PETERSON'S
GRADUATE
PROGRAMS IN
ENGINEERING &
APPLIED SCIENCES

2 0 1 1

PETERSON'S
Publishing

PETERSON'S
Publishing

About Peterson's Publishing
To succeed on your lifelong educational journey, you will need accurate, dependable, and practical tools and resources. That is why Peterson's is everywhere education happens. Because whenever and however you need education content delivered, you can rely on Peterson's to provide the information, know-how, and guidance to help you reach your goals. Tools to match the right students with the right school. It's here. Personalized resources and expert guidance. It's here. Comprehensive and dependable education content—delivered whenever and however you need it. It's all here.

For more information, contact Peterson's, 2000 Lenox Drive, Lawrenceville, NJ 08648; 800-338-3282 Ext. 54229; or find us online at www.petersonspublishing.com.

© 2011 Peterson's, a Nelnet company

Previous editions © 1966, 1967, 1968, 1969, 1970, 1971, 1972, 1973, 1974, 1975, 1976, 1977, 1978, 1979, 1980, 1981, 1982, 1983, 1984, 1985, 1986, 1987, 1988, 1989, 1990, 1991, 1992, 1993, 1994, 1995, 1996, 1997, 1998, 1999, 2000, 2001, 2002, 2003, 2004, 2005, 2006, 2007, 2008, 2009, 2010

Facebook® and Facebook logos are registered trademarks of Facebook, Inc. Twitter™ and Twitter logos are registered trademarks of Twitter, Inc. Neither Facebook, Inc. nor Twitter, Inc. were involved in the production of this book and make no endorsement of this product.

Stephen Clemente, Managing Director, Publishing and Institutional Research; Bernadette Webster, Director of Publishing; Jill C. Schwartz, Editor; Ken Britschge, Research Project Manager; Courtney Foust, Amy L. Weber, Research Associates; Phyllis Johnson, Programmer; Ray Golaszewski, Manufacturing Manager; Linda M. Williams, Composition Manager; Karen Mount, Danielle Vreeland, Shannon White, Client Relations Representatives

ISSN 1097-1068
ISBN-13: 978-0-7689-2856-3
ISBN-10: 0-7689-2856-7

Printed in the United States of America

10 9 8 7 6 5 4 3 2 1   13 12 11

Forty-fifth Edition

By producing this book on recycled paper (40% post consumer waste) 80 trees were saved.

CONTENTS

A Note from the Peterson's Editors

The six volumes of Peterson's *Graduate and Professional Programs*, the only annually updated reference work of its kind, provide wide-ranging information on the graduate and professional programs offered by accredited colleges and universities in the United States, U.S. territories, and Canada and by those institutions outside the United States that are accredited by U.S. accrediting bodies. More than 44,000 individual academic and professional programs at more than 2,200 institutions are listed. Peterson's *Graduate and Professional Programs* have been used for more than forty years by prospective graduate and professional students, placement counselors, faculty advisers, and all others interested in postbaccalaureate education.

Graduate & Professional Programs: An Overview contains information on institutions as a whole, while the other books in the series are devoted to specific academic and professional fields:

Graduate Programs in the Humanities, Arts & Social Sciences
Graduate Programs in the Biological Sciences
Graduate Programs in the Physical Sciences, Mathematics, Agricultural Sciences, the Environment & Natural Resources
Graduate Programs in Engineering & Applied Sciences
Graduate Programs in Business, Education, Health, Information Studies, Law & Social Work

The books may be used individually or as a set. For example, if you have chosen a field of study but do not know what institution you want to attend or if you have a college or university in mind but have not chosen an academic field of study, it is best to begin with the Overview guide.

Graduate & Professional Programs: An Overview presents several directories to help you identify programs of study that might interest you; you can then research those programs further in the other books in the series by using the Directory of Graduate and Professional Programs by Field, which lists 500 fields and gives the names of those institutions that offer graduate degree programs in each.

For geographical or financial reasons, you may be interested in attending a particular institution and will want to know what it has to offer. You should turn to the Directory of Institutions and Their Offerings, which lists the degree programs available at each institution. As in the Directory of Graduate and Professional Programs by Field, the level of degrees offered is also indicated.

All books in the series include advice on graduate education, including topics such as admissions tests, financial aid, and accreditation. **The Graduate Adviser** includes two essays and information about accreditation. The first essay, "The Admissions Process," discusses general admission requirements, admission tests, factors to consider when selecting a graduate school or program, when and how to apply, and how admission decisions are made. Special information for international students and tips for minority students are also included. The second essay, "Financial Support," is an overview of the broad range of support available at the graduate level. Fellowships, scholarships, and grants; assistantships and internships; federal and private loan programs, as well as Federal Work-Study; and the GI bill are detailed. This essay concludes with advice on applying for need-based financial aid. "Accreditation and Accrediting Agencies" gives information on accreditation and its purpose and lists institutional accrediting agencies first and then specialized accrediting agencies relevant to each volume's specific fields of study.

With information on more than 44,000 graduate programs in 500 disciplines, Peterson's *Graduate and Professional Programs* give you all the information you need about the programs that are of interest to you in three formats: **Profiles** (capsule summaries of basic information), **Displays** (information that an institution or program wants to emphasize), and **Close-Ups** (written by administrators, with more expansive information than the **Profiles**, emphasizing different aspects of the programs). By using these various formats of program information, coupled with **Appendixes** and **Indexes** covering directories and subject areas for all six books, you will find that these guides provide the most comprehensive, accurate, and up-to-date graduate study information available.

Find Us on Facebook® and Follow Us on Twitter™

Join the grad school conversation on Facebook® and Twitter™ at www.facebook.com/usgradschools and www.twitter.com/usgradschools. Peterson's expert resources are available to help you as you search for the right graduate program for you.

Peterson's publishes a full line of resources with information you need to guide you through the graduate admissions process. Peterson's publications can be found at college libraries and career centers and your local bookstore or library—or visit us on the Web at www.petersonspublishing.com. Peterson's books are now also available as eBooks.

Colleges and universities will be pleased to know that Peterson's helped you in your selection. Admissions staff members are more than happy to answer questions, address specific problems, and help in any way they can. The editors at Peterson's wish you great success in your graduate program search!

THE GRADUATE ADVISER

The Admissions Process

Generalizations about graduate admissions practices are not always helpful because each institution has its own set of guidelines and procedures. Nevertheless, some broad statements can be made about the admissions process that may help you plan your strategy.

Factors Involved in Selecting a Graduate School or Program

Selecting a graduate school and a specific program of study is a complex matter. Quality of the faculty; program and course offerings; the nature, size, and location of the institution; admission requirements; cost; and the availability of financial assistance are among the many factors that affect one's choice of institution. Other considerations are job placement and achievements of the program's graduates and the institution's resources, such as libraries, laboratories, and computer facilities. If you are to make the best possible choice, you need to learn as much as you can about the schools and programs you are considering before you apply.

The following steps may help you narrow your choices.

- Talk to alumni of the programs or institutions you are considering to get their impressions of how well they were prepared for work in their fields of study.
- Remember that graduate school requirements change, so be sure to get the most up-to-date information possible.
- Talk to department faculty members and the graduate adviser at your undergraduate institution. They often have information about programs of study at other institutions.
- Visit the Web sites of the graduate schools in which you are interested to request a graduate catalog. Contact the department chair in your chosen field of study for additional information about the department and the field.
- Visit as many campuses as possible. Call ahead for an appointment with the graduate adviser in your field of interest and be sure to check out the facilities and talk to students.

General Requirements

Graduate schools and departments have requirements that applicants for admission must meet. Typically, these requirements include undergraduate transcripts (which provide information about undergraduate grade point average and course work applied toward a major), admission test scores, and letters of recommendation. Most graduate programs also ask for an essay or personal statement that describes your personal reasons for seeking graduate study. In some fields, such as art and music, portfolios or auditions may be required in addition to other evidence of talent. Some institutions require that the applicant have an undergraduate degree in the same subject as the intended graduate major.

Most institutions evaluate each applicant on the basis of the applicant's total record, and the weight accorded any given factor varies widely from institution to institution and from program to program.

The Application Process

You should begin the application process at least one year before you expect to begin your graduate study. Find out the application deadline for each institution (many are provided in the **Profile** section of this guide). Go to the institution's Web site and find out if you can apply online. If not, request a paper application form. Fill out this form thoroughly and neatly. Assume that the school needs all the information it is requesting and that the admissions officer will be sensitive to the neatness and overall quality of what you submit. Do not supply more information than the school requires.

The institution may ask at least one question that will require a three- or four-paragraph answer. Compose your response on the assumption that the admissions officer is interested in both what you think and how you express yourself. Keep your statement brief and to the point, but, at the same time, include all pertinent information about your past experiences and your educational goals. Individual statements vary greatly in style and content, which helps admissions officers differentiate among applicants. Many graduate departments give considerable weight to the statement in making their admissions decisions, so be sure to take the time to prepare a thoughtful and concise statement.

If recommendations are a part of the admissions requirements, carefully choose the individuals you ask to write them. It is generally best to ask current or former professors to write the recommendations, provided they are able to attest to your intellectual ability and motivation for doing the work required of a graduate student. It is advisable to provide stamped, preaddressed envelopes to people being asked to submit recommendations on your behalf.

Completed applications, including references, transcripts, and admission test scores, should be received at the institution by the specified date.

Be advised that institutions do not usually make admissions decisions until all materials have been received. Enclose a self-addressed postcard with your application, requesting confirmation of receipt. Allow at least ten days for the return of the postcard before making further inquiries.

If you plan to apply for financial support, it is imperative that you file your application early.

ADMISSION TESTS

The major testing program used in graduate admissions is the Graduate Record Examinations (GRE) testing program, sponsored by the GRE Board and administered by Educational Testing Service, Princeton, New Jersey.

The Graduate Record Examinations testing program consists of a General Test and eight Subject Tests. The General Test measures critical thinking, verbal reasoning, quantitative reasoning, and analytical writing skills. It is offered as an Internet-based test (iBT) in the United States, Canada, and many other countries.

The typical computer-based General Test consists of one 30-minute verbal reasoning section, one 45-minute quantitative reasoning sections, one 45-minute issue analysis (writing) section, and one 30-minute argument analysis (writing) section. In addition, an unidentified verbal or quantitative section that doesn't count toward a score may be included and an identified research section that is not scored may also be included.

The Subject Tests measure achievement and assume undergraduate majors or extensive background in the following eight disciplines:

- Biochemistry, Cell and Molecular Biology
- Biology
- Chemistry
- Computer Science
- Literature in English
- Mathematics
- Physics
- Psychology

The Subject Tests are available three times per year as paper-based administrations around the world. Testing time is approximately 2 hours and 50 minutes. You can obtain more information about the GRE by visiting the ETS Web site at www.ets.org or consulting the *GRE Information and Registration Bulletin*. The *Bulletin* can be obtained at many undergraduate colleges. You can also download it from the ETS Web site or obtain it by contacting Graduate Record Examinations, Educational Testing Service, P.O. Box 6000, Princeton, NJ 08541-6000; phone: 609-771-7670.

If you expect to apply for admission to a program that requires any of the GRE tests, you should select a test date well in advance of the application deadline. Scores on the computer-based General Test are reported within ten to fifteen days; scores on the paper-based Subject Tests are reported within six weeks.

Another testing program, the Miller Analogies Test (MAT), is administered at more than 500 Controlled Testing Centers, licensed by Harcourt Assessment, Inc., in the United States, Canada, and other countries. The MAT computer-based test is now available. Testing time is 60 minutes. The test consists of 120 partial analogies. You can obtain the *Candidate Information Booklet,* which contains a list of test centers and instructions for taking the test, from http://www.milleranalogies.com or by calling 800-622-3231 (toll-free).

Check the specific requirements of the programs to which you are applying.

How Admission Decisions Are Made

The program you apply to is directly involved in the admissions process. Although the final decision is usually made by the graduate dean (or an associate) or the faculty admissions committee, recommendations from faculty members in your intended field are important. At some institutions, an interview is incorporated into the decision process.

A Special Note for International Students

In addition to the steps already described, there are some special considerations for international students who intend to apply for graduate study in the United States. All graduate schools require an indication of competence in English. The purpose of the Test of English as a Foreign Language (TOEFL) is to evaluate the English proficiency of people who are nonnative speakers of English and want to study at colleges and universities where English is the language of instruction. The TOEFL is administered by Educational Testing Service (ETS) under the general direction of a policy board established by the College Board and the Graduate Record Examinations Board.

The TOEFL iBT assesses the four basic language skills: listening, reading, writing, and speaking. It was administered for the first time in September 2005, and ETS continues to introduce the TOEFL iBT in selected cities. The Internet-based test is administered at secure, official test centers. The testing time is approximately 4 hours. Because the TOEFL iBT includes a speaking section, the Test of Spoken English (TSE) is no longer needed.

The TOEFL is also offered in the paper-based format in areas of the world where Internet-based testing is not available. The paper-based TOEFL consists of three sections—listening comprehension, structure and written expression, and reading comprehension. The testing time is approximately 3 hours. The Test of Written English (TWE) is also given. The TWE is a 30-minute essay that measures the examinee's ability to compose in English. Examinees receive a TWE score separate from their TOEFL score. The *Information Bulletin* contains information on local fees and registration procedures.

Additional information and registration materials are available from TOEFL Services, Educational Testing Service, P.O. Box 6151, Princeton, New Jersey 08541-6151. Phone: 609-771-7100. Web site: www.toefl.org.

International students should apply especially early because of the number of steps required to complete the admissions process. Furthermore, many United States graduate schools have a limited number of spaces for international students, and many more students apply than the schools can accommodate.

International students may find financial assistance from institutions very limited. The U.S. government requires international applicants to submit a certification of support, which is a statement attesting to the applicant's financial resources. In addition, international students *must* have health insurance coverage.

Tips for Minority Students

Indicators of a university's values in terms of diversity are found both in its recruitment programs and its resources directed to student success. Important questions: Does the institution vigorously recruit minorities for its graduate programs? Is there funding available to help with the costs associated with visiting the school? Are minorities represented in the institution's brochures or Web site or on their faculty rolls? What campus-based resources or services (including assistance in locating housing or career counseling and placement) are available? Is funding available to members of underrepresented groups?

At the program level, it is particularly important for minority students to investigate the "climate" of a program under consideration. How many minority students are enrolled and how many have graduated? What opportunities are there to work with diverse faculty and mentors whose research interests match yours? How are conflicts resolved or concerns addressed? How interested are faculty in building strong and supportive relations with students? "Climate" concerns should be addressed by posing questions to various individuals, including faculty members, current students, and alumni.

Information is also available through various organizations, such as the Hispanic Association of Colleges & Universities (HACU), and publications such as *Diverse Issues in Higher Education* and *Hispanic Outlook* magazine. There are also books devoted to this topic, such as *The Multicultural Student's Guide to Colleges* by Robert Mitchell.

Financial Support

The range of financial support at the graduate level is very broad. The following descriptions will give you a general idea of what you might expect and what will be expected of you as a financial support recipient.

Fellowships, Scholarships, and Grants

These are usually outright awards of a few hundred to many thousands of dollars with no service to the institution required in return. Fellowships and scholarships are usually awarded on the basis of merit and are highly competitive. Grants are made on the basis of financial need or special talent in a field of study. Many fellowships, scholarships, and grants not only cover tuition, fees, and supplies but also include stipends for living expenses with allowances for dependents. However, the terms of each should be examined because some do not permit recipients to supplement their income with outside work. Fellowships, scholarships, and grants may vary in the number of years for which they are awarded.

In addition to the availability of these funds at the university or program level, many excellent fellowship programs are available at the national level and may be applied for before and during enrollment in a graduate program. A listing of many of these programs can be found at the Council of Graduate Schools' Web site: http://www.cgsnet.org. There is a wealth of information in the "Programs" and "Awards" sections.

Assistantships and Internships

Many graduate students receive financial support through assistantships, particularly involving teaching or research duties. It is important to recognize that such appointments should not be viewed simply as employment relationships but rather should constitute an integral and important part of a student's graduate education. As such, the appointments should be accompanied by strong faculty mentoring and increasingly responsible apprenticeship experiences. The specific nature of these appointments in a given program should be considered in selecting that graduate program.

TEACHING ASSISTANTSHIPS

These usually provide a salary and full or partial tuition remission and may also provide health benefits. Unlike fellowships, scholarships, and grants, which require no service to the institution, teaching assistantships require recipients to provide the institution with a specific amount of undergraduate teaching, ideally related to the student's field of study. Some teaching assistants are limited to grading papers, compiling bibliographies, taking notes, or monitoring laboratories. At some graduate schools, teaching assistants must carry lighter course loads than regular full-time students.

RESEARCH ASSISTANTSHIPS

These are very similar to teaching assistantships in the manner in which financial assistance is provided. The difference is that recipients are given basic research assignments in their disciplines rather than teaching responsibilities. The work required is normally related to the student's field of study; in most instances, the assistantship supports the student's thesis or dissertation research.

ADMINISTRATIVE INTERNSHIPS

These are similar to assistantships in application of financial assistance funds, but the student is given an assignment on a part-time basis, usually as a special assistant with one of the university's administrative offices. The assignment may not necessarily be directly related to the recipient's discipline.

RESIDENCE HALL AND COUNSELING ASSISTANTSHIPS

These assistantships are frequently assigned to graduate students in psychology, counseling, and social work, but they may be offered to students in other disciplines, especially if the student has worked in this capacity during his or her undergraduate years. Duties can vary from being available in a dean's office for a specific number of hours for consultation with undergraduates to living in campus residences and being responsible for both counseling and administrative tasks or advising student activity groups. Residence hall assistantships often include a room and board allowance and, in some cases, tuition assistance and stipends. Contact the Housing and Student Life Office for more information.

Health Insurance

The availability and affordability of health insurance is an important issue and one that should be considered in an applicant's choice of institution and program. While often included with assistantships and fellowships, this is not always the case and, even if provided, the benefits may be limited. It is important to note that the U.S. government requires international students to have health insurance.

The GI Bill

This provides financial assistance for students who are veterans of the United States armed forces. If you are a veteran, contact your local Veterans Administration office to determine your eligibility and to get full details about benefits. There are a number of programs that offer educational benefits to current military enlistees. Some states have tuition assistance programs for members of the National Guard. Contact the VA office at the college for more information.

Federal Work-Study Program (FWS)

Employment is another way some students finance their graduate studies. The federally funded Federal Work-Study Program provides eligible students with employment opportunities, usually in public and private nonprofit organizations. Federal funds pay up to 75 percent of the wages, with the remainder paid by the employing agency. FWS is available to graduate students who demonstrate financial need. Not all schools have these funds, and some only award them to undergraduates. Each school sets its application deadline and work-study earnings limits. Wages vary and are related to the type of work done. You must file the Free Application for Federal Student Aid (FAFSA) to be eligible for this program.

Loans

Many graduate students borrow to finance their graduate programs when other sources of assistance (which do not have to be repaid) prove insufficient. You should always read and understand the terms of any loan program before submitting your application.

FEDERAL DIRECT LOANS

Federal Direct Stafford Loans. The Federal Direct Stafford Loan Program offers low-interest loans to students with the Department of Education acting as the lender.

There are two components of the Federal Stafford Loan program. Under the *subsidized* component of the program, the federal government pays the interest on the loan while you are enrolled in graduate school on at least a half-time basis, during the six-month grace period after you drop below half-time enrollment, as well as during any period of deferment. Under the *unsubsidized* component of the program, you pay the interest on the loan from the day proceeds are issued. Eligibility for the federal subsidy is based on demonstrated financial need as determined by the financial aid office from the information you provide on the FAFSA. A cosigner is not required, since the loan is not based on creditworthiness.

Although *unsubsidized* Federal Direct Stafford Loans may not be as desirable as *subsidized* Federal Direct Stafford Loans from the student's perspective, they are a useful source of support for those who may not qualify for the subsidized loans or who need additional financial assistance.

Graduate students may borrow up to $20,500 per year through the Direct Stafford Loan Program, up to a cumulative maximum of $138,500, including undergraduate borrowing. This may include up to $8500 in *subsidized* Direct Stafford Loans annually, depending on eligibility, up to a cumulative maximum of $65,500, including undergraduate borrowing. The amount of the loan borrowed through the *unsubsidized* Direct Stafford Loan Program equals the total amount of the loan (as much as $20,500) minus your eligibility for a *subsidized* Direct Stafford Loan (as much as $8500). You may borrow up to the cost of attendance at the school in which you are enrolled or will attend, minus estimated financial assistance from other federal, state, and private sources, up to a maximum of $20,500.

Direct Stafford Loans made on or after July 1, 2006, carry a fixed interest rate of 6.8% both for in-school and in-repayment borrowers.

A fee is deducted from the loan proceeds upon disbursement. Loans with a first disbursement on or after July 1, 2010 have a borrower origination fee of 1 percent. The Department of Education offers a 0.5 percent origination fee rebate incentive. Borrowers must make their first twelve payments on time in order to retain the rebate.

Under the *subsidized* Federal Direct Stafford Loan Program, repayment begins six months after your last date of enrollment on at least a half-time basis. Under the *unsubsidized* program, repayment of interest begins within thirty days from disbursement of the loan proceeds, and repayment of the principal begins six months after your last enrollment on at least a half-time basis. Some borrowers may choose to defer interest payments while they are in school. The accrued interest is added to the loan balance when the borrower begins repayment. There are several repayment options.

Federal Perkins Loans. The Federal Perkins Loan is available to students demonstrating financial need and is administered directly by the school. Not all schools have these funds, and some may award them to undergraduates only. Eligibility is determined from the information you provide on the FAFSA. The school will notify you of your eligibility.

Eligible graduate students may borrow up to $6000 per year, up to a maximum of $40,000, including undergraduate borrowing (even if your previous Perkins Loans have been repaid). The interest rate for Federal Perkins Loans is 5 percent, and no interest accrues while you remain in school at least half-time. There are no guarantee, loan, or disbursement fees. Repayment begins nine months after your last date of enrollment on at least a half-time basis and may extend over a maximum of ten years with no prepayment penalty.

Federal Direct Graduate PLUS Loans. Effective July 1, 2006, graduate and professional students are eligible for Graduate PLUS loans. This program allows students to borrow up to the cost of attendance, less any other aid received. These loans have a fixed interest rate of 7.9 percent, and interest begins to accrue at the time of disbursement. The PLUS loans do involve a credit check; a PLUS borrower may obtain a loan with a cosigner if his or her credit is not good enough. Grad PLUS loans may be deferred while a student in school and for the six months following a drop below half-time enrollment. For more information, contact your college financial aid office.

Deferring Your Federal Loan Repayments. If you borrowed under the Federal Direct Stafford Loan Program, Federal Direct Loan Program, or the Federal Perkins Loan Program for previous undergraduate or graduate study, your repayments may be deferred when you return to graduate school, depending on when you borrowed and under which program.

There are other deferment options available if you are temporarily unable to repay your loan. Information about these deferments is provided at your entrance and exit interviews. If you believe you are eligible for a deferment of your loan repayments, you must contact your lender or loan servicer to request a deferment form. The deferment must be filed prior to the time your repayment is due, and it must be refiled when it expires if you remain eligible for deferment at that time.

SUPPLEMENTAL (PRIVATE) LOANS

Many lending institutions offer supplemental loan programs and other financing plans, such as the ones described here, to students seeking additional assistance in meeting their education expenses. Some loan programs target all types of graduate students; others are designed specifically for business, law, or medical students. In addition, you can use private loans not specifically designed for education to help finance your graduate degree.

If you are considering borrowing through a supplemental or private loan program, you should carefully consider the terms and be sure to "read the fine print." Check with the program sponsor for the most current terms that will be applicable to the amounts you intend to borrow for graduate study. Most supplemental loan programs for graduate study offer unsubsidized, credit-based loans. In general, a credit-ready borrower is one who has a satisfactory credit history or no credit history at all. A creditworthy borrower generally must pass a credit test to be eligible to borrow or act as a cosigner for the loan funds.

Many supplemental loan programs have minimum and maximum annual loan limits. Some offer amounts equal to the cost of attendance minus any other aid you will receive for graduate study. If you are planning to borrow for several years of graduate study, consider whether there is a cumulative or aggregate limit on the amount you may borrow. Often this cumulative or aggregate limit will include any amounts you borrowed and have not repaid for undergraduate or previous graduate study.

The combination of the annual interest rate, loan fees, and the repayment terms you choose will determine how much you will repay over time. Compare these features in combination before you decide which loan program to use. Some loans offer interest rates that are adjusted monthly, some quarterly, some annually. Some offer interest rates that are lower during the in-school, grace, and deferment periods and then increase when you begin repayment. Some programs include a loan "origination" fee, which is usually deducted from the principal amount you receive when the loan is disbursed and must be repaid along with the interest and other principal when you graduate, withdraw from school, or drop below half-time study. Sometimes the loan fees are reduced if you borrow with a qualified cosigner. Some programs allow you to defer interest and/or principal payments while you are enrolled in graduate school. Many programs allow you to capitalize your interest payments; the interest due on your loan is added to the outstanding balance of your loan, so you don't have to repay immediately, but this increases the amount you owe. Other programs allow you to pay the interest as you go, which reduces the amount you later have to repay. The private loan market is very competitive, and your financial aid office can help you evaluate these programs.

Applying for Need-Based Financial Aid

Schools that award federal and institutional financial assistance based on need will require you to complete the FAFSA and, in some cases, an institutional financial aid application.

If you are applying for federal student assistance, you **must** complete the FAFSA. A service of the U.S. Department of Education, the FAFSA is free to all applicants. Most applicants apply online at www.fafsa.ed.gov. Paper applications are available at the financial aid office of your local college.

After your FAFSA information has been processed, you will receive a Student Aid Report (SAR). If you provided an e-mail address on the FAFSA, this will be sent to you electronically; otherwise, it will be mailed to your home address.

Follow the instructions on the SAR if you need to correct information reported on your original application. If your situation changes after you file your FAFSA, contact your financial aid officer to discuss amending your information. You can also appeal your financial aid award if you have extenuating circumstances.

If you would like more information on federal student financial aid, visit the FAFSA Web site or download the most recent version of *Funding Education Beyond High School: The Guide to Federal Student Aid* at http://studentaid.ed.gov/students/publications/student_guide/index.html. This guide is also available in Spanish.

The U.S. Department of Education also has a toll-free number for questions concerning federal student aid programs. The number is 1-800-4-FED AID (1-800-433-3243). If you are hearing impaired, call toll-free, 1-800-730-8913.

Summary

Remember that these are generalized statements about financial assistance at the graduate level. Because each institution allots its aid differently, you should communicate directly with the school and the specific department of interest to you. It is not unusual, for example, to find that an endowment vested within a specific department supports one or more fellowships. You may fit its requirements and specifications precisely.

Accreditation and Accrediting Agencies

Colleges and universities in the United States, and their individual academic and professional programs, are accredited by nongovernmental agencies concerned with monitoring the quality of education in this country. Agencies with both regional and national jurisdictions grant accreditation to institutions as a whole, while specialized bodies acting on a nationwide basis—often national professional associations—grant accreditation to departments and programs in specific fields.

Institutional and specialized accrediting agencies share the same basic concerns: the purpose an academic unit—whether university or program—has set for itself and how well it fulfills that purpose, the adequacy of its financial and other resources, the quality of its academic offerings, and the level of services it provides. Agencies that grant institutional accreditation take a broader view, of course, and examine university-wide or college-wide services with which a specialized agency may not concern itself.

Both types of agencies follow the same general procedures when considering an application for accreditation. The academic unit prepares a self-evaluation, focusing on the concerns mentioned above and usually including an assessment of both its strengths and weaknesses; a team of representatives of the accrediting body reviews this evaluation, visits the campus, and makes its own report; and finally, the accrediting body makes a decision on the application. Often, even when accreditation is granted, the agency makes a recommendation regarding how the institution or program can improve. All institutions and programs are also reviewed every few years to determine whether they continue to meet established standards; if they do not, they may lose their accreditation.

Accrediting agencies themselves are reviewed and evaluated periodically by the U.S. Department of Education and the Council for Higher Education Accreditation (CHEA). Recognized agencies adhere to certain standards and practices, and their authority in matters of accreditation is widely accepted in the educational community.

This does not mean, however, that accreditation is a simple matter, either for schools wishing to become accredited or for students deciding where to apply. Indeed, in certain fields the very meaning and methods of accreditation are the subject of a good deal of debate. For their part, those applying to graduate school should be aware of the safeguards provided by regional accreditation, especially in terms of degree acceptance and institutional longevity. Beyond this, applicants should understand the role that specialized accreditation plays in their field, as this varies considerably from one discipline to another. In certain professional fields, it is necessary to have graduated from a program that is accredited in order to be eligible for a license to practice, and in some fields the federal government also makes this a hiring requirement. In other disciplines, however, accreditation is not as essential, and there can be excellent programs that are not accredited. In fact, some programs choose not to seek accreditation, although most do.

Institutions and programs that present themselves for accreditation are sometimes granted the status of candidate for accreditation, or what is known as "preaccreditation." This may happen, for example, when an academic unit is too new to have met all the requirements for accreditation. Such status signifies initial recognition and indicates that the school or program in question is working to fulfill all requirements; it does not, however, guarantee that accreditation will be granted.

Institutional Accrediting Agencies—Regional

MIDDLE STATES ASSOCIATION OF COLLEGES AND SCHOOLS
Accredits institutions in Delaware, District of Columbia, Maryland, New Jersey, New York, Pennsylvania, Puerto Rico, and the Virgin Islands.
Dr. Elizabeth Sibolski, Acting President
Middle States Commission on Higher Education
3624 Market Street, Second Floor West
Philadelphia, Pennsylvania 19104
Phone: 267-284-5000
Fax: 215-662-5501
E-mail: info@msche.org
Web: www.msche.org

NEW ENGLAND ASSOCIATION OF SCHOOLS AND COLLEGES
Accredits institutions in Connecticut, Maine, Massachusetts, New Hampshire, Rhode Island, and Vermont.
Barbara E. Brittingham, Director
Commission on Institutions of Higher Education
209 Burlington Road, Suite 201
Bedford, Massachusetts 01730-1433
Phone: 781-271-0022
Fax: 781-271-0950
E-mail: CIHE@neasc.org
Web: www.neasc.org

NORTH CENTRAL ASSOCIATION OF COLLEGES AND SCHOOLS
Accredits institutions in Arizona, Arkansas, Colorado, Illinois, Indiana, Iowa, Kansas, Michigan, Minnesota, Missouri, Nebraska, New Mexico, North Dakota, Ohio, Oklahoma, South Dakota, West Virginia, Wisconsin, and Wyoming.
Dr. Sylvia Manning, President
The Higher Learning Commission
230 South LaSalle Street, Suite 7-500
Chicago, Illinois 60604-1413
Phone: 312-263-0456
Fax: 312-263-7462
E-mail: smanning@hlcommission.org
Web: www.ncahigherlearningcommission.org

NORTHWEST COMMISSION ON COLLEGES AND UNIVERSITIES
Accredits institutions in Alaska, Idaho, Montana, Nevada, Oregon, Utah, and Washington.
Dr. Sandra E. Elman, President
8060 165th Avenue, NE, Suite 100
Redmond, Washington 98052
Phone: 425-558-4224
Fax: 425-376-0596
E-mail: selman@nwccu.org
Web: www.nwccu.org

SOUTHERN ASSOCIATION OF COLLEGES AND SCHOOLS
Accredits institutions in Alabama, Florida, Georgia, Kentucky, Louisiana, Mississippi, North Carolina, South Carolina, Tennessee, Texas, and Virginia.
Belle S. Wheelan, President
Commission on Colleges
1866 Southern Lane
Decatur, Georgia 30033-4097
Phone: 404-679-4500
Fax: 404-679-4558
E-mail: questions@sacscoc.org
Web: www.sacsoc.org

WESTERN ASSOCIATION OF SCHOOLS AND COLLEGES
Accredits institutions in California, Guam, and Hawaii.
Ralph A. Wolff, President and Executive Director
Accrediting Commission for Senior Colleges and Universities
985 Atlantic Avenue, Suite 100
Alameda, California 94501
Phone: 510-748-9001
Fax: 510-748-9797
E-mail: www.wascsenior.org
Web: www.wascweb.org/contact

Institutional Accrediting Agencies—Other

ACCREDITING COUNCIL FOR INDEPENDENT COLLEGES AND SCHOOLS
Albert C. Gray, Ph.D., Executive Director and CEO
750 First Street, NE, Suite 980
Washington, DC 20002-4241
Phone: 202-336-6780
Fax: 202-842-2593
E-mail: info@acics.org
Web: www.acics.org

DISTANCE EDUCATION AND TRAINING COUNCIL (DETC)
Accrediting Commission
Michael P. Lambert, Executive Director
1601 18th Street, NW, Suite 2
Washington, DC 20009
Phone: 202-234-5100
Fax: 202-332-1386
E-mail: detc@detc.org
Web: www.detc.org

Specialized Accrediting Agencies

[Only *Graduate & Professional Programs: An Overview* of *Peterson's Graduate and Professional Programs* Series includes the complete list of specialized accrediting groups recognized by the U.S. Department of Education and the Council on Higher Education Accreditation (CHEA). The list in this book is abridged.]

ENGINEERING
Michael Milligan, Ph.D., PE, Executive Director
Accreditation Board for Engineering and Technology, Inc. (ABET)
111 Market Place, Suite 1050
Baltimore, Maryland 21202
Phone: 410-347-7700
Fax: 410-625-2238
E-mail: info@abet.org
Web: www.abet.org

TECHNOLOGY
Michale S. McComis, Ed.D., Executive Director
Accrediting Commission of Career Schools and Colleges
2101 Wilson Boulevard, Suite 302
Arlington, Virginia 22201
Phone: 703-247-4212
Fax: 703-247-4533
E-mail: mccomis@accsct.org
Web: www.accs.org

How to Use These Guides

As you identify the particular programs and institutions that interest you, you can use both the *Graduate & Professional Programs: An Overview* volume and the specialized volumes in the series to obtain detailed information.

- *Graduate Programs in the Physical Sciences, Mathematics, Agricultural Sciences, the Environment & Natural Resources*
- *Graduate Programs in Engineering & Applied Sciences*
- *Graduate Programs the Humanities, Arts & Social Sciences*
- *Graduate Programs in the Biological Sciences*
- *Graduate Programs in Business, Education, Health, Information Studies, Law & Social Work*

Each of the specialized volumes in the series is divided into sections that contain one or more directories devoted to programs in a particular field. If you do not find a directory devoted to your field of interest in a specific volume, consult "Directories and Subject Areas" (located at the end of each volume). After you have identified the correct volume, consult the "Directories and Subject Areas in This Book" index, which shows (as does the more general directory) what directories cover subjects not specifically named in a directory or section title.

Each of the specialized volumes in the series has a number of general directories. These directories have entries for the largest unit at an institution granting graduate degrees in that field. For example, the general Engineering and Applied Sciences directory in the *Graduate Programs in Engineering & Applied Sciences* volume consists of **Profiles** for colleges, schools, and departments of engineering and applied sciences.

General directories are followed by other directories, or sections, that give more detailed information about programs in particular areas of the general field that has been covered. The general Engineering and Applied Sciences directory, in the previous example, is followed by nineteen sections with directories in specific areas of engineering, such as Chemical Engineering, Industrial/Management Engineering, and Mechanical Engineering.

Because of the broad nature of many fields, any system of organization is bound to involve a certain amount of overlap. Environmental studies, for example, is a field whose various aspects are studied in several types of departments and schools. Readers interested in such studies will find information on relevant programs in the *Graduate Programs in the Biological Sciences* volume under Ecology and Environmental Biology; in the *Graduate Programs in the Physical Sciences, Mathematics, Agricultural Sciences, the Environment & Natural Resources* volume under Environmental Management and Policy and Natural Resources; in the *Graduate Programs in Engineering & Applied Sciences* volume under Energy Management and Policy and Environmental Engineering; and in the *Graduate Programs in Business, Education, Health, Information Studies, Law & Social Work* volume under Environmental and Occupational Health. To help you find all of the programs of interest to you, the introduction to each section within the specialized volumes includes, if applicable, a paragraph suggesting other sections and directories with information on related areas of study.

Directory of Institutions with Programs in Engineering and Applied Sciences

This directory lists institutions in alphabetical order and includes beneath each name the academic fields in which each institution offers graduate programs. The degree level in each field is also indicated, provided that the institution has supplied that information in response to Peterson's Annual Survey of Graduate and Professional Institutions. An M indicates that a master's degree program is offered; a D indicates that a doctoral degree program is offered; a P indicates that the first professional degree is offered; an O signifies that other advanced degrees (e.g., certificates or specialist degrees) are offered; and an *

(asterisk) indicates that a **Close-Up** and/or **Display** is located in this volume. See the index, "Close-Ups and Displays," for the specific page number.

Profiles of Academic and Professional Programs in the Specialized Volumes

Each section of **Profiles** has a table of contents that lists the Program Directories, **Displays**, and **Close-Ups**. Program Directories consist of the **Profiles** of programs in the relevant fields, with **Displays** following if programs have chosen to include them. **Close-Ups**, which are more individualized statements, again if programs have chosen to submit them, are also listed.

The **Profiles** found in the 500 directories in the specialized volumes provide basic data about the graduate units in capsule form for quick reference. To make these directories as useful as possible, **Profiles** are generally listed for an institution's smallest academic unit within a subject area. In other words, if an institution has a College of Liberal Arts that administers many related programs, the **Profile** for the individual program (e.g., Program in History), not the entire College, appears in the directory.

There are some programs that do not fit into any current directory and are not given individual **Profiles**. The directory structure is reviewed annually in order to keep this number to a minimum and to accommodate major trends in graduate education.

The following outline describes the **Profile** information found in the guides and explains how best to use that information. Any item that does not apply to or was not provided by a graduate unit is omitted from its listing. The format of the **Profiles** is constant, making it easy to compare one institution with another and one program with another.

Identifying Information. The institution's name, in boldface type, is followed by a complete listing of the administrative structure for that field of study. (For example, University of Akron, Buchtel College of Arts and Sciences, Department of Theoretical and Applied Mathematics, Program in Mathematics.) The last unit listed is the one to which all information in the **Profile** pertains. The institution's city, state, and zip code follow.

Offerings. Each field of study offered by the unit is listed with all postbaccalaureate degrees awarded. Degrees that are not preceded by a specific concentration are awarded in the general field listed in the unit name. Frequently, fields of study are broken down into subspecializations, and those appear following the degrees awarded; for example, "Offerings in secondary education (M.Ed.), including English education, mathematics education, science education." Students enrolled in the M.Ed. program would be able to specialize in any of the three fields mentioned.

Professional Accreditation. Some **Profiles** indicate whether a program is professionally accredited. Because it is possible for a program to receive or lose professional accreditation at any time, students entering fields in which accreditation is important to a career should verify the status of programs by contacting either the chairperson or the appropriate accrediting association.

Jointly Offered Degrees. Explanatory statements concerning programs that are offered in cooperation with other institutions are included in the list of degrees offered. This occurs most commonly on a regional basis (for example, two state universities offering a cooperative Ph.D. in special education) or where the specialized nature of the institutions encourages joint efforts (a J.D./M.B.A. offered by a law school at an institution with no formal business programs and an institution with a business school but lacking a law school). Only programs that are truly cooperative are listed; those involving only limited course work at another institution are not. Interested students should contact the heads of such units for further information.

Part-Time and Evening/Weekend Programs. When information regarding the availability of part-time or evening/weekend study appears in the **Profile**, it means that students are able to earn a degree exclusively through such study.

Postbaccalaureate Distance Learning Degrees. A postbaccalaureate distance learning degree program signifies that course requirements can be fulfilled with minimal or no on-campus study.

Faculty. Figures on the number of faculty members actively involved with graduate students through teaching or research are separated into full-and part-time as well as men and women whenever the information has been supplied.

Students. Figures for the number of students enrolled in graduate and professional programs pertain to the semester of highest enrollment from the 2009–10 academic year. These figures are broken down into full-and part-time and men and women whenever the data have been supplied. Information on the number of matriculated students enrolled in the unit who are members of a minority group or are international students appears here. The average age of the matriculated students is followed by the number of applicants, the percentage accepted, and the number enrolled for fall 2009.

Degrees Awarded. The number of degrees awarded in the calendar year is listed. Many doctoral programs offer a terminal master's degree if students leave the program after completing only part of the requirements for a doctoral degree; that is indicated here. All degrees are classified into one of four types: master's, doctoral, first professional, and other advanced degrees. A unit may award one or several degrees at a given level; however, the data are only collected by type and may therefore represent several different degree programs.

Degree Requirements. The information in this section is also broken down by type of degree, and all information for a degree level pertains to all degrees of that type unless otherwise specified. Degree requirements are collected in a simplified form to provide some very basic information on the nature of the program and on foreign language, thesis or dissertation, comprehensive exam, and registration requirements. Many units also provide a short list of additional requirements, such as fieldwork or an internship. For complete information on graduation requirements, contact the graduate school or program directly.

Entrance Requirements. Entrance requirements are broken down into the four degree levels of master's, doctoral, first professional, and other advanced degrees. Within each level, information may be provided in two basic categories: entrance exams and other requirements. The entrance exams are identified by the standard acronyms used by the testing agencies, unless they are not well known. Other entrance requirements are quite varied, but they often contain an undergraduate or graduate grade point average (GPA). Unless otherwise stated, the GPA is calculated on a 4.0 scale and is listed as a minimum required for admission. Additional exam requirements/recommendations for international students may be listed here. Application deadlines for domestic and international students, the application fee, and whether electronic applications are accepted may be listed here. Note that the deadline should be used for reference only; these dates are subject to change, and students interested in applying should always contact the graduate unit directly about application procedures and deadlines.

Expenses. The typical cost of study for the 2009–10 academic year is given in two basic categories: tuition and fees. Cost of study may be quite complex at a graduate institution. There are often sliding scales for part-time study, a different cost for first-year students, and other variables that make it impossible to completely cover the cost of study for each graduate program. To provide the most usable information, figures are given for full-time study for a full year where available and for part-time study in terms of a per-unit rate (per credit, per semester hour, etc.). Occasionally, variances may be noted in tuition and fees for reasons such as the type of program, whether courses are taken during the day or evening, whether courses are at the master's or doctoral level, or other institution-specific reasons. Expenses are usually subject to change; for exact costs at any given time, contact your chosen schools and programs directly. Keep in mind that the tuition of Canadian institutions is usually given in Canadian dollars.

Financial Support. This section contains data on the number of awards administered by the institution and given to graduate students during the 2009–10 academic year. The first figure given represents the total number of students receiving financial support enrolled in that unit. If the unit has provided information on graduate appointments, these are broken down into three major categories: fellowships give money to graduate students to cover the cost of study and living expenses and are not based on a work obligation or research commitment, research assistantships provide stipends to graduate students for assistance in a formal research project with a faculty member, and teaching assistantships provide stipends to graduate students for teaching or for assisting faculty members in teaching undergraduate classes. Within each category, figures are given for the total number of awards, the average yearly amount per award, and whether full or partial tuition reimbursements are awarded. In addition to graduate appointments, the availability of several other financial aid sources is covered in this section. Tuition waivers are routinely part of a graduate appointment, but units sometimes waive part or all of a student's tuition even if a graduate appointment is not available. Federal Work-Study is made available to students who demonstrate need and meet the federal guidelines; this form of aid normally includes 10 or more hours of work per week in an office of the institution. Institutionally sponsored loans are low-interest loans available to graduate students to cover both educational and living expenses. Career-related internships or fieldwork offer money to students who are participating in a formal off-campus research project or practicum. Grants, scholarships, traineeships, unspecified assistantships, and other awards may also be noted. The availability of financial support to part-time students is also indicated here.

Some programs list the financial aid application deadline and the forms that need to be completed for students to be eligible for financial awards. There are two forms: FAFSA, the Free Application for Federal Student Aid, which is required for federal aid, and the CSS PROFILE®.

Faculty Research. Each unit has the opportunity to list several keyword phrases describing the current research involving faculty members and graduate students. Space limitations prevent the unit from listing complete information on all research programs. The total expenditure for funded research from the previous academic year may also be included.

Unit Head and Application Contact. The head of the graduate program for each unit is listed with academic title and telephone and fax numbers and e-mail address if available. In addition to the unit head, many graduate programs list a separate contact for application and admission information, which follows the listing for the unit head. If no unit head or application contact is given, you should contact the overall institution for information on graduate admissions.

Displays and Close-Ups

The **Displays** and **Close-Ups** are supplementary insertions submitted by deans, chairs, and other administrators who wish to offer an additional, more individualized statement to readers. A number of graduate school and program administrators have attached a **Display** ad near the **Profile** listing. Here you will find information that an institution or program wants to emphasize. The **Close-Ups** are by their very nature more expansive and flexible than the **Profiles**, and the administrators who have written them may emphasize different aspects of their programs. All of the **Close-Ups** are organized in the same way (with the exception of a few that describe research and training opportunities instead of degree programs), and in each one you will find information on the same basic topics, such as programs of study, research facilities, tuition and fees, financial aid, and application procedures. If an institution or program has submitted a **Close-Up**, a boldface cross-reference appears below its **Profile**. As with the **Displays**, all of the **Close-Ups** in the guides have been submitted by choice; the absence of a **Display** or **Close-Up** does not reflect any type of editorial judgment on the part of Peterson's, and their presence in the guides should not be taken as an indication of status, quality, or approval. Statements regarding a university's objectives and accomplishments are a reflection of its own beliefs and are not the opinions of the Peterson's editors.

Appendixes

This section contains two appendixes. The first, "Institutional Changes Since the 2010 Edition," lists institutions that have closed, merged, or changed their name or status since the last edition of the guides. The second, "Abbreviations Used in the Guides," gives abbreviations of degree names, along with what those abbreviations stand for. These appendixes are identical in all six volumes of *Peterson's Graduate and Professional Programs*.

Indexes

There are three indexes presented here. The first index, "Close-Ups and Displays," gives page references for all programs that have chosen to place **Close-Ups** and **Displays** in this volume. It is arranged alphabetically by institution; within institutions, the arrangement is alphabetical by subject area. It is not an index to all programs in the book's directories of **Profiles**; readers must refer to the directories themselves for **Profile** information on programs that have not submitted the additional, more individualized statements. The second index, "Directories and Subject Areas in Other Books in This Series", gives book references for the directories in the specialized volumes and also includes cross-references for subject area names not used in the directory structure, for example, "Computing Technology (see Computer Science)." The third index, "Directories and Subject Areas in This Book," gives page references for the directories in this volume and cross-references for subject area names not used in this volume's directory structure.

Data Collection Procedures

The information published in the directories and **Profiles** of all the books is collected through Peterson's Annual Survey of Graduate and Professional Institutions. The survey is sent each spring to more than 2,200 institutions offering postbaccalaureate degree programs, including accredited institutions in the United States, U.S. territories, and Canada and those institutions outside the United States that are accredited by U.S. accrediting bodies. Deans and other administrators complete these surveys, providing information on programs in the 500 academic and professional fields covered in the guides as well as overall institutional information. While every effort has been made to ensure the accuracy and completeness of the data, information is sometimes unavailable or changes occur after publication deadlines. All usable information received in time for publication has been included. The omission of any particular item from a directory or **Profile** signifies either that the item is not applicable to the institution or program or that information was not available. **Profiles** of programs scheduled to begin during the 2010–11 academic year cannot, obviously, include statistics on enrollment or, in many cases, the number of faculty members. If no usable data were submitted by an institution, its name, address, and program name appear in order to indicate the availability of graduate work.

Criteria for Inclusion in This Guide

To be included in this guide, an institution must have full accreditation or be a candidate for accreditation (preaccreditation) status by an institutional or specialized accrediting body recognized by the U.S. Department of Education or the Council for Higher Education Accreditation (CHEA). Institutional accrediting bodies, which review each institution as a whole, include the six regional associations of schools and colleges (Middle States, New England, North Central, Northwest, Southern, and Western), each of which is responsible for a specified portion of the United States and its territories. Other institutional accrediting bodies are national in scope and accredit specific kinds of institutions (e.g., Bible colleges, independent colleges, and rabbinical and Talmudic schools). Program registration by the New York State Board of Regents is considered to be the equivalent of institutional accreditation, since the board requires that all programs offered by an institution meet its standards before recognition is granted. A Canadian institution must be chartered and authorized to grant degrees by the provincial government, affiliated with a chartered institution, or accredited by a recognized U.S. accrediting body. This guide also includes institutions outside the United States that are accredited by these U.S. accrediting bodies. There are recognized specialized or professional accrediting bodies in more than fifty different fields, each of which is authorized to accredit institutions or specific programs in its particular field. For specialized institutions that offer programs in one field only, we designate this to be the equivalent of institutional accreditation. A full explanation of the accrediting process and complete information on recognized institutional (regional and national) and specialized accrediting bodies can be found online at www.chea.org or at www.ed.gov/admins/finaid/accred/index.html.

DIRECTORY OF INSTITUTIONS WITH PROGRAMS IN ENGINEERING & APPLIED SCIENCES

ACADEMY OF ART UNIVERSITY

Game Design and Development	M

ACADIA UNIVERSITY

Computer Science	M

AIR FORCE INSTITUTE OF TECHNOLOGY

Aerospace/Aeronautical Engineering	M,D
Computer Engineering	M,D
Computer Science	M,D
Electrical Engineering	M,D
Engineering and Applied Sciences—General	M,D
Engineering Management	M
Engineering Physics	M,D
Environmental Engineering	M
Management of Technology	M,D
Materials Sciences	M,D
Nuclear Engineering	M,D
Operations Research	M,D
Systems Engineering	M,D

ALABAMA AGRICULTURAL AND MECHANICAL UNIVERSITY

Computer Science	M
Engineering and Applied Sciences—General	M
Materials Sciences	M,D

ALASKA PACIFIC UNIVERSITY

Telecommunications Management	M

ALCORN STATE UNIVERSITY

Computer Science	M
Information Science	M

ALFRED UNIVERSITY

Bioengineering	M,D
Ceramic Sciences and Engineering	M,D
Electrical Engineering	M,D
Engineering and Applied Sciences—General	M,D
Materials Sciences	M,D
Mechanical Engineering	M,D

ALLIANT INTERNATIONAL UNIVERSITY–SAN DIEGO

Management of Technology	M,D

AMERICAN INTERCONTINENTAL UNIVERSITY DUNWOODY CAMPUS

Information Science	M

AMERICAN INTERCONTINENTAL UNIVERSITY ONLINE

Computer and Information Systems Security	M
Information Science	M

AMERICAN INTERCONTINENTAL UNIVERSITY SOUTH FLORIDA

Computer and Information Systems Security	M
Information Science	M

AMERICAN PUBLIC UNIVERSITY SYSTEM

Fire Protection Engineering	M

AMERICAN SENTINEL UNIVERSITY

Computer Science	M
Health Informatics	M

AMERICAN UNIVERSITY

Applied Science and Technology	M
Computer Science	M,O

THE AMERICAN UNIVERSITY IN CAIRO

Biotechnology	M
Computer Science	M
Construction Engineering	M

THE AMERICAN UNIVERSITY IN DUBAI

Construction Management	M

THE AMERICAN UNIVERSITY OF ATHENS

Computer Science	M
Engineering and Applied Sciences—General	M
Systems Engineering	M
Telecommunications	M

AMERICAN UNIVERSITY OF BEIRUT

Civil Engineering	M,D
Computer Engineering	M,D
Computer Science	M
Electrical Engineering	M,D
Engineering and Applied Sciences—General	M,D
Engineering Management	M,D
Mechanical Engineering	M,D
Water Resources Engineering	M,D

AMERICAN UNIVERSITY OF SHARJAH

Chemical Engineering	M
Civil Engineering	M
Computer Engineering	M
Electrical Engineering	M
Mechanical Engineering	M

ANDREWS UNIVERSITY

Engineering and Applied Sciences—General	M
Software Engineering	M

ANNA MARIA COLLEGE

Fire Protection Engineering	M

APPALACHIAN STATE UNIVERSITY

Computer Science	M
Engineering Physics	M

ARIZONA STATE UNIVERSITY

Aerospace/Aeronautical Engineering	M,D
Bioengineering	M,D
Bioinformatics	M,D
Biotechnology	P,M
Chemical Engineering	M,D
Civil Engineering	M,D
Computer Engineering	M
Computer Science	M,D
Construction Engineering	M
Construction Management	M
Electrical Engineering	M,D
Engineering and Applied Sciences—General	M,D
Environmental Engineering	M,D
Geological Engineering	M,D
Industrial/Management Engineering	M,D
Information Science	M
Manufacturing Engineering	M,D
Materials Engineering	M,D
Materials Sciences	M,D
Mechanical Engineering	M,D
Medical Informatics	M,D
Nanotechnology	M,D
Reliability Engineering	M
Software Engineering	M
Systems Engineering	M
Systems Science	M

ARKANSAS STATE UNIVERSITY— JONESBORO

Computer Science	M
Engineering and Applied Sciences—General	M

ARKANSAS TECH UNIVERSITY

Engineering and Applied Sciences—General	M
Health Informatics	M
Information Science	M

ARMSTRONG ATLANTIC STATE UNIVERSITY

Computer Science	M

ASPEN UNIVERSITY

Information Science	M,O

ATHABASCA UNIVERSITY

Information Science	M
Management of Technology	M,O

AUBURN UNIVERSITY

Aerospace/Aeronautical Engineering	M,D
Chemical Engineering	M,D
Civil Engineering	M,D
Computer Engineering	M,D
Computer Science	M,D
Construction Engineering	M,D
Construction Management	M
Electrical Engineering	M,D
Engineering and Applied Sciences—General	M,D
Environmental Engineering	M,D
Geotechnical Engineering	M,D
Hydraulics	M,D
Industrial/Management Engineering	M,D
Materials Engineering	M,D
Mechanical Engineering	M,D
Software Engineering	M,D
Structural Engineering	M,D
Systems Engineering	M,D
Textile Sciences and Engineering	D
Transportation and Highway Engineering	M,D

BALL STATE UNIVERSITY

Computer Science	M
Information Science	M
Telecommunications	M

BARRY UNIVERSITY

Health Informatics	O
Information Science	M

BAYLOR COLLEGE OF MEDICINE

Bioengineering	D
Biomedical Engineering	D

BAYLOR UNIVERSITY

Biomedical Engineering	M
Computer Engineering	M
Computer Science	M
Electrical Engineering	M
Engineering and Applied Sciences—General	M
Mechanical Engineering	M

BELLEVUE UNIVERSITY

Information Science	M

BENEDICTINE UNIVERSITY

Computer and Information Systems Security	M
Health Informatics	M

BENTLEY UNIVERSITY

Ergonomics and Human Factors	M
Information Science	M

BOISE STATE UNIVERSITY

Civil Engineering	M
Computer Engineering	M,D
Computer Science	M
Electrical Engineering	M,D
Engineering and Applied Sciences—General	M,D
Materials Engineering	M
Mechanical Engineering	M

BOSTON UNIVERSITY

Bioinformatics	M,D
Biomedical Engineering	M,D
Computer Engineering	M,D
Computer Science	M,D
Electrical Engineering	M,D
Engineering and Applied Sciences—General	M,D
Management of Technology	M
Materials Engineering	M,D
Materials Sciences	M,D
Mechanical Engineering	M,D
Systems Engineering	M,D
Telecommunications	M

BOWIE STATE UNIVERSITY

Computer Science	M,D

BOWLING GREEN STATE UNIVERSITY

Computer Science	M
Construction Management	M
Manufacturing Engineering	M
Operations Research	M
Software Engineering	M

BRADLEY UNIVERSITY

Civil Engineering	M

Computer Science	M
Construction Engineering	M
Electrical Engineering	M
Engineering and Applied Sciences—General	M
Industrial/Management Engineering	M
Information Science	M
Manufacturing Engineering	M
Mechanical Engineering	M

BRANDEIS UNIVERSITY

Bioinformatics	M,O
Biotechnology	M
Computer and Information Systems Security	M,O
Computer Science	M,D,O
Software Engineering	M,O

BRIDGEWATER STATE UNIVERSITY

Computer Science	M

BRIGHAM YOUNG UNIVERSITY

Biotechnology	M,D
Chemical Engineering	M,D
Civil Engineering	M,D
Computer Engineering	M,D
Computer Science	M,D
Construction Management	M
Electrical Engineering	M,D
Engineering and Applied Sciences—General	M,D
Information Science	M
Mechanical Engineering	M,D

BROCK UNIVERSITY

Biotechnology	M,D
Computer Science	M

BROOKLYN COLLEGE OF THE CITY UNIVERSITY OF NEW YORK

Computer Science	M,D,O
Information Science	M,D,O

BROWN UNIVERSITY

Biomedical Engineering	M,D
Biotechnology	M,D
Chemical Engineering	M,D
Computer Engineering	M,D
Computer Science	M,D
Electrical Engineering	M,D
Engineering and Applied Sciences—General	M,D
Materials Sciences	M,D
Mechanical Engineering	M,D
Mechanics	M,D

BUCKNELL UNIVERSITY

Chemical Engineering	M
Civil Engineering	M
Electrical Engineering	M
Engineering and Applied Sciences—General	M
Mechanical Engineering	M

BUFFALO STATE COLLEGE, STATE UNIVERSITY OF NEW YORK

Industrial/Management Engineering	M

CALIFORNIA INSTITUTE OF TECHNOLOGY

Aerospace/Aeronautical Engineering	M,D,O
Bioengineering	M,D
Chemical Engineering	M,D

Civil Engineering	M,D,O
Computer Science	M,D
Electrical Engineering	M,D,O
Engineering and Applied Sciences—General	M,D,O
Environmental Engineering	M,D
Materials Sciences	M,D
Mechanical Engineering	M,D,O
Mechanics	M,D
Systems Engineering	M,D

CALIFORNIA LUTHERAN UNIVERSITY

Management of Technology	M,O

CALIFORNIA NATIONAL UNIVERSITY FOR ADVANCED STUDIES

Engineering and Applied Sciences—General	M
Engineering Management	M

CALIFORNIA POLYTECHNIC STATE UNIVERSITY, SAN LUIS OBISPO

Aerospace/Aeronautical Engineering	M
Civil Engineering	M
Computer Science	M
Electrical Engineering	M
Engineering and Applied Sciences—General	M
Environmental Engineering	M
Industrial/Management Engineering	M
Mechanical Engineering	M
Polymer Science and Engineering	M

CALIFORNIA STATE POLYTECHNIC UNIVERSITY, POMONA

Civil Engineering	M
Computer Science	M
Electrical Engineering	M
Engineering and Applied Sciences—General	M
Engineering Management	M
Mechanical Engineering	M

CALIFORNIA STATE UNIVERSITY CHANNEL ISLANDS

Bioinformatics	M
Biotechnology	M
Computer Science	M

CALIFORNIA STATE UNIVERSITY, CHICO

Computer Engineering	M
Computer Science	M
Electrical Engineering	M
Engineering and Applied Sciences—General	M

CALIFORNIA STATE UNIVERSITY, DOMINGUEZ HILLS

Bioinformatics	M
Computer Science	M

CALIFORNIA STATE UNIVERSITY, EAST BAY

Computer Science	M
Construction Management	M
Engineering and Applied Sciences—General	M

Engineering Management	M
Operations Research	M

CALIFORNIA STATE UNIVERSITY, FRESNO

Civil Engineering	M
Computer Science	M
Electrical Engineering	M
Engineering and Applied Sciences—General	M
Industrial/Management Engineering	M
Mechanical Engineering	M

CALIFORNIA STATE UNIVERSITY, FULLERTON

Civil Engineering	M
Computer Science	M
Electrical Engineering	M
Engineering and Applied Sciences—General	M
Information Science	M
Mechanical Engineering	M
Mechanics	M
Software Engineering	M
Systems Engineering	M

CALIFORNIA STATE UNIVERSITY, LONG BEACH

Aerospace/Aeronautical Engineering	M
Chemical Engineering	M
Civil Engineering	M
Computer Engineering	M
Computer Science	M
Electrical Engineering	M
Engineering Management	M,D
Ergonomics and Human Factors	M
Mechanical Engineering	M,D

CALIFORNIA STATE UNIVERSITY, LOS ANGELES

Civil Engineering	M
Computer Science	M
Electrical Engineering	M
Engineering and Applied Sciences—General	M
Management of Technology	M
Mechanical Engineering	M

CALIFORNIA STATE UNIVERSITY, NORTHRIDGE

Artificial Intelligence/Robotics	M
Civil Engineering	M
Computer Science	M
Electrical Engineering	M
Engineering and Applied Sciences—General	M
Engineering Management	M
Ergonomics and Human Factors	M
Industrial/Management Engineering	M
Manufacturing Engineering	M
Materials Engineering	M
Mechanical Engineering	M
Software Engineering	M
Structural Engineering	M
Systems Engineering	M

CALIFORNIA STATE UNIVERSITY, SACRAMENTO

Civil Engineering	M
Computer Science	M
Electrical Engineering	M

Engineering and Applied Sciences—General	M
Mechanical Engineering	M
Software Engineering	M

CALIFORNIA STATE UNIVERSITY, SAN BERNARDINO

Computer Science	M

CALIFORNIA STATE UNIVERSITY, SAN MARCOS

Computer Science	M

CAMBRIDGE COLLEGE

Management of Technology	M
Medical Informatics	M

CAPELLA UNIVERSITY

Computer and Information Systems Security	M,D,O
Management of Technology	M,D,O

CAPITOL COLLEGE

Computer and Information Systems Security	M
Computer Science	M
Electrical Engineering	M
Information Science	M
Telecommunications Management	M

CARLETON UNIVERSITY

Aerospace/Aeronautical Engineering	M,D
Biomedical Engineering	M
Civil Engineering	M,D
Computer Science	M,D
Electrical Engineering	M,D
Engineering and Applied Sciences—General	M,D
Environmental Engineering	M,D
Information Science	M,D
Management of Technology	M
Materials Engineering	M,D
Mechanical Engineering	M,D
Systems Engineering	M,D
Systems Science	M,D

CARNEGIE MELLON UNIVERSITY

Architectural Engineering	M,D
Artificial Intelligence/Robotics	M,D
Bioengineering	M,D
Biomedical Engineering	M,D
Biotechnology	M,D
Chemical Engineering	M,D
Civil Engineering	M,D
Computer and Information Systems Security	M
Computer Engineering	M,D*
Computer Science	M,D*
Construction Management	M,D
Electrical Engineering	M,D
Environmental Engineering	M,D
Human-Computer Interaction	M,D
Information Science	M,D
Management of Technology	M,D
Materials Engineering	M,D
Materials Sciences	M,D
Mechanical Engineering	M,D
Mechanics	M,D
Operations Research	D

Polymer Science and Engineering	M,D
Software Engineering	M,D
Systems Engineering	M
Technology and Public Policy	M,D*
Telecommunications Management	M

CARROLL UNIVERSITY

Software Engineering	M

CASE WESTERN RESERVE UNIVERSITY

Aerospace/Aeronautical Engineering	M,D
Biomedical Engineering	M,D*
Chemical Engineering	M,D
Civil Engineering	M,D
Computer Engineering	M,D
Computer Science	M,D
Electrical Engineering	M,D
Engineering and Applied Sciences—General	M,D
Engineering Management	M
Information Science	M,D
Materials Engineering	M,D
Materials Sciences	M,D
Mechanical Engineering	M,D
Operations Research	M
Polymer Science and Engineering	M,D
Systems Engineering	M,D

THE CATHOLIC UNIVERSITY OF AMERICA

Bioinformatics	M,D
Biomedical Engineering	M,D
Civil Engineering	M,D,O
Computer and Information Systems Security	M,D
Computer Science	M,D
Construction Management	M,D,O
Electrical Engineering	M,D
Engineering and Applied Sciences—General	M,D,O
Engineering Management	M,O
Environmental Engineering	M,D,O
Ergonomics and Human Factors	M,D
Geotechnical Engineering	M,D,O
Mechanical Engineering	M,D
Mechanics	M,D,O
Structural Engineering	M,D,O
Systems Engineering	M,D,O
Telecommunications	M,D

CENTRAL CONNECTICUT STATE UNIVERSITY

Computer Science	M,O
Construction Management	M,O
Engineering and Applied Sciences—General	M,O
Management of Technology	M,O

CENTRAL MICHIGAN UNIVERSITY

Automotive Engineering	M,O
Computer Science	M
Engineering and Applied Sciences—General	M
Materials Sciences	D

CENTRAL WASHINGTON UNIVERSITY

Engineering and Applied Sciences—General	M

Industrial/Management Engineering	M

CHAMPLAIN COLLEGE

Management of Technology	M

CHICAGO STATE UNIVERSITY

Computer Science	M

CHRISTIAN BROTHERS UNIVERSITY

Engineering and Applied Sciences—General	M

CHRISTOPHER NEWPORT UNIVERSITY

Computer Science	M

THE CITADEL, THE MILITARY COLLEGE OF SOUTH CAROLINA

Computer Science	M
Information Science	M

CITY COLLEGE OF THE CITY UNIVERSITY OF NEW YORK

Biomedical Engineering	M,D
Chemical Engineering	M,D
Civil Engineering	M,D
Computer Science	M,D
Electrical Engineering	M,D
Engineering and Applied Sciences—General	M,D*
Mechanical Engineering	M,D

CITY UNIVERSITY OF SEATTLE

Computer and Information Systems Security	M,O
Management of Technology	M,O

CLAFLIN UNIVERSITY

Biotechnology	M

CLAREMONT GRADUATE UNIVERSITY

Financial Engineering	M*
Health Informatics	M,D,O
Information Science	M,D,O
Operations Research	M,D
Systems Science	M,D,O
Telecommunications	M,D,O

CLARK ATLANTA UNIVERSITY

Computer Science	M
Information Science	M

CLARKSON UNIVERSITY

Chemical Engineering	M,D
Civil Engineering	M
Computer Engineering	M,D
Computer Science	M
Electrical Engineering	M,D
Engineering and Applied Sciences—General	M,D*
Engineering Management	M
Environmental Engineering	M,D
Information Science	M*
Mechanical Engineering	M,D

CLARK UNIVERSITY

Information Science	M

CLEMSON UNIVERSITY

Automotive Engineering	M,D
Bioengineering	M,D
Biosystems Engineering	M,D
Chemical Engineering	M,D
Civil Engineering	M,D
Computer Engineering	M,D
Computer Science	M,D
Construction Management	M
Electrical Engineering	M,D
Engineering and Applied Sciences—General	M,D
Environmental Engineering	M,D
Ergonomics and Human Factors	D
Industrial/Management Engineering	M,D
Manufacturing Engineering	M
Materials Engineering	M,D
Materials Sciences	M,D
Mechanical Engineering	M,D
Operations Research	M,D

CLEVELAND STATE UNIVERSITY

Biomedical Engineering	D
Chemical Engineering	M,D
Civil Engineering	M,D
Computer Science	M,D
Electrical Engineering	M,D
Engineering and Applied Sciences—General	M,D
Environmental Engineering	M,D
Industrial/Management Engineering	M,D
Information Science	M,D
Mechanical Engineering	M,D
Software Engineering	M,D

COLEMAN UNIVERSITY

Information Science	M
Management of Technology	M

COLLEGE OF CHARLESTON

Computer Science	M

THE COLLEGE OF SAINT ROSE

Computer Science	M
Information Science	M

THE COLLEGE OF ST. SCHOLASTICA

Health Informatics	M,O

COLLEGE OF STATEN ISLAND OF THE CITY UNIVERSITY OF NEW YORK

Computer Science	M

THE COLLEGE OF WILLIAM AND MARY

Applied Science and Technology	M,D
Computer Science	M,D
Operations Research	M

COLORADO SCHOOL OF MINES

Chemical Engineering	M,D
Computer Science	M,D
Electronic Materials	M,D
Engineering and Applied Sciences—General	M,D,O
Engineering Management	M,D

Environmental Engineering	M,D
Geological Engineering	M,D
Management of Technology	M,D
Materials Engineering	M,D
Materials Sciences	M,D
Metallurgical Engineering and Metallurgy	M,D
Mineral/Mining Engineering	M,D
Nuclear Engineering	M,D
Petroleum Engineering	M,D
Systems Engineering	M,D

COLORADO STATE UNIVERSITY

Biomedical Engineering	M,D
Chemical Engineering	M,D
Civil Engineering	M,D
Computer Science	M,D
Construction Management	M
Electrical Engineering	M,D
Engineering and Applied Sciences—General	M,D
Mechanical Engineering	M,D

COLORADO STATE UNIVERSITY– PUEBLO

Applied Science and Technology	M
Engineering and Applied Sciences—General	M
Industrial/Management Engineering	M
Systems Engineering	M

COLORADO TECHNICAL UNIVERSITY COLORADO SPRINGS

Computer and Information Systems Security	M,D
Computer Engineering	M
Computer Science	M,D
Database Systems	M,D
Electrical Engineering	M
Management of Technology	M,D
Software Engineering	M,D
Systems Engineering	M

COLORADO TECHNICAL UNIVERSITY DENVER

Computer and Information Systems Security	M
Computer Engineering	M
Computer Science	M
Database Systems	M
Electrical Engineering	M
Management of Technology	M
Software Engineering	M
Systems Engineering	M

COLORADO TECHNICAL UNIVERSITY SIOUX FALLS

Computer and Information Systems Security	M
Computer Science	M
Management of Technology	M
Software Engineering	M

COLUMBIA UNIVERSITY

Biomedical Engineering	M,D
Chemical Engineering	M,D
Civil Engineering	M,D,O
Computer Engineering	M,D,O
Computer Science	M,D,O*
Construction Engineering	M,D,O

M—master's degree; P—first professional degree; D—doctorate; O—other advanced degree; *—Close-Up and / or Display

Construction Management	M,D,O
Electrical Engineering	M,D,O*
Engineering and Applied Sciences—General	M,D,O
Engineering Management	M,D,O
Environmental Engineering	M,D,O
Financial Engineering	M,D,O
Industrial/Management Engineering	M,D,O
Management of Technology	M
Materials Engineering	M,D,O
Materials Sciences	M,D,O
Mechanical Engineering	M,D,O
Mechanics	M,D,O
Medical Informatics	M,D,O
Metallurgical Engineering and Metallurgy	M,D,O
Mineral/Mining Engineering	M,D,O
Operations Research	M,D,O

COLUMBUS STATE UNIVERSITY

Computer Science	M

CONCORDIA UNIVERSITY (CANADA)

Aerospace/Aeronautical Engineering	M
Biotechnology	M,D,O
Civil Engineering	M,D,O
Computer and Information Systems Security	M,O
Computer Engineering	M,D
Computer Science	M,D,O
Construction Engineering	M,D,O
Electrical Engineering	M,D
Engineering and Applied Sciences—General	M,D,O
Environmental Engineering	M,D,O
Game Design and Development	M,O
Industrial/Management Engineering	M,D,O
Mechanical Engineering	M,D,O
Software Engineering	M,D,O
Systems Engineering	M,O
Telecommunications Management	M,O

COOPER UNION FOR THE ADVANCEMENT OF SCIENCE AND ART

Chemical Engineering	M
Civil Engineering	M
Electrical Engineering	M
Engineering and Applied Sciences—General	M
Mechanical Engineering	M

CORNELL UNIVERSITY

Aerospace/Aeronautical Engineering	M,D
Agricultural Engineering	M,D
Artificial Intelligence/ Robotics	M,D
Biochemical Engineering	M,D
Bioengineering	M,D
Biomedical Engineering	M,D
Chemical Engineering	M,D
Civil Engineering	M,D
Computer Engineering	M,D
Computer Science	M,D
Electrical Engineering	M,D
Engineering and Applied Sciences—General	M,D
Engineering Management	M,D
Engineering Physics	M,D

Environmental Engineering	M,D
Ergonomics and Human Factors	M
Geotechnical Engineering	M,D
Human-Computer Interaction	D
Industrial/Management Engineering	M,D
Information Science	D
Manufacturing Engineering	M,D
Materials Engineering	M,D
Materials Sciences	M,D
Mechanical Engineering	M,D
Mechanics	M,D
Operations Research	M,D
Polymer Science and Engineering	M,D
Structural Engineering	M,D
Systems Engineering	M
Textile Sciences and Engineering	M,D
Transportation and Highway Engineering	M,D
Water Resources Engineering	M,D

DAKOTA STATE UNIVERSITY

Information Science	M,D*

DALHOUSIE UNIVERSITY

Agricultural Engineering	M,D
Bioengineering	M,D
Bioinformatics	M,D
Biomedical Engineering	M,D
Chemical Engineering	M,D
Civil Engineering	M,D
Computer Engineering	M,D
Computer Science	M,D
Electrical Engineering	M,D
Engineering and Applied Sciences—General	M,D
Environmental Engineering	M,D
Human-Computer Interaction	M
Industrial/Management Engineering	M,D
Materials Engineering	M,D
Mechanical Engineering	M,D
Medical Informatics	M,D
Mineral/Mining Engineering	M,D

DALLAS BAPTIST UNIVERSITY

Engineering Management	M
Management of Technology	M

DARTMOUTH COLLEGE

Biochemical Engineering	M,D
Biomedical Engineering	M,D
Biotechnology	M,D
Computer Engineering	M,D
Computer Science	M,D
Electrical Engineering	M,D
Engineering and Applied Sciences—General	M,D
Engineering Management	M
Engineering Physics	M,D
Environmental Engineering	M,D
Manufacturing Engineering	M,D
Materials Engineering	M,D
Materials Sciences	M,D
Mechanical Engineering	M,D

DAVENPORT UNIVERSITY

Computer and Information Systems Security	M

DAVENPORT UNIVERSITY

Computer and Information Systems Security	M

DAVENPORT UNIVERSITY

Computer and Information Systems Security	M

DEPAUL UNIVERSITY

Computer and Information Systems Security	M,D
Computer Science	M,D
Game Design and Development	M,D
Human-Computer Interaction	M,D
Information Science	M,D
Management of Technology	M,D
Polymer Science and Engineering	M
Software Engineering	M,D
Telecommunications	M,D

DESALES UNIVERSITY

Information Science	M

DIGIPEN INSTITUTE OF TECHNOLOGY

Computer Science	M

DREXEL UNIVERSITY

Architectural Engineering	M,D
Biochemical Engineering	M
Biomedical Engineering	M,D
Chemical Engineering	M,D
Civil Engineering	M,D
Computer Engineering	M
Computer Science	M,D
Construction Management	M
Electrical Engineering	M*
Engineering and Applied Sciences—General	M,D,O
Engineering Management	M,O
Environmental Engineering	M,D
Geotechnical Engineering	M,D
Hydraulics	M,D
Information Science	M,D
Materials Engineering	M,D
Mechanical Engineering	M,D
Mechanics	M,D
Medical Informatics	M,D,O
Software Engineering	M,D,O
Structural Engineering	M,D
Telecommunications	M

DUKE UNIVERSITY

Bioinformatics	D
Biomedical Engineering	M,D
Civil Engineering	M,D
Computer Engineering	M,D
Computer Science	M,D
Electrical Engineering	M,D*
Engineering and Applied Sciences—General	M,D
Engineering Management	M
Environmental Engineering	M,D
Materials Sciences	M,D
Mechanical Engineering	M,D

DUQUESNE UNIVERSITY

Biotechnology	M

EAST CAROLINA UNIVERSITY

Biotechnology	M
Computer Science	M,D,O

Industrial/Management Engineering	M,D,O
Information Science	M
Management of Technology	M,D,O
Manufacturing Engineering	M,D,O

EASTERN ILLINOIS UNIVERSITY

Computer and Information Systems Security	M,O
Computer Science	M,O
Engineering and Applied Sciences—General	M,O
Systems Science	M,O

EASTERN KENTUCKY UNIVERSITY

Industrial/Management Engineering	M
Manufacturing Engineering	M

EASTERN MICHIGAN UNIVERSITY

Artificial Intelligence/ Robotics	M,O
Bioinformatics	M,O
Computer and Information Systems Security	M,O
Computer Science	M,O
Construction Management	M
Engineering and Applied Sciences—General	M
Engineering Management	M
Management of Technology	D
Polymer Science and Engineering	M
Technology and Public Policy	M

EASTERN WASHINGTON UNIVERSITY

Computer Science	M

EAST STROUDSBURG UNIVERSITY OF PENNSYLVANIA

Computer Science	M

EAST TENNESSEE STATE UNIVERSITY

Computer Science	M
Information Science	M
Manufacturing Engineering	M
Software Engineering	M

ÉCOLE POLYTECHNIQUE DE MONTRÉAL

Aerospace/Aeronautical Engineering	M,D,O
Biomedical Engineering	M,D,O
Chemical Engineering	M,D,O
Civil Engineering	M,D,O
Computer Engineering	M,D,O
Computer Science	M,D,O
Electrical Engineering	M,D,O
Engineering and Applied Sciences—General	M,D,O
Engineering Physics	M,D,O
Environmental Engineering	M,D,O
Geotechnical Engineering	M,D,O
Hydraulics	M,D,O
Industrial/Management Engineering	M,D,O
Management of Technology	M,D,O
Mechanical Engineering	M,D,O
Mechanics	M,D,O
Nuclear Engineering	M,D,O
Operations Research	M,D,O
Structural Engineering	M,D,O

Transportation and Highway Engineering	M,D,O

ELMHURST COLLEGE

Computer Science	M

EMBRY-RIDDLE AERONAUTICAL UNIVERSITY (AZ)

Safety Engineering	M

EMBRY-RIDDLE AERONAUTICAL UNIVERSITY (FL)

Aerospace/Aeronautical Engineering	M
Ergonomics and Human Factors	M
Mechanical Engineering	M
Software Engineering	M
Systems Engineering	M

EMBRY-RIDDLE AERONAUTICAL UNIVERSITY WORLDWIDE

Aerospace/Aeronautical Engineering	M
Management of Technology	M,O

EMORY UNIVERSITY

Biomedical Engineering	D
Computer Science	M,D
Health Informatics	M,D

EVERGLADES UNIVERSITY

Aviation	M
Information Science	M

EXCELSIOR COLLEGE

Medical Informatics	O

FAIRFIELD UNIVERSITY

Computer Engineering	M
Electrical Engineering	M
Engineering and Applied Sciences—General	M
Management of Technology	M
Mechanical Engineering	M
Software Engineering	M

FAIRLEIGH DICKINSON UNIVERSITY, COLLEGE AT FLORHAM

Chemical Engineering	M,O
Management of Technology	M,O

FAIRLEIGH DICKINSON UNIVERSITY, METROPOLITAN CAMPUS

Computer Engineering	M
Computer Science	M
Electrical Engineering	M
Engineering and Applied Sciences—General	M
Systems Science	M

FERRIS STATE UNIVERSITY

Computer Science	M
Database Systems	M

FITCHBURG STATE UNIVERSITY

Computer Science	M

FLORIDA AGRICULTURAL AND MECHANICAL UNIVERSITY

Biomedical Engineering	M,D
Chemical Engineering	M,D
Civil Engineering	M,D
Electrical Engineering	M,D
Engineering and Applied Sciences—General	M,D
Environmental Engineering	M,D
Industrial/Management Engineering	M,D
Mechanical Engineering	M,D
Software Engineering	M

FLORIDA ATLANTIC UNIVERSITY

Civil Engineering	M
Computer Engineering	M,D
Computer Science	M,D
Electrical Engineering	M,D
Engineering and Applied Sciences—General	M,D
Mechanical Engineering	M,D
Ocean Engineering	M,D

FLORIDA GULF COAST UNIVERSITY

Computer Science	M
Information Science	M

FLORIDA INSTITUTE OF TECHNOLOGY

Aerospace/Aeronautical Engineering	M,D*
Aviation	M
Biotechnology	M,D
Chemical Engineering	M,D
Civil Engineering	M,D*
Computer Engineering	M,D
Computer Science	M,D*
Electrical Engineering	M,D*
Engineering and Applied Sciences—General	M,D
Engineering Management	M*
Ergonomics and Human Factors	M
Management of Technology	M
Mechanical Engineering	M,D*
Ocean Engineering	M,D*
Operations Research	M,D
Software Engineering	M,D
Systems Engineering	M

FLORIDA INTERNATIONAL UNIVERSITY

Biomedical Engineering	M,D
Civil Engineering	M,D
Computer Engineering	M
Computer Science	M,D
Construction Management	M
Electrical Engineering	M,D
Engineering and Applied Sciences—General	M,D
Environmental Engineering	M
Information Science	M,D
Materials Engineering	M,D
Mechanical Engineering	M,D
Telecommunications	M,D

FLORIDA STATE UNIVERSITY

Biomedical Engineering	M,D

Chemical Engineering	M,D
Civil Engineering	M,D
Computer and Information Systems Security	M,D
Computer Science	M,D
Electrical Engineering	M,D
Engineering and Applied Sciences—General	M,D
Environmental Engineering	M,D
Industrial/Management Engineering	M,D
Manufacturing Engineering	M,D
Materials Sciences	M,D
Mechanical Engineering	M,D
Polymer Science and Engineering	M
Software Engineering	M,D

FORDHAM UNIVERSITY

Computer Science	M

FRANKLIN PIERCE UNIVERSITY

Telecommunications	M,D,O

FRANKLIN UNIVERSITY

Computer Science	M

FROSTBURG STATE UNIVERSITY

Computer Science	M

FULL SAIL UNIVERSITY

Game Design and Development	M

GANNON UNIVERSITY

Computer Science	M
Electrical Engineering	M
Engineering Management	M
Environmental Engineering	M
Information Science	M
Mechanical Engineering	M
Software Engineering	M

GEORGE MASON UNIVERSITY

Bioinformatics	M,D,O
Civil Engineering	M,D,O
Computer and Information Systems Security	M,D,O
Computer Engineering	M,D,O
Computer Science	M,D,O
Database Systems	M,D,O
Electrical Engineering	M,D,O
Engineering and Applied Sciences—General	M,D,O
Engineering Physics	M
Game Design and Development	M,D,O
Health Informatics	M,O
Information Science	M,D,O
Management of Technology	M,D
Nanotechnology	M,D,O
Operations Research	M,D,O
Software Engineering	M,D,O
Systems Engineering	M,D,O
Telecommunications Management	M,D,O
Telecommunications	M,D,O
Water Resources Engineering	M,D,O

GEORGETOWN UNIVERSITY

Bioinformatics	M
Computer Science	M
Materials Sciences	D

THE GEORGE WASHINGTON UNIVERSITY

Aerospace/Aeronautical Engineering	M,D,O
Bioinformatics	M
Biotechnology	M
Civil Engineering	M,D,O
Computer Engineering	M,D
Computer Science	M,D
Electrical Engineering	M,D
Engineering and Applied Sciences—General	M,D,O*
Engineering Management	M,D,O
Environmental Engineering	M,D,O
Management of Technology	M,D
Materials Sciences	M,D
Mechanical Engineering	M,D,O
Systems Engineering	M,D,O
Technology and Public Policy	M
Telecommunications	M,D

GEORGIA INSTITUTE OF TECHNOLOGY

Aerospace/Aeronautical Engineering	M,D
Bioengineering	M,D
Bioinformatics	M,D
Biomedical Engineering	D
Chemical Engineering	M,D
Civil Engineering	M,D
Computer and Information Systems Security	M,D
Computer Engineering	M,D
Computer Science	M,D
Electrical Engineering	M,D
Engineering and Applied Sciences—General	M,D
Environmental Engineering	M,D
Ergonomics and Human Factors	M,D
Human-Computer Interaction	M
Industrial/Management Engineering	M,D
Management of Technology	M,O
Materials Engineering	M,D
Mechanical Engineering	M,D
Mechanics	M,D
Nuclear Engineering	M,D
Operations Research	M,D
Polymer Science and Engineering	M,D
Systems Engineering	M,D
Textile Sciences and Engineering	M,D

GEORGIA SOUTHERN UNIVERSITY

Electrical Engineering	M
Mechanical Engineering	M

GEORGIA SOUTHWESTERN STATE UNIVERSITY

Computer Science	M
Information Science	M

---

*M—master's degree; P—first professional degree; D—doctorate; O—other advanced degree; *—Close-Up and/or Display*

GEORGIA STATE UNIVERSITY

Computer Science	M,D
Information Science	M
Operations Research	M,D

GOLDEN GATE UNIVERSITY

Management of Technology	M,D,O

GOVERNORS STATE UNIVERSITY

Computer Science	M

GRADUATE SCHOOL AND UNIVERSITY CENTER OF THE CITY UNIVERSITY OF NEW YORK

Biomedical Engineering	D
Chemical Engineering	D
Civil Engineering	D
Computer Science	D
Electrical Engineering	D
Engineering and Applied Sciences—General	D*
Mechanical Engineering	D

GRAND VALLEY STATE UNIVERSITY

Bioinformatics	M
Computer Engineering	M
Computer Science	M
Electrical Engineering	M
Engineering and Applied Sciences—General	M
Information Science	M
Manufacturing Engineering	M
Mechanical Engineering	M
Medical Informatics	M
Software Engineering	M

HAMPTON UNIVERSITY

Computer Science	M

HARDING UNIVERSITY

Management of Technology	M

HARRISBURG UNIVERSITY OF SCIENCE AND TECHNOLOGY

Construction Management	M
Management of Technology	M
Systems Engineering	M

HARVARD UNIVERSITY

Applied Science and Technology	M,O
Biomedical Engineering	M,D
Biotechnology	M,O
Computer Science	M,D
Engineering and Applied Sciences—General	M,D
Information Science	M,D,O
Management of Technology	D
Medical Informatics	M

HAWAI'I PACIFIC UNIVERSITY

Software Engineering	M
Telecommunications Management	M

HEC MONTREAL

Financial Engineering	M
Operations Research	M

HODGES UNIVERSITY

Management of Technology	M

HOFSTRA UNIVERSITY

Computer Science	M

HOLY NAMES UNIVERSITY

Energy Management and Policy	M

HOOD COLLEGE

Biotechnology	M,O
Computer Science	M
Information Science	M
Systems Science	M

HOWARD UNIVERSITY

Biotechnology	M,D
Chemical Engineering	M
Civil Engineering	M
Computer Science	M
Electrical Engineering	M,D
Engineering and Applied Sciences—General	M,D
Mechanical Engineering	M,D

HUMBOLDT STATE UNIVERSITY

Hazardous Materials Management	M

IDAHO STATE UNIVERSITY

Civil Engineering	M
Engineering and Applied Sciences—General	M,D,O
Environmental Engineering	M
Hazardous Materials Management	M
Management of Technology	M
Mechanical Engineering	M
Nuclear Engineering	M,D,O
Operations Research	M

ILLINOIS INSTITUTE OF TECHNOLOGY

Aerospace/Aeronautical Engineering	M,D
Agricultural Engineering	M,D
Architectural Engineering	M,D
Bioengineering	M,D
Biomedical Engineering	D
Chemical Engineering	M,D
Civil Engineering	M,D
Computer Engineering	M,D
Computer Science	M,D
Construction Engineering	M,D
Electrical Engineering	M,D
Engineering and Applied Sciences—General	M,D
Environmental Engineering	M,D
Geotechnical Engineering	M,D
Manufacturing Engineering	M,D
Materials Engineering	M,D
Materials Sciences	M,D
Mechanical Engineering	M,D
Software Engineering	M,D
Structural Engineering	M,D
Telecommunications	M,D
Transportation and Highway Engineering	M,D

ILLINOIS STATE UNIVERSITY

Biotechnology	M
Industrial/Management Engineering	M

Management of Technology	M

INDIANA STATE UNIVERSITY

Computer Engineering	M
Computer Science	M
Engineering and Applied Sciences—General	M
Industrial/Management Engineering	M
Management of Technology	D

INDIANA UNIVERSITY BLOOMINGTON

Bioinformatics	M,D
Biotechnology	M,D
Computer Science	M,D
Ergonomics and Human Factors	M,D
Health Informatics	M,D
Human-Computer Interaction	M,D
Information Science	M,D,O
Safety Engineering	M,D
Telecommunications	M

INDIANA UNIVERSITY–PURDUE UNIVERSITY FORT WAYNE

Computer Engineering	M
Computer Science	M
Construction Management	M
Electrical Engineering	M
Engineering and Applied Sciences—General	M,O
Industrial/Management Engineering	M
Information Science	M
Mechanical Engineering	M
Operations Research	M,O
Systems Engineering	M

INDIANA UNIVERSITY–PURDUE UNIVERSITY INDIANAPOLIS

Artificial Intelligence/Robotics	M,D
Biomedical Engineering	M,D,O
Computer Engineering	M,D
Computer Science	M,D
Electrical Engineering	M,D
Information Science	M,D
Mechanical Engineering	M,D,O

INDIANA UNIVERSITY SOUTH BEND

Computer Science	M

INSTITUTO TECNOLOGICO DE SANTO DOMINGO

Construction Management	M
Engineering and Applied Sciences—General	M
Environmental Engineering	M
Industrial/Management Engineering	M
Structural Engineering	M
Telecommunications	M

INSTITUTO TECNOLÓGICO Y DE ESTUDIOS SUPERIORES DE MONTERREY, CAMPUS CENTRAL DE VERACRUZ

Computer Science	M
Management of Technology	M

INSTITUTO TECNOLÓGICO Y DE ESTUDIOS SUPERIORES DE MONTERREY, CAMPUS CHIHUAHUA

Computer Engineering	M,O
Electrical Engineering	M,O
Engineering Management	M,O
Industrial/Management Engineering	M,O
Mechanical Engineering	M,O
Systems Engineering	M,O

INSTITUTO TECNOLÓGICO Y DE ESTUDIOS SUPERIORES DE MONTERREY, CAMPUS CIUDAD DE MÉXICO

Computer Science	M,D
Environmental Engineering	M,D
Industrial/Management Engineering	M,D
Telecommunications Management	M

INSTITUTO TECNOLÓGICO Y DE ESTUDIOS SUPERIORES DE MONTERREY, CAMPUS CIUDAD OBREGÓN

Engineering and Applied Sciences—General	M
Telecommunications Management	M

INSTITUTO TECNOLÓGICO Y DE ESTUDIOS SUPERIORES DE MONTERREY, CAMPUS CUERNAVACA

Computer Science	M,D
Information Science	M,D
Management of Technology	M,D

INSTITUTO TECNOLÓGICO Y DE ESTUDIOS SUPERIORES DE MONTERREY, CAMPUS ESTADO DE MÉXICO

Computer Science	M,D
Information Science	M,D
Materials Engineering	M,D
Materials Sciences	M,D
Telecommunications Management	M,D

INSTITUTO TECNOLÓGICO Y DE ESTUDIOS SUPERIORES DE MONTERREY, CAMPUS IRAPUATO

Computer Science	M,D
Information Science	M,D
Management of Technology	M,D
Telecommunications Management	M,D

INSTITUTO TECNOLÓGICO Y DE ESTUDIOS SUPERIORES DE MONTERREY, CAMPUS LAGUNA

Industrial/Management Engineering	M

INSTITUTO TECNOLÓGICO Y DE ESTUDIOS SUPERIORES DE MONTERREY, CAMPUS MONTERREY

Agricultural Engineering	M,D
Artificial Intelligence/Robotics	M,D
Biotechnology	M,D
Chemical Engineering	M,D

Civil Engineering — M,D
Computer Science — M,D
Electrical Engineering — M,D
Engineering and Applied
  Sciences—General — M,D
Environmental
  Engineering — M,D
Industrial/Management
  Engineering — M,D
Information Science — M,D
Manufacturing Engineering — M,D
Mechanical Engineering — M,D
Systems Engineering — M,D

INSTITUTO TECNOLÓGICO Y DE ESTUDIOS SUPERIORES DE MONTERREY, CAMPUS SONORA NORTE
Information Science — M

INTER AMERICAN UNIVERSITY OF PUERTO RICO, BAYAMÓN CAMPUS
Biotechnology — M

INTER AMERICAN UNIVERSITY OF PUERTO RICO, GUAYAMA CAMPUS
Computer and Information
  Systems Security — M
Computer Science — M

INTER AMERICAN UNIVERSITY OF PUERTO RICO, METROPOLITAN CAMPUS
Computer Science — M

INTERNATIONAL TECHNOLOGICAL UNIVERSITY
Computer Engineering — M
Computer Science — M
Electrical Engineering — M,D
Engineering Management — M
Software Engineering — M,D

THE INTERNATIONAL UNIVERSITY OF MONACO
Financial Engineering — M

IONA COLLEGE
Computer Science — M
Management of
  Technology — M,O
Telecommunications — M

IOWA STATE UNIVERSITY OF SCIENCE AND TECHNOLOGY
Aerospace/Aeronautical
  Engineering — M,D
Agricultural Engineering — M,D
Bioengineering — M,D
Bioinformatics — M,D
Biosystems Engineering — M,D
Chemical Engineering — M,D
Civil Engineering — M,D
Computer Engineering — M,D
Computer Science — M,D
Construction Engineering — M,D
Electrical Engineering — M,D
Engineering and Applied
  Sciences—General — M,D
Environmental
  Engineering — M,D
Geotechnical Engineering — M,D
Human-Computer
  Interaction — M,D

Industrial/Management
  Engineering — M,D
Information Science — M
Materials Engineering — M,D
Materials Sciences — M,D
Mechanical Engineering — M,D
Mechanics — M,D
Operations Research — M,D
Structural Engineering — M,D
Systems Engineering — M
Transportation and
  Highway Engineering — M,D

JACKSON STATE UNIVERSITY
Computer Science — M
Materials Sciences — M

JACKSONVILLE STATE UNIVERSITY
Computer Science — M
Software Engineering — M

JAMES MADISON UNIVERSITY
Applied Science and
  Technology — M
Computer Science — M

THE JOHNS HOPKINS UNIVERSITY
Bioengineering — M,D
Bioinformatics — M,D,O
Biomedical Engineering — M,D,O
Biotechnology — M
Chemical Engineering — M,D
Civil Engineering — M,D
Computer and Information
  Systems Security — M,O
Computer Engineering — M,D,O
Computer Science — M,D,O
Electrical Engineering — M,D,O
Engineering and Applied
  Sciences—General — M,D,O
Engineering Management — M
Environmental
  Engineering — M,D,O
Health Informatics — M
Information Science — M
Management of
  Technology — M,O
Materials Engineering — M,D
Materials Sciences — M,D
Mechanical Engineering — M,D
Mechanics — M
Nanotechnology — M
Operations Research — M,D
Systems Engineering — M,O
Telecommunications — M,O

JONES INTERNATIONAL UNIVERSITY
Computer and Information
  Systems Security — M
Management of
  Technology — M

KANSAS STATE UNIVERSITY
Agricultural Engineering — M,D
Architectural Engineering — M
Bioengineering — M,D
Chemical Engineering — M,D
Civil Engineering — M,D
Computer Science — M,D
Electrical Engineering — M,D
Engineering and Applied
  Sciences—General — M,D*
Engineering Management — M,D
Industrial/Management
  Engineering — M,D
Information Science — M,D

Manufacturing Engineering — M,D
Mechanical Engineering — M,D
Nuclear Engineering — M,D
Operations Research — M,D
Software Engineering — M,D

KAPLAN UNIVERSITY, DAVENPORT CAMPUS
Computer and Information
  Systems Security — M

KEAN UNIVERSITY
Biotechnology — M

KENNESAW STATE UNIVERSITY
Computer Science — M
Information Science — M

KENT STATE UNIVERSITY
Computer Science — M,D
Engineering and Applied
  Sciences—General — M
Financial Engineering — M
Information Science — M

KENTUCKY STATE UNIVERSITY
Computer and Information
  Systems Security — M
Computer Science — M
Information Science — M

KETTERING UNIVERSITY
Automotive Engineering — M
Electrical Engineering — M
Energy and Power
  Engineering — M
Engineering Design — M
Engineering Management — M
Information Science — M
Manufacturing Engineering — M
Mechanical Engineering — M

KNOWLEDGE SYSTEMS INSTITUTE
Computer Science — M
Information Science — M

KUTZTOWN UNIVERSITY OF PENNSYLVANIA
Computer Science — M

LAKEHEAD UNIVERSITY
Computer Engineering — M
Computer Science — M
Electrical Engineering — M
Engineering and Applied
  Sciences—General — M
Environmental
  Engineering — M

LAMAR UNIVERSITY
Chemical Engineering — M,D
Civil Engineering — M,D
Computer Science — M
Electrical Engineering — M,D
Engineering and Applied
  Sciences—General — M,D
Engineering Management — M,D
Environmental
  Engineering — M,D
Industrial/Management
  Engineering — M,D
Information Science — M
Mechanical Engineering — M,D

LA SALLE UNIVERSITY
Computer Science — M
Management of
  Technology — M

LAURENTIAN UNIVERSITY
Engineering and Applied
  Sciences—General — M,D
Mineral/Mining
  Engineering — M,D

LAWRENCE TECHNOLOGICAL UNIVERSITY
Automotive Engineering — M,D
Civil Engineering — M,D
Computer Engineering — M,D
Computer Science — M
Construction Engineering — M,D
Electrical Engineering — M,D
Engineering and Applied
  Sciences—General — M,D
Engineering Management — M,D
Industrial/Management
  Engineering — M,D
Management of
  Technology — M,D
Manufacturing Engineering — M,D
Mechanical Engineering — M,D

LEBANESE AMERICAN UNIVERSITY
Computer Science — M

LEHIGH UNIVERSITY
Bioengineering — M,D
Chemical Engineering — M,D
Civil Engineering — M,D
Computer Engineering — M,D
Computer Science — M,D
Electrical Engineering — M,D
Energy and Power
  Engineering — M
Engineering and Applied
  Sciences—General — M,D
Environmental
  Engineering — M,D
Industrial/Management
  Engineering — M,D
Information Science — M
Manufacturing Engineering — M
Materials Engineering — M,D
Materials Sciences — M,D
Mechanical Engineering — M,D
Mechanics — M,D
Polymer Science and
  Engineering — M,D
Structural Engineering — M,D
Systems Engineering — M,D

LEHMAN COLLEGE OF THE CITY UNIVERSITY OF NEW YORK
Computer Science — M

LEWIS UNIVERSITY
Aviation — M
Computer and Information
  Systems Security — M
Management of
  Technology — M

LONG ISLAND UNIVERSITY, BROOKLYN CAMPUS
Computer Science — M

---

*M—master's degree; P—first professional degree; D—doctorate; O—other advanced degree; *—Close-Up and/or Display*

LONG ISLAND UNIVERSITY, C.W. POST CAMPUS

Computer Science	M
Engineering Management	M
Information Science	M

LOUISIANA STATE UNIVERSITY AND AGRICULTURAL AND MECHANICAL COLLEGE

Agricultural Engineering	M,D
Applied Science and Technology	M
Bioengineering	M,D
Chemical Engineering	M,D
Civil Engineering	M,D
Computer Engineering	M,D
Computer Science	M,D
Electrical Engineering	M,D
Engineering and Applied Sciences—General	M,D
Environmental Engineering	M,D
Geotechnical Engineering	M,D
Industrial/Management Engineering	M,D
Mechanical Engineering	M,D
Mechanics	M,D
Petroleum Engineering	M,D
Structural Engineering	M,D
Systems Science	M,D
Transportation and Highway Engineering	M,D
Water Resources Engineering	M,D

LOUISIANA STATE UNIVERSITY IN SHREVEPORT

Computer Science	M
Systems Science	M

LOUISIANA TECH UNIVERSITY

Biomedical Engineering	M,D
Chemical Engineering	M,D
Civil Engineering	M,D
Computer Science	M
Electrical Engineering	M,D
Engineering and Applied Sciences—General	M,D
Industrial/Management Engineering	M
Mechanical Engineering	M,D

LOYOLA MARYMOUNT UNIVERSITY

Civil Engineering	M
Computer Science	M
Electrical Engineering	M
Engineering Management	M
Environmental Engineering	M
Mechanical Engineering	M
Systems Engineering	M

LOYOLA UNIVERSITY CHICAGO

Computer Science	M
Information Science	M
Software Engineering	M

LOYOLA UNIVERSITY MARYLAND

Computer Science	M
Software Engineering	M

MAHARISHI UNIVERSITY OF MANAGEMENT

Computer Science	M

MANHATTAN COLLEGE

Chemical Engineering	M
Civil Engineering	M
Computer Engineering	M
Electrical Engineering	M
Engineering and Applied Sciences—General	M
Environmental Engineering	M
Mechanical Engineering	M

MARIST COLLEGE

Computer Science	M,O
Management of Technology	M,Q
Software Engineering	M,O

MARLBORO COLLEGE

Information Science	M

MARQUETTE UNIVERSITY

Bioinformatics	M,D
Biomedical Engineering	M,D
Civil Engineering	M,D
Computer Engineering	M,D
Computer Science	M,D
Construction Management	M,D
Electrical Engineering	M,D
Engineering and Applied Sciences—General	M,D
Engineering Management	M,D
Environmental Engineering	M,D
Geotechnical Engineering	M,D
Management of Technology	M,D
Manufacturing Engineering	M,D
Mechanical Engineering	M,D
Structural Engineering	M,D
Transportation and Highway Engineering	M,D
Water Resources Engineering	M,D

MARSHALL UNIVERSITY

Engineering and Applied Sciences—General	M
Engineering Management	M
Environmental Engineering	M
Information Science	M
Management of Technology	M

MARYLHURST UNIVERSITY

Energy and Power Engineering	M

MARYMOUNT UNIVERSITY

Computer and Information Systems Security	M,O
Medical Informatics	M,O

MARYWOOD UNIVERSITY

Biotechnology	M
Information Science	M,O

MASSACHUSETTS INSTITUTE OF TECHNOLOGY

Aerospace/Aeronautical Engineering	M,D,O
Bioengineering	M,D*
Biomedical Engineering	M,D
Chemical Engineering	M,D
Civil Engineering	M,D,O
Computer Science	M,D,O
Construction Engineering	M,D,O
Electrical Engineering	M,D,O
Electronic Materials	M,D,O
Engineering and Applied Sciences—General	M,D,O
Engineering Management	M,D
Environmental Engineering	M,D,O
Geotechnical Engineering	M,D,O
Information Science	M,D,O
Manufacturing Engineering	M,D,O
Materials Engineering	M,D,O
Materials Sciences	M,D,O
Mechanical Engineering	M,D,O
Medical Informatics	M
Metallurgical Engineering and Metallurgy	M,D,O
Nuclear Engineering	M,D,O
Ocean Engineering	M,D,O
Operations Research	M,D
Polymer Science and Engineering	M,D,O
Structural Engineering	M,D,O
Systems Engineering	M,D
Technology and Public Policy	M,D
Transportation and Highway Engineering	M,D,O

MAYO GRADUATE SCHOOL

Biomedical Engineering	D

MCGILL UNIVERSITY

Aerospace/Aeronautical Engineering	M,D
Agricultural Engineering	M,D
Bioengineering	M,D
Bioinformatics	M,D
Biomedical Engineering	M,D
Biotechnology	M,D,O
Chemical Engineering	M,D
Civil Engineering	M,D
Computer Engineering	M,D
Computer Science	M,D
Electrical Engineering	M,D
Engineering and Applied Sciences—General	M,D,O
Environmental Engineering	M,D
Geotechnical Engineering	M,D
Hydraulics	M,D
Materials Engineering	M,D,O
Mechanical Engineering	M,D
Mechanics	M,D
Mineral/Mining Engineering	M,D,O
Structural Engineering	M,D
Water Resources Engineering	M,D

MCMASTER UNIVERSITY

Chemical Engineering	M,D
Civil Engineering	M,D
Computer Science	M,D
Electrical Engineering	M,D
Engineering and Applied Sciences—General	M,D
Engineering Physics	M,D
Materials Engineering	M,D
Materials Sciences	M,D
Mechanical Engineering	M,D
Nuclear Engineering	M,D
Software Engineering	M,D

MCNEESE STATE UNIVERSITY

Chemical Engineering	M
Civil Engineering	M
Computer Science	M
Electrical Engineering	M
Engineering and Applied Sciences—General	M
Engineering Management	M
Mechanical Engineering	M

MEDICAL COLLEGE OF GEORGIA

Health Informatics	M

MEDICAL COLLEGE OF WISCONSIN

Bioinformatics	M
Medical Informatics	M

MEMORIAL UNIVERSITY OF NEWFOUNDLAND

Civil Engineering	M,D
Computer Engineering	M,D
Computer Science	M,D
Electrical Engineering	M,D
Engineering and Applied Sciences—General	M,D
Environmental Engineering	M
Mechanical Engineering	M,D
Ocean Engineering	M,D

MERCER UNIVERSITY

Biomedical Engineering	M
Computer Engineering	M
Electrical Engineering	M
Engineering and Applied Sciences—General	M
Engineering Management	M
Environmental Engineering	M
Management of Technology	M
Mechanical Engineering	M
Software Engineering	M

MERCY COLLEGE

Computer and Information Systems Security	M

MERITUS UNIVERSITY

Management of Technology	M

METROPOLITAN STATE UNIVERSITY

Computer and Information Systems Security	M,O
Computer Science	M

MIAMI UNIVERSITY

Engineering and Applied Sciences—General	M,O
Paper and Pulp Engineering	M
Software Engineering	M,O
Systems Science	M

MICHIGAN STATE UNIVERSITY

Biosystems Engineering	M,D
Chemical Engineering	M,D
Civil Engineering	M,D
Computer Science	M,D
Construction Management	M,D
Electrical Engineering	M,D
Engineering and Applied Sciences—General	M,D
Environmental Engineering	M,D
Game Design and Development	M
Manufacturing Engineering	M,D
Materials Engineering	M,D
Materials Sciences	M,D
Mechanical Engineering	M,D
Mechanics	M,D
Telecommunications	M

MICHIGAN TECHNOLOGICAL UNIVERSITY

Biomedical Engineering	D
Chemical Engineering	M,D
Civil Engineering	M,D
Computer Engineering	D
Computer Science	M,D
Electrical Engineering	M,D
Engineering and Applied Sciences—General	M,D
Engineering Physics	D
Environmental Engineering	M,D
Geological Engineering	M,D
Materials Engineering	M,D
Mechanical Engineering	M,D
Mechanics	M
Metallurgical Engineering and Metallurgy	M,D
Mineral/Mining Engineering	M,D

MIDDLE TENNESSEE STATE UNIVERSITY

Aerospace/Aeronautical Engineering	M
Computer Science	M
Medical Informatics	M

MIDWESTERN STATE UNIVERSITY

Computer Science	M

MILLS COLLEGE

Computer Science	M,O

MILWAUKEE SCHOOL OF ENGINEERING

Engineering and Applied Sciences—General	M
Engineering Management	M
Environmental Engineering	M
Medical Informatics	M
Structural Engineering	M

MINNESOTA STATE UNIVERSITY MANKATO

Automotive Engineering	M
Computer Science	M,O
Database Systems	M,O
Electrical Engineering	M
Manufacturing Engineering	M

MISSISSIPPI COLLEGE

Computer Science	M

MISSISSIPPI STATE UNIVERSITY

Aerospace/Aeronautical Engineering	M,D
Bioengineering	M,D
Biomedical Engineering	M,D
Chemical Engineering	M,D
Civil Engineering	M,D
Computer Engineering	M,D
Computer Science	M,D
Electrical Engineering	M,D
Engineering and Applied Sciences—General	M,D
Industrial/Management Engineering	M,D
Mechanical Engineering	M,D
Systems Engineering	M,D

MISSISSIPPI VALLEY STATE UNIVERSITY

Bioinformatics	M

MISSOURI STATE UNIVERSITY

Applied Science and Technology	M
Computer Science	M
Construction Management	M
Materials Sciences	M

MISSOURI UNIVERSITY OF SCIENCE AND TECHNOLOGY

Aerospace/Aeronautical Engineering	M,D
Ceramic Sciences and Engineering	M,D
Chemical Engineering	M,D
Civil Engineering	M,D
Computer Engineering	M,D
Computer Science	M,D
Construction Engineering	M,D
Electrical Engineering	M,D
Engineering and Applied Sciences—General	M,D
Engineering Management	M,D
Environmental Engineering	M,D
Geological Engineering	M,D
Geotechnical Engineering	M,D
Hydraulics	M,D
Information Science	M
Manufacturing Engineering	M,D
Mechanical Engineering	M,D
Mechanics	M,D
Metallurgical Engineering and Metallurgy	M,D
Mineral/Mining Engineering	M,D
Nuclear Engineering	M,D
Petroleum Engineering	M,D
Systems Engineering	M,D

MONMOUTH UNIVERSITY

Computer Science	M,O
Software Engineering	M,O

MONTANA STATE UNIVERSITY

Chemical Engineering	M,D
Civil Engineering	M,D
Computer Engineering	M,D
Computer Science	M,D
Construction Engineering	M,D
Electrical Engineering	M,D
Engineering and Applied Sciences—General	M,D
Environmental Engineering	M,D
Industrial/Management Engineering	M,D
Mechanical Engineering	M,D
Mechanics	M,D

MONTANA TECH OF THE UNIVERSITY OF MONTANA

Electrical Engineering	M
Engineering and Applied Sciences—General	M
Environmental Engineering	M
Geological Engineering	M
Industrial/Management Engineering	M
Metallurgical Engineering and Metallurgy	M
Mineral/Mining Engineering	M
Petroleum Engineering	M

MONTCLAIR STATE UNIVERSITY

Computer Science	M,D,O
Information Science	M,O

MOREHEAD STATE UNIVERSITY

Industrial/Management Engineering	M

MORGAN STATE UNIVERSITY

Bioinformatics	M
Civil Engineering	M,D
Electrical Engineering	M,D
Engineering and Applied Sciences—General	M,D
Industrial/Management Engineering	M,D
Telecommunications Management	M
Transportation and Highway Engineering	M

MURRAY STATE UNIVERSITY

Management of Technology	M
Safety Engineering	M
Telecommunications Management	M

NATIONAL UNIVERSITY

Computer Science	M
Database Systems	M
Engineering and Applied Sciences—General	M
Engineering Management	M
Environmental Engineering	M
Game Design and Development	M
Information Science	M
Management of Technology	M
Safety Engineering	M
Software Engineering	M
Systems Engineering	M
Telecommunications	M

NAVAL POSTGRADUATE SCHOOL

Aerospace/Aeronautical Engineering	M
Applied Science and Technology	M
Computer Engineering	M,D,O
Computer Science	M,D
Electrical Engineering	M,D,O
Human-Computer Interaction	M,D
Information Science	M,O
Mechanical Engineering	M,D,O
Operations Research	M,D
Software Engineering	M,D
Systems Engineering	M,D,O

NEW JERSEY INSTITUTE OF TECHNOLOGY

Bioinformatics	M,D
Biomedical Engineering	M,D
Chemical Engineering	M,D
Civil Engineering	M,D
Computer Engineering	M,D
Computer Science	M,D
Electrical Engineering	M,D
Energy and Power Engineering	M
Engineering and Applied Sciences—General	M,D,O
Engineering Management	M
Environmental Engineering	M,D
Industrial/Management Engineering	M,D
Information Science	M,D
Internet Engineering	M

Management of Technology

	M
Manufacturing Engineering	M
Materials Engineering	M,D
Materials Sciences	M,D
Mechanical Engineering	M,D,O
Pharmaceutical Engineering	M
Safety Engineering	M
Software Engineering	M,D
Transportation and Highway Engineering	M,D

NEW MEXICO HIGHLANDS UNIVERSITY

Computer Science	M

NEW MEXICO INSTITUTE OF MINING AND TECHNOLOGY

Computer Science	M,D
Electrical Engineering	M
Engineering Management	M
Environmental Engineering	M
Hazardous Materials Management	M
Materials Engineering	M,D
Mechanics	M
Mineral/Mining Engineering	M
Operations Research	M,D
Petroleum Engineering	M,D
Water Resources Engineering	M

NEW MEXICO STATE UNIVERSITY

Bioinformatics	M,D
Chemical Engineering	M,D
Civil Engineering	M,D
Computer Engineering	M,D
Computer Science	M,D
Electrical Engineering	M,D
Engineering and Applied Sciences—General	M,D
Environmental Engineering	M,D
Industrial/Management Engineering	M,D
Mechanical Engineering	M,D

NEW YORK INSTITUTE OF TECHNOLOGY

Computer and Information Systems Security	M
Computer Engineering	M
Computer Science	M
Electrical Engineering	M
Energy and Power Engineering	M,O
Energy Management and Policy	M,O
Engineering and Applied Sciences—General	M,O
Environmental Engineering	M

NEW YORK UNIVERSITY

Agricultural Engineering	M,D
Computer Science	M,D
Construction Management	M,O
Database Systems	M,O
Ergonomics and Human Factors	M,D

NICHOLLS STATE UNIVERSITY

Computer Science	M

*M—master's degree; P—first professional degree; D—doctorate; O—other advanced degree; *—Close-Up and / or Display*

NORFOLK STATE UNIVERSITY

Computer Engineering	M
Computer Science	M
Electrical Engineering	M
Materials Sciences	M

NORTH CAROLINA AGRICULTURAL AND TECHNICAL STATE UNIVERSITY

Chemical Engineering	M,D
Civil Engineering	M
Computer Engineering	M,D
Computer Science	M
Construction Management	M
Electrical Engineering	M,D
Energy and Power Engineering	M,D
Engineering and Applied Sciences—General	M,D
Industrial/Management Engineering	M,D
Management of Technology	M,D
Mechanical Engineering	M,D
Systems Engineering	M,D

NORTH CAROLINA STATE UNIVERSITY

Aerospace/Aeronautical Engineering	M,D
Agricultural Engineering	M,D,O
Bioengineering	M,D,O
Bioinformatics	M,D
Biomedical Engineering	M,D
Biotechnology	M
Chemical Engineering	M,D
Civil Engineering	M,D
Computer Engineering	M,D
Computer Science	M,D
Electrical Engineering	M,D
Engineering and Applied Sciences—General	M,D*
Ergonomics and Human Factors	D
Financial Engineering	M
Industrial/Management Engineering	M,D
Management of Technology	D
Manufacturing Engineering	M
Materials Engineering	M,D
Materials Sciences	M,D
Mechanical Engineering	M,D*
Nuclear Engineering	M,D
Operations Research	M,D
Paper and Pulp Engineering	M,D
Polymer Science and Engineering	D
Textile Sciences and Engineering	M,D

NORTH CENTRAL COLLEGE

Computer Science	M

NORTH DAKOTA STATE UNIVERSITY

Agricultural Engineering	M,D
Bioinformatics	M,D
Biosystems Engineering	M,D
Civil Engineering	M,D
Computer Engineering	M,D
Computer Science	M,D,O
Construction Management	M
Electrical Engineering	M,D
Engineering and Applied Sciences—General	M,D
Environmental Engineering	M,D

Industrial/Management Engineering	M,D
Manufacturing Engineering	M,D
Materials Sciences	D
Mechanical Engineering	M,D
Mechanics	M,D
Nanotechnology	D
Operations Research	M,D,O
Polymer Science and Engineering	M,D
Software Engineering	M,D,O

NORTHEASTERN ILLINOIS UNIVERSITY

Computer Science	M

NORTHEASTERN UNIVERSITY

Bioinformatics	M
Biotechnology	M,D
Chemical Engineering	M,D
Civil Engineering	M,D
Computer Engineering	M,D
Computer Science	M,D
Electrical Engineering	M,D
Energy and Power Engineering	M
Engineering and Applied Sciences—General	M,D,O
Engineering Management	M,D
Environmental Engineering	M,D
Health Informatics	M,D
Industrial/Management Engineering	M,D
Information Science	M,D,O
Manufacturing Engineering	M,D
Mechanical Engineering	M,D
Operations Research	M,D
Telecommunications Management	M

NORTHERN ARIZONA UNIVERSITY

Civil Engineering	M
Computer Science	M
Electrical Engineering	M
Engineering and Applied Sciences—General	M,D
Environmental Engineering	M
Mechanical Engineering	M

NORTHERN ILLINOIS UNIVERSITY

Computer Science	M
Electrical Engineering	M
Engineering and Applied Sciences—General	M
Industrial/Management Engineering	M
Mechanical Engineering	M

NORTHERN KENTUCKY UNIVERSITY

Computer and Information Systems Security	M,O
Computer Science	M,O
Health Informatics	M,O
Information Science	M,O
Management of Technology	M
Software Engineering	M,O

NORTHWESTERN POLYTECHNIC UNIVERSITY

Computer Engineering	M
Computer Science	M
Electrical Engineering	M
Engineering and Applied Sciences—General	M

NORTHWESTERN UNIVERSITY

Bioinformatics	M
Biomedical Engineering	M,D
Biotechnology	D
Chemical Engineering	M,D
Civil Engineering	M,D
Computer and Information Systems Security	M
Computer Engineering	M,D,O
Computer Science	M,D,O
Database Systems	M
Electrical Engineering	M,D,O
Electronic Materials	M,D,O
Engineering and Applied Sciences—General	M,D,O
Engineering Design	M
Engineering Management	M
Environmental Engineering	M,D
Geotechnical Engineering	M,D
Industrial/Management Engineering	M,D
Information Science	M
Manufacturing Engineering	M
Materials Engineering	M,D,O
Materials Sciences	M,D,O
Mechanical Engineering	M,D
Mechanics	M,D
Medical Informatics	M
Operations Research	M,D
Software Engineering	M
Structural Engineering	M,D
Transportation and Highway Engineering	M,D

NORTHWEST MISSOURI STATE UNIVERSITY

Computer Science	M,O

NORWICH UNIVERSITY

Civil Engineering	M
Computer and Information Systems Security	M

NOVA SOUTHEASTERN UNIVERSITY

Bioinformatics	M,O
Computer and Information Systems Security	M,D
Computer Science	M,D
Health Informatics	M,O
Information Science	M,D
Medical Informatics	M,O

OAKLAND UNIVERSITY

Computer Engineering	M
Computer Science	M
Electrical Engineering	M
Engineering and Applied Sciences—General	M,D
Engineering Management	M
Mechanical Engineering	M,D
Software Engineering	M
Systems Engineering	M,D
Systems Science	M

OGI SCHOOL OF SCIENCE & ENGINEERING AT OREGON HEALTH & SCIENCE UNIVERSITY

Biomedical Engineering	M,D
Computer Engineering	M,D
Computer Science	M,D
Electrical Engineering	M,D
Environmental Engineering	M,D
Management of Technology	M,O
Ocean Engineering	M,D

THE OHIO STATE UNIVERSITY

Aerospace/Aeronautical Engineering	M,D
Agricultural Engineering	M,D
Bioengineering	M,D
Biomedical Engineering	M,D
Chemical Engineering	M,D
Civil Engineering	M,D
Computer Engineering	M,D
Computer Science	M,D
Electrical Engineering	M,D
Engineering and Applied Sciences—General	M,D
Engineering Physics	M,D
Industrial/Management Engineering	M,D
Information Science	M,D
Materials Engineering	M,D
Materials Sciences	M,D
Mechanical Engineering	M,D
Mechanics	M,D
Metallurgical Engineering and Metallurgy	M,D
Nuclear Engineering	M,D
Surveying Science and Engineering	M,D
Systems Engineering	M,D

OHIO UNIVERSITY

Biomedical Engineering	M,D
Chemical Engineering	M,D
Civil Engineering	M,D
Computer Science	M,D
Construction Engineering	M,D
Electrical Engineering	M,D
Engineering and Applied Sciences—General	M,D
Environmental Engineering	M,D
Geotechnical Engineering	M,D
Industrial/Management Engineering	M,D
Mechanical Engineering	M,D
Mechanics	M,D
Structural Engineering	M,D
Systems Engineering	M
Telecommunications	M
Transportation and Highway Engineering	M,D
Water Resources Engineering	M,D

OKLAHOMA CITY UNIVERSITY

Computer Science	M

OKLAHOMA STATE UNIVERSITY

Agricultural Engineering	M,D
Applied Science and Technology	M,D,O
Bioengineering	M,D
Chemical Engineering	M,D
Civil Engineering	M,D
Computer Engineering	M,D
Computer Science	M,D
Electrical Engineering	M,D
Engineering and Applied Sciences—General	M,D
Environmental Engineering	M,D
Fire Protection Engineering	M,D
Industrial/Management Engineering	M,D
Information Science	M,D
Mechanical Engineering	M,D
Telecommunications Management	M,D

OLD DOMINION UNIVERSITY

Aerospace/Aeronautical Engineering	M,D
Automotive Engineering	M
Civil Engineering	M,D
Computer Engineering	M,D
Computer Science	M,D
Electrical Engineering	M,D
Engineering and Applied Sciences—General	M,D
Engineering Management	M,D
Environmental Engineering	M,D
Ergonomics and Human Factors	D
Human-Computer Interaction	M,D
Information Science	D
Management of Technology	M
Manufacturing Engineering	M,D
Mechanical Engineering	M,D
Systems Engineering	M,D

OREGON HEALTH & SCIENCE UNIVERSITY

Bioinformatics	M,D,O
Biomedical Engineering	M,D
Computer Engineering	M,D
Computer Science	M,D
Electrical Engineering	M,D
Environmental Engineering	M,D
Management of Technology	M
Medical Informatics	M,D,O

OREGON STATE UNIVERSITY

Bioengineering	M,D
Chemical Engineering	M,D
Civil Engineering	M,D
Computer Engineering	M,D
Computer Science	M,D
Construction Engineering	M,D
Electrical Engineering	M,D
Engineering and Applied Sciences—General	M,D*
Environmental Engineering	M,D
Geotechnical Engineering	M,D
Industrial/Management Engineering	M,D
Manufacturing Engineering	M,D
Materials Sciences	M,D
Mechanical Engineering	M,D
Nanotechnology	M,D
Nuclear Engineering	M,D
Ocean Engineering	M,D
Operations Research	M,D
Paper and Pulp Engineering	M,D
Structural Engineering	M,D
Systems Engineering	M,D
Transportation and Highway Engineering	M,D
Water Resources Engineering	M,D

OUR LADY OF THE LAKE UNIVERSITY OF SAN ANTONIO

Computer and Information Systems Security	M

PACE UNIVERSITY

Computer and Information Systems Security	M,D,O
Computer Science	M,D,O
Information Science	M,D,O

Software Engineering	M,D,O
Telecommunications	M,D,O

PACIFIC LUTHERAN UNIVERSITY

Management of Technology	M

PACIFIC STATES UNIVERSITY

Computer Science	M
Management of Technology	M

PENN STATE GREAT VALLEY

Engineering and Applied Sciences—General	M

PENN STATE HARRISBURG

Engineering and Applied Sciences—General	M

PENN STATE HERSHEY MEDICAL CENTER

Bioengineering	M,D

PENN STATE UNIVERSITY PARK

Aerospace/Aeronautical Engineering	M,D
Agricultural Engineering	M,D
Architectural Engineering	M,D
Bioengineering	M,D
Biomedical Engineering	M,D
Chemical Engineering	M,D
Civil Engineering	M,D
Computer Engineering	M,D
Computer Science	M,D*
Electrical Engineering	M,D
Engineering and Applied Sciences—General	M,D
Environmental Engineering	M,D
Geotechnical Engineering	M,D
Industrial/Management Engineering	M,D
Manufacturing Engineering	M,D
Materials Engineering	M,D
Materials Sciences	M,D
Mechanical Engineering	M,D
Mechanics	M,D
Nuclear Engineering	M,D
Operations Research	M,D

PHILADELPHIA UNIVERSITY

Construction Management	M
Textile Sciences and Engineering	M,D

PITTSBURG STATE UNIVERSITY

Engineering and Applied Sciences—General	M

POINT PARK UNIVERSITY

Engineering Management	M

POLYTECHNIC INSTITUTE OF NYU

Bioengineering	M
Bioinformatics	M
Biomedical Engineering	M,D
Biotechnology	M
Chemical Engineering	M,D
Civil Engineering	M,D
Computer and Information Systems Security	O
Computer Engineering	M,O
Computer Science	M,D

Construction Management	M,D,O
Electrical Engineering	M,D
Engineering Physics	M
Environmental Engineering	M
Financial Engineering	M,O
Industrial/Management Engineering	M
Management of Technology	M,D,O
Manufacturing Engineering	M
Materials Sciences	M
Mechanical Engineering	M,D
Polymer Science and Engineering	M
Software Engineering	O
Systems Engineering	M
Telecommunications Management	M
Telecommunications	M
Transportation and Highway Engineering	M,D

POLYTECHNIC INSTITUTE OF NYU, LONG ISLAND GRADUATE CENTER

Aerospace/Aeronautical Engineering	M
Bioinformatics	M
Chemical Engineering	M
Civil Engineering	M
Computer Engineering	M
Computer Science	M
Construction Management	M
Electrical Engineering	M
Engineering Design	M
Engineering Physics	M
Environmental Engineering	M
Financial Engineering	M,O
Industrial/Management Engineering	M
Management of Technology	M
Manufacturing Engineering	M
Mechanical Engineering	M
Software Engineering	M
Systems Engineering	M
Telecommunications	M
Transportation and Highway Engineering	M

POLYTECHNIC INSTITUTE OF NYU, WESTCHESTER GRADUATE CENTER

Bioinformatics	M
Chemical Engineering	M
Computer Engineering	M
Computer Science	M
Electrical Engineering	M
Financial Engineering	M,O
Industrial/Management Engineering	M
Information Science	M
Management of Technology	M
Manufacturing Engineering	M
Telecommunications	M

POLYTECHNIC UNIVERSITY OF PUERTO RICO

Civil Engineering	M
Computer Engineering	M
Computer Science	M
Electrical Engineering	M
Engineering Management	M
Management of Technology	M
Manufacturing Engineering	M

POLYTECHNIC UNIVERSITY OF THE AMERICAS–MIAMI CAMPUS

Engineering Management	M

POLYTECHNIC UNIVERSITY OF THE AMERICAS–ORLANDO CAMPUS

Civil Engineering	M
Computer Engineering	M
Electrical Engineering	M
Engineering Management	M

PONTIFICIA UNIVERSIDAD CATOLICA MADRE Y MAESTRA

Construction Engineering	M
Energy and Power Engineering	M
Environmental Engineering	M

PORTLAND STATE UNIVERSITY

Artificial Intelligence/Robotics	M,D,O
Civil Engineering	M,D,O
Computer Engineering	M,D
Computer Science	M,D
Electrical Engineering	M,D
Engineering and Applied Sciences—General	M,D,O
Engineering Management	M,D,O
Environmental Engineering	M,D
Management of Technology	M,D
Manufacturing Engineering	M
Mechanical Engineering	M,D,O
Software Engineering	M,D
Systems Engineering	M,O
Systems Science	M,D,O

PRAIRIE VIEW A&M UNIVERSITY

Computer Science	M,D
Electrical Engineering	M,D
Engineering and Applied Sciences—General	M,D

PRINCETON UNIVERSITY

Aerospace/Aeronautical Engineering	M,D
Chemical Engineering	M,D
Civil Engineering	M,D
Computer Science	M,D
Electrical Engineering	M,D
Electronic Materials	D
Engineering and Applied Sciences—General	M,D
Financial Engineering	M,D
Materials Sciences	D
Mechanical Engineering	M,D
Ocean Engineering	D
Operations Research	M,D

PURDUE UNIVERSITY

Aerospace/Aeronautical Engineering	M,D
Agricultural Engineering	M,D
Biomedical Engineering	M,D
Chemical Engineering	M,D
Civil Engineering	M,D
Computer and Information Systems Security	M
Computer Engineering	M,D
Computer Science	M,D
Electrical Engineering	M,D
Engineering and Applied Sciences—General	M,D,O
Industrial/Management Engineering	M,D

*M—master's degree; P—first professional degree; D—doctorate; O—other advanced degree; *—Close-Up and/or Display*

Materials Engineering	M,D
Mechanical Engineering	M,D,O
Nuclear Engineering	M,D

PURDUE UNIVERSITY CALUMET

Biotechnology	M
Computer Engineering	M
Electrical Engineering	M
Engineering and Applied Sciences—General	M
Mechanical Engineering	M

QUEENS COLLEGE OF THE CITY UNIVERSITY OF NEW YORK

Computer Science	M

QUEEN'S UNIVERSITY AT KINGSTON

Chemical Engineering	M,D
Civil Engineering	M,D
Computer Engineering	M,D
Computer Science	M,D
Electrical Engineering	M,D
Engineering and Applied Sciences—General	M,D
Mechanical Engineering	M,D
Mineral/Mining Engineering	M,D

REGIS COLLEGE (MA)

Biotechnology	M

REGIS UNIVERSITY

Computer and Information Systems Security	M,O
Computer Science	M,O
Database Systems	M,O
Information Science	M,O
Management of Technology	M,O
Software Engineering	M,O
Systems Engineering	M,O

RENSSELAER AT HARTFORD

Computer Engineering	M
Computer Science	M
Electrical Engineering	M
Engineering and Applied Sciences—General	M
Information Science	M
Mechanical Engineering	M
Systems Science	M

RENSSELAER POLYTECHNIC INSTITUTE

Aerospace/Aeronautical Engineering	M,D
Applied Science and Technology	M
Bioengineering	M,D
Biomedical Engineering	M,D
Ceramic Sciences and Engineering	M,D
Chemical Engineering	M,D
Civil Engineering	M,D
Computer Engineering	M,D
Computer Science	M,D
Electrical Engineering	M,D
Energy and Power Engineering	M,D
Engineering and Applied Sciences—General	M,D
Engineering Management	M,D
Engineering Physics	M,D
Environmental Engineering	M,D
Financial Engineering	
Geotechnical Engineering	M,D

Human-Computer Interaction	M
Industrial/Management Engineering	M,D
Information Science	M
Materials Engineering	M,D
Materials Sciences	M,D
Mechanical Engineering	M,D
Metallurgical Engineering and Metallurgy	M,D
Nuclear Engineering	M,D
Polymer Science and Engineering	M,D
Structural Engineering	M,D
Systems Engineering	M,D
Technology and Public Policy	M,D
Transportation and Highway Engineering	M,D

RICE UNIVERSITY

Bioengineering	M,D
Bioinformatics	M,D
Biomedical Engineering	M,D
Chemical Engineering	M,D
Civil Engineering	M,D
Computer Engineering	M,D
Computer Science	M,D
Electrical Engineering	M,D
Engineering and Applied Sciences—General	M,D
Environmental Engineering	M,D
Materials Sciences	M,D
Mechanical Engineering	M,D

RIVIER COLLEGE

Computer Science	M

ROBERT MORRIS UNIVERSITY

Computer and Information Systems Security	M,D
Engineering and Applied Sciences—General	M
Engineering Management	M
Information Science	M,D

ROCHESTER INSTITUTE OF TECHNOLOGY

Bioinformatics	M
Computer and Information Systems Security	M,O
Computer Engineering	M
Computer Science	M,D,O
Database Systems	M,O
Electrical Engineering	M
Engineering and Applied Sciences—General	M,D,O
Engineering Design	M
Engineering Management	M
Game Design and Development	M
Human-Computer Interaction	M
Industrial/Management Engineering	M
Information Science	M,D
Manufacturing Engineering	M
Materials Engineering	M
Materials Sciences	M
Mechanical Engineering	M
Software Engineering	M
Systems Engineering	M,D
Technology and Public Policy	M
Telecommunications	M

ROGER WILLIAMS UNIVERSITY

Construction Management	M

ROLLINS COLLEGE

Management of Technology	M

ROOSEVELT UNIVERSITY

Biotechnology	M
Computer Science	M
Telecommunications	M

ROSE-HULMAN INSTITUTE OF TECHNOLOGY

Biomedical Engineering	M
Chemical Engineering	M
Civil Engineering	M
Computer Engineering	M
Electrical Engineering	M
Engineering and Applied Sciences—General	M*
Engineering Management	M
Environmental Engineering	M
Mechanical Engineering	M

ROWAN UNIVERSITY

Chemical Engineering	M
Civil Engineering	M
Construction Management	M
Electrical Engineering	M
Engineering and Applied Sciences—General	M
Engineering Management	M
Mechanical Engineering	M

ROYAL MILITARY COLLEGE OF CANADA

Chemical Engineering	M,D
Civil Engineering	M,D
Computer Engineering	M,D
Computer Science	M
Electrical Engineering	M,D
Engineering and Applied Sciences—General	M,D
Environmental Engineering	M,D
Materials Sciences	M,D
Mechanical Engineering	M,D
Nuclear Engineering	M,D
Software Engineering	M,D

RUTGERS, THE STATE UNIVERSITY OF NEW JERSEY, CAMDEN

Computer Science	M

RUTGERS, THE STATE UNIVERSITY OF NEW JERSEY, NEW BRUNSWICK

Aerospace/Aeronautical Engineering	M,D
Biochemical Engineering	M,D
Biomedical Engineering	M,D
Chemical Engineering	M,D
Civil Engineering	M,D
Computer Engineering	M,D
Computer Science	M,D
Electrical Engineering	M,D*
Environmental Engineering	M,D
Hazardous Materials Management	M,D
Industrial/Management Engineering	M,D
Materials Engineering	M,D
Materials Sciences	M,D
Mechanical Engineering	M,D
Mechanics	M,D
Operations Research	D
Systems Engineering	M,D

SACRED HEART UNIVERSITY

Computer and Information Systems Security	M,O
Computer Science	M,O
Database Systems	M,O
Information Science	M,O

ST. AMBROSE UNIVERSITY

Management of Technology	M

ST. CLOUD STATE UNIVERSITY

Biomedical Engineering	M
Computer and Information Systems Security	M
Computer Science	M
Electrical Engineering	M
Engineering and Applied Sciences—General	M
Engineering Management	M
Mechanical Engineering	M
Technology and Public Policy	M

ST. FRANCIS XAVIER UNIVERSITY

Computer Science	M

ST. JOHN'S UNIVERSITY (NY)

Biotechnology	M
Computer Science	M

SAINT JOSEPH'S UNIVERSITY

Computer Science	M,O
Health Informatics	M,O

SAINT LEO UNIVERSITY

Computer and Information Systems Security	M

SAINT LOUIS UNIVERSITY

Biomedical Engineering	M,D

SAINT MARTIN'S UNIVERSITY

Civil Engineering	M
Engineering Management	M

SAINT MARY'S UNIVERSITY (CANADA)

Applied Science and Technology	M

ST. MARY'S UNIVERSITY (UNITED STATES)

Computer Engineering	M
Computer Science	M
Electrical Engineering	M
Engineering and Applied Sciences—General	M
Engineering Management	M
Industrial/Management Engineering	M
Information Science	M
Operations Research	M
Software Engineering	M

SAINT MARY'S UNIVERSITY OF MINNESOTA

Telecommunications	M

SAINT XAVIER UNIVERSITY

Computer Science	M
Information Science	M

SALEM INTERNATIONAL UNIVERSITY

Computer and Information Systems Security	M

SAM HOUSTON STATE UNIVERSITY

Computer Science	M
Industrial/Management Engineering	M
Information Science	M

SAN DIEGO STATE UNIVERSITY

Aerospace/Aeronautical Engineering	M,D
Civil Engineering	M
Computer Science	M
Electrical Engineering	M
Engineering and Applied Sciences—General	M,D
Engineering Design	M,D
Mechanical Engineering	M,D
Mechanics	M,D
Telecommunications Management	M

SAN FRANCISCO STATE UNIVERSITY

Computer Science	M
Engineering and Applied Sciences—General	M
Software Engineering	M

SAN JOSE STATE UNIVERSITY

Aerospace/Aeronautical Engineering	M
Chemical Engineering	M
Civil Engineering	M
Computer Engineering	M
Computer Science	M
Electrical Engineering	M
Engineering and Applied Sciences—General	M
Industrial/Management Engineering	M
Materials Engineering	M
Mechanical Engineering	M
Software Engineering	M
Systems Engineering	M

SANTA CLARA UNIVERSITY

Civil Engineering	M
Computer Engineering	M,D,O
Computer Science	M,D,O
Electrical Engineering	M,D,O
Engineering and Applied Sciences—General	M,D,O
Engineering Design	M,D,O
Engineering Management	M
Management of Technology	M
Materials Engineering	M,D,O
Mechanical Engineering	M,D,O
Software Engineering	M,D,O
Telecommunications Management	M,D,O

SAVANNAH COLLEGE OF ART AND DESIGN

Game Design and Development	M

SCHOOL OF THE ART INSTITUTE OF CHICAGO

Materials Sciences	M

SEATTLE UNIVERSITY

Engineering and Applied Sciences—General	M
Software Engineering	M

SETON HALL UNIVERSITY

Management of Technology	M

SHIPPENSBURG UNIVERSITY OF PENNSYLVANIA

Computer Science	M

SILICON VALLEY UNIVERSITY

Computer Engineering	M
Computer Science	M

SIMON FRASER UNIVERSITY

Biotechnology	M,D
Computer Science	M,D
Engineering and Applied Sciences—General	M,D
Information Science	M,D
Management of Technology	M,D

SOUTH CAROLINA STATE UNIVERSITY

Civil Engineering	M
Mechanical Engineering	M
Transportation and Highway Engineering	M

SOUTH DAKOTA SCHOOL OF MINES AND TECHNOLOGY

Artificial Intelligence/Robotics	M
Bioengineering	M,D
Biomedical Engineering	M,D
Chemical Engineering	M
Civil Engineering	M
Computer Science	M
Construction Management	M
Electrical Engineering	M
Engineering and Applied Sciences—General	M,D
Geological Engineering	M,D
Management of Technology	M
Materials Engineering	M,D
Materials Sciences	M,D
Mechanical Engineering	M
Metallurgical Engineering and Metallurgy	M
Nanotechnology	D

SOUTH DAKOTA STATE UNIVERSITY

Agricultural Engineering	M,D
Biosystems Engineering	M,D
Civil Engineering	M
Electrical Engineering	M,D
Engineering and Applied Sciences—General	M,D
Industrial/Management Engineering	M
Mechanical Engineering	M

SOUTHEASTERN LOUISIANA UNIVERSITY

Applied Science and Technology	M

SOUTHEASTERN OKLAHOMA STATE UNIVERSITY

Aviation	M
Biotechnology	M

SOUTHEAST MISSOURI STATE UNIVERSITY

Management of Technology	M

SOUTHERN ARKANSAS UNIVERSITY–MAGNOLIA

Computer Science	M

SOUTHERN CONNECTICUT STATE UNIVERSITY

Computer Science	M

SOUTHERN ILLINOIS UNIVERSITY CARBONDALE

Biomedical Engineering	M
Civil Engineering	M
Computer Engineering	M,D
Computer Science	M,D
Electrical Engineering	M,D
Energy and Power Engineering	D
Engineering and Applied Sciences—General	M,D
Manufacturing Engineering	M
Mechanical Engineering	M
Mechanics	M,D
Mineral/Mining Engineering	M

SOUTHERN ILLINOIS UNIVERSITY EDWARDSVILLE

Biotechnology	M
Civil Engineering	M
Computer Science	M
Electrical Engineering	M
Engineering and Applied Sciences—General	M
Industrial/Management Engineering	M
Mechanical Engineering	M

SOUTHERN METHODIST UNIVERSITY

Applied Science and Technology	M,D
Civil Engineering	M,D
Computer Engineering	M,D
Computer Science	M,D
Electrical Engineering	M,D
Engineering and Applied Sciences—General	M,D
Engineering Management	M,D
Environmental Engineering	M,D
Hazardous Materials Management	M,D
Information Science	M,D
Manufacturing Engineering	M,D
Mechanical Engineering	M,D
Operations Research	M,D
Software Engineering	M,D
Systems Engineering	M,D
Systems Science	M,D
Telecommunications	M,D

SOUTHERN OREGON UNIVERSITY

Computer Science	M

SOUTHERN POLYTECHNIC STATE UNIVERSITY

Computer and Information Systems Security	M,O
Computer Engineering	M
Computer Science	M,O
Construction Management	M
Electrical Engineering	M
Engineering and Applied Sciences—General	M,O
Industrial/Management Engineering	M,O
Information Science	M,O
Software Engineering	M,O
Systems Engineering	M,O

SOUTHERN UNIVERSITY AND AGRICULTURAL AND MECHANICAL COLLEGE

Computer Science	M
Engineering and Applied Sciences—General	M

STANFORD UNIVERSITY

Aerospace/Aeronautical Engineering	M,D,O
Bioengineering	M,D
Biomedical Engineering	M
Chemical Engineering	M,D,O
Civil Engineering	M,D,O
Computer Science	M,D
Electrical Engineering	M,D,O
Engineering and Applied Sciences—General	M,D,O
Engineering Design	M
Engineering Management	M,D
Environmental Engineering	M,D,O
Industrial/Management Engineering	M,D
Materials Engineering	M,D,O
Materials Sciences	M,D,O
Mechanical Engineering	M,D,O*
Medical Informatics	M,D
Petroleum Engineering	M,D,O

STATE UNIVERSITY OF NEW YORK AT BINGHAMTON

Biomedical Engineering	M,D
Computer Science	M,D
Electrical Engineering	M,D
Engineering and Applied Sciences—General	M,D
Industrial/Management Engineering	M,D
Materials Engineering	M,D
Materials Sciences	M,D
Mechanical Engineering	M,D
Systems Science	M,D

STATE UNIVERSITY OF NEW YORK AT NEW PALTZ

Computer Engineering	M
Computer Science	M
Electrical Engineering	M

STATE UNIVERSITY OF NEW YORK AT OSWEGO

Human-Computer Interaction	M

STATE UNIVERSITY OF NEW YORK COLLEGE OF ENVIRONMENTAL SCIENCE AND FORESTRY

Construction Management	M,D
Environmental Engineering	M,D

---

*M—master's degree; P—first professional degree; D—doctorate; O—other advanced degree; *—Close-Up and/or Display*

Paper and Pulp Engineering	M,D

STATE UNIVERSITY OF NEW YORK DOWNSTATE MEDICAL CENTER

Biomedical Engineering	M,D

STATE UNIVERSITY OF NEW YORK INSTITUTE OF TECHNOLOGY

Computer Science	M
Engineering and Applied Sciences—General	M
Information Science	M
Management of Technology	M
Telecommunications	M

STEPHEN F. AUSTIN STATE UNIVERSITY

Biotechnology	M
Computer Science	M

STEPHENS COLLEGE

Health Informatics	M,O

STEVENS INSTITUTE OF TECHNOLOGY

Aerospace/Aeronautical Engineering	M,O
Bioinformatics	M,D,O
Biomedical Engineering	M,O
Chemical Engineering	M,D,O
Civil Engineering	M,D,O
Computer and Information Systems Security	M,D,O
Computer Engineering	M,D,O
Computer Science	M,D,O
Construction Engineering	M,O
Construction Management	M,O
Database Systems	M,D,O
Electrical Engineering	M,D,O
Engineering and Applied Sciences—General	M,D,O
Engineering Design	M
Engineering Management	M,D
Engineering Physics	M,D,O
Environmental Engineering	M,D,O
Financial Engineering	M
Health Informatics	M,D,O
Information Science	M,O
Management of Technology	M,D,O
Manufacturing Engineering	M
Materials Engineering	,M,D
Mechanical Engineering	M,D,O
Ocean Engineering	M,D
Polymer Science and Engineering	M,D,O
Software Engineering	M,D,O
Structural Engineering	M,D,O
Systems Engineering	M,D,O
Systems Science	M,D
Telecommunications Management	M,D,O
Telecommunications	M,D,O
Water Resources Engineering	M,D,O

STEVENSON UNIVERSITY

Information Science	M
Management of Technology	M

STONY BROOK UNIVERSITY, STATE UNIVERSITY OF NEW YORK

Biomedical Engineering	M,D,O
Computer Engineering	M,D,O
Computer Science	M,D,O

Electrical Engineering	M,D
Engineering and Applied Sciences—General	M,D,O
Hazardous Materials Management	M,O
Management of Technology	M
Materials Engineering	M,D
Materials Sciences	M,D
Mechanical Engineering	M,D
Software Engineering	M,D,O
Systems Engineering	M
Technology and Public Policy	D

STRATFORD UNIVERSITY

Computer and Information Systems Security	M
Software Engineering	M
Telecommunications	M

STRAYER UNIVERSITY

Computer and Information Systems Security	M
Information Science	M
Software Engineering	M
Systems Science	M
Telecommunications Management	M

SUFFOLK UNIVERSITY

Computer Science	M

SULLIVAN UNIVERSITY

Management of Technology	P,M

SYRACUSE UNIVERSITY

Aerospace/Aeronautical Engineering	M,D
Bioengineering	M,D
Chemical Engineering	M,D
Civil Engineering	M,D
Computer and Information Systems Security	O
Computer Engineering	M,D,O
Computer Science	M
Electrical Engineering	M,D,O
Engineering and Applied Sciences—General	M,D,O*
Engineering Management	M
Environmental Engineering	M,D
Information Science	D
Mechanical Engineering	M,D
Telecommunications Management	M,O
Telecommunications	M

TEACHERS COLLEGE, COLUMBIA UNIVERSITY

Management of Technology	M

TÉLÉ-UNIVERSITÉ

Computer Science	M,D

TEMPLE UNIVERSITY

Civil Engineering	M
Computer Engineering	M
Computer Science	M,D
Electrical Engineering	M
Engineering and Applied Sciences—General	M,D
Financial Engineering	M
Information Science	M,D
Mechanical Engineering	M

TENNESSEE STATE UNIVERSITY

Engineering and Applied Sciences—General	M,D

TENNESSEE TECHNOLOGICAL UNIVERSITY

Chemical Engineering	M,D
Civil Engineering	M,D
Computer Science	M
Electrical Engineering	M,D
Engineering and Applied Sciences—General	M,D
Mechanical Engineering	M,D

TEXAS A&M HEALTH SCIENCE CENTER

Materials Sciences	M

TEXAS A&M UNIVERSITY

Aerospace/Aeronautical Engineering	M,D
Agricultural Engineering	M,D
Bioengineering	M,D
Biomedical Engineering	M,D
Chemical Engineering	M,D
Civil Engineering	M,D
Computer Engineering	M,D
Computer Science	M,D
Construction Engineering	M,D
Construction Management	M,D
Electrical Engineering	M,D
Engineering and Applied Sciences—General	M,D
Environmental Engineering	M,D
Geotechnical Engineering	M,D
Industrial/Management Engineering	M,D
Manufacturing Engineering	M
Materials Engineering	M,D
Mechanical Engineering	M,D
Nuclear Engineering	M,D
Ocean Engineering	M,D
Petroleum Engineering	M,D
Structural Engineering	M,D
Transportation and Highway Engineering	M,D
Water Resources Engineering	M,D

TEXAS A&M UNIVERSITY–COMMERCE

Computer Science	M
Industrial/Management Engineering	M
Management of Technology	M

TEXAS A&M UNIVERSITY–CORPUS CHRISTI

Computer Science	M

TEXAS A&M UNIVERSITY–KINGSVILLE

Chemical Engineering	M
Civil Engineering	M
Computer Science	M
Electrical Engineering	M
Engineering and Applied Sciences—General	M,D
Environmental Engineering	M,D
Industrial/Management Engineering	M
Mechanical Engineering	M
Petroleum Engineering	M

TEXAS SOUTHERN UNIVERSITY

Computer Science	M
Industrial/Management Engineering	M
Transportation and Highway Engineering	M

TEXAS STATE UNIVERSITY–SAN MARCOS

Computer Science	M
Industrial/Management Engineering	M
Management of Technology	M
Software Engineering	M

TEXAS TECH UNIVERSITY

Bioinformatics	M,D
Biotechnology	M,D
Chemical Engineering	M,D
Civil Engineering	M,D
Computer Science	M,D
Electrical Engineering	M,D
Engineering and Applied Sciences—General	M,D
Engineering Management	M,D
Environmental Engineering	M,D
Industrial/Management Engineering	M,D
Manufacturing Engineering	M,D
Mechanical Engineering	M,D
Petroleum Engineering	M,D
Software Engineering	M,D
Systems Engineering	M,D

TEXAS TECH UNIVERSITY HEALTH SCIENCES CENTER

Biotechnology	M

THOMAS EDISON STATE COLLEGE

Applied Science and Technology	O

THOMAS JEFFERSON UNIVERSITY

Biomedical Engineering	D
Biotechnology	D

TOWSON UNIVERSITY

Computer and Information Systems Security	D,O
Computer Science	M
Database Systems	D,O
Information Science	M,D,O
Software Engineering	D,O

TRENT UNIVERSITY

Computer Science	M
Materials Sciences	M

TREVECCA NAZARENE UNIVERSITY

Information Science	M

TRINE UNIVERSITY

Civil Engineering	M
Engineering and Applied Sciences—General	M
Mechanical Engineering	M

TROY UNIVERSITY

Computer Science	M

TUFTS UNIVERSITY

Bioengineering	M,D,O
Biomedical Engineering	M,D
Biotechnology	O
Chemical Engineering	M,D
Civil Engineering	M,D
Computer Science	M,D,O
Electrical Engineering	M,D,O
Engineering and Applied Sciences—General	M,D
Engineering Management	M
Environmental Engineering	M,D
Ergonomics and Human Factors	M,D
Geotechnical Engineering	M,D
Hazardous Materials Management	M,D
Human-Computer Interaction	O
Manufacturing Engineering	O
Mechanical Engineering	M,D
Structural Engineering	M,D
Water Resources Engineering	M,D

TUI UNIVERSITY

Computer and Information Systems Security	M,D
Health Informatics	M,D,O

TULANE UNIVERSITY

Biomedical Engineering	M,D
Chemical Engineering	D

TUSKEGEE UNIVERSITY

Electrical Engineering	M
Engineering and Applied Sciences—General	M,D
Materials Engineering	D
Mechanical Engineering	M

UNION GRADUATE COLLEGE

Computer Science	M
Electrical Engineering	M
Engineering and Applied Sciences—General	M
Engineering Management	M
Mechanical Engineering	M

UNIVERSIDAD AUTONOMA DE GUADALAJARA

Computer Science	M,D
Energy and Power Engineering	M,D
Manufacturing Engineering	M,D
Systems Science	M,D

UNIVERSIDAD CENTRAL DEL ESTE

Environmental Engineering	P,M,D

UNIVERSIDAD DE LAS AMÉRICAS–PUEBLA

Biotechnology	M
Chemical Engineering	M
Computer Science	M,D
Construction Management	M
Electrical Engineering	M
Engineering and Applied Sciences—General	M,D
Industrial/Management Engineering	M
Manufacturing Engineering	M

UNIVERSIDAD DEL ESTE

Computer and Information Systems Security	M

UNIVERSIDAD DEL TURABO

Telecommunications	M

UNIVERSIDAD NACIONAL PEDRO HENRIQUEZ URENA

Construction Engineering	P,M,D
Environmental Engineering	P,M,D

UNIVERSITÉ DE MONCTON

Civil Engineering	M
Computer Science	M,O
Electrical Engineering	M
Engineering and Applied Sciences—General	M
Industrial/Management Engineering	M
Mechanical Engineering	M

UNIVERSITÉ DE MONTRÉAL

Biomedical Engineering	M,D,O
Computer Science	M,D
Ergonomics and Human Factors	O

UNIVERSITÉ DE SHERBROOKE

Biotechnology	P,M,D,O
Chemical Engineering	M,D
Civil Engineering	M,D
Electrical Engineering	M,D
Engineering and Applied Sciences—General	M,D,O
Engineering Management	M,O
Environmental Engineering	M
Information Science	M,D
Mechanical Engineering	M,D

UNIVERSITÉ DU QUÉBEC À CHICOUTIMI

Engineering and Applied Sciences—General	M,D

UNIVERSITÉ DU QUÉBEC À MONTRÉAL

Ergonomics and Human Factors	O

UNIVERSITÉ DU QUÉBEC À RIMOUSKI

Engineering and Applied Sciences—General	M

UNIVERSITÉ DU QUÉBEC À TROIS-RIVIÈRES

Computer Science	M
Electrical Engineering	M,D
Industrial/Management Engineering	M,O

UNIVERSITÉ DU QUÉBEC, ÉCOLE DE TECHNOLOGIE SUPÉRIEURE

Engineering and Applied Sciences—General	M,D,O

UNIVERSITÉ DU QUÉBEC EN ABITIBI-TÉMISCAMINGUE

Engineering and Applied Sciences—General	M,O

Mineral/Mining Engineering	M,O

UNIVERSITÉ DU QUÉBEC EN OUTAOUAIS

Computer Science	M,D
Software Engineering	O

UNIVERSITÉ DU QUÉBEC, INSTITUT NATIONAL DE LA RECHERCHE SCIENTIFIQUE

Energy Management and Policy	M,D
Materials Sciences	M,D
Telecommunications	M,D

UNIVERSITÉ LAVAL

Aerospace/Aeronautical Engineering	M
Agricultural Engineering	M
Chemical Engineering	M,D
Civil Engineering	M,D,O
Computer Science	M,D
Electrical Engineering	M,D
Engineering and Applied Sciences—General	M,D,O
Environmental Engineering	M,D
Industrial/Management Engineering	O
Mechanical Engineering	M,D
Metallurgical Engineering and Metallurgy	M,D
Mineral/Mining Engineering	M,D
Software Engineering	O

UNIVERSITY AT ALBANY, STATE UNIVERSITY OF NEW YORK

Computer Science	M,D
Information Science	M,D,O
Management of Technology	M
Nanotechnology	M,D

UNIVERSITY AT BUFFALO, THE STATE UNIVERSITY OF NEW YORK

Aerospace/Aeronautical Engineering	M,D
Bioengineering	M,D
Biotechnology	M
Chemical Engineering	M,D
Civil Engineering	M,D
Computer Science	M,D
Electrical Engineering	M,D
Engineering and Applied Sciences—General	M,D*
Environmental Engineering	M,D
Financial Engineering	M,D,O
Industrial/Management Engineering	M,D
Materials Sciences	M
Mechanical Engineering	M,D
Structural Engineering	M,D

UNIVERSITY OF ADVANCING TECHNOLOGY

Computer and Information Systems Security	M
Computer Science	M
Game Design and Development	M
Management of Technology	M

THE UNIVERSITY OF AKRON

Biomedical Engineering	M,D
Chemical Engineering	M,D
Civil Engineering	M,D
Computer Engineering	M,D
Computer Science	M
Electrical Engineering	M,D
Engineering and Applied Sciences—General	M,D
Engineering Management	M
Management of Technology	M
Mechanical Engineering	M,D
Polymer Science and Engineering	M,D

THE UNIVERSITY OF ALABAMA

Aerospace/Aeronautical Engineering	M,D
Chemical Engineering	M,D
Civil Engineering	M,D
Computer Engineering	M,D
Computer Science	M,D
Construction Engineering	M,D
Electrical Engineering	M,D
Engineering and Applied Sciences—General	M,D
Environmental Engineering	M,D
Ergonomics and Human Factors	M
Materials Engineering	M,D
Materials Sciences	D
Mechanical Engineering	M,D
Mechanics	M,D
Metallurgical Engineering and Metallurgy	M,D

THE UNIVERSITY OF ALABAMA AT BIRMINGHAM

Biomedical Engineering	M,D
Civil Engineering	M,D
Computer Engineering	D
Computer Science	M,D
Electrical Engineering	M
Engineering and Applied Sciences—General	M,D
Health Informatics	M
Information Science	M,D
Materials Engineering	M,D
Materials Sciences	D
Mechanical Engineering	M

THE UNIVERSITY OF ALABAMA IN HUNTSVILLE

Aerospace/Aeronautical Engineering	M,D
Biotechnology	D
Chemical Engineering	M
Civil Engineering	M,D
Computer Engineering	M,D
Computer Science	M,D,O
Electrical Engineering	M,D
Engineering and Applied Sciences—General	M,D
Engineering Management	M,D
Environmental Engineering	M,D
Geotechnical Engineering	M,D
Industrial/Management Engineering	M,D
Materials Sciences	M,D
Mechanical Engineering	M,D
Operations Research	M
Software Engineering	M,D,O
Structural Engineering	M,D
Systems Engineering	M,D
Transportation and Highway Engineering	M,D

*M—master's degree; P—first professional degree; D—doctorate; O—other advanced degree; *—Close-Up and / or Display*

Water Resources
  Engineering — M,D

UNIVERSITY OF ALASKA ANCHORAGE

Civil Engineering — M,O
Engineering and Applied
  Sciences—General — M,O
Engineering Management — M
Environmental
  Engineering — M
Geological Engineering — M
Ocean Engineering — M,O

UNIVERSITY OF ALASKA FAIRBANKS

Civil Engineering — M,D
Computer Engineering — M,D
Computer Science — M
Electrical Engineering — M,D
Engineering and Applied
  Sciences—General — M,D
Engineering Management — M,D
Environmental
  Engineering — M,D
Geological Engineering — M,D
Mechanical Engineering — M,D
Mineral/Mining
  Engineering — M
Petroleum Engineering — M,D
Software Engineering — M

UNIVERSITY OF ALBERTA

Biomedical Engineering — M,D
Biotechnology — M,D
Chemical Engineering — M,D
Civil Engineering — M,D
Computer Engineering — M,D
Computer Science — M,D
Construction Engineering — M,D
Electrical Engineering — M,D
Energy and Power
  Engineering — M,D
Engineering Management — M,D
Environmental
  Engineering — M,D
Geotechnical Engineering — M,D
Materials Engineering — M,D
Mechanical Engineering — M,D
Mineral/Mining
  Engineering — M,D
Nanotechnology — M,D
Petroleum Engineering — M,D
Structural Engineering — M,D
Systems Engineering — M,D
Telecommunications — M,D
Water Resources
  Engineering — M,D

THE UNIVERSITY OF ARIZONA

Aerospace/Aeronautical
  Engineering — M,D
Agricultural Engineering — M,D
Biomedical Engineering — M,D
Biosystems Engineering — M,D
Chemical Engineering — M,D
Civil Engineering — M,D
Computer Engineering — M,D
Computer Science — M,D
Electrical Engineering — M,D
Engineering and Applied
  Sciences—General — M,D,O
Environmental
  Engineering — M,D
Geological Engineering — M,D,O
Industrial/Management
  Engineering — M,D
Materials Engineering — M,D
Materials Sciences — M,D
Mechanical Engineering — M,D
Mechanics — M,D

Medical Informatics — M,D,O
Mineral/Mining
  Engineering — M,O
Reliability Engineering — M
Systems Engineering — M,D

UNIVERSITY OF ARKANSAS

Agricultural Engineering — M,D
Bioengineering — M
Biomedical Engineering — M
Chemical Engineering — M,D
Civil Engineering — M,D
Computer Engineering — M,D
Computer Science — M,D
Electrical Engineering — M,D
Electronic Materials — M,D
Engineering and Applied
  Sciences—General — M,D
Environmental
  Engineering — M
Industrial/Management
  Engineering — M,D
Mechanical Engineering — M,D
Operations Research — M,D
Telecommunications — M,D
Transportation and
  Highway Engineering — M

UNIVERSITY OF ARKANSAS AT LITTLE ROCK

Applied Science and
  Technology — M,D
Bioinformatics — M,D
Computer Science — M
Construction Management — M,O
Information Science — M
Management of
  Technology — M,O
Systems Engineering — O

UNIVERSITY OF ATLANTA

Computer Science — P,M,D,O

UNIVERSITY OF BALTIMORE

Human-Computer
  Interaction — M,D
Information Science — M,D

UNIVERSITY OF BRIDGEPORT

Computer Engineering — M,D
Computer Science — M,D
Electrical Engineering — M
Engineering and Applied
  Sciences—General — M,D
Management of
  Technology — M
Mechanical Engineering — M

THE UNIVERSITY OF BRITISH COLUMBIA

Chemical Engineering — M,D
Civil Engineering — M,D
Computer Engineering — M,D
Computer Science — M,D
Electrical Engineering — M,D
Engineering and Applied
  Sciences—General — M,D
Engineering Physics — M
Geological Engineering — M,D
Materials Engineering — M,D
Materials Sciences — M,D
Mechanical Engineering — M,D
Metallurgical Engineering
  and Metallurgy — M,D
Mineral/Mining
  Engineering — M,D
Operations Research — M
Software Engineering — M

UNIVERSITY OF CALGARY

Biomedical Engineering — M,D
Biotechnology — M
Chemical Engineering — M,D
Civil Engineering — M,D
Computer Engineering — M,D
Computer Science — M,D
Electrical Engineering — M,D
Engineering and Applied
  Sciences—General — M,D
Geotechnical Engineering — M,D
Manufacturing Engineering — M,D
Mechanical Engineering — M,D
Petroleum Engineering — M,D
Software Engineering — M,D

UNIVERSITY OF CALIFORNIA, BERKELEY

Applied Science and
  Technology — D
Bioengineering — D
Chemical Engineering — M,D
Civil Engineering — M,D
Computer Science — M,D
Construction Management — O
Electrical Engineering — M,D
Energy Management and
  Policy — M,D
Engineering and Applied
  Sciences—General — M,D,O
Engineering Management — M,D
Environmental
  Engineering — M,D
Financial Engineering — M
Geotechnical Engineering — M,D
Industrial/Management
  Engineering — M,D
Materials Engineering — M,D
Materials Sciences — M,D
Mechanical Engineering — M,D
Mechanics — M,D
Nuclear Engineering — M,D
Operations Research — M,D
Structural Engineering — M,D
Transportation and
  Highway Engineering — M,D
Water Resources
  Engineering — M,D

UNIVERSITY OF CALIFORNIA, DAVIS

Aerospace/Aeronautical
  Engineering — M,D,O
Applied Science and
  Technology — M,D
Bioengineering — M,D
Biomedical Engineering — M,D
Chemical Engineering — M,D
Civil Engineering — M,D,O
Computer Engineering — M,D
Computer Science — M,D
Electrical Engineering — M,D
Engineering and Applied
  Sciences—General — M,D,O
Environmental
  Engineering — M,D,O
Materials Engineering — M,D
Materials Sciences — M,D
Mechanical Engineering — M,D,O
Medical Informatics — M
Transportation and
  Highway Engineering — M,D

UNIVERSITY OF CALIFORNIA, IRVINE

Aerospace/Aeronautical
  Engineering — M,D
Biochemical Engineering — M,D
Biomedical Engineering — M,D
Biotechnology — M
Chemical Engineering — M,D

Civil Engineering — M,D
Computer Science — M,D
Electrical Engineering — M,D
Engineering and Applied
  Sciences—General — M,D
Environmental
  Engineering — M,D
Information Science — M,D
Materials Engineering — M,D
Materials Sciences — M,D
Mechanical Engineering — M,D
Transportation and
  Highway Engineering — M,D

UNIVERSITY OF CALIFORNIA, LOS ANGELES

Aerospace/Aeronautical
  Engineering — M,D
Biomedical Engineering — M,D
Chemical Engineering — M,D
Civil Engineering — M,D
Computer Science — M,D
Electrical Engineering — M,D
Engineering and Applied
  Sciences—General — M,D
Environmental
  Engineering — M,D
Manufacturing Engineering — M
Materials Engineering — M,D
Materials Sciences — M,D
Mechanical Engineering — M,D

UNIVERSITY OF CALIFORNIA, MERCED

Bioengineering — M,D
Computer Science — M,D
Electrical Engineering — M,D
Engineering and Applied
  Sciences—General — M,D
Mechanical Engineering — M,D
Mechanics — M,D

UNIVERSITY OF CALIFORNIA, RIVERSIDE

Artificial Intelligence/
  Robotics — M,D
Bioengineering — M,D
Bioinformatics — D
Chemical Engineering — M,D
Computer Engineering — M,D
Computer Science — M,D*
Electrical Engineering — M,D
Environmental
  Engineering — M,D
Materials Engineering — M,D
Materials Sciences — M,D
Mechanical Engineering — M,D
Nanotechnology — M,D

UNIVERSITY OF CALIFORNIA, SAN DIEGO

Aerospace/Aeronautical
  Engineering — M,D
Artificial Intelligence/
  Robotics — M,D
Bioengineering — M,D*
Bioinformatics — D*
Chemical Engineering — M,D
Computer Engineering — M,D
Computer Science — M,D*
Electrical Engineering — M,D*
Engineering Physics — M,D
Materials Sciences — M,D
Mechanical Engineering — M,D
Mechanics — M,D
Ocean Engineering — M,D
Structural Engineering — M,D
Telecommunications — M,D

UNIVERSITY OF CALIFORNIA, SAN FRANCISCO

Bioengineering	D
Medical Informatics	D

UNIVERSITY OF CALIFORNIA, SANTA BARBARA

Chemical Engineering	M,D
Computer Engineering	M,D
Computer Science	M,D
Electrical Engineering	M,D
Engineering and Applied Sciences—General	M,D
Materials Engineering	M,D
Materials Sciences	M,D
Mechanical Engineering	M,D

UNIVERSITY OF CALIFORNIA, SANTA CRUZ

Bioinformatics	M,D
Computer Engineering	M,D
Computer Science	M,D
Electrical Engineering	M,D
Engineering and Applied Sciences—General	M,D
Telecommunications	M,D

UNIVERSITY OF CENTRAL ARKANSAS

Computer Science	M

UNIVERSITY OF CENTRAL FLORIDA

Aerospace/Aeronautical Engineering	M
Civil Engineering	M,D,O
Computer Engineering	M,D
Computer Science	M,D
Construction Engineering	M,D,O
Electrical Engineering	M,D,O
Engineering and Applied Sciences—General	M,D,O
Engineering Design	M,D,O
Environmental Engineering	M,D
Ergonomics and Human Factors	M,D,O
Industrial/Management Engineering	M,D,O
Materials Engineering	M,D
Materials Sciences	M,D
Mechanical Engineering	M,D,O
Operations Research	M,D,O
Structural Engineering	M,D,O
Systems Engineering	M,D,O
Transportation and Highway Engineering	M,D,O

UNIVERSITY OF CENTRAL MISSOURI

Aerospace/Aeronautical Engineering	M,D
Computer Science	M,D
Information Science	M,D,O
Management of Technology	M,D

UNIVERSITY OF CENTRAL OKLAHOMA

Computer Science	M
Engineering and Applied Sciences—General	M

UNIVERSITY OF CHICAGO

Computer Science	M

UNIVERSITY OF CINCINNATI

Aerospace/Aeronautical Engineering	M,D
Bioinformatics	D
Biomedical Engineering	D
Ceramic Sciences and Engineering	M,D
Chemical Engineering	M,D
Civil Engineering	M,D
Computer Engineering	M,D
Computer Science	M,D
Electrical Engineering	M,D
Engineering and Applied Sciences—General	M,D
Environmental Engineering	M,D
Ergonomics and Human Factors	M,D
Industrial/Management Engineering	M,D
Materials Engineering	M,D
Materials Sciences	M,D
Mechanical Engineering	M,D
Mechanics	M,D
Metallurgical Engineering and Metallurgy	M,D
Nuclear Engineering	M,D
Polymer Science and Engineering	M,D

UNIVERSITY OF COLORADO AT BOULDER

Aerospace/Aeronautical Engineering	M,D
Architectural Engineering	M,D
Chemical Engineering	M,D
Civil Engineering	M,D
Computer Engineering	M,D
Computer Science	M,D
Construction Engineering	M,D
Electrical Engineering	M,D
Engineering and Applied Sciences—General	M,D
Engineering Management	M
Environmental Engineering	M,D
Geotechnical Engineering	M,D
Mechanical Engineering	M,D
Operations Research	M
Structural Engineering	M,D
Telecommunications Management	M
Telecommunications	M
Water Resources Engineering	M,D

UNIVERSITY OF COLORADO AT COLORADO SPRINGS

Aerospace/Aeronautical Engineering	M
Computer Science	M,D
Electrical Engineering	M,D
Engineering and Applied Sciences—General	M,D
Engineering Management	M
Information Science	M
Manufacturing Engineering	M
Mechanical Engineering	M
Software Engineering	M

UNIVERSITY OF COLORADO DENVER

Applied Science and Technology	M
Civil Engineering	M,D
Computer Engineering	M,D
Computer Science	M,D
Electrical Engineering	M
Information Science	D
Mechanical Engineering	M

UNIVERSITY OF CONNECTICUT

Biomedical Engineering	M,D
Chemical Engineering	M,D
Civil Engineering	M,D
Computer Science	M,D
Electrical Engineering	M,D
Engineering and Applied Sciences—General	M,D
Environmental Engineering	M,D
Materials Engineering	M,D
Materials Sciences	M,D
Mechanical Engineering	M,D
Metallurgical Engineering and Metallurgy	M,D
Polymer Science and Engineering	M,D
Software Engineering	M,D

UNIVERSITY OF DALLAS

Management of Technology	M

UNIVERSITY OF DAYTON

Aerospace/Aeronautical Engineering	M,D
Agricultural Engineering	M
Chemical Engineering	M
Civil Engineering	M
Computer Engineering	M,D
Computer Science	M
Electrical Engineering	M,D
Engineering and Applied Sciences—General	M,D
Engineering Management	M
Environmental Engineering	M
Materials Engineering	M,D
Mechanical Engineering	M,D
Mechanics	M
Structural Engineering	M
Transportation and Highway Engineering	M
Water Resources Engineering	M

UNIVERSITY OF DELAWARE

Biotechnology	M,D
Chemical Engineering	M,D
Civil Engineering	M,D
Computer Engineering	M,D
Computer Science	M,D*
Electrical Engineering	M,D
Energy Management and Policy	M,D
Engineering and Applied Sciences—General	M,D
Environmental Engineering	M,D
Geotechnical Engineering	M,D
Information Science	M,D
Management of Technology	M
Materials Engineering	M,D
Materials Sciences	M,D
Mechanical Engineering	M,D
Ocean Engineering	M,D
Operations Research	M,D
Structural Engineering	M,D
Transportation and Highway Engineering	M,D
Water Resources Engineering	M,D

UNIVERSITY OF DENVER

Bioengineering	M,D
Computer Engineering	M
Computer Science	M,D,O
Construction Management	M

Electrical Engineering	M
Management of Technology	M,O
Materials Engineering	M,D
Mechanical Engineering	M,D
Telecommunications Management	M,O
Telecommunications	M,O

UNIVERSITY OF DETROIT MERCY

Architectural Engineering	M
Civil Engineering	M,D
Computer Engineering	M,D
Computer Science	M
Electrical Engineering	M,D
Engineering and Applied Sciences—General	M,D
Engineering Management	M
Environmental Engineering	M,D
Information Science	M
Mechanical Engineering	M,D
Software Engineering	M

UNIVERSITY OF EVANSVILLE

Computer Science	M
Electrical Engineering	M
Engineering and Applied Sciences—General	M

UNIVERSITY OF FLORIDA

Aerospace/Aeronautical Engineering	M,D,O
Agricultural Engineering	M,D,O
Bioengineering	M,D,O
Biomedical Engineering	M,D,O
Chemical Engineering	M,D
Civil Engineering	M,D,O
Computer Engineering	M,D,O
Computer Science	M,D
Construction Engineering	M,D
Electrical Engineering	M,D,O
Engineering and Applied Sciences—General	M,D,O
Environmental Engineering	M,D,O
Industrial/Management Engineering	M,D,O
Information Science	M,D
Materials Engineering	M,D,O
Materials Sciences	M,D,O
Mechanical Engineering	M,D,O
Nuclear Engineering	M,D,O
Ocean Engineering	M,D,O
Systems Engineering	M,D,O

UNIVERSITY OF GEORGIA

Agricultural Engineering	M,D
Artificial Intelligence/Robotics	M
Bioengineering	M,D
Computer Science	M,D
Internet Engineering	M

UNIVERSITY OF GUELPH

Bioengineering	M,D
Biotechnology	M,D
Computer Science	M,D
Engineering and Applied Sciences—General	M,D
Environmental Engineering	M,D
Water Resources Engineering	M,D

UNIVERSITY OF HARTFORD

Engineering and Applied Sciences—General	M

---

*M—master's degree; P—first professional degree; D—doctorate; O—other advanced degree; *—Close-Up and/or Display*

UNIVERSITY OF HAWAII AT MANOA

Bioengineering	M
Civil Engineering	M,D
Computer Science	M,D,O
Electrical Engineering	M,D
Engineering and Applied Sciences—General	M,D
Environmental Engineering	M,D
Financial Engineering	M
Geological Engineering	M,D
Information Science	M,D
Mechanical Engineering	M,D
Ocean Engineering	M,D
Telecommunications	O

UNIVERSITY OF HOUSTON

Biomedical Engineering	M
Chemical Engineering	M,D
Civil Engineering	M,D
Computer and Information Systems Security	M
Computer Engineering	M,D
Computer Science	M,D*
Construction Management	M
Electrical Engineering	M,D
Engineering and Applied Sciences—General	M,D
Environmental Engineering	M,D
Industrial/Management Engineering	M,D
Information Science	M,D
Mechanical Engineering	M,D
Telecommunications	M

UNIVERSITY OF HOUSTON–CLEAR LAKE

Biotechnology	M
Computer Engineering	M
Computer Science	M
Information Science	M
Software Engineering	M
Systems Engineering	M

UNIVERSITY OF HOUSTON–VICTORIA

Computer Science	M

UNIVERSITY OF IDAHO

Agricultural Engineering	M,D
Bioengineering	M,D
Bioinformatics	M,D
Chemical Engineering	M,D
Civil Engineering	M,D
Computer Engineering	M
Computer Science	M,D
Electrical Engineering	M,D
Engineering and Applied Sciences—General	M,D
Engineering Management	M
Environmental Engineering	M
Geological Engineering	M
Materials Engineering	M,D
Materials Sciences	M,D
Metallurgical Engineering and Metallurgy	M,D
Mineral/Mining Engineering	M,D
Nuclear Engineering	M,D

UNIVERSITY OF ILLINOIS AT CHICAGO

Bioengineering	M,D
Biotechnology	D
Chemical Engineering	M,D
Civil Engineering	M,D
Computer Engineering	M,D

Computer Science	M,D
Electrical Engineering	M,D
Engineering and Applied Sciences—General	M,D
Health Informatics	M
Industrial/Management Engineering	M,D
Materials Engineering	M,D
Mechanical Engineering	M,D
Operations Research	D

UNIVERSITY OF ILLINOIS AT SPRINGFIELD

Computer Science	M

UNIVERSITY OF ILLINOIS AT URBANA–CHAMPAIGN

Aerospace/Aeronautical Engineering	M,D
Agricultural Engineering	M,D
Aviation	M
Bioengineering	M,D
Bioinformatics	M,D,O
Chemical Engineering	M,D
Civil Engineering	M,D
Computer Engineering	M,D
Computer Science	M,D
Electrical Engineering	M,D
Energy Management and Policy	M,D
Engineering and Applied Sciences—General	M,D
Environmental Engineering	M,D
Ergonomics and Human Factors	M
Financial Engineering	M,D
Health Informatics	M,D,O
Human-Computer Interaction	M,D,O
Industrial/Management Engineering	M,D
Information Science	M,D,O
Management of Technology	M,D
Materials Engineering	M,D
Materials Sciences	M,D
Mechanical Engineering	M,D
Mechanics	M,D
Medical Informatics	M,D,O
Nuclear Engineering	M,D*
Systems Engineering	M,D

THE UNIVERSITY OF IOWA

Biochemical Engineering	M,D
Biomedical Engineering	M,D
Chemical Engineering	M,D
Civil Engineering	M,D
Computer Engineering	M,D
Computer Science	M,D
Electrical Engineering	M,D
Engineering and Applied Sciences—General	M,D*
Environmental Engineering	M,D
Ergonomics and Human Factors	M,D
Health Informatics	M,D,O
Industrial/Management Engineering	M,D
Information Science	M,D,O
Manufacturing Engineering	M,D
Mechanical Engineering	M,D
Operations Research	M,D

THE UNIVERSITY OF KANSAS

Aerospace/Aeronautical Engineering	M,D
Architectural Engineering	M
Bioengineering	M,D
Biotechnology	M

Chemical Engineering	M,D
Civil Engineering	M,D
Computer Engineering	M
Computer Science	M,D
Construction Management	M
Electrical Engineering	M,D
Engineering and Applied Sciences—General	M,D
Engineering Management	M
Environmental Engineering	M,D
Mechanical Engineering	M,D
Medical Informatics	M,D,O
Petroleum Engineering	M,D

UNIVERSITY OF KENTUCKY

Agricultural Engineering	M,D
Biomedical Engineering	M,D
Chemical Engineering	M,D
Civil Engineering	M,D
Computer Science	M,D
Electrical Engineering	M,D
Engineering and Applied Sciences—General	M,D
Manufacturing Engineering	M
Materials Sciences	M,D
Mechanical Engineering	M,D
Mineral/Mining Engineering	M,D

UNIVERSITY OF LA VERNE

Health Informatics	M

UNIVERSITY OF LETHBRIDGE

Computer Science	M,D

UNIVERSITY OF LOUISIANA AT LAFAYETTE

Architectural Engineering	M
Chemical Engineering	M
Civil Engineering	M
Computer Engineering	M,D
Computer Science	M,D
Engineering Management	M
Mechanical Engineering	M
Petroleum Engineering	M
Telecommunications	M

UNIVERSITY OF LOUISVILLE

Chemical Engineering	M,D
Civil Engineering	M,D
Computer and Information Systems Security	M,D,O
Computer Engineering	M,D,O
Computer Science	M,D,O
Electrical Engineering	M,D
Engineering and Applied Sciences—General	M,D,O
Engineering Management	M,D,O
Environmental Engineering	M,D
Industrial/Management Engineering	M,D,O
Mechanical Engineering	M,D

UNIVERSITY OF MAINE

Bioengineering	M
Chemical Engineering	M,D
Civil Engineering	M,D
Computer Engineering	M,D
Computer Science	M,D
Electrical Engineering	M,D
Engineering and Applied Sciences—General	M,D
Engineering Physics	M
Environmental Engineering	M,D
Geotechnical Engineering	M,D

Mechanical Engineering	M,D
Structural Engineering	M,D

UNIVERSITY OF MANAGEMENT AND TECHNOLOGY

Computer Science	M,O
Information Science	M,O
Software Engineering	M,O

UNIVERSITY OF MANITOBA

Biosystems Engineering	M,D
Civil Engineering	M,D
Computer Engineering	M,D
Computer Science	M,D
Electrical Engineering	M,D
Engineering and Applied Sciences—General	M,D
Industrial/Management Engineering	M,D
Manufacturing Engineering	M,D
Mechanical Engineering	M,D

UNIVERSITY OF MARYLAND, BALTIMORE COUNTY

Biochemical Engineering	M,D,O
Biotechnology	O
Chemical Engineering	M,D
Civil Engineering	M,D
Computer Engineering	M,D
Computer Science	M,D
Electrical Engineering	M,D
Engineering and Applied Sciences—General	M,D,O
Engineering Management	M,O
Environmental Engineering	M,D
Information Science	M,D
Mechanical Engineering	M,D,O
Systems Engineering	M,O

UNIVERSITY OF MARYLAND, COLLEGE PARK

Aerospace/Aeronautical Engineering	M,D,O
Bioengineering	M,D
Chemical Engineering	M,D,O
Civil Engineering	M,D,O
Computer Engineering	M,D
Computer Science	M,D
Electrical Engineering	M,D,O
Engineering and Applied Sciences—General	M
Environmental Engineering	M,D
Fire Protection Engineering	M,O
Manufacturing Engineering	M,D
Materials Engineering	M,D,O
Materials Sciences	M,D,O
Mechanical Engineering	M,D,O
Mechanics	M,D
Nuclear Engineering	M,D
Reliability Engineering	M,D,O
Systems Engineering	M,O
Telecommunications	M*

UNIVERSITY OF MARYLAND EASTERN SHORE

Computer Science	M

UNIVERSITY OF MARYLAND UNIVERSITY COLLEGE

Biotechnology	M,O
Health Informatics	M,O
Information Science	M,O
Management of Technology	M,O

UNIVERSITY OF MASSACHUSETTS AMHERST

Biotechnology	M,D
Chemical Engineering	M,D
Civil Engineering	M,D
Computer Engineering	M,D
Computer Science	M,D
Electrical Engineering	M,D
Engineering and Applied Sciences—General	M,D
Engineering Management	
Environmental Engineering	M
Industrial/Management Engineering	M,D
Mechanical Engineering	M,D
Operations Research	M,D
Polymer Science and Engineering	M,D

UNIVERSITY OF MASSACHUSETTS BOSTON

Biotechnology	M
Computer Science	M,D

UNIVERSITY OF MASSACHUSETTS DARTMOUTH

Biomedical Engineering	D
Biotechnology	D
Civil Engineering	M
Computer Engineering	M,D,O
Computer Science	M,O
Electrical Engineering	M,D,O
Engineering and Applied Sciences—General	M,D,O
Environmental Engineering	M
Mechanical Engineering	M
Software Engineering	M,O
Telecommunications	M,D,O
Textile Sciences and Engineering	M

UNIVERSITY OF MASSACHUSETTS LOWELL

Biotechnology	M,D
Chemical Engineering	M,D
Civil Engineering	M,D,O
Computer Engineering	M
Computer Science	M,D
Electrical Engineering	M,D
Energy and Power Engineering	M,D
Engineering and Applied Sciences—General	M,D,O
Environmental Engineering	M,D,O
Ergonomics and Human Factors	M,D,O
Health Informatics	M,O
Industrial/Management Engineering	M,D,O
Materials Engineering	M,D,O
Mechanical Engineering	M,D
Mechanics	M,D
Nuclear Engineering	M,D
Polymer Science and Engineering	M,D,O

UNIVERSITY OF MASSACHUSETTS WORCESTER

Biomedical Engineering	D

UNIVERSITY OF MEDICINE AND DENTISTRY OF NEW JERSEY

Bioinformatics	M,D
Biomedical Engineering	M,D,O
Medical Informatics	M,D,O

UNIVERSITY OF MEMPHIS

Biomedical Engineering	M,D
Civil Engineering	M,D
Computer Engineering	M,D
Computer Science	M,D
Electrical Engineering	M,D
Energy and Power Engineering	M,D
Engineering and Applied Sciences—General	M,D
Environmental Engineering	M,D
Industrial/Management Engineering	M,D
Manufacturing Engineering	M
Mechanical Engineering	M,D
Structural Engineering	M,D
Transportation and Highway Engineering	M,D
Water Resources Engineering	M,D

UNIVERSITY OF MIAMI

Aerospace/Aeronautical Engineering	M,D
Architectural Engineering	M,D
Biomedical Engineering	M,D
Civil Engineering	M,D
Computer Engineering	M,D
Computer Science	M,D
Electrical Engineering	M,D
Engineering and Applied Sciences—General	M,D
Ergonomics and Human Factors	M
Industrial/Management Engineering	M,D
Management of Technology	M,D
Mechanical Engineering	M,D

UNIVERSITY OF MICHIGAN

Aerospace/Aeronautical Engineering	M,D
Bioinformatics	M,D
Biomedical Engineering	M,D
Chemical Engineering	M,D,O
Civil Engineering	M,D,O
Computer Engineering	M,D
Computer Science	M,D
Construction Engineering	M,D,O
Electrical Engineering	M,D
Engineering and Applied Sciences—General	M,D,O
Environmental Engineering	M,D,O
Human-Computer Interaction	M,D
Industrial/Management Engineering	M,D
Information Science	M,D
Materials Engineering	M,D
Materials Sciences	M,D*
Mechanical Engineering	M,D
Nuclear Engineering	M,D,O
Ocean Engineering	M,D,O
Operations Research	M,D
Structural Engineering	M,D,O

UNIVERSITY OF MICHIGAN–DEARBORN

Automotive Engineering	M,D
Computer Engineering	M
Computer Science	M
Electrical Engineering	M
Engineering and Applied Sciences—General	M,D*
Engineering Management	M,D
Industrial/Management Engineering	M,D

Information Science	M,D
Manufacturing Engineering	M
Mechanical Engineering	M
Software Engineering	M
Systems Engineering	M,D*
Systems Science	M,D

UNIVERSITY OF MICHIGAN–FLINT

Computer Science	M
Information Science	M

UNIVERSITY OF MINNESOTA, DULUTH

Computer Engineering	M
Computer Science	M
Electrical Engineering	M
Engineering Management	M
Safety Engineering	M

UNIVERSITY OF MINNESOTA, TWIN CITIES CAMPUS

Aerospace/Aeronautical Engineering	M,D
Biomedical Engineering	M,D
Biosystems Engineering	M,D
Biotechnology	M
Chemical Engineering	M,D
Civil Engineering	M,D
Computer and Information Systems Security	M
Computer Engineering	M,D
Computer Science	M,D
Electrical Engineering	M,D
Engineering and Applied Sciences—General	M,D
Geological Engineering	M,D
Health Informatics	M,D
Industrial/Management Engineering	M,D
Information Science	M,D
Management of Technology	M
Materials Engineering	M,D
Materials Sciences	M,D
Mechanical Engineering	M,D
Mechanics	M,D
Systems Engineering	M
Technology and Public Policy	M

UNIVERSITY OF MISSISSIPPI

Applied Science and Technology	M,D
Engineering and Applied Sciences—General	M,D

UNIVERSITY OF MISSOURI

Aerospace/Aeronautical Engineering	M,D
Agricultural Engineering	M,D
Bioengineering	M,D
Bioinformatics	D
Chemical Engineering	M,D
Civil Engineering	M,D
Computer Science	M,D
Electrical Engineering	M,D
Engineering and Applied Sciences—General	M,D
Environmental Engineering	M,D
Geotechnical Engineering	M,D
Health Informatics	M
Industrial/Management Engineering	M,D
Manufacturing Engineering	M,D
Mechanical Engineering	M,D
Nuclear Engineering	M,D
Structural Engineering	M,D

Transportation and Highway Engineering	M,D
Water Resources Engineering	M,D

UNIVERSITY OF MISSOURI–KANSAS CITY

Bioinformatics	M,D
Civil Engineering	M,D
Computer Engineering	M,D
Computer Science	M,D
Electrical Engineering	M,D
Engineering and Applied Sciences—General	M,D
Mechanical Engineering	M,D
Polymer Science and Engineering	M,D
Software Engineering	M,D
Telecommunications	M,D

UNIVERSITY OF MISSOURI–ST. LOUIS

Biotechnology	M,D,O
Computer Science	M,D

THE UNIVERSITY OF MONTANA

Computer Science	M

UNIVERSITY OF NEBRASKA AT OMAHA

Computer Science	M
Information Science	M,D,O

UNIVERSITY OF NEBRASKA–LINCOLN

Agricultural Engineering	M,D
Architectural Engineering	M,D
Bioengineering	M,D
Bioinformatics	M,D
Chemical Engineering	M,D
Civil Engineering	M,D
Computer Engineering	M,D
Computer Science	M,D
Electrical Engineering	M,D
Engineering and Applied Sciences—General	M,D
Engineering Management	M,D
Environmental Engineering	M,D
Industrial/Management Engineering	M,D
Information Science	M,D
Manufacturing Engineering	M,D
Materials Engineering	M,D
Materials Sciences	M,D
Mechanical Engineering	M,D*
Mechanics	M,D
Metallurgical Engineering and Metallurgy	M,D

UNIVERSITY OF NEVADA, LAS VEGAS

Aerospace/Aeronautical Engineering	M,D
Biomedical Engineering	M,D
Civil Engineering	M,D
Computer Engineering	M,D
Computer Science	M,D
Construction Management	M
Electrical Engineering	M,D
Engineering and Applied Sciences—General	M,D
Information Science	M,D
Materials Engineering	M,D
Mechanical Engineering	M,D
Nuclear Engineering	M,D
Transportation and Highway Engineering	M,D

*M—master's degree; P—first professional degree; D—doctorate; O—other advanced degree; *—Close-Up and/or Display*

UNIVERSITY OF NEVADA, RENO

Biomedical Engineering	M,D
Biotechnology	M
Chemical Engineering	M,D
Civil Engineering	M,D
Computer Engineering	M,D
Computer Science	M,D
Electrical Engineering	M,D
Engineering and Applied Sciences—General	M,D
Geological Engineering	M,D
Materials Engineering	M,D
Mechanical Engineering	M,D
Metallurgical Engineering and Metallurgy	M,D
Mineral/Mining Engineering	M

UNIVERSITY OF NEW BRUNSWICK FREDERICTON

Chemical Engineering	M,D
Civil Engineering	M,D
Computer Engineering	M,D
Computer Science	M,D
Construction Engineering	M,D
Electrical Engineering	M,D
Engineering and Applied Sciences—General	M,D,O
Engineering Management	M
Environmental Engineering	M,D
Geotechnical Engineering	M,D
Materials Sciences	M,D
Mechanical Engineering	M,D
Mechanics	M,D
Structural Engineering	M,D
Surveying Science and Engineering	M,D,O
Transportation and Highway Engineering	M,D

UNIVERSITY OF NEW HAMPSHIRE

Chemical Engineering	M,D
Civil Engineering	M,D
Computer Science	M,D
Electrical Engineering	M,D
Management of Technology	M,O
Materials Sciences	M,D
Mechanical Engineering	M,D
Ocean Engineering	M,D,O

UNIVERSITY OF NEW HAVEN

Computer and Information Systems Security	M,O
Computer Engineering	M
Computer Science	M,O
Database Systems	M,O
Electrical Engineering	M
Engineering and Applied Sciences—General	M,O
Engineering Management	M
Environmental Engineering	M,O
Fire Protection Engineering	M,O
Hazardous Materials Management	M,O
Industrial/Management Engineering	M,O
Information Science	M,O
Mechanical Engineering	M
Software Engineering	M,O
Systems Engineering	M,O
Telecommunications Management	M,O
Water Resources Engineering	M,O

UNIVERSITY OF NEW MEXICO

Chemical Engineering	M,D

Civil Engineering	M,D
Computer and Information Systems Security	M
Computer Engineering	M,D,O
Computer Science	M,D
Construction Management	M
Electrical Engineering	M,D,O*
Engineering and Applied Sciences—General	M,D,O
Management of Technology	M
Manufacturing Engineering	M
Mechanical Engineering	M,D
Nanotechnology	M,D
Nuclear Engineering	M,D

UNIVERSITY OF NEW ORLEANS

Computer Science	M
Engineering and Applied Sciences—General	M,D,O
Engineering Management	M,O
Mechanical Engineering	M

THE UNIVERSITY OF NORTH CAROLINA AT CHAPEL HILL

Biomedical Engineering	M,D
Computer Science	M,D*
Environmental Engineering	M,D
Materials Sciences	M,D
Operations Research	M,D

THE UNIVERSITY OF NORTH CAROLINA AT CHARLOTTE

Bioinformatics	M
Civil Engineering	M,D
Computer Engineering	M,D
Computer Science	M
Electrical Engineering	M,D
Engineering and Applied Sciences—General	M,D
Engineering Management	M
Environmental Engineering	D
Health Informatics	M
Information Science	M,D
Mechanical Engineering	M,D
Systems Engineering	D

THE UNIVERSITY OF NORTH CAROLINA AT GREENSBORO

Computer Science	M

THE UNIVERSITY OF NORTH CAROLINA WILMINGTON

Computer Science	M
Systems Science	M

UNIVERSITY OF NORTH DAKOTA

Aviation	M
Chemical Engineering	M
Civil Engineering	M
Computer Science	M
Electrical Engineering	M
Engineering and Applied Sciences—General	D
Environmental Engineering	M
Geological Engineering	M
Mechanical Engineering	M
Mineral/Mining Engineering	M
Structural Engineering	M

UNIVERSITY OF NORTHERN BRITISH COLUMBIA

Computer Science	M,D,O

UNIVERSITY OF NORTHERN IOWA

Computer Science	M

UNIVERSITY OF NORTH FLORIDA

Civil Engineering	M
Computer Science	M
Electrical Engineering	M
Information Science	M
Mechanical Engineering	M

UNIVERSITY OF NORTH TEXAS

Computer Engineering	M,D
Computer Science	M,D
Electrical Engineering	M
Engineering and Applied Sciences—General	M
Materials Sciences	M,D

UNIVERSITY OF NORTH TEXAS HEALTH SCIENCE CENTER AT FORT WORTH

Biotechnology	M,D

UNIVERSITY OF NOTRE DAME

Aerospace/Aeronautical Engineering	M,D
Bioengineering	M,D
Chemical Engineering	M,D
Civil Engineering	M,D
Computer Engineering	M,D
Computer Science	M,D
Electrical Engineering	M,D*
Engineering and Applied Sciences—General	M,D
Environmental Engineering	M,D
Mechanical Engineering	M,D

UNIVERSITY OF OKLAHOMA

Aerospace/Aeronautical Engineering	M,D
Bioengineering	M,D
Chemical Engineering	M,D
Civil Engineering	M,D
Computer Engineering	M,D
Computer Science	M,D
Electrical Engineering	M,D
Engineering and Applied Sciences—General	M,D
Engineering Physics	M,D
Environmental Engineering	M,D
Geological Engineering	M,D
Geotechnical Engineering	M,D
Hazardous Materials Management	M,D
Industrial/Management Engineering	M,D
Mechanical Engineering	M,D
Petroleum Engineering	M,D
Structural Engineering	M,D
Telecommunications	M

UNIVERSITY OF OKLAHOMA—TULSA

Telecommunications	M

UNIVERSITY OF OREGON

Computer Science	M,D
Information Science	M,D

UNIVERSITY OF OTTAWA

Aerospace/Aeronautical Engineering	M,D
Biomedical Engineering	M
Chemical Engineering	M,D
Civil Engineering	M,D
Computer Engineering	M,D

Computer Science	M,D
Electrical Engineering	M,D
Engineering and Applied Sciences—General	M,D,O
Engineering Management	M,O
Information Science	M,O
Mechanical Engineering	M,D
Systems Science	M,D,O

UNIVERSITY OF PENNSYLVANIA

Bioengineering	M,D
Biotechnology	M
Chemical Engineering	M,D
Computer Science	M,D
Electrical Engineering	M,D
Engineering and Applied Sciences—General	M,D,O*
Information Science	M,D
Management of Technology	M
Materials Engineering	M,D
Materials Sciences	M,D
Mechanical Engineering	M,D
Mechanics	M,D
Systems Engineering	M,D
Telecommunications Management	M
Telecommunications	M

UNIVERSITY OF PHOENIX

Health Informatics	M
Management of Technology	M

UNIVERSITY OF PHOENIX–ATLANTA CAMPUS

Management of Technology	M

UNIVERSITY OF PHOENIX–AUGUSTA CAMPUS

Management of Technology	M

UNIVERSITY OF PHOENIX–AUSTIN CAMPUS

Management of Technology	M

UNIVERSITY OF PHOENIX–BAY AREA CAMPUS

Management of Technology	M

UNIVERSITY OF PHOENIX–BIRMINGHAM CAMPUS

Health Informatics	M
Management of Technology	M

UNIVERSITY OF PHOENIX–BOSTON CAMPUS

Management of Technology	M

UNIVERSITY OF PHOENIX–CENTRAL FLORIDA CAMPUS

Management of Technology	M

UNIVERSITY OF PHOENIX–CENTRAL MASSACHUSETTS CAMPUS

Management of Technology	M

**UNIVERSITY OF PHOENIX–
CENTRAL VALLEY CAMPUS**

Management of
Technology   M

**UNIVERSITY OF PHOENIX–
CHARLOTTE CAMPUS**

Management of
Technology   M

**UNIVERSITY OF PHOENIX–
CHATTANOOGA CAMPUS**

Management of
Technology   M

**UNIVERSITY OF PHOENIX–
CHEYENNE CAMPUS**

Management of
Technology   M

**UNIVERSITY OF PHOENIX–
CHICAGO CAMPUS**

Management of
Technology   M

**UNIVERSITY OF PHOENIX–
CINCINNATI CAMPUS**

Information Science   M
Management of
Technology   M

**UNIVERSITY OF PHOENIX–
CLEVELAND CAMPUS**

Management of
Technology   M

**UNIVERSITY OF PHOENIX–
COLUMBIA CAMPUS**

Management of
Technology   M

**UNIVERSITY OF PHOENIX–
COLUMBUS GEORGIA CAMPUS**

Management of
Technology   M

**UNIVERSITY OF PHOENIX–
COLUMBUS OHIO CAMPUS**

Management of
Technology   M

**UNIVERSITY OF PHOENIX–
DALLAS CAMPUS**

Management of
Technology   M

**UNIVERSITY OF PHOENIX–
DENVER CAMPUS**

Management of
Technology   M

**UNIVERSITY OF PHOENIX–DES
MOINES CAMPUS**

Management of
Technology   M

**UNIVERSITY OF PHOENIX–
EASTERN WASHINGTON CAMPUS**

Management of
Technology   M

**UNIVERSITY OF PHOENIX–
HARRISBURG CAMPUS**

Management of
Technology   M

**UNIVERSITY OF PHOENIX–HAWAII
CAMPUS**

Management of
Technology   M

**UNIVERSITY OF PHOENIX–
HOUSTON CAMPUS**

Management of
Technology   M

**UNIVERSITY OF PHOENIX–IDAHO
CAMPUS**

Management of
Technology   M

**UNIVERSITY OF PHOENIX–
INDIANAPOLIS CAMPUS**

Management of
Technology   M

**UNIVERSITY OF PHOENIX–JERSEY
CITY CAMPUS**

Management of
Technology   M

**UNIVERSITY OF PHOENIX–
KANSAS CITY CAMPUS**

Management of
Technology   M

**UNIVERSITY OF PHOENIX–LAS
VEGAS CAMPUS**

Management of
Technology   M

**UNIVERSITY OF PHOENIX–
LOUISIANA CAMPUS**

Management of
Technology   M

**UNIVERSITY OF PHOENIX–
LOUISVILLE CAMPUS**

Management of
Technology   M

**UNIVERSITY OF PHOENIX–
MADISON CAMPUS**

Management of
Technology   M

**UNIVERSITY OF PHOENIX–
MADISON CAMPUS**

Management of
Technology   M

**UNIVERSITY OF PHOENIX–
MARYLAND CAMPUS**

Management of
Technology   M

**UNIVERSITY OF PHOENIX–
MEMPHIS CAMPUS**

Management of
Technology   M

**UNIVERSITY OF PHOENIX–METRO
DETROIT CAMPUS**

Management of
Technology   M

**UNIVERSITY OF PHOENIX–
MINNEAPOLIS/ST. LOUIS PARK
CAMPUS**

Management of
Technology   M

**UNIVERSITY OF PHOENIX–
NASHVILLE CAMPUS**

Management of
Technology   M

**UNIVERSITY OF PHOENIX–NEW
MEXICO CAMPUS**

Management of
Technology   M

**UNIVERSITY OF PHOENIX–
NORTHERN NEVADA CAMPUS**

Management of
Technology   M

**UNIVERSITY OF PHOENIX–
NORTHERN VIRGINIA CAMPUS**

Management of
Technology   M

**UNIVERSITY OF PHOENIX–
NORTHWEST ARKANSAS CAMPUS**

Management of
Technology   M

**UNIVERSITY OF PHOENIX–
OKLAHOMA CITY CAMPUS**

Management of
Technology   M

**UNIVERSITY OF PHOENIX–OMAHA
CAMPUS**

Management of
Technology   M

**UNIVERSITY OF PHOENIX–
OREGON CAMPUS**

Management of
Technology   M

**UNIVERSITY OF PHOENIX–
PHILADELPHIA CAMPUS**

Management of
Technology   M

**UNIVERSITY OF PHOENIX–
PHOENIX CAMPUS**

Health Informatics   M,O
Information Science   M
Management of
Technology   M

**UNIVERSITY OF PHOENIX–
PITTSBURGH CAMPUS**

Management of
Technology   M

**UNIVERSITY OF PHOENIX–
PUERTO RICO CAMPUS**

Management of
Technology   M

**UNIVERSITY OF PHOENIX–
RALEIGH CAMPUS**

Management of
Technology   M

**UNIVERSITY OF PHOENIX–
RICHMOND CAMPUS**

Management of
Technology   M

**UNIVERSITY OF PHOENIX–
SACRAMENTO VALLEY CAMPUS**

Management of
Technology   M

**UNIVERSITY OF PHOENIX–
SAN ANTONIO CAMPUS**

Management of
Technology   M

**UNIVERSITY OF PHOENIX–
SAN DIEGO CAMPUS**

Management of
Technology   M

**UNIVERSITY OF PHOENIX–
SAVANNAH CAMPUS**

Management of
Technology   M

**UNIVERSITY OF PHOENIX–
SOUTHERN ARIZONA CAMPUS**

Management of
Technology   M

**UNIVERSITY OF PHOENIX–
SOUTHERN COLORADO CAMPUS**

Management of
Technology   M

**UNIVERSITY OF PHOENIX–
SPRINGFIELD CAMPUS**

Management of
Technology   M

**UNIVERSITY OF PHOENIX–TULSA
CAMPUS**

Management of
Technology   M

**UNIVERSITY OF PHOENIX–UTAH
CAMPUS**

Management of
Technology   M

**UNIVERSITY OF PHOENIX–
VANCOUVER CAMPUS**

Management of
Technology   M

**UNIVERSITY OF PHOENIX–
WESTERN WASHINGTON CAMPUS**

Management of
Technology   M

**UNIVERSITY OF PHOENIX–
WEST FLORIDA CAMPUS**

Management of
Technology   M

*M—master's degree; P—first professional degree; D—doctorate; O—other advanced degree; *—Close-Up and/or Display*

UNIVERSITY OF PITTSBURGH

Artificial Intelligence/ Robotics	D
Bioengineering	M,D
Bioinformatics	M,D,O
Chemical Engineering	M,D
Civil Engineering	M,D
Computer Science	M,D
Electrical Engineering	M,D
Engineering and Applied Sciences—General	M,D
Environmental Engineering	M,D
Health Informatics	M
Industrial/Management Engineering	M,D
Information Science	M,D,O
Materials Sciences	M,D
Mechanical Engineering	M,D
Petroleum Engineering	M,D
Telecommunications	M,D,O

UNIVERSITY OF PORTLAND

Engineering and Applied Sciences—General	M

UNIVERSITY OF PUERTO RICO, MAYAGÜEZ CAMPUS

Chemical Engineering	M,D
Civil Engineering	M,D
Computer Engineering	M
Electrical Engineering	M
Engineering and Applied Sciences—General	M,D
Industrial/Management Engineering	M
Information Science	D
Mechanical Engineering	M

UNIVERSITY OF PUERTO RICO, MEDICAL SCIENCES CAMPUS

Health Informatics	M

UNIVERSITY OF REGINA

Computer Engineering	M,D
Computer Science	M,D
Engineering and Applied Sciences—General	M,D
Environmental Engineering	M,D
Industrial/Management Engineering	M,D
Manufacturing Engineering	M
Petroleum Engineering	M,D
Systems Engineering	M,D

UNIVERSITY OF RHODE ISLAND

Biomedical Engineering	M,D,O
Biotechnology	M,D
Chemical Engineering	M,D
Civil Engineering	M,D
Computer Engineering	M,D,O
Computer Science	M,D,O
Electrical Engineering	M,D,O
Engineering and Applied Sciences—General	M,D,O
Environmental Engineering	M,D
Ocean Engineering	M,D

UNIVERSITY OF ROCHESTER

Biomedical Engineering	M,D
Chemical Engineering	M,D*
Computer Engineering	M,D
Computer Science	M,D*
Electrical Engineering	M,D
Engineering and Applied Sciences—General	M,D*

Materials Sciences	M,D
Mechanical Engineering	M,D

UNIVERSITY OF ST. THOMAS (MN)

Computer and Information Systems Security	M,O
Engineering and Applied Sciences—General	M,O
Engineering Management	M,O
Management of Technology	M,O
Manufacturing Engineering	M,O
Software Engineering	M,O
Systems Engineering	M,O

UNIVERSITY OF SAN FRANCISCO

Computer Science	M
Internet Engineering	M
Telecommunications Management	M

UNIVERSITY OF SASKATCHEWAN

Agricultural Engineering	M,D
Biomedical Engineering	M,D
Biotechnology	M
Chemical Engineering	M,D
Civil Engineering	M,D
Computer Science	M,D
Electrical Engineering	M,D
Engineering and Applied Sciences—General	M,D,O
Engineering Physics	M,D
Environmental Engineering	M,D,O
Mechanical Engineering	M,D

THE UNIVERSITY OF SCRANTON

Software Engineering	M

UNIVERSITY OF SOUTH AFRICA

Chemical Engineering	M
Engineering and Applied Sciences—General	M
Information Science	M,D
Technology and Public Policy	M,D
Telecommunications Management	M,D

UNIVERSITY OF SOUTH ALABAMA

Chemical Engineering	M
Civil Engineering	M
Computer Science	M
Electrical Engineering	M
Engineering and Applied Sciences—General	M
Information Science	M
Mechanical Engineering	M

UNIVERSITY OF SOUTH CAROLINA

Chemical Engineering	M,D
Civil Engineering	M,D
Computer Engineering	M,D
Computer Science	M,D
Electrical Engineering	M,D
Engineering and Applied Sciences—General	M,D
Hazardous Materials Management	M,D
Mechanical Engineering	M,D
Nuclear Engineering	M,D
Software Engineering	M,D

THE UNIVERSITY OF SOUTH DAKOTA

Computer Science	M,D

UNIVERSITY OF SOUTHERN CALIFORNIA

Aerospace/Aeronautical Engineering	M,D,O
Artificial Intelligence/ Robotics	M,D
Bioinformatics	D
Biomedical Engineering	M,D
Chemical Engineering	M,D,O
Civil Engineering	M,D,O
Computer and Information Systems Security	M,D
Computer Engineering	M,D,O
Computer Science	M,D
Construction Management	M,D,O
Electrical Engineering	M,D,O
Engineering and Applied Sciences—General	M,D,O
Engineering Management	M,D,O
Environmental Engineering	M,D,O
Game Design and Development	M,D
Industrial/Management Engineering	M,D,O
Manufacturing Engineering	M,D,O
Materials Sciences	M,D,O
Mechanical Engineering	M,D,O
Mechanics	M,D,O
Operations Research	M,D,O
Petroleum Engineering	M,D,O
Safety Engineering	M,D,O
Software Engineering	M,D
Systems Engineering	M,D,O
Telecommunications	M,D,O
Transportation and Highway Engineering	M,D,O

UNIVERSITY OF SOUTHERN INDIANA

Engineering and Applied Sciences—General	M

UNIVERSITY OF SOUTHERN MAINE

Computer Science	M
Manufacturing Engineering	M

UNIVERSITY OF SOUTHERN MISSISSIPPI

Computer Science	M,D
Construction Engineering	M
Construction Management	M
Engineering and Applied Sciences—General	M,D
Polymer Science and Engineering	M,D

UNIVERSITY OF SOUTH FLORIDA

Chemical Engineering	M,D
Civil Engineering	M,D
Computer Engineering	M,D
Computer Science	M,D
Electrical Engineering	M,D
Engineering and Applied Sciences—General	M,D
Engineering Management	M,D
Environmental Engineering	M,D
Industrial/Management Engineering	M,D
Mechanical Engineering	M,D
Polymer Science and Engineering	M,D

THE UNIVERSITY OF TENNESSEE

Aerospace/Aeronautical Engineering	M,D
Agricultural Engineering	M

Artificial Intelligence/ Robotics	M,D
Aviation	M
Biomedical Engineering	M,D
Biosystems Engineering	M,D
Chemical Engineering	M,D
Civil Engineering	M,D
Computer Engineering	M,D
Computer Science	M,D
Electrical Engineering	M,D
Engineering and Applied Sciences—General	M,D
Engineering Management	M,D
Environmental Engineering	M
Industrial/Management Engineering	M,D
Information Science	M,D
Materials Engineering	M,D
Materials Sciences	M,D
Mechanical Engineering	M,D
Mechanics	M,D
Nuclear Engineering	M,D
Polymer Science and Engineering	M,D
Reliability Engineering	M,D

THE UNIVERSITY OF TENNESSEE AT CHATTANOOGA

Chemical Engineering	M
Civil Engineering	M
Computer Science	M,O
Electrical Engineering	M
Energy and Power Engineering	M,O
Engineering and Applied Sciences—General	M,D,O
Engineering Management	M,O
Industrial/Management Engineering	M
Mechanical Engineering	M
Medical Informatics	M,O

THE UNIVERSITY OF TENNESSEE HEALTH SCIENCE CENTER

Biomedical Engineering	M,D

THE UNIVERSITY OF TENNESSEE SPACE INSTITUTE

Aerospace/Aeronautical Engineering	M,D
Aviation	M
Computer Science	M,D
Electrical Engineering	M,D
Engineering and Applied Sciences—General	M,D
Engineering Management	M,D
Materials Engineering	M
Materials Sciences	M
Mechanical Engineering	M,D
Mechanics	M,D

THE UNIVERSITY OF TEXAS AT ARLINGTON

Aerospace/Aeronautical Engineering	M,D
Bioengineering	M,D
Civil Engineering	M,D
Computer Engineering	M,D
Computer Science	M,D
Electrical Engineering	M,D
Engineering and Applied Sciences—General	M,D
Industrial/Management Engineering	M
Materials Engineering	M,D
Materials Sciences	M,D
Mechanical Engineering	M,D
Software Engineering	M,D
Systems Engineering	M

THE UNIVERSITY OF TEXAS AT AUSTIN

Aerospace/Aeronautical Engineering	M,D
Architectural Engineering	M
Biomedical Engineering	M,D
Chemical Engineering	M,D
Civil Engineering	M,D
Computer Engineering	M,D
Computer Science	M,D
Electrical Engineering	M,D
Engineering and Applied Sciences—General	M,D
Environmental Engineering	M,D
Geotechnical Engineering	M,D
Industrial/Management Engineering	M,D
Materials Engineering	M,D
Materials Sciences	M,D
Mechanical Engineering	M,D
Mechanics	M,D
Mineral/Mining Engineering	M
Operations Research	M,D
Petroleum Engineering	M,D
Technology and Public Policy	M
Textile Sciences and Engineering	M
Water Resources Engineering	M,D

THE UNIVERSITY OF TEXAS AT DALLAS

Biotechnology	M,D
Computer and Information Systems Security	M
Computer Engineering	M,D
Computer Science	M,D
Electrical Engineering	M,D
Engineering and Applied Sciences—General	M,D
Materials Engineering	M,D
Materials Sciences	M,D
Mechanical Engineering	M
Software Engineering	M,D
Telecommunications	M,D

THE UNIVERSITY OF TEXAS AT EL PASO

Bioinformatics	M,D
Civil Engineering	M,D,O
Computer Engineering	M,D
Computer Science	M,D
Construction Management	M,D,O
Electrical Engineering	M,D
Engineering and Applied Sciences—General	M,D
Environmental Engineering	M,D,O
Industrial/Management Engineering	M,O
Information Science	M,D
Manufacturing Engineering	M,O
Materials Engineering	M,D
Materials Sciences	M,D
Mechanical Engineering	M
Metallurgical Engineering and Metallurgy	M,D
Systems Engineering	M,O

THE UNIVERSITY OF TEXAS AT SAN ANTONIO

Biomedical Engineering	M,D
Biotechnology	M,D
Civil Engineering	M,D
Computer Engineering	M,D
Computer Science	M,D
Electrical Engineering	M,D

Engineering and Applied Sciences—General	M,D
Environmental Engineering	M,D
Information Science	M,D
Mechanical Engineering	M

THE UNIVERSITY OF TEXAS AT TYLER

Civil Engineering	M
Computer Science	M
Electrical Engineering	M
Environmental Engineering	M
Mechanical Engineering	M
Structural Engineering	M
Transportation and Highway Engineering	M
Water Resources Engineering	M

THE UNIVERSITY OF TEXAS HEALTH SCIENCE CENTER AT HOUSTON

Health Informatics	M,D,O

THE UNIVERSITY OF TEXAS MEDICAL BRANCH

Bioinformatics	D

THE UNIVERSITY OF TEXAS OF THE PERMIAN BASIN

Computer Science	M

THE UNIVERSITY OF TEXAS–PAN AMERICAN

Computer Science	M
Electrical Engineering	M
Manufacturing Engineering	M
Mechanical Engineering	M

THE UNIVERSITY OF TEXAS SOUTHWESTERN MEDICAL CENTER AT DALLAS

Biomedical Engineering	M,D

UNIVERSITY OF THE DISTRICT OF COLUMBIA

Computer Science	M
Engineering and Applied Sciences—General	M

UNIVERSITY OF THE SACRED HEART

Information Science	O

UNIVERSITY OF THE SCIENCES IN PHILADELPHIA

Bioinformatics	M
Biotechnology	M,D

THE UNIVERSITY OF TOLEDO

Bioengineering	M,D
Bioinformatics	M,O
Biomedical Engineering	D
Chemical Engineering	M,D
Civil Engineering	M,D
Computer Science	M,D
Electrical Engineering	M,D
Engineering and Applied Sciences—General	M
Industrial/Management Engineering	M,D
Mechanical Engineering	M,D

UNIVERSITY OF TORONTO

Aerospace/Aeronautical Engineering	M,D
Biomedical Engineering	M,D
Chemical Engineering	M,D
Civil Engineering	M,D
Computer Engineering	M,D
Computer Science	M,D
Electrical Engineering	M,D
Engineering and Applied Sciences—General	M,D
Industrial/Management Engineering	M,D
Materials Engineering	M,D
Materials Sciences	M,D
Mechanical Engineering	M,D

UNIVERSITY OF TULSA

Chemical Engineering	M,D
Computer Science	M,D
Electrical Engineering	M
Energy Management and Policy	M
Engineering and Applied Sciences—General	M,D
Engineering Physics	M
Financial Engineering	M
Mechanical Engineering	M,D
Petroleum Engineering	M,D

UNIVERSITY OF UTAH

Bioengineering	M,D
Bioinformatics	M,D,O
Biotechnology	M
Chemical Engineering	M,D
Civil Engineering	M,D
Computer Science	M,D
Electrical Engineering	M,D,O
Engineering and Applied Sciences—General	M,D,O
Environmental Engineering	M,D
Geological Engineering	M,D
Materials Engineering	M,D
Materials Sciences	M,D
Mechanical Engineering	M,D
Metallurgical Engineering and Metallurgy	M,D
Mineral/Mining Engineering	M,D
Nuclear Engineering	M,D

UNIVERSITY OF VERMONT

Biomedical Engineering	M
Civil Engineering	M,D
Computer Science	M,D
Electrical Engineering	M,D
Engineering and Applied Sciences—General	M,D
Environmental Engineering	M,D
Materials Sciences	M,D
Mechanical Engineering	M,D

UNIVERSITY OF VICTORIA

Computer Engineering	M,D
Computer Science	M,D
Electrical Engineering	M,D
Engineering and Applied Sciences—General	M,D
Health Informatics	M
Mechanical Engineering	M,D

UNIVERSITY OF VIRGINIA

Aerospace/Aeronautical Engineering	M,D
Biomedical Engineering	M,D
Chemical Engineering	M,D

Civil Engineering	M,D
Computer Engineering	M,D
Computer Science	M,D
Electrical Engineering	M,D
Engineering and Applied Sciences—General	M,D
Engineering Physics	M,D
Health Informatics	M
Materials Sciences	M,D
Mechanical Engineering	M,D
Systems Engineering	M,D

UNIVERSITY OF WASHINGTON

Aerospace/Aeronautical Engineering	M,D
Bioengineering	M,D
Bioinformatics	M,D
Biotechnology	D
Chemical Engineering	M,D*
Civil Engineering	M,D
Computer Science	M,D
Construction Engineering	M,D
Construction Management	M
Electrical Engineering	M,D
Energy Management and Policy	M,D
Environmental Engineering	M,D
Geotechnical Engineering	M,D
Health Informatics	M,D
Industrial/Management Engineering	M,D
Information Science	M,D
Management of Technology	M,D
Materials Engineering	M,D
Materials Sciences	M,D
Mechanical Engineering	M,D
Medical Informatics	M,D
Nanotechnology	M,D
Structural Engineering	M,D
Transportation and Highway Engineering	M,D
Water Resources Engineering	M,D

UNIVERSITY OF WASHINGTON, BOTHELL

Computer Engineering	M
Software Engineering	M

UNIVERSITY OF WASHINGTON, TACOMA

Computer Engineering	M
Software Engineering	M

UNIVERSITY OF WATERLOO

Chemical Engineering	M,D
Civil Engineering	M,D
Computer Engineering	M,D
Computer Science	M,D
Electrical Engineering	M,D
Engineering and Applied Sciences—General	M,D
Engineering Management	M,D
Environmental Engineering	M,D
Information Science	M,D
Management of Technology	M,D
Mechanical Engineering	M,D
Operations Research	M,D
Software Engineering	M,D
Systems Engineering	M,D

THE UNIVERSITY OF WESTERN ONTARIO

Biochemical Engineering	M,D
Chemical Engineering	M,D

Civil Engineering	M,D
Computer Engineering	M,D
Computer Science	M,D
Electrical Engineering	M,D
Engineering and Applied Sciences—General	M,D
Environmental Engineering	M,D
Materials Engineering	M,D
Mechanical Engineering	M,D

UNIVERSITY OF WEST FLORIDA

Biotechnology	M
Computer Science	M
Database Systems	M
Software Engineering	M

UNIVERSITY OF WEST GEORGIA

Computer Science	M,O
Software Engineering	M,O

UNIVERSITY OF WINDSOR

Civil Engineering	M,D
Computer Science	M,D
Electrical Engineering	M,D
Engineering and Applied Sciences—General	M,D
Environmental Engineering	M,D
Industrial/Management Engineering	M,D
Manufacturing Engineering	M,D
Materials Engineering	M,D
Mechanical Engineering	M,D

UNIVERSITY OF WISCONSIN–LA CROSSE

Software Engineering	M

UNIVERSITY OF WISCONSIN–MADISON

Agricultural Engineering	M,D
Bioengineering	M,D
Biomedical Engineering	M,D
Chemical Engineering	M,D
Civil Engineering	M,D
Computer and Information Systems Security	M
Computer Science	M,D
Electrical Engineering	M,D
Energy and Power Engineering	M,D
Engineering and Applied Sciences—General	M,D
Engineering Management	M
Engineering Physics	M,D
Environmental Engineering	M,D
Geological Engineering	M,D
Industrial/Management Engineering	M,D
Management of Technology	M
Manufacturing Engineering	M
Materials Engineering	M,D
Materials Sciences	M,D
Mechanical Engineering	M,D
Mechanics	M,D
Nuclear Engineering	M,D
Polymer Science and Engineering	M,D
Systems Engineering	M,D

UNIVERSITY OF WISCONSIN–MILWAUKEE

Civil Engineering	M,D,O
Computer Engineering	M,D,O
Computer Science	M,D
Electrical Engineering	M,D,O

Engineering and Applied Sciences—General	M,D,O
Engineering Management	M,D,O
Ergonomics and Human Factors	M,D,O
Health Informatics	M,O
Industrial/Management Engineering	M,D,O
Manufacturing Engineering	M,D,O
Materials Engineering	M,D,O
Mechanical Engineering	M,D,O
Mechanics	M,D,O
Medical Informatics	D

UNIVERSITY OF WISCONSIN–PARKSIDE

Computer Science	M
Information Science	M

UNIVERSITY OF WISCONSIN–PLATTEVILLE

Computer Science	M
Engineering and Applied Sciences—General	M

UNIVERSITY OF WISCONSIN–STOUT

Industrial/Management Engineering	M
Information Science	M
Management of Technology	M
Manufacturing Engineering	M
Telecommunications Management	M

UNIVERSITY OF WISCONSIN–WHITEWATER

Management of Technology	M

UNIVERSITY OF WYOMING

Biotechnology	D
Chemical Engineering	M,D
Civil Engineering	M,D
Computer Science	M,D
Electrical Engineering	M,D
Engineering and Applied Sciences—General	M,D
Environmental Engineering	M
Mechanical Engineering	M,D
Petroleum Engineering	M,D

UTAH STATE UNIVERSITY

Aerospace/Aeronautical Engineering	M,D
Agricultural Engineering	M,D
Civil Engineering	M,D,O
Computer Science	M,D
Electrical Engineering	M,D
Engineering and Applied Sciences—General	M,D,O
Environmental Engineering	M,D,O
Mechanical Engineering	M,D
Water Resources Engineering	M,D

VALPARAISO UNIVERSITY

Engineering Management	M,O

VANDERBILT UNIVERSITY

Bioinformatics	M,D
Biomedical Engineering	M,D
Chemical Engineering	M,D
Civil Engineering	M,D
Computer Science	M,D

Electrical Engineering	M,D
Engineering and Applied Sciences—General	M,D
Environmental Engineering	M,D
Materials Sciences	M,D
Mechanical Engineering	M,D

VILLANOVA UNIVERSITY

Artificial Intelligence/Robotics	M,O
Chemical Engineering	M
Civil Engineering	M
Computer Engineering	M,O
Computer Science	M,O*
Electrical Engineering	M,O
Engineering and Applied Sciences—General	M,D,O
Environmental Engineering	M
Manufacturing Engineering	M,O
Mechanical Engineering	M,O
Software Engineering	M
Transportation and Highway Engineering	M
Water Resources Engineering	M

VIRGINIA COMMONWEALTH UNIVERSITY

Bioengineering	M,D
Bioinformatics	M
Biomedical Engineering	M,D
Chemical Engineering	M,D
Computer Science	M,D,O
Electrical Engineering	M,D
Engineering and Applied Sciences—General	M,D,O
Mechanical Engineering	M,D
Nanotechnology	D
Nuclear Engineering	M
Operations Research	M,O

VIRGINIA INTERNATIONAL UNIVERSITY

Computer Science	M

VIRGINIA POLYTECHNIC INSTITUTE AND STATE UNIVERSITY

Aerospace/Aeronautical Engineering	M,D,O
Agricultural Engineering	M,D
Bioengineering	M,D
Bioinformatics	D
Biomedical Engineering	M,D
Biotechnology	M
Chemical Engineering	M,D
Civil Engineering	M,D
Computer and Information Systems Security	M,O
Computer Engineering	M,D,O
Computer Science	M,D,O
Construction Engineering	M
Electrical Engineering	M,D,O
Engineering and Applied Sciences—General	M,D
Engineering Management	M,D,O
Environmental Engineering	M,D
Industrial/Management Engineering	M,D
Information Science	M
Materials Engineering	M,D
Materials Sciences	M,D
Mechanical Engineering	M,D
Mechanics	M,D
Mineral/Mining Engineering	M,D
Ocean Engineering	M,D,O
Operations Research	M,D

Electrical Engineering	M,D
Engineering and Applied Sciences—General	M,D
Environmental Engineering	M,D
Materials Sciences	M,D
Mechanical Engineering	M,D

VIRGINIA STATE UNIVERSITY

Computer Science	M

WAKE FOREST UNIVERSITY

Biomedical Engineering	M,D
Computer Science	M

WALDEN UNIVERSITY

Engineering and Applied Sciences—General	M,O
Engineering Management	M,D,O
Health Informatics	M,D
Management of Technology	M,D,O
Software Engineering	M,O
Systems Engineering	M,O

WASHINGTON STATE UNIVERSITY

Agricultural Engineering	M,D
Bioengineering	M,D
Chemical Engineering	M,D
Civil Engineering	M,D
Computer Engineering	M,D
Computer Science	M,D
Electrical Engineering	M,D
Engineering and Applied Sciences—General	M,D
Environmental Engineering	M
Materials Engineering	M
Materials Sciences	M,D
Mechanical Engineering	M,D

WASHINGTON STATE UNIVERSITY SPOKANE

Engineering Management	M

WASHINGTON STATE UNIVERSITY TRI-CITIES

Computer Engineering	M,D
Computer Science	M,D
Electrical Engineering	M,D
Engineering and Applied Sciences—General	M,D
Mechanical Engineering	M,D

WASHINGTON STATE UNIVERSITY VANCOUVER

Computer Science	M
Engineering and Applied Sciences—General	M
Mechanical Engineering	M

WASHINGTON UNIVERSITY IN ST. LOUIS

Aerospace/Aeronautical Engineering	M,D
Biomedical Engineering	M,D
Chemical Engineering	M,D
Computer Engineering	M,D
Computer Science	M,D
Electrical Engineering	M,D
Engineering and Applied Sciences—General	M,D
Environmental Engineering	M,D
Mechanical Engineering	M,D
Structural Engineering	M,D
Systems Science	M,D

WAYNE STATE UNIVERSITY

Biomedical Engineering	M,D
Chemical Engineering	M,D
Civil Engineering	M,D

Computer Engineering	M,D
Computer Science	M,D,O
Electrical Engineering	M,D
Engineering and Applied Sciences—General	M,D,O
Engineering Management	M
Hazardous Materials Management	M,O
Industrial/Management Engineering	M,D
Manufacturing Engineering	M
Materials Engineering	M,D,O
Materials Sciences	M,D,O
Mechanical Engineering	M,D
Metallurgical Engineering and Metallurgy	M,D,O
Polymer Science and Engineering	M,D,O

WEBSTER UNIVERSITY

Aerospace/Aeronautical Engineering	M,D,O
Computer Science	M,O
Engineering Management	M
Telecommunications Management	M,D,O

WESLEYAN UNIVERSITY

Bioinformatics	D

WEST CHESTER UNIVERSITY OF PENNSYLVANIA

Computer and Information Systems Security	M,O
Computer Science	M,O
Management of Technology	M

WESTERN CAROLINA UNIVERSITY

Computer Science	M
Construction Management	M
Industrial/Management Engineering	M

WESTERN GOVERNORS UNIVERSITY

Computer and Information Systems Security	M

WESTERN ILLINOIS UNIVERSITY

Computer Science	M
Manufacturing Engineering	M
Technology and Public Policy	M

WESTERN INTERNATIONAL UNIVERSITY

Systems Engineering	M

WESTERN KENTUCKY UNIVERSITY

Computer Science	M

WESTERN MICHIGAN UNIVERSITY

Biotechnology	M,D

Chemical Engineering	M,D
Civil Engineering	M
Computer Engineering	M,D
Computer Science	M
Construction Engineering	M
Construction Management	M
Electrical Engineering	M,D
Engineering and Applied Sciences—General	M,D
Engineering Management	M
Industrial/Management Engineering	M
Manufacturing Engineering	M
Mechanical Engineering	M,D
Nanotechnology	M,D
Paper and Pulp Engineering	M,D
Structural Engineering	M
Transportation and Highway Engineering	M

WESTERN NEW ENGLAND COLLEGE

Electrical Engineering	M
Engineering and Applied Sciences—General	M
Industrial/Management Engineering	M
Manufacturing Engineering	M
Mechanical Engineering	M

WESTERN WASHINGTON UNIVERSITY

Computer Science	M

WESTMINSTER COLLEGE (UT)

Management of Technology	M,O

WEST TEXAS A&M UNIVERSITY

Engineering and Applied Sciences—General	M

WEST VIRGINIA STATE UNIVERSITY

Biotechnology	M

WEST VIRGINIA UNIVERSITY

Aerospace/Aeronautical Engineering	M,D
Chemical Engineering	M,D
Civil Engineering	M,D
Computer Engineering	D
Computer Science	M,D
Electrical Engineering	M,D
Engineering and Applied Sciences—General	M,D
Environmental Engineering	M,D
Industrial/Management Engineering	M,D
Mechanical Engineering	M,D
Mineral/Mining Engineering	M,D
Petroleum Engineering	M,D
Safety Engineering	M
Software Engineering	M

WEST VIRGINIA UNIVERSITY INSTITUTE OF TECHNOLOGY

Engineering and Applied Sciences—General	M
Systems Engineering	M

WICHITA STATE UNIVERSITY

Aerospace/Aeronautical Engineering	M,D
Computer Engineering	M,D
Computer Science	M,D
Electrical Engineering	M,D
Engineering and Applied Sciences—General	M,D
Industrial/Management Engineering	M,D
Manufacturing Engineering	M,D
Mechanical Engineering	M,D

WIDENER UNIVERSITY

Chemical Engineering	M
Civil Engineering	M
Computer Engineering	M
Engineering and Applied Sciences—General	M
Engineering Management	M
Mechanical Engineering	M
Software Engineering	M
Telecommunications	M

WILKES UNIVERSITY

Electrical Engineering	M
Engineering and Applied Sciences—General	M

WILLIAM PATERSON UNIVERSITY OF NEW JERSEY

Biotechnology	M

WILMINGTON UNIVERSITY

Computer and Information Systems Security	M
Internet Engineering	M

WINSTON-SALEM STATE UNIVERSITY

Computer Science	M

WINTHROP UNIVERSITY

Software Engineering	M,O

WOODS HOLE OCEANOGRAPHIC INSTITUTION

Civil Engineering	M,D,O
Electrical Engineering	M,D,O
Mechanical Engineering	M,D,O
Ocean Engineering	M,D,O

WORCESTER POLYTECHNIC INSTITUTE

Biomedical Engineering	M,D,O
Biotechnology	M,D
Chemical Engineering	M,D
Civil Engineering	M,D,O

Computer Engineering	M,D,O
Computer Science	M,D,O
Construction Management	M,D,O
Electrical Engineering	M,D,O
Energy and Power Engineering	M,D
Engineering and Applied Sciences—General	M,D,O
Engineering Design	M,O
Environmental Engineering	M,D,O
Fire Protection Engineering	M,D,O
Manufacturing Engineering	M,D
Materials Engineering	M,D
Materials Sciences	M,D
Mechanical Engineering	M,D
Systems Science	M,D,O

WORCESTER STATE COLLEGE

Biotechnology	M

WRIGHT STATE UNIVERSITY

Biomedical Engineering	M
Computer Engineering	M,D
Computer Science	M,D
Electrical Engineering	M
Engineering and Applied Sciences—General	M,D
Ergonomics and Human Factors	M,D
Materials Engineering	M
Materials Sciences	M
Mechanical Engineering	M

YALE UNIVERSITY

Bioinformatics	D
Biomedical Engineering	M,D
Chemical Engineering	M,D
Computer Science	M,D
Electrical Engineering	M,D
Engineering and Applied Sciences—General	M,D*
Engineering Physics	M,D
Environmental Engineering	M,D
Mechanical Engineering	M,D

YORK UNIVERSITY

Computer Science	M,D

YOUNGSTOWN STATE UNIVERSITY

Civil Engineering	M
Computer Engineering	M
Computer Science	M
Electrical Engineering	M
Engineering and Applied Sciences—General	M
Environmental Engineering	M
Industrial/Management Engineering	M
Information Science	M
Mechanical Engineering	M

---

*M—master's degree; P—first professional degree; D—doctorate; O—other advanced degree; *—Close-Up and/or Display*

ACADEMIC AND PROFESSIONAL PROGRAMS IN ENGINEERING & APPLIED SCIENCES

Section 1
Engineering and Applied Sciences

This section contains a directory of institutions offering graduate work in engineering and applied sciences, followed by in-depth entries submitted by institutions that chose to prepare detailed program descriptions. Additional information about programs listed in the directory but not augmented by an in-depth entry may be obtained by writing directly to the dean of a graduate school or chair of a department at the address given in the directory.

For programs in specific areas of engineering, see all other sections in this book. In the other guides in this series:

Graduate Programs in the Humanities, Arts & Social Sciences
See *Applied Arts and Design (Industrial Design)* and *Architecture (Environmental Design)*

Graduate Programs in the Biological Sciences
See *Ecology, Environmental Biology,* and *Evolutionary Biology*

Graduate Programs in the Physical Sciences, Mathematics, Agricultural Sciences, the Environment & Natural Resources
See *Agricultural and Food Sciences* and *Natural Resources*

CONTENTS

Engineering and Applied Sciences—General

Air Force Institute of Technology, Graduate School of Engineering and Management, Dayton, OH 45433-7765. Offers MS, PhD. *Accreditation:* ABET (one or more programs are accredited). Part-time programs available. *Degree requirements:* For master's, thesis; for doctorate, thesis/dissertation. *Entrance requirements:* For master's, GRE General Test, minimum GPA of 3.0; for doctorate, GRE General Test.

Alabama Agricultural and Mechanical University, School of Graduate Studies, School of Engineering and Technology, Huntsville, AL 35811. Offers M Ed, MS. Part-time and evening/weekend programs available. *Degree requirements:* For master's, comprehensive exam, thesis optional. *Entrance requirements:* For master's, GRE General Test. Additional exam requirements/recommendations for international students: Required—TOEFL (minimum score 500 paper-based; 173 computer-based; 61 iBT). Electronic applications accepted. *Faculty research:* Ionized gases, hypersonic flow phenomenology, robotics systems development.

Alfred University, Graduate School, New York State College of Ceramics, School of Engineering, Alfred, NY 14802-1205. Offers biomedical materials engineering science (MS); ceramic engineering (MS); ceramics (PhD); electrical engineering (MS); glass science (MS, PhD); materials science and engineering (MS, PhD); mechanical engineering (MS). *Degree requirements:* For master's, thesis; for doctorate, thesis/dissertation. *Entrance requirements:* Additional exam requirements/recommendations for international students: Required—TOEFL (minimum score 590 paper-based; 243 computer-based). Electronic applications accepted. *Expenses:* Contact institution. *Faculty research:* Fine-particle technology, x-ray diffraction, superconductivity, electronic materials.

The American University of Athens, The School of Graduate Studies, Athens, Greece. Offers biomedical sciences (MS); business (MBA); business communication (MA); computer sciences (MS); engineering and applied sciences (MS); politics and policy making (MA); systems engineering (MS); telecommunications (MS). *Entrance requirements:* For master's, resum&e, 2 recommendation letters. Additional exam requirements/recommendations for international students: Required—TOEFL (minimum score 550 paper-based; 213 computer-based). *Faculty research:* Nanotechnology, environmental sciences, rock mechanics, human skin studies, Monte Carlo algorithms and software.

American University of Beirut, Graduate Programs, Faculty of Engineering and Architecture, Beirut, Lebanon. Offers civil engineering (ME, PhD); electrical and computer engineering (ME, PhD); engineering management (MEM); environmental and water resources (ME); environmental and water resources engineering (PhD); environmental technology (MSES); mechanical engineering (ME, PhD); urban design (MUD); urban planning and policy (MUP). Part-time programs available. *Degree requirements:* For master's, one foreign language, comprehensive exam, thesis (for some programs); for doctorate, one foreign language, comprehensive exam, thesis/dissertation, publications. *Entrance requirements:* For master's, letters of recommendation; for doctorate, letters of recommendation, master's degree, transcripts, curriculum vitae, interview. Additional exam requirements/recommendations for international students: Required—TOEFL (minimum score 600 paper-based; 250 computer-based; 100 iBT), IELTS (minimum score 7.5). Electronic applications accepted.

Andrews University, School of Graduate Studies, College of Technology, Berrien Springs, MI 49104. Offers MS. *Faculty:* 6 full-time (1 woman). *Students:* 7 full-time (1 woman), 2 part-time (0 women); includes 1 minority (African American), 6 international. Average age 31. 9 applicants, 56% accepted, 4 enrolled. In 2009, 3 master's awarded. *Entrance requirements:* For master's, minimum GPA of 2.6. Additional exam requirements/recommendations for international students: Required—TOEFL (minimum score 550 paper-based). *Application deadline:* Applications are processed on a rolling basis. Application fee: $40. *Unit head:* Dr. Verlyn Benson, Head, 269-471-3413. *Application contact:* Carolyn Hurst, Supervisor of Graduate Admission, 800-253-2874, Fax: 269-471-6321, E-mail: graduate@andrews.edu.

Arizona State University, Graduate College, College of Technology and Innovation, Tempe, AZ 85287. Offers MCST, MS. Part-time and evening/weekend programs available. *Degree requirements:* For master's, thesis or applied project and oral defense. *Entrance requirements:* For master's, 3 letters of recommendation, minimum GPA of 3.0, resume. Additional exam requirements/recommendations for international students: Required—TOEFL (minimum score 550 paper-based; 213 computer-based; 83 iBT); Recommended—TWE. Electronic applications accepted.

Arizona State University, Graduate College, Ira A. Fulton School of Engineering, Tempe, AZ 85287. Offers M Eng, MCS, MS, MSE, PhD, MSE/MIMOT. Part-time programs available. *Degree requirements:* For doctorate, thesis/dissertation.

Arkansas State University—Jonesboro, Graduate School, College of Engineering, Jonesboro, State University, AR 72467. Offers MEM. Part-time programs available. *Faculty:* 3 part-time/adjunct (0 women). *Students:* 4 full-time (1 woman), 15 part-time (3 women); includes 1 minority (African American), 11 international. Average age 27. 17 applicants, 88% accepted, 10 enrolled. *Degree requirements:* For master's, comprehensive exam. *Entrance requirements:* For master's, GRE, appropriate bachelor's degree, official transcript, letters of recommendation, resume, immunization records. Additional exam requirements/recommendations for international students: Required—TOEFL (minimum score 550 paper-based; 213 computer-based; 79 iBT), IELTS (minimum score 6). *Application deadline:* For fall admission, 6/1 for domestic and international students; for spring admission, 10/15 for domestic and international students. Applications are processed on a rolling basis. Application fee: $30 ($40 for international students). Electronic applications accepted. *Expenses:* Tuition, state resident: full-time $3744; part-time $208 per credit hour. Tuition, nonresident: full-time $9540; part-time $530 per credit hour. Required fees: $896; $47 per credit hour. $25 per term. One-time fee: $50. Tuition and fees vary according to course load and program. *Financial support:* In 2009–10, 4 students received support. Career-related internships or fieldwork, scholarships/grants, and unspecified assistantships available. Financial award application deadline: 7/1; financial award applicants required to submit FAFSA. *Unit head:* Dr. David Beasley, Dean, 870-972-2088, Fax: 870-972-3948, E-mail: dbbeasley@astate.edu. *Application contact:* Dr. Andrew Sustich, Dean of the Graduate School, 870-972-3029, Fax: 870-972-3857, E-mail: sustich@astate.edu.

Arkansas Tech University, Graduate College, College of Applied Sciences, Russellville, AR 72801. Offers emergency management (MS); engineering (M Engr); information technology (MS). Part-time programs available. *Students:* 73 full-time (17 women), 50 part-time (22 women); includes 8 minority (4 African Americans, 1 American Indian/Alaska Native, 1 Asian American or Pacific Islander, 2 Hispanic Americans), 55 international. Average age 29. In 2009, 38 master's awarded. *Degree requirements:* For master's, comprehensive exam (for some programs), thesis (for some programs), internship. *Entrance requirements:* For master's, GRE General Test. Additional exam requirements/recommendations for international students: Required—TOEFL (minimum score 550 paper-based; 213 computer-based; 79 iBT), IELTS (minimum score 6). *Application deadline:* For fall admission, 3/1 priority date for domestic students, 5/1 priority date for international students; for spring admission, 10/1 priority date for domestic and international students. Applications are processed on a rolling basis. Application fee: $0 ($30 for international students). Electronic applications accepted. *Expenses:* Tuition, state resident: full-time $3438; part-time $191 per hour. Tuition, nonresident: full-time $6876; part-time $382 per hour. Required fees: $482; $9 per credit hour. $140 per semester. Tuition and fees vary according to course load. *Financial support:* In 2009–10, teaching assistantships with full tuition reimbursements (averaging $4,000 per year); research assistantships, career-related internships or fieldwork, Federal Work-Study, scholarships/grants, health care benefits, and unspecified assistantships also available. Support available to part-time students. Financial award application deadline: 4/15; financial award applicants required to submit FAFSA. *Unit head:* Dr. William Hoefler, Dean, 479-968-0353 Ext. 501, E-mail: whoeflerjr@atu.edu. *Application*

contact: Dr. Mary B. Gunter, Dean of Graduate College, 479-968-0398, Fax: 479-964-0542, E-mail: graduate.school@atu.edu.

Auburn University, Graduate School, Ginn College of Engineering, Auburn University, AL 36849. Offers M Ch E, M Mtl E, MAE, MCE, MEE, MISE, MME, MS, MSWE, PhD. Part-time programs available. *Faculty:* 146 full-time (12 women), 17 part-time/adjunct (2 women). *Students:* 407 full-time (96 women), 347 part-time (70 women); includes 65 minority (40 African Americans, 2 American Indian/Alaska Native, 15 Asian Americans or Pacific Islanders, 8 Hispanic Americans), 385 international. Average age 28. 1,512 applicants, 44% accepted, 162 enrolled. In 2009, 125 master's, 48 doctorates awarded. *Degree requirements:* For master's, thesis (for some programs); for doctorate, thesis/dissertation. *Entrance requirements:* For master's and doctorate, GRE General Test. *Application deadline:* For fall admission, 7/7 for domestic students; for spring admission, 11/24 for domestic students. Applications are processed on a rolling basis. Application fee: $50 ($60 for international students). Electronic applications accepted. *Expenses:* Tuition, state resident: full-time $6240. Tuition, nonresident: full-time $18,720. International tuition: $18,938 full-time. Required fees: $492. Tuition and fees vary according to course load, program and reciprocity agreements. *Financial support:* Fellowships, research assistantships, teaching assistantships, Federal Work-Study available. Support available to part-time students. Financial award application deadline: 3/15; financial award applicants required to submit FAFSA. *Unit head:* Dr. Larry Benefield, Dean, 334-844-2308. *Application contact:* Dr. George Flowers, Dean of the Graduate School, 334-844-2125.

Baylor University, Graduate School, School of Engineering and Computer Science, Waco, TX 76798. Offers computer science (MS); engineering (ME, MSBE, MSECE, MSME), including biomedical engineering (MSBE), electrical and computer engineering (MSECE), engineering (ME), mechanical engineering (MSME). Part-time programs available. *Students:* 40 full-time (6 women), 6 part-time (1 woman); includes 7 minority (1 African American, 1 Asian American or Pacific Islander, 5 Hispanic Americans), 19 international. In 2009, 18 master's awarded. *Degree requirements:* For master's, thesis optional. *Entrance requirements:* For master's, GRE General Test. *Application deadline:* For fall admission, 8/1 for domestic students; for spring admission, 12/1 for domestic students. Applications are processed on a rolling basis. Application fee: $25. *Financial support:* Teaching assistantships available. Financial award application deadline: 3/15. *Faculty research:* Database systems, advanced architecture, operations research. *Unit head:* Dr. Greg Speegle, Graduate Program Director, 254-710-3876, Fax: 254-710-3839, E-mail: greg_speegle@baylor.edu. *Application contact:* Suzanne Keener, Administrative Assistant, 254-710-3588, Fax: 254-710-3870.

Boise State University, Graduate College, College of Engineering, Boise, ID 83725-0399. Offers M Engr, MS, PhD. Part-time programs available. Postbaccalaureate distance learning degree programs offered (no on-campus study). *Entrance requirements:* For master's, minimum GPA of 3.0. Electronic applications accepted. *Expenses:* Tuition, state resident: full-time $3106; part-time $209 per credit. Tuition, nonresident: part-time $284 per credit.

Boston University, College of Engineering, Boston, MA 02215. Offers M Eng, MS, PhD, MD/PhD, MS/MBA. Part-time programs available. Postbaccalaureate distance learning degree programs offered (no on-campus study). *Faculty:* 114 full-time (13 women), 1 part-time/adjunct (0 women). *Students:* 505 full-time (121 women), 48 part-time (16 women); includes 67 minority (8 African Americans, 1 American Indian/Alaska Native, 47 Asian Americans or Pacific Islanders, 11 Hispanic Americans), 245 international. Average age 25. 1,574 applicants, 30% accepted, 188 enrolled. In 2009, 114 master's, 44 doctorates awarded. Terminal master's awarded for partial completion of doctoral program. *Degree requirements:* For master's, thesis (for some programs); for doctorate, comprehensive exam, thesis/dissertation. *Entrance requirements:* For master's and doctorate, GRE General Test. Additional exam requirements/recommendations for international students: Required—TOEFL (minimum score 550 paper-based; 213 computer-based; 84 iBT) or IELTS (minimum score 6.5). *Application deadline:* For fall admission, 4/1 for domestic and international students; for spring admission, 10/1 for domestic and international students. Applications are processed on a rolling basis. Application fee: $70. Electronic applications accepted. *Expenses:* Tuition: Full-time $37,910; part-time $1184 per credit hour. Required fees: $386; $40 per semester. Part-time tuition and fees vary according to class time, course level, degree level and program. *Financial support:* In 2009–10, 424 students received support, including 66 fellowships with full tuition reimbursements available (averaging $27,600 per year), 247 research assistantships with full tuition reimbursements available (averaging $18,200 per year), 49 teaching assistantships with full tuition reimbursements available (averaging $18,200 per year); career-related internships or fieldwork, Federal Work-Study, institutionally sponsored loans, scholarships/grants, traineeships, health care benefits, and tuition waivers (full and partial) also available. Financial award application deadline: 1/15; financial award applicants required to submit FAFSA. *Faculty research:* Photonics, bioengineering, computer and information systems, nanotechnology, materials science and engineering. *Unit head:* Dr. Kenneth R. Lutchen, Dean, 617-353-2800, Fax: 617-358-3468, E-mail: klutch@bu.edu. *Application contact:* Cheryl Kelley, Director of Graduate Programs, 617-353-9760, Fax: 617-353-0259, E-mail: enggrad@bu.edu.

Bradley University, Graduate School, College of Engineering and Technology, Peoria, IL 61625-0002. Offers MSCE, MSEE, MSIE, MSME, MSMFE. Part-time and evening/weekend programs available. *Degree requirements:* For master's, comprehensive exam, thesis optional. *Entrance requirements:* For master's, minimum GPA of 3.0, 2 letters of recommendation. Additional exam requirements/recommendations for international students: Required—TOEFL (minimum score 550 paper-based; 213 computer-based; 79 iBT). *Expenses:* Contact institution.

Brigham Young University, Graduate Studies, Ira A. Fulton College of Engineering and Technology, Provo, UT 84602. Offers MS, PhD. *Faculty:* 104 full-time (1 woman), 16 part-time/adjunct (0 women). *Students:* 291 full-time (31 women), 86 part-time (7 women); includes 37 minority (2 African Americans, 1 American Indian/Alaska Native, 24 Asian Americans or Pacific Islanders, 10 Hispanic Americans), 35 international. Average age 26. 203 applicants, 77% accepted, 120 enrolled. In 2009, 88 master's, 22 doctorates awarded. *Degree requirements:* For master's, comprehensive exam (for some programs), thesis; for doctorate, comprehensive exam, thesis/dissertation. *Entrance requirements:* For master's, GRE, at least 3 letters of recommendation; transcripts from each institution attended; ecclesiastical endorsement; for doctorate, GRE, at least 3 letters of recommendation; ecclesiastical endorsement. Additional exam requirements/recommendations for international students: Required—TOEFL (minimum score 580 paper-based; 237 computer-based; 85 iBT). *Application deadline:* For fall admission, 1/15 for domestic and international students; for winter admission, 6/15 for domestic and international students; for spring admission, 2/15 for domestic and international students. Application fee: $50. Electronic applications accepted. *Expenses:* Tuition: Full-time $5580; part-time $301 per credit hour. Tuition and fees vary according to student's religious affiliation. *Financial support:* In 2009–10, 13 fellowships with full and partial tuition reimbursements (averaging $46,500 per year), 202 research assistantships with full and partial tuition reimbursements (averaging $63,974 per year), 88 teaching assistantships with full and partial tuition reimbursements (averaging $55,001 per year) were awarded; career-related internships or fieldwork, institutionally sponsored loans, scholarships/grants, and unspecified assistantships also available. Support available to part-time students. Financial award application deadline: 6/30; financial award applicants required to submit FAFSA. *Faculty research:* Combustion, microwave remote sensing, structural optimization, biomedical engineering, networking. Total annual research expenditures: $7.5 million. *Unit head:* Dr. Alan R. Parkinson, Dean, 801-422-4327, Fax: 801-422-0218, E-mail: college@et.byu.edu. *Application contact:* Claire A. DeWitt, Adviser, 801-422-4541, Fax: 801-378-5238, E-mail: gradstudies@byu.edu.

Brown University, Graduate School, Division of Engineering, Providence, RI 02912. Offers biomedical engineering (Sc M, PhD); electrical sciences and computer engineering (Sc M, PhD); fluid, thermal and chemical processes (Sc M, PhD); materials science and engineering

(Sc M, PhD); mechanics of solids (Sc M, PhD). *Degree requirements:* For doctorate, thesis/dissertation, preliminary exam.

Bucknell University, Graduate Studies, College of Engineering, Lewisburg, PA 17837. Offers MS, MS Ch E, MSCE, MSEE, MSEV, MSME. Part-time programs available. *Degree requirements:* For master's, thesis. *Entrance requirements:* For master's, GRE General Test, GRE Subject Test, minimum GPA of 2.8. Additional exam requirements/recommendations for international students: Required—TOEFL.

California Institute of Technology, Division of Engineering and Applied Science, Pasadena, CA 91125-0001. Offers aeronautics (MS, PhD, Engr); applied and computational mathematics (MS, PhD); applied mechanics (MS, PhD); applied physics (MS, PhD); bioengineering (MS, PhD); civil engineering (MS, PhD, Engr); computation and neural systems (MS, PhD); computer science (MS, PhD); control and dynamical systems (MS, PhD); electrical engineering (MS, PhD, Engr); environmental science and engineering (MS, PhD); materials science (MS, PhD); mechanical engineering (MS, PhD, Engr). *Faculty:* 92 full-time (15 women). *Students:* 476 full-time (101 women). 2,364 applicants, 10% accepted, 114 enrolled. In 2009, 63 master's, 74 doctorates awarded. Terminal master's awarded for partial completion of doctoral program. *Degree requirements:* For doctorate, thesis/dissertation. *Entrance requirements:* For master's and doctorate, GRE (strongly recommended), minimum GPA of 3.5. Additional exam requirements/recommendations for international students: Required—TOEFL; Recommended—TWE (minimum score 5). *Application deadline:* For fall admission, 1/1 for domestic students. Application fee: $50. Electronic applications accepted. *Financial support:* In 2009–10, 134 fellowships, 267 research assistantships, 95 teaching assistantships were awarded; Federal Work-Study and institutionally sponsored loans also available. Support available to part-time students. *Unit head:* Dr. Ares J. Rosakis, Chair to Division of Engineering and Applied Science, 626-395-4100, E-mail: arosakis@caltech.edu. *Application contact:* Natalie Gilmore, Assistant Dean of Graduate Studies, 626-395-3812, Fax: 626-577-9246, E-mail: ngilmore@caltech.edu.

California National University for Advanced Studies, College of Engineering, Northridge, CA 91325. Offers MS Eng. Part-time programs available. Postbaccalaureate distance learning degree programs offered (no on-campus study). *Degree requirements:* For master's, thesis or alternative, project. *Entrance requirements:* For master's, minimum GPA of 3.0. Electronic applications accepted.

California Polytechnic State University, San Luis Obispo, College of Engineering, Department of Biomedical and General Engineering, San Luis Obispo, CA 93407. Offers MS, MBA/MS, MCRP/MS. Part-time programs available. *Faculty:* 12 full-time (4 women), 1 part-time/adjunct (0 women). *Students:* 89 full-time (23 women), 33 part-time (4 women); includes 37 minority (2 African Americans, 1 American Indian/Alaska Native, 23 Asian Americans or Pacific Islanders, 11 Hispanic Americans), 4 international. Average age 26. 86 applicants, 72% accepted, 46 enrolled. In 2009, 44 master's awarded. *Degree requirements:* For master's, comprehensive exam (for some programs), thesis (for some programs). *Entrance requirements:* For master's, minimum GPA of 2.5 in last 90 quarter units of course work. Additional exam requirements/recommendations for international students: Required—TOEFL (minimum score 550 paper-based; 213 computer-based), TWE (minimum score 4.5). *Application deadline:* For fall admission, 7/1 for domestic students, 11/30 for international students; for winter admission, 11/1 for domestic students, 6/30 for international students; for spring admission, 2/1 for domestic students. Applications are processed on a rolling basis. Application fee: $55. Electronic applications accepted. *Expenses:* Tuition, nonresident: full-time $11,160; part-time $248 per unit. Required fees: $7134; $1553 per quarter. *Financial support:* Fellowships, research assistantships, teaching assistantships, Federal Work-Study and scholarships/grants available. Support available to part-time students. Financial award application deadline: 3/2; financial award applicants required to submit FAFSA. *Faculty research:* Biomedical engineering, materials engineering, water engineering. *Unit head:* Dr. Lanny Griffin, Graduate Coordinator, 805-756-2575, Fax: 805-756-6424, E-mail: lgriffin@calpoly.edu. *Application contact:* Dr. Lanny Griffin, Graduate Coordinator, 805-756-2575, Fax: 805-756-6424, E-mail: lgriffin@calpoly.edu.

California State Polytechnic University, Pomona, Academic Affairs, College of Engineering, Pomona, CA 91768-2557. Offers civil engineering (MS); electrical engineering (MSEE); engineering (MSE); engineering management (MS); mechanical engineering (MS). Part-time programs available. *Faculty:* 95 full-time (17 women), 71 part-time/adjunct (6 women). *Students:* 36 full-time (3 women), 198 part-time (33 women); includes 104 minority (1 African American, 2 American Indian/Alaska Native, 69 Asian Americans or Pacific Islanders, 32 Hispanic Americans), 42 international. Average age 28. 237 applicants, 49% accepted, 73 enrolled. In 2009, 46 master's awarded. *Degree requirements:* For master's, thesis or comprehensive exam. *Entrance requirements:* For master's, GRE General Test or minimum GPA of 3.0 in upper-level course work. Additional exam requirements/recommendations for international students: Required—TOEFL. *Application deadline:* For fall admission, 5/1 priority date for domestic students; for winter admission, 10/15 priority date for domestic students; for spring admission, 1/2 priority date for domestic students. Applications are processed on a rolling basis. Application fee: $55. Electronic applications accepted. *Expenses:* Tuition, nonresident: full-time $6696; part-time $248 per credit. Required fees: $5487; $3237 per term. Tuition and fees vary according to course load, degree level and program. *Financial support:* In 2009–10, 1 fellowship, 6 research assistantships, 5 teaching assistantships were awarded; career-related internships or fieldwork, Federal Work-Study, institutionally sponsored loans, and unspecified assistantships also available. Support available to part-time students. Financial award application deadline: 3/2; financial award applicants required to submit FAFSA. *Faculty research:* Aerospace; alternative vehicles; communications, computers, and controls; engineering management. Total annual research expenditures: $650,000. *Unit head:* Dr. Edward Hohmann, Dean, 909-869-2472, Fax: 909-869-4370, E-mail: echohmann@csupomona.edu. *Application contact:* Dr. Edward Hohmann, Dean, 909-869-2472, Fax: 909-869-4370, E-mail: echohmann@csupomona.edu.

California State University, Chico, Graduate School, College of Engineering, Computer Science, and Technology, Chico, CA 95929-0722. Offers MS. Part-time programs available. Postbaccalaureate distance learning degree programs offered. *Students:* 22 full-time (0 women), 28 part-time (4 women); includes 5 minority (all Asian Americans or Pacific Islanders), 31 international. Average age 27. 140 applicants, 71% accepted, 16 enrolled. In 2009, 73 master's awarded. *Entrance requirements:* Additional exam requirements/recommendations for international students: Required—TOEFL (minimum score 550 paper-based; 213 computer-based; 80 iBT), IELTS (minimum score 6.5). *Application deadline:* For fall admission, 3/1 priority date for domestic students, 3/1 for international students; for spring admission, 9/15 priority date for domestic students, 9/15 for international students. Applications are processed on a rolling basis. Application fee: $55. Electronic applications accepted. *Financial support:* Fellowships, research assistantships, teaching assistantships, career-related internships or fieldwork and Federal Work-Study available. Support available to part-time students. *Unit head:* Dr. Kenneth Derucher, Dean, 530-898-5963. *Application contact:* School of Graduate, International, and Interdisciplinary Studies, 530-898-6880, Fax: 530-898-6889, E-mail: grin@csuchico.edu.

California State University, East Bay, Academic Programs and Graduate Studies, College of Science, Engineering Department, Hayward, CA 94542-3000. Offers construction management (MS); engineering management (MS). *Faculty:* 4 full-time (2 women). *Students:* 24 full-time (9 women), 61 part-time (17 women); includes 27 minority (6 African Americans, 14 Asian Americans or Pacific Islanders, 7 Hispanic Americans), 33 international. Average age 31. 124 applicants, 59% accepted, 36 enrolled. In 2009, 5 master's awarded. *Entrance requirements:* For master's, GRE or GMAT, minimum GPA of 2.5. Additional exam requirements/recommendations for international students: Required—TOEFL (minimum score 550 paper-based; 213 computer-based). *Application deadline:* For fall admission, 6/30 for domestic and international students. Application fee: $55. Electronic applications accepted. *Financial support:* Federal Work-Study and institutionally sponsored loans available. Support available to part-time students. *Unit head:* Dr. Saeid Motavalli, Chair, 510-885-2654, Fax: 510-885-2678, E-mail: saeid.motavalli@csueastbay.edu. *Application contact:* Donna Wiley, Interim Associate Director, 510-885-2928, Fax: 510-885-4777, E-mail: donna.wiley@csueastbay.edu.

California State University, Fresno, Division of Graduate Studies, College of Engineering and Computer Science, Fresno, CA 93740-8027. Offers MS. Part-time and evening/weekend programs available. *Degree requirements:* For master's, thesis or alternative. *Entrance requirements:* For master's, GRE General Test, minimum GPA of 2.7. Additional exam requirements/recommendations for international students: Required—TOEFL. Electronic applications accepted. *Faculty research:* Exhaust emission, blended fuel testing, waste management.

California State University, Fullerton, Graduate Studies, College of Engineering and Computer Science, Fullerton, CA 92834-9480. Offers MS. Part-time programs available. *Students:* 200 full-time (53 women), 483 part-time (99 women); includes 226 minority (11 African Americans, 1 American Indian/Alaska Native, 180 Asian Americans or Pacific Islanders, 34 Hispanic Americans), 280 international. Average age 29. 815 applicants, 61% accepted, 214 enrolled. In 2009, 212 master's awarded. *Degree requirements:* For master's, comprehensive exam, project or thesis. *Entrance requirements:* For master's, minimum undergraduate GPA of 2.5. Application fee: $55. *Expenses:* Tuition, nonresident: full-time $11,160; part-time $373 per credit. Required fees: $1440 per term. Tuition and fees vary according to course load, degree level and program. *Financial support:* Career-related internships or fieldwork, Federal Work-Study, institutionally sponsored loans, and scholarships/grants available. Support available to part-time students. Financial award application deadline: 3/1; financial award applicants required to submit FAFSA. *Unit head:* Dr. Raman Unnikrishnan, Dean, 657-278-3362. *Application contact:* Admissions/Applications, 657-278-2371.

California State University, Los Angeles, Graduate Studies, College of Engineering, Computer Science, and Technology, Los Angeles, CA 90032-8530. Offers MA, MS. Part-time and evening/weekend programs available. *Faculty:* 13 full-time (4 women), 13 part-time/adjunct (4 women). *Students:* 162 full-time (48 women), 378 part-time (68 women); includes 163 minority (23 African Americans, 80 Asian Americans or Pacific Islanders, 60 Hispanic Americans), 312 international. Average age 28. 274 applicants, 100% accepted, 91 enrolled. In 2009, 117 master's awarded. *Entrance requirements:* Additional exam requirements/recommendations for international students: Required—TOEFL (minimum score 550 paper-based). *Application deadline:* For fall admission, 5/1 for domestic and international students. Applications are processed on a rolling basis. Application fee: $55. Electronic applications accepted. *Financial support:* Federal Work-Study available. Support available to part-time students. Financial award application deadline: 3/1. *Unit head:* Dr. Keith Moo-Young, Dean, 323-343-4500, Fax: 323-343-4555, E-mail: kmooyou@exchange.calstatela.edu. *Application contact:* Dr. Cheryl L. Ney, Associate Vice President for Academic Affairs and Dean of Graduate Studies, 323-343-3820, Fax: 323-343-5653, E-mail: cney@cslanet.calstatela.edu.

California State University, Northridge, Graduate Studies, College of Engineering and Computer Science, Northridge, CA 91330. Offers MS. Part-time and evening/weekend programs available. *Faculty:* 53 full-time (7 women), 84 part-time/adjunct (24 women). *Students:* 357 full-time (46 women), 366 part-time (63 women); includes 9 African Americans, 74 Asian Americans or Pacific Islanders, 58 Hispanic Americans, 372 international. Average age 28. 1,179 applicants, 57% accepted, 256 enrolled. In 2009, 177 master's awarded. *Entrance requirements:* For master's, GRE General Test, minimum GPA of 2.5. Additional exam requirements/recommendations for international students: Required—TOEFL. *Application deadline:* For fall admission, 11/30 for domestic students. Application fee: $55. *Financial support:* Teaching assistantships, career-related internships or fieldwork and Federal Work-Study available. Support available to part-time students. Financial award application deadline: 3/1. *Unit head:* Dr. S. K. Ramesh, Dean, 818-677-4501, E-mail: s.ramesh@csun.edu. *Application contact:* Dr. S. K. Ramesh, Dean, 818-677-4501, E-mail: s.ramesh@csun.edu.

California State University, Sacramento, Graduate Studies, College of Engineering and Computer Science, Sacramento, CA 95819. Offers MS. Part-time and evening/weekend programs available. *Degree requirements:* For master's, writing proficiency exam. *Entrance requirements:* Additional exam requirements/recommendations for international students: Required—TOEFL. Electronic applications accepted.

Carleton University, Faculty of Graduate Studies, Faculty of Engineering and Design, Ottawa, ON K1S 5B6, Canada. Offers M Arch, M Des, M Eng, M Sc, MA Sc, PhD. *Degree requirements:* For doctorate, thesis/dissertation. *Entrance requirements:* For master's, honors degree; for doctorate, MA Sc or M Eng. Additional exam requirements/recommendations for international students: Required—TOEFL.

Case Western Reserve University, School of Graduate Studies, The Case School of Engineering, Cleveland, OH 44106. Offers ME, MEM, MS, PhD, MD/MS, MD/PhD. Part-time and evening/weekend programs available. Postbaccalaureate distance learning degree programs offered (minimal on-campus study). *Faculty:* 106 full-time (12 women). *Students:* 527 full-time (116 women), 93 part-time (18 women); includes 65 minority (17 African Americans, 3 American Indian/Alaska Native, 40 Asian Americans or Pacific Islanders, 5 Hispanic Americans), 288 international. 1,359 applicants, 32% accepted, 171 enrolled. In 2009, 118 master's, 61 doctorates awarded. Terminal master's awarded for partial completion of doctoral program. *Degree requirements:* For master's, thesis (for some programs); for doctorate, thesis/dissertation, qualifying exam, teaching experience. *Entrance requirements:* For master's and doctorate, GRE General Test. Additional exam requirements/recommendations for international students: Required—TOEFL (minimum score 550 paper-based; 213 computer-based; 79 iBT), IELTS (minimum score 6.5). *Application deadline:* Applications are processed on a rolling basis. Application fee: $50. Electronic applications accepted. *Financial support:* Fellowships with full and partial tuition reimbursements, research assistantships with full and partial tuition reimbursements, teaching assistantships, career-related internships or fieldwork, Federal Work-Study, and institutionally sponsored loans available. Support available to part-time students. Financial award applicants required to submit FAFSA. *Faculty research:* Advanced materials, biomedical engineering and human health, electrical engineering and computer science, civil engineering, engineering management. Total annual research expenditures: $4.3 million. *Unit head:* Norman C. Tien, Dean and Nord Professor of Engineering, 216-368-4436, Fax: 216-368-6939, E-mail: norman.tien@case.edu. *Application contact:* Dr. Patrick Crago, Associate Dean and Professor of Biomedical Engineering, 216-368-4436, Fax: 216-368-6939, E-mail: cseinfo@case.edu.

The Catholic University of America, School of Engineering, Washington, DC 20064. Offers MBE, MCE, MEE, MME, MSCS, MSE, D Engr, PhD, Certificate. Part-time programs available. *Faculty:* 24 full-time (3 women), 23 part-time/adjunct (1 woman). *Students:* 54 full-time (20 women), 112 part-time (23 women); includes 29 minority (12 African Americans, 7 Asian Americans or Pacific Islanders, 10 Hispanic Americans), 48 international. Average age 32. 173 applicants, 57% accepted, 55 enrolled. In 2009, 58 master's, 3 doctorates, 2 other advanced degrees awarded. *Degree requirements:* For master's, thesis optional; for doctorate, comprehensive exam, thesis/dissertation, 53 semester hours, approval and successful defense of the dissertation in an oral exam, approval of a dissertation proposal. *Entrance requirements:* For master's, statement of purpose, official copies of academic transcripts, three letters of recommendation, minimum GPA of 3.0 for undergraduate courses; for doctorate, statement of purpose; official copies of academic transcripts; three letters of recommendation; minimum GPA of 3.0 for undergraduate courses, 3.4 for master's-level courses. Additional exam requirements/recommendations for international students: Required—TOEFL (minimum score 580 paper-based; 237 computer-based). *Application deadline:* For fall admission, 8/1 priority date for domestic students, 7/15 for international students; for spring admission, 12/1 priority date for domestic students, 10/15 for international students. Applications are processed on a rolling basis. Application fee: $55. Electronic applications accepted. *Expenses:* Contact institution. *Financial support:* Fellowships, research assistantships, teaching assistantships, Federal Work-Study, scholarships/grants, tuition waivers (full and partial), and unspecified assistantships available. Financial award application deadline: 2/1; financial award applicants required to submit FAFSA. *Faculty research:* Rehabilitation engineering, cardiopulmonary biomechanics, geotechnical engineering, signal and image processing, fluid mechanics. Total annual research

Engineering and Applied Sciences—General

The Catholic University of America (continued)

expenditures: $2.9 million. *Unit head:* Dr. Charles C. Nguyen, Dean, 202-319-5160, Fax: 202-319-4499, E-mail: nguyen@cua.edu. *Application contact:* Julie Schwing, Director of Graduate Admissions, 202-319-5057, Fax: 202-319-6533, E-mail: cua-admissions@cua.edu.

Central Connecticut State University, School of Graduate Studies, School of Technology, Department of Engineering, New Britain, CT 06050-4010. Offers MS. Part-time and evening/weekend programs available. *Faculty:* 12 full-time (1 woman), 8 part-time/adjunct (1 woman). *Students:* 2 full-time (0 women), 25 part-time (4 women); includes 6 minority (4 Asian Americans or Pacific Islanders, 2 Hispanic Americans), 2 international. Average age 34. 10 applicants, 60% accepted, 5 enrolled. In 2009, 7 master's awarded. *Degree requirements:* For master's, comprehensive exam, thesis or alternative. *Entrance requirements:* For master's, minimum undergraduate GPA of 2.7. Additional exam requirements/recommendations for international students: Required—TOEFL. *Application deadline:* For fall admission, 7/1 for domestic students; for spring admission, 12/1 for domestic students. Applications are processed on a rolling basis. Application fee: $50. Electronic applications accepted. *Expenses:* Tuition, area resident: Full-time $4662; part-time $440 per credit. Tuition, state resident: full-time $6994; part-time $440 per credit. Tuition, nonresident: full-time $12,988; part-time $440 per credit. Required fees: $3606. One-time fee: $62 part-time. *Financial support:* In 2009–10, 2 students received support. Career-related internships or fieldwork, Federal Work-Study, scholarships/grants, and unspecified assistantships available. Support available to part-time students. Financial award application deadline: 3/1; financial award applicants required to submit FAFSA. *Unit head:* Dr. Alfred Gates, Chair, 860-832-1815. *Application contact:* Dr. Alfred Gates, Chair, 860-832-1815.

Central Connecticut State University, School of Graduate Studies, School of Technology, Department of Technology Engineering Education, New Britain, CT 06050-4010. Offers MS, Certificate. Part-time and evening/weekend programs available. *Faculty:* 5 full-time (1 woman), 2 part-time/adjunct (0 women). *Students:* 6 full-time (0 women), 26 part-time (0 women); includes 2 minority (1 American Indian/Alaska Native, 1 Hispanic American). Average age 38. 17 applicants, 76% accepted, 7 enrolled. In 2009, 3 master's, 3 other advanced degrees awarded. *Degree requirements:* For master's, comprehensive exam, thesis or alternative; for Certificate, qualifying exam. *Entrance requirements:* For master's, minimum undergraduate GPA of 2.7. Additional exam requirements/recommendations for international students: Required—TOEFL. *Application deadline:* For fall admission, 7/1 for domestic students; for spring admission, 12/1 for domestic students. Applications are processed on a rolling basis. Application fee: $50. Electronic applications accepted. *Expenses:* Tuition, area resident: Full-time $4662; part-time $440 per credit. Tuition, state resident: full-time $6994; part-time $440 per credit. Tuition, nonresident: full-time $12,988; part-time $440 per credit. Required fees: $3606. One-time fee: $62 part-time. *Financial support:* In 2009–10, 1 student received support. Career-related internships or fieldwork, Federal Work-Study, scholarships/grants, and unspecified assistantships available. Support available to part-time students. Financial award application deadline: 3/1; financial award applicants required to submit FAFSA. *Faculty research:* Instruction, curriculum development, administration, occupational training. *Unit head:* Dr. James DeLaura, Chair, 860-832-1850. *Application contact:* Dr. James DeLaura, Chair, 860-832-1850.

Central Michigan University, College of Graduate Studies, College of Science and Technology, Department of Engineering Technology, Mount Pleasant, MI 48859. Offers industrial management and technology (MA). Part-time programs available. *Degree requirements:* For master's, thesis or alternative. Electronic applications accepted. *Faculty research:* Computer applications, manufacturing process control, mechanical engineering automation, industrial technology.

Central Washington University, Graduate Studies and Research, College of Education and Professional Studies, Department of Industrial and Engineering Technology, Ellensburg, WA 98926. Offers engineering technology (MS). Part-time programs available. *Faculty:* 15 full-time (0 women). *Students:* 6 full-time (2 women), 14 part-time (0 women); includes 3 minority (1 African American, 2 Asian Americans or Pacific Islanders). 10 applicants, 90% accepted, 9 enrolled. In 2009, 11 master's awarded. *Degree requirements:* For master's, thesis or alternative. *Entrance requirements:* For master's, minimum GPA of 3.0. Additional exam requirements/recommendations for international students: Required—TOEFL (minimum score 550 paper-based; 213 computer-based; 79 iBT). *Application deadline:* For fall admission, 2/1 priority date for domestic students; for winter admission, 10/1 for domestic students; for spring admission, 1/1 for domestic students. Applications are processed on a rolling basis. Application fee: $50. Electronic applications accepted. *Expenses:* Tuition, state resident: full-time $7353; part-time $245 per credit. Tuition, nonresident: full-time $16,383; part-time $546 per credit. Required fees: $882. Tuition and fees vary according to degree level. *Financial support:* In 2009–10, 3 teaching assistantships with full and partial tuition reimbursements (averaging $9,145 per year) were awarded; career-related internships or fieldwork, Federal Work-Study, and health care benefits also available. *Unit head:* Dr. Michael Whelan, Chair, 509-963-1756. *Application contact:* Justine Eason, Admissions Program Coordinator, 509-963-3103, Fax: 509-963-1799, E-mail: masters@cwu.edu.

Christian Brothers University, School of Engineering, Memphis, TN 38104-5581. Offers MEM, MSEM. Part-time and evening/weekend programs available. Postbaccalaureate distance learning degree programs offered (no on-campus study). *Faculty:* 1 full-time (0 women), 3 part-time/adjunct (0 women). *Students:* 1 (woman) full-time, 89 part-time (21 women); includes 19 minority (12 African Americans, 4 Asian Americans or Pacific Islanders, 3 Hispanic Americans), 43 international. Average age 32. In 2009, 12 master's awarded. *Degree requirements:* For master's, engineering management project. *Entrance requirements:* For master's, GRE. Additional exam requirements/recommendations for international students: Required—TOEFL. Application fee: $50. *Financial support:* Institutionally sponsored loans available. *Unit head:* Dr. Eric B. Welch, Dean, 901-321-3425, Fax: 901-321-3402, E-mail: ewelch@cbu.edu. *Application contact:* Dr. Neal Jackson, Director, 901-321-3283, Fax: 901-321-3494, E-mail: njackson@cbu.edu.

City College of the City University of New York, Graduate School, Grove School of Engineering, New York, NY 10031-9198. Offers ME, MS, PhD. Part-time programs available. *Students:* 30 full-time (5 women), 126 part-time (33 women); includes 80 minority (22 African Americans, 40 Asian Americans or Pacific Islanders, 18 Hispanic Americans), 57 international. 309 applicants, 66% accepted. In 2009, 108 master's awarded. Terminal master's awarded for partial completion of doctoral program. *Degree requirements:* For master's, thesis optional; for doctorate, one foreign language, comprehensive exam, thesis/dissertation. *Entrance requirements:* For master's, GRE General Test, minimum B average in undergraduate coursework; for doctorate, GRE General Test, minimum GPA of 3.5. Additional exam requirements/recommendations for international students: Required—TOEFL (minimum score 500 paper-based; 173 computer-based; 61 iBT). *Application deadline:* For fall admission, 5/1 for domestic and international students; for spring admission, 11/15 for domestic and international students. Applications are processed on a rolling basis. Application fee: $125. *Financial support:* In 2009–10, fellowships with partial tuition reimbursements (averaging $20,000 per year), research assistantships with full tuition reimbursements (averaging $20,000 per year), teaching assistantships (averaging $12,000 per year) were awarded; Federal Work-Study, institutionally sponsored loans, and tuition waivers (full and partial) also available. Support available to part-time students. Financial award applicants required to submit CSS PROFILE or FAFSA. *Faculty research:* Robotics, network systems, structures. Total annual research expenditures: $8.5 million. *Unit head:* Dr. Muntaz G. Kassir, Associate Dean for Graduate Studies, 212-650-8030, Fax: 212-650-8024, E-mail: kassir@ccny.cuny.edu. *Application contact:* 212-650-6977, Fax: 212-650-6417, E-mail: gradadm@ccny.cuny.edu.

See Close-Up on page 69.

Clarkson University, Graduate School, Wallace H. Coulter School of Engineering, Potsdam, NY 13699. Offers ME, MS, PhD. Part-time programs available. *Faculty:* 86 full-time (18 women), 7 part-time/adjunct (3 women). *Students:* 216 full-time (51 women), 3 part-time (all women); includes 5 minority (1 American Indian/Alaska Native, 2 Asian Americans or Pacific Islanders, 2 Hispanic Americans), 129 international. Average age 28. 426 applicants, 56% accepted, 58 enrolled. In 2009, 39 master's, 25 doctorates awarded. Terminal master's awarded for partial completion of doctoral program. *Degree requirements:* For master's, thesis (for some programs); for doctorate, comprehensive exam, thesis/dissertation, departmental qualifying exam. *Entrance requirements:* For master's, GRE, resume, 3 letters of recommendation; for doctorate, GRE, transcripts of all college coursework, resume, personal statement, three letters of recommendation. Additional exam requirements/recommendations for international students: Required—TOEFL (minimum score 550 paper-based; 213 computer-based; 80 iBT), IELTS (minimum score 6.5). *Application deadline:* For fall admission, 1/30 priority date for domestic and international students; for spring admission, 9/1 priority date for domestic and international students. Applications are processed on a rolling basis. Application fee: $25 ($35 for international students). Electronic applications accepted. *Expenses:* Tuition: Part-time $1074 per credit hour. *Financial support:* In 2009–10, 180 students received support, including 8 fellowships (averaging $30,000 per year), 107 research assistantships (averaging $20,190 per year), 41 teaching assistantships (averaging $20,190 per year); scholarships/grants, tuition waivers (partial), and unspecified assistantships also available. *Faculty research:* Advanced materials processing, renewable energy rehabilitation, environmental. Total annual research expenditures: $8.7 million. *Unit head:* Dr. Goodarz Ahmadi, Dean, 315-268-6446, Fax: 315-268-4494, E-mail: ahmadi@clarkson.edu. *Application contact:* Kelly Sharlow, Assistant to the Dean, 315-268-7929, Fax: 315-268-4494, E-mail: ksharlow@clarkson.edu.

See Close-Up on page 71.

Clemson University, Graduate School, College of Engineering and Science, Clemson, SC 29634. Offers M Engr, MFA, MS, PhD. Part-time programs available. *Faculty:* 293 full-time (42 women), 37 part-time/adjunct (9 women). *Students:* 1,106 full-time (285 women), 223 part-time (61 women); includes 85 minority (47 African Americans, 4 American Indian/Alaska Native, 27 Asian Americans or Pacific Islanders, 7 Hispanic Americans), 675 international. Average age 27. 2,379 applicants, 55% accepted, 396 enrolled. In 2009, 225 master's, 74 doctorates awarded. *Degree requirements:* For doctorate, thesis/dissertation. *Entrance requirements:* For master's and doctorate, GRE General Test. Additional exam requirements/recommendations for international students: Required—TOEFL. Application fee: $70 ($80 for international students). Electronic applications accepted. *Expenses:* Tuition, state resident: full-time $8684; part-time $528 per credit hour. Tuition, nonresident: full-time $15,330; part-time $1078 per credit hour. Required fees: $736; $37 per semester. Part-time tuition and fees vary according to course load and program. *Financial support:* In 2009–10, 834 students received support, including 45 fellowships with full and partial tuition reimbursements available (averaging $11,291 per year), 408 research assistantships with partial tuition reimbursements available (averaging $18,200 per year), 283 teaching assistantships with partial tuition reimbursements available (averaging $17,985 per year); career-related internships or fieldwork, institutionally sponsored loans, scholarships/grants, health care benefits, and unspecified assistantships also available. Support available to part-time students. Financial award applicants required to submit FAFSA. Total annual research expenditures: $27.9 million. *Unit head:* Dr. Esin Gulari, Dean, 864-656-3202. *Application contact:* Dr. R. Larry Dooley, Associate Dean for Research and Graduate Studies, 864-656-3200, Fax: 864-656-4466, E-mail: dooley@eng.clemson.edu.

Cleveland State University, College of Graduate Studies, Fenn College of Engineering, Cleveland, OH 44115. Offers MS, D Eng. Part-time and evening/weekend programs available. *Degree requirements:* For master's, thesis or alternative; for doctorate, thesis/dissertation, candidacy and qualifying exams. *Entrance requirements:* For master's, GRE General Test, BS in engineering, minimum GPA of 3.0 (2.75 for students from ABET/EAC-accredited programs from the U. S. and Canada); for doctorate, GRE General Test, MS in engineering, minimum GPA of 3.25. Additional exam requirements/recommendations for international students: Required—TOEFL (minimum score 525 paper-based; 197 computer-based). Electronic applications accepted. *Faculty research:* Structural analysis and design, dynamic system and controls, applied biomedical engineering, transportation, water resources, telecommunication, power electronics, computer engineering, industrial automation, engineering management, mechanical design, thermodynamics and fluid mechanics, material engineering, tribology.

Colorado School of Mines, Graduate School, Golden, CO 80401. Offers ME, MIPER, MS, PMS, PhD, Graduate Certificate. Part-time programs available. *Faculty:* 326 full-time (75 women), 92 part-time/adjunct (23 women). *Students:* 919 full-time (253 women), 166 part-time (42 women); includes 96 minority (14 African Americans, 6 American Indian/Alaska Native, 39 Asian Americans or Pacific Islanders, 37 Hispanic Americans), 278 international. Average age 30. 1,503 applicants, 61% accepted, 393 enrolled. In 2009, 280 master's, 46 doctorates awarded. *Degree requirements:* For master's, thesis (for some programs); for doctorate, comprehensive exam, thesis/dissertation. *Entrance requirements:* For master's, doctorate, and Graduate Certificate, GRE General Test. Additional exam requirements/recommendations for international students: Required—TOEFL (minimum score 550 paper-based; 213 computer-based; 80 iBT). *Application deadline:* For fall admission, 1/15 priority date for domestic and international students; for spring admission, 9/1 priority date for domestic and international students. Application fee: $50 ($70 for international students). Electronic applications accepted. *Expenses:* Tuition, state resident: full-time $10,584; part-time $588 per credit hour. Tuition, nonresident: full-time $24,750; part-time $1375 per credit hour. Required fees: $1654; $827.10 per semester. *Financial support:* In 2009–10, 547 students received support, including 36 fellowships with full tuition reimbursements available (averaging $20,000 per year), 355 research assistantships with full tuition reimbursements available (averaging $20,000 per year), 156 teaching assistantships with full tuition reimbursements available (averaging $20,000 per year); career-related internships or fieldwork, Federal Work-Study, institutionally sponsored loans, scholarships/grants, health care benefits, and unspecified assistantships also available. Financial award application deadline: 1/15; financial award applicants required to submit FAFSA. *Faculty research:* Energy, environment, materials, minerals, engineering systems. Total annual research expenditures: $32.3 million. *Unit head:* Dr. Tom M. Boyd, Dean of Graduate Studies, 303-273-3020, Fax: 303-273-3244, E-mail: tboyd@mines.edu. *Application contact:* Kay Leaman, Graduate Admissions Coordinator, 303-273-3249, Fax: 303-273-3244, E-mail: grad-app@mines.edu.

Colorado State University, Graduate School, College of Engineering, Fort Colllins, CO 80523-1301. Offers ME, MEE, MS, PhD. *Accreditation:* ABET. Part-time programs available. *Faculty:* 96 full-time (10 women), 11 part-time/adjunct (1 woman). *Students:* 252 full-time (57 women), 295 part-time (51 women); includes 45 minority (4 African Americans, 8 American Indian/Alaska Native, 13 Asian Americans or Pacific Islanders, 20 Hispanic Americans), 168 international. Average age 30. 844 applicants, 37% accepted, 126 enrolled. In 2009, 92 master's, 40 doctorates awarded. *Degree requirements:* For doctorate, thesis/dissertation. *Entrance requirements:* For master's, GRE General Test, minimum GPA of 3.0, 3 letters of recommendation; for doctorate, GRE General Test, minimum GPA of 3.0, transcripts, 3 letters of recommendation, statement of purpose with interests. Additional exam requirements/recommendations for international students: Required—TOEFL. *Application deadline:* For fall admission, 2/1 priority date for domestic and international students; for spring admission, 10/1 priority date for domestic and international students. Applications are processed on a rolling basis. Application fee: $50. Electronic applications accepted. *Expenses:* Tuition, state resident: full-time $6434; part-time $359.10 per credit. Tuition, nonresident: full-time $18,116; part-time $1006.45 per credit. Required fees: $1496; $83 per credit. *Financial support:* In 2009–10, 259 students received support, including 26 fellowships with full tuition reimbursements available (averaging $29,223 per year), 200 research assistantships with full tuition reimbursements available (averaging $17,091 per year), 33 teaching assistantships with full tuition reimbursements available (averaging $9,379 per year); career-related internships or fieldwork, Federal Work-Study, institutionally sponsored loans, scholarships/grants, traineeships, health care benefits, and unspecified assistantships also available. Financial award application deadline: 1/15. *Faculty research:* Atmospheric science, biological engineering, civil and environmental engineering, electrical and computer engineering, mechanical and biomedical engineering. Total annual research expenditures: $57.4 million. *Unit head:* Dr. Sandra L. Woods, Dean,

970-491-3366, Fax: 970-491-5569, E-mail: sandra.woods@colostate.edu. *Application contact:* Dr. Tom Siller, Associate Dean, 970-491-6220, Fax: 970-491-3429, E-mail: thomas.siller@colostate.edu.

Colorado State University–Pueblo, College of Education, Engineering and Professional Studies, Pueblo, CO 81001-4901. Offers M Ed, MS. Part-time and evening/weekend programs available. *Degree requirements:* For master's, thesis optional. *Entrance requirements:* For master's, GRE General Test. Additional exam requirements/recommendations for international students: Required—TOEFL (minimum score 500 paper-based; 173 computer-based). Electronic applications accepted. *Expenses:* Contact institution. *Faculty research:* Nanotechnology, applied operations, research transportation, decision analysis.

Columbia University, Fu Foundation School of Engineering and Applied Science, New York, NY 10027. Offers MS, Eng Sc D, PhD, Engr, MS/MBA. Part-time programs available. Postbaccalaureate distance learning degree programs offered (no on-campus study). *Faculty:* 127 full-time (10 women), 35 part-time/adjunct (7 women). *Students:* 1,242 full-time (298 women), 599 part-time (135 women); includes 172 minority (17 African Americans, 2 American Indian/Alaska Native, 130 Asian Americans or Pacific Islanders, 23 Hispanic Americans), 1,168 international. Average age 27. 4,232 applicants, 34% accepted, 667 enrolled. In 2009, 603 master's, 77 doctorates awarded. Terminal master's awarded for partial completion of doctoral program. *Degree requirements:* For master's, comprehensive exam (for some programs), thesis (for some programs); for doctorate, comprehensive exam (for some programs), thesis/dissertation, qualifying exam; for Engr, thesis optional. *Entrance requirements:* For master's and Engr, GRE General Test; for doctorate, GRE General Test, GRE Subject Test (computer science and applied physics). Additional exam requirements/recommendations for international students: Required—TOEFL. *Application deadline:* For fall admission, 12/1 priority date for domestic and international students; for spring admission, 10/1 priority date for domestic and international students. Application fee: $70. Electronic applications accepted. *Financial support:* In 2009–10, 528 students received support, including 57 fellowships with full and partial tuition reimbursements available (averaging $26,430 per year), 349 research assistantships with full and partial tuition reimbursements available (averaging $28,263 per year), 158 teaching assistantships with full and partial tuition reimbursements available (averaging $24,640 per year); career-related internships or fieldwork, traineeships, health care benefits, and unspecified assistantships also available. Support available to part-time students. Financial award application deadline: 12/1; financial award applicants required to submit FAFSA. Total annual research expenditures: $110.8 million. *Unit head:* Dr. Feniosky Pena-Mora, Dean, 212-854-2993, Fax: 212-864-0104, E-mail: dean@seas.columbia.edu. *Application contact:* Olga Tymejczyk, Admissions Coordinator, 212-854-6456, Fax: 212-854-5900, E-mail: seasgradmit@columbia.edu.

Concordia University, School of Graduate Studies, Faculty of Engineering and Computer Science, Montréal, QC H3G 1M8, Canada. Offers M App Comp Sc, M Comp Sc, M Eng, MA Sc, PhD, Certificate, Diploma. *Degree requirements:* For doctorate, comprehensive exam, thesis/dissertation. *Expenses:* Contact institution.

Cooper Union for the Advancement of Science and Art, Albert Nerken School of Engineering, New York, NY 10003-7120. Offers chemical engineering (ME); civil engineering (ME); electrical engineering (ME); mechanical engineering (ME). Part-time programs available. *Faculty:* 27 full-time (1 woman), 15 part-time/adjunct (2 women). *Students:* 66 full-time (8 women), 20 part-time (1 woman); includes 30 minority (2 African Americans, 1 American Indian/Alaska Native, 19 Asian Americans or Pacific Islanders, 8 Hispanic Americans), 10 international. Average age 24. 80 applicants, 90% accepted, 56 enrolled. In 2009, 18 master's awarded. *Degree requirements:* For master's, thesis. *Entrance requirements:* For master's, GRE, BE, minimum GPA of 3.5. Additional exam requirements/recommendations for international students: Required—TOEFL (minimum score 600 paper-based; 250 computer-based; 100 iBT). *Application deadline:* For fall admission, 5/1 for domestic and international students. Applications are processed on a rolling basis. Application fee: $65. *Expenses:* Tuition: Full-time $35,000. Required fees: $1650. *Financial support:* Fellowships with tuition reimbursements, career-related internships or fieldwork, Federal Work-Study, tuition waivers (full), and all admitted students receive full-tuition scholarships available. Support available to part-time students. Financial award application deadline: 5/1; financial award applicants required to submit CSS PROFILE or FAFSA. *Faculty research:* Civil infrastructure, imaging and sensing technology, biomedical engineering, encryption technology, process engineering. *Unit head:* Dr. Simon Ben-Avi, Dean, 212-353-4285, E-mail: benavi@cooper.edu. *Application contact:* Student Contact, 212-353-4120, E-mail: admissions@cooper.edu.

Cornell University, Graduate School, Graduate Fields of Engineering, Ithaca, NY 14853-0001. Offers M Eng, MPS, MS, PhD, M Eng/MBA. *Faculty:* 347 full-time (46 women). *Students:* 1,560 full-time (387 women); includes 222 minority (23 African Americans, 1 American Indian/Alaska Native, 145 Asian Americans or Pacific Islanders, 53 Hispanic Americans), 686 international. Average age 26. 5,090 applicants, 35% accepted, 735 enrolled. In 2009, 596 master's, 115 doctorates awarded. *Degree requirements:* For doctorate, comprehensive exam, thesis/dissertation. *Entrance requirements:* Additional exam requirements/recommendations for international students: Required—TOEFL. Application fee: $70. Electronic applications accepted. *Expenses:* Tuition: Full-time $29,500. Required fees: $70. Full-time tuition and fees vary according to degree level, program and student level. *Financial support:* In 2009–10, 740 students received support, including 113 fellowships with full tuition reimbursements available, 49 research assistantships with full tuition reimbursements available, 41 teaching assistantships with full tuition reimbursements available; career-related internships or fieldwork, institutionally sponsored loans, scholarships/grants, health care benefits, tuition waivers (full and partial), and unspecified assistantships also available. Financial award applicants required to submit FAFSA. *Application contact:* Graduate School Application Requests, Caldwell Hall, 607-255-5816.

Dalhousie University, Faculty of Engineering, Halifax, NS B3H 4R2, Canada. Offers M Eng, M Sc, MA Sc, PhD, M Eng/M Plan, MA Sc/M Plan, MBA/M Eng. *Entrance requirements:* Additional exam requirements/recommendations for international students: Required—TOEFL, IELTS, 1 of 5 approved tests: TOEFL, IELTS, CANTEST, CAEL, Michigan English Language Assessment Battery.

Dartmouth College, Thayer School of Engineering, Hanover, NH 03755. Offers MEM, MS, PhD, MBA/MEM. *Faculty:* 47 full-time (8 women), 21 part-time/adjunct (3 women). *Students:* 189 full-time (55 women); includes 11 minority (1 African American, 1 American Indian/Alaska Native, 8 Asian Americans or Pacific Islanders, 1 Hispanic American), 87 international. Average age 24. 606 applicants, 28% accepted, 97 enrolled. In 2009, 58 master's, 10 doctorates awarded. *Degree requirements:* For doctorate, thesis/dissertation, candidacy oral exam. *Entrance requirements:* For master's and doctorate, GRE General Test. Additional exam requirements/recommendations for international students: Required—TOEFL. *Application deadline:* For fall admission, 1/1 priority date for domestic and international students. Applications are processed on a rolling basis. Application fee: $45. Electronic applications accepted. *Financial support:* In 2009–10, 187 students received support, including 10 fellowships with full tuition reimbursements available (averaging $22,920 per year), 89 research assistantships with full tuition reimbursements available (averaging $22,920 per year), 33 teaching assistantships with partial tuition reimbursements available (averaging $7,200 per year); career-related internships or fieldwork, institutionally sponsored loans, scholarships/grants, and tuition waivers (full and partial) also available. Financial award application deadline: 2/15; financial award applicants required to submit CSS PROFILE. *Faculty research:* Biomedical engineering, biotechnology and biochemical engineering, electrical and computer engineering, engineering physics, environmental engineering, materials science and engineering, mechanical systems engineering. Total annual research expenditures: $16.6 million. *Unit head:* Dr. Joseph J. Helbie, Dean, 603-646-2238, Fax: 603-646-2580, E-mail: joseph.j.helbie@dartmouth.edu. *Application contact:* Candace S. Potter, Graduate Admissions Administrator, 603-646-3844, Fax: 603-646-1620, E-mail: candace.potter@dartmouth.edu.

Drexel University, College of Engineering, Philadelphia, PA 19104-2875. Offers MS, MSEE, MSSE, PhD, Certificate. Part-time and evening/weekend programs available. *Degree requirements:* For doctorate, thesis/dissertation. *Entrance requirements:* Additional exam requirements/recommendations for international students: Required—TOEFL. Electronic applications accepted.

Drexel University, School of Technology and Professional Studies, Philadelphia, PA 19104-2875. Offers construction management (MS); engineering technology (MS); food science (MS); hospitality management (MS); professional studies: creativity studies (MS); professional studies: e-learning leadership (MS); professional studies: homeland security management (MS); project management (MS); property management (MS); sport management (MS). Postbaccalaureate distance learning degree programs offered.

Duke University, Graduate School, Pratt School of Engineering, Durham, NC 27708-0586. Offers MEM, MS, PhD, JD/MS, MBA/MS. Part-time programs available. *Degree requirements:* For doctorate, thesis/dissertation. *Entrance requirements:* For master's and doctorate, GRE General Test.

Eastern Illinois University, Graduate School, Lumpkin College of Business and Applied Sciences, School of Technology, Charleston, IL 61920-3099. Offers computer technology (Certificate); quality systems (Certificate); technology (MS); technology security (Certificate); work performance improvement (Certificate). Part-time and evening/weekend programs available. *Faculty:* 14 full-time (2 women). In 2009, 39 master's, 14 other advanced degrees awarded. *Application deadline:* For fall admission, 3/31 priority date for domestic students. Applications are processed on a rolling basis. Application fee: $30. *Expenses:* Tuition, state resident: full-time $9434; part-time $239 per credit hour. Tuition, nonresident: full-time $23,774; part-time $717 per credit hour. Required fees: $802.63. *Financial support:* In 2009–10, 3 research assistantships with tuition reimbursements (averaging $8,100 per year), 3 teaching assistantships with tuition reimbursements (averaging $8,100 per year) were awarded. *Unit head:* Dr. Mahyar Izadi, Chairperson, 217-581-6269, Fax: 217-581-6607, E-mail: mizadi@eiu.edu. *Application contact:* Dr. Peter Ping Liu, Coordinator, 217-581-6267, Fax: 217-581-6607, E-mail: pliu@eiu.edu.

Eastern Michigan University, Graduate School, College of Technology, School of Engineering Technology, Programs in Computer Aided Engineering, Ypsilanti, MI 48197. Offers CAD/CAM (MS); computer aided technology (MS). Part-time and evening/weekend programs available. Postbaccalaureate distance learning degree programs offered (minimal on-campus study). *Students:* 3 full-time (1 woman), 31 part-time (6 women); includes 2 minority (1 African American, 1 Asian American or Pacific Islander), 28 international. Average age 26. In 2009, 16 master's awarded. *Entrance requirements:* Additional exam requirements/recommendations for international students: Required—TOEFL. *Application deadline:* Applications are processed on a rolling basis. Application fee: $35. Tuition and fees vary according to course level. *Financial support:* Fellowships, research assistantships with full tuition reimbursements, teaching assistantships with full tuition reimbursements, tuition waivers (partial) available. Financial award applicants required to submit FAFSA. *Unit head:* Dr. Tony Fukuo Shay, Program Coordinator, 734-487-2040, Fax: 734-487-8755, E-mail: tony.shay@emich.edu. *Application contact:* Dr. Tony Fukuo Shay, Program Coordinator, 734-487-2040, Fax: 734-487-8755, E-mail: tony.shay@emich.edu.

École Polytechnique de Montréal, Graduate Programs, Montréal, QC H3C 3A7, Canada. Offers M Eng, M Sc A, PhD, DESS. Part-time and evening/weekend programs available. Terminal master's awarded for partial completion of doctoral program. *Degree requirements:* For master's, one foreign language, thesis; for doctorate, one foreign language, thesis/dissertation. *Entrance requirements:* For master's, minimum GPA of 2.75; for doctorate, minimum GPA of 3.0. Electronic applications accepted. *Faculty research:* Chemical engineering, environmental engineering, microelectronics and communications, biomedical engineering, engineering physics.

Fairfield University, School of Engineering, Fairfield, CT 06824-5195. Offers electrical and computer engineering (MS); management of technology (MS); mechanical engineering (MS); software engineering (MS). Part-time and evening/weekend programs available. *Degree requirements:* For master's, thesis, capstone course. *Entrance requirements:* For master's, interview, minimum GPA of 2.8, resume, 2 recommendations. Additional exam requirements/recommendations for international students: Required—TOEFL (minimum score 550 paper-based; 213 computer-based; 80 iBT). Electronic applications accepted. *Expenses:* Contact institution. *Faculty research:* Vehicle dynamics, image processing, multimedia in instruction, thermal packaging, character recognition, photovoltaics and nanotechnology, Web technology.

Fairleigh Dickinson University, Metropolitan Campus, University College: Arts, Sciences, and Professional Studies, School of Computer Sciences and Engineering, Teaneck, NJ 07666-1914. Offers computer engineering (MS); computer science (MS); e-commerce (MS); electrical engineering (MSEE); management information systems (MS); mathematical foundation (MS). *Students:* 130 full-time (45 women), 88 part-time (42 women), 146 international. Average age 28. 489 applicants, 63% accepted, 56 enrolled. In 2009, 124 master's awarded. *Application deadline:* Applications are processed on a rolling basis. Application fee: $40. *Unit head:* Dr. Alfredo Tan, Director, 201-692-2000. *Application contact:* Susan Brooman, University Director of Graduate Admissions, 201-692-2554, Fax: 201-692-2560, E-mail: globaleducation@fdu.edu.

Florida Agricultural and Mechanical University, Division of Graduate Studies, Research, and Continuing Education, College of Engineering Science, Technology, and Agriculture, Division of Agricultural Sciences, Tallahassee, FL 32307-3200. Offers agribusiness (MS); animal science (MS); engineering technology (MS); entomology (MS); food science (MS); international programs (MS); plant science (MS). *Faculty:* 31 full-time (2 women). *Students:* 14 full-time (8 women), 8 part-time (4 women); includes 17 minority (16 African Americans, 1 Asian American or Pacific Islander), 3 international. In 2009, 7 master's awarded. *Degree requirements:* For master's, thesis. *Entrance requirements:* For master's, GRE General Test, minimum GPA of 3.0. Additional exam requirements/recommendations for international students: Required—TOEFL (minimum score 500 paper-based). *Application deadline:* For fall admission, 5/18 for domestic students, 12/18 for international students; for spring admission, 11/12 for domestic students, 5/12 for international students. Application fee: $20. *Financial support:* Application deadline: 2/15. *Unit head:* Dr. Mitwe N. Musingo, Graduate Coordinator, 850-561-2309, Fax: 850-599-8821. *Application contact:* Dr. Chanta M. Haywood, Dean of Graduate Studies, Research, and Continuing Education, 850-599-3315, Fax: 850-599-3727.

Florida Agricultural and Mechanical University, Division of Graduate Studies, Research, and Continuing Education, FAMU-FSU College of Engineering, Tallahassee, FL 32307-3200. Offers MS, PhD. College administered jointly by Florida State University. *Faculty:* 23 full-time (2 women). *Students:* 24 full-time (10 women), 14 part-time (2 women); includes 31 African Americans, 1 Asian American or Pacific Islander, 6 international. In 2009, 4 master's, 4 doctorates awarded. *Entrance requirements:* For master's, GRE General Test, minimum GPA of 3.0. Additional exam requirements/recommendations for international students: Required—TOEFL (minimum score 550 paper-based; 213 computer-based). *Application deadline:* For fall admission, 7/1 for domestic students, 3/1 for international students. Application fee: $30. *Financial support:* Fellowships, research assistantships, teaching assistantships, tuition waivers (full) available. *Unit head:* Dr. C. J. Chen, Dean, 850-410-6100, Fax: 850-487-6486. *Application contact:* Dr. Chanta M. Haywood, Dean of Graduate Studies, Research, and Continuing Education, 850-599-3315, Fax: 850-599-3727.

Florida Atlantic University, College of Engineering and Computer Science, Boca Raton, FL 33431-0991. Offers MS, PhD. Part-time and evening/weekend programs available. Postbaccalaureate distance learning degree programs offered (minimal on-campus study). *Faculty:* 70 full-time (9 women), 3 part-time/adjunct (1 woman). *Students:* 162 full-time (38 women), 149 part-time (34 women); includes 90 minority (20 African Americans, 25 Asian Americans or

Engineering and Applied Sciences—General

Florida Atlantic University (continued)
Pacific Islanders, 45 Hispanic Americans), 107 international. Average age 31. 267 applicants, 58% accepted, 75 enrolled. In 2009, 82 master's, 10 doctorates awarded. Terminal master's awarded for partial completion of doctoral program. *Degree requirements:* For master's, thesis optional; for doctorate, thesis/dissertation, qualifying exam. *Entrance requirements:* For master's, GRE General Test, minimum GPA of 3.0; for doctorate, GRE General Test. Additional exam requirements/recommendations for international students: Required—TOEFL. *Application deadline:* For fall admission, 7/1 for domestic students, 2/15 for international students; for spring admission, 11/1 for domestic students, 7/15 for international students. Applications are processed on a rolling basis. Application fee: $30. *Expenses:* Tuition, state resident: full-time $7055; part-time $293.94 per credit hour. Tuition, nonresident: full-time $22,096; part-time $920.66 per credit hour. *Financial support:* In 2009–10, research assistantships with partial tuition reimbursements (averaging $15,000 per year), teaching assistantships with partial tuition reimbursements (averaging $15,000 per year) were awarded; fellowships, career-related internships or fieldwork, Federal Work-Study, and unspecified assistantships also available. Support available to part-time students. Financial award applicants required to submit FAFSA. *Faculty research:* Automated underwater vehicles, communication systems, computer networks, materials, neural networks. *Unit head:* Dr. Karl K. Stevens, Dean, 561-297-3400, Fax: 561-297-2659, E-mail: stevens@fau.edu. *Application contact:* Dr. Karl K. Stevens, Dean, 561-297-3400, Fax: 561-297-2659, E-mail: stevens@fau.edu.

Florida Institute of Technology, Graduate Programs, College of Engineering, Melbourne, FL 32901-6975. Offers MS, PhD. Part-time and evening/weekend programs available. *Faculty:* 60 full-time (4 women), 5 part-time/adjunct (0 women). *Students:* 287 full-time (53 women), 305 part-time (64 women); includes 57 minority (18 African Americans, 18 Asian Americans or Pacific Islanders, 21 Hispanic Americans), 231 international. Average age 28. 1,032 applicants, 59% accepted, 156 enrolled. In 2009, 235 master's, 9 doctorates awarded. Terminal master's awarded for partial completion of doctoral program. *Degree requirements:* For master's, comprehensive exam (for some programs), thesis (for some programs); for doctorate, comprehensive exam, thesis/dissertation. *Entrance requirements:* For master's, GRE, minimum GPA of 3.0; for doctorate, GRE, minimum GPA of 3.2, 3 letters of recommendation, resume, statement of objectives. Additional exam requirements/recommendations for international students: Required—TOEFL (minimum score 550 paper-based; 213 computer-based; 79 iBT). *Application deadline:* For fall admission, 4/1 for international students; for spring admission, 9/30 for international students. Applications are processed on a rolling basis. Application fee: $50. Electronic applications accepted. *Expenses:* Tuition: Part-time $1015 per credit. Tuition and fees vary according to campus/location and program. *Financial support:* In 2009–10, 88 students received support, including 5 fellowships with full and partial tuition reimbursements available (averaging $7,240 per year), 34 research assistantships with full and partial tuition reimbursements available (averaging $5,349 per year), 54 teaching assistantships with full and partial tuition reimbursements available (averaging $5,976 per year); career-related internships or fieldwork, institutionally sponsored loans, unspecified assistantships, and tuition remissions also available. Support available to part-time students. Financial award application deadline: 3/1; financial award applicants required to submit FAFSA. *Faculty research:* Electrical and computer science and engineering; aerospace, chemical, civil, mechanical, and ocean engineering; environmental science and oceanography. Total annual research expenditures: $4.5 million. *Unit head:* Dr. Thomas D. Waite, Dean, 321-674-8020, Fax: 321-674-7270, E-mail: twaite@fit.edu. *Application contact:* Thomas M. Shea, Director of Graduate Admissions, 321-674-7577, Fax: 321-723-9468, E-mail: tshea@fit.edu.

Florida International University, College of Engineering and Computing, Miami, FL 33175. Offers MS, PhD. Part-time and evening/weekend programs available. Postbaccalaureate distance learning degree programs offered. *Faculty:* 98 full-time (9 women). *Students:* 469 full-time (129 women), 347 part-time (94 women); includes 320 minority (53 African Americans, 33 Asian Americans or Pacific Islanders, 234 Hispanic Americans), 376 international. Average age 29. 1,013 applicants, 22% accepted, 191 enrolled. In 2009, 347 master's, 42 doctorates awarded. Terminal master's awarded for partial completion of doctoral program. *Degree requirements:* For master's, thesis (for some programs); for doctorate, comprehensive exam, thesis/dissertation. *Entrance requirements:* For master's, GRE (depending on program), minimum GPA of 3.0; for doctorate, GRE General Test, minimum GPA of 3.0. Additional exam requirements/recommendations for international students: Required—TOEFL (minimum score 550 paper-based; 80 iBT). *Application deadline:* For fall admission, 6/1 for domestic students, 4/1 for international students; for spring admission, 10/1 for domestic students, 9/1 for international students. Applications are processed on a rolling basis. Application fee: $30. Electronic applications accepted. *Expenses:* Tuition, state resident: full-time $8008; part-time $4004 per year. Tuition, nonresident: full-time $20,104; part-time $10,052 per year. Required fees: $298; $149 per term. *Financial support:* In 2009–10, 27 fellowships (averaging $25,000 per year), 95 research assistantships (averaging $20,000 per year), 137 teaching assistantships (averaging $20,000 per year) were awarded; career-related internships or fieldwork, Federal Work-Study, institutionally sponsored loans, scholarships/grants, and unspecified assistantships also available. Financial award application deadline: 3/1; financial award applicants required to submit FAFSA. *Faculty research:* Databases, informatics, computing systems, software engineering, security, biosensors, imaging, tissue engineering, biomaterials and bionanotechnology, transportation, wind engineering, hydrology, environmental engineering, engineering management, sustainability and green construction, risk management and decision systems, infrastructure systems, digital signal processing, power systems, nanophotonics, embedded systems, image processing, nanotechnology. Total annual research expenditures: $14.9 million. *Unit head:* Dr. Amir Mirmiran, Dean, 305-348-2522, Fax: 305-348-1401, E-mail: amir.mirmiran@fiu.edu. *Application contact:* Maria Parrilla, Assistant Director of Graduate Admissions, 305-348-1890, Fax: 305-348-6142, E-mail: grad_eng@fiu.edu.

Florida State University, The Graduate School, FAMU-FSU College of Engineering, Tallahassee, FL 32306. Offers MS, PhD. Part-time programs available. Postbaccalaureate distance learning degree programs offered (minimal on-campus study). *Faculty:* 77 full-time (9 women), 6 part-time/adjunct (1 woman). *Students:* 295 full-time (68 women); includes 206 minority (71 African Americans, 113 Asian Americans or Pacific Islanders, 22 Hispanic Americans). Average age 29. 440 applicants, 50% accepted, 73 enrolled. In 2009, 47 master's, 22 doctorates awarded. *Degree requirements:* For master's, thesis (for some programs); for doctorate, comprehensive exam, thesis/dissertation, preliminary exam, diagnostic examination. *Entrance requirements:* For master's and doctorate, GRE General Test. Additional exam requirements/recommendations for international students: Required—TOEFL (minimum score 550 paper-based; 213 computer-based). *Application deadline:* For fall admission, 7/1 for domestic and international students; for spring admission, 11/1 for domestic and international students. Applications are processed on a rolling basis. Application fee: $30. *Expenses:* Tuition, state resident: full-time $7413.36. Tuition, nonresident: full-time $22,567. *Financial support:* In 2009–10, 177 students received support, including 6 fellowships with full tuition reimbursements available (averaging $18,000 per year), 123 research assistantships with full tuition reimbursements available, 49 teaching assistantships with full tuition reimbursements available; career-related internships or fieldwork, institutionally sponsored loans, scholarships/grants, tuition waivers (full), and unspecified assistantships also available. Financial award application deadline: 6/15. *Faculty research:* Fluid mechanics, aerodynamics, electromagnetics, digital signal processing, polymer processing. Total annual research expenditures: $10.7 million. *Unit head:* Dr. Ching-Jen Chen, Dean and Professor, 850-410-6439, Fax: 850-410-6546, E-mail: cjchen@eng.fsu.edu. *Application contact:* Dr. Ching-Jen Chen, Dean and Professor, 850-410-6439, Fax: 850-410-6546, E-mail: cjchen@eng.fsu.edu.

George Mason University, Volgenau School of Information Technology and Engineering, Fairfax, VA 22030. Offers MS, PhD, Certificate, Engr. Part-time and evening/weekend programs available. *Faculty:* 142 full-time (29 women), 139 part-time/adjunct (21 women). *Students:* 334 full-time (71 women), 1,326 part-time (296 women); includes 297 minority (63 African Americans, 4 American Indian/Alaska Native, 182 Asian Americans or Pacific Islanders, 48 Hispanic Americans), 499 international. Average age 31. 1,704 applicants, 62% accepted, 408 enrolled. In 2009, 425 master's, 28 doctorates, 94 other advanced degrees awarded. *Degree requirements:* For master's, thesis optional; for doctorate, thesis/dissertation, comprehensive oral and written exams. *Entrance requirements:* For master's, minimum GPA of 3.0 in last 60 hours of course work; for doctorate, GRE General Test, minimum graduate GPA of 3.5. Additional exam requirements/recommendations for international students: Required—TOEFL. Application fee: $75. Electronic applications accepted. *Expenses:* Tuition, state resident: full-time $7568; part-time $315.33 per credit hour. Tuition, nonresident: full-time $21,704; part-time $904.33 per credit hour. Required fees: $2184; $91 per credit hour. *Financial support:* In 2009–10, 244 students received support, including 8 fellowships with full tuition reimbursements available (averaging $18,000 per year), 99 research assistantships with full and partial tuition reimbursements available (averaging $10,697 per year), 142 teaching assistantships with full and partial tuition reimbursements available (averaging $7,713 per year); career-related internships or fieldwork, Federal Work-Study, scholarships/grants, unspecified assistantships, and health care benefits (full-time research or teaching assistantship recipients) also available. Support available to part-time students. Financial award application deadline: 3/1; financial award applicants required to submit FAFSA. *Faculty research:* Systems management, quality assurance, decision support systems, cognitive ergonomics. Total annual research expenditures: $16.3 million. *Unit head:* Lloyd Griffiths, Dean, 703-993-1500, Fax: 703-993-1734, E-mail: lgriff@gmu.edu. *Application contact:* Nicole Sealey, Graduate Admission & Enrollment Services Director, 703-993-3932, E-mail: nsealey@gmu.edu.

The George Washington University, School of Engineering and Applied Science, Washington, DC 20052. Offers MS, D Sc, App Sc, Engr, Graduate Certificate. Part-time and evening/weekend programs available. *Faculty:* 80 full-time (9 women), 72 part-time/adjunct (8 women). *Students:* 379 full-time (92 women), 1,564 part-time (359 women); includes 455 minority (188 African Americans, 13 American Indian/Alaska Native, 187 Asian Americans or Pacific Islanders, 67 Hispanic Americans), 432 international. Average age 33. 1,361 applicants, 86% accepted, 506 enrolled. In 2009, 599 master's, 61 doctorates, 345 other advanced degrees awarded. *Degree requirements:* For master's, thesis optional; for doctorate, thesis/dissertation, qualifying exam. *Entrance requirements:* For master's, appropriate bachelor's degree; for doctorate, appropriate bachelor's or master's degree, GRE if highest earned degree is BS; for other advanced degree, appropriate master's degree. Additional exam requirements/recommendations for international students: Required—TOEFL or George Washington University English as a Foreign Language Test. *Application deadline:* For fall admission, 3/1 for domestic students; for spring admission, 10/1 for domestic students. Applications are processed on a rolling basis. Application fee: $60. *Financial support:* In 2009–10, 216 students received support; fellowships with full and partial tuition reimbursements available, research assistantships with full and partial tuition reimbursements available, teaching assistantships with full and partial tuition reimbursements available, career-related internships or fieldwork, Federal Work-Study, institutionally sponsored loans, and tuition waivers (full and partial) available. Financial award application deadline: 3/1; financial award applicants required to submit FAFSA. *Faculty research:* Fatigue fracture and structural reliability, computer-integrated manufacturing, materials engineering, artificial intelligence and expert systems, quality assurance. Total annual research expenditures: $6.3 million. *Unit head:* David S. Dolling, Dean, 202-994-6080, E-mail: dolling@gwu.edu. *Application contact:* Adina Lav, Marketing, Recruiting and Admissions, 202-994-5827, Fax: 202-994-0909, E-mail: engineering@gwu.edu.

See Close-Up on page 73.

Georgia Institute of Technology, Graduate Studies and Research, College of Engineering, Atlanta, GA 30332-0001. Offers MS, MS Bio E, MS Ch E, MS Env E, MS Poly, MS Stat, MSAE, MSCE, MSEE, MSESM, MSHS, MSIE, MSME, MSNE, MSOR, PhD, MD/PhD. *Accreditation:* ABET (one or more programs are accredited). Part-time programs available. Postbaccalaureate distance learning degree programs offered. Terminal master's awarded for partial completion of doctoral program. *Degree requirements:* For doctorate, thesis/dissertation. *Entrance requirements:* Additional exam requirements/recommendations for international students: Required—TOEFL. Electronic applications accepted.

Graduate School and University Center of the City University of New York, Graduate Studies, Program in Engineering, New York, NY 10016-4039. Offers biomedical engineering (PhD); chemical engineering (PhD); civil engineering (PhD); electrical engineering (PhD); mechanical engineering (PhD). *Faculty:* 68 full-time (1 woman). *Students:* 115 full-time (33 women), 8 part-time (2 women); includes 17 minority (5 African Americans, 8 Asian Americans or Pacific Islanders, 4 Hispanic Americans), 68 international. Average age 34. 119 applicants, 48% accepted, 26 enrolled. In 2009, 30 doctorates awarded. *Degree requirements:* For doctorate, thesis/dissertation. *Entrance requirements:* For doctorate, GRE General Test. Additional exam requirements/recommendations for international students: Required—TOEFL. Application fee: $125. Electronic applications accepted. *Financial support:* In 2009–10, 61 fellowships, 10 teaching assistantships were awarded; research assistantships, Federal Work-Study, institutionally sponsored loans, and tuition waivers (full and partial) also available. Financial award application deadline: 2/1; financial award applicants required to submit FAFSA. *Unit head:* Dr. Mumtaz Kassir, Executive Officer, 212-650-8031, Fax: 212-650-8029, E-mail: kassir@ce-mail.engr.ccny.cuny.edu. *Application contact:* Les Gribben, Director of Admissions, 212-817-7470, Fax: 212-817-1624, E-mail: lgribben@gc.cuny.edu.

See Close-Up on page 69.

Grand Valley State University, Padnos College of Engineering and Computing, School of Engineering, Allendale, MI 49401-9403. Offers electrical and computer engineering (MSE); manufacturing operations (MSE); mechanical engineering (MSE); product design and manufacturing engineering (MSE). Part-time and evening/weekend programs available. *Faculty:* 6 full-time (0 women). *Students:* 8 full-time (1 woman), 37 part-time (4 women), 4 international. Average age 30. 21 applicants, 86% accepted, 10 enrolled. In 2009, 12 master's awarded. *Degree requirements:* For master's, project or thesis. *Entrance requirements:* For master's, engineering degree, minimum GPA of 3.0. Additional exam requirements/recommendations for international students: Required—TOEFL. *Application deadline:* Applications are processed on a rolling basis. Application fee: $30. Electronic applications accepted. *Financial support:* In 2009–10, 11 students received support, including 3 fellowships (averaging $1,083 per year), 9 research assistantships with full tuition reimbursements available (averaging $7,304 per year); career-related internships or fieldwork, Federal Work-Study, institutionally sponsored loans, scholarships/grants, and unspecified assistantships also available. *Faculty research:* Digital signal processing, computer aided design, computer aided manufacturing, manufacturing simulation, biomechanics, product design. Total annual research expenditures: $300,000. *Unit head:* Dr. Charles Standridge, Acting Director, 616-331-6750, Fax: 616-331-7215, E-mail: standric@gvsu.edu. *Application contact:* Dr. Pranod Chaphalkar, Graduate Director, 616-331-6843, Fax: 616-331-7215, E-mail: chaphalp@gvsu.edu.

Harvard University, Graduate School of Arts and Sciences, School of Engineering and Applied Sciences, Cambridge, MA 02138. Offers applied mathematics (ME, SM, PhD); applied physics (ME, SM, PhD); computer science (ME, SM, PhD); engineering science (ME); engineering sciences (SM, PhD). Part-time programs available. *Faculty:* 57 full-time (9 women), 9 part-time/adjunct (1 woman). *Students:* 355 full-time (89 women), 3 part-time (0 women); includes 50 minority (4 African Americans, 40 Asian Americans or Pacific Islanders, 6 Hispanic Americans), 166 international. 1,617 applicants, 11% accepted, 88 enrolled. In 2009, 67 master's, 53 doctorates awarded. Terminal master's awarded for partial completion of doctoral program. *Degree requirements:* For master's, thesis optional; for doctorate, comprehensive exam, thesis/dissertation. *Entrance requirements:* For master's and doctorate, GRE General Test, GRE Subject Test (recommended), 3 letters of recommendation. Additional exam requirements/recommendations for international students: Required—TOEFL (minimum score 80 iBT). *Application deadline:* For fall admission, 12/31 priority date for domestic and international students. Application fee: $105. Electronic applications accepted. *Expenses:* Tuition: Full-time $33,696. Required fees: $1126. Full-time tuition and fees vary according to program. *Financial support:* In 2009–10, 115 fellowships with full tuition reimbursements (averaging $21,375 per year), 184 research assistantships with full and partial tuition reimbursements (averaging $28,500 per year), 76 teaching assistantships with full and partial tuition reimbursements (averaging $5,563 per year) were awarded; Federal Work-Study, institutionally sponsored loans, traineeships, and health care benefits also available. *Faculty research:* Applied mathematics, applied physics, computer science and electrical engineering, environmental engineering, mechanical and biomedical engineering. Total annual research expenditures: $43.8 million. *Unit head:* Cherry Murray, Dean, 617-495-5829, Fax: 617-495-5264, E-mail: dean@seas.harvard.edu. *Application contact:* Office of Admissions and Financial Aid, 617-495-5315, E-mail: admissions@seas.harvard.edu.

Howard University, College of Engineering, Architecture, and Computer Sciences, School of Engineering and Computer Science, Washington, DC 20059-0002. Offers M Eng, MCS, MS, PhD. Part-time programs available. Terminal master's awarded for partial completion of doctoral program. *Degree requirements:* For doctorate, one foreign language, thesis/dissertation, preliminary exam. *Entrance requirements:* For master's and doctorate, GRE General Test, minimum GPA of 3.0. Additional exam requirements/recommendations for international students: Required—TOEFL. Electronic applications accepted. *Faculty research:* Environmental engineering, solid-state electronics, dynamics and control of large flexible space structures, power systems, reaction kinetics.

Idaho State University, Office of Graduate Studies, College of Engineering, Pocatello, ID 83209-8060. Offers MS, PhD, Postbaccalaureate Certificate. *Accreditation:* ABET. Part-time programs available. *Faculty:* 17 full-time (1 woman). *Students:* 48 full-time (8 women), 58 part-time (12 women); includes 5 minority (1 African American, 4 Asian Americans or Pacific Islanders), 41 international. Average age 33. 46 applicants, 52% accepted, 11 enrolled. In 2009, 16 master's, 2 doctorates, 1 other advanced degree awarded. *Degree requirements:* For master's, comprehensive exam (for some programs), thesis, thesis project, 2 semesters of seminar; for doctorate, comprehensive exam, thesis/dissertation, oral presentation and defense of research, oral examination; for Postbaccalaureate Certificate, comprehensive exam (for some programs), thesis optional, oral exam or thesis defense. *Entrance requirements:* For master's, GRE General Test, minimum GPA of 3.0 in upper-division undergraduate classes; for doctorate, GRE General Test, master's degree in engineering or physics, 1-page statement of research interests, resume, 3 letters of reference, 1-page statement of career interests; for Postbaccalaureate Certificate, GRE (if GPA between 2.0 and 3.0), bachelor's degree, minimum GPA of 3.0 in upper-division courses. Additional exam requirements/recommendations for international students: Required—TOEFL (minimum score 550 paper-based; 213 computer-based; 80 iBT). *Application deadline:* For fall admission, 7/1 for domestic students, 6/1 for international students; for spring admission, 12/1 for domestic students, 11/1 for international students. Applications are processed on a rolling basis. Application fee: $55. Electronic applications accepted. *Expenses:* Tuition, state resident: full-time $3318; part-time $297 per credit hour. Tuition, nonresident: full-time $13,120; part-time $437 per credit hour. Required fees: $2530. Tuition and fees vary according to program. *Financial support:* In 2009–10, 13 research assistantships with full and partial tuition reimbursements (averaging $9,320 per year), 7 teaching assistantships with full and partial tuition reimbursements (averaging $10,841 per year) were awarded; career-related internships or fieldwork, Federal Work-Study, institutionally sponsored loans, scholarships/grants, health care benefits, tuition waivers (full and partial), and unspecified assistantships also available. Support available to part-time students. Financial award application deadline: 1/1; financial award applicants required to submit FAFSA. *Faculty research:* Nuclear engineering, biomedical engineering, robotics, measurement and control, structural systems. *Unit head:* Dr. Richard Jacobsen, Dean, 208-282-2902, Fax: 208-282-4538, E-mail: jacorich@isu.edu. *Application contact:* Tami Carson, Graduate School Technical Records Specialist, 208-282-2150, Fax: 208-282-4847, E-mail: carstami@isu.edu.

Illinois Institute of Technology, Graduate College, Armour College of Engineering, Chicago, IL 60616-3793. Offers M Arch E, M Ch E, M Env E, M Geoenv E, M Trans E, MBE, MBMI, MCEM, MECE, MEM, MFPE, MGE, MGE, MMAE, MME, MMME, MNE, MPE, MPW, MS, MSE, MTSE, MVM, PhD, MS/M Ch E. Part-time and evening/weekend programs available. Postbaccalaureate distance learning degree programs offered (no on-campus study). Terminal master's awarded for partial completion of doctoral program. *Degree requirements:* For master's, comprehensive exam (for some programs), thesis (for some programs); for doctorate, comprehensive exam, thesis/dissertation. *Entrance requirements:* For master's and doctorate, GRE General Test, minimum undergraduate GPA of 3.0. Additional exam requirements/recommendations for international students: Required—TOEFL (minimum score 550 paper-based; 213 computer-based; 80 iBT). Electronic applications accepted. *Expenses:* Tuition: Full-time $17,550; part-time $888 per credit hour. Required fees: $850; $7.50 per credit hour. One-time fee: $50 full-time. Full-time tuition and fees vary according to program.

Indiana State University, School of Graduate Studies, College of Technology, Terre Haute, IN 47809. Offers MS, MA/MS. *Entrance requirements:* For master's, bachelor's degree in industrial technology or related field. Additional exam requirements/recommendations for international students: Required—TOEFL. Electronic applications accepted.

Indiana University–Purdue University Fort Wayne, College of Engineering, Technology, and Computer Science, Fort Wayne, IN 46805-1499. Offers MS, Certificate. Part-time programs available. *Faculty:* 37 full-time (11 women), 3 part-time/adjunct (0 women). *Students:* 22 full-time (10 women), 96 part-time (28 women); includes 17 minority (8 African Americans, 7 Asian Americans or Pacific Islanders, 2 Hispanic Americans), 12 international. Average age 33. 60 applicants, 87% accepted, 42 enrolled. In 2009, 11 master's awarded. *Entrance requirements:* For master's, GRE General Test, minimum GPA of 3.0. Additional exam requirements/recommendations for international students: Required—TOEFL (minimum score 550 paper-based; 213 computer-based; 77 iBT); Recommended—TWE. *Application deadline:* For fall admission, 7/15 for domestic students, 5/15 for international students; for spring admission, 12/1 for domestic students, 10/15 for international students. Applications are processed on a rolling basis. Application fee: $55 ($60 for international students). Electronic applications accepted. *Expenses:* Tuition, state resident: full-time $4595; part-time $255 per credit. Tuition, nonresident: full-time $10,963; part-time $609 per credit. Required fees: $528; $29.35 per credit. Tuition and fees vary according to course load. *Financial support:* In 2009–10, 1 research assistantship with partial tuition reimbursement (averaging $12,740 per year), 7 teaching assistantships with partial tuition reimbursements (averaging $12,740 per year) were awarded; career-related internships or fieldwork, scholarships/grants, and unspecified assistantships also available. Support available to part-time students. Financial award application deadline: 3/1; financial award applicants required to submit FAFSA. *Faculty research:* Anomalous traffic detection, video streaming, pedagogical implication. Total annual research expenditures: $113,890. *Unit head:* Dr. Gerard Voland, Dean, 260-481-6839, Fax: 260-481-5734, E-mail: volandg@ipfw.edu. *Application contact:* Dr. Gerard Voland, Dean, 260-481-6839, Fax: 260-481-5734, E-mail: volandg@ipfw.edu.

Instituto Tecnologico de Santo Domingo, Graduate School, Santo Domingo, Dominican Republic. Offers applied linguistics (MA); construction administration (M Mgmt); corporate finance (M Mgmt); education (M Ed); engineering (M Eng), including data telecommunications, industrial engineering, logistics and supply chain, maintenance engineering, sanitary and environmental engineering, structural engineering; environmental science (M En S), including environmental education, environmental management, marine and coastal ecosystems, natural resources management; family therapy (MA); food science and technology (MS); human development (MA); human resources administration (M Mgmt); international business (M Mgmt); labor risks (M Mgmt); management (M Mgmt); marketing (M Mgmt); mathematics (MS); organizational development (M Mgmt); planning and taxation (M Mgmt); psychology (MA); social science (M Ed); upper management (M Mgmt). *Entrance requirements:* For master's, birth certificate, minimum GPA of 2.0.

Instituto Tecnológico y de Estudios Superiores de Monterrey, Campus Ciudad Obregón, Program in Engineering, Ciudad Obregón, Mexico. Offers ME.

Instituto Tecnológico y de Estudios Superiores de Monterrey, Campus Monterrey, Graduate and Research Division, Programs in Engineering, Monterrey, Mexico. Offers applied

statistics (M Eng); artificial intelligence (PhD); automation engineering (M Eng); chemical engineering (M Eng); civil engineering (M Eng); electrical engineering (M Eng); electronic engineering (M Eng); environmental engineering (M Eng); industrial engineering (M Eng, PhD); manufacturing engineering (M Eng); mechanical engineering (M Eng); systems and quality engineering (M Eng). Part-time and evening/weekend programs available. Terminal master's awarded for partial completion of doctoral program. *Degree requirements:* For master's, one foreign language, thesis; for doctorate, one foreign language, thesis/dissertation. *Entrance requirements:* For master's, EXADEP; for doctorate, GRE, master's degree in related field. Additional exam requirements/recommendations for international students: Required—TOEFL. *Faculty research:* Flexible manufacturing cells, materials, statistical methods, environmental prevention, control and evaluation.

Iowa State University of Science and Technology, Graduate College, College of Engineering, Ames, IA 50011. Offers M Eng, MS, PhD. Part-time programs available. *Faculty:* 201 full-time (22 women), 16 part-time/adjunct (3 women). *Students:* 691 full-time (149 women), 291 part-time (46 women); includes 61 minority (16 African Americans, 4 American Indian/Alaska Native, 26 Asian Americans or Pacific Islanders, 15 Hispanic Americans), 495 international. 2,152 applicants, 18% accepted, 235 enrolled. In 2009, 192 master's, 89 doctorates awarded. *Degree requirements:* For doctorate, thesis/dissertation. *Entrance requirements:* Additional exam requirements/recommendations for international students: Required—TOEFL. Application fee: $40 ($90 for international students). Electronic applications accepted. *Expenses:* Tuition, state resident: full-time $6716. Tuition, nonresident: full-time $8908. Tuition and fees vary according to course level, course load, program and student level. *Financial support:* In 2009–10, 484 research assistantships with full and partial tuition reimbursements (averaging $16,000 per year), 101 teaching assistantships with full and partial tuition reimbursements (averaging $14,500 per year) were awarded; fellowships, Federal Work-Study, scholarships/grants, health care benefits, and unspecified assistantships also available. Support available to part-time students. *Unit head:* Dr. Jonathan Wickert, Dean, 515-294-9988. *Application contact:* Dr. Jonathan Wickert, Dean, 515-294-9988.

The Johns Hopkins University, Engineering for Professionals, Elkridge, MD 21075. Offers M Ch E, M Mat SE, MCE, MEE, MME, MS, MSE, Graduate Certificate, Post-Master's Certificate. Part-time and evening/weekend programs available. *Faculty:* 235 part-time/adjunct (30 women). *Students:* 79 full-time (19 women), 1,849 part-time (412 women); includes 497 minority (176 African Americans, 3 American Indian/Alaska Native, 233 Asian Americans or Pacific Islanders, 85 Hispanic Americans), 42 international. Average age 32. In 2009, 623 master's, 9 other advanced degrees awarded. *Application deadline:* Applications are processed on a rolling basis. Application fee: $75. Electronic applications accepted. *Unit head:* Dr. Allan Bjerkaas, Associate Dean, 410-516-2300, Fax: 410-579-8049, E-mail: bjerkaas@jhu.edu. *Application contact:* Priyanka Dwivedi, Admissions Manager, 410-516-2300, Fax: 410-579-8049, E-mail: pdwived1@jhu.edu.

The Johns Hopkins University, G. W. C. Whiting School of Engineering, Baltimore, MD 21218-2699. Offers M Ch E, M Mat SE, MA, MCE, MEE, MME, MS, MSE, MSEM, MSSI, PhD, Certificate, Post-Master's Certificate. *Faculty:* 190 full-time (37 women), 94 part-time/adjunct (16 women). *Students:* 889 full-time (245 women), 45 part-time (9 women); includes 130 minority (20 African Americans, 87 Asian Americans or Pacific Islanders, 23 Hispanic Americans), 482 international. Average age 26. 2,443 applicants, 37% accepted, 289 enrolled. In 2009, 196 master's, 73 doctorates awarded. Terminal master's awarded for partial completion of doctoral program. *Degree requirements:* For master's, comprehensive exam (for some programs), thesis (for some programs); for doctorate, comprehensive exam, thesis/dissertation, oral exam. *Entrance requirements:* For master's, GRE General Test, letters of recommendation, transcripts; for doctorate, GRE General Test, letters of recommendation. Additional exam requirements/recommendations for international students: Required—TOEFL (minimum score 600 paper-based; 250 computer-based; 100 iBT) or IELTS (minimum score 7). Application fee: $75. Electronic applications accepted. *Financial support:* In 2009–10, 67 fellowships with full tuition reimbursements (averaging $25,085 per year), 497 research assistantships with full tuition reimbursements (averaging $25,085 per year), 36 teaching assistantships with full tuition reimbursements (averaging $19,154 per year) were awarded; Federal Work-Study, institutionally sponsored loans, scholarships/grants, health care benefits, tuition waivers (full and partial), and unspecified assistantships also available. Support available to part-time students. Financial award applicants required to submit FAFSA. *Faculty research:* Biomedical engineering, environmental systems and engineering, materials science and engineering, signal and image processing, structural dynamics and geomechanics. Total annual research expenditures: $64 million. *Unit head:* Dr. Nicholas P. Jones, Interim Dean, 410-516-8350 Ext. 3, Fax: 410-516-8627. *Application contact:* Dennis McIver, Coordinator of Graduate Admissions, 410-516-8174, Fax: 410-516-0780, E-mail: graduateadmissions@jhu.edu.

Kansas State University, Graduate School, College of Engineering, Manhattan, KS 66506. Offers MEM, MS, MSE, PhD. Part-time programs available. Postbaccalaureate distance learning degree programs offered (minimal on-campus study). *Faculty:* 99 full-time (11 women), 21 part-time/adjunct (2 women). *Students:* 280 full-time (67 women), 287 part-time (67 women); includes 23 minority (3 African Americans, 2 American Indian/Alaska Native, 10 Asian Americans or Pacific Islanders, 8 Hispanic Americans), 219 international. 734 applicants, 41% accepted, 202 enrolled. In 2009, 131 master's, 23 doctorates awarded. *Degree requirements:* For doctorate, thesis/dissertation. *Entrance requirements:* For master's and doctorate, GRE. Additional exam requirements/recommendations for international students: Required—TOEFL. *Application deadline:* For fall admission, 2/1 priority date for domestic and international students; for spring admission, 8/1 priority date for domestic and international students. Applications are processed on a rolling basis. Application fee: $40 ($55 for international students). Electronic applications accepted. *Financial support:* In 2009–10, 197 research assistantships (averaging $14,634 per year), 34 teaching assistantships (averaging $14,843 per year) were awarded; career-related internships or fieldwork, Federal Work-Study, institutionally sponsored loans, and scholarships/grants also available. Support available to part-time students. Financial award application deadline: 3/1; financial award applicants required to submit FAFSA. Total annual research expenditures: $10.3 million. *Unit head:* John English, Dean, 785-532-5590, Fax: 785-532-7810, E-mail: jenglish@ksu.edu. *Application contact:* Maureen Lockhart, Administrative Assistant to the Dean, 785-532-5441, Fax: 785-532-7810, E-mail: maureen@ksu.edu.

See Close-Up on page 75.

Kent State University, College of Technology, Kent, OH 44242-0001. Offers MT. Part-time programs available. Postbaccalaureate distance learning degree programs offered. *Degree requirements:* For master's, thesis optional. *Entrance requirements:* For master's, GRE, minimum GPA of 2.75. Electronic applications accepted. *Faculty research:* Automation, robotics, CAD, CAM, CIM.

Lakehead University, Graduate Studies, Faculty of Engineering, Thunder Bay, ON P7B 5E1, Canada. Offers control engineering (M Sc Engr); electrical/computer engineering (M Sc Engr); environmental engineering (M Sc Engr). Part-time programs available. *Degree requirements:* For master's, thesis. *Entrance requirements:* For master's, bachelor's degree in chemical, electrical or mechanical engineering, minimum B average. Additional exam requirements/recommendations for international students: Required—TOEFL. *Faculty research:* Pulp and paper, adaptive/process control, robust/interactive learning control, vibration control.

Lamar University, College of Graduate Studies, College of Engineering, Beaumont, TX 77710. Offers ME, MEM, MES, MS, DE, PhD. Part-time and evening/weekend programs available. *Faculty:* 38 full-time (2 women). *Students:* 390 full-time (68 women), 125 part-time (17 women); includes 16 minority (6 African Americans, 8 Asian Americans or Pacific Islanders, 2 Hispanic Americans), 344 international. Average age 24. 708 applicants, 31% accepted, 138 enrolled. In 2009, 236 master's, 6 doctorates awarded. Terminal master's awarded for partial completion of doctoral program. *Degree requirements:* For doctorate, thesis/dissertation. *Entrance requirements:* For master's and doctorate, GRE General Test. Additional exam

Engineering and Applied Sciences—General

Lamar University (continued)
requirements/recommendations for international students: Required—TOEFL. *Application deadline:* For fall admission, 5/15 priority date for domestic students; for spring admission, 10/1 priority date for domestic students. Applications are processed on a rolling basis. Application fee: $25 ($50 for international students). *Financial support:* In 2009–10, fellowships with partial tuition reimbursements (averaging $6,000 per year), research assistantships with partial tuition reimbursements (averaging $7,500 per year), teaching assistantships with partial tuition reimbursements (averaging $7,500 per year) were awarded; career-related internships or fieldwork, Federal Work-Study, institutionally sponsored loans, scholarships/grants, tuition waivers (full and partial), and laboratory assistantships, graders also available. Support available to part-time students. Financial award application deadline: 4/1. *Faculty research:* Energy alternatives; process analysis, design, and control; pollution prevention. *Unit head:* Dr. Jack Hopper, Chair, 409-880-8784, Fax: 409-880-2197, E-mail: che_dept@hal.lamar.edu. *Application contact:* Sandy Drane, Coordinator of Graduate Admissions, 409-880-8356, Fax: 409-880-8414, E-mail: gradmissions@hal.lamar.edu.

Laurentian University, School of Graduate Studies and Research, School of Engineering, Sudbury, ON P3E 2C6, Canada. Offers mineral resources engineering (M Eng, MA Sc); natural resources engineering (PhD). Part-time programs available. *Faculty research:* Mining engineering, rock mechanics (tunneling, rockbursts, rock support), metallurgy (mineral processing, hydro and pyrometallurgy), simulations and remote mining, simulations and scheduling.

Lawrence Technological University, College of Engineering, Southfield, MI 48075-1058. Offers automotive engineering (MAE); civil engineering (MCE); construction engineering management (MS); electrical and computer engineering (MS); engineering management (ME); industrial engineering (MSIE); manufacturing systems (MEMS, DE); mechanical engineering (MS); mechatronic systems engineering (MS). Part-time and evening/weekend programs available. *Faculty:* 20 full-time (4 women), 12 part-time/adjunct (0 women). *Students:* 15 full-time (4 women), 389 part-time (50 women); includes 57 minority (22 African Americans, 1 American Indian/Alaska Native, 30 Asian Americans or Pacific Islanders, 4 Hispanic Americans), 137 international. Average age 31. 361 applicants, 52% accepted, 108 enrolled. In 2009, 161 master's, 1 doctorate awarded. *Degree requirements:* For master's, thesis (for some programs). *Entrance requirements:* Additional exam requirements/recommendations for international students: Required—TOEFL (minimum score 550 paper-based; 213 computer-based; 79 iBT). *Application deadline:* For fall admission, 8/1 priority date for domestic students, 6/1 for international students; for winter admission, 12/1 priority date for domestic students, 10/1 for international students; for spring admission, 5/1 priority date for domestic students, 3/1 for international students. Applications are processed on a rolling basis. Application fee: $50. Electronic applications accepted. *Expenses:* Tuition: Full-time $11,320; part-time $798 per credit hour. *Financial support:* Federal Work-Study and institutionally sponsored loans available. Support available to part-time students. Financial award application deadline: 4/1; financial award applicants required to submit FAFSA. *Faculty research:* Advanced composite materials in bridges, strengthening existing bridges with carbon and glass fiber sheets, development of drive shafts using composite materials. *Unit head:* Dr. Nabil Grace, Interim Dean, 248-204-2500, Fax: 248-204-2509, E-mail: engrdean@ltu.edu. *Application contact:* Jane Rohrback, Director of Admissions, 248-204-3160, Fax: 248-204-3188, E-mail: admissions@ltu.edu.

Lehigh University, P.C. Rossin College of Engineering and Applied Science, Bethlehem, PA 18015. Offers M Eng, MS, PhD, MBA/E. Part-time and evening/weekend programs available. Postbaccalaureate distance learning degree programs offered (no on-campus study). *Faculty:* 114 full-time (14 women), 5 part-time/adjunct (0 women). *Students:* 439 full-time (99 women), 156 part-time (39 women); includes 28 minority (4 African Americans, 18 Asian Americans or Pacific Islanders, 6 Hispanic Americans), 311 international. Average age 27. 1,984 applicants, 20% accepted, 203 enrolled. In 2009, 115 master's, 41 doctorates awarded. Terminal master's awarded for partial completion of doctoral program. *Degree requirements:* For master's, comprehensive exam (for some programs), thesis (for some programs); for doctorate, comprehensive exam (for some programs), thesis/dissertation. *Entrance requirements:* For master's and doctorate, GRE General Test, BS. Additional exam requirements/recommendations for international students: Required—TOEFL (minimum score 550 paper-based; 213 computer-based; 79 iBT). *Application deadline:* For fall admission, 7/15 for domestic and international students; for spring admission, 12/1 for domestic and international students. Applications are processed on a rolling basis. Application fee: $75. Electronic applications accepted. *Expenses:* Contact institution. *Financial support:* In 2009–10, 312 students received support, including 35 fellowships with full and partial tuition reimbursements available (averaging $15,795 per year), 199 research assistantships with full and partial tuition reimbursements available (averaging $21,060 per year), 57 teaching assistantships with full and partial tuition reimbursements available (averaging $15,795 per year); career-related internships or fieldwork, institutionally sponsored loans, scholarships/grants, and tuition waivers (full and partial) also available. Support available to part-time students. Financial award application deadline: 1/15. *Faculty research:* Advanced materials and nanotechnology, life sciences and bioengineering, environmental science and energy, information science and technology, large structural systems, optical technologies. *Unit head:* Dr. John P. Coulter, Associate Dean of Graduate Studies and Research, 610-758-6310, Fax: 610-758-5623, E-mail: john.coulter@lehigh.edu. *Application contact:* Brianne Lisk, Administrative Coordinator of Graduate Studies and Research, 610-758-6310, Fax: 610-758-5623, E-mail: brc3@lehigh.edu.

Louisiana State University and Agricultural and Mechanical College, Graduate School, College of Agriculture, Department of Biological and Agricultural Engineering, Baton Rouge, LA 70803. Offers biological and agricultural engineering (MSBAE); engineering science (MS, PhD). Part-time programs available. *Faculty:* 13 full-time (2 women). *Students:* 16 full-time (2 women), 4 part-time (2 women); includes 2 African Americans, 3 Asian Americans or Pacific Islanders, 8 international. Average age 26. 9 applicants, 78% accepted, 4 enrolled. In 2009, 5 master's awarded. Terminal master's awarded for partial completion of doctoral program. *Degree requirements:* For master's, thesis; for doctorate, thesis/dissertation. *Entrance requirements:* For master's and doctorate, GRE General Test, minimum GPA of 3.0. Additional exam requirements/recommendations for international students: Required—TOEFL (minimum score 550 paper-based; 213 computer-based; 79 iBT) or IELTS (minimum score 6.5). *Application deadline:* For fall admission, 1/25 priority date for domestic students, 5/15 for international students; for spring admission, 10/15 for international students. Applications are processed on a rolling basis. Application fee: $50 ($70 for international students). Electronic applications accepted. *Financial support:* In 2009–10, 19 students received support, including 1 fellowship (averaging $35,195 per year), 14 research assistantships with partial tuition reimbursements available (averaging $14,723 per year); teaching assistantships with partial tuition reimbursements available, career-related internships or fieldwork, Federal Work-Study, institutionally sponsored loans, scholarships/grants, health care benefits, and unspecified assistantships also available. Financial award application deadline: 7/1; financial award applicants required to submit FAFSA. *Faculty research:* Bioenergy, bioprocess engineering, cellular and molecular engineering, drug delivery using nanotechnology, environmental engineering. Total annual research expenditures: $25,277. *Unit head:* Dr. Dan Thomas, Head, 225-578-3153, Fax: 225-578-3492, E-mail: dthomas@agcenter.lsu.edu. *Application contact:* Dr. Steven Hall, Graduate Coordinator, 225-578-1058, Fax: 225-578-3492, E-mail: sghall@agcenter.lsu.edu.

Louisiana State University and Agricultural and Mechanical College, Graduate School, College of Engineering, Department of Construction Management and Industrial Engineering, Baton Rouge, LA 70803. Offers engineering science (PhD); industrial engineering (MSIE). *Faculty:* 13 full-time (5 women). *Students:* 14 full-time (1 woman), 9 part-time (2 women), 19 international. Average age 27. 30 applicants, 73% accepted, 6 enrolled. In 2009, 5 master's awarded. Terminal master's awarded for partial completion of doctoral program. *Degree requirements:* For master's, thesis; for doctorate, thesis/dissertation. *Entrance requirements:* For master's and doctorate, GRE General Test, minimum GPA of 3.0. Additional exam requirements/recommendations for international students: Required—TOEFL (minimum score 550 paper-based; 213 computer-based; 79 iBT) or IELTS (minimum score 6.5). *Application deadline:* For fall admission, 1/25 priority date for domestic students, 5/15 for international students; for spring admission, 10/15 for international students. Applications are processed on a rolling basis. Application fee: $50 ($70 for international students). Electronic applications accepted. *Financial support:* In 2009–10, 17 students received support, including 9 research assistantships with partial tuition reimbursements available (averaging $11,242 per year), 4 teaching assistantships with partial tuition reimbursements available (averaging $8,380 per year); fellowships, Federal Work-Study, institutionally sponsored loans, health care benefits, and unspecified assistantships also available. Financial award application deadline: 5/1; financial award applicants required to submit FAFSA. *Faculty research:* Ergonomics and occupational health, information technology, production systems, supply management, construction safety and methods. Total annual research expenditures: $178,060. *Unit head:* Dr. Thomas Ray, Chair, 225-578-5369, Fax: 225-578-5109, E-mail: tray@lsu.edu. *Application contact:* Dr. Fereydoun Aghazadeh, Graduate Adviser, 225-578-5112, Fax: 225-578-5109, E-mail: aghazadeh@lsu.edu.

Louisiana State University and Agricultural and Mechanical College, Graduate School, College of Engineering, Interdepartmental Programs in Engineering, Baton Rouge, LA 70803. Offers engineering science (MSES, PhD). Part-time and evening/weekend programs available. *Students:* 53 full-time (18 women), 27 part-time (10 women); includes 6 minority (5 African Americans, 1 American Indian/Alaska Native), 58 international. Average age 29. 45 applicants, 64% accepted, 8 enrolled. In 2009, 16 master's, 4 doctorates awarded. Terminal master's awarded for partial completion of doctoral program. *Degree requirements:* For master's, thesis optional; for doctorate, thesis/dissertation. *Entrance requirements:* For master's and doctorate, GRE General Test, minimum GPA of 3.0. Additional exam requirements/recommendations for international students: Required—TOEFL (minimum score 550 paper-based, 213 computer-based, 79 iBT) or IELTS (minimum score 6.5). *Application deadline:* For fall admission, 1/25 priority date for domestic students, 5/15 for international students; for spring admission, 10/15 for international students. Applications are processed on a rolling basis. Application fee: $50 ($70 for international students). *Financial support:* In 2009–10, 57 students received support, including 5 fellowships (averaging $25,874 per year), 23 research assistantships with full and partial tuition reimbursements available (averaging $16,330 per year), 13 teaching assistantships with full and partial tuition reimbursements available (averaging $10,801 per year); Federal Work-Study, scholarships/grants, health care benefits, tuition waivers (full and partial), and unspecified assistantships also available. Support available to part-time students. Financial award application deadline: 3/1; financial award applicants required to submit FAFSA. *Faculty research:* Environmental engineering, transportation engineering, enhanced oil recovery, microelectrical-mechanical systems, manufacturing. Total annual research expenditures: $1.2 million. *Unit head:* Dr. Kelly Rusch, Associate Dean for Research and Graduate Studies, 225-578-4845, Fax: 225-578-9162, E-mail: krusch@lsu.edu. *Application contact:* Dr. Kelly Rusch, Associate Dean for Research and Graduate Studies, 225-578-4845, Fax: 225-578-9162, E-mail: krusch@lsu.edu.

Louisiana Tech University, Graduate School, College of Engineering and Science, Ruston, LA 71272. Offers MS, PhD. Part-time programs available. Terminal master's awarded for partial completion of doctoral program. *Degree requirements:* For doctorate, thesis/dissertation. *Entrance requirements:* For master's, GRE General Test, minimum GPA of 3.0 in last 60 hours. Additional exam requirements/recommendations for international students: Required—TOEFL. *Faculty research:* Trenchless technology, micromanufacturing, radionuclide transport, microbial liquefaction, hazardous waste treatment.

Manhattan College, Graduate Division, School of Engineering, Riverdale, NY 10471. Offers chemical engineering (MS); civil engineering (MS); computer engineering (MS); electrical engineering (MS); environmental engineering (ME, MS); mechanical engineering (MS). Part-time and evening/weekend programs available. *Degree requirements:* For master's, thesis or alternative. *Entrance requirements:* For master's, GRE (recommended), minimum GPA of 3.0. Additional exam requirements/recommendations for international students: Required—TOEFL (minimum score 550 paper-based; 213 computer-based). *Expenses:* Contact institution. *Faculty research:* Environmental/water, nucleation, environmental/management, heat transfer.

Marquette University, Graduate School, College of Engineering, Milwaukee, WI 53201-1881. Offers MS, PhD. Part-time and evening/weekend programs available. *Faculty:* 61 full-time (8 women), 23 part-time/adjunct (14 women). *Students:* 133 full-time (35 women), 113 part-time (21 women); includes 19 minority (5 African Americans, 9 Asian Americans or Pacific Islanders, 5 Hispanic Americans), 82 international. Average age 28. 301 applicants, 62% accepted, 63 enrolled. In 2009, 62 master's, 11 doctorates awarded. *Degree requirements:* For doctorate, thesis/dissertation. *Entrance requirements:* For master's, minimum GPA of 3.0; for doctorate, GRE General Test, minimum GPA of 3.0. Additional exam requirements/recommendations for international students: Required—TOEFL. *Application deadline:* Applications are processed on a rolling basis. Application fee: $40. Electronic applications accepted. *Financial support:* In 2009–10, 115 students received support, including 30 fellowships with tuition reimbursements available (averaging $16,866 per year), 53 research assistantships with tuition reimbursements available (averaging $14,861 per year), 32 teaching assistantships with tuition reimbursements available (averaging $13,790 per year); Federal Work-Study, institutionally sponsored loans, scholarships/grants, and tuition waivers (full and partial) also available. Support available to part-time students. Financial award application deadline: 2/15. *Faculty research:* Urban watershed management, microsensors for environmental pollutants, orthopedic rehabilitation engineering, telemedicine, ergonomics. *Unit head:* Dr. Stan V. Jaskolski, Dean, 414-288-6591, Fax: 414-288-7082, E-mail: stan.jaskolski@marquette.edu. *Application contact:* Craig Pierce, Director of Admissions, 414-288-7137, Fax: 414-288-1902, E-mail: mugs@vms.csd.mu.edu.

Marshall University, Academic Affairs Division, College of Information Technology and Engineering, Huntington, WV 25755. Offers MS, MSE. Part-time and evening/weekend programs available. *Faculty:* 23 full-time (3 women), 9 part-time/adjunct (0 women). *Students:* 66 full-time (18 women), 106 part-time (23 women); includes 5 minority (2 African Americans, 2 Asian Americans or Pacific Islanders, 1 Hispanic American), 36 international. Average age 32. In 2009, 42 master's awarded. *Degree requirements:* For master's, final project, oral exam. Application fee: $40. *Expenses:* Contact institution. *Financial support:* Fellowships, tuition waivers (full) available. Support available to part-time students. Financial award application deadline: 8/1; financial award applicants required to submit FAFSA. *Unit head:* Dr. Betsy Dulin, Dean, 304-746-2087, E-mail: bdulin@marshall.edu. *Application contact:* Information Contact, 304-746-1900, Fax: 304-746-1902, E-mail: services@marshall.edu.

Massachusetts Institute of Technology, School of Engineering, Cambridge, MA 02139-4307. Offers M Eng, SM, PhD, Sc D, CE, EAA, ECS, EE, Mat E, Mech E, Met E, NE, Naval E, SM/MBA. *Faculty:* 369 full-time (54 women), 1 part-time/adjunct (0 women). *Students:* 2,696 full-time (651 women), 6 part-time (0 women); includes 419 minority (46 African Americans, 8 American Indian/Alaska Native, 279 Asian Americans or Pacific Islanders, 86 Hispanic Americans), 1,170 international. Average age 27. 7,064 applicants, 18% accepted, 872 enrolled. In 2009, 708 master's, 302 doctorates, 11 other advanced degrees awarded. Terminal master's awarded for partial completion of doctoral program. *Degree requirements:* For master's, thesis (for some programs); for doctorate, comprehensive exam, thesis/dissertation; for other advanced degree, thesis. Application fee: $75. Electronic applications accepted. *Financial support:* In 2009–10, 2,587 students received support, including 584 fellowships with tuition reimbursements available (averaging $26,773 per year), research assistantships with tuition reimbursements available (averaging $28,054 per year), 230 teaching assistantships with tuition reimbursements available (averaging $28,878 per year); career-related internships or fieldwork, Federal Work-Study, institutionally sponsored loans, scholarships/grants, traineeships, health care benefits, and unspecified assistantships also available. Total annual research expenditures: $273.9 million. *Unit head:* Prof. Subra Suresh, Dean, 617-253-3291, Fax: 617-253-8549. *Application contact:* Graduate Admissions, 617-253-2917, Fax: 617-258-8304, E-mail: mitgrad@mit.edu.

McGill University, Faculty of Graduate and Postdoctoral Studies, Faculty of Engineering, Montréal, QC H3A 2T5, Canada. Offers M Arch I, M Arch II, M Eng, M Sc, MMM, MUP, PhD, Diploma.

McGill University, Faculty of Graduate and Postdoctoral Studies, Faculty of Science, Department of Mathematics and Statistics, Montréal, QC H3A 2T5, Canada. Offers computational science and engineering (M Sc); mathematics and statistics (M Sc, MA, PhD), including applied mathematics (M Sc, MA), pure mathematics (M Sc, MA), statistics (M Sc, MA).

McMaster University, School of Graduate Studies, Faculty of Engineering, Hamilton, ON L8S 4M2, Canada. Offers M Eng, M Sc, MA Sc, PhD. Part-time programs available. *Degree requirements:* For doctorate, comprehensive exam, thesis/dissertation. *Entrance requirements:* Additional exam requirements/recommendations for international students: Required—TOEFL (minimum score 550 paper-based; 213 computer-based). *Faculty research:* Computer process control, water resources engineering, elasticity, flow induced vibrations, microelectronics.

McNeese State University, Doré School of Graduate Studies, College of Engineering and Engineering Technology, Lake Charles, LA 70609. Offers chemical engineering (M Eng); civil engineering (M Eng); electrical engineering (M Eng); engineering management (M Eng); mechanical engineering (M Eng). Part-time and evening/weekend programs available. *Degree requirements:* For master's, thesis or alternative. *Entrance requirements:* For master's, GRE, minimum undergraduate GPA of 3.0. Additional exam requirements/recommendations for international students: Required—TOEFL.

Memorial University of Newfoundland, School of Graduate Studies, Faculty of Engineering and Applied Science, St. John's, NL A1C 5S7, Canada. Offers civil engineering (M Eng, PhD); electrical and computer engineering (M Eng, PhD); mechanical engineering (M Eng, PhD); ocean and naval architecture engineering (M Eng, PhD). Part-time programs available. *Degree requirements:* For master's, thesis; for doctorate, comprehensive exam, thesis/dissertation, oral thesis defense. *Entrance requirements:* For master's, 2nd class degree; for doctorate, master's degree in engineering. Electronic applications accepted. *Faculty research:* Engineering analysis, environmental and hydrotechnical studies, manufacturing and robotics, mechanics, structures and materials.

Mercer University, Graduate Studies, Macon Campus, School of Engineering, Macon, GA 31207-0003. Offers biomedical engineering (MSE); computer engineering (MSE); electrical engineering (MSE); engineering management (MSE); environmental engineering (MSE); environmental systems (MS); mechanical engineering (MSE); software engineering (MSE); software systems (MS); technical communications management (MS); technical management (MS). Part-time and evening/weekend programs available. Postbaccalaureate distance learning degree programs offered (no on-campus study). *Faculty:* 19 full-time (4 women), 1 part-time/adjunct (0 women). *Students:* 6 full-time (1 woman), 95 part-time (22 women); includes 22 minority (5 African Americans, 13 Asian Americans or Pacific Islanders, 4 Hispanic Americans), 3 international. Average age 33. In 2009, 42 master's awarded. *Degree requirements:* For master's, thesis or alternative. *Entrance requirements:* For master's, minimum undergraduate GPA of 3.0. Additional exam requirements/recommendations for international students: Required—TOEFL. *Application deadline:* For fall admission, 7/1 for domestic students; for spring admission, 11/15 for domestic students. Applications are processed on a rolling basis. Application fee: $35 ($50 for international students). Electronic applications accepted. *Expenses:* Contact institution. *Financial support:* Federal Work-Study available. *Unit head:* Dr. Wade H. Shaw, Dean, 478-301-2459, Fax: 478-301-5593, E-mail: shaw_wh@mercer.edu. *Application contact:* Greg Lofton, Graduate Program Coordinator, 478-301-5480, Fax: 478-301-5434, E-mail: lofton_g@mercer.edu.

Miami University, Graduate School, School of Engineering and Applied Science, Oxford, OH 45056. Offers computational science and engineering (MS); computer science and software engineering (MCS), including computer science; paper and chemical engineering (MS); software development (Certificate). *Students:* 35 full-time (14 women), 9 part-time (2 women); includes 4 minority (all Asian Americans or Pacific Islanders), 25 international. *Entrance requirements:* For master's, GRE, minimum undergraduate GPA of 3.0 during previous 2 years or 2.75 overall. Additional exam requirements/recommendations for international students: Required—TOEFL. Application fee: $50. *Expenses:* Tuition, state resident: full-time $11,280. Tuition, nonresident: full-time $24,912. Required fees: $516. *Financial support:* Fellowships with full tuition reimbursements, research assistantships, teaching assistantships, Federal Work-Study, health care benefits, tuition waivers (full), and unspecified assistantships available. Financial award application deadline: 3/1. *Unit head:* Dr. Marek Dollar, Dean, 513-529-0700, E-mail: seasfyi@muohio.edu. *Application contact:* Mary York, Domestic Graduate Admission Coordinator or Janet Miller, International Graduate Admission Coordinator, 513-529-3734, Fax: 513-529-3734, E-mail: gradschool@muohio.edu.

Michigan State University, The Graduate School, College of Engineering, East Lansing, MI 48824. Offers MS, PhD. Part-time programs available. Electronic applications accepted.

Michigan Technological University, Graduate School, College of Engineering, Houghton, MI 49931. Offers ME, MS, PhD. Part-time programs available. Postbaccalaureate distance learning degree programs offered (minimal on-campus study). Terminal master's awarded for partial completion of doctoral program. *Degree requirements:* For master's, comprehensive exam (for some programs), thesis (for some programs); for doctorate, comprehensive exam, thesis/dissertation. *Entrance requirements:* For master's, GRE. Additional exam requirements/recommendations for international students: Required—TOEFL (minimum score 550 paper-based; 213 computer-based). Electronic applications accepted.

Milwaukee School of Engineering, Department of Electrical Engineering and Computer Science, Program in Engineering, Milwaukee, WI 53202-3109. Offers MS. Part-time and evening/weekend programs available. *Faculty:* 3 full-time (0 women), 3 part-time/adjunct (1 woman). *Students:* 2 full-time (0 women), 38 part-time (5 women); includes 5 minority (2 African Americans, 2 Asian Americans or Pacific Islanders, 1 Hispanic American), 1 international. Average age 23. 20 applicants, 75% accepted, 7 enrolled. In 2009, 5 master's awarded. *Degree requirements:* For master's, design project. *Entrance requirements:* For master's, GRE General Test, BS in engineering. Additional exam requirements/recommendations for international students: Required—TOEFL (minimum score 79 iBT). *Application deadline:* Applications are processed on a rolling basis. Application fee: $30. Electronic applications accepted. *Expenses:* Tuition: Part-time $603 per credit. *Financial support:* In 2009–10, 14 students received support, including 4 research assistantships (averaging $15,000 per year); career-related internships or fieldwork also available. Support available to part-time students. Financial award applicants required to submit FAFSA. *Faculty research:* Microprocessors, materials, thermodynamics, artificial intelligence, fluid power/hydraulics. *Unit head:* Dr. Subha Kumpaty, Director, 414-277-7466, Fax: 414-277-2222, E-mail: kumpaty@msoe.edu. *Application contact:* David E. Tietyen, Graduate Admissions Director, 800-332-6763, Fax: 414-277-7475, E-mail: wp@msoe.edu.

Mississippi State University, Bagley College of Engineering, MS State, MS 39762. Offers MS, PhD. Part-time programs available. Postbaccalaureate distance learning degree programs offered (no on-campus study). *Faculty:* 98 full-time (12 women), 5 part-time/adjunct (0 women). *Students:* 375 full-time (72 women), 208 part-time (45 women); includes 66 minority (43 African Americans, 16 Asian Americans or Pacific Islanders, 7 Hispanic Americans), 243 international. Average age 29. 614 applicants, 36% accepted, 132 enrolled. In 2009, 96 master's, 35 doctorates awarded. *Degree requirements:* For master's, comprehensive exam (for some programs), thesis; for doctorate, comprehensive exam (for some programs), thesis/dissertation. *Entrance requirements:* For master's, GRE General Test, minimum GPA of 2.75; for doctorate, GRE General Test. Additional exam requirements/recommendations for international students: Required—TOEFL (minimum score 475 paper-based; 153 computer-based; 53 iBT); Recommended—IELTS (minimum score 4.5). *Application deadline:* For fall admission, 7/1 for domestic students, 5/1 for international students; for spring admission, 11/1 for domestic students, 9/1 for international students. Applications are processed on a rolling basis. Application fee: $40. Electronic applications accepted. *Expenses:* Tuition, state resident: full-time $2575.50; part-time $286.25 per credit hour. Tuition, nonresident: full-time $6510; part-time $723.50 per credit hour. Tuition and fees vary according to course load. *Financial support:* In 2009–10, 239 research assistantships with full tuition reimbursements (averaging $12,340 per year), 43 teaching assistantships with full tuition reimbursements (averaging $12,707 per year) were awarded; fellowships, Federal Work-Study, institutionally sponsored loans, scholarships/grants, and unspecified assistantships also available. Financial award application deadline: 4/1; financial award applicants required to submit FAFSA. *Faculty research:* Fluid dynamics, combustion, composite materials, computer design, high-voltage phenomena. Total annual research expenditures: $58.2 million. *Unit head:* Dr. Sarah A. Rajala, Dean, 662-325-2270, Fax: 662-325-8573, E-mail: rajala@bagley.msstate.edu. *Application contact:* Dr. Lori Bruce, Associate Dean for Research and Graduate Studies, 662-325-2270, Fax: 662-325-8573, E-mail: rburrell@bagley.msstate.edu.

Mississippi State University, College of Arts and Sciences, Department of Physics and Astronomy, Mississippi State, MS 39762. Offers engineering (PhD), including applied physics; physics (MS). Part-time programs available. *Faculty:* 13 full-time (0 women). *Students:* 25 full-time (5 women); includes 2 minority (1 African American, 1 Hispanic American), 20 international. Average age 26. 45 applicants, 24% accepted, 9 enrolled. In 2009, 7 master's awarded. *Degree requirements:* For master's, thesis optional, comprehensive oral or written exam; for doctorate, thesis/dissertation, comprehensive oral or written exam. *Entrance requirements:* For master's, GRE, minimum GPA of 2.75 on last two year's of undergraduate courses; for doctorate, GRE. Additional exam requirements/recommendations for international students: Required—TOEFL (minimum score 475 paper-based; 153 computer-based; 53 iBT); Recommended—IELTS (minimum score 4.5). *Application deadline:* For fall admission, 7/1 priority date for domestic students, 5/1 for international students; for spring admission, 11/1 priority date for domestic students, 9/1 for international students. Applications are processed on a rolling basis. Application fee: $40. Electronic applications accepted. *Expenses:* Tuition, state resident: full-time $2575.50; part-time $286.25 per credit hour. Tuition, nonresident: full-time $6510; part-time $723.50 per credit hour. Tuition and fees vary according to course load. *Financial support:* In 2009–10, 22 research assistantships with full tuition reimbursements (averaging $12,719 per year), 16 teaching assistantships with full tuition reimbursements (averaging $12,139 per year) were awarded; Federal Work-Study, institutionally sponsored loans, and unspecified assistantships also available. Financial award application deadline: 3/15; financial award applicants required to submit FAFSA. *Faculty research:* Atomic/molecular spectroscopy, theoretical optics, gamma-ray astronomy, experimental nuclear physics, computational physics. Total annual research expenditures: $2.3 million. *Unit head:* Dr. Mark A. Novotny, Department Head and Professor, 662-325-2806, Fax: 662-325-8898, E-mail: man40@ra.msstate.edu. *Application contact:* Dr. David Monts, Professor and Graduate Coordinator, 662-325-2931, Fax: 662-325-8898, E-mail: physics@msstate.edu.

Missouri University of Science and Technology, Graduate School, School of Engineering, Rolla, MO 65409. Offers M Eng, MS, DE, PhD. Part-time and evening/weekend programs available. Electronic applications accepted.

Montana State University, College of Graduate Studies, College of Engineering, Department of Chemical and Biological Engineering, Bozeman, MT 59717. Offers chemical engineering (MS); engineering (PhD), including chemical engineering option, environmental engineering option; environmental engineering (MS). Part-time programs available. *Faculty:* 9 full-time (2 women), 1 part-time/adjunct (0 women). *Students:* 1 full-time (0 women), 23 part-time (9 women); includes 2 minority (1 American Indian/Alaska Native, 1 Asian American or Pacific Islander), 3 international. Average age 27. 7 applicants. In 2009, 4 master's awarded. *Degree requirements:* For master's, comprehensive exam, thesis (for some programs); for doctorate, comprehensive exam, thesis/dissertation. *Entrance requirements:* For master's, GRE General Test, BS in chemical engineering or related scientific field; for doctorate, GRE General Test, BS or MS in chemical engineering or related scientific field. Additional exam requirements/recommendations for international students: Required—TOEFL (minimum score 550 paper-based; 213 computer-based). *Application deadline:* For fall admission, 7/15 priority date for domestic students, 5/15 priority date for international students; for spring admission, 12/1 priority date for domestic students, 10/1 priority date for international students. Applications are processed on a rolling basis. Application fee: $30. Electronic applications accepted. *Expenses:* Tuition, state resident: full-time $5635; part-time $3492 per year. Tuition, nonresident: full-time $17,212; part-time $7865.10 per year. Required fees: $1441.05; $153.15 per credit. Tuition and fees vary according to course load and program. *Financial support:* In 2009–10, 3 fellowships with full tuition reimbursements (averaging $25,000 per year), 20 research assistantships with full tuition reimbursements (averaging $18,000 per year), 2 teaching assistantships with full tuition reimbursements (averaging $18,000 per year) were awarded. Financial award application deadline: 3/1; financial award applicants required to submit FAFSA. *Faculty research:* The effects of variable permeability on the resistance to flow through the tissues and biofilms; development of protective coatings on planar solid oxide fuel cell (SOFC) metallic interconnects; carbon sequestration; zero emissions research and technology; research in the areas of biofuels, extremophilic bioprocessing, and in situ biocatalyzed heavy metal transformations; subsurface biofilm barriers; magnetic resonance microscopy. Total annual research expenditures: $1.8 million. *Unit head:* Dr. Ron W. Larson, Head, 406-994-2221, Fax: 406-994-5308, E-mail: ronl@coe.montana.edu. *Application contact:* Dr. Carl A. Fox, Vice Provost for Graduate Education, 406-994-4145, Fax: 406-994-7433, E-mail: gradstudy@montana.edu.

Montana State University, College of Graduate Studies, College of Engineering, Department of Civil Engineering, Bozeman, MT 59717. Offers civil engineering (MS); construction engineering management (MCEM); engineering (PhD), including applied mechanics option, civil engineering option. Part-time programs available. *Faculty:* 19 full-time (2 women), 2 part-time/adjunct (0 women). *Students:* 24 full-time (7 women), 16 part-time (3 women); includes 1 minority (American Indian/Alaska Native), 1 international. Average age 26. 36 applicants, 50% accepted, 16 enrolled. In 2009, 15 master's, 2 doctorates awarded. *Degree requirements:* For master's, comprehensive exam, thesis (for some programs); for doctorate, comprehensive exam, thesis/dissertation. *Entrance requirements:* For master's and doctorate, GRE General Test. Additional exam requirements/recommendations for international students: Required—TOEFL (minimum score 550 paper-based; 213 computer-based). *Application deadline:* For fall admission, 7/15 priority date for domestic students, 5/15 priority date for international students; for spring admission, 12/1 priority date for domestic students, 10/1 priority date for international students. Applications are processed on a rolling basis. Application fee: $30. Electronic applications accepted. *Expenses:* Tuition, state resident: full-time $5635; part-time $3492 per year. Tuition, nonresident: full-time $17,212; part-time $7865.10 per year. Required fees: $1441.05; $153.15 per credit. Tuition and fees vary according to course load and program. *Financial support:* In 2009–10, 15 students received support, including 1 research assistantship with partial tuition reimbursement available (averaging $24,000 per year), 5 teaching assistantships with partial tuition reimbursements available (averaging $8,000 per year); scholarships/grants and tuition waivers (partial) also available. Financial award application deadline: 3/1; financial award applicants required to submit FAFSA. *Faculty research:* Snow and ice mechanics, biofilm engineering, transportation, structural and geo materials, water resources. Total annual research expenditures: $714,709. *Unit head:* Dr. Brett Gunnick, Head, 406-994-2111, Fax: 406-994-6105, E-mail: bgunnick@ce.montana.edu. *Application contact:* Dr. Carl A. Fox, Vice Provost for Graduate Education, 406-994-4145, Fax: 406-994-7433, E-mail: gradstudy@montana.edu.

Montana State University, College of Graduate Studies, College of Engineering, Department of Mechanical and Industrial Engineering, Bozeman, MT 59717. Offers engineering (PhD), including industrial engineering option, mechanical engineering option; industrial and management engineering (MS); mechanical engineering (MS). Part-time programs available. *Faculty:* 18 full-time (2 women), 4 part-time/adjunct (1 woman). *Students:* 20 full-time (3 women), 21 part-time (1 woman); includes 2 minority (1 American Indian/Alaska Native, 1 Asian American or Pacific Islander), 9 international. Average age 26. 44 applicants, 48% accepted, 8 enrolled. In 2009, 13 master's awarded. *Degree requirements:* For master's,

Engineering and Applied Sciences—General

Montana State University (continued)
comprehensive exam, thesis, oral exams; for doctorate, comprehensive exam, thesis/dissertation, qualifying exam. *Entrance requirements:* For master's and doctorate, GRE General Test. Additional exam requirements/recommendations for international students: Required—TOEFL (minimum score 550 paper-based; 213 computer-based). *Application deadline:* For fall admission, 7/15 priority date for domestic students, 5/15 priority date for international students; for spring admission, 12/1 priority date for domestic students, 10/1 priority date for international students. Applications are processed on a rolling basis. Application fee: $30. Electronic applications accepted. *Expenses:* Tuition, state resident: full-time $5635; part-time $3492 per year. Tuition, nonresident: full-time $17,212; part-time $7865.10 per year. Required fees: $1441.05; $153.15 per credit. Tuition and fees vary according to course load and program. *Financial support:* In 2009–10, 30 students received support, including 2 fellowships with full tuition reimbursements available (averaging $18,000 per year), 14 research assistantships with full and partial tuition reimbursements available (averaging $9,493 per year), 22 teaching assistantships with full and partial tuition reimbursements available (averaging $4,782 per year); scholarships/grants and unspecified assistantships also available. Financial award application deadline: 3/1; financial award applicants required to submit FAFSA. *Faculty research:* Design and manufacture; energy systems, materials and structures, measurement systems, systems modeling. Total annual research expenditures: $1.3 million. *Unit head:* Dr. Chris Jenkins, Head, 406-994-2203, Fax: 406-994-6292, E-mail: cjenkins@me.montana.edu. *Application contact:* Dr. Carl A. Fox, Vice Provost for Graduate Education, 406-994-4145, Fax: 406-994-7433, E-mail: gradstudy@montana.edu.

Montana Tech of The University of Montana, Graduate School, Department of General Engineering, Butte, MT 59701-8997. Offers MS. Part-time programs available. *Faculty:* 8 full-time (0 women), 4 part-time/adjunct (0 women). *Students:* 4 full-time (1 woman). 4 applicants, 50% accepted, 0 enrolled. In 2009, 2 master's awarded. *Degree requirements:* For master's, comprehensive exam (for some programs), thesis optional. *Entrance requirements:* For master's, minimum GPA of 3.0. Additional exam requirements/recommendations for international students: Required—TOEFL (minimum score 525 paper-based; 195 computer-based; 71 iBT). *Application deadline:* For fall admission, 4/1 priority date for domestic students, 3/1 priority date for international students; for spring admission, 10/1 priority date for domestic students, 7/1 priority date for international students. Applications are processed on a rolling basis. Application fee: $30. Electronic applications accepted. *Expenses:* Tuition, state resident: full-time $5068; part-time $319 per credit. Tuition, nonresident: full-time $14,815; part-time $875 per credit. Tuition and fees vary according to course load and campus/location. *Financial support:* In 2009–10, 3 students received support, including 3 teaching assistantships with partial tuition reimbursements available (averaging $8,000 per year); research assistantships with partial tuition reimbursements available, career-related internships or fieldwork, tuition waivers (full and partial), and unspecified assistantships also available. Financial award application deadline: 4/1; financial award applicants required to submit FAFSA. *Faculty research:* Wind energy and power controls, robotics, concurrent engineering, remotely piloted aircraft, composite materials. *Unit head:* Dr. Butch Gerbrandt, Head, 406-496-4109, Fax: 406-496-4650, E-mail: bgerbrandt@mtech.edu. *Application contact:* Cindy Dunstan, Administrator, Graduate School, 406-496-4304, Fax: 406-496-4710, E-mail: cdunstan@mtech.edu.

Morgan State University, School of Graduate Studies, Clarence M. Mitchell, Jr. School of Engineering, Baltimore, MD 21251. Offers civil engineering (M Eng, D Eng); electrical engineering (M Eng, D Eng); industrial engineering (M Eng, D Eng); transportation (MS). Part-time and evening/weekend programs available. *Degree requirements:* For master's, thesis, comprehensive exam or equivalent; for doctorate, thesis/dissertation, comprehensive exam or equivalent. *Entrance requirements:* For master's, GRE, minimum undergraduate GPA of 2.5; for doctorate, GRE, minimum GPA of 3.0. Additional exam requirements/recommendations for international students: Required—TOEFL (minimum score 550 paper-based; 213 computer-based).

National University, Academic Affairs, School of Engineering and Technology, Department of Applied Engineering, La Jolla, CA 92037-1011. Offers database administration (MS); engineering management (MS); environmental engineering (MS); homeland security and safety engineering (MS); system engineering (MS); wireless communications (MS). Part-time and evening/weekend programs available. Postbaccalaureate distance learning degree programs offered (no on-campus study). *Faculty:* 6 full-time (1 woman), 7 part-time/adjunct (1 woman). *Students:* 61 full-time (16 women), 176 part-time (35 women); includes 54 minority (11 African Americans, 1 American Indian/Alaska Native, 23 Asian Americans or Pacific Islanders, 19 Hispanic Americans), 117 international. Average age 31. 133 applicants, 100% accepted, 83 enrolled. In 2009, 34 master's awarded. *Degree requirements:* For master's, thesis. *Entrance requirements:* For master's, interview, minimum GPA of 2.5. Additional exam requirements/recommendations for international students: Required—TOEFL (minimum score 550 paper-based; 213 computer-based; 79 iBT), IELTS (minimum score 6). *Application deadline:* Applications are processed on a rolling basis. Application fee: $60 ($65 for international students). Electronic applications accepted. *Expenses:* Tuition: Part-time $338 per quarter hour. *Financial support:* Career-related internships or fieldwork, institutionally sponsored loans, scholarships/grants, and tuition waivers (partial) available. Support available to part-time students. Financial award application deadline: 6/30; financial award applicants required to submit FAFSA. *Unit head:* Dr. Shekar Viswanathan, Chair and Associate Professor, 858-309-8416, Fax: 858-309-3420, E-mail: sviswana@nu.edu. *Application contact:* Dominick Giovanniello, Associate Regional Dean—San Diego, 800-NAT-UNIV, Fax: 858-541-7792, E-mail: dgiovann@nu.edu.

New Jersey Institute of Technology, Office of Graduate Studies, Newark, NJ 07102. Offers M Arch, MA, MAT, MBA, MIP, MS, PhD, Engineer, M Arch/MIP, M Arch/MS. Part-time and evening/weekend programs available. Terminal master's awarded for partial completion of doctoral program. *Degree requirements:* For master's, thesis optional; for doctorate, thesis/dissertation. *Entrance requirements:* For master's and doctorate, GRE General Test. Additional exam requirements/recommendations for international students: Required—TOEFL (minimum score 550 paper-based; 213 computer-based; 79 iBT). Electronic applications accepted. *Faculty research:* Toxic and hazardous waste management, transportation, biomedical engineering, computer-integrated manufacturing, management of technology.

New Jersey Institute of Technology, Office of Graduate Studies, Newark College of Engineering, Interdisciplinary Program in Engineering Science, Newark, NJ 07102. Offers MS. Part-time and evening/weekend programs available. *Entrance requirements:* For master's, GRE General Test. Additional exam requirements/recommendations for international students: Required—TOEFL (minimum score 550 paper-based; 213 computer-based; 79 iBT). Electronic applications accepted.

New Mexico State University, Graduate School, College of Engineering, Las Cruces, NM 88003-8001. Offers MS Ch E, MS Env E, MSCE, MSEE, MSIE, MSME, PhD. Part-time programs available. *Faculty:* 53 full-time (7 women). *Students:* 267 full-time (66 women), 149 part-time (34 women); includes 95 minority (10 African Americans, 4 American Indian/Alaska Native, 6 Asian Americans or Pacific Islanders, 75 Hispanic Americans), 197 international. Average age 29. 496 applicants, 74% accepted, 131 enrolled. In 2009, 101 master's, 13 doctorates awarded. *Degree requirements:* For doctorate, thesis/dissertation. *Application deadline:* For fall admission, 7/1 priority date for domestic students; for spring admission, 11/1 for domestic students. Applications are processed on a rolling basis. Application fee: $30 ($50 for international students). Electronic applications accepted. *Expenses:* Tuition, state resident: full-time $4080; part-time $223 per credit. Tuition, nonresident: full-time $14,256; part-time $647 per credit. Required fees: $1278; $639 per semester. *Financial support:* In 2009–10, 95 research assistantships (averaging $9,915 per year), 91 teaching assistantships (averaging $8,158 per year) were awarded; fellowships, career-related internships or fieldwork, Federal Work-Study, and health care benefits also available. Support available to part-time students. Financial award application deadline: 3/1. *Faculty research:* Structures and nondestructive testing, environmental science and engineering, telecommunication theory and systems, manufacturing methods and systems, high performance computing and software engineering. *Unit head:* Dr. Ken White, Interim Dean, 575-646-2914, Fax: 575-646-3549, E-mail: krwhite@nmsu.edu. *Application contact:* Dr. Ken White, Interim Dean, 575-646-2914, Fax: 575-646-3549, E-mail: krwhite@nmsu.edu.

New York Institute of Technology, Graduate Division, School of Engineering and Computing Sciences, Old Westbury, NY 11568-8000. Offers MS, Advanced Certificate. Part-time and evening/weekend programs available. Postbaccalaureate distance learning degree programs offered. *Students:* 373 full-time (87 women), 336 part-time (66 women); includes 91 minority (34 African Americans, 2 American Indian/Alaska Native, 30 Asian Americans or Pacific Islanders, 25 Hispanic Americans), 377 international. Average age 28. In 2009, 226 master's, 15 other advanced degrees awarded. *Entrance requirements:* Additional exam requirements/recommendations for international students: Required—TOEFL (minimum score 550 paper-based; 213 computer-based). *Application deadline:* For fall admission, 7/1 priority date for domestic students; for spring admission, 12/1 priority date for domestic students. Applications are processed on a rolling basis. Application fee: $50. Electronic applications accepted. *Expenses:* Tuition: Part-time $825 per credit. *Financial support:* Fellowships, research assistantships with partial tuition reimbursements, career-related internships or fieldwork, institutionally sponsored loans, tuition waivers (full and partial), and unspecified assistantships available. Support available to part-time students. Financial award applicants required to submit FAFSA. *Faculty research:* Hybrid vehicle development, system design of photovoltaic cells, prototype module of DTV application environment, adaptive target detection in nonhomogeneous environment. *Unit head:* Dr. Nada Anid, Dean, 516-686-7931, Fax: 516-625-7933, E-mail: nanid@nyit.edu. *Application contact:* Dr. Jacquelyn Nealon, Vice President for Enrollment Services, 516-686-7925, Fax: 516-686-7597, E-mail: jnealon@nyit.edu.

North Carolina Agricultural and Technical State University, Graduate School, College of Engineering, Greensboro, NC 27411. Offers MS Ch E, MSCE, MSCS, MSE, MSEE, MSIE, MSME, PhD. Part-time programs available.

North Carolina State University, Graduate School, College of Engineering, Raleigh, NC 27695. Offers M Ch E, M Eng, MC Sc, MCE, MIE, MIMS, MMSE, MNE, MOR, MS, PhD. Part-time programs available. Terminal master's awarded for partial completion of doctoral program. *Degree requirements:* For doctorate, thesis/dissertation. Electronic applications accepted.

See Display on page 53 and Close-Up on page 77.

North Dakota State University, College of Graduate and Interdisciplinary Studies, College of Engineering and Architecture, Fargo, ND 58108. Offers MS, PhD. Part-time programs available. *Faculty:* 72 full-time (9 women), 11 part-time/adjunct (0 women). *Students:* 49 full-time (10 women), 105 part-time (11 women); includes 72 minority (1 African American, 8 American Indian/Alaska Native, 62 Asian Americans or Pacific Islanders, 1 Hispanic American), 47 international. Average age 27. 225 applicants, 47% accepted. In 2009, 32 master's, 5 doctorates awarded. Terminal master's awarded for partial completion of doctoral program. *Degree requirements:* For master's, thesis; for doctorate, comprehensive exam, thesis/dissertation. *Entrance requirements:* For master's and doctorate, minimum GPA of 3.0. Additional exam requirements/recommendations for international students: Required—TOEFL. *Application deadline:* For fall admission, 4/1 priority date for domestic and international students; for spring admission, 10/1 priority date for domestic and international students. Applications are processed on a rolling basis. Application fee: $45 ($60 for international students). *Expenses:* Contact institution. *Financial support:* In 2009–10, 150 students received support, including fellowships with full tuition reimbursements available (averaging $15,000 per year), research assistantships with full tuition reimbursements available (averaging $9,000 per year), teaching assistantships with full tuition reimbursements available (averaging $8,000 per year); career-related internships or fieldwork, Federal Work-Study, institutionally sponsored loans, scholarships/grants, and tuition waivers (full) also available. Support available to part-time students. Financial award application deadline: 4/15. *Faculty research:* Theoretical mechanics, robotics, automation, environmental engineering, man-made materials. Total annual research expenditures: $2.6 million. *Unit head:* Dr. Gary R. Smith, Dean, 701-231-7494, Fax: 701-231-8957, E-mail: gary.smith@ndsu.edu. *Application contact:* Dr. David A. Wittrock, Dean, 701-231-7033, Fax: 701-231-6524.

Northeastern University, College of Engineering, Boston, MA 02115-5096. Offers MS, PhD, Certificate. Part-time programs available. *Students:* 1,006 full-time (133 women), 311 part-time (62 women); includes 8 African Americans, 13 Asian Americans or Pacific Islanders, 6 Hispanic Americans, 676 international. 2,136 applicants, 62% accepted, 401 enrolled. In 2009, 299 master's, 34 doctorates awarded. *Entrance requirements:* For master's and doctorate, GRE General Test. Additional exam requirements/recommendations for international students: Required—TOEFL. *Application deadline:* For fall admission, 1/15 priority date for domestic and international students. Applications are processed on a rolling basis. Application fee: $50. Electronic applications accepted. *Expenses:* Contact institution. *Financial support:* In 2009–10, 268 students received support, including 4 fellowships with full tuition reimbursements available, 146 research assistantships with full tuition reimbursements available (averaging $18,320 per year), 117 teaching assistantships with full tuition reimbursements available (averaging $18,320 per year); career-related internships or fieldwork, Federal Work-Study, scholarships/grants, tuition waivers (full), and unspecified assistantships also available. Support available to part-time students. Financial award application deadline: 1/15; financial award applicants required to submit FAFSA. *Unit head:* Dr. Yaman Yener, Associate Dean of Engineering for Research and Graduate Studies, 617-373-2711, Fax: 617-373-2501. *Application contact:* Stephen L. Gibson, Associate Director, 617-373-2711, Fax: 617-373-2501, E-mail: grad-eng@coe.neu.edu.

Northern Arizona University, Graduate College, College of Engineering, Forestry and Natural Sciences, Flagstaff, AZ 86011. Offers M Ed, MAST, MAT, MF, MS, MSE, MSF, PhD. *Faculty:* 195 full-time (62 women). *Students:* 239 full-time (116 women), 102 part-time (61 women); includes 31 minority (1 African American, 10 American Indian/Alaska Native, 8 Asian Americans or Pacific Islanders, 12 Hispanic Americans), 19 international. 283 applicants, 50% accepted, 104 enrolled. In 2009, 84 master's, 13 doctorates awarded. *Entrance requirements:* For master's, minimum GPA of 3.0 in final 60 hours of undergraduate course work. Application fee: $65. *Financial support:* In 2009–10, 32 students received support, including 66 research assistantships, 150 teaching assistantships. *Unit head:* Paul W. Jagodzinski, Dean, 928-523-2701. *Application contact:* Paul W. Jagodzinski, Dean, 928-523-2701.

Northern Illinois University, Graduate School, College of Engineering and Engineering Technology, De Kalb, IL 60115-2854. Offers MS. Part-time and evening/weekend programs available. *Faculty:* 36 full-time (2 women), 2 part-time/adjunct (0 women). *Students:* 141 full-time (27 women), 133 part-time (27 women); includes 17 minority (3 African Americans, 1 American Indian/Alaska Native, 6 Asian Americans or Pacific Islanders, 7 Hispanic Americans), 175 international. Average age 26. 551 applicants, 42% accepted, 76 enrolled. In 2009, 88 master's awarded. *Degree requirements:* For master's, comprehensive exam, thesis optional. *Entrance requirements:* For master's, GRE General Test, minimum GPA of 2.75. Additional exam requirements/recommendations for international students: Required—TOEFL (minimum score 550 paper-based; 213 computer-based). *Application deadline:* For fall admission, 6/1 for domestic students, 5/1 for international students; for spring admission, 11/1 for domestic students, 10/1 for international students. Applications are processed on a rolling basis. Application fee: $30. Electronic applications accepted. *Expenses:* Tuition, state resident: full-time $6576; part-time $274 per credit hour. Tuition, nonresident: full-time $13,152; part-time $548 per credit hour. Required fees: $1813; $75.53 per credit hour. Part-time tuition and fees vary according to course load. *Financial support:* In 2009–10, 8 research assistantships with full tuition reimbursements were awarded; fellowships with full tuition reimbursements, teaching assistantships with full tuition reimbursements, career-related internships or fieldwork, Federal Work-Study, scholarships/grants, tuition waivers (full), and unspecified assistantships also available. Support available to part-time students. Financial award applicants required to submit FAFSA.

Unit head: Dr. Promod Vohra, Dean, 815-753-1281, Fax: 815-753-1310, E-mail: pvohra@niu.edu. *Application contact:* Graduate School Office, 815-753-0395, E-mail: gradsch@niu.edu.

Northwestern Polytechnic University, School of Engineering, Fremont, CA 94539-7482. Offers computer science (MS); computer systems engineering (MS); electrical engineering (MS). Part-time and evening/weekend programs available. *Degree requirements:* For master's, thesis optional. *Entrance requirements:* For master's, minimum GPA of 3.0. Additional exam requirements/recommendations for international students: Required—TOEFL (minimum score 550 paper-based; 213 computer-based; 79 iBT). *Faculty research:* Computer networking, database design, Internet technology, software engineering, digital signal processing.

Northwestern University, McCormick School of Engineering and Applied Science, Evanston, IL 60208. Offers MEM, MIT, MME, MMM, MPD, MS, PhD, Certificate. MS and PhD admissions and degrees offered through The Graduate School. Part-time and evening/weekend programs available. *Degree requirements:* For doctorate, thesis/dissertation. *Entrance requirements:* For master's and doctorate, GRE General Test. Additional exam requirements/recommendations for international students: Required—TOEFL. Electronic applications accepted.

Oakland University, Graduate Study and Lifelong Learning, School of Engineering and Computer Science, Rochester, MI 48309-4401. Offers MS, PhD. Part-time and evening/weekend programs available. *Degree requirements:* For doctorate, thesis/dissertation. *Entrance requirements:* For master's and doctorate, minimum GPA of 3.0 for unconditional admission. Additional exam requirements/recommendations for international students: Required—TOEFL (minimum score 550 paper-based; 213 computer-based). Electronic applications accepted. *Expenses:* Contact institution. *Faculty research:* Acquisition of automotive antenna measurements instrumentation, high fidelity antenna model, development for LAAS Cat-1 siting criteria, cyber security, 3D imaging of neurochemical in rat brains.

The Ohio State University, Graduate School, College of Engineering, Columbus, OH 43210. Offers M Arch, M Land Arch, MAS, MCRP, MS, MWE, PhD. Part-time and evening/weekend programs available. *Faculty:* 475. *Students:* 1,241 full-time (280 women), 411 part-time (86 women); includes 108 minority (27 African Americans, 2 American Indian/Alaska Native, 49 Asian Americans or Pacific Islanders, 30 Hispanic Americans), 848 international. Average age 27. In 2009, 380 master's, 135 doctorates awarded. *Degree requirements:* For doctorate, thesis/dissertation. *Entrance requirements:* Additional exam requirements/recommendations for international students: Recommended—TOEFL (minimum score 600 paper-based; 250 computer-based). *Application deadline:* For fall admission, 8/15 priority date for domestic students, 7/1 priority date for international students; for winter admission, 12/1 priority date for domestic students, 11/1 priority date for international students; for spring admission, 3/1 priority date for domestic students, 2/1 priority date for international students. Applications are processed on a rolling basis. Application fee: $40 ($50 for international students). Electronic applications accepted. *Expenses:* Tuition, state resident: full-time $10,683. Tuition, nonresident: full-time $25,923. Tuition and fees vary according to course load and program. *Financial support:* Fellowships, research assistantships, teaching assistantships, career-related internships or fieldwork, Federal Work-Study, institutionally sponsored loans, and unspecified assistantships available. Support available to part-time students. *Unit head:* Dr. Gregory N. Washington, Interim Dean, 614-292-2836, Fax: 614-292-9379, E-mail: washington.88@osu.edu. *Application contact:* 614-292-9444, Fax: 614-292-3895, E-mail: domestic.grad@osu.edu.

Ohio University, Graduate College, Russ College of Engineering and Technology, Athens, OH 45701-2979. Offers M Eng Mgt, MS, PhD. Part-time programs available. *Faculty:* 114 full-time (6 women), 15 part-time/adjunct (3 women). *Students:* 221 full-time (49 women), 81 part-time (11 women); includes 5 minority (3 African Americans, 2 Hispanic Americans), 188 international. 312 applicants, 57% accepted, 47 enrolled. In 2009, 65 master's, 12 doctorates awarded. *Degree requirements:* For master's, comprehensive exam (for some programs), thesis (for some programs); for doctorate, comprehensive exam, thesis/dissertation. *Entrance requirements:* For master's, GRE General Test, BS in engineering or related field; for doctorate, GRE General Test, MS in engineering or related field. Additional exam requirements/recommendations for international students: Required—TOEFL or IELTS Academic. *Application deadline:* Applications are processed on a rolling basis. Application fee: $50 ($55 for international students). Electronic applications accepted. *Expenses:* Contact institution. *Financial support:* Fellowships with full tuition reimbursements, research assistantships with full tuition reimbursements, teaching assistantships with full tuition reimbursements, career-related internships or fieldwork, Federal Work-Study, institutionally sponsored loans, and unspecified assistantships available. Financial award application deadline: 3/15. *Faculty research:* Avionics engineering, coal research, transportation engineering, software systems integration, materials processing. Total annual research expenditures: $14.7 million. *Unit head:* Dr. Dennis Irwin, Dean, 740-593-1482, Fax: 740-593-0659, E-mail: irwind@ohio.edu. *Application contact:* Dr. James Rankin, Associate Dean for Research and Graduate Studies, 740-593-1482, Fax: 740-593-0659, E-mail: rankinj@ohio.edu.

Oklahoma State University, College of Engineering, Architecture and Technology, Stillwater, OK 74078. Offers MS, PhD. Postbaccalaureate distance learning degree programs offered. *Faculty:* 111 full-time (12 women), 10 part-time/adjunct (1 woman). *Students:* 341 full-time (60 women), 417 part-time (62 women); includes 44 minority (7 African Americans, 11 American Indian/Alaska Native, 18 Asian Americans or Pacific Islanders, 8 Hispanic Americans), 490 international. Average age 28. 1,246 applicants, 34% accepted, 170 enrolled. In 2009, 179 master's, 18 doctorates awarded. *Degree requirements:* For master's, thesis (for some programs); for doctorate, comprehensive exam, thesis/dissertation. *Entrance requirements:* For master's and doctorate, GRE or GMAT. Additional exam requirements/recommendations for international students: Required—TOEFL (minimum score 550 paper-based; 79 iBT). *Application deadline:* For fall admission, 3/1 priority date for international students; for spring admission, 8/1 priority date for international students. Applications are processed on a rolling basis. Application fee: $40 ($75 for international students). Electronic applications accepted. *Expenses:* Tuition, state resident: full-time $3716; part-time $154.85 per credit hour. Tuition, nonresident: full-time $14,448; part-time $602 per credit hour. Required fees: $1772; $73.85 per credit hour. One-time fee: $50. Tuition and fees vary according to course load and campus/location. *Financial support:* In 2009–10, 259 research assistantships (averaging $10,610 per year), 160 teaching assistantships (averaging $8,194 per year) were awarded; career-related internships or fieldwork, Federal Work-Study, scholarships/grants, health care benefits, tuition waivers (partial), and unspecified assistantships also available. Support available to part-time students. Financial award application deadline: 3/1; financial award applicants required to submit FAFSA. *Unit head:* Dr. Karl N. Reid, Dean, 405-744-5140. *Application contact:* Dr. Gordon Emslie, Dean, 405-744-6368, Fax: 405-744-0355, E-mail: grad-i@okstate.edu.

Old Dominion University, Frank Batten College of Engineering and Technology, Norfolk, VA 23529. Offers ME, MEM, MS, D Eng, PhD. Part-time and evening/weekend programs available. Postbaccalaureate distance learning degree programs offered. *Faculty:* 93 full-time (12 women), 32 part-time/adjunct (5 women). *Students:* 237 full-time (45 women), 516 part-time (100 women); includes 100 minority (45 African Americans, 4 American Indian/Alaska Native, 32 Asian Americans or Pacific Islanders, 19 Hispanic Americans), 236 international. Average age 32. 558 applicants, 63% accepted, 144 enrolled. In 2009, 243 master's, 18 doctorates awarded. *Degree requirements:* For master's, comprehensive exam, thesis (for some programs); for doctorate, thesis/dissertation, candidacy exam. *Entrance requirements:* For master's, GRE, minimum GPA of 3.0; for doctorate, GRE, minimum GPA of 3.5. Additional exam requirements/recommendations for international students: Required—TOEFL (minimum score 550 paper-based). *Application deadline:* For fall admission, 6/1 for domestic students, 2/15 priority date for international students; for spring admission, 11/1 for domestic students, 10/1 for international students. Applications are processed on a rolling basis. Application fee: $40. Electronic applications accepted. *Expenses:* Tuition, state resident: full-time $8112; part-time $338 per credit. Tuition, nonresident: full-time $20,256; part-time $844 per credit. Required fees: $119 per semester. One-time fee: $50. *Financial support:* In 2009–10, 168 students received

Engineering and Applied Sciences—General

Old Dominion University *(continued)*
support, including 8 fellowships with full and partial tuition reimbursements available (averaging $15,000 per year), 92 research assistantships with full and partial tuition reimbursements available (averaging $15,000 per year), 68 teaching assistantships with full and partial tuition reimbursements available (averaging $15,000 per year); career-related internships or fieldwork, Federal Work-Study, institutionally sponsored loans, scholarships/grants, and unspecified assistantships also available. Support available to part-time students. Financial award applicants required to submit FAFSA. *Faculty research:* Physical electronics, computational applied mechanics, structural dynamics, computational fluid dynamics, coastal engineering of water resources. Total annual research expenditures: $28.3 million. *Unit head:* Dr. Oktay Baysal, Dean, 757-683-3789, Fax: 757-683-4898, E-mail: obaysal@odu.edu. *Application contact:* Dr. Linda Vahala, Associate Dean, 757-683-3789, Fax: 757-683-4898, E-mail: lvahala@odu.edu.

Oregon State University, Graduate School, College of Engineering, Corvallis, OR 97331. Offers M Eng, M Engr, M Oc E, MA, MAIS, MBE, MHP, MS, PhD. Part-time programs available. *Faculty:* 117 full-time (17 women), 8 part-time/adjunct (4 women). *Students:* 563 full-time (118 women), 150 part-time (32 women); includes 67 minority (7 African Americans, 2 American Indian/Alaska Native, 39 Asian Americans or Pacific Islanders, 19 Hispanic Americans), 261 international. Average age 29. In 2009, 136 master's, 36 doctorates awarded. Terminal master's awarded for partial completion of doctoral program. *Degree requirements:* For doctorate, thesis/dissertation. *Entrance requirements:* For master's and doctorate, minimum GPA of 3.0 in last 90 hours. Additional exam requirements/recommendations for international students: Required—TOEFL (minimum score 550 paper-based; 213 computer-based). *Application deadline:* Applications are processed on a rolling basis. Application fee: $50. *Expenses:* Tuition, state resident: full-time $9774; part-time $362 per credit. Tuition, nonresident: full-time $15,849; part-time $587 per credit. Required fees: $1639. Full-time tuition and fees vary according to course load and program. *Financial support:* In 2009–10, 20 fellowships with full tuition reimbursements (averaging $11,608 per year), 192 research assistantships with full tuition reimbursements (averaging $12,639 per year), 129 teaching assistantships with full tuition reimbursements (averaging $9,965 per year) were awarded; career-related internships or fieldwork, Federal Work-Study, institutionally sponsored loans, and instructorships also available. Support available to part-time students. Financial award application deadline: 2/1. *Faculty research:* Molecular beam epitaxy, wave-structure interaction, pavement materials, toxic wastes, mechanical design methodology. Total annual research expenditures: $22.8 million. *Unit head:* Dr. Ronald L. Adams, Dean, 541-737-7722, Fax: 541-737-1805, E-mail: ronald.lynn.adams@orst.edu. *Application contact:* Chris A. Bell, Associate Dean, 541-737-1598, Fax: 541-737-1805, E-mail: chris.a.bell@oregonstate.edu.

See Close-Up on page 79.

Penn State Great Valley, Graduate Studies, Engineering Division, Malvern, PA 19355-1488. Offers ME, MEM, MS, MSE. *Unit head:* Dr. James A. Nemes, Division Head, 610-648-3335 Ext. 610, Fax: 648-648-3377, E-mail: jan16@psu.edu. *Application contact:* Dr. James A. Nemes, Division Head, 610-648-3335 Ext. 610, Fax: 648-648-3377, E-mail: jan16@psu.edu.

Penn State Harrisburg, Graduate School, School of Science, Engineering and Technology, Middletown, PA 17057-4898. Offers M Eng, MEPC, MPS, MS, MEPC/JD. Evening/weekend programs available. *Unit head:* Dr. Omid Ansary, Director, 717-948-6353, E-mail: axa8@psu.edu. *Application contact:* Robert Coffman, Director of Admissions, 717-948-6250, Fax: 717-948-6325, E-mail: ric1@psu.edu.

Penn State University Park, Graduate School, College of Engineering, State College, University Park, PA 16802-1503. Offers M Eng, MAE, MMM, MS, PhD. *Students:* 1,174 full-time (237 women), 155 part-time (25 women). Average age 27. 3,578 applicants, 29% accepted, 340 enrolled. In 2009, 319 master's, 124 doctorates awarded. *Entrance requirements:* Additional exam requirements/recommendations for international students: Required—TOEFL (minimum score 550 paper-based; 213 computer-based; 80 iBT). *Application deadline:* Applications are processed on a rolling basis. Application fee: $65. Electronic applications accepted. *Financial support:* Fellowships, research assistantships, teaching assistantships available. Financial award applicants required to submit FAFSA. *Unit head:* Dr. David N. Wormley, Dean, 814-865-7537, Fax: 814-865-8767, E-mail: dnw2@engr.psu.edu. *Application contact:* Cynthia E. Nicosia, Director, Graduate Enrollment Services, 814-865-1834, E-mail: cey1@psu.edu.

Pittsburg State University, Graduate School, College of Technology, Department of Engineering Technology, Pittsburg, KS 66762. Offers MET. *Degree requirements:* For master's, thesis or alternative. *Expenses:* Tuition, state resident: full-time $4212; part-time $176 per credit. Tuition, nonresident: full-time $11,530; part-time $480 per credit. Required fees: $940; $43 per credit. Tuition and fees vary according to course level, course load, degree level, campus/location, reciprocity agreements and student level.

Pittsburg State University, Graduate School, College of Technology, Department of Technology Studies, Pittsburg, KS 66762. Offers technical teacher education (MS); technology education (MS). *Degree requirements:* For master's, thesis or alternative. *Expenses:* Tuition, state resident: full-time $4212; part-time $176 per credit. Tuition, nonresident: full-time $11,530; part-time $480 per credit. Required fees: $940; $43 per credit. Tuition and fees vary according to course level, course load, degree level, campus/location, reciprocity agreements and student level.

Portland State University, Graduate Studies, Maseeh College of Engineering and Computer Science, Portland, OR 97207-0751. Offers M Eng, ME, MS, MSE, PhD, Certificate, MS/MBA, MS/MS. Part-time and evening/weekend programs available. *Degree requirements:* For doctorate, one foreign language, thesis/dissertation, oral and written exams. *Entrance requirements:* For master's, minimum GPA of 3.0 in upper-division course work or 2.75 overall; for doctorate, GRE General Test, GRE Subject Test, minimum GPA of 3.0 in upper-division course work. Additional exam requirements/recommendations for international students: Required—TOEFL (minimum score 550 paper-based; 213 computer-based).

Prairie View A&M University, College of Engineering, Prairie View, TX 77446-0519. Offers computer information systems (MSCIS); computer science (MSCS); electrical engineering (MSEE, PhDEE); engineering (MS Engr). Part-time and evening/weekend programs available. *Faculty:* 19 full-time (0 women). *Students:* 64 full-time (18 women), 47 part-time (14 women); includes 43 minority (36 African Americans, 4 Asian Americans or Pacific Islanders, 3 Hispanic Americans), 51 international. Average age 24. 50 applicants, 84% accepted, 33 enrolled. In 2009, 26 master's, 3 doctorates awarded. *Degree requirements:* For master's, thesis (for some programs); for doctorate, comprehensive exam, thesis/dissertation. *Entrance requirements:* For master's, GRE General Test, bachelor's degree in engineering from an ABET accredited institution; for doctorate, GRE. Additional exam requirements/recommendations for international students: Required—TOEFL (minimum score 550 paper-based). *Application deadline:* For fall admission, 7/1 priority date for domestic and international students; for spring admission, 11/1 priority date for domestic and international students. Application fee: $50. Electronic applications accepted. *Expenses:* Tuition, state resident: full-time $2200. Tuition, nonresident: full-time $5600. Required fees: $1720. Tuition and fees vary according to course load. *Financial support:* In 2009–10, 80 students received support, including 14 fellowships (averaging $1,050 per year), 16 research assistantships (averaging $16,150 per year), 13 teaching assistantships (averaging $14,000 per year); career-related internships or fieldwork, institutionally sponsored loans, scholarships/grants, health care benefits, tuition waivers (partial), and unspecified assistantships also available. Financial award application deadline: 3/1; financial award applicants required to submit FAFSA. *Faculty research:* Applied radiation research, thermal science, computational fluid dynamics, analog mixed signal, aerial space battlefield. Total annual research expenditures: $439,054. *Unit head:* Dr. Kendall T. Harris, Dean, 936-261-9956, Fax: 936-261-9869, E-mail: tharris@pvamu.edu. *Application contact:* Barbara A. Thompson, Administrative Assistant, 936-261-9896, Fax: 936-261-9869, E-mail: bathompson@pvamu.edu.

Princeton University, Graduate School, School of Engineering and Applied Science, Princeton, NJ 08544-1019. Offers M Eng, MSE, PhD. Terminal master's awarded for partial completion of doctoral program. *Degree requirements:* For master's, thesis (for some programs); for doctorate, thesis/dissertation, Ph.D. (Doctor of Philosophy) ??? fully funded, typically 5-year program, entailing coursework, research, teaching and a dissertation. Passing of general exam required. *Entrance requirements:* For master's and doctorate, GRE General Test; GRE Subject Test recommended for Department of Computer Science, official transcript(s), 3 letters of recommendation, personal statement. Additional exam requirements/recommendations for international students: Required—TOEFL. Electronic applications accepted. *Financial support:* Fellowships with full tuition reimbursements, research assistantships with full tuition reimbursements, teaching assistantships with full tuition reimbursements, institutionally sponsored loans and health care benefits available. *Unit head:* Dr. Stephen Friedfeld, Associate Dean, Graduate Affairs, 609-258-6740, Fax: 609-258-6744, E-mail: egrad@princeton.edu. *Application contact:* Michelle Carman, Manager of Graduate Admissions, 609-258-3034, Fax: 609-258-7262, E-mail: gsadmit@princeton.edu.

Purdue University, College of Engineering, West Lafayette, IN 47907-2045. Offers MS, MSAAE, MSABE, MSBME, MSCE, MSChE, MSE, MSECE, MSIE, MSME, MSMSE, MSNE, PhD, Certificate, MD/PhD. *Accreditation:* ABET. Part-time programs available. Postbaccalaureate distance learning degree programs offered (no on-campus study). *Faculty:* 327 full-time (51 women), 101 part-time/adjunct (16 women). *Students:* 1,813 full-time (351 women), 701 part-time (125 women); includes 206 minority (48 African Americans, 3 American Indian/Alaska Native, 102 Asian Americans or Pacific Islanders, 53 Hispanic Americans), 1,315 international. 5,253 applicants, 31% accepted, 658 enrolled. In 2009, 398 master's, 210 doctorates awarded. Terminal master's awarded for partial completion of doctoral program. *Degree requirements:* For master's, thesis (for some programs); for doctorate, comprehensive exam, thesis/dissertation. *Entrance requirements:* Additional exam requirements/recommendations for international students: Required—TOEFL, TOEFL (minimum score 550 paper-based; 213 computer-based) or IELTS (minimum score 6.5); Recommended—TWE. *Application deadline:* Applications are processed on a rolling basis. Application fee: $55. Electronic applications accepted. *Expenses:* Contact institution. *Financial support:* Fellowships with full tuition reimbursements, research assistantships with partial tuition reimbursements, teaching assistantships with partial tuition reimbursements, career-related internships or fieldwork, health care benefits, and unspecified assistantships available. *Faculty research:* Nanotechnology, advanced materials manufacturing, tissue and cell engineering, intelligent infrastructures, global sustainable industrial systems. Total annual research expenditures: $147.3 million. *Unit head:* Dr. Audeen Fentiman, Associate Dean, 765-494-5340, E-mail: engrad@purdue.edu. *Application contact:* Susan K. Fisher, Director of Graduate Programs, 765-494-0600, E-mail: engrad@purdue.edu.

Purdue University Calumet, Graduate School, School of Engineering, Mathematics, and Science, Department of Engineering, Hammond, IN 46323-2094. Offers computer engineering (MSE); electrical engineering (MSE); engineering (MS); mechanical engineering (MSE). Evening/weekend programs available. *Entrance requirements:* Additional exam requirements/recommendations for international students: Required—TOEFL.

Queen's University at Kingston, School of Graduate Studies and Research, Faculty of Applied Science, Kingston, ON K7L 3N6, Canada. Offers M Eng, M Sc, M Sc Eng, PhD. Part-time programs available. *Degree requirements:* For doctorate, comprehensive exam, thesis/dissertation. *Entrance requirements:* Additional exam requirements/recommendations for international students: Required—TOEFL. Electronic applications accepted.

Rensselaer at Hartford, Department of Engineering, Hartford, CT 06120-2991. Offers ME, MS. Part-time and evening/weekend programs available. *Faculty:* 6 full-time (0 women), 20 part-time/adjunct (0 women). *Students:* 4 full-time (0 women), 370 part-time (61 women); includes 80 minority (17 African Americans, 35 Asian Americans or Pacific Islanders, 28 Hispanic Americans), 3 international. Average age 34. 140 applicants, 54% accepted, 76 enrolled. In 2009, 81 master's awarded. *Entrance requirements:* For master's, GRE. Additional exam requirements/recommendations for international students: Required—TOEFL (minimum score 600 paper-based; 250 computer-based; 100 iBT). *Application deadline:* For fall admission, 8/30 priority date for domestic students, 8/1 priority date for international students. Applications are processed on a rolling basis. Application fee: $75. Electronic applications accepted. *Expenses:* Tuition: Full-time $31,800; part-time $1325 per credit hour. *Financial support:* Research assistantships, career-related internships or fieldwork, tuition waivers (full and partial), and unspecified assistantships available. Support available to part-time students. Financial award applicants required to submit FAFSA. *Unit head:* Dr. Ernesto Gutierrez-Miravete, 860-548-2464, E-mail: gutiee@rpi.edu. *Application contact:* Kristin Galligan, Director, Enrollment Management and Marketing, 860-548-2480, E-mail: info@ewp.rpi.edu.

Rensselaer Polytechnic Institute, Graduate School, School of Engineering, Troy, NY 12180-3590. Offers M Eng, MS, PhD. Part-time and evening/weekend programs available. Postbaccalaureate distance learning degree programs offered (no on-campus study). *Faculty:* 131 full-time (15 women), 15 part-time/adjunct (0 women). *Students:* 494 full-time (95 women), 59 part-time (10 women); includes 51 minority (5 African Americans, 24 Asian Americans or Pacific Islanders, 22 Hispanic Americans). Average age 27. 1,805 applicants, 27% accepted, 203 enrolled. In 2009, 131 master's, 66 doctorates awarded. Terminal master's awarded for partial completion of doctoral program. *Degree requirements:* For master's, comprehensive exam (for some programs), thesis (for some programs); for doctorate, comprehensive exam (for some programs), thesis/dissertation. *Entrance requirements:* For master's and doctorate, GRE. Additional exam requirements/recommendations for international students: Required—TOEFL (minimum score 570 paper-based; 230 computer-based). *Application deadline:* For fall admission, 1/1 priority date for domestic and international students; for spring admission, 8/15 priority date for domestic and international students. Applications are processed on a rolling basis. Application fee: $75. Electronic applications accepted. *Expenses:* Tuition: Full-time $38,100. *Financial support:* In 2009–10, 25 fellowships with full tuition reimbursements (averaging $22,000 per year), 282 research assistantships with full and partial tuition reimbursements (averaging $20,000 per year), 125 teaching assistantships with full and partial tuition reimbursements (averaging $17,600 per year) were awarded; career-related internships or fieldwork, institutionally sponsored loans, scholarships/grants, tuition waivers (full and partial), and unspecified assistantships also available. Financial award application deadline: 2/1. *Faculty research:* Computer networking, materials, computational mechanics and modeling, microelectronic technology, data mining. Total annual research expenditures: $24.4 million. *Unit head:* Dr. Joe Chow, Acting Dean, 518-276-6374, Fax: 518-276-6261, E-mail: chowj@rpi.edu. *Application contact:* James G. Nondorf, Vice President for Enrollment, 518-276-6216, Fax: 518-276-4072, E-mail: admissions@rpi.edu.

Rice University, Graduate Programs, George R. Brown School of Engineering, Houston, TX 77251-1892. Offers M Ch E, M Stat, MA, MBE, MCAM, MCE, MCS, MCSE, MEE, MEE, MES, MME, MMS, MS, PhD, MBA/M Stat, MBA/ME, MBA/MEE, MD/PhD. Part-time programs available. Terminal master's awarded for partial completion of doctoral program. *Degree requirements:* For master's, comprehensive exam (for some programs), thesis (for some programs); for doctorate, comprehensive exam (for some programs), thesis/dissertation. *Entrance requirements:* For master's and doctorate, GRE General Test. Additional exam requirements/recommendations for international students: Required—TOEFL (minimum score 600 paper-based; 250 computer-based). Electronic applications accepted. *Faculty research:* Digital signal processing, tissue engineering, groundwater remediation, computational engineering and high performance computing, nanoscale science and technology.

Robert Morris University, Graduate Studies, School of Engineering, Mathematics and Science, Moon Township, PA 15108-1189. Offers engineering management (MS). Part-time and evening/weekend programs available. *Faculty:* 3 full-time (0 women). *Students:* 36 part-time (3 women); includes 2 minority (1 African American, 1 American Indian/Alaska Native), 9 international. Average age 33. 11 applicants, 73% accepted, 7 enrolled. In 2009, 9 master's awarded.

Entrance requirements: For master's, letters of recommendation. Additional exam requirements/recommendations for international students: Required—TOEFL (minimum score 550 paper-based; 213 computer-based; 79 iBT). *Application deadline:* For fall admission, 7/1 priority date for domestic and international students; for spring admission, 11/1 priority date for domestic and international students. Applications are processed on a rolling basis. Application fee: $35. Electronic applications accepted. *Expenses:* Contact institution. *Financial support:* Federal Work-Study, institutionally sponsored loans, and unspecified assistantships available. Financial award application deadline: 5/1; financial award applicants required to submit FAFSA. *Unit head:* Dr. Joe Iannelli, Department Head, Engineering, 412-397-2514, Fax: 412-397-2593, E-mail: iannelli@rmu.edu. *Application contact:* Deborah Roach, Assistant Dean, Graduate Admissions, 412-397-5200, Fax: 412-397-2425, E-mail: graduateadmissions@rmu.edu.

Rochester Institute of Technology, Graduate Enrollment Services, College of Applied Science and Technology, Department of Electrical, Computer and Telecommunications Engineering Technology, Rochester, NY 14623-5603. Offers facility management (MS); manufacturing and mechanical systems integration (MS); telecommunications engineering technology (MS). Part-time and evening/weekend programs available. Postbaccalaureate distance learning degree programs offered (no on-campus study). *Students:* 59 full-time (21 women), 48 part-time (6 women); includes 5 minority (2 African Americans, 3 Hispanic Americans), 54 international. Average age 31. 154 applicants, 53% accepted, 33 enrolled. In 2009, 36 master's awarded. *Degree requirements:* For master's, thesis. *Entrance requirements:* For master's, GRE, minimum GPA of 3.0. Additional exam requirements/recommendations for international students: Required—TOEFL (minimum score 550 paper-based; 213 computer-based; 79 iBT), or IELTS (minimum score 6.5). *Application deadline:* For fall admission, 2/15 priority date for domestic and international students; for winter admission, 11/1 for domestic and international students; for spring admission, 2/1 for domestic and international students. Applications are processed on a rolling basis. Application fee: $50. *Expenses:* Tuition: Full-time $31,533; part-time $876 per credit hour. Required fees: $210. *Financial support:* In 2009–10, 84 students received support; research assistantships with partial tuition reimbursements available, teaching assistantships with partial tuition reimbursements available, career-related internships or fieldwork and unspecified assistantships available. Support available to part-time students. Financial award application deadline: 2/15; financial award applicants required to submit FAFSA. *Faculty research:* Fiber optic networks, next generation networks, project management. *Unit head:* Michael Eastman, Department Chair, 585-475-7787, Fax: 585-475-2178, E-mail: mgeiee@rit.edu. *Application contact:* Diane Ellison, Assistant Vice President, Graduate Enrollment Services, 585-475-2229, Fax: 585-475-7164, E-mail: gradinfo@rit.edu.

Rochester Institute of Technology, Graduate Enrollment Services, Kate Gleason College of Engineering, Rochester, NY 14623-5603. Offers ME, MS, MSEE, PhD, AC. Part-time and evening/weekend programs available. Postbaccalaureate distance learning degree programs offered (no on-campus study). *Students:* 305 full-time (62 women), 174 part-time (32 women); includes 41 minority (10 African Americans, 2 American Indian/Alaska Native, 17 Asian Americans or Pacific Islanders, 12 Hispanic Americans), 184 international. Average age 28. 802 applicants, 52% accepted, 168 enrolled. In 2009, 231 master's, 5 other advanced degrees awarded. Terminal master's awarded for partial completion of doctoral program. *Entrance requirements:* For master's, minimum GPA of 3.0. Additional exam requirements/recommendations for international students: Required—TOEFL (minimum score 570 paper-based; 230 computer-based; 88 iBT), or IELTS (minimum score 6.5). *Application deadline:* For fall admission, 2/15 priority date for domestic and international students. Applications are processed on a rolling basis. Application fee: $50. Electronic applications accepted. *Expenses:* Tuition: Full-time $31,533; part-time $876 per credit hour. Required fees: $210. *Financial support:* In 2009–10, 346 students received support; fellowships with partial tuition reimbursements available, research assistantships with partial tuition reimbursements available, teaching assistantships with partial tuition reimbursements available, career-related internships or fieldwork, institutionally sponsored loans, scholarships/grants, tuition waivers (partial), and unspecified assistantships available. Support available to part-time students. Financial award applicants required to submit FAFSA. *Faculty research:* Microprocessors, energy, communication systems. *Unit head:* Dr. Harvey Palmer, Dean, 585-475-2145, Fax: 585-475-6879, E-mail: coe@rit.edu. *Application contact:* Diane Ellison, Assistant Vice President, Graduate Enrollment Services, 585-475-2229, Fax: 585-475-7164, E-mail: gradinfo@rit.edu.

Rose-Hulman Institute of Technology, Faculty of Engineering and Applied Sciences, Terre Haute, IN 47803-3999. Offers M Eng, MS, MD/MS. Part-time and evening/weekend programs available. Postbaccalaureate distance learning degree programs offered (minimal on-campus study). *Faculty:* 91 full-time (20 women), 4 part-time/adjunct (1 woman). *Students:* 61 full-time (13 women), 59 part-time (12 women); includes 8 minority (1 African American, 5 Asian Americans or Pacific Islanders, 2 Hispanic Americans), 34 international. Average age 27. 91 applicants, 90% accepted, 50 enrolled. In 2009, 42 master's awarded. *Degree requirements:* For master's, thesis (for some programs). *Entrance requirements:* For master's, GRE, minimum GPA of 3.0. Additional exam requirements/recommendations for international students: Required—TOEFL (minimum score 580 paper-based; 237 computer-based). *Application deadline:* For fall admission, 2/1 priority date for domestic students. Applications are processed on a rolling basis. Application fee: $0. *Expenses:* Tuition: Full-time $33,900; part-time $987 per credit hour. *Financial support:* In 2009–10, 36 students received support; fellowships with full and partial tuition reimbursements available, research assistantships with full and partial tuition reimbursements available, institutionally sponsored loans, scholarships/grants, and tuition waivers (full and partial) available. *Faculty research:* Optical instrument design and prototypes, biomaterials, adsorption and adsorption-based separations, image and speech processing, groundwater, solid and hazardous waste. Total annual research expenditures: $2.8 million. *Unit head:* Dr. Daniel J. Moore, Associate Dean of the Faculty, 812-877-8110, Fax: 812-877-8061, E-mail: daniel.j.moore@rose-hulman.edu. *Application contact:* Dr. Daniel J. Moore, Associate Dean of the Faculty, 812-877-8110, Fax: 812-877-8061, E-mail: daniel.j.moore@rose-hulman.edu.

See Close-Up on page 81.

Rowan University, Graduate School, College of Engineering, Program in Engineering, Glassboro, NJ 08028-1701. Offers MS. Part-time and evening/weekend programs available. *Students:* 2 full-time (1 woman); both minorities (both Asian Americans or Pacific Islanders). Average age 24. 1 applicant, 100% accepted, 1 enrolled. *Degree requirements:* For master's, thesis (for some programs). *Entrance requirements:* For master's, GRE General Test. Additional exam requirements/recommendations for international students: Required—TOEFL. *Application deadline:* Applications are processed on a rolling basis. Application fee: $50. Electronic applications accepted. *Expenses:* Tuition, state resident: full-time $10,624; part-time $590 per semester hour. Tuition, nonresident: full-time $10,624; part-time $590 per semester hour. Required fees: $2320; $125 per semester hour. *Financial support:* Career-related internships or fieldwork, scholarships/grants, health care benefits, and unspecified assistantships available. *Unit head:* Dr. Mira Lalovic-Hand, Interim Associate Provost/Director of Graduate School, 856-256-5120, E-mail: lalovic-hand@rowan.edu. *Application contact:* Karen Haynes, Graduate Coordinator, 856-256-4052, E-mail: haynes@rowan.edu.

Royal Military College of Canada, Division of Graduate Studies and Research, Engineering Division, Kingston, ON K7K 7B4, Canada. Offers M Eng, M Sc, MA Sc, PhD. *Degree requirements:* For master's, thesis; for doctorate, comprehensive exam, thesis/dissertation. *Entrance requirements:* For master's, honours degree with second-class standing; for doctorate, master's degree. Electronic applications accepted.

St. Cloud State University, School of Graduate Studies, College of Science and Engineering, St. Cloud, MN 56301-4498. Offers MA, MEM, MS. *Faculty:* 85 full-time (19 women). *Students:* 100 full-time (25 women), 171 part-time (53 women); includes 22 minority (4 African Americans, 16 Asian Americans or Pacific Islanders, 2 Hispanic Americans), 171 international. 179 applicants, 66% accepted. In 2009, 31 master's awarded. *Degree requirements:* For master's, thesis or alternative. *Entrance requirements:* For master's, GRE General Test, minimum GPA of 2.75. Additional exam requirements/recommendations for international students: Required—TOEFL (minimum score 550 paper-based; 213 computer-based). Application fee: $35. Electronic applications accepted. *Financial support:* Federal Work-Study and unspecified assistantships available. Financial award application deadline: 3/1. *Unit head:* Dr. David DeGroote, Chairperson, 320-308-2036, Fax: 320-308-4166. *Application contact:* Linda Lou Krueger, School of Graduate Studies, 320-308-2113, Fax: 320-308-5371, E-mail: lekrueger@stcloudstate.edu.

St. Mary's University, Graduate School, Department of Engineering, San Antonio, TX 78228-8507. Offers electrical engineering (MS), including electrical engineering, electrical/computer engineering; engineering administration (MS); engineering systems management (MS); industrial engineering (MS), including engineering computer applications, engineering management, industrial engineering, operations research; software engineering (MS); JD/MS. Part-time programs available. *Degree requirements:* For master's, comprehensive exam. *Entrance requirements:* For master's, GRE General Test. Additional exam requirements/recommendations for international students: Required—TOEFL (minimum score 550 paper-based; 213 computer-based). Electronic applications accepted. *Expenses:* Tuition: Full-time $8004. Required fees: $536. One-time fee: $5 full-time. Full-time tuition and fees vary according to program. *Faculty research:* Image processing, control, communication, artificial intelligence, robotics.

San Diego State University, Graduate and Research Affairs, College of Engineering, San Diego, CA 92182. Offers MS, PhD. Part-time and evening/weekend programs available. Terminal master's awarded for partial completion of doctoral program. *Degree requirements:* For master's, thesis optional; for doctorate, thesis/dissertation. *Entrance requirements:* For master's, GRE General Test; for doctorate, GRE, 3 letters of recommendation. Additional exam requirements/recommendations for international students: Required—TOEFL. Electronic applications accepted.

San Francisco State University, Division of Graduate Studies, College of Science and Engineering, School of Engineering, San Francisco, CA 94132-1722. Offers embedded electrical and computer systems (MS); engineering (MS); structural/earthquake engineering (MS). Part-time programs available. Electronic applications accepted.

San Jose State University, Graduate Studies and Research, Charles W. Davidson College of Engineering, Department of General Engineering, San Jose, CA 95192-0001. Offers MS. *Students:* 71 full-time (40 women), 148 part-time (56 women); includes 64 minority (3 African Americans, 58 Asian Americans or Pacific Islanders, 3 Hispanic Americans), 127 international. Average age 28. 142 applicants, 51% accepted, 31 enrolled. In 2009, 97 master's awarded. *Application deadline:* For fall admission, 6/29 for domestic students; for spring admission, 11/30 for domestic students. Applications are processed on a rolling basis. Application fee: $59. Electronic applications accepted. *Financial support:* Applicants required to submit FAFSA. *Unit head:* Dr. Leonard Wesley, Graduate Advisor, 408-924-3968, Fax: 408-924-3818. *Application contact:* Dr. Leonard Wesley, Graduate Advisor, 408-924-3968, Fax: 408-924-3818.

Santa Clara University, School of Engineering, Santa Clara, CA 95053. Offers MS, MSE, PhD, Certificate, Engineer. Part-time and evening/weekend programs available. *Faculty:* 44 full-time (14 women), 59 part-time/adjunct (10 women). *Students:* 287 full-time (86 women), 497 part-time (109 women); includes 244 minority (13 African Americans, 1 American Indian/Alaska Native, 204 Asian Americans or Pacific Islanders, 26 Hispanic Americans), 301 international. Average age 29. 439 applicants, 75% accepted, 179 enrolled. In 2009, 154 master's, 3 doctorates awarded. *Degree requirements:* For master's, thesis (for some programs); for doctorate, thesis/dissertation; for other advanced degree, thesis. *Entrance requirements:* For master's, GRE (waiver may be available); for doctorate, GRE, master's degree or equivalent; for other advanced degree, master's degree, published paper. Additional exam requirements/recommendations for international students: Required—TOEFL (minimum score 550 paper-based; 213 computer-based; 79 iBT). *Application deadline:* For fall admission, 8/13 for domestic students, 7/16 for international students; for winter admission, 10/29 for domestic students, 9/24 for international students; for spring admission, 2/25 for domestic students, 1/21 for international students. Applications are processed on a rolling basis. Application fee: $60. *Expenses:* Contact institution. *Financial support:* Research assistantships, teaching assistantships available. Financial award application deadline: 3/2; financial award applicants required to submit FAFSA. *Faculty research:* Development of Small Satellite Design, Tests and Operations Technology, Thermal and Electrical Nanoscale Transport (TENT). Total annual research expenditures: $1.9 million. *Unit head:* Dr. Alex Zecevic, Associate Dean for Graduate Studies, 408-554-2394, E-mail: azecevic@scu.edu. *Application contact:* Stacey Tinker, Director of Enrollment Management, 408-554-4748, Fax: 408-554-4323, E-mail: stinker@scu.edu.

Seattle University, College of Science and Engineering, Seattle, WA 98122-1090. Offers MSE. Part-time and evening/weekend programs available. *Degree requirements:* For master's, thesis. *Entrance requirements:* For master's, GRE General Test, 2 years of related work experience. *Expenses:* Contact institution.

Simon Fraser University, Graduate Studies, Faculty of Applied Sciences, School of Engineering Science, Burnaby, BC V5A 1S6, Canada. Offers M Eng, MA Sc, PhD. *Degree requirements:* For master's, thesis (for some programs); for doctorate, thesis/dissertation, qualifying exam. *Entrance requirements:* For master's, GRE, minimum GPA of 3.0; for doctorate, GRE, minimum GPA of 3.5. Additional exam requirements/recommendations for international students: Required—TOEFL or IELTS. *Faculty research:* Signal processing, electronics, communications, systems and control.

South Dakota School of Mines and Technology, Graduate Division, College of Engineering, Rapid City, SD 57701-3995. Offers MS, PhD. Part-time programs available. *Faculty:* 59 full-time (4 women), 15 part-time/adjunct (4 women). *Students:* 16 full-time (4 women), 16 part-time (3 women). In 2009, 4 master's, 5 doctorates awarded. *Degree requirements:* For doctorate, thesis/dissertation. *Entrance requirements:* For doctorate, minimum graduate GPA of 3.0. Additional exam requirements/recommendations for international students: Required—TOEFL, TWE. *Application deadline:* For fall admission, 7/1 priority date for domestic students, 4/1 for international students; for spring admission, 11/1 for domestic students, 9/1 for international students. Applications are processed on a rolling basis. Application fee: $35. Electronic applications accepted. *Expenses:* Tuition, state resident: full-time $3340; part-time $139 per credit hour. Tuition, nonresident: full-time $7060; part-time $294 per credit hour. Required fees: $3270. *Financial support:* Fellowships, research assistantships, teaching assistantships, Federal Work-Study and institutionally sponsored loans available. Support available to part-time students. Financial award application deadline: 5/15. *Unit head:* Dr. Duane Abata, Dean, 605-394-5264, E-mail: duane.abata@sdsmt.edu. *Application contact:* Jeannette R. Nilson, Administrative Support Coordinator, Graduate Education, 800-454-8162 Ext. 1206, Fax: 605-394-5360, E-mail: graduate_admissions@sdsmt.edu.

South Dakota State University, Graduate School, College of Engineering, Brookings, SD 57007. Offers MS, PhD. Part-time programs available. *Degree requirements:* For master's, thesis, oral exam; for doctorate, thesis/dissertation, preliminary oral and written exams. *Entrance requirements:* Additional exam requirements/recommendations for international students: Required—TOEFL. *Faculty research:* Process control and management, ground source heat pumps, water quality, heat transfer, power systems.

Southern Illinois University Carbondale, Graduate School, College of Engineering, Carbondale, IL 62901-4701. Offers ME, MS, PhD. *Degree requirements:* For master's, comprehensive exam; for doctorate, thesis/dissertation. *Entrance requirements:* For master's, minimum GPA of 2.7; for doctorate, GRE General Test, minimum GPA of 3.5. Additional exam requirements/recommendations for international students: Required—TOEFL. *Faculty research:* Electrical systems, all facets of fossil energy, mechanics.

Southern Illinois University Edwardsville, Graduate Studies and Research, School of Engineering, Edwardsville, IL 62026-0001. Offers MS. Part-time programs available. *Faculty:* 46 full-time (4 women). *Students:* 78 full-time (16 women), 143 part-time (30 women); includes 7 minority (3 African Americans, 4 Asian Americans or Pacific Islanders), 126 international.

Engineering and Applied Sciences—General

Southern Illinois University Edwardsville (continued)
Average age 26. 447 applicants, 52% accepted. In 2009, 65 master's awarded. *Degree requirements:* For master's, thesis or research paper, final exam. *Entrance requirements:* For master's, GRE. Additional exam requirements/recommendations for international students: Required—TOEFL (minimum score 550 paper-based; 213 computer-based; 79 iBT), IELTS (minimum score 6.5). *Application deadline:* For fall admission, 7/23 for domestic students, 6/1 for international students; for spring admission, 12/11 for domestic students, 10/1 for international students. Applications are processed on a rolling basis. Application fee: $30. Electronic applications accepted. *Expenses:* Tuition, state resident: part-time $1252.50 per semester. Tuition, nonresident: part-time $3131.25 per semester. Required fees: $586.85 per semester. Tuition and fees vary according to course load. *Financial support:* In 2009–10, 4 fellowships with full tuition reimbursements (averaging $8,370 per year), 15 research assistantships with full tuition reimbursements (averaging $8,064 per year), 72 teaching assistantships with full tuition reimbursements (averaging $8,064 per year) were awarded; career-related internships or fieldwork, Federal Work-Study, institutionally sponsored loans, scholarships/grants, traineeships, and unspecified assistantships also available. Support available to part-time students. Financial award application deadline: 3/1; financial award applicants required to submit FAFSA. *Unit head:* Dr. Hasan Sevim, Dean, 618-650-2541, E-mail: hsevim@siue.edu. *Application contact:* Dr. Hasan Sevim, Dean, 618-650-2541, E-mail: hsevim@siue.edu.

Southern Methodist University, Bobby B. Lyle School of Engineering, Dallas, TX 75275. Offers MS, MS Cp E, MSEE, MSEM, MSIEM, MSME, DE, PhD. Part-time and evening/weekend programs available. Postbaccalaureate distance learning degree programs offered (no on-campus study). *Faculty:* 57 full-time (10 women), 63 part-time/adjunct (6 women). *Students:* 218 full-time (70 women), 659 part-time (136 women); includes 211 minority (65 African Americans, 3 American Indian/Alaska Native, 86 Asian Americans or Pacific Islanders, 57 Hispanic Americans), 216 international. Average age 32. 672 applicants, 54% accepted, 226 enrolled. In 2009, 265 master's, 18 doctorates awarded. Terminal master's awarded for partial completion of doctoral program. *Degree requirements:* For master's, thesis optional; for doctorate, thesis/dissertation, oral and written qualifying exams. *Entrance requirements:* For master's, GRE General Test, minimum GPA of 3.0 in last 2 years; bachelor's degree in engineering, mathematics, or sciences; for doctorate, bachelor's degree in related field. Additional exam requirements/recommendations for international students: Required—TOEFL (minimum score 550 paper-based; 213 computer-based). *Application deadline:* For fall admission, 7/1 for domestic students, 5/15 for international students; for spring admission, 11/15 for domestic students, 9/1 for international students. Applications are processed on a rolling basis. Application fee: $75. *Expenses:* Contact institution. *Financial support:* In 2009–10, 72 students received support, including 35 research assistantships with full tuition reimbursements available (averaging $16,800 per year), 33 teaching assistantships with full tuition reimbursements available (averaging $12,600 per year); fellowships, career-related internships or fieldwork, Federal Work-Study, institutionally sponsored loans, scholarships/grants, and tuition waivers (full and partial) also available. Financial award applicants required to submit FAFSA. *Faculty research:* Mobile and fault-tolerant computing, manufacturing systems, telecommunications, solid state devices and materials, fluid and thermal sciences. Total annual research expenditures: $3 million. *Unit head:* Dr. Geoffrey Orsak, Dean, 214-768-3050, Fax: 214-768-3845. *Application contact:* Marc Valerin, Director of Graduate and Executive Admissions, 214-768-3042, E-mail: valerin@engr.smu.edu.

Southern Polytechnic State University, Division of Engineering, Marietta, GA 30060-2896. Offers systems engineering (MS, Advanced Certificate, Graduate Certificate). Part-time and evening/weekend programs available. *Faculty:* 3 full-time (2 women), 2 part-time/adjunct (0 women). *Students:* 6 full-time (2 women), 44 part-time (10 women); includes 12 African Americans, 1 Asian American or Pacific Islander, 5 Hispanic Americans, 1 international. Average age 37. 24 applicants, 92% accepted, 18 enrolled. In 2009, 4 master's awarded. *Entrance requirements:* Additional exam requirements/recommendations for international students: Required—TOEFL (minimum score 550 paper-based; 213 computer-based; 79 iBT), IELTS (minimum score 6.5). *Application deadline:* For fall admission, 7/1 priority date for domestic students, 5/1 priority date for international students; for spring admission, 11/1 priority date for domestic students, 9/1 priority date for international students. Applications are processed on a rolling basis. Application fee: $20. Electronic applications accepted. *Expenses:* Tuition, state resident: full-time $2896; part-time $181 per credit hour. Tuition, nonresident: full-time $11,552; part-time $722 per credit hour. Required fees: $1096; $1096 per year. *Financial support:* In 2009–10, 6 students received support. *Unit head:* Dr. Tom Currin, Associate Dean, 678-915-7482, Fax: 678-915-5527, E-mail: tcurrin@spsu.edu. *Application contact:* Nikki Palamiotis, Director of Graduate Studies, 678-915-4276, Fax: 678-915-7292, E-mail: npalamio@spsu.edu.

Southern Polytechnic State University, School of Engineering Technology and Management, Marietta, GA 30060-2896. Offers MBA, MS, MSA, Graduate Certificate, Graduate Transition Certificate. Part-time and evening/weekend programs available. Postbaccalaureate distance learning degree programs offered. *Faculty:* 20 full-time (7 women), 10 part-time/adjunct (4 women). *Students:* 103 full-time (44 women), 169 part-time (58 women); includes 98 minority (66 African Americans, 1 American Indian/Alaska Native, 21 Asian Americans or Pacific Islanders, 10 Hispanic Americans), 75 international. Average age 34. 127 applicants, 92% accepted, 81 enrolled. In 2009, 79 master's awarded. *Entrance requirements:* For master's, GRE, GMAT. Additional exam requirements/recommendations for international students: Required—TOEFL (minimum score 550 paper-based; 213 computer-based; 79 iBT), IELTS (minimum score 6.5). *Application deadline:* For fall admission, 7/1 priority date for domestic students, 5/1 priority date for international students; for spring admission, 11/1 priority date for domestic students, 9/1 priority date for international students. Applications are processed on a rolling basis. Application fee: $20. Electronic applications accepted. *Expenses:* Tuition, state resident: full-time $2896; part-time $181 per credit hour. Tuition, nonresident: full-time $11,552; part-time $722 per credit hour. Required fees: $1096; $1096 per year. *Financial support:* In 2009–10, 42 students received support; research assistantships with tuition reimbursements available, teaching assistantships with tuition reimbursements available, career-related internships or fieldwork, scholarships/grants, and unspecified assistantships available. Support available to part-time students. Financial award application deadline: 5/1; financial award applicants required to submit FAFSA. *Faculty research:* Ethics, virtual reality, sustainability, management of technology, quality management, capacity planning, human-computer interaction/interface, enterprise integration planning, economic impact of educational institutions, behavioral accounting, accounting ethics, taxation, information security, visualizational simulation, human-computer interaction, analog and digital communications, computer networking, analog and low power electronics design, control systems and digital signal processing. *Unit head:* Dr. Jeff Ray, Dean, 678-915-7205, Fax: 678-915-7134, E-mail: jray@spsu.edu. *Application contact:* Nikki Palamiotis, Director of Graduate Studies, 678-915-4276, Fax: 678-915-7292, E-mail: npalamio@spsu.edu.

Southern University and Agricultural and Mechanical College, Graduate School, College of Engineering, Baton Rouge, LA 70813. Offers ME. *Degree requirements:* For master's, thesis. *Entrance requirements:* For master's, GRE General Test. Additional exam requirements/recommendations for international students: Required—TOEFL (minimum score 525 paper-based; 193 computer-based).

Stanford University, School of Engineering, Stanford, CA 94305-9991. Offers MS, PhD, Eng. *Degree requirements:* For doctorate, thesis/dissertation; for Eng, thesis. *Entrance requirements:* For master's, doctorate, and Eng, GRE General Test. Additional exam requirements/recommendations for international students: Required—TOEFL. Electronic applications accepted. *Expenses:* Contact institution.

State University of New York at Binghamton, Graduate School, Thomas J. Watson School of Engineering and Applied Science, Binghamton, NY 13902-6000. Offers M Eng, MS, MSAT, PhD. Part-time and evening/weekend programs available. *Faculty:* 50 full-time (6 women), 24 part-time/adjunct (6 women). *Students:* 359 full-time (71 women), 362 part-time (56 women); includes 64 minority (11 African Americans, 2 American Indian/Alaska Native, 37 Asian Americans or Pacific Islanders, 14 Hispanic Americans), 480 international. Average age 27. 865 applicants, 67% accepted, 191 enrolled. In 2009, 134 master's, 28 doctorates awarded. Terminal master's awarded for partial completion of doctoral program. *Degree requirements:* For doctorate, thesis/dissertation. *Entrance requirements:* For master's and doctorate, GRE General Test, GRE Subject Test. Additional exam requirements/recommendations for international students: Required—TOEFL (minimum score 550 paper-based; 213 computer-based; 80 iBT). *Application deadline:* Applications are processed on a rolling basis. Application fee: $60. Electronic applications accepted. *Financial support:* In 2009–10, 259 students received support, including 2 fellowships with full tuition reimbursements available (averaging $16,500 per year), 143 research assistantships with full tuition reimbursements available (averaging $16,500 per year), 81 teaching assistantships with full tuition reimbursements available (averaging $16,500 per year); career-related internships or fieldwork, Federal Work-Study, institutionally sponsored loans, scholarships/grants, health care benefits, tuition waivers (full and partial), and unspecified assistantships also available. Financial award application deadline: 2/15; financial award applicants required to submit FAFSA. *Unit head:* Dr. Hari Srihari, Dean, 607-777-2871, E-mail: hsrihari@binghamton.edu. *Application contact:* Victoria Williams, Recruiting and Admissions Coordinator, 607-777-2151, Fax: 607-777-2501, E-mail: vwilliam@binghamton.edu.

State University of New York Institute of Technology, School of Information Systems and Engineering Technology, Utica, NY 13504-3050. Offers advanced technology (MS); computer and information science (MS); telecommunications (MS). Part-time and evening/weekend programs available. *Entrance requirements:* For master's, GRE General Test, minimum GPA of 3.0. Additional exam requirements/recommendations for international students: Required—TOEFL (minimum score 550 paper-based; 213 computer-based). *Faculty research:* Systems security, operating systems, traffic management, nanotechnology, rehabilitation technology.

Stevens Institute of Technology, Graduate School, Charles V. Schaefer Jr. School of Engineering, Hoboken, NJ 07030. Offers M Eng, MS, PhD, Certificate, Engr. Part-time and evening/weekend programs available. Postbaccalaureate distance learning degree programs offered. Terminal master's awarded for partial completion of doctoral program. *Degree requirements:* For doctorate, thesis/dissertation. *Entrance requirements:* Additional exam requirements/recommendations for international students: Required—TOEFL. Electronic applications accepted. *Expenses:* Tuition: Full-time $9900; part-time $1100 per credit. Required fees: $286 per semester.

Stony Brook University, State University of New York, Graduate School, College of Engineering and Applied Sciences, Stony Brook, NY 11794. Offers MS, PhD, Advanced Certificate, Certificate. Part-time and evening/weekend programs available. *Faculty:* 140 full-time (26 women), 20 part-time/adjunct (2 women). *Students:* 735 full-time (213 women), 223 part-time (74 women); includes 102 minority (17 African Americans, 71 Asian Americans or Pacific Islanders, 14 Hispanic Americans), 665 international. 2,318 applicants, 36% accepted. In 2009, 250 master's, 82 doctorates awarded. *Degree requirements:* For doctorate, comprehensive exam, thesis/dissertation. *Entrance requirements:* For doctorate, GRE General Test. Additional exam requirements/recommendations for international students: Required—TOEFL. *Application deadline:* For fall admission, 1/15 for domestic students. Application fee: $60. *Expenses:* Tuition, state resident: full-time $8370; part-time $349 per credit. Tuition, nonresident: full-time $13,250; part-time $552 per credit. Required fees: $933. *Financial support:* In 2009–10, 211 research assistantships, 139 teaching assistantships were awarded; fellowships, career-related internships or fieldwork also available. Total annual research expenditures: $25.7 million. *Unit head:* Dr. Yacov Shamash, Dean, 631-632-8380. *Application contact:* Dr. Kent Marks, Assistant Dean, Admissions and Records, 631-632-4723, Fax: 631-632-7243, E-mail: kmarks@notes.cc.sunysb.edu.

Syracuse University, L. C. Smith College of Engineering and Computer Science, Syracuse, NY 13244. Offers ME, MS, PhD, CAS, CE, EE. Part-time and evening/weekend programs available. *Faculty:* 66 full-time (6 women), 19 part-time/adjunct (1 woman). *Students:* 550 full-time (139 women), 162 part-time (20 women); includes 28 minority (7 African Americans, 19 Asian Americans or Pacific Islanders, 2 Hispanic Americans), 453 international. Average age 26. 1,472 applicants, 49% accepted, 215 enrolled. In 2009, 297 master's, 22 doctorates, 4 other advanced degrees awarded. *Degree requirements:* For doctorate, thesis/dissertation. *Entrance requirements:* For master's and doctorate, GRE General Test. Additional exam requirements/recommendations for international students: Required—TOEFL (minimum score 100 iBT). *Application deadline:* For fall admission, 6/1 priority date for domestic and international students. Applications are processed on a rolling basis. Application fee: $75. Electronic applications accepted. *Expenses:* Tuition: Full-time $26,808; part-time $1117 per credit. Required fees: $1024. *Financial support:* Fellowships with full and partial tuition reimbursements, research assistantships with full and partial tuition reimbursements, teaching assistantships with full and partial tuition reimbursements, scholarships/grants and tuition waivers (full and partial) available. Financial award application deadline: 1/1; financial award applicants required to submit FAFSA. *Faculty research:* Environmental systems, information assurance, biomechanics, solid mechanics and materials, software engineering. *Unit head:* Dr. Laura J. Steinberg, Dean, 315-443-2545, E-mail: ljs@syr.edu. *Application contact:* Kathleen Joyce, Director of Graduate Recruitment, 314-443-2219, E-mail: topgrads@syr.edu.

See Close-Up on page 83.

Temple University, Graduate School, College of Engineering, Philadelphia, PA 19122-6096. Offers MS, MSE, PhD. Part-time programs available. *Degree requirements:* For master's, thesis optional; for doctorate, comprehensive exam, thesis/dissertation, 2 published papers. *Entrance requirements:* For master's, GRE General Test, minimum undergraduate GPA of 3.0; for doctorate, GRE General Test, minimum graduate GPA of 3.5, MS. Additional exam requirements/recommendations for international students: Required—TOEFL (minimum score 550 paper-based; 213 computer-based; 79 iBT). Electronic applications accepted. *Faculty research:* Computer engineering, digital systems, bioengineering, transportation, materials.

Tennessee State University, The School of Graduate Studies and Research, College of Engineering, Technology, and Computer Science, Nashville, TN 37209-1561. Offers computer and information systems engineering (MS, PhD); engineering (ME). Part-time and evening/weekend programs available. *Degree requirements:* For master's, project; for doctorate, comprehensive exam, thesis/dissertation. *Entrance requirements:* For doctorate, minimum GPA of 3.3. *Faculty research:* Robotics, intelligent systems, human-computer interaction software systems, biomedical engineering, signal/image processing, probabilistic design, intelligent manufacturing, cooperative mobile robots, condition based maintenance, sensor fusion.

Tennessee Technological University, Graduate School, College of Engineering, Cookeville, TN 38505. Offers MS, PhD. Part-time programs available. *Faculty:* 76 full-time (2 women). *Students:* 102 full-time (19 women), 40 part-time (9 women); includes 86 minority (16 African Americans, 69 Asian Americans or Pacific Islanders, 1 Hispanic American). Average age 28. 255 applicants, 53% accepted, 41 enrolled. In 2009, 43 master's, 10 doctorates awarded. *Degree requirements:* For master's, comprehensive exam, thesis; for doctorate, comprehensive exam, thesis/dissertation. *Entrance requirements:* For master's, GRE General Test; for doctorate, GRE, minimum GPA of 3.5. Additional exam requirements/recommendations for international students: Required—TOEFL (minimum score 550 paper-based; 79 iBT), IELTS (minimum score 5.5). *Application deadline:* For fall admission, 8/1 for domestic students, 5/1 for international students; for spring admission, 12/1 for domestic students, 10/1 for international students. Application fee: $25 ($30 for international students). Electronic applications accepted. *Expenses:* Tuition, state resident: full-time $7034; part-time $368 per credit hour. *Financial support:* In 2009–10, 3 fellowships (averaging $8,000 per year), 71 research assistantships (averaging $9,293 per year), 41 teaching assistantships (averaging $7,223 per year) were awarded; career-related internships or fieldwork also available. Support available to part-time students. Financial award application deadline: 4/1. *Unit head:* Dr. David Huddleston, Interim

Dean. *Application contact:* Shelia K. Kendrick, Coordinator of Graduate Studies, 931-372-3808, Fax: 931-372-3497, E-mail: skendrick@tntech.edu.

Texas A&M University, College of Engineering, College Station, TX 77843. Offers M En, M Eng, MCS, MID, MS, D Eng, PhD. Part-time programs available. Postbaccalaureate distance learning degree programs offered (minimal on-campus study). *Faculty:* 372. *Students:* 2,520 full-time (498 women), 333 part-time (67 women); includes 243 minority (48 African Americans, 5 American Indian/Alaska Native, 82 Asian Americans or Pacific Islanders, 108 Hispanic Americans), 1,914 international. In 2009, 540 master's, 178 doctorates awarded. Terminal master's awarded for partial completion of doctoral program. *Entrance requirements:* For master's and doctorate, GRE General Test. Additional exam requirements/recommendations for international students: Required—TOEFL. Application fee: $50 ($75 for international students). Electronic applications accepted. *Expenses:* Tuition, state resident: full-time $3991.32; part-time $221.74 per credit hour. Tuition, nonresident: full-time $9049; part-time $502.74 per credit hour. *Financial support:* Fellowships, research assistantships, teaching assistantships, career-related internships or fieldwork, institutionally sponsored loans, scholarships/grants, and unspecified assistantships available. Financial award applicants required to submit FAFSA. *Unit head:* Dr. G. Kemble Bennett, Dean, 979-845-7203, Fax: 979-845-8986, E-mail: kem-bennett@tamu.edu. *Application contact:* Karen Butler-Purry, Assistant Dean, 979-845-7200, Fax: 979-847-8654, E-mail: eapo@tamu.edu.

Texas A&M University–Kingsville, College of Graduate Studies, College of Engineering, Kingsville, TX 78363. Offers ME, MS, PhD. Part-time and evening/weekend programs available. *Degree requirements:* For master's, comprehensive exam. *Entrance requirements:* For master's, GRE General Test. Additional exam requirements/recommendations for international students: Required—TOEFL.

Texas Tech University, Graduate School, College of Engineering, Lubbock, TX 79409. Offers M Engr, MENVEGR, MS, MS Ch E, MSCE, MSEE, MSETM, MSIE, MSME, MSMSE, MSPE, MSSEM, PhD. *Accreditation:* ABET. Part-time programs available. *Faculty:* 100 full-time (18 women), 5 part-time/adjunct (0 women). *Students:* 523 full-time (118 women), 187 part-time (30 women); includes 29 minority (9 African Americans, 5 Asian Americans or Pacific Islanders, 15 Hispanic Americans), 490 international. Average age 27. 1,818 applicants, 37% accepted, 162 enrolled. In 2009, 171 master's, 31 doctorates awarded. *Degree requirements:* For master's, thesis (for some programs); for doctorate, thesis/dissertation. *Entrance requirements:* For master's and doctorate, GRE General Test, minimum GPA of 3.0. Additional exam requirements/recommendations for international students: Required—TOEFL (minimum score 550 paper-based; 213 computer-based). *Application deadline:* For fall admission, 3/1 priority date for international students; for spring admission, 11/1 priority date for international students. Applications are processed on a rolling basis. Application fee: $50 ($75 for international students). Electronic applications accepted. *Expenses:* Contact institution. *Financial support:* In 2009–10, 152 research assistantships with partial tuition reimbursements (averaging $22,650 per year), 76 teaching assistantships with partial tuition reimbursements (averaging $12,388 per year) were awarded; career-related internships or fieldwork, Federal Work-Study, and institutionally sponsored loans also available. Support available to part-time students. Financial award application deadline: 4/15; financial award applicants required to submit FAFSA. *Faculty research:* Pulsed power and power electronics; water resources; energy (wind, star, petroleum, etc.); nanophotonics and nanotechnology. Total annual research expenditures: $17.1 million. *Unit head:* Dr. Jon C. Strauss, Interim Dean, 806-742-3451, Fax: 806-742-3493. *Application contact:* Dr. John E. Kobza, Senior Associate Dean, 806-742-3451, Fax: 806-742-3493, E-mail: john.kobza@ttu.edu.

Trine University, Allen School of Engineering and Technology, Angola, IN 46703-1764. Offers civil engineering (ME); mechanical engineering (ME). Part-time and evening/weekend programs available. *Degree requirements:* For master's, comprehensive exam, thesis. *Faculty research:* CAD, computer aided MFG, computer numerical control, parametric modeling, megatronics.

Tufts University, School of Engineering, Medford, MA 02155. Offers ME, MS, MSEM, PhD. Part-time programs available. *Faculty:* 74 full-time, 22 part-time/adjunct. *Students:* 481 (145 women); includes 43 minority (6 African Americans, 34 Asian Americans or Pacific Islanders, 3 Hispanic Americans), 112 international. 735 applicants, 51% accepted, 156 enrolled. In 2009, 174 master's, 21 doctorates awarded. Terminal master's awarded for partial completion of doctoral program. *Degree requirements:* For master's, thesis (for some programs); for doctorate, thesis/dissertation. *Entrance requirements:* For master's and doctorate, GRE General Test. Additional exam requirements/recommendations for international students: Required—TOEFL (minimum score 550 paper-based; 213 computer-based; 80 iBT). *Application deadline:* For fall admission, 1/15 priority date for domestic students, 12/15 for international students; for spring admission, 10/15 for domestic students, 9/15 for international students. Applications are processed on a rolling basis. Application fee: $75. Electronic applications accepted. *Expenses:* Tuition: Full-time $38,096; part-time $3962 per credit. Required fees: $686; $40 per year. Tuition and fees vary according to course level, course load, degree level, program and student level. *Financial support:* Fellowships with full tuition reimbursements, research assistantships with full and partial tuition reimbursements, teaching assistantships with full and partial tuition reimbursements, Federal Work-Study, scholarships/grants, tuition waivers (partial), and unspecified assistantships available. Financial award application deadline: 1/15; financial award applicants required to submit FAFSA. *Unit head:* Linda Abriola, Dean, 617-627-3237, Fax: 617-627-3819. *Application contact:* Linda Abriola, Dean, 617-627-3237, Fax: 617-627-3819.

Tuskegee University, Graduate Programs, College of Engineering, Architecture and Physical Sciences, Tuskegee, AL 36088. Offers MSEE, MSME, PhD. *Faculty:* 19 full-time (0 women). *Students:* 67 full-time (22 women), 4 part-time (0 women); includes 32 minority (30 African Americans, 1 Asian American or Pacific Islander, 1 Hispanic American), 31 international. Average age 28. 104 applicants, 59% accepted. In 2009, 15 master's awarded. *Degree requirements:* For master's, thesis or alternative. *Entrance requirements:* For master's, GRE General Test, GRE Subject Test. Additional exam requirements/recommendations for international students: Required—TOEFL (minimum score 500 paper-based; 69 computer-based). *Application deadline:* For fall admission, 7/15 for domestic students. Applications are processed on a rolling basis. Application fee: $25 ($35 for international students). *Expenses:* Tuition: Full-time $15,630; part-time $940 per credit hour. Required fees: $650. *Financial support:* Fellowships, research assistantships, teaching assistantships, career-related internships or fieldwork, Federal Work-Study, and institutionally sponsored loans available. Support available to part-time students. Financial award application deadline: 4/15. *Unit head:* Dr. Legand L. Burge, Acting Dean, 334-727-8356. *Application contact:* Dr. Robert L. Laney, Vice President/Director of Admissions and Enrollment Management, 334-727-8580, Fax: 334-727-5750, E-mail: planey@tuskegee.edu.

Union Graduate College, School of Engineering and Computer Science, Schenectady, NY 12308-3107. Offers computer science (MS); electrical engineering (MS); engineering and management systems (MS); mechanical engineering (MS). Part-time and evening/weekend programs available. *Faculty:* 24 part-time/adjunct (1 woman). *Students:* 10 full-time (0 women), 60 part-time (7 women); includes 5 minority (1 African American, 1 American Indian/Alaska Native, 2 Asian Americans or Pacific Islanders, 1 Hispanic American), 5 international. Average age 27. 47 applicants, 55% accepted, 25 enrolled. In 2009, 28 master's awarded. *Degree requirements:* For master's, capstone course. *Entrance requirements:* For master's, minimum GPA of 3.0, letters of recommendation. Additional exam requirements/recommendations for international students: Required—TOEFL (minimum score 550 paper-based; 213 computer-based). *Application deadline:* Applications are processed on a rolling basis. Application fee: $60. Electronic applications accepted. *Expenses:* Contact institution. *Financial support:* Research assistantships, Federal Work-Study, scholarships/grants, health care benefits, and tuition waivers (full and partial) available. Support available to part-time students. Financial award applicants required to submit FAFSA. *Unit head:* Robert Kozik, Dean, 515-631-9881, Fax: 518-631-9902, E-mail: kozikr@union.edu. *Application contact:* Diane Trzaskos, Coordinator, Admissions, 518-631-9837, Fax: 518-631-9901, E-mail: trzaskod@uniongraduatecollege.edu.

Universidad de las Américas–Puebla, Division of Graduate Studies, School of Engineering, Puebla, Mexico. Offers M Adm, MS, PhD. Part-time and evening/weekend programs available. *Degree requirements:* For master's, one foreign language, thesis. *Faculty research:* Artificial intelligence, food technology, construction, telecommunications, computers in education, operations research.

Université de Moncton, Faculty of Engineering, Moncton, NB E1A 3E9, Canada. Offers civil engineering (M Sc A); electrical engineering (M Sc A); industrial engineering (M Sc A); mechanical engineering (M Sc A). *Degree requirements:* For master's, thesis, proficiency in French. *Faculty research:* Structures, energy, composite materials, quality control, geo-environment, telecommunications, instrumentation, analog and digital electronics.

Université de Sherbrooke, Faculty of Engineering, Sherbrooke, QC J1K 2R1, Canada. Offers M Eng, M Env, M Sc A, PhD, Diploma. Part-time programs available. *Degree requirements:* For master's, one foreign language, thesis; for doctorate, comprehensive exam, thesis/dissertation. *Entrance requirements:* For master's, bachelor's degree in engineering or equivalent. Electronic applications accepted.

Université du Québec à Chicoutimi, Graduate Programs, Program in Engineering, Chicoutimi, QC G7H 2B1, Canada. Offers M Sc A, PhD. Part-time programs available. *Degree requirements:* For master's, thesis; for doctorate, thesis/dissertation. *Entrance requirements:* For master's, appropriate bachelor's degree, proficiency in French.

Université du Québec à Rimouski, Graduate Programs, Program in Engineering, Rimouski, QC G5L 3A1, Canada. Offers M Sc A.

Université du Québec, École de technologie supérieure, Graduate Programs, Montréal, QC H3C 1K3, Canada. Offers M Eng, PhD, Diploma. Postbaccalaureate distance learning degree programs offered (minimal on-campus study). *Entrance requirements:* For master's and Diploma, appropriate bachelor's degree, proficiency in French; for doctorate, appropriate master's degree, proficiency in French.

Université du Québec en Abitibi-Témiscamingue, Graduate Programs, Program in Engineering, Rouyn-Noranda, QC J9X 5E4, Canada. Offers engineering (ME); mineral engineering (ME); mining engineering (DESS).

Université Laval, Faculty of Sciences and Engineering, Québec, QC G1K 7P4, Canada. Offers M Sc, PhD, Diploma. Part-time programs available. *Degree requirements:* For doctorate, thesis/dissertation. Electronic applications accepted.

University at Buffalo, the State University of New York, Graduate School, School of Engineering and Applied Sciences, Buffalo, NY 14260. Offers M Eng, MS, PhD. Part-time and evening/weekend programs available. Postbaccalaureate distance learning degree programs offered (minimal on-campus study). *Faculty:* 143 full-time (19 women), 21 part-time/adjunct (4 women). *Students:* 1,091 full-time (217 women), 154 part-time (23 women); includes 57 minority (13 African Americans, 1 American Indian/Alaska Native, 31 Asian Americans or Pacific Islanders, 12 Hispanic Americans), 905 international. Average age 27. 4,903 applicants, 29% accepted, 477 enrolled. In 2009, 277 master's, 56 doctorates awarded. Terminal master's awarded for partial completion of doctoral program. *Degree requirements:* For doctorate, thesis/dissertation. *Entrance requirements:* For master's and doctorate, GRE General Test. Additional exam requirements/recommendations for international students: Required—TOEFL (minimum score 550 paper-based; 217 computer-based; 79 iBT). *Application deadline:* Applications are processed on a rolling basis. Application fee: $50. Electronic applications accepted. *Financial support:* In 2009–10, 61 fellowships with full tuition reimbursements (averaging $28,908 per year), 201 research assistantships with full and partial tuition reimbursements (averaging $21,300 per year), 149 teaching assistantships with full tuition reimbursements (averaging $20,900 per year) were awarded; career-related internships or fieldwork, Federal Work-Study, institutionally sponsored loans, scholarships/grants, tuition waivers (full and partial), and unspecified assistantships also available. Support available to part-time students. Financial award applicants required to submit FAFSA. *Faculty research:* Bioengineering, infrastructure and environmental engineering, electronic and photonic materials, simulation and visualization, information technology and computing. Total annual research expenditures: $54.8 million. *Unit head:* Dr. Harvey G. Stenger, Dean, 716-645-2771, Fax: 716-645-2495, E-mail: dean@.buffalo.edu. *Application contact:* Dr. Rajan Batta, Associate Dean for Graduate Education, 716-645-2772, Fax: 716-645-2495, E-mail: batta@buffalo.edu.

See Close-Up on page 85.

The University of Akron, Graduate School, College of Engineering, Akron, OH 44325. Offers MS, PhD, MD/PhD. Part-time and evening/weekend programs available. *Faculty:* 96 full-time (11 women), 16 part-time/adjunct (0 women). *Students:* 237 full-time (57 women), 80 part-time (16 women); includes 13 minority (4 African Americans, 8 Asian Americans or Pacific Islanders, 1 Hispanic American), 181 international. Average age 27. 412 applicants, 43% accepted, 74 enrolled. In 2009, 40 master's, 23 doctorates awarded. Terminal master's awarded for partial completion of doctoral program. *Degree requirements:* For master's, thesis optional; for doctorate, one foreign language, thesis/dissertation, candidacy exam, qualifying exam. *Entrance requirements:* For master's, GRE, minimum GPA of 2.75, letters of recommendation, resume; for doctorate, GRE, minimum GPA of 3.0 with bachelor's degree, 3.5 with master's degree; letters of recommendation; personal statement, resume. Additional exam requirements/recommendations for international students: Required—TOEFL (minimum score 550 paper-based; 213 computer-based; 79 iBT). *Application deadline:* Applications are processed on a rolling basis. Application fee: $30 ($40 for international students). Electronic applications accepted. *Expenses:* Tuition, state resident: full-time $6570; part-time $365 per credit hour. Tuition, nonresident: full-time $11,250; part-time $625 per credit hour. *Financial support:* In 2009–10, 4 fellowships with full tuition reimbursements, 46 research assistantships with full tuition reimbursements, 139 teaching assistantships with full tuition reimbursements were awarded; career-related internships or fieldwork and Federal Work-Study also available. *Faculty research:* Engineering materials, energy research, NEMS and MEMS, bio-engineering, computational methods. Total annual research expenditures: $6.3 million. *Unit head:* Dr. George Haritos, Dean, 330-972-6978, E-mail: haritos@uakron.edu. *Application contact:* Dr. Craig Menzemer, Director of Graduate Studies, 330-972-5536, E-mail: ccmenze@uakron.edu.

The University of Alabama, Graduate School, College of Engineering, Tuscaloosa, AL 35487. Offers MAE, MES, MS, MS Ch E, MS Met E, MSCE, PhD. Part-time programs available. Postbaccalaureate distance learning degree programs offered (no on-campus study). *Faculty:* 96 full-time (13 women). *Students:* 255 full-time (45 women), 50 part-time (13 women); includes 25 minority (16 African Americans, 1 American Indian/Alaska Native, 6 Asian Americans or Pacific Islanders, 2 Hispanic Americans), 159 international. Average age 30. 450 applicants, 33% accepted, 90 enrolled. In 2009, 62 master's, 11 doctorates awarded. Terminal master's awarded for partial completion of doctoral program. *Median time to degree:* Of those who began their doctoral program in fall 2001, 58% received their degree in 8 years or less. *Degree requirements:* For master's, comprehensive exam; for doctorate, thesis/dissertation. *Entrance requirements:* For master's and doctorate, minimum GPA of 3.0. Additional exam requirements/recommendations for international students: Required—TOEFL (minimum score 550 paper-based; 213 computer-based). *Application deadline:* For fall admission, 7/1 for domestic students, 4/15 for international students; for spring admission, 11/15 for domestic students, 9/1 for international students. Applications are processed on a rolling basis. Application fee: $50 ($60 for international students). Electronic applications accepted. *Expenses:* Tuition, state resident: full-time $7000. Tuition, nonresident: full-time $19,200. *Financial support:* In 2009–10, 188 students received support, including 23 fellowships with full tuition reimbursements available (averaging $16,022 per year), 85 research assistantships with full tuition reimbursements available (averaging $16,022 per year), 73 teaching assistantships with full tuition reimburse-

Engineering and Applied Sciences—General

The University of Alabama (continued)

ments available (averaging $16,022 per year); career-related internships or fieldwork, Federal Work-Study, and institutionally sponsored loans also available. Financial award application deadline: 2/15. *Faculty research:* Materials and biomaterials networks and sensors, transportation, energy. Total annual research expenditures: $14.2 million. *Unit head:* Dr. Charles Karr, Dean, 205-348-6405, Fax: 205-348-8573. *Application contact:* Dr. David A. Francko, Dean, 205-348-8280, Fax: 205-348-0400, E-mail: dfrancko@ua.edu.

The University of Alabama at Birmingham, School of Engineering, Birmingham, AL 35294. Offers MS Mt E, MSBME, MSCE, MSEE, MSME, PhD. Evening/weekend programs available. *Degree requirements:* For doctorate, thesis/dissertation. *Entrance requirements:* For master's, GRE General Test. Electronic applications accepted.

The University of Alabama in Huntsville, School of Graduate Studies, College of Engineering, Huntsville, AL 35899. Offers MSE, MSOR, MSSE, PhD. Part-time and evening/weekend programs available. Postbaccalaureate distance learning degree programs offered (minimal on-campus study). *Faculty:* 57 full-time (8 women), 6 part-time/adjunct (0 women). *Students:* 107 full-time (21 women), 414 part-time (73 women); includes 49 minority (28 African Americans, 2 American Indian/Alaska Native, 10 Asian Americans or Pacific Islanders, 9 Hispanic Americans), 63 international. Average age 32. 440 applicants, 57% accepted, 147 enrolled. In 2009, 132 master's, 16 doctorates awarded. *Degree requirements:* For master's, comprehensive exam, thesis or alternative, oral and written exams; for doctorate, comprehensive exam, thesis/dissertation, oral and written exams. *Entrance requirements:* For master's and doctorate, GRE General Test, minimum GPA of 3.0. Additional exam requirements/recommendations for international students: Required—TOEFL (minimum score 500 paper-based; 173 computer-based; 62 iBT). *Application deadline:* For fall admission, 7/15 for domestic students, 4/1 for international students; for spring admission, 11/30 for domestic students, 9/1 for international students. Applications are processed on a rolling basis. Application fee: $40 ($50 for international students). Electronic applications accepted. *Expenses:* Tuition, state resident: part-time $355.75 per credit hour. Tuition, nonresident: part-time $847.10 per credit hour. Required fees: $210.80 per semester. Tuition and fees vary according to course load and program. *Financial support:* In 2009–10, 74 students received support, including 30 research assistantships with full and partial tuition reimbursements available (averaging $12,100 per year), 43 teaching assistantships with full and partial tuition reimbursements available (averaging $10,488 per year); career-related internships or fieldwork, Federal Work-Study, institutionally sponsored loans, scholarships/grants, health care benefits, tuition waivers, and unspecified assistantships also available. Support available to part-time students. Financial award application deadline: 4/1; financial award applicants required to submit FAFSA. *Faculty research:* Propulsion, missile systems, automation, robotics, plasma. Total annual research expenditures: $29.4 million. *Unit head:* Dr. Phillip Farrington, Acting Dean, 256-824-6474, Fax: 256-824-6843, E-mail: phillip.farrington@uah.edu. *Application contact:* Kathy Biggs, Graduate Studies Admissions Manager, 256-824-6199, Fax: 256-824-6405, E-mail: deangrad@uah.edu.

University of Alaska Anchorage, School of Engineering, Anchorage, AK 99508. Offers M AEST, MCE, MS, Certificate. Part-time and evening/weekend programs available. *Degree requirements:* For master's, comprehensive exam (for some programs), thesis (for some programs). *Entrance requirements:* For master's, GRE General Test. Additional exam requirements/recommendations for international students: Required—TOEFL (minimum score 550 paper-based; 213 computer-based).

University of Alaska Fairbanks, College of Engineering and Mines, Department of Civil and Environmental Engineering, Program in Environmental Engineering, Fairbanks, AK 99775-5900. Offers engineering (PhD), including environmental engineering; environmental engineering (MS), including environmental contaminants, environmental science and management, water supply and waste treatment. Part-time programs available. *Students:* 4 full-time (3 women), 3 part-time (2 women). Average age 28. 5 applicants, 60% accepted, 1 enrolled. In 2009, 3 master's, 1 doctorate awarded. *Degree requirements:* For master's, comprehensive exam, thesis or alternative; for doctorate, comprehensive exam, thesis/dissertation, oral exam, oral defense. *Entrance requirements:* For master's, basic computer techniques; for doctorate, GRE General Test. Additional exam requirements/recommendations for international students: Required—TOEFL (minimum score 575 paper-based; 213 computer-based). *Application deadline:* For fall admission, 5/1 for domestic students, 3/1 for international students; for spring admission, 10/15 for domestic students, 9/1 for international students. Applications are processed on a rolling basis. Application fee: $60. Electronic applications accepted. *Expenses:* Tuition, state resident: full-time $7584; part-time $316 per credit. Tuition, nonresident: full-time $15,504; part-time $646 per credit. Required fees: $23 per credit. $135 per semester. Tuition and fees vary according to course level, course load and reciprocity agreements. *Financial support:* In 2009–10, 4 research assistantships (averaging $13,290 per year), 1 teaching assistantship (averaging $7,088 per year) were awarded; fellowships, career-related internships or fieldwork, Federal Work-Study, scholarships/grants, health care benefits, and unspecified assistantships also available. Support available to part-time students. Financial award application deadline: 7/1; financial award applicants required to submit FAFSA. *Unit head:* Dr. David Barnes, Department Chair, 907-474-7241, Fax: 907-474-6087, E-mail: fyeqe@uaf.edu. *Application contact:* Dr. David Barnes, Department Chair, 907-474-7241, Fax: 907-474-6087, E-mail: fyeqe@uaf.edu.

University of Alaska Fairbanks, College of Engineering and Mines, Department of Electrical and Computer Engineering, Fairbanks, AK 99775-5915. Offers electrical engineering (MEE, MS, PhD); engineering (PhD). Part-time programs available. *Faculty:* 7 full-time (2 women). *Students:* 14 full-time (3 women), 2 part-time (1 woman), 10 international. Average age 29. 11 applicants, 36% accepted, 4 enrolled. In 2009, 5 master's awarded. Terminal master's awarded for partial completion of doctoral program. *Degree requirements:* For master's, comprehensive exam, thesis or alternative; for doctorate, comprehensive exam, thesis/dissertation, oral exam, oral defense. *Entrance requirements:* For master's and doctorate, GRE General Test. Additional exam requirements/recommendations for international students: Required—TOEFL (minimum score 550 paper-based; 213 computer-based; 80 iBT). *Application deadline:* For fall admission, 6/1 for domestic students, 3/1 for international students; for spring admission, 10/15 for domestic students, 9/1 for international students. Applications are processed on a rolling basis. Application fee: $60. Electronic applications accepted. *Expenses:* Tuition, state resident: full-time $7584; part-time $316 per credit. Tuition, nonresident: full-time $15,504; part-time $646 per credit. Required fees: $23 per credit. $135 per semester. Tuition and fees vary according to course level, course load and reciprocity agreements. *Financial support:* In 2009–10, 2 fellowships (averaging $6,749 per year), 6 research assistantships (averaging $15,656 per year), 2 teaching assistantships (averaging $8,087 per year) were awarded; career-related internships or fieldwork, Federal Work-Study, scholarships/grants, health care benefits, and unspecified assistantships also available. Support available to part-time students. Financial award application deadline: 7/1; financial award applicants required to submit FAFSA. *Faculty research:* Geomagnetically-induced currents in power lines, electromagnetic wave propagation, laser radar systems, bioinformatics, distributed sensor networks. *Unit head:* Dr. Charles Mayer, Chair, 907-474-7137, Fax: 907-474-5135, E-mail: fyee@uaf.edu. *Application contact:* Dr. Charles Mayer, Chair, 907-474-7137, Fax: 907-474-5135, E-mail: fyee@uaf.edu.

University of Alaska Fairbanks, College of Engineering and Mines, Department of Mechanical Engineering, Fairbanks, AK 99775-5905. Offers engineering (PhD); mechanical engineering (MS). Part-time programs available. *Faculty:* 9 full-time (0 women), 1 part-time/adjunct (0 women). *Students:* 9 full-time (3 women), 3 part-time (1 woman); includes 2 minority (1 African American, 1 Asian American or Pacific Islander), 6 international. Average age 29. 17 applicants, 29% accepted, 5 enrolled. In 2009, 3 master's, 1 doctorate awarded. Terminal master's awarded for partial completion of doctoral program. *Degree requirements:* For master's, comprehensive exam, thesis or alternative; for doctorate, comprehensive exam, thesis/dissertation, oral exam, oral defense. *Entrance requirements:* For master's and doctorate, GRE General Test. Additional exam requirements/recommendations for international students: Required—TOEFL (minimum score 550 paper-based; 213 computer-based; 80 iBT). *Application deadline:* For fall admission, 6/1 for domestic students, 3/1 for international students; for spring admission, 10/15 for domestic students, 9/1 for international students. Applications are processed on a rolling basis. Application fee: $60. Electronic applications accepted. *Expenses:* Tuition, state resident: full-time $7584; part-time $316 per credit. Tuition, nonresident: full-time $15,504; part-time $646 per credit. Required fees: $23 per credit. $135 per semester. Tuition and fees vary according to course level, course load and reciprocity agreements. *Financial support:* In 2009–10, 2 research assistantships (averaging $13,004 per year), 5 teaching assistantships (averaging $7,088 per year) were awarded; fellowships, career-related internships or fieldwork, Federal Work-Study, scholarships/grants, health care benefits, and unspecified assistantships also available. Support available to part-time students. Financial award application deadline: 7/1; financial award applicants required to submit FAFSA. *Faculty research:* Cold regions engineering, fluid mechanics, heat transfer, energy systems, indoor air quality. *Unit head:* Dr. Jonah Lee, Department Chair, 907-474-7136, Fax: 907-474-6141, E-mail: fymech@uaf.edu. *Application contact:* Dr. Jonah Lee, Department Chair, 907-474-7136, Fax: 907-474-6141, E-mail: fymech@uaf.edu.

The University of Arizona, Graduate College, College of Engineering, Tucson, AZ 85721. Offers M Eng, ME, MS, PhD, Certificate. Part-time programs available. Postbaccalaureate distance learning degree programs offered (no on-campus study). *Faculty:* 108. *Students:* 375 full-time (103 women), 215 part-time (50 women); includes 35 minority (1 African American, 3 American Indian/Alaska Native, 17 Asian Americans or Pacific Islanders, 14 Hispanic Americans), 310 international. Average age 30. 1,006 applicants, 31% accepted, 117 enrolled. In 2009, 101 master's, 50 doctorates awarded. *Degree requirements:* For doctorate, thesis/dissertation. *Entrance requirements:* Additional exam requirements/recommendations for international students: Required—TOEFL (minimum score 550 paper-based; 213 computer-based; 79 iBT). Application fee: $75. *Expenses:* Tuition, state resident: full-time $9028. Tuition, nonresident: full-time $24,890. *Financial support:* In 2009–10, 182 research assistantships with full tuition reimbursements (averaging $18,239 per year), 48 teaching assistantships with full tuition reimbursements (averaging $18,101 per year) were awarded; institutionally sponsored loans, scholarships/grants, health care benefits, and unspecified assistantships also available. Total annual research expenditures: $18.4 million. *Unit head:* Dr. Thomas W. Peterson, Dean, 520-621-6594, Fax: 520-621-2232, E-mail: twp@engr.arizona.edu. *Application contact:* General Information, 520-621-3471, Fax: 520-621-7112, E-mail: gradadm@grad.arizona.edu.

University of Arkansas, Graduate School, College of Engineering, Fayetteville, AR 72701-1201. Offers MS, MS Cmp E, MS Ch E, MS En E, MS Tc E, MSBE, MSBME, MSCE, MSE, MSEE, MSIE, MSME, MSOR, MSTE, PhD. *Students:* 142 full-time (30 women), 542 part-time (120 women); includes 102 minority (67 African Americans, 6 American Indian/Alaska Native, 16 Asian Americans or Pacific Islanders, 13 Hispanic Americans), 177 international. In 2009, 259 master's, 23 doctorates awarded. *Degree requirements:* For doctorate, one foreign language, thesis/dissertation. Application fee: $40 ($50 for international students). *Expenses:* Tuition, state resident: full-time $7355; part-time $356.58 per hour. Tuition, nonresident: full-time $17,401; part-time $775.17 per hour. Required fees: $1203. *Financial support:* In 2009–10, 32 fellowships with tuition reimbursements, 180 research assistantships, 26 teaching assistantships were awarded; career-related internships or fieldwork and Federal Work-Study also available. Support available to part-time students. Financial award application deadline: 4/1; financial award applicants required to submit FAFSA. *Unit head:* Ashok Saxena, Dean, 479-575-4153, Fax: 479-575-4346, E-mail: asaxena@uark.edu. *Application contact:* Dr. Terry Martin, Associate Dean for Academic Affairs, 479-575-3052, E-mail: tmartin@uark.edu.

University of Bridgeport, School of Engineering, Bridgeport, CT 06604. Offers MS, PhD. Part-time and evening/weekend programs available. Postbaccalaureate distance learning degree programs offered (no on-campus study). *Degree requirements:* For master's, thesis optional; for doctorate, thesis/dissertation. *Entrance requirements:* Additional exam requirements/recommendations for international students: Recommended—TOEFL (minimum score 550 paper-based; 213 computer-based; 80 iBT), IELTS (minimum score 6.5). Electronic applications accepted. *Expenses:* Contact institution. *Faculty research:* Atmospheric chemistry, minicomputers, heat transfer.

The University of British Columbia, Faculty of Applied Science, Vancouver, BC V6T 1Z1, Canada. Offers M Arch, M Eng, M Sc, MA Sc, MASA, MASLA, MLA, MSN, MSS, PhD. Part-time programs available. *Degree requirements:* For master's, comprehensive exam (for some programs), thesis (for some programs); for doctorate, comprehensive exam, thesis/dissertation. *Entrance requirements:* Additional exam requirements/recommendations for international students: Required—TOEFL (minimum score 550 paper-based; 213 computer-based). Electronic applications accepted. *Faculty research:* Architecture, nursing, engineering, landscape architecture.

University of Calgary, Faculty of Graduate Studies, Schulich School of Engineering, Calgary, AB T2N 1N4, Canada. Offers M Eng, M Sc, MPM, PhD. Part-time and evening/weekend programs available. *Degree requirements:* For doctorate, comprehensive exam, thesis/dissertation, candidacy exam. *Entrance requirements:* For master's, minimum GPA of 3.0; for doctorate, minimum GPA of 3.5. Additional exam requirements/recommendations for international students: Required—TOEFL, IELTS. *Faculty research:* Chemical and petroleum engineering, civil engineering, electrical and computer engineering, geomatics engineering, mechanical engineering and computer-integrated manufacturing.

University of California, Berkeley, Graduate Division, College of Engineering, Berkeley, CA 94720-1500. Offers M Eng, MS, D Eng, PhD, M Arch/MS, MCP/MS, MPP/MS. *Students:* 1,579 full-time (367 women); includes 351 minority (30 African Americans, 7 American Indian/Alaska Native, 248 Asian Americans or Pacific Islanders, 66 Hispanic Americans), 557 international. Average age 27. 5,943 applicants, 406 enrolled. In 2009, 368 master's, 206 doctorates awarded. *Degree requirements:* For doctorate, thesis/dissertation, exam. *Entrance requirements:* For master's and doctorate, GRE General Test, minimum GPA of 3.0, 3 letters of recommendation. Application fee: $70 ($90 for international students). *Financial support:* Fellowships, research assistantships, teaching assistantships, career-related internships or fieldwork, Federal Work-Study, institutionally sponsored loans, scholarships/grants, tuition waivers (full and partial), and unspecified assistantships available. *Unit head:* Dr. Shankar Sastry, Dean, 510-642-5771, E-mail: sastry@coe.berkeley.edu. *Application contact:* Dr. Shankar Sastry, Dean, 510-642-5771, E-mail: sastry@coe.berkeley.edu.

University of California, Berkeley, UC Berkeley Extension, Certificate Programs in Engineering, Construction and Facilities Management, Berkeley, CA 94720-1500. Offers construction management (Certificate); HVAC (Certificate); integrated circuit design and techniques (online) (Certificate). Postbaccalaureate distance learning degree programs offered. *Unit head:* Diana Wu, Dean, 510-642-4181. *Application contact:* Engineering, Construction, and Facilities Management, 510-642-4151, E-mail: course@unex.berkeley.edu.

University of California, Davis, College of Engineering, Davis, CA 95616. Offers M Engr, MS, D Engr, PhD, Certificate, M Engr/MBA. Part-time programs available. Terminal master's awarded for partial completion of doctoral program. *Degree requirements:* For master's, comprehensive exam (for some programs), thesis (for some programs); for doctorate, comprehensive exam, thesis/dissertation. *Entrance requirements:* For doctorate, GRE. Additional exam requirements/recommendations for international students: Required—TOEFL (minimum score 550 paper-based; 213 computer-based). Electronic applications accepted.

University of California, Irvine, Office of Graduate Studies, School of Engineering, Irvine, CA 92697. Offers MS, PhD. Part-time programs available. *Students:* 630 full-time (139 women), 74 part-time (19 women); includes 161 minority (2 African Americans, 1 American Indian/Alaska Native, 141 Asian Americans or Pacific Islanders, 17 Hispanic Americans), 349 international. Average age 27. 2,300 applicants, 25% accepted, 213 enrolled. In 2009, 171 master's, 70 doctorates awarded. Terminal master's awarded for partial completion of doctoral program. *Degree requirements:* For doctorate, thesis/dissertation. *Entrance requirements:* For master's and doctorate, GRE General Test, minimum GPA of 3.0, 3 letters of recommendation. Additional exam requirements/recommendations for international students: Required—TOEFL (minimum score 550 paper-based; 213 computer-based). *Application deadline:* For fall admission, 1/15 priority date for domestic students, 1/15 for international students. Applications are processed on a rolling basis. Application fee: $70 ($90 for international students). Electronic applications accepted. *Financial support:* In 2009–10, fellowships with tuition reimbursements (averaging $14,656 per year); research assistantships with full tuition reimbursements, teaching assistantships with tuition reimbursements, institutionally sponsored loans, traineeships, health care benefits, and unspecified assistantships also available. Financial award application deadline: 3/1; financial award applicants required to submit FAFSA. *Faculty research:* Biomedical engineering, chemical and biochemical engineering, civil and environmental engineering, electrical and computer engineering, mechanical and aerospace engineering. *Unit head:* Dr. Nicolaos G. Alexopoulos, Dean, 949-824-6002, Fax: 949-824-7966, E-mail: alfios@uci.edu. *Application contact:* Thomas Cahoon, Graduate Counselor, 949-824-3562, Fax: 949-824-3440, E-mail: tcahoon@uci.edu.

University of California, Los Angeles, Graduate Division, Henry Samueli School of Engineering and Applied Science, Los Angeles, CA 90095-1601. Offers MS, PhD, MBA/MS. Evening/weekend programs available. Postbaccalaureate distance learning degree programs offered (no on-campus study). *Faculty:* 157 full-time (17 women). *Students:* 1,635 full-time (295 women); includes 528 minority (22 African Americans, 440 Asian Americans or Pacific Islanders, 66 Hispanic Americans), 627 international. 3,380 applicants, 39% accepted, 552 enrolled. In 2009, 307 master's, 143 doctorates awarded. Terminal master's awarded for partial completion of doctoral program. *Degree requirements:* For master's, comprehensive exam or thesis; for doctorate, thesis/dissertation, qualifying exams. *Entrance requirements:* For master's, GRE General Test, minimum GPA of 3.0; for doctorate, GRE General Test, minimum GPA of 3.25. Additional exam requirements/recommendations for international students: Required—TOEFL (minimum score 560 paper-based; 220 computer-based). *Application deadline:* For fall admission, 12/15 for domestic and international students. Application fee: $70 ($90 for international students). Electronic applications accepted. *Financial support:* In 2009–10, 479 fellowships, 497 teaching assistantships were awarded; research assistantships, career-related internships or fieldwork, Federal Work-Study, institutionally sponsored loans, and tuition waivers (full and partial) also available. Financial award application deadline: 3/2; financial award applicants required to submit FAFSA. Total annual research expenditures: $93.3 million. *Unit head:* Dr. Richard D. Wesel, Associate Dean, Academic and Student Affairs, 310-825-2942. *Application contact:* Jan Labuda, Student Affairs Officer, 310-825-2514, Fax: 301-825-2473, E-mail: jan@ea.ucla.edu.

University of California, Merced, Division of Graduate Studies, School of Engineering, Merced, CA 95343. Offers electrical engineering and computer science (MS, PhD). *Expenses:* Tuition, nonresident: full-time $15,102. Required fees: $10,919.

University of California, Santa Barbara, Graduate Division, College of Engineering, Santa Barbara, CA 93106-5130. Offers MS, PhD, MS/PhD. *Students:* 672 full-time (142 women); includes 77 minority (6 African Americans, 2 American Indian/Alaska Native, 56 Asian Americans or Pacific Islanders, 13 Hispanic Americans), 322 international. Average age 26. 2,474 applicants, 21% accepted, 141 enrolled. In 2009, 92 master's, 90 doctorates awarded. Terminal master's awarded for partial completion of doctoral program. *Degree requirements:* For doctorate, thesis/dissertation. *Entrance requirements:* For master's, GRE, 3 letters of recommendation, resume/curriculum vitae; for doctorate, GRE, 3 letters of recommendation, statement of purpose, personal achievements/contributions statement, resume/curriculum vitae, transcripts for post-secondary institutions attended. Additional exam requirements/recommendations for international students: Required—TOEFL (minimum score 550 paper-based; 213 computer-based; 80 iBT) or IELTS (minimum score 7). Application fee: $70 ($90 for international students). Electronic applications accepted. *Financial support:* Fellowships with full and partial tuition reimbursements, research assistantships with full and partial tuition reimbursements, teaching assistantships with partial tuition reimbursements, career-related internships or fieldwork, Federal Work-Study, institutionally sponsored loans, scholarships/grants, traineeships, health care benefits, tuition waivers (full and partial), and unspecified assistantships available. Financial award applicants required to submit FAFSA. *Unit head:* Dr. Matthew Tirrell, Dean, 805-893-3141. *Application contact:* 805-893-3207, E-mail: engrdean@engineering.ucsb.edu.

University of California, Santa Cruz, Division of Graduate Studies, Jack Baskin School of Engineering, Santa Cruz, CA 95064. Offers MS, PhD. *Entrance requirements:* For master's and doctorate, GRE General Test.

University of Central Florida, College of Engineering and Computer Science, Orlando, FL 32816. Offers MS, MS Cp E, MS Env E, MSAE, MSCE, MSEE, MSIE, MSME, MSMSE, PhD, Certificate. Part-time and evening/weekend programs available. *Faculty:* 127 full-time (13 women), 37 part-time/adjunct (1 woman). *Students:* 635 full-time (120 women), 615 part-time (135 women); includes 266 minority (58 African Americans, 5 American Indian/Alaska Native, 74 Asian Americans or Pacific Islanders, 129 Hispanic Americans), 384 international. Average age 30. 1,184 applicants, 60% accepted, 409 enrolled. In 2009, 234 master's, 65 doctorates, 14 other advanced degrees awarded. *Degree requirements:* For doctorate, thesis/dissertation, candidacy exam, departmental qualifying exam. *Entrance requirements:* For master's, GRE General Test, minimum GPA of 3.0 in last 60 hours; for doctorate, minimum GPA of 3.5 in last 60 hours, resume. Additional exam requirements/recommendations for international students: Required—TOEFL. *Application deadline:* For fall admission, 7/15 for domestic students; for spring admission, 12/1 for domestic students. Application fee: $30. Electronic applications accepted. *Expenses:* Tuition, state resident: part-time $306.31 per credit hour. Tuition, nonresident: part-time $1099.01 per credit hour. Part-time tuition and fees vary according to degree level and program. *Financial support:* In 2009–10, 331 students received support, including 79 fellowships with partial tuition reimbursements available (averaging $7,200 per year), 269 research assistantships with partial tuition reimbursements available (averaging $9,700 per year), 91 teaching assistantships with partial tuition reimbursements available (averaging $8,600 per year); career-related internships or fieldwork, Federal Work-Study, institutionally sponsored loans, tuition waivers (partial), and unspecified assistantships also available. Financial award application deadline: 3/1; financial award applicants required to submit FAFSA. *Faculty research:* Electro-optics, lasers, materials, simulation, microelectronics. *Unit head:* Dr. Marwan Simaan, IDean, 407-823-2156, E-mail: simaan@eecs.ucf.edu. *Application contact:* Dr. Marwan Simaan, IDean, 407-823-2156, E-mail: simaan@eecs.ucf.edu.

University of Central Oklahoma, College of Graduate Studies and Research, College of Mathematics and Science, Department of Physics and Engineering, Edmond, OK 73034-5209. Offers MS. Part-time programs available. *Degree requirements:* For master's, thesis optional. *Entrance requirements:* For master's, 24 hours of course work in physics. Additional exam requirements/recommendations for international students: Required—TOEFL (minimum score 550 paper-based; 213 computer-based). Electronic applications accepted. *Faculty research:* Acoustics, solid-state physics/optical properties, molecular dynamics, nuclear physics, crystallography.

University of Cincinnati, Graduate School, College of Engineering, Cincinnati, OH 45221. Offers MS, PhD, MBA/MS. *Accreditation:* ABET (one or more programs are accredited). Part-time and evening/weekend programs available. Terminal master's awarded for partial completion of doctoral program. *Degree requirements:* For master's, thesis or alternative; for doctorate, comprehensive exam, thesis/dissertation. *Entrance requirements:* For master's and doctorate, GRE General Test. Additional exam requirements/recommendations for international students: Required—TOEFL (minimum score 520 paper-based; 190 computer-based).

University of Colorado at Boulder, Graduate School, College of Engineering and Applied Science, Boulder, CO 80309. Offers ME, MS, PhD, JD/MS, MBA/MS. Part-time programs available. Postbaccalaureate distance learning degree programs offered. *Faculty:* 178 full-time (31 women). *Students:* 1,039 full-time (217 women), 440 part-time (101 women); includes 150 minority (15 African Americans, 9 American Indian/Alaska Native, 82 Asian Americans or Pacific Islanders, 44 Hispanic Americans), 437 international. Average age 28. 2,227 applicants, 36% accepted, 365 enrolled. In 2009, 385 master's, 68 doctorates awarded. *Degree requirements:* For doctorate, thesis/dissertation. Application fee: $50 ($60 for international students). Electronic applications accepted. *Expenses:* Contact institution. *Financial support:* In 2009–10, 247 fellowships with full tuition reimbursements (averaging $12,287 per year), 413 research assistantships with full tuition reimbursements (averaging $15,375 per year), 70 teaching assistantships with full tuition reimbursements (averaging $17,591 per year) were awarded; career-related internships or fieldwork, scholarships/grants, traineeships, and tuition waivers (full) also available. Total annual research expenditures: $47.2 million.

University of Colorado at Colorado Springs, Graduate School, College of Engineering and Applied Science, Colorado Springs, CO 80933-7150. Offers ME, MS, PhD. Part-time and evening/weekend programs available. *Faculty:* 29 full-time (5 women), 2 part-time/adjunct (0 women). *Students:* 90 full-time (14 women), 145 part-time (28 women); includes 38 minority (2 African Americans, 1 American Indian/Alaska Native, 22 Asian Americans or Pacific Islanders, 13 Hispanic Americans), 14 international. Average age 32. 83 applicants, 81% accepted, 36 enrolled. In 2009, 43 master's, 4 doctorates awarded. *Degree requirements:* For doctorate, comprehensive exam, thesis/dissertation. *Entrance requirements:* For master's, GRE General Test, minimum GPA of 3.0; for doctorate, GRE General Test, minimum GPA of 3.3. Additional exam requirements/recommendations for international students: Required—TOEFL. *Application deadline:* For fall admission, 5/1 for domestic students; for spring admission, 10/1 for domestic students. Applications are processed on a rolling basis. Application fee: $60 ($75 for international students). *Expenses:* Contact institution. *Financial support:* Fellowships, research assistantships, teaching assistantships, career-related internships or fieldwork, Federal Work-Study, and scholarships/grants available. Support available to part-time students. Financial award application deadline: 3/1; financial award applicants required to submit FAFSA. *Faculty research:* Ferroelectronics, electronics communication, computer-aided design, electromagnetics. Total annual research expenditures: $1.6 million. *Unit head:* Dr. Ramaswami Dandapani, Dean, 719-255-3543, Fax: 719-255-3542, E-mail: rdan@cas.uccs.edu. *Application contact:* Tina Moore, Director, Office of Student Support, 719-255-3347, E-mail: tmoore@uccs.edu.

University of Connecticut, Graduate School, School of Engineering, Storrs, CT 06269. Offers M Eng, MS, PhD. *Faculty:* 192 full-time (25 women). *Students:* 530 full-time (143 women), 146 part-time (25 women); includes 62 minority (16 African Americans, 29 Asian Americans or Pacific Islanders, 17 Hispanic Americans), 360 international. Average age 28. 1,248 applicants, 15% accepted, 106 enrolled. In 2009, 94 master's, 37 doctorates awarded. Terminal master's awarded for partial completion of doctoral program. *Degree requirements:* For master's, comprehensive exam; for doctorate, thesis/dissertation. *Entrance requirements:* For master's and doctorate, GRE General Test. Additional exam requirements/recommendations for international students: Required—TOEFL (minimum score 550 paper-based; 213 computer-based). *Application deadline:* For fall admission, 2/1 priority date for domestic and international students; for spring admission, 11/1 for domestic students, 10/1 for international students. Applications are processed on a rolling basis. Application fee: $55. Electronic applications accepted. *Expenses:* Tuition, state resident: full-time $4725; part-time $525 per credit. Tuition, nonresident: full-time $12,267; part-time $1363 per credit. Required fees: $346 per semester. Tuition and fees vary according to course load. *Financial support:* In 2009–10, 414 research assistantships with full tuition reimbursements, 53 teaching assistantships with full tuition reimbursements were awarded; fellowships, career-related internships or fieldwork, Federal Work-Study, scholarships/grants, health care benefits, and unspecified assistantships also available. Financial award application deadline: 2/1; financial award applicants required to submit FAFSA. *Unit head:* Mun Y. Choi, Dean, 860-486-2221, Fax: 860-486-0318, E-mail: choi@engr.uconn.edu. *Application contact:* Mun Y. Choi, Dean, 860-486-2221, Fax: 860-486-0318, E-mail: choi@engr.uconn.edu.

University of Dayton, Graduate School, School of Engineering, Dayton, OH 45469-0228. Offers MS, MS Ch E, MS Mat E, MSAE, MSCE, MSE, MSEE, MSEM, MSEM, MSEO, MSME, MSMS, DE, PhD. Part-time and evening/weekend programs available. Postbaccalaureate distance learning degree programs offered (no on-campus study). *Faculty:* 50 full-time (4 women), 36 part-time/adjunct (3 women). *Students:* 307 full-time (78 women), 144 part-time (18 women); includes 55 minority (32 African Americans, 14 Asian Americans or Pacific Islanders, 9 Hispanic Americans), 165 international. Average age 29. 682 applicants, 38% accepted, 104 enrolled. In 2009, 111 master's, 18 doctorates awarded. *Degree requirements:* For master's, thesis optional; for doctorate, thesis/dissertation, departmental qualifying exam. *Entrance requirements:* For doctorate, MS. Additional exam requirements/recommendations for international students: Required—TOEFL (minimum score 550 paper-based; 213 computer-based; 80 iBT). *Application deadline:* For fall admission, 8/1 priority date for domestic students, 3/1 priority date for international students; for winter admission, 7/1 priority date for international students; for spring admission, 1/1 priority date for international students. Applications are processed on a rolling basis. Application fee: $0 ($50 for international students). Electronic applications accepted. *Expenses:* Tuition: Full-time $8412; part-time $701 per credit hour. Required fees: $325; $65 per course. $25 per semester. Tuition and fees vary according to course load, degree level and program. *Financial support:* In 2009–10, 105 students received support, including 7 fellowships with full tuition reimbursements available (averaging $28,000 per year), 84 research assistantships with full tuition reimbursements available (averaging $15,000 per year), 14 teaching assistantships with full tuition reimbursements available (averaging $9,000 per year); career-related internships or fieldwork, institutionally sponsored loans, health care benefits, tuition waivers (full and partial), and unspecified assistantships also available. Financial award applicants required to submit FAFSA. Total annual research expenditures: $6.1 million. *Unit head:* Dr. Malcolm W. Daniels, Interim Dean, 937-229-2736, Fax: 937-229-2756, E-mail: malcolm.daniels@notes.udayton.edu. *Application contact:* Graduate Admissions, 937-229-4411, Fax: 937-229-4729, E-mail: gradadmission@udayton.edu.

University of Delaware, College of Engineering, Newark, DE 19716. Offers M Ch E, MAS, MCE, MEM, MMSE, MS, MSECE, MSME, PhD. Part-time and evening/weekend programs available. Postbaccalaureate distance learning degree programs offered (minimal on-campus study). Terminal master's awarded for partial completion of doctoral program. *Degree requirements:* For master's, thesis (for some programs); for doctorate, thesis/dissertation. *Entrance requirements:* For master's and doctorate, GRE General Test. Additional exam requirements/recommendations for international students: Required—TOEFL (minimum score 550 paper-based; 213 computer-based). Electronic applications accepted. *Faculty research:* Biotechnology, photonics, transportation, composite materials, materials science.

University of Detroit Mercy, College of Engineering and Science, Detroit, MI 48221. Offers M Eng Mgt, MATM, ME, MS, MSCS, DE. Part-time and evening/weekend programs available. *Degree requirements:* For doctorate, thesis/dissertation. *Expenses:* Contact institution.

University of Evansville, College of Engineering and Computer Science, Evansville, IN 47722. Offers MS. Part-time programs available. *Faculty:* 2 full-time (1 woman). *Students:* 2 part-time (1 woman). Average age 30. In 2009, 1 master's awarded. *Degree requirements:* For master's, thesis. *Entrance requirements:* For master's, GRE, minimum undergraduate GPA of 2.8, 2 letters of recommendation, BS in electrical engineering or computer science. Additional exam requirements/recommendations for international students: Required—TOEFL (minimum score 530 paper-based; 71 iBT), IELTS (minimum score 6). *Application deadline:* For fall admission, 5/1 priority date for domestic and international students. Applications are processed on a rolling basis. Application fee: $25 ($50 for international students). *Expenses:* Contact institution. *Financial support:* In 2009–10, 1 student received support. Scholarships/grants available. Financial award application deadline: 6/1; financial award applicants required to submit FAFSA. *Faculty research:* Digital signal processing, computer algorithms, distributed systems, microcontrollers. *Unit head:* Dr. Philip Gerhart, Dean, 812-488-2651, Fax: 812-488-2780, E-mail: pg3@evansville.edu. *Application contact:* Dr. Dick Blandford, Department Chair, 812-488-2570, Fax: 812-488-2662, E-mail: blandford@evansville.edu.

Engineering and Applied Sciences—General

University of Florida, Graduate School, College of Engineering, Gainesville, FL 32611. Offers MCE, ME, MS, PhD, Certificate, Engr, JD/MS, MD/PhD. *Accreditation:* ABET (one or more programs are accredited). Part-time programs available. *Degree requirements:* For doctorate, thesis/dissertation. *Entrance requirements:* For master's, GRE General Test, minimum GPA of 3.0; for doctorate and other advanced degree, GRE General Test. Additional exam requirements/recommendations for international students: Required—TOEFL (minimum score 550 paper-based; 213 computer-based). Electronic applications accepted.

University of Guelph, Graduate Program Services, College of Physical and Engineering Science, School of Engineering, Guelph, ON N1G 2W1, Canada. Offers biological engineering (M Eng, M Sc, MA Sc, PhD); engineering systems and computing (M Eng, M Sc, MA Sc, PhD); environmental engineering (M Eng, M Sc, MA Sc, PhD); water resources engineering (M Eng, M Sc, MA Sc, PhD). Part-time programs available. *Degree requirements:* For master's, thesis (for some programs); for doctorate, comprehensive exam, thesis/dissertation. *Entrance requirements:* For master's, minimum B- average during previous 2 years of course work; for doctorate, minimum B average. Additional exam requirements/recommendations for international students: Required—TOEFL (minimum score 550 paper-based; 213 computer-based; 89 iBT), IELTS (minimum score 6.5). Electronic applications accepted. *Faculty research:* Water and food safety, environmental contaminant fates and mechanisms, computer systems, robotics and mechatronics, waste treatment.

University of Hartford, College of Engineering, Technology and Architecture, Program in Engineering, West Hartford, CT 06117-1599. Offers M Eng. *Entrance requirements:* Additional exam requirements/recommendations for international students: Required—TOEFL.

University of Hawaii at Manoa, Graduate Division, College of Engineering, Honolulu, HI 96822. Offers MS, PhD. *Accreditation:* ABET (one or more programs are accredited). Part-time programs available. *Entrance requirements:* Additional exam requirements/recommendations for international students: Required—TOEFL or IELTS. *Expenses:* Tuition, state resident: full-time $8900; part-time $372 per credit. Tuition, nonresident: full-time $21,400; part-time $898 per credit. Required fees: $207 per semester.

University of Houston, Cullen College of Engineering, Houston, TX 77204. Offers M Pet E, MCE, MCHE, MEE, MIE, MME, MS, MS Ch E, MS Pet E, MSBE, MSCE, MSEE, MSIE, MSME, PhD. Part-time and evening/weekend programs available. *Faculty:* 81 full-time (6 women), 32 part-time/adjunct (4 women). *Students:* 555 full-time (145 women), 237 part-time (41 women); includes 111 minority (18 African Americans, 1 American Indian/Alaska Native, 64 Asian Americans or Pacific Islanders, 28 Hispanic Americans), 538 international. Average age 27. 1,198 applicants, 54% accepted, 234 enrolled. In 2009, 164 master's, 38 doctorates awarded. Terminal master's awarded for partial completion of doctoral program. *Degree requirements:* For master's, thesis (for some programs); for doctorate, thesis/dissertation, departmental qualifying exam. *Entrance requirements:* For master's and doctorate, GRE General Test. *Application deadline:* For fall admission, 2/1 for domestic and international students; for spring admission, 10/1 for domestic and international students. Applications are processed on a rolling basis. Application fee: $25 ($75 for international students). Electronic applications accepted. *Expenses:* Tuition, state resident: full-time $7676; part-time $320 per credit hour. Tuition, nonresident: full-time $14,324; part-time $597 per credit hour. Required fees: $3034. *Financial support:* In 2009–10, 33 fellowships with full tuition reimbursements (averaging $16,500 per year), 185 research assistantships with full tuition reimbursements (averaging $12,500 per year), 79 teaching assistantships with full tuition reimbursements (averaging $12,500 per year) were awarded; career-related internships or fieldwork, Federal Work-Study, institutionally sponsored loans, scholarships/grants, health care benefits, and unspecified assistantships also available. Support available to part-time students. Financial award application deadline: 2/1. *Faculty research:* Superconducting materials, microantennas for space packs, direct numerical simulation of pairing vortices. *Unit head:* Dr. Joseph Tedesco, Dean, 713-743-4200, Fax: 713-743-4214, E-mail: jtedesco@uh.edu. *Application contact:* Dr. Joseph Tedesco, Dean, 713-743-4200, Fax: 713-743-4214, E-mail: jtedesco@uh.edu.

University of Idaho, College of Graduate Studies, College of Engineering, Moscow, ID 83844-2282. Offers M Engr, MS, PhD. *Faculty:* 72 full-time, 16 part-time/adjunct. *Students:* 176 full-time (23 women), 242 part-time (32 women). In 2009, 90 master's, 12 doctorates awarded. *Degree requirements:* For doctorate, thesis/dissertation. *Entrance requirements:* For doctorate, minimum undergraduate GPA of 2.8, graduate 3.0. *Application deadline:* For fall admission, 8/1 for domestic students; for spring admission, 12/15 for domestic students. Application fee: $55 ($60 for international students). *Expenses:* Tuition, state resident: full-time $6120. Tuition, nonresident: full-time $17,712. *Financial support:* Fellowships, research assistantships, teaching assistantships, career-related internships or fieldwork and Federal Work-Study available. Support available to part-time students. Financial award application deadline: 2/15. *Faculty research:* Robotics, micro-electronic packaging, water resources engineering and science, oscillating flows in macro- and micro-scale methods of mechanical separation, nuclear energy. *Unit head:* Dr. Donald Blackketter, Dean, 208-885-6470. *Application contact:* Dr. Donald Blackketter, Dean, 208-885-6470.

University of Illinois at Chicago, Graduate College, College of Engineering, Chicago, IL 60607-7128. Offers M Eng, MEE, MS, PhD. Part-time and evening/weekend programs available. Terminal master's awarded for partial completion of doctoral program. *Degree requirements:* For doctorate, thesis/dissertation. *Entrance requirements:* For doctorate, GRE. Additional exam requirements/recommendations for international students: Required—TOEFL. Electronic applications accepted. *Expenses:* Contact institution.

University of Illinois at Urbana–Champaign, Graduate College, College of Engineering, Champaign, IL 61820. Offers MCS, MS, PhD, M Arch/MS, MBA/MS, MCS/JD, MCS/M Arch, MCS/MBA, MS/MBA, PhD/MBA. *Faculty:* 389 full-time (38 women), 19 part-time/adjunct (3 women). *Students:* 2,056 full-time (357 women), 438 part-time (76 women); includes 237 minority (24 African Americans, 171 Asian Americans or Pacific Islanders, 42 Hispanic Americans), 1,353 international. 5,598 applicants, 20% accepted, 572 enrolled. In 2009, 347 master's, 230 doctorates awarded. *Application deadline:* Applications are processed on a rolling basis. Application fee: $60 ($75 for international students). Electronic applications accepted. *Expenses:* Contact institution. *Financial support:* In 2009–10, 258 fellowships, 686 teaching assistantships were awarded; research assistantships, tuition waivers (full and partial) also available. *Unit head:* Dr. Ilesanmi Adesida, Dean, 217-333-2150, Fax: 217-244-7705, E-mail: iadesida@illinois.edu. *Application contact:* Dr. Ilesanmi Adesida, Dean, 217-333-2150, Fax: 217-244-7705, E-mail: iadesida@illinois.edu.

The University of Iowa, Graduate College, College of Engineering, Iowa City, IA 52242-1316. Offers MS, PhD. *Faculty:* 87 full-time (10 women), 2 part-time/adjunct (1 woman). *Students:* 354 full-time (108 women); includes 24 minority (10 African Americans, 10 Asian Americans or Pacific Islanders, 4 Hispanic Americans), 171 international. Average age 27. 630 applicants, 27% accepted, 77 enrolled. In 2009, 51 master's, 35 doctorates awarded. *Degree requirements:* For master's, thesis optional, exam; for doctorate, comprehensive exam, thesis/dissertation. *Entrance requirements:* For master's and doctorate, GRE, Official academic records/transcripts, 3 letters of recommendation, a resume, a statement of purpose and once admitted a financial statement. Additional exam requirements/recommendations for international students: Required—TOEFL (minimum score 550 paper-based; 213 computer-based; 81 iBT). *Application deadline:* For fall admission, 7/15 for domestic students, 4/15 for international students; for spring admission, 12/1 for domestic students, 10/1 for international students. Applications are processed on a rolling basis. Application fee: $60 ($100 for international students). Electronic applications accepted. *Financial support:* In 2009–10, 20 fellowships with partial tuition reimbursements (averaging $20,678 per year), 274 research assistantships with partial tuition reimbursements (averaging $20,739 per year), 81 teaching assistantships with partial tuition reimbursements (averaging $17,174 per year) were awarded; scholarships/grants, health care benefits, and unspecified assistantships also available. Financial award application deadline: 2/1; financial award applicants required to submit FAFSA. Total annual research expenditures: $43.6 million. *Unit head:* Dr. P. Barry Butler, Dean, 319-335-5766, Fax: 319-335-6086, E-mail: patrick-butler@uiowa.edu. *Application contact:* Betty Wood, Associate Director of Admissions, 319-335-1525, Fax: 319-335-1535, E-mail: admissions@uiowa.edu.

See Close-Up on page 87.

The University of Kansas, Graduate Studies, School of Engineering, Lawrence, KS 66045. Offers MCE, MCM, ME, MS, DE, PhD. Part-time and evening/weekend programs available. Postbaccalaureate distance learning degree programs offered (no on-campus study). *Students:* 346 full-time (95 women), 304 part-time (58 women); includes 57 minority (13 African Americans, 5 American Indian/Alaska Native, 29 Asian Americans or Pacific Islanders, 10 Hispanic Americans), 247 international. Average age 29. 650 applicants, 43% accepted, 130 enrolled. In 2009, 134 master's, 25 doctorates awarded. Terminal master's awarded for partial completion of doctoral program. *Degree requirements:* For doctorate, comprehensive exam, thesis/dissertation. *Entrance requirements:* For master's, GRE, minimum GPA of 3.0; for doctorate, GRE, minimum GPA of 3.5. Additional exam requirements/recommendations for international students: Required—TOEFL. *Application deadline:* Applications are processed on a rolling basis. Application fee: $45 ($55 for international students). Electronic applications accepted. *Expenses:* Contact institution. *Financial support:* Fellowships, research assistantships with full and partial tuition reimbursements, teaching assistantships with full and partial tuition reimbursements, career-related internships or fieldwork, Federal Work-Study, scholarships/grants, and unspecified assistantships available. *Faculty research:* Telecommunications, oil recovery, airplane design, structured materials, robotics. *Unit head:* Dr. Stuart R. Bell, Dean, 785-864-3881, E-mail: kuengr@ku.edu. *Application contact:* Dr. Glen Marotz, Associate Dean, 785-864-2980, Fax: 785-864-5445, E-mail: gama@ku.edu.

University of Kentucky, Graduate School, College of Engineering, Lexington, KY 40506-0032. Offers M Eng, MCE, MME, MS, MS Ch E, MS Min, MSCE, MSEE, MSEM, MSMAE, MSME, MSMSE, PhD. Part-time programs available. *Degree requirements:* For master's, comprehensive exam; for doctorate, comprehensive exam, thesis/dissertation. *Entrance requirements:* For master's, GRE General Test, minimum undergraduate GPA of 2.75; for doctorate, GRE General Test, minimum undergraduate GPA of 3.0. Additional exam requirements/recommendations for international students: Required—TOEFL (minimum score 550 paper-based; 213 computer-based). Electronic applications accepted.

University of Louisville, J.B. Speed School of Engineering, Louisville, KY 40292-0001. Offers M Eng, MS, PhD, Certificate, M Eng/MBA. *Accreditation:* ABET (one or more programs are accredited). Part-time programs available. Postbaccalaureate distance learning degree programs offered (no on-campus study). *Faculty:* 81 full-time (12 women), 3 part-time/adjunct (0 women). *Students:* 349 full-time (69 women), 143 part-time (27 women); includes 50 minority (22 African Americans, 23 Asian Americans or Pacific Islanders, 5 Hispanic Americans), 146 international. Average age 28. 258 applicants, 56% accepted, 78 enrolled. In 2009, 185 master's, 24 doctorates, 14 other advanced degrees awarded. Terminal master's awarded for partial completion of doctoral program. *Degree requirements:* For master's, comprehensive exam (for some programs), thesis or alternative; for doctorate, comprehensive exam, thesis/dissertation, minimum GPA of 3.0. *Entrance requirements:* For master's, doctorate, and Certificate, GRE General Test. Additional exam requirements/recommendations for international students: Required—TOEFL (minimum score 550 paper-based; 213 computer-based; 80 iBT). *Application deadline:* For fall admission, 7/12 priority date for domestic and international students; for winter admission, 11/29 priority date for domestic and international students; for spring admission, 3/28 priority date for domestic and international students. Applications are processed on a rolling basis. Application fee: $50. Electronic applications accepted. *Financial support:* In 2009–10, 133 students received support, including 32 fellowships with full tuition reimbursements available (averaging $20,000 per year), 52 research assistantships with full tuition reimbursements available (averaging $20,000 per year), 40 teaching assistantships with full tuition reimbursements available (averaging $20,000 per year); scholarships/grants also available. Financial award application deadline: 1/25; financial award applicants required to submit FAFSA. *Faculty research:* Bioengineering, civil infrastructure, computer engineering and computer science, logistics and distribution, materials management. Total annual research expenditures: $12.4 million. *Unit head:* Dr. Mickey R. Wilhelm, Dean, 502-852-6281, Fax: 502-852-7033, E-mail: wilhelm@louisville.edu. *Application contact:* Dr. Michael Day, Associate Dean, 502-852-6195, Fax: 502-852-7294, E-mail: day@louisville.edu.

University of Maine, Graduate School, College of Engineering, Orono, ME 04469. Offers MS, PhD. Part-time programs available. *Faculty:* 65 full-time (6 women), 8 part-time/adjunct (0 women). *Students:* 96 full-time (15 women), 56 part-time (11 women); includes 8 minority (2 American Indian/Alaska Native, 6 Asian Americans or Pacific Islanders), 47 international. Average age 29. 131 applicants, 38% accepted, 30 enrolled. In 2009, 15 master's, 8 doctorates awarded. Terminal master's awarded for partial completion of doctoral program. *Degree requirements:* For doctorate, thesis/dissertation. *Entrance requirements:* For master's and doctorate, GRE General Test. Additional exam requirements/recommendations for international students: Required—TOEFL. *Application deadline:* For fall admission, 2/1 priority date for domestic students. Applications are processed on a rolling basis. Application fee: $65. Electronic applications accepted. *Financial support:* In 2009–10, 1 research assistantship with tuition reimbursement (averaging $12,790 per year) was awarded; Federal Work-Study, institutionally sponsored loans, scholarships/grants, and tuition waivers (full and partial) also available. Financial award application deadline: 3/1. *Unit head:* Dr. Dana Humphrey, Interim Dean, 207-581-2216, Fax: 207-581-2220. *Application contact:* Scott G. Delcourt, Associate Dean of the Graduate School, 207-581-3291, Fax: 207-581-3232, E-mail: graduate@maine.edu.

University of Manitoba, Faculty of Graduate Studies, Faculty of Engineering, Winnipeg, MB R3T 2N2, Canada. Offers M Eng, M Sc, PhD.

University of Maryland, Baltimore County, Graduate School, College of Engineering and Information Technology, Baltimore, MD 21250. Offers MS, PhD, Postbaccalaureate Certificate. Part-time and evening/weekend programs available. Postbaccalaureate distance learning degree programs offered (no on-campus study). *Faculty:* 79 full-time (21 women), 102 part-time/adjunct (35 women). *Students:* 343 full-time (105 women), 613 part-time (172 women); includes 247 minority (128 African Americans, 3 American Indian/Alaska Native, 97 Asian Americans or Pacific Islanders, 19 Hispanic Americans), 237 international. Average age 31. 890 applicants, 65% accepted, 251 enrolled. In 2009, 162 master's, 38 doctorates, 18 other advanced degrees awarded. *Degree requirements:* For master's, comprehensive exam (for some programs), thesis (for some programs); for doctorate, comprehensive exam, thesis/dissertation. *Entrance requirements:* For master's and doctorate, GRE General Test, minimum GPA of 3.0. Additional exam requirements/recommendations for international students: Required—TOEFL (minimum score 550 paper-based; 213 computer-based; 80 iBT). *Application deadline:* For fall admission, 6/1 for domestic students, 1/1 for international students; for spring admission, 11/1 for domestic students, 6/1 for international students. Applications are processed on a rolling basis. Application fee: $50. Electronic applications accepted. *Financial support:* In 2009–10, 4 fellowships with full tuition reimbursements (averaging $19,500 per year), 100 research assistantships with full tuition reimbursements (averaging $21,100 per year), 78 teaching assistantships with full tuition reimbursements (averaging $18,500 per year) were awarded; career-related internships or fieldwork, Federal Work-Study, scholarships/grants, health care benefits, tuition waivers (partial), and unspecified assistantships also available. Support available to part-time students. Financial award application deadline: 6/30; financial award applicants required to submit FAFSA. *Faculty research:* Biomaterials engineering, water resources engineering, security and information assurance, human-centered computing, design and manufacturing. Total annual research expenditures: $14.6 million. *Unit head:* Dr. Warren R. DeVries, Dean, 410-455-3270, Fax: 410-455-3559, E-mail: wdevries@umbc.edu. *Application contact:* Graduate School, 410-455-2537, E-mail: umbcgrad@umbc.edu.

University of Maryland, College Park, Academic Affairs, A. James Clark School of Engineering and School of Public Policy, Program in Engineering and Public Policy, College Park, MD 20742. Offers MS. *Students:* 4 full-time (1 woman), 8 part-time (4 women); includes 4 minority (2 African Americans, 2 Hispanic Americans), 1 international. 31 applicants, 58% accepted, 3 enrolled. In 2009, 3 master's awarded. *Application deadline:* For fall admission, 4/1 for domestic students, 2/1 for international students; for spring admission, 10/15 for domestic students, 6/1 for international students. Application fee: $60. *Expenses:* Tuition, area resident: Part-time $471 per credit hour. Tuition, state resident: part-time $471 per credit hour. Tuition, nonresident: part-time $1016 per credit hour. Required fees: $337.04 per term. *Financial support:* In 2009–10, 2 teaching assistantships (averaging $15,909 per year) were awarded. *Unit head:* Dr. Steven Gabriel, Co-Director, 301-405-6331, E-mail: mepp@umd.edu. *Application contact:* Dr., Dean of the Graduate School, 301-405-0376, Fax: 301-314-9305, E-mail: ccaramel@umd.edu.

University of Massachusetts Amherst, Graduate School, College of Engineering, Amherst, MA 01003. Offers MS, PhD. *Accreditation:* ABET (one or more programs are accredited). Part-time programs available. *Faculty:* 117 full-time (11 women). *Students:* 375 full-time (88 women), 60 part-time (17 women); includes 26 minority (5 African Americans, 12 Asian Americans or Pacific Islanders, 9 Hispanic Americans), 262 international. Average age 26. 1,343 applicants, 32% accepted, 162 enrolled. In 2009, 69 master's, 24 doctorates awarded. Terminal master's awarded for partial completion of doctoral program. *Degree requirements:* For master's, thesis (for some programs); for doctorate, comprehensive exam, thesis/dissertation. *Entrance requirements:* For master's and doctorate, GRE General Test. Additional exam requirements/recommendations for international students: Required—TOEFL (minimum score 550 paper-based; 213 computer-based; 80 iBT), IELTS (minimum score 6.5). *Application deadline:* Applications are processed on a rolling basis. Application fee: $50 ($65 for international students). Electronic applications accepted. *Expenses:* Tuition, state resident: full-time $2640; part-time $110 per credit. Tuition, nonresident: full-time $9936; part-time $414 per credit. Tuition and fees vary according to course load. *Financial support:* In 2009–10, 13 fellowships with full tuition reimbursements (averaging $18,620 per year), 318 research assistantships with full tuition reimbursements (averaging $14,387 per year), 66 teaching assistantships with full tuition reimbursements (averaging $6,946 per year) were awarded; career-related internships or fieldwork, Federal Work-Study, scholarships/grants, traineeships, health care benefits, tuition waivers, and unspecified assistantships also available. Support available to part-time students. Financial award applicants required to submit FAFSA. *Unit head:* Dr. Michael Malone, Dean, 413-545-6388, Fax: 413-545-6388. *Application contact:* Jean M. Ames, Supervisor of Admissions, 413-545-0722, Fax: 413-577-0010, E-mail: gradadm@grad.umass.edu.

University of Massachusetts Dartmouth, Graduate School, College of Engineering, North Dartmouth, MA 02747-2300. Offers MS, PhD, Postbaccalaureate Certificate. Part-time programs available. *Faculty:* 62 full-time (8 women), 10 part-time/adjunct (0 women). *Students:* 129 full-time (34 women), 112 part-time (19 women); includes 12 minority (2 African Americans, 6 Asian Americans or Pacific Islanders, 4 Hispanic Americans), 144 international. Average age 26. 283 applicants, 82% accepted, 81 enrolled. In 2009, 75 master's, 2 doctorates, 3 other advanced degrees awarded. *Degree requirements:* For master's, thesis or alternative; for doctorate, comprehensive exam, thesis/dissertation. *Entrance requirements:* For doctorate, GRE. Additional exam requirements/recommendations for international students: Required—TOEFL (minimum score 500 paper-based). *Application deadline:* Applications are processed on a rolling basis. Application fee: $40 ($60 for international students). Electronic applications accepted. *Expenses:* Tuition, state resident: full-time $2071; part-time $86.29 per credit. Tuition, nonresident: full-time $8099; part-time $337.46 per credit. Required fees: $9446. Tuition and fees vary according to class time, course load and reciprocity agreements. *Financial support:* In 2009–10, 5 fellowships with full tuition reimbursements (averaging $12,707 per year), 52 research assistantships with full tuition reimbursements (averaging $9,501 per year), 37 teaching assistantships with full tuition reimbursements (averaging $10,140 per year) were awarded; Federal Work-Study and unspecified assistantships also available. Support available to part-time students. Financial award application deadline: 3/1; financial award applicants required to submit FAFSA. *Faculty research:* Soil-geosynthetic systems, signals and systems, heat exchanger optimization, tracking of mesoscale features, blue light cures. Total annual research expenditures: $4.2 million. *Unit head:* Dr. Robert Peck, Dean, 508-999-8539, Fax: 508-999-9137, E-mail: rpeck@umassd.edu. *Application contact:* Elan Turcotte-Shamski, Graduate Admissions Officer, 508-999-8604, Fax: 508-999-8183, E-mail: graduate@umassd.edu.

University of Massachusetts Lowell, James B. Francis College of Engineering, Lowell, MA 01854-2881. Offers MS Eng, MSES, D Eng, PhD, Certificate, Graduate Certificate. Part-time and evening/weekend programs available. Terminal master's awarded for partial completion of doctoral program. *Degree requirements:* For doctorate, thesis/dissertation. *Entrance requirements:* For master's and doctorate, GRE General Test.

University of Memphis, Graduate School, Herff College of Engineering, Memphis, TN 38152. Offers MS, PhD. Part-time programs available. *Faculty:* 40 full-time (3 women), 4 part-time/adjunct (1 woman). *Students:* 117 full-time (35 women), 57 part-time (13 women); includes 13 African Americans, 3 Asian Americans or Pacific Islanders, 1 Hispanic American, 80 international. Average age 29. 77 applicants, 84% accepted, 62 enrolled. In 2009, 34 master's, 7 doctorates awarded. *Degree requirements:* For master's, comprehensive exam, thesis optional, 30-36 hours of course work, completion of course work within 6 years, continuous enrollment; for doctorate, comprehensive exam, thesis/dissertation, completion of degree within 12 years, residency, continuous enrollment. *Entrance requirements:* For master's, GRE, MAT, GMAT or PRAXIS; for doctorate, GRE, MAT, GMAT. Additional exam requirements/recommendations for international students: Required—TOEFL (minimum score 550 paper-based; 210 computer-based; 79 iBT). *Application deadline:* For fall admission, 7/1 for domestic students, 5/1 for international students; for spring admission, 12/1 for domestic students, 9/15 for international students. Application fee: $35 ($60 for international students). Electronic applications accepted. *Expenses:* Tuition, state resident: full-time $6246; part-time $347 per credit hour. Tuition, nonresident: full-time $15,894; part-time $883 per credit hour. Required fees: $1160. Full-time tuition and fees vary according to course load, degree level and program. *Financial support:* In 2009–10, 30 students received support; fellowships with full tuition reimbursements available, research assistantships with full tuition reimbursements available, teaching assistantships with full tuition reimbursements available, career-related internships or fieldwork, Federal Work-Study, scholarships/grants, tuition waivers (full and partial), and unspecified assistantships available. Financial award application deadline: 2/15; financial award applicants required to submit FAFSA. *Faculty research:* Medical and biological applications of engineering; infrastructure, including transportation, ground water and GPS studies; computational intelligence and modeling; sensors. Total annual research expenditures: $4.5 million. *Unit head:* Dr. Richard C. Warder, Dean, 901-678-4306, Fax: 901-678-4180, E-mail: rcwarder@memphis.edu. *Application contact:* Dr. Deborah Hochstein, Associate Dean, 901-678-3298, Fax: 901-678-5030, E-mail: dhochstn@memphis.edu.

University of Miami, Graduate School, College of Engineering, Coral Gables, FL 33124. Offers MS, MSAE, MSBE, MSCE, MSECE, MSEVH, MSIE, MSME, MSOES, PhD, MBA/MSIE. Part-time and evening/weekend programs available. *Degree requirements:* For master's, thesis (for some programs); for doctorate, comprehensive exam, thesis/dissertation. *Entrance requirements:* For master's and doctorate, GRE General Test, minimum GPA of 3.0. Additional exam requirements/recommendations for international students: Required—TOEFL (minimum score 550 paper-based; 213 computer-based; 59 iBT). Electronic applications accepted.

University of Michigan, Horace H. Rackham School of Graduate Studies, College of Engineering, Ann Arbor, MI 48109. Offers M Eng, MS, MSE, D Eng, PhD, CE, Certificate, Ch E, Mar Eng, Nav Arch, Nuc E, M Arch/M Eng, M Arch/MSE, MBA/M Eng, MBA/MS, MBA/MSE. Part-time programs available. Postbaccalaureate distance learning degree programs offered (no on-campus study). *Faculty:* 348 full-time (55 women). *Students:* 2,218 full-time (467 women), 300 part-time (50 women); includes 318 minority (71 African Americans, 1 American Indian/Alaska Native, 182 Asian Americans or Pacific Islanders, 64 Hispanic Americans), 1,293 international. Average age 27. 5,643 applicants, 33% accepted, 724 enrolled. In 2009, 758 master's, 255 doctorates awarded. *Application deadline:* Applications are processed on a rolling basis. Application fee: $60 ($75 for international students). Electronic applications accepted. *Expenses:* Contact institution. *Financial support:* Fellowships, research assistantships, teaching assistantships, career-related internships or fieldwork, Federal Work-Study, institutionally sponsored loans, scholarships/grants, traineeships, health care benefits, tuition waivers (full and partial), and unspecified assistantships available. Support available to part-time students. Financial award applicants required to submit FAFSA. Total annual research expenditures: $155.3 million. *Unit head:* Prof. David C. Munson, Chair, 734-647-7010, Fax: 734-647-7009, E-mail: munson@umich.edu. *Application contact:* Mike Nazareth, Recruiting Contact, 734-647-7030, Fax: 734-647-7045, E-mail: mikenaz@umich.edu.

University of Michigan–Dearborn, College of Engineering and Computer Science, Dearborn, MI 48128-1491. Offers MS, MSE, PhD, MBA/MSE. Part-time and evening/weekend programs available. *Faculty:* 52 full-time (3 women), 12 part-time/adjunct (1 woman). *Students:* 63 full-time (9 women), 431 part-time (86 women); includes 106 minority (23 African Americans, 64 Asian Americans or Pacific Islanders, 19 Hispanic Americans), 84 international. Average age 31. 230 applicants, 61% accepted, 105 enrolled. In 2009, 121 master's awarded. *Degree requirements:* For master's, thesis optional; for doctorate, thesis/dissertation. *Entrance requirements:* Additional exam requirements/recommendations for international students: Required—TOEFL (minimum score 560 paper-based; 220 computer-based; 84 iBT). *Application deadline:* For fall admission, 6/15 for domestic students, 4/1 for international students; for winter admission, 12/1 for domestic students, 10/15 for international students; for spring admission, 2/15 for domestic and international students. Applications are processed on a rolling basis. Application fee: $60 ($75 for international students). Electronic applications accepted. *Expenses:* Tuition, area resident: Part-time $504.10 per credit hour. Tuition, state resident: part-time $504.10 per credit hour. Tuition, nonresident: part-time $957.90 per credit hour. *Financial support:* In 2009–10, 12 students received support, including 7 fellowships (averaging $18,331 per year), 27 research assistantships with full tuition reimbursements available (averaging $56,894 per year), 12 teaching assistantships (averaging $3,400 per year); career-related internships or fieldwork and Federal Work-Study also available. Financial award application deadline: 4/1; financial award applicants required to submit FAFSA. *Faculty research:* CAD/CAM, expert systems, acoustics, vehicle electronics, engines and fuels. *Unit head:* Dr. Subrata Sengupta, Dean, 313-593-5290, Fax: 313-593-9967, E-mail: razal@engin.umd.umich.edu. *Application contact:* Dr. Keshav Varde, Associate Dean, 313-593-5117, Fax: 313-593-9967, E-mail: varde@engin.umd.umich.edu.

See Close-Ups on pages 89 and 431.

University of Minnesota, Twin Cities Campus, Institute of Technology, Minneapolis, MN 55455-0213. Offers M Aero E, M Ch E, M Comp E, M Geo E, M Mat SE, MA, MCE, MCIS, MCS, MEE, MS, MS Ch E, MS Mat SE, MSEE, MSIE, MSISE, MSME, MSMOT, MSST, PhD, MD/PhD. Part-time and evening/weekend programs available. Postbaccalaureate distance learning degree programs offered (minimal on-campus study). Electronic applications accepted.

University of Mississippi, Graduate School, School of Engineering, Oxford, University, MS 38677. Offers computational engineering science (MS, PhD); engineering science (MS, PhD). *Faculty:* 46 full-time (3 women), 2 part-time/adjunct (1 woman). *Students:* 122 full-time (31 women), 37 part-time (7 women); includes 14 minority (9 African Americans, 4 Asian Americans or Pacific Islanders, 1 Hispanic American), 82 international. In 2009, 36 master's, 14 doctorates awarded. *Degree requirements:* For master's, thesis (for some programs); for doctorate, thesis/dissertation. *Entrance requirements:* For master's, GRE General Test, minimum GPA of 3.0; for doctorate, GRE General Test. Additional exam requirements/recommendations for international students: Required—TOEFL. *Application deadline:* For fall admission, 4/1 for domestic students; for spring admission, 10/1 for domestic students. Applications are processed on a rolling basis. Application fee: $25. Electronic applications accepted. *Financial support:* Scholarships/grants available. Financial award application deadline: 3/1; financial award applicants required to submit FAFSA. *Unit head:* Alexander Cheng, 662-915-7407, Fax: 662-915-1287, E-mail: engineer@olemiss.edu. *Application contact:* Dr. Christy M. Wyandt, Associate Dean, 662-915-7474, Fax: 662-915-7577, E-mail: cwyandt@olemiss.edu.

University of Missouri, Graduate School, College of Engineering, Columbia, MO 65211. Offers ME, MS, PhD. Part-time programs available. *Degree requirements:* For doctorate, thesis/dissertation. *Entrance requirements:* For master's and doctorate, GRE General Test. Additional exam requirements/recommendations for international students: Required—TOEFL.

University of Missouri–Kansas City, School of Computing and Engineering, Kansas City, MO 64110-2499. Offers civil engineering (MS); computer and electrical engineering (PhD); computer science (MS), including bioinformatics, software engineering, telecommunications networking; computer science and informatics (PhD); computing (PhD); electrical engineering (MS); engineering (PhD); mechanical engineering (MS); telecommunications (PhD). PhD (interdisciplinary) offered through the School of Graduate Studies. Part-time programs available. *Faculty:* 40 full-time (5 women), 28 part-time/adjunct (0 women). *Students:* 230 full-time (46 women), 158 part-time (31 women); includes 20 minority (5 African Americans, 12 Asian Americans or Pacific Islanders, 3 Hispanic Americans), 313 international. Average age 24. 484 applicants, 64% accepted, 106 enrolled. In 2009, 144 master's awarded. *Degree requirements:* For doctorate, thesis/dissertation. *Entrance requirements:* For master's, GRE General Test, minimum GPA of 3.0, 3 letters of recommendations from professors; for doctorate, GRE General Test, minimum GPA of 3.5. Additional exam requirements/recommendations for international students: Required—TOEFL (minimum score 550 paper-based; 213 computer-based; 80 iBT). *Application deadline:* For fall admission, 1/15 priority date for domestic students, 1/15 for international students. Applications are processed on a rolling basis. Application fee: $45 ($50 for international students). *Expenses:* Tuition, state resident: full-time $5378; part-time $299 per credit hour. Tuition, nonresident: full-time $13,881; part-time $771 per credit hour. Required fees: $641; $71 per credit hour. Tuition and fees vary according to course load and program. *Financial support:* In 2009–10, 29 research assistantships with partial tuition reimbursements (averaging $15,040 per year), 10 teaching assistantships with partial tuition reimbursements (averaging $12,118 per year) were awarded; career-related internships or fieldwork, Federal Work-Study, scholarships/grants, tuition waivers (partial), and unspecified assistantships also available. Support available to part-time students. Financial award application deadline: 3/1; financial award applicants required to submit FAFSA. *Faculty research:* Algorithms, bioinformatics and medical informatics, biomechanics/biomaterials, civil engineering materials, networking and telecommunications, thermal science. Total annual research expenditures: $1.4 million. *Unit head:* Dr. Kevin Z. Truman, Dean, 816-235-2399, Fax: 816-235-5159. *Application contact:* Dr. Kevin Z. Truman, Dean, 816-235-2399, Fax: 816-235-5159.

University of Nebraska–Lincoln, Graduate College, College of Engineering, Lincoln, NE 68588. Offers M Eng, MAE, MEE, MS, PhD. *Degree requirements:* For doctorate, comprehensive exam, thesis/dissertation. *Entrance requirements:* For master's and doctorate, GRE General Test. Additional exam requirements/recommendations for international students: Required—TOEFL. Electronic applications accepted.

University of Nevada, Las Vegas, Graduate College, Howard R. Hughes College of Engineering, Las Vegas, NV 89154-4005. Offers MS, MSE, PhD. Part-time programs available. *Faculty:* 67 full-time (9 women), 18 part-time/adjunct (0 women). *Students:* 131 full-time (23 women), 100 part-time (23 women); includes 36 minority (5 African Americans, 1 American Indian/Alaska Native, 24 Asian Americans or Pacific Islanders, 6 Hispanic Americans), 105 international. Average age 32. 246 applicants, 72% accepted, 85 enrolled. In 2009, 64 master's, 13 doctorates awarded. *Degree requirements:* For master's, comprehensive exam (for some programs), thesis (for some programs), final project; for doctorate, comprehensive exam, thesis/dissertation. *Entrance requirements:* Additional exam requirements/recommendations for international students: Required—TOEFL (minimum score 550 paper-based; 213 computer-based; 80 iBT), IELTS (minimum score 7). *Application deadline:* For fall admission, 8/1 for domestic students, 5/1 for international students; for spring admission, 12/1 for domestic students, 10/1 for international students. Applications are processed on a rolling basis. Application fee: $60 ($95 for international students). Electronic applications accepted. *Financial support:* In 2009–10, 121 students received support, including 57 research assistantships with partial

Engineering and Applied Sciences—General

University of Nevada, Las Vegas *(continued)*
tuition reimbursements available (averaging $12,288 per year), 64 teaching assistantships with partial tuition reimbursements available (averaging $10,751 per year); institutionally sponsored loans, scholarships/grants, health care benefits, and unspecified assistantships also available. Financial award application deadline: 3/1. Total annual research expenditures: $11.6 million. *Unit head:* Dr. Eric Sandgren, Dean, 702-895-3699, Fax: 702-895-4059, E-mail: eric.sandgren@unlv.edu. *Application contact:* Graduate College Admissions Evaluator, 702-895-3320, Fax: 702-895-4180, E-mail: gradcollege@unlv.edu.

University of Nevada, Reno, Graduate School, College of Engineering, Reno, NV 89557. Offers MS, PhD. Terminal master's awarded for partial completion of doctoral program. *Degree requirements:* For master's, thesis optional; for doctorate, thesis/dissertation. *Entrance requirements:* For master's, GRE General Test, minimum GPA of 2.75; for doctorate, GRE General Test, minimum GPA of 3.0. Additional exam requirements/recommendations for international students: Required—TOEFL (minimum score 500 paper-based; 173 computer-based; 61 iBT), IELTS (minimum score 6). Electronic applications accepted. *Faculty research:* Fabrication, development of new materials, structural and earthquake engineering, computer vision/virtual reality, acoustics, smart materials.

University of New Brunswick Fredericton, School of Graduate Studies, Faculty of Engineering, Fredericton, NB E3B 5A3, Canada. Offers M Eng, M Sc E, PhD, Certificate, Diploma. Part-time programs available. *Faculty:* 68 full-time (10 women), 17 part-time/adjunct (1 woman). *Students:* 216 full-time (49 women), 41 part-time (5 women). In 2009, 48 master's, 15 doctorates awarded. *Degree requirements:* For master's, thesis; for doctorate, comprehensive exam, thesis/dissertation, qualifying exam. *Entrance requirements:* For master's, minimum GPA of 3.0. Additional exam requirements/recommendations for international students: Required—TOEFL, TWE. *Application deadline:* For fall admission, 3/1 priority date for domestic students. Applications are processed on a rolling basis. Application fee: $50 Canadian dollars. Tuition and fees charges are reported in Canadian dollars. *Expenses:* Tuition, area resident: Full-time $5562 Canadian dollars; part-time $2781 Canadian dollars per year. Required fees: $49.75 Canadian dollars per term. *Financial support:* In 2009–10, 142 research assistantships, 188 teaching assistantships were awarded; career-related internships or fieldwork also available. *Unit head:* Dr. David Coleman, Dean, 506-453-4570, Fax: 506-453-4569, E-mail: dcoleman@unb.ca. *Application contact:* Dr. David Coleman, Dean, 506-453-4570, Fax: 506-453-4569, E-mail: dcoleman@unb.ca.

University of New Haven, Graduate School, Tagliatela College of Engineering, West Haven, CT 06516-1916. Offers EMS, MS, MSIE, Certificate. Part-time and evening/weekend programs available. *Faculty:* 17 full-time (4 women), 14 part-time/adjunct (2 women). *Students:* 108 full-time (26 women), 92 part-time (16 women); includes 23 minority (12 African Americans, 6 Asian Americans or Pacific Islanders, 5 Hispanic Americans), 104 international. Average age 29. 485 applicants, 89% accepted, 66 enrolled. In 2009, 118 master's, 11 other advanced degrees awarded. *Degree requirements:* For master's, thesis or alternative. *Entrance requirements:* Additional exam requirements/recommendations for international students: Required—TOEFL (minimum score 520 paper-based; 190 computer-based; 70 iBT); Recommended—IELTS (minimum score 5.5). *Application deadline:* For fall admission, 5/30 for international students; for winter admission, 10/15 for international students; for spring admission, 1/15 for international students. Applications are processed on a rolling basis. Application fee: $50. Electronic applications accepted. *Expenses:* Tuition: Part-time $700 per credit. Required fees: $45 per term. One-time fee: $390 part-time. *Financial support:* Research assistantships with partial tuition reimbursements, teaching assistantships with partial tuition reimbursements, career-related internships or fieldwork, Federal Work-Study, scholarships/grants, tuition waivers, and unspecified assistantships available. Support available to part-time students. Financial award applicants required to submit FAFSA. *Unit head:* Dr. Barry Farbrother, Dean, 203-932-7167. *Application contact:* Eloise Gormley, Director of Graduate Admissions, 203-932-7449, Fax: 203-932-7137, E-mail: gradinfo@newhaven.edu.

University of New Mexico, Graduate School, School of Engineering, Albuquerque, NM 87131-2039. Offers MCM, MEME, MS, PhD, Post-Doctoral Certificate, MBA/MEME. Part-time and evening/weekend programs available. *Faculty:* 136 full-time (21 women), 24 part-time/adjunct (3 women). *Students:* 413 full-time (85 women), 205 part-time (33 women); includes 98 minority (4 African Americans, 6 American Indian/Alaska Native, 10 Asian Americans or Pacific Islanders, 78 Hispanic Americans), 261 international. Average age 30. 647 applicants, 38% accepted, 139 enrolled. In 2009, 96 master's, 32 doctorates, 2 other advanced degrees awarded. *Entrance requirements:* Additional exam requirements/recommendations for international students: Required—TSE. *Application deadline:* Applications are processed on a rolling basis. Application fee: $50. Electronic applications accepted. *Expenses:* Tuition, state resident: full-time $2098.80; part-time $233.20 per credit hour. Tuition, nonresident: full-time $6650. Required fees: $25 per semester. Tuition and fees vary according to course load, program and reciprocity agreements. *Financial support:* In 2009–10, 4 fellowships (averaging $12,250 per year), 204 research assistantships (averaging $16,959 per year), 20 teaching assistantships (averaging $13,110 per year) were awarded. Financial award application deadline: 3/1; financial award applicants required to submit FAFSA. Total annual research expenditures: $12.6 million. *Unit head:* Dr. Joseph L. Cecchi, Dean, 505-277-5522, Fax: 505-277-1422, E-mail: cecchi@unm.edu. *Application contact:* Dr. Joseph L. Cecchi, Dean, 505-277-5522, Fax: 505-277-1422, E-mail: cecchi@unm.edu.

University of New Orleans, Graduate School, College of Engineering, New Orleans, LA 70148. Offers MS, PhD, Certificate. Part-time programs available. Terminal master's awarded for partial completion of doctoral program. *Degree requirements:* For master's, comprehensive exam, thesis optional; for doctorate, comprehensive exam, thesis/dissertation. *Entrance requirements:* For master's, GRE General Test, minimum GPA of 3.0; for doctorate, GRE General Test. Additional exam requirements/recommendations for international students: Required—TOEFL (minimum score 550 paper-based; 213 computer-based; 79 iBT). Electronic applications accepted. *Faculty research:* Electrical, civil, environmental, mechanical, naval architecture, and marine engineering.

The University of North Carolina at Charlotte, Graduate School, The William States Lee College of Engineering, Charlotte, NC 28223-0001. Offers MS, MSCE, MSE, MSEE, MSME, PhD. Part-time and evening/weekend programs available. *Faculty:* 98 full-time (12 women), 2 part-time/adjunct (0 women). *Students:* 232 full-time (48 women), 139 part-time (26 women); includes 19 African Americans, 8 American Indian/Alaska Native, 5 Hispanic Americans, 204 international. Average age 27. 652 applicants, 54% accepted, 104 enrolled. In 2009, 88 master's, 14 doctorates awarded. *Entrance requirements:* For master's, GRE General Test. Additional exam requirements/recommendations for international students: Required—TOEFL (minimum score 557 paper-based; 220 computer-based; 83 iBT). *Application deadline:* For fall admission, 7/1 for domestic students, 5/1 for international students; for spring admission, 11/1 for domestic students, 10/1 for international students. Applications are processed on a rolling basis. Application fee: $55. Electronic applications accepted. *Financial support:* In 2009–10, 159 students received support, including 5 fellowships (averaging $32,506 per year), 35 research assistantships (averaging $7,834 per year), 118 teaching assistantships (averaging $8,695 per year); career-related internships or fieldwork, Federal Work-Study, institutionally sponsored loans, scholarships/grants, and administrative assistantship also available. Support available to part-time students. Financial award application deadline: 4/1; financial award applicants required to submit FAFSA. *Faculty research:* Environmental engineering, structures and geotechnical engineering, precision engineering and precision metrology, optoelectronics and microelectronics, communications. Total annual research expenditures: $5.4 million. *Unit head:* Dr. Robert E. Johnson, Dean, 704-687-2301, Fax: 704-687-2352, E-mail: robejohn@uncc.edu. *Application contact:* Kathy B. Giddings, Director of Graduate Admissions, 704-687-5503, Fax: 704-687-3279, E-mail: gradadm@uncc.edu.

University of North Dakota, Graduate School, School of Engineering and Mines, Program in Engineering, Grand Forks, ND 58202. Offers PhD. *Degree requirements:* For doctorate,

comprehensive exam, thesis/dissertation, final exam. *Entrance requirements:* For doctorate, minimum GPA of 3.0. Additional exam requirements/recommendations for international students: Required—TOEFL (minimum score 550 paper-based; 213 computer-based; 79 iBT), IELTS (minimum score 6.5). Electronic applications accepted. *Faculty research:* Combustion science, energy conversion, power transmission, environmental engineering.

University of North Texas, Robert B. Toulouse School of Graduate Studies, College of Engineering, Department of Engineering Technology, Denton, TX 76207. Offers MS. Part-time programs available. *Degree requirements:* For master's, comprehensive exam (for some programs), project or thesis. *Entrance requirements:* For master's, GRE General Test, BS in related field. Additional exam requirements/recommendations for international students: Required—proof of English language proficiency required for non-native English speakers; Recommended—TOEFL (minimum score 550 paper-based; 213 computer-based; 79 iBT), IELTS (minimum score 6.5). *Application deadline:* For fall admission, 2/1 for international students; for spring admission, 4/1 for international students. Applications are processed on a rolling basis. Application fee: $50 ($75 for international students). Electronic applications accepted. *Expenses:* Tuition, state resident: full-time $4298; part-time $239 per contact hour. Tuition, nonresident: full-time $9878; part-time $549 per contact hour. Required fees: $265 per contact hour. *Financial support:* Fellowships, research assistantships with partial tuition reimbursements, teaching assistantships with partial tuition reimbursements available. Financial award application deadline: 4/15; financial award applicants required to submit FAFSA. *Faculty research:* Green design, steel structures, Piezoelectric system modeling, biophotonics, concrete pavement cracking. *Application contact:* Graduate Adviser, 940-565-2022, Fax: 940-565-2666, E-mail: kozak@unt.edu.

University of Notre Dame, Graduate School, College of Engineering, Notre Dame, IN 46556. Offers M Eng, MEME, MS, MS Aero E, MS Bio E, MS Ch E, MS Env E, MSCE, MSCSE, MSEE, MSME, PhD. Terminal master's awarded for partial completion of doctoral program. *Degree requirements:* For master's, comprehensive exam; for doctorate, thesis/dissertation. *Entrance requirements:* For master's and doctorate, GRE General Test. Additional exam requirements/recommendations for international students: Required—TOEFL. Electronic applications accepted.

University of Oklahoma, Graduate College, College of Engineering, Program in Engineering, Norman, OK 73019-0390. Offers MS, D Engr, PhD. Part-time programs available. *Faculty:* 2 full-time (1 woman). *Students:* 5 full-time (1 woman), 3 part-time (0 women); includes 2 minority (1 American Indian/Alaska Native, 1 Hispanic American), 1 international. In 2009, 1 master's, 2 doctorates awarded. *Degree requirements:* For doctorate, comprehensive exam, thesis/dissertation, oral and qualifying exams. *Entrance requirements:* For doctorate, GRE. Additional exam requirements/recommendations for international students: Required—TOEFL (minimum score 550 paper-based; 213 computer-based). *Application deadline:* For fall admission, 6/1 for domestic students, 4/1 for international students; for spring admission, 11/1 for domestic students, 9/1 for international students. Applications are processed on a rolling basis. Application fee: $40 ($90 for international students). Electronic applications accepted. *Expenses:* Tuition, state resident: full-time $3744; part-time $156 per credit hour. Tuition, nonresident: full-time $13,577; part-time $565.70 per credit hour. Required fees: $2415; $90.10 per credit hour. *Financial support:* In 2009–10, 5 students received support. Federal Work-Study, scholarships/grants, health care benefits, and unspecified assistantships available. Support available to part-time students. Financial award application deadline: 3/1; financial award applicants required to submit FAFSA. *Faculty research:* Bioengineering, energy, engineering education, infrastructure environment, nanotechnology and weather technology.

University of Ottawa, Faculty of Graduate and Postdoctoral Studies, Faculty of Engineering, Ottawa, ON K1N 6N5, Canada. Offers M Eng, MA Sc, MCS, PhD, Certificate. *Degree requirements:* For master's, thesis or alternative; for doctorate, thesis/dissertation. *Entrance requirements:* For master's, honors degree or equivalent, minimum B average. Electronic applications accepted.

University of Pennsylvania, School of Engineering and Applied Science, Philadelphia, PA 19104. Offers EMBA, MCIT, MS, MSE, PhD, AC, M Arch/MSE, MD/PhD, MSE/MBA, MSE/MCP, VMD/PhD. Part-time and evening/weekend programs available. *Faculty:* 106 full-time (14 women), 26 part-time/adjunct (1 woman). *Students:* 818 full-time (223 women), 310 part-time (65 women); includes 161 minority (25 African Americans, 121 Asian Americans or Pacific Islanders, 15 Hispanic Americans), 508 international. 3,076 applicants, 31% accepted, 516 enrolled. In 2009, 353 master's, 74 doctorates awarded. *Degree requirements:* For doctorate, thesis/dissertation. *Entrance requirements:* Additional exam requirements/recommendations for international students: Required—TOEFL. *Application deadline:* For fall admission, 6/1 priority date for domestic students, 5/1 priority date for international students; for spring admission, 11/1 priority date for domestic students, 10/1 priority date for international students. Applications are processed on a rolling basis. Application fee: $70. Electronic applications accepted. *Expenses:* Tuition: Full-time $25,660; part-time $4758 per course. Required fees: $2152; $270 per course. Tuition and fees vary according to course load, degree level and program. *Financial support:* In 2009–10, 393 students received support; fellowships, research assistantships, teaching assistantships, institutionally sponsored loans, scholarships/grants, traineeships, health care benefits, and unspecified assistantships available. Financial award application deadline: 12/15. *Unit head:* Eduardo D. Glandt, Dean, 215-898-7244, Fax: 215-573-2018, E-mail: seasdean@seas.upenn.edu. *Application contact:* Academic Programs Office, 215-898-4542, Fax: 215-573-5577, E-mail: engstats@seas.upenn.edu.

See Close-Up on page 91.

University of Pittsburgh, Katz Graduate School of Business, MBA/Master of Science in Engineering Dual-Degree Program, Pittsburgh, PA 15260. Offers MBA/MSE. Part-time and evening/weekend programs available. *Students:* 9 full-time (2 women), 20 part-time (2 women); includes 4 minority (all Hispanic Americans). Average age 26. 26 applicants, 81% accepted, 13 enrolled. *Entrance requirements:* Additional exam requirements/recommendations for international students: Required—TOEFL (minimum score 600 paper-based; 250 computer-based; 100 iBT), or IELTS. *Application deadline:* For fall admission, 7/1 for domestic and international students; for winter admission, 11/1 for domestic and international students; for spring admission, 3/1 for domestic and international students. Applications are processed on a rolling basis. Application fee: $50. Electronic applications accepted. *Expenses:* Tuition, state resident: full-time $16,402; part-time $665 per credit. Tuition, nonresident: full-time $28,694; part-time $1175 per credit. Required fees: $690; $175 per term. Tuition and fees vary according to program. *Financial support:* In 2009–10, 4 students received support. Career-related internships or fieldwork and scholarships/grants available. Financial award application deadline: 6/1; financial award applicants required to submit FAFSA. *Faculty research:* Diffusion of technology-driven innovation, customer-focused development of engineered and high-tech products and services, logistics and operations research, global supply chains, value innovation and sustainable innovation—green products for the planet's population. *Unit head:* William T. Valenta, Assistant Dean/Director of MBA Programs, 412-648-1610, Fax: 412-648-1659, E-mail: wtvalenta@katz.pitt.edu. *Application contact:* Cliff McCormick, Director of MBA Admissions, 412-648-1700, Fax: 412-648-1659, E-mail: mba@katz.pitt.edu.

University of Pittsburgh, School of Engineering, Pittsburgh, PA 15260. Offers MS Ch E, MSBENG, MSCEE, MSEE, MSIE, MSME, MSPE, PhD, MD/PhD, MS Ch E/MSPE. Part-time programs available. *Faculty:* 104 full-time (16 women), 211 part-time/adjunct (21 women). *Students:* 469 full-time (128 women), 282 part-time (44 women); includes 60 minority (18 African Americans, 2 American Indian/Alaska Native, 25 Asian Americans or Pacific Islanders, 15 Hispanic Americans), 250 international. 1,841 applicants, 36% accepted, 194 enrolled. In 2009, 94 master's, 44 doctorates awarded. Terminal master's awarded for partial completion of doctoral program. *Degree requirements:* For doctorate, comprehensive exam, thesis/dissertation, final oral exams. *Entrance requirements:* Additional exam requirements/recommendations for international students: Required—TOEFL (minimum score 550 paper-based; 213 computer-based; 80 iBT). *Application deadline:* For fall admission, 3/1 priority date for domestic students;

for spring admission, 7/1 priority date for domestic students. Applications are processed on a rolling basis. Application fee: $50. Electronic applications accepted. *Expenses:* Contact institution. *Financial support:* In 2009–10, 397 students received support, including 72 fellowships with full tuition reimbursements available (averaging $20,772 per year), 247 research assistantships with full tuition reimbursements available (averaging $22,000 per year), 78 teaching assistantships with full tuition reimbursements available (averaging $21,000 per year); scholarships/grants, traineeships, and tuition waivers (full and partial) also available. Financial award application deadline: 4/15. *Faculty research:* Artificial organs, biotechnology, signal processing, construction management, fluid dynamics. Total annual research expenditures: $68.1 million. *Unit head:* Dr. Gerald D. Holder, Dean, 412-624-9811, Fax: 412-624-0412, E-mail: holder@engrng.pitt.edu. *Application contact:* 412-624-9800, Fax: 412-624-9808, E-mail: admin@engrng.pitt.edu.

University of Portland, School of Engineering, Portland, OR 97203-5798. Offers ME. Part-time and evening/weekend programs available. *Faculty:* 16 full-time (0 women). *Students:* 1 full-time (0 women), all international. Average age 28. In 2009, 1 master's awarded. *Entrance requirements:* For master's, GRE General Test, minimum GPA of 3.0, 3 letters of recommendation, resume, statement of goals, official transcripts. Additional exam requirements/recommendations for international students: Required—TOEFL (minimum score 550 paper-based; 80 iBT), IELTS (minimum score 7). *Application deadline:* For fall admission, 7/15 priority date for domestic and international students; for spring admission, 12/15 priority date for domestic and international students. Applications are processed on a rolling basis. Application fee: $50. *Expenses:* Contact institution. *Financial support:* Teaching assistantships, career-related internships or fieldwork, Federal Work-Study, and scholarships/grants available. Support available to part-time students. Financial award application deadline: 3/1; financial award applicants required to submit FAFSA. *Unit head:* Dr. Zia Yamayee, Dean, 503-943-7314. *Application contact:* Dr. Khalid Khan, Director, 503-943-7276, E-mail: khan@up.edu.

University of Puerto Rico, Mayagüez Campus, Graduate Studies, College of Engineering, Mayagüez, PR 00681-9000. Offers ME, MS, PhD. Part-time programs available. *Degree requirements:* For master's, comprehensive exam; for doctorate, one foreign language, thesis/dissertation. *Entrance requirements:* Additional exam requirements/recommendations for international students: Required—TOEFL or IELTS.

University of Regina, Faculty of Graduate Studies and Research, Faculty of Engineering and Applied Science, Regina, SK S4S 0A2, Canada. Offers M Eng, MA Sc, PhD. *Faculty:* 39 full-time (7 women), 37 part-time/adjunct (10 women). *Students:* 155 full-time (37 women), 22 part-time (8 women). 295 applicants, 46% accepted. In 2009, 27 master's, 13 doctorates awarded. *Degree requirements:* For master's, project or thesis; for doctorate, comprehensive exam, thesis/dissertation. *Entrance requirements:* Additional exam requirements/recommendations for international students: Required—TOEFL (minimum score 550 paper-based; 213 computer-based; 80 iBT). *Application deadline:* Applications are processed on a rolling basis. Application fee: $90 ($100 for international students). Electronic applications accepted. *Expenses:* Contact institution. *Financial support:* In 2009–10, 42 fellowships (averaging $19,000 per year), 17 research assistantships (averaging $16,910 per year), 57 teaching assistantships (averaging $6,650 per year) were awarded; career-related internships or fieldwork and scholarships/grants also available. Financial award application deadline: 6/15. *Unit head:* Dr. Paitoon Tontiwachwuthikul, Dean, 306-585-4160, Fax: 306-585-4855, E-mail: paitoon.tontiwachwuthikul@uregina.ca. *Application contact:* Crystal Pick, Information Contact, 306-337-2603, E-mail: crystal.pick@uregina.ca.

University of Rhode Island, Graduate School, College of Engineering, Kingston, RI 02881. Offers MS, PhD, Graduate Certificate. *Accreditation:* ABET (one or more programs are accredited). Part-time programs available. *Faculty:* 54 full-time (9 women), 10 part-time/adjunct (0 women). *Students:* 107 full-time (28 women), 92 part-time (19 women); includes 19 minority (7 African Americans, 6 Asian Americans or Pacific Islanders, 6 Hispanic Americans), 53 international. In 2009, 48 master's, 7 doctorates awarded. *Entrance requirements:* Additional exam requirements/recommendations for international students: Required—TOEFL (minimum score 550 paper-based; 213 computer-based). Application fee: $65. Electronic applications accepted. *Expenses:* Tuition, state resident: full-time $8828; part-time $490 per credit hour. Tuition, nonresident: full-time $22,100; part-time $1228 per credit hour. Required fees: $1118; $57 per semester. Tuition and fees vary according to program. *Financial support:* In 2009–10, 31 research assistantships with full and partial tuition reimbursements (averaging $8,698 per year), 21 teaching assistantships with full and partial tuition reimbursements (averaging $9,443 per year) were awarded. Financial award applicants required to submit FAFSA. Total annual research expenditures: $6 million. *Unit head:* Dr. Raymond Wright, Dean, 401-874-2186, Fax: 401-782-1066, E-mail: dean@egr.uri.edu. *Application contact:* Dr. Raymond Wright, Dean, 401-874-2186, Fax: 401-782-1066, E-mail: dean@egr.uri.edu.

University of Rochester, The College, School of Engineering and Applied Sciences, Rochester, NY 14627. Offers MS, PhD. Part-time programs available. Terminal master's awarded for partial completion of doctoral program. *Degree requirements:* For master's, comprehensive exam, thesis optional; for doctorate, thesis/dissertation, preliminary and oral exams. *Entrance requirements:* For master's and doctorate, GRE. Additional exam requirements/recommendations for international students: Required—TOEFL.

See Close-Up on page 93.

University of St. Thomas, Graduate Studies, School of Engineering, St. Paul, MN 55105-1096. Offers engineering and technology management (Certificate); manufacturing systems (MS); manufacturing systems engineering (MMSE); systems engineering (MS); technology management (MS). *Accreditation:* ABET (one or more programs are accredited). Electronic applications accepted. *Expenses:* Contact institution.

University of Saskatchewan, College of Graduate Studies and Research, College of Engineering, Saskatoon, SK S7N 5A2, Canada. Offers M Eng, M Sc, PhD, Diploma. *Degree requirements:* For doctorate, thesis/dissertation. *Entrance requirements:* For master's and doctorate, GRE. Additional exam requirements/recommendations for international students: Required—TOEFL. Tuition and fees charges are reported in Canadian dollars. *Expenses:* Tuition, area resident: Full-time $3000 Canadian dollars; part-time $500 Canadian dollars per term. Required fees: $700 Canadian dollars; $100 Canadian dollars per term.

University of South Africa, College of Science, Engineering and Technology, Pretoria, South Africa. Offers chemical engineering (M Tech); information technology (M Tech).

University of South Alabama, Graduate School, College of Engineering, Mobile, AL 36688-0002. Offers MS Ch E, MSCE, MSEE, MSME. Part-time programs available. *Degree requirements:* For master's, project or thesis. *Entrance requirements:* For master's, GRE General Test, BS in engineering, minimum GPA of 3.0. *Expenses:* Tuition, state resident: part-time $218 per contact hour. Required fees: $1102 per year.

University of South Carolina, The Graduate School, College of Engineering and Computing, Columbia, SC 29208. Offers ME, MS, PhD. Part-time and evening/weekend programs available. Postbaccalaureate distance learning degree programs offered (minimal on-campus study). *Degree requirements:* For master's, thesis (for some programs); for doctorate, thesis/dissertation. *Entrance requirements:* For master's and doctorate, GRE General Test. Additional exam requirements/recommendations for international students: Required—TOEFL. Electronic applications accepted. *Faculty research:* Electrochemical engineering/fuel cell technology, fracture mechanics and nondestructive evaluation, virtual prototyping for electric power systems, wideband-gap electronics materials behavior/composites and smart materials.

University of Southern California, Graduate School, Viterbi School of Engineering, Los Angeles, CA 90089. Offers MCM, ME, MS, PhD, Engr, Graduate Certificate, MS/MBA. Part-time programs available. Postbaccalaureate distance learning degree programs offered (no on-campus study). *Faculty:* 164 full-time (15 women), 66 part-time/adjunct (12 women). *Students:* 2,598 full-time (566 women), 1,833 part-time (361 women); includes 709 minority (65 African Americans, 8 American Indian/Alaska Native, 500 Asian Americans or Pacific Islanders, 136 Hispanic Americans), 2,555 international. 6,123 applicants, 46% accepted, 1221 enrolled. In 2009, 1,205 master's, 139 doctorates, 16 other advanced degrees awarded. Terminal master's awarded for partial completion of doctoral program. *Degree requirements:* For doctorate, comprehensive exam, thesis/dissertation. *Entrance requirements:* For master's and doctorate, GRE. *Application deadline:* For fall admission, 4/1 priority date for domestic and international students; for spring admission, 10/1 priority date for domestic and international students. Applications are processed on a rolling basis. Application fee: $85. Electronic applications accepted. *Expenses:* Contact institution. *Financial support:* In 2009–10, 858 students received support, including 103 fellowships with full tuition reimbursements available (averaging $30,000 per year), 492 research assistantships with full tuition reimbursements available (averaging $18,800 per year), 263 teaching assistantships with full tuition reimbursements available (averaging $18,800 per year); institutionally sponsored loans and scholarships/grants also available. Financial award application deadline: 12/1. *Faculty research:* Mechanics and materials, aerodynamics of air/ground vehicles, gas dynamics, aerosols, astronautics and space science, geophysical and microgravity flows, planetary physics, power MEMs and MEMS vacuum pumps, heat transfer and combustion, health systems, transportation and logistics, manufacturing and automation, engineering systems design, risk and economic analysis, electromagnetic devices circuits and VLSI, MEMS and nanotechnology, electromagnetics and plasmas. Total annual research expenditures: $168 million. *Unit head:* Dr. Yannis C. Yortsos, Dean, 213-740-0617, Fax: 213-740-8493, E-mail: engrdean@usc.edu. *Application contact:* Margery Berti, Associate Dean, 213-740-6241, Fax: 213-740-2367, E-mail: berti@usc.edu.

University of Southern Indiana, Graduate Studies, College of Science and Engineering, Evansville, IN 47712-3590. Offers MS. Part-time and evening/weekend programs available. *Faculty:* 6 full-time (3 women), 1 (woman) part-time/adjunct. *Students:* 12 part-time (4 women). Average age 33. 1 applicant, 100% accepted, 1 enrolled. In 2009, 2 master's awarded. *Degree requirements:* For master's, project. *Entrance requirements:* For master's, minimum GPA of 2.5, BS in engineering or engineering technology. Additional exam requirements/recommendations for international students: Required—TOEFL (minimum score 550 paper-based; 213 computer-based; 79 iBT), IELTS (minimum score 6). *Application deadline:* For fall admission, 8/15 priority date for domestic students, 3/1 priority date for international students. Applications are processed on a rolling basis. Application fee: $25. Electronic applications accepted. *Expenses:* Tuition, state resident: full-time $4592; part-time $255 per credit hour. Tuition, nonresident: full-time $9060; part-time $503 per credit hour. Required fees: $220; $22.75 per term. Tuition and fees vary according to course load and reciprocity agreements. *Financial support:* In 2009–10, 2 students received support. Federal Work-Study, scholarships/grants, tuition waivers (full and partial), and unspecified assistantships available. Financial award application deadline: 3/1; financial award applicants required to submit FAFSA. *Unit head:* Dr. Scott A. Gordon, Dean, 812-465-7137, E-mail: sgordon@usi.edu. *Application contact:* Dr. Peggy F. Harrel, Director, Graduate Studies, 812-465-7015, Fax: 812-464-1956, E-mail: pharrel@usi.edu.

University of Southern Mississippi, Graduate School, College of Science and Technology, School of Computing, Hattiesburg, MS 39406-0001. Offers computational science (MS, PhD); computer science (MS, PhD); engineering technology (MS). *Faculty:* 18 full-time (3 women), 1 (woman) part-time/adjunct. *Students:* 72 full-time (20 women), 21 part-time (6 women); includes 7 minority (5 African Americans, 2 Hispanic Americans), 51 international. Average age 29. 101 applicants, 61% accepted, 24 enrolled. In 2009, 15 master's awarded. *Degree requirements:* For master's, comprehensive exam, thesis; for doctorate, comprehensive exam, thesis/dissertation. *Entrance requirements:* For master's, GRE General Test, minimum GPA of 2.75 in last 60 hours. Additional exam requirements/recommendations for international students: Required—TOEFL. *Application deadline:* For fall admission, 3/15 priority date for domestic students, 3/15 for international students. Applications are processed on a rolling basis. Application fee: $35. *Expenses:* Tuition, state resident: full-time $5096; part-time $284 per hour. Tuition, nonresident: full-time $13,052; part-time $726 per hour. Required fees: $402. Tuition and fees vary according to course level and course load. *Financial support:* In 2009–10, 29 research assistantships with full tuition reimbursements (averaging $8,750 per year), 7 teaching assistantships with full tuition reimbursements (averaging $9,944 per year) were awarded; Federal Work-Study and institutionally sponsored loans also available. Financial award application deadline: 3/15; financial award applicants required to submit FAFSA. *Faculty research:* Satellite telecommunications, advanced life-support systems, artificial intelligence. *Unit head:* Dr. Adel Ali, Chair, 601-266-4949, Fax: 601-266-6452. *Application contact:* Shonna Breland, Manager of Graduate Admissions, 601-266-6563, Fax: 601-266-5138.

University of South Florida, Graduate School, College of Engineering, Tampa, FL 33620-9951. Offers MCE, MCH, ME, MIE, MME, MSBE, MSBE, MSCE, MSCP, MSCS, MSEE, MSEM, MSES, MSIE, MSME, PhD. Part-time and evening/weekend programs available. *Faculty:* 92 full-time (11 women), 10 part-time/adjunct (1 woman). *Students:* 474 full-time (138 women), 294 part-time (58 women); includes 178 minority (60 African Americans, 1 American Indian/Alaska Native, 50 Asian Americans or Pacific Islanders, 67 Hispanic Americans), 288 international. Average age 32. 760 applicants, 59% accepted, 220 enrolled. In 2009, 211 master's, 37 doctorates awarded. Terminal master's awarded for partial completion of doctoral program. *Degree requirements:* For master's, comprehensive exam, thesis; for doctorate, comprehensive exam, thesis/dissertation. *Entrance requirements:* For master's, GRE General Test, minimum GPA of 3.0 in last 60 hours of coursework; for doctorate, GRE General Test, minimum GPA of 3.3 in last 60 hours of coursework. Additional exam requirements/recommendations for international students: Required—TOEFL (minimum score 550 paper-based; 213 computer-based). *Application deadline:* For fall admission, 2/15 for domestic students, 1/2 priority date for international students; for spring admission, 10/15 for domestic students, 6/1 priority date for international students. Applications are processed on a rolling basis. Application fee: $30. Electronic applications accepted. *Financial support:* Career-related internships or fieldwork, Federal Work-Study, scholarships/grants, health care benefits, and unspecified assistantships available. Financial award application deadline: 3/1; financial award applicants required to submit FAFSA. Total annual research expenditures: $64,893. *Unit head:* Dr. John Wieneck, Dean, 813-974-2530, Fax: 813-974-5094, E-mail: wieneck@eng.usf.edu. *Application contact:* Marsha L. Brett, Administrative Assistant, 813-974-3782, Fax: 813-974-5094, E-mail: brett@eng.usf.edu.

The University of Tennessee, Graduate School, College of Engineering, Knoxville, TN 37996. Offers MS, PhD, MS/MBA, MS/PhD. Part-time and evening/weekend programs available. Postbaccalaureate distance learning degree programs offered. *Faculty:* 143 full-time (10 women), 63 part-time/adjunct (4 women). *Students:* 501 full-time (91 women), 325 part-time (44 women); includes 59 minority (31 African Americans, 3 American Indian/Alaska Native, 18 Asian Americans or Pacific Islanders, 7 Hispanic Americans), 307 international. Average age 25. 1,336 applicants, 28% accepted, 167 enrolled. In 2009, 204 master's, 59 doctorates awarded. *Degree requirements:* For master's, thesis or alternative; for doctorate, comprehensive exam, thesis/dissertation. *Entrance requirements:* For master's and doctorate, GRE, minimum GPA of 2.7. Additional exam requirements/recommendations for international students: Required—TOEFL (minimum score 550 paper-based; 213 computer-based). *Application deadline:* For fall admission, 2/1 priority date for domestic and international students; for spring admission, 6/15 priority date for international students. Applications are processed on a rolling basis. Application fee: $35. Electronic applications accepted. *Expenses:* Tuition, state resident: full-time $6826; part-time $380 per semester hour. Tuition, nonresident: full-time $21,844; part-time $1147 per semester hour. Tuition and fees vary according to program. *Financial support:* In 2009–10, 278 students received support, including 54 fellowships with full tuition reimbursements available (averaging $9,897 per year), 391 research assistantships with full tuition reimbursements available (averaging $16,881 per year), 154 teaching assistantships with full tuition reimbursements available (averaging $11,694 per year); career-related internships or fieldwork, Federal Work-Study, institutionally sponsored loans, health care benefits, and unspecified assistantships also available. Financial award application deadline: 2/1; financial award applicants required to

Engineering and Applied Sciences—General

The University of Tennessee (continued)
submit FAFSA. Total annual research expenditures: $42 million. *Unit head:* Dr. Wayne T. Davis, Dean, 865-974-5321, Fax: 865-974-8890, E-mail: way@utk.edu. *Application contact:* Dr. Masood Parang, Associate Dean of Student Affairs, 865-974-2454, Fax: 865-974-9871, E-mail: mparang@utk.edu.

The University of Tennessee at Chattanooga, Graduate School, College of Engineering and Computer Science, Chattanooga, TN 37403. Offers MS, MS Engr, PhD, Graduate Certificate. Part-time and evening/weekend programs available. Postbaccalaureate distance learning degree programs offered (no on-campus study). *Faculty:* 22 full-time (3 women), 2 part-time/adjunct (1 woman). *Students:* 64 full-time (20 women), 120 part-time (20 women); includes 44 minority (17 African Americans, 22 Asian Americans or Pacific Islanders, 5 Hispanic Americans), 26 international. Average age 33. 150 applicants, 60% accepted, 52 enrolled. In 2009, 37 master's, 4 doctorates, 8 other advanced degrees awarded. *Degree requirements:* For master's, comprehensive exam, thesis or alternative, capstone project; for doctorate, comprehensive exam, thesis/dissertation. *Entrance requirements:* For master's, GRE. Additional exam requirements/recommendations for international students: Required—TOEFL (minimum score 550 paper-based; 213 computer-based; 79 iBT), IELTS (minimum score 6). *Application deadline:* For fall admission, 8/1 priority date for domestic students, 6/1 for international students; for spring admission, 12/1 priority date for domestic students, 10/1 for international students. Applications are processed on a rolling basis. Application fee: $35. Electronic applications accepted. *Expenses:* Tuition, state resident: full-time $5404; part-time $300 per credit hour. Tuition, nonresident: full-time $16,702; part-time $928 per credit hour. Required fees: $1150; $130 per credit hour. *Financial support:* In 2009–10, 39 research assistantships with full and partial tuition reimbursements (averaging $5,500 per year) were awarded; career-related internships or fieldwork, scholarships/grants, and unspecified assistantships also available. Support available to part-time students. *Faculty research:* Quality control and project management, aerodynamics, artificial intelligence, computational design, network security. Total annual research expenditures: $6.9 million. *Unit head:* Dr. William Sutton, Dean, 423-425-2256, Fax: 423-425-5229, E-mail: will-sutton@utc.edu. *Application contact:* Dr. Stephanie Bellar, Dean of Graduate Studies, 423-425-4666, Fax: 423-425-5223, E-mail: stephanie-bellar@utc.edu.

The University of Tennessee Space Institute, Graduate Programs, Tullahoma, TN 37388-9700. Offers MS, PhD. Part-time programs available. Postbaccalaureate distance learning degree programs offered. *Faculty:* 23 full-time (3 women), 37 part-time/adjunct (2 women). *Students:* 46 full-time (5 women), 120 part-time (19 women); includes 17 minority (10 African Americans, 3 American Indian/Alaska Native, 2 Asian Americans or Pacific Islanders, 2 Hispanic Americans), 12 international. 49 applicants, 71% accepted, 14 enrolled. In 2009, 47 master's, 2 doctorates awarded. Terminal master's awarded for partial completion of doctoral program. *Degree requirements:* For doctorate, one foreign language, thesis/dissertation. *Entrance requirements:* Additional exam requirements/recommendations for international students: Required—TOEFL (minimum score 550 paper-based; 213 computer-based; 80 iBT), IELTS (minimum score 6.5). *Application deadline:* For fall admission, 2/1 for international students; for spring admission, 6/15 for international students. Applications are processed on a rolling basis. Application fee: $35. Electronic applications accepted. *Expenses:* Tuition, state resident: full-time $6826; part-time $380 per hour. Tuition, nonresident: full-time $20,622; part-time $1147 per hour. Required fees: $10 per hour. One-time fee: $90 full-time. *Financial support:* In 2009–10, 6 fellowships with full and partial tuition reimbursements (averaging $2,500 per year), 39 research assistantships with full tuition reimbursements (averaging $17,791 per year) were awarded; career-related internships or fieldwork, Federal Work-Study, institutionally sponsored loans, health care benefits, tuition waivers (full and partial), and unspecified assistantships also available. *Faculty research:* Materials processing, computational fluid dynamics, aerodynamics, laser applications. *Unit head:* Dr. Gregory Sedrick, Dean and Professor, 931-393-7318, Fax: 931-393-7201, E-mail: gsedrick@utsi.edu. *Application contact:* Dee Merriman, Coordinator III, 931-393-7293, Fax: 931-393-7201, E-mail: dmerrima@utsi.edu.

The University of Texas at Arlington, Graduate School, College of Engineering, Arlington, TX 76019. Offers M Engr, M Sw En, MS, PhD. Part-time and evening/weekend programs available. Postbaccalaureate distance learning degree programs offered (minimal on-campus study). *Faculty:* 118 full-time (9 women), 133 part-time/adjunct (12 women). *Students:* 984 full-time (218 women), 607 part-time (129 women); includes 135 minority (22 African Americans, 72 Asian Americans or Pacific Islanders, 41 Hispanic Americans), 1,182 international. Average age 27. 1,629 applicants, 98% accepted, 378 enrolled. In 2009, 428 master's, 45 doctorates awarded. Terminal master's awarded for partial completion of doctoral program. *Degree requirements:* For master's, thesis optional; for doctorate, thesis/dissertation. *Entrance requirements:* For master's, GRE General Test, minimum GPA of 3.0 in last 60 hours of coursework; for doctorate, GRE General Test. Additional exam requirements/recommendations for international students: Required—TOEFL (minimum score 550 paper-based; 213 computer-based). *Application deadline:* For fall admission, 6/6 for domestic students, 4/4 for international students; for spring admission, 10/17 for domestic students, 9/5 for international students. Applications are processed on a rolling basis. Application fee: $35 ($50 for international students). *Financial support:* Fellowships, research assistantships, teaching assistantships, career-related internships or fieldwork, Federal Work-Study, institutionally sponsored loans, scholarships/grants, and tuition waivers (partial) available. Financial award application deadline: 6/1; financial award applicants required to submit FAFSA. *Faculty research:* Nanotechnology, mobile pervasive computing, bioinformatics intelligent systems. *Unit head:* Dr. Bill D. Carroll, Dean, 817-272-2571, Fax: 817-272-5110, E-mail: carroll@uta.edu. *Application contact:* Dr. Lynn L. Peterson, Associate Dean for Academic Affairs, 817-272-2571, Fax: 817-272-2548, E-mail: peterson@uta.edu.

The University of Texas at Austin, Graduate School, Cockrell School of Engineering, Austin, TX 78712-1111. Offers MA, MS, MSE, PhD, MBA/MSE, MD/PhD, MP Aff/MSE. *Accreditation:* ABET (one or more programs are accredited). Part-time and evening/weekend programs available. *Entrance requirements:* For master's and doctorate, GRE General Test. Additional exam requirements/recommendations for international students: Required—TOEFL (minimum score 550 paper-based; 213 computer-based). Electronic applications accepted.

The University of Texas at Dallas, Erik Jonsson School of Engineering and Computer Science, Richardson, TX 75080. Offers MS, MSEE, MSME, MSTE, PhD. Part-time and evening/weekend programs available. *Faculty:* 96 full-time (12 women), 5 part-time/adjunct (1 woman). *Students:* 859 full-time (204 women), 355 part-time (65 women); includes 138 minority (17 African Americans, 1 American Indian/Alaska Native, 97 Asian Americans or Pacific Islanders, 23 Hispanic Americans), 868 international. Average age 27. 2,229 applicants, 40% accepted, 320 enrolled. In 2009, 372 master's, 30 doctorates awarded. *Degree requirements:* For master's, thesis optional; for doctorate, thesis/dissertation. *Entrance requirements:* For master's, GRE General Test, minimum GPA of 3.0 in related bachelor's course work; for doctorate, GRE General Test, minimum GPA of 3.5. Additional exam requirements/recommendations for international students: Required—TOEFL (minimum score 550 paper-based; 213 computer-based). *Application deadline:* For fall admission, 7/15 for domestic students, 5/1 priority date for international students; for spring admission, 11/15 for domestic students, 9/1 priority date for international students. Applications are processed on a rolling basis. Application fee: $50 ($100 for international students). Electronic applications accepted. *Expenses:* Tuition, state resident: full-time $11,068; part-time $461 per credit hour. Tuition, nonresident: full-time $21,178; part-time $882 per credit hour. Tuition and fees vary according to course load. *Financial support:* In 2009–10, 12 fellowships with full tuition reimbursements (averaging $18,650 per year), 220 research assistantships with full tuition reimbursements (averaging $17,528 per year), 84 teaching assistantships with full tuition reimbursements (averaging $17,670 per year) were awarded; career-related internships or fieldwork, Federal Work-Study, institutionally sponsored loans, scholarships/grants, and unspecified assistantships also available. Support available to part-time students. Financial award application deadline: 4/30; financial award applicants required to submit FAFSA. *Faculty research:* Telecommunications, optical devices, software engineering, materials and systems, artificial intelligence. Total annual research expenditures: $18.6 million. *Unit head:* Dr. Mark Spong, Dean, 972-883-2974, Fax: 972-883-2813, E-mail: ecsdean@utdallas.edu. *Application contact:* Dr. Cy Cantrell, Senior Associate Dean, 972-883-6234, Fax: 972-883-2813, E-mail: gradecs@utdallas.edu.

The University of Texas at El Paso, Graduate School, College of Engineering, El Paso, TX 79968-0001. Offers MEENE, MS, MSENE, MSIT, PhD. Part-time and evening/weekend programs available. *Students:* 431 (97 women); includes 161 minority (3 African Americans, 8 Asian Americans or Pacific Islanders, 150 Hispanic Americans), 250 international. Average age 28. 338 applicants, 49% accepted. In 2009, 116 master's, 8 doctorates awarded. *Degree requirements:* For master's, thesis optional; for doctorate, thesis/dissertation. *Entrance requirements:* For master's, GRE, minimum GPA of 3.0, letters of reference; for doctorate, GRE, Statement of Purpose, Letters of Reference. Additional exam requirements/recommendations for international students: Required—TOEFL; Recommended—IELTS. *Application deadline:* For fall admission, 8/1 priority date for domestic students, 3/1 for international students; for spring admission, 11/1 priority date for domestic students, 9/1 for international students. Applications are processed on a rolling basis. Application fee: $45 ($80 for international students). Electronic applications accepted. *Expenses:* Contact institution. *Financial support:* In 2009–10, research assistantships with partial tuition reimbursements (averaging $21,125 per year), teaching assistantships with partial tuition reimbursements (averaging $16,900 per year) were awarded; fellowships with partial tuition reimbursements, institutionally sponsored loans, scholarships/grants, health care benefits, tuition waivers (partial), and unspecified assistantships also available. Support available to part-time students. Financial award application deadline: 3/15; financial award applicants required to submit FAFSA. *Unit head:* Dr. Richard Schoephoerster, Dean, 915-747-6444, Fax: 915-747-5437, E-mail: schoephoerster@utep.edu. *Application contact:* Dr. Patricia D. Witherspoon, Dean of the Graduate School, 915-747-5491, Fax: 915-747-5788, E-mail: withersp@utep.edu.

The University of Texas at San Antonio, College of Engineering, San Antonio, TX 78249-0617. Offers MS, MSCE, MSEE, MSME, PhD. Part-time and evening/weekend programs available. *Faculty:* 51 full-time (7 women), 6 part-time/adjunct (0 women). *Students:* 194 full-time (53 women), 165 part-time (36 women); includes 81 minority (11 African Americans, 19 Asian Americans or Pacific Islanders, 51 Hispanic Americans), 182 international. Average age 28. 378 applicants, 74% accepted, 117 enrolled. In 2009, 37 master's, 19 doctorates awarded. *Degree requirements:* For master's, comprehensive exam (for some programs), thesis (for some programs); for doctorate, comprehensive exam, thesis/dissertation. *Entrance requirements:* For master's, GRE General Test, minimum GPA of 3.0 in last 60 hours of bachelor's degree; for doctorate, GRE. Additional exam requirements/recommendations for international students: Required—TOEFL (minimum score 500 paper-based; 173 computer-based), IELTS (minimum score 5). *Application deadline:* For fall admission, 7/1 for domestic students, 4/1 for international students; for spring admission, 11/1 for domestic students, 9/1 for international students. Applications are processed on a rolling basis. Application fee: $45 ($80 for international students). Electronic applications accepted. *Expenses:* Tuition, state resident: full-time $3975; part-time $221 per contact hour. Tuition, nonresident: full-time $13,947; part-time $775 per contact hour. Required fees: $1853. *Financial support:* In 2009–10, 144 students received support, including 23 fellowships (averaging $28,879 per year), 110 research assistantships (averaging $12,699 per year), 41 teaching assistantships (averaging $11,243 per year); career-related internships or fieldwork, institutionally sponsored loans, scholarships/grants, tuition waivers, and unspecified assistantships also available. Support available to part-time students. Financial award application deadline: 3/31. Total annual research expenditures: $2.5 million. *Unit head:* Dr. C. Mauli Agarwal, Dean, 210-458-5526, Fax: 210-458-5556, E-mail: mauli.agarwal@utsa.edu. *Application contact:* Dr. Dorothy A. Flannagan, Dean of the Graduate School, 210-458-4330, Fax: 210-458-4332, E-mail: dorothy.flannagan@utsa.edu.

University of the District of Columbia, School of Engineering and Applied Science, Washington, DC 20008-1175. Offers MS. *Expenses:* Tuition, state resident: full-time $7580. Tuition, nonresident: full-time $14,580. Required fees: $620. *Unit head:* Dr. Ben O. Latigo, Dean, 202-274-5220, E-mail: blatigo@udc.edu. *Application contact:* Ann Marie Waterman, Associate Vice President for Admission, Recruitment and Financial Aid, 202-274-6110.

The University of Toledo, College of Graduate Studies, College of Engineering, Program in Engineering, Toledo, OH 43606-3390. Offers general engineering (MS). *Accreditation:* ABET. *Entrance requirements:* For master's, GRE General Test, minimum GPA of 2.7, industrial experience.

University of Toronto, School of Graduate Studies, Physical Sciences Division, Faculty of Applied Science and Engineering, Toronto, ON M5S 1A1, Canada. Offers M Eng, MA Sc, MH Sc, PhD. Part-time programs available. *Degree requirements:* For doctorate, thesis/dissertation. *Expenses:* Contact institution.

University of Tulsa, Graduate School, College of Engineering and Natural Sciences, Tulsa, OK 74104-3189. Offers ME, MS, MSE, MTA, PhD, JD/MS, MBA/MS, MSF/MSAM. Part-time programs available. *Faculty:* 90 full-time (13 women), 13 part-time/adjunct (3 women). *Students:* 239 full-time (65 women), 66 part-time (22 women); includes 15 minority (3 African Americans, 5 American Indian/Alaska Native, 4 Asian Americans or Pacific Islanders, 3 Hispanic Americans), 169 international. Average age 26. 563 applicants, 44% accepted, 118 enrolled. In 2009, 81 master's, 9 doctorates awarded. *Degree requirements:* For master's, thesis (for some programs); for doctorate, comprehensive exam, thesis/dissertation. *Entrance requirements:* For master's and doctorate, GRE General Test. Additional exam requirements/recommendations for international students: Required—TOEFL (minimum score 550 paper-based; 213 computer-based), IELTS (minimum score 6). *Application deadline:* Applications are processed on a rolling basis. Application fee: $40. Electronic applications accepted. *Expenses:* Tuition: Full-time $16,182; part-time $899 per credit hour. Required fees: $4 per credit hour. Tuition and fees vary according to course load. *Financial support:* In 2009–10, 182 students received support, including 38 fellowships with full and partial tuition reimbursements available (averaging $4,872 per year), 111 research assistantships with full and partial tuition reimbursements available (averaging $11,007 per year), 66 teaching assistantships with full and partial tuition reimbursements available (averaging $11,105 per year); career-related internships or fieldwork, Federal Work-Study, scholarships/grants, health care benefits, tuition waivers (full and partial), and unspecified assistantships also available. Support available to part-time students. Financial award application deadline: 2/1; financial award applicants required to submit FAFSA. Total annual research expenditures: $15.5 million. *Unit head:* Dr. Steve J. Bellovich, Dean, 918-631-2288, E-mail: steven-bellovich@utulsa.edu. *Application contact:* Graduate School, 918-631-2336, Fax: 918-631-2156, E-mail: grad@utulsa.edu.

University of Utah, The Graduate School, College of Engineering, Salt Lake City, UT 84112. Offers M Phil, ME, MS, PhD, EE. *Accreditation:* ABET. Part-time programs available. *Faculty:* 149 full-time (19 women), 14 part-time/adjunct (1 woman). *Students:* 626 full-time (92 women), 299 part-time (38 women); includes 41 minority (2 African Americans, 1 American Indian/Alaska Native, 23 Asian Americans or Pacific Islanders, 15 Hispanic Americans), 385 international. Average age 28. 657 applicants, 60% accepted, 245 enrolled. In 2009, 236 master's, 62 doctorates awarded. *Entrance requirements:* For master's and doctorate, minimum GPA of 3.0. Additional exam requirements/recommendations for international students: Required—TOEFL (minimum score 500 paper-based; 173 computer-based). *Application deadline:* For fall admission, 4/1 for domestic and international students; for spring admission, 11/1 for domestic and international students. Applications are processed on a rolling basis. Application fee: $55 ($65 for international students). *Expenses:* Tuition, state resident: full-time $4004; part-time $1674 per semester. Tuition, nonresident: full-time $14,134; part-time $5915 per semester. Required fees: $324 per semester. Tuition and fees vary according to course load, degree level and program. *Financial support:* Fellowships with full tuition reimbursements, research assistantships with full tuition reimbursements, teaching assistantships with full tuition reimbursements, career-related internships or fieldwork, Federal Work-Study, institutionally sponsored loans, scholarships/grants, traineeships, health care benefits, and unspecified assistantships available. Support available to part-time students. Financial award application deadline: 2/1; financial award applicants required to submit FAFSA. *Faculty research:* Biomaterials, wastewater treatment, computer-aided graphics design, semiconductors, polymers. Total annual research expenditures: $53.9 million. *Unit head:* Dr. Richard B. Brown, Dean, 801-581-6912, E-mail: brown@coe.utah.edu. *Application contact:* Dianne Leonard, Coordinator, Administrative Program, 801-585-7769, Fax: 801-581-8692, E-mail: dleonard@coe.utah.edu.

University of Vermont, Graduate College, College of Engineering and Mathematics, Burlington, VT 05405. Offers MS, MST, PhD. Part-time programs available. *Students:* 180 (51 women); includes 7 minority (6 Asian Americans or Pacific Islanders, 1 Hispanic American), 57 international. 274 applicants, 51% accepted, 49 enrolled. In 2009, 23 master's, 5 doctorates awarded. *Degree requirements:* For doctorate, thesis/dissertation. *Entrance requirements:* Additional exam requirements/recommendations for international students: Required—TOEFL (minimum score 550 paper-based; 213 computer-based; 80 iBT). *Application deadline:* For fall admission, 4/1 priority date for domestic students. Applications are processed on a rolling basis. Application fee: $40. Electronic applications accepted. *Expenses:* Tuition, area resident: Part-time $508 per credit hour. Tuition, state resident: part-time $508 per credit hour. Tuition, nonresident: part-time $1281 per credit hour. *Financial support:* Fellowships, research assistantships, teaching assistantships, Federal Work-Study available. Financial award application deadline: 3/1. *Unit head:* Prof. Jason Bates, Interim Director, 802-656-3333. *Application contact:* Prof. Jason Bates, Interim Director, 802-656-3333.

University of Victoria, Faculty of Graduate Studies, Faculty of Engineering, Victoria, BC V8W 2Y2, Canada. Offers M Eng, M Sc, MA Sc, PhD.

University of Virginia, School of Engineering and Applied Science, Charlottesville, VA 22903. Offers MCS, ME, MEP, MMSE, MS, PhD, ME/MBA. Part-time programs available. Post-baccalaureate distance learning degree programs offered (no on-campus study). *Faculty:* 165 full-time (20 women), 4 part-time/adjunct (1 woman). *Students:* 631 full-time (161 women), 22 part-time (5 women); includes 72 minority (16 African Americans, 45 Asian Americans or Pacific Islanders, 11 Hispanic Americans), 261 international. Average age 27. 1,690 applicants, 18% accepted, 138 enrolled. In 2009, 157 master's, 63 doctorates awarded. Terminal master's awarded for partial completion of doctoral program. *Degree requirements:* For doctorate, comprehensive exam, thesis/dissertation. *Entrance requirements:* For master's, GRE General Test, 3 letters of recommendation; for doctorate, GRE General Test, 3 letters of recommendation, essay. Additional exam requirements/recommendations for international students: Required—TOEFL (minimum score 600 paper-based; 250 computer-based; 90 iBT), IELTS (minimum score 7). *Application deadline:* For fall admission, 8/1 for domestic students, 4/1 for international students; for winter admission, 12/1 for domestic students, 8/1 for international students; for spring admission, 5/1 for domestic students, 1/1 for international students. Applications are processed on a rolling basis. Application fee: $60. Electronic applications accepted. *Financial support:* Fellowships with full tuition reimbursements, research assistantships with full tuition reimbursements, teaching assistantships with full tuition reimbursements, career-related internships or fieldwork available. Financial award application deadline: 1/15; financial award applicants required to submit FAFSA. *Unit head:* James H. Aylor, Dean, 434-924-3072, Fax: 434-243-2083. *Application contact:* Kathryn C. Thornton, Associate Dean for Graduate Programs, 434-924-3897, Fax: 434-982-3044, E-mail: seas-grad-admission@virginia.edu.

University of Waterloo, Graduate Studies, Faculty of Engineering, Waterloo, ON N2L 3G1, Canada. Offers M Arch, M Eng, MA Sc, MBET, MMS, PhD. Part-time and evening/weekend programs available. Postbaccalaureate distance learning degree programs offered (no on-campus study). *Degree requirements:* For master's, research paper or thesis; for doctorate, comprehensive exam, thesis/dissertation. *Entrance requirements:* For master's, honors degree; for doctorate, master's degree, minimum A- average. Additional exam requirements/recommendations for international students: Required—TOEFL, TWE. Electronic applications accepted.

The University of Western Ontario, Faculty of Graduate Studies, Physical Sciences Division, Faculty of Engineering, London, ON N6A 5B8, Canada. Offers chemical and biochemical engineering (ME Sc, PhD); civil and environmental engineering (M Eng, ME Sc, PhD); electrical and computer engineering (M Eng, ME Sc, PhD); mechanical and materials engineering (M Eng, ME Sc, PhD). Part-time programs available. Terminal master's awarded for partial completion of doctoral program. *Degree requirements:* For master's, thesis; for doctorate, thesis/dissertation. *Entrance requirements:* For master's, minimum B average; for doctorate, minimum B+ average. *Faculty research:* Wind, geotechnical, chemical reactor engineering, applied electrostatics, biochemical engineering.

University of Windsor, Faculty of Graduate Studies, Faculty of Engineering, Windsor, ON N9B 3P4, Canada. Offers M Eng, MA Sc, PhD. Part-time programs available. *Degree requirements:* For doctorate, comprehensive exam, thesis/dissertation. *Entrance requirements:* For master's, minimum B average; for doctorate, master's degree. Additional exam requirements/recommendations for international students: Required—TOEFL. Electronic applications accepted.

University of Wisconsin–Madison, Graduate School, College of Engineering, Madison, WI 53706-1380. Offers ME, MS, PhD. Part-time programs available. Postbaccalaureate distance learning degree programs offered (minimal on-campus study). *Faculty:* 214 full-time (32 women), 80 part-time/adjunct (19 women). *Students:* 1,108 full-time (230 women), 98 part-time (16 women); includes 104 minority (15 African Americans, 3 American Indian/Alaska Native, 56 Asian Americans or Pacific Islanders, 30 Hispanic Americans), 286 international. 3,109 applicants, 35% accepted, 371 enrolled. In 2009, 172 master's, 94 doctorates awarded. *Degree requirements:* For doctorate, thesis/dissertation. *Application deadline:* Applications are processed on a rolling basis. Application fee: $56. Electronic applications accepted. *Expenses:* Tuition, state resident: part-time $594 per credit. Tuition, nonresident: part-time $1504 per credit. Required fees: $65 per credit. Tuition and fees vary according to course load, program and reciprocity agreements. *Financial support:* Fellowships with full and partial tuition reimbursements, research assistantships with full tuition reimbursements, teaching assistantships with full tuition reimbursements, career-related internships or fieldwork, Federal Work-Study, institutionally sponsored loans, scholarships/grants, and unspecified assistantships available. Support available to part-time students. Total annual research expenditures: $85.2 million. *Unit head:* Paul S. Peercy, Dean, 608-262-3482, Fax: 608-262-6400, E-mail: peercy@engr.wisc.edu. *Application contact:* 608-262-2433, Fax: 608-262-5134, E-mail: gradadmiss@mail.bascom.wisc.edu.

University of Wisconsin–Madison, Graduate School, Department of Engineering Professional Development, Madison, WI 53706. Offers engine systems (ME); professional practice (ME). *Expenses:* Tuition, state resident: part-time $594 per credit. Tuition, nonresident: part-time $1504 per credit. Required fees: $65 per credit. Tuition and fees vary according to course load, program and reciprocity agreements.

University of Wisconsin–Milwaukee, Graduate School, College of Engineering and Applied Science, Milwaukee, WI 53201. Offers MS, PhD, Certificate, MUP/MS. Part-time programs available. *Faculty:* 81 full-time (10 women). *Students:* 142 full-time (28 women), 159 part-time (27 women); includes 29 minority (3 African Americans, 18 Asian Americans or Pacific Islanders, 8 Hispanic Americans), 142 international. Average age 32. 305 applicants, 64% accepted, 39 enrolled. In 2009, 46 master's, 14 doctorates awarded. *Degree requirements:* For master's, comprehensive exam (for some programs), thesis or alternative; for doctorate, thesis/dissertation, internship. *Entrance requirements:* For master's, GRE, minimum GPA of 2.75; for doctorate, GRE, minimum GPA of 3.5. Additional exam requirements/recommendations for international students: Required—TOEFL (minimum score 550 paper-based; 79 iBT), IELTS (minimum score 6.5). *Application deadline:* For fall admission, 1/1 priority date for domestic students; for spring admission, 9/1 for domestic students. Applications are processed on a rolling basis. Application fee: $45 ($75 for international students). *Expenses:* Tuition, state

resident: full-time $8800. Tuition, nonresident: full-time $20,760. Tuition and fees vary according to program and reciprocity agreements. *Financial support:* In 2009–10, 31 research assistantships, 82 teaching assistantships were awarded; fellowships, career-related internships or fieldwork, Federal Work-Study, and unspecified assistantships also available. Support available to part-time students. Financial award application deadline: 4/15. Total annual research expenditures: $3.6 million. *Unit head:* Dr. Michael R. Lovell, Dean, 414-229-4126, E-mail: mlovell@uwm.edu. *Application contact:* David Yu, General Information Contact, 414-229-4982, Fax: 414-229-6169, E-mail: yu@uwm.edu.

University of Wisconsin–Platteville, School of Graduate Studies, Distance Learning Center, Online Master of Science in Engineering Program, Platteville, WI 53818-3099. Offers MS. Part-time and evening/weekend programs available. Postbaccalaureate distance learning degree programs offered (no on-campus study). *Students:* 2 full-time (0 women), 118 part-time (17 women); includes 9 minority (4 African Americans, 3 Asian Americans or Pacific Islanders, 2 Hispanic Americans), 12 international. 19 applicants, 100% accepted, 19 enrolled. In 2009, 33 master's awarded. *Degree requirements:* For master's, thesis or alternative. *Entrance requirements:* Additional exam requirements/recommendations for international students: Required—TOEFL (minimum score 500 paper-based; 173 computer-based; 61 iBT). *Application deadline:* For fall admission, 7/1 priority date for domestic students; for spring admission, 11/1 priority date for domestic students. Applications are processed on a rolling basis. Application fee: $56. Electronic applications accepted. *Expenses:* Contact institution. *Financial support:* Scholarships/grants available. Support available to part-time students. *Unit head:* Dr. Lisa Riedle, Coordinator, 608-342-1686, Fax: 608-342-1566, E-mail: riedle@uwplatt.edu. *Application contact:* Information Contact, 608-342-1158, Fax: 608-342-1566, E-mail: engineering@uwplatt.edu.

University of Wyoming, College of Engineering and Applied Sciences, Laramie, WY 82070. Offers MS, PhD. Part-time programs available. *Entrance requirements:* For master's and doctorate, GRE General Test, minimum GPA of 3.0. Additional exam requirements/recommendations for international students: Required—TOEFL. Electronic applications accepted.

Utah State University, School of Graduate Studies, College of Engineering, Logan, UT 84322. Offers ME, MS, PhD, CE. Part-time and evening/weekend programs available. Terminal master's awarded for partial completion of doctoral program. *Degree requirements:* For master's, thesis (for some programs); for doctorate, thesis/dissertation. *Entrance requirements:* For master's and doctorate, GRE General Test, minimum GPA of 3.0. Additional exam requirements/recommendations for international students: Required—TOEFL. Electronic applications accepted. *Faculty research:* Crop-yield modeling, earthquake engineering, digital signal processing, technology and the public school, cryogenic cooling.

Vanderbilt University, School of Engineering, Nashville, TN 37235. Offers M Eng, MS, PhD, MD/PhD. MS and PhD offered through the Graduate School. Part-time programs available. *Faculty:* 121 full-time (22 women), 25 part-time/adjunct (2 women). *Students:* 398 full-time (115 women); includes 38 minority (18 African Americans, 2 American Indian/Alaska Native, 12 Asian Americans or Pacific Islanders, 6 Hispanic Americans), 144 international. Average age 26. 1,645 applicants, 11% accepted, 99 enrolled. In 2009, 73 master's, 56 doctorates awarded. Terminal master's awarded for partial completion of doctoral program. *Degree requirements:* For master's, comprehensive exam (for some programs), thesis (for some programs); for doctorate, comprehensive exam (for some programs), thesis/dissertation. *Entrance requirements:* For master's and doctorate, GRE General Test. Additional exam requirements/recommendations for international students: Required—TOEFL. *Application deadline:* For fall admission, 1/15 for domestic and international students; for spring admission, 11/1 for domestic and international students. Application fee: $0. Electronic applications accepted. *Financial support:* Fellowships with full tuition reimbursements, research assistantships with full tuition reimbursements, teaching assistantships with full tuition reimbursements, career-related internships or fieldwork, Federal Work-Study, institutionally sponsored loans, scholarships/grants, traineeships, health care benefits, and tuition waivers (full and partial) available. Support available to part-time students. Financial award application deadline: 1/15; financial award applicants required to submit CSS PROFILE or FAFSA. *Faculty research:* Robotics, microelectronics, reliability in design, software engineering, medical imaging. Total annual research expenditures: $54.6 million. *Unit head:* Dean Kenneth F. Galloway, Dean, 615-322-0720, Fax: 615-343-8006, E-mail: kenneth.f.galloway@vanderbilt.edu. *Application contact:* Dolores A. Black, Coordinator, Graduate Student Recruiting, 615-343-3308, Fax: 615-343-8006, E-mail: dolores.black@vanderbilt.edu.

Villanova University, College of Engineering, Villanova, PA 19085-1699. Offers MSCPE, MSChE, MSEE, MSME, MSTE, MSWREE, PhD, Certificate. Part-time and evening/weekend programs available. Postbaccalaureate distance learning degree programs offered (minimal on-campus study). Terminal master's awarded for partial completion of doctoral program. *Degree requirements:* For master's, thesis optional; for doctorate, thesis/dissertation. *Entrance requirements:* For master's, GRE General Test (for applicants with degrees from foreign universities), minimum GPA of 3.0; for doctorate, GRE General Test. Additional exam requirements/recommendations for international students: Required—TOEFL (minimum score 600 paper-based; 250 computer-based; 100 iBT). Electronic applications accepted. *Expenses:* Contact institution. *Faculty research:* Composite materials, economy and risk, heat transfer, signal detection.

Virginia Commonwealth University, Graduate School, School of Engineering, Richmond, VA 23284-9005. Offers MS, PhD, Certificate, MD/PhD. *Degree requirements:* For doctorate, thesis/dissertation, comprehensive oral and written exams. *Entrance requirements:* For master's and doctorate, GRE General Test. *Faculty research:* Artificial hearts, orthopedic implants, medical imaging, medical instrumentation and sensors, cardiac monitoring.

Virginia Polytechnic Institute and State University, Graduate School, College of Engineering, Blacksburg, VA 24061. Offers M Eng, MEA, MIS, MS, PhD. *Accreditation:* ABET (one or more programs are accredited). *Entrance requirements:* Additional exam requirements/recommendations for international students: Required—TOEFL. Electronic applications accepted.

Walden University, Graduate Programs, NTU School of Engineering and Applied Science, Minneapolis, MN 55401. Offers competitive product management (Postbaccalaureate Certificate); engineering management (Postbaccalaureate Certificate); software engineering (MS); software project management (Postbaccalaureate Certificate); software testing (Postbaccalaureate Certificate); systems engineering (MS, Postbaccalaureate Certificate); technical project management (Postbaccalaureate Certificate). Part-time and evening/weekend programs available. Postbaccalaureate distance learning degree programs offered (no on-campus study). *Faculty:* 31 part-time/adjunct. *Students:* 22 full-time (6 women), 120 part-time (14 women); includes 26 minority (19 African Americans, 7 Asian Americans or Pacific Islanders). Average age 38. In 2009, 41 master's awarded. *Degree requirements:* For master's, thesis optional. *Entrance requirements:* For master's, bachelor's degree or equivalent in related field, minimum GPA of 2.5. Additional exam requirements/recommendations for international students: Required—TOEFL (minimum score 550 paper-based; 213 computer-based), IELTS (minimum score 6.5), or Michigan English Language Assessment Battery (minimum score 82). *Application deadline:* Applications are processed on a rolling basis. Application fee: $50. Electronic applications accepted. *Expenses:* Tuition: Full-time $13,665; part-time $560 per credit. Required fees: $1375. Tuition and fees vary according to course load, degree level and program. *Financial support:* Fellowships, Federal Work-Study, scholarships/grants, unspecified assistantships, and family tuition reduction, active duty/veteran tuition reduction, group tuition reduction, interest-free payment plans available. Support available to part-time students. Financial award applicants required to submit FAFSA. *Unit head:* Colin Wightman, Interim Associate Dean, 800-925-3368. *Application contact:* Jennifer Hall, Director of Enrollment, 866-4-WALDEN, E-mail: info@walden.edu.

Washington State University, Graduate School, College of Engineering and Architecture, Pullman, WA 99164. Offers M Arch, MS, PhD. Terminal master's awarded for partial completion

Engineering and Applied Sciences—General

Washington State University (continued)

of doctoral program. *Degree requirements:* For master's, comprehensive exam (for some programs), thesis (for some programs), oral exam; for doctorate, comprehensive exam, thesis/dissertation, oral exam. *Entrance requirements:* For master's, GRE, minimum GPA of 3.0, 3 letters of recommendation; for doctorate, GRE, minimum GPA of 3.4, 3 letters of recommendation. Additional exam requirements/recommendations for international students: Required—TOEFL (minimum score 520 paper-based; 190 computer-based).

Washington State University Tri-Cities, Graduate Programs, College of Engineering and Computer Science, Richland, WA 99352. Offers computer science (MS, PhD); electrical and computer engineering (PhD); electrical engineering (MS); mechanical engineering (MS, PhD). Part-time programs available. *Faculty:* 28. *Students:* 4 full-time (0 women), 25 part-time (8 women); includes 2 minority (both African Americans), 1 international. *Degree requirements:* For master's, comprehensive exam, thesis (for some programs); for doctorate, comprehensive exam, thesis/dissertation, oral exam. *Entrance requirements:* For master's and doctorate, GRE, minimum GPA of 3.0, 3 letters of recommendation. Additional exam requirements/recommendations for international students: Required—TOEFL (minimum score 550 paper-based; 213 computer-based). *Application deadline:* For fall admission, 1/10 priority date for domestic students, 1/10 for international students; for spring admission, 7/1 priority date for domestic students, 7/1 for international students. Application fee: $50. *Expenses:* Tuition, state resident: part-time $423 per credit. Tuition, nonresident: part-time $1032 per credit. *Financial support:* Application deadline: 3/1. *Faculty research:* Positive ion track structure, biological systems computer simulations. *Unit head:* Dr. Ali Saberi, Chair, 509-372-7178, E-mail: sidra@eecs.wsu.edu. *Application contact:* Dr. Scott Hudson, Associate Director, 509-372-7254, Fax: 509-335-1949, E-mail: hudson@tricity.wsu.edu.

Washington State University Vancouver, Graduate Programs, School of Engineering and Computer Science, Vancouver, WA 98686. Offers computer science (MS); mechanical engineering (MS). Part-time programs available. *Faculty:* 9. *Students:* 14 full-time (1 woman), 5 part-time (1 woman); includes 1 minority (Asian American or Pacific Islander), 5 international. In 2009, 4 master's awarded. *Degree requirements:* For master's, comprehensive exam (for some programs), thesis, research project. *Entrance requirements:* For master's, minimum GPA of 3.0, 3 letters of recommendation with evaluation forms, resume. Additional exam requirements/recommendations for international students: Required—TOEFL (minimum score 550 paper-based). *Application deadline:* For fall admission, 1/10 priority date for domestic students, 1/10 for international students; for spring admission, 7/1 priority date for domestic students, 7/1 for international students. Applications are processed on a rolling basis. Application fee: $50. *Expenses:* Tuition, state resident: full-time $4228; part-time $423 per credit. Tuition, nonresident: full-time $10,322; part-time $1032 per credit. *Financial support:* In 2009–10, research assistantships with full tuition reimbursements (averaging $14,634 per year), teaching assistantships with full tuition reimbursements (averaging $13,383 per year) were awarded; health care benefits and unspecified assistantships also available. Financial award application deadline: 2/15. *Faculty research:* Software design, artificial intelligence, sensor networks, robotics, nanotechnology. Total annual research expenditures: $3.4 million. *Unit head:* Dr. Hakan Gurocak, Director, 360-546-9637, Fax: 360-546-9438, E-mail: hgurocak@vancouver.wsu.edu. *Application contact:* Peggy Moore, Academic Coordinator, 360-546-9638, Fax: 360-546-9438, E-mail: moorep@vancouver.wsu.edu.

Washington University in St. Louis, Henry Edwin Sever Graduate School of Engineering and Applied Science, St. Louis, MO 63130-4899. Offers M Eng, MCE, MCM, MEM, MIM, MPM, MS, MSEE, MSEE, D Sc, PhD. Part-time and evening/weekend programs available. *Faculty:* 78 full-time, 69 part-time/adjunct. *Students:* 359 full-time (83 women), 324 part-time (69 women); includes 83 minority (29 African Americans, 2 American Indian/Alaska Native, 42 Asian Americans or Pacific Islanders, 10 Hispanic Americans), 209 international. 1,304 applicants, 34% accepted, 248 enrolled. In 2009, 187 master's, 50 doctorates awarded. Terminal master's awarded for partial completion of doctoral program. *Degree requirements:* For master's, comprehensive exam (for some programs), thesis (for some programs); for doctorate, comprehensive exam, thesis/dissertation. *Entrance requirements:* For master's and doctorate, GRE. Additional exam requirements/recommendations for international students: Required—TOEFL (minimum score 550 paper-based; 213 computer-based; 90 iBT), TWE. *Application deadline:* For fall admission, 1/15 for domestic and international students. Applications are processed on a rolling basis. Application fee: $60. Electronic applications accepted. *Financial support:* In 2009–10, 281 students received support, including 31 fellowships with full tuition reimbursements available, 241 research assistantships with full tuition reimbursements available, 5 teaching assistantships with full tuition reimbursements available; career-related internships or fieldwork, Federal Work-Study, institutionally sponsored loans, scholarships/grants, health care benefits, tuition waivers (full and partial), and unspecified assistantships also available. Financial award applicants required to submit FAFSA. Total annual research expenditures: $41.5 million. *Unit head:* Salvatore Sutera, Dean, 314-935-6166. *Application contact:* Beth Schnettler, Director of Graduate Admissions, 314-935-7974, Fax: 314-719-4703, E-mail: bethschnettler@seas.wustl.edu.

Wayne State University, College of Engineering, Detroit, MI 48202. Offers MS, PhD, Certificate. Part-time programs available. Terminal master's awarded for partial completion of doctoral program. *Degree requirements:* For master's, thesis optional; for doctorate, thesis/dissertation. *Entrance requirements:* Additional exam requirements/recommendations for international students: Required—TOEFL (minimum score 550 paper-based; 213 computer-based); Recommended—TWE (minimum score 6). *Faculty research:* Smart sensors and integrated micro systems, biomedical engineering, civil infrastructures, nanotechnology, manufacturing and automotive engineering.

Western Michigan University, Graduate College, College of Engineering and Applied Sciences, Kalamazoo, MI 49008. Offers MS, MSE, PhD. Part-time programs available. *Degree requirements:* For doctorate, thesis/dissertation, oral exam. *Entrance requirements:* For master's, minimum GPA of 3.0; for doctorate, GRE General Test, minimum GPA of 3.0.

Western New England College, School of Engineering, Springfield, MA 01119. Offers MSE, MSEM. Part-time and evening/weekend programs available. *Students:* 37 part-time (8 women); includes 2 African Americans, 4 Asian Americans or Pacific Islanders, 2 Hispanic Americans. In 2009, 7 master's awarded. *Degree requirements:* For master's, comprehensive exam, thesis optional. *Entrance requirements:* For master's, GRE, bachelor's degree in engineering or related field, Letters of Recommendation and Resume. *Application deadline:* Applications are processed on a rolling basis. Application fee: $30. *Expenses:* Tuition: Part-time $552 per credit hour. Part-time tuition and fees vary according to program. *Financial support:* Available to part-time students. Applicants required to submit FAFSA. *Faculty research:* Fluid mechanics, control systems. *Unit head:* Dr. S. Hossein Cheraghi, Dean, 413-782-1272, E-mail: cheraghi@wnec.edu. *Application contact:* Matt Fox, Director of Recruiting and Marketing for Adult Learners, 413-782-1517, Fax: 413-782-1777, E-mail: study@wnec.edu.

West Texas A&M University, College of Agriculture, Nursing, and Natural Sciences, Department of Mathematics, Physical Sciences and Engineering Technology, Program in Engineering Technology, Canyon, TX 79016-0001. Offers MS. Part-time programs available. *Degree requirements:* For master's, comprehensive exam, thesis optional. *Entrance requirements:* For master's, GRE General Test. Additional exam requirements/recommendations for international students: Required—TOEFL (minimum score 550 paper-based). Electronic applications accepted. *Faculty research:* Composites, firearms technology, small arms research and development.

West Virginia University, College of Engineering and Mineral Resources, Morgantown, WV 26506. Offers MS, MS Ch E, MS Min E, MSAE, MSCE, MSCS, MSE, MSEE, MSIE, MSME, MSPNGE, MSSE, PhD. *Accreditation:* ABET (one or more programs are accredited). Part-time programs available. Terminal master's awarded for partial completion of doctoral program. *Degree requirements:* For master's, thesis optional; for doctorate, comprehensive exam, thesis/dissertation. *Entrance requirements:* Additional exam requirements/recommendations for international students: Required—TOEFL (minimum score 550 paper-based; 213 computer-based). *Expenses:* Contact institution. *Faculty research:* Composite materials, software engineering, information systems, aerodynamics, vehicle propulsion and emission.

West Virginia University Institute of Technology, College of Engineering, Montgomery, WV 25136. Offers MS. Part-time programs available. *Degree requirements:* For master's, thesis or alternative, fieldwork. *Entrance requirements:* For master's, GRE General Test, minimum GPA of 3.0. Additional exam requirements/recommendations for international students: Required—TOEFL.

Wichita State University, Graduate School, College of Engineering, Wichita, KS 67260. Offers MEM, MS, PhD. Part-time and evening/weekend programs available. *Expenses:* Tuition, state resident: full-time $4247; part-time $235.95 per credit hour. Tuition, nonresident: full-time $11,171; part-time $620.60 per credit hour. Required fees: $34; $3.60 per credit hour. $17 per term. Tuition and fees vary according to campus/location and program. *Unit head:* Dr. Zulma Toro-Ramos, Dean, 316-978-3400, Fax: 316-978-3853, E-mail: zulma.toro-ramos@wichita.edu. *Application contact:* Dr. Zulma Toro-Ramos, Dean, 316-978-3400, Fax: 316-978-3853, E-mail: zulma.toro-ramos@wichita.edu.

Widener University, Graduate Programs in Engineering, Chester, PA 19013-5792. Offers chemical engineering (M Eng); civil engineering (M Eng); computer and software engineering (M Eng); engineering management (M Eng); management and technology (MSMT); mechanical engineering (M Eng); telecommunications engineering (M Eng); ME/MBA. Part-time and evening/weekend programs available. *Faculty:* 10 full-time (1 woman), 4 part-time/adjunct (0 women). *Students:* 25 full-time (3 women), 18 part-time (1 woman); includes 3 minority (1 American Indian/Alaska Native, 2 Asian Americans or Pacific Islanders), 17 international. Average age 29. 439 applicants, 46% accepted, 23 enrolled. In 2009, 22 master's awarded. *Degree requirements:* For master's, thesis optional. *Entrance requirements:* Additional exam requirements/recommendations for international students: Required—TOEFL (minimum score 550 paper-based; 213 computer-based). *Application deadline:* For fall admission, 8/1 priority date for domestic students, 4/1 priority date for international students; for winter admission, 2/1 priority date for international students; for spring admission, 12/1 priority date for domestic students, 9/1 priority date for international students. Applications are processed on a rolling basis. Application fee: $25 ($300 for international students). *Expenses:* Contact institution. *Financial support:* In 2009–10, 5 teaching assistantships with partial tuition reimbursements (averaging $8,000 per year) were awarded; research assistantships, unspecified assistantships also available. Financial award application deadline: 3/15. *Faculty research:* Collagen, geosynthetics, mobile computing, image and signal processing. Total annual research expenditures: $490,773. *Unit head:* Nora J. Kogut, Assistant Dean, 610-499-4037, Fax: 610-499-4059, E-mail: njkogut@widener.edu. *Application contact:* Christine M. Weist, Assistant to Associate Provost for Graduate Studies, 610-499-4351, Fax: 610-499-4277, E-mail: christine.m.weist@widener.edu.

Wilkes University, College of Graduate and Professional Studies, College of Science and Engineering, Wilkes-Barre, PA 18766-0002. Offers MS, MS Ed, MSEE. Part-time programs available. *Students:* 16 full-time (2 women), 20 part-time (2 women), 25 international. Average age 27. In 2009, 28 master's awarded. *Entrance requirements:* Additional exam requirements/recommendations for international students: Required—TOEFL (minimum score 500 paper-based; 173 computer-based). Application fee: $45. *Unit head:* Dr. Dale Bruns, Dean, 570-408-4600, Fax: 570-408-7860, E-mail: dale.bruns@wilkes.edu. *Application contact:* Kathleen Houlihan, Director of Graduate Studies, 570-408-3235, Fax: 570-408-7846, E-mail: kathleen.houlihan@wilkes.edu.

Worcester Polytechnic Institute, Graduate Studies and Research, Worcester, MA 01609-2280. Offers M Eng, MBA, ME, MME, MS, PhD, Advanced Certificate, Graduate Certificate. Part-time and evening/weekend programs available. Postbaccalaureate distance learning degree programs offered (no on-campus study). *Faculty:* 140 full-time (28 women), 32 part-time/adjunct (5 women). *Students:* 437 full-time (145 women), 716 part-time (161 women). Average age 29. 2,178 applicants, 64% accepted, 575 enrolled. In 2009, 299 master's, 25 doctorates awarded. Terminal master's awarded for partial completion of doctoral program. *Degree requirements:* For master's, thesis (for some programs); for doctorate, thesis/dissertation. *Entrance requirements:* For master's and doctorate, 3 letters of recommendation. Additional exam requirements/recommendations for international students: Required—TOEFL (minimum score 550 paper-based; 213 computer-based; 79 iBT), IELTS (minimum score 6.5). *Application deadline:* For fall admission, 1/15 priority date for domestic and international students; for spring admission, 10/15 priority date for domestic and international students. Applications are processed on a rolling basis. Application fee: $70. Electronic applications accepted. *Financial support:* Institutionally sponsored loans, scholarships/grants, tuition waivers, and unspecified assistantships available. Financial award application deadline: 1/15. *Unit head:* Richard Sisson, Dean of Graduate Studies, 508-831-5633, Fax: 508-831-5178, E-mail: grad@wpi.edu. *Application contact:* Lynne Dougherty, Administrative Assistant, 508-831-5301, Fax: 508-831-5717, E-mail: grad@wpi.edu.

Wright State University, School of Graduate Studies, College of Engineering and Computer Science, Dayton, OH 45435. Offers MS, MSCE, MSE, PhD. Part-time and evening/weekend programs available. *Degree requirements:* For master's, thesis optional; for doctorate, thesis/dissertation, candidacy and general exams. *Entrance requirements:* For doctorate, GRE General Test, minimum GPA of 3.3. Additional exam requirements/recommendations for international students: Required—TOEFL. *Faculty research:* Robotics, heat transfer, fluid dynamics, microprocessors, mechanical vibrations.

Yale University, Graduate School of Arts and Sciences, School of Engineering and Applied Science, New Haven, CT 06520. Offers MS, PhD. Part-time programs available. Terminal master's awarded for partial completion of doctoral program. *Degree requirements:* For doctorate, thesis/dissertation, exam. *Entrance requirements:* For master's and doctorate, GRE General Test. Additional exam requirements/recommendations for international students: Required—TOEFL.

See Close-Up on page 95.

Youngstown State University, Graduate School, College of Science, Technology, Engineering and Mathematics, Youngstown, OH 44555-0001. Offers MCIS, MSE. Part-time and evening/weekend programs available. *Degree requirements:* For master's, thesis optional. *Entrance requirements:* For master's, minimum GPA of 2.75 in field. Additional exam requirements/recommendations for international students: Required—TOEFL. *Faculty research:* Structural mechanics, water quality, wetlands engineering, control systems, power systems, heat transfer, kinematics and dynamics.

Applied Science and Technology

American University, College of Arts and Sciences, Department of Biology, Program in Applied Science, Washington, DC 20016-8007. Offers MS. *Students:* 6 full-time (3 women), 2 international. Average age 23. 20 applicants, 50% accepted, 3 enrolled. *Entrance requirements:* Additional exam requirements/recommendations for international students: Required—TOEFL. Application fee: $80. *Expenses:* Tuition: Full-time $22,266; part-time $1237 per credit hour. Required fees: $430. Tuition and fees vary according to program. *Unit head:* Victoria Connaughton, Chair, 202-885-2194, Fax: 202-885-2182, E-mail: vconn@american.edu. *Application contact:* Kathleen Clowery, Director, Graduate Admissions, 202-885-3621, Fax: 202-885-1505.

The College of William and Mary, Faculty of Arts and Sciences, Department of Applied Science, Williamsburg, VA 23187-8795. Offers MS, PhD. *Faculty:* 10 full-time (2 women), 2 part-time/adjunct (0 women). *Students:* 31 full-time (10 women); includes 1 minority (Asian American or Pacific Islander), 22 international. Average age 26. 45 applicants, 49% accepted, 9 enrolled. In 2009, 9 master's, 1 doctorate awarded. *Degree requirements:* For master's, comprehensive exam, thesis; for doctorate, comprehensive exam, thesis/dissertation, 4 core courses. *Entrance requirements:* For master's and doctorate, GRE General Test, GRE Subject Test. Additional exam requirements/recommendations for international students: Required—TOEFL, TWE. *Application deadline:* For fall admission, 2/5 priority date for domestic students, 2/5 for international students; for spring admission, 10/8 priority date for domestic students, 10/8 for international students. Applications are processed on a rolling basis. Application fee: $45. Electronic applications accepted. *Expenses:* Tuition, state resident: full-time $6400; part-time $315 per credit hour. Tuition, nonresident: full-time $19,720; part-time $840 per credit hour. Required fees: $4114. *Financial support:* In 2009–10, 30 students received support, including 12 fellowships, 29 research assistantships, 1 teaching assistantship; Federal Work-Study, health care benefits, tuition waivers (full), and unspecified assistantships also available. Financial award application deadline: 4/15; financial award applicants required to submit FAFSA. *Faculty research:* Computational biology, non-destructive evaluation, neurophysiology, lasers 8 optics, solid state FTNMR. Total annual research expenditures: $2.5 million. *Unit head:* Dr. Mark Hinders, Chair, 757-221-1519, Fax: 757-221-2050, E-mail: hinders@as.wm.edu. *Application contact:* Destiny D. Elliott, Graduate Studies Administrator, 757-221-2563, Fax: 757-221-2050, E-mail: ddelli@wm.edu.

Colorado State University–Pueblo, College of Science and Mathematics, Pueblo, CO 81001-4901. Offers applied natural science (MS), including biochemistry, biology, chemistry. Part-time and evening/weekend programs available. *Degree requirements:* For master's, comprehensive exam (for some programs), thesis (for some programs), internship report (if non-thesis). *Entrance requirements:* For master's, GRE General Test (minimum score 1000), 2 letters of reference, minimum GPA of 3.0. Additional exam requirements/recommendations for international students: Required—TOEFL (minimum score 500 paper-based; 173 computer-based), IELTS (minimum score 5). *Faculty research:* Fungal cell walls, molecular biology, bioactive materials synthesis, atomic force microscopy-surface chemistry, nanoscience.

Harvard University, Extension School, Cambridge, MA 02138-3722. Offers applied sciences (CAS); biotechnology (ALM); educational technologies (ALM); educational technology (CET); English for graduate and professional studies (DGP); environmental management (ALM, CEM); information technology (ALM); journalism (ALM); liberal arts (ALM); management (ALM, CM); mathematics for teaching (ALM); museum studies (ALM); premedical studies (Diploma); publication and communication (CPC). Part-time and evening/weekend programs available. *Degree requirements:* For master's, thesis. *Entrance requirements:* For master's, 3 completed graduate courses with grade of B or higher. Additional exam requirements/recommendations for international students: Required—TOEFL (minimum score 600 paper-based; 250 computer-based), TWE (minimum score 5). *Expenses:* Contact institution.

James Madison University, The Graduate School, College of Integrated Science and Technology, Department of Integrated Science and Technology, Harrisonburg, VA 22807. Offers MS. *Faculty:* 18 full-time (4 women). *Students:* 35 full-time (17 women), 9 part-time (1 woman); includes 3 minority (1 African American, 1 Asian American or Pacific Islander, 1 Hispanic American), 16 international. Average age 27. In 2009, 10 master's awarded. *Degree requirements:* For master's, thesis or alternative. *Entrance requirements:* For master's, GRE General Test. Additional exam requirements/recommendations for international students: Required—TOEFL. *Application deadline:* For fall admission, 5/1 priority date for domestic students; for spring admission, 9/1 priority date for domestic students. Applications are processed on a rolling basis. Application fee: $55. Electronic applications accepted. *Expenses:* Tuition, area resident: Part-time $305 per credit hour. Tuition, state resident: part-time $305 per credit hour. Tuition, nonresident: part-time $890 per credit hour. *Financial support:* In 2009–10, 21 students received support. Federal Work-Study available. Financial award application deadline: 3/1; financial award applicants required to submit FAFSA. *Unit head:* Dr. Pauline K. Cushman, Interim Academic Unit Head, 540-568-2740. *Application contact:* Lynette M. Bible, Director of Graduate Admissions, 540-568-6395, Fax: 540-568-7860, E-mail: biblelm@jmu.edu.

Louisiana State University and Agricultural and Mechanical College, Graduate School, College of Basic Sciences, Master of Natural Sciences Program, Baton Rouge, LA 70803. Offers MNS. Part-time programs available. *Students:* 2 full-time (1 woman), 5 part-time (3 women); includes 1 Asian American or Pacific Islander. Average age 39. 3 applicants, 67% accepted, 1 enrolled. In 2009, 10 master's awarded. *Degree requirements:* For master's, comprehensive exam. *Entrance requirements:* For master's, GRE General Test, minimum GPA of 3.0. Additional exam requirements/recommendations for international students: Required—TOEFL (minimum score 550 paper-based; 213 computer-based; 79 iBT) or IELTS (minimum score 6.5). *Application deadline:* For fall admission, 5/15 priority date for domestic students, 5/15 for international students; for spring admission, 10/15 for international students. Applications are processed on a rolling basis. Application fee: $50 ($70 for international students). Electronic applications accepted. *Financial support:* In 2009–10, 1 student received support, including 1 research assistantship (averaging $17,500 per year); fellowships, teaching assistantships with partial tuition reimbursements available, Federal Work-Study, institutionally sponsored loans, and health care benefits also available. Financial award applicants required to submit FAFSA. Total annual research expenditures: $193,063. *Unit head:* Dr. Gary Byerly, Director, 225-578-4200, Fax: 225-578-8826. *Application contact:* Dr. Fred Rainey, Associate Dean, 225-578-4200, Fax: 225-578-8826, E-mail: frainey@lsu.edu.

Missouri State University, Graduate College, College of Natural and Applied Sciences, Department of Agriculture, Springfield, MO 65897. Offers natural and applied science (MNAS), including agriculture (MNAS, MS Ed); plant science (MS); secondary education (MS Ed), including agriculture (MNAS, MS Ed). Part-time programs available. *Faculty:* 16 full-time (3 women). *Students:* 10 full-time (7 women), 16 part-time (10 women), 2 international. Average age 31. 7 applicants, 71% accepted, 3 enrolled. In 2009, 9 master's awarded. *Degree requirements:* For master's, comprehensive exam, thesis or alternative. *Entrance requirements:* For master's, GRE (MS plant science, MNAS), 9-12 teacher certification (MS Ed), minimum GPA of 3.0 (MS plant science, MNAS). Additional exam requirements/recommendations for international students: Required—TOEFL (minimum score 550 paper-based; 213 computer-based; 79 iBT). *Application deadline:* For fall admission, 7/20 priority date for domestic students, 5/1 for international students; for spring admission, 12/20 priority date for domestic students, 9/1 for international students. Applications are processed on a rolling basis. Application fee: $35 ($50 for international students). Electronic applications accepted. *Expenses:* Tuition, state resident: full-time $3852; part-time $214 per credit hour. Tuition, nonresident: full-time $7524; part-time $418 per credit hour. Required fees: $696; $172 per semester. Tuition and fees vary according to course level, course load, degree level and program. *Financial support:* In 2009–10, 6 research assistantships with full tuition reimbursements (averaging $8,535 per year), 6 teaching assistantships with full tuition reimbursements (averaging $8,535 per year) were awarded; Federal Work-Study, institutionally sponsored loans, scholarships/grants, and unspecified assistantships also available. Financial award application deadline: 3/31; financial award applicants required to submit FAFSA. *Faculty research:* Grapevine biotechnology, agricultural marketing, Asian elephant reproduction, poultry science, integrated pest management. *Unit head:* Dr. W. Anson Elliott, Head, 417-836-5638, E-mail: ansonelliot@missouristate.edu. *Application contact:* Eric Eckert, Coordinator of Graduate Admissions and Recruitment, 417-836-5331, Fax: 417-836-6200.

Missouri State University, Graduate College, College of Natural and Applied Sciences, Department of Biology, Springfield, MO 65897. Offers biology (MS); natural and applied science (MNAS), including biology (MNAS, MS Ed); secondary education (MS Ed), including biology (MNAS, MS Ed). *Faculty:* 18 full-time (3 women), 6 part-time/adjunct (1 woman). *Students:* 25 full-time (13 women), 22 part-time (10 women); includes 2 minority (1 American Indian/Alaska Native, 1 Asian American or Pacific Islander), 3 international. Average age 26. 17 applicants, 94% accepted, 10 enrolled. In 2009, 20 master's awarded. *Degree requirements:* For master's, comprehensive exam, thesis or alternative. *Entrance requirements:* For master's, GRE (MS, MNAS), 24 hours of course work in biology (MS); minimum GPA of 3.0 (MS, MNAS), 9-12 teacher certification (MS Ed). Additional exam requirements/recommendations for international students: Required—TOEFL (minimum score 550 paper-based; 213 computer-based; 79 iBT). *Application deadline:* For fall admission, 7/20 priority date for domestic students, 5/1 for international students; for spring admission, 12/20 priority date for domestic students, 9/1 for international students. Applications are processed on a rolling basis. Application fee: $35 ($50 for international students). Electronic applications accepted. *Expenses:* Tuition, state resident: full-time $3852; part-time $214 per credit hour. Tuition, nonresident: full-time $7524; part-time $418 per credit hour. Required fees: $696; $172 per semester. Tuition and fees vary according to course level, course load, degree level and program. *Financial support:* In 2009–10, 4 research assistantships with full tuition reimbursements (averaging $9,730 per year), 23 teaching assistantships with full tuition reimbursements (averaging $8,372 per year) were awarded; Federal Work-Study, institutionally sponsored loans, scholarships/grants, and unspecified assistantships also available. Financial award application deadline: 3/31; financial award applicants required to submit FAFSA. *Faculty research:* Hibernation physiology of bats, behavioral ecology of salamanders, mussel conservation, plant evolution and systematics, cellular/molecular mechanisms involved in migraine pathology. *Unit head:* Dr. S. Alicia Mathis, Head, 417-836-5126, Fax: 417-836-6934, E-mail: biology@missouristate.edu. *Application contact:* Dr. Eric Eckert, Coordinator of Graduate Admissions and Recruitment, 417-836-5331, Fax: 417-836-6200, E-mail: ericeckert@missouristate.edu.

Missouri State University, Graduate College, College of Natural and Applied Sciences, Department of Chemistry, Springfield, MO 65897. Offers chemistry (MS); natural and applied science (MNAS), including chemistry (MNAS, MS Ed); secondary education (MS Ed), including chemistry (MNAS, MS Ed). Part-time programs available. *Faculty:* 14 full-time (1 woman). *Students:* 7 full-time (4 women), 9 part-time (3 women), 1 international. Average age 28. 10 applicants, 90% accepted, 5 enrolled. In 2009, 3 master's awarded. *Degree requirements:* For master's, comprehensive exam, thesis. *Entrance requirements:* For master's, GRE General Test (MS, MNAS), minimum undergraduate GPA of 3.0 (MS and MNAS), 9-12 teacher certification (MS Ed). Additional exam requirements/recommendations for international students: Required—TOEFL (minimum score 550 paper-based; 213 computer-based; 79 iBT). *Application deadline:* For fall admission, 7/20 priority date for domestic students, 5/1 for international students; for spring admission, 12/20 priority date for domestic students, 9/1 for international students. Applications are processed on a rolling basis. Application fee: $35 ($50 for international students). Electronic applications accepted. *Expenses:* Tuition, state resident: full-time $3852; part-time $214 per credit hour. Tuition, nonresident: full-time $7524; part-time $418 per credit hour. Required fees: $696; $172 per semester. Tuition and fees vary according to course level, course load, degree level and program. *Financial support:* In 2009–10, 1 research assistantship with full tuition reimbursement (averaging $9,730 per year), 9 teaching assistantships with full tuition reimbursements (averaging $9,730 per year) were awarded; Federal Work-Study, institutionally sponsored loans, scholarships/grants, and unspecified assistantships also available. Financial award application deadline: 3/31; financial award applicants required to submit FAFSA. *Faculty research:* Polyethylene glycol derivatives, electrochemiluminescence of environmental systems, enzymology, environmental organic pollutants, DNA repair via NMR. *Unit head:* Dr. Alan Schick, Department Head, 417-836-5506, Fax: 417-836-5507, E-mail: chemistry@missouristate.edu. *Application contact:* Eric Eckert, Coordinator of Admissions and Recruitment, 417-836-5331, Fax: 417-836-6200, E-mail: ericeckert@missouristate.edu.

Missouri State University, Graduate College, College of Natural and Applied Sciences, Department of Geography, Geology, and Planning, Springfield, MO 65897. Offers geospatial sciences (MS); natural and applied science (MNAS), including geography, geology and planning; secondary education (MS Ed), including earth science, geography. *Accreditation:* ACSP. Part-time and evening/weekend programs available. *Faculty:* 20 full-time (4 women). *Students:* 19 full-time (10 women), 12 part-time (5 women); includes 1 minority (American Indian/Alaska Native), 1 international. Average age 29. 19 applicants, 100% accepted, 13 enrolled. In 2009, 4 master's awarded. *Degree requirements:* For master's, comprehensive exam, thesis (for some programs). *Entrance requirements:* For master's, GRE General Test (MS, MNAS), minimum undergraduate GPA of 3.0 (MS, MNAS), 9-12 teacher certification (MS Ed). Additional exam requirements/recommendations for international students: Required—TOEFL (minimum score 550 paper-based; 213 computer-based; 79 iBT). *Application deadline:* For fall admission, 7/20 priority date for domestic students, 5/1 for international students; for spring admission, 12/20 priority date for domestic students, 9/1 for international students. Applications are processed on a rolling basis. Application fee: $35 ($50 for international students). Electronic applications accepted. *Expenses:* Tuition, state resident: full-time $3852; part-time $214 per credit hour. Tuition, nonresident: full-time $7524; part-time $418 per credit hour. Required fees: $696; $172 per semester. Tuition and fees vary according to course level, course load, degree level and program. *Financial support:* In 2009–10, 7 research assistantships with full tuition reimbursements (averaging $8,933 per year), 8 teaching assistantships with full tuition reimbursements (averaging $8,236 per year) were awarded; career-related internships or fieldwork, Federal Work-Study, institutionally sponsored loans, scholarships/grants, and unspecified assistantships also available. Financial award application deadline: 3/31; financial award applicants required to submit FAFSA. *Faculty research:* Stratigraphy and ancient meteorite impacts, environmental geochemistry of karst, hyperspectral image processing, water quality, small town planning. *Unit head:* Dr. Thomas Plymate, Head, 417-836-5800, Fax: 417-836-6934, E-mail: tomplymate@missouristate.edu. *Application contact:* Eric Eckert, Coordinator of Graduate Admissions and Recruitment, 417-836-5331, Fax: 417-836-6200, E-mail: ericeckert@missouristate.edu.

Missouri State University, Graduate College, College of Natural and Applied Sciences, Department of Mathematics, Springfield, MO 65897. Offers mathematics (MS); natural and applied science (MNAS), including mathematics (MNAS, MS Ed); secondary education (MS Ed), including mathematics (MNAS, MS Ed). Part-time programs available. *Faculty:* 23 full-time (5 women). *Students:* 15 full-time (1 woman), 7 part-time (1 woman), 1 international. Average age 25. 12 applicants, 100% accepted, 9 enrolled. In 2009, 4 master's awarded. *Degree requirements:* For master's, comprehensive exam, thesis or alternative. *Entrance requirements:* For master's, GRE (MS, MNAS), minimum undergraduate GPA of 3.0 (MS, MNAS), 9-12 teacher certification (MS Ed). Additional exam requirements/recommendations for international students: Required—TOEFL (minimum score 550 paper-based; 213 computer-based; 79 iBT). *Application deadline:* For fall admission, 7/20 priority date for domestic students, 5/1 for international students; for spring admission, 12/20 priority date for domestic students, 9/1 for international students. Applications are processed on a rolling basis. Application fee: $35 ($50 for international students). Electronic applications accepted. *Expenses:* Tuition, state resident: full-time $3852; part-time $214 per credit hour. Tuition, nonresident: full-time $7524; part-time

Applied Science and Technology

Missouri State University *(continued)*
$418 per credit hour. Required fees: $696; $172 per semester. Tuition and fees vary according to course level, course load, degree level and program. *Financial support:* In 2009–10, 7 teaching assistantships with full tuition reimbursements (averaging $9,730 per year) were awarded; Federal Work-Study, institutionally sponsored loans, scholarships/grants, and unspecified assistantships also available. Financial award application deadline: 3/31; financial award applicants required to submit FAFSA. *Faculty research:* Harmonic analysis, commutative algebra, number theory, K-theory, probability. *Unit head:* Dr. Yungchen Cheng, Head, 417-836-5112, Fax: 417-836-6966, E-mail: yungchencheng@missouristate.edu. *Application contact:* Eric Eckert, Coordinator of Admissions and Recruitment, 417-836-5331, Fax: 417-836-6200, E-mail: ericeckert@missouristate.edu.

Naval Postgraduate School, Graduate Programs, Program in Undersea Warfare, Monterey, CA 93943. Offers applied science (MS); electrical engineering (MS); engineering acoustics (MS); operations research (MS); physical oceanography (MS). Program only open to commissioned officers of the United States and friendly nations and selected United States federal civilian employees. Part-time programs available. *Degree requirements:* For master's, thesis.

Oklahoma State University, Graduate College, Stillwater, OK 74078. Offers environmental science (MS); international studies (MS); natural and applied science (MS); photonics (PhD); plant science (PhD). Programs are interdisciplinary. *Faculty:* 2 full-time (0 women). *Students:* 82 full-time (47 women), 156 part-time (75 women); includes 49 minority (15 African Americans, 17 American Indian/Alaska Native, 10 Asian Americans or Pacific Islanders, 7 Hispanic Americans), 68 international. Average age 32. 779 applicants, 68% accepted, 87 enrolled. In 2009, 77 master's, 8 doctorates awarded. *Degree requirements:* For master's, thesis (for some programs); for doctorate, comprehensive exam, thesis/dissertation. *Entrance requirements:* For master's and doctorate, GRE or GMAT. Additional exam requirements/recommendations for international students: Required—TOEFL (minimum score 550 paper-based; 79 iBT). *Application deadline:* For fall admission, 3/1 priority date for international students; for spring admission, 8/1 priority date for international students. Applications are processed on a rolling basis. Application fee: $40 ($75 for international students). Electronic applications accepted. *Expenses:* Tuition, state resident: full-time $3716; part-time $154.85 per credit hour. Tuition, nonresident: full-time $14,448; part-time $602 per credit hour. Required fees: $1772; $73.85 per credit hour. One-time fee: $50. Tuition and fees vary according to course load and campus/location. *Financial support:* In 2009–10, 2 research assistantships (averaging $10,200 per year) were awarded; career-related internships or fieldwork, Federal Work-Study, scholarships/grants, health care benefits, tuition waivers (partial), and unspecified assistantships also available. Support available to part-time students. Financial award application deadline: 3/1; financial award applicants required to submit FAFSA. *Unit head:* Dr. Gordon Emslie, Dean, 405-744-6368, Fax: 405-744-0355, E-mail: grad-i@okstate.edu. *Application contact:* Dr. Susan Mathew, Coordinator of Admissions, 405-744-6368, Fax: 405-744-0355, E-mail: grad-i@okstate.edu.

Rensselaer Polytechnic Institute, Graduate School, School of Science, Master's Program in Applied Science, Troy, NY 12180-3590. Offers MS. Part-time programs available. *Students:* 2 part-time (1 woman). Average age 25. 4 applicants, 25% accepted, 0 enrolled. In 2009, 1 master's awarded. Terminal master's awarded for partial completion of doctoral program. *Degree requirements:* For master's, comprehensive exam (for some programs), thesis optional. *Entrance requirements:* Additional exam requirements/recommendations for international students: Required—TOEFL. *Application deadline:* For fall admission, 1/15 priority date for domestic and international students. Applications are processed on a rolling basis. Application fee: $75. Electronic applications accepted. *Expenses:* Tuition: Full-time $38,100. *Financial support:* Career-related internships or fieldwork and institutionally sponsored loans available. Financial award application deadline: 2/1. *Faculty research:* Bioinformatics, polymer science, scientific computation, database systems. *Unit head:* Dr. William L. Siegmann, Associate Dean for Graduate Education and Research, 518-276-6905, Fax: 518-276-2825, E-mail: siegmw@rpi.edu. *Application contact:* Dr. William L. Siegmann, Associate Dean for Graduate Education and Research, 518-276-6905, Fax: 518-276-2825, E-mail: siegmw@rpi.edu.

Saint Mary's University, Faculty of Science, Interdisciplinary Program in Applied Science, Halifax, NS B3H 3C3, Canada. Offers M Sc. *Application deadline:* For fall admission, 2/1 for domestic students. *Financial support:* Fellowships, teaching assistantships available. *Unit head:* Dr. Malcolm N. Butler, Dean, 902-420-5494, Fax: 902-420-5261, E-mail: malcolm.butler@smu.ca. *Application contact:* Dr. Malcolm N. Butler, Dean, 902-420-5494, Fax: 902-420-5261, E-mail: malcolm.butler@smu.ca.

Southeastern Louisiana University, College of Science and Technology, Program in Integrated Science and Technology, Hammond, LA 70402. Offers MS. Part-time and evening/weekend programs available. *Faculty:* 6 full-time (0 women). *Students:* 15 full-time (5 women), 12 part-time (3 women); includes 2 minority (1 African American, 1 Asian American or Pacific Islander), 10 international. Average age 32. 8 applicants, 88% accepted, 5 enrolled. In 2009, 6 master's awarded. *Degree requirements:* For master's, thesis optional. *Entrance requirements:* For master's, GRE (minimum combined score 850), 2 letters of reference; minimum GPA of 2.75; 30 hours of course work including chemistry, physics, industrial technology, or mathematics. Additional exam requirements/recommendations for international students: Required—TOEFL (minimum score 500 paper-based; 173 computer-based; 61 iBT). *Application deadline:* For fall admission, 7/15 priority date for domestic students, 6/1 priority date for international students; for spring admission, 12/1 priority date for domestic students, 10/1 priority date for international students. Applications are processed on a rolling basis. Application fee: $20 ($30 for international students). Electronic applications accepted. *Expenses:* Tuition, state resident: full-time $3086; part-time $225 per credit hour. Tuition, nonresident: part-time $529 per credit hour. Required fees: $1195. Tuition and fees vary according to course level and course load. *Financial support:* In 2009–10, 4 students received support, including 4 research assistantships (averaging $10,100 per year); career-related internships or fieldwork, Federal Work-Study, institutionally sponsored loans, and administrative assistantships also available. Support available to part-time students. Financial award application deadline: 5/1; financial award applicants required to submit FAFSA. *Faculty research:* Chemistry, physics, industrial technology, mathematics, computer science. *Unit head:* Dr. Ken Li, Coordinator, 985-549-3822, Fax: 985-549-2099, E-mail: kli@selu.edu. *Application contact:* Sandra Meyers, Graduate Admissions Analyst, 985-549-5620, Fax: 985-549-5632, E-mail: admissions@selu.edu.

Southern Methodist University, Bobby B. Lyle School of Engineering, Department of Engineering Management, Information, and Systems, Dallas, TX 75275. Offers applied science (MS); engineering management (MSEM, DE); information engineering and management (MSIEM); operations research (MS, PhD); systems engineering (MS, PhD). Part-time and evening/weekend programs available. Postbaccalaureate distance learning degree programs offered. *Faculty:* 10 full-time (3 women), 22 part-time/adjunct (2 women). *Students:* 54 full-time (24 women), 288 part-time (68 women); includes 96 minority (30 African Americans, 2 American Indian/Alaska Native, 35 Asian Americans or Pacific Islanders, 29 Hispanic Americans), 38 international. Average age 33. 125 applicants, 74% accepted, 60 enrolled. In 2009, 128 master's, 3 doctorates awarded. Terminal master's awarded for partial completion of doctoral program. *Degree requirements:* For master's, thesis optional; for doctorate, thesis/dissertation, oral and written qualifying exams. *Entrance requirements:* For master's, minimum GPA of 3.0 in last 2 years; bachelor's degree in engineering, mathematics, sciences, or technical area; for doctorate, GRE General Test (operations research, engineering management), bachelor's degree in related field. Additional exam requirements/recommendations for international students: Required—TOEFL. *Application deadline:* For fall admission, 7/1 for domestic students, 5/15 for international students; for spring admission, 11/15 for domestic students, 9/1 for international students. Applications are processed on a rolling basis. Application fee: $75. *Financial*

support: In 2009–10, 8 students received support, including 3 research assistantships with full tuition reimbursements available (averaging $18,000 per year), 9 teaching assistantships with full tuition reimbursements available (averaging $18,000 per year); tuition waivers (full) also available. *Faculty research:* Telecommunications, decision systems, information engineering, operations research, software. Total annual research expenditures: $172,823. *Unit head:* Dr. Richard S. Barr, Chair, 214-768-1772, Fax: 214-768-1112, E-mail: emis@lyle.smu.edu. *Application contact:* Marc Valerin, Director of Graduate and Executive Admissions, 214-768-3042, E-mail: valerin@lyle.smu.edu.

Southern Methodist University, Bobby B. Lyle School of Engineering, Department of Environmental and Civil Engineering, Dallas, TX 75275-0340. Offers applied science (MS, PhD); civil engineering (MS, PhD); environmental engineering (MS); environmental science (MS), including environmental systems management, hazardous and waste materials management; facilities management (MS). Part-time and evening/weekend programs available. Postbaccalaureate distance learning degree programs offered (no on-campus study). *Faculty:* 7 full-time (0 women), 13 part-time/adjunct (4 women). *Students:* 19 full-time (8 women), 50 part-time (17 women); includes 13 minority (9 African Americans, 2 Asian Americans or Pacific Islanders, 2 Hispanic Americans), 7 international. Average age 34. 50 applicants, 86% accepted, 28 enrolled. In 2009, 17 master's, 1 doctorate awarded. Terminal master's awarded for partial completion of doctoral program. *Degree requirements:* For master's, thesis optional; for doctorate, thesis/dissertation, oral and written qualifying exams. *Entrance requirements:* For master's, GRE General Test, minimum GPA of 3.0 in last 2 years; bachelor's degree in engineering, mathematics, or sciences; for doctorate, GRE, BS and MS in related field, minimum GPA of 3.3. Additional exam requirements/recommendations for international students: Required—TOEFL. *Application deadline:* For fall admission, 7/1 for domestic students, 5/15 for international students; for spring admission, 11/15 for domestic students, 9/1 for international students. Applications are processed on a rolling basis. Application fee: $75. Electronic applications accepted. *Financial support:* In 2009–10, 9 students received support, including 2 research assistantships with full tuition reimbursements available (averaging $18,000 per year), 7 teaching assistantships with full tuition reimbursements available (averaging $18,000 per year); career-related internships or fieldwork, tuition waivers (full and partial), and unspecified assistantships also available. *Faculty research:* Human and environmental health effects of endocrine disrupters, development of air pollution control systems for diesel engines, structural analysis and design, modeling and design of waste treatment systems. Total annual research expenditures: $100,000. *Unit head:* Prof. Bijan Mohraz, Chair, 214-768-3894, Fax: 214-768-2164, E-mail: bmohraz@lyle.smu.edu. *Application contact:* Marc Valerin, Director of Graduate and Executive Admissions, 214-768-3042, Fax: 214-768-3778, E-mail: valerin@lyle.smu.edu.

Thomas Edison State College, School of Applied Science and Technology, Trenton, NJ 08608-1176. Offers Graduate Certificate. Part-time programs available. Postbaccalaureate distance learning degree programs offered (no on-campus study). *Students:* 25 part-time (17 women); includes 5 minority (3 African Americans, 1 Asian American or Pacific Islander, 1 Hispanic American). Average age 42. In 2009, 7 Graduate Certificates awarded. *Entrance requirements:* Additional exam requirements/recommendations for international students: Required—TOEFL (minimum score 550 paper-based; 213 computer-based; 79 iBT). *Application deadline:* For fall admission, 8/15 priority date for domestic and international students; for winter admission, 11/15 priority date for domestic and international students; for spring admission, 2/15 priority date for domestic students, 1/15 priority date for international students. Applications are processed on a rolling basis. Application fee: $75. Electronic applications accepted. *Expenses:* Tuition, area resident: Part-time $479 per credit. Tuition, state resident: part-time $479 per credit. Tuition, nonresident: part-time $479 per credit. *Financial support:* Applicants required to submit FAFSA. *Unit head:* Dr. Marcus Tillery, Dean, School of Applied Science and Technology, 609-984-1130, Fax: 609-984-3898, E-mail: info@tesc.edu. *Application contact:* David Hoftiezer, Director of Admissions, 888-442-8372, Fax: 609-984-8447, E-mail: admissions@tesc.edu.

University of Arkansas at Little Rock, Graduate School, George W. Donughey College of Engineering and Information Technology, Department of Applied Science, Little Rock, AR 72204-1099. Offers MS, PhD. Part-time programs available. *Degree requirements:* For master's, comprehensive exam, thesis optional, oral exams; for doctorate, thesis/dissertation, 2 semesters of residency, candidacy exams. *Entrance requirements:* For master's, GRE General Test, interview, minimum GPA of 3.0; for doctorate, GRE General Test, interview, minimum graduate GPA of 3.5. Additional exam requirements/recommendations for international students: Required—TOEFL. *Faculty research:* Particle and powder science and technology, optical sensors, process control and automation, signal and image processing, biomedical measurement systems.

University of California, Berkeley, Graduate Division, College of Engineering, Group in Applied Science and Technology, Berkeley, CA 94720-1500. Offers PhD. *Students:* 37 full-time (7 women). Average age 28. 76 applicants, 3 enrolled. In 2009, 14 doctorates awarded. *Degree requirements:* For doctorate, thesis/dissertation, preliminary exam, qualifying exam. *Entrance requirements:* For doctorate, GRE General Test, BA or BS in engineering, physics, mathematics, chemistry, or related field; minimum GPA of 3.0, 3 letters of recommendation. *Application deadline:* For fall admission, 12/15 for domestic students. Application fee: $70 ($90 for international students). *Financial support:* Fellowships, research assistantships, teaching assistantships, career-related internships or fieldwork and unspecified assistantships available. Financial award applicants required to submit FAFSA. *Unit head:* Ronald Gronsky, Head, 510-642-8790, Fax: 510-643-6103. *Application contact:* Patricia M. Berumen, Student Affairs Officer, 510-642-8790, Fax: 510-643-6103, E-mail: ast.program@coe.berkeley.edu.

University of California, Davis, College of Engineering, Program in Applied Science, Davis, CA 95616. Offers MS, PhD. Terminal master's awarded for partial completion of doctoral program. *Degree requirements:* For master's, comprehensive exam (for some programs), thesis (for some programs); for doctorate, thesis/dissertation. *Entrance requirements:* For master's and doctorate, GRE General Test, minimum GPA of 3.3. Additional exam requirements/recommendations for international students: Required—TOEFL (minimum score 550 paper-based; 213 computer-based). Electronic applications accepted. *Faculty research:* Plasma physics, scientific computing, fusion technology, laser physics and nonlinear optics.

University of Colorado Denver, College of Liberal Arts and Sciences, Program in Integrated Sciences, Denver, CO 80217-3364. Offers applied science (MIS); computer science (MIS); mathematics (MIS). *Students:* 3 part-time (1 woman); includes 1 minority (African American). 1 applicant, 0% accepted, 0 enrolled. In 2009, 4 master's awarded. *Financial support:* Research assistantships, teaching assistantships available. Financial award application deadline: 4/1; financial award applicants required to submit FAFSA. *Application contact:* Tammy Stone, Associate Dean, Curriculum and Student Affairs, 303-556-3063, Fax: 303-556-4861.

University of Mississippi, Graduate School, School of Applied Sciences, Oxford, University, MS 38677. Offers MA, MS, MSW, PhD. *Students:* 150 full-time (111 women), 47 part-time (27 women); includes 33 minority (29 African Americans, 1 American Indian/Alaska Native, 2 Asian Americans or Pacific Islanders, 1 Hispanic American), 8 international. In 2009, 27 master's, 3 doctorates awarded. *Entrance requirements:* For master's, GRE General Test, minimum GPA of 3.0. Additional exam requirements/recommendations for international students: Required—TOEFL. *Application deadline:* For fall admission, 4/1 for domestic students; for spring admission, 10/1 for domestic students. Applications are processed on a rolling basis. Application fee: $25. Electronic applications accepted. *Financial support:* Scholarships/grants available. Financial award application deadline: 3/1; financial award applicants required to submit FAFSA. *Unit head:* Dr. Linda Chitwood, Dean, 662-915-7916, Fax: 662-915-5717, E-mail: lchitwoo@olemiss.edu. *Application contact:* Dr. Christy M. Wyandt, Associate Dean, 662-915-7474, Fax: 662-915-7577, E-mail: cwyandt@olemiss.edu.

THE CITY COLLEGE AND THE GRADUATE CENTER OF THE CITY UNIVERSITY OF NEW YORK

Grove School of Engineering

Programs of Study

The Grove School of Engineering (GSOE) of the City College of New York offers programs of study leading to Master of Science, Master of Engineering, and Doctor of Philosophy degrees in six areas: biomedical engineering, chemical engineering, civil engineering, computer science*, electrical engineering, and mechanical engineering. (*The Ph.D. program in computer science is offered through the Graduate Center.) Two 12-credit advanced certificate programs are also offered: in civil engineering and in engineering management.

The Master of Engineering (M.E.) degree is offered in chemical engineering, civil engineering, electrical engineering, and mechanical engineering. The Master of Science (M.S.) degree is offered in biomedical engineering, computer science, and engineering (interdisciplinary). Certificates of Advanced Study are offered in civil engineering and engineering management.

The master's degree is awarded upon completion of 30 credits of approved graduate courses with a minimum average grade of B. Students are also required to complete any one of the following: a thesis (up to 6 credits), a project (3 credits), a report (no credit), or seminars (1 credit). The advanced certificate is awarded upon completion of 12 credits of approved graduate courses with a minimum average grade of B. The doctoral degree requires satisfactory completion of 60 credits of approved graduate work beyond the bachelor's degree, of which a minimum of 30 credits must be taken at the City College. It also requires the successful passing of the comprehensive first examination (the qualifying examination) and second examination in the field of dissertation research, proficiency in a tool of research, and the passing of an oral defense of the dissertation. One full year of residence on the campus is required.

Research Facilities

Each department is equipped with substantial, up-to-date research facilities to conduct its research programs. Additional interdisciplinary research facilities are also available. Some of the facilities and research groups are administered as research institutes, centers, and laboratories. These include the Benjamin Levich Institute for Physicochemical Hydrodynamics, the New York Center for Biomedical Engineering, the Institute for Transportation Systems, the Center for Water Resources and Environmental Research, the Institute for Municipal Waste Research, the Institute for Ultrafast Spectroscopy and Lasers, the Photonics Engineering Center, the Telecommunications Laboratory, the Optical Signal Processing Laboratory, the Biomechanics Laboratory, the Biosignal Processing Laboratory, the Tissue Engineering Laboratory, the Turbomachinery/Aerospace Laboratories, the Micro Electronic Heat Transfer and Materials Laboratory, the Theory of Machines Laboratory, the Solid Mechanics Research Laboratory, and the Roads and Airfields Materials Laboratory. The Grove School of Engineering provides a wide range of networked computer facilities for both teaching and research, which amount to approximately 300 engineering workstations and various PC facilities.

Financial Aid

New Ph.D. students are awarded fellowships and/or research assistantships consisting of $24,000 stipends plus tuition plus health benefits. Continuing students are supported through research and/or teaching assistantships. Special fellowships are available for minority students, including women. Summer support is also available to augment a student's fellowship and/or assistantship.

Cost of Study

In 2009–10, tuition for entering New York State residents was $360 per credit to a maximum of approximately $4315 per semester. Non–state residents, including international students, paid $640 per credit. Student fees are approximately $180 per year. The tuition for students who have passed the Ph.D. qualifying examination is significantly lower. (More information is available in the graduate bulletin, available online at http://www.ccny.cuny.edu.)

Living and Housing Costs

A brand new residence hall, the Towers, is located on the City College campus. The Towers houses 600 students in fully furnished air-conditioned units complete with state-of-the-art features, such as card access and wireless Internet lounges. For more information, students should visit http://www.ccnytowers.com/ccny.

Rent in private housing near the City College campus varies from $8000 to $10,000 per year.

Student Group

The average graduate enrollment in all engineering departments at the master's level is more than 450 students. At the doctoral level, enrollment exceeds 200. This includes computer science students doing research work with mentors at CCNY.

Student Outcomes

All Ph.D. graduates from 2002 to 2008 have found desirable positions. Approximately 15 percent are in academia, 60 percent are in industry, 15 percent are in government, and 10 percent hold postdoctoral research positions.

Location

The City College occupies a 35-acre modern campus in historic St. Nicholas Heights, which is only a few blocks from the Hudson River. Some of its buildings are impressive New York City landmarks.

The College and The School

The City College was founded in 1847. In 1866, it was named College of the City of New York (CCNY). The College was committed to expanding opportunities for all who sought a higher education, while maintaining and enhancing academic excellence. From 1944 to 1961, a wide range of master's programs were introduced. In 1961, doctoral-level programs were introduced. Today, the City College is a comprehensive teaching and research institution dedicated to excellence in graduate education. The City College is financed by New York State, student fees, and gifts. The Grove School of Engineering was formally established as a separate school in 1919. Steinman Hall, which houses the GSOE, was fully renovated in 1994. In the fiscal year 2007–08, the Grove School of Engineering had research expenditures of approximately $22.5 million.

Applying

The deadlines for application for admission to the master's program for the fall and spring semesters are April 15 and November 1, respectively. The deadlines for application for admission to the Ph.D. program for the fall and spring semesters are April 15 and November 15, respectively.

Correspondence and Information

For master's and doctoral programs:
Office of Admissions
The City College of New York
Convent Avenue at 138th Street
New York, New York 10031
Phone: 212-650-6853
Fax: 212-650-6417
E-mail: admissions@ccny.cuny.edu
Web site: http://www.ccny.cuny.edu

For additional information:
Dr. Mumtaz K. Kassir
Associate Dean for Graduate Studies and Executive Officer
Grove School of Engineering
The City College of New York
New York, New York 10031
Phone: 212-650-8030
Fax: 212-650-8029
E-mail: gp@engr.ccny.cuny.edu
Web site: http://www.engr.cuny.cuny

The City College and the Graduate Center of the City University of New York

THE DEPARTMENTS AND THEIR RESEARCH

Biomedical Engineering

Professor John Tarbell, Chairman (phone: 212-650-6841, fax: 212-650-6727). This department of 9 faculty members has major research activities in cardiovascular engineering; molecular, cell, and tissue engineering; nanotechnology and biomaterials; musculoskeletal biomechanics; and neural engineering and imaging. Special arrangements for research in eight preeminent medical institutions in New York City are made possible through the New York Center for Bioengineering (NYCBE), a consortium directed by the Biomedical Engineering Department. Graduate students have the unique opportunity to conduct their dissertation research with mentors from either the Biomedical Engineering Department or the hospital partners in the NYCBE or with dual mentors. Further information can be found at the Biomedical Engineering Department Web site at http://www.bme.ccny.cuny.edu.

Chemical Engineering

Professor Alexander Couzis, Chairman (phone: 212-650-7135, fax: 212-650-6660). Major areas of research include multiphase fluid mechanics (suspension rheology, sedimentation, hydrodynamic stability, interfacial phenomena, two-phase jet and pore flows, flow of near-critical binary mixtures, and high-velocity fluidization), effective properties of materials (flow in porous media, thermocapillarity, electrophoresis, and thermal and electronic properties of semiconductors), process control and simulation (combined cycle power generation), reaction engineering (multiphase reactor analysis), biomedical engineering (controlled drug release, study of the mechanism of artery disease, and liquid extraction of fermentation broths), polymer science (hydrogel technology, thin organic films, adsorption and self-assembly phenomena at solid-polymer interface, and viscoelasticity), powder technology (granulation, fluidization, and electrostatic effects of powders), and environmental engineering (air pollution control; soil remediation of organic, metallic, and radioactive contaminants).

Civil Engineering

Professor Claire McKnight, Chairman (phone: 212-650-8010, fax: 212-650-6965). Areas of research in the three specialization options are structures (wave propagation in solids, fracture mechanics, nonlinear behavior of structures, safety evaluation of bridges, structural reliability, earthquake engineering, soil-structure interaction, seismic risk assessment, and durability mechanics in concrete structures), transportation (traffic engineering; traffic safety; advanced traffic information systems; advanced traffic management systems; travel demand modeling; transportation infrastructure management; pavement design, construction, and maintenance; nondestructive testing of pavement; transportation finance; pricing; funding and institutions; transit planning, including rail, bus, ferry, and telecommuting; pedestrian and bicycle transportation; and sustainable urban transportation systems), and environmental engineering/water resources (remote sensing, satellite data analysis, algorithm development, and hydrological processing, with an emphasis on water resources and environmental monitoring; municipal and industrial wastewater treatment process development; biological nutrient removal; drinking water quality and stability; disinfection by-products; erosion-controlled transport of radioactive and agrochemical pollutants; and modeling of contaminants in freezing/thawing soils). Research is also done in air pollution engineering (management practices; ambient and source measurement methods; control and prevention from mobile, point, and area sources; tropospheric chemistry and fluid dynamics; and modeling, analysis, and assessment approaches).

Computer Science

Professor Douglas Troeger, Chairman (phone: 212-650-6631, fax: 212-650-6184). The department's active research reflects its position in the School of Engineering and encompasses diverse areas of computer science and engineering. Primary research concentrations are in computational geometry and vision, information security and assurance, data systems and information retrieval, distributed computing systems and algorithms, combinatorial mathematics and optimization, Web-based human-computer interaction, information management and e-commerce, multimedia networks and digital libraries, computational methods for image and speech processing, remote sensing, and programming systems and language paradigms. Further information can be found via the department's Web site at http://www-cs.engr.ccny.cuny.edu.

Electrical Engineering

Professor Roger Dorsinville, Chairman (phone: 212-650-7248, fax: 212-650-8249). The principal areas of research are photonics engineering (quantum optics and electronics, nonlinear optics, new laser sources, optical computing, ultrafast phenomena and devices, new optical materials, microstructures, laser remote sensing, and optical imaging), signal processing (signal detection and estimation theory, filter design, stability analysis, algorithms for extraction of parameters from radar and X-ray signals, development of fast algorithms, image processing, pattern recognition, and underwater acoustic signal processing), communication and networking engineering (data and digital communication, computer and local area networks, high-speed and multimedia communication networks, and optical communication), biomedical engineering (laser applications in medicine, biomedical signal and image processing, and medical instrumentation and optical diagnostic instruments), and control and systems theory (adaptive, modal, nonlinear, and robust control in control of discrete event systems and in-flight control applications).

Mechanical Engineering

Professor Feridun Delale, Chairman (phone: 212-650-5218, fax: 212-650-8013). Students and faculty members are engaged in research that includes fluid dynamics, turbulence and shock wave interaction, blast waves and composites interaction, advanced laser diagnostics, vortex dynamics, near-wall turbulence, spatiotemporal nonlinear dynamics, vibration and control, chaotic motions, hydrodynamics and interfacial phenomena, fire dynamics, superfluids, MEMS, nanomechanics, micro heat transfer, material processing with lasers, dynamics of porous media, laser techniques, composite materials, fracture mechanics, adhesive bonding, elasticity of nonhomogeneous materials, biological materials, orthopedic biomechanics, bone remodeling, heat and mass transfer, bioheat transfer, image processing and electron microscopy, CAD/CAM/CIM, computational mechanics (including finite-element and boundary-element methods), machine dynamics, turbomachinery, wakes and corner flows, biofluid dynamics, and biotransport phenomena.

CLARKSON UNIVERSITY

Coulter School of Engineering

Programs of Study

The Coulter School of Engineering, comprising departments of chemical and biomolecular, civil and environmental, electrical and computer, and mechanical and aeronautical engineering, offers programs of study leading to the Doctor of Philosophy (Ph.D.), Master of Science (M.S.), and Master of Engineering (M.E.) degrees. Interdisciplinary programs allow the student to specialize in such areas as materials processing, information technology, computer science, and environmental science and engineering. Descriptions of these programs can be found at http://www.clarkson.edu/engineering/graduate.

The Master of Science degree is awarded upon completion of 30 credit hours of graduate work, including a thesis. The Master of Engineering degree can be obtained in one calendar year; it includes the completion of a design-oriented project. In addition, Clarkson has initiated a two-year, two-degree program whereby students may obtain an M.E. degree in one year and continue on for an additional year to obtain an M.B.A.

The Ph.D. is awarded upon completion of a minimum of 90 credit hours of graduate work, corresponding to a minimum of three academic years of full-time study beyond the bachelor's degree. The candidacy procedure for the Ph.D. requires the presentation and defense of a proposal for the Ph.D. research. Candidates for the Ph.D. are required to prepare an original dissertation in an advanced research area and defend it in an oral examination.

The academic year consists of two semesters of fifteen weeks each. There is no formal summer session for graduate classes; graduate students and faculty members devote the summer entirely to research.

Research Facilities

The Department of Chemical and Biomolecular Engineering houses research labs for chemical-mechanical planarization (CMP); thin-film processing; bioengineering; nucleation; chemical metallurgy; chemical kinetics; process design; electrochemistry and electrochemical engineering; process intensification; experimental and computational fluid mechanics, including two research-grade wind tunnels; heat and mass transfer; and interfacial fluid mechanics, including a bubble column equipped with a motorized camera platform. The Department has a fuel-cell test laboratory and facilities for conducting research on alternate energy sources. In addition, excellent facilities are available for aerosol generation and ambient and indoor air pollution sampling and analysis, as well as tools for advanced data analysis.

The Department of Civil and Environmental Engineering has well-equipped environmental engineering laboratories with pilot plant facilities, walk-in constant-temperature rooms, and modern research instrumentation for organic and inorganic analyses; a hydraulics laboratory with a large automated tilting flume; temperature-controlled cold rooms and ice mechanics laboratories; a geomechanics laboratory with a wide array of laboratory and field testing equipment for geotechnical problems, including a number of specialized sensors, and a variety of loading systems, such as 200-kip closed-loop controlled stepping motor system and a 20-kip hydraulic closed-loop controlled servo-valve controlled axial-torsional system; structural and materials testing laboratories, including a unique strong floor and strong wall testing facility and an Instron 220-kip UTM; and soil mechanics and materials laboratories.

The Department of Electrical and Computer Engineering has laboratories for distributed computing networks, intelligent information processing, microelectronics, motion control, robotics, power electronics, electric machines and drives, liquid dielectric breakdown, biomedical signal and image processing, advanced visualization and networked multimedia and networked systems, and a 1-million-volt high-voltage measurement laboratory.

The Department of Mechanical and Aeronautical Engineering houses three wind tunnels, a clean room for microcontamination and nanotechnology research, and labs for fluid mechanics, heat transfer, aerosol and multiphase flow, CAD, image processing, energy conversion, vibrations, combustion, materials processing, manufacturing, and welding.

Much of the research work is conducted in conjunction with the University's interdisciplinary research centers: the New York State Center for Advanced Materials Processing (CAMP), Institute for the Sustainable Environment (ISE), Center for Sustainable Energy Systems (CRES), Center for Rehabilitation Engineering Science and Technology (CREST), and Center for Air Resources Engineering and Science (CARES). Computing facilities within the School of Engineering include an IBM series and a variety of Sun and IBM workstations, all interconnected to each office and laboratory by a high-speed wide-band network. Clarkson's Campus Information Services houses modern information storage and retrieval facilities, the computing center, and the library.

Financial Aid

Several forms of financial assistance are available, which permit a full-time program of study and provide a stipend plus tuition. Instructional assistantships involve an obligation of 12 hours per week of assistance in courses or laboratories. Research assistantships require research activity that is also used to satisfy thesis requirements. Partial-tuition scholarships are available for all degree programs.

Cost of Study

Tuition for graduate work is $1136 per credit hour in 2010–11. Fees are about $440 per year.

Living and Housing Costs

Graduate students can find rooms or apartments near the campus. The University maintains single and married student housing units. Off-campus apartments for 2 students rent for approximately $300 per month and up.

Student Group

There are approximately 200 students on campus pursuing graduate work in engineering. The total Graduate School enrollment is 400, and the undergraduate enrollment is 2,600.

Location

Potsdam, New York, is an attractive village located along the banks of the Raquette River on a rolling plain between the Adirondack Mountains and the St. Lawrence River. Three other colleges (one in Potsdam) provide a total college student body of 11,000 within a 12-mile radius. Potsdam is 100 miles from Montreal, 80 miles from Ottawa and Lake Placid, and 140 miles from Syracuse. The St. Lawrence Seaway, the Thousand Islands, and Adirondack resort areas are within a short drive. Opportunities for fishing, hiking, boating, golfing, camping, swimming, and skiing abound throughout the area.

The University

Clarkson University is a privately endowed school of science, engineering, and business. Master's degrees are offered in the engineering departments and in business administration, chemistry, computer science, mathematics, management systems, and physics; Ph.D. degrees are offered in chemical engineering, chemistry, civil and environmental engineering, electrical and computer engineering, engineering science, environmental science and engineering, materials science and engineering, mathematics, mechanical engineering, and physics.

Applying

It is recommended that applications be submitted by January 30 for the fall semester and September 15 for the spring semester to allow for full financial aid consideration. Study may begin in August, January, or June. Scores on the General Test of the GRE are required for all applications except those of Clarkson students. TOEFL scores of at least 550 (paper-based test), 213 (computer-based test), or 80 (Internet-based test) are required for all international applications.

Correspondence and Information

Wallace H. Coulter
School of Engineering
Graduate Studies Office
Box 5700
Clarkson University
Potsdam, New York 13699-5700

Phone: 315-268-7929
Fax: 315-268-4494
E-mail: enggrad@clarkson.edu
Web site: http://www.clarkson.edu/engineering/graduate

Clarkson University

THE FACULTY AND THEIR RESEARCH

Department of Chemical and Biomolecular Engineering
S. V. Babu, Professor; Ph.D., SUNY at Stony Brook. Chemical-mechanical planarization of metal and dielectric films and thin films for photovoltaic applications.
Ruth E. Baltus, Professor; Ph.D., Carnegie Mellon. Transport in porous media, membrane separations, membrane characterization, room temperature ionic liquids and biosensors.
Sandra L. Harris, Associate Professor; Ph.D., California, Santa Barbara. Adaptive control, process control, and process identification; periodic processing; the control of systems having varying dead-times; the generation of input signals for efficient process identification.
Philip K. Hopke, Professor; Ph.D., Princeton. Multivariate statistical methods for data analysis; characterization of source/receptor relationships for ambient air pollutants; sampling, chemical, and physical characterization of airborne particles; experimental studies of homogeneous, heterogeneous, and ion-induced nucleation; indoor air quality; exposure and risk assessment.
R. J. J. Jachuck, Research Associate Professor; Ph.D., Newcastle Upon Tyne. Process intensification and miniaturization, intensified heat and mass transfer, polymerization.
Sitaraman Krishnan, Assistant Professor; Ph.D., Lehigh. Antifouling and biocompatible polymers, biomaterials, responsive materials, nanostructured material design using self-assembly, X-ray techniques for nanoscale materials characterization, multiphase polymerization kinetics.
Richard J. McCluskey, Associate Professor; Ph.D., Minnesota. Reaction kinetics and thermodynamics.
John B. McLaughlin, Professor; Ph.D., Harvard. Fluid mechanics, modeling of protective textiles, self-healing composite materials and the flow of air and suspended particles, electrostatic precipitator.
Don H. Rasmussen, Professor; Ph.D., Wisconsin–Madison. Nucleation and phase transformations, metal reduction, colloidal and interfacial phenomena.
R. Shankar Subramanian, Professor; Ph.D., Clarkson. Transport phenomena, colloidal and interfacial phenomena.
Ian Ivar Suni, Professor; Ph.D., Harvard. Electrochemical and electrochemical engineering with applications to biosensors, thin film growth and nanotechnology.
Ross Taylor, Professor; Ph.D., Manchester. Multicomponent mass transfer, separation process simulation, engineering applications of computer algebra.
Selma Mededovic Thagard, Assistant Professor; Ph.D., Florida State. Nonthermal plasma for air and wastewater treatment, plasma-assisted material synthesis, plasma chemistry, mathematical modeling of electrical discharges in gases and liquids.
William R. Wilcox, Professor and Co-Director, International Center for Gravity Materials Science and Applications; Ph.D., Berkeley. Materials processing, crystal growth.

Department of Civil and Environmental Engineering
Norbert L. Ackermann, Professor; Ph.D., Carnegie Tech. Mechanics of granular flow, river hydraulics.
James S. Bonner, Professor and Director, Center for the Environment; Ph.D., Clarkson. Water quality and spill monitoring.
John P. Dempsey, Professor and Shipley Center for Innovation Fellow; Ph.D., Auckland (New Zealand). Fracture mechanics, tribology, ice-structure interaction.
Andrea Ferro, Associate Professor; Ph.D., Stanford. Air pollution, indoor air quality.
Stefan J. Grimberg, Associate Professor and Chair; Ph.D., North Carolina at Chapel Hill. Bioremediation, bioavailability of organic environmental pollutants.
Thomas M. Holsen, Professor; Ph.D., Berkeley. Fate and transport of chemicals in the environment.
Kerop Janoyan, Associate Professor and Executive Officer; Ph.D., UCLA. Geotechnical and structural engineering, soil-structural interactions, structural health monitoring.
Feng-Bor Lin, Professor; Ph.D., Carnegie Mellon. Modeling traffic operations, systems analysis.
Yongming Liu, Assistant Professor; Ph.D., Vanderbilt. Structural durability, multiscale damage modeling of materials.
Levon Minnetyan, Professor; Ph.D., Duke. Structural analysis and design.
Narayanan Neithalath, Associate Professor; Ph.D., Purdue. Advanced concrete material.
Sulapha Peethamparan, Assistant Professor; Ph.D, Purdue. Characterization and control of cement and concrete materials.
Susan E. Powers, Professor and Associate Dean; Ph.D., Michigan. Multiphase fluid flow; hazardous-waste management.
Shane Rogers, Assistant Professor; Ph.D., Iowa State. Fate and transport of etiological agents and anthropogenic compounds.
Hayley H. Shen, Professor; Ph.D., Clarkson; Ph.D., Iowa. Granular flow, sea ice processes.
Hung Tao Shen, Professor; Ph.D., Iowa. River hydraulics, river ice processes, mathematical modeling.
Poojitha Yapa, Professor; Ph.D., Clarkson. Mathematical modeling of oil spills.

Department of Electrical and Computer Engineering
James J. Carroll, Associate Professor; Ph.D., Clemson. High-performance motion control, nonlinear control, control strategies.
Ming-Cheng Cheng, Associate Professor; Ph.D., Polytechnic. Device physics and modeling and simulation of electronic and thermal characteristics for advanced solid state devices.
Susan E. Conry, Associate Professor; Ph.D., Rice. Multiagent systems, distributed problem solving, design of coordination strategies.
Daqing Hou, Assistant Professor; Ph.D., Alberta. Software design, program analysis, semantics of programming languages, software development environments and tools, software reuse, documentation, software evolution, formal methods.
William Jemison, Professor and Chair; Ph.D. Drexel. Microwave photonic systems and substations, microwave/mm-wave antenna design and measurement, radar systems, wireless and optical communications systems, lidar systems, biological applications of microwaves and photonics.
Abul N. Khondker, Associate Professor; Ph.D., Rice. Solid-state materials and device theory, modeling and characterization of semiconductor devices.
Jack Koplowitz, Associate Professor; Ph.D., Colorado. Image and signal processing, computer vision, pattern recognition.
Paul B. McGrath, Professor; Ph.D., London. Dielectric materials and high-voltage engineering, insulation problems.
Robert A. Meyer, Associate Professor; Ph.D., Rice. Artificial intelligence and distributed problem solving, verification of hardware designs, software engineering.
Thomas H. Ortmeyer, Professor; Ph.D., Iowa State. Power electronics, power quality, power system operation.
Pragasen Pillay, Professor; Ph.D., Virginia Tech. Modeling, analysis, design, and control of electric machines; electric motor drive systems.
Vladimir Privman, Professor; D.Sci., Technion (Israel). Quantum devices: quantum computing, spintronics, nanoscale electronics; colloids and nanoparticles; synthesis and properties.
Liya L. Regel, Research Professor and Director, International Center for Gravity Materials Science and Applications; Ph.D., Irkutsk State (Russia); Doctorat, Ioffe Institute (Russia). Materials science and its influence on properties and device performance.
Jeremiah Remus, Assistant Professor; Ph.D., Duke. Statistical signal processing, model inversion and optimization, pattern recognition.
Charles J. Robinson, Founding Director, Center for Rehabilitation Engineering, Science, and Technology (CREST), and Herman L. Shulman Chair Professor; D.Sc., Washington (St. Louis). Combining the development of microdevices and nanodevices capable of measuring stroke sequences with fundamental research that characterizes the behavior of the nervous system, quantification of tremor through signal processing analysis of graphical drawings, and determining and describing the control systems employed in health and disease to permit upright standing in humans.
Edward Sazonov, Research Associate Professor; Ph.D., West Virginia. Computational intelligence, biomedical engineering, nondestructive testing.
Robert J. Schilling, Professor; Ph.D., Berkeley. Control, nonlinear systems, robotics, active control of acoustic noise, motion planning.
Stephanie Schuckers, Associate Professor; Ph.D., Michigan. Biomedical signal processing, medical devices, pattern recognition, large datasets.
James A. Svoboda, Associate Professor and Associate Chair; Ph.D., Wisconsin. Circuit theory, system theory, electronics, digital signal processing.
Lei Wu, Assistant Professor, Ph.D., IIT. Stochastic modeling and optimization of large-scale power systems, smart grid, high-penetration renewable energy applications, power systems reliability and economics, market power analysis and risk management.

Department of Mechanical and Aeronautical Engineering
Goodarz Ahmadi, Clarkson Distinguished Professor, Robert R. Hill '48 Professor, and Dean, Coulter School of Engineering; Ph.D., Purdue. Fluid mechanics, solid mechanics, multiphase flows, aerosols, microcontamination, surface cleaning.
Ajit Achuthan, Assistant Professor; Ph.D., Purdue. Solid mechanics, ferroelectrics, nanomechanics and smart structures and materials, fiber optic sensors.
Daryush Aidun, Professor and Chair; Ph.D., Rensselaer. Welding metallurgy and automation, corrosion, materials processing and solidification, reliability analysis of engineering components/systems.
Douglas Bohl, Assistant Professor; Ph.D., Michigan State. Experimental fluid mechanics and thermal science.
Frederick Carlson, Associate Professor; Ph.D., Connecticut. Heat transfer, crystal growth.
Cetin Cetinkaya, Professor; Ph.D., Illinois at Urbana-Champaign. Solid mechanics, stress wave propagation, surface cleaning and nanotechnology.
Suresh Dhaniyala, Associate Professor; Ph.D., Minnesota. Aerosols, nanoparticles, particle instrumentation, atmospheric aerosols, aircraft and ground-based sampling, fluid mechanics.
Weiqiang Ding, Assistant Professor; Ph.D., Northwestern. Solid mechanics and nanocomposite materials.
Kevin Fite, Assistant Professor; Ph.D., Vanderbilt. Dynamic systems and controls, robotics and mechatronics.
Brian Helenbrook, Associate Professor; Ph.D., Princeton. Computational fluid dynamics and combustion.
Kathleen Issen, Associate Professor; Ph.D., Northwestern. Solid mechanics, inelastic behavior and failure of geomaterials.
Ratneshwar Jha, Associate Professor; Ph.D., Arizona State. Solid mechanics, optimization, smart materials.
James Kane, Associate Professor; Ph.D., Connecticut. Solid mechanics, boundary-element methods.
Laurel Kuxhaus, Assistant Professor; Ph.D., Pittsburgh. Biomechanics; mechanics and control of the upper extremity, especially the elbow; elbow joint stiffness and its application to arthritis; prosthetic upper limb control and the diagnosis of Parkinson's disease; mathematical modeling of ligaments; mechanical properties of vertebral bone.
Ronald LaFleur, Associate Professor; Ph.D., Connecticut. Fluid mechanics, thermofluid design.
Sung P. Lin, Professor Emeritus; Ph.D., Michigan. Fluid mechanics, fluid dynamic stability.
Pier Marzocca, Associate Professor; Ph.D., Virginia Tech. Solid mechanics, nonlinear systems control.
John Moosbrugger, Professor and Associate Dean; Ph.D., Georgia Tech. Solid mechanics, plasticity.
David Morrison, Associate Professor; Ph.D., Michigan. Materials science, fracture mechanics.
Eric Thacher, Professor Emeritus and Senior Research Professor; Ph.D., New Mexico State. Thermal sciences, solar energy.
Daniel Valentine, Associate Professor and Executive Officer; Ph.D., Catholic University. Fluid mechanics, hydrodynamics.
Kenneth Visser, Associate Professor; Ph.D., Notre Dame. Experimental aerodynamics.
Kenneth Willmert, Professor; Ph.D., Case Western Reserve. Solid mechanics, optimal design.
Steven W. Yurgartis, Associate Professor; Ph.D., Rensselaer. Solid mechanics, composite materials.

THE GEORGE WASHINGTON UNIVERSITY

School of Engineering and Applied Science

Programs of Study

The School of Engineering and Applied Science (SEAS) at the George Washington University (GW) offers the graduate degrees of Master of Science, Applied Scientist, Engineer, and Doctor of Philosophy as well as graduate-level certificate programs. The fields of study include civil and environmental engineering, computer engineering, computer science, electrical engineering (including biomedical engineering), engineering management, mechanical and aerospace engineering, systems engineering, and telecommunications and computers. Interdisciplinary study is encouraged, especially at the doctoral level. Within most fields, students may design their degree programs to pursue their own professional goals and academic interests, following curricular guidelines of the School and in consultation with their academic adviser. The minimum master's program consists of 24 credit hours plus a 6-credit-hour thesis; the nonthesis option consists of 30 to 36 credit hours, depending on the field of study. The professional degree programs (Applied Scientist and Engineer) require a minimum of 30 hours of courses beyond the master's degree. A technical project may be required. Course work done for the professional degree may be transferred to the Doctor of Philosophy, and vice versa, under certain conditions. The Doctor of Philosophy program requires a minimum of 30 hours of course work beyond the master's degree or 54 hours beyond the bachelor's degree, followed by a doctoral qualifying examination. The dissertation, requiring a minimum of 24 credit hours of work under the guidance of an adviser, is also presented orally in the final examination. The School's dissertations have had application in industry, such as an evaluation model of an oil spill contingency plan or an analysis of red blood cell flow; in government, for example, in projecting risks associated with nuclear reactors; and in higher education, through refined theoretical formulations of traditional problems.

Research Facilities

The University's three libraries hold more than 2 million volumes. Students have access to the Library of Congress and may consult GW's computerized catalog of holdings, those of six other local university libraries, and selected online periodical indexes. SEAS students may use laboratories that are well equipped as facilities for course work, experimentation, and research. Laboratories focus, for example, on artificial intelligence, biomedical systems, communications, computational simulation of complex physical systems, computer-aided design, computer-aided manufacturing, decision support systems, digital electronics, earthquake engineering, energy technology, environmental engineering, fiber optics and lasers, fluid mechanics, magnetics, materials science, propulsion, robotics, soil mechanics, and VLSI design and testing. Research institutes organized by the faculty as sites for advancing their research are described in the Areas of Research section. The Washington, D.C., area has the second-largest concentration of research and development activity in the United States, and many national laboratories are available to SEAS students for research.

Financial Aid

Teaching assistantships may provide tuition for full-time graduate study and a salary for each section taught or supervised per semester. Research assistants may receive salaries or stipends for both academic- and calendar-year appointments. School Fellowship awards range from $7500 to $19,000 per year for eligible full-time students and may be augmented by up to 18 semester hours of tuition credit. Full-time students who are U.S. citizens or permanent residents may be eligible for half-tuition Graduate Engineering Honors Fellowships.

Cost of Study

Tuition is charged at the rate of $1175 per credit hour for the 2010–11 academic year and is payable on a course-by-course basis. Information on all other fees and charges is available on the GW Web site at http://www.gwu.edu/apply/graduateprofessional/costshousingfunding.

Living and Housing Costs

Apartments for students are available in the surrounding area at a wide range of costs, starting at approximately $1000 per month, on average.

Student Group

SEAS students include graduates from the majority of U.S. colleges and universities and from seventy countries around the world. Approximately 900 students are working on master's degrees, 25 on professional degrees, and 400 on doctorates. Approximately 60 percent of SEAS students are international, and 30 percent are women.

Location

SEAS offers most programs at the main campus in the Foggy Bottom historic district of Washington, D.C., and selected programs at off-campus sites and the GW Virginia campus near Washington Dulles International Airport. Within a couple of hours' drive east of the University lie the beaches of Virginia, Maryland, and Delaware, and west to the mountains are U.S. national forests and parks, where recreation includes skiing, fishing, hiking, and camping. Cultural activities in Washington, D.C., frequently free of charge, include the rich resources of the Smithsonian and other museums, performing art in numerous local and national theaters such as Wolf Trap Farm Park and the Kennedy Center for the Performing Arts, seasonal events and athletics along the Potomac River and the C&O Canal, and scores of restaurants featuring ethnic-American and international foods.

The University and The School

The George Washington University was chartered as a private university in 1821, in response to the hope of President George Washington that a national university would be established in the federal city. GW has two colleges and six schools in addition to the School of Engineering and Applied Science. The others, which offer collaborative opportunities for engineering students, include arts and sciences, business, education, international affairs, law, medicine, and public health and health services. Organized at GW in 1884, the School of Engineering and Applied Science is one of the oldest engineering schools in America and was one of the first to admit women.

Applying

For all graduate programs, except the Doctor of Science in engineering management, applications are processed as they are received, and admission is granted while space is available; May 1 and October 1 are the priority deadlines for fall and spring respectively (January 15 and September 1 for fellowship/assistantship applicants, doctoral applicants, and applicants requiring a student visa). International applicants must submit scores on the TOEFL; 550 on the paper-based test (80 on the Internet-based test) is the minimum for admission directly to graduate study. SEAS accepts the IELTS test with an overall minimum band score of 6.0, with no individual band score below 5.0. Submission of Graduate Record Examinations scores is required when admission is sought to the doctoral program and/or when an assistantship or fellowship is desired. It is recommended for all other applicants.

Correspondence and Information

Office of Graduate Admissions
School of Engineering and Applied Science
Tompkins Hall 103
The George Washington University
725 23rd Street, NW
Washington, D.C. 20052
Phone: 202-596-7239
      800-537-7327 (toll-free)
Fax: 202-994-1651
E-mail: engineering@gwu.edu
Web site: http://www.graduate.seas.gwu.edu

The George Washington University

AREAS OF RESEARCH

Civil and Environmental Engineering. Research activities include advanced crash-analysis simulations, biomechanics, and security design at the GW/Department of Transportation National Crash Analysis Center located at the GW Virginia campus and Intelligent Transportation System research within the Intelligent Systems Center at the same location. Other areas of research being conducted at both the Foggy Bottom and Virginia campuses include biosystems processing of wastewater, electro-coagulation for water and wastewater applications, concrete and steel bridge design and retrofit, geotechnical constitutive modeling, and state-of-the-art earthquake engineering using GW's "6 degrees of freedom" shake table.

Computer Science. Areas of research in biomedical computing and bioinformatics include image-guided surgery, surgical simulations, medical informatics, medical imaging, and computational biology. In the area of computer security and information assurance, the emphasis is on network security, information warfare, cryptography, information policy, and computer forensics. Digital media research is concentrated on motion control, rendering, and information visualization. In networking and mobile computing, research is being conducted in wireless LAN, mobile ad hoc and sensor networks, distributed and high-performance cluster computing, and peer-to-peer networks. Pervasive computing and embedded systems research addresses issues in wearable computer architecture and applications, sensor networks, real-time embedded operating systems, embedded system networking, smart spaces, dynamic service discovery, security and privacy, and mobility. Software engineering and systems research involves use of various concepts and techniques to specify, verify, and test large software systems. Included are formal methods, collaborative computing paradigms, peer-to-peer systems, and component-based enterprise systems. Current research in algorithms and theory includes algorithms for networks and distributed systems, data structures, semantics of programming languages, optimizing compilers, and data compression and image processing.

Electrical and Computer Engineering. Active research groups of the faculty members and graduate students are working in biomedical engineering—medical instrumentation, telemedicine, medical image analysis, and bioinformatics; communication and networking—theoretical problems of modulations and coding, mobile communication systems and networks, all-optical networking, and high-speed telecommunication networks and Internet; computer architecture and networking—high-performance processor architecture, embedded systems, high-performance computing systems, and reconfigurable computing; electromagnetics—magnetics (memories and devices), fibers and integrated optics, antennas, propagation and microwave devices, and radar and remote sensing systems; microelectronics and VLSI—designing and testing VLSI digital/analog circuits, MEMS (microelectromechanical systems), VLSI circuits with applications to signal processing and communications, numerical device modeling, sensor design and applications, and nanotechnology; multimedia processing—image analysis and understanding, video and audio processing, and multimedia algorithms; and signal processing and systems—digital signal processing, real-time DSP algorithms, control systems, radar and sonar signal processing, and power generation, transmission, and distribution.

Engineering Management and Systems Engineering. Active research areas of the faculty members and graduate students encompass construction and facilities management; cost effectiveness; crisis and emergency management; decision support systems; emergency health and medical management systems; engineering and project management; environmental management; information management; information security and assurance; knowledge management; modeling and simulation of complex, adaptive systems; maritime safety systems and risk management; evaluating and monitoring risk; privacy and technology; systems and software engineering; strategic planning; and systems engineering processes. Current research in stochastic modeling includes simulation, Bayesian statistics applied to decision analysis and quality assurance, practical concerns in reliability, reliability and risk assessment, and stress models for accelerated reliability testing. Other research deals with applications of optimization; sensitivity analysis for finitely constrained problems; integer, nonlinear, and nonconvex algorithmic development and applications, including health-care, defense, and economic modeling; nonparametric discriminant analysis via optimization; and game theoretic models and applications to societal problems.

Mechanical and Aerospace Engineering. Research encompasses design of mechanical engineering systems, including computer-aided design and manufacturing, computer-integrated manufacturing, and robotics; fluid mechanics, thermal sciences, and energy; aerospace engineering, including aeronautics and flight dynamics, astronautics, and propulsion; and solid mechanics and materials science. Major research investigations are under way in biomimetics and bioinspired design, composite materials and testing, computational fluid dynamics, controls, finite-element analysis and finite-element models for biomechanical analysis, fracture mechanics, numerical optimization and artificial intelligence, vehicle dynamics (including a space station modal identification experiment), computational aeroacoustics, high-Knudsen-number gasdynamics and wind tunnel design, laser diagnostics for supersonic and combustion flows (including experiments on fuel mixing and combustion in scramjets), nanometrology, nonsteady flow induction, plasma-based nanotechnology, spacecraft control (including advanced flight deck technology research), spacecraft propulsion, strong vortex/boundary layer and launch vehicle/payload interactions, and vortex dynamics.

RESEARCH CENTERS, RESEARCH INSTITUTES, AND SPECIAL PROGRAMS

Biomedical Engineering Laboratory
Center for Biomimetics and Bioinspired Engineering (COBRE)
Center for Intelligent Systems Research
Center for the Study of Combustion and the Environment
Communications and Electronics
Computer-aided Design Laboratory
Computer-aided Engineering Laboratory
Computer Engineering and Design Laboratory
Computer Science Lab
Computer Science Special Projects Laboratory
Computer Security and Information Assurance Research Laboratory
Cooperative Vehicle Systems Laboratory
Crisis, Emergency, and Risk Management Laboratory
Cyber Security Laboratory
Cyberspace Security and Policy Research Institute
Decision Support Laboratory
Digital Media and RF Laboratory
Electromagnetic Research Laboratory
Embedded Systems Laboratory
Engineering Design Lab/PC Laboratory
Environmental Engineering Laboratory
Experimental Networked Systems Laboratory
Flow Simulation and Analysis Group
Fluid Mechanics Laboratory
Fluid Mechanics and Hydraulics Laboratory
FSAG Lab (Flow Simulation and Analysis Group)
General Computer Laboratory
GW Aviation Institute
GW Center for Networks Research
GW Institute for Biomedical Engineering
GW Transportation Research Institute
High Assurance Computing and Communications Laboratory
High Performance Computing Laboratory (HPCL)
Human Computer Interaction Group
Imaging Laboratory
Institute for Biomedical Engineering
Institute for Computer Graphics
Institute for Crisis, Disaster and Risk Management
Institute for Knowledge and Innovation (joint with GW's School of Business)

Institute for Massively Parallel Applications and Computing Technologies (IMPACT)
Institute for Materials Science (joint with GW's Columbian College of Arts and Sciences)
Institute for Magnetics Research
Institute for Medical Imaging and Image Analysis
Institute for MEMS and VLSI Technology
Instructional Laboratory
Instrumentation, Networks & Devices Laboratory
Jones Design Center
Laboratory for Advanced Computer Applications in Medicine
Laboratory for Infrastructure Safety and Reliability
Laser Cutter Laboratory
Linux Computer Laboratory
Machine Shop
Magnetic Material Testing Laboratory
Magnetic Refrigeration Research Laboratory
Manufacturing and Metrology Laboratory
Materials Testing Laboratory
Medical Instrumentation and Research Laboratory
Motion Capture and Analysis Laboratory (MOCA)
National Crash Analysis Center
Power Systems Laboratory
Precision Systems Laboratory
Project Alisa: Adaptive Learning Image and Signal Analysis
Propulsion Laboratory
Senior Design Laboratory
Simulations and Robotics Laboratory
Software Development Laboratory
Soil Mechanics Laboratory
Space and Advanced Communications Research Institute
Structural Testing/Materials Science Laboratory
Telecommunications Research Laboratory
Thin Film and Vapor Deposition Laboratory
UNIX Workstation Lab
VLSI Design and Testing Laboratory
Wind Tunnel
Wireless Sensor Network Laboratory

KANSAS STATE UNIVERSITY

College of Engineering

Programs of Study

The College of Engineering offers programs leading to the M.S. and Ph.D. degrees. The College has eight academic departments: Architectural Engineering and Construction Science, Biological and Agricultural Engineering, Chemical Engineering, Civil Engineering, Computing and Information Sciences, Electrical and Computer Engineering, Industrial and Manufacturing Systems Engineering, and Mechanical and Nuclear Engineering. The M.S. degree is offered in all departments. An M.S. degree in operations research and a Master of Software Engineering are also offered. The College offers Ph.D. degrees in all of the academic departments except the Department of Architectural Engineering and Construction Science.

Candidates for the M.S. degree are normally required to spend one academic year in residence; however, some M.S. degree programs are available partially or fully by distance. Subject to the approval of the major department, the candidate may choose one of the following options: (1) a minimum of 30 semester hours of graduate credit, including a master's thesis of 6 to 8 semester hours; (2) a minimum of 30 semester hours of graduate credit, including a written report of 2 semester hours, either of research or of problem work on a topic in the major field; or (3) a minimum of 30 semester hours of graduate credit in course work only, but including evidence of scholarly effort such as term papers and production of creative work, as determined by the student's supervisory committee.

Candidates for the Ph.D. degree normally devote at least three years of two semesters each to graduate study, or about 90 semester hours beyond the bachelor's degree. A dissertation is required. Ph.D. candidates must complete a year of full-time study in residence at Kansas State University. Furthermore, a minimum registration of 30 hours in research is required, not including work done toward a master's degree. Each candidate also must have completed at least 24 hours of course work at the University. The foreign language requirement is determined as a matter of policy by the graduate faculty in each department.

Research Facilities

Each of the eight departments in the College of Engineering has modern and fully equipped teaching and research laboratories. In addition, the College has several centers and institutes, including the Civil Infrastructure Systems Laboratory, the Advanced Manufacturing Institute, the Center for Sustainable Energy, the Center for Hazardous Substance Research, the Pollution Prevention Institute, the Institute for Environmental Research, and the National Gas Machinery Laboratory.

Financial Aid

The College of Engineering offers approximately 300 fellowships, traineeships, and assistantships each year. These awards are administered by individual departments.

Cost of Study

Fees for 2009–10 were $280 per credit hour for residents and $644 per credit hour for nonresidents. In addition, an $81 campus fee was charged for the first credit hour, with $24 charged for each additional credit hour, up to a maximum fee of $342 per semester. Students enrolled in the College of Engineering were assessed an engineering equipment fee of $19 per credit hour and a tuition surcharge of $20 per credit hour for engineering courses. Students with graduate assistantships may qualify for resident fees.

Living and Housing Costs

Residence hall rates for room and board for a double room with a fifteen-meal plan were $3332 per semester per student in 2009–10. A variety of apartments is also available at the Jardine complex, with monthly rent ranging from $367 for a one-bedroom unfurnished traditional apartment to $530 for a one-bedroom newly constructed apartment. In addition, there are scholarship housing units available that function as cooperatives in which students provide their own services. Complete information for Housing and Dining Services is available at http://housing.k-state.edu/. There are numerous privately owned apartments with a wide range of rental rates in the community.

Student Group

Kansas State University enrolls more than 23,000 students. The College of Engineering has approximately 3,000 undergraduate and 500 graduate students.

Location

The University's 664-acre campus is located in Manhattan, Kansas, a community of about 50,000 residents located in the scenic Flint Hills of northeast Kansas.

The University

Kansas State University was established in 1863 as the first land-grant institution under the Morrill Act. The University is composed of the Graduate School and the Colleges of Agriculture, Architecture and Design, Arts and Sciences, Business Administration, Education, Engineering, Human Ecology, Technology, and Veterinary Medicine. The College of Technology is located at Kansas State in Salina.

There are numerous cultural and entertainment activities associated with the University and the community. One of the most noteworthy is the Alfred M. Landon Lecture Series on Public Issues, which regularly brings outstanding speakers to the campus. The list of notables has included Tom Brokaw, George H. W. Bush, George W. Bush, Jimmy Carter, Bill Clinton, Bob Dole, Elizabeth Dole, Gerald Ford, Mikhail Gorbachev, Billy Graham, Nancy Landon Kassebaum, Robert Kennedy, Richard Myers, Richard Nixon, Sandra Day O'Connor, Colin Powell, Dan Rather, Ronald Reagan, Sheikh Yamani, and many others.

The University is a member of the Big Twelve Conference and provides numerous facilities for athletic activities.

Applying

The Graduate School has a nonrefundable application fee of $40 for domestic students and $55 for international students. Requirements vary according to department. Students interested in graduate study in the College of Engineering are invited to write to the Dean of Engineering, stating their area of interest.

Correspondence and Information

John R. English, Dean of Engineering
1046 Rathbone Hall
Kansas State University
Manhattan, Kansas 66506-5201

Phone: 785-532-5590
E-mail: ees@ksu.edu
Web site: http://www.ksu.edu

Kansas State University

FACULTY HEADS AND AREAS OF RESEARCH

Architectural Engineering. David R. Fritchen, Head; M.S., Washington (Seattle). (16 faculty members) Structural, mechanical, and electrical systems design for buildings: domestic water-supply and sanitation systems, fire protection, heating and air-conditioning systems, lighting and electrical systems, environmental control systems in buildings, communication and energy management systems for buildings. Building design and construction: integration of structural, mechanical, and electrical systems in buildings.

Biological and Agricultural Engineering. Joseph P. Harner, Head; Ph.D., Virginia Tech. (16 faculty members) Grain processing, handling, drying, and storage. Water and soil resources: irrigation systems, movement of pesticides and other chemicals in surface water and groundwater, improved water management techniques, erosion and sedimentation control, water quality and nonpoint pollution control, animal waste management. Off-highway vehicle systems: chemical application systems, site-specific and precision agriculture. Energy use in agriculture: efficient internal-combustion engine operation. Control systems: instrumentation and controls, sensor development, image processing, chemical spray metering and control. Animal environment: air quality, environmental modification, ventilation-fan performance. Process engineering: process design, cereal-based product development, properties of biological products, biobased fuels. Environmental engineering: constructed wetlands, vegetative filters, watershed modeling, bioremediation.

Chemical Engineering. James H. Edgar, Head; Ph.D., Florida. (10 faculty members) Bioconversion and bioprocessing: enzyme manipulation and reactor design, biomass conversion, biobased industrial products, separation and purification of biological systems, environmental engineering. Sensors and advanced materials: microelectronic materials, polymer science, adsorbents, catalysts, graphene technologies, bionanotechnology, and nanoelectronics. Alternative energy: catalysts and reactor design for hydrogen production, process synthesis, hydrogen and natural gas storage, artificial membranes for separation and purification.

Civil Engineering. Alok Bhandari, Head; Ph.D., Virginia Tech. (15 faculty members) Hydrology and hydraulic engineering: hydraulic and hydrologic modeling, overland flow hydraulics. Environmental engineering: physical, chemical, and biological processes for water, wastewater, and hazardous-waste treatment. Soil mechanics and foundation engineering: physical and mechanical properties of soil, soil stabilization, earth pressures and reactions, environmental geotechnology. Structural engineering: behavior and load-carrying capacity of steel and reinforced concrete members, fracture mechanics of concrete, finite-element methods, optimization applied to civil engineering structures, structural dynamics and earthquake engineering. Transportation engineering: urban transportation planning, transportation systems, analysis and simulation, geometric design of highways, highway safety, pavements and highway materials.

Computing and Information Sciences. Gurdip Singh, Head; Ph.D., SUNY at Stony Brook. (17 faculty members) Languages and software: high assurance software, software verification and certification, programming language and programming environment design. Cyber-security: language-based security, information assurance, enterprise systems security. Parallel and distributed computing systems: distributed mutual exclusion, real-time embedded systems, cluster computing, synchronization and concurrency, construction, distributed algorithms and protocols, operating systems, parallel programming languages and systems. Database systems: database design, object-oriented databases, artificial intelligence, data mining, bioinformatics. Software engineering: software life cycle, software environments and tools, software metrics, software specification, software testing, large software systems, computational science and engineering, agent-oriented software engineering.

Electrical and Computer Engineering. Don M. Gruenbacher, Head; Ph.D., Kansas State. (20 faculty members) Bioengineering: biomedicine, light-based bioinstrumentation, telemedicine. Communication systems: detection and estimation, analog/digital/RF circuits and systems, wireless telecommunications. Computer systems: computer vision, testing of digital systems, neural networks, computer architecture, noncontact sensing. Electromagnetics: device modeling and simulation, bioelectromagnetics. Instrumentation: computer-based instrumentation, sensors, intelligent instrumentation, microcontroller applications. Power systems: renewable energy, power system and stability, nonlinear dynamic systems, load management, distribution automation, power electronics, power devices, high-voltage circuits. Signal processing: adaptive signal processing, image processing. Solid-state electronics: sensors, device and process modeling, analog and digital integrated circuit design, infrared emitters and detectors, wide-bandgap semiconductors.

Industrial and Manufacturing Systems Engineering. Bradley A. Kramer, Head; Ph.D., Kansas State. (11 faculty members) Operations research: network optimization, graph theory, mathematical programming, health systems modeling and control, disaster recovery logistics, stochastic processes and queuing, fuzzy and uncertainty reasoning. Manufacturing systems engineering: advanced manufacturing processes, machining difficult materials, energy manufacturing, quality control. Ergonomics: highway safety, work environments. Engineering management: project management, management decision making.

Mechanical and Nuclear Engineering. Donald L. Fenton, Head; Ph.D., Illinois at Urbana-Champaign. (23 faculty members) Heat and mass transfer: fluid mechanics, room air diffusion. Machine design and materials science: acoustics, dynamics, kinematics, rock mechanics, stress analysis, vibrations. Control systems: dynamic system modeling, stability, robust control, instrumentation and measurements, simulation and control, aircraft navigation and control. Heating, air conditioning, human comfort. Computer-assisted design and graphics. Nuclear reactor physics and engineering: radiation transport theory, neutron spectroscopy. Radiation detection and measurement: neutron activation analysis, X-ray and gamma-ray spectroscopy, nondestructive assay of fissile materials. Radiation protection: radiation shielding, environmental monitoring. Controlled thermonuclear power: radiation damage and materials problems.

Advanced Manufacturing Institute. Bradley A. Kramer, Director; Ph.D., Kansas State. The Advanced Manufacturing Institute (AMI) is dedicated to providing innovative and cost-effective engineering and business solutions. AMI offers a full spectrum of capabilities that integrate business and creative insight with design and engineering expertise. AMI works with entrepreneurs and businesses of all sizes—from startups to Fortune 500 companies—in every market imaginable, including manufacturing, transportation, aerospace, consumer products, agriculture, food, chemicals, plastics, bioprocessing, equipment, and machinery. AMI also manages a highly successful intern program that allows undergraduate and graduate students to gain real work experience in the company of experienced professionals. The program helps students increase their skills and knowledge and be more productive in the workplace upon graduation.

Center for Sustainable Energy. Mary Rezac, Co-director; Ph.D., Texas at Austin. The center is focused on efforts related to assessment, conversion, and/or utilization of sustainable energy resources such as biomass, wind, and solar. Faculty from the Colleges of Engineering, Agriculture, Arts and Sciences, and Business are involved in research and educational outreach efforts with biomass resource assessment, plant genetics for efficient biofuel production, and conversion and utilization of renewable resources to fuels for transportation and electricity.

Center for Hazardous Substance Research. Larry E. Erickson, Director; Ph.D., Kansas State. Handling and processing hazardous waste/materials; protection of water supplies: resource recovery, treatment, disposal, and storage of hazardous materials.

Pollution Prevention Institute. Nancy Larson, Director; B.S., Montana State. Provides technical assistance and training in source reduction and environmental compliance to businesses, institutions, technical assistance groups, and private citizens throughout the Midwest. The institute also supports engineering interns, hosts an environmental management system (EMS) peer center, and serves as a meeting ground for KSU faculty members involved in pollution prevention and other related activities.

Institute for Environmental Research. Steven Eckels, Director; Ph.D., Iowa State. Study of the interaction of humans and their thermal environment: thermal comfort, humidification, air movement, clothing, physical activity, heat stress, cold stress, protective apparel, biothermal modeling, automobile environmental systems, aircraft cabin environmental quality.

National Gas Machinery Laboratory. Kirby S. Chapman, Director; Ph.D., Purdue. This laboratory provides the natural gas industry with independent testing and research capabilities, knowledge databases, and educational programs. A premier turbocharger test and research facility has been developed through acquisition of gas turbine engines, instrumentation, and a laboratory building.

Civil Infrastructure Systems Laboratory. Yacoub "Jacob" M. Najjar, Acting Supervisor; Ph.D., Oklahoma. The Testing Facility includes a pavement accelerated testing lab, a falling weight deflectometer state calibration station, and facilities for structural testing of bridge components and prestressed concrete girders. The facility is a center for cooperation between academia, industry, and state departments of transportation. The pavement research and testing activity is sponsored by a consortium called the Midwest States Accelerated Testing Pooled Funds Program that fulfills the needs of the surrounding states for full-scale testing and addresses research topics of national and international importance.

University Transportation Center. Robert W. Stokes, Director; Ph.D., Texas A&M. The University Transportation Center (UTC) coordinates interdisciplinary transportation education, research, training, and outreach efforts at K-State. The UTC's theme, "The sustainability and safety of rural transportation systems and infrastructure," emphasizes the unique needs of rural transportation systems. The UTC conducts research concerning local, state, regional, national, and international transportation problems through a coordinated effort between K-State, the Kansas Department of Transportation (KDOT), and the Research and Innovative Technology Administration (RITA) of the US Department of Transportation (USDOT). Dissemination of research information is achieved through the Center's Web site (http://transport.ksu.edu/), publication of reports, and through seminars for members of industry, government, and academia. Continuing education is also provided on transportation-related issues for licensed professional engineers. Training includes the development of short courses, handbooks, manuals, and other training materials developed under the Traffic Assistance Services for Kansas (TASK) Program and the American Concrete Institute (ACI) and Superpave certification training programs for personnel engaged in the construction of Kansas's highways. The Center also sponsors the annual Kansas Transportation Engineering Conference.

NORTH CAROLINA STATE UNIVERSITY

College of Engineering

Programs of Study

The College of Engineering comprises eleven degree-granting departments which are authorized to award the Master of Science, the Master of Engineering in a designated field, and the Doctor of Philosophy. Programs of graduate study leading to the M.S. and Ph.D. are aerospace engineering, biological and agricultural engineering, biomedical engineering (jointly with School of Medicine at the University of North Carolina at Chapel Hill), chemical engineering, civil engineering, computer science, electrical and computer engineering, industrial and systems engineering, materials science and engineering, mechanical engineering, and nuclear engineering; textile engineering offers the M.S. degree. Nonthesis master's degrees are also offered in most of the discipline areas and in the interdisciplinary program of integrated manufacturing systems engineering. Most nonthesis degrees require project or research work and a written technical report. The M.S. and Ph.D. degrees as well as the nonthesis master's degree are offered in the interdisciplinary program of operations research. Master's degrees are offered via distance learning through Engineering Online in aerospace engineering, chemical engineering, civil engineering, computer engineering, computer science, electrical engineering, industrial and systems engineering, integrated manufacturing systems engineering, materials science and engineering, mechanical engineering, and nuclear engineering. The Master of Engineering degree can be earned via distance education as well.

In most departments, the Master of Science degree is awarded for completing 30 credits of work, including a thesis. The Master of Engineering in a designated field is awarded for completing 30–36 course credits. A Ph.D. degree is awarded for completing a program of work, passing the oral preliminary examination, completing a research dissertation, and passing a final examination on the dissertation.

Research Facilities

Special research facilities and equipment include RAMAN and FIIR facilities; transmission electron microscopes; computerized SEM with full X-ray and image analysis capabilities; electron beam–induced current and cathodoluminescence microscopy equipment; a scanning laser microscope; laser MBE and pulsed laser depositions systems with full diagnostics; field emission electron beam lithography equipment; an imaging ion microscope for SIMS and 3-D ion imaging; a scanning Auger microprobe; an electron microprobe; complete X-ray analysis facilities including equipment for diffraction, topography, and radiography; a photoluminescence laboratory; MBE systems with in situ surface analysis; focused ion beam micromachinery; atomic resolution scanning tunneling microscopes; a precision engineering laboratory including diamond turning, ductile regime grinding, and surface metrology capabilities; a nuclear reactor with radiographic and neutron activation analysis; an applied energy laboratory; a plasma studies laboratory; a Freon simulator of a PWR fission reactor; a synthesis laboratory for III–V semiconductor materials; an organometallic chemical vapor deposition system; a semiconductor device fabrication laboratory, a deep UV mask aligner, and oxidation diffusion furnaces; a plasma and chemical etching and vapor deposition facility; computer systems for research in communications and signal processing and in microelectronics; a commercial computer design system for large integrated circuits; an EPA automated pollution and combustion gas facility; anechoic and reverberation chambers; a computer-controlled gas chromatograph–mass spectrometer; a robotics and automation laboratory; state-of-the-art multimedia, voice I/O, and software engineering labs; UNIX, Linux, and Windows workstations linked through Ethernet; a large structures-testing system; pavement wheel-track testing; superpave asphalt testing; a shake table; geotechnical test pits; plasmas for fusion; plasma propulsion; and laser-ablated plasmas for thin-film deposition. An engineering graduate research center features more than 120,000 square feet of dedicated laboratory facilities, including a class-10 clean room for processing.

Financial Aid

Approximately half of the engineering graduate students are provided assistantships with full support for studies, including tuition and health insurance.

Cost of Study

Tuition and fees for full-time study in 2010–11 are $3522 per semester for North Carolina residents and $9546 per semester for nonresidents. Students taking fewer than 9 credits pay reduced amounts. Most students appointed as teaching or research assistants qualify for tuition and health insurance support.

Living and Housing Costs

On-campus dormitory facilities are provided for unmarried graduate students. In 2009–10, the rent for double rooms started at $2555 per semester. Apartments for married students in King Village rented for $545 per month for a studio, $605 for a one-bedroom apartment, and $695 for a two-bedroom apartment.

Student Group

The College of Engineering had an enrollment of 6,050 undergraduate students and 2,399 graduate students in 2009–10. Most graduate students find full- or part-time support through fellowships, assistantships, and special duties with research organizations in the area. During the 2009–10 academic year, the College conferred 157 doctoral degrees, 539 master's degrees, and 1,011 Bachelor of Science degrees.

Location

Raleigh, the state capital, has a metropolitan population of over 500,000 and is ranked among the best places to live and work. Nearby is Research Triangle Park, one of the largest and fastest-growing research parks in the nation. The area offers numerous opportunities for recreation, sports, the arts, and other entertainment.

The University and The College

North Carolina State University is the principal technological institution of the University of North Carolina System. It is the home of the nationally acclaimed Centennial Campus, a model industry–government–university research park where students and professors work alongside industry leaders. The University's largest schools are the Colleges of Engineering; Agriculture and Life Sciences; Physical and Mathematical Sciences; and Humanities and Social Sciences. Total enrollment is more than 32,000. A cooperative relationship with Duke University and the University of North Carolina at Chapel Hill contributes to a rich academic and research atmosphere, as does the University's association with the Research Triangle Park and the Oak Ridge National Lab. The College has 300 faculty members with professorial rank.

Applying

Applications may be submitted at any time. Although the GRE General Test is not always required, it is helpful in making decisions concerning financial aid. An applicant desiring to visit the campus may request information concerning travel allowances by writing to the graduate administrator of the preferred program of study. Students may apply for fellowships or assistantships in their application for admission. Applications for all students are only accepted online at http://www2.acs.ncsu.edu/grad/applygrad.htm.

Correspondence and Information

Dean of the Graduate School
North Carolina State University
P.O. Box 7102
Raleigh, North Carolina 27695-7102

Phone: 919-515-2872
Web site: http://www.ncstate.edu

North Carolina State University

THE FACULTY AND THEIR RESEARCH

BIOLOGICAL AND AGRICULTURAL ENGINEERING. R. Evans, Department Head. **Faculty:** D. Beasley, F. Birgand, M. Boyette, M. Burchell, L. Cartee, J. Cheng, G. Chescheir, M. Chinn, J. Classen, C. Daubert, B. Farkas, G. Grabow, S. Hale, R. Huffman, W. Hunt, G. Jennings, P. Kolar, T. Losordo, P. Mente, G. Roberson, S. Roe, K. Sandeep, S. Shah, R. Sharma, R. Skaggs, O. Simmons, J. Spooner, L. Stikeleather, K. Swartzel, M. Veal, L. Wang, P. Westerman, T. Whitaker, D. Willits, M. Youssef. **Research areas:** Bioinstrumentation, bioprocessing, materials handling, energy conservation and alternative fuels, environmental control, machine systems, microprocessor applications, water and waste management, hydrology, ecological and environmental engineering.

BIOMEDICAL ENGINEERING. N. Allbritton, Department Head. **Faculty:** A. Banes, T. Bateman, L. Cartee, P. Dayton, R. Dennis, O. Favorov, C. Finley, G. Forest, C. Gallippi, M. Gamcsik, M. Giddings, R. Goldberg, S. Gomez, E. Grant, D. Lalush, W. Lin, E. Loboa, J. Macdonald, T. Magnuson, G. McCarty, M. McCord, P. Mente, H. Troy Nagle, R. Narayan, H. Ozturk, H. Pillsbury, J. Ramsey, B. Steele, M. Tommerdahl, A. Veleva, G. Walker, P. Weinhold. **Affiliated Faculty:** A. Aleksandrov, N. Allen, D. Bitzer, M. Bourham, J. Brickley Jr., G. Buckner, B. Button, J. Cavanagh, E. Chaney, M. Chow, L. Clarke, S. Cooper, D. Cormier, S. Franzen, H. Fuchs, R. Gardner, R. Gorga, R. Grossfeld, M. Haider, A. Hale, O. Harrysson, A. Hickey, W. Holton, T. Johnson, J. Kimbell, C. Kleinstreuer, K. Kocis, H. Krim, A. Kuznetsov, G. Lazzi, S. Lubkin, N. Monteiro-Riviere, J. Muth, B. Oberhardt, T. O'Connell, A. Oldenburg, M. Olufsen, D. Padua, S. Pizer, B. Pourdeyhimi, J. Qi, A. Rabiei, M. Ramasubramanian, L. Reid, S. Roe, J. Rubin, M. Schoenfisch, S. Seelecke, D. Shen, C. Smith, W. Snyder, A. Spagnoli, L. Stikeleather, A. Stomp, M. Stoskopf, R. Superfine, J. Thompson, D. Thrall, A. Tonelli, A. Tropsha, B. Vaughn, M. Vouk, S. Washburn, D. Woodward, B. Yu. **Research areas:** Biomedical imaging, micro- and nano-systems engineering, rehabilitation engineering.

CHEMICAL AND BIOMOLECULAR ENGINEERING. P. Fedklw, Department Head. **Faculty:** R. Carbonell, J. DeSimone, M. Dickey, J. Genzer, C. Grant, K. Gubbins, C. Hall, J. Haugh, W. Henderson, R. Kelly, S. Khan, H. Lamb, P. Lim, D. Ollis, G. Parsons, S. Peretti, B. Rao, G. Reeves, R. Spontak, O. Velev, P. Westmoreland. **Research areas:** Biomolecular engineering, biotechnology, biofuels and biomass conversion, electrochemical and reaction engineering, electronic materials, energy, green chemistry and engineering, innovative textiles, molecular simulations, nanotechnology and interfacial science, polymers and colloids, supercritical fluids.

CIVIL ENGINEERING. M. Barlaz, Department Head. V. Matzen, Director of Graduate Programs. **Faculty:** S. Arumugam, J. Baugh, C. Bobko, R. C. Borden, R. H. Borden, E. Downey Brill Jr., J. DeCarolis, F. de los Reyes, J. Ducoste, B. Edge, M. Evans, C. Frey, M. Gabr, M. Guddati, A. Gupta, T. Hassan, J. Hummer, D. Johnston, N. Khosla, Y. Kim, D. Knappe, M. Kowalsky, M. Leming, G. List, M. Liu, G. Mahinthakumar, J. Nau, M. Overton, S. Rahman, S. Ranjithan, W. Rasdorf, S. Rizkalla, N. Rouphail, R. Seracino, J. Stone, A. Tayebali, B. Williams, J. Yu. **Research areas:** Civil engineering systems, computer-aided engineering, construction engineering and management, construction materials, energy modeling, environmental engineering, geotechnical engineering, transportation systems and materials, solid mechanics, structural engineering, water resources and coastal engineering.

COMPUTER SCIENCE. M. Vouk, Department Head. **Faculty:** A. Anton, K. Anyanwu, D. Bahler, D. Bitzer, F. Brglez, R. Chirkova, J. Doyle, R. Dutta, R. Fornaro, V. Freeh, E. Gehringer, X. Gu, K. Harfoush, C. Healey, S. Heber, S. Heckman, T. Honeycutt, S. Iyer, X. Jiang, J. Lester, X. Ma, F. Mueller, E. Murphy-Hill, P. Ning, H. Perros, M. Rappa, D. Reeves, I. Rhee, D. Roberts, R. Rodman, G. Rouskas, N. Samatova, R. St. Amant, C. Savage, M. Singh, M. Stallmann, W. Stewart, A. Tharp, D. Thuente, B. Watson, L. Williams, T. Xie, R. Young, T. Yu. **Research areas:** Theory (algorithms, theory of computation), systems (computer architectures and operating systems, embedded and real-time systems, parallel and distributed systems, scientific and high performance computing), artificial intelligence (intelligent agents; data-mining, information and knowledge discovery, engineering and management; ecommerce technologies; information visualization, graphics and human-computer interaction), networks (networking and performance evaluation), security (software and network systems security, information assurance, privacy), software engineering (requirements, formal methods, reliability engineering, process and methods, programming languages), computer-based education.

ELECTRICAL AND COMPUTER ENGINEERING. D. Stancil, Department Head. **Faculty:** T. Alexander, W. Alexander, J. Baliga, M. Baran, D. Baron, S. Bedair, S. Bhattacharya, G. Bilbro, A. Bozkurt, J. Brickley, G. Byrd, A. Chakrabortty, M. Chow, H. Dai, R. Davis, A. Dean, M. Devetsikiotis, A. Duel-Hallen, M. Escuti, D. Eun, B. Floyd, P. Franzon, E. Gehringer, J. Grainger, E. Grant, B. Greene, A. Huang, B. Hughes, K. Kim, R. Kolbas, H. Krim, S. Lukic, L. Lunardi, N. Masnari, T. Miller, V. Misra, T. Mitchell, J. Muth, T. Nagle, A. Nilsson, H. Ozturk, M. Ozturk, E. Rotenberg, D. Schurig, M. Sichitiu, W. Snyder, Y. Solihin, M. Steer, C. Townsend, K. Townsend, R. Trew, J. Trussell, I. Viniotis, S. Walsh, W. Wang, C. Williams, G. Yu, H. Zhou. **Research areas:** Bioelectronics engineering; communications and digital signal processing; computer architecture and systems; control, robotics, and mechatronics; electronic circuits and systems; nanoelectronics and photonics; networking; power electronics and power systems.

INDUSTRIAL AND SYSTEMS ENGINEERING. P. Cohen, Department Head. **Faculty:** M. Ayoub, R. Bernhard, D. Cormier, T. Culbreth, B. Denton, J. Dong, S. Elmaghraby, S.-C. Fang, Y. Fathi, O. Harrysson, T. Hodgson, S. Hsiang, J. Ivy, D. Kaber, M. Kay, R. King, Y.-S. Lee, S. Roberts, E. Sanii, R. Uzsoy, J. Wilson, R. Young. **Research areas:** Medical device manufacturing; health systems; investment science; ergonomics; occupational safety; facilities design; production planning, scheduling, and control; logistics systems; supply chain design and management; material handling; concurrent engineering; manufacturing processes; rapid prototyping; optimization; soft computing; stochastic processes and simulation.

INTEGRATED MANUFACTURING SYSTEMS ENGINEERING. T. J. Hodgson, Director. S. D. Jackson, Associate Director. **Associate Faculty:** D. R. Bahler, P. Banks-Lee, R. L. Barker, K. Barletta, M. D. Boyette, C. Bozarth, G. D. Buckner, S. Chapman, Y. A. Chen, T. Clapp, T. Culbreth, B. Denton, M. Devetsikiotis, Y. Fathi, T. K. Ghosh, R. Handfield, O. L. A. Harrysson, G. L. Hodge, J. Ivy, M. G. Kay, R. E. King, J. P. Lavelle, J. W. Leach, Y.-S. Lee, R. L. Lemaster, K. Mitchell, M. Montoya-Weiss, M. K. Ramasubramanian, M. Rappa, W. J. Rasdorf, P. Ro, S. Roberts, R. Rodman, C. Rossetti, J. P. Rust, D. Saloni, E. T. Sanii, A. M. Seyam, L. M. Silverberg, E. Sumner, K. A. Thoney, J. R. Wilson, R. E. Young, C. F. Zorowski. **Adjunct Faculty:** J. A. Janet, J. Taheri. The Integrated Manufacturing Systems Engineering (IMSE) Institute was established in 1984. IMSE provides multidisciplinary graduate-level education and practical training opportunities in the theory and practice of integrated manufacturing systems engineering at the master's level. IMSE focuses on providing a manufacturing presence and a program environment in the College of Engineering where faculty, graduate students, and industry can engage cooperatively in multidisciplinary graduate education, basic and applied research, and technology transfer in areas of common interest related to modern manufacturing systems technology. The objective of the IMSE program is to offer students with traditional discipline backgrounds in engineering and the physical sciences an opportunity to broaden their understanding of the multidisciplinary area of manufacturing systems. Core areas of concentration are offered in manufacturing systems, logistics, mechatronics, and biomanufacturing. **Research areas:** Automation, CAD, CAM, CIM and advanced information technology, logistics, manufacturing system simulations, material handling, mechatronics, part fabrication, quality assurance and testing, process and facilities planning, product assembly, product design, robotics, scheduling and operations management, supply chain management.

MATERIALS SCIENCE AND ENGINEERING. J. Schwartz, Department Head. **Faculty:** C. M. Balik, D. Brenner, J. Cuomo, N. El-Masry, D. Irving, M. Johnson, J. Kasichainula, C. Koch, T. Luo, J. P. Maria, A. Melechko, K. L. Murty, J. Narayan, T. Rawanowicz, C. L. Reynolds, J. M. Rigsbee, G. Rozgonyi, R. Scattergood, Z. Sitar, R. Spontak, J. Tracy, Y. Yingling, Y. Zhu. **Emeritus Faculty:** K. Bachman, R. Benson Jr., C. Chiklis, H. Conrad, R. F. Davis, A. Fahmy, J. Hren, H. Palmour III, H. Stadelmaier. **Research areas:** Atomic resolution electronic microscopy and analytical techniques, advanced materials and processing methods, composite materials, computer simulation techniques, electronic materials, electrical and mechanical properties, metals, nanostructured materials, nonequilibrium processing, nuclear materials, polymers, biomaterials, structure-property relations, surface phenomena, thin-film processing and characterization.

MECHANICAL AND AEROSPACE ENGINEERING. R. Gould, Department Head. **Faculty:** G. Buckner, F. DeJarnette, T. Dow, T. Echekki, H. Eckerlin, J. Edwards Jr., J. Eischen, T. Fang, S. Ferguson, A. Gopalarathnam, C. Hall Jr., H. Hassan, H. Y. Huang, R. Keltie, E. Klang, C. Kleinstreuer, A. Kuznetsov, H. Luo, K. Lyons, A. Mazzoleni, R. Nagel, G. Ngaile, K. Peters, A. Rabiei, M. Ramasubramanian, P. Ro, W. Roberts, A. Saveliev, S. Seelecke, L. Silverberg, J. Strenkowski, R. Tolson, J. Tu, T. Ward, F. Wu, F. Yuan, Y. Zhu, M. Zikry. **Research areas:** Aerothermodynamics, autoadaptive systems, biofluid dynamics, biomechanics, combustion, composite structures, computational fluid dynamics, control systems, electromechanics, energy conversion, environmental engineering, flight dynamics and aircraft design, fluid/aero dynamics, fluid mechanics and two-phase flow, fracture mechanics, heat transfer, hypersonics, manufacturing, materials processing, mechanical and random vibrations, mechatronics, micro/nano mechanical and electrical systems, nano thermosystems, precision engineering, probabilistic mechanics, propulsion, risk and reliability, robotics, solid mechanics, space systems and dynamics, structural health monitoring, thermal management, theoretical and structural acoustics.

NUCLEAR ENGINEERING. Y. Y. Azmy, Department Head. **Faculty:** H. S. Abdel-Khalik, D. Anistratov, M. A. Bourham, D. G. Cacuci, J. M. Doster, J. Eapen, R. P. Gardner, J. G. Gilligan, A. I. Hawari, K. L. Murty, S. C. Shannon, P. J. Turinsky, M.-S. Yim. **Research areas:** Computational reactor physics; fuel management; plasma engineering; radiation effects in nuclear materials; nuclear power systems modeling; plasma-surface interactions; radiation transport; reactor dynamics, control, and safety; computational thermal hydraulics; nuclear waste management; radiological engineering; industrial radiation applications; medical radiation physics; plasmas for fusion; plasma propulsion; laser-ablated plasmas for thin-film deposition; nuclear environmental risk analysis; radiation measurements; neutron scattering and imaging; advanced nuclear fuel cycles; multiscale and multiphysics modeling.

OPERATIONS RESEARCH. T. J. Hodgson, Co-Director; N. Medhin, Co-Director. **Faculty:** J. Baugh, R. Bernhard, B. Bhattacharyya, J. Bishir, E. Brill Jr., R. Buche, S. Campbell, R. Chirkova, W. Chou, B. Denton, M. Devetsikiotis, J. Dunn, B. Edge, S. Elmaghraby, S. Fang, Y. Fathi, R. Funderlic, S. Ghosal, H. Gold, R. Handfield, R. Hartwig, P. Hersh, T. Hodgson, D. Holthausen, T. Honeycutt, S. Hsiang, I. Ipsen, K. Ito, J. Ivy, J. Joines, M. Kang, M. Kay, C. Kelley, R. King, J. Lavery, Z. Li, M. Liu, G. List, D. McAllister, C. Meyer Jr., A. Nilsson, H. Nuttle, T. Pang, H. Perros, K. Pollock, S. Ranjithan, M. Rappa, T. Reiland, S. Roberts, J. Roise, G. Rouskas, C. Savage, J. Scroggs, M. Singh, C. Smith, R. Smith, M. Stallmann, J. Stape, W. Stewart, J. Stone, M. Suh, W. Sun, J. Taheri, K. Thoney-Barletta, H. Tran, R. Uzsoy, I. Viniotis, M. Vouk, W. Wang, D. Warsing, J. Wilson, F. Wu, R. Young, T. Yu, Z. Zeng, D. Zenkov. **Research areas:** Mathematical programming, fuzzy optimization and decision making, networks, queuing, production planning, scheduling, project management, routing, simulation, stochastic processes and modeling, systems theory and optimal control, facilities layout and planning, logistics, inventory theory, supply chain management, financial engineering.

TEXTILE ENGINEERING. J. Rust, Department Head. H. Hamouda, Program Director. **Faculty:** R. Barker, K. Beck, T. Clapp, R. Gorga, B. Gupta, J. Hinestroza, W. Jasper, J. Joines, W. Krause, M. McCord, G. Mock, J. Rust. **Research areas:** Electromechanical design, real-time monitoring and control, studies in thermal and fluid sciences, polymer and fiber science, biomedical application of textiles, design and fabrication, process optimization, product/machine/system design, nanocomposites, nanolayer electrostatic self-assemblies, mathematical modeling of transport phenomena, rheology, polyelectrolytes, semi-crystalline polymers, carbon nanotube composite extrusion for enhanced mechanical/thermal/electrical properties, barrier fabrics, biopolymers, structure-property relationships.

OREGON STATE UNIVERSITY

College of Engineering

Programs of Study

The College of Engineering, one of eleven colleges in Oregon State University, offers the Master of Science (M.S.) and Doctor of Philosophy (Ph.D.) degrees in the Schools of Chemical, Biological, and Environmental Engineering; Civil and Construction Engineering; Electrical Engineering and Computer Science; and Mechanical, Industrial, and Manufacturing Engineering; and the Departments of Biological and Ecological Engineering and Nuclear Engineering and Radiation Health Physics.

An M.S. and Ph.D. are also available in materials science. Master of Engineering degrees (nonthesis) are offered in most departments. Master of Ocean Engineering, Master of Business and Engineering, and Master of Health Physics are also available. M.S. degrees can be completed in a minimum of one year, but they normally take 1½ to 2 years and can include a project or a thesis. The Ph.D. degree entails the successful completion of at least three academic years of residence subsequent to the bachelor's degree, a thesis describing the results of independent research, and an oral examination based on the thesis and research. Most graduate students are involved with funded research projects.

Research Facilities

Extensive research facilities are located in each unit and at the Oregon Nanoscience and Microtechnologies Institute, a signature research center located on the Hewlett-Packard campus near the University. OSU engineering researchers place a high priority on collaboration with faculty members in other colleges and departments and have access to major analytical instruments. Faculty members also collaborate with other universities, national laboratories, and industry partners, gaining access to facilities throughout the world. Faculty members collaborate in teams and in research clusters that facilitate research in the following strategic areas: mixed-signal integration (including mixed-signal, wireless, and integrated circuit design), nanoscience and microtechnology (including design, manufacture, and testing of microtechnology-based energy and chemical systems (MECS)), usability engineering (including mining large scientific databases, Internet2, and supercomputing), biological and environmental systems (including environmental remediation and sustainability), energy systems (including passive nuclear systems and renewable energy), and infrastructure and transportation technology (including sustainable infrastructure, earthquake engineering, natural disaster mitigation, and transportation systems).

Financial Aid

Fellowships, along with research and teaching assistantships, are available from various departments. Students who are granted such support also receive a tuition waiver. In the academic year 2009–10, stipends varied from $15,000 to $31,000, depending upon duties and experience. Teaching and research assistantships typically require 13 to 20 hours a week. Fellowships do not require duties. Additional financial support may be provided during the summer months.

Cost of Study

Estimated tuition and other fees for the 2009–10 academic year were $11,413 for residents and $17,488 for nonresidents. The cost of books and supplies was estimated at $1603. Figures are subject to change without notice.

Living and Housing Costs

For 2009–10, the rate for double occupancy in University dormitories and a full meal plan was approximately $8388 for the academic year. A few University apartments are available for married students with rents starting at about $430 per month. Off-campus one-bedroom apartments rent for about $495 to $600 per month.

Student Group

Of the 21,969 students enrolled at Oregon State University in fall 2009, 4,399 were in the College of Engineering. Of these, 422 were enrolled in the M.S. degree program and 291 in the Ph.D. degree program.

Student Outcomes

Graduates of the College's programs find employment in industry (e.g., Intel, Tektronix, Hewlett-Packard, and Boeing), government (e.g., EPA, Federal Laboratories, and the Department of Defense), and at universities.

Location

Oregon State University is located in Corvallis, Oregon, 80 miles south of Portland, Oregon's largest and most dynamic city. A community of approximately 50,000, Corvallis is located at the confluence of the Marys River and the Willamette River. With the Pacific Ocean 50 miles to the west and the Cascade Mountains 60 miles to the east, outdoor activities, such as skiing, hiking, surfing, and fishing, are easily accessible. The Corvallis community and the University offer concerts, plays, movies, art exhibits, and natural areas.

The University and The College

Oregon State University is one of only two American universities to hold land-grant, sea-grant, sun-grant, and space-grant designations and is the only Oregon institution recognized for its "very high research activity" (RU/VH) by the Carnegie Foundation for the Advancement of Teaching. Since its origin in 1893, the College has graduated more than 30,000 engineers. Each year it awards about 500 B.S., 175 M.S., and 40 Ph.D. degrees. The faculty currently numbers 124. Interdisciplinary programs with departments in the Colleges of Science, Forestry, and Agriculture are also available.

Applying

The School of Electrical Engineering and Computer Science accepts applications only for fall term, and they must be submitted by January 15. All other college units accept applications at any time. Prospective students should contact each department directly for complete information. Detailed requirements for each program are also available on the College of Engineering Web site. Application forms may be obtained by writing to the Office of Admissions and Orientation or from its Web site.

Correspondence and Information

College of Engineering
101 Covell Hall
Oregon State University
Corvallis, Oregon 97331-2409
Phone: 541-737-3101
   877-257-5182 (toll-free)
Fax: 541-737-1805
E-mail: info@engr.oregonstate.edu
Web site: http://engr.oregonstate.edu/

Office of Admissions and Orientation
104 Kerr Administration Building
Oregon State University
Corvallis, Oregon 97331-2106
Phone: 541-737-4411
   800-291-4192 (toll-free)
Fax: 541-737-2482
E-mail: osuadmit@oregonstate.edu
Web site: http://oregonstate.edu/admissions/graduate.html

Oregon State University

SCHOOL HEADS AND RESEARCH AREAS

School of Biological and Ecological Engineering
School Head: John P. Bolte, Ph.D., Auburn. Thirteen faculty members. The program focuses on the interface between biological and ecological sciences and engineering. Emphasis areas include water resources engineering, watershed analysis, hydrologic systems modeling, groundwater monitoring and irrigation management; biological and ecological systems analysis and modeling; biobased products and energy; and metabolic engineering. Inquiries: 541-737-2041; fax: 541-737-2082; e-mail: info-bee@engr.orst.edu; Web site: http://www.bee.oregonstate.edu

School of Chemical, Biological, and Environmental Engineering
School Head: Kenneth J. Williamson, Ph.D., Stanford. Nineteen faculty members. Major areas for study and research include chemical reactor engineering, mass and heat transport, electronic materials processing, microreactor technology, nanotechnology, bioprocessing, environmental technologies, and environmental systems. Inquiries: 541-737-4791; fax: 541-737-4600; e-mail: cbee@oregonstate.edu; Web site: http://www.cbee.oregonstate.edu

School of Civil and Construction Engineering
School Head: Scott Ashford, Ph.D., Berkeley. Twenty-four faculty members. Programs of study and research include construction engineering management in the areas of equipment and methods, productivity, and project control and management; geomatics engineering in the area of coastal monitoring and construction applications; geotechnical engineering in the areas of slope stability, cold regions engineering, earthquake engineering, and innovative earth structures; coastal and ocean engineering in the areas of coastal/ocean structures, wave and wave/structure interaction modeling, and coastal erosion mitigation; structural engineering in the areas of dynamics, wood and steel structures, seismic response of structures, and advanced computational analysis; transportation engineering in the areas of materials, pavement evaluation and performance, traffic engineering, truck size and weight impacts, mobility of the handicapped and elderly, and safety; and water resources in the areas of hydrology and hydraulic issues related to environmental problems and storm-water management. Inquiries: 541-737-4934; fax: 541-737-3052; e-mail: cce@engr.oregonstate.edu; Web site: http://www.cce.oregonstate.edu

School of Electrical Engineering and Computer Science
School Head: Terri Fiez, Ph.D., Oregon State. Fifty faculty members. Areas of study and research in the electrical and computer engineering programs include analog and mixed signal; artificial intelligence and machine learning; communication, signal processing, and control; computer systems, electronic materials, and devices; and energy systems, RF/microwaves, and optics. Areas of study and research in the computer science program include artificial intelligence and machine learning; computer graphics, vision, visualization, and computational geometry; computer systems; human-computer interaction; programming languages; software engineering; and theoretical computer science. Inquiries: 541-737-2889; fax: 541-737-1300; e-mail: eecs.gradinfo@oregonstate.edu; Web site: http://eecs.oregonstate.edu.

School of Mechanical, Industrial, and Manufacturing Engineering (MIME)
School Head: Belinda B. Batten, Ph.D., Clemson. Thirty faculty members. Current MIME research clusters include complex systems; energy systems; human systems engineering; manufacturing, production, and service systems; materials science and biomaterials; micro- and nano-scale processes; and robotics and autonomous systems. Inquiries: 541-737-3441; fax: 541-737-2600; e-mail: info-mime@engr.oregonstate.edu; Web site: http://mime.oregonstate.edu

School of Nuclear Engineering and Radiation Health Physics
School Head: Kathryn A. Higley, Ph.D., Colorado State. Eleven faculty members. Graduate degrees are offered in nuclear engineering, radiation health physics, and medical physics. Research in the department is focused in eight primary areas: nuclear reactor safety, thermal hydraulics, environmental health physics, radiation detection, scientific computing, numerical methods development, radiochemistry, and therapeutic radiologic physics. In nuclear engineering, particular attention is directed toward the application of scientific principles to the safe design and operation of nuclear installations, with emphasis in system safety and thermal hydraulic testing; high-performance computational methods development; nuclear reactor engineering; nuclear instrumentation; particle transport methods; arms control technology; space nuclear power systems; and radioisotope production. Areas of emphasis in radiation health physics include environmental transport modeling and monitoring, radiological risk assessment, radiation protection, radiochemistry, radioecology, emergency response planning, radioactive waste management and transport, facilities decommissioning, medical radioisotopes, radiation shielding, radiation dosimetry, and radiation detection methods. Emphasis areas in medical physics include radiation therapy and medical health physics. Specialized facilities include a TRIGA Mark II nuclear reactor, the Advanced Thermal Hydraulic Research Laboratory, the APEX nuclear safety scaled testing facility, the Advanced Nuclear Systems Engineering Laboratory, and laboratories to accommodate the use of radiation and radioactive materials. Inquiries: 541-737-2343; fax: 541-737-0480; e-mail: nuc_engr@ne.oregonstate.edu; Web site: http://ne.oregonstate.edu.

ROSE-HULMAN INSTITUTE OF TECHNOLOGY

Faculty of Engineering and Applied Sciences

Programs of Study

Graduate programs leading to the degree of Master of Science are authorized in biomedical, chemical, civil, electrical, environmental, mechanical, and optical engineering as well as in engineering management, mathematics, and physics. Applicants are currently being accepted only for work leading to the M.S. degree in biomedical engineering, chemical engineering, civil engineering, electrical engineering, engineering management, environmental engineering, mechanical engineering, and optical engineering.

A thesis is considered to be a normal part of the master's degree program. A nonthesis option is now available to electrical engineering students who choose the Master of Electrical and Computer Engineering degree. The degree program is tailored to the needs of each of the students, who develop a specific plan of study jointly with their individual advisory committee. A minimum of 51 quarter credits and an average grade of B are required. A maximum of 12 quarter credits may be earned by thesis research.

Research Facilities

Moench Hall, Olin Hall, and Crapo Hall house laboratories, classrooms, and offices for all the academic departments. The Computing Center supports three major logical networks: an AFS-based UNIX network, a Novell NetWare–based PC/Mao network, and an Open VMS Cluster. Project work with industry is supported in the 4,000-square-foot John T. Myers Center for Technological Research with Industry building.

Financial Aid

In general, Rose-Hulman has three types of financial aid available to graduate students. Assistantships—both graduate and research appointments—are awarded by the president of the Institute upon the recommendation of the Graduate Studies Committee. Tuition grants are also awarded by the president upon the recommendation of the Graduate Studies Committee. Loans are applied for through the Office of Student Life. Assistantships carry a stipend for the academic year and normally include a full tuition grant; payment is made in installments beginning in September.

Cost of Study

The 2010–11 tuition for a full-time graduate student is $11,865 per quarter. Part-time students enroll at $1038 per quarter hour. Book costs, student insurance, and expenses for reproducing the thesis are the responsibility of the student.

Living and Housing Costs

On-campus housing is not currently available for graduate students.

Student Group

There are approximately 1,900 students at the Institute, all majoring in engineering or science. There are about 85 students in the on-campus graduate program and 90 in Rose-Hulman's off-campus graduate program.

Location

The city of Terre Haute is located approximately 70 miles west of Indianapolis, near the Indiana-Illinois state line. The campus consists of 200 rolling acres in a suburban/residential setting east of Terre Haute. It is within easy driving distance of many major midwestern cities and universities. Numerous parks and recreational areas are close by.

The Institute

Rose-Hulman Institute of Technology is one of the select few independent colleges of engineering and science in the United States. It was founded in 1874 by Chauncey Rose, a pioneer industrialist and entrepreneur. The college's mission is to educate Renaissance scientists and engineers—people who can change the times, who understand the importance of their technical knowledge in relation to society, and who maintain their appreciation for the arts and humanities. Some of the most academically talented students in the nation are enrolled at Rose-Hulman.

Applying

Applications for admission to graduate work and information may be obtained from the Institute address. Regular admission requires that the applicant have both a bachelor's degree in an appropriate undergraduate field from an accredited educational institution and at least a B average. International applicants who are not graduates of an accredited bachelor's program offered by a U.S. college or university must provide official copies of the results of the Graduate Record Examinations and the Test of English as a Foreign Language (TOEFL). The minimum acceptable score on the TOEFL is 580 (237 on the computer-based test and 92 on the Internet-based test) divided equally among test sections.

Correspondence and Information

Associate Dean of the Faculty
Rose-Hulman Institute of Technology
5500 Wabash Avenue
Terre Haute, Indiana 47803

Phone: 812-877-8403
E-mail: gradadmis@rose-hulman.edu
Web site: http://www.rose-hulman.edu

Rose-Hulman Institute of Technology

THE FACULTY AND THEIR RESEARCH

Biomedical Engineering. Jameel Ahmed, Associate Professor; Ph.D., Northwestern, 1997: retinal blood flow, signal processing in the retina. Christine A. Buckley, Associate Professor; Ph.D., Northwestern, 1994: orthopedic biomaterials, corrosion of biomaterials, tissue engineering. Robert M. Bunch, Professor, Ph.D., Kansas, 1981; PE: optical instrument design, fiber-optic sensors, light scattering. Phillip J. Cornwell, Professor; Ph.D., Princeton, 1989: femoral component monitoring, structural dynamics. Kay C. Dee, Associate Professor; Ph.D., Rensselaer, 1996: tissue engineering, cell-biomaterial interactions, cellular responses to chemical and mechanical stimuli. Keith E. Hoover, Professor; Ph.D., Illinois, 1976: development of digital radio direction-finding and radio-locating techniques, ionospheric modeling, digital signal processing. Tina A. Hudson, Assistant Professor; Ph.D., Georgia Tech, 2000: neuromorphic engineering, analog and digital integrated circuit design. Charles Joenathan, Professor and Head of the Department of Physics and Applied Optics; Ph.D., Indian Institute of Technology, 1986; PE: speckle techniques, holography, fiber-optic sensors. Glen A. Livesay, Associate Professor; Ph.D., Pittsburgh, 1996: experimental and theoretical biomechanics, soft tissue mechanics, sports mechanics, morphometrics. Lorraine G. Olson, Professor; Ph.D., MIT, 1985: inverse electrocardiography. Renee Rogge, Assistant Professor; Ph.D., Iowa, 2000: orthopedic biomechanics, upper extremity biomechanics, finite element modeling. Mario F. Simoni, Assistant Professor; Ph.D., Georgia Tech, 2002: neuroengineering; analog, digital, and RF integrated circuits. Richard E. Stamper, Associate Professor; Ph.D., Maryland, 1997; PE: halo orthosis constraint systems, parallel manipulators, product design methodologies. Robert Throne, Associate Professor; Ph.D., Michigan, 1990: inverse problems, biomedical signal processing, control systems. Luanne Tilstra, Associate Professor; Ph.D., LSU, 1987; PE: physical chemistry/polymer physical chemistry, using light scattering and fluorescence to monitor peptide aggregation. Lee R. Waite, Professor of Mechanical and Biomedical Engineering and Head of the Department of Applied Biology and Biomedical Engineering; Ph.D., Iowa State, 1987; PE: biomedical fluid mechanics, biomedical instrumentation. William W. Weiner, Associate Professor; Ph.D., Syracuse, 2000; PE: invertebrate vision, circadian rhythms. Arthur B. Western Jr., Professor of Physics and Applied Optics, Vice President of Academic Affairs, and Dean of Faculty; Ph.D., Montana State, 1976; PE: optical holographic interferometry. Huihui Xu, Assistant Professor; Ph.D., Illinois at Chicago, 2005: magnetic resonance imaging, bone tissue engineering. **Chemical Engineering.** Mark R. Anklam, Associate Professor; Ph.D., Princeton, 1997: emulsification and emulsion stability, surfactant-based separations, gas hydrate formation and control, polymer-surfactant interactions. Ronald S. Artigue, Professor; D.E., Tulane, 1980: process control, computer simulation physical and biological systems, micro/ultra filtration. Alfred Carlson, Professor; Ph.D., Wisconsin, 1982: biotechnology, bioseparations, fermentation design, chromatography, protein refolding, protein engineering. Daniel G. Coronell, Associate Professor; Ph.D., MIT, 1993: chemical vapor deposition of thin films, numerical simulation of reaction and transport/applications to the microelectronics and combustion industries. M. Hossein Hariri, Professor and Head of the Department of Chemical Engineering; Ph.D., Manchester, 1979: air-pollution control, petroleum engineering, sorption of NOx and SOx, mass transfer. Scott J. McClellan, Assistant Professor; Ph.D., Purdue, 2005: Interfacial engineering, protein/surfactant adsorption, thin film characterization, photocatalysis. David C. Miller, Associate Professor; Ph.D., Ohio State, 1998: process synthesis and design, especially with respect to batch processes and pharmaceutical production; applied intelligent systems and process optimization. Sharon G. Sauer, Assistant Professor; Ph.D., Rice, 2001: physical property methods, including molecularly based equations of state using statistical mechanics and molecular simulation with applications to petrochemical and biochemical separations. Atanas Serbezov, Associate Professor; Ph.D., Rochester, 1997: adsorption and adsorption-based separations, porous materials, modeling and simulation, process control. **Civil/Environmental Engineering.** Richard A. Anthony, Associate Professor; Ph.D., Illinois at Chicago, 1995; PE: yeast genetics and molecular biology, ribosome structure and function. M. Hossein Hariri, Professor; Ph.D., Manchester, 1979; PE: air pollution control, petroleum engineering, sorption of NOx and SOx, mass transfer. Ella L. Ingram, Assistant Professor; Ph.D., Indiana University, 2004: ecology of temperate forests, plant/fungi interactions. Thomas W. Mason, Professor of Economics; Ph.D., Pittsburgh, 1972; PE: entrepreneurship, managerial economics and impact assessment. Howard McLean, Associate Professor; Ph.D., Wyoming, 1988; PE: geochemical and environmental analysis, lacustrine and plume modeling, bioremediation strategies. Sue L. Niezgoda, Assistant Professor; Ph.D., Penn State, 2004; PE: hydraulics, river engineering, stream restoration, stormwater management. Terry Schumacher, Assistant Professor; Ph.D., Portland State, 1992: technology forecasting, organizational culture and culture change, project management, new product development. **Electrical and Computer Engineering.** Frederick C. Berry, Professor; D.E., Louisiana Tech, 1988; PE: controls, parallel processing. Carlotta A. Berry, Assistant Professor; Ph.D., Vanderbilt, 2003: mobile robotics, human-robot interfaces, controls. Bruce A. Black, Professor; Ph.D., Berkeley, 1971; PE: spread spectrum communications, wireless systems. Edward R. Doering, Professor; Ph.D., Iowa State, 1992: image and signal processing, embedded systems. William J. Eccles, Professor; Ph.D., Purdue, 1965; PE: circuits and systems. Clifford H. Grigg, Professor; Ph.D., Manchester (England), 1977; PE: power system operation, control, and economics. Marc E. Herniter, Professor; Ph.D., Michigan, 1989: analog circuits, power electronics, circuit simulation, alternative energy, model-based design, hybrid electric vehicles. Keith E. Hoover, Professor; Ph.D., Illinois, 1976: digital radio direction-finding and radio-locating techniques, ionospheric modeling, digital signal processing, neural networks. Tina A. Hudson, Associate Professor; Ph.D., Georgia Tech, 2000: analog and digital integrated circuit design, subthreshold MOSFET neuromorphic design, linear-threshold circuits. Daniel J. Moore, Professor; Ph.D., North Carolina State, 1989: semiconductor optical and electronic devices, materials, analog electronics. Xiaoyan Mu, Assistant Professor; Ph.D., Wayne State, 2004: pattern recognition, artificial intelligence, neural networks, image processing and computer vision. Wayne T. Padgett, Associate Professor; Ph.D., Georgia Tech, 1994: digital signal processing, fixed point algorithms, sensor arrays processing, image processing. Mihaela Elena Radu, Associate Professor; Ph.D., Technical University of Cluj-Napoca (Romania), 2000: digital design, fault-tolerance and testability of digital systems, analog and digital electronics. Niusha Rostamkolai, Professor; Ph.D., Virginia Tech, 1986; PE: power system dynamics and control, power system protection, flexible AC transmission. Mario F. Simoni, Associate Professor; Ph.D., Georgia Tech, 2002: analog, digital, and RF integrated circuits; bioengineering; neuroscience. Jianjian Song, Associate Professor; Ph.D., Minnesota, 1991: electromagnetic compatibility, high-speed digital system design, microcontroller-based system design, embedded and real-time systems, electronics design automation, algorithms and architecture for parallel and cluster computing. Robert Throne, Professor; Ph.D., Michigan, 1990: inverse problems, biomedical signal processing, control systems. David R. Voltmer, Professor Emeritus; Ph.D., Ohio State, 1970; PE: microwave CAD and metrology, computational electromagnetics, GPS applications. Deborah J. Walter, Assistant Professor; Ph.D., Penn State, 1999: medical imaging systems, optimization of systems, electromagnetics. Phillip B. Walter, Visiting Professor; Ph.D., Penn State, 1997: control systems, intelligent and autonomous systems, nuclear power and propulsion, robotics. Edward D. Wheeler, Associate Professor; Ph.D., Missouri–Rolla, 1996: electronic and optical properties of materials, electromagnetics. Mark A. Yoder, Professor; Ph.D., Purdue, 1984: image and speech processing, digital signal processing, software defined radio. **Mechanical Engineering.** Thomas M. Adams, Associate Professor; Ph.D., Georgia Tech, 1998: heat transfer in microchannels; numerical modeling of two-phase, two-component fluid flow and heat transfer. M. Patricia Brackin, Professor; Ph.D., Georgia Tech, 1996; PE: design processes and optimization, quality management. April M. Bryan, Assistant Professor; Ph.D., Michigan, 2008: product development, design optimization, manufacturing systems. Bradley T. Burchett, Associate Professor; Ph.D., Oregon State, 2001: controls, dynamics, estimation. Zachariah Chambers, Associate Professor; Ph.D., Tennessee, Knoxville, 2000: finite element analysis, computational fluid dynamics. Phillip J. Cornwell, Professor; Ph.D., Princeton, 1989: structural dynamics, structural health monitoring. Patrick J. Cunningham, Assistant Professor; Ph.D., Purdue, 2006: controls and signal processing, internal combustion engine and exhaust after treatment monitoring and control. Patrick D. Ferro, Assistant Professor; Ph.D., Colorado School of Mines, 1994, PE: materials and manufacturing processes, superalloy and titanium casting, directional solidification, hydrogen storage. Jerry M. Fine, Associate Professor; Ph.D., Texas at Austin, 1984: Runge-Kutta-Nystrom methods with interpolants, finite-element analysis. David S. Fisher, Assistant Professor; Ph.D., Stanford, 2005: gait interventions relating to knee osteoarthritis. J. Darrell Gibson, Professor; Ph.D., New Mexico, 1968; PE: noise and vibration analysis, mechanical design. Frederick L. Haan, Jr., Associate Professor; Ph.D., Notre Dame, 2000: fluid mechanics, structural dynamics, bluff body aerodynamics, wind engineering. Richard A. Layton, Associate Professor; Ph.D., Washington (Seattle), 1995; PE: dynamic systems modeling, simulation, analysis, and design. Calvin Lui, Associate Professor; Stanford, 2003: computational methods, aeroacoustics, compressible turbulence. James E. Mayhew, Associate Professor; Ph.D., California, Davis, 1999: gas turbine film cooling, convection heat transfer, thermochromic liquid crystals. Andrew R. Mech, Professor; Ph.D., Illinois, 1986; PE: system simulation and optimization, gas turbines, power production. Michael S. Moorhead, Assistant Professor; Ph.D., Cornell, 2009: aerospace engineering, thermal and fluid sciences. Lorraine G. Olson, Professor; Ph.D., MIT, 1985: application of finite-element methodology to nontraditional areas. Richard M. Onyancha, Assistant Professor; Ph.D., New Hampshire, 2007: manufacturing, mechanics, finite element analysis and metrology with emphasis in micromanufacturing and micrometrology. David J. Purdy, Professor and Head of the Department of Mechanical Engineering; Ph.D., Purdue, 1981: dynamics, simulation, control system design and analysis. Donald E. Richards, Professor; Ph.D., Ohio State, 1981; PE: heat exchanger design, absorption heat pump technology, multifluid heat exchangers. L. Wayne Sanders, Professor; Ph.D., SMU, 1974; PE: internal-combustion engines, finite-element computational heat transfer, waste heat recovery in gas turbines. David Stienstra, Associate Professor; Ph.D., Texas A&M, 1990: fracture mechanics and fatigue, mechanical behavior of materials. Allen R. White, Assistant Professor; Ph.D., Ohio State, 2007: molecular energy transfer. **Optical Engineering.** Robert M. Bunch, Professor; Ph.D., Kansas, 1981: development of optics-based products, fiber-optic components, light scattering. Richard Ditteon, Professor and Director of the Oakley Observatory; Ph.D., UCLA, 1981: astronomy, geometrical optics, computer-aided optical system design. Galen C. Duree Jr., Associate Professor; Ph.D., Arkansas, 1995: ultrashort pulse lasers and applications, laser physics, nonlinear optics, fiber laser technology, photorefractive phenomena. Sergio C. Granieri, Assistant Professor; Ph.D., La Plata (Argentina), 1998: optical signal processing, RF-photonics, fiber Bragg gratings and fiber-optic components. Charles Joenathan, Professor and Head of Physics and Optical Engineering; Ph.D., Indian Institute of Technology (Madras), 1986: speckle techniques, holography, fiber-optic sensors, phase-measuring interferometry. Elaine M. Kirkpatrick, Assistant Professor; Ph.D., Carnegie Mellon, 1997: structural and magnetic properties of materials, nanostructured and nanoparticulate magnetic materials. Richard S. Lepkowicz, Assistant Professor; Ph.D., Central Florida, 2004: nonlinear and ultrafast spectroscopy, gradient refractive index optics, photonic crystals. Renat R. Letfullin, Assistant Professor; Ph.D., Saratov State (Russia), 1992: laser physics, wave optics, quantum optics, nano-optics, biophotonics, nano-medicine, aerosol physics. Michael F. McInerney, Professor; Ph.D., Kent (England), 1978: solid state, materials, electronic packaging; image processing; complexity. Sudipa Mitra-Kirtley, Professor; Ph.D., Kentucky, 1991: X-ray absorption studies with synchrotron radiation, UV-visible absorption and fluorescence studies of organic molecules, innovative teaching methods in physics classes. Michael J. Moloney, Professor; Ph.D., Maryland, 1966: small-scale acoustics experimentation, scientific uses of Excel. Azad Siahmakoun, Professor and Director of Micro-Nanoscale Devices and Systems (MiNDS) Facilities; Ph.D., Arkansas, 1987: nonlinear photorefractive materials and their applications, RF-photonics, nanophotonics, micronanofabrication and semiconductor devices. Maarij Syed, Associate Professor; Ph.D., Notre Dame, 1998: ellipsometric and magneto-optical studies of semiconductors and photorefractive materials. Jerome F. Wagner, Professor; Ph.D., Ohio, 1971: infrared detectors coupled with guided-wave optics and optical lithography. Arthur B. Western Jr., Professor, Vice President for Academic Affairs, and Dean of Faculty; Ph.D., Montana State, 1976: optical holographic interferometry, solid-state physics.

SYRACUSE UNIVERSITY

College of Engineering and Computer Science

Programs of Study

The L. C. Smith College of Engineering and Computer Science (LCS) offers programs leading to the following degrees: bioengineering, M.S. and Ph.D.; chemical engineering, M.S. and Ph.D.; civil engineering, M.S. and Ph.D.; computer and information science and engineering (CISE), Ph.D.; computer engineering, M.S.; computer science, M.S.; electrical and computer engineering (ECE), Ph.D.; electrical engineering, M.S.; engineering management, M.S.; environmental engineering, M.S.; environmental engineering science, M.S.; mechanical and aerospace engineering, M.S. and Ph.D.; and mechanical systems, M.Eng.

In general, the Master of Science degree requires a minimum of 30 credit hours except for the Master of Science degree in engineering management, which requires 36 credit hours. The thesis option requires 24 credits of course work and 6 hours accounted for by a research-related thesis. Most departments offer a nonthesis option that substitutes 6 hours of course work for the thesis and requires a comprehensive examination and/or project. Requirements for the Ph.D. vary among the academic units. Depending on the program, a minimum of 48–78 credit hours beyond the baccalaureate is required, including graduate course work, independent study, and a dissertation.

Research Facilities

The College of Engineering and Computer Science is located on the main campus quadrangle and shares space in the Center for Science and Technology and in the recently completed headquarters building for the Syracuse Center of Excellence in Environmental and Energy Systems located in downtown Syracuse. A new Syracuse Biomaterials Institute facility occupying space on the main campus quadrangle is slated to open in the fall of 2010. Located just 2 miles away on the South Campus are several research facilities including the Green Data Center which is a unique facility allowing for cutting-edge research related to improving energy efficiency for such centers; the large anechoic jet lab and wind tunnel facility for research on high-speed jet noise and wind turbine noise and efficiency; and the Institute for Sensory Research, a lab facility uniquely suited to sensory research and other advanced research. Each building has modern, fully equipped laboratories for research, as well as study laboratories, classrooms, and seminar rooms. Major research laboratory facilities include a high-performance distributed computing laboratory; distributed information systems laboratory; scalable concurrent processing laboratory; a composite materials manufacturing and testing laboratory; a structural testing lab; a polymer processing lab; geotechnical labs; a microwave laboratory; a printed-circuits facility; a VLSI design laboratory; a signal processing laboratory; a robotics laboratory; low-speed, supersonic, and hypersonic wind tunnels; indoor air quality laboratory; structure/material testing laboratories; and a biomechanics laboratory. In addition, the College maintains biochemical engineering labs; environmental engineering core labs that include microbiology, soil, analytical, acid wash, and trace metals laboratories; and supercritical extraction and absorption and filtration labs.

The College of Engineering and Computer Science maintains excellent computer facilities available for use by graduate students. The College's Computer Information Technologies Group provides each student with both a Windows LAN account and a UNIX account. Within LCS, there a number of Windows and UNIX clusters. These facilities complement dedicated computer labs maintained by individual faculty members for their research teams. Computer resources at LCS include high-performance Sun Microsystems machines that support file and application services, Web page development and hosting, and a general purpose time-sharing compute server. A rich suite of software that is unique to LCS studies is provided on the respective systems. In addition, students in the College can readily access facilities operated by the University's central Computing and Media Services (CMS) organization. Detailed information is available via the World Wide Web concerning computer facilities available at the University (http://cms.syr.edu).

Financial Aid

Financial assistance is available to highly qualified graduate students, particularly at the doctoral level. Merit-based awards are given in the form of University fellowships, research assistantships, and teaching assistantships, all of which include a stipend/salary and tuition scholarships. Each year, a limited number of additional full or partial tuition scholarships are also made available. Applicants who wish to be considered for these awards should submit all materials by December 1 for admission to the following fall semester.

Cost of Study

Tuition for graduate students at Syracuse University is charged per credit hour. For 2010–11, graduate tuition is $1162 per credit hour.

Living and Housing Costs

Academic-year living expenses are about $19,000 for single students.

Student Group

The graduate community within the College of Engineering and Computer Science is broad and diverse, with students drawn from across the country and around the world. Currently, there are 619 full- and part-time graduate students, about 12 percent of whom are pursuing Ph.D. degrees.

Location

Syracuse is the hub of a metropolitan area of more than 500,000 people. Located in the center of New York State, it lies near the lake and mountain areas of the Finger Lakes, the Thousand Islands, the Adirondacks, and Canada; and offers a wide range of cultural and recreational activities. Downtown Syracuse is only a 20-minute walk from the University, yet the campus is spacious and attractive. Winters are snowy; summers are pleasant. An international airport and interstate highways provide easy access to many major cities.

The University

Syracuse University is a major private institution founded in 1870. A member of both the Association of American Universities and the Council of Graduate Schools, Syracuse University is considered one of the nation's major institutions of higher learning. The academic breadth of the University is particularly notable, with a total of eleven academic schools and colleges enrolling 12,981 full-time undergraduate and 3,841 full-time graduate students. The University has a growing stature in the sciences and engineering, and maintains outstanding traditions in music, art, drama, communications, and public affairs.

Applying

Most students start their studies in August; however, students may also start in January or May. The verbal, quantitative, and analytical writing tests of the Graduate Record Examinations are required for admission. International applicants are required to take the TOEFL. Applications can be completed or application forms may be obtained online at the College's Web site. If that is not practical for the applicant, forms may be requested by writing to the College.

Correspondence and Information

Sue Karlik
College of Engineering and Computer Science
223 Link Hall
Syracuse University
Syracuse, New York 13244
E-mail: skarlik@syr.edu
Web site: http://www.lcs.syr.edu

Syracuse University

THE FACULTY AND AREAS OF RESEARCH

Biomedical and Chemical Engineering

Radhakrishna Sureshkumar (Chair), Rebecca Bader, Andrew L. Darling, Jeremy L. Gilbert, Julie Hasenwinkel, James Henderson, John Heydweiller, George Martin, Patrick Mather, Dacheng Ren, Ashok Sangani, Lawrence Tavlarides.

The faculty members of the department work together to bring the respective strengths of programs in bioengineering and chemical engineering to bear on research of real-world relevance.

Faculty members are engaged in advanced multidisciplinary research in bioengineering that combines engineering and life sciences in the study of biomaterials, biomechanics, and bioinstrumentation. Current research interests include the development and characterization of novel biomaterials and smart materials; degradation and corrosion in biological environments; micromechanics of biological tissues and materials; cellular biomechanics; tissue engineering; nerve regeneration; localized drug delivery; bacterial pathogenesis; bacteria-surface interactions; control of biomedical device-related infections; and development of novel medical devices.

They are also engaged in a broad spectrum of research in chemical engineering. Current research interests are in the areas of biochemical engineering, chemical equilibria and kinetics, supercritical extraction and chemical reaction of hazardous wastes, biofuel production and combustion, process optimization, chemical reaction and transport in biological systems, bioremediation, fluid mechanics in multiphase systems, catalysis and surface chemistry, chemistry-property relations in polymers and polymer-based composites, systems biology, functional genomics, and biofilm engineering.

Civil and Environmental Engineering

Riyad S. Aboutaha, Shobha K. Bhatia, Samuel P. Clemence, Charles T. Driscoll Jr., Chris E. Johnson, Swiatoslav W. Kaczmar, Raymond D. Letterman, Eric M. Lui, Belal Mousa, Dawit Negussey, Emmet M. Owens Jr., Suresh Santanam, Andria Costello Staniec, Laura J. Steinberg, David S. Wazenkewitz.

Major areas of study are environmental engineering, geotechnical engineering, and structural engineering. Current research activities are in the areas of aquatic, soil, and applied surface chemistry; biogeochemistry; water quality modeling; solid-liquid separation processes; problems related to water supply; water-treatment and waste-treatment systems; bioremediation; biotechnology; ecosystem modeling; soil dynamics; geotextiles; geofoams; geotubes; erosion control; soil mechanics and helical anchors; fiber optic sensors; critical infrastructure protection; natural disaster mitigation; damage detection and assessment; analytical and numerical modeling of construction materials; experimental evaluations; structural dynamics; earthquake engineering; structural rehabilitation; failure analysis; computer-aided analysis and design of structural systems; bridge engineering; and performance-based seismic design. (Web site: http://www.lcs.syr.edu/academic/civilenvironment_eng/index.aspx).

Electrical Engineering and Computer Science

Ercument Arvas, Howard A. Blair, Stephen J. Chapin, Biao Chen, C. Y. Roger Chen, Hao Chen, Shiu-Kai Chin, Wenliang (Kevin) Du, Mahmoud EL Sabbagh, Ehat Ercanli, Makan Fardad, James W. Fawcett, Prasanta K. Ghosh, Amrit L. Goel, Carlos R. P. Hartmann, Can Isik, Kaveh Jokar Deris, Philipp Kornreich, Andrew C.-Y. Lee, Jay Kyoon Lee, Yingbin Liang, Duane L. Marcy, Roman Markowski, Kishan Mehrotra, James H. Michels, Chilukuri K. Mohan, Ruixin Niu, Jae C. Oh, Susan Older, Daniel J. Pease, Leonard J. Popyack Jr., James S. Royer, Tapan K. Sarkar, Ernest Sibert, Q. Wang Song, Pramod K. Varshney, Hong Wang, Heng Yin.

Current faculty member research interests include artificial intelligence, communications and signal processing, complex systems, distributed information systems, electromagnetic fields and antennas, high-confidence design, logic in computer science, microelectronics, neural networks, optics and wave phenomena, photonics and optical engineering, programming languages, RF and wireless engineering, software engineering, systems assurance, theory of computation, VLSI.

Mechanical and Aerospace Engineering

Edward Bogucz, Frederick J. Carranti, Thong Q. Dang, John Dannenhoffer, Barry D. Davidson, Mark N. Glauser, Hiroshi Higuchi, Ezzat Khalifa, Alan J. Levy, Jacques Lewalle, Young B. Moon, Vadrevu R. Murthy, Harish Palanthandalam-Madapusi, Utpal Roy, Eric F. Spina, Jianshun S. Zhang, Archille Messac, Jeongmin Ahn.

Major fields of study are fluid dynamics, solid mechanics, energy systems, and manufacturing engineering. A major research focus is indoor environmental quality and building energy efficiency. Current areas of research activity include experimental aerodynamics, turbulence modeling, computational fluid dynamics, gas turbine flows, turbomachinery, flow control, mechanics of composite materials, micromechanics, fracture mechanics, biomechanics, manufacturing processes, geometric tolerancing, intelligent manufacturing systems, and helicopter rotor dynamics.

University at Buffalo
The State University of New York

UNIVERSITY AT BUFFALO, THE STATE UNIVERSITY OF NEW YORK
School of Engineering and Applied Sciences

Programs of Study

The University at Buffalo offers degrees in all major fields of engineering through the School of Engineering and Applied Sciences (SEAS). Students may pursue master's and doctoral degrees in the departments of chemical and biological engineering; civil, structural, and environmental engineering; computer science and engineering; electrical engineering; industrial and systems engineering; and mechanical and aerospace engineering. In the top 15 percent of the nation's 300 engineering schools, the School of Engineering and Applied Sciences offers a wide variety of excellent instruction, research opportunities, resources, and facilities to its students.

SEAS faculty members participate in many research activities, including extensive involvement in two major Integrative Graduate Education Research and Traineeship (IGERT) grants funded by the National Science Foundation.

Research Facilities

Research facilities are supported by the School of Engineering and Applied Sciences to give students the opportunity to conduct research specific to their area of study. The Center for Biomedical Engineering coordinates research in biomedical engineering through cooperation among engineering departments and other schools, especially medicine and pharmacy. Research at the Center of Excellence for Document Analysis and Recognition focuses on the theory and applications of pattern recognition, machine learning, and information retrieval. The Center for Excellence in Global Enterprise Management was established in 1998 to deliver leading-edge research driven by industrial need with results that have immediate practical impact. The Center for Unified Biometrics is focused on advancing the fundamental science of biometrics and providing key enabling technologies to build engineered systems. The goals of the Center for Excellence in Information Systems Assurance Research and Education are graduate education and coordinated research in computer security and information assurance by faculty members from several schools and departments at the University at Buffalo. Founded in 1987 as the New York State Center for Hazardous Waste Management, the Center for Integrated Waste Management was established by the New York State Legislation to initiate and coordinate research and technology development in the areas of toxic substances and hazardous wastes. The Center for Multisource Information Fusion serves as one focal point for the conduct of research and development in information fusion and as an incubation center for small businesses and professional and individual entrepreneurial activities. The research focus of the Energy Systems Institute is the development of mechanisms to predict failure in electronic systems.

The mission of the Great Lakes Program is to develop, evaluate, and synthesize scientific and technical knowledge on the Great Lakes Ecosystem in support of public education and policy formation. The Multidisciplinary Center for Earthquake Engineering Research's overall goal is to enhance the seismic resiliency of communities through improved engineering and management tools for critical infrastructure systems (water supply, electric power, hospitals, and transportation systems). The New York State Center for Engineering Design and Industrial Innovation carries out research to develop state-of-the-art simulation techniques and tools for the design of products, complex systems, and scientific applications. The Center for Industrial Effectiveness forges a link between the University at Buffalo's technical resources and the business community.

Financial Aid

For highly qualified applicants, a variety of research appointments are available, as are University-supported assistantships and fellowships. Tuition scholarships are also available. Summer support is available for most research appointments. Work done as a research assistant is generally applicable to the student's thesis or dissertation.

Cost of Study

Tuition for in-state residents is $8370 per academic year for full-time study. The comprehensive fee is $1406.50 and the student activity fee is $106. Out-of-state students must add an additional $4880.

Living and Housing Costs

The University at Buffalo offers students residence hall accommodations as well as apartments at several complexes surrounding the campus. Housing costs vary, depending upon location.

Student Group

More than 1,200 graduate students are enrolled in degree programs through the School of Engineering and Applied Sciences. Approximately 420 students are enrolled in doctoral programs, while the remaining students are enrolled as master's degree candidates.

Location

The city of Buffalo, New York, is located on the banks of Lake Erie, within an hour's drive of Lake Ontario and just minutes from the majestic scenery of Niagara Falls. It is within easy driving distance of Toronto and lies directly in the middle of the Northeastern trade corridor that runs from Chicago to Boston. With more than 9 million residents, it is the third-largest trade market in North America and is home to several professional sports franchises, museums, art galleries, and numerous areas for outdoor recreation throughout the year.

The University and The School

The School of Engineering and Applied Sciences is part of the University at Buffalo, the largest comprehensive public university in the state of New York, and is located on the North Campus in Amherst, New York.

Applying

The fastest and easiest way to apply is through the University's interactive graduate application Web site at http://www.gradmit. buffalo.edu/grenglinks.htm. The deadline for application materials varies by each department. The academic year begins in August. Applicants must hold a bachelor's degree in a science or engineering-related field. All international applicants must be able to document their ability to meet all educational and living expenses for their entire length of study.

Applications for graduate study and other related information may be obtained via e-mail (seasgrad@eng.buffalo.edu).

Correspondence and Information

The School of Engineering and Applied Sciences
412 Bonner Hall
University at Buffalo, the State University of New York
Buffalo, New York 14260
Phone: 716-645-0956
E-mail: seasgrad@eng.buffalo.edu
Web site: http://www.eng.buffalo.edu

University at Buffalo, the State University of New York

FACULTY HEADS AND AREAS OF RESEARCH

Chemical and Biological Engineering
Paschalis Alexandridis, Director of Graduate Study; Ph.D., MIT.

The Department of Chemical and Biological Engineering has attained international recognition for its research and teaching programs. Research projects focus primarily on fluid mechanics, polymer processing and rheology, biochemical engineering, chemical reactors and catalysis, surface science, ceramics, and materials science. These projects are supported by federal agencies such as the National Science Foundation and the Department of Energy, and by industry. (Web site: http://www.cbe.buffalo.edu)

Civil, Structural, and Environmental Engineering
Amjad Aref, Director of Graduate Study; Ph.D., Illinois.

Current research in the Department of Civil, Structural, and Environmental Engineering includes active and passive control of structures, artificial intelligence applications in transportation, aseismic base isolation, biological process analysis, bioremediation, computational mechanics, drinking water, dynamic network modeling and control, earthquake engineering, ecosystem restoration, fiber reinforced polymeric structures, freight modeling, geotechnical engineering, Great Lakes research, groundwater, infrastructure repair and management, integrated transportation and land-use modeling, intelligent transportation systems, reinforced concrete structures, seismic behavior, soil dynamics, steel structures, toxic substances fate, traffic simulation, traveler behavior modeling, volatile organics, and wastewater treatment. (Web site: http://www.csee.buffalo.edu/)

Computer Science and Engineering
Jan Chomicki, Director of Graduate Study; Ph.D., Rutgers.

The Department of Computer Science and Engineering conducts research in algorithms and theory of computing, augmentative technology for the handicapped, bioinformatics and computational biology, computational linguistics and cognitive science, computer networks and distributed systems, computer science education, computer security and information assurance, computer vision, cyberinfrastructure and computational science, databases, data fusion, data mining, embedded systems and computer architecture, high-performance and grid computing, information visualization, knowledge representation and reasoning, medical image processing and applications, multimedia databases and information retrieval, pattern recognition and machine learning, pervasive computing, programming languages and software systems, VLSI circuits and systems, and wireless and sensor networks. (Web site: http://www.cse.buffalo.edu/)

Electrical Engineering
Wayne A. Anderson, Director of Graduate Study; Ph.D., SUNY at Buffalo.

The Department of Electrical Engineering conducts research in the following areas: microelectronics, photonics, and materials (bio MEMS, computational photonics, electromagnetic compatibility, MEMS, nanotechnology, micromachined microwave systems, microfluidics, MIR and THz devices, molecular beam epitaxy, optoelectronics, photonics, photovoltaics, superconductivity, and TFT's), communications and signal processing (adaptive signal processing, coding and sequences, communication theory and systems, detection and estimation, robust communications, secure communications, space-time signal processing, and wireless communications), and energy systems (batteries, electrochemical power, power electronics, power packaging, and plasma processing). (Web site: http://www.ee.buffalo.edu)

Industrial and Systems Engineering
Victor Paquet, Director of Graduate Study; Ph.D., Massachusetts Lowell.

The Department of Industrial and Systems Engineering offers three areas of specialization for the Ph.D.: human factors (applications of engineering, psychology, computer science, and physical ergonomics to the modeling, analysis, and design of various environments and other systems), operations research (applies math and engineering principles to formulate models and solve problems in long range planning, energy and urban systems, and manufacturing), and production systems (focuses on production planning and scheduling, computer-integrated manufacturing, quality assurance, and related topics). In addition to the three areas of specialization mentioned above, there are two other programs (for a total of five) at the master's level: service systems engineering (applies industrial engineering principles to the growing service sector) and engineering management (focuses on leadership practices for a variety of engineering areas). (Web site: http://www.ise.buffalo.edu/index.shtml.)

Mechanical and Aerospace Engineering
Susan Hua, Director of Graduate Study; Ph.D., Maryland.

Faculty members and students in the Department of Mechanical and Aerospace Engineering are involved in a wide range of research activities in the fluid and thermal sciences, system dynamics, design, materials engineering, biomedical engineering, and applied mechanics. Faculty interests include computer and mathematical modeling as well as laboratory and experimental efforts in both basic and applied research. (Web site: http://www.mae.buffalo.edu/)

THE UNIVERSITY OF IOWA

College of Engineering

Programs of Study

The College of Engineering (http://www.engineering.uiowa.edu) at The University of Iowa (http://www.uiowa.edu) offers M.S. and Ph.D. programs in biomedical engineering, chemical and biochemical engineering, civil and environmental engineering, electrical and computer engineering, industrial engineering, and mechanical engineering. The College excels nationally and internationally in several specialty and interdisciplinary research areas, including computer-aided design and simulation, human factors, environmental health solutions, biotechnology, bioinformatics, medical imaging, photopolymerization, hydraulics and water/air resources, and nanotechnology. Master's candidates must maintain at least a 3.0 grade point average and may choose either a thesis or nonthesis program. Students must also successfully complete a minimum of 30 semester hours, 24 of which must be taken at The University of Iowa. Doctoral candidates must complete three years beyond the bachelor's degree, with a minimum of 72 semester hours. One academic year must be in residence. Research tools may be required as specified by the individual program. Those interested should contact the specific department for additional requirements. Graduate students often do interdisciplinary research work in a variety of programs and facilities contained in this description.

Research Facilities

The College of Engineering has twenty research locations in eastern Iowa, covering its six academic programs, four research centers reporting to the College, and interdisciplinary research efforts. IIHR–Hydroscience and Engineering (http://www.iihr.uiowa.edu) is unique for its state-of-the-art in-house capabilities in both computational simulations and laboratory modeling and for field observational research. Today IIHR pioneers high-speed computational analysis and simulation of complex flow phenomena while maintaining exceptional experimental laboratory capabilities and facilities. Observational facilities include a Mississippi River environmental research station (http://www.iihr.uiowa.edu/projects/mrers) and a wide range of remote sensing equipment. Experimental facilities include hydraulic flumes, air- and water-flow units, sediment labs, and advanced instruments for laboratory and field measurements. Engineers in IIHR's mechanical and electronic shops provide in-house expertise for construction of models and instruments. Active academic and research programs at IIHR are supported by a diverse set of computing resources and facilities. For high performance computing (HPC) IIHR is acquiring a parallel, distributed memory compute cluster comprised of over 800 2.67 GHz Intel Xeon (Nahalem) cores, 2.4 TB memory, 60 TB of scratch space running Linux, MPI, OpenMP, and the Intel and GNU compiler and tool suites. The computing nodes feature an Infiniband Quad Data Rate (fully unblocked at DDR) interconnect for high-speed, low-latency message passing. Two head nodes provide access to the cluster for compiling and launching jobs. This system will replace the current Sun cluster featuring 128 processors running at 3.06 GHz, 256 GB memory, and 8 TB of temporary storage for computation, and a Myranet interconnect.

Other engineering research-related facilities include the Engineering Research Facility, Iowa Advanced Technology Laboratories, Iowa Injury Prevention Research Center (http://www.public-health.uiowa.edu/IPRC), University of Iowa Hospitals and Clinics (http://www.uihealthcare.com/uihospitalsandclinics/index.html), National Advanced Driving Simulator (http://www.nads-sc.uiowa.edu), Center for Biocatalysis and Bioprocessing (http://www.uiowa.edu/~biocat), and Chemistry Building, which support laboratories devoted to such areas as biomechanics, biotechnology, molecular and computational biology, bioinformatics, environmental contamination, and remote sensing. The Center for Computer-Aided Design (http://www.ccad.uiowa.edu) is housed in the Engineering Research Facility and has 7,500 square feet of office space for staff researchers, student assistants, and program administration. The eight on-site laboratories house research facilities for two state-of-the-art motion capture research laboratories, one of which includes a 6-DOF shaker table motion platform, a fully immersive virtual reality environment, automobile driving simulation, robotic systems, materials testing fixtures, and equipment for individual student research in various engineering disciplines. An off-site facility is maintained at the Iowa City Regional Airport that includes three flight simulation capabilities (a high-performance, functional Boeing 737-800 mockup for high-workload simulation and analysis as well as functional Boeing 777 and F-15 mock-ups). CCAD's Iowa City airport facility also houses two dedicated research aircraft, including a single-engine Beechcraft A-36 Bonanza aircraft, outfitted to create the CCAD Computerized Airborne Research Platform (CARP) in support of airborne human factors research for advanced flight deck technology, and a single-engine tandem seat I-29 jet trainer aircraft, to provide flight testing for additional avionics systems research programs. The center maintains in-house electrical and machine shops. The center's computer infrastructure incorporates high-performance workstations, servers, and PC network in support of intensive computation, geometric modeling and analysis, software development, and visualization and simulation. The National Advanced Driving Simulator (NADS) is located at the University of Iowa Research Park (http://enterprise.uiowa.edu/researchpark). The NADS conducts groundbreaking research and development in the field of driving simulation. Utilizing one of the world's most advanced driving simulator capabilities, researchers at the University have defined the state-of-the-art in driving simulation, vehicle performance, and cognitive systems engineering. The NADS houses the NADS-1 driving simulator as well as several lower-fidelity driving simulators primarily used to support development, testing, and refinement of experimental procedures at lower cost to the client. These include the NADS-2, a static-base simulator with a limited field of view, and several portable PC-based mini-simulators. All simulation platforms at the center share a common software architecture with the NADS-1, ensuring compatibility of scenarios and data across all NADS simulators.

Engineering Computer Systems Support (http://css.engineering.uiowa.edu) provides the curricular and research computing needs of the College through state-of-the-art hardware, the same commercial software used by engineers in the industry, and a dedicated professional support staff. All engineering students receive computer accounts and maintain those accounts throughout their college careers. Full Internet and Web access complement local educational resources, which include enhanced classroom instruction, online classes, engineering design and simulation packages, programming languages, and productivity software. There are twenty-eight Linux and approximately 300 Windows workstations, supported by more than $10 million worth of professional software dedicated for student use 24 hours a day. The H. William Lichtenberger Engineering Library provides Internet access to indexes and abstracts, more than 125,000 volumes, ANSI standards, and electronic access to thousands of engineering and science journals.

Financial Aid

Financial aid is available to graduate students in the form of research and teaching assistantships as well as fellowships from federal agencies and industry. Support includes a competitive stipend reduction in tuition and partial payment of tuition. Specific information is available from individual departments.

Cost of Study

For 2010–11, tuition per semester was $3625 for Iowa residents and $10,835 for nonresidents. There is a technology fee of $313.50 per semester, which allows students the use of Computer Systems Support. In addition, there are, per semester, a mandatory student health fee of $113, a student activities fee of $32.50, a student services fee of $34.50, a student union fee of $56, a building fee of $59.50, an arts and cultural events fee of $12, recreation fee of $112.50, and a professional enhancement fee of $30.

Living and Housing Costs

Housing is available in apartments or private homes within walking distance of the campus.

Student Group

Total enrollment at the University for fall 2009 was 30,328 students. Students come from all fifty states, three U.S. possessions, and 104 other countries. Engineering enrollment for fall 2009 was 1,412 undergraduate students and 354 graduate students.

Student Outcomes

Nearly half of the graduates accept positions in Iowa and Illinois, though companies and academic institutions from across the country present offers. Recent graduates have taken positions with companies such as 3M, Accenture, Cargill, Caterpillar, Deere & Company, General Mills, Hewlett-Packard, HNI, Monsanto, Motorola, Pella, and Rockwell Collins.

Location

The University is located in Iowa City, known as the "Athens of the Midwest" because of the many cultural, intellectual, and diverse opportunities available. The Iowa City metropolitan area is a community of 139,600 people, approximately 25 miles from Cedar Rapids, Iowa's second-largest city, with nearly 246,400 people.

The University

The University of Iowa, established in 1847, comprises eleven colleges. The University was the first state university to admit women on an equal basis with men. The University founded the first law school west of the Mississippi River, established one of the first university-based medical centers in the Midwest, and was the first state university in the nation to establish an interfaith school of religion. It was an innovator in accepting creative work—fine art, musical compositions, poetry, drama, and fiction—for academic credit. The University established Iowa City as a national college-prospect testing center. It was a leader in the development of actuarial science as an essential tool of business administration. As a pioneering participant in space exploration, it has become a center for education and research in astrophysical science.

Applying

The application fee is $60 ($100 for international students). Admission requirements differ in each department; students should contact the department in which they are interested for additional requirements.

Correspondence and Information

Admissions
107 Calvin Hall
The University of Iowa
Iowa City, Iowa 52242
Web site: http://www.grad.uiowa.edu/ (Graduate College)
http://www.engineering.uiowa.edu/research (College of Engineering)
http://www.engineering.uiowa.edu/future-students.html (College of Engineering)

The University of Iowa

DEPARTMENTS, CHAIRS, AND AREAS OF FACULTY RESEARCH

STUDIES BY ENGINEERING DISCIPLINE

Biomedical Engineering (http://www.bme.engineering.uiowa.edu). Joseph M. Reinhardt, Departmental Executive Officer. Biomechanics of the spine, low back pain and scoliosis, upper-extremity biomechanics, articular joint contact mechanics, total joint replacement, computational simulation of artificial heart valve dynamics, hemodynamics of arterial disease, mechanical properties of diseased arteries, biomechanics and rupture predication of abdominal aorta aneurysms, solution-perfused tubes for preventing blood-materials interaction, control and coordination of the cardiovascular and respiratory systems, controlled drug delivery, medical image acquisition, processing and quantitative analysis, wire coil–reinforced bone cement, models of cellular processes based on nonequilibrium thermodynamics, tissue engineered vascular grafts, bioinformatics and computational biology, drug/target discovery, gene therapy, development of genomic resources.

Chemical and Biochemical Engineering (http://www.cbe.engineering.uiowa.edu). David W. Murhammer, Departmental Executive Officer. Air pollution engineering, atmospheric aerosol particles, atmospheric chemistry, biocatalysis, biochemical engineering, biofilms, biofuels, biomaterials, biotechnological applications of extremophiles, controlled release, drug delivery, engineering education, fermentation, high-speed computing, insect and mammalian cell culture, medical aerosols, microlithography, nanotechnology, oxidative stress in cell culture, photopolymerization, polymer reaction engineering, polymer science, polymer/liquid crystal composites, process scale protein purification, protein crystallography, reversible emulsifiers, spectroscopy, supercritical fluids, surface science, vaccines, virus infection, chemicals from biomass, green chemistry, and sustainable energy.

Civil and Environmental Engineering (http://www.cee.engineering.uiowa.edu). Keri C. Hornbuckle, Departmental Executive Officer. Environmental remediation, sustainability, water quality, air pollution, drinking water quality, bioremediation, biogeochemistry, computational solid mechanics, constitutive modeling, design of hydraulics structures, design simulation, hydropower, optimal control of nonlinear systems, optimal design of nonlinear structures, diverse aspects of water resources engineering, rainfall and flood forecasting, thermal pollution/power plant operation, transportation-infrastructure modeling, highway pavements, water-quality modeling, winter highway maintenance.

Electrical and Computer Engineering (http://www.ece.engineering.uiowa.edu). Milan Sonka, Departmental Executive Officer. Sustainable energy, quantitative medical image processing, communication systems and computer networks, sensors and sensor networks, wireless communication, controls, signal processing, parallel and distributed computing systems, large-scale intelligent systems, bioinformatics, photonics, plasma waves, software engineering, design and testing of very-large-scale integrated circuits, nanotechnology, materials, and devices.

Industrial Engineering (http://www.mie.engineering.uiowa.edu/IEProgram/IEMain.php). Andrew Kusiak, Departmental Executive Officer. Computational intelligence, informatics, engineering economics, engineering management, financial engineering, human factors and ergonomics, human-computer interfaces, flight simulation, driver behavior, manufacturing processes control and operations, operations research and applied statistics, telerobotics, quality control and reliability, health-care systems, wind energy, and optimization of energy systems.

Mechanical Engineering (http://www.mie.engineering.uiowa.edu/MEProgram/MEMain.php). Andrew Kusiak, Departmental Executive Officer. Biomechanics and biofluids, biology-based design, biorenewable and alternative fuels, bioengineering, combustion, chemically reactive flows, computer-aided analysis and design, dynamics, fatigue and fracture mechanics, fluid mechanics and ship hydrodynamics, fluid mechanics, heat transfer, casting and solidification, materials processing and behavior, reliability-based design, robotics, structural mechanics, composite materials, system simulation, thermal systems, vehicle dynamics and simulation, virtual prototyping, multiscale modeling and simulation, computational mechanics, nanotechnology, and wind energy.

COLLEGE RESEARCH CENTERS, INSTITUTES, AND LABORATORIES

Center for Bioinformatics and Computational Biology (http://genome.uiowa.edu). Thomas L. Casavant, Director. A multidisciplinary research center dedicated to applying high-performance networking and computing to basic life science and applied biomedical research.

Center for Computer-Aided Design (http://www.ccad.uiowa.edu). Karim Abdel-Malek, Director. Virtual Soldier Research (musculoskeletal model, whole body vibration, validation, motion capture, intuitive interface, immersive virtual reality, physiology, standard ergonomic assessments, zone differentiation, posture and motion prediction, hand model, spine modeling, gait: walking and running, predictive dynamics, dynamic strength and fatigue, modeling of clothing, human performance, armor and soldier performance); Cognitive Systems Laboratory (ergonomics, human interaction with advanced technology and automation, cognitive processing burden assessment/sensory and data input cognitive impact, human-machine interaction optimization for operational control and safety, driving simulation supporting automotive operation and warning-systems effectiveness, computational modeling of human performance); Operator Performance Laboratory (optimal aircraft instrumentation configuration, rotorcraft, flight simulation supporting aircraft operation task analysis, warning-system effectiveness, roadway markings and illumination analysis, driver performance measurement); Reliability and Sensor Prognostic Systems (mesh-free methods for structural analysis and design-sensitivity analysis, composite materials, probabilistic mechanics and reliability, reliability-based design optimization, topology optimization, multidisciplinary design optimization, sensor technologies, sensor-based process monitoring optimization); National Advanced Driving Simulator (highway safety and transportation efficiency, equipment product development effectiveness enhancement via virtual prototyping, vehicle dynamics and simulation, simulator technology and virtual reality environment and human factors); Musculoskeletal Imaging Modeling and Experimentation Program (computational modeling of anatomic structures, with emphasis on finite modeling); Biomechanics of Soft Tissue (soft tissue mechanics, biomechanics of the heart, cardiovascular system, aneurysm formation, CFD, nonlinear FEA).

IIHR–Hydroscience and Engineering (http://www.iihr.uiowa.edu). Larry J. Weber, Director. A leading institute in fluids-related fundamental and applied research. Cutting-edge research activities incorporate computational fluid dynamics with laboratory modeling and field observational studies. Research includes: fluid dynamics (ship hydrodynamics, turbulent flows, biological fluid flow); environmental hydraulics (structures, river and dam hydraulics, fish passage at dams, sediment management, heat dispersal in water bodies and power production, water-quality monitoring, air-water exchange processes); water and air resources (atmospheric boundary layer, air pollution, hydrogeology, hydrology, hydrometeorology, remote sensing).

Iowa Institute for Biomedical Imaging (http://www.biomed-imaging.uiowa.edu). Milan Sonka, Codirector. Knowledge-based analysis of biomedical images from a variety of imaging modalities (e.g., CT, MR, and ultrasound). Current focus areas include development of computer-aided and automated techniques for quantitative analysis of human, animal, and cellular image data.

INTERDISCIPLINARY RESEARCH CENTERS AND INSTITUTES

Medicine and Bioengineering

Center for Biocatalysis and Bioprocessing (http://www.uiowa.edu/~biocat). Mani Subramanian, Director. Biocatalyst fundamental properties, bioremediation, bioprocessing, new biocatalyst discovery, novel biocatalyst applications, biosensing technology, reactive agent development.

Center for International Rural and Environmental Health (http://www.public-health.uiowa.edu/cireh). Tom Cook, Director. Rural and environmental health, with special emphasis on adverse health effects that threaten agricultural and other rural populations; promotes greater understanding and awareness of the causes, consequences, and prevention of communicable, chronic, environmental, and occupational diseases in all regions of the globe, focusing on nations with substantial agrarian economies.

Iowa Injury Prevention Research Center (http://www.public-health.uiowa.edu/IPRC). Corinne Peek-Asa, Director. Prevention, acute care, rehabilitation, surveillance, and biomechanics, including examining causes of delay in Iowa's trauma system, identifying risk factors for injuries to farmers and their families, domestic violence in rural populations, and studying the driving abilities of individuals with sleep disorders and epilepsy.

Orthopaedic Biomechanics Laboratory (http://poppy.obrl.uiowa.edu). Thomas D. Brown, Director. Application of advanced innovative computational formulations and novel experimental approaches to clinically-oriented problems across the diverse spectrum of musculoskeletal biomechanical research; total joint replacement (hip, spine, knee, ankle), posttraumatic arthritis, osteonecrosis of the hip, high-energy limb trauma, carpal tunnel syndrome, and articular contact stresses as they relate to joint degeneration.

Environmental and Hydroscience

NSF Center for Environmentally Beneficial Catalysis (http://www.erc-assoc.org/factsheets/09/09-Fact%20Sheet%202005.htm). Mani Subramanian, Director. A multidisciplinary, multi-university research center. Catalyst design, synthesis, and characterization; biocatalyst preparation and characterization; synthesis of catalyst supports with controlled pore structure; benign media, including carbon dioxide–based solvents and ionic liquids; probing reaction mechanisms with advanced analytical tools; advanced molecular modeling of chemical, physical, and thermodynamic properties involving reactions and media; multiphase reactor design and analysis; economic and environmental impact analysis; computational fluid dynamics.

Center for Global and Regional Environmental Research (http://www.cgrer.uiowa.edu). Gregory R. Carmichael and Jerald L. Schnoor, Co-directors. Multiple aspects of global environmental change, including the regional effects on natural ecosystems, environments, and resources and on human health, culture, and social systems.

Center for Health Effects of Environmental Contamination (http://www.cheec.uiowa.edu). Gene F. Parkin, Director. Conducts and supports research on the identification and measurement of environmental toxins, particularly water contaminants, and possible associations between exposure to environmental contaminants and adverse health effects. Provides environmental database design and development and systems support for environmental health research.

Environmental Health Sciences Research Center (http://www.ehsrc.uiowa.edu). Peter S. Thorne, Director. Agricultural and rural environmental exposures and health effects, agricultural chemical exposures and health effects.

Science and Technology

Iowa Alliance for Wind Innovation and Novel Development (http://www.iawind.org). P. Barry Butler, Principal Investigator. The Iowa Alliance for Wind Innovation and Novel Development (IAWIND) is a partnership with state and local governments, community colleges, Regents Universities, independent Iowa colleges, the private sector, and the federal government. It is designed to serve as a catalyst for the growth of wind energy and to support and to facilitate the research and training needs of wind energy companies.

Nanoscience and Nanotechnology Institute (http://research.uiowa.edu/nniui). Vicki Grassian, Director. Environment and health (air quality, natural environment, workplace environment, human and animal toxicity, environmental health, drug delivery, disease detection, imaging, bioanalytical assays, environmental remediation and decontamination, green chemistry, fuel cells, energy, sustainability, sensors); nanomaterials (quantum theory, understanding condensed-phase matter at the nanoscale, synthesis and characterization of nanomaterials, defense-related applications).

Optical Science and Technology Center (http://www.ostc.uiowa.edu). Mark Arnold, Director. Laser spectroscopy and photochemistry, photonics and optoelectronics, ultrafast laser development, condensed-matter physics, materials growth techniques, device physics/engineering, surface chemistry, chemical sensors, environmental chemistry, polymer science, plasma physics, nonlinear optics.

NSF IUCRC Photopolymerization Center (http://css.engineering.uiowa.edu/~cfap). Alec Scranton, Director. Kinetics and mechanisms of photopolymerizations and their impact on the structure and properties of photopolymerized materials.

Public Policy Center (http://ppc.uiowa.edu). Peter C. Damiano, Director. Transportation, environmental quality, health care, economic growth and development.

Water Sustainability Initiative (http://watersustainability.uiowa.edu). Jerald Schnoor, Chair, Steering Committee. The University of Iowa has expanded its existing strength in interdisciplinary research on water including its availability, quality, reuse, health impact, and its relationship to a changing climate. Economics, policy, and law, as well as the natural sciences and engineering, are all engaged to solve the problems of water. The faculty alliance on water sustainability encompasses the Colleges of Liberal Arts and Sciences, Public Health, Law, Engineering, the Graduate College, and the Public Policy Center. Among the various resources already developed to advance the initiative are the new Iowa Flood Center and the University of Iowa Office of Sustainability.

UNIVERSITY OF MICHIGAN–DEARBORN

College of Engineering and Computer Science

Programs of Study

The postbaccalaureate programs in engineering at the University of Michigan–Dearborn (U of M–Dearborn) are geared to the demands of the student and the needs of industry and are designed to further the theoretical and technical background of the engineer. The College offers programs leading to the Master of Science in Automotive Engineering, Master of Science in Computer Engineering, Master of Science in Computer and Information Science, Master of Science in Electrical Engineering, Master of Science in Engineering Management, Master of Science in Industrial and Systems Engineering, Master of Science in Manufacturing Systems Engineering, Master of Science in Mechanical Engineering, and joint M.S./M.B.A. degrees through the School of Management.

U of M–Dearborn College of Engineering and Computer Science (CECS) offer two Ph.D. programs: Information Systems Engineering and Automotive Systems Engineering. These are 50-credit-hour programs that feature full-time or part-time enrollment, interdisciplinary curriculum, a wide range of specialization courses and research topics, and convenient evening classes.

Working students are accommodated by course offerings late in the afternoon and evening in automotive engineering, computer engineering, computer and information science, electrical and computer engineering, engineering management, industrial and systems engineering, manufacturing systems engineering, and mechanical engineering.

All programs in graduate studies in engineering at the University of Michigan–Dearborn, except the M.B.A. part of the I.S.E./M.B.A. degrees, are offered through the Horace H. Rackham School of Graduate Studies in Ann Arbor.

A master's degree is awarded after completion of a minimum of 30 credit hours, although each program has individual requirements that must be met prior to graduation.

Research Facilities

The College of Engineering and Computer Science built the Engineering Complex in 1997, adding 53,000 square feet of laboratory, classroom, office, and study space. The complex houses a rapid prototype laboratory, a human factors laboratory, a design studio, a hypermedia laboratory, and CAD, PC, Macintosh, networking, and Sun computer laboratories. The Manufacturing Systems Engineering Laboratory building is equipped with laboratories that include metrology, machine dynamics and diagnostics, precision machining, and computer-integrated manufacturing. This component of manufacturing research is supplemented by an extensive array of computers dedicated to the engineering disciplines. In addition, the College has several other experimental laboratories available for research: machine vision and intelligence, design and fatigue, acoustics and vibrations, combustion engines and fuels, vehicle electronics, plastics and composites, circuits, electronic control systems, energy conversion, manufacturing simulation, 3-D imaging, applied thermodynamics, fluid mechanics, heat transfer, computer automation, robotics, data communications, and digital systems. Combined, the College's facilities provide effective and comprehensive areas for teaching, student projects, research, and faculty projects that affect curriculum and build strong partnerships with industry, government, and the community.

The College also features several centers and institutes—the Institute for Advanced Vehicle Systems, the Center for Lightweight Automotive Materials and Processing, the Henry W. Patton Center for Engineering Education & Practice, and the Vetronics Institute—to further facilitate advanced research objectives.

Financial Aid

Scholarships, fellowships, and other grants-in-aid, as well as financial assistance through departmental employment, are often available to qualified students in engineering. In keeping with University practice and policy, such assistance is available without regard to race, color, creed, sex, or national origin.

The number of awards available each year varies, as does the amount of the stipend. Recipients are appointed by, or upon the nomination of, the departments in which the applicants are enrolled. Application forms for students who will be registered at the University of Michigan–Dearborn can be obtained from the College of Engineering. When submitted to the College of Engineering, this application form, titled "Application for Graduate School Fellowship, Teaching, or Research Assistantship," serves as the vehicle for obtaining consideration for all awards administered by the College.

Cost of Study

The tuition for full-time graduate students (8 credit hours) working toward a master's degree is about $5500 for Michigan residents and about $7553 for out-of-state residents. In addition, students are assessed a $77.25 fee per credit hour and a per-semester technology assessment of $157.95.

Living and Housing Costs

The local living costs are somewhat dependent upon the availability of housing. An estimation of living costs beyond the cost of study is $1400 per month.

Student Group

Enrollment at the University of Michigan–Dearborn is 8,700 students. Of this figure, 2,500 students are enrolled in the College of Engineering and Computer Science: 1,500 are undergraduates and 1,000 are graduate students.

Location

The University of Michigan–Dearborn is located in the heart of Michigan's largest urban area, just 10 miles from downtown Detroit and a wide variety of cultural, athletic, and recreational opportunities. Many outdoor recreation facilities, including rivers, lakes, beaches, and ski areas are within a short driving distance.

The University

The University of Michigan–Dearborn is one of three campuses governed by the University of Michigan Board of Regents. As a regional campus of the University of Michigan system, it shares in the tradition of excellence in teaching, research, and service. The campus, which is located on 202 acres of the former estate of the late Henry Ford, is primarily a commuter campus. It was founded in 1959 as a senior-level institution offering only junior, senior, and graduate courses. Since 1971, the Dearborn campus has offered full four-year degree programs and expanded its graduate offerings. As part of the University of Michigan System, U of M–Dearborn enjoys the resources of a large multiuniversity and the advantages of moderate size.

Applying

Applications for graduate admission, accompanied by a nonrefundable fee of $60 for domestic students ($75 for international students), transcripts, and letters of recommendation, should reach the department by August 1 for the fall term, December 1 for the winter term, or April 1 for the spring term. Application materials can be downloaded via the College's Web site at http://www.engin.umd.umich.edu.

Correspondence and Information

For information about the various engineering programs at the University, students should contact Graduate Student Services.

College of Engineering and Computer Science
2201 Engineering Complex
University of Michigan–Dearborn
4901 Evergreen Road
Dearborn, Michigan 48128-1491

Phone: 313-593-0897
Fax: 313-593-9967
E-mail: gradprog@engin.umd.umich.edu
Web site: http://www.engin.umd.umich.edu/

University of Michigan–Dearborn

THE FACULTY AND THEIR RESEARCH

Kuimi Akingbehin, Professor of Computer and Information Science; Ph.D., Wayne State, 1985. Intelligent systems, real-time computing.

Alan Argento, Professor of Mechanical Engineering; Ph.D., Michigan, 1989. Structural dynamics, vibration.

Adnan Aswad, Professor of Industrial and manufacturing Systems Engineering; Ph.D., Michigan, 1972. Quality engineering and product and process design and development.

Selim Awad, Professor of Electrical and Computer Engineering; Ph.D., Polytechnic Institute of Grenoble (France), 1983. DSP, education technology and distance learning.

Vivek Bhise, Professor of Industrial and Manufacturing Systems Engineering; Ph.D., Ohio State, 1971. Human factors engineering, vehicle ergonomics, total quality management.

Chia-hao Chang, Professor of Industrial and Manufacturing Systems Engineering; Ph.D., Oregon State, 1978. Information systems.

Yubao Chen, Professor of Industrial and Manufacturing Systems Engineering; Ph.D., Wisconsin–Madison, 1986. Intelligent manufacturing.

John Cherng, Professor of Mechanical Engineering; Ph.D., Tennessee, 1978. Vibrations, acoustics, NVH.

Chi L. Chow, Professor of Mechanical Engineering; Ph.D., London, 1965. Fatigue, fracture and damage mechanics.

Bruce Elenbogen, Associate Professor of Computer and Information Science; Ph.D., Northwestern, 1981. Theory of computation.

William Grosky, Professor and Chairperson, Computer and Information Science; Ph.D., Yale, 1971. Multimedia databases.

Jinhua Guo, Assistant Professor of Computer and Information Science; Ph.D., Georgia, 2002. Networking, wireless networks, vehicular networks, security and privacy.

Afzal Hossain, Assistant Professor of Electrical and Computer Engineering; Ph.D., Syracuse, 2002. High performance computer architecture, semiconductor chip design, and mobile systems architecture.

Hugh E. Huntley, Associate Professor of Mechanical Engineering; Ph.D., Michigan, 1992. Engineering materials and manufacturing design.

Dohoy Jung, Assistant Professor of Mechanical Engineering; Ph.D., Michigan–Dearborn, 2001. Advanced energy conversion in automotive systems including internal combustion engine processes, hybrid powertrain, PEM fuel cell, vehicle thermal management, system integration.

Swatantra K. Kachhal, Professor; Industrial and Manufacturing Systems Engineering; Ph.D., Minnesota, 1974. Health-care system.

Roberto R. Kampfner, Associate Professor of Computer and Information Science; Ph.D., Michigan, 1981. Information systems, intelligent systems.

HongTae Kang, Assistant Professor of Mechanical Engineering; Ph.D., Alabama, 1999. Fatigue, automotive structural durability, road load prediction.

Ali El Kateeb, Associate Professor of Electrical and Computer Engineering; Ph.D., Concordia (Montreal), 1992. Reconfigurable computing.

Sang-Hwan Kim, Assistant Professor of Industrial and Manufacturing Systems Engineering; Ph.D , North Carolina State, 2009. Human factors, cognitive engineering, aviation psychology, human-computer interaction, user interface/interation/experience design.

Taehyung Kim, Assistant Professor of Electrical and Computer Engineering; Ph.D., Texas A&M, 2003. Power electronics, motor drives and hybrid electric vehicles.

James W. Knight, Associate Professor of Industrial and Manufacturing Systems Engineering; Ph.D., Ohio State, 1977. Ergonomics, statistical design of experiments.

Ghassan Kridli, Associate Professor of Industrial and Manufacturing Systems Engineering; Ph.D., Missouri–Columbia, 1997. Intelligent manufacturing and metal forming.

Shridhar Lakshmanan, Associate Professor of Electrical and Computer Engineering; Ph.D., Massachusetts Amherst, 1991. Signal and image processing.

Cheol Lee, Assistant Professor of Industrial and Manufacturing Systems Engineering; Ph.D., Purdue, 2000. Manufacturing processes, control, neural networks.

Ben Q. Li, Professor and Chairperson, Mechanical Engineering; Ph.D., Berkeley, 1989. Computational study of multiscale and multiphysical phenomena in thermal fluids, materials processing and manufacturing.

Xiangyang (Sean) Li, Assistant Professor of Industrial and Manufacturing Systems Engineering; Ph.D., Arizona State, 2001. Information systems and quality, data mining, human-computer interaction, simulation.

Robert E. Little, Professor of Mechanical Engineering; Ph.D., Michigan, 1963. Reliability, modes of failure, fatigue, mechanical design.

Yung-wen Liu, Assistant Professor of Industrial and Manufacturing Systems Engineering; Ph.D., Washington (Seattle), 2006. Reliability and quality engineering, stochastic process modeling, applied statistics, health-care modeling.

Di Ma, Assistant Professor of Computer and Information Science; Ph.D., California, Irvine, 2009. Digital forensics, applied cryptography, multimedia security, date and storage security, computer and network security and privacy.

Hafiz Malik, Assistant Professor of Electrical and Computer Engineering; Ph.D., Illinois, 2006. Digital forensics, information security, information fusion, multimedia processing, diometric security, steganalysis and information hiding.

P. K. Mallick, Professor of Mechanical Engineering and Director of Interdisciplinary Programs; Ph.D., IIT, 1973. Materials and manufacturing processes, solid mechanics, failure analysis/design, composites.

Bruce Maxim, Associate Professor of Computer and Information Science; Ph.D., Michigan, 1982. Software engineering.

Brahim Medjahed, Assistant Professor of Computer and Information Science; Ph.D., Virginia Tech, 2004. Databases, semantic Web, Internet computing, workflows.

Carole Mei, Associate Professor of Mechanical Engineering; Ph.D., Auckland (New Zealand), 1999. Vibration analysis and vibration control.

Chris Mi, Assistant Professor of Electrical and Computer Engineering; Ph.D., Toronto, 2000. Power electronics.

John Miller, Associate Professor of Electrical and Computer Engineering; Ph.D., Toledo, 1983. Machine vision systems and image processing.

Pravansu Mohanty, Associate Professor of Mechanical Engineering; Ph.D., McGill, 1994. Engineering materials and manufacturing design.

Yi Lu Murphey, Professor of Electrical and Computer Engineering; Ph.D., Michigan, 1989. Character segmentation and recognition.

Natarajian Narasimhamurthi, Associate Professor of Electrical and Computer Engineering; Ph.D., Berkeley, 1979. Hybrid vehicles and electric vehicles.

Elsayed A. Orady, Professor of Industrial and Manufacturing Systems Engineering; Ph.D., McMaster, 1982. Intelligent manufacturing.

Eric Ratts, Associate Professor of Mechanical Engineering; Ph.D., MIT, 1993. Thermodynamics, heat transfer and cryogenics.

Paul C. Richardson, Associate Professor of Electrical and Computer Engineering; Ph.D., Oakland, 1999. Wireless communications, target tracking.

German Reyes-Villanueva, Assistant Professor of Mechanical Engineering; Ph.D., Liverpool (England), 2002. Lightweight fiber-reinforced composite materials and metal alloys.

Paul C. Richardson, Associate Professor of Electrical and Computer Engineering; Ph.D., Oakland, 1999. Real-time networks.

David Rodick, Assistant Professor of Industrial and Manufacturing Systems Engineering; Ph.D., Louisville. Physical/occupational ergonomics, occupational health, and safety and applied cognition.

Naeem Seliya, Assistant Professor of Computer and Information Science; Ph.D., Florida Atlantic, 2005. Software engineering, data mining, machine learning, application and data security, computational intelligence.

Subrata Sengupta, Professor of Mechanical Engineering and Dean of the College of Engineering and Computer Science; Ph.D., Case Western Reserve, 1974. Waste heat management and utilization.

Tariq Shamim, Associate Professor of Mechanical Engineering; Ph.D., Michigan, 1997. Combustion, emissions and heat transfer.

Adnan K. Shaout, Professor of Electrical and Computer Engineering; Ph.D., Syracuse, 1987. Fuzzy logic and industrial application.

Jie Shen, Assistant Professor of Computer and Information Science; Ph.D., Saskatchewan, 2000. Computational geometry and graphics.

Taehyun Shim, Assistant Professor of Mechanical Engineering; Ph.D., California, Davis, 2000. Vehicle dynamics.

Malayappan Shridhar, Professor and Chairperson, Electrical and Computer Engineering; Ph.D., Aston (England), 1969. Speech and image processing, pattern recognition.

Yuqing Song, Assistant Professor of Computer and Information Science; Ph.D., Buffalo, SUNY, 2002. Multimedia information retrieval.

Louis Y. Tsui, Associate Professor of Computer and Information Science; Ph.D., Michigan, 1984. Operating systems.

Onur Ulgen, Professor of Industrial and Manufacturing Systems Engineering; Ph.D., Texas Tech, 1979. Discrete and continuous simulation, modeling of production systems, material handling systems, ARIMA and other time-series techniques.

Keshav S. Varde, Professor of Mechanical Engineering and Associate Dean of the College of Engineering and Computer Science; Ph.D., Rochester, 1971. Thermal/fluid sciences, thermodynamics, combustion, alternative energy sources/fuels.

Shengquan Wang, Assistant Professor of Computer and Information Science; Ph.D., Texas A & M, 2006. Networking and distributed systems.

Paul Watta, Associate Professor of Electrical and Computer Engineering; Ph.D., Wayne State, 1994. Artificial neural networks.

Weidong Xiang, Assistant Professor of Electrical and Computer Engineering; Ph.D., Tsinghua (China), 1999. Software radio, smart antenna, OFDM, MIMO, Wireless LAN.

Zhiwei Xu, Assistant Professor of Computer and Information Science; Ph.D., Florida Atlantic, 2001. Software metrices, quality modeling, software V&V, data mining, pattern recognition, artificial intelligence, cost modeling and optimization.

David Yoon, Associate Professor of Computer and Information Science; Ph.D., Wayne State, 1989. Computer graphics.

Armen Zakarian, Associate Professor and Chairperson of Industrial and Manufacturing Systems Engineering; Ph.D., Iowa, 1997. Modeling and analysis of manufacturing systems, intelligent simulation environments.

Yi Zhang, Professor of Mechanical Engineering; Ph.D., Illinois, 1989. Design and manufacturing of gearing systems.

Dongming Zhao, Associate Professor of Electrical and Computer Engineering; Ph.D., Rutgers, 1990. Image processing and machine vision.

Qiang Zhu, Assistant Professor of Computer and Information Science; Ph.D., Waterloo, 1995. Database query optimization.

Oleg Zikanov, Associate Professor of Mechanical Engineering; Ph.D., Moscow State (Russia), 1993. Fluid mechanics.

UNIVERSITY OF PENNSYLVANIA

School of Engineering and Applied Science

Programs of Study

Research and education form the creative graduate mission of Penn Engineering. The excitement and discovery of research is open to all students and is the keystone of the School's world-renowned Ph.D. programs. These programs are augmented by a diverse array of master's degree offerings.

Penn Engineering's collaborative research and learning environment truly distinguishes the School from its peers. Students work with and learn from faculty mentors within the core disciplinary programs as well as through scholarly interactions involving the School of Medicine, the School of Arts and Sciences, and the Wharton School of Business, to note a few. This environment is further enriched by Penn's many institutes, centers, and laboratories. For more than 100 years, Penn Engineering has been at the forefront of innovation, just like the University's founder: America's first scientist and engineer—Benjamin Franklin.

The six Doctor of Philosophy (Ph.D.) programs are research-oriented degree programs for students of superior caliber who will make original contributions to theory and practice in their fields of interest. The programs prepare them for a research career in academe, government, or industry. Curricula are purposely designed to develop the intellectual skills essential for the rapidly changing character of research.

Penn Engineering's fifteen master's programs serve a wide range of highly qualified students such as working professionals seeking greater expertise to advance their careers and students expanding on their undergraduate training for professional engineering practice, preparing for doctoral studies, or pursuing an entirely new field of interest. The School's constantly evolving curricula, grounded in up-to-the-minute research findings and industrial priorities, and focused on practical applications of knowledge, are designed to be responsive to career and professional interests, as well as to the needs of today's high-tech society and economy.

Research Facilities

Shared research laboratories and facilities are an integral part of research and education at Penn Engineering. From nanotechnology to fluid mechanics to robotics to entrepreneurship, dedicated space exists for all forms of research in which students and faculty engage. The School's collection of labs and facilities include the Mechanical Engineering and Applied Mechanics Design and Prototyping Laboratories, SIG Center for Computer Graphics, Nano Probe Innovation Facility, Penn Regional Nanotechnology Facility, the Weiss Tech House, and Wolf Nanofabrication Facility.

Interdisciplinary research centers and institutes span all departments in Penn Engineering and foster collaborations across different schools throughout the university. The physical connectivity of engineering buildings and the proximity to each of the other schools enables exciting collaborations with faculty, students, and postdoctoral scholars across Penn. From biotechnology and robotics to computer animation and nanotechnology, Penn Engineering's centers and institutes are at the forefront of research on each scientific and technological frontier. (http://www.seas.upenn.edu/research/centers-institutes)

Financial Aid

A number of fellowships, assistantships, and scholarships are available on a yearly competitive basis, mainly for doctoral candidates. Provisions of these awards vary; the maximum benefits include payment of tuition and the general and technology fees plus a stipend and health insurance.

Cost of Study

Tuition for eight courses in the academic year 2009–10 was $36,920, and there was a general fee of $2080 and a technology fee of $622 for full-time study. For part-time study, the tuition was $4615 per course unit (one course), the general fee was $260, and the technology fee was $78.

Living and Housing Costs

On-campus housing is available for both single and married students. Residences for single students cost $685 and up per month. For a shared situation and for a private apartment the cost is $1195 and up per month. There are numerous privately owned apartments for rent in the immediate area.

Student Group

There are approximately 20,000 students at the University, around 10,000 of whom are enrolled in graduate and professional schools. Of these, approximately 1,000 are in graduate engineering programs.

Location

The University of Pennsylvania is located in West Philadelphia, just a few blocks from the heart of the city. Philadelphia is a twenty-first-century city with seventeenth-century origins. Renowned museums, concert halls, theaters, and sports arenas provide cultural and recreational outlets for students. Fairmount Park extends through large sections of Philadelphia, occupying both banks of the Schuylkill River. Not far away are the Jersey shore to the east, Pennsylvania Dutch country to the west, and the Pocono Mountains to the north. Less than a 3-hour drive from New York City and Washington, D.C., the city of Philadelphia is a patchwork of distinctive neighborhoods ranging from Colonial Society Hill to Chinatown.

The School

The School of Engineering and Applied Science has a distinguished reputation for the quality of its programs. Its alumni have achieved international distinction in research, higher education, management, entrepreneurship and industrial development, and government service. Its faculty leads a research program that is at the forefront of modern technology and has made major contributions in a wide variety of fields.

The University of Pennsylvania was founded in 1740 by Benjamin Franklin. A member of the Ivy League and one of the world's leading universities, Penn is renowned for its graduate schools, faculty, research centers, and institutes. Conveniently situated on a compact and attractive campus, Penn offers an abundance of multidisciplinary and cross-school educational programs with exceptional opportunities for individually tailored graduate education. It also offers students all the amenities of a 20,000-student university.

Applying

Candidates may apply directly to the School of Engineering through an online application system. Visit http://www.seas.upenn.edu/prospective-students/graduate/admissions for detailed application requirements and access to the online application system. Ph.D. applications for fall matriculation must be received by December 15 or January 2 (varies by department) to ensure consideration for financial aid. Master's applications are considered on a rolling basis with a final deadline of June 1. Admission is based on the student's past record as well as on letters of recommendation. Scores on the Graduate Record Examinations are required. All students whose native language is not English must arrange to take the Test of English as a Foreign Language (TOEFL) prior to the application process; the minimum score accepted on the Internet-based test is 100.

Correspondence and Information

Office of Graduate Admissions
School of Engineering and Applied Science
Towne Building
University of Pennsylvania
Philadelphia, Pennsylvania 19104-6391

Phone: 215-898-4542
E-mail: gradstudies@seas.upenn.edu
Web site: http://www.seas.upenn.edu

University of Pennsylvania

AREAS OF RESEARCH

Bioengineering. The nation's first Ph.D. in bioengineering was granted at the University of Pennsylvania, and today the department consists of 15 primary faculty members and more than 60 secondary and associated faculty members. The Bioengineering Ph.D. Program is designed to train individuals for academic, government, or industrial research careers. Research interests include cellular biomechanics, bioactive biomaterials, cell and tissue engineering, neuroengineering, orthopedic bioengineering, neurorehabilitation, respiratory mechanics and transport, molecular and cellular aspects of bioengineering, and biomedical imaging. Penn's interdisciplinary research training laboratories are in the Department of Bioengineering, the School of Engineering and Applied Science, and the new Institute for Medicine and Engineering; the University's medical, dental, and veterinary schools; and four research-oriented hospitals, all of which are located on campus. Students are exposed to clinical applications of bioengineering. The department also offers an M.S.E. in bioengineering and a professional master's program as a medical engineering track in the master's of biotechnology program. (http://www.seas.upenn.edu/be)

Biotechnology. The Master of Biotechnology degree is offered jointly by the School of Arts and Sciences and the School of Engineering and Applied Science. This interdisciplinary program prepares both full- and part-time students for productive and creative careers in the biotechnology and pharmaceutical industries. Students can specialize in one of the following tracks: bioinformatics/computational biology, biopharmaceuticals/engineering biotechnology, biomedical technologies, or molecular biotechnology. These tracks, in combination with core courses, ensure that the students get a uniquely broad exposure to the entire field of biotechnology. (http://www.upenn.edu/biotech)

Chemical and Biomolecular Engineering. The department was one of the first in the United States to offer a degree in chemical engineering. Courses and research programs are offered in applied mathematics, adsorption, biochemical and biomedical engineering, computer-aided design, transport and interfacial phenomena, thermodynamics, polymer engineering, semiconductor and ceramic materials processing, reaction kinetics, catalysis, artificial intelligence, and process control. Many research projects are collaborative and take advantage of other strong programs in the University. Ongoing research includes joint projects with faculty members from the medical school and Wistar Institute, from the Department of Biology, from the Department of Chemistry, from Computer Science and Engineering, and from Materials Science and Engineering. (http://www.seas.upenn.edu/cheme)

Computer and Information Science. The program is intended for students from many disciplines and backgrounds who normally have had substantial course work in mathematics and computer science. Research and teaching covers a wide range of topics in theory and applications, including algorithms, architecture, programming languages, operating systems, logic and computation, software engineering, databases, parallel and distributed systems, real-time systems, high-speed networks, graphics, computational biology, artificial intelligence, natural language processing, machine learning, data-mining, vision, and robotics. Much of this research involves multidisciplinary collaborations with other graduate programs in the School of Engineering, as well as the Schools of Mathematics, Linguistics, Philosophy, Psychology, Biology, and Neuroscience. The department also has a number of ongoing research collaborations with national and international organizations and laboratories. The CIS faculty seeks students who, whether pursuing a master's degree or doctoral studies, will be actively involved at the leading edge of computer science research. (http://www.cis.upenn.edu)

Computer and Information Technology. The program is designed for candidates who have a strong academic background in areas other than computer science but who have a need for graduate education in computer science. Completion of the M.C.I.T. program gives the graduate a solid foundation in computer science, providing the advanced expertise needed to meet the demands of a rapidly growing field of information technology (IT). The program is also suitable for IT professionals who wish to augment their practical skills with an understanding of the foundations of computing. (http://www.cis.upenn.edu/mcit/index.shtml)

Computer Graphics and Game Technology. The goal of the program is to expose recent graduates as well as students returning from industry to state-of-the-art graphics and animation technologies, interactive media design principles, product development methodologies, and engineering entrepreneurship. This degree program prepares students for those positions that require multi-disciplinary skills, such as designers, technical animators, directors, and game programmers. Opportunities for specialization are provided in such core areas as art and animation, creative design, animation and simulation technology, human/computer interfaces, and production management. (http://cis.upenn.edu/cggt/cggt-overview.shtml)

Electrical and Systems Engineering. The new graduate group in electrical and systems engineering offers the following programs: Ph.D. in electrical and systems engineering (ESE), M.S.E. in Electrical Engineering (EE), and a M.S.E. in Systems Engineering (SE). The department's research foci are the three main areas of electroscience, systems science, and network systems and telecommunications. Electrosciences includes electromagnetics and photonics, sensors and MEMS, LSI, and nanotechnology. Systems science covers signal processing, optimization, simulation, control and cybernetics, complex adaptive systems, stochastic processes, and decision sciences. Most of the research activities are interdisciplinary in nature and electrical and systems engineering faculty members and students typically interact or collaborate with professors and students from other departments in SEAS, the School of Arts and Sciences, and the Wharton School. (http://www.seas.upenn.edu/ese)

Embedded Systems. The Master of Science in Engineering in Embedded Systems (E.M.B.S.) spans the core topics of embedded control, real-time operating systems, model-based design and verification, and implementation of embedded systems. This innovative and unique degree program is offered jointly by Computer and Information Science and Electrical and Systems Engineering and is integrated with the PRECISE Center for Research in Embedded Systems. The program is ideally suited for students with either computer science or electrical engineering academic background who wish to pursue industrial jobs in automotive, aerospace, defense, and consumer electronics, as well as for practicing engineers in the embedded systems industry who want to gain knowledge in state-of-the-art tools and theories. (http://www.cis.upenn.edu/grad/embedded.shtml)

Integrated Product Design. The IPD program is intended to cultivate design professionals who possess both a breadth of knowledge and a depth of expertise in a specialty to bridge the domains of technology, manufacturing, business, aesthetics, and human-product interaction. The guiding philosophy of the program is not only to teach students to create products but to understand and address the social, environmental, and experiential contexts of those products, so that product design can be harnessed as a force for the greater good. The program builds the skills to investigate, imagine, conceptualize, and model a wide range of products and their complementary business models. The program draws on the strengths of three internationally recognized schools within the University: the School of Engineering and Applied Science, the Wharton School, and the School of Design. The graduate courses that make up the program create an interdisciplinary point of view and are taught by professors from all three schools. Studio classes accompany classroom studies, providing creative and analytical approaches and shifting students between rigorous technical and explorative processes in the development of both experiential and theoretical knowledge. Collaborative team projects and student-driven independent projects complement the core courses to give students both a solid grasp of the fundamentals and a deep understanding of the nuances of these fields. (http://www.me.upenn.edu/ipd/)

Materials Science and Engineering. The department conducts an extensive program of graduate education and research aimed at understanding the physical origins of the behavior of ceramics, polymers, metals, and alloys in electronic, structural, magnetic, and interfacial applications. Students have access to a broad range of state-of-the-art instrumentation in the department and the Laboratory for Research on the Structure of Matter (LRSM), which is housed in the same building. The LRSM is one of the largest NSF-supported Materials Research Science and Engineering Centers in the country and includes central facilities for surface studies, ion scattering, electron microscopy, X-ray diffraction, computer simulation, mechanical testing, and materials synthesis and processing. Access to synchrotron radiation (X-ray and UV) and neutron-scattering facilities is also available at nearby National Labs. Research within the department can be grouped under four general headings: surfaces and interfaces (polymer-polymer, metal-ceramic, and grain boundaries in metallic materials), complex materials (carbon-based nanotubes, copolymers, intermetallic alloys, and nanomaterials), failure mechanisms (plastic deformation, fatigue, embrittlement, corrosion, and predictive modeling), and novel electronic ceramics (ferroelectrics, microwave materials, batteries and fuel cells, superconductors, and catalysts). (http://www.seas.upenn.edu/mse)

Mechanical Engineering and Applied Mechanics. The research in the department combines theory, computation, and experiments with applications. It is often interdisciplinary in nature and is done in collaboration with material sciences, computer sciences, electrical and systems engineering, chemical and biomolecular engineering, and the medical school. The areas of focus are thermal and fluid sciences, mechanics of materials, computational science and engineering, mechanical systems and robotics, and biomechanics. Research in thermal fluids focuses on energy conversion, advanced power generation, Second-Law (energy) analysis, combustion, water desalination, microelectronic device fabrication and cooling, inorganic and organic (macromolecular) crystal growth, active control of flow patterns, transport processes associated with mesodevices and microdevices and with sensors, material processing, multiphase flows, computational fluid dynamics, and micro- and nano-scale thermofluid transport. The research in mechanics of materials focuses on crystal plasticity, effective properties of nonlinear composites, intermetallic compounds, localization studies, metal-forming processes, interfacial fracture, fatigue and high-temperature fracture, soft material, phase transitions in thermoelastic solids, nano-scale mechanics and tribology (friction, adhesion, and wear), and cell mechanics. Research in computational science and engineering focuses on parallel algorithms for the solution of differential and integral equations, inverse problems in nonlinear transport and wave propagation, and numerical study of systems with coupled multiple physics domains and multiple scales. Research in mechanical systems focuses on robotics, computational design, compliant mechanisms, optimization, computer vision, hybrid systems, dynamics, controls, virtual and rapid prototyping, and microelectromechanical systems (MEMS). Robotics research addresses control of multi-robot systems, active sensor networks, micromanipulation, and distributed control and sensing, flying robots, modular reconfigurable robots, robotic locomotion, haptic interfaces, teleoperation, and medical robotics. Biomechanics research spans scales from the tissue level through the molecular, with major efforts in cell mechanics, tendon and ligament properties, biomolecular network simulation, and gravity effects on cells and tissues. (http://www.me.upenn.edu)

Nanotechnology. The new master's program in nanotechnology prepares students for this profession with a solid foundation in the three technical core areas: nanofabrication; devices and properties; and biotechnology; as well as commercialization and societal impacts of technology. Courses are offered by the School of Engineering and Applied Science, the School of Arts and Sciences, and the Wharton School. (http://www.masters.nano.upenn.edu/program/)

Robotics. This new and unique program educates students in the interdisciplinary aspects of the science and technology of robotic and intelligent machines. The modern expert in robotics and intelligent systems must be proficient in artificial intelligence, computer vision, controls systems, dynamics, and machine learning as well as in design, programming, and prototyping of robotic systems. This multidepartmental, multidisciplinary program provides an ideal foundation for industrial jobs in robotics, defense, aerospace, and automotive industries and various government agencies. (http://www.grasp.upenn.edu/education/mse.htm)

Telecommunications and Networking. This interdisciplinary program draws its faculty members and courses from two SEAS departments—electrical and systems engineering and computer and information science—and from the Wharton School of Business. Two required courses cover the theory and practice of modern data and voice networking as well as future broadband-integrated networking; five telecommunications electives provide breadth and depth in the field. Two additional free electives allow students to further deepen their technical proficiency or address the increasingly complex managerial and business demands placed on telecommunications professionals. The program's interdisciplinary nature offers full- and part-time students the flexibility to tailor the curriculum to their specific interests, backgrounds, and career goals. (http://www.ese.upenn.edu)

UNIVERSITY OF ROCHESTER

Edmund A. Hajim School of Engineering and Applied Sciences

Programs of Study
The Edmund A. Hajim School of Engineering and Applied Sciences offers programs leading to M.S. and Ph.D. degrees in biomedical engineering, chemical engineering, computer science, electrical engineering, materials science, mechanical engineering, and optics. Additional master's programs include alternative energy, and technical entrepreneurship and management. Each department's M.S. degree requires a minimum of 30 semester hours of graduate credit and may be earned with or without a thesis. Thesis research can involve up to 12 hours of graduate credit. The M.S. option without a thesis may include up to 6 credits of independent study or project work and requires a comprehensive final examination. Programs are open to both full-time and part-time students. The Ph.D. degree is offered to prepare individuals for careers in research and teaching. The requirements include 90 semester hours of credit beyond the bachelor's degree and at least one academic year of full-time study in residence. A typical academic program is divided between course work and research credits to provide Ph.D. candidates with a broad exposure to their fields of interest, the requisite training for mastery of their area of specialization, and experience in conducting scholarly research. Ph.D. students must pass a preliminary examination and an oral qualifying examination and must present and defend an original thesis that contributes to knowledge in the field.

Research Facilities
The academic departments of the Hajim School are located on the River Campus, the University's main campus. Each department has extensive laboratories with modern equipment for research and instruction. Research centers within the academic units include the Center for Emerging and Innovative Sciences, the Center for Future Health, and the Rochester Center for Biomedical Ultrasound. An additional research center located on campus is the Laboratory for Laser Energetics, which houses the world's most powerful ultraviolet laser system and conducts research in high-energy-density phenomena and laser physics.
The University's library system contains more than 3.5 million volumes, and the Carlson Science and Engineering Library maintains complete collections in the research areas of the Hajim School. A campuswide network connects the extensive computing facilities.

Financial Aid
Research and teaching assistantships, department fellowships, and other fellowships and scholarships are available. Graduate assistantships provide a stipend of $22,000 to $26,000 per year plus a full-tuition scholarship. This support includes the summer months. University fellowships for outstanding candidates and special honors fellowships are also offered for up to $26,000 per year. Nearly all full-time graduate students receive financial aid.

Cost of Study
Tuition for 2010–11 is $1234 per credit. The mandatory health fee for 2010–11 is $552 per year.

Living and Housing Costs
University-owned apartments near the River Campus accommodate about 25 percent of the graduate students. This housing ranges from studio apartments to three-bedroom town houses, both furnished and unfurnished. Rents range from about $450 per month for a room adjoining the campus to approximately $890 per month for a furnished, two-bedroom, two-bathroom apartment in an on-campus housing complex. Off-campus (private) housing is plentiful. Food and other living costs in Rochester are moderate.

Student Group
The University's total enrollment is about 9,400, including 5,200 full-time undergraduates, 3,100 full-time graduate students, and 1,000 part-time students. There are approximately 430 full-time graduate students and 30 part-time graduate students in the Hajim School of Engineering and Applied Sciences.

Student Outcomes
Students completing engineering graduate studies at the University of Rochester (UR) have many options available to them. Recent graduates have found positions in a wide range of industrial, government laboratory, academic, and business sectors. A sampling of companies where graduates work includes Bausch & Lomb, National Rehabilitation Hospital, Intel, Trison Business Solutions, Bell Labs, IBM, Xerox, Philips Laboratories, Lockheed Martin, Microsoft, Martin Marietta, Siemens, Google, Yahoo, Optipro, Corning, Delphi, Laboratory for Laser Energetics, Thorlabs, QED Technologies, NASA, Beckman Laser Institute, and Optimax. Some graduates have gone on to faculty positions in prestigious engineering departments and medical centers around the country. Opportunities for UR graduate students remain abundant.

Location
The greater Rochester metropolitan area has a population of approximately 1 million. Its economy is based primarily on high-technology industries. Eastman Kodak and Xerox are major employers. The area is unusually strong in the quality of its public institutions and cultural life and is the home of the Rochester Philharmonic Orchestra, the Eastman School of Music, the Memorial Art Gallery, the Museum and Science Center, and the International Museum of Photography. Recreational opportunities include boating and fishing on Lake Ontario and the nearby Finger Lakes, skiing in the Bristol Hills, touring the Finger Lakes wineries, and camping and hiking in the Adirondacks (only a 4-hour drive from Rochester).

The University
Founded in 1850, the University of Rochester is an independent, nonsectarian, coeducational institution of higher learning and research. It is one of the nation's smallest distinguished universities. Academic and research programs are conducted by seven schools and colleges on three campuses. Programs ranging from the undergraduate to the postdoctoral level are offered in the humanities, social sciences, natural sciences, and professional fields of business, education, engineering, medicine, music, and nursing.
The River Campus, which includes the Hajim School of Engineering and Applied Sciences and the School of Arts and Sciences, is situated on the tree-lined bank of the Genesee River about 3 miles south of downtown Rochester. The Medical Center is adjacent to the River Campus; the Eastman School of Music is in the heart of the cultural district of downtown Rochester. The University offers excellent facilities for sports and recreation, including the multimillion-dollar Robert B. Goergen Athletic Center.

Applying
Admission to graduate study normally begins in the fall semester. Applicants seeking financial aid beginning in the fall semester should submit complete applications by the preceding January 15. Students not requesting financial aid should submit applications by June 30 for fall admission. There is no application fee for those who apply online at https://its-w2ks08.acs.rochester.edu/admgrad/. The exception to this is the department of biomedical engineering, which charges $60 for Ph.D. and M.S. applicants. TOEFL or IELTS scores are required for international students whose native language is not English. GRE scores are strongly recommended for all applicants. Direct contact with the department of interest is encouraged.

Correspondence and Information
Edmund A. Hajim School of Engineering and Applied Sciences
Box 270076
University of Rochester
Rochester, New York 14627-0076

Phone: 585-275-4151
Fax: 585-461-4735
E-mail: gradstudies@mail.rochester.edu (general information)
　　　　bme_gradinfo@seas.rochester.edu (biomedical engineering)
　　　　eagan@che.rochester.edu (chemical engineering)
　　　　admissions@cs.rochester.edu (computer science)
　　　　gradinfo@ece.rochester.edu (electrical engineering)
　　　　megrinfo@me.rochester.edu (materials science)
　　　　megrinfo@me.rochester.edu (mechanical engineering)
　　　　gradinfo@optics.rochester.edu (The Institute of Optics)
Web site: http://www.hajim.rochester.edu/

University of Rochester

THE FACULTY AND THEIR RESEARCH

BIOMEDICAL ENGINEERING: H. Awad, D. Benoit, E. Brown, L. Carney, D. Dalecki, K. Davis, G. Gdowski, M. Jacobs, N. Kuzma, A. Lerner, A. Luebke, K. Madden, S. McAleavey, J. L. McGrath, D. Pinto, S. Seidman, R. Waugh (Chair), A. Wismueller. **Research Areas: Molecular cell and tissue engineering:** cellular mechanics and adhesion, especially of the vascular system; microvascular flow and its regulation; extracellular matrix interactions; nanoscale materials and biosensors. **Biomedical imaging:** computer-aided diagnostics, nuclear spin spectroscopy for cardiovascular diagnostics, applications and technological developments of ultrasound, imaging of growth and repair of musculoskeletal tissues, medical image processing and functional imaging, optical devices incorporating state-of-the-art optical technology, vision research, molecular imaging, computational radiology, magnetic resonance imaging. **Neuroengineering:** systems modeling and neurophysiological analysis; cell and molecular engineering applied to vestibular, auditory, and visual systems. **Biomedical optics:** multiphoton microscopy for tissue characterization, principles of physical optics and optics design for clinical applications, confocal microscopy for clinical diagnosis, spectroscopic analysis of biological fluids, advanced microscopy for cell and molecular measurements. **Biomechanics:** musculoskeletal tissue engineering, analysis of bone stresses during movement, analysis of gait, bone growth and development, mechanics of vascular cells.

CHEMICAL ENGINEERING: M. L. Anthamatten, S. H. Chen, E. H. Chimowitz (Associate Chair), J. Jorné, A. A. Shestopalov, C. W. Tang, J. H. D. Wu, H Yang, M. Z. Yates (Chair). **Research Areas: Biotechnology and bioengineering:** bone marrow tissue engineering, genome approach to molecular and cellular modulation of hematopoiesis, adaptive cellular immunotherapy, molecular engineering of protein biocatalysts for biotechnological and biomaterial applications, genetic and protein engineering, molecular biology and biophysics, pulmonary physiology, biomedical applications of transport processes, interfacial phenomena, methods to study impacts of nanomaterials to human health, the rational design, synthesis, characterization, and employment of materials to treat diseases or control cell behavior for applications in drug therapy, regenerative medicine, and tissue engineering. **Inorganic materials:** material synthesis in microemulsions, phase transition and critical behavior of fluids in disordered porous materials, supercritical fluid phenomena, statistical mechanics and molecular simulation, microelectronics, transport and reaction in porous media, complex reaction systems, chemical vapor deposition, membrane separations and pollution control, fuel storage and gas sensor technology, magnetorheology. **Nanostructured materials:** block copolymers, ordering transitions in nanostructured and mesostructured materials, nanoparticle synthesis, self-assembly and processing, monodispersed nanoparticles and their applications, dimensionality of nanostructured materials, nanoparticle/polymer composites, layer-by-layer deposition, multiple-component and functional nanoparticles, core-shell nanoparticles, mesoporous materials, magnetic nanoparticles, magnetic nanoparticle carriers, self-assembled monolayer in nanofabrication, fabrication of functional nanostructured materials, inorganic quantum dot solar cells, photonic and biophotonic components and devices. **Particle technology:** functionalization of particle surfaces, colloidal crystallization, electrostatic self-assembly, microencapsulation, environmentally friendly synthesis and processing using ionic liquids and supercritical fluids, morphological control, particles and particle assemblies for optoelectronics, drug delivery, membranes, biological labeling. **Organic materials and devices:** organic light-emitting diodes; solar cells; photoconductors; image sensors; photoreceptors; charge injection, transport, recombination, and luminescence properties; liquid crystals and liquid crystalline polymers; reversibility associating polymers; conjugated polymers; self-assembled organic thin films; vapor deposition polymerization; materials for flat-panel displays. **Fuel cell technology:** electrocatalysts, platinum alloy and intermetallic catalysts, low-platinum and high-active nanomaterial in catalyst electrodes, new materials and structures for proton exchange membranes, alignment in nanocomposites membranes, MEA assembly, small-molecule (hydrogen, methanol, and formic acid) fuel cells, water management.

COMPUTER SCIENCE:J. Allen, J. Bigham, C. Brown, C. Ding, S. Dwarkadas, D. Gildea, L. Hemaspaandra, E. Ipek, H. Kautz (Chair), R. Nelson, L. Schubert, M. Scott, J. Seiferas, K. Shen, D. Stefankovic, M. Venkitasubramanian. **Research Areas:** artificial intelligence, systems, and theory; natural language processing; human-computer interaction; machine vision; machine learning; computer architecture; programming languages; parallel computing; cryptography; social choice theory; complexity theory; and algorithms.

ELECTRICAL AND COMPUTER ENGINEERING: P. Ampadu, M. F. Bocko, H. Dery, M. Doyley, P. M. Fauchet (Chair), E. G. Friedman, W. Heinzelman, T. Y. Hsiang, M. Huang, Z. Ignjatovic, T. B. Jones, J. G. Mottley, K. J. Parker, G. Sharma, R. Sobolewski, A. Vosoughi, R. C. Waag, H. Wu. **Research Areas: Computer systems and microelectronics:** computer architecture, computer organization, microprocessor design, high-speed adaptive architectures, multiprocessor systems, computer systems performance analysis, digital systems design, VLSI circuits and systems, CMOS circuits, synchronization, clock distribution, pipelining, signal integrity, speed/power/area tradeoffs, WSI, VLSI systems, routing and placement, CAD tools, analog IC design, analog to digital converters, CMOS image sensors, integrated sensors, fault-tolerant VLSI design, reliability of VLSI circuits, VLSI signal processing circuits, nanoscale integrated circuits, RF circuit design, microwave engineering, device modeling. **Optoelectronics and nanoelectronics:** optoelectronic and photonic materials and devices, light-emitting porous silicon, silicon nanodevices and nanotechnologies, biosensors, single-electron devices, femtosecond lasers, optical diagnostics, ultrafast phenomena, superconducting thin films and devices, nonequilibrium effects, high-temperature superconductors, optoelectronic switching, magnetic thin films, infrared detection, electronic noise, solid-state and quantum electronics, nonequilibrium and ultrafast phenomena in condensed matter, nanodevices and nanotechnologies, spintronics. **Signal processing and biomedical imaging:** digital image processing, genomic signal processing, multimedia data security, color reproduction, audio and music signal processing, ultrasonic scattering, biomedical ultrasound, bioelectric phenomena, interaction of acoustic and electric fields with biological materials, quantitative ultrasonic tissue and materials characterization, anisotropy of ultrasonic parameters, ultrasonic contrast agents, medical imaging, Doppler imaging techniques, digital half-toning, 3-D/4-D medical imaging, tissue characterization, inverse problems, breast imaging, elastography, cardiovascular disease, molecular imaging, ultrasound, and MRI. **Communications:** wireless communication, wireless networking, protocol design, mobile ad hoc networking, sensor networks, mobile computing, code design, media access protocols, routing protocols, mobility management, error control, protocols to ensure quality of service, joint source coding, distributed data compression, transceiver design in wireless communications systems, multiple-access communications, radar, sonar, signal design and coding, psychoacoustics, echolocation. **Electromechanics and electrostatics:** electromechanics of particles, microfluidics, microelectromechanics, biological dielectrophoresis, industrial electrostatic hazards.

MATERIALS SCIENCE: Research Areas: Materials synthesis: new nonlinear optical crystals; glasses and polymers; liquid crystal polymers; organic and inorganic polymers made with transition-metal catalysts; block and conjugated copolymers; magneto-optical materials; polymer LEDs; fluorescent materials; nanocomposites; epitaxial semiconductors and optoelectronic devices; III–V and group IV compounds and semiconductors; fuel cell materials, membranes, and catalysts. **Materials processing:** chemical vapor deposition of ceramics; deterministic optical fabrication and manufacturing; microgrinding; mechanical and electrochemical polishing; high-intensity laser-matter interactions; piezoelectric materials; sputtering and thin-film deposition and processing; lithography; powder ceramics and metals; bulk and thin-film ceramic superconductors; electrohydrodynamic fabrication and electrospinning for biomedical, drug delivery, and engineered materials. **Materials characterization:** high-resolution X-ray diffraction, scanning and transmission electron microscopy, atomic-force microscopy, nanoindentation, near-field and Nomarski optical microscopy, Raman spectroscopy, extensive facilities for optical property measurements. **Materials testing:** nanoindentation and scratching, AFMs for indentation, impression creep, fatigue and recovery, acoustic and optical damping, laser damage testing, thermomechanical and fracture toughness facilities, fuel cell polarization measurements. **Analytic and computational studies:** deformation; dislocation mechanics; nucleation; phase transitions; cyclic and statistical thermodynamics of solids; adhesion; fluctuations, especially in superconductors; molecular dynamics; laser physics; fracture mechanics and failure analysis.

MECHANICAL ENGINEERING: R. Betti, S. J. Burns, R. L. Clark, P. D. Funkenbusch, R. F. Gans, S. M. Gracewski, J. C. Lambropoulos (Chair), J. C. M. Li, D. D. Meyerhofer, J. Nam, R. L. Perucchio, D. J. Quesnel, C. Ren, J. H. Thomas. **Research Areas (Solid mechanics and materials): Mechanics of materials:** Mechanical properties of materials: fracture and fatigue, scratch resistance and impression creep, nanoscale contact, thermomechanical deformation of materials, indentation and adhesion, piezoelectric failures. **Microstructure Characterization:** atomic-force microscopy, nanoindentation, optical and scanning electron microscopy, surface profilometry, X-ray and electron diffraction. **Materials processing:** laser damage of materials; electrospinning; mechanics and material problems in deterministic microgrinding and optical manufacturing; processing of powder materials; thermal and deformation processing of metals and alloys, especially metal aluminides. **Special materials:** piezoelectrics, corrosion, biological and biomedical materials, nonlinear optical materials, adaptive structures. **Applied dynamics:** dynamic systems and controls, adaptive acoustic materials and structures, active structural and acoustic control, elastic waves in layered media, mechanics of bonded interfaces and whisker failures in microelectronic solders, thermal and mechanical properties of thin films, expansion and collapse of bubbles. **Biological applications:** *Mechanics of cardiac growth and development:* elasticity, poroelasticity, material properties, nonlinear finite-element modeling of the developing heart. **Biomedical ultrasound:** imaging and lithotripsy, fracture mechanics and failure of kidney and gall stones. **Bone growth and orthopedics:** medical image-based modeling. **Mechanical properties of fusion energy research:** inertial and magnetic confinement fusion; hydrodynamic theory and simulations of inertial fusion implosions; experimental studies of laser driven implosions; hydrodynamic stability and nonlinear waves with both Rayleigh-Taylor and parametric instabilities; experimental studies of the scattering of radiation from laser-produced plasma; plasma diagnostics; the investigation of intense X-ray sources; experimental studies of the interaction of very short pulse, high-intensity lasers with matter; measurements of equation of state at ultrahigh pressures and densities; particle acceleration in plasmas; magnetohydrodynamic equilibrium and stability of tokamak plasmas; plasma dynamics, kinetic theory and wave-particle interaction. **Fluid mechanics:** Astrophysical fluid dynamics and magnetohydrodynamics: the physics of sunspots, dynamos in the Sun and other stars, the formation of planetary nebulae, hydrodynamic lubrication, non-Newtonian fluids, magneto-rheological fluids, numerical modeling (CFD).

THE INSTITUTE OF OPTICS: G. P. Agrawal, M. A. Alonso, A. Berger, T. G. Brown, J. R. Fienup, N. George, C. Guo, W. H. Knox (Director), D. T. Moore, L. Novotny, J. Rolland, C. R. Stroud, K. J. Teegarden, G. W. Wicks (Associate Director), D. R. Williams, J. M. Zavislan. **Research Areas: Component technologies:** diffractive optics, gradient-index optics, holographic optical elements. **Guided-wave optics:** fiber optics, integrated optics, optical waveguide phenomena, fiber gratings, fiber amplifiers. **Image science:** diffractive theory, electronic imaging, pattern recognition, Fourier optics, phase retrieval, wavefront sensing, image reconstruction and restoration, biological imaging. **Lasers:** solid-state lasers, semiconductor lasers, fiber lasers, laser instabilities, high-intensity lasers, laser fusion, ultrafast laser physics and engineering. **Medical optics:** human visual system, mechanisms of vision, laser-tissue interactions, Raman spectroscopy, spectroscopy of turbid systems, measurement of chemical concentrations in intact biological specimens, biological imaging. **Nanoscale optics:** optical interactions and devices involving structures with nanometer dimensions. **Nonlinear optics:** nonlinear interactions, phase conjugation, nonlinear optical materials. **Optical materials:** glasses, III–V and group IV semiconductors, epitaxial growth, nonlinear materials, liquid crystals, materials processing, polishing science, optical thin-film coatings. **Optical system design:** design algorithms, novel optical systems, optical aberration theory, optical systems without symmetry, nonimaging optics, design using anisotropic optical materials. **Photonics:** optoelectronics, quantum electronics. **Quantum optics:** resonant interaction of light with matter, Rydberg atoms, electron and atomic wavepackets, multiphoton processes, ultrafast phenomena. **Telecommunications:** solitons, optical-fiber communications. **Theoretical foundations:** coherence theory, quantum and classical electrodynamics, propagation of light, statistical optics, radiation theory, mathematical models of wave propagation.

YALE UNIVERSITY

School of Engineering & Applied Science

Programs of Study

All research and instructional programs in engineering and applied science are coordinated by the School of Engineering & Applied Science, which consists of the Departments of Biomedical, Chemical and Environmental, Electrical, and Mechanical Engineering and Materials Science. These four units have autonomous faculty appointments and instructional programs, and students may obtain degrees designated according to different disciplines. A Director of Graduate Studies in each department oversees all graduate student matters. Students have considerable freedom in selecting programs to suit their interests and may choose programs of study that draw upon the resources of science departments that are not within the School of Engineering & Applied Science, including the Departments of Applied Physics, Physics, Chemistry, Mathematics, Statistics, Astronomy, Geology and Geophysics, Molecular Biophysics and Biochemistry, and Computer Science, and departments of the School of Medicine and the School of Management.

The student plans his or her course of study in consultation with faculty advisers (the student's advisory committee). A minimum of ten term courses is required and they must be completed in the first two years. Mastery of the mathematical topics is expected, and the core courses, as identified by each department/program, should be taken in the first year. No more than two courses should be Special Investigations, and at least two should be outside the area of the dissertation. Periodically, the faculty reviews the overall performance of the student to determine whether he or she may continue working toward the Ph.D. degree. At the end of the first year, a faculty member typically agrees to accept the student as a research assistant. By December 5 of the third year, an area examination must be passed and a written prospectus submitted before dissertation research is begun. These events result in the student's admission to candidacy. Subsequently, students report orally each year to the full advisory committee on their progress. When the research is nearing completion, but before the thesis writing has commenced, the full advisory committee advises the student on the thesis plan. A final oral presentation of the dissertation research is required during term time. There is no foreign language requirement.

M.S. degrees are offered and require the successful completion of at least eight term courses, two of which may be special projects. Although this program can normally be completed in one year of full-time study, a part-time M.S. program is available for practicing engineers and others. Its requirements are the successful completion of eight term courses in a time period not to exceed four calendar years.

Research Facilities

Department facilities are equipped with state-of-the-art experimental and computational equipment in support of the research activity described above. They are centrally located on campus in Mason and Becton Laboratories and in the Malone Engineering Center, adjacent to the Departments of Mathematics and Computer Science and near the complex of facilities for physics, chemistry, and the biological sciences. The School of Engineering & Applied Science has a rich computing environment, including servers, UNIX workstations, and Macintosh and Microsoft Windows personal computers. A high-speed data network interconnects engineering and extends to the campus network. Yale has long been connected to the Internet and is now participating in vBNS and the emerging Internet2. In addition, advanced instrumentation, computing, and networking are combined in a number of laboratories.

Financial Aid

Almost all first-year Ph.D. students receive a University fellowship paying full tuition and an adjusted stipend. Support thereafter is generally provided by research assistantships, which pay $29,000 plus full tuition in 2010–11. Prize fellowships are available to exceptional students. Fellowship support is not available for master's degree or part-time students.

Cost of Study

Tuition is $33,500 for the 2010–11 academic year.

Living and Housing Costs

On-campus graduate dormitory housing units range from $4200 to $7160 per academic year. Graduate apartment units range from $794 to $1114 per month. More housing details can be found at http://www.yale.edu/gradhousing.

Student Group

Yale has 11,250 students—5,300 are undergraduates and the remainder are graduate and professional students. About 200 graduate students are in engineering, most of them working toward the Ph.D.

Location

Situated on Long Island Sound, among the scenic attractions of southern New England, New Haven provides outstanding cultural and recreational opportunities. The greater New Haven area has a population of more than 350,000 and is only 1½ hours from New York by train or car.

The University

Yale is the third-oldest university in the United States, and its engineering program is also one of the oldest. The administrative organization for engineering has changed through the years, but the intention has always been to give students a high degree of flexibility in arranging their programs, with close interaction between individual students and faculty members.

Applying

Students with a bachelor's degree in any field of engineering or in mathematics, physics, or chemistry may apply for admission to graduate study, as may other students prepared to do graduate-level work in any of the study areas of the chosen department, regardless of their specific undergraduate field. Students are admitted only at the beginning of the fall term. Application should be initiated about a year in advance of desired admission, and the application should be filed preferably before December 25; the file, including letters of reference, should be completed before January 2. Notifications of admission and award of financial aid are sent by April 1. Applicants must take the General Test of the Graduate Record Examinations; the exam should be taken in October. International applicants must submit scores on the TOEFL unless the undergraduate degree is from an institution in which English is the primary language of instruction. The school's Web site provides information on the faculty members and degree programs.

Correspondence and Information

Office of Graduate Studies
School of Engineering & Applied Science
Yale University
P.O. Box 208267
New Haven, Connecticut 06520-8267
Phone: 203-432-4250
Fax: 203-432-7736
Web site: http://www.seas.yale.edu/

Yale University

THE FACULTY AND AREAS OF RESEARCH

APPLIED MECHANICS/MECHANICAL ENGINEERING/MATERIALS SCIENCE. A. Dollar, E. Dufresne, J. Fernández de la Mora, A. Gomez, M. B. Long, J. Morrell, C. S. O'Hern, N. Ouellette, A. G. Ramirez, J. Schroers, U. D. Schwarz, M. D. Smooke, H. Tang. Joint appointments (with primary appointment in another department): D. Bercovici, S.-I. Karato, D. E. Rosner, R. B. Smith. Adjunct faculty: A. Liñan-Martinez, F. A. Williams. Emeritus faculty: I. B. Bernstein.

Mechanics of Fluids. Dynamics and stability of drops and bubbles; dynamics of thin liquid films; macroscopic and particle-scale dynamics of emulsions, foams, and colloidal suspensions; electrospray theory and applications; electrical propulsion applications; properties of nanoparticles and nanodrops; combustion and flames; computational methods for fluid dynamics and reacting flows; turbulence; particle tracking in fluid mechanics; laser diagnostics of reacting and nonreacting flows.

Mechanics of Solids/Material Science/Soft Matter. Characterization of crystallization and other phase transformations; studies of thin films, MEMS, smart materials such as shape memory alloys, amorphous metals, and nanomaterials including nanocomposites; jamming and slow dynamics in glasses and granular materials; mechanical properties of soft and biological materials; self assembly; dynamics of macromolecules; NEMS; nano-imprinting; classical and quantum optomechanics; atomic-scale investigations of surface interactions and properties; classical and quantum nanomechanics; and nanotribology.

Robotics/Mechatronics. Machine and mechanism design; dynamics and control; robotic grasping and manipulation; human-machine interface; rehabilitation robotics; haptics; electromechanical energy conversion; biomechanics of human movement; human powered vehicles.

BIOMEDICAL ENGINEERING. R. E. Carson, R. T. Constable, J. Duncan, T. Fahmy, R. Fan, A. Gonzalez, J. Humphrey, F. Hyder, T. Kyriakides, M. Levene, K. Miller-Jensen, D. Rothman, M. Saltzman, L. Staib, S. Zucker. Joint appointments (with primary appointment in another department): R. de Graaf, E. Morris, L. Niklason, X. Papademetris, S. Sampath, E. Shapiro, F. Sigworth, H. Tagare.

Biomedical Imaging and Biosignals. Formation of anatomical and functional medical images; magnetic resonance spectroscopy; analysis and processing of medical image data, including functional MRI (fMRI); diffusion tensor imaging; imaging of brain biochemical processes; image-guided neurosurgery; using biomechanical models to guide recovery of left ventricular strain from medical images; biomedical signal processing; relating EEG and fMRI information.

Biomechanics. Simulation and loading of the lumbar spine in regard to tissue loads during heavy lifting, low-back pain and mechanical instability of the spine, muscle mechanics and electromyography, mechanical performance of implants, microcirculation in skeletal muscle, mechanisms of blood-flow control, cell-to-cell communication in vascular resistance networks.

Biomolecular Engineering and Biotechnology. Drug delivery and tissue engineering, drug delivery systems, polymers as biomaterials, tissue engineering, spinal cord regeneration, drug delivery and repair in retina and optic nerve, new biomaterials for drug delivery and tissue engineering, bioseparations, chromatography and electrophoresis, electrical recording (patch clamp) and signal processing of ion channel currents, studies of structure and function of ion channel proteins, cryoelectron microscopy methods for macromolecular structure determination.

CHEMICAL AND ENVIRONMENTAL ENGINEERING. E. I. Altman, G. Benoit, M. Elimelech, G. L. Haller, M. Loewenberg, W. Mitch, C. Osuji, J. Peccia, L. D. Pfefferle, D. E. Rosner, M. Saltzman, A. D. Taylor, P. Van Tassel (Department Chair), T. K. Vanderlick, C. Wilson, J. Zimmerman. Adjunct faculty: A. Firoozabadi, Y. Khalil, J. Pignatello. Joint appointments (with primary appointment in another department): M. Bell, R. Blake, E. Dufresne, T. E. Graedel, E. Kaplan, J. Saiers, K. W. Zilm.

Nanomaterials. Carbon and inorganic nanotubes, nanoscale polymer films, nanoscale devices, nanomaterials and biomolecules in engineered and natural aquatic systems.

Soft Matter and Interfacial Phenomena. Colloidal and interfacial phenomena, surface science, physics of synthetic and biological macromolecules, microfluidic biosensors, self-assembled soft materials for biomedical applications.

Biomolecular Engineering. Biomolecules at interfaces, nanofilm biomaterials, bioaerosol detection and source tracking, microarrays and other high throughput measurements, production of functional binding biomolecules, biological production of sustainable fuels, transport and fate of microbial pathogens in aquatic environments, membrane separations for desalination and water quality control.

Energy. Biofuels, energy extraction from waste materials, efficient water treatment and delivery, integration of science and engineering with economics and policy.

Water. Sustainable and culturally appropriate technologies for low-quality-source water reclamation in the developing world.

Sustainability. Green solvents, bio-based materials, safer nanotechnology and systems optimization for reduced environmental impact and enhanced economic competitiveness.

ELECTRICAL ENGINEERING. E. Culurciello, J. Han, H. Koser, R. Kuc, M. Lee, T. P. Ma, Y. Makris, A. S. Morse, K. S. Narendra, M. A. Reed, A. Savvides, H. Tang, S. Tatikonda, J. R. Vaisnys, E. Yeh. Joint appointments (with primary appointment in another department): J. Duncan, L. Staib, H. D. Tagare, R. Yang. Adjunct faculty: P. J. Kindlmann, R. Lethin. Emeritus faculty: R. C. Barker, P. M. Schultheiss.

Signal Processing, Control, and Communications. Linear system models, automatic control systems, representation of information in signals, transmission and storage of information, processing information by computers, networking, communication theory. Applications include bioengineering, digital signal processing, image processing, neural networks, robotics, sensors, and telecommunication systems.

Computer Engineering, Sensor Networks, Circuits and Systems. Study and design of digital circuits and computer systems; computer architecture; sensor networks; very-large-scale integrated (VLSI) circuit design, implementation, and testing. Applications include computing networks, computer design, biomedical instrumentation, bio-inspired circuits and systems.

Electronics, Photonics, and Nanodevices. Design, fabrication, and characterization of novel electronic, photonic, and nano devices; study of structure-property relationships in electronic and photonic materials. Applications include chem./bio-sensing, solid-state lighting, solar cells, micro/nano-electromechanical systems, non-volatile memory, and ultrafast devices.

Section 2
Aerospace/Aeronautical Engineering

This section contains a directory of institutions offering graduate work in aerospace/aeronautical engineering, followed by an in-depth entry submitted by an institution that chose to prepare a detailed program description. Additional information about programs listed in the directory but not augmented by an in-depth entry may be obtained by writing directly to the dean of a graduate school or chair of a department at the address given in the directory.

For programs offering related work, see also in this book *Engineering and Applied Sciences* and *Mechanical Engineering and Mechanics*. In another guide in this series:

Graduate Programs in the Physical Sciences, Mathematics, Agricultural Sciences, the Environment & Natural Resources
See *Geosciences* and *Physics*

CONTENTS

Program Directories

Close-Up

Aerospace/Aeronautical Engineering

Air Force Institute of Technology, Graduate School of Engineering and Management, Department of Aeronautics and Astronautics, Dayton, OH 45433-7765. Offers aeronautical engineering (MS, PhD); astronautical engineering (MS, PhD); materials science (MS, PhD); space operations (MS); systems engineering (MS, PhD). *Accreditation:* ABET (one or more programs are accredited). Part-time programs available. *Degree requirements:* For master's, thesis; for doctorate, thesis/dissertation. *Entrance requirements:* For master's and doctorate, GRE General Test, minimum GPA of 3.0, U.S. citizenship. *Faculty research:* Computational fluid dynamics, experimental aerodynamics, computational structural mechanics, experimental structural mechanics, aircraft and spacecraft stability and control.

Arizona State University, Graduate College, College of Technology and Innovation, Department of Aeronautical Management Technology, Tempe, AZ 85287. Offers MS. Part-time and evening/weekend programs available. *Degree requirements:* For master's, thesis or applied project and oral defense. *Entrance requirements:* For master's, minimum GPA of 3.0, 30 semester hours in technology or equivalent, 16 hours of physical science and mathematics. Additional exam requirements/recommendations for international students: Required—TOEFL (minimum score 550 paper-based; 213 computer-based; 83 iBT); Recommended—TWE. Electronic applications accepted. *Faculty research:* Aviation training and education, human factors, aviation psychology, high altitude flight physiology, women in aviation, safety, aerospace medicine, metacognition, self regulation, learning strategies of pilots, aviation law, airline management.

Arizona State University, Graduate College, Ira A. Fulton School of Engineering, Department of Mechanical and Aerospace Engineering, Tempe, AZ 85287. Offers aerospace engineering (MS, MSE, PhD); mechanical engineering (MS, MSE, PhD). *Degree requirements:* For master's, thesis or alternative; for doctorate, thesis/dissertation. *Entrance requirements:* For master's and doctorate, GRE General Test.

Auburn University, Graduate School, Ginn College of Engineering, Department of Aerospace Engineering, Auburn University, AL 36849. Offers MAE, MS, PhD. Part-time programs available. *Faculty:* 10 full-time (0 women), 3 part-time/adjunct (0 women). *Students:* 21 full-time (3 women), 16 part-time (2 women); includes 3 minority (2 Asian Americans or Pacific Islanders, 1 Hispanic American), 8 international. Average age 27. 76 applicants, 38% accepted, 10 enrolled. In 2009, 15 master's, 1 doctorate awarded. *Degree requirements:* For master's, thesis (MS), exam; for doctorate, thesis/dissertation, exams. *Entrance requirements:* For master's and doctorate, GRE General Test. *Application deadline:* For fall admission, 7/7 for domestic students; for spring admission, 11/24 for domestic students. Applications are processed on a rolling basis. Application fee: $50 ($60 for international students). Electronic applications accepted. *Expenses:* Tuition, state resident: full-time $6240. Tuition, nonresident: full-time $18,720. International tuition: $18,938 full-time. Required fees: $492. Tuition and fees vary according to course load, program and reciprocity agreements. *Financial support:* Fellowships, research assistantships, teaching assistantships, Federal Work-Study available. Support available to part-time students. Financial award application deadline: 3/15; financial award applicants required to submit FAFSA. *Faculty research:* Aerodynamics, flight dynamics and simulation, propulsion, structures and aeroelasticity, aerospace smart structures. *Unit head:* Dr. John E. Cochran, Head, 334-844-4874. *Application contact:* Dr. George Flowers, Dean of the Graduate School, 334-844-2125.

California Institute of Technology, Division of Engineering and Applied Science, Option in Aeronautics, Pasadena, CA 91125-0001. Offers MS, PhD, Engr. *Faculty:* 10 full-time (2 women). *Students:* 49 full-time (14 women). 220 applicants, 16% accepted, 19 enrolled. In 2009, 10 master's, 7 doctorates awarded. *Degree requirements:* For doctorate, thesis/dissertation. *Application deadline:* For fall admission, 1/15 for domestic students. Application fee: $0. *Financial support:* In 2009–10, 22 fellowships, 39 research assistantships, 9 teaching assistantships were awarded. *Faculty research:* Computational fluid dynamics, technical fluid dynamics, structural mechanics, mechanics of fracture, aeronautical engineering and propulsion. *Unit head:* Dr. Guruswami Ravichandran, Director, 626-395-4523, E-mail: ravi@aero.caltech.edu. *Application contact:* Natalie Gilmore, Assistant Dean of Graduate Studies, 626-395-3812, Fax: 626-577-9246, E-mail: ngilmore@caltech.edu.

California Polytechnic State University, San Luis Obispo, College of Engineering, Department of Aerospace Engineering, San Luis Obispo, CA 93407. Offers MS. Part-time programs available. *Faculty:* 8 full-time (2 women), 1 part-time/adjunct (0 women). *Students:* 20 full-time (0 women), 18 part-time (1 woman); includes 8 minority (6 Asian Americans or Pacific Islanders, 2 Hispanic Americans). Average age 26. 21 applicants, 76% accepted, 13 enrolled. In 2009, 22 master's awarded. *Degree requirements:* For master's, thesis. *Entrance requirements:* For master's, GRE General Test, minimum GPA of 3.0 in last 90 quarter units. Additional exam requirements/recommendations for international students: Required—TOEFL (minimum score 550 paper-based; 213 computer-based), or IELTS (minimum score 6). *Application deadline:* For fall admission, 7/1 for domestic students, 11/30 for international students; for winter admission, 11/1 for domestic students, 6/30 for international students; for spring admission, 2/1 for domestic students. Applications are processed on a rolling basis. Application fee: $55. Electronic applications accepted. *Expenses:* Tuition, nonresident: full-time $11,160; part-time $248 per unit. Required fees: $7134; $1553 per quarter. *Financial support:* Research assistantships, teaching assistantships, career-related internships or fieldwork, Federal Work-Study, scholarships/grants, and unspecified assistantships available. Support available to part-time students. Financial award application deadline: 3/2; financial award applicants required to submit FAFSA. *Faculty research:* Space systems engineering, space vehicle design, aerodynamics, aerospace propulsion, dynamics and control. *Unit head:* Dr. Jin Tso, Graduate Coordinator/Department Chair, 805-756-1391, Fax: 805-756-2376, E-mail: jtso@calpoly.edu. *Application contact:* Dr. Jin Tso, Graduate Coordinator/Department Chair, 805-756-1391, Fax: 805-756-2376, E-mail: jtso@calpoly.edu.

California State University, Long Beach, Graduate Studies, College of Engineering, Department of Mechanical and Aerospace Engineering, Program in Aerospace Engineering, Long Beach, CA 90840. Offers MSAE. Part-time programs available. *Students:* 18 full-time (2 women), 30 part-time (4 women); includes 19 minority (1 African American, 13 Asian Americans or Pacific Islanders, 5 Hispanic Americans), 11 international. Average age 29. *Degree requirements:* For master's, thesis or alternative. *Entrance requirements:* Additional exam requirements/recommendations for international students: Required—TOEFL. *Application deadline:* For fall admission, 7/1 for domestic students. Application fee: $55. Electronic applications accepted. *Expenses:* Required fees: $1802 per semester. Part-time tuition and fees vary according to course load. *Financial support:* Career-related internships or fieldwork, Federal Work-Study, institutionally sponsored loans, scholarships/grants, and unspecified assistantships available. Financial award application deadline: 3/2. *Faculty research:* Aerodynamic flows, ice accretion, stability and transition. *Unit head:* Dr. Hamid Hefazi, Chairman, 562-985-1563, Fax: 562-985-4408, E-mail: hefazi@csulb.edu. *Application contact:* Dr. Hsin-Piao Chen, Graduate Advisor, 562-985-1563.

Carleton University, Faculty of Graduate Studies, Faculty of Engineering and Design, Department of Mechanical and Aerospace Engineering, Ottawa, ON K1S 5B6, Canada. Offers aerospace engineering (M Eng, MA Sc, PhD); materials engineering (M Eng, MA Sc); mechanical engineering (M Eng, MA Sc, PhD). *Degree requirements:* For master's, thesis optional; for doctorate, thesis/dissertation. *Entrance requirements:* For master's, honors degree; for doctorate, MA Sc or M Eng. Additional exam requirements/recommendations for international students: Required—TOEFL. *Faculty research:* Thermal fluids engineering, heat transfer, vehicle engineering.

Case Western Reserve University, School of Graduate Studies, The Case School of Engineering, Department of Mechanical and Aerospace Engineering, Cleveland, OH 44106. Offers MS, PhD, MD/PhD. Part-time programs available. Postbaccalaureate distance learning degree programs offered (no on-campus study). *Faculty:* 13 full-time (3 women). *Students:* 60 full-time (9 women), 16 part-time (2 women); includes 6 minority (2 African Americans, 1 American Indian/Alaska Native, 3 Asian Americans or Pacific Islanders), 26 international. In 2009, 11 master's, 5 doctorates awarded. *Degree requirements:* For master's, thesis (for some programs); for doctorate, thesis/dissertation, qualifying exam, teaching experience. *Entrance requirements:* For master's and doctorate, GRE General Test. Additional exam requirements/recommendations for international students: Required—TOEFL. *Application deadline:* For fall admission, 7/1 priority date for domestic students. Applications are processed on a rolling basis. Application fee: $50. *Financial support:* Fellowships with full and partial tuition reimbursements, research assistantships with full and partial tuition reimbursements, teaching assistantships, institutionally sponsored loans and tuition waivers (full and partial) available. Financial award application deadline: 3/1; financial award applicants required to submit FAFSA. *Faculty research:* Musculoskeletal biomechanics, combustion diagnostics and computation, mechanical behavior of advanced materials and nanostructures, biorobotics. Total annual research expenditures: $7.8 million. *Unit head:* Dr. Iwan Alexander, Department Chair, 216-368-6045, Fax: 216-368-6445, E-mail: ida2@case.edu. *Application contact:* Carla Wilson, Student Affairs Coordinator, 216-368-4580, Fax: 216-368-3007, E-mail: cxw75@case.edu.

Concordia University, School of Graduate Studies, Faculty of Engineering and Computer Science, Program in Aerospace Engineering, Montréal, QC H3G 1M8, Canada. Offers M Eng. *Degree requirements:* For master's, thesis or alternative. *Faculty research:* Aeronautics and propulsion avionics and control, structures and materials, space engineering.

Cornell University, Graduate School, Graduate Fields of Engineering, Field of Aerospace Engineering, Ithaca, NY 14853-0001. Offers M Eng, MS, PhD. *Faculty:* 41 full-time (6 women). *Students:* 48 full-time (7 women); includes 6 minority (1 African American, 5 Hispanic Americans), 16 international. Average age 25. 110 applicants, 43% accepted, 26 enrolled. In 2009, 21 master's, 3 doctorates awarded. Terminal master's awarded for partial completion of doctoral program. *Degree requirements:* For master's, thesis (MS); for doctorate, one foreign language, comprehensive exam, thesis/dissertation. *Entrance requirements:* For master's and doctorate, GRE General Test, 3 letters of recommendation. Additional exam requirements/recommendations for international students: Required—TOEFL (minimum score 550 paper-based; 213 computer-based; 77 iBT). *Application deadline:* For fall admission, 1/15 for domestic students; for spring admission, 11/1 for domestic students. Application fee: $70. Electronic applications accepted. *Expenses:* Tuition: Full-time $29,500. Required fees: $70. Full-time tuition and fees vary according to degree level, program and student level. *Financial support:* In 2009–10, 22 students received support, including 6 fellowships with full tuition reimbursements available, 2 research assistantships with full tuition reimbursements available; teaching assistantships with full tuition reimbursements available, institutionally sponsored loans, scholarships/grants, health care benefits, tuition waivers (full and partial), and unspecified assistantships also available. Financial award applicants required to submit FAFSA. *Faculty research:* Aerodynamics, fluid mechanics, turbulence, combustion/propulsion, aeroacoustics. *Unit head:* Director of Graduate Studies, 607-255-5250. *Application contact:* Graduate Field Assistant, 607-255-5250, E-mail: maegrad@cornell.edu.

École Polytechnique de Montréal, Graduate Programs, Department of Mechanical Engineering, Montréal, QC H3C 3A7, Canada. Offers aerothermics (M Eng, M Sc A, PhD); applied mechanics (M Eng, M Sc A, PhD); tool design (M Eng, M Sc A, PhD). Part-time and evening/weekend programs available. *Degree requirements:* For master's, one foreign language, thesis; for doctorate, one foreign language, thesis/dissertation. *Entrance requirements:* For master's, minimum GPA of 2.75; for doctorate, minimum GPA of 3.0. *Faculty research:* Noise control and vibration, fatigue and creep, aerodynamics, composite materials, biomechanics, robotics.

Embry-Riddle Aeronautical University, Daytona Beach Campus Graduate Program, Department of Aeronautics, Daytona Beach, FL 32114-3900. Offers MSA. Part-time and evening/weekend programs available. *Faculty:* 1 part-time/adjunct (0 women). *Students:* 88 full-time (27 women), 26 part-time (7 women); includes 21 minority (6 African Americans, 6 Asian Americans or Pacific Islanders, 9 Hispanic Americans), 25 international. Average age 27. 93 applicants, 69% accepted, 33 enrolled. In 2009, 20 master's awarded. *Degree requirements:* For master's, thesis optional. *Entrance requirements:* For master's, minimum GPA of 2.5. Additional exam requirements/recommendations for international students: Required—TOEFL (minimum score 550 paper-based; 213 computer-based; 79 iBT). *Application deadline:* For fall admission, 8/1 priority date for domestic students; for spring admission, 12/1 priority date for domestic students. Applications are processed on a rolling basis. Application fee: $50. Electronic applications accepted. *Expenses:* Tuition: Full-time $13,740; part-time $1145 per credit hour. *Financial support:* In 2009–10, 26 students received support, including 7 research assistantships with full and partial tuition reimbursements available (averaging $5,566 per year); teaching assistantships with full and partial tuition reimbursements available, career-related internships or fieldwork, Federal Work-Study, and unspecified assistantships also available. Support available to part-time students. Financial award application deadline: 4/15; financial award applicants required to submit FAFSA. *Unit head:* Dr. Marvin Smith, Program Coordinator, 386-226-6448, Fax: 386-226-6012, E-mail: smithm@erau.edu. *Application contact:* Keith Deaton, Director, International and Graduate Admissions, 800-388-3728, Fax: 386-226-7070, E-mail: graduate.admissions@erau.edu.

Embry-Riddle Aeronautical University, Daytona Beach Campus Graduate Program, Department of Aerospace Engineering, Daytona Beach, FL 32114-3900. Offers MSAE. Part-time and evening/weekend programs available. *Faculty:* 8 full-time (0 women). *Students:* 92 full-time (10 women), 14 part-time (3 women); includes 12 minority (2 African Americans, 6 Asian Americans or Pacific Islanders, 4 Hispanic Americans), 49 international. Average age 24. 107 applicants, 62% accepted, 36 enrolled. In 2009, 33 master's awarded. *Degree requirements:* For master's, thesis optional. *Entrance requirements:* For master's, BS in aeronautical engineering or equivalent; minimum GPA of 3.0 in last 2 undergraduate years, 2.5 overall. Additional exam requirements/recommendations for international students: Required—TOEFL (minimum score 550 paper-based; 213 computer-based; 79 iBT). *Application deadline:* For fall admission, 8/1 priority date for domestic students; for spring admission, 12/1 priority date for domestic students. Applications are processed on a rolling basis. Application fee: $50. Electronic applications accepted. *Expenses:* Tuition: Full-time $13,740; part-time $1145 per credit hour. *Financial support:* In 2009–10, 54 students received support, including 5 research assistantships with full and partial tuition reimbursements available (averaging $6,542 per year), 15 teaching assistantships with full and partial tuition reimbursements available (averaging $6,542 per year); career-related internships or fieldwork, Federal Work-Study, and unspecified assistantships also available. Support available to part-time students. Financial award application deadline: 4/15; financial award applicants required to submit FAFSA. *Faculty research:* Propulsion research: CFD research, composite torque research, establishing software engineering domain expertise, assessment of software tools for safety critical real-time systems, student NASA eagle eye satellite, structural blade testing support, remote airport lighting system (RALS). Total annual research expenditures: $377,487. *Unit head:* Dr. Y. Zhao, Program Coordinator, 386-226-6746, Fax: 386-226-6747. *Application contact:* Keith Deaton, Director, International and Graduate Admissions, 800-388-3728, Fax: 386-226-7070, E-mail: graduate.admissions@erau.edu.

Embry-Riddle Aeronautical University Worldwide, Worldwide Headquarters, Program in Aeronautics, Daytona Beach, FL 32114-3900. Offers MAS. Part-time and evening/weekend programs available. Postbaccalaureate distance learning degree programs offered (minimal on-campus study). *Faculty:* 16 full-time (0 women), 39 part-time/adjunct (4 women). *Students:* 1,140 full-time (149 women), 1,808 part-time (254 women); includes 495 minority (198 African Americans, 28 American Indian/Alaska Native, 98 Asian Americans or Pacific Islanders, 171 Hispanic Americans), 17 international. Average age 34. 1,010 applicants, 82% accepted, 684 enrolled. In 2009, 805 master's awarded. *Degree requirements:* For master's, thesis optional.

Application deadline: Applications are processed on a rolling basis. Application fee: $50. Electronic applications accepted. *Financial support:* In 2009–10, 97 students received support. Available to part-time students. Applicants required to submit FAFSA. *Unit head:* Dr. Katherine Moran, Chair, 360-597-4560, E-mail: morank@erau.edu. *Application contact:* Linda Dammer, Director of Admissions, 386-226-6910, Fax: 386-226-6984, E-mail: ecinfo@erau.edu.

Florida Institute of Technology, Graduate Programs, College of Aeronautics, Melbourne, FL 32901-6975. Offers airport development and management (MSA); applied aviation safety option (MSA); aviation human factors (MS). Part-time and evening/weekend programs available. *Faculty:* 6 full-time (0 women), 2 part-time/adjunct (0 women). *Students:* 22 full-time (6 women), 21 part-time (5 women); includes 1 minority (Asian American or Pacific Islander), 21 international. Average age 27. 34 applicants, 53% accepted, 9 enrolled. In 2009, 8 master's awarded. *Degree requirements:* For master's, thesis (for some programs). *Entrance requirements:* For master's, GRE, minimum GPA of 3.0. Additional exam requirements/recommendations for international students: Required—TOEFL (minimum score 550 paper-based; 213 computer-based; 79 iBT). *Application deadline:* For fall admission, 4/1 for international students; for spring admission, 9/30 for international students. Applications are processed on a rolling basis. Application fee: $50. Electronic applications accepted. *Expenses:* Tuition: Part-time $1015 per credit. Tuition and fees vary according to campus/location and program. *Financial support:* Career-related internships or fieldwork, institutionally sponsored loans, tuition waivers (partial), and tuition remissions available. Support available to part-time students. Financial award application deadline: 3/1; financial award applicants required to submit FAFSA. *Faculty research:* Aircraft cockpit design, medical human factors, operating room human factors, hypobaric chamber operations and effects, aviation professional education. Total annual research expenditures: $49,349. *Unit head:* Dr. Winston E. Scott, Dean, 321-674-8971, Fax: 321-674-7368, E-mail: wscott@fit.edu. *Application contact:* Thomas M. Shea, Director of Graduate Admissions, 321-674-7577, Fax: 321-723-9468, E-mail: tshea@fit.edu.

See Close-Up on page 107.

Florida Institute of Technology, Graduate Programs, College of Business, Extended Studies Division, Melbourne, FL 32901-6975. Offers acquisition and contract management (PMBA); business administration (PMBA); computer information systems (MS); e-business (PMBA); human resource management (PMBA); human resources management (MS); logistics management (MS), including humanitarian and disaster relief logistics; management (MS), including acquisition and contract management, e-business, human resource management, information systems, logistics management, management, transportation management; material acquisition management (MS); project management (MS), including information systems, operations research; public administration (MPA); quality management (MS); space management (MS); space systems (MS); systems management (MS), including information systems, operations research, systems management. Part-time and evening/weekend programs available. Postbaccalaureate distance learning degree programs offered (no on-campus study). *Faculty:* 12 full-time (3 women), 117 part-time/adjunct (20 women). *Students:* 74 full-time (32 women), 1,041 part-time (484 women); includes 343 minority (240 African Americans, 12 American Indian/Alaska Native, 44 Asian Americans or Pacific Islanders, 47 Hispanic Americans), 22 international. Average age 35. 520 applicants, 72% accepted, 279 enrolled. In 2009, 509 master's awarded. *Degree requirements:* For master's, capstone course. *Entrance requirements:* For master's, GMAT or resume showing 8 years of supervised experience, minimum GPA of 3.0, 2 letters of recommendation, resume. Additional exam requirements/recommendations for international students: Required—TOEFL (minimum score 550 paper-based; 213 computer-based; 79 iBT). *Application deadline:* For fall admission, 4/1 for international students; for spring admission, 9/30 for international students. Applications are processed on a rolling basis. Application fee: $50. Electronic applications accepted. *Expenses:* Tuition: Part-time $1015 per credit. Tuition and fees vary according to campus/location and program. *Financial support:* Application deadline: 3/1; *Unit head:* Dr. Clifford Bragdon, Dean, 321-674-8821, Fax: 321-674-7597, E-mail: cbragdon@fit.edu. *Application contact:* Carolyn Farrior, Director of Graduate Admissions Online Learning and Off Campus Programs, 321-674-7118, Fax: 321-674-8216, E-mail: cfarrior@fit.edu.

Florida Institute of Technology, Graduate Programs, College of Engineering, Mechanical and Aerospace Engineering Department, Melbourne, FL 32901-6975. Offers aerospace engineering (MS, PhD); mechanical engineering (MS, PhD). Part-time programs available. *Faculty:* 13 full-time (1 woman). *Students:* 58 full-time (1 woman), 34 part-time (3 women); includes 7 minority (1 African American, 3 Asian Americans or Pacific Islanders, 3 Hispanic Americans), 42 international. Average age 27. 206 applicants, 59% accepted, 43 enrolled. In 2009, 14 master's, 1 doctorate awarded. *Degree requirements:* For master's, comprehensive exam (for some programs), thesis optional; for doctorate, comprehensive exam, thesis/dissertation, oral section of written exam, complete program of significant original research. *Entrance requirements:* For master's, GRE General Test, minimum GPA of 3.0, bachelor's degree from an ABET-accredited program; for doctorate, GRE General Test, 3 letters of recommendation, minimum GPA of 3.5, resume, statement of objectives. Additional exam requirements/recommendations for international students: Required—TOEFL (minimum score 550 paper-based; 213 computer-based; 79 iBT). *Application deadline:* For fall admission, 4/1 for international students; for spring admission, 9/30 for international students. Applications are processed on a rolling basis. Application fee: $50. Electronic applications accepted. *Expenses:* Tuition: Part-time $1015 per credit. Tuition and fees vary according to campus/location and program. *Financial support:* In 2009–10, 15 students received support, including 4 research assistantships with full and partial tuition reimbursements available (averaging $3,002 per year), 11 teaching assistantships with full and partial tuition reimbursements available (averaging $3,041 per year); career-related internships or fieldwork, institutionally sponsored loans, tuition waivers (partial), unspecified assistantships, and tuition remissions also available. Support available to part-time students. Financial award application deadline: 3/1; financial award applicants required to submit FAFSA. *Faculty research:* Dynamic systems, robotics, and controls; structures, solid mechanics, and materials; thermal-fluid sciences, optical tomography, composite/recycled materials. Total annual research expenditures: $731,514. *Unit head:* Dr. Pei-feng Hsu, Department Head, 321-674-8092, Fax: 321-674-8813, E-mail: phsu@fit.edu. *Application contact:* Thomas M. Shea, Director of Graduate Admissions, 321-674-7577, Fax: 321-723-9468, E-mail: tshea@fit.edu.

See Close-Up on page 521.

The George Washington University, School of Engineering and Applied Science, Department of Mechanical and Aerospace Engineering, Washington, DC 20052. Offers MS, D Sc, App Sc, Engr, Graduate Certificate. Part-time and evening/weekend programs available. *Faculty:* 11 full-time (0 women), 10 part-time/adjunct (1 woman). *Students:* 30 full-time (6 women), 36 part-time (7 women); includes 9 minority (2 African Americans, 1 American Indian/Alaska Native, 6 Asian Americans or Pacific Islanders), 27 international. Average age 29. 84 applicants, 93% accepted, 18 enrolled. In 2009, 11 master's, 6 doctorates awarded. *Degree requirements:* For master's, thesis optional; for doctorate, thesis/dissertation, final and qualifying exams. *Entrance requirements:* For master's, appropriate bachelor's degree, minimum GPA of 3.0; for doctorate, appropriate bachelor's or master's degree, minimum GPA of 3.4, GRE if highest earned degree is BS; for other advanced degree, appropriate master's degree, minimum GPA of 3.0. Additional exam requirements/recommendations for international students: Required—TOEFL or George Washington University English as a Foreign Language Test. *Application deadline:* For fall admission, 3/1 priority date for domestic students; for spring admission, 10/1 for domestic students. Applications are processed on a rolling basis. Application fee: $60. *Financial support:* In 2009–10, 51 students received support; fellowships with tuition reimbursements available, research assistantships, teaching assistantships with tuition reimbursements available, career-related internships or fieldwork and institutionally sponsored loans available. Financial award application deadline: 3/1; financial award applicants required to submit FAFSA. *Unit head:* Dr. Michael Plesniak, Chairman, 202-994-6749, E-mail: maeng@gwu.edu. *Application contact:* Adina Lav, Marketing, Recruiting and Admissions, 202-994-5827, Fax: 202-994-0909, E-mail: engineering@gwu.edu.

Georgia Institute of Technology, Graduate Studies and Research, College of Engineering, School of Aerospace Engineering, Atlanta, GA 30332-0001. Offers MS, MSAE, PhD. Part-time programs available. Terminal master's awarded for partial completion of doctoral program. *Degree requirements:* For master's, thesis optional; for doctorate, thesis/dissertation. *Entrance requirements:* For master's, GRE, minimum GPA of 3.0; for doctorate, GRE, minimum GPA of 3.25. Additional exam requirements/recommendations for international students: Required—TOEFL. *Faculty research:* Structural mechanics and dynamics, fluid mechanics, flight mechanics and controls, combustion and propulsion, system design and optimization.

Illinois Institute of Technology, Graduate College, Armour College of Engineering, Department of Mechanical, Materials and Aerospace Engineering, Chicago, IL 60616-3793. Offers manufacturing engineering (MME, MS); materials science and engineering (MMME, MS, PhD); mechanical and aerospace engineering (MMAE, MS, PhD). Part-time programs available. Terminal master's awarded for partial completion of doctoral program. *Degree requirements:* For master's, comprehensive exam (for some programs), thesis (for some programs); for doctorate, comprehensive exam, thesis/dissertation. *Entrance requirements:* For master's and doctorate, GRE General Test, minimum undergraduate GPA of 3.0. Additional exam requirements/recommendations for international students: Required—TOEFL (minimum score 550 paper-based; 213 computer-based; 80 iBT). Electronic applications accepted. *Expenses:* Tuition: Full-time $17,550; part-time $888 per credit hour. Required fees: $850; $7.50 per credit hour. One-time fee: $50 full-time. Full-time tuition and fees vary according to program. *Faculty research:* Active flow control, bio-fluid dynamics, acoustics and separated flows, digital design and manufacturing and high performance materials, two-phase flows in micro scales and combustion-driven MEMS, global positioning systems, experimental and computational solid mechanics.

Iowa State University of Science and Technology, Graduate College, College of Engineering, Department of Aerospace Engineering and Engineering Mechanics, Ames, IA 50011. Offers aerospace engineering (M Eng, MS, PhD); engineering mechanics (M Eng, MS, PhD). *Faculty:* 28 full-time (1 woman), 3 part-time/adjunct (0 women). *Students:* 50 full-time (7 women), 2 part-time (0 women); includes 4 minority (3 Asian Americans or Pacific Islanders, 1 Hispanic American), 33 international. 121 applicants, 24% accepted, 18 enrolled. In 2009, 15 master's, 8 doctorates awarded. *Degree requirements:* For master's, thesis (for some programs); for doctorate, thesis/dissertation. *Entrance requirements:* For master's and doctorate, GRE General Test, resume. Additional exam requirements/recommendations for international students: Required—TOEFL (minimum score 550 paper-based; 80 iBT) or IELTS (minimum score 6.5). *Application deadline:* For fall admission, 1/1 priority date for domestic and international students; for spring admission, 9/1 priority date for domestic and international students. Application fee: $40 ($90 for international students). Electronic applications accepted. *Expenses:* Tuition, state resident: full-time $6716. Tuition, nonresident: full-time $8908. Tuition and fees vary according to course level, course load, program and student level. *Financial support:* In 2009–10, 30 research assistantships with full and partial tuition reimbursements (averaging $15,000 per year), 18 teaching assistantships with full and partial tuition reimbursements (averaging $15,000 per year) were awarded; fellowships, scholarships/grants, health care benefits, and unspecified assistantships also available. *Unit head:* Dr. Thomas Rudolphi, Interim Chair, 515-294-5666, E-mail: aere_@iastate.edu. *Application contact:* Dr. Alric Rothmayer, Director of Graduate Education, 515-294-8851, E-mail: aere_info@iastate.edu.

Massachusetts Institute of Technology, School of Engineering, Department of Aeronautics and Astronautics, Cambridge, MA 02139-4307. Offers aeronautics and astronautics (SM, PhD, Sc D, EAA); aerospace computational engineering (PhD, Sc D); air transportation systems (PhD, Sc D); air-breathing propulsion (PhD, Sc D); aircraft systems engineering (PhD, Sc D); autonomous systems (PhD, Sc D); communications and networks (PhD, Sc D); controls (PhD, Sc D); humans in aerospace (PhD, Sc D); materials and structures (PhD, Sc D); space propulsion (PhD, Sc D); space systems (PhD, Sc D); SM/MBA. *Faculty:* 32 full-time (7 women). *Students:* 227 full-time (49 women), 2 part-time (0 women); includes 36 minority (4 African Americans, 1 American Indian/Alaska Native, 25 Asian Americans or Pacific Islanders, 6 Hispanic Americans), 88 international. Average age 26. 358 applicants, 20% accepted, 39 enrolled. In 2009, 54 master's, 23 doctorates awarded. *Degree requirements:* For master's and EAA, thesis; for doctorate, comprehensive exam, thesis/dissertation. *Entrance requirements:* For master's and doctorate, GRE General Test. Additional exam requirements/recommendations for international students: Required—TOEFL (minimum score 600 paper-based; 250 computer-based; 100 iBT), IELTS (minimum score 7). *Application deadline:* For fall admission, 12/15 for domestic and international students. Application fee: $75. Electronic applications accepted. *Financial support:* In 2009–10, 221 students received support, including 28 fellowships with tuition reimbursements available (averaging $24,767 per year), 156 research assistantships with tuition reimbursements available (averaging $27,050 per year), 17 teaching assistantships with tuition reimbursements available (averaging $29,530 per year); Federal Work-Study, institutionally sponsored loans, scholarships/grants, health care benefits, and unspecified assistantships also available. *Faculty research:* Aerospace information engineering, aerospace systems engineering, aerospace vehicles engineering. Total annual research expenditures: $19.3 million. *Unit head:* Prof. Ian A. Waitz, Department Head, 617-258-7537, Fax: 617-258-7566. *Application contact:* Graduate Administrator, 617-253-0043, Fax: 617-253-0823, E-mail: aa-studentservices@mit.edu.

McGill University, Faculty of Graduate and Postdoctoral Studies, Faculty of Engineering, Department of Mechanical Engineering, Montréal, QC H3A 2T5, Canada. Offers aerospace (M Eng); manufacturing management (MMM); mechanical engineering (M Eng, M Sc, PhD).

Middle Tennessee State University, College of Graduate Studies, College of Basic and Applied Sciences, Department of Aerospace, Murfreesboro, TN 37132. Offers aerospace education (M Ed); aviation administration (MS). Part-time and evening/weekend programs available. Postbaccalaureate distance learning degree programs offered. *Faculty:* 4 full-time (1 woman). *Students:* 9 full-time (3 women), 13 part-time (3 women); includes 8 minority (6 African Americans, 2 Asian Americans or Pacific Islanders). Average age 28. 15 applicants, 67% accepted, 10 enrolled. *Degree requirements:* For master's, one foreign language, comprehensive exam. *Entrance requirements:* For master's, GRE General Test or MAT. Additional exam requirements/recommendations for international students: Required—TOEFL (minimum score 525 paper-based; 195 computer-based; 71 iBT) or IELTS (minimum score 6). *Application deadline:* For fall admission, 6/1 for domestic and international students. Applications are processed on a rolling basis. Application fee: $25 ($30 for international students). Electronic applications accepted. *Expenses:* Tuition, state resident: full-time $4404. Tuition, nonresident: full-time $10,956. *Financial support:* In 2009–10, 4 students received support. Institutionally sponsored loans available. Support available to part-time students. Financial award application deadline: 5/1. *Unit head:* Dr. Wayne Dornan, Chair, 615-898-2788, E-mail: wdornan@mtsu.edu. *Application contact:* Dr. Wayne Dornan, Chair, 615-898-2788, E-mail: wdornan@mtsu.edu.

Mississippi State University, Bagley College of Engineering, Department of Aerospace Engineering, Mississippi State, MS 39762. Offers aerospace engineering (MS); engineering (PhD), including aerospace engineering. Part-time programs available. *Faculty:* 10 full-time (0 women), 1 part-time/adjunct (0 women). *Students:* 25 full-time (2 women), 7 part-time (1 woman); includes 2 minority (both African Americans), 13 international. Average age 28. 24 applicants, 46% accepted, 2 enrolled. In 2009, 9 master's, 2 doctorates awarded. *Degree requirements:* For master's, comprehensive exam, thesis; for doctorate, comprehensive exam, thesis/dissertation. *Entrance requirements:* For master's, GRE, bachelor's degree in engineering; for doctorate, GRE, bachelor's or master's degree in engineering. Additional exam requirements/recommendations for international students: Required—TOEFL (minimum score 550 paper-based; 213 computer-based; 79 iBT); Recommended—IELTS (minimum score 6.5). *Application deadline:* For fall admission, 7/1 for domestic students, 5/1 for international students; for spring admission, 11/1 for domestic students, 9/1 for international students. Applications are processed on a rolling basis. Application fee: $40. Electronic applications accepted. *Expenses:* Tuition, state resident: full-time $2575.50; part-time $286.25 per credit hour. Tuition, nonresident:

Aerospace/Aeronautical Engineering

Mississippi State University (continued)
full-time $6510; part-time $723.50 per credit hour. Tuition and fees vary according to course load. *Financial support:* In 2009–10, 17 research assistantships with partial tuition reimbursements (averaging $11,000 per year), 3 teaching assistantships with partial tuition reimbursements (averaging $14,435 per year) were awarded; Federal Work-Study, institutionally sponsored loans, and unspecified assistantships also available. Financial award application deadline: 4/4; financial award applicants required to submit FAFSA. *Faculty research:* Computational fluid dynamics, flight mechanics, aerodynamics, composite structures, prototype development. Total annual research expenditures: $1.1 million. *Unit head:* Dr. Pasquale J. Cinnella, Department Head, 662-325-3623, Fax: 662-325-7730, E-mail: cinnella@ae.msstate.edu. *Application contact:* Dr. Mark Janus, Professor and Graduate Coordinator, 662-325-2463, Fax: 662-325-7730, E-mail: mark@hpc.msstate.edu.

Missouri University of Science and Technology, Graduate School, Department of Mechanical and Aerospace Engineering, Rolla, MO 65409. Offers aerospace engineering (MS, PhD); mechanical engineering (MS, DE, PhD). Part-time and evening/weekend programs available. Terminal master's awarded for partial completion of doctoral program. *Degree requirements:* For master's, thesis optional; for doctorate, comprehensive exam, thesis/dissertation. *Entrance requirements:* For master's, GRE General Test (minimum score 1100 verbal and quantitative, writing 3.5), minimum GPA of 3.0; for doctorate, GRE General Test (minimum score: verbal and quantitative 1100, writing 3.5), minimum GPA of 3.5. Additional exam requirements/recommendations for international students: Required—TOEFL. Electronic applications accepted. *Faculty research:* Dynamics and controls, acoustics, computational fluid dynamics, space mechanics, hypersonics.

Naval Postgraduate School, Graduate Programs, Space Systems Academic Group, Monterey, CA 93943. Offers space systems operations (MS). Program only open to commissioned officers of the United States and friendly nations and selected United States federal civilian employees. Part-time programs available. *Degree requirements:* For master's, thesis.

North Carolina State University, Graduate School, College of Engineering, Department of Mechanical and Aerospace Engineering, Program in Aerospace Engineering, Raleigh, NC 27695. Offers MS, PhD. Postbaccalaureate distance learning degree programs offered (no on-campus study). *Degree requirements:* For master's, thesis (for some programs), oral exam; for doctorate, thesis/dissertation, oral and preliminary exams. *Entrance requirements:* For master's and doctorate, GRE General Test. Additional exam requirements/recommendations for international students: Required—TOEFL (minimum score 550 paper-based; 213 computer-based). Electronic applications accepted. *Faculty research:* Aerodynamics, computational fluid dynamics, flight research, smart structures, propulsion.

See Close-Up on page 523.

The Ohio State University, Graduate School, College of Engineering, Program in Aeronautical and Astronautical Engineering, Columbus, OH 43210. Offers MS, PhD. *Faculty:* 14. *Students:* 26 full-time (2 women), 16 part-time (3 women); includes 4 minority (all Asian Americans or Pacific Islanders), 8 international. Average age 26. In 2009, 17 master's, 2 doctorates awarded. *Degree requirements:* For master's, thesis optional; for doctorate, thesis/dissertation. *Entrance requirements:* For master's and doctorate, GRE General Test. Additional exam requirements/recommendations for international students: Recommended—TOEFL (minimum score 600 paper-based; 250 computer-based). *Application deadline:* For fall admission, 8/15 priority date for domestic students, 7/1 priority date for international students; for winter admission, 12/1 priority date for domestic students, 11/1 priority date for international students; for spring admission, 3/1 priority date for domestic students, 2/1 priority date for international students. Applications are processed on a rolling basis. Application fee: $40 ($50 for international students). Electronic applications accepted. *Expenses:* Tuition, state resident: full-time $10,683. Tuition, nonresident: full-time $25,923. Tuition and fees vary according to course load and program. *Financial support:* Fellowships, research assistantships, teaching assistantships, career-related internships or fieldwork, Federal Work-Study, institutionally sponsored loans, and unspecified assistantships also available. *Unit head:* Mo-How Shen, Graduate Studies Committee Chair, E-mail: shen.1@osu.edu. *Application contact:* 614-292-9444, Fax: 614-292-3895, E-mail: domestic.grad@osu.edu.

Old Dominion University, Frank Batten College of Engineering and Technology, Programs in Aerospace Engineering, Norfolk, VA 23529. Offers ME, MS, D Eng, PhD. Part-time and evening/weekend programs available. Postbaccalaureate distance learning degree programs offered (no on-campus study). *Faculty:* 10 full-time (0 women), 8 part-time/adjunct (0 women). *Students:* 41 full-time (3 women), 26 part-time (7 women); includes 6 minority (3 African Americans, 2 Asian Americans or Pacific Islanders, 1 Hispanic American), 35 international. Average age 26. 50 applicants, 60% accepted, 10 enrolled. In 2009, 9 master's, 4 doctorates awarded. *Degree requirements:* For master's, comprehensive exam, thesis (MS), exam/project (ME); for doctorate, thesis/dissertation, candidacy exam, proposal, exam. *Entrance requirements:* For master's, GRE, minimum GPA of 3.0; for doctorate, GRE, minimum GPA of 3.5. Additional exam requirements/recommendations for international students: Required—TOEFL (minimum score 550 paper-based; 230 computer-based; 79 iBT). *Application deadline:* For fall admission, 7/1 priority date for domestic students, 5/1 priority date for international students; for spring admission, 10/1 priority date for domestic students, 9/1 priority date for international students. Applications are processed on a rolling basis. Application fee: $40. Electronic applications accepted. *Expenses:* Tuition, state resident: full-time $8112; part-time $338 per credit. Tuition, nonresident: full-time $20,256; part-time $844 per credit. Required fees: $119 per semester. One-time fee: $50. *Financial support:* In 2009–10, 4 students received support, including 3 fellowships with full and partial tuition reimbursements available (averaging $17,000 per year), 30 research assistantships with full and partial tuition reimbursements available (averaging $17,000 per year); career-related internships or fieldwork, scholarships/grants, and unspecified assistantships also available. Financial award application deadline: 2/15; financial award applicants required to submit FAFSA. *Faculty research:* Computational fluid dynamics, experimental fluid dynamics, structural mechanics, dynamics and control, maglev, microfluidics. Total annual research expenditures: $1.6 million. *Unit head:* Dr. Colin Britcher, Chair, 757-683-4916, Fax: 757-683-3200, E-mail: britcher@aero.odu.edu. *Application contact:* Dr. Brett Newman, Graduate Program Director, 757-683-5860, Fax: 757-683-3200, E-mail: aeroinfo@odu.edu.

Penn State University Park, Graduate School, College of Engineering, Department of Aerospace Engineering, State College, University Park, PA 16802-1503. Offers M Eng, MS, PhD.

Polytechnic Institute of NYU, Long Island Graduate Center, Graduate Programs, Department of Mechanical and Aerospace Engineering, Melville, NY 11747. Offers aeronautics and astronautics (MS); industrial engineering (MS); manufacturing engineering (MS); mechanical engineering (MS). Part-time and evening/weekend programs available. *Students:* 1 (woman) part-time. Average age 25. In 2009, 2 master's awarded. *Degree requirements:* For master's, comprehensive exam (for some programs), thesis (for some programs). *Entrance requirements:* Additional exam requirements/recommendations for international students: Required—TOEFL (minimum score 550 paper-based; 213 computer-based; 80 iBT); Recommended—IELTS (minimum score 6.5). *Application deadline:* For fall admission, 7/31 priority date for domestic students, 4/30 priority date for international students; for spring admission, 12/31 priority date for domestic students, 11/30 priority date for international students. Applications are processed on a rolling basis. Application fee: $75. Electronic applications accepted. *Financial support:* In 2009–10, 16 fellowships with tuition reimbursements (averaging $1,394 per year) were awarded; research assistantships with tuition reimbursements, institutionally sponsored loans, scholarships/grants, and unspecified assistantships also available. Support available to part-time students. Financial award applicants required to submit FAFSA. *Faculty research:* UV filter, fuel efficient hydrodynamic containment for gas core fission, turbulent boundary layer research. *Unit head:* Dr. George Vradis, Department Head, 718-260-3875, E-mail: gvradis@duke.poly.edu. *Application contact:* JeanCarlo Bonilla, Director of Graduate Enrollment Management, 718-260-3182, Fax: 718-260-3624, E-mail: gradinfo@poly.edu.

Princeton University, Graduate School, School of Engineering and Applied Science, Department of Mechanical and Aerospace Engineering, Princeton, NJ 08544. Offers M Eng, MSE, PhD. *Faculty:* 23 full-time (2 women). Terminal master's awarded for partial completion of doctoral program. *Degree requirements:* For master's, thesis (MSE); for doctorate, thesis/dissertation, general exam. *Entrance requirements:* For master's, GRE General Test, 3 letters of recommendation; for doctorate, GRE General Test, official transcript(s), 3 letters of recommendation, personal statement. Additional exam requirements/recommendations for international students: Required—TOEFL. *Application deadline:* For fall admission, 12/15 for domestic and international students. Application fee: $90. Electronic applications accepted. *Financial support:* Fellowships with full tuition reimbursements, research assistantships with full tuition reimbursements, teaching assistantships with full tuition reimbursements, institutionally sponsored loans and health care benefits available. *Faculty research:* Bioengineering and bio-mechanics; combustion, energy conversion, and climate; fluid mechanics, dynamics, and control systems; lasers and applied physics; materials and mechanical systems. *Unit head:* Jessica O'Leary, Graduate Program Administrator, 609-258-4683, Fax: 609-258-6109, E-mail: maegrad@princeton.edu. *Application contact:* Michelle Carman, Manager of Graduate Admissions, 609-258-3034, Fax: 609-258-7262, E-mail: gsadmit@princeton.edu.

Purdue University, College of Engineering, School of Aeronautics and Astronautics Engineering, West Lafayette, IN 47907. Offers MS, MSAAE, MSE, PhD. Part-time programs available. Postbaccalaureate distance learning degree programs offered (no on-campus study). Terminal master's awarded for partial completion of doctoral program. *Entrance requirements:* For master's, GRE General Test, minimum GPA of 3.2; for doctorate, GRE General Test, minimum GPA of 3.5. Additional exam requirements/recommendations for international students: Required—TOEFL (minimum score 550 paper-based; 213 computer-based; 77 iBT), IELTS (minimum score 6.5); Recommended—TWE. Electronic applications accepted. *Faculty research:* Structures and materials, propulsion, aerodynamics, dynamics and control.

Rensselaer Polytechnic Institute, Graduate School, School of Engineering, Department of Mechanical, Aerospace, and Nuclear Engineering, Program in Aerospace Engineering, Troy, NY 12180-3590. Offers M Eng, MS, PhD. Part-time programs available. *Faculty:* 4 full-time (0 women), 1 part-time/adjunct (0 women). *Students:* 23 full-time (0 women), 7 international. Average age 27. 30 applicants, 53% accepted, 4 enrolled. In 2009, 1 master's, 1 doctorate awarded. *Degree requirements:* For master's, thesis (for some programs); for doctorate, thesis/dissertation. *Entrance requirements:* For master's and doctorate, GRE. Additional exam requirements/recommendations for international students: Required—TOEFL (minimum score 600 paper-based; 250 computer-based; 100 iBT); Recommended—IELTS. *Application deadline:* For fall admission, 1/15 priority date for domestic and international students; for spring admission, 1/15 for domestic and international students. Applications are processed on a rolling basis. Application fee: $75. Electronic applications accepted. *Expenses:* Tuition: Full-time $38,100. *Financial support:* In 2009–10, 7 students received support, including 1 fellowship with full tuition reimbursement available (averaging $22,000 per year), 13 research assistantships with full tuition reimbursements available (averaging $16,500 per year), 6 teaching assistantships with full tuition reimbursements available (averaging $16,500 per year); career-related internships or fieldwork, tuition waivers, and unspecified assistantships also available. Financial award application deadline: 2/1. *Faculty research:* Vehicular performance and flight mechanics, gas dynamics, aerodynamics, structural dynamics, advanced propulsion, fluids. Total annual research expenditures: $937,713. *Unit head:* Dr. Timothy Wei, Head, 518-276-6351, Fax: 518-276-6025, E-mail: weit@rpi.edu. *Application contact:* Dr. Thierry A. Blanchet, Associate Chair for Graduate Studies, 518-276-8697, Fax: 518-276-2623, E-mail: blanct@rpi.edu.

Rutgers, The State University of New Jersey, New Brunswick, Graduate School-New Brunswick, Program in Mechanical and Aerospace Engineering, Piscataway, NJ 08854-8097. Offers design and control (MS, PhD); fluid mechanics (MS, PhD); solid mechanics (MS, PhD); thermal sciences (MS, PhD). Part-time and evening/weekend programs available. *Degree requirements:* For master's, thesis (for some programs); for doctorate, thesis/dissertation. *Entrance requirements:* For master's, GRE General Test, BS in mechanical/aerospace engineering or related field; for doctorate, GRE General Test, MS in mechanical/aerospace engineering or related field. Additional exam requirements/recommendations for international students: Required—TOEFL. Electronic applications accepted. *Faculty research:* Combustion, propulsion, thermal transport, crystal plasticity, optimization, fabrication, nanoidentation.

San Diego State University, Graduate and Research Affairs, College of Engineering, Department of Aerospace Engineering and Engineering Mechanics, San Diego, CA 92182. Offers aerospace engineering (MS); engineering mechanics (MS); engineering sciences and applied mechanics (PhD); flight dynamics (MS); fluid dynamics (MS). Terminal master's awarded for partial completion of doctoral program. *Degree requirements:* For master's, comprehensive exam (for some programs), thesis (for some programs); for doctorate, thesis/dissertation. *Entrance requirements:* For master's, GRE General Test; for doctorate, GRE, 3 letters of recommendation. Additional exam requirements/recommendations for international students: Required—TOEFL. Electronic applications accepted. *Faculty research:* Organized structures in post-stall flow over wings/three dimensional separated flow, airfoil growth effect, probabilities, structural mechanics.

San Jose State University, Graduate Studies and Research, Charles W. Davidson College of Engineering, Department of Mechanical and Aerospace Engineering, Program in Aerospace Engineering, San Jose, CA 95192-0001. Offers MS. *Students:* 17 full-time (1 woman), 9 part-time (1 woman); includes 11 minority (1 American Indian/Alaska Native, 8 Asian Americans or Pacific Islanders, 2 Hispanic Americans), 6 international. Average age 27. 29 applicants, 76% accepted, 14 enrolled. In 2009, 7 master's awarded. *Entrance requirements:* For master's, GRE. *Application deadline:* For fall admission, 6/29 for domestic students; for spring admission, 11/30 for domestic students. Applications are processed on a rolling basis. Application fee: $59. Electronic applications accepted. *Financial support:* Applicants required to submit FAFSA. *Unit head:* Dr. Raghu Agarwal, Graduate Coordinator, 408-924-3845. *Application contact:* Dr. Raghu Agarwal, Graduate Coordinator, 408-924-3845.

Stanford University, School of Engineering, Department of Aeronautics and Astronautics, Stanford, CA 94305-9991. Offers MS, PhD, Eng. Terminal master's awarded for partial completion of doctoral program. *Degree requirements:* For doctorate, thesis/dissertation; for Eng, thesis. *Entrance requirements:* For master's and Eng, GRE General Test, GRE Subject Test; for doctorate, GRE General Test, GRE Engineering Subject Test. Additional exam requirements/recommendations for international students: Required—TOEFL. Electronic applications accepted. *Expenses:* Tuition: Full-time $37,380; part-time $2760 per quarter. Required fees: $501.

Stevens Institute of Technology, Graduate School, School of Systems and Enterprises, Program in Space Systems Engineering, Hoboken, NJ 07030. Offers M Eng, Certificate. *Expenses:* Tuition: Full-time $9900; part-time $1100 per credit. Required fees: $286 per semester.

Syracuse University, L. C. Smith College of Engineering and Computer Science, Program in Mechanical and Aerospace Engineering, Syracuse, NY 13244. Offers MS, PhD. *Students:* 67 full-time (14 women), 16 part-time (2 women); includes 6 minority (4 Asian Americans or Pacific Islanders, 2 Hispanic Americans), 59 international. Average age 27. 143 applicants, 48% accepted, 28 enrolled. In 2009, 27 master's, 3 doctorates awarded. *Degree requirements:* For master's, project or thesis; for doctorate, thesis/dissertation. *Entrance requirements:* For master's and doctorate, GRE General Test. Additional exam requirements/recommendations for international students: Required—TOEFL (minimum score 100 iBT). *Application deadline:* For fall admission, 6/1 priority date for domestic and international students. Applications are processed on a rolling basis. Application fee: $75. Electronic applications accepted. *Expenses:* Tuition: Full-time $26,808; part-time $1117 per credit. Required fees: $1024. *Financial support:* Fellowships with full tuition reimbursements, research assistantships with full and partial tuition reimbursements, teaching assistantships with full and partial tuition reimbursements, scholarships/grants and tuition waivers (partial) available. Financial award application deadline: 1/1. *Faculty research:* Solid mechanics and materials, fluid mechanics, thermal sciences, controls and robotics. *Unit head:* Dr. Alan Levy, Chair, 315-443-4311, Fax: 315-443-9099. *Application contact:* Kathy Datthyn-Madigan, Information Contact, 315-443-4367, E-mail: kjdatthy@syr.edu.

Texas A&M University, College of Engineering, Department of Aerospace Engineering, College Station, TX 77843. Offers M Eng, MS, PhD. *Faculty:* 26. *Students:* 128 full-time (22 women), 14 part-time (1 woman); includes 15 minority (2 African Americans, 3 Asian Americans or Pacific Islanders, 10 Hispanic Americans), 48 international. Average age 27. In 2009, 15 master's, 10 doctorates awarded. *Degree requirements:* For master's, thesis (MS); for doctorate, thesis/dissertation. *Entrance requirements:* For master's and doctorate, GRE General Test. Additional exam requirements/recommendations for international students: Required—TOEFL. *Application deadline:* For fall admission, 1/15 priority date for domestic students; for spring admission, 9/15 for domestic students. Applications are processed on a rolling basis. Application fee: $50 ($75 for international students). Electronic applications accepted. *Expenses:* Tuition, state resident: full-time $3991.32; part-time $221.74 per credit hour. Tuition, nonresident: full-time $9049; part-time $502.74 per credit hour. *Financial support:* Fellowships, research assistantships, teaching assistantships available. Financial award application deadline: 3/1; financial award applicants required to submit FAFSA. *Faculty research:* Materials and structures, aerodynamics and CFD, flight dynamics and control. *Unit head:* Dr. Walter Haisler, Head, 979-854-7261, E-mail: haisler@tamu.edu. *Application contact:* Dr., Graduate Adviser, 979-845-5520, Fax: 979-845-6051.

Université Laval, Faculty of Sciences and Engineering, Department of Mechanical Engineering, Program in Aerospace Engineering, Québec, QC G1K 7P4, Canada. Offers M Sc. Part-time programs available. *Entrance requirements:* For master's, knowledge of French and English. Electronic applications accepted.

University at Buffalo, the State University of New York, Graduate School, School of Engineering and Applied Sciences, Department of Mechanical and Aerospace Engineering, Buffalo, NY 14260. Offers aerospace engineering (MS, PhD); mechanical engineering (MS, PhD). Part-time programs available. *Faculty:* 26 full-time (4 women), 8 part-time/adjunct (0 women). *Students:* 204 full-time (19 women), 66 part-time (8 women); includes 17 minority (3 African Americans, 11 Asian Americans or Pacific Islanders, 3 Hispanic Americans), 148 international. Average age 27. 773 applicants, 17% accepted, 90 enrolled. In 2009, 59 master's, 10 doctorates awarded. Terminal master's awarded for partial completion of doctoral program. *Degree requirements:* For master's, comprehensive exam, project or thesis; for doctorate, thesis/dissertation. *Entrance requirements:* For master's and doctorate, GRE General Test, GRE Subject Test. Additional exam requirements/recommendations for international students: Required—TOEFL (minimum score 79 iBT). *Application deadline:* For fall admission, 1/15 for domestic and international students; for spring admission, 9/15 for domestic and international students. Applications are processed on a rolling basis. Application fee: $50. *Financial support:* In 2009–10, 157 students received support, including 5 fellowships with full tuition reimbursements available (averaging $28,900 per year), 25 research assistantships with full tuition reimbursements available (averaging $24,000 per year), 30 teaching assistantships with full tuition reimbursements available (averaging $20,900 per year); Federal Work-Study, institutionally sponsored loans, tuition waivers (partial), and unspecified assistantships also available. Financial award application deadline: 1/15; financial award applicants required to submit FAFSA. *Faculty research:* Fluid and thermal sciences, systems and design, mechanics and materials. Total annual research expenditures: $6.2 million. *Unit head:* Dr. Gary Dargush, Chair, 716-645-2593, Fax: 716-645-2883, E-mail: gdargush@buffalo.edu. *Application contact:* Dr. Zonglu (Susan) Hua, Director of Graduate Studies, 716-645-1471, Fax: 716-645-3875, E-mail: zhua@buffalo.edu.

The University of Alabama, Graduate School, College of Engineering, Department of Aerospace Engineering and Mechanics, Tuscaloosa, AL 35487. Offers aerospace engineering (MAE); engineering science and mechanics (MES, PhD). Part-time programs available. Post-baccalaureate distance learning degree programs offered (no on-campus study). *Faculty:* 14 full-time (1 woman). *Students:* 26 full-time (5 women), 21 part-time (4 women); includes 1 minority (Hispanic American), 19 international. Average age 27. 52 applicants, 52% accepted, 20 enrolled. In 2009, 8 degrees awarded. Terminal master's awarded for partial completion of doctoral program. *Degree requirements:* For master's, comprehensive exam (for some programs), thesis (for some programs); for doctorate, comprehensive exam, thesis/dissertation, 1 year residency. *Entrance requirements:* For master's and doctorate, GRE, minimum undergraduate GPA of 3.0. Additional exam requirements/recommendations for international students: Required—TOEFL (minimum score 550 paper-based). *Application deadline:* For fall admission, 7/1 priority date for domestic students, 1/15 priority date for international students; for spring admission, 11/1 priority date for domestic students, 6/1 priority date for international students. Applications are processed on a rolling basis. Application fee: $50 ($60 for international students). Electronic applications accepted. *Expenses:* Tuition, state resident: full-time $7000. Tuition, nonresident: full-time $19,200. *Financial support:* In 2009–10, 18 students received support, including fellowships with full tuition reimbursements available (averaging $20,000 per year), research assistantships with full tuition reimbursements available (averaging $18,375 per year), teaching assistantships with full tuition reimbursements available (averaging $18,375 per year); Federal Work-Study, institutionally sponsored loans, scholarships/grants, health care benefits, and unspecified assistantships also available. Financial award application deadline: 2/15. *Faculty research:* Intelligent computer systems, genetic algorithms, neural networks, impact and penetration mechanics, spacecraft dynamics and controls. Total annual research expenditures: $753,882. *Unit head:* Dr. Stanley E. Jones, Interim Department Head and Cudworth Professor, 205-348-7242, Fax: 205-348-7240, E-mail: sejones@eng.ua.edu. *Application contact:* Dr. John E. Jackson, Professor, 205-348-7306, Fax: 208-348-7240, E-mail: johnjackson@eng.ua.edu.

The University of Alabama in Huntsville, School of Graduate Studies, College of Engineering, Department of Mechanical and Aerospace Engineering, Huntsville, AL 35899. Offers aerospace engineering (MSE), including missile systems engineering, rotorcraft systems engineering; mechanical engineering (MSE, PhD). Part-time and evening/weekend programs available. *Faculty:* 17 full-time (2 women), 3 part-time/adjunct (0 women). *Students:* 44 full-time (8 women), 109 part-time (13 women); includes 11 minority (4 African Americans, 1 American Indian/Alaska Native, 3 Asian Americans or Pacific Islanders, 3 Hispanic Americans), 19 international. Average age 30. 112 applicants, 71% accepted, 47 enrolled. In 2009, 25 master's, 4 doctorates awarded. *Degree requirements:* For master's, comprehensive exam, thesis or alternative, oral and written exams; for doctorate, comprehensive exam, thesis/dissertation, oral and written exams. *Entrance requirements:* For master's, GRE General Test, BSE, minimum GPA of 3.0; for doctorate, GRE General Test, minimum GPA of 3.0. Additional exam requirements/recommendations for international students: Required—TOEFL (minimum score 500 paper-based; 173 computer-based; 62 iBT). *Application deadline:* For fall admission, 7/15 for domestic students, 4/1 for international students; for spring admission, 1/30 for domestic students, 9/1 for international students. Applications are processed on a rolling basis. Application fee: $40 ($50 for international students). Electronic applications accepted. *Expenses:* Tuition, state resident: part-time $355.75 per credit hour. Tuition, nonresident: part-time $847.10 per credit hour. Required fees: $210.80 per semester. Tuition and fees vary according to course load and program. *Financial support:* In 2009–10, 29 students received support, including 14 research assistantships with full and partial tuition reimbursements available (averaging $12,975 per year), 15 teaching assistantships with full and partial tuition reimbursements available (averaging $10,400 per year); career-related internships or fieldwork, Federal Work-Study, institutionally sponsored loans, scholarships/grants, health care benefits, and unspecified assistantships also available. Support available to part-time students. Financial award application deadline: 4/1; financial award applicants required to submit FAFSA. *Faculty research:* Combustion, fluid dynamics, materials and structures, propulsion, laser diagnostics. Total annual research expenditures: $4.7 million. *Unit head:* Dr. Kader Frendi, Chair, 256-824-6154,

Fax: 256-824-6758, E-mail: frendi@mae.uah.edu. *Application contact:* Kathy Biggs, Graduate Studies Admissions Manager, 256-824-6199, Fax: 256-824-6405, E-mail: deangrad@uah.edu.

The University of Arizona, Graduate College, College of Engineering, Department of Aerospace and Mechanical Engineering, Program in Aerospace Engineering, Tucson, AZ 85721. Offers MS, PhD. Part-time programs available. *Students:* 27 full-time (3 women), 12 part-time (2 women), 21 international. Average age 27. 37 applicants, 68% accepted, 17 enrolled. In 2009, 6 master's, 1 doctorate awarded. *Degree requirements:* For master's, thesis or alternative; for doctorate, thesis/dissertation. *Entrance requirements:* For master's and doctorate, GRE General Test, minimum GPA of 3.25. Additional exam requirements/recommendations for international students: Required—TOEFL (minimum score 550 paper-based; 213 computer-based; 79 iBT). *Application deadline:* For fall admission, 6/1 for domestic students, 12/1 for international students; for spring admission, 10/1 for domestic students, 6/1 for international students. Applications are processed on a rolling basis. Application fee: $75. Electronic applications accepted. *Expenses:* Tuition, state resident: full-time $9028. Tuition, nonresident: full-time $24,890. *Financial support:* Research assistantships, teaching assistantships, unspecified assistantships available. *Faculty research:* Fluid mechanics, structures, computer-aided design, stability and control, combustion. *Unit head:* Dr. Ara Arabyan, Interim Department Head, 520-621-2116, Fax: 520-621-8191, E-mail: arabyan@email.arizona.edu. *Application contact:* Barbara Heefner, Graduate Secretary, 520-621-4692, Fax: 520-621-8191, E-mail: heefner@email.arizona.edu.

University of California, Davis, College of Engineering, Program in Mechanical and Aeronautical Engineering, Davis, CA 95616. Offers aeronautical engineering (M Engr, MS, D Engr, PhD, Certificate); mechanical engineering (M Engr, MS, D Engr, PhD, Certificate); M Engr/MBA. *Degree requirements:* For master's, comprehensive exam (for some programs), thesis (for some programs); for doctorate, thesis/dissertation. *Entrance requirements:* For master's and doctorate, GRE General Test, minimum GPA of 3.0. Additional exam requirements/recommendations for international students: Required—TOEFL (minimum score 550 paper-based; 213 computer-based). Electronic applications accepted.

University of California, Irvine, Office of Graduate Studies, School of Engineering, Department of Mechanical and Aerospace Engineering, Irvine, CA 92697. Offers MS, PhD. Part-time programs available. *Students:* 113 full-time (21 women), 11 part-time (2 women); includes 32 minority (23 Asian Americans or Pacific Islanders, 9 Hispanic Americans), 52 international. Average age 27. 343 applicants, 27% accepted, 38 enrolled. In 2009, 31 master's, 17 doctorates awarded. Terminal master's awarded for partial completion of doctoral program. *Degree requirements:* For doctorate, thesis/dissertation. *Entrance requirements:* For master's, GRE General Test, minimum GPA of 3.0. 3 letters of recommendation; for doctorate, GRE General Test, minimum GPA of 3.0, 3 letters of recommendation. Additional exam requirements/recommendations for international students: Required—TOEFL (minimum score 550 paper-based; 213 computer-based). *Application deadline:* For fall admission, 1/15 priority date for domestic students, 1/15 for international students. Applications are processed on a rolling basis. Application fee: $70 ($90 for international students). Electronic applications accepted. *Financial support:* In 2009–10, fellowships with tuition reimbursements (averaging $14,656 per year); research assistantships with full tuition reimbursements, teaching assistantships with tuition reimbursements, institutionally sponsored loans, traineeships, health care benefits, and unspecified assistantships also available. Financial award application deadline: 3/1; financial award applicants required to submit FAFSA. *Faculty research:* Thermal and fluid sciences, combustion and propulsion, control systems, robotics, lightweight structures. *Unit head:* Dr. Simitri Papamoschoy, Chair, 949-824-6590, Fax: 949-824-3726. *Application contact:* Leslie Noel, Graduate Coordinator, 949-824-7984, Fax: 949-824-8585, E-mail: lknoel@uci.edu.

University of California, Los Angeles, Graduate Division, Henry Samueli School of Engineering and Applied Science, Department of Mechanical and Aerospace Engineering, Program in Aerospace Engineering, Los Angeles, CA 90095-1597. Offers MS, PhD. *Students:* 54 full-time (4 women); includes 21 minority (1 African American, 17 Asian Americans or Pacific Islanders, 3 Hispanic Americans), 8 international. 77 applicants, 64% accepted, 19 enrolled. In 2009, 13 master's, 6 doctorates awarded. *Degree requirements:* For master's, comprehensive exam or thesis; for doctorate, thesis/dissertation, qualifying exams. *Entrance requirements:* For master's, GRE General Test, minimum GPA of 3.0; for doctorate, GRE General Test, minimum GPA of 3.25. Additional exam requirements/recommendations for international students: Required—TOEFL (minimum score 560 paper-based; 220 computer-based). *Application deadline:* For fall admission, 1/5 for domestic and international students; for winter admission, 10/1 for domestic students; for spring admission, 12/31 for domestic students. Application fee: $70 ($90 for international students). Electronic applications accepted. *Financial support:* Fellowships, research assistantships, teaching assistantships, Federal Work-Study, institutionally sponsored loans, and tuition waivers (full and partial) available. Financial award application deadline: 1/5; financial award applicants required to submit FAFSA. *Unit head:* Dr. Adrienne Lavine, Chair, 310-825-7468. *Application contact:* Angie Castillo, Student Affairs Officer, 310-825-7793, Fax: 310-206-4830, E-mail: angie@ea.ucla.edu.

University of California, San Diego, Office of Graduate Studies, Department of Mechanical and Aerospace Engineering, Program in Aerospace Engineering, La Jolla, CA 92093. Offers MS, PhD. Part-time programs available. *Degree requirements:* For master's, comprehensive exam or thesis; for doctorate, thesis/dissertation, qualifying exam. *Entrance requirements:* For master's and doctorate, GRE General Test, minimum GPA of 3.0. Additional exam requirements/recommendations for international students: Required—TOEFL. *Faculty research:* Aerospace structures, turbulence, gas dynamics and combustion.

University of Central Florida, College of Engineering and Computer Science, Department of Mechanical, Materials, and Aerospace Engineering, Program in Aerospace Engineering, Orlando, FL 32816. Offers MSAE. *Students:* 10 full-time (2 women), 10 part-time (1 woman); includes 5 minority (2 African Americans, 1 Asian American or Pacific Islander, 2 Hispanic Americans), 1 international. Average age 26. 20 applicants, 45% accepted, 8 enrolled. In 2009, 4 master's awarded. *Degree requirements:* For master's, thesis or alternative. *Application deadline:* For fall admission, 7/15 priority date for domestic students; for spring admission, 12/1 priority date for domestic students. Application fee: $30. Electronic applications accepted. *Expenses:* Tuition, state resident: part-time $306.31 per credit hour. Tuition, nonresident: part-time $1099.01 per credit hour. Part-time tuition and fees vary according to degree level and program. *Financial support:* In 2009–10, 4 students received support, including 1 research assistantship (averaging $10,800 per year), 3 teaching assistantships (averaging $9,000 per year); career-related internships or fieldwork, institutionally sponsored loans, scholarships/grants, tuition waivers (partial), and unspecified assistantships also available.

University of Central Missouri, The Graduate School, College of Science and Technology, Warrensburg, MO 64093. Offers applied mathematics (MS); aviation safety (MS); biology (MS); computer science (MS); environmental studies (MA); industrial management (MS); mathematics (MS); technology (MS); technology management (PhD). Part-time programs available. Postbaccalaureate distance learning degree programs offered. *Faculty:* 59. *Students:* 99 full-time (31 women), 85 part-time (37 women). Average age 33. 45 applicants, 96% accepted, 42 enrolled. In 2009, 68 master's awarded. *Entrance requirements:* Additional exam requirements/recommendations for international students: Required—TOEFL (minimum score 550 paper-based; 79 computer-based). *Application deadline:* For fall admission, 6/1 priority date for domestic students, 5/1 for international students; for spring admission, 10/1 priority date for domestic students, 10/1 for international students. Applications are processed on a rolling basis. Application fee: $30 ($75 for international students). Electronic applications accepted. *Expenses:* Tuition, area resident: Part-time $245.80 per credit hour. Tuition, nonresident: part-time $491.60 per credit hour. Required fees: $24.20 per credit hour. Full-time tuition and fees vary according to course load, degree level, campus/location and reciprocity agreements. *Financial support:* In 2009–10, 15 students received support; fellowships with full and partial tuition reimbursements available, research assistantships with full and partial tuition reimbursements available, teaching assistantships with full and partial tuition reimbursements

Aerospace/Aeronautical Engineering

University of Central Missouri *(continued)*
available, career-related internships or fieldwork, Federal Work-Study, scholarships/grants, and administrative and laboratory assistantships available. Support available to part-time students. Financial award application deadline: 3/1; financial award applicants required to submit FAFSA. *Unit head:* Dr. Alice Greife, Dean, 660-543-4450, Fax: 660-543-8031, E-mail: greife@ucmo.edu. *Application contact:* Laurie Delap, Admissions Coordinator, 660-543-4621, Fax: 660-543-4778, E-mail: gradinfo@ucmo.edu.

University of Cincinnati, Graduate School, College of Engineering, Department of Aerospace Engineering and Engineering Mechanics, Cincinnati, OH 45221. Offers MS, PhD. Part-time programs available. Terminal master's awarded for partial completion of doctoral program. *Degree requirements:* For master's, project or thesis; for doctorate, thesis/dissertation. *Entrance requirements:* For master's and doctorate, GRE General Test. Additional exam requirements/recommendations for international students: Required—TOEFL (minimum score 550 paper-based; 213 computer-based). Electronic applications accepted. *Faculty research:* Computational fluid mechanics/propulsion, large space structures, dynamics and guidance of VTOL vehicles.

University of Colorado at Boulder, Graduate School, College of Engineering and Applied Science, Department of Aerospace Engineering Sciences, Boulder, CO 80309. Offers MS, PhD. Postbaccalaureate distance learning degree programs offered. *Faculty:* 27 full-time (3 women). *Students:* 139 full-time (23 women), 51 part-time (13 women); includes 21 minority (2 African Americans, 2 American Indian/Alaska Native, 12 Asian Americans or Pacific Islanders, 5 Hispanic Americans), 27 international. Average age 27. 187 applicants, 52% accepted, 54 enrolled. In 2009, 35 master's, 11 doctorates awarded. Terminal master's awarded for partial completion of doctoral program. *Degree requirements:* For master's, comprehensive exam, thesis or alternative; for doctorate, comprehensive exam, thesis/dissertation. *Entrance requirements:* For master's, GRE General Test, minimum undergraduate GPA of 3.0; for doctorate, minimum undergraduate GPA of 3.25. *Application deadline:* For fall admission, 2/1 priority date for domestic students, 12/1 for international students; for spring admission, 10/1 for domestic students, 8/1 for international students. Applications are processed on a rolling basis. Application fee: $50 ($60 for international students). *Financial support:* In 2009–10, 38 fellowships (averaging $14,348 per year), 71 research assistantships with full tuition reimbursements (averaging $15,952 per year), 13 teaching assistantships with full tuition reimbursements (averaging $17,431 per year) were awarded; career-related internships or fieldwork, Federal Work-Study, and scholarships/grants also available. Support available to part-time students. Financial award application deadline: 2/1. *Faculty research:* Aerodynamics, gasdynamics and fluid mechanics; astrodynamics; atmospheric and oceanic sciences; bioengineering; computational fluid dynamics; global positioning; guidance and control. Total annual research expenditures: $11.2 million.

University of Colorado at Colorado Springs, Graduate School, College of Engineering and Applied Science, Department of Mechanical and Aerospace Engineering, Colorado Springs, CO 80933-7150. Offers engineering management (ME); information operations (ME); manufacturing (ME); mechanical engineering (MS); software engineering (ME); space operations (ME); space systems (MS). Part-time and evening/weekend programs available. *Faculty:* 10 full-time (2 women). *Students:* 14 full-time (4 women), 13 part-time (2 women); includes 3 minority (2 Asian Americans or Pacific Islanders, 1 Hispanic American). Average age 30. 39 applicants, 82% accepted, 16 enrolled. In 2009, 6 master's awarded. *Degree requirements:* For master's, thesis optional. *Entrance requirements:* For master's, GRE General Test, bachelor's degree in engineering or related degree, minimum GPA of 3.0. Additional exam requirements/recommendations for international students: Required—TOEFL. *Application deadline:* For fall admission, 5/1 for domestic students; for spring admission, 10/1 for domestic students. Applications are processed on a rolling basis. Application fee: $60 ($75 for international students). *Expenses:* Tuition, state resident: full-time $8922; part-time $639 per credit hour. Tuition, nonresident: full-time $19,372; part-time $1154 per credit hour. Tuition and fees vary according to course level, course load, degree level, program, reciprocity agreements and student level. *Financial support:* Federal Work-Study and scholarships/grants available. Support available to part-time students. Financial award application deadline: 3/1; financial award applicants required to submit FAFSA. *Faculty research:* Neural networks, artificial intelligence, robust control, space operations, space propulsion. *Unit head:* Dr. T. S. Kalkur, Chair, 719-255-3147, Fax: 719-255-3042, E-mail: kalkur@eas.uccs.edu. *Application contact:* Siew Nylund, Academic Adviser, 719-255-3243, Fax: 719-255-3589, E-mail: snylund@eas.uccs.edu.

University of Dayton, Graduate School, School of Engineering, Department of Mechanical and Aerospace Engineering, Dayton, OH 45469-1300. Offers aerospace engineering (MSAE, DE, PhD); mechanical engineering (MSME, DE, PhD); renewable and clean energy (MS). Part-time programs available. Postbaccalaureate distance learning degree programs offered (no on-campus study). *Faculty:* 15 full-time (2 women), 13 part-time/adjunct (1 woman). *Students:* 83 full-time (16 women), 29 part-time (5 women); includes 13 minority (6 African Americans, 3 Asian Americans or Pacific Islanders, 4 Hispanic Americans), 32 international. Average age 30. 80 applicants, 50% accepted, 24 enrolled. In 2009, 24 master's, 5 doctorates awarded. Terminal master's awarded for partial completion of doctoral program. *Degree requirements:* For master's, thesis optional; for doctorate, variable foreign language requirement, thesis/dissertation, departmental qualifying exam. *Entrance requirements:* Additional exam requirements/recommendations for international students: Required—TOEFL (minimum score 550 paper-based; 213 computer-based; 80 iBT). *Application deadline:* For fall admission, 8/1 priority date for domestic students, 6/1 priority date for international students; for winter admission, 9/1 priority date for international students; for spring admission, 3/1 priority date for international students. Applications are processed on a rolling basis. Application fee: $0. Electronic applications accepted. *Expenses:* Tuition: Full-time $8412; part-time $701 per credit hour. Required fees: $325; $65 per course. $25 per semester. Tuition and fees vary according to course load, degree level and program. *Financial support:* In 2009–10, 25 students received support, including 2 fellowships with full tuition reimbursements available (averaging $27,500 per year), 22 research assistantships with full tuition reimbursements available (averaging $12,000 per year), 1 teaching assistantship (averaging $9,000 per year). Financial award applicants required to submit FAFSA. *Faculty research:* Jet engine combustion, surface coating friction and wear, aircraft thermal management, aerospace fuels, energy efficient buildings, energy efficient manufacturing, renewable energy. Total annual research expenditures: $1.2 million. *Unit head:* Dr. Kevin Hallinan, Chair, 937-229-2835, Fax: 937-229-4766, E-mail: kevin.hallinan@udayton.edu. *Application contact:* Graduate Admissions, 937-229-4411, Fax: 937-229-4729, E-mail: gradadmission@udayton.edu.

University of Florida, Graduate School, College of Engineering, Department of Mechanical and Aerospace Engineering, Gainesville, FL 32611. Offers aerospace engineering (ME, MS, PhD, Engr); mechanical engineering (ME, MS, PhD, Engr). Part-time programs available. *Degree requirements:* For master's, thesis (for some programs); for doctorate, thesis/dissertation; for Engr, thesis. *Entrance requirements:* For master's and doctorate, GRE General Test, minimum GPA of 3.0; for Engr, GRE General Test. Additional exam requirements/recommendations for international students: Required—TOEFL (minimum score 550 paper-based; 213 computer-based). Electronic applications accepted. *Faculty research:* Thermal sciences, design, controls and robotics, manufacturing, energy transport and utilization.

University of Illinois at Urbana–Champaign, Graduate College, College of Engineering, Department of Aerospace Engineering, Champaign, IL 61820. Offers MS, PhD. *Faculty:* 18 full-time (2 women). *Students:* 108 full-time (11 women), 17 part-time (1 woman); includes 20 minority (2 African Americans, 15 Asian Americans or Pacific Islanders, 3 Hispanic Americans), 46 international. 238 applicants, 63% accepted, 50 enrolled. In 2009, 20 master's, 2 doctorates awarded. *Entrance requirements:* For master's and doctorate, GRE General Test. Additional exam requirements/recommendations for international students: Required—TOEFL (minimum score 613 paper-based; 257 computer-based; 103 iBT), or IELTS (minimum score 7). *Application deadline:* Applications are processed on a rolling basis. Application fee: $60 ($75 for international students). Electronic applications accepted. *Financial support:* In 2009–10, 16 fellow-

ships, 79 research assistantships, 32 teaching assistantships were awarded; tuition waivers (full and partial) also available. *Unit head:* Dr. J. Craig Dutton, Head, 217-333-8580, Fax: 217-244-0720, E-mail: jcdutton@illinois.edu. *Application contact:* Staci L. Tankersley, Coordinator of Academic Programs, 217-333-3674, Fax: 217-244-0720, E-mail: tank@illinois.edu.

The University of Kansas, Graduate Studies, School of Engineering, Department of Aerospace Engineering, Lawrence, KS 66045. Offers ME, MS, DE, PhD. *Faculty:* 8 full-time (0 women), 1 part-time/adjunct (0 women). *Students:* 34 full-time (5 women), 7 part-time (1 woman); includes 1 minority (American Indian/Alaska Native), 22 international. Average age 27. 46 applicants, 43% accepted, 8 enrolled. In 2009, 5 master's, 4 doctorates awarded. *Degree requirements:* For master's, comprehensive exam, thesis; for doctorate, comprehensive exam, thesis/dissertation, Foreign Language or Research Requirement, Doctoral Qualifying Exam. *Entrance requirements:* For master's, GRE, minimum GPA of 3.0; for doctorate, GRE, minimum GPA of 3.5. Additional exam requirements/recommendations for international students: Required—TOEFL (minimum score 570 paper-based; 80 computer-based; 80 iBT). *Application deadline:* For fall admission, 5/1 for domestic students, 5/1 priority date for international students; for spring admission, 12/1 priority date for domestic and international students. Applications are processed on a rolling basis. Application fee: $45 ($55 for international students). Electronic applications accepted. *Expenses:* Tuition, state resident: full-time $6492; part-time $270.50 per credit hour. Tuition, nonresident: full-time $15,510; part-time $646.25 per credit hour. Required fees: $847; $70.56 per credit hour. Tuition and fees vary according to course load and program. *Financial support:* Fellowships with full and partial tuition reimbursements, research assistantships with full and partial tuition reimbursements, teaching assistantships with full and partial tuition reimbursements, career-related internships or fieldwork, scholarships/grants, tuition waivers (full and partial), and unspecified assistantships available. Financial award application deadline: 1/1. *Faculty research:* Aerodynamics, propulsion, astronautics, fluid mechanics, flight dynamics and control, structures, flight vehicle design, flight testing, orbital mechanics, space craft attitude determination and control. *Unit head:* Dr. Mark Ewing, Chair and Associate Professor, 785-864-4267, Fax: 785-864-3597, E-mail: aerohawk@ku.edu. *Application contact:* Amy Borton, Graduate Secretary, 785-864-4267, Fax: 785-864-3597, E-mail: aerohawk@ku.edu.

University of Maryland, College Park, Academic Affairs, A. James Clark School of Engineering, Department of Aerospace Engineering, College Park, MD 20742. Offers M Eng, MS, PhD. Part-time and evening/weekend programs available. Postbaccalaureate distance learning degree programs offered. *Faculty:* 41 full-time (2 women), 11 part-time/adjunct (0 women). *Students:* 124 full-time (19 women), 43 part-time (6 women); includes 26 minority (10 African Americans, 1 American Indian/Alaska Native, 11 Asian Americans or Pacific Islanders, 4 Hispanic Americans), 45 international. 214 applicants, 41% accepted, 51 enrolled. In 2009, 28 master's, 11 doctorates awarded. *Degree requirements:* For master's, thesis optional; for doctorate, thesis/dissertation. *Entrance requirements:* For master's and doctorate, GRE General Test (recommended), 3 letters of recommendation. *Application deadline:* For fall admission, 5/15 for domestic students, 2/1 for international students; for spring admission, 10/31 for domestic students, 6/1 for international students. Applications are processed on a rolling basis. Application fee: $60. Electronic applications accepted. *Expenses:* Tuition, area resident: Part-time $471 per credit hour. Tuition, state resident: part-time $471 per credit hour. Tuition, nonresident: part-time $1016 per credit hour. Required fees: $337.04 per term. *Financial support:* In 2009–10, 14 fellowships with full and partial tuition reimbursements (averaging $11,666 per year), 102 research assistantships with tuition reimbursements (averaging $23,615 per year), 13 teaching assistantships with tuition reimbursements (averaging $18,290 per year) were awarded; Federal Work-Study and scholarships/grants also available. Support available to part-time students. Financial award applicants required to submit FAFSA. *Faculty research:* Aerodynamics and propulsion, structural mechanics, flight dynamics, rotor craft, space robotics. Total annual research expenditures: $13.5 million. *Unit head:* Mark Lewis, Chair, 301-405-0263, E-mail: lewis@umd.edu. *Application contact:* Dr. Charles Caramello, Dean of Graduate School, 301-405-0376, Fax: 301-314-9305.

University of Maryland, College Park, Academic Affairs, A. James Clark School of Engineering, Department of Continuing and Distance Learning in Engineering, Professional Program in Engineering, College Park, MD 20742. Offers aerospace engineering (M Eng); chemical engineering (M Eng); civil engineering (M Eng); electrical engineering (M Eng); engineering (Certificate); fire protection engineering (M Eng); materials science and engineering (M Eng); mechanical engineering (M Eng); reliability engineering (M Eng); systems engineering (M Eng). Part-time and evening/weekend programs available. Postbaccalaureate distance learning degree programs offered. *Students:* 50 full-time (15 women), 234 part-time (41 women); includes 91 minority (36 African Americans, 39 Asian Americans or Pacific Islanders, 16 Hispanic Americans), 45 international. 137 applicants, 69% accepted, 77 enrolled. In 2009, 103 master's awarded. *Entrance requirements:* For master's, 3 letters of recommendation. *Application deadline:* For fall admission, 8/15 for domestic students, 1/10 for international students; for spring admission, 12/15 for domestic students, 6/1 for international students. Applications are processed on a rolling basis. Application fee: $60. Electronic applications accepted. *Expenses:* Tuition, area resident: Part-time $471 per credit hour. Tuition, state resident: part-time $471 per credit hour. Tuition, nonresident: part-time $1016 per credit hour. Required fees: $337.04 per term. *Financial support:* In 2009–10, 2 research assistantships with tuition reimbursements (averaging $19,561 per year), 9 teaching assistantships with tuition reimbursements (averaging $16,849 per year) were awarded; fellowships, Federal Work-Study and scholarships/grants also available. Support available to part-time students. Financial award applicants required to submit FAFSA. *Unit head:* Dr. George Syrmos, Director, 301-405-3633, Fax: 301-314-3305, E-mail: syrmos@umd.edu. *Application contact:* Dean of Graduate School, 301-405-0376, Fax: 301-314-9305.

University of Miami, Graduate School, College of Engineering, Department of Mechanical and Aerospace Engineering, Coral Gables, FL 33124. Offers MSME, PhD. Part-time programs available. *Degree requirements:* For master's, thesis (for some programs); for doctorate, comprehensive exam, thesis/dissertation. *Entrance requirements:* For master's and doctorate, GRE General Test, minimum GPA of 3.0. Additional exam requirements/recommendations for international students: Required—TOEFL (minimum score 550 paper-based; 213 computer-based). Electronic applications accepted. *Faculty research:* Internal combustion engines, heat transfer, hydrogen energy, controls, fuel cells.

University of Michigan, Horace H. Rackham School of Graduate Studies, College of Engineering, Department of Aerospace Engineering, Ann Arbor, MI 48109. Offers M Eng, MS, MSE, PhD. Part-time programs available. *Faculty:* 26 full-time (3 women). *Students:* 164 full-time (19 women), 4 part-time (1 woman); includes 27 minority (4 African Americans, 18 Asian Americans or Pacific Islanders, 5 Hispanic Americans), 70 international. 373 applicants, 55% accepted, 80 enrolled. In 2009, 56 master's, 22 doctorates awarded. *Degree requirements:* For doctorate, thesis/dissertation, oral defense of dissertation, preliminary exams. *Entrance requirements:* For master's, GRE General Test; for doctorate, GRE General Test, master's degree. *Application deadline:* Applications are processed on a rolling basis. Application fee: $60 ($75 for international students). Electronic applications accepted. *Expenses:* Tuition, state resident: full-time $17,286; part-time $1099 per credit hour. Tuition, nonresident: full-time $34,944; part-time $2080 per credit hour. Required fees: $95 per semester. Tuition and fees vary according to course load, degree level and program. *Financial support:* Fellowships, research assistantships, teaching assistantships, Federal Work-Study and tuition waivers (full and partial) available. *Faculty research:* Turbulent flows and combustion, advanced spacecraft control, helicopter aeroelasticity, experimental fluid dynamics, space propulsion, optimal structural design, interactive materials, computational fluid and solid dynamics. *Unit head:* Dr. Wei Shyy, Chair, 734-764-3310, Fax: 734-763-0578, E-mail: weishyy@umich.edu. *Application contact:* Denise Phelps, Graduate Admissions Coordinator, 734-615-4406, Fax: 734-763-0578, E-mail: dphelps@umich.edu.

University of Michigan, Horace H. Rackham School of Graduate Studies, College of Engineering, Department of Atmospheric, Oceanic, and Space Sciences, Ann Arbor, MI 48109. Offers atmospheric (MS); atmospheric and space sciences (PhD); geoscience and remote sensing (PhD); space and planetary sciences (PhD); space engineering (M Eng); space sciences (MS). Part-time programs available. *Faculty:* 22 full-time (4 women). *Students:* 74 full-time (30 women), 1 part-time (0 women); includes 4 minority (1 African American, 2 Asian Americans or Pacific Islanders, 1 Hispanic American), 29 international. 62 applicants, 48% accepted, 17 enrolled. In 2009, 38 master's, 4 doctorates awarded. Terminal master's awarded for partial completion of doctoral program. *Degree requirements:* For master's, thesis (for some programs); for doctorate, thesis/dissertation, oral defense of dissertation, preliminary exams. *Entrance requirements:* For master's and doctorate, GRE General Test. Additional exam requirements/recommendations for international students: Required—TOEFL. *Application deadline:* Applications are processed on a rolling basis. Application fee: $60 ($75 for international students). Electronic applications accepted. *Expenses:* Tuition, state resident: full-time $17,286; part-time $1099 per credit hour. Tuition, nonresident: full-time $34,944; part-time $2080 per credit hour. Required fees: $95 per semester. Tuition and fees vary according to course load, degree level and program. *Financial support:* Fellowships, research assistantships, teaching assistantships, career-related internships or fieldwork, Federal Work-Study, institutionally sponsored loans, and health care benefits available. Support available to part-time students. Financial award applicants required to submit FAFSA. *Faculty research:* Planetary environments, space instrumentation, air pollution meteorology, global climate change, sun-earth connection, space weather. *Unit head:* Tamas Gombosi, Chair, 734-764-7222, Fax: 734-615-4645, E-mail: tamas@umich.edu. *Application contact:* Margaret Reid, Student Services Associate, 734-936-0482, Fax: 734-763-0437, E-mail: aoss.um@umich.edu.

University of Minnesota, Twin Cities Campus, Institute of Technology, Department of Aerospace Engineering and Mechanics, Minneapolis, MN 55455-0213. Offers aerospace engineering (M Aero E); aerospace engineering and mechanics (MS, PhD). Part-time programs available. *Degree requirements:* For doctorate, thesis/dissertation. *Entrance requirements:* Additional exam requirements/recommendations for international students: Required—TOEFL (minimum score 550 paper-based; 213 computer-based). Electronic applications accepted. *Faculty research:* Fluid mechanics, solid and continuum fluid mechanics, computational mechanics, aerospace systems.

University of Missouri, Graduate School, College of Engineering, Department of Mechanical and Aerospace Engineering, Columbia, MO 65211. Offers MS, PhD. *Degree requirements:* For master's, thesis; for doctorate, one foreign language, thesis/dissertation. *Entrance requirements:* For master's and doctorate, GRE General Test, minimum GPA of 3.0. Additional exam requirements/recommendations for international students: Required—TOEFL (minimum score 500 paper-based; 173 computer-based; 61 iBT).

University of Nevada, Las Vegas, Graduate College, Howard R. Hughes College of Engineering, Department of Mechanical Engineering, Las Vegas, NV 89154-4027. Offers aerospace engineering (MS); biomedical engineering (MS); materials and nuclear engineering (MS); mechanical engineering (MS, PhD). Part-time programs available. *Faculty:* 17 full-time (0 women), 10 part-time/adjunct (0 women). *Students:* 39 full-time (4 women), 28 part-time (6 women); includes 10 minority (1 African American, 8 Asian Americans or Pacific Islanders, 1 Hispanic American), 28 international. Average age 30. 64 applicants, 83% accepted, 22 enrolled. In 2009, 13 master's, 7 doctorates awarded. *Degree requirements:* For master's, comprehensive exam, thesis (for some programs), project; for doctorate, comprehensive exam, thesis/dissertation. *Entrance requirements:* For master's and doctorate, GRE General Test. Additional exam requirements/recommendations for international students: Required—TOEFL (minimum score 550 paper-based; 213 computer-based; 80 iBT), IELTS (minimum score 7). *Application deadline:* For fall admission, 5/1 priority date for domestic and international students; for spring admission, 10/1 priority date for domestic and international students. Applications are processed on a rolling basis. Application fee: $60 ($95 for international students). Electronic applications accepted. *Financial support:* In 2009–10, 37 students received support, including 21 research assistantships with partial tuition reimbursements available (averaging $13,335 per year), 16 teaching assistantships with partial tuition reimbursements available (averaging $11,000 per year); institutionally sponsored loans, scholarships/grants, health care benefits, and unspecified assistantships also available. Financial award application deadline: 3/1. *Unit head:* Dr. Woosoon Yim, Chair/Professor, 702-895-0956, Fax: 702-895-3936, E-mail: wy@me.unlv.edu. *Application contact:* Graduate College Admissions Evaluator, 702-895-3320, Fax: 702-895-4180, E-mail: gradcollege@unlv.edu.

University of Notre Dame, Graduate School, College of Engineering, Department of Aerospace and Mechanical Engineering, Notre Dame, IN 46556. Offers aerospace and mechanical engineering (M Eng, PhD); aerospace engineering (MS Aero E); mechanical engineering (MEME, MSME). Terminal master's awarded for partial completion of doctoral program. *Degree requirements:* For master's, comprehensive exam, thesis or alternative; for doctorate, thesis/dissertation, candidacy exam. *Entrance requirements:* For master's and doctorate, GRE General Test. Additional exam requirements/recommendations for international students: Required—TOEFL (minimum score 600 paper-based; 250 computer-based; 80 iBT). Electronic applications accepted. *Faculty research:* Aerodynamics/fluid dynamics, design and manufacturing, controls/robotics, solid mechanics or biomechanics/biomaterials.

University of Oklahoma, Graduate College, College of Engineering, School of Aerospace and Mechanical Engineering, Program in Aerospace Engineering, Norman, OK 73019. Offers MS, PhD. Part-time programs available. *Students:* 6 full-time (1 woman), 13 part-time (0 women); includes 3 minority (1 American Indian/Alaska Native, 2 Asian Americans or Pacific Islanders), 4 international. 3 applicants, 100% accepted, 1 enrolled. In 2009, 6 master's awarded. Terminal master's awarded for partial completion of doctoral program. *Degree requirements:* For master's, comprehensive exam, thesis or alternative; for doctorate, comprehensive exam, thesis/dissertation, combined general and qualifying exam. *Entrance requirements:* For master's, GRE General Test, BS in engineering or physical sciences; for doctorate, GRE General Test, MS in aerospace engineering or equivalent. Additional exam requirements/recommendations for international students: Required—TOEFL (minimum score 600 paper-based; 250 computer-based). *Application deadline:* For fall admission, 6/1 priority date for domestic students, 4/1 for international students; for spring admission, 11/1 for domestic students, 9/1 for international students. Applications are processed on a rolling basis. Application fee: $40 ($90 for international students). Electronic applications accepted. *Expenses:* Tuition, state resident: full-time $3744; part-time $156 per credit hour. Tuition, nonresident: full-time $13,577; part-time $565.70 per credit hour. Required fees: $2415; $90.10 per credit hour. *Financial support:* In 2009–10, 7 students received support. Career-related internships or fieldwork, health care benefits, and unspecified assistantships available. Financial award application deadline: 3/1; financial award applicants required to submit FAFSA. *Faculty research:* Dynamics, controls and robotics, materials, design and manufacturing, structures, thermal-fluid systems. *Unit head:* Farrokh Mistree, Director, 405-325-5011, Fax: 405-325-1088, E-mail: farrokh.mistree@ou.edu. *Application contact:* Dr. Ramkumar Parthasarathy, Graduate Liaison, 405-325-1735, Fax: 405-325-1088, E-mail: rparthasarathy@ou.edu.

University of Ottawa, Faculty of Graduate and Postdoctoral Studies, Faculty of Engineering, Ottawa-Carleton Institute for Mechanical and Aerospace Engineering, Ottawa, ON K1N 6N5, Canada. Offers M Eng, MA Sc, PhD. *Degree requirements:* For master's, thesis or alternative; for doctorate, thesis/dissertation, seminar series, qualifying exam. *Entrance requirements:* For master's, honors degree or equivalent, minimum B average; for doctorate, master's degree, minimum B+ average. Electronic applications accepted. *Faculty research:* Fluid mechanics-heat transfer, solid mechanics, design, manufacturing and control.

University of Southern California, Graduate School, Viterbi School of Engineering, Department of Aerospace and Mechanical Engineering, Los Angeles, CA 90089. Offers aerospace and mechanical engineering: computational fluid and solid mechanics (MS); aerospace and mechanical engineering: dynamics and control (MS); aerospace engineering (MS, PhD, Engr), including aerospace engineering (PhD, Engr); mechanical engineering (MS, PhD, Engr), including mechanical engineering (PhD, Engr); product development engineering (MS). Part-time programs available. Postbaccalaureate distance learning degree programs offered. *Faculty:*

24 full-time (3 women), 19 part-time/adjunct (2 women). *Students:* 186 full-time (22 women), 192 part-time (35 women); includes 89 minority (9 African Americans, 60 Asian Americans or Pacific Islanders, 20 Hispanic Americans), 119 international. 499 applicants, 48% accepted, 107 enrolled. In 2009, 107 master's, 11 doctorates, 1 other advanced degree awarded. Terminal master's awarded for partial completion of doctoral program. *Degree requirements:* For doctorate, thesis/dissertation. *Entrance requirements:* For master's and doctorate, General GRE Test. *Application deadline:* For fall admission, 3/1 priority date for domestic and international students; for spring admission, 10/1 priority date for domestic and international students. Applications are processed on a rolling basis. Application fee: $85. Electronic applications accepted. *Expenses:* Tuition: Full-time $25,980; part-time $1315 per unit. Required fees: $554. One-time fee: $35 full-time. Full-time tuition and fees vary according to degree level and program. *Financial support:* In 2009–10, fellowships with full tuition reimbursements (averaging $30,000 per year), research assistantships with full tuition reimbursements (averaging $19,250 per year), teaching assistantships with full tuition reimbursements (averaging $19,250 per year) were awarded; career-related internships or fieldwork, scholarships/grants, traineeships, health care benefits, and unspecified assistantships also available. Financial award application deadline: 12/1; financial award applicants required to submit CSS PROFILE or FAFSA. *Faculty research:* Mechanics and materials, aerodynamics of air/ground vehicles, gas dynamics; aerosols, astronautics and space science, geophysical and microgravity flows, planetary physics, power MEMs and MEMS vacuum pumps, heat transfer and combustion. Total annual research expenditures: $3.9 million. *Unit head:* Dr. Geoffrey Spedding, Chair, 213-740-4132, Fax: 213-740-8071, E-mail: geoff@usc.edu. *Application contact:* Samantha Graves, Student Service Advisor, 213-740-1735, Fax: 213-740-7774, E-mail: smgraves@usc.edu.

University of Southern California, Graduate School, Viterbi School of Engineering, Division of Astronautics and Space Technology, Los Angeles, CA 90089. Offers astronautical engineering (MS, PhD, Engr, Graduate Certificate). Part-time and evening/weekend programs available. Postbaccalaureate distance learning degree programs offered (no on-campus study). *Faculty:* 4 full-time (0 women), 14 part-time/adjunct (0 women). *Students:* 23 full-time (3 women), 84 part-time (17 women); includes 16 minority (3 African Americans, 8 Asian Americans or Pacific Islanders, 5 Hispanic Americans), 11 international. 63 applicants, 68% accepted, 23 enrolled. In 2009, 49 master's, 1 doctorate, 1 other advanced degree awarded. *Degree requirements:* For doctorate, thesis/dissertation. *Entrance requirements:* For master's and doctorate, General GRE Test. *Application deadline:* For fall admission, 3/1 priority date for domestic and international students; for spring admission, 10/1 priority date for domestic and international students. Applications are processed on a rolling basis. Application fee: $85. Electronic applications accepted. *Expenses:* Tuition: Full-time $25,980; part-time $1315 per unit. Required fees: $554. One-time fee: $35 full-time. Full-time tuition and fees vary according to degree level and program. *Financial support:* In 2009–10, fellowships with full tuition reimbursements (averaging $30,000 per year), research assistantships with full tuition reimbursements (averaging $19,250 per year), teaching assistantships with full tuition reimbursements (averaging $19,250 per year) were awarded; career-related internships or fieldwork, scholarships/grants, health care benefits, and unspecified assistantships also available. Financial award application deadline: 12/1; financial award applicants required to submit CSS PROFILE or FAFSA. *Faculty research:* Space technology, space science and applications, space instrumentation, advanced propulsion, fundamental processes in gases and plasmas. Total annual research expenditures: $353,651. *Unit head:* Dr. Daniel A. Erwin, Chair, 213-740-5358, Fax: 213-740-5819, E-mail: erwin@usc.edu. *Application contact:* Dell Cuason, Department Administrator, 213-740-5817, Fax: 213-740-5819, E-mail: cuason@usc.edu.

The University of Tennessee, Graduate School, College of Engineering, Department of Mechanical, Aerospace and Biomedical Engineering, Program in Aerospace Engineering, Knoxville, TN 37996. Offers MS, PhD, MS/MBA. Part-time programs available. *Faculty:* 5 full-time (0 women), 1 part-time/adjunct (0 women). *Students:* 25 full-time (2 women), 15 part-time (0 women); includes 5 minority (2 African Americans, 3 Hispanic Americans), 7 international. Average age 26. 22 applicants, 27% accepted, 3 enrolled. In 2009, 7 master's, 1 doctorate awarded. *Degree requirements:* For master's, thesis or alternative; for doctorate, comprehensive exam, thesis/dissertation. *Entrance requirements:* For master's and doctorate, GRE, minimum GPA of 2.7. Additional exam requirements/recommendations for international students: Required—TOEFL (minimum score 550 paper-based; 213 computer-based). *Application deadline:* For fall admission, 2/1 priority date for domestic and international students; for spring admission, 6/15 priority date for international students. Applications are processed on a rolling basis. Application fee: $35. Electronic applications accepted. *Expenses:* Tuition, state resident: full-time $6826; part-time $380 per semester hour. Tuition, nonresident: full-time $21,844; part-time $1147 per semester hour. Tuition and fees vary according to program. *Financial support:* In 2009–10, 1 student received support, including 2 fellowships with full tuition reimbursements available (averaging $13,692 per year), 14 research assistantships with full tuition reimbursements available (averaging $14,628 per year), 5 teaching assistantships with full tuition reimbursements available (averaging $10,104 per year); career-related internships or fieldwork, Federal Work-Study, institutionally sponsored loans, health care benefits, and unspecified assistantships also available. Financial award application deadline: 2/1; financial award applicants required to submit FAFSA. *Faculty research:* Control engineering, thermal science, robotics and automation. Total annual research expenditures: $550,000. *Unit head:* Dr. William Hamel, Head, 865-974-5115, Fax: 865-974-5274, E-mail: whamel@utk.edu. *Application contact:* Dr. Gary V. Smith, Chair, Graduate Programs Committee, 865-974-5271, E-mail: gvsmith@utk.edu.

The University of Tennessee Space Institute, Graduate Programs, Program in Aerospace Engineering, Tullahoma, TN 37388-9700. Offers MS, PhD. Part-time programs available. *Faculty:* 4 full-time (0 women), 11 part-time/adjunct (1 woman). *Students:* 12 full-time (2 women), 15 part-time (0 women); includes 3 minority (2 African Americans, 1 Hispanic American), 3 international. 12 applicants, 67% accepted, 1 enrolled. In 2009, 7 master's, 1 doctorate awarded. *Degree requirements:* For master's, thesis (for some programs); for doctorate, one foreign language, thesis/dissertation. *Entrance requirements:* For master's and doctorate, GRE General Test. Additional exam requirements/recommendations for international students: Required—TOEFL (minimum score 550 paper-based; 213 computer-based), IELTS (minimum score 6.5). *Application deadline:* For fall admission, 2/1 for international students; for spring admission, 6/15 for international students. Applications are processed on a rolling basis. Application fee: $35. Electronic applications accepted. *Expenses:* Tuition, state resident: full-time $6826; part-time $380 per hour. Tuition, nonresident: full-time $20,622; part-time $1147 per hour. Required fees: $10 per hour. One-time fee: $90 full-time. *Financial support:* In 2009–10, 1 fellowship (averaging $3,000 per year), 13 research assistantships with full tuition reimbursements (averaging $17,791 per year) were awarded; career-related internships or fieldwork, Federal Work-Study, institutionally sponsored loans, health care benefits, tuition waivers (full and partial), and unspecified assistantships also available. Financial award applicants required to submit FAFSA. *Faculty research:* Air and space vehicles, flight mechanics, propulsion, fluid mechanics, gas dynamics, energy conversion, structures. *Unit head:* Dr. Basil Antar, Degree Program Chairman, 931-393-7471, Fax: 931-393-7444, E-mail: bantar@utsi.edu. *Application contact:* Dee Merriman, Coordinator III, 931-393-7293, Fax: 931-393-7201, E-mail: dmerrima@utsi.edu.

The University of Texas at Arlington, Graduate School, College of Engineering, Department of Mechanical and Aerospace Engineering, Program in Aerospace Engineering, Arlington, TX 76019. Offers M Engr, MS, PhD. Part-time and evening/weekend programs available. Postbaccalaureate distance learning degree programs offered (minimal on-campus study). *Students:* 56 full-time (12 women), 44 part-time (5 women); includes 16 minority (2 African Americans, 9 Asian Americans or Pacific Islanders, 5 Hispanic Americans), 49 international. 46 applicants, 98% accepted, 21 enrolled. In 2009, 12 master's, 1 doctorate awarded. Terminal master's awarded for partial completion of doctoral program. *Degree requirements:* For master's, thesis optional; for doctorate, comprehensive exam, thesis/dissertation. *Entrance requirements:* For master's, GRE General Test, minimum GPA of 3.3; for doctorate, GRE General Test, minimum GPA of 3.5. Additional exam requirements/recommendations for international students:

Aerospace/Aeronautical Engineering

The University of Texas at Arlington (continued)

Required—TOEFL (minimum score 550 paper-based; 213 computer-based). *Application deadline:* For fall admission, 6/6 for domestic students, 4/4 for international students; for spring admission, 10/17 for domestic students, 9/5 for international students. Applications are processed on a rolling basis. Application fee: $25 ($50 for international students). *Financial support:* In 2009–10, 8 fellowships (averaging $1,000 per year), 13 research assistantships (averaging $12,000 per year), 6 teaching assistantships (averaging $14,000 per year) were awarded; institutionally sponsored loans, scholarships/grants, health care benefits, and unspecified assistantships also available. Financial award application deadline: 6/1; financial award applicants required to submit FAFSA. *Unit head:* Dr. Erian Armanios, Chair, 817-272-2062, Fax: 817-272-5010, E-mail: armanios@uta.edu. *Application contact:* Dr. Donald R. Wilson, Graduate Advisor, 817-272-2072, Fax: 817-272-5010, E-mail: wilson@uta.edu.

The University of Texas at Austin, Graduate School, Cockrell School of Engineering, Department of Aerospace Engineering and Engineering Mechanics, Program in Aerospace Engineering, Austin, TX 78712-1111. Offers MSE, PhD. *Entrance requirements:* For master's and doctorate, GRE General Test. Electronic applications accepted.

University of Toronto, School of Graduate Studies, Physical Sciences Division, Faculty of Applied Science and Engineering, Institute for Aerospace Science and Engineering, Toronto, ON M5S 1A1, Canada. Offers M Eng, MA Sc, PhD. Part-time programs available. *Degree requirements:* For master's, thesis (for some programs); for doctorate, thesis/dissertation, formal manuscript for publication. *Entrance requirements:* For master's, BA Sc degree or equivalent in engineering (M Eng); bachelor's degree in physics, mathematics, engineering or chemistry (MA Sc); 2 letters of reference; for doctorate, master's degree in applied science, engineering, mathematics, physics, or chemistry; demonstrated ability to perform advanced research, 2 letters of reference. Additional exam requirements/recommendations for international students: Required—TOEFL (minimum score 580 paper-based; 237 computer-based), TWE (minimum score 5), GRE.

University of Virginia, School of Engineering and Applied Science, Department of Mechanical and Aerospace Engineering, Charlottesville, VA 22903. Offers ME, MS, PhD. Postbaccalaureate distance learning degree programs offered (no on-campus study). *Faculty:* 24 full-time (3 women). *Students:* 77 full-time (11 women), 5 part-time (0 women); includes 4 minority (1 African American, 2 Asian Americans or Pacific Islanders, 1 Hispanic American), 24 international. Average age 27. 190 applicants, 15% accepted, 22 enrolled. In 2009, 17 master's, 9 doctorates awarded. *Degree requirements:* For master's, thesis (MS); for doctorate, comprehensive exam, thesis/dissertation. *Entrance requirements:* For master's and doctorate, GRE General Test, 3 letters of recommendation. Additional exam requirements/recommendations for international students: Required—TOEFL (minimum score 650 paper-based; 250 computer-based; 90 iBT), IELTS (minimum score 7). *Application deadline:* For fall admission, 8/1 for domestic students, 4/1 for international students; for winter admission, 12/1 for domestic students, 8/1 for international students; for spring admission, 5/1 for domestic students, 1/1 for international students. Applications are processed on a rolling basis. Application fee: $60. Electronic applications accepted. *Financial support:* Fellowships, research assistantships, teaching assistantships available. Financial award application deadline: 1/15; financial award applicants required to submit FAFSA. *Faculty research:* Solid mechanics, dynamical systems and control, thermofluids. *Unit head:* Hossein Haj-Hariri, Chair, 434-924-7424, Fax: 434-982-2037, E-mail: mae-adm@virginia.edu. *Application contact:* Graduate Secretary, 434-924-7425, Fax: 434-982-2037, E-mail: mae-adm@virginia.edu.

University of Washington, Graduate School, College of Engineering, Department of Aeronautics and Astronautics, Seattle, WA 98195-2400. Offers aeronautics and astronautics (MSAA, PhD); composite materials and structures (MAE, MAECMS). Part-time programs available. Postbaccalaureate distance learning degree programs offered (no on-campus study). *Faculty:* 19 full-time (1 woman), 4 part-time/adjunct (0 women). *Students:* 66 full-time (12 women), 80 part-time (7 women); includes 20 minority (1 African American, 10 Asian Americans or Pacific Islanders, 9 Hispanic Americans), 26 international. Average age 27. 187 applicants, 65% accepted, 65 enrolled. In 2009, 26 master's, 5 doctorates awarded. *Degree requirements:* For master's, thesis optional; for doctorate, comprehensive exam, thesis/dissertation. *Entrance requirements:* For master's, GRE General Test, minimum GPA of 3.0; for doctorate, GRE General Test, minimum GPA of 3.4, research advisor. Additional exam requirements/recommendations for international students: Required—TOEFL (minimum score 580 paper-based; 237 computer-based; 70 iBT), TOEFL iBT (listening, writing and reading sections). *Application deadline:* For fall admission, 1/15 priority date for domestic students, 11/1 priority date for international students; for winter admission, 10/1 priority date for domestic students; for spring admission, 2/1 priority date for domestic students. Applications are processed on a rolling basis. Application fee: $65. Electronic applications accepted. *Financial support:* In 2009–10, 2 students received support, including 9 fellowships (averaging $15,624 per year), 35 research assistantships with full tuition reimbursements available (averaging $17,217 per year), 9 teaching assistantships with full tuition reimbursements available (averaging $13,725 per year); career-related internships or fieldwork, Federal Work-Study, health care benefits, tuition waivers (full), and unspecified assistantships also available. Financial award application deadline: 1/15. *Faculty research:* Space systems, aircraft systems, energy systems, composites/structures, fluid dynamics, controls. Total annual research expenditures: $7 million. *Unit head:* Dr. Adam P. Bruckner, Professor and Chair, 206-543-1950, Fax: 206-543-0217, E-mail: bruckner@aa.washington.edu. *Application contact:* Wanda Frederick, Manager of Graduate Programs and External Relations, 206-616-1113, Fax: 206-543-0217, E-mail: wanda@aa.washington.edu.

Utah State University, School of Graduate Studies, College of Engineering, Department of Mechanical and Aerospace Engineering, Logan, UT 84322. Offers aerospace engineering (MS, PhD); mechanical engineering (ME, MS, PhD). Terminal master's awarded for partial completion of doctoral program. *Degree requirements:* For master's, thesis (for some programs); for doctorate, thesis/dissertation. *Entrance requirements:* For master's, GRE General Test, minimum GPA of 3.0; for doctorate, GRE General Test, minimum GPA of 3.3. Additional exam requirements/recommendations for international students: Required—TOEFL. *Faculty research:* In-space instruments, cryogenic cooling, thermal science, space structures, composite materials.

Virginia Polytechnic Institute and State University, Graduate School, College of Engineering, Department of Aerospace and Ocean Engineering, Blacksburg, VA 24061. Offers aerospace engineering (M Eng, MS, PhD); ocean engineering (MS). *Entrance requirements:* For master's and doctorate, GRE. Additional exam requirements/recommendations for international students: Required—TOEFL (minimum score 550 paper-based; 213 computer-based), GRE. Electronic applications accepted. *Faculty research:* Aerodynamics, flight mechanics, vehicle structures, space mechanics and design.

Virginia Polytechnic Institute and State University, VT Online, Blacksburg, VA 24061. Offers aerospace engineering (MS); business information systems (Graduate Certificate); career and technical education (MS); computer engineering (M Eng, MS); decision support systems (Graduate Certificate); eLearning leadership (MA); electrical engineering (M Eng, MS); engineering administration (MEA); environmental politics and policy (Graduate Certificate); foundations of political analysis (Graduate Certificate); health product risk management (Graduate Certificate); information policy and society (Graduate Certificate); information security (Graduate Certificate); instructional technology (MA); liberal arts (Graduate Certificate); life sciences: health product risk management (MS); natural resources (MNR, Graduate Certificate); networking (Graduate Certificate); nonprofit and nongovernmental organization management (Graduate Certificate); ocean engineering (MS); political science (MA); security studies (Graduate Certificate); software development (Graduate Certificate).

Washington University in St. Louis, Henry Edwin Sever Graduate School of Engineering and Applied Science, Department of Mechanical, Aerospace and Structural Engineering, St. Louis, MO 63130-4899. Offers MS, D Sc, PhD. Part-time programs available. Terminal master's awarded for partial completion of doctoral program. *Degree requirements:* For master's, thesis optional; for doctorate, thesis/dissertation optional. *Entrance requirements:* For master's, GRE; for doctorate, GRE General Test, departmental qualifying exam. *Faculty research:* Aerosols science and technology, applied mechanics, biomechanics and biomedical engineering, design, dynamic systems, combustion science, composite materials, materials science.

Webster University, George Herbert Walker School of Business and Technology, Department of Management, St. Louis, MO 63119-3194. Offers business and organizational security management (MA); computer resources and information management (MA); environmental management (MS); government contracting (Certificate); health care management (MA); health services management (MA); human resources development (MA); human resources management (MA); management (DM); management and leadership (MA); marketing (MA); nonprofit management (Certificate); procurement and acquisitions management (MA); public administration (MA); quality management (MA); space systems operations management (MS); telecommunications management (MA). Part-time and evening/weekend programs available. Postbaccalaureate distance learning degree programs offered (no on-campus study). *Faculty:* 16 full-time, 781 part-time/adjunct. *Students:* 1,369 full-time (610 women), 5,182 part-time (3,047 women); includes 3,460 minority (2,835 African Americans, 38 American Indian/Alaska Native, 169 Asian Americans or Pacific Islanders, 418 Hispanic Americans), 80 international. Average age 37. In 2009, 2,491 master's, 13 doctorates, 68 other advanced degrees awarded. *Degree requirements:* For master's, thesis (for some programs); for doctorate, thesis/dissertation, written exam. *Entrance requirements:* For doctorate, GMAT, 3 years of work experience, MBA. Additional exam requirements/recommendations for international students: Required—TOEFL. *Application deadline:* Applications are processed on a rolling basis. Application fee: $25 ($50 for international students). *Expenses:* Tuition: Part-time $565 per credit hour. Tuition and fees vary according to degree level, campus/location and program. *Financial support:* Federal Work-Study available. Support available to part-time students. Financial award application deadline: 4/1; financial award applicants required to submit FAFSA. *Unit head:* Jim Brasfield, Chair, 314-961-2660 Ext. 7063, Fax: 314-968-7077, E-mail: mgtchair@webster.edu. *Application contact:* Matt Nolan, Assoc. V.P.—Enrollment Management / Dean of Admissions, Fax: 314-968-7116, E-mail: gadmit@webster.edu.

West Virginia University, College of Engineering and Mineral Resources, Department of Mechanical and Aerospace Engineering, Program in Aerospace Engineering, Morgantown, WV 26506. Offers MSAE, PhD. Part-time programs available. Terminal master's awarded for partial completion of doctoral program. *Degree requirements:* For master's, thesis; for doctorate, comprehensive exam, thesis/dissertation, qualifying exams, proposal defense. *Entrance requirements:* For master's and doctorate, GRE General Test, minimum GPA of 3.0, 3 reference letters. Additional exam requirements/recommendations for international students: Required—TOEFL (minimum score 550 paper-based; 213 computer-based; 79 iBT). *Faculty research:* Transonic flight controls and simulations, thermal science, composite materials, aerospace design.

Wichita State University, Graduate School, College of Engineering, Department of Aerospace Engineering, Wichita, KS 67260. Offers MS, PhD. Part-time programs available. *Expenses:* Tuition, state resident: full-time $4247; part-time $235.95 per credit hour. Tuition, nonresident: full-time $11,171; part-time $620.60 per credit hour. Required fees: $34; $3.60 per credit hour. $17 per term. Tuition and fees vary according to campus/location and program. *Unit head:* Dr. L. Scott Miller, Chairperson, 316-978-3410, E-mail: scott.miller@wichita.edu. *Application contact:* Dr. L. Scott Miller, Chairperson, 316-978-3410, E-mail: scott.miller@wichita.edu.

Aviation

Everglades University, Graduate Programs, Program in Aviation Science, Boca Raton, FL 33431. Offers MSA. *Entrance requirements:* Additional exam requirements/recommendations for international students: Recommended—TOEFL (minimum score 500 paper-based; 173 computer-based). Electronic applications accepted.

Lewis University, College of Arts and Sciences, Program in Aviation and Transportation, Romeoville, IL 60446. Offers administration (MS); safety and security (MS). Part-time and evening/weekend programs available. *Faculty:* 2 full-time (0 women), 1 part-time/adjunct (0 women). *Students:* 2 full-time (0 women), 10 part-time (1 woman); includes 2 minority (1 African American, 1 Hispanic American). Average age 37. In 2009, 2 master's awarded. *Entrance requirements:* For master's, bachelor's degree, minimum GPA of 3.0, personal statement, 3 letters of recommendation. Additional exam requirements/recommendations for international students: Required—TOEFL (minimum score 550 paper-based; 213 computer-based). *Application deadline:* For fall admission, 5/1 priority date for international students; for spring admission, 11/15 priority date for international students. Applications are processed on a rolling basis. Application fee: $40. Electronic applications accepted. *Expenses:* Tuition: Full-time $6480; part-time $720 per credit. One-time fee: $40. Tuition and fees vary according to course load, degree level and program. *Financial support:* Application deadline: 5/1; *Unit head:* Dr. Randal DeMik, Head, 815-838-0500 Ext. 5559, E-mail: demikra@lewisu.edu. *Application contact:* Diane Blazevich, Information Contact, 815-838-0500 Ext. 5434, E-mail: blazevdi@lewisu.edu.

Southeastern Oklahoma State University, Department of Aviation Science, Durant, OK 74701-0609. Offers aerospace administration and logistics (MS). Part-time and evening/weekend programs available. *Students:* 33 full-time (4 women), 53 part-time (13 women); includes 16 minority (5 African Americans, 2 American Indian/Alaska Native, 3 Asian Americans or Pacific Islanders, 6 Hispanic Americans), 1 international. Average age 30. 86 applicants, 100% accepted, 86 enrolled. *Entrance requirements:* For master's, minimum GPA of 3.0 in last 60 hours or 2.75 overall. Additional exam requirements/recommendations for international students: Required—TOEFL (minimum score 550 paper-based; 213 computer-based). *Application deadline:* For fall admission, 8/1 for domestic students, 6/1 for international students; for spring admission, 1/5 for domestic students, 11/1 for international students. Application fee: $20 ($55 for international students). Electronic applications accepted. *Financial support:* Federal Work-Study and institutionally sponsored loans available. Support available to part-time students. Financial award application deadline: 6/15. *Unit head:* Dr. David Conway, Director, 580-745-3240, Fax: 580-924-0741, E-mail: dconway@se.edu. *Application contact:* Carrie Williamson, Administrative Assistant-Graduate Office, 580-745-2200, Fax: 580-745-7474, E-mail: cwilliamson@se.edu.

University of Illinois at Urbana–Champaign, Institute of Aviation, Champaign, IL 61820. Offers human factors (MS). *Faculty:* 5 full-time (1 woman). *Students:* 11 full-time (8 women), 6 international. 18 applicants, 28% accepted, 4 enrolled. In 2009, 3 master's awarded. *Entrance requirements:* For master's, GRE, minimum undergraduate GPA of 3.0 for last 60 hours.

Additional exam requirements/recommendations for international students: Required—TOEFL. *Application deadline:* Applications are processed on a rolling basis. Application fee: $60 ($75 for international students). Electronic applications accepted. *Financial support:* In 2009–10, 9 research assistantships, 4 teaching assistantships were awarded; fellowships, tuition waivers (full and partial) also available. *Unit head:* Alex Kirlik, Acting Head, 217-244-8972, E-mail: kirlik@illinois.edu. *Application contact:* Peter Vlach, Information Systems Specialist, 217-265-9456, E-mail: pvlach@illinois.edu.

University of North Dakota, Graduate School, John D. Odegard School of Aerospace Sciences, Department of Aviation, Grand Forks, ND 58202. Offers MS. Part-time programs available. Postbaccalaureate distance learning degree programs offered (minimal on-campus study). *Degree requirements:* For master's, comprehensive exam. *Entrance requirements:* For master's, GRE General Test, FAA private pilot certificate or foreign equivalent. Additional exam requirements/recommendations for international students: Required—TOEFL (minimum score 550 paper-based; 213 computer-based; 79 iBT), IELTS (minimum score 6.5). Electronic applications accepted.

The University of Tennessee, Graduate School, Intercollegiate Programs, Program in Aviation Systems, Knoxville, TN 37996. Offers MS. Part-time programs available. Postbaccalaureate distance learning degree programs offered (no on-campus study). *Degree requirements:* For master's, thesis optional. *Entrance requirements:* For master's, minimum GPA of 2.7. Additional exam requirements/recommendations for international students: Required—TOEFL. Electronic applications accepted. *Expenses:* Tuition, state resident: full-time $6826; part-time $380 per semester hour. Tuition, nonresident: full-time $21,844; part-time $1147 per semester hour. Tuition and fees vary according to program.

The University of Tennessee Space Institute, Graduate Programs, Program in Aviation Systems, Tullahoma, TN 37388-9700. Offers MS. *Faculty:* 4 full-time (0 women), 3 part-time/adjunct (0 women). *Students:* 6 full-time (0 women), 29 part-time (3 women); includes 1 minority (Hispanic American), 2 international. 8 applicants, 100% accepted, 3 enrolled. In 2009, 25 master's awarded. *Degree requirements:* For master's, thesis (for some programs). *Entrance requirements:* Additional exam requirements/recommendations for international students: Required—TOEFL (minimum score 550 paper-based; 213 computer-based), IELTS (minimum score 6.5). *Application deadline:* For fall admission, 2/1 for international students; for spring admission, 6/15 for international students. Applications are processed on a rolling basis. Application fee: $35. Electronic applications accepted. *Expenses:* Tuition, state resident: full-time $6826; part-time $380 per hour. Tuition, nonresident: full-time $20,622; part-time $1147 per hour. Required fees: $10 per hour. One-time fee: $90 full-time. *Financial support:* In 2009–10, 1 fellowship (averaging $3,000 per year), 2 research assistantships with full tuition reimbursements (averaging $17,791 per year) were awarded; career-related internships or fieldwork, Federal Work-Study, institutionally sponsored loans, health care benefits, tuition waivers (full and partial), and unspecified assistantships also available. Financial award applicants required to submit FAFSA. *Faculty research:* Aircraft performance and flying qualities, atmospheric and earth/ocean science, flight systems and human factors, aircraft design, advanced flight test instrumentation. *Unit head:* Dr. Stephen Corda, Chairman, 931-393-7413, Fax: 931-393-7533, E-mail: scorda@utsi.edu. *Application contact:* Dee Merriman, Coordinator III, 931-393-7293, Fax: 931-393-7201, E-mail: dmerrima@utsi.edu.

FLORIDA INSTITUTE OF TECHNOLOGY

College of Aeronautics
Division of Aviation Studies
Master of Science in Aviation Program
Master of Science in Aviation Human Factors Program

Program of Study

The Master of Science in Aviation (M.S.A.) is designed for the professional growth needs of persons interested in a wide range of aviation careers. The degree is relevant for those who have earned a baccalaureate degree in aviation and those who have worked in the aviation field and now require more advanced knowledge. Two areas of emphasis are currently being offered: the airport development and management option and the applied aviation safety option. Persons interested in careers in airport or airline management, airport consulting, and governmental organizations involved in airport management or regulation will be interested in this option, which is designed to offer specialization in airport operations and management. Modern airport management requires a unique skill set that crosses traditional corporate lines into government regulation and oversight, public finance, public administration, urban planning, environmental protection, security, flight safety, contract management, airspace management, and a host of other disciplines. This degree option helps place all of these disciplines in context and prepares professionals for demanding but uniquely rewarding careers.

The applied aviation safety option places emphasis on aviation safety, accident investigation, technical aviation consulting, and educational, regulatory, or investigative positions in governmental or trade organizations. This option is designed to broaden knowledge in a variety of technical areas of aviation. Modern accident investigators, consultants, government employees, teachers, and researchers often need to be able to assimilate and interpret aviation information from a variety of specialists and to apply this information to the resolution of complex problems and issues. The degree option prepares professionals to understand, integrate, and use information derived from such diverse fields as aviation physiology, avionics, electronics, human factors, and meteorology.

The College of Aeronautics also offers the Master of Science (M.S.) degree with a major in aviation human factors. Human factors refers to the study of human-machine interaction to optimize the design and operation of aviation systems. This degree prepares individuals to assume critical positions in the design, fabrication, maintenance, investigation, and evaluation of aviation systems. The program is offered through resident instruction or online. It is also a strong preparatory degree for entry into human factors Ph.D. programs.

In cooperation with Florida Tech's outstanding Science Education Department, the College of Aeronautics sponsors a Ph.D. in science education–aeronautics. The program is designed to prepare exceptional individuals for faculty positions at universities and colleges offering aviation programs.

Research Facilities

The program offers modern computer laboratories for weather, air traffic control, advanced airport and airspace planning applications, statistical analyses, and word processing. The College of Aeronautics is housed in the Skurla Building located on the main campus of Florida Tech. Modern conference rooms and classrooms are available for meetings, program courses, and content-specific seminars. All rooms have access to audiovisual equipment, including projectors, VCR equipment, projection screens, movie projectors, and engine mock-up and avionics equipment. Library resources contain major, general-purpose magazines and newspapers as well as professional reference books, dictionaries, and indexes. There is also electronic library search capability on the Internet and access to the Web.

A complete flight training facility consisting of over thirty-five single and multiengine aircraft, flight simulators, classrooms with appropriate flight instructional aids, and a comprehensive maintenance facility are located minutes away at the Melbourne International Airport for students' use. Single-engine, multiengine, and flight-training device (FTD) simulators are also available on the main campus.

Financial Aid

Awards are based on academic promise, need, college costs, and the availability of funding. Inquiries should be sent to the Director of Financial Aid. Students eligible for Veterans Administration (VA) benefits may contact the VA representative on the Melbourne campus. Some flight, airport, and human factors internship may be available.

Cost of Study

Tuition for the academic year 2010–11 is $1040 per credit hour. Graduate student teaching and research awards may include tuition remission and a stipend.

Living and Housing Costs

Room and board on campus cost approximately $4500 per semester in 2010–11. On-campus housing (dormitories and apartments) is available for full-time single and married graduate students, but priority for dormitory rooms is given to undergraduate students. Many apartment complexes and rental houses are available near the campus.

Student Group

Florida Tech has an active student government that acts as a vital link between the administration and the student body, as the liaison between the university and the community, and as the catalyst for social events. The organization promotes new ideas and encourages student participation at all levels of university activity. The College of Aeronautics specifically has a student-organized Aeronautics Committee, the National Association of Women in Aviation (NAWA), Florida Institute of Technology College of Aeronautics Alumni organization (FITSA), Alpha Eta Rho, the Falcons Flight Team, the American Association of Airport Executives (AAEE), and the first student chapter of the International Society of Aviation Safety Investigators (ISASI).

Student Outcomes

Graduates of the program obtain positions in various areas and companies, such as airport management; the FAA; Airborne Express; K-C Aviation; Molex Inc.; UXB International; Collier County Airport Authority; U.S. Air Force Civilian Personnel; Pittsburgh International Airport; City of Houston, Department of Aviation; San Francisco International Airport; NASA; Hoyle, Tanner & Associates, Inc.; Flight Data Inc.; Kenton County Airport Board; Hanover County Municipal Airport; Greiner Inc.; and the New Piper Aircraft.

Location

Melbourne, Florida, is a medium-sized community with a subtropical climate. Shopping centers and a major hospital are nearby. Melbourne International Airport serves the community and campus with flights from all major cities. There are beaches approximately 3 miles from the campus for surfing, sailing, skin diving, and water-skiing. The Kennedy Space Center and Disney World are also nearby.

The Institute and The College

Florida Tech is an accredited, coeducational, independent university. Since its founding in 1958, along with the U.S. space program, the university has grown rapidly. Today nearly 4,000 students are enrolled in undergraduate and graduate programs. The university offers doctoral degrees in eighteen disciplines, while master's degrees are offered in more than forty areas of study. The College of Aeronautics is also accredited by the Council on Aviation Accreditation.

Applying

A strong background in aviation or its related fields and scores on the GRE General Test are recommended. Applications should be received at the Graduate Admissions Office by early January. Students are selected on the basis of undergraduate records and interviews with several members of the faculty.

Correspondence and Information

Dr. John Cain
Program Chairman of Graduate Studies
College of Aeronautics
Florida Institute of Technology
150 West University Boulevard
Melbourne, Florida 32901-6988

Phone: 321-674-8120
Fax: 321-674-8057
E-mail: jcain@fit.edu
Web site: http://www.fit.edu/acadres/aero

For a catalog and an application:

Graduate Admissions Office
Florida Institute of Technology
150 West University Boulevard
Melbourne, Florida 32901

Phone: 321-674-8027
  800-944-4348 (toll-free)
Fax: 321-723-9468
E-mail: grad-admissions@fit.edu
Web site: http://www.fit.edu/grad

Florida Institute of Technology

THE FACULTY AND THEIR RESEARCH

Winston E. Scott, Dean, College of Aeronautics. Captain Scott is a retired naval aviator with more than 5000 hours of flight experience in over twenty different aircraft. He holds a Master of Science degree in aeronautical engineering with avionics and honorary doctorate degrees from Florida Atlantic University and Michigan State University. Captain Scott served a tour of duty with Fighter Squadron Eighty Four at NAS Oceana, Virginia, served as a production test pilot at the Naval Aviation Depot with NAS in Jacksonville, and was later assigned as a test pilot and as the Deputy Director of the Tactical Aircraft Systems Department in Warminster, Pennsylvania. He served as Vice President for Student Affairs and Associate Dean, College of Engineering at Florida State University. He was also an Associate Instructor of electrical engineering at Florida A&M University and Florida Community College at Jacksonville. Captain Scott was selected as an astronaut by NASA in 1992. Serving as a mission specialist on two space flights, he logged over 24 days; including three spacewalks totaling over 19 hours. He is a published author, has appeared on national TV news as an expert commentator, and advised elected officials on matters related to space and aeronautics.

Ballard Barker, Ph.D., Oklahoma. Planning, design, operation, and management of airports and other aviation facilities.

John Cain, Ed.S., Ph.D., Florida Tech. Develops curriculum and instructs aviation science and aviation management academics; instructs aeronautical science courses in aerodynamics, computer systems, aviation math, aircraft systems, aircraft performance, and accident investigation.

Kenneth Crooks, J.D., Florida; M.P.A., Golden Gate. Corporate finance, decision theory, investments, business law, management, transportation, and labor relations with an emphasis on the legal environment of aviation management.

Stephe Cusick, J.D., Louisville. Corporate attorney and former navy pilot. Teaches aviation technology, aviation safety, and aviation law courses.

John Deaton, Ph.D., Catholic University. An Applied Experimental Psychologist, former Navy Commander with more than 800 flight hours, served as an Aerospace Experimental Psychologist, was a semifinalist for NASA's astronaut training program.

Korhan Oyman, Ph.D., Anadolu (Turkey). Former international airport manager, works on airport- and airline-related subjects. Consults aviation institutions and corporations worldwide.

Thomas Utley, Ph.D., Florida Tech. Certified meteorologist with more than thirty years of aviation meteorology experience, former director of several governmental meteorological organizations.

Nathaniel Villaire, Ed.D., William and Mary; M.P.A., Golden Gate. High-altitude pulmonary physiology, human factors in ATC, airspace management and safety.

Section 3
Agricultural Engineering and Bioengineering

This section contains a directory of institutions offering graduate work in agricultural engineering and bioengineering, followed by in-depth entries submitted by institutions that chose to prepare detailed program descriptions. Additional information about programs listed in the directory but not augmented by an in-depth entry may be obtained by writing directly to the dean of a graduate school or chair of a department at the address given in the directory.

For programs offering related work, see also in this book *Biomedical Engineering and Biotechnology; Civil and Environmental Engineering; Engineering and Applied Sciences;* and *Management of Engineering and Technology.* In the other guides in this series:

Graduate Programs in the Biological Sciences

See *Biological and Biomedical Sciences; Ecology, Environmental Biology, and Evolutionary Biology; Marine Biology; Nutrition;* and *Zoology*

Graduate Programs in the Physical Sciences, Mathematics, Agricultural Sciences, the Environment & Natural Resources

See *Agricultural and Food Sciences* and *Natural Resources*

CONTENTS

Agricultural Engineering

Cornell University, Graduate School, Graduate Fields of Agriculture and Life Sciences and Graduate Fields of Engineering, Field of Biological and Environmental Engineering, Ithaca, NY 14853-0001. Offers biological engineering (M Eng, MPS, MS, PhD); energy (M Eng, MPS, MS, PhD); environmental engineering (M Eng, MPS, MS, PhD); environmental management (MPS); food processing engineering (M Eng, MPS, MS, PhD); international agriculture (M Eng, MPS, MS, PhD); local roads (M Eng, MPS, MS, PhD); machine systems (M Eng, MPS, MS, PhD); soil and water engineering (M Eng, MPS, MS, PhD); structures and environment (M Eng, MPS, MS, PhD). *Faculty:* 34 full-time (6 women). *Students:* 61 full-time (23 women); includes 5 minority (2 African Americans, 2 Asian Americans or Pacific Islanders, 1 Hispanic American), 23 international. Average age 29. 88 applicants, 43% accepted, 24 enrolled. In 2009, 13 master's, 9 doctorates awarded. Terminal master's awarded for partial completion of doctoral program. *Degree requirements:* For master's, thesis (MS); for doctorate, comprehensive exam, thesis/dissertation. *Entrance requirements:* For master's, 3 letters of recommendation (MS), 2 letters of recommentdaion (M Eng, MPS); for doctorate, GRE General Test, 3 letters of recommendation. Additional exam requirements/recommendations for international students: Required—TOEFL (minimum score 550 paper-based; 213 computer-based; 77 iBT). *Application deadline:* For fall admission, 1/15 priority date for domestic students; for spring admission, 10/1 for domestic students. Applications are processed on a rolling basis. Application fee: $70. Electronic applications accepted. *Expenses:* Tuition: Full-time $29,500. Required fees: $70. Full-time tuition and fees vary according to degree level, program and student level. *Financial support:* In 2009–10, 45 students received support, including 3 fellowships with full tuition reimbursements available, 8 research assistantships with full tuition reimbursements available, 2 teaching assistantships with full tuition reimbursements available; institutionally sponsored loans, scholarships/grants, health care benefits, tuition waivers (full and partial), and unspecified assistantships also available. Financial award applicants required to submit FAFSA. *Faculty research:* Biological and food engineering, environmental, soil and water engineering, international agricultural engineering, structures and controlled environments, machine systems and energy. *Unit head:* Director of Graduate Studies, 607-255-2173, Fax: 607-255-4080, E-mail: abengradfield@cornell.edu. *Application contact:* Graduate Field Assistant, 607-255-2173, Fax: 607-255-4080, E-mail: abengradfield@cornell.edu.

Dalhousie University, Faculty of Engineering, Department of Biological Engineering, Halifax, NS B3J 2X4, Canada. Offers M Eng, MA Sc, PhD. *Faculty:* 5 full-time (0 women), 1 part-time/adjunct (0 women). *Students:* 10 full-time (1 woman), 1 part-time (0 women). Average age 33. 17 applicants, 76% accepted. In 2009, 1 master's awarded. *Degree requirements:* For master's, thesis; for doctorate, thesis/dissertation. *Entrance requirements:* Additional exam requirements/recommendations for international students: Required—TOEFL, IELTS, CANTEST, CAEL, or Michigan English Language Assessment Battery. *Application deadline:* For fall admission, 6/1 for domestic students, 4/1 for international students; for winter admission, 10/31 for domestic students, 8/31 for international students; for spring admission, 2/28 for domestic students, 12/31 for international students. Applications are processed on a rolling basis. Application fee: $70. *Financial support:* In 2009–10, 1 research assistantship (averaging $1,600 per year), 4 teaching assistantships (averaging $4,000 per year) were awarded; fellowships, scholarships/grants and unspecified assistantships also available. *Faculty research:* Waste management, energy and environment, bio-machinery and robotics, soil and water, aquacultural and food engineering. *Unit head:* Dr. Michael Pegg, Unit Head, 902-494-3252, Fax: 902-423-0219, E-mail: michael.pegg@dal.ca. *Application contact:* Dr. Georges Kipouros, Graduate Coordinator, 902-494-6100, Fax: 902-423-0219, E-mail: peas.grad@dal.ca.

Illinois Institute of Technology, Graduate College, Armour College of Engineering, Department of Chemical and Biological Engineering, Chicago, IL 60616-3793. Offers biological engineering (MBE); chemical engineering (M Ch E, MS, PhD); food process engineering (MFPE); food processing engineering (MS); gas engineering (MGE); manufacturing engineering (MME, MS); MS/M Ch E. Part-time and evening/weekend programs available. Postbaccalaureate distance learning degree programs offered. Terminal master's awarded for partial completion of doctoral program. *Degree requirements:* For master's, comprehensive exam, thesis (for some programs); for doctorate, comprehensive exam, thesis/dissertation. *Entrance requirements:* For master's and doctorate, GRE General Test, minimum undergraduate GPA of 3.0. Additional exam requirements/recommendations for international students: Required—TOEFL (minimum score 550 paper-based; 213 computer-based; 80 iBT). Electronic applications accepted. *Expenses:* Tuition: Full-time $17,550; part-time $888 per credit hour. Required fees: $850; $7.50 per credit hour. One-time fee: $50 full-time. Full-time tuition and fees vary according to program. *Faculty research:* Biochemical, bioenergy, biosensors, tissue engineering, fuel cells, batteries, renewable energy, gas cleaning, particle technology, fluidization, colloid and interfacial engineering complex fluids, polymers, complex systems and dynamics.

Instituto Tecnológico y de Estudios Superiores de Monterrey, Campus Monterrey, Graduate and Research Division, Program in Agriculture, Monterrey, Mexico. Offers agricultural parasitology (PhD); agricultural sciences (MS); farming productivity (MS); food processing engineering (MS); phytopathology (MS). Part-time programs available. *Degree requirements:* For master's, one foreign language, thesis; for doctorate, one foreign language, thesis/dissertation. *Entrance requirements:* For master's, EXADEP; for doctorate, GMAT or GRE, master's degree in related field. Additional exam requirements/recommendations for international students: Required—TOEFL. *Faculty research:* Animal embryos and reproduction, crop entomology, tropical agriculture, agricultural productivity, induced mutation in oleaginous plants.

Iowa State University of Science and Technology, Graduate College, College of Engineering, Department of Agricultural and Biosystems Engineering, Ames, IA 50011. Offers M Eng, MS, PhD. *Faculty:* 30 full-time (2 women), 3 part-time/adjunct (0 women). *Students:* 54 full-time (21 women), 9 part-time (2 women); includes 3 minority (1 African American, 1 Asian American or Pacific Islander, 1 Hispanic American), 30 international. 47 applicants, 49% accepted, 20 enrolled. In 2009, 8 master's, 5 doctorates awarded. *Degree requirements:* For master's, thesis (for some programs); for doctorate, thesis/dissertation. *Entrance requirements:* Additional exam requirements/recommendations for international students: Required—TOEFL (minimum score 550 paper-based; 79 iBT) or IELTS (minimum score 6.5). *Application deadline:* For fall admission, 2/1 priority date for domestic and international students; for spring admission, 7/1 priority date for domestic and international students. Applications are processed on a rolling basis. Application fee: $40 ($90 for international students). Electronic applications accepted. *Expenses:* Tuition, state resident: full-time $6716. Tuition, nonresident: full-time $8908. Tuition and fees vary according to course level, course load, program and student level. *Financial support:* In 2009–10, 43 research assistantships with full and partial tuition reimbursements (averaging $15,410 per year), 1 teaching assistantship with full and partial tuition reimbursement (averaging $14,160 per year) were awarded; fellowships, scholarships/grants, health care benefits, and unspecified assistantships also available. *Faculty research:* Grain processing and quality, tillage systems, simulation and controls, water management, environmental quality. *Unit head:* Dr. Ramesh Kanwar, Chair, 515-294-1434. *Application contact:* Dr. Steven Freeman, Director of Graduate Education, 515-294-9541, E-mail: sfreeman@iastate.edu.

Kansas State University, Graduate School, College of Agriculture, Department of Grain Science and Industry, Manhattan, KS 66506. Offers MS, PhD. Part-time programs available. *Faculty:* 15 full-time (3 women), 10 part-time/adjunct (2 women). *Students:* 44 full-time (23 women), 2 part-time (0 women); includes 3 minority (2 African Americans, 1 Hispanic American), 28 international. Average age 27. 36 applicants, 64% accepted, 7 enrolled. In 2009, 9 master's, 2 doctorates awarded. Terminal master's awarded for partial completion of doctoral program. *Degree requirements:* For master's, thesis, oral exam; for doctorate, thesis/dissertation, preliminary exam. *Entrance requirements:* For master's and doctorate, GRE General Test, minimum undergraduate GPA of 3.0. Additional exam requirements/recommendations for international students: Required—TOEFL (minimum score 550 paper-based; 213 computer-based). *Application deadline:* For fall admission, 2/1 priority date for domestic and international students; for spring admission, 8/1 priority date for domestic and international students. Applications are processed on a rolling basis. Application fee: $40 ($55 for international students). Electronic applications accepted. *Financial support:* In 2009–10, 33 research assistantships (averaging $15,064 per year), 3 teaching assistantships with partial tuition reimbursements (averaging $16,410 per year) were awarded; fellowships, Federal Work-Study, institutionally sponsored loans, and scholarships/grants also available. Support available to part-time students. Financial award application deadline: 3/1; financial award applicants required to submit FAFSA. *Faculty research:* Particle management, grain and cereal product research, industrial value added products from cereals and legumes, grain stored wheat and pest management, biosecurity and global tracing. Total annual research expenditures: $1.4 million. *Unit head:* Dirk Maier, Head, 785-532-6161, Fax: 785-532-7010, E-mail: dmaier@ksu.edu. *Application contact:* David Wetzel, Director, 785-532-6005, Fax: 785-532-7010, E-mail: dwetzel@ksu.edu.

Kansas State University, Graduate School, College of Engineering, Department of Biological and Agricultural Engineering, Manhattan, KS 66506. Offers MS, PhD. *Faculty:* 14 full-time (1 woman), 6 part-time/adjunct (0 women). *Students:* 24 full-time (5 women), 6 part-time (4 women); includes 1 minority (Asian American or Pacific Islander), 20 international. Average age 31. 27 applicants, 26% accepted, 7 enrolled. In 2009, 3 master's, 3 doctorates awarded. Terminal master's awarded for partial completion of doctoral program. *Degree requirements:* For master's, thesis; for doctorate, thesis/dissertation. *Entrance requirements:* For master's, GRE (recommended), bachelor's degree in agricultural engineering; for doctorate, GRE (recommended). Additional exam requirements/recommendations for international students: Required—TOEFL (minimum score 600 paper-based; 250 computer-based). *Application deadline:* For fall admission, 2/1 priority date for domestic and international students; for spring admission, 8/1 priority date for domestic and international students. Applications are processed on a rolling basis. Application fee: $40 ($55 for international students). Electronic applications accepted. *Financial support:* In 2009–10, 24 research assistantships (averaging $13,992 per year) were awarded; fellowships, teaching assistantships, Federal Work-Study, institutionally sponsored loans, and scholarships/grants also available. Support available to part-time students. Financial award application deadline: 3/1; financial award applicants required to submit FAFSA. *Faculty research:* Ecological engineering, watershed modeling, air quality, bioprocessing, sensors and controls. Total annual research expenditures: $2.1 million. *Unit head:* Joseph Harner, Interim Head, 785-532-5580, Fax: 785-532-5825, E-mail: jharner@ksu.edu. *Application contact:* Naiqian Zhang, Director, 785-532-2910, Fax: 785-532-5825, E-mail: zhangn@ksu.edu.

Louisiana State University and Agricultural and Mechanical College, Graduate School, College of Agriculture, Department of Biological and Agricultural Engineering, Baton Rouge, LA 70803. Offers biological and agricultural engineering (MSBAE); engineering science (MS, PhD). Part-time programs available. *Faculty:* 13 full-time (2 women). *Students:* 16 full-time (2 women), 4 part-time (2 women); includes 2 African Americans, 3 Asian Americans or Pacific Islanders, 8 international. Average age 26. 9 applicants, 78% accepted, 4 enrolled. In 2009, 5 master's awarded. Terminal master's awarded for partial completion of doctoral program. *Degree requirements:* For master's, thesis; for doctorate, thesis/dissertation. *Entrance requirements:* For master's and doctorate, GRE General Test, minimum GPA of 3.0. Additional exam requirements/recommendations for international students: Required—TOEFL (minimum score 550 paper-based; 213 computer-based; 79 iBT) or IELTS (minimum score 6.5). *Application deadline:* For fall admission, 1/25 priority date for domestic students, 5/15 for international students; for spring admission, 10/15 for international students. Applications are processed on a rolling basis. Application fee: $50 ($70 for international students). Electronic applications accepted. *Financial support:* In 2009–10, 19 students received support, including 1 fellowship (averaging $35,195 per year), 14 research assistantships with partial tuition reimbursements available (averaging $14,723 per year); teaching assistantships with partial tuition reimbursements available, career-related internships or fieldwork, Federal Work-Study, institutionally sponsored loans, scholarships/grants, health care benefits, and unspecified assistantships also available. Financial award application deadline: 7/1; financial award applicants required to submit FAFSA. *Faculty research:* Bioenergy, bioprocess engineering, cellular and molecular engineering, drug delivery using nanotechnology, environmental engineering. Total annual research expenditures: $25,277. *Unit head:* Dr. Dan Thomas, Head, 225-578-3153, Fax: 225-578-3492, E-mail: dthomas@agcenter.lsu.edu. *Application contact:* Dr. Steven Hall, Graduate Coordinator, 225-578-1058, Fax: 225-578-3492, E-mail: sghall@agcenter.lsu.edu.

McGill University, Faculty of Graduate and Postdoctoral Studies, Faculty of Agricultural and Environmental Sciences, Department of Bioresource Engineering, Montréal, QC H3A 2T5, Canada. Offers computer applications (M Sc, M Sc A, PhD); food engineering (M Sc, M Sc A, PhD); grain drying (M Sc, M Sc A, PhD); irrigation and drainage (M Sc, M Sc A, PhD); machinery (M Sc, M Sc A, PhD); pollution control (M Sc, M Sc A, PhD); post-harvest technology (M Sc, M Sc A, PhD); soil dynamics (M Sc, M Sc A, PhD); structure and environment (M Sc, M Sc A, PhD); vegetable and fruit storage (M Sc, M Sc A, PhD).

New York University, Graduate School of Arts and Science, Department of Environmental Medicine, New York, NY 10012-1019. Offers environmental health sciences (MS, PhD), including biostatistics (PhD), environmental hygiene (MS), epidemiology (PhD), ergonomics and biomechanics (PhD), exposure assessment and health effects (PhD), molecular toxicology/carcinogenesis (PhD), toxicology. Part-time programs available. *Faculty:* 26 full-time (7 women). *Students:* 45 full-time (37 women), 15 part-time (8 women); includes 9 minority (3 African Americans, 3 Asian Americans or Pacific Islanders, 3 Hispanic Americans), 23 international. Average age 31. 60 applicants, 48% accepted, 14 enrolled. In 2009, 11 master's, 10 doctorates awarded. Terminal master's awarded for partial completion of doctoral program. *Degree requirements:* For master's, thesis or alternative; for doctorate, one foreign language, thesis/dissertation, oral and written exams. *Entrance requirements:* For master's and doctorate, GRE General Test, GRE Subject Test, minimum GPA of 3.0; bachelor's degree in biological, physical, or engineering science. Additional exam requirements/recommendations for international students: Required—TOEFL. *Application deadline:* For fall admission, 12/12 for domestic students. Application fee: $90. *Expenses:* Tuition: Full-time $30,528; part-time $1272 per credit. Required fees: $2177. *Financial support:* Fellowships with tuition reimbursements, teaching assistantships with tuition reimbursements, career-related internships or fieldwork, Federal Work-Study, institutionally sponsored loans, and health care benefits available. Financial award application deadline: 12/12; financial award applicants required to submit FAFSA. *Unit head:* Dr. Max Costa, Chair, 845-731-3661, Fax: 845-351-4510, E-mail: ehs@env.med.nyu.edu. *Application contact:* Dr. Jerome J. Solomon, Director of Graduate Studies, 845-731-3661, Fax: 845-351-4510, E-mail: ehs@env.med.nyu.edu.

North Carolina State University, Graduate School, College of Agriculture and Life Sciences, Department of Biological and Agricultural Engineering, Raleigh, NC 27695. Offers MBAE, MS, PhD, Certificate. Part-time programs available. Postbaccalaureate distance learning degree programs offered. *Degree requirements:* For master's, thesis (for some programs); for doctorate, thesis/dissertation. *Entrance requirements:* For master's and doctorate, GRE. Additional exam requirements/recommendations for international students: Required—TOEFL. Electronic applications accepted. *Faculty research:* Bioinstrumentation, animal waste management, water quality engineering, machine systems, controlled environment agriculture.

North Dakota State University, College of Graduate and Interdisciplinary Studies, College of Engineering and Architecture, Department of Agricultural and Biosystems Engineering, Fargo, ND 58108. Offers agricultural and biosystems engineering (MS, PhD); engineering (PhD); natural resource management (MS); natural resources management (PhD). Part-time programs available. *Faculty:* 6 full-time (1 woman). *Students:* 9 full-time (5 women), 2 part-time (0 women); includes 3 Hispanic Americans, 8 international. Average age 28. 22 applicants, 36% accepted, 7 enrolled. *Degree requirements:* For master's, thesis; for doctorate, thesis/

dissertation. *Entrance requirements:* For master's and doctorate, BS in engineering or the equivalent, minimum undergraduate GPA of 3.0. Additional exam requirements/recommendations for international students: Required—TOEFL (minimum score 550 paper-based; 213 computer-based; 79 iBT). *Application deadline:* For fall admission, 7/1 priority date for domestic and international students; for spring admission, 10/1 priority date for domestic and international students. Applications are processed on a rolling basis. Application fee: $45 ($60 for international students). Electronic applications accepted. *Financial support:* In 2009–10, 9 research assistantships with full tuition reimbursements (averaging $15,000 per year) were awarded; career-related internships or fieldwork, Federal Work-Study, institutionally sponsored loans, and unspecified assistantships also available. Support available to part-time students. Financial award application deadline: 4/15. *Faculty research:* Irrigation, crop processing, food engineering, environmental resources, sensors and instrumentation. Total annual research expenditures: $158,309. *Unit head:* Leslie F. Backer, Chair, 701-231-7261, Fax: 701-231-1008, E-mail: leslie.backer@ndsu.edu. *Application contact:* Dr. David A. Wittrock, Dean, 701-231-7033, Fax: 701-231-6524.

The Ohio State University, Graduate School, College of Food, Agricultural, and Environmental Sciences, Department of Food, Agricultural, and Biological Engineering, Columbus, OH 43210. Offers MS, PhD. *Faculty:* 31. *Students:* 22 full-time (12 women), 10 part-time (1 woman); includes 3 minority (1 African American, 2 Hispanic Americans), 18 international. Average age 29. In 2009, 5 master's, 3 doctorates awarded. *Degree requirements:* For master's, thesis optional; for doctorate, thesis/dissertation. *Entrance requirements:* For master's and doctorate, GRE General Test, GRE Subject Test in engineering (recommended). Additional exam requirements/recommendations for international students: Required—TOEFL (minimum score 550 paper-based; 213 computer-based) or IELTS (minimum score 7) or Michigan English Language Assessment Battery (minimum score 85). *Application deadline:* For fall admission, 8/15 priority date for domestic students, 7/1 priority date for international students; for winter admission, 12/1 priority date for domestic students, 11/1 priority date for international students; for spring admission, 3/1 priority date for domestic students, 2/1 priority date for international students. Applications are processed on a rolling basis. Application fee: $40 ($50 for international students). Electronic applications accepted. *Expenses:* Tuition, state resident: full-time $10,683. Tuition, nonresident: full-time $25,923. Tuition and fees vary according to course load and program. *Financial support:* Fellowships, research assistantships, teaching assistantships, career-related internships or fieldwork, Federal Work-Study, and institutionally sponsored loans available. Support available to part-time students. *Application contact:* Graduate Admissions, 614-292-9444, Fax: 614-292-3895, E-mail: domestic.grad@osu.edu.

Oklahoma State University, College of Agricultural Science and Natural Resources, Department of Biosystems and Agricultural Engineering, Stillwater, OK 74078. Offers biosystems engineering (MS, PhD); environmental and natural resources (MS, PhD). *Faculty:* 25 full-time (4 women), 1 part-time/adjunct (0 women). *Students:* 15 full-time (5 women), 31 part-time (10 women); includes 3 minority (1 African American, 1 American Indian/Alaska Native, 1 Hispanic American), 26 international. Average age 29. 57 applicants, 32% accepted, 12 enrolled. In 2009, 13 master's, 1 doctorate awarded. *Degree requirements:* For master's, thesis; for doctorate, comprehensive exam, thesis/dissertation. *Entrance requirements:* For master's and doctorate, GRE or GMAT. Additional exam requirements/recommendations for international students: Required—TOEFL (minimum score 550 paper-based; 79 iBT). *Application deadline:* For fall admission, 3/1 priority date for international students; for spring admission, 8/1 priority date for international students. Applications are processed on a rolling basis. Application fee: $40 ($75 for international students). Electronic applications accepted. *Expenses:* Tuition, state resident: full-time $3716; part-time $154.85 per credit hour. Tuition, nonresident: full-time $14,448; part-time $602 per credit hour. Required fees: $1772; $73.85 per credit hour. One-time fee: $50. Tuition and fees vary according to course load and campus/location. *Financial support:* In 2009–10, 50 research assistantships (averaging $15,858 per year), 4 teaching assistantships (averaging $9,900 per year) were awarded; career-related internships or fieldwork, Federal Work-Study, scholarships/grants, health care benefits, tuition waivers (partial), and unspecified assistantships also available. Support available to part-time students. Financial award application deadline: 3/1; financial award applicants required to submit FAFSA. *Unit head:* Dr. Ronald L. Elliot, Head, 405-744-5431, Fax: 405-744-6059. *Application contact:* Dr. Gordon Emslie, Dean, 405-744-6368, Fax: 405-744-0355, E-mail: grad-i@okstate.edu.

Penn State University Park, Graduate School, College of Agricultural Sciences, Department of Agricultural and Biological Engineering, State College, University Park, PA 16802-1503. Offers MS, PhD.

Purdue University, College of Engineering, Department of Agricultural and Biological Engineering, West Lafayette, IN 47907-2093. Offers MS, MSABE, MSE, PhD. Part-time programs available. Terminal master's awarded for partial completion of doctoral program. *Degree requirements:* For master's, thesis (for some programs); for doctorate, thesis/dissertation. *Entrance requirements:* For master's and doctorate, GRE General Test. Additional exam requirements/recommendations for international students: Required—TOEFL (minimum score 550 paper-based; 213 computer-based; 77 iBT). Electronic applications accepted. *Faculty research:* Food and biological engineering, environmental engineering, machine systems, biotechnology, machine intelligence.

South Dakota State University, Graduate School, College of Engineering, Department of Agricultural and Biosystems Engineering, Brookings, SD 57007. Offers biological sciences (MS, PhD); engineering (MS). Part-time programs available. *Degree requirements:* For master's, thesis (for some programs), oral exam; for doctorate, thesis/dissertation, preliminary oral and written exams. *Entrance requirements:* For master's and doctorate, engineering degree. Additional exam requirements/recommendations for international students: Required—TOEFL (minimum score 550 paper-based; 213 computer-based; 79 iBT). *Faculty research:* Water resources, food engineering, natural resources engineering, machine design, bioprocess engineering.

Texas A&M University, College of Agriculture and Life Sciences and College of Engineering, Department of Biological and Agricultural Engineering, College Station, TX 77843. Offers M Agr, M Eng, MS, DE, PhD. Part-time programs available. *Faculty:* 18. *Students:* 66 full-time (22 women), 10 part-time (2 women); includes 9 minority (3 African Americans, 3 Asian Americans or Pacific Islanders, 3 Hispanic Americans), 43 international. Average age 29. In 2009, 9 master's, 3 doctorates awarded. *Degree requirements:* For master's, thesis (MS), preliminary and final exams; for doctorate, thesis/dissertation, preliminary and final exams. *Entrance requirements:* For master's and doctorate, GRE General Test. Additional exam requirements/recommendations for international students: Required—TOEFL (minimum score 550 paper-based; 213 computer-based). *Application deadline:* For fall admission, 2/1 priority date for domestic students; for spring admission, 10/1 for domestic students. Applications are processed on a rolling basis. Application fee: $50 ($75 for international students). Electronic applications accepted. *Expenses:* Tuition, state resident: full-time $3991.32; part-time $221.74 per credit hour. Tuition, nonresident: full-time $9049; part-time $502.74 per credit hour. *Financial support:* In 2009–10, 3 fellowships with full and partial tuition reimbursements (averaging $15,000 per year), 17 research assistantships with full and partial tuition reimbursements (averaging $18,150 per year), 12 teaching assistantships with partial tuition reimbursements (averaging $19,590 per year) were awarded; career-related internships or fieldwork, institutionally sponsored loans, scholarships/grants, tuition waivers, and unspecified assistantships also available. Financial award application deadline: 3/1; financial award applicants required to submit FAFSA. *Faculty research:* Water quality and quantity; air quality; biological, food, ecological engineering; off-road equipment; mechatronics. *Unit head:* Head, 979-854-3931, Fax: 979-862-3442, E-mail: info@baen.tamu.edu. *Application contact:* Academic Programs Assistant, 979-845-0609, Fax: 979-862-3442, E-mail: info@baen.tamu.edu.

Université Laval, Faculty of Agricultural and Food Sciences, Department of Soils and Agricultural Engineering, Programs in Agri-Food Engineering, Québec, QC G1K 7P4, Canada. Offers agri-food engineering (M Sc); environmental technology (M Sc). *Degree requirements:* For master's, thesis (for some programs). *Entrance requirements:* For master's, knowledge of French. Electronic applications accepted.

The University of Arizona, Graduate College, College of Agriculture and Life Sciences, Department of Agricultural and Biosystems Engineering, Tucson, AZ 85721. Offers MS, PhD. *Faculty:* 11. *Students:* 18 full-time (3 women), 11 part-time (1 woman); includes 2 minority (both Asian Americans or Pacific Islanders), 16 international. Average age 32. 19 applicants, 74% accepted, 6 enrolled. In 2009, 6 master's, 5 doctorates awarded. Terminal master's awarded for partial completion of doctoral program. *Degree requirements:* For master's, thesis; for doctorate, thesis/dissertation. *Entrance requirements:* For master's, minimum GPA of 3.0 in last 2 years of undergraduate study, 3 letters of recommendation; for doctorate, minimum GPA of 3.0 in last 2 years of undergraduate study, 3 letters of recommendation, statement of purpose. Additional exam requirements/recommendations for international students: Required—TOEFL (minimum score 213 computer-based). *Application deadline:* For fall admission, 6/1 for domestic students, 2/1 for international students; for spring admission, 9/1 for domestic students, 8/1 for international students. Applications are processed on a rolling basis. Application fee: $75. Electronic applications accepted. *Expenses:* Tuition, state resident: full-time $9028. Tuition, nonresident: full-time $24,890. *Financial support:* In 2009–10, 4 research assistantships with full and partial tuition reimbursements (averaging $24,714 per year), 1 teaching assistantship with full and partial tuition reimbursement (averaging $18,724 per year) were awarded; fellowships, career-related internships or fieldwork, Federal Work-Study, institutionally sponsored loans, scholarships/grants, traineeships, health care benefits, tuition waivers (full and partial), and unspecified assistantships also available. Financial award application deadline: 5/1. *Faculty research:* Irrigation system design, energy-use management, equipment for alternative crops, food properties enhancement. Total annual research expenditures: $452,871. *Unit head:* Donald Slack, Head, 520-621-3691, Fax: 520-621-3963, E-mail: slackd@u.arizona.edu. *Application contact:* Daniela Ibarra, Senior Office Specialist, 520-621-1753, Fax: 520-621-3963, E-mail: dcastro@email.arizona.edu.

University of Arkansas, Graduate School, College of Engineering, Department of Biological and Agricultural Engineering, Fayetteville, AR 72701-1201. Offers biological and agricultural engineering (MSE, PhD); biological engineering (MSBE); biomedical engineering (MSBME). *Students:* 5 full-time (2 women), 18 part-time (4 women); includes 2 minority (1 African American, 1 Asian American or Pacific Islander), 16 international. In 2009, 8 master's awarded. *Degree requirements:* For master's, thesis; for doctorate, one foreign language, thesis/dissertation. Application fee: $40 ($50 for international students). *Expenses:* Tuition, state resident: full-time $7355; part-time $356.58 per hour. Tuition, nonresident: full-time $17,401; part-time $775.17 per hour. Required fees: $1203. *Financial support:* In 2009–10, 1 fellowship with tuition reimbursement, 17 research assistantships, 1 teaching assistantship were awarded; career-related internships or fieldwork and Federal Work-Study also available. Support available to part-time students. Financial award application deadline: 4/1; financial award applicants required to submit FAFSA. *Unit head:* Dr. Carl Griffis, Department Head, 479-575-2351, Fax: 479-575-2846, E-mail: clg@uark.edu. *Application contact:* Dr. Jin-Woo Kim, Program Coordinator, 479-575-2351, Fax: 479-575-2846, E-mail: jwkim@uark.edu.

University of Dayton, Graduate School, School of Engineering, Department of Civil and Environmental Engineering, Dayton, OH 45469-1300. Offers engineering mechanics (MSEM); environmental engineering (MSCE); geotechnical engineering (MSCE); structural engineering (MSCE); transport engineering (MSCE); water resources engineering (MSCE). Part-time programs available. *Faculty:* 8 full-time (2 women), 1 part-time/adjunct (0 women). *Students:* 10 full-time (6 women), 8 part-time (1 woman); includes 3 minority (all African Americans), 7 international. Average age 29. 35 applicants, 49% accepted, 6 enrolled. In 2009, 3 master's awarded. *Degree requirements:* For master's, thesis optional. *Entrance requirements:* Additional exam requirements/recommendations for international students: Required—TOEFL (minimum score 550 paper-based; 213 computer-based; 80 iBT). *Application deadline:* For fall admission, 8/1 for domestic students, 3/1 priority date for international students; for winter admission, 7/1 priority date for international students; for spring admission, 1/1 priority date for international students. Applications are processed on a rolling basis. Application fee: $0 ($50 for international students). Electronic applications accepted. *Expenses:* Tuition: Full-time $8412; part-time $701 per credit hour. Required fees: $325; $65 per course. $25 per semester. Tuition and fees vary according to course load, degree level and program. *Financial support:* In 2009–10, 3 research assistantships (averaging $10,780 per year), 4 teaching assistantships with partial tuition reimbursements (averaging $5,110 per year) were awarded. Financial award applicants required to submit FAFSA. *Faculty research:* Physical modeling of hydraulic systems, finite element methods, mechanics of composite materials, transportation systems safety, high-velocity wear. Total annual research expenditures: $421,839. *Unit head:* Dr. Donald V. Chase, Interim Chair, 937-229-3847, Fax: 937-229-3491, E-mail: donald.chase@notes.udayton.edu. *Application contact:* Graduate Admissions, 937-229-4411, Fax: 937-229-4729, E-mail: gradadmission@udayton.edu.

University of Florida, Graduate School, College of Engineering and College of Agricultural and Life Sciences, Department of Agricultural and Biological Engineering, Gainesville, FL 32611. Offers ME, MS, PhD, Engr. Part-time programs available. Terminal master's awarded for partial completion of doctoral program. *Degree requirements:* For master's and Engr, thesis optional; for doctorate, thesis/dissertation. *Entrance requirements:* For master's and doctorate, GRE General Test, minimum GPA of 3.0; for Engr, GRE General Test. Additional exam requirements/recommendations for international students: Required—TOEFL (minimum score 550 paper-based; 213 computer-based). Electronic applications accepted. *Faculty research:* Soil and water engineering, structures and environments, power and machinery, biological processing, food engineering.

University of Georgia, Graduate School, College of Agricultural and Environmental Sciences, Department of Biological and Agricultural Engineering, Athens, GA 30602. Offers agricultural engineering (MS); biological and agricultural engineering (PhD); biological engineering (MS). *Faculty:* 29 full-time (3 women), 2 part-time/adjunct (0 women). *Students:* 38 full-time (11 women), 6 part-time (0 women); includes 4 minority (all African Americans), 25 international. 26 applicants, 69% accepted, 15 enrolled. In 2009, 3 master's, 3 doctorates awarded. *Degree requirements:* For master's, thesis; for doctorate, one foreign language, thesis/dissertation. *Entrance requirements:* For master's and doctorate, GRE General Test. *Application deadline:* For fall admission, 7/1 priority date for domestic students; for spring admission, 11/15 for domestic students. Application fee: $50. Electronic applications accepted. *Expenses:* Tuition, state resident: full-time $6000; part-time $250 per credit hour. Tuition, nonresident: full-time $20,904; part-time $871 per credit hour. Required fees: $730 per semester. *Financial support:* Fellowships, research assistantships, teaching assistantships, unspecified assistantships available. *Unit head:* Dr. E. Dale Threadgill, Head, 706-542-1653, Fax: 706-542-8806, E-mail: tgill@engr.uga.edu. *Application contact:* Dr. William S. Kisaalita, Graduate Coordinator, 706-542-0835, Fax: 706-542-8806, E-mail: williamk@engr.uga.edu.

University of Idaho, College of Graduate Studies, College of Engineering, Department of Biological and Agricultural Engineering, Moscow, ID 83844-2282. Offers agricultural engineering (M Engr, MS); biological and agricultural engineering (PhD). *Faculty:* 5 full-time, 1 part-time/adjunct. *Students:* 8 full-time, 5 part-time. In 2009, 3 master's awarded. *Degree requirements:* For master's, thesis or alternative; for doctorate, one foreign language, thesis/dissertation. *Entrance requirements:* For master's, minimum GPA of 2.8; for doctorate, minimum undergraduate GPA of 2.8, 3.0 graduate. *Application deadline:* For fall admission, 8/1 for domestic students; for spring admission, 12/15 for domestic students. Application fee: $55 ($60 for international students). *Expenses:* Tuition, state resident: full-time $6120. Tuition, nonresident: full-time $17,712. *Financial support:* Research assistantships, teaching assistantships, career-related internships or fieldwork available. Financial award application deadline: 2/15. *Faculty research:* Water and environmental research, alternative fuels/biodiesel, agricultural safety health, biological processes for agricultural/food waste. *Unit head:* Dr. Jon Harlan Van Gerpen, Department Head, 208-885-7891. *Application contact:* Dr. Jon Harlan Van Gerpen, Department Head, 208-885-7891.

Agricultural Engineering

University of Illinois at Urbana–Champaign, Graduate College, College of Agricultural, Consumer and Environmental Sciences, Department of Agricultural and Biological Engineering, Champaign, IL 61820. Offers agricultural engineering (MS, PhD); bioenergy (MS), including professional science. *Faculty:* 19 full-time (2 women). *Students:* 38 full-time (11 women), 10 part-time (1 woman); includes 1 minority (Hispanic American), 33 international. 44 applicants, 18% accepted, 6 enrolled. In 2009, 10 master's, 6 doctorates awarded. *Entrance requirements:* For master's and doctorate, minimum GPA of 3.0. Additional exam requirements/recommendations for international students: Required—TOEFL (minimum score 570 paper-based; 230 computer-based; 88 iBT), or IELTS (minimum score 6.5). *Application deadline:* Applications are processed on a rolling basis. Application fee: $60 ($75 for international students). Electronic applications accepted. *Financial support:* In 2009–10, 6 fellowships, 47 research assistantships were awarded; teaching assistantships, tuition waivers (full and partial) also available. *Unit head:* Kuan Chong Ting, Head, 217-333-3570, Fax: 217-244-0323, E-mail: kcting@illinois.edu. *Application contact:* Ronda Sullivan, Assistant to the Head, 217-333-3570, Fax: 217-244-0323, E-mail: rsully@illinois.edu.

University of Kentucky, Graduate School, College of Agriculture, Program in Biosystems and Agricultural Engineering, Lexington, KY 40506-0032. Offers MS, PhD. Part-time programs available. *Degree requirements:* For master's, comprehensive exam, thesis optional; for doctorate, comprehensive exam, thesis/dissertation. *Entrance requirements:* For master's, GRE General Test, minimum undergraduate GPA of 2.75; for doctorate, GRE General Test, minimum graduate GPA of 3.0. Additional exam requirements/recommendations for international students: Required—TOEFL (minimum score 550 paper-based; 213 computer-based). Electronic applications accepted. *Faculty research:* Machine systems, food engineering, fermentation, hydrology, water quality.

University of Missouri, Graduate School, College of Engineering, Department of Biological Engineering, Columbia, MO 65211. Offers agricultural engineering (MS); biological engineering (MS, PhD). *Degree requirements:* For master's, thesis; for doctorate, thesis/dissertation. *Entrance requirements:* For master's and doctorate, GRE General Test, minimum GPA of 3.0. Additional exam requirements/recommendations for international students: Required—TOEFL (minimum score 550 paper-based; 213 computer-based; 80 iBT).

University of Nebraska–Lincoln, Graduate College, College of Engineering, Department of Biological Systems Engineering, Interdepartmental Area of Agricultural and Biological Systems Engineering, Lincoln, NE 68588. Offers MS, PhD. *Degree requirements:* For master's, thesis optional. *Entrance requirements:* Additional exam requirements/recommendations for international students: Required—TOEFL (minimum score 550 paper-based; 213 computer-based). Electronic applications accepted. *Faculty research:* Hydrological engineering, tractive performance, biomedical engineering, irrigation systems.

University of Saskatchewan, College of Graduate Studies and Research, College of Engineering, Department of Agricultural and Bioresource Engineering, Saskatoon, SK S7N 5A2, Canada. Offers M Eng, M Sc, PhD. *Degree requirements:* For master's, thesis (for some programs); for doctorate, thesis/dissertation. *Entrance requirements:* For master's and doctorate, GRE. Additional exam requirements/recommendations for international students: Required—TOEFL. Tuition and fees charges are reported in Canadian dollars. *Expenses:* Tuition, area resident: Full-time $3000 Canadian dollars; part-time $500 Canadian dollars per term. Required fees: $700 Canadian dollars; $100 Canadian dollars per term.

The University of Tennessee, Graduate School, College of Agricultural Sciences and Natural Resources, Department of Biosystems Engineering and Environmental Science, Program in Biosystems Engineering Technology, Knoxville, TN 37996. Offers MS. *Degree requirements:* For master's, thesis or alternative. *Entrance requirements:* For master's, GRE General Test, minimum GPA of 2.7. Additional exam requirements/recommendations for international students: Required—TOEFL. Electronic applications accepted. *Expenses:* Tuition, state resident: full-time $6826; part-time $380 per semester hour. Tuition, nonresident: full-time $21,844; part-time $1147 per semester hour. Tuition and fees vary according to program.

University of Wisconsin–Madison, Graduate School, College of Agricultural and Life Sciences, Department of Biological Systems Engineering, Madison, WI 53706. Offers MS, PhD. Part-time programs available. Terminal master's awarded for partial completion of doctoral program. *Degree requirements:* For master's, thesis optional; for doctorate, thesis/dissertation. *Entrance requirements:* For master's, GRE. Additional exam requirements/recommendations for international students: Required—TOEFL. Electronic applications accepted. *Expenses:* Tuition, state resident: part-time $594 per credit. Tuition, nonresident: part-time $1504 per credit. Required fees: $65 per credit. Tuition and fees vary according to course load, program and reciprocity agreements. *Faculty research:* Waste systems, food engineering, power and machinery, structures and environment, construction management.

Utah State University, School of Graduate Studies, College of Engineering, Department of Biological and Irrigation Engineering, Logan, UT 84322. Offers biological and agricultural engineering (MS, PhD); irrigation engineering (MS, PhD). Part-time programs available. Terminal master's awarded for partial completion of doctoral program. *Degree requirements:* For master's, thesis (for some programs); for doctorate, thesis/dissertation. *Entrance requirements:* For master's and doctorate, GRE General Test, minimum GPA of 3.0. Additional exam requirements/recommendations for international students: Required—TOEFL. *Faculty research:* On-farm water management, crop-water yield modeling, irrigation, biosensors, biological engineering.

Virginia Polytechnic Institute and State University, Graduate School, College of Engineering, Department of Biological Systems Engineering, Blacksburg, VA 24061. Offers M Eng, MS, PhD. *Entrance requirements:* Additional exam requirements/recommendations for international students: Required—TOEFL (minimum score 550 paper-based; 213 computer-based). Electronic applications accepted. *Faculty research:* Soil and water engineering, alternative energy sources for agriculture and agricultural mechanization.

Washington State University, Graduate School, College of Engineering and Architecture, Department of Biological Systems Engineering, Pullman, WA 99164. Offers biological and agricultural engineering (MS, PhD). *Degree requirements:* For master's, comprehensive exam, thesis (for some programs), written and oral exam; for doctorate, comprehensive exam, thesis/dissertation, written and oral exam. *Entrance requirements:* For master's, GRE General Test, GRE Subject Test, minimum GPA of 3.0, bachelor's degree in engineering or closely related subject; for doctorate, minimum GPA of 3.0, bachelor's degree in engineering or closely related subject. Additional exam requirements/recommendations for international students: Required—TOEFL. *Faculty research:* Social issues and engineering education, electronic instrument design, prediction, technology for dust from agricultural lands.

Bioengineering

Alfred University, Graduate School, New York State College of Ceramics, School of Engineering, Alfred, NY 14802-1205. Offers biomedical materials engineering science (MS); ceramic engineering (MS); ceramics (PhD); electrical engineering (MS); glass science (MS, PhD); materials science and engineering (MS, PhD); mechanical engineering (MS). *Degree requirements:* For master's, thesis; for doctorate, thesis/dissertation. *Entrance requirements:* Additional exam requirements/recommendations for international students: Required—TOEFL (minimum score 590 paper-based; 243 computer-based). Electronic applications accepted. *Expenses:* Contact institution. *Faculty research:* Fine-particle technology, x-ray diffraction, superconductivity, electronic materials.

Arizona State University, Graduate College, Ira A. Fulton School of Engineering, Harrington Department of Bioengineering, Tempe, AZ 85287. Offers MS, PhD. *Degree requirements:* For doctorate, thesis/dissertation. *Entrance requirements:* For master's and doctorate, GRE General Test.

Baylor College of Medicine, Graduate School of Biomedical Sciences, Program in Translational Biology and Molecular Medicine, Houston, TX 77030-3498. Offers PhD. *Faculty:* 151 full-time (48 women). *Students:* 48 full-time (23 women); includes 13 minority (4 African Americans, 4 Asian Americans or Pacific Islanders, 5 Hispanic Americans), 14 international. Average age 24. *Degree requirements:* For doctorate, thesis/dissertation, public defense. *Entrance requirements:* For doctorate, GRE, minimum GPA of 3.0. Additional exam requirements/recommendations for international students: Required—TOEFL. *Application deadline:* For fall admission, 1/1 for domestic students. Application fee: $0. Electronic applications accepted. *Financial support:* In 2009–10, 48 students received support; fellowships, research assistantships, career-related internships or fieldwork, Federal Work-Study, health care benefits, and students receive a scholarship unless there are grant funds available to pay tuition available. Financial award applicants required to submit FAFSA. *Unit head:* Dr. Mary Estes, Director, 713-798-3585, Fax: 713-798-3586, E-mail: tbmm@bcm.edu. *Application contact:* Wanda Waguespack, Graduate Program Administrator, 713-798-1077, Fax: 713-798-3586, E-mail: wandaw@bcm.edu.

California Institute of Technology, Division of Engineering and Applied Science, Option in Bioengineering, Pasadena, CA 91125-0001. Offers MS, PhD. *Faculty:* 4 full-time (0 women). *Students:* 35 full-time (6 women). 152 applicants, 11% accepted, 8 enrolled. In 2009, 3 master's, 4 doctorates awarded. *Degree requirements:* For master's, thesis; for doctorate, thesis/dissertation. *Application deadline:* For fall admission, 1/1 for domestic students. *Financial support:* In 2009–10, 11 fellowships, 12 research assistantships, 1 teaching assistantship were awarded. *Faculty research:* Biosynthesis and analysis, biometrics. *Unit head:* Dr. Niles Pierce, Executive Officer, 626-395-8086, E-mail: niles@caltech.edu. *Application contact:* Natalie Gilmore, Assistant Dean of Graduate Studies, 626-395-3812, Fax: 626-577-9246, E-mail: ngilmore@caltech.edu.

Carnegie Mellon University, Carnegie Institute of Technology, Biomedical and Health Engineering Program, Pittsburgh, PA 15213-3891. Offers bioengineering (MS, PhD); MD/PhD. *Degree requirements:* For master's, thesis; for doctorate, thesis/dissertation, qualifying exam. *Entrance requirements:* For master's and doctorate, GRE General Test. Additional exam requirements/recommendations for international students: Required—TOEFL. Electronic applications accepted. *Faculty research:* Cellular and molecular systematics, signal and image processing, materials and mechanics.

Clemson University, Graduate School, College of Engineering and Science, Department of Bioengineering, Clemson, SC 29634. Offers MS, PhD. Part-time programs available. *Faculty:* 19 full-time (5 women), 3 part-time/adjunct (all women). *Students:* 87 full-time (32 women), 16 part-time (5 women); includes 14 minority (4 African Americans, 1 American Indian/Alaska Native, 7 Asian Americans or Pacific Islanders, 2 Hispanic Americans), 38 international. Average age 27. 119 applicants, 52% accepted, 21 enrolled. In 2009, 6 master's, 9 doctorates awarded. *Degree requirements:* For master's, thesis optional; for doctorate, thesis/dissertation. *Entrance requirements:* For master's and doctorate, GRE General Test. Additional exam requirements/recommendations for international students: Required—TOEFL. *Application deadline:* For fall admission, 6/1 for domestic students, 4/15 for international students; for spring admission, 11/1 for domestic students, 9/15 for international students. Applications are processed on a rolling basis. Application fee: $70 ($80 for international students). Electronic applications accepted. *Expenses:* Tuition, state resident: full-time $8684; part-time $528 per credit hour. Tuition, nonresident: full-time $15,330; part-time $1078 per credit hour. Required fees: $736; $37 per semester. Part-time tuition and fees vary according to course load and program. *Financial support:* In 2009–10, 70 students received support, including 5 fellowships with full and partial tuition reimbursements available (averaging $17,400 per year), 55 research assistantships with partial tuition reimbursements available (averaging $17,480 per year), 12 teaching assistantships with partial tuition reimbursements available (averaging $16,847 per year); career-related internships or fieldwork, institutionally sponsored loans, scholarships/grants, health care benefits, and unspecified assistantships also available. Support available to part-time students. Financial award application deadline: 2/15; financial award applicants required to submit FAFSA. *Faculty research:* Biomaterials, biomechanics. Total annual research expenditures: $4.5 million. *Unit head:* Dr. Martine LaBerge, Interim Chair, 864-656-5556, Fax: 864-656-4466, E-mail: laberge@eng.clemson.edu. *Application contact:* Dr. Robert Latour, Graduate Student Coordinator, 864-656-5552, Fax: 864-656-4466, E-mail: latourr@eng.clemson.edu.

Cornell University, Graduate School, Graduate Fields of Agriculture and Life Sciences and Graduate Fields of Engineering, Field of Biological and Environmental Engineering, Ithaca, NY 14853-0001. Offers biological engineering (M Eng, MPS, MS, PhD); energy (M Eng, MPS, MS, PhD); environmental engineering (M Eng, MPS, MS, PhD); environmental management (MPS); food processing engineering (M Eng, MPS, MS, PhD); international agriculture (M Eng, MPS, MS, PhD); local roads (M Eng, MPS, MS, PhD); machine systems (M Eng, MPS, MS, PhD); soil and water engineering (M Eng, MPS, MS, PhD); structures and environment (M Eng, MPS, MS, PhD). *Faculty:* 34 full-time (6 women). *Students:* 61 full-time (23 women); includes 5 minority (2 African Americans, 2 Asian Americans or Pacific Islanders, 1 Hispanic American), 23 international. Average age 29. 88 applicants, 43% accepted, 24 enrolled. In 2009, 13 master's, 9 doctorates awarded. Terminal master's awarded for partial completion of doctoral program. *Degree requirements:* For master's, thesis (MS); for doctorate, comprehensive exam, thesis/dissertation. *Entrance requirements:* For master's, 3 letters of recommendation (MS), 2 letters of recommendaion (M Eng, MPS); for doctorate, GRE General Test, 3 letters of recommendation. Additional exam requirements/recommendations for international students: Required—TOEFL (minimum score 550 paper-based; 213 computer-based; 77 iBT). *Application deadline:* For fall admission, 1/15 priority date for domestic students; for spring admission, 10/1 for domestic students. Applications are processed on a rolling basis. Application fee: $70. Electronic applications accepted. *Expenses:* Tuition: Full-time $29,500. Required fees: $70. Full-time tuition and fees vary according to degree level, program and student level. *Financial support:* In 2009–10, 45 students received support, including 3 fellowships with full tuition reimbursements available, 8 research assistantships with full tuition reimbursements available, 2 teaching assistantships with full tuition reimbursements available; institutionally sponsored loans, scholarships/grants, health care benefits, tuition waivers (full and partial), and unspecified assistantships also available. Financial award applicants required to submit FAFSA. *Faculty research:* Biological and food engineering, environmental, soil and water engineering, international agricultural engineering, structures and controlled environments, machine systems and energy. *Unit head:* Director of Graduate Studies, 607-255-2173, Fax: 607-255-4080, E-mail: abengradfield@cornell.edu. *Application contact:* Graduate Field Assistant, 607-255-2173, Fax: 607-255-4080, E-mail: abengradfield@cornell.edu.

Dalhousie University, Faculty of Engineering, Department of Biological Engineering, Halifax, NS B3J 2X4, Canada. Offers M Eng, MA Sc, PhD. *Faculty:* 5 full-time (0 women), 1 part-time/adjunct (0 women). *Students:* 10 full-time (1 woman), 1 part-time (0 women). Average age 33. 17 applicants, 76% accepted. In 2009, 1 master's awarded. *Degree requirements:* For master's, thesis; for doctorate, thesis/dissertation. *Entrance requirements:* Additional exam requirements/recommendations for international students: Required—TOEFL, IELTS, CANTEST, CAEL, or Michigan English Language Assessment Battery. *Application deadline:* For fall admission, 6/1 for domestic students, 4/1 for international students; for winter admission, 10/31 for domestic students, 8/31 for international students; for spring admission, 2/28 for domestic students, 12/31 for international students. Applications are processed on a rolling basis. Application fee: $70. *Financial support:* In 2009–10, 1 research assistantship (averaging $1,600 per year), 4 teaching assistantships (averaging $4,000 per year) were awarded; fellowships, scholarships/grants and unspecified assistantships also available. *Faculty research:* Waste management, energy and environment, bio-machinery and robotics, soil and water, aquacultural and food engineering. *Unit head:* Dr. Michael Pegg, Unit Head, 902-494-3252, Fax: 902-423-0219, E-mail: michael.pegg@dal.ca. *Application contact:* Dr. Georges Kipouros, Graduate Coordinator, 902-494-6100, Fax: 902-423-0219, E-mail: peas.grad@dal.ca.

Georgia Institute of Technology, Graduate Studies and Research, College of Engineering, School of Chemical and Biomolecular Engineering, Atlanta, GA 30332-0001. Offers bioengineering (MS Bio E, PhD); chemical engineering (MS Ch E, PhD); paper science and engineering (MS, PhD); polymers (MS Poly). *Degree requirements:* For master's, thesis; for doctorate, comprehensive exam, thesis/dissertation. *Entrance requirements:* For master's and doctorate, GRE, minimum GPA of 3.0. Additional exam requirements/recommendations for international students: Required—TOEFL (minimum score 550 paper-based; 213 computer-based). Electronic applications accepted. *Faculty research:* Biochemical engineering; process modeling, synthesis, and control; polymer science and engineering; thermodynamics and separations; surface and particle science.

Georgia Institute of Technology, Graduate Studies and Research, College of Engineering, The Wallace H. Coulter Department of Biomedical Engineering at Georgia Tech and Emory University, Atlanta, GA 30332-0001. Offers bioengineering (PhD); bioinformatics (PhD); biomedical engineering (PhD); MD/PhD. PhD in biomedical engineering program jointly offered with Emory University (Georgia) and Peking University (China). Terminal master's awarded for partial completion of doctoral program. *Degree requirements:* For doctorate, thesis/dissertation. *Entrance requirements:* Additional exam requirements/recommendations for international students: Required—TOEFL. *Faculty research:* Biomechanics and tissue engineering, bioinstrumentation and medical imaging.

Illinois Institute of Technology, Graduate College, Armour College of Engineering, Department of Chemical and Biological Engineering, Chicago, IL 60616-3793. Offers biological engineering (MBE); chemical engineering (M Ch E, MS, PhD); food process engineering (MFPE); food processing engineering (MS); gas engineering (MGE); manufacturing engineering (MME, MS); MS/M Ch E. Part-time and evening/weekend programs available. Postbaccalaureate distance learning degree programs offered. Terminal master's awarded for partial completion of doctoral program. *Degree requirements:* For master's, comprehensive exam, thesis (for some programs); for doctorate, comprehensive exam, thesis/dissertation. *Entrance requirements:* For master's and doctorate, GRE General Test, minimum undergraduate GPA of 3.0. Additional exam requirements/recommendations for international students: Required—TOEFL (minimum score 550 paper-based; 213 computer-based; 80 iBT). Electronic applications accepted. *Expenses:* Tuition: Full-time $17,550; part-time $888 per credit hour. Required fees: $850; $7.50 per credit hour. One-time fee: $50 full-time. Full-time tuition and fees vary according to program. *Faculty research:* Biochemical, bioenergy, biosensors, tissue engineering, fuel cells, batteries, renewable energy, gas cleaning, particle technology, fluidization, colloid and interfacial engineering complex fluids, polymers, complex systems and dynamics.

Iowa State University of Science and Technology, Graduate College, College of Engineering, Department of Chemical and Biological Engineering, Ames, IA 50011. Offers M Eng, MS, PhD. *Faculty:* 19 full-time (5 women). *Students:* 54 full-time (17 women), 1 part-time (0 women); includes 5 minority (2 Asian Americans or Pacific Islanders, 3 Hispanic Americans), 28 international. 136 applicants, 17% accepted, 10 enrolled. In 2009, 6 master's, 11 doctorates awarded. *Degree requirements:* For master's, thesis (for some programs); for doctorate, thesis/dissertation. *Entrance requirements:* For master's and doctorate, GRE General Test. Additional exam requirements/recommendations for international students: Required—TOEFL (minimum score 587 paper-based; 94 iBT) or IELTS (minimum score 7). *Application deadline:* For fall admission, 1/15 priority date for domestic and international students; for spring admission, 10/1 for domestic and international students. Application fee: $40 ($90 for international students). Electronic applications accepted. *Expenses:* Tuition, state resident: full-time $6716. Tuition, nonresident: full-time $8908. Tuition and fees vary according to course level, course load, program and student level. *Financial support:* In 2009–10, 45 research assistantships with full and partial tuition reimbursements (averaging $19,410 per year), 8 teaching assistantships with full and partial tuition reimbursements (averaging $19,410 per year) were awarded; scholarships/grants, health care benefits, and unspecified assistantships also available. *Unit head:* Dr. Surya Mallaragada, Chair, 515-294-8472, Fax: 515-294-2689, E-mail: suryakm@iastate.edu. *Application contact:* Dr. Monica Lamm, Director of Graduate Education, 515-294-7643, E-mail: chemengr@iastate.edu.

The Johns Hopkins University, G. W. C. Whiting School of Engineering and School of Medicine, Department of Biomedical Engineering, Baltimore, MD 21205. Offers bioengineering innovation and design (MSE); biomedical engineering (MSE, PhD). *Faculty:* 45 full-time (7 women). *Students:* 224 full-time (79 women); includes 62 minority (5 African Americans, 48 Asian Americans or Pacific Islanders, 9 Hispanic Americans), 97 international. Average age 24. 569 applicants, 20% accepted, 51 enrolled. In 2009, 15 master's, 17 doctorates awarded. Terminal master's awarded for partial completion of doctoral program. *Degree requirements:* For master's, thesis; for doctorate, comprehensive exam, thesis/dissertation, oral exam. *Entrance requirements:* For master's and doctorate, GRE General Test. Additional exam requirements/recommendations for international students: Required—TOEFL or IELTS. *Application deadline:* For fall admission, 1/15 for domestic and international students. Application fee: $75. Electronic applications accepted. *Financial support:* In 2009–10, 208 students received support, including 206 research assistantships with full tuition reimbursements available (averaging $24,553 per year); fellowships with partial tuition reimbursements available, teaching assistantships with full and partial tuition reimbursements available, Federal Work-Study, institutionally sponsored loans, scholarships/grants, tuition waivers (full), and unspecified assistantships also available. Support available to part-time students. *Faculty research:* Cell and tissue engineering, systems neuroscience, imaging, cardiovascular systems physiology, theoretical and computational biology. Total annual research expenditures: $12 million. *Unit head:* Dr. Elliot R. McVeigh, Director, 410-516-5282, Fax: 410-516-4771. *Application contact:* Samuel Bourne, Academic Master's Program Coordinator, 410-516-8482, Fax: 410-516-4771, E-mail: sbourne@jhu.edu.

The Johns Hopkins University, G. W. C. Whiting School of Engineering, Department of Chemical and Biomolecular Engineering, Baltimore, MD 21218. Offers MSE, PhD. Part-time programs available. *Faculty:* 21 full-time (6 women), 3 part-time/adjunct (0 women). *Students:* 82 full-time (31 women); includes 15 minority (3 African Americans, 8 Asian Americans or Pacific Islanders, 4 Hispanic Americans), 27 international. Average age 26. 186 applicants, 18% accepted, 24 enrolled. In 2009, 13 master's, 8 doctorates awarded. *Degree requirements:* For doctorate, thesis/dissertation, oral exam. *Entrance requirements:* For doctorate, GRE General Test. Additional exam requirements/recommendations for international students: Required—TOEFL (minimum score 600 paper-based; 250 computer-based; 100 iBT). *Application deadline:* For fall admission, 1/15 for domestic and international students. Applications are processed on a rolling basis. Application fee: $75. Electronic applications accepted. *Financial support:* In 2009–10, 12 fellowships with full and partial tuition reimbursements (averaging $25,000 per year), 42 research assistantships with full tuition reimbursements (averaging $25,000 per year) were awarded; teaching assistantships with full and partial tuition reimbursements, scholarships/grants, health care benefits, tuition waivers (partial), and unspecified assistantships also available. Financial award application deadline: 1/15. *Faculty research:* Polymers and complex fluids, nucleation, bioengineering and biotechnology, computational biology and genomics, cell and molecular biotechnology. Total annual research expenditures: $3.1 million. *Unit head:* Dr. Konstantinos Konstantopoulos, Chair and Professor, 410-516-7170, Fax: 410-516-5510, E-mail: kkonsta1@jhu.edu. *Application contact:* Lindsay Spivey, Academic Program Coordinator, 410-516-4166, Fax: 410-516-5510, E-mail: spivey@jhu.edu.

Kansas State University, Graduate School, College of Engineering, Department of Biological and Agricultural Engineering, Manhattan, KS 66506. Offers MS, PhD. *Faculty:* 14 full-time (1 woman), 6 part-time/adjunct (0 women). *Students:* 24 full-time (5 women), 6 part-time (4 women); includes 1 minority (Asian American or Pacific Islander), 20 international. Average age 31. 27 applicants, 26% accepted, 7 enrolled. In 2009, 3 master's, 3 doctorates awarded. Terminal master's awarded for partial completion of doctoral program. *Degree requirements:* For master's, thesis; for doctorate, thesis/dissertation. *Entrance requirements:* For master's, GRE (recommended), bachelor's degree in agricultural engineering; for doctorate, GRE (recommended). Additional exam requirements/recommendations for international students: Required—TOEFL (minimum score 600 paper-based; 250 computer-based). *Application deadline:* For fall admission, 2/1 priority date for domestic and international students; for spring admission, 8/1 priority date for domestic and international students. Applications are processed on a rolling basis. Application fee: $40 ($55 for international students). Electronic applications accepted. *Financial support:* In 2009–10, 24 research assistantships (averaging $13,992 per year) were awarded; fellowships, teaching assistantships, Federal Work-Study, institutionally sponsored loans, and scholarships/grants also available. Support available to part-time students. Financial award application deadline: 3/1; financial award applicants required to submit FAFSA. *Faculty research:* Ecological engineering, watershed modeling, air quality, bioprocessing, sensors and controls. Total annual research expenditures: $2.1 million. *Unit head:* Joseph Harner, Interim Head, 785-532-5580, Fax: 785-532-5825, E-mail: jharner@ksu.edu. *Application contact:* Naiqian Zhang, Director, 785-532-2910, Fax: 785-532-5825, E-mail: zhangn@ksu.edu.

Lehigh University, P.C. Rossin College of Engineering and Applied Science, Department of Chemical Engineering, Bethlehem, PA 18015. Offers biological chemical engineering (M Eng); chemical engineering (M Eng, PhD); MBA/E. Part-time programs available. Postbaccalaureate distance learning degree programs offered (no on-campus study). *Faculty:* 17 full-time (2 women), 2 part-time/adjunct (0 women). *Students:* 45 full-time (11 women), 26 part-time (11 women); includes 9 minority (2 African Americans, 4 Asian Americans or Pacific Islanders, 3 Hispanic Americans), 32 international. Average age 27. 113 applicants, 24% accepted, 21 enrolled. In 2009, 4 master's, 6 doctorates awarded. Terminal master's awarded for partial completion of doctoral program. *Degree requirements:* For master's, thesis (for some programs); for doctorate, comprehensive exam, thesis/dissertation. *Entrance requirements:* For master's and doctorate, GRE General Test. Additional exam requirements/recommendations for international students: Required—TOEFL (minimum score 570 paper-based; 230 computer-based; 85 iBT). *Application deadline:* For fall admission, 7/15 for domestic students, 1/15 priority date for international students; for spring admission, 12/1 for domestic and international students. Applications are processed on a rolling basis. Application fee: $65. Electronic applications accepted. *Financial support:* In 2009–10, 41 students received support, including 5 fellowships with full tuition reimbursements available (averaging $20,400 per year), 32 research assistantships with full tuition reimbursements available (averaging $20,400 per year), 7 teaching assistantships with full and partial tuition reimbursements available (averaging $20,400 per year); career-related internships or fieldwork, institutionally sponsored loans, scholarships/grants, health care benefits, and unspecified assistantships also available. Financial award application deadline: 1/15. *Faculty research:* Emulsion polymers, process control, energy, biotechnology, catalysis. Total annual research expenditures: $2.6 million. *Unit head:* Dr. Anthony J. McHugh, Chairman, 610-758-4260, Fax: 610-758-5057, E-mail: ajm8@lehigh.edu. *Application contact:* Barbara A. Kessler, Graduate Secretary, 610-758-4261, Fax: 610-758-5057, E-mail: inchegs@mail.lehigh.edu.

Louisiana State University and Agricultural and Mechanical College, Graduate School, College of Agriculture, Department of Biological and Agricultural Engineering, Baton Rouge, LA 70803. Offers biological and agricultural engineering (MSBAE); engineering science (MS, PhD). Part-time programs available. *Faculty:* 13 full-time (2 women). *Students:* 16 full-time (2 women), 4 part-time (2 women); includes 2 African Americans, 3 Asian Americans or Pacific Islanders, 8 international. Average age 26. 9 applicants, 78% accepted, 4 enrolled. In 2009, 5 master's awarded. Terminal master's awarded for partial completion of doctoral program. *Degree requirements:* For master's, thesis; for doctorate, thesis/dissertation. *Entrance requirements:* For master's and doctorate, GRE General Test, minimum GPA of 3.0. Additional exam requirements/recommendations for international students: Required—TOEFL (minimum score 550 paper-based; 213 computer-based; 79 iBT) or IELTS (minimum score 6.5). *Application deadline:* For fall admission, 1/25 priority date for domestic students, 5/15 for international students; for spring admission, 10/15 for international students. Applications are processed on a rolling basis. Application fee: $50 ($70 for international students). Electronic applications accepted. *Financial support:* In 2009–10, 19 students received support, including 1 fellowship (averaging $35,195 per year), 14 research assistantships with partial tuition reimbursements available (averaging $14,723 per year); teaching assistantships with partial tuition reimbursements available, career-related internships or fieldwork, Federal Work-Study, institutionally sponsored loans, scholarships/grants, health care benefits, and unspecified assistantships also available. Financial award application deadline: 7/1; financial award applicants required to submit FAFSA. *Faculty research:* Bioenergy, bioprocess engineering, cellular and molecular engineering, drug delivery using nanotechnology, environmental engineering. Total annual research expenditures: $25,277. *Unit head:* Dr. Dan Thomas, Head, 225-578-3153, Fax: 225-578-3492, E-mail: dthomas@agcenter.lsu.edu. *Application contact:* Dr. Steven Hall, Graduate Coordinator, 225-578-1058, Fax: 225-578-3492, E-mail: sghall@agcenter.lsu.edu.

Massachusetts Institute of Technology, School of Engineering, Department of Biological Engineering, Cambridge, MA 02139-4307. Offers applied biosciences (PhD, Sc D); bioengineering (PhD, Sc D); biological engineering (PhD, Sc D); biomedical engineering (M Eng); toxicology (SM); SM/MBA. *Faculty:* 18 full-time (2 women). *Students:* 105 full-time (51 women); includes 24 minority (3 African Americans, 16 Asian Americans or Pacific Islanders, 5 Hispanic Americans), 29 international. Average age 26. 371 applicants, 9% accepted, 22 enrolled. In 2009, 5 master's, 20 doctorates awarded. Terminal master's awarded for partial completion of doctoral program. *Degree requirements:* For master's, thesis; for doctorate, comprehensive exam, thesis/dissertation. *Entrance requirements:* For master's and doctorate, GRE General Test. Additional exam requirements/recommendations for international students: Required—TOEFL (minimum score 600 paper-based; 250 computer-based), IELTS (minimum score 7). *Application deadline:* For fall admission, 12/31 for domestic and international students. Application fee: $75. Electronic applications accepted. *Financial support:* In 2009–10, 105 students received support, including 51 fellowships with tuition reimbursements available (averaging $35,187 per year), 49 research assistantships with tuition reimbursements available (averaging $31,622 per year); teaching assistantships with tuition reimbursements available, Federal Work-Study, institutionally sponsored loans, scholarships/grants, traineeships, health care benefits, and unspecified assistantships also available. *Faculty research:* Bioinformatics, computational, systems, and synthetic biology, biological materials, cancer initiation, progression, and therapeutics, genomics, proteomics, glycomics, imaging, transport phenomena, biomolecular and cell engineering, nanoscale engineering of biological systems, neurobiological systems. Total annual research expenditures: $35.2 million. *Unit head:* Prof. Douglas A. Lauffenburger, Department Head, 617-253-1712, E-mail: be-acad@mit.edu. *Application contact:* Biological Engineering Academic Office, 617-253-1712, Fax: 617-258-8676, E-mail: be-acad@mit.edu.

See Close-Up on page 119.

McGill University, Faculty of Graduate and Postdoctoral Studies, Faculty of Agricultural and Environmental Sciences, Department of Bioresource Engineering, Montréal, QC H3A 2T5,

Bioengineering

McGill University (continued)
Canada. Offers computer applications (M Sc, M Sc A, PhD); food engineering (M Sc, M Sc A, PhD); grain drying (M Sc, M Sc A, PhD); irrigation and drainage (M Sc, M Sc A, PhD); machinery (M Sc, M Sc A, PhD); pollution control (M Sc, M Sc A, PhD); post-harvest technology (M Sc, M Sc A, PhD); soil dynamics (M Sc, M Sc A, PhD); structure and environment (M Sc, M Sc A, PhD); vegetable and fruit storage (M Sc, M Sc A, PhD).

Mississippi State University, College of Agriculture and Life Sciences, Department of Agricultural and Biological Engineering, Mississippi State, MS 39762. Offers biological engineering (MS); biomedical engineering (MS, PhD); engineering (PhD), including biological engineering. *Faculty:* 8 full-time (1 woman). *Students:* 22 full-time (6 women), 9 part-time (5 women); includes 7 minority (4 African Americans, 3 Asian Americans or Pacific Islanders), 7 international. Average age 27. 20 applicants, 50% accepted, 7 enrolled. In 2009, 4 master's, 2 doctorates awarded. *Degree requirements:* For master's, thesis; for doctorate, thesis/dissertation, preliminary exam. *Entrance requirements:* For master's, GRE General Test, minimum undergraduate GPA of 2.75 (3.0 for biomedical engineering); for doctorate, GRE General Test, minimum GPA of 3.0 (biomedical engineering). Additional exam requirements/recommendations for international students: Required—TOEFL (minimum score 550 paper-based; 213 computer-based; 79 iBT); Recommended—IELTS (minimum score 6.5). *Application deadline:* For fall admission, 7/1 for domestic students, 5/1 for international students; for spring admission, 11/1 for domestic students, 9/1 for international students. Applications are processed on a rolling basis. Application fee: $40. Electronic applications accepted. *Expenses:* Tuition, state resident: full-time $2575.50; part-time $286.25 per credit hour. Tuition, nonresident: full-time $6510; part-time $723.50 per credit hour. Tuition and fees vary according to course load. *Financial support:* In 2009–10, 19 research assistantships with partial tuition reimbursements (averaging $12,530 per year) were awarded; Federal Work-Study, institutionally sponsored loans, and unspecified assistantships also available. Financial award applicants required to submit FAFSA. *Faculty research:* Bioenvironmental engineering, bioinstrumentation, biomechanics/biomaterials, precision agriculture, tissue engineering, ergonomics human factors, biosimulation and modeling. Total annual research expenditures: $1.6 million. *Unit head:* Dr. William D. Batchelor, Department Head and Professor, 662-325-3280, Fax: 662-325-3853, E-mail: batchelor@abe.msstate.edu. *Application contact:* Dr. Jeremiah Davis, Assistant Professor and Graduate Coordinator, 662-325-3282, Fax: 662-325-3853, E-mail: jdavis@abe.msstate.edu.

North Carolina State University, Graduate School, College of Agriculture and Life Sciences, Department of Biological and Agricultural Engineering, Raleigh, NC 27695. Offers MBAE, MS, PhD, Certificate. Part-time programs available. Postbaccalaureate distance learning degree programs offered. *Degree requirements:* For master's, thesis (for some programs); for doctorate, thesis/dissertation. *Entrance requirements:* For master's and doctorate, GRE. Additional exam requirements/recommendations for international students: Required—TOEFL. Electronic applications accepted. *Faculty research:* Bioinstrumentation, animal waste management, water quality engineering, machine systems, controlled environment agriculture.

The Ohio State University, Graduate School, College of Food, Agricultural, and Environmental Sciences, Department of Food, Agricultural, and Biological Engineering, Columbus, OH 43210. Offers MS, PhD. *Faculty:* 31. *Students:* 22 full-time (12 women), 10 part-time (1 woman); includes 3 minority (1 African American, 2 Hispanic Americans), 18 international. Average age 29. In 2009, 5 master's, 3 doctorates awarded. *Degree requirements:* For master's, thesis optional; for doctorate, thesis/dissertation. *Entrance requirements:* For master's and doctorate, GRE General Test, GRE Subject Test in engineering (recommended). Additional exam requirements/recommendations for international students: Required—TOEFL (minimum score 550 paper-based; 213 computer-based) or IELTS (minimum score 7) or Michigan English Language Assessment Battery (minimum score 85). *Application deadline:* For fall admission, 8/15 priority date for domestic students, 7/1 priority date for international students; for winter admission, 12/1 priority date for domestic students, 11/1 priority date for international students; for spring admission, 3/1 priority date for domestic students, 2/1 priority date for international students. Applications are processed on a rolling basis. Application fee: $40 ($50 for international students). Electronic applications accepted. *Expenses:* Tuition, state resident: full-time $10,683. Tuition, nonresident: full-time $25,923. Tuition and fees vary according to course load and program. *Financial support:* Fellowships, research assistantships, teaching assistantships, career-related internships or fieldwork, Federal Work-Study, and institutionally sponsored loans available. Support available to part-time students. *Application contact:* Graduate Admissions, 614-292-9444, Fax: 614-292-3895, E-mail: domestic.grad@osu.edu.

Oklahoma State University, College of Agricultural Science and Natural Resources, Department of Biosystems and Agricultural Engineering, Stillwater, OK 74078. Offers biosystems engineering (MS, PhD); environmental and natural resources (MS, PhD). *Faculty:* 25 full-time (4 women), 1 part-time/adjunct (0 women). *Students:* 15 full-time (5 women), 31 part-time (10 women); includes 3 minority (1 African American, 1 American Indian/Alaska Native, 1 Hispanic American), 26 international. Average age 29. 57 applicants, 32% accepted, 12 enrolled. In 2009, 13 master's, 1 doctorate awarded. *Degree requirements:* For master's, thesis; for doctorate, comprehensive exam, thesis/dissertation. *Entrance requirements:* For master's and doctorate, GRE or GMAT. Additional exam requirements/recommendations for international students: Required—TOEFL (minimum score 550 paper-based; 79 iBT). *Application deadline:* For fall admission, 3/1 priority date for international students; for spring admission, 8/1 priority date for international students. Applications are processed on a rolling basis. Application fee: $40 ($75 for international students). Electronic applications accepted. *Expenses:* Tuition, state resident: full-time $3716; part-time $154.85 per credit hour. Tuition, nonresident: full-time $14,448; part-time $602 per credit hour. Required fees: $1772; $73.85 per credit hour. One-time fee: $50. Tuition and fees vary according to course load and campus/location. *Financial support:* In 2009–10, 50 research assistantships (averaging $15,858 per year), 4 teaching assistantships (averaging $9,900 per year) were awarded; career-related internships or fieldwork, Federal Work-Study, scholarships/grants, health care benefits, tuition waivers (partial), and unspecified assistantships also available. Support available to part-time students. Financial award application deadline: 3/1; financial award applicants required to submit FAFSA. *Unit head:* Dr. Ronald L. Elliot, Head, 405-744-5431, Fax: 405-744-6059. *Application contact:* Dr. Gordon Emslie, Dean, 405-744-6368, Fax: 405-744-0355, E-mail: grad-i@okstate.edu.

Oregon State University, Graduate School, College of Engineering, Department of Biological and Ecological Engineering, Corvallis, OR 97331. Offers M Eng, MS, PhD. *Students:* 23. 8 applicants, 50% accepted, 2 enrolled. In 2009, 1 doctorate awarded. Terminal master's awarded for partial completion of doctoral program. *Degree requirements:* For master's, thesis or alternative; for doctorate, thesis/dissertation. *Entrance requirements:* For master's and doctorate, minimum GPA of 3.0 in last 90 hours. Additional exam requirements/recommendations for international students: Required—TOEFL (minimum score 550 paper-based; 213 computer-based). *Application deadline:* For fall admission, 3/1 for domestic students. Applications are processed on a rolling basis. Application fee: $50. *Expenses:* Contact institution. *Financial support:* In 2009–10, 3 fellowships with full tuition reimbursements (averaging $13,041 per year), 10 research assistantships with full tuition reimbursements (averaging $13,041 per year) were awarded; teaching assistantships, Federal Work-Study and institutionally sponsored loans also available. Support available to part-time students. Financial award application deadline: 2/1. *Faculty research:* Bioengineering, water resources engineering, food engineering, cell culture and fermentation, vadose zone transport. Total annual research expenditures: $827,438. *Unit head:* Dr. John P. Bolte, Head, 541-737-6303, Fax: 541-737-2082, E-mail: info-bee@engr.orst.edu. *Application contact:* Elena Maus, Information Contact, 541-737-2041, Fax: 541-737-2082, E-mail: info-bee@engr.orst.edu.

Oregon State University, Graduate School, College of Engineering, School of Mechanical, Industrial, and Manufacturing Engineering, Corvallis, OR 97331. Offers human systems engineering (MS, PhD); industrial engineering (MS, PhD); information systems engineering (MS, PhD); manufacturing engineering (M Engr); manufacturing systems engineering (MS, PhD); materials science (MAIS, MS, PhD); mechanical engineering (MS, PhD); nano/micro fabrication (MS, PhD). Part-time programs available. Postbaccalaureate distance learning degree programs offered (minimal on-campus study). *Faculty:* 26 full-time (2 women), 2 part-time/adjunct (1 woman). *Students:* 136 full-time (25 women), 12 part-time (2 women); includes 11 minority (3 African Americans, 4 Asian Americans or Pacific Islanders, 4 Hispanic Americans), 46 international. Average age 29. 53 applicants, 42% accepted, 13 enrolled. In 2009, 26 master's, 10 doctorates awarded. *Degree requirements:* For master's, thesis or alternative; for doctorate, thesis/dissertation. *Entrance requirements:* For master's, placement exam, minimum GPA of 3.0 in last 90 hours of course work; for doctorate, GRE, placement exam, minimum GPA of 3.0 in last 90 hours of course work. Additional exam requirements/recommendations for international students: Required—TOEFL (minimum score 550 paper-based; 213 computer-based). *Application deadline:* For fall admission, 3/1 for domestic students. Applications are processed on a rolling basis. Application fee: $50. *Expenses:* Tuition, state resident: full-time $9774; part-time $362 per credit. Tuition, nonresident: full-time $15,849; part-time $587 per credit. Required fees: $1639. Full-time tuition and fees vary according to course load and program. *Financial support:* In 2009–10, 10 research assistantships with full tuition reimbursements (averaging $11,124 per year), 8 teaching assistantships with full tuition reimbursements (averaging $7,020 per year) were awarded; fellowships with full tuition reimbursements, institutionally sponsored loans and instructorships also available. Support available to part-time students. Financial award application deadline: 2/1. *Faculty research:* Computer-integrated manufacturing, human factors, robotics, decision support systems, simulation modeling and analysis. Total annual research expenditures: $1.3 million. *Unit head:* Dr. Belinda A. Batten, Head, 541-737-3441, Fax: 541-737-2600, E-mail: info-mime@oregonstate.edu. *Application contact:* Jean Robinson, Graduate Records Specialist, 541-737-7009, Fax: 541-737-2600, E-mail: jean.robinson@oregonstate.edu.

Penn State Hershey Medical Center, College of Medicine, Graduate School Programs in the Biomedical Sciences, Intercollege Bioengineering Graduate Program, Hershey, PA 17033-2360. Offers MS, PhD, MD/PhD. Terminal master's awarded for partial completion of doctoral program. *Degree requirements:* For master's, thesis; for doctorate, comprehensive exam, thesis/dissertation, oral exam. *Entrance requirements:* For master's, GRE; for doctorate, GRE, minimum GPA of 3.0. Additional exam requirements/recommendations for international students: Required—TOEFL (minimum score 500 paper-based; 213 computer-based). *Application deadline:* Applications are processed on a rolling basis. Application fee: $65. Electronic applications accepted. *Expenses:* Tuition, state resident: part-time $644 per credit. Tuition, nonresident: part-time $1142 per credit. Required fees: $22 per semester. *Financial support:* In 2009–10, 8 research assistantships with full tuition reimbursements were awarded; fellowships with full tuition reimbursements, scholarships/grants, health care benefits, and unspecified assistantships also available. Financial award applicants required to submit FAFSA. *Faculty research:* Artificial organs, cardiovascular and orthopedic biomaterials, magnetic resonance imaging, bio-degradable responsive polymers for drug delivery. *Unit head:* Program Director. *Application contact:* Program Director.

Penn State University Park, Graduate School, College of Agricultural Sciences, Department of Agricultural and Biological Engineering, State College, University Park, PA 16802-1503. Offers MS, PhD.

Penn State University Park, Graduate School, Intercollege Graduate Programs, Intercollege Graduate Program in Bioengineering, State College, University Park, PA 16802-1503. Offers MS, PhD. *Unit head:* Dr. Herbert H. Lipowsky, Head, 814-865-1407, Fax: 814-863-0490, E-mail: hhlbio@engr.psu.edu. *Application contact:* Dr. Herbert H. Lipowsky, Head, 814-865-1407, Fax: 814-863-0490, E-mail: hhlbio@engr.psu.edu.

Polytechnic Institute of NYU, Department of Chemical and Biological Sciences, Major in Bioengineering, Brooklyn, NY 11201-2990. Offers MS. Part-time programs available. *Students:* 1 part-time (0 women). 1 applicant, 0% accepted, 0 enrolled. *Entrance requirements:* Additional exam requirements/recommendations for international students: Required—TOEFL (minimum score 550 paper-based; 213 computer-based; 80 iBT); Recommended—IELTS (minimum score 6.5). *Application deadline:* For fall admission, 7/31 priority date for domestic students, 4/30 priority date for international students; for spring admission, 12/31 priority date for domestic students, 11/30 priority date for international students. Applications are processed on a rolling basis. Application fee: $75. Electronic applications accepted. *Expenses:* Tuition: Full-time $21,492; part-time $1194 per credit hour. Required fees: $1160; $204 per course. *Financial support:* Institutionally sponsored loans, scholarships/grants, and unspecified assistantships available. Support available to part-time students. *Unit head:* Dr. Bruce Garetz, Department Head, 718-260-3600. *Application contact:* JeanCarlo Bonilla, Director of Graduate Enrollment Management, 718-260-3182, Fax: 718-260-3624, E-mail: gradinfo@poly.edu.

Rensselaer Polytechnic Institute, Graduate School, School of Engineering, Howard P. Isermann Department of Chemical and Biological Engineering, Troy, NY 12180-3590. Offers M Eng, MS, PhD. Part-time programs available. *Faculty:* 13 full-time (1 woman). *Students:* 67 full-time (15 women), 2 part-time (1 woman); includes 7 minority (1 African American, 5 Asian Americans or Pacific Islanders, 1 Hispanic American), 39 international. Average age 24. 161 applicants, 33% accepted, 19 enrolled. In 2009, 4 master's, 16 doctorates awarded. Terminal master's awarded for partial completion of doctoral program. *Entrance requirements:* For master's, GRE (minimum score 550 verbal); for doctorate, GRE (Verbal minimum score of 550). Additional exam requirements/recommendations for international students: Required—TOEFL (minimum score 570 paper-based). *Application deadline:* For fall admission, 1/1 priority date for domestic students, 1/1 for international students; for spring admission, 8/15 for domestic and international students. Applications are processed on a rolling basis. Application fee: $75. Electronic applications accepted. *Expenses:* Tuition: Full-time $38,100. *Financial support:* In 2009–10, 65 students received support, including 2 fellowships with full tuition reimbursements available (averaging $23,000 per year), 53 research assistantships with full tuition reimbursements available (averaging $22,000 per year), 10 teaching assistantships with full tuition reimbursements available (averaging $16,500 per year); institutionally sponsored loans and scholarships/grants also available. Financial award application deadline: 1/1. *Faculty research:* Biocatalysis, bioseparations, biotechnology, molecular modeling and simulation, advanced materials, interfacial phenomena, systems biology. Total annual research expenditures: $4.7 million. *Unit head:* Dr. Shekhar Garde, Department Head, 518-276-2511, Fax: 518-276-4030, E-mail: gardes@rpi.edu. *Application contact:* Dr. B. Wayne Bequette, Chairman, Graduate Affairs Committee, 518-276-6683, Fax: 518-276-4030, E-mail: bequette@rpi.edu.

Rice University, Graduate Programs, George R. Brown School of Engineering, Department of Bioengineering, Houston, TX 77251-1892. Offers MBE, MS, PhD, MD/PhD. Terminal master's awarded for partial completion of doctoral program. *Degree requirements:* For master's, thesis; for doctorate, thesis/dissertation, qualifying exam, internship. *Entrance requirements:* For master's and doctorate, GRE General Test. Additional exam requirements/recommendations for international students: Required—TOEFL (minimum score 600 paper-based; 250 computer-based; 90 iBT). Electronic applications accepted. *Faculty research:* Biomaterials, tissue engineering, laser-tissue interactions, biochemical engineering, gene therapy.

Rice University, Graduate Programs, George R. Brown School of Engineering, Department of Electrical and Computer Engineering, Houston, TX 77251-1892. Offers bioengineering (MS, PhD); circuits, controls, and communication systems (MS, PhD); computer science and engineering (MS, PhD); electrical engineering (MEE); lasers, microwaves, and solid-state electronics (MS, PhD); MBA/MEE. Part-time programs available. *Degree requirements:* For master's, thesis (for some programs); for doctorate, thesis/dissertation. *Entrance requirements:* For master's and doctorate, GRE General Test, GRE Subject Test, minimum GPA of 3.0. Additional exam requirements/recommendations for international students: Required—TOEFL (minimum score 600 paper-based; 250 computer-based; 90 iBT). Electronic applications accepted. *Faculty research:* Physical electronics, systems, computer engineering, bioengineering.

South Dakota School of Mines and Technology, Graduate Division, College of Engineering, Department of Chemical and Biological Engineering, Rapid City, SD 57701-3995. Offers chemical and biological engineering (PhD); chemical engineering (MS). *Students:* 17 full-time

(6 women); includes 1 Hispanic American, 9 international. Average age 28. 18 applicants, 56% accepted, 7 enrolled. *Expenses:* Tuition, state resident: full-time $3340; part-time $139 per credit hour. Tuition, nonresident: full-time $7060; part-time $294 per credit hour. Required fees: $3270. *Unit head:* Dr. David Dixon, Chair, 605-394-1235, E-mail: david.dixon@sdsmt.edu. *Application contact:* Jeannette R. Nilson, Administrative Support Coordinator, Graduate Education, 800-454-8162 Ext. 1206, Fax: 605-394-5360, E-mail: graduate_admissions@sdsmt.edu.

Stanford University, School of Medicine, Department of Bioengineering, Stanford, CA 94305-9991. Offers MS, PhD. *Degree requirements:* For master's, thesis optional; for doctorate, comprehensive exam, thesis/dissertation. *Entrance requirements:* For master's and doctorate, GRE General Test. Additional exam requirements/recommendations for international students: Required—TOEFL. Electronic applications accepted. *Expenses:* Tuition: Full-time $37,380; part-time $2760 per quarter. Required fees: $501. *Faculty research:* Biomedical computation, regenerative medicine/tissue engineering, molecular and cell bioengineering, biomedical imaging, biomedical devices.

Syracuse University, L. C. Smith College of Engineering and Computer Science, Program in Bioengineering, Syracuse, NY 13244. Offers ME, MS, PhD. *Students:* 35 full-time (16 women), 6 part-time (1 woman); includes 2 minority (1 African American, 1 Asian American or Pacific Islander), 23 international. Average age 25. 48 applicants, 52% accepted, 13 enrolled. In 2009, 5 master's, 1 doctorate awarded. *Entrance requirements:* For master's and doctorate, GRE General Test. Additional exam requirements/recommendations for international students: Required—TOEFL (minimum score 100 iBT). *Application deadline:* For fall admission, 6/1 priority date for domestic and international students. Applications are processed on a rolling basis. Application fee: $75. Electronic applications accepted. *Expenses:* Tuition: Full-time $26,808; part-time $1117 per credit. Required fees: $1024. *Financial support:* Fellowships with full tuition reimbursements, research assistantships with full tuition reimbursements, teaching assistantships with full tuition reimbursements, tuition waivers (full and partial) available. Financial award application deadline: 1/1; financial award applicants required to submit FAFSA. *Faculty research:* Computational neuroscience. *Unit head:* Dr. Radhakrishna Sureshkumar, Chair, 315-443-3194, Fax: 315-443-9175, E-mail: rsureshk@syr.edu. *Application contact:* Kathleen Joyce, Director of Graduate Recruitment, 314-443-2219, E-mail: topgrads@syr.edu.

Texas A&M University, College of Agriculture and Life Sciences and College of Engineering, Department of Biological and Agricultural Engineering, College Station, TX 77843. Offers M Agr, M Eng, MS, DE, PhD. Part-time programs available. *Faculty:* 18. *Students:* 66 full-time (22 women), 10 part-time (2 women); includes 9 minority (3 African Americans, 3 Asian Americans or Pacific Islanders, 3 Hispanic Americans), 43 international. Average age 29. In 2009, 9 master's, 3 doctorates awarded. *Degree requirements:* For master's, thesis (MS), preliminary and final exams; for doctorate, thesis/dissertation, preliminary and final exams. *Entrance requirements:* For master's and doctorate, GRE General Test. Additional exam requirements/recommendations for international students: Required—TOEFL (minimum score 550 paper-based; 213 computer-based). *Application deadline:* For fall admission, 2/1 priority date for domestic students; for spring admission, 10/1 for domestic students. Applications are processed on a rolling basis. Application fee: $50 ($75 for international students). Electronic applications accepted. *Expenses:* Tuition, state resident: full-time $3991.32; part-time $221.74 per credit hour. Tuition, nonresident: full-time $9049; part-time $502.74 per credit hour. *Financial support:* In 2009–10, 3 fellowships with full and partial tuition reimbursements (averaging $15,000 per year), 17 research assistantships with full and partial tuition reimbursements (averaging $18,150 per year), 12 teaching assistantships with partial tuition reimbursements (averaging $19,590 per year) were awarded; career-related internships or fieldwork, institutionally sponsored loans, scholarships/grants, tuition waivers, and unspecified assistantships also available. Financial award application deadline: 3/1; financial award applicants required to submit FAFSA. *Faculty research:* Water quality and quantity; air quality; biological, food, ecological engineering; off-road equipment; mechatronics. *Unit head:* Head, 979-854-3931, Fax: 979-862-3442, E-mail: info@baen.tamu.edu. *Application contact:* Academic Programs Assistant, 979-845-0609, Fax: 979-862-3442, E-mail: info@baen.tamu.edu.

Tufts University, Graduate School of Arts and Sciences, Graduate Certificate Programs, Program in Bioengineering, Medford, MA 02155. Offers Certificate. Part-time and evening/weekend programs available. Electronic applications accepted. *Expenses:* Tuition: Full-time $38,096; part-time $3962 per credit. Required fees: $686; $40 per year. Tuition and fees vary according to course level, course load, degree level, program and student level.

Tufts University, School of Engineering, Department of Chemical and Biological Engineering, Medford, MA 02155. Offers ME, MS, PhD. Part-time programs available. *Faculty:* 8 full-time, 2 part-time/adjunct. *Students:* 42 (16 women); includes 4 minority (all Asian Americans or Pacific Islanders), 18 international. Average age 27. 68 applicants, 40% accepted, 8 enrolled. In 2009, 8 master's, 3 doctorates awarded. Terminal master's awarded for partial completion of doctoral program. *Degree requirements:* For master's, thesis (for some programs); for doctorate, thesis/dissertation. *Entrance requirements:* For master's and doctorate, GRE General Test. Additional exam requirements/recommendations for international students: Required—TOEFL (minimum score 550 paper-based; 213 computer-based; 80 iBT). *Application deadline:* For fall admission, 1/15 priority date for domestic students, 12/15 for international students; for spring admission, 10/15 for domestic students, 9/15 for international students. Applications are processed on a rolling basis. Application fee: $75. Electronic applications accepted. *Expenses:* Tuition: Full-time $38,096; part-time $3962 per credit. Required fees: $686; $40 per year. Tuition and fees vary according to course level, course load, degree level, program and student level. *Financial support:* Fellowships with full tuition reimbursements, research assistantships with full and partial tuition reimbursements, teaching assistantships with full and partial tuition reimbursements, Federal Work-Study, scholarships/grants, tuition waivers (partial), and unspecified assistantships available. Financial award application deadline: 1/15; financial award applicants required to submit FAFSA. *Unit head:* Dr. Kyongbum Lee, Chair, 617-627-3900. *Application contact:* Erin Quigley, Staff, 617-627-3900.

University at Buffalo, the State University of New York, Graduate School, School of Engineering and Applied Sciences, Department of Chemical and Biological Engineering, Buffalo, NY 14260. Offers M Eng, MS, PhD. Part-time programs available. *Faculty:* 18 full-time (1 woman), 4 part-time/adjunct (1 woman). *Students:* 95 full-time (36 women), 7 part-time (3 women); includes 6 minority (4 Asian Americans or Pacific Islanders, 2 Hispanic Americans), 81 international. Average age 26. 324 applicants, 20% accepted, 42 enrolled. In 2009, 13 master's, 7 doctorates awarded. *Degree requirements:* For master's, thesis (for some programs); for doctorate, comprehensive exam, thesis/dissertation. *Entrance requirements:* For master's and doctorate, GRE General Test. Additional exam requirements/recommendations for international students: Required—TOEFL (minimum score 550 paper-based; 213 computer-based; 79 iBT). *Application deadline:* For fall admission, 2/1 priority date for domestic and international students; for spring admission, 10/1 priority date for domestic and international students. Applications are processed on a rolling basis. Application fee: $50. Electronic applications accepted. *Financial support:* In 2009–10, 50 students received support, including 13 fellowships (averaging $30,000 per year), 34 research assistantships with full tuition reimbursements available (averaging $24,000 per year), 9 teaching assistantships with full tuition reimbursements available (averaging $20,900 per year); institutionally sponsored loans, scholarships/grants, health care benefits, tuition waivers (partial), and unspecified assistantships also available. Support available to part-time students. Financial award application deadline: 2/28; financial award applicants required to submit FAFSA. *Faculty research:* Transport, polymers, nanomaterials, biochemical engineering, catalysis. Total annual research expenditures: $9.6 million. *Unit head:* Dr. David A. Kofke, Chairman, 716-645-2911, Fax: 716-645-3822, E-mail: kofke@buffalo.edu. *Application contact:* Dr. Paschalis Alexandridis, Director of Graduate Studies, 716-645-1183, Fax: 716-645-3822, E-mail: palexand@buffalo.edu.

University of Arkansas, Graduate School, College of Engineering, Department of Biological and Agricultural Engineering, Program in Biological Engineering, Fayetteville, AR 72701-1201. Offers MSBE. *Accreditation:* ABET. *Students:* 3 full-time (2 women), 17 part-time (3 women); includes 2 minority (1 African American, 1 Asian American or Pacific Islander), 13 international. In 2009, 3 master's awarded. Application fee: $40 ($50 for international students). *Expenses:* Tuition, state resident: full-time $7355; part-time $356.58 per hour. Tuition, nonresident: full-time $17,401; part-time $775.17 per hour. Required fees: $1203. *Financial support:* In 2009–10, 1 fellowship, 16 research assistantships were awarded; teaching assistantships. *Unit head:* Dr. Carl Griffis, Department Head, 479-575-2351, Fax: 479-575-2846, E-mail: clg@uark.edu. *Application contact:* Dr. Jin-Woo Kim, Program Coordinator, 479-575-2351, Fax: 479-575-2846, E-mail: jwkim@uark.edu.

University of California, Berkeley, Graduate Division, Bioengineering Graduate Program Berkeley/UCSF, Berkeley, CA 94720-1762. Offers PhD. *Degree requirements:* For doctorate, comprehensive exam, thesis/dissertation. *Entrance requirements:* For doctorate, GRE General Test, minimum GPA of 3.0. Additional exam requirements/recommendations for international students: Required—TOEFL (minimum score 570 paper-based; 230 computer-based; 68 iBT). Electronic applications accepted. *Faculty research:* Biomedical imaging, tissue engineering, biomechanics, computational biology, synthetic and systems biology, neuroscience, vision science, biomedical instrumentation, drug delivery, nanotechnology.

University of California, Davis, College of Engineering, Program in Biological Systems Engineering, Davis, CA 95616. Offers M Engr, MS, D Engr, PhD, M Engr/MBA. Terminal master's awarded for partial completion of doctoral program. *Degree requirements:* For master's, thesis; for doctorate, thesis/dissertation. *Entrance requirements:* For master's, minimum GPA of 3.0; for doctorate, GRE, minimum graduate GPA of 3.25. Additional exam requirements/recommendations for international students: Required—TOEFL (minimum score 550 paper-based; 213 computer-based). Electronic applications accepted. *Faculty research:* Forestry, irrigation and drainage, power and machinery, structures and environment, information and energy technologies.

University of California, Merced, Division of Graduate Studies, School of Natural Sciences, Merced, CA 95343. Offers applied mathematics (MS, PhD); biological engineering and small-scale technologies (MS, PhD); environmental systems (MS, PhD); mechanical engineering and applied mechanics (MS, PhD); physics and chemistry (PhD); quantitative and systems biology (MS, PhD). *Expenses:* Tuition, nonresident: full-time $15,102. Required fees: $10,919.

University of California, Riverside, Graduate Division, Department of Bioengineering, Riverside, CA 92521-0102. Offers MS, PhD. *Degree requirements:* For doctorate, thesis/dissertation, qualifying exams. *Entrance requirements:* Additional exam requirements/recommendations for international students: Required—TOEFL (minimum score 550 paper-based; 213 computer-based; 80 iBT).

University of California, San Diego, Office of Graduate Studies, Department of Bioengineering, La Jolla, CA 92093. Offers M Eng, MS, PhD. *Entrance requirements:* For master's and doctorate, GRE General Test, minimum GPA of 3.0. Additional exam requirements/recommendations for international students: Required—TOEFL. Electronic applications accepted.

See Close-Up on page 121.

University of California, San Francisco, Graduate Division, Program in Bioengineering, Berkeley, CA 94720-1762. Offers PhD. *Degree requirements:* For doctorate, thesis/dissertation, qualifying exam. *Entrance requirements:* For doctorate, GRE General Test, minimum GPA of 3.0. Additional exam requirements/recommendations for international students: Required—TOEFL (minimum score 570 paper-based). Electronic applications accepted. *Faculty research:* Imaging, biomechanics, modeling, neuroscience, biomedical computing, vision.

University of Denver, School of Engineering and Computer Science, Department of Mechanical and Materials Engineering, Denver, CO 80208. Offers bioengineering (MS); engineering (MS, PhD); materials science (PhD); mechanical engineering (MS); mechatronics (MS). *Faculty:* 9 full-time (1 woman), 2 part-time/adjunct (1 woman). *Students:* 1 full-time (0 women), 17 part-time (12 women), 3 international. Average age 31. 46 applicants, 61% accepted, 12 enrolled. In 2009, 9 master's awarded. *Expenses:* Tuition: Full-time $34,596; part-time $961 per quarter hour. Required fees: $4 per quarter hour. Tuition and fees vary according to course load, campus/location and program. *Financial support:* In 2009–10, 3 research assistantships (averaging $11,000 per year), 5 teaching assistantships (averaging $11,000 per year) were awarded. *Faculty research:* Aerosols, biomechanics, composite materials, photo optics, drug delivery. Total annual research expenditures: $565,000. *Unit head:* Dr. Maciej Kumosa, Chair, 303-871-3807. *Application contact:* Dr. Maciej Kumosa, Chair, 303-871-3807.

University of Florida, Graduate School, College of Engineering and College of Agricultural and Life Sciences, Department of Agricultural and Biological Engineering, Gainesville, FL 32611. Offers ME, MS, PhD, Engr. Part-time programs available. Terminal master's awarded for partial completion of doctoral program. *Degree requirements:* For master's and Engr, thesis optional; for doctorate, thesis/dissertation. *Entrance requirements:* For master's and doctorate, GRE General Test, minimum GPA of 3.0; for Engr, GRE General Test. Additional exam requirements/recommendations for international students: Required—TOEFL (minimum score 550 paper-based; 213 computer-based). Electronic applications accepted. *Faculty research:* Soil and water engineering, structures and environments, power and machinery, biological processing, food engineering.

University of Georgia, Graduate School, College of Agricultural and Environmental Sciences, Department of Biological and Agricultural Engineering, Athens, GA 30602. Offers agricultural engineering (MS); biological and agricultural engineering (PhD); biological engineering (MS). *Faculty:* 29 full-time (3 women), 2 part-time/adjunct (0 women). *Students:* 38 full-time (11 women), 6 part-time (0 women); includes 4 minority (all African Americans), 25 international. 26 applicants, 69% accepted, 15 enrolled. In 2009, 3 master's, 3 doctorates awarded. *Degree requirements:* For master's, thesis; for doctorate, one foreign language, thesis/dissertation. *Entrance requirements:* For master's and doctorate, GRE General Test. *Application deadline:* For fall admission, 7/1 priority date for domestic students; for spring admission, 11/15 for domestic students. Application fee: $50. Electronic applications accepted. *Expenses:* Tuition, state resident: full-time $6000; part-time $250 per credit hour. Tuition, nonresident: full-time $20,904; part-time $871 per credit hour. Required fees: $730 per semester. *Financial support:* Fellowships, research assistantships, teaching assistantships, unspecified assistantships available. *Unit head:* Dr. E. Dale Threadgill, Head, 706-542-1653, Fax: 706-542-8806, E-mail: tgill@engr.uga.edu. *Application contact:* Dr. William S. Kisaalita, Graduate Coordinator, 706-542-0835, Fax: 706-542-8806, E-mail: williamk@engr.uga.edu.

University of Guelph, Graduate Program Services, College of Physical and Engineering Science, School of Engineering, Guelph, ON N1G 2W1, Canada. Offers biological engineering (M Eng, M Sc, MA Sc, PhD); engineering systems and computing (M Eng, M Sc, MA Sc, PhD); environmental engineering (M Eng, M Sc, MA Sc, PhD); water resources engineering (M Eng, M Sc, MA Sc, PhD). Part-time programs available. *Degree requirements:* For master's, thesis (for some programs); for doctorate, comprehensive exam, thesis/dissertation. *Entrance requirements:* For master's, minimum B- average during previous 2 years of course work; for doctorate, minimum B average. Additional exam requirements/recommendations for international students: Required—TOEFL (minimum score 550 paper-based; 213 computer-based; 89 iBT), IELTS (minimum score 6.5). Electronic applications accepted. *Faculty research:* Water and food safety, environmental contaminant fates and mechanisms, computer systems, robotics and mechatronics, waste treatment.

University of Hawaii at Manoa, Graduate Division, College of Tropical Agriculture and Human Resources, Department of Molecular Biosciences and Bioengineering, Program in Bioengineering, Honolulu, HI 96822. Offers MS. Part-time programs available. *Faculty:* 6 full-time (0 women). *Students:* 8 full-time (3 women); includes 2 minority (both Asian Americans or Pacific Islanders), 3 international. Average age 28. 14 applicants, 71% accepted, 6 enrolled. In 2009, 1 master's awarded. *Degree requirements:* For master's, thesis optional. *Entrance*

Bioengineering

University of Hawaii at Manoa (continued)
requirements: For master's, GRE General Test. Additional exam requirements/recommendations for international students: Required—TOEFL (minimum score 500 paper-based; 173 computer-based; 61 iBT), IELTS (minimum score 5). *Application deadline:* For fall admission, 5/1 for domestic students, 3/1 for international students; for spring admission, 9/1 for domestic students, 8/1 for international students. Application fee: $50. *Expenses:* Tuition, state resident: full-time $8900; part-time $372 per credit. Tuition, nonresident: full-time $21,400; part-time $898 per credit. Required fees: $207 per semester. *Financial support:* In 2009–10, 1 student received support, including 1 fellowship (averaging $1,250 per year), 6 research assistantships (averaging $19,609 per year). *Application contact:* Dr. Samir Khanal, Graduate Chairperson, 808-956-8384, Fax: 808-956-3542, E-mail: khanal@hawaii.edu.

University of Idaho, College of Graduate Studies, College of Engineering, Department of Biological and Agricultural Engineering, Moscow, ID 83844-2282. Offers agricultural engineering (M Engr, MS); biological and agricultural engineering (PhD). *Faculty:* 5 full-time, 1 part-time/adjunct. *Students:* 8 full-time, 5 part-time. In 2009, 3 master's awarded. *Degree requirements:* For master's, thesis or alternative; for doctorate, one foreign language, thesis/dissertation. *Entrance requirements:* For master's, minimum GPA of 2.8; for doctorate, minimum undergraduate GPA of 2.8, 3.0 graduate. *Application deadline:* For fall admission, 8/1 for domestic students; for spring admission, 12/15 for domestic students. Application fee: $55 ($60 for international students). *Expenses:* Tuition, state resident: full-time $6120. Tuition, nonresident: full-time $17,712. *Financial support:* Research assistantships, teaching assistantships, career-related internships or fieldwork available. Financial award application deadline: 2/15. *Faculty research:* Water and environmental research, alternative fuels/biodiesel, agricultural safety health, biological processes for agricultural/food waste. *Unit head:* Dr. Jon Harlan Van Gerpen, Department Head, 208-885-7891. *Application contact:* Dr. Jon Harlan Van Gerpen, Department Head, 208-885-7891.

University of Illinois at Chicago, Graduate College, College of Engineering, Department of Bioengineering, Chicago, IL 60607-7128. Offers MS, PhD. Terminal master's awarded for partial completion of doctoral program. *Degree requirements:* For master's, thesis; for doctorate, thesis/dissertation. *Entrance requirements:* For master's and doctorate, GRE Subject Test, minimum GPA of 3.0. Additional exam requirements/recommendations for international students: Required—TOEFL. Electronic applications accepted. *Faculty research:* Imaging systems, bioinstrumentation, electrophysiology, biological control, laser scattering.

University of Illinois at Urbana–Champaign, Graduate College, College of Agricultural, Consumer and Environmental Sciences, Department of Agricultural and Biological Engineering, Champaign, IL 61820. Offers agricultural engineering (MS, PhD); bioenergy (MS), including professional science. *Faculty:* 19 full-time (2 women). *Students:* 38 full-time (11 women), 10 part-time (1 woman); includes 1 minority (Hispanic American), 33 international. 44 applicants, 18% accepted, 6 enrolled. In 2009, 10 master's, 6 doctorates awarded. *Entrance requirements:* For master's and doctorate, minimum GPA of 3.0. Additional exam requirements/recommendations for international students: Required—TOEFL (minimum score 570 paper-based; 230 computer-based; 88 iBT), or IELTS (minimum score 6.5). *Application deadline:* Applications are processed on a rolling basis. Application fee: $60 ($75 for international students). Electronic applications accepted. *Financial support:* In 2009–10, 6 fellowships, 47 research assistantships were awarded; teaching assistantships, tuition waivers (full and partial) also available. *Unit head:* Kuan Chong Ting, Head, 217-333-3570, Fax: 217-244-0323, E-mail: kcting@illinois.edu. *Application contact:* Ronda Sullivan, Assistant to the Head, 217-333-3570, Fax: 217-244-0323, E-mail: rsully@illinois.edu.

University of Illinois at Urbana–Champaign, Graduate College, College of Engineering, Department of Bioengineering, Champaign, IL 61820. Offers MS, PhD. *Faculty:* 7 full-time (1 woman). *Students:* 40 full-time (16 women), 1 (woman) part-time; includes 9 minority (1 African American, 8 Asian Americans or Pacific Islanders), 17 international. 90 applicants, 8% accepted, 7 enrolled. In 2009, 5 master's, 1 doctorate awarded. *Entrance requirements:* For doctorate, GRE. Additional exam requirements/recommendations for international students: Required—TOEFL (minimum score 590 paper-based; 243 computer-based; 96 iBT), or IELTS (minimum score 6.5). *Application deadline:* Applications are processed on a rolling basis. Application fee: $60 ($75 for international students). Electronic applications accepted. *Financial support:* In 2009–10, 8 fellowships, 26 research assistantships, 7 teaching assistantships were awarded; tuition waivers (full and partial) also available. *Unit head:* Michael Insana, Interim Head, 217-244-0739, Fax: 217-265-0246, E-mail: mfi@illinois.edu. *Application contact:* Sam Smucker, Graduate Programs Research Coordinator, 217-244-6389, Fax: 217-265-0246, E-mail: ssmucker@illinois.edu.

University of Illinois at Urbana–Champaign, Graduate College, College of Liberal Arts and Sciences, School of Chemical Sciences, Department of Chemical and Biomolecular Engineering, Champaign, IL 61820. Offers bioinformatics: chemical and biomolecular engineering (MS); chemical engineering (MS, PhD). *Faculty:* 16 full-time (2 women). *Students:* 115 full-time (47 women), 4 part-time (0 women); includes 15 minority (3 African Americans, 9 Asian Americans or Pacific Islanders, 3 Hispanic Americans), 63 international. 381 applicants, 21% accepted, 28 enrolled. In 2009, 6 master's, 20 doctorates awarded. *Entrance requirements:* For master's and doctorate, GRE, minimum GPA of 3.0. Additional exam requirements/recommendations for international students: Required—TOEFL (minimum score 610 paper-based; 257 computer-based). *Application deadline:* Applications are processed on a rolling basis. Application fee: $60 ($75 for international students). Electronic applications accepted. *Financial support:* In 2009–10, 23 fellowships, 106 research assistantships, 40 teaching assistantships were awarded; tuition waivers (full and partial) also available. *Unit head:* Edmund Seebauer, Head, 217-244-9214, Fax: 217-333-5052, E-mail: eseebaue@illinois.edu. *Application contact:* Cathy Paceley, Office Manager, 217-333-3640, Fax: 217-333-5052, E-mail: paceley@illinois.edu.

The University of Kansas, Graduate Studies, School of Engineering, Program in Bioengineering, Lawrence, KS 66045. Offers MS, PhD. *Faculty:* 7. *Students:* 33 full-time (12 women), 2 part-time (1 woman); includes 2 minority (1 American Indian/Alaska Native, 1 Asian American or Pacific Islander), 14 international. Average age 25. 34 applicants, 68% accepted, 11 enrolled. *Degree requirements:* For master's, thesis; for doctorate, comprehensive exam, thesis/dissertation. *Entrance requirements:* For master's and doctorate, GRE. Additional exam requirements/recommendations for international students: Required—TOEFL. *Application deadline:* For fall admission, 12/15 for domestic and international students; for spring admission, 10/31 for domestic students, 9/30 for international students. Application fee: $45 ($55 for international students). Electronic applications accepted. *Expenses:* Tuition, state resident: full-time $6492; part-time $270.50 per credit hour. Tuition, nonresident: full-time $15,510; part-time $646.25 per credit hour. Required fees: $847; $70.56 per credit hour. Tuition and fees vary according to course load and program. *Financial support:* Fellowships, research assistantships with full and partial tuition reimbursements, teaching assistantships available. Financial award application deadline: 12/15. *Faculty research:* Bioimaging, bioinformatics, biomaterials and tissue engineering, biomechanics and neural engineering, biomedical product design and development, biomolecular engineering. *Unit head:* Dr. Carl W. Luchies, Director, 785-864-2993, Fax: 785-864-5254, E-mail: luchies@ku.edu. *Application contact:* Glen Marotz, Associate Dean, 785-864-2941, Fax: 785-864-5445, E-mail: gama@ku.edu.

University of Maine, Graduate School, College of Engineering, Department of Chemical and Biological Engineering, Program in Biological Engineering, Orono, ME 04469. Offers MS. Part-time programs available. *Students:* 3 full-time (1 woman), 1 part-time (0 women), 2 international. Average age 24. 6 applicants, 33% accepted, 2 enrolled. *Degree requirements:* For master's, thesis (for some programs). *Entrance requirements:* For master's, GRE General Test. Additional exam requirements/recommendations for international students: Required—TOEFL. *Application deadline:* For fall admission, 2/1 priority date for domestic students. Applications are processed on a rolling basis. Application fee: $65. Electronic applications accepted. *Financial support:* Federal Work-Study available. Financial award application deadline: 3/1. *Unit head:* Dr. Douglas Bousfield, Coordinator, 207-581-2300, Fax: 207-581-2725. *Application contact:* Scott G. Delcourt, Associate Dean of the Graduate School, 207-581-3291, Fax: 207-581-3232, E-mail: graduate@maine.edu.

University of Maryland, College Park, Academic Affairs, A. James Clark School of Engineering, Department of Chemical and Biomolecular Engineering, Program in Bioengineering, College Park, MD 20742. Offers MS, PhD. *Students:* 57 full-time (25 women), 5 part-time (2 women); includes 12 minority (1 African American, 10 Asian Americans or Pacific Islanders, 1 Hispanic American), 12 international. 186 applicants, 17% accepted, 13 enrolled. In 2009, 1 master's, 5 doctorates awarded. *Degree requirements:* For master's, thesis; for doctorate, thesis/dissertation, qualifying exam, oral defense. *Entrance requirements:* Additional exam requirements/recommendations for international students: Required—TOEFL. *Application deadline:* For fall admission, 1/15 for domestic students, 2/1 for international students. Application fee: $60. *Expenses:* Tuition, area resident: Part-time $471 per credit hour. Tuition, state resident: part-time $471 per credit hour. Tuition, nonresident: part-time $1016 per credit hour. Required fees: $337.04 per term. *Financial support:* In 2009–10, 5 fellowships (averaging $106,199 per year), 22 research assistantships (averaging $20,129 per year), 20 teaching assistantships (averaging $22,920 per year) were awarded. *Unit head:* Dr. William Bentley, Chairman, 301-405-4321, Fax: 301-405-9023, E-mail: bentley@umd.edu. *Application contact:* Dean of Graduate School, 301-405-0358, Fax: 301-314-9305, E-mail: admociti@umd.edu.

University of Maryland, College Park, Academic Affairs, A. James Clark School of Engineering, Fischell Department of Bioengineering, College Park, MD 20742. Offers MS, PhD. *Faculty:* 71 full-time (11 women), 4 part-time/adjunct (0 women). *Students:* 57 full-time (25 women), 5 part-time (2 women); includes 12 minority (1 African American, 10 Asian Americans or Pacific Islanders, 1 Hispanic American), 12 international. 186 applicants, 17% accepted, 13 enrolled. In 2009, 1 master's, 5 doctorates awarded. *Degree requirements:* For master's, thesis optional; for doctorate, thesis/dissertation. *Entrance requirements:* For master's, GRE General Test, minimum GPA of 3.0, 3 letters of recommendation. *Application deadline:* For fall admission, 1/15 for domestic students, 2/1 for international students; for spring admission, 6/1 for international students. Applications are processed on a rolling basis. Application fee: $60. Electronic applications accepted. *Expenses:* Tuition, area resident: Part-time $471 per credit hour. Tuition, state resident: part-time $471 per credit hour. Tuition, nonresident: part-time $1016 per credit hour. Required fees: $337.04 per term. *Financial support:* In 2009–10, 11 fellowships with partial tuition reimbursements (averaging $9,839 per year), 29 research assistantships with tuition reimbursements (averaging $25,338 per year), 16 teaching assistantships with tuition reimbursements (averaging $25,046 per year) were awarded; career-related internships or fieldwork also available. Financial award applicants required to submit FAFSA. *Faculty research:* Bioengineering, bioenvironmental and water resources engineering, natural resources management. Total annual research expenditures: $1.7 million. *Unit head:* Dr. William Bentley, Chairman, 301-405-4321, Fax: 301-405-9023, E-mail: bentley@umd.edu. *Application contact:* Dean of Graduate School, 301-405-0376, Fax: 301-314-9305.

University of Missouri, Graduate School, College of Engineering, Department of Biological Engineering, Columbia, MO 65211. Offers agricultural engineering (MS); biological engineering (MS, PhD). *Degree requirements:* For master's, thesis; for doctorate, thesis/dissertation. *Entrance requirements:* For master's and doctorate, GRE General Test, minimum GPA of 3.0. Additional exam requirements/recommendations for international students: Required—TOEFL (minimum score 550 paper-based; 213 computer-based; 80 iBT).

University of Nebraska–Lincoln, Graduate College, College of Engineering, Department of Biological Systems Engineering, Interdepartmental Area of Agricultural and Biological Systems Engineering, Lincoln, NE 68588. Offers MS, PhD. *Degree requirements:* For master's, thesis optional. *Entrance requirements:* Additional exam requirements/recommendations for international students: Required—TOEFL (minimum score 550 paper-based; 213 computer-based). Electronic applications accepted. *Faculty research:* Hydrological engineering, tractive performance, biomedical engineering, irrigation systems.

University of Nebraska–Lincoln, Graduate College, College of Engineering, Department of Chemical and Biomolecular Engineering, Lincoln, NE 68588. Offers MS, PhD. *Degree requirements:* For master's, thesis; for doctorate, comprehensive exam, thesis/dissertation. *Entrance requirements:* For master's and doctorate, GRE. Additional exam requirements/recommendations for international students: Required—TOEFL (minimum score 550 paper-based; 213 computer-based). Electronic applications accepted. *Faculty research:* Fermentation, radioactive waste remediation, chemical fuels from renewable feedstocks.

University of Notre Dame, Graduate School, College of Engineering, Department of Civil Engineering and Geological Sciences, Notre Dame, IN 46556. Offers bioengineering (MS Bio E); civil engineering (MSCE); civil engineering and geological sciences (PhD); environmental engineering (MS Env E); geological sciences (MS). Terminal master's awarded for partial completion of doctoral program. *Degree requirements:* For master's, comprehensive exam; for doctorate, thesis/dissertation, candidacy exam. *Entrance requirements:* For master's and doctorate, GRE General Test. Additional exam requirements/recommendations for international students: Required—TOEFL (minimum score 600 paper-based; 250 computer-based; 80 iBT). Electronic applications accepted. *Faculty research:* Environmental modeling, biological-waste treatment, petrology, environmental geology, geochemistry.

University of Oklahoma, Graduate College, College of Engineering, Center for Bioengineering, Norman, OK 73019. Offers MS, PhD. *Students:* 22 full-time (7 women), 10 part-time (3 women); includes 6 minority (1 African American, 4 Asian Americans or Pacific Islanders, 1 Hispanic American), 14 international. 2 applicants, 100% accepted, 1 enrolled. In 2009, 2 master's, 4 doctorates awarded. Terminal master's awarded for partial completion of doctoral program. *Degree requirements:* For master's, thesis; for doctorate, thesis/dissertation, oral exam. *Entrance requirements:* For master's and doctorate, minimum GPA of 3.0. Additional exam requirements/recommendations for international students: Required—TOEFL (minimum score 550 paper-based; 213 computer-based; 79 iBT). *Application deadline:* For fall admission, 6/1 priority date for domestic students, 4/1 priority date for international students; for spring admission, 11/1 priority date for domestic students, 9/1 priority date for international students. Application fee: $40 ($90 for international students). Electronic applications accepted. *Expenses:* Tuition, state resident: full-time $3744; part-time $156 per credit hour. Tuition, nonresident: full-time $13,577; part-time $565.70 per credit hour. Required fees: $2415; $90.10 per credit hour. *Financial support:* In 2009–10, 26 students received support. Unspecified assistantships available. Financial award applicants required to submit FAFSA. *Faculty research:* Assistive devices, biomechanics, medical imaging, targeted therapeutics, tissue engineering and biomaterials. *Unit head:* Dr. Lance Lobban, Director, 405-325-5811, Fax: 405-325-5813, E-mail: llobban@ou.edu. *Application contact:* Dr. Ulli Nollert, Graduate Program Coordinator and Associate Professor, 405-325-4366, Fax: 405-325-5813, E-mail: nollert@ou.edu.

University of Pennsylvania, School of Engineering and Applied Science, Department of Bioengineering, Philadelphia, PA 19104. Offers MSE, PhD, MD/PhD, VMD/PhD. *Faculty:* 40 full-time (6 women), 13 part-time/adjunct (0 women). *Students:* 137 full-time (60 women), 9 part-time (5 women); includes 35 minority (5 African Americans, 25 Asian Americans or Pacific Islanders, 5 Hispanic Americans), 27 international. 382 applicants, 25% accepted, 53 enrolled. In 2009, 18 master's, 22 doctorates awarded. Terminal master's awarded for partial completion of doctoral program. *Degree requirements:* For master's, thesis optional; for doctorate, thesis/dissertation. *Entrance requirements:* For master's and doctorate, GRE General Test. Additional exam requirements/recommendations for international students: Required—TOEFL. *Application deadline:* For fall admission, 6/1 priority date for domestic students, 5/1 priority date for international students. Applications are processed on a rolling basis. Application fee: $70. Electronic applications accepted. *Expenses:* Tuition: Full-time $25,660; part-time $4758 per course. Required fees: $2152; $270 per course. Tuition and fees vary according to course load, degree level and program. *Financial support:* Fellowships, research assistantships, teaching assistantships, institutionally sponsored loans, scholarships/grants, traineeships, health care benefits, and unspecified assistantships available. *Faculty research:* Biomaterials and biomechanics, biofluid mechanics and transport, bioelectric phenomena, computational neuroscience.

University of Pittsburgh, School of Engineering, Department of Bioengineering, Pittsburgh, PA 15260. Offers MSBENG, PhD, MD/PhD. Part-time programs available. *Faculty:* 20 full-time (2 women), 94 part-time/adjunct (8 women). *Students:* 132 full-time (48 women), 14 part-time (5 women); includes 18 minority (3 African Americans, 1 American Indian/Alaska Native, 10 Asian Americans or Pacific Islanders, 4 Hispanic Americans), 32 international. Average age 23. 300 applicants, 26% accepted, 35 enrolled. In 2009, 19 master's, 17 doctorates awarded. Terminal master's awarded for partial completion of doctoral program. *Degree requirements:* For master's, thesis; for doctorate, comprehensive exam, thesis/dissertation, final oral exams. *Entrance requirements:* For master's and doctorate, GRE General Test, minimum QPA of 3.0. Additional exam requirements/recommendations for international students: Required—TOEFL (minimum score 550 paper-based; 213 computer-based; 80 iBT). *Application deadline:* For fall admission, 3/1 priority date for domestic students; for spring admission, 7/1 for domestic students. Applications are processed on a rolling basis. Application fee: $50. Electronic applications accepted. *Expenses:* Tuition, state resident: full-time $16,402; part-time $665 per credit. Tuition, nonresident: full-time $28,694; part-time $1175 per credit. Required fees: $690; $175 per term. Tuition and fees vary according to program. *Financial support:* In 2009–10, 125 students received support, including 33 fellowships with full tuition reimbursements available (averaging $20,772 per year), 80 research assistantships with full tuition reimbursements available (averaging $24,000 per year), 12 teaching assistantships with full tuition reimbursements available (averaging $22,000 per year); scholarships/grants and traineeships also available. Financial award application deadline: 4/15. *Faculty research:* Artificial organs, biomechanics, biomaterials, signal processing, biotechnology. Total annual research expenditures: $38.6 million. *Unit head:* Harvey S. Borovetz, Chairman, 412-383-9713, Fax: 412-383-8788, E-mail: borovetzhs@msx.upmc.edu. *Application contact:* Harvey S. Borovetz, Chairman, 412-383-9713, Fax: 412-383-8788, E-mail: borovetzhs@msx.upmc.edu.

The University of Texas at Arlington, Graduate School, College of Engineering, Bioengineering Department, Arlington, TX 76019. Offers MS, PhD. Part-time programs available. *Faculty:* 11 full-time (2 women), 1 (woman) part-time/adjunct. *Students:* 90 full-time (34 women), 61 part-time (27 women); includes 18 minority (4 African Americans, 11 Asian Americans or Pacific Islanders, 3 Hispanic Americans), 113 international. 80 applicants, 96% accepted, 36 enrolled. In 2009, 49 master's, 1 doctorate awarded. *Degree requirements:* For master's, thesis optional; for doctorate, thesis/dissertation, qualifying exam. *Entrance requirements:* For master's, GRE General Test, minimum GPA of 3.0 in last 60 hours of course work; for doctorate, GRE General Test, minimum GPA of 3.4 in last 60 hours of course work. Additional exam requirements/recommendations for international students: Required—TOEFL. *Application deadline:* For fall admission, 6/6 for domestic students, 4/4 for international students; for spring admission, 10/17 for domestic students, 9/5 for international students. Applications are processed on a rolling basis. Application fee: $35 ($50 for international students). *Financial support:* In 2009–10, 4 fellowships (averaging $1,000 per year), 5 research assistantships (averaging $10,000 per year), 9 teaching assistantships (averaging $18,000 per year) were awarded; career-related internships or fieldwork, Federal Work-Study, institutionally sponsored loans, scholarships/grants, and tuition waivers (partial) also available. Financial award application deadline: 6/1; financial award applicants required to submit FAFSA. *Faculty research:* Instrumentation, mechanics, materials. *Unit head:* Dr. Khosrow Behbehani, Chair, 817-272-2249, Fax: 817-272-2251, E-mail: kb@uta.edu. *Application contact:* Suzanne Despres, Academic Advisor, 817-272-0783, Fax: 817-272-2251, E-mail: sdespres@uta.edu.

The University of Toledo, College of Graduate Studies, College of Engineering, Department of Bioengineering, Toledo, OH 43606-3390. Offers MS, PhD. Terminal master's awarded for partial completion of doctoral program. *Degree requirements:* For master's, thesis optional; for doctorate, thesis/dissertation, qualifying exam. *Entrance requirements:* For master's, GRE General Test, minimum GPA of 3.0; for doctorate, GRE General Test, minimum GPA of 3.3. Additional exam requirements/recommendations for international students: Required—TOEFL (minimum score 550 paper-based; 213 computer-based; 80 iBT). Electronic applications accepted. *Faculty research:* Artificial organs, biochemical engineering, bioelectrical systems, biomechanics, cellular engineering.

University of Utah, The Graduate School, College of Engineering, Department of Bioengineering, Salt Lake City, UT 84112-9202. Offers MS, PhD. *Faculty:* 21 full-time (2 women), 2 part-time/adjunct (1 woman). *Students:* 108 full-time (27 women), 18 part-time (5 women); includes 8 minority (all Asian Americans or Pacific Islanders), 30 international. Average age 28. 39 applicants, 100% accepted, 29 enrolled. In 2009, 13 master's, 14 doctorates awarded. Terminal master's awarded for partial completion of doctoral program. *Degree requirements:* For master's, comprehensive exam, thesis (MS), written project, oral presentation, course option (MS); for doctorate, thesis/dissertation, Dissertation (PhD). *Entrance requirements:* For master's and doctorate, GRE General Test, minimum GPA of 3.0. Additional exam requirements/recommendations for international students: Required—TOEFL (minimum score 500 paper-based; 173 computer-based; 61 iBT), IELTS. *Application deadline:* For fall admission, 4/1 for domestic and international students. Application fee: $55 ($65 for international students). Electronic applications accepted. *Expenses:* Tuition, state resident: full-time $4004; part-time $1674 per semester. Tuition, nonresident: full-time $14,134; part-time $5915 per semester. Required fees: $324 per semester. Tuition and fees vary according to course load, degree level and program. *Financial support:* In 2009–10, 6 fellowships with full tuition reimbursements (averaging $20,000 per year), 84 research assistantships with full tuition reimbursements (averaging $23,000 per year), 10 teaching assistantships with full tuition reimbursements (averaging $23,000 per year) were awarded; traineeships, health care benefits, tuition waivers (full), and unspecified assistantships also available. Financial award application deadline: 2/15; financial award applicants required to submit FAFSA. *Faculty research:* Ultrasonic bioinstrumentation, medical imaging, neuroprosthesis, biomaterials and tissue engineering, biomechanic biomedical computing/modeling. Total annual research expenditures: $7.2 million. *Unit head:* Dr. Richard D. Rabbit, Chair, 801-581-6968, Fax: 801-585-5151, E-mail: r.rabbit@utah.edu. *Application contact:* Karen Lynn Terry, Graduate Program Advisor and Coordinator, 801-581-8559, Fax: 801-585-5151, E-mail: karen.terry@utah.edu.

University of Washington, Graduate School, College of Engineering and School of Medicine, Department of Bioengineering, Seattle, WA 98195-5061. Offers MME, MS, PhD. Evening/weekend programs available. *Faculty:* 27 full-time (8 women), 53 part-time/adjunct (4 women). *Students:* 93 full-time (41 women), 23 part-time (9 women); includes 34 minority (4 African Americans, 1 American Indian/Alaska Native, 24 Asian Americans or Pacific Islanders, 5 Hispanic Americans), 22 international. Average age 26. 300 applicants, 18% accepted, 23 enrolled. In 2009, 11 master's, 11 doctorates awarded. *Degree requirements:* For master's, thesis; for doctorate, thesis/dissertation, qualifying exam, general exam, thesis defense. *Entrance requirements:* For master's and doctorate, GRE General Test, minimum GPA of 3.0. Additional exam requirements/recommendations for international students: Required—TOEFL (minimum score 580 paper-based; 237 computer-based; 70 iBT). *Application deadline:* For fall admission, 12/15 for domestic students, 12/1 for international students. Application fee: $65. Electronic applications accepted. *Financial support:* In 2009–10, 2 students received support, including 26 fellowships with full tuition reimbursements available (averaging $23,886 per year), 99 research assistantships with full tuition reimbursements available (averaging $19,224 per year), 16 teaching assistantships with full tuition reimbursements available (averaging $19,224 per year); Federal Work-Study, institutionally sponsored loans, traineeships, health care benefits, and tuition waivers (full) also available. Support available to part-time students. Financial award application deadline: 12/15. *Faculty research:* Biomaterials and tissue engineering; global health, distributed diagnosis and home healthcare; bioinstrumentation; molecular bioengineering; imaging and image-guided therapy. Total annual research expenditures: $18.8 million. *Unit head:* Dr. Paul Yager, Professor and Chair, 206-685-2000, Fax: 206-685-3300, E-mail: yagerp@u.washington.edu. *Application contact:* Dorian Taylor, Senior Academic Counselor, 206-685-2000, Fax: 206-685-3300, E-mail: bioeng@u.washington.edu.

University of Wisconsin–Madison, Graduate School, College of Engineering, Department of Chemical and Biological Engineering, Madison, WI 53706-1380. Offers chemical engineering (MS, PhD). *Faculty:* 19 full-time (2 women), 1 part-time/adjunct (0 women). *Students:* 122 full-time (34 women); includes 13 minority (9 Asian Americans or Pacific Islanders, 4 Hispanic Americans), 51 international. Average age 26. 405 applicants, 21% accepted, 30 enrolled. In 2009, 3 master's, 16 doctorates awarded. Terminal master's awarded for partial completion of doctoral program. *Degree requirements:* For master's, thesis or alternative; for doctorate, thesis/dissertation, 2 semesters of teaching assistantship. *Entrance requirements:* For master's and doctorate, GRE General Test. Additional exam requirements/recommendations for international students: Required—TOEFL (minimum score 550 paper-based; 213 computer-based; 80 iBT). *Application deadline:* For fall admission, 1/15 for domestic and international students; for spring admission, 10/15 for domestic and international students. Application fee: $56. Electronic applications accepted. *Expenses:* Tuition, state resident: part-time $594 per credit. Tuition, nonresident: part-time $1504 per credit. Required fees: $65 per credit. Tuition and fees vary according to course load, program and reciprocity agreements. *Financial support:* In 2009–10, 122 students received support, including 14 fellowships with full tuition reimbursements available (averaging $29,065 per year), 108 research assistantships with full tuition reimbursements available (averaging $24,000 per year), 46 teaching assistantships with full tuition reimbursements available (averaging $25,195 per year); traineeships and health care benefits also available. Financial award application deadline: 1/15. *Faculty research:* Biotechnology, nanotechnology, complex fluids, molecular and systems modeling, alternative energy: materials and processes. Total annual research expenditures: $17.7 million. *Unit head:* Prof. Nicholas L. Abbott, Chair, 608-265-5278, Fax: 608-262-5434, E-mail: abbott@engr.wisc.edu. *Application contact:* Donna M. Bell, Graduate Coordinator, 608-263-3138, Fax: 608-262-5434, E-mail: gradoffice@che.wisc.edu.

Virginia Commonwealth University, Graduate School, School of Engineering, Department of Chemical and Life Science Engineering, Richmond, VA 23284-9005. Offers MS, PhD.

Virginia Polytechnic Institute and State University, Graduate School, College of Engineering, Department of Biological Systems Engineering, Blacksburg, VA 24061. Offers M Eng, MS, PhD. *Entrance requirements:* Additional exam requirements/recommendations for international students: Required—TOEFL (minimum score 550 paper-based; 213 computer-based). Electronic applications accepted. *Faculty research:* Soil and water engineering, alternative energy sources for agriculture and agricultural mechanization.

Washington State University, Graduate School, College of Engineering and Architecture, Department of Biological Systems Engineering, Pullman, WA 99164. Offers biological and agricultural engineering (MS, PhD). *Degree requirements:* For master's, comprehensive exam, thesis (for some programs), written and oral exam; for doctorate, comprehensive exam, thesis/dissertation, written and oral exam. *Entrance requirements:* For master's, GRE General Test, GRE Subject Test, minimum GPA of 3.0, bachelor's degree in engineering or closely related subject; for doctorate, minimum GPA of 3.0, bachelor's degree in engineering or closely related subject. Additional exam requirements/recommendations for international students: Required—TOEFL. *Faculty research:* Social issues and engineering education, electronic instrument design, prediction, technology for dust from agricultural lands.

Biosystems Engineering

Clemson University, Graduate School, College of Agriculture, Forestry and Life Sciences, Department of Agricultural and Biological Engineering and College of Engineering and Science, Program in Biosystems Engineering, Clemson, SC 29634. Offers MS, PhD. Part-time programs available. *Students:* 15 full-time (7 women), 3 part-time (1 woman); includes 1 minority (African American), 7 international. Average age 28. 23 applicants, 43% accepted, 2 enrolled. In 2009, 4 master's, 1 doctorate awarded. *Degree requirements:* For master's, thesis (for some programs); for doctorate, thesis/dissertation. *Entrance requirements:* For master's and doctorate, GRE General Test, minimum GPA of 3.0. Additional exam requirements/recommendations for international students: Required—TOEFL. *Application deadline:* For fall admission, 6/1 for domestic students, 4/15 for international students; for spring admission, 9/15 for international students. Applications are processed on a rolling basis. Application fee: $70 ($80 for international students). Electronic applications accepted. *Expenses:* Tuition, state resident: full-time $8684; part-time $528 per credit hour. Tuition, nonresident: full-time $15,330; part-time $1078 per credit hour. Required fees: $736; $37 per semester. Part-time tuition and fees vary according to course load and program. *Financial support:* In 2009–10, 14 students received support, including 3 fellowships with full and partial tuition reimbursements available (averaging $13,111 per year), 9 research assistantships with partial tuition reimbursements available (averaging $18,344 per year), 7 teaching assistantships with partial tuition reimbursements available (averaging $9,092 per year); career-related internships or fieldwork, institutionally sponsored loans, scholarships/grants, health care benefits, and unspecified assistantships also available. Support available to part-time students. *Unit head:* Dr. Young Jo Han, Chair, 864-656-3250, Fax: 864-656-0338, E-mail: yhan@clemson.edu. *Application contact:* Dr. Caye Drapcho, Graduate Coordinator, 864-656-0378, Fax: 864-656-0338, E-mail: cdrapch@clemson.edu.

Iowa State University of Science and Technology, Graduate College, College of Engineering, Department of Agricultural and Biosystems Engineering, Ames, IA 50011. Offers M Eng, MS, PhD. *Faculty:* 30 full-time (2 women), 3 part-time/adjunct (0 women). *Students:* 54 full-time (21 women), 9 part-time (2 women); includes 3 minority (1 African American, 1 Asian American or Pacific Islander, 1 Hispanic American), 30 international. 47 applicants, 49% accepted, 20 enrolled. In 2009, 8 master's, 5 doctorates awarded. *Degree requirements:* For master's, thesis (for some programs); for doctorate, thesis/dissertation. *Entrance requirements:* Additional exam requirements/recommendations for international students: Required—TOEFL (minimum score 550 paper-based; 79 iBT) or IELTS (minimum score 6.5). *Application deadline:* For fall admission, 2/1 priority date for domestic and international students; for spring admission, 7/1 priority date for domestic and international students. Applications are processed on a rolling basis. Application fee: $40 ($90 for international students). Electronic applications accepted. *Expenses:* Tuition, state resident: full-time $6716. Tuition, nonresident: full-time $8908. Tuition and fees vary according to course level, course load, program and student level. *Financial support:* In 2009–10, 43 research assistantships with full and partial tuition reimbursements (averaging $15,410 per year), 1 teaching assistantship with full and partial tuition reimbursement (averaging $14,160 per year) were awarded; fellowships, scholarships/grants, health care benefits, and unspecified assistantships also available. *Faculty research:* Grain processing and quality, tillage systems, simulation and controls, water management, environmental quality.

Biosystems Engineering

Iowa State University of Science and Technology *(continued)*
Unit head: Dr. Ramesh Kanwar, Chair, 515-294-1434. *Application contact:* Dr. Steven Freeman, Director of Graduate Education, 515-294-9541, E-mail: sfreeman@iastate.edu.

Michigan State University, The Graduate School, College of Agriculture and Natural Resources and College of Engineering, Department of Biosystems and Agricultural Engineering, East Lansing, MI 48824. Offers biosystems engineering (MS, PhD). *Entrance requirements:* Additional exam requirements/recommendations for international students: Required—TOEFL. Electronic applications accepted.

North Dakota State University, College of Graduate and Interdisciplinary Studies, College of Engineering and Architecture, Department of Agricultural and Biosystems Engineering, Fargo, ND 58108. Offers agricultural and biosystems engineering (MS, PhD); engineering (PhD); natural resource management (MS); natural resources management (PhD). Part-time programs available. *Faculty:* 6 full-time (1 woman). *Students:* 9 full-time (5 women), 2 part-time (0 women); includes 3 Hispanic Americans, 8 international. Average age 28. 22 applicants, 36% accepted, 7 enrolled. *Degree requirements:* For master's, thesis; for doctorate, thesis/dissertation. *Entrance requirements:* For master's and doctorate, BS in engineering or the equivalent, minimum undergraduate GPA of 3.0. Additional exam requirements/recommendations for international students: Required—TOEFL (minimum score 550 paper-based; 213 computer-based; 79 iBT). *Application deadline:* For fall admission, 7/1 priority date for domestic and international students; for spring admission, 10/1 priority date for domestic and international students. Applications are processed on a rolling basis. Application fee: $45 ($60 for international students). Electronic applications accepted. *Financial support:* In 2009–10, 9 research assistantships with full tuition reimbursements (averaging $15,000 per year) were awarded; career-related internships or fieldwork, Federal Work-Study, institutionally sponsored loans, and unspecified assistantships also available. Support available to part-time students. Financial award application deadline: 4/15. *Faculty research:* Irrigation, crop processing, food engineering, environmental resources, sensors and instrumentation. Total annual research expenditures: $158,309. *Unit head:* Leslie F. Backer, Chair, 701-231-7261, Fax: 701-231-1008, E-mail: leslie.backer@ndsu.edu. *Application contact:* Dr. David A. Wittrock, Dean, 701-231-7033, Fax: 701-231-6524.

South Dakota State University, Graduate School, College of Agriculture and Biological Sciences, Department of Agriculture and Biosystems Engineering, Brookings, SD 57007. Offers MS, PhD. Part-time programs available. *Degree requirements:* For master's, thesis; for doctorate, comprehensive exam, thesis/dissertation, preliminary oral and written exams. *Entrance requirements:* Additional exam requirements/recommendations for international students: Required—TOEFL (minimum score 525 paper-based; 197 computer-based; 71 iBT).

South Dakota State University, Graduate School, College of Engineering, Department of Agricultural and Biosystems Engineering, Brookings, SD 57007. Offers biological sciences (MS, PhD); engineering (MS). Part-time programs available. *Degree requirements:* For master's, thesis (for some programs), oral exam; for doctorate, thesis/dissertation, preliminary oral and written exams. *Entrance requirements:* For master's and doctorate, engineering degree. Additional exam requirements/recommendations for international students: Required—TOEFL (minimum score 550 paper-based; 213 computer-based; 79 iBT). *Faculty research:* Water resources, food engineering, natural resources engineering, machine design, bioprocess engineering.

The University of Arizona, Graduate College, College of Agriculture and Life Sciences, Department of Agricultural and Biosystems Engineering, Tucson, AZ 85721. Offers MS, PhD. *Faculty:* 11. *Students:* 18 full-time (3 women), 11 part-time (1 woman); includes 2 minority (both Asian Americans or Pacific Islanders), 16 international. Average age 32. 19 applicants, 74% accepted, 6 enrolled. In 2009, 6 master's, 5 doctorates awarded. Terminal master's awarded for partial completion of doctoral program. *Degree requirements:* For master's, thesis; for doctorate, thesis/dissertation. *Entrance requirements:* For master's, minimum GPA of 3.0 in last 2 years of undergraduate study, 3 letters of recommendation; for doctorate, minimum GPA of 3.0 in last 2 years of undergraduate study, 3 letters of recommendation, statement of purpose. Additional exam requirements/recommendations for international students: Required—TOEFL (minimum score 213 computer-based). *Application deadline:* For fall admission, 6/1 for domestic students, 2/1 for international students; for spring admission, 9/1 for domestic students, 8/1 for international students. Applications are processed on a rolling basis. Application fee: $75. Electronic applications accepted. *Expenses:* Tuition, state resident: full-time $9028. Tuition, nonresident: full-time $24,890. *Financial support:* In 2009–10, 4 research assistantships with full and partial tuition reimbursements (averaging $24,714 per year), 1 teaching assistantship with full and partial tuition reimbursement (averaging $18,724 per year) were awarded; fellowships, career-related internships or fieldwork, Federal Work-Study, institutionally sponsored loans, scholarships/grants, traineeships, health care benefits, tuition waivers (full and partial), and unspecified assistantships also available. Financial award application deadline: 5/1. *Faculty research:* Irrigation system design, energy-use management, equipment for alternative crops, food properties enhancement. Total annual research expenditures: $452,871. *Unit head:* Donald Slack, Head, 520-621-3691, Fax: 520-621-3963, E-mail: slackd@u.arizona.edu. *Application contact:* Daniela Ibarra, Senior Office Specialist, 520-621-1753, Fax: 520-621-3963, E-mail: dcastro@email.arizona.edu.

University of Manitoba, Faculty of Graduate Studies, Faculty of Engineering, Department of Biosystems Engineering, Winnipeg, MB R3T 2N2, Canada. Offers M Eng, M Sc, PhD.

University of Minnesota, Twin Cities Campus, Graduate School, College of Food, Agricultural and Natural Resource Sciences, Program in Bioproducts and Biosystems Science Engineering and Management, Minneapolis, MN 55455-0213. Offers MS, PhD. Part-time programs available. *Degree requirements:* For master's, comprehensive exam, thesis (for some programs), seminar; for doctorate, comprehensive exam, thesis/dissertation, seminar. *Entrance requirements:* For master's and doctorate, BS in engineering, mathematics, physical or biological sciences, or related field. Additional exam requirements/recommendations for international students: Required—TOEFL (minimum score 550 paper-based; 213 computer-based; 79 iBT). *Faculty research:* Water quality, bioprocessing, food engineering, terramechanics, process and machine control.

The University of Tennessee, Graduate School, College of Agricultural Sciences and Natural Resources, Department of Biosystems Engineering and Environmental Science, Program in Biosystems Engineering, Knoxville, TN 37996. Offers MS, PhD. *Degree requirements:* For master's, thesis; for doctorate, thesis/dissertation. *Entrance requirements:* For master's and doctorate, GRE General Test, minimum GPA of 2.7. Additional exam requirements/recommendations for international students: Required—TOEFL. Electronic applications accepted. *Expenses:* Tuition, state resident: full-time $6826; part-time $380 per semester hour. Tuition, nonresident: full-time $21,844; part-time $1147 per semester hour. Tuition and fees vary according to program.

The University of Tennessee, Graduate School, College of Agricultural Sciences and Natural Resources, Department of Biosystems Engineering and Environmental Science, Program in Biosystems Engineering Technology, Knoxville, TN 37996. Offers MS. *Degree requirements:* For master's, thesis or alternative. *Entrance requirements:* For master's, GRE General Test, minimum GPA of 2.7. Additional exam requirements/recommendations for international students: Required—TOEFL. Electronic applications accepted. *Expenses:* Tuition, state resident: full-time $6826; part-time $380 per semester hour. Tuition, nonresident: full-time $21,844; part-time $1147 per semester hour. Tuition and fees vary according to program.

MASSACHUSETTS INSTITUTE OF TECHNOLOGY

Department of Biological Engineering
Graduate Program in Bioengineering and Applied Bioscience

Program of Study

A program leading to the Ph.D. in the bioengineering track or the applied biosciences track is offered within the Biological Engineering Department. The purpose of this program is to educate the next generation of researchers in the fusion of molecular and cellular biosciences and engineering, bringing together a powerful combination of measurement, modeling, and manipulation approaches towards the objectives of understanding how biological systems operate, especially when perturbed by genetic, chemical, or materials interventions or subjected to pathogens or toxins; and designing innovative technologies in biology-based diagnostics, therapeutics, materials, and devices for broad application to medicine and human health. This education should prepare students for careers in biotechnology, pharmaceutical, and medical diagnostic and device industries as well as in academic departments across a broad spectrum of engineering and science disciplines.

Students admitted to the program may have a B.S. or an M.S. degree in any of a broad spectrum of science or engineering disciplines. During their first year they pursue a core curriculum, including basic and applied biological science subjects along with bioengineering subjects, with integrated but diverging curricula for the parallel bioengineering and applied biosciences tracks. Electives in basic and applied sciences and in engineering are generally pursued during the second year and beyond as desired.

The written part of the doctoral qualifying examinations is centered on the core curriculum and is taken at the end of the first year. Students also select a research adviser during the first year. The oral part of the doctoral qualifying examinations focuses on the student's thesis research proposal and is taken by the end of the second year. Approximately five years of total residence are needed to complete the doctoral thesis and other degree requirements.

The faculty members associated with the program have a wide range of research interests within biological engineering. Areas in which students may specialize include bioinformatics and computational biology; biological transport phenomena; biological imaging; biological routes to energy production; biomaterials; biomolecular engineering; cell and tissue engineering; discovery and delivery of molecular therapeutics; drug metabolism; environmental microbiology; genetic toxicology; macromolecular biochemistry and biophysics; microbial pathogenesis; molecular, cell, and tissue biomechanics; molecular, chemical, and environmental carcinogenesis; molecular epidemiology and dosimetry; molecular pharmacology; physical biology; systems biology; synthetic biology; and new tools for genomics, functional genomics, proteomics, and glycomics.

Most of the faculty members are associated with one or more interdisciplinary research centers at the Massachusetts Institute of Technology (MIT), including the Biotechnology Process Engineering Center, the Center for Biomedical Engineering, the Center for Environmental Health Sciences, the Computational and Systems Biology Initiative, the Division of Comparative Medicine, the Broad Institute for Genomic Medicine, the Koch Institute for Integrative Cancer Research, and the Whitehead Institute for Biomedical Research.

Research Facilities

Laboratories of faculty members are equipped in accordance with their particular research interests. Shared resources include cell and tissue culture facilities associated with quantitative microscopy and imaging equipment (including fluorescence, two-photon, and laser-confocal) and equipment for studying chemical and mechanical interactions among cells and biomolecules (BIACore, Cytosensor, optical trap, radiolabeling facility). Graduate students also have access to resources and facilities of other departments as provided by bioengineering faculty appointments.

Financial Aid

Financial support (full tuition and stipend) is provided for all admitted students. The stipend for 2010–11 is $2520 per month for all Department students. Employment opportunities are usually available for students' spouses both on campus and in the community. International students and their spouses may find work permits difficult to obtain and should plan accordingly.

Cost of Study

In 2010–11, tuition is $19,470 per regular term ($38,940 for fall and spring); summer tuition may be waived in the future for "research only" registration. Hospital and accident insurance is approximately $1740 per year, with additional coverage available for dependents. The cost of textbooks is estimated at $1000 to $1500 per year. All students in the program receive a stipend, full tuition support, and single student health insurance (family rates are available for students to purchase separately).

Living and Housing Costs

On-campus rooms are available for single graduate students. Rates range from approximately $900 to $2500 per month. Rents for Institute housing for married students vary from $900 to $2500 per month, including utilities, for efficiency and one- and two-bedroom apartments. Off-campus apartments may be available at considerably higher rates.

Student Group

The Department of Biological Engineering is made up of 104 graduate students. Of these, 45 are women and 31 are international students. Most students enter immediately after completion of study elsewhere.

Location

MIT is located on the banks of the Charles River, which separates Cambridge and Boston, cities with a combined metropolitan population of 2.5 million. Numerous concerts, museums, exhibits, and other cultural resources are readily available. The large concentration of universities in the metropolitan area—Harvard, MIT, Boston University, Tufts, and others—provides a stimulating intellectual environment. MIT offers the combined advantages of New England's largest metropolitan center with easy access to the Atlantic Ocean beaches and the New England countryside. As one of the earliest communities established in the United States, Boston also has a wide variety of historical sites and traditions.

The Institute

Massachusetts Institute of Technology was founded in 1861 to teach "exactly and thoroughly the fundamental principles of positive science." Its goals include the education of men and women with sound capabilities in science, but whose abilities and goals are shaped by nonscientific influences as well. These objectives are maintained for the current enrollment of about 4,500 undergraduate and 5,300 graduate students. At present the Institute's involvement in the community is growing through expanding tutoring and community service projects. Its primary objectives, however, remain the education of its students and the advancement of scientific research.

Applying

Applicants must have a B.S. degree or the equivalent in some field across the spectrum of engineering and science disciplines. Applicants admitted without having satisfied all of the prerequisite course work are expected to make up for academic deficiencies by taking appropriate courses during the first year. Transcripts, three letters of recommendation, and scores from the GRE General Test must be submitted. In addition, a minimum score of 600 on the TOEFL or a minimun score of 7 on the IELTS is required of applicants whose first language is not English. Applications should be completed by December 31 for entrance in September. Applicants are generally notified of the outcome by April 1.

Correspondence and Information

Biological Engineering Department
Massachusetts Institute of Technology
Building 56-651
Cambridge, Massachusetts 02139-4307
Phone: 617-253-1712
Fax: 617-258-8676
Web site: http://web.mit.edu/be/

Massachusetts Institute of Technology

THE BIOLOGICAL ENGINEERING FACULTY AND THEIR RESEARCH

Eric Alm, Assistant Professor of Biological and Environmental Engineering; Ph.D., Washington (Seattle). Computational and experimental approaches to understanding the evolution of gene regulatory networks in environmental microorganisms.

Mark Bathe, Assistant Professor of Biological Engineering; Ph.D., MIT. Integration of high resolution light and electron microscopy data with mechanistic models of cytoskeletal function.

Angela Belcher, Professor of Biological Engineering and Materials Science; Ph.D., California, Santa Barbara. Biomaterials, biological materials.

Edward Boyden, Benesse Career Development Professor of the Media Lab and of Biological Engineering; Ph.D., Stanford. Neurotechnology, neural circuit analysis and engineering, novel neurological disease treatments, optical and molecular tools for neuroscience.

Christopher B. Burge, Associate Professor of Biology and Biological Engineering; Ph.D., Stanford. Mechanisms of gene regulation.

Arup Chakraborty, Professor of Chemical Engineering, Chemistry, and Biological Engineering; Ph.D., Delaware. Computational modeling of biological and physiological processes.

Peter C. Dedon, Underwood-Prescott Professor of Toxicology and Biological Engineering; M.D., Ph.D., Rochester. Biological chemistry of RNA and DNA modification, chemical mechanisms linking inflammation and cancer.

Edward F. DeLong, Professor of Environmental and Biological Engineering; Ph.D., California, San Diego. Environmental genomics, microbial diversity, photobiology, integrating microbial systems biology with systems ecology.

C. Forbes Dewey Jr., Professor of Mechanical Engineering and Bioengineering; Ph.D., Caltech. Cell mechanics, biological imaging.

Bevin P. Engelward, Associate Professor of Biological Engineering; Sc.D., Harvard. Genetic toxicology: mechanisms of DNA damage and repair.

John M. Essigmann, Leitch Professor of Toxicology and Chemistry and Biological Engineering; Ph.D., MIT. Genetic toxicology, molecular pharmacology, oncology.

James G. Fox, Professor of Toxicology and Director of the Division of Comparative Medicine; D.V.M., Colorado. Host/pathogen interactions and endogenous carcinogens.

Ernest Fraenkel, Assistant Professor of Biological Engineering; Ph.D. MIT. Computational biology, systems biology, transcriptional regulation.

Linda G. Griffith, Professor of Biological and Mechanical Engineering; Ph.D., Berkeley. Tissue engineering, biomaterials.

Alan J. Grodzinsky, Professor of Electrical, Mechanical, and Biological Engineering; Sc.D., MIT. Cell mechanotransduction, molecular and tissue electromechanics, tissue engineering.

Kimberly Hamad-Schifferli, Assistant Professor of Mechanical and Biological Engineering, Ph.D., Berkeley. Bioengineering, manufacturing, manipulation of biological molecules, chemistry, nanotechnology, materials science.

Jongyoon Han, Associate Professor of Electrical and Biological Engineering; Ph.D., Cornell. Microfabrication and nanofabrication technology, including separation and analysis of biomolecules.

Darrell J. Irvine, Associate Professor of Biological Engineering and Materials Science; Ph.D., MIT. Biomaterials, tissue engineering, immunology.

Alan P. Jasanoff, Associate Professor of Nuclear Science and Engineering, Biological Engineering, and Brain and Cognitive Science; Ph.D. Harvard. Molecular imaging in neurobiology, functional MRI, systems neuroscience.

Roger D. Kamm, Professor of Mechanical and Biological Engineering; Ph.D., MIT. Cell and tissue mechanics.

Alexander M. Klibanov, Novartis Professor of Chemistry and Biological Engineering; Ph.D., Moscow. Enzyme engineering, pharmaceutical proteins, bactericidal materials.

Robert S. Langer, Germeshausen Professor of Chemical and Biological Engineering; Sc.D., MIT. Biomaterials, drug delivery, tissue engineering.

Douglas A. Lauffenburger, Whitaker Professor of Biological Engineering, Biology, and Chemical Engineering and Department Head; Ph.D., Minnesota. Molecular cell engineering.

Harvey F. Lodish, Professor of Biology and Biological Engineering; Ph.D., Rockefeller. Molecular and cell therapeutics.

Scott R. Manalis, Associate Professor of Media Arts and Biological Engineering; Ph.D., Stanford. Nanotechnology and microtechnology.

Jacquin C. Niles, Assistant Professor of Biological Engineering; Ph.D., MIT; M.D., Harvard. Synthetic biology, macromolecular biochemistry and biophysics, microbial systems and pathogenesis.

Katharina Ribbeck, Assistant Professor of Biological Engineering; Ph.D., Harvard. Mucus: A model system to study biological permeability filters.

Leona D. Samson, American Cancer Society Professor of Toxicology and Biological Engineering; Ph.D., London. DNA repair, genomic analysis of cellular responses.

Ram Sasisekharan, Professor of Biological Engineering and E. H. Taplin Professor of Health Sciences and Technology; Ph.D., Harvard. Extracellular matrix regulation of cell function.

Peter T. So, Professor of Mechanical and Biological Engineering; Ph.D., Princeton. Biological imaging, optical spectroscopy, tissue/cellular/molecular mechanics.

Steven R. Tannenbaum, Underwood-Prescott Professor of Toxicology and Chemistry; Ph.D., MIT. Chemical and biological aspects of cancer etiology.

William G. Thilly, Professor of Toxicology and Biological Engineering; Sc.D., MIT. Mutational spectra: mechanisms of mutation and genetic epidemiology.

Bruce Tidor, Professor of Biological Engineering and Computer Science; Ph.D., Harvard. Computational biology, molecular modeling, bioinformatics.

Krystyn Van Vliet, Associate Professor of Material Science and Engineering and Biological Engineering; Ph.D., MIT. Mechanics of molecules, cells, and materials.

Ron Weiss, Associate Professor of Biological Engineering; Ph.D., MIT. Synthetic biology, construction and analysis of synthetic gene networks.

Forest White, Associate Professor of Biological Engineering; Ph.D., Florida State. Mass spectrometry, proteomic studies of cancer biology and toxicology.

K. Dane Wittrup, Mares Professor of Chemical Engineering and Biological Engineering; Ph.D., Caltech. Protein engineering, directed evolution, combinatorial screening.

Gerald N. Wogan, Professor Emeritus of Toxicology, Biological Engineering, and Chemistry; Ph.D., Illinois. DNA adducts and genetic change in carcinogenesis.

Michael Yaffe, Professor of Biology and Biological Engineering; Ph.D., M.D., Case Western Reserve. Regulation of protein-protein interactions, structure and function of modular signaling domains, design of bioinformatics tools for proteomic analysis.

Jacquelyn C. Yanch, Professor of Nuclear Science and Engineering and Biological Engineering; Ph.D., London. Radiation production, radiation applications in biology and medicine, particle accelerator applications, radiation transport.

Mehmet Fatih Yanik, Associate Professor of Electrical and Biological Engineering; Ph.D., Stanford. Biological imaging and functional measurement; new tools for genomics, functional genomics, proteomics, and glycomics; discovery and delivery of molecular therapeutics.

Ioannis Yannas, Professor of Polymer Science and Bioengineering; Ph.D., Princeton. Tissue engineering, tissue and organ regeneration.

UNIVERSITY OF CALIFORNIA, SAN DIEGO

Department of Bioengineering

Programs of Study	The Department of Bioengineering at the University of California, San Diego (UCSD), offers graduate instruction leading to the Master of Engineering (M.Eng.), Master of Science (M.S.), and Doctorate of Philosophy (Ph.D.) degrees. The bioengineering graduate program began in 1966, and the Department was established in the Jacobs School of Engineering in 1994. The graduate programs provide an excellent education, integrating the fields of engineering and biomedical sciences. Students with an undergraduate education in engineering or in physical or biological sciences learn how to use engineering concepts and methodology to analyze and solve biological problems associated with genes, molecules, cells, tissues, organs, and systems, with applications to clinical medicine and biology. Education and research in bioengineering has been facilitated by the establishment of the Whitaker Institute of Biomedical Engineering and the receipt of Whitaker Foundation Development and Leadership Awards.

The M.S. program is intended to equip the student with fundamental knowledge in bioengineering. The degree may be terminal or obtained on the way to earning the Ph.D. degree. It requires successful completion of 48 quarter units of credit combining course work and research, culminating in a thesis. In addition to the M.S. degree, the Department offers the M.Eng. degree. The degree is intended to prepare design and project engineers for careers in the biomedical and biotechnology industries within the framework of the graduate program of the bioengineering department. It is a terminal professional degree in engineering.

The Ph.D. program is designed to prepare students for a career in research and/or teaching in bioengineering. Each student, in conjunction with a faculty adviser, develops a course program that prepares him or her for the Departmental Ph.D. qualifying examination, which tests students' capabilities in three areas of specialization, and ascertains their potential for independent study and research. The degree requires the completion of a dissertation and defense of that research.

The Department of Bioengineering also participates in a new interdisciplinary graduate training program at the interfaces between the biological, medical, physical, and engineering sciences. UCSD is one of ten universities selected through the Howard Hughes Medical Institute (HHMI) to initiate this new program. To learn more about the UCSD Interfaces Training Program, students should visit http://interfaces.ucsd.edu/.

There is also an M.D./Ph.D. degree offered in conjunction with the UCSD Medical School, pending independent admission to the Medical School.

Research Facilities   The Department is housed in a modern research building constructed in 2003 with funds from the Whitaker and Powell Foundations. This building houses a majority of the bioengineering research laboratories in addition to premier core and instructional facilities. The research laboratories in the Department are fully equipped for modern bioengineering research. The Department houses several state-of-the-art core facilities, including biotechnology, microfabrication, cell engineering, and microscopy, and a vivarium. The state-of-the-art instrumentation includes access to high-throughput (Solexa) sequencers, mass spectrometry for proteomics and metabolomics, live-cell imaging, and new-generation cell-sorting/selection equipment. The Department maintains excellent computing and network facilities, including a graduate workstation lab, a multimedia laboratory, and two 105-node Linux clusters.

Financial Aid   The Department supports domestic full-time graduate students at the Ph.D. level. Financial support is available in the form of fellowships, traineeships, teaching assistantships, and research assistantships. Awarding of financial support is competitive, and stipends average $25,000 for the academic year, plus tuition and fees. Sources of funding include University fellowships and traineeships from an NIH training grant. Funds for support of international students are extremely limited, and the selection process is highly competitive. International students are encouraged to come with their own funding to gain admission.

Cost of Study   In 2010–11, full-time students who are California residents are expected to pay $4211 per quarter in registration and incidental fees. Nonresidents pay a total of $9245 per quarter in registration and incidental fees. There is a reduced fee structure for students enrolled on a half-time basis. Fees are subject to change.

Living and Housing Costs   UCSD provides 1,625 apartments for graduate students. Current monthly rates range from $405 for a single student to $1430 for a family. In fall 2010, UCSD Affiliated Housing is scheduled to open Arris Verde, which is designed to house an additional 450 graduate students. There is also a variety of off-campus housing in the surrounding communities. Prevailing rents range from $613 per month for a room in a private home to $1500 or more per month for a two-bedroom apartment. Information may be obtained from the UCSD Affiliated Housing Office.

Student Group   The current campus enrollment is 26,500 students, of whom 22,500 are undergraduates and 4,000 are graduate students. The Department of Bioengineering has an undergraduate enrollment of 843 and a graduate enrollment of 163.

Location   The 2,040-acre campus spreads from the coastline, where the Scripps Institution of Oceanography is located, across a large wooded portion of the Torrey Pines Mesa overlooking the Pacific Ocean. To the east and north lie mountains, and to the south are Mexico and the almost uninhabited seacoast of Baja, California.

The University   One of ten campuses in the University of California System, UCSD comprises the general campus, the School of Medicine, and the Scripps Institution of Oceanography. Established in La Jolla in 1960, UCSD is one of the newer campuses, but in this short time, it has become one of the major universities in the country.

Applying   A minimum GPA of 3.4 (on a 4.0 scale) is required for Ph.D. and M.S. admission. For the M.Eng. degree, a minimum GPA of 3.0 (on a 4.0 scale) is required for admission. The average GPA for students offered support in 2009–10 was 3.80. All applicants are required to take the GRE General Test. International applicants whose native language is not English are required to take the TOEFL and obtain a minimum score of 550 on the paper-based version, 213 on the computer-based version, or 80 on the Internet-based version. In addition to test scores, applicants must submit a completed Graduate Admission Application, all official transcripts (English translation must accompany official transcripts written in other languages), a statement of purpose, and three letters of recommendation. The deadline for filing applications for both international students and U.S. residents is December 15, 2010. Applicants are considered for admission for the fall quarter only.

Correspondence and Information
Department of Bioengineering 0419
University of California, San Diego
La Jolla, California 92093-0419

Phone: 858-822-1604
E-mail: be-gradinfo@bioeng.ucsd.edu
Web site: http://be.uscd.edu

University of California, San Diego

THE FACULTY AND THEIR RESEARCH

Shu Chien, M.D., Ph.D., University Professor of Bioengineering and Medicine. Effects of mechanical forces on endothelial gene expression and signal transduction, molecular bioengineering, DNA microarrays, nanotechnology, circulatory regulation in health and disease, energy balance and molecular basis of leukocyte-endothelial interactions, vascular tissue engineering.

Pedro Cabrales, Ph.D., Assistant Professor. Transport of biological gases and their ability to regulate or affect cardiovascular function and cellular metabolism in order to design novel therapeutic interventions to treat, manage, and ultimately prevent disease using an integrative analysis of physical and chemical phenomena, based on engineering sciences principles and methods.

Gert Cauwenberghs, Ph.D., Professor of Biological Sciences. Cross-cutting advances at the interface between in vivo and in silico neural information processing; silicon adaptive microsystems and emerging nanotechnologies as tools for basic neuroscience research and clinical biomedical applications, and the insights they provide regarding the inner workings of nervous systems; facilitating the development of sensory and neural prostheses and brain-machine interfaces.

Karen Christman, Ph.D., Assistant Professor. Regeneration of injured and diseased cardiovascular tissues in vivo, using polymer chemistry and nanotechnology methods to develop novel biomaterials for tissue implantation and cell delivery.

Adam Engler, Ph.D., Assistant Professor. Interactions between cells and their extracellular matrix (ECM), especially the role of mechanical properties of the matrix in regulating stem cell differentiation; applying basic studies of cell-matrix interactions and mechanobiology to design new models for studying cancer progress and new strategies for engineering nerve and muscle tissues.

David A. Gough, Ph.D., Professor. Implantable glucose sensor for diabetes; glucose and oxygen transport through tissues, sensor biocompatibility; dynamic models of the natural pancreas on based glucose input and insulin output; machine learning for prediction of protein-protein interactions.

Jeff M. Hasty, Ph.D., Associate Professor. Computational genomics and the dynamics of gene regulatory networks: Dissection and analysis of the complex dynamical interactions involved in gene regulation using techniques from nonlinear dynamics, statistical physics, and molecular biology to model, design, and construct synthetic gene networks.

Michael J. Heller, Ph.D., Professor. Development of high-performance bioanalytical techniques and technologies for genomic, proteomic, and pharmacogenomic applications, including novel devices (DNA array/lab-on-a-chip) and systems for mutation scanning, ultrafast DNA sequencing, single molecule detection, and combinatorial selection processes; nanotechnology and research related to the development of biomolecular-based mechanisms for photonic/electronic energy transfer, chemical to mechanical energy conversions, and DNA-based self-organizing nanostructures for data storage and computation; development of nanofabrication processes for the assembly of highly integrated macroscopic 2-D and 3-D structures from molecular and nanoscale components.

Xiaohua Huang, Ph.D., Assistant Professor. Genomics, molecular biotechnology, and bioinformatics, including chemistry and biophysics of protein and DNA molecules and technologies to uncover greater information regarding the human genome and genetics.

Trey Ideker, Ph.D., Associate Professor. Development of large-scale, computer-aided models of cellular signaling and regulatory pathways; new types of models and statistical frameworks for integrating the enormous amount of data on gene expression, protein expression, and protein interactions arising in the wake of the Human Genome Project.

Marcos Intaglietta, Ph.D., Professor. Development of plasma expanders and artificial blood, theory of tissue oxygenation at the microvascular level, optical methods for the study of microcirculation.

Ratnesh Lal, Ph.D., Professor. Nano-bio-interface science and technology; atomic force microscopy-based multimodality imaging and functional mapping to study protein misfolding, cell-cell, and cell-surround interactions; design and application of biosensors and devices to study normal and pathophysiology, preventive strategies, and therapeutics.

Andrew D. McCulloch, Ph.D., Professor. In vivo, in vitro, and in silico studies of the normal and diseased heart in model organisms and humans; cardiac phenotyping in gene-targeted animal models; cardiac muscle tissue engineering; myocyte mechanotransduction and mechanoelectric feedback; computational modeling of cardiac electromechanics; excitation-contraction coupling; metabolism and cell signaling; systems biology of cardiac function in *Drosophila*.

Bernhard Palsson, Ph.D., Professor. Hematopoietic tissue engineering, stem cell technology, bioreactor design, metabolic dynamics and regulation, whole cell simulators, metabolic engineering, genetic circuits.

Robert L. Sah, M.D., Sc.D., Professor of Bioengineering and HHMI Professor. Bioengineering of cartilage tissue and synovial fluid at the molecular, cellular, tissue, and joint scales; cartilage growth, aging, degeneration, and repair; cartilage biophysics, biomechanics, and transport; chondrocyte and cartilage mechanoregulation.

Geert W. Schmid-Schönbein, Ph.D., Professor of Bioengineering and Medicine. Microcirculation, biomechanics, molecular, and cellular mechanisms for transport in living tissues; mechanisms for cell activation in cardiovascular disease with applications to shock, ischemia, inflammation, and hypertension.

Gabriel A. Silva, Ph.D., Associate Professor. Retinal and central nervous system neural engineering; use of microtechnology and nanotechnology applied to molecular neurobiology and cell biology for regeneration of the neural retina and central nervous system; theoretical and computational neuroscience applied to understanding the retinal neural code; focus on retinal neurophysiology and pathophysiology of degenerative retinal disorders, tissue engineering and cellular replacement theories, adult stem cell biology for neuroscience applications.

Shankar Subramaniam, Ph.D., Professor and Chair. Bioinformatics and systems biology and bioengineering; measurement and integration of cellular data to reconstruct context-specific metabolic, signaling, and regulatory pathways; development of quantitative systems models for deciphering phenotypes in mammalian cells.

Lanping Amy Sung, Ph.D., Professor. Molecular structure and control of gene expression of membrane skeletal proteins in relation to the mechanical properties of cells and tissues in differentiation, aging, and disease; molecular defects of membrane skeletal proteins in hereditary diseases; protein 4.2 as a pseudozyme in maintaining the stability and flexibility of erythrocyte membranes; mechanical function of tropomodulin (a tropomyosin-binding protein) in the heart, muscles, and erythrocytes.

Shyni Varghese, Ph.D., Assistant Professor. Application of novel and rational biomaterial design and synthesis to the repair and regeneration of injured and diseased tissues, especially for developing embryonic stem cell–based therapies for cartilage defects and osteoarthritis; the interface between stem cell differentiation, cell-matrix interactions, and biopolymers with the translational science of orthopedic surgery.

John T. Watson, Ph.D., Professor-in-Residence of Bioengineering and Vice Chair, External Relations. Heart failure and mechanical circulatory support; biomaterials; medical implant design; bioimaging; creativity, innovation, and technology transfer.

Kun Zhang, Ph.D., Assistant Professor. Development and scientific application of new genomic technologies, with an emphasis on high-throughput genomic analyses of single DNA molecules.

Bioengineering Adjunct Faculty

Michael Berns, Professor. Application of lasers and associated optical technologies in biology, medicine, and biomedical engineering: Laser-tissue interactions, laser microbeam studies on cell structure and function, development of photonics-based biomedical instrumentation, and clinical research in oncology, fertility, and ophthalmology.

Lars M. Bjursten, M.D., Ph.D., Professor.

Charles Cantor, Ph.D., Professor. Genomics, biochemical assays, protein immobilization, and pharmacology; biophysical chemistry and bioassays.

Paul Citron, Professor.

J. S. Lee, Ph.D., Professor.

G. Paternostro, Ph.D., M.D., Professor. Cardiac imaging and noninvasive study of metabolism, applications to high-throughput screening, apoptosis, genetic and genomic analysis of cardiac aging, *Drosophila melanogaster* as a model of chronic heart dysfunction.

P. Tong, Ph.D., Professor.

Bioengineering Affiliate Faculty

Richard Buxton, Ph.D., Professor of Radiology. Recently developed functional MRI (fMRI) techniques to measure patterns of activation in the brain, including basic studies of the physiological mechanisms that underlie fMRI, novel approaches to the design and analysis of fMRI experiments, and development of new imaging techniques to directly measure tissue blood flow.

Pao C. Chau, Ph.D., Professor of Chemical Engineering. Biotechnology and cellular engineering; development of a hollow fiber bioreactor to produce human monoclonal antibodies or binding fragments specific to tumor-associated antigens; cell-cycle kinetics research to understand the basic phenomena of antibody synthesis, especially under serum-free conditions; uses of flow cytometry to measure cell-cycle parameters; molecular biology techniques to probe transcriptional and posttranscriptional regulations; complementation of data and system analyses by mathematical models.

James W. Covell, M.D., Professor Emeritus of Medicine. Cardiovascular physiology and pharmacology; biomedical computing; mechanisms of diseased cardiac muscle contraction in the intact animal, the function of ischemic and hypertrophied cardiac muscle, and the role of the extracellular matrix in hypertrophy and heart failure; high-resolution measurements of finite deformation and finite-element modeling to explore these relationships; role of the extracellular matrix linking adjacent myocardial laminae in ischemia and heart failure.

Mark H. Ellisman, Ph.D., Professor of Neurosciences. Development and application of advanced imaging technologies to obtain new information about cell structure and function, structural correlates of nerve impulse conduction and axonal transport, cellular interactions during nervous system regeneration, cellular mechanisms regulating transient changes in cytoplasmic calcium, aging in the central nervous system.

David Hall, Ph.D., Assistant Adjunct Professor of Radiology. Using optical imaging approaches to interrogate tissue in vivo.

Andrew Kummel, Ph.D., Professor of Chemistry and Biochemistry.

Juan Lasheras, Ph.D., Distinguished Professor of Mechanical and Aerospace Engineering. Turbulent flows, two-phase flows, biomedical fluid mechanics, biomechanics.

Richard L. Lieber, Ph.D., Professor of Orthopedics. Musculoskeletal system design and plasticity, skeletal muscle architecture and its relation to tendon transfer surgery, development of intraoperative and rehabilitative measuring devices, skeletal muscle mechanics, sarcomere length measurement in isolated fibers and whole muscles, myosin expression in skeletal muscle after exercise-induced injury, immobilization, spinal cord injury and electrical stimulation.

Thomas Liu, Ph.D., Associate Professor of Radiology. Design and analysis of experiments for functional MRI (fMRI), with emphasis on statistical optimization, nonlinear signal processing, and physiological noise reduction; characterization and modeling of hemodynamic response to neural activity, including effects of drugs such as caffeine; development of novel imaging methods to measure cerebral blood flow and volume; characterization of cerebral blood flow in Alzheimer's disease and glaucoma.

Thomas Nelson, Ph.D., Professor of Radiology.

Sanjay Nigam, M.D., Professor of Medicine.

Jeffrey H. Omens, Ph.D., Professor of Medicine. Regional mechanics of the normal and diseased heart; miniaturization of functional measurement techniques for rat and mouse hearts; role of mechanical factors in cardiac hypertrophy, remodeling and growth; residual stress in the heart; computer-assisted analysis of cardiac mechanics.

Michael Sailor, Ph.D., Professor of Chemistry and Biochemistry

Scott Thomson, M.D., Ph.D., Professor-in-Residence of Orthopedics. Kidney physiology, using animal models; studies of regulation of kidney function by the juxtaglomerular apparatus, using a variety of adaptations on the technique of renal micropuncture.

Peter D. Wagner, M.D., Professor of Medicine. Theoretical and experimental basis of oxygen transport in the lungs and skeletal muscles; muscle capillary growth regulation using molecular biological approaches in integrated systems—the role of oxygen, microvascular hemodynamics, physical factors, and inflammatory mediators; mechanisms of exercise limitation in health and disease, especially the role of muscle dysfunction in heart failure, emphysema, and renal failure.

Sam Ward, Ph.D., Assistant Professor of Radiology.

John B. West, M.D., Ph.D., D.Sc., Professor Emeritus of Medicine. Bioengineering aspects of the lung; stress failure and physiology of pulmonary capillaries when exposed to high transmural pressures; distribution of ventilation and blood flow in the lung; effect of gravity on the lung; measurements of pulmonary function during sustained weightlessness; distortion of the lung resulting from its weight; regulation of the structure of capillary walls, including changes of gene expression as the result of stress; high-altitude physiology, especially extreme altitude.

Section 4
Architectural Engineering

This section contains a directory of institutions offering graduate work in architectural engineering. Additional information about programs listed in the directory but not augmented by an in-depth entry may be obtained by writing directly to the dean of a graduate school or chair of a department at the address given in the directory.

For programs offering related work, see also in this book *Engineering and Applied Sciences* and *Management of Engineering and Technology.* In the other guides in this series:

Graduate Programs in the Humanities, Arts & Social Sciences
See *Applied Arts and Design (Industrial Design* and *Interior Design), Architecture (Environmental Design), Political Science and International Affairs,* and *Public, Regional, and Industrial Affairs (Urban and Regional Planning* and *Urban Studies)*

Graduate Programs in the Physical Sciences, Mathematics, Agricultural Sciences, the Environment & Natural Resources
See *Environmental Sciences and Management*

CONTENTS

Program Directory

Architectural Engineering

Carnegie Mellon University, College of Fine Arts, School of Architecture, Pittsburgh, PA 15213-3891. Offers architectural engineering construction management (M Sc); architecture (MSA); architecture, engineering, and construction management (PhD); building performance and diagnostics (M Sc, PhD); computational design (M Sc, PhD); sustainable design (M Sc); urban design (M Sc). Terminal master's awarded for partial completion of doctoral program. *Degree requirements:* For doctorate, thesis/dissertation. *Entrance requirements:* For master's and doctorate, GRE General Test. Additional exam requirements/recommendations for international students: Required—TOEFL.

Drexel University, College of Engineering, Department of Civil, Architectural, and Environmental Engineering, Philadelphia, PA 19104-2875. Offers architectural / building systems engineering (MS, PhD); civil engineering (MS, PhD); environmental engineering (MS, PhD); geotechnical, geoenvironmental and geosynthetics engineering (MS, PhD); hydraulics, hydrology and water resources engineering (MS, PhD); structures (MS). Part-time and evening/weekend programs available. *Degree requirements:* For master's, thesis optional; for doctorate, thesis/dissertation. *Entrance requirements:* For master's, minimum GPA of 3.0; for doctorate, minimum GPA of 3.5, MS in civil engineering. Additional exam requirements/recommendations for international students: Required—TOEFL. Electronic applications accepted. *Faculty research:* Structural dynamics, hazardous wastes, water resources, pavement materials, groundwater.

Illinois Institute of Technology, Graduate College, Armour College of Engineering, Department of Civil, Architectural and Environmental Engineering, Chicago, IL 60616-3793. Offers architectural engineering (M Arch E); civil engineering (MS, PhD); construction engineering and management (MCEM); environmental engineering (M Env E, MS, PhD); geoenvironmental engineering (M Geoenv E); geotechnical engineering (MGE); public works (MPW); structural engineering (MSE); transportation engineering (M Trans E). Part-time and evening/weekend programs available. Terminal master's awarded for partial completion of doctoral program. *Degree requirements:* For master's, thesis (for some programs); for doctorate, comprehensive exam, thesis/dissertation. *Entrance requirements:* For master's and doctorate, GRE General Test, minimum undergraduate GPA of 3.0. Additional exam requirements/recommendations for international students: Required—TOEFL (minimum score 550 paper-based; 213 computer-based; 80 iBT). Electronic applications accepted. *Expenses:* Tuition: Full-time $17,550; part-time $888 per credit hour. Required fees: $850; $7.50 per credit hour. One-time fee: $50 full-time. Full-time tuition and fees vary according to program. *Faculty research:* Seismic analysis of buildings and bridges, fatigue analysis and materials of construction, construction zone safety and construction productivity, architectural acoustics and building energy efficiency, environmental engineering, air and water quality.

Kansas State University, Graduate School, College of Engineering, Department of Architectural Engineering and Construction Science, Manhattan, KS 66506. Offers architectural engineering (MS). *Faculty:* 10 full-time (2 women). *Students:* 18 full-time (7 women), 3 part-time (2 women). Average age 24. 8 applicants, 75% accepted. In 2009, 13 master's awarded. *Degree requirements:* For master's, thesis or alternative. *Entrance requirements:* For master's, GRE, minimum GPA of 3.25. Additional exam requirements/recommendations for international students: Required—TOEFL. *Application deadline:* For fall admission, 2/1 priority date for domestic and international students; for spring admission, 8/1 priority date for domestic and international students. Applications are processed on a rolling basis. Application fee: $40 ($55 for international students). Electronic applications accepted. *Financial support:* Fellowships, research assistantships, teaching assistantships, career-related internships or fieldwork, Federal Work-Study, institutionally sponsored loans, and scholarships/grants available. Support available to part-time students. Financial award application deadline: 3/1; financial award applicants required to submit FAFSA. *Faculty research:* Construction sciences, sustainable engineering, building electrical and lighting systems, building HVAC and plumbing systems, structural systems design and analysis. *Unit head:* David Fritchen, Head, 785-532-3566, Fax: 785-532-6944, E-mail: dfritch@ksu.edu. *Application contact:* Kimberly Kramer, Director, 785-532-3576, Fax: 785-532-6944, E-mail: kramer@ksu.edu.

Penn State University Park, Graduate School, College of Engineering, Department of Architectural Engineering, State College, University Park, PA 16802-1503. Offers M Eng, MAE, MS, PhD.

University of Colorado at Boulder, Graduate School, College of Engineering and Applied Science, Department of Civil, Environmental, and Architectural Engineering, Boulder, CO 80309. Offers building systems (MS, PhD); construction engineering management (MS, PhD); environmental engineering (MS, PhD); geotechnical engineering and geomechanics (MS, PhD); hydrology, water resources and environmental fluid mechanics (MS, PhD); structural engineering and structural mechanics (MS, PhD). *Faculty:* 39 full-time (5 women). *Students:* 202 full-time (62 women), 29 part-time (6 women); includes 34 minority (3 African Americans, 3 American Indian/Alaska Native, 12 Asian Americans or Pacific Islanders, 16 Hispanic Americans), 53 international. Average age 29. 384 applicants, 44% accepted, 80 enrolled. In 2009, 60 master's, 7 doctorates awarded. *Degree requirements:* For master's, comprehensive exam, thesis or alternative; for doctorate, thesis/dissertation. *Entrance requirements:* For master's, GRE General Test, minimum undergraduate GPA of 3.0. *Application deadline:* For fall admission, 3/1 for domestic students, 12/1 for international students; for spring admission, 10/31 for domestic students, 10/1 for international students. Application fee: $50 ($60 for international students). *Financial support:* In 2009–10, 45 fellowships (averaging $7,876 per year), 68 research assistantships (averaging $15,204 per year) were awarded. Financial award application deadline: 1/15. *Faculty research:* Building systems engineering, construction engineering and management, environmental engineering, geoenvironmental engineering, geotechnical engineering, materials and mechanics, structural engineering, water resources engineering, life-cycle engineering. Total annual research expenditures: $6.1 million.

University of Detroit Mercy, School of Architecture, Detroit, MI 48221. Offers M Arch. *Entrance requirements:* For master's, BS in architecture, minimum GPA of 3.0, portfolio.

The University of Kansas, Graduate Studies, School of Engineering, Department of Civil, Environmental, and Architectural Engineering, Program in Architectural Engineering, Lawrence, KS 66045. Offers MS. Part-time programs available. *Faculty:* 11 full-time (2 women). *Students:* 5 full-time (3 women), 1 (woman) part-time, 4 international. Average age 26. 17 applicants, 47% accepted, 2 enrolled. In 2009, 3 master's awarded. *Degree requirements:* For master's, thesis or alternative, exam. *Entrance requirements:* For master's, GRE, BS in engineering. Additional exam requirements/recommendations for international students: Required—TOEFL. *Application deadline:* For fall admission, 7/1 priority date for domestic students, 3/15 priority date for international students; for spring admission, 12/1 priority date for domestic students, 8/15 priority date for international students. Applications are processed on a rolling basis. Application fee: $45 ($55 for international students). Electronic applications accepted. *Expenses:* Tuition, state resident: full-time $6492; part-time $270.50 per credit hour. Tuition, nonresident: full-time $15,510; part-time $646.25 per credit hour. Required fees: $847; $70.56 per credit hour. Tuition and fees vary according to course load and program. *Financial support:* Fellowships with full tuition reimbursements, research assistantships with full tuition reimbursements, teaching assistantships with full tuition reimbursements, career-related internships or fieldwork available. Financial award application deadline: 2/7. *Faculty research:* Structural engineering, construction engineering, building mechanical systems, energy management. *Unit head:* Craig D. Adams, Chair, 785-864-2700, Fax: 785-864-5631, E-mail: adamscd@ku.edu. *Application contact:* Bruce M. McEnroe, Graduate Advisor, 785-864-2925, Fax: 785-864-5631, E-mail: mcenroe@ku.edu.

University of Louisiana at Lafayette, College of the Arts, School of Architecture, Lafayette, LA 70504. Offers M Arch. *Degree requirements:* For master's, thesis. *Entrance requirements:* For master's, GRE General Test. Additional exam requirements/recommendations for international students: Required—TOEFL (minimum score 550 paper-based; 213 computer-based). Electronic applications accepted.

University of Miami, Graduate School, College of Engineering, Department of Civil, Architectural, and Environmental Engineering, Coral Gables, FL 33124. Offers architectural engineering (MSAE); civil engineering (MSCE, PhD). Part-time programs available. Terminal master's awarded for partial completion of doctoral program. *Degree requirements:* For master's, thesis (for some programs); for doctorate, comprehensive exam, thesis/dissertation. *Entrance requirements:* For master's, GRE General Test (minimum score 1000 verbal and quantitative), minimum GPA of 3.0; for doctorate, GRE General Test, minimum GPA of 3.5 in preceding degree. Additional exam requirements/recommendations for international students: Required—TOEFL (minimum score 550 paper-based; 213 computer-based). Electronic applications accepted. *Faculty research:* Structural assessment and wind engineering, sustainable construction and materials, moisture transport and management, wastewater and waste engineering, water management and risk analysis.

University of Nebraska–Lincoln, Graduate College, College of Engineering, Program in Architectural Engineering, Lincoln, NE 68588. Offers M Eng, MAE, MS, PhD. *Accreditation:* ABET. *Entrance requirements:* Additional exam requirements/recommendations for international students: Required—TOEFL (minimum score 550 paper-based; 213 computer-based), GRE.

The University of Texas at Austin, Graduate School, Cockrell School of Engineering, Department of Civil, Architectural and Environmental Engineering, Program in Architectural Engineering, Austin, TX 78712-1111. Offers MSE. Part-time programs available. *Degree requirements:* For master's, thesis. *Entrance requirements:* For master's, GRE General Test. Additional exam requirements/recommendations for international students: Required—TOEFL. Electronic applications accepted. *Faculty research:* Materials engineering, structural engineering, construction engineering, project management.

Section 5
Biomedical Engineering and Biotechnology

This section contains a directory of institutions offering graduate work in biomedical engineering and biotechnology, followed by an in-depth entry submitted by an institution that chose to prepare a detailed program description. Additional information about programs listed in the directory but not augmented by an in-depth entry may be obtained by writing directly to the dean of a graduate school or chair of a department at the address given in the directory.

For programs offering related work, see also in this book *Aerospace/ Aeronautical Engineering, Engineering and Applied Sciences, Engineering Design, Engineering Physics, Management of Engineering and Technology,* and *Mechanical Engineering and Mechanics.* In the other guides in this series:

Graduate Programs in the Biological Sciences
See *Biological and Biomedical Sciences* and *Physiology*
Graduate Programs in the Physical Sciences, Mathematics, Agricultural Sciences, the Environment & Natural Resources
See *Mathematical Sciences (Biometrics and Biostatistics)*
Graduate Programs in Business, Education, Health, Information Studies, Law & Social Work
See *Allied Health*

CONTENTS

Biomedical Engineering

Baylor College of Medicine, Graduate School of Biomedical Sciences, Program in Translational Biology and Molecular Medicine, Houston, TX 77030-3498. Offers PhD. *Faculty:* 151 full-time (48 women). *Students:* 48 full-time (23 women); includes 13 minority (4 African Americans, 4 Asian Americans or Pacific Islanders, 5 Hispanic Americans), 14 international. Average age 24. *Degree requirements:* For doctorate, thesis/dissertation, public defense. *Entrance requirements:* For doctorate, GRE, minimum GPA of 3.0. Additional exam requirements/recommendations for international students: Required—TOEFL. *Application deadline:* For fall admission, 1/1 for domestic students. Application fee: $0. Electronic applications accepted. *Financial support:* In 2009–10, 48 students received support; fellowships, research assistantships, career-related internships or fieldwork, Federal Work-Study, health care benefits, and students receive a scholarship unless there are grant funds available to pay tuition available. Financial award applicants required to submit FAFSA. *Unit head:* Dr. Mary Estes, Director, 713-798-3585, Fax: 713-798-3586, E-mail: tbmm@bcm.edu. *Application contact:* Wanda Waguespack, Graduate Program Administrator, 713-798-1077, Fax: 713-798-3586, E-mail: wandaw@bcm.edu.

Baylor University, Graduate School, School of Engineering and Computer Science, Department of Engineering, Waco, TX 76798. Offers biomedical engineering (MSBE); electrical and computer engineering (MSECE); engineering (ME); mechanical engineering (MSME). *Faculty:* 14 full-time (1 woman). *Students:* 19 full-time (1 woman), 5 part-time (1 woman); includes 4 minority (1 African American, 1 Asian American or Pacific Islander, 2 Hispanic Americans), 8 international. In 2009, 8 master's awarded. *Unit head:* Dr. Mike Thompson, Graduate Director, 254-710-4188. *Application contact:* Linda Keer, Administrative Assistant, 254-710-4188, Fax: 254-710-3870, E-mail: linda_kerr@baylor.edu.

Boston University, College of Engineering, Department of Biomedical Engineering, Boston, MA 02215. Offers M Eng, MS, PhD, MD/PhD. Part-time programs available. *Faculty:* 31 full-time (3 women), 1 part-time/adjunct (0 women). *Students:* 150 full-time (49 women), 4 part-time (1 woman); includes 18 minority (2 African Americans, 14 Asian Americans or Pacific Islanders, 2 Hispanic Americans), 41 international. Average age 24. 469 applicants, 27% accepted, 43 enrolled. In 2009, 18 master's, 14 doctorates awarded. Terminal master's awarded for partial completion of doctoral program. *Degree requirements:* For master's, thesis (for some programs); for doctorate, comprehensive exam, thesis/dissertation. *Entrance requirements:* For master's and doctorate, GRE General Test. Additional exam requirements/recommendations for international students: Required—TOEFL (minimum score 550 paper-based; 213 computer-based; 84 iBT), IELTS (minimum score 6). *Application deadline:* For fall admission, 4/1 for domestic and international students; for spring admission, 10/1 for domestic and international students. Applications are processed on a rolling basis. Application fee: $70. Electronic applications accepted. *Expenses:* Tuition: Full-time $37,910; part-time $1184 per credit hour. Required fees: $386; $40 per semester. Part-time tuition and fees vary according to class time, course level, degree level and program. *Financial support:* In 2009–10, 142 students received support, including 39 fellowships with full tuition reimbursements available (averaging $27,600 per year), 84 research assistantships with full tuition reimbursements available (averaging $18,400 per year), 7 teaching assistantships with full tuition reimbursements available (averaging $18,400 per year); career-related internships or fieldwork, Federal Work-Study, institutionally sponsored loans, scholarships/grants, traineeships, and health care benefits also available. Financial award application deadline: 1/15; financial award applicants required to submit FAFSA. *Faculty research:* Biomaterials, tissue engineering and drug delivery; modeling of biological systems; molecular bioengineering and biophysics; neuroscience and neural disease; synthetic biology and systems biology. Total annual research expenditures: $18.7 million. *Unit head:* Dr. Solomon Eisenberg, Chairman, 617-353-2805, Fax: 617-353-6766, E-mail: sre@bu.edu. *Application contact:* Cheryl Kelley, Director of Graduate Programs, 617-353-9760, Fax: 617-353-0259, E-mail: enggrad@bu.edu.

Brown University, Graduate School, Division of Biology and Medicine, Program in Artificial Organs, Biomaterials, and Cell Technology, Providence, RI 02912. Offers MA, Sc M, PhD. Terminal master's awarded for partial completion of doctoral program. *Degree requirements:* For doctorate, thesis/dissertation, preliminary exam. *Entrance requirements:* For master's and doctorate, GRE General Test, GRE Subject Test. Additional exam requirements/recommendations for international students: Required—TOEFL. Electronic applications accepted.

Brown University, Graduate School, Division of Biology and Medicine and Division of Engineering, Program in Biomedical Engineering, Providence, RI 02912. Offers MS, PhD. *Entrance requirements:* For master's and doctorate, GRE General Test, interview. Additional exam requirements/recommendations for international students: Required—TOEFL.

Brown University, Graduate School, Division of Engineering and Division of Biology and Medicine, Center for Biomedical Engineering, Providence, RI 02912. Offers Sc M, PhD. *Degree requirements:* For master's, thesis.

Carleton University, Faculty of Graduate Studies, Faculty of Engineering and Design, Ottawa-Carleton Institute for Biomedical Engineering, Ottawa, ON K1S 5B6, Canada. Offers MA Sc. *Degree requirements:* For master's, thesis optional. *Entrance requirements:* For master's, honours degree. Additional exam requirements/recommendations for international students: Required—TOEFL.

Carnegie Mellon University, Carnegie Institute of Technology, Biomedical and Health Engineering Program, Pittsburgh, PA 15213-3891. Offers bioengineering (MS, PhD); MD/PhD. *Degree requirements:* For master's, thesis; for doctorate, thesis/dissertation, qualifying exam. *Entrance requirements:* For master's and doctorate, GRE General Test. Additional exam requirements/recommendations for international students: Required—TOEFL. Electronic applications accepted. *Faculty research:* Cellular and molecular systematics, signal and image processing, materials and mechanics.

Carnegie Mellon University, Carnegie Institute of Technology, Department of Electrical and Computer Engineering, Concentration in Biomedical Engineering, Pittsburgh, PA 15213-3891. Offers MS. Part-time programs available. *Degree requirements:* For master's, thesis. *Entrance requirements:* For master's, GRE General Test. Additional exam requirements/recommendations for international students: Required—TOEFL.

Case Western Reserve University, School of Graduate Studies, The Case School of Engineering, Department of Biomedical Engineering, Cleveland, OH 44106. Offers MS, PhD, MD/MS, MD/PhD. *Faculty:* 19 full-time (2 women). *Students:* 105 full-time (35 women), 25 part-time (6 women); includes 31 minority (6 African Americans, 1 American Indian/Alaska Native, 20 Asian Americans or Pacific Islanders, 4 Hispanic Americans), 48 international. In 2009, 11 master's, 21 doctorates awarded. Terminal master's awarded for partial completion of doctoral program. *Degree requirements:* For master's, thesis (for some programs); for doctorate, thesis/dissertation, qualifying exam, teaching experience. *Entrance requirements:* For master's and doctorate, GRE General Test. Additional exam requirements/recommendations for international students: Required—TOEFL. *Application deadline:* For fall admission, 2/1 priority date for domestic students; for spring admission, 10/1 priority date for domestic students. Applications are processed on a rolling basis. Application fee: $50. *Financial support:* Fellowships with full tuition reimbursements, research assistantships with full and partial tuition reimbursements, traineeships available. Financial award application deadline: 2/15; financial award applicants required to submit FAFSA. *Faculty research:* Neuroengineering, biomaterials/tissue engineering, biomedical imaging, biomedical sensors/systems. Total annual research expenditures: $12.5 million. *Unit head:* Dr. Jeffrey Duerk, Department Chair, 216-368-6047, Fax: 216-368-4969, E-mail: duerk@case.edu. *Application contact:* Carol Adrine, Academic Operations Coordinator, 216-368-4094, Fax: 216-368-4969, E-mail: caa7@case.edu.

See Close-Up on page 141.

The Catholic University of America, School of Engineering, Department of Biomedical Engineering, Washington, DC 20064. Offers bioinstrumentation (MBE, MSE, D Engr); biomechanics (MBE, D Engr, PhD); biosignal processing and medical imaging (MBE, MSE, PhD); home care technologies (MBE, MSE, D Engr); rehabilitation engineering (MBE, MSE, D Engr); telemedicine (MBE, MSE, D Engr). Part-time programs available. *Faculty:* 6 full-time (1 woman), 1 part-time/adjunct (0 women). *Students:* 13 full-time (6 women), 10 part-time (4 women); includes 6 minority (3 African Americans, 3 Hispanic Americans), 6 international. Average age 29. 30 applicants, 63% accepted, 12 enrolled. In 2009, 15 master's awarded. *Degree requirements:* For master's, thesis or alternative; for doctorate, comprehensive exam, thesis/dissertation, oral exams. *Entrance requirements:* For master's, GRE (minimum score: 1250), minimum GPA of 3.0, statement of purpose, official copies of academic transcripts, three letters of recommendation; for doctorate, GRE (minimum score 1300), minimum GPA of 3.5, 3 letters of recommendation. Additional exam requirements/recommendations for international students: Required—TOEFL (minimum score 580 paper-based; 237 computer-based). *Application deadline:* For fall admission, 8/1 priority date for domestic students, 7/15 for international students; for spring admission, 12/1 priority date for domestic students, 10/15 for international students. Applications are processed on a rolling basis. Application fee: $55. Electronic applications accepted. *Expenses:* Contact institution. *Financial support:* Fellowships, research assistantships, teaching assistantships, Federal Work-Study, scholarships/grants, tuition waivers (full and partial), and unspecified assistantships available. Financial award application deadline: 2/1; financial award applicants required to submit FAFSA. *Faculty research:* Cardiopulmonary biomechanics, robotics and human motor control, cell and tissue engineering, biomechanics, rehabilitation engineering. Total annual research expenditures: $780,403. *Unit head:* Dr. Binh Q. Tran, Chair, 202-319-5181, Fax: 202-319-4287, E-mail: tran@cua.edu. *Application contact:* Julie Schwing, Director of Graduate Admissions, 202-319-5057, Fax: 202-319-6533, E-mail: cua-admissions@cua.edu.

City College of the City University of New York, Graduate School, Grove School of Engineering, Department of Biomedical Engineering, New York, NY 10031-9198. Offers ME, PhD. *Entrance requirements:* For master's, GRE. Additional exam requirements/recommendations for international students: Required—TOEFL (minimum score 550 paper-based; 213 computer-based).

Cleveland State University, College of Graduate Studies, Fenn College of Engineering, Department of Chemical and Biomedical Engineering, Program in Applied Biomedical Engineering, Cleveland, OH 44115. Offers D Eng. Part-time and evening/weekend programs available. *Degree requirements:* For doctorate, thesis/dissertation. *Entrance requirements:* For doctorate, GRE, minimum undergraduate GPA of 2.75, minimum MS or MD GPA of 3.25, 1 degree in engineering. Additional exam requirements/recommendations for international students: Required—TOEFL (minimum score 525 paper-based; 197 computer-based). *Faculty research:* Biomechanics, drug delivery systems, medical imaging, tissue engineering, artificial heart valves.

Colorado State University, Graduate School, School of Biomedical Engineering, Fort Collins, CO 80523-1376. Offers ME, MS, PhD. Part-time and evening/weekend programs available. *Students:* 19 full-time (5 women), 4 part-time (3 women); includes 5 minority (2 Asian Americans or Pacific Islanders, 3 Hispanic Americans), 1 international. Average age 26. 72 applicants, 46% accepted, 12 enrolled. In 2009, 1 master's awarded. *Degree requirements:* For master's, thesis; for doctorate, comprehensive exam, thesis/dissertation. *Entrance requirements:* For master's, GRE General Test, minimum GPA of 3.0, 3 letters of recommendation, resume; for doctorate, GRE General Test, minimum GPA of 3.0, 3 letters of recommendation, resume, official transcripts, statement of purpose. Additional exam requirements/recommendations for international students: Required—TOEFL (minimum score 550 paper-based; 213 computer-based; 95 iBT). *Application deadline:* For fall admission, 1/15 priority date for domestic and international students; for spring admission, 9/1 priority date for domestic students, 8/1 priority date for international students. Application fee: $50. *Expenses:* Tuition, state resident: full-time $6434; part-time $359.10 per credit. Tuition, nonresident: full-time $18,116; part-time $1006.45 per credit. Required fees: $1496; $83 per credit. *Financial support:* In 2009–10, 16 students received support, including 13 research assistantships with full tuition reimbursements available (averaging $9,639 per year), 3 teaching assistantships with full tuition reimbursements available (averaging $7,529 per year); fellowships, unspecified assistantships also available. Financial award application deadline: 3/1; financial award applicants required to submit FAFSA. *Faculty research:* Biomechanics and biomaterials; molecular, cellular and tissues engineering; medical diagnostics, devices and imaging. *Unit head:* Dr. Susan James, Director, 970-491-2842, Fax: 970-491-3827, E-mail: susan.james@colostate.edu. *Application contact:* Sara Neys, Academic Advisor, 970-491-7157, E-mail: sara.neys@colostate.edu.

Columbia University, Fu Foundation School of Engineering and Applied Science, Department of Biomedical Engineering, New York, NY 10027. Offers MS, Eng Sc D, PhD. Part-time programs available. Postbaccalaureate distance learning degree programs offered (no on-campus study). *Faculty:* 17 full-time (3 women), 4 part-time/adjunct (1 woman). *Students:* 98 full-time (36 women), 20 part-time (9 women); includes 22 minority (20 Asian Americans or Pacific Islanders, 2 Hispanic Americans), 49 international. Average age 27. 285 applicants, 25% accepted, 39 enrolled. In 2009, 25 master's, 11 doctorates awarded. *Degree requirements:* For doctorate, thesis/dissertation, qualifying exam. *Entrance requirements:* For master's and doctorate, GRE General Test. Additional exam requirements/recommendations for international students: Required—TOEFL. *Application deadline:* For fall admission, 12/1 priority date for domestic and international students; for spring admission, 10/1 priority date for domestic and international students. Application fee: $70. Electronic applications accepted. *Financial support:* In 2009–10, 36 students received support, including 12 fellowships with full tuition reimbursements available (averaging $32,500 per year), 44 research assistantships with full tuition reimbursements available (averaging $29,000 per year), 14 teaching assistantships with full tuition reimbursements available (averaging $29,000 per year); traineeships, health care benefits, and unspecified assistantships also available. Financial award application deadline: 12/1; financial award applicants required to submit FAFSA. *Faculty research:* Orthopedic biomechanics and osteoarthritis research, biomedical optical and ultrasound imaging, neurocomputational modeling and neuroengineering including mechanical injury to brain tissue, cellular and tissue engineering and regenerative medicine, magnetic resonance imaging and spectroscopy. *Unit head:* Dr. Van C. Mow, Department Chair, Stanley Dicker Professor of Biomedical Engineering and Orthopedic Bioengineering, 212-854-8462, Fax: 212-854-5117, E-mail: vcm1@columbia.edu. *Application contact:* Jarmaine Lomax, Administrative Coordinator, 212-854-4460, Fax: 212-854-8725, E-mail: jl432@columbia.edu.

Cornell University, Graduate School, Graduate Fields of Engineering, Field of Biomedical Engineering, Ithaca, NY 14853-0001. Offers M Eng, MS, PhD. *Faculty:* 50 full-time (11 women). *Students:* 156 full-time (52 women); includes 49 minority (8 African Americans, 30 Asian Americans or Pacific Islanders, 11 Hispanic Americans), 39 international. Average age 24. 332 applicants, 51% accepted, 90 enrolled. In 2009, 59 master's, 4 doctorates awarded. *Degree requirements:* For master's, thesis; for doctorate, comprehensive exam, thesis/dissertation. *Entrance requirements:* For master's and doctorate, GRE General Test, GRE Subject Test (engineering), 3 letters of recommendation. Additional exam requirements/recommendations for international students: Required—TOEFL (minimum score 77 iBT). *Application deadline:* For fall admission, 1/15 priority date for domestic students. Application fee: $70. Electronic applications accepted. *Expenses:* Tuition: Full-time $29,500. Required fees: $70. Full-time tuition and fees vary according to degree level, program and student level. *Financial support:* In 2009–10, 57 students received support, including 13 fellowships with full tuition reimbursements available, 7 research assistantships with full tuition reimbursements available, 1 teaching assistantship; institutionally sponsored loans, scholarships/grants, health care benefits, tuition waivers (full and partial), and unspecified assistantships also available. *Faculty research:* Biomaterials; biomedical instrumentation and diagnostics; biomedical mechanics; drug delivery, design, and metabolism. *Unit head:* Director of Graduate Studies, 607-255-1003, Fax: 607-255-1136. *Application contact:* Graduate Field Assistant, 607-255-2573, Fax: 607-255-1136, E-mail: biomedgrad@cornell.edu.

Dalhousie University, Faculty of Engineering and Faculty of Medicine, Department of Biomedical Engineering, Halifax, NS B3H3J5, Canada. Offers MA Sc, PhD. *Entrance requirements:* Additional exam requirements/recommendations for international students: Required—TOEFL, IELTS, CANTEST, CAEL, or Michigan English Language Assessment Battery. *Application deadline:* For fall admission, 6/1 for domestic students, 4/1 for international students; for winter admission, 11/15 for domestic students, 8/31 for international students; for spring admission, 2/28 for domestic students, 12/31 for international students. Application fee: $70. Electronic applications accepted. *Unit head:* Dr. Cheryl Kozey, Director, 902-494-3427, Fax: 902-494-6621, E-mail: bme@dal.ca. *Application contact:* Dr. Sarah Wells, Graduate Coordinator, 902-494-2320, Fax: 902-494-6621, E-mail: sarah.wells@dal.ca.

Dartmouth College, Thayer School of Engineering, Program in Biomedical Engineering, Hanover, NH 03755. Offers MS, PhD. *Faculty research:* Imaging, physiological modeling, cancer hyperthermia and radiation therapy, bioelectromagnetics, biomedical optics and lasers. *Unit head:* Dr. Joseph J. Helbie, Dean, 603-646-2238, Fax: 603-646-2580, E-mail: joseph.j.helbie@dartmouth.edu. *Application contact:* Candace S. Potter, Graduate Admissions Administrator, 603-646-3844, Fax: 603-646-1620, E-mail: candace.potter@dartmouth.edu.

Drexel University, School of Biomedical Engineering, Science and Health Systems, Program in Biomedical Engineering, Philadelphia, PA 19104-2875. Offers MS, PhD. *Degree requirements:* For master's, thesis (for some programs); for doctorate, thesis/dissertation. Electronic applications accepted.

Duke University, Graduate School, Pratt School of Engineering, Department of Biomedical Engineering, Durham, NC 27708. Offers MS, PhD. *Faculty:* 37 full-time. *Students:* 210 full-time (68 women); includes 46 minority (5 African Americans, 2 American Indian/Alaska Native, 31 Asian Americans or Pacific Islanders, 8 Hispanic Americans), 70 international. 476 applicants, 25% accepted, 61 enrolled. In 2009, 19 master's, 21 doctorates awarded. *Degree requirements:* For doctorate, thesis/dissertation. *Entrance requirements:* For master's and doctorate, GRE General Test. Additional exam requirements/recommendations for international students: Required—TOEFL (minimum score 550 paper-based; 213 computer-based; 83 iBT), IELTS (minimum score 7). *Application deadline:* For fall admission, 12/8 priority date for domestic and international students; for spring admission, 11/1 for domestic students. Application fee: $75. *Financial support:* Fellowships, research assistantships, teaching assistantships, Federal Work-Study available. Financial award application deadline: 12/31. *Unit head:* Dr. Ashutosh Chilkoti, Director of Graduate Studies, 919-660-5132, Fax: 919-684-4488, E-mail: kwb@acpub.duke.edu. *Application contact:* Cynthia Robertson, Associate Dean for Enrollment Services, 919-684-3913, E-mail: grad-admissions@duke.edu.

École Polytechnique de Montréal, Graduate Programs, Institute of Biomedical Engineering, Montréal, QC H3C 3A7, Canada. Offers M Sc A, PhD, DESS. Part-time programs available. *Degree requirements:* For master's, one foreign language, thesis; for doctorate, one foreign language, thesis/dissertation. *Entrance requirements:* For master's, minimum GPA of 2.75; for doctorate, minimum GPA of 3.0. *Faculty research:* Cardiac electrophysiology, biomedical instrumentation, biomechanics, biomaterials, medical imagery.

Emory University, School of Medicine, The Wallace H. Coulter Department of Biomedical Engineering, Atlanta, GA 30322-1100. Offers PhD. Offered as joint program with Georgia Institute of Technology and Peking University (China).

Florida Agricultural and Mechanical University, Division of Graduate Studies, Research, and Continuing Education, FAMU-FSU College of Engineering, Department of Biomedical Engineering, Tallahassee, FL 32307-3200. Offers MS, PhD. *Faculty:* 16 full-time (1 woman). *Students:* 1 (woman) full-time; minority (African American). In 2009, 1 master's awarded. *Degree requirements:* For master's, thesis optional; for doctorate, thesis/dissertation, paper presentation at professional meeting. *Entrance requirements:* For master's, GRE General Test, minimum GPA of 3.3, letters of recommendation (3); for doctorate, minimum GPA of 3.3. Additional exam requirements/recommendations for international students: Required—TOEFL (minimum score 550 paper-based; 213 computer-based). *Application deadline:* For fall admission, 7/1 for domestic students, 3/1 for international students. Application fee: $20. *Faculty research:* Cellular signaling, cancer therapy, drug delivery, cellular and tissue engineering, brain physiology. *Unit head:* Dr. Michael H. Peters, Program Director, 850-410-6151. *Application contact:* Dr. Chanta M. Haywood, Dean of Graduate Studies, Research, and Continuing Education, 850-599-3315, Fax: 850-599-3727.

Florida International University, College of Engineering and Computing, Department of Biomedical Engineering, Miami, FL 33175. Offers MS, PhD. Part-time and evening/weekend programs available. *Faculty:* 7 full-time (1 woman). *Students:* 39 full-time (15 women), 8 part-time (4 women); includes 14 minority (2 African Americans, 4 Asian Americans or Pacific Islanders, 8 Hispanic Americans), 27 international. Average age 25. 82 applicants, 15% accepted, 12 enrolled. In 2009, 20 master's, 2 doctorates awarded. *Degree requirements:* For master's, thesis; for doctorate, comprehensive exam, thesis/dissertation. *Entrance requirements:* For master's, GRE General Test minimum 1000 verbal >=350 Quantitative >=650, minimum GPA of 3.0; for doctorate, GRE General Test minimum score 1150, 450 verbal, 700 quantitative), minimum GPA of 3.0, letter of intent, letters of recommendation. Additional exam requirements/recommendations for international students: Required—TOEFL (minimum score 550 paper-based; 80 iBT). *Application deadline:* For fall admission, 6/1 for domestic students, 4/1 for international students; for spring admission, 10/1 for domestic students, 9/1 for international students. Applications are processed on a rolling basis. Application fee: $30. Electronic applications accepted. *Expenses:* Tuition, state resident: full-time $8008; part-time $4004 per year. Tuition, nonresident: full-time $20,104; part-time $10,052 per year. Required fees: $298; $149 per term. *Financial support:* In 2009–10, 4 fellowships (averaging $25,000 per year), 9 research assistantships (averaging $20,474 per year), 14 teaching assistantships (averaging $20,474 per year) were awarded; institutionally sponsored loans, scholarships/grants, and unspecified assistantships also available. Financial award application deadline: 3/1; financial award applicants required to submit FAFSA. *Faculty research:* Bio-imaging and bio-signal processing, bio-instrumentation, devices and sensors, biomaterials and bio-nano technology, cellular and tissue engineering. *Unit head:* Dr. Anthony McGoron, Acting Chair, Biomedical Engineering Department, 305-348-1352, Fax: 305-348-6954, E-mail: anthony.mcgoron@fiu.edu. *Application contact:* Maria Parrilla, Graduate Admissions Assistant, 305-348-1890, Fax: 305-348-6140, E-mail: grad_eng@fiu.edu.

Florida State University, The Graduate School, FAMU-FSU College of Engineering, Department of Chemical and Biomedical Engineering, Tallahassee, FL 32310-6046. Offers biomedical engineering (MS, PhD); chemical engineering (MS, PhD). Part-time programs available. *Faculty:* 13 full-time (1 woman). *Students:* 29 full-time (15 women); includes 20 minority (4 African Americans, 15 Asian Americans or Pacific Islanders, 1 Hispanic American). Average age 25. 69 applicants, 14% accepted, 9 enrolled. In 2009, 2 master's awarded. *Degree requirements:* For master's, thesis (for some programs); for doctorate, comprehensive exam, thesis/dissertation, preliminary exam, qualifying exam. *Entrance requirements:* For master's, GRE General Test (minimum score 1200), BS in chemical engineering, minimum GPA of 3.0; for doctorate, GRE General Test (minimum score: 1200), BS in chemical engineering, minimum GPA of 3.0, or MS in chemical engineering or biomedical engineering. Additional exam requirements/recommendations for international students: Required—TOEFL (minimum score 550 paper-based; 213 computer-based). *Application deadline:* For fall admission, 7/1 priority date for domestic students, 7/1 for international students; for spring admission, 11/1 for domestic and international students. Applications are processed on a rolling basis. Application fee: $30. *Expenses:* Contact institution. *Financial support:* In 2009–10, 21 students received support, including 4 fellowships with full tuition reimbursements available (averaging $18,500 per year), 12 research assistantships with full tuition reimbursements available (averaging $18,500 per year), 10 teaching assistantships with full tuition reimbursements available (averaging $18,500 per year); scholarships/grants also available. Financial award application deadline: 3/1. *Faculty research:* Macromolecular transport, polymer processing, biochemical engineering, environmental engineering, transport and reaction, NMR-MRI, fuel cells. Total annual research expenditures: $734,000. *Unit head:* Dr. Bruce R. Locke, Chair and Professor, 850-410-6149, Fax: 850-410-6150, E-mail: locke@eng.fsu.edu. *Application contact:* Becky Culp, Office Administrator, 850-410-6151, Fax: 850-410-6150, E-mail: bculp@eng.fsu.edu.

Georgia Institute of Technology, Graduate Studies and Research, College of Engineering, The Wallace H. Coulter Department of Biomedical Engineering at Georgia Tech and Emory University, Atlanta, GA 30332-0001. Offers bioengineering (PhD); bioinformatics (PhD); biomedical engineering (PhD); MD/PhD. PhD in biomedical engineering program jointly offered with Emory University (Georgia) and Peking University (China). Terminal master's awarded for partial completion of doctoral program. *Degree requirements:* For doctorate, thesis/dissertation. *Entrance requirements:* Additional exam requirements/recommendations for international students: Required—TOEFL. *Faculty research:* Biomechanics and tissue engineering, bioinstrumentation and medical imaging.

Graduate School and University Center of the City University of New York, Graduate Studies, Program in Engineering, New York, NY 10016-4039. Offers biomedical engineering (PhD); chemical engineering (PhD); civil engineering (PhD); electrical engineering (PhD); mechanical engineering (PhD). *Faculty:* 68 full-time (1 woman). *Students:* 115 full-time (33 women), 8 part-time (2 women); includes 17 minority (5 African Americans, 8 Asian Americans or Pacific Islanders, 4 Hispanic Americans), 68 international. Average age 34. 119 applicants, 48% accepted, 26 enrolled. In 2009, 30 doctorates awarded. *Degree requirements:* For doctorate, thesis/dissertation. *Entrance requirements:* For doctorate, GRE General Test. Additional exam requirements/recommendations for international students: Required—TOEFL. Application fee: $125. Electronic applications accepted. *Financial support:* In 2009–10, 61 fellowships, 10 teaching assistantships were awarded; research assistantships, Federal Work-Study, institutionally sponsored loans, and tuition waivers (full and partial) also available. Financial award application deadline: 2/1; financial award applicants required to submit FAFSA. *Unit head:* Dr. Mumtaz Kassir, Executive Officer, 212-650-8031, Fax: 212-650-8029, E-mail: kassir@ce-mail.engr.ccny.cuny.edu. *Application contact:* Les Gribben, Director of Admissions, 212-817-7470, Fax: 212-817-1624, E-mail: lgribben@gc.cuny.edu.

See Close-Up on page 69.

Harvard University, Graduate School of Arts and Sciences, Department of Physics, Cambridge, MA 02138. Offers experimental physics (PhD); medical engineering/medical physics (PhD), including applied physics, engineering sciences, physics; theoretical physics (PhD). *Degree requirements:* For doctorate, thesis/dissertation, final exams, laboratory experience. *Entrance requirements:* For doctorate, GRE General Test, GRE Subject Test. Additional exam requirements/recommendations for international students: Required—TOEFL. *Expenses:* Tuition: Full-time $33,696. Required fees: $1126. Full-time tuition and fees vary according to program. *Faculty research:* Particle physics, condensed matter physics, atomic physics.

Harvard University, Harvard Medical School and Graduate School of Arts and Sciences, Division of Health Sciences and Technology, Program in Biomedical Engineering, Cambridge, MA 02138. Offers M Eng. *Students:* 3 applicants, 0% accepted, 0 enrolled. In 2009, 1 master's awarded. *Degree requirements:* For master's, thesis. *Entrance requirements:* For master's, candidate must be current MIT undergraduate. *Application deadline:* For spring admission, 5/31 for domestic and international students. Application fee: $70. *Expenses:* Contact institution. *Financial support:* Health care benefits and unspecified assistantships available. Financial award application deadline: 12/15; financial award applicants required to submit FAFSA. *Unit head:* Dr. Roger G. Mark, Director, 617-495-1000. *Application contact:* Andrea Santp, Admissions Coordinator, 617-258-7084, E-mail: asanto@mit.edu.

Harvard University, Harvard Medical School and Graduate School of Arts and Sciences, Division of Health Sciences and Technology and Department of Physics and School of Engineering and Applied Sciences, Program in Medical Engineering/Medical Physics, Cambridge, MA 02138. Offers medical engineering (PhD); medical engineering/medical physics (Sc D); medical physics (PhD). *Students:* 118 full-time (38 women); includes 31 minority (5 African Americans, 21 Asian Americans or Pacific Islanders, 5 Hispanic Americans), 35 international. Average age 26. 240 applicants, 11% accepted, 21 enrolled. In 2009, 17 doctorates awarded. *Degree requirements:* For doctorate, comprehensive exam, thesis/dissertation, oral and written qualifying exams. *Entrance requirements:* For doctorate, GRE, bachelor's degree in engineering or science. Additional exam requirements/recommendations for international students: Required—TOEFL; Recommended—IELTS. *Application deadline:* For fall admission, 12/15 for domestic and international students. Application fee: $70. *Expenses:* Contact institution. *Financial support:* In 2009–10, 96 students received support, including 61 fellowships with full and partial tuition reimbursements available (averaging $48,526 per year), 47 research assistantships with full and partial tuition reimbursements available (averaging $42,576 per year), 9 teaching assistantships with full and partial tuition reimbursements available (averaging $15,463 per year); career-related internships or fieldwork, institutionally sponsored loans, traineeships, health care benefits, and unspecified assistantships also available. Financial award application deadline: 12/15; financial award applicants required to submit FAFSA. *Faculty research:* Regenerative biomedical technologies, biomedical imaging and optics, biophysics, systems physiology, bioinstrumentation, biomedical informatics/integrative genomics. *Unit head:* Dr. Ram Sasisekharan, Director, 617-258-7282. *Application contact:* Laurie Ward, Graduate Administrator, 617-253-3609, Fax: 617-253-6692, E-mail: laurie@mit.edu.

Illinois Institute of Technology, Graduate College, Armour College of Engineering, Department of Biomedical Engineering, Chicago, IL 60616-3793. Offers PhD. Part-time programs available. *Degree requirements:* For doctorate, comprehensive exam, thesis/dissertation. *Entrance requirements:* For doctorate, GRE General Test. Additional exam requirements/recommendations for international students: Required—TOEFL (minimum score 550 paper-based; 213 computer-based; 80 iBT). Electronic applications accepted. *Expenses:* Tuition: Full-time $17,550; part-time $888 per credit hour. Required fees: $850; $7.50 per credit hour. One-time fee: $50 full-time. Full-time tuition and fees vary according to program. *Faculty research:* Medical imaging, cell and tissue engineering, neural engineering, diabetes research.

Indiana University–Purdue University Indianapolis, School of Engineering and Technology, Department of Electrical Engineering, Indianapolis, IN 46202-2896. Offers biomedical engineering (MS, PhD); electrical and computer engineering (MS, MSECE, PhD), including biomedical engineering (MSECE), control and automation (MSECE), signal processing (MSECE); engineering (interdisciplinary) (MSE). *Students:* 41 full-time (10 women), 27 part-time (2 women); includes 11 minority (5 African Americans, 4 Asian Americans or Pacific Islanders, 2 Hispanic Americans), 38 international. Average age 27. 178 applicants, 56% accepted, 54 enrolled. In 2009, 28 master's awarded. Application fee: $55 ($65 for international students). *Unit head:* Yaobin Chen, Unit Head, 317-274-4032, Fax: 317-274-4493. *Application contact:* Valerie Diemer, Graduate Program, 317-278-4960, Fax: 317-278-1671, E-mail: grad@engr.iupui.edu.

Indiana University–Purdue University Indianapolis, School of Engineering and Technology, Department of Mechanical Engineering, Indianapolis, IN 46202-2896. Offers biomedical engineering (MS Bm E); computer-aided mechanical engineering (Certificate); mechanical engineering (MSME, PhD). Part-time programs available. *Students:* 11 full-time (0 women), 43 part-time (13 women); includes 5 minority (1 African American, 2 Asian Americans or Pacific Islanders, 2 Hispanic Americans), 29 international. Average age 27. 6 applicants, 0% accepted, 0 enrolled. In 2009, 13 master's awarded. *Degree requirements:* For master's, thesis optional. *Entrance requirements:* For master's, GRE. Additional exam requirements/recommendations for international students: Required—TOEFL. *Application deadline:* For fall admission, 7/1 for domestic students. Application fee: $55 ($65 for international students). *Financial support:* Fellowships with tuition reimbursements, research assistantships with full and partial tuition

Biomedical Engineering

Indiana University–Purdue University Indianapolis (continued)
reimbursements, tuition waivers (full and partial) available. Financial award application deadline: 3/1. *Faculty research:* Computational fluid dynamics, heat transfer, finite-element methods, composites, biomechanics. *Unit head:* Dr. Hasan Akay, Chairman, 317-274-9717, Fax: 317-274-9744. *Application contact:* Valerie Diemer, Graduate Program, 317-278-4960, Fax: 317-278-1671, E-mail: grad@engr.iupui.edu.

The Johns Hopkins University, Engineering for Professionals, Part-time Program in Applied Biomedical Engineering, Baltimore, MD 21218-2699. Offers MS, Post-Master's Certificate. Part-time and evening/weekend programs available. *Faculty:* 6 part-time/adjunct (0 women). *Students:* 4 full-time (2 women), 37 part-time (12 women); includes 10 minority (2 African Americans, 1 American Indian/Alaska Native, 5 Asian Americans or Pacific Islanders, 2 Hispanic Americans), 4 international. Average age 31. In 2009, 9 master's awarded. *Application deadline:* Applications are processed on a rolling basis. Application fee: $75. Electronic applications accepted. *Financial support:* Institutionally sponsored loans available. *Unit head:* Dr. Russell McCally, Program Chair, 443-778-6201, E-mail: russell.mccally@jhuapl.edu. *Application contact:* Priyanka Dwivedi, Admissions Manager, 410-516-2300, Fax: 410-579-8049, E-mail: pdwived1@jhu.edu.

The Johns Hopkins University, G. W. C. Whiting School of Engineering and School of Medicine, Department of Biomedical Engineering, Baltimore, MD 21205. Offers bioengineering innovation and design (MSE); biomedical engineering (MSE, PhD). *Faculty:* 45 full-time (7 women). *Students:* 224 full-time (79 women); includes 62 minority (5 African Americans, 48 Asian Americans or Pacific Islanders, 9 Hispanic Americans), 97 international. Average age 24. 569 applicants, 20% accepted, 51 enrolled. In 2009, 15 master's, 17 doctorates awarded. Terminal master's awarded for partial completion of doctoral program. *Degree requirements:* For master's, thesis; for doctorate, comprehensive exam, thesis/dissertation, oral exam. *Entrance requirements:* For master's and doctorate, GRE General Test. Additional exam requirements/recommendations for international students: Required—TOEFL or IELTS. *Application deadline:* For fall admission, 1/15 for domestic and international students. Application fee: $75. Electronic applications accepted. *Financial support:* In 2009–10, 208 students received support, including 206 research assistantships with full tuition reimbursements available (averaging $24,553 per year); fellowships with partial tuition reimbursements available, teaching assistantships with full and partial tuition reimbursements available, Federal Work-Study, institutionally sponsored loans, scholarships/grants, tuition waivers (full), and unspecified assistantships also available. Support available to part-time students. *Faculty research:* Cell and tissue engineering, systems neuroscience, imaging, cardiovascular systems physiology, theoretical and computational biology. Total annual research expenditures: $12 million. *Unit head:* Dr. Elliot R. McVeigh, Director, 410-516-5282, Fax: 410-516-4771. *Application contact:* Samuel Bourne, Academic Master's Program Coordinator, 410-516-8482, Fax: 410-516-4771, E-mail: sbourne@jhu.edu.

Louisiana Tech University, Graduate School, College of Engineering and Science, Department of Biomedical Engineering, Ruston, LA 71272. Offers MS, PhD. Part-time programs available. Terminal master's awarded for partial completion of doctoral program. *Degree requirements:* For master's, thesis; for doctorate, thesis/dissertation. *Entrance requirements:* For master's, GRE General Test, minimum GPA of 3.0 in last 60 hours; for doctorate, minimum graduate GPA of 3.25 (MS) or GRE General Test. Additional exam requirements/recommendations for international students: Required—TOEFL. *Faculty research:* Microbiosensors and microcirculatory transport, speech recognition, artificial intelligence, rehabilitation engineering, bioelectromagnetics.

Marquette University, Graduate School, College of Engineering, Department of Biomedical Engineering, Milwaukee, WI 53201-1881. Offers bioinstrumentation/computers (MS, PhD); biomechanics/biomaterials (MS, PhD); functional imaging (PhD); healthcare technologies management (MS); systems physiology (MS, PhD). Part-time and evening/weekend programs available. *Faculty:* 16 full-time (6 women), 3 part-time/adjunct (2 women). *Students:* 64 full-time (21 women), 22 part-time (8 women); includes 6 minority (5 Asian Americans or Pacific Islanders, 1 Hispanic American), 33 international. Average age 27. 132 applicants, 45% accepted, 22 enrolled. In 2009, 19 master's, 3 doctorates awarded. Terminal master's awarded for partial completion of doctoral program. *Degree requirements:* For master's, comprehensive exam, thesis; for doctorate, comprehensive exam, thesis/dissertation, dissertation defense, qualifying exam. *Entrance requirements:* For master's and doctorate, GRE General Test, minimum GPA of 3.0. Additional exam requirements/recommendations for international students: Required—TOEFL. *Application deadline:* For fall admission, 2/15 priority date for domestic students; for spring admission, 11/15 priority date for domestic students. Applications are processed on a rolling basis. Application fee: $40. Electronic applications accepted. *Financial support:* In 2009–10, 50 students received support, including 9 fellowships with full tuition reimbursements available (averaging $24,600 per year), 34 research assistantships with full tuition reimbursements available (averaging $14,500 per year), 7 teaching assistantships with full tuition reimbursements available (averaging $12,306 per year); Federal Work-Study, institutionally sponsored loans, and scholarships/grants also available. Support available to part-time students. Financial award application deadline: 2/15. *Faculty research:* Cell and organ physiology, signal processing, gait analysis, orthopedic rehabilitation engineering, telemedicine. *Unit head:* Dr. Kristina Ropella, Chair, 414-288-3375, Fax: 414-288-7938, E-mail: kristina.ropella@marquette.edu. *Application contact:* Dr. Dean Jeutter, Assistant Chair, 414-288-3375, Fax: 414-288-7938, E-mail: dean.jeutter@marquette.edu.

Massachusetts Institute of Technology, Harvard-MIT Division of Health Sciences and Technology, Medical Engineering/Medical Physics Program, Cambridge, MA 02139-4307. Offers medical engineering (PhD); medical engineering and medical physics (Sc D); medical physics (PhD). *Students:* 118 full-time (38 women); includes 33 minority (5 African Americans, 1 American Indian/Alaska Native, 21 Asian Americans or Pacific Islanders, 6 Hispanic Americans), 35 international. Average age 26. 240 applicants, 11% accepted, 21 enrolled. In 2009, 17 doctorates awarded. *Degree requirements:* For doctorate, comprehensive exam, thesis/dissertation, oral and written departmental qualifying exams. *Entrance requirements:* For doctorate, GRE, bachelor's degree in engineering or science. Additional exam requirements/recommendations for international students: Required—TOEFL; Recommended—IELTS. *Application deadline:* For fall admission, 12/15 for domestic and international students. Application fee: $70. Electronic applications accepted. *Expenses:* Contact institution. *Financial support:* In 2009–10, 96 students received support, including 61 fellowships with full and partial tuition reimbursements available (averaging $48,526 per year), 47 research assistantships with full and partial tuition reimbursements available (averaging $42,576 per year), 9 teaching assistantships with full and partial tuition reimbursements available (averaging $15,463 per year); career-related internships or fieldwork, institutionally sponsored loans, traineeships, health care benefits, and unspecified assistantships also available. Financial award application deadline: 12/15. *Faculty research:* Regenerative biomedical technologies, biomedical imaging and optics, biophysics, systems physiology, bioinstrumentation, biomedical informatics/integrative genomics. *Unit head:* Dr. Ram Sasisekharan, Director, E-mail: mgray@mit.edu. *Application contact:* Laurie Ward, Graduate Administrator, 617-253-3609, Fax: 617-253-6692, E-mail: laurie@mit.edu.

Massachusetts Institute of Technology, Harvard-MIT Division of Health Sciences and Technology, Program in Biomedical Engineering, Cambridge, MA 02139-4307. Offers M Eng. *Students:* 3 applicants, 0% accepted, 0 enrolled. In 2009, 1 master's awarded. *Degree requirements:* For master's, thesis. *Entrance requirements:* For master's, current status as MIT student. *Application deadline:* For spring admission, 5/31 for domestic and international students. Application fee: $70. *Expenses:* Contact institution. *Financial support:* Health care benefits and unspecified assistantships available. Financial award application deadline: 12/15. *Unit head:* Dr. Roger G. Mark, Director, 617-253-7818. *Application contact:* Andrea Santo, Admissions Coordinator, 617-258-7084, Fax: 617-253-6692, E-mail: asanto@mit.edu.

Massachusetts Institute of Technology, School of Engineering, Department of Biological Engineering, Cambridge, MA 02139-4307. Offers applied biosciences (PhD, Sc D); bioengineering (PhD, Sc D); biological engineering (PhD, Sc D); biomedical engineering (M Eng); toxicology (SM); SM/MBA. *Faculty:* 18 full-time (2 women). *Students:* 105 full-time (51 women); includes 24 minority (3 African Americans, 16 Asian Americans or Pacific Islanders, 5 Hispanic Americans), 29 international. Average age 26. 371 applicants, 9% accepted, 22 enrolled. In 2009, 5 master's, 20 doctorates awarded. Terminal master's awarded for partial completion of doctoral program. *Degree requirements:* For master's, thesis; for doctorate, comprehensive exam, thesis/dissertation. *Entrance requirements:* For master's and doctorate, GRE General Test. Additional exam requirements/recommendations for international students: Required—TOEFL (minimum score 600 paper-based; 250 computer-based), IELTS (minimum score 7). *Application deadline:* For fall admission, 12/31 for domestic and international students. Application fee: $75. Electronic applications accepted. *Financial support:* In 2009–10, 105 students received support, including 51 fellowships with tuition reimbursements available (averaging $35,187 per year), 49 research assistantships with tuition reimbursements available (averaging $31,622 per year); teaching assistantships with tuition reimbursements available, Federal Work-Study, institutionally sponsored loans, scholarships/grants, traineeships, health care benefits, and unspecified assistantships also available. *Faculty research:* Bioinformatics, computational, systems, and synthetic biology, biological materials, cancer initiation, progression, and therapeutics, genomics, proteomics, glycomics, imaging, transport phenomena, biomolecular and cell engineering, nanoscale engineering of biological systems, neurobiological systems. Total annual research expenditures: $35.2 million. *Unit head:* Prof. Douglas A. Lauffenburger, Department Head, 617-253-1712, E-mail: be-acad@mit.edu. *Application contact:* Biological Engineering Academic Office, 617-253-1712, Fax: 617-258-8676, E-mail: be-acad@mit.edu.

See Close-Up on page 119.

Mayo Graduate School, Graduate Programs in Biomedical Sciences, Program in Biomedical Engineering, Rochester, MN 55905. Offers PhD. *Degree requirements:* For doctorate, oral defense of dissertation, qualifying oral and written exam. *Entrance requirements:* For doctorate, GRE, 1 year of chemistry, biology, calculus, and physics. Additional exam requirements/recommendations for international students: Required—TOEFL. Electronic applications accepted.

McGill University, Faculty of Graduate and Postdoctoral Studies, Faculty of Medicine, Department of Biomedical Engineering, Montréal, QC H3A 2T5, Canada. Offers M Eng, PhD.

Mercer University, Graduate Studies, Macon Campus, School of Engineering, Macon, GA 31207-0003. Offers biomedical engineering (MSE); computer engineering (MSE); electrical engineering (MSE); engineering management (MSE); environmental engineering (MSE); environmental systems (MS); mechanical engineering (MSE); software engineering (MSE); software systems (MS); technical communications management (MS); technical management (MS). Part-time and evening/weekend programs available. Postbaccalaureate distance learning degree programs offered (no on-campus study). *Faculty:* 19 full-time (4 women), 1 part-time/adjunct (0 women). *Students:* 6 full-time (1 woman), 95 part-time (22 women); includes 22 minority (5 African Americans, 13 Asian Americans or Pacific Islanders, 4 Hispanic Americans), 3 international. Average age 33. In 2009, 42 master's awarded. *Degree requirements:* For master's, thesis or alternative. *Entrance requirements:* For master's, minimum undergraduate GPA of 3.0. Additional exam requirements/recommendations for international students: Required—TOEFL. *Application deadline:* For fall admission, 7/1 for domestic students; for spring admission, 11/15 for domestic students. Applications are processed on a rolling basis. Application fee: $35 ($50 for international students). Electronic applications accepted. *Expenses:* Contact institution. *Financial support:* Federal Work-Study available. *Unit head:* Dr. Wade H. Shaw, Dean, 478-301-2459, Fax: 478-301-5593, E-mail: shaw_wh@mercer.edu. *Application contact:* Greg Lofton, Graduate Program Coordinator, 478-301-5480, Fax: 478-301-5434, E-mail: lofton_g@mercer.edu.

Michigan Technological University, Graduate School, College of Engineering, Department of Biomedical Engineering, Houghton, MI 49931. Offers PhD. Part-time programs available. *Degree requirements:* For doctorate, comprehensive exam, thesis/dissertation. *Entrance requirements:* For doctorate, GRE. Additional exam requirements/recommendations for international students: Required—TOEFL (minimum score 550 paper-based; 213 computer-based). Electronic applications accepted. *Expenses:* Contact institution. *Faculty research:* Biomaterials/tissue engineering; physiology measurement; biomechanics; mechanotransduction; bone metabolism.

Mississippi State University, College of Agriculture and Life Sciences, Department of Agricultural and Biological Engineering, Mississippi State, MS 39762. Offers biological engineering (MS); biomedical engineering (MS, PhD); engineering (PhD), including biological engineering. *Faculty:* 8 full-time (1 woman). *Students:* 22 full-time (6 women), 9 part-time (5 women); includes 7 minority (4 African Americans, 3 Asian Americans or Pacific Islanders), 7 international. Average age 27. 20 applicants, 50% accepted, 7 enrolled. In 2009, 4 master's, 2 doctorates awarded. *Degree requirements:* For master's, thesis; for doctorate, thesis/dissertation, preliminary exam. *Entrance requirements:* For master's, GRE General Test, minimum undergraduate GPA of 2.75 (3.0 for biomedical engineering); for doctorate, GRE General Test, minimum GPA of 3.0 (biomedical engineering). Additional exam requirements/recommendations for international students: Required—TOEFL (minimum score 550 paper-based; 213 computer-based; 79 iBT); Recommended—IELTS (minimum score 6.5). *Application deadline:* For fall admission, 7/1 for domestic students, 5/1 for international students; for spring admission, 11/1 for domestic students, 9/1 for international students. Applications are processed on a rolling basis. Application fee: $40. Electronic applications accepted. *Expenses:* Tuition, state resident: full-time $2575.50; part-time $286.25 per credit hour. Tuition, nonresident: full-time $6510; part-time $723.50 per credit hour. Tuition and fees vary according to course load. *Financial support:* In 2009–10, 19 research assistantships with partial tuition reimbursements (averaging $12,530 per year) were awarded; Federal Work-Study, institutionally sponsored loans, and unspecified assistantships also available. Financial award applicants required to submit FAFSA. *Faculty research:* Bioenvironmental engineering, bioinstrumentation, biomechanics/biomaterials, precision agriculture, tissue engineering, ergonomics human factors, biosimulation and modeling. Total annual research expenditures: $1.6 million. *Unit head:* Dr. William D. Batchelor, Department Head and Professor, 662-325-3280, Fax: 662-325-3853, E-mail: batchelor@abe.msstate.edu. *Application contact:* Dr. Jeremiah Davis, Assistant Professor and Graduate Coordinator, 662-325-3282, Fax: 662-325-3853, E-mail: jdavis@abe.msstate.edu.

New Jersey Institute of Technology, Office of Graduate Studies, Newark College of Engineering, Department of Biomedical Engineering, Newark, NJ 07102. Offers MS, PhD. Part-time and evening/weekend programs available. Terminal master's awarded for partial completion of doctoral program. *Degree requirements:* For master's, thesis optional; for doctorate, thesis/dissertation. *Entrance requirements:* For master's and doctorate, GRE General Test. Additional exam requirements/recommendations for international students: Required—TOEFL (minimum score 550 paper-based; 213 computer-based; 79 iBT). Electronic applications accepted.

North Carolina State University, Graduate School, College of Engineering, Joint Department of Biomedical Engineering UNC-Chapel Hill and NC State, Raleigh, NC 27695. Offers MS, PhD. Programs offered jointly with the University of North Carolina at Chapel Hill. Terminal master's awarded for partial completion of doctoral program. *Degree requirements:* For master's, comprehensive exam, thesis, research laboratory experience; for doctorate, one foreign language, comprehensive exam, thesis/dissertation, written and oral examinations, dissertation defense, teaching experience, research laboratory experience. *Entrance requirements:* For master's and doctorate, GRE General Test. Additional exam requirements/recommendations for international students: Required—TOEFL. Electronic applications accepted.

Northwestern University, McCormick School of Engineering and Applied Science, Department of Biomedical Engineering, Evanston, IL 60208. Offers MS, PhD. Admissions and degrees offered through The Graduate School. Part-time programs available. Terminal master's awarded for partial completion of doctoral program. *Degree requirements:* For master's, thesis or alternative; for doctorate, thesis/dissertation. *Faculty research:* Biomechanics and transport, rehabilitation engineering, neuroscience, biomaterials, cellular engineering.

OGI School of Science & Engineering at Oregon Health & Science University, Graduate Studies, Department of Biomedical Engineering, Beaverton, OR 97006-8921. Offers MS, PhD. *Degree requirements:* For doctorate, comprehensive exam, thesis/dissertation. *Entrance requirements:* For master's and doctorate, GRE General Test, minimum GPA of 3.5, 3 letters of recommendation. Additional exam requirements/recommendations for international students: Required—TOEFL (minimum score 620 paper-based; 250 computer-based). Electronic applications accepted. *Expenses:* Contact institution. *Faculty research:* Biomedical optics, genetic engineering, neuroengineering, tissue engineering and biomaterials.

The Ohio State University, Graduate School, College of Engineering, Program in Biomedical Engineering, Columbus, OH 43210. Offers MS, PhD. Evening/weekend programs available. *Faculty:* 86. *Students:* 28 full-time (11 women), 19 part-time (4 women); includes 9 minority (2 African Americans, 5 Asian Americans or Pacific Islanders, 2 Hispanic Americans), 16 international. Average age 27. In 2009, 9 master's, 8 doctorates awarded. *Degree requirements:* For master's, thesis optional; for doctorate, thesis/dissertation. *Entrance requirements:* For master's and doctorate, GRE General Test. Additional exam requirements/recommendations for international students: Recommended—TOEFL (minimum score 600 paper-based; 250 computer-based). *Application deadline:* For fall admission, 8/15 priority date for domestic students, 7/1 priority date for international students; for winter admission, 12/1 priority date for domestic students, 11/1 priority date for international students; for spring admission, 3/1 priority date for domestic students, 2/1 priority date for international students. Applications are processed on a rolling basis. Application fee: $40 ($50 for international students). Electronic applications accepted. *Expenses:* Tuition, state resident: full-time $10,683. Tuition, nonresident: full-time $25,923. Tuition and fees vary according to course load and program. *Financial support:* Fellowships, research assistantships, career-related internships or fieldwork, Federal Work-Study, and institutionally sponsored loans available. Support available to part-time students. *Unit head:* Alan S. Litsky, Graduate Studies Committee Chair, 614-292-1285, Fax: 614-292-7301, E-mail: litsky.1@osu.edu. *Application contact:* 614-292-9444, Fax: 614-292-3895, E-mail: domestic.grad@osu.edu.

Ohio University, Graduate College, Russ College of Engineering and Technology, Department of Chemical and Biomolecular Engineering, Program in Biomedical Engineering, Athens, OH 45701-2979. Offers MS. Part-time programs available. *Faculty:* 21 full-time (5 women). *Students:* 3 full-time (1 woman); includes 1 minority (Asian American or Pacific Islander). Average age 27. 9 applicants, 44% accepted, 3 enrolled. *Degree requirements:* For master's, thesis. *Entrance requirements:* For master's, GRE General Test. Additional exam requirements/recommendations for international students: Required—TOEFL (minimum score 590 paper-based; 243 computer-based; 96 iBT), IELTS (minimum score 7). *Application deadline:* For fall admission, 2/1 priority date for domestic and international students. Applications are processed on a rolling basis. Application fee: $50 ($55 for international students). Electronic applications accepted. *Expenses:* Tuition, state resident: full-time $7839; part-time $323 per quarter hour. Tuition, nonresident: full-time $15,831; part-time $654 per quarter hour. Required fees: $2931. *Financial support:* In 2009–10, 1 fellowship with full tuition reimbursement (averaging $18,000 per year), 2 research assistantships with full tuition reimbursements (averaging $18,000 per year) were awarded; institutionally sponsored loans also available. Financial award application deadline: 2/1. *Faculty research:* Molecular mechanisms of human disease, molecular therapeutics, biomedical information analysis and management, image analysis, biomechanics. Total annual research expenditures: $1.5 million. *Unit head:* Dr. Douglas J. Goetz, Director, 740-593-1000. *Application contact:* Tom Riggs, Assistant, 740-597-2797, Fax: 740-593-0873, E-mail: biomed@ohio.edu.

Ohio University, Graduate College, Russ College of Engineering and Technology, Department of Mechanical Engineering, Athens, OH 45701-2979. Offers biomedical engineering (MS); mechanical engineering (MS, PhD), including CAD/CAM (MS), design (MS), energy (MS), manufacturing (MS), materials (MS), robotics (MS), thermofluids (MS). Part-time programs available. *Faculty:* 12 full-time (1 woman). *Students:* 24 full-time (2 women), 4 part-time (0 women); includes 1 minority (Hispanic American), 9 international. 34 applicants, 47% accepted, 8 enrolled. In 2009, 7 master's awarded. *Degree requirements:* For master's, comprehensive exam (for some programs), thesis; for doctorate, comprehensive exam, thesis/dissertation. *Entrance requirements:* For master's, GRE, BS in engineering or science, minimum GPA of 2.8; for doctorate, GRE. Additional exam requirements/recommendations for international students: Required—TOEFL (minimum score 550 paper-based; 80 iBT) or IELTS Academic (minimum score 6.5). *Application deadline:* For fall admission, 2/15 priority date for domestic and international students. Applications are processed on a rolling basis. Application fee: $50 ($55 for international students). Electronic applications accepted. *Expenses:* Tuition, state resident: full-time $7839; part-time $323 per quarter hour. Tuition, nonresident: full-time $15,831; part-time $654 per quarter hour. Required fees: $2931. *Financial support:* In 2009–10, research assistantships with tuition reimbursements (averaging $14,000 per year), teaching assistantships with tuition reimbursements (averaging $14,000 per year) were awarded; career-related internships or fieldwork, Federal Work-Study, institutionally sponsored loans, tuition waivers (full and partial), and unspecified assistantships also available. Financial award application deadline: 2/15; financial award applicants required to submit FAFSA. *Faculty research:* Biomedical, energy and the environment, materials and manufacturing, bioengineering. *Unit head:* Dr. Greg Kremer, Chairman, 740-593-1561, Fax: 740-593-0476, E-mail: kremer@bobcat.ent.ohiou.edu. *Application contact:* Dr. Frank F. Kraft, Graduate Chairman, 740-597-1478, Fax: 740-593-0476, E-mail: kraft@ohio.edu.

Oregon Health & Science University, OGI School of Science and Engineering, Department of Biomedical Engineering, Portland, OR 97239-3098. Offers MS, PhD. Tuition and fees vary according to course level, course load, degree level, program and reciprocity agreements.

Penn State University Park, Graduate School, Intercollege Graduate Programs, State College, University Park, PA 16802-1503. Offers acoustics (M Eng, MS, PhD); bioengineering (MS, PhD); biogeochemistry (dual) (PhD); business administration (MBA); cell and developmental biology (PhD); demography (dual) (MA); ecology (MS, PhD); environmental pollution control (MEPC, MS); genetics (MS, PhD); human dimensions of natural resources and the environment (dual) (MA, MS, PhD); immunology and infectious diseases (MS); integrative biosciences (MS, PhD), including integrative biosciences; materials science and engineering (PhD); operations research (dual) (M Eng, MA, MS, PhD); physiology (MS, PhD); plant physiology (MS, PhD); quality and manufacturing management (MMM). *Students:* 371 full-time (157 women), 22 part-time (7 women). Average age 27. 1,074 applicants, 18% accepted, 130 enrolled. *Entrance requirements:* Additional exam requirements/recommendations for international students: Required—TOEFL (minimum score 550 paper-based; 213 computer-based; 80 iBT). *Application deadline:* Applications are processed on a rolling basis. Application fee: $45. Electronic applications accepted. *Financial support:* Fellowships, research assistantships, teaching assistantships available. Financial award applicants required to submit FAFSA. *Unit head:* Dr. Regina Vasilatos-Younken, Senior Associate Dean, 814-865-2516, Fax: 814-863-4627, E-mail: rxv@psu.edu. *Application contact:* Cynthia E. Nicosia, Director, Graduate Enrollment Services, 814-865-1795, Fax: 814-865-4627, E-mail: cey1@psu.edu.

Polytechnic Institute of NYU, Department of Chemical and Biological Sciences, Major in Biomedical Engineering, Brooklyn, NY 11201-2990. Offers MS, PhD. *Students:* 48 full-time (18 women), 28 part-time (10 women); includes 14 minority (5 African Americans, 9 Asian Americans or Pacific Islanders), 42 international. 124 applicants, 58% accepted, 29 enrolled. In 2009, 29 master's, 1 doctorate awarded. *Degree requirements:* For master's, comprehensive exam (for some programs), thesis (for some programs); for doctorate, comprehensive exam, thesis/dissertation. *Entrance requirements:* Additional exam requirements/recommendations for international students: Required—TOEFL (minimum score 550 paper-based; 213 computer-based; 80 iBT); Recommended—IELTS (minimum score 6.5). *Application deadline:* For fall admission, 7/31 priority date for domestic students, 4/30 priority date for international students; for spring admission, 12/31 priority date for domestic students, 10/30 priority date for international students. Applications are processed on a rolling basis. Application fee: $75. Electronic applications accepted. *Expenses:* Tuition: Full-time $21,492; part-time $1194 per credit hour. Required

fees: $1160; $204 per course. *Unit head:* Dr. Bruce Garetz, Department Head, 718-260-3600. *Application contact:* JeanCarlo Bonilla, Director of Graduate Enrollment Management, 718-260-3182, Fax: 718-260-3624, E-mail: gradinfo@poly.edu.

Purdue University, College of Engineering, Weldon School of Biomedical Engineering, West Lafayette, IN 47907-2032. Offers MSBME, PhD, MD/PhD. Degree programs offered jointly with School of Mechanical Engineering, School of Electrical and Computer Engineering, and School of Chemical Engineering. *Entrance requirements:* For master's and doctorate, GRE General Test, minimum GPA of 3.25. Additional exam requirements/recommendations for international students: Required—TOEFL (minimum score 550 paper-based; 213 computer-based; 77 iBT); Recommended—TWE. Electronic applications accepted. *Faculty research:* Biomaterials, biomechanics, medical image and signal processing, medical instrumentation, tissue engineering.

Rensselaer Polytechnic Institute, Graduate School, School of Engineering, Department of Biomedical Engineering, Troy, NY 12180-3590. Offers MS, PhD. *Faculty:* 7 full-time (1 woman). *Students:* 28 full-time (12 women), 2 part-time (1 woman); includes 4 minority (all Asian Americans or Pacific Islanders). Average age 23. 94 applicants, 22% accepted, 12 enrolled. In 2009, 12 master's, 2 doctorates awarded. Terminal master's awarded for partial completion of doctoral program. *Degree requirements:* For master's, thesis optional; for doctorate, thesis/dissertation. *Entrance requirements:* For master's and doctorate, GRE, minimum GPA of 3.0. Additional exam requirements/recommendations for international students: Required—TOEFL (minimum score 620 paper-based; 260 computer-based; 106 iBT). *Application deadline:* For fall admission, 1/1 priority date for domestic students. Applications are processed on a rolling basis. Application fee: $75. Electronic applications accepted. *Expenses:* Tuition: Full-time $38,100. *Financial support:* In 2009–10, 20 students received support, including 2 fellowships with full tuition reimbursements available (averaging $22,000 per year), 12 research assistantships with full tuition reimbursements available (averaging $16,500 per year), 6 teaching assistantships with full tuition reimbursements available (averaging $16,500 per year); career-related internships or fieldwork and institutionally sponsored loans also available. Financial award application deadline: 2/1. *Faculty research:* Computational biomechanics, cellular and tissue bioengineering, biofluids and cellular bioengineering, functional tissue engineering, orthopedic biomechanics. *Unit head:* Dr. Stanley Dunn, Graduate Program Director, 518-276-8433, Fax: 518-276-2256, E-mail: dunns6@rpi.edu. *Application contact:* Ronnie Rowe, Senior Services Administrator, 518-276-2347, Fax: 518-276-2256, E-mail: rower@rpi.edu.

Rice University, Graduate Programs, George R. Brown School of Engineering, Department of Chemical and Biomolecular Engineering, Houston, TX 77251-1892. Offers chemical and biomolecular engineering (MS, PhD); chemical engineering (M Ch E). Part-time programs available. *Faculty:* 12 full-time (2 women). *Students:* 69 full-time (19 women), 1 part-time (0 women); includes 5 minority (2 Asian Americans or Pacific Islanders, 3 Hispanic Americans), 49 international. Average age 24. 175 applicants, 23% accepted, 17 enrolled. In 2009, 2 master's, 9 doctorates awarded. *Degree requirements:* For master's, thesis (for some programs); for doctorate, thesis/dissertation. *Entrance requirements:* For master's and doctorate, GRE General Test, minimum GPA of 3.0. Additional exam requirements/recommendations for international students: Required—TOEFL (minimum score 600 paper-based; 250 computer-based; 90 iBT). *Application deadline:* For fall admission, 1/15 for domestic and international students. Application fee: $35. Electronic applications accepted. *Financial support:* In 2009–10, fellowships (averaging $24,000 per year), research assistantships (averaging $24,000 per year) were awarded; tuition waivers (full) also available. *Faculty research:* Thermodynamics, phase equilibria, rheology, fluid mechanics, polymers, biomedical engineering, interfacial phenomena, process control, petroleum engineering, reaction engineering and catalysis, biomaterials, metabolic engineering. *Unit head:* Christine Hughes, Department Administrator, 713-348-3424, Fax: 713-348-5478, E-mail: chbe@rice.edu. *Application contact:* Sharrm Kinnaird, Department Coordinator, 713-348-3424, Fax: 713-348-5478, E-mail: kinnaird@rice.edu.

Rose-Hulman Institute of Technology, Faculty of Engineering and Applied Sciences, Department of Applied Biology and Biomedical Engineering, Terre Haute, IN 47803-3999. Offers biomedical engineering (MD/MS); MD/MS. Part-time programs available. *Faculty:* 12 full-time (6 women). *Students:* 2 full-time (1 woman), 1 part-time (0 women), 1 international. Average age 28. 1 applicant, 0% accepted, 0 enrolled. In 2009, 3 master's awarded. *Degree requirements:* For master's, thesis. *Entrance requirements:* For master's, GRE, minimum GPA of 3.0. Additional exam requirements/recommendations for international students: Required—TOEFL (minimum score 580 paper-based; 237 computer-based; 92 iBT). *Application deadline:* For fall admission, 2/1 priority date for domestic students. Applications are processed on a rolling basis. Application fee: $0. *Expenses:* Tuition: Full-time $33,900; part-time $987 per credit hour. *Financial support:* Fellowships with full and partial tuition reimbursements, research assistantships with full and partial tuition reimbursements, institutionally sponsored loans, scholarships/grants, and tuition waivers (full and partial) available. *Faculty research:* Soft tissue biomechanics, tissue-biomaterial interaction, biomaterials, biomedical instrumentation, biomedical fluid mechanics. Total annual research expenditures: $468,158. *Unit head:* Dr. Lee Waite, Chairman, 812-877-8404, Fax: 812-877-3198, E-mail: lee.waite@rose-hulman.edu. *Application contact:* Dr. Daniel J. Moore, Associate Dean of the Faculty, 812-877-8110, Fax: 812-877-8061, E-mail: daniel.j.moore@rose-hulman.edu.

Rutgers, The State University of New Jersey, New Brunswick, Graduate School-New Brunswick, Program in Biomedical Engineering, Piscataway, NJ 08854-8097. Offers MS, PhD. Part-time programs available. Terminal master's awarded for partial completion of doctoral program. *Degree requirements:* For master's, thesis optional; for doctorate, comprehensive exam, thesis/dissertation. *Entrance requirements:* For master's and doctorate, GRE General Test, minimum GPA of 3.0. Additional exam requirements/recommendations for international students: Required—TOEFL. Electronic applications accepted. *Faculty research:* Molecular, cellular and nanosystems bioengineering; biomaterials and tissue engineering; biomechanics and rehabilitation engineering; integrative systems physiology and biomedical instrumentation; computational bioengineering and biomedical imaging.

St. Cloud State University, School of Graduate Studies, College of Science and Engineering, Academic Center for Regulatory Affairs and Services, St. Cloud, MN 56301-4498. Offers MS. Part-time programs available. *Faculty:* 2 full-time (0 women). *Students:* 1 full-time (0 women), 39 part-time (22 women); includes 7 minority (1 African American, 5 Asian Americans or Pacific Islanders, 1 Hispanic American), 1 international. 16 applicants, 100% accepted, 0 enrolled. *Degree requirements:* For master's, final paper. *Entrance requirements:* For master's, GRE General Test, minimum GPA of 2.75. *Application deadline:* Applications are processed on a rolling basis. Application fee: $35. *Expenses:* Contact institution. *Unit head:* Dr. Bruce Jacobson, Interim Director, 320-308-2192, Fax: 320-308-5124, E-mail: cose@stcloudstate.edu. *Application contact:* Linda Lou Krueger, School of Graduate Studies, 320-308-2113, Fax: 320-308-5371, E-mail: lekrueger@stcloudstate.edu.

Saint Louis University, Graduate School, Parks College of Engineering, Aviation, and Technology and Graduate School, Department of Biomedical Engineering, St. Louis, MO 63103-2097. Offers MS, MS-R, PhD. *Degree requirements:* For master's, thesis optional; for doctorate, thesis/dissertation. *Entrance requirements:* For master's, GRE General Test, letters of recommendation, resume, interview; for doctorate, GRE General Test, letters of recommendation, resumé, interview, transcripts, goal statement. Additional exam requirements/recommendations for international students: Required—TOEFL (minimum score 525 paper-based; 194 computer-based). *Faculty research:* Tissue engineering and biomaterialsûneural cardiovascular and orthopedic tissue engineering; tissue engineeringûairway remodeling, vasculopathy, and elastic, biodegradable scaffolds; biomechanicsûorthopedics, trauma biomechanics and biomechanical modeling; biosignalsûelectrophysiology, signal processing, and biomechanical instrumentation.

South Dakota School of Mines and Technology, Graduate Division, College of Engineering, Program in Biomedical Engineering, Rapid City, SD 57701-3995. Offers MS, PhD. *Students:* 17 full-time (5 women), 3 part-time (0 women), 8 international. Average age 27. 18 applicants,

Biomedical Engineering

South Dakota School of Mines and Technology (continued)
83% accepted, 9 enrolled. *Entrance requirements:* For doctorate, GRE General Test, 3 letters of recommendation, minimum GPA of 3.0. Additional exam requirements/recommendations for international students: Required—TOEFL. *Expenses:* Tuition, state resident: full-time $3340; part-time $139 per credit hour. Tuition, nonresident: full-time $7060; part-time $294 per credit hour. Required fees: $3270. *Unit head:* Dr. Mano Thubrikar, Director, 605-394-1775, E-mail: mano.thubrikar@sdsmt.edu. *Application contact:* Jeannette R. Nilson, Administrative Support Coordinator, Graduate Education, 800-454-8162 Ext. 1206, Fax: 605-394-5360, E-mail: graduate_admissions@sdsmt.edu.

Southern Illinois University Carbondale, Graduate School, College of Engineering, Program in Biomedical Engineering, Carbondale, IL 62901-4701. Offers ME, MS.

Stanford University, School of Engineering, Department of Mechanical Engineering, Program in Biomechanical Engineering, Stanford, CA 94305-9991. Offers MS. *Entrance requirements:* For master's, GRE General Test, undergraduate degree in engineering, math or sciences. Additional exam requirements/recommendations for international students: Required—TOEFL. *Expenses:* Tuition: Full-time $37,380; part-time $2760 per quarter. Required fees: $501.

See Close-Up on page 525.

State University of New York at Binghamton, Graduate School, Thomas J. Watson School of Engineering and Applied Science, Department of Bioengineering, Binghamton, NY 13902-6000. Offers biomedical engineering (MS, PhD). *Students:* 9 full-time (5 women), 1 part-time (0 women); includes 1 minority (Asian American or Pacific Islander), 5 international. Average age 25. 28 applicants, 43% accepted, 7 enrolled. In 2009, 2 master's, 3 doctorates awarded. *Financial support:* In 2009–10, 5 students received support, including 5 teaching assistantships with full tuition reimbursements available (averaging $16,500 per year). *Unit head:* Dr. Ken McLeod, Chair, 607-777-5778, Fax: 607-777-5780, E-mail: kmcleod@binghamton.edu. *Application contact:* Victoria Williams, Recruiting and Admissions Coordinator, 607-777-2151, Fax: 607-777-2501, E-mail: vwilliam@binghamton.edu.

State University of New York Downstate Medical Center, School of Graduate Studies, Program in Biomedical Engineering, Brooklyn, NY 11203-2098. Offers bioimaging and neuroengineering (PhD); biomedical engineering (MS); MD/PhD. *Degree requirements:* For doctorate, comprehensive exam, thesis/dissertation.

Stevens Institute of Technology, Graduate School, Charles V. Schaefer Jr. School of Engineering, Department of Chemistry, Chemical Biology and Biomedical Engineering, Program in Biomedical Engineering, Hoboken, NJ 07030. Offers M Eng, Certificate. *Expenses:* Tuition: Full-time $9900; part-time $1100 per credit. Required fees: $286 per semester.

Stony Brook University, State University of New York, Graduate School, College of Engineering and Applied Sciences, Department of Biomedical Engineering, Stony Brook, NY 11794. Offers biomedical engineering (MS, PhD, Certificate); medical physics (MS, PhD). *Faculty:* 15 full-time (3 women). *Students:* 70 full-time (26 women), 3 part-time (0 women); includes 11 minority (1 African American, 7 Asian Americans or Pacific Islanders, 3 Hispanic Americans), 31 international. Average age 26. 179 applicants, 27% accepted. In 2009, 14 master's, 13 doctorates awarded. *Degree requirements:* For doctorate, thesis/dissertation, qualifying exams. *Entrance requirements:* For master's and doctorate, GRE General Test. Additional exam requirements/recommendations for international students: Required—TOEFL. *Application deadline:* For fall admission, 1/15 for domestic students. Application fee: $60. *Expenses:* Tuition, state resident: full-time $8370; part-time $349 per credit. Tuition, nonresident: full-time $13,250; part-time $552 per credit. Required fees: $933. *Financial support:* In 2009–10, 42 research assistantships, 15 teaching assistantships were awarded; fellowships also available. Total annual research expenditures: $6.8 million. *Unit head:* Dr. Helene Benveniste, Chair, 631-632-8521, Fax: 631-632-8577. *Application contact:* Graduate Director, 631-444-2303, Fax: 631-444-6646.

Texas A&M University, College of Engineering, Department of Biomedical Engineering, College Station, TX 77843. Offers M Eng, MS, D Eng, PhD. Part-time programs available. *Faculty:* 20. *Students:* 76 full-time (25 women), 9 part-time (5 women); includes 11 minority (2 African Americans, 5 Asian Americans or Pacific Islanders, 4 Hispanic Americans), 37 international. Average age 27. In 2009, 14 master's, 5 doctorates awarded. *Degree requirements:* For master's, thesis (MS); for doctorate, dissertation (PhD). *Entrance requirements:* For master's and doctorate, GRE General Test, leveling courses if non-engineering undergraduate major. Additional exam requirements/recommendations for international students: Required—TOEFL. *Application deadline:* For fall admission, 7/1 priority date for domestic students, 6/1 for international students; for winter admission, 11/1 priority date for domestic students, 3/1 for international students; for spring admission, 4/1 priority date for domestic students, 10/1 for international students. Applications are processed on a rolling basis. Application fee: $50 ($75 for international students). Electronic applications accepted. *Expenses:* Tuition, state resident: full-time $3991.32; part-time $221.74 per credit hour. Tuition, nonresident: full-time $9049; part-time $502.74 per credit hour. *Financial support:* In 2009–10, research assistantships with partial tuition reimbursements (averaging $12,600 per year), teaching assistantships (averaging $11,400 per year) were awarded; fellowships with partial tuition reimbursements, career-related internships or fieldwork, scholarships/grants, and unspecified assistantships also available. Financial award application deadline: 4/15; financial award applicants required to submit FAFSA. *Faculty research:* Medical lasers, optical biosensors, medical instrumentation, cardiovascular mechanics, orthopedic mechanics. *Unit head:* Dr. James Moore, Head, 979-845-4196, Fax: 979-845-4450, E-mail: jmoorejr@tamu.edu. *Application contact:* Dr., Graduate Advisor, 979-845-5532, Fax: 979-845-4450, E-mail: bmengrad@iemail.tamu.edu.

Thomas Jefferson University, Jefferson College of Graduate Studies, PhD Program in Tissue Engineering and Regenerative Medicine, Philadelphia, PA 19107. Offers PhD. *Faculty:* 18 full-time (6 women). *Students:* 4 full-time (3 women); includes 1 minority (Asian American or Pacific Islander). 3 applicants, 0% accepted, 0 enrolled. In 2009, 2 doctorates awarded. *Degree requirements:* For doctorate, comprehensive exam, thesis/dissertation. *Entrance requirements:* For doctorate, GRE General Test, minimum GPA of 3.2. Additional exam requirements/recommendations for international students: Required—TOEFL (minimum score 250 computer-based; 100 iBT), or IELTS. *Application deadline:* For fall admission, 1/15 priority date for domestic and international students. Applications are processed on a rolling basis. Application fee: $50. Electronic applications accepted. *Expenses:* Tuition: Full-time $26,858; part-time $879 per credit. Required fees: $525. *Financial support:* In 2009–10, 4 students received support, including 4 fellowships with full tuition reimbursements available (averaging $52,883 per year); Federal Work-Study, institutionally sponsored loans, traineeships, and stipend also available. Financial award application deadline: 5/1; financial award applicants required to submit FAFSA. *Faculty research:* Skeletal development, biomaterials, bone implant interaction, tissue engineering, high resolution imaging. Total annual research expenditures: $8 million. *Unit head:* Dr. Irving Shapiro, Program Director, 215-955-7217, Fax: 215-955-9159, E-mail: irving.shapiro@jefferson.edu. *Application contact:* Marc E. Stearns, Director of Admissions, 215-503-0155, Fax: 215-503-9920, E-mail: jcgs-info@jefferson.edu.

Tufts University, School of Engineering, Department of Biomedical Engineering, Medford, MA 02155. Offers ME, MS, PhD. Part-time programs available. *Faculty:* 7 full-time, 4 part-time/adjunct. *Students:* 63 (28 women); includes 9 minority (all Asian Americans or Pacific Islanders), 10 international. 127 applicants, 28% accepted, 14 enrolled. In 2009, 17 master's, 6 doctorates awarded. Terminal master's awarded for partial completion of doctoral program. *Degree requirements:* For master's, thesis (for some programs); for doctorate, thesis/dissertation. *Entrance requirements:* For master's and doctorate, GRE General Test. Additional exam requirements/recommendations for international students: Required—TOEFL (minimum score 550 paper-based; 213 computer-based; 80 iBT). *Application deadline:* For fall admission, 1/15 priority date for domestic students, 12/15 for international students; for spring admission, 10/15 for domestic students, 9/15 for international students. Applications are processed on a rolling basis. Application fee: $75. Electronic applications accepted. *Expenses:* Tuition: Full-time $38,096; part-time $3962 per credit. Required fees: $686; $40 per year. Tuition and fees vary according to course level, course load, degree level, program and student level. *Financial support:* Fellowships with full tuition reimbursements, research assistantships with full and partial tuition reimbursements, teaching assistantships with full and partial tuition reimbursements, Federal Work-Study, scholarships/grants, tuition waivers (partial), and unspecified assistantships available. Financial award application deadline: 1/15; financial award applicants required to submit FAFSA. *Unit head:* David Kaplan, Chair, 617-627-2580. *Application contact:* David Kaplan, Chair, 617-627-2580.

Tulane University, School of Science and Engineering, Department of Biomedical Engineering, New Orleans, LA 70118-5669. Offers MS, PhD. MS and PhD offered through the Graduate School. Part-time programs available. Terminal master's awarded for partial completion of doctoral program. *Degree requirements:* For master's, thesis (for some programs); for doctorate, thesis/dissertation. *Entrance requirements:* For master's and doctorate, GRE General Test, minimum B average in undergraduate course work. Additional exam requirements/recommendations for international students: Required—TOEFL. Electronic applications accepted. *Faculty research:* Pulmonary and biofluid mechanics and biomechanics of bone, biomaterials science, finite element analysis, electric fields of the brain.

Université de Montréal, Faculty of Medicine, Institute of Biomedical Engineering, Montréal, QC H3C 3J7, Canada. Offers M Sc A, PhD, DESS. *Degree requirements:* For master's, thesis; for doctorate, thesis/dissertation, general exam. *Entrance requirements:* For master's and doctorate, proficiency in French, knowledge of English. Electronic applications accepted. *Faculty research:* Electrophysiology, biomechanics, instrumentation, imaging, simulation.

The University of Akron, Graduate School, College of Engineering, Department of Biomedical Engineering, Akron, OH 44325. Offers MS, PhD. Part-time and evening/weekend programs available. *Faculty:* 8 full-time (2 women). *Students:* 21 full-time (7 women), 10 part-time (4 women); includes 1 minority (African American), 14 international. Average age 26. 56 applicants, 36% accepted, 6 enrolled. In 2009, 6 master's awarded. *Degree requirements:* For master's, thesis optional; for doctorate, one foreign language, thesis/dissertation, candidacy exam, qualifying exam. *Entrance requirements:* For master's, GRE General Test, minimum GPA of 2.75, letters of recommendation, resume; for doctorate, GRE General Test, minimum GPA of 3.0 with bachelor's degree, 3.5 with master's degree; letters of recommendation; personal statement, resume. Additional exam requirements/recommendations for international students: Required—TOEFL (minimum score 590 paper-based; 243 computer-based; 96 iBT). *Application deadline:* Applications are processed on a rolling basis. Application fee: $30 ($40 for international students). Electronic applications accepted. *Expenses:* Tuition, state resident: full-time $6570; part-time $365 per credit hour. Tuition, nonresident: full-time $11,250; part-time $625 per credit hour. *Financial support:* In 2009–10, 7 research assistantships with full tuition reimbursements, 6 teaching assistantships with full tuition reimbursements were awarded; career-related internships or fieldwork, Federal Work-Study, and scholarships/grants also available. *Faculty research:* Signal and image processing, physiological controls and instrumentation, biomechanics—orthopaedic and hemodynamic, biomaterials for gene and drug delivery systems, telemedicine. Total annual research expenditures: $227,395. *Unit head:* Dr. Daniel Sheffer, Chair, 330-972-6977, E-mail: dsheffer@uakron.edu. *Application contact:* Dr. Daniel Sheffer, Chair, 330-972-6977, E-mail: dsheffer@uakron.edu.

The University of Akron, Graduate School, College of Engineering, Program in Engineering (Biomedical Engineering Specialization), Akron, OH 44325. Offers MS. *Students:* 1 applicant, 100% accepted, 0 enrolled. In 2009, 1 master's awarded. *Entrance requirements:* For master's, GRE, minimum GPA of 2.75, letters of recommendation, resume. Additional exam requirements/recommendations for international students: Required—TOEFL (minimum score 590 paper-based; 243 computer-based; 96 iBT). *Application deadline:* Applications are processed on a rolling basis. Application fee: $30 ($40 for international students). Electronic applications accepted. *Expenses:* Tuition, state resident: full-time $6570; part-time $365 per credit hour. Tuition, nonresident: full-time $11,250; part-time $625 per credit hour. *Unit head:* Dr. Daniel Sheffer, Chair, 330-972-6977, E-mail: sheffer@uakron.edu. *Application contact:* Dr. Craig Menzemer, Director of Graduate Studies, 330-972-5536, E-mail: ccmenze@uakron.edu.

The University of Alabama at Birmingham, School of Engineering, Program in Biomedical Engineering, Birmingham, AL 35294. Offers MSBME, PhD. *Degree requirements:* For master's, thesis or alternative, oral exam; for doctorate, comprehensive exam, thesis/dissertation. *Entrance requirements:* For master's and doctorate, GRE General Test. Additional exam requirements/recommendations for international students: Required—TOEFL. Electronic applications accepted.

University of Alberta, Faculty of Medicine and Dentistry and Faculty of Graduate Studies and Research, Graduate Programs in Medicine, Department of Biomedical Engineering, Edmonton, AB T6G 2E1, Canada. Offers biomedical engineering (M Sc); medical sciences (PhD). *Faculty:* 7 full-time (2 women), 9 part-time/adjunct (0 women). *Students:* 22 full-time (6 women). Average age 23. 14 applicants, 43% accepted. In 2009, 3 master's awarded. *Degree requirements:* For master's, thesis; for doctorate, thesis/dissertation. *Application deadline:* For fall admission, 7/1 for domestic students; for winter admission, 11/1 for domestic students. Applications are processed on a rolling basis. Application fee: $0 Canadian dollars. Electronic applications accepted. Tuition and fees charges are reported in Canadian dollars. *Expenses:* Tuition, area resident: Full-time $4626.24 Canadian dollars; part-time $99.72 Canadian dollars per unit. International tuition: $8216 Canadian dollars full-time. Required fees: $3589.92 Canadian dollars; $99.72 Canadian dollars per unit. $215 Canadian dollars per term. *Financial support:* In 2009–10, 15 students received support, including 2 research assistantships (averaging $14,865 per year), 4 teaching assistantships (averaging $14,865 per year); fellowships with tuition reimbursements available, institutionally sponsored loans, scholarships/grants, and unspecified assistantships also available. Financial award application deadline: 3/1. *Faculty research:* Medical imaging, rehabilitation engineering, biomaterials and tissue engineering, biomechanics, cryobiology. Total annual research expenditures: $5 million Canadian dollars. *Unit head:* Dr. Robert E. Burrell, Chair, 780-492-6397, Fax: 780-492-8259. *Application contact:* Maisie Goh, Department Administrator, 780-492-2541, Fax: 780-492-8259.

The University of Arizona, Graduate College, Graduate Interdisciplinary Programs, Graduate Interdisciplinary Program in Biomedical Engineering, Tucson, AZ 85721. Offers MS, PhD. *Faculty:* 5 full-time (1 woman). *Students:* 23 full-time (10 women), 5 part-time (1 woman); includes 8 minority (1 American Indian/Alaska Native, 6 Asian Americans or Pacific Islanders, 1 Hispanic American), 2 international. Average age 27. 46 applicants, 20% accepted, 7 enrolled. In 2009, 1 master's, 3 doctorates awarded. *Entrance requirements:* For master's, GRE, 3 letters of recommendation; for doctorate, GRE, 3 letters of recommendation, statement of purpose. Additional exam requirements/recommendations for international students: Required—TOEFL (minimum score 600 paper-based; 250 computer-based). *Application deadline:* For fall admission, 2/1 for domestic students, 12/1 for international students. Application fee: $65. Electronic applications accepted. *Expenses:* Tuition, state resident: full-time $9028. Tuition, nonresident: full-time $24,890. *Financial support:* In 2009–10, 6 research assistantships with full tuition reimbursements (averaging $18,773 per year) were awarded; institutionally sponsored loans, scholarships/grants, traineeships, health care benefits, tuition waivers (full), and unspecified assistantships also available. *Unit head:* Jennifer Barton, Chair, 520-621-4116, E-mail: barton@u.arizona.edu. *Application contact:* Debbi Howard, Program Coordinator, 520-626-8726, Fax: 520-626-8726, E-mail: dhoward@u.arizona.edu.

University of Arkansas, Graduate School, College of Engineering, Department of Biological and Agricultural Engineering, Program in Biomedical Engineering, Fayetteville, AR 72701-1201. Offers MSBME. *Students:* 2 full-time (0 women), 1 (woman) part-time, all international. In 2009, 5 master's awarded. Application fee: $40 ($50 for international students). *Expenses:* Tuition, state resident: full-time $7355; part-time $356.58 per hour. Tuition, nonresident: full-time $17,401; part-time $775.17 per hour. Required fees: $1203. *Financial support:* In 2009–10, 1 research assistantship, 1 teaching assistantship were awarded; fellowships also available. *Unit head:* Dr. Carl Griffis, Department Head, 479-575-2351, Fax: 479-575-2846, E-mail:

clg@uark.edu. *Application contact:* Dr. Jin-Woo Kim, Program Coordinator, 479-575-2351, Fax: 479-575-2846, E-mail: jwkim@uark.edu.

University of Calgary, Faculty of Graduate Studies, Faculty of Kinesiology, Calgary, AB T2N 1N4, Canada. Offers biomedical engineering (M Sc, PhD); kinesiology (M Kin, M Sc, PhD), including biomechanics (PhD), health and exercise physiology (PhD). *Degree requirements:* For master's, thesis (M Sc); for doctorate, thesis/dissertation. *Entrance requirements:* Additional exam requirements/recommendations for international students: Required—TOEFL. Electronic applications accepted. *Faculty research:* Load acting on the human body, muscle mechanics and physiology, optimizing high performance athlete performance, eye movement in sports, analysis of body composition.

University of Calgary, Faculty of Graduate Studies, Schulich School of Engineering, Graduate Program in Biomedical Engineering, Calgary, AB T2N 1N4, Canada. Offers M Eng, M Sc, PhD. *Degree requirements:* For master's, thesis; for doctorate, comprehensive exam, thesis/dissertation. *Faculty research:* Bioinstrumentation and imaging, clinical engineering, biomechanics, biomaterials, systems physiology.

University of California, Davis, College of Engineering, Graduate Group in Biomedical Engineering, Davis, CA 95616. Offers MS, PhD. *Degree requirements:* For master's, thesis; for doctorate, thesis/dissertation. *Entrance requirements:* For master's and doctorate, GRE General Test, minimum GPA of 3.25. Additional exam requirements/recommendations for international students: Required—TOEFL (minimum score 550 paper-based; 213 computer-based), IELTS (minimum score 7). Electronic applications accepted. *Faculty research:* Orthopedic biomechanics, cell/molecular biomechanics and transport, biosensors and instrumentation, human movement, biomedical image analysis, spectroscopy.

University of California, Irvine, Office of Graduate Studies, School of Engineering, Department of Biomedical Engineering, Irvine, CA 92697. Offers MS, PhD. Part-time programs available. *Students:* 92 full-time (28 women), 5 part-time (1 woman); includes 34 minority (1 African American, 31 Asian Americans or Pacific Islanders, 2 Hispanic Americans), 22 international. Average age 26. 224 applicants, 38% accepted, 30 enrolled. In 2009, 30 master's, 19 doctorates awarded. Terminal master's awarded for partial completion of doctoral program. *Degree requirements:* For doctorate, thesis/dissertation. *Entrance requirements:* For master's and doctorate, GRE General Test, minimum GPA of 3.0, 3 letters of recommendation. Additional exam requirements/recommendations for international students: Required—TOEFL (minimum score 550 paper-based; 213 computer-based). *Application deadline:* For fall admission, 1/15 priority date for domestic students, 1/15 for international students. Applications are processed on a rolling basis. Application fee: $70 ($90 for international students). Electronic applications accepted. *Financial support:* In 2009–10, fellowships (averaging $14,656 per year); research assistantships with full tuition reimbursements, teaching assistantships, institutionally sponsored loans, traineeships, health care benefits, and unspecified assistantships also available. Financial award application deadline: 3/1; financial award applicants required to submit FAFSA. *Faculty research:* Biomedical photonics, biomedical imaging, biomedical nano- and micro-scale systems, biomedical computation/modeling, neuroengineering, tissue engineering. *Unit head:* Dr. Steven George, Director, 949-824-3941, Fax: 949-824-3440, E-mail: scgeorge@uci.edu. *Application contact:* Abe Lee, Graduate Advisor, 949-824-3494, Fax: 949-824-1727, E-mail: aplee@uci.edu.

University of California, Los Angeles, Graduate Division, Henry Samueli School of Engineering and Applied Science, Interdepartmental Graduate Program in Biomedical Engineering, Los Angeles, CA 90095-1600. Offers MS, PhD. *Faculty:* 7 full-time (1 woman). *Students:* 140 full-time (46 women); includes 54 minority (49 Asian Americans or Pacific Islanders, 5 Hispanic Americans), 42 international. 219 applicants, 55% accepted, 46 enrolled. In 2009, 23 master's, 15 doctorates awarded. *Degree requirements:* For master's, comprehensive exam or thesis; for doctorate, thesis/dissertation, qualifying exams. *Entrance requirements:* For master's, GRE General Test, minimum GPA of 3.0; for doctorate, GRE General Test, minimum GPA of 3.25. Additional exam requirements/recommendations for international students: Required—TOEFL (minimum score 560 paper-based; 220 computer-based). *Application deadline:* For fall admission, 12/15 for domestic and international students. Application fee: $70 ($90 for international students). Electronic applications accepted. *Financial support:* In 2009–10, 30 fellowships, 66 research assistantships, 41 teaching assistantships were awarded; career-related internships or fieldwork, Federal Work-Study, institutionally sponsored loans, and tuition waivers (full and partial) also available. Financial award application deadline: 1/15; financial award applicants required to submit FAFSA. Total annual research expenditures: $2.2 million. *Unit head:* Dr. Timothy J. Deming, Chair, 310-794-4450. *Application contact:* Larry Nadeau, Student Affairs Officer, 310-794-5945, Fax: 310-794-5956, E-mail: nadeau@ea.ucla.edu.

University of Cincinnati, Graduate School, College of Engineering, Department of Biomedical Engineering, Cincinnati, OH 45221. Offers bioinformatics (PhD); biomechanics (PhD); medical imaging (PhD); tissue engineering (PhD). Part-time programs available. *Degree requirements:* For doctorate, one foreign language, thesis/dissertation. *Entrance requirements:* For doctorate, GRE General Test. Additional exam requirements/recommendations for international students: Required—TOEFL (minimum score 600 paper-based; 250 computer-based).

University of Connecticut, Graduate School, School of Engineering, Department of Electrical and Computer Engineering, Field of Biomedical Engineering, Storrs, CT 06269. Offers MS, PhD. *Faculty:* 53 full-time (8 women). *Students:* 63 full-time (19 women), 14 part-time (5 women); includes 9 minority (3 African Americans, 6 Asian Americans or Pacific Islanders), 34 international. Average age 28. 135 applicants, 24% accepted, 17 enrolled. In 2009, 17 master's awarded. Terminal master's awarded for partial completion of doctoral program. *Degree requirements:* For master's, comprehensive exam, thesis or alternative; for doctorate, thesis/dissertation. *Entrance requirements:* For master's and doctorate, GRE General Test. Additional exam requirements/recommendations for international students: Required—TOEFL (minimum score 550 paper-based; 213 computer-based). *Application deadline:* For fall admission, 2/1 priority date for domestic and international students; for spring admission, 11/1 for domestic students, 10/1 for international students. Applications are processed on a rolling basis. Application fee: $55. Electronic applications accepted. *Expenses:* Tuition, state resident: full-time $4725; part-time $525 per credit. Tuition, nonresident: full-time $12,267; part-time $1363 per credit. Required fees: $346 per semester. Tuition and fees vary according to course load. *Financial support:* In 2009–10, 33 research assistantships with full tuition reimbursements, 12 teaching assistantships with full tuition reimbursements were awarded; fellowships, career-related internships or fieldwork, Federal Work-Study, scholarships/grants, health care benefits, and unspecified assistantships also available. Financial award application deadline: 2/1; financial award applicants required to submit FAFSA. *Unit head:* Dr. John D. Enderle, Director, 860-486-5521, Fax: 860-486-2500, E-mail: jenderle@bme.uconn.edu. *Application contact:* Lisa Ephraim, Academic Advisor, 860-486-5838, E-mail: lisae@engr.uconn.edu.

University of Florida, Graduate School, College of Engineering, Department of Biomedical Engineering, Gainesville, FL 32611. Offers ME, MS, PhD, Certificate. *Degree requirements:* For master's, thesis optional; for doctorate, thesis/dissertation. *Entrance requirements:* For master's, GRE General Test, minimum GPA of 3.1; for doctorate, GRE General Test, minimum GPA of 3.3. Additional exam requirements/recommendations for international students: Required—TOEFL (minimum score 550 paper-based; 213 computer-based). Electronic applications accepted.

University of Houston, Cullen College of Engineering, Department of Biomedical Engineering, Houston, TX 77204. Offers MSBE. Part-time and evening/weekend programs available. *Students:* 3 full-time (1 woman), 1 (woman) part-time; includes 2 minority (1 Asian American or Pacific Islander, 1 Hispanic American). Average age 23. 2 applicants, 100% accepted, 2 enrolled. In 2009, 1 master's awarded. *Entrance requirements:* For master's, GRE. Additional exam requirements/recommendations for international students: Required—TOEFL. *Application deadline:* For fall admission, 2/1 for domestic and international students; for spring admission, 10/1 for domestic and international students. Application fee: $25 ($75 for international students).

Electronic applications accepted. *Expenses:* Tuition, state resident: full-time $7676; part-time $320 per credit hour. Tuition, nonresident: full-time $14,324; part-time $597 per credit hour. Required fees: $3034. *Unit head:* Dr. Metin Akay, Chair, 832-842-8860, E-mail: makay@uh.edu. *Application contact:* Dr. Larry Witte, Associate Dean, Graduate Programs, 713-743-4205, Fax: 713-743-4214, E-mail: witte@uh.edu.

The University of Iowa, Graduate College, College of Engineering, Department of Biomedical Engineering, Iowa City, IA 52242-1316. Offers MS, PhD. Part-time programs available. *Faculty:* 15 full-time (2 women). *Students:* 72 full-time (34 women); includes 4 minority (1 African American, 3 Asian Americans or Pacific Islanders), 36 international. Average age 26. 92 applicants, 38% accepted, 15 enrolled. In 2009, 18 master's, 7 doctorates awarded. *Degree requirements:* For master's, thesis (for some programs), written and oral exam; for doctorate, comprehensive exam, thesis/dissertation, written and oral exam. *Entrance requirements:* For master's, GRE, minimum undergraduate GPA of 3.0; for doctorate, GRE. Additional exam requirements/recommendations for international students: Required—TOEFL (minimum score 600 paper-based; 250 computer-based; 100 iBT). *Application deadline:* For fall admission, 3/1 for domestic and international students; for spring admission, 8/1 for domestic and international students. Applications are processed on a rolling basis. Application fee: $60 ($100 for international students). Electronic applications accepted. *Financial support:* In 2009–10, 5 fellowships with partial tuition reimbursements (averaging $17,236 per year), 60 research assistantships with partial tuition reimbursements (averaging $23,776 per year), 11 teaching assistantships with partial tuition reimbursements (averaging $16,635 per year) were awarded; scholarships/grants, health care benefits, and unspecified assistantships also available. Support available to part-time students. Financial award application deadline: 3/1. *Faculty research:* Biomaterials, tissue engineering and cellular mechanics; cell motion analysis and modeling; spinal and joint biomechanics, digital human modeling, and biomedical imaging; bioinformatics and computational biology; fluid and cardiovascular biomechanics. Total annual research expenditures: $11.5 million. *Unit head:* Dr. Joseph M. Reinhardt, Departmental Executive Officer, 319-335-5634, Fax: 319-335-5631, E-mail: joe-reinhardt@uiowa.edu. *Application contact:* Lorena Lovetinsky, Secretary, 319-384-0671, Fax: 319-335-5631, E-mail: bme@engineering.uiowa.edu.

The University of Iowa, Roy J. and Lucille A. Carver College of Medicine and Graduate College, Biosciences Program, Iowa City, IA 52242-1316. Offers anatomy and biology (PhD); biochemistry (PhD); biology (PhD); biomedical engineering (PhD); chemistry (PhD); free radical and radiation biology (PhD); genetics (PhD); human toxicology (PhD); immunology (PhD); microbiology (PhD); molecular and cellular biology (PhD); molecular physiology and biophysics (PhD); neuroscience (PhD); pharmacology (PhD); physical therapy and rehabilitation science (PhD); speech and hearing (PhD). *Faculty:* 310 full-time. *Students:* 25 full-time (13 women); includes 1 African American, 2 Asian Americans or Pacific Islanders, 4 international. 225 applicants. *Degree requirements:* For doctorate, thesis/dissertation. *Entrance requirements:* For doctorate, GRE General Test, minimum GPA of 3.0. Additional exam requirements/recommendations for international students: Required—TOEFL (minimum score 600 paper-based; 250 computer-based; 100 iBT). *Application deadline:* For fall admission, 1/15 priority date for domestic and international students. Applications are processed on a rolling basis. Application fee: $60 ($100 for international students). Electronic applications accepted. *Expenses:* Contact institution. *Financial support:* In 2009–10, 25 students received support, including 25 research assistantships with full tuition reimbursements available (averaging $24,250 per year); fellowships, teaching assistantships, health care benefits also available. *Unit head:* Dr. Andrew F. Russo, Director, 319-335-7872, Fax: 319-335-7656, E-mail: andrew-russo@uiowa.edu. *Application contact:* Jodi M. Graff, Program Associate, 319-335-8305, Fax: 319-335-7656, E-mail: biosciences-admissions@uiowa.edu.

University of Kentucky, Graduate School, Program in Biomedical Engineering, Lexington, KY 40506-0032. Offers MSBE, PBME, PhD. *Degree requirements:* For master's, comprehensive exam, thesis optional; for doctorate, comprehensive exam, thesis/dissertation. *Entrance requirements:* For master's, GRE General Test, minimum undergraduate GPA of 2.75; for doctorate, GRE General Test, minimum graduate GPA of 3.0. Additional exam requirements/recommendations for international students: Required—TOEFL (minimum score 550 paper-based; 213 computer-based). Electronic applications accepted. *Faculty research:* Signal processing and dynamical systems, cardiopulmonary mechanics and systems, bioelectromagnetics, neuromotor control and electrical stimulation, biomaterials and musculoskeletal biomechanics.

University of Massachusetts Dartmouth, Graduate School, Program in Biomedical Engineering and Biotechnology, North Dartmouth, MA 02747-2300. Offers PhD. Part-time programs available. *Students:* 16 full-time (8 women), 6 part-time (2 women); includes 1 minority (Hispanic American), 13 international. Average age 29. 19 applicants, 79% accepted, 9 enrolled. In 2009, 1 doctorate awarded. *Degree requirements:* For doctorate, comprehensive exam, thesis/dissertation. *Entrance requirements:* For doctorate, GRE, minimum GPA of 3.0, 3 letters of recommendation. Additional exam requirements/recommendations for international students: Required—TOEFL (minimum score 550 paper-based; 213 computer-based). *Application deadline:* For fall admission, 4/20 for domestic students, 2/20 for international students; for spring admission, 11/15 for domestic students, 9/15 for international students. Application fee: $40 ($60 for international students). Electronic applications accepted. *Expenses:* Tuition, state resident: full-time $2071; part-time $86.29 per credit. Tuition, nonresident: full-time $8099; part-time $337.46 per credit. Required fees: $9446. Tuition and fees vary according to class time, course load and reciprocity agreements. *Financial support:* In 2009–10, 3 fellowships with full tuition reimbursements (averaging $10,512 per year), 10 research assistantships with full tuition reimbursements (averaging $10,868 per year), 1 teaching assistantship with full tuition reimbursement (averaging $3,000 per year) were awarded; unspecified assistantships also available. Financial award application deadline: 3/1; financial award applicants required to submit FAFSA. *Faculty research:* Tetracycline-encapsulated chitosan microspheres, artificial tissues, sensor arrays for orthopedic rehab, blue light cures, healing bandages. Total annual research expenditures: $28,000. *Unit head:* Dr. Vijay Chalivendra, Co-Director, 508-910-6572, E-mail: vchalivendra@umassd.edu. *Application contact:* Elan Turcotte-Shamski, Graduate Admissions Officer, 508-999-8604, Fax: 508-999-8183, E-mail: graduate@umassd.edu.

University of Massachusetts Worcester, Graduate School of Biomedical Sciences, Program in Biomedical Engineering and Medical Physics, Worcester, MA 01655-0115. Offers PhD. *Degree requirements:* For doctorate, comprehensive exam, thesis/dissertation. *Entrance requirements:* For doctorate, GRE General Test. Additional exam requirements/recommendations for international students: Required—TOEFL (minimum score 600 paper-based; 250 computer-based). Electronic applications accepted. *Faculty research:* Tissue engineering, imaging, bioinstrumentation.

University of Medicine and Dentistry of New Jersey, Graduate School of Biomedical Sciences, Graduate Programs in Biomedical Sciences–Newark, Department of Biomedical Engineering, Newark, NJ 07107. Offers Certificate. *Students:* 9 full-time (2 women); includes 3 Asian Americans or Pacific Islanders, 2 international. *Entrance requirements:* Additional exam requirements/recommendations for international students: Required—TOEFL. *Application deadline:* For fall admission, 2/1 for domestic students. Applications are processed on a rolling basis. Application fee: $40. Electronic applications accepted. *Unit head:* Dr. Kevin Pang, Program Director, 973-676-1000 Ext. 1277, E-mail: kevin.pang@va.gov. *Application contact:* Dr. Kevin Pang, Program Director, 973-676-1000 Ext. 1277, E-mail: kevin.pang@va.gov.

University of Medicine and Dentistry of New Jersey, Graduate School of Biomedical Sciences, Graduate Programs in Biomedical Sciences–Piscataway, Program in Biomedical Engineering, Piscataway, NJ 08854-5635. Offers MS, PhD, MD/PhD. *Degree requirements:* For master's, thesis, qualifying exam; for doctorate, thesis/dissertation, qualifying exam. *Entrance requirements:* For master's and doctorate, GRE General Test. Additional exam requirements/recommendations for international students: Required—TOEFL. *Application deadline:* For fall admission, 1/5 for domestic students. Applications are processed on a rolling basis. Application fee: $40. Electronic applications accepted. *Financial support:* Fellowships, research assistant-

Biomedical Engineering

University of Medicine and Dentistry of New Jersey (continued)

ships, teaching assistantships available. Financial award application deadline: 5/1. *Unit head:* Dr. Prabhas Moghe, Director, 732-445-4500 Ext. 6315, Fax: 732-445-3753, E-mail: moghe@rcj.rutgers.edu. *Application contact:* University Registrar, 973-972-5338.

University of Memphis, Graduate School, Herff College of Engineering, Program in Biomedical Engineering, Memphis, TN 38152. Offers MS, PhD. *Faculty:* 7 full-time (1 woman), 2 part-time/adjunct (1 woman). *Students:* 37 full-time (15 women), 13 part-time (3 women); includes 4 minority (2 African Americans, 1 Asian American or Pacific Islander, 1 Hispanic American), 11 international. Average age 29. 19 applicants, 68% accepted, 13 enrolled. In 2009, 6 master's awarded. *Degree requirements:* For master's, thesis or alternative, oral exam; for doctorate, thesis/dissertation, exams. *Entrance requirements:* For master's, GRE General Test or MAT, minimum undergraduate GPA of 3.0; for doctorate, GRE General Test, minimum undergraduate GPA of 3.25 or master's degree in biomedical engineering. *Application deadline:* For fall admission, 8/1 priority date for domestic students; for spring admission, 12/1 for domestic students. Applications are processed on a rolling basis. Application fee: $35 ($60 for international students). Electronic applications accepted. *Expenses:* Tuition, state resident: full-time $6246; part-time $347 per credit hour. Tuition, nonresident: full-time $15,894; part-time $883 per credit hour. Required fees: $1160. Full-time tuition and fees vary according to course load, degree level and program. *Financial support:* In 2009–10, 8 students received support; fellowships with full tuition reimbursements available, research assistantships with full tuition reimbursements available, career-related internships or fieldwork, Federal Work-Study, scholarships/grants, and unspecified assistantships available. Financial award application deadline: 2/15; financial award applicants required to submit FAFSA. *Faculty research:* Biomaterials and cell/tissue engineering, especially for orthopedic applications; biosensors; biomechanics (hemodynamics, soft tissue, lung, gait); electrophysiology; novel medical image-acquisition devices. *Unit head:* Dr. Eugene C. Eckstein, Chairman, 901-678-3733, Fax: 901-678-5281, E-mail: eckstein@memphis.edu. *Application contact:* Dr. Steven M. Slack, Associate Dean, 901-678-4791, Fax: 901-678-5281, E-mail: sslack@memphis.edu.

University of Miami, Graduate School, College of Engineering, Department of Biomedical Engineering, Coral Gables, FL 33124. Offers MSBE, PhD. Part-time programs available. *Degree requirements:* For master's, thesis (for some programs); for doctorate, comprehensive exam, thesis/dissertation. *Entrance requirements:* For master's and doctorate, GRE General Test, minimum GPA of 3.0. Additional exam requirements/recommendations for international students: Required—TOEFL (minimum score 550 paper-based; 213 computer-based). Electronic applications accepted. *Faculty research:* Biomedical signal processing and instrumentation, cardiovascular engineering, optics and lasers, rehabilitation engineering, tissue mechanics.

University of Michigan, Horace H. Rackham School of Graduate Studies, College of Engineering, Department of Biomedical Engineering, Ann Arbor, MI 48109. Offers MS, MSE, PhD. Part-time programs available. *Faculty:* 16 full-time (3 women). *Students:* 193 full-time (76 women), 4 part-time (0 women); includes 50 minority (10 African Americans, 31 Asian Americans or Pacific Islanders, 9 Hispanic Americans), 59 international. 369 applicants, 51% accepted, 83 enrolled. In 2009, 63 master's, 32 doctorates awarded. *Degree requirements:* For master's, thesis optional; for doctorate, comprehensive exam, oral defense of dissertation. *Entrance requirements:* For master's, GRE General Test; for doctorate, GRE General Test, master's degree. Additional exam requirements/recommendations for international students: Required—TOEFL. *Application deadline:* Applications are processed on a rolling basis. Application fee: $60 ($75 for international students). Electronic applications accepted. *Expenses:* Tuition, state resident: full-time $17,286; part-time $1099 per credit hour. Tuition, nonresident: full-time $34,944; part-time $2080 per credit hour. Required fees: $95 per semester. Tuition and fees vary according to course load, degree level and program. *Financial support:* Fellowships, research assistantships, teaching assistantships, Federal Work-Study, scholarships/grants, traineeships, and tuition waivers (partial) available. Financial award applicants required to submit FAFSA. *Faculty research:* Cellular and tissue engineering, biotechnology, biomedical materials, biomechanics, biomedical imaging, rehabilitation engineering. *Unit head:* Douglas Noll, Chair, Biomedical Engineering, 734-647-1091, Fax: 734-936-1905, E-mail: biomede@umich.edu. *Application contact:* Maria E. Steele, Senior Student Administration Assistant, 734-647-1091, Fax: 734-936-1905, E-mail: msteele@umich.edu.

University of Minnesota, Twin Cities Campus, Institute of Technology and Medical School, Department of Biomedical Engineering, Minneapolis, MN 55455-0213. Offers MS, PhD, MD/PhD. Part-time programs available. Terminal master's awarded for partial completion of doctoral program. *Degree requirements:* For master's, thesis optional; for doctorate, thesis/dissertation. *Entrance requirements:* For master's and doctorate, GRE General Test. *Faculty research:* Biomedical microelectromechanical systems, tissue engineering, biomechanics and blood/fluid dynamics, biomaterials, soft tissue mechanics, biomedical imaging.

University of Nevada, Las Vegas, Graduate College, Howard R. Hughes College of Engineering, Department of Mechanical Engineering, Las Vegas, NV 89154-4027. Offers aerospace engineering (MS); biomedical engineering (MS); materials and nuclear engineering (MS); mechanical engineering (MS, PhD). Part-time programs available. *Faculty:* 17 full-time (0 women), 10 part-time/adjunct (0 women). *Students:* 39 full-time (4 women), 28 part-time (6 women); includes 10 minority (1 African American, 8 Asian Americans or Pacific Islanders, 1 Hispanic American), 28 international. Average age 30. 64 applicants, 83% accepted, 22 enrolled. In 2009, 13 master's, 7 doctorates awarded. *Degree requirements:* For master's, comprehensive exam, thesis (for some programs), project; for doctorate, comprehensive exam, thesis/dissertation. *Entrance requirements:* For master's and doctorate, GRE General Test. Additional exam requirements/recommendations for international students: Required—TOEFL (minimum score 550 paper-based; 213 computer-based; 80 iBT), IELTS (minimum score 7). *Application deadline:* For fall admission, 5/1 priority date for domestic and international students; for spring admission, 10/1 priority date for domestic and international students. Applications are processed on a rolling basis. Application fee: $60 ($95 for international students). Electronic applications accepted. *Financial support:* In 2009–10, 37 students received support, including 21 research assistantships with partial tuition reimbursements available (averaging $13,335 per year), 16 teaching assistantships with partial tuition reimbursements available (averaging $11,000 per year); institutionally sponsored loans, scholarships/grants, health care benefits, and unspecified assistantships also available. Financial award application deadline: 3/1. *Unit head:* Dr. Woosoon Yim, Chair/Professor, 702-895-0956, Fax: 702-895-3936, E-mail: wy@me.unlv.edu. *Application contact:* Graduate College Admissions Evaluator, 702-895-3320, Fax: 702-895-4180, E-mail: gradcollege@unlv.edu.

University of Nevada, Reno, Graduate School, Interdisciplinary Program in Biomedical Engineering, Reno, NV 89557. Offers MS, PhD. Terminal master's awarded for partial completion of doctoral program. *Degree requirements:* For master's, thesis optional; for doctorate, thesis/dissertation. *Entrance requirements:* For master's, GRE General Test (recommended), minimum GPA of 2.75; for doctorate, GRE General Test (recommended), minimum GPA of 3.0. Additional exam requirements/recommendations for international students: Required—TOEFL (minimum score 500 paper-based; 173 computer-based; 61 iBT), IELTS (minimum score 6). Electronic applications accepted. *Faculty research:* Bioengineering, biophysics, biomedical instrumentation, biosensors.

The University of North Carolina at Chapel Hill, School of Medicine and Graduate School, Graduate Programs in Medicine, Joint Department of Biomedical Engineering UNC-Chapel Hill and NC State, Chapel Hill, NC 27599. Offers MS, PhD. *Faculty:* 24 full-time (5 women), 76 part-time/adjunct (15 women). *Students:* 88 full-time (31 women); includes 16 minority (7 African Americans, 8 Asian Americans or Pacific Islanders, 1 Hispanic American), 13 international. 312 applicants, 14% accepted, 20 enrolled. In 2009, 5 master's, 8 doctorates awarded. Terminal master's awarded for partial completion of doctoral program. *Degree requirements:* For master's, comprehensive exam, thesis, ethics seminar; for doctorate, comprehensive exam, thesis/dissertation, qualifying exam, teaching and ethics seminar. *Entrance requirements:* For master's and doctorate, GRE General Test, minimum GPA of 3.0. Additional exam requirements/recommendations for international students: Required—TOEFL. *Application deadline:* For fall admission, 1/15 for domestic and international students. Application fee: $77. Electronic applications accepted. *Financial support:* In 2009–10, 10 students received support, including 10 fellowships with full tuition reimbursements available (averaging $25,750 per year), 53 research assistantships with full tuition reimbursements available (averaging $23,400 per year), 11 teaching assistantships with full tuition reimbursements available (averaging $16,000 per year); Federal Work-Study, scholarships/grants, traineeships, health care benefits, and unspecified assistantships also available. Financial award applicants required to submit FAFSA. *Faculty research:* Biomedical imaging, rehabilitation engineering, microsystems engineering. *Unit head:* Dr. Nancy L. Allbritton, Chair and Professor, 919-966-1175, Fax: 919-966-2963, E-mail: nlallbri@unc.edu. *Application contact:* Nancy D. McKinney, Graduate Coordinator, 919-966-8088, Fax: 919-966-2963, E-mail: nancy_mckinney@unc.edu.

University of Ottawa, Faculty of Graduate and Postdoctoral Studies, Ottawa—Carlton Joint Program in Biomedical Engineering, Ottawa, ON K1N 6N5, Canada. Offers MA Sc. *Degree requirements:* For master's, thesis or alternative. *Entrance requirements:* For master's, honors degree or equivalent, minimum B average.

University of Rhode Island, Graduate School, College of Engineering, Department of Electrical, Computer and Biomedical Engineering, Kingston, RI 02881. Offers MS, PhD, Graduate Certificate. Part-time programs available. *Faculty:* 18 full-time (3 women), 2 part-time/adjunct (0 women). *Students:* 27 full-time (7 women), 17 part-time (2 women); includes 7 minority (2 African Americans, 2 Asian Americans or Pacific Islanders, 3 Hispanic Americans), 13 international. In 2009, 13 master's, 3 doctorates awarded. *Degree requirements:* For master's, comprehensive exam (for some programs), thesis optional; for doctorate, comprehensive exam, thesis/dissertation. *Entrance requirements:* For master's and doctorate, 2 letters of recommendation. Additional exam requirements/recommendations for international students: Required—TOEFL (minimum score 550 paper-based; 213 computer-based). *Application deadline:* For fall admission, 7/15 for domestic students, 2/1 for international students; for spring admission, 11/15 for domestic students, 7/15 for international students. Application fee: $65. Electronic applications accepted. *Expenses:* Tuition, state resident: full-time $8828; part-time $490 per credit hour. Tuition, nonresident: full-time $22,100; part-time $1228 per credit hour. Required fees: $1118; $57 per semester. Tuition and fees vary according to program. *Financial support:* In 2009–10, 5 research assistantships with full and partial tuition reimbursements (averaging $4,888 per year), 4 teaching assistantships with full and partial tuition reimbursements (averaging $6,726 per year) were awarded. Financial award application deadline: 7/15; financial award applicants required to submit FAFSA. *Faculty research:* Biomedical Instrumentation, cardiac physiology and computational modeling, analog/digital CMOS circuits, neural-machine interface, digital circuit design and VLSI testing. Total annual research expenditures: $744,413. *Unit head:* Dr. G. Faye Boudreaux-Bartels, Chair, 401-874-5805, Fax: 401-782-6422, E-mail: boud@ele.uri.edu. *Application contact:* Dr. Godi Fischer, Director of Graduate Studies, 401-874-5879, Fax: 401-782-6422, E-mail: fischer@ele.uri.edu.

University of Rochester, The College, School of Engineering and Applied Sciences, Department of Biomedical Engineering, Rochester, NY 14627. Offers MS, PhD. Part-time programs available. Terminal master's awarded for partial completion of doctoral program. *Degree requirements:* For master's, comprehensive exam; for doctorate, thesis/dissertation, qualifying exam. *Entrance requirements:* For doctorate, GRE General Test. Additional exam requirements/recommendations for international students: Required—TOEFL. *Faculty research:* Biomechanics, biomedical optics, cell and tissue engineering, medical imaging, neuroengineering.

University of Saskatchewan, College of Graduate Studies and Research, College of Engineering, Division of Biomedical Engineering, Saskatoon, SK S7N 5A2, Canada. Offers M Eng, M Sc, PhD. *Degree requirements:* For master's, thesis (for some programs); for doctorate, thesis/dissertation. *Entrance requirements:* For master's and doctorate, GRE. Additional exam requirements/recommendations for international students: Required—TOEFL. Tuition and fees charges are reported in Canadian dollars. *Expenses:* Tuition, area resident: Full-time $3000 Canadian dollars; part-time $500 Canadian dollars per term. Required fees: $700 Canadian dollars; $100 Canadian dollars per term.

University of Southern California, Graduate School, Viterbi School of Engineering, Department of Biomedical Engineering, Los Angeles, CA 90089. Offers biomedical engineering (MS, PhD), including medical imaging and imaging informatics (MS); medical device and diagnostic engineering (MS). Postbaccalaureate distance learning degree programs offered. *Faculty:* 11 full-time (1 woman), 13 part-time/adjunct (2 women). *Students:* 186 full-time (65 women), 44 part-time (14 women); includes 70 minority (4 African Americans, 1 American Indian/Alaska Native, 56 Asian Americans or Pacific Islanders, 9 Hispanic Americans), 110 international. 339 applicants, 51% accepted, 69 enrolled. In 2009, 61 master's, 18 doctorates awarded. Terminal master's awarded for partial completion of doctoral program. *Degree requirements:* For doctorate, thesis/dissertation. *Entrance requirements:* For master's and doctorate, General GRE. *Application deadline:* For fall admission, 3/1 priority date for domestic and international students; for spring admission, 10/1 priority date for domestic and international students. Applications are processed on a rolling basis. Application fee: $85. Electronic applications accepted. *Expenses:* Tuition: Full-time $25,980; part-time $1315 per unit. Required fees: $554. One-time fee: $35 full-time. Full-time tuition and fees vary according to degree level and program. *Financial support:* In 2009–10, fellowships with full tuition reimbursements (averaging $30,000 per year), research assistantships with full tuition reimbursements (averaging $19,250 per year), teaching assistantships with full tuition reimbursements (averaging $19,250 per year) were awarded; career-related internships or fieldwork, scholarships/grants, health care benefits, and unspecified assistantships also available. Financial award application deadline: 12/1; financial award applicants required to submit CSS PROFILE or FAFSA. *Faculty research:* Medical ultrasound, BioMEMS, neural prosthetics, computational bioengineering, bioengineering of vision, medical devices. Total annual research expenditures: $11.4 million. *Unit head:* Dr. Michael C. K. Khoo, Chair, 213-740-0347, Fax: 213-740-0343, E-mail: khoo@bmsr.usc.edu. *Application contact:* Mischal C. Diasanta, Graduate Student Affairs Advisor, 213-740-0344, Fax: 213-821-3897, E-mail: diasanta@usc.edu.

The University of Tennessee, Graduate School, College of Engineering, Department of Mechanical, Aerospace and Biomedical Engineering, Program in Biomedical Engineering, Knoxville, TN 37996. Offers MS, PhD, MS/PhD. Part-time programs available. *Faculty:* 6 full-time (1 woman), 1 part-time/adjunct (0 women). *Students:* 23 full-time (5 women), 13 part-time (2 women); includes 3 minority (all Asian Americans or Pacific Islanders), 11 international. Average age 29. 55 applicants, 45% accepted, 8 enrolled. In 2009, 10 master's, 2 doctorates awarded. *Degree requirements:* For master's, thesis or alternative; for doctorate, comprehensive exam, thesis/dissertation. *Entrance requirements:* Additional exam requirements/recommendations for international students: Required—TOEFL (minimum score 550 paper-based; 213 computer-based). *Application deadline:* For fall admission, 2/1 priority date for domestic and international students; for spring admission, 6/15 priority date for international students. Applications are processed on a rolling basis. Application fee: $35. Electronic applications accepted. *Expenses:* Tuition, state resident: full-time $6826; part-time $380 per semester hour. Tuition, nonresident: full-time $21,844; part-time $1147 per semester hour. Tuition and fees vary according to program. *Financial support:* In 2009–10, 4 students received support, including 1 fellowship with full tuition reimbursement available (averaging $13,692 per year), 13 research assistantships with full tuition reimbursements available (averaging $14,628 per year), 5 teaching assistantships with full tuition reimbursements available (averaging $10,104 per year); career-related internships or fieldwork, Federal Work-Study, institutionally sponsored loans, health care benefits, and unspecified assistantships also available. Financial award application deadline: 2/1; financial award applicants required to submit FAFSA. *Faculty research:* Bioimaging, biomechanics, biorobotics, biosensors, biomaterials. Total annual research expenditures: $636,000. *Unit head:* Dr. William Hamel, Head, 865-974-5115, Fax: 865-974-5274, E-mail: whamel@utk.edu. *Application contact:* Dr. Gary V. Smith, Chair, Graduate Programs Committee, 865-974-5271, E-mail: gvsmith@utk.edu.

The University of Tennessee, Graduate School, College of Engineering, Department of Mechanical, Aerospace and Biomedical Engineering, Program in Engineering Science, Knoxville, TN 37996. Offers applied artificial intelligence (MS); composite materials (MS, PhD); computational mechanics (MS, PhD); engineering science (MS, PhD); fluid mechanics (MS, PhD); industrial engineering (PhD); optical engineering (MS, PhD); solid mechanics (MS, PhD); MS/MBA. Part-time programs available. *Students:* 9 full-time (0 women), 4 part-time (1 woman); includes 2 minority (both African Americans), 2 international. Average age 34. 5 applicants, 60% accepted, 1 enrolled. In 2009, 2 master's awarded. *Degree requirements:* For master's, thesis or alternative; for doctorate, comprehensive exam, thesis/dissertation. *Entrance requirements:* For master's and doctorate, GRE, minimum GPA of 2.7. Additional exam requirements/recommendations for international students: Required—TOEFL (minimum score 550 paper-based; 213 computer-based). *Application deadline:* For fall admission, 2/1 priority date for domestic and international students; for spring admission, 6/15 priority date for international students. Applications are processed on a rolling basis. Application fee: $35. Electronic applications accepted. *Expenses:* Tuition, state resident: full-time $6826; part-time $380 per semester hour. Tuition, nonresident: full-time $21,844; part-time $1147 per semester hour. Tuition and fees vary according to program. *Financial support:* In 2009–10, 1 student received support, including 5 research assistantships with full tuition reimbursements available (averaging $14,628 per year), 2 teaching assistantships with full tuition reimbursements available (averaging $10,104 per year); fellowships, career-related internships or fieldwork, Federal Work-Study, institutionally sponsored loans, health care benefits, and unspecified assistantships also available. Financial award application deadline: 2/1; financial award applicants required to submit FAFSA. *Faculty research:* Thermal science, computational mechanics, computational fluid dynamics, micro/nano-scale science and engineering for bio-systems. *Unit head:* Dr. William Hamel, Head, 865-974-5115, Fax: 865-974-5274, E-mail: whamel@utk.edu. *Application contact:* Dr. Gary V. Smith, Chair, Graduate Programs Committee, 865-974-5271, E-mail: gvsmith@utk.edu.

The University of Tennessee Health Science Center, College of Medicine, Department of Biomedical Engineering and Imaging, Memphis, TN 38163-0002. Offers MS, PhD. Part-time programs available. Terminal master's awarded for partial completion of doctoral program. *Degree requirements:* For master's, comprehensive exam, thesis; for doctorate, thesis/dissertation, oral and written preliminary and comprehensive exams. *Entrance requirements:* For master's and doctorate, GRE General Test, minimum B average with bachelor's degree in engineering, physics, chemistry, computer or mathematical science, biology, or a closely related field. Additional exam requirements/recommendations for international students: Required—TOEFL. Electronic applications accepted. *Faculty research:* Bioinformatics, drug delivery, medical imaging, orthopedics.

The University of Texas at Austin, Graduate School, Cockrell School of Engineering, Department of Biomedical Engineering, Austin, TX 78712-1111. Offers MS, PhD, MD/PhD. Part-time programs available. *Degree requirements:* For master's, thesis optional; for doctorate, comprehensive exam, thesis/dissertation. *Entrance requirements:* For master's and doctorate, GRE General Test. Additional exam requirements/recommendations for international students: Required—TOEFL (minimum score 550 paper-based; 213 computer-based). Electronic applications accepted. *Faculty research:* Biomechanics, bioengineering, tissue engineering, tissue optics, biothermal studies.

The University of Texas at San Antonio, College of Engineering, Department of Biomedical Engineering, San Antonio, TX 78249-0617. Offers MS, PhD. Part-time and evening/weekend programs available. *Faculty:* 7 full-time (2 women). *Students:* 13 full-time (9 women), 38 part-time (16 women); includes 20 minority (3 African Americans, 3 Asian Americans or Pacific Islanders, 14 Hispanic Americans), 12 international. Average age 28. 56 applicants, 57% accepted, 17 enrolled. In 2009, 3 master's awarded. *Degree requirements:* For master's, comprehensive exam (for some programs), thesis (for some programs); for doctorate, comprehensive exam, thesis/dissertation (for some programs). *Entrance requirements:* For master's, GRE, minimum GPA of 3.0 in last 60 hours; for doctorate, GRE. Additional exam requirements/recommendations for international students: Required—TOEFL (minimum score 500 paper-based; 173 computer-based; 61 iBT), IELTS (minimum score 5). *Application deadline:* For fall admission, 7/1 for domestic students, 4/1 for international students; for spring admission, 11/1 for domestic students, 9/1 for international students. Applications are processed on a rolling basis. Application fee: $45 ($80 for international students). Electronic applications accepted. *Expenses:* Tuition, state resident: full-time $3975; part-time $221 per contact hour. Tuition, nonresident: full-time $13,947; part-time $775 per contact hour. Required fees: $1853. *Financial support:* In 2009–10, 21 students received support, including 1 fellowship (averaging $15,998 per year), 3 research assistantships (averaging $6,344 per year); career-related internships or fieldwork, scholarships/grants, tuition waivers, and unspecified assistantships also available. Support available to part-time students. Total annual research expenditures: $115,470. *Unit head:* Dr. Anson J. Ong, Head, 210-458-7149, Fax: 210-458-7007, E-mail: anson.ong@utsa.edu. *Application contact:* Mark Appleford, Graduate Advisor, 210-458-6840, E-mail: mark.appleford@utsa.edu.

The University of Texas Southwestern Medical Center at Dallas, Southwestern Graduate School of Biomedical Sciences, Division of Applied Science, Biomedical Engineering Program, Dallas, TX 75390. Offers MS, PhD. *Faculty:* 46 full-time (6 women), 22 part-time/adjunct (3 women). *Students:* 15 full-time (4 women), 15 part-time (5 women); includes 3 minority (all Asian Americans or Pacific Islanders), 21 international. Average age 27. 89 applicants, 4% accepted, 1 enrolled. In 2009, 5 doctorates awarded. *Degree requirements:* For master's, comprehensive exam or thesis; for doctorate, comprehensive exam, thesis/dissertation. *Entrance requirements:* For master's, GRE General Test, minimum GPA of 3.0; for doctorate, GRE General Test, minimum GPA of 3.4. Additional exam requirements/recommendations for international students: Required—TOEFL. *Application deadline:* For fall admission, 1/5 priority date for domestic students. Applications are processed on a rolling basis. Application fee: $0. Electronic applications accepted. *Financial support:* Fellowships with partial tuition reimbursements, research assistantships, career-related internships or fieldwork, institutionally sponsored loans, scholarships/grants, and tuition waivers (partial) available. Financial award application deadline: 3/1; financial award applicants required to submit FAFSA. *Faculty research:* Noninvasive image analysis, biomaterials development, rehabilitation engineering, biomechanics, bioinstrumentation. *Unit head:* Dr. Peter P. Antich, Chair, 214-648-2856, Fax: 214-648-2991, E-mail: peter.antich@utsouthwestern.edu. *Application contact:* Kay Emerson, Program Assistant, 214-648-2503, Fax: 214-648-2991, E-mail: kay.emerson@utsouthwestern.edu.

The University of Toledo, College of Graduate Studies, College of Engineering and College of Medicine, PhD Program in Biomedical Engineering, Toledo, OH 43606-3390. Offers PhD. *Degree requirements:* For doctorate, thesis/dissertation, qualifying exam. *Entrance requirements:* For doctorate, GRE General Test, minimum GPA of 3.3. Additional exam requirements/recommendations for international students: Required—TOEFL (minimum score 550 paper-based; 213 computer-based; 80 iBT). Electronic applications accepted. *Faculty research:* Biomechanics, biomaterials, tissue engineering, artificial organs, biosensors.

University of Toronto, School of Graduate Studies, Physical Sciences Division, Faculty of Applied Science and Engineering, Institute of Biomaterials and Biomedical Engineering, Toronto, ON M5S 1A1, Canada. Offers biomedical engineering (MA Sc, PhD); clinical biomedical engineering (MH Sc). Part-time programs available. *Degree requirements:* For master's, thesis (for some programs), research project (MH Sc), oral presentation (MA Sc); for doctorate, thesis/dissertation, qualifying exam. *Entrance requirements:* For master's, bachelor's degree or equivalent in engineering, physical or biological science (MA Sc), minimum A– average; bachelor's degree or equivalent in applied science or engineering (MH Sc); for doctorate, master's degree in engineering, engineering science, medicine, dentistry, or a physical or biological science. Additional exam requirements/recommendations for international students: Required—TOEFL (minimum score 600 paper-based; 260 computer-based), TWE (minimum score 4), Michigan English Language Assessment Battery, IELTS, or COPE.

University of Vermont, Graduate College, College of Engineering and Mathematics, Program in Biomedical Engineering, Burlington, VT 05405. Offers MS. *Students:* 6 (3 women); includes 1 minority (Asian American or Pacific Islander), 2 international. 10 applicants, 10% accepted, 1 enrolled. *Degree requirements:* For master's, thesis. *Entrance requirements:* For master's, GRE General Test. Additional exam requirements/recommendations for international students: Required—TOEFL (minimum score 550 paper-based; 213 computer-based; 80 iBT). *Application deadline:* For fall admission, 2/1 priority date for domestic students. Applications are processed on a rolling basis. Application fee: $40. Electronic applications accepted. *Expenses:* Tuition, area resident: part-time $508 per credit hour. Tuition, state resident: part-time $508 per credit hour. Tuition, nonresident: part-time $1281 per credit hour. *Financial support:* Fellowships, research assistantships, teaching assistantships available. Financial award application deadline: 3/1. *Unit head:* Dr. J. Iatridis, Coordinator, 802-656-3343. *Application contact:* Dr. J. Iatridis, Coordinator, 802-656-3343.

University of Virginia, School of Engineering and Applied Science, Department of Biomedical Engineering, Charlottesville, VA 22903. Offers ME, MS, PhD. *Faculty:* 19 full-time (3 women), 1 part-time/adjunct (0 women). *Students:* 84 full-time (29 women); includes 10 minority (1 African American, 8 Asian Americans or Pacific Islanders, 1 Hispanic American), 14 international. Average age 26. 260 applicants, 20% accepted, 17 enrolled. In 2009, 6 master's, 11 doctorates awarded. *Degree requirements:* For master's, project or thesis; for doctorate, thesis/dissertation. *Entrance requirements:* For master's, GRE General Test, 3 letters of recommendation; for doctorate, GRE General Test, 3 letters of recommendation, essay. Additional exam requirements/recommendations for international students: Required—TOEFL (minimum score 600 paper-based; 250 computer-based; 90 iBT), IELTS (minimum score 7). *Application deadline:* For fall admission, 8/1 for domestic students, 4/1 for international students; for winter admission, 12/1 for domestic students, 8/1 for international students; for spring admission, 5/1 for domestic students, 1/1 for international students. Applications are processed on a rolling basis. Application fee: $60. Electronic applications accepted. *Financial support:* Fellowships, research assistantships, teaching assistantships available. Financial award application deadline: 1/15; financial award applicants required to submit FAFSA. *Faculty research:* Cardiopulmonary and neural engineering, cellular engineering, image processing, orthopedics and rehabilitation engineering. *Unit head:* Michael B. Lawrence, Interim Chair, 434-924-5101, Fax: 434-982-3870, E-mail: bme-dept@virginia.edu. *Application contact:* Jeffrey Holmes, Director of Graduate Programs, E-mail: bmegrad@virginia.edu.

University of Wisconsin–Madison, Graduate School, College of Engineering, Department of Biomedical Engineering, Madison, WI 53706. Offers MS, PhD. Part-time programs available. *Faculty:* 22 full-time (6 women), 55 part-time/adjunct (13 women). *Students:* 101 full-time (39 women), 5 part-time (3 women); includes 19 minority (5 African Americans, 1 American Indian/Alaska Native, 9 Asian Americans or Pacific Islanders, 4 Hispanic Americans), 24 international. Average age 25. 200 applicants, 30% accepted, 40 enrolled. In 2009, 20 master's, 6 doctorates awarded. Terminal master's awarded for partial completion of doctoral program. *Degree requirements:* For master's, thesis optional; for doctorate, comprehensive exam, thesis/dissertation, 32 credits of coursework beyond MS degree. *Entrance requirements:* For master's, GRE, bachelor's degree in engineering or a physical science (chemistry or physics); for doctorate, GRE. Additional exam requirements/recommendations for international students: Recommended—TOEFL (minimum score 550 paper-based; 213 computer-based; 80 iBT), IELTS (minimum score 7). *Application deadline:* For fall admission, 12/31 for domestic and international students; for spring admission, 10/1 for domestic and international students. Application fee: $56. Electronic applications accepted. *Expenses:* Tuition, state resident: part-time $594 per credit. Tuition, nonresident: part-time $1504 per credit. Required fees: $65 per credit. Tuition and fees vary according to course load, program and reciprocity agreements. *Financial support:* In 2009–10, 54 students received support, including 2 fellowships with full tuition reimbursements available (averaging $22,260 per year), 35 research assistantships with full tuition reimbursements available.(averaging $40,368 per year), 14 teaching assistantships with full tuition reimbursements available (averaging $28,175 per year); career-related internships or fieldwork, Federal Work-Study, scholarships/grants, traineeships, and health care benefits also available. *Faculty research:* Biomaterials, bioinstrumentation, cellular scale, biomechanics, biomedical imaging, ergonomics; design, fabrication, and testing of novel micro fabrication techniques; magnetic resonance; tissue engineering; biomedical optics. Total annual research expenditures: $10.5 million. *Unit head:* Dr. Robert G. Radwin, Professor and Chair, 608-263-4660, Fax: 608-265-9239, E-mail: bme@engr.wisc.edu. *Application contact:* Anne Duchek, Graduate Admissions Coordinator, 608-890-2765, Fax: 608-890-2204, E-mail: amduchek@engr.wisc.edu.

Vanderbilt University, School of Engineering and Graduate School, Department of Biomedical Engineering, Nashville, TN 37240-1001. Offers M Eng, MS, PhD, MD/PhD. *Faculty:* 16 full-time (1 woman), 10 part-time/adjunct (0 women). *Students:* 51 full-time (24 women); includes 9 minority (2 African Americans, 1 American Indian/Alaska Native, 4 Asian Americans or Pacific Islanders, 2 Hispanic Americans), 8 international. Average age 26. 172 applicants, 12% accepted, 8 enrolled. In 2009, 8 master's, 9 doctorates awarded. *Degree requirements:* For master's, thesis (for some programs); for doctorate, thesis/dissertation. *Entrance requirements:* For master's, GRE General Test (for all except M Eng); for doctorate, GRE General Test. Additional exam requirements/recommendations for international students: Required—TOEFL. *Application deadline:* For fall admission, 1/15 for domestic and international students; for spring admission, 11/1 for domestic and international students. Application fee: $0. Electronic applications accepted. *Financial support:* In 2009–10, 2 fellowships with full tuition reimbursements (averaging $26,665 per year), 31 research assistantships with full tuition reimbursements (averaging $22,527 per year), 17 teaching assistantships with full tuition reimbursements (averaging $19,000 per year) were awarded; institutionally sponsored loans, scholarships/grants, traineeships, and tuition waivers (partial) also available. Support available to part-time students. Financial award application deadline: 1/15. *Faculty research:* Bio-medical imaging, cell bioengineering, biomedical optics, technology-guided therapy, laser-tissue interaction and spectroscopy. Total annual research expenditures: $10.5 million. *Unit head:* Dr. Todd D. Giorgio, Chair, 615-322-3756, Fax: 615-343-7919, E-mail: todd.d.giorgio@vanderbilt.edu. *Application contact:* Dr. E. Duco Jansen, Director of Graduate Studies, 615-343-1911, Fax: 615-343-7919, E-mail: duco.jansen@vanderbilt.edu.

Virginia Commonwealth University, Graduate School, School of Engineering, Department of Biomedical Engineering, Richmond, VA 23284-9005. Offers MS, PhD, MD/PhD. *Degree requirements:* For master's, thesis; for doctorate, thesis/dissertation, comprehensive oral and written exams. *Entrance requirements:* For master's and doctorate, GRE General Test. *Faculty research:* Clinical instrumentation, mathematical modeling, neurosciences, radiation physics and rehabilitation.

Virginia Polytechnic Institute and State University, Graduate School, Intercollege, Virginia Tech-Wake Forest University School of Biomedical Engineering and Sciences, Blacksburg, VA 24061. Offers MS, PhD. Terminal master's awarded for partial completion of doctoral program. *Degree requirements:* For master's, comprehensive exam, thesis; for doctorate, comprehensive exam, thesis/dissertation, clinical rotation. *Entrance requirements:* For master's and doctorate, GRE. Additional exam requirements/recommendations for international students: Required—TOEFL (minimum score 550 paper-based; 213 computer-based). Electronic applications accepted. *Faculty research:* Biomechanics, cell and tissue engineering, imaging and signal analysis.

Wake Forest University, Virginia Tech-Wake Forest University School of Biomedical Engineering and Sciences, Winston-Salem, NC 27109. Offers biomedical engineering (MS, PhD); DVM/PhD; MD/PhD. Terminal master's awarded for partial completion of doctoral program. *Degree requirements:* For master's, comprehensive exam, thesis; for doctorate, comprehensive exam, thesis/dissertation. *Entrance requirements:* For master's and doctorate, GRE, 3 letters of recommendation. Additional exam requirements/recommendations for international students: Required—TOEFL (minimum score 603 paper-based; 250 computer-based). Electronic applica-

Biomedical Engineering

Wake Forest University (continued)
tions accepted. *Faculty research:* Biomechanics, cell and tissue engineering, medical imaging, medical physics.

Washington University in St. Louis, Henry Edwin Sever Graduate School of Engineering and Applied Science, Department of Biomedical Engineering, St. Louis, MO 63130-4899. Offers MS, D Sc, PhD. Terminal master's awarded for partial completion of doctoral program. *Degree requirements:* For master's, thesis optional; for doctorate, thesis/dissertation. *Entrance requirements:* For master's, GRE, minimum GPA of 3.0; for doctorate, GRE General Test, minimum GPA of 3.5. Additional exam requirements/recommendations for international students: Required—TOEFL. Electronic applications accepted. *Faculty research:* Cell and tissue engineering, molecular engineering, neural engineering.

Wayne State University, College of Engineering, Department of Biomedical Engineering, Detroit, MI 48202. Offers MS, PhD. *Degree requirements:* For master's, thesis optional; for doctorate, thesis/dissertation. *Entrance requirements:* For master's, GRE (optional); for doctorate, GRE, personal statement. Additional exam requirements/recommendations for international students: Required—TOEFL (minimum score 550 paper-based; 213 computer-based); Recommended—TWE (minimum score 6). Electronic applications accepted. *Faculty research:* Injury and orthopedic biomechanics; neurophysiology of pain; smart sensors; biomaterials and imaging.

Worcester Polytechnic Institute, Graduate Studies and Research, Department of Biomedical Engineering, Worcester, MA 01609-2280. Offers biomedical engineering (M Eng, MS, PhD, Graduate Certificate). Part-time and evening/weekend programs available. *Faculty:* 6 full-time (1 woman). *Students:* 22 full-time (11 women), 19 part-time (11 women). 125 applicants, 42% accepted, 19 enrolled. In 2009, 17 master's, 2 doctorates awarded. Terminal master's awarded for partial completion of doctoral program. *Degree requirements:* For master's, thesis optional; for doctorate, comprehensive exam, thesis/dissertation. *Entrance requirements:* For master's, GRE General Test, 3 letters of recommendation; for doctorate, GRE General Test, 3 letters of recommendation, statement of purpose. Additional exam requirements/recommendations for international students: Required—TOEFL (minimum score 550 paper-based; 213 computer-based; 79 iBT), IELTS (minimum score 6.5). *Application deadline:* For fall admission, 1/15 priority date for domestic and international students. Application fee: $70. Electronic applications accepted. *Financial support:* Career-related internships or fieldwork, institutionally sponsored loans, scholarships/grants, and unspecified assistantships available. Financial award application deadline: 1/15. *Faculty research:* Biomedical sensors and instrumentation, biomechanics, nuclear magnetic resonance image and spectroscopy, medical imaging, biomaterial/tissue interactions, engineering and regenerative medicine, biosignal processing. *Unit head:* Dr. Yitzhak Mendelson, Interim Head, 508-831-5447, Fax: 508-831-5541, E-mail: ym@wpi.edu. *Application contact:* Dr. Glenn Gaudette, Graduate Coordinator, 508-831-5447, Fax: 508-831-5541, E-mail: gaudette@wpi.edu.

Wright State University, School of Graduate Studies, College of Engineering and Computer Science, Programs in Engineering, Program in Biomedical and Human Factors Engineering, Dayton, OH 45435. Offers biomedical engineering (MSE); human factors engineering (MSE). Part-time programs available. *Degree requirements:* For master's, thesis or course option alternative. *Entrance requirements:* Additional exam requirements/recommendations for international students: Required—TOEFL. *Faculty research:* Medical imaging, functional electrical stimulation, implantable aids, man-machine interfaces, expert systems.

Yale University, Graduate School of Arts and Sciences, School of Engineering and Applied Science, Department of Biomedical Engineering, New Haven, CT 06520. Offers MS, PhD. *Faculty research:* Biomedical imaging and biosignals; biomechanics; biomolecular engineering and biotechnology.

Biotechnology

The American University in Cairo, Graduate Studies and Research, School of Sciences and Engineering, Program in Biotechnology, Cairo, Egypt. Offers MS.

Arizona State University, Sandra Day O'Connor College of Law, Tempe, AZ 85287-7906. Offers biotechnology and genomics (LL M); law (JD); legal studies (MLS); tribal policy, law and government (LL M); JD/MBA; JD/MD; JD/PhD. *Accreditation:* ABA. *Faculty:* 57 full-time (20 women), 46 part-time/adjunct (12 women). *Students:* 591 full-time (258 women), 35 part-time (21 women); includes 131 minority (12 African Americans, 41 American Indian/Alaska Native, 19 Asian Americans or Pacific Islanders, 59 Hispanic Americans), 16 international. Average age 27. 2,400 applicants, 28% accepted, 184 enrolled. In 2009, 177 first professional degrees awarded. *Degree requirements:* For JD, comprehensive exam, paper. *Entrance requirements:* For JD, LSAT; for master's, bachelor's degree; JD (for LL M). Additional exam requirements/recommendations for international students: Required—TOEFL (minimum score 550 paper-based; 213 computer-based; 80 iBT). *Application deadline:* For fall admission, 11/15 priority date for domestic and international students; for spring admission, 2/1 for domestic and international students. Applications are processed on a rolling basis. Application fee: $60. Electronic applications accepted. *Expenses:* Contact institution. *Financial support:* In 2009–10, 490 students received support; research assistantships, teaching assistantships, career-related internships or fieldwork, Federal Work-Study, institutionally sponsored loans, scholarships/grants, tuition waivers (full and partial), and unspecified assistantships available. Financial award application deadline: 3/5; financial award applicants required to submit FAFSA. *Faculty research:* Emerging technologies and the law, Indian law, law and philosophy, international law, intellectual property. Total annual research expenditures: $514,610. *Unit head:* Dean Paul Schiff Berman, Dean and Foundation Professor of Law, 480-965-6188, Fax: 480-965-6521, E-mail: paul.berman@asu.edu. *Application contact:* Chitra Damania, Director of Operations, 480-965-1474, Fax: 480-727-7930, E-mail: law.admissions@asu.edu.

Brandeis University, Graduate School of Arts and Sciences, Program in Biotechnology, Waltham, MA 02454-9110. Offers MS. *Degree requirements:* For master's, poster presentation. *Entrance requirements:* For master's, GRE, official transcript(s), 3 recommendation letters, CV or resume, statement of purpose. Additional exam requirements/recommendations for international students: Required—TOEFL (minimum score 600 paper-based; 250 computer-based; 100 iBT); Recommended—IELTS (minimum score 7). *Application deadline:* Applications are processed on a rolling basis. Application fee: $75. Electronic applications accepted. *Financial support:* Scholarships/grants available. Financial award application deadline: 4/15; financial award applicants required to submit FAFSA. *Faculty research:* Managing technology and regulatory affairs in biosciences, business and biology, molecular biology, microbiology, molecular pharmacology, protein structure and disease, biostatistics, human genetics, neurobiology of human disease, growth control and cancer, stem cells, human reproductive and developmental biology, enzyme mechanisms, and quantitative approaches to biochemistry. *Unit head:* Prof. Neil Simister, Director of Graduate Studies, 781-736-4952, E-mail: simister@brandeis.edu. *Application contact:* David F. Cotter, Assistant Dean, Graduate School of Arts and Sciences, 781-736-3410, Fax: 781-736-3412, E-mail: gradschool@brandeis.edu.

Brigham Young University, Graduate Studies, College of Life Sciences, Department of Plant and Wildlife Sciences, Provo, UT 84602-1001. Offers environmental science (MS); genetics and biotechnology (MS); wildlife and wildlands conservation (MS, PhD). *Faculty:* 21 full-time (1 woman), 15 part-time/adjunct (3 women). *Students:* 35 full-time (13 women), 18 part-time (5 women); includes 7 minority (2 Asian Americans or Pacific Islanders, 5 Hispanic Americans), 5 international. Average age 29. 34 applicants, 68% accepted, 21 enrolled. In 2009, 9 master's, 1 doctorate awarded. *Degree requirements:* For master's, thesis; for doctorate, comprehensive exam, thesis/dissertation, minimum GPA of 3.0, 54 hours (18 dissertation, 36 coursework). *Entrance requirements:* For master's, GRE General Test, minimum GPA of 3.0 during last 60 hours of course work; for doctorate, GRE, minimum GPA of 3.0. Additional exam requirements/recommendations for international students: Required—TOEFL (minimum score 580 paper-based; 237 computer-based; 85 iBT). *Application deadline:* 2/1 for domestic and international students. Applications are processed on a rolling basis. Application fee: $50. Electronic applications accepted. *Expenses:* Tuition: Full-time $5580; part-time $301 per credit hour. Tuition and fees vary according to student's religious affiliation. *Financial support:* In 2009–10, 22 students received support, including 2 research assistantships with partial tuition reimbursements available (averaging $16,650 per year), 37 teaching assistantships with partial tuition reimbursements available (averaging $16,650 per year); scholarships/grants and tuition waivers (partial) also available. Financial award application deadline: 2/1. *Faculty research:* environmental science, plant genetics, plant ecology, plant nutrition and pathology, wildlife and wildlands conservation. Total annual research expenditures: $1.1 million. *Unit head:* Dr. Val J. Anderson, Chair, 801-422-3527, Fax: 801-422-0008, E-mail: val_anderson@byu.edu. *Application contact:* Dr. Loreen Allphin, Graduate Coordinator, 801-422-5603, Fax: 801-422-0008, E-mail: loreen_allphin@byu.edu.

Brock University, Faculty of Graduate Studies, Faculty of Mathematics and Science, Program in Biotechnology, St. Catharines, ON L2S 3A1, Canada. Offers M Sc, PhD. Part-time programs available. *Degree requirements:* For master's, thesis; for doctorate, thesis/dissertation. *Entrance requirements:* For master's, honors B Sc; for doctorate, M Sc. Additional exam requirements/recommendations for international students: Required—TOEFL (minimum score 550 paper-based; 213 computer-based; 80 iBT), IELTS (minimum score 6.5), TWE (minimum score 4). Electronic applications accepted. *Faculty research:* Bioorganic chemistry, structural chemistry, electrochemistry, cell and molecular biology, plant sciences, oenology, and viticulture.

Brown University, Graduate School, Division of Biology and Medicine, Program in Artificial Organs, Biomaterials, and Cell Technology, Providence, RI 02912. Offers MA, Sc M, PhD. Terminal master's awarded for partial completion of doctoral program. *Degree requirements:* For doctorate, thesis/dissertation, preliminary exam. *Entrance requirements:* For master's and doctorate, GRE General Test, GRE Subject Test. Additional exam requirements/recommendations for international students: Required—TOEFL. Electronic applications accepted.

California State University Channel Islands, Extended Education, Programs in Biotechnology, Camarillo, CA 93012. Offers biotechnology and bioinformatics (MS); MS/MBA. *Entrance requirements:* Additional exam requirements/recommendations for international students: Required—TOEFL (minimum score 550 paper-based).

Carnegie Mellon University, H. John Heinz III College, School of Public Policy and Management, Program in Biotechnology and Management, Pittsburgh, PA 15213-3891. Offers MS. *Accreditation:* AACSB.

Carnegie Mellon University, Mellon College of Science, Department of Chemistry, Pittsburgh, PA 15213-3891. Offers biotechnology and management (MS); chemistry (PhD), including bioinorganic, bioorganic, organic and materials, biophysics and spectroscopy, computational and theoretical, polymer; colloids, polymers and surfaces (MS). Part-time programs available. Terminal master's awarded for partial completion of doctoral program. *Degree requirements:* For doctorate, thesis/dissertation, departmental qualifying and oral exams, teaching experience. *Entrance requirements:* For master's, GRE General Test; for doctorate, GRE General Test, GRE Subject Test. Additional exam requirements/recommendations for international students: Required—TOEFL. Electronic applications accepted. *Faculty research:* Physical and theoretical chemistry, chemical synthesis, biophysical/bioinorganic chemistry.

Claflin University, Graduate Programs, Orangeburg, SC 29115. Offers biotechnology (MS); business administration (MBA); educational studies (M Ed). Part-time programs available. *Entrance requirements:* For master's, GRE, GMAT, baccalaureate degree, 3 letters of recommendation. Additional exam requirements/recommendations for international students: Recommended—TOEFL (minimum score 550 paper-based; 213 computer-based).

Concordia University, School of Graduate Studies, Faculty of Arts and Science, Department of Biology, Montréal, QC H3G 1M8, Canada. Offers biology (M Sc, PhD); biotechnology and genomics (Diploma). *Degree requirements:* For master's, thesis; for doctorate, thesis/dissertation, pedagogical training. *Entrance requirements:* For master's, honors degree in biology; for doctorate, M Sc in life science. *Faculty research:* Cell biology, animal physiology, ecology, microbiology/molecular biology, plant physiology/biochemistry and biotechnology.

Dartmouth College, Thayer School of Engineering, Program in Biotechnology and Biochemical Engineering, Hanover, NH 03755. Offers MS, PhD. *Degree requirements:* For master's, thesis; for doctorate, thesis/dissertation, candidacy oral exam. *Entrance requirements:* For master's and doctorate, GRE General Test. *Application deadline:* For fall admission, 1/1 priority date for domestic students. Application fee: $45. *Financial support:* Fellowships, research assistantships, teaching assistantships, career-related internships or fieldwork, Federal Work-Study, institutionally sponsored loans, and tuition waivers (full and partial) available. Financial award application deadline: 1/15. *Faculty research:* Biomass processing, metabolic engineering, kinetics and reactor design, applied microbiology, resource and environmental analysis. Total annual research expenditures: $3.1 million. *Unit head:* Dr. Joseph J. Helbie, Dean, 603-646-2238, Fax: 603-646-2580, E-mail: joseph.j.helbie@dartmouth.edu. *Application contact:* Candace S. Potter, Graduate Admissions Administrator, 603-646-3844, Fax: 603-646-1620, E-mail: candace.potter@dartmouth.edu.

Duquesne University, Bayer School of Natural and Environmental Sciences, Program in Biotechnology, Pittsburgh, PA 15282-0001. Offers MS. Part-time programs available. *Faculty:* 1 full-time (0 women). *Students:* 4 full-time (1 woman), 6 part-time (3 women), 1 international. Average age 23. 18 applicants, 50% accepted, 5 enrolled. In 2009, 4 master's awarded. *Entrance requirements:* For master's, GRE General Test, 3 letters of recommendation. Additional exam requirements/recommendations for international students: Required—TOEFL (minimum score 80 iBT). *Application deadline:* For fall admission, 5/1 priority date for domestic students, 5/1 for international students; for spring admission, 10/1 priority date for domestic students, 10/1 for international students. Applications are processed on a rolling basis. Application fee: $0 ($40 for international students). Electronic applications accepted. *Expenses:* Tuition: Part-time $851 per credit. Required fees: $81 per credit. *Financial support:* Career-related internships or fieldwork available. *Unit head:* Dr. Alan W. Seadler, Director, 412-396-1568, E-mail: seadlera@duq.edu. *Application contact:* Heather Costello, Graduate Academic Advisor, 412-396-6339, Fax: 412-396-4881, E-mail: costelloh@duq.edu.

East Carolina University, Graduate School, Thomas Harriot College of Arts and Sciences, Department of Biology, Greenville, NC 27858-4353. Offers biology (MS); molecular biology/biotechnology (MS). Part-time programs available. *Degree requirements:* For master's, one foreign language, comprehensive exam, thesis. *Entrance requirements:* For master's, GRE General Test, GRE Subject Test. Additional exam requirements/recommendations for international students: Required—TOEFL. *Faculty research:* Biochemistry, microbiology, cell biology.

Florida Institute of Technology, Graduate Programs, College of Science, Department of Biological Sciences, Melbourne, FL 32901-6975. Offers biological sciences (PhD); biotechnology (MS); cell and molecular biology (MS, PhD); ecology (MS); marine biology (MS). Part-time programs available. *Faculty:* 15 full-time (1 woman). *Students:* 60 full-time (35 women), 6 part-time (4 women); includes 4 minority (all Hispanic Americans), 28 international. Average age 27. 188 applicants, 43% accepted, 20 enrolled. In 2009, 16 master's, 4 doctorates awarded. *Degree requirements:* For master's, thesis (for some programs), thesis seminar of publication quality; for doctorate, thesis/dissertation, dissertations seminar, publications. *Entrance requirements:* For master's, GRE General Test, 3 letters of recommendation, minimum GPA of 3.0, resume; for doctorate, GRE General Test, GRE Subject Test, resume, 3 letters of recommendation, minimum GPA of 3.2, statement of objectives. Additional exam requirements/recommendations for international students: Required—TOEFL (minimum score 550 paper-based; 213 computer-based; 79 iBT). *Application deadline:* For fall admission, 3/1 for domestic and international students; for spring admission, 9/1 for domestic and international students. Applications are processed on a rolling basis. Application fee: $50. Electronic applications accepted. *Expenses:* Tuition: Part-time $1015 per credit. Tuition and fees vary according to campus/location and program. *Financial support:* In 2009–10, 35 students received support, including 14 research assistantships with full and partial tuition reimbursements available (averaging $12,417 per year), 21 teaching assistantships with full and partial tuition reimbursements available (averaging $14,255 per year); career-related internships or fieldwork, institutionally sponsored loans, tuition waivers (partial), unspecified assistantships, and tuition remissions also available. Support available to part-time students. Financial award application deadline: 3/1; financial award applicants required to submit FAFSA. *Faculty research:* Initiation of protein synthesis in eukaryotic cells, fixation of radioactive carbon, changes in DNA molecule, endangered or threatened avian and mammalian species, hydroacoustics and feeding preference of the West Indian manatee. Total annual research expenditures: $1.2 million. *Unit head:* Dr. Richard B. Aronson, Department Head, 321-674-8034, Fax: 321-674-7238, E-mail: raronson@fit.edu. *Application contact:* Thomas M. Shea, Director of Graduate Admissions, 321-674-7577, Fax: 321-723-9468, E-mail: tshea@fit.edu.

The George Washington University, College of Professional Studies, Program in Molecular Biotechnology, Washington, DC 20052. Offers MPS. *Students:* 8 full-time (6 women), 2 part-time (1 woman); includes 3 minority (1 Asian American or Pacific Islander, 2 Hispanic Americans), 4 international. Average age 28. 25 applicants, 76% accepted, 5 enrolled. In 2009, 7 master's awarded. *Application deadline:* For fall admission, 4/1 for domestic and international students. Application fee: $25. Electronic applications accepted. *Financial support:* In 2009–10, 8 students received support. Tuition waivers available. *Unit head:* Dr. Mark Reeves, Director, 202-994-6279, Fax: 202-994-3001, E-mail: reevesme@gwu.edu. *Application contact:* Kristin Williams, Assistant Vice President for Graduate and Special Enrollment Management, 202-994-0467, Fax: 202-994-0371, E-mail: ksw@gwu.edu.

Harvard University, Extension School, Cambridge, MA 02138-3722. Offers applied sciences (CAS); biotechnology (ALM); educational technologies (ALM); educational technology (CET); English for graduate and professional studies (DGP); environmental management (ALM, CEM); information technology (ALM); journalism (ALM); liberal arts (ALM); management (ALM, CM); mathematics for teaching (ALM); museum studies (ALM); premedical studies (Diploma); publication and communication (CPC). Part-time and evening/weekend programs available. *Degree requirements:* For master's, thesis. *Entrance requirements:* For master's, 3 completed graduate courses with grade of B or higher. Additional exam requirements/recommendations for international students: Required—TOEFL (minimum score 600 paper-based; 250 computer-based), TWE (minimum score 5). *Expenses:* Contact institution.

Hood College, Graduate School, Program in Biomedical Science, Frederick, MD 21701-8575. Offers biomedical science (MS), including biotechnology/molecular biology, microbiology/immunology/virology, regulatory compliance; regulatory compliance (Certificate). Part-time and evening/weekend programs available. *Faculty:* 3 full-time (1 woman), 4 part-time/adjunct (2 women). *Students:* 9 full-time (2 women), 82 part-time (54 women); includes 23 minority (17 African Americans, 2 Asian Americans or Pacific Islanders, 4 Hispanic Americans), 7 international. Average age 29. 51 applicants, 67% accepted, 28 enrolled. In 2009, 11 master's, 10 other advanced degrees awarded. *Degree requirements:* For master's, comprehensive exam, thesis or alternative. *Entrance requirements:* For master's, bachelor's degree in biology; minimum GPA of 2.75; undergraduate course work in cell biology, chemistry, organic chemistry, and genetics. Additional exam requirements/recommendations for international students: Required—TOEFL (minimum score 575 paper-based; 231 computer-based; 89 iBT). *Application deadline:* For fall admission, 7/15 for domestic and international students; for spring admission, 12/15 for domestic and international students. Applications are processed on a rolling basis. Application fee: $35. Electronic applications accepted. *Expenses:* Tuition: Full-time $6480; part-time $360 per credit. Required fees: $100; $50 per term. *Financial support:* In 2009–10, 3 research assistantships with full tuition reimbursements (averaging $10,609 per year) were awarded. Financial award applicants required to submit FAFSA. *Unit head:* Dr. Oney Smith, Director, 301-696-3653, Fax: 301-696-3597, E-mail: osmith@hood.edu. *Application contact:* Dr. Allen P. Flora, Dean of Graduate School, 301-696-3811, Fax: 301-696-3597, E-mail: gofurther@hood.edu.

Howard University, College of Medicine, Department of Biochemistry and Molecular Biology, Washington, DC 20059-0002. Offers biochemistry and molecular biology (PhD); biotechnology (MS); MD/PhD. Part-time programs available. *Degree requirements:* For master's, externship; for doctorate, comprehensive exam, thesis/dissertation. *Entrance requirements:* For master's and doctorate, GRE General Test, minimum GPA of 3.0. *Faculty research:* Cellular and molecular biology of olfaction, gene regulation and expression, enzymology, NMR spectroscopy of molecular structure, hormone regulation/metabolism.

Illinois State University, Graduate School, College of Arts and Sciences, Department of Biological Sciences, Program in Biotechnology, Normal, IL 61790-2200. Offers MS. *Degree requirements:* For master's, thesis or alternative. *Entrance requirements:* For master's, GRE General Test, minimum GPA of 2.6 in last 60 hours of course work.

Indiana University Bloomington, University Graduate School, College of Arts and Sciences, Department of Biology, Bloomington, IN 47405. Offers biology teaching (MAT); biotechnology (MA); evolution, ecology, and behavior (MA, PhD); genetics (PhD); microbiology (MA, PhD); molecular, cellular, and developmental biology (PhD); plant sciences (MA, PhD); zoology (MA, PhD). *Faculty:* 58 full-time (15 women), 21 part-time/adjunct (6 women). *Students:* 165 full-time (95 women); includes 14 minority (6 African Americans, 1 American Indian/Alaska Native, 7 Asian Americans or Pacific Islanders), 56 international. Average age 27. 312 applicants, 19% accepted, 24 enrolled. In 2009, 4 master's, 22 doctorates awarded. Terminal master's awarded for partial completion of doctoral program. *Degree requirements:* For master's, thesis, oral defense; for doctorate, thesis/dissertation, oral defense. *Entrance requirements:* For master's and doctorate, GRE General Test. Additional exam requirements/recommendations for international students: Required—TOEFL (minimum score 100 iBT). *Application deadline:* For fall admission, 1/5 priority date for domestic students, 12/1 priority date for international students. Application fee: $55 ($65 for international students). Electronic applications accepted. *Financial support:* In 2009–10, 165 students received support, including 62 fellowships with tuition reimbursements available (averaging $19,484 per year), 27 research assistantships with tuition reimbursements available (averaging $22,605 per year), 76 teaching assistantships with tuition reimbursements available (averaging $20,528 per year); scholarships/grants, traineeships, health care benefits, and unspecified assistantships also available. Financial award application deadline: 1/5. *Faculty research:* Evolution, ecology and behavior; microbiology; molecular biology and genetics; plant biology. *Unit head:* Dr. Roger Innes, Chair, 812-855-2219, Fax: 812-855-6082, E-mail: rinnes@indiana.edu. *Application contact:* Tracey D. Stohr, Graduate Student Recruitment Coordinator, 812-856-6303, Fax: 812-855-6082, E-mail: gradbio@indiana.edu.

Instituto Tecnológico y de Estudios Superiores de Monterrey, Campus Monterrey, Graduate and Research Division, Program in Natural and Social Sciences, Monterrey, Mexico. Offers biotechnology (MS); chemistry (MS, PhD); communications (MS); education (MA). Part-time programs available. *Degree requirements:* For master's, one foreign language, thesis; for doctorate, one foreign language, thesis/dissertation. *Entrance requirements:* For master's, EXADEP; for doctorate, EXADEP, master's degree in related field. Additional exam requirements/recommendations for international students: Required—TOEFL. *Faculty research:* Cultural industries, mineral substances, bioremediation, food processing, CQ in industrial chemical processing.

Inter American University of Puerto Rico, Bayamón Campus, Graduate School, Bayamón, PR 00957. Offers biology (MS), including environmental sciences and ecology, molecular biotechnology; electronic commerce (MBA); human resources (MBA). Part-time and evening/weekend programs available. *Faculty:* 6 full-time (1 woman), 5 part-time/adjunct (2 women). *Students:* 99 part-time (61 women); includes all Hispanic Americans. Average age 31. *Degree requirements:* For master's, comprehensive exam, research project. *Entrance requirements:* For master's, EXADEP, GRE General Test, letters of recommendation. *Application deadline:* For fall admission, 7/1 for domestic students, 5/1 priority date for international students; for winter admission, 11/15 priority date for domestic and international students; for spring admission, 2/15 priority date for domestic and international students. Application fee: $31. *Expenses:* Tuition: Part-time $195 per credit. Required fees: $148 per trimester. *Unit head:* Prof. Juan F. Martinez, Rector, 787-279-1200 Ext. 2295, Fax: 787-279-2205, E-mail: jmartinez@bc.inter.edu. *Application contact:* Carlos Alicea, Director of Admission, 787-279-1200 Ext. 2017, Fax: 787-279-2205, E-mail: calicea@bc.inter.edu.

The Johns Hopkins University, G. W. C. Whiting School of Engineering, Program in Engineering Management, Baltimore, MD 21218-2699. Offers biomaterials (MSEM); communications science (MSEM); computer science (MSEM); fluid mechanics (MSEM); materials science and engineering (MSEM); mechanical engineering (MSEM); mechanics and materials (MSEM); nano-biotechnology (MSEM); nanomaterials and nanotechnology (MSEM); probability and statistics (MSEM); smart product and device design (MSEM); systems analysis, management and environmental policy (MSEM). *Students:* 12 full-time (0 women), 3 international. Average age 23. 66 applicants, 67% accepted. *Entrance requirements:* For master's, GRE, 3 letters of recommendation, resume. Additional exam requirements/recommendations for international students: Required—TOEFL (minimum score 600 paper-based; 250 computer-based; 100 iBT) or IELTS (minimum score 7). *Application deadline:* For fall admission, 1/15 priority date for domestic students, 1/15 for international students; for spring admission, 9/15 priority date for domestic students, 9/15 for international students. Applications are processed on a rolling basis. Application fee: $75. Electronic applications accepted. *Financial support:* Fellowships, health care benefits available. *Unit head:* Dr. Edward R. Scheinerman, Interim Director/Vice Dean for Education, School of Engineering/Professor, Applied Mathematics and Statistics, 410-516-7395, Fax: 410-516-4880, E-mail: ers@jhu.edu. *Application contact:* Dennis McIver, Coordinator of Graduate Admissions, 410-516-8174, Fax: 410-516-0780, E-mail: graduateadmissions@jhu.edu.

The Johns Hopkins University, Zanvyl Krieger School of Arts and Sciences, Advanced Academic Programs, Program in Biotechnology, Baltimore, MD 21218-2699. Offers MS, MS/MBA. Part-time and evening/weekend programs available. Postbaccalaureate distance learning degree programs offered (minimal on-campus study). *Faculty:* 8 full-time (4 women), 99 part-time/adjunct (21 women). *Students:* 107 full-time (62 women), 463 part-time (281 women); includes 148 minority (47 African Americans, 2 American Indian/Alaska Native, 77 Asian Americans or Pacific Islanders, 22 Hispanic Americans), 77 international. Average age 31. 368 applicants, 57% accepted, 182 enrolled. In 2009, 163 master's awarded. *Degree requirements:* For master's, thesis (for some programs). *Entrance requirements:* For master's, minimum GPA of 3.0; coursework in biology and chemistry. Additional exam requirements/recommendations for international students: Required—TOEFL (minimum score 250 computer-based; 100 iBT). *Application deadline:* For fall admission, 5/31 priority date for domestic students, 4/30 priority date for international students; for spring admission, 10/31 priority date for domestic and international students. Applications are processed on a rolling basis. Application fee: $75. Electronic applications accepted. *Financial support:* Applicants required to submit FAFSA. *Unit head:* Dr. Lynn Johnson Langer, Senior Associate Program Chair, 301-294-7063, Fax: 301-294-7000. *Application contact:* Valana M. McMickens, Director of Admissions/Student Services, 202-452-1941, Fax: 202-452-1970, E-mail: aapadmissions@jhu.edu.

Kean University, Nathan Weiss Graduate College, Program in Biotechnology, Union, NJ 07083. Offers MS. Part-time and evening/weekend programs available. *Faculty:* 6 full-time (3 women). *Students:* 7 full-time (3 women), 19 part-time (13 women); includes 7 minority (1 African American, 4 Asian Americans or Pacific Islanders, 2 Hispanic Americans), 6 international. Average age 30. 18 applicants, 89% accepted, 9 enrolled. In 2009, 8 master's awarded. *Degree requirements:* For master's, internship or externship, presentation of research. *Entrance requirements:* For master's, GRE General Test, minimum GPA of 3.0 overall and in all science and math courses, 3 letters of recommendation, departmental interview. *Application deadline:* For fall admission, 5/1 for domestic students. Application fee: $60 ($150 for international students). Electronic applications accepted. *Expenses:* Tuition, state resident: full-time $10,440; part-time $435 per credit. Tuition, nonresident: full-time $14,160; part-time $590 per credit. Required fees: $2642; $110 per credit. Part-time tuition and fees vary according to course load and degree level. *Financial support:* In 2009–10, 2 research assistantships with full tuition reimbursements (averaging $3,263 per year) were awarded; unspecified assistantships also available. *Unit head:* Dr. Dil Ramanathan, Program Coordinator, 908-737-3426, Fax: 908-737-3425, E-mail: ramanatd@kean.edu. *Application contact:* Reenat Hasan, Pre-Admissions Coordinator, 908-737-5923, Fax: 908-737-5965, E-mail: rhasan@exchange.kean.edu.

Marywood University, Academic Affairs, College of Liberal Arts and Sciences, Science Department, Program in Biotechnology, Scranton, PA 18509-1598. Offers MS. *Students:* 3 full-time (all women), 5 part-time (3 women), 2 international. Average age 24. In 2009, 6 master's awarded. *Entrance requirements:* Additional exam requirements/recommendations for international students: Required—TOEFL (minimum score 550 paper-based; 213 computer-based; 79 iBT). *Application deadline:* For fall admission, 1/9 priority date for domestic and international students. Application fee: $35. Electronic applications accepted. *Expenses:* Tuition: Part-time $715 per credit. Required fees: $270 per semester. Tuition and fees vary according to degree level, campus/location and program. *Financial support:* Career-related internships or fieldwork, scholarships/grants, and unspecified assistantships available. Support available to part-time students. Financial award application deadline: 6/30; financial award applicants required to submit FAFSA. *Faculty research:* Microbiology, molecular biology, genetics. *Application contact:* Tammy Manka, Assistant Director of Graduate Admissions, 866-279-9663, E-mail: tmanka@marywood.edu.

McGill University, Faculty of Graduate and Postdoctoral Studies, Faculty of Agricultural and Environmental Sciences, Institute of Parasitology, Montréal, QC H3A 2T5, Canada. Offers biotechnology (M Sc A, Certificate); parasitology (M Sc, PhD).

North Carolina State University, Graduate School, College of Agriculture and Life Sciences, Department of Microbiology, Program in Microbial Biotechnology, Raleigh, NC 27695. Offers MMB. *Entrance requirements:* For master's, GRE. Electronic applications accepted.

Northeastern University, Bouvé College of Health Sciences Graduate School and College of Arts and Sciences and College of Engineering, Program in Biotechnology, Boston, MA 02115-5096. Offers MS, PSM. Part-time and evening/weekend programs available. *Students:* 56 full-time (33 women), 16 part-time (5 women); includes 1 African American, 1 Asian American or Pacific Islander, 42 international. 190 applicants, 58% accepted, 41 enrolled. In 2009, 16

Biotechnology

Northeastern University (continued)

master's awarded. *Entrance requirements:* For master's, GRE. Additional exam requirements/recommendations for international students: Required—TOEFL (minimum score 600 paper-based; 250 computer-based; 100 iBT). *Application deadline:* For fall admission, 4/1 for domestic students. Application fee: $50. Electronic applications accepted. *Expenses:* Contact institution. *Financial support:* Teaching assistantships, scholarships/grants available. *Faculty research:* Genomics, proteomics, gene expression analysis (molecular biotechnology), drug discovery, development, delivery (pharmaceutical biotechnology), bioprocess development and optimization (process development). *Unit head:* Prof. Thomas Gilbert, Professor, 617-373-4505, E-mail: t.gilbert@neu.edu. *Application contact:* Cynthia Bainton, Administrative Manager, 617-373-2627, Fax: 617-373-8795, E-mail: c.bainton@neu.edu.

Northeastern University, College of Science, Department of Biology, Boston, MA 02115-5096. Offers bioinformatics (PMS); biology (MS, PhD); biotechnology (MS); marine biology (MS). Part-time programs available. *Faculty:* 27 full-time (10 women), 5 part-time/adjunct (all women). *Students:* 111 full-time (67 women); includes 2 African Americans, 3 Asian Americans or Pacific Islanders, 3 Hispanic Americans, 39 international. 178 applicants, 28% accepted, 35 enrolled. In 2009, 31 master's, 5 doctorates awarded. Terminal master's awarded for partial completion of doctoral program. *Degree requirements:* For master's, thesis (for some programs); for doctorate, thesis/dissertation, qualifying exam. *Entrance requirements:* For master's and doctorate, GRE General Test. Additional exam requirements/recommendations for international students: Required—TOEFL (minimum score 250 computer-based). *Application deadline:* For fall admission, 1/1 priority date for domestic and international students. Applications are processed on a rolling basis. Application fee: $50. Electronic applications accepted. *Financial support:* In 2009–10, 19 research assistantships with tuition reimbursements (averaging $18,285 per year), 41 teaching assistantships with tuition reimbursements (averaging $18,285 per year) were awarded; fellowships with tuition reimbursements, career-related internships or fieldwork, Federal Work-Study, tuition waivers (full and partial), and unspecified assistantships also available. Financial award application deadline: 3/1; financial award applicants required to submit FAFSA. *Faculty research:* Biochemistry, marine sciences, molecular biology, microbiology and immunology neurobiology, cellular and molecular biology, biochemistry, marine biochemistry and ecology, microbiology, neurobiology, biotechnology. *Unit head:* Dr. Wendy Smith, Graduate Coordinator, 617-373-2260, Fax: 617-373-3724, E-mail: gradbio@neu.edu. *Application contact:* Jo-Anne Dickinson, Admissions Assistant, 617-373-5990, Fax: 617-373-7281, E-mail: gsas@neu.edu.

Northwestern University, The Graduate School and Judd A. and Marjorie Weinberg College of Arts and Sciences, Interdepartmental Biological Sciences Program (IBiS), Evanston, IL 60208. Offers biochemistry, molecular biology, and cell biology (PhD), including biochemistry, cell and molecular biology, molecular biophysics, structural biology; biotechnology (PhD); cell and molecular biology (PhD); developmental biology and genetics (PhD); hormone action and signal transduction (PhD); neuroscience (PhD); structural biology, biochemistry, and biophysics (PhD). Program participants include the Departments of Biochemistry, Molecular Biology, and Cell Biology; Chemistry; Neurobiology and Physiology; Chemical Engineering; Civil Engineering; and Evanston Hospital. *Degree requirements:* For doctorate, thesis/dissertation, qualifying exam. *Entrance requirements:* For doctorate, GRE General Test. Additional exam requirements/recommendations for international students: Required—TOEFL (minimum score 600 paper-based). Electronic applications accepted. *Faculty research:* Developmental genetics, gene regulation, DNA-protein interactions, biological clocks, bioremediation.

Polytechnic Institute of NYU, Department of Chemical and Biological Sciences, Major in Biotechnology, Brooklyn, NY 11201-2990. Offers MS. *Students:* 76 full-time (26 women), 16 part-time (6 women); includes 3 minority (1 African American, 2 Asian Americans or Pacific Islanders), 85 international. 153 applicants, 56% accepted, 30 enrolled. In 2009, 14 master's awarded. *Entrance requirements:* Additional exam requirements/recommendations for international students: Required—TOEFL (minimum score 550 paper-based; 213 computer-based; 80 iBT); Recommended—IELTS (minimum score 6.5). *Application deadline:* For fall admission, 7/31 priority date for domestic students, 4/30 priority date for international students; for spring admission, 12/31 priority date for domestic students, 10/30 priority date for international students. Applications are processed on a rolling basis. Application fee: $75. Electronic applications accepted. *Expenses:* Tuition: Full-time $21,492; part-time $1194 per credit hour. Required fees: $1160; $204 per course. *Unit head:* Dr. Bruce Garetz, Department Head, 718-260-3600. *Application contact:* JeanCarlo Bonilla, Director of Graduate Enrollment Management, 718-260-3182, Fax: 718-260-3624, E-mail: gradinfo@poly.edu.

Polytechnic Institute of NYU, Department of Chemical and Biological Sciences, Major in Biotechnology and Entrepreneurship, Brooklyn, NY 11201-2990. Offers MS. *Students:* 25 full-time (6 women), 7 part-time (1 woman); includes 1 minority (Asian American or Pacific Islander), 31 international. 80 applicants, 46% accepted, 8 enrolled. In 2009, 14 master's awarded. *Entrance requirements:* Additional exam requirements/recommendations for international students: Required—TOEFL (minimum score 550 paper-based; 213 computer-based; 80 iBT); Recommended—IELTS (minimum score 6.5). *Application deadline:* For fall admission, 7/31 priority date for domestic students, 4/30 priority date for international students; for spring admission, 12/31 priority date for domestic students, 10/30 priority date for international students. Applications are processed on a rolling basis. Application fee: $75. Electronic applications accepted. *Expenses:* Tuition: Full-time $21,492; part-time $1194 per credit hour. Required fees: $1160; $204 per course. *Financial support:* Institutionally sponsored loans, scholarships/grants, and unspecified assistantships available. Support available to part-time students. *Unit head:* Dr. Bruce Garetz, Department Head, 718-260-3600. *Application contact:* JeanCarlo Bonilla, Director of Graduate Enrollment Management, 718-260-3182, Fax: 718-260-3624, E-mail: gradinfo@poly.edu.

Purdue University Calumet, Graduate School, School of Engineering, Mathematics, and Science, Department of Biological Sciences, Program in Biotechnology, Hammond, IN 46323-2094. Offers MS. *Degree requirements:* For master's, thesis (for some programs). *Entrance requirements:* For master's, GRE General Test, 3 letters of recommendation.

Regis College, Department of Health Product Regulation and Clinical Research, Weston, MA 02493. Offers MS. Part-time and evening/weekend programs available. *Faculty:* 1 full-time (0 women), 7 part-time/adjunct (2 women). *Students:* 1 (woman) full-time, 26 part-time (21 women); includes 2 minority (both Asian Americans or Pacific Islanders). Average age 37. 10 applicants, 100% accepted, 8 enrolled. In 2009, 15 master's awarded. *Degree requirements:* For master's, thesis optional, internship. *Entrance requirements:* For master's, GRE or MAT. Additional exam requirements/recommendations for international students: Required—TOEFL (minimum score 550 paper-based; 213 computer-based). *Application deadline:* Applications are processed on a rolling basis. Application fee: $50. *Expenses:* Contact institution. *Financial support:* In 2009–10, 7 students received support. Career-related internships or fieldwork and scholarships/grants available. Financial award applicants required to submit FAFSA. *Faculty research:* FDA regulatory affairs medical device. *Unit head:* Charles Burr, Director, 781-768-7008, E-mail: charles.burr@regiscollege.edu. *Application contact:* Christine Petherick, Administrative Coordinator, Graduate Admission, 866-438-7344, Fax: 781-768-7071, E-mail: christine.petherick@regiscollege.edu.

Roosevelt University, Graduate Division, College of Arts and Sciences, Department of Biological, Chemical, and Physical Sciences, Chicago, IL 60605. Offers biotechnology and chemical science (MS). Part-time and evening/weekend programs available. *Degree requirements:* For master's, thesis optional. *Entrance requirements:* For master's, minimum GPA of 2.7, undergraduate course work in science and mathematics. *Faculty research:* Phase-transfer catalysts, bioinorganic chemistry, long chain dicarboxylic acids, organosilicon compounds, spectroscopic studies.

St. John's University, Institute for Biotechnology, Queens, NY 11439. Offers biological/pharmaceutical biotechnology (MS). *Students:* 14 full-time (8 women), 7 part-time (5 women); includes 6 minority (1 African American, 5 Asian Americans or Pacific Islanders), 12 international. Average age 24. 91 applicants, 38% accepted, 8 enrolled. In 2009, 3 master's awarded. *Entrance requirements:* For master's, GRE General and Subject Tests, minimum GPA of 3.0. Additional exam requirements/recommendations for international students: Required—TOEFL (minimum score 500 paper-based; 173 computer-based; 61 iBT), IELTS (minimum score 5.5). *Application deadline:* For fall admission, 5/1 priority date for domestic and international students; for spring admission, 11/1 priority date for domestic and international students. Applications are processed on a rolling basis. Application fee: $70. Electronic applications accepted. *Expenses:* Contact institution. *Financial support:* In 2009–10, 7 students received support, including 4 teaching assistantships with full tuition reimbursements available (averaging $9,650 per year). Financial award application deadline: 3/1; financial award applicants required to submit FAFSA. *Unit head:* Dr. Diana Bartelt, Director, 718-990-1654, E-mail: barteltd@stjohns.edu. *Application contact:* Kathleen Davis, Director of Graduate Admission, 718-990-2790, E-mail: gradhelp@stjohns.edu.

Simon Fraser University, Graduate Studies, Faculty of Business Administration, Burnaby, BC V5A 1S6, Canada. Offers business administration (EMBA, PhD); financial management (MA); general business (MBA); global asset and wealth management (MBA); management of technology/biotechnology (MBA); MBA/MRM. *Accreditation:* AACSB. Postbaccalaureate distance learning degree programs offered. *Degree requirements:* For master's, thesis or written project. *Entrance requirements:* For master's, minimum GPA of 3.0. Additional exam requirements/recommendations for international students: Required—TOEFL. *Expenses:* Contact institution. *Faculty research:* Leadership, marketing and technology, wealth management.

Southeastern Oklahoma State University, School of Arts and Sciences, Durant, OK 74701-0609. Offers biology (MT); computer information systems (MT). Part-time and evening/weekend programs available. *Faculty:* 12 full-time (4 women), 1 part-time/adjunct (0 women). *Students:* 10 full-time (5 women), 7 part-time (1 woman); includes 5 minority (4 American Indian/Alaska Native, 1 Hispanic American). Average age 28. 1 applicant, 100% accepted, 1 enrolled. *Degree requirements:* For master's, thesis optional. *Entrance requirements:* For master's, minimum GPA of 3.0 in last 60 hours or 2.75 overall. Additional exam requirements/recommendations for international students: Required—TOEFL (minimum score 550 paper-based; 213 computer-based). *Application deadline:* For fall admission, 8/1 for domestic students, 6/1 for international students; for spring admission, 1/5 for domestic students, 11/1 for international students. Application fee: $20 ($55 for international students). Electronic applications accepted. *Financial support:* In 2009–10, 8 students received support; fellowships, research assistantships, teaching assistantships, Federal Work-Study and institutionally sponsored loans available. Support available to part-time students. Financial award application deadline: 6/15; financial award applicants required to submit FAFSA. *Unit head:* Dr. Teresa Golden, Graduate Coordinator, 580-745-2286, E-mail: tgolden@se.edu. *Application contact:* Carrie Williamson, Graduate Secretary, 580-745-2200, Fax: 580-745-7474, E-mail: cwilliamson@se.edu.

Southern Illinois University Edwardsville, Graduate Studies and Research, College of Arts and Sciences, Department of Biological Sciences, Program in Biotechnology Management, Edwardsville, IL 62026-0001. Offers MS. Part-time programs available. *Students:* 2 full-time (1 woman), 5 part-time (3 women), 4 international. Average age 26. 51 applicants, 31% accepted. In 2009, 3 master's awarded. *Degree requirements:* For master's, thesis or alternative, internship, research paper. *Entrance requirements:* For master's, GRE. Additional exam requirements/recommendations for international students: Required—TOEFL (minimum score 550 paper-based; 213 computer-based; 79 iBT), IELTS (minimum score 6.5). *Application deadline:* For fall admission, 2/28 for domestic students, 6/1 for international students. Application fee: $30. Electronic applications accepted. *Expenses:* Tuition, state resident: part-time $1252.50 per semester. Tuition, nonresident: part-time $3131.25 per semester. Required fees: $586.85 per semester. Tuition and fees vary according to course load. *Financial support:* Fellowships with full tuition reimbursements, research assistantships with full tuition reimbursements, teaching assistantships with full tuition reimbursements available. Financial award application deadline: 3/1; financial award applicants required to submit FAFSA. *Unit head:* Dr. Steve McCommas, Director, 618-650-3406, E-mail: smccomm@siue.edu. *Application contact:* Dr. Steve McCommas, Director, 618-650-3406, E-mail: smccomm@siue.edu.

Stephen F. Austin State University, Graduate School, College of Sciences and Mathematics, Division of Biotechnology, Nacogdoches, TX 75962. Offers MS. *Degree requirements:* For master's, comprehensive exam, thesis. *Entrance requirements:* For master's, GRE General Test, minimum GPA of 2.8 in last 60 hours, 2.5 overall. Additional exam requirements/recommendations for international students: Required—TOEFL.

Texas Tech University, Center for Biotechnology and Genomics, Lubbock, TX 79409. Offers biotechnology (MS); science and agricultural biotechnology (MS); JD/MS. Part-time programs available. *Faculty:* 2 full-time (1 woman). *Students:* 22 full-time (10 women), 2 part-time (1 woman), 23 international. Average age 23. 114 applicants, 61% accepted, 16 enrolled. In 2009, 8 master's awarded. *Degree requirements:* For master's, thesis or alternative. *Entrance requirements:* For master's, GRE General Test. Additional exam requirements/recommendations for international students: Required—TOEFL (minimum score 550 paper-based; 213 computer-based). *Application deadline:* For fall admission, 3/1 priority date for international students; for spring admission, 11/1 priority date for international students. Application fee: $50 ($75 for international students). *Expenses:* Tuition, state resident: full-time $5100; part-time $213 per credit hour. Tuition, nonresident: full-time $11,748; part-time $490 per credit hour. Required fees: $2298; $50 per credit hour. $555 per semester. *Financial support:* In 2009–10, 4 students received support, including 2 research assistantships with partial tuition reimbursements available (averaging $15,037 per year). Financial award application deadline: 4/15. *Faculty research:* Biotechnology and applied science. *Unit head:* Dr. David B. Knaff, Advisor, 806-742-0288, Fax: 806-742-1289, E-mail: david.knaff@ttu.edu. *Application contact:* Jatindra Tripathy, Senior Research Associate, 806-742-3722 Ext. 229, Fax: 806-742-3788, E-mail: jatindra.tripathy@ttu.edu.

Texas Tech University, Graduate School, College of Arts and Sciences, Department of Chemistry and Biochemistry, Lubbock, TX 79409. Offers biotechnology (MS); biotechnology: science and agricultural biotechnology (MS); chemistry (MS, PhD); JD/MS. Part-time programs available. *Faculty:* 21 full-time (2 women), 1 (woman) part-time/adjunct. *Students:* 92 full-time (33 women), 3 part-time (0 women); includes 3 minority (1 African American, 1 Asian American or Pacific Islander, 1 Hispanic American), 69 international. Average age 27. 157 applicants, 31% accepted, 15 enrolled. In 2009, 8 doctorates awarded. *Degree requirements:* For master's, thesis; for doctorate, thesis/dissertation. *Entrance requirements:* For master's and doctorate, GRE General Test. Additional exam requirements/recommendations for international students: Required—TOEFL (minimum score 550 paper-based; 213 computer-based). *Application deadline:* For fall admission, 3/1 priority date for international students; for spring admission, 11/1 priority date for international students. Applications are processed on a rolling basis. Application fee: $50 ($75 for international students). Electronic applications accepted. *Expenses:* Tuition, state resident: full-time $5100; part-time $213 per credit hour. Tuition, nonresident: full-time $11,748; part-time $490 per credit hour. Required fees: $2298; $50 per credit hour. $555 per semester. *Financial support:* In 2009–10, 39 research assistantships with partial tuition reimbursements (averaging $32,533 per year), 56 teaching assistantships with partial tuition reimbursements (averaging $18,612 per year) were awarded; career-related internships or fieldwork, Federal Work-Study, and institutionally sponsored loans also available. Support available to part-time students. Financial award application deadline: 4/15; financial award applicants required to submit FAFSA. *Faculty research:* Theoretical and computational chemistry, plant biochemistry and chemical biology, materials and supramolecular chemistry, nanotechnology, spectroscopic analysis. Total annual research expenditures: $3.7 million. *Unit head:* Dr. Dominick J. Casadonte, Chair, 806-742-3067, Fax: 806-742-1289, E-mail: chemchair@ttu.edu. *Application* contact: Carly Jenkins, Senior Business Assistant, 806-742-3057, Fax: 806-742-4890, E-mail: carly.jenkins@ttu.edu.

Texas Tech University Health Sciences Center, Graduate School of Biomedical Sciences, Department of Cell Biology and Biochemistry, Program in Biotechnology, Lubbock, TX 79430. Offers MS. *Entrance requirements:* For master's, GRE General Test, minimum GPA of 3.0. Additional exam requirements/recommendations for international students: Required—TOEFL. *Faculty research:* Reproductive endocrinology, immunology, molecular biology and developmental biochemistry, biology of developing systems.

Thomas Jefferson University, Jefferson College of Graduate Studies, PhD Program in Tissue Engineering and Regenerative Medicine, Philadelphia, PA 19107. Offers PhD. *Faculty:* 18 full-time (6 women). *Students:* 4 full-time (3 women); includes 1 minority (Asian American or Pacific Islander). 3 applicants, 0% accepted, 0 enrolled. In 2009, 2 doctorates awarded. *Degree requirements:* For doctorate, comprehensive exam, thesis/dissertation. *Entrance requirements:* For doctorate, GRE General Test, minimum GPA of 3.2. Additional exam requirements/recommendations for international students: Required—TOEFL (minimum score 250 computer-based; 100 iBT), or IELTS. *Application deadline:* For fall admission, 1/15 priority date for domestic and international students. Applications are processed on a rolling basis. Application fee: $50. Electronic applications accepted. *Expenses:* Tuition: Full-time $26,858; part-time $879 per credit. Required fees: $525. *Financial support:* In 2009–10, 4 students received support, including 4 fellowships with full tuition reimbursements available (averaging $52,883 per year); Federal Work-Study, institutionally sponsored loans, traineeships, and stipend also available. Financial award application deadline: 5/1; financial award applicants required to submit FAFSA. *Faculty research:* Skeletal development, biomaterials, bone implant interaction, tissue engineering, high resolution imaging. Total annual research expenditures: $8 million. *Unit head:* Dr. Irving Shapiro, Program Director, 215-955-7217, Fax: 215-955-9159, E-mail: irving.shapiro@jefferson.edu. *Application contact:* Marc E. Stearns, Director of Admissions, 215-503-0155, Fax: 215-503-9920, E-mail: jcgs-info@jefferson.edu.

Tufts University, Graduate School of Arts and Sciences, Graduate Certificate Programs, Biotechnology Engineering Program, Medford, MA 02155. Offers Certificate. Part-time and evening/weekend programs available. Electronic applications accepted. *Expenses:* Tuition: Full-time $38,096; part-time $3962 per credit. Required fees: $686; $40 per year. Tuition and fees vary according to course level, course load, degree level, program and student level.

Tufts University, Graduate School of Arts and Sciences, Graduate Certificate Programs, Biotechnology Program, Medford, MA 02155. Offers Certificate. Part-time and evening/weekend programs available. Electronic applications accepted. *Expenses:* Tuition: Full-time $38,096; part-time $3962 per credit. Required fees: $686; $40 per year. Tuition and fees vary according to course level, course load, degree level, program and student level.

Universidad de las Américas–Puebla, Division of Graduate Studies, School of Sciences, Program in Biotechnology, Puebla, Mexico. Offers MS. *Degree requirements:* For master's, one foreign language, thesis.

Université de Sherbrooke, Faculty of Law, Sherbrooke, QC J1K 2R1, Canada. Offers alternative dispute resolution (LL M, Diploma); biotechnology (LL B); business administration (LL B); business law (Diploma); health law (LL M, Diploma); law (LL B, LL D); legal management (Diploma); notarial law (DDN); transnational law (Diploma). Part-time and evening/weekend programs available. *Degree requirements:* For master's, thesis; for other advanced degree, one foreign language. *Entrance requirements:* For master's and other advanced degree, LL B. Electronic applications accepted.

University at Buffalo, the State University of New York, Graduate School, School of Medicine and Biomedical Sciences, Graduate Programs in Medicine and Biomedical Sciences, Department of Biotechnical and Clinical Laboratory Sciences, Buffalo, NY 14260. Offers biotechnology (MS). *Accreditation:* NAACLS. Part-time programs available. *Faculty:* 9 full-time (6 women), 5 part-time/adjunct (3 women). *Students:* 27 full-time (11 women), 1 (woman) part-time, 24 international. Average age 24. 115 applicants, 63% accepted, 10 enrolled. In 2009, 12 master's awarded. *Degree requirements:* For master's, thesis. *Entrance requirements:* For master's, GRE General Test, background in biology, chemistry or related field. Additional exam requirements/recommendations for international students: Required—TOEFL (minimum score 233 computer-based; 79 iBT). *Application deadline:* For fall admission, 3/1 priority date for domestic students, 2/1 for international students. Applications are processed on a rolling basis. Application fee: $50. Electronic applications accepted. *Financial support:* In 2009–10, 15 students received support, including research assistantships with full and partial tuition reimbursements available (averaging $10,000 per year), 15 teaching assistantships with full tuition reimbursements available (averaging $9,000 per year); Federal Work-Study and unspecified assistantships also available. Financial award application deadline: 3/1. *Faculty research:* Endocrine-immune interaction, tumor immunology, molecular biology, oxidative stress, cell differentiation. Total annual research expenditures: $1.1 million. *Unit head:* Dr. Paul Kostyniak, Chair, 716-829-3630 Ext. 107, Fax: 716-829-3601. *Application contact:* Dr. Stephen T. Koury, Director of Graduate Studies, 716-829-3630 Ext. 111, Fax: 716-829-3601, E-mail: stvkoury@buffalo.edu.

The University of Alabama in Huntsville, School of Graduate Studies, Interdisciplinary Studies, Interdisciplinary Program in Biotechnology Science and Engineering, Huntsville, AL 35899. Offers PhD. Part-time and evening/weekend programs available. *Faculty:* 28 full-time (5 women). *Students:* 25 full-time (13 women), 2 part-time (1 woman); includes 5 minority (4 African Americans, 1 American Indian/Alaska Native), 12 international. Average age 29. 15 applicants, 60% accepted, 6 enrolled. In 2009, 2 doctorates awarded. *Degree requirements:* For doctorate, comprehensive exam, thesis/dissertation, oral and written exams. *Entrance requirements:* For doctorate, GRE General Test, bachelor's degree in science or engineering, minimum of GPA of 3.0. Additional exam requirements/recommendations for international students: Required—TOEFL (minimum score 550 paper-based; 213 computer-based; 62 iBT). *Application deadline:* For fall admission, 7/15 for domestic students, 4/1 for international students; for spring admission, 11/30 for domestic students, 9/1 for international students. Applications are processed on a rolling basis. Application fee: $40 ($50 for international students). Electronic applications accepted. *Expenses:* Tuition, state resident: part-time $355.75 per credit hour. Tuition, nonresident: part-time $847.10 per credit hour. Required fees: $210.80 per semester. Tuition and fees vary according to course load and program. *Financial support:* In 2009–10, 23 students received support, including 7 research assistantships with full and partial tuition reimbursements available (averaging $12,420 per year), 16 teaching assistantships with full and partial tuition reimbursements available (averaging $11,297 per year); career-related internships or fieldwork, Federal Work-Study, institutionally sponsored loans, scholarships/grants, health care benefits, and unspecified assistantships also available. Support available to part-time students. Financial award application deadline: 4/1; financial award applicants required to submit FAFSA. *Unit head:* Dr. Joseph Ng, Coordinator, 256-824-3715, Fax: 256-824-3469, E-mail: ngj@uah.edu. *Application contact:* Kathy Biggs, Graduate Studies Admissions Manager, 256-824-6199, Fax: 256-824-6405, E-mail: deangrad@uah.edu.

University of Alberta, Faculty of Graduate Studies and Research, Department of Biological Sciences, Edmonton, AB T6G 2E1, Canada. Offers environmental biology and ecology (M Sc, PhD); microbiology and biotechnology (M Sc, PhD); molecular biology and genetics (M Sc, PhD); physiology and cell biology (M Sc, PhD); plant biology (M Sc, PhD); systematics and evolution (M Sc, PhD). *Faculty:* 72 full-time (15 women), 15 part-time/adjunct (4 women). *Students:* 238 full-time (117 women), 32 part-time (15 women), 31 international. 206 applicants, 42% accepted. In 2009, 29 master's, 31 doctorates awarded. Terminal master's awarded for partial completion of doctoral program. *Degree requirements:* For master's, thesis; for doctorate, thesis/dissertation. *Entrance requirements:* Additional exam requirements/recommendations for international students: Required—TOEFL. *Application deadline:* For fall admission, 3/1 priority date for domestic students. Applications are processed on a rolling basis. Application fee: $0. Tuition and fees charges are reported in Canadian dollars. *Expenses:* Tuition, area

resident: Full-time $4626.24 Canadian dollars; part-time $99.72 Canadian dollars per unit. International tuition: $8216 Canadian dollars full-time. Required fees: $3589.92 Canadian dollars; $99.72 Canadian dollars per unit. $215 Canadian dollars per term. *Financial support:* In 2009–10, 4 research assistantships with partial tuition reimbursements (averaging $12,000 per year), 103 teaching assistantships with partial tuition reimbursements (averaging $12,300 per year) were awarded; career-related internships or fieldwork and scholarships/grants also available. *Unit head:* Laura Frost, Chair, 780-492-1904. *Application contact:* Dr. John P. Chang, Associate Chair for Graduate Studies, 780-492-1257, Fax: 780-492-9457, E-mail: bio.grad.coordinator@ualberta.ca.

University of Calgary, Faculty of Medicine and Faculty of Graduate Studies, Program in Biomedical Technology, Calgary, AB T2N 1N4, Canada. Offers MBT. Part-time programs available. *Degree requirements:* For master's, comprehensive exam, practicum. *Entrance requirements:* For master's, minimum GPA of 3.2 in last 2 years, B Sc in biological science. Additional exam requirements/recommendations for international students: Required—TOEFL (minimum score 600 paper-based; 250 computer-based). Electronic applications accepted. *Expenses:* Contact institution. *Faculty research:* Patent law, intellectual proprietorship.

University of California, Irvine, Office of Graduate Studies, School of Biological Sciences, Department of Molecular Biology and Biochemistry, Program in Biotechnology, Irvine, CA 92697. Offers MS. *Students:* 28 full-time (14 women); includes 8 minority (6 Asian Americans or Pacific Islanders, 2 Hispanic Americans), 9 international. Average age 25. 126 applicants, 20% accepted, 14 enrolled. In 2009, 12 master's awarded. *Entrance requirements:* For master's, GRE General Test, GRE Subject Test, minimum GPA of 3.0. *Application deadline:* For fall admission, 3/1 priority date for domestic and international students. Applications are processed on a rolling basis. Application fee: $70 ($90 for international students). Electronic applications accepted. *Financial support:* Application deadline: 3/1; *Unit head:* Krishna Tewari, Graduate Adviser, 949-824-4738, Fax: 949-824-8551, E-mail: kktewari@uci.edu. *Application contact:* Krishna Tewari, Graduate Adviser, 949-824-4738, Fax: 949-824-8551, E-mail: kktewari@uci.edu.

University of Delaware, College of Arts and Sciences, Department of Biological Sciences, Newark, DE 19716. Offers biotechnology (MS); cancer biology (MS, PhD); cell and extracellular matrix biology (MS, PhD); cell and systems physiology (MS, PhD); developmental biology (MS, PhD); ecology and evolution (MS, PhD); microbiology (MS, PhD); molecular biology and genetics (MS, PhD). Terminal master's awarded for partial completion of doctoral program. *Degree requirements:* For master's, thesis, preliminary exam; for doctorate, comprehensive exam, thesis/dissertation, preliminary exam. *Entrance requirements:* For master's and doctorate, GRE General Test. Additional exam requirements/recommendations for international students: Required—TOEFL (minimum score 600 paper-based; 250 computer-based); Recommended—TWE. Electronic applications accepted. *Faculty research:* Microorganisms, bone, cancer metastasis, developmental biology, cell biology, DNA.

University of Guelph, Graduate Program Services, Ontario Agricultural College, Department of Environmental Biology, Guelph, ON N1G 2W1, Canada. Offers entomology (M Sc, PhD); environmental microbiology and biotechnology (M Sc, PhD); environmental toxicology (M Sc, PhD); plant and forest systems (M Sc, PhD); plant pathology (M Sc, PhD). Part-time programs available. *Degree requirements:* For master's, thesis; for doctorate, comprehensive exam, thesis/dissertation. *Entrance requirements:* For master's, minimum 75% average during previous 2 years of course work; for doctorate, minimum 75% average. Additional exam requirements/recommendations for international students: Required—TOEFL or IELTS. Electronic applications accepted. *Faculty research:* Entomology, environmental microbiology and biotechnology, environmental toxicology, forest ecology, plant pathology.

University of Houston–Clear Lake, School of Science and Computer Engineering, Program in Biotechnology, Houston, TX 77058-1098. Offers MS.

University of Illinois at Chicago, College of Pharmacy, Center for Pharmaceutical Biotechnology, Chicago, IL 60607-7173. Offers PhD.

The University of Kansas, University of Kansas Medical Center, School of Allied Health, Program in Molecular Biotechnology, Lawrence, KS 66045. Offers MS. *Faculty:* 4 full-time (2 women), 1 (woman) part-time/adjunct. *Students:* 2 full-time (both women), 4 part-time (3 women), 1 international. Average age 28. 18 applicants, 28% accepted, 4 enrolled. In 2009, 2 master's awarded. *Degree requirements:* For master's, comprehensive exam. *Entrance requirements:* For master's, GRE General Test. Additional exam requirements/recommendations for international students: Required—TOEFL. *Application deadline:* For fall admission, 2/1 priority date for domestic and international students. Application fee: $60. Electronic applications accepted. *Expenses:* Tuition, state resident: full-time $6492; part-time $270.50 per credit hour. Tuition, nonresident: full-time $15,510; part-time $646.25 per credit hour. Required fees: $847; $70.56 per credit hour. Tuition and fees vary according to course load and program. *Financial support:* In 2009–10, 2 students received support. Applicants required to submit FAFSA. *Faculty research:* Diabetes, obesity, polycystic kidney disease, protein structure and function, cell signaling pathways. Total annual research expenditures: $184,687. *Unit head:* Dr. Eric Elsinghorst, Director of Graduate Studies, 913-588-1089, E-mail: eelsinghorst@kumc.edu. *Application contact:* Moffett Ferguson, Student Affairs Coordinator, 913-588-5275, Fax: 913-588-5254, E-mail: mfergus1@kumc.edu.

University of Maryland, Baltimore County, Graduate School, Continuing and Professional Studies, Program in Biotechnology Management, Baltimore, MD 21250. Offers Graduate Certificate. *Faculty:* 10 part-time/adjunct (4 women). *Students:* 13 full-time (9 women), 26 part-time (16 women); includes 6 African Americans, 7 Asian Americans or Pacific Islanders, 1 Hispanic American, 7 international. 59 applicants, 66% accepted, 18 enrolled. *Entrance requirements:* Additional exam requirements/recommendations for international students: Required—TOEFL (minimum score 597 paper-based; 247 computer-based; 99 iBT). *Application deadline:* For fall admission, 8/15 for domestic students, 1/1 for international students; for spring admission, 12/15 for domestic students. *Financial support:* Career-related internships or fieldwork available. Financial award applicants required to submit FAFSA. *Unit head:* Dr. Chris Morris, Associate Vice Provost, Continuing and Professional Studies, 410-455-1570, E-mail: morrisc@umbc.edu. *Application contact:* Nancy Clements, Program Specialist, 410-455-5536, E-mail: nancyc@umbc.edu.

University of Maryland University College, Graduate School of Management and Technology, Program in Biotechnology Studies, Adelphi, MD 20783. Offers MS, Certificate. Part-time and evening/weekend programs available. Postbaccalaureate distance learning degree programs offered (no on-campus study). *Students:* 7 full-time (4 women), 350 part-time (209 women); includes 137 minority (84 African Americans, 1 American Indian/Alaska Native, 35 Asian Americans or Pacific Islanders, 17 Hispanic Americans), 9 international. Average age 34. 120 applicants, 100% accepted, 75 enrolled. In 2009, 54 master's, 11 other advanced degrees awarded. *Degree requirements:* For master's, thesis or alternative. *Application deadline:* Applications are processed on a rolling basis. Application fee: $50. Electronic applications accepted. *Expenses:* Tuition, state resident: full-time $7704; part-time $428 per credit hour. Tuition, nonresident: full-time $11,862; part-time $659 per credit hour. *Financial support:* Federal Work-Study and scholarships/grants available. Support available to part-time students. Financial award application deadline: 6/1; financial award applicants required to submit FAFSA. *Unit head:* Dr. Rana Khan, Director, 240-684-2400, Fax: 240-684-2401, E-mail: rkhan@umuc.edu. *Application contact:* Coordinator, Graduate Admissions, 800-888-UMUC, Fax: 240-684-2151, E-mail: newgrad@umuc.edu.

University of Massachusetts Amherst, Graduate School, College of Natural Sciences, Department of Animal Biotechnology and Biomedical Sciences, Amherst, MA 01003. Offers MS, PhD. Part-time programs available. *Faculty:* 21 full-time (8 women). *Students:* 22 full-time (15 women); includes 2 minority (1 African American, 1 Hispanic American), 8 international. Average age 30. 41 applicants, 7% accepted, 3 enrolled. In 2009, 1 master's, 4 doctorates

University of Massachusetts Amherst (continued)
awarded. Terminal master's awarded for partial completion of doctoral program. *Degree requirements:* For master's, thesis or alternative; for doctorate, comprehensive exam, thesis/dissertation. *Entrance requirements:* For master's and doctorate, GRE General Test. Additional exam requirements/recommendations for international students: Required—TOEFL (minimum score 550 paper-based; 213 computer-based; 80 iBT), IELTS (minimum score 6.5). *Application deadline:* For fall admission, 2/1 for domestic and international students; for spring admission, 10/1 for domestic and international students. Applications are processed on a rolling basis. Application fee: $50 ($65 for international students). Electronic applications accepted. *Expenses:* Tuition, state resident: full-time $2640; part-time $110 per credit. Tuition, nonresident: full-time $9936; part-time $414 per credit. Tuition and fees vary according to course load. *Financial support:* In 2009–10, 42 research assistantships with full tuition reimbursements (averaging $11,650 per year), 11 teaching assistantships with full tuition reimbursements (averaging $11,217 per year) were awarded; fellowships, career-related internships or fieldwork, Federal Work-Study, scholarships/grants, traineeships, health care benefits, tuition waivers (full), and unspecified assistantships also available. Support available to part-time students. Financial award application deadline: 2/1. *Unit head:* Dr. Pablo E. Visconti, Graduate Program Director, 413-577-1193, Fax: 413-577-1150. *Application contact:* Jean M. Ames, Supervisor of Admissions, 413-545-0722, Fax: 413-577-0010, E-mail: gradadm@grad.umass.edu.

University of Massachusetts Boston, Office of Graduate Studies, College of Science and Mathematics, Program in Biotechnology and Biomedical Science, Boston, MA 02125-3393. Offers MS. Part-time and evening/weekend programs available. *Degree requirements:* For master's, comprehensive exam, thesis optional, oral exams. *Entrance requirements:* For master's, GRE General Test, GRE Subject Test, minimum GPA of 2.75, 3.0 in science and math. *Faculty research:* Evolutionary and molecular immunology, molecular genetics, tissue culture, computerized laboratory technology.

University of Massachusetts Dartmouth, Graduate School, Program in Biomedical Engineering and Biotechnology, North Dartmouth, MA 02747-2300. Offers PhD. Part-time programs available. *Students:* 16 full-time (8 women), 6 part-time (2 women); includes 1 minority (Hispanic American), 13 international. Average age 29. 19 applicants, 79% accepted, 9 enrolled. In 2009, 1 doctorate awarded. *Degree requirements:* For doctorate, comprehensive exam, thesis/dissertation. *Entrance requirements:* For doctorate, GRE, minimum GPA of 3.0, 3 letters of recommendation. Additional exam requirements/recommendations for international students: Required—TOEFL (minimum score 550 paper-based; 213 computer-based). *Application deadline:* For fall admission, 4/20 for domestic students, 2/20 for international students; for spring admission, 11/15 for domestic students, 9/15 for international students. Application fee: $40 ($60 for international students). Electronic applications accepted. *Expenses:* Tuition, state resident: full-time $2071; part-time $86.29 per credit. Tuition, nonresident: full-time $8099; part-time $337.46 per credit. Required fees: $9446. Tuition and fees vary according to class time, course load and reciprocity agreements. *Financial support:* In 2009–10, 3 fellowships with full tuition reimbursements (averaging $10,512 per year), 10 research assistantships with full tuition reimbursements (averaging $10,868 per year), 1 teaching assistantship with full tuition reimbursement (averaging $3,000 per year) were awarded; unspecified assistantships also available. Financial award application deadline: 3/1; financial award applicants required to submit FAFSA. *Faculty research:* Tetracycline-encapsulated chitosan microspheres, artificial tissues, sensor arrays for orthopedic rehab, blue light cures, healing bandages. Total annual research expenditures: $28,000. *Unit head:* Dr. Vijay Chalivendra, Co-Director, 508-910-6572, E-mail: vchalivendra@umassd.edu. *Application contact:* Elan Turcotte-Shamski, Graduate Admissions Officer, 508-999-8604, Fax: 508-999-8183, E-mail: graduate@umassd.edu.

University of Massachusetts Lowell, College of Arts and Sciences, Department of Biological Sciences, Lowell, MA 01854-2881. Offers biochemistry (PhD); biological sciences (MS); biotechnology (MS). Part-time programs available. *Degree requirements:* For master's, thesis; for doctorate, thesis/dissertation. *Entrance requirements:* For master's and doctorate, GRE General Test. Electronic applications accepted.

University of Minnesota, Twin Cities Campus, Graduate School, Program in Microbial Engineering, Minneapolis, MN 55455-0213. Offers MS. Part-time programs available. *Degree requirements:* For master's, thesis. *Entrance requirements:* For master's, GRE General Test. Additional exam requirements/recommendations for international students: Required—TOEFL. *Faculty research:* Microbial genetics, oncogenesis, gene transfer, fermentation, bioreactors, genetics of antibiotic biosynthesis.

University of Missouri–St. Louis, College of Arts and Sciences, Department of Biology, St. Louis, MO 63121. Offers biology (MS, PhD), including animal behavior (MS), biochemistry, biochemistry and biotechnology (MS), biotechnology (MS), conservation biology (MS), development (MS), ecology (MS), environmental studies (PhD), evolution (MS), genetics (MS), molecular biology and biochemistry (PhD), molecular/cellular biology (MS), physiology (MS), plant systematics, population biology (MS), tropical biology (MS); biotechnology (Certificate); tropical biology and conservation (Certificate). Part-time programs available. *Faculty:* 43 full-time (13 women), 2 part-time/adjunct (1 woman). *Students:* 54 full-time (27 women), 79 part-time (43 women); includes 15 minority (6 African Americans, 7 Asian Americans or Pacific Islanders, 2 Hispanic Americans), 47 international. Average age 29. 193 applicants, 44% accepted, 44 enrolled. In 2009, 30 master's, 7 doctorates, 9 other advanced degrees awarded. *Degree requirements:* For master's, thesis or alternative; for doctorate, thesis/dissertation, 1 semester of teaching experience. *Entrance requirements:* For master's, 3 letters of recommendation; for doctorate, GRE General Test, 3 letters of recommendation. Additional exam requirements/recommendations for international students: Required—TOEFL. *Application deadline:* For fall admission, 12/1 priority date for domestic and international students; for spring admission, 10/15 priority date for domestic and international students. Applications are processed on a rolling basis. Application fee: $35 ($40 for international students). Electronic applications accepted. *Expenses:* Tuition, state resident: full-time $5377; part-time $297.70 per credit hour. Tuition, nonresident: full-time $13,882; part-time $771.20 per credit hour. Required fees: $220; $12.20 per credit hour. One-time fee: $12. Tuition and fees vary according to course level, campus/location and program. *Financial support:* In 2009–10, 22 research assistantships with full and partial tuition reimbursements (averaging $16,300 per year), 14 teaching assistantships with full and partial tuition reimbursements (averaging $16,727 per year) were awarded; fellowships with full tuition reimbursements, career-related internships or fieldwork and Federal Work-Study also available. Support available to part-time students. Financial award application deadline: 2/1. *Faculty research:* Molecular biology, microbial genetics, animal behavior, tropical ecology, plant systematics. *Unit head:* Dr. Elizabeth Kellogg, Director of Graduate Studies, 314-516-6200, Fax: 314-516-6233, E-mail: tkellogg@umsl.edu. *Application contact:* 314-516-5458, Fax: 314-516-6996, E-mail: gradadm@umsl.edu.

University of Nevada, Reno, Graduate School, College of Agriculture, Biotechnology and Natural Resources, Program in Biotechnology, Reno, NV 89557. Offers MS. 5 year degree; students are admitted to as undergraduates. *Degree requirements:* For master's, thesis. *Entrance requirements:* For master's, GRE, minimum GPA of 2.75. Additional exam requirements/recommendations for international students: Required—TOEFL (minimum score 500 paper-based; 173 computer-based; 61 iBT), IELTS (minimum score 6). Electronic applications accepted. *Faculty research:* Cancer biology, plant virology.

University of North Texas Health Science Center at Fort Worth, Graduate School of Biomedical Sciences, Fort Worth, TX 76107-2699. Offers anatomy and cell biology (MS, PhD); biochemistry and molecular biology (MS, PhD); biomedical sciences (MS, PhD); biotechnology (MS); forensic genetics (MS); integrative physiology (MS, PhD); medical science (MS); microbiology and immunology (MS, PhD); pharmacology (MS, PhD); science education (MS); DO/MS; DO/PhD. Terminal master's awarded for partial completion of doctoral program. *Degree requirements:* For master's, thesis; for doctorate, thesis/dissertation. *Entrance requirements:* For master's and doctorate, GRE General Test. Additional exam requirements/recommendations for international students: Required—TOEFL. *Expenses:* Contact institution. *Faculty research:* Alzheimer's disease, aging, eye diseases, cancer, cardiovascular disease.

University of Pennsylvania, School of Engineering and Applied Science, Program in Biotechnology, Philadelphia, PA 19104. Offers MS. Part-time programs available. *Students:* 70 full-time (40 women), 35 part-time (15 women); includes 24 minority (3 African Americans, 18 Asian Americans or Pacific Islanders, 3 Hispanic Americans), 48 international. 150 applicants, 51% accepted, 54 enrolled. In 2009, 72 master's awarded. *Entrance requirements:* For master's, GRE General Test, bachelor's degree in science or undergraduate course work in molecular biology. Additional exam requirements/recommendations for international students: Required—TOEFL. *Application deadline:* For fall admission, 6/1 priority date for domestic students, 5/1 priority date for international students. Applications are processed on a rolling basis. Application fee: $70. Electronic applications accepted. *Expenses:* Tuition: Full-time $25,660; part-time $4758 per course. Required fees: $2152; $270 per course. Tuition and fees vary according to course load, degree level and program.

University of Rhode Island, Graduate School, College of the Environment and Life Sciences, Department of Cell and Molecular Biology, Kingston, RI 02881. Offers biochemistry (MS, PhD); clinical laboratory sciences (MS), including biotechnology, clinical laboratory science, cytopathology; microbiology (MS, PhD); molecular genetics (MS, PhD). Part-time programs available. *Faculty:* 12 full-time (4 women). *Students:* 29 full-time (17 women), 43 part-time (31 women); includes 13 minority (5 African Americans, 4 Asian Americans or Pacific Islanders, 4 Hispanic Americans), 3 international. In 2009, 5 master's, 2 doctorates awarded. *Degree requirements:* For master's, comprehensive exam (for some programs); for doctorate, comprehensive exam. *Entrance requirements:* For master's and doctorate, GRE, 2 letters of recommendation. Additional exam requirements/recommendations for international students: Required—TOEFL (minimum score 550 paper-based; 213 computer-based). *Application deadline:* For fall admission, 7/15 for domestic students, 2/1 for international students; for spring admission, 11/15 for domestic students, 7/15 for international students. Application fee: $65. Electronic applications accepted. *Expenses:* Tuition, state resident: full-time $8828; part-time $490 per credit hour. Tuition, nonresident: full-time $22,100; part-time $1228 per credit hour. Required fees: $1118; $57 per semester. Tuition and fees vary according to program. *Financial support:* In 2009–10, 2 research assistantships with full and partial tuition reimbursements (averaging $10,535 per year), 10 teaching assistantships with full and partial tuition reimbursements (averaging $13,449 per year) were awarded. Financial award application deadline: 7/15; financial award applicants required to submit FAFSA. *Faculty research:* Genomics and Sequencing Center: an interdisciplinary genomics research and undergraduate and graduate student training program which provides researchers access to cutting-edge technologies in the field of genomics. Total annual research expenditures: $1.2 million. *Unit head:* Dr. Jay Sperry, Chairperson, 401-874-2201, Fax: 401-874-2202, E-mail: jsperry@mail.uri.edu. *Application contact:* Dr. Jay Sperry, Chairperson, 401-874-2201, Fax: 401-874-2202, E-mail: jsperry@mail.uri.edu.

University of Saskatchewan, College of Graduate Studies and Research, Edwards School of Business, Program in Business Administration, Saskatoon, SK S7N 5A2, Canada. Offers agribusiness management (MBA); biotechnology management (MBA); health services management (MBA); indigenous management (MBA); international business management (MBA). Tuition and fees charges are reported in Canadian dollars. *Expenses:* Tuition, area resident: Full-time $3000 Canadian dollars; part-time $500 Canadian dollars per term. Required fees: $700 Canadian dollars; $100 Canadian dollars per term.

The University of Texas at Dallas, School of Natural Sciences and Mathematics, Program in Biology, Richardson, TX 75080. Offers bioinformatics and computational biology (MS); biotechnology (MS); molecular and cell biology (MS, PhD). Part-time and evening/weekend programs available. *Faculty:* 16 full-time (3 women). *Students:* 89 full-time (50 women), 16 part-time (11 women); includes 19 minority (16 Asian Americans or Pacific Islanders, 3 Hispanic Americans), 62 international. Average age 26. 313 applicants, 31% accepted, 42 enrolled. In 2009, 36 master's, 4 doctorates awarded. *Degree requirements:* For master's, thesis optional; for doctorate, thesis/dissertation, publishable paper. *Entrance requirements:* For master's and doctorate, GRE General Test. Additional exam requirements/recommendations for international students: Required—TOEFL (minimum score 550 paper-based; 213 computer-based). *Application deadline:* For fall admission, 7/15 for domestic students, 5/1 priority date for international students; for spring admission, 11/15 for domestic students, 9/1 priority date for international students. Applications are processed on a rolling basis. Application fee: $50 ($100 for international students). Electronic applications accepted. *Expenses:* Tuition, state resident: full-time $11,068; part-time $461 per credit hour. Tuition, nonresident: full-time $21,178; part-time $882 per credit hour. Tuition and fees vary according to course load. *Financial support:* In 2009–10, 15 research assistantships with full tuition reimbursements (averaging $14,347 per year), 27 teaching assistantships with full tuition reimbursements (averaging $13,511 per year) were awarded; fellowships, career-related internships or fieldwork, Federal Work-Study, institutionally sponsored loans, scholarships/grants, and unspecified assistantships also available. Support available to part-time students. Financial award application deadline: 4/30; financial award applicants required to submit FAFSA. *Faculty research:* DNA replication, regulation of gene expression, subcellular organelles, physical chemistry of macromolecules, damage and repair of cellular DNA. *Unit head:* Dr. Li Zhang, Department Head, 972-883-6032, Fax: 972-883-2502, E-mail: li.zhang@utdallas.edu. *Application contact:* Dr. Lawrence Reitzer, Graduate Advisor, 972-883-2502, Fax: 972-883-2402, E-mail: reitzer@utdallas.edu.

The University of Texas at San Antonio, College of Sciences, Department of Biology, San Antonio, TX 78249-0617. Offers biology (MS, PhD), including cellular and molecular biology (PhD), neurobiology (PhD); biotechnology (MS). Part-time programs available. *Faculty:* 37 full-time (6 women), 7 part-time/adjunct (1 woman). *Students:* 144 full-time (82 women), 45 part-time (28 women); includes 57 minority (6 African Americans, 13 Asian Americans or Pacific Islanders, 38 Hispanic Americans), 69 international. Average age 28. 263 applicants, 58% accepted, 72 enrolled. In 2009, 40 master's, 6 doctorates awarded. *Degree requirements:* For master's, comprehensive exam, thesis; for doctorate, comprehensive exam, thesis/dissertation. *Entrance requirements:* For master's, GRE General Test, minimum GPA of 3.0; for doctorate, GRE General Test, minimum GPA of 3.3. Additional exam requirements/recommendations for international students: Required—TOEFL (minimum score 500 paper-based; 173 computer-based; 61 iBT), IELTS (minimum score 5). *Application deadline:* For fall admission, 7/1 for domestic students, 4/1 for international students; for spring admission, 11/1 for domestic students, 9/1 for international students. Applications are processed on a rolling basis. Application fee: $45 ($80 for international students). Electronic applications accepted. *Expenses:* Tuition, state resident: full-time $3975; part-time $221 per contact hour. Tuition, nonresident: full-time $13,947; part-time $775 per contact hour. Required fees: $1853. *Financial support:* In 2009–10, 66 students received support, including 13 fellowships (averaging $31,063 per year), 87 research assistantships (averaging $15,279 per year), 66 teaching assistantships (averaging $10,368 per year); career-related internships or fieldwork, scholarships/grants, and unspecified assistantships also available. Support available to part-time students. *Faculty research:* Cell and molecular biology, neurobiology, microbiology, integrative biology, environmental science. Total annual research expenditures: $1.7 million. *Unit head:* Dr. Edwin J. Barea-Rodriguez, Interim Chair, 210-458-5481, Fax: 210-458-7498, E-mail: edwin.barea@utsa.edu. *Application contact:* Dr. Dorothy A. Flannagan, Dean of the Graduate School, 210-458-4330, Fax: 210-458-4332, E-mail: dorothy.flannagan@utsa.edu.

University of the Sciences in Philadelphia, College of Graduate Studies, Program in Cell Biology and Biotechnology, Philadelphia, PA 19104-4495. Offers cell and molecular biology (PhD); cell biology (MS). Part-time and evening/weekend programs available. *Degree requirements:* For master's, thesis (for some programs). *Entrance requirements:* For master's, GRE General Test. Additional exam requirements/recommendations for international students: Required—TOEFL, TWE. *Expenses:* Contact institution. *Faculty research:* Invertebrate cell adhesion, plant-microbe interactions, natural product mechanisms, cell signal transduction, gene regulation and organization.

University of Utah, The Graduate School, Professional Master of Science and Technology Program, Salt Lake City, UT 84112-1107. Offers biotechnology (PSM); computational science (PSM); environmental science (PSM); science instrumentation (PSM). Part-time programs available. *Students:* 32 full-time (17 women), 38 part-time (13 women); includes 5 minority (1 African American, 3 Asian Americans or Pacific Islanders, 1 Hispanic American), 19 international. Average age 31. 84 applicants, 33% accepted, 16 enrolled. In 2009, 7 master's awarded. *Degree requirements:* For master's, internship. *Entrance requirements:* For master's, GRE (recommended), minimum undergraduate GPA of 3.0, bachelor's degree from accredited university or college. Additional exam requirements/recommendations for international students: Required—TOEFL (minimum score 500 paper-based; 173 computer-based). *Application deadline:* For fall admission, 3/1 for domestic and international students. Application fee: $55 ($65 for international students). Electronic applications accepted. *Expenses:* Tuition, state resident: full-time $4004; part-time $1674 per semester. Tuition, nonresident: full-time $14,134; part-time $5915 per semester. Required fees: $324 per semester. Tuition and fees vary according to course load, degree level and program. *Financial support:* In 2009–10, 4 fellowships with full and partial tuition reimbursements (averaging $12,000 per year), 3 research assistantships with full tuition reimbursements (averaging $13,000 per year) were awarded; unspecified assistantships also available. Financial award applicants required to submit FAFSA. *Unit head:* Jennifer Schmidt, Program Director, 801-585-5630, E-mail: jennifer.schmidt@gradschool.utah.edu. *Application contact:* Francine Stirling, Project Coordinator, 801-585-3650, Fax: 801-585-6749, E-mail: francine.stirling@gradschool.utah.edu.

University of Washington, Graduate School, School of Medicine and Graduate School, Graduate Programs in Medicine, Department of Genome Sciences, Seattle, WA 98195. Offers PhD. *Degree requirements:* For doctorate, thesis/dissertation, general exam. *Entrance requirements:* For doctorate, GRE General Test, minimum GPA of 3.0. Additional exam requirements/recommendations for international students: Required—TOEFL. Electronic applications accepted. *Faculty research:* Model organism genetics, human and medical genetics, genomics and proteomics, computational biology.

University of West Florida, College of Arts and Sciences: Sciences, School of Allied Health and Life Sciences, Department of Biology, Pensacola, FL 32514-5750. Offers biological chemistry (MS); biology (MS); biology education (MST); biotechnology (MS); coastal zone studies (MS); environmental biology (MS). *Faculty:* 7 full-time (2 women), 1 (woman) part-time/adjunct. *Students:* 5 full-time (1 woman), 21 part-time (14 women); includes 2 minority (1 Asian American or Pacific Islander, 1 Hispanic American), 1 international. Average age 28. 19 applicants, 58% accepted, 7 enrolled. In 2009, 12 master's awarded. *Degree requirements:* For master's, thesis. *Entrance requirements:* For master's, GRE General Test. Additional exam requirements/recommendations for international students: Required—TOEFL (minimum score 550 paper-based; 213 computer-based). *Application deadline:* For fall admission, 6/1 for domestic students, 5/15 for international students; for spring admission, 11/1 for domestic students, 10/1 for international students. Applications are processed on a rolling basis. Application fee: $30. *Expenses:* Tuition, state resident: full-time $4982; part-time $260 per credit hour. Tuition, nonresident: full-time $20,059; part-time $919 per credit hour. Required fees: $1247; $52 per credit hour. *Financial support:* In 2009–10, 2 research assistantships with partial tuition reimbursements (averaging $8,500 per year), 10 teaching assistantships with partial tuition reimbursements (averaging $8,176 per year) were awarded; unspecified assistantships also available. Financial award application deadline: 4/15; financial award applicants required to submit FAFSA. *Unit head:* Dr. George L. Stewart, Chairperson, 850-474-2748. *Application contact:* Terry McCray, Assistant Director of Graduate Admissions, 850-473-7718, Fax: 850-473-7714, E-mail: gradadmissions@uwf.edu.

University of Wyoming, Graduate Program in Molecular and Cellular Life Sciences, Laramie, WY 82070. Offers PhD. *Degree requirements:* For doctorate, thesis/dissertation, four eight-week laboratory rotations, comprehensive basic practical exam, two-part qualifying exam, seminars, symposium.

Virginia Polytechnic Institute and State University, Graduate School, College of Science, Program in Biomedical Technology Development and Management, Blacksburg, VA 24061. Offers MS.

Western Michigan University, Graduate College, College of Arts and Sciences, Department of Biological Sciences, Kalamazoo, MI 49008. Offers biological sciences (MS, PhD); electron microscopy (MS); molecular biotechnology (MS). *Degree requirements:* For master's, thesis,

oral exam; for doctorate, thesis/dissertation, oral exam. *Entrance requirements:* For master's and doctorate, GRE General Test.

West Virginia State University, Graduate Programs, Institute, WV 25112-1000. Offers biotechnology (MA, MS); media studies (MA). *Students:* 41 full-time (19 women), 8 part-time (6 women); includes 7 minority (5 African Americans, 1 Asian American or Pacific Islander, 1 Hispanic American), 8 international. *Entrance requirements:* For master's, GRE General Test, minimum GPA of 3.0, 3 letters of recommendation. Additional exam requirements/recommendations for international students: Required—TOEFL (minimum score 550 paper-based). *Financial support:* Research assistantships with tuition reimbursements, teaching assistantships with tuition reimbursements available. *Application contact:* Dr. John Teeuwissen, Assistant Vice President, Academic Affairs, 304-766-3147, E-mail: johntee@wvstateu.edu.

William Paterson University of New Jersey, College of Science and Health, Wayne, NJ 07470-8420. Offers biotechnology (MS); communication disorders (MS); general biology (MS); nursing (MSN). Part-time and evening/weekend programs available. *Students:* 53 full-time (48 women), 135 part-time (126 women); includes 27 minority (7 African Americans, 11 Asian Americans or Pacific Islanders, 9 Hispanic Americans), 4 international. *Entrance requirements:* For master's, GRE General Test, minimum GPA of 2.75. *Application deadline:* Applications are processed on a rolling basis. Application fee: $50. Electronic applications accepted. *Financial support:* Research assistantships with full tuition reimbursements, career-related internships or fieldwork and unspecified assistantships available. Support available to part-time students. Financial award application deadline: 4/1; financial award applicants required to submit FAFSA. *Faculty research:* Plant tissue culture, DNA cloning, cellular structure, language development, speech and hearing science. *Unit head:* Dr. Sandra DeYoung, Dean, College of Science and Health, 973-720-2432, E-mail: deyoungs@wpunj.edu. *Application contact:* Christina Aiello, Assistant Director, Graduate Admissions, 973-720-2506, Fax: 973-720-2035, E-mail: aielloc@wpunj.edu.

Worcester Polytechnic Institute, Graduate Studies and Research, Department of Biology and Biotechnology, Worcester, MA 01609-2280. Offers biology and biotechnology (MS); biotechnology (PhD). *Faculty:* 7 full-time (3 women). *Students:* 17 full-time (13 women), 3 part-time (all women). 102 applicants, 8% accepted, 6 enrolled. In 2009, 4 master's awarded. Terminal master's awarded for partial completion of doctoral program. *Degree requirements:* For master's, thesis; for doctorate, comprehensive exam, thesis/dissertation, qualifying exam. *Entrance requirements:* For master's, GRE General Test, 3 letters of recommendation; for doctorate, GRE General Test, 3 letters of recommendation, statement of purpose. Additional exam requirements/recommendations for international students: Required—TOEFL (minimum score 550 paper-based; 213 computer-based; 79 iBT), IELTS (minimum score 6.5). *Application deadline:* For fall admission, 1/15 priority date for domestic and international students. Application fee: $70. Electronic applications accepted. *Financial support:* Teaching assistantships, career-related internships or fieldwork, institutionally sponsored loans, scholarships/grants, and unspecified assistantships available. *Faculty research:* Developmental/regenerative biology, plant cell biology/biotechnology, immunobiology/pathogenesis, molecular ecology/evolution, genetics, cell and molecular biology, bioprocess technology. *Unit head:* Dr. Eric Overstrom, Head, 508-831-5538, Fax: 508-831-5936, E-mail: ewo@wpi.edu. *Application contact:* Dr. Joseph Duffy, Graduate Coordinator, 508-831-5538, Fax: 508-831-5936, E-mail: jduffy@wpi.edu.

Worcester State College, Graduate Studies, Program in Biotechnology, Worcester, MA 01602-2597. Offers MS. Part-time and evening/weekend programs available. *Faculty:* 7 full-time (2 women), 2 part-time/adjunct (0 women). *Students:* 3 full-time (0 women), 23 part-time (15 women); includes 4 minority (2 African Americans, 1 Asian American or Pacific Islander, 1 Hispanic American), 1 international. Average age 30. 23 applicants, 65% accepted, 9 enrolled. In 2009, 6 master's awarded. *Degree requirements:* For master's, comprehensive exam, thesis. *Entrance requirements:* For master's, GRE General Test or MAT, minimum undergraduate GPA of 3.0 in biology. Additional exam requirements/recommendations for international students: Required—TOEFL (minimum score 550 paper-based; 213 computer-based; 79 iBT). *Application deadline:* Applications are processed on a rolling basis. Application fee: $30. *Expenses:* Tuition, area resident: Part-time $150 per credit. Tuition, state resident: part-time $150 per credit. Tuition, nonresident: part-time $150 per credit. Required fees: $85. *Financial support:* In 2009–10, 2 students received support, including 2 research assistantships with full tuition reimbursements available (averaging $4,800 per year); career-related internships or fieldwork, scholarships/grants, and unspecified assistantships also available. Financial award application deadline: 3/1; financial award applicants required to submit FAFSA. *Faculty research:* Effects of insulin in invertebrates, ecology of freshwater turtles, symbiotic relations of plants and animals. *Unit head:* Dr. Peter Bradley, Coordinator, 508-929-8571, Fax: 508-929-8171, E-mail: pbradley@worcester.edu. *Application contact:* Nicole Brown, Assistant Dean of Graduate and Continuing Education, 508-929-8787, Fax: 508-929-8100, E-mail: nbrown@worcester.edu.

Nanotechnology

Arizona State University, Graduate College, College of Liberal Arts and Sciences, Division of Natural Sciences, Department of Physics, Tempe, AZ 85287. Offers nanoscience (PSM); physics (MNS, MS, PhD). *Degree requirements:* For master's, thesis, oral and written exams; for doctorate, thesis/dissertation. *Entrance requirements:* For master's and doctorate, GRE.

George Mason University, College of Science, Fairfax, VA 22030. Offers biodefense (MS, PhD); bioinformatics and computational biology (MS, PhD, Certificate); biology (MS, PhD), including bioinformatics (MS), ecology, systematics and evolution (MS), interpretive biology (MS), molecular and cellular biology (MS), molecular and microbiology (PhD), organismal biology (MS); chemistry and biochemistry (MS), including chemistry; climate dynamics (PhD); computational and data sciences (MS, PhD, Certificate); computational social science (PhD); computational techniques and applications (Certificate); earth systems and geoinformation sciences (MS, PhD, Certificate); environmental science and policy (MS, PhD); geography (MS), including geographic and cartographic sciences; mathematical sciences (MS, PhD), including mathematics; nanotechnology and nanoscience (Certificate); neuroscience (PhD); physical sciences (PhD); physics and astronomy (MS), including applied and engineering physics; remote sensing and earth image processing (Certificate). Part-time and evening/weekend programs available. *Degree requirements:* For doctorate, comprehensive exam, thesis/dissertation. *Entrance requirements:* For master's and doctorate, GRE General Test, minimum GPA of 3.0 in last 60 hours. Additional exam requirements/recommendations for international students: Required—TOEFL. Electronic applications accepted. *Expenses:* Tuition, state resident: full-time $7568; part-time $315.33 per credit hour. Tuition, nonresident: full-time $21,704; part-time $904.33 per credit hour. Required fees: $2184; $91 per credit hour. *Faculty research:* Space sciences and astrophysics, fluid dynamics, materials modeling and simulation, bioinformatics, global changes and statistics.

The Johns Hopkins University, G. W. C. Whiting School of Engineering, Program in Engineering Management, Baltimore, MD 21218-2699. Offers biomaterials (MSEM); communications science (MSEM); computer science (MSEM); fluid mechanics (MSEM); materials science and engineering (MSEM); mechanical engineering (MSEM); mechanics and materials (MSEM); nano-biotechnology (MSEM); nanomaterials and nanotechnology (MSEM); probability and statistics (MSEM); smart product and device design (MSEM); systems analysis, management and environmental policy (MSEM). *Students:* 12 full-time (0 women), 3 international. Average age 23. 66 applicants, 67% accepted. *Entrance requirements:* For master's, GRE, 3 letters of recommendation, resume. Additional exam requirements/recommendations for inter-

national students: Required—TOEFL (minimum score 600 paper-based; 250 computer-based; 100 iBT) or IELTS (minimum score 7). *Application deadline:* For fall admission, 1/15 priority date for domestic students, 1/15 for international students; for spring admission, 9/15 priority date for domestic students, 9/15 for international students. Applications are processed on a rolling basis. Application fee: $75. Electronic applications accepted. *Financial support:* Fellowships, health care benefits available. *Unit head:* Dr. Edward R. Scheinerman, Interim Director/Vice Dean for Education, School of Engineering/Professor, Applied Mathematics and Statistics, 410-516-7395, Fax: 410-516-4880, E-mail: ers@jhu.edu. *Application contact:* Dennis McIver, Coordinator of Graduate Admissions, 410-516-8174, Fax: 410-516-0780, E-mail: graduateadmissions@jhu.edu.

North Dakota State University, College of Graduate and Interdisciplinary Studies, Interdisciplinary Program in Materials and Nanotechnology, Fargo, ND 58108. Offers PhD. *Students:* 3 full-time (0 women), 2 part-time (0 women), all international. In 2009, 1 doctorate awarded. *Entrance requirements:* For doctorate, GRE General Test. Additional exam requirements/recommendations for international students: Required—TOEFL (minimum score 525 paper-based; 197 computer-based; 71 iBT). Application fee: $45 ($60 for international students). *Unit head:* Dr. Daniel Kroll, Director, 701-231-8968, E-mail: daniel.kroll@ndsu.edu. *Application contact:* Dr. Daniel Kroll, Director, 701-231-8968, E-mail: daniel.kroll@ndsu.edu.

Oregon State University, Graduate School, College of Engineering, School of Mechanical, Industrial, and Manufacturing Engineering, Corvallis, OR 97331. Offers human systems engineering (MS, PhD); industrial engineering (MS, PhD); information systems engineering (MS, PhD); manufacturing engineering (M Engr); manufacturing systems engineering (MS, PhD); materials science (MAIS, MS, PhD); mechanical engineering (MS, PhD); nano/micro fabrication (MS, PhD). Part-time programs available. Postbaccalaureate distance learning degree programs offered (minimal on-campus study). *Faculty:* 26 full-time (2 women), 2 part-time/adjunct (1 woman). *Students:* 136 full-time (25 women), 12 part-time (2 women); includes 11 minority (3 African Americans, 4 Asian Americans or Pacific Islanders, 4 Hispanic Americans), 46 international. Average age 29. 53 applicants, 42% accepted, 13 enrolled. In 2009, 26 master's, 10 doctorates awarded. *Degree requirements:* For master's, thesis or alternative; for doctorate, thesis/dissertation. *Entrance requirements:* For master's, placement exam, minimum GPA of 3.0 in last 90 hours of course work; for doctorate, GRE, placement exam, minimum GPA of 3.0 in last 90 hours of course work. Additional exam requirements/recommendations for international students: Required—TOEFL (minimum score 550 paper-

Nanotechnology

Oregon State University *(continued)*
based; 213 computer-based). *Application deadline:* For fall admission, 3/1 for domestic students. Applications are processed on a rolling basis. Application fee: $50. *Expenses:* Tuition, state resident: full-time $9774; part-time $362 per credit. Tuition, nonresident: full-time $15,849; part-time $587 per credit. Required fees: $1639. Full-time tuition and fees vary according to course load and program. *Financial support:* In 2009–10, 10 research assistantships with full tuition reimbursements (averaging $11,124 per year), 8 teaching assistantships with full tuition reimbursements (averaging $7,020 per year) were awarded; fellowships with full tuition reimbursements, institutionally sponsored loans and instructorships also available. Support available to part-time students. Financial award application deadline: 2/1. *Faculty research:* Computer-integrated manufacturing, human factors, robotics, decision support systems, simulation modeling and analysis. Total annual research expenditures: $1.3 million. *Unit head:* Dr. Belinda A. Batten, Head, 541-737-3441, Fax: 541-737-2600, E-mail: info-mime@oregonstate.edu. *Application contact:* Jean Robinson, Graduate Records Specialist, 541-737-7009, Fax: 541-737-2600, E-mail: jean.robinson@oregonstate.edu.

South Dakota School of Mines and Technology, Graduate Division, College of Engineering, Program in Nanoscience and Nanoengineering, Rapid City, SD 57701-3995. Offers PhD. *Faculty:* 7 full-time (0 women). *Students:* 24 full-time (7 women), 16 international. Average age 27. 15 applicants, 53% accepted, 7 enrolled. *Expenses:* Tuition, state resident: full-time $3340; part-time $139 per credit hour. Tuition, nonresident: full-time $7060; part-time $294 per credit hour. Required fees: $3270. *Financial support:* In 2009–10, research assistantships (averaging $15,800 per year), teaching assistantships (averaging $5,350 per year) were awarded; fellowships also available. *Unit head:* Dr. Steve Smith, Director, 605-394-5268, E-mail: steve.smith@sdsmt.edu. *Application contact:* Jeannette R. Nilson, Administrative Support Coordinator, Graduate Education, 800-454-8162 Ext. 1206, Fax: 605-394-5360, E-mail: graduate_admissions@sdsmt.edu.

University at Albany, State University of New York, College of Nanoscale Science and Engineering, Albany, NY 12222-0001. Offers MS, PhD. *Entrance requirements:* Additional exam requirements/recommendations for international students: Required—TOEFL (minimum score 550 paper-based; 213 computer-based). *Faculty research:* Thin film material structures, optoelectronic materials, design and fabrication of nano-mechanical systems, materials characterization.

University of Alberta, Faculty of Graduate Studies and Research, Department of Electrical and Computer Engineering, Edmonton, AB T6G 2E1, Canada. Offers communications (M Eng, M Sc, PhD); computer engineering (M Eng, M Sc, PhD); electromagnetics (M Eng, M Sc, PhD); nanotechnology and microdevices (M Eng, M Sc, PhD); power/power electronics (M Eng, M Sc, PhD); systems (M Eng, M Sc, PhD). *Faculty:* 42 full-time (3 women), 12 part-time/adjunct (0 women). *Students:* 252 full-time (28 women), 65 part-time (10 women). Average age 26. 1,500 applicants, 5% accepted. Terminal master's awarded for partial completion of doctoral program. *Degree requirements:* For master's, thesis; for doctorate, thesis/dissertation. *Entrance requirements:* Additional exam requirements/recommendations for international students: Required—TOEFL. *Application deadline:* For fall admission, 4/30 for domestic students; for winter admission, 8/30 for domestic students. Applications are processed on a rolling basis. Application fee: $0 Canadian dollars. Electronic applications accepted. Tuition and fees charges are reported in Canadian dollars. *Expenses:* Tuition, area resident: Full-time $4626.24 Canadian dollars; part-time $99.72 Canadian dollars per unit. International tuition: $8216 Canadian dollars full-time. Required fees: $3589.92 Canadian dollars; $99.72 Canadian dollars per unit. $215 Canadian dollars per term. *Financial support:* In 2009–10, 80 students received support; fellowships, research assistantships, teaching assistantships, scholarships/grants available. *Faculty research:* Controls, communications, microelectronics, electromagnetics. Total annual research expenditures: $3 million Canadian dollars. *Unit head:* Dr. H. J. Marquez, Chair, 780-492-0161, Fax: 780-492-1811. *Application contact:* Michelle Vaage, Graduate Student Advisor, 780-492-0161, Fax: 780-492-1811, E-mail: gradinfo@ece.ualberta.ca.

University of California, Riverside, Graduate Division, Graduate Materials Science and Engineering Program, Riverside, CA 92521-0102. Offers MS, PhD.

University of New Mexico, Graduate School, Program in Nanoscience and Microsystems, Albuquerque, NM 87131-2039. Offers MS, PhD. Part-time programs available. *Students:* 20 full-time (8 women), 4 part-time (0 women); includes 6 minority (1 American Indian/Alaska Native, 2 Asian Americans or Pacific Islanders, 3 Hispanic Americans), 2 international. Average age 31. 18 applicants, 78% accepted, 11 enrolled. In 2009, 1 master's awarded. *Degree requirements:* For master's, comprehensive exam, thesis; for doctorate, comprehensive exam, thesis/dissertation. *Entrance requirements:* For master's and doctorate, GRE. Additional exam requirements/recommendations for international students: Required—TOEFL. *Application deadline:* For fall admission, 7/30 for domestic students, 2/1 for international students; for spring admission, 11/30 for domestic students, 6/1 for international students. Application fee: $50. Electronic applications accepted. *Expenses:* Tuition, nonresident: full-time $6650. Required fees: $25 per semester. Tuition and fees vary according to course load, program and reciprocity agreements. *Unit head:* Dr. Abhaya Datye, Distinguished Professor, 505-277-0477, Fax: 505-277-1024, E-mail: datye@unm.edu. *Application contact:* Heather Elizabeth Armstrong, Program Specialist, 505-277-6824, Fax: 505-277-1024, E-mail: heathera@unm.edu.

University of Washington, Graduate School, College of Engineering, Department of Materials Science and Engineering, Seattle, WA 98195-2120. Offers materials science and engineering (MS, MSE, MSMSE, PhD); materials science and engineering nanotechnology (PhD). Part-time programs available. *Faculty:* 15 full-time (2 women), 6 part-time/adjunct (1 woman). *Students:* 95 full-time (32 women), 8 part-time (2 women); includes 18 minority (2 African Americans, 1 American Indian/Alaska Native, 12 Asian Americans or Pacific Islanders, 3 Hispanic Americans), 48 international. Average age 30. 194 applicants, 12% accepted, 9 enrolled. In 2009, 4 master's, 10 doctorates awarded. *Degree requirements:* For master's, comprehensive exam, thesis; for doctorate, comprehensive exam, thesis/dissertation. *Entrance requirements:* For master's and doctorate, GRE General Test, minimum GPA of 3.0. Additional exam requirements/recommendations for international students: Required—TOEFL (minimum score 600 paper-based; 250 computer-based; 70 iBT). *Application deadline:* For fall admission, 1/15 priority date for domestic and international students. Application fee: $65. Electronic applications accepted. *Financial support:* In 2009–10, 3 students received support, including 12 fellowships with full tuition reimbursements available, 42 research assistantships with full tuition reimbursements available (averaging $16,380 per year), 13 teaching assistantships with full tuition reimbursements available (averaging $16,380 per year); career-related internships or fieldwork, Federal Work-Study, institutionally sponsored loans, scholarships/grants, health care benefits, unspecified assistantships, and stipend supplements also available. Financial award application deadline: 1/15. *Faculty research:* Biomimetics and biomaterials; electronic, optical and magnetic materials; eco-materials and materials for energy applications; ceramics, metals, composites, and polymers. Total annual research expenditures: $7.4 million. *Unit head:* Dr. Alex Jen, Professor and Chair, 206-543-2600, Fax: 206-543-3100, E-mail: ajen@uw.edu. *Application contact:* Kathleen A. Elkins, Academic Counselor, 206-616-6581, Fax: 206-543-3100, E-mail: kelkins@uw.edu.

Virginia Commonwealth University, Graduate School, College of Humanities and Sciences, Program in Nanosciences, Richmond, VA 23284-9005. Offers PhD.

Western Michigan University, Graduate College, College of Arts and Sciences, Department of Biological Sciences, Kalamazoo, MI 49008. Offers biological sciences (MS, PhD); electron microscopy (MS); molecular biotechnology (MS). *Degree requirements:* For master's, thesis, oral exam; for doctorate, thesis/dissertation, oral exam. *Entrance requirements:* For master's and doctorate, GRE General Test.

CASE WESTERN RESERVE UNIVERSITY

Department of Biomedical Engineering

Programs of Study

The Department offers many exceptional and innovative educational programs leading to career opportunities in biomedical engineering (BME) research, development, and design in industry, medical centers, and academic institutions. Graduate degrees offered include the M.S. and Ph.D. in BME, a combined M.D./M.S. degree offered to students admitted to the School of Medicine, and combined M.D./Ph.D. degrees in BME offered through the Physician Engineer Training Program or the Medical Scientist Training Program. Individualized BME programs of study allow students to develop strength in an engineering specialty and apply this expertise to an important biomedical problem under the supervision of a Faculty Guidance Committee. Students can choose from more than forty-three courses regularly taught in BME, as well as many courses in other departments. Typically, an M.S. program consists of seven to nine courses, and a Ph.D. program consists of about thirteen courses beyond the B.S. Students can select research projects from among the many strengths of the Department, including neural engineering and neural prostheses, biomaterials, tissue engineering, drug and gene delivery, biomedical imaging, sensors, optical imaging and diagnostics, the cardiovascular system, biomechanics, mass and heat transport, and metabolic systems. Collaborative research and training in basic biomedical sciences, as well as clinical and translational research, are available through primary faculty members, associated faculty members, and researchers in the nearby major medical centers.

Research Facilities

The primary faculty members have laboratories focusing on cardiovascular and skeletal biomaterials; cardiovascular, orthopaedic, and neural tissue engineering; materials and nanoparticles for drug and gene delivery, biomedical image processing, biomedical imaging in several modalities, cellular and tissue cardiac bioelectricity, ion channel function, electrochemical and fiber-optic sensors, neural engineering and brain electrophysiology, and neural prostheses. BME faculty members and students also make extensive use of campus research centers for special purposes such as microelectronic fabrication, biomedical imaging, and material analyses. Associated faculty members have labs devoted to eye movement control, gait analysis, implantable sensors/actuators, biomedical imaging, metabolism, and tissue pathology. These are located at four major medical centers and teaching hospitals that (with one exception) are within walking distance.

Financial Aid

Graduate students pursuing the Ph.D. may receive financial support from faculty members as research assistants, from training grants (NIH, NSF, DoE GAANN), or from the School of Medicine (M.D./Ph.D. only). These positions are awarded on a competitive basis. There are also opportunities for research assistantships in order to pursue the M.S.

Cost of Study

Tuition at Case in 2009–10 for graduate students was $1430 per credit hour. A full load for graduate students is a minimum of 9 credits per semester. Fees for health insurance and activities are estimated at $500 per semester.

Living and Housing Costs

Within a 2-mile radius of the campus, numerous apartments are available for married and single graduate students at rents ranging from $450 to $900 per month.

Student Group

The Department of Biomedical Engineering has 150 graduate students, of whom about 85 percent are advancing toward the Ph.D. At Case Western Reserve University, approximately 4,356 students are enrolled as undergraduates, 3,182 in graduate studies, and 2,276 in the professional schools.

Location

Case is located on the eastern boundary of Cleveland in University Circle, which is the city's cultural center. The area includes Severance Hall (home of the Cleveland Orchestra), the Museum of Art, the Museum of Natural History, the Garden Center, the Institute of Art, the Institute of Music, the Western Reserve Historical Society, and the Crawford Auto-Aviation Museum. Metropolitan Cleveland has a population of almost 2 million. The Cleveland Hopkins International Airport is 30 minutes away by rail transit. A network of parks encircles the greater Cleveland area. Opportunities are available for sailing on Lake Erie and for hiking and skiing nearby in Ohio, Pennsylvania, and New York. Major-league sports, theater, and all types of music provide a full range of entertainment.

The University and The Department

The Department of Biomedical Engineering at Case Western Reserve University is part of both the Case School of Engineering and the School of Medicine, which are located on the same campus. Established in 1967, the Department is one of the pioneers in biomedical engineering education and is currently among the nation's largest and highest rated (according to *U.S. News & World Report*). Case Western Reserve University was formed in 1967 by a federation of Western Reserve College and Case Institute of Technology. Numerous interdisciplinary programs exist with the professional Schools of Medicine, Dentistry, Nursing, Law, Social Work, and Management.

Applying

Applications that request financial aid should be submitted before February 1. The completed application requires official transcripts, scores on the GRE General Test, and three letters of reference. Application forms are available from the BME Admissions Coordinator or can be downloaded from the Case Web site (http://www.case.edu). Applicants for the M.D./M.S. and M.D./Ph.D. programs can apply through the School of Medicine.

Correspondence and Information

Admissions Coordinator
Department of Biomedical Engineering
Wickenden Building 310
Case Western Reserve University
10900 Euclid Avenue
Cleveland, Ohio 44106-7207

Phone: 216-368-4094
Fax: 216-368-4969
Web site: http://bme.case.edu

Case Western Reserve University

THE FACULTY AND THEIR RESEARCH

Primary Faculty

Eben Alsberg, Ph.D., Assistant Professor. Biomimetic tissue engineering, innovative biomaterials and drug delivery vehicles for functional tissue regeneration and cancer therapy, control of stem cell differentiation, mechanotransduction and the influence of mechanics on cell and tissue function, cell-cell interactions.

James P. Basilion, Ph.D., Associate Professor of BME and Radiology. Molecular imaging, biomarkers, diagnosis and treatment of cancer.

Harihara Baskaran, Ph.D., Assistant Professor of BME and Chemical Engineering. Tissue engineering; cell/cellular transport processes in inflammation, wound healing, and cancer metastasis.

Patrick E. Crago, Ph.D., Professor. Control of neuroprostheses for motor function, neuromuscular control systems.

Jeffrey L. Duerk, Ph.D., Professor and Chairman. Radiology, MRI, fast MRI pulse sequence design, interventional MRI, MRI reconstruction.

Dominique M. Durand, Ph.D., Professor. Neural engineering, neuroprostheses, neural dynamics, magnetic and electric stimulation of the nervous system, neural interfaces with electronic devices, analysis and control of epilepsy.

Steven J. Eppell, Ph.D., Associate Professor. Nanoscale instrumentation for biomaterials, bone and cartilage structure and function.

Miklos Gratzl, Ph.D., Associate Professor. Fine chemical manipulation of microdroplets and single cells, cancer research and neurochemistry at the single-cell level, cost-effective biochemical diagnostics in microliter body fluids.

Kenneth Gustafson, Ph.D., Assistant Professor. Neural engineering, neural prostheses, neurophysiology and neural control of genitourinary function, devices to restore genitourinary function, functional neuromuscular stimulation.

Efstathios Karathanasis, Ph.D., Assistant Professor. Fabricating multifunctional agents that facilitate diagnosing, treating, and monitoring of therapies in a patient-specific manner.

J. Lawrence Katz, Ph.D., Professor Emeritus. Structure-property relationships in bone, osteophilic biomaterials, ultrasonic studies of tissue anisotropy, scanning acoustic microscopy.

Robert Kirsch, Ph.D., Professor. Functional neuromuscular stimulation, biomechanics and neural control of human movement, modeling and simulation of musculoskeletal systems, identification of physiological systems.

Melissa Knothe-Tate, Ph.D., Professor of BME and Mechanical and Aerospace Engineering. Etiology and innovative treatment modalities for osteoporosis, fracture healing, osteolysis, and osteonecrosis.

Erin Lavik, Sc.D., Associate Professor. Biomaterials and synthesis of new degradable polymers, tissue engineering, spinal cord repair, retinal regeneration, drug delivery for optic nerve preservation and repair.

Zheng-Rong Lu, Ph.D., Professor. Molecular imaging and drug delivery using novel nanotechnology.

Roger E. Marchant, Ph.D., Professor and Director of the Center for Cardiovascular Biomaterials. Surface modification of cardiovascular devices, molecular-level structure and function of plasma proteins, liposome drug delivery systems, mechanisms of bacterial adhesion to biomaterials.

J. Thomas Mortimer, Ph.D., Professor Emeritus. Neural prostheses, electrical activation of the nervous system, bowel and bladder assist device, respiratory assist device, selective stimulation and electrode development, electrochemical aspects of electrical stimulation.

P. Hunter Peckham, Ph.D., Professor and Director of the Functional Electrical Stimulation Center. Neural prostheses, implantable stimulation and control of movement, rehabilitation engineering.

Andrew M. Rollins, Ph.D., Assistant Professor. Biomedical diagnosis; novel optical methods for high-resolution, minimally invasive imaging; tissue characterization and analyte sensing; real-time microstructural and functional imaging using coherence tomography; endoscopy.

Gerald M. Saidel, Ph.D., Professor and Director of the Center for Modeling Integrated Metabolic Systems. Mass and heat transport and metabolic analysis in cells, tissues, and organs; mathematical modeling, simulation, and parameter estimation; optimal experimental design; metabolic dynamics; minimally invasive thermal tumor ablation; slow-release drug delivery.

Anirban Sen Gupta, Ph.D., Assistant Professor. Targeted drug delivery, targeted molecular imaging, image-guided therapy, platelet substitutes, novel polymeric biomaterials for tissue engineering scaffolds.

Dustin Tyler, Ph.D., Assistant Professor. Neuromimetic neuroprostheses, laryngeal neuroprostheses, clinical implementation of nerve electrodes, cortical neuroprostheses, minimally invasive implantation techniques, modeling of neural stimulation and neuroprostheses.

Horst von Recum, Ph.D., Assistant Professor. Tissue-engineered epithelia, prevascularized polymer scaffolds, directed stem cell differentiation, novel stimuli-responsive biomaterials for gene and drug delivery, systems biology approaches to the identification of angiogenic factors.

David L. Wilson, Ph.D., Professor. In vivo microscopic and molecular imaging; medical image processing; image segmentation, registration, and analysis; quantitative image quality of X-ray fluoroscopy and fast MRI; interventional MRI treatment of cancer.

Xin Yu, Sc.D., Associate Professor. Cardiovascular physiology, magnetic resonance imaging and spectroscopy, characterization of the structure-function and energy-function relationships in normal and diseased hearts, small-animal imaging and spectroscopy.

Associated Faculty (partial list)

Jay Alberts, Ph.D., Assistant Professor (BME, Cleveland Clinic Foundation). Neural basis of upper-extremity motor function and deep-brain stimulation in Parkinson's disease.

James M. Anderson, M.D./Ph.D., Professor (Pathology, University Hospitals). Biocompatibility of implants, human vascular grafts.

Richard C. Burgess, M.D./Ph.D., Adjunct Professor (Staff Physician, Neurology, Cleveland Clinic Foundation). Electrophysiological monitoring, EEG processing.

Arnold Caplan, Ph.D., Professor of Biology. Tissue engineering.

Peter R. Cavanagh, Ph.D., Adjunct Professor (Academic Director, Diabetic Foot Care Program, and Virginia Lois Kennedy Chairman of Biomedical Engineering, Cleveland Clinic Foundation). Foot complications of diabetes, bone biomechanics.

John Chae, M.D., Associate Professor (Neural Rehabilitation, MetroHealth Medical Center). Application of neuroprostheses in hemiplegia.

Yuanna Cheng, M.D./Ph.D., Adjunct Associate Professor (Cardiovascular Medicine, Cleveland Clinic Foundation). Cardiac imaging, mechanisms of arrhythmias, implantable defibrillators, cardiac remodeling, antiarrhythmic therapy.

Hillel J. Chiel, Ph.D., Professor. Biomechanical and neural basis of feeding behavior in *Aplysia californica,* neuromechanical system modeling.

Guy Chisolm, Ph.D., Adjunct Professor (Vice Chairman, Lerner Research Institute, and Staff, Cell Biology, Cleveland Clinic Foundation). Cell and molecular mechanisms in vascular disease and vascular biology; role of lipoprotein oxidation in atherosclerosis; lipoprotein transport into, accumulation in, and injury to arterial tissue.

Janis J. Daly, Ph.D., Adjunct Associate Professor (Neurology, VA Medical Center). Cognitive and motor processes involved in motor control.

Margot Damaser, Ph.D., Assistant Professor of Molecular Medicine (BME, Cleveland Clinic Foundation). Biomechanics as it relates to function and dysfunction of the lower urinary tract.

Brian Davis, Ph.D., Adjunct Associate Professor (BME, Cleveland Clinic Foundation). Human locomotion, diabetic foot pathology, space flight–induced osteoporosis, biomedical instrumentation.

David Dean, Ph.D., Assistant Professor (Neurological Surgery, University Hospitals). 3-D medical imaging and morphometrics; skull, brain, soft tissue face.

Louis F. Dell'Osso, Ph.D., Professor (Neurology, VA Medical Center). Neurophysiological control, ocular motor control and oscillations.

Kathleen Derwin, Ph.D., Assistant Professor (BME, Cleveland Clinic Foundation). Tendon mechanobiology and tissue engineering.

Isabelle Deschenes, Ph.D., Assistant Professor (Cardiology, MetroHealth Medical Center). Molecular imaging, ion channel structure and function, genetic regulation of ion channels, cellular and molecular mechanisms of cardiac arrhythmias.

Claire M. Doerschuk, M.D., Associate Professor (Pediatrics, RB&C, University Hospitals). Regulation of the inflammatory response in the lungs.

Agata Exner, Ph.D., Assistant Professor (Radiology, University Hospitals). Image-guided drug delivery, polymers for interventional radiology, models of cancer.

Baowei Fei, Ph.D., Assistant Professor (Radiology, University Hospitals). Quantitative image analysis, multimodality image registration, fusion visualization, image-guided minimally invasive therapy, prostate cancer, photodynamic therapy.

Elizabeth Fisher, Ph.D., Assistant Staff (BME, Cleveland Clinic Foundation). Quantitative image analysis for monitoring multiple sclerosis.

Marc Griswold, Ph.D., Associate Professor (Radiology, University Hospitals). Rapid magnetic resonance imaging, image reconstruction and processing, MRI hardware/instrumentation.

Elizabeth C. Hardin, Ph.D., Adjunct Assistant Professor (Rehabilitation Research and Development, VA Medical Center). Neural prostheses and gait mechanics, improving gait performance with neural prostheses using strategies developed in conjunction with forward dynamics musculoskeletal models.

Michael W. Keith, M.D., Professor (Orthopaedics, MetroHealth Medical Center). Restoration of motor function in hands.

Kevin Kilgore, Ph.D., Adjunct Assistant Professor (MetroHealth Medical Center). Functional electrical stimulation, restoration of hand function.

Kandice Kottke-Marchant, M.D./Ph.D., Adjunct Associate Professor (Staff, Clinical Pathology, Cleveland Clinic Foundation). Interaction of blood and materials, endothelial cell function on biomaterials.

Kenneth R. Laurita, Ph.D., Assistant Professor (Heart and Vascular Research Center, MetroHealth Medical Center). Cardiac electrophysiology, arrhythmia mechanisms, intracellular calcium homeostasis, fluorescence imaging, instrumentation and software for potential mapping.

Zhenghong Lee, Ph.D., Assistant Professor (Radiology, University Hospitals). Quantitative PET and SPECT imaging, multimodal image registration, 3-D visualization, molecular imaging, small-animal imaging systems.

R. John Leigh, M.D., Professor (Neurology, VA Medical Center). Normal and abnormal motor control, eye movements.

Cameron McIntyre, Ph.D., Adjunct Assistant Professor (BME, Cleveland Clinic Foundation). Electric field modeling in the nervous system, deep brain stimulation.

George Muschler, M.D., Professor (Staff, BME, Cleveland Clinic Foundation). Musculoskeletal oncology, adult reconstructive orthopaedic surgery, fracture nonunion, research in bone healing and bone-grafting materials.

Raymond Muzic, Ph.D., Assistant Professor (Radiology, University Hospitals). Modeling and experiment design for PET, image reconstruction.

Sherif G. Nour, M.D., Assistant Professor (Radiology, University Hospitals). Interventional MRI.

Marc Penn, M.D., Ph.D., Adjunct Assistant Professor (Assistant Staff, Cardiology and Cell Biology, Cleveland Clinic Foundation). Myocardial ischemia, remodeling, gene regulation and therapy.

Clare Rimnac, Ph.D., Associate Professor and Director of the Musculoskeletal Mechanics and Materials Laboratories, Mechanical and Aerospace Engineering. Orthopaedic implant performance and design, mechanical behavior of hand tissues.

David S. Rosenbaum, M.D., Associate Professor (Director, Heart and Vascular Research Center, MetroHealth Medical Center). High-resolution cardiac optical mapping, arrhythmia mechanisms, ECG signal processing.

Mark S. Rzeszotarski, Ph.D., Assistant Professor (Radiology, MetroHealth Medical Center). Computers in radiology: MRI/CT/nuclear medicine, ultrasound.

Dawn Taylor, Ph.D., Assistant Professor (BME, Cleveland Clinic Foundation). Brain-computer interfaces for control of computers, neural prostheses, and robotic devices; invasive and noninvasive brain signal acquisition; adaptive decoding algorithms for retraining the brain to control alternative devices after paralysis.

Ronald Triolo, Ph.D., Associate Professor (Orthopaedics, VA Medical Center). Rehabilitation engineering, neuroprostheses, orthopaedic biomechanics.

Antonie J. van den Bogert, Ph.D., Adjunct Assistant Professor (Assistant Staff, BME, Cleveland Clinic Foundation). Biomechanics of human movement.

D. Geoffrey Vince, Ph.D., Adjunct Assistant Professor (Assistant Staff, BME, Cleveland Clinic Foundation). Image and signal processing of intravascular ultrasound images, coronary plaque rupture, cellular aspects of atherosclerosis.

Albert L. Waldo, M.D., Professor (Medicine, University Hospitals). Cardiac electrophysiology, cardiac excitation mapping, mechanisms of cardiac arrhythmias and conduction.

Barry W. Wessels, Ph.D., Professor (Radiation Oncology, University Hospitals). Radio-labeled antibody therapy (dosimeter and clinical trials); image-guided radiotherapy; intensity-modulated radiation therapy; image fusion of CT, MR, SPECT, and PET for adaptive radiation therapy treatment planning.

Guang H. Yue, Ph.D., Adjunct Assistant Professor (Assistant Staff, BME, Cleveland Clinic Foundation). Neural control of movement, electrophysiology, MRI.

Marcie Zborowski, Ph.D., Adjunct Assistant Professor (Assistant Staff, BME, Cleveland Clinic Foundation). High-speed magnetic cell sorting.

Nicholas P. Ziats, Ph.D., Assistant Professor (Pathology, University Hospitals). Vascular grafts, cell-material interactions, extracellular matrix, tissue engineering, blood compatibility.

Section 6
Chemical Engineering

This section contains a directory of institutions offering graduate work in chemical engineering, followed by an in-depth entry submitted by an institution that chose to prepare a detailed program description. Additional information about programs listed in the directory but not augmented by an in-depth entry may be obtained by writing directly to the dean of a graduate school or chair of a department at the address given in the directory.

For programs offering related work, see also in this book *Engineering and Applied Sciences; Geological, Mineral/Mining, and Petroleum Engineering; Management of Engineering and Technology;* and *Materials Sciences and Engineering.* In the other guides in this series:

Graduate Programs in the Humanities, Arts & Social Sciences
See *Family and Consumer Sciences (Clothing and Textiles)*
Graduate Programs in the Biological Sciences
See *Biochemistry*
Graduate Programs in the Physical Sciences, Mathematics, Agricultural Sciences, the Environment & Natural Resources
See *Chemistry and Geosciences (Geochemistry and Geology)*

CONTENTS

Program Directories

Close-Up and Display

Biochemical Engineering

Cornell University, Graduate School, Graduate Fields of Engineering, Field of Chemical Engineering, Ithaca, NY 14853-0001. Offers advanced materials processing (M Eng, MS, PhD); applied mathematics and computational methods (M Eng, MS, PhD); biochemical engineering (M Eng, MS, PhD); chemical reaction engineering (M Eng, MS, PhD); classical and statistical thermodynamics (M Eng, MS, PhD); fluid dynamics, rheology and biorheology (M Eng, MS, PhD); heat and mass transfer (M Eng, MS, PhD); kinetics and catalysis (M Eng, MS, PhD); polymers (M Eng, MS, PhD); surface science (M Eng, MS, PhD). *Faculty:* 29 full-time (2 women). *Students:* 95 full-time (30 women); includes 9 minority (1 African American, 5 Asian Americans or Pacific Islanders, 3 Hispanic Americans), 41 international. Average age 25. 317 applicants, 38% accepted, 46 enrolled. In 2009, 22 master's, 17 doctorates awarded. *Degree requirements:* For master's, thesis (MS); for doctorate, comprehensive exam, thesis/dissertation. *Entrance requirements:* For master's and doctorate, GRE General Test, 2 letters of recommendation. Additional exam requirements/recommendations for international students: Required—TOEFL (minimum score 600 paper-based; 237 computer-based; 77 iBT). *Application deadline:* For fall admission, 1/15 priority date for domestic students. Application fee: $70. Electronic applications accepted. *Expenses:* Tuition: Full-time $29,500. Required fees: $70. Full-time tuition and fees vary according to degree level, program and student level. *Financial support:* In 2009–10, 67 students received support, including 3 fellowships with full tuition reimbursements available, 3 research assistantships with full tuition reimbursements available; teaching assistantships with full tuition reimbursements available, institutionally sponsored loans, scholarships/grants, health care benefits, tuition waivers (full and partial), and unspecified assistantships also available. Financial award applicants required to submit FAFSA. *Faculty research:* Biochemical, biomedical and metabolic engineering; fluid and polymer dynamics; surface science and chemical kinetics; electronics materials; microchemical systems and nanotechnology. *Unit head:* Director of Graduate Studies, 607-255-4550. *Application contact:* Graduate Field Assistant, 607-255-4550, E-mail: dgs@cheme.cornell.edu.

Dartmouth College, Thayer School of Engineering, Program in Biotechnology and Biochemical Engineering, Hanover, NH 03755. Offers MS, PhD. *Degree requirements:* For master's, thesis; for doctorate, thesis/dissertation, candidacy oral exam. *Entrance requirements:* For master's and doctorate, GRE General Test. *Application deadline:* For fall admission, 1/1 priority date for domestic students. Application fee: $45. *Financial support:* Fellowships, research assistantships, teaching assistantships, career-related internships or fieldwork, Federal Work-Study, institutionally sponsored loans, and tuition waivers (full and partial) available. Financial award application deadline: 1/15. *Faculty research:* Biomass processing, metabolic engineering, kinetics and reactor design, applied microbiology, resource and environmental analysis. Total annual research expenditures: $3.1 million. *Unit head:* Dr. Joseph J. Helbie, Dean, 603-646-2238, Fax: 603-646-2580, E-mail: joseph.j.helbie@dartmouth.edu. *Application contact:* Candace S. Potter, Graduate Admissions Administrator, 603-646-3844, Fax: 603-646-1620, E-mail: candace.potter@dartmouth.edu.

Drexel University, College of Engineering, Department of Chemical and Biological Engineering, Program in Biochemical Engineering, Philadelphia, PA 19104-2875. Offers MS. Part-time and evening/weekend programs available. *Degree requirements:* For master's, thesis. *Entrance requirements:* For master's, minimum GPA of 3.0 in chemical engineering or biological sciences. Additional exam requirements/recommendations for international students: Required—TOEFL. Electronic applications accepted. *Faculty research:* Monitoring and control of bioreactors, sensors for bioreactors, large-scale production of monoclonal antibodies.

Rutgers, The State University of New Jersey, New Brunswick, Graduate School-New Brunswick, Program in Chemical and Biochemical Engineering, Piscataway, NJ 08854-8097. Offers MS, PhD. Part-time and evening/weekend programs available. Terminal master's awarded for partial completion of doctoral program. *Degree requirements:* For master's, thesis or alternative; for doctorate, thesis/dissertation. *Entrance requirements:* For master's and doctorate, GRE General Test. Additional exam requirements/recommendations for international students: Required—TOEFL. *Faculty research:* Biotechnology, pharmaceutical engineering, nanotechnology, process system engineering, materials and polymer science, chemical engineering sciences.

University of California, Irvine, Office of Graduate Studies, School of Engineering, Department of Chemical Engineering and Materials Science, Irvine, CA 92697. Offers chemical and biochemical engineering (MS, PhD); materials science and engineering (MS, PhD). Part-time programs available. *Students:* 78 full-time (24 women), 7 part-time (2 women); includes 22 minority (1 American Indian/Alaska Native, 19 Asian Americans or Pacific Islanders, 2 Hispanic Americans), 37 international. Average age 27. 281 applicants, 25% accepted, 25 enrolled. In 2009, 26 master's, 4 doctorates awarded. Terminal master's awarded for partial completion of doctoral program. *Degree requirements:* For doctorate, thesis/dissertation. *Entrance requirements:* For master's and doctorate, GRE General Test, minimum GPA of 3.0, 3 letters of recommendation. Additional exam requirements/recommendations for international students: Required—TOEFL (minimum score 550 paper-based; 213 computer-based). *Application deadline:* For fall admission, 1/15 priority date for domestic students, 1/15 for international students. Applications are processed on a rolling basis. Application fee: $70 ($90 for international students). Electronic applications accepted. *Financial support:* In 2009–10, fellowships with tuition reimbursements (averaging $14,656 per year); research assistantships with full tuition reimbursements, teaching assistantships with tuition reimbursements, institutionally sponsored loans, traineeships, health care benefits, and unspecified assistantships also available. Financial award application deadline: 3/1; financial award applicants required to submit FAFSA. *Faculty research:* Molecular biotechnology, nano-bio-materials, biophotonics,

synthesis, superplasticity and mechanical behavior, characterization of advanced and nanostructural materials. *Unit head:* Dr. Stanley Grant, Director, 949-824-8277, Fax: 949-824-2541, E-mail: sbgrant@uci.edu. *Application contact:* Beatrice Mei, Graduate Coordinator, 949-824-3887, Fax: 949-824-2541, E-mail: bmei@uci.edu.

The University of Iowa, Graduate College, College of Engineering, Department of Chemical and Biochemical Engineering, Iowa City, IA 52242-1316. Offers MS, PhD. Part-time programs available. *Faculty:* 11 full-time (3 women), 1 (woman) part-time/adjunct. *Students:* 40 full-time (16 women); includes 5 minority (4 African Americans, 1 Asian American or Pacific Islander), 17 international. Average age 28. 67 applicants, 22% accepted, 11 enrolled. In 2009, 5 master's, 6 doctorates awarded. *Degree requirements:* For master's, comprehensive exam (for some programs), thesis (for some programs); for doctorate, comprehensive exam, thesis/dissertation. *Entrance requirements:* For master's and doctorate, GRE, minimum undergraduate GPA of 3.0. Additional exam requirements/recommendations for international students: Required—TOEFL (minimum score 550 paper-based; 213 computer-based). *Application deadline:* For fall admission, 2/1 for domestic and international students; for spring admission, 10/1 for domestic and international students. Applications are processed on a rolling basis. Application fee: $60 ($100 for international students). Electronic applications accepted. *Financial support:* In 2009–10, 4 fellowships with partial tuition reimbursements (averaging $16,300 per year), 30 research assistantships with partial tuition reimbursements (averaging $21,368 per year), 12 teaching assistantships with partial tuition reimbursements (averaging $19,493 per year) were awarded; unspecified assistantships also available. Financial award applicants required to submit FAFSA. *Faculty research:* Polymeric materials; photopolymerization; atmospheric chemistry and air pollution; biochemical engineering; bioprocessing and biomedical engineering. Total annual research expenditures: $2.2 million. *Unit head:* Dr. David W. Murhammer, Departmental Executive Officer, 319-335-1228, Fax: 319-335-1415, E-mail: david-murhammer@uiowa.edu. *Application contact:* Natalie Potter, Secretary, 319-335-1215, Fax: 319-335-1415, E-mail: chemeng@engineering.uiowa.edu.

University of Maryland, Baltimore County, Graduate School, College of Engineering and Information Technology, Department of Chemical and Biochemical Engineering, Post Baccalaureate Certificate Program in Biochemical Regulatory Engineering, Baltimore, MD 21250. Offers Postbaccalaureate Certificate. Part-time programs available. *Students:* 4 part-time (1 woman); includes 1 minority (African American). Average age 43. 3 applicants, 100% accepted, 2 enrolled. In 2009, 3 Postbaccalaureate Certificates awarded. *Application deadline:* For fall admission, 7/1 for domestic and international students; for spring admission, 2/1 for domestic students, 12/1 for international students. Applications are processed on a rolling basis. Application fee: $50. Electronic applications accepted. *Unit head:* Dr. Antonio Moreira, Vice Provost for Academic Affairs, 410-455-6576, E-mail: moreira@umbc.edu. *Application contact:* Dr. Mark Marten, Professor and Graduate Program Director, 410-455-3439, Fax: 410-455-1049, E-mail: marten@umbc.edu.

University of Maryland, Baltimore County, Graduate School, College of Engineering and Information Technology, Department of Chemical and Biochemical Engineering, Program in Chemical and Biochemical Engineering, Baltimore, MD 21250. Offers MS, PhD. Part-time programs available. *Students:* 24 full-time (12 women), 5 part-time (3 women); includes 5 minority (1 African American, 3 Asian Americans or Pacific Islanders, 1 Hispanic American), 20 international. Average age 25. 38 applicants, 39% accepted, 9 enrolled. In 2009, 10 master's, 3 doctorates awarded. *Degree requirements:* For master's, comprehensive exam (for some programs), thesis (for some programs); for doctorate, comprehensive exam, thesis/dissertation. *Entrance requirements:* For master's, GRE General Test, minimum GPA of 3.0; for doctorate, GRE General Test (within last 5 years), GRE Subject Test, minimum GPA of 3.0. Additional exam requirements/recommendations for international students: Required—TOEFL (minimum score 550 paper-based; 213 computer-based; 80 iBT). *Application deadline:* For fall admission, 6/1 for domestic students, 1/1 for international students; for spring admission, 11/1 for domestic students, 6/1 for international students. Applications are processed on a rolling basis. Application fee: $50. Electronic applications accepted. *Financial support:* In 2009–10, 3 students received support, including 1 fellowship with full tuition reimbursement available (averaging $24,000 per year), 14 research assistantships with full tuition reimbursements available (averaging $22,000 per year), 8 teaching assistantships with full tuition reimbursements available (averaging $21,000 per year); career-related internships or fieldwork, Federal Work-Study, scholarships/grants, health care benefits, tuition waivers (partial), and unspecified assistantships also available. Support available to part-time students. Financial award application deadline: 6/30; financial award applicants required to submit FAFSA. *Faculty research:* Biomaterials engineering, cellular engineering, sensor technology, systems biology and functional genomics, engineering education and outreach. *Unit head:* Dr. Julia M. Ross, Professor and Chair. *Application contact:* Dr. Mark Marten, Professor and Graduate Program Director, 410-455-3439, Fax: 410-455-1049, E-mail: marten@umbc.edu.

The University of Western Ontario, Faculty of Graduate Studies, Physical Sciences Division, Faculty of Engineering, London, ON N6A 5B8, Canada. Offers chemical and biochemical engineering (ME Sc, PhD); civil and environmental engineering (M Eng, ME Sc, PhD); electrical and computer engineering (M Eng, ME Sc, PhD); mechanical and materials engineering (M Eng, ME Sc, PhD). Part-time programs available. Terminal master's awarded for partial completion of doctoral program. *Degree requirements:* For master's, thesis; for doctorate, thesis/dissertation. *Entrance requirements:* For master's, minimum B average; for doctorate, minimum B+ average. *Faculty research:* Wind, geotechnical, chemical reactor engineering, applied electrostatics, biochemical engineering.

Chemical Engineering

American University of Sharjah, Graduate Programs, Sharjah, United Arab Emirates. Offers business (EMBA, GEMPA, MBA); chemical engineering (MS Ch E); civil engineering (MSCE); computer engineering (MS); electrical engineering (MSEE); mechanical engineering (MSME); mechatronics engineering (MS); public administration (MPA); teaching English to speakers of other languages (MA); translation and interpreting (MA); urban planning (MUP). Part-time and evening/weekend programs available. *Faculty:* 59 full-time (4 women), 5 part-time/adjunct (1 woman). *Students:* 101 full-time (44 women), 218 part-time (95 women). Average age 27. 184 applicants, 83% accepted, 92 enrolled. In 2009, 97 master's awarded. *Entrance requirements:* For master's, GMAT (MBA). Additional exam requirements/recommendations for international students: Required—TOEFL (minimum score 550 paper-based; 213 computer-based; 80 iBT), TWE (minimum score 5). *Application deadline:* For fall admission, 7/30 priority date for domestic students, 7/15 priority date for international students; for spring admission, 12/31 priority date for domestic students, 12/16 for international students. Applications are processed on a rolling basis. Application fee: $300. Electronic applications accepted. Tuition charges are reported in United Arab Emirates dirhams. *Expenses:* Tuition: Part-time 3250 United Arab Emirates dirhams per credit hour. *Financial support:* In 2009–10, 63 students received support, including 28 research assistantships with tuition reimbursements available, 35 teaching assistantships with tuition reimbursements available. *Faculty research:* Chemical engineering, civil engineering, computer engineering, electrical engineering, linguistics, translation. *Unit head:* Ghada S. Sami, Admissions Manager, 971-65151006 Ext. 1006, Fax: 971-65151020, E-mail:

graduateadmission@aus.edu. *Application contact:* Ghada S. Sami, Admissions Manager, 971-65151006 Ext. 1006, Fax: 971-65151020, E-mail: graduateadmission@aus.edu.

Arizona State University, Graduate College, Ira A. Fulton School of Engineering, Department of Chemical Engineering, Tempe, AZ 85287. Offers MS, MSE, PhD. *Degree requirements:* For doctorate, thesis/dissertation. *Entrance requirements:* For master's and doctorate, GRE General Test.

Auburn University, Graduate School, Ginn College of Engineering, Department of Chemical Engineering, Auburn University, AL 36849. Offers M Ch E, MS, PhD. Part-time programs available. *Faculty:* 17 full-time (3 women), 1 part-time/adjunct (0 women). *Students:* 47 full-time (17 women), 44 part-time (13 women); includes 8 minority (4 African Americans, 2 Asian Americans or Pacific Islanders, 2 Hispanic Americans), 52 international. Average age 27. 216 applicants, 19% accepted, 16 enrolled. In 2009, 6 master's, 7 doctorates awarded. *Degree requirements:* For master's, thesis (for some programs); for doctorate, comprehensive exam, thesis/dissertation. *Entrance requirements:* For master's and doctorate, GRE General Test. *Application deadline:* For fall admission, 7/7 for domestic students; for spring admission, 11/24 for domestic students. Applications are processed on a rolling basis. Application fee: $50 ($60 for international students). Electronic applications accepted. *Expenses:* Tuition, state resident: full-time $6240. Tuition, nonresident: full-time $18,720. International tuition: $18,938 full-time. Required fees: $492. Tuition and fees vary according to course load, program and reciprocity agreements. *Financial support:* Fellowships, research assistantships, teaching assistantships,

Federal Work-Study available. Support available to part-time students. Financial award application deadline: 3/15; financial award applicants required to submit FAFSA. *Faculty research:* Coal liquefaction, asphalt research, pulp and paper engineering, surface science, biochemical engineering. *Unit head:* Dr. Christopher Roberts, Chair, 334-844-4827. *Application contact:* Dr. George Flowers, Dean of the Graduate School, 334-844-2125.

Brigham Young University, Graduate Studies, Ira A. Fulton College of Engineering and Technology, Department of Chemical Engineering, Provo, UT 84602. Offers MS, PhD. *Faculty:* 13 full-time (0 women), 8 part-time/adjunct (0 women). *Students:* 39 full-time (8 women), 1 part-time (0 women); includes 12 minority (all Asian Americans or Pacific Islanders). Average age 25. 11 applicants, 55% accepted, 4 enrolled. In 2009, 2 master's, 5 doctorates awarded. *Degree requirements:* For master's, comprehensive exam, thesis; for doctorate, comprehensive exam, thesis/dissertation. *Entrance requirements:* For master's, GRE, minimum GPA of 3.0 in upper-division course work in major; for doctorate, GRE, minimum GPA of 3.3. Additional exam requirements/recommendations for international students: Required—TOEFL (minimum score 580 paper-based; 85 iBT), IELTS (minimum score 7). *Application deadline:* For fall admission, 2/15 for domestic and international students; for winter admission, 6/15 for domestic and international students; for spring admission, 10/15 for domestic and international students. Application fee: $50. Electronic applications accepted. *Expenses:* Tuition: Full-time $5580; part-time $301 per credit hour. Tuition and fees vary according to student's religious affiliation. *Financial support:* In 2009–10, 40 students received support, including 1 fellowship (averaging $22,000 per year), 34 research assistantships with full and partial tuition reimbursements available (averaging $22,000 per year), 9 teaching assistantships with full and partial tuition reimbursements available (averaging $21,000 per year); career-related internships or fieldwork and tuition scholarships for students receiving teaching or research assistantships also available. Financial award application deadline: 6/30; financial award applicants required to submit FAFSA. *Faculty research:* Biomedical engineering, oil reservoir simulation, electrochemical engineering, energy and combustion, molecular modeling, thermodynamics. Total annual research expenditures: $2.2 million. *Unit head:* Dr. Richard L. Rowley, Chair, 801-422-2586, Fax: 801-422-0151, E-mail: cheme@byu.edu. *Application contact:* Dr. Dean R. Wheeler, Graduate Coordinator, 801-422-2588, Fax: 801-422-0151, E-mail: dean_wheeler@byu.edu.

Brown University, Graduate School, Division of Engineering, Program in Fluid, Thermal and Chemical Processes, Providence, RI 02912. Offers Sc M, PhD. *Degree requirements:* For doctorate, thesis/dissertation, preliminary exam.

Bucknell University, Graduate Studies, College of Engineering, Department of Chemical Engineering, Lewisburg, PA 17837. Offers MS, MS Ch E. Part-time programs available. *Degree requirements:* For master's, thesis. *Entrance requirements:* For master's, GRE General Test, GRE Subject Test, minimum GPA of 2.8. Additional exam requirements/recommendations for international students: Required—TOEFL. *Faculty research:* Computer-aided design, software engineering, applied mathematics and modeling, polymer science, digital process control.

California Institute of Technology, Division of Chemistry and Chemical Engineering, Program in Chemical Engineering, Pasadena, CA 91125-0001. Offers MS, PhD. Part-time and evening/weekend programs available. Postbaccalaureate distance learning degree programs offered (minimal on-campus study). Terminal master's awarded for partial completion of doctoral program. *Degree requirements:* For master's, thesis; for doctorate, thesis/dissertation. *Entrance requirements:* Additional exam requirements/recommendations for international students: Required—TOEFL; Recommended—IELTS, TWE. Electronic applications accepted.

California State University, Long Beach, Graduate Studies, College of Engineering, Department of Chemical Engineering, Long Beach, CA 90840. Offers MS. *Faculty:* 2 full-time (0 women). *Students:* 33 full-time (12 women), 48 part-time (13 women); includes 42 minority (5 African Americans, 29 Asian Americans or Pacific Islanders, 8 Hispanic Americans), 11 international. Average age 33. *Expenses:* Required fees: $1802 per semester. Part-time tuition and fees vary according to course load. *Unit head:* Dr. Larry Jang, Chair/Graduate Advisor, 562-985-7533, E-mail: jang@csulb.edu. *Application contact:* Dr. Sandra Cynar, Associate Dean for Instruction, 562-985-1512, Fax: 562-985-7561, E-mail: cynar@csulb.edu.

Carnegie Mellon University, Carnegie Institute of Technology, Department of Chemical Engineering, Pittsburgh, PA 15213-3891. Offers chemical engineering (M Ch E, MS, PhD); colloids, polymers and surfaces (MS). Part-time and evening/weekend programs available. Terminal master's awarded for partial completion of doctoral program. *Degree requirements:* For doctorate, thesis/dissertation, qualifying exam. *Entrance requirements:* For master's and doctorate, GRE General Test, GRE Subject Test. Additional exam requirements/recommendations for international students: Required—TOEFL. *Faculty research:* Computer-aided design in process engineering, biomedical engineering, biotechnology, complex fluids.

Case Western Reserve University, School of Graduate Studies, The Case School of Engineering, Department of Chemical Engineering, Cleveland, OH 44106. Offers MS, PhD. Part-time and evening/weekend programs available. Postbaccalaureate distance learning degree programs offered. *Faculty:* 11 full-time (1 woman). *Students:* 35 full-time (9 women); includes 4 minority (all Asian Americans or Pacific Islanders), 18 international. In 2009, 3 master's, 6 doctorates awarded. Terminal master's awarded for partial completion of doctoral program. *Degree requirements:* For master's, thesis (for some programs); for doctorate, thesis/dissertation, qualifying exam, research proposal, teaching experience. *Entrance requirements:* For master's and doctorate, GRE General Test. Additional exam requirements/recommendations for international students: Required—TOEFL. *Application deadline:* For fall admission, 2/15 priority date for domestic students; for spring admission, 11/1 for domestic students. Applications are processed on a rolling basis. Application fee: $50. *Financial support:* Fellowships with full and partial tuition reimbursements, research assistantships with full and partial tuition reimbursements, teaching assistantships, Federal Work-Study and institutionally sponsored loans available. Financial award application deadline: 3/1; financial award applicants required to submit FAFSA. *Faculty research:* Biotransport and bioprocessing, electrochemical engineering, materials engineering, energy storage and fuel cells. Total annual research expenditures: $4 million. *Unit head:* Uziel Landau, Department Chair, 216-368-4132, Fax: 216-368-3016. *Application contact:* Kathleen Bates, Academic Administrator Manager, 216-368-3840, Fax: 216-368-3209, E-mail: kmb4@case.edu.

City College of the City University of New York, Graduate School, Grove School of Engineering, Department of Chemical Engineering, New York, NY 10031-9198. Offers ME, MS, PhD. Part-time programs available. *Degree requirements:* For master's, thesis optional; for doctorate, one foreign language, comprehensive exam, thesis/dissertation. *Entrance requirements:* For master's and doctorate, GRE General Test. Additional exam requirements/recommendations for international students: Required—TOEFL (minimum score 500 paper-based; 173 computer-based; 61 iBT). *Faculty research:* Theoretical turbulences, bio-fluid dynamics, polymers, fluidization, transport phenomena.

Clarkson University, Graduate School, Wallace H. Coulter School of Engineering, Department of Chemical and Biomolecular Engineering, Potsdam, NY 13699. Offers chemical engineering (ME, MS, PhD). Part-time programs available. *Faculty:* 18 full-time (5 women), 2 part-time/adjunct (1 woman). *Students:* 26 full-time (5 women), 23 international. Average age 27. 57 applicants, 39% accepted, 3 enrolled. In 2009, 6 master's, 5 doctorates awarded. Terminal master's awarded for partial completion of doctoral program. *Degree requirements:* For master's, thesis; for doctorate, comprehensive exam, thesis/dissertation. *Entrance requirements:* For master's, GRE, resume, 3 letters of recommendation; for doctorate, GRE, transcripts of all college coursework, resume, personal statement, three letters of recommendation. Additional exam requirements/recommendations for international students: Required—TOEFL (minimum score 550 paper-based; 213 computer-based; 80 iBT), IELTS (minimum score 6.5). *Application deadline:* For fall admission, 1/30 priority date for domestic and international students; for spring admission, 9/1 priority date for domestic and international students. Applications are processed on a rolling basis. Application fee: $25 ($35 for international students). Electronic applications accepted. *Expenses:* Tuition: Part-time $1074 per credit hour. *Financial support:* In 2009–10, 24 students received support, including 1 fellowship (averaging $30,000 per year), 15 research assistantships (averaging $20,190 per year), 9 teaching assistantships (averaging $20,190 per year); scholarships/grants, tuition waivers (partial), and unspecified assistantships also available. *Faculty research:* Fuel cells, polymer colloids, coating of particles, multivariate statistical methods for data analysis, electronic manufacturing. Total annual research expenditures: $1.9 million. *Unit head:* Dr. Ruth E. Baltus, Department Chair, 315-268-2368, Fax: 315-268-6654, E-mail: baltus@clarkson.edu. *Application contact:* Kelly Sharlow, Assistant to the Dean, 315-268-7929, Fax: 315-268-4494, E-mail: ksharlow@clarkson.edu.

Clemson University, Graduate School, College of Engineering and Science, Department of Chemical and Biomolecular Engineering, Clemson, SC 29634. Offers MS, PhD. *Faculty:* 9 full-time (0 women). *Students:* 30 full-time (11 women), 2 part-time (0 women); includes 2 minority (1 African American, 1 Asian American or Pacific Islander), 23 international. Average age 26. 61 applicants, 11% accepted, 4 enrolled. In 2009, 1 master's, 4 doctorates awarded. *Degree requirements:* For master's, thesis; for doctorate, thesis/dissertation. *Entrance requirements:* For master's and doctorate, GRE General Test. Additional exam requirements/recommendations for international students: Required—TOEFL. *Application deadline:* For fall admission, 6/1 for domestic students, 4/15 for international students; for spring admission, 9/15 for international students. Applications are processed on a rolling basis. Application fee: $70 ($80 for international students). Electronic applications accepted. *Expenses:* Tuition, state resident: full-time $8684; part-time $528 per credit hour. Tuition, nonresident: full-time $15,330; part-time $1078 per credit hour. Required fees: $736; $37 per semester. Part-time tuition and fees vary according to course load and program. *Financial support:* In 2009–10, 30 students received support, including 24 research assistantships with partial tuition reimbursements available (averaging $26,191 per year), 6 teaching assistantships with partial tuition reimbursements available (averaging $25,667 per year); fellowships with full and partial tuition reimbursements available, career-related internships or fieldwork, institutionally sponsored loans, scholarships/grants, health care benefits, and unspecified assistantships also available. Support available to part-time students. Financial award applicants required to submit FAFSA. *Faculty research:* Polymer processing, catalysis, process automation, thermodynamics, separation processes. Total annual research expenditures: $2 million. *Unit head:* Dr. Douglas E. Hirt, Chair, 864-656-0822, Fax: 864-656-0784, E-mail: hirtd@clemson.edu. *Application contact:* Dr. Scott M. Husson, Coordinator, 864-656-4502, Fax: 864-656-0784, E-mail: shusson@clemson.edu.

Cleveland State University, College of Graduate Studies, Fenn College of Engineering, Department of Chemical and Biomedical Engineering, Cleveland, OH 44115. Offers applied biomedical engineering (D Eng); chemical engineering (MS, D Eng). Part-time and evening/weekend programs available. *Degree requirements:* For master's, project or thesis; for doctorate, thesis/dissertation, candidacy and qualifying exams. *Entrance requirements:* For master's, GRE General Test, minimum GPA of 2.75; for doctorate, GRE General Test, minimum GPA of 3.25. Additional exam requirements/recommendations for international students: Required—TOEFL (minimum score 550 paper-based; 213 computer-based; 78 iBT). *Faculty research:* Absorption equilibrium and dynamics, advanced materials processing, biomaterials surface characterization, bioprocessing, cardiovascular mechanics, magnetic resonance imaging, mechanics of biomolecules, metabolic modeling, molecular simulation, process systems engineering, statistical mechanics.

Colorado School of Mines, Graduate School, Department of Chemical Engineering, Golden, CO 80401. Offers MS, PhD. Part-time programs available. *Faculty:* 41 full-time (9 women), 7 part-time/adjunct (1 woman). *Students:* 53 full-time (10 women), 3 part-time (1 woman); includes 3 minority (all Asian Americans or Pacific Islanders), 19 international. Average age 31. 115 applicants, 41% accepted, 27 enrolled. In 2009, 8 master's, 7 doctorates awarded. *Degree requirements:* For master's, thesis (for some programs); for doctorate, comprehensive exam, thesis/dissertation. *Entrance requirements:* For master's and doctorate, GRE General Test. Additional exam requirements/recommendations for international students: Required—TOEFL (minimum score 550 paper-based; 213 computer-based; 80 iBT). *Application deadline:* For fall admission, 1/15 for domestic and international students; for spring admission, 9/1 for domestic and international students. Application fee: $50 ($70 for international students). Electronic applications accepted. *Expenses:* Tuition, state resident: full-time $10,584; part-time $588 per credit hour. Tuition, nonresident: full-time $24,750; part-time $1375 per credit hour. Required fees: $1654; $827.10 per semester. *Financial support:* In 2009–10, 44 students received support, including fellowships with full tuition reimbursements available (averaging $20,000 per year), 41 research assistantships with full tuition reimbursements available (averaging $20,000 per year), 3 teaching assistantships with full tuition reimbursements available (averaging $20,000 per year); scholarships/grants, health care benefits, and unspecified assistantships also available. Financial award application deadline: 1/15; financial award applicants required to submit FAFSA. *Faculty research:* Liquid fuels for the future, responsible management of hazardous substances, surface and interfacial engineering, advanced computational methods and process control, gas hydrates. Total annual research expenditures: $4.5 million. *Unit head:* Dr. James F. Ely, Department Head, 303-273-3885, E-mail: jely@mines.edu. *Application contact:* Dr. Sumit Agarwal, Professor, 303-273-3508, Fax: 303-273-3730, E-mail: sagarwal@mines.edu.

Colorado State University, Graduate School, College of Engineering, Department of Chemical and Biological Engineering, Fort Collins, CO 80523-1370. Offers chemical engineering (MS, PhD); engineering (ME). Part-time programs available. *Faculty:* 12 full-time (1 woman). *Students:* 13 full-time (1 woman), 12 part-time (1 woman); includes 3 minority (1 American Indian/Alaska Native, 1 Asian American or Pacific Islander, 1 Hispanic American), 11 international. Average age 28. 62 applicants, 11% accepted, 6 enrolled. In 2009, 4 master's, 1 doctorate awarded. Terminal master's awarded for partial completion of doctoral program. *Degree requirements:* For master's, comprehensive exam (for some programs), thesis (for some programs), preliminary exam (first year); for doctorate, comprehensive exam, thesis/dissertation, exams. *Entrance requirements:* For master's and doctorate, GRE General Test, minimum GPA of 3.0. Additional exam requirements/recommendations for international students: Required—TOEFL (minimum score 550 paper-based; 213 computer-based; 80 iBT). *Application deadline:* For fall admission, 1/15 priority date for domestic and international students; for spring admission, 9/15 priority date for domestic and international students. Applications are processed on a rolling basis. Application fee: $50. Electronic applications accepted. *Expenses:* Tuition, state resident: full-time $6434; part-time $359.10 per credit. Tuition, nonresident: full-time $18,116; part-time $1006.45 per credit. Required fees: $1496; $83 per credit. *Financial support:* In 2009–10, 13 students received support, including 6 fellowships (averaging $28,340 per year), 7 research assistantships with full tuition reimbursements available (averaging $18,185 per year); teaching assistantships with full tuition reimbursements available, scholarships/grants and unspecified assistantships also available. Financial award application deadline: 1/15; financial award applicants required to submit FAFSA. *Faculty research:* Biochemical and biomedical engineering, nanostructured materials, polymer science, transport phenomena, mathematical modeling. Total annual research expenditures: $2 million. *Unit head:* Dr. David S. Dandy, Department Head, 970-491-7437, Fax: 970-491-7369, E-mail: david.dandy@colostate.edu. *Application contact:* Dr. S. Ranil Wickramasinghe, Associate Professor, 970-491-5276, Fax: 970-491-7369, E-mail: ranil.wickramasinghe@colostate.edu.

Columbia University, Fu Foundation School of Engineering and Applied Science, Department of Chemical Engineering, New York, NY 10027. Offers MS, Eng Sc D, PhD. PhD offered through the Graduate School of Arts and Sciences. Part-time programs available. Postbaccalaureate distance learning degree programs offered (no on-campus study). *Faculty:* 8 full-time (0 women), 2 part-time/adjunct (1 woman). *Students:* 50 full-time (16 women), 13 part-time (7 women); includes 8 minority (1 African American, 6 Asian Americans or Pacific Islanders, 1 Hispanic American), 30 international. Average age 26. 112 applicants, 44% accepted, 21 enrolled. In 2009, 17 master's, 6 doctorates awarded. *Degree requirements:* For doctorate, thesis/dissertation, qualifying exam. *Entrance requirements:* For master's and doctorate, GRE General Test. Additional exam requirements/recommendations for international students: Required—TOEFL. *Application deadline:* For fall admission, 12/1 priority

Chemical Engineering

Columbia University (continued)

date for domestic and international students; for spring admission, 10/1 priority date for domestic and international students. Application fee: $70. Electronic applications accepted. *Financial support:* In 2009–10, 39 students received support, including 2 fellowships with full tuition reimbursements available (averaging $30,000 per year), 26 research assistantships with full tuition reimbursements available (averaging $28,000 per year), 11 teaching assistantships with full tuition reimbursements available (averaging $22,000 per year); career-related internships or fieldwork, health care benefits, and unspecified assistantships also available. Financial award application deadline: 12/1; financial award applicants required to submit FAFSA. *Faculty research:* Polymer physics and science, genomics, colloids, protein, metabolic and biomedical engineering, electrochemical engineering. *Unit head:* Dr. Alan C. West, Samuel Ruben-Peter G. Viele Professor of Electrochemistry; Department Chair, 212-854-4452, Fax: 212-854-3054, E-mail: acw17@columbia.edu. *Application contact:* Teresa Colaizzo, Departmental Administrator, 212-854-4415, Fax: 212-854-3054; E-mail: tc16@columbia.edu.

Cooper Union for the Advancement of Science and Art, Albert Nerken School of Engineering, New York, NY 10003-7120. Offers chemical engineering (ME); civil engineering (ME); electrical engineering (ME); mechanical engineering (ME). Part-time programs available. *Faculty:* 27 full-time (1 woman), 15 part-time/adjunct (2 women). *Students:* 66 full-time (8 women), 20 part-time (1 woman); includes 30 minority (2 African Americans, 1 American Indian/Alaska Native, 19 Asian Americans or Pacific Islanders, 8 Hispanic Americans), 10 international. Average age 24. 80 applicants, 90% accepted, 56 enrolled. In 2009, 18 master's awarded. *Degree requirements:* For master's, thesis. *Entrance requirements:* For master's, GRE, BE, minimum GPA of 3.5. Additional exam requirements/recommendations for international students: Required—TOEFL (minimum score 600 paper-based; 250 computer-based; 100 iBT). *Application deadline:* For fall admission, 5/1 for domestic and international students. Applications are processed on a rolling basis. Application fee: $65. *Expenses:* Tuition: Full-time $35,000. Required fees: $1650. *Financial support:* Fellowships with tuition reimbursements, career-related internships or fieldwork, Federal Work-Study, tuition waivers (full), and all admitted students receive full-tuition scholarships available. Support available to part-time students. Financial award application deadline: 5/1; financial award applicants required to submit CSS PROFILE or FAFSA. *Faculty research:* Civil infrastructure, imaging and sensing technology, biomedical engineering, encryption technology, process engineering. *Unit head:* Dr. Simon Ben-Avi, Dean, 212-353-4285, E-mail: benavi@cooper.edu. *Application contact:* Student Contact, 212-353-4120, E-mail: admissions@cooper.edu.

Cornell University, Graduate School, Graduate Fields of Engineering, Field of Chemical Engineering, Ithaca, NY 14853-0001. Offers advanced materials processing (M Eng, MS, PhD); applied mathematics and computational methods (M Eng, MS, PhD); biochemical engineering (M Eng, MS, PhD); chemical reaction engineering (M Eng, MS, PhD); classical and statistical thermodynamics (M Eng, MS, PhD); fluid dynamics, rheology and biorheology (M Eng, MS, PhD); heat and mass transfer (M Eng, MS, PhD); kinetics and catalysis (M Eng, MS, PhD); polymers (M Eng, MS, PhD); surface science (M Eng, MS, PhD). *Faculty:* 29 full-time (2 women). *Students:* 95 full-time (30 women); includes 9 minority (1 African American, 5 Asian Americans or Pacific Islanders, 3 Hispanic Americans), 41 international. Average age 25. 317 applicants, 38% accepted, 46 enrolled. In 2009, 22 master's, 17 doctorates awarded. *Degree requirements:* For master's, thesis (MS); for doctorate, comprehensive exam, thesis/dissertation. *Entrance requirements:* For master's and doctorate, GRE General Test, 2 letters of recommendation. Additional exam requirements/recommendations for international students: Required—TOEFL (minimum score 600 paper-based; 237 computer-based; 77 iBT). *Application deadline:* For fall admission, 1/15 priority date for domestic students. Application fee: $70. Electronic applications.accepted. *Expenses:* Tuition: Full-time $29,500. Required fees: $70. Full-time tuition and fees vary according to degree level, program and student level. *Financial support:* In 2009–10, 67 students received support, including 3 fellowships with full tuition reimbursements available, 3 research assistantships with full tuition reimbursements available; teaching assistantships with full tuition reimbursements available, institutionally sponsored loans, scholarships/grants, health care benefits, tuition waivers (full and partial), and unspecified assistantships also available. Financial award applicants required to submit FAFSA. *Faculty research:* Biochemical, biomedical and metabolic engineering; fluid and polymer dynamics; surface science and chemical kinetics; electronics materials; microchemical systems and nanotechnology. *Unit head:* Director of Graduate Studies, 607-255-4550. *Application contact:* Graduate Field Assistant, 607-255-4550, E-mail: dgs@cheme.cornell.edu.

Dalhousie University, Faculty of Engineering, Department of Chemical Engineering, Halifax, NS B3J 1Z1, Canada. Offers M Eng, MA Sc, PhD. *Faculty:* 6 full-time (0 women), 2 part-time/adjunct (0 women). *Students:* 20 full-time (4 women). 31 applicants, 61% accepted. In 2009, 1 master's awarded. *Degree requirements:* For master's, thesis; for doctorate, thesis/dissertation. *Entrance requirements:* Additional exam requirements/recommendations for international students: Required—TOEFL, IELTS, CANTEST, CAEL, or Michigan English Language Assessment Battery. *Application deadline:* For fall admission, 6/1 for domestic students, 4/1 for international students; for winter admission, 11/15 for domestic students, 8/31 for international students; for spring admission, 2/28 for domestic students, 12/31 for international students. Applications are processed on a rolling basis. Application fee: $60. Electronic applications accepted. *Financial support:* Fellowships, research assistantships, teaching assistantships available. *Faculty research:* Explosions, process optimization, combustion synthesis of materials, waste minimization, treatment of industrial wastewater. *Unit head:* Dr. Michael Pegg, Head, 902-494-3252, Fax: 902-420-0219, E-mail: michael.pegg@dal.ca. *Application contact:* Dr. Georges Kipouros, Graduate Coordinator, 902-494-6100, Fax: 902-494-0219, E-mail: peas.grad@dal.ca.

Drexel University, College of Engineering, Department of Chemical and Biological Engineering, Program in Chemical Engineering, Philadelphia, PA 19104-2875. Offers MS, PhD. *Degree requirements:* For doctorate, thesis/dissertation. *Entrance requirements:* For master's, minimum GPA of 3.0; for doctorate, minimum GPA of 3.5, MS in chemical engineering. Additional exam requirements/recommendations for international students: Required—TOEFL. Electronic applications accepted.

École Polytechnique de Montréal, Graduate Programs, Department of Chemical Engineering, Montréal, QC H3C 3A7, Canada. Offers M Eng, M Sc A, PhD, DESS. Part-time and evening/weekend programs available. Terminal master's awarded for partial completion of doctoral program. *Degree requirements:* For master's, one foreign language, thesis; for doctorate, one foreign language, thesis/dissertation. *Entrance requirements:* For master's, minimum GPA of 2.75; for doctorate, minimum GPA of 3.0. Electronic applications accepted. *Faculty research:* Polymer engineering, biochemical and food engineering, reactor engineering and industrial processes pollution control engineering, gas technology.

Fairleigh Dickinson University, College at Florham, Silberman College of Business, Program in Pharmaceutical Studies, Madison, NJ 07940-1099. Offers MBA, Certificate. *Students:* 11 full-time (4 women), 26 part-time (13 women), 7 international. Average age 33. 30 applicants, 57% accepted, 4 enrolled. In 2009, 15 master's awarded. *Application deadline:* Applications are processed on a rolling basis. Application fee: $40.

Florida Agricultural and Mechanical University, Division of Graduate Studies, Research, and Continuing Education, FAMU-FSU College of Engineering, Department of Chemical Engineering, Tallahassee, FL 32310-6046. Offers MS, PhD. *Students:* 1 (woman) full-time, 2 part-time (1 woman); all minorities (all African Americans). *Degree requirements:* For master's, thesis (for some programs); for doctorate, thesis/dissertation, presentation of research topic at professional meeting. *Entrance requirements:* For master's, GRE General Test, minimum GPA of 3.0; for doctorate, GRE General Test, minimum GPA of 3.3. Additional exam requirements/recommendations for international students: Required—TOEFL (minimum score 550 paper-based; 213 computer-based). *Application deadline:* For fall admission, 7/1 for domestic students, 5/1 for international students. Application fee: $30. *Expenses:* Contact institution. *Financial support:* Research assistantships, teaching assistantships, tuition waivers (full) available.

Faculty research: Macromolecular transport, polymer processing, biochemical engineering, process control, environmental engineering. *Unit head:* Dr. Michael H. Peters, Program Director, 850-410-6151. *Application contact:* Dr. Bruce R. Locke, Graduate Coordinator, 850-599-3000.

Florida Institute of Technology, Graduate Programs, College of Engineering, Chemical Engineering Department, Melbourne, FL 32901-6975. Offers MS, PhD. Part-time programs available. *Faculty:* 5 full-time (1 woman). *Students:* 16 full-time (8 women), 5 part-time (1 woman); includes 1 minority (African American), 13 international. Average age 25. 49 applicants, 53% accepted, 4 enrolled. In 2009, 1 master's awarded. Terminal master's awarded for partial completion of doctoral program. *Degree requirements:* For master's, thesis, seminar, independent research project; for doctorate, comprehensive exam, thesis/dissertation, oral exam, original research project, written exam. *Entrance requirements:* For master's, minimum GPA of 3.0; for doctorate, GRE General Test, GRE Subject Test, minimum GPA of 3.5, resume, 3 letters of recommendation, statement of objectives. Additional exam requirements/recommendations for international students: Required—TOEFL (minimum score 550 paper-based; 213 computer-based; 79 iBT). *Application deadline:* For fall admission, 4/1 for international students; for spring admission, 9/30 for international students. Applications are processed on a rolling basis. Application fee: $50. Electronic applications accepted. *Expenses:* Tuition: Part-time $1015 per credit. Tuition and fees vary according to campus/location and program. *Financial support:* In 2009–10, 4 students received support, including 2 research assistantships with full and partial tuition reimbursements available (averaging $7,500 per year), 2 teaching assistantships with full and partial tuition reimbursements available (averaging $11,600 per year); career-related internships or fieldwork, institutionally sponsored loans, tuition waivers (partial), unspecified assistantships, and tuition remissions also available. Support available to part-time students. Financial award application deadline: 3/1; financial award applicants required to submit FAFSA. *Faculty research:* Space technology, biotechnology, materials synthesis and processing, super-critical fluids, water treatment, process control. Total annual research expenditures: $175,467. *Unit head:* Dr. Paul A. Jennings, Department Head, 321-674-7561, Fax: 321-674-7565, E-mail: jennings@fit.edu. *Application contact:* Thomas M. Shea, Director of Graduate Admissions, 321-674-7577, Fax: 321-723-9468, E-mail: tshea@fit.edu.

Florida State University, The Graduate School, FAMU-FSU College of Engineering, Department of Chemical and Biomedical Engineering, Tallahassee, FL 32310-6046. Offers biomedical engineering (MS, PhD); chemical engineering (MS, PhD). Part-time programs available. *Faculty:* 13 full-time (1 woman). *Students:* 29 full-time (15 women); includes 20 minority (4 African Americans, 15 Asian Americans or Pacific Islanders, 1 Hispanic American). Average age 25. 69 applicants, 14% accepted, 9 enrolled. In 2009, 2 master's awarded. *Degree requirements:* For master's, thesis (for some programs); for doctorate, comprehensive exam, thesis/dissertation, preliminary exam, qualifying exam. *Entrance requirements:* For master's, GRE General Test (minimum score 1200), BS in chemical engineering, minimum GPA of 3.0; for doctorate, GRE General Test (minimum score: 1200), BS in chemical engineering, minimum GPA of 3.0, or MS in chemical engineering or biomedical engineering. Additional exam requirements/recommendations for international students: Required—TOEFL (minimum score 550 paper-based; 213 computer-based). *Application deadline:* For fall admission, 7/1 priority date for domestic students, 7/1 for international students; for spring admission, 11/1 for domestic and international students. Applications are processed on a rolling basis. Application fee: $30. *Expenses:* Contact institution. *Financial support:* In 2009–10, 21 students received support, including 4 fellowships with full tuition reimbursements available (averaging $18,500 per year), 12 research assistantships with full tuition reimbursements available (averaging $18,500 per year), 10 teaching assistantships with full tuition reimbursements available (averaging $18,500 per year); scholarships/grants also available. Financial award application deadline: 3/1. *Faculty research:* Macromolecular transport, polymer processing, biochemical engineering, environmental engineering, transport and reaction, NMR-MRI, fuel cells. Total annual research expenditures: $734,000. *Unit head:* Dr. Bruce R. Locke, Chair and Professor, 850-410-6149, Fax: 850-410-6150, E-mail: locke@eng.fsu.edu. *Application contact:* Becky Culp, Office Administrator, 850-410-6151, Fax: 850-410-6150, E-mail: bculp@eng.fsu.edu.

Georgia Institute of Technology, Graduate Studies and Research, College of Engineering, School of Chemical and Biomolecular Engineering, Atlanta, GA 30332-0001. Offers bioengineering (MS Bio E, PhD); chemical engineering (MS Ch E, PhD); paper science and engineering (MS, PhD); polymers (MS Poly). *Degree requirements:* For master's, thesis; for doctorate, comprehensive exam, thesis/dissertation. *Entrance requirements:* For master's and doctorate, GRE, minimum GPA of 3.0. Additional exam requirements/recommendations for international students: Required—TOEFL (minimum score 550 paper-based; 213 computer-based). Electronic applications accepted. *Faculty research:* Biochemical engineering; process modeling, synthesis, and control; polymer science and engineering; thermodynamics and separations; surface and particle science.

Graduate School and University Center of the City University of New York, Graduate Studies, Program in Engineering, New York, NY 10016-4039. Offers biomedical engineering (PhD); chemical engineering (PhD); civil engineering (PhD); electrical engineering (PhD); mechanical engineering (PhD). *Faculty:* 68 full-time (1 woman). *Students:* 115 full-time (33 women), 8 part-time (2 women); includes 17 minority (5 African Americans, 8 Asian Americans or Pacific Islanders, 4 Hispanic Americans), 68 international. Average age 34. 119 applicants, 48% accepted, 26 enrolled. In 2009, 30 doctorates awarded. *Degree requirements:* For doctorate, thesis/dissertation. *Entrance requirements:* For doctorate, GRE General Test. Additional exam requirements/recommendations for international students: Required—TOEFL. Application fee: $125. Electronic applications accepted. *Financial support:* In 2009–10, 61 fellowships, 10 teaching assistantships were awarded; research assistantships, Federal Work-Study, institutionally sponsored loans, and tuition waivers (full and partial) also available. Financial award application deadline: 2/1; financial award applicants required to submit FAFSA. *Unit head:* Dr. Mumtaz Kassir, Executive Officer, 212-650-8031, Fax: 212-650-8029, E-mail: kassir@ce-mail.engr.ccny.cuny.edu. *Application contact:* Les Gribben, Director of Admissions, 212-817-7470, Fax: 212-817-1624, E-mail: lgribben@gc.cuny.edu.

See Close-Up on page 69.

Howard University, College of Engineering, Architecture, and Computer Sciences, School of Engineering and Computer Science, Department of Chemical Engineering, Washington, DC 20059-0002. Offers MS. Offered through the Graduate School of Arts and Sciences. Part-time programs available. *Degree requirements:* For master's, thesis. *Entrance requirements:* For master's, GRE General Test, minimum GPA of 2.75. Additional exam requirements/recommendations for international students: Required—TOEFL. *Faculty research:* Bioengineering, reactor modeling, environmental engineering, nanotechnology, fuel cells.

Illinois Institute of Technology, Graduate College, Armour College of Engineering, Department of Chemical and Biological Engineering, Chicago, IL 60616-3793. Offers biological engineering (MBE); chemical engineering (M Ch E, MS, PhD); food process engineering (MFPE); food processing engineering (MS); gas engineering (MGE); manufacturing engineering (MME, MS); MS/M Ch E. Part-time and evening/weekend programs available. Postbaccalaureate distance learning degree programs offered. Terminal master's awarded for partial completion of doctoral program. *Degree requirements:* For master's, comprehensive exam, thesis (for some programs); for doctorate, comprehensive exam, thesis/dissertation. *Entrance requirements:* For master's and doctorate, GRE General Test, minimum undergraduate GPA of 3.0. Additional exam requirements/recommendations for international students: Required—TOEFL (minimum score 550 paper-based; 213 computer-based; 80 iBT). Electronic applications accepted. *Expenses:* Tuition: Full-time $17,550; part-time $888 per credit hour. Required fees: $850; $7.50 per credit hour. One-time fee: $50 full-time. Full-time tuition and fees vary according to program. *Faculty research:* Biochemical, bioenergy, biosensors, tissue engineering, fuel cells, batteries, renewable energy, gas cleaning, particle technology, fluidization, colloid and interfacial engineering complex fluids, polymers, complex systems and dynamics.

Instituto Tecnológico y de Estudios Superiores de Monterrey, Campus Monterrey, Graduate and Research Division, Programs in Engineering, Monterrey, Mexico. Offers applied statistics (M Eng); artificial intelligence (PhD); automation engineering (M Eng); chemical engineering (M Eng); civil engineering (M Eng); electrical engineering (M Eng); electronic engineering (M Eng); environmental engineering (M Eng); industrial engineering (M Eng, PhD); manufacturing engineering (M Eng); mechanical engineering (M Eng); systems and quality engineering (M Eng). Part-time and evening/weekend programs available. Terminal master's awarded for partial completion of doctoral program. *Degree requirements:* For master's, one foreign language, thesis; for doctorate, one foreign language, thesis/dissertation. *Entrance requirements:* For master's, EXADEP; for doctorate, GRE, master's degree in related field. Additional exam requirements/recommendations for international students: Required—TOEFL. *Faculty research:* Flexible manufacturing cells, materials, statistical methods, environmental prevention, control and evaluation.

Iowa State University of Science and Technology, Graduate College, College of Engineering, Department of Chemical and Biological Engineering, Ames, IA 50011. Offers M Eng, MS, PhD. *Faculty:* 19 full-time (5 women). *Students:* 54 full-time (17 women), 1 part-time (0 women); includes 5 minority (2 Asian Americans or Pacific Islanders, 3 Hispanic Americans), 28 international. 136 applicants, 17% accepted, 10 enrolled. In 2009, 6 master's, 11 doctorates awarded. *Degree requirements:* For master's, thesis (for some programs); for doctorate, thesis/dissertation. *Entrance requirements:* For master's and doctorate, GRE General Test. Additional exam requirements/recommendations for international students: Required—TOEFL (minimum score 587 paper-based; 94 iBT) or IELTS (minimum score 7). *Application deadline:* For fall admission, 1/15 priority date for domestic and international students; for spring admission, 10/1 for domestic and international students. Application fee: $40 ($90 for international students). Electronic applications accepted. *Expenses:* Tuition, state resident: full-time $6716. Tuition, nonresident: full-time $8908. Tuition and fees vary according to course level, course load, program and student level. *Financial support:* In 2009–10, 45 research assistantships with full and partial tuition reimbursements (averaging $19,410 per year), 8 teaching assistantships with full and partial tuition reimbursements (averaging $19,410 per year) were awarded; scholarships/grants, health care benefits, and unspecified assistantships also available. *Unit head:* Dr. Surya Mallaragada, Chair, 515-294-8472, Fax: 515-294-2689, E-mail: suryakm@iastate.edu. *Application contact:* Dr. Monica Lamm, Director of Graduate Education, 515-294-7643, E-mail: chemengr@iastate.edu.

The Johns Hopkins University, Engineering for Professionals, Part-time Program in Chemical and Biomolecular Engineering, Baltimore, MD 21218-2699. Offers M Ch E. Part-time and evening/weekend programs available. *Faculty:* 2 part-time/adjunct (both women). *Students:* 2 full-time (both women), 8 part-time (1 woman); includes 2 minority (1 African American, 1 Asian American or Pacific Islander), 1 international. Average age 31. *Application deadline:* Applications are processed on a rolling basis. Application fee: $75. Electronic applications accepted. *Financial support:* Institutionally sponsored loans available. *Unit head:* Dr. Dilip Asthagiri, Program Chair, 410-516-3475, E-mail: dilipa@jhu.edu. *Application contact:* Priyanka Dwivedi, Admissions Manager, 410-516-2300, Fax: 410-579-8049, E-mail: pdwived1@jhu.edu.

The Johns Hopkins University, G. W. C. Whiting School of Engineering, Department of Chemical and Biomolecular Engineering, Baltimore, MD 21218. Offers MSE, PhD. Part-time programs available. *Faculty:* 21 full-time (6 women), 3 part-time/adjunct (0 women). *Students:* 82 full-time (31 women); includes 15 minority (3 African Americans, 8 Asian Americans or Pacific Islanders, 4 Hispanic Americans), 27 international. Average age 26. 186 applicants, 18% accepted, 24 enrolled. In 2009, 13 master's, 8 doctorates awarded. *Degree requirements:* For doctorate, thesis/dissertation, oral exam. *Entrance requirements:* For doctorate, GRE General Test. Additional exam requirements/recommendations for international students: Required—TOEFL (minimum score 600 paper-based; 250 computer-based; 100 iBT). *Application deadline:* For fall admission, 1/15 for domestic and international students. Applications are processed on a rolling basis. Application fee: $75. Electronic applications accepted. *Financial support:* In 2009–10, 12 fellowships with full and partial tuition reimbursements (averaging $25,000 per year), 42 research assistantships with full tuition reimbursements (averaging $25,000 per year) were awarded; teaching assistantships with full and partial tuition reimbursements, scholarships/grants, health care benefits, tuition waivers (partial), and unspecified assistantships also available. Financial award application deadline: 1/15. *Faculty research:* Polymers and complex fluids, nucleation, bioengineering and biotechnology, computational biology and genomics, cell and molecular biotechnology. Total annual research expenditures: $3.1 million. *Unit head:* Dr. Konstantinos Konstantopoulos, Chair and Professor, 410-516-7170, Fax: 410-516-5510, E-mail: kkonsta1@jhu.edu. *Application contact:* Lindsay Spivey, Academic Program Coordinator, 410-516-4166, Fax: 410-516-5510, E-mail: spivey@jhu.edu.

Kansas State University, Graduate School, College of Engineering, Department of Chemical Engineering, Manhattan, KS 66506. Offers MS, PhD. Postbaccalaureate distance learning degree programs offered. *Faculty:* 8 full-time (2 women), 5 part-time/adjunct (0 women). *Students:* 20 full-time (7 women), 17 part-time (4 women); includes 3 minority (2 Asian Americans or Pacific Islanders, 1 Hispanic American), 15 international. Average age 28. 48 applicants, 19% accepted, 9 enrolled. In 2009, 3 master's, 3 doctorates awarded. *Degree requirements:* For master's, thesis or alternative; for doctorate, thesis/dissertation. *Entrance requirements:* For master's and doctorate, GRE. Additional exam requirements/recommendations for international students: Required—TOEFL. *Application deadline:* For fall admission, 2/1 priority date for domestic and international students; for spring admission, 8/1 priority date for domestic and international students. Applications are processed on a rolling basis. Application fee: $40 ($55 for international students). Electronic applications accepted. *Financial support:* In 2009–10, 21 research assistantships (averaging $17,679 per year), 4 teaching assistantships with partial tuition reimbursements (averaging $18,220 per year) were awarded; fellowships with partial tuition reimbursements, institutionally sponsored loans and scholarships/grants also available. Support available to part-time students. Financial award application deadline: 3/1; financial award applicants required to submit FAFSA. *Faculty research:* Renewable sustainable energy, molecular engineering, advanced materials. Total annual research expenditures: $1.1 million. *Unit head:* James Edgar, Head, 785-532-4320, Fax: 785-532-7372, E-mail: edgarjh@ksu.edu. *Application contact:* James Edgar, Director, 785-532-4320, Fax: 785-532-7372, E-mail: edgarjh@ksu.edu.

Lamar University, College of Graduate Studies, College of Engineering, Department of Chemical Engineering, Beaumont, TX 77710. Offers ME, MES, DE, PhD. *Faculty:* 12 full-time (1 woman). *Students:* 99 full-time (27 women), 21 part-time (2 women); includes 5 minority (2 African Americans, 2 Asian Americans or Pacific Islanders, 1 Hispanic American), 87 international. Average age 25. 108 applicants, 33% accepted, 29 enrolled. In 2009, 57 master's, 1 doctorate awarded. *Degree requirements:* For master's, comprehensive exam (for some programs), thesis (for some programs); for doctorate, comprehensive exam, thesis/dissertation. *Entrance requirements:* For master's and doctorate, GRE General Test. Additional exam requirements/recommendations for international students: Required—TOEFL. *Application deadline:* For fall admission, 5/15 priority date for domestic students; for spring admission, 10/1 priority date for domestic students. Applications are processed on a rolling basis. Application fee: $25 ($50 for international students). *Financial support:* In 2009–10, 49 fellowships with partial tuition reimbursements (averaging $1,000 per year), 15 research assistantships with partial tuition reimbursements (averaging $6,000 per year), 8 teaching assistantships with partial tuition reimbursements (averaging $12,600 per year) were awarded; tuition waivers (full and partial) also available. Financial award application deadline: 4/1. *Faculty research:* Flare minimization, process optimization, process integration. *Unit head:* Dr. Kuyen Li, Chair, 409-880-8784, Fax: 409-880-2197, E-mail: che_dept@hal.lamar.edu. *Application contact:* Sandy Drane, Coordinator of Graduate Admissions, 409-880-8356, Fax: 409-880-8414, E-mail: gradmissions@hal.lamar.edu.

Lehigh University, P.C. Rossin College of Engineering and Applied Science, Department of Chemical Engineering, Bethlehem, PA 18015. Offers biological chemical engineering (M Eng); chemical engineering (M Eng, PhD); MBA/E. Part-time programs available. Postbaccalaureate distance learning degree programs offered (no on-campus study). *Faculty:* 17 full-time (2 women), 2 part-time/adjunct (0 women). *Students:* 45 full-time (11 women), 26 part-time (11 women); includes 9 minority (2 African Americans, 4 Asian Americans or Pacific Islanders, 3 Hispanic Americans), 32 international. Average age 27. 113 applicants, 24% accepted, 21 enrolled. In 2009, 4 master's, 6 doctorates awarded. Terminal master's awarded for partial completion of doctoral program. *Degree requirements:* For master's, thesis (for some programs); for doctorate, comprehensive exam, thesis/dissertation. *Entrance requirements:* For master's and doctorate, GRE General Test. Additional exam requirements/recommendations for international students: Required—TOEFL (minimum score 570 paper-based; 230 computer-based; 85 iBT). *Application deadline:* For fall admission, 7/15 for domestic students, 1/15 priority date for international students; for spring admission, 12/1 for domestic and international students. Applications are processed on a rolling basis. Application fee: $65. Electronic applications accepted. *Financial support:* In 2009–10, 41 students received support, including 5 fellowships with full tuition reimbursements available (averaging $20,400 per year), 32 research assistantships with full tuition reimbursements available (averaging $20,400 per year), 7 teaching assistantships with full and partial tuition reimbursements available (averaging $20,400 per year); career-related internships or fieldwork, institutionally sponsored loans, scholarships/grants, health care benefits, and unspecified assistantships also available. Financial award application deadline: 1/15. *Faculty research:* Emulsion polymers, process control, energy, biotechnology, catalysis. Total annual research expenditures: $2.6 million. *Unit head:* Dr. Anthony J. McHugh, Chairman, 610-758-4260, Fax: 610-758-5057, E-mail: ajm8@lehigh.edu. *Application contact:* Barbara A. Kessler, Graduate Secretary, 610-758-4261, Fax: 610-758-5057, E-mail: inchegs@mail.lehigh.edu.

Louisiana State University and Agricultural and Mechanical College, Graduate School, College of Engineering, Cain Department of Chemical Engineering, Baton Rouge, LA 70803. Offers MS Ch E, PhD. Part-time and evening/weekend programs available. *Faculty:* 16 full-time (1 woman). *Students:* 53 full-time (13 women), 8 part-time (2 women); includes 4 minority (3 Asian Americans or Pacific Islanders, 1 Hispanic American), 41 international. Average age 26. 131 applicants, 23% accepted, 13 enrolled. In 2009, 4 master's, 6 doctorates awarded. Terminal master's awarded for partial completion of doctoral program. *Degree requirements:* For master's, comprehensive exam or thesis; for doctorate, thesis/dissertation, general exam, qualifying exam. *Entrance requirements:* For master's and doctorate, GRE General Test, minimum GPA of 3.0. Additional exam requirements/recommendations for international students: Required—TOEFL (minimum score 550 paper-based; 213 computer-based; 79 iBT) or IELTS (minimum score 6.5). *Application deadline:* For fall admission, 1/25 priority date for domestic students, 5/15 priority date for international students; for spring admission, 10/15 for international students. Applications are processed on a rolling basis. Application fee: $50 ($70 for international students). Electronic applications accepted. *Financial support:* In 2009–10, 55 students received support, including 2 fellowships (averaging $30,940 per year), 46 research assistantships with full and partial tuition reimbursements available (averaging $24,091 per year); teaching assistantships, Federal Work-Study, health care benefits, and tuition waivers (full and partial) also available. Financial award application deadline: 4/15; financial award applicants required to submit FAFSA. *Faculty research:* Reaction engineering, control, thermodynamic and transport phenomena, polymer processing and properties, biochemical engineering. Total annual research expenditures: $2.8 million. *Unit head:* Dr. K. T. Valsaraj, Chair, 225-578-1426, Fax: 225-578-1476, E-mail: valsaraj@lsu.edu. *Application contact:* Dr. Judy Wornat, Coordinator, 225-578-1426, Fax: 225-578-1476, E-mail: mjwornat@lsu.edu.

Louisiana Tech University, Graduate School, College of Engineering and Science, Department of Chemical Engineering, Ruston, LA 71272. Offers MS, PhD. Part-time programs available. Terminal master's awarded for partial completion of doctoral program. *Degree requirements:* For master's, thesis; for doctorate, thesis/dissertation. *Entrance requirements:* For master's, GRE General Test, minimum GPA of 3.0 in last 60 hours; for doctorate, minimum graduate GPA of 3.25 (with MS) or GRE General Test. Additional exam requirements/recommendations for international students: Required—TOEFL. *Faculty research:* Artificial intelligence, biotechnology, hazardous waste process safety.

Manhattan College, Graduate Division, School of Engineering, Program in Chemical Engineering, Riverdale, NY 10471. Offers MS. Postbaccalaureate distance learning degree programs offered (no on-campus study). *Degree requirements:* For master's, thesis or alternative. *Entrance requirements:* For master's, GRE (recommended), minimum GPA of 3.0. Additional exam requirements/recommendations for international students: Required—TOEFL (minimum score 550 paper-based; 213 computer-based). *Faculty research:* Advanced separation processes, environmental management, combustion, pollution prevention.

Massachusetts Institute of Technology, School of Engineering, Department of Chemical Engineering, Cambridge, MA 02139-4307. Offers chemical engineering (SM, PhD, Sc D); chemical engineering practice (SM, PhD); SM/MBA. *Faculty:* 31 full-time (4 women). *Students:* 241 full-time (70 women); includes 34 minority (1 African American, 29 Asian Americans or Pacific Islanders, 4 Hispanic Americans), 96 international. Average age 25. 443 applicants, 15% accepted, 50 enrolled. In 2009, 49 master's, 43 doctorates awarded. Terminal master's awarded for partial completion of doctoral program. *Degree requirements:* For master's, thesis (for some programs), semester of practice school (SM in chemical engineering practice); for doctorate, comprehensive exam, thesis/dissertation. *Entrance requirements:* For master's and doctorate, GRE General Test. Additional exam requirements/recommendations for international students: Required—TOEFL (minimum score 600 paper-based; 250 computer-based) or IELTS (minimum score 7). *Application deadline:* For fall admission, 1/2 for domestic and international students. Application fee: $75. Electronic applications accepted. *Financial support:* In 2009–10, 241 students received support, including 95 fellowships with tuition reimbursements available (averaging $26,244 per year), 124 research assistantships with tuition reimbursements available (averaging $31,510 per year), 16 teaching assistantships with tuition reimbursements available (averaging $32,215 per year); career-related internships or fieldwork, Federal Work-Study, institutionally sponsored loans, scholarships/grants, traineeships, health care benefits, and unspecified assistantships also available. *Faculty research:* Catalysis and reaction engineering, biological engineering, materials and polymers, surfaces and nanostructures, thermodynamics and molecular computation. Total annual research expenditures: $35.2 million. *Unit head:* Prof. Klavs F. Jensen, Department Head, 617-253-4561, Fax: 617-258-8992. *Application contact:* Suzanne Easterly, Academic Administrator, 617-253-4577, Fax: 617-253-9695, E-mail: easterly@mit.edu.

McGill University, Faculty of Graduate and Postdoctoral Studies, Faculty of Engineering, Department of Chemical Engineering, Montréal, QC H3A 2T5, Canada. Offers chemical engineering (M Eng, PhD); environmental engineering (M Eng).

McMaster University, School of Graduate Studies, Faculty of Engineering, Department of Chemical Engineering, Hamilton, ON L8S 4M2, Canada. Offers M Eng, MA Sc, PhD. *Degree requirements:* For master's, thesis; for doctorate, comprehensive exam, thesis/dissertation. *Entrance requirements:* For master's, minimum B average in the last two years. Additional exam requirements/recommendations for international students: Required—TOEFL (minimum score 550 paper-based; 213 computer-based). *Faculty research:* Biomaterials, computer process control, polymer processing, environmental biotechnology, reverse osmosis.

McNeese State University, Doré School of Graduate Studies, College of Engineering and Engineering Technology, Lake Charles, LA 70609. Offers chemical engineering (M Eng); civil engineering (M Eng); electrical engineering (M Eng); engineering management (M Eng); mechanical engineering (M Eng). Part-time and evening/weekend programs available. *Degree requirements:* For master's, thesis or alternative. *Entrance requirements:* For master's, GRE, minimum undergraduate GPA of 3.0. Additional exam requirements/recommendations for international students: Required—TOEFL.

Michigan State University, The Graduate School, College of Engineering, Department of Chemical Engineering and Materials Science, East Lansing, MI 48824. Offers chemical engineering (MS, PhD); materials science and engineering (MS, PhD). *Entrance requirements:* Additional exam requirements/recommendations for international students: Required—TOEFL. Electronic applications accepted.

Chemical Engineering

Michigan Technological University, Graduate School, College of Engineering, Department of Chemical Engineering, Houghton, MI 49931. Offers MS, PhD. Part-time programs available. Terminal master's awarded for partial completion of doctoral program. *Degree requirements:* For master's, comprehensive exam; for doctorate, comprehensive exam, thesis/dissertation. *Entrance requirements:* For master's, GRE. Additional exam requirements/recommendations for international students: Required—TOEFL (minimum score 575 paper-based; 230 computer-based). Electronic applications accepted. *Expenses:* Contact institution. *Faculty research:* Polymer engineering, thermodynamics, chemical process safety, surface science/catalysis, environmental chemical engineering.

Mississippi State University, Bagley College of Engineering, David C. Swalm School of Chemical Engineering, MS State, MS 39762. Offers chemical engineering (MS); engineering (PhD), including chemical engineering. *Faculty:* 11 full-time (4 women), 1 part-time/adjunct (0 women). *Students:* 24 full-time (8 women), 12 part-time (2 women); includes 4 minority (3 African Americans, 1 Asian American or Pacific Islander), 15 international. Average age 28. 28 applicants, 18% accepted, 4 enrolled. In 2009, 2 master's awarded. *Degree requirements:* For master's, comprehensive exam, thesis optional, comprehensive oral or written exam; for doctorate, comprehensive exam, thesis/dissertation. *Entrance requirements:* For master's and doctorate, GRE, minimum GPA of 3.0. Additional exam requirements/recommendations for international students: Required—TOEFL (minimum score 550 paper-based; 213 computer-based; 79 iBT); Recommended—IELTS (minimum score 6.5). *Application deadline:* For fall admission, 4/1 priority date for domestic students, 5/1 for international students; for spring admission, 8/1 priority date for domestic students, 9/1 for international students. Applications are processed on a rolling basis. Application fee: $40. Electronic applications accepted. *Expenses:* Tuition, state resident: full-time $2575.50; part-time $286.25 per credit hour. Tuition, nonresident: full-time $6510; part-time $723.50 per credit hour. Tuition and fees vary according to course load. *Financial support:* In 2009–10, 21 research assistantships with full tuition reimbursements (averaging $13,134 per year) were awarded; Federal Work-Study, institutionally sponsored loans, and unspecified assistantships also available. Financial award application deadline: 4/1; financial award applicants required to submit FAFSA. *Faculty research:* Thermodynamics, composite materials, catalysis, surface science, environmental engineering. Total annual research expenditures: $4.6 million. *Unit head:* Dr. Mark White, Director, 662-325-2480, Fax: 662-325-2482, E-mail: white@che.msstate.edu. *Application contact:* Dr. Mark White, Director, 662-325-2480, Fax: 662-325-2482, E-mail: white@che.msstate.edu.

Missouri University of Science and Technology, Graduate School, Department of Chemical and Biological Engineering, Rolla, MO 65409. Offers chemical engineering (MS, DE, PhD). *Degree requirements:* For master's, thesis optional; for doctorate, comprehensive exam. *Entrance requirements:* For master's, GRE (minimum score 1100 verbal and quantitative, 4 writing); for doctorate, GRE (minimum score: verbal and quantitative 1200, writing 4). Additional exam requirements/recommendations for international students: Required—TOEFL (minimum score 550 paper-based; 213 computer-based). *Faculty research:* Mixing, fluid mechanics, bioengineering, freeze-drying, extraction.

Montana State University, College of Graduate Studies, College of Engineering, Department of Chemical and Biological Engineering, Bozeman, MT 59717. Offers chemical engineering (MS); engineering (PhD), including chemical engineering option, environmental engineering option; environmental engineering (MS). Part-time programs available. *Faculty:* 9 full-time (2 women), 1 part-time/adjunct (0 women). *Students:* 1 full-time (0 women), 23 part-time (9 women); includes 2 minority (1 American Indian/Alaska Native, 1 Asian American or Pacific Islander), 3 international. Average age 27. 7 applicants. In 2009, 4 master's awarded. *Degree requirements:* For master's, comprehensive exam, thesis (for some programs); for doctorate, comprehensive exam, thesis/dissertation. *Entrance requirements:* For master's, GRE General Test, BS in chemical engineering or related scientific field; for doctorate, GRE General Test, BS or MS in chemical engineering or related scientific field. Additional exam requirements/recommendations for international students: Required—TOEFL (minimum score 550 paper-based; 213 computer-based). *Application deadline:* For fall admission, 7/15 priority date for domestic students, 5/15 priority date for international students; for spring admission, 12/1 priority date for domestic students, 10/1 priority date for international students. Applications are processed on a rolling basis. Application fee: $30. Electronic applications accepted. *Expenses:* Tuition, state resident: full-time $5635; part-time $3492 per year. Tuition, nonresident: full-time $17,212; part-time $7865.10 per year. Required fees: $1441.05; $153.15 per credit. Tuition and fees vary according to course load and program. *Financial support:* In 2009–10, 3 fellowships with full tuition reimbursements (averaging $25,000 per year), 20 research assistantships with full tuition reimbursements (averaging $18,000 per year), 2 teaching assistantships with full tuition reimbursements (averaging $18,000 per year) were awarded. Financial award application deadline: 3/1; financial award applicants required to submit FAFSA. *Faculty research:* The effects of variable permeability on the resistance to flow through the tissues and biofilms; development of protective coatings on planar solid oxide fuel cell (SOFC) metallic interconnects; carbon sequestration; zero emissions research and technology; research in the areas of biofuels, extremophilic bioprocessing, and in situ biocatalyzed heavy metal transformations; subsurface biofilm barriers; magnetic resonance microscopy. Total annual research expenditures: $1.8 million. *Unit head:* Dr. Ron W. Larson, Head, 406-994-2221, Fax: 406-994-5308, E-mail: ronl@coe.montana.edu. *Application contact:* Dr. Carl A. Fox, Vice Provost for Graduate Education, 406-994-4145, Fax: 406-994-7433, E-mail: gradstudy@montana.edu.

New Jersey Institute of Technology, Office of Graduate Studies, Newark College of Engineering, Department of Chemical Engineering, Program in Chemical Engineering, Newark, NJ 07102. Offers MS, PhD. Part-time and evening/weekend programs available. Terminal master's awarded for partial completion of doctoral program. *Degree requirements:* For master's, thesis optional; for doctorate, thesis/dissertation, residency. *Entrance requirements:* For master's, GRE General Test; for doctorate, GRE General Test, minimum graduate GPA of 3.5. Additional exam requirements/recommendations for international students: Required—TOEFL (minimum score 550 paper-based; 213 computer-based; 79 iBT). Electronic applications accepted.

New Mexico State University, Graduate School, College of Engineering, Department of Chemical Engineering, Las Cruces, NM 88003-8001. Offers MS Ch E, PhD. Part-time programs available. *Faculty:* 6 full-time (2 women). *Students:* 21 full-time (6 women), 2 part-time (0 women), 20 international. Average age 26. 48 applicants, 79% accepted, 9 enrolled. In 2009, 4 master's, 1 doctorate awarded. Terminal master's awarded for partial completion of doctoral program. *Degree requirements:* For master's, thesis (for some programs); for doctorate, comprehensive exam, thesis/dissertation. *Entrance requirements:* For master's and doctorate, GRE General Test. Additional exam requirements/recommendations for international students: Required—TOEFL. *Application deadline:* For fall admission, 3/1 priority date for domestic and international students; for spring admission, 11/1 priority date for domestic and international students. Applications are processed on a rolling basis. Application fee: $30 ($50 for international students). Electronic applications accepted. *Expenses:* Tuition, state resident: full-time $4080; part-time $223 per credit. Tuition, nonresident: full-time $14,256; part-time $647 per credit. Required fees: $1278; $639 per semester. *Financial support:* In 2009–10, 8 research assistantships with full and partial tuition reimbursements (averaging $5,531 per year), 10 teaching assistantships with full and partial tuition reimbursements (averaging $4,964 per year) were awarded; fellowships with full tuition reimbursements, career-related internships or fieldwork, Federal Work-Study, scholarships/grants, health care benefits, and unspecified assistantships also available. Support available to part-time students. Financial award application deadline: 3/1. *Faculty research:* Advanced materials, environmental engineering, food technology, computer-aided design, bioengineering. *Unit head:* Dr. Martha C. Mitchell, Head, 575-646-2093, Fax: 575-646-7706, E-mail: martmitc@nmsu.edu. *Application contact:* Dr. David A. Rockstraw, Professor, 575-646-7705, Fax: 575-646-7706, E-mail: drockstr@nmsu.edu.

North Carolina Agricultural and Technical State University, Graduate School, College of Engineering, Department of Mechanical and Chemical Engineering, Greensboro, NC 27411. Offers chemical engineering (MS Ch E); mechanical engineering (MSME, PhD). Part-time programs available. *Degree requirements:* For master's, comprehensive exam, thesis optional,

dual exam, qualifying exam, thesis defense; for doctorate, thesis/dissertation. *Entrance requirements:* For doctorate, GRE. *Faculty research:* Composites, smart materials and sensors, mechanical systems modeling and finite element analysis, computational fluid dynamics and engine research, design and manufacturing.

North Carolina State University, Graduate School, College of Engineering, Department of Chemical and Biomolecular Engineering, Raleigh, NC 27695. Offers chemical engineering (M Ch E, MS, PhD). Part-time programs available. Terminal master's awarded for partial completion of doctoral program. *Degree requirements:* For master's, thesis optional; for doctorate, thesis/dissertation. *Entrance requirements:* For master's and doctorate, GRE General Test. Additional exam requirements/recommendations for international students: Required—TOEFL. Electronic applications accepted. *Faculty research:* Molecular themodynamics and computer simulation, catalysis, kinetics, electrochemical reaction engineering, biochemical engineering.

Northeastern University, College of Engineering, Department of Chemical Engineering, Boston, MA 02115-5096. Offers MS, PhD. Part-time programs available. *Faculty:* 8 full-time (5 women). *Students:* 39 full-time (21 women), 6 part-time (2 women); includes 4 minority (3 Asian Americans or Pacific Islanders, 1 Hispanic American), 24 international. 102 applicants, 24% accepted, 10 enrolled. In 2009, 9 master's, 1 doctorate awarded. *Degree requirements:* For master's, thesis optional; for doctorate, thesis/dissertation, departmental qualifying exam. *Entrance requirements:* For master's and doctorate, GRE General Test. Additional exam requirements/recommendations for international students: Required—TOEFL (minimum score 550 paper-based; 213 computer-based; 80 iBT). *Application deadline:* For fall admission, 1/15 priority date for domestic and international students. Applications are processed on a rolling basis. Application fee: $50. Electronic applications accepted. *Financial support:* In 2009–10, 21 students received support, including 1 fellowship with full tuition reimbursement available, 13 research assistantships with full tuition reimbursements available, 17 teaching assistantships with full tuition reimbursements available (averaging $18,320 per year); career-related internships or fieldwork, Federal Work-Study, scholarships/grants, tuition waivers (full), and unspecified assistantships also available. Support available to part-time students. Financial award application deadline: 1/15; financial award applicants required to submit FAFSA. *Faculty research:* Aerogel, catalysts, advanced microgravity materials processing, biomaterials, catalyst development, biochemical reactions. *Unit head:* Dr. Laura H. Lewis, Chair, 617-373-2989, Fax: 617-373-8504. *Application contact:* Stephen L. Gibson, Associate Director, 617-373-2711, Fax: 617-373-2501, E-mail: grad-eng@coe.neu.edu.

Northwestern University, McCormick School of Engineering and Applied Science, Department of Chemical Engineering, Evanston, IL 60208. Offers MS, PhD. Admissions and degrees offered through The Graduate School. Part-time programs available. Terminal master's awarded for partial completion of doctoral program. *Degree requirements:* For master's, thesis optional; for doctorate, thesis/dissertation. *Entrance requirements:* Additional exam requirements/recommendations for international students: Required—TOEFL (minimum score 600 paper-based). *Faculty research:* Biotechnology and bioengineering; complex systems; environmental catalysis, kinetics and reaction engineering; modeling, theory, and simulation; polymer science and engineering; transport process.

The Ohio State University, Graduate School, College of Engineering, Department of Chemical and Biomolecular Engineering, Columbus, OH 43210. Offers chemical engineering (MS, PhD). *Faculty:* 13. *Students:* 69 full-time (21 women), 25 part-time (10 women); includes 7 minority (5 Asian Americans or Pacific Islanders, 2 Hispanic Americans), 61 international. Average age 26. In 2009, 16 master's, 15 doctorates awarded. *Degree requirements:* For master's, thesis; for doctorate, thesis/dissertation. *Entrance requirements:* For master's and doctorate, GRE General Test. Additional exam requirements/recommendations for international students: Recommended—TOEFL (minimum score 600 paper-based; 250 computer-based). *Application deadline:* For fall admission, 8/15 priority date for domestic students, 7/1 priority date for international students; for winter admission, 12/1 priority date for domestic students, 11/1 priority date for international students; for spring admission, 3/1 priority date for domestic students, 2/1 priority date for international students. Applications are processed on a rolling basis. Application fee: $40 ($50 for international students). Electronic applications accepted. *Expenses:* Tuition, state resident: full-time $10,683. Tuition, nonresident: full-time $25,923. Tuition and fees vary according to course load and program. *Financial support:* Fellowships, research assistantships, teaching assistantships, career-related internships or fieldwork, Federal Work-Study, institutionally sponsored loans, and unspecified assistantships available. Support available to part-time students. *Unit head:* Kurt W. Koelling, Graduate Studies Committee Chair, 614-292-7907, Fax: 614-292-3769, E-mail: koelling.1@osu.edu. *Application contact:* 614-292-9444, Fax: 614-292-3895, E-mail: domestic.grad@osu.edu.

Ohio University, Graduate College, Russ College of Engineering and Technology, Department of Chemical and Biomolecular Engineering, Athens, OH 45701-2979. Offers biomedical engineering (MS); chemical engineering (MS, PhD). Part-time programs available. *Faculty:* 10 full-time (3 women), 4 part-time/adjunct (0 women). *Students:* 44 full-time (17 women), 14 part-time (3 women), 48 international. 53 applicants, 26% accepted, 6 enrolled. In 2009, 6 master's, 4 doctorates awarded. *Degree requirements:* For master's, comprehensive exam (for some programs), thesis; for doctorate, comprehensive exam, thesis/dissertation, qualifying exams. *Entrance requirements:* For master's and doctorate, GRE General Test. Additional exam requirements/recommendations for international students: Required—TOEFL (minimum score 590 paper-based; 96 iBT) or IELTS Academic (minimum score 7). *Application deadline:* For fall admission, 3/1 priority date for domestic and international students. Applications are processed on a rolling basis. Application fee: $50 ($55 for international students). Electronic applications accepted. *Expenses:* Tuition, state resident: full-time $7839; part-time $323 per quarter hour. Tuition, nonresident: full-time $15,831; part-time $654 per quarter hour. Required fees: $2931. *Financial support:* In 2009–10, fellowships with full tuition reimbursements (averaging $19,000 per year), research assistantships with full tuition reimbursements (averaging $17,000 per year), teaching assistantships with full tuition reimbursements (averaging $15,000 per year) were awarded; Federal Work-Study, institutionally sponsored loans, and unspecified assistantships also available. Financial award application deadline: 3/1; financial award applicants required to submit FAFSA. *Faculty research:* Corrosion and multiphase flow, biochemical engineering, thin film materials, air pollution modeling and control, biomedical engineering. Total annual research expenditures: $1.8 million. *Unit head:* Dr. Valerie L. Young, Chair, 740-593-1496, Fax: 740-593-0873, E-mail: youngv@ohio.edu. *Application contact:* Dr. Daniel A. Gulino, Assistant Chair for Graduate Studies, 740-593-1495, Fax: 740-593-0873, E-mail: gulino@ohio.edu.

Oklahoma State University, College of Engineering, Architecture and Technology, School of Chemical Engineering, Stillwater, OK 74078. Offers MS, PhD. *Faculty:* 14 full-time (2 women), 1 part-time/adjunct (0 women). *Students:* 38 full-time (11 women), 17 part-time (4 women), 53 international. Average age 26. 100 applicants, 46% accepted, 17 enrolled. In 2009, 5 master's, 2 doctorates awarded. *Degree requirements:* For master's, thesis or alternative; for doctorate, comprehensive exam, thesis/dissertation. *Entrance requirements:* For master's and doctorate, GRE or GMAT. Additional exam requirements/recommendations for international students: Required—TOEFL (minimum score 550 paper-based; 79 iBT). *Application deadline:* For fall admission, 3/1 priority date for international students; for spring admission, 8/1 priority date for international students. Applications are processed on a rolling basis. Application fee: $40 ($75 for international students). Electronic applications accepted. *Expenses:* Tuition, state resident: full-time $3716; part-time $154.85 per credit hour. Tuition, nonresident: full-time $14,448; part-time $602 per credit hour. Required fees: $1772; $73.85 per credit hour. One-time fee: $50. Tuition and fees vary according to course load and campus/location. *Financial support:* In 2009–10, 39 research assistantships (averaging $10,942 per year), 25 teaching assistantships (averaging $10,495 per year) were awarded; fellowships, career-related internships or fieldwork, Federal Work-Study, scholarships/grants, health care benefits, tuition waivers (partial), and unspecified assistantships also available. Support available to part-time students. Financial award application deadline: 3/1; financial award applicants required to submit FAFSA. *Unit* *head:* Dr. Khaled A. M. Gasem, Head, 405-744-5280, Fax: 405-744-6338. *Application contact:* Dr. Gordon Emslie, Dean, 405-744-6368, Fax: 405-744-0355, E-mail: grad-i@okstate.edu.

Oregon State University, Graduate School, College of Engineering, School of Chemical, Biological and Environmental Engineering, Department of Chemical Engineering, Corvallis, OR 97331. Offers M Eng, MS, PhD. *Students:* 56 full-time (20 women), 7 part-time (3 women); includes 7 minority (1 African American, 5 Asian Americans or Pacific Islanders, 1 Hispanic American), 17 international. Average age 29. In 2009, 13 master's, 1 doctorate awarded. *Expenses:* Tuition, state resident: full-time $9774; part-time $362 per credit. Tuition, nonresident: full-time $15,849; part-time $587 per credit. Required fees: $1639. Full-time tuition and fees vary according to course load and program. *Unit head:* Dr. Kenneth J. Williamson, Head, 541-737-6836, Fax: 541-737-4600, E-mail: kenneth.williamson@oregonstate.edu. *Application contact:* Karen Kelly, Information Contact, 541-737-2491, Fax: 541-737-4600, E-mail: cbee@oregonstate.edu.

Penn State University Park, Graduate School, College of Engineering, Department of Chemical Engineering, State College, University Park, PA 16802-1503. Offers MS, PhD.

Polytechnic Institute of NYU, Department of Chemical and Biological Engineering, Major in Chemical Engineering, Brooklyn, NY 11201-2990. Offers MS, PhD. Part-time and evening/weekend programs available. *Students:* 26 full-time (8 women), 15 part-time (7 women); includes 8 minority (3 African Americans, 1 American Indian/Alaska Native, 2 Asian Americans or Pacific Islanders, 2 Hispanic Americans), 23 international. 82 applicants, 29% accepted, 10 enrolled. In 2009, 4 master's, 6 doctorates awarded. *Degree requirements:* For master's, comprehensive exam (for some programs), thesis (for some programs); for doctorate, comprehensive exam, thesis/dissertation. *Entrance requirements:* For master's, GRE General Test, BS in chemical engineering; for doctorate, GRE General Test. Additional exam requirements/recommendations for international students: Required—TOEFL (minimum score 550 paper-based; 213 computer-based; 80 iBT); Recommended—IELTS (minimum score 6.5). *Application deadline:* For fall admission, 7/31 priority date for domestic students, 4/30 priority date for international students; for spring admission, 12/31 priority date for domestic students, 11/30 priority date for international students. Applications are processed on a rolling basis. Application fee: $75. Electronic applications accepted. *Expenses:* Tuition: Full-time $21,492; part-time $1194 per credit hour. Required fees: $1160; $204 per course. *Financial support:* Fellowships, research assistantships, teaching assistantships, institutionally sponsored loans, scholarships/grants, and unspecified assistantships available. Support available to part-time students. Financial award applicants required to submit FAFSA. *Faculty research:* Plasma polymerization, crystallization of organic compounds, dipolar relaxations in reactive polymers. *Unit head:* Dr. Walter Zurawsky, Head, 718-260-3725, Fax: 718-260-3125, E-mail: zurawsky@poly.edu. *Application contact:* JeanCarlo Bonilla, Dir. Graduate Enrollment Management, 718-260-3182, Fax: 718-260-3624, E-mail: gradinfo@poly.edu.

Polytechnic Institute of NYU, Long Island Graduate Center, Graduate Programs, Department of Chemical and Biological Engineering, Major in Chemical Engineering, Melville, NY 11747. Offers MS. *Degree requirements:* For master's, comprehensive exam (for some programs), thesis (for some programs). *Entrance requirements:* Additional exam requirements/recommendations for international students: Required—TOEFL (minimum score 550 paper-based; 213 computer-based; 80 iBT); Recommended—IELTS (minimum score 6.5). *Application deadline:* For fall admission, 7/31 priority date for domestic students, 4/30 priority date for international students; for spring admission, 12/31 priority date for domestic students, 11/30 priority date for international students. Applications are processed on a rolling basis. Application fee: $75. Electronic applications accepted. *Financial support:* Institutionally sponsored loans, scholarships/grants, and unspecified assistantships available. Support available to part-time students. *Unit head:* Dr. Walter Zurawsky, Department Head, 718-260-3725, E-mail: zurawsky@poly.edu. *Application contact:* JeanCarlo Bonilla, Director of Graduate Enrollment Management, 718-260-3182, Fax: 718-260-3624, E-mail: gradinfo@poly.edu.

Polytechnic Institute of NYU, Westchester Graduate Center, Graduate Programs, Department of Chemical and Biological Engineering, Major in Chemical Engineering, Hawthorne, NY 10532-1507. Offers MS. *Degree requirements:* For master's, comprehensive exam (for some programs), thesis (for some programs). *Entrance requirements:* Additional exam requirements/recommendations for international students: Required—TOEFL (minimum score 550 paper-based; 213 computer-based; 80 iBT); Recommended—IELTS (minimum score 6.5). *Application deadline:* For fall admission, 7/31 priority date for domestic students, 4/30 priority date for international students; for spring admission, 12/31 priority date for domestic students, 11/30 priority date for international students. Applications are processed on a rolling basis. Application fee: $75. Electronic applications accepted. *Financial support:* Institutionally sponsored loans, scholarships/grants, and unspecified assistantships available. Support available to part-time students. *Unit head:* Dr. Walter Zurawsky, Department Head, 718-260-3725, E-mail: zurawsky@poly.edu. *Application contact:* JeanCarlo Bonilla, Director of Graduate Enrollment Management, 718-260-3182, Fax: 718-260-3624, E-mail: gradinfo@poly.edu.

Princeton University, Graduate School, School of Engineering and Applied Science, Department of Chemical Engineering, Princeton, NJ 08544-1019. Offers M Eng, MSE, PhD. *Faculty:* 17 full-time (2 women). Terminal master's awarded for partial completion of doctoral program. *Degree requirements:* For master's, thesis (MSE); for doctorate, thesis/dissertation, general exam. *Entrance requirements:* For master's, GRE General Test, 3 letters of recommendation; for doctorate, GRE General Test, official transcript(s), 3 letters of recommendation, personal statement. Additional exam requirements/recommendations for international students: Required—TOEFL. *Application deadline:* For fall admission, 12/31 for domestic and international students. Application fee: $90. Electronic applications accepted. *Financial support:* Fellowships with full tuition reimbursements, research assistantships with full tuition reimbursements, teaching assistantships with full tuition reimbursements, institutionally sponsored loans and health care benefits available. *Faculty research:* Applied and computational mathematics, bioengineering, environmental and energy science and technology, fluid mechanics and transport phenomena, materials science. *Unit head:* Karen Oliver, Graduate Program Administrator, 800-238-6169, Fax: 609-258-0211, E-mail: chegrad@princeton.edu. *Application contact:* Michelle Carman, Manager of Graduate Admissions, 609-258-3034, Fax: 609-258-7262, E-mail: gsadmit@princeton.edu.

Purdue University, College of Engineering, School of Chemical Engineering, West Lafayette, IN 47907-2050. Offers MSChE, PhD. Terminal master's awarded for partial completion of doctoral program. *Entrance requirements:* For master's and doctorate, GRE, minimum GPA of 3.0. Additional exam requirements/recommendations for international students: Required—TOEFL (minimum score 550 paper-based; 213 computer-based); Recommended—TWE. Electronic applications accepted. *Faculty research:* Biochemical and biomedical processes, polymer materials, interfacial and surface phenomena, applied thermodynamics, process systems engineering.

Queen's University at Kingston, School of Graduate Studies and Research, Faculty of Applied Science, Department of Chemical Engineering, Kingston, ON K7L 3N6, Canada. Offers M Sc, PhD. Part-time programs available. *Degree requirements:* For master's, thesis or alternative; for doctorate, comprehensive exam, thesis/dissertation. *Entrance requirements:* Additional exam requirements/recommendations for international students: Required—TOEFL (minimum score 580 paper-based; 237 computer-based). Electronic applications accepted. *Faculty research:* Polymers and reaction engineering, process control and applied statistics, combustion, fermentation and bioremediation, biomaterials.

Rensselaer Polytechnic Institute, Graduate School, School of Engineering, Howard P. Isermann Department of Chemical and Biological Engineering, Troy, NY 12180-3590. Offers M Eng, MS, PhD. Part-time programs available. *Faculty:* 13 full-time (1 woman). *Students:* 67 full-time (15 women), 2 part-time (1 woman); includes 7 minority (1 African American, 5 Asian Americans or Pacific Islanders, 1 Hispanic American), 39 international. Average age 24. 161 applicants, 33% accepted, 19 enrolled. In 2009, 4 master's, 16 doctorates awarded. Terminal master's awarded for partial completion of doctoral program. *Entrance requirements:* For master's, GRE (minimum score 550 verbal); for doctorate, GRE (Verbal minimum score of 550). Additional exam requirements/recommendations for international students: Required—TOEFL (minimum score 570 paper-based). *Application deadline:* For fall admission, 1/1 priority date for domestic students, 1/1 for international students; for spring admission, 8/15 for domestic and international students. Applications are processed on a rolling basis. Application fee: $75. Electronic applications accepted. *Expenses:* Tuition: Full-time $38,100. *Financial support:* In 2009–10, 65 students received support, including 2 fellowships with full tuition reimbursements available (averaging $23,000 per year), 53 research assistantships with full tuition reimbursements available (averaging $22,000 per year), 10 teaching assistantships with full tuition reimbursements available (averaging $16,500 per year); institutionally sponsored loans and scholarships/grants also available. Financial award application deadline: 1/1. *Faculty research:* Biocatalysis, bioseparations, biotechnology, molecular modeling and simulation, advanced materials, interfacial phenomena, systems biology. Total annual research expenditures: $4.7 million. *Unit head:* Dr. Shekhar Garde, Department Head, 518-276-2511, Fax: 518-276-4030, E-mail: gardes@rpi.edu. *Application contact:* Dr. B. Wayne Bequette, Chairman, Graduate Affairs Committee, 518-276-6683, Fax: 518-276-4030, E-mail: bequette@rpi.edu.

Rice University, Graduate Programs, George R. Brown School of Engineering, Department of Chemical and Biomolecular Engineering, Houston, TX 77251-1892. Offers chemical and biomolecular engineering (MS, PhD); chemical engineering (M Ch E). Part-time programs available. *Faculty:* 12 full-time (2 women). *Students:* 69 full-time (19 women), 1 part-time (0 women); includes 5 minority (2 Asian Americans or Pacific Islanders, 3 Hispanic Americans), 49 international. Average age 24. 175 applicants, 23% accepted, 17 enrolled. In 2009, 2 master's, 9 doctorates awarded. *Degree requirements:* For master's, thesis (for some programs); for doctorate, thesis/dissertation. *Entrance requirements:* For master's and doctorate, GRE General Test, minimum GPA of 3.0. Additional exam requirements/recommendations for international students: Required—TOEFL (minimum score 600 paper-based; 250 computer-based; 90 iBT). *Application deadline:* For fall admission, 1/15 for domestic and international students. Application fee: $35. Electronic applications accepted. *Financial support:* In 2009–10, fellowships (averaging $24,000 per year), research assistantships (averaging $24,000 per year) were awarded; tuition waivers (full) also available. *Faculty research:* Thermodynamics, phase equilibria, rheology, fluid mechanics, polymers, biomedical engineering, interfacial phenomena, process control, petroleum engineering, reaction engineering and catalysis, biomaterials, metabolic engineering. *Unit head:* Christine Hughes, Department Administrator, 713-348-3424, Fax: 713-348-5478, E-mail: chbe@rice.edu. *Application contact:* Sharrm Kinnaird, Department Coordinator, 713-348-3424, Fax: 713-348-5478, E-mail: kinnaird@rice.edu.

Rose-Hulman Institute of Technology, Faculty of Engineering and Applied Sciences, Department of Chemical Engineering, Terre Haute, IN 47803-3999. Offers MS. Part-time programs available. *Faculty:* 9 full-time (2 women), 2 part-time/adjunct (0 women). *Students:* 2 full-time (1 woman). Average age 25. 2 applicants, 100% accepted, 2 enrolled. In 2009, 2 master's awarded. *Degree requirements:* For master's, thesis. *Entrance requirements:* For master's, GRE, minimum GPA of 3.0. Additional exam requirements/recommendations for international students: Required—TOEFL (minimum score 580 paper-based; 237 computer-based; 92 iBT). *Application deadline:* For fall admission, 2/1 priority date for domestic students. Applications are processed on a rolling basis. Application fee: $0. *Expenses:* Tuition: Full-time $33,900; part-time $987 per credit hour. *Financial support:* In 2009–10, 2 students received support; fellowships with full and partial tuition reimbursements available, research assistantships with full and partial tuition reimbursements available, institutionally sponsored loans, scholarships/grants, and tuition waivers (full and partial) available. *Faculty research:* Emulsification and emulsion stability, fermentation technology, adsorption and adsorption-based separations, process control. Total annual research expenditures: $108,503. *Unit head:* Dr. Mark Anklam, Chairman, 812-877-8098, Fax: 812-877-8992, E-mail: mark.r.anklam@rose-hulman.edu. *Application contact:* Dr. Daniel J. Moore, Associate Dean of the Faculty, 812-877-8110, Fax: 812-877-8061, E-mail: daniel.j.moore@rose-hulman.edu.

Rowan University, Graduate School, College of Engineering, Department of Chemical Engineering, Glassboro, NJ 08028-1701. Offers MS. Part-time and evening/weekend programs available. *Faculty:* 4 full-time (2 women). *Students:* 3 full-time (1 woman), 1 (woman) part-time; includes 1 minority (African American). Average age 23. 7 applicants, 71% accepted, 3 enrolled. In 2009, 3 master's awarded. *Degree requirements:* For master's, thesis optional. *Entrance requirements:* For master's, GRE General Test. Additional exam requirements/recommendations for international students: Required—TOEFL. *Application deadline:* Applications are processed on a rolling basis. Application fee: $50. Electronic applications accepted. *Expenses:* Tuition, state resident: full-time $10,624; part-time $590 per semester hour. Tuition, nonresident: full-time $10,624; part-time $590 per semester hour. Required fees: $2320; $125 per semester hour. *Financial support:* Research assistantships, scholarships/grants available. *Unit head:* Robert Hesketh, Chair, 856-256-5313, E-mail: hesketh@rowan.edu. *Application contact:* Dr. Ralph Dusseau, Program Adviser, 856-256-5332.

Royal Military College of Canada, Division of Graduate Studies and Research, Science Division, Department of Chemistry and Chemical and Materials Engineering, Kingston, ON K7K 7B4, Canada. Offers chemical engineering (M Eng, MA Sc, PhD); chemistry (M Sc, PhD). *Degree requirements:* For master's, thesis; for doctorate, comprehensive exam, thesis/dissertation. *Entrance requirements:* For master's, honour's degree with second-class standing; for doctorate, master's degree. Electronic applications accepted.

Rutgers, The State University of New Jersey, New Brunswick, Graduate School-New Brunswick, Program in Chemical and Biochemical Engineering, Piscataway, NJ 08854-8097. Offers MS, PhD. Part-time and evening/weekend programs available. Terminal master's awarded for partial completion of doctoral program. *Degree requirements:* For master's, thesis or alternative; for doctorate, thesis/dissertation. *Entrance requirements:* For master's and doctorate, GRE General Test. Additional exam requirements/recommendations for international students: Required—TOEFL. *Faculty research:* Biotechnology, pharmaceutical engineering, nanotechnology, process system engineering, materials and polymer science, chemical engineering sciences.

San Jose State University, Graduate Studies and Research, Charles W. Davidson College of Engineering, Department of Chemical and Materials Engineering, Program in Chemical Engineering, San Jose, CA 95192-0001. Offers MS. *Students:* 16 full-time (7 women), 48 part-time (19 women); includes 26 minority (23 Asian Americans or Pacific Islanders, 3 Hispanic Americans), 20 international. Average age 26. 61 applicants, 43% accepted, 14 enrolled. In 2009, 15 master's awarded. *Degree requirements:* For master's, thesis or alternative. *Application deadline:* For fall admission, 6/29 for domestic students; for spring admission, 11/30 for domestic students. Applications are processed on a rolling basis. Application fee: $59. Electronic applications accepted. *Financial support:* Applicants required to submit FAFSA.

South Dakota School of Mines and Technology, Graduate Division, College of Engineering, Department of Chemical and Biological Engineering, Program in Chemical Engineering, Rapid City, SD 57701-3995. Offers MS. Part-time programs available. *Faculty:* 12 full-time (2 women), 2 part-time/adjunct (0 women). *Students:* 14 full-time (3 women), 2 part-time (0 women); includes 1 minority (Hispanic American), 9 international. Average age 24. 14 applicants, 64% accepted, 7 enrolled. In 2009, 7 master's awarded. *Degree requirements:* For master's, thesis. *Entrance requirements:* For master's, GRE General Test. Additional exam requirements/recommendations for international students: Required—TOEFL, TWE. *Application deadline:* For fall admission, 7/1 priority date for domestic students, 4/1 for international students; for spring admission, 11/1 for domestic students, 9/1 for international students. Applications are processed on a rolling basis. Application fee: $35. Electronic applications accepted. *Expenses:* Tuition, state resident: full-time $3340; part-time $139 per credit hour. Tuition, nonresident: full-time $7060; part-time $294 per credit hour. Required fees: $3270. *Financial support:* In 2009–10, 2 fellowships (averaging $1,725 per year), 6 research assistantships with partial tuition reimbursements (averaging $9,950 per year), 16 teaching assistantships with partial tuition reimbursements (averaging $3,502 per year) were awarded; Federal Work-Study and

Chemical Engineering

South Dakota School of Mines and Technology (continued)
institutionally sponsored loans also available. Support available to part-time students. Financial award application deadline: 5/15. *Faculty research:* Incineration chemistry, environmental chemistry, polymer surface chemistry. Total annual research expenditures: $79,357. *Application contact:* Jeannette R. Nilson, Administrative Support Coordinator, Graduate Education, 800-454-8162 Ext. 1206, Fax: 605-394-5360, E-mail: graduate_admissions@sdsmt.edu.

Stanford University, School of Engineering, Department of Chemical Engineering, Stanford, CA 94305-9991. Offers MS, PhD, Eng. Terminal master's awarded for partial completion of doctoral program. *Degree requirements:* For doctorate, thesis/dissertation; for Eng, thesis. *Entrance requirements:* For master's, doctorate, and Eng GRE General Test. Additional exam requirements/recommendations for international students: Required—TOEFL. Electronic applications accepted. *Expenses:* Tuition: Full-time $37,380; part-time $2760 per quarter. Required fees: $501.

Stevens Institute of Technology, Graduate School, Charles V. Schaefer Jr. School of Engineering, Department of Chemical Engineering and Materials Science, Program in Chemical Engineering, Hoboken, NJ 07030. Offers M Eng, PhD, Engr. *Expenses:* Tuition: Full-time $9900; part-time $1100 per credit. Required fees: $286 per semester.

Syracuse University, L. C. Smith College of Engineering and Computer Science, Program in Chemical Engineering, Syracuse, NY 13244. Offers MS, PhD. Part-time programs available. *Students:* 17 full-time (12 women), 4 part-time (0 women); includes 1 minority (Asian American or Pacific Islander), 16 international. Average age 28. 47 applicants, 32% accepted, 6 enrolled. In 2009, 11 master's, 2 doctorates awarded. *Entrance requirements:* For master's, GRE General Test. Additional exam requirements/recommendations for international students: Required—TOEFL (minimum score 100 iBT). *Application deadline:* For fall admission, 6/1 priority date for domestic and international students. Applications are processed on a rolling basis. Application fee: $75. Electronic applications accepted. *Expenses:* Tuition: Full-time $26,808; part-time $1117 per credit. Required fees: $1024. *Financial support:* Fellowships with tuition reimbursements, research assistantships with tuition reimbursements, teaching assistantships with tuition reimbursements, tuition waivers (partial) available. Financial award application deadline: 1/1. *Unit head:* Dr. John Heydweiller, Interim Dean, 315-443-3064, E-mail: jcheydwe@syr.edu. *Application contact:* Kathleen Joyce, Director of Graduate Recruitment, 314-443-2219, E-mail: topgrads@syr.edu.

Tennessee Technological University, Graduate School, College of Engineering, Department of Chemical Engineering, Cookeville, TN 38505. Offers MS, PhD. Part-time programs available. *Faculty:* 8 full-time (0 women). *Students:* 9 full-time (2 women), 2 part-time (both women); includes 7 minority (2 African Americans, 5 Asian Americans or Pacific Islanders). Average age 26. 20 applicants, 55% accepted, 4 enrolled. In 2009, 4 master's awarded. *Degree requirements:* For master's, thesis. *Entrance requirements:* For master's, GRE General Test. Additional exam requirements/recommendations for international students: Required—TOEFL (minimum score 550 paper-based; 79 iBT), IELTS (minimum score 5.5). *Application deadline:* For fall admission, 8/1 for domestic students, 5/1 for international students; for spring admission, 12/1 for domestic students, 10/1 for international students. Application fee: $25 ($30 for international students). Electronic applications accepted. *Expenses:* Tuition, state resident: full-time $7034; part-time $368 per credit hour. *Financial support:* In 2009–10, fellowships (averaging $8,000 per year), 7 research assistantships (averaging $7,000 per year), 5 teaching assistantships (averaging $5,433 per year) were awarded; career-related internships or fieldwork also available. Financial award application deadline: 4/1. *Faculty research:* Biochemical conversion, insulation, fuel reprocessing. *Unit head:* Dr. Pedro Arce, Chairperson, 931-372-3297, Fax: 931-372-6372. *Application contact:* Shelia K. Kendrick, Coordinator of Graduate Studies, 931-372-3808, Fax: 931-372-3497, E-mail: skendrick@tntech.edu.

Texas A&M University, College of Engineering, Artie McFerrin Department of Chemical Engineering, College Station, TX 77843. Offers M Eng, MS, PhD. *Faculty:* 24. *Students:* 170 full-time (59 women), 7 part-time (2 women); includes 12 minority (4 African Americans, 1 American Indian/Alaska Native, 1 Asian American or Pacific Islander, 6 Hispanic Americans), 130 international. Average age 27. In 2009, 13 master's, 8 doctorates awarded. Terminal master's awarded for partial completion of doctoral program. *Degree requirements:* For master's, thesis (MS); for doctorate, thesis/dissertation. *Entrance requirements:* For master's and doctorate, GRE General Test. Additional exam requirements/recommendations for international students: Required—TOEFL. *Application deadline:* For fall admission, 3/1 priority date for domestic and international students; for spring admission, 10/1 priority date for domestic students, 10/1 for international students. Applications are processed on a rolling basis. Application fee: $50 ($75 for international students). Electronic applications accepted. *Expenses:* Tuition, state resident: full-time $3991.32; part-time $221.74 per credit hour. Tuition, nonresident: full-time $9049; part-time $502.74 per credit hour. *Financial support:* In 2009–10, fellowships with full tuition reimbursements (averaging $18,240 per year), research assistantships with full tuition reimbursements (averaging $17,000 per year), teaching assistantships with full tuition reimbursements (averaging $17,132 per year) were awarded; career-related internships or fieldwork, scholarships/grants, and tuition waivers (full) also available. Financial award application deadline: 3/31; financial award applicants required to submit FAFSA. *Faculty research:* Reaction engineering, interface phenomena, environmental applications, biochemical engineering, polymers. *Unit head:* Dr. Daniel Shantz, Head, 979-845-3348, E-mail: shantz@che.tamu.edu. *Application contact:* Towanna H. Hubacek, Staff Assistant, 979-845-3364, Fax: 979-845-6446, E-mail: towanna@tamu.edu.

Texas A&M University–Kingsville, College of Graduate Studies, College of Engineering, Department of Chemical Engineering and Natural Gas Engineering, Program in Chemical Engineering, Kingsville, TX 78363. Offers ME, MS. Part-time and evening/weekend programs available. *Degree requirements:* For master's, comprehensive exam, thesis or alternative. *Entrance requirements:* For master's, GRE General Test, minimum GPA of 3.0. Additional exam requirements/recommendations for international students: Required—TOEFL. *Faculty research:* Process control, error detection and reconciliation, fluid mechanics, handling of solids.

Texas Tech University, Graduate School, College of Engineering, Department of Chemical Engineering, Lubbock, TX 79409. Offers MS Ch E, PhD. Part-time programs available. *Faculty:* 8 full-time (2 women). *Students:* 48 full-time (20 women), 2 part-time (0 women); includes 1 minority (African American), 46 international. Average age 26. 117 applicants, 29% accepted, 18 enrolled. In 2009, 1 master's, 5 doctorates awarded. *Degree requirements:* For master's, thesis or alternative; for doctorate, thesis/dissertation. *Entrance requirements:* For master's and doctorate, GRE General Test, minimum GPA of 3.0. Additional exam requirements/recommendations for international students: Required—TOEFL (minimum score 550 paper-based; 213 computer-based). *Application deadline:* For fall admission, 3/1 priority date for international students; for spring admission, 11/1 priority date for international students. Applications are processed on a rolling basis. Application fee: $50 ($75 for international students). Electronic applications accepted. *Expenses:* Tuition, state resident: full-time $5100; part-time $213 per credit hour. Tuition, nonresident: full-time $11,748; part-time $490 per credit hour. Required fees: $2298; $50 per credit hour. $555 per semester. *Financial support:* In 2009–10, 4 research assistantships with tuition reimbursements (averaging $27,647 per year), 2 teaching assistantships with partial tuition reimbursements (averaging $24,975 per year) were awarded; fellowships, Federal Work-Study and institutionally sponsored loans also available. Support available to part-time students. Financial award application deadline: 4/15; financial award applicants required to submit FAFSA. *Faculty research:* Chemical process control, polymers and materials science, computational methods, bioengineering, renewable resources. Total annual research expenditures: $1.7 million. *Unit head:* Dr. M. Nazmul Karim, Chair, 806-742-3553, Fax: 806-742-3552, E-mail: naz.karim@ttu.edu. *Application contact:* Dr. M. Nazmul Karim, Chair, 806-742-3553, Fax: 806-742-3552, E-mail: naz.karim@ttu.edu.

Tufts University, School of Engineering, Department of Chemical and Biological Engineering, Medford, MA 02155. Offers ME, MS, PhD. Part-time programs available. *Faculty:* 8 full-time, 2 part-time/adjunct. *Students:* 42 (16 women); includes 4 minority (all Asian Americans or Pacific Islanders), 18 international. Average age 27. 68 applicants, 40% accepted, 8 enrolled. In 2009, 8 master's, 3 doctorates awarded. Terminal master's awarded for partial completion of doctoral program. *Degree requirements:* For master's, thesis (for some programs); for doctorate, thesis/dissertation. *Entrance requirements:* For master's and doctorate, GRE General Test. Additional exam requirements/recommendations for international students: Required—TOEFL (minimum score 550 paper-based; 213 computer-based; 80 iBT). *Application deadline:* For fall admission, 1/15 priority date for domestic students, 12/15 for international students; for spring admission, 10/15 for domestic students, 9/15 for international students. Applications are processed on a rolling basis. Application fee: $75. Electronic applications accepted. *Expenses:* Tuition: Full-time $38,096; part-time $3962 per credit. Required fees: $686; $40 per year. Tuition and fees vary according to course level, course load, degree level, program and student level. *Financial support:* Fellowships with full tuition reimbursements, research assistantships with full and partial tuition reimbursements, teaching assistantships with full and partial tuition reimbursements, Federal Work-Study, scholarships/grants, tuition waivers (partial), and unspecified assistantships available. Financial award application deadline: 1/15; financial award applicants required to submit FAFSA. *Unit head:* Dr. Kyongbum Lee, Chair, 617-627-3900. *Application contact:* Erin Quigley, Staff, 617-627-3900.

Tulane University, School of Science and Engineering, Department of Chemical and Biomolecular Engineering, New Orleans, LA 70118-5669. Offers PhD. Part-time programs available. Terminal master's awarded for partial completion of doctoral program. *Degree requirements:* For doctorate, thesis/dissertation. *Entrance requirements:* For doctorate, GRE General Test, minimum B average in undergraduate course work. Additional exam requirements/recommendations for international students: Required—TOEFL. Electronic applications accepted. *Faculty research:* Interfacial phenomena catalysis, electrochemical engineering, environmental science.

Universidad de las Américas–Puebla, Division of Graduate Studies, School of Engineering, Program in Chemical Engineering, Puebla, Mexico. Offers chemical engineering (MS); food technology (MS). Part-time and evening/weekend programs available. *Degree requirements:* For master's, one foreign language, thesis. *Faculty research:* Food science, reactors, oil industry, biotechnology.

Université de Sherbrooke, Faculty of Engineering, Department of Chemical Engineering, Sherbrooke, QC J1K 2R1, Canada. Offers M Sc A, PhD. *Degree requirements:* For master's, one foreign language, thesis; for doctorate, comprehensive exam, thesis/dissertation. *Entrance requirements:* For doctorate, master's degree in engineering or equivalent. Electronic applications accepted. *Faculty research:* Conversion processes, high-temperature plasma technologies, system engineering, environmental engineering, textile technologies.

Université Laval, Faculty of Sciences and Engineering, Department of Chemical Engineering, Programs in Chemical Engineering, Québec, QC G1K 7P4, Canada. Offers M Sc, PhD. Terminal master's awarded for partial completion of doctoral program. *Degree requirements:* For master's, thesis (for some programs); for doctorate, comprehensive exam, thesis/dissertation. *Entrance requirements:* Additional exam requirements/recommendations for international students: Required—TOEFL (minimum score 500 paper-based). Electronic applications accepted.

University at Buffalo, the State University of New York, Graduate School, School of Engineering and Applied Sciences, Department of Chemical and Biological Engineering, Buffalo, NY 14260. Offers M Eng, MS, PhD. Part-time programs available. *Faculty:* 18 full-time (1 woman), 4 part-time/adjunct (1 woman). *Students:* 95 full-time (36 women), 7 part-time (3 women); includes 6 minority (4 Asian Americans or Pacific Islanders, 2 Hispanic Americans), 81 international. Average age 26. 324 applicants, 20% accepted, 42 enrolled. In 2009, 13 master's, 7 doctorates awarded. *Degree requirements:* For master's, thesis (for some programs); for doctorate, comprehensive exam, thesis/dissertation. *Entrance requirements:* For master's and doctorate, GRE General Test. Additional exam requirements/recommendations for international students: Required—TOEFL (minimum score 550 paper-based; 213 computer-based; 79 iBT). *Application deadline:* For fall admission, 2/1 priority date for domestic and international students; for spring admission, 10/1 priority date for domestic and international students. Applications are processed on a rolling basis. Application fee: $50. Electronic applications accepted. *Financial support:* In 2009–10, 50 students received support, including 13 fellowships (averaging $30,000 per year), 34 research assistantships with full tuition reimbursements available (averaging $24,000 per year), 9 teaching assistantships with full tuition reimbursements available (averaging $20,900 per year); institutionally sponsored loans, scholarships/grants, health care benefits, tuition waivers (partial), and unspecified assistantships also available. Support available to part-time students. Financial award application deadline: 2/28; financial award applicants required to submit FAFSA. *Faculty research:* Transport, polymers, nanomaterials, biochemical engineering, catalysis. Total annual research expenditures: $9.6 million. *Unit head:* Dr. David A. Kofke, Chairman, 716-645-2911, Fax: 716-645-3822, E-mail: kofke@buffalo.edu. *Application contact:* Dr. Paschalis Alexandridis, Director of Graduate Studies, 716-645-1183, Fax: 716-645-3822, E-mail: palexand@buffalo.edu.

The University of Akron, Graduate School, College of Engineering, Department of Chemical and Biomolecular Engineering, Akron, OH 44325. Offers MS, PhD. Part-time and evening/weekend programs available. *Faculty:* 13 full-time (3 women), 1 part-time/adjunct (0 women). *Students:* 57 full-time (18 women), 9 part-time (3 women); includes 5 minority (4 Asian Americans or Pacific Islanders, 1 Hispanic American), 50 international. Average age 24. 55 applicants, 62% accepted, 8 enrolled. In 2009, 3 master's, 10 doctorates awarded. *Degree requirements:* For master's, thesis optional; for doctorate, one foreign language, thesis/dissertation, candidacy exam, qualifying exam. *Entrance requirements:* For master's, GRE General Test, minimum GPA of 2.75, letter of recommendation; for doctorate, GRE General Test, minimum GPA of 3.0 with bachelor's degree, 3.5 with master's degree; letters of recommendation; personal statement. Additional exam requirements/recommendations for international students: Required—TOEFL (minimum score 550 paper-based; 213 computer-based; 79 iBT). *Application deadline:* For fall admission, 4/1 for domestic and international students; for spring admission, 10/1 for domestic and international students. Application fee: $30 ($40 for international students). Electronic applications accepted. *Expenses:* Tuition, state resident: full-time $6570; part-time $365 per credit hour. Tuition, nonresident: full-time $11,250; part-time $625 per credit hour. *Financial support:* In 2009–10, 21 research assistantships with full tuition reimbursements, 30 teaching assistantships with full tuition reimbursements were awarded; career-related internships or fieldwork and scholarships/grants also available. *Faculty research:* Renewable energy, fuel cell and CO12 sequestration, nanofiber synthesis and applications, materials for biomedical applications, engineering, surface characterization and modification. Total annual research expenditures: $1.7 million. *Unit head:* Dr. Lu-Kwang Ju, Chair, 330-972-7252, E-mail: lukeju@uakron.edu. *Application contact:* Dr. Lu-Kwang Ju, Chair, 330-972-7252, E-mail: lukeju@uakron.edu.

The University of Alabama, Graduate School, College of Engineering, Department of Chemical and Biological Engineering, Tuscaloosa, AL 35487. Offers MS Ch E, PhD. *Faculty:* 11 full-time (3 women). *Students:* 17 full-time (4 women), 2 part-time (1 woman); includes 1 minority (Asian American or Pacific Islander), 13 international. Average age 26. 48 applicants, 29% accepted, 6 enrolled. In 2009, 3 master's, 1 doctorate awarded. Terminal master's awarded for partial completion of doctoral program. *Median time to degree:* Of those who began their doctoral program in fall 2001, 100% received their degree in 8 years or less. *Degree requirements:* For master's, comprehensive exam, thesis; for doctorate, comprehensive exam, thesis/dissertation. *Entrance requirements:* For master's, GRE, minimum GPA of 3.0 overall; for doctorate, GRE General Test or minimum GPA of 3.0. Additional exam requirements/recommendations for international students: Required—TOEFL (minimum score 550 paper-based; 213 computer-based); Recommended—IELTS (minimum score 6.5). *Application deadline:*

Applications are processed on a rolling basis. Application fee: $50 ($60 for international students). Electronic applications accepted. *Expenses:* Tuition, state resident: full-time $7000. Tuition, nonresident: full-time $19,200. *Financial support:* In 2009–10, 2 fellowships with full tuition reimbursements (averaging $22,000 per year), 14 research assistantships with full tuition reimbursements, 4 teaching assistantships with full tuition reimbursements were awarded; Federal Work-Study also available. *Faculty research:* Nanostructured materials, catalysis, alternative energy. Total annual research expenditures: $1.1 million. *Unit head:* Dr. Viola L. Acoff, Interim Head, 205-348-2080, Fax: 205-348-6579, E-mail: vacoff@eng.ua.edu. *Application contact:* Dr. Stephen M. C. Ritchie, Associate Professor, 205-348-2712, Fax: 205-348-6579, E-mail: sritchie@eng.ua.edu.

The University of Alabama in Huntsville, School of Graduate Studies, College of Engineering, Department of Chemical and Materials Engineering, Huntsville, AL 35899. Offers chemical engineering (MSE). Part-time and evening/weekend programs available. *Faculty:* 6 full-time (1 woman). *Students:* 3 full-time (0 women), 6 part-time (1 woman), 2 international. Average age 30. 12 applicants, 50% accepted, 2 enrolled. In 2009, 4 master's awarded. *Degree requirements:* For master's, comprehensive exam, thesis or alternative, oral and written exams. *Entrance requirements:* For master's, GRE General Test, appropriate bachelor's degree, minimum GPA of 3.0. Additional exam requirements/recommendations for international students: Required—TOEFL (minimum score 500 paper-based; 173 computer-based; 62 iBT). *Application deadline:* For fall admission, 7/15 for domestic students, 4/1 for international students; for spring admission, 11/30 for domestic students, 9/1 for international students. Applications are processed on a rolling basis. Application fee: $40 ($50 for international students). Electronic applications accepted. *Expenses:* Tuition, state resident: part-time $355.75 per credit hour. Tuition, nonresident: part-time $847.10 per credit hour. Required fees: $210.80 per semester. Tuition and fees vary according to course load and program. *Financial support:* In 2009–10, 3 students received support, including 1 research assistantship with full and partial tuition reimbursement available (averaging $13,000 per year), 2 teaching assistantships with full and partial tuition reimbursements available (averaging $11,174 per year); career-related internships or fieldwork, Federal Work-Study, institutionally sponsored loans, scholarships/grants, health care benefits, and unspecified assistantships also available. Support available to part-time students. Financial award application deadline: 4/1; financial award applicants required to submit FAFSA. *Faculty research:* Ultrathin films for optical, sensor and biological applications; materials processing including low gravity; hypergolic reactants; computational fluid dynamics; biofuels and renewable resources. Total annual research expenditures: $190,330. *Unit head:* Dr. Ramon Cerro, Chair, 256-824-7313, Fax: 256-824-6839, E-mail: rlc@eng.uah.edu. *Application contact:* Kathy Biggs, Graduate Studies Admissions Manager, 256-824-6199, Fax: 256-824-6405, E-mail: deangrad@uah.edu.

University of Alberta, Faculty of Graduate Studies and Research, Department of Chemical and Materials Engineering, Edmonton, AB T6G 2E1, Canada. Offers chemical engineering (M Eng, M Sc, PhD); materials engineering (M Eng, M Sc, PhD); process control (M Eng, M Sc, PhD); welding (M Eng). Part-time programs available. Postbaccalaureate distance learning degree programs offered (minimal on-campus study). *Faculty:* 30 full-time (3 women), 16 part-time/adjunct (0 women). *Students:* 60 full-time (14 women), 19 part-time (2 women). Terminal master's awarded for partial completion of doctoral program. *Degree requirements:* For master's, thesis; for doctorate, thesis/dissertation. *Application deadline:* For fall admission, 2/1 priority date for domestic students. Tuition and fees charges are reported in Canadian dollars. *Expenses:* Tuition, area resident: Full-time $4626.24 Canadian dollars; part-time $99.72 Canadian dollars per unit. International tuition: $8216 Canadian dollars full-time. Required fees: $3589.92 Canadian dollars; $99.72 Canadian dollars per unit. $215 Canadian dollars per term. *Financial support:* In 2009–10, 79 students received support, including 35 research assistantships (averaging $18,000 per year); career-related internships or fieldwork and scholarships/grants also available. *Faculty research:* Advanced materials and polymers, catalytic and reaction engineering, mineral processing, physical metallurgy, fluid mechanics. Total annual research expenditures: $4.2 million. *Unit head:* Dr. William McCaffrey, Graduate Coordinator, 780-492-1823, Fax: 403-492-2881, E-mail: chemical.materials@ualberta.ca. *Application contact:* Dr. William McCaffrey, Graduate Coordinator, 780-492-1823, Fax: 403-492-2881, E-mail: chemical.materials@ualberta.ca.

The University of Arizona, Graduate College, College of Engineering, Department of Chemical and Environmental Engineering, Program in Chemical Engineering, Tucson, AZ 85721. Offers MS, PhD. *Students:* 29 full-time (10 women), 3 part-time (0 women); includes 3 minority (1 Asian American or Pacific Islander, 2 Hispanic Americans), 23 international. Average age 27. 72 applicants, 15% accepted, 8 enrolled. In 2009, 1 master's, 7 doctorates awarded. *Entrance requirements:* For master's and doctorate, GRE, 3 letters of recommendation, resume, statement of purpose. Additional exam requirements/recommendations for international students: Required—TOEFL (minimum score 550 paper-based; 213 computer-based; 79 iBT). *Application deadline:* Applications are processed on a rolling basis. Application fee: $75. Electronic applications accepted. *Expenses:* Tuition, state resident: full-time $9028. Tuition, nonresident: full-time $24,890. *Financial support:* Unspecified assistantships available. *Unit head:* Dr. Glenn L. Schrader, Department Head, 520-621-2591, Fax: 520-621-6048, E-mail: schrader@email.arizona.edu. *Application contact:* Jo Leeming, Program Coordinator, 520-621-6044, Fax: 520-621-6048, E-mail: leeming@email.arizona.edu.

University of Arkansas, Graduate School, College of Engineering, Department of Chemical Engineering, Fayetteville, AR 72701-1201. Offers MS Ch E, MSE, PhD. Part-time programs available. *Students:* 12 full-time (6 women), 11 part-time (1 woman); includes 1 minority (American Indian/Alaska Native), 10 international. In 2009, 1 master's, 2 doctorates awarded. *Degree requirements:* For master's, thesis optional; for doctorate, one foreign language, thesis/dissertation. *Entrance requirements:* For master's and doctorate, GRE General Test. Application fee: $40 ($50 for international students). *Expenses:* Tuition, state resident: full-time $7355; part-time $356.58 per hour. Tuition, nonresident: full-time $17,401; part-time $775.17 per hour. Required fees: $1203. *Financial support:* In 2009–10, 10 fellowships with tuition reimbursements, 17 research assistantships, 1 teaching assistantship were awarded; career-related internships or fieldwork and Federal Work-Study also available. Support available to part-time students. Financial award application deadline: 4/1; financial award applicants required to submit FAFSA. *Unit head:* Dr. Tom Spicer, Department Chair, 479-575-4951, E-mail: tos@uark.edu. *Application contact:* Dr. Richard Ulrich, Graduate Coordinator, 479-575-5645, E-mail: rulrich@uark.edu.

The University of British Columbia, Faculty of Applied Science, Program in Chemical and Biological Engineering, Vancouver, BC V6T 1Z1, Canada. Offers chemical engineering (M Eng, M Sc, MA Sc, PhD). Part-time and evening/weekend programs available. *Degree requirements:* For master's, thesis (for some programs); for doctorate, thesis/dissertation. *Entrance requirements:* Additional exam requirements/recommendations for international students: Required—TOEFL, IELTS. Electronic applications accepted. *Faculty research:* Biotechnology, catalysis, polymers, fluidization, pulp and paper.

University of Calgary, Faculty of Graduate Studies, Schulich School of Engineering, Department of Chemical and Petroleum Engineering, Calgary, AB T2N 1N4, Canada. Offers M Eng, M Sc, PhD. Part-time programs available. *Degree requirements:* For master's, thesis (for some programs); for doctorate, comprehensive exam, thesis/dissertation, candidacy exam. *Entrance requirements:* For master's, minimum GPA of 3.0; for doctorate, minimum GPA of 3.5. Additional exam requirements/recommendations for international students: Required—TOEFL (minimum score 550 paper-based; 213 computer-based; 80 iBT), IELTS (minimum score 7). Electronic applications accepted. *Faculty research:* Environmental engineering, biomedical engineering modeling, simulation and control, petroleum recovery and reservoir engineering, phase equilibria and transport properties.

University of California, Berkeley, Graduate Division, College of Chemistry, Department of Chemical Engineering, Berkeley, CA 94720-1500. Offers MS, PhD. *Faculty:* 17 full-time, 2 part-time/adjunct. *Students:* 118 full-time (34 women). Average age 26. 372 applicants, 30 enrolled. In 2009, 12 master's, 14 doctorates awarded. *Degree requirements:* For master's, thesis; for doctorate, thesis/dissertation, qualifying exam. *Entrance requirements:* For master's and doctorate, GRE General Test, minimum GPA of 3.0, 3 letters of recommendation. Additional exam requirements/recommendations for international students: Required—TOEFL. *Application deadline:* For fall admission, 1/8 for domestic students. Application fee: $70 ($90 for international students). *Financial support:* Unspecified assistantships available. *Faculty research:* Biochemical engineering, electrochemical engineering, electronic materials, heterogeneous catalysis and reaction engineering, complex fluids. *Unit head:* Jeffery Reimer, Chair, 510-642-8011, E-mail: reimer@berkeley.edu. *Application contact:* Aileen Harris, Graduate Student Affairs Officer, 510-642-5882, Fax: 510-642-9675, E-mail: aileenak@berkeley.edu.

University of California, Davis, College of Engineering, Program in Chemical Engineering, Davis, CA 95616. Offers MS, PhD. Terminal master's awarded for partial completion of doctoral program. *Degree requirements:* For master's, comprehensive exam (for some programs), thesis (for some programs); for doctorate, thesis/dissertation. *Entrance requirements:* For master's and doctorate, GRE General Test, minimum GPA of 3.0. Additional exam requirements/recommendations for international students: Required—TOEFL (minimum score 550 paper-based; 213 computer-based). Electronic applications accepted. *Faculty research:* Transport phenomena, colloid science, catalysis, biotechnology, materials.

University of California, Irvine, Office of Graduate Studies, School of Engineering, Department of Chemical Engineering and Materials Science, Irvine, CA 92697. Offers chemical and biochemical engineering (MS, PhD); materials science and engineering (MS, PhD). Part-time programs available. *Students:* 78 full-time (24 women), 7 part-time (2 women); includes 22 minority (1 American Indian/Alaska Native, 19 Asian Americans or Pacific Islanders, 2 Hispanic Americans), 37 international. Average age 27. 281 applicants, 25% accepted, 25 enrolled. In 2009, 26 master's, 4 doctorates awarded. Terminal master's awarded for partial completion of doctoral program. *Degree requirements:* For doctorate, thesis/dissertation. *Entrance requirements:* For master's and doctorate, GRE General Test, minimum GPA of 3.0, 3 letters of recommendation. Additional exam requirements/recommendations for international students: Required—TOEFL (minimum score 550 paper-based; 213 computer-based). *Application deadline:* For fall admission, 1/15 priority date for domestic students, 1/15 for international students. Applications are processed on a rolling basis. Application fee: $70 ($90 for international students). Electronic applications accepted. *Financial support:* In 2009–10, fellowships with tuition reimbursements (averaging $14,656 per year); research assistantships with full tuition reimbursements, teaching assistantships with tuition reimbursements, institutionally sponsored loans, traineeships, health care benefits, and unspecified assistantships also available. Financial award application deadline: 3/1; financial award applicants required to submit FAFSA. *Faculty research:* Molecular biotechnology, nano-bio-materials, biophotonics, synthesis, superplasticity and mechanical behavior, characterization of advanced and nanostructural materials. *Unit head:* Dr. Stanley Grant, Director, 949-824-8277, Fax: 949-824-2541, E-mail: sbgrant@uci.edu. *Application contact:* Beatrice Mei, Graduate Coordinator, 949-824-3887, Fax: 949-824-2541, E-mail: bmei@uci.edu.

University of California, Los Angeles, Graduate Division, Henry Samueli School of Engineering and Applied Science, Department of Chemical and Biomolecular Engineering, Los Angeles, CA 90095-1592. Offers MS, PhD. *Faculty:* 12 full-time (2 women). *Students:* 77 full-time (28 women); includes 24 minority (1 African American, 18 Asian Americans or Pacific Islanders, 5 Hispanic Americans), 31 international. 215 applicants, 17% accepted, 20 enrolled. In 2009, 1 master's, 15 doctorates awarded. *Degree requirements:* For master's, comprehensive exam (for some programs), thesis (for some programs); for doctorate, thesis/dissertation, qualifying exams. *Entrance requirements:* For master's, GRE General Test, minimum GPA of 3.0; for doctorate, GRE General Test, minimum GPA of 3.25. Additional exam requirements/recommendations for international students: Required—TOEFL (minimum score 560 paper-based; 220 computer-based). *Application deadline:* For fall admission, 1/15 for domestic and international students. Application fee: $70 ($90 for international students). Electronic applications accepted. *Financial support:* In 2009–10, 60 fellowships, 91 research assistantships, 59 teaching assistantships were awarded; Federal Work-Study, institutionally sponsored loans, and tuition waivers (full and partial) also available. Financial award application deadline: 1/15; financial award applicants required to submit FAFSA. Total annual research expenditures: $4.8 million. *Unit head:* Dr. Harold G. Monbouquette, Chair, 310-825-8946. *Application contact:* John Berger, Student Affairs Officer, 310-825-9063, Fax: 310-206-4107, E-mail: jpberger@ea.ucla.edu.

University of California, Riverside, Graduate Division, Department of Chemical and Environmental Engineering, Riverside, CA 92521-0102. Offers MS, PhD. Part-time programs available. *Faculty:* 13 full-time (2 women), 2 part-time/adjunct (0 women). *Students:* 72 full-time (38 women); includes 6 minority (1 African American, 4 Asian Americans or Pacific Islanders, 1 Hispanic American), 52 international. Average age 27. 140 applicants, 31% accepted, 18 enrolled. In 2009, 5 master's, 13 doctorates awarded. Terminal master's awarded for partial completion of doctoral program. *Degree requirements:* For master's, thesis (for some programs); for doctorate, comprehensive exam, thesis/dissertation. *Entrance requirements:* For master's and doctorate, GRE General Test, minimum GPA of 3.0. Additional exam requirements/recommendations for international students: Required—TOEFL (minimum score 550 paper-based; 213 computer-based; 80 iBT). *Application deadline:* For fall admission, 1/5 for domestic and international students; for winter admission, 9/1 for domestic students, 7/1 for international students; for spring admission, 12/1 for domestic students, 10/1 for international students. Applications are processed on a rolling basis. Application fee: $60 ($100 for international students). Electronic applications accepted. *Financial support:* In 2009–10, fellowships with tuition reimbursements (averaging $12,000 per year), research assistantships with tuition reimbursements (averaging $18,000 per year), 2 teaching assistantships with partial tuition reimbursements (averaging $16,500 per year) were awarded; scholarships/grants, health care benefits, and unspecified assistantships also available. Financial award application deadline: 1/5; financial award applicants required to submit FAFSA. *Faculty research:* Air quality systems, water quality systems, advanced materials and nanotechnology, energy systems/alternative fuels, theory and molecular modeling. *Unit head:* Dr. Jianzhong Wu, Graduate Advisor, 951-827-2859, Fax: 951-827-5696, E-mail: gradcee@engr.ucr.edu. *Application contact:* William Suh, Graduate Student Affairs Officer, 951-827-2859, Fax: 951-827-2859, E-mail: gradcee@engr.ucr.edu.

University of California, San Diego, Office of Graduate Studies, Chemical Engineering Program, La Jolla, CA 92093. Offers MS, PhD. Part-time programs available. *Degree requirements:* For master's, thesis; for doctorate, thesis/dissertation. *Entrance requirements:* For master's and doctorate, GRE General Test. Additional exam requirements/recommendations for international students: Required—TOEFL (minimum score 550 paper-based). Electronic applications accepted. *Faculty research:* Semiconductor and composite materials processing, biochemical processing, electrochemistry and catalysis.

University of California, Santa Barbara, Graduate Division, College of Engineering, Department of Chemical Engineering, Santa Barbara, CA 93106-5080. Offers chemical engineering (MS, PhD); computational science and engineering (PhD). *Faculty:* 21 full-time (1 woman). *Students:* 69 full-time (18 women). Average age 25. 285 applicants, 23% accepted, 16 enrolled. In 2009, 2 master's, 15 doctorates awarded. Terminal master's awarded for partial completion of doctoral program. *Degree requirements:* For master's, thesis or comprehensive exam; for doctorate, thesis/dissertation, candidacy exam, dissertation defense, defense exam, seminar presentation. *Entrance requirements:* For master's, GRE General Test, 3 letters of recommendation, resume/curriculum vitae; for doctorate, GRE General Test, 3 letters of recommendation, statement of purpose, personal achievements/contributions statement, resume/curriculum vitae, transcripts for post-secondary institutions attended. Additional exam requirements/recommendations for international students: Required—TOEFL (minimum score 560 paper-based; 220 computer-based; 83 iBT) or IELTS (minimum score 7). *Application deadline:* For fall admission, 1/15 priority date for domestic and international students. Application fee: $70 ($90 for international students). Electronic applications accepted. *Financial support:*

Chemical Engineering

University of California, Santa Barbara (continued)
In 2009–10, 68 students received support, including 32 fellowships with full and partial tuition reimbursements available (averaging $8,200 per year), 63 research assistantships with full and partial tuition reimbursements available (averaging $10,800 per year), 41 teaching assistantships with partial tuition reimbursements available (averaging $3,400 per year); Federal Work-Study, institutionally sponsored loans, scholarships/grants, health care benefits, tuition waivers (full and partial), and unspecified assistantships also available. Financial award application deadline: 1/15; financial award applicants required to submit FAFSA. *Faculty research:* Fluid transport, complex fluid and polymers, biomaterials/bioengineering, catalysis and reaction engineering, systems process design and control. Total annual research expenditures: $7.4 million. *Unit head:* Prof. Michael Doherty, Chair, 805-893-5309, Fax: 805-893-4731, E-mail: mfd@engineering.ucsb.edu. *Application contact:* Laura Crownover, Student Affairs Officer, 805-893-8671, Fax: 805-893-4731, E-mail: laura@engineering.ucsb.edu.

University of Cincinnati, Graduate School, College of Engineering, Department of Chemical and Materials Engineering, Program in Chemical Engineering, Cincinnati, OH 45221. Offers MS, PhD. Part-time and evening/weekend programs available. Terminal master's awarded for partial completion of doctoral program. *Degree requirements:* For master's, thesis; for doctorate, thesis/dissertation. *Entrance requirements:* For master's and doctorate, GRE General Test. Additional exam requirements/recommendations for international students: Required—TOEFL (minimum score 600 paper-based; 250 computer-based).

University of Colorado at Boulder, Graduate School, College of Engineering and Applied Science, Department of Chemical and Biological Engineering, Boulder, CO 80309. Offers ME, MS, PhD. Part-time programs available. *Faculty:* 21 full-time (5 women). *Students:* 112 full-time (46 women), 8 part-time (3 women); includes 11 minority (1 African American, 1 American Indian/Alaska Native, 5 Asian Americans or Pacific Islanders, 4 Hispanic Americans), 19 international. Average age 26. 268 applicants, 25% accepted, 38 enrolled. In 2009, 26 master's, 15 doctorates awarded. Terminal master's awarded for partial completion of doctoral program. *Degree requirements:* For master's, comprehensive exam, thesis; for doctorate, thesis/dissertation. *Entrance requirements:* For master's, minimum undergraduate GPA of 3.0. *Application deadline:* Applications are processed on a rolling basis. Application fee: $50 ($60 for international students). Electronic applications accepted. *Financial support:* In 2009–10, 49 fellowships (averaging $18,993 per year), 43 research assistantships (averaging $13,187 per year), 34 teaching assistantships (averaging $19,546 per year) were awarded; career-related internships or fieldwork, scholarships/grants, traineeships, and tuition waivers (full) also available. *Faculty research:* Bioengineering and biotechnology, ceramic materials, fluid dynamics and fluid-article technology, heterogeneous catalysis, interfacial and surface phenomena, low-gravity fluid mechanics and materials. Total annual research expenditures: $11.2 million.

University of Connecticut, Graduate School, School of Engineering, Department of Chemical, Materials and Biomolecular Engineering, Field of Chemical Engineering, Storrs, CT 06269. Offers MS, PhD. *Faculty:* 18 full-time (1 woman). *Students:* 35 full-time (14 women), 12 part-time (3 women); includes 5 minority (1 African American, 3 Asian Americans or Pacific Islanders, 1 Hispanic American), 26 international. Average age 27. 121 applicants, 11% accepted, 7 enrolled. In 2009, 8 master's, 6 doctorates awarded. Terminal master's awarded for partial completion of doctoral program. *Degree requirements:* For master's, comprehensive exam, thesis or alternative; for doctorate, thesis/dissertation. *Entrance requirements:* For master's and doctorate, GRE General Test. Additional exam requirements/recommendations for international students: Required—TOEFL (minimum score 550 paper-based; 213 computer-based). *Application deadline:* For fall admission, 2/1 priority date for domestic and international students; for spring admission, 11/1 for domestic students, 10/1 for international students. Applications are processed on a rolling basis. Application fee: $55. Electronic applications accepted. *Expenses:* Tuition, state resident: full-time $4725; part-time $525 per credit. Tuition, nonresident: full-time $12,267; part-time $1363 per credit. Required fees: $346 per semester. Tuition and fees vary according to course load. *Financial support:* In 2009–10, 28 research assistantships with full tuition reimbursements, 3 teaching assistantships with full tuition reimbursements were awarded; fellowships, Federal Work-Study, scholarships/grants, health care benefits, and unspecified assistantships also available. Financial award application deadline: 2/1; financial award applicants required to submit FAFSA. *Unit head:* Richard Parnas, Program Director, 860-486-9060, E-mail: rparnas@mail.ims.uconn.edu. *Application contact:* Susan Soucy, Administrative Assistant, 860-486-4020, E-mail: chenginfo@enr.uconn.edu.

University of Dayton, Graduate School, School of Engineering, Department of Chemical Engineering, Dayton, OH 45469-1300. Offers MS Ch E. Part-time and evening/weekend programs available. *Faculty:* 6 full-time (0 women), 5 part-time/adjunct (1 woman). *Students:* 12 full-time (2 women), 6 part-time (0 women); includes 4 minority (2 African Americans, 1 Asian American or Pacific Islander, 1 Hispanic American), 9 international. Average age 27. 18 applicants, 44% accepted, 6 enrolled. In 2009, 4 master's awarded. *Degree requirements:* For master's, thesis optional. *Entrance requirements:* Additional exam requirements/recommendations for international students: Required—TOEFL. *Application deadline:* For fall admission, 8/1 priority date for domestic students. Applications are processed on a rolling basis. Application fee: $0. Electronic applications accepted. *Expenses:* Tuition: Full-time $8412; part-time $701 per credit hour. Required fees: $325; $65 per course. $25 per semester. Tuition and fees vary according to course load, degree level and program. *Financial support:* In 2009–10, 6 research assistantships with full tuition reimbursements (averaging $12,000 per year) were awarded. Financial award applicants required to submit FAFSA. *Faculty research:* Vertically-aligned carbon nanotubes infiltrated with temperature-responsive polymers: smart nanocomposite films for self-cleaning and controlled release, bilayer and bulk heterojunction solar cells using liquid crystalline porphyrins as donors by solution processing, DNA damage induced by multiwalled carbon nanotubes in mouse embryonic stem cells. Total annual research expenditures: $1.5 million. *Unit head:* Dr. Robert Wilkins, Chair, 937-229-2627, E-mail: robert.wilkins@notes.udayton.edu. *Application contact:* Graduate Admissions, 937-229-4411, Fax: 937-229-4729, E-mail: gradadmission@udayton.edu.

University of Delaware, College of Engineering, Department of Chemical Engineering, Newark, DE 19716. Offers M Ch E, PhD. Part-time and evening/weekend programs available. Postbaccalaureate distance learning degree programs offered (minimal on-campus study). Terminal master's awarded for partial completion of doctoral program. *Degree requirements:* For master's, thesis (for some programs); for doctorate, thesis/dissertation. *Entrance requirements:* For master's and doctorate, GRE General Test. Additional exam requirements/recommendations for international students: Required—TOEFL. Electronic applications accepted. *Faculty research:* Biochemical/biomedical engineer, thermodynamics, polymers/composites, materials, catalysis/reactions, colloid/interfaces, expert systems/process control.

University of Florida, Graduate School, College of Engineering, Department of Chemical Engineering, Gainesville, FL 32611. Offers ME, MS, PhD. Part-time programs available. *Degree requirements:* For master's, thesis (for some programs); for doctorate, thesis/dissertation. *Entrance requirements:* For master's and doctorate, GRE General Test, minimum GPA of 3.0. Additional exam requirements/recommendations for international students: Required—TOEFL (minimum score 550 paper-based; 213 computer-based). Electronic applications accepted. *Faculty research:* Microelectronics, polymeric and biochemical materials, applied control theory, electrochemical and surface sciences.

University of Houston, Cullen College of Engineering, Chemical and Biomolecular Engineering, Houston, TX 77204. Offers M Pet E, MCHE, MS Ch E, MS Pet E, PhD. Part-time and evening/weekend programs available. *Faculty:* 14 full-time (1 woman), 14 part-time/adjunct (0 women). *Students:* 98 full-time (28 women), 56 part-time (10 women); includes 33 minority (6 African Americans, 20 Asian Americans or Pacific Islanders, 7 Hispanic Americans), 86 international. Average age 28. 322 applicants, 27% accepted, 39 enrolled. In 2009, 35 master's, 11 doctorates awarded. Terminal master's awarded for partial completion of doctoral program. *Entrance requirements:* For master's and doctorate, GRE General Test. Additional exam requirements/recommendations for international students: Required—TOEFL (minimum score 550 paper-based; 79 iBT), IELTS (minimum score 6.5). *Application deadline:* For fall admission, 2/15 for domestic and international students. Application fee: $25 ($75 for international students). *Expenses:* Tuition, state resident: full-time $7676; part-time $320 per credit hour. Tuition, nonresident: full-time $14,324; part-time $597 per credit hour. Required fees: $3034. *Financial support:* In 2009–10, 1 fellowship with full tuition reimbursement (averaging $19,800 per year), 44 research assistantships with full tuition reimbursements (averaging $15,800 per year), 16 teaching assistantships with full tuition reimbursements (averaging $15,800 per year) were awarded; career-related internships or fieldwork, Federal Work-Study, institutionally sponsored loans, scholarships/grants, health care benefits, and unspecified assistantships also available. Support available to part-time students. Financial award application deadline: 2/1. *Faculty research:* Chemical engineering. *Unit head:* Dr. Ramanan Krishnamoorti, Chairman, 713-743-4304, Fax: 713-743-4323, E-mail: ramanan@uh.edu. *Application contact:* Yolanda Thomas, Academic Advisor, 713-743-4311, Fax: 713-743-4323, E-mail: ythomas@uh.edu.

University of Idaho, College of Graduate Studies, College of Engineering, Department of Chemical Engineering, Moscow, ID 83844-2282. Offers M Engr, MS, PhD. *Faculty:* 10 full-time. *Students:* 10 full-time, 6 part-time. In 2009, 4 master's, 1 doctorate awarded. *Degree requirements:* For master's, thesis; for doctorate, one foreign language, thesis/dissertation. *Entrance requirements:* For master's, GRE, minimum GPA of 2.8; for doctorate, GRE, minimum undergraduate GPA of 2.8, 3.0 graduate. *Application deadline:* For fall admission, 8/1 for domestic students; for spring admission, 12/15 for domestic students. Application fee: $55 ($60 for international students). *Expenses:* Tuition, state resident: full-time $6120. Tuition, nonresident: full-time $17,712. *Financial support:* Fellowships, research assistantships, teaching assistantships available. Financial award application deadline: 2/15. *Faculty research:* Geothermal energy utilization, alcohol production from agriculture waste material, energy conservation in pulp and paper mills. *Unit head:* Dr. Wudneh Admassu, 208-885-7572. *Application contact:* Dr. Wudneh Admassu, 208-885-7572.

University of Illinois at Chicago, Graduate College, College of Engineering, Department of Chemical Engineering, Chicago, IL 60607-7128. Offers MS, PhD. Part-time programs available. *Degree requirements:* For master's, thesis or project; for doctorate, thesis/dissertation, departmental qualifying exam. *Entrance requirements:* For master's and doctorate, GRE General Test, minimum GPA of 2.75. Additional exam requirements/recommendations for international students: Required—TOEFL. *Faculty research:* Multiphase flows, interfacial transport, heterogeneous catalysis, coal technology, molecular and static thermodynamics.

University of Illinois at Urbana–Champaign, Graduate College, College of Liberal Arts and Sciences, School of Chemical Sciences, Department of Chemical and Biomolecular Engineering, Champaign, IL 61820. Offers bioinformatics: chemical and biomolecular engineering (MS); chemical engineering (MS, PhD). *Faculty:* 16 full-time (2 women). *Students:* 115 full-time (47 women), 4 part-time (0 women); includes 15 minority (3 African Americans, 9 Asian Americans or Pacific Islanders, 3 Hispanic Americans), 63 international. 381 applicants, 21% accepted, 28 enrolled. In 2009, 6 master's, 20 doctorates awarded. *Entrance requirements:* For master's and doctorate, GRE, minimum GPA of 3.0. Additional exam requirements/recommendations for international students: Required—TOEFL (minimum score 610 paper-based; 257 computer-based). *Application deadline:* Applications are processed on a rolling basis. Application fee: $60 ($75 for international students). Electronic applications accepted. *Financial support:* In 2009–10, 23 fellowships, 106 research assistantships, 40 teaching assistantships were awarded; tuition waivers (full and partial) also available. *Unit head:* Edmund Seebauer, Head, 217-244-9214, Fax: 217-333-5052, E-mail: eseebaue@illinois.edu. *Application contact:* Cathy Paceley, Office Manager, 217-333-3640, Fax: 217-333-5052, E-mail: paceley@illinois.edu.

The University of Iowa, Graduate College, College of Engineering, Department of Chemical and Biochemical Engineering, Iowa City, IA 52242-1316. Offers MS, PhD. Part-time programs available. *Faculty:* 11 full-time (3 women), 1 (woman) part-time/adjunct. *Students:* 40 full-time (16 women); includes 5 minority (4 African Americans, 1 Asian American or Pacific Islander), 17 international. Average age 28. 67 applicants, 22% accepted, 11 enrolled. In 2009, 5 master's, 6 doctorates awarded. *Degree requirements:* For master's, comprehensive exam (for some programs), thesis (for some programs); for doctorate, comprehensive exam, thesis/dissertation. *Entrance requirements:* For master's and doctorate, GRE, minimum undergraduate GPA of 3.0. Additional exam requirements/recommendations for international students: Required—TOEFL (minimum score 550 paper-based; 213 computer-based). *Application deadline:* For fall admission, 2/1 for domestic and international students; for spring admission, 10/1 for domestic and international students. Applications are processed on a rolling basis. Application fee: $60 ($100 for international students). Electronic applications accepted. *Financial support:* In 2009–10, 4 fellowships with partial tuition reimbursements (averaging $16,300 per year), 30 research assistantships with partial tuition reimbursements (averaging $21,368 per year), 12 teaching assistantships with partial tuition reimbursements (averaging $19,493 per year) were awarded; unspecified assistantships also available. Financial award applicants required to submit FAFSA. *Faculty research:* Polymeric materials; photopolymerization; atmospheric chemistry and air pollution; biochemical engineering; bioprocessing and biomedical engineering. Total annual research expenditures: $2.2 million. *Unit head:* Dr. David W. Murhammer, Departmental Executive Officer, 319-335-1228, Fax: 319-335-1415, E-mail: david-murhammer@uiowa.edu. *Application contact:* Natalie Potter, Secretary, 319-335-1215, Fax: 319-335-1415, E-mail: chemeng@engineering.uiowa.edu.

The University of Kansas, Graduate Studies, School of Engineering, Department of Chemical and Petroleum Engineering, Lawrence, KS 66045. Offers chemical engineering (MS); chemical/petroleum engineering (PhD); petroleum engineering (MS). Part-time programs available. *Faculty:* 15 full-time (3 women). *Students:* 55 full-time (25 women); includes 2 minority (1 Asian American or Pacific Islander, 1 Hispanic American), 41 international. Average age 28. 70 applicants, 30% accepted, 16 enrolled. In 2009, 6 master's, 7 doctorates awarded. *Degree requirements:* For master's, thesis (for some programs), exam; for doctorate, comprehensive exam, thesis/dissertation, qualifying exams. *Entrance requirements:* For master's, GRE General Test, minimum GPA of 3.0; for doctorate, GRE General Test, minimum GPA of 3.5. Additional exam requirements/recommendations for international students: Required—TOEFL. *Application deadline:* For fall admission, 1/10 priority date for domestic students, 1/10 for international students; for spring admission, 6/10 priority date for domestic students, 6/10 for international students. Applications are processed on a rolling basis. Application fee: $45 ($55 for international students). Electronic applications accepted. *Expenses:* Tuition, state resident: full-time $6492; part-time $270.50 per credit hour. Tuition, nonresident: full-time $15,510; part-time $646.25 per credit hour. Required fees: $847; $70.56 per credit hour. Tuition and fees vary according to course load and program. *Financial support:* Fellowships, research assistantships with full and partial tuition reimbursements, teaching assistantships with full and partial tuition reimbursements, career-related internships or fieldwork, Federal Work-Study, scholarships/grants, traineeships, and unspecified assistantships available. Financial award application deadline: 1/31; financial award applicants required to submit FAFSA. *Faculty research:* Enhanced oil recovery, catalysis and kinetics, electrochemical engineering, biomedical engineering, semiconductor materials processing. *Unit head:* Prof. Laurence Weatherley, Chairperson, 785-864-4965, Fax: 785-864-4967, E-mail: lweather@ku.edu. *Application contact:* Prof. Marylee Southard, Graduate Recruiting Officer, 785-864-4965, Fax: 785-864-4967, E-mail: marylee@ku.edu.

University of Kentucky, Graduate School, College of Engineering, Program in Chemical Engineering, Lexington, KY 40506-0032. Offers MS, PhD. *Degree requirements:* For master's, comprehensive exam, thesis optional; for doctorate, comprehensive exam, thesis/dissertation. *Entrance requirements:* For master's, GRE General Test, minimum undergraduate GPA of 2.75; for doctorate, GRE General Test, minimum undergraduate GPA of 3.0. Additional exam requirements/recommendations for international students: Required—TOEFL (minimum score 550 paper-based; 213 computer-based). Electronic applications accepted. *Faculty research:* Aerosol physics and chemistry, biocellular engineering fuel science, poly and membrane science.

University of Louisiana at Lafayette, College of Engineering, Department of Chemical Engineering, Lafayette, LA 70504. Offers MSE. Evening/weekend programs available. *Degree requirements:* For master's, comprehensive exam, thesis or alternative. *Entrance requirements:* For master's, GRE General Test, BS in chemical engineering, minimum GPA of 2.85. Additional exam requirements/recommendations for international students: Required—TOEFL (minimum score 550 paper-based; 213 computer-based). Electronic applications accepted. *Faculty research:* Corrosion, transport phenomena and thermodynamics in the oil and gas industry.

University of Louisville, J.B. Speed School of Engineering, Department of Chemical Engineering, Louisville, KY 40292-0001. Offers M Eng, MS, PhD. *Accreditation:* ABET (one or more programs are accredited). Part-time programs available. *Faculty:* 8 full-time (1 woman). *Students:* 36 full-time (9 women), 8 part-time (3 women); includes 3 minority (2 African Americans, 1 Asian American or Pacific Islander), 18 international. Average age 26. 25 applicants, 52% accepted, 4 enrolled. In 2009, 15 master's, 3 doctorates awarded. Terminal master's awarded for partial completion of doctoral program. *Degree requirements:* For master's, comprehensive exam (for some programs), thesis or alternative; for doctorate, comprehensive exam, thesis/dissertation, minimum GPA of 3.0. *Entrance requirements:* For master's and doctorate, GRE General Test. Additional exam requirements/recommendations for international students: Required—TOEFL (minimum score 550 paper-based; 213 computer-based; 80 iBT). *Application deadline:* For fall admission, 7/12 priority date for domestic and international students; for winter admission, 11/29 priority date for domestic and international students; for spring admission, 3/28 priority date for domestic and international students. Applications are processed on a rolling basis. Application fee: $50. Electronic applications accepted. *Financial support:* In 2009–10, 18 students received support, including 5 fellowships with full tuition reimbursements available (averaging $20,000 per year), 8 research assistantships with full tuition reimbursements available (averaging $20,000 per year), 5 teaching assistantships with full tuition reimbursements available (averaging $20,000 per year). Financial award application deadline: 1/25; financial award applicants required to submit FAFSA. *Faculty research:* Mixing in chemical and biochemical systems; nanomaterials processing; nanoparticles; surface science; materials including polymers, thin films, and rapid prototyping. Total annual research expenditures: $1.7 million. *Unit head:* Dr. James C. Waters, Chair, 502-852-6347, Fax: 502-852-6355, E-mail: jcwatt01@louisville.edu. *Application contact:* Dr. Michael Day, Associate Dean, 502-852-6195, Fax: 502-852-7294, E-mail: day@louisville.edu.

University of Maine, Graduate School, College of Engineering, Department of Chemical and Biological Engineering, Program in Chemical Engineering, Orono, ME 04469. Offers MS, PhD. Part-time programs available. *Students:* 9 full-time (1 woman), 8 part-time (2 women); includes 1 minority (American Indian/Alaska Native), 11 international. Average age 28. 24 applicants, 29% accepted, 2 enrolled. In 2009, 3 doctorates awarded. Terminal master's awarded for partial completion of doctoral program. *Degree requirements:* For master's, thesis; for doctorate, thesis/dissertation. *Entrance requirements:* For master's and doctorate, GRE General Test. Additional exam requirements/recommendations for international students: Required—TOEFL. *Application deadline:* For fall admission, 2/1 priority date for domestic students. Applications are processed on a rolling basis. Application fee: $65. Electronic applications accepted. *Financial support:* Federal Work-Study and tuition waivers (full and partial) available. Financial award application deadline: 3/1. *Unit head:* Dr. Douglas Bousfield, Coordinator, 207-581-2300, Fax: 207-581-2725. *Application contact:* Scott G. Delcourt, Associate Dean of the Graduate School, 207-581-3291, Fax: 207-581-3232, E-mail: graduate@maine.edu.

University of Maryland, Baltimore County, Graduate School, College of Engineering and Information Technology, Department of Chemical and Biochemical Engineering, Program in Chemical and Biochemical Engineering, Baltimore, MD 21250. Offers MS, PhD. Part-time programs available. *Students:* 24 full-time (12 women), 5 part-time (3 women); includes 5 minority (1 African American, 3 Asian Americans or Pacific Islanders, 1 Hispanic American), 20 international. Average age 25. 38 applicants, 39% accepted, 9 enrolled. In 2009, 10 master's, 3 doctorates awarded. *Degree requirements:* For master's, comprehensive exam (for some programs), thesis (for some programs); for doctorate, comprehensive exam, thesis/dissertation. *Entrance requirements:* For master's, GRE General Test, minimum GPA of 3.0; for doctorate, GRE General Test (within last 5 years), GRE Subject Test, minimum GPA of 3.0. Additional exam requirements/recommendations for international students: Required—TOEFL (minimum score 550 paper-based; 213 computer-based; 80 iBT). *Application deadline:* For fall admission, 6/1 for domestic students, 1/1 for international students; for spring admission, 11/1 for domestic students, 6/1 for international students. Applications are processed on a rolling basis. Application fee: $50. Electronic applications accepted. *Financial support:* In 2009–10, 3 students received support, including 1 fellowship with full tuition reimbursement available (averaging $24,000 per year), 14 research assistantships with full tuition reimbursements available (averaging $22,000 per year), 8 teaching assistantships with full tuition reimbursements available (averaging $21,000 per year); career-related internships or fieldwork, Federal Work-Study, scholarships/grants, health care benefits, tuition waivers (partial), and unspecified assistantships also available. Support available to part-time students. Financial award application deadline: 6/30; financial award applicants required to submit FAFSA. *Faculty research:* Biomaterials engineering, cellular engineering, sensor technology, systems biology and functional genomics, engineering education and outreach. *Unit head:* Dr. Julia M. Ross, Professor and Chair. *Application contact:* Dr. Mark Marten, Professor and Graduate Program Director, 410-455-3439, Fax: 410-455-1049, E-mail: marten@umbc.edu.

University of Maryland, College Park, Academic Affairs, A. James Clark School of Engineering, Department of Chemical and Biomolecular Engineering, College Park, MD 20742. Offers bioengineering (MS, PhD); chemical engineering (M Eng, MS, PhD). Part-time and evening/weekend programs available. *Faculty:* 21 full-time (3 women). *Students:* 45 full-time (14 women), 5 part-time (2 women); includes 8 minority (3 African Americans, 3 Asian Americans or Pacific Islanders, 2 Hispanic Americans), 34 international. 152 applicants, 17% accepted, 10 enrolled. In 2009, 1 master's, 8 doctorates awarded. *Degree requirements:* For master's, thesis optional; for doctorate, variable foreign language requirement, thesis/dissertation, exam, oral presentation. *Entrance requirements:* For master's and doctorate, GRE General Test, 3 letters of recommendation. Additional exam requirements/recommendations for international students: Required—TOEFL. *Application deadline:* For fall admission, 1/15 for domestic students, 2/1 for international students; for spring admission, 6/1 for domestic and international students. Applications are processed on a rolling basis. Application fee: $60. Electronic applications accepted. *Expenses:* Tuition, area resident: Part-time $471 per credit hour. Tuition, state resident: part-time $471 per credit hour. Tuition, nonresident: part-time $1016 per credit hour. Required fees: $337.04 per term. *Financial support:* In 2009–10, 1 fellowship with partial tuition reimbursement (averaging $10,341 per year), 26 research assistantships with tuition reimbursements (averaging $23,318 per year), 6 teaching assistantships with tuition reimbursements (averaging $22,152 per year) were awarded; Federal Work-Study and scholarships/grants also available. Support available to part-time students. Financial award applicants required to submit FAFSA. *Faculty research:* Applied polymer science, biochemical engineering, thermal properties, bioprocess monitoring. Total annual research expenditures: $1.1 million. *Unit head:* Francis Joseph Schork, Chair and Professor, 301-405-1074, E-mail: fjschork@umd.edu. *Application contact:* Dr., Dean of Graduate School, 301-405-0376, Fax: 301-314-9305, E-mail: admociti@umd.edu.

University of Maryland, College Park, Academic Affairs, A. James Clark School of Engineering, Department of Continuing and Distance Learning in Engineering, Professional Program in Engineering, College Park, MD 20742. Offers aerospace engineering (M Eng); chemical engineering (M Eng); civil engineering (M Eng); electrical engineering (M Eng); engineering (Certificate); fire protection engineering (M Eng); materials science and engineering (M Eng); mechanical engineering (M Eng); reliability engineering (M Eng); systems engineering (M Eng). Part-time and evening/weekend programs available. Postbaccalaureate distance learning degree programs offered. *Students:* 50 full-time (15 women), 234 part-time (41 women); includes 91 minority (36 African Americans, 39 Asian Americans or Pacific Islanders, 16 Hispanic Americans), 45 international. 137 applicants, 69% accepted, 77 enrolled. In 2009, 103 master's awarded. *Entrance requirements:* For master's, 3 letters of recommendation. *Application deadline:* For fall admission, 8/15 for domestic students, 1/10 for international students; for spring admission, 12/15 for domestic students, 6/1 for international students. Applications are processed on a rolling basis. Application fee: $60. Electronic applications accepted. *Expenses:* Tuition, area resident: Part-time $471 per credit hour. Tuition, state resident: part-time $471 per credit hour. Tuition, nonresident: part-time $1016 per credit hour. Required fees: $337.04 per term. *Financial support:* In 2009–10, 2 research assistantships with tuition reimbursements (averaging $19,561 per year), 9 teaching assistantships with tuition reimbursements (averaging $16,849 per year) were awarded; fellowships, Federal Work-Study and scholarships/grants also available. Support available to part-time students. Financial award applicants required to submit FAFSA. *Unit head:* Dr. George Syrmos, Director, 301-405-3633, Fax: 301-314-3305, E-mail: syrmos@umd.edu. *Application contact:* Dean of Graduate School, 301-405-0376, Fax: 301-314-9305.

University of Massachusetts Amherst, Graduate School, College of Engineering, Department of Chemical Engineering, Amherst, MA 01003. Offers MS, PhD. Part-time programs available. *Faculty:* 18 full-time (2 women). *Students:* 71 full-time (19 women), 4 part-time (1 woman); includes 2 minority (both Asian Americans or Pacific Islanders), 45 international. Average age 26. 207 applicants, 20% accepted, 21 enrolled. In 2009, 1 master's, 10 doctorates awarded. Terminal master's awarded for partial completion of doctoral program. *Degree requirements:* For master's, thesis; for doctorate, comprehensive exam, thesis/dissertation. *Entrance requirements:* For master's and doctorate, GRE General Test. Additional exam requirements/recommendations for international students: Required—TOEFL (minimum score 550 paper-based; 213 computer-based; 80 iBT), IELTS (minimum score 6.5). *Application deadline:* For fall admission, 1/15 for domestic and international students. Applications are processed on a rolling basis. Application fee: $50 ($65 for international students). Electronic applications accepted. *Expenses:* Tuition, state resident: full-time $2640; part-time $110 per credit. Tuition, nonresident: full-time $9936; part-time $414 per credit. Tuition and fees vary according to course load. *Financial support:* In 2009–10, 5 fellowships with full tuition reimbursements (averaging $25,620 per year), 58 research assistantships with full tuition reimbursements (averaging $20,504 per year), 6 teaching assistantships with full tuition reimbursements (averaging $9,469 per year) were awarded; career-related internships or fieldwork, Federal Work-Study, scholarships/grants, traineeships, health care benefits, tuition waivers, and unspecified assistantships also available. Support available to part-time students. Financial award application deadline: 1/15; financial award applicants required to submit FAFSA. *Unit head:* Dr. T. J. Mountziaris, Graduate Program Director, 413-545-6164, Fax: 413-545-1647. *Application contact:* Jean M. Ames, Supervisor of Admissions, 413-545-0722, Fax: 413-577-0010, E-mail: gradadm@grad.umass.edu.

University of Massachusetts Lowell, James B. Francis College of Engineering, Department of Chemical Engineering, Lowell, MA 01854-2881. Offers MS Eng; D Eng, PhD. Part-time programs available. *Degree requirements:* For master's, thesis; for doctorate, thesis/dissertation, seminar, qualifying examination. *Entrance requirements:* For master's, GRE General Test. Electronic applications accepted. *Faculty research:* Biotechnology/bioprocessing, nanomaterials, ceramic materials, materials characterization.

University of Michigan, Horace H. Rackham School of Graduate Studies, College of Engineering, Department of Chemical Engineering, Ann Arbor, MI 48109. Offers MSE, PhD, Ch E. Part-time programs available. Postbaccalaureate distance learning degree programs offered (no on-campus study). *Faculty:* 20 full-time (4 women). *Students:* 100 full-time (29 women), 5 part-time (0 women); includes 16 minority (3 African Americans, 11 Asian Americans or Pacific Islanders, 2 Hispanic Americans), 39 international. 209 applicants, 33% accepted, 16 enrolled. In 2009, 17 master's, 9 doctorates awarded. Terminal master's awarded for partial completion of doctoral program. *Degree requirements:* For doctorate, thesis/dissertation, oral defense of dissertation, preliminary exams. *Entrance requirements:* For master's and doctorate, GRE General Test. Additional exam requirements/recommendations for international students: Required—TOEFL (minimum score 600 paper-based; 250 computer-based). *Application deadline:* Applications are processed on a rolling basis. Application fee: $60 ($75 for international students). Electronic applications accepted. *Expenses:* Tuition, state resident: full-time $17,286; part-time $1099 per credit hour. Tuition, nonresident: full-time $34,944; part-time $2080 per credit hour. Required fees: $95 per semester. Tuition and fees vary according to course load, degree level and program. *Financial support:* Fellowships, research assistantships, teaching assistantships, scholarships/grants, traineeships, health care benefits, tuition waivers (partial), and unspecified assistantships available. Financial award applicants required to submit FAFSA. *Faculty research:* Life sciences and biotechnology, energy and environment, complex fluids and nanostructured materials. *Unit head:* Mark Burns, Department Chair, 734-764-1516, E-mail: maburns@umich.edu. *Application contact:* Sue Hamlin, Department Office, 734-763-1148, Fax: 734-764-7453, E-mail: hamlins@umich.edu.

University of Minnesota, Twin Cities Campus, Institute of Technology, Department of Chemical Engineering and Materials Science, Program in Chemical Engineering, Minneapolis, MN 55455-0132. Offers M Ch E, MS Ch E, PhD. Part-time programs available. Terminal master's awarded for partial completion of doctoral program. *Degree requirements:* For master's, thesis; for doctorate, thesis/dissertation. *Entrance requirements:* For master's and doctorate, GRE General Test. *Faculty research:* Chemical kinetics, reaction engineering and modeling, gas and membrane separation processes, biochemical engineering, nonequilibrium statistical mechanics.

University of Missouri, Graduate School, College of Engineering, Department of Chemical Engineering, Columbia, MO 65211. Offers MS, PhD. *Degree requirements:* For master's, thesis; for doctorate, thesis/dissertation. *Entrance requirements:* For master's and doctorate, GRE General Test, minimum GPA of 3.0. Additional exam requirements/recommendations for international students: Required—TOEFL (minimum score 550 paper-based; 213 computer-based; 80 iBT).

University of Nebraska–Lincoln, Graduate College, College of Engineering, Department of Chemical and Biomolecular Engineering, Lincoln, NE 68588. Offers MS, PhD. *Degree requirements:* For master's, thesis; for doctorate, comprehensive exam, thesis/dissertation. *Entrance requirements:* For master's and doctorate, GRE. Additional exam requirements/recommendations for international students: Required—TOEFL (minimum score 550 paper-based; 213 computer-based). Electronic applications accepted. *Faculty research:* Fermentation, radioactive waste remediation, chemical fuels from renewable feedstocks.

University of Nebraska–Lincoln, Graduate College, College of Engineering, Department of Mechanical Engineering, Lincoln, NE 68588. Offers chemical and materials engineering (PhD); mechanical engineering (MS, PhD), including materials science engineering (MS), metallurgical engineering (MS). *Degree requirements:* For master's, thesis optional; for doctorate, comprehensive exam, thesis/dissertation. *Entrance requirements:* For master's and doctorate, GRE General Test. Additional exam requirements/recommendations for international students: Required—TOEFL (minimum score 550 paper-based; 213 computer-based). Electronic applications accepted. *Faculty research:* Robotics for planetary exploration, vehicle crashworthiness, transient heat conduction, laser beam/particle interactions.

See Close-Up on page 527.

University of Nevada, Reno, Graduate School, College of Engineering, Department of Chemical and Materials Engineering, Program in Chemical Engineering, Reno, NV 89557. Offers MS, PhD. Terminal master's awarded for partial completion of doctoral program. *Degree requirements:* For master's, comprehensive exam, thesis optional; for doctorate, thesis/dissertation. *Entrance requirements:* For master's, GRE General Test, minimum GPA of 2.75; for doctorate, GRE General Test, minimum GPA of 3.0. Additional exam requirements/recommendations for international students: Required—TOEFL (minimum score 500 paper-based; 173 computer-based; 61 iBT), IELTS (minimum score 6). Electronic applications accepted. *Faculty research:* Energy conservation, fuel efficiency, development and fabrication of new materials.

Chemical Engineering

University of New Brunswick Fredericton, School of Graduate Studies, Faculty of Engineering, Department of Chemical Engineering, Fredericton, NB E3B 5A3, Canada. Offers M Eng, M Sc E, PhD. Part-time programs available. *Faculty:* 10 full-time (3 women), 6 part-time/adjunct (0 women). *Students:* 47 full-time (22 women), 9 part-time (0 women). In 2009, 7 master's, 1 doctorate awarded. *Degree requirements:* For master's, thesis; for doctorate, comprehensive exam, thesis/dissertation, qualifying exam. *Entrance requirements:* For master's, minimum GPA of 3.0; for doctorate, Ph.D. Qualifying Exam, minimum GPA of 3.0. Additional exam requirements/recommendations for international students: Required—TOEFL (minimum score 580 paper-based), TWE (minimum score 4). *Application deadline:* For fall admission, 3/1 priority date for domestic students. Application fee: $50 Canadian dollars. Electronic applications accepted. Tuition and fees charges are reported in Canadian dollars. *Expenses:* Tuition, area resident: Full-time $5562 Canadian dollars; part-time $2781 Canadian dollars per year. Required fees: $49.75 Canadian dollars per term. *Financial support:* In 2009–10, 19 research assistantships with tuition reimbursements (averaging $18,000 per year), 47 teaching assistantships (averaging $1,500 per year) were awarded. *Faculty research:* Processing and characterizing nanoengineered composite materials based on carbon nanotubes; enhanced oil recovery processes and oil sweep strategies for conventional and heavy oils; pulp and paper; wastewater treatment; chemistry and corrosion of high and lower temperature water systems. *Unit head:* Dr. Yonghao Ni, Director of Graduate Studies, 506-451-6857, Fax: 506-453-3591, E-mail: yonghao@unb.ca. *Application contact:* Sylvia Demerson, Graduate Secretary, 506-453-4520, Fax: 506-453-3591, E-mail: sdemerso@unb.ca.

University of New Hampshire, Graduate School, College of Engineering and Physical Sciences, Department of Chemical Engineering, Durham, NH 03824. Offers MS, PhD. *Faculty:* 7 full-time (1 woman). *Students:* 3 full-time (1 woman), 9 part-time (2 women); includes 1 minority (African American), 6 international. Average age 27. 17 applicants, 76% accepted, 5 enrolled. In 2009, 5 master's awarded. *Degree requirements:* For master's, thesis; for doctorate, thesis/dissertation. *Entrance requirements:* For master's and doctorate, GRE. Additional exam requirements/recommendations for international students: Required—TOEFL (minimum score 550 paper-based; 213 computer-based). *Application deadline:* For fall admission, 6/1 priority date for domestic students, 4/1 for international students; for spring admission, 12/1 for domestic students. Applications are processed on a rolling basis. Application fee: $65. Electronic applications accepted. *Expenses:* Tuition, state resident: full-time $10,380; part-time $577 per credit hour. Tuition, nonresident: full-time $24,350; part-time $1002 per credit hour. Required fees: $1550; $387.50 per semester. Tuition and fees vary according to course load and program. *Financial support:* In 2009–10, 8 students received support, including 1 research assistantship, 7 teaching assistantships; fellowships, Federal Work-Study, scholarships/grants, and tuition waivers (full and partial) also available. Support available to part-time students. Financial award application deadline: 2/15. *Unit head:* Dr. P. T. Vasudevan, Chairperson, 603-862-3654. *Application contact:* Nancy Littlefield, Administrative Assistant, 603-862-3654, E-mail: chemeng.grad@unh.edu.

University of New Mexico, Graduate School, School of Engineering, Department of Chemical and Nuclear Engineering, Program in Chemical Engineering, Albuquerque, NM 87131-2039. Offers MS, PhD. Part-time programs available. *Students:* 37 full-time (11 women), 13 part-time (6 women); includes 12 minority (1 African American, 1 Asian American or Pacific Islander, 10 Hispanic Americans), 11 international. Average age 30. 36 applicants, 44% accepted, 9 enrolled. In 2009, 6 master's, 2 doctorates awarded. Terminal master's awarded for partial completion of doctoral program. *Degree requirements:* For master's, thesis (for some programs); for doctorate, comprehensive exam, thesis/dissertation, qualifying exam. *Entrance requirements:* For master's, GRE General Test, minimum GPA of 3.0, 3 letters of reference, letter of intent; for doctorate, GRE General Test, 3 letters of reference, minimum GPA of 3.0, letter of intent. Additional exam requirements/recommendations for international students: Required—TOEFL. *Application deadline:* For fall admission, 1/15 priority date for domestic and international students; for spring admission, 7/15 priority date for domestic and international students. Application fee: $50. Electronic applications accepted. *Expenses:* Tuition, state resident: full-time $2098.80; part-time $233.20 per credit hour. Tuition, nonresident: full-time $6650. Required fees: $25 per semester. Tuition and fees vary according to course load, program and reciprocity agreements. *Financial support:* In 2009–10, 10 students received support, including 33 research assistantships with full tuition reimbursements available (averaging $21,600 per year); teaching assistantships, scholarships/grants, traineeships, and health care benefits also available. Financial award application deadline: 1/15; financial award applicants required to submit FAFSA. *Faculty research:* Bioanalytical systems, ceramics, catalysis, colloidal science, bioengineering, biomaterials, fuel cells, protein engineering, semiconductors, tissue engineering. Total annual research expenditures: $7.6 million. *Unit head:* Dr. Timothy Ward, Chair, 505-277-5431, Fax: 505-277-5433, E-mail: tward@unm.edu. *Application contact:* Jocelyn White, Coordinator, Program Advisor, 505-277-5606, Fax: 505-277-5433, E-mail: jowhite@unm.edu.

University of North Dakota, Graduate School, School of Engineering and Mines, Department of Chemical Engineering, Grand Forks, ND 58202. Offers M Engr, MS. Part-time programs available. *Degree requirements:* For master's, comprehensive exam, thesis or alternative. *Entrance requirements:* For master's, GRE General Test, minimum GPA of 3.0 (MS), minimum GPA of 2.5 (M Engr). Additional exam requirements/recommendations for international students: Required—TOEFL (minimum score 550 paper-based; 213 computer-based; 79 iBT), IELTS (minimum score 6.5). Electronic applications accepted. *Faculty research:* Catalysis, fluid flow and heat transfer, application of fractals, modeling and simulation, reaction engineering.

University of Notre Dame, Graduate School, College of Engineering, Department of Chemical and Biomolecular Engineering, Notre Dame, IN 46556. Offers MS Ch E, PhD. *Degree requirements:* For master's, comprehensive exam, thesis; for doctorate, comprehensive exam, thesis/dissertation, candidacy exam. *Entrance requirements:* For master's, GRE General Test; for doctorate, GRE General Test, GRE Subject Test (strongly recommended). Additional exam requirements/recommendations for international students: Required—TOEFL (minimum score 600 paper-based; 250 computer-based; 80 iBT). Electronic applications accepted. *Faculty research:* Biomolecular engineering, green chemistry and engineering for the environment, advanced materials, nanoengineering, catalysis and reaction engineering.

University of Oklahoma, Graduate College, College of Engineering, School of Chemical, Biological and Materials Engineering, Norman, OK 73019. Offers chemical engineering (MS, PhD). *Faculty:* 18 full-time (1 woman), 2 part-time/adjunct (0 women). *Students:* 49 full-time (16 women), 6 part-time (1 woman); includes 2 minority (both Hispanic Americans), 42 international. 13 applicants, 100% accepted, 9 enrolled. In 2009, 5 master's, 2 doctorates awarded. Terminal master's awarded for partial completion of doctoral program. *Degree requirements:* For master's, thesis, oral exams; for doctorate, thesis/dissertation, oral exam, qualifying exams. *Entrance requirements:* For master's and doctorate, minimum GPA of 3.0. Additional exam requirements/recommendations for international students: Required—TOEFL (minimum score 600 paper-based; 250 computer-based; 79 iBT). *Application deadline:* For fall admission, 6/1 priority date for domestic students, 4/1 for international students; for spring admission, 11/1 for domestic students, 9/1 for international students. Applications are processed on a rolling basis. Application fee: $40 ($90 for international students). Electronic applications accepted. *Expenses:* Tuition, state resident: full-time $3744; part-time $156 per credit hour. Tuition, nonresident: full-time $13,577; part-time $565.70 per credit hour. Required fees: $2415; $90.10 per credit hour. *Financial support:* In 2009–10, 53 students received support, including 1 fellowship (averaging $2,500 per year), 56 research assistantships with partial tuition reimbursements available (averaging $16,145 per year); unspecified assistantships also available. Financial award application deadline: 3/1; financial award applicants required to submit FAFSA. *Faculty research:* Renewable energy and catalysis, surface modification and surfactants, biomedical and biochemical engineering, polymers and nanostructured materials, process design optimization. Total annual research expenditures: $3.6 million. *Unit head:* Dr. Lance Lobban, Director, 405-325-5811, Fax: 405-325-5813, E-mail: llobban@ou.edu. *Application contact:* Dr. Ulli Nollert, Graduate Program Coordinator and Associate Professor, 405-325-4366, Fax: 405-325-5813, E-mail: nollert@ou.edu.

University of Ottawa, Faculty of Graduate and Postdoctoral Studies, Faculty of Engineering, Department of Chemical Engineering, Ottawa, ON K1N 6N5, Canada. Offers M Eng, MA Sc, PhD. *Degree requirements:* For master's, thesis or alternative; for doctorate, comprehensive exam, thesis/dissertation. *Entrance requirements:* For master's, honors degree or equivalent, minimum B average; for doctorate, master's degree, minimum B+ average. Electronic applications accepted. *Faculty research:* Material development, process engineering, clean technologies.

University of Pennsylvania, School of Engineering and Applied Science, Department of Chemical Engineering, Philadelphia, PA 19104. Offers MSE, PhD, MSE/MBA. Part-time programs available. *Faculty:* 21 full-time (3 women), 2 part-time/adjunct (0 women). *Students:* 69 full-time (22 women), 6 part-time (2 women); includes 7 minority (6 Asian Americans or Pacific Islanders, 1 Hispanic American), 34 international. 227 applicants, 35% accepted, 30 enrolled. In 2009, 11 master's, 10 doctorates awarded. Terminal master's awarded for partial completion of doctoral program. *Degree requirements:* For doctorate, thesis/dissertation. *Entrance requirements:* Additional exam requirements/recommendations for international students: Required—TOEFL. *Application deadline:* For fall admission, 6/1 priority date for domestic students. Applications are processed on a rolling basis. Application fee: $70. Electronic applications accepted. *Expenses:* Tuition: Full-time $25,660; part-time $4758 per course. Required fees: $2152; $270 per course. Tuition and fees vary according to course load, degree level and program. *Financial support:* Fellowships, research assistantships, teaching assistantships, institutionally sponsored loans, scholarships/grants, traineeships, health care benefits, and unspecified assistantships available. *Faculty research:* Biochemical engineering, surface and interfacial phenomena, process and design control, zeolites, molecular dynamics.

University of Pittsburgh, School of Engineering, Department of Chemical and Petroleum Engineering, Pittsburgh, PA 15260. Offers chemical engineering (MS Ch E, PhD); petroleum engineering (MSPE); MS Ch E/MSPE. Part-time programs available. Postbaccalaureate distance learning degree programs offered. *Faculty:* 16 full-time (2 women), 25 part-time/adjunct (4 women). *Students:* 41 full-time (9 women), 6 part-time (2 women); includes 4 minority (2 Asian Americans or Pacific Islanders, 2 Hispanic Americans), 25 international. 171 applicants, 12% accepted, 5 enrolled. In 2009, 2 master's, 4 doctorates awarded. *Degree requirements:* For master's, thesis; for doctorate, comprehensive exam, thesis/dissertation, final oral exams. *Entrance requirements:* For master's and doctorate, GRE General Test, minimum QPA of 3.2. Additional exam requirements/recommendations for international students: Required—TOEFL (minimum score 550 paper-based; 213 computer-based; 80 iBT). *Application deadline:* For fall admission, 3/1 priority date for domestic students; for spring admission, 7/1 priority date for domestic students. Applications are processed on a rolling basis. Application fee: $50. Electronic applications accepted. *Expenses:* Tuition, state resident: full-time $16,402; part-time $665 per credit. Tuition, nonresident: full-time $28,694; part-time $1175 per credit. Required fees: $690; $175 per term. Tuition and fees vary according to program. *Financial support:* In 2009–10, 38 students received support, including 1 fellowship with full tuition reimbursement available (averaging $20,772 per year), 26 research assistantships with full tuition reimbursements available (averaging $24,000 per year), 6 teaching assistantships with full tuition reimbursements available (averaging $22,000 per year); scholarships/grants, traineeships, and tuition waivers (full and partial) also available. Financial award application deadline: 4/15. *Faculty research:* Biotechnology, polymers, catalysis, energy and environment, computational modeling. Total annual research expenditures: $5.1 million. *Unit head:* Dr. J. Karl Johnson, Chairman, 412-624-5644, Fax: 412-624-9639, E-mail: johnson@engr.pitt.edu. *Application contact:* William Federspiel, Associate Professor and Graduate Coordinator, 412-624-9499, Fax: 412-624-9639, E-mail: federspiel@engrng.pitt.edu.

University of Puerto Rico, Mayagüez Campus, Graduate Studies, College of Engineering, Department of Chemical Engineering, Mayagüez, PR 00681-9000. Offers ME, MS, PhD. Part-time programs available. *Degree requirements:* For master's, comprehensive exam, thesis; for doctorate, comprehensive exam, thesis/dissertation. *Entrance requirements:* For master's, BS degree in chemical engineering or its equivalent. Additional exam requirements/recommendations for international students: Required—TOEFL. *Faculty research:* Process simulation and optimization, air and water pollution control, mass transport, biochemical engineering.

University of Rhode Island, Graduate School, College of Engineering, Department of Chemical Engineering, Kingston, RI 02881. Offers MS, PhD. Part-time programs available. *Faculty:* 7 full-time (1 woman), 3 part-time/adjunct (0 women). *Students:* 16 full-time (6 women), 5 part-time (0 women); includes 5 minority (3 African Americans, 2 Asian Americans or Pacific Islanders), 8 international. In 2009, 1 master's, 2 doctorates awarded. *Degree requirements:* For master's, comprehensive exam (for some programs), thesis optional; for doctorate, comprehensive exam, thesis/dissertation. *Entrance requirements:* For master's and doctorate, 3 letters of recommendation. Additional exam requirements/recommendations for international students: Required—TOEFL (minimum score 550 paper-based; 213 computer-based). *Application deadline:* For fall admission, 7/15 for domestic students, 2/1 for international students; for spring admission, 11/15 for domestic students, 7/15 for international students. Application fee: $65. Electronic applications accepted. *Expenses:* Tuition, state resident: full-time $8828; part-time $490 per credit hour. Tuition, nonresident: full-time $22,100; part-time $1228 per credit hour. Required fees: $1118; $57 per semester. Tuition and fees vary according to program. *Financial support:* In 2009–10, 7 research assistantships with full and partial tuition reimbursements (averaging $8,987 per year), 2 teaching assistantships with partial tuition reimbursements (averaging $7,004 per year) were awarded. Financial award application deadline: 7/15; financial award applicants required to submit FAFSA. *Faculty research:* Photobioreactors, colloidal and interfacial engineering, biomembrane thermodynamics and transport, degradation of materials, closed loop recycling systems. Total annual research expenditures: $1.4 million. *Unit head:* Dr. Arijit Bose, Chair, 401-874-2804, Fax: 401-874-4689, E-mail: bosea@egr.uri.edu. *Application contact:* Dr. Richard Brown, Director of Graduate Studies, 401-874-2707, Fax: 401-874-4689, E-mail: rbrown@uri.edu.

University of Rochester, The College, School of Engineering and Applied Sciences, Department of Chemical Engineering, Rochester, NY 14627. Offers MS, PhD. Part-time programs available. Terminal master's awarded for partial completion of doctoral program. *Degree requirements:* For master's, comprehensive exam; for doctorate, thesis/dissertation, preliminary and oral exams. *Entrance requirements:* For master's and doctorate, GRE. Additional exam requirements/recommendations for international students: Required—TOEFL.

See Close-Up on page 159.

University of Saskatchewan, College of Graduate Studies and Research, College of Engineering, Department of Chemical Engineering, Saskatoon, SK S7N 5A2, Canada. Offers M Eng, M Sc, PhD. *Degree requirements:* For master's, thesis (for some programs); for doctorate, thesis/dissertation. *Entrance requirements:* For master's and doctorate, GRE. Additional exam requirements/recommendations for international students: Required—TOEFL. Tuition and fees charges are reported in Canadian dollars. *Expenses:* Tuition, area resident: Full-time $3000 Canadian dollars; part-time $500 Canadian dollars per term. Required fees: $700 Canadian dollars; $100 Canadian dollars per term.

University of South Africa, College of Science, Engineering and Technology, Pretoria, South Africa. Offers chemical engineering (M Tech); information technology (M Tech).

University of South Alabama, Graduate School, College of Engineering, Department of Chemical Engineering, Mobile, AL 36688-0002. Offers MS Ch E. *Degree requirements:* For master's, project or thesis. *Entrance requirements:* For master's, GRE General Test, BS in engineering, minimum GPA of 3.0. *Expenses:* Tuition, state resident: part-time $218 per contact hour. Required fees: $1102 per year.

University of South Carolina, The Graduate School, College of Engineering and Computing, Department of Chemical Engineering, Columbia, SC 29208. Offers ME, MS, PhD. Part-time and evening/weekend programs available. Postbaccalaureate distance learning degree programs offered (minimal on-campus study). *Degree requirements:* For master's, comprehensive exam, thesis (for some programs); for doctorate, comprehensive exam, thesis/dissertation. *Entrance requirements:* For master's and doctorate, GRE General Test. Additional exam requirements/recommendations for international students: Required—TOEFL. Electronic applications accepted. *Faculty research:* Rheology, liquid and supercritical extractions, electrochemistry, corrosion, heterogeneous and homogeneous catalysis.

University of Southern California, Graduate School, Viterbi School of Engineering, Mork Family Department of Chemical Engineering and Materials Science, Los Angeles, CA 90089. Offers chemical engineering (MS, PhD, Engr); materials science (MS, PhD, Engr); petroleum engineering (MS, PhD, Engr); smart oilfield technologies (MS, Graduate Certificate). Part-time programs available. Postbaccalaureate distance learning degree programs offered (no on-campus study). *Faculty:* 17 full-time (3 women), 14 part-time/adjunct (1 woman). *Students:* 182 full-time (63 women), 70 part-time (23 women); includes 33 minority (8 African Americans, 18 Asian Americans or Pacific Islanders, 7 Hispanic Americans), 170 international. 443 applicants, 37% accepted, 72 enrolled. In 2009, 37 master's, 19 doctorates, 4 other advanced degrees awarded. Terminal master's awarded for partial completion of doctoral program. *Degree requirements:* For doctorate, thesis/dissertation. *Entrance requirements:* For master's, GRE General Test; for doctorate, General GRE. *Application deadline:* For fall admission, 3/1 priority date for domestic and international students; for spring admission, 10/1 priority date for domestic and international students. Applications are processed on a rolling basis. Application fee: $85. Electronic applications accepted. *Expenses:* Contact institution. *Financial support:* In 2009–10, 12 fellowships with full tuition reimbursements (averaging $30,000 per year), 70 research assistantships with full tuition reimbursements (averaging $19,250 per year), 29 teaching assistantships with full tuition reimbursements (averaging $19,250 per year) were awarded; career-related internships or fieldwork, scholarships/grants, health care benefits, and unspecified assistantships also available. Financial award application deadline: 12/1; financial award applicants required to submit CSS PROFILE or FAFSA. *Faculty research:* Heterogeneous materials and porous media, statistical mechanics, molecular simulation, polymer science and engineering, advanced materials, reaction engineering and catalysis, membrane processes and separation, biochemical engineering, cell culture, bioreactor modeling, petroleum engineering. Total annual research expenditures: $8.8 million. *Unit head:* Dr. Theodore Tsotsis, Chair, 213-740-2069, Fax: 213-740-8053, E-mail: tsotsis@usc.edu. *Application contact:* Petra P. Sapir, Student Service Advisor, 213-740-6011, Fax: 213-740-7797, E-mail: ppearce@usc.edu.

University of South Florida, Graduate School, College of Engineering, Department of Chemical and Biomedical Engineering, Tampa, FL 33620. Offers biological engineering (MSBE, PhD); chemical and biological engineering (MCH, ME, MSES, PhD); chemical engineering (PhD). Part-time programs available. *Faculty:* 13 full-time (1 woman). *Students:* 68 full-time (32 women), 6 part-time (2 women); includes 26 minority (12 African Americans, 8 Asian Americans or Pacific Islanders, 6 Hispanic Americans), 26 international. Average age 32. 75 applicants, 49% accepted, 14 enrolled. In 2009, 36 master's, 4 doctorates awarded. Terminal master's awarded for partial completion of doctoral program. *Degree requirements:* For master's, comprehensive exam, thesis (for some programs); for doctorate, comprehensive exam, thesis/dissertation. *Entrance requirements:* For master's, GRE General Test, minimum GPA of 3.0 in last 60 hours of course work; for doctorate, GRE General Test. Additional exam requirements/recommendations for international students: Required—TOEFL (minimum score 550 paper-based; 213 computer-based; 79 iBT). *Application deadline:* For fall admission, 2/15 for domestic students, 1/2 priority date for international students; for spring admission, 10/15 for domestic students, 6/1 priority date for international students. Application fee: $30. Electronic applications accepted. *Financial support:* In 2009–10, 35 students received support, including teaching assistantships with tuition reimbursements available (averaging $15,000 per year); unspecified assistantships also available. Financial award applicants required to submit FAFSA. *Faculty research:* Biomedical engineering, supercritical fluid technology, advanced materials, surface and interfacial science, alternative and renewable energy. Total annual research expenditures: $1.7 million. *Unit head:* Dr. Venkat R. Bhethanabotla, Chair, 813-974-3997. *Application contact:* Dr. Vinay Gupta, Graduate Admissions Coordinator for Chemical Engineering, 813-974-0851, Fax: 813-974-3651.

The University of Tennessee, Graduate School, College of Engineering, Department of Chemical Engineering, Knoxville, TN 37996. Offers chemical engineering (MS, PhD); reliability and maintainability engineering (MS); MS/MBA. *Faculty:* 12 full-time (1 woman), 12 part-time/adjunct (0 women). *Students:* 25 full-time (7 women), 10 part-time (3 women); includes 3 minority (1 American Indian/Alaska Native, 2 Asian Americans or Pacific Islanders), 24 international. Average age 23. 73 applicants, 23% accepted, 8 enrolled. In 2009, 4 master's, 1 doctorate awarded. *Degree requirements:* For master's, thesis or alternative; for doctorate, comprehensive exam, thesis/dissertation. *Entrance requirements:* For master's and doctorate, GRE General Test, minimum GPA of 2.7, 2 reference forms. Additional exam requirements/recommendations for international students: Required—TOEFL (minimum score 550 paper-based; 213 computer-based). *Application deadline:* For fall admission, 2/1 priority date for domestic and international students; for spring admission, 6/15 priority date for international students. Applications are processed on a rolling basis. Application fee: $35. Electronic applications accepted. *Expenses:* Tuition, state resident: full-time $6826; part-time $380 per semester hour. Tuition, nonresident: full-time $21,844; part-time $1147 per semester hour. Tuition and fees vary according to program. *Financial support:* In 2009–10, 10 students received support, including 26 research assistantships with full tuition reimbursements available (averaging $21,612 per year), 9 teaching assistantships with full tuition reimbursements available (averaging $17,520 per year); career-related internships or fieldwork, Federal Work-Study, institutionally sponsored loans, health care benefits, and unspecified assistantships also available. Financial award application deadline: 2/1; financial award applicants required to submit FAFSA. *Faculty research:* Molecular and cellular bioengineering; engineering of soft, functional and structural materials; bio-fuels; molecular modeling and simulations; fuel cells and energy storage devices. Total annual research expenditures: $2.3 million. *Unit head:* Dr. Bamin Khomami, Head, 865-974-2421, Fax: 865-974-7076, E-mail: bkhomami@utk.edu. *Application contact:* Dr. Paul Frymier, Graduate Program Coordinator, 865-974-4961, Fax: 865-974-7076, E-mail: pdf@utk.edu.

The University of Tennessee at Chattanooga, Graduate School, College of Engineering and Computer Science, Program in Engineering, Chattanooga, TN 37403. Offers chemical (MS Engr); civil (MS Engr); computational (MS Engr); electrical (MS Engr); industrial (MS Engr); mechanical (MS Engr). Part-time and evening/weekend programs available. *Faculty:* 8 full-time (0 women). *Students:* 22 full-time (7 women), 30 part-time (3 women); includes 9 minority (4 African Americans, 4 Asian Americans or Pacific Islanders, 1 Hispanic American), 9 international. Average age 29. 59 applicants, 59% accepted, 19 enrolled. In 2009, 9 master's awarded. *Degree requirements:* For master's, comprehensive exam, thesis or alternative, engineering project. *Entrance requirements:* For master's, GRE General Test, minimum undergraduate GPA of 2.5 or 3.0 in last 30 hours of coursework. Additional exam requirements/recommendations for international students: Required—TOEFL (minimum score 550 paper-based; 213 computer-based; 79 iBT), IELTS (minimum score 6). *Application deadline:* For fall admission, 8/1 priority date for domestic students, 6/1 for international students; for spring admission, 12/1 priority date for domestic students, 10/1 for international students. Applications are processed on a rolling basis. Application fee: $35. Electronic applications accepted. *Expenses:* Tuition, state resident: full-time $5404; part-time $300 per credit hour. Tuition, nonresident: full-time $16,702; part-time $928 per credit hour. Required fees: $1150; $130 per credit hour. *Financial support:* In 2009–10, 23 research assistantships with full and partial tuition reimbursements (averaging $5,500 per year) were awarded; career-related internships or fieldwork, scholarships/grants, and unspecified assistantships also available. Support available to part-time students. *Faculty research:* Quality control and reliability engineering, financial management, thermal science, energy conservation, structural analysis. Total annual research expenditures: $2.6 million. *Unit head:* Dr. Neslihan Alp, Director, 423-425-4032, Fax: 423-425-5229, E-mail: neslihan-alp@utc.edu. *Application contact:* Dr. Stephanie Bellar, Dean of Graduate Studies, 423-425-4666, Fax: 423-425-5223, E-mail: stephanie-bellar@utc.edu.

The University of Texas at Austin, Graduate School, Cockrell School of Engineering, Department of Chemical Engineering, Austin, TX 78712-1111. Offers MSE, PhD. Terminal master's awarded for partial completion of doctoral program. *Degree requirements:* For master's, thesis (for some programs); for doctorate, comprehensive exam, thesis/dissertation. *Entrance requirements:* For master's and doctorate, GRE General Test. Electronic applications accepted.

The University of Toledo, College of Graduate Studies, College of Engineering, Department of Chemical and Environmental Engineering, Toledo, OH 43606-3390. Offers chemical engineering (MS, PhD). Part-time and evening/weekend programs available. *Degree requirements:* For master's, thesis optional; for doctorate, thesis/dissertation, qualifying exam. *Entrance requirements:* For master's, GRE General Test, minimum GPA of 3.0; for doctorate, GRE General Test, minimum GPA of 3.3. Additional exam requirements/recommendations for international students: Required—TOEFL (minimum score 550 paper-based; 213 computer-based; 80 iBT). Electronic applications accepted. *Faculty research:* Polymers, applied computing, membranes, alternative energy (fuel cells).

University of Toronto, School of Graduate Studies, Physical Sciences Division, Faculty of Applied Science and Engineering, Department of Chemical Engineering and Applied Chemistry, Toronto, ON M5S 1A1, Canada. Offers M Eng, MA Sc, PhD. Part-time programs available. *Degree requirements:* For master's, thesis (for some programs); for doctorate, thesis/dissertation. *Entrance requirements:* For master's, minimum B+ average in final 2 years, four-year degree in engineering (M Eng, MA Sc) or physical sciences (MA Sc), 2 letters of reference; for doctorate, research master's degree, minimum B+ average, 2 letters of reference. Additional exam requirements/recommendations for international students: Required—TOEFL (minimum score 580 paper-based; 237 computer-based), TWE (minimum score 4).

University of Tulsa, Graduate School, College of Engineering and Natural Sciences, Department of Chemical Engineering, Tulsa, OK 74104-3189. Offers ME, MSE, PhD. Part-time programs available. *Faculty:* 10 full-time (3 women). *Students:* 17 full-time (8 women), 3 part-time (1 woman), 15 international. Average age 25. 41 applicants, 59% accepted, 8 enrolled. In 2009, 7 master's, 2 doctorates awarded. *Degree requirements:* For master's, thesis (for some programs); for doctorate, comprehensive exam, thesis/dissertation. *Entrance requirements:* For master's and doctorate, GRE General Test. Additional exam requirements/recommendations for international students: Required—TOEFL (minimum score 550 paper-based; 213 computer-based; 80 iBT), IELTS (minimum score 6). *Application deadline:* Applications are processed on a rolling basis. Application fee: $40. Electronic applications accepted. *Expenses:* Tuition: Full-time $16,182; part-time $899 per credit hour. Required fees: $4 per credit hour. Tuition and fees vary according to course load. *Financial support:* In 2009–10, 17 students received support, including 10 fellowships (averaging $2,352 per year), 12 research assistantships with full and partial tuition reimbursements available (averaging $10,818 per year), 5 teaching assistantships with full and partial tuition reimbursements available (averaging $18,666 per year); career-related internships or fieldwork, Federal Work-Study, scholarships/grants, health care benefits, tuition waivers (full and partial), and unspecified assistantships also available. Support available to part-time students. Financial award application deadline: 2/1; financial award applicants required to submit FAFSA. *Faculty research:* Environment, surface science, catalysis, transport phenomena, process systems engineering, bioengineering, alternative energy, petrochemical processes. Total annual research expenditures: $2.6 million. *Unit head:* Dr. Geoffrey Price, Chairperson, 918-631-2575, Fax: 918-631-3268, E-mail: chegradadvisor@utulsa.edu. *Application contact:* Dr. Daniel Crunkleton, Advisor, 918-631-2644, Fax: 918-631-3268, E-mail: chegradadvisor@utulsa.edu.

University of Utah, The Graduate School, College of Engineering, Department of Chemical Engineering, Salt Lake City, UT 84112-1107. Offers chemical engineering (ME, MS, PhD); environmental engineering (ME, MS, PhD). Part-time and evening/weekend programs available. Postbaccalaureate distance learning degree programs offered. *Faculty:* 15 full-time (1 woman), 1 part-time/adjunct (0 women). *Students:* 43 full-time (8 women), 23 part-time (4 women); includes 3 minority (1 Asian American or Pacific Islander, 2 Hispanic Americans), 26 international. Average age 28. 93 applicants, 13% accepted, 8 enrolled. In 2009, 9 master's, 8 doctorates awarded. Terminal master's awarded for partial completion of doctoral program. *Degree requirements:* For master's, comprehensive exam, thesis (for some programs); for doctorate, comprehensive exam, thesis/dissertation. *Entrance requirements:* For master's and doctorate, GRE General Test, minimum GPA of 3.0, degree or course work in chemical engineering. Additional exam requirements/recommendations for international students: Required—TOEFL (minimum score 500 paper-based; 173 computer-based). *Application deadline:* For fall admission, 4/1 priority date for domestic students, 2/1 for international students; for spring admission, 11/1 priority date for domestic students, 10/1 priority date for international students. Applications are processed on a rolling basis. Application fee: $55 ($65 for international students). Electronic applications accepted. *Expenses:* Tuition, state resident: full-time $4004; part-time $1674 per semester. Tuition, nonresident: full-time $14,134; part-time $5915 per semester. Required fees: $324 per semester. Tuition and fees vary according to course load, degree level and program. *Financial support:* In 2009–10, 1 fellowship with tuition reimbursement (averaging $30 per year), 44 research assistantships with tuition reimbursements (averaging $24,750 per year) were awarded; teaching assistantships with tuition reimbursements, Federal Work-Study, institutionally sponsored loans, scholarships/grants, health care benefits, and unspecified assistantships also available. Financial award application deadline: 4/1; financial award applicants required to submit FAFSA. *Faculty research:* Vaccine and drug delivery, biosorption, fossil fuel and biomass combustion and gasification, polymer structure and dynamics, oil and gas reservoir characteristics and management. Total annual research expenditures: $5.4 million. *Unit head:* Dr. JoAnn S. Lighty, Chair, 801-581-6715, Fax: 801-585-9291, E-mail: jlighty@utah.edu. *Application contact:* Jenny Jones, Academic Advisor, 801-581-6915, Fax: 801-585-9291, E-mail: jones.jenny@eng.utah.edu.

University of Virginia, School of Engineering and Applied Science, Department of Chemical Engineering, Charlottesville, VA 22903. Offers ME, MS, PhD. Postbaccalaureate distance learning degree programs offered (no on-campus study). *Faculty:* 12 full-time (2 women). *Students:* 51 full-time (17 women), 1 part-time (0 women); includes 6 minority (1 African American, 3 Asian Americans or Pacific Islanders, 2 Hispanic Americans), 29 international. Average age 25. 113 applicants, 29% accepted, 12 enrolled. In 2009, 12 master's, 6 doctorates awarded. *Degree requirements:* For master's, thesis (for some programs); for doctorate, thesis/dissertation. *Entrance requirements:* For master's, GRE General Test, 3 recommendations; for doctorate, GRE General Test, 3 recommendations, essay. Additional exam requirements/recommendations for international students: Required—TOEFL (minimum score 600 paper-based; 250 computer-based; 90 iBT), IELTS (minimum score 7). *Application deadline:* For fall admission, 8/1 for domestic students, 4/1 for international students; for winter admission, 12/1 for domestic students, 8/1 for international students; for spring admission, 5/1 for domestic students, 1/1 for international students. Applications are processed on a rolling basis. Application fee: $60. Electronic applications accepted. *Financial support:* Fellowships, research assistantships, teaching assistantships available. Financial award application deadline: 1/15; financial award applicants required to submit FAFSA. *Faculty research:* Fluid mechanics, heat and mass transfer, chemical reactor analysis and engineering, biochemical engineering and biotechnology. *Unit head:* Robert Davis, Chair, 434-924-7778, Fax: 434-982-2658, E-mail: cheadmis@virginia.edu. *Application contact:* Steven McIntosh, Graduate Program Coordinator, 434-924-7778, Fax: 434-982-2658, E-mail: mcintosh@virginia.edu.

University of Washington, Graduate School, College of Engineering, Department of Chemical Engineering, Seattle, WA 98195-1750. Offers MS Ch E, MSE, PhD. *Faculty:* 14 full-time (2 women), 14 part-time/adjunct (3 women). *Students:* 66 full-time (24 women); includes 13 minority (2 African Americans, 1 American Indian/Alaska Native, 10 Asian Americans or Pacific Islanders), 18 international. Average age 25. 167 applicants, 32% accepted, 15 enrolled. In 2009, 11 master's, 8 doctorates awarded. Terminal master's awarded for partial completion of doctoral program. *Degree requirements:* For master's, thesis or alternative; for doctorate, thesis/dissertation. *Entrance requirements:* For master's and doctorate, GRE, minimum GPA of 3.0. Additional exam requirements/recommendations for international students: Required—

Chemical Engineering

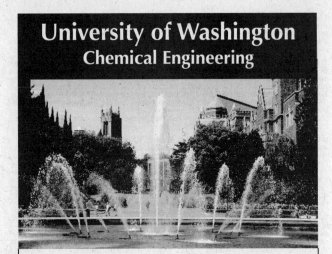
TOEFL (minimum score 600 paper-based; 250 computer-based; 100 iBT). *Application deadline:* For fall admission, 1/15 priority date for domestic students, 12/1 priority date for international students. Applications are processed on a rolling basis. Application fee: $65. Electronic applications accepted. *Financial support:* In 2009–10, 3 students received support, including 22 fellowships with full tuition reimbursements available (averaging $22,500 per year), 32 research assistantships with full tuition reimbursements available (averaging $19,035 per year), 11 teaching assistantships with full tuition reimbursements available (averaging $19,035 per year); career-related internships or fieldwork, Federal Work-Study, health care benefits, and unspecified assistantships also available. Financial award application deadline: 1/15. *Faculty research:* Molecular energy processes, living systems and biomolecular processes, molecular aspects of materials and interfaces, molecular/organic electronics. Total annual research expenditures: $7.7 million. *Unit head:* Dr. Daniel T. Schwartz, Professor and Chair, 206-543-2250, Fax: 206-543-3778, E-mail: dts@uw.edu. *Application contact:* Dave Drischell, Lead Academic Counselor, 206-543-2252, Fax: 206-543-3778, E-mail: rdd@u.washington.edu.

See Display on this page.

University of Waterloo, Graduate Studies, Faculty of Engineering, Department of Chemical Engineering, Waterloo, ON N2L 3G1, Canada. Offers M Eng, MA Sc, PhD. Part-time programs available. *Degree requirements:* For master's, research project or thesis, seminar; for doctorate, comprehensive exam, thesis/dissertation. *Entrance requirements:* For master's, honors degree, minimum B average; for doctorate, master's degree, minimum A- average. Additional exam requirements/recommendations for international students: Required—TOEFL, TWE. Electronic applications accepted. *Faculty research:* Biotechnical and environmental engineering, mathematical analysis, statistics and control, polymer science and engineering.

The University of Western Ontario, Faculty of Graduate Studies, Physical Sciences Division, Faculty of Engineering, London, ON N6A 5B8, Canada. Offers chemical and biochemical engineering (ME Sc, PhD); civil and environmental engineering (M Eng, ME Sc, PhD); electrical and computer engineering (M Eng, ME Sc, PhD); mechanical and materials engineering (M Eng, ME Sc, PhD). Part-time programs available. Terminal master's awarded for partial completion of doctoral program. *Degree requirements:* For master's, thesis; for doctorate, thesis/dissertation. *Entrance requirements:* For master's, minimum B average; for doctorate, minimum B+ average. *Faculty research:* Wind, geotechnical, chemical reactor engineering, applied electrostatics, biochemical engineering.

University of Wisconsin–Madison, Graduate School, College of Engineering, Department of Chemical and Biological Engineering, Madison, WI 53706-1380. Offers chemical engineering (MS, PhD). *Faculty:* 19 full-time (2 women), 1 part-time/adjunct (0 women). *Students:* 122 full-time (34 women); includes 13 minority (9 Asian Americans or Pacific Islanders, 4 Hispanic Americans), 51 international. Average age 26. 405 applicants, 21% accepted, 30 enrolled. In 2009, 3 master's, 16 doctorates awarded. Terminal master's awarded for partial completion of doctoral program. *Degree requirements:* For master's, thesis or alternative; for doctorate, thesis/dissertation, 2 semesters of teaching assistantship. *Entrance requirements:* For master's and doctorate, GRE General Test. Additional exam requirements/recommendations for international students: Required—TOEFL (minimum score 550 paper-based; 213 computer-based; 80 iBT). *Application deadline:* For fall admission, 1/15 for domestic and international students; for spring admission, 10/15 for domestic and international students. Application fee: $56. Electronic applications accepted. *Expenses:* Tuition, state resident: part-time $594 per credit. Tuition, nonresident: part-time $1504 per credit. Required fees: $65 per credit. Tuition and fees vary according to course load, program and reciprocity agreements. *Financial support:* In 2009–10, 122 students received support, including 14 fellowships with full tuition reimbursements available (averaging $29,065 per year), 108 research assistantships with full tuition reimbursements available (averaging $24,000 per year), 46 teaching assistantships with full tuition reimbursements available (averaging $25,195 per year); traineeships and health care benefits also available. Financial award application deadline: 1/15. *Faculty research:* Biotechnology, nanotechnology, complex fluids, molecular and systems modeling, alternative energy: materials and processes. Total annual research expenditures: $17.7 million. *Unit head:* Prof. Nicholas L. Abbott, Chair, 608-265-5278, Fax: 608-262-5434, E-mail: abbott@engr.wisc.edu. *Application contact:* Donna M. Bell, Graduate Coordinator, 608-263-3138, Fax: 608-262-5434, E-mail: gradoffice@che.wisc.edu.

University of Wyoming, College of Engineering and Applied Sciences, Department of Chemical and Petroleum Engineering, Program in Chemical Engineering, Laramie, WY 82070. Offers MS, PhD. Part-time programs available. Terminal master's awarded for partial completion of doctoral program. *Degree requirements:* For master's, thesis; for doctorate, thesis/dissertation. *Entrance requirements:* For master's and doctorate, GRE General Test, minimum GPA of 3.0. Additional exam requirements/recommendations for international students: Required—TOEFL (minimum score 600 paper-based; 250 computer-based; 76 iBT). Electronic applications accepted. *Faculty research:* Microwave reactor systems, synthetic fuels, fluidization, coal combustion/gasification, flue-gas cleanup.

Vanderbilt University, School of Engineering, Department of Chemical and Biomolecular Engineering, Nashville, TN 37240-1001. Offers M Eng, MS, PhD. MS and PhD offered through the Graduate School. Part-time programs available. *Faculty:* 9 full-time (2 women), 6 part-time/adjunct (1 woman). *Students:* 34 full-time (11 women); includes 1 minority (African American), 15 international. Average age 26. 131 applicants, 21% accepted, 12 enrolled. In 2009, 1 master's, 6 doctorates awarded. *Degree requirements:* For master's, thesis; for doctorate, thesis/dissertation. *Entrance requirements:* For master's and doctorate, GRE General Test. Additional exam requirements/recommendations for international students: Required—TOEFL. *Application deadline:* For fall admission, 1/15 for domestic students; for spring admission, 11/1 for domestic students. Application fee: $0. Electronic applications accepted. *Financial support:* In 2009–10, 8 fellowships with full tuition reimbursements (averaging $26,400 per year), 25 research assistantships with full tuition reimbursements (averaging $20,604 per year), 11 teaching assistantships with full tuition reimbursements (averaging $20,604 per year) were awarded; Federal Work-Study, institutionally sponsored loans, and tuition waivers (partial) also available. Support available to part-time students. Financial award application deadline: 1/15; financial award applicants required to submit CSS PROFILE or FAFSA. *Faculty research:* Adsorption and surface chemistry; biochemical engineering and biotechnology; chemical reaction engineering, environment, materials, process modeling and control; molecular modeling and thermodynamics. Total annual research expenditures: $2.9 million. *Unit head:* Dr. Peter N. Pintauro, Chair, 615-343-6918, Fax: 615-343-7951, E-mail: peter.n.pintauro@vanderbilt.edu. *Application contact:* Dr. G. Kane Jennings, Director of Graduate Studies, 615-322-2441, Fax: 615-343-7951, E-mail: jenningk@vuse.vanderbilt.edu.

Villanova University, College of Engineering, Department of Chemical Engineering, Villanova, PA 19085-1699. Offers MSChE. Part-time and evening/weekend programs available. *Degree requirements:* For master's, comprehensive exam, thesis optional. *Entrance requirements:* For master's, GRE General Test (for applicants with degrees from foreign universities), B Ch E, minimum GPA of 3.0. Additional exam requirements/recommendations for international students: Required—TOEFL (minimum score 600 paper-based; 250 computer-based; 100 iBT). *Expenses:* Tuition: Part-time $630 per credit. Required fees: $60 per credit. Part-time tuition and fees vary according to degree level and program. *Faculty research:* Heat transfer, advanced materials, chemical vapor deposition, pyrolysis and combustion chemistry, industrial waste treatment.

Virginia Commonwealth University, Graduate School, School of Engineering, Department of Chemical and Life Science Engineering, Richmond, VA 23284-9005. Offers MS, PhD.

Virginia Polytechnic Institute and State University, Graduate School, College of Engineering, Department of Chemical Engineering, Blacksburg, VA 24061. Offers M Eng, MS, PhD. *Entrance requirements:* For master's and doctorate, GRE. Additional exam requirements/recommendations for international students: Required—TOEFL (minimum score 550 paper-based; 213 computer-based). Electronic applications accepted.

Washington State University, Graduate School, College of Engineering and Architecture, School of Chemical Engineering and Bioengineering, Program in Chemical Engineering, Pullman, WA 99164. Offers MS, PhD. Terminal master's awarded for partial completion of doctoral program. *Degree requirements:* For master's, comprehensive exam (for some programs), thesis, oral exam; for doctorate, one foreign language, comprehensive exam, thesis/dissertation, oral exam. *Entrance requirements:* For master's and doctorate, GRE, minimum GPA of 3.0, 3 letters of recommendation by faculty. Additional exam requirements/recommendations for international students: Required—TOEFL (minimum score 580 paper-based; 190 computer-based). *Faculty research:* Bioprocessing, kinetics and catalysis, hazardous waste remediation.

Washington University in St. Louis, Henry Edwin Sever Graduate School of Engineering and Applied Science, Department of Energy, Environmental and Chemical Engineering, St. Louis, MO 63130-4899. Offers chemical engineering (MS, D Sc); environmental engineering (MS, D Sc). Part-time programs available. Terminal master's awarded for partial completion of doctoral program. *Degree requirements:* For master's, thesis optional; for doctorate, thesis/dissertation, preliminary exam, qualifying exam. *Entrance requirements:* For master's and doctorate, GRE, minimum B average during final 2 years of course work. Additional exam requirements/recommendations for international students: Required—TOEFL, TWE. Electronic applications accepted. *Faculty research:* Reaction engineering, materials processing, catalysis, process control, air pollution control.

Wayne State University, College of Engineering, Department of Chemical Engineering and Materials Science, Program in Chemical Engineering, Detroit, MI 48202. Offers MS, PhD. *Degree requirements:* For master's, thesis optional; for doctorate, thesis/dissertation. *Entrance requirements:* For master's, GRE (if applying for financial support), letter of recommendations, resume; for doctorate, GRE (if applying for financial support), recommendations; resumé, personal statement. Additional exam requirements/recommendations for international students: Required—TOEFL (minimum score 550 paper-based; 213 computer-based), TWE (minimum score 6). Electronic applications accepted. *Faculty research:* Environmental management, biochemical engineering, supercritical technology, polymer process catalysis.

Western Michigan University, Graduate College, College of Engineering and Applied Sciences, Department of Paper Engineering, Chemical Engineering, and Imaging, Kalamazoo, MI 49008. Offers paper and imaging science and engineering (MS, PhD). *Degree requirements:* For master's, thesis optional; for doctorate, one foreign language, comprehensive exam, thesis/dissertation. *Entrance requirements:* For master's, minimum GPA of 3.0. *Faculty research:* Fiber recycling, paper machine wet end operations, paper coating.

West Virginia University, College of Engineering and Mineral Resources, Department of Chemical Engineering, Morgantown, WV 26506. Offers MS Ch E, PhD. Part-time programs available. Terminal master's awarded for partial completion of doctoral program. *Degree requirements:* For master's, thesis; for doctorate, comprehensive exam, thesis/dissertation, original research proposal, dissertation research proposal. *Entrance requirements:* For master's and doctorate, minimum GPA of 3.0. Additional exam requirements/recommendations for international students: Required—TOEFL (minimum score 550 paper-based; 213 computer-based; 80 iBT). Electronic applications accepted. *Faculty research:* Biocatalysis and catalysis,

fluid-particle systems, high-value non-fuel uses of coal, opto-electronic materials processing, polymer and polymer-composite nanotechnology.

Widener University, Graduate Programs in Engineering, Program in Chemical Engineering, Chester, PA 19013-5792. Offers M Eng. Part-time and evening/weekend programs available. *Students:* 3 full-time (1 woman), 2 part-time (1 woman); includes 1 minority (Asian American or Pacific Islander), 2 international. Average age 28. In 2009, 13 master's awarded. *Degree requirements:* For master's, thesis optional. *Application deadline:* For fall admission, 8/1 priority date for domestic students; for spring admission, 12/1 for domestic students. Applications are processed on a rolling basis. Application fee: $25 ($300 for international students). *Financial support:* Teaching assistantships with full tuition reimbursements, unspecified assistantships available. Financial award application deadline: 3/15. *Faculty research:* Biotechnology, environmental engineering, computational fluid mechanics, reaction kinetics, process design. *Unit head:* Dr. Charles R. Nippert, Chairman, 610-499-4050, Fax: 610-499-4059, E-mail: crnippert@widener.edu. *Application contact:* Dr. Charles R. Nippert, Chairman, 610-499-4050, Fax: 610-499-4059, E-mail: crnippert@widener.edu.

Worcester Polytechnic Institute, Graduate Studies and Research, Department of Chemical Engineering, Worcester, MA 01609-2280. Offers MS, PhD. Part-time and evening/weekend programs available. *Faculty:* 6 full-time (2 women). *Students:* 17 full-time (7 women), 7 part-time (6 women). 69 applicants, 57% accepted, 12 enrolled. In 2009, 4 master's, 1 doctorate awarded. Terminal master's awarded for partial completion of doctoral program. *Degree requirements:* For master's, thesis; for doctorate, comprehensive exam, thesis/dissertation. *Entrance requirements:* For master's and doctorate, GRE (recommended), 3 letters of recommendation. Additional exam requirements/recommendations for international students: Required—TOEFL (minimum score 550 paper-based; 213 computer-based; 79 iBT), IELTS (minimum score 6.5). *Application deadline:* For fall admission, 1/15 priority date for domestic and international students; for spring admission, 10/15 priority date for domestic and international students. Applications are processed on a rolling basis. Application fee: $70. Electronic applications accepted. *Financial support:* Career-related internships or fieldwork, institutionally sponsored loans, scholarships/grants, and unspecified assistantships available. Financial award application deadline: 1/15. *Faculty research:* Biochemical/medical engineering; inorganic membranes; computational analysis in transport/reaction engineering; process analysis, control and safety; water remediation chemistry and engineering; hydrogen energy and fuel cells. *Unit head:* Dr. David DiBiasio, Head, 508-831-5250, Fax: 508-831-5853, E-mail: dibiasio@wpi.edu. *Application contact:* Dr. Nikolaos Kazantzis, Graduate Coordinator, 508-831-5250, Fax: 508-831-5853, E-mail: nikolas@wp.edu.

Yale University, Graduate School of Arts and Sciences, School of Engineering and Applied Science, Department of Chemical Engineering, New Haven, CT 06520. Offers MS, PhD. Terminal master's awarded for partial completion of doctoral program. *Degree requirements:* For doctorate, thesis/dissertation, exam. *Entrance requirements:* For master's and doctorate, GRE General Test. Additional exam requirements/recommendations for international students: Required—TOEFL. *Faculty research:* Biochemical engineering, heterogeneous catalysis, high-temperature chemical reaction engineering, separation science and technology, colloids and complex fluids.

UNIVERSITY OF ROCHESTER

Edmund A. Hajim School of Engineering and Applied Sciences
Department of Chemical Engineering

Program of Study

The interdisciplinary nature of the University of Rochester's chemical engineering program manifests itself in active collaborations with other departments at the school. The faculty enjoys generous research support from government agencies and private industries.

To earn a Ph.D., students must complete 90 credit hours. It typically takes five years to complete the program, which includes successful defense of a dissertation. The first two semesters are devoted to graduate courses in chemical engineering and other sciences. Students are expected to provide undergraduate teaching assistance during this time. At the end of this period, students take a first-year examination as a transition from classroom to full-time research.

Students without prior backgrounds in chemical engineering are encouraged to apply. The Department has a graduate curriculum devised for students with a background in science, such as chemistry, physics, and biology. The curriculum combines courses at the undergraduate and graduate levels and is designed to foster interdisciplinary research in advanced materials, nanotechnology, clean energy, and biotechnology.

The Master of Science degree may be obtained through either a full-time or a part-time program. Graduate students may complete a thesis (Plan A) or choose a nonthesis (Plan B) option. All students who pursue Plan A are expected to earn 30 hours of credit, of which a minimum of 18 and a maximum of 24 hours should be formal course work. The balance of credit hours required for the degree is earned through M.S. research and/or reading courses. Satisfactory completion of the master's thesis is also required. All students who pursue Plan B must earn a minimum of 32 credits of course work. At least 18 credits should be taken from courses within the Department. Overall, no more than 6 credits toward a degree may be earned by research and/or reading courses. Plan B students are required to pass a comprehensive oral exam toward the end of their program.

The Department's 3/2 B.S./M.S. program leads to both the B.S. and M.S. degrees in five years. Students are granted a 75 percent tuition scholarship for their fifth year of study and may earn a stipend in return for their research assistance.

Research Facilities

The River Campus Libraries hold approximately 2.5 million volumes and provide access to an extensive collection of electronic, multimedia, and interlibrary loan resources. Miner Library includes more than 230,000 volumes of journals, books, theses, and government documents for health-care and medical research. Located at the Medical Center, the library also maintains access to online databases and electronic resources.

The Laboratory for Laser Energetics and the Center for Optoelectronics and Imaging are two state-of-the-art facilities in which specialized material science research is conducted. The Laboratory for Laser Energetics was established in 1970 for the investigation of the interaction of intense radiation with matter, to conduct experiments in support of the National Inertial Confinement Fusion (ICF) program; develop new laser and materials technologies; provide education in electrooptics, high-power lasers, high-energy-density physics, plasma physics, and nuclear fusion technology; operate the National Laser User's Facility; and conduct research in advanced technology related to high-energy-density phenomena.

The renowned Medical Center, which is a few minutes' walk from the River Campus, houses the Peptide Sequencing/Mass Spectrometry Facilities, Cell Sorting Facility, Nucleic Acid Laboratory, Real-Time and Static Confocal Imaging Facility, Functional Genomics Center, and a network of nearly 1,000 investigators providing research, clinical trial, and education services. In addition, a recently founded research institute, the Aab Institute of Biomedical Sciences, is the centerpiece of a ten-year, $400 million strategic plan to expand the Medical Center's research programs in the basic sciences. It is headquartered in a 240,000-square-foot research building on the Medical Center campus.

Financial Aid

The University offers fellowships, scholarships, and assistantships for full-time graduate students, and individual departments provide support through research assistantships. Applicants are encouraged to apply for outside funding such as NSF or New York State fellowships. Full-time Ph.D. students receive an annual stipend of $24,000 plus full graduate tuition.

Cost of Study

In the 2010–11 academic year, tuition is $39,000. Students must also pay additional fees for health services ($552) and health insurance ($1560). These fee amounts are subject to change.

Living and Housing Costs

Students are eligible to lease a University apartment if enrolled as a full-time graduate student or postgraduate trainee. In the 2010–11 academic year, rent, utilities, food, and supplies are estimated at $17,795 per year; books at $1100; and personal expenses at $2400. These fee amounts are subject to change.

Student Group

The chemical engineering discipline appeals to students who are proficient at both analytical and descriptive sciences, and are intrigued by the prospect of investigating new phenomena, and devising new materials and devices for the technologies of the future. Students in the master's degree program should have acquired technical background in chemistry, mathematics, and physics. For students interested in biotechnology, a technical background in biology is desirable.

Student Outcomes

In addition to the traditional jobs in the chemical process and petrochemical industries, chemical engineers work in pharmaceuticals, health care, pulp and paper, food processing, polymers, biotechnology, and environmental health and safety industries. Their expertise is also applied in law, education, publishing, finance, and medicine. Chemical engineers also are well equipped to analyze environmental issues and develop solutions to environmental problems, such as pollution control and remediation.

Location

Located at a bend of the Genesee River, the 85-acre River Campus is about 2 miles south of downtown Rochester, New York. Recently ranked as one of the Northeast's ten "Best Places to Live in America" by *Money* magazine, Rochester has also been listed as one of the "Most Livable Cities" in America by the Partners for Livable Communities. Rochester claims more sites on the National Register of Historic Places than any other city its size. With Lake Ontario on its northern border and the scenic Finger Lakes to the south, the Rochester area of about 1 million people offers a wide variety of cultural and recreational opportunities through its museums, parks, orchestras, planetarium, theater companies, and professional sports teams.

The University

Founded in 1850, the University of Rochester ranks among the most highly regarded universities in the country, offering degree programs at the bachelor's, master's, and doctoral levels, as well as in several professional disciplines. In the last eighteen years, 27 faculty members have been named Guggenheim Fellows. Present faculty members include a MacArthur Foundation fellowship recipient and 6 National Endowment for the Humanities Senior Fellows. Past alumni have included 7 Nobel Prize winners and 11 Pulitzer Prize winners. The University's Eastman School of Music is consistently ranked as one of the top music schools in the nation.

Applying

The official graduate application can be found online at https://its-w2ks08.acs.rochester.edu/admgrad/. The entire application must be received by January 15 for fall admission. Late applications are considered for exceptional applicants only if scholarship slots are available. Applicants are required to send college transcripts, letters of recommendation, personal/research statement, curriculum vitae, and standardized test results to the Department of Chemical Engineering.

Correspondence and Information

Graduate Program Coordinator
Department of Chemical Engineering
206 Gavett Hall, Box 270166
University of Rochester
Rochester, New York 14627-0166

Phone: 585-275-4913
Fax: 585-273-1348
E-mail: chegradinfo@che.rochester.edu
Web site: http://www.che.rochester.edu

University of Rochester

THE FACULTY AND THEIR RESEARCH

Mitchell Anthamatten, Associate Professor and Scientist, LLE; Ph.D., MIT, 2001. Macromolecular self-assembly, associative and functional polymers, nanostructured materials, liquid crystals, interfacial phenomena, optoelectronic materials, vapor deposition polymerization, fuel cell membranes.

Danielle Benoit, Assistant Professor, Biomedical Engineering and Chemical Engineering; Ph.D., Colorado, 2006. The rational design, synthesis, characterization, and employment of materials to treat diseases or control cell behavior for applications in drug therapy, regenerative medicine, and tissue engineering.

Shaw H. Chen, Professor, Chair, and Senior Scientist, LLE; Ph.D., Minnesota, 1981. Organic semiconductors, glassy liquid crystals, photoalignment of conjugated molecules, bipolar hosts for phosphorescent OLEDs, geometric surfactancy for bulk heterojunction solar cells.

Eldred H. Chimowitz, Professor and Associate Chair; Ph.D., Connecticut, 1982. Critical phenomena, statistical mechanics of fluids, computer-aided design.

David Harding, Professor of Chemical Engineering and Senior Scientist, LLE; Ph.D., Cambridge, 1986. Thin-film deposition, properties of films and composite structures, and developing cryogenic fuel capsules for nuclear fusion experiments.

Stephen Jacobs, Professor of Optics and Chemical Engineering and Senior Scientist, LLE; Ph.D., Rochester, 1975. Optical materials for laser applications, liquid crystal optics, electrooptic devices, optics manufacturing processes, magnetorheological finishing, polishing abrasives and slurries, optical glass.

Jacob Jornè, Professor; Ph.D., Berkeley, 1972. Electrochemical engineering, microelectronics processing, fuel cells, polymer electrolyte membrane fuel cell.

F. Douglas Kelley, Associate Professor; Ph.D., Rochester, 1990. Ways to exploit the divergent transport properties of fluids near the critical point, energy storage technologies that can be useful in balancing energy demand with sustainable energy generation, polymer mixtures and composites.

Lewis Rothberg, Professor of Chemistry and Chemical Engineering; Ph.D., Harvard, 1984. Polymer electronics, optoelectronic devices, light-emitting diodes, thin-film transistors, organic photovoltaics and solar cells, biomolecular sensors, plasmon-enhanced devices.

Yonathon Shapir, Professor of Physics and Chemical Engineering; Ph.D., Tel-Aviv, 1981. Critical phenomena in ordered and disordered systems, classical and quantum transport in dirty metals and the metal-insulator transition, statistical properties of different polymer configurations, fractal properties of percolation and other clusters, kinetic models of growth and aggregation.

Alexander A. Shestopalov, Assistant Professor; Ph.D., Duke, 2009. Development of new unconventional fabrication and patterning techniques and their use in preparation of functional micro- and nanostructured devices.

Ching Tang, Professor of Chemical Engineering, Chemistry, and Physics; Ph.D., Cornell, 1975. Applications of organic electronic devices—organic light-emitting diodes, solar cells, photoconductors, image sensors, photoreceptors; basic studies of organic thin-film devices: charge injection, transport, recombination and luminescence properties; metal-organic and organic-organic junction phenomena; development of flat-panel display technology based on organic light-emitting diodes.

J. H. David Wu, Professor of Chemical Engineering and Biomedical Engineering and Associate Professor of Microbiology and Immunology; Ph.D., MIT, 1987. Biofuels development, molecular enzymology, transcriptional network, genomics and systems biology of biomass degradation for bioenergy conversion, artificial bone marrow and lymphoid tissue engineering, molecular control of hematopoiesis and immune response, stem cell and lymphocyte culture, biochemical engineering, fermentation, molecular biology.

Hong Yang, Associate Professor and Scientist, LLE; Ph.D., Toronto, 1998. Nanostructured materials, fuel cell catalysts, magnetic nanoparticles and nanocomposites, nanoparticles in ionic liquid, porous solids, microfabrication and nanofabrication, functional nanomaterials for biological applications.

Matthew Yates, Associate Professor and Scientist, LLE; Ph.D., Texas, 1999. Particle synthesis and assembly, crystallization, fuel cell membranes, microemulsions, supercritical fluids, microencapsulation.

Section 7
Civil and Environmental Engineering

This section contains a directory of institutions offering graduate work in civil and environmental engineering, followed by an in-depth entry submitted by an institution that chose to prepare a detailed program description. Additional information about programs listed in the directory but not augmented by an in-depth entry may be obtained by writing directly to the dean of a graduate school or chair of a department at the address given in the directory.

For programs offering related work, see also in this book *Agricultural Engineering and Bioengineering, Biomedical Engineering and Biotechnology, Engineering and Applied Sciences, Management of Engineering and Technology,* and *Ocean Engineering.* In the other guides in this series:

Graduate Programs in the Humanities, Arts & Social Sciences
See *Public, Regional, and Industrial Affairs (Urban and Regional Planning* and *Urban Studies)*
Graduate Programs in the Biological Sciences
See *Ecology, Environmental Biology,* and *Evolutionary Biology*
Graduate Programs in the Physical Sciences, Mathematics, Agricultural Sciences, the Environment & Natural Resources
See *Agricultural and Food Sciences, Environmental Sciences and Management, Geosciences,* and *Marine Sciences and Oceanography*

CONTENTS

Program Directories

Close-Up

See also:

Civil Engineering

American University of Beirut, Graduate Programs, Faculty of Engineering and Architecture, Beirut, Lebanon. Offers civil engineering (ME, PhD); electrical and computer engineering (ME, PhD); engineering management (MEM); environmental and water resources (ME); environmental and water resources engineering (PhD); environmental technology (MSES); mechanical engineering (ME, PhD); urban design (MUD); urban planning and policy (MUP). Part-time programs available. *Degree requirements:* For master's, one foreign language, comprehensive exam, thesis (for some programs); for doctorate, one foreign language, comprehensive exam, thesis/dissertation, publications. *Entrance requirements:* For master's, letters of recommendation; for doctorate, letters of recommendation, master's degree, transcripts, curriculum vitae, interview. Additional exam requirements/recommendations for international students: Required—TOEFL (minimum score 600 paper-based; 250 computer-based; 100 iBT), IELTS (minimum score 7.5). Electronic applications accepted.

American University of Sharjah, Graduate Programs, Sharjah, United Arab Emirates. Offers business (EMBA, GEMPA, MBA); chemical engineering (MS Ch E); civil engineering (MSCE); computer engineering (MS); electrical engineering (MSEE); mechanical engineering (MSME); mechatronics engineering (MS); public administration (MPA); teaching English to speakers of other languages (MA); translation and interpreting (MA); urban planning (MUP). Part-time and evening/weekend programs available. *Faculty:* 59 full-time (4 women), 5 part-time/adjunct (1 woman). *Students:* 101 full-time (44 women), 218 part-time (95 women). Average age 27. 184 applicants, 83% accepted, 92 enrolled. In 2009, 97 master's awarded. *Entrance requirements:* For master's, GMAT (MBA). Additional exam requirements/recommendations for international students: Required—TOEFL (minimum score 550 paper-based; 213 computer-based; 80 iBT), TWE (minimum score 5). *Application deadline:* For fall admission, 7/30 priority date for domestic students, 7/15 priority date for international students; for spring admission, 12/31 priority date for domestic students, 12/16 for international students. Applications are processed on a rolling basis. Application fee: $300. Electronic applications accepted. Tuition charges are reported in United Arab Emirates dirhams. *Expenses:* Tuition: Part-time 3250 United Arab Emirates dirhams per credit hour. *Financial support:* In 2009–10, 63 students received support, including 28 research assistantships with tuition reimbursements available, 35 teaching assistantships with tuition reimbursements available. *Faculty research:* Chemical engineering, civil engineering, computer engineering, electrical engineering, linguistics, translation. *Unit head:* Ghada S. Sami, Admissions Manager, 971-65151006 Ext. 1006, Fax: 971-65151020, E-mail: graduateadmission@aus.edu. *Application contact:* Ghada S. Sami, Admissions Manager, 971-65151006 Ext. 1006, Fax: 971-65151020, E-mail: graduateadmission@aus.edu.

Arizona State University, Graduate College, Ira A. Fulton School of Engineering, Department of Civil and Environmental Engineering, Tempe, AZ 85287. Offers MS, MSE, PhD. *Degree requirements:* For master's, thesis or alternative; for doctorate, thesis/dissertation. *Entrance requirements:* For master's and doctorate, GRE General Test (recommended).

Auburn University, Graduate School, Ginn College of Engineering, Department of Civil Engineering, Auburn University, AL 36849. Offers construction engineering and management (MCE, MS, PhD); environmental engineering (MCE, MS, PhD); geotechnical/materials engineering (MCE, MS, PhD); hydraulics/hydrology (MCE, MS, PhD); structural engineering (MCE, MS, PhD); transportation engineering (MCE, MS, PhD). Part-time programs available. *Faculty:* 21 full-time (1 woman), 3 part-time/adjunct (1 woman). *Students:* 46 full-time (15 women), 39 part-time (5 women); includes 4 minority (3 African Americans, 1 Asian American or Pacific Islander), 29 international. Average age 26. 136 applicants, 43% accepted, 26 enrolled. In 2009, 19 master's, 4 doctorates awarded. *Degree requirements:* For master's, project (MCE), thesis (MS); for doctorate, comprehensive exam, thesis/dissertation. *Entrance requirements:* For master's and doctorate, GRE General Test. *Application deadline:* For fall admission, 7/7 for domestic students; for spring admission, 11/24 for domestic students. Applications are processed on a rolling basis. Application fee: $50 ($60 for international students). Electronic applications accepted. *Expenses:* Tuition, state resident: full-time $6240. Tuition, nonresident: full-time $18,720. International tuition: $18,938 full-time. Required fees: $492. Tuition and fees vary according to course load, program and reciprocity agreements. *Financial support:* Fellowships, research assistantships, teaching assistantships, Federal Work-Study available. Support available to part-time students. Financial award application deadline: 3/15; financial award applicants required to submit FAFSA. *Unit head:* Dr. J. Michael Stallings, Head, 334-844-4320. *Application contact:* Dr. George Flowers, Dean of the Graduate School, 334-844-2125.

Boise State University, Graduate College, College of Engineering, Department of Civil Engineering, Boise, ID 83725-0399. Offers M Engr, MS. Part-time and evening/weekend programs available. *Degree requirements:* For master's, thesis. *Entrance requirements:* For master's, GRE General Test, minimum GPA of 3.0. Additional exam requirements/recommendations for international students: Required—TOEFL. Electronic applications accepted. *Expenses:* Tuition, state resident: full-time $3106; part-time $209 per credit. Tuition, nonresident: part-time $284 per credit.

Bradley University, Graduate School, College of Engineering and Technology, Department of Civil Engineering and Construction, Peoria, IL 61625-0002. Offers MSCE. Part-time and evening/weekend programs available. *Degree requirements:* For master's, comprehensive exam. *Entrance requirements:* For master's, minimum GPA of 3.0, 2 letters of recommendation. Additional exam requirements/recommendations for international students: Required—TOEFL (minimum score 550 paper-based; 213 computer-based; 79 iBT).

Brigham Young University, Graduate Studies, Ira A. Fulton College of Engineering and Technology, Department of Civil and Environmental Engineering, Provo, UT 84602. Offers civil engineering (MS, PhD). Part-time programs available. *Faculty:* 16 full-time (0 women), 7 part-time/adjunct (0 women). *Students:* 79 full-time (10 women), 23 part-time (1 woman); includes 19 minority (2 African Americans, 10 Asian Americans or Pacific Islanders, 7 Hispanic Americans), 1 international. Average age 28. 62 applicants, 90% accepted, 47 enrolled. In 2009, 37 master's, 1 doctorate awarded. *Degree requirements:* For master's, thesis (for some programs), Fundamentals of Engineering (FE) Exam; for doctorate, comprehensive exam, thesis/dissertation. *Entrance requirements:* For master's, GRE General Test, minimum GPA of 3.0 in last 60 hours of course work; for doctorate, GRE General Test, minimum graduate GPA of 3.4. Additional exam requirements/recommendations for international students: Required—TOEFL (minimum score 580 paper-based; 237 computer-based; 85 iBT), IELTS (minimum score 7). *Application deadline:* For fall admission, 2/15 for domestic and international students; for winter admission, 8/15 for domestic students, 6/15 for international students; for spring admission, 2/15 for domestic students, 10/15 for international students. Applications are processed on a rolling basis. Application fee: $50. Electronic applications accepted. *Expenses:* Tuition: Full-time $5580; part-time $301 per credit hour. Tuition and fees vary according to student's religious affiliation. *Financial support:* In 2009–10, 56 students received support, including 43 research assistantships (averaging $6,700 per year), 26 teaching assistantships (averaging $5,300 per year); career-related internships or fieldwork and scholarships/grants also available. Support available to part-time students. Financial award application deadline: 3/15; financial award applicants required to submit FAFSA. *Faculty research:* Structural optimization, finite element modeling and earthquake resistant analysis, groundwater, surface water, watershed and hydrologic modeling and visualization, subsurface environmental issues including transport, remediation, monitoring and characterization, capacity of deep foundations under static and dynamic loading and the behavior and mitigation of liquefiable soils, traffic planning, operations, safety, pavements and materials. Total annual research expenditures: $894,357. *Unit head:* Dr. Steven E. Benzley, Department Chair, 801-422-2811, Fax: 801-422-0159, E-mail: seb@byu.edu. *Application contact:* Dr. E. James Nelson, Graduate Coordinator, 801-422-2811, Fax: 801-422-0159, E-mail: jimn@byu.edu.

Bucknell University, Graduate Studies, College of Engineering, Department of Civil and Environmental Engineering, Lewisburg, PA 17837. Offers MS, MSCE, MSEV. Part-time programs available. *Degree requirements:* For master's, thesis. *Entrance requirements:* For master's, GRE General Test, GRE Subject Test, minimum GPA of 2.8. Additional exam requirements/recommendations for international students: Required—TOEFL. *Faculty research:* Pile foundations, rehabilitation of bridges, deep-shaft biological-waste treatment, pre-cast concrete structures.

California Institute of Technology, Division of Engineering and Applied Science, Option in Civil Engineering, Pasadena, CA 91125-0001. Offers MS, PhD, Engr. *Faculty:* 2 full-time (0 women). *Students:* 11 full-time (2 women). 69 applicants, 6% accepted, 2 enrolled. In 2009, 6 master's, 3 doctorates awarded. *Degree requirements:* For doctorate, thesis/dissertation. *Application deadline:* For fall admission, 1/1 for domestic students. Application fee: $0. *Financial support:* In 2009–10, 7 fellowships, 4 research assistantships, 3 teaching assistantships were awarded. *Faculty research:* Earthquake engineering, soil mechanics, finite-element analysis, hydraulics, coastal engineering. *Unit head:* Dr. Thomas H. Heaton, Option Representative, 626-395-4232, E-mail: heaton@caltech.edu. *Application contact:* Natalie Gilmore, Assistant Dean of Graduate Studies, 626-395-3812, Fax: 626-577-9246, E-mail: ngilmore@caltech.edu.

California Polytechnic State University, San Luis Obispo, College of Engineering, Department of Civil and Environmental Engineering, San Luis Obispo, CA 93407. Offers MS. Part-time programs available. *Faculty:* 11 full-time (1 woman), 2 part-time/adjunct (0 women). *Students:* 40 full-time (7 women), 4 part-time (1 woman); includes 5 minority (2 Asian Americans or Pacific Islanders, 3 Hispanic Americans). Average age 24. 58 applicants, 57% accepted, 28 enrolled. In 2009, 17 master's awarded. *Degree requirements:* For master's, comprehensive exam (for some programs), thesis (for some programs). *Entrance requirements:* For master's, GRE General Test, minimum GPA of 3.0 in last 90 quarter units, 3 letters of recommendation. Additional exam requirements/recommendations for international students: Required—TOEFL (minimum score 550 paper-based; 213 computer-based). *Application deadline:* For fall admission, 7/1 for domestic students, 11/30 for international students; for winter admission, 11/1 for domestic students, 6/30 for international students; for spring admission, 2/1 for domestic students. Applications are processed on a rolling basis. Application fee: $55. Electronic applications accepted. *Expenses:* Tuition, nonresident: full-time $11,160; part-time $248 per unit. Required fees: $7134; $1553 per quarter. *Financial support:* Fellowships, research assistantships, teaching assistantships, career-related internships or fieldwork, Federal Work-Study, and scholarships/grants available. Support available to part-time students. Financial award application deadline: 3/2; financial award applicants required to submit FAFSA. *Faculty research:* Soils, structures, transportation, traffic, environmental protection. *Unit head:* Dr. Robb Moss, Graduate Coordinator, 805-756-6427, Fax: 805-756-6330, E-mail: rmoss@calpoly.edu. *Application contact:* Dr. Robb Moss, Graduate Coordinator, 805-756-6427, Fax: 805-756-6330, E-mail: rmoss@calpoly.edu.

California State Polytechnic University, Pomona, Academic Affairs, College of Engineering, Pomona, CA 91768-2557. Offers civil engineering (MS); electrical engineering (MSEE); engineering (MSE); engineering management (MS); mechanical engineering (MS). Part-time programs available. *Faculty:* 95 full-time (17 women), 71 part-time/adjunct (6 women). *Students:* 36 full-time (3 women), 198 part-time (33 women); includes 104 minority (1 African American, 2 American Indian/Alaska Native, 69 Asian Americans or Pacific Islanders, 32 Hispanic Americans), 42 international. Average age 28. 237 applicants, 49% accepted, 73 enrolled. In 2009, 46 master's awarded. *Degree requirements:* For master's, thesis or comprehensive exam. *Entrance requirements:* For master's, GRE General Test or minimum GPA of 3.0 in upper-level course work. Additional exam requirements/recommendations for international students: Required—TOEFL. *Application deadline:* For fall admission, 5/1 priority date for domestic students; for winter admission, 10/15 priority date for domestic students; for spring admission, 1/2 priority date for domestic students. Applications are processed on a rolling basis. Application fee: $55. Electronic applications accepted. *Expenses:* Tuition, nonresident: full-time $6696; part-time $248 per credit. Required fees: $5487; $3237 per term. Tuition and fees vary according to course load, degree level and program. *Financial support:* In 2009–10, 1 fellowship, 6 research assistantships, 5 teaching assistantships were awarded; career-related internships or fieldwork, Federal Work-Study, institutionally sponsored loans, and unspecified assistantships also available. Support available to part-time students. Financial award application deadline: 3/2; financial award applicants required to submit FAFSA. *Faculty research:* Aerospace; alternative vehicles; communications, computers, and controls; engineering management. Total annual research expenditures: $650,000. *Unit head:* Dr. Edward Hohmann, Dean, 909-869-2472, Fax: 909-869-4370, E-mail: echohmann@csupomona.edu. *Application contact:* Dr. Edward Hohmann, Dean, 909-869-2472, Fax: 909-869-4370, E-mail: echohmann@csupomona.edu.

California State University, Fresno, Division of Graduate Studies, College of Engineering and Computer Science, Department of Civil Engineering, Fresno, CA 93740-8027. Offers MS. Part-time and evening/weekend programs available. *Degree requirements:* For master's, thesis or alternative. *Entrance requirements:* For master's, GRE General Test, minimum GPA of 2.75. Additional exam requirements/recommendations for international students: Required—TOEFL. Electronic applications accepted. *Faculty research:* Surveying, water damage, instrumentation equipment, agricultural drainage, aerial triangulation, dairy manure particles.

California State University, Fullerton, Graduate Studies, College of Engineering and Computer Science, Department of Civil Engineering and Engineering Mechanics, Fullerton, CA 92834-9480. Offers MS. Part-time programs available. *Students:* 63 full-time (15 women), 61 part-time (14 women); includes 55 minority (2 African Americans, 44 Asian Americans or Pacific Islanders, 9 Hispanic Americans), 20 international. Average age 30. 136 applicants, 66% accepted, 42 enrolled. In 2009, 27 master's awarded. *Degree requirements:* For master's, comprehensive exam, project or thesis. *Entrance requirements:* For master's, minimum undergraduate GPA of 2.5. Application fee: $55. *Expenses:* Tuition, nonresident: full-time $11,160; part-time $373 per credit. Required fees: $1440 per term. Tuition and fees vary according to course load, degree level and program. *Financial support:* Career-related internships or fieldwork, Federal Work-Study, institutionally sponsored loans, and scholarships/grants available. Support available to part-time students. Financial award application deadline: 3/1; financial award applicants required to submit FAFSA. *Faculty research:* Soil-structure interaction, finite-element analysis, computer-aided analysis and design. *Unit head:* Dr. Pinaki Chakrabarti, Chair, 657-278-3016. *Application contact:* Admissions/Applications, 657-278-2371.

California State University, Long Beach, Graduate Studies, College of Engineering, Department of Civil Engineering and Construction Engineering Management, Long Beach, CA 90840. Offers civil engineering (MSCE). Part-time programs available. *Faculty:* 6 full-time (4 women). *Students:* 34 full-time (10 women), 68 part-time (15 women); includes 45 minority (2 African Americans, 27 Asian Americans or Pacific Islanders, 16 Hispanic Americans), 24 international. Average age 30. *Degree requirements:* For master's, comprehensive exam or thesis. *Entrance requirements:* Additional exam requirements/recommendations for international students: Required—TOEFL. *Application deadline:* For fall admission, 3/1 for domestic students. Application fee: $55. Electronic applications accepted. *Expenses:* Required fees: $1802 per semester. Part-time tuition and fees vary according to course load. *Financial support:* Career-related internships or fieldwork, Federal Work-Study, institutionally sponsored loans, scholarships/grants, and unspecified assistantships available. Financial award application deadline: 3/2. *Faculty research:* Soils, hydraulics, seismic structures, composite metals, computer-aided manufacturing. *Unit head:* Dr. Emelinda Parentela, Chair, 562-985-4932, Fax: 562-985-2380, E-mail: parent@csulb.edu. *Application contact:* Dr. Jeremy Redman, Graduate Advisor, 562-985-5135, Fax: 562-985-2380, E-mail: jredman@csulb.edu.

California State University, Los Angeles, Graduate Studies, College of Engineering, Computer Science, and Technology, Department of Civil Engineering, Los Angeles, CA 90032-8530. Offers MS. Part-time and evening/weekend programs available. *Faculty:* 3 part-time/adjunct (0 women). *Students:* 20 full-time (6 women), 46 part-time (7 women); includes 43 minority (9 African Americans, 21 Asian Americans or Pacific Islanders, 13 Hispanic Americans), 10 international. Average age 30. 25 applicants, 100% accepted, 13 enrolled. In 2009, 14 master's awarded. *Degree requirements:* For master's, comprehensive exam or thesis. *Entrance requirements:* For master's, GRE or minimum GPA of 2.4. Additional exam requirements/recommendations for international students: Required—TOEFL (minimum score 550 paper-based). *Application deadline:* For fall admission, 5/1 for domestic and international students. Applications are processed on a rolling basis. Application fee: $55. *Financial support:* Federal Work-Study available. Support available to part-time students. Financial award application deadline: 3/1. *Faculty research:* Structure, hydraulics, hydrology, soil mechanics. *Unit head:* Dr. Rupa Purasinghe, Chair, 323-343-4450, Fax: 323-343-6316, E-mail: rpurasi@calstatela.edu. *Application contact:* Dr. Cheryl L. Ney, Associate Vice President for Academic Affairs and Dean of Graduate Studies, 323-343-3820, Fax: 323-343-5653, E-mail: cney@cslanet.calstatela.edu.

California State University, Northridge, Graduate Studies, College of Engineering and Computer Science, Department of Civil Engineering and Applied Mechanics, Northridge, CA 91330. Offers engineering (MS), including structural engineering. Part-time and evening/weekend programs available. *Faculty:* 8 full-time (0 women), 13 part-time/adjunct (4 women). *Students:* 17 full-time (3 women), 19 part-time (6 women); includes 1 Asian American or Pacific Islander, 6 Hispanic Americans. Average age 29. 51 applicants, 67% accepted, 20 enrolled. *Degree requirements:* For master's, thesis. *Entrance requirements:* Additional exam requirements/recommendations for international students: Required—TOEFL. *Application deadline:* For fall admission, 11/30 for domestic students. Application fee: $55. *Financial support:* Teaching assistantships available. Financial award application deadline: 3/1. *Faculty research:* Composite study. *Unit head:* Prof. Stephen Gadomski, Chair, 818-677-2166. *Application contact:* Prof. Stephen Gadomski, Chair, 818-677-2166.

California State University, Sacramento, Graduate Studies, College of Engineering and Computer Science, Department of Civil Engineering, Sacramento, CA 95819. Offers MS. Part-time and evening/weekend programs available. *Degree requirements:* For master's, thesis or alternative, writing proficiency exam. *Entrance requirements:* Additional exam requirements/recommendations for international students: Required—TOEFL. Electronic applications accepted.

Carleton University, Faculty of Graduate Studies, Faculty of Engineering and Design, Department of Civil and Environmental Engineering, Ottawa, ON K1S 5B6, Canada. Offers M Eng, MA Sc, PhD. *Degree requirements:* For master's, thesis optional; for doctorate, thesis/dissertation. *Entrance requirements:* For master's, honors degree; for doctorate, MA Sc or M Eng. Additional exam requirements/recommendations for international students: Required—TOEFL. *Faculty research:* Pollution and wastewater management, fire safety engineering, earthquake engineering, structural design, bridge engineering.

Carnegie Mellon University, Carnegie Institute of Technology, Department of Civil and Environmental Engineering, Pittsburgh, PA 15213. Offers civil and environmental engineering (PhD); advanced infrastructure systems (MS, PhD); civil and environmental engineering (MS); civil and environmental engineering/engineering and public policy (PhD); civil engineering (MS, PhD); computational mechanics (MS, PhD); computational science and engineering (MS, PhD); environmental engineering (MS, PhD); environmental management and science (MS, PhD). Part-time programs available. *Faculty:* 19 full-time (3 women), 13 part-time/adjunct (3 women). *Students:* 118 full-time (48 women), 12 part-time (6 women); includes 15 minority (4 African Americans, 10 Asian Americans or Pacific Islanders, 1 Hispanic American), 78 international. Average age 26. 294 applicants, 75% accepted, 78 enrolled. In 2009, 55 master's, 10 doctorates awarded. Terminal master's awarded for partial completion of doctoral program. *Degree requirements:* For master's, thesis optional; for doctorate, comprehensive exam, thesis/dissertation, qualifying exam, public defense of dissertation. *Entrance requirements:* For master's and doctorate, GRE General Test. Additional exam requirements/recommendations for international students: Required—TOEFL (minimum score 550 paper-based; 213 computer-based; 82 iBT). *Application deadline:* For fall admission, 1/15 priority date for domestic and international students; for spring admission, 9/30 priority date for domestic and international students. Application fee: $65. Electronic applications accepted. *Financial support:* In 2009–10, 102 students received support, including 18 fellowships with full and partial tuition reimbursements available (averaging $22,853 per year), 34 research assistantships with full and partial tuition reimbursements available (averaging $23,661 per year); tuition waivers (partial) and unspecified assistantships also available. Financial award application deadline: 1/15. *Faculty research:* Advanced infrastructure systems; environmental engineering science and management; mechanics, materials, and computing; green design; global sustainable construction. Total annual research expenditures: $4.5 million. *Unit head:* Dr. James H. Garrett, Head, 412-268-2941, Fax: 412-268-7813, E-mail: garrett@cmu.edu. *Application contact:* Maxine A. Leffard, Graduate Program Administrator, 412-268-5673, Fax: 412-268-7813, E-mail: ce-admissions@andrew.cmu.edu.

Case Western Reserve University, School of Graduate Studies, The Case School of Engineering, Department of Civil Engineering, Cleveland, OH 44106. Offers civil engineering (MS, PhD). Part-time programs available. Postbaccalaureate distance learning degree programs offered (minimal on-campus study). *Faculty:* 7 full-time (0 women). *Students:* 18 full-time (6 women), 1 part-time (0 women), 11 international. In 2009, 4 master's, 3 doctorates awarded. *Degree requirements:* For master's, thesis (for some programs); for doctorate, thesis/dissertation, qualifying exam, teaching experience. *Entrance requirements:* For master's and doctorate, GRE General Test. Additional exam requirements/recommendations for international students: Required—TOEFL. *Application deadline:* For fall admission, 8/1 priority date for domestic students; for spring admission, 1/1 for domestic students. Application fee: $50. *Financial support:* Fellowships with full and partial tuition reimbursements, research assistantships with full and partial tuition reimbursements, teaching assistantships, institutionally sponsored loans available. Financial award application deadline: 8/1; financial award applicants required to submit FAFSA. *Faculty research:* Environmental, geotechnical, infrastructure reliability, mechanics, structures. Total annual research expenditures: $439,000. *Unit head:* Dr. David Zeng, Chairman and Frank H. Neff Professor, 216-368-2923, Fax: 216-368-5229, E-mail: xxz16@case.edu. *Application contact:* Carla Wilson, Student Affairs Coordinator, 216-368-4580, Fax: 216-368-3007, E-mail: cxw75@case.edu.

The Catholic University of America, School of Engineering, Department of Civil Engineering, Washington, DC 20064. Offers environmental engineering (MCE, MSE, D Engr, PhD, Certificate); environmental engineering and management (MCE, MSE, PhD, Certificate); environmental engineering and management (D Engr); fluid and solid mechanics (MCE, MSE, PhD, Certificate); geotechnical engineering (MCE, MSE, PhD, Certificate); management of construction (MCE, MSE, D Engr, PhD); structural engineering (MSE, D Engr, PhD); systems engineering (MSE, D Engr, PhD, Certificate). Part-time programs available. *Faculty:* 5 full-time (0 women), 7 part-time/adjunct (1 woman). *Students:* 7 full-time (3 women), 18 part-time (5 women); includes 6 minority (3 African Americans, 3 Hispanic Americans), 11 international. Average age 32. 36 applicants, 47% accepted, 9 enrolled. In 2009, 8 master's, 2 doctorates awarded. *Degree requirements:* For master's, thesis optional; for doctorate, comprehensive exam, thesis/dissertation. *Entrance requirements:* For master's and doctorate, statement of purpose, official copies of academic transcripts, three letters of recommendation. Additional exam requirements/recommendations for international students: Required—TOEFL (minimum score 580 paper-based; 237 computer-based). *Application deadline:* For fall admission, 8/1 priority date for domestic students, 7/15 for international students; for spring admission, 12/1 priority date for domestic students, 10/15 for international students. Applications are processed on a rolling basis. Application fee: $55. Electronic applications accepted. *Expenses:* Contact institution. *Financial support:* Fellowships, research assistantships, teaching assistantships, Federal Work-Study, scholarships/grants, tuition waivers (full and partial), and unspecified assistantships available. Financial award application deadline: 2/1; financial award applicants required to submit FAFSA. *Faculty research:* Geotechnical engineering, solid mechanics, construction engineering and management, environmental engineering, structural engineering. Total annual research expenditures: $438,834. *Unit head:* Dr. Lu Sun, Chair, 202-319-5164, Fax: 202-319-

6677, E-mail: sunl@cua.edu. *Application contact:* Julie Schwing, Director of Graduate Admissions, 202-319-5057, Fax: 202-319-6533, E-mail: cua-admissions@cua.edu.

City College of the City University of New York, Graduate School, Grove School of Engineering, Department of Civil Engineering, New York, NY 10031-9198. Offers ME, MS, PhD. Part-time programs available. *Degree requirements:* For master's, thesis optional; for doctorate, one foreign language, comprehensive exam, thesis/dissertation. *Entrance requirements:* For master's and doctorate, GRE General Test. Additional exam requirements/recommendations for international students: Required—TOEFL (minimum score 500 paper-based; 173 computer-based; 61 iBT). *Faculty research:* Earthquake engineering, transportation systems, groundwater, environmental systems, highway systems.

Clarkson University, Graduate School, Wallace H. Coulter School of Engineering, Department of Civil and Environmental Engineering, Potsdam, NY 13699. Offers civil engineering (ME, MS). Part-time programs available. *Faculty:* 24 full-time (5 women), 3 part-time/adjunct (0 women). *Students:* 43 full-time (12 women); includes 2 minority (1 Asian American or Pacific Islander, 1 Hispanic American), 32 international. Average age 26. 95 applicants, 65% accepted, 12 enrolled. In 2009, 10 master's awarded. Terminal master's awarded for partial completion of doctoral program. *Degree requirements:* For master's, thesis. *Entrance requirements:* For master's, GRE, resume, 3 letters of recommendation. Additional exam requirements/recommendations for international students: Required—TOEFL (minimum score 550 paper-based; 213 computer-based; 80 iBT), IELTS (minimum score 6.5). *Application deadline:* For fall admission, 1/30 priority date for domestic and international students; for spring admission, 9/1 priority date for domestic and international students. Applications are processed on a rolling basis. Application fee: $25 ($35 for international students). Electronic applications accepted. *Expenses:* Tuition: Part-time $1074 per credit hour. *Financial support:* In 2009–10, 39 students received support, including 27 research assistantships (averaging $20,190 per year), 7 teaching assistantships (averaging $20,190 per year); scholarships/grants, tuition waivers (partial), and unspecified assistantships also available. *Faculty research:* Granular flows, bioremediation, elasticity, soil-structure interaction, geotechnical structural dynamics. Total annual research expenditures: $3.7 million. *Unit head:* Dr. Hung Tao Shen, Department Chair, 315-268-6606, Fax: 315-268-7985, E-mail: htshen@clarkson.edu. *Application contact:* Kelly Sharlow, Assistant to the Dean, 315-268-7929, Fax: 315-268-4494, E-mail: ksharlow@clarkson.edu.

Clemson University, Graduate School, College of Engineering and Science, Department of Civil Engineering, Clemson, SC 29634. Offers MS, PhD. Part-time programs available. *Faculty:* 20 full-time (1 woman), 2 part-time/adjunct (0 women). *Students:* 86 full-time (26 women), 7 part-time (1 woman); includes 4 minority (all African Americans), 40 international. Average age 27. 163 applicants, 61% accepted, 19 enrolled. In 2009, 27 master's, 4 doctorates awarded. *Degree requirements:* For master's, thesis or alternative, oral exam, seminar; for doctorate, thesis/dissertation, oral exam, seminar. *Entrance requirements:* For master's and doctorate, GRE General Test, minimum GPA of 3.0. Additional exam requirements/recommendations for international students: Required—TOEFL. *Application deadline:* For fall admission, 6/1 for domestic students, 4/15 for international students; for spring admission, 9/15 for international students. Applications are processed on a rolling basis. Application fee: $70 ($80 for international students). Electronic applications accepted. *Expenses:* Tuition, state resident: full-time $8684; part-time $528 per credit hour. Tuition, nonresident: full-time $15,330; part-time $1078 per credit hour. Required fees: $736; $37 per semester. Part-time tuition and fees vary according to course load and program. *Financial support:* In 2009–10, 69 students received support, including 5 fellowships with full and partial tuition reimbursements available (averaging $7,157 per year), 29 research assistantships with partial tuition reimbursements available (averaging $14,906 per year), 11 teaching assistantships with partial tuition reimbursements available (averaging $17,674 per year); career-related internships or fieldwork, institutionally sponsored loans, scholarships/grants, health care benefits, and unspecified assistantships also available. Support available to part-time students. Financial award application deadline: 2/15; financial award applicants required to submit FAFSA. *Faculty research:* Applied fluid mechanics, construction materials, project management, structural engineering. Total annual research expenditures: $2.2 million. *Unit head:* Dr. Nadim Aziz, Chair, 864-656-3300, Fax: 864-656-2670, E-mail: aziz@clemson.edu. *Application contact:* Dr. Ron D. Andrus, Graduate Program Coordinator, 864-656-0488, Fax: 864-656-2670, E-mail: randrus@clemson.edu.

Cleveland State University, College of Graduate Studies, Fenn College of Engineering, Department of Civil and Environmental Engineering, Cleveland, OH 44115. Offers accelerated program civil engineering (MS); accelerated program environmental engineering (MS); civil engineering (MS, D Eng); engineering mechanics (MS); environmental engineering (MS). Part-time and evening/weekend programs available. *Degree requirements:* For master's, project or thesis; for doctorate, comprehensive exam, thesis/dissertation, candidacy and qualifying exams. *Entrance requirements:* For master's, GRE General Test, GRE Subject Test, minimum GPA of 2.75; for doctorate, GRE General Test, GRE Subject Test, minimum GPA of 3.25. Additional exam requirements/recommendations for international students: Required—TOEFL (minimum score 525 paper-based; 197 computer-based). *Faculty research:* Solid-waste disposal, constitutive modeling, transportation, safety engineering.

Colorado State University, Graduate School, College of Engineering, Department of Civil and Environmental Engineering, Fort Collins, CO 80523-1372. Offers civil engineering (ME, MS, PhD). Part-time programs available. Postbaccalaureate distance learning degree programs offered (no on-campus study). *Faculty:* 28 full-time (3 women), 7 part-time/adjunct (1 woman). *Students:* 67 full-time (16 women), 102 part-time (22 women); includes 3 minority (1 African American, 2 Asian Americans or Pacific Islanders), 64 international. Average age 31. 165 applicants, 67% accepted, 39 enrolled. In 2009, 24 master's, 12 doctorates awarded. Terminal master's awarded for partial completion of doctoral program. *Degree requirements:* For master's, thesis (for some programs); for doctorate, comprehensive exam, thesis/dissertation. *Entrance requirements:* For master's, GRE General Test, minimum GPA of 3.0, letters of recommendation, resume; for doctorate, GRE General Test, minimum GPA of 3.0, MS, letters of recommendation, statement of purpose, resume. Additional exam requirements/recommendations for international students: Required—TOEFL (minimum score 550 paper-based; 213 computer-based; 80 iBT); Recommended—IELTS (minimum score 6.5). *Application deadline:* For fall admission, 5/1 priority date for domestic and international students; for spring admission, 11/1 priority date for domestic and international students. Applications are processed on a rolling basis. Application fee: $50. Electronic applications accepted. *Expenses:* Tuition, state resident: full-time $6434; part-time $359.10 per credit. Tuition, nonresident: full-time $18,116; part-time $1006.45 per credit. Required fees: $1496; $83 per credit. *Financial support:* In 2009–10, 58 students received support, including 1 fellowship (averaging $43,000 per year), 45 research assistantships with tuition reimbursements available (averaging $11,012 per year), 12 teaching assistantships with tuition reimbursements available (averaging $10,286 per year); scholarships/grants and unspecified assistantships also available. Financial award application deadline: 2/15; financial award applicants required to submit FAFSA. *Faculty research:* Wind and fluid mechanics, structural engineering and mechanics, hydraulic engineering, geotechnical engineering, environmental and geoenvironmental engineering. Total annual research expenditures: $9.4 million. *Unit head:* Dr. Luis Garcia, Head, 970-491-5048, Fax: 970-491-7727, E-mail: luis.garcia@colostate.edu. *Application contact:* Kathy Stencel, Student Advisor, 970-491-7425, Fax: 970-491-7727, E-mail: kathleen.stencel@colostate.edu.

Columbia University, Fu Foundation School of Engineering and Applied Science, Department of Civil Engineering and Engineering Mechanics, New York, NY 10027. Offers civil engineering (MS, Eng Sc D, PhD, Engr); construction engineering and management (MS); engineering mechanics (MS, Eng Sc D, PhD, Engr). Part-time programs available. Postbaccalaureate distance learning degree programs offered (no on-campus study). *Faculty:* 10 full-time (1 woman), 4 part-time/adjunct (0 women). *Students:* 89 full-time (24 women), 48 part-time (16 women); includes 17 minority (2 African Americans, 8 Asian Americans or Pacific Islanders, 7 Hispanic Americans), 72 international. Average age 27. 221 applicants, 54% accepted, 48 enrolled. In 2009, 38 master's, 1 doctorate awarded. Terminal master's awarded for partial

Civil Engineering

Columbia University (continued)
completion of doctoral program. *Degree requirements:* For doctorate, thesis/dissertation, qualifying exam. *Entrance requirements:* For master's, doctorate, and Engr, GRE General Test. Additional exam requirements/recommendations for international students: Required—TOEFL. *Application deadline:* For fall admission, 12/1 priority date for domestic and international students; for spring admission, 10/1 priority date for domestic and international students. Application fee: $70. Electronic applications accepted. *Financial support:* In 2009–10, 29 students received support, including 5 fellowships with full tuition reimbursements available (averaging $33,518 per year), 12 research assistantships with full tuition reimbursements available (averaging $32,761 per year), 12 teaching assistantships with full tuition reimbursements available (averaging $32,761 per year); health care benefits also available. Financial award application deadline: 12/1; financial award applicants required to submit FAFSA. *Faculty research:* Motion monitoring of Manhattan Bridge, lightweight concrete panels, simulation of life of well sealant, intercultural knowledge system dynamics, corrosion monitoring of New York City bridges. *Unit head:* Dr. Upmanu Lall, Interim Chairman and Professor, 212-854-8905, Fax: 212-854-7081, E-mail: lall@civil.columbia.edu. *Application contact:* Rene B. Testa, Professor, 212-854-3143, Fax: 212-854-6267, E-mail: testa@civil.columbia.edu.

Concordia University, School of Graduate Studies, Faculty of Engineering and Computer Science, Department of Building, Civil and Environmental Engineering, Montréal, QC H3G 1M8, Canada. Offers building engineering (M Eng, MA Sc, PhD, Certificate); civil engineering (M Eng, MA Sc, PhD); environmental engineering (Certificate). *Degree requirements:* For master's, thesis or alternative; for doctorate, comprehensive exam, thesis/dissertation. *Faculty research:* Structural engineering, geotechnical engineering, water resources and fluid engineering, transportation engineering, systems engineering.

Cooper Union for the Advancement of Science and Art, Albert Nerken School of Engineering, New York, NY 10003-7120. Offers chemical engineering (ME); civil engineering (ME); electrical engineering (ME); mechanical engineering (ME). Part-time programs available. *Faculty:* 27 full-time (1 woman), 15 part-time/adjunct (2 women). *Students:* 66 full-time (8 women), 20 part-time (1 woman); includes 30 minority (2 African Americans, 1 American Indian/Alaska Native, 19 Asian Americans or Pacific Islanders, 8 Hispanic Americans), 10 international. Average age 24. 80 applicants, 90% accepted, 56 enrolled. In 2009, 18 master's awarded. *Degree requirements:* For master's, thesis. *Entrance requirements:* For master's, GRE, BE, minimum GPA of 3.5. Additional exam requirements/recommendations for international students: Required—TOEFL (minimum score 600 paper-based; 250 computer-based; 100 iBT). *Application deadline:* For fall admission, 5/1 for domestic and international students. Applications are processed on a rolling basis. Application fee: $65. *Expenses:* Tuition: Full-time $35,000. Required fees: $1650. *Financial support:* Fellowships with tuition reimbursements, career-related internships or fieldwork, Federal Work-Study, tuition waivers (full), and all admitted students receive full-tuition scholarships available. Support available to part-time students. Financial award application deadline: 5/1; financial award applicants required to submit CSS PROFILE or FAFSA. *Faculty research:* Civil infrastructure, imaging and sensing technology, biomedical engineering, encryption technology, process engineering. *Unit head:* Dr. Simon Ben-Avi, Dean, 212-353-4285, E-mail: benavi@cooper.edu. *Application contact:* Student Contact, 212-353-4120, E-mail: admissions@cooper.edu.

Cornell University, Graduate School, Graduate Fields of Engineering, Field of Civil and Environmental Engineering, Ithaca, NY 14853-0001. Offers engineering management (M Eng, MS, PhD); environmental engineering (M Eng, MS, PhD); environmental fluid mechanics and hydrology (M Eng, MS, PhD); environmental systems engineering (M Eng, MS, PhD); geotechnical engineering (M Eng, MS, PhD); remote sensing (M Eng, MS, PhD); structural engineering (M Eng, MS, PhD); structural mechanics (M Eng, MS); transportation engineering (MS, PhD); transportation systems engineering (M Eng); water resource systems (M Eng, MS, PhD). *Faculty:* 40 full-time (7 women). *Students:* 144 full-time (48 women); includes 12 minority (2 African Americans, 1 American Indian/Alaska Native, 5 Asian Americans or Pacific Islanders, 4 Hispanic Americans), 58 international. Average age 25. 454 applicants, 57% accepted, 86 enrolled. In 2009, 69 master's, 5 doctorates awarded. Terminal master's awarded for partial completion of doctoral program. *Degree requirements:* For master's, thesis (MS); for doctorate, comprehensive exam, thesis/dissertation. *Entrance requirements:* For master's and doctorate, GRE General Test (recommended), 2 letters of recommendation. Additional exam requirements/recommendations for international students: Required—TOEFL (minimum score 600 paper-based; 250 computer-based; 77 iBT). *Application deadline:* For fall admission, 1/15 priority date for domestic students; for spring admission, 10/15 for domestic students. Application fee: $70. Electronic applications accepted. *Expenses:* Tuition: Full-time $29,500. Required fees: $70. Full-time tuition and fees vary according to degree level, program and student level. *Financial support:* In 2009–10, 50 students received support, including 6 fellowships with full tuition reimbursements available, 5 research assistantships with full tuition reimbursements available, 1 teaching assistantship with full tuition reimbursement available; institutionally sponsored loans, scholarships/grants, health care benefits, tuition waivers (full and partial), and unspecified assistantships also available. Financial award applicants required to submit FAFSA. *Faculty research:* Environmental engineering, geotechnical engineering remote sensing, environmental fluid mechanics and hydrology, structural engineering. *Unit head:* Director of Graduate Studies, 607-255-7560, Fax: 607-255-9004. *Application contact:* Graduate Field Assistant, 607-255-7560, Fax: 607-255-9004, E-mail: cee_grad@cornell.edu.

Dalhousie University, Faculty of Engineering, Department of Civil and Resource Engineering, Halifax, NS B3J 2X4, Canada. Offers M Eng, MA Sc, PhD. *Faculty:* 11 full-time (1 woman), 2 part-time/adjunct (0 women). *Students:* 25 full-time (7 women), 5 part-time (1 woman). Average age 30. 41 applicants, 78% accepted. In 2009, 10 master's, 2 doctorates awarded. *Degree requirements:* For master's, thesis; for doctorate, thesis/dissertation. *Entrance requirements:* Additional exam requirements/recommendations for international students: Required—TOEFL, IELTS, CANTEST, CAEL, or Michigan English Language Assessment Battery. *Application deadline:* For fall admission, 6/1 priority date for domestic students, 4/1 for international students; for winter admission, 11/15 priority date for domestic students, 8/31 for international students; for spring admission, 2/28 priority date for domestic students, 12/31 for international students. Applications are processed on a rolling basis. Application fee: $70. Electronic applications accepted. *Financial support:* Fellowships, research assistantships, teaching assistantships, career-related internships or fieldwork and scholarships/grants available. *Faculty research:* Environmental/water resources, bridge engineering, geotechnical engineering, pavement design and management/highway materials, composite materials. *Unit head:* Dr. Steve Zou, Head, 902-494-3960, Fax: 902-494-3108, E-mail: civil.engineering@dal.ca. *Application contact:* Dr. Margaret Walsh, Graduate Coordinator, 902-494-8430, Fax: 902-494-3108, E-mail: mwalsh2@dal.ca.

Drexel University, College of Engineering, Department of Civil, Architectural, and Environmental Engineering, Program in Civil Engineering, Philadelphia, PA 19104-2875. Offers MS, PhD. Part-time and evening/weekend programs available. *Degree requirements:* For master's, thesis optional; for doctorate, thesis/dissertation. *Entrance requirements:* For master's, minimum GPA of 3.0; for doctorate, minimum GPA of 3.5, MS in civil engineering. Additional exam requirements/recommendations for international students: Required—TOEFL. Electronic applications accepted.

Duke University, Graduate School, Pratt School of Engineering, Department of Civil and Environmental Engineering, Durham, NC 27708. Offers civil and environmental engineering (MS, PhD); environmental engineering (MS, PhD). Part-time programs available. *Faculty:* 21 full-time. *Students:* 51 full-time (13 women); includes 2 minority (1 African American, 1 Hispanic American), 30 international. 124 applicants, 31% accepted, 12 enrolled. In 2009, 2 master's, 7 doctorates awarded. Terminal master's awarded for partial completion of doctoral program. *Degree requirements:* For doctorate, thesis/dissertation. *Entrance requirements:* For master's and doctorate, GRE General Test. Additional exam requirements/recommendations for international students: Required—TOEFL (minimum score 550 paper-based; 213 computer-based;

83 iBT), IELTS (minimum score 7). *Application deadline:* For fall admission, 12/8 priority date for domestic and international students; for spring admission, 11/1 for domestic students. Application fee: $75. Electronic applications accepted. *Financial support:* Fellowships, research assistantships, Federal Work-Study available. Financial award application deadline: 12/31. *Unit head:* Dolbow John, Director of Graduate Studies, 919-660-5200, Fax: 919-660-5219, E-mail: ruby.carpenter@duke.edu. *Application contact:* Cynthia Robertson, Associate Dean for Enrollment Services, 919-684-3913, E-mail: grad-admissions@duke.edu.

École Polytechnique de Montréal, Graduate Programs, Department of Civil, Geological and Mining Engineering, Montréal, QC H3C 3A7, Canada. Offers civil, geological and mining engineering (DESS); environmental engineering (M Eng, M Sc A, PhD); geotechnical engineering (M Eng, M Sc A, PhD); hydraulics engineering (M Eng, M Sc A, PhD); structural engineering (M Eng, M Sc A, PhD); transportation engineering (M Eng, M Sc A, PhD). Part-time programs available. *Degree requirements:* For master's, one foreign language, thesis; for doctorate, one foreign language, thesis/dissertation. *Entrance requirements:* For master's, minimum GPA of 2.75; for doctorate, minimum GPA of 3.0. *Faculty research:* Water resources management, characteristics of building materials, aging of dams, pollution control.

Florida Agricultural and Mechanical University, Division of Graduate Studies, Research, and Continuing Education, FAMU-FSU College of Engineering, Department of Civil and Environmental Engineering, Tallahassee, FL 32307-3200. Offers civil engineering (MS, PhD); environmental engineering (MS, PhD). *Faculty:* 20 full-time (6 women). *Students:* 24 full-time (10 women), 14 part-time (2 women); includes 32 minority (31 African Americans, 1 Asian American or Pacific Islander), 6 international. In 2009, 1 doctorate awarded. *Degree requirements:* For master's, comprehensive exam, thesis optional; for doctorate, comprehensive exam, thesis/dissertation. *Entrance requirements:* For master's, GRE General Test, minimum GPA of 3.0; for doctorate, GRE General Test, minimum GPA of 3.0, letters of recommendation (3). Additional exam requirements/recommendations for international students: Required—TOEFL (minimum score 550 paper-based; 213 computer-based). *Application deadline:* For fall admission, 7/1 for domestic students, 3/1 for international students. Application fee: $30. *Faculty research:* Geotechnical, environmental, hydraulic, construction materials, and structures. *Unit head:* Dr. Jerry Wekezer, Chairperson, 850-410-6100. *Application contact:* Dr. Chanta M. Haywood, Dean of Graduate Studies, Research, and Continuing Education, 850-599-3315, Fax: 850-599-3727.

Florida Atlantic University, College of Engineering and Computer Science, Department of Civil, Environmental and Geomatics Engineering, Boca Raton, FL 33431-0991. Offers civil engineering (MS). Part-time and evening/weekend programs available. *Faculty:* 10 full-time (0 women). *Students:* 14 full-time (2 women), 17 part-time (4 women); includes 13 minority (4 African Americans, 2 Asian Americans or Pacific Islanders, 7 Hispanic Americans), 4 international. Average age 31. 27 applicants, 56% accepted, 8 enrolled. In 2009, 8 master's awarded. *Degree requirements:* For master's, thesis optional. *Entrance requirements:* For master's, GRE General Test, minimum GPA of 3.0 in last 60 hours of undergraduate course work. Additional exam requirements/recommendations for international students: Required—TOEFL (minimum score 550 paper-based; 213 computer-based). *Application deadline:* For fall admission, 7/1 priority date for domestic students, 2/15 for international students; for spring admission, 11/1 for domestic students, 7/15 for international students. Applications are processed on a rolling basis. Application fee: $30. *Expenses:* Tuition, state resident: full-time $7055; part-time $293.94 per credit hour. Tuition, nonresident: full-time $22,096; part-time $920.66 per credit hour. *Financial support:* Research assistantships with full tuition reimbursements, teaching assistantships with full tuition reimbursements, career-related internships or fieldwork, Federal Work-Study, scholarships/grants, and unspecified assistantships available. Financial award applicants required to submit FAFSA. *Faculty research:* Structures, geotechnical engineering, environmental and water resources engineering, transportation engineering, materials. *Unit head:* Dr. Pete D. Scarlatos, Chair, 561-297-0466, Fax: 561-297-0493, E-mail: scarlatos@fau.edu. *Application contact:* Dr. Frederick Bloetscher, Assistant Professor, 561-297-0744, E-mail: fbloetscher@civil.fau.edu.

Florida Institute of Technology, Graduate Programs, College of Engineering, Civil Engineering Department, Melbourne, FL 32901-6975. Offers MS, PhD. Part-time programs available. *Faculty:* 5 full-time (0 women), 1 part-time/adjunct (0 women). *Students:* 15 full-time (2 women), 6 part-time (1 woman); includes 2 minority (both Asian Americans or Pacific Islanders), 13 international. Average age 28. 59 applicants, 51% accepted, 6 enrolled. In 2009, 7 master's awarded. *Degree requirements:* For master's, comprehensive exam (for some programs), thesis, teaching or final examinations; for doctorate, comprehensive exam, thesis/dissertation, research project, written and/or oral exam. *Entrance requirements:* For master's, 2 letters of recommendation, minimum GPA of 3.0; for doctorate, 3 letters of recommendation, minimum GPA of 3.2, resume, statement of objectives. Additional exam requirements/recommendations for international students: Required—TOEFL (minimum score 550 paper-based; 213 computer-based; 79 iBT). *Application deadline:* For fall admission, 4/1 for international students; for spring admission, 9/30 for international students. Applications are processed on a rolling basis. Application fee: $50. Electronic applications accepted. *Expenses:* Tuition: Part-time $1015 per credit. Tuition and fees vary according to campus/location and program. *Financial support:* In 2009–10, 9 students received support, including 6 research assistantships with full and partial tuition reimbursements available (averaging $6,692 per year), 3 teaching assistantships with full and partial tuition reimbursements available (averaging $4,367 per year); career-related internships or fieldwork, institutionally sponsored loans, tuition waivers (partial), unspecified assistantships, and tuition remissions also available. Support available to part-time students. Financial award application deadline: 3/1; financial award applicants required to submit FAFSA. *Faculty research:* Groundwater and surface water modeling, pavements, waste materials, in situ soil testing, fiber optic sensors. Total annual research expenditures: $329,289. *Unit head:* Dr. Ashok Pandit, Department Head, 321-674-7151, Fax: 321-768-7565, E-mail: apandit@fit.edu. *Application contact:* Thomas M. Shea, Director of Graduate Admissions, 321-674-7577, Fax: 321-723-9468, E-mail: tshea@fit.edu.

See Close-Up on page 213.

Florida International University, College of Engineering and Computing, Department of Civil and Environmental Engineering, Program in Civil Engineering, Miami, FL 33175. Offers MS, PhD. Part-time and evening/weekend programs available. Postbaccalaureate distance learning degree programs offered (no on-campus study). *Students:* 71 full-time (19 women), 41 part-time (10 women); includes 42 minority (9 African Americans, 4 Asian Americans or Pacific Islanders, 29 Hispanic Americans), 59 international. Average age 30. 85 applicants, 27% accepted, 23 enrolled. In 2009, 30 master's, 8 doctorates awarded. *Degree requirements:* For master's, thesis optional; for doctorate, comprehensive exam, thesis/dissertation. *Entrance requirements:* For master's, bachelor's degree in related field, minimum GPA of 3.0; for doctorate, GRE General Test, minimum graduate GPA of 3.3, master's degree, resume, letters of recommendation, statement of objectives. Additional exam requirements/recommendations for international students: Required—TOEFL (minimum score 550 paper-based; 80 iBT). *Application deadline:* For fall admission, 6/1 for domestic students, 4/1 for international students; for spring admission, 10/1 for domestic students, 9/1 for international students. Applications are processed on a rolling basis. Application fee: $30. Electronic applications accepted. *Expenses:* Tuition, state resident: full-time $8008; part-time $4004 per year. Tuition, nonresident: full-time $20,104; part-time $10,052 per year. Required fees: $298; $149 per term. *Financial support:* In 2009–10, 15 research assistantships (averaging $20,000 per year), 24 teaching assistantships (averaging $20,000 per year) were awarded; Federal Work-Study, institutionally sponsored loans, scholarships/grants, health care benefits, and unspecified assistantships also available. Financial award application deadline: 3/1; financial award applicants required to submit FAFSA. *Faculty research:* Structural engineering, wind engineering, sustainable infrastructure engineering, water resources engineering, transportation engineering. *Unit head:* Dr. Fang Zhao, Chair, Civil and Environmental Engineering Department, 305-348-3821, Fax: 305-348-2802, E-mail: fang.zhao@fiu.edu. *Application contact:* Maria Parrilla, Graduate Admissions Assistant, 305-348-1890, Fax: 305-348-6142, E-mail: grad_eng@fiu.edu.

Florida State University, The Graduate School, FAMU-FSU College of Engineering, Department of Civil and Environmental Engineering, Tallahassee, FL 32306. Offers MS, PhD. Part-time programs available. *Faculty:* 16 full-time (3 women). *Students:* 33 full-time (9 women), 10 part-time (3 women); includes 23 minority (12 African Americans, 7 Asian Americans or Pacific Islanders, 4 Hispanic Americans). Average age 23. 48 applicants, 48% accepted, 7 enrolled. In 2009, 11 master's, 4 doctorates awarded. *Degree requirements:* For master's, thesis optional; for doctorate, thesis/dissertation. *Entrance requirements:* For master's, GRE General Test (minimum score 1000), BS in engineering or related field, minimum GPA of 3.0; for doctorate, GRE General Test (minimum score 1100), Master's degree in engineering or related field, minimum GPA of 3.0. Additional exam requirements/recommendations for international students: Required—TOEFL (minimum score 550 paper-based; 213 computer-based). *Application deadline:* For fall admission, 7/1 for domestic and international students; for spring admission, 11/1 for domestic and international students. Applications are processed on a rolling basis. Application fee: $30. *Expenses:* Tuition, state resident: full-time $7413.36. Tuition, nonresident: full-time $22,567. *Financial support:* In 2009–10, 25 students received support, including 15 research assistantships with full tuition reimbursements available (averaging $15,000 per year), 10 teaching assistantships with full tuition reimbursements available (averaging $15,000 per year); fellowships, Federal Work-Study, tuition waivers (full), and unspecified assistantships also available. Financial award application deadline: 6/15; financial award applicants required to submit FAFSA. *Faculty research:* Tidal hydraulics, temperature effects on bridge girders, codes for coastal construction, field performance of pine bridges, river basin management, transportation pavement design, soil dynamics, structural analysis. Total annual research expenditures: $1.3 million. *Unit head:* Dr. Kamal S. Tawfiq, Chair and Professor, 850-410-6143, Fax: 850-410-6142, E-mail: tawfiq@eng.fsu.edu. *Application contact:* Johnnye Belinda Morris, Office Manager, 850-410-6139, Fax: 850-410-6142, E-mail: bmorris@eng.fsu.edu.

George Mason University, Volgenau School of Information Technology and Engineering, Department of Civil, Environmental, and Infrastructure Engineering, Fairfax, VA 22030. Offers civil and infrastructure engineering (MS, PhD); civil infrastructure and security engineering (Certificate); leading technical enterprises (Certificate); sustainability and the environment (Certificate); water resources engineering (Certificate). Part-time and evening/weekend programs available. *Faculty:* 9 full-time (3 women), 15 part-time/adjunct (0 women). *Students:* 19 full-time (3 women), 61 part-time (18 women); includes 16 minority (5 African Americans, 7 Asian Americans or Pacific Islanders, 4 Hispanic Americans), 8 international. Average age 33. 102 applicants, 58% accepted, 43 enrolled. In 2009, 13 master's, 2 other advanced degrees awarded. *Degree requirements:* For master's, thesis (for some programs), 30 credits, departmental seminars; for doctorate, thesis/dissertation, qualifying exams. *Entrance requirements:* For master's, GRE or GMAT. Additional exam requirements/recommendations for international students: Required—TOEFL (minimum score 575 paper-based; 230 computer-based; 88 iBT). *Application deadline:* For fall admission, 3/15 priority date for domestic students, 3/15 for international students; for spring admission, 11/1 for domestic students, 10/1 for international students. Application fee: $75. Electronic applications accepted. *Expenses:* Tuition, state resident: full-time $7568; part-time $315.33 per credit hour. Tuition, nonresident: full-time $21,704; part-time $904.33 per credit hour. Required fees: $2184; $91 per credit hour. *Financial support:* In 2009–10, 12 students received support, including 2 research assistantships with full and partial tuition reimbursements available (averaging $15,000 per year), 10 teaching assistantships with full and partial tuition reimbursements available (averaging $4,557 per year); career-related internships or fieldwork, scholarships/grants, unspecified assistantships, and health care benefits (full-time research or teaching assistantship recipients) also available. Support available to part-time students. Financial award application deadline: 3/1; financial award applicants required to submit FAFSA. *Faculty research:* Evolutionary design, infrastructure security, intelligent transportation systems, national transportation networks, water quality modeling. Total annual research expenditures: $67,461. *Unit head:* Dr. Michael Bronzini, Chair, 703-993-1504, Fax: 703-993-1521. *Application contact:* Lisa Nolder, Graduate Student Services Director, 703-993-1499, E-mail: snolder@gmu.edu.

The George Washington University, School of Engineering and Applied Science, Department of Civil and Environmental Engineering, Washington, DC 20052. Offers MS, D Sc, App Sc, Engr. Part-time and evening/weekend programs available. *Faculty:* 12 full-time (3 women), 10 part-time/adjunct (1 woman). *Students:* 18 full-time (5 women), 36 part-time (12 women); includes 5 minority (2 African Americans, 2 Asian Americans or Pacific Islanders, 1 Hispanic American), 33 international. Average age 31. 79 applicants, 56% accepted, 12 enrolled. In 2009, 12 master's, 6 doctorates awarded. *Degree requirements:* For master's, thesis optional; for doctorate, thesis/dissertation, final and qualifying exams. *Entrance requirements:* For master's, appropriate bachelor's degree, minimum GPA of 3.0; for doctorate, appropriate bachelor's or master's degree, minimum GPA of 3.4, GRE if highest earned degree is BS; for other advanced degree, appropriate master's degree, minimum GPA of 3.0. Additional exam requirements/recommendations for international students: Required—TOEFL or George Washington University English as a Foreign Language Test. *Application deadline:* For fall admission, 3/1 priority date for domestic students; for spring admission, 10/1 for domestic students. Applications are processed on a rolling basis. Application fee: $60. *Financial support:* In 2009–10, 42 students received support; fellowships with tuition reimbursements available, research assistantships, teaching assistantships with tuition reimbursements available, career-related internships or fieldwork, Federal Work-Study, institutionally sponsored loans, and tuition waivers available. Financial award application deadline: 3/1; financial award applicants required to submit FAFSA. *Faculty research:* Computer-integrated manufacturing, materials engineering, electronic materials, fatigue and fracture, reliability. *Unit head:* Dr. Kim Roddis, Chair, 202-994-8515, Fax: 202-994-0127, E-mail: roddis@gwu.edu. *Application contact:* Adina Lav, Marketing, Recruiting and Admissions, 202-994-5827, Fax: 202-994-0909, E-mail: engineering@gwu.edu.

Georgia Institute of Technology, Graduate Studies and Research, College of Engineering, School of Civil and Environmental Engineering, Program in Civil Engineering, Atlanta, GA 30332-0001. Offers MS, MSCE, PhD. Part-time programs available. Terminal master's awarded for partial completion of doctoral program. *Degree requirements:* For doctorate, thesis/dissertation. *Entrance requirements:* For master's, GRE, minimum GPA of 3.0; for doctorate, GRE, minimum GPA of 3.2. Additional exam requirements/recommendations for international students: Required—TOEFL. *Faculty research:* Structural analysis, fluid mechanics, geotechnical engineering, construction management, transportation engineering.

Graduate School and University Center of the City University of New York, Graduate Studies, Program in Engineering, New York, NY 10016-4039. Offers biomedical engineering (PhD); chemical engineering (PhD); civil engineering (PhD); electrical engineering (PhD); mechanical engineering (PhD). *Faculty:* 68 full-time (1 woman). *Students:* 115 full-time (33 women), 8 part-time (2 women); includes 17 minority (5 African Americans, 8 Asian Americans or Pacific Islanders, 4 Hispanic Americans), 68 international. Average age 34. 119 applicants, 48% accepted, 26 enrolled. In 2009, 30 doctorates awarded. *Degree requirements:* For doctorate, thesis/dissertation. *Entrance requirements:* For doctorate, GRE General Test. Additional exam requirements/recommendations for international students: Required—TOEFL. Application fee: $125. Electronic applications accepted. *Financial support:* In 2009–10, 61 fellowships, 10 teaching assistantships were awarded; research assistantships, Federal Work-Study, institutionally sponsored loans, and tuition waivers (full and partial) also available. Financial award application deadline: 2/1; financial award applicants required to submit FAFSA. *Unit head:* Dr. Mumtaz Kassir, Executive Officer, 212-650-8031, Fax: 212-650-8029, E-mail: kassir@ce-mail.engr.ccny.cuny.edu. *Application contact:* Les Gribben, Director of Admissions, 212-817-7470, Fax: 212-817-1624, E-mail: lgribben@gc.cuny.edu.

See Close-Up on page 69.

Howard University, College of Engineering, Architecture, and Computer Sciences, School of Engineering and Computer Science, Department of Civil Engineering, Washington, DC 20059-0002. Offers M Eng. Offered through the Graduate School of Arts and Sciences. *Degree requirements:* For master's, comprehensive exam (for some programs), thesis (for some programs). *Entrance requirements:* For master's, GRE General Test, minimum GPA of 3.0, bachelor's degree in engineering or related field. Additional exam requirements/recommendations for international students: Required—TOEFL. Electronic applications accepted. *Faculty research:* Modeling of concrete, structures, transportation planning, structural analysis, environmental and water resources.

Idaho State University, Office of Graduate Studies, College of Engineering, Civil and Environmental Engineering Department, Pocatello, ID 83209-8060. Offers civil engineering (MS); environmental engineering (MS); environmental science and management (MS). Part-time programs available. *Faculty:* 1 full-time (0 women). *Students:* 9 full-time (1 woman), 17 part-time (6 women); includes 2 minority (both Asian Americans or Pacific Islanders), 12 international. Average age 31. In 2009, 9 master's awarded. *Degree requirements:* For master's, comprehensive exam (for some programs), thesis optional, thesis project, 2 semesters of seminar. *Entrance requirements:* For master's, GRE. Additional exam requirements/recommendations for international students: Required—TOEFL (minimum score 550 paper-based; 213 computer-based; 80 iBT). *Application deadline:* For fall admission, 7/1 for domestic students, 6/1 for international students; for spring admission, 12/1 for domestic students, 11/1 for international students. Applications are processed on a rolling basis. Application fee: $55. Electronic applications accepted. *Expenses:* Tuition, state resident: full-time $3318; part-time $297 per credit hour. Tuition, nonresident: full-time $13,120; part-time $437 per credit hour. Required fees: $2530. Tuition and fees vary according to program. *Financial support:* Research assistantships with full and partial tuition reimbursements, teaching assistantships with full and partial tuition reimbursements, career-related internships or fieldwork, Federal Work-Study, institutionally sponsored loans, scholarships/grants, traineeships, health care benefits, tuition waivers (full and partial), and unspecified assistantships available. Support available to part-time students. Financial award application deadline: 1/1; financial award applicants required to submit FAFSA. *Faculty research:* Floor vibration investigations, earthquake engineering, base isolation systems and seismic risk assessment, infrastructure revitalization (building foundations and damage, bridge structures, highways, and dams), slope stability and soil erosion, pavement rehabilitation, computational fluid dynamics and flood control structures, microbial fuel cells, water treatment and water quality modeling, environmental risk assessment, biotechnology, nanotechnology. *Unit head:* Dr. Arya Ebrahimpour, Chair, 208-282-4695, Fax: 208-282-4538, E-mail: ebraaryai@isu.edu. *Application contact:* Tami Carson, Graduate School Technical Records Specialist, 208-282-2150, Fax: 208-282-4847, E-mail: carstami@isu.edu.

Illinois Institute of Technology, Graduate College, Armour College of Engineering, Department of Civil, Architectural and Environmental Engineering, Chicago, IL 60616-3793. Offers architectural engineering (M Arch E); civil engineering (MS, PhD); construction engineering and management (MCEM); environmental engineering (M Env E, MS, PhD); geoenvironmental engineering (M Geoenv E); geotechnical engineering (MGE); public works (MPW); structural engineering (MSE); transportation engineering (M Trans E). Part-time and evening/weekend programs available. Terminal master's awarded for partial completion of doctoral program. *Degree requirements:* For master's, thesis (for some programs); for doctorate, comprehensive exam, thesis/dissertation. *Entrance requirements:* For master's and doctorate, GRE General Test, minimum undergraduate GPA of 3.0. Additional exam requirements/recommendations for international students: Required—TOEFL (minimum score 550 paper-based; 213 computer-based; 80 iBT). Electronic applications accepted. *Expenses:* Tuition: Full-time $17,550; part-time $888 per credit hour. Required fees: $850; $7.50 per credit hour. One-time fee: $50 full-time. Full-time tuition and fees vary according to program. *Faculty research:* Seismic analysis of buildings and bridges, fatigue analysis and materials of construction, construction zone safety and construction productivity, architectural acoustics and building energy efficiency, environmental engineering. air and water quality.

Instituto Tecnológico y de Estudios Superiores de Monterrey, Campus Monterrey, Graduate and Research Division, Programs in Engineering, Monterrey, Mexico. Offers applied statistics (M Eng); artificial intelligence (PhD); automation engineering (M Eng); chemical engineering (M Eng); civil engineering (M Eng); electrical engineering (M Eng); electronic engineering (M Eng); environmental engineering (M Eng); industrial engineering (M Eng, PhD); manufacturing engineering (M Eng); mechanical engineering (M Eng); systems and quality engineering (M Eng). Part-time and evening/weekend programs available. Terminal master's awarded for partial completion of doctoral program. *Degree requirements:* For master's, one foreign language, thesis; for doctorate, one foreign language, thesis/dissertation. *Entrance requirements:* For master's, EXADEP; for doctorate, GRE, master's degree in related field. Additional exam requirements/recommendations for international students: Required—TOEFL. *Faculty research:* Flexible manufacturing cells, materials, statistical methods, environmental prevention, control and evaluation.

Iowa State University of Science and Technology, Graduate College, College of Engineering, Department of Civil and Construction Engineering, Ames, IA 50011. Offers civil engineering (MS, PhD), including civil engineering materials, construction engineering and management, environmental engineering, geometronics, geotechnical engineering, structural engineering, transportation engineering. *Faculty:* 32 full-time (5 women), 6 part-time/adjunct (0 women). *Students:* 87 full-time (20 women), 33 part-time (8 women); includes 2 minority (1 American Indian/Alaska Native, 1 Asian American or Pacific Islander), 48 international. 204 applicants, 29% accepted, 27 enrolled. In 2009, 6 master's, 11 doctorates awarded. *Degree requirements:* For master's, thesis or alternative; for doctorate, thesis/dissertation. *Entrance requirements:* For master's and doctorate, GRE General Test. Additional exam requirements/recommendations for international students: Required—TOEFL (minimum score 550 paper-based; 82 iBT) or IELTS (minimum score 6.5). *Application deadline:* For fall admission, 2/1 priority date for domestic students, 2/1 for international students; for spring admission, 8/1 priority date for domestic students, 8/1 for international students. Application fee: $40 ($90 for international students). Electronic applications accepted. *Expenses:* Tuition, state resident: full-time $6716. Tuition, nonresident: full-time $8908. Tuition and fees vary according to course level, course load, program and student level. *Financial support:* In 2009–10, 70 research assistantships with full and partial tuition reimbursements (averaging $16,000 per year), 4 teaching assistantships with full and partial tuition reimbursements (averaging $18,000 per year) were awarded; fellowships, scholarships/grants, health care benefits, and unspecified assistantships also available. *Unit head:* Dr. James Alleman, Chair, 515-294-3892, E-mail: ccee-grad-inquiry@iastate.edu. *Application contact:* Dr. Sri Srithanan, Director of Graduate Education, 515-294-5328, E-mail: ccee-grad-inquiry@iastate.edu.

The Johns Hopkins University, Engineering for Professionals, Part-time Program in Civil Engineering, Baltimore, MD 21218-2699. Offers MCE. Part-time and evening/weekend programs available. *Faculty:* 3 part-time/adjunct (1 woman). *Students:* 19 part-time (6 women); includes 3 minority (2 African Americans, 1 Asian American or Pacific Islander), 1 international. Average age 27. In 2009, 3 master's awarded. *Application deadline:* Applications are processed on a rolling basis. Application fee: $75. Electronic applications accepted. *Financial support:* Institutionally sponsored loans available. *Unit head:* Dr. A. Rajah Anandarajah, Chair, 410-516-8682, E-mail: rajah@jhu.edu. *Application contact:* Priyanka Dwivedi, Admissions Manager, 410-516-2300, Fax: 410-579-8049, E-mail: pdwived1@jhu.edu.

The Johns Hopkins University, G. W. C. Whiting School of Engineering, Department of Civil Engineering, Baltimore, MD 21218. Offers MCE, MSE, PhD. *Faculty:* 11 full-time (3 women), 3 part-time/adjunct (0 women). *Students:* 31 full-time (8 women); includes 1 minority (Asian American or Pacific Islander), 24 international. Average age 28. 83 applicants, 37% accepted, 9 enrolled. In 2009, 9 master's, 4 doctorates awarded. Terminal master's awarded for partial completion of doctoral program. *Degree requirements:* For master's, thesis (for some programs); for doctorate, comprehensive exam, thesis/dissertation, Departmental Qualifying Exam, Graduate Board Oral exam. *Entrance requirements:* For master's and doctorate, GRE General Test. Additional exam requirements/recommendations for international students: Required—TOEFL. *Application deadline:* For fall admission, 2/16 for domestic and international students. Application fee: $25. Electronic applications accepted. *Financial support:* In 2009–10, 9 fellowships with

Civil Engineering

The Johns Hopkins University (continued)

full tuition reimbursements (averaging $24,940 per year), 18 research assistantships with full tuition reimbursements (averaging $22,699 per year) were awarded; teaching assistantships with tuition reimbursements, scholarships/grants, health care benefits, tuition waivers (partial), and unspecified assistantships also available. Financial award application deadline: 2/1. *Faculty research:* Geotechnical engineering, structural engineering, structural mechanics, geomechanics, probabilistic modeling1. Total annual research expenditures: $1.6 million. *Unit head:* Prof. Benjamin Schafer, Chair, 410-516-6265, E-mail: schafer@jhu.edu. *Application contact:* Lisa Wetzelberger, Academic Coordinator, 410-516-8680, Fax: 410-516-7473, E-mail: lawetzel@jhu.edu.

Kansas State University, Graduate School, College of Engineering, Department of Civil Engineering, Manhattan, KS 66506. Offers MS, PhD. Postbaccalaureate distance learning degree programs offered (no on-campus study). *Faculty:* 14 full-time (2 women), 2 part-time/adjunct (0 women). *Students:* 37 full-time (8 women), 52 part-time (11 women); includes 3 minority (1 American Indian/Alaska Native, 2 Hispanic Americans), 33 international. Average age 30. 63 applicants, 75% accepted, 36 enrolled. In 2009, 11 master's, 4 doctorates awarded. *Degree requirements:* For master's, thesis or alternative; for doctorate, thesis/dissertation. *Entrance requirements:* For master's, GRE General Test, bachelor's degree or course work in civil engineering; for doctorate, GRE General Test. Additional exam requirements/recommendations for international students: Required—TOEFL. *Application deadline:* For fall admission, 2/1 priority date for domestic and international students; for spring admission, 8/1 priority date for domestic and international students. Applications are processed on a rolling basis. Application fee: $40 ($55 for international students). Electronic applications accepted. *Financial support:* In 2009–10, 33 research assistantships (averaging $10,722 per year) were awarded; institutionally sponsored loans, scholarships/grants, and tuition waivers also available. Support available to part-time students. Financial award application deadline: 3/1; financial award applicants required to submit FAFSA. *Faculty research:* Transportation and materials engineering, water resources engineering, environmental engineering, geotechnical engineering, structural engineering. Total annual research expenditures: $2 million. *Unit head:* Yacoub Najjar, Interim Head, 785-532-1586, Fax: 785-532-7717, E-mail: ea4146@ksu.edu. *Application contact:* Hayder Rasheed, Director, 785-532-1589, Fax: 785-532-7717, E-mail: hayder@ksu.edu.

Lamar University, College of Graduate Studies, College of Engineering, Department of Civil Engineering, Beaumont, TX 77710. Offers civil engineering (ME, MES, DE); environmental engineering (MS); environmental studies (MS). Part-time programs available. *Faculty:* 6 full-time (1 woman), 3 part-time/adjunct (0 women). *Students:* 55 full-time (12 women), 16 part-time (4 women); includes 2 minority (both African Americans), 41 international. Average age 26. 94 applicants, 40% accepted, 17 enrolled. In 2009, 49 master's, 2 doctorates awarded. *Degree requirements:* For master's, thesis optional; for doctorate, thesis/dissertation. *Entrance requirements:* For master's and doctorate, GRE General Test. Additional exam requirements/recommendations for international students: Required—TOEFL. *Application deadline:* For fall admission, 5/15 priority date for domestic students; for spring admission, 10/1 priority date for domestic students. Applications are processed on a rolling basis. Application fee: $25 ($50 for international students). *Financial support:* In 2009–10, 45 fellowships with partial tuition reimbursements (averaging $1,000 per year), 10 research assistantships with partial tuition reimbursements (averaging $7,200 per year), 3 teaching assistantships with partial tuition reimbursements (averaging $7,200 per year) were awarded; scholarships/grants and tuition waivers (partial) also available. Financial award application deadline: 4/1. *Faculty research:* Environmental remediations, construction productivity, geotechnical soil stabilization, lake/reservoir hydrodynamics, air pollution. *Unit head:* Dr. Enno Koehn, Chair, 409-880-8759, Fax: 409-880-8121, E-mail: koehneu@hal.lamar.edu. *Application contact:* Sandy Drane, Coordinator of Graduate Admissions, 409-880-8356, Fax: 409-880-8414, E-mail: gradmissions@hal.lamar.edu.

Lawrence Technological University, College of Engineering, Southfield, MI 48075-1058. Offers automotive engineering (MAE); civil engineering (MCE); construction engineering management (MS); electrical and computer engineering (MS); engineering management (ME); industrial engineering (MSIE); manufacturing systems (MEMS, DE); mechanical engineering (MS); mechatronic systems engineering (MS). Part-time and evening/weekend programs available. *Faculty:* 20 full-time (4 women), 12 part-time/adjunct (0 women). *Students:* 15 full-time (4 women), 389 part-time (50 women); includes 57 minority (22 African Americans, 1 American Indian/Alaska Native, 30 Asian Americans or Pacific Islanders, 4 Hispanic Americans), 137 international. Average age 31. 361 applicants, 52% accepted, 108 enrolled. In 2009, 161 master's, 1 doctorate awarded. *Degree requirements:* For master's, thesis (for some programs). *Entrance requirements:* Additional exam requirements/recommendations for international students: Required—TOEFL (minimum score 550 paper-based; 213 computer-based; 79 iBT). *Application deadline:* For fall admission, 8/1 priority date for domestic students, 6/1 for international students; for winter admission, 12/1 priority date for domestic students, 10/1 for international students; for spring admission, 5/1 priority date for domestic students, 3/1 for international students. Applications are processed on a rolling basis. Application fee: $50. Electronic applications accepted. *Expenses:* Tuition: Full-time $11,320; part-time $798 per credit hour. *Financial support:* Federal Work-Study and institutionally sponsored loans available. Support available to part-time students. Financial award application deadline: 4/1; financial award applicants required to submit FAFSA. *Faculty research:* Advanced composite materials in bridges, strengthening existing bridges with carbon and glass fiber sheets, development of drive shafts using composite materials. *Unit head:* Dr. Nabil Grace, Interim Dean, 248-204-2500, Fax: 248-204-2509, E-mail: engrdean@ltu.edu. *Application contact:* Jane Rohrback, Director of Admissions, 248-204-3160, Fax: 248-204-3188, E-mail: admissions@ltu.edu.

Lehigh University, P.C. Rossin College of Engineering and Applied Science, Department of Civil and Environmental Engineering, Bethlehem, PA 18015-3094. Offers civil engineering (M Eng, MS, PhD); environmental engineering (MS, PhD); structural engineering (M Eng, MS, PhD). Part-time programs available. *Faculty:* 17 full-time (3 women). *Students:* 68 full-time (14 women), 11 part-time (2 women); includes 6 minority (4 Asian Americans or Pacific Islanders, 2 Hispanic Americans), 39 international. Average age 26. 284 applicants, 21% accepted, 39 enrolled. In 2009, 26 master's, 2 doctorates awarded. Terminal master's awarded for partial completion of doctoral program. *Degree requirements:* For master's, thesis (for some programs); for doctorate, comprehensive exam, thesis/dissertation. *Entrance requirements:* For master's and doctorate, GRE. Additional exam requirements/recommendations for international students: Required—TOEFL (minimum score 550 paper-based; 213 computer-based; 79 iBT). *Application deadline:* For fall admission, 7/15 priority date for domestic and international students; for spring admission, 12/1 priority date for domestic and international students. Applications are processed on a rolling basis. Application fee: $75. Electronic applications accepted. *Expenses:* Contact institution. *Financial support:* In 2009–10, 46 students received support, including 12 fellowships with full tuition reimbursements available (averaging $15,795 per year), 29 research assistantships with full tuition reimbursements available (averaging $20,500 per year), 5 teaching assistantships with full tuition reimbursements available (averaging $15,795 per year); institutionally sponsored loans, scholarships/grants, tuition waivers, and unspecified assistantships also available. Financial award application deadline: 1/15. *Faculty research:* Structural engineering, geotechnical engineering, water resources engineering, environmental engineering. Total annual research expenditures: $8 million. *Unit head:* Dr. Stephen Pessiki, Chairman, 610-758-3494, Fax: 610-758-6405, E-mail: pessiki@lehigh.edu. *Application contact:* Prisca Vidanage, Graduate Coordinator, 610-758-3530, Fax: 610-758-6405, E-mail: pmv1@lehigh.edu.

Louisiana State University and Agricultural and Mechanical College, Graduate School, College of Engineering, Department of Civil and Environmental Engineering, Baton Rouge, LA 70803. Offers environmental engineering (MSCE, PhD); geotechnical engineering (MSCE, PhD); structural engineering and mechanics (MSCE, PhD); transportation engineering (MSCE, PhD); water resources (MSCE, PhD). Part-time programs available. *Faculty:* 28 full-time (2 women). *Students:* 74 full-time (18 women), 37 part-time (6 women); includes 9 minority (1 American Indian/Alaska Native, 5 Asian Americans or Pacific Islanders, 3 Hispanic Americans), 59 international. Average age 31. 104 applicants, 63% accepted, 31 enrolled. In 2009, 16 master's, 13 doctorates awarded. *Degree requirements:* For master's, thesis optional; for doctorate, one foreign language, thesis/dissertation. *Entrance requirements:* For master's and doctorate, GRE General Test, minimum GPA of 3.0. Additional exam requirements/recommendations for international students: Required—TOEFL (minimum score 550 paper-based; 213 computer-based; 79 iBT) or IELTS (minimum score 6.5). *Application deadline:* For fall admission, 1/25 priority date for domestic students, 5/15 for international students; for spring admission, 10/15 for international students. Applications are processed on a rolling basis. Application fee: $50 ($70 for international students). Electronic applications accepted. *Financial support:* In 2009–10, 74 students received support, including 2 fellowships with full and partial tuition reimbursements available (averaging $16,672 per year), 65 research assistantships with full and partial tuition reimbursements available (averaging $11,242 per year); teaching assistantships with full and partial tuition reimbursements available, career-related internships or fieldwork, institutionally sponsored loans, scholarships/grants, and health care benefits also available. Financial award application deadline: 3/1; financial award applicants required to submit FAFSA. *Faculty research:* Mechanics and structures, environmental, geotechnical transportation, water resources. Total annual research expenditures: $2.4 million. *Unit head:* Dr. George Z. Voyiadjis, Chair/Boyd Professor, 225-578-8668, Fax: 225-578-9176, E-mail: cegzv@lsu.edu. *Application contact:* Dr. Donald Dean Adrian, Professor, 225-578-8636, E-mail: dadrian@lsu.edu.

Louisiana Tech University, Graduate School, College of Engineering and Science, Department of Civil Engineering, Ruston, LA 71272. Offers MS, PhD. Part-time programs available. Terminal master's awarded for partial completion of doctoral program. *Degree requirements:* For master's, thesis or alternative; for doctorate, thesis/dissertation. *Entrance requirements:* For master's, GRE General Test, minimum GPA of 3.0 in last 60 hours; for doctorate, minimum graduate GPA of 3.25 (with MS) or GRE General Test. Additional exam requirements/recommendations for international students: Required—TOEFL. *Faculty research:* Environmental engineering, trenchless excavation construction, structural mechanics, transportation materials and planning, water quality modeling.

Loyola Marymount University, College of Science and Engineering, Department of Civil Engineering and Environmental Science, Programs in Civil Engineering, Los Angeles, CA 90045. Offers environmental engineering (MSE). Part-time programs available. *Faculty:* 6 full-time (1 woman), 3 part-time/adjunct (0 women). *Students:* 2 full-time (0 women), 14 part-time (3 women); includes 10 minority (1 African American, 4 Asian Americans or Pacific Islanders, 5 Hispanic Americans), 1 international. Average age 30. 10 applicants, 30% accepted, 3 enrolled. In 2009, 2 master's awarded. *Degree requirements:* For master's, comprehensive exam. *Entrance requirements:* For master's, 2 letters of recommendation; bachelor of science degree or undergraduate engineering degree; 3 semester hours of general chemistry; course work in mathematics through one year of college calculus; 12 semester hours or 4 courses in science including biology, microbiology, chemistry, or physics. Additional exam requirements/recommendations for international students: Required—TOEFL (minimum score 550 paper-based; 213 computer-based; 80 iBT). *Application deadline:* Applications are processed on a rolling basis. Application fee: $50. Electronic applications accepted. *Financial support:* In 2009–10, 2 students received support. Scholarships/grants and laboratory assistantships available. Support available to part-time students. Financial award application deadline: 6/1; financial award applicants required to submit FAFSA. Total annual research expenditures: $14,321. *Unit head:* Prof. Joe Reichenberger, Graduate Director, 310-338-2830, E-mail: jreichenberger@lmu.edu. *Application contact:* Chake H. Kouyoumjian, Associate Dean of Graduate Studies, 310-338-2721, Fax: 310-338-6086, E-mail: ckouyoum@lmu.edu.

Manhattan College, Graduate Division, School of Engineering, Program in Civil Engineering, Riverdale, NY 10471. Offers MS. Part-time and evening/weekend programs available. *Degree requirements:* For master's, thesis or alternative. *Entrance requirements:* For master's, GRE (recommended), minimum GPA of 3.0. Additional exam requirements/recommendations for international students: Required—TOEFL (minimum score 550 paper-based; 213 computer-based). Electronic applications accepted. *Faculty research:* Compressible-inclusion function for geofoams used with rigid walls under static loading, validation of sediment criteria.

Marquette University, Graduate School, College of Engineering, Department of Civil and Environmental Engineering, Milwaukee, WI 53201-1881. Offers construction and public works management (MS, PhD); environmental/water resources engineering (MS, PhD); structural/geotechnical engineering (MS, PhD); transportation planning and engineering (MS, PhD). Part-time and evening/weekend programs available. *Faculty:* 13 full-time (0 women), 2 part-time/adjunct (1 woman). *Students:* 16 full-time (4 women), 17 part-time (2 women); includes 2 minority (1 Asian American or Pacific Islander, 1 Hispanic American), 13 international. Average age 27. 47 applicants, 85% accepted, 11 enrolled. In 2009, 8 master's, 1 doctorate awarded. Terminal master's awarded for partial completion of doctoral program. *Degree requirements:* For master's, comprehensive exam, thesis or alternative; for doctorate, thesis/dissertation. *Entrance requirements:* For master's and doctorate, GRE General Test, minimum GPA of 3.0. Additional exam requirements/recommendations for international students: Required—TOEFL. *Application deadline:* For fall admission, 6/1 priority date for domestic students. Applications are processed on a rolling basis. Application fee: $40. Electronic applications accepted. *Financial support:* In 2009–10, 13 students received support, including 5 fellowships with tuition reimbursements available (averaging $7,697 per year), 3 research assistantships with tuition reimbursements available (averaging $24,570 per year), 5 teaching assistantships with tuition reimbursements available (averaging $24,804 per year); Federal Work-Study, institutionally sponsored loans, scholarships/grants, and tuition waivers (full and partial) also available. Support available to part-time students. Financial award application deadline: 2/15. *Faculty research:* Highway safety, highway performance, and intelligent transportation systems; surface mount technology; watershed management. Total annual research expenditures: $138,209. *Unit head:* Dr. Michael S. Switzenbaum, Chair, 414-288-7030, Fax: 414-288-7521, E-mail: michael.switzenbaum@marquette.edu. *Application contact:* Dr. Stephen M. Heinrich, Director of Graduate Studies, 414-288-5466, E-mail: stephen.heinrich@marquette.edu.

Massachusetts Institute of Technology, School of Engineering, Department of Civil and Environmental Engineering, Cambridge, MA 02139-4307. Offers biological oceanography (PhD, Sc D); chemical oceanography (PhD, Sc D); civil and environmental engineering (M Eng, SM, PhD, Sc D); civil and environmental systems (PhD, Sc D); civil engineering (PhD, Sc D, CE); coastal engineering (PhD, Sc D); construction engineering and management (PhD, Sc D); environmental biology (PhD, Sc D); environmental chemistry (PhD, Sc D); environmental engineering (PhD, Sc D); environmental fluid mechanics (PhD, Sc D); geotechnical and geoenvironmental engineering (PhD, Sc D); hydrology (PhD, Sc D); information technology (PhD, Sc D); oceanographic engineering (PhD, Sc D); structures and materials (PhD, Sc D); transportation (PhD, Sc D); SM/MBA. *Faculty:* 36 full-time (5 women). *Students:* 190 full-time (59 women); includes 22 minority (2 African Americans, 14 Asian Americans or Pacific Islanders, 6 Hispanic Americans), 103 international. Average age 26. 478 applicants, 25% accepted, 76 enrolled. In 2009, 72 master's, 14 doctorates awarded. *Degree requirements:* For master's and CE, thesis; for doctorate, comprehensive exam, thesis/dissertation. *Entrance requirements:* For master's and doctorate, GRE General Test. Additional exam requirements/recommendations for international students: Required—TOEFL (minimum score 577 paper-based; 233 computer-based; 90 iBT), IELTS (minimum score 7). *Application deadline:* For fall admission, 1/2 for domestic and international students. Application fee: $75. Electronic applications accepted. *Financial support:* In 2009–10, 185 students received support, including 40 fellowships with tuition reimbursements available (averaging $27,725 per year), 97 research assistantships with tuition reimbursements available (averaging $28,035 per year), 21 teaching assistantships with tuition reimbursements available (averaging $24,802 per year); career-related internships or fieldwork, Federal Work-Study, institutionally sponsored loans, scholarships/grants, health care benefits, and unspecified assistantships also available. *Faculty research:* Environmental chemistry, environmental microbiology, environmental fluid mechanics and coastal engineering, geotechnical engineering and geomechanics, hydrology and hydroclimatology, mechanics of materials and structures, operations research/supply chain, transportation. Total annual research expenditures: $16.6 million. *Unit head:* Prof. Andrew Whittle, Department Head, 617-253-7101. *Application contact:* Patricia Glidden, Graduate Admissions Coordinator, 617-253-7119, Fax: 617-258-6775, E-mail: cee-admissions@mit.edu.

McGill University, Faculty of Graduate and Postdoctoral Studies, Faculty of Engineering, Department of Civil Engineering and Applied Mechanics, Montréal, QC H3A 2T5, Canada. Offers environmental engineering (M Eng, M Sc, PhD); fluid mechanics (M Sc); fluid mechanics and hydraulic engineering (M Eng, PhD); materials engineering (M Eng, PhD); rehabilitation of urban infrastructure (M Eng, PhD); soil behavior (M Eng, PhD); soil mechanics and foundations (M Eng, PhD); structures and structural mechanics (M Eng, PhD); water resources (M Sc); water resources engineering (M Eng, PhD).

McMaster University, School of Graduate Studies, Faculty of Engineering, Department of Civil Engineering, Hamilton, ON L8S 4M2, Canada. Offers M Eng, MA Sc, PhD. *Degree requirements:* For master's, thesis; for doctorate, comprehensive exam, thesis/dissertation. *Entrance requirements:* Additional exam requirements/recommendations for international students: Required—TOEFL (minimum score 550 paper-based; 213 computer-based). *Faculty research:* Building science, environmental hydrology, bolted steel connections, research on highway materials, earthquake engineering.

McNeese State University, Doré School of Graduate Studies, College of Engineering and Engineering Technology, Lake Charles, LA 70609. Offers chemical engineering (M Eng); civil engineering (M Eng); electrical engineering (M Eng); engineering management (M Eng); mechanical engineering (M Eng). Part-time and evening/weekend programs available. *Degree requirements:* For master's, thesis or alternative. *Entrance requirements:* For master's, GRE, minimum undergraduate GPA of 3.0. Additional exam requirements/recommendations for international students: Required—TOEFL.

Memorial University of Newfoundland, School of Graduate Studies, Faculty of Engineering and Applied Science, St. John's, NL A1C 5S7, Canada. Offers civil engineering (M Eng, PhD); electrical and computer engineering (M Eng, PhD); mechanical engineering (M Eng, PhD); ocean and naval architecture engineering (M Eng, PhD). Part-time programs available. *Degree requirements:* For master's, thesis; for doctorate, comprehensive exam, thesis/dissertation, oral thesis defense. *Entrance requirements:* For master's, 2nd class degree; for doctorate, master's degree in engineering. Electronic applications accepted. *Faculty research:* Engineering analysis, environmental and hydrotechnical studies, manufacturing and robotics, mechanics, structures and materials.

Michigan State University, The Graduate School, College of Engineering, Department of Civil and Environmental Engineering, East Lansing, MI 48824. Offers civil engineering (MS, PhD); environmental engineering (MS, PhD); environmental engineering-environmental toxicology (PhD). Part-time programs available. *Entrance requirements:* Additional exam requirements/recommendations for international students: Required—TOEFL. Electronic applications accepted.

Michigan Technological University, Graduate School, College of Engineering, Department of Civil and Environmental Engineering, Program in Civil Engineering, Houghton, MI 49931. Offers ME, MS, PhD. Part-time programs available. Terminal master's awarded for partial completion of doctoral program. *Degree requirements:* For master's, comprehensive exam (for some programs), thesis (for some programs); for doctorate, comprehensive exam, thesis/dissertation. *Entrance requirements:* For master's, GRE (to be considered for university assistantship); for doctorate, GRE. Additional exam requirements/recommendations for international students: Required—TOEFL (minimum score 600 paper-based; 250 computer-based). Electronic applications accepted. *Expenses:* Contact institution.

Mississippi State University, Bagley College of Engineering, Department of Civil and Environmental Engineering, Mississippi State, MS 39762. Offers civil engineering (MS); engineering (PhD), including civil engineering. Part-time programs available. Postbaccalaureate distance learning degree programs offered (no on-campus study). *Faculty:* 10 full-time (0 women), 2 part-time/adjunct (0 women). *Students:* 29 full-time (7 women), 37 part-time (8 women); includes 6 minority (3 African Americans, 3 Hispanic Americans), 10 international. Average age 29. 35 applicants, 49% accepted, 12 enrolled. In 2009, 10 master's, 2 doctorates awarded. Terminal master's awarded for partial completion of doctoral program. *Degree requirements:* For master's, thesis (for some programs); for doctorate, thesis/dissertation, research on an approved topic. *Entrance requirements:* For master's and doctorate, GRE, minimum GPA of 3.0. Additional exam requirements/recommendations for international students: Required—TOEFL (minimum score 550 paper-based; 213 computer-based; 79 iBT); Recommended—IELTS (minimum score 6.5). *Application deadline:* For fall admission, 7/1 for domestic students, 5/1 for international students; for spring admission, 11/1 for domestic students, 9/1 for international students. Applications are processed on a rolling basis. Application fee: $40. Electronic applications accepted. *Expenses:* Tuition, state resident: full-time $2575.50; part-time $286.25 per credit hour. Tuition, nonresident: full-time $6510; part-time $723.50 per credit hour. Tuition and fees vary according to course load. *Financial support:* In 2009–10, 15 research assistantships with full tuition reimbursements (averaging $11,295 per year), 3 teaching assistantships with full tuition reimbursements (averaging $10,112 per year) were awarded; Federal Work-Study, institutionally sponsored loans, and unspecified assistantships also available. Financial award application deadline: 4/1; financial award applicants required to submit FAFSA. *Faculty research:* Transportation, water modeling, construction materials, structures. Total annual research expenditures: $4.6 million. *Unit head:* Dr. Dennis D. Truax, Department Head, 662-325-7187, Fax: 662-325-7189, E-mail: truax@cee.msstate.edu. *Application contact:* Dr. James L. Martin, Professor and Graduate Coordinator, 662-325-7194, Fax: 662-325-7189, E-mail: jmartin@cee.msstate.edu.

Missouri University of Science and Technology, Graduate School, Department of Civil, Architectural, and Environmental Engineering, Rolla, MO 65409. Offers civil engineering (MS, DE, PhD); construction engineering (MS, DE, PhD); environmental engineering (MS); fluid mechanics (MS, DE, PhD); geotechnical engineering (MS, DE, PhD); hydrology and hydraulic engineering (MS, DE, PhD). Part-time and evening/weekend programs available. Terminal master's awarded for partial completion of doctoral program. *Degree requirements:* For master's, thesis optional; for doctorate, comprehensive exam, thesis/dissertation. *Entrance requirements:* For master's, GRE General Test (minimum combined score 1100), minimum GPA of 3.0; for doctorate, GRE General Test (minimum score: verbal and quantitative 400, writing 3.5), minimum GPA of 3.0. Additional exam requirements/recommendations for international students: Required—TOEFL. Electronic applications accepted. *Faculty research:* Earthquake engineering, structural optimization and control systems, structural health monitoring/damage detection, soil-structure interaction, soil mechanics and foundation engineering.

Montana State University, College of Graduate Studies, College of Engineering, Department of Civil Engineering, Bozeman, MT 59717. Offers civil engineering (MS); construction engineering management (MCEM); engineering (PhD), including applied mechanics option, civil engineering option. Part-time programs available. *Faculty:* 19 full-time (2 women), 2 part-time/adjunct (0 women). *Students:* 24 full-time (7 women), 16 part-time (3 women); includes 1 minority (American Indian/Alaska Native), 1 international. Average age 26. 36 applicants, 50% accepted, 16 enrolled. In 2009, 15 master's, 2 doctorates awarded. *Degree requirements:* For master's, comprehensive exam, thesis (for some programs); for doctorate, comprehensive exam, thesis/dissertation. *Entrance requirements:* For master's and doctorate, GRE General Test. Additional exam requirements/recommendations for international students: Required—TOEFL (minimum score 550 paper-based; 213 computer-based). *Application deadline:* For fall admission, 7/15 priority date for domestic students, 5/15 priority date for international students; for spring admission, 12/1 priority date for domestic students, 10/1 priority date for international students. Applications are processed on a rolling basis. Application fee: $30. Electronic applications accepted. *Expenses:* Tuition, state resident: full-time $5635; part-time $3492 per year. Tuition, nonresident: full-time $17,212; part-time $7865.10 per year. Required fees: $1441.05; $153.15 per credit. Tuition and fees vary according to course load and program. *Financial support:* In 2009–10, 15 students received support, including 1 research assistantship with partial tuition reimbursement available (averaging $24,000 per year), 5 teaching assistantships with partial tuition reimbursements available (averaging $8,000 per year); scholarships/grants and tuition waivers (partial) also available. Financial award application deadline: 3/1; financial award applicants required to submit FAFSA. *Faculty research:* Snow and ice mechanics, biofilm engineering, transportation, structural and geo materials, water resources. Total annual research expenditures: $714,709. *Unit head:* Dr. Brett Gunnick, Head, 406-994-2111, Fax: 406-994-6105, E-mail: bgunnick@ce.montana.edu. *Application contact:* Dr. Carl A. Fox, Vice Provost for Graduate Education, 406-994-4145, Fax: 406-994-7433, E-mail: gradstudy@montana.edu.

Morgan State University, School of Graduate Studies, Clarence M. Mitchell, Jr. School of Engineering, Baltimore, MD 21251. Offers civil engineering (M Eng, D Eng); electrical engineering (M Eng, D Eng); industrial engineering (M Eng, D Eng); transportation (MS). Part-time and evening/weekend programs available. *Degree requirements:* For master's, thesis, comprehensive exam or equivalent; for doctorate, thesis/dissertation, comprehensive exam or equivalent. *Entrance requirements:* For master's, GRE, minimum undergraduate GPA of 2.5; for doctorate, GRE, minimum GPA of 3.0. Additional exam requirements/recommendations for international students: Required—TOEFL (minimum score 550 paper-based; 213 computer-based).

New Jersey Institute of Technology, Office of Graduate Studies, Newark College of Engineering, Department of Civil and Environmental Engineering, Program in Civil Engineering, Newark, NJ 07102. Offers MS, PhD. Part-time and evening/weekend programs available. Terminal master's awarded for partial completion of doctoral program. *Degree requirements:* For master's, thesis optional; for doctorate, thesis/dissertation. *Entrance requirements:* For master's and doctorate, GRE General Test. Additional exam requirements/recommendations for international students: Required—TOEFL (minimum score 550 paper-based; 213 computer-based; 79 iBT). Electronic applications accepted.

New Mexico State University, Graduate School, College of Engineering, Department of Civil Engineering, Las Cruces, NM 88003-8001. Offers civil engineering (MSCE, PhD); environmental engineering (MS Env E). Part-time programs available. Postbaccalaureate distance learning degree programs offered. *Faculty:* 11 full-time (2 women). *Students:* 52 full-time (16 women), 20 part-time (7 women); includes 21 minority (2 Asian Americans or Pacific Islanders, 19 Hispanic Americans), 35 international. Average age 30. 57 applicants, 74% accepted, 23 enrolled. In 2009, 21 master's, 3 doctorates awarded. *Degree requirements:* For master's, thesis (for some programs); for doctorate, thesis/dissertation. *Entrance requirements:* For master's and doctorate, BS in engineering, minimum GPA of 3.0. Additional exam requirements/recommendations for international students: Required—TOEFL. *Application deadline:* For fall admission, 4/1 priority date for domestic and international students; for spring admission, 9/1 priority date for domestic and international students. Applications are processed on a rolling basis. Application fee: $30 ($50 for international students). Electronic applications accepted. *Expenses:* Tuition, state resident: full-time $4080; part-time $223 per credit. Tuition, nonresident: full-time $14,256; part-time $647 per credit. Required fees: $1278; $639 per semester. *Financial support:* In 2009–10, 26 research assistantships (averaging $10,619 per year), 19 teaching assistantships (averaging $11,291 per year) were awarded; fellowships, career-related internships or fieldwork, Federal Work-Study, and health care benefits also available. Support available to part-time students. Financial award application deadline: 3/1. *Faculty research:* Structural engineering, water resources engineering, environmental engineering, geotechnical engineering, hydraulics/hydrology. *Unit head:* Dr. Adrian Hanson, Interim Head, 575-646-3801, E-mail: athanson@nmsu.edu. *Application contact:* Dr. Adrian Hanson, Interim Head, 575-646-3801, E-mail: athanson@nmsu.edu.

North Carolina Agricultural and Technical State University, Graduate School, College of Engineering, Department of Civil, Architectural, Agricultural, Environmental, and Geomatics Engineering, Greensboro, NC 27411. Offers civil engineering (MSCE). Part-time programs available. *Degree requirements:* For master's, thesis defense. *Entrance requirements:* For master's, GRE General Test, GRE Subject Test (recommended). Additional exam requirements/recommendations for international students: Required—TOEFL (MSCE). *Faculty research:* Lightning, indoor air quality, material behavior HVAC controls, structural masonry systems.

North Carolina State University, Graduate School, College of Engineering, Department of Civil, Construction, and Environmental Engineering, Raleigh, NC 27695. Offers civil engineering (MCE, MS, PhD). Part-time programs available. Postbaccalaureate distance learning degree programs offered. *Degree requirements:* For master's, thesis optional, oral exams; for doctorate, thesis/dissertation, oral exams. *Entrance requirements:* For master's, GRE General Test, minimum B average in major; for doctorate, GRE General Test. Additional exam requirements/recommendations for international students: Required—TOEFL. Electronic applications accepted. *Faculty research:* Materials; systems, environmental, geotechnical, structural, transportation and water rescue engineering.

North Dakota State University, College of Graduate and Interdisciplinary Studies, College of Engineering and Architecture, Department of Civil Engineering, Fargo, ND 58108. Offers civil engineering (MS, PhD); environmental engineering (MS, PhD); transportation and logistics (PhD). PhD in transportation and logistics offered jointly with Upper Great Plains Transportation Institute. Part-time programs available. Postbaccalaureate distance learning degree programs offered (minimal on-campus study). *Students:* 20 full-time (4 women), 12 part-time (0 women); includes 2 minority (both Asian Americans or Pacific Islanders), 21 international. In 2009, 7 master's, 1 doctorate awarded. *Degree requirements:* For master's, thesis; for doctorate, comprehensive exam, thesis/dissertation. *Entrance requirements:* Additional exam requirements/recommendations for international students: Required—TOEFL (minimum score 525 paper-based; 197 computer-based; 71 iBT). *Application deadline:* For fall admission, 7/1 priority date for domestic students, 1/15 priority date for international students; for spring admission, 5/1 priority date for international students. Applications are processed on a rolling basis. Application fee: $45 ($60 for international students). *Financial support:* Fellowships with full tuition reimbursements, research assistantships with full tuition reimbursements, teaching assistantships with full tuition reimbursements, career-related internships or fieldwork, Federal Work-Study, and institutionally sponsored loans available. Support available to part-time students. Financial award application deadline: 1/15. *Faculty research:* Wastewater, solid waste, composites, nanotechnology. Total annual research expenditures: $800,000. *Unit head:* Dr. Dinesh R. Katti, Chair, 701-231-7244, Fax: 701-231-6185, E-mail: dinesh.katti@ndsu.edu. *Application contact:* Dr. Kalpana Katti, Associate Professor and Graduate Program Coordinator, 701-231-9504, Fax: 701-231-6185, E-mail: kalpana.katti@ndsu.edu.

Northeastern University, College of Engineering, Department of Civil and Environmental Engineering, Boston, MA 02115-5096. Offers MS, PhD. Part-time programs available. *Faculty:* 15 full-time (2 women), 2 part-time/adjunct (0 women). *Students:* 74 full-time (27 women), 39 part-time (13 women); includes 2 minority (1 African American, 1 Asian American or Pacific Islander), 53 international. 185 applicants, 70% accepted, 37 enrolled. In 2009, 23 master's, 6 doctorates awarded. *Degree requirements:* For master's, thesis optional; for doctorate, thesis/dissertation, departmental qualifying exam. *Entrance requirements:* For master's and doctorate, GRE General Test. Additional exam requirements/recommendations for international students: Required—TOEFL (minimum score 550 paper-based; 213 computer-based; 80 iBT). *Application deadline:* For fall admission, 1/15 priority date for domestic and international students. Applications are processed on a rolling basis. Application fee: $50. Electronic applications accepted. *Financial support:* In 2009–10, 33 students received support, including 18 research assistantships with full tuition reimbursements available (averaging $18,320 per year), 15 teaching assistantships with full tuition reimbursements available (averaging $18,320 per year); career-related internships or fieldwork, Federal Work-Study, scholarships/grants, tuition waivers (full), and unspecified assistantships also available. Support available to part-time students. Financial award application deadline: 1/15; financial award applicants required to submit FAFSA. *Faculty research:* Earthquake engineering, geotechnical and geoenvironmental engineering, structural

Civil Engineering

Northeastern University (continued)

engineering, transportation engineering, environmental engineering. *Unit head:* Dr. Jerome Jaffar, Chairman, 617-373-2444, Fax: 617-373-4419. *Application contact:* Stephen L. Gibson, Associate Director, 617-373-2711, Fax: 617-373-2501, E-mail: grad-eng@coe.neu.edu.

Northern Arizona University, Graduate College, College of Engineering, Forestry and Natural Sciences, Programs in Engineering, Flagstaff, AZ 86011. Offers civil engineering (MSE); computer science (MSE); electrical engineering (MSE); environmental engineering (MSE); mechanical engineering (MSE). Postbaccalaureate distance learning degree programs offered (no on-campus study). *Faculty:* 43 full-time (11 women). *Students:* 30 full-time (4 women), 9 part-time (0 women); includes 6 minority (4 American Indian/Alaska Native, 1 Asian American or Pacific Islander, 1 Hispanic American), 10 international. Average age 28. 42 applicants, 55% accepted, 12 enrolled. In 2009, 4 master's awarded. *Degree requirements:* For master's, thesis. *Entrance requirements:* Additional exam requirements/recommendations for international students: Required—TOEFL (minimum score 550 paper-based; 213 computer-based; 80 iBT), IELTS (minimum score 7). *Application deadline:* For fall admission, 3/1 priority date for domestic students, 9/1 priority date for international students; for spring admission, 9/15 priority date for domestic students. Applications are processed on a rolling basis. Application fee: $65. Electronic applications accepted. *Financial support:* In 2009–10, 9 research assistantships with partial tuition reimbursements, 9 teaching assistantships with partial tuition reimbursements were awarded; career-related internships or fieldwork, Federal Work-Study, scholarships/grants, health care benefits, and unspecified assistantships also available. Support available to part-time students. Financial award application deadline: 3/30; financial award applicants required to submit FAFSA. *Unit head:* Dr. Ernesto Penado, Chair, 928-523-9453, Fax: 928-523-2300, E-mail: ernesto.penado@nau.edu. *Application contact:* Dieter Otte, Coordinator, 928-523-0876, Fax: 928-523-2300, E-mail: dieter.otte@nau.edu.

Northwestern University, McCormick School of Engineering and Applied Science, Department of Civil and Environmental Engineering, Evanston, IL 60208-3109. Offers environmental engineering and science (MS, PhD); geotechnical engineering (MS, PhD); mechanics of materials and solids (MS, PhD); project management (MS, PhD); structural engineering and materials (MS, PhD); theoretical and applied mechanics (MS, PhD), including fluid mechanics, solid mechanics; transportation systems analysis and planning (MS, PhD). MS and PhD admissions and degrees offered through The Graduate School. Part-time programs available. *Faculty:* 25 full-time (2 women), 3 part-time/adjunct (1 woman). *Students:* 63 full-time (19 women), 3 part-time (0 women); includes 7 minority (1 African American, 3 Asian Americans or Pacific Islanders, 3 Hispanic Americans), 34 international. Average age 22. 149 applicants, 30% accepted, 23 enrolled. In 2009, 11 master's, 11 doctorates awarded. Terminal master's awarded for partial completion of doctoral program. *Degree requirements:* For master's, thesis (for some programs); for doctorate, thesis/dissertation. *Entrance requirements:* For master's and doctorate, GRE General Test, minimum 2 letters of recommendation, transcripts from all academic institutions attended. Additional exam requirements/recommendations for international students: Required—TOEFL (minimum score 600 paper-based; 250 computer-based; 100 iBT), IELTS (minimum score 7), TOEFL (minimum score iBT 26). *Application deadline:* For fall admission, 12/31 for domestic and international students. Application fee: $75. Electronic applications accepted. *Financial support:* In 2009–10, 55 students received support, including fellowships with full tuition reimbursements available (averaging $15,390 per year), research assistantships with full tuition reimbursements available (averaging $17,892 per year), 23 teaching assistantships with full tuition reimbursements available (averaging $15,867 per year); career-related internships or fieldwork, institutionally sponsored loans, scholarships/grants, and health care benefits also available. Financial award application deadline: 12/31; financial award applicants required to submit FAFSA. *Faculty research:* Environmental engineering and science, geotechnics, mechanics of materials and solids, structural engineering and materials, transportation systems analysis and planning. Total annual research expenditures: $5.8 million. *Unit head:* Jianmin Qu, Chair, 847-467-4528, Fax: 847-491-4011, E-mail: j-qu@northwestern.edu. *Application contact:* Janet Soule, Academic Coordinator, 847-491-7462, Fax: 847-491-4011, E-mail: civil-info@northwestern.edu.

Norwich University, School of Graduate and Continuing Studies, Program in Civil Engineering, Northfield, VT 05663. Offers MCE. Evening/weekend programs available. *Faculty:* 140 full-time (38 women). *Students:* 140 full-time (38 women); includes 21 minority (10 African Americans, 8 Asian Americans or Pacific Islanders, 3 Hispanic Americans). Average age 35. 189 applicants, 88% accepted, 140 enrolled. In 2009, 136 master's awarded. *Entrance requirements:* For master's, minimum GPA of 2.75. Additional exam requirements/recommendations for international students: Required—TOEFL (minimum score 550 paper-based; 213 computer-based; 83 iBT). *Application deadline:* For fall admission, 8/10 for domestic and international students; for spring admission, 2/6 for domestic and international students. Application fee: $50. Full-time tuition and fees vary according to course level and course load. *Financial support:* Scholarships/grants available. Financial award applicants required to submit FAFSA. *Unit head:* Dr. Thomas Descoteaux, Program Director, 802-485-2730. *Application contact:* Shelley W. Brown, Director of Marketing & Business Partnership, 802-485-2784, Fax: 802-485-2533, E-mail: sbrown@norwich.edu.

The Ohio State University, Graduate School, College of Engineering, Program in Civil Engineering, Columbus, OH 43210. Offers MS, PhD. *Faculty:* 32. *Students:* 47 full-time (11 women), 13 part-time (0 women); includes 3 minority (1 African American, 2 Asian Americans or Pacific Islanders), 28 international. Average age 28. In 2009, 24 master's, 4 doctorates awarded. *Degree requirements:* For master's, thesis optional; for doctorate, thesis/dissertation. *Entrance requirements:* For master's, GRE General Test or engineering degree from ABET or CAB accredited U. S. or Canadian institution; for doctorate, GRE General Test or engineering degree from ABET or CAB accredited US or Canadian institution. Additional exam requirements/recommendations for international students: Recommended—TOEFL (minimum score 600 paper-based; 250 computer-based). *Application deadline:* For fall admission, 8/15 priority date for domestic students, 7/1 priority date for international students; for winter admission, 12/1 priority date for domestic students, 11/1 priority date for international students; for spring admission, 3/1 priority date for domestic students, 2/1 priority date for international students. Applications are processed on a rolling basis. Application fee: $40 ($50 for international students). Electronic applications accepted. *Expenses:* Tuition, state resident: full-time $10,683. Tuition, nonresident: full-time $25,923. Tuition and fees vary according to course load and program. *Financial support:* Fellowships, research assistantships, teaching assistantships, career-related internships or fieldwork, Federal Work-Study, institutionally sponsored loans, and unspecified assistantships available. Support available to part-time students. *Unit head:* Fabian Hadipriono Tan, Graduate Studies Committee Chair, 614-292-0790, Fax: 614-292-3780, E-mail: tan.184@osu.edu. *Application contact:* 614-292-9444, Fax: 614-292-3895, E-mail: domestic.grad@osu.edu.

Ohio University, Graduate College, Russ College of Engineering and Technology, Department of Civil Engineering, Athens, OH 45701-2979. Offers civil engineering (PhD); construction (MS); environmental (MS); geotechnical and geoenvironmental (MS); mechanics (MS); structures (MS); transportation (MS); water resources and structures (MS). Part-time programs available. *Faculty:* 13 full-time (3 women), 3 part-time/adjunct (0 women). *Students:* 18 full-time (2 women), 2 part-time (1 woman), 13 international. 22 applicants, 68% accepted, 1 enrolled. In 2009, 7 master's awarded. *Degree requirements:* For master's, comprehensive exam (for some programs), thesis or alternative; for doctorate, comprehensive exam, thesis/dissertation. *Entrance requirements:* For master's, GRE General Test, minimum GPA of 3.0, 3 letters of recommendation; for doctorate, GRE General Test. Additional exam requirements/recommendations for international students: Required—TOEFL (minimum score 550 paper-based; 80 iBT) or IELTS Academic (minimum score 6.5). *Application deadline:* For fall admission, 5/1 priority date for domestic students, 2/1 priority date for international students; for winter admission, 8/1 priority date for domestic students, 4/1 priority date for international students; for spring admission, 2/1 priority date for domestic students, 7/1 priority date for international students. Applications are processed on a rolling basis. Application fee: $50 ($55 for international students). Electronic applications accepted. *Expenses:* Tuition, state resident: full-time $7839; part-time $323 per quarter hour. Tuition, nonresident: full-time $15,831; part-time $654 per quarter hour. Required fees: $2931. *Financial support:* Research assistantships with full tuition reimbursements, teaching assistantships with full tuition reimbursements, Federal Work-Study, institutionally sponsored loans, scholarships/grants, and unspecified assistantships available. Financial award application deadline: 3/15; financial award applicants required to submit FAFSA. *Faculty research:* Noise abatement, materials and environment, highway infrastructure, subsurface investigation, (pavements, pipes, bridges, etc.). Total annual research expenditures: $1.2 million. *Unit head:* Dr. Gayle F. Mitchell, Chair, 740-593-0430, Fax: 740-593-0625, E-mail: mitchelg@ohio.edu. *Application contact:* Dr. Shad M. Sargand, Graduate Chair, 740-593-1465, Fax: 740-593-0625, E-mail: sargand@ohio.edu.

Oklahoma State University, College of Engineering, Architecture and Technology, School of Civil and Environmental Engineering, Stillwater, OK 74078. Offers civil engineering (MS); environmental engineering (PhD). *Faculty:* 15 full-time (1 woman), 3 part-time/adjunct (0 women). *Students:* 43 full-time (12 women), 34 part-time (10 women); includes 6 minority (3 American Indian/Alaska Native, 2 Asian Americans or Pacific Islanders, 1 Hispanic American), 48 international. Average age 28. 137 applicants, 31% accepted, 19 enrolled. In 2009, 14 master's, 1 doctorate awarded. *Degree requirements:* For master's, thesis or alternative; for doctorate, comprehensive exam, thesis/dissertation. *Entrance requirements:* For master's and doctorate, GRE or GMAT. Additional exam requirements/recommendations for international students: Required—TOEFL (minimum score 550 paper-based; 79 iBT). *Application deadline:* For fall admission, 3/1 priority date for international students; for spring admission, 8/1 priority date for international students. Applications are processed on a rolling basis. Application fee: $40 ($75 for international students). Electronic applications accepted. *Expenses:* Tuition, state resident: full-time $3716; part-time $154.85 per credit hour. Tuition, nonresident: full-time $14,448; part-time $602 per credit hour. Required fees: $1772; $73.85 per credit hour. One-time fee: $50. Tuition and fees vary according to course load and campus/location. *Financial support:* In 2009–10, 20 research assistantships (averaging $13,708 per year), 16 teaching assistantships (averaging $9,319 per year) were awarded; career-related internships or fieldwork, Federal Work-Study, scholarships/grants, health care benefits, tuition waivers (partial), and unspecified assistantships also available. Support available to part-time students. Financial award application deadline: 3/1; financial award applicants required to submit FAFSA. *Unit head:* Dr. John Veenstra, Head, 405-744-5190, Fax: 405-744-7554. *Application contact:* Dr. Gordon Emslie, Dean, 405-744-6368, Fax: 405-744-0355, E-mail: grad-i@okstate.edu.

Old Dominion University, Frank Batten College of Engineering and Technology, Program in Civil and Environmental Engineering, Norfolk, VA 23529. Offers D Eng, PhD. Part-time and evening/weekend programs available. Postbaccalaureate distance learning degree programs offered (minimal on-campus study). *Faculty:* 11 full-time (2 women), 7 part-time/adjunct (2 women). *Students:* 1 full-time (0 women), 2 part-time (0 women); includes 1 minority (African American). Average age 48. *Degree requirements:* For doctorate, thesis/dissertation, candidacy exam. *Entrance requirements:* For doctorate, GRE, minimum GPA of 3.5 for regular admission. Additional exam requirements/recommendations for international students: Required—TOEFL (minimum score 550 paper-based; 213 computer-based; 80 iBT). *Application deadline:* For fall admission, 6/1 priority date for domestic students, 4/15 priority date for international students; for spring admission, 11/1 priority date for domestic students, 10/1 priority date for international students. Applications are processed on a rolling basis. Application fee: $40. Electronic applications accepted. *Expenses:* Tuition, state resident: full-time $8112; part-time $338 per credit. Tuition, nonresident: full-time $20,256; part-time $844 per credit. Required fees: $119 per semester. One-time fee: $50. *Financial support:* Scholarships/grants and unspecified assistantships available. Support available to part-time students. Financial award application deadline: 4/1. *Faculty research:* Structural engineering, coastal engineering, environmental engineering, geotechnical engineering, water resources, transportation engineering. Total annual research expenditures: $474,605. *Unit head:* Dr. Isao Ishibashi, Graduate Program Director, 757-683-4641, Fax: 757-683-5354, E-mail: cegpd@odu.edu. *Application contact:* Dr. Isao Ishibashi, Graduate Program Director, 757-683-4641, Fax: 757-683-5354, E-mail: cegpd@odu.edu.

Old Dominion University, Frank Batten College of Engineering and Technology, Program in Civil Engineering, Norfolk, VA 23529. Offers ME, MS. Part-time and evening/weekend programs available. Postbaccalaureate distance learning degree programs offered (minimal on-campus study). *Faculty:* 11 full-time (2 women), 7 part-time/adjunct (2 women). *Students:* 22 full-time (4 women), 39 part-time (6 women); includes 9 minority (3 African Americans, 1 American Indian/Alaska Native, 2 Asian Americans or Pacific Islanders, 3 Hispanic Americans), 17 international. Average age 31. 18 applicants, 100% accepted, 13 enrolled. In 2009, 8 master's awarded. *Degree requirements:* For master's, comprehensive exam, thesis optional. *Entrance requirements:* For master's, GRE, minimum GPA of 3.0 for regular admission. Additional exam requirements/recommendations for international students: Required—TOEFL (minimum score 550 paper-based; 213 computer-based; 80 iBT). *Application deadline:* For fall admission, 6/1 priority date for domestic students, 4/15 priority date for international students; for spring admission, 11/1 priority date for domestic students, 10/1 priority date for international students. Applications are processed on a rolling basis. Application fee: $40. Electronic applications accepted. *Expenses:* Tuition, state resident: full-time $8112; part-time $338 per credit. Tuition, nonresident: full-time $20,256; part-time $844 per credit. Required fees: $119 per semester. One-time fee: $50. *Financial support:* In 2009–10, 1 fellowship with partial tuition reimbursement (averaging $14,633 per year), 4 research assistantships with full and partial tuition reimbursements (averaging $11,463 per year), 4 teaching assistantships with full and partial tuition reimbursements (averaging $12,920 per year) were awarded; scholarships/grants and unspecified assistantships also available. Support available to part-time students. Financial award application deadline: 4/1; financial award applicants required to submit FAFSA. *Faculty research:* Structural engineering, coastal engineering, environmental engineering, geotechnical engineering, water resources, transportation engineering. Total annual research expenditures: $474,605. *Unit head:* Dr. Isao Ishibashi, Graduate Program Director, 757-683-4641, Fax: 757-683-5354, E-mail: cegpd@odu.edu. *Application contact:* Dr. Isao Ishibashi, Graduate Program Director, 757-683-4641, Fax: 757-683-5354, E-mail: cegpd@odu.edu.

Oregon State University, Graduate School, College of Engineering, School of Civil and Construction Engineering, Corvallis, OR 97331. Offers civil engineering (MS, PhD); coastal and ocean engineering (M Oc E, PhD); coastal engineering (MS); construction engineering management (MBE, PhD); engineering (M Eng, MAIS); geotechnical engineering (MS, PhD); structural engineering (MS, PhD); transportation engineering (MS, PhD); water engineering (MS, PhD). Part-time programs available. *Faculty:* 25 full-time (5 women), 1 part-time/adjunct (0 women). *Students:* 71 full-time (17 women), 12 part-time (2 women); includes 4 minority (all Asian Americans or Pacific Islanders), 34 international. Average age 28. 75 applicants, 87% accepted, 31 enrolled. In 2009, 26 master's, 7 doctorates awarded. Terminal master's awarded for partial completion of doctoral program. *Degree requirements:* For master's, thesis or alternative; for doctorate, one foreign language, thesis/dissertation. *Entrance requirements:* For master's, GRE General Test, minimum GPA of 3.0 in last 90 hours (3.5 for MS); for doctorate, GRE General Test, minimum GPA of 3.0 in last 90 hours of undergraduate course work. Additional exam requirements/recommendations for international students: Required—TOEFL (minimum score 580 paper-based; 237 computer-based). *Application deadline:* For fall admission, 3/1 priority date for domestic students. Applications are processed on a rolling basis. Application fee: $50. *Expenses:* Tuition, state resident: full-time $9774; part-time $362 per credit. Tuition, nonresident: full-time $15,849; part-time $587 per credit. Required fees: $1639. Full-time tuition and fees vary according to course load and program. *Financial support:* Fellowships, research assistantships with full tuition reimbursements, teaching assistantships with full tuition reimbursements, career-related internships or fieldwork and institutionally sponsored loans available. Support available to part-time students. Financial award application deadline: 2/1. *Faculty research:* Hazardous waste management, carbon cycling, wave forces on structures, pavement design, seismic analysis. Total annual research expenditures: $7.1 million. *Unit head:* Dr. Scott A. Ashford, Head, 541-737-4934. *Application contact:* Kathy Westberg, CCE Graduate Advising School Operations Manager, 541-737-1786, Fax: 541-737-3052, E-mail: kathy.westberg@oregonstate.edu.

Penn State University Park, Graduate School, College of Engineering, Department of Civil and Environmental Engineering, State College, University Park, PA 16802-1503. Offers M Eng, MS, PhD.

Polytechnic Institute of NYU, Department of Civil Engineering, Major in Civil Engineering, Brooklyn, NY 11201-2990. Offers MS, PhD. Part-time and evening/weekend programs available. *Students:* 35 full-time (7 women), 52 part-time (12 women); includes 21 minority (7 African Americans, 11 Asian Americans or Pacific Islanders, 3 Hispanic Americans), 25 international. 117 applicants, 63% accepted, 26 enrolled. In 2009, 22 master's, 5 doctorates awarded. *Degree requirements:* For master's, comprehensive exam (for some programs), thesis (for some programs); for doctorate, comprehensive exam, thesis/dissertation. *Entrance requirements:* For doctorate, qualifying exam, MS in civil engineering. Additional exam requirements/recommendations for international students: Required—TOEFL (minimum score 550 paper-based; 213 computer-based; 80 iBT); Recommended—IELTS (minimum score 6.5). *Application deadline:* For fall admission, 7/31 priority date for domestic students, 4/30 priority date for international students; for spring admission, 12/31 priority date for domestic students, 10/30 priority date for international students. Applications are processed on a rolling basis. Application fee: $75. Electronic applications accepted. *Expenses:* Tuition: Full-time $21,492; part-time $1194 per credit hour. Required fees: $1160; $204 per course. *Financial support:* Fellowships, research assistantships, teaching assistantships, institutionally sponsored loans, scholarships/grants, and unspecified assistantships available. Support available to part-time students. Financial award applicants required to submit FAFSA. *Unit head:* Dr. Lawrence Chiarelli, Department Head, 718-260-4040, Fax: 718-260-3433, E-mail: lchiarel@poly.edu. *Application contact:* JeanCarlo Bonilla, Director of Graduate Enrollment Management, 718-260-3182, Fax: 718-260-3624, E-mail: gradinfo@poly.edu.

Polytechnic Institute of NYU, Long Island Graduate Center, Graduate Programs, Department of Civil Engineering, Major in Civil Engineering, Melville, NY 11747. Offers MS. *Students:* 2 full-time (0 women), 1 (woman) part-time, 2 international. 2 applicants, 100% accepted, 0 enrolled. *Degree requirements:* For master's, comprehensive exam (for some programs), thesis (for some programs). *Entrance requirements:* Additional exam requirements/recommendations for international students: Required—TOEFL (minimum score 550 paper-based; 213 computer-based; 80 iBT); Recommended—IELTS (minimum score 6.5). *Application deadline:* For fall admission, 7/31 priority date for domestic students, 4/30 priority date for international students; for spring admission, 12/31 priority date for domestic students, 11/30 priority date for international students. Applications are processed on a rolling basis. Application fee: $75. Electronic applications accepted. *Financial support:* Institutionally sponsored loans, scholarships/grants, and unspecified assistantships available. Support available to part-time students. Financial award applicants required to submit FAFSA. *Unit head:* Dr. Roger Peter Roess, Department Head, 718-260-3018, E-mail: rroess@poly.edu. *Application contact:* JeanCarlo Bonilla, Director of Graduate Enrollment Management, 718-260-3182, Fax: 718-260-3624, E-mail: gradinfo@poly.edu.

Polytechnic University of Puerto Rico, Graduate School, Hato Rey, PR 00919. Offers business administration (MBA), including general studies, management of information systems, management of international enterprises; civil engineering (ME, MS); computer engineering (ME, MS); computer science (MS); electrical engineering (ME, MS); engineering management (MEM); environmental management (MEPM); landscape architecture (M Land Arch); manufacturing competitiveness (MMC, MS); manufacturing engineering (ME, MS). Part-time and evening/weekend programs available. *Entrance requirements:* For master's, 3 letters of recommendation.

Polytechnic University of the Americas–Orlando Campus, Graduate School, Winter Park, FL 32792. Offers business administration (MBA); civil engineering (MS); computer engineering (MS); electrical engineering (MS); engineering management (MEM). Part-time and evening/weekend programs available. Postbaccalaureate distance learning degree programs offered (no on-campus study). *Entrance requirements:* For master's, minimum GPA of 3.0. Electronic applications accepted.

Portland State University, Graduate Studies, Maseeh College of Engineering and Computer Science, Department of Civil and Environmental Engineering, Portland, OR 97207-0751. Offers civil and environmental engineering (M Eng, MS, PhD); civil and environmental engineering management (M Eng); environmental sciences and resources (PhD); systems science (PhD). Part-time and evening/weekend programs available. *Degree requirements:* For master's, thesis or alternative, oral exam; for doctorate, one foreign language, thesis/dissertation, oral and written exams. *Entrance requirements:* For master's, minimum GPA of 3.0 in upper-division course work, BS in civil engineering or allied field; for doctorate, GRE General Test, GRE Subject Test, minimum GPA of 3.0 in upper-division course work, master's in civil and environmental engineering, 2 years full-time graduate work beyond master's degree. Additional exam requirements/recommendations for international students: Required—TOEFL (minimum score 550 paper-based; 213 computer-based). *Faculty research:* Structures, water resources, geotechnical engineering, environmental engineering, transportation.

Portland State University, Graduate Studies, Systems Science Program, Portland, OR 97207-0751. Offers computational intelligence (Certificate); computer modeling and simulation (Certificate); systems science (MS); systems science/anthropology (PhD); systems science/business administration (PhD); systems science/civil engineering (PhD); systems science/economics (PhD); systems science/engineering management (PhD); systems science/general (PhD); systems science/mathematical sciences (PhD); systems science/mechanical engineering (PhD); systems science/psychology (PhD); systems science/sociology (PhD). *Degree requirements:* For doctorate, variable foreign language requirement, thesis/dissertation. *Entrance requirements:* For master's, 2 letters of recommendation; for doctorate, GMAT, GRE General Test, minimum undergraduate GPA of 3.0. Additional exam requirements/recommendations for international students: Required—TOEFL. *Faculty research:* Systems theory and methodology, artificial intelligence neural networks, information theory, nonlinear dynamics/chaos, modeling and simulation.

Princeton University, Graduate School, School of Engineering and Applied Science, Department of Civil and Environmental Engineering, Princeton, NJ 08544-1019. Offers civil and environmental engineering (MSE). *Faculty:* 16 full-time (3 women). Terminal master's awarded for partial completion of doctoral program. *Degree requirements:* For master's, thesis (MSE); for doctorate, thesis/dissertation, general exam. *Entrance requirements:* For master's, GRE General Test, 3 letters of recommendation; for doctorate, GRE General Test, official transcript(s), 3 letters of recommendation, personal statement. Additional exam requirements/recommendations for international students: Required—TOEFL. *Application deadline:* For fall admission, 12/31 for domestic and international students. Application fee: $90. Electronic applications accepted. *Financial support:* Fellowships with full tuition reimbursements, research assistantships with full tuition reimbursements, teaching assistantships with full tuition reimbursements, institutionally sponsored loans and health care benefits available. *Faculty research:* Carbon mitigation; civil engineering materials and structures; climate and atmospheric dynamics; computational mechanics and risk assessment; hydrology, remote sensing, and sustainability. *Unit head:* Tiffany Sirois, Graduate Program Administrator, 609-258-5539, Fax: 609-258-2760, E-mail: cee@princeton.edu. *Application contact:* Michelle Carman, Manager of Graduate Admissions, 609-258-3034, Fax: 609-258-7262, E-mail: gsadmit@princeton.edu.

Purdue University, College of Engineering, School of Civil Engineering, West Lafayette, IN 47907-2051. Offers MS, MSCE, MSE, PhD. Part-time programs available. Terminal master's awarded for partial completion of doctoral program. *Degree requirements:* For master's, thesis (for some programs); for doctorate, thesis/dissertation. *Entrance requirements:* For master's and doctorate, GRE General Test, minimum GPA of 3.0. Additional exam requirements/recommendations for international students: Required—TOEFL (minimum score 575 paper-based; 233 computer-based; 90 iBT); Recommended—TWE. Electronic applications accepted. *Faculty research:* Environmental and hydraulic engineering, geotechnical and materials engineering, structural engineering, construction engineering, infrastructure and transportation systems engineering.

Queen's University at Kingston, School of Graduate Studies and Research, Faculty of Applied Science, Department of Civil Engineering, Kingston, ON K7L 3N6, Canada. Offers M Eng, M Sc Eng, PhD. Part-time programs available. *Degree requirements:* For master's, thesis (for some programs); for doctorate, comprehensive exam, thesis/dissertation. *Entrance requirements:* Additional exam requirements/recommendations for international students: Required—TOEFL. *Faculty research:* Structural, geotechnical, transportation, hydrotechnical, and environmental engineering.

Rensselaer Polytechnic Institute, Graduate School, School of Engineering, Department of Civil and Environmental Engineering, Program in Civil Engineering, Troy, NY 12180-3590. Offers geotechnical engineering (M Eng, MS, PhD); mechanics of composite materials and structures (M Eng, MS, PhD); structural engineering (M Eng, MS, PhD); transportation engineering (M Eng, MS, PhD). Part-time programs available. *Faculty:* 6 full-time (0 women), 5 part-time/adjunct (0 women). *Students:* 27 full-time (2 women); includes 4 minority (3 Asian Americans or Pacific Islanders, 1 Hispanic American), 3 international. Average age 24. 70 applicants, 14% accepted, 7 enrolled. In 2009, 5 master's, 1 doctorate awarded. Terminal master's awarded for partial completion of doctoral program. *Degree requirements:* For master's, thesis (for some programs); for doctorate, thesis/dissertation. *Entrance requirements:* For master's and doctorate, GRE. Additional exam requirements/recommendations for international students: Required—TOEFL (minimum score 570 paper-based; 230 computer-based; 89 iBT), IELTS (minimum score 6.5). *Application deadline:* For fall admission, 1/15 priority date for domestic and international students; for spring admission, 8/15 priority date for domestic and international students. Applications are processed on a rolling basis. Application fee: $75. Electronic applications accepted. *Expenses:* Tuition: Full-time $38,100. *Financial support:* In 2009–10, 1 fellowship with full tuition reimbursement (averaging $16,500 per year), 3 research assistantships with full tuition reimbursements (averaging $16,500 per year), 4 teaching assistantships with full tuition reimbursements (averaging $16,500 per year) were awarded; career-related internships or fieldwork and institutionally sponsored loans also available. Financial award application deadline: 2/1. *Faculty research:* Computational mechanics, earthquake engineering, geo-environmental engineering. Total annual research expenditures: $2.7 million. *Unit head:* Dr. Tarek Abdoun, Acting Chair, 518-276-6362, Fax: 518-276-4833, E-mail: abdout@rpi.edu. *Application contact:* Kimberly Boyce, Administrative Assistant, 518-276-6941, Fax: 518-276-4833, E-mail: boycek@rpi.edu.

Rice University, Graduate Programs, George R. Brown School of Engineering, Department of Civil and Environmental Engineering, Houston, TX 77251-1892. Offers civil engineering (MCE, MS, PhD); environmental engineering (MEE, MES, MS, PhD); environmental science (MEE, MES, MS, PhD). Part-time programs available. *Degree requirements:* For master's, thesis (for some programs); for doctorate, thesis/dissertation. *Entrance requirements:* For master's and doctorate, GRE General Test, GRE Subject Test, minimum GPA of 3.25. Additional exam requirements/recommendations for international students: Required—TOEFL (minimum score 600 paper-based; 250 computer-based; 90 iBT). Electronic applications accepted. *Faculty research:* Biology and chemistry of groundwater, pollutant fate in groundwater systems, water quality monitoring, urban storm water runoff, urban air quality.

Rose-Hulman Institute of Technology, Faculty of Engineering and Applied Sciences, Department of Civil Engineering, Terre Haute, IN 47803-3999. Offers civil engineering (MS); environmental engineering (MS). Part-time programs available. *Faculty:* 6 full-time (1 woman). *Students:* 1 (woman) full-time. Average age 22. 5 applicants, 60% accepted. *Degree requirements:* For master's, thesis. *Entrance requirements:* For master's, GRE, minimum GPA of 3.0. Additional exam requirements/recommendations for international students: Required—TOEFL (minimum score 580 paper-based; 237 computer-based; 92 iBT). *Application deadline:* For fall admission, 2/1 priority date for domestic students. Applications are processed on a rolling basis. Application fee: $0. *Expenses:* Tuition: Full-time $33,900; part-time $987 per credit hour. *Financial support:* In 2009–10, 1 student received support; fellowships with full and partial tuition reimbursements available, research assistantships with full and partial tuition reimbursements available, institutionally sponsored loans, scholarships/grants, and tuition waivers (full and partial) available. Financial award application deadline: 2/1. *Faculty research:* Urban stormwater management, groundwater and surface water models, solid and hazardous waste, risk and decision analysis. *Unit head:* Dr. Kevin G. Sutterer, Chairman, 812-877-8959, Fax: 812-877-8440, E-mail: kevin.g.sutterer@rose-hulman.edu. *Application contact:* Dr. Daniel J. Moore, Associate Dean of the Faculty, 812-877-8110, Fax: 812-877-8061, E-mail: daniel.j.moore@rose-hulman.edu.

Rowan University, Graduate School, College of Engineering, Department of Civil and Environmental Engineering, Program in Civil Engineering, Glassboro, NJ 08028-1701. Offers MS. *Students:* 7 full-time (1 woman), 3 part-time (1 woman); includes 6 minority (5 Asian Americans or Pacific Islanders, 1 Hispanic American). Average age 26. 7 applicants, 100% accepted, 3 enrolled. In 2009, 3 master's awarded. *Entrance requirements:* For master's, GRE General Test. Additional exam requirements/recommendations for international students: Required—TOEFL. *Application deadline:* Applications are processed on a rolling basis. Electronic applications accepted. *Expenses:* Tuition, state resident: full-time $10,624; part-time $590 per semester hour. Tuition, nonresident: full-time $10,624; part-time $590 per semester hour. Required fees: $2320; $125 per semester hour. *Unit head:* Kauser Jahan, Chair, 856-256-5323, E-mail: jahan@rowan.edu. *Application contact:* Dr. Ralph Dusseau, Program Adviser, 856-256-5332.

Royal Military College of Canada, Division of Graduate Studies and Research, Engineering Division, Department of Civil Engineering, Kingston, ON K7K 7B4, Canada. Offers M Eng, MA Sc, PhD. *Degree requirements:* For master's, thesis; for doctorate, comprehensive exam, thesis/dissertation. *Entrance requirements:* For master's, honours degree with second-class standing; for doctorate, master's degree. Electronic applications accepted.

Rutgers, The State University of New Jersey, New Brunswick, Graduate School-New Brunswick, Department of Civil and Environmental Engineering, Piscataway, NJ 08854-8097. Offers MS, PhD. Part-time and evening/weekend programs available. Terminal master's awarded for partial completion of doctoral program. *Degree requirements:* For master's, comprehensive exam, thesis or alternative; for doctorate, comprehensive exam, thesis/dissertation. *Entrance requirements:* For master's and doctorate, GRE General Test. Additional exam requirements/recommendations for international students: Required—TOEFL (minimum score 580 paper-based; 237 computer-based). Electronic applications accepted. *Faculty research:* Civil engineering materials research, non-destructive evaluation of transportation infrastructure, transportation planning, intelligent transportation systems.

Saint Martin's University, Graduate Programs, Program in Civil Engineering, Lacey, WA 98503. Offers MCE. Part-time and evening/weekend programs available. *Faculty:* 4 full-time (0 women), 1 part-time/adjunct (0 women). *Students:* 3 full-time (0 women), 3 part-time (0 women); includes 1 minority (Asian American or Pacific Islander), 1 international. Average age 40. 1 applicant, 100% accepted, 1 enrolled. In 2009, 3 master's awarded. *Degree requirements:* For master's, thesis optional. *Entrance requirements:* For master's, minimum GPA of 2.8; BS in civil engineering or other engineering/science with completion of calculus, differential equations, physics, chemistry. Additional exam requirements/recommendations for international students: Required—TOEFL (minimum score 525 paper-based; 210 computer-based). *Application deadline:* For fall admission, 6/30 priority date for domestic students, 4/30 for international students; for spring admission, 9/30 priority date for domestic students, 6/30 for international students. Applications are processed on a rolling basis. Application fee: $35. *Expenses:* Tuition: Full-time $12,440; part-time $827 per credit hour. *Financial support:* Scholarships/grants and tuition waivers (partial) available. Support available to part-time students. Financial award application deadline: 2/5. *Faculty research:* Transportation engineering, metal fatigue and fracture, environmental engineering. *Unit head:* Dr. Pius O. Igharo, Program Chair, 360-438-4322, Fax: 360-438-4548, E-mail: pigharo@stmartin.edu. *Application contact:* Hopie Lopez, Administrative Assistant, 360-438-4320, Fax: 360-438-4548, E-mail: hlopez@stmartin.edu.

Civil Engineering

San Diego State University, Graduate and Research Affairs, College of Engineering, Department of Civil and Environmental Engineering, San Diego, CA 92182. Offers civil engineering (MS). Part-time and evening/weekend programs available. *Degree requirements:* For master's, thesis optional. *Entrance requirements:* For master's, GRE General Test. Additional exam requirements/recommendations for international students: Required—TOEFL. Electronic applications accepted. *Faculty research:* Hydraulics, hydrology, transportation, smart material, concrete material.

San Jose State University, Graduate Studies and Research, Charles W. Davidson College of Engineering, Department of Civil and Environmental Engineering, San Jose, CA 95192-0001. Offers civil engineering (MS). *Students:* 52 full-time (19 women), 58 part-time (15 women); includes 51 minority (6 African Americans, 40 Asian Americans or Pacific Islanders, 5 Hispanic Americans), 32 international. Average age 30. 146 applicants, 34% accepted, 26 enrolled. In 2009, 45 master's awarded. *Degree requirements:* For master's, thesis or alternative. *Entrance requirements:* For master's, minimum GPA of 2.7. *Application deadline:* For fall admission, 6/29 for domestic students; for spring admission, 11/30 for domestic students. Applications are processed on a rolling basis. Application fee: $59. Electronic applications accepted. *Financial support:* Applicants required to submit FAFSA. *Unit head:* Udeme J. Ndon, Chair, 408-924-3900, Fax: 408-924-4004. *Application contact:* Udeme J. Ndon, Chair, 408-924-3900, Fax: 408-924-4004.

Santa Clara University, School of Engineering, Department of Civil Engineering, Santa Clara, CA 95053. Offers MS. Part-time and evening/weekend programs available. *Students:* 4 full-time (3 women), 3 international. Average age 25. *Degree requirements:* For master's, thesis (for some programs). *Entrance requirements:* For master's, GRE (waiver may be available). Additional exam requirements/recommendations for international students: Required—TOEFL (minimum score 550 paper-based; 213 computer-based; 79 iBT). *Application deadline:* For fall admission, 7/13 for domestic students, 7/16 for international students; for winter admission, 10/29 for domestic students, 9/24 for international students; for spring admission, 2/25 for domestic students, 1/21 for international students. Applications are processed on a rolling basis. Application fee: $60. *Expenses:* Contact institution. *Financial support:* Research assistantships, teaching assistantships available. Financial award application deadline: 3/2; financial award applicants required to submit FAFSA. *Unit head:* Dr. Alex Zecevic, Associate Dean for Graduate Studies, 408-554-2394, Fax: 408-554-4323, E-mail: azecevic@scu.edu. *Application contact:* Stacey Tinker, 408-554-4748, Fax: 408-554-4323, E-mail: stinker@scu.edu.

South Carolina State University, School of Graduate Studies, Department of Civil and Mechanical Engineering Technology, Orangeburg, SC 29117-0001. Offers transportation (MS). Part-time and evening/weekend programs available. *Degree requirements:* For master's, comprehensive exam, thesis, departmental qualifying exam. *Entrance requirements:* For master's, GRE. Electronic applications accepted. *Expenses:* Tuition, state resident: part-time $470 per credit hour. Tuition, nonresident: part-time $924 per credit hour. *Faculty research:* Societal competence, relationship of parent-child interaction to adult, rehabilitation evaluation, vocation, language assessment of rural children.

South Dakota School of Mines and Technology, Graduate Division, College of Engineering, Department of Civil and Environmental Engineering, Rapid City, SD 57701-3995. Offers civil engineering (MS); construction management (MS). Part-time programs available. *Faculty:* 12 full-time (2 women), 1 (woman) part-time/adjunct. *Students:* 26 full-time (6 women), 6 part-time (5 women), 8 international. Average age 25. 28 applicants, 89% accepted, 15 enrolled. In 2009, 26 master's awarded. *Entrance requirements:* Additional exam requirements/recommendations for international students: Required—TOEFL, TWE. *Application deadline:* For fall admission, 7/1 priority date for domestic students, 4/1 for international students; for spring admission, 11/1 for domestic students, 9/1 for international students. Applications are processed on a rolling basis. Application fee: $35. Electronic applications accepted. *Expenses:* Tuition, state resident: full-time $3340; part-time $139 per credit hour. Tuition, nonresident: full-time $7060; part-time $294 per credit hour. Required fees: $3270. *Financial support:* In 2009–10, 5 fellowships (averaging $4,050 per year), 9 research assistantships with partial tuition reimbursements (averaging $12,388 per year), 21 teaching assistantships with partial tuition reimbursements (averaging $4,520 per year) were awarded; Federal Work-Study and institutionally sponsored loans also available. Support available to part-time students. Financial award application deadline: 5/15. *Faculty research:* Concrete technology, environmental and sanitation engineering, water resources engineering, composite materials, geotechnical engineering. Total annual research expenditures: $356,502. *Unit head:* Dr. Henry Mott, Chair, 605-394-5170, E-mail: henry.mott@sdsmt.edu. *Application contact:* Jeannette R. Nilson, Administrative Support Coordinator, Graduate Education, 800-454-8162 Ext. 1206, Fax: 605-394-5360, E-mail: graduate_admissions@sdsmt.edu.

South Dakota State University, Graduate School, College of Engineering, Department of Civil and Environmental Engineering, Brookings, SD 57007. Offers engineering (MS). Part-time programs available. Postbaccalaureate distance learning degree programs offered (minimal on-campus study). *Degree requirements:* For master's, thesis (for some programs), oral exam. *Entrance requirements:* Additional exam requirements/recommendations for international students: Required—TOEFL (minimum score 525 paper-based). *Faculty research:* Structural, environmental, geotechnical, transportation engineering and water resources.

Southern Illinois University Carbondale, Graduate School, College of Engineering, Department of Civil and Environmental Engineering, Carbondale, IL 62901-4701. Offers civil engineering (MS). *Degree requirements:* For master's, comprehensive exam, thesis. *Entrance requirements:* For master's, minimum GPA of 2.7. Additional exam requirements/recommendations for international students: Required—TOEFL. *Faculty research:* Composite materials, wastewater treatment, solid waste disposal, slurry transport, geotechnical engineering.

Southern Illinois University Edwardsville, Graduate Studies and Research, School of Engineering, Department of Civil Engineering, Edwardsville, IL 62026-0001. Offers MS. Part-time and evening/weekend programs available. *Faculty:* 8 full-time (1 woman). *Students:* 9 full-time (2 women), 41 part-time (5 women); includes 1 minority (Asian American or Pacific Islander), 9 international. Average age 26. 45 applicants, 62% accepted. In 2009, 10 master's awarded. *Degree requirements:* For master's, thesis or research paper. *Entrance requirements:* For master's, minimum undergraduate GPA of 2.75 in science, math, and engineering courses. Additional exam requirements/recommendations for international students: Required—TOEFL (minimum score 550 paper-based; 213 computer-based; 79 iBT), IELTS (minimum score 6.5). *Application deadline:* For fall admission, 7/23 for domestic students, 6/1 for international students; for spring admission, 12/11 for domestic students, 10/1 for international students. Applications are processed on a rolling basis. Application fee: $30. Electronic applications accepted. *Expenses:* Tuition, state resident: part-time $1252.50 per semester. Tuition, nonresident: part-time $3131.25 per semester. Required fees: $586.85 per semester. Tuition and fees vary according to course load. *Financial support:* In 2009–10, 1 fellowship with full tuition reimbursement (averaging $8,370 per year), 3 research assistantships with full tuition reimbursements (averaging $8,064 per year), 8 teaching assistantships with full tuition reimbursements (averaging $8,064 per year) were awarded; career-related internships or fieldwork, Federal Work-Study, institutionally sponsored loans, scholarships/grants, traineeships, and unspecified assistantships also available. Support available to part-time students. Financial award application deadline: 3/1; financial award applicants required to submit FAFSA. *Unit head:* Dr. Susan Morgan, Chair, 618-650-2533, E-mail: smorgan@siue.edu. *Application contact:* Dr. Jianpeng Zhou, Director, 618-650-3221, E-mail: jzhou@siue.edu.

Southern Methodist University, Bobby B. Lyle School of Engineering, Department of Environmental and Civil Engineering, Dallas, TX 75275-0340. Offers applied science (MS, PhD); civil engineering (MS, PhD); environmental engineering (MS); environmental science (MS), including environmental systems management, hazardous and waste materials management; facilities management (MS). Part-time and evening/weekend programs available. Postbaccalaureate distance learning degree programs offered (no on-campus study). *Faculty:* 7 full-time (0 women), 13 part-time/adjunct (4 women). *Students:* 19 full-time (8 women), 50 part-time (17 women); includes 13 minority (9 African Americans, 2 Asian Americans or Pacific Islanders, 2 Hispanic Americans), 7 international. Average age 34. 50 applicants, 86% accepted, 28 enrolled. In 2009, 17 master's, 1 doctorate awarded. Terminal master's awarded for partial completion of doctoral program. *Degree requirements:* For master's, thesis optional; for doctorate, thesis/dissertation, oral and written qualifying exams. *Entrance requirements:* For master's, GRE General Test, minimum GPA of 3.0 in last 2 years; bachelor's degree in engineering, mathematics, or sciences; for doctorate, GRE, BS and MS in related field, minimum GPA of 3.3. Additional exam requirements/recommendations for international students: Required—TOEFL. *Application deadline:* For fall admission, 7/1 for domestic students, 5/15 for international students; for spring admission, 11/15 for domestic students, 9/1 for international students. Applications are processed on a rolling basis. Application fee: $75. Electronic applications accepted. *Financial support:* In 2009–10, 9 students received support, including 2 research assistantships with full tuition reimbursements available (averaging $18,000 per year), 7 teaching assistantships with full tuition reimbursements available (averaging $18,000 per year); career-related internships or fieldwork, tuition waivers (full and partial), and unspecified assistantships also available. *Faculty research:* Human and environmental health effects of endocrine disrupters, development of air pollution control systems for diesel engines, structural analysis and design, modeling and design of waste treatment systems. Total annual research expenditures: $100,000. *Unit head:* Prof. Bijan Mohraz, Chair, 214-768-3894, Fax: 214-768-2164, E-mail: bmohraz@lyle.smu.edu. *Application contact:* Marc Valerin, Director of Graduate and Executive Admissions, 214-768-3042, Fax: 214-768-3778, E-mail: valerin@lyle.smu.edu.

Stanford University, School of Engineering, Department of Civil and Environmental Engineering, Stanford, CA 94305-9991. Offers MS, PhD, Eng. Terminal master's awarded for partial completion of doctoral program. *Degree requirements:* For doctorate, thesis/dissertation, qualifying exam; for Eng, thesis. *Entrance requirements:* For master's, doctorate, and Eng, GRE General Test. Additional exam requirements/recommendations for international students: Required—TOEFL. Electronic applications accepted. *Expenses:* Tuition: Full-time $37,380; part-time $2760 per quarter. Required fees: $501.

Stevens Institute of Technology, Graduate School, Charles V. Schaefer Jr. School of Engineering, Department of Civil, Environmental, and Ocean Engineering, Program in Civil Engineering, Hoboken, NJ 07030. Offers civil engineering (PhD); geotechnical engineering (Certificate); geotechnical/geoenvironmental engineering (M Eng, Engr); hydrologic modeling (M Eng); stormwater management (M Eng); structural engineering (M Eng, Engr); water resources engineering (M Eng). *Degree requirements:* For master's, thesis optional; for doctorate, variable foreign language requirement, thesis/dissertation; for other advanced degree, project or thesis. *Entrance requirements:* For doctorate, GRE. Additional exam requirements/recommendations for international students: Required—TOEFL. Electronic applications accepted. *Expenses:* Tuition: Full-time $9900; part-time $1100 per credit. Required fees: $286 per semester.

Syracuse University, L. C. Smith College of Engineering and Computer Science, Program in Civil Engineering, Syracuse, NY 13244. Offers MS, PhD. Part-time programs available. *Students:* 35 full-time (4 women), 3 part-time (0 women); includes 4 minority (1 African American, 3 Asian Americans or Pacific Islanders), 28 international. Average age 27. 49 applicants, 69% accepted, 17 enrolled. In 2009, 8 master's, 2 doctorates awarded. *Degree requirements:* For doctorate, thesis/dissertation. *Entrance requirements:* For master's and doctorate, GRE General Test. Additional exam requirements/recommendations for international students: Required—TOEFL (minimum score 100 iBT). *Application deadline:* For fall admission, 6/1 priority date for domestic and international students. Applications are processed on a rolling basis. Application fee: $75. Electronic applications accepted. *Expenses:* Tuition: Full-time $26,808; part-time $1117 per credit. Required fees: $1024. *Financial support:* Fellowships with full tuition reimbursements, research assistantships with full tuition reimbursements, teaching assistantships with full tuition reimbursements, tuition waivers (partial) available. Financial award application deadline: 1/1. *Faculty research:* Fate and transport of pollutants, methods for characterization and remediation of hazardous wastes, response of eco-systems to disturbances, water quality and engineering. *Unit head:* Dr. Chris E. Johnson, Interim Chair, 315-443-2311, E-mail: cejohns@syr.edu. *Application contact:* Elizabeth Buchanan, Information Contact, 315-443-2558, E-mail: ebuchana@syr.edu.

Temple University, Graduate School, College of Engineering, Department of Civil and Environmental Engineering, Philadelphia, PA 19122-6096. Offers civil engineering (MSE). Part-time programs available. *Degree requirements:* For master's, thesis optional. *Entrance requirements:* For master's, GRE General Test, minimum GPA of 3.0. Additional exam requirements/recommendations for international students: Required—TOEFL (minimum score 550 paper-based; 213 computer-based; 79 iBT). *Faculty research:* Prestressed masonry structure, recycling processes and products, finite element analysis of highways and runways.

Tennessee Technological University, Graduate School, College of Engineering, Department of Civil Engineering, Cookeville, TN 38505. Offers MS, PhD. Part-time programs available. *Faculty:* 17 full-time (0 women). *Students:* 13 full-time (2 women), 2 part-time (1 woman); includes 4 minority (1 African American, 3 Asian Americans or Pacific Islanders). Average age 27. 19 applicants, 79% accepted, 9 enrolled. In 2009, 7 master's awarded. *Degree requirements:* For master's, thesis. *Entrance requirements:* For master's, GRE. Additional exam requirements/recommendations for international students: Required—TOEFL (minimum score 550 paper-based; 79 iBT), IELTS (minimum score 5.5). *Application deadline:* For fall admission, 8/1 for domestic students, 5/1 for international students; for spring admission, 12/1 for domestic students, 10/1 for international students. Application fee: $25 ($30 for international students). Electronic applications accepted. *Expenses:* Tuition, state resident: full-time $7034; part-time $368 per credit hour. *Financial support:* In 2009–10, 6 research assistantships (averaging $8,227 per year), 5 teaching assistantships (averaging $7,200 per year) were awarded; career-related internships or fieldwork also available. Financial award application deadline: 4/1. *Faculty research:* Environmental engineering, transportation, structural engineering, water resources. *Unit head:* Dr. Sharon Huo, Interim Chairperson, 931-372-3454, Fax: 931-372-6352. *Application contact:* Shelia K. Kendrick, Coordinator of Graduate Studies, 931-372-3808, Fax: 931-372-3497, E-mail: skendrick@tntech.edu.

Texas A&M University, College of Engineering, Zachry Department of Civil Engineering, College Station, TX 77843. Offers construction engineering and management (M Eng, MS, D Eng, PhD); environmental engineering (M Eng, MS, D Eng, PhD); geotechnical engineering (M Eng, MS, D Eng, PhD); materials engineering (M Eng, MS, D Eng, PhD); ocean engineering (M Eng, MS, D Eng, PhD); structural engineering (M Eng, MS, D Eng, PhD); transportation engineering (M Eng, MS, D Eng, PhD); water resources engineering (M Eng, MS, D Eng, PhD). Part-time programs available. *Faculty:* 61. *Students:* 390 full-time (89 women), 42 part-time (6 women); includes 23 minority (2 African Americans, 11 Asian Americans or Pacific Islanders, 10 Hispanic Americans), 281 international. Average age 29. In 2009, 100 master's, 36 doctorates awarded. *Degree requirements:* For master's, thesis (MS); for doctorate, dissertation (PhD), internship (D Eng). *Entrance requirements:* For master's and doctorate, GRE General Test. Additional exam requirements/recommendations for international students: Required—TOEFL. *Application deadline:* Applications are processed on a rolling basis. Application fee: $50 ($75 for international students). Electronic applications accepted. *Expenses:* Tuition, state resident: full-time $3991.32; part-time $221.74 per credit hour. Tuition, nonresident: full-time $9049; part-time $502.74 per credit hour. *Financial support:* In 2009–10, fellowships (averaging $4,500 per year), research assistantships (averaging $14,000 per year), teaching assistantships (averaging $14,400 per year) were awarded; career-related internships or fieldwork and institutionally sponsored loans also available. Financial award application deadline: 4/15; financial award applicants required to submit FAFSA. *Unit head:* Dr. Tony Cahill, Head, 979-845-2438, E-mail: t-cahill@civil.tamu.edu. *Application contact:* Graduate Advisor, 979-845-2498, Fax: 979-862-2800, E-mail: ce-grad@tamu.edu.

Texas A&M University–Kingsville, College of Graduate Studies, College of Engineering, Department of Civil Engineering, Kingsville, TX 78363. Offers ME, MS. Part-time and evening/

weekend programs available. *Degree requirements:* For master's, comprehensive exam, thesis or alternative. *Entrance requirements:* For master's, GRE General Test. Additional exam requirements/recommendations for international students: Required—TOEFL. *Faculty research:* Geotechnical engineering, structural mechanics, structural design, transportation engineering.

Texas Tech University, Graduate School, College of Engineering, Department of Civil and Environmental Engineering, Lubbock, TX 79409. Offers civil engineering (MSCE, PhD); environmental engineering (MENVEGR); environmental technology management (MSETM). *Accreditation:* ABET. Part-time programs available. *Faculty:* 21 full-time (2 women), 1 part-time/adjunct (0 women). *Students:* 47 full-time (11 women), 18 part-time (3 women); includes 3 minority (1 African American, 1 Asian American or Pacific Islander, 1 Hispanic American), 42 international. Average age 27. 94 applicants, 60% accepted, 11 enrolled. In 2009, 27 master's, 2 doctorates awarded. *Degree requirements:* For master's, thesis or alternative; for doctorate, thesis/dissertation. *Entrance requirements:* For master's and doctorate, GRE General Test, minimum GPA of 3.0. Additional exam requirements/recommendations for international students: Required—TOEFL (minimum score 550 paper-based; 213 computer-based). *Application deadline:* For fall admission, 3/1 priority date for international students; for spring admission, 11/1 priority date for international students. Applications are processed on a rolling basis. Application fee: $50 ($75 for international students). Electronic applications accepted. *Expenses:* Tuition, state resident: full-time $5100; part-time $213 per credit hour. Tuition, nonresident: full-time $11,748; part-time $490 per credit hour. Required fees: $2298; $50 per credit hour. $555 per semester. *Financial support:* In 2009–10, 31 research assistantships with partial tuition reimbursements (averaging $19,861 per year), 11 teaching assistantships with partial tuition reimbursements (averaging $12,241 per year) were awarded; Federal Work-Study and institutionally sponsored loans also available. Support available to part-time students. Financial award application deadline: 4/15; financial award applicants required to submit FAFSA. *Faculty research:* Wind load/engineering on structures, fluid mechanics, structural dynamics, water resource management, transportation engineering. Total annual research expenditures: $998,329. *Unit head:* Dr. H. Scott Norville, Chair, 806-742-3523, Fax: 806-742-3488, E-mail: scott.norville@ttu.edu. *Application contact:* Dr. Priyantha Jayawickrama, Graduate Adviser, 806-742-3523, Fax: 806-742-3488, E-mail: priyantha.jayawickrama@ttu.edu.

Trine University, Allen School of Engineering and Technology, Angola, IN 46703-1764. Offers civil engineering (ME); mechanical engineering (ME). Part-time and evening/weekend programs available. *Degree requirements:* For master's, comprehensive exam, thesis. *Faculty research:* CAD, computer aided MFG, computer numerical control, parametric modeling, megatronics.

Tufts University, School of Engineering, Department of Civil and Environmental Engineering, Medford, MA 02155. Offers civil engineering (ME, MS, PhD), including geotechnical engineering, structural engineering; environmental engineering (ME, MS, PhD), including environmental engineering and environmental sciences, environmental geotechnology, environmental health, environmental science and management, hazardous materials management, water resources engineering. Part-time programs available. *Faculty:* 17 full-time, 7 part-time/adjunct. *Students:* 72 (33 women); includes 6 minority (2 African Americans, 4 Asian Americans or Pacific Islanders), 17 international. Average age 27. 170 applicants, 59% accepted, 20 enrolled. In 2009, 17 master's, 3 doctorates awarded. Terminal master's awarded for partial completion of doctoral program. *Degree requirements:* For master's, thesis or alternative; for doctorate, thesis/dissertation. *Entrance requirements:* For master's and doctorate, GRE General Test. Additional exam requirements/recommendations for international students: Required—TOEFL (minimum score 550 paper-based; 213 computer-based; 80 iBT). *Application deadline:* For fall admission, 1/15 priority date for domestic students, 12/15 for international students; for spring admission, 10/15 for domestic students, 9/15 for international students. Applications are processed on a rolling basis. Application fee: $75. Electronic applications accepted. *Expenses:* Tuition: Full-time $38,096; part-time $3962 per credit. Required fees: $686; $40 per year. Tuition and fees vary according to course level, course load, degree level, program and student level. *Financial support:* Fellowships with full tuition reimbursements, research assistantships with full and partial tuition reimbursements, teaching assistantships with full and partial tuition reimbursements, Federal Work-Study, scholarships/grants, tuition waivers (partial), and unspecified assistantships available. Financial award application deadline: 1/15; financial award applicants required to submit FAFSA. *Unit head:* Dr. Kurt Penell, Chair, 617-627-3211, Fax: 617-627-3994. *Application contact:* Laura Sacco, Information Contact, 617-627-3211.

Université de Moncton, Faculty of Engineering, Program in Civil Engineering, Moncton, NB E1A 3E9, Canada. Offers M Sc A. *Degree requirements:* For master's, thesis, proficiency in French. *Faculty research:* Structures and materials, hydrology and water resources, soil mechanics and statistical analysis, environment, transportation.

Université de Sherbrooke, Faculty of Engineering, Department of Civil Engineering, Sherbrooke, QC J1K 2R1, Canada. Offers M Sc A, PhD. *Degree requirements:* For master's, one foreign language, thesis; for doctorate, comprehensive exam, thesis/dissertation. *Entrance requirements:* For master's, bachelor's degree in engineering or equivalent; for doctorate, master's degree in engineering or equivalent. Electronic applications accepted. *Faculty research:* High-strength concrete, dynamics of structures, solid mechanics, geotechnical engineering, wastewater treatment.

Université Laval, Faculty of Sciences and Engineering, Department of Civil Engineering, Program in Urban Infrastructure Engineering, Québec, QC G1K 7P4, Canada. Offers Diploma. Part-time and evening/weekend programs available. *Entrance requirements:* For degree, knowledge of French. Electronic applications accepted.

Université Laval, Faculty of Sciences and Engineering, Department of Civil Engineering, Programs in Civil Engineering, Québec, QC G1K 7P4, Canada. Offers civil engineering (M Sc, PhD); environmental technology (M Sc). Terminal master's awarded for partial completion of doctoral program. *Degree requirements:* For master's, thesis (for some programs); for doctorate, comprehensive exam, thesis/dissertation. *Entrance requirements:* For master's and doctorate, knowledge of French and English. Electronic applications accepted.

University at Buffalo, the State University of New York, Graduate School, School of Engineering and Applied Sciences, Department of Civil, Structural, and Environmental Engineering, Buffalo, NY 14260. Offers civil engineering (M Eng, MS, PhD); engineering science (MS). Part-time programs available. Postbaccalaureate distance learning degree programs offered (minimal on-campus study). *Faculty:* 27 full-time (4 women), 3 part-time/adjunct (2 women). *Students:* 136 full-time (26 women), 14 part-time (3 women); includes 10 minority (1 American Indian/Alaska Native, 4 Asian Americans or Pacific Islanders, 5 Hispanic Americans), 100 international. Average age 28. 514 applicants, 40% accepted, 59 enrolled. In 2009, 25 master's, 8 doctorates awarded. Terminal master's awarded for partial completion of doctoral program. *Degree requirements:* For master's, thesis optional, project, thesis, or comprehensive exam; for doctorate, thesis/dissertation. *Entrance requirements:* For master's and doctorate, GRE General Test, letters of reference. Additional exam requirements/recommendations for international students: Required—TOEFL (minimum score 550 paper-based; 213 computer-based; 79 iBT). *Application deadline:* For fall admission, 1/15 priority date for domestic and international students; for spring admission, 9/15 for domestic and international students. Applications are processed on a rolling basis. Application fee: $50. Electronic applications accepted. *Financial support:* In 2009–10, 79 students received support, including 18 fellowships with full tuition reimbursements available (averaging $17,200 per year), 34 research assistantships with full tuition reimbursements available (averaging $14,000 per year), 27 teaching assistantships with full tuition reimbursements available (averaging $14,700 per year); career-related internships or fieldwork, Federal Work-Study, institutionally sponsored loans, scholarships/grants, traineeships, health care benefits, tuition waivers (full and partial), and unspecified assistantships also available. Support available to part-time students. Financial award application deadline: 1/15; financial award applicants required to submit FAFSA. *Faculty research:* Environmental engineering and fluid mechanics, structural dynamics, geomechanics, earthquake engineering computational mechanics. Total annual research expenditures: $7.3 million. *Unit head:* Dr. A. Scott Weber, Chairman, 716-645-2114, Fax: 716-645-3733, E-mail: sweber@eng.buffalo.edu. *Application contact:* Dr. Amjad J. Aref, Director of Graduate Studies, 716-645-4369, Fax: 716-645-3733, E-mail: cjb@buffalo.edu.

The University of Akron, Graduate School, College of Engineering, Department of Civil Engineering, Akron, OH 44325. Offers MS, PhD. Evening/weekend programs available. *Faculty:* 16 full-time (3 women), 3 part-time/adjunct (0 women). *Students:* 48 full-time (9 women), 13 part-time (2 women); includes 1 African American, 33 international. Average age 28. 47 applicants, 70% accepted, 18 enrolled. In 2009, 11 master's, 7 doctorates awarded. *Degree requirements:* For master's, thesis optional; for doctorate, thesis/dissertation, candidacy exam, qualifying exam. *Entrance requirements:* For master's, GRE, minimum GPA of 2.75, letters of recommendation, resume; for doctorate, GRE, minimum GPA of 3.0 with bachelor's degree, 3.5 with master's degree; letters of recommendation; personal statement, resume. Additional exam requirements/recommendations for international students: Required—TOEFL (minimum score 550 paper-based; 213 computer-based; 79 iBT). *Application deadline:* Applications are processed on a rolling basis. Application fee: $30 ($40 for international students). Electronic applications accepted. *Expenses:* Tuition, state resident: full-time $6570; part-time $365 per credit hour. Tuition, nonresident: full-time $11,250; part-time $625 per credit hour. *Financial support:* In 2009–10, 2 fellowships with full tuition reimbursements, 2 research assistantships with full tuition reimbursements, 37 teaching assistantships with full tuition reimbursements were awarded; career-related internships or fieldwork and Federal Work-Study also available. *Faculty research:* Development of constitutive laws for numerical analysis of nonlinear problems in structural mechanics, multiscale modeling and simulation of novel materials, water quality and distribution system analysis, safety related traffic control, dynamic pile testing and analysis. Total annual research expenditures: $1.6 million. *Unit head:* Dr. Wieslaw K. Binienda, Chair, 330-972-6693, E-mail: wbinienda@uakron.edu. *Application contact:* Dr. Wieslaw K. Binienda, Chair, 330-972-6693, E-mail: wbinienda@uakron.edu.

The University of Alabama, Graduate School, College of Engineering, Department of Civil, Construction and Environmental Engineering, Tuscaloosa, AL 35487-0205. Offers civil engineering (MSCE, PhD); environmental engineering (MS). Part-time programs available. *Faculty:* 20 full-time (2 women). *Students:* 39 full-time (11 women), 10 part-time (4 women); includes 9 minority (7 African Americans, 1 American Indian/Alaska Native, 1 Asian American or Pacific Islander), 18 international. Average age 30. 68 applicants, 26% accepted, 12 enrolled. In 2009, 16 master's, 1 doctorate awarded. Terminal master's awarded for partial completion of doctoral program. *Median time to degree:* Of those who began their doctoral program in fall 2001, 100% received their degree in 8 years or less. *Degree requirements:* For master's, thesis or alternative; for doctorate, one foreign language, thesis/dissertation. *Entrance requirements:* For master's and doctorate, GRE General Test, minimum GPA of 3.0 in last 60 hours of course work. Additional exam requirements/recommendations for international students: Required—TOEFL (minimum score 550 paper-based; 213 computer-based), IELTS (minimum score 6.5). *Application deadline:* For fall admission, 7/6 for domestic students, 1/15 for international students; for spring admission, 11/1 for domestic students, 6/1 for international students. Applications are processed on a rolling basis. Application fee: $50 ($60 for international students). Electronic applications accepted. *Expenses:* Tuition, state resident: full-time $7000. Tuition, nonresident: full-time $19,200. *Financial support:* In 2009–10, 40 students received support, including 32 research assistantships with full tuition reimbursements available (averaging $10,489 per year), 12 teaching assistantships with full tuition reimbursements available (averaging $10,489 per year); fellowships, scholarships/grants, tuition waivers (partial), and unspecified assistantships also available. Financial award application deadline: 3/15. *Faculty research:* Experimental structures, modeling of structures, bridge management systems, geotechnological engineering, environmental remediation. Total annual research expenditures: $2.3 million. *Unit head:* Dr. Kenneth J. Fridley, Head and Professor, 205-348-6550, Fax: 205-348-0783, E-mail: kfridley@coe.eng.ua.edu. *Application contact:* Dr. David A. Francko, Dean, 205-348-8280, Fax: 205-348-0400, E-mail: dfrancko@ua.edu.

The University of Alabama at Birmingham, School of Engineering, Program in Civil Engineering, Birmingham, AL 35294. Offers MSCE, PhD.

The University of Alabama in Huntsville, School of Graduate Studies, College of Engineering, Department of Civil and Environmental Engineering, Huntsville, AL 35899. Offers civil and environmental engineering (PhD); civil engineering (MSE), including environmental and water resource engineering, geotechnical engineering, structural engineering and structural mechanics, transportation engineering. Part-time and evening/weekend programs available. *Faculty:* 6 full-time (1 woman). *Students:* 12 full-time (3 women), 7 part-time (1 woman); includes 3 minority (2 African Americans, 1 Asian American or Pacific Islander), 5 international. Average age 33. 26 applicants, 58% accepted, 9 enrolled. In 2009, 10 master's, 2 doctorates awarded. *Degree requirements:* For master's, comprehensive exam, thesis or alternative, oral and written exams; for doctorate, comprehensive exam, thesis/dissertation, oral and written exams. *Entrance requirements:* For master's, GRE General Test, BSE, minimum GPA of 3.0; for doctorate, GRE General Test, minimum GPA of 3.0. Additional exam requirements/recommendations for international students: Required—TOEFL (minimum score 500 paper-based; 173 computer-based; 62 iBT). *Application deadline:* For fall admission, 7/15 for domestic students, 4/1 for international students; for spring admission, 11/30 for domestic students, 9/1 for international students. Applications are processed on a rolling basis. Application fee: $40 ($50 for international students). Electronic applications accepted. *Expenses:* Tuition, state resident: part-time $355.75 per credit hour. Tuition, nonresident: part-time $847.10 per credit hour. Required fees: $210.80 per semester. Tuition and fees vary according to course load and program. *Financial support:* In 2009–10, 10 students received support, including 4 research assistantships with full and partial tuition reimbursements available (averaging $11,525 per year), 6 teaching assistantships with full and partial tuition reimbursements available (averaging $9,678 per year); career-related internships or fieldwork, Federal Work-Study, institutionally sponsored loans, scholarships/grants, health care benefits, and unspecified assistantships also available. Support available to part-time students. Financial award application deadline: 4/1; financial award applicants required to submit FAFSA. *Faculty research:* Hydrologic modeling, orbital debris impact, hydrogeology, environmental engineering, transportation engineering. Total annual research expenditures: $1.5 million. *Unit head:* Dr. Houssam Toutanji, Chair, 256-824-7361, Fax: 256-824-6724, E-mail: toutanji@cee.uah.edu. *Application contact:* Kathy Biggs, Graduate Studies Admissions Manager, 256-824-6199, Fax: 256-824-6405, E-mail: deangrad@uah.edu.

University of Alaska Anchorage, School of Engineering, Program in Civil Engineering, Anchorage, AK 99508. Offers civil engineering (MCE, MS); port and coastal engineering (Certificate). Part-time and evening/weekend programs available. *Degree requirements:* For master's, thesis (for some programs). *Entrance requirements:* For master's, bachelor's degree in engineering. Additional exam requirements/recommendations for international students: Required—TOEFL (minimum score 550 paper-based; 213 computer-based). *Faculty research:* Structural engineering, engineering education, astronomical observations related to engineering.

University of Alaska Fairbanks, College of Engineering and Mines, Department of Civil and Environmental Engineering, Fairbanks, AK 99775-5900. Offers arctic engineering (MS, PhD); civil engineering (MCE, MS, PhD); engineering (PhD); engineering and science management (MS, PhD), including engineering management, science management (MS); environmental engineering (MS, PhD), including engineering (PhD), environmental engineering (MS); environmental quality science (MS), including environmental contaminants, environmental quality science, environmental science and management, water supply and waste treatment. Part-time programs available. *Faculty:* 13 full-time (4 women), 5 part-time/adjunct (0 women). *Students:* 32 full-time (13 women), 17 part-time (9 women); includes 4 minority (1 African American, 2 American Indian/Alaska Native, 1 Asian American or Pacific Islander), 15 international. Average age 30. 28 applicants, 57% accepted, 11 enrolled. In 2009, 8 master's, 3 doctorates awarded. Terminal master's awarded for partial completion of doctoral program. *Degree requirements:* For master's, comprehensive exam, thesis or alternative; for doctorate, comprehensive exam, thesis/dissertation, oral exam, oral defense. *Entrance requirements:* For doctorate, GRE General Test. Additional exam requirements/recommendations for international students: Required—

Civil Engineering

University of Alaska Fairbanks *(continued)*
TOEFL (minimum score 550 paper-based; 213 computer-based; 80 iBT). *Application deadline:* For fall admission, 6/1 for domestic students, 3/1 for international students; for spring admission, 10/15 for domestic students, 9/1 for international students. Applications are processed on a rolling basis. Application fee: $60. Electronic applications accepted. *Expenses:* Tuition, state resident: full-time $7584; part-time $316 per credit. Tuition, nonresident: full-time $15,504; part-time $646 per credit. Required fees: $23 per credit; $135 per semester. Tuition and fees vary according to course level, course load and reciprocity agreements. *Financial support:* In 2009–10, 21 research assistantships (averaging $14,368 per year), 7 teaching assistantships (averaging $6,202 per year) were awarded; fellowships, career-related internships or fieldwork, Federal Work-Study, scholarships/grants, health care benefits, and unspecified assistantships also available. Support available to part-time students. Financial award application deadline: 7/1; financial award applicants required to submit FAFSA. *Faculty research:* Soils, structures, culvert thawing with solar power, pavement drainage, contaminant hydrogeology. *Unit head:* Dr. David Barnes, Department Chair, 907-474-7241, Fax: 907-474-6087, E-mail: fycee@uaf.edu. *Application contact:* Dr. David Barnes, Department Chair, 907-474-7241, Fax: 907-474-6087, E-mail: fycee@uaf.edu.

University of Alberta, Faculty of Graduate Studies and Research, Department of Civil and Environmental Engineering, Edmonton, AB T6G 2E1, Canada. Offers construction engineering and management (M Eng, M Sc, PhD); environmental engineering (M Eng, M Sc, PhD); environmental science (M Sc, PhD); geoenvironmental engineering (M Eng, M Sc, PhD); geotechnical engineering (M Eng, M Sc, PhD); mining engineering (M Eng, M Sc, PhD); petroleum engineering (M Eng, M Sc, PhD); structural engineering (M Eng, M Sc, PhD); water resources (M Eng, M Sc, PhD). Part-time programs available. Postbaccalaureate distance learning degree programs offered (minimal on-campus study). *Faculty:* 44 full-time (3 women), 2 part-time/adjunct (0 women). *Students:* 215 full-time (49 women), 99 part-time (19 women). 1,428 applicants, 15% accepted, 123 enrolled. In 2009, 124 master's, 34 doctorates awarded. *Degree requirements:* For master's, thesis (for some programs); for doctorate, thesis/dissertation. *Entrance requirements:* For master's, minimum GPA of 3.0 in last 2 years of undergraduate studies; for doctorate, minimum GPA of 3.0. Additional exam requirements/recommendations for international students: Required—TOEFL (minimum score 550 paper-based; 213 computer-based). *Application deadline:* For fall admission, 6/1 priority date for domestic students, 6/1 for international students; for winter admission, 11/1 for domestic students, 9/15 for international students. Applications are processed on a rolling basis. Application fee: $0 Canadian dollars. Electronic applications accepted. Tuition and fees charges are reported in Canadian dollars. *Expenses:* Tuition, area resident: Full-time $4626.24 Canadian dollars; part-time $99.72 Canadian dollars per unit. International tuition: $8216 Canadian dollars full-time. Required fees: $3589.92 Canadian dollars; $99.72 Canadian dollars per unit. $215 Canadian dollars per term. *Financial support:* In 2009–10, 88 research assistantships with full and partial tuition reimbursements, 134 teaching assistantships with full and partial tuition reimbursements were awarded; scholarships/grants and tuition waivers (full and partial) also available. Financial award application deadline: 4/1. *Faculty research:* Mining. Total annual research expenditures: $6,791 Canadian dollars. *Unit head:* Dr. David Zhu, Associate Chair, Graduate Studies, 780-492-1198, Fax: 403-492-8198. *Application contact:* Gwen Mendoza, Student Services Officer, 403-492-1539, Fax: 403-492-0249, E-mail: civegrad@ualberta.ca.

The University of Arizona, Graduate College, College of Engineering, Department of Civil Engineering and Engineering Mechanics, Program in Civil Engineering, Tucson, AZ 85721. Offers MS, PhD. Part-time programs available. *Students:* 38 full-time (11 women), 23 part-time (3 women); includes 9 minority (3 American Indian/Alaska Native, 3 Asian Americans or Pacific Islanders, 3 Hispanic Americans), 33 international. Average age 30. 74 applicants, 46% accepted, 7 enrolled. In 2009, 7 master's, 6 doctorates awarded. *Degree requirements:* For master's, thesis; for doctorate, thesis/dissertation, departmental qualifying exam. *Entrance requirements:* For master's, GRE General Test, 3 letters of recommendation, statement of purpose; for doctorate, GRE General Test, minimum GPA of 3.5, 3 letters of recommendation, statement of purpose. Additional exam requirements/recommendations for international students: Required—TOEFL (minimum score 550 paper-based; 213 computer-based; 79 iBT). *Application deadline:* For fall admission, 6/1 for domestic students, 12/1 for international students; for spring admission, 10/1 for domestic students, 6/1 for international students. Applications are processed on a rolling basis. Application fee: $75. Electronic applications accepted. *Expenses:* Tuition, state resident: full-time $9028. Tuition, nonresident: full-time $24,890. *Financial support:* Institutionally sponsored loans and unspecified assistantships available. Financial award application deadline: 4/6. *Faculty research:* Soil-structure interaction, water resources, waste disposal, concrete and steel structures. *Unit head:* Kevin E. Lansey, Department Head, 520-621-6564, E-mail: lansey@engr.arizona.edu. *Application contact:* Graduate Coordinator, 520-621-2266, Fax: 520-621-2550, E-mail: ceem@engr.arizona.edu.

University of Arkansas, Graduate School, College of Engineering, Department of Civil Engineering, Program in Civil Engineering, Fayetteville, AR 72701-1201. Offers MSCE, MSE, PhD. *Students:* 19 full-time (3 women), 10 part-time (5 women); includes 3 minority (1 African American, 1 Asian American or Pacific Islander, 1 Hispanic American), 4 international. In 2009, 11 master's, 4 doctorates awarded. *Degree requirements:* For master's, thesis optional; for doctorate, one foreign language, thesis/dissertation. Application fee: $40 ($50 for international students). *Expenses:* Tuition, state resident: full-time $7355; part-time $356.58 per hour. Tuition, nonresident: full-time $17,401; part-time $775.17 per hour. Required fees: $1203. *Financial support:* In 2009–10, 4 fellowships, 19 research assistantships were awarded; teaching assistantships, career-related internships or fieldwork and Federal Work-Study also available. Support available to part-time students. Financial award application deadline: 4/1; financial award applicants required to submit FAFSA. *Unit head:* Dr. Kevin Hall, Departmental Chair, 479-575-4954, Fax: 479-575-7168, E-mail: kdhall@uark.edu. *Application contact:* Dr. Kelvin Wang, Graduate Coordinator, 479-575-4954, Fax: 479-575-7168, E-mail: kcw@uark.edu.

The University of British Columbia, Faculty of Applied Science, Department of Civil Engineering, Vancouver, BC V6T 1Z1, Canada. Offers M Eng, MA Sc, PhD. Part-time programs available. *Degree requirements:* For master's, thesis; for doctorate, thesis/dissertation. *Entrance requirements:* Additional exam requirements/recommendations for international students: Required—TOEFL (minimum score 600 paper-based; 250 computer-based), IELTS (minimum score 7), TWE (minimum score 5). Electronic applications accepted. *Faculty research:* Geotechnology; structural, water, and environmental engineering; transportation; materials and construction engineering.

University of Calgary, Faculty of Graduate Studies, Schulich School of Engineering, Department of Civil Engineering, Calgary, AB T2N 1N4, Canada. Offers M Eng, M Sc, MPM, PhD. Part-time and evening/weekend programs available. *Degree requirements:* For master's, thesis (for some programs); for doctorate, thesis/dissertation, candidacy exam. *Entrance requirements:* For master's, minimum GPA of 3.0; for doctorate, minimum GPA of 3.5. Additional exam requirements/recommendations for international students: Required—TOEFL (minimum score 580 paper-based; 230 computer-based). *Faculty research:* Structures, including structural materials; transportation; project management and biomechanics; geotechnical engineering; environmental engineering.

University of California, Berkeley, Graduate Division, College of Engineering, Department of Civil and Environmental Engineering, Berkeley, CA 94720-1500. Offers engineering and project management (M Eng, MS, D Eng, PhD); environmental engineering (M Eng, MS, D Eng, PhD); geoengineering (M Eng, MS, D Eng, PhD); structural engineering, mechanics and materials (M Eng, MS, D Eng, PhD); transportation engineering (M Eng, MS, D Eng, PhD); M Arch/MS; MCP/MS; MPP/MS. *Students:* 368 full-time (125 women). Average age 27. 921 applicants, 179 enrolled. In 2009, 158 master's, 39 doctorates awarded. *Degree requirements:* For master's, comprehensive exam or thesis (MS); for doctorate, thesis/dissertation, qualifying exam. *Entrance requirements:* For master's, GRE General Test, minimum GPA of 3.0, 3 letters of recommendation; for doctorate, GRE General Test, minimum GPA of 3.5, 3 letters of recommendation. Additional exam requirements/recommendations for international students: Required—TOEFL (minimum score 570 paper-based; 230 computer-based). *Application deadline:* For fall admission, 2/3 for domestic students. Application fee: $70 ($90 for international students). Electronic applications accepted. *Financial support:* Fellowships, research assistantships, teaching assistantships, unspecified assistantships available. *Unit head:* Prof. Lisa Alvarez-Cohen, Chair, 510-643-8739, Fax: 510-643-5264, E-mail: chair@ce.berkeley.edu. *Application contact:* Shelly Okimoto, Graduate Advisor, 510-642-6464, Fax: 510-643-5264, E-mail: aao@ce.berkeley.edu.

University of California, Davis, College of Engineering, Program in Civil and Environmental Engineering, Davis, CA 95616. Offers M Engr, MS, D Engr, PhD, Certificate, M Engr/MBA. *Degree requirements:* For master's, comprehensive exam (for some programs), thesis (for some programs); for doctorate, thesis/dissertation. *Entrance requirements:* For master's, GRE General Test, minimum GPA of 3.0; for doctorate, GRE, minimum graduate GPA of 3.5. Additional exam requirements/recommendations for international students: Required—TOEFL (minimum score 550 paper-based; 213 computer-based). Electronic applications accepted. *Faculty research:* Environmental water resources, transportation, structural mechanics, structural engineering, geotechnical engineering.

University of California, Irvine, Office of Graduate Studies, School of Engineering, Department of Civil and Environmental Engineering, Irvine, CA 92697. Offers MS, PhD. Part-time programs available. *Students:* 112 full-time (29 women), 16 part-time (9 women); includes 25 minority (22 Asian Americans or Pacific Islanders, 3 Hispanic Americans), 63 international. Average age 27. 254 applicants, 43% accepted, 37 enrolled. In 2009, 34 master's, 8 doctorates awarded. Terminal master's awarded for partial completion of doctoral program. *Degree requirements:* For doctorate, thesis/dissertation. *Entrance requirements:* For master's and doctorate, GRE General Test, minimum GPA of 3.0, 3 letters of recommendation. Additional exam requirements/recommendations for international students: Required—TOEFL (minimum score 550 paper-based; 213 computer-based). *Application deadline:* For fall admission, 1/15 priority date for domestic students, 1/15 for international students. Applications are processed on a rolling basis. Application fee: $70 ($90 for international students). Electronic applications accepted. *Financial support:* In 2009–10, fellowships (averaging $14,656 per year); research assistantships with full tuition reimbursements, teaching assistantships, institutionally sponsored loans, traineeships, health care benefits, and unspecified assistantships also available. Financial award application deadline: 3/1; financial award applicants required to submit FAFSA. *Faculty research:* Intelligent transportation systems and transportation economics, risk and reliability, fluid mechanics, environmental hydrodynamics, hydrological and climate systems, water resources. *Unit head:* Dr. Masanobu Shinozuka, Chair, 949-824-9379, Fax: 949-824-3672, E-mail: shino@uci.edu. *Application contact:* Lorrie Aguirre, Administrative Assistant, 949-824-2120, Fax: 949-824-2117, E-mail: llaguirr@uci.edu.

University of California, Los Angeles, Graduate Division, Henry Samueli School of Engineering and Applied Science, Department of Civil and Environmental Engineering, Los Angeles, CA 90095-1593. Offers MS, PhD. *Faculty:* 15 full-time (3 women). *Students:* 138 full-time (47 women); includes 41 minority (2 African Americans, 29 Asian Americans or Pacific Islanders, 10 Hispanic Americans), 48 international. 281 applicants, 62% accepted, 78 enrolled. In 2009, 52 master's, 10 doctorates awarded. *Degree requirements:* For master's, comprehensive exam or thesis; for doctorate, thesis/dissertation, qualifying exams. *Entrance requirements:* For master's, GRE General Test, minimum GPA of 3.0; for doctorate, GRE General Test, minimum GPA of 3.25. Additional exam requirements/recommendations for international students: Required—TOEFL (minimum score 560 paper-based; 220 computer-based). *Application deadline:* For fall admission, 1/15 for domestic and international students. Application fee: $70 ($90 for international students). Electronic applications accepted. *Financial support:* In 2009–10, 98 fellowships, 95 research assistantships, 45 teaching assistantships were awarded; Federal Work-Study, institutionally sponsored loans, and tuition waivers (full and partial) also available. Financial award application deadline: 12/15; financial award applicants required to submit FAFSA. Total annual research expenditures: $3.9 million. *Unit head:* Dr. Jiun-Shyan Chen, Chair, 310-267-4620. *Application contact:* Maida Bassili, Graduate Affairs Officer, 310-825-1851, Fax: 310-206-2222, E-mail: maida@ea.ucla.edu.

University of Central Florida, College of Engineering and Computer Science, Department of Civil, Environmental, and Construction Engineering, Program in Civil Engineering, Orlando, FL 32816. Offers civil engineering (MS, MSCE, PhD); construction engineering (Certificate); structural engineering (Certificate); transportation engineering (Certificate). Part-time and evening/weekend programs available. *Students:* 53 full-time (8 women), 68 part-time (20 women); includes 22 minority (4 African Americans, 1 American Indian/Alaska Native, 5 Asian Americans or Pacific Islanders, 12 Hispanic Americans), 34 international. Average age 29. 90 applicants, 73% accepted, 45 enrolled. In 2009, 30 master's, 2 doctorates awarded. *Degree requirements:* For master's, thesis or alternative; for doctorate, thesis/dissertation, departmental qualifying exam, candidacy exam. *Entrance requirements:* For master's, GRE General Test, minimum GPA of 3.0 in last 60 hours; for doctorate, GRE General Test, minimum GPA of 3.5 in last 60 hours. Additional exam requirements/recommendations for international students: Required—TOEFL. *Application deadline:* For fall admission, 7/15 priority date for domestic students; for spring admission, 12/15 priority date for domestic students. Application fee: $30. Electronic applications accepted. *Expenses:* Tuition, state resident: part-time $306.31 per credit hour. Tuition, nonresident: part-time $1099.01 per credit hour. Part-time tuition and fees vary according to degree level and program. *Financial support:* In 2009–10, 30 students received support, including 7 fellowships with partial tuition reimbursements available (averaging $7,100 per year), 19 research assistantships with partial tuition reimbursements available (averaging $11,600 per year), 12 teaching assistantships with partial tuition reimbursements available (averaging $9,700 per year); career-related internships or fieldwork, Federal Work-Study, institutionally sponsored loans, tuition waivers (partial), and unspecified assistantships also available. Financial award application deadline: 3/1; financial award applicants required to submit FAFSA.

University of Cincinnati, Graduate School, College of Engineering, Department of Civil and Environmental Engineering, Program in Civil Engineering, Cincinnati, OH 45221. Offers MS, PhD. Part-time programs available. Terminal master's awarded for partial completion of doctoral program. *Degree requirements:* For master's, project or thesis; for doctorate, one foreign language, thesis/dissertation. *Entrance requirements:* For master's and doctorate, GRE General Test. Additional exam requirements/recommendations for international students: Required—TOEFL (minimum score 580 paper-based; 237 computer-based; 92 iBT). Electronic applications accepted. *Faculty research:* Soil mechanics and foundations, structures, transportation, water resources systems and hydraulics.

University of Colorado at Boulder, Graduate School, College of Engineering and Applied Science, Department of Civil, Environmental, and Architectural Engineering, Boulder, CO 80309. Offers building systems (MS, PhD); construction engineering management (MS, PhD); environmental engineering (MS, PhD); geotechnical engineering and geomechanics (MS, PhD); hydrology, water resources and environmental fluid mechanics (MS, PhD); structural engineering and structural mechanics (MS, PhD). *Faculty:* 39 full-time (5 women). *Students:* 202 full-time (62 women), 29 part-time (6 women); includes 34 minority (3 African Americans, 3 American Indian/Alaska Native, 12 Asian Americans or Pacific Islanders, 16 Hispanic Americans), 53 international. Average age 29. 384 applicants, 44% accepted, 80 enrolled. In 2009, 60 master's, 7 doctorates awarded. *Degree requirements:* For master's, comprehensive exam, thesis or alternative; for doctorate, thesis/dissertation. *Entrance requirements:* For master's, GRE General Test, minimum undergraduate GPA of 3.0. *Application deadline:* For fall admission, 3/1 for domestic students, 12/1 for international students; for spring admission, 10/31 for domestic students, 10/1 for international students. Application fee: $50 ($60 for international students). *Financial support:* In 2009–10, 45 fellowships (averaging $7,876 per year), 68 research assistantships (averaging $15,204 per year) were awarded. Financial award application deadline: 1/15. *Faculty research:* Building systems engineering, construction engineering and management, environmental engineering, geoenvironmental engineering, geotechnical engineering, materials and mechanics, structural engineering, water resources engineering, life-cycle engineering. Total annual research expenditures: $6.1 million.

University of Colorado Denver, College of Engineering and Applied Science, Department of Civil Engineering, Denver, CO 80217-3364. Offers civil engineering (MS, PhD); geographic information systems (M Eng). Part-time and evening/weekend programs available. *Students:* 22 full-time (5 women), 139 part-time (39 women); includes 31 minority (11 African Americans, 11 Asian Americans or Pacific Islanders, 9 Hispanic Americans), 15 international. 83 applicants, 64% accepted, 36 enrolled. In 2009, 35 master's, 6 doctorates awarded. *Degree requirements:* For master's, comprehensive exam, thesis or alternative; for doctorate, comprehensive exam, thesis/dissertation. *Entrance requirements:* For master's and doctorate, GRE. Additional exam requirements/recommendations for international students: Required—TOEFL (minimum score 525 paper-based; 197 computer-based). *Application deadline:* For fall admission, 4/1 for domestic students; for spring admission, 10/1 for domestic students. Applications are processed on a rolling basis. Application fee: $50 ($75 for international students). Electronic applications accepted. *Financial support:* Research assistantships, teaching assistantships, career-related internships or fieldwork and Federal Work-Study available. Financial award application deadline: 4/1; financial award applicants required to submit FAFSA. *Unit head:* Dr. Nien-Yin Chang, Acting Chair, 303-556-2810, Fax: 303-556-2368, E-mail: nien.chang@ucdenver.edu. *Application contact:* Mindy Gewuerz, Program Assistant, 303-556-6712, Fax: 303-556-2368, E-mail: mindy.gewuerz@ucdenver.edu.

University of Connecticut, Graduate School, School of Engineering, Department of Civil and Environmental Engineering, Field of Civil Engineering, Storrs, CT 06269. Offers MS, PhD. *Faculty:* 22 full-time (4 women). *Students:* 36 full-time (8 women), 15 part-time (3 women); includes 6 minority (2 African Americans, 2 Asian Americans or Pacific Islanders, 2 Hispanic Americans), 21 international. Average age 27. 53 applicants, 38% accepted, 12 enrolled. In 2009, 9 master's, 5 doctorates awarded. Terminal master's awarded for partial completion of doctoral program. *Degree requirements:* For master's, comprehensive exam, thesis or alternative; for doctorate, thesis/dissertation. *Entrance requirements:* Additional exam requirements/recommendations for international students: Required—TOEFL (minimum score 550 paper-based; 213 computer-based). *Application deadline:* For fall admission, 2/1 priority date for domestic and international students; for spring admission, 11/1 for domestic students, 10/1 for international students. Applications are processed on a rolling basis. Application fee: $55. Electronic applications accepted. *Expenses:* Tuition, state resident: full-time $4725; part-time $525 per credit. Tuition, nonresident: full-time $12,267; part-time $1363 per credit. Required fees: $346 per semester. Tuition and fees vary according to course load. *Financial support:* In 2009–10, 30 research assistantships with full tuition reimbursements, 3 teaching assistantships with full tuition reimbursements were awarded; fellowships, Federal Work-Study, scholarships/grants, health care benefits, and unspecified assistantships also available. Financial award application deadline: 2/1; financial award applicants required to submit FAFSA. *Application contact:* Kristina Ashley, Administrative Assistant, 860-486-4018, E-mail: lazz@engr.uconn.edu.

University of Dayton, Graduate School, School of Engineering, Department of Civil and Environmental Engineering, Dayton, OH 45469-1300. Offers engineering mechanics (MSEM); environmental engineering (MSCE); geotechnical engineering (MSCE); structural engineering (MSCE); transport engineering (MSCE); water resources engineering (MSCE). Part-time programs available. *Faculty:* 8 full-time (2 women), 1 part-time/adjunct (0 women). *Students:* 10 full-time (6 women), 8 part-time (1 woman); includes 3 minority (all African Americans), 7 international. Average age 29. 35 applicants, 49% accepted, 6 enrolled. In 2009, 3 master's awarded. *Degree requirements:* For master's, thesis optional. *Entrance requirements:* Additional exam requirements/recommendations for international students: Required—TOEFL (minimum score 550 paper-based; 213 computer-based; 80 iBT). *Application deadline:* For fall admission, 8/1 for domestic students, 3/1 priority date for international students; for winter admission, 7/1 priority date for international students; for spring admission, 1/1 priority date for international students. Applications are processed on a rolling basis. Application fee: $0 ($50 for international students). Electronic applications accepted. *Expenses:* Tuition: Full-time $8412; part-time $701 per credit hour. Required fees: $325; $65 per course. $25 per semester. Tuition and fees vary according to course load, degree level and program. *Financial support:* In 2009–10, 3 research assistantships (averaging $10,780 per year), 4 teaching assistantships with partial tuition reimbursements (averaging $5,110 per year) were awarded. Financial award applicants required to submit FAFSA. *Faculty research:* Physical modeling of hydraulic systems, finite element methods, mechanics of composite materials, transportation systems safety, high-velocity wear. Total annual research expenditures: $421,839. *Unit head:* Dr. Donald V. Chase, Interim Chair, 937-229-3847, Fax: 937-229-3491, E-mail: donald.chase@notes.udayton.edu. *Application contact:* Graduate Admissions, 937-229-4411, Fax: 937-229-4729, E-mail: gradadmission@udayton.edu.

University of Delaware, College of Engineering, Department of Civil and Environmental Engineering, Newark, DE 19716. Offers environmental engineering (MAS, MCE, PhD); geotechnical engineering (MAS, MCE, PhD); ocean engineering (MAS, MCE, PhD); structural engineering (MAS, MCE, PhD); transportation engineering (MAS, MCE, PhD); water resource engineering (MAS, MCE, PhD). Part-time programs available. Terminal master's awarded for partial completion of doctoral program. *Degree requirements:* For master's, thesis; for doctorate, thesis/dissertation. *Entrance requirements:* For master's and doctorate, GRE General Test. Additional exam requirements/recommendations for international students: Required—TOEFL. Electronic applications accepted. *Faculty research:* Structural engineering and mechanics; transportation engineering; ocean engineering; soil mechanics and foundation; water resources and environmental engineering.

University of Detroit Mercy, College of Engineering and Science, Department of Civil and Environmental Engineering, Detroit, MI 48221. Offers ME, DE. Evening/weekend programs available. *Faculty research:* Geotechnical engineering.

University of Florida, Graduate School, College of Engineering, Department of Civil and Coastal Engineering, Gainesville, FL 32611. Offers civil engineering (MCE, MS, PhD, Engr); coastal and oceanographic engineering (ME, MS, PhD, Engr). Part-time programs available. *Degree requirements:* For master's and Engr, thesis optional; for doctorate, thesis/dissertation. *Entrance requirements:* For master's and doctorate, GRE General Test, minimum GPA of 3.0. Additional exam requirements/recommendations for international students: Required—TOEFL (minimum score 550 paper-based; 213 computer-based). Electronic applications accepted.

University of Hawaii at Manoa, Graduate Division, College of Engineering, Department of Civil and Environmental Engineering, Honolulu, HI 96822. Offers MS, PhD. Part-time programs available. *Faculty:* 24 full-time (1 woman), 1 part-time/adjunct (0 women). *Students:* 59 full-time (14 women), 11 part-time (2 women); includes 30 minority (all Asian Americans or Pacific Islanders), 26 international. Average age 27. 63 applicants, 62% accepted, 24 enrolled. In 2009, 14 master's, 2 doctorates awarded. *Degree requirements:* For master's, comprehensive exam, thesis; for doctorate, comprehensive exam, thesis/dissertation. *Entrance requirements:* For master's and doctorate, GRE General Test or EIT Exam. Additional exam requirements/recommendations for international students: Required—TOEFL (minimum score 540 paper-based; 207 computer-based; 76 iBT), IELTS (minimum score 5). *Application deadline:* For fall admission, 5/1 for domestic and international students; for spring admission, 9/1 for domestic and international students. Application fee: $60. *Expenses:* Tuition, state resident: full-time $8900; part-time $372 per credit. Tuition, nonresident: full-time $21,400; part-time $898 per credit. Required fees: $207 per semester. *Financial support:* In 2009–10, 1 student received support, including 5 fellowships (averaging $1,800 per year), 36 research assistantships (averaging $18,389 per year), 5 teaching assistantships (averaging $14,852 per year); career-related internships or fieldwork, Federal Work-Study, and tuition waivers (full and partial) also available. *Faculty research:* Structures, transportation, environmental engineering, geotechnical engineering, construction. Total annual research expenditures: $1.2 million. *Application contact:* Roger Babcock, Graduate Chair, 808-956-7449, Fax: 808-956-5014, E-mail: rbabcock@eng.hawaii.edu.

University of Houston, Cullen College of Engineering, Department of Civil and Environmental Engineering, Houston, TX 77204. Offers MCE, MSCE, PhD. Part-time and evening/weekend programs available. *Faculty:* 12 full-time (1 woman), 5 part-time/adjunct (1 woman). *Students:* 39 full-time (9 women), 49 part-time (11 women); includes 26 minority (3 African Americans, 16 Asian Americans or Pacific Islanders, 7 Hispanic Americans), 36 international. Average age 30. 80 applicants, 70% accepted, 19 enrolled. In 2009, 13 master's, 3 doctorates awarded. Terminal master's awarded for partial completion of doctoral program. *Entrance requirements:* For master's and doctorate, GRE General Test. Additional exam requirements/recommendations for international students: Required—TOEFL (minimum score 550 paper-based; 213 computer-based; 79 iBT), IELTS (minimum score 6.5). *Application deadline:* For fall admission, 6/1 for domestic students, 5/1 for international students; for spring admission, 10/1 for domestic and international students. Applications are processed on a rolling basis. Application fee: $25 ($75 for international students). Electronic applications accepted. *Expenses:* Tuition, state resident: full-time $7676; part-time $320 per credit hour. Tuition, nonresident: full-time $14,324; part-time $597 per credit hour. Required fees: $3034. *Financial support:* In 2009–10, 16 research assistantships with full tuition reimbursements (averaging $11,400 per year), 23 teaching assistantships with full tuition reimbursements (averaging $11,400 per year) were awarded; career-related internships or fieldwork, Federal Work-Study, institutionally sponsored loans, scholarships/grants, health care benefits, and unspecified assistantships also available. Support available to part-time students. Financial award application deadline: 2/1. *Faculty research:* Civil engineering. *Unit head:* Dr. Dennis Clifford, Chairperson, 713-743-4266, Fax: 713-743-4260, E-mail: daclifford@uh.edu. *Application contact:* Charlene Holliday, Graduate Admissions Assistant, 713-743-4254, Fax: 713-743-4260, E-mail: civilgrad@egr.uh.edu.

University of Idaho, College of Graduate Studies, College of Engineering, Department of Civil Engineering, Moscow, ID 83844-2282. Offers civil engineering (MS, PhD); engineering management (M Engr); geological engineering (MS). *Faculty:* 16 full-time, 9 part-time/adjunct. *Students:* 30 full-time (6 women), 74 part-time (16 women). In 2009, 25 master's, 3 doctorates awarded. *Degree requirements:* For master's, thesis; for doctorate, thesis/dissertation. *Entrance requirements:* For master's, minimum GPA of 2.8; for doctorate, minimum undergraduate GPA of 2.8, 3.0 graduate. *Application deadline:* For fall admission, 8/1 for domestic students; for spring admission, 12/15 for domestic students. Application fee: $55 ($60 for international students). *Expenses:* Tuition, state resident: full-time $6120. Tuition, nonresident: full-time $17,712. *Financial support:* Fellowships, research assistantships, teaching assistantships, career-related internships or fieldwork available. Financial award application deadline: 2/15. *Faculty research:* Water resources systems, structural analysis and design, soil mechanics, transportation technology. *Unit head:* Richard J. Nielsen, Chair, 208-885-8961. *Application contact:* Richard J. Nielsen, Chair, 208-885-8961.

University of Illinois at Chicago, Graduate College, College of Engineering, Department of Civil and Materials Engineering, Chicago, IL 60607-7128. Offers civil engineering (MS, PhD); materials engineering (MS, PhD). Evening/weekend programs available. *Degree requirements:* For master's, thesis (for some programs); for doctorate, thesis/dissertation, preliminary and qualifying exams. *Entrance requirements:* For master's and doctorate, GRE General Test, minimum GPA of 3.0. Additional exam requirements/recommendations for international students: Required—TOEFL. Electronic applications accepted. *Faculty research:* Transportation and geotechnical engineering, damage and anisotropic behavior, steel processing.

University of Illinois at Urbana–Champaign, Graduate College, College of Engineering, Department of Civil and Environmental Engineering, Champaign, IL 61820. Offers civil engineering (MS); environmental engineering in civil engineering (MS, PhD); environmental science in civil engineering (MS, PhD); M Arch/MS; MBA/MS. *Faculty:* 48 full-time (6 women), 4 part-time/adjunct (1 woman). *Students:* 349 full-time (88 women), 69 part-time (23 women); includes 37 minority (3 African Americans, 22 Asian Americans or Pacific Islanders, 12 Hispanic Americans), 212 international. 803 applicants, 35% accepted, 140 enrolled. In 2009, 83 master's, 24 doctorates awarded. *Entrance requirements:* For master's and doctorate, GRE. Additional exam requirements/recommendations for international students: Required—TOEFL (minimum score 550 paper-based; 213 computer-based; 79 iBT), or IELTS (minimum score 6.5). *Application deadline:* Applications are processed on a rolling basis. Application fee: $60 ($75 for international students). Electronic applications accepted. *Financial support:* In 2009–10, 58 fellowships, 253 research assistantships, 66 teaching assistantships were awarded; tuition waivers (full and partial) also available. *Unit head:* Amr S. Elnashai, Head, 217-265-5497, Fax: 217-265-8040, E-mail: aelnash@illinois.edu. *Application contact:* Mary Pearson, Administrative Secretary, 217-333-3811, Fax: 217-333-9464, E-mail: mkpearso@illinois.edu.

The University of Iowa, Graduate College, College of Engineering, Department of Civil and Environmental Engineering, Iowa City, IA 52242-1316. Offers MS, PhD. Part-time programs available. *Faculty:* 21 full-time (3 women). *Students:* 83 full-time (25 women); includes 3 minority (1 Asian American or Pacific Islander, 2 Hispanic Americans), 35 international. Average age 28. 177 applicants, 29% accepted, 19 enrolled. In 2009, 17 master's, 11 doctorates awarded. Terminal master's awarded for partial completion of doctoral program. *Degree requirements:* For master's, thesis optional, exam; for doctorate, comprehensive exam, thesis/dissertation, exam. *Entrance requirements:* For master's, GRE, A minimum undergraduate grade point average of 3.0; for doctorate, GRE, The completion of a Master's degree or equivalent, with a 3.20 minimum grade point average on completed graduate work. Additional exam requirements/recommendations for international students: Required—TOEFL (minimum score 550 paper-based; 213 computer-based; 81 iBT). *Application deadline:* For fall admission, 2/1 priority date for domestic and international students; for spring admission, 12/1 for domestic students, 10/1 for international students. Applications are processed on a rolling basis. Application fee: $60 ($100 for international students). Electronic applications accepted. *Financial support:* In 2009–10, 5 fellowships with partial tuition reimbursements (averaging $23,480 per year), 58 research assistantships with partial tuition reimbursements (averaging $22,553 per year), 22 teaching assistantships with partial tuition reimbursements (averaging $16,575 per year) were awarded; career-related internships or fieldwork, Federal Work-Study, scholarships/grants, traineeships, and unspecified assistantships also available. Support available to part-time students. Financial award application deadline: 2/1; financial award applicants required to submit FAFSA. *Faculty research:* Water resources; environmental engineering and science; hydraulics and hydrology; structures, mechanics, and materials; transportation engineering. Total annual research expenditures: $10.4 million. *Unit head:* Dr. Keri C. Hornbuckle, Departmental Executive Officer, 319-384-0789, Fax: 319-335-5660, E-mail: keri-hornbuckle@uiowa.edu. *Application contact:* Judy Holland, Secretary, 319-335-5647, Fax: 319-335-5660, E-mail: cee@engineering.uiowa.edu.

The University of Kansas, Graduate Studies, School of Engineering, Department of Civil, Environmental, and Architectural Engineering, Program in Civil Engineering, Lawrence, KS 66045. Offers MCE, MS, DE, PhD. Part-time and evening/weekend programs available. *Faculty:* 25 full-time (3 women), 2 part-time/adjunct (0 women). *Students:* 45 full-time (13 women), 59 part-time (10 women); includes 6 minority (1 African American, 2 Asian Americans or Pacific Islanders, 3 Hispanic Americans), 33 international. Average age 29. 68 applicants, 74% accepted, 24 enrolled. In 2009, 20 master's, 5 doctorates awarded. *Degree requirements:* For master's, thesis or alternative, exam; for doctorate, comprehensive exam, thesis/dissertation. *Entrance requirements:* For master's and doctorate, GRE, BS in engineering. Additional exam requirements/recommendations for international students: Required—TOEFL. *Application deadline:* For fall admission, 7/1 priority date for domestic students, 3/15 priority date for international students; for spring admission, 12/1 priority date for domestic students, 8/15 priority date for international students. Applications are processed on a rolling basis. Application fee: $45 ($55 for international students). Electronic applications accepted. *Expenses:* Tuition, state resident: full-time $6492; part-time $270.50 per credit hour. Tuition, nonresident: full-time $15,510; part-time $646.25 per credit hour. Required fees: $847; $70.56 per credit hour. Tuition and fees vary according to course load and program. *Financial support:* Fellowships with full tuition reimbursements, research assistantships with full tuition reimbursements, teaching assistantships with full and partial tuition reimbursements, career-related internships

Civil Engineering

The University of Kansas (continued)
or fieldwork available. Financial award application deadline: 2/7. *Faculty research:* Structural engineering, geotechnical engineering, transportation engineering, water resources engineering, construction engineering. *Unit head:* Craig D. Adams, Chair, 785-864-2700, Fax: 785-864-5631, E-mail: adamscd@ku.edu. *Application contact:* Bruce M. McEnroe, Graduate Advisor, 785-864-2925, Fax: 785-864-5631, E-mail: mcenroe@ku.edu.

University of Kentucky, Graduate School, College of Engineering, Program in Civil Engineering, Lexington, KY 40506-0032. Offers MCE, MSCE, PhD. *Degree requirements:* For master's, comprehensive exam, thesis optional; for doctorate, comprehensive exam, thesis/dissertation. *Entrance requirements:* For master's, GRE General Test, minimum undergraduate GPA of 2.75; for doctorate, GRE General Test, minimum undergraduate GPA of 3.0. Additional exam requirements/recommendations for international students: Required—TOEFL (minimum score 550 paper-based; 213 computer-based). Electronic applications accepted. *Faculty research:* Geotechnical engineering, structures, construction engineering and management, environmental engineering and water resources, transportation and materials.

University of Louisiana at Lafayette, College of Engineering, Department of Civil Engineering, Lafayette, LA 70504. Offers MSE. Evening/weekend programs available. *Degree requirements:* For master's, comprehensive exam, thesis or alternative. *Entrance requirements:* For master's, GRE General Test, BS in civil engineering, minimum GPA of 2.85. *Faculty research:* Structural mechanics, computer-aided design, environmental engineering.

University of Louisville, J.B. Speed School of Engineering, Department of Civil and Environmental Engineering, Louisville, KY 40292-0001. Offers civil engineering (M Eng, MS, PhD). *Accreditation:* ABET (one or more programs are accredited). Part-time programs available. Postbaccalaureate distance learning degree programs offered (no on-campus study). *Faculty:* 12 full-time (1 woman), 1 part-time/adjunct (0 women). *Students:* 43 full-time (10 women), 11 part-time (2 women); includes 4 minority (2 Asian Americans or Pacific Islanders, 2 Hispanic Americans), 9 international. Average age 26. 23 applicants, 57% accepted, 7 enrolled. In 2009, 37 master's, 2 doctorates awarded. Terminal master's awarded for partial completion of doctoral program. *Degree requirements:* For master's, comprehensive exam (for some programs), thesis or alternative; for doctorate, comprehensive exam, thesis/dissertation, minimum GPA of 3.0. *Entrance requirements:* For master's and doctorate, GRE General Test. Additional exam requirements/recommendations for international students: Required—TOEFL (minimum score 550 paper-based; 213 computer-based; 80 iBT). *Application deadline:* For fall admission, 7/12 priority date for domestic and international students; for winter admission, 11/29 priority date for domestic and international students; for spring admission, 3/28 priority date for domestic and international students. Applications are processed on a rolling basis. Application fee: $50. Electronic applications accepted. *Financial support:* In 2009–10, 9 students received support, including 2 fellowships with full tuition reimbursements available (averaging $20,000 per year), 2 research assistantships with full tuition reimbursements available (averaging $20,000 per year), 5 teaching assistantships with full tuition reimbursements available (averaging $20,000 per year). Financial award application deadline: 1/25; financial award applicants required to submit FAFSA. *Faculty research:* Structures, hydraulics, transportation, environmental engineering, geomechanics. Total annual research expenditures: $1.8 million. *Unit head:* Dr. J. P. Mohsen, Chair, 502-852-6276, Fax: 502-852-8851, E-mail: jpmohs01@louisville.edu. *Application contact:* Dr. Michael Day, Associate Dean, 502-852-6195, Fax: 502-852-7294, E-mail: day@louisville.edu.

University of Maine, Graduate School, College of Engineering, Department of Civil and Environmental Engineering, Orono, ME 04469. Offers civil engineering (MS, PhD), including environmental engineering, geotechnical engineering, structural engineering. *Faculty:* 10 full-time (2 women), 2 part-time/adjunct (0 women). *Students:* 28 full-time (7 women), 15 part-time (2 women); includes 2 minority (both American Indian/Alaska Native), 3 international. Average age 27. 31 applicants, 35% accepted, 7 enrolled. In 2009, 6 master's, 1 doctorate awarded. *Degree requirements:* For doctorate, thesis/dissertation. *Entrance requirements:* For master's and doctorate, GRE General Test. Additional exam requirements/recommendations for international students: Required—TOEFL. *Application deadline:* For fall admission, 2/1 priority date for domestic students. Applications are processed on a rolling basis. Application fee: $65. Electronic applications accepted. *Financial support:* In 2009–10, 15 research assistantships with tuition reimbursements (averaging $15,815 per year), 3 teaching assistantships with tuition reimbursements (averaging $12,790 per year) were awarded; Federal Work-Study, institutionally sponsored loans, scholarships/grants, and tuition waivers (full and partial) also available. Financial award application deadline: 3/1. *Unit head:* Dr. Eric Landis, Chair. *Application contact:* Scott G. Delcourt, Associate Dean of the Graduate School, 207-581-3291, Fax: 207-581-3232, E-mail: graduate@maine.edu.

University of Maine, Graduate School, College of Engineering, Department of Spatial Information Science and Engineering, Orono, ME 04469. Offers MS, PhD. *Faculty:* 6 full-time (1 woman). *Students:* 11 full-time (1 woman), 11 part-time (4 women), 7 international. Average age 36. 15 applicants, 47% accepted, 2 enrolled. In 2009, 3 master's, 3 doctorates awarded. *Degree requirements:* For master's, thesis (for some programs); for doctorate, thesis/dissertation. *Entrance requirements:* For master's and doctorate, GRE General Test. Additional exam requirements/recommendations for international students: Required—TOEFL. *Application deadline:* For fall admission, 2/1 priority date for domestic students. Applications are processed on a rolling basis. Application fee: $65. Electronic applications accepted. *Financial support:* In 2009–10, 16 research assistantships with tuition reimbursements (averaging $26,470 per year) were awarded; Federal Work-Study, institutionally sponsored loans, and tuition waivers (full and partial) also available. Financial award application deadline: 3/1. *Faculty research:* Geographic information systems, analytical photogrammetry, geodesy, global positioning systems, remote sensing. *Unit head:* Dr. Michael Worboys, Chair, 207-581-3679. *Application contact:* Scott G. Delcourt, Associate Dean of the Graduate School, 207-581-3291, Fax: 207-581-3232, E-mail: graduate@maine.edu.

University of Manitoba, Faculty of Graduate Studies, Faculty of Engineering, Department of Civil Engineering, Winnipeg, MB R3T 2N2, Canada. Offers M Eng, M Sc, PhD. *Degree requirements:* For master's, thesis.

University of Maryland, Baltimore County, Graduate School, College of Engineering and Information Technology, Department of Civil and Environmental Engineering, Program in Civil Engineering, Baltimore, MD 21250. Offers MS, PhD. Part-time programs available. *Faculty:* 2 full-time (0 women), 1 part-time/adjunct (0 women). *Students:* 8 full-time (5 women), 6 part-time (3 women); includes 4 minority (1 African American, 3 Asian Americans or Pacific Islanders), 7 international. Average age 28. 11 applicants, 36% accepted, 3 enrolled. In 2009, 2 master's awarded. *Degree requirements:* For master's, comprehensive exam (for some programs), thesis (for some programs); for doctorate, comprehensive exam, thesis/dissertation. *Entrance requirements:* For master's and doctorate, GRE General Test, BS in civil and environmental engineering or related field of engineering. Additional exam requirements/recommendations for international students: Required—TOEFL (minimum score 550 paper-based; 213 computer-based; 80 iBT). *Application deadline:* For fall admission, 6/1 for domestic students, 1/1 for international students; for spring admission, 11/1 for domestic students, 6/1 for international students. Applications are processed on a rolling basis. Application fee: $50. Electronic applications accepted. *Financial support:* In 2009–10, 9 research assistantships with full tuition reimbursements (averaging $24,000 per year) were awarded; career-related internships or fieldwork, Federal Work-Study, scholarships/grants, health care benefits, tuition waivers (partial), and unspecified assistantships also available. Support available to part-time students. Financial award application deadline: 6/30; financial award applicants required to submit FAFSA. *Faculty research:* Environmental engineering, water resources engineering. *Unit head:* Dr. Brian Reed, Professor and Chair, 410-455-8646, Fax: 410-455-6500, E-mail: reedb@umbc.edu. *Application contact:* Dr. Upal Ghosh, Associate Professor and Graduate Program Director, 410-455-8665, Fax: 410-455-6500, E-mail: ughosh@umbc.edu.

University of Maryland, College Park, Academic Affairs, A. James Clark School of Engineering, Department of Civil and Environmental Engineering, College Park, MD 20742. Offers M Eng, MS, PhD. Part-time and evening/weekend programs available. Postbaccalaureate distance learning degree programs offered. *Faculty:* 65 full-time (10 women), 24 part-time/adjunct (5 women). *Students:* 151 full-time (61 women), 51 part-time (17 women); includes 30 minority (13 African Americans, 1 American Indian/Alaska Native, 12 Asian Americans or Pacific Islanders, 4 Hispanic Americans), 108 international. 307 applicants, 42% accepted, 64 enrolled. In 2009, 29 master's, 10 doctorates awarded. *Degree requirements:* For master's, thesis optional; for doctorate, thesis/dissertation, qualifying exam. *Entrance requirements:* For master's and doctorate, GRE General Test, 3 letters of recommendation. *Application deadline:* For fall admission, 5/1 for domestic students, 2/1 for international students; for spring admission, 10/15 for domestic students, 6/1 for international students. Applications are processed on a rolling basis. Application fee: $60. Electronic applications accepted. *Expenses:* Tuition, area resident: Part-time $471 per credit hour. Tuition, state resident: part-time $471 per credit hour. Tuition, nonresident: part-time $1016 per credit hour. Required fees: $337.04 per term. *Financial support:* In 2009–10, 13 fellowships with full and partial tuition reimbursements (averaging $13,868 per year), 59 research assistantships with tuition reimbursements (averaging $18,990 per year), 17 teaching assistantships with tuition reimbursements (averaging $19,112 per year) were awarded; Federal Work-Study and scholarships/grants also available. Support available to part-time students. Financial award applicants required to submit FAFSA. *Faculty research:* Transportation and urban systems, environmental engineering, geotechnical engineering, construction engineering and management, hydraulics. Total annual research expenditures: $15.7 million. *Unit head:* Dr. Ali Haghani, Chairman, 301-405-1974, Fax: 301-405-2585, E-mail: haghani@umd.edu. *Application contact:* Dean of Graduate School, 301-405-0376, Fax: 301-314-9305.

University of Maryland, College Park, Academic Affairs, A. James Clark School of Engineering, Department of Continuing and Distance Learning in Engineering, Professional Program in Engineering, College Park, MD 20742. Offers aerospace engineering (M Eng); chemical engineering (M Eng); civil engineering (M Eng); electrical engineering (M Eng); engineering (Certificate); fire protection engineering (M Eng); materials science and engineering (M Eng); mechanical engineering (M Eng); reliability engineering (M Eng); systems engineering (M Eng). Part-time and evening/weekend programs available. Postbaccalaureate distance learning degree programs offered. *Students:* 50 full-time (15 women), 234 part-time (41 women); includes 91 minority (36 African Americans, 39 Asian Americans or Pacific Islanders, 16 Hispanic Americans), 45 international. 137 applicants, 69% accepted, 77 enrolled. In 2009, 103 master's awarded. *Entrance requirements:* For master's, 3 letters of recommendation. *Application deadline:* For fall admission, 8/15 for domestic students, 1/10 for international students; for spring admission, 12/15 for domestic students, 6/1 for international students. Applications are processed on a rolling basis. Application fee: $60. Electronic applications accepted. *Expenses:* Tuition, area resident: Part-time $471 per credit hour. Tuition, state resident: part-time $471 per credit hour. Tuition, nonresident: part-time $1016 per credit hour. Required fees: $337.04 per term. *Financial support:* In 2009–10, 2 research assistantships with tuition reimbursements (averaging $19,561 per year), 9 teaching assistantships with tuition reimbursements (averaging $16,849 per year) were awarded; fellowships, Federal Work-Study and scholarships/grants also available. Support available to part-time students. Financial award applicants required to submit FAFSA. *Unit head:* Dr. George Syrmos, Director, 301-405-3633, Fax: 301-314-3305, E-mail: syrmos@umd.edu. *Application contact:* Dean of Graduate School, 301-405-0376, Fax: 301-314-9305.

University of Massachusetts Amherst, Graduate School, College of Engineering, Department of Civil and Environmental Engineering, Program in Civil Engineering, Amherst, MA 01003. Offers MS, PhD. Part-time programs available. *Faculty:* 27 full-time (5 women). *Students:* 53 full-time (14 women), 11 part-time (6 women); includes 6 minority (3 Asian Americans or Pacific Islanders, 3 Hispanic Americans), 30 international. Average age 27. 154 applicants, 45% accepted, 26 enrolled. In 2009, 8 master's, 3 doctorates awarded. Terminal master's awarded for partial completion of doctoral program. *Degree requirements:* For master's, thesis or alternative, project; for doctorate, comprehensive exam, thesis/dissertation. *Entrance requirements:* For master's and doctorate, GRE General Test. Additional exam requirements/recommendations for international students: Required—TOEFL (minimum score 550 paper-based; 213 computer-based; 80 iBT), IELTS (minimum score 6.5). *Application deadline:* For fall admission, 2/1 for domestic and international students; for spring admission, 10/1 for domestic and international students. Applications are processed on a rolling basis. Application fee: $50 ($65 for international students). Electronic applications accepted. *Expenses:* Tuition, state resident: full-time $2640; part-time $110 per credit. Tuition, nonresident: full-time $9936; part-time $414 per credit. Tuition and fees vary according to course load. *Financial support:* Fellowships with full tuition reimbursements, research assistantships with full tuition reimbursements, teaching assistantships with full tuition reimbursements, career-related internships or fieldwork, Federal Work-Study, scholarships/grants, traineeships, health care benefits, tuition waivers, and unspecified assistantships available. Support available to part-time students. Financial award application deadline: 2/1; financial award applicants required to submit FAFSA. *Unit head:* Dr. Richard Palmer, Graduate Program Director, 413-545-0686, Fax: 413-545-2840. *Application contact:* Jean M. Ames, Supervisor of Admissions, 413-545-0722, Fax: 413-577-0100, E-mail: gradadm@grad.umass.edu.

University of Massachusetts Amherst, Graduate School, Interdisciplinary Programs, Program in Civil Engineering and Business Administration, Amherst, MA 01003. Offers MSCE/MBA. Part-time programs available. *Entrance requirements:* Additional exam requirements/recommendations for international students: Required—TOEFL (minimum score 600 paper-based; 250 computer-based; 100 iBT), IELTS (minimum score 7). *Application deadline:* For fall admission, 2/1 for domestic and international students. Applications are processed on a rolling basis. Application fee: $50 ($65 for international students). Electronic applications accepted. *Expenses:* Tuition, state resident: full-time $2640; part-time $110 per credit. Tuition, nonresident: full-time $9936; part-time $414 per credit. Tuition and fees vary according to course load. *Financial support:* Career-related internships or fieldwork, Federal Work-Study, scholarships/grants, traineeships, health care benefits, tuition waivers (full), and unspecified assistantships available. Support available to part-time students. *Unit head:* Dr. Richard N. Palmer, Graduate Program Director, 413-545-0686, Fax: 413-545-2840. *Application contact:* Jean M. Ames, Supervisor of Admissions, 413-545-0722, Fax: 413-577-0010, E-mail: gradadm@grad.umass.edu.

University of Massachusetts Dartmouth, Graduate School, College of Engineering, Program in Civil and Environmental Engineering, North Dartmouth, MA 02747-2300. Offers MS. Part-time programs available. *Faculty:* 6 full-time (1 woman), 4 part-time/adjunct (0 women). *Students:* 4 full-time (0 women), 7 part-time (1 woman); includes 1 minority (Hispanic American), 1 international. Average age 24. 9 applicants, 89% accepted, 4 enrolled. In 2009, 2 master's awarded. *Degree requirements:* For master's, thesis or alternative. *Entrance requirements:* For master's, GRE, minimum GPA of 3.0, 3 letters of recommendation. Additional exam requirements/recommendations for international students: Required—TOEFL (minimum score 550 paper-based). *Application deadline:* For fall admission, 4/20 priority date for domestic students, 2/20 priority date for international students; for spring admission, 11/15 priority date for domestic students, 9/15 priority date for international students. Application fee: $40 ($60 for international students). *Expenses:* Tuition, state resident: full-time $2071; part-time $86.29 per credit. Tuition, nonresident: full-time $8099; part-time $337.46 per credit. Required fees: $9446. Tuition and fees vary according to class time, course load and reciprocity agreements. *Financial support:* In 2009–10, 5 teaching assistantships with full tuition reimbursements (averaging $12,500 per year) were awarded. Financial award application deadline: 3/1; financial award applicants required to submit FAFSA. *Faculty research:* Evaluation of road system in Massachusetts, physico-chemical treatment of hazardous waste, soil-geosynthetic systems, waste water treatment systems, concrete analysis. Total annual research expenditures: $883,000. *Unit head:* Dr. Heather Miller, Graduate Director, 508-999-8481, E-mail: hmiller@umassd.edu. *Application contact:* Elan Turcotte-Shamski, Graduate Admissions Officer, 508-999-8604, Fax: 508-999-8183, E-mail: graduate@umassd.edu.

University of Massachusetts Lowell, James B. Francis College of Engineering, Department of Civil and Environmental Engineering, Lowell, MA 01854-2881. Offers civil and environmental engineering (MS Eng, Certificate); environmental engineering (D Eng); environmental studies (MSES, PhD, Certificate), including environmental engineering (MSES), environmental studies (PhD, Certificate); sustainable infrastructure for developing nations (Certificate). Part-time programs available. *Degree requirements:* For master's, thesis optional. *Entrance requirements:* For master's, GRE General Test. *Faculty research:* Bridge design, traffic control, groundwater remediation, pile capacity.

University of Memphis, Graduate School, Herff College of Engineering, Department of Civil Engineering, Memphis, TN 38152. Offers civil engineering (PhD); environmental engineering (MS); foundation engineering (MS); structural engineering (MS); transportation engineering (MS); water resources engineering (MS). *Faculty:* 12 full-time (1 woman), 1 part-time/adjunct (0 women). *Students:* 12 full-time (3 women), 16 part-time (6 women); includes 2 minority (1 African American, 1 Asian American or Pacific Islander), 9 international. Average age 28. 18 applicants, 94% accepted, 8 enrolled. In 2009, 11 master's awarded. *Degree requirements:* For master's, comprehensive exam, thesis or alternative; for doctorate, thesis/dissertation. *Entrance requirements:* For master's, GRE General Test or MAT, minimum undergraduate GPA of 2.5. *Application deadline:* For fall admission, 8/1 for domestic students; for spring admission, 12/1 for domestic students. Application fee: $35 ($60 for international students). *Expenses:* Tuition, state resident: full-time $6246; part-time $347 per credit hour. Tuition, nonresident: full-time $15,894; part-time $883 per credit hour. Required fees: $1160. Full-time tuition and fees vary according to course load, degree level and program. *Financial support:* In 2009–10, 6 students received support; fellowships with full tuition reimbursements available, research assistantships with full tuition reimbursements available, career-related internships or fieldwork, Federal Work-Study, scholarships/grants, and unspecified assistantships available. Financial award application deadline: 2/15; financial award applicants required to submit FAFSA. *Faculty research:* Structural response to earthquakes, pavement design, water quality, transportation safety, intermodal transportation. *Unit head:* Dr. Sharam Pezeshk, Interim Chair, 901-678-2746, Fax: 901-678-3026. *Application contact:* Dr. Roger Meier, Coordinator of Graduate Studies, 901-678-3284.

University of Miami, Graduate School, College of Engineering, Department of Civil, Architectural, and Environmental Engineering, Coral Gables, FL 33124. Offers architectural engineering (MSAE); civil engineering (MSCE, PhD). Part-time programs available. Terminal master's awarded for partial completion of doctoral program. *Degree requirements:* For master's, thesis (for some programs); for doctorate, comprehensive exam, thesis/dissertation. *Entrance requirements:* For master's, GRE General Test (minimum score 1000 verbal and quantitative), minimum GPA of 3.0; for doctorate, GRE General Test, minimum GPA of 3.5 in preceding degree. Additional exam requirements/recommendations for international students: Required—TOEFL (minimum score 550 paper-based; 213 computer-based). Electronic applications accepted. *Faculty research:* Structural assessment and wind engineering, sustainable construction and materials, moisture transport and management, wastewater and waste engineering, water management and risk analysis.

University of Michigan, Horace H. Rackham School of Graduate Studies, College of Engineering, Department of Civil and Environmental Engineering, Ann Arbor, MI 48109. Offers civil engineering (MSE, PhD, CE); construction engineering and management (M Eng, MSE); environmental engineering (MSE, PhD); structural engineering (M Eng); MBA/MSE. Part-time programs available. *Faculty:* 28 full-time (8 women). *Students:* 104 full-time (34 women), 1 part-time (0 women); includes 9 minority (2 African Americans, 5 Asian Americans or Pacific Islanders, 2 Hispanic Americans), 49 international. 413 applicants, 29% accepted, 40 enrolled. In 2009, 47 master's, 18 doctorates awarded. *Degree requirements:* For master's, thesis optional; for doctorate, comprehensive exam, thesis/dissertation, oral defense of dissertation, preliminary and written exams. *Entrance requirements:* For master's and doctorate, GRE General Test. Additional exam requirements/recommendations for international students: Required—TOEFL (minimum score 560 paper-based; 220 computer-based). *Application deadline:* Applications are processed on a rolling basis. Application fee: $60 ($75 for international students). Electronic applications accepted. *Expenses:* Tuition, state resident: full-time $17,286; part-time $1099 per credit hour. Tuition, nonresident: full-time $34,944; part-time $2080 per credit hour. Required fees: $95 per semester. Tuition and fees vary according to course load, degree level and program. *Financial support:* Fellowships, research assistantships, teaching assistantships, institutionally sponsored loans and tuition waivers (partial) available. Financial award application deadline: 1/19. *Faculty research:* Construction engineering and management; geotechnical engineering; earthquake-resistant design of structures; environmental chemistry and microbiology; cost engineering; environmental and water resources engineering. *Unit head:* Nancy Love, Chair, 734-764-8405, Fax: 734-764-4292, E-mail: nglove@umich.edu. *Application contact:* Kimberly Smith, Student Advisor, 734-764-8405, Fax: 734-647-2127, E-mail: kansmith@umich.edu.

University of Michigan, Horace H. Rackham School of Graduate Studies, College of Engineering, Department of Naval Architecture and Marine Engineering, Ann Arbor, MI 48109. Offers concurrent marine design (M Eng); naval architecture and marine engineering (MS, MSE, PhD, Mar Eng, Nav Arch); MBA/MSE. Part-time programs available. *Faculty:* 12 full-time (2 women). *Students:* 74 full-time (13 women), 1 part-time (0 women); includes 3 minority (1 African American, 1 Asian American or Pacific Islander, 1 Hispanic American), 32 international. 104 applicants, 64% accepted, 37 enrolled. In 2009, 12 master's, 6 doctorates awarded. Terminal master's awarded for partial completion of doctoral program. *Degree requirements:* For master's, thesis (for some programs); for doctorate, comprehensive exam, thesis/dissertation, oral defense of dissertation, preliminary exams (written and oral); for other advanced degree, comprehensive exam, thesis, oral defense of thesis. *Entrance requirements:* For master's, GRE General Test (for financial award applicants); for doctorate, GRE General Test, master's degree; for other advanced degree, GRE General Test. Additional exam requirements/recommendations for international students: Required—TOEFL (minimum score 560 paper-based; 220 computer-based). *Application deadline:* Applications are processed on a rolling basis. Application fee: $60 ($75 for international students). Electronic applications accepted. *Expenses:* Tuition, state resident: full-time $17,286; part-time $1099 per credit hour. Tuition, nonresident: full-time $34,944; part-time $2080 per credit hour. Required fees: $95 per semester. Tuition and fees vary according to course load, degree level and program. *Financial support:* Fellowships, research assistantships, teaching assistantships, career-related internships or fieldwork, Federal Work-Study, institutionally sponsored loans, scholarships/grants, and unspecified assistantships available. *Faculty research:* System and structural reliability, design and analysis of offshore structures and vehicles, marine systems design, remote sensing of ship wakes and sea surfaces, marine hydrodynamics, nonlinear seakeeping analysis. *Unit head:* Dr. Armin W. Troesch, Chair, 734-763-6644, Fax: 734-936-8820, E-mail: kdrake@engin.umich.edu. *Application contact:* Nathalie Fiveland, Unit Administrator, 734-936-0566, Fax: 734-936-8820, E-mail: fiveland@umich.edu.

University of Minnesota, Twin Cities Campus, Institute of Technology, Department of Civil Engineering, Minneapolis, MN 55455-0213. Offers civil engineering (MCE, MS, PhD); geological engineering (M Geo E, MS, PhD). Part-time programs available. *Degree requirements:* For master's, thesis optional; for doctorate, thesis/dissertation. *Entrance requirements:* For master's and doctorate, GRE General Test. Additional exam requirements/recommendations for international students: Required—TOEFL. *Faculty research:* Environmental engineering, rock mechanics, water resources, structural engineering, transportation.

University of Missouri, Graduate School, College of Engineering, Department of Civil and Environmental Engineering, Columbia, MO 65211. Offers civil engineering (MS, PhD); environmental engineering (MS, PhD); geotechnical engineering (MS, PhD); structural engineering (MS, PhD); transportation and highway engineering (MS); water resources (MS, PhD). *Degree requirements:* For master's, report or thesis; for doctorate, thesis/dissertation. *Entrance requirements:* For master's and doctorate, GRE General Test. Additional exam requirements/recommendations for international students: Required—TOEFL (minimum score 550 paper-based; 213 computer-based; 79 iBT).

University of Missouri–Kansas City, School of Computing and Engineering, Kansas City, MO 64110-2499. Offers civil engineering (MS); computer and electrical engineering (PhD); computer science (MS), including bioinformatics, software engineering, telecommunications networking; computer science and informatics (PhD); computing (PhD); electrical engineering (MS); engineering (PhD); mechanical engineering (MS); telecommunications (PhD). PhD (interdisciplinary) offered through the School of Graduate Studies. Part-time programs available. *Faculty:* 40 full-time (5 women), 28 part-time/adjunct (0 women). *Students:* 230 full-time (46 women), 158 part-time (31 women); includes 20 minority (5 African Americans, 12 Asian Americans or Pacific Islanders, 3 Hispanic Americans), 313 international. Average age 24. 484 applicants, 64% accepted, 106 enrolled. In 2009, 144 master's awarded. *Degree requirements:* For doctorate, thesis/dissertation. *Entrance requirements:* For master's, GRE General Test, minimum GPA of 3.0, 3 letters of recommendations from professors; for doctorate, GRE General Test, minimum GPA of 3.5. Additional exam requirements/recommendations for international students: Required—TOEFL (minimum score 550 paper-based; 213 computer-based; 80 iBT). *Application deadline:* For fall admission, 1/15 priority date for domestic students, 1/15 for international students. Applications are processed on a rolling basis. Application fee: $45 ($50 for international students). *Expenses:* Tuition, state resident: full-time $5378; part-time $299 per credit hour. Tuition, nonresident: full-time $13,881; part-time $771 per credit hour. Required fees: $641; $71 per credit hour. Tuition and fees vary according to course load and program. *Financial support:* In 2009–10, 29 research assistantships with partial tuition reimbursements (averaging $15,040 per year), 10 teaching assistantships with partial tuition reimbursements (averaging $12,118 per year) were awarded; career-related internships or fieldwork, Federal Work-Study, scholarships/grants, tuition waivers (partial), and unspecified assistantships also available. Support available to part-time students. Financial award application deadline: 3/1; financial award applicants required to submit FAFSA. *Faculty research:* Algorithms, bioinformatics and medical informatics, biomechanics/biomaterials, civil engineering materials, networking and telecommunications, thermal science. Total annual research expenditures: $1.4 million. *Unit head:* Dr. Kevin Z. Truman, Dean, 816-235-2399, Fax: 816-235-5159. *Application contact:* Dr. Kevin Z. Truman, Dean, 816-235-2399, Fax: 816-235-5159.

University of Nebraska–Lincoln, Graduate College, College of Engineering, Department of Civil Engineering, Lincoln, NE 68588. Offers MS, PhD. *Degree requirements:* For master's, thesis optional; for doctorate, comprehensive exam, thesis/dissertation. *Entrance requirements:* For master's and doctorate, GRE General Test. Additional exam requirements/recommendations for international students: Required—TOEFL (minimum score 550 paper-based; 213 computer-based). Electronic applications accepted. *Faculty research:* Water resources engineering, sediment transport, steel bridge systems, highway safety.

University of Nevada, Las Vegas, Graduate College, Howard R. Hughes College of Engineering, Department of Civil and Environmental Engineering, Las Vegas, NV 89154-4015. Offers civil and environmental engineering (MS, PhD); transportation (MS). Part-time programs available. *Faculty:* 16 full-time (3 women), 4 part-time/adjunct (0 women). *Students:* 25 full-time (6 women), 28 part-time (6 women); includes 7 minority (2 African Americans, 3 Asian Americans or Pacific Islanders, 2 Hispanic Americans), 16 international. Average age 37. 51 applicants, 55% accepted, 25 enrolled. In 2009, 14 master's, 5 doctorates awarded. *Degree requirements:* For master's, comprehensive exam (for some programs), thesis (for some programs); for doctorate, comprehensive exam, thesis/dissertation. *Entrance requirements:* For master's and doctorate, GRE General Test. Additional exam requirements/recommendations for international students: Required—TOEFL (minimum score 550 paper-based; 213 computer-based; 80 iBT), IELTS (minimum score 7). *Application deadline:* For fall admission, 3/15 priority date for domestic and international students; for spring admission, 11/15 priority date for domestic students, 8/30 priority date for international students. Applications are processed on a rolling basis. Application fee: $60 ($95 for international students). Electronic applications accepted. *Financial support:* In 2009–10, 38 students received support, including 23 research assistantships with partial tuition reimbursements available (averaging $13,595 per year), 15 teaching assistantships with partial tuition reimbursements available (averaging $11,200 per year); institutionally sponsored loans, scholarships/grants, health care benefits, and unspecified assistantships also available. Financial award application deadline: 3/1. *Unit head:* Dr. Edward Neumann, Chair/Professor, 702-895-1072, Fax: 702-895-3936, E-mail: neumann@ce.unlv.edu. *Application contact:* Graduate College Admissions Evaluator, 702-895-3320, Fax: 702-895-4180, E-mail: gradcollege@unlv.edu.

University of Nevada, Reno, Graduate School, College of Engineering, Department of Civil and Environmental Engineering, Reno, NV 89557. Offers MS, PhD. Terminal master's awarded for partial completion of doctoral program. *Degree requirements:* For master's, thesis optional; for doctorate, thesis/dissertation. *Entrance requirements:* For master's, GRE General Test, minimum GPA of 3.0; for doctorate, GRE General Test, minimum GPA of 3.25. Additional exam requirements/recommendations for international students: Required—TOEFL (minimum score 500 paper-based; 173 computer-based; 61 iBT), IELTS (minimum score 6). Electronic applications accepted. *Faculty research:* Structural and earthquake engineering, geotechnical engineering, environmental engineering, transportation, pavements/materials.

University of New Brunswick Fredericton, School of Graduate Studies, Faculty of Engineering, Department of Civil Engineering, Fredericton, NB E3B 5A3, Canada. Offers construction engineering and management (M Eng, M Sc E, PhD); environmental engineering (M Eng, M Sc E, PhD); environmental studies (M Eng); geotechnical engineering (M Eng, M Sc E, PhD); groundwater/hydrology (M Eng, M Sc E, PhD); materials (M Eng, M Sc E, PhD); pavements (M Eng, M Sc E, PhD); structures (M Eng, M Sc E, PhD); transportation (M Eng, M Sc E, PhD). Part-time programs available. *Faculty:* 18 full-time (1 woman), 1 (woman) part-time/adjunct. *Students:* 42 full-time (9 women), 18 part-time (2 women). In 2009, 11 master's, 4 doctorates awarded. *Degree requirements:* For master's, thesis, proposal; for doctorate, comprehensive exam, thesis/dissertation, Qualifying exam; Proposal; 27 credit hours of courses. *Entrance requirements:* For master's, Minimum GPA of 3.0; BScE in Civil Engineering or related engineering degree.; for doctorate, Minimum GPA of 3.0; Candidates are normally required to have a graduate degree in engineering or applied science. Additional exam requirements/recommendations for international students: Required—TOEFL (minimum score 580 paper-based; 237 computer-based), TWE (minimum score 4), or IELTS (minimum score 7.5). *Application deadline:* For fall admission, 5/1 priority date for domestic students; for winter admission, 11/1 priority date for domestic students. Applications are processed on a rolling basis. Application fee: $50 Canadian dollars. Tuition and fees charges are reported in Canadian dollars. *Expenses:* Tuition, area resident: Full-time $5562 Canadian dollars; part-time $2781 Canadian dollars per year. Required fees: $49.75 Canadian dollars per term. *Financial support:* In 2009–10, 51 research assistantships (averaging $7,000 per year), 43 teaching assistantships (averaging $2,000 per year) were awarded; career-related internships or fieldwork and scholarships/grants also available. *Faculty research:* Construction engineering and management, concrete materials and structural engineering, transportation and asset management, geotechnical engineering, water and environmental engineering. *Unit head:* Dr. Eric Hildebrand, Director of Graduate Studies, 506-453-5113, Fax: 506-453-3568, E-mail: ktm@unb.ca. *Application contact:* Joyce Moore, Graduate Secretary, 506-452-6127, Fax: 506-453-3568, E-mail: civil-grad@unb.ca.

University of New Hampshire, Graduate School, College of Engineering and Physical Sciences, Department of Civil Engineering, Durham, NH 03824. Offers MS, PhD. Part-time programs available. *Faculty:* 17 full-time (5 women). *Students:* 26 full-time (5 women), 41 part-time (16 women); includes 1 minority (American Indian/Alaska Native), 6 international. Average age 32. 40 applicants, 90% accepted, 21 enrolled. In 2009, 11 master's, 3 doctorates awarded. *Degree requirements:* For master's, thesis or alternative; for doctorate, thesis/dissertation. *Entrance requirements:* For master's and doctorate, GRE. Additional exam requirements/recommendations for international students: Required—TOEFL (minimum score 550 paper-based; 213 computer-based; 80 iBT). *Application deadline:* For fall admission, 4/1

Civil Engineering

University of New Hampshire (continued)
priority date for domestic students, 4/1 for international students; for spring admission, 12/1 for domestic students. Applications are processed on a rolling basis. Application fee: $65. *Expenses:* Tuition, state resident: full-time $10,380; part-time $577 per credit hour. Tuition, nonresident: full-time $24,350; part-time $1002 per credit hour. Required fees: $1550; $387.50 per semester. Tuition and fees vary according to course load and program. *Financial support:* In 2009–10, 40 students received support, including 1 fellowship, 22 research assistantships, 15 teaching assistantships; Federal Work-Study, scholarships/grants, and tuition waivers (full and partial) also available. Support available to part-time students. Financial award application deadline: 2/15. *Faculty research:* Environmental, structural materials, geotechnical engineering, water resources, systems analysis. *Unit head:* Dr. Jean Benoit, Chairperson, 603-862-1419. *Application contact:* Robin Collins, Administrative Assistant, 603-862-1353, E-mail: civil.engineering@unh.edu.

University of New Mexico, Graduate School, School of Engineering, Department of Civil Engineering, Albuquerque, NM 87131-2039. Offers civil engineering (MS); construction management (MCM); engineering (PhD). Part-time programs available. *Faculty:* 15 full-time (2 women), 6 part-time/adjunct (1 woman). *Students:* 57 full-time (18 women), 25 part-time (5 women); includes 12 minority (all Hispanic Americans), 37 international. Average age 30. 61 applicants, 46% accepted, 17 enrolled. In 2009, 11 master's, 2 doctorates awarded. Terminal master's awarded for partial completion of doctoral program. *Degree requirements:* For master's, comprehensive exam, thesis (for some programs); for doctorate, comprehensive exam, thesis/dissertation. *Entrance requirements:* For master's, GRE General Test for MSCE; GMAT for MCM, minimum GPA of 3.0; for doctorate, GRE General Test, minimum GPA of 3.0. Additional exam requirements/recommendations for international students: Required—TOEFL (minimum score 550 paper-based; 213 computer-based; 79 iBT). *Application deadline:* For fall admission, 7/15 for domestic students, 3/1 for international students; for spring admission, 11/10 for domestic students, 8/1 for international students. Applications are processed on a rolling basis. Application fee: $50. Electronic applications accepted. *Expenses:* Tuition, state resident: full-time $2098.80; part-time $233.20 per credit hour. Tuition, nonresident: full-time $6650. Required fees: $25 per semester. Tuition and fees vary according to course load, program and reciprocity agreements. *Financial support:* In 2009–10, 8 students received support, including 136 research assistantships with full and partial tuition reimbursements available (averaging $19,100 per year), 3 teaching assistantships with full and partial tuition reimbursements available (averaging $19,200 per year); scholarships/grants, health care benefits, and unspecified assistantships also available. Support available to part-time students. Financial award application deadline: 3/1; financial award applicants required to submit FAFSA. *Faculty research:* Application of artificial intelligence in structural engineering and bio-mechanics, blast resistant composite materials, construction engineering, ecohydrology and ecohydraulics, environmental engineering, geotechnical engineering, structural acoustics, hydraulics and water resources, hybrid biofilm systems, open channel hydraulics, pavement materials and foundations, evaluation of groundwater contamination from on-site waste water disposal systems, structural engineering. Total annual research expenditures: $3.1 million. *Unit head:* Dr. John C. Stormont, Chair, 505-277-2722, Fax: 505-277-1988, E-mail: jcstorm@unm.edu. *Application contact:* Josie Gibson, Professional Academic Advisor, 505-277-2722, Fax: 505-277-1988, E-mail: civil@unm.edu.

The University of North Carolina at Charlotte, Graduate School, The William States Lee College of Engineering, Department of Civil and Environmental Engineering, Charlotte, NC 28223-0001. Offers civil engineering (MSCE); infrastructure and environmental systems (PhD), including infrastructure and environmental systems design, infrastructure and environmental systems management. Part-time and evening/weekend programs available. *Faculty:* 17 full-time (2 women), 1 part-time/adjunct (0 women). *Students:* 34 full-time (8 women), 18 part-time (6 women); includes 3 African Americans, 1 Asian American or Pacific Islander, 2 Hispanic Americans, 12 international. Average age 25. 41 applicants, 80% accepted, 20 enrolled. In 2009, 17 master's awarded. Terminal master's awarded for partial completion of doctoral program. *Degree requirements:* For master's, thesis or project. *Entrance requirements:* For master's, GRE General Test, minimum GPA of 3.0 in undergraduate major, 2.75 overall. Additional exam requirements/recommendations for international students: Required—TOEFL (minimum score 550 paper-based; 220 computer-based; 83 iBT). *Application deadline:* For fall admission, 7/1 for domestic students, 5/1 for international students; for spring admission, 11/1 for domestic students, 10/1 for international students. Applications are processed on a rolling basis. Application fee: $55. Electronic applications accepted. *Financial support:* In 2009–10, 48 students received support, including 14 research assistantships (averaging $7,026 per year), 33 teaching assistantships (averaging $7,986 per year); career-related internships or fieldwork, Federal Work-Study, institutionally sponsored loans, scholarships/grants, and administrative assistantship also available. Support available to part-time students. Financial award application deadline: 4/1; financial award applicants required to submit FAFSA. *Faculty research:* Structural composite materials, storm water systems, natural and man-made disaster reduction engineering, older drivers and nighttime driving, soil contamination and transport. Total annual research expenditures: $968,217. *Unit head:* Dr. David T. Young, Chair, 704-687-4175, Fax: 704-687-6953, E-mail: dyoung@uncc.edu. *Application contact:* Kathy B. Giddings, Director of Graduate Admissions, 704-687-5503, Fax: 704-687-3279, E-mail: gradadm@uncc.edu.

University of North Dakota, Graduate School, School of Engineering and Mines, Department of Civil Engineering, Grand Forks, ND 58202. Offers civil engineering (M Engr); sanitary engineering (M Engr), including soils and structures engineering, surface mining engineering. Part-time programs available. *Degree requirements:* For master's, comprehensive exam, thesis or alternative. *Entrance requirements:* For master's, GRE General Test, minimum GPA of 2.5. Additional exam requirements/recommendations for international students: Required—TOEFL (minimum score 550 paper-based; 213 computer-based; 79 iBT), IELTS (minimum score 6.5). Electronic applications accepted. *Faculty research:* Soil-structures, environmental-water resources.

University of North Florida, College of Computing, Engineering, and Construction, Jacksonville, FL 32224. Offers civil engineering (MSCE); computer and information sciences (MS); electrical engineering (MSEE); mechanical engineering (MSME). Part-time programs available. *Faculty:* 35 full-time (6 women). *Students:* 21 full-time (4 women), 64 part-time (11 women); includes 22 minority (6 African Americans, 9 Asian Americans or Pacific Islanders, 7 Hispanic Americans), 10 international. Average age 31. 82 applicants, 45% accepted, 14 enrolled. In 2009, 6 master's awarded. *Degree requirements:* For master's, thesis optional. *Entrance requirements:* For master's, GRE General Test, minimum GPA of 3.0 in last 60 hours of course work. Additional exam requirements/recommendations for international students: Required—TOEFL (minimum score 500 paper-based; 173 computer-based). *Application deadline:* For fall admission, 7/1 priority date for domestic students, 5/1 for international students; for spring admission, 11/1 priority date for domestic students, 10/1 for international students. Applications are processed on a rolling basis. Application fee: $30. Electronic applications accepted. *Expenses:* Tuition, state resident: full-time $6649.20; part-time $277.05 per credit hour. Tuition, nonresident: full-time $22,970; part-time $957.08 per credit hour. Required fees: $985; $41.03 per credit hour. *Financial support:* In 2009–10, 20 students received support, including 5 research assistantships (averaging $5,009 per year), 3 teaching assistantships (averaging $2,844 per year); Federal Work-Study and tuition waivers (partial) also available. Support available to part-time students. Financial award application deadline: 4/1; financial award applicants required to submit FAFSA. *Faculty research:* Parallel and distributed computing, networks, generic programming, algorithms, artificial intelligence. Total annual research expenditures: $2.2 million. *Unit head:* Dr. Neal Coulter, Dean, 904-620-1350, E-mail: ncoulter@unf.edu. *Application contact:* Dr. Roger Eggen, Director of Graduate Studies for Computer Science, 904-320-2985, Fax: 904-620-2988, E-mail: ree@unf.edu.

University of Notre Dame, Graduate School, College of Engineering, Department of Civil Engineering and Geological Sciences, Notre Dame, IN 46556. Offers bioengineering (MS Bio E); civil engineering (MSCE); civil engineering and geological sciences (PhD); environmental engineering (MS Env E); geological sciences (MS). Terminal master's awarded for partial completion of doctoral program. *Degree requirements:* For master's, comprehensive exam; for doctorate, thesis/dissertation, candidacy exam. *Entrance requirements:* For master's and doctorate, GRE General Test. Additional exam requirements/recommendations for international students: Required—TOEFL (minimum score 600 paper-based; 250 computer-based; 80 iBT). Electronic applications accepted. *Faculty research:* Environmental modeling, biological-waste treatment, petrology, environmental geology, geochemistry.

University of Oklahoma, Graduate College, College of Engineering, School of Civil Engineering and Environmental Science, Program in Civil Engineering, Norman, OK 73019-0390. Offers civil engineering (MS, PhD); geotechnical engineering (MS); structures (MS). Part-time programs available. *Students:* 42 full-time (8 women), 9 part-time (1 woman); includes 4 minority (1 African American, 1 American Indian/Alaska Native, 1 Asian American or Pacific Islander, 1 Hispanic American), 28 international. 18 applicants, 100% accepted, 6 enrolled. In 2009, 13 master's, 3 doctorates awarded. *Degree requirements:* For master's, comprehensive exam, oral exams; for doctorate, thesis/dissertation, oral and qualifying exams. *Entrance requirements:* For master's, minimum GPA of 3.0; for doctorate, minimum graduate GPA of 3.5. Additional exam requirements/recommendations for international students: Required—TOEFL (minimum score 600 paper-based). *Application deadline:* For fall admission, 4/1 priority date for domestic students, 4/1 for international students; for spring admission, 11/1 for domestic students, 9/1 for international students. Applications are processed on a rolling basis. Application fee: $40 ($90 for international students). Electronic applications accepted. *Expenses:* Tuition, state resident: full-time $3744; part-time $156 per credit hour. Tuition, nonresident: full-time $13,577; part-time $565.70 per credit hour. Required fees: $2415; $90.10 per credit hour. *Financial support:* Scholarships/grants and unspecified assistantships available. Financial award application deadline: 3/1; financial award applicants required to submit FAFSA. *Faculty research:* Structural engineering, environmental modeling, natural hazards, transport and fate of chemicals, geotechnical engineering. *Unit head:* Robert C. Knox, Director, 405-325-5911, Fax: 405-325-4217, E-mail: rknox@ou.edu. *Application contact:* Robert C. Knox, Director, 405-325-5911, Fax: 405-325-4217, E-mail: rknox@ou.edu.

University of Ottawa, Faculty of Graduate and Postdoctoral Studies, Faculty of Engineering, Ottawa-Carleton Institute for Civil Engineering, Ottawa, ON K1N 6N5, Canada. Offers M Eng, MA Sc, PhD. *Degree requirements:* For master's, thesis or alternative; for doctorate, comprehensive exam, thesis/dissertation, seminar series. *Entrance requirements:* For master's, honors degree or equivalent, minimum B average; for doctorate, master's degree, minimum B+ average. Electronic applications accepted. *Faculty research:* Environmental engineering, geotechnical engineering, structural engineering, transportation engineering, water resources engineering.

University of Pittsburgh, School of Engineering, Department of Civil and Environmental Engineering, Pittsburgh, PA 15260. Offers MSCEE, PhD. Part-time programs available. Post-baccalaureate distance learning degree programs offered. *Faculty:* 16 full-time (3 women), 21 part-time/adjunct (1 woman). *Students:* 75 full-time (23 women), 45 part-time (8 women); includes 9 minority (5 African Americans, 4 Asian Americans or Pacific Islanders), 45 international. 205 applicants, 83% accepted, 42 enrolled. In 2009, 17 master's awarded. Terminal master's awarded for partial completion of doctoral program. *Degree requirements:* For master's, thesis optional; for doctorate, comprehensive exam, thesis/dissertation, final oral exams. *Entrance requirements:* For master's and doctorate, minimum QPA of 3.0. Additional exam requirements/recommendations for international students: Required—TOEFL (minimum score 550 paper-based; 213 computer-based; 80 iBT). *Application deadline:* For fall admission, 3/1 priority date for domestic students; for spring admission, 7/1 priority date for domestic students. Applications are processed on a rolling basis. Application fee: $50. Electronic applications accepted. *Expenses:* Tuition, state resident: full-time $16,402; part-time $665 per credit. Tuition, nonresident: full-time $28,694; part-time $1175 per credit. Required fees: $690; $175 per term. Tuition and fees vary according to program. *Financial support:* In 2009–10, 44 students received support, including 3 fellowships with tuition reimbursements available (averaging $20,772 per year), 35 research assistantships with full tuition reimbursements available (averaging $22,000 per year), 23 teaching assistantships with full tuition reimbursements available (averaging $21,000 per year); scholarships/grants, traineeships, and tuition waivers (full and partial) also available. Financial award application deadline: 4/15. *Faculty research:* Environmental and water resources, structures and infrastructures, construction management. Total annual research expenditures: $2.7 million. *Unit head:* Dr. Radisav Vidic, Chairman, 412-624-9870, Fax: 412-624-0135. *Application contact:* Amir Kouboa, Academic Coordinator, 412-624-9869, Fax: 412-624-0135, E-mail: amk59@pitt.edu.

University of Puerto Rico, Mayagüez Campus, Graduate Studies, College of Engineering, Department of Civil Engineering and Surveying, Mayagüez, PR 00681-9000. Offers civil engineering (ME, MS, PhD). Part-time programs available. *Degree requirements:* For master's, comprehensive exam, thesis (MS); for doctorate, one foreign language, thesis/dissertation. *Entrance requirements:* For master's, proficiency in English and Spanish, BS degree in civil engineering or its equivalent; for doctorate, proficiency in English and Spanish. *Faculty research:* Structural design, concrete structure, finite elements, dynamic analysis, transportation, soils.

University of Rhode Island, Graduate School, College of Engineering, Department of Civil and Environmental Engineering, Kingston, RI 02881. Offers MS, PhD. Part-time programs available. *Faculty:* 6 full-time (2 women), 1 part-time/adjunct (0 women). *Students:* 14 full-time (7 women), 17 part-time (5 women); includes 2 minority (1 Asian American or Pacific Islander, 1 Hispanic American), 7 international. In 2009, 17 master's, 1 doctorate awarded. *Degree requirements:* For master's, comprehensive exam (for some programs), thesis optional; for doctorate, comprehensive exam, thesis/dissertation. *Entrance requirements:* For master's and doctorate, 2 letters of recommendation. Additional exam requirements/recommendations for international students: Required—TOEFL (minimum score 550 paper-based; 213 computer-based). *Application deadline:* For fall admission, 7/15 for domestic students, 2/1 for international students; for spring admission, 11/15 for domestic students, 7/15 for international students. Application fee: $65. Electronic applications accepted. *Expenses:* Tuition, state resident: full-time $8828; part-time $490 per credit hour. Tuition, nonresident: full-time $22,100; part-time $1228 per credit hour. Required fees: $1118; $57 per semester. Tuition and fees vary according to program. *Financial support:* In 2009–10, 4 research assistantships with full and partial tuition reimbursements (averaging $8,760 per year), 5 teaching assistantships with full and partial tuition reimbursements (averaging $12,687 per year) were awarded. Financial award application deadline: 7/15; financial award applicants required to submit FAFSA. *Faculty research:* Industrial waste treatment, structural health monitoring, traffic and transit system operations, computational mechanics, engineering materials design. Total annual research expenditures: $422,735. *Unit head:* Dr. George E. Tsiatas, Chair, 401-874-5117, Fax: 401-874-2786, E-mail: gt@uri.edu. *Application contact:* Dr. Mayrai Gindy, Director of Graduate Studies, 401-874-5587, Fax: 401-874-2786, E-mail: gindy@egr.uri.edu.

University of Saskatchewan, College of Graduate Studies and Research, College of Engineering, Department of Civil and Geological Engineering, Saskatoon, SK S7N 5A2, Canada. Offers M Eng, M Sc, PhD. *Degree requirements:* For master's, thesis (for some programs); for doctorate, thesis/dissertation. *Entrance requirements:* For master's, GRE, minimum GPA of 5.0 on an 8.0 scale; for doctorate, GRE. Additional exam requirements/recommendations for international students: Required—TOEFL. Tuition and fees charges are reported in Canadian dollars. *Expenses:* Tuition, area resident: Full-time $3000 Canadian dollars; part-time $500 Canadian dollars per term. Required fees: $700 Canadian dollars; $100 Canadian dollars per term. *Faculty research:* Geotechnical engineering, structures, water sciences.

University of South Alabama, Graduate School, College of Engineering, Department of Civil Engineering, Mobile, AL 36688-0002. Offers MSCE. *Expenses:* Tuition, state resident: part-time $218 per contact hour. Required fees: $1102 per year.

University of South Carolina, The Graduate School, College of Engineering and Computing, Department of Civil and Environmental Engineering, Columbia, SC 29208. Offers civil engineering (ME, MS, PhD). Part-time and evening/weekend programs available. Post-baccalaureate distance learning degree programs offered (minimal on-campus study). *Degree requirements:* For master's, comprehensive exam, thesis (for some programs); for doctorate, thesis/dissertation. *Entrance requirements:* For master's and doctorate, GRE General Test, 2 letters of recommendation. Additional exam requirements/recommendations for international students: Required—TOEFL (minimum score 570 paper-based; 230 computer-based). Electronic applications accepted. *Faculty research:* Structures, Water Resources, Environmental, Geo-technical and Transportation.

University of Southern California, Graduate School, Viterbi School of Engineering, Sonny Astani Department of Civil Engineering, Los Angeles, CA 90089. Offers applied mechanics (MS); civil engineering (MS, PhD); computer-aided engineering (ME, Graduate Certificate); construction management (MCM); engineering technology commercialization (Graduate Certificate); environmental engineering (MS, PhD); environmental quality management (ME); structural design (ME); sustainable cities (Graduate Certificate); transportation systems (Graduate Certificate). Part-time programs available. Postbaccalaureate distance learning degree programs offered (no on-campus study). *Faculty:* 16 full-time (2 women), 35 part-time/adjunct (5 women). *Students:* 165 full-time (48 women), 65 part-time (16 women); includes 54 minority (40 Asian Americans or Pacific Islanders, 14 Hispanic Americans), 108 international. 451 applicants, 41% accepted, 73 enrolled. In 2009, 74 master's, 10 doctorates awarded. Terminal master's awarded for partial completion of doctoral program. *Degree requirements:* For doctorate, thesis/dissertation. *Entrance requirements:* For master's, GRE General Test; for doctorate, General GRE. *Application deadline:* For fall admission, 3/1 priority date for domestic and international students; for spring admission, 10/1 priority date for domestic and international students. Applications are processed on a rolling basis. Application fee: $85. Electronic applications accepted. *Expenses:* Tuition: Full-time $25,980; part-time $1315 per unit. Required fees: $554. One-time fee: $35 full-time. Full-time tuition and fees vary according to degree level and program. *Financial support:* In 2009–10, fellowships with full tuition reimbursements (averaging $30,000 per year), research assistantships with full tuition reimbursements (averaging $19,250 per year), teaching assistantships with full tuition reimbursements (averaging $19,250 per year) were awarded; career-related internships or fieldwork, scholarships/grants, health care benefits, and unspecified assistantships also available. Financial award application deadline: 12/1; financial award applicants required to submit CSS PROFILE or FAFSA. *Faculty research:* Geotechnical engineering, transportation engineering, structural engineering, construction management, environmental engineering, water resources. Total annual research expenditures: $4.2 million. *Unit head:* Dr. Jean-Pierre Bardet, Chair, 213-740-0609, Fax: 213-744-1426, E-mail: bardet@usc.edu. *Application contact:* Jennifer A. Gerson, Director of Student Services, 213-740-0573, Fax: 213-740-8662, E-mail: jgerson@usc.edu.

University of South Florida, Graduate School, College of Engineering, Department of Civil and Environmental Engineering, Tampa, FL 33620-9951. Offers civil and environmental engineering (MSES); civil engineering (MCE, MSCE, PhD). Part-time programs available. *Faculty:* 19 full-time (3 women), 1 part-time/adjunct (0 women). *Students:* 91 full-time (33 women), 54 part-time (13 women); includes 26 minority (9 African Americans, 9 Asian Americans or Pacific Islanders, 8 Hispanic Americans), 44 international. Average age 32. 124 applicants, 69% accepted, 46 enrolled. In 2009, 41 master's, 7 doctorates awarded. Terminal master's awarded for partial completion of doctoral program. *Degree requirements:* For master's, comprehensive exam, thesis (for some programs); for doctorate, comprehensive exam, thesis/dissertation. *Entrance requirements:* For master's, GRE General Test, minimum GPA of 3.0 in last 60 hours of coursework; for doctorate, GRE General Test, minimum GPA of 3.3 in last 60 hours of coursework. Additional exam requirements/recommendations for international students: Required—TOEFL (minimum score 550 paper-based; 213 computer-based; 79 iBT). *Application deadline:* For fall admission, 2/15 for domestic students, 1/2 priority date for international students; for spring admission, 10/15 for domestic students, 6/1 priority date for international students. Application fee: $30. Electronic applications accepted. *Financial support:* In 2009–10, teaching assistantships with tuition reimbursements (averaging $26,422 per year). *Faculty research:* Water resources, structures and materials, transportation, geotechnical engineering, mechanics. Total annual research expenditures: $2 million. *Application contact:* Dr. Sarina Ergas, Director, 813-974-1119, Fax: 813-974-2957, E-mail: sergas@usf.edu.

The University of Tennessee, Graduate School, College of Engineering, Department of Civil and Environmental Engineering, Program in Civil Engineering, Knoxville, TN 37996. Offers MS, PhD, MS/MBA. Part-time programs available. Postbaccalaureate distance learning degree programs offered (minimal on-campus study). *Faculty:* 13 full-time (1 woman), 4 part-time/adjunct (0 women). *Students:* 55 full-time (14 women), 46 part-time (4 women); includes 5 minority (4 African Americans, 1 Asian American or Pacific Islander), 32 international. Average age 23. 78 applicants, 71% accepted, 22 enrolled. In 2009, 32 master's, 4 doctorates awarded. *Degree requirements:* For master's, thesis or alternative; for doctorate, comprehensive exam, thesis/dissertation. *Entrance requirements:* For master's, GRE, minimum GPA of 2.7; for doctorate, GRE, minimum GPA of 3.0. Additional exam requirements/recommendations for international students: Required—TOEFL (minimum score 550 paper-based; 213 computer-based). *Application deadline:* For fall admission, 2/1 priority date for domestic and international students; for spring admission, 6/15 priority date for international students. Applications are processed on a rolling basis. Application fee: $35. Electronic applications accepted. *Expenses:* Tuition, state resident: full-time $6826; part-time $380 per semester hour. Tuition, nonresident: full-time $21,844; part-time $1147 per semester hour. Tuition and fees vary according to program. *Financial support:* In 2009–10, 35 students received support, including 48 research assistantships with full tuition reimbursements available (averaging $13,608 per year), 24 teaching assistantships with full tuition reimbursements available (averaging $6,624 per year); career-related internships or fieldwork, Federal Work-Study, institutionally sponsored loans, health care benefits, and unspecified assistantships also available. Financial award application deadline: 2/1; financial award applicants required to submit FAFSA. *Faculty research:* Multi-functional composites and mechanics of materials; geohydrologic investigations and monitoring; structures and vibrations; geotechnical and earthquake engineering; transportation system planning and design. Total annual research expenditures: $3.7 million. *Unit head:* Dr. Dayakar Penumadu, Head, 865-974-2355, Fax: 865-974-2355, E-mail: dpenumad@utk.edu. *Application contact:* Dr. Masood Parang, Associate Dean of Student Affairs, 865-974-2454, Fax: 865-974-9871, E-mail: mparang@utk.edu.

The University of Tennessee at Chattanooga, Graduate School, College of Engineering and Computer Science, Program in Engineering, Chattanooga, TN 37403. Offers chemical (MS Engr); civil (MS Engr); computational (MS Engr); electrical (MS Engr); industrial (MS Engr); mechanical (MS Engr). Part-time and evening/weekend programs available. *Faculty:* 8 full-time (0 women). *Students:* 22 full-time (7 women), 30 part-time (3 women); includes 9 minority (4 African Americans, 4 Asian Americans or Pacific Islanders, 1 Hispanic American), 9 international. Average age 29. 59 applicants, 59% accepted, 19 enrolled. In 2009, 9 master's awarded. *Degree requirements:* For master's, comprehensive exam, thesis or alternative, engineering project. *Entrance requirements:* For master's, GRE General Test, minimum undergraduate GPA of 2.5 or 3.0 in last 30 hours of coursework. Additional exam requirements/recommendations for international students: Required—TOEFL (minimum score 550 paper-based; 213 computer-based; 79 iBT), IELTS (minimum score 6). *Application deadline:* For fall admission, 8/1 priority date for domestic students, 6/1 for international students; for spring admission, 12/1 priority date for domestic students, 10/1 for international students. Applications are processed on a rolling basis. Application fee: $35. Electronic applications accepted. *Expenses:* Tuition, state resident: full-time $5404; part-time $300 per credit hour. Tuition, nonresident: full-time $16,702; part-time $928 per credit hour. Required fees: $1150; $130 per credit hour. *Financial support:* In 2009–10, 23 research assistantships with full and partial tuition reimbursements (averaging $5,500 per year) were awarded; career-related internships or fieldwork, scholarships/grants, and unspecified assistantships also available. Support available to part-time students. *Faculty research:* Quality control and reliability engineering, financial management, thermal science, energy conservation, structural analysis. Total annual research expenditures: $2.6 million. *Unit head:* Dr. Neslihan Alp, Director, 423-425-4032, Fax: 423-425-5229, E-mail: neslihan-alp@utc.edu. *Application contact:* Dr. Stephanie Bellar, Dean of Graduate Studies, 423-425-4666, Fax: 423-425-5223, E-mail: stephanie-bellar@utc.edu.

The University of Texas at Arlington, Graduate School, College of Engineering, Department of Civil Engineering, Arlington, TX 76019. Offers M Engr, MS, PhD. Part-time and evening/weekend programs available. Postbaccalaureate distance learning degree programs offered (minimal on-campus study). *Faculty:* 17 full-time (1 woman). *Students:* 95 full-time (25 women), 99 part-time (28 women); includes 33 minority (10 African Americans, 11 Asian Americans or Pacific Islanders, 12 Hispanic Americans), 105 international. 100 applicants, 98% accepted, 48 enrolled. In 2009, 43 master's, 8 doctorates awarded. Terminal master's awarded for partial completion of doctoral program. *Degree requirements:* For master's, comprehensive exam, thesis (for some programs), oral and written exams; for doctorate, comprehensive exam, thesis/dissertation, oral and written defense of dissertation. *Entrance requirements:* For master's, GRE General Test, minimum GPA of 3.0 in last 60 hours of undergraduate course work; for doctorate, GRE General Test. Additional exam requirements/recommendations for international students: Required—TOEFL. *Application deadline:* For fall admission, 6/6 for domestic students, 4/4 for international students; for spring admission, 10/17 for domestic students, 9/5 for international students. Applications are processed on a rolling basis. Application fee: $35 ($50 for international students). *Financial support:* In 2009–10, 29 fellowships with partial tuition reimbursements (averaging $1,000 per year), 15 research assistantships with partial tuition reimbursements (averaging $13,200 per year), 14 teaching assistantships with partial tuition reimbursements (averaging $12,000 per year) were awarded; career-related internships or fieldwork, Federal Work-Study, scholarships/grants, tuition waivers (partial), and unspecified assistantships also available. Financial award application deadline: 6/1; financial award applicants required to submit FAFSA. *Faculty research:* Environmental and water resources structures, geotechnical, transportation. *Unit head:* Dr. Nur Yazdani, Chair, 817-272-5055, Fax: 817-272-2630, E-mail: yazdani@uta.edu. *Application contact:* Dr. Mostafa Ghandehari, Graduate Advisor, 817-272-2201, Fax: 817-272-2630, E-mail: ghandeha@uta.edu.

The University of Texas at Austin, Graduate School, Cockrell School of Engineering, Department of Civil, Architectural and Environmental Engineering, Austin, TX 78712-1111. Offers architectural engineering (MSE); civil engineering (MS, PhD); environmental and water resources engineering (MS, PhD). *Accreditation:* ABET (one or more programs are accredited). Part-time programs available. *Degree requirements:* For master's, thesis or alternative; for doctorate, comprehensive exam, thesis/dissertation. *Entrance requirements:* For master's and doctorate, GRE General Test. Additional exam requirements/recommendations for international students: Required—TOEFL. Electronic applications accepted. *Faculty research:* Geotechnical structural engineering, transportation engineering, construction enginering/project management.

The University of Texas at El Paso, Graduate School, College of Engineering, Department of Civil Engineering, El Paso, TX 79968-0001. Offers civil engineering (MS, PhD); construction mangement (Certificate); environmental engineering (MEENE, MSENE). Part-time and evening/weekend programs available. *Degree requirements:* For master's, thesis optional. *Entrance requirements:* For master's, GRE General Test, minimum GPA of 3.0. Additional exam requirements/recommendations for international students: Required—TOEFL. Electronic applications accepted. *Faculty research:* On-site wastewater treatment systems, wastewater reuse, disinfection by-product control, water resources, membrane filtration.

The University of Texas at San Antonio, College of Engineering, Department of Civil and Environmental Engineering, San Antonio, TX 78249-0617. Offers civil engineering (MSCE); environmental science and engineering (PhD). Part-time and evening/weekend programs available. *Faculty:* 11 full-time (1 woman), 1 part-time/adjunct (0 women). *Students:* 34 full-time (8 women), 28 part-time (5 women); includes 16 minority (4 African Americans, 4 Asian Americans or Pacific Islanders, 8 Hispanic Americans), 24 international. Average age 33. 56 applicants, 55% accepted, 19 enrolled. In 2009, 12 master's, 4 doctorates awarded. *Degree requirements:* For master's, comprehensive exam (for some programs), thesis (for some programs); for doctorate, comprehensive exam, thesis/dissertation. *Entrance requirements:* For master's, GRE General Test, minimum GPA of 3.0 in last 60 hours of undergraduate degree. Additional exam requirements/recommendations for international students: Required—TOEFL (minimum score 500 paper-based; 173 computer-based; 61 iBT), IELTS (minimum score 5). *Application deadline:* For fall admission, 7/1 for domestic students, 4/1 for international students; for spring admission, 11/1 for domestic students, 9/1 for international students. Applications are processed on a rolling basis. Application fee: $45 ($80 for international students). Electronic applications accepted. *Expenses:* Tuition, state resident: full-time $3975; part-time $221 per contact hour. Tuition, nonresident: full-time $13,947; part-time $775 per contact hour. Required fees: $1853. *Financial support:* In 2009–10, 29 students received support, including 15 research assistantships (averaging $18,213 per year); career-related internships or fieldwork, scholarships/grants, tuition waivers, and unspecified assistantships also available. Support available to part-time students. Financial award application deadline: 3/31. Total annual research expenditures: $475,434. *Unit head:* Dr. Athanassio T. Papagiannakis, Chair, 210-458-7071, Fax: 210-458-6475, E-mail: at.papagiannakis@utsa.edu. *Application contact:* Dr. Dorothy A. Flannagan, Dean of the Graduate School, 210-458-4330, Fax: 210-458-4332, E-mail: dorothy.flannagan@utsa.edu.

The University of Texas at Tyler, College of Engineering and Computer Science, Department of Civil Engineering, Tyler, TX 75799-0001. Offers environmental engineering (MS); industrial safety (MS); structural engineering (MS); transportation engineering (MS); water resources engineering (MS). Part-time and evening/weekend programs available. *Faculty:* 6 full-time (0 women). *Students:* 5 full-time (1 woman), 7 part-time (1 woman); includes 1 African American, 1 Asian American or Pacific Islander, 1 Hispanic American, 1 international. Average age 26. 5 applicants, 80% accepted, 3 enrolled. *Degree requirements:* For master's, thesis optional. *Entrance requirements:* For master's, GRE General Test, bachelor's degree in engineering, associated science degree. Additional exam requirements/recommendations for international students: Required—TOEFL (minimum score 79 computer-based). *Application deadline:* For fall admission, 8/17 priority date for domestic students, 7/1 priority date for international students; for spring admission, 12/21 priority date for domestic students, 11/1 priority date for international students. Application fee: $25 ($50 for international students). *Expenses:* Tuition, state resident: part-time $665 per semester hour. Tuition, nonresident: part-time $942 per semester hour. Part-time tuition and fees vary according to degree level and program. *Financial support:* Application deadline: 7/1. *Faculty research:* Non-destructive strength testing, indoor air quality, transportation routing and signaling, pavement replacement criteria, flood water routing, construction and long-term behavior of innovative geotechnical foundation and embankment construction used in highway construction, engineering education. *Unit head:* Dr. Ron Welch, Chair, 903-566-7002, Fax: 903-566-7337, E-mail: rwelch@uttyler.edu. *Application contact:* Dr. Torey Nalbone, Program Chair, 903-565-5520, Fax: 903-566-7337, E-mail: tnalbone@uttyler.edu.

The University of Toledo, College of Graduate Studies, College of Engineering, Department of Civil Engineering, Toledo, OH 43606-3390. Offers MS, PhD. Part-time programs available. Terminal master's awarded for partial completion of doctoral program. *Degree requirements:* For master's, thesis or alternative; for doctorate, thesis/dissertation, qualifying exam. *Entrance requirements:* For master's, GRE General Test, minimum GPA of 3.0; for doctorate, GRE General Test, minimum GPA of 3.3. Additional exam requirements/recommendations for international students: Required—TOEFL (minimum score 550 paper-based; 213 computer-based; 80 iBT). Electronic applications accepted. *Faculty research:* Environmental modeling, soil/pavement interaction, structural mechanics, earthquakes, transportation engineering.

University of Toronto, School of Graduate Studies, Physical Sciences Division, Faculty of Applied Science and Engineering, Department of Civil Engineering, Toronto, ON M5S 1A1, Canada. Offers M Eng, MA Sc, PhD. Part-time programs available. *Degree requirements:* For

Civil Engineering

University of Toronto (continued)
master's, thesis (for some programs), thesis and oral presentation (MA Sc); for doctorate, thesis/dissertation, oral presentation. *Entrance requirements:* For master's, bachelor's degree in civil engineering, proficiency in computer usage, minimum B average in final 2 years, 3 letters of reference; for doctorate, proficiency in computer usage, minimum B average in final 2 years, 3 letters of reference.

University of Utah, The Graduate School, College of Engineering, Department of Civil and Environmental Engineering, Salt Lake City, UT 84112. Offers civil engineering (MS, PhD); environmental engineering (ME, MS, PhD); nuclear engineering (ME, MS, PhD). Part-time and evening/weekend programs available. Postbaccalaureate distance learning degree programs offered. *Faculty:* 19 full-time (5 women), 3 part-time/adjunct (0 women). *Students:* 66 full-time (14 women), 58 part-time (11 women); includes 5 minority (all Hispanic Americans), 35 international. Average age 30. 127 applicants, 58% accepted, 33 enrolled. In 2009, 33 master's, 9 doctorates awarded. Terminal master's awarded for partial completion of doctoral program. *Degree requirements:* For master's, comprehensive exam (for some programs), thesis (for some programs); for doctorate, comprehensive exam, thesis/dissertation, departmental qualifying exam. *Entrance requirements:* For master's and doctorate, GRE General Test, minimum GPA of 3.0. Additional exam requirements/recommendations for international students: Required—TOEFL (minimum score 550 paper-based; 213 computer-based). *Application deadline:* For fall admission, 4/1 for domestic and international students; for spring admission, 11/1 for domestic and international students. Applications are processed on a rolling basis. Application fee: $55 ($65 for international students). Electronic applications accepted. *Expenses:* Tuition, state resident: full-time $4004; part-time $1674 per semester. Tuition, nonresident: full-time $14,134; part-time $5915 per semester. Required fees: $324 per semester. Tuition and fees vary according to course load, degree level and program. *Financial support:* In 2009–10, 55 students received support, including 2 fellowships with full tuition reimbursements available (averaging $22,000 per year), 42 research assistantships with full tuition reimbursements available (averaging $20,016 per year), 11 teaching assistantships with full tuition reimbursements available (averaging $19,200 per year); career-related internships or fieldwork, Federal Work-Study, institutionally sponsored loans, scholarships/grants, health care benefits, tuition waivers (full and partial), and unspecified assistantships also available. Support available to part-time students. Financial award application deadline: 2/1; financial award applicants required to submit FAFSA. *Faculty research:* Structural engineering, geotechnical engineering, transportation engineering, environmental engineering, water resources. Total annual research expenditures: $2.1 million. *Unit head:* Dr. Paul J. Tikalsky, Chair, 801-581-6931, Fax: 801-585-5477, E-mail: tikalsky@civil.utah.edu. *Application contact:* Amanda May, Academic Program Specialist, 801-581-6931, Fax: 801-585-5477, E-mail: amandam@civil.utah.edu.

University of Vermont, Graduate College, College of Engineering and Mathematics, Department of Civil and Environmental Engineering, Burlington, VT 05405. Offers MS, PhD. *Students:* 25 (10 women), 6 international. 25 applicants, 52% accepted, 4 enrolled. In 2009, 1 master's, 1 doctorate awarded. *Degree requirements:* For master's, thesis or alternative; for doctorate, thesis/dissertation. *Entrance requirements:* For master's and doctorate, GRE General Test. Additional exam requirements/recommendations for international students: Required—TOEFL (minimum score 550 paper-based; 213 computer-based; 80 iBT). *Application deadline:* For fall admission, 2/1 priority date for domestic students. Applications are processed on a rolling basis. Application fee: $40. Electronic applications accepted. *Expenses:* Tuition, area resident: Part-time $508 per credit hour. Tuition, state resident: part-time $508 per credit hour. Tuition, nonresident: part-time $1281 per credit hour. *Financial support:* Research assistantships, teaching assistantships available. Financial award application deadline: 3/1. *Unit head:* Dr. J. Marshall, Director, 802-656-3800. *Application contact:* Dr. Britt Holmen, Coordinator, 802-656-3800.

University of Virginia, School of Engineering and Applied Science, Department of Civil Engineering, Charlottesville, VA 22903. Offers ME, MS, PhD. Part-time programs available. Postbaccalaureate distance learning degree programs offered (no on-campus study). *Faculty:* 15 full-time (3 women), 2 part-time/adjunct (0 women). *Students:* 45 full-time (13 women), 3 part-time (0 women); includes 9 minority (3 African Americans, 5 Asian Americans or Pacific Islanders, 1 Hispanic American), 18 international. Average age 28. 136 applicants, 26% accepted, 11 enrolled. In 2009, 19 master's, 4 doctorates awarded. Terminal master's awarded for partial completion of doctoral program. *Degree requirements:* For master's, thesis (for some programs); for doctorate, comprehensive exam, thesis/dissertation. *Entrance requirements:* For master's and doctorate, GRE General Test, 3 letters of recommendation. Additional exam requirements/recommendations for international students: Required—TOEFL (minimum score 600 paper-based; 250 computer-based; 90 iBT), IELTS (minimum score 7). *Application deadline:* For fall admission, 8/1 for domestic students, 4/1 for international students; for winter admission, 12/1 for domestic students, 8/1 for international students; for spring admission, 5/1 for domestic students, 1/1 for international students. Applications are processed on a rolling basis. Application fee: $60. Electronic applications accepted. *Financial support:* Fellowships with full tuition reimbursements, research assistantships with full tuition reimbursements, teaching assistantships with full tuition reimbursements available. Financial award application deadline: 1/15. *Faculty research:* Groundwater, surface water, traffic engineering, composite materials. *Unit head:* Michael J. Demetsky, Chair, 434-924-7464, Fax: 434-982-2951, E-mail: civil@virginia.edu. *Application contact:* Michael J. Demetsky, Chair, 434-924-7464, Fax: 434-982-2951, E-mail: civil@virginia.edu.

University of Washington, Graduate School, College of Engineering, Department of Civil and Environmental Engineering, Seattle, WA 98195-2700. Offers construction engineering (MSCE); environmental engineering (MS, MSCE, MSE, PhD); hydrology, water resources, and environmental fluid mechanics (MS, MSCE, MSE, PhD); structural and geotechnical engineering and mechanics (MS, MSCE, MSE, PhD); transportation and construction engineering (MS, MSE, PhD); transportation engineering (MSCE). Part-time programs available. Postbaccalaureate distance learning degree programs offered (no on-campus study). *Faculty:* 36 full-time (9 women), 16 part-time/adjunct (6 women). *Students:* 186 full-time (62 women), 57 part-time (10 women); includes 35 minority (24 Asian Americans or Pacific Islanders, 11 Hispanic Americans), 58 international. 360 applicants, 68% accepted, 98 enrolled. In 2009, 74 master's, 8 doctorates awarded. Terminal master's awarded for partial completion of doctoral program. *Degree requirements:* For master's, thesis (for some programs); for doctorate, comprehensive exam, thesis/dissertation. *Entrance requirements:* For master's, GRE General Test, minimum GPA of 3.0; for doctorate, GRE, minimum GPA of 3.5. Additional exam requirements/recommendations for international students: Required—TOEFL (minimum score 580 paper-based; 237 computer-based; 70 iBT). *Application deadline:* For fall admission, 1/15 priority date for domestic and international students. Applications are processed on a rolling basis. Application fee: $65. Electronic applications accepted. *Financial support:* In 2009–10, 5 students received support, including 13 fellowships with full and partial tuition reimbursements available (averaging $16,173 per year), 68 research assistantships with full tuition reimbursements available (averaging $16,173 per year), 12 teaching assistantships with full tuition reimbursements available (averaging $16,173 per year); scholarships/grants also available. Financial award application deadline: 1/15. *Faculty research:* Environmental/water resources, hydrology; construction/transportation; structures/ geotechnical. Total annual research expenditures: $11.4 million. *Unit head:* Dr. Gregory R. Miller, Professor and Chair, 206-543-0350, Fax: 206-543-1543, E-mail: gmiller@uw.edu. *Application contact:* Lorna Latal, Graduate Adviser, 206-543-2574, Fax: 206-543-1543, E-mail: llatal@u.washington.edu.

University of Waterloo, Graduate Studies, Faculty of Engineering, Department of Civil and Environmental Engineering, Waterloo, ON N2L 3G1, Canada. Offers M Eng, MA Sc, PhD. Part-time programs available. *Degree requirements:* For master's, research paper or thesis; for doctorate, comprehensive exam, thesis/dissertation. *Entrance requirements:* For master's, honors degree, minimum B average; for doctorate, master's degree, minimum A- average. Additional exam requirements/recommendations for international students: Required—TOEFL,

TWE. Electronic applications accepted. *Faculty research:* Water resources, structures, construction management, transportation, geotechnical engineering.

The University of Western Ontario, Faculty of Graduate Studies, Physical Sciences Division, Faculty of Engineering, London, ON N6A 5B8, Canada. Offers chemical and biochemical engineering (ME Sc, PhD); civil and environmental engineering (M Eng, ME Sc, PhD); electrical and computer engineering (M Eng, ME Sc, PhD); mechanical and materials engineering (M Eng, ME Sc, PhD). Part-time programs available. Terminal master's awarded for partial completion of doctoral program. *Degree requirements:* For master's, thesis; for doctorate, thesis/dissertation. *Entrance requirements:* For master's, minimum B average; for doctorate, minimum B+ average. *Faculty research:* Wind, geotechnical, chemical reactor engineering, applied electrostatics, biochemical engineering.

University of Windsor, Faculty of Graduate Studies, Faculty of Engineering, Department of Civil and Environmental Engineering, Windsor, ON N9B 3P4, Canada. Offers civil engineering (M Eng, MA Sc, PhD); environmental engineering (M Eng, MA Sc, PhD). Part-time programs available. *Degree requirements:* For master's, thesis; for doctorate, comprehensive exam, thesis/dissertation. *Entrance requirements:* For master's, minimum B average; for doctorate, master's degree, minimum A average. Additional exam requirements/recommendations for international students: Required—TOEFL (minimum score 580 paper-based; 237 computer-based). Electronic applications accepted. *Faculty research:* Odors: sampling, measurement, control; drinking water disinfection, hydrocarbon contaminated soil remediation, structural dynamics, numerical simulation of piezoelectric materials.

University of Wisconsin–Madison, Graduate School, College of Engineering, Department of Civil and Environmental Engineering, Madison, WI 53706-1380. Offers MS, PhD. Part-time programs available. *Faculty:* 31 full-time (3 women), 2 part-time/adjunct (0 women). *Students:* 113 full-time (32 women), 40 part-time (8 women); includes 6 minority (1 Asian American or Pacific Islander, 5 Hispanic Americans), 78 international. Average age 29. 383 applicants, 37% accepted, 43 enrolled. In 2009, 15 master's, 2 doctorates awarded. Terminal master's awarded for partial completion of doctoral program. *Degree requirements:* For master's, thesis or alternative; for doctorate, thesis/dissertation, preliminary exam, qualifying exams. *Entrance requirements:* For master's and doctorate, GRE General Test, minimum GPA of 3.0 for last 60 credits of course work. Additional exam requirements/recommendations for international students: Required—TOEFL (minimum score 550 paper-based; 213 computer-based; 80 iBT). *Application deadline:* For fall admission, 3/15 for domestic and international students; for spring admission, 10/15 for domestic and international students. Applications are processed on a rolling basis. Application fee: $56. Electronic applications accepted. *Expenses:* Tuition, state resident: part-time $594 per credit. Tuition, nonresident: part-time $1504 per credit. Required fees: $65 per credit. Tuition and fees vary according to course load, program and reciprocity agreements. *Financial support:* In 2009–10, 63 students received support, including 9 fellowships with full tuition reimbursements available (averaging $22,224 per year), 76 research assistantships with full tuition reimbursements available (averaging $40,368 per year), 12 teaching assistantships with full tuition reimbursements available (averaging $28,175 per year); Federal Work-Study, scholarships/grants, health care benefits, and unspecified assistantships also available. Support available to part-time students. Financial award application deadline: 12/15. *Faculty research:* Environmental geotechnics and soil mechanics, design and analysis of structures, traffic engineering and intelligent transport systems, industrial pollution control, hydrological monitoring. Total annual research expenditures: $7.4 million. *Unit head:* Jeffrey S. Russell, Chair, 608-262-3542, Fax: 608-262-5199, E-mail: russell@engr.wisc.edu. *Application contact:* Marc Nowak, Student Status Examiner, 608-265-5570, Fax: 608-890-1174, E-mail: mrnowak@wisc.edu.

University of Wisconsin–Milwaukee, Graduate School, College of Engineering and Applied Science, Program in Engineering, Milwaukee, WI 53201-0413. Offers civil engineering (MS); electrical and computer engineering (MS); energy engineering (Certificate); engineering (PhD); engineering management (MS); engineering mechanics (MS); ergonomics (Certificate); industrial and management engineering (MS); manufacturing engineering (MS); materials engineering (MS); mechanical engineering (MS); MUP/MS. Part-time programs available. *Faculty:* 44 full-time (6 women). *Students:* 119 full-time (22 women), 130 part-time (22 women); includes 23 minority (2 African Americans, 14 Asian Americans or Pacific Islanders, 7 Hispanic Americans), 126 international. Average age 32. 231 applicants, 67% accepted, 33 enrolled. In 2009, 29 master's, 14 doctorates awarded. *Degree requirements:* For master's, comprehensive exam (for some programs), thesis or alternative; for doctorate, comprehensive exam, thesis/dissertation, internship. *Entrance requirements:* For master's, GRE, minimum GPA of 2.75; for doctorate, GRE, minimum GPA of 3.5. Additional exam requirements/recommendations for international students: Required—TOEFL (minimum score 550 paper-based; 79 iBT), IELTS (minimum score 6.5). *Application deadline:* For fall admission, 1/1 priority date for domestic students; for spring admission, 9/1 for domestic students. Applications are processed on a rolling basis. Application fee: $45 ($75 for international students). *Expenses:* Tuition, state resident: full-time $8800. Tuition, nonresident: full-time $20,760. Tuition and fees vary according to program and reciprocity agreements. *Financial support:* In 2009–10, 18 research assistantships, 51 teaching assistantships were awarded; fellowships, career-related internships or fieldwork, Federal Work-Study, and unspecified assistantships also available. Support available to part-time students. Financial award application deadline: 4/15. Total annual research expenditures: $2.9 million. *Unit head:* David Yu, Head, 414-229-6169, E-mail: yu@uwm.edu. *Application contact:* Betty Warras, General Information Contact, 414-229-4982, Fax: 414-229-6967, E-mail: bwarras@uwm.edu.

University of Wyoming, College of Engineering and Applied Sciences, Department of Civil and Architectural Engineering, Program in Civil Engineering, Laramie, WY 82070. Offers MS, PhD. Part-time programs available. Terminal master's awarded for partial completion of doctoral program. *Degree requirements:* For master's, thesis (for some programs); for doctorate, variable foreign language requirement, comprehensive exam, thesis/dissertation. *Entrance requirements:* For master's, GRE General Test (minimum score 900), minimum GPA of 3.0; for doctorate, GRE General Test (minimum score: 1000), minimum GPA of 3.0. Additional exam requirements/recommendations for international students: Required—TOEFL. Electronic applications accepted. *Faculty research:* Structures, water, resources, geotechnical, transportation.

Utah State University, School of Graduate Studies, College of Engineering, Department of Civil and Environmental Engineering, Logan, UT 84322. Offers ME, MS, PhD, CE. *Degree requirements:* For master's, thesis (for some programs); for doctorate, thesis/dissertation. *Entrance requirements:* For master's and doctorate, GRE General Test, minimum GPA of 3.0. Additional exam requirements/recommendations for international students: Required—TOEFL. Electronic applications accepted. *Faculty research:* Hazardous waste treatment, large space structures, river basin management, earthquake engineering, environmental impact.

Vanderbilt University, School of Engineering, Department of Civil and Environmental Engineering, Program in Civil Engineering, Nashville, TN 37240-1001. Offers M Eng, MS, PhD. MS and PhD offered through the Graduate School. Part-time programs available. *Faculty:* 12 full-time (1 woman), 1 (woman) part-time/adjunct. *Students:* 50 full-time (7 women); includes 6 minority (3 African Americans, 3 Hispanic Americans), 14 international. Average age 28. 75 applicants, 19% accepted, 9 enrolled. In 2009, 19 master's, 2 doctorates awarded. Terminal master's awarded for partial completion of doctoral program. *Degree requirements:* For master's, thesis; for doctorate, thesis/dissertation. *Entrance requirements:* For master's and doctorate, GRE General Test. Additional exam requirements/recommendations for international students: Required—TOEFL. *Application deadline:* For fall admission, 1/15 for domestic students; for spring admission, 11/1 for domestic students. Applications are processed on a rolling basis. Application fee: $0. Electronic applications accepted. *Financial support:* In 2009–10, 12 fellowships with full tuition reimbursements (averaging $30,000 per year), 15 research assistantships with full tuition reimbursements (averaging $25,200 per year), 7 teaching assistantships with full tuition reimbursements (averaging $21,600 per year) were awarded; career-related internships or fieldwork, institutionally sponsored loans, scholarships/grants, traineeships, and tuition waivers (full and partial) also available. Financial award application deadline: 1/15. *Faculty research:* Structural mechanics, finite element analysis, urban transportation, hazardous material transport. *Unit head:* Dr. David S. Kosson, Chair, 615-322-2697, Fax: 615-322-3365, E-mail: david.kosson@vanderbilt.edu. *Application contact:* Dr. P. K. Basu, Director of Graduate Studies, 615-322-7477, Fax: 615-322-3365, E-mail: p.k.basu@vanderbilt.edu.

Villanova University, College of Engineering, Department of Civil and Environmental Engineering, Program in Civil Engineering, Villanova, PA 19085-1699. Offers MSCE. Part-time and evening/weekend programs available. *Degree requirements:* For master's, thesis optional. *Entrance requirements:* For master's, GRE General Test (for applicants with degrees from foreign universities), minimum GPA of 3.0. Additional exam requirements/recommendations for international students: Required—TOEFL (minimum score 600 paper-based; 250 computer-based; 100 iBT). Electronic applications accepted. *Expenses:* Tuition: Part-time $630 per credit. Required fees: $60 per credit. Part-time tuition and fees vary according to degree level and program. *Faculty research:* Bridge inspection, environment maintenance, economy and risk.

Virginia Polytechnic Institute and State University, Graduate School, College of Engineering, Department of Civil and Environmental Engineering, Blacksburg, VA 24061. Offers civil engineering (M Eng, MS, PhD); environmental engineering (M Eng, MS); environmental sciences and engineering (MS). *Accreditation:* ABET (one or more programs are accredited). *Entrance requirements:* For master's and doctorate, GRE. Additional exam requirements/recommendations for international students: Required—TOEFL (minimum score 570 paper-based; 230 computer-based). Electronic applications accepted. *Faculty research:* Construction, environmental geotechnical hydrosystems, structures and transportation engineering.

Washington State University, Graduate School, College of Engineering and Architecture, Department of Civil and Environmental Engineering, Program in Civil Engineering, Pullman, WA 99164. Offers MS, PhD. *Faculty:* 25. *Students:* 68 full-time (17 women), 6 part-time (1 woman); includes 4 minority (1 American Indian/Alaska Native, 3 Asian Americans or Pacific Islanders), 32 international. Average age 29. 146 applicants, 32% accepted, 30 enrolled. In 2009, 20 master's, 6 doctorates awarded. Terminal master's awarded for partial completion of doctoral program. *Degree requirements:* For master's, comprehensive exam (for some programs), thesis (for some programs), oral exam; for doctorate, comprehensive exam, thesis/dissertation, oral exam, written exam. *Entrance requirements:* For master's and doctorate, GRE General Test, Official transcripts from all colleges and universities attended; one-page statement of purpose; three letters of recommendation; copy of application and assistantship forms. Additional exam requirements/recommendations for international students: Required—TOEFL, IELTS. *Application deadline:* For fall admission, 1/10 priority date for domestic students, 1/10 for international students; for spring admission, 7/1 for domestic and international students. Applications are processed on a rolling basis. Application fee: $50. Electronic applications accepted. *Financial support:* In 2009–10, 4 fellowships (averaging $2,875 per year), 31 research assistantships with full and partial tuition reimbursements (averaging $13,917 per year), 13 teaching assistantships with full and partial tuition reimbursements (averaging $13,056 per year) were awarded; career-related internships or fieldwork, Federal Work-Study, and institutionally sponsored loans also available. Financial award application deadline: 4/1; financial award applicants required to submit FAFSA. *Faculty research:* Environmental geotechnical, hydraulics transportation, structures, wood. Total annual research expenditures: $3.6 million. *Unit head:* Dr. David McLean, Chair, 509-335-9578, Fax: 509-335-7632, E-mail: mclean@wsu.edu. *Application contact:* Graduate School Admissions, 800-GRADWSU, Fax: 509-335-1949, E-mail: gradsch@wsu.edu.

Wayne State University, College of Engineering, Department of Civil Engineering, Detroit, MI 48202. Offers MS, PhD. *Degree requirements:* For master's, thesis optional; for doctorate, thesis/dissertation. *Entrance requirements:* For master's, BS in civil engineering with minimum honor-point average of 2.8; for doctorate, GRE if BS in engineering is not from an ABET accredited institution in the US, MS in civil engineering with minimum honor-point average of 3.5, international: letters of recommendation. Additional exam requirements/recommendations for international students: Required—TOEFL (minimum score 550 paper-based; 213 computer-based); Recommended—TWE (minimum score 6). Electronic applications accepted. *Faculty research:* Environmental geotechnics, civil infrastructure systems and materials, seismic analysis of structures and foundations, traffic and construction safety, transportation planning and economics.

Western Michigan University, Graduate College, College of Engineering and Applied Sciences, Department of Civil and Construction Engineering, Kalamazoo, MI 49008. Offers civil engineering (MS), including construction engineering and management, structural engineering, transportation engineering. *Entrance requirements:* For master's, minimum GPA of 3.0.

West Virginia University, College of Engineering and Mineral Resources, Department of Civil and Environmental Engineering, Morgantown, WV 26506. Offers civil engineering (MSCE, MSE, PhD). Part-time programs available. *Degree requirements:* For master's, thesis; for doctorate, comprehensive exam, thesis/dissertation. *Entrance requirements:* For master's and doctorate, minimum GPA of 3.0. Additional exam requirements/recommendations for international students: Required—TOEFL, GRE. *Faculty research:* Habitat restoration, advanced materials for civil infrastructure, pavement modeling, infrastructure condition assessment.

Widener University, Graduate Programs in Engineering, Program in Civil Engineering, Chester, PA 19013-5792. Offers M Eng. Part-time and evening/weekend programs available. *Students:* 4 full-time (0 women), 3 part-time (0 women), 2 international. Average age 30. In 2009, 1 master's awarded. *Degree requirements:* For master's, thesis optional. *Application deadline:* For fall admission, 8/1 priority date for domestic students; for spring admission, 12/1 for domestic students. Applications are processed on a rolling basis. Application fee: $25 ($300 for international students). *Financial support:* Teaching assistantships with full tuition reimbursements, unspecified assistantships available. Financial award application deadline: 3/15. *Faculty research:* Environmental engineering, laws and water supply, structural analysis and design. *Unit head:* Dr. Vicki L. Brown, Chairman, 610-499-4249, E-mail: vicki.l.brown@widener.edu. *Application contact:* Dr. Vicki L. Brown, Chairman, 610-499-4249, E-mail: vicki.l.brown@widener.edu.

Woods Hole Oceanographic Institution, MIT/WHOI Joint Program in Oceanography/Applied Ocean Science and Engineering, Woods Hole, MA 02543-1541. Offers applied ocean sciences (PhD); biological oceanography (PhD, Sc D); chemical oceanography (PhD, Sc D); civil and environmental and oceanographic engineering (PhD); electrical and oceanographic engineering (PhD); geochemistry (PhD); geophysics (PhD); marine biology (PhD); marine geochemistry (PhD, Sc D); marine geology (PhD, Sc D); marine geophysics (PhD); mechanical and oceanographic engineering (PhD); ocean engineering (PhD); oceanographic engineering (M Eng, MS, PhD, Sc D, Eng); paleoceanography (PhD); physical oceanography (PhD, Sc D). Terminal master's awarded for partial completion of doctoral program. *Degree requirements:* For master's and Eng, thesis (for some programs); for doctorate, thesis/dissertation. *Entrance requirements:* For master's, GRE General Test; for doctorate, GRE General Test, GRE Subject Test. Additional exam requirements/recommendations for international students: Required—TOEFL. Electronic applications accepted.

Worcester Polytechnic Institute, Graduate Studies and Research, Department of Civil and Environmental Engineering, Worcester, MA 01609-2280. Offers civil and environmental engineering (Advanced Certificate, Graduate Certificate); civil engineering (ME, MS, PhD); construction project management (MS); environmental engineering (MS); master builder environmental engineering (M Eng). Part-time and evening/weekend programs available. Post-baccalaureate distance learning degree programs offered (no on-campus study). *Faculty:* 10 full-time (1 woman), 1 part-time/adjunct (0 women). *Students:* 23 full-time (10 women), 53 part-time (14 women). 121 applicants, 79% accepted, 28 enrolled. In 2009, 18 master's, 2 doctorates awarded. *Degree requirements:* For master's, thesis optional; for doctorate, comprehensive exam, thesis/dissertation. *Entrance requirements:* For master's and doctorate, GRE (recommended), 3 letters of recommendation. Additional exam requirements/recommendations for international students: Required—TOEFL (minimum score 550 paper-based; 213 computer-based; 79 iBT), IELTS (minimum score 6.5). *Application deadline:* For fall admission, 1/15 priority date for domestic and international students; for spring admission, 10/15 priority date for domestic and international students. Applications are processed on a rolling basis. Application fee: $70. Electronic applications accepted. *Financial support:* Career-related internships or fieldwork, institutionally sponsored loans, scholarships/grants, and unspecified assistantships available. Financial award application deadline: 1/15. *Faculty research:* Environmental engineering and sustainability, pavement engineering technology, impact mechanics and engineering. *Unit head:* Dr. Tahar El-Korchi, Interim Head, 508-831-5530, Fax: 508-831-5808, E-mail: tek@wpi.edu. *Application contact:* Dr. Paul Mathisen, Graduate Coordinator, 508-831-5530, Fax: 508-831-5808, E-mail: mathisen@wpi.edu.

Youngstown State University, Graduate School, College of Science, Technology, Engineering and Mathematics, Department of Civil and Environmental Engineering, Youngstown, OH 44555-0001. Offers MSE. Part-time and evening/weekend programs available. *Degree requirements:* For master's, thesis optional. *Entrance requirements:* For master's, minimum GPA of 2.75 in field. Additional exam requirements/recommendations for international students: Required—TOEFL. *Faculty research:* Structural mechanics, water quality modeling, surface and ground water hydrology, physical and chemical processes in aquatic systems.

Construction Engineering

The American University in Cairo, Graduate Studies and Research, School of Sciences and Engineering, Department of Construction Engineering, Cairo, Egypt. Offers M Eng, MS. *Degree requirements:* For master's, thesis. *Entrance requirements:* Additional exam requirements/recommendations for international students: Required—English entrance exam and/or TOEFL. *Faculty research:* Composite materials, superelasticity, expert systems, materials selection.

Arizona State University, Graduate College, Ira A. Fulton School of Engineering, Del E. Webb School of Construction, Tempe, AZ 85287. Offers MS. *Entrance requirements:* For master's, GRE General Test (recommended), minimum GPA of 3.0. Additional exam requirements/recommendations for international students: Required—TOEFL.

Auburn University, Graduate School, College of Architecture, Design, and Construction, Department of Building Science, Auburn University, AL 36849. Offers building science (MBS); construction management (MBS). *Faculty:* 18 full-time (1 woman), 3 part-time/adjunct (1 woman). *Students:* 23 full-time (6 women), 25 part-time (3 women); includes 3 minority (1 African American, 2 Hispanic Americans), 4 international. Average age 27. 83 applicants, 60% accepted, 42 enrolled. In 2009, 7 master's awarded. *Entrance requirements:* For master's, GRE General Test. *Application deadline:* For fall admission, 7/17 for domestic students; for spring admission, 11/24 for domestic students. Applications are processed on a rolling basis. Application fee: $50 ($60 for international students). Electronic applications accepted. *Expenses:* Tuition, state resident: full-time $6240. Tuition, nonresident: full-time $18,720. International tuition: $18,938 full-time. Required fees: $492. Tuition and fees vary according to course load, program and reciprocity agreements. *Financial support:* Application deadline: 3/15; *Unit head:* John D. Murphy, Head, 334-844-4518. *Application contact:* Dr. George Flowers, Dean of the Graduate School, 334-844-2125.

Auburn University, Graduate School, Ginn College of Engineering, Department of Civil Engineering, Auburn University, AL 36849. Offers construction engineering and management (MCE, MS, PhD); environmental engineering (MCE, MS, PhD); geotechnical/materials engineering (MCE, MS, PhD); hydraulics/hydrology (MCE, MS, PhD); structural engineering (MCE, MS, PhD); transportation engineering (MCE, MS, PhD). Part-time programs available. *Faculty:* 21 full-time (1 woman), 3 part-time/adjunct (1 woman). *Students:* 46 full-time (15 women), 39 part-time (5 women); includes 4 minority (3 African Americans, 1 Asian American or Pacific Islander), 29 international. Average age 26. 136 applicants, 43% accepted, 26 enrolled. In 2009, 19 master's, 4 doctorates awarded. *Degree requirements:* For master's, project (MCE), thesis (MS); for doctorate, comprehensive exam, thesis/dissertation. *Entrance requirements:* For master's and doctorate, GRE General Test. *Application deadline:* For fall admission, 7/7 for domestic students; for spring admission, 11/24 for domestic students. Applications are processed on a rolling basis. Application fee: $50 ($60 for international students). Electronic applications accepted. *Expenses:* Tuition, state resident: full-time $6240. Tuition, nonresident: full-time $18,720. International tuition: $18,938 full-time. Required fees: $492. Tuition and fees vary according to course load, program and reciprocity agreements. *Financial support:* Fellowships, research assistantships, teaching assistantships, Federal Work-Study available. Support available to part-time students. Financial award application deadline: 3/15; financial award applicants required to submit FAFSA. *Unit head:* Dr. J. Michael Stallings, Head, 334-844-4320. *Application contact:* Dr. George Flowers, Dean of the Graduate School, 334-844-2125.

Bradley University, Graduate School, College of Engineering and Technology, Department of Civil Engineering and Construction, Peoria, IL 61625-0002. Offers MSCE. Part-time and evening/weekend programs available. *Degree requirements:* For master's, comprehensive exam. *Entrance requirements:* For master's, minimum GPA of 3.0, 2 letters of recommendation. Additional exam requirements/recommendations for international students: Required—TOEFL (minimum score 550 paper-based; 213 computer-based; 79 iBT).

Columbia University, Fu Foundation School of Engineering and Applied Science, Department of Civil Engineering and Engineering Mechanics, New York, NY 10027. Offers civil engineering (MS, Eng Sc D, PhD, Engr); construction engineering and management (MS); engineering mechanics (MS, Eng Sc D, PhD, Engr). Part-time programs available. Postbaccalaureate distance learning degree programs offered (no on-campus study). *Faculty:* 10 full-time (1 woman), 4 part-time/adjunct (0 women). *Students:* 89 full-time (24 women), 48 part-time (16 women); includes 17 minority (2 African Americans, 8 Asian Americans or Pacific Islanders, 7 Hispanic Americans), 72 international. Average age 27. 221 applicants, 54% accepted, 48 enrolled. In 2009, 38 master's, 1 doctorate awarded. Terminal master's awarded for partial completion of doctoral program. *Degree requirements:* For doctorate, thesis/dissertation, qualifying exam. *Entrance requirements:* For master's, doctorate, and Engr, GRE General Test. Additional exam requirements/recommendations for international students: Required—TOEFL. *Application deadline:* For fall admission, 12/1 priority date for domestic and international students; for spring admission, 10/1 priority date for domestic and international students. Application fee: $70. Electronic applications accepted. *Financial support:* In 2009–10, 29 students received support, including 5 fellowships with full tuition reimbursements available

Construction Engineering

Columbia University (continued)
(averaging $33,518 per year), 12 research assistantships with full tuition reimbursements available (averaging $32,761 per year), 12 teaching assistantships with full tuition reimbursements available (averaging $32,761 per year); health care benefits also available. Financial award application deadline: 12/1; financial award applicants required to submit FAFSA. *Faculty research:* Motion monitoring of Manhattan Bridge, lightweight concrete panels, simulation of life of well sealant, intercultural knowledge system dynamics, corrosion monitoring of New York City bridges. *Unit head:* Dr. Upmanu Lall, Interim Chairman and Professor, 212-854-8905, Fax: 212-854-7081, E-mail: lall@civil.columbia.edu. *Application contact:* Rene B. Testa, Professor, 212-854-3143, Fax: 212-854-6267, E-mail: testa@civil.columbia.edu.

Concordia University, School of Graduate Studies, Faculty of Engineering and Computer Science, Department of Building, Civil and Environmental Engineering, Montréal, QC H3G 1M8, Canada. Offers building engineering (M Eng, MA Sc, PhD, Certificate); civil engineering (M Eng, MA Sc, PhD); environmental engineering (Certificate). *Degree requirements:* For master's, thesis or alternative; for doctorate, comprehensive exam, thesis/dissertation. *Faculty research:* Structural engineering, geotechnical engineering, water resources and fluid engineering, transportation engineering, systems engineering.

Illinois Institute of Technology, Graduate College, Armour College of Engineering, Department of Civil, Architectural and Environmental Engineering, Chicago, IL 60616-3793. Offers architectural engineering (M Arch E); civil engineering (MS, PhD); construction engineering and management (MCEM); environmental engineering (M Env E, MS, PhD); geoenvironmental engineering (M Geoenv E); geotechnical engineering (MGE); public works (MPW); structural engineering (MSE); transportation engineering (M Trans E). Part-time and evening/weekend programs available. Terminal master's awarded for partial completion of doctoral program. *Degree requirements:* For master's, thesis (for some programs); for doctorate, comprehensive exam, thesis/dissertation. *Entrance requirements:* For master's and doctorate, GRE General Test, minimum undergraduate GPA of 3.0. Additional exam requirements/recommendations for international students: Required—TOEFL (minimum score 550 paper-based; 213 computer-based; 80 iBT). Electronic applications accepted. *Expenses:* Tuition: Full-time $17,550; part-time $888 per credit hour. Required fees: $850; $7.50 per credit hour. One-time fee: $50 full-time. Full-time tuition and fees vary according to program. *Faculty research:* Seismic analysis of buildings and bridges, fatigue analysis and materials of construction, construction zone safety and construction productivity, architectural acoustics and building energy efficiency, environmental engineering. air and water quality.

Iowa State University of Science and Technology, Graduate College, College of Engineering, Department of Civil and Construction Engineering, Ames, IA 50011. Offers civil engineering (MS, PhD), including civil engineering materials, construction engineering and management, environmental engineering, geometronics, geotechnical engineering, structural engineering, transportation engineering. *Faculty:* 32 full-time (5 women), 6 part-time/adjunct (0 women). *Students:* 87 full-time (20 women), 33 part-time (8 women); includes 2 minority (1 American Indian/Alaska Native, 1 Asian American or Pacific Islander), 48 international. 204 applicants, 29% accepted, 27 enrolled. In 2009, 6 master's, 11 doctorates awarded. *Degree requirements:* For master's, thesis or alternative; for doctorate, thesis/dissertation. *Entrance requirements:* For master's and doctorate, GRE General Test. Additional exam requirements/recommendations for international students: Required—TOEFL (minimum score 550 paper-based; 82 iBT) or IELTS (minimum score 6.5). *Application deadline:* For fall admission, 2/1 priority date for domestic students, 2/1 for international students; for spring admission, 8/1 priority date for domestic students, 8/1 for international students. Application fee: $40 ($90 for international students). Electronic applications accepted. *Expenses:* Tuition, state resident: full-time $6716. Tuition, nonresident: full-time $8908. Tuition and fees vary according to course level, course load, program and student level. *Financial support:* In 2009–10, 70 research assistantships with full and partial tuition reimbursements (averaging $16,000 per year), 4 teaching assistantships with full and partial tuition reimbursements (averaging $18,000 per year) were awarded; fellowships, scholarships/grants, health care benefits, and unspecified assistantships also available. *Unit head:* Dr. James Alleman, Chair, 515-294-3892, E-mail: ccee-grad-inquiry@iastate.edu. *Application contact:* Dr. Sri Srithanan, Director of Graduate Education, 515-294-5328, E-mail: ccee-grad-inquiry@iastate.edu.

Lawrence Technological University, College of Engineering, Southfield, MI 48075-1058. Offers automotive engineering (MAE); civil engineering (MCE); construction engineering management (MS); electrical and computer engineering (MS); engineering management (ME); industrial engineering (MSIE); manufacturing systems (MEMS, DE); mechanical engineering (MS); mechatronic systems engineering (MS). Part-time and evening/weekend programs available. *Faculty:* 20 full-time (4 women), 12 part-time/adjunct (0 women). *Students:* 15 full-time (4 women), 389 part-time (50 women); includes 57 minority (22 African Americans, 1 American Indian/Alaska Native, 30 Asian Americans or Pacific Islanders, 4 Hispanic Americans), 137 international. Average age 31. 361 applicants, 52% accepted, 108 enrolled. In 2009, 161 master's, 1 doctorate awarded. *Degree requirements:* For master's, thesis (for some programs). *Entrance requirements:* Additional exam requirements/recommendations for international students: Required—TOEFL (minimum score 550 paper-based; 213 computer-based; 79 iBT). *Application deadline:* For fall admission, 8/1 priority date for domestic students, 6/1 for international students; for winter admission, 12/1 priority date for domestic students, 10/1 for international students; for spring admission, 5/1 priority date for domestic students, 3/1 for international students. Applications are processed on a rolling basis. Application fee: $50. Electronic applications accepted. *Expenses:* Tuition: Full-time $11,320; part-time $798 per credit hour. *Financial support:* Federal Work-Study and institutionally sponsored loans available. Support available to part-time students. Financial award application deadline: 4/1; financial award applicants required to submit FAFSA. *Faculty research:* Advanced composite materials in bridges, strengthening existing bridges with carbon and glass fiber sheets, development of drive shafts using composite materials. *Unit head:* Dr. Nabil Grace, Interim Dean, 248-204-2500, Fax: 248-204-2509, E-mail: engrdean@ltu.edu. *Application contact:* Jane Rohrback, Director of Admissions, 248-204-3160, Fax: 248-204-3188, E-mail: admissions@ltu.edu.

Massachusetts Institute of Technology, School of Engineering, Department of Civil and Environmental Engineering, Cambridge, MA 02139-4307. Offers biological oceanography (PhD, Sc D); chemical oceanography (PhD, Sc D); civil and environmental engineering (M Eng, SM, PhD, Sc D); civil and environmental systems (PhD, Sc D); civil engineering (PhD, Sc D, CE); coastal engineering (PhD, Sc D); construction engineering and management (PhD, Sc D); environmental biology (PhD, Sc D); environmental chemistry (PhD, Sc D); environmental engineering (PhD, Sc D); environmental fluid mechanics (PhD, Sc D); geotechnical and geoenvironmental engineering (PhD, Sc D); hydrology (PhD, Sc D); information technology (PhD, Sc D); oceanographic engineering (PhD, Sc D); structures and materials (PhD, Sc D); transportation (PhD, Sc D); SM/MBA. *Faculty:* 36 full-time (5 women). *Students:* 190 full-time (59 women); includes 22 minority (2 African Americans, 14 Asian Americans or Pacific Islanders, 6 Hispanic Americans), 103 international. Average age 26. 478 applicants, 25% accepted, 76 enrolled. In 2009, 72 master's, 14 doctorates awarded. *Degree requirements:* For master's and CE, thesis; for doctorate, comprehensive exam, thesis/dissertation. *Entrance requirements:* For master's and doctorate, GRE General Test. Additional exam requirements/recommendations for international students: Required—TOEFL (minimum score 577 paper-based; 233 computer-based; 90 iBT), IELTS (minimum score 7). *Application deadline:* For fall admission, 1/2 for domestic and international students. Application fee: $75. Electronic applications accepted. *Financial support:* In 2009–10, 185 students received support, including 40 fellowships with tuition reimbursements available (averaging $27,725 per year), 97 research assistantships with tuition reimbursements available (averaging $28,035 per year), 21 teaching assistantships with tuition reimbursements available (averaging $24,802 per year); career-related internships or fieldwork, Federal Work-Study, institutionally sponsored loans, scholarships/grants, health care benefits, and unspecified assistantships also available. *Faculty research:* Environmental chemistry, environmental microbiology, environmental fluid mechanics and coastal engineering, geotechnical engineering and geomechanics, hydrology and hydroclimatology, mechanics of materials and structures, operations research/supply chain, transportation. Total annual research expenditures: $16.6 million. *Unit head:* Prof. Andrew Whittle, Department Head, 617-253-7101. *Application contact:* Patricia Glidden, Graduate Admissions Coordinator, 617-253-7119, Fax: 617-258-6775, E-mail: cee-admissions@mit.edu.

Missouri University of Science and Technology, Graduate School, Department of Civil, Architectural, and Environmental Engineering, Rolla, MO 65409. Offers civil engineering (MS, DE, PhD); construction engineering (MS, DE, PhD); environmental engineering (MS); fluid mechanics (MS, DE, PhD); geotechnical engineering (MS, DE, PhD); hydrology and hydraulic engineering (MS, DE, PhD). Part-time and evening/weekend programs available. Terminal master's awarded for partial completion of doctoral program. *Degree requirements:* For master's, thesis optional; for doctorate, comprehensive exam, thesis/dissertation. *Entrance requirements:* For master's, GRE General Test (minimum combined score 1100), minimum GPA of 3.0; for doctorate, GRE General Test (minimum score: verbal and quantitative 400, writing 3.5), minimum GPA of 3.0. Additional exam requirements/recommendations for international students: Required—TOEFL. Electronic applications accepted. *Faculty research:* Earthquake engineering, structural optimization and control systems, structural health monitoring/damage detection, soil-structure interaction, soil mechanics and foundation engineering.

Montana State University, College of Graduate Studies, College of Engineering, Department of Civil Engineering, Bozeman, MT 59717. Offers civil engineering (MS); construction engineering management (MCEM); engineering (PhD), including applied mechanics option, civil engineering option. Part-time programs available. *Faculty:* 19 full-time (2 women), 2 part-time/adjunct (0 women). *Students:* 24 full-time (7 women), 16 part-time (3 women); includes 1 minority (American Indian/Alaska Native), 1 international. Average age 26. 36 applicants, 50% accepted, 16 enrolled. In 2009, 15 master's, 2 doctorates awarded. *Degree requirements:* For master's, comprehensive exam, thesis (for some programs); for doctorate, comprehensive exam, thesis/dissertation. *Entrance requirements:* For master's and doctorate, GRE General Test. Additional exam requirements/recommendations for international students: Required—TOEFL (minimum score 550 paper-based; 213 computer-based). *Application deadline:* For fall admission, 7/15 priority date for domestic students, 5/15 priority date for international students; for spring admission, 12/1 priority date for domestic students, 10/1 priority date for international students. Applications are processed on a rolling basis. Application fee: $30. Electronic applications accepted. *Expenses:* Tuition, state resident: full-time $5635; part-time $3492 per year. Tuition, nonresident: full-time $17,212; part-time $7865.10 per year. Required fees: $1441.05; $153.15 per credit. Tuition and fees vary according to course load and program. *Financial support:* In 2009–10, 15 students received support, including 1 research assistantship with partial tuition reimbursement available (averaging $24,000 per year), 5 teaching assistantships with partial tuition reimbursements available (averaging $8,000 per year); scholarships/grants and tuition waivers (partial) also available. Financial award application deadline: 3/1; financial award applicants required to submit FAFSA. *Faculty research:* Snow and ice mechanics, biofilm engineering, transportation, structural and geo materials, water resources. Total annual research expenditures: $714,709. *Unit head:* Dr. Brett Gunnick, Head, 406-994-2111, Fax: 406-994-6105, E-mail: bgunnick@ce.montana.edu. *Application contact:* Dr. Carl A. Fox, Vice Provost for Graduate Education, 406-994-4145, Fax: 406-994-7433, E-mail: gradstudy@montana.edu.

Ohio University, Graduate College, Russ College of Engineering and Technology, Department of Civil Engineering, Athens, OH 45701-2979. Offers civil engineering (PhD); construction (MS); environmental (MS); geotechnical and geoenvironmental (MS); mechanics (MS); structures (MS); transportation (MS); water resources and structures (MS). Part-time programs available. *Faculty:* 13 full-time (3 women), 3 part-time/adjunct (0 women). *Students:* 18 full-time (2 women), 2 part-time (1 woman), 13 international. 22 applicants, 68% accepted, 1 enrolled. In 2009, 7 master's awarded. *Degree requirements:* For master's, comprehensive exam (for some programs), thesis or alternative; for doctorate, comprehensive exam, thesis/dissertation. *Entrance requirements:* For master's, GRE General Test, minimum GPA of 3.0, 3 letters of recommendation; for doctorate, GRE General Test. Additional exam requirements/recommendations for international students: Required—TOEFL (minimum score 550 paper-based; 80 iBT) or IELTS Academic (minimum score 6.5). *Application deadline:* For fall admission, 5/1 priority date for domestic students, 2/1 priority date for international students; for winter admission, 8/1 priority date for domestic students, 4/1 priority date for international students; for spring admission, 2/1 priority date for domestic students, 7/1 priority date for international students. Applications are processed on a rolling basis. Application fee: $50 ($55 for international students). Electronic applications accepted. *Expenses:* Tuition, state resident: full-time $7839; part-time $323 per quarter hour. Tuition, nonresident: full-time $15,831; part-time $654 per quarter hour. Required fees: $2931. *Financial support:* Research assistantships with full tuition reimbursements, teaching assistantships with full tuition reimbursements, Federal Work-Study, institutionally sponsored loans, scholarships/grants, and unspecified assistantships available. Financial award application deadline: 3/15; financial award applicants required to submit FAFSA. *Faculty research:* Noise abatement, materials and environment, highway infrastructure, subsurface investigation, (pavements, pipes, bridges, etc.). Total annual research expenditures: $1.2 million. *Unit head:* Dr. Gayle F. Mitchell, Chair, 740-593-0430, Fax: 740-593-0625, E-mail: mitchelg@ohio.edu. *Application contact:* Dr. Shad M. Sargand, Graduate Chair, 740-593-1465, Fax: 740-593-0625, E-mail: sargand@ohio.edu.

Oregon State University, Graduate School, College of Engineering, School of Civil and Construction Engineering, Corvallis, OR 97331. Offers civil engineering (MS, PhD); coastal and ocean engineering (M Oc E, PhD); coastal engineering (MS); construction engineering management (MBE, PhD); engineering (M Eng, MAIS); geotechnical engineering (MS, PhD); structural engineering (MS, PhD); transportation engineering (MS, PhD); water engineering (MS, PhD). Part-time programs available. *Faculty:* 25 full-time (5 women), 1 part-time/adjunct (0 women). *Students:* 71 full-time (17 women), 12 part-time (2 women); includes 4 minority (all Asian Americans or Pacific Islanders), 34 international. Average age 28. 75 applicants, 87% accepted, 31 enrolled. In 2009, 26 master's, 7 doctorates awarded. Terminal master's awarded for partial completion of doctoral program. *Degree requirements:* For master's, thesis or alternative; for doctorate, one foreign language, thesis/dissertation. *Entrance requirements:* For master's, GRE General Test, minimum GPA of 3.0 in last 90 hours (3.5 for MS); for doctorate, GRE General Test, minimum GPA of 3.0 in last 90 hours of undergraduate course work. Additional exam requirements/recommendations for international students: Required—TOEFL (minimum score 580 paper-based; 237 computer-based). *Application deadline:* For fall admission, 3/1 priority date for domestic students. Applications are processed on a rolling basis. Application fee: $50. *Expenses:* Tuition, state resident: full-time $9774; part-time $362 per credit. Tuition, nonresident: full-time $15,849; part-time $587 per credit. Required fees: $1639. Full-time tuition and fees vary according to course load and program. *Financial support:* Fellowships, research assistantships with full tuition reimbursements, teaching assistantships with full tuition reimbursements, career-related internships or fieldwork and institutionally sponsored loans available. Support available to part-time students. Financial award application deadline: 2/1. *Faculty research:* Hazardous waste management, carbon cycling, wave forces on structures, pavement design, seismic analysis. Total annual research expenditures: $7.1 million. *Unit head:* Dr. Scott A. Ashford, Head, 541-737-4934. *Application contact:* Kathy Westberg, CCE Graduate Advising School Operations Manager, 541-737-1786, Fax: 541-737-3052, E-mail: kathy.westberg@oregonstate.edu.

Pontificia Universidad Catolica Madre y Maestra, Graduate School, Santiago, Dominican Republic. Offers administration (M Adm); architecture of interiors (M Arch); architecture of tourist lodgings (M Arch); banking and financial management (M Mgmt); civil law (LL M); construction administration (ME); corporate business law (LL M); criminal procedure law (LL M); environmental engineering (ME, MEE); finance (M Mgmt); history applied to education (M Ed); human resources (EMBA); insurance (M Mgmt); international business (M Mgmt); labor law and Social Security (LL M); logistics management (ME); marketing (M Mgmt); renewable energy (ME); strategic cost management (M Mgmt). *Entrance requirements:* For master's, curriculum vitae, interview.

Stevens Institute of Technology, Graduate School, Charles V. Schaefer Jr. School of Engineering, Department of Civil, Environmental, and Ocean Engineering, Program in

Construction Management, Hoboken, NJ 07030. Offers construction accounting/estimating (Certificate); construction engineering (Certificate); construction law/disputes (Certificate); construction management (MS); construction/quality management (Certificate). *Degree requirements:* For master's, thesis optional. *Entrance requirements:* For master's, GMAT, GRE General Test. Additional exam requirements/recommendations for international students: Required—TOEFL. Electronic applications accepted. *Expenses:* Tuition: Full-time $9900; part-time $1100 per credit. Required fees: $286 per semester.

Texas A&M University, College of Architecture, Department of Construction Science, College Station, TX 77843. Offers construction management (MS). *Faculty:* 15. *Students:* 85 full-time (26 women), 5 part-time (1 woman); includes 2 minority (both Asian Americans or Pacific Islanders), 76 international. Average age 30. In 2009, 42 master's awarded. *Degree requirements:* For master's, comprehensive exam. *Entrance requirements:* For master's, GRE General Test. Additional exam requirements/recommendations for international students: Required—TOEFL. *Application deadline:* For fall admission, 4/1 priority date for domestic students; for winter admission, 1/1 priority date for domestic students; for spring admission, 9/1 priority date for domestic students. Applications are processed on a rolling basis. Application fee: $50 ($75 for international students). Electronic applications accepted. *Expenses:* Tuition, state resident: full-time $3991.32; part-time $221.74 per credit hour. Tuition, nonresident: full-time $9049; part-time $502.74 per credit hour. *Financial support:* In 2009–10, fellowships with partial tuition reimbursements (averaging $1,000 per year), research assistantships with partial tuition reimbursements (averaging $9,000 per year), teaching assistantships with partial tuition reimbursements (averaging $9,000 per year) were awarded. Financial award application deadline: 4/1; financial award applicants required to submit FAFSA. *Faculty research:* Fire safety, housing foundations, construction project management, quality management.

Texas A&M University, College of Engineering, Zachry Department of Civil Engineering, College Station, TX 77843. Offers construction engineering and management (M Eng, MS, D Eng, PhD); environmental engineering (M Eng, MS, D Eng, PhD); geotechnical engineering (M Eng, MS, D Eng, PhD); materials engineering (M Eng, MS, D Eng, PhD); ocean engineering (M Eng, MS, D Eng, PhD); structural engineering (M Eng, MS, D Eng, PhD); transportation engineering (M Eng, MS, D Eng, PhD); water resources engineering (M Eng, MS, D Eng, PhD). Part-time programs available. *Faculty:* 61. *Students:* 390 full-time (89 women), 42 part-time (6 women); includes 23 minority (2 African Americans, 11 Asian Americans or Pacific Islanders, 10 Hispanic Americans), 281 international. Average age 29. In 2009, 100 master's, 36 doctorates awarded. *Degree requirements:* For master's, thesis (MS); for doctorate, dissertation (PhD), internship (D Eng). *Entrance requirements:* For master's and doctorate, GRE General Test. Additional exam requirements/recommendations for international students: Required—TOEFL. *Application deadline:* Applications are processed on a rolling basis. Application fee: $50 ($75 for international students). Electronic applications accepted. *Expenses:* Tuition, state resident: full-time $3991.32; part-time $221.74 per credit hour. Tuition, nonresident: full-time $9049; part-time $502.74 per credit hour. *Financial support:* In 2009–10, fellowships (averaging $4,500 per year), research assistantships (averaging $14,000 per year), teaching assistantships (averaging $14,400 per year) were awarded; career-related internships or fieldwork and institutionally sponsored loans also available. Financial award application deadline: 4/15; financial award applicants required to submit FAFSA. *Unit head:* Dr. Tony Cahill, Head, 979-845-2438, E-mail: t-cahill@civil.tamu.edu. *Application contact:* Graduate Advisor, 979-845-2498, Fax: 979-862-2800, E-mail: ce-grad@tamu.edu.

Universidad Nacional Pedro Henriquez Urena, Graduate School, Santo Domingo, Dominican Republic. Offers administrative sciences (PhD); business administration (MBA); environmental engineering (MEE); project management (M Man, MPM); sanitation engineering (ME); veterinary medicine (DVM).

The University of Alabama, Graduate School, College of Engineering, Department of Civil, Construction and Environmental Engineering, Tuscaloosa, AL 35487-0205. Offers civil engineering (MSCE, PhD); environmental engineering (MS). Part-time programs available. *Faculty:* 20 full-time (2 women). *Students:* 39 full-time (11 women), 10 part-time (4 women); includes 9 minority (7 African Americans, 1 American Indian/Alaska Native, 1 Asian American or Pacific Islander), 18 international. Average age 30. 68 applicants, 26% accepted, 12 enrolled. In 2009, 16 master's, 1 doctorate awarded. Terminal master's awarded for partial completion of doctoral program. *Median time to degree:* Of those who began their doctoral program in fall 2001, 100% received their degree in 8 years or less. *Degree requirements:* For master's, thesis or alternative; for doctorate, one foreign language, thesis/dissertation. *Entrance requirements:* For master's and doctorate, GRE General Test, minimum GPA of 3.0 in last 60 hours of course work. Additional exam requirements/recommendations for international students: Required—TOEFL (minimum score 550 paper-based; 213 computer-based), IELTS (minimum score 6.5). *Application deadline:* For fall admission, 7/6 for domestic students, 1/15 for international students; for spring admission, 11/1 for domestic students, 6/1 for international students. Applications are processed on a rolling basis. Application fee: $50 ($60 for international students). Electronic applications accepted. *Expenses:* Tuition, state resident: full-time $7000. Tuition, nonresident: full-time $19,200. *Financial support:* In 2009–10, 40 students received support, including 32 research assistantships with full tuition reimbursements available (averaging $10,489 per year), 12 teaching assistantships with full tuition reimbursements available (averaging $10,489 per year); fellowships, scholarships/grants, tuition waivers (partial), and unspecified assistantships also available. Financial award application deadline: 3/15. *Faculty research:* Experimental structures, modeling of structures, bridge management systems, geotechnological engineering, environmental remediation. Total annual research expenditures: $2.3 million. *Unit head:* Dr. Kenneth J. Fridley, Head and Professor, 205-348-6550, Fax: 205-348-0783, E-mail: kfridley@coe.eng.ua.edu. *Application contact:* Dr. David A. Francko, Dean, 205-348-8280, Fax: 205-348-0400, E-mail: dfrancko@ua.edu.

University of Alberta, Faculty of Graduate Studies and Research, Department of Civil and Environmental Engineering, Edmonton, AB T6G 2E1, Canada. Offers construction engineering and management (M Eng, M Sc, PhD); environmental engineering (M Eng, M Sc, PhD); environmental science (M Sc, PhD); geoenvironmental engineering (M Eng, M Sc, PhD); geotechnical engineering (M Eng, M Sc, PhD); mining engineering (M Eng, M Sc, PhD); petroleum engineering (M Eng, M Sc, PhD); structural engineering (M Eng, M Sc, PhD); water resources (M Eng, M Sc, PhD). Part-time programs available. Postbaccalaureate distance learning degree programs offered (minimal on-campus study). *Faculty:* 44 full-time (3 women), 2 part-time/adjunct (0 women). *Students:* 215 full-time (49 women), 99 part-time (19 women). 1,428 applicants, 15% accepted, 123 enrolled. In 2009, 124 master's, 34 doctorates awarded. *Degree requirements:* For master's, thesis (for some programs); for doctorate, thesis/dissertation. *Entrance requirements:* For master's, minimum GPA of 3.0 in last 2 years of undergraduate studies; for doctorate, minimum GPA of 3.0. Additional exam requirements/recommendations for international students: Required—TOEFL (minimum score 550 paper-based; 213 computer-based). *Application deadline:* For fall admission, 6/1 priority date for domestic students, 6/1 for international students; for winter admission, 11/1 for domestic students, 9/15 for international students. Applications are processed on a rolling basis. Application fee: $0 Canadian dollars. Electronic applications accepted. Tuition and fees charges are reported in Canadian dollars. *Expenses:* Tuition, area resident: Full-time $4626.24 Canadian dollars; part-time $99.72 Canadian dollars per unit. International tuition: $8216 Canadian dollars full-time. Required fees: $3589.92 Canadian dollars; $99.72 Canadian dollars per unit. $215 Canadian dollars per term. *Financial support:* In 2009–10, 88 research assistantships with full and partial tuition reimbursements, 134 teaching assistantships with full and partial tuition reimbursements were awarded; scholarships/grants and tuition waivers (full and partial) also available. Financial award application deadline: 4/1. *Faculty research:* Mining. Total annual research expenditures: $6,791 Canadian dollars. *Unit head:* Dr. David Zhu, Associate Chair, Graduate Studies, 780-492-1198, Fax: 403-492-8198. *Application contact:* Gwen Mendoza, Student Services Officer, 403-492-1539, Fax: 403-492-0249, E-mail: civegrad@ualberta.ca.

University of Central Florida, College of Engineering and Computer Science, Department of Civil, Environmental, and Construction Engineering, Program in Civil Engineering, Orlando, FL 32816. Offers civil engineering (MS, MSCE, PhD); construction engineering (Certificate); structural engineering (Certificate); transportation engineering (Certificate). Part-time and evening/weekend programs available. *Students:* 53 full-time (8 women), 68 part-time (20 women); includes 22 minority (4 African Americans, 1 American Indian/Alaska Native, 5 Asian Americans or Pacific Islanders, 12 Hispanic Americans), 34 international. Average age 29. 90 applicants, 73% accepted, 45 enrolled. In 2009, 30 master's, 2 doctorates awarded. *Degree requirements:* For master's, thesis or alternative; for doctorate, thesis/dissertation, departmental qualifying exam, candidacy exam. *Entrance requirements:* For master's, GRE General Test, minimum GPA of 3.0 in last 60 hours; for doctorate, GRE General Test, minimum GPA of 3.5 in last 60 hours. Additional exam requirements/recommendations for international students: Required—TOEFL. *Application deadline:* For fall admission, 7/15 priority date for domestic students; for spring admission, 12/15 priority date for domestic students. Application fee: $30. Electronic applications accepted. *Expenses:* Tuition, state resident: part-time $306.31 per credit hour. Tuition, nonresident: part-time $1099.01 per credit hour. Part-time tuition and fees vary according to degree level and program. *Financial support:* In 2009–10, 30 students received support, including 7 fellowships with partial tuition reimbursements available (averaging $7,100 per year), 19 research assistantships with partial tuition reimbursements available (averaging $11,600 per year), 12 teaching assistantships with partial tuition reimbursements available (averaging $9,700 per year); career-related internships or fieldwork, Federal Work-Study, institutionally sponsored loans, tuition waivers (partial), and unspecified assistantships also available. Financial award application deadline: 3/1; financial award applicants required to submit FAFSA.

University of Colorado at Boulder, Graduate School, College of Engineering and Applied Science, Department of Civil, Environmental, and Architectural Engineering, Boulder, CO 80309. Offers building systems (MS, PhD); construction engineering management (MS, PhD); environmental engineering (MS, PhD); geotechnical engineering and geomechanics (MS, PhD); hydrology, water resources and environmental fluid mechanics (MS, PhD); structural engineering and structural mechanics (MS, PhD). *Faculty:* 39 full-time (5 women). *Students:* 202 full-time (62 women), 29 part-time (6 women); includes 34 minority (3 African Americans, 3 American Indian/Alaska Native, 12 Asian Americans or Pacific Islanders, 16 Hispanic Americans), 53 international. Average age 29. 384 applicants, 44% accepted, 80 enrolled. In 2009, 60 master's, 7 doctorates awarded. *Degree requirements:* For master's, comprehensive exam, thesis or alternative; for doctorate, thesis/dissertation. *Entrance requirements:* For master's, GRE General Test, minimum undergraduate GPA of 3.0. *Application deadline:* For fall admission, 3/1 for domestic students, 12/1 for international students; for spring admission, 10/31 for domestic students, 10/1 for international students. Application fee: $50 ($60 for international students). *Financial support:* In 2009–10, 45 fellowships (averaging $7,876 per year), 68 research assistantships (averaging $15,204 per year) were awarded. Financial award application deadline: 1/15. *Faculty research:* Building systems engineering, construction engineering and management, environmental engineering, geoenvironmental engineering, geotechnical engineering, materials and mechanics, structural engineering, water resources engineering, life-cycle engineering. Total annual research expenditures: $6.1 million.

University of Florida, Graduate School, College of Design, Construction and Planning, M. E. Rinker, Sr. School of Building Construction, Gainesville, FL 32611. Offers MBC, MICM, MSBC, PhD. Part-time programs available. *Degree requirements:* For master's, thesis. *Entrance requirements:* For master's, GRE General Test, minimum GPA of 3.0. Additional exam requirements/recommendations for international students: Required—TOEFL. Electronic applications accepted. *Faculty research:* Safety, affordable housing, construction management, environmental issues, sustainable construction.

University of Michigan, Horace H. Rackham School of Graduate Studies, College of Engineering, Department of Civil and Environmental Engineering, Ann Arbor, MI 48109. Offers civil engineering (MSE, PhD, CE); construction engineering and management (M Eng, MSE); environmental engineering (MSE, PhD); structural engineering (M Eng); MBA/MSE. Part-time programs available. *Faculty:* 28 full-time (8 women). *Students:* 104 full-time (34 women), 1 part-time (0 women); includes 9 minority (2 African Americans, 5 Asian Americans or Pacific Islanders, 2 Hispanic Americans), 49 international. 413 applicants, 29% accepted, 40 enrolled. In 2009, 47 master's, 18 doctorates awarded. *Degree requirements:* For master's, thesis optional; for doctorate, comprehensive exam, thesis/dissertation, oral defense of dissertation, preliminary and written exams. *Entrance requirements:* For master's and doctorate, GRE General Test. Additional exam requirements/recommendations for international students: Required—TOEFL (minimum score 560 paper-based; 220 computer-based). *Application deadline:* Applications are processed on a rolling basis. Application fee: $60 ($75 for international students). Electronic applications accepted. *Expenses:* Tuition, state resident: full-time $17,286; part-time $1099 per credit hour. Tuition, nonresident: full-time $34,944; part-time $2080 per credit hour. Required fees: $95 per semester. Tuition and fees vary according to course load, degree level and program. *Financial support:* Fellowships, research assistantships, teaching assistantships, institutionally sponsored loans and tuition waivers (partial) available. Financial award application deadline: 1/19. *Faculty research:* Construction engineering and management; geotechnical engineering; earthquake-resistant design of structures; environmental chemistry and microbiology; cost engineering; environmental and water resources engineering. *Unit head:* Nancy Love, Chair, 734-764-8405, Fax: 734-764-4292, E-mail: nglove@umich.edu. *Application contact:* Kimberly Smith, Student Advisor, 734-764-8405, Fax: 734-647-2127, E-mail: kansmith@umich.edu.

University of New Brunswick Fredericton, School of Graduate Studies, Faculty of Engineering, Department of Civil Engineering, Fredericton, NB E3B 5A3, Canada. Offers construction engineering and management (M Eng, M Sc E, PhD); environmental engineering (M Eng, M Sc E, PhD); environmental studies (M Eng); geotechnical engineering (M Eng, M Sc E, PhD); groundwater/hydrology (M Eng, M Sc E, PhD); materials (M Eng, M Sc E, PhD); pavements (M Eng, M Sc E, PhD); structures (M Eng, M Sc E, PhD); transportation (M Eng, M Sc E, PhD). Part-time programs available. *Faculty:* 18 full-time (1 woman), 1 (woman) part-time/adjunct. *Students:* 42 full-time (9 women), 18 part-time (2 women). In 2009, 11 master's, 4 doctorates awarded. *Degree requirements:* For master's, thesis, proposal; for doctorate, comprehensive exam, thesis/dissertation, Qualifying exam; Proposal; 27 credit hours of courses. *Entrance requirements:* For master's, Minimum GPA of 3.0; BScE in Civil Engineering or related engineering degree.; for doctorate, Minimum GPA of 3.0; Candidates are normally required to have a graduate degree in engineering or applied science. Additional exam requirements/recommendations for international students: Required—TOEFL (minimum score 580 paper-based; 237 computer-based), TWE (minimum score 4), or IELTS (minimum score 7.5). *Application deadline:* For fall admission, 5/1 priority date for domestic students; for winter admission, 11/1 priority date for domestic students. Applications are processed on a rolling basis. Application fee: $50 Canadian dollars. Tuition and fees charges are reported in Canadian dollars. *Expenses:* Tuition, area resident: Full-time $5562 Canadian dollars; part-time $2781 Canadian dollars per year. Required fees: $49.75 Canadian dollars per term. *Financial support:* In 2009–10, 51 research assistantships (averaging $7,000 per year), 43 teaching assistantships (averaging $2,000 per year) were awarded; career-related internships or fieldwork and scholarships/grants also available. *Faculty research:* Construction engineering and management, concrete materials and structural engineering, transportation and asset management, geotechnical engineering, water and environmental engineering. *Unit head:* Dr. Eric Hildebrand, Director of Graduate Studies, 506-453-5113, Fax: 506-453-3568, E-mail: ktm@unb.ca. *Application contact:* Joyce Moore, Graduate Secretary, 506-452-6127, Fax: 506-453-3568, E-mail: civil-grad@unb.ca.

University of Southern Mississippi, Graduate School, College of Science and Technology, School of Construction, Hattiesburg, MS 39406-0001. Offers architecture and construction visualization (MS); construction management and technology (MS); logistics management and technology (MS). Part-time programs available. *Faculty:* 6 full-time (0 women). *Students:* 13 full-time (4 women), 7 part-time (2 women); includes 3 minority (all African Americans), 2 international. Average age 31. 19 applicants, 74% accepted, 9 enrolled. In 2009, 13 master's awarded. *Degree requirements:* For master's, comprehensive exam, thesis optional. *Entrance*

Construction Engineering

University of Southern Mississippi (continued)

requirements: For master's, GMAT or GRE General Test, minimum GPA of 2.75 in last 60 hours. Additional exam requirements/recommendations for international students: Required—TOEFL. *Application deadline:* For fall admission, 3/1 priority date for domestic students, 3/1 for international students. Applications are processed on a rolling basis. Application fee: $35. *Expenses:* Tuition, state resident: full-time $5096; part-time $284 per hour. Tuition, nonresident: full-time $13,052; part-time $726 per hour. Required fees: $402. Tuition and fees vary according to course level and course load. *Financial support:* In 2009–10, 7 teaching assistantships (averaging $6,947 per year) were awarded; research assistantships, career-related internships or fieldwork and Federal Work-Study also available. Financial award application deadline: 3/15; financial award applicants required to submit FAFSA. *Faculty research:* Robotics; CAD/CAM; simulation; computer-integrated manufacturing processes; construction scheduling, estimating, and computer systems. *Unit head:* Dr. Desmond Fletcher, Director, 601-266-5185. *Application contact:* Shonna Breland, Graduate Admissions, 601-266-6563.

University of Washington, Graduate School, College of Engineering, Department of Civil and Environmental Engineering, Seattle, WA 98195-2700. Offers construction engineering (MSCE); environmental engineering (MS, MSCE, MSE, PhD); hydrology, water resources, and environmental fluid mechanics (MS, MSCE, MSE, PhD); structural and geotechnical engineering and mechanics (MS, MSCE, MSE, PhD); transportation and construction engineering (MS, MSE, PhD); transportation engineering (MSCE). Part-time programs available. Postbaccalaureate distance learning degree programs offered (no on-campus study). *Faculty:* 36 full-time (9 women), 16 part-time/adjunct (6 women). *Students:* 186 full-time (62 women), 57 part-time (10 women); includes 35 minority (24 Asian Americans or Pacific Islanders, 11 Hispanic Americans), 58 international. 360 applicants, 68% accepted, 98 enrolled. In 2009, 74 master's, 8 doctorates awarded. Terminal master's awarded for partial completion of doctoral program. *Degree requirements:* For master's, thesis (for some programs); for doctorate, comprehensive exam, thesis/dissertation. *Entrance requirements:* For master's, GRE General Test, minimum GPA of 3.0; for doctorate, GRE, minimum GPA of 3.5. Additional exam requirements/recommendations for international students: Required—TOEFL (minimum score 580 paper-based; 237 computer-based; 70 iBT). *Application deadline:* For fall admission, 1/15 priority date for domestic and international students. Applications are processed on a rolling basis. Application fee: $65. Electronic applications accepted. *Financial support:* In 2009–10, 5 students received support, including 13 fellowships with full and partial tuition reimbursements available (averaging $16,173 per year), 68 research assistantships with full tuition reimbursements available (averaging $16,173 per year), 12 teaching assistantships with full tuition reimbursements available (averaging $16,173 per year); scholarships/grants also available. Financial award application deadline: 1/15. *Faculty research:* Environmental/water resources, hydrology; construction/transportation; structures/ geotechnical. Total annual research expenditures: $11.4 million. *Unit head:* Dr. Gregory R. Miller, Professor and Chair, 206-543-0350, Fax: 206-543-1543, E-mail: gmiller@uw.edu. *Application contact:* Lorna Latal, Graduate Adviser, 206-543-2574, Fax: 206-543-1543, E-mail: llatal@u.washington.edu.

Virginia Polytechnic Institute and State University, Graduate School, College of Architecture and Urban Studies, Department of Building Construction, Blacksburg, VA 24061. Offers MS. *Entrance requirements:* Additional exam requirements/recommendations for international students: Required—TOEFL. Electronic applications accepted.

Western Michigan University, Graduate College, College of Engineering and Applied Sciences, Department of Civil and Construction Engineering, Kalamazoo, MI 49008. Offers civil engineering (MS), including construction engineering and management, structural engineering, transportation engineering. *Entrance requirements:* For master's, minimum GPA of 3.0.

Environmental Engineering

Air Force Institute of Technology, Graduate School of Engineering and Management, Department of Systems and Engineering Management, Dayton, OH 45433-7765. Offers cost analysis (MS); environmental and engineering management (MS); environmental engineering science (MS); information resource/systems management (MS). *Accreditation:* ABET. Part-time programs available. *Degree requirements:* For master's, thesis. *Entrance requirements:* For master's, GRE, GMAT, minimum GPA of 3.0.

Arizona State University, Graduate College, Ira A. Fulton School of Engineering, Department of Civil and Environmental Engineering, Tempe, AZ 85287. Offers MS, MSE, PhD. *Degree requirements:* For master's, thesis or alternative; for doctorate, thesis/dissertation. *Entrance requirements:* For master's and doctorate, GRE General Test (recommended).

Auburn University, Graduate School, Ginn College of Engineering, Department of Civil Engineering, Auburn University, AL 36849. Offers construction engineering and management (MCE, MS, PhD); environmental engineering (MCE, MS, PhD); geotechnical/materials engineering (MCE, MS, PhD); hydraulics/hydrology (MCE, MS, PhD); structural engineering (MCE, MS, PhD); transportation engineering (MCE, MS, PhD). Part-time programs available. *Faculty:* 21 full-time (1 woman), 3 part-time/adjunct (1 woman). *Students:* 46 full-time (15 women), 39 part-time (5 women); includes 4 minority (3 African Americans, 1 Asian American or Pacific Islander), 29 international. Average age 26. 136 applicants, 43% accepted, 26 enrolled. In 2009, 19 master's, 4 doctorates awarded. *Degree requirements:* For master's, project (MCE), thesis (MS); for doctorate, comprehensive exam, thesis/dissertation. *Entrance requirements:* For master's and doctorate, GRE General Test. *Application deadline:* For fall admission, 7/7 for domestic students; for spring admission, 11/24 for domestic students. Applications are processed on a rolling basis. Application fee: $50 ($60 for international students). Electronic applications accepted. *Expenses:* Tuition, state resident: full-time $6240. Tuition, nonresident: full-time $18,720. International tuition: $18,938 full-time. Required fees: $492. Tuition and fees vary according to course load, program and reciprocity agreements. *Financial support:* Fellowships, research assistantships, teaching assistantships, Federal Work-Study available. Support available to part-time students. Financial award application deadline: 3/15; financial award applicants required to submit FAFSA. *Unit head:* Dr. J. Michael Stallings, Head, 334-844-4320. *Application contact:* Dr. George Flowers, Dean of the Graduate School, 334-844-2125.

California Institute of Technology, Division of Engineering and Applied Science, Option in Environmental Science and Engineering, Pasadena, CA 91125-0001. Offers MS, PhD. *Faculty:* 5 full-time (1 woman). *Students:* 23 full-time (9 women). 57 applicants, 18% accepted, 3 enrolled. In 2009, 6 master's, 2 doctorates awarded. *Degree requirements:* For doctorate, thesis/dissertation. *Application deadline:* For fall admission, 1/1 for domestic students. Application fee: $0. Electronic applications accepted. *Financial support:* In 2009–10, 6 fellowships, 14 research assistantships, 4 teaching assistantships were awarded. *Faculty research:* Chemistry of natural waters, physics and chemistry of particulates, fluid mechanics of the natural environment, pollutant formation and control, environmental modeling systems. *Unit head:* Dr. Paul O. Wennberg, Executive Officer, 626-395-2447, E-mail: wennberg@gps.caltech.edu. *Application contact:* Natalie Gilmore, Assistant Dean of Graduate Studies, 626-395-3812, Fax: 626-577-9246, E-mail: ngilmore@caltech.edu.

California Polytechnic State University, San Luis Obispo, College of Engineering, Department of Civil and Environmental Engineering, San Luis Obispo, CA 93407. Offers MS. Part-time programs available. *Faculty:* 11 full-time (1 woman), 2 part-time/adjunct (0 women). *Students:* 40 full-time (7 women), 4 part-time (1 woman); includes 5 minority (2 Asian Americans or Pacific Islanders, 3 Hispanic Americans). Average age 24. 58 applicants, 57% accepted, 28 enrolled. In 2009, 17 master's awarded. *Degree requirements:* For master's, comprehensive exam (for some programs), thesis (for some programs). *Entrance requirements:* For master's, GRE General Test, minimum GPA of 3.0 in last 90 quarter units, 3 letters of recommendation. Additional exam requirements/recommendations for international students: Required—TOEFL (minimum score 550 paper-based; 213 computer-based). *Application deadline:* For fall admission, 7/1 for domestic students, 11/30 for international students; for winter admission, 11/1 for domestic students, 6/30 for international students; for spring admission, 2/1 for domestic students. Applications are processed on a rolling basis. Application fee: $55. Electronic applications accepted. *Expenses:* Tuition, nonresident: full-time $11,160; part-time $248 per unit. Required fees: $7134; $1553 per quarter. *Financial support:* Fellowships, research assistantships, teaching assistantships, career-related internships or fieldwork, Federal Work-Study, and scholarships/grants available. Support available to part-time students. Financial award application deadline: 3/2; financial award applicants required to submit FAFSA. *Faculty research:* Soils, structures, transportation, traffic, environmental protection. *Unit head:* Dr. Robb Moss, Graduate Coordinator, 805-756-6427, Fax: 805-756-6330, E-mail: rmoss@calpoly.edu. *Application contact:* Dr. Robb Moss, Graduate Coordinator, 805-756-6427, Fax: 805-756-6330, E-mail: rmoss@calpoly.edu.

Carleton University, Faculty of Graduate Studies, Faculty of Engineering and Design, Department of Civil and Environmental Engineering, Ottawa, ON K1S 5B6, Canada. Offers M Eng, MA Sc, PhD. *Degree requirements:* For master's, thesis optional; for doctorate, thesis/dissertation. *Entrance requirements:* For master's, honors degree; for doctorate, MA Sc or M Eng. Additional exam requirements/recommendations for international students: Required—TOEFL. *Faculty research:* Pollution and wastewater management, fire safety engineering, earthquake engineering, structural design, bridge engineering.

Carnegie Mellon University, Carnegie Institute of Technology, Department of Civil and Environmental Engineering, Pittsburgh, PA 15213. Offers civil and environmental engineering (PhD); advanced infrastructure systems (MS, PhD); civil and environmental engineering (MS); civil and environmental engineering/engineering and public policy (PhD); civil engineering (MS, PhD); computational mechanics (MS, PhD); computational science and engineering (MS, PhD); environmental engineering (MS, PhD); environmental management and science (MS, PhD). Part-time programs available. *Faculty:* 19 full-time (3 women), 13 part-time/adjunct (3 women). *Students:* 118 full-time (48 women), 12 part-time (6 women); includes 15 minority (4 African Americans, 10 Asian Americans or Pacific Islanders, 1 Hispanic American), 78 international. Average age 26. 294 applicants, 75% accepted, 78 enrolled. In 2009, 55 master's, 10 doctorates awarded. Terminal master's awarded for partial completion of doctoral program. *Degree requirements:* For master's, thesis optional; for doctorate, comprehensive exam, thesis/dissertation, qualifying exam, public defense of dissertation. *Entrance requirements:* For master's and doctorate, GRE General Test. Additional exam requirements/recommendations for international students: Required—TOEFL (minimum score 550 paper-based; 213 computer-based; 82 iBT). *Application deadline:* For fall admission, 1/15 priority date for domestic and international students; for spring admission, 9/30 priority date for domestic and international students. Application fee: $65. Electronic applications accepted. *Financial support:* In 2009–10, 102 students received support, including 18 fellowships with full and partial tuition reimbursements available (averaging $22,853 per year), 34 research assistantships with full and partial tuition reimbursements available (averaging $23,661 per year); tuition waivers (partial) and unspecified assistantships also available. Financial award application deadline: 1/15. *Faculty research:* Advanced infrastructure systems; environmental engineering science and management; mechanics, materials, and computing; green design; global sustainable construction. Total annual research expenditures: $4.5 million. *Unit head:* Dr. James H. Garrett, Head, 412-268-2941, Fax: 412-268-7813, E-mail: garrett@cmu.edu. *Application contact:* Maxine A. Leffard, Graduate Program Administrator, 412-268-5673, Fax: 412-268-7813, E-mail: ce-admissions@andrew.cmu.edu.

Carnegie Mellon University, Tepper School of Business, Pittsburgh, PA 15213-3891. Offers accounting (PhD); algorithms, combinatorics, and optimization (MS, PhD); business management and software engineering (MBMSE); civil engineering and industrial management (MS); computational finance (MSCF); economics (MS, PhD); electronic commerce (MS); environmental engineering and management (MEEM); finance (PhD); financial economics (PhD); industrial administration (MBA), including administration and public management; information systems (PhD); management of manufacturing and automation (PhD); marketing (PhD); mathematical finance (PhD); operations research (PhD); organizational behavior and theory (PhD); political economy (PhD); production and operations management (PhD); public policy and management (MS, MSED); software engineering and business management (MS); JD/MS; JD/MSIA; M Div/MS; MOM/MSIA; MSCF/MSIA. Part-time programs available. Terminal master's awarded for partial completion of doctoral program. *Degree requirements:* For doctorate, thesis/dissertation. *Entrance requirements:* For master's, GMAT. Additional exam requirements/recommendations for international students: Required—TOEFL. *Expenses:* Contact institution.

The Catholic University of America, School of Engineering, Department of Civil Engineering, Washington, DC 20064. Offers environmental engineering (MCE, MSE, D Engr, PhD, Certificate); environmental engineering and management (MCE, MSE, PhD, Certificate); environmental engineering and management (D Engr); fluid and solid mechanics (MCE, MSE, PhD, Certificate); geotechnical engineering (MCE, MSE, PhD, Certificate); management of construction (MCE, MSE, D Engr, PhD); structural engineering (MSE, D Engr, PhD); systems engineering (MSE, D Engr, PhD, Certificate). Part-time programs available. *Faculty:* 5 full-time (0 women), 7 part-time/adjunct (1 woman). *Students:* 7 full-time (3 women), 18 part-time (5 women); includes 6 minority (3 African Americans, 3 Hispanic Americans), 11 international. Average age 32. 36 applicants, 47% accepted, 9 enrolled. In 2009, 8 master's, 2 doctorates awarded. *Degree requirements:* For master's, thesis optional; for doctorate, comprehensive exam, thesis/dissertation. *Entrance requirements:* For master's and doctorate, statement of purpose, official copies of academic transcripts, three letters of recommendation. Additional exam requirements/recommendations for international students: Required—TOEFL (minimum score 580 paper-based; 237 computer-based). *Application deadline:* For fall admission, 8/1 priority date for domestic students, 7/15 for international students; for spring admission, 12/1 priority date for domestic students, 10/15 for international students. Applications are processed on a rolling basis. Application fee: $55. Electronic applications accepted. *Expenses:* Contact institution. *Financial support:* Fellowships, research assistantships, teaching assistantships, Federal Work-Study, scholarships/grants, tuition waivers (full and partial), and unspecified assistantships available. Financial award application deadline: 2/1; financial award applicants required to submit FAFSA. *Faculty research:* Geotechnical engineering, solid mechanics, construction engineering and management, environmental engineering, structural engineering. Total annual research expenditures: $438,834. *Unit head:* Dr. Lu Sun, Chair, 202-319-5164, Fax: 202-319-6677, E-mail: sunl@cua.edu. *Application contact:* Julie Schwing, Director of Graduate Admissions, 202-319-5057, Fax: 202-319-6533, E-mail: cua-admissions@cua.edu.

Clarkson University, Graduate School, Wallace H. Coulter School of Engineering, Program in Environmental Science and Engineering, Potsdam, NY 13699. Offers MS, PhD. Part-time programs available. *Students:* 28 full-time (12 women), 2 part-time (both women), 16 international. Average age 28. 68 applicants, 44% accepted, 10 enrolled. In 2009, 3 master's, 1 doctorate awarded. Terminal master's awarded for partial completion of doctoral program. *Degree requirements:* For master's, thesis; for doctorate, comprehensive exam, thesis/dissertation, proposal/defense. *Entrance requirements:* For master's, GRE, transcripts of all college coursework, resume, personal statement, three letters of recommendation; for doctorate, GRE, resume, 3 letters of recommendation. Additional exam requirements/recommendations for international students: Required—TOEFL (minimum score 550 paper-based; 213 computer-based; 80 iBT), IELTS (minimum score 6.5). *Application deadline:* For fall admission, 1/30 priority date for domestic and international students; for spring admission, 9/1 priority date for domestic and international students. Applications are processed on a rolling basis. Application fee: $25 ($35 for international students). Electronic applications accepted. *Expenses:* Tuition: Part-time $1074 per credit hour. *Financial support:* In 2009–10, 26 students received support, including 1 fellowship (averaging $30,000 per year), 18 research assistantships (averaging $20,190 per year), 4 teaching assistantships (averaging $20,190 per year); scholarships/grants, tuition waivers (partial), and unspecified assistantships also available. *Faculty research:* Biological, chemical, physical and social systems, renewable energy, environmental health. *Unit head:* Dr. Susan E. Powers, Associate Dean, 315-268-6542, Fax: 315-268-4291, E-mail: sep@clarkson.edu. *Application contact:* Kelly Sharlow, Assistant to the Dean, 315-268-7929, Fax: 315-268-4494, E-mail: ksharlow@clarkson.edu.

Clemson University, Graduate School, College of Engineering and Science, Department of Environmental Engineering and Earth Sciences, Programs in Environmental Engineering and Science, Clemson, SC 29634. Offers environmental engineering and science (M Engr, MS, PhD); environmental health physics (MS). *Accreditation:* ABET. *Students:* 52 full-time (16 women), 11 part-time (6 women); includes 2 minority (1 African American, 1 American Indian/Alaska Native), 26 international. Average age 30. 117 applicants, 47% accepted, 16 enrolled. In 2009, 8 master's, 4 doctorates awarded. *Degree requirements:* For master's, thesis; for doctorate, thesis/dissertation. *Entrance requirements:* For master's and doctorate, GRE General Test, minimum GPA of 3.0. Additional exam requirements/recommendations for international students: Required—TOEFL. *Application deadline:* For fall admission, 3/1 priority date for domestic and international students; for spring admission, 9/15 for international students. Applications are processed on a rolling basis. Application fee: $70 ($80 for international students). Electronic applications accepted. *Expenses:* Tuition, state resident: full-time $8684; part-time $528 per credit hour. Tuition, nonresident: full-time $15,330; part-time $1078 per credit hour. Required fees: $736; $37 per semester. Part-time tuition and fees vary according to course load and program. *Financial support:* In 2009–10, 41 students received support, including 6 fellowships with full and partial tuition reimbursements available (averaging $12,785 per year), 23 research assistantships with partial tuition reimbursements available (averaging $18,370 per year), 11 teaching assistantships with partial tuition reimbursements available (averaging $17,304 per year); career-related internships or fieldwork, institutionally sponsored loans, scholarships/grants, health care benefits, and unspecified assistantships also available. Support available to part-time students. Financial award applicants required to submit FAFSA. *Faculty research:* Water and air pollution control, hazardous waste and environmental management, environmental chemistry and biology, containment transport modeling, risk assessment. *Unit head:* Dr. Tanju Karanfil, Chair, 864-656-1005, Fax: 864-656-5973, E-mail: tkaranf@clemson.edu. *Application contact:* Dr. Cindy Lee, Graduate Program Coordinator, 864-656-1006, Fax: 864-656-5973, E-mail: lc@clemson.edu.

Cleveland State University, College of Graduate Studies, Fenn College of Engineering, Department of Civil and Environmental Engineering, Cleveland, OH 44115. Offers accelerated program civil engineering (MS); accelerated program environmental engineering (MS); civil engineering (MS, D Eng); engineering mechanics (MS); environmental engineering (MS). Part-time and evening/weekend programs available. *Degree requirements:* For master's, project or thesis; for doctorate, comprehensive exam, thesis/dissertation, candidacy and qualifying exams. *Entrance requirements:* For master's, GRE General Test, GRE Subject Test, minimum GPA of 2.75; for doctorate, GRE General Test, GRE Subject Test, minimum GPA of 3.25. Additional exam requirements/recommendations for international students: Required—TOEFL (minimum score 525 paper-based; 197 computer-based). *Faculty research:* Solid-waste disposal, constitutive modeling, transportation, safety engineering.

Colorado School of Mines, Graduate School, Division of Environmental Science and Engineering, Golden, CO 80401. Offers MS, PhD. Part-time programs available. *Faculty:* 27 full-time (8 women), 6 part-time/adjunct (1 woman). *Students:* 74 full-time (44 women), 21 part-time (6 women); includes 15 minority (4 African Americans, 4 Asian Americans or Pacific Islanders, 7 Hispanic Americans), 5 international. Average age 30. 127 applicants, 65% accepted, 38 enrolled. In 2009, 34 master's, 1 doctorate awarded. *Degree requirements:* For master's, thesis (for some programs); for doctorate, comprehensive exam, thesis/dissertation. *Entrance requirements:* For master's and doctorate, GRE General Test. Additional exam requirements/recommendations for international students: Required—TOEFL (minimum score 550 paper-based; 213 computer-based; 80 iBT). *Application deadline:* For fall admission, 1/15 priority date for domestic and international students; for spring admission, 9/1 priority date for domestic and international students. Application fee: $50 ($70 for international students). Electronic applications accepted. *Expenses:* Tuition, state resident: full-time $10,584; part-time $588 per credit hour. Tuition, nonresident: full-time $24,750; part-time $1375 per credit hour. Required fees: $1654; $827.10 per semester. *Financial support:* In 2009–10, 35 students received support, including 2 fellowships with full tuition reimbursements available (averaging $20,000 per year), 30 research assistantships with full tuition reimbursements available (averaging $20,000 per year), 3 teaching assistantships with full tuition reimbursements available (averaging $20,000 per year); scholarships/grants, health care benefits, and unspecified assistantships also available. Financial award application deadline: 1/15; financial award applicants required to submit FAFSA. *Faculty research:* Treatment of water and wastes, environmental law: policy and practice, natural environment systems, hazardous waste management, environmental data analysis. Total annual research expenditures: $5.3 million. *Unit head:* Dr. Robert Siegrist, Division Director, 303-384-2158, Fax: 303-273-3413, E-mail: siegrist@mines.edu. *Application contact:* Tim VanHaverbeke, Research Faculty, 303-273-3467, Fax: 303-273-3413, E-mail: tvanhave@mines.edu.

Columbia University, Fu Foundation School of Engineering and Applied Science, Department of Earth and Environmental Engineering, New York, NY 10027. Offers earth and environmental engineering (MS, Eng Sc D, PhD); metallurgical engineering (Engr); mining engineering (Engr); MS/MBA. Part-time programs available. Postbaccalaureate distance learning degree programs offered (minimal on-campus study). *Faculty:* 7 full-time (0 women), 4 part-time/adjunct (1 woman). *Students:* 50 full-time (19 women), 20 part-time (7 women); includes 3 minority (1 African American, 1 American Indian/Alaska Native, 1 Asian American or Pacific Islander), 33 international. Average age 28. 149 applicants, 25% accepted, 18 enrolled. In 2009, 12 master's, 4 doctorates awarded. Terminal master's awarded for partial completion of doctoral program. *Degree requirements:* For master's, thesis; for doctorate, thesis/dissertation, qualifying exam. *Entrance requirements:* For master's, doctorate, and Engr, GRE General Test. Additional exam requirements/recommendations for international students: Required—TOEFL. *Application deadline:* For fall admission, 12/1 priority date for domestic and international students; for spring admission, 10/1 priority date for domestic and international students. Application fee: $70. Electronic applications accepted. *Financial support:* In 2009–10, 39 students received support, including 6 fellowships with full and partial tuition reimbursements available (averaging $16,478 per year), 26 research assistantships with full tuition reimbursements available (averaging $27,733 per year), 7 teaching assistantships with full tuition reimbursements available (averaging $22,500 per year); health care benefits and unspecified assistantships also available. Financial award application deadline: 12/1; financial award applicants required to submit FAFSA. *Faculty research:* Sustainable energy and materials, waste to energy, water resources and climate risks, environmental health engineering, life cycle analysis. *Unit head:* Dr. Klaus S. Lackner, Department Chair; Maurice Ewing and J. Lamar Worzel Professor of Geophysics, 212-854-0304, Fax: 212-854-7081, E-mail: kl2010@columbia.edu. *Application contact:* Peter

Rennee, Department Administrator, 212-854-7065, Fax: 212-854-7081, E-mail: pr99@columbia.edu.

Concordia University, School of Graduate Studies, Faculty of Engineering and Computer Science, Department of Building, Civil and Environmental Engineering, Montréal, QC H3G 1M8, Canada. Offers building engineering (M Eng, MA Sc, PhD, Certificate); civil engineering (M Eng, MA Sc, PhD); environmental engineering (Certificate). *Degree requirements:* For master's, thesis or alternative; for doctorate, comprehensive exam, thesis/dissertation. *Faculty research:* Structural engineering, geotechnical engineering, water resources and fluid engineering, transportation engineering, systems engineering.

Cornell University, Graduate School, Graduate Fields of Engineering, Field of Civil and Environmental Engineering, Ithaca, NY 14853-0001. Offers engineering management (M Eng, MS, PhD); environmental engineering (M Eng, MS, PhD); environmental fluid mechanics and hydrology (M Eng, MS, PhD); environmental systems engineering (M Eng, MS, PhD); geotechnical engineering (M Eng, MS, PhD); remote sensing (M Eng, MS, PhD); structural engineering (M Eng, MS, PhD); structural mechanics (M Eng, MS); transportation engineering (MS, PhD); transportation systems engineering (M Eng); water resource systems (M Eng, MS, PhD). *Faculty:* 40 full-time (7 women). *Students:* 144 full-time (48 women); includes 12 minority (2 African Americans, 1 American Indian/Alaska Native, 5 Asian Americans or Pacific Islanders, 4 Hispanic Americans), 58 international. Average age 25. 454 applicants, 57% accepted, 86 enrolled. In 2009, 69 master's, 5 doctorates awarded. Terminal master's awarded for partial completion of doctoral program. *Degree requirements:* For master's, thesis (MS); for doctorate, comprehensive exam, thesis/dissertation. *Entrance requirements:* For master's and doctorate, GRE General Test (recommended), 2 letters of recommendation. Additional exam requirements/recommendations for international students: Required—TOEFL (minimum score 600 paper-based; 250 computer-based; 77 iBT). *Application deadline:* For fall admission, 1/15 priority date for domestic students; for spring admission, 10/15 for domestic students. Application fee: $70. Electronic applications accepted. *Expenses:* Tuition: Full-time $29,500. Required fees: $70. Full-time tuition and fees vary according to degree level, program and student level. *Financial support:* In 2009–10, 50 students received support, including 6 fellowships with full tuition reimbursements available, 5 research assistantships with full tuition reimbursements available, 1 teaching assistantship with full tuition reimbursement available; institutionally sponsored loans, scholarships/grants, health care benefits, tuition waivers (full and partial), and unspecified assistantships also available. Financial award applicants required to submit FAFSA. *Faculty research:* Environmental engineering, geotechnical engineering remote sensing, environmental fluid mechanics and hydrology, structural engineering. *Unit head:* Director of Graduate Studies, 607-255-7560, Fax: 607-255-9004. *Application contact:* Graduate Field Assistant, 607-255-7560, Fax: 607-255-9004, E-mail: cee_grad@cornell.edu.

Dalhousie University, Faculty of Engineering, Department of Environmental Engineering, Halifax, NS B3J 2X4, Canada. Offers M Eng, MA Sc, PhD. *Entrance requirements:* Additional exam requirements/recommendations for international students: Required—TOEFL, IELTS, CANTEST, CAEL, or Michigan English Language Assessment Battery. *Application deadline:* For fall admission, 6/1 for domestic students, 4/1 for international students; for winter admission, 11/15 for domestic students, 8/31 for international students; for spring admission, 1/28 for domestic students, 12/31 for international students. Application fee: $70. Electronic applications accepted. *Unit head:* Dr. John Hill, Director, 902-494-3957, Fax: 902-425-1037, E-mail: john.hill@dal.ca. *Application contact:* Heather Hillyard, Admissions Coordinator, Graduate Studies and Research, 902-494-1288, Fax: 902-494-3011, E-mail: heather.hillyard@dal.ca.

Dartmouth College, Thayer School of Engineering, Program in Environmental Engineering, Hanover, NH 03755. Offers MS, PhD. Application fee: $45. *Faculty research:* Resource and environmental analysis, decision theory, risk assessment and public policy, environmental fluid mechanics. Total annual research expenditures: $742,498. *Unit head:* Dr. Joseph J. Helbie, Dean, 603-646-2238, Fax: 603-646-2580, E-mail: joseph.j.helbie@dartmouth.edu. *Application contact:* Candace S. Potter, Graduate Admissions Administrator, 603-646-3844, Fax: 603-646-1620, E-mail: candace.potter@dartmouth.edu.

Drexel University, College of Engineering, Department of Civil, Architectural, and Environmental Engineering, Program in Environmental Engineering, Philadelphia, PA 19104-2875. Offers MS, PhD. Part-time and evening/weekend programs available. Terminal master's awarded for partial completion of doctoral program. *Degree requirements:* For master's, thesis optional; for doctorate, thesis/dissertation. Electronic applications accepted.

Drexel University, College of Engineering, Department of Civil, Architectural, and Environmental Engineering, Program in Geotechnical, Geoenvironmental and Geosynthetics Engineering, Philadelphia, PA 19104-2875. Offers MS, PhD.

Duke University, Graduate School, Pratt School of Engineering, Department of Civil and Environmental Engineering, Durham, NC 27708. Offers civil and environmental engineering (MS, PhD); environmental engineering (MS, PhD). Part-time programs available. *Faculty:* 21 full-time. *Students:* 51 full-time (13 women); includes 2 minority (1 African American, 1 Hispanic American), 30 international. 124 applicants, 31% accepted, 12 enrolled. In 2009, 2 master's, 7 doctorates awarded. Terminal master's awarded for partial completion of doctoral program. *Degree requirements:* For doctorate, thesis/dissertation. *Entrance requirements:* For master's and doctorate, GRE General Test. Additional exam requirements/recommendations for international students: Required—TOEFL (minimum score 550 paper-based; 213 computer-based; 83 iBT), IELTS (minimum score 7). *Application deadline:* For fall admission, 12/8 priority date for domestic and international students; for spring admission, 11/1 for domestic students. Application fee: $75. Electronic applications accepted. *Financial support:* Fellowships, research assistantships, Federal Work-Study available. Financial award application deadline: 12/31. *Unit head:* Dolbow John, Director of Graduate Studies, 919-660-5200, Fax: 919-660-5219, E-mail: ruby.carpenter@duke.edu. *Application contact:* Cynthia Robertson, Associate Dean for Enrollment Services, 919-684-3913, E-mail: grad-admissions@duke.edu.

École Polytechnique de Montréal, Graduate Programs, Department of Civil, Geological and Mining Engineering, Montréal, QC H3C 3A7, Canada. Offers civil, geological and mining engineering (DESS); environmental engineering (M Eng, M Sc A, PhD); geotechnical engineering (M Eng, M Sc A, PhD); hydraulics engineering (M Eng, M Sc A, PhD); structural engineering (M Eng, M Sc A, PhD); transportation engineering (M Eng, M Sc A, PhD). Part-time programs available. *Degree requirements:* For master's, one foreign language, thesis; for doctorate, one foreign language, thesis/dissertation. *Entrance requirements:* For master's, minimum GPA of 2.75; for doctorate, minimum GPA of 3.0. *Faculty research:* Water resources management, characteristics of building materials, aging of dams, pollution control.

Florida Agricultural and Mechanical University, Division of Graduate Studies, Research, and Continuing Education, FAMU-FSU College of Engineering, Department of Civil and Environmental Engineering, Tallahassee, FL 32307-3200. Offers civil engineering (MS, PhD); environmental engineering (MS, PhD). *Faculty:* 20 full-time (6 women). *Students:* 24 full-time (10 women), 14 part-time (2 women); includes 32 minority (31 African Americans, 1 Asian American or Pacific Islander), 6 international. In 2009, 1 doctorate awarded. *Degree requirements:* For master's, comprehensive exam, thesis optional; for doctorate, comprehensive exam, thesis/dissertation. *Entrance requirements:* For master's, GRE General Test, minimum GPA of 3.0; for doctorate, GRE General Test, minimum GPA of 3.0, letters of recommendation (3). Additional exam requirements/recommendations for international students: Required—TOEFL (minimum score 550 paper-based; 213 computer-based). *Application deadline:* For fall admission, 7/1 for domestic students, 3/1 for international students. Application fee: $30. *Faculty research:* Geotechnical, environmental, hydraulic, construction materials, and structures. *Unit head:* Dr. Jerry Wekezer, Chairperson, 850-410-6100. *Application contact:* Dr. Chanta M. Haywood, Dean of Graduate Studies, Research, and Continuing Education, 850-599-3315, Fax: 850-599-3727.

Environmental Engineering

Florida International University, College of Engineering and Computing, Department of Civil and Environmental Engineering, Program in Environmental Engineering, Miami, FL 33175. Offers MS. Part-time and evening/weekend programs available. Postbaccalaureate distance learning degree programs offered (no on-campus study). *Students:* 19 full-time (8 women), 9 part-time (4 women); includes 12 minority (1 African American, 11 Hispanic Americans), 15 international. Average age 26. 24 applicants, 25% accepted, 6 enrolled. In 2009, 5 master's awarded. *Degree requirements:* For master's, thesis optional. *Entrance requirements:* For master's, minimum GPA of 3.0; resume, 3 letters of recommendation. Additional exam requirements/recommendations for international students: Required—TOEFL (minimum score 550 paper-based; 80 iBT). *Application deadline:* For fall admission, 6/1 for domestic students, 4/1 for international students; for spring admission, 10/1 for domestic students, 9/1 for international students. Applications are processed on a rolling basis. Application fee: $30. Electronic applications accepted. *Expenses:* Tuition, state resident: full-time $8008; part-time $4004 per year. Tuition, nonresident: full-time $20,104; part-time $10,052 per year. Required fees: $298; $149 per term. *Financial support:* In 2009–10, 6 research assistantships (averaging $13,333 per year), 4 teaching assistantships (averaging $13,333 per year) were awarded; institutionally sponsored loans and scholarships/grants also available. Financial award application deadline: 3/1; financial award applicants required to submit FAFSA. *Faculty research:* Water and wastewater treatment, water quality, solid and hazardous waste, sustainability and green engineering, clean up, remediation and restoration. *Unit head:* Dr. Fang Zhao, Chair, Environmental Engineering Department, 305-348-3821, Fax: 305-348-2802, E-mail: fang.zhao@fiu.edu. *Application contact:* Maria Parrila, Graduate Admissions Assistant, 305-348-1890, Fax: 305-348-6142, E-mail: grad_eng@fiu.edu.

Florida State University, The Graduate School, FAMU-FSU College of Engineering, Department of Civil and Environmental Engineering, Tallahassee, FL 32306. Offers MS, PhD. Part-time programs available. *Faculty:* 16 full-time (3 women). *Students:* 33 full-time (9 women), 10 part-time (3 women); includes 23 minority (12 African Americans, 7 Asian Americans or Pacific Islanders, 4 Hispanic Americans). Average age 23. 48 applicants, 48% accepted, 7 enrolled. In 2009, 11 master's, 4 doctorates awarded. *Degree requirements:* For master's, thesis optional; for doctorate, thesis/dissertation. *Entrance requirements:* For master's, GRE General Test (minimum score 1000), BS in engineering or related field, minimum GPA of 3.0; for doctorate, GRE General Test (minimum score 1100), Master's degree in engineering or related field, minimum GPA of 3.0. Additional exam requirements/recommendations for international students: Required—TOEFL (minimum score 550 paper-based; 213 computer-based). *Application deadline:* For fall admission, 7/1 for domestic and international students; for spring admission, 11/1 for domestic and international students. Applications are processed on a rolling basis. Application fee: $30. *Expenses:* Tuition, state resident: full-time $7413.36. Tuition, nonresident: full-time $22,567. *Financial support:* In 2009–10, 25 students received support, including 15 research assistantships with full tuition reimbursements available (averaging $15,000 per year), 10 teaching assistantships with full tuition reimbursements available (averaging $15,000 per year); fellowships, Federal Work-Study, tuition waivers (full), and unspecified assistantships also available. Financial award application deadline: 6/15; financial award applicants required to submit FAFSA. *Faculty research:* Tidal hydraulics, temperature effects on bridge girders, codes for coastal construction, field performance of pine bridges, river basin management, transportation pavement design, soil dynamics, structural analysis. Total annual research expenditures: $1.3 million. *Unit head:* Dr. Kamal S. Tawfiq, Chair and Professor, 850-410-6143, Fax: 850-410-6142, E-mail: tawfiq@eng.fsu.edu. *Application contact:* Johnnye Belinda Morris, Office Manager, 850-410-6139, Fax: 850-410-6142, E-mail: bmorris@eng.fsu.edu.

Gannon University, School of Graduate Studies, College of Engineering and Business, School of Engineering and Computer Science, Program in Environmental Science and Engineering, Erie, PA 16541-0001. Offers MS. Part-time and evening/weekend programs available. *Students:* 8 full-time (2 women), 4 part-time (2 women); includes 1 minority (African American), 1 international. Average age 28. 24 applicants, 42% accepted, 1 enrolled. In 2009, 4 master's awarded. *Degree requirements:* For master's, thesis, internship, research paper or project. *Entrance requirements:* For master's, GRE. Additional exam requirements/recommendations for international students: Required—TOEFL (minimum score 79 iBT). *Application deadline:* Applications are processed on a rolling basis. Application fee: $25. Electronic applications accepted. *Expenses:* Tuition: Full-time $13,590; part-time $755 per credit. Required fees: $524; $17 per credit. Tuition and fees vary according to course load, degree level, campus/location and program. *Financial support:* Scholarships/grants and unspecified assistantships available. Financial award application deadline: 7/1; financial award applicants required to submit FAFSA. *Unit head:* Dr. Harry Diz, Chair, 814-871-7633, E-mail: diz001@gannon.edu. *Application contact:* Kara Morgan, Assistant Director of Graduate Admissions, 814-871-5831, Fax: 814-871-5827, E-mail: graduate@gannon.edu.

The George Washington University, School of Engineering and Applied Science, Department of Civil and Environmental Engineering, Washington, DC 20052. Offers MS, D Sc, App Sc, Engr. Part-time and evening/weekend programs available. *Faculty:* 12 full-time (3 women), 10 part-time/adjunct (1 woman). *Students:* 18 full-time (5 women), 36 part-time (12 women); includes 5 minority (2 African Americans, 2 Asian Americans or Pacific Islanders, 1 Hispanic American), 33 international. Average age 31. 79 applicants, 56% accepted, 12 enrolled. In 2009, 12 master's, 6 doctorates awarded. *Degree requirements:* For master's, thesis optional; for doctorate, thesis/dissertation, final and qualifying exams. *Entrance requirements:* For master's, appropriate bachelor's degree, minimum GPA of 3.0; for doctorate, appropriate bachelor's or master's degree, minimum GPA of 3.4, GRE if highest earned degree is BS; for other advanced degree, appropriate master's degree, minimum GPA of 3.0. Additional exam requirements/recommendations for international students: Required—TOEFL or George Washington University English as a Foreign Language Test. *Application deadline:* For fall admission, 3/1 priority date for domestic students; for spring admission, 10/1 for domestic students. Applications are processed on a rolling basis. Application fee: $60. *Financial support:* In 2009–10, 42 students received support; fellowships with tuition reimbursements available, research assistantships, teaching assistantships with tuition reimbursements available, career-related internships or fieldwork, Federal Work-Study, institutionally sponsored loans, and tuition waivers available. Financial award application deadline: 3/1; financial award applicants required to submit FAFSA. *Faculty research:* Computer-integrated manufacturing, materials engineering, electronic materials, fatigue and fracture, reliability. *Unit head:* Dr. Kim Roddis, Chair, 202-994-8515, Fax: 202-994-0127, E-mail: roddis@gwu.edu. *Application contact:* Adina Lav, Marketing, Recruiting and Admissions, 202-994-5827, Fax: 202-994-0909, E-mail: engineering@gwu.edu.

Georgia Institute of Technology, Graduate Studies and Research, College of Engineering, School of Civil and Environmental Engineering, Program in Environmental Engineering, Atlanta, GA 30332-0001. Offers MS, MS Env E, PhD. *Accreditation:* ABET (one or more programs are accredited). Part-time programs available. Postbaccalaureate distance learning degree programs offered (no on-campus study). *Degree requirements:* For master's, research report or thesis; for doctorate, thesis/dissertation. *Entrance requirements:* For master's and doctorate, GRE, minimum GPA of 3.2. Additional exam requirements/recommendations for international students: Required—TOEFL. *Faculty research:* Advanced microbiology of water and wastes, industrial waste treatment and disposal, air pollution measurements and control.

Idaho State University, Office of Graduate Studies, College of Engineering, Civil and Environmental Engineering Department, Pocatello, ID 83209-8060. Offers civil engineering (MS); environmental engineering (MS); environmental science and management (MS). Part-time programs available. *Faculty:* 1 full-time (0 women). *Students:* 9 full-time (1 woman), 17 part-time (6 women); includes 2 minority (both Asian Americans or Pacific Islanders), 12 international. Average age 31. In 2009, 9 master's awarded. *Degree requirements:* For master's, comprehensive exam (for some programs), thesis optional, thesis project, 2 semesters of seminar. *Entrance requirements:* For master's, GRE. Additional exam requirements/recommendations for international students: Required—TOEFL (minimum score 550 paper-based; 213 computer-based; 80 iBT). *Application deadline:* For fall admission, 7/1 for domestic students, 6/1 for international students; for spring admission, 12/1 for domestic students, 11/1 for international students. Applications are processed on a rolling basis. Application fee: $55. Electronic applications accepted. *Expenses:* Tuition, state resident: full-time $3318; part-time $297 per credit hour. Tuition, nonresident: full-time $13,120; part-time $437 per credit hour. Required fees: $2530. Tuition and fees vary according to program. *Financial support:* Research assistantships with full and partial tuition reimbursements, teaching assistantships with full and partial tuition reimbursements, career-related internships or fieldwork, Federal Work-Study, institutionally sponsored loans, scholarships/grants, traineeships, health care benefits, tuition waivers (full and partial), and unspecified assistantships available. Support available to part-time students. Financial award application deadline: 1/1; financial award applicants required to submit FAFSA. *Faculty research:* Floor vibration investigations, earthquake engineering, base isolation systems and seismic risk assessment, infrastructure revitalization (building foundations and damage, bridge structures, highways, and dams), slope stability and soil erosion, pavement rehabilitation, computational fluid dynamics and flood control structures, microbial fuel cells, water treatment and water quality modeling, environmental risk assessment, biotechnology, nanotechnology. *Unit head:* Dr. Arya Ebrahimpour, Chair, 208-282-4695, Fax: 208-282-4538, E-mail: ebraarya@isu.edu. *Application contact:* Tami Carson, Graduate School Technical Records Specialist, 208-282-2150, Fax: 208-282-4847, E-mail: carstami@isu.edu.

Illinois Institute of Technology, Graduate College, Armour College of Engineering, Department of Chemical and Biological Engineering, Chicago, IL 60616-3793. Offers biological engineering (MBE); chemical engineering (M Ch E, MS, PhD); food process engineering (MFPE); food processing engineering (MS); gas engineering (MGE); manufacturing engineering (MME, MS); MS/M Ch E. Part-time and evening/weekend programs available. Postbaccalaureate distance learning degree programs offered. Terminal master's awarded for partial completion of doctoral program. *Degree requirements:* For master's, comprehensive exam, thesis (for some programs); for doctorate, comprehensive exam, thesis/dissertation. *Entrance requirements:* For master's and doctorate, GRE General Test, minimum undergraduate GPA of 3.0. Additional exam requirements/recommendations for international students: Required—TOEFL (minimum score 550 paper-based; 213 computer-based; 80 iBT). Electronic applications accepted. *Expenses:* Tuition: Full-time $17,550; part-time $888 per credit hour. Required fees: $850; $7.50 per credit hour. One-time fee: $50 full-time. Full-time tuition and fees vary according to program. *Faculty research:* Biochemical, bioenergy, biosensors, tissue engineering, fuel cells, batteries, renewable energy, gas cleaning, particle technology, fluidization, colloid and interfacial engineering complex fluids, polymers, complex systems and dynamics.

Illinois Institute of Technology, Graduate College, Armour College of Engineering, Department of Civil, Architectural and Environmental Engineering, Chicago, IL 60616-3793. Offers architectural engineering (M Arch E); civil engineering (MS, PhD); construction engineering and management (MCEM); environmental engineering (M Env E, MS, PhD); geoenvironmental engineering (M Geoenv E); geotechnical engineering (MGE); public works (MPW); structural engineering (MSE); transportation engineering (M Trans E). Part-time and evening/weekend programs available. Terminal master's awarded for partial completion of doctoral program. *Degree requirements:* For master's, thesis (for some programs); for doctorate, comprehensive exam, thesis/dissertation. *Entrance requirements:* For master's and doctorate, GRE General Test, minimum undergraduate GPA of 3.0. Additional exam requirements/recommendations for international students: Required—TOEFL (minimum score 550 paper-based; 213 computer-based; 80 iBT). Electronic applications accepted. *Expenses:* Tuition: Full-time $17,550; part-time $888 per credit hour. Required fees: $850; $7.50 per credit hour. One-time fee: $50 full-time. Full-time tuition and fees vary according to program. *Faculty research:* Seismic analysis of buildings and bridges, fatigue analysis and materials of construction, construction zone safety and construction productivity, architectural acoustics and building energy efficiency, environmental engineering. air and water quality.

Instituto Tecnologico de Santo Domingo, Graduate School, Santo Domingo, Dominican Republic. Offers applied linguistics (MA); construction administration (M Mgmt); corporate finance (M Mgmt); education (M Ed); engineering (M Eng), including data telecommunications, industrial engineering, logistics and supply chain, maintenance engineering, sanitary and environmental engineering, structural engineering; environmental science (M En S), including environmental education, environmental management, marine and coastal ecosystems, natural resources management; family therapy (MA); food science and technology (MS); human development (MA); human resources administration (M Mgmt); international business (M Mgmt); labor risks (M Mgmt); management (M Mgmt); marketing (M Mgmt); mathematics (MS); organizational development (M Mgmt); planning and taxation (M Mgmt); psychology (MA); social science (M Ed); upper management (M Mgmt). *Entrance requirements:* For master's, birth certificate, minimum GPA of 2.0.

Instituto Tecnológico y de Estudios Superiores de Monterrey, Campus Ciudad de México, Virtual University Division, Ciudad de Mexico, Mexico. Offers administration of information technologies (MA); computer sciences (MA); education (MA, PhD); educational technology (MA); environmental engineering (MA); environmental systems (MA); humanistic studies (MA); industrial engineering (MA); international business for Latin America (MA); quality systems (MA); quality systems and productivity (MA). Part-time and evening/weekend programs available. Postbaccalaureate distance learning degree programs offered (minimal on-campus study). *Entrance requirements:* For master's and doctorate, Instituto entrance exam. Additional exam requirements/recommendations for international students: Required—TOEFL.

Instituto Tecnológico y de Estudios Superiores de Monterrey, Campus Monterrey, Graduate and Research Division, Programs in Engineering, Monterrey, Mexico. Offers applied statistics (M Eng); artificial intelligence (PhD); automation engineering (M Eng); chemical engineering (M Eng); civil engineering (M Eng); electrical engineering (M Eng); electronic engineering (M Eng); environmental engineering (M Eng); industrial engineering (M Eng, PhD); manufacturing engineering (M Eng); mechanical engineering (M Eng); systems and quality engineering (M Eng). Part-time and evening/weekend programs available. Terminal master's awarded for partial completion of doctoral program. *Degree requirements:* For master's, one foreign language, thesis; for doctorate, one foreign language, thesis/dissertation. *Entrance requirements:* For master's, EXADEP; for doctorate, GRE, master's degree in related field. Additional exam requirements/recommendations for international students: Required—TOEFL. *Faculty research:* Flexible manufacturing cells, materials, statistical methods, environmental prevention, control and evaluation.

Iowa State University of Science and Technology, Graduate College, College of Engineering, Department of Civil and Construction Engineering, Ames, IA 50011. Offers civil engineering (MS, PhD), including civil engineering materials, construction engineering and management, environmental engineering, geometronics, geotechnical engineering; structural engineering, transportation engineering. *Faculty:* 32 full-time (5 women), 6 part-time/adjunct (0 women). *Students:* 87 full-time (20 women), 33 part-time (8 women); includes 2 minority (1 American Indian/Alaska Native, 1 Asian American or Pacific Islander), 48 international. 204 applicants, 29% accepted, 27 enrolled. In 2009, 6 master's, 11 doctorates awarded. *Degree requirements:* For master's, thesis or alternative; for doctorate, thesis/dissertation. *Entrance requirements:* For master's and doctorate, GRE General Test. Additional exam requirements/recommendations for international students: Required—TOEFL (minimum score 550 paper-based; 82 iBT) or IELTS (minimum score 6.5). *Application deadline:* For fall admission, 2/1 priority date for domestic students, 2/1 for international students; for spring admission, 8/1 priority date for domestic students, 8/1 for international students. Application fee: $40 ($90 for international students). Electronic applications accepted. *Expenses:* Tuition, state resident: full-time $6716. Tuition, nonresident: full-time $8908. Tuition and fees vary according to course level, course load, program and student level. *Financial support:* In 2009–10, 70 research assistantships with full and partial tuition reimbursements (averaging $16,000 per year), 4 teaching assistantships with full and partial tuition reimbursements (averaging $18,000 per year) were awarded; fellowships, scholarships/grants, health care benefits, and unspecified assistantships also available. *Unit head:* Dr. James Alleman, Chair, 515-294-3892, E-mail: ccee-grad-inquiry@

iastate.edu. *Application contact:* Dr. Sri Srithanan, Director of Graduate Education, 515-294-5328, E-mail: ccee-grad-inquiry@iastate.edu.

The Johns Hopkins University, Bloomberg School of Public Health, Department of Environmental Health Sciences, Baltimore, MD 21218-2699. Offers environmental health engineering (PhD); environmental health sciences (MHS, Dr PH); occupational and environmental health (PhD); occupational and environmental hygiene (MHS, MHS); physiology (PhD); toxicology (PhD). Postbaccalaureate distance learning degree programs offered (minimal on-campus study). *Faculty:* 71 full-time (27 women), 58 part-time/adjunct (26 women). *Students:* 65 full-time (43 women), 17 part-time (12 women); includes 22 minority (4 African Americans, 1 American Indian/Alaska Native, 13 Asian Americans or Pacific Islanders, 4 Hispanic Americans), 11 international. Average age 31. 101 applicants, 49% accepted, 31 enrolled. In 2009, 22 master's, 13 doctorates awarded. *Degree requirements:* For master's, essay, presentation; for doctorate, comprehensive exam, thesis/dissertation, 1 year full-time residency, oral and written exams. *Entrance requirements:* For master's, GRE General Test or MCAT, 3 letters of recommendation, transcripts; for doctorate, GRE General Test or MCAT, 3 letters of recommendation. Additional exam requirements/recommendations for international students: Required—TOEFL (minimum score 600 paper-based; 250 computer-based). *Application deadline:* For fall admission, 12/15 priority date for domestic and international students. Applications are processed on a rolling basis. Application fee: $45. Electronic applications accepted. *Financial support:* In 2009–10, 5 fellowships with full tuition reimbursements (averaging $26,500 per year) were awarded; Federal Work-Study, institutionally sponsored loans, scholarships/grants, traineeships, health care benefits, and stipends also available. Support available to part-time students. Financial award application deadline: 3/15; financial award applicants required to submit FAFSA. *Faculty research:* Chemical carcinogenesis/toxicology, lung disease, occupational and environmental health, nuclear imaging, molecular epidemiology. Total annual research expenditures: $23.7 million. *Unit head:* Dr. John Davis Groopman, Chair, 410-955-3720, Fax: 410-955-0617, E-mail: jgroopma@jhsph.edu. *Application contact:* Nina J. Kulacki, Academic Program Manager, 410-955-2212, Fax: 410-955-0617, E-mail: nkulacki@jhsph.edu.

The Johns Hopkins University, Engineering for Professionals, Part-Time Program in Environmental Engineering, Baltimore, MD 21218-2699. Offers MS, Graduate Certificate, Post-Master's Certificate. Part-time and evening/weekend programs available. *Faculty:* 9 part-time/adjunct (1 woman). *Students:* 22 part-time (11 women); includes 4 minority (1 African American, 1 Asian American or Pacific Islander, 2 Hispanic Americans), 2 international. Average age 30. In 2009, 6 master's awarded. Application fee: $75. *Unit head:* Dr. Hedy Alavi, Program Chair, 410-516-7091, Fax: 410-516-8996, E-mail: hedy.alavi@jhu.edu. *Application contact:* Priyanka Dwivedi, Admissions Manager, 410-516-2300, Fax: 410-579-8049, E-mail: dwived1@jhu.edu.

The Johns Hopkins University, Engineering for Professionals, Part-time Program in Environmental Engineering and Science, Baltimore, MD 21218-2699. Offers MEE, MS, Graduate Certificate, Post-Master's Certificate. Part-time and evening/weekend programs available. *Faculty:* 8 part-time/adjunct (2 women). *Students:* 40 part-time (17 women); includes 8 minority (2 African Americans, 2 Asian Americans or Pacific Islanders, 4 Hispanic Americans). Average age 29. In 2009, 6 master's awarded. *Application deadline:* Applications are processed on a rolling basis. Application fee: $75. Electronic applications accepted. *Financial support:* Institutionally sponsored loans available. *Unit head:* Dr. Hedy Alavi, Program Chair, 410-516-7091, Fax: 410-516-8996, E-mail: hedy.alavi@jhu.edu. *Application contact:* Priyanka Dwivedi, Admissions Manager, 410-516-2300, Fax: 410-579-8049, E-mail: pdwived1@jhu.edu.

The Johns Hopkins University, G. W. C. Whiting School of Engineering, Department of Geography and Environmental Engineering, Baltimore, MD 21218-2699. Offers MA, MS, MSE, PhD. *Faculty:* 15 full-time (4 women), 4 part-time/adjunct (0 women). *Students:* 55 full-time (25 women), 5 part-time (4 women); includes 4 minority (1 African American, 1 Asian American or Pacific Islander, 2 Hispanic Americans), 29 international. Average age 27. 118 applicants, 73% accepted, 25 enrolled. In 2009, 27 master's, 7 doctorates awarded. Terminal master's awarded for partial completion of doctoral program. *Degree requirements:* For master's, thesis (for some programs), 1 year full-time residency; for doctorate, comprehensive exam, thesis/dissertation, oral exam, 2 year full-time residency. *Entrance requirements:* For master's and doctorate, GRE General Test. Additional exam requirements/recommendations for international students: Required—TOEFL (minimum score 670 paper-based; 300 computer-based; 120 iBT); Recommended—IELTS. *Application deadline:* For fall admission, 1/15 priority date for domestic and international students. Applications are processed on a rolling basis. Application fee: $75. Electronic applications accepted. *Financial support:* In 2009–10, 3 fellowships with full tuition reimbursements (averaging $27,000 per year), 24 research assistantships with full tuition reimbursements (averaging $24,000 per year) were awarded; teaching assistantships with full tuition reimbursements, Federal Work-Study, institutionally sponsored loans, scholarships/grants, health care benefits, tuition waivers (partial), and unspecified assistantships also available. *Faculty research:* Environmental engineering; environmental chemistry; water resources engineering; systems analysis and economics for public decision making; geomorphology, hydrology and ecology. Total annual research expenditures: $1.2 million. *Unit head:* Dr. Edward J. Bouwer, Chair, 410-516-7102, Fax: 410-516-8996, E-mail: bouwer@jhu.edu. *Application contact:* Dr. Edward J. Bouwer, Chair, 410-516-7102, Fax: 410-516-8996, E-mail: bouwer@jhu.edu.

Lakehead University, Graduate Studies, Faculty of Engineering, Thunder Bay, ON P7B 5E1, Canada. Offers control engineering (M Sc Engr); electrical/computer engineering (M Sc Engr); environmental engineering (M Sc Engr). Part-time programs available. *Degree requirements:* For master's, thesis. *Entrance requirements:* For master's, bachelor's degree in chemical, electrical or mechanical engineering, minimum B average. Additional exam requirements/recommendations for international students: Required—TOEFL. *Faculty research:* Pulp and paper, adaptive/process control, robust/interactive learning control, vibration control.

Lamar University, College of Graduate Studies, College of Engineering, Department of Civil Engineering, Beaumont, TX 77710. Offers civil engineering (ME, MES, DE); environmental engineering (MS); environmental studies (MS). Part-time programs available. *Faculty:* 6 full-time (1 woman), 3 part-time/adjunct (0 women). *Students:* 55 full-time (12 women), 16 part-time (4 women); includes 2 minority (both African Americans), 41 international. Average age 26. 94 applicants, 40% accepted, 17 enrolled. In 2009, 49 master's, 2 doctorates awarded. *Degree requirements:* For master's, thesis optional; for doctorate, thesis/dissertation. *Entrance requirements:* For master's and doctorate, GRE General Test. Additional exam requirements/recommendations for international students: Required—TOEFL. *Application deadline:* For fall admission, 5/15 priority date for domestic students; for spring admission, 10/1 priority date for domestic students. Applications are processed on a rolling basis. Application fee: $25 ($50 for international students). *Financial support:* In 2009–10, 45 fellowships with partial tuition reimbursements (averaging $1,000 per year), 10 research assistantships with partial tuition reimbursements (averaging $7,200 per year), 3 teaching assistantships with partial tuition reimbursements (averaging $7,200 per year) were awarded; scholarships/grants and tuition waivers (partial) also available. Financial award application deadline: 4/1. *Faculty research:* Environmental remediations, construction productivity, geotechnical soil stabilization, lake/reservoir hydrodynamics, air pollution. *Unit head:* Dr. Enno Koehn, Chair, 409-880-8759, Fax: 409-880-8121, E-mail: koehneu@hal.lamar.edu. *Application contact:* Sandy Drane, Coordinator of Graduate Admissions, 409-880-8356, Fax: 409-880-8414, E-mail: gradmissions@hal.lamar.edu.

Lehigh University, P.C. Rossin College of Engineering and Applied Science, Department of Civil and Environmental Engineering, Bethlehem, PA 18015-3094. Offers civil engineering (M Eng, MS, PhD); environmental engineering (MS, PhD); structural engineering (M Eng, MS, PhD). Part-time programs available. *Faculty:* 17 full-time (3 women). *Students:* 68 full-time (14 women), 11 part-time (2 women); includes 6 minority (4 Asian Americans or Pacific Islanders, 2 Hispanic Americans), 39 international. Average age 26. 284 applicants, 21% accepted, 39 enrolled. In 2009, 26 master's, 2 doctorates awarded. Terminal master's awarded for partial completion of doctoral program. *Degree requirements:* For master's, thesis (for some programs); for doctorate, comprehensive exam, thesis/dissertation. *Entrance requirements:* For master's and doctorate, GRE. Additional exam requirements/recommendations for international students: Required—TOEFL (minimum score 550 paper-based; 213 computer-based; 79 iBT). *Application deadline:* For fall admission, 7/15 priority date for domestic and international students; for spring admission, 12/1 priority date for domestic and international students. Applications are processed on a rolling basis. Application fee: $75. Electronic applications accepted. *Expenses:* Contact institution. *Financial support:* In 2009–10, 46 students received support, including 12 fellowships with full tuition reimbursements available (averaging $15,795 per year), 29 research assistantships with full tuition reimbursements available (averaging $20,500 per year), 5 teaching assistantships with full tuition reimbursements available (averaging $15,795 per year); institutionally sponsored loans, scholarships/grants, tuition waivers, and unspecified assistantships also available. Financial award application deadline: 1/15. *Faculty research:* Structural engineering, geotechnical engineering, water resources engineering, environmental engineering. Total annual research expenditures: $8 million. *Unit head:* Dr. Stephen Pessiki, Chairman, 610-758-3494, Fax: 610-758-6405, E-mail: pessiki@lehigh.edu. *Application contact:* Prisca Vidanage, Graduate Coordinator, 610-758-3530, Fax: 610-758-6405, E-mail: pmv1@lehigh.edu.

Louisiana State University and Agricultural and Mechanical College, Graduate School, College of Engineering, Department of Civil and Environmental Engineering, Baton Rouge, LA 70803. Offers environmental engineering (MSCE, PhD); geotechnical engineering (MSCE, PhD); structural engineering and mechanics (MSCE, PhD); transportation engineering (MSCE, PhD); water resources (MSCE, PhD). Part-time programs available. *Faculty:* 28 full-time (2 women). *Students:* 74 full-time (18 women), 37 part-time (6 women); includes 9 minority (1 American Indian/Alaska Native, 5 Asian Americans or Pacific Islanders, 3 Hispanic Americans), 59 international. Average age 31. 104 applicants, 63% accepted, 31 enrolled. In 2009, 16 master's, 13 doctorates awarded. *Degree requirements:* For master's, thesis optional; for doctorate, one foreign language, thesis/dissertation. *Entrance requirements:* For master's and doctorate, GRE General Test, minimum GPA of 3.0. Additional exam requirements/recommendations for international students: Required—TOEFL (minimum score 550 paper-based; 213 computer-based; 79 iBT) or IELTS (minimum score 6.5). *Application deadline:* For fall admission, 1/25 priority date for domestic students, 5/15 for international students; for spring admission, 10/15 for international students. Applications are processed on a rolling basis. Application fee: $50 ($70 for international students). Electronic applications accepted. *Financial support:* In 2009–10, 74 students received support, including 2 fellowships with full and partial tuition reimbursements available (averaging $16,672 per year), 65 research assistantships with full and partial tuition reimbursements available (averaging $11,242 per year); teaching assistantships with full and partial tuition reimbursements available, career-related internships or fieldwork, institutionally sponsored loans, scholarships/grants, and health care benefits also available. Financial award application deadline: 3/1; financial award applicants required to submit FAFSA. *Faculty research:* Mechanics and structures, environmental, geotechnical transportation, water resources. Total annual research expenditures: $2.4 million. *Unit head:* Dr. George Z. Voyiadjis, Chair/Boyd Professor, 225-578-8668, Fax: 225-578-9176, E-mail: cegzv@lsu.edu. *Application contact:* Dr. Donald Dean Adrian, Professor, 225-578-8636, E-mail: dadrian@lsu.edu.

Loyola Marymount University, College of Science and Engineering, Department of Civil Engineering and Environmental Science, Programs in Civil Engineering, Los Angeles, CA 90045. Offers environmental engineering (MSE). Part-time programs available. *Faculty:* 6 full-time (1 woman), 3 part-time/adjunct (0 women). *Students:* 2 full-time (0 women), 14 part-time (3 women); includes 10 minority (1 African American, 4 Asian Americans or Pacific Islanders, 5 Hispanic Americans), 1 international. Average age 30. 10 applicants, 30% accepted, 3 enrolled. In 2009, 2 master's awarded. *Degree requirements:* For master's, comprehensive exam. *Entrance requirements:* For master's, 2 letters of recommendation; bachelor of science degree or undergraduate engineering degree; 3 semester hours of general chemistry; course work in mathematics through one year of college calculus; 12 semester hours or 4 courses in science including biology, microbiology, chemistry, or physics. Additional exam requirements/recommendations for international students: Required—TOEFL (minimum score 550 paper-based; 213 computer-based; 80 iBT). *Application deadline:* Applications are processed on a rolling basis. Application fee: $50. Electronic applications accepted. *Financial support:* In 2009–10, 2 students received support. Scholarships/grants and laboratory assistantships available. Support available to part-time students. Financial award application deadline: 6/1; financial award applicants required to submit FAFSA. Total annual research expenditures: $14,321. *Unit head:* Prof. Joe Reichenberger, Graduate Director, 310-338-2830, E-mail: jreichenberger@lmu.edu. *Application contact:* Chake H. Kouyoumjian, Associate Dean of Graduate Studies, 310-338-2721, Fax: 310-338-6086, E-mail: ckouyoum@lmu.edu.

Manhattan College, Graduate Division, School of Engineering, Program in Environmental Engineering, Riverdale, NY 10471. Offers ME, MS. *Accreditation:* ABET. Part-time and evening/weekend programs available. *Degree requirements:* For master's, thesis or alternative. *Entrance requirements:* For master's, GRE (recommended), minimum GPA of 3.0. Additional exam requirements/recommendations for international students: Required—TOEFL (minimum score 550 paper-based; 213 computer-based). *Faculty research:* Water quality modeling, environmental chemistry, air modeling, biological treatment, water quality modeling, environmental chemistry, air modeling.

Marquette University, Graduate School, College of Engineering, Department of Civil and Environmental Engineering, Milwaukee, WI 53201-1881. Offers construction and public works management (MS, PhD); environmental/water resources engineering (MS, PhD); structural/geotechnical engineering (MS, PhD); transportation planning and engineering (MS, PhD). Part-time and evening/weekend programs available. *Faculty:* 13 full-time (0 women), 2 part-time/adjunct (1 woman). *Students:* 16 full-time (4 women), 17 part-time (2 women); includes 2 minority (1 Asian American or Pacific Islander, 1 Hispanic American), 13 international. Average age 27. 47 applicants, 85% accepted, 11 enrolled. In 2009, 8 master's, 1 doctorate awarded. Terminal master's awarded for partial completion of doctoral program. *Degree requirements:* For master's, comprehensive exam, thesis or alternative; for doctorate, thesis/dissertation. *Entrance requirements:* For master's and doctorate, GRE General Test, minimum GPA of 3.0. Additional exam requirements/recommendations for international students: Required—TOEFL. *Application deadline:* For fall admission, 6/1 priority date for domestic students. Applications are processed on a rolling basis. Application fee: $40. Electronic applications accepted. *Financial support:* In 2009–10, 13 students received support, including 5 fellowships with tuition reimbursements available (averaging $7,697 per year), 3 research assistantships with tuition reimbursements available (averaging $24,570 per year), 5 teaching assistantships with tuition reimbursements available (averaging $24,804 per year); Federal Work-Study, institutionally sponsored loans, scholarships/grants, and tuition waivers (full and partial) also available. Support available to part-time students. Financial award application deadline: 2/15. *Faculty research:* Highway safety, highway performance, and intelligent transportation systems; surface mount technology; watershed management. Total annual research expenditures: $138,209. *Unit head:* Dr. Michael S. Switzenbaum, Chair, 414-288-7030, Fax: 414-288-7521, E-mail: michael.switzenbaum@marquette.edu. *Application contact:* Dr. Stephen M. Heinrich, Director of Graduate Studies, 414-288-5466, E-mail: stephen.heinrich@marquette.edu.

Marshall University, Academic Affairs Division, College of Information Technology and Engineering, Weisberg Division of Engineering and Computer Science, Huntington, WV 25755. Offers engineering (MSE); information systems (MS). Part-time and evening/weekend programs available. *Faculty:* 6 full-time (0 women). *Students:* 20 full-time (6 women), 31 part-time (6 women); includes 3 minority (2 African Americans, 1 Asian American or Pacific Islander), 15 international. Average age 30. In 2009, 15 master's awarded. *Degree requirements:* For master's, final project, oral exam. *Entrance requirements:* For master's, GMAT or GRE General Test, minimum undergraduate GPA of 2.75. Application fee: $40. *Financial support:* Tuition waivers (full) available. Support available to part-time students. Financial award application deadline: 8/1; financial award applicants required to submit FAFSA. *Unit head:* Dr. Bill Pierson,

Environmental Engineering

Marshall University (continued)
Chair, 304-696-2695, E-mail: pierson@marshall.edu. *Application contact:* Information Contact, 304-746-1900, Fax: 304-746-1902, E-mail: services@marshall.edu.

Massachusetts Institute of Technology, School of Engineering, Department of Civil and Environmental Engineering, Cambridge, MA 02139-4307. Offers biological oceanography (PhD, Sc D); chemical oceanography (PhD, Sc D); civil and environmental engineering (M Eng, SM, PhD, Sc D); civil and environmental systems (PhD, Sc D); civil engineering (PhD, Sc D, CE); coastal engineering (PhD, Sc D); construction engineering and management (PhD, Sc D); environmental biology (PhD, Sc D); environmental chemistry (PhD, Sc D); environmental engineering (PhD, Sc D); environmental fluid mechanics (PhD, Sc D); geotechnical and geoenvironmental engineering (PhD, Sc D); hydrology (PhD, Sc D); information technology (PhD, Sc D); oceanographic engineering (PhD, Sc D); structures and materials (PhD, Sc D); transportation (PhD, Sc D); SM/MBA. *Faculty:* 36 full-time (5 women). *Students:* 190 full-time (59 women); includes 22 minority (2 African Americans, 14 Asian Americans or Pacific Islanders, 6 Hispanic Americans), 103 international. Average age 26. 478 applicants, 25% accepted, 76 enrolled. In 2009, 72 master's, 14 doctorates awarded. *Degree requirements:* For master's and CE, thesis; for doctorate, comprehensive exam, thesis/dissertation. *Entrance requirements:* For master's and doctorate, GRE General Test. Additional exam requirements/recommendations for international students: Required—TOEFL (minimum score 577 paper-based; 233 computer-based; 90 iBT), IELTS (minimum score 7). *Application deadline:* For fall admission, 1/2 for domestic and international students. Application fee: $75. Electronic applications accepted. *Financial support:* In 2009–10, 185 students received support, including 40 fellowships with tuition reimbursements available (averaging $27,725 per year), 97 research assistantships with tuition reimbursements available (averaging $28,035 per year), 21 teaching assistantships with tuition reimbursements available (averaging $24,802 per year); career-related internships or fieldwork, Federal Work-Study, institutionally sponsored loans, scholarships/grants, health care benefits, and unspecified assistantships also available. *Faculty research:* Environmental chemistry, environmental microbiology, environmental fluid mechanics and coastal engineering, geotechnical engineering and geomechanics, hydrology and hydroclimatology, mechanics of materials and structures, operations research/supply chain, transportation. Total annual research expenditures: $16.6 million. *Unit head:* Prof. Andrew Whittle, Department Head, 617-253-7101. *Application contact:* Patricia Glidden, Graduate Admissions Coordinator, 617-253-7119, Fax: 617-258-6775, E-mail: cee-admissions@mit.edu.

McGill University, Faculty of Graduate and Postdoctoral Studies, Faculty of Engineering, Department of Chemical Engineering, Montréal, QC H3A 2T5, Canada. Offers chemical engineering (M Eng, PhD); environmental engineering (M Eng).

McGill University, Faculty of Graduate and Postdoctoral Studies, Faculty of Engineering, Department of Civil Engineering and Applied Mechanics, Montréal, QC H3A 2T5, Canada. Offers environmental engineering (M Eng, M Sc, PhD); fluid mechanics (M Sc); fluid mechanics and hydraulic engineering (M Eng, PhD); materials engineering (M Eng, PhD); rehabilitation of urban infrastructure (M Eng, PhD); soil behavior (M Eng, PhD); soil mechanics and foundations (M Eng, PhD); structures and structural mechanics (M Eng, PhD); water resources (M Sc); water resources engineering (M Eng, PhD).

Memorial University of Newfoundland, School of Graduate Studies, Interdisciplinary Program in Environmental Systems Engineering and Management, St. John's, NL A1C 5S7, Canada. Offers MA Sc. *Degree requirements:* For master's, project course. *Entrance requirements:* For master's, 2nd class engineering degree.

Mercer University, Graduate Studies, Macon Campus, School of Engineering, Macon, GA 31207-0003. Offers biomedical engineering (MSE); computer engineering (MSE); electrical engineering (MSE); engineering management (MSE); environmental engineering (MSE); environmental systems (MS); mechanical engineering (MSE); software engineering (MSE); software systems (MS); technical communications management (MS); technical management (MS). Part-time and evening/weekend programs available. Postbaccalaureate distance learning degree programs offered (no on-campus study). *Faculty:* 19 full-time (4 women), 1 part-time/adjunct (0 women). *Students:* 6 full-time (1 woman), 95 part-time (22 women); includes 22 minority (5 African Americans, 13 Asian Americans or Pacific Islanders, 4 Hispanic Americans), 3 international. Average age 33. In 2009, 42 master's awarded. *Degree requirements:* For master's, thesis or alternative. *Entrance requirements:* For master's, minimum undergraduate GPA of 3.0. Additional exam requirements/recommendations for international students: Required—TOEFL. *Application deadline:* For fall admission, 7/1 for domestic students; for spring admission, 11/15 for domestic students. Applications are processed on a rolling basis. Application fee: $35 ($50 for international students). Electronic applications accepted. *Expenses:* Contact institution. *Financial support:* Federal Work-Study available. *Unit head:* Dr. Wade H. Shaw, Dean, 478-301-2459, Fax: 478-301-5593, E-mail: shaw_wh@mercer.edu. *Application contact:* Greg Lofton, Graduate Program Coordinator, 478-301-5480, Fax: 478-301-5434, E-mail: lofton_g@mercer.edu.

Michigan State University, The Graduate School, College of Engineering, Department of Civil and Environmental Engineering, East Lansing, MI 48824. Offers civil engineering (MS, PhD); environmental engineering (MS, PhD); environmental engineering-environmental toxicology (PhD). Part-time programs available. *Entrance requirements:* Additional exam requirements/recommendations for international students: Required—TOEFL. Electronic applications accepted.

Michigan Technological University, Graduate School, College of Engineering, Department of Civil and Environmental Engineering, Program in Environmental Engineering, Houghton, MI 49931. Offers ME, MS, PhD. Part-time programs available. Terminal master's awarded for partial completion of doctoral program. *Degree requirements:* For master's, comprehensive exam (for some programs), thesis (for some programs); for doctorate, comprehensive exam, thesis/dissertation. *Entrance requirements:* For master's, GRE (to be considered for university assistantship); for doctorate, GRE. Additional exam requirements/recommendations for international students: Required—TOEFL (minimum score 600 paper-based; 250 computer-based). Electronic applications accepted. *Expenses:* Contact institution.

Michigan Technological University, Graduate School, College of Engineering, Department of Civil and Environmental Engineering, Program in Environmental Engineering Science, Houghton, MI 49931. Offers MS. Part-time programs available. *Degree requirements:* For master's, comprehensive exam (for some programs), thesis (for some programs). *Entrance requirements:* For master's, GRE (to be considered for university assistantship). Additional exam requirements/recommendations for international students: Required—TOEFL (minimum score 600 paper-based; 250 computer-based). Electronic applications accepted. *Expenses:* Contact institution.

Milwaukee School of Engineering, Department of Architectural Engineering and Building Construction, Program in Environmental Engineering, Milwaukee, WI 53202-3109. Offers MS. Part-time and evening/weekend programs available. *Faculty:* 2 full-time (1 woman), 4 part-time/adjunct (0 women). *Students:* 3 full-time (1 woman), 4 part-time (2 women). Average age 22. 11 applicants, 73% accepted, 3 enrolled. In 2009, 3 master's awarded. *Degree requirements:* For master's, design project. *Entrance requirements:* For master's, GRE General Test or GMAT, 2 letters of recommendation, BS in architectural, chemical, civil or mechanical engineering or a related field. Additional exam requirements/recommendations for international students: Required—TOEFL (minimum score 79 iBT). *Application deadline:* Applications are processed on a rolling basis. Application fee: $30. Electronic applications accepted. *Expenses:* Tuition: Part-time $603 per credit. *Financial support:* In 2009–10, 4 students received support. Career-related internships or fieldwork available. Support available to part-time students. Financial award applicants required to submit FAFSA. *Faculty research:* Environmental systems. *Unit head:* Dr. Francis Manhuta, Director, 414-277-7599. *Application contact:* David E. Tietyen, Graduate Admissions Director, 800-332-6763, Fax: 414-277-7475, E-mail: wp@msoe.edu.

Missouri University of Science and Technology, Graduate School, Department of Civil, Architectural, and Environmental Engineering, Rolla, MO 65409. Offers civil engineering (MS, DE, PhD); construction engineering (MS, DE, PhD); environmental engineering (MS); fluid mechanics (MS, DE, PhD); geotechnical engineering (MS, DE, PhD); hydrology and hydraulic engineering (MS, DE, PhD). Part-time and evening/weekend programs available. Terminal master's awarded for partial completion of doctoral program. *Degree requirements:* For master's, thesis optional; for doctorate, comprehensive exam, thesis/dissertation. *Entrance requirements:* For master's, GRE General Test (minimum combined score 1100), minimum GPA of 3.0; for doctorate, GRE General Test (minimum score: verbal and quantitative 400, writing 3.5), minimum GPA of 3.0. Additional exam requirements/recommendations for international students: Required—TOEFL. Electronic applications accepted. *Faculty research:* Earthquake engineering, structural optimization and control systems, structural health monitoring/damage detection, soil-structure interaction, soil mechanics and foundation engineering.

Montana State University, College of Graduate Studies, College of Engineering, Department of Chemical and Biological Engineering, Bozeman, MT 59717. Offers chemical engineering (MS); engineering (PhD), including chemical engineering option, environmental engineering option; environmental engineering (MS). Part-time programs available. *Faculty:* 9 full-time (2 women), 1 part-time/adjunct (0 women). *Students:* 1 full-time (0 women), 23 part-time (9 women); includes 2 minority (1 American Indian/Alaska Native, 1 Asian American or Pacific Islander), 3 international. Average age 27. 7 applicants. In 2009, 4 master's awarded. *Degree requirements:* For master's, comprehensive exam, thesis (for some programs); for doctorate, comprehensive exam, thesis/dissertation. *Entrance requirements:* For master's, GRE General Test, BS in chemical engineering or related scientific field; for doctorate, GRE General Test, BS or MS in chemical engineering or related scientific field. Additional exam requirements/recommendations for international students: Required—TOEFL (minimum score 550 paper-based; 213 computer-based). *Application deadline:* For fall admission, 7/15 priority date for domestic students, 5/15 priority date for international students; for spring admission, 12/1 priority date for domestic students, 10/1 priority date for international students. Applications are processed on a rolling basis. Application fee: $30. Electronic applications accepted. *Expenses:* Tuition, state resident: full-time $5635; part-time $3492 per year. Tuition, nonresident: full-time $17,212; part-time $7865.10 per year. Required fees: $1441.05; $153.15 per credit. Tuition and fees vary according to course load and program. *Financial support:* In 2009–10, 3 fellowships with full tuition reimbursements (averaging $25,000 per year), 20 research assistantships with full tuition reimbursements (averaging $18,000 per year), 2 teaching assistantships with full tuition reimbursements (averaging $18,000 per year) were awarded. Financial award application deadline: 3/1; financial award applicants required to submit FAFSA. *Faculty research:* The effects of variable permeability on the resistance to flow through the tissues and biofilms; development of protective coatings on planar solid oxide fuel cell (SOFC) metallic interconnects; carbon sequestration; zero emissions research and technology; research in the areas of biofuels, extremophilic bioprocessing, and in situ biocatalyzed heavy metal transformations; subsurface biofilm barriers; magnetic resonance microscopy. Total annual research expenditures: $1.8 million. *Unit head:* Dr. Ron W. Larson, Head, 406-994-2221, Fax: 406-994-5308, E-mail: ronl@coe.montana.edu. *Application contact:* Dr. Carl A. Fox, Vice Provost for Graduate Education, 406-994-4145, Fax: 406-994-7433, E-mail: gradstudy@montana.edu.

Montana Tech of The University of Montana, Graduate School, Department of Environmental Engineering, Butte, MT 59701-8997. Offers MS. Part-time programs available. *Faculty:* 7 full-time (2 women). *Students:* 5 full-time (2 women), 1 part-time (0 women); includes 1 minority (American Indian/Alaska Native). 7 applicants, 57% accepted, 1 enrolled. *Degree requirements:* For master's, thesis. *Entrance requirements:* For master's, GRE General Test, minimum GPA of 3.0. Additional exam requirements/recommendations for international students: Required—TOEFL (minimum score 525 paper-based; 195 computer-based; 71 iBT). *Application deadline:* For fall admission, 4/1 priority date for domestic students, 3/1 priority date for international students; for spring admission, 10/1 priority date for domestic students, 7/1 priority date for international students. Applications are processed on a rolling basis. Application fee: $30. Electronic applications accepted. *Expenses:* Tuition, state resident: full-time $5068; part-time $319 per credit. Tuition, nonresident: full-time $14,815; part-time $875 per credit. Tuition and fees vary according to course load and campus/location. *Financial support:* In 2009–10, 5 students received support, including 3 teaching assistantships with partial tuition reimbursements available (averaging $4,333 per year); research assistantships with full tuition reimbursements available, career-related internships or fieldwork, tuition waivers (full and partial), and unspecified assistantships also available. Financial award application deadline: 4/1; financial award applicants required to submit FAFSA. *Faculty research:* Mine waste reclamation, modeling, air pollution control, wetlands, water pollution control. *Unit head:* Dr. Kumar Ganesan, Head, 406-496-4239, Fax: 406-496-4650, E-mail: kganesan@mtech.edu. *Application contact:* Cindy Dunstan, Administrator, Graduate School, 406-496-4304, Fax: 406-496-4710, E-mail: cdunstan@mtech.edu.

National University, Academic Affairs, School of Engineering and Technology, Department of Applied Engineering, La Jolla, CA 92037-1011. Offers database administration (MS); engineering management (MS); environmental engineering (MS); homeland security and safety engineering (MS); system engineering (MS); wireless communications (MS). Part-time and evening/weekend programs available. Postbaccalaureate distance learning degree programs offered (no on-campus study). *Faculty:* 6 full-time (1 woman), 7 part-time/adjunct (1 woman). *Students:* 61 full-time (16 women), 176 part-time (35 women); includes 54 minority (11 African Americans, 1 American Indian/Alaska Native, 23 Asian Americans or Pacific Islanders, 19 Hispanic Americans), 117 international. Average age 31. 133 applicants, 100% accepted, 83 enrolled. In 2009, 34 master's awarded. *Degree requirements:* For master's, thesis. *Entrance requirements:* For master's, interview, minimum GPA of 2.5. Additional exam requirements/recommendations for international students: Required—TOEFL (minimum score 550 paper-based; 213 computer-based; 79 iBT), IELTS (minimum score 6). *Application deadline:* Applications are processed on a rolling basis. Application fee: $60 ($65 for international students). Electronic applications accepted. *Expenses:* Tuition: Part-time $338 per quarter hour. *Financial support:* Career-related internships or fieldwork, institutionally sponsored loans, scholarships/grants, and tuition waivers (partial) available. Support available to part-time students. Financial award application deadline: 6/30; financial award applicants required to submit FAFSA. *Unit head:* Dr. Shekar Viswanathan, Chair and Associate Professor, 858-309-8416, Fax: 858-309-3420, E-mail: sviswana@nu.edu. *Application contact:* Dominick Giovanniello, Associate Regional Dean—San Diego, 800-NAT-UNIV, Fax: 858-541-7792, E-mail: dgiovann@nu.edu.

New Jersey Institute of Technology, Office of Graduate Studies, Newark College of Engineering, Department of Civil and Environmental Engineering, Program in Environmental Engineering, Newark, NJ 07102. Offers MS, PhD. Part-time and evening/weekend programs available. Terminal master's awarded for partial completion of doctoral program. *Degree requirements:* For master's, thesis or alternative; for doctorate, thesis/dissertation, residency. *Entrance requirements:* For master's, GRE General Test; for doctorate, GRE General Test, minimum graduate GPA of 3.5. Additional exam requirements/recommendations for international students: Required—TOEFL (minimum score 550 paper-based; 213 computer-based; 79 iBT). Electronic applications accepted. *Faculty research:* Water resources engineering, solid and hazardous waste management.

New Mexico Institute of Mining and Technology, Graduate Studies, Department of Environmental Engineering, Socorro, NM 87801. Offers environmental engineering (MS), including air quality engineering and science, hazardous waste engineering, water quality engineering and science. *Degree requirements:* For master's, thesis. *Entrance requirements:* For master's, GRE General Test. Additional exam requirements/recommendations for international students: Required—TOEFL (minimum score 540 paper-based; 207 computer-based). *Faculty research:* Air quality, hazardous waste management, wastewater management and treatment, site remediation.

New Mexico State University, Graduate School, College of Engineering, Department of Civil Engineering, Las Cruces, NM 88003-8001. Offers civil engineering (MSCE, PhD); environ-

Environmental Engineering

Oklahoma State University (continued)
award application deadline: 3/1; financial award applicants required to submit FAFSA. *Unit head:* Dr. John Veenstra, Head, 405-744-5190, Fax: 405-744-7554. *Application contact:* Dr. Gordon Emslie, Dean, 405-744-6368, Fax: 405-744-0355, E-mail: grad-i@okstate.edu.

Old Dominion University, Frank Batten College of Engineering and Technology, Program in Civil and Environmental Engineering, Norfolk, VA 23529. Offers D Eng, PhD. Part-time and evening/weekend programs available. Postbaccalaureate distance learning degree programs offered (minimal on-campus study). *Faculty:* 11 full-time (2 women), 7 part-time/adjunct (2 women). *Students:* 1 full-time (0 women), 2 part-time (0 women); includes 1 minority (African American). Average age 48. *Degree requirements:* For doctorate, thesis/dissertation, candidacy exam. *Entrance requirements:* For doctorate, GRE, minimum GPA of 3.5 for regular admission. Additional exam requirements/recommendations for international students: Required—TOEFL (minimum score 550 paper-based; 213 computer-based; 80 iBT). *Application deadline:* For fall admission, 6/1 priority date for domestic students, 4/15 priority date for international students; for spring admission, 11/1 priority date for domestic students, 10/1 priority date for international students. Applications are processed on a rolling basis. Application fee: $40. Electronic applications accepted. *Expenses:* Tuition, state resident: full-time $8112; part-time $338 per credit. Tuition, nonresident: full-time $20,256; part-time $844 per credit. Required fees: $119 per semester. One-time fee: $50. *Financial support:* Scholarships/grants and unspecified assistantships available. Support available to part-time students. Financial award application deadline: 4/1. *Faculty research:* Structural engineering, coastal engineering, environmental engineering, geotechnical engineering, water resources, transportation engineering. Total annual research expenditures: $474,605. *Unit head:* Dr. Isao Ishibashi, Graduate Program Director, 757-683-4641, Fax: 757-683-5354, E-mail: cegpd@odu.edu. *Application contact:* Dr. Isao Ishibashi, Graduate Program Director, 757-683-4641, Fax: 757-683-5354, E-mail: cegpd@odu.edu.

Old Dominion University, Frank Batten College of Engineering and Technology, Program in Environmental Engineering, Norfolk, VA 23529. Offers ME, MS. Part-time and evening/weekend programs available. Postbaccalaureate distance learning degree programs offered (minimal on-campus study). *Faculty:* 11 full-time (2 women), 7 part-time/adjunct (2 women). *Students:* 10 full-time (4 women), 28 part-time (11 women); includes 5 minority (4 African Americans, 1 Asian American or Pacific Islander), 12 international. Average age 31. 22 applicants, 95% accepted, 11 enrolled. In 2009, 13 master's awarded. *Degree requirements:* For master's, comprehensive exam, thesis optional. *Entrance requirements:* For master's, GRE, minimum GPA of 3.0 for regular admission. Additional exam requirements/recommendations for international students: Required—TOEFL (minimum score 550 paper-based; 213 computer-based; 80 iBT). *Application deadline:* For fall admission, 6/1 priority date for domestic students, 4/15 priority date for international students; for spring admission, 11/1 priority date for domestic students, 10/1 priority date for international students. Applications are processed on a rolling basis. Application fee: $40. Electronic applications accepted. *Expenses:* Tuition, state resident: full-time $8112; part-time $338 per credit. Tuition, nonresident: full-time $20,256; part-time $844 per credit. Required fees: $119 per semester. One-time fee: $50. *Financial support:* In 2009–10, 1 fellowship with full tuition reimbursement (averaging $15,000 per year), 1 research assistantship with full and partial tuition reimbursement (averaging $13,714 per year), 2 teaching assistantships with full tuition reimbursements (averaging $13,500 per year) were awarded; scholarships/grants and unspecified assistantships also available. Support available to part-time students. Financial award application deadline: 4/1; financial award applicants required to submit FAFSA. *Faculty research:* Aquatic chemistry, physiochemical treatment, waste water treatment, hazardous waste treatment, environmental microbiology. Total annual research expenditures: $474,605. *Unit head:* Dr. Isao Ishibashi, Graduate Program Director, 757-683-4641, Fax: 757-683-5354, E-mail: cegpd@odu.edu. *Application contact:* Dr. Linda Vahala, Associate Dean, 757-683-3789, Fax: 757-683-4898, E-mail: lvahala@odu.edu.

Oregon Health & Science University, OGI School of Science and Engineering, Department of Environmental and Biomolecular Systems, Portland, OR 97239-3098. Offers biochemistry and molecular biology (MS, PhD); environmental science and engineering (MS, PhD). Tuition and fees vary according to course level, course load, degree level, program and reciprocity agreements.

Oregon State University, Graduate School, College of Engineering, School of Civil and Construction Engineering, Corvallis, OR 97331. Offers civil engineering (MS, PhD); coastal and ocean engineering (M Oc E, PhD); coastal engineering (MS); construction engineering management (MBE, PhD); engineering (M Eng, MAIS); geotechnical engineering (MS, PhD); structural engineering (MS, PhD); transportation engineering (MS, PhD); water engineering (MS, PhD). Part-time programs available. *Faculty:* 25 full-time (5 women), 1 part-time/adjunct (0 women). *Students:* 71 full-time (17 women), 12 part-time (2 women); includes 4 minority (all Asian Americans or Pacific Islanders), 34 international. Average age 28. 75 applicants, 87% accepted, 31 enrolled. In 2009, 26 master's, 7 doctorates awarded. Terminal master's awarded for partial completion of doctoral program. *Degree requirements:* For master's, thesis or alternative; for doctorate, one foreign language, thesis/dissertation. *Entrance requirements:* For master's, GRE General Test, minimum GPA of 3.0 in last 90 hours (3.5 for MS); for doctorate, GRE General Test, minimum GPA of 3.0 in last 90 hours of undergraduate course work. Additional exam requirements/recommendations for international students: Required—TOEFL (minimum score 580 paper-based; 237 computer-based). *Application deadline:* For fall admission, 3/1 priority date for domestic students. Applications are processed on a rolling basis. Application fee: $50. *Expenses:* Tuition, state resident: full-time $9774; part-time $362 per credit. Tuition, nonresident: full-time $15,849; part-time $587 per credit. Required fees: $1639. Full-time tuition and fees vary according to course load and program. *Financial support:* Fellowships, research assistantships with full tuition reimbursements, teaching assistantships with full tuition reimbursements, career-related internships or fieldwork and institutionally sponsored loans available. Support available to part-time students. Financial award application deadline: 2/1. *Faculty research:* Hazardous waste management, carbon cycling, wave forces on structures, pavement design, seismic analysis. Total annual research expenditures: $7.1 million. *Unit head:* Dr. Scott A. Ashford, Head, 541-737-4934. *Application contact:* Kathy Westberg, CCE Graduate Advising School Operations Manager, 541-737-1786, Fax: 541-737-3052, E-mail: kathy.westberg@oregonstate.edu.

Penn State University Park, Graduate School, College of Engineering, Department of Civil and Environmental Engineering, State College, University Park, PA 16802-1503. Offers M Eng, MS, PhD.

Polytechnic Institute of NYU, Department of Civil Engineering, Major in Environmental Engineering, Brooklyn, NY 11201-2990. Offers MS. Part-time and evening/weekend programs available. *Students:* 10 full-time (4 women), 2 part-time (1 woman), 10 international. 32 applicants, 63% accepted, 7 enrolled. In 2009, 5 master's awarded. *Degree requirements:* For master's, comprehensive exam (for some programs), thesis (for some programs). *Entrance requirements:* Additional exam requirements/recommendations for international students: Required—TOEFL (minimum score 550 paper-based; 213 computer-based; 80 iBT); Recommended—IELTS (minimum score 6.5). *Application deadline:* For fall admission, 7/31 priority date for domestic students, 4/30 priority date for international students; for spring admission, 12/31 priority date for domestic students, 10/30 priority date for international students. Applications are processed on a rolling basis. Application fee: $75. Electronic applications accepted. *Expenses:* Tuition: Full-time $21,492; part-time $1194 per credit hour. Required fees: $1160; $204 per course. *Financial support:* Fellowships, research assistantships, teaching assistantships, institutionally sponsored loans, scholarships/grants, and unspecified assistantships available. Support available to part-time students. Financial award applicants required to submit FAFSA. *Unit head:* Dr. Lawrence Chiarelli, Head, 718-260-4040, Fax: 718-260-3433, E-mail: lchiarel@poly.edu. *Application contact:* JeanCarlo Bonilla, Director of Graduate Enrollment Management, 718-260-3182, Fax: 718-260-3684, E-mail: gradinfo@poly.edu.

Polytechnic Institute of NYU, Long Island Graduate Center, Graduate Programs, Department of Civil Engineering, Major in Environmental Engineering, Melville, NY 11747. Offers MS.

Degree requirements: For master's, comprehensive exam (for some programs), thesis (for some programs). *Entrance requirements:* Additional exam requirements/recommendations for international students: Required—TOEFL (minimum score 550 paper-based; 213 computer-based; 80 iBT); Recommended—IELTS (minimum score 6.5). *Application deadline:* For fall admission, 7/31 priority date for domestic students, 4/30 priority date for international students; for spring admission, 12/31 priority date for domestic students, 11/30 priority date for international students. Applications are processed on a rolling basis. Application fee: $75. Electronic applications accepted. *Financial support:* Institutionally sponsored loans, scholarships/grants, and unspecified assistantships available. Support available to part-time students. Financial award applicants required to submit FAFSA. *Unit head:* Dr. Roger Peter Roess, Department Head, 718-260-3018, E-mail: rroess@poly.edu. *Application contact:* JeanCarlo Bonilla, Director of Graduate Enrollment Management, 718-260-3182, Fax: 718-260-3624, E-mail: gradinfo@poly.edu.

Pontificia Universidad Catolica Madre y Maestra, Graduate School, Santiago, Dominican Republic. Offers administration (M Adm); architecture of interiors (M Arch); architecture of tourist lodgings (M Arch); banking and financial management (M Mgmt); civil law (LL M); construction administration (ME); corporate business law (LL M); criminal procedure law (LL M); environmental engineering (ME, MEE); finance (M Mgmt); history applied to education (M Ed); human resources (EMBA); insurance (M Mgmt); international business (M Mgmt); labor law and Social Security (LL M); logistics management (ME); marketing (M Mgmt); renewable energy (ME); strategic cost management (M Mgmt). *Entrance requirements:* For master's, curriculum vitae, interview.

Portland State University, Graduate Studies, Maseeh College of Engineering and Computer Science, Department of Civil and Environmental Engineering, Portland, OR 97207-0751. Offers civil and environmental engineering (M Eng, MS, PhD); civil and environmental engineering management (M Eng); environmental sciences and resources (PhD); systems science (PhD). Part-time and evening/weekend programs available. *Degree requirements:* For master's, thesis or alternative, oral exam; for doctorate, one foreign language, thesis/dissertation, oral and written exams. *Entrance requirements:* For master's, minimum GPA of 3.0 in upper-division course work, BS in civil engineering or allied field; for doctorate, GRE General Test, GRE Subject Test, minimum GPA of 3.0 in upper-division course work, master's in civil and environmental engineering, 2 years full-time graduate work beyond master's degree. Additional exam requirements/recommendations for international students: Required—TOEFL (minimum score 550 paper-based; 213 computer-based). *Faculty research:* Structures, water resources, geotechnical engineering, environmental engineering, transportation.

Rensselaer Polytechnic Institute, Graduate School, School of Engineering, Department of Civil and Environmental Engineering, Program in Environmental Engineering, Troy, NY 12180-3590. Offers M Eng, MS, PhD. Part-time programs available. *Faculty:* 2 full-time (1 woman), 1 part-time/adjunct (0 women). *Students:* 6 full-time (2 women), 1 part-time (0 women); includes 1 Hispanic American, 1 international. Average age 25. 20 applicants, 15% accepted, 1 enrolled. In 2009, 1 master's, 2 doctorates awarded. Terminal master's awarded for partial completion of doctoral program. *Degree requirements:* For master's, thesis (for some programs); for doctorate, thesis/dissertation. *Entrance requirements:* For master's and doctorate, GRE. Additional exam requirements/recommendations for international students: Required—TOEFL (minimum score 570 paper-based; 230 computer-based; 89 iBT), IELTS (minimum score 6.5). *Application deadline:* For fall admission, 1/15 priority date for domestic students, 1/15 for international students; for spring admission, 8/15 for domestic and international students. Applications are processed on a rolling basis. Application fee: $75. Electronic applications accepted. *Expenses:* Tuition: Full-time $38,100. *Financial support:* In 2009–10, 1 fellowship with full tuition reimbursement (averaging $16,500 per year), 3 research assistantships with full tuition reimbursements (averaging $16,500 per year), 4 teaching assistantships with full tuition reimbursements (averaging $16,500 per year) were awarded; career-related internships or fieldwork, institutionally sponsored loans, and tuition waivers (full and partial) also available. Financial award application deadline: 2/1. *Faculty research:* Water treatment, bioremediation of hazardous wastes, environmental systems. Total annual research expenditures: $44,940. *Unit head:* Dr. Tarek Abdoun, Acting Chair, 518-276-6362, Fax: 518-276-4833, E-mail: abdout@rpi.edu. *Application contact:* Kimberly Boyce, Administrative Assistant II, 518-276-6941, Fax: 518-276-4833, E-mail: boycek@rpi.edu.

Rice University, Graduate Programs, George R. Brown School of Engineering, Department of Civil and Environmental Engineering, Houston, TX 77251-1892. Offers civil engineering (MCE, MS, PhD); environmental engineering (MEE, MES, MS, PhD); environmental science (MEE, MES, MS, PhD). Part-time programs available. *Degree requirements:* For master's, thesis (for some programs); for doctorate, thesis/dissertation. *Entrance requirements:* For master's and doctorate, GRE General Test, GRE Subject Test, minimum GPA of 3.25. Additional exam requirements/recommendations for international students: Required—TOEFL (minimum score 600 paper-based; 250 computer-based; 90 iBT). Electronic applications accepted. *Faculty research:* Biology and chemistry of groundwater, pollutant fate in groundwater systems, water quality monitoring, urban storm water runoff, urban air quality.

Rose-Hulman Institute of Technology, Faculty of Engineering and Applied Sciences, Department of Civil Engineering, Terre Haute, IN 47803-3999. Offers civil engineering (MS); environmental engineering (MS). Part-time programs available. *Faculty:* 6 full-time (1 woman). *Students:* 1 (woman) full-time. Average age 22. 5 applicants, 60% accepted. *Degree requirements:* For master's, thesis. *Entrance requirements:* For master's, GRE, minimum GPA of 3.0. Additional exam requirements/recommendations for international students: Required—TOEFL (minimum score 580 paper-based; 237 computer-based; 92 iBT). *Application deadline:* For fall admission, 2/1 priority date for domestic students. Applications are processed on a rolling basis. Application fee: $0. *Expenses:* Tuition: Full-time $33,900; part-time $987 per credit hour. *Financial support:* In 2009–10, 1 student received support; fellowships with full and partial tuition reimbursements available, research assistantships with full and partial tuition reimbursements available, institutionally sponsored loans, scholarships/grants, and tuition waivers (full and partial) available. Financial award application deadline: 2/1. *Faculty research:* Urban stormwater management, groundwater and surface water models, solid and hazardous waste, risk and decision analysis. *Unit head:* Dr. Kevin G. Sutterer, Chairman, 812-877-8959, Fax: 812-877-8440, E-mail: kevin.g.sutterer@rose-hulman.edu. *Application contact:* Dr. Daniel J. Moore, Associate Dean of the Faculty, 812-877-8110, Fax: 812-877-8061, E-mail: daniel.j.moore@rose-hulman.edu.

Royal Military College of Canada, Division of Graduate Studies and Research, Engineering Division, Department of Chemistry and Chemical Engineering, Program in Environmental Engineering, Kingston, ON K7K 7B4, Canada. Offers chemical and materials (M Eng); chemistry (M Eng); environmental (PhD); nuclear (PhD). *Degree requirements:* For master's, thesis; for doctorate, comprehensive exam, thesis/dissertation. *Entrance requirements:* For master's, honours degree with second-class standing; for doctorate, master's degree. Electronic applications accepted.

Rutgers, The State University of New Jersey, New Brunswick, Graduate School-New Brunswick, Department of Civil and Environmental Engineering, Piscataway, NJ 08854-8097. Offers MS, PhD. Part-time and evening/weekend programs available. Terminal master's awarded for partial completion of doctoral program. *Degree requirements:* For master's, comprehensive exam, thesis or alternative; for doctorate, comprehensive exam, thesis/dissertation. *Entrance requirements:* For master's and doctorate, GRE General Test. Additional exam requirements/recommendations for international students: Required—TOEFL (minimum score 580 paper-based; 237 computer-based). Electronic applications accepted. *Faculty research:* Civil engineering materials research, non-destructive evaluation of transportation infrastructure, transportation planning, intelligent transportation systems.

Southern Methodist University, Bobby B. Lyle School of Engineering, Department of Environmental and Civil Engineering, Dallas, TX 75275-0340. Offers applied science (MS, PhD); civil engineering (MS, PhD); environmental engineering (MS); environmental science (MS), including

mental engineering (MS Env E). Part-time programs available. Postbaccalaureate distance learning degree programs offered. *Faculty:* 11 full-time (2 women). *Students:* 52 full-time (16 women), 20 part-time (7 women); includes 21 minority (2 Asian Americans or Pacific Islanders, 19 Hispanic Americans), 35 international. Average age 30. 57 applicants, 74% accepted, 23 enrolled. In 2009, 21 master's, 3 doctorates awarded. *Degree requirements:* For master's, thesis (for some programs); for doctorate, thesis/dissertation. *Entrance requirements:* For master's and doctorate, BS in engineering, minimum GPA of 3.0. Additional exam requirements/recommendations for international students: Required—TOEFL. *Application deadline:* For fall admission, 4/1 priority date for domestic and international students; for spring admission, 9/1 priority date for domestic and international students. Applications are processed on a rolling basis. Application fee: $30 ($50 for international students). Electronic applications accepted. *Expenses:* Tuition, state resident: full-time $4080; part-time $223 per credit. Tuition, nonresident: full-time $14,256; part-time $647 per credit. Required fees: $1278; $639 per semester. *Financial support:* In 2009–10, 26 research assistantships (averaging $10,619 per year), 19 teaching assistantships (averaging $11,291 per year) were awarded; fellowships, career-related internships or fieldwork, Federal Work-Study, and health care benefits also available. Support available to part-time students. Financial award application deadline: 3/1. *Faculty research:* Structural engineering, water resources engineering, environmental engineering, geotechnical engineering, hydraulics/hydrology. *Unit head:* Dr. Adrian Hanson, Interim Head, 575-646-3801, E-mail: athanson@nmsu.edu. *Application contact:* Dr. Adrian Hanson, Interim Head, 575-646-3801, E-mail: athanson@nmsu.edu.

New York Institute of Technology, Graduate Division, School of Engineering and Computing Sciences, Program in Environmental Technology, Old Westbury, NY 11568-8000. Offers MS. Part-time and evening/weekend programs available. *Students:* 22 full-time (9 women), 26 part-time (12 women); includes 6 minority (3 African Americans, 1 Asian American or Pacific Islander, 2 Hispanic Americans), 23 international. Average age 30. In 2009, 18 master's awarded. *Degree requirements:* For master's, thesis or alternative. *Entrance requirements:* For master's, minimum QPA of 2.85. Additional exam requirements/recommendations for international students: Required—TOEFL (minimum score 550 paper-based; 213 computer-based). *Application deadline:* For fall admission, 7/1 priority date for domestic students; for spring admission, 12/1 priority date for domestic students. Applications are processed on a rolling basis. Application fee: $50. Electronic applications accepted. *Expenses:* Tuition: Part-time $825 per credit. *Financial support:* Fellowships, research assistantships with partial tuition reimbursements, career-related internships or fieldwork, institutionally sponsored loans, tuition waivers (full and partial), and unspecified assistantships available. Support available to part-time students. Financial award applicants required to submit FAFSA. *Faculty research:* Development and testing of methodology to assess health risks and environmental impacts from separate sanitary sewage, introduction of technology innovation (including geographical information systems). *Unit head:* Stanley Greenwald, Chair, 516-686-7969, Fax: 516-686-7919, E-mail: sgreenwa@nyit.edu. *Application contact:* Dr. Jacquelyn Nealon, Vice President for Enrollment Services, 516-686-7925, Fax: 516-686-7597, E-mail: jnealon@nyit.edu.

North Dakota State University, College of Graduate and Interdisciplinary Studies, College of Engineering and Architecture, Department of Civil Engineering, Fargo, ND 58108. Offers civil engineering (MS, PhD); environmental engineering (MS, PhD); transportation and logistics (PhD). PhD in transportation and logistics offered jointly with Upper Great Plains Transportation Institute. Part-time programs available. Postbaccalaureate distance learning degree programs offered (minimal on-campus study). *Students:* 20 full-time (4 women), 12 part-time (0 women); includes 2 minority (both Asian Americans or Pacific Islanders), 21 international. In 2009, 7 master's, 1 doctorate awarded. *Degree requirements:* For master's, thesis; for doctorate, comprehensive exam, thesis/dissertation. *Entrance requirements:* Additional exam requirements/recommendations for international students: Required—TOEFL (minimum score 525 paper-based; 197 computer-based; 71 iBT). *Application deadline:* For fall admission, 7/1 priority date for domestic students, 1/15 priority date for international students; for spring admission, 5/1 priority date for international students. Applications are processed on a rolling basis. Application fee: $45 ($60 for international students). *Financial support:* Fellowships with full tuition reimbursements, research assistantships with full tuition reimbursements, teaching assistantships with full tuition reimbursements, career-related internships or fieldwork, Federal Work-Study, and institutionally sponsored loans available. Support available to part-time students. Financial award application deadline: 1/15. *Faculty research:* Wastewater, solid waste, composites, nanotechnology. Total annual research expenditures: $800,000. *Unit head:* Dr. Dinesh R. Katti, Chair, 701-231-7244, Fax: 701-231-6185, E-mail: dinesh.katti@ndsu.edu. *Application contact:* Dr. Kalpana Katti, Associate Professor and Graduate Program Coordinator, 701-231-9504, Fax: 701-231-6185, E-mail: kalpana.katti@ndsu.edu.

Northeastern University, College of Engineering, Department of Civil and Environmental Engineering, Boston, MA 02115-5096. Offers MS, PhD. Part-time programs available. *Faculty:* 15 full-time (2 women), 2 part-time/adjunct (0 women). *Students:* 74 full-time (27 women), 39 part-time (13 women); includes 2 minority (1 African American, 1 Asian American or Pacific Islander), 53 international. 185 applicants, 70% accepted, 37 enrolled. In 2009, 23 master's, 6 doctorates awarded. *Degree requirements:* For master's, thesis optional; for doctorate, thesis/dissertation, departmental qualifying exam. *Entrance requirements:* For master's and doctorate, GRE General Test. Additional exam requirements/recommendations for international students: Required—TOEFL (minimum score 550 paper-based; 213 computer-based; 80 iBT). *Application deadline:* For fall admission, 1/15 priority date for domestic and international students. Applications are processed on a rolling basis. Application fee: $50. Electronic applications accepted. *Financial support:* In 2009–10, 33 students received support, including 18 research assistantships with full tuition reimbursements available (averaging $18,320 per year), 15 teaching assistantships with full tuition reimbursements available (averaging $18,320 per year); career-related internships or fieldwork, Federal Work-Study, scholarships/grants, tuition waivers (full), and unspecified assistantships also available. Support available to part-time students. Financial award application deadline: 1/15; financial award applicants required to submit FAFSA. *Faculty research:* Earthquake engineering, geotechnical and geoenvironmental engineering, structural engineering, transportation engineering, environmental engineering. *Unit head:* Dr. Jerome Jaffar, Chairman, 617-373-2444, Fax: 617-373-4419. *Application contact:* Stephen L. Gibson, Associate Director, 617-373-2711, Fax: 617-373-2501, E-mail: grad-eng@coe.neu.edu.

Northern Arizona University, Graduate College, College of Engineering, Forestry and Natural Sciences, Programs in Engineering, Flagstaff, AZ 86011. Offers civil engineering (MSE); computer science (MSE); electrical engineering (MSE); environmental engineering (MSE); mechanical engineering (MSE). Postbaccalaureate distance learning degree programs offered (no on-campus study). *Faculty:* 43 full-time (11 women). *Students:* 30 full-time (4 women), 9 part-time (0 women); includes 6 minority (4 American Indian/Alaska Native, 1 Asian American or Pacific Islander, 1 Hispanic American), 10 international. Average age 28. 42 applicants, 55% accepted, 12 enrolled. In 2009, 4 master's awarded. *Degree requirements:* For master's, thesis. *Entrance requirements:* Additional exam requirements/recommendations for international students: Required—TOEFL (minimum score 550 paper-based; 213 computer-based; 80 iBT), IELTS (minimum score 7). *Application deadline:* For fall admission, 3/1 priority date for domestic students, 9/1 priority date for international students; for spring admission, 9/15 priority date for domestic students. Applications are processed on a rolling basis. Application fee: $65. Electronic applications accepted. *Financial support:* In 2009–10, 9 research assistantships with partial tuition reimbursements, 9 teaching assistantships with partial tuition reimbursements were awarded; career-related internships or fieldwork, Federal Work-Study, scholarships/grants, health care benefits, and unspecified assistantships also available. Support available to part-time students. Financial award application deadline: 3/30; financial award applicants required to submit FAFSA. *Unit head:* Dr. Ernesto Penado, Chair, 928-523-9453, Fax: 928-523-2300, E-mail: ernesto.penado@nau.edu. *Application contact:* Dieter Otte, Coordinator, 928-523-0876, Fax: 928-523-2300, E-mail: dieter.otte@nau.edu.

Northwestern University, McCormick School of Engineering and Applied Science, Department of Civil and Environmental Engineering, Evanston, IL 60208-3109. Offers environmental engineering and science (MS, PhD); geotechnical engineering (MS, PhD); mechanics of materials and solids (MS, PhD); project management (MS, PhD); structural engineering and materials (MS, PhD); theoretical and applied mechanics (MS, PhD), including fluid mechanics, solid mechanics; transportation systems analysis and planning (MS, PhD). MS and PhD admissions and degrees offered through The Graduate School. Part-time programs available. *Faculty:* 25 full-time (2 women), 3 part-time/adjunct (1 woman). *Students:* 63 full-time (19 women), 3 part-time (0 women); includes 7 minority (1 African American, 3 Asian Americans or Pacific Islanders, 3 Hispanic Americans), 34 international. Average age 22. 149 applicants, 30% accepted, 23 enrolled. In 2009, 11 master's, 11 doctorates awarded. Terminal master's awarded for partial completion of doctoral program. *Degree requirements:* For master's, thesis (for some programs); for doctorate, thesis/dissertation. *Entrance requirements:* For master's and doctorate, GRE General Test, minimum 2 letters of recommendation, transcripts from all academic institutions attended. Additional exam requirements/recommendations for international students: Required—TOEFL (minimum score 600 paper-based; 250 computer-based; 100 iBT), IELTS (minimum score 7), TOEFL (minimum score iBT 26). *Application deadline:* For fall admission, 12/31 for domestic and international students. Application fee: $75. Electronic applications accepted. *Financial support:* In 2009–10, 55 students received support, including fellowships with full tuition reimbursements available (averaging $15,390 per year), research assistantships with full tuition reimbursements available (averaging $17,892 per year), 23 teaching assistantships with full tuition reimbursements available (averaging $15,867 per year); career-related internships or fieldwork, institutionally sponsored loans, scholarships/grants, and health care benefits also available. Financial award application deadline: 12/31; financial award applicants required to submit FAFSA. *Faculty research:* Environmental engineering and science, geotechnics, mechanics of materials and solids, structural engineering and materials, transportation systems analysis and planning. Total annual research expenditures: $5.8 million. *Unit head:* Jianmin Qu, Chair, 847-467-4528, Fax: 847-491-4011, E-mail: j-qu@northwestern.edu. *Application contact:* Janet Soule, Academic Coordinator, 847-491-7462, Fax: 847-491-4011, E-mail: civil-info@northwestern.edu.

OGI School of Science & Engineering at Oregon Health & Science University, Graduate Studies, Department of Environmental and Biomolecular Systems, Beaverton, OR 97006-8921. Offers biochemistry and molecular biology (MS, PhD); environmental health systems (MS); environmental information technology (MS, PhD); environmental science and engineering (MS, PhD). Part-time programs available. Terminal master's awarded for partial completion of doctoral program. *Degree requirements:* For master's, thesis optional; for doctorate, comprehensive exam, oral defense of dissertation. *Entrance requirements:* For master's and doctorate, GRE General Test. Additional exam requirements/recommendations for international students: Required—TOEFL. Electronic applications accepted. *Faculty research:* Air and water science, hydrogeology, estuarine and coastal modeling, environmental microbiology, contaminant transport, biochemistry, biomolecular systems.

Ohio University, Graduate College, Russ College of Engineering and Technology, Department of Civil Engineering, Athens, OH 45701-2979. Offers civil engineering (PhD); construction (MS); environmental (MS); geotechnical and geoenvironmental (MS); mechanics (MS); structures (MS); transportation (MS); water resources and structures (MS). Part-time programs available. *Faculty:* 13 full-time (3 women), 3 part-time/adjunct (0 women). *Students:* 18 full-time (2 women), 2 part-time (1 woman), 13 international. 22 applicants, 68% accepted, 1 enrolled. In 2009, 7 master's awarded. *Degree requirements:* For master's, comprehensive exam (for some programs), thesis or alternative; for doctorate, comprehensive exam, thesis/dissertation. *Entrance requirements:* For master's, GRE General Test, minimum GPA of 3.0, 3 letters of recommendation; for doctorate, GRE General Test. Additional exam requirements/recommendations for international students: Required—TOEFL (minimum score 550 paper-based; 80 iBT) or IELTS Academic (minimum score 6.5). *Application deadline:* For fall admission, 5/1 priority date for domestic students, 2/1 priority date for international students; for winter admission, 8/1 priority date for domestic students, 4/1 priority date for international students; for spring admission, 2/1 priority date for domestic students, 7/1 priority date for international students. Applications are processed on a rolling basis. Application fee: $50 ($55 for international students). Electronic applications accepted. *Expenses:* Tuition, state resident: full-time $7839; part-time $323 per quarter hour. Tuition, nonresident: full-time $15,831; part-time $654 per quarter hour. Required fees: $2931. *Financial support:* Research assistantships with full tuition reimbursements, teaching assistantships with full tuition reimbursements, Federal Work-Study, institutionally sponsored loans, scholarships/grants, and unspecified assistantships available. Financial award application deadline: 3/15; financial award applicants required to submit FAFSA. *Faculty research:* Noise abatement, materials and environment, highway infrastructure, subsurface investigation, (pavements, pipes, bridges, etc.). Total annual research expenditures: $1.2 million. *Unit head:* Dr. Gayle F. Mitchell, Chair, 740-593-0430, Fax: 740-593-0625, E-mail: mitchelg@ohio.edu. *Application contact:* Dr. Shad M. Sargand, Graduate Chair, 740-593-1465, Fax: 740-593-0625, E-mail: sargand@ohio.edu.

Oklahoma State University, College of Agricultural Science and Natural Resources, Department of Biosystems and Agricultural Engineering, Stillwater, OK 74078. Offers biosystems engineering (MS, PhD); environmental and natural resources (MS, PhD). *Faculty:* 25 full-time (4 women), 1 part-time/adjunct (0 women). *Students:* 15 full-time (5 women), 31 part-time (10 women); includes 3 minority (1 African American, 1 American Indian/Alaska Native, 1 Hispanic American), 26 international. Average age 29. 57 applicants, 32% accepted, 12 enrolled. In 2009, 13 master's, 1 doctorate awarded. *Degree requirements:* For master's, thesis; for doctorate, comprehensive exam, thesis/dissertation. *Entrance requirements:* For master's and doctorate, GRE or GMAT. Additional exam requirements/recommendations for international students: Required—TOEFL (minimum score 550 paper-based; 79 iBT). *Application deadline:* For fall admission, 3/1 priority date for international students; for spring admission, 8/1 priority date for international students. Applications are processed on a rolling basis. Application fee: $40 ($75 for international students). Electronic applications accepted. *Expenses:* Tuition, state resident: full-time $3716; part-time $154.85 per credit hour. Tuition, nonresident: full-time $14,448; part-time $602 per credit hour. Required fees: $1772; $73.85 per credit hour. One-time fee: $50. Tuition and fees vary according to course load and campus/location. *Financial support:* In 2009–10, 50 research assistantships (averaging $15,858 per year), 4 teaching assistantships (averaging $9,900 per year) were awarded; career-related internships or fieldwork, Federal Work-Study, scholarships/grants, health care benefits, tuition waivers (partial), and unspecified assistantships also available. Support available to part-time students. Financial award application deadline: 3/1; financial award applicants required to submit FAFSA. *Unit head:* Dr. Ronald L. Elliot, Head, 405-744-5431, Fax: 405-744-6059. *Application contact:* Dr. Gordon Emslie, Dean, 405-744-6368, Fax: 405-744-0355, E-mail: grad-i@okstate.edu.

Oklahoma State University, College of Engineering, Architecture and Technology, School of Civil and Environmental Engineering, Stillwater, OK 74078. Offers civil engineering (MS); environmental engineering (PhD). *Faculty:* 15 full-time (1 woman), 3 part-time/adjunct (0 women). *Students:* 43 full-time (12 women), 34 part-time (10 women); includes 6 minority (3 American Indian/Alaska Native, 2 Asian Americans or Pacific Islanders, 1 Hispanic American), 48 international. Average age 28. 137 applicants, 31% accepted, 19 enrolled. In 2009, 14 master's, 1 doctorate awarded. *Degree requirements:* For master's, thesis or alternative; for doctorate, comprehensive exam, thesis/dissertation. *Entrance requirements:* For master's and doctorate, GRE or GMAT. Additional exam requirements/recommendations for international students: Required—TOEFL (minimum score 550 paper-based; 79 iBT). *Application deadline:* For fall admission, 3/1 priority date for international students; for spring admission, 8/1 priority date for international students. Applications are processed on a rolling basis. Application fee: $40 ($75 for international students). Electronic applications accepted. *Expenses:* Tuition, state resident: full-time $3716; part-time $154.85 per credit hour. Tuition, nonresident: full-time $14,448; part-time $602 per credit hour. Required fees: $1772; $73.85 per credit hour. One-time fee: $50. Tuition and fees vary according to course load and campus/location. *Financial support:* In 2009–10, 20 research assistantships (averaging $13,708 per year), 16 teaching assistantships (averaging $9,319 per year) were awarded; career-related internships or fieldwork, Federal Work-Study, scholarships/grants, health care benefits, tuition waivers (partial), and unspecified assistantships also available. Support available to part-time students. Financial

environmental systems management, hazardous and waste materials management; facilities management (MS). Part-time and evening/weekend programs available. Postbaccalaureate distance learning degree programs offered (no on-campus study). *Faculty:* 7 full-time (0 women), 13 part-time/adjunct (4 women). *Students:* 19 full-time (8 women), 50 part-time (17 women); includes 13 minority (9 African Americans, 2 Asian Americans or Pacific Islanders, 2 Hispanic Americans), 7 international. Average age 34. 50 applicants, 86% accepted, 28 enrolled. In 2009, 17 master's, 1 doctorate awarded. Terminal master's awarded for partial completion of doctoral program. *Degree requirements:* For master's, thesis optional; for doctorate, thesis/dissertation, oral and written qualifying exams. *Entrance requirements:* For master's, GRE General Test, minimum GPA of 3.0 in last 2 years; bachelor's degree in engineering, mathematics, or sciences; for doctorate, GRE, BS and MS in related field, minimum GPA of 3.3. Additional exam requirements/recommendations for international students: Required—TOEFL. *Application deadline:* For fall admission, 7/1 for domestic students, 5/15 for international students; for spring admission, 11/15 for domestic students, 9/1 for international students. Applications are processed on a rolling basis. Application fee: $75. Electronic applications accepted. *Financial support:* In 2009–10, 9 students received support, including 2 research assistantships with full tuition reimbursements available (averaging $18,000 per year), 7 teaching assistantships with full tuition reimbursements available (averaging $18,000 per year); career-related internships or fieldwork, tuition waivers (full and partial), and unspecified assistantships also available. *Faculty research:* Human and environmental health effects of endocrine disrupters, development of air pollution control systems for diesel engines, structural analysis and design, modeling and design of waste treatment systems. Total annual research expenditures: $100,000. *Unit head:* Prof. Bijan Mohraz, Chair, 214-768-3894, Fax: 214-768-2164, E-mail: bmohraz@lyle.smu.edu. *Application contact:* Marc Valerin, Director of Graduate and Executive Admissions, 214-768-3042, Fax: 214-768-3778, E-mail: valerin@lyle.smu.edu.

Stanford University, School of Engineering, Department of Civil and Environmental Engineering, Stanford, CA 94305-9991. Offers MS, PhD, Eng. Terminal master's awarded for partial completion of doctoral program. *Degree requirements:* For doctorate, thesis/dissertation, qualifying exam; for Eng, thesis. *Entrance requirements:* For master's, doctorate, and Eng, GRE General Test. Additional exam requirements/recommendations for international students: Required—TOEFL. Electronic applications accepted. *Expenses:* Tuition: Full-time $37,380; part-time $2760 per quarter. Required fees: $501.

State University of New York College of Environmental Science and Forestry, Department of Construction Management and Wood Products Engineering, Syracuse, NY 13210-2779. Offers environmental and resources engineering (MPS, MS, PhD). *Degree requirements:* For master's, thesis (for some programs); for doctorate, comprehensive exam, thesis/dissertation. *Entrance requirements:* For master's and doctorate, GRE General Test, minimum GPA of 3.0. Additional exam requirements/recommendations for international students: Required—TOEFL (minimum score 550 paper-based; 213 computer-based; 80 iBT), IELTS (minimum score 6).

State University of New York College of Environmental Science and Forestry, Department of Environmental Resources and Forest Engineering, Syracuse, NY 13210-2779. Offers environmental and resources engineering (MPS, MS, PhD). *Degree requirements:* For master's, thesis (for some programs); for doctorate, comprehensive exam, thesis/dissertation. *Entrance requirements:* For master's and doctorate, GRE General Test, minimum GPA of 3.0. Additional exam requirements/recommendations for international students: Required—TOEFL (minimum score 550 paper-based; 213 computer-based; 80 iBT), IELTS (minimum score 6). *Faculty research:* Forest engineering, paper science and engineering, wood products engineering.

State University of New York College of Environmental Science and Forestry, Department of Paper and Bioprocess Engineering, Syracuse, NY 13210-2779. Offers environmental and resources engineering (MPS, MS, PhD). *Degree requirements:* For master's, thesis; for doctorate, comprehensive exam, thesis/dissertation. *Entrance requirements:* For master's and doctorate, GRE General Test, minimum GPA of 3.0. Additional exam requirements/recommendations for international students: Required—TOEFL (minimum score 550 paper-based; 213 computer-based; 80 iBT), IELTS (minimum score 6).

Stevens Institute of Technology, Graduate School, Charles V. Schaefer Jr. School of Engineering, Department of Civil, Environmental, and Ocean Engineering, Program in Environmental Engineering, Hoboken, NJ 07030. Offers environmental compatibility in engineering (Certificate); environmental engineering (PhD); environmental processes (M Eng, Certificate); groundwater and soil pollution control (M Eng, Certificate); inland and coastal environmental hydrodynamics (M Eng, Certificate); water quality control (Certificate). *Degree requirements:* For master's, thesis optional; for doctorate, variable foreign language requirement, thesis/dissertation; for Certificate, project or thesis. *Entrance requirements:* For doctorate, GRE. Additional exam requirements/recommendations for international students: Required—TOEFL. Electronic applications accepted. *Expenses:* Tuition: Full-time $9900; part-time $1100 per credit. Required fees: $286 per semester.

Syracuse University, L. C. Smith College of Engineering and Computer Science, Program in Environmental Engineering, Syracuse, NY 13244. Offers environmental engineering (MS, PhD); environmental science (MS). Part-time programs available. *Students:* 8 full-time (5 women), 1 part-time (0 women), 8 international. Average age 24. 23 applicants, 57% accepted, 4 enrolled. In 2009, 2 master's awarded. *Entrance requirements:* For master's and doctorate, GRE General Test. Additional exam requirements/recommendations for international students: Required—TOEFL (minimum score 100 iBT). *Application deadline:* For fall admission, 6/1 priority date for domestic students, 5/1 priority date for international students. Applications are processed on a rolling basis. Application fee: $75. Electronic applications accepted. *Expenses:* Tuition: Full-time $26,808; part-time $1117 per credit. Required fees: $1024. *Financial support:* Fellowships with tuition reimbursements, research assistantships with tuition reimbursements, teaching assistantships with tuition reimbursements, tuition waivers (partial) available. Financial award application deadline: 1/1. *Unit head:* Dr. Chris E. Johnson, Interim Chair, 315-443-4425, E-mail: cejohns@syr.edu. *Application contact:* Elizabeth Buchanan, Information Contact, 314-443-2558, E-mail: topgrads@syr.edu.

Texas A&M University, College of Engineering, Zachry Department of Civil Engineering, College Station, TX 77843. Offers construction engineering and management (M Eng, MS, D Eng, PhD); environmental engineering (M Eng, MS, D Eng, PhD); geotechnical engineering (M Eng, MS, D Eng, PhD); materials engineering (M Eng, MS, D Eng, PhD); ocean engineering (M Eng, MS, D Eng, PhD); structural engineering (M Eng, MS, D Eng, PhD); transportation engineering (M Eng, MS, D Eng, PhD); water resources engineering (M Eng, MS, D Eng, PhD). Part-time programs available. *Faculty:* 61. *Students:* 390 full-time (89 women), 42 part-time (6 women); includes 23 minority (2 African Americans, 11 Asian Americans or Pacific Islanders, 10 Hispanic Americans), 281 international. Average age 29. In 2009, 100 master's, 36 doctorates awarded. *Degree requirements:* For master's, thesis (MS); for doctorate, dissertation (PhD), internship (D Eng). *Entrance requirements:* For master's and doctorate, GRE General Test. Additional exam requirements/recommendations for international students: Required—TOEFL. *Application deadline:* Applications are processed on a rolling basis. Application fee: $50 ($75 for international students). Electronic applications accepted. *Expenses:* Tuition, state resident: full-time $3991.32; part-time $221.74 per credit hour. Tuition, nonresident: full-time $9049; part-time $502.74 per credit hour. *Financial support:* In 2009–10, fellowships (averaging $4,500 per year), research assistantships (averaging $14,000 per year), teaching assistantships (averaging $14,400 per year) were awarded; career-related internships or fieldwork and institutionally sponsored loans also available. Financial award application deadline: 4/15; financial award applicants required to submit FAFSA. *Unit head:* Dr. Tony Cahill, Head, 979-845-2438, E-mail: t-cahill@civil.tamu.edu. *Application contact:* Graduate Advisor, 979-845-2498, Fax: 979-862-2800, E-mail: ce-grad@tamu.edu.

Texas A&M University–Kingsville, College of Graduate Studies, College of Engineering, Department of Environmental Engineering, Kingsville, TX 78363. Offers ME, MS, PhD. Part-time and evening/weekend programs available. *Degree requirements:* For master's, comprehensive exam, thesis. *Entrance requirements:* For master's, GRE General Test, bachelor's degree in engineering or physical science, minimum undergraduate GPA of 2.7. Additional exam requirements/recommendations for international students: Required—TOEFL. *Faculty research:* Biodegradation of hazardous waste, air modeling, toxicology and industrial hygiene, water waste treating.

Texas Tech University, Graduate School, College of Engineering, Department of Civil and Environmental Engineering, Lubbock, TX 79409. Offers civil engineering (MSCE, PhD); environmental engineering (MENVEGR); environmental technology management (MSETM). *Accreditation:* ABET. Part-time programs available. *Faculty:* 21 full-time (2 women), 1 part-time/adjunct (0 women). *Students:* 47 full-time (11 women), 18 part-time (3 women); includes 3 minority (1 African American, 1 Asian American or Pacific Islander, 1 Hispanic American), 42 international. Average age 27. 94 applicants, 60% accepted, 11 enrolled. In 2009, 27 master's, 2 doctorates awarded. *Degree requirements:* For master's, thesis or alternative; for doctorate, thesis/dissertation. *Entrance requirements:* For master's and doctorate, GRE General Test, minimum GPA of 3.0. Additional exam requirements/recommendations for international students: Required—TOEFL (minimum score 550 paper-based; 213 computer-based). *Application deadline:* For fall admission, 3/1 priority date for international students; for spring admission, 11/1 priority date for international students. Applications are processed on a rolling basis. Application fee: $50 ($75 for international students). Electronic applications accepted. *Expenses:* Tuition, state resident: full-time $5100; part-time $213 per credit hour. Tuition, nonresident: full-time $11,748; part-time $490 per credit hour. Required fees: $2298; $50 per credit hour. $555 per semester. *Financial support:* In 2009–10, 31 research assistantships with partial tuition reimbursements (averaging $19,861 per year), 11 teaching assistantships with partial tuition reimbursements (averaging $12,241 per year) were awarded; Federal Work-Study and institutionally sponsored loans also available. Support available to part-time students. Financial award application deadline: 4/15; financial award applicants required to submit FAFSA. *Faculty research:* Wind load/engineering on structures, fluid mechanics, structural dynamics, water resource management, transportation engineering. Total annual research expenditures: $998,329. *Unit head:* Dr. H. Scott Norville, Chair, 806-742-3523, Fax: 806-742-3488, E-mail: scott.norville@ttu.edu. *Application contact:* Dr. Priyantha Jayawickrama, Graduate Adviser, 806-742-3523, Fax: 806-742-3488, E-mail: priyantha.jayawickrama@ttu.edu.

Tufts University, School of Engineering, Department of Civil and Environmental Engineering, Medford, MA 02155. Offers civil engineering (ME, MS, PhD), including geotechnical engineering, structural engineering; environmental engineering (ME, MS, PhD), including environmental engineering and environmental sciences, environmental geotechnology, environmental health, environmental science and management, hazardous materials management, water resources engineering. Part-time programs available. *Faculty:* 17 full-time, 7 part-time/adjunct. *Students:* 72 (33 women); includes 6 minority (2 African Americans, 4 Asian Americans or Pacific Islanders), 17 international. Average age 27. 170 applicants, 59% accepted, 20 enrolled. In 2009, 17 master's, 3 doctorates awarded. Terminal master's awarded for partial completion of doctoral program. *Degree requirements:* For master's, thesis or alternative; for doctorate, thesis/dissertation. *Entrance requirements:* For master's and doctorate, GRE General Test. Additional exam requirements/recommendations for international students: Required—TOEFL (minimum score 550 paper-based; 213 computer-based; 80 iBT). *Application deadline:* For fall admission, 1/15 priority date for domestic students, 12/15 for international students; for spring admission, 10/15 for domestic students, 9/15 for international students. Applications are processed on a rolling basis. Application fee: $75. Electronic applications accepted. *Expenses:* Tuition: Full-time $38,096; part-time $3962 per credit. Required fees: $686; $40 per year. Tuition and fees vary according to course level, course load, degree level, program and student level. *Financial support:* Fellowships with full tuition reimbursements, research assistantships with full and partial tuition reimbursements, teaching assistantships with full and partial tuition reimbursements, Federal Work-Study, scholarships/grants, tuition waivers (partial), and unspecified assistantships available. Financial award application deadline: 1/15; financial award applicants required to submit FAFSA. *Unit head:* Dr. Kurt Penell, Chair, 617-627-3211, Fax: 617-627-3994. *Application contact:* Laura Sacco, Information Contact, 617-627-3211.

Universidad Central del Este, Graduate School, San Pedro de Macoris, Dominican Republic. Offers administration (M Ad); dentistry (DMD); development of educational and social policies (PhD); environmental engineering (ME); financial management (M Ad); higher education (M Ed); human resources (M Ad); public health (MPH). *Entrance requirements:* For master's, letters of recommendation.

Universidad Nacional Pedro Henriquez Urena, Graduate School, Santo Domingo, Dominican Republic. Offers administrative sciences (PhD); business administration (MBA); environmental engineering (MEE); project management (M Man, MPM); sanitation engineering (ME); veterinary medicine (DVM).

Université de Sherbrooke, Faculty of Engineering, Program in the Environment, Sherbrooke, QC J1K 2R1, Canada. Offers M Env. *Degree requirements:* For master's, thesis.

Université Laval, Faculty of Sciences and Engineering, Department of Civil Engineering, Programs in Civil Engineering, Québec, QC G1K 7P4, Canada. Offers civil engineering (M Sc, PhD); environmental technology (M Sc). Terminal master's awarded for partial completion of doctoral program. *Degree requirements:* For master's, thesis (for some programs); for doctorate, comprehensive exam, thesis/dissertation. *Entrance requirements:* For master's and doctorate, knowledge of French and English. Electronic applications accepted.

University at Buffalo, the State University of New York, Graduate School, School of Engineering and Applied Sciences, Department of Civil, Structural, and Environmental Engineering, Buffalo, NY 14260. Offers civil engineering (M Eng, MS, PhD); engineering science (MS). Part-time programs available. Postbaccalaureate distance learning degree programs offered (minimal on-campus study). *Faculty:* 27 full-time (4 women), 3 part-time/adjunct (2 women). *Students:* 136 full-time (26 women), 14 part-time (3 women); includes 10 minority (1 American Indian/Alaska Native, 4 Asian Americans or Pacific Islanders, 5 Hispanic Americans), 100 international. Average age 28. 514 applicants, 40% accepted, 59 enrolled. In 2009, 25 master's, 8 doctorates awarded. Terminal master's awarded for partial completion of doctoral program. *Degree requirements:* For master's, thesis optional, project, thesis, or comprehensive exam; for doctorate, thesis/dissertation. *Entrance requirements:* For master's and doctorate, GRE General Test, letters of reference. Additional exam requirements/recommendations for international students: Required—TOEFL (minimum score 550 paper-based; 213 computer-based; 79 iBT). *Application deadline:* For fall admission, 1/15 priority date for domestic and international students; for spring admission, 9/15 for domestic and international students. Applications are processed on a rolling basis. Application fee: $50. Electronic applications accepted. *Financial support:* In 2009–10, 79 students received support, including 18 fellowships with full tuition reimbursements available (averaging $17,200 per year), 34 research assistantships with full tuition reimbursements available (averaging $14,000 per year), 27 teaching assistantships with full tuition reimbursements available (averaging $14,700 per year); career-related internships or fieldwork, Federal Work-Study, institutionally sponsored loans, scholarships/grants, traineeships, health care benefits, tuition waivers (full and partial), and unspecified assistantships also available. Support available to part-time students. Financial award application deadline: 1/15; financial award applicants required to submit FAFSA. *Faculty research:* Environmental engineering and fluid mechanics, structural dynamics, geomechanics, earthquake engineering computational mechanics. Total annual research expenditures: $7.3 million. *Unit head:* Dr. A. Scott Weber, Chairman, 716-645-2114, Fax: 716-645-3733, E-mail: sweber@eng.buffalo.edu. *Application contact:* Dr. Amjad J. Aref, Director of Graduate Studies, 716-645-4369, Fax: 716-645-3733, E-mail: cjb@buffalo.edu.

The University of Alabama, Graduate School, College of Engineering, Department of Civil, Construction and Environmental Engineering, Tuscaloosa, AL 35487-0205. Offers civil engineering (MSCE, PhD); environmental engineering (MS). Part-time programs available. *Faculty:* 20 full-time (2 women). *Students:* 39 full-time (11 women), 10 part-time (4 women); includes 9 minority (7 African Americans, 1 American Indian/Alaska Native, 1 Asian American or Pacific Islander), 18 international. Average age 30. 68 applicants, 26% accepted, 12

Environmental Engineering

The University of Alabama (continued)

enrolled. In 2009, 16 master's, 1 doctorate awarded. Terminal master's awarded for partial completion of doctoral program. *Median time to degree:* Of those who began their doctoral program in fall 2001, 100% received their degree in 8 years or less. *Degree requirements:* For master's, thesis or alternative; for doctorate, one foreign language, thesis/dissertation. *Entrance requirements:* For master's and doctorate, GRE General Test, minimum GPA of 3.0 in last 60 hours of course work. Additional exam requirements/recommendations for international students: Required—TOEFL (minimum score 550 paper-based; 213 computer-based), IELTS (minimum score 6.5). *Application deadline:* For fall admission, 7/6 for domestic students, 1/15 for international students; for spring admission, 11/1 for domestic students, 6/1 for international students. Applications are processed on a rolling basis. Application fee: $50 ($60 for international students). Electronic applications accepted. *Expenses:* Tuition, state resident: full-time $7000. Tuition, nonresident: full-time $19,200. *Financial support:* In 2009–10, 40 students received support, including 32 research assistantships with full tuition reimbursements available (averaging $10,489 per year), 12 teaching assistantships with full tuition reimbursements available (averaging $10,489 per year); fellowships, scholarships/grants, tuition waivers (partial), and unspecified assistantships also available. Financial award application deadline: 3/15. *Faculty research:* Experimental structures, modeling of structures, bridge management systems, geotechnological engineering, environmental remediation. Total annual research expenditures: $2.3 million. *Unit head:* Dr. Kenneth J. Fridley, Head and Professor, 205-348-6550, Fax: 205-348-0783, E-mail: kfridley@coe.eng.ua.edu. *Application contact:* Dr. David A. Francko, Dean, 205-348-8280, Fax: 205-348-0400, E-mail: dfrancko@ua.edu.

The University of Alabama in Huntsville, School of Graduate Studies, College of Engineering, Department of Civil and Environmental Engineering, Huntsville, AL 35899. Offers civil and environmental engineering (PhD); civil engineering (MSE), including environmental and water resource engineering, geotechnical engineering, structural engineering and structural mechanics, transportation engineering. Part-time and evening/weekend programs available. *Faculty:* 6 full-time (1 woman). *Students:* 12 full-time (3 women), 7 part-time (1 woman); includes 3 minority (2 African Americans, 1 Asian American or Pacific Islander), 5 international. Average age 33. 26 applicants, 58% accepted, 9 enrolled. In 2009, 10 master's, 2 doctorates awarded. *Degree requirements:* For master's, comprehensive exam, thesis or alternative, oral and written exams; for doctorate, comprehensive exam, thesis/dissertation, oral and written exams. *Entrance requirements:* For master's, GRE General Test, BSE, minimum GPA of 3.0; for doctorate, GRE General Test, minimum GPA of 3.0. Additional exam requirements/recommendations for international students: Required—TOEFL (minimum score 500 paper-based; 173 computer-based; 62 iBT). *Application deadline:* For fall admission, 7/15 for domestic students, 4/1 for international students; for spring admission, 11/30 for domestic students, 9/1 for international students. Applications are processed on a rolling basis. Application fee: $40 ($50 for international students). Electronic applications accepted. *Expenses:* Tuition, state resident: part-time $355.75 per credit hour. Tuition, nonresident: part-time $847.10 per credit hour. Required fees: $210.80 per semester. Tuition and fees vary according to course load and program. *Financial support:* In 2009–10, 10 students received support, including 4 research assistantships with full and partial tuition reimbursements available (averaging $11,525 per year), 6 teaching assistantships with full and partial tuition reimbursements available (averaging $9,678 per year); career-related internships or fieldwork, Federal Work-Study, institutionally sponsored loans, scholarships/grants, health care benefits, and unspecified assistantships also available. Support available to part-time students. Financial award application deadline: 4/1; financial award applicants required to submit FAFSA. *Faculty research:* Hydrologic modeling, orbital debris impact, hydrogeology, environmental engineering, transportation engineering. Total annual research expenditures: $1.5 million. *Unit head:* Dr. Houssam Toutanji, Chair, 256-824-7361, Fax: 256-824-6724, E-mail: toutanji@cee.uah.edu. *Application contact:* Kathy Biggs, Graduate Studies Admissions Manager, 256-824-6199, Fax: 256-824-6405, E-mail: deangrad@uah.edu.

University of Alaska Anchorage, School of Engineering, Program in Applied Environmental Science and Technology, Anchorage, AK 99508. Offers M AEST, MS. Part-time and evening/weekend programs available. *Degree requirements:* For master's, comprehensive exam, thesis (for some programs). *Entrance requirements:* For master's, GRE General Test. Additional exam requirements/recommendations for international students: Required—TOEFL (minimum score 550 paper-based; 213 computer-based). *Faculty research:* Wastewater treatment, environmental regulations, water resources management, justification of public facilities, rural sanitation, biological treatment process.

University of Alaska Fairbanks, College of Engineering and Mines, Department of Civil and Environmental Engineering, Program in Environmental Engineering, Fairbanks, AK 99775-5900. Offers engineering (PhD), including environmental engineering; environmental engineering (MS), including environmental contaminants, environmental science and management, water supply and waste treatment. Part-time programs available. *Students:* 4 full-time (3 women), 3 part-time (2 women). Average age 28. 5 applicants, 60% accepted, 1 enrolled. In 2009, 3 master's, 1 doctorate awarded. *Degree requirements:* For master's, comprehensive exam, thesis or alternative; for doctorate, comprehensive exam, thesis/dissertation, oral exam, oral defense. *Entrance requirements:* For master's, basic computer techniques; for doctorate, GRE General Test. Additional exam requirements/recommendations for international students: Required—TOEFL (minimum score 575 paper-based; 213 computer-based). *Application deadline:* For fall admission, 5/1 for domestic students, 3/1 for international students; for spring admission, 10/15 for domestic students, 9/1 for international students. Applications are processed on a rolling basis. Application fee: $60. Electronic applications accepted. *Expenses:* Tuition, state resident: full-time $7584; part-time $316 per credit. Tuition, nonresident: full-time $15,504; part-time $646 per credit. Required fees: $23 per credit. $135 per semester. Tuition and fees vary according to course level, course load and reciprocity agreements. *Financial support:* In 2009–10, 4 research assistantships (averaging $13,290 per year), 1 teaching assistantship (averaging $7,088 per year) were awarded; fellowships, career-related internships or fieldwork, Federal Work-Study, scholarships/grants, health care benefits, and unspecified assistantships also available. Support available to part-time students. Financial award application deadline: 7/1; financial award applicants required to submit FAFSA. *Unit head:* Dr. David Barnes, Department Chair, 907-474-7241, Fax: 907-474-6087, E-mail: fyeqe@uaf.edu. *Application contact:* Dr. David Barnes, Department Chair, 907-474-7241, Fax: 907-474-6087, E-mail: fyeqe@uaf.edu.

University of Alberta, Faculty of Graduate Studies and Research, Department of Civil and Environmental Engineering, Edmonton, AB T6G 2E1, Canada. Offers construction engineering and management (M Eng, M Sc, PhD); environmental engineering (M Eng, M Sc, PhD); environmental science (M Sc, PhD); geoenvironmental engineering (M Eng, M Sc, PhD); geotechnical engineering (M Eng, M Sc, PhD); mining engineering (M Eng, M Sc, PhD); petroleum engineering (M Eng, M Sc, PhD); structural engineering (M Eng, M Sc, PhD); water resources (M Eng, M Sc, PhD). Part-time programs available. Postbaccalaureate distance learning degree programs offered (minimal on-campus study). *Faculty:* 44 full-time (3 women), 2 part-time/adjunct (0 women). *Students:* 215 full-time (49 women), 99 part-time (19 women). 1,428 applicants, 15% accepted, 123 enrolled. In 2009, 124 master's, 34 doctorates awarded. *Degree requirements:* For master's, thesis (for some programs); for doctorate, thesis/dissertation. *Entrance requirements:* For master's, minimum GPA of 3.0 in last 2 years of undergraduate studies; for doctorate, minimum GPA of 3.0. Additional exam requirements/recommendations for international students: Required—TOEFL (minimum score 550 paper-based; 213 computer-based). *Application deadline:* For fall admission, 6/1 priority date for domestic students, 6/1 for international students; for winter admission, 11/1 for domestic students, 9/15 for international students. Applications are processed on a rolling basis. Application fee: $0 Canadian dollars. Electronic applications accepted. Tuition and fees charges are reported in Canadian dollars. *Expenses:* Tuition, area resident: Full-time $4626.24 Canadian dollars; part-time $99.72 Canadian dollars per unit. International tuition: $8216 Canadian dollars full-time. Required fees: $3589.92 Canadian dollars; $99.72 Canadian dollars per unit. $215 Canadian dollars per term. *Financial support:* In 2009–10, 88 research assistantships with full and partial tuition reimbursements, 134 teaching assistantships with full and partial tuition reimbursements were awarded; scholarships/grants and tuition waivers (full and partial) also available. Financial award application deadline: 4/1. *Faculty research:* Mining. Total annual research expenditures: $6,791 Canadian dollars. *Unit head:* Dr. David Zhu, Associate Chair, Graduate Studies, 780-492-1198, Fax: 403-492-8198. *Application contact:* Gwen Mendoza, Student Services Officer, 403-492-1539, Fax: 403-492-0249, E-mail: civegrad@ualberta.ca.

The University of Arizona, Graduate College, College of Engineering, Department of Chemical and Environmental Engineering, Program in Environmental Engineering, Tucson, AZ 85721. Offers MS, PhD. *Students:* 23 full-time (11 women), 3 part-time (1 woman); includes 2 minority (1 African American, 1 Hispanic American), 14 international. Average age 30. 54 applicants, 24% accepted, 5 enrolled. In 2009, 6 master's, 6 doctorates awarded. *Entrance requirements:* For master's and doctorate, GRE, 3 letters of recommendation, resume, statement of purpose. Additional exam requirements/recommendations for international students: Required—TOEFL (minimum score 550 paper-based; 213 computer-based; 79 iBT). *Application deadline:* Applications are processed on a rolling basis. Application fee: $75. Electronic applications accepted. *Expenses:* Tuition, state resident: full-time $9028. Tuition, nonresident: full-time $24,890. *Unit head:* Dr. Glenn L. Schrader, Department Head, 520-621-2591, Fax: 520-621-6048, E-mail: schrader@email.arizona.edu. *Application contact:* Jo Leeming, Program Coordinator, 520-621-6044, Fax: 520-621-6048, E-mail: leeming@email.arizona.edu.

University of Arkansas, Graduate School, College of Engineering, Department of Civil Engineering, Program in Environmental Engineering, Fayetteville, AR 72701-1201. Offers MS En E, MSE. *Accreditation:* ABET. *Students:* 2 part-time (0 women). In 2009, 2 master's awarded. *Degree requirements:* For master's, thesis optional. Application fee: $40 ($50 for international students). *Expenses:* Tuition, state resident: full-time $7355; part-time $356.58 per hour. Tuition, nonresident: full-time $17,401; part-time $775.17 per hour. Required fees: $1203. *Financial support:* In 2009–10, 2 research assistantships were awarded; fellowships, teaching assistantships, career-related internships or fieldwork and Federal Work-Study also available. Support available to part-time students. Financial award application deadline: 4/1; financial award applicants required to submit FAFSA. *Unit head:* Dr. Kevin Hall, Departmental Chair, 479-575-4954, Fax: 479-575-7168, E-mail: kdhall@uark.edu. *Application contact:* Dr. Kelvin Wang, Graduate Coordinator, 479-575-4954, Fax: 479-575-7168, E-mail: kcw@uark.edu.

University of California, Berkeley, Graduate Division, College of Engineering, Department of Civil and Environmental Engineering, Berkeley, CA 94720-1500. Offers engineering and project management (M Eng, MS, D Eng, PhD); environmental engineering (M Eng, MS, D Eng, PhD); geoengineering (M Eng, MS, D Eng, PhD); structural engineering, mechanics and materials (M Eng, MS, D Eng, PhD); transportation engineering (M Eng, MS, D Eng, PhD); M Arch/MS; MCP/MS; MPP/MS. *Students:* 368 full-time (125 women). Average age 27. 921 applicants, 179 enrolled. In 2009, 158 master's, 39 doctorates awarded. *Degree requirements:* For master's, comprehensive exam or thesis (MS); for doctorate, thesis/dissertation, qualifying exam. *Entrance requirements:* For master's, GRE General Test, minimum GPA of 3.0, 3 letters of recommendation; for doctorate, GRE General Test, minimum GPA of 3.5, 3 letters of recommendation. Additional exam requirements/recommendations for international students: Required—TOEFL (minimum score 570 paper-based; 230 computer-based). *Application deadline:* For fall admission, 2/3 for domestic students. Application fee: $70 ($90 for international students). Electronic applications accepted. *Financial support:* Fellowships, research assistantships, teaching assistantships, unspecified assistantships available. *Unit head:* Prof. Lisa Alvarez-Cohen, Chair, 510-643-8739, Fax: 510-643-5264, E-mail: chair@ce.berkeley.edu. *Application contact:* Shelly Okimoto, Graduate Advisor, 510-642-6464, Fax: 510-643-5264, E-mail: aao@ce.berkeley.edu.

University of California, Davis, College of Engineering, Program in Civil and Environmental Engineering, Davis, CA 95616. Offers M Engr, MS, D Engr, PhD, Certificate, M Engr/MBA. *Degree requirements:* For master's, comprehensive exam (for some programs), thesis (for some programs); for doctorate, thesis/dissertation. *Entrance requirements:* For master's, GRE General Test, minimum GPA of 3.0; for doctorate, GRE, minimum graduate GPA of 3.5. Additional exam requirements/recommendations for international students: Required—TOEFL (minimum score 550 paper-based; 213 computer-based). Electronic applications accepted. *Faculty research:* Environmental water resources, transportation, structural mechanics, structural engineering, geotechnical engineering.

University of California, Irvine, Office of Graduate Studies, School of Engineering, Department of Civil and Environmental Engineering, Irvine, CA 92697. Offers MS, PhD. Part-time programs available. *Students:* 112 full-time (29 women), 16 part-time (9 women); includes 25 minority (22 Asian Americans or Pacific Islanders, 3 Hispanic Americans), 63 international. Average age 27. 254 applicants, 43% accepted, 37 enrolled. In 2009, 34 master's, 8 doctorates awarded. Terminal master's awarded for partial completion of doctoral program. *Degree requirements:* For doctorate, thesis/dissertation. *Entrance requirements:* For master's and doctorate, GRE General Test, minimum GPA of 3.0, 3 letters of recommendation. Additional exam requirements/recommendations for international students: Required—TOEFL (minimum score 550 paper-based; 213 computer-based). *Application deadline:* For fall admission, 1/15 priority date for domestic students, 1/15 for international students. Applications are processed on a rolling basis. Application fee: $70 ($90 for international students). Electronic applications accepted. *Financial support:* In 2009–10, fellowships (averaging $14,656 per year); research assistantships with full tuition reimbursements, teaching assistantships, institutionally sponsored loans, traineeships, health care benefits, and unspecified assistantships also available. Financial award application deadline: 3/1; financial award applicants required to submit FAFSA. *Faculty research:* Intelligent transportation systems and transportation economics, risk and reliability, fluid mechanics, environmental hydrodynamics, hydrological and climate systems, water resources. *Unit head:* Dr. Masanobu Shinozuka, Chair, 949-824-9379, Fax: 949-824-3672, E-mail: shino@uci.edu. *Application contact:* Lorrie Aguirre, Administrative Assistant, 949-824-2120, Fax: 949-824-2117, E-mail: llaguirr@uci.edu.

University of California, Irvine, Office of Graduate Studies, School of Engineering, Program in Environmental Engineering, Irvine, CA 92697. Offers engineering (MS, PhD). Part-time programs available. *Students:* 28 full-time (8 women), 2 part-time (both women); includes 12 minority (11 Asian Americans or Pacific Islanders, 1 Hispanic American), 8 international. Average age 26. 63 applicants, 35% accepted, 9 enrolled. In 2009, 5 master's awarded. Terminal master's awarded for partial completion of doctoral program. *Degree requirements:* For doctorate, thesis/dissertation. *Entrance requirements:* For master's and doctorate, GRE General Test, 3 letters of recommendation, minimum GPA of 3.0. Additional exam requirements/recommendations for international students: Required—TOEFL (minimum score 550 paper-based; 213 computer-based). *Application deadline:* For fall admission, 1/15 priority date for domestic students, 1/15 for international students. Applications are processed on a rolling basis. Application fee: $70 ($90 for international students). Electronic applications accepted. *Financial support:* In 2009–10, fellowships (averaging $14,656 per year); research assistantships with full tuition reimbursements, teaching assistantships, institutionally sponsored loans, traineeships, health care benefits, and unspecified assistantships also available. Financial award application deadline: 3/1; financial award applicants required to submit FAFSA. *Faculty research:* Air and water chemistry, environmental microbiology, combustion technologies, aerosol science, transport phenomena. *Unit head:* Dr. Stanley Grant, Director, 949-824-8277, Fax: 949-824-2541, E-mail: sbgrant@uci.edu. *Application contact:* Thomas Cahoon, Graduate Counselor, 949-824-3562, Fax: 949-824-3440, E-mail: tcahoon@uci.edu.

University of California, Los Angeles, Graduate Division, Henry Samueli School of Engineering and Applied Science, Department of Civil and Environmental Engineering, Los Angeles, CA 90095-1593. Offers MS, PhD. *Faculty:* 15 full-time (3 women). *Students:* 138 full-time (47 women); includes 41 minority (2 African Americans, 29 Asian Americans or Pacific Islanders, 10 Hispanic Americans), 48 international. 281 applicants, 62% accepted, 78 enrolled. In 2009, 52 master's, 10 doctorates awarded. *Degree requirements:* For master's, comprehensive exam or thesis; for doctorate, thesis/dissertation, qualifying exams. *Entrance requirements:* For master's, GRE General Test, minimum GPA of 3.0; for doctorate, GRE General Test, minimum GPA of 3.25. Additional exam requirements/recommendations for international students: Required—TOEFL (minimum score 560 paper-based; 220 computer-based). *Application deadline:* For fall admission, 1/15 for domestic and international students. Application fee: $70 ($90 for international students). Electronic applications accepted. *Financial support:* In 2009–10, 98 fellowships, 95 research assistantships, 45 teaching assistantships were awarded; Federal Work-Study, institutionally sponsored loans, and tuition waivers (full and partial) also available. Financial award application deadline: 12/15; financial award applicants required to submit FAFSA. Total annual research expenditures: $3.9 million. *Unit head:* Dr. Jiun-Shyan Chen, Chair, 310-267-4620. *Application contact:* Maida Bassili, Graduate Affairs Officer, 310-825-1851, Fax: 310-206-2222, E-mail: maida@ea.ucla.edu.

University of California, Los Angeles, Graduate Division, School of Public Health, Department of Environmental Health Sciences, Los Angeles, CA 90095. Offers environmental health sciences (MS, PhD); environmental science and engineering (D Env); molecular toxicology (PhD); JD/MPH. *Accreditation:* ABET (one or more programs are accredited). *Degree requirements:* For master's, comprehensive exam or thesis; for doctorate, thesis/dissertation, oral and written qualifying exams. *Entrance requirements:* For master's, GRE General Test, minimum GPA of 3.0; for doctorate, GRE General Test, minimum undergraduate GPA of 3.0. Electronic applications accepted.

University of California, Los Angeles, Graduate Division, School of Public Health, Program in Environmental Science and Engineering, Los Angeles, CA 90095. Offers D Env. *Degree requirements:* For doctorate, thesis/dissertation, oral and written qualifying exams. *Entrance requirements:* For doctorate, GRE General Test, minimum undergraduate GPA of 3.0, master's degree or equivalent in a natural science, engineering, or public health. *Faculty research:* Toxic and hazardous substances, air and water pollution, risk assessment/management, water resources, marine science.

University of California, Riverside, Graduate Division, Department of Chemical and Environmental Engineering, Riverside, CA 92521-0102. Offers MS, PhD. Part-time programs available. *Faculty:* 13 full-time (2 women), 2 part-time/adjunct (0 women). *Students:* 72 full-time (38 women); includes 6 minority (1 African American, 4 Asian Americans or Pacific Islanders, 1 Hispanic American), 52 international. Average age 27. 140 applicants, 31% accepted, 18 enrolled. In 2009, 5 master's, 13 doctorates awarded. Terminal master's awarded for partial completion of doctoral program. *Degree requirements:* For master's, thesis (for some programs); for doctorate, comprehensive exam, thesis/dissertation. *Entrance requirements:* For master's and doctorate, GRE General Test, minimum GPA of 3.0. Additional exam requirements/recommendations for international students: Required—TOEFL (minimum score 550 paper-based; 213 computer-based; 80 iBT). *Application deadline:* For fall admission, 1/5 for domestic and international students; for winter admission, 9/1 for domestic students, 7/1 for international students; for spring admission, 12/1 for domestic students, 10/1 for international students. Applications are processed on a rolling basis. Application fee: $60 ($100 for international students). Electronic applications accepted. *Financial support:* In 2009–10, fellowships with tuition reimbursements (averaging $12,000 per year), research assistantships with tuition reimbursements (averaging $18,000 per year), 2 teaching assistantships with partial tuition reimbursements (averaging $16,500 per year) were awarded; scholarships/grants, health care benefits, and unspecified assistantships also available. Financial award application deadline: 1/5; financial award applicants required to submit FAFSA. *Faculty research:* Air quality systems, water quality systems, advanced materials and nanotechnology, energy systems/alternative fuels, theory and molecular modeling. *Unit head:* Dr. Jianzhong Wu, Graduate Advisor, 951-827-2859, Fax: 951-827-5696, E-mail: gradcee@engr.ucr.edu. *Application contact:* William Suh, Graduate Student Affairs Officer, 951-827-2859, Fax: 951-827-2859, E-mail: gradcee@engr.ucr.edu.

University of Central Florida, College of Engineering and Computer Science, Department of Civil, Environmental, and Construction Engineering, Program in Environmental Engineering, Orlando, FL 32816. Offers MS, MS Env E, PhD. Part-time and evening/weekend programs available. *Students:* 23 full-time (7 women), 11 part-time (2 women); includes 4 minority (2 African Americans, 2 Hispanic Americans), 12 international. Average age 29. 27 applicants, 63% accepted, 9 enrolled. In 2009, 13 master's, 5 doctorates awarded. *Degree requirements:* For master's, thesis or alternative; for doctorate, thesis/dissertation, departmental qualifying exam, candidacy exam. *Entrance requirements:* For master's, GRE General Test, minimum GPA of 3.0 in last 60 hours of course work; for doctorate, GRE General Test, minimum GPA of 3.5 in last 60 hours of course work, interview. Additional exam requirements/recommendations for international students: Required—TOEFL. *Application deadline:* For fall admission, 7/15 priority date for domestic students; for spring admission, 12/15 priority date for domestic students. Application fee: $30. Electronic applications accepted. *Expenses:* Tuition, state resident: part-time $306.31 per credit hour. Tuition, nonresident: part-time $1099.01 per credit hour. Part-time tuition and fees vary according to degree level and program. *Financial support:* In 2009–10, 13 students received support, including 3 fellowships with partial tuition reimbursements available (averaging $3,800 per year), 14 research assistantships with partial tuition reimbursements available (averaging $8,500 per year), 2 teaching assistantships with partial tuition reimbursements available (averaging $12,800 per year); career-related internships or fieldwork, Federal Work-Study, institutionally sponsored loans, tuition waivers (partial), and unspecified assistantships also available. Financial award application deadline: 3/1; financial award applicants required to submit FAFSA.

University of Cincinnati, Graduate School, College of Engineering, Department of Civil and Environmental Engineering, Program in Environmental Engineering, Cincinnati, OH 45221. Offers MS, PhD. *Accreditation:* ABET (one or more programs are accredited). Part-time programs available. *Degree requirements:* For master's, project or thesis; for doctorate, one foreign language, thesis/dissertation. *Entrance requirements:* For master's and doctorate, GRE General Test. Additional exam requirements/recommendations for international students: Required—TOEFL (minimum score 580 paper-based; 237 computer-based; 92 iBT). Electronic applications accepted. *Faculty research:* Environmental microbiology, solid-waste management, air pollution control, water pollution control, aerosols.

University of Colorado at Boulder, Graduate School, College of Engineering and Applied Science, Department of Civil, Environmental, and Architectural Engineering, Boulder, CO 80309. Offers building systems (MS, PhD); construction engineering management (MS, PhD); environmental engineering (MS, PhD); geotechnical engineering and geomechanics (MS, PhD); hydrology, water resources and environmental fluid mechanics (MS, PhD); structural engineering and structural mechanics (MS, PhD). *Faculty:* 39 full-time (5 women). *Students:* 202 full-time (62 women), 29 part-time (6 women); includes 34 minority (3 African Americans, 3 American Indian/Alaska Native, 12 Asian Americans or Pacific Islanders, 16 Hispanic Americans), 53 international. Average age 29. 384 applicants, 44% accepted, 80 enrolled. In 2009, 60 master's, 7 doctorates awarded. *Degree requirements:* For master's, comprehensive exam, thesis or alternative; for doctorate, thesis/dissertation. *Entrance requirements:* For master's, GRE General Test, minimum undergraduate GPA of 3.0. *Application deadline:* For fall admission, 3/1 for domestic students, 12/1 for international students; for spring admission, 10/31 for domestic students, 10/1 for international students. Application fee: $50 ($60 for international students). *Financial support:* In 2009–10, 45 fellowships (averaging $7,876 per year), 68 research assistantships (averaging $15,204 per year) were awarded. Financial award application deadline: 1/15. *Faculty research:* Building systems engineering, construction engineering and management, environmental engineering, geoenvironmental engineering, geotechnical engineering, materials and mechanics, structural engineering, water resources engineering, life-cycle engineering. Total annual research expenditures: $6.1 million.

University of Connecticut, Graduate School, School of Engineering, Department of Civil and Environmental Engineering, Field of Environmental Engineering, Storrs, CT 06269. Offers MS, PhD. *Faculty:* 21 full-time (6 women). *Students:* 28 full-time (9 women), 6 part-time (2 women); includes 3 minority (1 Asian American or Pacific Islander, 2 Hispanic Americans), 20 international. Average age 28. 32 applicants, 31% accepted, 5 enrolled. In 2009, 5 master's, 1 doctorate awarded. *Degree requirements:* For master's, comprehensive exam; for doctorate, thesis/dissertation. *Entrance requirements:* For master's and doctorate, GRE General Test. Additional exam requirements/recommendations for international students: Required—TOEFL (minimum score 550 paper-based; 213 computer-based). *Application deadline:* For fall admission, 2/1 priority date for domestic and international students; for spring admission, 11/1 for domestic students, 10/1 for international students. Applications are processed on a rolling basis. Application fee: $55. Electronic applications accepted. *Expenses:* Tuition, state resident: full-time $4725; part-time $525 per credit. Tuition, nonresident: full-time $12,267; part-time $1363 per credit. Required fees: $346 per semester. Tuition and fees vary according to course load. *Financial support:* In 2009–10, 25 research assistantships with full tuition reimbursements, 2 teaching assistantships with full tuition reimbursements were awarded; fellowships, Federal Work-Study, scholarships/grants, health care benefits, and unspecified assistantships also available. Financial award application deadline: 2/1; financial award applicants required to submit FAFSA. *Unit head:* Guiling Wang, Chairperson, 860-486-5648, E-mail: wang@engr.uconn.edu. *Application contact:* Kristina Ashley, Administrative Assistant, 860-486-4018, E-mail: lazz@engr.uconn.edu.

University of Dayton, Graduate School, School of Engineering, Department of Civil and Environmental Engineering, Dayton, OH 45469-1300. Offers engineering mechanics (MSEM); environmental engineering (MSCE); geotechnical engineering (MSCE); structural engineering (MSCE); transport engineering (MSCE); water resources engineering (MSCE). Part-time programs available. *Faculty:* 8 full-time (2 women), 1 part-time/adjunct (0 women). *Students:* 10 full-time (6 women), 8 part-time (1 woman); includes 3 minority (all African Americans), 7 international. Average age 29. 35 applicants, 49% accepted, 6 enrolled. In 2009, 3 master's awarded. *Degree requirements:* For master's, thesis optional. *Entrance requirements:* Additional exam requirements/recommendations for international students: Required—TOEFL (minimum score 550 paper-based; 213 computer-based; 80 iBT). *Application deadline:* For fall admission, 8/1 for domestic students, 3/1 priority date for international students; for winter admission, 7/1 priority date for international students; for spring admission, 1/1 priority date for international students. Applications are processed on a rolling basis. Application fee: $0 ($50 for international students). Electronic applications accepted. *Expenses:* Tuition: Full-time $8412; part-time $701 per credit hour. Required fees: $325; $65 per course. $25 per semester. Tuition and fees vary according to course load, degree level and program. *Financial support:* In 2009–10, 3 research assistantships (averaging $10,780 per year), 4 teaching assistantships with partial tuition reimbursements (averaging $5,110 per year) were awarded. Financial award applicants required to submit FAFSA. *Faculty research:* Physical modeling of hydraulic systems, finite element methods, mechanics of composite materials, transportation systems safety, high-velocity wear. Total annual research expenditures: $421,839. *Unit head:* Dr. Donald V. Chase, Interim Chair, 937-229-3847, Fax: 937-229-3491, E-mail: donald.chase@notes.udayton.edu. *Application contact:* Graduate Admissions, 937-229-4411, Fax: 937-229-4729, E-mail: gradadmission@udayton.edu.

University of Delaware, College of Engineering, Department of Civil and Environmental Engineering, Newark, DE 19716. Offers environmental engineering (MAS, MCE, PhD); geotechnical engineering (MAS, MCE, PhD); ocean engineering (MAS, MCE, PhD); structural engineering (MAS, MCE, PhD); transportation engineering (MAS, MCE, PhD); water resource engineering (MAS, MCE, PhD). Part-time programs available. Terminal master's awarded for partial completion of doctoral program. *Degree requirements:* For master's, thesis; for doctorate, thesis/dissertation. *Entrance requirements:* For master's and doctorate, GRE General Test. Additional exam requirements/recommendations for international students: Required—TOEFL. Electronic applications accepted. *Faculty research:* Structural engineering and mechanics; transportation engineering; ocean engineering; soil mechanics and foundation; water resources and environmental engineering.

University of Detroit Mercy, College of Engineering and Science, Department of Civil and Environmental Engineering, Detroit, MI 48221. Offers ME, DE. Evening/weekend programs available. *Faculty research:* Geotechnical engineering.

University of Florida, Graduate School, College of Engineering, Department of Environmental Engineering Sciences, Gainesville, FL 32611. Offers ME, MS, PhD, Engr, JD/MS. Terminal master's awarded for partial completion of doctoral program. *Degree requirements:* For master's and Engr, project or thesis; for doctorate, thesis/dissertation. *Entrance requirements:* For master's and doctorate, GRE General Test, minimum GPA of 3.0; for Engr, GRE General Test. Additional exam requirements/recommendations for international students: Required—TOEFL (minimum score 550 paper-based; 213 computer-based). Electronic applications accepted. *Faculty research:* Air pollution, potable water supply system, water pollution control, hazardous waste, aquatic ecology and chemistry.

University of Guelph, Graduate Program Services, College of Physical and Engineering Science, School of Engineering, Guelph, ON N1G 2W1, Canada. Offers biological engineering (M Eng, M Sc, MA Sc, PhD); engineering systems and computing (M Eng, M Sc, MA Sc, PhD); environmental engineering (M Eng, M Sc, MA Sc, PhD); water resources engineering (M Eng, M Sc, MA Sc, PhD). Part-time programs available. *Degree requirements:* For master's, thesis (for some programs); for doctorate, comprehensive exam, thesis/dissertation. *Entrance requirements:* For master's, minimum B- average during previous 2 years of course work; for doctorate, minimum B average. Additional exam requirements/recommendations for international students: Required—TOEFL (minimum score 550 paper-based; 213 computer-based; 89 iBT), IELTS (minimum score 6.5). Electronic applications accepted. *Faculty research:* Water and food safety, environmental contaminant fates and mechanisms, computer systems, robotics and mechatronics, waste treatment.

University of Hawaii at Manoa, Graduate Division, College of Engineering, Department of Civil and Environmental Engineering, Honolulu, HI 96822. Offers MS, PhD. Part-time programs available. *Faculty:* 24 full-time (1 woman), 1 part-time/adjunct (0 women). *Students:* 59 full-time (14 women), 11 part-time (2 women); includes 30 minority (all Asian Americans or Pacific Islanders), 26 international. Average age 27. 63 applicants, 62% accepted, 24 enrolled. In 2009, 14 master's, 2 doctorates awarded. *Degree requirements:* For master's, comprehensive exam, thesis; for doctorate, comprehensive exam, thesis/dissertation. *Entrance requirements:* For master's and doctorate, GRE General Test or EIT Exam. Additional exam requirements/recommendations for international students: Required—TOEFL (minimum score 540 paper-based; 207 computer-based; 76 iBT), IELTS (minimum score 5). *Application deadline:* For fall admission, 5/1 for domestic and international students; for spring admission, 9/1 for domestic and international students. Application fee: $60. *Expenses:* Tuition, state resident: full-time $8900; part-time $372 per credit. Tuition, nonresident: full-time $21,400; part-time $898 per credit. Required fees: $207 per semester. *Financial support:* In 2009–10, 1 student received support, including 5 fellowships (averaging $1,800 per year), 36 research assistantships (averaging $18,389 per year), 5 teaching assistantships (averaging $14,852 per year); career-related internships or fieldwork, Federal Work-Study, and tuition waivers (full and partial) also available. *Faculty research:* Structures, transportation, environmental engineering, geotechnical engineering, construction. Total annual research expenditures: $1.2 million. *Application contact:* Roger Babcock, Graduate Chair, 808-956-7449, Fax: 808-956-5014, E-mail: rbabcock@eng.hawaii.edu.

University of Houston, Cullen College of Engineering, Department of Civil and Environmental Engineering, Houston, TX 77204. Offers MCE, MSCE, PhD. Part-time and evening/weekend programs available. *Faculty:* 12 full-time (1 woman), 5 part-time/adjunct (1 woman). *Students:* 39 full-time (9 women), 49 part-time (11 women); includes 26 minority (3 African Americans, 16 Asian Americans or Pacific Islanders, 7 Hispanic Americans), 36 international. Average age 30. 80 applicants, 70% accepted, 19 enrolled. In 2009, 13 master's, 3 doctorates awarded. Terminal master's awarded for partial completion of doctoral program. *Entrance requirements:* For master's and doctorate, GRE General Test. Additional exam requirements/

Environmental Engineering

University of Houston (continued)
recommendations for international students: Required—TOEFL (minimum score 550 paper-based; 213 computer-based; 79 iBT), IELTS (minimum score 6.5). *Application deadline:* For fall admission, 6/1 for domestic students, 5/1 for international students; for spring admission, 10/1 for domestic and international students. Applications are processed on a rolling basis. Application fee: $25 ($75 for international students). Electronic applications accepted. *Expenses:* Tuition, state resident: full-time $7676; part-time $320 per credit hour. Tuition, nonresident: full-time $14,324; part-time $597 per credit hour. Required fees: $3034. *Financial support:* In 2009–10, 16 research assistantships with full tuition reimbursements (averaging $11,400 per year), 23 teaching assistantships with full tuition reimbursements (averaging $11,400 per year) were awarded; career-related internships or fieldwork, Federal Work-Study, institutionally sponsored loans, scholarships/grants, health care benefits, and unspecified assistantships also available. Support available to part-time students. Financial award application deadline: 2/1. *Faculty research:* Civil engineering. *Unit head:* Dr. Dennis Clifford, Chairperson, 713-743-4266, Fax: 713-743-4260, E-mail: daclifford@uh.edu. *Application contact:* Charlene Holliday, Graduate Admissions Assistant, 713-743-4254, Fax: 713-743-4260, E-mail: civilgrad@egr.uh.edu.

University of Idaho, College of Graduate Studies, College of Engineering, Department of Engineering, Program in Environmental Engineering, Moscow, ID 83844-2282. Offers M Engr, MS. *Students:* 1 full-time, 1 part-time. In 2009, 1 master's awarded. *Application deadline:* For fall admission, 8/1 for domestic students; for spring admission, 12/15 for domestic students. Applications are processed on a rolling basis. Application fee: $55 ($60 for international students). *Expenses:* Tuition, state resident: full-time $6120. Tuition, nonresident: full-time $17,712. *Unit head:* Dr. Wudneh Admassu, Director, 208-885-7461, E-mail: enve@uidaho.edu. *Application contact:* Dr. Wudneh Admassu, Director, 208-885-7461, E-mail: enve@uidaho.edu.

University of Illinois at Urbana–Champaign, Graduate College, College of Engineering, Department of Civil and Environmental Engineering, Champaign, IL 61820. Offers civil engineering (MS); environmental engineering in civil engineering (MS, PhD); environmental science in civil engineering (MS, PhD); M Arch/MS; MBA/MS. *Faculty:* 48 full-time (6 women), 4 part-time/adjunct (1 woman). *Students:* 349 full-time (88 women), 69 part-time (23 women); includes 37 minority (3 African Americans, 22 Asian Americans or Pacific Islanders, 12 Hispanic Americans), 212 international. 803 applicants, 35% accepted, 140 enrolled. In 2009, 83 master's, 24 doctorates awarded. *Entrance requirements:* For master's and doctorate, GRE. Additional exam requirements/recommendations for international students: Required—TOEFL (minimum score 550 paper-based; 213 computer-based; 79 iBT), or IELTS (minimum score 6.5). *Application deadline:* Applications are processed on a rolling basis. Application fee: $60 ($75 for international students). Electronic applications accepted. *Financial support:* In 2009–10, 58 fellowships, 253 research assistantships, 66 teaching assistantships were awarded; tuition waivers (full and partial) also available. *Unit head:* Amr S. Elnashai, Head, 217-265-5497, Fax: 217-265-8040, E-mail: aelnash@illinois.edu. *Application contact:* Mary Pearson, Administrative Secretary, 217-333-3811, Fax: 217-333-9464, E-mail: mkpearso@illinois.edu.

The University of Iowa, Graduate College, College of Engineering, Department of Civil and Environmental Engineering, Iowa City, IA 52242-1316. Offers MS, PhD. Part-time programs available. *Faculty:* 21 full-time (3 women). *Students:* 83 full-time (25 women); includes 3 minority (1 Asian American or Pacific Islander, 2 Hispanic Americans), 35 international. Average age 28. 177 applicants, 29% accepted, 19 enrolled. In 2009, 17 master's, 11 doctorates awarded. Terminal master's awarded for partial completion of doctoral program. *Degree requirements:* For master's, thesis optional, exam; for doctorate, comprehensive exam, thesis/dissertation, exam. *Entrance requirements:* For master's, GRE, A minimum undergraduate grade point average of 3.0; for doctorate, GRE, The completion of a Master's degree or equivalent, with a 3.20 minimum grade point average on completed graduate work. Additional exam requirements/recommendations for international students: Required—TOEFL (minimum score 550 paper-based; 213 computer-based; 81 iBT). *Application deadline:* For fall admission, 2/1 priority date for domestic and international students; for spring admission, 12/1 for domestic students, 10/1 for international students. Applications are processed on a rolling basis. Application fee: $60 ($100 for international students). Electronic applications accepted. *Financial support:* In 2009–10, 5 fellowships with partial tuition reimbursements (averaging $23,480 per year), 58 research assistantships with partial tuition reimbursements (averaging $22,553 per year), 22 teaching assistantships with partial tuition reimbursements (averaging $16,575 per year) were awarded; career-related internships or fieldwork, Federal Work-Study, scholarships/grants, traineeships, and unspecified assistantships also available. Support available to part-time students. Financial award application deadline: 2/1; financial award applicants required to submit FAFSA. *Faculty research:* Water resources; environmental engineering and science; hydraulics and hydrology; structures, mechanics, and materials; transportation engineering. Total annual research expenditures: $10.4 million. *Unit head:* Dr. Keri C. Hornbuckle, Departmental Executive Officer, 319-384-0789, Fax: 319-335-5660, E-mail: keri-hornbuckle@uiowa.edu. *Application contact:* Judy Holland, Secretary, 319-335-5647, Fax: 319-335-5660, E-mail: cee@engineering.uiowa.edu.

The University of Kansas, Graduate Studies, School of Engineering, Department of Civil, Environmental, and Architectural Engineering, Program in Environmental Engineering, Lawrence, KS 66045. Offers MS, PhD. Part-time programs available. *Faculty:* 9 full-time (1 woman), 1 part-time/adjunct (0 women). *Students:* 9 full-time (4 women), 7 part-time (4 women); includes 1 minority (Hispanic American), 6 international. Average age 29. 22 applicants, 50% accepted, 4 enrolled. In 2009, 5 master's awarded. *Degree requirements:* For master's, thesis or alternative, exam; for doctorate, comprehensive exam, thesis/dissertation. *Entrance requirements:* For master's and doctorate, GRE, BS in engineering. Additional exam requirements/recommendations for international students: Required—TOEFL. *Application deadline:* For fall admission, 3/1 priority date for domestic students, 3/15 priority date for international students; for spring admission, 12/1 priority date for domestic students, 8/15 priority date for international students. Applications are processed on a rolling basis. Application fee: $45 ($55 for international students). Electronic applications accepted. *Expenses:* Tuition, state resident: full-time $6492; part-time $270.50 per credit hour. Tuition, nonresident: full-time $15,510; part-time $646.25 per credit hour. Required fees: $847; $70.56 per credit hour. Tuition and fees vary according to course load and program. *Financial support:* Fellowships with full tuition reimbursements, research assistantships with full tuition reimbursements, teaching assistantships with full and partial tuition reimbursements, career-related internships or fieldwork available. Financial award application deadline: 2/7. *Faculty research:* Water quality, water treatment, wastewater treatment, air quality, air pollution control, solid waste, hazardous waste, water resources engineering. *Unit head:* Craig D. Adams, Chair, 785-864-2700, Fax: 785-864-5631, E-mail: adamscd@ku.edu. *Application contact:* Bruce M. McEnroe, Graduate Advisor, 785-864-2925, Fax: 785-864-5631, E-mail: mcenroe@ku.edu.

University of Louisville, J.B. Speed School of Engineering, Department of Civil and Environmental Engineering, Louisville, KY 40292-0001. Offers civil engineering (M Eng, MS, PhD). *Accreditation:* ABET (one or more programs are accredited). Part-time programs available. Postbaccalaureate distance learning degree programs offered (no on-campus study). *Faculty:* 12 full-time (1 woman), 1 part-time/adjunct (0 women). *Students:* 43 full-time (10 women), 11 part-time (2 women); includes 4 minority (2 Asian Americans or Pacific Islanders, 2 Hispanic Americans), 9 international. Average age 26. 23 applicants, 57% accepted, 7 enrolled. In 2009, 37 master's, 2 doctorates awarded. Terminal master's awarded for partial completion of doctoral program. *Degree requirements:* For master's, comprehensive exam (for some programs), thesis or alternative; for doctorate, comprehensive exam, thesis/dissertation, minimum GPA of 3.0. *Entrance requirements:* For master's and doctorate, GRE General Test. Additional exam requirements/recommendations for international students: Required—TOEFL (minimum score 550 paper-based; 213 computer-based; 80 iBT). *Application deadline:* For fall admission, 7/12 priority date for domestic and international students; for winter admission, 11/29 priority date for domestic and international students; for spring admission, 3/28 priority date for domestic and international students. Applications are processed on a rolling basis. Application fee: $50. Electronic applications accepted. *Financial support:* In 2009–10, 9 students received support, including 2 fellowships with full tuition reimbursements available (averaging $20,000 per year), 2 research assistantships with full tuition reimbursements available (averaging $20,000 per year), 5 teaching assistantships with full tuition reimbursements available (averaging $20,000 per year). Financial award application deadline: 1/25; financial award applicants required to submit FAFSA. *Faculty research:* Structures, hydraulics, transportation, environmental engineering, geomechanics. Total annual research expenditures: $1.8 million. *Unit head:* Dr. J. P. Mohsen, Chair, 502-852-6276, Fax: 502-852-8851, E-mail: jpmohs01@louisville.edu. *Application contact:* Dr. Michael Day, Associate Dean, 502-852-6195, Fax: 502-852-7294, E-mail: day@louisville.edu.

University of Maine, Graduate School, College of Engineering, Department of Civil and Environmental Engineering, Orono, ME 04469. Offers civil engineering (MS, PhD), including environmental engineering, geotechnical engineering, structural engineering. *Faculty:* 10 full-time (2 women), 2 part-time/adjunct (0 women). *Students:* 28 full-time (7 women), 15 part-time (2 women); includes 2 minority (both American Indian/Alaska Native), 3 international. Average age 27. 31 applicants, 35% accepted, 7 enrolled. In 2009, 6 master's, 1 doctorate awarded. *Degree requirements:* For doctorate, thesis/dissertation. *Entrance requirements:* For master's and doctorate, GRE General Test. Additional exam requirements/recommendations for international students: Required—TOEFL. *Application deadline:* For fall admission, 2/1 priority date for domestic students. Applications are processed on a rolling basis. Application fee: $65. Electronic applications accepted. *Financial support:* In 2009–10, 15 research assistantships with tuition reimbursements (averaging $15,815 per year), 3 teaching assistantships with tuition reimbursements (averaging $12,790 per year) were awarded; Federal Work-Study, institutionally sponsored loans, scholarships/grants, and tuition waivers (full and partial) also available. Financial award application deadline: 3/1. *Unit head:* Dr. Eric Landis, Chair. *Application contact:* Scott G. Delcourt, Associate Dean of the Graduate School, 207-581-3291, Fax: 207-581-3232, E-mail: graduate@maine.edu.

University of Maryland, Baltimore County, Graduate School, College of Engineering and Information Technology, Department of Civil and Environmental Engineering, Baltimore, MD 21250. Offers civil engineering (MS, PhD). Part-time programs available. *Faculty:* 2 full-time (0 women), 1 part-time/adjunct (0 women). *Students:* 8 full-time (5 women), 6 part-time (3 women); includes 4 minority (1 African American, 3 Asian Americans or Pacific Islanders), 7 international. Average age 28. 11 applicants, 36% accepted, 3 enrolled. In 2009, 2 master's awarded. *Degree requirements:* For master's, comprehensive exam (for some programs), thesis (for some programs); for doctorate, comprehensive exam, thesis/dissertation. *Entrance requirements:* For master's and doctorate, GRE General Test, BS in civil and environmental engineering or related field of engineering. Additional exam requirements/recommendations for international students: Required—TOEFL (minimum score 550 paper-based; 213 computer-based; 80 iBT). *Application deadline:* For fall admission, 6/1 for domestic students, 1/1 for international students; for spring admission, 11/1 for domestic students, 6/1 for international students. Applications are processed on a rolling basis. Application fee: $50. Electronic applications accepted. *Financial support:* In 2009–10, 9 research assistantships with full tuition reimbursements (averaging $24,000 per year) were awarded; career-related internships or fieldwork, Federal Work-Study, scholarships/grants, health care benefits, tuition waivers (partial), and unspecified assistantships also available. Support available to part-time students. Financial award application deadline: 6/30; financial award applicants required to submit FAFSA. *Faculty research:* Environmental engineering, water resources engineering. Total annual research expenditures: $2.6 million. *Unit head:* Dr. Brian Reed, Professor and Chair, 410-455-8646, Fax: 410-455-6500, E-mail: reedb@umbc.edu. *Application contact:* Dr. Upal Ghosh, Associate Professor and Graduate Program Director, 410-455-8665, Fax: 410-455-6500, E-mail: ughosh@umbc.edu.

University of Maryland, College Park, Academic Affairs, A. James Clark School of Engineering, Department of Civil and Environmental Engineering, College Park, MD 20742. Offers M Eng, MS, PhD. Part-time and evening/weekend programs available. Postbaccalaureate distance learning degree programs offered. *Faculty:* 65 full-time (10 women), 24 part-time/adjunct (5 women). *Students:* 151 full-time (61 women), 51 part-time (17 women); includes 30 minority (13 African Americans, 1 American Indian/Alaska Native, 12 Asian Americans or Pacific Islanders, 4 Hispanic Americans), 108 international. 307 applicants, 42% accepted, 64 enrolled. In 2009, 29 master's, 10 doctorates awarded. *Degree requirements:* For master's, thesis optional; for doctorate, thesis/dissertation, qualifying exam. *Entrance requirements:* For master's and doctorate, GRE General Test, 3 letters of recommendation. *Application deadline:* For fall admission, 5/1 for domestic students, 2/1 for international students; for spring admission, 10/15 for domestic students, 6/1 for international students. Applications are processed on a rolling basis. Application fee: $60. Electronic applications accepted. *Expenses:* Tuition, area resident: Part-time $471 per credit hour. Tuition, state resident: part-time $471 per credit hour. Tuition, nonresident: part-time $1016 per credit hour. Required fees: $337.04 per term. *Financial support:* In 2009–10, 13 fellowships with full and partial tuition reimbursements (averaging $13,868 per year), 59 research assistantships with tuition reimbursements (averaging $18,990 per year), 17 teaching assistantships with tuition reimbursements (averaging $19,112 per year) were awarded; Federal Work-Study and scholarships/grants also available. Support available to part-time students. Financial award applicants required to submit FAFSA. *Faculty research:* Transportation and urban systems, environmental engineering, geotechnical engineering, construction engineering and management, hydraulics. Total annual research expenditures: $15.7 million. *Unit head:* Dr. Ali Haghani, Chairman, 301-405-1974, Fax: 301-405-2585, E-mail: haghani@umd.edu. *Application contact:* Dean of Graduate School, 301-405-0376, Fax: 301-314-9305.

University of Massachusetts Amherst, Graduate School, College of Engineering, Department of Civil and Environmental Engineering, Program in Environmental Engineering, Amherst, MA 01003. Offers MS. *Accreditation:* ABET. Part-time programs available. *Students:* 16 full-time (8 women), 2 part-time (1 woman); includes 1 minority (Hispanic American), 2 international. Average age 25. 60 applicants, 27% accepted, 9 enrolled. In 2009, 5 master's awarded. *Degree requirements:* For master's, thesis or alternative, project. *Entrance requirements:* For master's, GRE General Test. Additional exam requirements/recommendations for international students: Required—TOEFL (minimum score 550 paper-based; 213 computer-based; 80 iBT), IELTS (minimum score 6.5). *Application deadline:* For fall admission, 2/1 for domestic and international students; for spring admission, 10/1 for domestic and international students. Applications are processed on a rolling basis. Application fee: $50 ($65 for international students). Electronic applications accepted. *Expenses:* Tuition, state resident: full-time $2640; part-time $110 per credit. Tuition, nonresident: full-time $9936; part-time $414 per credit. Tuition and fees vary according to course load. *Financial support:* Fellowships with full tuition reimbursements, research assistantships with full tuition reimbursements, teaching assistantships with full tuition reimbursements, career-related internships or fieldwork, Federal Work-Study, scholarships/grants, traineeships, health care benefits, tuition waivers, and unspecified assistantships available. Support available to part-time students. Financial award application deadline: 2/1; financial award applicants required to submit FAFSA. *Unit head:* Dr. John E. Tobiason, Graduate Program Director, 413-545-0686, Fax: 413-545-2840. *Application contact:* Jean M. Ames, Supervisor of Admissions, 413-545-0722, Fax: 413-577-0100, E-mail: gradadm@grad.umass.edu.

University of Massachusetts Amherst, Graduate School, Interdisciplinary Programs, Program in Environmental Engineering and Business Administration, Amherst, MA 01003. Offers MS Envr E/MBA. Part-time programs available. *Students:* 1 applicant, 0% accepted, 0 enrolled. *Entrance requirements:* Additional exam requirements/recommendations for international students: Required—TOEFL (minimum score 600 paper-based; 250 computer-based; 100 iBT), IELTS (minimum score 7). *Application deadline:* For fall admission, 2/1 for domestic and international students. Applications are processed on a rolling basis. Application fee: $50 ($65 for international students). Electronic applications accepted. *Expenses:* Tuition, state resident: full-time $2640; part-time $110 per credit. Tuition, nonresident: full-time $9936; part-time $414 per credit. Tuition and fees vary according to course load. *Financial support:* Career-related internships or fieldwork, Federal Work-Study, scholarships/grants, traineeships, health care benefits, tuition waivers (full), and unspecified assistantships available. Support available to part-time students. *Unit head:* Dr. John E. Tobiason, Graduate Program Director, 413-545-2681, Fax: 413-545-2840. *Application contact:* Jean M. Ames, Supervisor of Admissions, 413-545-0722, Fax: 413-577-0010, E-mail: gradadm@grad.umass.edu.

University of Massachusetts Dartmouth, Graduate School, College of Engineering, Program in Civil and Environmental Engineering, North Dartmouth, MA 02747-2300. Offers MS. Part-time programs available. *Faculty:* 6 full-time (1 woman), 4 part-time/adjunct (0 women). *Students:* 4 full-time (0 women), 7 part-time (1 woman); includes 1 minority (Hispanic American), 1 international. Average age 24. 9 applicants, 89% accepted, 4 enrolled. In 2009, 2 master's awarded. *Degree requirements:* For master's, thesis or alternative. *Entrance requirements:* For master's, GRE, minimum GPA of 3.0, 3 letters of recommendation. Additional exam requirements/recommendations for international students: Required—TOEFL (minimum score 550 paper-based). *Application deadline:* For fall admission, 4/20 priority date for domestic students, 2/20 priority date for international students; for spring admission, 11/15 priority date for domestic students, 9/15 priority date for international students. Application fee: $40 ($60 for international students). *Expenses:* Tuition, state resident: full-time $2071; part-time $86.29 per credit. Tuition, nonresident: full-time $8099; part-time $337.46 per credit. Required fees: $9446. Tuition and fees vary according to class time, course load and reciprocity agreements. *Financial support:* In 2009–10, 5 teaching assistantships with full tuition reimbursements (averaging $12,500 per year) were awarded. Financial award application deadline: 3/1; financial award applicants required to submit FAFSA. *Faculty research:* Evaluation of road system in Massachusetts, physico-chemical treatment of hazardous waste, soil-geosynthetic systems, waste water treatment systems, concrete analysis. Total annual research expenditures: $883,000. *Unit head:* Dr. Heather Miller, Graduate Director, 508-999-8481, E-mail: hmiller@umassd.edu. *Application contact:* Elan Turcotte-Shamski, Graduate Admissions Officer, 508-999-8604, Fax: 508-999-8183, E-mail: graduate@umassd.edu.

University of Massachusetts Lowell, James B. Francis College of Engineering, Department of Civil and Environmental Engineering and College of Arts and Sciences, Program in Environmental Studies, Lowell, MA 01854-2881. Offers environmental engineering (MSES); environmental studies (PhD, Certificate). Part-time programs available. *Degree requirements:* For master's, thesis optional. *Entrance requirements:* For master's, GRE General Test. *Faculty research:* Remote sensing of air pollutants, atmospheric deposition of toxic metals, contaminant transport in groundwater, soil remediation.

University of Memphis, Graduate School, Herff College of Engineering, Department of Civil Engineering, Memphis, TN 38152. Offers civil engineering (PhD); environmental engineering (MS); foundation engineering (MS); structural engineering (MS); transportation engineering (MS); water resources engineering (MS). *Faculty:* 12 full-time (1 woman), 1 part-time/adjunct (0 women). *Students:* 12 full-time (3 women), 16 part-time (6 women); includes 2 minority (1 African American, 1 Asian American or Pacific Islander), 9 international. Average age 28. 18 applicants, 94% accepted, 8 enrolled. In 2009, 11 master's awarded. *Degree requirements:* For master's, comprehensive exam, thesis or alternative; for doctorate, thesis/dissertation. *Entrance requirements:* For master's, GRE General Test or MAT, minimum undergraduate GPA of 2.5. *Application deadline:* For fall admission, 8/1 for domestic students; for spring admission, 12/1 for domestic students. Application fee: $35 ($60 for international students). *Expenses:* Tuition, state resident: full-time $6246; part-time $347 per credit hour. Tuition, nonresident: full-time $15,894; part-time $883 per credit hour. Required fees: $1160. Full-time tuition and fees vary according to course load, degree level and program. *Financial support:* In 2009–10, 6 students received support; fellowships with full tuition reimbursements available, research assistantships with full tuition reimbursements available, career-related internships or fieldwork, Federal Work-Study, scholarships/grants, and unspecified assistantships available. Financial award application deadline: 2/15; financial award applicants required to submit FAFSA. *Faculty research:* Structural response to earthquakes, pavement design, water quality, transportation safety, intermodal transportation. *Unit head:* Dr. Sharam Pezeshk, Interim Chair, 901-678-2746, Fax: 901-678-3026. *Application contact:* Dr. Roger Meier, Coordinator of Graduate Studies, 901-678-3284.

University of Michigan, Horace H. Rackham School of Graduate Studies, College of Engineering, Department of Civil and Environmental Engineering, Ann Arbor, MI 48109. Offers civil engineering (MSE, PhD, CE); construction engineering and management (M Eng, MSE); environmental engineering (MSE, PhD); structural engineering (M Eng); MBA/MSE. Part-time programs available. *Faculty:* 28 full-time (8 women). *Students:* 104 full-time (34 women), 1 part-time (0 women); includes 9 minority (2 African Americans, 5 Asian Americans or Pacific Islanders, 2 Hispanic Americans), 49 international. 413 applicants, 29% accepted, 40 enrolled. In 2009, 47 master's, 18 doctorates awarded. *Degree requirements:* For master's, thesis optional; for doctorate, comprehensive exam, thesis/dissertation, oral defense of dissertation, preliminary and written exams. *Entrance requirements:* For master's and doctorate, GRE General Test. Additional exam requirements/recommendations for international students: Required—TOEFL (minimum score 560 paper-based; 220 computer-based). *Application deadline:* Applications are processed on a rolling basis. Application fee: $60 ($75 for international students). Electronic applications accepted. *Expenses:* Tuition, state resident: full-time $17,286; part-time $1099 per credit hour. Tuition, nonresident: full-time $34,944; part-time $2080 per credit hour. Required fees: $95 per semester. Tuition and fees vary according to course load, degree level and program. *Financial support:* Fellowships, research assistantships, teaching assistantships, institutionally sponsored loans and tuition waivers (partial) available. Financial award application deadline: 1/19. *Faculty research:* Construction engineering and management; geotechnical engineering; earthquake-resistant design of structures; environmental chemistry and microbiology; cost engineering; environmental and water resources engineering. *Unit head:* Nancy Love, Chair, 734-764-8405, Fax: 734-764-4292, E-mail: nglove@umich.edu. *Application contact:* Kimberly Smith, Student Advisor, 734-764-8405, Fax: 734-647-2127, E-mail: kansmith@umich.edu.

University of Missouri, Graduate School, College of Engineering, Department of Civil and Environmental Engineering, Columbia, MO 65211. Offers civil engineering (MS, PhD); environmental engineering (MS, PhD); geotechnical engineering (MS, PhD); structural engineering (MS, PhD); transportation and highway engineering (MS); water resources (MS, PhD). *Degree requirements:* For master's, report or thesis; for doctorate, thesis/dissertation. *Entrance requirements:* For master's and doctorate, GRE General Test. Additional exam requirements/recommendations for international students: Required—TOEFL (minimum score 550 paper-based; 213 computer-based; 79 iBT).

University of Nebraska–Lincoln, Graduate College, College of Engineering, Interdepartmental Area of Environmental Engineering, Lincoln, NE 68588. Offers MS, PhD. *Degree requirements:* For master's, thesis optional; for doctorate, comprehensive exam, thesis/dissertation. *Entrance requirements:* For master's and doctorate, GRE General Test. Additional exam requirements/recommendations for international students: Required—TOEFL (minimum score 550 paper-based; 213 computer-based). Electronic applications accepted. *Faculty research:* Wastewater engineering, hazardous waste management, solid waste management, groundwater engineering.

University of New Brunswick Fredericton, School of Graduate Studies, Faculty of Engineering, Department of Civil Engineering, Fredericton, NB E3B 5A3, Canada. Offers construction engineering and management (M Eng, M Sc E, PhD); environmental engineering (M Eng, M Sc E, PhD); environmental studies (M Eng); geotechnical engineering (M Eng, M Sc E, PhD); groundwater/hydrology (M Eng, M Sc E, PhD); materials (M Eng, M Sc E, PhD); pavements (M Eng, M Sc E, PhD); structures (M Eng, M Sc E, PhD); transportation (M Eng, M Sc E, PhD). Part-time programs available. *Faculty:* 18 full-time (1 woman), 1 (woman) part-time/adjunct. *Students:* 42 full-time (9 women), 18 part-time (2 women). In 2009, 11 master's, 4 doctorates awarded. *Degree requirements:* For master's, thesis, proposal; for doctorate, comprehensive exam, thesis/dissertation, Qualifying exam; Proposal; 27 credit hours of courses. *Entrance requirements:* For master's, Minimum GPA of 3.0; BScE in Civil Engineering or related engineering degree.; for doctorate, Minimum GPA of 3.0; Candidates are normally required to have a graduate degree in engineering or applied science. Additional exam requirements/recommendations for international students: Required—TOEFL (minimum score 580 paper-based; 237 computer-based), TWE (minimum score 4), or IELTS (minimum score 7.5). *Application deadline:* For fall admission, 5/1 priority date for domestic students; for winter admission, 11/1 priority date for domestic students. Applications are processed on a rolling basis. Application fee: $50 Canadian dollars. Tuition and fees charges are reported in Canadian dollars. *Expenses:* Tuition, area resident: Full-time $5562 Canadian dollars; part-time $2781 Canadian dollars per year. Required fees: $49.75 Canadian dollars per term. *Financial support:* In 2009–10, 51 research assistantships (averaging $7,000 per year), 43 teaching assistantships (averaging $2,000 per year) were awarded; career-related internships or fieldwork and scholarships/grants also available. *Faculty research:* Construction engineering and management, concrete materials and structural engineering, transportation and asset management, geotechnical engineering, water and environmental engineering. *Unit head:* Dr. Eric Hildebrand, Director of Graduate Studies, 506-453-5113, Fax: 506-453-3568, E-mail: ktm@unb.ca. *Application contact:* Joyce Moore, Graduate Secretary, 506-452-6127, Fax: 506-453-3568, E-mail: civil-grad@unb.ca.

University of New Haven, Graduate School, Tagliatela College of Engineering, Program in Environmental Engineering, West Haven, CT 06516-1916. Offers environmental engineering (MS); industrial and hazardous wastes (MS); water and wastewater treatment (MS); water resources (Certificate). Part-time and evening/weekend programs available. *Faculty:* 6 full-time (1 woman), 2 part-time/adjunct (0 women). *Students:* 15 full-time (4 women), 6 part-time (1 woman); includes 2 African Americans, 14 international. Average age 29. 35 applicants, 97% accepted, 7 enrolled. In 2009, 10 master's awarded. *Degree requirements:* For master's, thesis or alternative. *Entrance requirements:* For master's, bachelor's degree in engineering. Additional exam requirements/recommendations for international students: Required—TOEFL (minimum score 520 paper-based; 190 computer-based; 70 iBT); Recommended—IELTS (minimum score 5.5). *Application deadline:* For fall admission, 5/31 for international students; for winter admission, 10/15 for international students; for spring admission, 1/15 for international students. Applications are processed on a rolling basis. Application fee: $50. Electronic applications accepted. *Expenses:* Tuition: Part-time $700 per credit. Required fees: $45 per term. One-time fee: $390 part-time. *Financial support:* Research assistantships with partial tuition reimbursements, teaching assistantships with partial tuition reimbursements, career-related internships or fieldwork, Federal Work-Study, scholarships/grants, tuition waivers, and unspecified assistantships available. Support available to part-time students. Financial award application deadline: 5/1; financial award applicants required to submit FAFSA. *Unit head:* Dr. Agamemnon D. Koutsospyros, Coordinator, 203-932-7398. *Application contact:* Eloise Gormley, Director of Graduate Admissions, 203-932-7449, Fax: 203-932-7137, E-mail: gradinfo@newhaven.edu.

The University of North Carolina at Chapel Hill, Graduate School, School of Public Health, Department of Environmental Sciences and Engineering, Chapel Hill, NC 27599. Offers air, radiation and industrial hygiene (MPH, MS, MSEE, MSPH, PhD); aquatic and atmospheric sciences (MPH, MS, MSPH, PhD); environmental engineering (MPH, MS, MSEE, MSPH, PhD); environmental health sciences (MPH, MS, MSPH, PhD); environmental management and policy (MPH, MS, MSPH, PhD). Terminal master's awarded for partial completion of doctoral program. *Degree requirements:* For master's, comprehensive exam, thesis (for some programs), research paper; for doctorate, comprehensive exam, thesis/dissertation. *Entrance requirements:* For master's and doctorate, GRE General Test, minimum GPA of 3.0. Additional exam requirements/recommendations for international students: Required—TOEFL. Electronic applications accepted. *Faculty research:* Air, radiation and industrial hygiene, aquatic and atmospheric sciences, environmental health sciences, environmental management and policy, water resources engineering.

The University of North Carolina at Charlotte, Graduate School, The William States Lee College of Engineering, Department of Civil and Environmental Engineering, Program in Infrastructure and Environmental Systems (INES), Charlotte, NC 28223-0001. Offers infrastructure and environmental systems design (PhD); infrastructure and environmental systems management (PhD). *Faculty:* 17 full-time (2 women), 1 part-time/adjunct (0 women). *Students:* 26 full-time (9 women), 9 part-time (2 women); includes 2 minority (both African Americans), 17 international. Average age 32. 13 applicants, 62% accepted, 6 enrolled. In 2009, 3 doctorates awarded. *Degree requirements:* For doctorate, thesis/dissertation, dissertation defense, qualifying exam. *Entrance requirements:* Additional exam requirements/recommendations for international students: Required—TOEFL (minimum score 557 paper-based; 220 computer-based; 83 iBT). *Application deadline:* For fall admission, 7/1 for domestic students, 5/1 for international students; for spring admission, 11/1 for domestic students, 10/1 for international students. Applications are processed on a rolling basis. Application fee: $55. Electronic applications accepted. *Financial support:* Research assistantships, teaching assistantships, career-related internships or fieldwork, Federal Work-Study, institutionally sponsored loans, scholarships/grants, and unspecified assistantships available. Support available to part-time students. Financial award application deadline: 4/1; financial award applicants required to submit FAFSA. Total annual research expenditures: $968,217. *Unit head:* Dr. David T. Young, Chair, Civil Engineering, 704-687-4178, Fax: 704-687-6953, E-mail: dyoung@uncc.edu. *Application contact:* Kathy B. Giddings, Director of Graduate Admissions, 704-687-5503, Fax: 704-687-3279, E-mail: gradadm@uncc.edu.

University of North Dakota, Graduate School, School of Engineering and Mines, Department of Environmental Engineering, Grand Forks, ND 58202. Offers M Engr, MS. *Degree requirements:* For master's, thesis. *Entrance requirements:* For master's, GRE General Test, minimum GPA of 3.0. Additional exam requirements/recommendations for international students: Required—TOEFL (minimum score 550 paper-based; 213 computer-based; 79 iBT), IELTS (minimum score 6.5). Electronic applications accepted.

University of Notre Dame, Graduate School, College of Engineering, Department of Civil Engineering and Geological Sciences, Notre Dame, IN 46556. Offers bioengineering (MS Bio E); civil engineering (MSCE); civil engineering and geological sciences (PhD); environmental engineering (MS Env E); geological sciences (MS). Terminal master's awarded for partial completion of doctoral program. *Degree requirements:* For master's, comprehensive exam; for doctorate, thesis/dissertation, candidacy exam. *Entrance requirements:* For master's and doctorate, GRE General Test. Additional exam requirements/recommendations for international students: Required—TOEFL (minimum score 600 paper-based; 250 computer-based; 80 iBT). Electronic applications accepted. *Faculty research:* Environmental modeling, biological-waste treatment, petrology, environmental geology, geochemistry.

University of Oklahoma, Graduate College, College of Earth and Energy, School of Petroleum and Geological Engineering, Program in Petroleum Engineering, Norman, OK 73019-0390. Offers natural gas engineering (MS); petroleum engineering (MS, PhD). Part-time programs available. Postbaccalaureate distance learning degree programs offered (minimal on-campus study). *Students:* 74 full-time (15 women), 13 part-time (1 woman); includes 4 minority (1 African American, 2 Asian Americans or Pacific Islanders, 1 Hispanic American), 73 international. 103 applicants, 25% accepted, 19 enrolled. In 2009, 11 master's, 2 doctorates awarded. Terminal master's awarded for partial completion of doctoral program. *Degree requirements:* For master's, thesis optional, industrial team project or thesis; for doctorate, thesis/dissertation. *Entrance requirements:* For master's, GRE General Test, bachelor's degree in engineering, 3 letters of recommendation, minimum GPA of 3.0 during final 60 hours of undergraduate course work; for doctorate, GRE General Test, minimum GPA of 3.0, 3 letters of recommendation. Additional exam requirements/recommendations for international students: Required—TOEFL (minimum score 550 paper-based; 213 computer-based). *Application deadline:* For fall admission, 6/1 priority date for domestic students, 4/1 for international students; for spring admission, 11/1 for domestic students, 9/1 for international students. Applications are processed on a rolling basis. Application fee: $40 ($90 for international students). Electronic applications accepted. *Expenses:* Tuition, state resident: full-time $3744; part-time $156 per credit hour. Tuition,

Environmental Engineering

University of Oklahoma (continued)

nonresident: full-time $13,577; part-time $565.70 per credit hour. Required fees: $2415; $90.10 per credit hour. *Financial support:* In 2009–10, 67 students received support. Career-related internships or fieldwork, health care benefits, and unspecified assistantships available. Financial award application deadline: 4/15; financial award applicants required to submit FAFSA. *Faculty research:* Petrophysics, history watching, well-bore stimulation, unconventional reservoirs. *Unit head:* Dr. Chandra Rai, Director, 405-325-2921, Fax: 405-325-7477, E-mail: crai@ou.edu. *Application contact:* Dr. Dean Oliver, Professor, 405-325-0189, Fax: 405-325-7477, E-mail: dsoliver@ou.edu.

University of Oklahoma, Graduate College, College of Engineering, School of Civil Engineering and Environmental Science, Program in Environmental Engineering, Norman, OK 73019-0390. Offers MS. *Students:* 8 full-time (3 women), 6 part-time (2 women); includes 1 minority (American Indian/Alaska Native), 3 international. 10 applicants, 80% accepted, 4 enrolled. In 2009, 2 master's awarded. *Entrance requirements:* For master's, undergraduate degree in a related engineering or science discipline. Additional exam requirements/recommendations for international students: Required—TOEFL (minimum score 600 paper-based; 250 computer-based). *Application deadline:* For fall admission, 4/1 priority date for domestic students, 4/1 for international students; for spring admission, 11/1 for domestic students, 9/1 for international students. Applications are processed on a rolling basis. Application fee: $40 ($90 for international students). Electronic applications accepted. *Expenses:* Tuition, state resident: full-time $3744; part-time $156 per credit hour. Tuition, nonresident: full-time $13,577; part-time $565.70 per credit hour. Required fees: $2415; $90.10 per credit hour. *Financial support:* In 2009–10, 12 students received support. Application deadline: 3/1. *Faculty research:* Hydrologic modeling, water treatment process, remediation process, transport and fate of chemicals. *Unit head:* Robert C. Knox, Director, 405-325-5911, Fax: 405-325-4217, E-mail: rknox@ou.edu. *Application contact:* Susan Williams, Graduate Programs Specialist, 405-325-2344, Fax: 405-325-4217, E-mail: srwilliams@ou.edu.

University of Pittsburgh, School of Engineering, Department of Civil and Environmental Engineering, Pittsburgh, PA 15260. Offers MSCEE, PhD. Part-time programs available. Postbaccalaureate distance learning degree programs offered. *Faculty:* 16 full-time (3 women), 21 part-time/adjunct (1 woman). *Students:* 75 full-time (23 women), 45 part-time (8 women); includes 9 minority (5 African Americans, 4 Asian Americans or Pacific Islanders), 45 international. 205 applicants, 83% accepted, 42 enrolled. In 2009, 17 master's awarded. Terminal master's awarded for partial completion of doctoral program. *Degree requirements:* For master's, thesis optional; for doctorate, comprehensive exam, thesis/dissertation, final oral exams. *Entrance requirements:* For master's and doctorate, minimum QPA of 3.0. Additional exam requirements/recommendations for international students: Required—TOEFL (minimum score 550 paper-based; 213 computer-based; 80 iBT). *Application deadline:* For fall admission, 3/1 priority date for domestic students; for spring admission, 7/1 priority date for domestic students. Applications are processed on a rolling basis. Application fee: $50. Electronic applications accepted. *Expenses:* Tuition, state resident: full-time $16,402; part-time $665 per credit. Tuition, nonresident: full-time $28,694; part-time $1175 per credit. Required fees: $690; $175 per term. Tuition and fees vary according to program. *Financial support:* In 2009–10, 44 students received support, including 3 fellowships with tuition reimbursements available (averaging $20,772 per year), 35 research assistantships with full tuition reimbursements available (averaging $22,000 per year), 23 teaching assistantships with full tuition reimbursements available (averaging $21,000 per year); scholarships/grants, traineeships, and tuition waivers (full and partial) also available. Financial award application deadline: 4/15. *Faculty research:* Environmental and water resources, structures and infrastructures, construction management. Total annual research expenditures: $2.7 million. *Unit head:* Dr. Radisav Vidic, Chairman, 412-624-9870, Fax: 412-624-0135. *Application contact:* Amir Kouboa, Academic Coordinator, 412-624-9869, Fax: 412-624-0135, E-mail: amk59@pitt.edu.

University of Regina, Faculty of Graduate Studies and Research, Faculty of Engineering and Applied Science, Program in Environmental Systems Engineering, Regina, SK S4S 0A2, Canada. Offers M Eng, MA Sc, PhD. *Faculty:* 8 full-time (3 women). *Students:* 49 full-time (18 women), 5 part-time (3 women). 57 applicants, 67% accepted. In 2009, 8 master's, 5 doctorates awarded. *Degree requirements:* For master's, thesis (for some programs). *Entrance requirements:* For doctorate, master's degree. Additional exam requirements/recommendations for international students: Required—TOEFL (minimum score 550 paper-based; 213 computer-based; 80 iBT). *Application deadline:* Applications are processed on a rolling basis. Application fee: $90 ($100 for international students). *Financial support:* In 2009–10, 14 fellowships (averaging $19,000 per year), 3 research assistantships (averaging $16,910 per year), 16 teaching assistantships (averaging $6,650 per year) were awarded; scholarships/grants also available. Financial award application deadline: 6/15. *Faculty research:* Flood control, groundwater contamination, transportation engineering, solid waste management, water and air pollution control. *Unit head:* Dr. Amy Veawab, Graduate Coordinator, 306-585-5665, Fax: 306-585-4855, E-mail: amy.veawab@uregina.ca. *Application contact:* Crystal Pick, 306-337-2603, E-mail: crystal.pick@uregina.ca.

University of Rhode Island, Graduate School, College of Engineering, Department of Civil and Environmental Engineering, Kingston, RI 02881. Offers MS, PhD. Part-time programs available. *Faculty:* 6 full-time (2 women), 1 part-time/adjunct (0 women). *Students:* 14 full-time (7 women), 17 part-time (5 women); includes 2 minority (1 Asian American or Pacific Islander, 1 Hispanic American), 7 international. In 2009, 17 master's, 1 doctorate awarded. *Degree requirements:* For master's, comprehensive exam (for some programs), thesis optional; for doctorate, comprehensive exam, thesis/dissertation. *Entrance requirements:* For master's and doctorate, 2 letters of recommendation. Additional exam requirements/recommendations for international students: Required—TOEFL (minimum score 550 paper-based; 213 computer-based). *Application deadline:* For fall admission, 7/15 for domestic students, 2/1 for international students; for spring admission, 11/15 for domestic students, 7/15 for international students. Application fee: $65. Electronic applications accepted. *Expenses:* Tuition, state resident: full-time $8828; part-time $490 per credit hour. Tuition, nonresident: full-time $22,100; part-time $1228 per credit hour. Required fees: $1118; $57 per semester. Tuition and fees vary according to program. *Financial support:* In 2009–10, 4 research assistantships with full and partial tuition reimbursements (averaging $8,760 per year), 5 teaching assistantships with full and partial tuition reimbursements (averaging $12,687 per year) were awarded. Financial award application deadline: 7/15; financial award applicants required to submit FAFSA. *Faculty research:* Industrial waste treatment, structural health monitoring, traffic and transit system operations, computational mechanics, engineering materials design. Total annual research expenditures: $422,735. *Unit head:* Dr. George E. Tsiatas, Chair, 401-874-5117, Fax: 401-874-2786, E-mail: gt@uri.edu. *Application contact:* Dr. Mayrai Gindy, Director of Graduate Studies, 401-874-5587, Fax: 401-874-2786, E-mail: gindy@egr.uri.edu.

University of Saskatchewan, College of Graduate Studies and Research, College of Engineering, Division of Environmental Engineering, Saskatoon, SK S7N 5A2, Canada. Offers M Eng, M Sc, PhD, Diploma. *Degree requirements:* For master's, thesis (for some programs); for doctorate, thesis/dissertation. *Entrance requirements:* For master's and doctorate, GRE. Additional exam requirements/recommendations for international students: Required—TOEFL. Tuition and fees charges are reported in Canadian dollars. *Expenses:* Tuition, area resident: Full-time $3000 Canadian dollars; part-time $500 Canadian dollars per term. Required fees: $700 Canadian dollars; $100 Canadian dollars per term.

University of Southern California, Graduate School, Viterbi School of Engineering, Sonny Astani Department of Civil Engineering, Los Angeles, CA 90089. Offers applied mechanics (MS); civil engineering (MS, PhD); computer-aided engineering (ME, Graduate Certificate); construction management (MCM); engineering technology commercialization (Graduate Certificate); environmental engineering (MS, PhD); environmental quality management (ME); structural design (ME); sustainable cities (Graduate Certificate); transportation systems (Graduate Certificate). Part-time programs available. Postbaccalaureate distance learning degree programs offered (no on-campus study). *Faculty:* 16 full-time (2 women), 35 part-time/adjunct (5 women). *Students:* 165 full-time (48 women), 65 part-time (16 women); includes 54 minority (40 Asian Americans or Pacific Islanders, 14 Hispanic Americans), 108 international. 451 applicants, 41% accepted, 73 enrolled. In 2009, 74 master's, 10 doctorates awarded. Terminal master's awarded for partial completion of doctoral program. *Degree requirements:* For doctorate, thesis/dissertation. *Entrance requirements:* For master's, GRE General Test; for doctorate, General GRE. *Application deadline:* For fall admission, 3/1 priority date for domestic and international students; for spring admission, 10/1 priority date for domestic and international students. Applications are processed on a rolling basis. Application fee: $85. Electronic applications accepted. *Expenses:* Tuition: Full-time $25,980; part-time $1315 per unit. Required fees: $554. One-time fee: $35 full-time. Full-time tuition and fees vary according to degree level and program. *Financial support:* In 2009–10, fellowships with full tuition reimbursements (averaging $30,000 per year), research assistantships with full tuition reimbursements (averaging $19,250 per year), teaching assistantships with full tuition reimbursements (averaging $19,250 per year) were awarded; career-related internships or fieldwork, scholarships/grants, health care benefits, and unspecified assistantships also available. Financial award application deadline: 12/1; financial award applicants required to submit CSS PROFILE or FAFSA. *Faculty research:* Geotechnical engineering, transportation engineering, structural engineering, construction management, environmental engineering, water resources. Total annual research expenditures: $4.2 million. *Unit head:* Dr. Jean-Pierre Bardet, Chair, 213-740-0609, Fax: 213-744-1426, E-mail: bardet@usc.edu. *Application contact:* Jennifer A. Gerson, Director of Student Services, 213-740-0573, Fax: 213-740-8662, E-mail: jgerson@usc.edu.

University of South Florida, Graduate School, College of Engineering, Department of Civil and Environmental Engineering, Tampa, FL 33620-9951. Offers civil and environmental engineering (MSES); civil engineering (MCE, MSCE, PhD). Part-time programs available. *Faculty:* 19 full-time (3 women), 1 part-time/adjunct (0 women). *Students:* 91 full-time (33 women), 54 part-time (13 women); includes 26 minority (9 African Americans, 9 Asian Americans or Pacific Islanders, 8 Hispanic Americans), 44 international. Average age 32. 124 applicants, 69% accepted, 46 enrolled. In 2009, 41 master's, 7 doctorates awarded. Terminal master's awarded for partial completion of doctoral program. *Degree requirements:* For master's, comprehensive exam, thesis (for some programs); for doctorate, comprehensive exam, thesis/dissertation. *Entrance requirements:* For master's, GRE General Test, minimum GPA of 3.0 in last 60 hours of coursework; for doctorate, GRE General Test, minimum GPA of 3.3 in last 60 hours of coursework. Additional exam requirements/recommendations for international students: Required—TOEFL (minimum score 550 paper-based; 213 computer-based; 79 iBT). *Application deadline:* For fall admission, 2/15 for domestic students, 1/2 priority date for international students; for spring admission, 10/15 for domestic students, 6/1 priority date for international students. Application fee: $30. Electronic applications accepted. *Financial support:* In 2009–10, teaching assistantships with tuition reimbursements (averaging $26,422 per year). *Faculty research:* Water resources, structures and materials, transportation, geotechnical engineering, mechanics. Total annual research expenditures: $2 million. *Application contact:* Dr. Sarina Ergas, Director, 813-974-1119, Fax: 813-974-2957, E-mail: sergas@usf.edu.

The University of Tennessee, Graduate School, College of Engineering, Department of Civil and Environmental Engineering, Program in Environmental Engineering, Knoxville, TN 37996. Offers MS, MS/MBA. Part-time programs available. Postbaccalaureate distance learning degree programs offered (minimal on-campus study). *Faculty:* 8 full-time (0 women). *Students:* 13 full-time (6 women), 5 part-time (2 women), 3 international. Average age 22. 43 applicants, 67% accepted, 14 enrolled. In 2009, 12 master's awarded. *Degree requirements:* For master's, thesis or alternative. *Entrance requirements:* For master's, GRE, minimum GPA of 2.7. Additional exam requirements/recommendations for international students: Required—TOEFL (minimum score 550 paper-based; 213 computer-based). *Application deadline:* For fall admission, 2/1 priority date for domestic and international students; for spring admission, 6/15 priority date for international students. Applications are processed on a rolling basis. Application fee: $35. Electronic applications accepted. *Expenses:* Tuition, state resident: full-time $6826; part-time $380 per semester hour. Tuition, nonresident: full-time $21,844; part-time $1147 per semester hour. Tuition and fees vary according to program. *Financial support:* In 2009–10, 18 students received support, including 9 research assistantships with full tuition reimbursements available (averaging $13,608 per year), 4 teaching assistantships with full tuition reimbursements available (averaging $6,624 per year); career-related internships or fieldwork, Federal Work-Study, institutionally sponsored loans, health care benefits, and unspecified assistantships also available. Financial award application deadline: 2/1; financial award applicants required to submit FAFSA. *Faculty research:* Air pollution control technologies; climate change and engineering impact on environment; environmental sampling, monitoring, and restoration; soil erosion prediction and control; waste management and utilization. Total annual research expenditures: $1.8 million. *Unit head:* Dr. Dayakar Penumadu, Head, 865-974-2355, Fax: 865-974-2355, E-mail: dpenumad@utk.edu. *Application contact:* Dr. Masood Parang, Associate Dean of Student Affairs, 865-974-2454, Fax: 865-974-9871, E-mail: mparang@utk.edu.

The University of Texas at Austin, Graduate School, Cockrell School of Engineering, Department of Civil, Architectural and Environmental Engineering, Program in Environmental and Water Resources Engineering, Austin, TX 78712-1111. Offers MS, PhD. *Accreditation:* ABET. Part-time programs available. *Degree requirements:* For master's, thesis or alternative. *Entrance requirements:* For master's, GRE General Test. Additional exam requirements/recommendations for international students: Required—TOEFL. Electronic applications accepted.

The University of Texas at El Paso, Graduate School, College of Engineering, Department of Civil Engineering, El Paso, TX 79968-0001. Offers civil engineering (MS, PhD); construction mangement (Certificate); environmental engineering (MEENE, MSENE). Part-time and evening/weekend programs available. *Degree requirements:* For master's, thesis optional. *Entrance requirements:* For master's, GRE General Test, minimum GPA of 3.0. Additional exam requirements/recommendations for international students: Required—TOEFL. Electronic applications accepted. *Faculty research:* On-site wastewater treatment systems, wastewater reuse, disinfection by-product control, water resources, membrane filtration.

The University of Texas at El Paso, Graduate School, Interdisciplinary Program in Environmental Science and Engineering, El Paso, TX 79968-0001. Offers PhD. Part-time and evening/weekend programs available. *Students:* 41 (15 women); includes 13 minority (3 Asian Americans or Pacific Islanders, 10 Hispanic Americans), 21 international. Average age 34. In 2009, 4 doctorates awarded. *Degree requirements:* For doctorate, thesis/dissertation. *Entrance requirements:* For doctorate, GRE, letters of recommendation. Additional exam requirements/recommendations for international students: Required—TOEFL; Recommended—IELTS. *Application deadline:* For fall admission, 8/1 for domestic students, 3/1 for international students; for spring admission, 11/1 for domestic students, 9/1 for international students. Applications are processed on a rolling basis. Application fee: $45 ($80 for international students). Electronic applications accepted. *Financial support:* In 2009–10, research assistantships with partial tuition reimbursements (averaging $22,500 per year), teaching assistantships with partial tuition reimbursements (averaging $18,000 per year) were awarded; fellowships with partial tuition reimbursements, institutionally sponsored loans, scholarships/grants, health care benefits, tuition waivers (partial), and unspecified assistantships also available. Support available to part-time students. Financial award application deadline: 3/15; financial award applicants required to submit FAFSA. *Unit head:* Dr. Barry A. Benedict, Director, 915-747-5604, Fax: 915-747-5145, E-mail: babenedict@utep.edu. *Application contact:* Dr. Patricia D. Witherspoon, Dean of the Graduate School, 915-747-5491, Fax: 915-747-5788, E-mail: withersp@utep.edu.

The University of Texas at San Antonio, College of Engineering, Department of Civil and Environmental Engineering, San Antonio, TX 78249-0617. Offers civil engineering (MSCE); environmental science and engineering (PhD). Part-time and evening/weekend programs available. *Faculty:* 11 full-time (1 woman), 1 part-time/adjunct (0 women). *Students:* 34 full-time (8 women), 28 part-time (5 women); includes 16 minority (4 African Americans, 4 Asian Americans or Pacific Islanders, 8 Hispanic Americans), 24 international. Average age 33. 56 applicants, 55% accepted, 19 enrolled. In 2009, 12 master's, 4 doctorates awarded. *Degree* *requirements:* For master's, comprehensive exam (for some programs), thesis (for some programs); for doctorate, comprehensive exam, thesis/dissertation. *Entrance requirements:* For master's, GRE General Test, minimum GPA of 3.0 in last 60 hours of undergraduate degree. Additional exam requirements/recommendations for international students: Required—TOEFL (minimum score 500 paper-based; 173 computer-based; 61 iBT), IELTS (minimum score 5). *Application deadline:* For fall admission, 7/1 for domestic students, 4/1 for international students; for spring admission, 11/1 for domestic students, 9/1 for international students. Applications are processed on a rolling basis. Application fee: $45 ($80 for international students). Electronic applications accepted. *Expenses:* Tuition, state resident: full-time $3975; part-time $221 per contact hour. Tuition, nonresident: full-time $13,947; part-time $775 per contact hour. Required fees: $1853. *Financial support:* In 2009–10, 29 students received support, including 15 research assistantships (averaging $18,213 per year); career-related internships or fieldwork, scholarships/grants, tuition waivers, and unspecified assistantships also available. Support available to part-time students. Financial award application deadline: 3/31. Total annual research expenditures: $475,434. *Unit head:* Dr. Athanassio T. Papagiannakis, Chair, 210-458-7071, Fax: 210-458-6475, E-mail: at.papagiannakis@utsa.edu. *Application contact:* Dr. Dorothy A. Flannagan, Dean of the Graduate School, 210-458-4330, Fax: 210-458-4332, E-mail: dorothy.flannagan@utsa.edu.

The University of Texas at Tyler, College of Engineering and Computer Science, Department of Civil Engineering, Tyler, TX 75799-0001. Offers environmental engineering (MS); industrial safety (MS); structural engineering (MS); transportation engineering (MS); water resources engineering (MS). Part-time and evening/weekend programs available. *Faculty:* 6 full-time (0 women). *Students:* 5 full-time (1 woman), 7 part-time (1 woman); includes 1 African American, 1 Asian American or Pacific Islander, 1 Hispanic American, 1 international. Average age 26. 5 applicants, 80% accepted, 3 enrolled. *Degree requirements:* For master's, thesis optional. *Entrance requirements:* For master's, GRE General Test, bachelor's degree in engineering, associated science degree. Additional exam requirements/recommendations for international students: Required—TOEFL (minimum score 79 computer-based). *Application deadline:* For fall admission, 8/17 priority date for domestic students, 7/1 priority date for international students; for spring admission, 12/21 priority date for domestic students, 11/1 priority date for international students. Application fee: $25 ($50 for international students). *Expenses:* Tuition, state resident: part-time $665 per semester hour. Tuition, nonresident: part-time $942 per semester hour. Part-time tuition and fees vary according to degree level and program. *Financial support:* Application deadline: 7/1. *Faculty research:* Non-destructive strength testing, indoor air quality, transportation routing and signaling, pavement replacement criteria, flood water routing, construction and long-term behavior of innovative geotechnical foundation and embankment construction used in highway construction, engineering education. *Unit head:* Dr. Ron Welch, Chair, 903-566-7002, Fax: 903-566-7337, E-mail: rwelch@uttyler.edu. *Application contact:* Dr. Torey Nalbone, Program Chair, 903-565-5520, Fax: 903-566-7337, E-mail: tnalbone@uttyler.edu.

University of Utah, The Graduate School, College of Engineering, Department of Chemical Engineering, Salt Lake City, UT 84112-1107. Offers chemical engineering (ME, MS, PhD); environmental engineering (ME, MS, PhD). Part-time and evening/weekend programs available. Postbaccalaureate distance learning degree programs offered. *Faculty:* 15 full-time (1 woman), 1 part-time/adjunct (0 women). *Students:* 43 full-time (8 women), 23 part-time (4 women); includes 3 minority (1 Asian American or Pacific Islander, 2 Hispanic Americans), 26 international. Average age 28. 93 applicants, 13% accepted, 8 enrolled. In 2009, 9 master's, 8 doctorates awarded. Terminal master's awarded for partial completion of doctoral program. *Degree requirements:* For master's, comprehensive exam, thesis (for some programs); for doctorate, comprehensive exam, thesis/dissertation. *Entrance requirements:* For master's and doctorate, GRE General Test, minimum GPA of 3.0, degree or course work in chemical engineering. Additional exam requirements/recommendations for international students: Required—TOEFL (minimum score 500 paper-based; 173 computer-based). *Application deadline:* For fall admission, 4/1 priority date for domestic students, 2/1 for international students; for spring admission, 11/1 priority date for domestic students, 10/1 priority date for international students. Applications are processed on a rolling basis. Application fee: $55 ($65 for international students). Electronic applications accepted. *Expenses:* Tuition, state resident: full-time $4004; part-time $1674 per semester. Tuition, nonresident: full-time $14,134; part-time $5915 per semester. Required fees: $324 per semester. Tuition and fees vary according to course load, degree level and program. *Financial support:* In 2009–10, 1 fellowship with tuition reimbursement (averaging $30 per year), 44 research assistantships with tuition reimbursements (averaging $24,750 per year) were awarded; teaching assistantships with tuition reimbursements, Federal Work-Study, institutionally sponsored loans, scholarships/grants, health care benefits, and unspecified assistantships also available. Financial award application deadline: 4/1; financial award applicants required to submit FAFSA. *Faculty research:* Vaccine and drug delivery, biosorption, fossil fuel and biomass combustion and gasification, polymer structure and dynamics, oil and gas reservoir characteristics and management. Total annual research expenditures: $5.4 million. *Unit head:* Dr. JoAnn S. Lighty, Chair, 801-581-6715, Fax: 801-585-9291, E-mail: jlighty@utah.edu. *Application contact:* Jenny Jones, Academic Advisor, 801-581-6915, Fax: 801-585-9291, E-mail: jones.jenny@eng.utah.edu.

University of Utah, The Graduate School, College of Engineering, Department of Civil and Environmental Engineering, Interdepartmental Program in Environmental Engineering, Salt Lake City, UT 84112-1107. Offers ME, MS, PhD. Part-time programs available. *Students:* 1 full-time (0 women), 2 part-time (both women), 2 international. Average age 33. 10 applicants, 50% accepted, 2 enrolled. In 2009, 1 master's awarded. Terminal master's awarded for partial completion of doctoral program. *Degree requirements:* For master's, comprehensive exam, thesis (for some programs); for doctorate, comprehensive exam, thesis/dissertation. *Entrance requirements:* For master's and doctorate, GRE, minimum undergraduate GPA of 3.0. Additional exam requirements/recommendations for international students: Required—TOEFL (minimum score 500 paper-based; 173 computer-based). *Application deadline:* For fall admission, 4/1 for domestic and international students; for spring admission, 11/1 for domestic and international students. Applications are processed on a rolling basis. Application fee: $55 ($65 for international students). Electronic applications accepted. *Expenses:* Tuition, state resident: full-time $4004; part-time $1674 per semester. Tuition, nonresident: full-time $14,134; part-time $5915 per semester. Required fees: $324 per semester. Tuition and fees vary according to course load, degree level and program. *Financial support:* In 2009–10, 2 research assistantships with full tuition reimbursements (averaging $18,000 per year) were awarded. Financial award application deadline: 2/15; financial award applicants required to submit FAFSA. *Unit head:* Dr. Paul J. Tikalsky, Chair and Professor in Civil and Environmental Engineering, 801-581-6931, Fax: 801-585-5477, E-mail: tikalsky@civil.utah.edu. *Application contact:* Amanda May, Academic Program Specialist, 801-581-6931, Fax: 850-585-5477, E-mail: amandam@civil.utah.edu.

University of Utah, The Graduate School, College of Mines and Earth Sciences, Department of Geology and Geophysics, Salt Lake City, UT 84112. Offers environmental engineering (ME, MS, PhD); geological engineering (ME, MS, PhD); geology (MS, PhD); geophysics (MS, PhD). *Faculty:* 20 full-time (3 women), 5 part-time/adjunct (1 woman). *Students:* 40 full-time (16 women), 27 part-time (9 women); includes 1 minority (Hispanic American), 17 international. Average age 32. 109 applicants, 23% accepted, 17 enrolled. In 2009, 18 master's, 5 doctorates awarded. Terminal master's awarded for partial completion of doctoral program. *Degree requirements:* For master's, comprehensive exam, thesis; for doctorate, thesis/dissertation, qualifying exam (written and oral). *Entrance requirements:* For master's and doctorate, GRE General Test, minimum GPA of 3.25. Additional exam requirements/recommendations for international students: Required—TOEFL (minimum score 500 paper-based; 173 computer-based). *Application deadline:* For fall admission, 1/15 priority date for domestic and international students. Applications are processed on a rolling basis. Application fee: $55 ($65 for international students). Electronic applications accepted. *Expenses:* Tuition, state resident: full-time $4004; part-time $1674 per semester. Tuition, nonresident: full-time $14,134; part-time $5915 per semester. Required fees: $324 per semester. Tuition and fees vary according to course load, degree level and program. *Financial support:* In 2009–10, 22 students received

support, including 11 fellowships with full tuition reimbursements available (averaging $13,450 per year), 45 research assistantships with full tuition reimbursements available (averaging $21,858 per year), 11 teaching assistantships with full tuition reimbursements available (averaging $13,450 per year); career-related internships or fieldwork, institutionally sponsored loans, scholarships/grants, unspecified assistantships, and stipends also available. Financial award application deadline: 1/15; financial award applicants required to submit FAFSA. *Faculty research:* Igneous, metamorphic, and sedimentary petrology; ore deposits; aqueous geochemistry; isotope geochemistry; heat flow. Total annual research expenditures: $2.2 million. *Unit head:* Dr. Marjorie A. Chan, Chair, 801-581-7162, Fax: 801-581-7065, E-mail: marjorie.chan@utah.edu. *Application contact:* Dr. Allan A. Ekdale, Director of Graduate Studies, 801-581-7266, Fax: 801-581-7065, E-mail: a.ekdale@utah.edu.

University of Vermont, Graduate College, College of Engineering and Mathematics, Department of Civil and Environmental Engineering, Burlington, VT 05405. Offers MS, PhD. *Students:* 25 (10 women), 6 international. 25 applicants, 52% accepted, 4 enrolled. In 2009, 1 master's, 1 doctorate awarded. *Degree requirements:* For master's, thesis or alternative; for doctorate, thesis/dissertation. *Entrance requirements:* For master's and doctorate, GRE General Test. Additional exam requirements/recommendations for international students: Required—TOEFL (minimum score 550 paper-based; 213 computer-based; 80 iBT). *Application deadline:* For fall admission, 2/1 priority date for domestic students. Applications are processed on a rolling basis. Application fee: $40. Electronic applications accepted. *Expenses:* Tuition, area resident: Part-time $508 per credit hour. Tuition, state resident: part-time $508 per credit hour. Tuition, nonresident: part-time $1281 per credit hour. *Financial support:* Research assistantships, teaching assistantships available. Financial award application deadline: 3/1. *Unit head:* Dr. J. Marshall, Director, 802-656-3800. *Application contact:* Dr. Britt Holmen, Coordinator, 802-656-3800.

University of Washington, Graduate School, College of Engineering, Department of Civil and Environmental Engineering, Seattle, WA 98195-2700. Offers construction engineering (MSCE); environmental engineering (MS, MSCE, MSE, PhD); hydrology, water resources, and environmental fluid mechanics (MS, MSCE, MSE, PhD); structural and geotechnical engineering and mechanics (MS, MSCE, MSE, PhD); transportation and construction engineering (MS, MSE, PhD); transportation engineering (MSCE). Part-time programs available. Postbaccalaureate distance learning degree programs offered (no on-campus study). *Faculty:* 36 full-time (9 women), 16 part-time/adjunct (6 women). *Students:* 186 full-time (62 women), 57 part-time (10 women); includes 35 minority (24 Asian Americans or Pacific Islanders, 11 Hispanic Americans), 58 international. 360 applicants, 68% accepted, 98 enrolled. In 2009, 74 master's, 8 doctorates awarded. Terminal master's awarded for partial completion of doctoral program. *Degree requirements:* For master's, thesis (for some programs); for doctorate, comprehensive exam, thesis/dissertation. *Entrance requirements:* For master's, GRE General Test, minimum GPA of 3.0; for doctorate, GRE, minimum GPA of 3.5. Additional exam requirements/recommendations for international students: Required—TOEFL (minimum score 580 paper-based; 237 computer-based; 70 iBT). *Application deadline:* For fall admission, 1/15 priority date for domestic and international students. Applications are processed on a rolling basis. Application fee: $65. Electronic applications accepted. *Financial support:* In 2009–10, 5 students received support, including 13 fellowships with full and partial tuition reimbursements available (averaging $16,173 per year), 68 research assistantships with full tuition reimbursements available (averaging $16,173 per year), 12 teaching assistantships with full tuition reimbursements available (averaging $16,173 per year); scholarships/grants also available. Financial award application deadline: 1/15. *Faculty research:* Environmental/water resources, hydrology; construction/transportation; structures/ geotechnical. Total annual research expenditures: $11.4 million. *Unit head:* Dr. Gregory R. Miller, Professor and Chair, 206-543-0350, Fax: 206-543-1543, E-mail: gmiller@uw.edu. *Application contact:* Lorna Latal, Graduate Adviser, 206-543-2574, Fax: 206-543-1543, E-mail: llatal@u.washington.edu.

University of Waterloo, Graduate Studies, Faculty of Engineering, Department of Civil and Environmental Engineering, Waterloo, ON N2L 3G1, Canada. Offers M Eng, MA Sc, PhD. Part-time programs available. *Degree requirements:* For master's, research paper or thesis; for doctorate, comprehensive exam, thesis/dissertation. *Entrance requirements:* For master's, honors degree, minimum B average; for doctorate, master's degree, minimum A- average. Additional exam requirements/recommendations for international students: Required—TOEFL, TWE. Electronic applications accepted. *Faculty research:* Water resources, structures, construction management, transportation, geotechnical engineering.

The University of Western Ontario, Faculty of Graduate Studies, Physical Sciences Division, Faculty of Engineering, London, ON N6A 5B8, Canada. Offers chemical and biochemical engineering (ME Sc, PhD); civil and environmental engineering (M Eng, ME Sc, PhD); electrical and computer engineering (M Eng, ME Sc, PhD); mechanical and materials engineering (M Eng, ME Sc, PhD). Part-time programs available. Terminal master's awarded for partial completion of doctoral program. *Degree requirements:* For master's, thesis; for doctorate, thesis/dissertation. *Entrance requirements:* For master's, minimum B average; for doctorate, minimum B+ average. *Faculty research:* Wind, geotechnical, chemical reactor engineering, applied electrostatics, biochemical engineering.

University of Windsor, Faculty of Graduate Studies, Faculty of Engineering, Department of Civil and Environmental Engineering, Windsor, ON N9B 3P4, Canada. Offers civil engineering (M Eng, MA Sc, PhD); environmental engineering (M Eng, MA Sc, PhD). Part-time programs available. *Degree requirements:* For master's, thesis; for doctorate, comprehensive exam, thesis/dissertation. *Entrance requirements:* For master's, minimum B average; for doctorate, master's degree, minimum A average. Additional exam requirements/recommendations for international students: Required—TOEFL (minimum score 580 paper-based; 237 computer-based). Electronic applications accepted. *Faculty research:* Odors: sampling, measurement, control; drinking water disinfection, hydrocarbon contaminated soil remediation, structural dynamics, numerical simulation of piezoelectric materials.

University of Wisconsin–Madison, Graduate School, College of Engineering, Department of Civil and Environmental Engineering, Madison, WI 53706-1380. Offers MS, PhD. Part-time programs available. *Faculty:* 31 full-time (3 women), 2 part-time/adjunct (0 women). *Students:* 113 full-time (32 women), 40 part-time (8 women); includes 6 minority (1 Asian American or Pacific Islander, 5 Hispanic Americans), 78 international. Average age 29. 383 applicants, 37% accepted, 43 enrolled. In 2009, 15 master's, 2 doctorates awarded. Terminal master's awarded for partial completion of doctoral program. *Degree requirements:* For master's, thesis or alternative; for doctorate, thesis/dissertation, preliminary exam, qualifying exams. *Entrance requirements:* For master's and doctorate, GRE General Test, minimum GPA of 3.0 for last 60 credits of course work. Additional exam requirements/recommendations for international students: Required—TOEFL (minimum score 550 paper-based; 213 computer-based; 80 iBT). *Application deadline:* For fall admission, 3/15 for domestic and international students; for spring admission, 10/15 for domestic and international students. Applications are processed on a rolling basis. Application fee: $56. Electronic applications accepted. *Expenses:* Tuition, state resident: part-time $594 per credit. Tuition, nonresident: part-time $1504 per credit. Required fees: $65 per credit. Tuition and fees vary according to course load, program and reciprocity agreements. *Financial support:* In 2009–10, 63 students received support, including 9 fellowships with full tuition reimbursements available (averaging $22,224 per year), 76 research assistantships with full tuition reimbursements available (averaging $40,368 per year), 12 teaching assistantships with full tuition reimbursements available (averaging $28,175 per year); Federal Work-Study, scholarships/grants, health care benefits, and unspecified assistantships also available. Support available to part-time students. Financial award application deadline: 12/15. *Faculty research:* Environmental geotechnics and soil mechanics, design and analysis of structures, traffic engineering and intelligent transport systems, industrial pollution control, hydrological monitoring. Total annual research expenditures: $7.4 million. *Unit head:* Jeffrey S. Russell, Chair, 608-262-3542, Fax: 608-262-5199, E-mail: russell@engr.wisc.edu. *Application contact:* Marc Nowak, Student Status Examiner, 608-265-5570, Fax: 608-890-1174, E-mail: mrnowak@wisc.edu.

Environmental Engineering

University of Wyoming, College of Engineering and Applied Sciences, Department of Civil and Architectural Engineering and Department of Chemical and Petroleum Engineering, Program in Environmental Engineering, Laramie, WY 82070. Offers MS. Part-time programs available. *Degree requirements:* For master's, thesis optional. *Entrance requirements:* For master's, GRE General Test, minimum GPA of 3.0. Additional exam requirements/recommendations for international students: Required—TOEFL (minimum score 550 paper-based; 213 computer-based). Electronic applications accepted. *Faculty research:* Water and waste water, solid and hazardous waste management, air pollution control, flue-gas cleanup.

Utah State University, School of Graduate Studies, College of Engineering, Department of Civil and Environmental Engineering, Logan, UT 84322. Offers ME, MS, PhD, CE. *Degree requirements:* For master's, thesis (for some programs); for doctorate, thesis/dissertation. *Entrance requirements:* For master's and doctorate, GRE General Test, minimum GPA of 3.0. Additional exam requirements/recommendations for international students: Required—TOEFL. Electronic applications accepted. *Faculty research:* Hazardous waste treatment, large space structures, river basin management, earthquake engineering, environmental impact.

Vanderbilt University, School of Engineering, Department of Civil and Environmental Engineering, Program in Environmental Engineering, Nashville, TN 37240-1001. Offers environmental engineering (M Eng); environmental management (MS, PhD). MS and PhD offered through Graduate School. Part-time programs available. *Faculty:* 9 full-time (0 women), 1 (woman) part-time/adjunct. *Students:* 24 full-time (13 women); includes 2 minority (1 African American, 1 Asian American or Pacific Islander), 4 international. Average age 30. 75 applicants, 17% accepted, 8 enrolled. In 2009, 5 master's awarded. Terminal master's awarded for partial completion of doctoral program. *Degree requirements:* For master's, thesis or alternative; for doctorate, thesis/dissertation. *Entrance requirements:* For master's and doctorate, GRE General Test. Additional exam requirements/recommendations for international students: Required—TOEFL. *Application deadline:* For fall admission, 1/15 for domestic students; for spring admission, 11/1 for domestic students. Applications are processed on a rolling basis. Application fee: $0. Electronic applications accepted. *Financial support:* In 2009–10, 5 fellowships with full tuition reimbursements (averaging $30,000 per year), 12 research assistantships with full tuition reimbursements (averaging $25,200 per year), 7 teaching assistantships with full tuition reimbursements (averaging $21,600 per year) were awarded; career-related internships or fieldwork, institutionally sponsored loans, scholarships/grants, traineeships, and tuition waivers (full and partial) also available. Financial award application deadline: 1/15. *Faculty research:* Waste treatment, hazardous waste management, chemical waste treatment, water quality. *Unit head:* Dr. David S. Kosson, Chair, 615-322-2697, Fax: 615-322-3365, E-mail: david.kosson@vanderbilt.edu. *Application contact:* Dr. James H. Clarke, Graduate Program Administrator, 615-322-3897, Fax: 615-322-3365.

Villanova University, College of Engineering, Department of Civil and Environmental Engineering, Program in Water Resources and Environmental Engineering, Villanova, PA 19085-1699. Offers MSWREE. Part-time and evening/weekend programs available. Postbaccalaureate distance learning degree programs offered (no on-campus study). *Degree requirements:* For master's, thesis optional. *Entrance requirements:* For master's, GRE General Test (for applicants with degrees from foreign universities), BCE or bachelor's degree in science or related engineering field, minimum GPA of 3.0. Additional exam requirements/recommendations for international students: Required—TOEFL (minimum score 600 paper-based; 250 computer-based; 100 iBT). Electronic applications accepted. *Expenses:* Tuition: Part-time $630 per credit. Required fees: $60 per credit. Part-time tuition and fees vary according to degree level and program. *Faculty research:* Photocatalytic decontamination and disinfection of water, urban storm water wetlands, economy and risk, removal and destruction of organic acids in water, sludge treatment.

Virginia Polytechnic Institute and State University, Graduate School, College of Engineering, Department of Civil and Environmental Engineering, Blacksburg, VA 24061. Offers civil engineering (M Eng, MS, PhD); environmental engineering (M Eng, MS); environmental sciences and engineering (MS). *Accreditation:* ABET (one or more programs are accredited). *Entrance requirements:* For master's and doctorate, GRE. Additional exam requirements/recommendations for international students: Required—TOEFL (minimum score 570 paper-based; 230 computer-based). Electronic applications accepted. *Faculty research:* Construction, environmental geotechnical hydrosystems, structures and transportation engineering.

Washington State University, Graduate School, College of Engineering and Architecture, Department of Civil and Environmental Engineering, Program in Environmental Engineering, Pullman, WA 99164. Offers MS. *Faculty:* 25. *Students:* 13 full-time (8 women), 3 part-time (1 woman); includes 1 minority (Hispanic American), 3 international. Average age 29. 44 applicants, 25% accepted, 3 enrolled. In 2009, 11 master's awarded. *Degree requirements:* For master's, comprehensive exam (for some programs), thesis (for some programs), oral exam. *Entrance requirements:* For master's, GRE General Test, Official transcripts from all colleges and universities attended; one-page statement of purpose; three letters of recommendation; copy of application and assistantship forms. Additional exam requirements/recommendations for international students: Required—TOEFL, IELTS. *Application deadline:* For fall admission, 1/10 priority date for domestic students, 1/10 for international students; for spring admission, 7/1 for domestic and international students. Applications are processed on a rolling basis. Application fee: $50. Electronic applications accepted. *Financial support:* In 2009–10, 7 students received support, including 3 research assistantships with full and partial tuition reimbursements available (averaging $13,917 per year), 2 teaching assistantships with full and partial

tuition reimbursements available (averaging $13,056 per year); fellowships, career-related internships or fieldwork, Federal Work-Study, and institutionally sponsored loans also available. Financial award application deadline: 4/1; financial award applicants required to submit FAFSA. *Faculty research:* Air quality, hazardous waste, soil and ground water contamination, acid precipitation, global climate. Total annual research expenditures: $3.6 million. *Unit head:* Dr. David McLean, Chair, 509-335-9578, Fax: 509-335-7632, E-mail: mclean@wsu.edu. *Application contact:* Graduate School Admissions, 800-GRADWSU, Fax: 509-335-1949, E-mail: gradsch@wsu.edu.

Washington University in St. Louis, Henry Edwin Sever Graduate School of Engineering and Applied Science, Department of Energy, Environmental and Chemical Engineering, St. Louis, MO 63130-4899. Offers chemical engineering (MS, D Sc); environmental engineering (MS, D Sc). Part-time programs available. Terminal master's awarded for partial completion of doctoral program. *Degree requirements:* For master's, thesis optional; for doctorate, thesis/dissertation, preliminary exam, qualifying exam. *Entrance requirements:* For master's and doctorate, GRE, minimum B average during final 2 years of course work. Additional exam requirements/recommendations for international students: Required—TOEFL, TWE. Electronic applications accepted. *Faculty research:* Reaction engineering, materials processing, catalysis, process control, air pollution control.

West Virginia University, College of Engineering and Mineral Resources, Department of Civil and Environmental Engineering, Morgantown, WV 26506. Offers civil engineering (MSCE, MSE, PhD). Part-time programs available. *Degree requirements:* For master's, thesis; for doctorate, comprehensive exam, thesis/dissertation. *Entrance requirements:* For master's and doctorate, minimum GPA of 3.0. Additional exam requirements/recommendations for international students: Required—TOEFL, GRE. *Faculty research:* Habitat restoration, advanced materials for civil infrastructure, pavement modeling, infrastructure condition assessment.

Worcester Polytechnic Institute, Graduate Studies and Research, Department of Civil and Environmental Engineering, Worcester, MA 01609-2280. Offers civil and environmental engineering (Advanced Certificate, Graduate Certificate); civil engineering (ME, MS, PhD); construction project management (MS); environmental engineering (MS); master builder environmental engineering (M Eng). Part-time and evening/weekend programs available. Postbaccalaureate distance learning degree programs offered (no on-campus study). *Faculty:* 10 full-time (1 woman), 1 part-time/adjunct (0 women). *Students:* 23 full-time (10 women), 53 part-time (14 women). 121 applicants, 79% accepted, 28 enrolled. In 2009, 18 master's, 2 doctorates awarded. *Degree requirements:* For master's, thesis optional; for doctorate, comprehensive exam, thesis/dissertation. *Entrance requirements:* For master's and doctorate, GRE (recommended), 3 letters of recommendation. Additional exam requirements/recommendations for international students: Required—TOEFL (minimum score 550 paper-based; 213 computer-based; 79 iBT), IELTS (minimum score 6.5). *Application deadline:* For fall admission, 1/15 priority date for domestic and international students; for spring admission, 10/15 priority date for domestic and international students. Applications are processed on a rolling basis. Application fee: $70. Electronic applications accepted. *Financial support:* Career-related internships or fieldwork, institutionally sponsored loans, scholarships/grants, and unspecified assistantships available. Financial award application deadline: 1/15. *Faculty research:* Environmental engineering and sustainability, pavement engineering technology, impact mechanics and engineering. *Unit head:* Dr. Tahar El-Korchi, Interim Head, 508-831-5530, Fax: 508-831-5808, E-mail: tek@wpi.edu. *Application contact:* Dr. Paul Mathisen, Graduate Coordinator, 508-831-5530, Fax: 508-831-5808, E-mail: mathisen@wpi.edu.

Worcester Polytechnic Institute, Graduate Studies and Research, Programs in Interdisciplinary Studies, Worcester, MA 01609-2280. Offers bioscience administration (MS); impact engineering (MS); manufacturing engineering management (MS); power systems management (MS); social science (PhD); systems modeling (MS). Part-time and evening/weekend programs available. *Faculty:* 1 part-time/adjunct (0 women). *Students:* 3 full-time (1 woman), 126 part-time (24 women). 184 applicants, 68% accepted, 100 enrolled. In 2009, 19 master's awarded. *Degree requirements:* For master's, thesis; for doctorate, comprehensive exam, thesis/dissertation. *Entrance requirements:* For master's and doctorate, 3 letters of recommendation. Additional exam requirements/recommendations for international students: Required—TOEFL (minimum score 550 paper-based; 213 computer-based; 79 iBT), IELTS (minimum score 6.5). *Application deadline:* For fall admission, 1/15 priority date for domestic students; for spring admission, 10/15 priority date for domestic students. Application fee: $70. *Financial support:* Institutionally sponsored loans, scholarships/grants, and unspecified assistantships available. Financial award application deadline: 1/15. *Unit head:* Dr. Fred J. Looft, Head, 508-831-5231, Fax: 508-831-5491, E-mail: fjlooft@wpi.edu. *Application contact:* Lynne Dougherty, Administrative Assistant, 508-831-5301, Fax: 508-831-5717, E-mail: grad@wpi.edu.

Yale University, Graduate School of Arts and Sciences, School of Engineering and Applied Science, Program in Environmental Engineering, New Haven, CT 06520. Offers MS, PhD.

Youngstown State University, Graduate School, College of Science, Technology, Engineering and Mathematics, Department of Civil and Environmental Engineering, Youngstown, OH 44555-0001. Offers MSE. Part-time and evening/weekend programs available. *Degree requirements:* For master's, thesis optional. *Entrance requirements:* For master's, minimum GPA of 2.75 in field. Additional exam requirements/recommendations for international students: Required—TOEFL. *Faculty research:* Structural mechanics, water quality modeling, surface and ground water hydrology, physical and chemical processes in aquatic systems.

Fire Protection Engineering

American Public University System, AMU/APU Graduate Programs, Charles Town, WV 25414. Offers air warfare (MA Military Studies); American Revolution (MA Military Studies); business administration (MBA); Civil War (MA Military Studies); criminal justice (MA); defense management (MA Military Studies); emergency and disaster management (MA); environmental policy and management (MS); fire science management (MA); global engagement (MA); history (MA); homeland security (MA); humanities (MA); intelligence (MA Military Studies, MA Strategic Intelligence); international peace and conflict resolution (MA); international relations and conflict resolution (MA); joint warfare (MA Military Studies); land warfare international perspective (MA Military Studies); management (MA); military history (MA); military leadership (MA Military Studies); national security studies (MA); naval warfare international (MA Military Studies); naval warfare US (MA Military Studies); political science (MA); public administration (MA); public health (MA); security management (MA); space studies (MS); special ops/LIC (MA Military Studies); sports management (MA); transportation and logistics management (MA); transportation management (MA); unconventional warfare (MA Military Studies); World War II (MA Military Studies). Programs offered via distance learning only. Part-time and evening/weekend programs available. Postbaccalaureate distance learning degree programs offered (no on-campus study). *Degree requirements:* For master's, comprehensive exam. *Entrance requirements:* For master's, bachelor's degree or equivalent, minimum GPA of 2.7 in last 60 hours of course work. Electronic applications accepted. *Faculty research:* Military history, criminal justice, management performance, national security.

Anna Maria College, Graduate Division, Program in Fire Science, Paxton, MA 01612. Offers fire science (MA). Part-time and evening/weekend programs available. *Degree requirements:* For master's, thesis, internship, research project. *Entrance requirements:* For master's, minimum

GPA of 2.7, resume, bachelor's degree in fire science or employment in a fire science organization. Additional exam requirements/recommendations for international students: Required—TOEFL (minimum score 500 paper-based). Electronic applications accepted.

Oklahoma State University, College of Arts and Sciences, Department of Political Science, Stillwater, OK 74078. Offers fire and emergency management administration (MS, PhD); political science (MA). *Faculty:* 19 full-time (5 women), 5 part-time/adjunct (1 woman). *Students:* 27 full-time (4 women), 54 part-time (8 women); includes 10 minority (2 African Americans, 6 American Indian/Alaska Native, 1 Asian American or Pacific Islander, 1 Hispanic American), 20 international. Average age 35. 77 applicants, 45% accepted, 27 enrolled. In 2009, 22 master's awarded. *Degree requirements:* For master's, comprehensive exam, thesis or creative component; for doctorate, comprehensive exam, thesis/dissertation. *Entrance requirements:* For master's, GRE; for doctorate, GRE. Additional exam requirements/recommendations for international students: Required—TOEFL (minimum score 550 paper-based; 79 iBT). *Application deadline:* For fall admission, 3/1 priority date for international students; for spring admission, 8/1 priority date for international students. Applications are processed on a rolling basis. Application fee: $40 ($75 for international students). Electronic applications accepted. *Expenses:* Tuition, state resident: full-time $3716; part-time $154.85 per credit hour. Tuition, nonresident: full-time $14,448; part-time $602 per credit hour. Required fees: $1772; $73.85 per credit hour. One-time fee: $50. Tuition and fees vary according to course load and campus/location. *Financial support:* In 2009–10, 3 research assistantships (averaging $11,090 per year), 11 teaching assistantships (averaging $10,767 per year) were awarded; career-related internships or fieldwork, Federal Work-Study, scholarships/grants, health care benefits, tuition waivers (partial), and unspecified assistantships also available. Support available to part-time students.

Financial award application deadline: 3/1; financial award applicants required to submit FAFSA. *Faculty research:* Fire and emergency management, environmental dispute resolution, voting and elections, women and politics, urban politics. *Unit head:* Dr. James Scott, Head, 405-744-5569, Fax: 405-744-6534. *Application contact:* Dr. Gordon Emslie, Dean, 405-744-6368, Fax: 405-744-0355, E-mail: grad-i@okstate.edu.

University of Maryland, College Park, Academic Affairs, A. James Clark School of Engineering, Department of Continuing and Distance Learning in Engineering, Professional Program in Engineering, College Park, MD 20742. Offers aerospace engineering (M Eng); chemical engineering (M Eng); civil engineering (M Eng); electrical engineering (M Eng); engineering (Certificate); fire protection engineering (M Eng); materials science and engineering (M Eng); mechanical engineering (M Eng); reliability engineering (M Eng); systems engineering (M Eng). Part-time and evening/weekend programs available. Postbaccalaureate distance learning degree programs offered. *Students:* 50 full-time (15 women), 234 part-time (41 women); includes 91 minority (36 African Americans, 39 Asian Americans or Pacific Islanders, 16 Hispanic Americans), 45 international. 137 applicants, 69% accepted, 77 enrolled. In 2009, 103 master's awarded. *Entrance requirements:* For master's, 3 letters of recommendation. *Application deadline:* For fall admission, 8/15 for domestic students, 1/10 for international students; for spring admission, 12/15 for domestic students, 6/1 for international students. Applications are processed on a rolling basis. Application fee: $60. Electronic applications accepted. *Expenses:* Tuition, area resident: Part-time $471 per credit hour. Tuition, state resident: part-time $471 per credit hour. Tuition, nonresident: part-time $1016 per credit hour. Required fees: $337.04 per term. *Financial support:* In 2009–10, 2 research assistantships with tuition reimbursements (averaging $19,561 per year), 9 teaching assistantships with tuition reimbursements (averaging $16,849 per year) were awarded; fellowships, Federal Work-Study and scholarships/grants also available. Support available to part-time students. Financial award applicants required to submit FAFSA. *Unit head:* Dr. George Syrmos, Director, 301-405-3633, Fax: 301-314-3305, E-mail: syrmos@umd.edu. *Application contact:* Dean of Graduate School, 301-405-0376, Fax: 301-314-9305.

University of Maryland, College Park, Academic Affairs, A. James Clark School of Engineering, Department of Fire Protection Engineering, College Park, MD 20742. Offers M Eng, MS. Part-time and evening/weekend programs available. *Faculty:* 6 full-time (0 women), 4 part-time/adjunct (0 women). *Students:* 16 full-time (4 women), 9 part-time (1 woman); includes 2 minority (1 Asian American or Pacific Islander, 1 Hispanic American), 3 international. Average age 26. 22 applicants, 32% accepted, 4 enrolled. In 2009, 8 master's awarded. *Degree requirements:* For master's, thesis optional. *Entrance requirements:* For master's, GRE General Test, minimum GPA of 3.0, BS in any engineering or physical science area, 3 letters of recommendation. *Application deadline:* For fall admission, 5/31 for domestic students, 2/1 for international students; for spring admission, 10/31 for domestic students, 6/1 for international students. Applications are processed on a rolling basis. Application fee: $60. Electronic applications accepted. *Expenses:* Tuition, area resident: Part-time $471 per credit hour. Tuition, state resident: part-time $471 per credit hour. Tuition, nonresident: part-time $1016 per credit hour. Required fees: $337.04 per term. *Financial support:* In 2009–10, 2 research assistantships with tuition reimbursements (averaging $23,247 per year), 7 teaching assistantships with tuition reimbursements (averaging $21,413 per year) were awarded; fellowships, career-related internships or fieldwork, Federal Work-Study, institutionally sponsored loans, and scholarships/grants also available. Financial award application deadline: 2/1; financial award applicants required to submit FAFSA. *Faculty research:* Fire and thermal degradation of materials, fire modeling, fire dynamics, smoke detection and management, fire resistance. Total annual research expenditures: $1.2 million. *Unit head:* Dr. Marino Dimarzo, Chair, 301-405-5257, Fax: 301-314-9477, E-mail: marino@eng.umd.edu. *Application contact:* Dr. James A. Milke, Graduate Director, 301-405-0376, Fax: 301-405-9383, E-mail: milke@eng.umd.edu.

University of New Haven, Graduate School, Henry C. Lee College of Criminal Justice and Forensic Sciences, Program in Fire Science, West Haven, CT 06516-1916. Offers emergency management (Certificate); fire administration (MS); fire science technology (Certificate); fire/arson investigation (MS, Certificate); forensic science/fire science (Certificate); public safety management (MS); public safety management (Certificate). Part-time and evening/weekend programs available. *Faculty:* 2 full-time (0 women). *Students:* 14 part-time (4 women); includes 1 minority (Hispanic American), 1 international. Average age 33. 6 applicants, 83% accepted, 3 enrolled. In 2009, 6 master's, 4 other advanced degrees awarded. *Degree requirements:* For master's, thesis or alternative. *Entrance requirements:* Additional exam requirements/recommendations for international students: Required—TOEFL (minimum score 520 paper-based; 190 computer-based; 70 iBT); Recommended—IELTS (minimum score 5.5). *Application deadline:* For fall admission, 5/31 for international students; for winter admission, 10/15 for international students; for spring admission, 1/15 for international students. Applications are processed on a rolling basis. Application fee: $50. Electronic applications accepted. *Expenses:* Tuition: Part-time $700 per credit. Required fees: $45 per term. One-time fee: $390 part-time. *Financial support:* Research assistantships with partial tuition reimbursements, teaching assistantships with partial tuition reimbursements, career-related internships or fieldwork, Federal Work-Study, scholarships/grants, tuition waivers, and unspecified assistantships available. Support available to part-time students. Financial award applicants required to submit FAFSA. *Unit head:* Robert E. Massicotte, Director, 203-932-7424. *Application contact:* Eloise Gormley, Director of Graduate Admissions, 203-932-7449, Fax: 203-932-7137, E-mail: gradinfo@newhaven.edu.

Worcester Polytechnic Institute, Graduate Studies and Research, Department of Fire Protection Engineering, Worcester, MA 01609-2280. Offers MS, PhD, Advanced Certificate, Graduate Certificate. Part-time and evening/weekend programs available. Postbaccalaureate distance learning degree programs offered (no on-campus study). *Faculty:* 4 full-time (1 woman). *Students:* 30 full-time (5 women), 82 part-time (14 women). 82 applicants, 85% accepted, 44 enrolled. In 2009, 32 master's awarded. *Degree requirements:* For master's, thesis optional; for doctorate, comprehensive exam, thesis/dissertation. *Entrance requirements:* For master's, GRE General Test (recommended), BS in engineering or physical sciences, 3 letters of recommendation, work experience or statement of purpose; for doctorate, GRE General Test, 3 letters of recommendation, statement of purpose. Additional exam requirements/recommendations for international students: Required—TOEFL (minimum score 550 paper-based; 213 computer-based; 79 iBT), IELTS (minimum score 6.5). *Application deadline:* For fall admission, 1/15 priority date for domestic students, 1/15 for international students; for spring admission, 10/15 priority date for domestic students, 10/15 for international students. Applications are processed on a rolling basis. Electronic applications accepted. *Financial support:* Career-related internships or fieldwork, institutionally sponsored loans, scholarships/grants, and unspecified assistantships available. Financial award application deadline: 1/15. *Faculty research:* Computer fire modeling, fire dynamics and material evaluation, structural systems and fire safety, explosions, risk assessment and regulatory reform, forest fires. *Unit head:* Dr. Kathy Notarianni, Head, 508-831-5593, Fax: 508-831-5862, E-mail: kanfpe@wpi.edu. *Application contact:* Dr. Ali Rangwala, Graduate Coordinator, 508-831-5593, Fax: 508-831-5862, E-mail: rangwala@wpi.edu.

Geotechnical Engineering

Auburn University, Graduate School, Ginn College of Engineering, Department of Civil Engineering, Auburn University, AL 36849. Offers construction engineering and management (MCE, MS, PhD); environmental engineering (MCE, MS, PhD); geotechnical/materials engineering (MCE, MS, PhD); hydraulics/hydrology (MCE, MS, PhD); structural engineering (MCE, MS, PhD); transportation engineering (MCE, MS, PhD). Part-time programs available. *Faculty:* 21 full-time (1 woman), 3 part-time/adjunct (1 woman). *Students:* 46 full-time (15 women), 39 part-time (5 women); includes 4 minority (3 African Americans, 1 Asian American or Pacific Islander), 29 international. Average age 26. 136 applicants, 43% accepted, 26 enrolled. In 2009, 19 master's, 4 doctorates awarded. *Degree requirements:* For master's, project (MCE), thesis (MS); for doctorate, comprehensive exam, thesis/dissertation. *Entrance requirements:* For master's and doctorate, GRE General Test. *Application deadline:* For fall admission, 7/7 for domestic students; for spring admission, 11/24 for domestic students. Applications are processed on a rolling basis. Application fee: $50 ($60 for international students). Electronic applications accepted. *Expenses:* Tuition, state resident: full-time $6240. Tuition, nonresident: full-time $18,720. International tuition: $18,938 full-time. Required fees: $492. Tuition and fees vary according to course load, program and reciprocity agreements. *Financial support:* Fellowships, research assistantships, teaching assistantships, Federal Work-Study available. Support available to part-time students. Financial award application deadline: 3/15; financial award applicants required to submit FAFSA. *Unit head:* Dr. J. Michael Stallings, Head, 334-844-4320. *Application contact:* Dr. George Flowers, Dean of the Graduate School, 334-844-2125.

The Catholic University of America, School of Engineering, Department of Civil Engineering, Washington, DC 20064. Offers environmental engineering (MCE, MSE, D Engr, PhD, Certificate); environmental engineering and management (MCE, MSE, PhD, Certificate); environmental engineering and management (D Engr); fluid and solid mechanics (MCE, MSE, PhD, Certificate); geotechnical engineering (MCE, MSE, PhD, Certificate); management of construction (MCE, MSE, D Engr, PhD); structural engineering (MSE, D Engr, PhD); systems engineering (MSE, D Engr, PhD, Certificate). Part-time programs available. *Faculty:* 5 full-time (0 women), 7 part-time/adjunct (1 woman). *Students:* 7 full-time (3 women), 18 part-time (5 women); includes 6 minority (3 African Americans, 3 Hispanic Americans), 11 international. Average age 32. 36 applicants, 47% accepted, 9 enrolled. In 2009, 8 master's, 2 doctorates awarded. *Degree requirements:* For master's, thesis optional; for doctorate, comprehensive exam, thesis/dissertation. *Entrance requirements:* For master's and doctorate, statement of purpose, official copies of academic transcripts, three letters of recommendation. Additional exam requirements/recommendations for international students: Required—TOEFL (minimum score 580 paper-based; 237 computer-based). *Application deadline:* For fall admission, 8/1 priority date for domestic students, 7/15 for international students; for spring admission, 12/1 priority date for domestic students, 10/15 for international students. Applications are processed on a rolling basis. Application fee: $55. Electronic applications accepted. *Expenses:* Contact institution. *Financial support:* Fellowships, research assistantships, teaching assistantships, Federal Work-Study, scholarships/grants, tuition waivers (full and partial), and unspecified assistantships available. Financial award application deadline: 2/1; financial award applicants required to submit FAFSA. *Faculty research:* Geotechnical engineering, solid mechanics, construction engineering and management, environmental engineering, structural engineering. Total annual research expenditures: $438,834. *Unit head:* Dr. Lu Sun, Chair, 202-319-5164, Fax: 202-319-6677, E-mail: sunl@cua.edu. *Application contact:* Julie Schwing, Director of Graduate Admissions, 202-319-5057, Fax: 202-319-6533, E-mail: cua-admissions@cua.edu.

Cornell University, Graduate School, Graduate Fields of Engineering, Field of Civil and Environmental Engineering, Ithaca, NY 14853-0001. Offers engineering management (M Eng, MS, PhD); environmental engineering (M Eng, MS, PhD); environmental fluid mechanics and hydrology (M Eng, MS, PhD); environmental systems engineering (M Eng, MS, PhD); geotechnical engineering (M Eng, MS, PhD); remote sensing (M Eng, MS, PhD); structural engineering (M Eng, MS, PhD); structural mechanics (M Eng, MS); transportation engineering (MS, PhD); transportation systems engineering (M Eng); water resource systems (M Eng, MS, PhD). *Faculty:* 40 full-time (7 women). *Students:* 144 full-time (48 women); includes 12 minority (2 African Americans, 1 American Indian/Alaska Native, 5 Asian Americans or Pacific Islanders, 4 Hispanic Americans), 58 international. Average age 25. 454 applicants, 57% accepted, 86 enrolled. In 2009, 69 master's, 5 doctorates awarded. Terminal master's awarded for partial completion of doctoral program. *Degree requirements:* For master's, thesis (MS); for doctorate, comprehensive exam, thesis/dissertation. *Entrance requirements:* For master's and doctorate, GRE General Test (recommended), 2 letters of recommendation. Additional exam requirements/recommendations for international students: Required—TOEFL (minimum score 600 paper-based; 250 computer-based; 77 iBT). *Application deadline:* For fall admission, 1/15 priority date for domestic students; for spring admission, 10/15 for domestic students. Application fee: $70. Electronic applications accepted. *Expenses:* Tuition: Full-time $29,500. Required fees: $70. Full-time tuition and fees vary according to degree level, program and student level. *Financial support:* In 2009–10, 50 students received support, including 6 fellowships with full tuition reimbursements available, 5 research assistantships with full tuition reimbursements available, 1 teaching assistantship with full tuition reimbursement available; institutionally sponsored loans, scholarships/grants, health care benefits, tuition waivers (full and partial), and unspecified assistantships also available. Financial award applicants required to submit FAFSA. *Faculty research:* Environmental engineering, geotechnical engineering remote sensing, environmental fluid mechanics and hydrology, structural engineering. *Unit head:* Director of Graduate Studies, 607-255-7560, Fax: 607-255-9004. *Application contact:* Graduate Field Assistant, 607-255-7560, Fax: 607-255-9004, E-mail: cee_grad@cornell.edu.

Drexel University, College of Engineering, Department of Civil, Architectural, and Environmental Engineering, Program in Geotechnical, Geoenvironmental and Geosynthetics Engineering, Philadelphia, PA 19104-2875. Offers MS, PhD.

École Polytechnique de Montréal, Graduate Programs, Department of Civil, Geological and Mining Engineering, Montréal, QC H3C 3A7, Canada. Offers civil, geological and mining engineering (DESS); environmental engineering (M Eng, M Sc A, PhD); geotechnical engineering (M Eng, M Sc A, PhD); hydraulics engineering (M Eng, M Sc A, PhD); structural engineering (M Eng, M Sc A, PhD); transportation engineering (M Eng, M Sc A, PhD). Part-time programs available. *Degree requirements:* For master's, one foreign language, thesis; for doctorate, one foreign language, thesis/dissertation. *Entrance requirements:* For master's, minimum GPA of 2.75; for doctorate, minimum GPA of 3.0. *Faculty research:* Water resources management, characteristics of building materials, aging of dams, pollution control.

Illinois Institute of Technology, Graduate College, Armour College of Engineering, Department of Civil, Architectural and Environmental Engineering, Chicago, IL 60616-3793. Offers architectural engineering (M Arch E); civil engineering (MS, PhD); construction engineering and management (MCEM); environmental engineering (M Env E, MS, PhD); geoenvironmental engineering (M Geoenv E); geotechnical engineering (MGE); public works (MPW); structural engineering (MSE); transportation engineering (M Trans E). Part-time and evening/weekend programs available. Terminal master's awarded for partial completion of doctoral program. *Degree requirements:* For master's, thesis (for some programs); for doctorate, comprehensive exam, thesis/dissertation. *Entrance requirements:* For master's and doctorate, GRE General Test, minimum undergraduate GPA of 3.0. Additional exam requirements/recommendations for international students: Required—TOEFL (minimum score 550 paper-based; 213 computer-based; 80 iBT). Electronic applications accepted. *Expenses:* Tuition: Full-time $17,550; part-time

Geotechnical Engineering

Illinois Institute of Technology (continued)

$888 per credit hour. Required fees: $850; $7.50 per credit hour. One-time fee: $50 full-time. Full-time tuition and fees vary according to program. *Faculty research:* Seismic analysis of buildings and bridges, fatigue analysis and materials of construction, construction zone safety and construction productivity, architectural acoustics and building energy efficiency, environmental engineering. air and water quality.

Iowa State University of Science and Technology, Graduate College, College of Engineering, Department of Civil and Construction Engineering, Ames, IA 50011. Offers civil engineering (MS, PhD), including civil engineering materials, construction engineering and management, environmental engineering, geometronics, geotechnical engineering, structural engineering, transportation engineering. *Faculty:* 32 full-time (5 women), 6 part-time/adjunct (0 women). *Students:* 87 full-time (20 women), 33 part-time (8 women); includes 2 minority (1 American Indian/Alaska Native, 1 Asian American or Pacific Islander), 48 international. 204 applicants, 29% accepted, 27 enrolled. In 2009, 6 master's, 11 doctorates awarded. *Degree requirements:* For master's, thesis or alternative; for doctorate, thesis/dissertation. *Entrance requirements:* For master's and doctorate, GRE General Test. Additional exam requirements/recommendations for international students: Required—TOEFL (minimum score 550 paper-based; 82 iBT) or IELTS (minimum score 6.5). *Application deadline:* For fall admission, 2/1 priority date for domestic students, 2/1 for international students; for spring admission, 8/1 priority date for domestic students, 8/1 for international students. Application fee: $40 ($90 for international students). Electronic applications accepted. *Expenses:* Tuition, state resident: full-time $6716. Tuition, nonresident: full-time $8908. Tuition and fees vary according to course level, course load, program and student level. *Financial support:* In 2009–10, 70 research assistantships with full and partial tuition reimbursements (averaging $16,000 per year), 4 teaching assistantships with full and partial tuition reimbursements (averaging $18,000 per year) were awarded; fellowships, scholarships/grants, health care benefits, and unspecified assistantships also available. *Unit head:* Dr. James Alleman, Chair, 515-294-3892, E-mail: ccee-grad-inquiry@iastate.edu. *Application contact:* Dr. Sri Srithanan, Director of Graduate Education, 515-294-5328, E-mail: ccee-grad-inquiry@iastate.edu.

Louisiana State University and Agricultural and Mechanical College, Graduate School, College of Engineering, Department of Civil and Environmental Engineering, Baton Rouge, LA 70803. Offers environmental engineering (MSCE, PhD); geotechnical engineering (MSCE, PhD); structural engineering and mechanics (MSCE, PhD); transportation engineering (MSCE, PhD); water resources (MSCE, PhD). Part-time programs available. *Faculty:* 28 full-time (2 women). *Students:* 74 full-time (18 women), 37 part-time (6 women); includes 9 minority (1 American Indian/Alaska Native, 5 Asian Americans or Pacific Islanders, 3 Hispanic Americans), 59 international. Average age 31. 104 applicants, 63% accepted, 31 enrolled. In 2009, 16 master's, 13 doctorates awarded. *Degree requirements:* For master's, thesis optional; for doctorate, one foreign language, thesis/dissertation. *Entrance requirements:* For master's and doctorate, GRE General Test, minimum GPA of 3.0. Additional exam requirements/recommendations for international students: Required—TOEFL (minimum score 550 paper-based; 213 computer-based; 79 iBT) or IELTS (minimum score 6.5). *Application deadline:* For fall admission, 1/25 priority date for domestic students, 5/15 for international students; for spring admission, 10/15 for international students. Applications are processed on a rolling basis. Application fee: $50 ($70 for international students). Electronic applications accepted. *Financial support:* In 2009–10, 74 students received support, including 2 fellowships with full and partial tuition reimbursements available (averaging $16,672 per year), 65 research assistantships with full and partial tuition reimbursements available (averaging $11,242 per year); teaching assistantships with full and partial tuition reimbursements available, career-related internships or fieldwork, institutionally sponsored loans, scholarships/grants, and health care benefits also available. Financial award application deadline: 3/1; financial award applicants required to submit FAFSA. *Faculty research:* Mechanics and structures, environmental, geotechnical transportation, water resources. Total annual research expenditures: $2.4 million. *Unit head:* Dr. George Z. Voyiadjis, Chair/Boyd Professor, 225-578-8668, Fax: 225-578-9176, E-mail: cegzv@lsu.edu. *Application contact:* Dr. Donald Dean Adrian, Professor, 225-578-8636, E-mail: dadrian@lsu.edu.

Marquette University, Graduate School, College of Engineering, Department of Civil and Environmental Engineering, Milwaukee, WI 53201-1881. Offers construction and public works management (MS, PhD); environmental/water resources engineering (MS, PhD); structural/geotechnical engineering (MS, PhD); transportation planning and engineering (MS, PhD). Part-time and evening/weekend programs available. *Faculty:* 13 full-time (0 women), 2 part-time/adjunct (1 woman). *Students:* 16 full-time (4 women), 17 part-time (2 women); includes 2 minority (1 Asian American or Pacific Islander, 1 Hispanic American), 13 international. Average age 27. 47 applicants, 85% accepted, 11 enrolled. In 2009, 8 master's, 1 doctorate awarded. Terminal master's awarded for partial completion of doctoral program. *Degree requirements:* For master's, comprehensive exam, thesis or alternative; for doctorate, thesis/dissertation. *Entrance requirements:* For master's and doctorate, GRE General Test, minimum GPA of 3.0. Additional exam requirements/recommendations for international students: Required—TOEFL. *Application deadline:* For fall admission, 6/1 priority date for domestic students. Applications are processed on a rolling basis. Application fee: $40. Electronic applications accepted. *Financial support:* In 2009–10, 13 students received support, including 5 fellowships with tuition reimbursements available (averaging $7,697 per year), 3 research assistantships with tuition reimbursements available (averaging $24,570 per year), 5 teaching assistantships with tuition reimbursements available (averaging $24,804 per year); Federal Work-Study, institutionally sponsored loans, scholarships/grants, and tuition waivers (full and partial) also available. Support available to part-time students. Financial award application deadline: 2/15. *Faculty research:* Highway safety, highway performance, and intelligent transportation systems; surface mount technology; watershed management. Total annual research expenditures: $138,209. *Unit head:* Dr. Michael S. Switzenbaum, Chair, 414-288-7030, Fax: 414-288-7521, E-mail: michael.switzenbaum@marquette.edu. *Application contact:* Dr. Stephen M. Heinrich, Director of Graduate Studies, 414-288-5466, E-mail: stephen.heinrich@marquette.edu.

Massachusetts Institute of Technology, School of Engineering, Department of Civil and Environmental Engineering, Cambridge, MA 02139-4307. Offers biological oceanography (PhD, Sc D); chemical oceanography (PhD, Sc D); civil and environmental engineering (M Eng, SM, PhD, Sc D); civil and environmental systems (PhD, Sc D); civil engineering (PhD, Sc D, CE); coastal engineering (PhD, Sc D); construction engineering and management (PhD, Sc D); environmental biology (PhD, Sc D); environmental chemistry (PhD, Sc D); environmental engineering (PhD, Sc D); environmental fluid mechanics (PhD, Sc D); geotechnical and geoenvironmental engineering (PhD, Sc D); hydrology (PhD, Sc D); information technology (PhD, Sc D); oceanographic engineering (PhD, Sc D); structures and materials (PhD, Sc D); transportation (PhD, Sc D); SM/MBA. *Faculty:* 36 full-time (5 women). *Students:* 190 full-time (59 women); includes 22 minority (2 African Americans, 14 Asian Americans or Pacific Islanders, 6 Hispanic Americans), 103 international. Average age 26. 478 applicants, 25% accepted, 76 enrolled. In 2009, 72 master's, 14 doctorates awarded. *Degree requirements:* For master's and CE, thesis; for doctorate, comprehensive exam, thesis/dissertation. *Entrance requirements:* For master's and doctorate, GRE General Test. Additional exam requirements/recommendations for international students: Required—TOEFL (minimum score 577 paper-based; 233 computer-based; 90 iBT), IELTS (minimum score 7). *Application deadline:* For fall admission, 1/2 for domestic and international students. Application fee: $75. Electronic applications accepted. *Financial support:* In 2009–10, 185 students received support, including 40 fellowships with tuition reimbursements available (averaging $27,725 per year), 97 research assistantships with tuition reimbursements available (averaging $28,035 per year), 21 teaching assistantships with tuition reimbursements available (averaging $24,802 per year); career-related internships or fieldwork, Federal Work-Study, institutionally sponsored loans, scholarships/grants, health care benefits, and unspecified assistantships also available. *Faculty research:* Environmental chemistry, environmental microbiology, environmental fluid mechanics and coastal engineering, geotechnical engineering and geomechanics, hydrology and hydroclimatology, mechanics of materials and structures, operations research/supply chain, transportation. Total annual research expenditures: $16.6 million. *Unit head:* Prof. Andrew Whittle, Department Head, 617-253-7101. *Application contact:* Patricia Glidden, Graduate Admissions Coordinator, 617-253-7119, Fax: 617-258-6775, E-mail: cee-admissions@mit.edu.

McGill University, Faculty of Graduate and Postdoctoral Studies, Faculty of Engineering, Department of Civil Engineering and Applied Mechanics, Montréal, QC H3A 2T5, Canada. Offers environmental engineering (M Eng, M Sc, PhD); fluid mechanics (M Sc); fluid mechanics and hydraulic engineering (M Eng, PhD); materials engineering (M Eng, PhD); rehabilitation of urban infrastructure (M Eng, PhD); soil behavior (M Eng, PhD); soil mechanics and foundations (M Eng, PhD); structures and structural mechanics (M Eng, PhD); water resources (M Sc); water resources engineering (M Eng, PhD).

Missouri University of Science and Technology, Graduate School, Department of Civil, Architectural, and Environmental Engineering, Rolla, MO 65409. Offers civil engineering (MS, DE, PhD); construction engineering (MS, DE, PhD); environmental engineering (MS); fluid mechanics (MS, DE, PhD); geotechnical engineering (MS, DE, PhD); hydrology and hydraulic engineering (MS, DE, PhD). Part-time and evening/weekend programs available. Terminal master's awarded for partial completion of doctoral program. *Degree requirements:* For master's, thesis optional; for doctorate, comprehensive exam, thesis/dissertation. *Entrance requirements:* For master's, GRE General Test (minimum combined score 1100), minimum GPA of 3.0; for doctorate, GRE General Test (minimum score: verbal and quantitative 400, writing 3.5), minimum GPA of 3.0. Additional exam requirements/recommendations for international students: Required—TOEFL. Electronic applications accepted. *Faculty research:* Earthquake engineering, structural optimization and control systems, structural health monitoring/damage detection, soil-structure interaction, soil mechanics and foundation engineering.

Northwestern University, McCormick School of Engineering and Applied Science, Department of Civil and Environmental Engineering, Evanston, IL 60208-3109. Offers environmental engineering and science (MS, PhD); geotechnical engineering (MS, PhD); mechanics of materials and solids (MS, PhD); project management (MS, PhD); structural engineering and materials (MS, PhD); theoretical and applied mechanics (MS, PhD), including fluid mechanics, solid mechanics; transportation systems analysis and planning (MS, PhD). MS and PhD admissions and degrees offered through The Graduate School. Part-time programs available. *Faculty:* 25 full-time (2 women), 3 part-time/adjunct (1 woman). *Students:* 63 full-time (19 women), 3 part-time (0 women); includes 7 minority (1 African American, 3 Asian Americans or Pacific Islanders, 3 Hispanic Americans), 34 international. Average age 22. 149 applicants, 30% accepted, 23 enrolled. In 2009, 11 master's, 11 doctorates awarded. Terminal master's awarded for partial completion of doctoral program. *Degree requirements:* For master's, thesis (for some programs); for doctorate, thesis/dissertation. *Entrance requirements:* For master's and doctorate, GRE General Test, minimum 2 letters of recommendation, transcripts from all academic institutions attended. Additional exam requirements/recommendations for international students: Required—TOEFL (minimum score 600 paper-based; 250 computer-based; 100 iBT), IELTS (minimum score 7), TOEFL (minimum score iBT 26). *Application deadline:* For fall admission, 12/31 for domestic and international students. Application fee: $75. Electronic applications accepted. *Financial support:* In 2009–10, 55 students received support, including fellowships with full tuition reimbursements available (averaging $15,390 per year), research assistantships with full tuition reimbursements available (averaging $17,892 per year), 23 teaching assistantships with full tuition reimbursements available (averaging $15,867 per year); career-related internships or fieldwork, institutionally sponsored loans, scholarships/grants, and health care benefits also available. Financial award application deadline: 12/31; financial award applicants required to submit FAFSA. *Faculty research:* Environmental engineering and science, geotechnics, mechanics of materials and solids, structural engineering and materials, transportation systems analysis and planning. Total annual research expenditures: $5.8 million. *Unit head:* Jianmin Qu, Chair, 847-467-4528, Fax: 847-491-4011, E-mail: j-qu@northwestern.edu. *Application contact:* Janet Soule, Academic Coordinator, 847-491-7462, Fax: 847-491-4011, E-mail: civil-info@northwestern.edu.

Ohio University, Graduate College, Russ College of Engineering and Technology, Department of Civil Engineering, Athens, OH 45701-2979. Offers civil engineering (PhD); construction (MS); environmental (MS); geotechnical and geoenvironmental (MS); mechanics (MS); structures (MS); transportation (MS); water resources and structures (MS). Part-time programs available. *Faculty:* 13 full-time (3 women), 3 part-time/adjunct (0 women). *Students:* 18 full-time (2 women), 2 part-time (1 woman), 13 international. 22 applicants, 68% accepted, 1 enrolled. In 2009, 7 master's awarded. *Degree requirements:* For master's, comprehensive exam (for some programs), thesis or alternative; for doctorate, comprehensive exam, thesis/dissertation. *Entrance requirements:* For master's, GRE General Test, minimum GPA of 3.0, 3 letters of recommendation; for doctorate, GRE General Test. Additional exam requirements/recommendations for international students: Required—TOEFL (minimum score 550 paper-based; 80 iBT) or IELTS Academic (minimum score 6.5). *Application deadline:* For fall admission, 5/1 priority date for domestic students, 2/1 priority date for international students; for winter admission, 8/1 priority date for domestic students, 4/1 priority date for international students; for spring admission, 2/1 priority date for domestic students, 7/1 priority date for international students. Applications are processed on a rolling basis. Application fee: $50 ($55 for international students). Electronic applications accepted. *Expenses:* Tuition, state resident: full-time $7839; part-time $323 per quarter hour. Tuition, nonresident: full-time $15,831; part-time $654 per quarter hour. Required fees: $2931. *Financial support:* Research assistantships with full tuition reimbursements, teaching assistantships with full tuition reimbursements, Federal Work-Study, institutionally sponsored loans, scholarships/grants, and unspecified assistantships available. Financial award application deadline: 3/15; financial award applicants required to submit FAFSA. *Faculty research:* Noise abatement, materials and environment, highway infrastructure, subsurface investigation, (pavements, pipes, bridges, etc.). Total annual research expenditures: $1.2 million. *Unit head:* Dr. Gayle F. Mitchell, Chair, 740-593-0430, Fax: 740-593-0625, E-mail: mitchelg@ohio.edu. *Application contact:* Dr. Shad M. Sargand, Graduate Chair, 740-593-1465, Fax: 740-593-0625, E-mail: sargand@ohio.edu.

Oregon State University, Graduate School, College of Engineering, School of Civil and Construction Engineering, Corvallis, OR 97331. Offers civil engineering (MS, PhD); coastal and ocean engineering (M Oc E, PhD); coastal engineering (MS); construction engineering management (MBE, PhD); engineering (M Eng, MAIS); geotechnical engineering (MS, PhD); structural engineering (MS, PhD); transportation engineering (MS, PhD); water engineering (MS, PhD). Part-time programs available. *Faculty:* 25 full-time (5 women), 1 part-time/adjunct (0 women). *Students:* 71 full-time (17 women), 12 part-time (2 women); includes 4 minority (all Asian Americans or Pacific Islanders), 34 international. Average age 28. 75 applicants, 87% accepted, 31 enrolled. In 2009, 26 master's, 7 doctorates awarded. Terminal master's awarded for partial completion of doctoral program. *Degree requirements:* For master's, thesis or alternative; for doctorate, one foreign language, thesis/dissertation. *Entrance requirements:* For master's, GRE General Test, minimum GPA of 3.0 in last 90 hours (3.5 for MS); for doctorate, GRE General Test, minimum GPA of 3.0 in last 90 hours of undergraduate course work. Additional exam requirements/recommendations for international students: Required—TOEFL (minimum score 580 paper-based; 237 computer-based). *Application deadline:* For fall admission, 3/1 priority date for domestic students. Applications are processed on a rolling basis. Application fee: $50. *Expenses:* Tuition, state resident: full-time $9774; part-time $362 per credit. Tuition, nonresident: full-time $15,849; part-time $587 per credit. Required fees: $1639. Full-time tuition and fees vary according to course load and program. *Financial support:* Fellowships, research assistantships with full tuition reimbursements, teaching assistantships with full tuition reimbursements, career-related internships or fieldwork and institutionally sponsored loans available. Support available to part-time students. Financial award application deadline: 2/1. *Faculty research:* Hazardous waste management, carbon cycling, wave forces on structures, pavement design, seismic analysis. Total annual research expenditures: $7.1 million. *Unit head:* Dr. Scott A. Ashford, Head, 541-737-4934. *Application contact:* Kathy Westberg, CCE Graduate Advising School Operations Manager, 541-737-1786, Fax: 541-737-3052, E-mail: kathy.westberg@oregonstate.edu.

Penn State University Park, Graduate School, College of Earth and Mineral Sciences, Department of Energy and Geo-Environmental Engineering, State College, University Park, PA 16802-1503. Offers MS, PhD.

Rensselaer Polytechnic Institute, Graduate School, School of Engineering, Department of Civil and Environmental Engineering, Program in Civil Engineering, Troy, NY 12180-3590. Offers geotechnical engineering (M Eng, MS, PhD); mechanics of composite materials and structures (M Eng, MS, PhD); structural engineering (M Eng, MS, PhD); transportation engineering (M Eng, MS, PhD). Part-time programs available. *Faculty:* 6 full-time (0 women), 5 part-time/adjunct (0 women). *Students:* 27 full-time (2 women); includes 4 minority (3 Asian Americans or Pacific Islanders, 1 Hispanic American), 3 international. Average age 24. 70 applicants, 14% accepted, 7 enrolled. In 2009, 5 master's, 1 doctorate awarded. Terminal master's awarded for partial completion of doctoral program. *Degree requirements:* For master's, thesis (for some programs); for doctorate, thesis/dissertation. *Entrance requirements:* For master's and doctorate, GRE. Additional exam requirements/recommendations for international students: Required—TOEFL (minimum score 570 paper-based; 230 computer-based; 89 iBT), IELTS (minimum score 6.5). *Application deadline:* For fall admission, 1/15 priority date for domestic and international students; for spring admission, 8/15 priority date for domestic and international students. Applications are processed on a rolling basis. Application fee: $75. Electronic applications accepted. *Expenses:* Tuition: Full-time $38,100. *Financial support:* In 2009–10, 1 fellowship with full tuition reimbursement (averaging $16,500 per year), 3 research assistantships with full tuition reimbursements (averaging $16,500 per year), 4 teaching assistantships with full tuition reimbursements (averaging $16,500 per year) were awarded; career-related internships or fieldwork and institutionally sponsored loans also available. Financial award application deadline: 2/1. *Faculty research:* Computational mechanics, earthquake engineering, geo-environmental engineering. Total annual research expenditures: $2.7 million. *Unit head:* Dr. Tarek Abdoun, Acting Chair, 518-276-6362, Fax: 518-276-4833, E-mail: abdout@rpi.edu. *Application contact:* Kimberly Boyce, Administrative Assistant, 518-276-6941, Fax: 518-276-4833, E-mail: boycek@rpi.edu.

Texas A&M University, College of Engineering, Zachry Department of Civil Engineering, College Station, TX 77843. Offers construction engineering and management (M Eng, MS, D Eng, PhD); environmental engineering (M Eng, MS, D Eng, PhD); geotechnical engineering (M Eng, MS, D Eng, PhD); materials engineering (M Eng, MS, D Eng, PhD); ocean engineering (M Eng, MS, D Eng, PhD); structural engineering (M Eng, MS, D Eng, PhD); transportation engineering (M Eng, MS, D Eng, PhD); water resources engineering (M Eng, MS, D Eng, PhD). Part-time programs available. *Faculty:* 61. *Students:* 390 full-time (89 women), 42 part-time (6 women); includes 23 minority (2 African Americans, 11 Asian Americans or Pacific Islanders, 10 Hispanic Americans), 281 international. Average age 29. In 2009, 100 master's, 36 doctorates awarded. *Degree requirements:* For master's, thesis (MS); for doctorate, dissertation (PhD), internship (D Eng). *Entrance requirements:* For master's and doctorate, GRE General Test. Additional exam requirements/recommendations for international students: Required—TOEFL. *Application deadline:* Applications are processed on a rolling basis. Application fee: $50 ($75 for international students). Electronic applications accepted. *Expenses:* Tuition, state resident: full-time $3991.32; part-time $221.74 per credit hour. Tuition, nonresident: full-time $9049; part-time $502.74 per credit hour. *Financial support:* In 2009–10, fellowships (averaging $4,500 per year), research assistantships (averaging $14,000 per year), teaching assistantships (averaging $14,400 per year) were awarded; career-related internships or fieldwork and institutionally sponsored loans also available. Financial award application deadline: 4/15; financial award applicants required to submit FAFSA. *Unit head:* Dr. Tony Cahill, Head, 979-845-2438, E-mail: t-cahill@civil.tamu.edu. *Application contact:* Graduate Advisor, 979-845-2498, Fax: 979-862-2800, E-mail: ce-grad@tamu.edu.

Tufts University, School of Engineering, Department of Civil and Environmental Engineering, Medford, MA 02155. Offers civil engineering (ME, MS, PhD), including geotechnical engineering, structural engineering; environmental engineering (ME, MS, PhD), including environmental engineering and environmental sciences, environmental geotechnology, environmental health, environmental science and management, hazardous materials management, water resources engineering. Part-time programs available. *Faculty:* 17 full-time, 7 part-time/adjunct. *Students:* 72 (33 women); includes 6 minority (2 African Americans, 4 Asian Americans or Pacific Islanders), 17 international. Average age 27. 170 applicants, 59% accepted, 20 enrolled. In 2009, 17 master's, 3 doctorates awarded. Terminal master's awarded for partial completion of doctoral program. *Degree requirements:* For master's, thesis or alternative; for doctorate, thesis/dissertation. *Entrance requirements:* For master's and doctorate, GRE General Test. Additional exam requirements/recommendations for international students: Required—TOEFL (minimum score 550 paper-based; 213 computer-based; 80 iBT). *Application deadline:* For fall admission, 1/15 priority date for domestic students, 12/15 for international students; for spring admission, 10/15 for domestic students, 9/15 for international students. Applications are processed on a rolling basis. Application fee: $75. Electronic applications accepted. *Expenses:* Tuition: Full-time $38,096; part-time $3962 per credit. Required fees: $686; $40 per year. Tuition and fees vary according to course level, course load, degree level, program and student level. *Financial support:* Fellowships with full tuition reimbursements, research assistantships with full and partial tuition reimbursements, teaching assistantships with full and partial tuition reimbursements, Federal Work-Study, scholarships/grants, tuition waivers (partial), and unspecified assistantships available. Financial award application deadline: 1/15; financial award applicants required to submit FAFSA. *Unit head:* Dr. Kurt Penell, Chair, 617-627-3211, Fax: 617-627-3994. *Application contact:* Laura Sacco, Information Contact, 617-627-3211.

The University of Alabama in Huntsville, School of Graduate Studies, College of Engineering, Department of Civil and Environmental Engineering, Huntsville, AL 35899. Offers civil and environmental engineering (PhD); civil engineering (MSE), including environmental and water resource engineering, geotechnical engineering, structural engineering and structural mechanics, transportation engineering. Part-time and evening/weekend programs available. *Faculty:* 6 full-time (1 woman). *Students:* 12 full-time (3 women), 7 part-time (1 woman); includes 3 minority (2 African Americans, 1 Asian American or Pacific Islander), 5 international. Average age 33. 26 applicants, 58% accepted, 9 enrolled. In 2009, 10 master's, 2 doctorates awarded. *Degree requirements:* For master's, comprehensive exam, thesis or alternative, oral and written exams; for doctorate, comprehensive exam, thesis/dissertation, oral and written exams. *Entrance requirements:* For master's, GRE General Test, BSE, minimum GPA of 3.0; for doctorate, GRE General Test, minimum GPA of 3.0. Additional exam requirements/recommendations for international students: Required—TOEFL (minimum score 500 paper-based; 173 computer-based; 62 iBT). *Application deadline:* For fall admission, 7/15 for domestic students, 4/1 for international students; for spring admission, 11/30 for domestic students, 9/1 for international students. Applications are processed on a rolling basis. Application fee: $40 ($50 for international students). Electronic applications accepted. *Expenses:* Tuition, state resident: part-time $355.75 per credit hour. Tuition, nonresident: part-time $847.10 per credit hour. Required fees: $210.80 per semester. Tuition and fees vary according to course load and program. *Financial support:* In 2009–10, 10 students received support, including 4 research assistantships with full and partial tuition reimbursements available (averaging $11,525 per year), 6 teaching assistantships with full and partial tuition reimbursements available (averaging $9,678 per year); career-related internships or fieldwork, Federal Work-Study, institutionally sponsored loans, scholarships/grants, health care benefits, and unspecified assistantships also available. Support available to part-time students. Financial award application deadline: 4/1; financial award applicants required to submit FAFSA. *Faculty research:* Hydrologic modeling, orbital debris impact, hydrogeology, environmental engineering, transportation engineering. Total annual research expenditures: $1.5 million. *Unit head:* Dr. Houssam Toutanji, Chair, 256-824-7361, Fax: 256-824-6724, E-mail: toutanji@cee.uah.edu. *Application contact:* Kathy Biggs, Graduate Studies Admissions Manager, 256-824-6199, Fax: 256-824-6405, E-mail: deangrad@uah.edu.

University of Alberta, Faculty of Graduate Studies and Research, Department of Civil and Environmental Engineering, Edmonton, AB T6G 2E1, Canada. Offers construction engineering and management (M Eng, M Sc, PhD); environmental engineering (M Eng, M Sc, PhD); environmental science (M Sc, PhD); geoenvironmental engineering (M Eng, M Sc, PhD); geotechnical engineering (M Eng, M Sc, PhD); mining engineering (M Eng, M Sc, PhD); petroleum engineering (M Eng, M Sc, PhD); structural engineering (M Eng, M Sc, PhD); water resources (M Eng, M Sc, PhD). Part-time programs available. Postbaccalaureate distance learning degree programs offered (minimal on-campus study). *Faculty:* 44 full-time (3 women), 2 part-time/adjunct (0 women). *Students:* 215 full-time (49 women), 99 part-time (19 women). 1,428 applicants, 15% accepted, 123 enrolled. In 2009, 124 master's, 34 doctorates awarded. *Degree requirements:* For master's, thesis (for some programs); for doctorate, thesis/dissertation. *Entrance requirements:* For master's, minimum GPA of 3.0 in last 2 years of undergraduate studies; for doctorate, minimum GPA of 3.0. Additional exam requirements/recommendations for international students: Required—TOEFL (minimum score 550 paper-based; 213 computer-based). *Application deadline:* For fall admission, 6/1 priority date for domestic students, 6/1 for international students; for winter admission, 11/1 for domestic students, 9/15 for international students. Applications are processed on a rolling basis. Application fee: $0 Canadian dollars. Electronic applications accepted. Tuition and fees charges are reported in Canadian dollars. *Expenses:* Tuition, area resident: Full-time $4626.24 Canadian dollars; part-time $99.72 Canadian dollars per unit. International tuition: $8216 Canadian dollars full-time. Required fees: $3589.92 Canadian dollars; $99.72 Canadian dollars per unit. $215 Canadian dollars per term. *Financial support:* In 2009–10, 88 research assistantships with full and partial tuition reimbursements, 134 teaching assistantships with full and partial tuition reimbursements were awarded; scholarships/grants and tuition waivers (full and partial) also available. Financial award application deadline: 4/1. *Faculty research:* Mining. Total annual research expenditures: $6,791 Canadian dollars. *Unit head:* Dr. David Zhu, Associate Chair, Graduate Studies, 780-492-1198, Fax: 403-492-8198. *Application contact:* Gwen Mendoza, Student Services Officer, 403-492-1539, Fax: 403-492-0249, E-mail: civegrad@ualberta.ca.

University of Calgary, Faculty of Graduate Studies, Schulich School of Engineering, Department of Geomatics Engineering, Calgary, AB T2N 1N4, Canada. Offers M Eng, M Sc, PhD. Part-time programs available. *Degree requirements:* For master's, thesis (for some programs); for doctorate, thesis/dissertation, candidacy exam. *Entrance requirements:* For master's, minimum GPA of 3.0; for doctorate, minimum GPA of 3.5. Additional exam requirements/recommendations for international students: Required—TOEFL (minimum score 550 paper-based; 213 computer-based). *Faculty research:* Gravity and geodynamics, digital imaging systems, engineering metrology, GIS and land tenure, positioning.

University of California, Berkeley, Graduate Division, College of Engineering, Department of Civil and Environmental Engineering, Berkeley, CA 94720-1500. Offers engineering and project management (M Eng, MS, D Eng, PhD); environmental engineering (M Eng, MS, D Eng, PhD); geoengineering (M Eng, MS, D Eng, PhD); structural engineering, mechanics and materials (M Eng, MS, D Eng, PhD); transportation engineering (M Eng, MS, D Eng, PhD); M Arch/MS; MCP/MS; MPP/MS. *Students:* 368 full-time (125 women). Average age 27. 921 applicants, 179 enrolled. In 2009, 158 master's, 39 doctorates awarded. *Degree requirements:* For master's, comprehensive exam or thesis (MS); for doctorate, thesis/dissertation, qualifying exam. *Entrance requirements:* For master's, GRE General Test, minimum GPA of 3.0, 3 letters of recommendation; for doctorate, GRE General Test, minimum GPA of 3.5, 3 letters of recommendation. Additional exam requirements/recommendations for international students: Required—TOEFL (minimum score 570 paper-based; 230 computer-based). *Application deadline:* For fall admission, 2/3 for domestic students. Application fee: $70 ($90 for international students). Electronic applications accepted. *Financial support:* Fellowships, research assistantships, teaching assistantships, unspecified assistantships available. *Unit head:* Prof. Lisa Alvarez-Cohen, Chair, 510-643-8739, Fax: 510-643-5264, E-mail: chair@ce.berkeley.edu. *Application contact:* Shelly Okimoto, Graduate Advisor, 510-642-6464, Fax: 510-643-5264, E-mail: aao@ce.berkeley.edu.

University of Colorado at Boulder, Graduate School, College of Engineering and Applied Science, Department of Civil, Environmental, and Architectural Engineering, Boulder, CO 80309. Offers building systems (MS, PhD); construction engineering management (MS, PhD); environmental engineering (MS, PhD); geotechnical engineering and geomechanics (MS, PhD); hydrology, water resources and environmental fluid mechanics (MS, PhD); structural engineering and structural mechanics (MS, PhD). *Faculty:* 39 full-time (5 women). *Students:* 202 full-time (62 women), 29 part-time (6 women); includes 34 minority (3 African Americans, 3 American Indian/Alaska Native, 12 Asian Americans or Pacific Islanders, 16 Hispanic Americans), 53 international. Average age 29. 384 applicants, 44% accepted, 80 enrolled. In 2009, 60 master's, 7 doctorates awarded. *Degree requirements:* For master's, comprehensive exam, thesis or alternative; for doctorate, thesis/dissertation. *Entrance requirements:* For master's, GRE General Test, minimum undergraduate GPA of 3.0. *Application deadline:* For fall admission, 3/1 for domestic students, 12/1 for international students; for spring admission, 10/31 for domestic students, 10/1 for international students. Application fee: $50 ($60 for international students). *Financial support:* In 2009–10, 45 fellowships (averaging $7,876 per year), 68 research assistantships (averaging $15,204 per year) were awarded. Financial award application deadline: 1/15. *Faculty research:* Building systems engineering, construction engineering and management, environmental engineering, geoenvironmental engineering, geotechnical engineering, materials and mechanics, structural engineering, water resources engineering, life-cycle engineering. Total annual research expenditures: $6.1 million.

University of Delaware, College of Engineering, Department of Civil and Environmental Engineering, Newark, DE 19716. Offers environmental engineering (MAS, MCE, PhD); geotechnical engineering (MAS, MCE, PhD); ocean engineering (MAS, MCE, PhD); structural engineering (MAS, MCE, PhD); transportation engineering (MAS, MCE, PhD); water resource engineering (MAS, MCE, PhD). Part-time programs available. Terminal master's awarded for partial completion of doctoral program. *Degree requirements:* For master's, thesis; for doctorate, thesis/dissertation. *Entrance requirements:* For master's and doctorate, GRE General Test. Additional exam requirements/recommendations for international students: Required—TOEFL. Electronic applications accepted. *Faculty research:* Structural engineering and mechanics; transportation engineering; ocean engineering; soil mechanics and foundation; water resources and environmental engineering.

University of Maine, Graduate School, College of Engineering, Department of Civil and Environmental Engineering, Orono, ME 04469. Offers civil engineering (MS, PhD), including environmental engineering, geotechnical engineering, structural engineering. *Faculty:* 10 full-time (2 women), 2 part-time/adjunct (0 women). *Students:* 28 full-time (7 women), 15 part-time (2 women); includes 2 minority (both American Indian/Alaska Native), 3 international. Average age 27. 31 applicants, 35% accepted, 7 enrolled. In 2009, 6 master's, 1 doctorate awarded. *Degree requirements:* For doctorate, thesis/dissertation. *Entrance requirements:* For master's and doctorate, GRE General Test. Additional exam requirements/recommendations for international students: Required—TOEFL. *Application deadline:* For fall admission, 2/1 priority date for domestic students. Applications are processed on a rolling basis. Application fee: $65. Electronic applications accepted. *Financial support:* In 2009–10, 15 research assistantships with tuition reimbursements (averaging $15,815 per year), 3 teaching assistantships with tuition reimbursements (averaging $12,790 per year) were awarded; Federal Work-Study, institutionally sponsored loans, scholarships/grants, and tuition waivers (full and partial) also available. Financial award application deadline: 3/1. *Unit head:* Dr. Eric Landis, Chair. *Application contact:* Scott G. Delcourt, Associate Dean of the Graduate School, 207-581-3291, Fax: 207-581-3232, E-mail: graduate@maine.edu.

University of Missouri, Graduate School, College of Engineering, Department of Civil and Environmental Engineering, Columbia, MO 65211. Offers civil engineering (MS, PhD); environmental engineering (MS, PhD); geotechnical engineering (MS, PhD); structural engineering (MS, PhD); transportation and highway engineering (MS); water resources (MS, PhD). *Degree requirements:* For master's, report or thesis; for doctorate, thesis/dissertation. *Entrance requirements:* For master's and doctorate, GRE General Test. Additional exam requirements/recommendations for international students: Required—TOEFL (minimum score 550 paper-based; 213 computer-based; 79 iBT).

Geotechnical Engineering

University of New Brunswick Fredericton, School of Graduate Studies, Faculty of Engineering, Department of Civil Engineering, Fredericton, NB E3B 5A3, Canada. Offers construction engineering and management (M Eng, M Sc E, PhD); environmental engineering (M Eng, M Sc E, PhD); environmental studies (M Eng); geotechnical engineering (M Eng, M Sc E, PhD); groundwater/hydrology (M Eng, M Sc E, PhD); materials (M Eng, M Sc E, PhD); pavements (M Eng, M Sc E, PhD); structures (M Eng, M Sc E, PhD); transportation (M Eng, M Sc E, PhD). Part-time programs available. *Faculty:* 18 full-time (1 woman), 1 (woman) part-time/adjunct. *Students:* 42 full-time (9 women), 18 part-time (2 women). In 2009, 11 master's, 4 doctorates awarded. *Degree requirements:* For master's, thesis, proposal; for doctorate, comprehensive exam, thesis/dissertation, Qualifying exam; Proposal; 27 credit hours of courses. *Entrance requirements:* For master's, Minimum GPA of 3.0; BScE in Civil Engineering or related engineering degree.; for doctorate, Minimum GPA of 3.0; Candidates are normally required to have a graduate degree in engineering or applied science. Additional exam requirements/recommendations for international students: Required—TOEFL (minimum score 580 paper-based; 237 computer-based), TWE (minimum score 4), or IELTS (minimum score 7.5). *Application deadline:* For fall admission, 5/1 priority date for domestic students; for winter admission, 11/1 priority date for domestic students. Applications are processed on a rolling basis. Application fee: $50 Canadian dollars. Tuition and fees charges are reported in Canadian dollars. *Expenses:* Tuition, area resident: Full-time $5562 Canadian dollars; part-time $2781 Canadian dollars per year. Required fees: $49.75 Canadian dollars per term. *Financial support:* In 2009–10, 51 research assistantships (averaging $7,000 per year), 43 teaching assistantships (averaging $2,000 per year) were awarded; career-related internships or fieldwork and scholarships/grants also available. *Faculty research:* Construction engineering and management, concrete materials and structural engineering, transportation and asset management, geotechnical engineering, water and environmental engineering. *Unit head:* Dr. Eric Hildebrand, Director of Graduate Studies, 506-453-5113, Fax: 506-453-3568, E-mail: ktm@unb.ca. *Application contact:* Joyce Moore, Graduate Secretary, 506-452-6127, Fax: 506-453-3568, E-mail: civil-grad@unb.ca.

University of Oklahoma, Graduate College, College of Engineering, School of Civil Engineering and Environmental Science, Program in Civil Engineering, Norman, OK 73019-0390. Offers civil engineering (MS, PhD); geotechnical engineering (MS); structures (MS). Part-time programs available. *Students:* 42 full-time (8 women), 9 part-time (1 woman); includes 4 minority (1 African American, 1 American Indian/Alaska Native, 1 Asian American or Pacific Islander, 1 Hispanic American), 28 international. 18 applicants, 100% accepted, 6 enrolled. In 2009, 13 master's, 3 doctorates awarded. *Degree requirements:* For master's, comprehensive exam, oral exams; for doctorate, thesis/dissertation, oral and qualifying exams. *Entrance requirements:* For master's, minimum GPA of 3.0; for doctorate, minimum graduate GPA of 3.5. Additional exam requirements/recommendations for international students: Required—TOEFL (minimum score 600 paper-based). *Application deadline:* For fall admission, 4/1 priority date for domestic students, 4/1 for international students; for spring admission, 11/1 for domestic students, 9/1 for international students. Applications are processed on a rolling basis. Application fee: $40 ($90 for international students). Electronic applications accepted. *Expenses:* Tuition, state resident: full-time $3744; part-time $156 per credit hour. Tuition, nonresident: full-time $13,577; part-time $565.70 per credit hour. Required fees: $2415; $90.10 per credit hour. *Financial support:* Scholarships/grants and unspecified assistantships available. Financial award application deadline: 3/1; financial award applicants required to submit FAFSA. *Faculty research:* Structural engineering, environmental modeling, natural hazards, transport and fate of chemicals, geotechnical engineering. *Unit head:* Robert C. Knox, Director, 405-325-5911, Fax: 405-325-4217, E-mail: rknox@ou.edu. *Application contact:* Robert C. Knox, Director, 405-325-5911, Fax: 405-325-4217, E-mail: rknox@ou.edu.

The University of Texas at Austin, Graduate School, Cockrell School of Engineering, Department of Petroleum and Geosystems Engineering, Austin, TX 78712-1111. Offers energy and earth resources (MA); petroleum engineering (MS, PhD). Evening/weekend programs available. Postbaccalaureate distance learning degree programs offered (no on-campus study). *Entrance requirements:* For master's and doctorate, GRE General Test. Electronic applications accepted.

University of Washington, Graduate School, College of Engineering, Department of Civil and Environmental Engineering, Seattle, WA 98195-2700. Offers construction engineering (MSCE); environmental engineering (MS, MSCE, MSE, PhD); hydrology, water resources, and environmental fluid mechanics (MS, MSCE, MSE, PhD); structural and geotechnical engineering and mechanics (MS, MSCE, MSE, PhD); transportation and construction engineering (MS, MSE, PhD); transportation engineering (MSCE). Part-time programs available. Postbaccalaureate distance learning degree programs offered (no on-campus study). *Faculty:* 36 full-time (9 women), 16 part-time/adjunct (6 women). *Students:* 186 full-time (62 women), 57 part-time (10 women); includes 35 minority (24 Asian Americans or Pacific Islanders, 11 Hispanic Americans), 58 international. 360 applicants, 68% accepted, 98 enrolled. In 2009, 74 master's, 8 doctorates awarded. Terminal master's awarded for partial completion of doctoral program. *Degree requirements:* For master's, thesis (for some programs); for doctorate, comprehensive exam, thesis/dissertation. *Entrance requirements:* For master's, GRE General Test, minimum GPA of 3.0; for doctorate, GRE, minimum GPA of 3.5. Additional exam requirements/recommendations for international students: Required—TOEFL (minimum score 580 paper-based; 237 computer-based; 70 iBT). *Application deadline:* For fall admission, 1/15 priority date for domestic and international students. Applications are processed on a rolling basis. Application fee: $65. Electronic applications accepted. *Financial support:* In 2009–10, 5 students received support, including 13 fellowships with full and partial tuition reimbursements available (averaging $16,173 per year), 68 research assistantships with full tuition reimbursements available (averaging $16,173 per year), 12 teaching assistantships with full tuition reimbursements available (averaging $16,173 per year); scholarships/grants also available. Financial award application deadline: 1/15. *Faculty research:* Environmental/water resources, hydrology; construction/transportation; structures/ geotechnical. Total annual research expenditures: $11.4 million. *Unit head:* Dr. Gregory R. Miller, Professor and Chair, 206-543-0350, Fax: 206-543-1543, E-mail: gmiller@uw.edu. *Application contact:* Lorna Latal, Graduate Adviser, 206-543-2574, Fax: 206-543-1543, E-mail: llatal@u.washington.edu.

Hazardous Materials Management

Humboldt State University, Graduate Studies, College of Natural Resources and Sciences, Programs in Natural Resources, Arcata, CA 95521-8299. Offers natural resources (MS), including fisheries, forestry, natural resources planning and interpretation, rangeland resources and wildland soils, wastewater utilization, watershed management, wildlife. *Students:* 51 full-time (22 women), 26 part-time (10 women); includes 4 minority (1 American Indian/Alaska Native, 1 Asian American or Pacific Islander, 2 Hispanic Americans), 1 international. Average age 31. 81 applicants, 26% accepted, 15 enrolled. In 2009, 25 master's awarded. *Degree requirements:* For master's, thesis or alternative. *Entrance requirements:* For master's, GRE, appropriate bachelor's degree, minimum GPA of 2.5, 3 letters of recommendation, resume. Additional exam requirements/recommendations for international students: Required—TOEFL (minimum score 500 paper-based; 173 computer-based). *Application deadline:* For fall admission, 2/1 for domestic and international students; for spring admission, 9/30 for domestic and international students. Applications are processed on a rolling basis. Application fee: $55. *Expenses:* Tuition, nonresident: full-time $8928. Required fees: $6102. Tuition and fees vary according to program. *Financial support:* Fellowships, career-related internships or fieldwork and Federal Work-Study available. Support available to part-time students. Financial award application deadline: 3/1; financial award applicants required to submit FAFSA. *Faculty research:* Spotted owl habitat, pre-settlement vegetation, hardwood utilization, tree physiology, fisheries. *Unit head:* Dr. Gary Hendrickson, Coordinator, 707-826-4233, E-mail: thiesfel@humboldt.edu. *Application contact:* Julie Tucker, Administrative Support Coordinator, 707-826-3256, E-mail: jlt7002@humboldt.edu.

Idaho State University, Office of Graduate Studies, Department of Interdisciplinary Studies, Pocatello, ID 83209. Offers general interdisciplinary (M Ed, MA, MNS); waste management and environmental science (MS). Part-time programs available. *Faculty:* 2 full-time (1 woman). In 2009, 2 master's awarded. *Degree requirements:* For master's, comprehensive exam, thesis optional. *Entrance requirements:* For master's, GRE General Test or MAT, minimum GPA of 3.0. Additional exam requirements/recommendations for international students: Required—TOEFL (minimum score 550 paper-based; 213 computer-based; 80 iBT). *Application deadline:* For fall admission, 7/1 for domestic students, 6/1 for international students; for spring admission, 12/1 for domestic students, 11/1 for international students. Applications are processed on a rolling basis. Application fee: $55. *Expenses:* Tuition, state resident: full-time $3318; part-time $297 per credit hour. Tuition, nonresident: full-time $13,120; part-time $437 per credit hour. Required fees: $2530. Tuition and fees vary according to program. *Financial support:* Career-related internships or fieldwork, Federal Work-Study, scholarships/grants, and unspecified assistantships available. Support available to part-time students. Financial award application deadline: 1/1; financial award applicants required to submit FAFSA. *Unit head:* Dr. Pamela Crowell, Vice President for Research, 208-282-2714, Fax: 208-282-4529. *Application contact:* Ellen Combs, Graduate School Technical Records Specialist, 208-282-2150, Fax: 208-282-4847.

New Mexico Institute of Mining and Technology, Graduate Studies, Department of Environmental Engineering, Socorro, NM 87801. Offers environmental engineering (MS), including air quality engineering and science, hazardous waste engineering, water quality engineering and science. *Degree requirements:* For master's, thesis. *Entrance requirements:* For master's, GRE General Test. Additional exam requirements/recommendations for international students: Required—TOEFL (minimum score 540 paper-based; 207 computer-based). *Faculty research:* Air quality, hazardous waste management, wastewater management and treatment, site remediation.

Rutgers, The State University of New Jersey, New Brunswick, Graduate School-New Brunswick, Department of Environmental Sciences, Piscataway, NJ 08854-8097. Offers air pollution and resources (MS, PhD); aquatic biology (MS, PhD); aquatic chemistry (MS, PhD); atmospheric science (MS, PhD); chemistry and physics of aerosol and hydrosol systems (MS, PhD); environmental chemistry (MS, PhD); environmental microbiology (MS, PhD); environmental toxicology (PhD); exposure assessment (PhD); fate and effects of pollutants (MS, PhD); pollution prevention and control (MS, PhD); water and wastewater treatment (MS, PhD); water resources (MS, PhD). Terminal master's awarded for partial completion of doctoral program. *Degree requirements:* For master's, comprehensive exam, thesis or alternative, oral final exam; for doctorate, comprehensive exam, thesis/dissertation, thesis defense, qualifying exam. *Entrance requirements:* For master's and doctorate, GRE General Test. Additional exam requirements/recommendations for international students: Required—TOEFL. Electronic applications accepted. *Faculty research:* Biological waste treatment; contaminant fate and transport; air, soil and water quality.

Southern Methodist University, Bobby B. Lyle School of Engineering, Department of Environmental and Civil Engineering, Dallas, TX 75275-0340. Offers applied science (MS, PhD); civil engineering (MS, PhD); environmental engineering (MS); environmental science (MS), including environmental systems management, hazardous and waste materials management; facilities management (MS). Part-time and evening/weekend programs available. Postbaccalaureate distance learning degree programs offered (no on-campus study). *Faculty:* 7 full-time (0 women), 13 part-time/adjunct (4 women). *Students:* 19 full-time (8 women), 50 part-time (17 women); includes 13 minority (9 African Americans, 2 Asian Americans or Pacific Islanders, 2 Hispanic Americans), 7 international. Average age 34. 50 applicants, 86% accepted, 28 enrolled. In 2009, 17 master's, 1 doctorate awarded. Terminal master's awarded for partial completion of doctoral program. *Degree requirements:* For master's, thesis optional; for doctorate, thesis/dissertation, oral and written qualifying exams. *Entrance requirements:* For master's, GRE General Test, minimum GPA of 3.0 in last 2 years; bachelor's degree in engineering, mathematics, or sciences; for doctorate, GRE, BS and MS in related field, minimum GPA of 3.3. Additional exam requirements/recommendations for international students: Required—TOEFL. *Application deadline:* For fall admission, 7/1 for domestic students, 5/15 for international students; for spring admission, 11/15 for domestic students, 9/1 for international students. Applications are processed on a rolling basis. Application fee: $75. Electronic applications accepted. *Financial support:* In 2009–10, 9 students received support, including 2 research assistantships with full tuition reimbursements available (averaging $18,000 per year), 7 teaching assistantships with full tuition reimbursements available (averaging $18,000 per year); career-related internships or fieldwork, tuition waivers (full and partial), and unspecified assistantships also available. *Faculty research:* Human and environmental health effects of endocrine disrupters, development of air pollution control systems for diesel engines, structural analysis and design, modeling and design of waste treatment systems. Total annual research expenditures: $100,000. *Unit head:* Prof. Bijan Mohraz, Chair, 214-768-3894, Fax: 214-768-2164, E-mail: bmohraz@lyle.smu.edu. *Application contact:* Marc Valerin, Director of Graduate and Executive Admissions, 214-768-3042, Fax: 214-768-3778, E-mail: valerin@lyle.smu.edu.

Stony Brook University, State University of New York, School of Professional Development, Stony Brook, NY 11794. Offers biology-grade 7-12 (MAT); chemistry-grade 7-12 (MAT); coaching (Graduate Certificate); computer integrated engineering (Graduate Certificate); earth science-grade 7-12 (MAT); educational computing (Graduate Certificate); educational leadership (Advanced Certificate); English-grade 7-12 (MAT); environmental management (Graduate Certificate); environmental/occupational health and safety (Graduate Certificate); French-grade 7-12 (MAT); German-grade 7-12 (MAT); human resource management (Graduate Certificate); information systems management (Graduate Certificate); Italian-grade 7-12 (MAT); liberal studies (MA); mathematics-grade 7-12 (MAT); operation research (Graduate Certificate); physics-grade 7-12 (MAT); school administration and supervision (Graduate Certificate); school building leadership (Graduate Certificate); school district administration (Graduate Certificate); school district business leadership (Advanced Certificate); school district leadership (Graduate Certificate); social science and the professions (MPS), including environmental waste management, human resource management; social studies-grade 7-12 (MAT); Spanish-grade 7-12 (MAT); waste management (Graduate Certificate). Part-time and evening/weekend programs available. Postbaccalaureate distance learning degree programs offered. *Faculty:* 5 full-time (3 women), 131 part-time/adjunct (53 women). *Students:* 317 full-time (187 women), 1,200 part-time (773 women); includes 187 minority (77 African Americans, 2 American Indian/Alaska Native, 22 Asian Americans or Pacific Islanders, 86 Hispanic Americans), 11 international. Average age 28. In 2009, 597 master's, 234 other advanced degrees awarded. *Degree requirements:* For master's, one foreign language, thesis or alternative. *Application deadline:* Applications are processed on a rolling basis. Application fee: $62. *Expenses:*

Tuition, state resident: full-time $8370; part-time $349 per credit. Tuition, nonresident: full-time $13,250; part-time $552 per credit. Required fees: $933. *Financial support:* Fellowships, research assistantships, teaching assistantships, career-related internships or fieldwork available. Support available to part-time students. *Unit head:* Dr. Paul J. Edelson, Dean, 631-632-7052, Fax: 631-632-9046, E-mail: paul.edelson@stonybrook.edu. *Application contact:* Dr. Paul J. Edelson, Dean, 631-632-7052, Fax: 631-632-9046, E-mail: paul.edelson@stonybrook.edu.

Tufts University, School of Engineering, Department of Civil and Environmental Engineering, Medford, MA 02155. Offers civil engineering (ME, MS, PhD), including geotechnical engineering, structural engineering; environmental engineering (ME, MS, PhD), including environmental engineering and environmental sciences, environmental geotechnology, environmental health, environmental science and management, hazardous materials management, water resources engineering. Part-time programs available. *Faculty:* 17 full-time, 7 part-time/adjunct. *Students:* 72 (33 women); includes 6 minority (2 African Americans, 4 Asian Americans or Pacific Islanders), 17 international. Average age 27. 170 applicants, 59% accepted, 20 enrolled. In 2009, 17 master's, 3 doctorates awarded. Terminal master's awarded for partial completion of doctoral program. *Degree requirements:* For master's, thesis or alternative; for doctorate, thesis/dissertation. *Entrance requirements:* For master's and doctorate, GRE General Test. Additional exam requirements/recommendations for international students: Required—TOEFL (minimum score 550 paper-based; 213 computer-based; 80 iBT). *Application deadline:* For fall admission, 1/15 priority date for domestic students, 12/15 for international students; for spring admission, 10/15 for domestic students, 9/15 for international students. Applications are processed on a rolling basis. Application fee: $75. Electronic applications accepted. *Expenses:* Tuition: Full-time $38,096; part-time $3962 per credit. Required fees: $686; $40 per year. Tuition and fees vary according to course level, course load, degree level, program and student level. *Financial support:* Fellowships with full tuition reimbursements, research assistantships with full and partial tuition reimbursements, teaching assistantships with full and partial tuition reimbursements, Federal Work-Study, scholarships/grants, tuition waivers (partial), and unspecified assistantships available. Financial award application deadline: 1/15; financial award applicants required to submit FAFSA. *Unit head:* Dr. Kurt Penell, Chair, 617-627-3211, Fax: 617-627-3994. *Application contact:* Laura Sacco, Information Contact, 617-627-3211.

University of New Haven, Graduate School, Tagliatela College of Engineering, Program in Environmental Engineering, West Haven, CT 06516-1916. Offers environmental engineering (MS); industrial and hazardous wastes (MS); water and wastewater treatment (MS); water resources (Certificate). Part-time and evening/weekend programs available. *Faculty:* 6 full-time (1 woman), 2 part-time/adjunct (0 women). *Students:* 15 full-time (4 women), 6 part-time (1 woman); includes 2 African Americans, 14 international. Average age 29. 35 applicants, 97% accepted, 7 enrolled. In 2009, 10 master's awarded. *Degree requirements:* For master's, thesis or alternative. *Entrance requirements:* For master's, bachelor's degree in engineering. Additional exam requirements/recommendations for international students: Required—TOEFL (minimum score 520 paper-based; 190 computer-based; 70 iBT); Recommended—IELTS (minimum score 5.5). *Application deadline:* For fall admission, 5/31 for international students; for winter admission, 10/15 for international students; for spring admission, 1/15 for international students. Applications are processed on a rolling basis. Application fee: $50. Electronic applications accepted. *Expenses:* Tuition: Part-time $700 per credit. Required fees: $45 per term. One-time fee: $390 part-time. *Financial support:* Research assistantships with partial tuition reimbursements, teaching assistantships with partial tuition reimbursements, career-related internships or fieldwork, Federal Work-Study, scholarships/grants, tuition waivers, and

unspecified assistantships available. Support available to part-time students. Financial award application deadline: 5/1; financial award applicants required to submit FAFSA. *Unit head:* Dr. Agamemnon D. Koutsospyros, Coordinator, 203-932-7398. *Application contact:* Eloise Gormley, Director of Graduate Admissions, 203-932-7449, Fax: 203-932-7137, E-mail: gradinfo@newhaven.edu.

University of Oklahoma, Graduate College, College of Engineering, School of Civil Engineering and Environmental Science, Program in Environmental Science, Norman, OK 73019-0390. Offers air (M Env Sc); environmental science (PhD); groundwater management (M Env Sc); hazardous solid waste (M Env Sc); occupational safety and health (M Env Sc); process design (M Env Sc); water quality resources (M Env Sc). *Students:* 9 full-time (4 women), 8 part-time (6 women); includes 3 minority (1 African American, 2 American Indian/Alaska Native), 2 international. 9 applicants, 67% accepted, 4 enrolled. In 2009, 4 master's, 2 doctorates awarded. Terminal master's awarded for partial completion of doctoral program. *Degree requirements:* For master's, comprehensive exam, oral exams; for doctorate, comprehensive exam, thesis/dissertation, oral and qualifying exams. *Entrance requirements:* For master's, minimum GPA of 3.0; for doctorate, minimum graduate GPA of 3.5. Additional exam requirements/recommendations for international students: Required—TOEFL (minimum score 600 paper-based; 250 computer-based). *Application deadline:* For fall admission, 4/1 priority date for domestic students, 4/1 for international students; for spring admission, 11/1 for domestic students, 9/1 for international students. Applications are processed on a rolling basis. Application fee: $40 ($90 for international students). Electronic applications accepted. *Expenses:* Tuition, state resident: full-time $3744; part-time $156 per credit hour. Tuition, nonresident: full-time $13,577; part-time $565.70 per credit hour. Required fees: $2415; $90.10 per credit hour. *Financial support:* In 2009–10, 10 students received support. Scholarships/grants available. Financial award application deadline: 3/1; financial award applicants required to submit FAFSA. *Faculty research:* Treatment wetlands, soil remediation, biomediation. *Unit head:* Robert C. Knox, Director, 405-325-5911, Fax: 405-325-4217, E-mail: rknox@ou.edu. *Application contact:* Robert C. Knox, Director, 405-325-5911, Fax: 405-325-4217, E-mail: rknox@ou.edu.

University of South Carolina, The Graduate School, Arnold School of Public Health, Department of Environmental Health Sciences, Program in Hazardous Materials Management, Columbia, SC 29208. Offers MPH, MSPH, PhD. *Degree requirements:* For master's, comprehensive exam, thesis (for some programs), practicum (MPH); for doctorate, one foreign language, comprehensive exam, thesis/dissertation. *Entrance requirements:* Additional exam requirements/recommendations for international students: Required—TOEFL (minimum score 570 paper-based; 230 computer-based). Electronic applications accepted. *Faculty research:* Environmental/human health protection; use and disposal of hazardous materials; site safety; exposure assessment; migration, fate and transformation of materials.

Wayne State University, College of Engineering, Department of Chemical Engineering and Materials Science, Programs in Hazardous Waste, Detroit, MI 48202. Offers environmental auditing (Certificate); hazardous materials management on public lands (Certificate); hazardous waste control (Certificate); hazardous waste management (MS). Part-time programs available. *Degree requirements:* For master's, thesis optional. *Entrance requirements:* For master's, GRE (if applying for financial support), certificate in hazardous waste control, recommendations, resume. Additional exam requirements/recommendations for international students: Required—TOEFL (minimum score 550 paper-based; 213 computer-based); Recommended—TWE (minimum score 6). Electronic applications accepted. *Faculty research:* Environmental management.

Hydraulics

Auburn University, Graduate School, Ginn College of Engineering, Department of Civil Engineering, Auburn University, AL 36849. Offers construction engineering and management (MCE, MS, PhD); environmental engineering (MCE, MS, PhD); geotechnical/materials engineering (MCE, MS, PhD); hydraulics/hydrology (MCE, MS, PhD); structural engineering (MCE, MS, PhD); transportation engineering (MCE, MS, PhD). Part-time programs available. *Faculty:* 21 full-time (1 woman), 3 part-time/adjunct (1 woman). *Students:* 46 full-time (15 women), 39 part-time (5 women); includes 4 minority (3 African Americans, 1 Asian American or Pacific Islander), 29 international. Average age 26. 136 applicants, 43% accepted, 26 enrolled. In 2009, 19 master's, 4 doctorates awarded. *Degree requirements:* For master's, project (MCE), thesis (MS); for doctorate, comprehensive exam, thesis/dissertation. *Entrance requirements:* For master's and doctorate, GRE General Test. *Application deadline:* For fall admission, 7/7 for domestic students; for spring admission, 11/24 for domestic students. Applications are processed on a rolling basis. Application fee: $50 ($60 for international students). Electronic applications accepted. *Expenses:* Tuition, state resident: full-time $6240. Tuition, nonresident: full-time $18,720. International tuition: $18,938 full-time. Required fees: $492. Tuition and fees vary according to course load, program and reciprocity agreements. *Financial support:* Fellowships, research assistantships, teaching assistantships, Federal Work-Study available. Support available to part-time students. Financial award application deadline: 3/15; financial award applicants required to submit FAFSA. *Unit head:* Dr. J. Michael Stallings, Head, 334-844-4320. *Application contact:* Dr. George Flowers, Dean of the Graduate School, 334-844-2125.

Drexel University, College of Engineering, Department of Civil, Architectural, and Environmental Engineering, Philadelphia, PA 19104-2875. Offers architectural / building systems engineering (MS, PhD); civil engineering (MS, PhD); environmental engineering (MS, PhD); geotechnical, geoenvironmental and geosynthetics engineering (MS, PhD); hydraulics, hydrology and water resources engineering (MS, PhD); structures (MS). Part-time and evening/weekend programs available. *Degree requirements:* For master's, thesis optional; for doctorate, thesis/dissertation. *Entrance requirements:* For master's, minimum GPA of 3.0; for doctorate, minimum GPA of 3.5, MS in civil engineering. Additional exam requirements/recommendations for international students: Required—TOEFL. Electronic applications accepted. *Faculty research:* Structural dynamics, hazardous wastes, water resources, pavement materials, groundwater.

École Polytechnique de Montréal, Graduate Programs, Department of Civil, Geological and Mining Engineering, Montréal, QC H3C 3A7, Canada. Offers civil, geological and mining engineering (DESS); environmental engineering (M Eng, M Sc A, PhD); geotechnical engineering (M Eng, M Sc A, PhD); hydraulics engineering (M Eng, M Sc A, PhD); structural engineering (M Eng, M Sc A, PhD); transportation engineering (M Eng, M Sc A, PhD). Part-time programs available. *Degree requirements:* For master's, one foreign language, thesis; for doctorate, one foreign language, thesis/dissertation. *Entrance requirements:* For master's, minimum GPA of 2.75; for doctorate, minimum GPA of 3.0. *Faculty research:* Water resources management, characteristics of building materials, aging of dams, pollution control.

McGill University, Faculty of Graduate and Postdoctoral Studies, Faculty of Engineering, Department of Civil Engineering and Applied Mechanics, Montréal, QC H3A 2T5, Canada. Offers environmental engineering (M Eng, M Sc, PhD); fluid mechanics (M Sc); fluid mechanics and hydraulic engineering (M Eng, PhD); materials engineering (M Eng, PhD); rehabilitation of urban infrastructure (M Eng, PhD); soil behavior (M Eng, PhD); soil mechanics and foundations (M Eng, PhD); structures and structural mechanics (M Eng, PhD); water resources (M Sc); water resources engineering (M Eng, PhD).

Missouri University of Science and Technology, Graduate School, Department of Civil, Architectural, and Environmental Engineering, Rolla, MO 65409. Offers civil engineering (MS, DE, PhD); construction engineering (MS, DE, PhD); environmental engineering (MS); fluid mechanics (MS, DE, PhD); geotechnical engineering (MS, DE, PhD); hydrology and hydraulic engineering (MS, DE, PhD). Part-time and evening/weekend programs available. Terminal master's awarded for partial completion of doctoral program. *Degree requirements:* For master's, thesis optional; for doctorate, comprehensive exam, thesis/dissertation. *Entrance requirements:* For master's, GRE General Test (minimum combined score 1100), minimum GPA of 3.0; for doctorate, GRE General Test (minimum score: verbal and quantitative 400, writing 3.5), minimum GPA of 3.0. Additional exam requirements/recommendations for international students: Required—TOEFL. Electronic applications accepted. *Faculty research:* Earthquake engineering, structural optimization and control systems, structural health monitoring/damage detection, soil-structure interaction, soil mechanics and foundation engineering.

Structural Engineering

Auburn University, Graduate School, Ginn College of Engineering, Department of Civil Engineering, Auburn University, AL 36849. Offers construction engineering and management (MCE, MS, PhD); environmental engineering (MCE, MS, PhD); geotechnical/materials engineering (MCE, MS, PhD); hydraulics/hydrology (MCE, MS, PhD); structural engineering (MCE, MS, PhD); transportation engineering (MCE, MS, PhD). Part-time programs available. *Faculty:* 21 full-time (1 woman), 3 part-time/adjunct (1 woman). *Students:* 46 full-time (15 women), 39 part-time (5 women); includes 4 minority (3 African Americans, 1 Asian American or Pacific Islander), 29 international. Average age 26. 136 applicants, 43% accepted, 26

enrolled. In 2009, 19 master's, 4 doctorates awarded. *Degree requirements:* For master's, project (MCE), thesis (MS); for doctorate, comprehensive exam, thesis/dissertation. *Entrance requirements:* For master's and doctorate, GRE General Test. *Application deadline:* For fall admission, 7/7 for domestic students; for spring admission, 11/24 for domestic students. Applications are processed on a rolling basis. Application fee: $50 ($60 for international students). Electronic applications accepted. *Expenses:* Tuition, state resident: full-time $6240. Tuition, nonresident: full-time $18,720. International tuition: $18,938 full-time. Required fees: $492. Tuition and fees vary according to course load, program and reciprocity agreements.

Structural Engineering

Auburn University (continued)

Financial support: Fellowships, research assistantships, teaching assistantships, Federal Work-Study available. Support available to part-time students. Financial award application deadline: 3/15; financial award applicants required to submit FAFSA. *Unit head:* Dr. J. Michael Stallings, Head, 334-844-4320. *Application contact:* Dr. George Flowers, Dean of the Graduate School, 334-844-2125.

California State University, Northridge, Graduate Studies, College of Engineering and Computer Science, Department of Civil Engineering and Applied Mechanics, Northridge, CA 91330. Offers engineering (MS), including structural engineering. Part-time and evening/weekend programs available. *Faculty:* 8 full-time (0 women), 13 part-time/adjunct (4 women). *Students:* 17 full-time (3 women), 19 part-time (6 women); includes 1 Asian American or Pacific Islander, 6 Hispanic Americans. Average age 29. 51 applicants, 67% accepted, 20 enrolled. *Degree requirements:* For master's, thesis. *Entrance requirements:* Additional exam requirements/recommendations for international students: Required—TOEFL. *Application deadline:* For fall admission, 11/30 for domestic students. Application fee: $55. *Financial support:* Teaching assistantships available. Financial award application deadline: 3/1. *Faculty research:* Composite study. *Unit head:* Prof. Stephen Gadomski, Chair, 818-677-2166. *Application contact:* Prof. Stephen Gadomski, Chair, 818-677-2166.

The Catholic University of America, School of Engineering, Department of Civil Engineering, Washington, DC 20064. Offers environmental engineering (MCE, MSE, D Engr, PhD, Certificate); environmental engineering and management (MCE, MSE, PhD, Certificate); environmental engineering and management (D Engr); fluid and solid mechanics (MCE, MSE, PhD, Certificate); geotechnical engineering (MCE, MSE, PhD, Certificate); management of construction (MCE, MSE, D Engr, PhD); structural engineering (MSE, D Engr, PhD); systems engineering (MSE, D Engr, PhD, Certificate). Part-time programs available. *Faculty:* 5 full-time (0 women), 7 part-time/adjunct (1 woman). *Students:* 7 full-time (3 women), 18 part-time (5 women); includes 6 minority (3 African Americans, 3 Hispanic Americans), 11 international. Average age 32. 36 applicants, 47% accepted, 9 enrolled. In 2009, 8 master's, 2 doctorates awarded. *Degree requirements:* For master's, thesis optional; for doctorate, comprehensive exam, thesis/dissertation. *Entrance requirements:* For master's and doctorate, statement of purpose, official copies of academic transcripts, three letters of recommendation. Additional exam requirements/recommendations for international students: Required—TOEFL (minimum score 580 paper-based; 237 computer-based). *Application deadline:* For fall admission, 8/1 priority date for domestic students, 7/15 for international students; for spring admission, 12/1 priority date for domestic students, 10/15 for international students. Applications are processed on a rolling basis. Application fee: $55. Electronic applications accepted. *Expenses:* Contact institution. *Financial support:* Fellowships, research assistantships, teaching assistantships, Federal Work-Study, scholarships/grants, tuition waivers (full and partial), and unspecified assistantships available. Financial award application deadline: 2/1; financial award applicants required to submit FAFSA. *Faculty research:* Geotechnical engineering, solid mechanics, construction engineering and management, environmental engineering, structural engineering. Total annual research expenditures: $438,834. *Unit head:* Dr. Lu Sun, Chair, 202-319-5164, Fax: 202-319-6677, E-mail: sunl@cua.edu. *Application contact:* Julie Schwing, Director of Graduate Admissions, 202-319-5057, Fax: 202-319-6533, E-mail: cua-admissions@cua.edu.

Cornell University, Graduate School, Graduate Fields of Engineering, Field of Civil and Environmental Engineering, Ithaca, NY 14853-0001. Offers engineering management (M Eng, MS, PhD); environmental engineering (M Eng, MS, PhD); environmental fluid mechanics and hydrology (M Eng, MS, PhD); environmental systems engineering (M Eng, MS, PhD); geotechnical engineering (M Eng, MS, PhD); remote sensing (M Eng, MS, PhD); structural engineering (M Eng, MS, PhD); structural mechanics (M Eng, MS); transportation engineering (MS, PhD); transportation systems engineering (M Eng); water resource systems (M Eng, MS, PhD). *Faculty:* 40 full-time (7 women). *Students:* 144 full-time (48 women); includes 12 minority (2 African Americans, 1 American Indian/Alaska Native, 5 Asian Americans or Pacific Islanders, 4 Hispanic Americans), 58 international. Average age 25. 454 applicants, 57% accepted, 86 enrolled. In 2009, 69 master's, 5 doctorates awarded. Terminal master's awarded for partial completion of doctoral program. *Degree requirements:* For master's, thesis (MS); for doctorate, comprehensive exam, thesis/dissertation. *Entrance requirements:* For master's and doctorate, GRE General Test (recommended), 2 letters of recommendation. Additional exam requirements/recommendations for international students: Required—TOEFL (minimum score 600 paper-based; 250 computer-based; 77 iBT). *Application deadline:* For fall admission, 1/15 priority date for domestic students; for spring admission, 10/15 for domestic students. Application fee: $70. Electronic applications accepted. *Expenses:* Tuition: Full-time $29,500. Required fees: $70. Full-time tuition and fees vary according to degree level, program and student level. *Financial support:* In 2009–10, 50 students received support, including 6 fellowships with full tuition reimbursements available, 5 research assistantships with full tuition reimbursements available, 1 teaching assistantship with full tuition reimbursement available; institutionally sponsored loans, scholarships/grants, health care benefits, tuition waivers (full and partial), and unspecified assistantships also available. Financial award applicants required to submit FAFSA. *Faculty research:* Environmental engineering, geotechnical engineering remote sensing, environmental fluid mechanics and hydrology, structural engineering. *Unit head:* Director of Graduate Studies, 607-255-7560, Fax: 607-255-9004. *Application contact:* Graduate Field Assistant, 607-255-7560, Fax: 607-255-9004, E-mail: cee_grad@cornell.edu.

Drexel University, College of Engineering, Department of Civil, Architectural, and Environmental Engineering, Philadelphia, PA 19104-2875. Offers architectural / building systems engineering (MS, PhD); civil engineering (MS, PhD); environmental engineering (MS, PhD); geotechnical, geoenvironmental and geosynthetics engineering (MS, PhD); hydraulics, hydrology and water resources engineering (MS, PhD); structures (MS). Part-time and evening/weekend programs available. *Degree requirements:* For master's, thesis optional; for doctorate, thesis/dissertation. *Entrance requirements:* For master's, minimum GPA of 3.0; for doctorate, minimum GPA of 3.5, MS in civil engineering. Additional exam requirements/recommendations for international students: Required—TOEFL. Electronic applications accepted. *Faculty research:* Structural dynamics, hazardous wastes, water resources, pavement materials, groundwater.

École Polytechnique de Montréal, Graduate Programs, Department of Civil, Geological and Mining Engineering, Montréal, QC H3C 3A7, Canada. Offers civil, geological and mining engineering (DESS); environmental engineering (M Eng, M Sc A, PhD); geotechnical engineering (M Eng, M Sc A, PhD); hydraulics engineering (M Eng, M Sc A, PhD); structural engineering (M Eng, M Sc A, PhD); transportation engineering (M Eng, M Sc A, PhD). Part-time programs available. *Degree requirements:* For master's, one foreign language, thesis; for doctorate, one foreign language, thesis/dissertation. *Entrance requirements:* For master's, minimum GPA of 2.75; for doctorate, minimum GPA of 3.0. *Faculty research:* Water resources management, characteristics of building materials, aging of dams, pollution control.

Illinois Institute of Technology, Graduate College, Armour College of Engineering, Department of Civil, Architectural and Environmental Engineering, Chicago, IL 60616-3793. Offers architectural engineering (M Arch E); civil engineering (MS, PhD); construction engineering and management (MCEM); environmental engineering (M Env E, MS, PhD); geoenvironmental engineering (M Geoenv E); geotechnical engineering (MGE); public works (MPW); structural engineering (MSE); transportation engineering (M Trans E). Part-time and evening/weekend programs available. Terminal master's awarded for partial completion of doctoral program. *Degree requirements:* For master's, thesis (for some programs); for doctorate, comprehensive exam, thesis/dissertation. *Entrance requirements:* For master's and doctorate, GRE General Test, minimum undergraduate GPA of 3.0. Additional exam requirements/recommendations for international students: Required—TOEFL (minimum score 550 paper-based; 213 computer-based; 80 iBT). Electronic applications accepted. *Expenses:* Tuition: Full-time $17,550; part-time $888 per credit hour. Required fees: $850; $7.50 per credit hour. One-time fee: $50 full-time. Full-time tuition and fees vary according to program. *Faculty research:* Seismic analysis of buildings and bridges, fatigue analysis and materials of construction, construction zone safety and construction productivity, architectural acoustics and building energy efficiency, environmental engineering. air and water quality.

Instituto Tecnologico de Santo Domingo, Graduate School, Santo Domingo, Dominican Republic. Offers applied linguistics (MA); construction administration (M Mgmt); corporate finance (M Mgmt); education (M Ed); engineering (M Eng), including data telecommunications, industrial engineering, logistics and supply chain, maintenance engineering, sanitary and environmental engineering, structural engineering; environmental science (M En S), including environmental education, environmental management, marine and coastal ecosystems, natural resources management; family therapy (MA); food science and technology (MS); human development (MA); human resources administration (M Mgmt); international business (M Mgmt); labor risks (M Mgmt); management (M Mgmt); marketing (M Mgmt); mathematics (MS); organizational development (M Mgmt); planning and taxation (M Mgmt); psychology (MA); social science (M Ed); upper management (M Mgmt). *Entrance requirements:* For master's, birth certificate, minimum GPA of 2.0.

Iowa State University of Science and Technology, Graduate College, College of Engineering, Department of Civil and Construction Engineering, Ames, IA 50011. Offers civil engineering (MS, PhD), including civil engineering materials, construction engineering and management, environmental engineering, geometronics, geotechnical engineering, structural engineering, transportation engineering. *Faculty:* 32 full-time (5 women), 6 part-time/adjunct (0 women). *Students:* 87 full-time (20 women), 33 part-time (8 women); includes 2 minority (1 American Indian/Alaska Native, 1 Asian American or Pacific Islander), 48 international. 204 applicants, 29% accepted, 27 enrolled. In 2009, 6 master's, 11 doctorates awarded. *Degree requirements:* For master's, thesis or alternative; for doctorate, thesis/dissertation. *Entrance requirements:* For master's and doctorate, GRE General Test. Additional exam requirements/recommendations for international students: Required—TOEFL (minimum score 550 paper-based; 82 iBT) or IELTS (minimum score 6.5). *Application deadline:* For fall admission, 2/1 priority date for domestic students, 2/1 for international students; for spring admission, 8/1 priority date for domestic students, 8/1 for international students. Application fee: $40 ($90 for international students). Electronic applications accepted. *Expenses:* Tuition, state resident: full-time $6716. Tuition, nonresident: full-time $8908. Tuition and fees vary according to course level, course load, program and student level. *Financial support:* In 2009–10, 70 research assistantships with full and partial tuition reimbursements (averaging $16,000 per year), 4 teaching assistantships with full and partial tuition reimbursements (averaging $18,000 per year) were awarded; fellowships, scholarships/grants, health care benefits, and unspecified assistantships also available. *Unit head:* Dr. James Alleman, Chair, 515-294-3892, E-mail: ccee-grad-inquiry@iastate.edu. *Application contact:* Dr. Sri Srithanan, Director of Graduate Education, 515-294-5328, E-mail: ccee-grad-inquiry@iastate.edu.

Lehigh University, P.C. Rossin College of Engineering and Applied Science, Department of Civil and Environmental Engineering, Bethlehem, PA 18015-3094. Offers civil engineering (M Eng, MS, PhD); environmental engineering (MS, PhD); structural engineering (M Eng, MS, PhD). Part-time programs available. *Faculty:* 17 full-time (3 women). *Students:* 68 full-time (14 women), 11 part-time (2 women); includes 6 minority (4 Asian Americans or Pacific Islanders, 2 Hispanic Americans), 39 international. Average age 26. 284 applicants, 21% accepted, 39 enrolled. In 2009, 26 master's, 2 doctorates awarded. Terminal master's awarded for partial completion of doctoral program. *Degree requirements:* For master's, thesis (for some programs); for doctorate, comprehensive exam, thesis/dissertation. *Entrance requirements:* For master's and doctorate, GRE. Additional exam requirements/recommendations for international students: Required—TOEFL (minimum score 550 paper-based; 213 computer-based; 79 iBT). *Application deadline:* For fall admission, 7/15 priority date for domestic and international students; for spring admission, 12/1 priority date for domestic and international students. Applications are processed on a rolling basis. Application fee: $75. Electronic applications accepted. *Expenses:* Contact institution. *Financial support:* In 2009–10, 46 students received support, including 12 fellowships with full tuition reimbursements available (averaging $15,795 per year), 29 research assistantships with full tuition reimbursements available (averaging $20,500 per year), 5 teaching assistantships with full tuition reimbursements available (averaging $15,795 per year); institutionally sponsored loans, scholarships/grants, tuition waivers, and unspecified assistantships also available. Financial award application deadline: 1/15. *Faculty research:* Structural engineering, geotechnical engineering, water resources engineering, environmental engineering. Total annual research expenditures: $8 million. *Unit head:* Dr. Stephen Pessiki, Chairman, 610-758-3494, Fax: 610-758-6405, E-mail: pessiki@lehigh.edu. *Application contact:* Prisca Vidanage, Graduate Coordinator, 610-758-3530, Fax: 610-758-6405, E-mail: pmv1@lehigh.edu.

Louisiana State University and Agricultural and Mechanical College, Graduate School, College of Engineering, Department of Civil and Environmental Engineering, Baton Rouge, LA 70803. Offers environmental engineering (MSCE, PhD); geotechnical engineering (MSCE, PhD); structural engineering and mechanics (MSCE, PhD); transportation engineering (MSCE, PhD); water resources (MSCE, PhD). Part-time programs available. *Faculty:* 28 full-time (2 women). *Students:* 74 full-time (18 women), 37 part-time (6 women); includes 9 minority (1 American Indian/Alaska Native, 5 Asian Americans or Pacific Islanders, 3 Hispanic Americans), 59 international. Average age 31. 104 applicants, 63% accepted, 31 enrolled. In 2009, 16 master's, 13 doctorates awarded. *Degree requirements:* For master's, thesis optional; for doctorate, one foreign language, thesis/dissertation. *Entrance requirements:* For master's and doctorate, GRE General Test, minimum GPA of 3.0. Additional exam requirements/recommendations for international students: Required—TOEFL (minimum score 550 paper-based; 213 computer-based; 79 iBT) or IELTS (minimum score 6.5). *Application deadline:* For fall admission, 1/25 priority date for domestic students, 5/15 for international students; for spring admission, 10/15 for international students. Applications are processed on a rolling basis. Application fee: $50 ($70 for international students). Electronic applications accepted. *Financial support:* In 2009–10, 74 students received support, including 2 fellowships with full and partial tuition reimbursements available (averaging $16,672 per year), 65 research assistantships with full and partial tuition reimbursements available (averaging $11,242 per year); teaching assistantships with full and partial tuition reimbursements available, career-related internships or fieldwork, institutionally sponsored loans, scholarships/grants, and health care benefits also available. Financial award application deadline: 3/1; financial award applicants required to submit FAFSA. *Faculty research:* Mechanics and structures, environmental, geotechnical transportation, water resources. Total annual research expenditures: $2.4 million. *Unit head:* Dr. George Z. Voyiadjis, Chair/Boyd Professor, 225-578-8668, Fax: 225-578-9176, E-mail: cegzv@lsu.edu. *Application contact:* Dr. Donald Dean Adrian, Professor, 225-578-8636, E-mail: dadrian@lsu.edu.

Marquette University, Graduate School, College of Engineering, Department of Civil and Environmental Engineering, Milwaukee, WI 53201-1881. Offers construction and public works management (MS, PhD); environmental/water resources engineering (MS, PhD); structural/geotechnical engineering (MS, PhD); transportation planning and engineering (MS, PhD). Part-time and evening/weekend programs available. *Faculty:* 13 full-time (0 women), 2 part-time/adjunct (1 woman). *Students:* 16 full-time (4 women), 17 part-time (2 women); includes 2 minority (1 Asian American or Pacific Islander, 1 Hispanic American), 13 international. Average age 27. 47 applicants, 85% accepted, 11 enrolled. In 2009, 8 master's, 1 doctorate awarded. Terminal master's awarded for partial completion of doctoral program. *Degree requirements:* For master's, comprehensive exam, thesis or alternative; for doctorate, thesis/dissertation. *Entrance requirements:* For master's and doctorate, GRE General Test, minimum GPA of 3.0. Additional exam requirements/recommendations for international students: Required—TOEFL. *Application deadline:* For fall admission, 6/1 priority date for domestic students. Applications are processed on a rolling basis. Application fee: $40. Electronic applications accepted. *Financial support:* In 2009–10, 13 students received support, including 5 fellowships with tuition reimbursements available (averaging $7,697 per year), 3 research assistantships with tuition reimbursements available (averaging $24,570 per year), 5 teaching assistantships with tuition reimbursements available (averaging $24,804 per year); Federal Work-Study, institutionally sponsored loans, scholarships/grants, and tuition waivers (full and partial) also available.

Support available to part-time students. Financial award application deadline: 2/15. *Faculty research:* Highway safety, highway performance, and intelligent transportation systems; surface mount technology; watershed management. Total annual research expenditures: $138,209. *Unit head:* Dr. Michael S. Switzenbaum, Chair, 414-288-7030, Fax: 414-288-7521, E-mail: michael.switzenbaum@marquette.edu. *Application contact:* Dr. Stephen M. Heinrich, Director of Graduate Studies, 414-288-5466, E-mail: stephen.heinrich@marquette.edu.

Massachusetts Institute of Technology, School of Engineering, Department of Civil and Environmental Engineering, Cambridge, MA 02139-4307. Offers biological oceanography (PhD, Sc D); chemical oceanography (PhD, Sc D); civil and environmental engineering (M Eng, SM, PhD, Sc D); civil and environmental systems (PhD, Sc D); civil engineering (PhD, Sc D, CE); coastal engineering (PhD, Sc D); construction engineering and management (PhD, Sc D); environmental biology (PhD, Sc D); environmental chemistry (PhD, Sc D); environmental engineering (PhD, Sc D); environmental fluid mechanics (PhD, Sc D); geotechnical and geoenvironmental engineering (PhD, Sc D); hydrology (PhD, Sc D); information technology (PhD, Sc D); oceanographic engineering (PhD, Sc D); structures and materials (PhD, Sc D); transportation (PhD, Sc D); SM/MBA. *Faculty:* 36 full-time (5 women). *Students:* 190 full-time (59 women); includes 22 minority (2 African Americans, 14 Asian Americans or Pacific Islanders, 6 Hispanic Americans), 103 international. Average age 26. 478 applicants, 25% accepted, 76 enrolled. In 2009, 72 master's, 14 doctorates awarded. *Degree requirements:* For master's and CE, thesis; for doctorate, comprehensive exam, thesis/dissertation. *Entrance requirements:* For master's and doctorate, GRE General Test. Additional exam requirements/recommendations for international students: Required—TOEFL (minimum score 577 paper-based; 233 computer-based; 90 iBT), IELTS (minimum score 7). *Application deadline:* For fall admission, 1/2 for domestic and international students. Application fee: $75. Electronic applications accepted. *Financial support:* In 2009–10, 185 students received support, including 40 fellowships with tuition reimbursements available (averaging $27,725 per year), 97 research assistantships with tuition reimbursements available (averaging $28,035 per year), 21 teaching assistantships with tuition reimbursements available (averaging $24,802 per year); career-related internships or fieldwork, Federal Work-Study, institutionally sponsored loans, scholarships/grants, health care benefits, and unspecified assistantships also available. *Faculty research:* Environmental chemistry, environmental microbiology, environmental fluid mechanics and coastal engineering, geotechnical engineering and geomechanics, hydrology and hydroclimatology, mechanics of materials and structures, operations research/supply chain, transportation. Total annual research expenditures: $16.6 million. *Unit head:* Prof. Andrew Whittle, Department Head, 617-253-7101. *Application contact:* Patricia Glidden, Graduate Admissions Coordinator, 617-253-7119, Fax: 617-258-6775, E-mail: cee-admissions@mit.edu.

Massachusetts Institute of Technology, School of Engineering, Department of Materials Science and Engineering, Cambridge, MA 02139-4307. Offers archaeological materials (PhD, Sc D); bio- and polymeric materials (PhD, Sc D); electronic, photonic and magnetic materials (PhD, Sc D); emerging, fundamental and computational studies in materials science (Sc D); emerging, fundamental, and computational studies in materials science (PhD); materials engineering (Mat E); materials science and engineering (M Eng, SM, PhD, Sc D); metallurgical engineering (Met E); structural and environmental materials (PhD, Sc D); SM/MBA. *Faculty:* 36 full-time (8 women). *Students:* 222 full-time (62 women); includes 32 minority (3 African Americans, 21 Asian Americans or Pacific Islanders, 8 Hispanic Americans), 125 international. Average age 26. 459 applicants, 23% accepted, 63 enrolled. In 2009, 35 master's, 28 doctorates awarded. Terminal master's awarded for partial completion of doctoral program. *Degree requirements:* For master's and other advanced degree, thesis; for doctorate, comprehensive exam, thesis/dissertation. *Entrance requirements:* For master's and doctorate, GRE General Test. Additional exam requirements/recommendations for international students: Required—IELTS (minimum score 5.5); Recommended—TOEFL (minimum score 577 paper-based; 233 computer-based; 90 iBT). *Application deadline:* For fall admission, 1/1 for domestic and international students. Application fee: $75. Electronic applications accepted. *Financial support:* In 2009–10, 222 students received support, including 55 fellowships with tuition reimbursements available (averaging $22,387 per year), 135 research assistantships with tuition reimbursements available (averaging $27,287 per year), 10 teaching assistantships with tuition reimbursements available (averaging $30,736 per year); career-related internships or fieldwork, Federal Work-Study, institutionally sponsored loans, scholarships/grants, health care benefits, and unspecified assistantships also available. *Faculty research:* Thermodynamics and kinetics of phase transformations, structure of all materials classes: metals, ceramics, semiconductors, polymers, biomaterials, influence of processing on materials structure, structure, property relationships (electrical, magnetic, optical, mechanical). Total annual research expenditures: $22.6 million. *Unit head:* Prof. Edwin L. Thomas, Department Head, 617-253-3300, Fax: 617-252-1775. *Application contact:* Angelita Mireles, Graduate Admissions, 617-253-3302, E-mail: dmse-admissions@mit.edu.

McGill University, Faculty of Graduate and Postdoctoral Studies, Faculty of Engineering, Department of Civil Engineering and Applied Mechanics, Montréal, QC H3A 2T5, Canada. Offers environmental engineering (M Eng, M Sc, PhD); fluid mechanics (M Sc); fluid mechanics and hydraulic engineering (M Eng, PhD); materials engineering (M Eng, PhD); rehabilitation of urban infrastructure (M Eng, PhD); soil behavior (M Eng, PhD); soil mechanics and foundations (M Eng, PhD); structures and structural mechanics (M Eng, PhD); water resources (M Sc); water resources engineering (M Eng, PhD).

Milwaukee School of Engineering, Department of Architectural Engineering and Building Construction, Program in Structural Engineering, Milwaukee, WI 53202-3109. Offers MS. Part-time and evening/weekend programs available. *Faculty:* 4 full-time (0 women), 1 (woman) part-time/adjunct. *Students:* 13 part-time (4 women); includes 1 minority (Asian American or Pacific Islander). Average age 22. 27 applicants, 74% accepted, 3 enrolled. In 2009, 23 master's awarded. *Degree requirements:* For master's, design project. *Entrance requirements:* For master's, GRE General Test or GMAT, 2 letters of recommendation, BS in architectural or structural engineering. Additional exam requirements/recommendations for international students: Required—TOEFL (minimum score 79 iBT). *Application deadline:* Applications are processed on a rolling basis. Application fee: $30. Electronic applications accepted. *Expenses:* Tuition: Part-time $603 per credit. *Financial support:* In 2009–10, 5 students received support; research assistantships, career-related internships or fieldwork available. Support available to part-time students. *Faculty research:* Steel, materials. *Unit head:* Dr. Richard DeVries, Director, 414-277-7596. *Application contact:* David E. Tietyen, Graduate Admissions Director, 800-332-6763, Fax: 414-277-7475, E-mail: wp@msoe.edu.

Northwestern University, McCormick School of Engineering and Applied Science, Department of Civil and Environmental Engineering, Evanston, IL 60208-3109. Offers environmental engineering and science (MS, PhD); geotechnical engineering (MS, PhD); mechanics of materials and solids (MS, PhD); project management (MS, PhD); structural engineering and materials (MS, PhD); theoretical and applied mechanics (MS, PhD), including fluid mechanics, solid mechanics; transportation systems analysis and planning (MS, PhD). MS and PhD admissions and degrees offered through The Graduate School. Part-time programs available. *Faculty:* 25 full-time (2 women), 3 part-time/adjunct (1 woman). *Students:* 63 full-time (19 women), 3 part-time (0 women); includes 7 minority (1 African American, 3 Asian Americans or Pacific Islanders, 3 Hispanic Americans), 34 international. Average age 22. 149 applicants, 30% accepted, 23 enrolled. In 2009, 11 master's, 11 doctorates awarded. Terminal master's awarded for partial completion of doctoral program. *Degree requirements:* For master's, thesis (for some programs); for doctorate, thesis/dissertation. *Entrance requirements:* For master's and doctorate, GRE General Test, minimum 2 letters of recommendation, transcripts from all academic institutions attended. Additional exam requirements/recommendations for international students: Required—TOEFL (minimum score 600 paper-based; 250 computer-based; 100 iBT), IELTS (minimum score 7), TOEFL (minimum score iBT 26). *Application deadline:* For fall admission, 12/31 for domestic and international students. Application fee: $75. Electronic applications accepted. *Financial support:* In 2009–10, 55 students received support, including fellowships with full tuition reimbursements available (averaging $15,390 per year), research assistantships with full tuition reimbursements available (averaging $17,892 per year), 23 teaching assistantships with full tuition reimbursements available (averaging $15,867 per year); career-related internships or fieldwork, institutionally sponsored loans, scholarships/grants, and health care benefits also available. Financial award application deadline: 12/31; financial award applicants required to submit FAFSA. *Faculty research:* Environmental engineering and science, geotechnics, mechanics of materials and solids, structural engineering and materials, transportation systems analysis and planning. Total annual research expenditures: $5.8 million. *Unit head:* Jianmin Qu, Chair, 847-467-4528, Fax: 847-491-4011, E-mail: j-qu@northwestern.edu. *Application contact:* Janet Soule, Academic Coordinator, 847-491-7462, Fax: 847-491-4011, E-mail: civil-info@northwestern.edu.

Ohio University, Graduate College, Russ College of Engineering and Technology, Department of Civil Engineering, Athens, OH 45701-2979. Offers civil engineering (PhD); construction (MS); environmental (MS); geotechnical and geoenvironmental (MS); mechanics (MS); structures (MS); transportation (MS); water resources and structures (MS). Part-time programs available. *Faculty:* 13 full-time (3 women), 3 part-time/adjunct (0 women). *Students:* 18 full-time (2 women), 2 part-time (1 woman), 13 international. 22 applicants, 68% accepted, 1 enrolled. In 2009, 7 master's awarded. *Degree requirements:* For master's, comprehensive exam (for some programs), thesis or alternative; for doctorate, comprehensive exam, thesis/dissertation. *Entrance requirements:* For master's, GRE General Test, minimum GPA of 3.0, 3 letters of recommendation; for doctorate, GRE General Test. Additional exam requirements/recommendations for international students: Required—TOEFL (minimum score 550 paper-based; 80 iBT) or IELTS Academic (minimum score 6.5). *Application deadline:* For fall admission, 5/1 priority date for domestic students, 2/1 priority date for international students; for winter admission, 8/1 priority date for domestic students, 4/1 priority date for international students; for spring admission, 2/1 priority date for domestic students, 7/1 priority date for international students. Applications are processed on a rolling basis. Application fee: $50 ($55 for international students). Electronic applications accepted. *Expenses:* Tuition, state resident: full-time $7839; part-time $323 per quarter hour. Tuition, nonresident: full-time $15,831; part-time $654 per quarter hour. Required fees: $2931. *Financial support:* Research assistantships with full tuition reimbursements, teaching assistantships with full tuition reimbursements, Federal Work-Study, institutionally sponsored loans, scholarships/grants, and unspecified assistantships available. Financial award application deadline: 3/15; financial award applicants required to submit FAFSA. *Faculty research:* Noise abatement, materials and environment, highway infrastructure, subsurface investigation, (pavements, pipes, bridges, etc.). Total annual research expenditures: $1.2 million. *Unit head:* Dr. Gayle F. Mitchell, Chair, 740-593-0430, Fax: 740-593-0625, E-mail: mitchelg@ohio.edu. *Application contact:* Dr. Shad M. Sargand, Graduate Chair, 740-593-1465, Fax: 740-593-0625, E-mail: sargand@ohio.edu.

Oregon State University, Graduate School, College of Engineering, School of Civil and Construction Engineering, Corvallis, OR 97331. Offers civil engineering (MS, PhD); coastal and ocean engineering (M Oc E, PhD); coastal engineering (MS); construction engineering management (MBE, PhD); engineering (M Eng, MAIS); geotechnical engineering (MS, PhD); structural engineering (MS, PhD); transportation engineering (MS, PhD); water engineering (MS, PhD). Part-time programs available. *Faculty:* 25 full-time (5 women), 1 part-time/adjunct (0 women). *Students:* 71 full-time (17 women), 12 part-time (2 women); includes 4 minority (all Asian Americans or Pacific Islanders), 34 international. Average age 28. 75 applicants, 87% accepted, 31 enrolled. In 2009, 26 master's, 7 doctorates awarded. Terminal master's awarded for partial completion of doctoral program. *Degree requirements:* For master's, thesis or alternative; for doctorate, one foreign language, thesis/dissertation. *Entrance requirements:* For master's, GRE General Test, minimum GPA of 3.0 in last 90 hours (3.5 for MS); for doctorate, GRE General Test, minimum GPA of 3.0 in last 90 hours of undergraduate course work. Additional exam requirements/recommendations for international students: Required—TOEFL (minimum score 580 paper-based; 237 computer-based). *Application deadline:* For fall admission, 3/1 priority date for domestic students. Applications are processed on a rolling basis. Application fee: $50. *Expenses:* Tuition, state resident: full-time $9774; part-time $362 per credit. Tuition, nonresident: full-time $15,849; part-time $587 per credit. Required fees: $1639. Full-time tuition and fees vary according to course load and program. *Financial support:* Fellowships, research assistantships with full tuition reimbursements, teaching assistantships with full tuition reimbursements, career-related internships or fieldwork and institutionally sponsored loans available. Support available to part-time students. Financial award application deadline: 2/1. *Faculty research:* Hazardous waste management, carbon cycling, wave forces on structures, pavement design, seismic analysis. Total annual research expenditures: $7.1 million. *Unit head:* Dr. Scott A. Ashford, Head, 541-737-4934. *Application contact:* Kathy Westberg, CCE Graduate Advising School Operations Manager, 541-737-1786, Fax: 541-737-3052, E-mail: kathy.westberg@oregonstate.edu.

Rensselaer Polytechnic Institute, Graduate School, School of Engineering, Department of Civil and Environmental Engineering, Program in Civil Engineering, Troy, NY 12180-3590. Offers geotechnical engineering (M Eng, MS, PhD); mechanics of composite materials and structures (M Eng, MS, PhD); structural engineering (M Eng, MS, PhD); transportation engineering (M Eng, MS, PhD). Part-time programs available. *Faculty:* 6 full-time (0 women), 5 part-time/adjunct (0 women). *Students:* 27 full-time (2 women); includes 4 minority (3 Asian Americans or Pacific Islanders, 1 Hispanic American), 3 international. Average age 24. 70 applicants, 14% accepted, 7 enrolled. In 2009, 5 master's, 1 doctorate awarded. Terminal master's awarded for partial completion of doctoral program. *Degree requirements:* For master's, thesis (for some programs); for doctorate, thesis/dissertation. *Entrance requirements:* For master's and doctorate, GRE. Additional exam requirements/recommendations for international students: Required—TOEFL (minimum score 570 paper-based; 230 computer-based; 89 iBT), IELTS (minimum score 6.5). *Application deadline:* For fall admission, 1/15 priority date for domestic and international students; for spring admission, 8/15 priority date for domestic and international students. Applications are processed on a rolling basis. Application fee: $75. Electronic applications accepted. *Expenses:* Tuition: Full-time $38,100. *Financial support:* In 2009–10, 1 fellowship with full tuition reimbursement (averaging $16,500 per year), 3 research assistantships with full tuition reimbursements (averaging $16,500 per year), 4 teaching assistantships with full tuition reimbursements (averaging $16,500 per year) were awarded; career-related internships or fieldwork and institutionally sponsored loans also available. Financial award application deadline: 2/1. *Faculty research:* Computational mechanics, earthquake engineering, geo-environmental engineering. Total annual research expenditures: $2.7 million. *Unit head:* Dr. Tarek Abdoun, Acting Chair, 518-276-6362, Fax: 518-276-4833, E-mail: abdout@rpi.edu. *Application contact:* Kimberly Boyce, Administrative Assistant, 518-276-6941, Fax: 518-276-4833, E-mail: boycek@rpi.edu.

Stevens Institute of Technology, Graduate School, Charles V. Schaefer Jr. School of Engineering, Department of Civil, Environmental, and Ocean Engineering, Program in Civil Engineering, Hoboken, NJ 07030. Offers civil engineering (PhD); geotechnical engineering (Certificate); geotechnical/geoenvironmental engineering (M Eng, Engr); hydrologic modeling (M Eng); stormwater management (M Eng); structural engineering (M Eng, Engr); water resources engineering (M Eng). *Degree requirements:* For master's, thesis optional; for doctorate, variable foreign language requirement, thesis/dissertation; for other advanced degree, project or thesis. *Entrance requirements:* For doctorate, GRE. Additional exam requirements/recommendations for international students: Required—TOEFL. Electronic applications accepted. *Expenses:* Tuition: Full-time $9900; part-time $1100 per credit. Required fees: $286 per semester.

Texas A&M University, College of Engineering, Zachry Department of Civil Engineering, College Station, TX 77843. Offers construction engineering and management (M Eng, MS, D Eng, PhD); environmental engineering (M Eng, MS, D Eng, PhD); geotechnical engineering (M Eng, MS, D Eng, PhD); materials engineering (M Eng, MS, D Eng, PhD); ocean engineering (M Eng, MS, D Eng, PhD); structural engineering (M Eng, MS, D Eng, PhD); transportation engineering (M Eng, MS, D Eng, PhD); water resources engineering (M Eng, MS, D Eng, PhD). Part-time programs available. *Faculty:* 61. *Students:* 390 full-time (89 women), 42 part-time (6 women); includes 23 minority (2 African Americans, 11 Asian Americans or Pacific Islanders, 10 Hispanic Americans), 281 international. Average age 29. In 2009, 100 master's,

Structural Engineering

Texas A&M University (continued)
36 doctorates awarded. *Degree requirements:* For master's, thesis (MS); for doctorate, dissertation (PhD), internship (D Eng). *Entrance requirements:* For master's and doctorate, GRE General Test. Additional exam requirements/recommendations for international students: Required—TOEFL. *Application deadline:* Applications are processed on a rolling basis. Application fee: $50 ($75 for international students). Electronic applications accepted. *Expenses:* Tuition, state resident: full-time $3991.32; part-time $221.74 per credit hour. Tuition, nonresident: full-time $9049; part-time $502.74 per credit hour. *Financial support:* In 2009–10, fellowships (averaging $4,500 per year), research assistantships (averaging $14,000 per year), teaching assistantships (averaging $14,400 per year) were awarded; career-related internships or fieldwork and institutionally sponsored loans also available. Financial award application deadline: 4/15; financial award applicants required to submit FAFSA. *Unit head:* Dr. Tony Cahill, Head, 979-845-2438, E-mail: t-cahill@civil.tamu.edu. *Application contact:* Graduate Advisor, 979-845-2498, Fax: 979-862-2800, E-mail: ce-grad@tamu.edu.

Tufts University, School of Engineering, Department of Civil and Environmental Engineering, Medford, MA 02155. Offers civil engineering (ME, MS, PhD), including geotechnical engineering, structural engineering; environmental engineering (ME, MS, PhD), including environmental engineering and environmental sciences, environmental geotechnology, environmental health, environmental science and management, hazardous materials management, water resources engineering. Part-time programs available. *Faculty:* 17 full-time, 7 part-time/adjunct. *Students:* 72 (33 women); includes 6 minority (2 African Americans, 4 Asian Americans or Pacific Islanders), 17 international. Average age 27. 170 applicants, 59% accepted, 20 enrolled. In 2009, 17 master's, 3 doctorates awarded. Terminal master's awarded for partial completion of doctoral program. *Degree requirements:* For master's, thesis or alternative; for doctorate, thesis/dissertation. *Entrance requirements:* For master's and doctorate, GRE General Test. Additional exam requirements/recommendations for international students: Required—TOEFL (minimum score 550 paper-based; 213 computer-based; 80 iBT). *Application deadline:* For fall admission, 1/15 priority date for domestic students, 12/15 for international students; for spring admission, 10/15 for domestic students, 9/15 for international students. Applications are processed on a rolling basis. Application fee: $75. Electronic applications accepted. *Expenses:* Tuition: Full-time $38,096; part-time $3962 per credit. Required fees: $686; $40 per year. Tuition and fees vary according to course level, course load, degree level, program and student level. *Financial support:* Fellowships with full tuition reimbursements, research assistantships with full and partial tuition reimbursements, teaching assistantships with full and partial tuition reimbursements, Federal Work-Study, scholarships/grants, tuition waivers (partial), and unspecified assistantships available. Financial award application deadline: 1/15; financial award applicants required to submit FAFSA. *Unit head:* Dr. Kurt Penell, Chair, 617-627-3211, Fax: 617-627-3994. *Application contact:* Laura Sacco, Information Contact, 617-627-3211.

University at Buffalo, the State University of New York, Graduate School, School of Engineering and Applied Sciences, Department of Civil, Structural, and Environmental Engineering, Buffalo, NY 14260. Offers civil engineering (M Eng, MS, PhD); engineering science (MS). Part-time programs available. Postbaccalaureate distance learning degree programs offered (minimal on-campus study). *Faculty:* 27 full-time (4 women), 3 part-time/adjunct (2 women). *Students:* 136 full-time (26 women), 14 part-time (3 women); includes 10 minority (1 American Indian/Alaska Native, 4 Asian Americans or Pacific Islanders, 5 Hispanic Americans), 100 international. Average age 28. 514 applicants, 40% accepted, 59 enrolled. In 2009, 25 master's, 8 doctorates awarded. Terminal master's awarded for partial completion of doctoral program. *Degree requirements:* For master's, thesis optional, project, thesis, or comprehensive exam; for doctorate, thesis/dissertation. *Entrance requirements:* For master's and doctorate, GRE General Test, letters of reference. Additional exam requirements/recommendations for international students: Required—TOEFL (minimum score 550 paper-based; 213 computer-based; 79 iBT). *Application deadline:* For fall admission, 1/15 priority date for domestic and international students; for spring admission, 9/15 for domestic and international students. Applications are processed on a rolling basis. Application fee: $50. Electronic applications accepted. *Financial support:* In 2009–10, 79 students received support, including 18 fellowships with full tuition reimbursements available (averaging $17,200 per year), 34 research assistantships with full tuition reimbursements available (averaging $14,000 per year), 27 teaching assistantships with full tuition reimbursements available (averaging $14,700 per year); career-related internships or fieldwork, Federal Work-Study, institutionally sponsored loans, scholarships/grants, traineeships, health care benefits, tuition waivers (full and partial), and unspecified assistantships also available. Support available to part-time students. Financial award application deadline: 1/15; financial award applicants required to submit FAFSA. *Faculty research:* Environmental engineering and fluid mechanics, structural dynamics, geomechanics, earthquake engineering computational mechanics. Total annual research expenditures: $7.3 million. *Unit head:* Dr. A. Scott Weber, Chairman, 716-645-2114, Fax: 716-645-3733, E-mail: sweber@eng.buffalo.edu. *Application contact:* Dr. Amjad J. Aref, Director of Graduate Studies, 716-645-4369, Fax: 716-645-3733, E-mail: cjb@buffalo.edu.

The University of Alabama in Huntsville, School of Graduate Studies, College of Engineering, Department of Civil and Environmental Engineering, Huntsville, AL 35899. Offers civil and environmental engineering (PhD); civil engineering (MSE), including environmental and water resource engineering, geotechnical engineering, structural engineering and structural mechanics, transportation engineering. Part-time and evening/weekend programs available. *Faculty:* 6 full-time (1 woman). *Students:* 12 full-time (3 women), 7 part-time (1 woman); includes 3 minority (2 African Americans, 1 Asian American or Pacific Islander), 5 international. Average age 33. 26 applicants, 58% accepted, 9 enrolled. In 2009, 10 master's, 2 doctorates awarded. *Degree requirements:* For master's, comprehensive exam, thesis or alternative, oral and written exams; for doctorate, comprehensive exam, thesis/dissertation, oral and written exams. *Entrance requirements:* For master's, GRE General Test, BSE, minimum GPA of 3.0; for doctorate, GRE General Test, minimum GPA of 3.0. Additional exam requirements/recommendations for international students: Required—TOEFL (minimum score 500 paper-based; 173 computer-based; 62 iBT). *Application deadline:* For fall admission, 7/15 for domestic students, 4/1 for international students; for spring admission, 11/30 for domestic students, 9/1 for international students. Applications are processed on a rolling basis. Application fee: $40 ($50 for international students). Electronic applications accepted. *Expenses:* Tuition, state resident: part-time $355.75 per credit hour. Tuition, nonresident: part-time $847.10 per credit hour. Required fees: $210.80 per semester. Tuition and fees vary according to course load and program. *Financial support:* In 2009–10, 10 students received support, including 4 research assistantships with full and partial tuition reimbursements available (averaging $11,525 per year), 6 teaching assistantships with full and partial tuition reimbursements available (averaging $9,678 per year); career-related internships or fieldwork, Federal Work-Study, institutionally sponsored loans, scholarships/grants, health care benefits, and unspecified assistantships also available. Support available to part-time students. Financial award application deadline: 4/1; financial award applicants required to submit FAFSA. *Faculty research:* Hydrologic modeling, orbital debris impact, hydrogeology, environmental engineering, transportation engineering. Total annual research expenditures: $1.5 million. *Unit head:* Dr. Houssam Toutanji, Chair, 256-824-7361, Fax: 256-824-6724, E-mail: toutanji@cee.uah.edu. *Application contact:* Kathy Biggs, Graduate Studies Admissions Manager, 256-824-6199, Fax: 256-824-6405, E-mail: deangrad@uah.edu.

University of Alberta, Faculty of Graduate Studies and Research, Department of Civil and Environmental Engineering, Edmonton, AB T6G 2E1, Canada. Offers construction engineering and management (M Eng, M Sc, PhD); environmental engineering (M Eng, M Sc, PhD); environmental science (M Sc, PhD); geoenvironmental engineering (M Eng, M Sc, PhD); geotechnical engineering (M Eng, M Sc, PhD); mining engineering (M Eng, M Sc, PhD); petroleum engineering (M Eng, M Sc, PhD); structural engineering (M Eng, M Sc, PhD); water resources (M Eng, M Sc, PhD). Part-time programs available. Postbaccalaureate distance learning degree programs offered (minimal on-campus study). *Faculty:* 44 full-time (3 women), 2 part-time/adjunct (0 women). *Students:* 215 full-time (49 women), 99 part-time (19 women). 1,428 applicants, 15% accepted, 123 enrolled. In 2009, 124 master's, 34 doctorates awarded. *Degree requirements:* For master's, thesis (for some programs); for doctorate, thesis/dissertation. *Entrance requirements:* For master's, minimum GPA of 3.0 in last 2 years of undergraduate studies; for doctorate, minimum GPA of 3.0. Additional exam requirements/recommendations for international students: Required—TOEFL (minimum score 550 paper-based; 213 computer-based). *Application deadline:* For fall admission, 6/1 priority date for domestic students, 6/1 for international students; for winter admission, 11/1 for domestic students, 9/15 for international students. Applications are processed on a rolling basis. Application fee: $0 Canadian dollars. Electronic applications accepted. Tuition and fees charges are reported in Canadian dollars. *Expenses:* Tuition, area resident: Full-time $4626.24 Canadian dollars; part-time $99.72 Canadian dollars per unit. International tuition: $8216 Canadian dollars full-time. Required fees: $3589.92 Canadian dollars; $99.72 Canadian dollars per unit. $215 Canadian dollars per term. *Financial support:* In 2009–10, 88 research assistantships with full and partial tuition reimbursements, 134 teaching assistantships with full and partial tuition reimbursements were awarded; scholarships/grants and tuition waivers (full and partial) also available. Financial award application deadline: 4/1. *Faculty research:* Mining. Total annual research expenditures: $6,791 Canadian dollars. *Unit head:* Dr. David Zhu, Associate Chair, Graduate Studies, 780-492-1198, Fax: 403-492-8198. *Application contact:* Gwen Mendoza, Student Services Officer, 403-492-1539, Fax: 403-492-0249, E-mail: civegrad@ualberta.ca.

University of California, Berkeley, Graduate Division, College of Engineering, Department of Civil and Environmental Engineering, Berkeley, CA 94720-1500. Offers engineering and project management (M Eng, MS, D Eng, PhD); environmental engineering (M Eng, MS, D Eng, PhD); geoengineering (M Eng, MS, D Eng, PhD); structural engineering, mechanics and materials (M Eng, MS, D Eng, PhD); transportation engineering (M Eng, MS, D Eng, PhD); M Arch/MS; MCP/MS; MPP/MS. *Students:* 368 full-time (125 women). Average age 27. 921 applicants, 179 enrolled. In 2009, 158 master's, 39 doctorates awarded. *Degree requirements:* For master's, comprehensive exam or thesis (MS); for doctorate, thesis/dissertation, qualifying exam. *Entrance requirements:* For master's, GRE General Test, minimum GPA of 3.0, 3 letters of recommendation; for doctorate, GRE General Test, minimum GPA of 3.5, 3 letters of recommendation. Additional exam requirements/recommendations for international students: Required—TOEFL (minimum score 570 paper-based; 230 computer-based). *Application deadline:* For fall admission, 2/3 for domestic students. Application fee: $70 ($90 for international students). Electronic applications accepted. *Financial support:* Fellowships, research assistantships, teaching assistantships, unspecified assistantships available. *Unit head:* Prof. Lisa Alvarez-Cohen, Chair, 510-643-8739, Fax: 510-643-5264, E-mail: chair@ce.berkeley.edu. *Application contact:* Shelly Okimoto, Graduate Advisor, 510-642-6464, Fax: 510-643-5264, E-mail: aao@ce.berkeley.edu.

University of California, San Diego, Office of Graduate Studies, Department of Structural Engineering, La Jolla, CA 92093. Offers MS, PhD. Part-time programs available. *Degree requirements:* For master's, comprehensive exam or thesis; for doctorate, thesis/dissertation, qualifying exam. *Entrance requirements:* For master's and doctorate, GRE General Test, minimum GPA of 3.0. Additional exam requirements/recommendations for international students: Required—TOEFL. *Faculty research:* Advanced large-scale civil, mechanical, and aerospace structures.

University of Central Florida, College of Engineering and Computer Science, Department of Civil, Environmental, and Construction Engineering, Program in Civil Engineering, Orlando, FL 32816. Offers civil engineering (MS, MSCE, PhD); construction engineering (Certificate); structural engineering (Certificate); transportation engineering (Certificate). Part-time and evening/weekend programs available. *Students:* 53 full-time (8 women), 68 part-time (20 women); includes 22 minority (4 African Americans, 1 American Indian/Alaska Native, 5 Asian Americans or Pacific Islanders, 12 Hispanic Americans), 34 international. Average age 29. 90 applicants, 73% accepted, 45 enrolled. In 2009, 30 master's, 2 doctorates awarded. *Degree requirements:* For master's, thesis or alternative; for doctorate, thesis/dissertation, departmental qualifying exam, candidacy exam. *Entrance requirements:* For master's, GRE General Test, minimum GPA of 3.0 in last 60 hours; for doctorate, GRE General Test, minimum GPA of 3.5 in last 60 hours. Additional exam requirements/recommendations for international students: Required—TOEFL. *Application deadline:* For fall admission, 7/15 priority date for domestic students; for spring admission, 12/15 priority date for domestic students. Application fee: $30. Electronic applications accepted. *Expenses:* Tuition, state resident: part-time $306.31 per credit hour. Tuition, nonresident: part-time $1099.01 per credit hour. Part-time tuition and fees vary according to degree level and program. *Financial support:* In 2009–10, 30 students received support, including 7 fellowships with partial tuition reimbursements available (averaging $7,100 per year), 19 research assistantships with partial tuition reimbursements available (averaging $11,600 per year), 12 teaching assistantships with partial tuition reimbursements available (averaging $9,700 per year); career-related internships or fieldwork, Federal Work-Study, institutionally sponsored loans, tuition waivers (partial), and unspecified assistantships also available. Financial award application deadline: 3/1; financial award applicants required to submit FAFSA.

University of Colorado at Boulder, Graduate School, College of Engineering and Applied Science, Department of Civil, Environmental, and Architectural Engineering, Boulder, CO 80309. Offers building systems (MS, PhD); construction engineering management (MS, PhD); environmental engineering (MS, PhD); geotechnical engineering and geomechanics (MS, PhD); hydrology, water resources and environmental fluid mechanics (MS, PhD); structural engineering and structural mechanics (MS, PhD). *Faculty:* 39 full-time (5 women). *Students:* 202 full-time (62 women), 29 part-time (6 women); includes 34 minority (3 African Americans, 3 American Indian/Alaska Native, 12 Asian Americans or Pacific Islanders, 16 Hispanic Americans), 53 international. Average age 29. 384 applicants, 44% accepted, 80 enrolled. In 2009, 60 master's, 7 doctorates awarded. *Degree requirements:* For master's, comprehensive exam, thesis or alternative; for doctorate, thesis/dissertation. *Entrance requirements:* For master's, GRE General Test, minimum undergraduate GPA of 3.0. *Application deadline:* For fall admission, 3/1 for domestic students, 12/1 for international students; for spring admission, 10/31 for domestic students, 10/1 for international students. Application fee: $50 ($60 for international students). *Financial support:* In 2009–10, 45 fellowships (averaging $7,876 per year), 68 research assistantships (averaging $15,204 per year) were awarded. Financial award application deadline: 1/15. *Faculty research:* Building systems engineering, construction engineering and management, environmental engineering, geoenvironmental engineering, geotechnical engineering, materials and mechanics, structural engineering, water resources engineering, life-cycle engineering. Total annual research expenditures: $6.1 million.

University of Dayton, Graduate School, School of Engineering, Department of Civil and Environmental Engineering, Dayton, OH 45469-1300. Offers engineering mechanics (MSEM); environmental engineering (MSCE); geotechnical engineering (MSCE); structural engineering (MSCE); transport engineering (MSCE); water resources engineering (MSCE). Part-time programs available. *Faculty:* 8 full-time (2 women), 1 part-time/adjunct (0 women). *Students:* 10 full-time (6 women), 8 part-time (1 woman); includes 3 minority (all African Americans), 7 international. Average age 29. 35 applicants, 49% accepted, 6 enrolled. In 2009, 3 master's awarded. *Degree requirements:* For master's, thesis optional. *Entrance requirements:* Additional exam requirements/recommendations for international students: Required—TOEFL (minimum score 550 paper-based; 213 computer-based; 80 iBT). *Application deadline:* For fall admission, 8/1 for domestic students, 3/1 priority date for international students; for winter admission, 7/1 priority date for international students; for spring admission, 1/1 priority date for international students. Applications are processed on a rolling basis. Application fee: $0 ($50 for international students). Electronic applications accepted. *Expenses:* Tuition: Full-time $8412; part-time $701 per credit hour. Required fees: $325; $65 per course. $25 per semester. Tuition and fees vary according to course load, degree level and program. *Financial support:* In 2009–10, 3 research assistantships (averaging $10,780 per year), 4 teaching assistantships with partial tuition reimbursements (averaging $5,110 per year) were awarded. Financial award applicants required to submit FAFSA. *Faculty research:* Physical modeling of hydraulic systems, finite element methods, mechanics of composite materials, transportation systems safety, high-velocity wear. Total annual research expenditures: $421,839. *Unit head:* Dr. Donald V. Chase,

Interim Chair, 937-229-3847, Fax: 937-229-3491, E-mail: donald.chase@notes.udayton.edu. *Application contact:* Graduate Admissions, 937-229-4411, Fax: 937-229-4729, E-mail: gradadmission@udayton.edu.

University of Delaware, College of Engineering, Department of Civil and Environmental Engineering, Newark, DE 19716. Offers environmental engineering (MAS, MCE, PhD); geotechnical engineering (MAS, MCE, PhD); ocean engineering (MAS, MCE, PhD); structural engineering (MAS, MCE, PhD); transportation engineering (MAS, MCE, PhD); water resource engineering (MAS, MCE, PhD). Part-time programs available. Terminal master's awarded for partial completion of doctoral program. *Degree requirements:* For master's, thesis; for doctorate, thesis/dissertation. *Entrance requirements:* For master's and doctorate, GRE General Test. Additional exam requirements/recommendations for international students: Required—TOEFL. Electronic applications accepted. *Faculty research:* Structural engineering and mechanics; transportation engineering; ocean engineering; soil mechanics and foundation; water resources and environmental engineering.

University of Maine, Graduate School, College of Engineering, Department of Civil and Environmental Engineering, Orono, ME 04469. Offers civil engineering (MS, PhD), including environmental engineering, geotechnical engineering, structural engineering. *Faculty:* 10 full-time (2 women), 2 part-time/adjunct (0 women). *Students:* 28 full-time (7 women), 15 part-time (2 women); includes 2 minority (both American Indian/Alaska Native), 3 international. Average age 27. 31 applicants, 35% accepted, 7 enrolled. In 2009, 6 master's, 1 doctorate awarded. *Degree requirements:* For doctorate, thesis/dissertation. *Entrance requirements:* For master's and doctorate, GRE General Test. Additional exam requirements/recommendations for international students: Required—TOEFL. *Application deadline:* For fall admission, 2/1 priority date for domestic students. Applications are processed on a rolling basis. Application fee: $65. Electronic applications accepted. *Financial support:* In 2009–10, 15 research assistantships with tuition reimbursements (averaging $15,815 per year), 3 teaching assistantships with tuition reimbursements (averaging $12,790 per year) were awarded; Federal Work-Study, institutionally sponsored loans, scholarships/grants, and tuition waivers (full and partial) also available. Financial award application deadline: 3/1. *Unit head:* Dr. Eric Landis, Chair. *Application contact:* Scott G. Delcourt, Associate Dean of the Graduate School, 207-581-3291, Fax: 207-581-3232, E-mail: graduate@maine.edu.

University of Memphis, Graduate School, Herff College of Engineering, Department of Civil Engineering, Memphis, TN 38152. Offers civil engineering (PhD); environmental engineering (MS); foundation engineering (MS); structural engineering (MS); transportation engineering (MS); water resources engineering (MS). *Faculty:* 12 full-time (1 woman), 1 part-time/adjunct (0 women). *Students:* 12 full-time (3 women), 16 part-time (6 women); includes 2 minority (1 African American, 1 Asian American or Pacific Islander), 9 international. Average age 28. 18 applicants, 94% accepted, 8 enrolled. In 2009, 11 master's awarded. *Degree requirements:* For master's, comprehensive exam, thesis or alternative; for doctorate, thesis/dissertation. *Entrance requirements:* For master's, GRE General Test or MAT, minimum undergraduate GPA of 2.5. *Application deadline:* For fall admission, 8/1 for domestic students; for spring admission, 12/1 for domestic students. Application fee: $35 ($60 for international students). *Expenses:* Tuition, state resident: full-time $6246; part-time $347 per credit hour. Tuition, nonresident: full-time $15,894; part-time $883 per credit hour. Required fees: $1160. Full-time tuition and fees vary according to course load, degree level and program. *Financial support:* In 2009–10, 6 students received support; fellowships with full tuition reimbursements available, research assistantships with full tuition reimbursements available, career-related internships or fieldwork, Federal Work-Study, scholarships/grants, and unspecified assistantships available. Financial award application deadline: 2/15; financial award applicants required to submit FAFSA. *Faculty research:* Structural response to earthquakes, pavement design, water quality, transportation safety, intermodal transportation. *Unit head:* Dr. Sharam Pezeshk, Interim Chair, 901-678-2746, Fax: 901-678-3026. *Application contact:* Dr. Roger Meier, Coordinator of Graduate Studies, 901-678-3284.

University of Michigan, Horace H. Rackham School of Graduate Studies, College of Engineering, Department of Civil and Environmental Engineering, Ann Arbor, MI 48109. Offers civil engineering (MSE, PhD, CE); construction engineering and management (M Eng, MSE); environmental engineering (MSE, PhD); structural engineering (M Eng); MBA/MSE. Part-time programs available. *Faculty:* 28 full-time (8 women). *Students:* 104 full-time (34 women), 1 part-time (0 women); includes 9 minority (2 African Americans, 5 Asian Americans or Pacific Islanders, 2 Hispanic Americans), 49 international. 413 applicants, 29% accepted, 40 enrolled. In 2009, 47 master's, 18 doctorates awarded. *Degree requirements:* For master's, thesis optional; for doctorate, comprehensive exam, thesis/dissertation, oral defense of dissertation, preliminary and written exams. *Entrance requirements:* For master's and doctorate, GRE General Test. Additional exam requirements/recommendations for international students: Required—TOEFL (minimum score 560 paper-based; 220 computer-based). *Application deadline:* Applications are processed on a rolling basis. Application fee: $60 ($75 for international students). Electronic applications accepted. *Expenses:* Tuition, state resident: full-time $17,286; part-time $1099 per credit hour. Tuition, nonresident: full-time $34,944; part-time $2080 per credit hour. Required fees: $95 per semester. Tuition and fees vary according to course load, degree level and program. *Financial support:* Fellowships, research assistantships, teaching assistantships, institutionally sponsored loans and tuition waivers (partial) available. Financial award application deadline: 1/19. *Faculty research:* Construction engineering and management; geotechnical engineering; earthquake-resistant design of structures; environmental chemistry and microbiology; cost engineering; environmental and water resources engineering. *Unit head:* Nancy Love, Chair, 734-764-8405, Fax: 734-764-4292, E-mail: nglove@umich.edu. *Application contact:* Kimberly Smith, Student Advisor, 734-764-8405, Fax: 734-647-2127, E-mail: kansmith@umich.edu.

University of Missouri, Graduate School, College of Engineering, Department of Civil and Environmental Engineering, Columbia, MO 65211. Offers civil engineering (MS, PhD); environmental engineering (MS, PhD); geotechnical engineering (MS, PhD); structural engineering (MS, PhD); transportation and highway engineering (MS); water resources (MS, PhD). *Degree requirements:* For master's, report or thesis; for doctorate, thesis/dissertation. *Entrance requirements:* For master's and doctorate, GRE General Test. Additional exam requirements/recommendations for international students: Required—TOEFL (minimum score 550 paper-based; 213 computer-based; 79 iBT).

University of New Brunswick Fredericton, School of Graduate Studies, Faculty of Engineering, Department of Civil Engineering, Fredericton, NB E3B 5A3, Canada. Offers construction engineering and management (M Eng, M Sc E, PhD); environmental engineering (M Eng, M Sc E, PhD); environmental studies (M Eng); geotechnical engineering (M Eng, M Sc E, PhD); groundwater/hydrology (M Eng, M Sc E, PhD); materials (M Eng, M Sc E, PhD); pavements (M Eng, M Sc E, PhD); structures (M Eng, M Sc E, PhD); transportation (M Eng, M Sc E, PhD). Part-time programs available. *Faculty:* 18 full-time (1 woman), 1 (woman) part-time/adjunct. *Students:* 42 full-time (9 women), 18 part-time (2 women). In 2009, 11 master's, 4 doctorates awarded. *Degree requirements:* For master's, thesis, proposal; for doctorate, comprehensive exam, thesis/dissertation, Qualifying exam; Proposal; 27 credit hours of courses. *Entrance requirements:* For master's, Minimum GPA of 3.0; BScE in Civil Engineering or related engineering degree.; for doctorate, Minimum GPA of 3.0; Candidates are normally required to have a graduate degree in engineering or applied science. Additional exam requirements/recommendations for international students: Required—TOEFL (minimum score 580 paper-based; 237 computer-based), TWE (minimum score 4), or IELTS (minimum score 7.5). *Application deadline:* For fall admission, 5/1 priority date for domestic students; for winter admission, 11/1 priority date for domestic students. Applications are processed on a rolling basis. Application fee: $50 Canadian dollars. Tuition and fees charges are reported in Canadian dollars. *Expenses:* Tuition, area resident: Full-time $5562 Canadian dollars; part-time $2781 Canadian dollars per year. Required fees: $49.75 Canadian dollars per term. *Financial support:* In 2009–10, 51 research assistantships (averaging $7,000 per year), 43 teaching assistantships (averaging $2,000 per year) were awarded; career-related internships or fieldwork and scholarships/grants also available. *Faculty research:* Construction engineering and management, concrete materials and structural engineering, transportation and asset management, geotechnical engineering, water and environmental engineering. *Unit head:* Dr. Eric Hildebrand, Director of Graduate Studies, 506-453-5113, Fax: 506-453-3568, E-mail: ktm@unb.ca. *Application contact:* Joyce Moore, Graduate Secretary, 506-452-6127, Fax: 506-453-3568, E-mail: civil-grad@unb.ca.

University of North Dakota, Graduate School, School of Engineering and Mines, Department of Civil Engineering, Grand Forks, ND 58202. Offers civil engineering (M Engr); sanitary engineering (M Engr), including soils and structures engineering, surface mining engineering. Part-time programs available. *Degree requirements:* For master's, comprehensive exam, thesis or alternative. *Entrance requirements:* For master's, GRE General Test, minimum GPA of 2.5. Additional exam requirements/recommendations for international students: Required—TOEFL (minimum score 550 paper-based; 213 computer-based; 79 iBT), IELTS (minimum score 6.5). Electronic applications accepted. *Faculty research:* Soil-structures, environmental-water resources.

University of Oklahoma, Graduate College, College of Engineering, School of Civil Engineering and Environmental Science, Program in Civil Engineering, Norman, OK 73019-0390. Offers civil engineering (MS, PhD); geotechnical engineering (MS); structures (MS). Part-time programs available. *Students:* 42 full-time (8 women), 9 part-time (1 woman); includes 4 minority (1 African American, 1 American Indian/Alaska Native, 1 Asian American or Pacific Islander, 1 Hispanic American), 28 international. 18 applicants, 100% accepted, 6 enrolled. In 2009, 13 master's, 3 doctorates awarded. *Degree requirements:* For master's, comprehensive exam, oral exams; for doctorate, thesis/dissertation, oral and qualifying exams. *Entrance requirements:* For master's, minimum GPA of 3.0; for doctorate, minimum graduate GPA of 3.5. Additional exam requirements/recommendations for international students: Required—TOEFL (minimum score 600 paper-based). *Application deadline:* For fall admission, 4/1 priority date for domestic students, 4/1 for international students; for spring admission, 11/1 for domestic students, 9/1 for international students. Applications are processed on a rolling basis. Application fee: $40 ($90 for international students). Electronic applications accepted. *Expenses:* Tuition, state resident: full-time $3744; part-time $156 per credit hour. Tuition, nonresident: full-time $13,577; part-time $565.70 per credit hour. Required fees: $2415; $90.10 per credit hour. *Financial support:* Scholarships/grants and unspecified assistantships available. Financial award application deadline: 3/1; financial award applicants required to submit FAFSA. *Faculty research:* Structural engineering, environmental modeling, natural hazards, transport and fate of chemicals, geotechnical engineering. *Unit head:* Robert C. Knox, Director, 405-325-5911, Fax: 405-325-4217, E-mail: rknox@ou.edu. *Application contact:* Robert C. Knox, Director, 405-325-5911, Fax: 405-325-4217, E-mail: rknox@ou.edu.

The University of Texas at Tyler, College of Engineering and Computer Science, Department of Civil Engineering, Tyler, TX 75799-0001. Offers environmental engineering (MS); industrial safety (MS); structural engineering (MS); transportation engineering (MS); water resources engineering (MS). Part-time and evening/weekend programs available. *Faculty:* 6 full-time (0 women). *Students:* 5 full-time (1 woman), 7 part-time (1 woman); includes 1 African American, 1 Asian American or Pacific Islander, 1 Hispanic American, 1 international. Average age 26. 5 applicants, 80% accepted, 3 enrolled. *Degree requirements:* For master's, thesis optional. *Entrance requirements:* For master's, GRE General Test, bachelor's degree in engineering, associated science degree. Additional exam requirements/recommendations for international students: Required—TOEFL (minimum score 79 computer-based). *Application deadline:* For fall admission, 8/17 priority date for domestic students, 7/1 priority date for international students; for spring admission, 12/21 priority date for domestic students, 11/1 priority date for international students. Application fee: $25 ($50 for international students). *Expenses:* Tuition, state resident: part-time $665 per semester hour. Tuition, nonresident: part-time $942 per semester hour. Part-time tuition and fees vary according to degree level and program. *Financial support:* Application deadline: 7/1. *Faculty research:* Non-destructive strength testing, indoor air quality, transportation routing and signaling, pavement replacement criteria, flood water routing, construction and long-term behavior of innovative geotechnical foundation and embankment construction used in highway construction, engineering education. *Unit head:* Dr. Ron Welch, Chair, 903-566-7002, Fax: 903-566-7337, E-mail: rwelch@uttyler.edu. *Application contact:* Dr. Torey Nalbone, Program Chair, 903-565-5520, Fax: 903-566-7337, E-mail: tnalbone@uttyler.edu.

University of Washington, Graduate School, College of Engineering, Department of Civil and Environmental Engineering, Seattle, WA 98195-2700. Offers construction engineering (MSCE); environmental engineering (MS, MSCE, MSE, PhD); hydrology, water resources, and environmental fluid mechanics (MS, MSCE, MSE, PhD); structural and geotechnical engineering and mechanics (MS, MSCE, MSE, PhD); transportation and construction engineering (MS, MSE, PhD); transportation engineering (MSCE). Part-time programs available. Postbaccalaureate distance learning degree programs offered (no on-campus study). *Faculty:* 36 full-time (9 women), 16 part-time/adjunct (6 women). *Students:* 186 full-time (62 women), 57 part-time (10 women); includes 35 minority (24 Asian Americans or Pacific Islanders, 11 Hispanic Americans), 58 international. 360 applicants, 68% accepted, 98 enrolled. In 2009, 74 master's, 8 doctorates awarded. Terminal master's awarded for partial completion of doctoral program. *Degree requirements:* For master's, thesis (for some programs); for doctorate, comprehensive exam, thesis/dissertation. *Entrance requirements:* For master's, GRE General Test, minimum GPA of 3.0; for doctorate, GRE, minimum GPA of 3.5. Additional exam requirements/recommendations for international students: Required—TOEFL (minimum score 580 paper-based; 237 computer-based; 70 iBT). *Application deadline:* For fall admission, 1/15 priority date for domestic and international students. Applications are processed on a rolling basis. Application fee: $65. Electronic applications accepted. *Financial support:* In 2009–10, 5 students received support, including 13 fellowships with full and partial tuition reimbursements available (averaging $16,173 per year), 68 research assistantships with full tuition reimbursements available (averaging $16,173 per year), 12 teaching assistantships with full tuition reimbursements available (averaging $16,173 per year); scholarships/grants also available. Financial award application deadline: 1/15. *Faculty research:* Environmental/water resources, hydrology; construction/transportation; structures/ geotechnical. Total annual research expenditures: $11.4 million. *Unit head:* Dr. Gregory R. Miller, Professor and Chair, 206-543-0350, Fax: 206-543-1543, E-mail: gmiller@uw.edu. *Application contact:* Lorna Latal, Graduate Adviser, 206-543-2574, Fax: 206-543-1543, E-mail: llatal@u.washington.edu.

Washington University in St. Louis, Henry Edwin Sever Graduate School of Engineering and Applied Science, Department of Mechanical, Aerospace and Structural Engineering, St. Louis, MO 63130-4899. Offers MS, D Sc, PhD. Part-time programs available. Terminal master's awarded for partial completion of doctoral program. *Degree requirements:* For master's, thesis optional; for doctorate, thesis/dissertation optional. *Entrance requirements:* For master's, GRE; for doctorate, GRE General Test, departmental qualifying exam. *Faculty research:* Aerosols science and technology, applied mechanics, biomechanics and biomedical engineering, design, dynamic systems, combustion science, composite materials, materials science.

Western Michigan University, Graduate College, College of Engineering and Applied Sciences, Department of Civil and Construction Engineering, Kalamazoo, MI 49008. Offers civil engineering (MS), including construction engineering and management, structural engineering, transportation engineering. *Entrance requirements:* For master's, minimum GPA of 3.0.

Surveying Science and Engineering

The Ohio State University, Graduate School, College of Engineering, Program in Geodetic Science and Surveying, Columbus, OH 43210. Offers MS, PhD. *Faculty:* 12. *Students:* 15 full-time (2 women), 1 (woman) part-time; includes 1 minority (African American), 12 international. Average age 28. In 2009, 1 doctorate awarded. *Degree requirements:* For master's, thesis optional; for doctorate, thesis/dissertation. *Entrance requirements:* For master's, GRE General Test (if overall GPA less than 3.0); for doctorate, GRE General Test (if GPA is below 3.0 overall). Additional exam requirements/recommendations for international students: Recommended—TOEFL (minimum score 600 paper-based; 250 computer-based). *Application deadline:* For fall admission, 8/15 priority date for domestic students, 7/1 priority date for international students; for winter admission, 12/1 priority date for domestic students, 11/1 priority date for international students; for spring admission, 3/1 priority date for domestic students, 2/1 priority date for international students. Applications are processed on a rolling basis. Application fee: $40 ($50 for international students). Electronic applications accepted. *Expenses:* Tuition, state resident: full-time $10,683. Tuition, nonresident: full-time $25,923. Tuition and fees vary according to course load and program. *Financial support:* Fellowships, research assistantships, teaching assistantships, Federal Work-Study and institutionally sponsored loans available. Support available to part-time students. *Faculty research:* Photogrammetry, cartography, geodesy, land information systems. *Unit head:* Alan S. Saalfeld, Graduate Studies Committee Chair, 614-292-8787, Fax: 614-292-3780, E-mail: soalfeld.1@osu.edu. *Application contact:* 614-292-944, Fax: 614-292-3895, E-mail: domestic.grad@osu.edu.

University of New Brunswick Fredericton, School of Graduate Studies, Faculty of Engineering, Department of Geodesy and Geomatics, Fredericton, NB E3B 5A3, Canada. Offers land information management (Diploma); mapping, charting and geodesy (Diploma); surveying engineering (M Eng, M Sc E, PhD). *Faculty:* 10 full-time (2 women). *Students:* 37 full-time (7 women), 4 part-time (1 woman). In 2009, 10 master's, 3 doctorates awarded. *Degree requirements:* For master's, thesis; for doctorate, comprehensive exam, thesis/dissertation, qualifying exam. *Entrance requirements:* For master's and doctorate, minimum GPA of 3.0. Additional exam requirements/recommendations for international students: Required—TOEFL (minimum score 580 paper-based), TWE (minimum score 4). *Application deadline:* For fall admission, 3/1 priority date for domestic students. Applications are processed on a rolling basis. Application fee: $50 Canadian dollars. Tuition and fees charges are reported in Canadian dollars. *Expenses:* Tuition, area resident: Full-time $5562 Canadian dollars; part-time $2781 Canadian dollars per year. Required fees: $49.75 Canadian dollars per term. *Financial support:* In 2009–10, 2 fellowships, 46 research assistantships, 23 teaching assistantships were awarded. *Faculty research:* Remote sensing, ocean mapping, land administration. *Unit head:* Dr. Sue Nichols, Director of Graduate Studies, 506-453-5141, Fax: 506-453-4943, E-mail: nichols@unb.ca. *Application contact:* Sylvia Whitaker, Graduate Secretary, 506-458-7085, Fax: 506-453-4943, E-mail: swhitake@unb.ca.

Transportation and Highway Engineering

Auburn University, Graduate School, Ginn College of Engineering, Department of Civil Engineering, Auburn University, AL 36849. Offers construction engineering and management (MCE, MS, PhD); environmental engineering (MCE, MS, PhD); geotechnical/materials engineering (MCE, MS, PhD); hydraulics/hydrology (MCE, MS, PhD); structural engineering (MCE, MS, PhD); transportation engineering (MCE, MS, PhD). Part-time programs available. *Faculty:* 21 full-time (1 woman), 3 part-time/adjunct (1 woman). *Students:* 46 full-time (15 women), 39 part-time (5 women); includes 4 minority (3 African Americans, 1 Asian American or Pacific Islander), 29 international. Average age 26. 136 applicants, 43% accepted, 26 enrolled. In 2009, 19 master's, 4 doctorates awarded. *Degree requirements:* For master's, project (MCE), thesis (MS); for doctorate, comprehensive exam, thesis/dissertation. *Entrance requirements:* For master's and doctorate, GRE General Test. *Application deadline:* For fall admission, 7/7 for domestic students; for spring admission, 11/24 for domestic students. Applications are processed on a rolling basis. Application fee: $50 ($60 for international students). Electronic applications accepted. *Expenses:* Tuition, state resident: full-time $6240. Tuition, nonresident: full-time $18,720. International tuition: $18,938 full-time. Required fees: $492. Tuition and fees vary according to course load, program and reciprocity agreements. *Financial support:* Fellowships, research assistantships, teaching assistantships, Federal Work-Study available. Support available to part-time students. Financial award application deadline: 3/15; financial award applicants required to submit FAFSA. *Unit head:* Dr. J. Michael Stallings, Head, 334-844-4320. *Application contact:* Dr. George Flowers, Dean of the Graduate School, 334-844-2125.

Cornell University, Graduate School, Graduate Fields of Engineering, Field of Civil and Environmental Engineering, Ithaca, NY 14853-0001. Offers engineering management (M Eng, MS, PhD); environmental engineering (M Eng, MS, PhD); environmental fluid mechanics and hydrology (M Eng, MS, PhD); environmental systems engineering (M Eng, MS, PhD); geotechnical engineering (M Eng, MS, PhD); remote sensing (M Eng, MS, PhD); structural engineering (M Eng, MS, PhD); structural mechanics (M Eng, MS); transportation engineering (MS, PhD); transportation systems engineering (M Eng); water resource systems (M Eng, MS, PhD). *Faculty:* 40 full-time (7 women). *Students:* 144 full-time (48 women); includes 12 minority (2 African Americans, 1 American Indian/Alaska Native, 5 Asian Americans or Pacific Islanders, 4 Hispanic Americans), 58 international. Average age 25. 454 applicants, 57% accepted, 86 enrolled. In 2009, 69 master's, 5 doctorates awarded. Terminal master's awarded for partial completion of doctoral program. *Degree requirements:* For master's, thesis (MS); for doctorate, comprehensive exam, thesis/dissertation. *Entrance requirements:* For master's and doctorate, GRE General Test (recommended), 2 letters of recommendation. Additional exam requirements/recommendations for international students: Required—TOEFL (minimum score 600 paper-based; 250 computer-based; 77 iBT). *Application deadline:* For fall admission, 1/15 priority date for domestic students; for spring admission, 10/15 for domestic students. Application fee: $70. Electronic applications accepted. *Expenses:* Tuition: Full-time $29,500. Required fees: $70. Full-time tuition and fees vary according to degree level, program and student level. *Financial support:* In 2009–10, 50 students received support, including 6 fellowships with full tuition reimbursements available, 5 research assistantships with full tuition reimbursements available, 1 teaching assistantship with full tuition reimbursement available; institutionally sponsored loans, scholarships/grants, health care benefits, tuition waivers (full and partial), and unspecified assistantships also available. Financial award applicants required to submit FAFSA. *Faculty research:* Environmental engineering, geotechnical engineering remote sensing, environmental fluid mechanics and hydrology, structural engineering. *Unit head:* Director of Graduate Studies, 607-255-7560, Fax: 607-255-9004. *Application contact:* Graduate Field Assistant, 607-255-7560, Fax: 607-255-9004, E-mail: cee_grad@cornell.edu.

École Polytechnique de Montréal, Graduate Programs, Department of Civil, Geological and Mining Engineering, Montréal, QC H3C 3A7, Canada. Offers civil, geological and mining engineering (DESS); environmental engineering (M Eng, M Sc A, PhD); geotechnical engineering (M Eng, M Sc A, PhD); hydraulics engineering (M Eng, M Sc A, PhD); structural engineering (M Eng, M Sc A, PhD); transportation engineering (M Eng, M Sc A, PhD). Part-time programs available. *Degree requirements:* For master's, one foreign language, thesis; for doctorate, one foreign language, thesis/dissertation. *Entrance requirements:* For master's, minimum GPA of 2.75; for doctorate, minimum GPA of 3.0. *Faculty research:* Water resources management, characteristics of building materials, aging of dams, pollution control.

Illinois Institute of Technology, Graduate College, Armour College of Engineering, Department of Civil, Architectural and Environmental Engineering, Chicago, IL 60616-3793. Offers architectural engineering (M Arch E); civil engineering (MS, PhD); construction engineering and management (MCEM); environmental engineering (M Env E, MS, PhD); geoenvironmental engineering (M Geoenv E); geotechnical engineering (MGE); public works (MPW); structural engineering (MSE); transportation engineering (M Trans E). Part-time and evening/weekend programs available. Terminal master's awarded for partial completion of doctoral program. *Degree requirements:* For master's, thesis (for some programs); for doctorate, comprehensive exam, thesis/dissertation. *Entrance requirements:* For master's and doctorate, GRE General Test, minimum undergraduate GPA of 3.0. Additional exam requirements/recommendations for international students: Required—TOEFL (minimum score 550 paper-based; 213 computer-based; 80 iBT). Electronic applications accepted. *Expenses:* Tuition: Full-time $17,550; part-time $888 per credit hour. Required fees: $850; $7.50 per credit hour. One-time fee: $50 full-time. Full-time tuition and fees vary according to program. *Faculty research:* Seismic analysis of buildings and bridges, fatigue analysis and materials of construction, construction zone safety and construction productivity, architectural acoustics and building energy efficiency, environmental engineering. air and water quality.

Iowa State University of Science and Technology, Graduate College, College of Engineering, Department of Civil and Construction Engineering, Ames, IA 50011. Offers civil engineering (MS, PhD), including civil engineering materials, construction engineering and management, environmental engineering, geometronics, geotechnical engineering, structural engineering, transportation engineering. *Faculty:* 32 full-time (5 women), 6 part-time/adjunct (0 women). *Students:* 87 full-time (20 women), 33 part-time (8 women); includes 2 minority (1 American Indian/Alaska Native, 1 Asian American or Pacific Islander), 48 international. 204 applicants, 29% accepted, 27 enrolled. In 2009, 6 master's, 11 doctorates awarded. *Degree requirements:* For master's, thesis or alternative; for doctorate, thesis/dissertation. *Entrance requirements:* For master's and doctorate, GRE General Test. Additional exam requirements/recommendations for international students: Required—TOEFL (minimum score 550 paper-based; 82 iBT) or IELTS (minimum score 6.5). *Application deadline:* For fall admission, 2/1 priority date for domestic students, 2/1 for international students; for spring admission, 8/1 priority date for domestic students, 8/1 for international students. Application fee: $40 ($90 for international students). Electronic applications accepted. *Expenses:* Tuition, state resident: full-time $6716. Tuition, nonresident: full-time $8908. Tuition and fees vary according to course level, course load, program and student level. *Financial support:* In 2009–10, 70 research assistantships with full and partial tuition reimbursements (averaging $16,000 per year), 4 teaching assistantships with full and partial tuition reimbursements (averaging $18,000 per year) were awarded; fellowships, scholarships/grants, health care benefits, and unspecified assistantships also available. *Unit head:* Dr. James Alleman, Chair, 515-294-3892, E-mail: ccee-grad-inquiry@iastate.edu. *Application contact:* Dr. Sri Srithanan, Director of Graduate Education, 515-294-5328, E-mail: ccee-grad-inquiry@iastate.edu.

Louisiana State University and Agricultural and Mechanical College, Graduate School, College of Engineering, Department of Civil and Environmental Engineering, Baton Rouge, LA 70803. Offers environmental engineering (MSCE, PhD); geotechnical engineering (MSCE, PhD); structural engineering and mechanics (MSCE, PhD); transportation engineering (MSCE, PhD); water resources (MSCE, PhD). Part-time programs available. *Faculty:* 28 full-time (2 women). *Students:* 74 full-time (18 women), 37 part-time (6 women); includes 9 minority (1 American Indian/Alaska Native, 5 Asian Americans or Pacific Islanders, 3 Hispanic Americans), 59 international. Average age 31. 104 applicants, 63% accepted, 31 enrolled. In 2009, 16 master's, 13 doctorates awarded. *Degree requirements:* For master's, thesis optional; for doctorate, one foreign language, thesis/dissertation. *Entrance requirements:* For master's and doctorate, GRE General Test, minimum GPA of 3.0. Additional exam requirements/recommendations for international students: Required—TOEFL (minimum score 550 paper-based; 213 computer-based; 79 iBT) or IELTS (minimum score 6.5). *Application deadline:* For fall admission, 1/25 priority date for domestic students, 5/15 for international students; for spring admission, 10/15 for international students. Applications are processed on a rolling basis. Application fee: $50 ($70 for international students). Electronic applications accepted. *Financial support:* In 2009–10, 74 students received support, including 2 fellowships with full and partial tuition reimbursements available (averaging $16,672 per year), 65 research assistantships with full and partial tuition reimbursements available (averaging $11,242 per year); teaching assistantships with full and partial tuition reimbursements available, career-related internships or fieldwork, institutionally sponsored loans, scholarships/grants, and health care benefits also available. Financial award application deadline: 3/1; financial award applicants required to submit FAFSA. *Faculty research:* Mechanics and structures, environmental, geotechnical transportation, water resources. Total annual research expenditures: $2.4 million. *Unit head:* Dr. George Z. Voyiadjis, Chair/Boyd Professor, 225-578-8668, Fax: 225-578-9176, E-mail: cegzv@lsu.edu. *Application contact:* Dr. Donald Dean Adrian, Professor, 225-578-8636, E-mail: dadrian@lsu.edu.

Marquette University, Graduate School, College of Engineering, Department of Civil and Environmental Engineering, Milwaukee, WI 53201-1881. Offers construction and public works management (MS, PhD); environmental/water resources engineering (MS, PhD); structural/geotechnical engineering (MS, PhD); transportation planning and engineering (MS, PhD). Part-time and evening/weekend programs available. *Faculty:* 13 full-time (0 women), 2 part-time/adjunct (1 woman). *Students:* 16 full-time (4 women), 17 part-time (2 women); includes 2 minority (1 Asian American or Pacific Islander, 1 Hispanic American), 13 international. Average age 27. 47 applicants, 85% accepted, 11 enrolled. In 2009, 8 master's, 1 doctorate awarded. Terminal master's awarded for partial completion of doctoral program. *Degree requirements:* For master's, comprehensive exam, thesis or alternative; for doctorate, thesis/dissertation. *Entrance requirements:* For master's and doctorate, GRE General Test, minimum GPA of 3.0. Additional exam requirements/recommendations for international students: Required—TOEFL. *Application deadline:* For fall admission, 6/1 priority date for domestic students. Applications are processed on a rolling basis. Application fee: $40. Electronic applications accepted. *Financial support:* In 2009–10, 13 students received support, including 5 fellowships with tuition reimbursements available (averaging $7,697 per year), 3 research assistantships with tuition reimbursements available (averaging $24,570 per year), 5 teaching assistantships with tuition reimbursements available (averaging $24,804 per year); Federal Work-Study, institutionally sponsored loans, scholarships/grants, and tuition waivers (full and partial) also available. Support available to part-time students. Financial award application deadline: 2/15. *Faculty research:* Highway safety, highway performance, and intelligent transportation systems; surface mount technology; watershed management. Total annual research expenditures: $138,209. *Unit head:* Dr. Michael S. Switzenbaum, Chair, 414-288-7030, Fax: 414-288-7521, E-mail: michael.switzenbaum@marquette.edu. *Application contact:* Dr. Stephen M. Heinrich, Director of Graduate Studies, 414-288-5466, E-mail: stephen.heinrich@marquette.edu.

Massachusetts Institute of Technology, School of Engineering, Department of Civil and Environmental Engineering, Cambridge, MA 02139-4307. Offers biological oceanography (PhD, Sc D); chemical oceanography (PhD, Sc D); civil and environmental engineering (M Eng, SM, PhD, Sc D); civil and environmental systems (PhD, Sc D); civil engineering (PhD, Sc D, CE); coastal engineering (PhD, Sc D); construction engineering and management (PhD, Sc D); environmental biology (PhD, Sc D); environmental chemistry (PhD, Sc D); environmental engineering (PhD, Sc D); environmental fluid mechanics (PhD, Sc D); geotechnical and geoenvironmental engineering (PhD, Sc D); hydrology (PhD, Sc D); information technology (PhD, Sc D); oceanographic engineering (PhD, Sc D); structures and materials (PhD, Sc D); transportation (PhD, Sc D); SM/MBA. *Faculty:* 36 full-time (5 women). *Students:* 190 full-time (59 women); includes 22 minority (2 African Americans, 14 Asian Americans or Pacific Islanders, 6 Hispanic Americans), 103 international. Average age 26. 478 applicants, 25% accepted, 76 enrolled. In 2009, 72 master's, 14 doctorates awarded. *Degree requirements:* For master's and CE, thesis; for doctorate, comprehensive exam, thesis/dissertation. *Entrance requirements:* For master's and doctorate, GRE General Test. Additional exam requirements/recommendations for international students: Required—TOEFL (minimum score 577 paper-based; 233 computer-based; 90 iBT), IELTS (minimum score 7). *Application deadline:* For fall admission, 1/2 for domestic and international students. Application fee: $75. Electronic applications accepted. *Financial support:* In 2009–10, 185 students received support, including 40 fellowships with tuition reimbursements available (averaging $27,725 per year), 97 research assistantships with tuition reimbursements available (averaging $28,035 per year), 21 teaching assistantships with tuition reimbursements available (averaging $24,802 per year); career-related internships or fieldwork, Federal Work-Study, institutionally sponsored loans, scholarships/grants, health care benefits, and unspecified assistantships also available. *Faculty research:* Environmental chemistry, environmental microbiology, environmental fluid mechanics and coastal engineering, geotechnical engineering and geomechanics, hydrology and hydroclimatology, mechanics of materials and structures, operations research/supply chain, transportation. Total annual research expenditures: $16.6 million. *Unit head:* Prof. Andrew Whittle, Department Head, 617-253-7101. *Application contact:* Patricia Glidden, Graduate Admissions Coordinator, 617-253-7119, Fax: 617-258-6775, E-mail: cee-admissions@mit.edu.

Morgan State University, School of Graduate Studies, Clarence M. Mitchell, Jr. School of Engineering, Department of Transportation, Baltimore, MD 21251. Offers MS. Part-time and evening/weekend programs available. *Degree requirements:* For master's, thesis optional, comprehensive exam or equivalent. *Entrance requirements:* For master's, minimum undergraduate GPA of 2.5. Additional exam requirements/recommendations for international students: Required—TOEFL (minimum score 550 paper-based; 213 computer-based). *Faculty research:* Distributional impacts of congestion, pricing education and training for intelligent vehicle highway systems.

New Jersey Institute of Technology, Office of Graduate Studies, Newark College of Engineering, Department of Civil and Environmental Engineering, Newark, NJ 07102. Offers civil engineering (MS, PhD); environmental engineering (MS, PhD); transportation (MS, PhD). Part-time and evening/weekend programs available. Terminal master's awarded for partial completion of doctoral program. *Degree requirements:* For master's, thesis optional; for doctorate, thesis/dissertation, residency. *Entrance requirements:* For master's, GRE General Test; for doctorate, GRE General Test, minimum graduate GPA of 3.5. Additional exam requirements/recommendations for international students: Required—TOEFL (minimum score 550 paper-based; 213 computer-based; 79 iBT). Electronic applications accepted. *Faculty research:* Geotechnical engineering, water resources engineering, construction engineering, transportation policy, traffic operations.

New Jersey Institute of Technology, Office of Graduate Studies, Newark College of Engineering, Interdisciplinary Program in Transportation, Newark, NJ 07102. Offers MS, PhD. Part-time and evening/weekend programs available. Terminal master's awarded for partial completion of doctoral program. *Degree requirements:* For master's, thesis or alternative; for doctorate, thesis/dissertation, residency. *Entrance requirements:* For master's, GRE General Test; for doctorate, GRE General Test, minimum graduate GPA of 3.5. Additional exam requirements/recommendations for international students: Required—TOEFL (minimum score 550 paper-based; 213 computer-based; 79 iBT). Electronic applications accepted. *Faculty research:* Transportation planning, administration, and policy; intelligent vehicle highway systems; bridge maintenance.

Northwestern University, McCormick School of Engineering and Applied Science, Department of Civil and Environmental Engineering, Evanston, IL 60208-3109. Offers environmental engineering and science (MS, PhD); geotechnical engineering (MS, PhD); mechanics of materials and solids (MS, PhD); project management (MS, PhD); structural engineering and materials (MS, PhD); theoretical and applied mechanics (MS, PhD), including fluid mechanics, solid mechanics; transportation systems analysis and planning (MS, PhD). MS and PhD admissions and degrees offered through The Graduate School. Part-time programs available. *Faculty:* 25 full-time (2 women), 3 part-time/adjunct (1 woman). *Students:* 63 full-time (19 women), 3 part-time (0 women); includes 7 minority (1 African American, 3 Asian Americans or Pacific Islanders, 3 Hispanic Americans), 34 international. Average age 22. 149 applicants, 30% accepted, 23 enrolled. In 2009, 11 master's, 11 doctorates awarded. Terminal master's awarded for partial completion of doctoral program. *Degree requirements:* For master's, thesis (for some programs); for doctorate, thesis/dissertation. *Entrance requirements:* For master's and doctorate, GRE General Test, minimum 2 letters of recommendation, transcripts from all academic institutions attended. Additional exam requirements/recommendations for international students: Required—TOEFL (minimum score 600 paper-based; 250 computer-based; 100 iBT), IELTS (minimum score 7), TOEFL (minimum score iBT 26). *Application deadline:* For fall admission, 12/31 for domestic and international students. Application fee: $75. Electronic applications accepted. *Financial support:* In 2009–10, 55 students received support, including fellowships with full tuition reimbursements available (averaging $15,390 per year), research assistantships with full tuition reimbursements available (averaging $17,892 per year), 23 teaching assistantships with full tuition reimbursements available (averaging $15,867 per year); career-related internships or fieldwork, institutionally sponsored loans, scholarships/grants, and health care benefits also available. Financial award application deadline: 12/31; financial award applicants required to submit FAFSA. *Faculty research:* Environmental engineering and science, geotechnics, mechanics of materials and solids, structural engineering and materials, transportation systems analysis and planning. Total annual research expenditures: $5.8 million. *Unit head:* Jianmin Qu, Chair, 847-467-4528, Fax: 847-491-4011, E-mail: j-qu@northwestern.edu. *Application contact:* Janet Soule, Academic Coordinator, 847-491-7462, Fax: 847-491-4011, E-mail: civil-info@northwestern.edu.

Ohio University, Graduate College, Russ College of Engineering and Technology, Department of Civil Engineering, Athens, OH 45701-2979. Offers civil engineering (PhD); construction (MS); environmental (MS); geotechnical and geoenvironmental (MS); mechanics (MS); structures (MS); transportation (MS); water resources and structures (MS). Part-time programs available. *Faculty:* 13 full-time (3 women), 3 part-time/adjunct (0 women). *Students:* 18 full-time (2 women), 2 part-time (1 woman), 13 international. 22 applicants, 68% accepted, 1 enrolled. In 2009, 7 master's awarded. *Degree requirements:* For master's, comprehensive exam (for some programs), thesis or alternative; for doctorate, comprehensive exam, thesis/dissertation. *Entrance requirements:* For master's, GRE General Test, minimum GPA of 3.0, 3 letters of recommendation; for doctorate, GRE General Test. Additional exam requirements/recommendations for international students: Required—TOEFL (minimum score 550 paper-based; 80 iBT) or IELTS Academic (minimum score 6.5). *Application deadline:* For fall admission, 5/1 priority date for domestic students, 2/1 priority date for international students; for winter admission, 8/1 priority date for domestic students, 4/1 priority date for international students; for spring admission, 2/1 priority date for domestic students, 7/1 priority date for international students. Applications are processed on a rolling basis. Application fee: $50 ($55 for international students). Electronic applications accepted. *Expenses:* Tuition, state resident: full-time $7839; part-time $323 per quarter hour. Tuition, nonresident: full-time $15,831; part-time $654 per quarter hour. Required fees: $2931. *Financial support:* Research assistantships with full tuition reimbursements, teaching assistantships with full tuition reimbursements, Federal Work-Study, institutionally sponsored loans, scholarships/grants, and unspecified assistantships available. Financial award application deadline: 3/15; financial award applicants required to submit FAFSA. *Faculty research:* Noise abatement, materials and environment, highway infrastructure, subsurface investigation, (pavements, pipes, bridges, etc.). Total annual research expenditures: $1.2 million. *Unit head:* Dr. Gayle F. Mitchell, Chair, 740-593-0430, Fax: 740-593-0625, E-mail: mitchelg@ohio.edu. *Application contact:* Dr. Shad M. Sargand, Graduate Chair, 740-593-1465, Fax: 740-593-0625, E-mail: sargand@ohio.edu.

Oregon State University, Graduate School, College of Engineering, School of Civil and Construction Engineering, Corvallis, OR 97331. Offers civil engineering (MS, PhD); coastal and ocean engineering (M Oc E, PhD); coastal engineering (MS); construction engineering management (MBE, PhD); engineering (M Eng, MAIS); geotechnical engineering (MS, PhD); structural engineering (MS, PhD); transportation engineering (MS, PhD); water engineering (MS, PhD). Part-time programs available. *Faculty:* 25 full-time (5 women), 1 part-time/adjunct (0 women). *Students:* 71 full-time (17 women), 12 part-time (2 women); includes 4 minority (all Asian Americans or Pacific Islanders), 34 international. Average age 28. 75 applicants, 87% accepted, 31 enrolled. In 2009, 26 master's, 7 doctorates awarded. Terminal master's awarded for partial completion of doctoral program. *Degree requirements:* For master's, thesis or alternative; for doctorate, one foreign language, thesis/dissertation. *Entrance requirements:* For master's, GRE General Test, minimum GPA of 3.0 in last 90 hours (3.5 for MS); for doctorate, GRE General Test, minimum GPA of 3.0 in last 90 hours of undergraduate course work. Additional exam requirements/recommendations for international students: Required—TOEFL (minimum score 580 paper-based; 237 computer-based). *Application deadline:* For fall admission, 3/1 priority date for domestic students. Applications are processed on a rolling basis. Application fee: $50. *Expenses:* Tuition, state resident: full-time $9774; part-time $362 per credit. Tuition, nonresident: full-time $15,849; part-time $587 per credit. Required fees: $1639. Full-time tuition and fees vary according to course load and program. *Financial support:* Fellowships, research assistantships with full tuition reimbursements, teaching assistantships with full tuition reimbursements, career-related internships or fieldwork and institutionally sponsored loans available. Support available to part-time students. Financial award application deadline: 2/1. *Faculty research:* Hazardous waste management, carbon cycling, wave forces on structures, pavement design, seismic analysis. Total annual research expenditures: $7.1 million. *Unit head:* Dr. Scott A. Ashford, Head, 541-737-4934. *Application contact:* Kathy Westberg, CCE Graduate Advising School Operations Manager, 541-737-1786, Fax: 541-737-3052, E-mail: kathy.westberg@oregonstate.edu.

Polytechnic Institute of NYU, Department of Civil Engineering, Major in Transportation Planning and Engineering, Brooklyn, NY 11201-2990. Offers MS, PhD. Part-time and evening/weekend programs available. *Students:* 8 full-time (4 women), 31 part-time (14 women); includes 13 minority (5 African Americans, 8 Asian Americans or Pacific Islanders), 6 international. 29 applicants, 79% accepted, 16 enrolled. In 2009, 7 master's, 1 doctorate awarded. *Degree requirements:* For master's, comprehensive exam (for some programs), thesis (for some programs); for doctorate, comprehensive exam, thesis/dissertation. *Entrance requirements:* Additional exam requirements/recommendations for international students: Required—TOEFL (minimum score 550 paper-based; 213 computer-based; 80 iBT); Recommended—IELTS (minimum score 6.5). *Application deadline:* For fall admission, 7/31 priority date for domestic students, 4/30 priority date for international students; for spring admission, 12/31 priority date for domestic students, 10/30 priority date for international students. Applications are processed on a rolling basis. Application fee: $75. Electronic applications accepted. *Expenses:* Tuition: Full-time $21,492; part-time $1194 per credit hour. Required fees: $1160; $204 per course. *Financial support:* Fellowships, research assistantships, teaching assistantships, institutionally sponsored loans, scholarships/grants, and unspecified assistantships available. Support available to part-time students. Financial award applicants required to submit FAFSA. *Unit head:* Dr. Lawrence Chiarelli, Head, 718-260-4040, Fax: 718-260-3433, E-mail: lchiarel@poly.edu. *Application contact:* JeanCarlo Bonilla, Director of Graduate Enrollment Management, 718-260-3182, Fax: 718-260-3624, E-mail: gradinfo@gmail.com.

Polytechnic Institute of NYU, Long Island Graduate Center, Graduate Programs, Department of Civil Engineering, Major in Transportation Planning and Engineering, Melville, NY 11747. Offers MS. *Students:* 1 part-time (0 women). 1 applicant, 100% accepted, 1 enrolled. *Degree requirements:* For master's, comprehensive exam (for some programs), thesis (for some programs). *Entrance requirements:* Additional exam requirements/recommendations for international students: Required—TOEFL (minimum score 550 paper-based; 213 computer-based; 80 iBT); Recommended—IELTS (minimum score 6.5). *Application deadline:* For fall admission, 7/31 priority date for domestic students, 4/30 priority date for international students; for spring admission, 12/31 priority date for domestic students, 11/30 priority date for international students. Applications are processed on a rolling basis. Application fee: $75. Electronic applications accepted. *Financial support:* Institutionally sponsored loans, scholarships/grants, and unspecified assistantships available. Support available to part-time students. Financial award applicants required to submit FAFSA. *Unit head:* Dr. Roger Peter Roess, Department Head, 718-260-3018, E-mail: rroess@poly.edu. *Application contact:* JeanCarlo Bonilla, Director of Graduate Enrollment Management, 718-260-3182, Fax: 718-260-3624, E-mail: gradinfo@poly.edu.

Rensselaer Polytechnic Institute, Graduate School, School of Engineering, Department of Civil and Environmental Engineering, Program in Civil Engineering, Troy, NY 12180-3590. Offers geotechnical engineering (M Eng, MS, PhD); mechanics of composite materials and structures (M Eng, MS, PhD); structural engineering (M Eng, MS, PhD); transportation engineering (M Eng, MS, PhD). Part-time programs available. *Faculty:* 6 full-time (0 women), 5 part-time/adjunct (0 women). *Students:* 27 full-time (2 women); includes 4 minority (3 Asian Americans or Pacific Islanders, 1 Hispanic American), 3 international. Average age 24. 70 applicants, 14% accepted, 7 enrolled. In 2009, 5 master's, 1 doctorate awarded. Terminal master's awarded for partial completion of doctoral program. *Degree requirements:* For master's, thesis (for some programs); for doctorate, thesis/dissertation. *Entrance requirements:* For master's and doctorate, GRE. Additional exam requirements/recommendations for international students: Required—TOEFL (minimum score 570 paper-based; 230 computer-based; 89 iBT), IELTS (minimum score 6.5). *Application deadline:* For fall admission, 1/15 priority date for domestic and international students; for spring admission, 8/15 priority date for domestic and international students. Applications are processed on a rolling basis. Application fee: $75. Electronic applications accepted. *Expenses:* Tuition: Full-time $38,100. *Financial support:* In 2009–10, 1 fellowship with full tuition reimbursement (averaging $16,500 per year), 3 research assistantships with full tuition reimbursements (averaging $16,500 per year), 4 teaching assistantships with full tuition reimbursements (averaging $16,500 per year) were awarded; career-related internships or fieldwork and institutionally sponsored loans also available. Financial award application deadline: 2/1. *Faculty research:* Computational mechanics, earthquake engineering, geo-environmental engineering. Total annual research expenditures: $2.7 million. *Unit head:* Dr. Tarek Abdoun, Acting Chair, 518-276-6362, Fax: 518-276-4833, E-mail: abdout@rpi.edu. *Application contact:* Kimberly Boyce, Administrative Assistant, 518-276-6941, Fax: 518-276-4833, E-mail: boycek@rpi.edu.

Rensselaer Polytechnic Institute, Graduate School, School of Engineering, Department of Civil and Environmental Engineering, Program in Transportation Engineering, Troy, NY 12180-3590. Offers M Eng, MS, PhD. Part-time programs available. *Faculty:* 3 full-time (0 women). *Students:* 13 full-time (3 women); includes 1 Asian American or Pacific Islander, 1 Hispanic American, 6 international. Average age 25. 30 applicants, 30% accepted, 5 enrolled. In 2009, 8 master's awarded. Terminal master's awarded for partial completion of doctoral program. *Degree requirements:* For master's, thesis (for some programs); for doctorate, thesis/dissertation. *Entrance requirements:* For master's and doctorate, GRE. Additional exam

Transportation and Highway Engineering

Rensselaer Polytechnic Institute (continued)

requirements/recommendations for international students: Required—TOEFL (minimum score 570 paper-based; 230 computer-based; 89 iBT), IELTS (minimum score 6.5). *Application deadline:* For fall admission, 1/15 priority date for domestic and international students; for spring admission, 8/15 priority date for domestic and international students. Applications are processed on a rolling basis. Application fee: $75. Electronic applications accepted. *Expenses:* Tuition: Full-time $38,100. *Financial support:* In 2009–10, 1 fellowship with full tuition reimbursement (averaging $16,500 per year), 3 research assistantships with full tuition reimbursements (averaging $16,500 per year), 4 teaching assistantships (averaging $16,500 per year) were awarded; institutionally sponsored loans also available. Financial award application deadline: 2/1. *Faculty research:* Intelligent transportation systems, routing algorithms, dynamic network management, user behavior. Total annual research expenditures: $919,337. *Unit head:* Dr. Tarek Abdoun, Acting Chair, 518-276-6362, Fax: 518-276-4833, E-mail: abdout@rpi.edu. *Application contact:* Kimberly Boyce, Assistant II, 518-276-6941, Fax: 518-276-4833, E-mail: boycek@rpi.edu.

South Carolina State University, School of Graduate Studies, Department of Civil and Mechanical Engineering Technology, Orangeburg, SC 29117-0001. Offers transportation (MS). Part-time and evening/weekend programs available. *Degree requirements:* For master's, comprehensive exam, thesis, departmental qualifying exam. *Entrance requirements:* For master's, GRE. Electronic applications accepted. *Expenses:* Tuition, state resident: part-time $470 per credit hour. Tuition, nonresident: part-time $924 per credit hour. *Faculty research:* Societal competence, relationship of parent-child interaction to adult, rehabilitation evaluation, vocation, language assessment of rural children.

Texas A&M University, College of Engineering, Zachry Department of Civil Engineering, College Station, TX 77843. Offers construction engineering and management (M Eng, MS, D Eng, PhD); environmental engineering (M Eng, MS, D Eng, PhD); geotechnical engineering (M Eng, MS, D Eng, PhD); materials engineering (M Eng, MS, D Eng, PhD); ocean engineering (M Eng, MS, D Eng, PhD); structural engineering (M Eng, MS, D Eng, PhD); transportation engineering (M Eng, MS, D Eng, PhD); water resources engineering (M Eng, MS, D Eng, PhD). Part-time programs available. *Faculty:* 61. *Students:* 390 full-time (89 women), 42 part-time (6 women); includes 23 minority (2 African Americans, 11 Asian Americans or Pacific Islanders, 10 Hispanic Americans), 281 international. Average age 29. In 2009, 100 master's, 36 doctorates awarded. *Degree requirements:* For master's, thesis (MS); for doctorate, dissertation (PhD), internship (D Eng). *Entrance requirements:* For master's and doctorate, GRE General Test. Additional exam requirements/recommendations for international students: Required—TOEFL. *Application deadline:* Applications are processed on a rolling basis. Application fee: $50 ($75 for international students). Electronic applications accepted. *Expenses:* Tuition, state resident: full-time $3991.32; part-time $221.74 per credit hour. Tuition, nonresident: full-time $9049; part-time $502.74 per credit hour. *Financial support:* In 2009–10, fellowships (averaging $4,500 per year), research assistantships (averaging $14,000 per year), teaching assistantships (averaging $14,400 per year) were awarded; career-related internships or fieldwork and institutionally sponsored loans also available. Financial award application deadline: 4/15; financial award applicants required to submit FAFSA. *Unit head:* Dr. Tony Cahill, Head, 979-845-2438, E-mail: t-cahill@civil.tamu.edu. *Application contact:* Graduate Advisor, 979-845-2498, Fax: 979-862-2800, E-mail: ce-grad@tamu.edu.

Texas Southern University, School of Science and Technology, Program in Transportation, Planning and Management, Houston, TX 77004-4584. Offers MS. Part-time and evening/weekend programs available. *Faculty:* 3 full-time (1 woman), 1 (woman) part-time/adjunct. *Students:* 27 full-time (15 women), 18 part-time (8 women); includes 39 minority (16 African Americans, 21 Asian Americans or Pacific Islanders, 2 Hispanic Americans), 2 international. Average age 30. 16 applicants, 100% accepted, 15 enrolled. In 2009, 8 master's awarded. *Degree requirements:* For master's, comprehensive exam, thesis optional. *Entrance requirements:* For master's, GRE General Test, minimum GPA of 2.5. Additional exam requirements/recommendations for international students: Required—TOEFL. *Application deadline:* For fall admission, 7/1 for domestic and international students; for spring admission, 11/1 for domestic and international students. Applications are processed on a rolling basis. Application fee: $50 ($75 for international students). Electronic applications accepted. *Expenses:* Tuition, state resident: full-time $1805; part-time $100 per credit hour. Tuition, nonresident: full-time $6470; part-time $343 per credit hour. Tuition and fees vary according to course level, course load and degree level. *Financial support:* In 2009–10, 23 research assistantships (averaging $7,485 per year), 2 teaching assistantships (averaging $2,525 per year) were awarded; fellowships with partial tuition reimbursements, career-related internships or fieldwork, scholarships/grants, and unspecified assistantships also available. Financial award application deadline: 5/1. *Faculty research:* Highway traffic operations, transportation and policy planning, air quality in transportation, transportation modeling. Total annual research expenditures: $500,000. *Unit head:* Dr. Lei Yu, Chair, 713-313-7282, Fax: 713-313-1856, E-mail: yu_lx@tsu.edu. *Application contact:* Paula Eakins, Administrative Assistant, 713-313-1841, E-mail: eakins_pl@tsu.edu.

The University of Alabama in Huntsville, School of Graduate Studies, College of Engineering, Department of Civil and Environmental Engineering, Huntsville, AL 35899. Offers civil and environmental engineering (PhD); civil engineering (MSE), including environmental and water resource engineering, geotechnical engineering, structural engineering and structural mechanics, transportation engineering. Part-time and evening/weekend programs available. *Faculty:* 6 full-time (1 woman). *Students:* 12 full-time (3 women), 7 part-time (1 woman); includes 3 minority (2 African Americans, 1 Asian American or Pacific Islander), 5 international. Average age 33. 26 applicants, 58% accepted, 9 enrolled. In 2009, 10 master's, 2 doctorates awarded. *Degree requirements:* For master's, comprehensive exam, thesis or alternative, oral and written exams; for doctorate, comprehensive exam, thesis/dissertation, oral and written exams. *Entrance requirements:* For master's, GRE General Test, BSE, minimum GPA of 3.0; for doctorate, GRE General Test, minimum GPA of 3.0. Additional exam requirements/recommendations for international students: Required—TOEFL (minimum score 500 paper-based; 173 computer-based; 62 iBT). *Application deadline:* For fall admission, 7/15 for domestic students, 4/1 for international students; for spring admission, 11/30 for domestic students, 9/1 for international students. Applications are processed on a rolling basis. Application fee: $40 ($50 for international students). Electronic applications accepted. *Expenses:* Tuition, state resident: part-time $355.75 per credit hour. Tuition, nonresident: part-time $847.10 per credit hour. Required fees: $210.80 per semester. Tuition and fees vary according to course load and program. *Financial support:* In 2009–10, 10 students received support, including 4 research assistantships with full and partial tuition reimbursements available (averaging $11,525 per year), 6 teaching assistantships with full and partial tuition reimbursements available (averaging $9,678 per year); career-related internships or fieldwork, Federal Work-Study, institutionally sponsored loans, scholarships/grants, health care benefits, and unspecified assistantships also available. Support available to part-time students. Financial award application deadline: 4/1; financial award applicants required to submit FAFSA. *Faculty research:* Hydrologic modeling, orbital debris impact, hydrogeology, environmental engineering, transportation engineering. Total annual research expenditures: $1.5 million. *Unit head:* Dr. Houssam Toutanji, Chair, 256-824-7361, Fax: 256-824-6724, E-mail: toutanji@cee.uah.edu. *Application contact:* Kathy Biggs, Graduate Studies Admissions Manager, 256-824-6199, Fax: 256-824-6405, E-mail: deangrad@uah.edu.

University of Arkansas, Graduate School, College of Engineering, Department of Civil Engineering, Program in Transportation Engineering, Fayetteville, AR 72701-1201. Offers MSE, MSTE. *Students:* 2 full-time (1 woman); both minorities (both African Americans). *Degree requirements:* For master's, thesis optional. Application fee: $40 ($50 for international students). *Expenses:* Tuition, state resident: full-time $7355; part-time $356.58 per hour. Tuition, nonresident: full-time $17,401; part-time $775.17 per hour. Required fees: $1203. *Financial support:* Fellowships, research assistantships, teaching assistantships available. Financial award application deadline: 4/1. *Unit head:* Dr. Kevin Hall, Departmental Chair, 479-575-4954, Fax: 479-575-7168, E-mail: kdhall@uark.edu. *Application contact:* Dr. Kelvin Wang, Graduate Coordinator, 479-575-4954, Fax: 479-575-7168, E-mail: kcw@uark.edu.

University of California, Berkeley, Graduate Division, College of Engineering, Department of Civil and Environmental Engineering, Berkeley, CA 94720-1500. Offers engineering and project management (M Eng, MS, D Eng, PhD); environmental engineering (M Eng, MS, D Eng, PhD); geoengineering (M Eng, MS, D Eng, PhD); structural engineering, mechanics and materials (M Eng, MS, D Eng, PhD); transportation engineering (M Eng, MS, D Eng, PhD); M Arch/MS; MCP/MS; MPP/MS. *Students:* 368 full-time (125 women). Average age 27. 921 applicants, 179 enrolled. In 2009, 158 master's, 39 doctorates awarded. *Degree requirements:* For master's, comprehensive exam or thesis (MS); for doctorate, thesis/dissertation, qualifying exam. *Entrance requirements:* For master's, GRE General Test, minimum GPA of 3.0, 3 letters of recommendation; for doctorate, GRE General Test, minimum GPA of 3.5, 3 letters of recommendation. Additional exam requirements/recommendations for international students: Required—TOEFL (minimum score 570 paper-based; 230 computer-based). *Application deadline:* For fall admission, 2/3 for domestic students. Application fee: $70 ($90 for international students). Electronic applications accepted. *Financial support:* Fellowships, research assistantships, teaching assistantships, unspecified assistantships available. *Unit head:* Prof. Lisa Alvarez-Cohen, Chair, 510-643-8739, Fax: 510-643-5264, E-mail: chair@ce.berkeley.edu. *Application contact:* Shelly Okimoto, Graduate Advisor, 510-642-6464, Fax: 510-643-5264, E-mail: aao@ce.berkeley.edu.

University of California, Davis, College of Engineering, Graduate Group in Transportation Technology and Policy, Davis, CA 95616. Offers MS, PhD. Terminal master's awarded for partial completion of doctoral program. *Degree requirements:* For master's, comprehensive exam (for some programs), thesis (for some programs); for doctorate, thesis/dissertation. *Entrance requirements:* For master's, GRE General Test, minimum GPA of 3.0; for doctorate, GRE General Test, minimum GPA of 3.5. Additional exam requirements/recommendations for international students: Required—TOEFL (minimum score 550 paper-based; 213 computer-based). Electronic applications accepted.

University of California, Irvine, Office of Graduate Studies, School of Social Sciences, Program in Transportation Science, Irvine, CA 92697. Offers MA, PhD. *Students:* 9 full-time (5 women); includes 5 minority (4 Asian Americans or Pacific Islanders, 1 Hispanic American). Average age 30. 10 applicants, 70% accepted, 4 enrolled. In 2009, 1 doctorate awarded. *Entrance requirements:* For master's and doctorate, GRE General Test, minimum GPA of 3.0. *Application deadline:* For fall admission, 1/15 for domestic and international students. Application fee: $70 ($90 for international students). *Financial support:* Fellowships, research assistantships with full tuition reimbursements, teaching assistantships, institutionally sponsored loans, traineeships, health care benefits, and unspecified assistantships available. Financial award application deadline: 3/1. *Unit head:* Dr. Michael G. McNally, Director, 949-824-5906, Fax: 949-824-8305. *Application contact:* Diane Enriquez, Graduate Counselor, 949-824-5924, Fax: 949-824-3548, E-mail: dmvargas@uci.edu.

University of Central Florida, College of Engineering and Computer Science, Department of Civil, Environmental, and Construction Engineering, Program in Civil Engineering, Orlando, FL 32816. Offers civil engineering (MS, MSCE, PhD); construction engineering (Certificate); structural engineering (Certificate); transportation engineering (Certificate). Part-time and evening/weekend programs available. *Students:* 53 full-time (8 women), 68 part-time (20 women); includes 22 minority (4 African Americans, 1 American Indian/Alaska Native, 5 Asian Americans or Pacific Islanders, 12 Hispanic Americans), 34 international. Average age 29. 90 applicants, 73% accepted, 45 enrolled. In 2009, 30 master's, 2 doctorates awarded. *Degree requirements:* For master's, thesis or alternative; for doctorate, thesis/dissertation, departmental qualifying exam, candidacy exam. *Entrance requirements:* For master's, GRE General Test, minimum GPA of 3.0 in last 60 hours; for doctorate, GRE General Test, minimum GPA of 3.5 in last 60 hours. Additional exam requirements/recommendations for international students: Required—TOEFL. *Application deadline:* For fall admission, 7/15 priority date for domestic students; for spring admission, 12/15 priority date for domestic students. Application fee: $30. Electronic applications accepted. *Expenses:* Tuition, state resident: part-time $306.31 per credit hour. Tuition, nonresident: part-time $1099.01 per credit hour. Part-time tuition and fees vary according to degree level and program. *Financial support:* In 2009–10, 30 students received support, including 7 fellowships with partial tuition reimbursements available (averaging $7,100 per year), 19 research assistantships with partial tuition reimbursements available (averaging $11,600 per year), 12 teaching assistantships with partial tuition reimbursements available (averaging $9,700 per year); career-related internships or fieldwork, Federal Work-Study, institutionally sponsored loans, tuition waivers (partial), and unspecified assistantships also available. Financial award application deadline: 3/1; financial award applicants required to submit FAFSA.

University of Dayton, Graduate School, School of Engineering, Department of Civil and Environmental Engineering, Dayton, OH 45469-1300. Offers engineering mechanics (MSEM); environmental engineering (MSCE); geotechnical engineering (MSCE); structural engineering (MSCE); transport engineering (MSCE); water resources engineering (MSCE). Part-time programs available. *Faculty:* 8 full-time (2 women), 1 part-time/adjunct (0 women). *Students:* 10 full-time (6 women), 8 part-time (1 woman); includes 3 minority (all African Americans), 7 international. Average age 29. 35 applicants, 49% accepted, 6 enrolled. In 2009, 3 master's awarded. *Degree requirements:* For master's, thesis optional. *Entrance requirements:* Additional exam requirements/recommendations for international students: Required—TOEFL (minimum score 550 paper-based; 213 computer-based; 80 iBT). *Application deadline:* For fall admission, 8/1 for domestic students, 3/1 priority date for international students; for winter admission, 7/1 priority date for international students; for spring admission, 1/1 priority date for international students. Applications are processed on a rolling basis. Application fee: $0 ($50 for international students). Electronic applications accepted. *Expenses:* Tuition: Full-time $8412; part-time $701 per credit hour. Required fees: $325; $65 per course. $25 per semester. Tuition and fees vary according to course load, degree level and program. *Financial support:* In 2009–10, 3 research assistantships (averaging $10,780 per year), 4 teaching assistantships with partial tuition reimbursements (averaging $5,110 per year) were awarded. Financial award applicants required to submit FAFSA. *Faculty research:* Physical modeling of hydraulic systems, finite element methods, mechanics of composite materials, transportation systems safety, high-velocity wear. Total annual research expenditures: $421,839. *Unit head:* Dr. Donald V. Chase, Interim Chair, 937-229-3847, Fax: 937-229-3491, E-mail: donald.chase@notes.udayton.edu. *Application contact:* Graduate Admissions, 937-229-4411, Fax: 937-229-4729, E-mail: gradadmission@udayton.edu.

University of Delaware, College of Engineering, Department of Civil and Environmental Engineering, Newark, DE 19716. Offers environmental engineering (MAS, MCE, PhD); geotechnical engineering (MAS, MCE, PhD); ocean engineering (MAS, MCE, PhD); structural engineering (MAS, MCE, PhD); transportation engineering (MAS, MCE, PhD); water resource engineering (MAS, MCE, PhD). Part-time programs available. Terminal master's awarded for partial completion of doctoral program. *Degree requirements:* For master's, thesis; for doctorate, thesis/dissertation. *Entrance requirements:* For master's and doctorate, GRE General Test. Additional exam requirements/recommendations for international students: Required—TOEFL. Electronic applications accepted. *Faculty research:* Structural engineering and mechanics; transportation engineering; ocean engineering; soil mechanics and foundation; water resources and environmental engineering.

University of Memphis, Graduate School, Herff College of Engineering, Department of Civil Engineering, Memphis, TN 38152. Offers civil engineering (PhD); environmental engineering (MS); foundation engineering (MS); structural engineering (MS); transportation engineering (MS); water resources engineering (MS). *Faculty:* 12 full-time (1 woman), 1 part-time/adjunct

(0 women). *Students:* 12 full-time (3 women), 16 part-time (6 women); includes 2 minority (1 African American, 1 Asian American or Pacific Islander), 9 international. Average age 28. 18 applicants, 94% accepted, 8 enrolled. In 2009, 11 master's awarded. *Degree requirements:* For master's, comprehensive exam, thesis or alternative; for doctorate, thesis/dissertation. *Entrance requirements:* For master's, GRE General Test or MAT, minimum undergraduate GPA of 2.5. *Application deadline:* For fall admission, 8/1 for domestic students; for spring admission, 12/1 for domestic students. Application fee: $35 ($60 for international students). *Expenses:* Tuition, state resident: full-time $6246; part-time $347 per credit hour. Tuition, nonresident: full-time $15,894; part-time $883 per credit hour. Required fees: $1160. Full-time tuition and fees vary according to course load, degree level and program. *Financial support:* In 2009–10, 6 students received support; fellowships with full tuition reimbursements available, research assistantships with full tuition reimbursements available, career-related internships or fieldwork, Federal Work-Study, scholarships/grants, and unspecified assistantships available. Financial award application deadline: 2/15; financial award applicants required to submit FAFSA. *Faculty research:* Structural response to earthquakes, pavement design, water quality, transportation safety, intermodal transportation. *Unit head:* Dr. Sharam Pezeshk, Interim Chair, 901-678-2746, Fax: 901-678-3026. *Application contact:* Dr. Roger Meier, Coordinator of Graduate Studies, 901-678-3284.

University of Missouri, Graduate School, College of Engineering, Department of Civil and Environmental Engineering, Columbia, MO 65211. Offers civil engineering (MS, PhD); environmental engineering (MS, PhD); geotechnical engineering (MS, PhD); structural engineering (MS, PhD); transportation and highway engineering (MS); water resources (MS, PhD). *Degree requirements:* For master's, report or thesis; for doctorate, thesis/dissertation. *Entrance requirements:* For master's and doctorate, GRE General Test. Additional exam requirements/recommendations for international students: Required—TOEFL (minimum score 550 paper-based; 213 computer-based; 79 iBT).

University of Nevada, Las Vegas, Graduate College, Howard R. Hughes College of Engineering, Department of Civil and Environmental Engineering, Las Vegas, NV 89154-4015. Offers civil and environmental engineering (MS, PhD); transportation (MS). Part-time programs available. *Faculty:* 16 full-time (3 women), 4 part-time/adjunct (0 women). *Students:* 25 full-time (6 women), 28 part-time (6 women); includes 7 minority (2 African Americans, 3 Asian Americans or Pacific Islanders, 2 Hispanic Americans), 16 international. Average age 37. 51 applicants, 55% accepted, 25 enrolled. In 2009, 14 master's, 5 doctorates awarded. *Degree requirements:* For master's, comprehensive exam (for some programs), thesis (for some programs); for doctorate, comprehensive exam, thesis/dissertation. *Entrance requirements:* For master's and doctorate, GRE General Test. Additional exam requirements/recommendations for international students: Required—TOEFL (minimum score 550 paper-based; 213 computer-based; 80 iBT), IELTS (minimum score 7). *Application deadline:* For fall admission, 3/15 priority date for domestic and international students; for spring admission, 11/15 priority date for domestic students, 8/30 priority date for international students. Applications are processed on a rolling basis. Application fee: $60 ($95 for international students). Electronic applications accepted. *Financial support:* In 2009–10, 38 students received support, including 23 research assistantships with partial tuition reimbursements available (averaging $13,595 per year), 15 teaching assistantships with partial tuition reimbursements available (averaging $11,200 per year); institutionally sponsored loans, scholarships/grants, health care benefits, and unspecified assistantships also available. Financial award application deadline: 3/1. *Unit head:* Dr. Edward Neumann, Chair/Professor, 702-895-1072, Fax: 702-895-3936, E-mail: neumann@ce.unlv.edu. *Application contact:* Graduate College Admissions Evaluator, 702-895-3320, Fax: 702-895-4180, E-mail: gradcollege@unlv.edu.

University of New Brunswick Fredericton, School of Graduate Studies, Faculty of Engineering, Department of Civil Engineering, Fredericton, NB E3B 5A3, Canada. Offers construction engineering and management (M Eng, M Sc E, PhD); environmental engineering (M Eng, M Sc E, PhD); environmental studies (M Eng); geotechnical engineering (M Eng, M Sc E, PhD); groundwater/hydrology (M Eng, M Sc E, PhD); materials (M Eng, M Sc E, PhD); pavements (M Eng, M Sc E, PhD); structures (M Eng, M Sc E, PhD); transportation (M Eng, M Sc E, PhD). Part-time programs available. *Faculty:* 18 full-time (1 woman), 1 (woman) part-time/adjunct. *Students:* 42 full-time (9 women), 18 part-time (2 women). In 2009, 11 master's, 4 doctorates awarded. *Degree requirements:* For master's, thesis, proposal; for doctorate, comprehensive exam, thesis/dissertation, Qualifying exam; Proposal; 27 credit hours of courses. *Entrance requirements:* For master's, Minimum GPA of 3.0; BScE in Civil Engineering or related engineering degree.; for doctorate, Minimum GPA of 3.0; Candidates are normally required to have a graduate degree in engineering or applied science. Additional exam requirements/recommendations for international students: Required—TOEFL (minimum score 580 paper-based; 237 computer-based), TWE (minimum score 4), or IELTS (minimum score 7.5). *Application deadline:* For fall admission, 5/1 priority date for domestic students; for winter admission, 11/1 priority date for domestic students. Applications are processed on a rolling basis. Application fee: $50 Canadian dollars. Tuition and fees charges are reported in Canadian dollars. *Expenses:* Tuition, area resident: Full-time $5562 Canadian dollars; part-time $2781 Canadian dollars per year. Required fees: $49.75 Canadian dollars per term. *Financial support:* In 2009–10, 51 research assistantships (averaging $7,000 per year), 43 teaching assistantships (averaging $2,000 per year) were awarded; career-related internships or fieldwork and scholarships/grants also available. *Faculty research:* Construction engineering and management, concrete materials and structural engineering, transportation and asset management, geotechnical engineering, water and environmental engineering. *Unit head:* Dr. Eric Hildebrand, Director of Graduate Studies, 506-453-5113, Fax: 506-453-3568, E-mail: ktm@unb.ca. *Application contact:* Joyce Moore, Graduate Secretary, 506-452-6127, Fax: 506-453-3568, E-mail: civil-grad@unb.ca.

University of Southern California, Graduate School, School of Policy, Planning, and Development, Master of Planning Program, Los Angeles, CA 90089. Offers sustainable cities (Graduate Certificate); transportation systems (Graduate Certificate); urban planning (M Pl); M Arch/M Pl; M Pl/MA; M Pl/MS; M Pl/MSW; MBA/M Pl; ML Arch/M Pl; MPA/M Pl. Part-time programs available. *Faculty:* 51 full-time (12 women), 74 part-time/adjunct (26 women). *Students:* 84 full-time (50 women), 6 part-time (4 women); includes 38 minority (5 African Americans, 21 Asian Americans or Pacific Islanders, 12 Hispanic Americans), 12 international. 260 applicants, 60% accepted, 62 enrolled. In 2009, 40 master's awarded. *Degree requirements:* For master's, comprehensive exam, internship. *Entrance requirements:* For master's, GRE or GMAT. Additional exam requirements/recommendations for international students: Required—TOEFL (minimum score 600 paper-based; 250 computer-based; 100 iBT). *Application deadline:* For fall admission, 12/15 priority date for domestic and international students; for spring admission, 11/1 for domestic students, 10/1 for international students. Application fee: $85. Electronic applications accepted. *Expenses:* Tuition: Full-time $25,980; part-time $1315 per unit. Required fees: $554. One-time fee: $35 full-time. Full-time tuition and fees vary according to degree level and program. *Financial support:* In 2009–10, 72 students received support, including 2 research assistantships with tuition reimbursements available (averaging $9,566 per year); scholarships/grants and tuition waivers (full and partial) also available. *Faculty research:* Transportation and infrastructure, comparative international development, healthy communities, socal economic development, sustainable community planning. Total annual research expenditures: $5 million. *Unit head:* Dr. Tridib Banerjee, Dean, 213-740-4724, Fax: 213-740-1801, E-mail: tbanerje@usc.edu. *Application contact:* Marisol R. Gonzalez, Director of Recruitment and Admission, 213-740-0550, Fax: 213-740-7573, E-mail: marisolr@usc.edu.

University of Southern California, Graduate School, Viterbi School of Engineering, Department of Industrial and Systems Engineering, Los Angeles, CA 90089. Offers digital supply chain management (MS); engineering management (MS); engineering technology communication (Graduate Certificate); health systems operations (Graduate Certificate); industrial and systems engineering (MS, PhD, Engr); manufacturing engineering (MS); operations research engineering (MS); optimization and supply chain management (Graduate Certificate); product development engineering (MS); safety systems and security (MS); systems architecting and engineering (MS, Graduate Certificate); systems safety and security (Graduate Certificate); transportation systems (Graduate Certificate); MS/MBA. Part-time programs available. Postbaccalaureate distance learning degree programs offered (minimal on-campus study). *Faculty:* 11 full-time (2 women), 39 part-time/adjunct (7 women). *Students:* 250 full-time (71 women), 145 part-time (37 women); includes 67 minority (6 African Americans, 2 American Indian/Alaska Native, 39 Asian Americans or Pacific Islanders, 20 Hispanic Americans), 253 international. 679 applicants, 58% accepted, 206 enrolled. In 2009, 98 master's, 7 doctorates awarded. Terminal master's awarded for partial completion of doctoral program. *Degree requirements:* For doctorate, thesis/dissertation. *Entrance requirements:* For master's, GRE General Test; for doctorate, General GRE. *Application deadline:* For fall admission, 3/1 priority date for domestic and international students; for spring admission, 10/1 for domestic students, 10/1 priority date for international students. Applications are processed on a rolling basis. Application fee: $85. Electronic applications accepted. *Expenses:* Tuition: Full-time $25,980; part-time $1315 per unit. Required fees: $554. One-time fee: $35 full-time. Full-time tuition and fees vary according to degree level and program. *Financial support:* In 2009–10, fellowships with full tuition reimbursements (averaging $30,000 per year), research assistantships with full tuition reimbursements (averaging $19,250 per year), teaching assistantships with full tuition reimbursements (averaging $19,250 per year) were awarded; career-related internships or fieldwork, scholarships/grants, health care benefits, and unspecified assistantships also available. Financial award application deadline: 12/1; financial award applicants required to submit CSS PROFILE or FAFSA. *Faculty research:* Health systems, music cognition and retrieval, transportation andlogistics, manufacturing and automation, engineering systems design, risk and economic analysis. Total annual research expenditures: $1.2 million. *Unit head:* Dr. James E. Moore, Chair, 213-740-4885, Fax: 213-740-1120, E-mail: jmoore@usc.edu. *Application contact:* Mary Ordaz, Student Service Advisor, 213-740-4886, Fax: 213-740-1120, E-mail: isedept@usc.edu.

University of Southern California, Graduate School, Viterbi School of Engineering, Sonny Astani Department of Civil Engineering, Los Angeles, CA 90089. Offers applied mechanics (MS); civil engineering (MS, PhD); computer-aided engineering (ME, Graduate Certificate); construction management (MCM); engineering technology commercialization (Graduate Certificate); environmental engineering (MS, PhD); environmental quality management (ME); structural design (ME); sustainable cities (Graduate Certificate); transportation systems (Graduate Certificate). Part-time programs available. Postbaccalaureate distance learning degree programs offered (no on-campus study). *Faculty:* 16 full-time (2 women), 35 part-time/adjunct (5 women). *Students:* 165 full-time (48 women), 65 part-time (16 women); includes 54 minority (40 Asian Americans or Pacific Islanders, 14 Hispanic Americans), 108 international. 451 applicants, 41% accepted, 73 enrolled. In 2009, 74 master's, 10 doctorates awarded. Terminal master's awarded for partial completion of doctoral program. *Degree requirements:* For doctorate, thesis/dissertation. *Entrance requirements:* For master's, GRE General Test; for doctorate, General GRE. *Application deadline:* For fall admission, 3/1 priority date for domestic and international students; for spring admission, 10/1 priority date for domestic and international students. Applications are processed on a rolling basis. Application fee: $85. Electronic applications accepted. *Expenses:* Tuition: Full-time $25,980; part-time $1315 per unit. Required fees: $554. One-time fee: $35 full-time. Full-time tuition and fees vary according to degree level and program. *Financial support:* In 2009–10, fellowships with full tuition reimbursements (averaging $30,000 per year), research assistantships with full tuition reimbursements (averaging $19,250 per year), teaching assistantships with full tuition reimbursements (averaging $19,250 per year) were awarded; career-related internships or fieldwork, scholarships/grants, health care benefits, and unspecified assistantships also available. Financial award application deadline: 12/1; financial award applicants required to submit CSS PROFILE or FAFSA. *Faculty research:* Geotechnical engineering, transportation engineering, structural engineering, construction management, environmental engineering, water resources. Total annual research expenditures: $4.2 million. *Unit head:* Dr. Jean-Pierre Bardet, Chair, 213-740-0609, Fax: 213-744-1426, E-mail: bardet@usc.edu. *Application contact:* Jennifer A. Gerson, Director of Student Services, 213-740-0573, Fax: 213-740-8662, E-mail: jgerson@usc.edu.

The University of Texas at Tyler, College of Engineering and Computer Science, Department of Civil Engineering, Tyler, TX 75799-0001. Offers environmental engineering (MS); industrial safety (MS); structural engineering (MS); transportation engineering (MS); water resources engineering (MS). Part-time and evening/weekend programs available. *Faculty:* 6 full-time (0 women). *Students:* 5 full-time (1 woman), 7 part-time (1 woman); includes 1 African American, 1 Asian American or Pacific Islander, 1 Hispanic American, 1 international. Average age 26. 5 applicants, 80% accepted, 3 enrolled. *Degree requirements:* For master's, thesis optional. *Entrance requirements:* For master's, GRE General Test, bachelor's degree in engineering, associated science degree. Additional exam requirements/recommendations for international students: Required—TOEFL (minimum score 79 computer-based). *Application deadline:* For fall admission, 8/17 priority date for domestic students, 7/1 priority date for international students; for spring admission, 12/21 priority date for domestic students, 11/1 priority date for international students. Application fee: $25 ($50 for international students). *Expenses:* Tuition, state resident: part-time $665 per semester hour. Tuition, nonresident: part-time $942 per semester hour. Part-time tuition and fees vary according to degree level and program. *Financial support:* Application deadline: 7/1. *Faculty research:* Non-destructive strength testing, indoor air quality, transportation routing and signaling, pavement replacement criteria, flood water routing, construction and long-term behavior of innovative geotechnical foundation and embankment construction used in highway construction, engineering education. *Unit head:* Dr. Ron Welch, Chair, 903-566-7002, Fax: 903-566-7337, E-mail: rwelch@uttyler.edu. *Application contact:* Dr. Torey Nalbone, Program Chair, 903-565-5520, Fax: 903-566-7337, E-mail: tnalbone@uttyler.edu.

University of Washington, Graduate School, College of Engineering, Department of Civil and Environmental Engineering, Seattle, WA 98195-2700. Offers construction engineering (MSCE); environmental engineering (MS, MSCE, MSE, PhD); hydrology, water resources, and environmental fluid mechanics (MS, MSCE, MSE, PhD); structural and geotechnical engineering and mechanics (MS, MSCE, MSE, PhD); transportation and construction engineering (MS, MSE, PhD); transportation engineering (MSCE). Part-time programs available. Postbaccalaureate distance learning degree programs offered (no on-campus study). *Faculty:* 36 full-time (9 women), 16 part-time/adjunct (6 women). *Students:* 186 full-time (62 women), 57 part-time (10 women); includes 35 minority (24 Asian Americans or Pacific Islanders, 11 Hispanic Americans), 58 international. 360 applicants, 68% accepted, 98 enrolled. In 2009, 74 master's, 8 doctorates awarded. Terminal master's awarded for partial completion of doctoral program. *Degree requirements:* For master's, thesis (for some programs); for doctorate, comprehensive exam, thesis/dissertation. *Entrance requirements:* For master's, GRE General Test, minimum GPA of 3.0; for doctorate, GRE, minimum GPA of 3.5. Additional exam requirements/recommendations for international students: Required—TOEFL (minimum score 580 paper-based; 237 computer-based; 70 iBT). *Application deadline:* For fall admission, 1/15 priority date for domestic and international students. Applications are processed on a rolling basis. Application fee: $65. Electronic applications accepted. *Financial support:* In 2009–10, 5 students received support, including 13 fellowships with full and partial tuition reimbursements available (averaging $16,173 per year), 68 research assistantships with full tuition reimbursements available (averaging $16,173 per year), 12 teaching assistantships with full tuition reimbursements available (averaging $16,173 per year); scholarships/grants also available. Financial award application deadline: 1/15. *Faculty research:* Environmental/water resources, hydrology; construction/transportation; structures/ geotechnical. Total annual research expenditures: $11.4 million. *Unit head:* Dr. Gregory R. Miller, Professor and Chair, 206-543-0350, Fax: 206-543-1543, E-mail: gmiller@uw.edu. *Application contact:* Lorna Latal, Graduate Adviser, 206-543-2574, Fax: 206-543-1543, E-mail: llatal@u.washington.edu.

Villanova University, College of Engineering, Department of Civil and Environmental Engineering, Program in Transportation Engineering, Villanova, PA 19085-1699. Offers MSTE. Part-time and evening/weekend programs available. *Degree requirements:* For master's, thesis

Transportation and Highway Engineering

Villanova University (continued)
optional. *Entrance requirements:* For master's, GRE General Test (for applicants with degrees from foreign universities), minimum GPA of 3.0; BCE or bachelor's degree in science, business, or related engineering field. Additional exam requirements/recommendations for international students: Required—TOEFL (minimum score 600 paper-based; 250 computer-based; 100 iBT). Electronic applications accepted. *Expenses:* Tuition: Part-time $630 per credit. Required fees: $60 per credit. Part-time tuition and fees vary according to degree level and program. *Faculty research:* Simulation of unsignalized intersections, services to the elderly and disabled, recycling of secondary materials into hot mix asphalt concrete pavements.

Western Michigan University, Graduate College, College of Engineering and Applied Sciences, Department of Civil and Construction Engineering, Kalamazoo, MI 49008. Offers civil engineering (MS), including construction engineering and management, structural engineering, transportation engineering. *Entrance requirements:* For master's, minimum GPA of 3.0.

Water Resources Engineering

American University of Beirut, Graduate Programs, Faculty of Engineering and Architecture, Beirut, Lebanon. Offers civil engineering (ME, PhD); electrical and computer engineering (ME, PhD); engineering management (MEM); environmental and water resources (ME); environmental and water resources engineering (PhD); environmental technology (MSES); mechanical engineering (ME, PhD); urban design (MUD); urban planning and policy (MUP). Part-time programs available. *Degree requirements:* For master's, one foreign language, comprehensive exam, thesis (for some programs); for doctorate, one foreign language, comprehensive exam, thesis/dissertation, publications. *Entrance requirements:* For master's, letters of recommendation; for doctorate, letters of recommendation, master's degree, transcripts, curriculum vitae, interview. Additional exam requirements/recommendations for international students: Required—TOEFL (minimum score 600 paper-based; 250 computer-based; 100 iBT), IELTS (minimum score 7.5). Electronic applications accepted.

Cornell University, Graduate School, Graduate Fields of Engineering, Field of Civil and Environmental Engineering, Ithaca, NY 14853-0001. Offers engineering management (M Eng, MS, PhD); environmental engineering (M Eng, MS, PhD); environmental fluid mechanics and hydrology (M Eng, MS, PhD); environmental systems engineering (M Eng, MS, PhD); geotechnical engineering (M Eng, MS, PhD); remote sensing (M Eng, MS, PhD); structural engineering (M Eng, MS, PhD); structural mechanics (M Eng, MS); transportation engineering (MS, PhD); transportation systems engineering (M Eng); water resource systems (M Eng, MS, PhD). *Faculty:* 40 full-time (7 women). *Students:* 144 full-time (48 women); includes 12 minority (2 African Americans, 1 American Indian/Alaska Native, 5 Asian Americans or Pacific Islanders, 4 Hispanic Americans), 58 international. Average age 25. 454 applicants, 57% accepted, 86 enrolled. In 2009, 69 master's, 5 doctorates awarded. Terminal master's awarded for partial completion of doctoral program. *Degree requirements:* For master's, thesis (MS); for doctorate, comprehensive exam, thesis/dissertation. *Entrance requirements:* For master's and doctorate, GRE General Test (recommended), 2 letters of recommendation. Additional exam requirements/recommendations for international students: Required—TOEFL (minimum score 600 paper-based; 250 computer-based; 77 iBT). *Application deadline:* For fall admission, 1/15 priority date for domestic students; for spring admission, 10/15 for domestic students. Application fee: $70. Electronic applications accepted. *Expenses:* Tuition: Full-time $29,500. Required fees: $70. Full-time tuition and fees vary according to degree level, program and student level. *Financial support:* In 2009–10, 50 students received support, including 6 fellowships with full tuition reimbursements available, 5 research assistantships with full tuition reimbursements available, 1 teaching assistantship with full tuition reimbursement available; institutionally sponsored loans, scholarships/grants, health care benefits, tuition waivers (full and partial), and unspecified assistantships also available. Financial award applicants required to submit FAFSA. *Faculty research:* Environmental engineering, geotechnical engineering remote sensing, environmental fluid mechanics and hydrology, structural engineering. *Unit head:* Director of Graduate Studies, 607-255-7560, Fax: 607-255-9004. *Application contact:* Graduate Field Assistant, 607-255-7560, Fax: 607-255-9004, E-mail: cee_grad@cornell.edu.

George Mason University, Volgenau School of Information Technology and Engineering, Department of Civil, Environmental, and Infrastructure Engineering, Fairfax, VA 22030. Offers civil and infrastructure engineering (MS, PhD); civil infrastructure and security engineering (Certificate); leading technical enterprises (Certificate); sustainability and the environment (Certificate); water resources engineering (Certificate). Part-time and evening/weekend programs available. *Faculty:* 9 full-time (3 women), 15 part-time/adjunct (0 women). *Students:* 19 full-time (3 women), 61 part-time (18 women); includes 16 minority (5 African Americans, 7 Asian Americans or Pacific Islanders, 4 Hispanic Americans), 8 international. Average age 33. 102 applicants, 58% accepted, 43 enrolled. In 2009, 13 master's, 2 other advanced degrees awarded. *Degree requirements:* For master's, thesis (for some programs), 30 credits, departmental seminars; for doctorate, thesis/dissertation, qualifying exams. *Entrance requirements:* For master's, GRE or GMAT. Additional exam requirements/recommendations for international students: Required—TOEFL (minimum score 575 paper-based; 230 computer-based; 88 iBT). *Application deadline:* For fall admission, 3/15 priority date for domestic students, 3/15 for international students; for spring admission, 11/1 for domestic students, 10/1 for international students. Application fee: $75. Electronic applications accepted. *Expenses:* Tuition, state resident: full-time $7568; part-time $315.33 per credit hour. Tuition, nonresident: full-time $21,704; part-time $904.33 per credit hour. Required fees: $2184; $91 per credit hour. *Financial support:* In 2009–10, 12 students received support, including 2 research assistantships with full and partial tuition reimbursements available (averaging $15,000 per year), 10 teaching assistantships with full and partial tuition reimbursements available (averaging $4,557 per year); career-related internships or fieldwork, scholarships/grants, unspecified assistantships, and health care benefits (full-time research or teaching assistantship recipients) also available. Support available to part-time students. Financial award application deadline: 3/1; financial award applicants required to submit FAFSA. *Faculty research:* Evolutionary design, infrastructure security, intelligent transportation systems, national transportation networks, water quality modeling. Total annual research expenditures: $67,461. *Unit head:* Dr. Michael Bronzini, Chair, 703-993-1504, Fax: 703-993-1521. *Application contact:* Lisa Nolder, Graduate Student Services Director, 703-993-1499, E-mail: snolder@gmu.edu.

Louisiana State University and Agricultural and Mechanical College, Graduate School, College of Engineering, Department of Civil and Environmental Engineering, Baton Rouge, LA 70803. Offers environmental engineering (MSCE, PhD); geotechnical engineering (MSCE, PhD); structural engineering and mechanics (MSCE, PhD); transportation engineering (MSCE, PhD); water resources (MSCE, PhD). Part-time programs available. *Faculty:* 28 full-time (2 women). *Students:* 74 full-time (18 women), 37 part-time (6 women); includes 9 minority (1 American Indian/Alaska Native, 5 Asian Americans or Pacific Islanders, 3 Hispanic Americans), 59 international. Average age 31. 104 applicants, 63% accepted, 31 enrolled. In 2009, 16 master's, 13 doctorates awarded. *Degree requirements:* For master's, thesis optional; for doctorate, one foreign language, thesis/dissertation. *Entrance requirements:* For master's and doctorate, GRE General Test, minimum GPA of 3.0. Additional exam requirements/recommendations for international students: Required—TOEFL (minimum score 550 paper-based; 213 computer-based; 79 iBT) or IELTS (minimum score 6.5). *Application deadline:* For fall admission, 1/25 priority date for domestic students, 5/15 for international students; for spring admission, 10/15 for international students. Applications are processed on a rolling basis. Application fee: $50 ($70 for international students). Electronic applications accepted. *Financial support:* In 2009–10, 74 students received support, including 2 fellowships with full and partial tuition reimbursements available (averaging $16,672 per year), 65 research assistantships with full and partial tuition reimbursements available (averaging $11,242 per year); teaching assistantships with full and partial tuition reimbursements available, career-related internships or fieldwork, institutionally sponsored loans, scholarships/grants, and health care benefits also available. Financial award application deadline: 3/1; financial award applicants required to submit FAFSA. *Faculty research:* Mechanics and structures, environmental, geotechnical transportation, water resources. Total annual research expenditures: $2.4 million. *Unit head:* Dr. George Z. Voyiadjis, Chair/Boyd Professor, 225-578-8668, Fax: 225-578-9176, E-mail: cegzv@lsu.edu. *Application contact:* Dr. Donald Dean Adrian, Professor, 225-578-8636, E-mail: dadrian@lsu.edu.

Marquette University, Graduate School, College of Engineering, Department of Civil and Environmental Engineering, Milwaukee, WI 53201-1881. Offers construction and public works management (MS, PhD); environmental/water resources engineering (MS, PhD); structural/geotechnical engineering (MS, PhD); transportation planning and engineering (MS, PhD). Part-time and evening/weekend programs available. *Faculty:* 13 full-time (0 women), 2 part-time/adjunct (1 woman). *Students:* 16 full-time (4 women), 17 part-time (2 women); includes 2 minority (1 Asian American or Pacific Islander, 1 Hispanic American), 13 international. Average age 27. 47 applicants, 85% accepted, 11 enrolled. In 2009, 8 master's, 1 doctorate awarded. Terminal master's awarded for partial completion of doctoral program. *Degree requirements:* For master's, comprehensive exam, thesis or alternative; for doctorate, thesis/dissertation. *Entrance requirements:* For master's and doctorate, GRE General Test, minimum GPA of 3.0. Additional exam requirements/recommendations for international students: Required—TOEFL. *Application deadline:* For fall admission, 6/1 priority date for domestic students. Applications are processed on a rolling basis. Application fee: $40. Electronic applications accepted. *Financial support:* In 2009–10, 13 students received support, including 5 fellowships with tuition reimbursements available (averaging $7,697 per year), 3 research assistantships with tuition reimbursements available (averaging $24,570 per year), 5 teaching assistantships with tuition reimbursements available (averaging $24,804 per year); Federal Work-Study, institutionally sponsored loans, scholarships/grants, and tuition waivers (full and partial) also available. Support available to part-time students. Financial award application deadline: 2/15. *Faculty research:* Highway safety, highway performance, and intelligent transportation systems; surface mount technology; watershed management. Total annual research expenditures: $138,209. *Unit head:* Dr. Michael S. Switzenbaum, Chair, 414-288-7030, Fax: 414-288-7521, E-mail: michael.switzenbaum@marquette.edu. *Application contact:* Dr. Stephen M. Heinrich, Director of Graduate Studies, 414-288-5466, E-mail: stephen.heinrich@marquette.edu.

McGill University, Faculty of Graduate and Postdoctoral Studies, Faculty of Engineering, Department of Civil Engineering and Applied Mechanics, Montréal, QC H3A 2T5, Canada. Offers environmental engineering (M Eng, M Sc, PhD); fluid mechanics (M Sc); fluid mechanics and hydraulic engineering (M Eng, PhD); materials engineering (M Eng, PhD); rehabilitation of urban infrastructure (M Eng, PhD); soil behavior (M Eng, PhD); soil mechanics and foundations (M Eng, PhD); structures and structural mechanics (M Eng, PhD); water resources (M Sc); water resources engineering (M Eng, PhD).

New Mexico Institute of Mining and Technology, Graduate Studies, Department of Environmental Engineering, Socorro, NM 87801. Offers environmental engineering (MS), including air quality engineering and science, hazardous waste engineering, water quality engineering and science. *Degree requirements:* For master's, thesis. *Entrance requirements:* For master's, GRE General Test. Additional exam requirements/recommendations for international students: Required—TOEFL (minimum score 540 paper-based; 207 computer-based). *Faculty research:* Air quality, hazardous waste management, wastewater management and treatment, site remediation.

Ohio University, Graduate College, Russ College of Engineering and Technology, Department of Civil Engineering, Athens, OH 45701-2979. Offers civil engineering (PhD); construction (MS); environmental (MS); geotechnical and geoenvironmental (MS); mechanics (MS); structures (MS); transportation (MS); water resources and structures (MS). Part-time programs available. *Faculty:* 13 full-time (3 women), 3 part-time/adjunct (0 women). *Students:* 18 full-time (2 women), 2 part-time (1 woman), 13 international. 22 applicants, 68% accepted, 1 enrolled. In 2009, 7 master's awarded. *Degree requirements:* For master's, comprehensive exam (for some programs), thesis or alternative; for doctorate, comprehensive exam, thesis/dissertation. *Entrance requirements:* For master's, GRE General Test, minimum GPA of 3.0, 3 letters of recommendation; for doctorate, GRE General Test. Additional exam requirements/recommendations for international students: Required—TOEFL (minimum score 550 paper-based; 80 iBT) or IELTS Academic (minimum score 6.5). *Application deadline:* For fall admission, 5/1 priority date for domestic students, 2/1 priority date for international students; for winter admission, 8/1 priority date for domestic students, 4/1 priority date for international students; for spring admission, 2/1 priority date for domestic students, 7/1 priority date for international students. Applications are processed on a rolling basis. Application fee: $50 ($55 for international students). Electronic applications accepted. *Expenses:* Tuition, state resident: full-time $7839; part-time $323 per quarter hour. Tuition, nonresident: full-time $15,831; part-time $654 per quarter hour. Required fees: $2931. *Financial support:* Research assistantships with full tuition reimbursements, teaching assistantships with full tuition reimbursements, Federal Work-Study, institutionally sponsored loans, scholarships/grants, and unspecified assistantships available. Financial award application deadline: 3/15; financial award applicants required to submit FAFSA. *Faculty research:* Noise abatement, materials and environment, highway infrastructure, subsurface investigation, (pavements, pipes, bridges, etc.). Total annual research expenditures: $1.2 million. *Unit head:* Dr. Gayle F. Mitchell, Chair, 740-593-0430, Fax: 740-593-0625, E-mail: mitchelg@ohio.edu. *Application contact:* Dr. Shad M. Sargand, Graduate Chair, 740-593-1465, Fax: 740-593-0625, E-mail: sargand@ohio.edu.

Oregon State University, Graduate School, College of Engineering, Department of Biological and Ecological Engineering, Corvallis, OR 97331. Offers M Eng, MS, PhD. *Students:* 23. 8 applicants, 50% accepted, 2 enrolled. In 2009, 1 doctorate awarded. Terminal master's awarded for partial completion of doctoral program. *Degree requirements:* For master's, thesis or alternative; for doctorate, thesis/dissertation. *Entrance requirements:* For master's and doctorate, minimum GPA of 3.0 in last 90 hours. Additional exam requirements/recommendations for international students: Required—TOEFL (minimum score 550 paper-based; 213 computer-based). *Application deadline:* For fall admission, 3/1 for domestic students. Applications are processed on a rolling basis. Application fee: $50. *Expenses:* Contact institution. *Financial support:* In 2009–10, 3 fellowships with full tuition reimbursements (averaging $13,041 per year), 10 research assistantships with full tuition reimbursements (averaging $13,041 per year) were awarded; teaching assistantships, Federal Work-Study and institutionally sponsored loans also available. Support available to part-time students. Financial award application deadline: 2/1. *Faculty research:* Bioengineering, water resources engineering, food engineering, cell culture and fermentation, vadose zone transport. Total annual research expenditures: $827,438. *Unit head:* Dr. John P. Bolte, Head, 541-737-6303, Fax: 541-737-2082, E-mail:

info-bee@engr.orst.edu. *Application contact:* Elena Maus, Information Contact, 541-737-2041, Fax: 541-737-2082, E-mail: info-bee@engr.orst.edu.

Oregon State University, Graduate School, College of Engineering, School of Civil and Construction Engineering, Corvallis, OR 97331. Offers civil engineering (MS, PhD); coastal and ocean engineering (M Oc E, PhD); coastal engineering (MS); construction engineering management (MBE, PhD); engineering (M Eng, MAIS); geotechnical engineering (MS, PhD); structural engineering (MS, PhD); transportation engineering (MS, PhD); water engineering (MS, PhD). Part-time programs available. *Faculty:* 25 full-time (5 women), 1 part-time/adjunct (0 women). *Students:* 71 full-time (17 women), 12 part-time (2 women); includes 4 minority (all Asian Americans or Pacific Islanders), 34 international. Average age 28. 75 applicants, 87% accepted, 31 enrolled. In 2009, 26 master's, 7 doctorates awarded. Terminal master's awarded for partial completion of doctoral program. *Degree requirements:* For master's, thesis or alternative; for doctorate, one foreign language, thesis/dissertation. *Entrance requirements:* For master's, GRE General Test, minimum GPA of 3.0 in last 90 hours (3.5 for MS); for doctorate, GRE General Test, minimum GPA of 3.0 in last 90 hours of undergraduate course work. Additional exam requirements/recommendations for international students: Required—TOEFL (minimum score 580 paper-based; 237 computer-based). *Application deadline:* For fall admission, 3/1 priority date for domestic students. Applications are processed on a rolling basis. Application fee: $50. *Expenses:* Tuition, state resident: full-time $9774; part-time $362 per credit. Tuition, nonresident: full-time $15,849; part-time $587 per credit. Required fees: $1639. Full-time tuition and fees vary according to course load and program. *Financial support:* Fellowships, research assistantships with full tuition reimbursements, teaching assistantships with full tuition reimbursements, career-related internships or fieldwork and institutionally sponsored loans available. Support available to part-time students. Financial award application deadline: 2/1. *Faculty research:* Hazardous waste management, carbon cycling, wave forces on structures, pavement design, seismic analysis. Total annual research expenditures: $7.1 million. *Unit head:* Dr. Scott A. Ashford, Head, 541-737-4934. *Application contact:* Kathy Westberg, CCE Graduate Advising School Operations Manager, 541-737-1786, Fax: 541-737-3052, E-mail: kathy.westberg@oregonstate.edu.

Oregon State University, Graduate School, Program in Water Resources Engineering, Corvallis, OR 97331. Offers MS, PhD. *Students:* 16 full-time (9 women), 2 part-time (1 woman); includes 2 minority (1 Asian American or Pacific Islander, 1 Hispanic American), 5 international. Average age 31. In 2009, 3 master's, 1 doctorate awarded. *Expenses:* Tuition, state resident: full-time $9774; part-time $362 per credit. Tuition, nonresident: full-time $15,849; part-time $587 per credit. Required fees: $1639. Full-time tuition and fees vary according to course load and program. *Unit head:* Dr. Mary Santelmann, Director, 541-737-1215, Fax: 541-737-1200, E-mail: santelmm@oregonstate.edu. *Application contact:* Rosemary Garagnani, Assistant Dean, 541-737-1465, Fax: 541-737-3313.

Stevens Institute of Technology, Graduate School, Charles V. Schaefer Jr. School of Engineering, Department of Civil, Environmental, and Ocean Engineering, Program in Civil Engineering, Hoboken, NJ 07030. Offers civil engineering (PhD); geotechnical engineering (Certificate); geotechnical/geoenvironmental engineering (M Eng, Engr); hydrologic modeling (M Eng); stormwater management (M Eng); structural engineering (M Eng, Engr); water resources engineering (M Eng). *Degree requirements:* For master's, thesis optional; for doctorate, variable foreign language requirement, thesis/dissertation; for other advanced degree, project or thesis. *Entrance requirements:* For doctorate, GRE. Additional exam requirements/recommendations for international students: Required—TOEFL. Electronic applications accepted. *Expenses:* Tuition: Full-time $9900; part-time $1100 per credit. Required fees: $286 per semester.

Texas A&M University, College of Engineering, Zachry Department of Civil Engineering, College Station, TX 77843. Offers construction engineering and management (M Eng, MS, D Eng, PhD); environmental engineering (M Eng, MS, D Eng, PhD); geotechnical engineering (M Eng, MS, D Eng, PhD); materials engineering (M Eng, MS, D Eng, PhD); ocean engineering (M Eng, MS, D Eng, PhD); structural engineering (M Eng, MS, D Eng, PhD); transportation engineering (M Eng, MS, D Eng, PhD); water resources engineering (M Eng, MS, D Eng, PhD). Part-time programs available. *Faculty:* 61. *Students:* 390 full-time (89 women), 42 part-time (6 women); includes 23 minority (2 African Americans, 11 Asian Americans or Pacific Islanders, 10 Hispanic Americans), 281 international. Average age 29. In 2009, 100 master's, 36 doctorates awarded. *Degree requirements:* For master's, thesis (MS); for doctorate, dissertation (PhD), internship (D Eng). *Entrance requirements:* For master's and doctorate, GRE General Test. Additional exam requirements/recommendations for international students: Required—TOEFL. *Application deadline:* Applications are processed on a rolling basis. Application fee: $50 ($75 for international students). Electronic applications accepted. *Expenses:* Tuition, state resident: full-time $3991.32; part-time $221.74 per credit hour. Tuition, nonresident: full-time $9049; part-time $502.74 per credit hour. *Financial support:* In 2009–10, fellowships (averaging $4,500 per year), research assistantships (averaging $14,000 per year), teaching assistantships (averaging $14,400 per year) were awarded; career-related internships or fieldwork and institutionally sponsored loans also available. Financial award application deadline: 4/15; financial award applicants required to submit FAFSA. *Unit head:* Dr. Tony Cahill, Head, 979-845-2438, E-mail: t-cahill@civil.tamu.edu. *Application contact:* Graduate Advisor, 979-845-2498, Fax: 979-862-2800, E-mail: ce-grad@tamu.edu.

Tufts University, School of Engineering, Department of Civil and Environmental Engineering, Medford, MA 02155. Offers civil engineering (ME, MS, PhD), including geotechnical engineering, structural engineering; environmental engineering (ME, MS, PhD), including environmental engineering and environmental sciences, environmental geotechnology, environmental health, environmental science and management, hazardous materials management, water resources engineering. Part-time programs available. *Faculty:* 17 full-time, 7 part-time/adjunct. *Students:* 72 (33 women); includes 6 minority (2 African Americans, 4 Asian Americans or Pacific Islanders), 17 international. Average age 27. 170 applicants, 59% accepted, 20 enrolled. In 2009, 17 master's, 3 doctorates awarded. Terminal master's awarded for partial completion of doctoral program. *Degree requirements:* For master's, thesis or alternative; for doctorate, thesis/dissertation. *Entrance requirements:* For master's and doctorate, GRE General Test. Additional exam requirements/recommendations for international students: Required—TOEFL (minimum score 550 paper-based; 213 computer-based; 80 iBT). *Application deadline:* For fall admission, 1/15 priority date for domestic students, 12/15 for international students; for spring admission, 10/15 for domestic students, 9/15 for international students. Applications are processed on a rolling basis. Application fee: $75. Electronic applications accepted. *Expenses:* Tuition: Full-time $38,096; part-time $3962 per credit. Required fees: $686; $40 per year. Tuition and fees vary according to course level, course load, degree level, program and student level. *Financial support:* Fellowships with full tuition reimbursements, research assistantships with full and partial tuition reimbursements, teaching assistantships with full and partial tuition reimbursements, Federal Work-Study, scholarships/grants, tuition waivers (partial), and unspecified assistantships available. Financial award application deadline: 1/15; financial award applicants required to submit FAFSA. *Unit head:* Dr. Kurt Penell, Chair, 617-627-3211, Fax: 617-627-3994. *Application contact:* Laura Sacco, Information Contact, 617-627-3211.

The University of Alabama in Huntsville, School of Graduate Studies, College of Engineering, Department of Civil and Environmental Engineering, Huntsville, AL 35899. Offers civil and environmental engineering (PhD); civil engineering (MSE), including environmental and water resource engineering, geotechnical engineering, structural engineering and structural mechanics, transportation engineering. Part-time and evening/weekend programs available. *Faculty:* 6 full-time (1 woman). *Students:* 12 full-time (3 women), 7 part-time (1 woman); includes 3 minority (2 African Americans, 1 Asian American or Pacific Islander), 5 international. Average age 33. 26 applicants, 58% accepted, 9 enrolled. In 2009, 10 master's, 2 doctorates awarded. *Degree requirements:* For master's, comprehensive exam, thesis or alternative, oral and written exams; for doctorate, comprehensive exam, thesis/dissertation, oral and written exams. *Entrance requirements:* For master's, GRE General Test, BSE, minimum GPA of 3.0; for doctorate, GRE General Test, minimum GPA of 3.0. Additional exam requirements/recommendations for international students: Required—TOEFL (minimum score 500 paper-based; 173 computer-based; 62 iBT). *Application deadline:* For fall admission, 7/15 for domestic students, 4/1 for international students; for spring admission, 11/30 for domestic students, 9/1 for international students. Applications are processed on a rolling basis. Application fee: $40 ($50 for international students). Electronic applications accepted. *Expenses:* Tuition, state resident: part-time $355.75 per credit hour. Tuition, nonresident: part-time $847.10 per credit hour. Required fees: $210.80 per semester. Tuition and fees vary according to course load and program. *Financial support:* In 2009–10, 10 students received support, including 4 research assistantships with full and partial tuition reimbursements available (averaging $11,525 per year), 6 teaching assistantships with full and partial tuition reimbursements available (averaging $9,678 per year); career-related internships or fieldwork, Federal Work-Study, institutionally sponsored loans, scholarships/grants, health care benefits, and unspecified assistantships also available. Support available to part-time students. Financial award application deadline: 4/1; financial award applicants required to submit FAFSA. *Faculty research:* Hydrologic modeling, orbital debris impact, hydrogeology, environmental engineering, transportation engineering. Total annual research expenditures: $1.5 million. *Unit head:* Dr. Houssam Toutanji, Chair, 256-824-7361, Fax: 256-824-6724, E-mail: toutanji@cee.uah.edu. *Application contact:* Kathy Biggs, Graduate Studies Admissions Manager, 256-824-6199, Fax: 256-824-6405, E-mail: deangrad@uah.edu.

University of Alberta, Faculty of Graduate Studies and Research, Department of Civil and Environmental Engineering, Edmonton, AB T6G 2E1, Canada. Offers construction engineering and management (M Eng, M Sc, PhD); environmental engineering (M Eng, M Sc, PhD); environmental science (M Sc, PhD); geoenvironmental engineering (M Eng, M Sc, PhD); geotechnical engineering (M Eng, M Sc, PhD); mining engineering (M Eng, M Sc, PhD); petroleum engineering (M Eng, M Sc, PhD); structural engineering (M Eng, M Sc, PhD); water resources (M Eng, M Sc, PhD). Part-time programs available. Postbaccalaureate distance learning degree programs offered (minimal on-campus study). *Faculty:* 44 full-time (3 women), 2 part-time/adjunct (0 women). *Students:* 215 full-time (49 women), 99 part-time (19 women). 1,428 applicants, 15% accepted, 123 enrolled. In 2009, 124 master's, 34 doctorates awarded. *Degree requirements:* For master's, thesis (for some programs); for doctorate, thesis/dissertation. *Entrance requirements:* For master's, minimum GPA of 3.0 in last 2 years of undergraduate studies; for doctorate, minimum GPA of 3.0. Additional exam requirements/recommendations for international students: Required—TOEFL (minimum score 550 paper-based; 213 computer-based). *Application deadline:* For fall admission, 6/1 priority date for domestic students, 6/1 for international students; for winter admission, 11/1 for domestic students, 9/15 for international students. Applications are processed on a rolling basis. Application fee: $0 Canadian dollars. Electronic applications accepted. Tuition and fees charges are reported in Canadian dollars. *Expenses:* Tuition, area resident: Full-time $4626.24 Canadian dollars; part-time $99.72 Canadian dollars per unit. International tuition: $8216 Canadian dollars full-time. Required fees: $3589.92 Canadian dollars; $99.72 Canadian dollars per unit. $215 Canadian dollars per term. *Financial support:* In 2009–10, 88 research assistantships with full and partial tuition reimbursements, 134 teaching assistantships with full and partial tuition reimbursements were awarded; scholarships/grants and tuition waivers (full and partial) also available. Financial award application deadline: 4/1. *Faculty research:* Mining. Total annual research expenditures: $6,791 Canadian dollars. *Unit head:* Dr. David Zhu, Associate Chair, Graduate Studies, 780-492-1198, Fax: 403-492-8198. *Application contact:* Gwen Mendoza, Student Services Officer, 403-492-1539, Fax: 403-492-0249, E-mail: civegrad@ualberta.ca.

University of California, Berkeley, Graduate Division, College of Engineering, Department of Civil and Environmental Engineering, Berkeley, CA 94720-1500. Offers engineering and project management (M Eng, MS, D Eng, PhD); environmental engineering (M Eng, MS, D Eng, PhD); geoengineering (M Eng, MS, D Eng, PhD); structural engineering, mechanics and materials (M Eng, MS, D Eng, PhD); transportation engineering (M Eng, MS, D Eng, PhD); M Arch/MS; MCP/MS; MPP/MS. *Students:* 368 full-time (125 women). Average age 27. 921 applicants, 179 enrolled. In 2009, 158 master's, 39 doctorates awarded. *Degree requirements:* For master's, comprehensive exam or thesis (MS); for doctorate, thesis/dissertation, qualifying exam. *Entrance requirements:* For master's, GRE General Test, minimum GPA of 3.0, 3 letters of recommendation; for doctorate, GRE General Test, minimum GPA of 3.5, 3 letters of recommendation. Additional exam requirements/recommendations for international students: Required—TOEFL (minimum score 570 paper-based; 230 computer-based). *Application deadline:* For fall admission, 2/3 for domestic students. Application fee: $70 ($90 for international students). Electronic applications accepted. *Financial support:* Fellowships, research assistantships, teaching assistantships, unspecified assistantships available. *Unit head:* Prof. Lisa Alvarez-Cohen, Chair, 510-643-8739, Fax: 510-643-5264, E-mail: chair@ce.berkeley.edu. *Application contact:* Shelly Okimoto, Graduate Advisor, 510-642-6464, Fax: 510-643-5264, E-mail: aao@ce.berkeley.edu.

University of Colorado at Boulder, Graduate School, College of Engineering and Applied Science, Department of Civil, Environmental, and Architectural Engineering, Boulder, CO 80309. Offers building systems (MS, PhD); construction engineering management (MS, PhD); environmental engineering (MS, PhD); geotechnical engineering and geomechanics (MS, PhD); hydrology, water resources and environmental fluid mechanics (MS, PhD); structural engineering and structural mechanics (MS, PhD). *Faculty:* 39 full-time (5 women). *Students:* 202 full-time (62 women), 29 part-time (6 women); includes 34 minority (3 African Americans, 3 American Indian/Alaska Native, 12 Asian Americans or Pacific Islanders, 16 Hispanic Americans), 53 international. Average age 29. 384 applicants, 44% accepted, 80 enrolled. In 2009, 60 master's, 7 doctorates awarded. *Degree requirements:* For master's, comprehensive exam, thesis or alternative; for doctorate, thesis/dissertation. *Entrance requirements:* For master's, GRE General Test, minimum undergraduate GPA of 3.0. *Application deadline:* For fall admission, 3/1 for domestic students, 12/1 for international students; for spring admission, 10/31 for domestic students, 10/1 for international students. Application fee: $50 ($60 for international students). *Financial support:* In 2009–10, 45 fellowships (averaging $7,876 per year), 68 research assistantships (averaging $15,204 per year) were awarded. Financial award application deadline: 1/15. *Faculty research:* Building systems engineering, construction engineering and management, environmental engineering, geoenvironmental engineering, geotechnical engineering, materials and mechanics, structural engineering, water resources engineering, life-cycle engineering. Total annual research expenditures: $6.1 million.

University of Dayton, Graduate School, School of Engineering, Department of Civil and Environmental Engineering, Dayton, OH 45469-1300. Offers engineering mechanics (MSEM); environmental engineering (MSCE); geotechnical engineering (MSCE); structural engineering (MSCE); transport engineering (MSCE); water resources engineering (MSCE). Part-time programs available. *Faculty:* 8 full-time (2 women), 1 part-time/adjunct (0 women). *Students:* 10 full-time (6 women), 8 part-time (1 woman); includes 3 minority (all African Americans), 7 international. Average age 29. 35 applicants, 49% accepted, 6 enrolled. In 2009, 3 master's awarded. *Degree requirements:* For master's, thesis optional. *Entrance requirements:* Additional exam requirements/recommendations for international students: Required—TOEFL (minimum score 550 paper-based; 213 computer-based; 80 iBT). *Application deadline:* For fall admission, 8/1 for domestic students, 3/1 priority date for international students; for winter admission, 7/1 priority date for international students; for spring admission, 1/1 priority date for international students. Applications are processed on a rolling basis. Application fee: $0 ($50 for international students). Electronic applications accepted. *Expenses:* Tuition: Full-time $8412; part-time $701 per credit hour. Required fees: $325; $65 per course. $25 per semester. Tuition and fees vary according to course load, degree level and program. *Financial support:* In 2009–10, 3 research assistantships (averaging $10,780 per year), 4 teaching assistantships with partial tuition reimbursements (averaging $5,110 per year) were awarded. Financial award applicants required to submit FAFSA. *Faculty research:* Physical modeling of hydraulic systems, finite element methods, mechanics of composite materials, transportation systems safety, high-velocity wear. Total annual research expenditures: $421,839. *Unit head:* Dr. Donald V. Chase, Interim Chair, 937-229-3847, Fax: 937-229-3491, E-mail: donald.chase@notes.udayton.edu. *Application contact:* Graduate Admissions, 937-229-4411, Fax: 937-229-4729, E-mail: gradadmission@udayton.edu.

Water Resources Engineering

University of Delaware, College of Engineering, Department of Civil and Environmental Engineering, Newark, DE 19716. Offers environmental engineering (MAS, MCE, PhD); geotechnical engineering (MAS, MCE, PhD); ocean engineering (MAS, MCE, PhD); structural engineering (MAS, MCE, PhD); transportation engineering (MAS, MCE, PhD); water resource engineering (MAS, MCE, PhD). Part-time programs available. Terminal master's awarded for partial completion of doctoral program. *Degree requirements:* For master's, thesis; for doctorate, thesis/dissertation. *Entrance requirements:* For master's and doctorate, GRE General Test. Additional exam requirements/recommendations for international students: Required—TOEFL. Electronic applications accepted. *Faculty research:* Structural engineering and mechanics; transportation engineering; ocean engineering; soil mechanics and foundation; water resources and environmental engineering.

University of Guelph, Graduate Program Services, College of Physical and Engineering Science, School of Engineering, Guelph, ON N1G 2W1, Canada. Offers biological engineering (M Eng, M Sc, MA Sc, PhD); engineering systems and computing (M Eng, M Sc, MA Sc, PhD); environmental engineering (M Eng, M Sc, MA Sc, PhD); water resources engineering (M Eng, M Sc, MA Sc, PhD). Part-time programs available. *Degree requirements:* For master's, thesis (for some programs); for doctorate, comprehensive exam, thesis/dissertation. *Entrance requirements:* For master's, minimum B- average during previous 2 years of course work; for doctorate, minimum B average. Additional exam requirements/recommendations for international students: Required—TOEFL (minimum score 550 paper-based; 213 computer-based; 89 iBT), IELTS (minimum score 6.5). Electronic applications accepted. *Faculty research:* Water and food safety, environmental contaminant fates and mechanisms, computer systems, robotics and mechatronics, waste treatment.

University of Memphis, Graduate School, Herff College of Engineering, Department of Civil Engineering, Memphis, TN 38152. Offers civil engineering (PhD); environmental engineering (MS); foundation engineering (MS); structural engineering (MS); transportation engineering (MS); water resources engineering (MS). *Faculty:* 12 full-time (1 woman), 1 part-time/adjunct (0 women). *Students:* 12 full-time (3 women), 16 part-time (6 women); includes 2 minority (1 African American, 1 Asian American or Pacific Islander), 9 international. Average age 28. 18 applicants, 94% accepted, 8 enrolled. In 2009, 11 master's awarded. *Degree requirements:* For master's, comprehensive exam, thesis or alternative; for doctorate, thesis/dissertation. *Entrance requirements:* For master's, GRE General Test or MAT, minimum undergraduate GPA of 2.5. *Application deadline:* For fall admission, 8/1 for domestic students; for spring admission, 12/1 for domestic students. Application fee: $35 ($60 for international students). *Expenses:* Tuition, state resident: full-time $6246; part-time $347 per credit hour. Tuition, nonresident: full-time $15,894; part-time $883 per credit hour. Required fees: $1160. Full-time tuition and fees vary according to course load, degree level and program. *Financial support:* In 2009–10, 6 students received support; fellowships with full tuition reimbursements available, research assistantships with full tuition reimbursements available, career-related internships or fieldwork, Federal Work-Study, scholarships/grants, and unspecified assistantships available. Financial award application deadline: 2/15; financial award applicants required to submit FAFSA. *Faculty research:* Structural response to earthquakes, pavement design, water quality, transportation safety, intermodal transportation. *Unit head:* Dr. Sharam Pezeshk, Interim Chair, 901-678-2746, Fax: 901-678-3026. *Application contact:* Dr. Roger Meier, Coordinator of Graduate Studies, 901-678-3284.

University of Missouri, Graduate School, College of Engineering, Department of Civil and Environmental Engineering, Columbia, MO 65211. Offers civil engineering (MS, PhD); environmental engineering (MS, PhD); geotechnical engineering (MS, PhD); structural engineering (MS, PhD); transportation and highway engineering (MS); water resources (MS, PhD). *Degree requirements:* For master's, report or thesis; for doctorate, thesis/dissertation. *Entrance requirements:* For master's and doctorate, GRE General Test. Additional exam requirements/recommendations for international students: Required—TOEFL (minimum score 550 paper-based; 213 computer-based; 79 iBT).

University of New Haven, Graduate School, Tagliatela College of Engineering, Program in Environmental Engineering, West Haven, CT 06516-1916. Offers environmental engineering (MS); industrial and hazardous wastes (MS); water and wastewater treatment (MS); water resources (Certificate). Part-time and evening/weekend programs available. *Faculty:* 6 full-time (1 woman), 2 part-time/adjunct (0 women). *Students:* 15 full-time (4 women), 6 part-time (1 woman); includes 2 African Americans, 14 international. Average age 29. 35 applicants, 97% accepted, 7 enrolled. In 2009, 10 master's awarded. *Degree requirements:* For master's, thesis or alternative. *Entrance requirements:* For master's, bachelor's degree in engineering. Additional exam requirements/recommendations for international students: Required—TOEFL (minimum score 520 paper-based; 190 computer-based; 70 iBT); Recommended—IELTS (minimum score 5.5). *Application deadline:* For fall admission, 5/31 for international students; for winter admission, 10/15 for international students; for spring admission, 1/15 for international students. Applications are processed on a rolling basis. Application fee: $50. Electronic applications accepted. *Expenses:* Tuition: Part-time $700 per credit. Required fees: $45 per term. One-time fee: $390 part-time. *Financial support:* Research assistantships with partial tuition reimbursements, teaching assistantships with partial tuition reimbursements, career-related internships or fieldwork, Federal Work-Study, scholarships/grants, tuition waivers, and unspecified assistantships available. Support available to part-time students. Financial award application deadline: 5/1; financial award applicants required to submit FAFSA. *Unit head:* Dr. Agamemnon D. Koutsospyros, Coordinator, 203-932-7398. *Application contact:* Eloise Gormley, Director of Graduate Admissions, 203-932-7449, Fax: 203-932-7137, E-mail: gradinfo@newhaven.edu.

The University of Texas at Austin, Graduate School, Cockrell School of Engineering, Department of Civil, Architectural and Environmental Engineering, Program in Environmental and Water Resources Engineering, Austin, TX 78712-1111. Offers MS, PhD. *Accreditation:* ABET. Part-time programs available. *Degree requirements:* For master's, thesis or alternative. *Entrance requirements:* For master's, GRE General Test. Additional exam requirements/recommendations for international students: Required—TOEFL. Electronic applications accepted.

The University of Texas at Tyler, College of Engineering and Computer Science, Department of Civil Engineering, Tyler, TX 75799-0001. Offers environmental engineering (MS); industrial safety (MS); structural engineering (MS); transportation engineering (MS); water resources engineering (MS). Part-time and evening/weekend programs available. *Faculty:* 6 full-time (0 women). *Students:* 5 full-time (1 woman), 7 part-time (1 woman); includes 1 African American, 1 Asian American or Pacific Islander, 1 Hispanic American, 1 international. Average age 26. 5 applicants, 80% accepted, 3 enrolled. *Degree requirements:* For master's, thesis optional. *Entrance requirements:* For master's, GRE General Test, bachelor's degree in engineering, associated science degree. Additional exam requirements/recommendations for international students: Required—TOEFL (minimum score 79 computer-based). *Application deadline:* For fall admission, 8/17 priority date for domestic students, 7/1 priority date for international students; for spring admission, 12/21 priority date for domestic students, 11/1 priority date for international students. Application fee: $25 ($50 for international students). *Expenses:* Tuition, state resident: part-time $665 per semester hour. Tuition, nonresident: part-time $942 per semester hour. Part-time tuition and fees vary according to degree level and program. *Financial support:* Application deadline: 7/1. *Faculty research:* Non-destructive strength testing, indoor air quality, transportation routing and signaling, pavement replacement criteria, flood water routing, construction and long-term behavior of innovative geotechnical foundation and embankment construction used in highway construction, engineering education. *Unit head:* Dr. Ron Welch, Chair, 903-566-7002, Fax: 903-566-7337, E-mail: rwelch@uttyler.edu. *Application contact:* Dr. Torey Nalbone, Program Chair, 903-565-5520, Fax: 903-566-7337, E-mail: tnalbone@uttyler.edu.

University of Washington, Graduate School, College of Engineering, Department of Civil and Environmental Engineering, Seattle, WA 98195-2700. Offers construction engineering (MSCE); environmental engineering (MS, MSCE, MSE, PhD); hydrology, water resources, and environmental fluid mechanics (MS, MSCE, MSE, PhD); structural and geotechnical engineering and mechanics (MS, MSCE, MSE, PhD); transportation and construction engineering (MS, MSE, PhD); transportation engineering (MSCE). Part-time programs available. Postbaccalaureate distance learning degree programs offered (no on-campus study). *Faculty:* 36 full-time (9 women), 16 part-time/adjunct (6 women). *Students:* 186 full-time (62 women), 57 part-time (10 women); includes 35 minority (24 Asian Americans or Pacific Islanders, 11 Hispanic Americans), 58 international. 360 applicants, 68% accepted, 98 enrolled. In 2009, 74 master's, 8 doctorates awarded. Terminal master's awarded for partial completion of doctoral program. *Degree requirements:* For master's, thesis (for some programs); for doctorate, comprehensive exam, thesis/dissertation. *Entrance requirements:* For master's, GRE General Test, minimum GPA of 3.0; for doctorate, GRE, minimum GPA of 3.5. Additional exam requirements/recommendations for international students: Required—TOEFL (minimum score 580 paper-based; 237 computer-based; 70 iBT). *Application deadline:* For fall admission, 1/15 priority date for domestic and international students. Applications are processed on a rolling basis. Application fee: $65. Electronic applications accepted. *Financial support:* In 2009–10, 5 students received support, including 13 fellowships with full and partial tuition reimbursements available (averaging $16,173 per year), 68 research assistantships with full tuition reimbursements available (averaging $16,173 per year), 12 teaching assistantships with full tuition reimbursements available (averaging $16,173 per year); scholarships/grants also available. Financial award application deadline: 1/15. *Faculty research:* Environmental/water resources, hydrology; construction/transportation; structures/ geotechnical. Total annual research expenditures: $11.4 million. *Unit head:* Dr. Gregory R. Miller, Professor and Chair, 206-543-0350, Fax: 206-543-1543, E-mail: gmiller@uw.edu. *Application contact:* Lorna Latal, Graduate Adviser, 206-543-2574, Fax: 206-543-1543, E-mail: llatal@u.washington.edu.

Utah State University, School of Graduate Studies, College of Engineering, Department of Biological and Irrigation Engineering, Logan, UT 84322. Offers biological and agricultural engineering (MS, PhD); irrigation engineering (MS, PhD). Part-time programs available. Terminal master's awarded for partial completion of doctoral program. *Degree requirements:* For master's, thesis (for some programs); for doctorate, thesis/dissertation. *Entrance requirements:* For master's and doctorate, GRE General Test, minimum GPA of 3.0. Additional exam requirements/recommendations for international students: Required—TOEFL. *Faculty research:* On-farm water management, crop-water yield modeling, irrigation, biosensors, biological engineering.

Villanova University, College of Engineering, Department of Civil and Environmental Engineering, Program in Water Resources and Environmental Engineering, Villanova, PA 19085-1699. Offers MSWREE. Part-time and evening/weekend programs available. Postbaccalaureate distance learning degree programs offered (no on-campus study). *Degree requirements:* For master's, thesis optional. *Entrance requirements:* For master's, GRE General Test (for applicants with degrees from foreign universities), BCE or bachelor's degree in science or related engineering field, minimum GPA of 3.0. Additional exam requirements/recommendations for international students: Required—TOEFL (minimum score 600 paper-based; 250 computer-based; 100 iBT). Electronic applications accepted. *Expenses:* Tuition: Part-time $630 per credit. Required fees: $60 per credit. Part-time tuition and fees vary according to degree level and program. *Faculty research:* Photocatalytic decontamination and disinfection of water, urban storm water wetlands, economy and risk, removal and destruction of organic acids in water, sludge treatment.

FLORIDA INSTITUTE OF TECHNOLOGY

College of Engineering
Graduate Programs in Civil Engineering

Programs of Study

Florida Institute of Technology offers programs of study leading to the Master of Science and Doctor of Philosophy in civil engineering. These programs are designed to provide opportunities for students' development of professional engineering competence and scholarly achievement.

The Master of Science in civil engineering provides specialization in the areas of construction, environmental, geoenvironmental, geotechnical, structures, and water resources engineering. The degree is conferred upon students who have successfully completed a minimum of 30 credit hours in either a thesis or a nonthesis program consisting of both required and elective course work. Students in the thesis program must successfully defend their thesis, while students in the nonthesis program are required to pass a comprehensive examination.

The Doctor of Philosophy degree program in civil engineering is offered for those students who wish to conduct advanced research in environmental/water resources or structural/geotechnical engineering. The program prepares students for conducting scientific engineering research, and completion of the doctoral dissertation leads to a significant contribution to the knowledge base of a particular area. A minimum of 24 credit hours of course work and 18 credit hours of dissertation beyond a master's degree are required.

Research Facilities

Laboratories and software for research are available in the areas of structures, materials, soils, solid waste, and water resources. Other campus laboratories may also be used by students conducting graduate research. Analytical capabilities are extended by means of cooperative projects with the academic programs in aerospace engineering, chemical engineering, mechanical engineering, ocean engineering, biology, chemistry, oceanography, and the Life Sciences Research Complex.

Financial Aid

Graduate teaching and research assistantships are available to qualified students. For the 2010–11 academic year, typical stipends for teaching assistants range from $10,000 upward for two semesters, for what are approximately half-time duties. Teaching assistants who are in the thesis option are granted partial or full tuition remission. Stipends for research students are usually higher than those for teaching assistants.

Cost of Study

For the 2010–11 academic year, tuition is $1040 per semester credit hour for all students. Tuition is waived for some graduate assistants.

Living and Housing Costs

Room and board on campus cost approximately $4500 per semester in 2010–11. On-campus housing (dormitories and apartments) is available for full-time single and married graduate students, but priority for dormitory rooms is given to undergraduate students. Many apartment complexes and rental houses are available near the campus.

Student Group

Approximately 20 students are enrolled in various areas of specialization in civil engineering. About 75 percent of the students are receiving some sort of financial support. Around 10 percent of the master's students have continued on to the Ph.D. degree.

Student Outcomes

Graduates of the graduate programs in civil engineering are employed by numerous counties, including Brevard, Collier, and Orange; by state agencies, such as the Florida Department of Environmental Protection, the Florida Department of Transportation, and the U.S. Army Corps of Engineers; and by numerous engineering and construction-related consulting firms, such as Agnoli, Barber & Brundage, Inc.; Bechtel; Berryman & Henigan; Camp, Dresser & McKee, Inc.; Centex-Rooney; CH2M Hill; Disney; GeoSyntec Consultants; HNTB; Kimley-Horn and Associates, Inc.; PBS&J; Technical Solutions; and many others. Students secure employment throughout the United States and internationally.

Location

The campus is located in Melbourne, on Florida's east coast. It is an area, located 3 miles from Atlantic Ocean beaches, with a year-round subtropical climate. The area's economy is supported by a well-balanced mix of industries in electronics, aviation, light manufacturing, optics, communications, agriculture, and tourism. Many industries support activities at the Kennedy Space Center.

The Institute

Florida Institute of Technology, founded in 1958, has developed into a distinctive independent university that provides undergraduate and graduate education in engineering and sciences for students from throughout the United States and many other countries. Florida Tech is supported by local industry and is the recipient of many research grants and contracts.

Applying

Applicants for graduate study in civil engineering should have an undergraduate degree in civil engineering. An applicant whose degree is in another field of engineering or in the applied sciences will be reviewed; however, undergraduate course work may be required prior to starting the Master of Science program.

Forms and instructions for applying for admission and assistantships are sent upon request. Applicants are asked to submit two letters of recommendation from academic references and a statement of purpose giving their reason for graduate study. Although the GRE is not required, it is considered for students with marginal undergraduate academic performance. International students applying for assistantships must have a TOEFL score greater than 600. International students without English proficiency and with a TOEFL score less than 550 are required to enroll in English studies before beginning their graduate studies. Separate application for an assistantship should be made on forms available from the graduate school.

Correspondence and Information

Office of Graduate Admission
Florida Institute of Technology
150 West University Boulevard
Melbourne, Florida 32901
Phone: 321-674-8027
      800-944-4348 (toll-free in the U.S.)
Fax: 321-723-9468
E-mail: grad-admissions@fit.edu
Web site: http://www.fit.edu

Dr. Ashok Pandit, Civil Engineering
Florida Institute of Technology
150 West University Boulevard
Melbourne, Florida 32901
Phone: 321-674-8048
Fax: 321-674-7565
E-mail: apandit@fit.edu
Web site: http://civil.fit.edu

Florida Institute of Technology

THE FACULTY AND THEIR RESEARCH

Paul J. Cosentino, Professor; Ph.D., Texas A&M; PE. Pavement design and evaluation; transportation planning; containment of hazardous wastes; geotechnical engineering, with emphasis on in situ testing of soils, instrumentation evaluation of pavements, and slope stability. Current funded research projects are the application of fiber-optic sensors for traffic monitoring, the development of a fiber-optic weigh-in-motion sensor, and the use of reclaimed asphalt pavement as a highway fill material.

Howell H. Heck, Associate Professor; Ph.D., Arkansas; PE. Solid-waste management, waste composition measurements, construction and demolition waste recycling, groundwater exchange with surface water. Current funded projects include modeling construction and demolition waste composition for the state of Florida and surface water and groundwater exchange in the Indian River Lagoon and St. Lucie River.

Edward H. Kalajian, Professor; Ph.D., Massachusetts; PE. Geotechnical engineering, foundations, stabilization of waste materials for beneficial uses. Current funded research projects are the use of reclaimed asphalt pavement as a highway material.

Ralph V. Locurcio, Professor; Ph.D. candidate, Purdue; PE. Project management, reconstruction management, mentoring and retention of young engineers.

Ashok Pandit, Professor; Ph.D., Clemson; PE. Groundwater hydraulics and hydrology, numerical groundwater modeling, storm water management. Current research projects are modeling of saltwater intrusion in aquifers, groundwater mounding below retention/detention basins, continuous simulation nonpoint source water quality models, BMP efficiency evaluation, and rainfall/runoff relationships.

Jean-Paul Pinelli, Associate Professor; Ph.D., Georgia Tech; PE. Structural dynamics, earthquake, and wind engineering. Current research projects are the effect of tornadic and hurricane winds and structures, the use of energy dissipative devices to dampen vibrations, and the use of structural physical models as teaching aids.

Section 8
Computer Science and Information Technology

This section contains a directory of institutions offering graduate work in computer science and information technology, followed by in-depth entries submitted by institutions that chose to prepare detailed program descriptions. Additional information about programs listed in the directory but not augmented by an in-depth entry may be obtained by writing directly to the dean of a graduate school or chair of a department at the address given in the directory.

For programs offering related work, see also in this book *Electrical and Computer Engineering, Engineering and Applied Sciences,* and *Industrial Engineering.* In the other guides in this series:

Graduate Programs in the Humanities, Arts & Social Sciences
See *Communication and Media*
Graduate Programs in the Physical Sciences, Mathematics, Agricultural Sciences, the Environment & Natural Resources
See *Mathematical Sciences*
Graduate Programs in Business, Education, Health, Information Studies, Law & Social Work, Allied Health
See *Business Administration and Management* and *Library and Information Studies*

CONTENTS

Program Directories

Close-Ups

Artificial Intelligence/Robotics

California State University, Northridge, Graduate Studies, College of Engineering and Computer Science, Department of Manufacturing Systems Engineering and Management, Northridge, CA 91330. Offers engineering automation (MS); engineering management (MS); manufacturing systems engineering (MS); materials engineering (MS). Postbaccalaureate distance learning degree programs offered. *Faculty:* 6 full-time (1 woman), 33 part-time/adjunct (12 women). *Students:* 137 full-time (18 women), 115 part-time (20 women); includes 4 African Americans, 22 Asian Americans or Pacific Islanders, 19 Hispanic Americans, 149 international. Average age 27. 210 applicants, 68% accepted, 69 enrolled. In 2009, 78 master's awarded. *Entrance requirements:* For master's, GRE (if cumulative undergraduate GPA less than 3.0). *Application deadline:* For fall admission, 3/30 for domestic students; for spring admission, 9/30 for domestic students. Application fee: $55. *Unit head:* Prof. Behzad Bavarian, Acting Chair, 818-677-2167. *Application contact:* Prof. Behzad Bavarian, Acting Chair, 818-677-2167.

Carnegie Mellon University, College of Humanities and Social Sciences, Department of Statistics, Pittsburgh, PA 15213-3891. Offers machine learning and statistics (PhD); mathematical finance (PhD); statistics (MS, PhD), including applied statistics (PhD), computational statistics (PhD), theoretical statistics (PhD); statistics and public policy (PhD). Terminal master's awarded for partial completion of doctoral program. *Degree requirements:* For doctorate, comprehensive exam, thesis/dissertation. *Entrance requirements:* For master's and doctorate, GRE General Test. Additional exam requirements/recommendations for international students: Required—TOEFL. *Faculty research:* Stochastic processes, Bayesian statistics, statistical computing, decision theory, psychiatric statistics.

Carnegie Mellon University, School of Computer Science, Department of Machine Learning, Pittsburgh, PA 15213-3891. Offers PhD.

Carnegie Mellon University, School of Computer Science and Carnegie Institute of Technology and Tepper School of Business, Robotics Institute, Pittsburgh, PA 15213-3891. Offers MS, PhD. *Degree requirements:* For doctorate, thesis/dissertation. *Entrance requirements:* For doctorate, GRE General Test, GRE Subject Test. Additional exam requirements/recommendations for international students: Required—TOEFL. *Faculty research:* Perception, cognition, manipulation, robot systems, manufacturing.

Cornell University, Graduate School, Graduate Fields of Engineering, Field of Computer Science, Ithaca, NY 14853-0001. Offers algorithms (M Eng, PhD); applied logic and automated reasoning (M Eng, PhD); artificial intelligence (M Eng, PhD); computer graphics (M Eng, PhD); computer science (M Eng, PhD); computer vision (M Eng, PhD); concurrency and distributed computing (M Eng, PhD); information organization and retrieval (M Eng, PhD); operating systems (M Eng, PhD); parallel computing (M Eng, PhD); programming environments (M Eng, PhD); programming languages and methodology (M Eng, PhD); robotics (M Eng, PhD); scientific computing (M Eng, PhD); theory of computation (M Eng, PhD). *Faculty:* 74 full-time (10 women). *Students:* 209 full-time (46 women); includes 18 minority (1 African American, 16 Asian Americans or Pacific Islanders, 1 Hispanic American), 119 international. Average age 26. 897 applicants, 26% accepted, 109 enrolled. In 2009, 97 master's, 14 doctorates awarded. *Degree requirements:* For doctorate, comprehensive exam, thesis/dissertation. *Entrance requirements:* For master's, GRE General Test, 2 letters of recommendation; for doctorate, GRE General Test, GRE Subject Test (computer science or mathematics), 3 letters of recommendation. Additional exam requirements/recommendations for international students: Required—TOEFL (minimum score 505 paper-based; 213 computer-based; 77 iBT). *Application deadline:* For fall admission, 1/1 for domestic students. Application fee: $70. Electronic applications accepted. *Expenses:* Tuition: Full-time $29,500. Required fees: $70. Full-time tuition and fees vary according to degree level, program and student level. *Financial support:* In 2009–10, 100 students received support, including 10 fellowships with full tuition reimbursements available, 4 research assistantships with full tuition reimbursements available, 18 teaching assistantships with full tuition reimbursements available; institutionally sponsored loans, scholarships/grants, health care benefits, tuition waivers (full and partial), and unspecified assistantships also available. Financial award applicants required to submit FAFSA. *Faculty research:* Artificial intelligence, operating systems and databases, programming languages and security, scientific computing, theory of computing, computational biology and graphics. *Unit head:* Director of Graduate Studies, 607-255-8593, Fax: 607-255-4428. *Application contact:* Graduate Field Assistant, 607-255-8593, Fax: 607-255-4428, E-mail: phd@cs.cornell.edu.

Eastern Michigan University, Graduate School, College of Arts and Sciences, Department of Computer Science, Ypsilanti, MI 48197. Offers artificial intelligence (Graduate Certificate); computer science (MS). Part-time and evening/weekend programs available. Postbaccalaureate distance learning degree programs offered (no on-campus study). *Faculty:* 15 full-time (5 women). *Students:* 16 full-time (6 women), 21 part-time (5 women); includes 6 minority (1 African American, 1 American Indian/Alaska Native, 4 Asian Americans or Pacific Islanders), 20 international. Average age 29. 88 applicants, 57% accepted, 10 enrolled. In 2009, 12 master's, 2 other advanced degrees awarded. *Degree requirements:* For master's, thesis or alternative. *Entrance requirements:* For master's, at least 18 credit hours of 200-level (or above) computer science courses including data structures, programming languages like java, C or C++, computer organization; courses in discrete mathematics, probability and statistics, linear algebra and calculus; minimum GPA of 2.75 in computer science. Additional exam requirements/recommendations for international students: Required—TOEFL. *Application deadline:* For fall admission, 8/1 for domestic students, 5/1 for international students; for winter admission, 12/1 for domestic students, 10/1 for international students; for spring admission, 4/1 for domestic students, 2/1 for international students. Application fee: $35. Tuition and fees vary according to course level. *Financial support:* Fellowships, research assistantships with full tuition reimbursements, teaching assistantships with full tuition reimbursements, career-related internships or fieldwork, Federal Work-Study, institutionally sponsored loans, scholarships/grants, tuition waivers (partial), and unspecified assistantships available. Support available to part-time students. Financial award applicants required to submit FAFSA. *Unit head:* Dr. William McMillan, Department Head, 734-487-1063, Fax: 734-487-6824, E-mail: wmcmillan@emich.edu. *Application contact:* Graduate Admissions, 734-487-3060, Fax: 734-487-6559, E-mail: graduate_admissions@emich.edu.

Eastern Michigan University, Graduate School, College of Arts and Sciences, Department of English Language and Literature, Program in Language Technology, Ypsilanti, MI 48197. Offers Graduate Certificate. Part-time and evening/weekend programs available. *Students:* 1 (woman) part-time, all international. Average age 27. *Entrance requirements:* Additional exam requirements/recommendations for international students: Required—TOEFL. Application fee: $35. Tuition and fees vary according to course level. *Financial support:* Research assistantships with full tuition reimbursements, teaching assistantships with full tuition reimbursements, career-related internships or fieldwork, Federal Work-Study, institutionally sponsored loans, scholarships/grants, tuition waivers (full and partial), and unspecified assistantships available. Support available to part-time students. *Unit head:* Dr. Rebecca Sipes, Department Head, 734-487-4220, Fax: 734-487-9744, E-mail: rebecca.sipe@emich.edu. *Application contact:* Dr. T. Daniel Seely, Program Advisor, 734-487-0145, Fax: 734-483-9744, E-mail: tseely@emich.edu.

Indiana University–Purdue University Indianapolis, School of Engineering and Technology, Department of Electrical Engineering, Indianapolis, IN 46202-2896. Offers biomedical engineering (MS, PhD); electrical and computer engineering (MS, MSECE, PhD), including biomedical engineering (MSECE), control and automation (MSECE), signal processing (MSECE); engineering (interdisciplinary) (MSE). *Students:* 41 full-time (10 women), 27 part-time (2 women); includes 11 minority (5 African Americans, 4 Asian Americans or Pacific Islanders, 2 Hispanic Americans), 38 international. Average age 27. 178 applicants, 56% accepted, 54 enrolled. In 2009, 28 master's awarded. Application fee: $55 ($65 for international students). *Unit head:* Yaobin Chen, Unit Head, 317-274-4032, Fax: 317-274-4493. *Application contact:* Valerie Diemer, Graduate Program, 317-278-4960, Fax: 317-278-1671, E-mail: grad@engr.iupui.edu.

Instituto Tecnológico y de Estudios Superiores de Monterrey, Campus Monterrey, Graduate and Research Division, Program in Computer Science, Monterrey, Mexico. Offers artificial intelligence (PhD); computer science (MS); information systems (MS); information technology (MS). Part-time programs available. *Degree requirements:* For master's, one foreign language, thesis; for doctorate, one foreign language, thesis/dissertation. *Entrance requirements:* For master's, EXADEP; for doctorate, master's degree in related field. Additional exam requirements/recommendations for international students: Required—TOEFL. *Faculty research:* Distributed systems, software engineering, decision support systems.

Instituto Tecnológico y de Estudios Superiores de Monterrey, Campus Monterrey, Graduate and Research Division, Programs in Engineering, Monterrey, Mexico. Offers applied statistics (M Eng); artificial intelligence (PhD); automation engineering (M Eng); chemical engineering (M Eng); civil engineering (M Eng); electrical engineering (M Eng); electronic engineering (M Eng); environmental engineering (M Eng); industrial engineering (M Eng, PhD); manufacturing engineering (M Eng); mechanical engineering (M Eng); systems and quality engineering (M Eng). Part-time and evening/weekend programs available. Terminal master's awarded for partial completion of doctoral program. *Degree requirements:* For master's, one foreign language, thesis; for doctorate, one foreign language, thesis/dissertation. *Entrance requirements:* For master's, EXADEP; for doctorate, GRE, master's degree in related field. Additional exam requirements/recommendations for international students: Required—TOEFL. *Faculty research:* Flexible manufacturing cells, materials, statistical methods, environmental prevention, control and evaluation.

Portland State University, Graduate Studies, Systems Science Program, Portland, OR 97207-0751. Offers computational intelligence (Certificate); computer modeling and simulation (Certificate); systems science (MS); systems science/anthropology (PhD); systems science/business administration (PhD); systems science/civil engineering (PhD); systems science/economics (PhD); systems science/engineering management (PhD); systems science/general (PhD); systems science/mathematical sciences (PhD); systems science/mechanical engineering (PhD); systems science/psychology (PhD); systems science/sociology (PhD). *Degree requirements:* For doctorate, variable foreign language requirement, thesis/dissertation. *Entrance requirements:* For master's, 2 letters of recommendation; for doctorate, GMAT, GRE General Test, minimum undergraduate GPA of 3.0. Additional exam requirements/recommendations for international students: Required—TOEFL. *Faculty research:* Systems theory and methodology, artificial intelligence neural networks, information theory, nonlinear dynamics/chaos, modeling and simulation.

South Dakota School of Mines and Technology, Graduate Division, College of Science and Letters, Department of Mathematics and Computer Science, Rapid City, SD 57701-3995. Offers computer science (MS); robotics and intelligent autonomous systems (MS). Part-time programs available. *Faculty:* 8 full-time (1 woman), 3 part-time/adjunct (0 women). *Students:* 6 full-time (3 women), 6 part-time (1 woman); includes 2 minority (1 American Indian/Alaska Native, 1 Asian American or Pacific Islander), 3 international. Average age 34. 21 applicants, 48% accepted, 7 enrolled. In 2009, 7 master's awarded. *Entrance requirements:* Additional exam requirements/recommendations for international students: Required—TOEFL, TWE. *Application deadline:* For fall admission, 7/1 priority date for domestic students, 4/1 for international students; for spring admission, 11/1 for domestic students, 9/1 for international students. Applications are processed on a rolling basis. Application fee: $35. Electronic applications accepted. *Expenses:* Tuition, state resident: full-time $3340; part-time $139 per credit hour. Tuition, nonresident: full-time $7060; part-time $294 per credit hour. Required fees: $3270. *Financial support:* In 2009–10, 4 research assistantships with partial tuition reimbursements (averaging $13,139 per year), 6 teaching assistantships with partial tuition reimbursements (averaging $6,610 per year) were awarded; fellowships, Federal Work-Study and institutionally sponsored loans also available. Support available to part-time students. Financial award application deadline: 5/15. *Faculty research:* Database systems, remote sensing, numerical modeling, artificial intelligence, neural networks. *Unit head:* Dr. Kyle Riley, Chair, 605-394-6147, E-mail: kyle.riley@sdsmt.edu. *Application contact:* Jeannette R. Nilson, Administrative Support Coordinator, Graduate Education, 800-454-8162 Ext. 1206, Fax: 605-394-5360, E-mail: graduate_admissions@sdsmt.edu.

University of California, Riverside, Graduate Division, Department of Electrical Engineering, Riverside, CA 92521-0102. Offers electrical engineering (MS, PhD), including computer engineering, control and robotics, intelligent systems, nano-materials, devices and circuits, signal processing and communications. Terminal master's awarded for partial completion of doctoral program. *Degree requirements:* For master's, thesis optional; for doctorate, thesis/dissertation, qualifying exams. *Entrance requirements:* For master's and doctorate, GRE General Test, minimum GPA of 3.25. Additional exam requirements/recommendations for international students: Required—TOEFL (minimum score 550 paper-based; 213 computer-based; 80 iBT). Electronic applications accepted. *Faculty research:* Solid state devices, integrated circuits, signal processing.

See Close-Up on page 375.

University of California, San Diego, Office of Graduate Studies, Department of Electrical and Computer Engineering, La Jolla, CA 92093. Offers applied ocean science (MS, PhD); applied physics (MS, PhD); communication theory and systems (MS, PhD); computer engineering (MS, PhD); electrical engineering (M Eng); electronic circuits and systems (MS, PhD); intelligent systems, robotics and control (MS, PhD); photonics (MS, PhD); signal and image processing (MS, PhD). MS only offered to students who have been admitted to the PhD program. *Entrance requirements:* For master's and doctorate, GRE General Test. Electronic applications accepted.

University of Georgia, Graduate School, College of Arts and Sciences, Artificial Intelligence Center, Athens, GA 30602. Offers MS. *Faculty:* 1 full-time (0 women). *Students:* 20 full-time (4 women), 6 part-time (2 women); includes 3 minority (2 African Americans, 1 Hispanic American), 10 international. 17 applicants, 59% accepted, 10 enrolled. In 2009, 5 master's awarded. *Degree requirements:* For master's, thesis. *Entrance requirements:* For master's, GRE General Test. *Application deadline:* For fall admission, 7/1 priority date for domestic students; for spring admission, 11/15 for domestic students. Application fee: $50. Electronic applications accepted. *Expenses:* Tuition, state resident: full-time $6000; part-time $250 per credit hour. Tuition, nonresident: full-time $20,904; part-time $871 per credit hour. Required fees: $730 per semester. *Financial support:* Unspecified assistantships available. *Unit head:* Dr. Walter Don Potter, Director, 706-542-0361, E-mail: potter@uga.edu. *Application contact:* Dr. Khaled M. Rasheed, Graduate Coordinator, 706-542-3444, Fax: 706-542-2966, E-mail: khaled@cs.uga.edu.

University of Pittsburgh, Katz Graduate School of Business, Doctoral Program in Business Administration, Pittsburgh, PA 15260. Offers accounting (PhD); finance (PhD); information systems (PhD); marketing (PhD); operations/decision sciences/artificial intelligence (PhD); organizational behavior and human resource management (PhD); strategic planning (PhD). *Accreditation:* AACSB. *Faculty:* 50 full-time (15 women). *Students:* 53 full-time (21 women); includes 8 minority (4 African Americans, 2 Asian Americans or Pacific Islanders, 2 Hispanic Americans), 22 international. 324 applicants, 4% accepted, 12 enrolled. In 2009, 11 doctorates awarded. *Degree requirements:* For doctorate, comprehensive exam, thesis/dissertation. *Entrance requirements:* For doctorate, GMAT or GRE, references, work experience relevant for individual program. Additional exam requirements/recommendations for international students: Required—TOEFL or IELTS. *Application deadline:* For fall admission, 2/1 priority date for domestic and international students. Applications are processed on a rolling basis. Application fee: $50. Electronic applications accepted. *Expenses:* Tuition, state resident: full-time $16,402; part-time $665 per credit. Tuition, nonresident: full-time $28,694; part-time $1175 per credit. Required fees: $690; $175 per term. Tuition and fees vary according to program. *Financial support:* In 2009–10, 36 students received support, including 31 research assistantships with full tuition reimbursements available (averaging $18,450 per year), 5 teaching assistantships with full tuition reimbursements available (averaging $23,511 per year); fellowships, Federal Work-Study, scholarships/grants, health care benefits, and unspecified assistantships also available. Financial award application deadline: 2/1. *Faculty research:* Accounting statements and reporting, incentives and governance; corporate finance, mergers and acquisitions; information systems processes, structures, OR, supply chain, and decision-making; organizational structure, knowledge management, and corporate strategy; consumer behavior and marketing models. Total annual research expenditures: $362,777. *Unit head:* Dr. John E. Hulland, Director, 412-648-1534, Fax: 412-624-3633, E-mail: jhulland@katz.pitt.edu. *Application contact:* Carrie Woods, Assistant Director, 412-648-1525, Fax: 412-624-3633, E-mail: cawoods@katz.pitt.edu.

University of Southern California, Graduate School, Viterbi School of Engineering, Department of Computer Science, Los Angeles, CA 90089. Offers computer networks (MS); computer science (MS, PhD); computer security (MS); game development (MS); high performance computing and simulations (MS); human language technology (MS); intelligent robotics (MS); multimedia and creative technologies (MS); software engineering (MS). Part-time programs available. Postbaccalaureate distance learning degree programs offered (no on-campus study). *Faculty:* 26 full-time (2 women), 56 part-time/adjunct (7 women). *Students:* 711 full-time (148 women), 304 part-time (55 women); includes 76 minority (5 African Americans, 59 Asian Americans or Pacific Islanders, 12 Hispanic Americans), 816 international. 2,017 applicants, 39% accepted, 382 enrolled. In 2009, 332 master's, 32 doctorates awarded. Terminal master's awarded for partial completion of doctoral program. *Degree requirements:* For doctorate, comprehensive exam, thesis/dissertation. *Entrance requirements:* For master's, GRE General Test; for doctorate, General GRE. *Application deadline:* For fall admission, 3/1 priority date for domestic and international students; for spring admission, 10/1 priority date for domestic and international students. Applications are processed on a rolling basis. Application fee: $85. Electronic applications accepted. *Expenses:* Tuition: Full-time $25,980; part-time $1315 per unit. Required fees: $554. One-time fee: $35 full-time. Full-time tuition and fees vary according to degree level and program. *Financial support:* In 2009–10, fellowships with full tuition reimbursements (averaging $30,000 per year), research assistantships with full tuition reimbursements (averaging $19,250 per year), teaching assistantships with full tuition reimbursements (averaging $19,250 per year) were awarded; career-related internships or fieldwork, scholarships/grants, health care benefits, and unspecified assistantships also available. Financial award application deadline: 12/1; financial award applicants required to submit CSS PROFILE or FAFSA. *Faculty research:* Databases, computer graphics and computer vision, software engineering, networks and security, robotics, multimedia and virtual reality. Total annual research expenditures: $10 million. *Unit head:* Dr. Shanghua Teng, Seeley G. Mudd Professor of Engineering and Department Chair, 213-740-4498, E-mail: shanghua@ usc.edu. *Application contact:* Steve Schrader, Director of Student Affairs, 213-740-4779, E-mail: steve.schrader@usc.edu.

The University of Tennessee, Graduate School, College of Engineering, Department of Mechanical, Aerospace and Biomedical Engineering, Program in Engineering Science, Knoxville, TN 37996. Offers applied artificial intelligence (MS); composite materials (MS, PhD); computational mechanics (MS, PhD); engineering science (MS, PhD); fluid mechanics (MS, PhD); industrial engineering (PhD); optical engineering (MS, PhD); solid mechanics (MS, PhD); MS/MBA. Part-time programs available. *Students:* 9 full-time (0 women), 4 part-time (1 woman); includes 2 minority (both African Americans), 2 international. Average age 34. 5 applicants, 60% accepted, 1 enrolled. In 2009, 2 master's awarded. *Degree requirements:* For master's, thesis or alternative; for doctorate, comprehensive exam, thesis/dissertation. *Entrance requirements:* For master's and doctorate, GRE, minimum GPA of 2.7. Additional exam requirements/recommendations for international students: Required—TOEFL (minimum score 550 paper-based; 213 computer-based). *Application deadline:* For fall admission, 2/1 priority date for domestic and international students; for spring admission, 6/15 priority date for international students. Applications are processed on a rolling basis. Application fee: $35. Electronic applications accepted. *Expenses:* Tuition, state resident: full-time $6826; part-time $380 per semester hour. Tuition, nonresident: full-time $21,844; part-time $1147 per semester hour. Tuition and fees vary according to program. *Financial support:* In 2009–10, 1 student received support, including 5 research assistantships with full tuition reimbursements available (averaging $14,628 per year), 2 teaching assistantships with full tuition reimbursements available (averaging $10,104 per year); fellowships, career-related internships or fieldwork, Federal Work-Study, institutionally sponsored loans, health care benefits, and unspecified assistantships also available. Financial award application deadline: 2/1; financial award applicants required to submit FAFSA. *Faculty research:* Thermal science, computational mechanics, computational fluid dynamics, micro/nano-scale science and engineering for bio-systems. *Unit head:* Dr. William Hamel, Head, 865-974-5115, Fax: 865-974-5274, E-mail: whamel@utk.edu. *Application contact:* Dr. Gary V. Smith, Chair, Graduate Programs Committee, 865-974-5271, E-mail: gvsmith@utk.edu.

Villanova University, College of Engineering, Department of Electrical and Computer Engineering, Program in Electrical Engineering, Villanova, PA 19085-1699. Offers communication systems engineering (Certificate); electric power systems (Certificate); electrical engineering (MSEE); electro mechanical systems (Certificate); high frequency systems (Certificate); intelligent systems (Certificate); wireless and digital communications (Certificate). Part-time and evening/weekend programs available. *Degree requirements:* For master's, thesis optional. *Entrance requirements:* For master's, GRE General Test (for applicants with degrees from foreign universities), BEE, minimum GPA of 3.0. Additional exam requirements/recommendations for international students: Required—TOEFL (minimum score 600 paper-based; 250 computer-based; 100 iBT). *Expenses:* Tuition: Part-time $630 per credit. Required fees: $60 per credit. Part-time tuition and fees vary according to degree level and program. *Faculty research:* Signal processing, communications, antennas, devices.

Bioinformatics

Arizona State University, Graduate College, Ira A. Fulton School of Engineering, Department of Biomedical Informatics, Tempe, AZ 85287. Offers MS, PhD.

Boston University, Graduate School of Arts and Sciences and College of Engineering, Intercollegiate Program in Bioinformatics, Boston, MA 02215. Offers MS, PhD. *Students:* 59 full-time (17 women), 15 part-time (5 women); includes 8 minority (1 African American, 5 Asian Americans or Pacific Islanders, 2 Hispanic Americans), 31 international. Average age 29. 145 applicants, 28% accepted, 22 enrolled. In 2009, 8 master's, 17 doctorates awarded. *Degree requirements:* For doctorate, thesis/dissertation. *Entrance requirements:* For master's and doctorate, GRE General Test, GRE Subject Test, 3 letters of recommendation, resume. Additional exam requirements/recommendations for international students: Required—TOEFL (minimum score 550 paper-based; 213 computer-based). *Application deadline:* For fall admission, 12/1 for domestic and international students; for spring admission, 10/1 for domestic and international students. Application fee: $70. Electronic applications accepted. *Expenses:* Tuition: Full-time $37,910; part-time $1184 per credit hour. Required fees: $386; $40 per semester. Part-time tuition and fees vary according to class time, course level, degree level and program. *Financial support:* In 2009–10, 27 students received support, including 4 fellowships with full tuition reimbursements available (averaging $18,900 per year), 23 research assistantships with full tuition reimbursements available (averaging $18,400 per year); career-related internships or fieldwork, Federal Work-Study, scholarships/grants, traineeships, and unspecified assistantships also available. Financial award application deadline: 12/1; financial award applicants required to submit FAFSA. *Unit head:* Tom Tullius, Director, 617-353-2482, E-mail: tullius@bu.edu. *Application contact:* David King, Graduate Administrator, 617-358-0751, Fax: 617-353-5929, E-mail: dking@bu.edu.

Brandeis University, Rabb School of Continuing Studies, Division of Graduate Professional Studies, Bioinformatics Program, Waltham, MA 02454-9110. Offers MS, Graduate Certificate. Part-time and evening/weekend programs available. *Faculty:* 2 full-time (both women), 32 part-time/adjunct (8 women). *Students:* 25 part-time (13 women); includes 3 minority (2 Asian Americans or Pacific Islanders, 1 Hispanic American). Average age 35. 4 applicants, 100% accepted, 4 enrolled. In 2009, 4 master's, 2 other advanced degrees awarded. *Entrance requirements:* For master's, resume, letter of recommendation; for Graduate Certificate, resume, official transcripts, letter of recommendation. Additional exam requirements/recommendations for international students: Recommended—TOEFL (minimum score 600 paper-based; 250 computer-based; 100 iBT). *Application deadline:* For fall admission, 6/15 priority date for domestic students; for winter admission, 10/15 priority date for domestic students; for spring admission, 2/15 priority date for domestic students. Applications are processed on a rolling basis. Application fee: $50. Electronic applications accepted. *Unit head:* Dr. Daniel Caffrey, Program Chair, 781-736-8787, Fax: 781-736-3420, E-mail: dcaffrey@brandeis.edu. *Application contact:* Frances Stearns, Associate Director of Admissions and Student Services, 781-736-8785, Fax: 781-736-3420, E-mail: fstearns@brandeis.edu.

California State University Channel Islands, Extended Education, Programs in Biotechnology, Camarillo, CA 93012. Offers biotechnology and bioinformatics (MS); MS/MBA. *Entrance requirements:* Additional exam requirements/recommendations for international students: Required—TOEFL (minimum score 550 paper-based).

California State University, Dominguez Hills, College of Natural and Behavioral Sciences, Department of Biology, Carson, CA 90747-0001. Offers MS. Part-time and evening/weekend programs available. *Faculty:* 7 full-time (2 women), 12 part-time/adjunct (5 women). *Students:* 10 full-time (6 women), 11 part-time (7 women); includes 11 minority (3 African Americans, 6 Asian Americans or Pacific Islanders, 2 Hispanic Americans). Average age 33. 12 applicants, 67% accepted, 6 enrolled. In 2009, 7 master's awarded. *Degree requirements:* For master's, thesis. *Entrance requirements:* For master's, minimum GPA of 2.75. Additional exam requirements/recommendations for international students: Required—TOEFL (minimum score 550 paper-based). *Application deadline:* For fall admission, 6/1 for domestic students, 5/1 for international students; for spring admission, 12/15 for domestic students, 10/1 for international students. Application fee: $55. Electronic applications accepted. *Expenses:* Tuition, nonresident: full-time $6696; part-time $372 per unit. Required fees: $5946; $1752 per semester. *Faculty research:* Cancer biology, infectious diseases, ecology of native plants, remediation, community ecology. *Unit head:* Dr. John Thomlinson, Chair, 310-243-3381, Fax: 310-243-2350, E-mail: jthomlinson@csudh.edu. *Application contact:* Dr. Getachew Kidane, Graduate Program Coordinator, 310-243-3564, Fax: 310-243-2350, E-mail: gkidane@csudh.edu.

The Catholic University of America, School of Engineering, Department of Electrical Engineering and Computer Science, Washington, DC 20064. Offers antennas and electromagnetic propagation (MEE, MSCS, D Engr); bioimaging (MEE, MSCS, PhD); bioinformatics and intelligent information systems (MEE, D Engr, PhD); distributed and real-time systems (MEE, MSCS, D Engr, PhD); high speed communications and networking (MSCS, D Engr, PhD); information security (MEE, MSCS, PhD); micro-optics (MEE, MSCS, D Engr, PhD); signal and image processing (MEE, MSCS, D Engr). Part-time programs available. *Faculty:* 7 full-time (2 women), 6 part-time/adjunct (0 women). *Students:* 10 full-time (4 women), 50 part-time (7 women); includes 10 minority (3 African Americans, 4 Asian Americans or Pacific Islanders, 3 Hispanic Americans), 12 international. Average age 34. 50 applicants, 54% accepted, 11 enrolled. In 2009, 10 master's awarded. *Degree requirements:* For master's, thesis or alternative; for doctorate, comprehensive exam, thesis/dissertation, qualifying exam, oral exams. *Entrance requirements:* For master's, statement of purpose, official copies of academic transcripts, three letters of recommendation; for doctorate, 3 letters of recommendation. Additional exam requirements/recommendations for international students: Required—TOEFL (minimum score 580 paper-based; 237 computer-based). *Application deadline:* For fall admission, 8/1 priority date for domestic students, 7/15 for international students; for spring admission, 12/1 priority date for domestic students, 10/15 for international students. Applications are processed on a rolling basis. Application fee: $55. Electronic applications accepted. *Expenses:* Contact institution. *Financial support:* Fellowships, research assistantships, teaching assistantships, Federal Work-Study, scholarships/grants, tuition waivers (full and partial), and unspecified assistantships available. Financial award application deadline: 2/1; financial award applicants required to submit FAFSA. *Faculty research:* Signal and image processing, computer communications, robotics, intelligent controls, bioelectromagnetics. Total annual research expenditures: $1.2 million. *Unit head:* Dr. Phillip Regalia, Chair, 202-319-5879, Fax: 202-319-5195, E-mail: regalia@cua.edu. *Application contact:* Julie Schwing, Director of Graduate Admissions, 202-319-5057, Fax: 202-319-6533, E-mail: cua-admissions@cua.edu.

Dalhousie University, Faculty of Computer Science, Halifax, NS B3H 1W5, Canada. Offers computational biology and bioinformatics (M Sc); computer science (PhD); computer science (project-based) (MA Sc); computer science (thesis-based) (MC Sc); electronic commerce (MEC); health informatics (MHI). *Degree requirements:* For master's, thesis (for some programs); for doctorate, thesis/dissertation. *Entrance requirements:* Additional exam requirements/recommendations for international students: Required—TOEFL, IELTS, 1 of the following 5 approved tests: TOEFL, IELTS, CANTEST, CAEL, Michigan English Language Assessment Battery. Electronic applications accepted.

Duke University, Graduate School, Department of Computational Biology and Bioinformatics, Durham, NC 27705. Offers PhD. *Faculty:* 39 full-time. *Students:* 28 full-time (10 women); includes 2 minority (1 African American, 1 Hispanic American), 14 international. 113 applicants, 17% accepted, 10 enrolled. In 2009, 4 doctorates awarded. *Degree requirements:* For doctorate, thesis/dissertation. *Entrance requirements:* Additional exam requirements/recommendations for international students: Required—TOEFL (minimum score 550 paper-based; 213 computer-based; 83 iBT), IELTS (minimum score 7). *Application deadline:* For fall admission, 12/8 priority date for domestic and international students. Application fee: $75. Electronic applications accepted. *Financial support:* Fellowships, research assistantships, teaching assistantships available. Financial award application deadline: 12/8. *Unit head:* Jeannette McCarthy, Director of Graduate Studies, 919-684-0881, Fax: 919-668-2465, E-mail: el81s@duke.edu. *Application contact:* Cynthia Robertson, Associate Dean for Academic Services, 919-684-3913, E-mail: grad-admissions@duke.edu.

Eastern Michigan University, Graduate School, College of Arts and Sciences, Interdisciplinary Studies Program in Bioinformatics, Ypsilanti, MI 48197. Offers MS, Graduate Certificate. Part-time and evening/weekend programs available. Postbaccalaureate distance learning degree

Bioinformatics

Eastern Michigan University (continued)
programs offered (minimal on-campus study). *Students:* 2 part-time (1 woman), 1 international. Average age 27. In 2009, 2 master's awarded. *Entrance requirements:* Additional exam requirements/recommendations for international students: Required—TOEFL. *Application deadline:* Applications are processed on a rolling basis. Application fee: $35. Tuition and fees vary according to course level. *Financial support:* Fellowships, research assistantships with full tuition reimbursements, teaching assistantships with full tuition reimbursements, career-related internships or fieldwork, Federal Work-Study, institutionally sponsored loans, scholarships/grants, tuition waivers (partial), and unspecified assistantships available. Support available to part-time students. Financial award applicants required to submit FAFSA. *Unit head:* Dr. Marianne Laporte, Program Administrator, 734-487-4242, Fax: 734-485-9592, E-mail: mlaporte@emich.edu. *Application contact:* Graduate Admissions, 734-487-3400, Fax: 734-487-6559, E-mail: graduate.admissions@emich.edu.

George Mason University, College of Science, Department of Bioinformatics and Computational Biology, Fairfax, VA 22030. Offers MS, PhD, Certificate. *Expenses:* Tuition, state resident: full-time $7568; part-time $315.33 per credit hour. Tuition, nonresident: full-time $21,704; part-time $904.33 per credit hour. Required fees: $2184; $91 per credit hour.

Georgetown University, Graduate School of Arts and Sciences, Programs in Biomedical Sciences, Department of Biostatistics, Bioinformatics and Biomathematics, Washington, DC 20057-1484. Offers biostatistics (MS), including bioinformatics, epidemiology. *Entrance requirements:* For master's, GRE General Test. Additional exam requirements/recommendations for international students: Required—TOEFL. *Faculty research:* Occupation epidemiology, cancer.

The George Washington University, School of Medicine and Health Sciences, Department of Biochemistry and Molecular Biology, Program in Genomics and Bioinformatics, Washington, DC 20052. Offers MS. Part-time programs available. *Students:* 13 full-time (8 women), 5 part-time (1 woman); includes 1 minority (Asian American or Pacific Islander), 11 international. Average age 26. 31 applicants, 84% accepted, 9 enrolled. In 2009, 7 master's awarded. *Entrance requirements:* For master's, GRE General Test, minimum GPA of 3.0. Additional exam requirements/recommendations for international students: Required—TOEFL (minimum score 550 paper-based; 213 computer-based). *Application deadline:* For fall admission, 4/1 priority date for domestic and international students; for spring admission, 10/1 priority date for domestic and international students. Applications are processed on a rolling basis. Application fee: $60. Electronic applications accepted. *Unit head:* Dr. Jack Vanderhoek, Director, 202-994-2929, E-mail: jyvdh@gwu.edu. *Application contact:* Dr. Fatah Kashanchi, Director, 202-994-1781, Fax: 202-994-6213, E-mail: bcmfxk@gwumc.edu.

Georgia Institute of Technology, Graduate Studies and Research, College of Engineering, The Wallace H. Coulter Department of Biomedical Engineering at Georgia Tech and Emory University, Atlanta, GA 30332-0001. Offers bioengineering (PhD); bioinformatics (PhD); biomedical engineering (PhD); MD/PhD. PhD in biomedical engineering program jointly offered with Emory University (Georgia) and Peking University (China). Terminal master's awarded for partial completion of doctoral program. *Degree requirements:* For doctorate, thesis/dissertation. *Entrance requirements:* Additional exam requirements/recommendations for international students: Required—TOEFL. *Faculty research:* Biomechanics and tissue engineering, bioinstrumentation and medical imaging.

Georgia Institute of Technology, Graduate Studies and Research, College of Sciences, School of Biology, Atlanta, GA 30332-0001. Offers applied biology (MS, PhD); bioinformatics (MS, PhD); biology (MS). Part-time programs available. Terminal master's awarded for partial completion of doctoral program. *Degree requirements:* For master's, thesis; for doctorate, thesis/dissertation, qualifying exam. *Entrance requirements:* For master's, GRE General Test, minimum GPA of 2.9; for doctorate, GRE General Test, minimum GPA of 3.0. Additional exam requirements/recommendations for international students: Required—TOEFL. Electronic applications accepted. *Faculty research:* Microbiology, molecular and cell biology, ecology.

Georgia Institute of Technology, Graduate Studies and Research, College of Sciences, School of Mathematics, Atlanta, GA 30332-0001. Offers algorithms, combinatorics, and optimization (PhD); applied mathematics (MS); bioinformatics (PhD); mathematics (PhD); quantitative and computational finance (MS); statistics (MS Stat). Terminal master's awarded for partial completion of doctoral program. *Degree requirements:* For master's, thesis or alternative; for doctorate, one foreign language, thesis/dissertation. *Entrance requirements:* For master's, GRE General Test, minimum GPA of 3.0; for doctorate, GRE General Test, GRE Subject Test, minimum GPA of 3.0. Additional exam requirements/recommendations for international students: Required—TOEFL. Electronic applications accepted. *Faculty research:* Dynamical systems, discrete mathematics, probability and statistics, mathematical physics.

Grand Valley State University, Padnos College of Engineering and Computing, Medical and Bioinformatics Program, Allendale, MI 49401-9403. Offers MS. Part-time and evening/weekend programs available. *Faculty:* 4 full-time (0 women). *Students:* 12 full-time (3 women), 7 part-time (4 women); includes 1 minority (Asian American or Pacific Islander), 12 international. Average age 28. 18 applicants, 72% accepted, 1 enrolled. In 2009, 6 master's awarded. *Degree requirements:* For master's, thesis or alternative. Application fee: $30. *Financial support:* In 2009–10, 9 students received support, including 1 fellowship (averaging $1,575 per year), 9 research assistantships with full and partial tuition reimbursements available (averaging $7,208 per year); career-related internships or fieldwork, tuition waivers (full), and unspecified assistantships also available. *Faculty research:* Biomedical informatics, information visualization, data mining, high-performance computing, computational biology. *Unit head:* Dr. Paul Leidig, Director, 616-331-2308, Fax: 616-331-2106, E-mail: leidigp@gvsu.edu. *Application contact:* Dr. David Elrod, PSM Coordinator, 616-331-8643, E-mail: elrod@gvsu.edu.

Indiana University Bloomington, School of Informatics, Bloomington, IN 47408. Offers bioinformatics (MS); chemical informatics (MS); computer science (MS, PhD); health informatics (MS); human computer interaction (MS); informatics (PhD); laboratory informatics (MS); media arts and science (MS); music informatics (MS); security informatics (MS); MS/PhD. PhD offered through University Graduate School. Part-time programs available. Postbaccalaureate distance learning degree programs offered (no on-campus study). *Faculty:* 63 full-time (12 women). *Students:* 367 full-time (93 women), 32 part-time (11 women); includes 18 minority (4 African Americans, 1 American Indian/Alaska Native, 11 Asian Americans or Pacific Islanders, 2 Hispanic Americans), 254 international. Average age 27. 676 applicants, 52% accepted, 146 enrolled. In 2009, 82 master's, 18 doctorates awarded. Terminal master's awarded for partial completion of doctoral program. *Degree requirements:* For master's, thesis optional; for doctorate, comprehensive exam, thesis/dissertation, oral and written exams. *Entrance requirements:* For master's and doctorate, GRE, letters of reference. Additional exam requirements/recommendations for international students: Required—TOEFL. *Application deadline:* For fall admission, 1/15 for domestic students, 12/1 for international students. Application fee: $55 ($65 for international students). Electronic applications accepted. *Financial support:* In 2009–10, 2 fellowships with full and partial tuition reimbursements (averaging $20,000 per year), 41 research assistantships (averaging $14,000 per year), 84 teaching assistantships (averaging $13,000 per year) were awarded; Federal Work-Study, institutionally sponsored loans, scholarships/grants, health care benefits, tuition waivers (full and partial), and unspecified assistantships also available. Support available to part-time students. Total annual research expenditures: $2 million. *Unit head:* Dr. David Leake, Associate Dean for Graduate Studies, 812-855-9756, E-mail: leake@cs.indiana.edu. *Application contact:* Rachel Lawmaster, Manager of Graduate Admissions and Studies, 812-856-3622, Fax: 812-856-3825, E-mail: raclee@indiana.edu.

Iowa State University of Science and Technology, Graduate College, Interdisciplinary Programs, Bioinformatics and Computational Biology Program, Ames, IA 50011. Offers MS, PhD. *Students:* 52 full-time (19 women), 2 part-time (1 woman); includes 3 minority (all Asian Americans or Pacific Islanders), 34 international. In 2009, 2 master's, 11 doctorates awarded. *Degree requirements:* For doctorate, thesis/dissertation. *Entrance requirements:* For doctorate, GRE General Test. Additional exam requirements/recommendations for international students: Required—TOEFL (minimum score 550 paper-based; 213 computer-based; 79 iBT) or IELTS (minimum score 6.5). *Application deadline:* For fall admission, 1/15 priority date for domestic students, 1/15 for international students; for spring admission, 10/15 for domestic and international students. Application fee: $40 ($90 for international students). Electronic applications accepted. *Expenses:* Tuition, state resident: full-time $6716. Tuition, nonresident: full-time $8908. Tuition and fees vary according to course level, course load, program and student level. *Financial support:* In 2009–10, 48 research assistantships with full and partial tuition reimbursements (averaging $18,330 per year), 3 teaching assistantships (averaging $17,000 per year) were awarded; fellowships with full tuition reimbursements, scholarships/grants, traineeships, health care benefits, and unspecified assistantships also available. *Faculty research:* Functional and structural genomics, genome evolution, macromolecular structure and function, mathematical biology and biological statistics, metabolic and developmental networks. *Unit head:* Dr. Volker Brendel, Chair, Supervising Committee, 515-294-5122, Fax: 515-294-6790, E-mail: bcb@iastate.edu. *Application contact:* Dr. Volker Brendel, Chair, Supervising Committee, 515-294-5122, Fax: 515-294-6790, E-mail: bcb@iastate.edu.

The Johns Hopkins University, Bloomberg School of Public Health, Department of Biostatistics, Baltimore, MD 21205-2179. Offers bioinformatics (MHS); biostatistics (MHS, Sc M, PhD). Part-time programs available. *Faculty:* 34 full-time (11 women), 16 part-time/adjunct (3 women). *Students:* 47 full-time (22 women), 2 part-time (1 woman); includes 9 minority (3 African Americans, 5 Asian Americans or Pacific Islanders, 1 Hispanic American), 20 international. Average age 25. 197 applicants, 22% accepted, 22 enrolled. In 2009, 18 master's, 5 doctorates awarded. *Degree requirements:* For master's, comprehensive exam (for some programs), thesis (for some programs), written exam, final project; for doctorate, comprehensive exam, thesis/dissertation, 1 year full-time residency, oral and written exams. *Entrance requirements:* For master's and doctorate, GRE General Test, course work in calculus and matrix algebra, 3 letters of recommendation, curriculum vitae. Additional exam requirements/recommendations for international students: Required—TOEFL (minimum score 600 paper-based; 250 computer-based). *Application deadline:* For fall admission, 1/15 for domestic and international students. Applications are processed on a rolling basis. Application fee: $45. Electronic applications accepted. *Financial support:* In 2009–10, 49 students received support, including 33 research assistantships (averaging $22,000 per year); fellowships, Federal Work-Study, institutionally sponsored loans, scholarships/grants, traineeships, health care benefits, and unspecified assistantships also available. Financial award application deadline: 3/15; financial award applicants required to submit FAFSA. *Faculty research:* Statistical genetics, bioinformatics, statistical computing, statistical methods, environmental statistics. Total annual research expenditures: $4.2 million. *Unit head:* Dr. Karen Bandeen-Roche, Chair, 410-955-3067, Fax: 410-955-0958, E-mail: kbandeen@jhsph.edu. *Application contact:* Mary Joy Argo, Academic Administrator, 410-614-4454, Fax: 410-955-0958, E-mail: margo@jhsph.edu.

The Johns Hopkins University, Engineering for Professionals and Advanced Academic Programs, Part-Time Program in Bioinformatics, Baltimore, MD 21218-2699. Offers MS, Post-Master's Certificate. Part-time and evening/weekend programs available. *Unit head:* Dr. Allan Bjerkaas, Associate Dean, 410-516-2300, Fax: 410-579-8049, E-mail: bjerkaas@jhu.edu. *Application contact:* Dr. Allan Bjerkaas, Associate Dean, 410-516-2300, Fax: 410-579-8049, E-mail: bjerkaas@jhu.edu.

The Johns Hopkins University, Engineering for Professionals, Part-Time Program in Computer Science, Baltimore, MD 21218-2699. Offers bioinformatics (MS); computer science (MS, Post-Master's Certificate); telecommunications and networking (MS). Part-time and evening/weekend programs available. Postbaccalaureate distance learning degree programs offered (no on-campus study). *Faculty:* 58 part-time/adjunct (5 women). *Students:* 25 full-time (3 women), 411 part-time (65 women); includes 103 minority (27 African Americans, 65 Asian Americans or Pacific Islanders, 11 Hispanic Americans), 8 international. Average age 29. In 2009, 174 master's, 2 other advanced degrees awarded. *Application deadline:* Applications are processed on a rolling basis. Application fee: $75. Electronic applications accepted. *Financial support:* Institutionally sponsored loans available. *Unit head:* Dr. Ralph D. Semmel, Program Chair, 443-778-6179, E-mail: ralph.semmel@jhuapl.edu. *Application contact:* Priyanka Dwivedi, Admissions Manager, 410-516-2300, Fax: 410-579-8049, E-mail: pdwived1@jhu.edu.

The Johns Hopkins University, Zanvyl Krieger School of Arts and Sciences, Advanced Academic Programs, Program in Bioinformatics, Baltimore, MD 21218-2699. Offers MS. Part-time and evening/weekend programs available. Postbaccalaureate distance learning degree programs offered (no on-campus study). *Faculty:* 8 full-time (4 women), 99 part-time/adjunct (21 women). *Students:* 10 full-time (4 women), 72 part-time (25 women); includes 17 minority (2 African Americans, 12 Asian Americans or Pacific Islanders, 3 Hispanic Americans), 13 international. Average age 33. 56 applicants, 41% accepted, 23 enrolled. In 2009, 14 master's awarded. *Degree requirements:* For master's, thesis (for some programs). *Entrance requirements:* For master's, minimum GPA of 3.0; coursework in programming and data structures, biology, and chemistry. Additional exam requirements/recommendations for international students: Required—TOEFL (minimum score 250 computer-based; 100 iBT). *Application deadline:* For fall admission, 5/31 priority date for domestic students, 4/30 priority date for international students; for spring admission, 10/31 priority date for domestic and international students. Applications are processed on a rolling basis. Application fee: $75. Electronic applications accepted. *Financial support:* Applicants required to submit FAFSA. *Unit head:* Dr. Kristina Obom, Associate Program Chair, 301-294-7159, E-mail: bioinformatics@jhu.edu. *Application contact:* Valana M. McMickens, Admissions Manager, 202-452-1941, Fax: 202-452-1970, E-mail: aapadmissions@jhu.edu.

Marquette University, Graduate School, College of Arts and Sciences, Department of Mathematics, Statistics, and Computer Science, Milwaukee, WI 53201-1881. Offers bioinformatics (MS); computational sciences (PhD); computers (MS); mathematics education (MS). Part-time programs available. *Faculty:* 28 full-time (12 women), 7 part-time/adjunct (2 women). *Students:* 20 full-time (4 women), 25 part-time (4 women); includes 2 minority (both Asian Americans or Pacific Islanders), 20 international. Average age 31. 68 applicants, 47% accepted, 15 enrolled. In 2009, 16 master's, 1 doctorate awarded. Terminal master's awarded for partial completion of doctoral program. *Degree requirements:* For master's, comprehensive exam, thesis or alternative; for doctorate, 2 foreign languages, comprehensive exam, thesis/dissertation. *Entrance requirements:* For doctorate, sample of scholarly writing. Additional exam requirements/recommendations for international students: Required—TOEFL. Application fee: $40. *Financial support:* In 2009–10, 2 research assistantships, 20 teaching assistantships were awarded; Federal Work-Study, institutionally sponsored loans, scholarships/grants, and tuition waivers (full and partial) also available. Support available to part-time students. Financial award application deadline: 2/15. *Faculty research:* Models of physiological systems, mathematical immunology, computational group theory, mathematical logic, computational science. *Unit head:* Dr. Peter Jones, Chair, 414-288-3263, Fax: 414-288-1578. *Application contact:* Dr. Gary Krenz, Director of Graduate Studies, 414-288-6345.

Marquette University, Graduate School, College of Arts and Sciences, Program in Bioinformatics, Milwaukee, WI 53201-1881. Offers MS. *Students:* 4 full-time (1 woman), 4 part-time (all women), 4 international. Average age 30. 28 applicants, 54% accepted, 4 enrolled. In 2009, 3 master's awarded. Application fee: $40. *Unit head:* Dr. Anne Clough, Head, 414-288-5238, E-mail: clough@mscs.mu.edu. *Application contact:* Erin Fox, Assistant Director for Recruitment, 414-288-5319, Fax: 414-288-1902, E-mail: erin.fox@marquette.edu.

McGill University, Faculty of Graduate and Postdoctoral Studies, Faculty of Science, Department of Biology, Montréal, QC H3A 2T5, Canada. Offers bioinformatics (M Sc, PhD); environment (M Sc, PhD); neo-tropical environment (M Sc, PhD).

Medical College of Wisconsin, Graduate School of Biomedical Sciences, Program in Bioinformatics, Milwaukee, WI 53226-0509. Offers MS.

Mississippi Valley State University, Department of Natural Science and Environmental Health, Itta Bena, MS 38941-1400. Offers bioinformatics (MS); environmental health (MS). Part-time and evening/weekend programs available. *Entrance requirements:* For master's, GRE, minimum GPA of 3.0. *Faculty research:* Toxicology, water equality, microbiology, ecology.

Morgan State University, School of Graduate Studies, School of Computer, Mathematical, and Natural Sciences, Department of Computer Science, Baltimore, MD 21251. Offers bioinformatics (MS). *Entrance requirements:* Additional exam requirements/recommendations for international students: Required—TOEFL (minimum score 550 paper-based; 213 computer-based).

New Jersey Institute of Technology, Office of Graduate Studies, College of Computing Science, Department of Computer Science, Newark, NJ 07102. Offers bioinformatics (MS); computer science (MS, PhD); computing and business (MS); software engineering (MS). Part-time and evening/weekend programs available. Terminal master's awarded for partial completion of doctoral program. *Degree requirements:* For master's, thesis optional; for doctorate, thesis/dissertation. *Entrance requirements:* For master's, GRE General Test; for doctorate, GRE General Test, minimum graduate GPA of 3.5. Additional exam requirements/recommendations for international students: Required—TOEFL (minimum score 550 paper-based; 213 computer-based; 79 iBT). Electronic applications accepted.

New Mexico State University, Graduate School, College of Arts and Sciences, Department of Computer Science, Las Cruces, NM 88003-8001. Offers bioinformatics (MS); computer science (MS, PhD). Part-time programs available. *Faculty:* 9 full-time (2 women), 1 part-time/adjunct (0 women). *Students:* 97 full-time (20 women), 18 part-time (3 women); includes 7 minority (2 Asian Americans or Pacific Islanders, 5 Hispanic Americans), 92 international. Average age 27. 232 applicants, 82% accepted, 34 enrolled. In 2009, 16 master's, 2 doctorates awarded. Terminal master's awarded for partial completion of doctoral program. *Degree requirements:* For master's, comprehensive exam, thesis or alternative; for doctorate, comprehensive exam, thesis/dissertation, qualifying examination, thesis proposal. *Entrance requirements:* For master's and doctorate, BS in computer science. Additional exam requirements/recommendations for international students: Required—TOEFL. *Application deadline:* For fall admission, 3/1 priority date for domestic and international students; for spring admission, 11/1 priority date for domestic and international students. Applications are processed on a rolling basis. Application fee: $30 ($50 for international students). Electronic applications accepted. *Expenses:* Tuition, state resident: full-time $4080; part-time $223 per credit. Tuition, nonresident: full-time $14,256; part-time $647 per credit. Required fees: $1278; $639 per semester. *Financial support:* In 2009–10, 36 research assistantships (averaging $9,586 per year), 26 teaching assistantships (averaging $5,340 per year) were awarded; fellowships, career-related internships or fieldwork, Federal Work-Study, scholarships/grants, health care benefits, and unspecified assistantships also available. Support available to part-time students. Financial award application deadline: 3/1; financial award applicants required to submit FAFSA. *Faculty research:* Programming languages, artificial intelligence, software engineering, bioinformatics, data mining, computer networks. *Unit head:* Dr. Enrico Pontelli, Head, 575-646-3723, Fax: 575-646-1002, E-mail: epontell@cs.nmsu.edu. *Application contact:* Dr. Mingzhou Song, Chair, Admissions Committee, 575-646-4299, Fax: 575-646-1002, E-mail: joemsong@cs.nmsu.edu.

North Carolina State University, Graduate School, College of Agriculture and Life Sciences and College of Engineering, Program in Bioinformatics, Raleigh, NC 27695. Offers MB, PhD. *Degree requirements:* For master's, thesis optional; for doctorate, thesis/dissertation. *Entrance requirements:* For master's and doctorate, GRE, minimum B average. Additional exam requirements/recommendations for international students: Required—TOEFL. Electronic applications accepted. *Faculty research:* Statistical genetics, molecular evolution, pedigree analysis, quantitative genetics, protein structure.

North Dakota State University, College of Graduate and Interdisciplinary Studies, Interdisciplinary Program in Genomics and Bioinformatics, Fargo, ND 58108. Offers MS, PhD. Part-time programs available. *Faculty:* 21 full-time (3 women). *Students:* 6 full-time (2 women), 7 part-time (5 women), 11 international. 2 applicants, 100% accepted, 2 enrolled. *Degree requirements:* For master's, thesis; for doctorate, comprehensive exam, thesis/dissertation. *Entrance requirements:* For master's and doctorate, minimum GPA of 3.0. Additional exam requirements/recommendations for international students: Required—TOEFL (minimum score 525 paper-based; 197 computer-based; 71 iBT). *Application deadline:* Applications are processed on a rolling basis. Application fee: $45 ($60 for international students). Electronic applications accepted. *Financial support:* In 2009–10, 12 research assistantships with full tuition reimbursements (averaging $15,000 per year) were awarded; unspecified assistantships also available. *Faculty research:* Genome evolution, genome mapping, genome expression, bioinformatics, data mining. Total annual research expenditures: $300,000. *Unit head:* Dr. Phillip E. McClean, Director, 701-231-8443, Fax: 701-231-8474. *Application contact:* Dr. Phillip E. McClean, Director, 701-231-8443, Fax: 701-231-8474.

Northeastern University, College of Science, Department of Biology, Professional Program in Bioinformatics, Boston, MA 02115-5096. Offers PMS. Part-time programs available. *Faculty:* 6 full-time (0 women). *Students:* 30 full-time (16 women); includes 1 Asian American or Pacific Islander, 19 international. 55 applicants, 76% accepted, 14 enrolled. In 2009, 8 master's awarded. *Degree requirements:* For master's, internship. *Entrance requirements:* For master's, GRE General Test. *Application deadline:* For fall admission, 2/1 priority date for domestic and international students. Application fee: $50. *Expenses:* Contact institution. *Financial support:* In 2009–10, research assistantships (averaging $18,285 per year); Federal Work-Study, scholarships/grants, and tuition waivers (partial) also available. Support available to part-time students. Financial award application deadline: 3/1; financial award applicants required to submit FAFSA. *Unit head:* Dr. Jacqueline Piret, Program Coordinator, 617-373-2260, Fax: 617-373-3724, E-mail: j.piret@neu.edu. *Application contact:* Jo-Anne Dickinson, Admissions Contact, 617-373-5990, Fax: 617-373-7281, E-mail: gsas@neu.edu.

Northwestern University, McCormick School of Engineering and Applied Science, Program in Computational Biology and Bioinformatics, Evanston, IL 60208. Offers MS. Part-time programs available. *Degree requirements:* For master's, thesis. *Entrance requirements:* For master's, GRE General Test, 2 letters of reference. Additional exam requirements/recommendations for international students: Required—TOEFL (minimum score 600 paper-based; 250 computer-based). Electronic applications accepted. *Faculty research:* Mathematical models of protein signaling, high throughput DNA sequencing, macromolecule interactions, chemoinformatics, genome DNA sequence evolution.

Nova Southeastern University, Health Professions Division, College of Osteopathic Medicine, Program in Biomedical Informatics, Fort Lauderdale, FL 33314-7796. Offers biomedical informatics (MS); clinical informatics (Graduate Certificate); public health informatics (Graduate Certificate). *Unit head:* Dr. Jennie Q. Lou, Director, 954-262-1619, E-mail: jlou@nova.edu. *Application contact:* Ellen Rondino, College of Osteopathic Medicine Admissions Counselor, 866-817-4068.

Oregon Health & Science University, School of Medicine, Graduate Programs in Medicine, Department of Medical Informatics and Clinical Epidemiology, Portland, OR 97239-3098. Offers biomedical informatics (MS, PhD, Certificate). Part-time programs available. Postbaccalaureate distance learning degree programs offered (minimal on-campus study). *Degree requirements:* For master's, thesis; for doctorate, comprehensive exam, thesis/dissertation. *Entrance requirements:* For master's and doctorate, GRE General Test, coursework in computer programming, human anatomy and physiology. Additional exam requirements/recommendations for international students: Required—TOEFL. Electronic applications accepted. *Expenses:* Contact institution. *Faculty research:* Information retrieval, telemedicine, consumer health informatics, information needs assessment, healthcare quality.

Polytechnic Institute of NYU, Department of Interdisciplinary Studies, Major in Bioinformatics, Brooklyn, NY 11201-2990. Offers MS. *Students:* 26 full-time (12 women), 36 part-time (16 women); includes 8 minority (2 African Americans, 4 Asian Americans or Pacific Islanders, 2 Hispanic Americans), 23 international. 92 applicants, 49% accepted, 27 enrolled. In 2009, 18 master's awarded. *Degree requirements:* For master's, comprehensive exam (for some programs), thesis (for some programs). *Entrance requirements:* Additional exam requirements/recommendations for international students: Required—TOEFL (minimum score 550 paper-based; 213 computer-based; 80 iBT); Recommended—IELTS (minimum score 6.5). *Application deadline:* For fall admission, 7/31 for domestic students, 4/30 priority date for international students; for spring admission, 12/31 for domestic students, 10/30 priority date for international students. Applications are processed on a rolling basis. Application fee: $75. Electronic applications accepted. *Expenses:* Tuition: Full-time $21,492; part-time $1194 per credit hour. Required fees: $1160; $204 per course. *Financial support:* Institutionally sponsored loans, scholarships/grants, and unspecified assistantships available. Support available to part-time students. *Application contact:* JeanCarlo Bonilla, Director of Graduate Enrollment Management, 718-260-3182, Fax: 718-260-3624, E-mail: gradinfo@poly.edu.

Polytechnic Institute of NYU, Long Island Graduate Center, Graduate Programs, Department of Interdisciplinary Studies, Major in Bioinformatics, Melville, NY 11747. Offers MS. Part-time and evening/weekend programs available. *Students:* 1 full-time (0 women), 4 part-time (all women); includes 1 minority (African American). *Entrance requirements:* Additional exam requirements/recommendations for international students: Required—TOEFL (minimum score 550 paper-based; 213 computer-based; 80 iBT); Recommended—IELTS (minimum score 6.5). *Application deadline:* For fall admission, 7/31 priority date for domestic students, 4/30 priority date for international students; for spring admission, 12/31 priority date for domestic students, 11/30 priority date for international students. Applications are processed on a rolling basis. Application fee: $75. Electronic applications accepted. *Financial support:* Institutionally sponsored loans, scholarships/grants, and unspecified assistantships available. Support available to part-time students. *Application contact:* JeanCarlo Bonilla, Director of Graduate Enrollment Management, 718-260-3182, Fax: 718-260-3624, E-mail: gradinfo@poly.edu.

Polytechnic Institute of NYU, Westchester Graduate Center, Graduate Programs, Department of Interdisciplinary Studies, Major in Bioinformatics, Hawthorne, NY 10532-1507. Offers MS. *Entrance requirements:* Additional exam requirements/recommendations for international students: Required—TOEFL (minimum score 550 paper-based; 213 computer-based; 80 iBT); Recommended—IELTS (minimum score 6.5). *Application deadline:* For fall admission, 7/31 priority date for domestic students, 4/30 priority date for international students; for spring admission, 12/31 priority date for domestic students, 11/30 priority date for international students. Applications are processed on a rolling basis. Application fee: $75. Electronic applications accepted. *Financial support:* Institutionally sponsored loans, scholarships/grants, and unspecified assistantships available. Support available to part-time students. *Application contact:* JeanCarlo Bonilla, Director of Graduate Enrollment Management, 718-260-3182, Fax: 718-260-3624, E-mail: gradinfo@poly.edu.

Rice University, Graduate Programs, George R. Brown School of Engineering, Department of Statistics, Houston, TX 77251-1892. Offers bioinformatics (PhD); biostatistics (PhD); computational finance (PhD); general statistics (PhD); statistics (M Stat, MA); MBA/M Stat. Part-time programs available. *Faculty:* 16 full-time (6 women), 1 part-time/adjunct (0 women). *Students:* 45 full-time (20 women), 3 part-time (2 women); includes 12 minority (1 African American, 5 Asian Americans or Pacific Islanders, 6 Hispanic Americans), 16 international. Average age 28. 112 applicants, 41% accepted, 20 enrolled. In 2009, 9 master's, 7 doctorates awarded. *Degree requirements:* For master's, comprehensive exam; for doctorate, comprehensive exam, thesis/dissertation. *Entrance requirements:* For master's and doctorate, GRE General Test, minimum GPA of 3.0. Additional exam requirements/recommendations for international students: Required—TOEFL (minimum score 630 paper-based; 250 computer-based; 90 iBT). *Application deadline:* For fall admission, 1/15 priority date for domestic and international students; for spring admission, 11/1 for international students. Applications are processed on a rolling basis. Application fee: $70. Electronic applications accepted. *Financial support:* In 2009–10, 13 students received support, including 1 fellowship with full tuition reimbursement available (averaging $15,000 per year), 19 research assistantships with full tuition reimbursements available (averaging $23,000 per year), 9 teaching assistantships with full tuition reimbursements available (averaging $17,250 per year); career-related internships or fieldwork, institutionally sponsored loans, scholarships/grants, traineeships, health care benefits, tuition waivers (full), and unspecified assistantships also available. *Faculty research:* Statistical genetics, non parametric function estimation, computational statistics and visualization, stochastic processes. Total annual research expenditures: $800,000. *Unit head:* Carolyn Duhon, Sr. Department Administrator, 713-348-6032, Fax: 713-348-5476, E-mail: stat@rice.edu. *Application contact:* Margaret Poon, Department Coordinator, 713-348-6032, Fax: 713-348-5476, E-mail: poon@rice.edu.

Rochester Institute of Technology, Graduate Enrollment Services, College of Science, Department of Biological Sciences, Program in Bioinformatics, Rochester, NY 14623-5603. Offers MS. Part-time programs available. *Students:* 15 full-time (5 women), 8 part-time (3 women); includes 2 American Indian/Alaska Native, 8 international. Average age 27. 75 applicants, 27% accepted, 6 enrolled. In 2009, 9 master's awarded. *Degree requirements:* For master's, thesis. *Entrance requirements:* For master's, GRE, minimum GPA of 3.2. Additional exam requirements/recommendations for international students: Required—TOEFL (minimum score 570 paper-based; 230 computer-based; 88 iBT), or IELTS (minimum score 6.5). *Application deadline:* For fall admission, 2/15 priority date for domestic and international students; for winter admission, 11/1 for domestic students; for spring admission, 2/1 for domestic students. Applications are processed on a rolling basis. Application fee: $50. Electronic applications accepted. *Expenses:* Tuition: Full-time $31,533; part-time $876 per credit hour. Required fees: $210. *Financial support:* In 2009–10, 17 students received support; fellowships with partial tuition reimbursements available, research assistantships with partial tuition reimbursements available, teaching assistantships with partial tuition reimbursements available, career-related internships or fieldwork, scholarships/grants, and unspecified assistantships available. Support available to part-time students. Financial award applicants required to submit FAFSA. *Unit head:* Dr. Gary R. Skuse, Director, 585-475-7577, Fax: 585-475-2533, E-mail: grssbi@rit.edu. *Application contact:* Diane Ellison, Assistant Vice President, Graduate Enrollment Services, 585-475-2229, Fax: 585-475-7164, E-mail: gradinfo@rit.edu.

Stevens Institute of Technology, Graduate School, Charles V. Schaefer Jr. School of Engineering, Department of Chemistry, Chemical Biology and Biomedical Engineering, Hoboken, NJ 07030. Offers analytical chemistry (PhD, Certificate); bioinformatics (PhD, Certificate); biomedical chemistry (Certificate); biomedical engineering (M Eng, Certificate); chemical biology (MS, PhD, Certificate); chemical physiology (Certificate); chemistry (MS, PhD); organic chemistry (PhD); physical chemistry (PhD); polymer chemistry (PhD, Certificate). Part-time and evening/weekend programs available. Postbaccalaureate distance learning degree programs offered (no on-campus study). Terminal master's awarded for partial completion of doctoral program. *Degree requirements:* For master's, thesis or alternative; for doctorate, one foreign language, thesis/dissertation; for Certificate, project or thesis. *Entrance requirements:* Additional exam requirements/recommendations for international students: Required—TOEFL. Electronic applications accepted. *Expenses:* Tuition: Full-time $9900; part-time $1100 per credit. Required fees: $286 per semester. *Faculty research:* Biochemical reaction engineering, polymerization engineering, reactor design, biochemical process control and synthesis.

Texas Tech University, Graduate School, College of Arts and Sciences, Department of Biological Sciences, Lubbock, TX 79409. Offers biological informatics (MS); biology (MS, PhD); microbiology (MS); zoology (MS, PhD). Part-time programs available. *Faculty:* 31 full-time (6 women). *Students:* 120 full-time (59 women), 5 part-time (3 women); includes 5 minority (1 Asian American or Pacific Islander, 4 Hispanic Americans), 65 international. Average age 29. 121 applicants, 42% accepted, 24 enrolled. In 2009, 17 master's, 6 doctorates awarded. *Degree requirements:* For master's, thesis or alternative; for doctorate, thesis/dissertation. *Entrance requirements:* For master's and doctorate, GRE General Test. Additional exam requirements/recommendations for international students: Required—TOEFL (minimum score

Bioinformatics

Texas Tech University (continued)
550 paper-based; 213 computer-based). *Application deadline:* For fall admission, 3/1 priority date for international students; for spring admission, 11/1 priority date for international students. Applications are processed on a rolling basis. Application fee: $50 ($75 for international students). Electronic applications accepted. *Expenses:* Tuition, state resident: full-time $5100; part-time $213 per credit hour. Tuition, nonresident: full-time $11,748; part-time $490 per credit hour. Required fees: $2298; $50 per credit hour. $555 per semester. *Financial support:* In 2009–10, 16 research assistantships with partial tuition reimbursements (averaging $21,854 per year), 11 teaching assistantships with partial tuition reimbursements (averaging $19,985 per year) were awarded; career-related internships or fieldwork, Federal Work-Study, and institutionally sponsored loans also available. Support available to part-time students. Financial award application deadline: 4/15; financial award applicants required to submit FAFSA. *Faculty research:* Biodiversity and evolution, climate change in arid ecosystems, plant biology and biotechnology, animal communication and behavior, zoonotic and emerging diseases. Total annual research expenditures: $2.1 million. *Unit head:* Dr. Llewellyn D. Densmore, Chair, 806-742-2715, Fax: 806-742-2963, E-mail: jlou.densmore@ttu.edu. *Application contact:* Dr. Randall M. Jeter, Graduate Adviser, 806-742-2710 Ext. 223, Fax: 806-742-2963, E-mail: randall.jeter@ttu.edu.

University of Arkansas at Little Rock, Graduate School, George W. Donughey College of Engineering and Information Technology, Program in Bioinformatics, Little Rock, AR 72204-1099. Offers MS, PhD.

University of California, Riverside, Graduate Division, Graduate Program in Genetics, Genomics, and Bioinformatics, Riverside, CA 92521-0102. Offers genomics and bioinformatics (PhD); molecular genetics (PhD); population and evolutionary genetics (PhD). *Degree requirements:* For doctorate, thesis/dissertation, qualifying exams, teaching experience. *Entrance requirements:* For doctorate, GRE General Test, minimum GPA of 3.2. Additional exam requirements/recommendations for international students: Required—TOEFL (minimum score 550 paper-based; 213 computer-based; 80 iBT). Electronic applications accepted. *Faculty research:* Molecular Genetics, Evolution and Population Genetics, Genomics and Bioinformatics.

University of California, San Diego, Office of Graduate Studies, Interdisciplinary Doctoral Program in Bioinformatics, La Jolla, CA 92093. Offers PhD. Offered through the Departments of Bioengineering, Biology, Biomedical Sciences, Chemistry and Biochemistry, Computer Sciences and Engineering, Mathematics, and Physics. *Entrance requirements:* For doctorate, GRE General Test. Electronic applications accepted.

See Close-Up on page 309.

University of California, San Diego, School of Medicine and Office of Graduate Studies, Molecular Pathology Program, La Jolla, CA 92093. Offers bioinformatics (PhD); cancer biology/oncology (PhD); cardiovascular sciences and disease (PhD); microbiology (PhD); molecular pathology (PhD); neurological disease (PhD); stem cell and developmental biology (PhD); structural biology/drug design (PhD). *Entrance requirements:* For doctorate, GRE General Test, GRE Subject Test. Additional exam requirements/recommendations for international students: Required—TOEFL. Electronic applications accepted.

University of California, Santa Cruz, Division of Graduate Studies, Jack Baskin School of Engineering, Program in Bioinformatics, Santa Cruz, CA 95064. Offers MS, PhD. *Degree requirements:* For master's, thesis; for doctorate, thesis/dissertation. *Entrance requirements:* For master's and doctorate, GRE General Test. Additional exam requirements/recommendations for international students: Required—TOEFL; Recommended—IELTS. Electronic applications accepted.

University of Cincinnati, Graduate School, College of Engineering, Department of Biomedical Engineering, Cincinnati, OH 45221. Offers bioinformatics (PhD); biomechanics (PhD); medical imaging (PhD); tissue engineering (PhD). Part-time programs available. *Degree requirements:* For doctorate, one foreign language, thesis/dissertation. *Entrance requirements:* For doctorate, GRE General Test. Additional exam requirements/recommendations for international students: Required—TOEFL (minimum score 600 paper-based; 250 computer-based).

University of Idaho, College of Graduate Studies, Program in Bioinformatics and Computational Biology, Moscow, ID 83844-2282. Offers MS, PhD. *Students:* 3 full-time, 1 part-time. In 2009, 1 master's awarded. *Entrance requirements:* For master's, GRE, minimum GPA of 2.8. *Application deadline:* For fall admission, 8/1 for domestic students; for spring admission, 12/15 for domestic students. Application fee: $55 ($60 for international students). *Expenses:* Tuition, state resident: full-time $6120. Tuition, nonresident: full-time $17,712. *Financial support:* Application deadline: 2/15. *Unit head:* Dr. Christopher Williams, Director, 208-885-6242, Fax: 208-885-6198, E-mail: bcb@uidaho.edu. *Application contact:* Dr. Christopher Williams, Director, 208-885-6242, Fax: 208-885-6198, E-mail: bcb@uidaho.edu.

University of Illinois at Urbana–Champaign, Graduate College, College of Agricultural, Consumer and Environmental Sciences, Department of Crop Sciences, Champaign, IL 61820. Offers agricultural production (MS), including professional science; bioinformatics: crop sciences (MS); crop sciences (MS, PhD). Postbaccalaureate distance learning degree programs offered (no on-campus study). *Faculty:* 46 full-time (6 women). *Students:* 56 full-time (17 women), 35 part-time (10 women); includes 4 minority (1 African American, 1 Asian American or Pacific Islander, 2 Hispanic Americans), 30 international. 64 applicants, 33% accepted, 15 enrolled. In 2009, 18 master's, 5 doctorates awarded. *Entrance requirements:* For master's and doctorate, GRE, minimum GPA of 3.0. Additional exam requirements/recommendations for international students: Required—TOEFL (minimum score 570 paper-based). *Application deadline:* Applications are processed on a rolling basis. Application fee: $60 ($75 for international students). Electronic applications accepted. *Financial support:* In 2009–10, 32 fellowships, 60 research assistantships, 17 teaching assistantships were awarded; tuition waivers (full and partial) also available. *Faculty research:* Plant breeding and genetics, molecular biology, crop production, plant physiology, weed science. *Unit head:* German A. Bollero, Head, 217-333-9475, Fax: 217-333-9817, E-mail: gbollero@illinois.edu. *Application contact:* S. Dianne Carson, Secretary, 217-244-0396, Fax: 217-333-9817, E-mail: sdcarson@illinois.edu.

University of Illinois at Urbana–Champaign, Graduate College, College of Engineering, Department of Computer Science, Champaign, IL 61820. Offers bioinformatics (MS); computer science (MCS, MS, PhD); MCS/JD; MCS/M Arch; MCS/MBA. Part-time programs available. Postbaccalaureate distance learning degree programs offered (no on-campus study). *Faculty:* 51 full-time (5 women), 1 part-time/adjunct (0 women). *Students:* 284 full-time (49 women), 174 part-time (23 women); includes 40 minority (4 African Americans, 35 Asian Americans or Pacific Islanders, 1 Hispanic American), 279 international. 1,288 applicants, 8% accepted, 87 enrolled. In 2009, 56 master's, 42 doctorates awarded. *Entrance requirements:* For master's and doctorate, minimum GPA of 3.0. Additional exam requirements/recommendations for international students: Required—TOEFL (minimum score 600 paper-based; 250 computer-based; 100 iBT), or IELTS (minimum score 6.5). *Application deadline:* Applications are processed on a rolling basis. Application fee: $60 ($75 for international students). Electronic applications accepted. *Financial support:* In 2009–10, 36 fellowships, 266 research assistantships, 100 teaching assistantships were awarded; tuition waivers (full and partial) also available. *Unit head:* Robin A. Rutenbar, Head, 217-333-3373, Fax: 217-333-3501, E-mail: rutenbar@illinois.edu. *Application contact:* Rhonda McElroy, Coordinator of Graduate Programs, 217-244-2745, Fax: 217-244-6073, E-mail: rmcelroy@illinois.edu.

University of Illinois at Urbana–Champaign, Graduate College, Graduate School of Library and Information Science, Champaign, IL 61820. Offers bioinformatics: library and information science (MS); library and information science (MS, PhD, CAS); library and information science: digital libraries (CAS). *Accreditation:* ALA (one or more programs are accredited). Postbaccalaureate distance learning degree programs offered. *Faculty:* 26 full-time (13 women), 9 part-time/adjunct (6 women). *Students:* 321 full-time (229 women), 310 part-time (230 women); includes 101 minority (34 African Americans, 4 American Indian/Alaska Native, 36 Asian Americans or Pacific Islanders, 27 Hispanic Americans), 35 international. 747 applicants, 53% accepted, 217 enrolled. In 2009, 240 master's, 7 doctorates, 6 other advanced degrees awarded. *Entrance requirements:* For master's, GRE General Test, minimum GPA of 3.0; for doctorate, minimum GPA of 3.0; for CAS, master's degree in library and information science or related field with minimum GPA of 3.0. Additional exam requirements/recommendations for international students: Required—TOEFL (minimum score 620 paper-based; 260 computer-based; 105 iBT), or IELTS (minimum score 7). *Application deadline:* Applications are processed on a rolling basis. Application fee: $60 ($75 for international students). Electronic applications accepted. *Financial support:* In 2009–10, 52 fellowships, 41 research assistantships, 27 teaching assistantships were awarded; tuition waivers (full and partial) also available. *Unit head:* John Unsworth, Dean, 217-333-3281, Fax: 217-244-3302, E-mail: unsworth@illinois.edu. *Application contact:* Valerie Youngen, Admissions and Records Representative, 217-333-0734, Fax: 217-244-3302, E-mail: vyoungen@illinois.edu.

University of Medicine and Dentistry of New Jersey, School of Health Related Professions, Department of Health Informatics, Program in Biomedical Informatics, Newark, NJ 07107-1709. Offers MS, PhD, DMD/MS, MD/MS. *Entrance requirements:* Additional exam requirements/recommendations for international students: Required—TOEFL. Electronic applications accepted.

University of Michigan, Horace H. Rackham School of Graduate Studies, Program in Biomedical Sciences (PIBS) and Horace H. Rackham School of Graduate Studies, Program in Bioinformatics, Ann Arbor, MI 48109. Offers MS, PhD. Part-time programs available. *Degree requirements:* For master's, thesis optional, summer internship or rotation; for doctorate, thesis/dissertation, oral defense of dissertation, preliminary exam. *Entrance requirements:* For master's and doctorate, GRE or MCAT. Additional exam requirements/recommendations for international students: Required—TOEFL (minimum score 84 iBT). Electronic applications accepted. *Expenses:* Tuition, state resident: full-time $17,286; part-time $1099 per credit hour. Tuition, nonresident: full-time $34,944; part-time $2080 per credit hour. Required fees: $95 per semester. Tuition and fees vary according to course load, degree level and program. *Faculty research:* Mathematical modeling, molecular modeling, statistical methods for computational biology.

University of Missouri, Graduate School, Informatics Institute, Columbia, MO 65211. Offers PhD. *Entrance requirements:* Additional exam requirements/recommendations for international students: Required—TOEFL (minimum score 577 paper-based; 233 computer-based; 90 iBT).

University of Missouri–Kansas City, School of Computing and Engineering, Kansas City, MO 64110-2499. Offers civil engineering (MS); computer and electrical engineering (PhD); computer science (MS), including bioinformatics, software engineering, telecommunications networking; computer science and informatics (PhD); computing (PhD); electrical engineering (MS); engineering (PhD); mechanical engineering (MS); telecommunications (PhD). PhD (interdisciplinary) offered through the School of Graduate Studies. Part-time programs available. *Faculty:* 40 full-time (5 women), 28 part-time/adjunct (0 women). *Students:* 230 full-time (46 women), 158 part-time (31 women); includes 20 minority (5 African Americans, 12 Asian Americans or Pacific Islanders, 3 Hispanic Americans), 313 international. Average age 24. 484 applicants, 64% accepted, 106 enrolled. In 2009, 144 master's awarded. *Degree requirements:* For doctorate, thesis/dissertation. *Entrance requirements:* For master's, GRE General Test, minimum GPA of 3.0, 3 letters of recommendations from professors; for doctorate, GRE General Test, minimum GPA of 3.5. Additional exam requirements/recommendations for international students: Required—TOEFL (minimum score 550 paper-based; 213 computer-based; 80 iBT). *Application deadline:* For fall admission, 1/15 priority date for domestic students, 1/15 for international students. Applications are processed on a rolling basis. Application fee: $45 ($50 for international students). *Expenses:* Tuition, state resident: full-time $5378; part-time $299 per credit hour. Tuition, nonresident: full-time $13,881; part-time $771 per credit hour. Required fees: $641; $71 per credit hour. Tuition and fees vary according to course load and program. *Financial support:* In 2009–10, 29 research assistantships with partial tuition reimbursements (averaging $15,040 per year), 10 teaching assistantships with partial tuition reimbursements (averaging $12,118 per year) were awarded; career-related internships or fieldwork, Federal Work-Study, scholarships/grants, tuition waivers (partial), and unspecified assistantships also available. Support available to part-time students. Financial award application deadline: 3/1; financial award applicants required to submit FAFSA. *Faculty research:* Algorithms, bioinformatics and medical informatics, biomechanics/biomaterials, civil engineering materials, networking and telecommunications, thermal science. Total annual research expenditures: $1.4 million. *Unit head:* Dr. Kevin Z. Truman, Dean, 816-235-2399, Fax: 816-235-5159. *Application contact:* Dr. Kevin Z. Truman, Dean, 816-235-2399, Fax: 816-235-5159.

University of Nebraska–Lincoln, Graduate College, College of Arts and Sciences and College of Engineering, Department of Computer Science and Engineering, Lincoln, NE 68588. Offers bioinformatics (MS, PhD); computer engineering (MS, PhD); computer science (MS, PhD); information technology (PhD). *Degree requirements:* For master's, thesis optional; for doctorate, comprehensive exam, thesis/dissertation. *Entrance requirements:* For master's and doctorate, GRE General Test. Additional exam requirements/recommendations for international students: Required—TOEFL (minimum score 600 paper-based; 250 computer-based). Electronic applications accepted. *Faculty research:* Software engineering, geo- and bio-informatics, scientific computation, secure communication.

The University of North Carolina at Charlotte, Graduate School, College of Computing and Informatics, Department of Bioinformatics and Genomics, Charlotte, NC 28223-0001. Offers bioinformatics (PMS). Part-time programs available. *Faculty:* 12 full-time (6 women). *Students:* 11 full-time (3 women), 5 part-time (3 women); includes 1 African American, 1 Asian American or Pacific Islander, 4 international. Average age 29. 35 applicants, 51% accepted, 9 enrolled. Terminal master's awarded for partial completion of doctoral program. *Degree requirements:* For master's, internship, research project, or thesis. *Entrance requirements:* For master's, GRE, minimum undergraduate GPA of 3.0, overall and in undergraduate major. Additional exam requirements/recommendations for international students: Required—TOEFL (minimum score 557 paper-based; 220 computer-based; 83 iBT). *Application deadline:* For fall admission, 7/15 for domestic students, 5/1 for international students; for spring admission, 11/15 for domestic students, 10/1 for international students. Applications are processed on a rolling basis. Application fee: $55. Electronic applications accepted. *Financial support:* In 2009–10, 9 fellowships (averaging $36,391 per year), 12 research assistantships (averaging $10,433 per year), 5 teaching assistantships (averaging $17,385 per year) were awarded; career-related internships or fieldwork, institutionally sponsored loans, scholarships/grants, and unspecified assistantships also available. Support available to part-time students. *Faculty research:* High-throughput studies, computational biophysics, structural bioinformatics, metagenomics, computational mass spectrometry. Total annual research expenditures: $13,917. *Unit head:* Dr. Larry Mays, Chairman, 704-687-8555, E-mail: lemays@uncc.edu. *Application contact:* Kathy B. Giddings, Director of Graduate Admissions, 704-687-5503, Fax: 704-687-3279, E-mail: gradadm@uncc.edu.

University of Pittsburgh, School of Medicine, Biomedical Informatics Training Program, Pittsburgh, PA 15260. Offers MS, PhD, Certificate. Part-time programs available. *Faculty:* 15 full-time (6 women), 13 part-time/adjunct (6 women). *Students:* 19 full-time (9 women), 9 part-time (2 women); includes 13 minority (12 Asian Americans or Pacific Islanders, 1 Hispanic American). Average age 28. 47 applicants, 32% accepted, 11 enrolled. In 2009, 3 master's, 3 doctorates awarded. Terminal master's awarded for partial completion of doctoral program. *Degree requirements:* For master's, comprehensive exam, written research report or thesis; for doctorate, comprehensive exam, thesis/dissertation; for Certificate, written research report or thesis. *Entrance requirements:* For master's, doctorate, and Certificate, GRE. Additional exam requirements/recommendations for international students: Required—TOEFL. *Application deadline:* For fall admission, 12/15 priority date for domestic and international students. Application fee: $40. *Expenses:* Tuition, state resident: full-time $16,402; part-time $665 per credit. Tuition, nonresident: full-time $28,694; part-time $1175 per credit. Required fees: $690; $175 per term. Tuition and fees vary according to program. *Financial support:* In 2009–10, 15 students received support, including 7 fellowships with full tuition reimbursements available (averaging $24,650 per year), 8 research assistantships with full tuition reimbursements available (averaging $24,650 per year); health care benefits also available. Financial award application deadline: 12/15. *Faculty research:* Artificial intelligence; probability theory; data mining; machine learning; evaluation methods; dental, radiology, and pathology imaging. *Unit head:* Dr. Rebecca Crowley, Program Director, 412-647-7176, Fax: 412-647-7190, E-mail: crowleyrs@upmc.edu. *Application contact:* Toni L. Porterfield, Training Coordinator, 412-647-7176, Fax: 412-647-7190, E-mail: tls18@pitt.edu.

University of Southern California, Graduate School, College of Letters, Arts and Sciences, Department of Biological Sciences, Program in Molecular and Computational Biology, Los Angeles, CA 90089. Offers computational biology and bioinformatics (PhD); molecular biology (PhD). *Faculty:* 43 full-time (8 women). *Students:* 131 full-time (67 women), 3 part-time (1 woman); includes 23 minority (2 African Americans, 1 American Indian/Alaska Native, 13 Asian Americans or Pacific Islanders, 7 Hispanic Americans), 53 international. 158 applicants, 29% accepted, 18 enrolled. In 2009, 15 doctorates awarded. Terminal master's awarded for partial completion of doctoral program. *Degree requirements:* For doctorate, thesis/dissertation, course work, qualifying examination, dissertation defense. *Entrance requirements:* For doctorate, General Record Exam, 3 letters of recommendation, personal statement, resume?, GPA >3.0. Additional exam requirements/recommendations for international students: Required—TOEFL (minimum score 600 paper-based; 250 computer-based; 100 iBT). *Application deadline:* For fall admission, 12/1 priority date for domestic students, 11/1 priority date for international students. Application fee: $85. Electronic applications accepted. *Expenses:* Tuition: Full-time $25,980; part-time $1315 per unit. Required fees: $554. One-time fee: $35 full-time. Full-time tuition and fees vary according to degree level and program. *Financial support:* In 2009–10, 57 students received support, including 8 fellowships with full tuition reimbursements available (averaging $27,000 per year), 44 research assistantships with full tuition reimbursements available (averaging $25,333 per year), 5 teaching assistantships with full tuition reimbursements available (averaging $25,333 per year); scholarships/grants, traineeships, health care benefits, and tuition waivers also available. *Faculty research:* Cell and developmental biology, cancer biology, computational biology and bioinformatics, genetics, computational neurobiology. *Unit head:* Dr. Myron Goodman, Professor of Biological Sciences and Chemistry, Director of the MCB Research Section, 213-740-5190, E-mail: mgoodman@usc.edu. *Application contact:* Catherine Atienza, Student Services Advisor I, 213-740-5188, E-mail: catherine.atienza@usc.edu.

The University of Texas at El Paso, Graduate School, College of Science, Department of Biological Sciences, El Paso, TX 79968-0001. Offers bioinformatics (MS); biological sciences (MS, PhD). Part-time and evening/weekend programs available. *Students:* 71 (32 women); includes 39 minority (4 African Americans, 4 Asian Americans or Pacific Islanders, 31 Hispanic Americans), 17 international. Average age 34. In 2009, 16 master's, 4 doctorates awarded. *Degree requirements:* For master's, thesis; for doctorate, thesis/dissertation. *Entrance requirements:* For master's, GRE, minimum GPA of 3.0, letters of recommendation; for doctorate, GRE, Statement of Purpose, Letters of Recommendation. Additional exam requirements/recommendations for international students: Required—TOEFL; Recommended—IELTS. *Application deadline:* For fall admission, 8/1 priority date for domestic students, 3/1 for international students; for spring admission, 11/1 priority date for domestic students, 9/1 for international students. Applications are processed on a rolling basis. Application fee: $45 ($80 for international students). Electronic applications accepted. *Financial support:* In 2009–10, research assistantships with partial tuition reimbursements (averaging $22,500 per year), teaching assistantships with partial tuition reimbursements (averaging $18,000 per year) were awarded; fellowships with partial tuition reimbursements, institutionally sponsored loans, scholarships/grants, health care benefits, tuition waivers (partial), and unspecified assistantships also available. Support available to part-time students. Financial award application deadline: 3/15; financial award applicants required to submit FAFSA. *Unit head:* Dr. Robert Kirken, Chair, 915-747-5844, Fax: 915-747-5808, E-mail: rkirken@utep.edu. *Application contact:* Dr. Patricia D. Witherspoon, Dean of Graduate School, 915-747-5491, Fax: 915-747-5788, E-mail: withersp@utep.edu.

The University of Texas at El Paso, Graduate School, College of Science, Program in Bioinformatics, El Paso, TX 79968-0001. Offers MS. *Entrance requirements:* For master's, GRE, minimum GPA of 3.0. Additional exam requirements/recommendations for international students: Required—TOEFL.

The University of Texas Medical Branch, Graduate School of Biomedical Sciences, Program in Biochemistry and Molecular Biology, Galveston, TX 77555. Offers biochemistry (PhD); bioinformatics (PhD); biophysics (PhD); cell biology (PhD); computational biology (PhD); structural biology (PhD). *Students:* 41 full-time (17 women); includes 6 minority (1 African American, 1 Asian American or Pacific Islander, 4 Hispanic Americans), 22 international. Average age 28. In 2009, 9 doctorates awarded. *Degree requirements:* For doctorate, thesis/dissertation. *Entrance requirements:* Additional exam requirements/recommendations for international students: Required—TOEFL (minimum score 550 paper-based; 213 computer-based). *Application deadline:* Applications are processed on a rolling basis. Application fee: $30 ($75 for international students). Electronic applications accepted. *Financial support:* In 2009–10, fellowships (averaging $25,000 per year), research assistantships (averaging $25,000 per year) were awarded. Financial award applicants required to submit FAFSA. *Unit head:* Dr. Sarita Sastry, Director, 409-747-1915, Fax: 409-747-1938, E-mail: sasastry@utmb.edu. *Application contact:* Debora Botting, Coordinator II Special Programs, 409-772-2769, Fax: 409-772-5102, E-mail: dmbottin@utmb.edu.

University of the Sciences in Philadelphia, College of Graduate Studies, Program in Bioinformatics, Philadelphia, PA 19104-4495. Offers MS. *Entrance requirements:* Additional exam requirements/recommendations for international students: Required—TOEFL, TWE. *Expenses:* Contact institution. *Faculty research:* Genomics, microarray analysis, computer aided drug design, molecular biophysics, cell structure, molecular dynamics, computational chemistry.

The University of Toledo, College of Graduate Studies, College of Medicine, Biomedical Science Programs, Program in Bioinformatics and Proteomics/Genomics, Toledo, OH 43606-3390. Offers MSBS, Certificate, MD/MSBS. Part-time programs available. *Degree requirements:* For master's, thesis, qualifying exam. *Entrance requirements:* For master's, GRE General Test, minimum Undergraduate GPA of 3.0.

University of Utah, School of Medicine and The Graduate School, Graduate Programs in Medicine, Department of Biomedical Informatics, Salt Lake City, UT 84112-1107. Offers MS, PhD, Certificate. Part-time programs available. Postbaccalaureate distance learning degree programs offered (minimal on-campus study). *Degree requirements:* For master's, comprehensive exam, thesis; for doctorate, comprehensive exam, thesis/dissertation, qualifying exam. *Entrance requirements:* For master's and doctorate, GRE General Test (minimum 60th percentile), minimum GPA of 3.3. Additional exam requirements/recommendations for international students: Required—TOEFL (minimum score 600 paper-based; 250 computer-based). Electronic applications accepted. *Expenses:* Tuition, state resident: full-time $4004; part-time $1674 per semester. Tuition, nonresident: full-time $14,134; part-time $5915 per semester. Required fees: $324 per semester. Tuition and fees vary according to course load, degree level and program. *Faculty research:* Health information systems and expert systems, genetic epidemiology, medical imaging, bioinformatics, public health informatics.

University of Washington, Graduate School, School of Medicine and Graduate School, Graduate Programs in Medicine, Department of Medical Education and Biomedical Informatics, Division of Biomedical and Health Informatics, Seattle, WA 98195. Offers MS, PhD. *Entrance requirements:* For master's and doctorate, GRE General Test, minimum GPA of 3.0; previous undergraduate course work in biology, computer programming, and mathematics. Additional exam requirements/recommendations for international students: Required—TOEFL (minimum score 580 paper-based; 237 computer-based; 70 iBT). Electronic applications accepted. *Faculty research:* Bio-clinical informatics, information retrieval, human-computer interaction, knowledge-based systems, telehealth.

University of Washington, Graduate School, School of Public Health, Department of Health Services, Seattle, WA 98195. Offers bioinformatics (PhD); cancer prevention and control (PhD); clinical research (MS); community oriented public health practice (MPH); economics or finance (PhD); evaluation sciences (PhD); executive program (MHA); health behavior and health promotion (PhD); health care and population health research (MPH); health policy analysis and process (PhD); health policy and analysis and process (MPH); health services (MS, PhD); health services administration (EMHA, MHA); in residence program (MHA); occupational health (PhD); population health and social determinants (PhD); social and behavioral sciences (MPH); sociology and demography (PhD); JD/MHA; MHA/MBA; MHA/MD; MHA/MPA; MPH/JD; MPH/MD; MPH/MN; MPH/MPA; MPH/MSD; MPH/MSW; MPH/PhD. Part-time and evening/weekend programs available. Postbaccalaureate distance learning degree programs offered (minimal on-campus study). *Faculty:* 52 full-time (24 women), 60 part-time/adjunct (28 women). *Students:* 104 full-time (83 women), 100 part-time (76 women); includes 21 minority (6 African Americans, 1 American Indian/Alaska Native, 11 Asian Americans or Pacific Islanders, 3 Hispanic Americans), 6 international. Average age 34. 375 applicants, 17% accepted, 24 enrolled. In 2009, 33 master's awarded. Terminal master's awarded for partial completion of doctoral program. *Degree requirements:* For master's, thesis (for some programs), practicum (MPH); for doctorate, comprehensive exam, thesis/dissertation. *Entrance requirements:* For master's and doctorate, GRE General Test, minimum GPA of 3.0. Additional exam requirements/recommendations for international students: Required—TOEFL. *Application deadline:* For fall admission, 1/15 for domestic students, 11/1 for international students. Application fee: 50 Albanian leks. Electronic applications accepted. *Financial support:* In 2009–10, 64 students received support, including 10 fellowships with full and partial tuition reimbursements available (averaging $21,000 per year), 10 research assistantships with full and partial tuition reimbursements available (averaging $18,000 per year), 3 teaching assistantships with full and partial tuition reimbursements available (averaging $18,000 per year); career-related internships or fieldwork, Federal Work-Study, institutionally sponsored loans, and traineeships also available. Financial award application deadline: 2/28; financial award applicants required to submit FAFSA. *Faculty research:* Health promotion and disease prevention, maternal and child health, health services research design, program evaluation, health policy. Total annual research expenditures: $10.5 million. *Unit head:* Dr. Larry Kessler, Chair, 206-543-616-2930. *Application contact:* Kitty A. Andert, MPH/MS/PhD Program Manager, 206-616-2926, Fax: 206-543-3964, E-mail: kitander@u.washington.edu.

Vanderbilt University, Graduate School, Department of Biomedical Informatics, Nashville, TN 37240-1001. Offers MS, PhD, MD/MS, MD/PhD. Part-time programs available. *Faculty:* 24 full-time (5 women). *Students:* 23 full-time (9 women), 1 (woman) part-time; includes 2 minority (1 African American, 1 Asian American or Pacific Islander), 5 international. Average age 34. 47 applicants, 21% accepted, 8 enrolled. In 2009, 5 master's, 3 doctorates awarded. Terminal master's awarded for partial completion of doctoral program. *Degree requirements:* For master's, thesis; for doctorate, thesis/dissertation, final and qualifying exams. *Entrance requirements:* For master's and doctorate, GRE General Test. Additional exam requirements/recommendations for international students: Required—TOEFL (minimum score 600 paper-based; 230 computer-based; 88 iBT). *Application deadline:* For fall admission, 1/15 for domestic and international students. Application fee: $0. Electronic applications accepted. *Financial support:* Fellowships with full and partial tuition reimbursements, research assistantships with full and partial tuition reimbursements, teaching assistantships with full and partial tuition reimbursements, Federal Work-Study, institutionally sponsored loans, scholarships/grants, traineeships, and health care benefits available. Financial award application deadline: 1/15; financial award applicants required to submit CSS PROFILE or FAFSA. *Faculty research:* Organizational informatics; the application of informatics to the role of information technology in organizational change; clinical research and translational informatics; applications of informatics to facilitating 'bench to bedside" translational research. *Unit head:* Dr. Daniel R. Masys, Chair, 615-936-1556, Fax: 615-936-1427, E-mail: dan.masys@vanderbilt.edu. *Application contact:* Dr. Cynthia S. Gadd, Director of Graduate Studies, 615-936-1556, Fax: 615-936-1427, E-mail: cindy.gadd@vanderbilt.edu.

Virginia Commonwealth University, Graduate School, School of Life Sciences, Center for the Study of Biological Complexity, Richmond, VA 23284-9005. Offers bioinformatics (MS). *Degree requirements:* For master's, thesis optional.

Virginia Polytechnic Institute and State University, Graduate School, Intercollege, Program in Genetics, Bioinformatics and Computational Biology, Blacksburg, VA 24061. Offers PhD. *Entrance requirements:* For doctorate, GRE. Additional exam requirements/recommendations for international students: Required—TOEFL (minimum score 550 paper-based; 213 computer-based). Electronic applications accepted.

Wesleyan University, Graduate Programs, Department of Biology, Middletown, CT 06459. Offers animal behavior (PhD); bioformatics/genomics (PhD); cell biology (PhD); developmental biology (PhD); evolution/ecology (PhD); genetics (PhD); neurobiology (PhD); population biology (PhD). *Faculty:* 13 full-time (4 women). *Students:* 23 full-time (11 women); includes 1 minority (African American), 3 international. Average age 26. 29 applicants, 10% accepted, 2 enrolled. In 2009, 3 doctorates awarded. *Degree requirements:* For doctorate, variable foreign language requirement, thesis/dissertation. *Entrance requirements:* For doctorate, GRE. Additional exam requirements/recommendations for international students: Required—TOEFL. *Application deadline:* For fall admission, 1/15 for domestic and international students. Applications are processed on a rolling basis. Application fee: $0. *Financial support:* In 2009–10, 3 research assistantships with full tuition reimbursements, 19 teaching assistantships with full tuition reimbursements were awarded; stipends also available. Financial award application deadline: 4/15; financial award applicants required to submit FAFSA. *Faculty research:* Microbial population genetics, genetic basis of evolutionary adaptation, genetic regulation of differentiation and pattern formation in *drosophila*. *Unit head:* Dr. Sonia E. Sultan, Chair/Professor, 860-685-3493, E-mail: jnaegele@wesleyan.edu. *Application contact:* Marjorie Fitzgibbons, Information Contact, 860-685-2140, E-mail: mfitzgibbons@wesleyan.edu.

Yale University, School of Medicine and Graduate School of Arts and Sciences, Combined Program in Biological and Biomedical Sciences (BBS), Computational Biology and Bioinformatics Track, New Haven, CT 06520. Offers PhD, MD/PhD. *Students:* 3 full-time. *Entrance requirements:* Additional exam requirements/recommendations for international students: Required—TOEFL. *Application deadline:* For fall admission, 12/6 for domestic and international students. *Unit head:* Dr. Perry Miller, Director of Graduate Studies, 203-737-2903. *Application contact:* Lisa Sobel, Graduate Registrar, 203-737-6029.

Computer and Information Systems Security

American InterContinental University Online, Program in Information Technology, Hoffman Estates, IL 60192. Offers Internet security (MIT); IT project management (MIT). Evening/weekend programs available. Postbaccalaureate distance learning degree programs offered (no on-campus study). *Entrance requirements:* Additional exam requirements/recommendations for international students: Required—TOEFL (minimum score 550 paper-based; 213 computer-based). Electronic applications accepted.

American InterContinental University South Florida, Program in Information Technology, Weston, FL 33326. Offers Internet security (MIT); wireless computer forensics (MIT). Part-time and evening/weekend programs available. *Entrance requirements:* Additional exam requirements/recommendations for international students: Required—TOEFL (minimum score 670 paper-based). Electronic applications accepted.

Benedictine University, Graduate Programs, Program in Business Administration, Lisle, IL 60532-0900. Offers accounting (MBA); entrepreneurship and managing innovation (MBA); financial management (MBA); health administration (MBA); human resource management (MBA); information systems security (MBA); international business (MBA); management consulting (MBA); management information systems (MBA); marketing management (MBA); operations management and logistics (MBA); organizational leadership (MBA); MBA/MPH; MBA/MS. Part-time and evening/weekend programs available. Postbaccalaureate distance learning degree programs offered (minimal on-campus study). *Entrance requirements:* For master's, GMAT. Additional exam requirements/recommendations for international students: Required—TOEFL (minimum score 550 paper-based; 213 computer-based). Electronic applications accepted. *Faculty research:* Strategic leadership in professional organizations, sociology of professions, organizational change, social identity theory, applications to change management.

Brandeis University, Rabb School of Continuing Studies, Division of Graduate Professional Studies, Information Assurance Program, Waltham, MA 02454-9110. Offers MS, Graduate Certificate. Part-time and evening/weekend programs available. Postbaccalaureate distance learning degree programs offered (no on-campus study). *Faculty:* 2 full-time (both women), 32 part-time/adjunct (8 women). *Students:* 10 part-time (0 women); includes 1 Asian American or Pacific Islander. Average age 35. 4 applicants, 100% accepted, 4 enrolled. *Entrance requirements:* For master's, resume, letter of recommendation; for Graduate Certificate, resume, official transcripts, recommendations. Additional exam requirements/recommendations for international students: Recommended—TOEFL (minimum score 600 paper-based; 250 computer-based; 100 iBT). *Application deadline:* For fall admission, 6/15 priority date for domestic students; for winter admission, 10/15 priority date for domestic students; for spring admission, 2/15 priority date for domestic students. Applications are processed on a rolling basis. Application fee: $50. Electronic applications accepted. *Unit head:* Dr. Cynthia Phillips, Program Chair, 781-736-8787, Fax: 781-736-3420, E-mail: cynthiap@brandeis.edu. *Application contact:* Frances Stearns, Associate Director of Admissions and Student Services, 781-736-8785, Fax: 781-736-3420, E-mail: fstearns@brandeis.edu.

Capella University, School of Business and Technology, Minneapolis, MN 55402. Offers accounting (MBA), including system design and programming; business (Certificate), including human resource management (MS, PhD, Certificate), information technology management (MS, PhD, Certificate), leadership (MBA, MS, PhD, Certificate); finance (MBA); general business (MBA); health care management (MBA); information technology (MS, Certificate), including general information technology (MS), information security, network architecture and design (MS), professional projects management (Certificate), project management and leadership (MS), system design and development (MS),); information technology management (MBA); marketing (MBA); organization and management (MBA, MS, PhD), including general business (PhD), general organization and management (MBA, MS), human resource management (MS, PhD, Certificate), information technology management (MS, PhD, Certificate), leadership (MBA, MS, PhD, Certificate); project management (MBA). Part-time and evening/weekend programs available. Postbaccalaureate distance learning degree programs offered (minimal on-campus study). Terminal master's awarded for partial completion of doctoral program. *Degree requirements:* For master's, thesis optional, integrative project; for doctorate, comprehensive exam, thesis/dissertation. *Entrance requirements:* Additional exam requirements/recommendations for international students: Required—TOEFL (minimum score 550 paper-based; 213 computer-based), TWE (minimum score 4). Electronic applications accepted. *Faculty research:* Business policies: strategic, corporate, and financial management; interplay of technological, organizational and social change.

Capitol College, Graduate Programs, Laurel, MD 20708-9759. Offers business administration (MBA); computer science (MS); electrical engineering (MS); information and telecommunications systems management (MS); information architecture (MS); network security (MS). Part-time and evening/weekend programs available. Postbaccalaureate distance learning degree programs offered (no on-campus study). *Entrance requirements:* For master's, minimum GPA of 3.0. Electronic applications accepted.

Carnegie Mellon University, Carnegie Institute of Technology, Information Networking Institute, Pittsburgh, PA 15213. Offers information networking (MS); information security technology and management (MS); information technology—information security (MS); information technology—mobility (MS); information technology—software management (MS). *Degree requirements:* For master's, thesis optional. *Entrance requirements:* For master's, GRE General Test, bachelor's degree in computer science, computer engineering, or electrical engineering, or related technology degree; programming skills (C/C++ fluency for some programs). Additional exam requirements/recommendations for international students: Required—TOEFL. *Faculty research:* Computer forensics and incident response; dependable systems, embedded systems, mobile systems, and sensor networks; computer and information networks, network and information security, human and socio-economic factors in secure system design; wireless sensor networks, survivable embedded systems, signal processing/compression; strategic management, international strategic management, group dynamics and decision-making structures, simulated competitive environments.

Carnegie Mellon University, H. John Heinz III College, School of Information Systems and Management, Program in Information Security Policy and Management, Pittsburgh, PA 15213-3891. Offers MSISPM.

The Catholic University of America, School of Engineering, Department of Electrical Engineering and Computer Science, Washington, DC 20064. Offers antennas and electromagnetic propagation (MEE, MSCS, D Engr); bioimaging (MEE, MSCS, PhD); bioinformatics and intelligent information systems (MEE, D Engr, PhD); distributed and real-time systems (MEE, MSCS, D Engr, PhD); high speed communications and networking (MSCS, D Engr, PhD); information security (MEE, MSCS, PhD); micro-optics (MEE, MSCS, D Engr, PhD); signal and image processing (MEE, MSCS, D Engr). Part-time programs available. *Faculty:* 7 full-time (2 women), 6 part-time/adjunct (0 women). *Students:* 10 full-time (4 women), 50 part-time (7 women); includes 10 minority (3 African Americans, 4 Asian Americans or Pacific Islanders, 3 Hispanic Americans), 12 international. Average age 34. 50 applicants, 54% accepted, 11 enrolled. In 2009, 10 master's awarded. *Degree requirements:* For master's, thesis or alternative; for doctorate, comprehensive exam, thesis/dissertation, qualifying exam, oral exams. *Entrance requirements:* For master's, statement of purpose, official copies of academic transcripts, three letters of recommendation; for doctorate, 3 letters of recommendation. Additional exam requirements/recommendations for international students: Required—TOEFL (minimum score 580 paper-based; 237 computer-based). *Application deadline:* For fall admission, 8/1 priority date for domestic students, 7/15 for international students; for spring admission, 12/1 priority date for domestic students, 10/15 for international students. Applications are processed on a rolling basis. Application fee: $55. Electronic applications accepted. *Expenses:* Contact institution. *Financial support:* Fellowships, research assistantships, teaching assistantships, Federal Work-Study, scholarships/grants, tuition waivers (full and partial), and unspecified assistantships available. Financial award application deadline: 2/1; financial award applicants required to submit FAFSA. *Faculty research:* Signal and image processing, computer communications, robotics, intelligent controls, bioelectromagnetics. Total annual research expenditures: $1.2 million. *Unit head:* Dr. Phillip Regalia, Chair, 202-319-5879, Fax: 202-319-5195, E-mail: regalia@cua.edu. *Application contact:* Julie Schwing, Director of Graduate Admissions, 202-319-5057, Fax: 202-319-6533, E-mail: cua-admissions@cua.edu.

City University of Seattle, Graduate Division, School of Management, Bellevue, WA 98005. Offers accounting (Certificate); change leadership (MBA, Certificate); financial management (MBA, Certificate); general management (MBA); general management-Europe (MBA); global leadership (Certificate); global marketing (MBA); individualized study (MBA); information security (MS); information systems (MBA); leadership (MA); marketing (MBA, Certificate); project management (MBA, MS, Certificate); sustainable business (Certificate); technology management (MBA, MS, Certificate). Part-time and evening/weekend programs available. Postbaccalaureate distance learning degree programs offered (no on-campus study). *Entrance requirements:* Additional exam requirements/recommendations for international students: Required—TOEFL (minimum score 540 paper-based; 207 computer-based); Recommended—IELTS. Electronic applications accepted. *Expenses:* Tuition: Full-time $14,760; part-time $615 per credit. Tuition and fees vary according to program.

Colorado Technical University Colorado Springs, Graduate Studies, Program in Computer Science, Colorado Springs, CO 80907-3896. Offers computer science (DCS); computer systems security (MSCS); database systems (MSCS); software engineering (MSCS). Part-time and evening/weekend programs available. Postbaccalaureate distance learning degree programs offered. *Degree requirements:* For master's, thesis or alternative; for doctorate, thesis/dissertation. *Entrance requirements:* For doctorate, minimum graduate GPA of 3.0, 5 years of related work experience. *Faculty research:* Software engineering, systems engineering.

Colorado Technical University Colorado Springs, Graduate Studies, Program in Information Science, Colorado Springs, CO 80907-3896. Offers information systems security (MSM). Postbaccalaureate distance learning degree programs offered.

Colorado Technical University Denver, Program in Computer Science, Greenwood Village, CO 80111. Offers computer systems security (MSCS); database systems (MSCS); software engineering (MSCS). Part-time and evening/weekend programs available. *Degree requirements:* For master's, thesis or alternative. *Entrance requirements:* For master's, minimum undergraduate GPA of 3.0, resume.

Colorado Technical University Denver, Program in Information Science, Greenwood Village, CO 80111. Offers information systems security (MSM).

Colorado Technical University Sioux Falls, Program in Computing, Sioux Falls, SD 57108. Offers computer systems security (MSCS); software engineering (MSCS).

Concordia University, School of Graduate Studies, Faculty of Engineering and Computer Science, Concordia Institute for Information Systems Engineering (CIISE), Montréal, QC H3G 1M8, Canada. Offers 3D graphics and game development (Certificate); information systems security (M Eng, MA Sc); quality systems engineering (M Eng, MA Sc); service engineering and network management (Certificate).

Davenport University, Sneden Graduate School, Grand Rapids, MI 49503. Offers accounting (MBA); business administration (EMBA); finance (MBA); health care management (MBA); human resources (MBA); information assurance (MS); public health (MPH); strategic management (MBA). Evening/weekend programs available. *Entrance requirements:* For master's, GMAT, minimum undergraduate GPA of 2.75. Additional exam requirements/recommendations for international students: Required—TOEFL. Electronic applications accepted. *Faculty research:* Leadership, management, marketing, organizational culture.

Davenport University, Sneden Graduate School, Warren, MI 48092-5209. Offers accounting (MBA); business administration (EMBA); finance (MBA); health care management (MBA); human resources management (MBA); information assurance (MS); public health (MPH); strategic management (MBA). *Entrance requirements:* For master's, minimum undergraduate GPA of 2.7.

Davenport University, Sneden Graduate School, Dearborn, MI 48126-3799. Offers accounting (MBA); business administration (EMBA); finance (MBA); health care management (MBA); human resources management (MBA); information assurance (MS); marketing (MBA); public health (MPH); strategic management (MBA). Part-time and evening/weekend programs available. Postbaccalaureate distance learning degree programs offered (no on-campus study). *Entrance requirements:* For master's, minimum GPA of 2.7, previous course work in accounting and statistics. *Faculty research:* Accounting, international accounting, social and environmental accounting, finance.

DePaul University, College of Computing and Digital Media, Chicago, IL 60604. Offers business information technology (MS); computational finance (MS); computer and information sciences (PhD); computer game development (MS); computer graphics and motion technology (MS); computer science (MS); computer, information and network security (MS), including applied technology; digital cinema (MFA, MS), including information technology project management (MS); e-commerce technology (MS); human-computer interaction (MS); information systems (MS); information technology (MA); information technology project management (MS); software engineering (MS); telecommunications systems (MS); JD/MS. Part-time and evening/weekend programs available. Postbaccalaureate distance learning degree programs offered (no on-campus study). *Faculty:* 78 full-time (16 women), 191 part-time/adjunct (51 women). *Students:* 922 full-time (239 women), 887 part-time (209 women); includes 466 minority (193 African Americans, 3 American Indian/Alaska Native, 162 Asian Americans or Pacific Islanders, 108 Hispanic Americans), 276 international. Average age 31. 853 applicants, 67% accepted, 294 enrolled. In 2009, 444 master's, 4 doctorates awarded. *Degree requirements:* For master's, thesis (for some programs); for doctorate, comprehensive exam, thesis/dissertation. *Entrance requirements:* For master's, GRE or GMAT (MS in computational finance only), bachelor's degree; for doctorate, GRE, master's degree in computer science. Additional exam requirements/recommendations for international students: Required—TOEFL (minimum score 550 paper-based; 213 computer-based), IELTS (minimum score 6.5), Pearson Test of English (minimum score 53). *Application deadline:* For fall admission, 8/15 priority date for domestic students, 6/1 priority date for international students; for winter admission, 12/15 priority date for domestic students, 9/15 priority date for international students; for spring admission, 3/1 priority date for domestic students, 12/15 priority date for international students. Applications are processed on a rolling basis. Application fee: $25. Electronic applications accepted. *Expenses:* Contact institution. *Financial support:* In 2009–10, 69 students received support, including 6 fellowships with full tuition reimbursements available (averaging $25,858 per year), 75 teaching assistantships with full and partial tuition reimbursements available (averaging $5,780 per year); research assistantships, Federal Work-Study, scholarships/grants, tuition waivers (full and partial), and unspecified assistantships also available. Support available to part-time students. Financial award application deadline: 4/30; financial award applicants required to submit FAFSA. *Faculty research:* Bioinformatics, visual computing, graphics and animation, high performance and scientific computing, databases. Total annual research expenditures: $790,000. *Unit head:* Dr. David Miller, Dean, 312-362-8381, Fax: 312-362-5185. *Application contact:* Dr. Liz Friedman, Assistant Dean of Student Services, 312-362-5384, Fax: 312-362-5327, E-mail: efriedm2@cdm.depaul.edu.

Eastern Illinois University, Graduate School, Lumpkin College of Business and Applied Sciences, School of Technology, Charleston, IL 61920-3099. Offers computer technology (Certificate); quality systems (Certificate); technology (MS); technology security (Certificate);

work performance improvement (Certificate). Part-time and evening/weekend programs available. *Faculty:* 14 full-time (2 women). In 2009, 39 master's, 14 other advanced degrees awarded. *Application deadline:* For fall admission, 3/31 priority date for domestic students. Applications are processed on a rolling basis. Application fee: $30. *Expenses:* Tuition, state resident: full-time $9434; part-time $239 per credit hour. Tuition, nonresident: full-time $23,774; part-time $717 per credit hour. Required fees: $802.63. *Financial support:* In 2009–10, 3 research assistantships with tuition reimbursements (averaging $8,100 per year), 3 teaching assistantships with tuition reimbursements (averaging $8,100 per year) were awarded. *Unit head:* Dr. Mahyar Izadi, Chairperson, 217-581-6269, Fax: 217-581-6607, E-mail: mizadi@eiu.edu. *Application contact:* Dr. Peter Ping Liu, Coordinator, 217-581-6267, Fax: 217-581-6607, E-mail: pliu@eiu.edu.

Eastern Michigan University, Graduate School, College of Technology, School of Technology Studies, Program in Information Assurance, Ypsilanti, MI 48197. Offers MLS, Graduate Certificate. Part-time and evening/weekend programs available. Postbaccalaureate distance learning degree programs offered (minimal on-campus study). *Students:* 12 full-time (4 women), 17 part-time (0 women); includes 21 minority (19 African Americans, 2 Hispanic Americans), 3 international. Average age 36. In 2009, 1 other advanced degree awarded. *Entrance requirements:* Additional exam requirements/recommendations for international students: Required—TOEFL. *Application deadline:* Applications are processed on a rolling basis. Application fee: $35. Tuition and fees vary according to course level. *Financial support:* Fellowships, research assistantships with full tuition reimbursements, teaching assistantships with full tuition reimbursements, career-related internships or fieldwork, Federal Work-Study, institutionally sponsored loans, scholarships/grants, tuition waivers (partial), and unspecified assistantships available. Support available to part-time students. Financial award applicants required to submit FAFSA. *Unit head:* Prof. Gerald Lawver, Program Coordinator, 734-487-3170, Fax: 734-487-7690, E-mail: skip.lawver@emich.edu. *Application contact:* Prof. Gerald Lawver, Program Coordinator, 734-487-3170, Fax: 734-487-7690, E-mail: skip.lawver@emich.edu.

Florida State University, The Graduate School, College of Arts and Sciences, Department of Computer Science, Tallahassee, FL 32306. Offers computer science (MS, PhD); information security (MS); software engineering (MS). Part-time programs available. *Faculty:* 17 full-time (1 woman), 2 part-time/adjunct (0 women). *Students:* 114 full-time (22 women), 16 part-time (3 women); includes 20 minority (4 African Americans, 1 American Indian/Alaska Native, 5 Asian Americans or Pacific Islanders, 10 Hispanic Americans), 66 international. Average age 28. 167 applicants, 72% accepted, 34 enrolled. In 2009, 29 master's, 2 doctorates awarded. Terminal master's awarded for partial completion of doctoral program. *Degree requirements:* For master's, thesis or alternative; for doctorate, comprehensive exam, thesis/dissertation. *Entrance requirements:* For master's, GRE General Test, minimum undergraduate GPA of 3.0; for doctorate, GRE General Test, minimum GPA of 3.5. Additional exam requirements/recommendations for international students: Required—TOEFL (minimum score 600 paper-based; 250 computer-based; 100 iBT). *Application deadline:* For fall admission, 3/1 priority date for domestic students, 3/1 for international students; for spring admission, 10/1 priority date for domestic students, 10/1 for international students. Application fee: $30. Electronic applications accepted. *Expenses:* Tuition, state resident: full-time $7413.36. Tuition, nonresident: full-time $22,567. *Financial support:* In 2009–10, 107 students received support, including 4 fellowships with full tuition reimbursements available (averaging $17,500 per year), 35 research assistantships with full tuition reimbursements available (averaging $17,000 per year), 62 teaching assistantships with full tuition reimbursements available (averaging $15,500 per year); career-related internships or fieldwork, scholarships/grants, health care benefits, and unspecified assistantships also available. Financial award application deadline: 3/1; financial award applicants required to submit FAFSA. *Faculty research:* Embedded systems, high performance computing, networking, operating systems, security. Total annual research expenditures: $1.4 million. *Unit head:* Dr. David Whalley, Chairman, 850-644-3506, Fax: 850-644-0058, E-mail: chair@cs.fsu.edu. *Application contact:* Matthew S. Claypool, Graduate Coordinator, 850-645-4975, Fax: 850-644-0058, E-mail: claypool@cs.fsu.edu.

George Mason University, Volgenau School of Information Technology and Engineering, Department of Computer Science, Fairfax, VA 22030. Offers biometrics (Certificate); computer games technology (Certificate); computer networking (Certificate); computer science (MS, PhD); data mining (Certificate); database management (Certificate); electronic commerce (Certificate); foundations of information systems (Certificate); information engineering (Certificate); information security and assurance (MS, Certificate); information systems (MS); intelligent agents (Certificate); software architecture (Certificate); software engineering (MS, Certificate); systems engineering (MS); Web-based software engineering (Certificate). Part-time and evening/weekend programs available. Postbaccalaureate distance learning degree programs offered. *Faculty:* 42 full-time (9 women), 18 part-time/adjunct (0 women). *Students:* 121 full-time (36 women), 489 part-time (118 women); includes 90 minority (11 African Americans, 70 Asian Americans or Pacific Islanders, 9 Hispanic Americans), 222 international. Average age 29. 882 applicants, 58% accepted, 147 enrolled. In 2009, 202 master's, 6 doctorates, 21 other advanced degrees awarded. *Degree requirements:* For master's, thesis optional; for doctorate, comprehensive exam, thesis/dissertation. *Entrance requirements:* For master's, GRE General Test, minimum GPA of 3.0 in last 60 hours, 3 letters of recommendation; for doctorate, GRE, 4-year BA degree, academic work in computer science, 3 letters of recommendation, statement of career goals and aspirations. Additional exam requirements/recommendations for international students: Required—TOEFL. *Application deadline:* For fall admission, 4/15 priority date for domestic students, 1/15 for international students; for spring admission, 11/15 for domestic students. Application fee: $75. Electronic applications accepted. *Expenses:* Tuition, state resident: full-time $7568; part-time $315.33 per credit hour. Tuition, nonresident: full-time $21,704; part-time $904.33 per credit hour. Required fees: $2184; $91 per credit hour. *Financial support:* In 2009–10, 106 students received support, including 3 fellowships (averaging $18,000 per year), 53 research assistantships (averaging $11,119 per year), 53 teaching assistantships (averaging $7,881 per year); unspecified assistantships and health care benefits (full-time research or teaching assistantship recipients) also available. Financial award application deadline: 3/1; financial award applicants required to submit FAFSA. *Faculty research:* Artificial intelligence, image processing/graphics, parallel/distributed systems, software engineering systems. Total annual research expenditures: $1.3 million. *Unit head:* Dr. Arun Sood, Director, 703-993-1524, Fax: 703-993-1710, E-mail: asood@gmu.edu. *Application contact:* Jay Shapiro, Professor, 703-993-1485, E-mail: jshapiro@gmu.edu.

Georgia Institute of Technology, Graduate Studies and Research, College of Computing, Atlanta, GA 30332-0001. Offers algorithms, combinatorics, and optimization (PhD); computational science and engineering (MS, PhD); computer science (MS, MSCS, PhD); human computer interaction (MSHCI); human-centered computing (PhD); information security (MS). Part-time programs available. Postbaccalaureate distance learning degree programs offered. Terminal master's awarded for partial completion of doctoral program. *Degree requirements:* For master's, thesis optional; for doctorate, comprehensive exam, thesis/dissertation. *Entrance requirements:* For master's, GRE General Test, GRE Subject Test, minimum GPA of 3.0; for doctorate, GRE General Test, GRE Subject Test, minimum GPA of 3.3. Additional exam requirements/recommendations for international students: Required—TOEFL. *Faculty research:* Computer systems, graphics, intelligent systems and artificial intelligence, networks and telecommunications, software engineering.

Inter American University of Puerto Rico, Guayama Campus, Department of Natural and Applied Sciences, Guayama, PR 00785. Offers computer security and networks (MS).

The Johns Hopkins University, Carey Business School, Information Technology Programs, Baltimore, MD 21218-2699. Offers competitive intelligence (Certificate); information security management (Certificate); information systems (MS); MBA/MSIS. Part-time and evening/weekend programs available. *Faculty:* 29 full-time (6 women), 135 part-time/adjunct (29 women). *Students:* 25 full-time (11 women), 171 part-time (57 women); includes 74 minority (35 African Americans, 34 Asian Americans or Pacific Islanders, 5 Hispanic Americans), 10 international.

Average age 34. 69 applicants, 77% accepted, 41 enrolled. In 2009, 131 master's, 45 other advanced degrees awarded. *Degree requirements:* For master's, MBA/MSIS—72 credits including Capstone project, MS—36 credits including final project. *Entrance requirements:* For master's and Certificate, minimum GPA of 3.0, resume, work experience, two letters of recommendation. Additional exam requirements/recommendations for international students: Required—TOEFL (minimum score 600 paper-based; 250 computer-based; 100 iBT). *Application deadline:* For fall admission, 5/1 for international students; for spring admission, 10/15 for international students. Applications are processed on a rolling basis. Application fee: $100. Electronic applications accepted. *Financial support:* Scholarships/grants available. Support available to part-time students. Financial award application deadline: 4/1; financial award applicants required to submit FAFSA. *Faculty research:* Information security, healthcare information systems. Total annual research expenditures: $89,653. *Unit head:* Dr. Dipankar Chakravarti, Vice Dean of Programs, 410-516-8561, E-mail: dipankar.chakravarti@jhu.edu. *Application contact:* Robin Greenberg, Admissions Coordinator, 410-516-4234, Fax: 410-516-0826, E-mail: carey.admissions@jhu.edu.

The Johns Hopkins University, Engineering for Professionals, Part-Time Program in Information Assurance, Baltimore, MD 21218-2699. Offers MS. Part-time and evening/weekend programs available. *Faculty:* 4 part-time/adjunct (0 women). *Students:* 2 full-time (1 woman), 8 part-time (1 woman); includes 3 minority (1 African American, 2 Asian Americans or Pacific Islanders). Average age 30. *Application deadline:* Applications are processed on a rolling basis. *Unit head:* Tom Longstaff, Vice Chair, 410-516-2300. *Application contact:* Priyanka Dwivedi, Admissions Manager, 410-516-2300, Fax: 410-579-8049, E-mail: pdwived1@jhu.edu.

The Johns Hopkins University, G. W. C. Whiting School of Engineering, Information Security Institute, Baltimore, MD 21218-2699. Offers MSSI. Part-time programs available. *Faculty:* 6 part-time/adjunct (0 women). *Students:* 23 full-time (2 women), 20 part-time (1 woman); includes 4 minority (2 African Americans, 1 Asian American or Pacific Islander, 1 Hispanic American), 24 international. Average age 25. 70 applicants, 93% accepted, 16 enrolled. In 2009, 13 master's awarded. *Degree requirements:* For master's, project. *Entrance requirements:* For master's, GRE, minimum GPA of 3.0. Additional exam requirements/recommendations for international students: Required—TOEFL (minimum score 600 paper-based; 250 computer-based). *Application deadline:* For fall admission, 6/15 priority date for domestic students, 3/15 for international students; for spring admission, 11/15 for domestic students, 11/1 for international students. Applications are processed on a rolling basis. Application fee: $25. Electronic applications accepted. *Financial support:* In 2009–10, 28 students received support, including 3 teaching assistantships with tuition reimbursements available (averaging $3,000 per year); fellowships with full tuition reimbursements available, career-related internships or fieldwork, Federal Work-Study, institutionally sponsored loans, scholarships/grants, traineeships, health care benefits, tuition waivers (partial), and unspecified assistantships also available. *Faculty research:* Critical infrastructure protection, insider/outsider cryptography and encryption methodologies, international policy protocols, web based intellectual property rights. Total annual research expenditures: $675,000. *Unit head:* Dr. Gerald M. Masson, Director, 410-516-7013, Fax: 410-516-3301, E-mail: masson@jhu.edu. *Application contact:* Deborah K. Higgins, Graduate Coordinator, 410-516-8521, Fax: 410-516-3301, E-mail: dhiggins@jhu.edu.

Jones International University, School of Business, Centennial, CO 80112. Offers accounting (MBA); business communication (MABC); entrepreneurship (MABC, MBA); finance (MBA); global enterprise management (MBA); health care management (MBA); information security management (MBA); information technology management (MBA); leadership and influence (MABC); leading the customer-driven organization (MABC); negotiation and conflict management (MBA); project management (MABC, MBA). Program only offered online. Part-time and evening/weekend programs available. Postbaccalaureate distance learning degree programs offered (no on-campus study). *Degree requirements:* For master's, capstone project. *Entrance requirements:* For master's, minimum cumulative GPA of 2.5. Additional exam requirements/recommendations for international students: Recommended—TOEFL (minimum score 550 paper-based; 213 computer-based). Electronic applications accepted.

Kaplan University, Davenport Campus, School of Information Technology, Davenport, IA 52807-2095. Offers decision support systems (MS); information security and assurance (MS). Part-time and evening/weekend programs available. Postbaccalaureate distance learning degree programs offered (no on-campus study). *Entrance requirements:* Additional exam requirements/recommendations for international students: Required—TOEFL (minimum score 550 paper-based; 218 computer-based; 80 iBT).

Kentucky State University, College of Mathematics, Sciences, Technology and Health, Frankfort, KY 40601. Offers aquaculture (MS); computer science (MS), including computer science theory, information assurance, information technology. Part-time and evening/weekend programs available. *Faculty:* 8 full-time (0 women), 1 part-time/adjunct (0 women). *Students:* 18 full-time (6 women), 18 part-time (4 women); includes 11 minority (8 African Americans, 1 Asian American or Pacific Islander, 2 Hispanic Americans), 7 international. Average age 35. 42 applicants, 55% accepted, 12 enrolled. In 2009, 8 master's awarded. *Degree requirements:* For master's, comprehensive exam, thesis optional. *Entrance requirements:* For master's, GRE, GMAT. Additional exam requirements/recommendations for international students: Required—TOEFL (minimum score 525 paper-based; 173 computer-based). *Application deadline:* For fall admission, 7/1 priority date for domestic students, 4/15 priority date for international students; for spring admission, 11/15 priority date for domestic students, 8/1 priority date for international students. Applications are processed on a rolling basis. Application fee: $30 ($100 for international students). Electronic applications accepted. *Expenses:* Tuition, state resident: full-time $5634; part-time $313 per credit hour. Tuition, nonresident: full-time $14,598; part-time $811 per credit hour. Required fees: $450; $25 per credit hour. *Financial support:* In 2009–10, 28 students received support, including 10 research assistantships (averaging $10,505 per year); career-related internships or fieldwork, scholarships/grants, tuition waivers (partial), and unspecified assistantships also available. Financial award application deadline: 4/15; financial award applicants required to submit FAFSA. *Unit head:* Dr. Charles Bennett, Dean, 502-597-6926, E-mail: charles.bennett@kysu.edu. *Application contact:* Cedric Cunningham, Administrative Assistant, Office of Graduate Studies, 502-597-6536, Fax: 502-597-6432, E-mail: cedric.cunningham@kysu.edu.

Lewis University, College of Business, Graduate School of Management, Program in Business Administration, Romeoville, IL 60446. Offers accounting (MBA); custom elective option (MBA); e-business (MBA); finance (MBA); healthcare management (MBA); human resources management (MBA); information security (MBA); international business (MBA); management information systems (MBA); marketing (MBA); project management (MBA); technology and operations management (MBA). Part-time and evening/weekend programs available. *Faculty:* 15 full-time (2 women), 18 part-time/adjunct (4 women). *Students:* 120 full-time (64 women), 222 part-time (103 women); includes 97 minority (62 African Americans, 4 Asian Americans or Pacific Islanders, 31 Hispanic Americans), 9 international. Average age 31. In 2009, 84 master's awarded. *Entrance requirements:* For master's, interview, bachelor's degree, resume, 2 recommendations. Additional exam requirements/recommendations for international students: Required—TOEFL (minimum score 550 paper-based; 213 computer-based). *Application deadline:* For fall admission, 8/15 priority date for domestic students, 5/1 priority date for international students; for spring admission, 11/15 priority date for international students. Applications are processed on a rolling basis. Application fee: $40. Electronic applications accepted. *Expenses:* Tuition: Full-time $6480; part-time $720 per credit. One-time fee: $40. Tuition and fees vary according to course load, degree level and program. *Financial support:* Career-related internships or fieldwork, Federal Work-Study, scholarships/grants, and unspecified assistantships available. Financial award application deadline: 5/1; financial award applicants required to submit FAFSA. *Unit head:* Dr. Maureen Culleeney, Academic Program Director, 815-838-0500 Ext. 5631, E-mail: culleema@lewisu.edu. *Application contact:* Michele King, Director of Admission, 815-838-0500 Ext. 5384, E-mail: gsm@lewisu.edu.

Lewis University, College of Business, Program in Information Security, Romeoville, IL 60446. Offers MS. Part-time and evening/weekend programs available. *Faculty:* 3 full-time (0

Computer and Information Systems Security

Lewis University (continued)

women), 4 part-time/adjunct (0 women). *Students:* 4 full-time (1 woman), 26 part-time (6 women); includes 5 minority (1 African American, 1 American Indian/Alaska Native, 3 Hispanic Americans), 5 international. Average age 31. In 2009, 13 master's awarded. *Entrance requirements:* For master's, bachelor's degree, minimum GPA of 3.0, resume, 2-page statement of purpose, 3 letters of recommendation. Additional exam requirements/recommendations for international students: Required—TOEFL (minimum score 550 paper-based; 213 computer-based). *Application deadline:* For fall admission, 5/1 priority date for international students; for spring admission, 11/15 priority date for international students. Applications are processed on a rolling basis. Application fee: $40. Electronic applications accepted. *Expenses:* Tuition: Full-time $6480; part-time $720 per credit. One-time fee: $40. Tuition and fees vary according to course load, degree level and program. *Financial support:* Application deadline: 5/1; *Unit head:* Dr. Rami Khasawneh, Dean, 815-838-0500 Ext. 5360. *Application contact:* Michele Ryan, Director of Admission, Graduate School of Management, 800-897-9000, E-mail: gsm@lewisu.edu.

Marymount University, School of Business Administration, Program in Information Technology, Arlington, VA 22207-4299. Offers computer security and information assurance (Certificate); health care informatics (Certificate); information technology (MS, Certificate); information technology project management: technology leadership (Certificate). Part-time and evening/weekend programs available. *Faculty:* 6 full-time (3 women), 4 part-time/adjunct (0 women). *Students:* 28 full-time (11 women), 23 part-time (6 women); includes 15 minority (9 African Americans, 1 American Indian/Alaska Native, 4 Asian Americans or Pacific Islanders, 1 Hispanic American), 21 international. Average age 31. 45 applicants, 100% accepted, 26 enrolled. In 2009, 19 master's, 1 other advanced degree awarded. *Degree requirements:* For master's, thesis or alternative. *Entrance requirements:* For master's, GMAT or GRE General Test, interview, resume, bachelor's degree in computer-related field or degree in another subject with a post-baccalaureate certificate in a computer-related field; for Certificate, resume. Additional exam requirements/recommendations for international students: Required—TOEFL (minimum score 600 paper-based; 250 computer-based; 96 iBT), IELTS (minimum score 6.5). *Application deadline:* For fall admission, 7/15 for domestic students, 7/1 for international students; for spring admission, 11/15 for domestic students, 10/15 for international students. Applications are processed on a rolling basis. Application fee: $40. Electronic applications accepted. *Expenses:* Tuition: Full-time $13,050; part-time $725 per credit hour. Required fees: $135; $7.50 per credit hour. *Financial support:* In 2009–10, 5 students received support; research assistantships with full tuition reimbursements available, career-related internships or fieldwork, Federal Work-Study, scholarships/grants, and unspecified assistantships available. Support available to part-time students. Financial award applicants required to submit FAFSA. *Unit head:* Dr. Diane Murphy, Chair, 703-284-5958, Fax: 703-527-3830, E-mail: diane.murphy@marymount.edu. *Application contact:* Francesca Reed, Director, Graduate Admissions, 703-284-5901, Fax: 703-527-3815, E-mail: grad.admissions@marymount.edu.

Mercy College, School of Liberal Arts, Program in Information Assurance and Security, Dobbs Ferry, NY 10522-1189. Offers MS. Part-time and evening/weekend programs available. Post-baccalaureate distance learning degree programs offered (no on-campus study). *Students:* 9 full-time (1 woman), 11 part-time (2 women); includes 6 African Americans, 2 Asian Americans or Pacific Islanders, 6 Hispanic Americans, 3 international. Average age 37. 11 applicants, 45% accepted, 5 enrolled. In 2009, 3 master's awarded. *Entrance requirements:* For master's, two letters of recommendation; two-page written personal statement; completion of undergraduate prerequisites in local area networks, database management systems, cryptographgy and computer security, operating systems, and statistics. Additional exam requirements/recommendations for international students: Required—TOEFL (minimum score 600 paper-based; 250 computer-based; 100 iBT). *Application deadline:* For fall admission, 8/1 for international students. Applications are processed on a rolling basis. Application fee: $40. Electronic applications accepted. *Expenses:* Contact institution. *Financial support:* Career-related internships or fieldwork, Federal Work-Study, scholarships/grants, and unspecified assistantships available. *Faculty research:* Information security theory, assurance, technical and analytical abilities. *Unit head:* Dr. Nagaraj Rao, Professor, Mathematics and Computer Information Science, 914-674-7593, E-mail: nrao@mercy.edu. *Application contact:* Dr. Nagaraj Rao, Professor, Mathematics and Computer Information Science, 914-674-7593, E-mail: nrao@mercy.edu.

Metropolitan State University, College of Management, St. Paul, MN 55106-5000. Offers business administration (MBA); information assurance security (Graduate Certificate); information management (MMIS); MIS generalist (Graduate Certificate); MIS systems analysis and design (Graduate Certificate); nonprofit management (MPNA); project management (Graduate Certificate); public administration (MPNA); systems management (MMIS). Part-time and evening/weekend programs available. *Degree requirements:* For master's, thesis optional, computer language (MMIS). *Entrance requirements:* For master's, GMAT (MBA), resume. Additional exam requirements/recommendations for international students: Required—TOEFL (minimum score 550 paper-based; 213 computer-based). *Expenses:* Tuition, state resident: full-time $5520; part-time $276 per credit hour. Tuition, nonresident: full-time $11,040; part-time $552 per credit hour. Required fees: $209; $10 per credit hour. Tuition and fees vary according to degree level. *Faculty research:* Yugoslav economic system, workers' cooperatives, participative management and job enrichment, global business systems.

New York Institute of Technology, Graduate Division, School of Engineering and Computing Sciences, Program in Information, Network, and Computer Security, Old Westbury, NY 11568-8000. Offers MS. Part-time and evening/weekend programs available. Postbaccalaureate distance learning degree programs offered. *Students:* 58 full-time (4 women), 58 part-time (11 women); includes 18 minority (8 African Americans, 1 American Indian/Alaska Native, 6 Asian Americans or Pacific Islanders, 3 Hispanic Americans), 38 international. Average age 28. In 2009, 33 master's awarded. *Entrance requirements:* Additional exam requirements/recommendations for international students: Required—TOEFL (minimum score 550 paper-based; 213 computer-based). *Application deadline:* For fall admission, 7/1 priority date for domestic students; for spring admission, 12/1 priority date for domestic students. Applications are processed on a rolling basis. Application fee: $50. Electronic applications accepted. *Expenses:* Tuition: Part-time $825 per credit. *Financial support:* Fellowships, research assistantships with partial tuition reimbursements, career-related internships or fieldwork, institutionally sponsored loans, tuition waivers (full and partial), and unspecified assistantships available. Support available to part-time students. Financial award applicants required to submit FAFSA. *Unit head:* Dr. Nada Anid, Dean, 516-686-7931, Fax: 516-625-7933, E-mail: nanid@nyit.edu. *Application contact:* Dr. Jacquelyn Nealon, Vice President for Enrollment Services, 516-686-7925, Fax: 516-686-7597, E-mail: jnealon@nyit.edu.

Northern Kentucky University, Office of Graduate Programs, College of Informatics, Department of Business Informatics, Highland Heights, KY 41099. Offers business informatics (MS, Certificate); corporate information security (Certificate); enterprise resource planning (Certificate). Part-time and evening/weekend programs available. Postbaccalaureate distance learning degree programs offered (no on-campus study). *Students:* 5 full-time (2 women), 30 part-time (13 women); includes 5 minority (3 African Americans, 2 Asian Americans or Pacific Islanders), 4 international. Average age 32. 23 applicants, 57% accepted, 7 enrolled. In 2009, 15 master's, 6 other advanced degrees awarded. *Degree requirements:* For master's, capstone and portfolio (some programs), internship. *Entrance requirements:* For master's, GMAT (minimum score 450), GRE General Test (minimum combined score 1000), resume, min 3.0 GPA, 3 letters of recommendation. Additional exam requirements/recommendations for international students: Required—TOEFL (minimum score 550 paper-based; 213 computer-based; 79 iBT); Recommended—IELTS (minimum score 6.5). *Application deadline:* For fall admission, 8/1 priority date for domestic students, 6/1 for international students; for spring admission, 12/1 priority date for domestic students, 10/1 for international students. Applications are processed on a rolling basis. Application fee: $40. Electronic applications accepted. *Expenses:* Tuition, state resident: full-time $6912; part-time $384 per credit hour. Tuition, nonresident: full-time $12,150; part-time $675 per credit hour. Tuition and fees vary according to course load, program and reciprocity agreements. *Financial support:* Unspecified assistantships available. Financial award applicants required to submit FAFSA. *Faculty research:* Information systems implementation, information systems security, business analytics, healthcare informatics. Total annual research expenditures: $50,000. *Unit head:* Dr. Vijay Raghavan, Director, 859-572-6358, E-mail: raghavan@nku.edu. *Application contact:* Dr. Peg Griffin, Director of Graduate Programs, 859-572-6934, Fax: 859-572-6670, E-mail: griffinp@nku.edu.

Northwestern University, School of Continuing Studies, Program in Information Systems, Evanston, IL 60208. Offers database and Internet technologies (MS); information systems management (MS); information systems security (MS); software project management and development (MS).

Norwich University, School of Graduate and Continuing Studies, Program in Information Assurance, Northfield, VT 05663. Offers business continuity management (MS); computer security incident response team management (MS); cyber forensic investigations (MS); managing cyber crime and digital incidents (MS). Evening/weekend programs available. *Faculty:* 18 part-time/adjunct (3 women). *Students:* 296 full-time (42 women); includes 31 minority (18 African Americans, 13 Hispanic Americans), 17 international. Average age 40. In 2009, 167 master's awarded. *Entrance requirements:* For master's, minimum undergraduate GPA of 2.75. Additional exam requirements/recommendations for international students: Required—TOEFL (minimum score 550 paper-based; 212 computer-based; 83 iBT). *Application deadline:* For fall admission, 8/10 for domestic and international students; for winter admission, 11/7 for domestic and international students; for spring admission, 2/6 for domestic and international students. Application fee: $50. Full-time tuition and fees vary according to course level and course load. *Financial support:* Scholarships/grants available. Financial award applicants required to submit FAFSA. *Unit head:* Dr. John Orlando, Program Director, 802-485-2730, E-mail: jorlando@norwich.edu. *Application contact:* Elizabeth Templeton, Administrative Director, 802-485-2757, Fax: 802-485-2533, E-mail: etemplet@norwich.edu.

Nova Southeastern University, Graduate School of Computer and Information Sciences, Program in Computer Information Systems, Fort Lauderdale, FL 33314-7796. Offers information security (MS). *Students:* 24 full-time (2 women), 176 part-time (31 women); includes 74 minority (23 African Americans, 3 American Indian/Alaska Native, 21 Asian Americans or Pacific Islanders, 27 Hispanic Americans), 3 international. In 2009, 19 master's, 6 doctorates awarded. *Degree requirements:* For master's, thesis optional; for doctorate, thesis/dissertation. *Application deadline:* Applications are processed on a rolling basis. Electronic applications accepted. *Unit head:* Dr. Amon Seagull, Interim Dean, 954-262-7300. *Application contact:* 954-262-2000, Fax: 954-262-2752, E-mail: scisinfo@nova.edu.

Nova Southeastern University, Graduate School of Computer and Information Sciences, Program in Information Security, Fort Lauderdale, FL 33314-7796. Offers MS. *Students:* 12 full-time (1 woman), 51 part-time (7 women); includes 28 minority (15 African Americans, 1 American Indian/Alaska Native, 2 Asian Americans or Pacific Islanders, 10 Hispanic Americans), 3 international. In 2009, 12 master's awarded. *Degree requirements:* For master's, thesis optional. *Application deadline:* Applications are processed on a rolling basis. Electronic applications accepted. *Unit head:* Dr. Amon Seagull, Interim Dean, 954-262-7300. *Application contact:* 954-262-2000, Fax: 954-262-2752, E-mail: scisinfo@nova.edu.

Nova Southeastern University, Graduate School of Computer and Information Sciences, Program in Management Information Systems, Fort Lauderdale, FL 33314-7796. Offers information security (MS); management information systems (MS). Part-time and evening/weekend programs available. Postbaccalaureate distance learning degree programs offered (no on-campus study). *Students:* 19 full-time (4 women), 120 part-time (42 women); includes 71 minority (36 African Americans, 8 Asian Americans or Pacific Islanders, 27 Hispanic Americans), 8 international. In 2009, 75 master's awarded. *Degree requirements:* For master's, thesis optional. *Application deadline:* Applications are processed on a rolling basis. Electronic applications accepted. *Financial support:* Application deadline: 5/1; *Unit head:* Dr. Amon Seagull, Interim Dean. *Application contact:* 954-262-2000, Fax: 954-262-2752, E-mail: scisinfo@nova.edu.

Our Lady of the Lake University of San Antonio, School of Business and Leadership, Program in Information Systems and Security, San Antonio, TX 78207-4689. Offers MS. *Students:* 7 part-time (3 women); includes 3 minority (all Hispanic Americans). Average age 32. In 2009, 6 master's awarded. *Expenses:* Tuition: Full-time $12,330; part-time $685 per contact hour. Required fees: $139; $12 per contact hour. $57 per semester. Tuition and fees vary according to campus/location. *Unit head:* Dr. Robert Bisking, Dean, 210-434-6711, Fax: 210-434-0821. *Application contact:* Dr. Robert Bisking, Dean, 210-434-6711, Fax: 210-434-0821.

Pace University, Seidenberg School of Computer Science and Information Systems, New York, NY 10038. Offers computer communications and networks (Certificate); computer science (MS); computing studies (DPS); information systems (MS); Internet technologies for e-commerce (MS); Internet technology (MS); object-oriented programming (Certificate); security and information assurance (Certificate); software development and engineering (MS); telecommunications (MS, Certificate). Part-time and evening/weekend programs available. *Students:* 122 full-time (37 women), 424 part-time (131 women); includes 188 minority (76 African Americans, 1 American Indian/Alaska Native, 65 Asian Americans or Pacific Islanders, 46 Hispanic Americans), 110 international. Average age 35. 352 applicants, 89% accepted, 128 enrolled. In 2009, 137 master's, 11 doctorates, 3 other advanced degrees awarded. *Entrance requirements:* For master's, GRE General Test. Additional exam requirements/recommendations for international students: Required—TOEFL. *Application deadline:* For fall admission, 7/31 priority date for domestic students; for spring admission, 11/30 for domestic students. Applications are processed on a rolling basis. Application fee: $70. Electronic applications accepted. *Expenses:* Contact institution. *Financial support:* Research assistantships, career-related internships or fieldwork available. Support available to part-time students. Financial award applicants required to submit FAFSA. *Unit head:* Dr. Constance Knapp, Interim Dean, 914-773-3750, Fax: 914-773-3533, E-mail: cknapp@pace.edu. *Application contact:* Joanna Broda, Director of Graduate Admissions, 914-422-4283, Fax: 914-422-4287, E-mail: gradwp@pace.edu.

Polytechnic Institute of NYU, Department of Computer Science and Engineering, Major in Cyber Security, Brooklyn, NY 11201-2990. Offers Graduate Certificate. *Students:* 2 part-time (0 women). 4 applicants, 50% accepted, 2 enrolled. *Application deadline:* For fall admission, 7/31 priority date for domestic students, 4/30 priority date for international students; for spring admission, 12/31 priority date for domestic students, 11/30 priority date for international students. Applications are processed on a rolling basis. Application fee: $75. Electronic applications accepted. *Expenses:* Tuition: Full-time $21,492; part-time $1194 per credit hour. Required fees: $1160; $204 per course. *Unit head:* Dr. Keith W. Ross, Head, 718-260-3859, Fax: 718-260-3609, E-mail: ross@poly.edu. *Application contact:* JeanCarlo Bonilla, Director of Graduate Enrollment Management, 718-260-3182, Fax: 718-260-3624, E-mail: gradinfo@poly.edu.

Purdue University, Graduate School, Center for Education and Research in Information Assurance and Security (CERIAS), Interdisciplinary Program in Information Security, West Lafayette, IN 47907. Offers MS. *Entrance requirements:* For master's, GRE. Additional exam requirements/recommendations for international students: Required—TOEFL. Electronic applications accepted.

Regis University, College for Professional Studies, School of Computer and Information Sciences, Denver, CO 80221-1099. Offers database administration with IBM DB2 (Certificate); database administration with Oracle (Certificate); database development (Certificate); database technologies (MA); enterprise Java software development (Certificate); executive information technologies (Certificate); information assurance (MA, Certificate); information technology management (MA); software and information systems (M Sc); software engineering (MA,

Certificate); storage area networks (Certificate); systems engineering (MA, Certificate). Offered at Boulder Campus, Northwest Denver Campus, Southeast Denver Campus, Fort Collins Campus, Colorado Springs Campus, and Broomfield Campus. Part-time and evening/weekend programs available. Postbaccalaureate distance learning degree programs offered (no on-campus study). *Degree requirements:* For master's, thesis, final research project. *Entrance requirements:* For master's, 2 years of related experience, resume, interview; for Certificate, 2 years of related experience, resumé. Additional exam requirements/recommendations for international students: Required—TOEFL (minimum score 213 computer-based), TWE (minimum score 5), TOEFL or university-based test. Electronic applications accepted. *Expenses:* Contact institution. *Faculty research:* Secure Virtual Laboratory Architecture, Joint IA project with W2C06 Institute, Information Policy, OLTP and OLAP Technologies, knowledge management, software architectures.

Robert Morris University, Graduate Studies, School of Communications and Information Systems, Moon Township, PA 15108-1189. Offers communication and information systems (MS); competitive intelligence systems (MS); information security and assurance (MS); information systems and communications (D Sc); information systems management (MS); information technology project management (MS); Internet information systems (MS); organizational studies (MS). Part-time and evening/weekend programs available. *Faculty:* 28 full-time (9 women), 9 part-time/adjunct (3 women). *Students:* 257 part-time (76 women); includes 41 minority (31 African Americans, 8 Asian Americans or Pacific Islanders, 2 Hispanic Americans), 16 international. Average age 33. 106 applicants, 100% accepted, 106 enrolled. In 2009, 84 master's, 8 doctorates awarded. *Degree requirements:* For doctorate, thesis/dissertation. *Entrance requirements:* For doctorate, employer letter of endorsement, interview. Additional exam requirements/recommendations for international students: Required—TOEFL (minimum score 550 paper-based; 213 computer-based; 79 iBT). *Application deadline:* For fall admission, 7/1 priority date for domestic and international students; for spring admission, 11/1 priority date for domestic and international students. Applications are processed on a rolling basis. Application fee: $35. Electronic applications accepted. *Expenses:* Contact institution. *Financial support:* Research assistantships with partial tuition reimbursements, institutionally sponsored loans and unspecified assistantships available. Support available to part-time students. Financial award application deadline: 5/1. *Unit head:* Dr. Barbara J. Levine, Dean, 412-397-2591, Fax: 412-397-2481, E-mail: levine@rmu.edu. *Application contact:* Deborah Roach, Assistant Dean, Graduate Admissions, 412-397-5200, Fax: 412-397-2425, E-mail: graduateadmissions@rmu.edu.

Rochester Institute of Technology, Graduate Enrollment Services, B. Thomas Golisano College of Computing and Information Sciences, Department of Information Technology, Rochester, NY 14623-5603. Offers database administration (AC); human computer interaction (MS); information assurance (AC); information technology (MS); interactive multimedia development (AC); software development and management (MS). Part-time and evening/weekend programs available. Postbaccalaureate distance learning degree programs offered (minimal on-campus study). *Students:* 95 full-time (32 women), 107 part-time (26 women); includes 16 minority (7 African Americans, 1 American Indian/Alaska Native, 5 Asian Americans or Pacific Islanders, 3 Hispanic Americans), 81 international. Average age 30. 162 applicants, 64% accepted, 52 enrolled. In 2009, 66 master's, 6 other advanced degrees awarded. *Degree requirements:* For master's, thesis or project. *Entrance requirements:* For master's, GRE, minimum GPA of 3.0. Additional exam requirements/recommendations for international students: Required—TOEFL (minimum score 570 paper-based; 230 computer-based; 99 iBT), or IELTS (minimum score 6.5). *Application deadline:* For fall admission, 8/1 for domestic students, 7/1 for international students; for spring admission, 2/1 for domestic students. Applications are processed on a rolling basis. Application fee: $50. Electronic applications accepted. *Expenses:* Tuition: Full-time $31,533; part-time $876 per credit hour. Required fees: $210. *Financial support:* In 2009–10, 137 students received support; research assistantships with partial tuition reimbursements available, teaching assistantships with partial tuition reimbursements available, career-related internships or fieldwork, scholarships/grants, and unspecified assistantships available. Support available to part-time students. Financial award applicants required to submit FAFSA. *Faculty research:* Human computer interaction: eye tracking, usability engineering, usability testing, ubiquitous computing, interface design and development; platform-independent Multiuser Online Virtual Environments (MOVEs); simulation; service computing, query optimization, data mining and integration; applications programming, interface designs, needs assessment, data modeling, database administration. *Unit head:* Prof. Jeffrey Lasky, Department Chair, 585-475-2284, Fax: 585-475-6584, E-mail: jalics@rit.edu. *Application contact:* Diane Ellison, Assistant Vice President, Graduate Enrollment Services, 585-475-2229, Fax: 585-475-7164, E-mail: gradinfo@rit.edu.

Rochester Institute of Technology, Graduate Enrollment Services, B. Thomas Golisano College of Computing and Information Sciences, Department of Networking, Security and Systems Administration, Program in Security and Information Assurance, Rochester, NY 14623-5603. Offers MS. Part-time and evening/weekend programs available. Postbaccalaureate distance learning degree programs offered (no on-campus study). *Students:* 16 full-time (3 women), 8 part-time (1 woman), 10 international. Average age 28. 49 applicants, 71% accepted, 15 enrolled. In 2009, 5 master's awarded. *Degree requirements:* For master's, thesis. *Entrance requirements:* For master's, GRE, minimum GPA of 3.0. Additional exam requirements/recommendations for international students: Required—TOEFL (minimum score 570 paper-based; 230 computer-based; 88 iBT), or IELTS (minimum score 6.5). *Application deadline:* For fall admission, 8/1 for domestic students, 7/1 for international students; for spring admission, 2/1 for domestic students. Applications are processed on a rolling basis. Application fee: $50. Electronic applications accepted. *Expenses:* Tuition: Full-time $31,533; part-time $876 per credit hour. Required fees: $210. *Financial support:* In 2009–10, 19 students received support; research assistantships with partial tuition reimbursements available, teaching assistantships with partial tuition reimbursements available, career-related internships or fieldwork, scholarships/grants, and unspecified assistantships available. Support available to part-time students. Financial award applicants required to submit FAFSA. *Unit head:* Prof. Dianne Bills, Graduate Coordinator, 585-475-2700, Fax: 585-475-6584, E-mail: informaticsgrad@rit.edu. *Application contact:* Diane Ellison, Assistant Vice President, Graduate Enrollment Services, 585-475-2229, Fax: 585-475-7164, E-mail: gradinfo@rit.edu.

Sacred Heart University, Graduate Programs, College of Arts and Sciences, Department of Computer Science and Information Technology, Fairfield, CT 06825-1000. Offers computer science (MS); database (CPS); information technology (MS, CPS); information technology and network security (CPS); interactive multimedia (CPS); Web development (CPS). Part-time and evening/weekend programs available. *Faculty:* 7 full-time (4 women). *Students:* 20 full-time (6 women), 79 part-time (25 women); includes 10 minority (2 African Americans, 1 American Indian/Alaska Native, 5 Asian Americans or Pacific Islanders, 2 Hispanic Americans), 30 international. Average age 33. 66 applicants, 97% accepted, 26 enrolled. In 2009, 17 master's awarded. *Degree requirements:* For master's, thesis optional. *Entrance requirements:* Additional exam requirements/recommendations for international students: Required—TOEFL (minimum score 550 paper-based; 213 computer-based). *Application deadline:* Applications are processed on a rolling basis. Application fee: $50 ($100 for international students). Electronic applications accepted. *Expenses:* Tuition: Full-time $24,000; part-time $650 per credit. Required fees: $248. *Financial support:* Career-related internships or fieldwork, institutionally sponsored loans, and unspecified assistantships available. Support available to part-time students. Financial award applicants required to submit FAFSA. *Faculty research:* Contemporary market software. *Unit head:* Domenick Pinto, Academic Director and Chairperson, 203-371-7789, Fax: 203-371-0506, E-mail: pintod@sacredheart.edu. *Application contact:* Dean Alexis Haakonsen, Office of Graduate Admissions, 203-365-7619, Fax: 203-365-4732, E-mail: gradstudies@sacredheart.edu.

St. Cloud State University, School of Graduate Studies, College of Science and Engineering, Program in Information Assurance, St. Cloud, MN 56301-4498. Offers MS. *Students:* 8 full-time (2 women), 1 part-time (0 women); includes 4 minority (1 African American, 3 Asian Americans or Pacific Islanders), 4 international. 7 applicants, 100% accepted. *Unit head:* Dr. Susantha Herath, Chairperson, 320-308-2174, Fax: 320-308-6074. *Application contact:* Linda Lou Krueger, School of Graduate Studies, 320-308-2113, Fax: 320-308-5371, E-mail: lekrueger@stcloudstate.edu.

St. Cloud State University, School of Graduate Studies, G.R. Herberger College of Business, Program in Business Administration, St. Cloud, MN 56301-4498. Offers business administration (MBA); information assurance (MS). Part-time and evening/weekend programs available. *Faculty:* 62 full-time (17 women), 4 part-time/adjunct (1 woman). *Students:* 67 full-time (24 women), 151 part-time (62 women); includes 19 minority (2 African Americans, 3 American Indian/Alaska Native, 14 Asian Americans or Pacific Islanders), 32 international. 58 applicants, 90% accepted. In 2009, 63 master's awarded. *Degree requirements:* For master's, thesis or alternative. *Entrance requirements:* For master's, GMAT, minimum GPA of 2.75. Additional exam requirements/recommendations for international students: Required—Michigan English Language Assessment Battery; Recommended—TOEFL (minimum score 550 paper-based; 213 computer-based), IELTS (minimum score 6.5). *Application deadline:* For fall admission, 6/1 priority date for domestic students, 4/1 for international students; for spring admission, 10/1 priority date for domestic students, 8/1 for international students. *Financial support:* Federal Work-Study, scholarships/grants, and unspecified assistantships available. Financial award application deadline: 3/1. *Unit head:* Michele Mumm, Graduate Director, 320-308-3212, E-mail: michelem@stcloudstate.edu. *Application contact:* Linda Lou Krueger, School of Graduate Studies, 320-308-2113, Fax: 320-308-5371, E-mail: lekrueger@stcloudstate.edu.

Saint Leo University, Graduate Business Studies, Saint Leo, FL 33574-6665. Offers accounting (MBA); business (MBA); criminal justice (MBA); health services management (MBA); human resource administration (MBA); information security management (MBA); marketing (MBA); sport business (MBA). Part-time and evening/weekend programs available. Postbaccalaureate distance learning degree programs offered (no on-campus study). *Faculty:* 31 full-time (5 women), 48 part-time/adjunct (17 women). *Students:* 1,433 full-time (856 women), 3 part-time (1 woman); includes 601 minority (429 African Americans, 8 American Indian/Alaska Native, 75 Asian Americans or Pacific Islanders, 89 Hispanic Americans), 11 international. Average age 37. In 2009, 405 master's awarded. *Entrance requirements:* For master's, GMAT (minimum score 500 if applicant does not have 5 years of professional work experience), bachelor's degree from regionally-accredited college or university with minimum GPA of 3.0 in the last 60 hours of coursework; 5 years of professional work experience; resume; 2 letters of recommendation. Additional exam requirements/recommendations for international students: Required—TOEFL (minimum score 550 paper-based; 213 computer-based; 80 iBT). *Application deadline:* For fall admission, 7/1 priority date for domestic students; for spring admission, 11/12 priority date for domestic students. Applications are processed on a rolling basis. Application fee: $75. Electronic applications accepted. *Expenses:* Contact institution. *Financial support:* In 2009–10, 1 student received support. Career-related internships or fieldwork, Federal Work-Study, and health care benefits available. Financial award application deadline: 3/1; financial award applicants required to submit FAFSA. *Unit head:* Dr. Robert Robertson, Director, 352-588-7390, Fax: 352-588-8585, E-mail: mba@saintleo.edu. *Application contact:* Jared Welling, Director, Graduate/Weekend and Evening Admission, 800-707-8846, Fax: 352-588-7873, E-mail: grad.admissions@saintleo.edu.

Salem International University, School of Business, Salem, WV 26426-0500. Offers information security (MBA); international business (MBA). Part-time programs available. Postbaccalaureate distance learning degree programs offered (no on-campus study). *Entrance requirements:* For master's, minimum undergraduate GPA of 2.5, course work in business, resume. Additional exam requirements/recommendations for international students: Recommended—TOEFL (minimum score 550 paper-based; 213 computer-based), IELTS (minimum score 6.5). Electronic applications accepted. *Expenses:* Contact institution. *Faculty research:* Organizational behavior strategy, marketing services.

Southern Polytechnic State University, School of Computing and Software Engineering, Department of Information Technology, Marietta, GA 30060-2896. Offers business continuity (Graduate Certificate); information security and assurance (Graduate Certificate); information technology (MSIT, Graduate Certificate); information technology fundamentals (Graduate Certificate). Part-time and evening/weekend programs available. Postbaccalaureate distance learning degree programs offered (minimal on-campus study). *Faculty:* 9 full-time (4 women), 3 part-time/adjunct (1 woman). *Students:* 32 full-time (10 women), 62 part-time (21 women); includes 32 African Americans, 9 Asian Americans or Pacific Islanders, 2 Hispanic Americans, 14 international. Average age 34. 53 applicants, 89% accepted, 36 enrolled. In 2009, 21 master's awarded. *Degree requirements:* For master's, thesis or alternative. *Entrance requirements:* For master's, minimum GPA of 2.75; for Graduate Certificate, bachelor's degree. Additional exam requirements/recommendations for international students: Required—TOEFL (minimum score 550 paper-based; 213 computer-based; 79 iBT), IELTS (minimum score 6.5). *Application deadline:* For fall admission, 7/1 priority date for domestic students, 5/1 priority date for international students; for spring admission, 11/1 priority date for domestic students, 9/1 priority date for international students. Applications are processed on a rolling basis. Application fee: $20. Electronic applications accepted. *Expenses:* Tuition, state resident: full-time $2896; part-time $181 per credit hour. Tuition, nonresident: full-time $11,552; part-time $722 per credit hour. Required fees: $1096; $1096 per year. *Financial support:* In 2009–10, 12 students received support, including 12 research assistantships with tuition reimbursements available (averaging $1,500 per year); career-related internships or fieldwork, scholarships/grants, and unspecified assistantships also available. Support available to part-time students. Financial award application deadline: 5/1; financial award applicants required to submit FAFSA. *Faculty research:* IT ethics, user interface design, IT security, IT integration, IT management. *Unit head:* Dr. Ju Au Wang, Chair, 678-915-3718, Fax: 678-915-5511, E-mail: jwang@spsu.edu. *Application contact:* Nikki Palamiotis, Director of Graduate Studies, 678-915-4276, Fax: 678-915-7292, E-mail: npalamio@spsu.edu.

Stevens Institute of Technology, Graduate School, Charles V. Schaefer Jr. School of Engineering, Department of Computer Science, Hoboken, NJ 07030. Offers computer graphics (Certificate); computer science (MS, PhD); computer systems (Certificate); database management systems (Certificate); distributed systems (Certificate); elements of computer science (Certificate); enterprise computing (Certificate); enterprise security and information assurance (Certificate); health informatics (Certificate); multimedia experience and management (Certificate); networks and systems administration (Certificate); security and privacy (Certificate); service oriented computing (Certificate); software design (Certificate); theoretical computer science (Certificate). Part-time and evening/weekend programs available. Terminal master's awarded for partial completion of doctoral program. *Degree requirements:* For master's, thesis optional; for doctorate, variable foreign language requirement, comprehensive exam, thesis/dissertation. *Entrance requirements:* For master's and doctorate, GRE, minimum GPA of 3.0. Additional exam requirements/recommendations for international students: Required—TOEFL. Electronic applications accepted. *Expenses:* Tuition: Full-time $9900; part-time $1100 per credit. Required fees: $286 per semester. *Faculty research:* Semantics, reliability theory, programming language, cyber security.

Stevens Institute of Technology, Graduate School, Wesley J. Howe School of Technology Management, Program in Information Systems, Hoboken, NJ 07030. Offers computer science (MS); e-commerce (MS); enterprise systems (MS); entrepreneurial information technology (MS); information architecture (MS); information management (MS, Certificate); information security (MS); information technology in financial services industry (MS); information technology in the pharmaceutical industry (MS); information technology outsourcing management (MS); project management (MS, Certificate); software engineering (MS); telecommunications (MS). *Degree requirements:* For master's, thesis optional. *Entrance requirements:* For master's, GMAT, GRE General Test. Additional exam requirements/recommendations for international students: Required—TOEFL. Electronic applications accepted. *Expenses:* Tuition: Full-time $9900; part-time $1100 per credit. Required fees: $286 per semester.

Stratford University, School of Graduate Studies, Falls Church, VA 22043. Offers accounting (MS); business administration (IMBA, MBA); enterprise business management (MS);

Computer and Information Systems Security

Stratford University (continued)
entrepreneurial management (MS); information assurance (MS); information systems (MS); software engineering (MS); telecommunications (MS). Part-time and evening/weekend programs available. Postbaccalaureate distance learning degree programs offered (no on-campus study). *Faculty:* 35 full-time (15 women), 115 part-time/adjunct (25 women). *Students:* 944 full-time (430 women), 15 part-time (5 women). Average age 26. 950 applicants, 45% accepted, 415 enrolled. In 2009, 412 master's awarded. *Degree requirements:* For master's, comprehensive exam, capstone project. *Entrance requirements:* For master's, baccalaureate degree. Additional exam requirements/recommendations for international students: Required—TOEFL (minimum score 500 paper-based; 173 computer-based; 61 iBT). *Application deadline:* Applications are processed on a rolling basis. Application fee: $50. Electronic applications accepted. *Expenses:* Tuition: Full-time $10,530; part-time $390 per credit. Tuition and fees vary according to course load. *Financial support:* Federal Work-Study available. Financial award applicants required to submit FAFSA. *Unit head:* Dr. Habib Khan, Chief Academic Officer, 703-821-8570 Ext. 3305, Fax: 703-734-5335, E-mail: hkhan@stratford.edu. *Application contact:* James Ray, Director of Admissions, 703-821-8570 Ext. 3021, Fax: 703-734-5339, E-mail: jray@stratford.edu.

Strayer University, Graduate Studies, Washington, DC 20005-2603. Offers accounting (MS); acquisition (MBA); business administration (MBA); communications technology (MS); educational management (M Ed); finance (MBA); health services administration (MHSA); hospitality and tourism management (MBA); human resource management (MBA); information systems (MS), including computer security management, decision support system management, enterprise resource management, network management, software engineering management, systems development management; management (MBA); management information systems (MS); marketing (MBA); professional accounting (MS), including accounting information systems, controllership, taxation; public administration (MPA); supply chain management (MBA); technology in education (M Ed). Programs also offered at campus locations in Birmingham, AL; Chamblee, GA; Cobb County, GA; Morrow, GA; White Marsh, MD; Charleston, SC; Columbia, SC; Greensboro, NC; Greenville, SC; Lexington, KY; Louisville, KY; Nashville, TN; North Raleigh, NC; Washington, DC. Part-time and evening/weekend programs available. Postbaccalaureate distance learning degree programs offered (minimal on-campus study). *Degree requirements:* For master's, thesis. *Entrance requirements:* For master's, GMAT, GRE General Test, bachelor's degree from an accredited college or university, minimum undergraduate GPA of 2.75. Electronic applications accepted.

Syracuse University, School of Information Studies, Program in Information Security Management, Syracuse, NY 13244. Offers CAS. Part-time and evening/weekend programs available. Postbaccalaureate distance learning degree programs offered. *Students:* 1 full-time (0 women), 15 part-time (3 women); includes 5 minority (2 African Americans, 1 Asian American or Pacific Islander, 2 Hispanic Americans). Average age 38. 49 applicants, 86% accepted, 7 enrolled. In 2009, 15 CASs awarded. *Entrance requirements:* Additional exam requirements/recommendations for international students: Required—TOEFL (minimum score 100 iBT). *Application deadline:* For fall admission, 2/1 priority date for domestic and international students; for spring admission, 10/15 priority date for domestic and international students. Applications are processed on a rolling basis. Application fee: $75. Electronic applications accepted. *Expenses:* Tuition: Full-time $26,808; part-time $1117 per credit. Required fees: $1024. *Financial support:* Application deadline: 1/1; *Unit head:* Dave Dischiave, Head, 315-443-4681, E-mail: ddischia@syr.edu. *Application contact:* Susan Corieri, Director of Enrollment Management, 315-443-2575, E-mail: ist@syr.edu.

Towson University, College of Graduate Studies and Research, Program in Applied Information Technology, Towson, MD 21252-0001. Offers applied information technology (D Sc); database management (Certificate); information security and assurance (Certificate); information systems management (Certificate); Internet application development (Certificate); networking technologies (Certificate); software engineering (Certificate). *Entrance requirements:* For doctorate, minimum GPA 3.0, letter of intent, resumé, 2 letters of recommendation, personal assessment forms, official transcripts. Additional exam requirements/recommendations for international students: Required—TOEFL (minimum score 550 paper-based). Electronic applications accepted.

Towson University, College of Graduate Studies and Research, Program in Information Security and Assurance, Towson, MD 21252-0001. Offers Certificate. Part-time and evening/weekend programs available.

TUI University, College of Business Administration, Program in Business Administration, Cypress, CA 90630. Offers business administration (PhD); conflict and negotiation management (MBA); criminal justice administration (MBA); entrepreneurship (MBA); finance (MBA); general management (MBA); government accounting (MBA); human resource management (MBA); information security and digital assurance management (MBA); information technology management (MBA); international business (MBA); logistics management (MBA); marketing (MBA); project management (MBA); public management (MBA); quality management (MBA); strategic leadership (MBA). Part-time and evening/weekend programs available. Postbaccalaureate distance learning degree programs offered (no on-campus study). *Degree requirements:* For doctorate, comprehensive exam, thesis/dissertation, defense of dissertation. *Entrance requirements:* For master's, minimum GPA of 2.5 (students with GPA 3.0 or greater may transfer up to 30% of graduate level credits); for doctorate, minimum GPA of 3.4, curriculum vitae, course work in research methods or statistics. Additional exam requirements/recommendations for international students: Required—TOEFL. Electronic applications accepted.

Universidad del Este, Graduate School, Carolina, PR 00984. Offers accounting (MBA); adult education (M Ed); agribusiness (MBA); bilingual education (M Ed); criminal justice and criminology (MA); early education (M Ed); elementary education (M Ed); human resources (MBA); information security management (MBA); information technology and Web business development (MBA); management (MBA); public policy (MPA); social work (MA), including clinical social work; special education (M Ed); strategic leadership (MBA); teaching English (M Ed); teaching Spanish (M Ed).

University of Advancing Technology, Master of Science Program in Technology, Tempe, AZ 85283-1042. Offers advancing computer science (MS); emerging technologies (MS); game production and management (MS); information assurance (MS); technology leadership (MS). *Degree requirements:* For master's, project or thesis. *Entrance requirements:* Additional exam requirements/recommendations for international students: Required—TOEFL (minimum score 550 paper-based). Electronic applications accepted. *Faculty research:* Artificial intelligence, fractals, organizational management.

University of Houston, College of Technology, Department of Information and Logistics Technology, Houston, TX 77204. Offers technology project management (MS), including information systems security, logistics. Part-time and evening/weekend programs available. *Faculty:* 6 full-time (3 women), 6 part-time/adjunct (2 women). *Students:* 59 full-time (18 women), 47 part-time (15 women); includes 18 minority (6 African Americans, 5 Asian Americans or Pacific Islanders, 7 Hispanic Americans), 58 international. Average age 29. 69 applicants, 87% accepted, 33 enrolled. In 2009, 25 master's awarded. *Degree requirements:* For master's, project or thesis (most programs). *Entrance requirements:* For master's, GMAT. Additional exam requirements/recommendations for international students: Required—TOEFL (minimum score 550 paper-based; 79 iBT). *Application deadline:* For fall admission, 7/1 for domestic students, 4/1 for international students; for spring admission, 12/1 for domestic students, 10/1 for international students. Applications are processed on a rolling basis. Application fee: $75 ($150 for international students). Electronic applications accepted. *Expenses:* Tuition, state resident: full-time $7676; part-time $320 per credit hour. Tuition, nonresident: full-time $14,324; part-time $597 per credit hour. Required fees: $3034. *Financial support:* In 2009–10, 11 fellowships with full tuition reimbursements (averaging $10,500 per year), 1 research assistantship with full tuition reimbursement (averaging $10,500 per year), 4 teaching assistantships with full tuition reimbursements (averaging $10,500 per year) were awarded. *Unit head:* Michael Gibson, Chairperson, 713-743-5116, E-mail: mlgibson@uh.edu. *Application contact:* Tiffany Roosa, Graduate Advisor, 713-743-2987, Fax: 713-743-4151, E-mail: troosa@uh.edu.

University of Louisville, J.B. Speed School of Engineering, Department of Computer Engineering and Computer Science, Louisville, KY 40292-0001. Offers computer engineering and computer science (M Eng, MS); computer science (MS); computer science and engineering (PhD); data mining (Certificate); network and information security (Certificate). *Accreditation:* ABET (one or more programs are accredited). Part-time programs available. Postbaccalaureate distance learning degree programs offered (no on-campus study). *Faculty:* 15 full-time (0 women). *Students:* 75 full-time (10 women), 42 part-time (10 women); includes 10 minority (7 African Americans, 2 Asian Americans or Pacific Islanders, 1 Hispanic American), 46 international. Average age 30. 66 applicants, 59% accepted, 21 enrolled. In 2009, 26 master's, 9 doctorates, 1 other advanced degree awarded. Terminal master's awarded for partial completion of doctoral program. *Degree requirements:* For master's, comprehensive exam (for some programs), thesis or alternative; for doctorate, comprehensive exam, thesis/dissertation, minimum GPA of 3.0. *Entrance requirements:* For master's, doctorate, and Certificate, GRE General Test. Additional exam requirements/recommendations for international students: Required—TOEFL (minimum score 550 paper-based; 213 computer-based; 80 iBT). *Application deadline:* For fall admission, 7/12 priority date for domestic and international students; for winter admission, 11/29 priority date for domestic and international students; for spring admission, 3/28 priority date for domestic and international students. Applications are processed on a rolling basis. Application fee: $50. Electronic applications accepted. *Financial support:* In 2009–10, 38 students received support, including 8 fellowships with full tuition reimbursements available (averaging $20,000 per year), 20 research assistantships with full tuition reimbursements available (averaging $20,700 per year), 6 teaching assistantships with full tuition reimbursements available (averaging $20,000 per year). Financial award application deadline: 1/25; financial award applicants required to submit FAFSA. *Faculty research:* Software systems engineering, information security and forensics, multimedia and vision, mobile and distributed computing, intelligent systems. Total annual research expenditures: $1.4 million. *Unit head:* Dr. Adel S. Elmaghraby, Chair, 502-852-6304, Fax: 502-852-4713, E-mail: adel@louisville.edu. *Application contact:* Dr. Michael Day, Associate Dean, 502-852-6195, Fax: 502-852-6294, E-mail: day@louisville.edu.

University of Minnesota, Twin Cities Campus, Institute of Technology, Technological Leadership Institute, Program in Security Technologies, Minneapolis, MN 55455-0213. Offers MSST. Part-time programs available. *Faculty:* 1 full-time (0 women), 23 part-time/adjunct (2 women). *Degree requirements:* For master's, capstone project. *Entrance requirements:* Additional exam requirements/recommendations for international students: Required—TOEFL (minimum score 580 paper-based; 240 computer-based; 90 iBT). *Application deadline:* For spring admission, 3/15 priority date for domestic students, 3/15 for international students. Applications are processed on a rolling basis. Application fee: $75 ($95 for international students). Electronic applications accepted. *Financial support:* Institutionally sponsored loans available. Financial award applicants required to submit FAFSA. *Unit head:* Dr. Massoud Amin, Director, 612-624-5747, Fax: 612-624-7510. *Application contact:* Jenna Egan, Student Services and Admissions, 612-624-4380, Fax: 612-624-7510, E-mail: tliss@umn.edu.

University of New Haven, Graduate School, Henry C. Lee College of Criminal Justice and Forensic Sciences, National Security and Public Safety Program, West Haven, CT 06516-1916. Offers information protection and security (MS); national security (Certificate); national security administration (Certificate). Part-time and evening/weekend programs available. *Faculty:* 8 full-time (2 women), 5 part-time/adjunct (0 women). *Students:* 34 full-time (10 women), 39 part-time (21 women); includes 19 minority (4 African Americans, 1 American Indian/Alaska Native, 4 Asian Americans or Pacific Islanders, 10 Hispanic Americans), 4 international. Average age 32. 39 applicants, 100% accepted, 33 enrolled. In 2009, 51 master's, 5 other advanced degrees awarded. *Entrance requirements:* Additional exam requirements/recommendations for international students: Required—TOEFL (minimum score 520 paper-based; 190 computer-based; 70 iBT); Recommended—IELTS (minimum score 5.5). *Application deadline:* For fall admission, 5/31 for international students; for winter admission, 10/15 for international students; for spring admission, 1/15 for international students. Applications are processed on a rolling basis. Application fee: $50. Electronic applications accepted. *Expenses:* Tuition: Part-time $700 per credit. Required fees: $45 per term. One-time fee: $390 part-time. *Financial support:* Research assistantships with partial tuition reimbursements, teaching assistantships with partial tuition reimbursements, career-related internships or fieldwork, Federal Work-Study, scholarships/grants, tuition waivers, and unspecified assistantships available. Support available to part-time students. Financial award applicants required to submit FAFSA. *Unit head:* Dr. William L. Tafoya, Dean, 203-932-7260. *Application contact:* Eloise Gormley, Director of Graduate Admissions, 203-932-7449, Fax: 203-932-7137, E-mail: gradinfo@newhaven.edu.

University of New Mexico, Robert O. Anderson Graduate School of Management, Department of Marketing, Information and Decision Sciences, Albuquerque, NM 87131. Offers information assurance (MBA); management information systems (MBA); marketing management (MBA); operations management (MBA). Part-time and evening/weekend programs available. *Faculty:* 14 full-time (3 women), 5 part-time/adjunct (0 women). *Students:* 39 full-time (18 women), 37 part-time (19 women); includes 31 minority (3 African Americans, 1 American Indian/Alaska Native, 3 Asian Americans or Pacific Islanders, 24 Hispanic Americans), 4 international. Average age 28. 40 applicants, 100% accepted, 36 enrolled. In 2009, 39 master's awarded. *Entrance requirements:* For master's, GMAT or GRE (can be waived in some instances). Additional exam requirements/recommendations for international students: Required—TOEFL (minimum score 550 paper-based; 213 computer-based; 79 iBT). *Application deadline:* For fall admission, 4/1 priority date for domestic students, 5/1 for international students; for spring admission, 10/1 priority date for domestic students, 10/1 for international students. Applications are processed on a rolling basis. Application fee: $50. Electronic applications accepted. *Expenses:* Tuition, state resident: full-time $2098.80; part-time $233.20 per credit hour. Tuition, nonresident: full-time $6650. Required fees: $25 per semester. Tuition and fees vary according to course load, program and reciprocity agreements. *Financial support:* Fellowships, research assistantships, teaching assistantships, career-related internships or fieldwork, Federal Work-Study, scholarships/grants, and unspecified assistantships available. Support available to part-time students. Financial award application deadline: 6/1. *Faculty research:* Marketing, operations, information science. *Unit head:* Dr. Steve Yourstone, Chair, 505-277-6471, Fax: 505-277-7108. *Application contact:* Megan Conner, Academic Advisement Manager, 505-277-3290, Fax: 505-277-8436, E-mail: mconner@mgt.unm.edu.

University of St. Thomas, Graduate Studies, Graduate Programs in Software, Saint Paul, MN 55105. Offers advanced studies in business analysis (Certificate); computer security (Certificate); information systems (Certificate); software design and development (Certificate); software engineering (MS); software management (MS); software systems (MSS); MS/MBA. Part-time and evening/weekend programs available. *Degree requirements:* For master's, thesis optional. *Entrance requirements:* Additional exam requirements/recommendations for international students: Required—TOEFL. *Application deadline:* For fall admission, 8/1 priority date for domestic students, 5/1 priority date for international students; for spring admission, 1/1 priority date for domestic students, 10/1 priority date for international students. Applications are processed on a rolling basis. Application fee: $30. *Expenses:* Contact institution. *Financial support:* Federal Work-Study, institutionally sponsored loans, and scholarships/grants available. Financial award application deadline: 4/1. *Faculty research:* Data mining, distributed databases, bioinformatics, computer security. *Unit head:* Dr. Bhabani Misra, Director, 651-962-5508, Fax: 651-962-5543, E-mail: bsmisra@stthomas.edu. *Application contact:* Douglas J. Stubeda, Assistant Director, 651-962-5503, Fax: 651-962-5543, E-mail: djstubeda@stthomas.edu.

University of Southern California, Graduate School, Viterbi School of Engineering, Department of Computer Science, Los Angeles, CA 90089. Offers computer networks (MS); computer science (MS, PhD); computer security (MS); game development (MS); high performance computing and simulations (MS); human language technology (MS); intelligent robotics (MS);

multimedia and creative technologies (MS); software engineering (MS). Part-time programs available. Postbaccalaureate distance learning degree programs offered (no on-campus study). *Faculty:* 26 full-time (2 women), 56 part-time/adjunct (7 women). *Students:* 711 full-time (148 women), 304 part-time (55 women); includes 76 minority (5 African Americans, 59 Asian Americans or Pacific Islanders, 12 Hispanic Americans), 816 international. 2,017 applicants, 39% accepted, 382 enrolled. In 2009, 332 master's, 32 doctorates awarded. Terminal master's awarded for partial completion of doctoral program. *Degree requirements:* For doctorate, comprehensive exam, thesis/dissertation. *Entrance requirements:* For master's, GRE General Test; for doctorate, General GRE. *Application deadline:* For fall admission, 3/1 priority date for domestic and international students; for spring admission, 10/1 priority date for domestic and international students. Applications are processed on a rolling basis. Application fee: $85. Electronic applications accepted. *Expenses:* Tuition: Full-time $25,980; part-time $1315 per unit. Required fees: $554. One-time fee: $35 full-time. Full-time tuition and fees vary according to degree level and program. *Financial support:* In 2009–10, fellowships with full tuition reimbursements (averaging $30,000 per year), research assistantships with full tuition reimbursements (averaging $19,250 per year), teaching assistantships with full tuition reimbursements (averaging $19,250 per year) were awarded; career-related internships or fieldwork, scholarships/grants, health care benefits, and unspecified assistantships also available. Financial award application deadline: 12/1; financial award applicants required to submit CSS PROFILE or FAFSA. *Faculty research:* Databases, computer graphics and computer vision, software engineering, networks and security, robotics, multimedia and virtual reality. Total annual research expenditures: $10 million. *Unit head:* Dr. Shanghua Teng, Seeley G. Mudd Professor of Engineering and Department Chair, 213-740-4498, E-mail: shanghua@ usc.edu. *Application contact:* Steve Schrader, Director of Student Affairs, 213-740-4779, E-mail: steve.schrader@usc.edu.

The University of Texas at Dallas, School of Management, Program in Information Systems and Operations Management, Richardson, TX 75080. Offers information technology management (MS), including enterprise systems, health care systems, information security; supply chain management (MS). Part-time and evening/weekend programs available. *Faculty:* 23 full-time (1 woman), 1 (woman) part-time/adjunct. *Students:* 153 full-time (54 women), 129 part-time (51 women); includes 36 minority (4 African Americans, 28 Asian Americans or Pacific Islanders, 4 Hispanic Americans), 212 international. Average age 27. 352 applicants, 74% accepted, 105 enrolled. In 2009, 67 master's awarded. *Degree requirements:* For master's, thesis optional. *Entrance requirements:* For master's, GMAT. Additional exam requirements/recommendations for international students: Required—TOEFL (minimum score 550 paper-based; 213 computer-based). *Application deadline:* For fall admission, 7/15 for domestic students, 5/1 priority date for international students; for spring admission, 11/15 for domestic students, 9/1 priority date for international students. Applications are processed on a rolling basis. Application fee: $50 ($100 for international students). Electronic applications accepted. *Expenses:* Tuition, state resident: full-time $11,068; part-time $461 per credit hour. Tuition, nonresident: full-time $21,178; part-time $882 per credit hour. Tuition and fees vary according to course load. *Financial support:* In 2009–10, 7 research assistantships with full tuition reimbursements (averaging $10,933 per year), 5 teaching assistantships with full tuition reimbursements (averaging $10,050 per year) were awarded; career-related internships or fieldwork, Federal Work-Study, institutionally sponsored loans, scholarships/grants, and unspecified assistantships also available. Support available to part-time students. Financial award application deadline: 4/30; financial award applicants required to submit FAFSA. *Faculty research:* Technology marketing, measuring information work productivity, electronic commerce, decision support systems, data quality. *Unit head:* Dr. Mark Thouin, Director, 972-883-4011, E-mail: mark.thouin@utdallas.edu. *Application contact:* James Parker, Assistant Director, 972-883-5842, E-mail: jparker@ utdallas.edu.

University of Wisconsin–Madison, Graduate School, Wisconsin School of Business, Wisconsin Full-Time MBA Program, Madison, WI 53706-1380. Offers applied corporate finance (MBA); applied security analysis (MBA); arts administration (MBA); brand and product management (MBA); entrepreneurial management (MBA); marketing research (MBA); operations and technology management (MBA); real estate (MBA); risk management and insurance (MBA); strategic human resource management (MBA); strategic management in the life and engineering sciences (MBA); supply chain management (MBA). *Faculty:* 32 full-time (5 women). *Students:* 242 full-time (74 women); includes 47 minority (16 African Americans, 3 American Indian/Alaska Native, 16 Asian Americans or Pacific Islanders, 12 Hispanic Americans), 29 international. Average age 28. 526 applicants, 32% accepted, 117 enrolled. In 2009, 106 master's awarded. *Entrance requirements:* For master's, GMAT, bachelor's or equivalent degree, 2 years of work experience, letters of recommendation. Additional exam requirements/recommendations for international students: Required—TOEFL (minimum score 600 paper-based; 250 computer-based; 100 iBT), IELTS. *Application deadline:* For fall admission, 11/4 for domestic and international students; for winter admission, 2/5 for domestic and international students; for spring admission, 5/26 for domestic students, 4/5 for international students. Applications are processed on a rolling basis. Application fee: $56. Electronic applications accepted. *Expenses:* Tuition, state resident: part-time $594 per credit. Tuition, nonresident: part-time $1504 per credit. Required fees: $65 per credit. Tuition and fees vary according to course load, program and reciprocity agreements. *Financial support:* In 2009–10, 103 students received support, including 13 fellowships with full and partial tuition reimbursements available (averaging $15,000 per year), 53 research assistantships with full tuition reimbursements available (averaging $8,000 per year), 35 teaching assistantships with full tuition reimbursements available (averaging $11,000 per year); scholarships/grants, health care benefits, and unspecified assistantships also available. Financial award application deadline: 4/5; financial award applicants required to submit FAFSA. *Unit head:* Prof. Kenneth A. Kavajecz, Associate Dean of Master's Programs, 608-265-3494, Fax: 608-265-4192, E-mail: kkavajecz@bus.wisc.edu. *Application contact:* Maria Reis, Assistant Director of MBA Marketing and Recruiting, 608-262-4000, Fax: 608-265-4192, E-mail: mreis@bus.wisc.edu.

Virginia Polytechnic Institute and State University, VT Online, Blacksburg, VA 24061. Offers aerospace engineering (MS); business information systems (Graduate Certificate); career and technical education (MS); computer engineering (M Eng, MS); decision support systems (Graduate Certificate); eLearning leadership (MA); electrical engineering (M Eng, MS); engineering administration (MEA); environmental politics and policy (Graduate Certificate); foundations of political analysis (Graduate Certificate); health product risk management (Graduate Certificate); information policy and society (Graduate Certificate); information security (Graduate Certificate); instructional technology (MA); liberal arts (Graduate Certificate); life sciences: health product risk management (MS); natural resources (MNR, Graduate Certificate); networking (Graduate Certificate); nonprofit and nongovernmental organization management (Graduate Certificate); ocean engineering (MS); political science (MA); security studies (Graduate Certificate); software development (Graduate Certificate).

West Chester University of Pennsylvania, Office of Graduate Studies, College of Arts and Sciences, Department of Computer Science, West Chester, PA 19383. Offers computer science (MS, Certificate); computer security (Certificate); information systems (Certificate); Web technology (Certificate). Part-time and evening/weekend programs available. *Students:* 4 full-time (3 women), 15 part-time (5 women); includes 3 minority (1 African American, 2 Asian Americans or Pacific Islanders), 8 international. Average age 26. 20 applicants, 85% accepted, 9 enrolled. In 2009, 11 master's awarded. *Degree requirements:* For master's, thesis optional. *Entrance requirements:* For master's, GRE, three letters of recommendation; for Certificate, GRE General Test. Additional exam requirements/recommendations for international students: Required—TOEFL (minimum score 550 paper-based; 213 computer-based; 80 iBT). *Application deadline:* For fall admission, 4/15 priority date for domestic students, 3/15 for international students; for spring admission, 10/15 for domestic students, 9/1 for international students. Applications are processed on a rolling basis. Application fee: $35. Electronic applications accepted. *Expenses:* Tuition, state resident: full-time $6666; part-time $370 per credit. Tuition, nonresident: full-time $10,666; part-time $593 per credit. Required fees: $122.56 per credit. *Financial support:* In 2009–10, 6 research assistantships with full and partial tuition reimbursements (averaging $5,000 per year) were awarded; unspecified assistantships also available. Support available to part-time students. Financial award application deadline: 2/15; financial award applicants required to submit FAFSA. *Faculty research:* Automata theory, compilers, non well-founded sets. *Unit head:* Dr. James Fabrey, Chair, 610-436-2204, E-mail: jfabrey@ wcupa.edu. *Application contact:* Dr. Afrand Agah, Graduate Coordinator, 610-436-4419, E-mail: aagah@wcupa.edu.

Western Governors University, Program in Information Security and Assurance, Salt Lake City, UT 84107. Offers MS. Postbaccalaureate distance learning degree programs offered. *Degree requirements:* For master's, capstone project.

Wilmington University, College of Technology, New Castle, DE 19720-6491. Offers corporate training (MS); information assurance (MS); information systems technologies (MS); Internet web design (MS); management information systems (MS). Part-time and evening/weekend programs available. *Entrance requirements:* Additional exam requirements/recommendations for international students: Required—TOEFL (minimum score 500 paper-based; 173 computer-based). Electronic applications accepted.

Computer Science

Acadia University, Faculty of Pure and Applied Science, Jodrey School of Computer Science, Wolfville, NS B4P 2R6, Canada. Offers M Sc. *Faculty:* 10 full-time (0 women), 1 part-time/adjunct (0 women). *Students:* 8 full-time (0 women), 3 part-time (0 women), all international. Average age 28. 31 applicants, 42% accepted, 2 enrolled. In 2009, 3 master's awarded. *Degree requirements:* For master's, thesis. *Entrance requirements:* For master's, honors degree in computer science. Additional exam requirements/recommendations for international students: Required—TOEFL (minimum score 580 paper-based; 237 computer-based; 93 iBT), IELTS (minimum score 6.5). *Application deadline:* For fall admission, 2/1 for domestic and international students. Applications are processed on a rolling basis. Application fee: $50. *Financial support:* Research assistantships, teaching assistantships, career-related internships or fieldwork, scholarships/grants, and unspecified assistantships available. Financial award application deadline: 2/1. *Faculty research:* Visual and object-oriented programming, concurrency, artificial intelligence, hypertext and multimedia, algorithm analysis, xml. *Unit head:* Dr. Daniel L. Silver, Director, 902-585-1331, Fax: 902-585-1067, E-mail: cs@acadiau.ca. *Application contact:* Dr. Tomasz Muldner, Graduate Chair, 902-585-1578, E-mail: tomasz.muldner@acadiau.ca.

Air Force Institute of Technology, Graduate School of Engineering and Management, Department of Electrical and Computer Engineering, Dayton, OH 45433-7765. Offers computer engineering (MS, PhD); computer systems/science (MS); electrical engineering (MS, PhD); electro-optics (MS, PhD). *Accreditation:* ABET (one or more programs are accredited). Part-time programs available. *Degree requirements:* For master's, thesis; for doctorate, thesis/dissertation. *Entrance requirements:* For master's and doctorate, GRE General Test, minimum GPA of 3.0, U.S. citizenship. *Faculty research:* Remote sensing, information survivability, microelectronics, computer networks, artificial intelligence.

Alabama Agricultural and Mechanical University, School of Graduate Studies, School of Engineering and Technology, Department of Computer Science, Huntsville, AL 35811. Offers MS. Evening/weekend programs available. *Degree requirements:* For master's, comprehensive exam, thesis optional. *Entrance requirements:* For master's, GRE General Test. Additional exam requirements/recommendations for international students: Required—TOEFL (minimum score 500 paper-based; 173 computer-based; 61 iBT). Electronic applications accepted. *Faculty research:* Computer-assisted instruction, database management, software engineering, operating systems, neural networks.

Alcorn State University, School of Graduate Studies, School of Arts and Sciences, Department of Mathematical Sciences, Alcorn State, MS 39096-7500. Offers computer and information sciences (MS).

American Sentinel University, Graduate Programs, Englewood, CO 80112. Offers business administration (MBA); business intelligence (MS); computer science (MSCS); health information management (MS); healthcare (MBA); information systems (MSIS); nursing (MSN). Part-time and evening/weekend programs available. Postbaccalaureate distance learning degree programs offered (no on-campus study). *Entrance requirements:* Additional exam requirements/recommendations for international students: Required—TOEFL (minimum score 600 paper-based; 215 computer-based). Electronic applications accepted.

American University, College of Arts and Sciences, Program in Computer Science, Washington, DC 20016-8058. Offers MS, Certificate. Part-time and evening/weekend programs available. *Faculty:* 4 full-time (1 woman), 2 part-time/adjunct (0 women). *Students:* 4 full-time (0 women), 3 part-time (2 women); includes 1 minority (African American), 2 international. Average age 30. 11 applicants, 9% accepted, 0 enrolled. In 2009, 3 master's awarded. *Degree requirements:* For master's, comprehensive exam, thesis or alternative. *Entrance requirements:* For master's, GRE, minimum GPA of 3.0, adequate undergraduate prep program; for Certificate, bachelor's degree. Additional exam requirements/recommendations for international students: Required—TOEFL. *Application deadline:* For fall admission, 2/1 priority date for domestic students; for spring admission, 10/1 for domestic students. Applications are processed on a rolling basis. Application fee: $80. *Expenses:* Tuition: Full-time $22,266; part-time $1237 per credit hour. Required fees: $430. Tuition and fees vary according to program. *Financial support:* Fellowships with full tuition reimbursements, career-related internships or fieldwork, Federal Work-Study, institutionally sponsored loans, tuition waivers (full and partial), and unspecified assistantships available. Financial award application deadline: 2/1. *Faculty research:* Artificial intelligence, database systems, software engineering, expert systems. *Unit head:* Dr. Angela Wu, Chair, 202-885-1476, Fax: 202-885-1479. *Application contact:* Dr. Angela Wu, Chair, 202-885-1476, Fax: 202-885-1479.

The American University in Cairo, Graduate Studies and Research, School of Sciences and Engineering, Department of Computer Science and Engineering, Cairo, Egypt. Offers MS. *Degree requirements:* For master's, thesis. *Entrance requirements:* Additional exam requirements/recommendations for international students: Required—English entrance exam and/or TOEFL. *Faculty research:* Software engineering, artificial intelligence, robotics, data and knowledge bases.

The American University of Athens, The School of Graduate Studies, Athens, Greece. Offers biomedical sciences (MS); business (MBA); business communication (MA); computer sciences (MS); engineering and applied sciences (MS); politics and policy making (MA);

Computer Science

The American University of Athens (continued)
systems engineering (MS); telecommunications (MS). *Entrance requirements:* For master's, resum&e, 2 recommendation letters. Additional exam requirements/recommendations for international students: Required—TOEFL (minimum score 550 paper-based; 213 computer-based). *Faculty research:* Nanotechnology, environmental sciences, rock mechanics, human skin studies, Monte Carlo algorithms and software.

American University of Beirut, Graduate Programs, Faculty of Arts and Sciences, Beirut, Lebanon. Offers anthropology (MA); Arabic language and literature (MA); archaeology (MA); biology (MS); chemistry (MS); computer science (MS); economics (MA); education (MA); English language (MA); English literature (MA); environmental policy planning (MSES); financial economics (MAFE); geology (MS); history (MA); mathematics (MA, MS); Middle Eastern studies (MA); philosophy (MA); physics (MS); political studies (MA); psychology (MA); public administration (MA); sociology (MA); statistics (MA, MS). Part-time programs available. *Degree requirements:* For master's, one foreign language, comprehensive exam, thesis (for some programs). *Entrance requirements:* For master's, GRE, letter of recommendation. Additional exam requirements/recommendations for international students: Required—TOEFL (minimum score 600 paper-based; 250 computer-based; 100 iBT), IELTS (minimum score 7.5). *Faculty research:* String theory and supergravity; computer graphics; algebra and number theory; popular Arabic literature; marine and freshwater biology; integrating science, math and technology.

Appalachian State University, Cratis D. Williams Graduate School, Department of Computer Science, Boone, NC 28608. Offers MS. Part-time programs available. *Faculty:* 10 full-time (3 women). *Students:* 14 full-time (3 women), 4 part-time (2 women); 4 international. 20 applicants, 80% accepted, 9 enrolled. In 2009, 8 master's awarded. *Degree requirements:* For master's, comprehensive exam, thesis. *Entrance requirements:* For master's, GRE General Test, 3 letters of recommendation. Additional exam requirements/recommendations for international students: Required—TOEFL (minimum score 570 paper-based; 230 computer-based; 79 iBT), IELTS (minimum score 6.5). *Application deadline:* For fall admission, 7/1 priority date for domestic students, 2/1 for international students; for spring admission, 11/1 for domestic students, 7/1 for international students. Applications are processed on a rolling basis. Application fee: $50. Electronic applications accepted. *Expenses:* Tuition, state resident: full-time $2960. Tuition, nonresident: full-time $14,051. Required fees: $2320. *Financial support:* In 2009–10, 8 teaching assistantships (averaging $9,500 per year) were awarded; fellowships, research assistantships, Federal Work-Study, scholarships/grants, and unspecified assistantships also available. Financial award application deadline: 4/1; financial award applicants required to submit FAFSA. *Faculty research:* Graph theory, compilers, parallel architecture, image processing. *Unit head:* Dr. James Wilkes, Chairperson, 828-262-2612. *Application contact:* Dr. Jay Fenwick, Advisor, 828-262-3050, Fax: 828-265-8617, E-mail: fenwickjb@appstate.edu.

Arizona State University, Graduate College, College of Technology and Innovation, Division of Computing Studies, Tempe, AZ 85287. Offers computing studies (MCST); technology (MS). Part-time programs available. *Degree requirements:* For master's, thesis or applied project. *Entrance requirements:* For master's, 30 semester hours or equivalent in technology, including course work applicable to computer systems; minimum of 16 semester hours in science and math. Additional exam requirements/recommendations for international students: Required—TOEFL (minimum score 550 paper-based; 213 computer-based; 83 iBT); Recommended—TWE. *Faculty research:* Software process and automated workflow, software architecture, dotal technologies, relational database systems, embedded systems.

Arizona State University, Graduate College, Ira A. Fulton School of Engineering, Department of Computer Science and Engineering, Tempe, AZ 85287. Offers computer science (MCS, MS, PhD). *Degree requirements:* For master's, thesis or alternative; for doctorate, thesis/dissertation. *Entrance requirements:* For master's and doctorate, GRE General Test (recommended).

Arkansas State University—Jonesboro, Graduate School, College of Sciences and Mathematics, Department of Computer Science, Jonesboro, State University, AR 72467. Offers MS. Part-time programs available. *Faculty:* 5 full-time (1 woman). *Students:* 21 full-time (5 women), 9 part-time (2 women); includes 1 minority (African American), 27 international. Average age 25. 56 applicants, 86% accepted, 12 enrolled. In 2009, 2 master's awarded. *Degree requirements:* For master's, comprehensive exam, thesis or alternative. *Entrance requirements:* For master's, GRE General Test or MAT, appropriate bachelor's degree. Additional exam requirements/recommendations for international students: Required—TOEFL (minimum score 550 paper-based; 213 computer-based; 79 iBT), IELTS (minimum score 6). *Application deadline:* For fall admission, 7/1 for domestic and international students; for spring admission, 11/15 for domestic students, 11/13 for international students. Applications are processed on a rolling basis. Application fee: $30 ($40 for international students). Electronic applications accepted. *Expenses:* Tuition, state resident: full-time $3744; part-time $208 per credit hour. Tuition, nonresident: full-time $9540; part-time $530 per credit hour. Required fees: $896; $47 per credit hour. $25 per term. One-time fee: $50. Tuition and fees vary according to course load and program. *Financial support:* In 2009–10, 11 students received support. Career-related internships or fieldwork, scholarships/grants, and unspecified assistantships available. Financial award application deadline: 7/1; financial award applicants required to submit FAFSA. *Unit head:* Dr. Jeff Jenness, Chair, 870-972-3978, Fax: 870-972-3950, E-mail: jeffj@astate.edu. *Application contact:* Dr. Andrew Sustich, Dean of the Graduate School, 870-972-3029, Fax: 870-972-3857, E-mail: sustich@astate.edu.

Armstrong Atlantic State University, School of Graduate Studies, Program in Computer Science, Savannah, GA 31419-1997. Offers MS. Part-time programs available. *Degree requirements:* For master's, project. *Entrance requirements:* For master's, GRE, minimum GPA of 2.7, letters of recommendation, BS in computer science. Additional exam requirements/recommendations for international students: Required—TOEFL (minimum score 523 paper-based; 193 computer-based). Electronic applications accepted.

Auburn University, Graduate School, Ginn College of Engineering, Department of Computer Science and Software Engineering, Auburn University, AL 36849. Offers MS, MSWE, PhD. Part-time programs available. *Faculty:* 19 full-time (3 women). *Students:* 58 full-time (15 women), 65 part-time (17 women); includes 19 minority (16 African Americans, 1 Asian American or Pacific Islander, 2 Hispanic Americans), 59 international. Average age 30. 214 applicants, 33% accepted, 19 enrolled. In 2009, 21 master's, 11 doctorates awarded. *Degree requirements:* For master's, thesis (for some programs); for doctorate, thesis/dissertation. *Entrance requirements:* For master's and doctorate, GRE General Test, GRE Subject Test. *Application deadline:* For fall admission, 7/7 for domestic students; for spring admission, 11/24 for domestic students. Applications are processed on a rolling basis. Application fee: $50 ($60 for international students). Electronic applications accepted. *Expenses:* Tuition, state resident: full-time $6240. Tuition, nonresident: full-time $18,720. International tuition: $18,938 full-time. Required fees: $492. Tuition and fees vary according to course load, program and reciprocity agreements. *Financial support:* Research assistantships, teaching assistantships, Federal Work-Study available. Support available to part-time students. Financial award application deadline: 3/15; financial award applicants required to submit FAFSA. *Faculty research:* Parallelizable, scalable software translations; graphical representations of algorithms, structures, and processes; graph drawing. Total annual research expenditures: $400,000. *Unit head:* Dr. Kai Chang, Chair, 334-844-6310. *Application contact:* Dr. George Flowers, Dean of the Graduate School, 334-844-2125.

Ball State University, Graduate School, College of Sciences and Humanities, Department of Computer Science, Muncie, IN 47306-1099. Offers MA, MS. *Entrance requirements:* For master's, GRE General Test. *Faculty research:* Numerical methods, programmer productivity, graphics.

Baylor University, Graduate School, School of Engineering and Computer Science, Department of Computer Science, Waco, TX 76798. Offers MS. Part-time programs available. *Faculty:* 10 full-time (1 woman). *Students:* 21 full-time (5 women), 1 part-time (0 women); includes 3 minority (all Hispanic Americans), 11 international. 27 applicants, 37% accepted, 10 enrolled. In 2009, 10 master's awarded. *Entrance requirements:* Additional exam requirements/recommendations for international students: Required—TOEFL (minimum score 550 paper-based; 213 computer-based). *Application deadline:* For fall admission, 2/15 priority date for domestic and international students; for spring admission, 9/1 priority date for domestic and international students. Applications are processed on a rolling basis. Application fee: $40. Electronic applications accepted. *Faculty research:* Bioinformatics, databases, machine learning, SWE, networking. *Unit head:* Dr. David Sturgill, Chair, 254-710-3876, E-mail: david_sturgill@baylor.edu. *Application contact:* Dr. Sharon Humphrey, Graduate Program Director, 254-710-6821, Fax: 254-710-3870, E-mail: sharon_humphrey@baylor.edu.

Boise State University, Graduate College, College of Engineering, Program in Computer Science, Boise, ID 83725-0399. Offers MS. Part-time programs available. *Degree requirements:* For master's, comprehensive exam, thesis. *Entrance requirements:* For master's, GRE General Test, minimum GPA of 3.0. Electronic applications accepted. *Expenses:* Tuition, state resident: full-time $3106; part-time $209 per credit. Tuition, nonresident: part-time $284 per credit.

Boston University, Graduate School of Arts and Sciences, Department of Computer Science, Boston, MA 02215. Offers MA, PhD. *Students:* 54 full-time (11 women), 9 part-time (2 women); includes 4 minority (all Asian Americans or Pacific Islanders), 41 international. Average age 29. 306 applicants, 20% accepted, 18 enrolled. In 2009, 72 master's, 7 doctorates awarded. *Degree requirements:* For master's, one foreign language, thesis optional, project; for doctorate, one foreign language, comprehensive exam, thesis/dissertation. *Entrance requirements:* For master's and doctorate, GRE General Test, 3 letters of recommendation. Additional exam requirements/recommendations for international students: Required—TOEFL (minimum score 550 paper-based; 213 computer-based). *Application deadline:* For fall admission, 12/15 for domestic and international students; for spring admission, 10/1 for domestic and international students. Application fee: $70. *Expenses:* Tuition: Full-time $37,910; part-time $1184 per credit hour. Required fees: $386; $40 per semester. Part-time tuition and fees vary according to class time, course level, degree level and program. *Financial support:* In 2009–10, 1 fellowship (averaging $18,900 per year), 21 research assistantships (averaging $18,400 per year), 16 teaching assistantships with full tuition reimbursements (averaging $18,400 per year) were awarded; Federal Work-Study and scholarships/grants also available. Support available to part-time students. Financial award application deadline: 12/15; financial award applicants required to submit FAFSA. *Unit head:* Stan Sclaroff, Chairman, 617-353-8919, Fax: 617-353-6457, E-mail: sclaroff@bu.edu. *Application contact:* Jennifer Streubel, Program Coordinator, 617-353-8919, Fax: 617-353-6457, E-mail: jenn4@bu.edu.

Boston University, Metropolitan College, Department of Computer Science, Boston, MA 02215. Offers computer information systems (MS); computer science (MS); telecommunications (MS). Part-time and evening/weekend programs available. Postbaccalaureate distance learning degree programs offered (no on-campus study). *Faculty:* 8 full-time (0 women), 31 part-time/adjunct (1 woman). *Students:* 25 full-time (9 women), 557 part-time (124 women); includes 97 minority (25 African Americans, 55 Asian Americans or Pacific Islanders, 17 Hispanic Americans), 68 international. Average age 35. 355 applicants, 77% accepted, 259 enrolled. In 2009, 173 master's awarded. *Degree requirements:* For master's, thesis optional. *Entrance requirements:* For master's, 3 letters of recommendation, professional resume. Additional exam requirements/recommendations for international students: Required—TOEFL (minimum score 550 paper-based; 213 computer-based; 80 iBT), or IELTS (minimum score 6). *Application deadline:* For fall admission, 7/1 priority date for international students; for winter admission, 11/1 priority date for international students; for spring admission, 3/1 priority date for international students. Applications are processed on a rolling basis. Application fee: $70. Electronic applications accepted. *Expenses:* Tuition: Full-time $37,910; part-time $1184 per credit hour. Required fees: $386; $40 per semester. Part-time tuition and fees vary according to class time, course level, degree level and program. *Financial support:* In 2009–10, 15 students received support, including 15 research assistantships with partial tuition reimbursements available; institutionally sponsored loans and unspecified assistantships also available. Support available to part-time students. Financial award applicants required to submit FAFSA. *Faculty research:* Medical informatics, Web technologies, telecom and networks, security and forensics, software engineering, programming languages, multimedia and AI, information systems and IT project management. *Unit head:* Dr. Lubomir Chitkushev, Chairman, 617-353-2566, Fax: 617-353-2367, E-mail: csinfo@bu.edu. *Application contact:* Kim Richards, Program Coordinator, 617-353-2566, Fax: 617-353-2367, E-mail: kimrich@bu.edu.

Bowie State University, Graduate Programs, Department of Computer Science, Bowie, MD 20715-9465. Offers MS. Part-time and evening/weekend programs available. *Degree requirements:* For master's, comprehensive exam, thesis optional, research paper. *Entrance requirements:* For master's, minimum undergraduate GPA of 2.5. Electronic applications accepted. *Faculty research:* Holographics, launch vehicle ground truth ephemera.

Bowie State University, Graduate Programs, Program in Computer Science, Bowie, MD 20715-9465. Offers App Sc D. Part-time and evening/weekend programs available. Electronic applications accepted.

Bowling Green State University, Graduate College, College of Arts and Sciences, Department of Computer Science, Bowling Green, OH 43403. Offers computer science (MS), including operations research, parallel and distributed computing, software engineering. Part-time programs available. *Degree requirements:* For master's, thesis or alternative. *Entrance requirements:* For master's, GRE General Test. Additional exam requirements/recommendations for international students: Required—TOEFL. Electronic applications accepted. *Faculty research:* Artificial intelligence, real time and concurrent programming languages, behavioral aspects of computing, network protocols.

Bradley University, Graduate School, College of Liberal Arts and Sciences, Department of Computer Science and Information Systems, Peoria, IL 61625-0002. Offers computer information systems (MS); computer science (MS). Part-time and evening/weekend programs available. *Degree requirements:* For master's, comprehensive exam, thesis or alternative, programming test. *Entrance requirements:* For master's, 2 letters of recommendation. Additional exam requirements/recommendations for international students: Required—TOEFL (minimum score 550 paper-based; 213 computer-based; 79 iBT).

Brandeis University, Graduate School of Arts and Sciences, Michtom School of Computer Science, Waltham, MA 02454-9110. Offers computer science (MA, PhD, Certificate); computer science and IT entrepreneurship (MA). Part-time programs available. *Faculty:* 12 full-time (3 women), 2 part-time/adjunct (1 woman). *Students:* 43 full-time (14 women), 5 part-time (2 women); includes 5 minority (1 African American, 4 Asian Americans or Pacific Islanders), 21 international. Average age 26. 76 applicants, 66% accepted, 18 enrolled. In 2009, 8 master's, 4 doctorates, 1 other advanced degree awarded. *Degree requirements:* For doctorate, thesis/dissertation, thesis proposal. *Entrance requirements:* For master's and doctorate, resume, 3 letters of recommendation. Additional exam requirements/recommendations for international students: Required—TOEFL (minimum score 600 paper-based; 250 computer-based; 100 iBT); Recommended—IELTS (minimum score 7). *Application deadline:* For fall admission, 1/15 for domestic students. Application fee: $75. Electronic applications accepted. *Financial support:* In 2009–10, 23 students received support, including 8 fellowships with full tuition reimbursements available (averaging $20,000 per year), 10 research assistantships with full tuition reimbursements available (averaging $20,000 per year), teaching assistantships with partial tuition reimbursements available (averaging $3,200 per year); scholarships/grants, health care benefits, and tuition waivers (full and partial) also available. Support available to part-time students. Financial award application deadline: 4/15; financial award applicants required to submit FAFSA. *Faculty research:* Artificial intelligence, programming languages, parallel computing, computational linguistics, data compression, technology and IT entrepreneurship. *Unit head:* Dr. Richard Alterman, Graduate Chair, 781-736-2700, Fax: 781-736-2741, E-mail:

ralterma@brandeis.edu. *Application contact:* Myrna Fox, Department Administrator, 781-736-2701, E-mail: maf@cs.brandeis.edu.

Brandeis University, Graduate School of Arts and Sciences, Program in Computational Linguistics, Waltham, MA 02454-9110. Offers MA. Part-time programs available. *Faculty:* 6 full-time (2 women), 1 part-time/adjunct (0 women). *Students:* 8 full-time (2 women), 1 part-time (0 women), 3 international. 14 applicants, 86% accepted, 8 enrolled. In 2009, 1 master's awarded. *Degree requirements:* For master's, thesis. *Entrance requirements:* For master's, statement of purpose, 2 letters of recommendation, official transcripts, resume or curriculum vitae. Additional exam requirements/recommendations for international students: Required—TOEFL (minimum score 650 paper-based; 250 computer-based; 100 iBT); Recommended—IELTS (minimum score 7). *Application deadline:* Applications are processed on a rolling basis. Application fee: $75. Electronic applications accepted. *Financial support:* In 2009–10, 3 teaching assistantships with partial tuition reimbursements (averaging $3,200 per year) were awarded; institutionally sponsored loans and scholarships/grants also available. Financial award application deadline: 4/15; financial award applicants required to submit FAFSA. *Faculty research:* Computer science (artificial intelligence, theory of computation, and programming methods), language and linguistics (phonology, syntax, semantics, and pragmatics). *Unit head:* Dr. James Pustejovsky, Program Chair, 781-736-2701, Fax: 781-736-2741, E-mail: jamesp@brandeis.edu. *Application contact:* David F. Cotter, Graduate School of Arts and Sciences, 781-736-3410, Fax: 781-736-3412, E-mail: gradschool@brandeis.edu.

Brandeis University, Graduate School of Arts and Sciences, Program in Computer Science and IT Entrepreneurship, Waltham, MA 02454-9110. Offers MA. Part-time programs available. *Entrance requirements:* For master's, official transcript(s), 3 letters of recommendation, CV or resume, statement of purpose. Additional exam requirements/recommendations for international students: Required—TOEFL (minimum score 600 paper-based; 250 computer-based; 100 iBT); Recommended—IELTS (minimum score 7). *Application deadline:* Applications are processed on a rolling basis. Application fee: $75. Electronic applications accepted. *Financial support:* Scholarships/grants available. Financial award application deadline: 4/15; financial award applicants required to submit FAFSA. *Faculty research:* Software development, IT entrepreneurship, business, computer science. *Unit head:* Prof. Fernando Colon Osorio, 781-736-4586, E-mail: fcco@brandeis.edu. *Application contact:* David F. Cotter, Assistant Dean, Graduate School of Arts and Sciences, 781-736-3410, Fax: 781-736-3412, E-mail: gradschool@brandeis.edu.

Bridgewater State University, School of Graduate Studies, School of Arts and Sciences, Department of Mathematics and Computer Science, Bridgewater, MA 02325-0001. Offers computer science (MS); mathematics (MAT). Part-time and evening/weekend programs available. *Entrance requirements:* For master's, GRE General Test.

Brigham Young University, Graduate Studies, College of Physical and Mathematical Sciences, Department of Computer Science, Provo, UT 84602-1001. Offers MS, PhD. *Faculty:* 27 full-time (0 women), 3 part-time/adjunct (0 women). *Students:* 101 full-time (8 women); includes 6 minority (4 Asian Americans or Pacific Islanders, 2 Hispanic Americans), 12 international. Average age 29. 45 applicants, 71% accepted, 28 enrolled. In 2009, 15 master's, 4 doctorates awarded. Terminal master's awarded for partial completion of doctoral program. *Degree requirements:* For master's, thesis; for doctorate, comprehensive exam, thesis/dissertation, residency. *Entrance requirements:* For master's, GRE General Test, minimum GPA of 3.25 in last 60 hours; for doctorate, GRE General Test, minimum GPA of 3.5 in last 60 hours, undergraduate degree in computer science. Additional exam requirements/recommendations for international students: Required—TOEFL (minimum score 600 paper-based; 250 computer-based; 85 iBT). *Application deadline:* For fall admission, 1/15 for domestic and international students; for winter admission, 8/15 for domestic and international students. Application fee: $50. Electronic applications accepted. *Expenses:* Tuition: Full-time $5580; part-time $301 per credit hour. Tuition and fees vary according to student's religious affiliation. *Financial support:* In 2009–10, 75 students received support, including fellowships with full tuition reimbursements available (averaging $22,000 per year), 66 research assistantships with full and partial tuition reimbursements available (averaging $15,000 per year), 17 teaching assistantships with partial tuition reimbursements available (averaging $12,000 per year); scholarships/grants and health care benefits also available. Financial award application deadline: 4/4. *Faculty research:* Graphics, image processing, neural networks and machine learning, formal methods. Total annual research expenditures: $728,000. *Unit head:* Dr. Parris K. Egbert, Chair, 801-422-4029, Fax: 801-422-0169, E-mail: egbert@cs.byu.edu. *Application contact:* Dr. Kent E. Seamons, Graduate Coordinator, 801-422-3722, Fax: 801-422-0169, E-mail: graduate@cs.byu.edu.

Brock University, Faculty of Graduate Studies, Faculty of Mathematics and Science, Program in Computer Science, St. Catharines, ON L2S 3A1, Canada. Offers M Sc. Part-time programs available. *Degree requirements:* For master's, thesis. *Entrance requirements:* For master's, honors degree. Additional exam requirements/recommendations for international students: Required—TOEFL (minimum score 550 paper-based; 213 computer-based; 80 iBT), IELTS (minimum score 6.5), TWE (minimum score 4).

Brooklyn College of the City University of New York, Division of Graduate Studies, Department of Computer and Information Science, Brooklyn, NY 11210-2889. Offers computer science (MA, PhD); computer science and health science (MS); information systems (MS); parallel and distributed computing (Advanced Certificate). The department offers courses at Brooklyn College that are creditable toward the CUNY doctoral degree. Part-time and evening/weekend programs available. *Degree requirements:* For master's, comprehensive exam, thesis or alternative. *Entrance requirements:* For master's, previous course work in computer science, 2 letters of recommendation. Additional exam requirements/recommendations for international students: Required—TOEFL (minimum score 525 paper-based; 195 computer-based; 70 iBT). Electronic applications accepted. *Faculty research:* Networks and distributed systems, programming languages, modeling and computer applications, algorithms, artificial intelligence, theoretical computer science.

Brown University, Graduate School, Department of Computer Science, Providence, RI 02912. Offers Sc M, PhD. *Degree requirements:* For master's, thesis or alternative; for doctorate, one foreign language, comprehensive exam, thesis/dissertation. *Entrance requirements:* For master's and doctorate, GRE General Test, GRE Subject Test.

California Institute of Technology, Division of Engineering and Applied Science, Option in Computer Science, Pasadena, CA 91125-0001. Offers MS, PhD. *Faculty:* 12 full-time (0 women). *Students:* 24 full-time (2 women). 289 applicants, 4% accepted, 5 enrolled. In 2009, 1 master's, 2 doctorates awarded. *Degree requirements:* For master's, thesis; for doctorate, thesis/dissertation. *Application deadline:* For fall admission, 1/1 for domestic students. Application fee: $0. Electronic applications accepted. *Financial support:* In 2009–10, 5 fellowships, 14 research assistantships, 4 teaching assistantships were awarded. *Faculty research:* VLSI systems, concurrent computation, high-level programming languages, signal and image processing, graphics. *Unit head:* Dr. Mathieu Desbrun, Director, 626-395-6230, E-mail: mathieu@cs.caltech.edu. *Application contact:* Natalie Gilmore, Assistant Dean of Graduate Studies, 626-395-3812, Fax: 626-577-9246, E-mail: ngilmore@caltech.edu.

California Polytechnic State University, San Luis Obispo, College of Engineering, Department of Computer Science, San Luis Obispo, CA 93407. Offers MS. Part-time programs available. *Faculty:* 10 full-time (2 women). *Students:* 16 full-time (0 women), 10 part-time (2 women); includes 4 minority (1 American Indian/Alaska Native, 2 Asian Americans or Pacific Islanders, 1 Hispanic American). Average age 25. 20 applicants, 35% accepted, 5 enrolled. In 2009, 13 master's awarded. *Degree requirements:* For master's, thesis. *Entrance requirements:* For master's, GRE General Test, minimum GPA of 3.0 in last 90 quarter units. Additional exam requirements/recommendations for international students: Required—TOEFL (minimum score 550 paper-based; 213 computer-based), or IELTS (minimum score 6). *Application deadline:* For fall admission, 4/1 for domestic students, 11/30 for international students; for winter admission, 9/1 for domestic students, 6/30 for international students. Applications are processed on a rolling basis. Application fee: $55. Electronic applications accepted. *Expenses:* Tuition, nonresident: full-time $11,160; part-time $248 per unit. Required fees: $7134; $1553 per quarter. *Financial support:* Teaching assistantships, career-related internships or fieldwork, Federal Work-Study, institutionally sponsored loans, scholarships/grants, and unspecified assistantships available. Support available to part-time students. Financial award application deadline: 3/2; financial award applicants required to submit FAFSA. *Faculty research:* Computer systems, software, graphics, hardware design, expert systems. *Unit head:* Dr. Hasmik Gharibyan, Graduate Coordinator, 805-756-7068, Fax: 805-756-2956, E-mail: hgharibу@calpoly.edu. *Application contact:* Dr. Hasmik Gharibyan, Graduate Coordinator, 805-756-7068, Fax: 805-756-2956, E-mail: hgharibу@calpoly.edu.

California State Polytechnic University, Pomona, Academic Affairs, College of Science, Program in Computer Science, Pomona, CA 91768-2557. Offers MS. Part-time programs available. *Students:* 15 full-time (2 women), 43 part-time (8 women); includes 22 minority (1 African American, 17 Asian Americans or Pacific Islanders, 4 Hispanic Americans), 19 international. Average age 28. 54 applicants, 39% accepted, 11 enrolled. In 2009, 7 master's awarded. *Degree requirements:* For master's, thesis. *Entrance requirements:* For master's, GRE General Test. *Application deadline:* For fall admission, 5/1 priority date for domestic students; for winter admission, 10/15 priority date for domestic students; for spring admission, 1/20 priority date for domestic students. Applications are processed on a rolling basis. Application fee: $55. Electronic applications accepted. *Expenses:* Tuition, nonresident: full-time $6696; part-time $248 per credit. Required fees: $5487; $3237 per term. Tuition and fees vary according to course load, degree level and program. *Financial support:* Career-related internships or fieldwork, Federal Work-Study, and institutionally sponsored loans available. Support available to part-time students. Financial award application deadline: 3/2; financial award applicants required to submit FAFSA. *Unit head:* Dr. Salam Salloum, Graduate Coordinator, 909-869-5317, E-mail: mscs@csupomona.edu. *Application contact:* Scott J. Duncan, Director, Admissions, 909-869-3258, Fax: 909-869-4529, E-mail: sjduncan@csupomona.edu.

California State University Channel Islands, Extended Education, Program in Computer Science, Camarillo, CA 93012. Offers MS. Part-time and evening/weekend programs available. *Entrance requirements:* Additional exam requirements/recommendations for international students: Required—TOEFL (minimum score 550 paper-based).

California State University, Chico, Graduate School, College of Engineering, Computer Science, and Technology, Department of Computer Science, Chico, CA 95929-0722. Offers MS. Postbaccalaureate distance learning degree programs offered. *Students:* 18 full-time (0 women), 11 part-time (1 woman); includes 2 minority (both Asian Americans or Pacific Islanders), 19 international. Average age 29. 88 applicants, 66% accepted, 9 enrolled. In 2009, 56 master's awarded. *Entrance requirements:* For master's, GRE General Test, 2 letters of recommendation. Additional exam requirements/recommendations for international students: Required—TOEFL (minimum score 550 paper-based; 213 computer-based; 80 iBT), IELTS (minimum score 6.5). *Application deadline:* For fall admission, 3/1 priority date for domestic students, 3/1 for international students; for spring admission, 9/15 priority date for domestic students, 9/15 for international students. Applications are processed on a rolling basis. Application fee: $55. Electronic applications accepted. *Financial support:* Fellowships, research assistantships, teaching assistantships, career-related internships or fieldwork available. *Unit head:* Dr. Moaty Fayek, Graduate Coordinator, 530-898-4010. *Application contact:* Dr. Moaty Fayek, Graduate Coordinator, 530-898-4010.

California State University, Dominguez Hills, College of Natural and Behavioral Sciences, Department of Computer Science, Carson, CA 90747-0001. Offers MSCS. *Faculty:* 5 full-time (1 woman), 1 part-time/adjunct (0 women). *Students:* 7 full-time (2 women), 9 part-time (3 women); includes 12 minority (2 African Americans, 3 Asian Americans or Pacific Islanders, 7 Hispanic Americans), 2 international. Average age 32. 11 applicants, 100% accepted, 4 enrolled. *Degree requirements:* For master's, comprehensive exam (for some programs), thesis (for some programs). *Entrance requirements:* For master's, GRE (minimum score 900), minimum GPA of 2.75. Additional exam requirements/recommendations for international students: Required—TOEFL (minimum score 550 paper-based). Application fee: $55. Electronic applications accepted. *Expenses:* Tuition, nonresident: full-time $6696; part-time $372 per unit. Required fees: $5946; $1752 per semester. *Unit head:* Dr. Mohsen Beheshti, Department Chair, 310-243-3398, E-mail: mbeheshti@csudh.edu. *Application contact:* Dr. Gayle Ball-Parker, Director of Admissions, 310-243-3654, E-mail: gball@csudh.edu.

California State University, East Bay, Academic Programs and Graduate Studies, College of Science, Department of Mathematics and Computer Science, Computer Science Program, Hayward, CA 94542-3000. Offers computer networks (MS); computer science (MS). Part-time programs available. *Faculty:* 15 full-time (4 women). *Students:* 67 full-time (35 women), 139 part-time (57 women); includes 34 minority (3 African Americans, 30 Asian Americans or Pacific Islanders, 1 Hispanic American), 143 international. Average age 27. 258 applicants, 67% accepted, 63 enrolled. In 2009, 38 master's awarded. *Degree requirements:* For master's, comprehensive exam or thesis. *Entrance requirements:* For master's, GRE, minimum GPA of 3.0 in field, 2.75 overall; upper-division course requirements. Additional exam requirements/recommendations for international students: Required—TOEFL (minimum score 550 paper-based; 213 computer-based). *Application deadline:* For fall admission, 6/30 for domestic and international students. Application fee: $55. Electronic applications accepted. *Financial support:* Fellowships, career-related internships or fieldwork, Federal Work-Study, institutionally sponsored loans, and scholarships/grants available. Support available to part-time students. Financial award application deadline: 3/1; financial award applicants required to submit FAFSA. *Unit head:* Dr. Kevin Callahan, Chair, 510-885-4011, Fax: 510-885-4169, E-mail: kevin.callahan@csueastbay.edu. *Application contact:* Donna Wiley, Interim Associate Director, 510-885-2928, Fax: 510-885-4777, E-mail: donna.wiley@csueastbay.edu.

California State University, Fresno, Division of Graduate Studies, College of Science and Mathematics, Department of Computer Science, Fresno, CA 93740-8027. Offers MS. Part-time and evening/weekend programs available. *Degree requirements:* For master's, thesis or alternative. *Entrance requirements:* For master's, GRE General Test, minimum GPA of 2.75. Additional exam requirements/recommendations for international students: Required—TOEFL. Electronic applications accepted. *Faculty research:* Software design, parallel processing, computer engineering, autoline research.

California State University, Fullerton, Graduate Studies, College of Engineering and Computer Science, Department of Computer Science, Fullerton, CA 92834-9480. Offers computer science (MS); software engineering (MS). Part-time programs available. Postbaccalaureate distance learning degree programs offered. *Students:* 71 full-time (28 women), 268 part-time (58 women); includes 120 minority (9 African Americans, 96 Asian Americans or Pacific Islanders, 15 Hispanic Americans), 134 international. Average age 30. 390 applicants, 60% accepted, 102 enrolled. In 2009, 126 master's awarded. *Degree requirements:* For master's, comprehensive exam, project or thesis. *Entrance requirements:* For master's, GRE General Test, minimum undergraduate GPA of 2.5. Application fee: $55. *Expenses:* Tuition, nonresident: full-time $11,160; part-time $373 per credit. Required fees: $1440 per term. Tuition and fees vary according to course load, degree level and program. *Financial support:* Career-related internships or fieldwork, Federal Work-Study, institutionally sponsored loans, and scholarships/grants available. Support available to part-time students. Financial award application deadline: 3/1; financial award applicants required to submit FAFSA. *Faculty research:* Software engineering, development of computer networks. *Unit head:* Dr. James Choi, Chair, 657-278-3700. *Application contact:* Admissions/Applications, 657-278-2371.

California State University, Long Beach, Graduate Studies, College of Engineering, Department of Computer Engineering and Computer Science, Long Beach, CA 90840. Offers computer engineering (MSCS); computer science (MSCS). Part-time programs available. *Faculty:* 17 full-time (9 women), 2 part-time/adjunct (0 women). *Students:* 104 full-time (20 women), 97 part-time (20 women); includes 48 minority (3 African Americans, 36 Asian Americans or Pacific Islanders, 9 Hispanic Americans), 99 international. Average age 28. 294

Computer Science

California State University, Long Beach (continued)
applicants, 69% accepted, 50 enrolled. *Degree requirements:* For master's, thesis or alternative. *Entrance requirements:* Additional exam requirements/recommendations for international students: Required—TOEFL. *Application deadline:* For fall admission, 3/1 for domestic students. Application fee: $55. Electronic applications accepted. *Expenses:* Required fees: $1802 per semester. Part-time tuition and fees vary according to course load. *Financial support:* Teaching assistantships, Federal Work-Study, institutionally sponsored loans, scholarships/grants, and unspecified assistantships available. Financial award application deadline: 3/2. *Faculty research:* Artificial intelligence, software engineering, computer simulation and modeling, user-interface design, networking. *Unit head:* Dr. Kenneth James, Chair, 562-985-5105, Fax: 562-985-7823, E-mail: james@csulb.edu. *Application contact:* Dr. Burkhard Englert, Graduate Advisor, 562-985-7987, Fax: 562-985-7823, E-mail: benglert@.csulb.edu.

California State University, Los Angeles, Graduate Studies, College of Engineering, Computer Science, and Technology, Department of Computer Science, Los Angeles, CA 90032-8530. Offers MS. *Faculty:* 4 full-time (1 woman), 4 part-time/adjunct (1 woman). *Students:* 45 full-time (20 women), 99 part-time (32 women); includes 27 minority (2 African Americans, 18 Asian Americans or Pacific Islanders, 7 Hispanic Americans), 93 international. Average age 28. 150 applicants, 99% accepted, 30 enrolled. In 2009, 21 master's awarded. *Entrance requirements:* Additional exam requirements/recommendations for international students: Required—TOEFL (minimum score 550 paper-based). *Application deadline:* For fall admission, 5/1 for domestic and international students. Applications are processed on a rolling basis. Application fee: $55. Electronic applications accepted. *Unit head:* Dr. Raj Pamula, Chair, 323-343-6690, Fax: 323-343-6672, E-mail: rpamula@calstatela.edu. *Application contact:* Dr. Cheryl L. Ney, Associate Vice President for Academic Affairs and Dean of Graduate Studies, 323-343-3820, Fax: 323-343-5653, E-mail: cney@cslanet.calstatela.edu.

California State University, Northridge, Graduate Studies, College of Engineering and Computer Science, Department of Computer Science, Northridge, CA 91330. Offers computer science (MS); software engineering (MS). Part-time and evening/weekend programs available. *Faculty:* 17 full-time (2 women), 11 part-time/adjunct (3 women). *Students:* 28 full-time (7 women), 45 part-time (6 women); includes 1 African American, 14 Asian Americans or Pacific Islanders, 4 Hispanic Americans, 18 international. Average age 31. 257 applicants, 23% accepted, 32 enrolled. In 2009, 11 master's awarded. *Degree requirements:* For master's, thesis. *Entrance requirements:* For master's, GRE General Test, minimum GPA of 2.5. Additional exam requirements/recommendations for international students: Required—TOEFL. *Application deadline:* For fall admission, 11/30 for domestic students. Application fee: $55. *Financial support:* Application deadline: 3/1. *Faculty research:* Radar data processing. *Unit head:* Prof. Steven G. Stepanek, Chair, 818-677-3398. *Application contact:* Prof. Steven G. Stepanek, Chair, 818-677-3398.

California State University, Sacramento, Graduate Studies, College of Engineering and Computer Science, Department of Computer Science, Sacramento, CA 95819. Offers computer systems (MS); software engineering (MS). Part-time and evening/weekend programs available. *Degree requirements:* For master's, thesis or alternative, writing proficiency exam. *Entrance requirements:* Additional exam requirements/recommendations for international students: Required—TOEFL. Electronic applications accepted.

California State University, San Bernardino, Graduate Studies, College of Natural Sciences, Department of Computer Science, San Bernardino, CA 92407-2397. Offers MS. *Faculty:* 7 full-time (1 woman). *Students:* 36 full-time (13 women), 20 part-time (4 women); includes 16 minority (4 African Americans, 6 Asian Americans or Pacific Islanders, 6 Hispanic Americans), 23 international. Average age 31. 47 applicants, 77% accepted, 18 enrolled. In 2009, 19 master's awarded. *Entrance requirements:* For master's, GRE. *Application deadline:* For fall admission, 8/31 priority date for domestic students. Application fee: $55. *Unit head:* Dr. George Georgiou, Chair, 909-537-5326, Fax: 909-537-7004, E-mail: georgiou@csusb.edu. *Application contact:* Olivia Rosas, Director of Admissions, 909-537-7577, Fax: 909-537-7034, E-mail: orosas@csusb.edu.

California State University, San Marcos, College of Arts and Sciences, Program in Computer Science, San Marcos, CA 92096-0001. Offers MS. Part-time programs available. *Entrance requirements:* For master's, GRE General Test, GRE Subject Test (recommended). Additional exam requirements/recommendations for international students: Required—TOEFL. *Faculty research:* Networks, multimedia, parallel algorithms, software engineering, artificial intelligence.

Capitol College, Graduate Programs, Laurel, MD 20708-9759. Offers business administration (MBA); computer science (MS); electrical engineering (MS); information and telecommunications systems management (MS); information architecture (MS); network security (MS). Part-time and evening/weekend programs available. Postbaccalaureate distance learning degree programs offered (no on-campus study). *Entrance requirements:* For master's, minimum GPA of 3.0. Electronic applications accepted.

Carleton University, Faculty of Graduate Studies, Faculty of Science, School of Computer Science, Ottawa, ON K1S 5B6, Canada. Offers computer science (MCS, PhD); information and system science (M Sc). Part-time programs available. *Degree requirements:* For master's, thesis optional, project; for doctorate, comprehensive exam, thesis/dissertation. *Entrance requirements:* For master's, honors degree. Additional exam requirements/recommendations for international students: Required—TOEFL. *Faculty research:* Programming systems, theory of computing, computer applications, computer systems.

Carnegie Mellon University, School of Computer Science, Department of Computer Science, Pittsburgh, PA 15213-3891. Offers algorithms, combinatorics, and optimization (PhD); computer science (MS, PhD); pure and applied logic (PhD). *Degree requirements:* For doctorate, thesis/dissertation. *Entrance requirements:* For doctorate, GRE General Test, GRE Subject Test, BS in computer science or equivalent. Additional exam requirements/recommendations for international students: Required—TOEFL. *Faculty research:* Software systems, theory of computations, artificial intelligence, computer systems, programming languages.

See Close-Up on page 293.

Carnegie Mellon University, School of Computer Science, Language Technologies Institute, Pittsburgh, PA 15213-3891. Offers MLT, PhD. Terminal master's awarded for partial completion of doctoral program. *Degree requirements:* For doctorate, thesis/dissertation. *Entrance requirements:* For master's and doctorate, GRE General Test, GRE Subject Test. Additional exam requirements/recommendations for international students: Required—TOEFL. *Faculty research:* Machine translation, natural language processing, speech and information retrieval, literacy.

Case Western Reserve University, School of Graduate Studies, The Case School of Engineering, Department of Electrical Engineering and Computer Science, Cleveland, OH 44106. Offers computer engineering (MS, PhD); computing and information sciences (MS, PhD); electrical engineering (MS, PhD); systems and control engineering (MS, PhD). Part-time and evening/weekend programs available. Postbaccalaureate distance learning degree programs offered (minimal on-campus study). *Faculty:* 32 full-time (2 women). *Students:* 175 full-time (26 women), 28 part-time (6 women); includes 9 minority (3 African Americans, 6 Asian Americans or Pacific Islanders), 107 international. In 2009, 29 master's, 15 doctorates awarded. Terminal master's awarded for partial completion of doctoral program. *Degree requirements:* For master's, thesis; for doctorate, thesis/dissertation, qualifying exam, teaching experience. *Entrance requirements:* For master's and doctorate, GRE General Test. Additional exam requirements/recommendations for international students: Required—TOEFL. *Application deadline:* For fall admission, 2/1 for domestic students; for spring admission, 11/1 for domestic students. Applications are processed on a rolling basis. Application fee: $50. *Financial support:* Fellowships with full and partial tuition reimbursements, research assistantships with full and partial tuition reimbursements, teaching assistantships, career-related internships or fieldwork, Federal Work-

Study, and institutionally sponsored loans available. Support available to part-time students. Financial award application deadline: 3/1; financial award applicants required to submit FAFSA. *Faculty research:* Applied artificial intelligence, automation, computer-aided design and testing of digital systems. Total annual research expenditures: $5.5 million. *Unit head:* Dwight Davy, Department Chair, 216-368-2802, E-mail: dtd@case.edu. *Application contact:* David Easler, Student Affairs Coordinator, 216-368-4080, Fax: 216-368-2801, E-mail: david.easler@case.edu.

The Catholic University of America, School of Engineering, Department of Electrical Engineering and Computer Science, Washington, DC 20064. Offers antennas and electromagnetic propagation (MEE, MSCS, D Engr); bioimaging (MEE, MSCS, PhD); bioinformatics and intelligent information systems (MEE, D Engr, PhD); distributed and real-time systems (MEE, MSCS, D Engr, PhD); high speed communications and networking (MSCS, D Engr, PhD); information security (MEE, MSCS, PhD); micro-optics (MEE, MSCS, D Engr, PhD); signal and image processing (MEE, MSCS, D Engr). Part-time programs available. *Faculty:* 7 full-time (2 women), 6 part-time/adjunct (0 women). *Students:* 10 full-time (4 women), 50 part-time (7 women); includes 10 minority (3 African Americans, 4 Asian Americans or Pacific Islanders, 3 Hispanic Americans), 12 international. Average age 34. 50 applicants, 54% accepted, 11 enrolled. In 2009, 10 master's awarded. *Degree requirements:* For master's, thesis or alternative; for doctorate, comprehensive exam, thesis/dissertation, qualifying exam, oral exams. *Entrance requirements:* For master's, statement of purpose, official copies of academic transcripts, three letters of recommendation; for doctorate, 3 letters of recommendation. Additional exam requirements/recommendations for international students: Required—TOEFL (minimum score 580 paper-based; 237 computer-based). *Application deadline:* For fall admission, 8/1 priority date for domestic students, 7/15 for international students; for spring admission, 12/1 priority date for domestic students, 10/15 for international students. Applications are processed on a rolling basis. Application fee: $55. Electronic applications accepted. *Expenses:* Contact institution. *Financial support:* Fellowships, research assistantships, teaching assistantships, Federal Work-Study, scholarships/grants, tuition waivers (full and partial), and unspecified assistantships available. Financial award application deadline: 2/1; financial award applicants required to submit FAFSA. *Faculty research:* Signal and image processing, computer communications, robotics, intelligent controls, bioelectromagnetics. Total annual research expenditures: $1.2 million. *Unit head:* Dr. Phillip Regalia, Chair, 202-319-5879, Fax: 202-319-5195, E-mail: regalia@cua.edu. *Application contact:* Julie Schwing, Director of Graduate Admissions, 202-319-5057, Fax: 202-319-6533, E-mail: cua-admissions@cua.edu.

Central Connecticut State University, School of Graduate Studies, School of Arts and Sciences, Department of Computer Science, New Britain, CT 06050-4010. Offers computer information technology (MS). Part-time and evening/weekend programs available. *Faculty:* 8 full-time (5 women), 7 part-time/adjunct (0 women). *Students:* 5 full-time (3 women), 43 part-time (11 women); includes 7 minority (3 African Americans, 4 Asian Americans or Pacific Islanders), 10 international. Average age 33. 61 applicants, 43% accepted, 23 enrolled. In 2009, 19 master's awarded. *Degree requirements:* For master's, comprehensive exam, thesis or alternative. *Entrance requirements:* For master's, minimum undergraduate GPA of 2.7. Additional exam requirements/recommendations for international students: Required—TOEFL. *Application deadline:* For fall admission, 7/1 for domestic students; for spring admission, 12/1 for domestic students. Applications are processed on a rolling basis. Application fee: $50. Electronic applications accepted. *Expenses:* Tuition, area resident: full-time $4662; part-time $440 per credit. Tuition, state resident: full-time $6994; part-time $440 per credit. Tuition, nonresident: full-time $12,988; part-time $440 per credit. Required fees: $3606. One-time fee: $62 part-time. *Financial support:* In 2009–10, 4 students received support, including 3 research assistantships; career-related internships or fieldwork, Federal Work-Study, scholarships/grants, and unspecified assistantships also available. Support available to part-time students. Financial award application deadline: 3/1; financial award applicants required to submit FAFSA. *Unit head:* Dr. Bradley Kjell, Chair, 860-832-2710. *Application contact:* Dr. Bradley Kjell, Chair, 860-832-2710.

Central Connecticut State University, School of Graduate Studies, School of Arts and Sciences, Department of Mathematical Sciences, New Britain, CT 06050-4010. Offers data mining (MS, Certificate); mathematics (MA, MS, Certificate, Sixth Year Certificate), including actuarial science (MA), computer science (MA), statistics (MA). Part-time and evening/weekend programs available. *Faculty:* 33 full-time (12 women), 60 part-time/adjunct (30 women). *Students:* 21 full-time (10 women), 129 part-time (76 women); includes 13 minority (4 African Americans, 1 American Indian/Alaska Native, 4 Asian Americans or Pacific Islanders, 4 Hispanic Americans), 13 international. Average age 37. 78 applicants, 64% accepted, 37 enrolled. In 2009, 27 master's, 13 other advanced degrees awarded. *Degree requirements:* For master's, comprehensive exam, thesis or alternative; for other advanced degree, qualifying exam. *Entrance requirements:* For master's, minimum undergraduate GPA of 2.7. Additional exam requirements/recommendations for international students: Required—TOEFL. *Application deadline:* For fall admission, 7/1 for domestic students; for spring admission, 12/1 for domestic students. Applications are processed on a rolling basis. Application fee: $50. Electronic applications accepted. *Expenses:* Tuition, area resident: Full-time $4662; part-time $440 per credit. Tuition, state resident: full-time $6994; part-time $440 per credit. Tuition, nonresident: full-time $12,988; part-time $440 per credit. Required fees: $3606. One-time fee: $62 part-time. *Financial support:* In 2009–10, 7 students received support, including 3 research assistantships; career-related internships or fieldwork, Federal Work-Study, scholarships/grants, and unspecified assistantships also available. Support available to part-time students. Financial award application deadline: 3/1; financial award applicants required to submit FAFSA. *Faculty research:* Statistics, actuarial mathematics, computer systems and engineering, computer programming techniques, operations research. *Unit head:* Dr. Jeffrey McGowan, Chair, 860-832-2835. *Application contact:* Dr. Jeffrey McGowan, Chair, 860-832-2835.

Central Michigan University, College of Graduate Studies, College of Science and Technology, Department of Computer Science, Mount Pleasant, MI 48859. Offers MS. Part-time programs available. *Degree requirements:* For master's, thesis or alternative. *Entrance requirements:* For master's, bachelor's degree from accredited institution with minimum GPA of 3.0 in last two years of study. Electronic applications accepted. *Faculty research:* Artificial intelligence, biocomputing, data mining, software engineering, operating systems.

Chicago State University, School of Graduate and Professional Studies, College of Arts and Sciences, Department of Mathematics and Computer Science, Chicago, IL 60628. Offers computer science (MS); mathematics (MS). *Degree requirements:* For master's, thesis optional, oral exam. *Entrance requirements:* For master's, minimum GPA of 2.75.

Christopher Newport University, Graduate Studies, Department of Physics, Computer Science, and Engineering, Newport News, VA 23606-2998. Offers applied physics and computer science (MS). Part-time and evening/weekend programs available. *Faculty:* 6 full-time (0 women), 3 part-time/adjunct (2 women). *Students:* 6 full-time (1 woman), 23 part-time (2 women); includes 2 minority (both African Americans). Average age 29. 10 applicants, 100% accepted, 7 enrolled. In 2009, 7 master's awarded. *Degree requirements:* For master's, comprehensive exam (for some programs), thesis optional. *Entrance requirements:* For master's, GRE General Test, minimum GPA of 3.0. Additional exam requirements/recommendations for international students: Required—TOEFL (minimum score 580 paper-based; 237 computer-based; 92 iBT). *Application deadline:* For fall admission, 8/15 priority date for domestic students, 4/1 for international students; for spring admission, 10/15 for domestic students, 10/1 for international students. Applications are processed on a rolling basis. Application fee: $45. Electronic applications accepted. *Expenses:* Tuition, area resident: Part-time $384 per credit hour. Tuition, state resident: part-time $384 per credit hour. Tuition, nonresident: part-time $701 per credit hour. *Financial support:* In 2009–10, 3 research assistantships with full and partial tuition reimbursements (averaging $2,000 per year) were awarded; fellowships with full tuition reimbursements, career-related internships or fieldwork, Federal Work-Study, and unspecified assistantships also available. Support available to part-time students. Financial award application deadline: 2/1; financial award applicants required to submit FAFSA. *Faculty research:* Advanced programming methodologies, experimental nuclear physics, computer architecture, semiconductor nanophysics, laser and optical fiber sensors. *Unit head:* Dr. Antonio Siochi, Coordinator, 757-594-7569, Fax: 757-594-7919, E-mail: siochi@cnu.edu. *Application contact:* Lyn Sawyer, Associate Director, Graduate Admissions and Records, 757-594-7544, Fax: 757-594-7649, E-mail: gradstdy@cnu.edu.

The Citadel, The Military College of South Carolina, Citadel Graduate College, Department of Mathematics and Computer Science, Charleston, SC 29409. Offers computer and information science (MS); mathematics education (MAE). *Accreditation:* NCATE (one or more programs are accredited). Part-time and evening/weekend programs available. *Faculty:* 3 full-time (0 women), 1 part-time/adjunct (0 women). *Students:* 1 (woman) full-time, 18 part-time (8 women); includes 1 minority (Asian American or Pacific Islander). Average age 35. In 2009, 3 master's awarded. *Degree requirements:* For master's, comprehensive exam (for some programs), thesis (for some programs). *Entrance requirements:* For master's, GRE (minimum score 1000 for MS; minimum score 900 verbal and quantitative for MAT, raw score of 396), minimum undergraduate GPA of 3.0 (MS) or 2.5 (MAT); competency, demonstrated through coursework, approved work experience, or a program-administrated competency exam, in the areas of basic computer architecture, object-oriented programming, discrete mathematics, and data structures (MS); successful completion of 7 courses (MAT). Additional exam requirements/recommendations for international students: Required—TOEFL (minimum score 550 paper-based; 213 computer-based; 79 iBT). *Application deadline:* Applications are processed on a rolling basis. Application fee: $30. Electronic applications accepted. *Expenses:* Tuition, state resident: part-time $400 per credit hour. Tuition, nonresident: part-time $657 per credit hour. Required fees: $40 per term. *Financial support:* Health care benefits and unspecified assistantships available. Support available to part-time students. Financial award application deadline: 7/1; financial award applicants required to submit FAFSA. *Unit head:* Dr. John I. Moore, Department Head, 843-953-5048, Fax: 843-953-7391, E-mail: john.moore@citadel.edu. *Application contact:* Dr. George L. Rudolph, Computer and Information Science Program Director, 843-953-5032, Fax: 843-953-7391, E-mail: george.rudolph@citadel.edu.

City College of the City University of New York, Graduate School, Grove School of Engineering, Department of Computer Sciences, New York, NY 10031-9198. Offers MS, PhD. *Degree requirements:* For master's, thesis optional; for doctorate, one foreign language, comprehensive exam, thesis/dissertation. *Entrance requirements:* For master's and doctorate, GRE General Test. Additional exam requirements/recommendations for international students: Required—TOEFL (minimum score 500 paper-based; 173 computer-based; 61 iBT). *Faculty research:* Complexities of algebraic research, human issues in computer science, scientific computing, supercompilers, parallel algorithms.

Clark Atlanta University, School of Arts and Sciences, Department of Computer and Information Science, Atlanta, GA 30314. Offers MS. Part-time programs available. *Faculty:* 5 full-time (1 woman). *Students:* 5 full-time (1 woman), 5 part-time (3 women); includes 9 minority (all African Americans), 1 international. Average age 31. 7 applicants, 100% accepted, 3 enrolled. In 2009, 3 master's awarded. *Degree requirements:* For master's, one foreign language, thesis. *Entrance requirements:* For master's, GRE General Test, minimum GPA of 2.5. Additional exam requirements/recommendations for international students: Required—TOEFL (minimum score 550 paper-based; 173 computer-based). *Application deadline:* For fall admission, 4/1 for domestic and international students; for spring admission, 11/1 for domestic and international students. Applications are processed on a rolling basis. Application fee: $40 ($55 for international students). *Expenses:* Tuition: Full-time $12,240; part-time $680 per credit hour. Required fees: $710; $355 per semester. *Financial support:* In 2009–10, 1 research assistantship, 3 teaching assistantships were awarded; career-related internships or fieldwork, Federal Work-Study, scholarships/grants, and unspecified assistantships also available. Support available to part-time students. Financial award application deadline: 4/30; financial award applicants required to submit FAFSA. *Unit head:* Dr. Roy George, Chairperson, 404-880-6945, E-mail: rgeorge@cau.edu. *Application contact:* Michelle Clark-Davis, Graduate Program Admissions, 404-880-6605, E-mail: cauadmissions@cau.edu.

Clarkson University, Graduate School, School of Arts and Sciences, Program in Computer Science, Potsdam, NY 13699. Offers MS. Part-time programs available. *Faculty:* 7 full-time (2 women). *Students:* 11 full-time (1 woman), 5 international. Average age 26. 28 applicants, 64% accepted, 5 enrolled. In 2009, 5 master's awarded. *Entrance requirements:* For master's, GRE, 3 letters of recommendation; resume (recommended). Additional exam requirements/recommendations for international students: Required—TOEFL, TSE (recommended). *Application deadline:* For fall admission, 1/30 priority date for domestic and international students; for spring admission, 9/1 priority date for domestic and international students. Applications are processed on a rolling basis. Application fee: $25 ($35 for international students). Electronic applications accepted. *Expenses:* Tuition: Part-time $1074 per credit hour. *Financial support:* In 2009–10, 6 students received support, including 1 fellowship (averaging $30,000 per year), 1 research assistantship (averaging $20,190 per year); scholarships/grants and unspecified assistantships also available. *Faculty research:* Theoretical computer science cryptography, computational complexity learning theory, applications to biology, networks and security. Total annual research expenditures: $187,733. *Unit head:* Dr. Peter Turner, Dean, 315-268-6544, Fax: 315-268-3983, E-mail: pturner@clarkson.edu. *Application contact:* Jennifer E. Reed, Graduate School Coordinator for School of Arts and Sciences, 315-268-3802, Fax: 315-268-3989, E-mail: jreed@clarkson.edu.

Clemson University, Graduate School, College of Engineering and Science, School of Computing, Program in Computer Science, Clemson, SC 29634. Offers MS, PhD. *Students:* 120 full-time (27 women), 31 part-time (8 women); includes 10 minority (all African Americans), 90 international. Average age 26. 238 applicants, 64% accepted, 53 enrolled. In 2009, 26 master's, 2 doctorates awarded. Terminal master's awarded for partial completion of doctoral program. *Degree requirements:* For master's, thesis optional; for doctorate, thesis/dissertation. *Entrance requirements:* For master's and doctorate, GRE General Test. Additional exam requirements/recommendations for international students: Required—TOEFL. *Application deadline:* Applications are processed on a rolling basis. Application fee: $70 ($80 for international students). Electronic applications accepted. *Expenses:* Tuition, state resident: full-time $8684; part-time $528 per credit hour. Tuition, nonresident: full-time $15,330; part-time $1078 per credit hour. Required fees: $736; $37 per semester. Part-time tuition and fees vary according to course load and program. *Financial support:* In 2009–10, 56 students received support, including 7 fellowships with full and partial tuition reimbursements available (averaging $11,238 per year), 32 research assistantships with partial tuition reimbursements available (averaging $17,525 per year), 18 teaching assistantships with partial tuition reimbursements available (averaging $14,968 per year); career-related internships or fieldwork, institutionally sponsored loans, scholarships/grants, health care benefits, and unspecified assistantships also available. Support available to part-time students. Financial award application deadline: 3/1; financial award applicants required to submit FAFSA. *Unit head:* Dr. Larry F. Hodges, Director, 864-656-7552, Fax: 864-656-0145, E-mail: lfh@clemson.edu. *Application contact:* Dr. Mark Smootherman, Director of Graduate Programs, 864-656-5878, Fax: 864-656-0145, E-mail: mark@clemson.edu.

Cleveland State University, College of Graduate Studies, Nance College of Business Administration, Department of Computer and Information Science, Cleveland, OH 44115. Offers computer and information science (MCIS); information systems (DBA). Part-time and evening/weekend programs available. Terminal master's awarded for partial completion of doctoral program. *Degree requirements:* For master's, thesis optional; for doctorate, comprehensive exam, thesis/dissertation. *Entrance requirements:* For master's, GRE or GMAT, minimum GPA of 2.75; for doctorate, GRE or GMAT, MBA, MCIS or equivalent. Additional exam requirements/recommendations for international students: Required—TOEFL (minimum score 525 paper-based; 197 computer-based; 78 iBT). Electronic applications accepted. *Faculty research:* Artificial intelligence, object oriented analysis, database design, software efficiency, distributed system, geographical information systems.

College of Charleston, Graduate School, School of Sciences and Mathematics, Program in Computer and Information Sciences, Charleston, SC 29424-0001. Offers MS. Part-time programs available. *Faculty:* 7 full-time (1 woman). *Students:* 9 full-time (2 women), 10 part-time (1 woman), 3 international. Average age 31. 10 applicants, 70% accepted, 7 enrolled. In 2009, 4 master's awarded. *Entrance requirements:* For master's, GRE. Additional exam requirements/recommendations for international students: Required—TOEFL. *Application deadline:* For fall admission, 7/1 for domestic students; for spring admission, 11/1 for domestic students. Application fee: $45. Electronic applications accepted. *Financial support:* Scholarships/grants and unspecified assistantships available. Financial award applicants required to submit FAFSA. *Unit head:* Dr. Paul Buhler, Director, 843-953-7146. *Application contact:* Susan Hallatt, Director of Graduate Admissions, 843-953-5614, Fax: 843-953-1434, E-mail: hallatts@cofc.edu.

The College of Saint Rose, Graduate Studies, School of Mathematics and Sciences, Program in Computer Information Systems, Albany, NY 12203-1419. Offers MS. Part-time and evening/weekend programs available. *Degree requirements:* For master's, comprehensive exam, research component. *Entrance requirements:* For master's, minimum GPA of 3.0, 9 undergraduate credits in math. Additional exam requirements/recommendations for international students: Required—TOEFL (minimum score 550 paper-based; 213 computer-based). Electronic applications accepted.

College of Staten Island of the City University of New York, Graduate Programs, Program in Computer Science, Staten Island, NY 10314-6600. Offers MS. Part-time and evening/weekend programs available. *Faculty:* 5 full-time (2 women). *Students:* 3 full-time (1 woman), 23 part-time (3 women); includes 3 minority (2 African Americans, 1 Asian American or Pacific Islander), 11 international. Average age 29. 18 applicants, 56% accepted, 6 enrolled. In 2009, 21 master's awarded. *Degree requirements:* For master's, thesis optional. *Entrance requirements:* For master's, GRE General Test, previous undergraduate course work in computer science, minimum GPA of 3.0. Additional exam requirements/recommendations for international students: Required—TOEFL (minimum score 550 paper-based; 213 computer-based; 79 iBT). *Application deadline:* Applications are processed on a rolling basis. Application fee: $125. Electronic applications accepted. *Expenses:* Tuition, state resident: full-time $7360; part-time $310 per credit. Tuition, nonresident: part-time $575 per credit. Required fees: $378; $113 per semester. *Financial support:* Research assistantships, teaching assistantships, career-related internships or fieldwork, Federal Work-Study, and unspecified assistantships available. Support available to part-time students. Financial award applicants required to submit FAFSA. Total annual research expenditures: $23,000. *Unit head:* Dr. Anatoliy Gordonov, Coordinator, 718-982-2852, Fax: 718-982-2856, E-mail: anatoliy.gordonov@csi.cuny.edu. *Application contact:* Sasha Spence, Assistant Director of Graduate Recruitment and Admissions, 718-982-2699, Fax: 718-982-2500, E-mail: sasha.spence@csi.cuny.edu.

The College of William and Mary, Faculty of Arts and Sciences, Department of Computer Science, Williamsburg, VA 23187-8795. Offers computational operations research (MS), including computer science; computer science (MS, PhD), including computational science (PhD). Part-time programs available. *Students:* 63 full-time (13 women), 11 part-time (5 women); includes 4 minority (2 African Americans, 1 Asian American or Pacific Islander, 1 Hispanic American), 33 international. Average age 27. 74 applicants, 74% accepted, 26 enrolled. In 2009, 14 master's, 6 doctorates awarded. *Degree requirements:* For master's, comprehensive exam, thesis optional, research project; for doctorate, comprehensive exam, thesis/dissertation. *Entrance requirements:* For master's, GRE General Test, minimum GPA of 2.5; for doctorate, GRE General Test, minimum GPA of 3.0. Additional exam requirements/recommendations for international students: Required—TOEFL, TWE. *Application deadline:* For fall admission, 3/1 priority date for domestic students, 3/1 for international students; for spring admission, 11/1 for domestic and international students. Applications are processed on a rolling basis. Application fee: $45. Electronic applications accepted. *Expenses:* Tuition, state resident: full-time $6400; part-time $315 per credit hour. Tuition, nonresident: full-time $19,720; part-time $840 per credit hour. Required fees: $4114. *Financial support:* In 2009–10, 2 fellowships with full tuition reimbursements (averaging $21,000 per year), 22 research assistantships with full tuition reimbursements (averaging $21,000 per year), 20 teaching assistantships with full tuition reimbursements (averaging $18,000 per year) were awarded; scholarships/grants and unspecified assistantships also available. Financial award application deadline: 3/1; financial award applicants required to submit FAFSA. *Faculty research:* High-performance computing, wireless computing, algorithms, computer systems and network computing, modeling and simulation. Total annual research expenditures: $897,620. *Unit head:* Dr. Phil Kearns, Chair, 757-221-3459, Fax: 757-221-1717, E-mail: chair@cs.wm.edu. *Application contact:* Vanessa Godwin, Administrative Director, 757-221-3455, Fax: 757-221-1717, E-mail: gradinfo@cs.wm.edu.

Colorado School of Mines, Graduate School, Department of Mathematical and Computer Sciences, Golden, CO 80401. Offers MS, PhD. Part-time programs available. *Faculty:* 33 full-time (15 women), 3 part-time/adjunct (0 women). *Students:* 42 full-time (12 women), 8 part-time (1 woman); includes 7 minority (1 American Indian/Alaska Native, 4 Asian Americans or Pacific Islanders, 2 Hispanic Americans), 8 international. Average age 30. 63 applicants, 60% accepted, 19 enrolled. In 2009, 10 master's, 2 doctorates awarded. *Degree requirements:* For master's, thesis (for some programs); for doctorate, comprehensive exam, thesis/dissertation. *Entrance requirements:* For master's and doctorate, GRE General Test. Additional exam requirements/recommendations for international students: Required—TOEFL (minimum score 550 paper-based; 213 computer-based; 80 iBT). *Application deadline:* For fall admission, 1/15 priority date for domestic and international students; for spring admission, 9/1 priority date for domestic and international students. Application fee: $50 ($70 for international students). Electronic applications accepted. *Expenses:* Tuition, state resident: full-time $10,584; part-time $588 per credit hour. Tuition, nonresident: full-time $24,750; part-time $1375 per credit hour. Required fees: $1654; $827.10 per semester. *Financial support:* In 2009–10, 30 students received support, including 2 fellowships with full tuition reimbursements available (averaging $20,000 per year), 15 research assistantships with full tuition reimbursements available (averaging $20,000 per year), 13 teaching assistantships with full tuition reimbursements available (averaging $20,000 per year); scholarships/grants, health care benefits, and unspecified assistantships also available. Financial award application deadline: 1/15; financial award applicants required to submit FAFSA. *Faculty research:* Applied statistics, numerical computation, artificial intelligence, linear optimization. Total annual research expenditures: $607,892. *Unit head:* Dr. Dinesh Mehta, Department Head, 303-273-3713, Fax: 303-273-3875, E-mail: dmehta@mines.edu. *Application contact:* William Navidi, Professor, 303-273-3489, Fax: 303-273-3875, E-mail: wnavidi@mines.edu.

Colorado State University, Graduate School, College of Natural Sciences, Department of Computer Science, Fort Collins, CO 80523-1873. Offers MCS, MS, PhD. Postbaccalaureate distance learning degree programs offered (no on-campus study). *Faculty:* 19 full-time (3 women), 1 part-time/adjunct (0 women). *Students:* 46 full-time (10 women), 130 part-time (15 women); includes 19 minority (2 African Americans, 1 American Indian/Alaska Native, 7 Asian Americans or Pacific Islanders, 9 Hispanic Americans), 65 international. Average age 32. 218 applicants, 57% accepted, 41 enrolled. In 2009, 42 master's, 3 doctorates awarded. Terminal master's awarded for partial completion of doctoral program. *Degree requirements:* For master's, comprehensive exam (for some programs), thesis (MS); for doctorate, comprehensive exam, thesis/dissertation, qualifying, preliminary, and final exams. *Entrance requirements:* For master's, GRE, computer science background, minimum GPA of 3.0, 3 letters of recommendation; for doctorate, GRE General Test, BSC or master's degree in computer science, minimum GPA of 3.0. Additional exam requirements/recommendations for international students: Required—TOEFL (minimum score 550 paper-based; 213 computer-based; 80 iBT). *Application deadline:* For fall admission, 9/15 priority date for domestic and international students; for spring admission, 1/15 priority date for domestic and international students. Applications are processed on a rolling basis. Application fee: $50. Electronic applications accepted. *Expenses:* Tuition, state resident: full-time $6434; part-time $359.10 per credit. Tuition, nonresident: full-time $18,116; part-time $1006.45 per credit. Required fees: $1496; $83 per credit. *Financial support:* In 2009–10, 57 students received support, including 27 research assistantships with full tuition reimbursements available (averaging $10,138 per year), 30 teaching assistantships with full tuition reimbursements available (averaging $11,012 per year); fellowships, health care benefits

Computer Science

Colorado State University (continued)

also available. Financial award application deadline: 1/15; financial award applicants required to submit FAFSA. *Faculty research:* Artificial intelligence, parallel and distributed computing, software engineering, computer vision/graphics, security. Total annual research expenditures: $2 million. *Unit head:* Dr. L. Darrell Whitley, Chairman, 970-491-5373, Fax: 970-491-2466, E-mail: whitley@cs.colostate.edu. *Application contact:* Carol Calliham, Graduate Coordinator, 970-491-1567, Fax: 970-491-2466, E-mail: gradinfo@cs.colostate.edu.

Colorado Technical University Colorado Springs, Graduate Studies, Program in Computer Science, Colorado Springs, CO 80907-3896. Offers computer science (DCS); computer systems security (MSCS); database systems (MSCS); software engineering (MSCS). Part-time and evening/weekend programs available. Postbaccalaureate distance learning degree programs offered. *Degree requirements:* For master's, thesis or alternative; for doctorate, thesis/dissertation. *Entrance requirements:* For doctorate, minimum graduate GPA of 3.0, 5 years of related work experience. *Faculty research:* Software engineering, systems engineering.

Colorado Technical University Denver, Program in Computer Science, Greenwood Village, CO 80111. Offers computer systems security (MSCS); database systems (MSCS); software engineering (MSCS). Part-time and evening/weekend programs available. *Degree requirements:* For master's, thesis or alternative. *Entrance requirements:* For master's, minimum undergraduate GPA of 3.0, resume.

Colorado Technical University Sioux Falls, Program in Computing, Sioux Falls, SD 57108. Offers computer systems security (MSCS); software engineering (MSCS).

Columbia University, Fu Foundation School of Engineering and Applied Science, Department of Computer Science, New York, NY 10027. Offers MS, Eng Sc D, PhD, Engr. PhD offered through the Graduate School of Arts and Sciences. Part-time programs available. Postbaccalaureate distance learning degree programs offered (no on-campus study). *Faculty:* 28 full-time (3 women), 6 part-time/adjunct (2 women). *Students:* 230 full-time (50 women), 136 part-time (22 women); includes 28 minority (4 African Americans, 21 Asian Americans or Pacific Islanders, 3 Hispanic Americans), 252 international. Average age 27. 849 applicants, 24% accepted, 110 enrolled. In 2009, 150 master's, 18 doctorates awarded. Terminal master's awarded for partial completion of doctoral program. *Degree requirements:* For master's and Engr, thesis optional; for doctorate, comprehensive exam, thesis/dissertation, candidacy exam. *Entrance requirements:* For master's and Engr, GRE General Test; for doctorate, GRE General Test, GRE Subject Test (computer science). Additional exam requirements/recommendations for international students: Required—TOEFL. *Application deadline:* For fall admission, 12/1 priority date for domestic and international students; for spring admission, 10/1 priority date for domestic and international students. Application fee: $70. Electronic applications accepted. *Financial support:* In 2009–10, 161 students received support, including 13 fellowships with full tuition reimbursements available (averaging $26,872 per year), 109 research assistantships with full tuition reimbursements available (averaging $24,372 per year), 39 teaching assistantships with full and partial tuition reimbursements available (averaging $3,000 per year); health care benefits and unspecified assistantships also available. Financial award application deadline: 12/1; financial award applicants required to submit FAFSA. *Faculty research:* Robotics, network security, graphics and user interfaces, computer vision, computational learning theory. *Unit head:* Dr. Shree K. Nayar, Department Chair; T.C. Chang Professor of Computer Science, 212-939-7092, E-mail: nayar@cs.columbia.edu. *Application contact:* Remiko O. Moss, Assistant Director, 212-939-7000, Fax: 212-666-0140, E-mail: ms-admissions@cs.columbia.edu;phd-admissions@cs.columbia.edu.

See Close-Up on page 299.

Columbus State University, Graduate Studies, D. Abbott Turner College of Business and Computer Science, Columbus, GA 31907-5645. Offers applied computer science (MS); business administration (MBA). *Accreditation:* AACSB. *Faculty:* 12 full-time (2 women). *Students:* 43 full-time (11 women), 122 part-time (47 women); includes 39 minority (25 African Americans, 2 American Indian/Alaska Native, 8 Asian Americans or Pacific Islanders, 4 Hispanic Americans), 10 international. Average age 34. 118 applicants, 55% accepted, 48 enrolled. In 2009, 44 master's awarded. *Entrance requirements:* For master's, GMAT, GRE. Additional exam requirements/recommendations for international students: Required—TOEFL (minimum score 550 paper-based; 213 computer-based; 79 iBT). *Application deadline:* For fall admission, 5/1 priority date for domestic students, 5/1 for international students; for spring admission, 11/1 for domestic and international students. Applications are processed on a rolling basis. Application fee: $30. Electronic applications accepted. *Financial support:* In 2009–10, 55 students received support, including 11 research assistantships (averaging $3,000 per year). Financial award application deadline: 5/1. *Unit head:* Dr. Linda U. Hadley, Dean, 706-568-2044, Fax: 706-568-2184, E-mail: hadley_linda@colstate.edu. *Application contact:* Katie Thornton, Graduate Admissions Specialist, 706-568-2035, Fax: 706-568-2462, E-mail: thornton_katie@colstate.edu.

Concordia University, School of Graduate Studies, Faculty of Engineering and Computer Science, Department of Computer Science and Software Engineering, Montréal, QC H3G 1M8, Canada. Offers computer science (M App Comp Sc, M Comp Sc, PhD, Diploma); software engineering (MA Sc). *Degree requirements:* For master's, one foreign language, thesis optional; for doctorate, one foreign language, comprehensive exam, thesis/dissertation. *Faculty research:* Computer systems and applications, mathematics of computation, pattern recognition, artificial intelligence and robotics.

Cornell University, Graduate School, Graduate Fields of Engineering, Field of Computer Science, Ithaca, NY 14853-0001. Offers algorithms (M Eng, PhD); applied logic and automated reasoning (M Eng, PhD); artificial intelligence (M Eng, PhD); computer graphics (M Eng, PhD); computer science (M Eng, PhD); computer vision (M Eng, PhD); concurrency and distributed computing (M Eng, PhD); information organization and retrieval (M Eng, PhD); operating systems (M Eng, PhD); parallel computing (M Eng, PhD); programming environments (M Eng, PhD); programming languages and methodology (M Eng, PhD); robotics (M Eng, PhD); scientific computing (M Eng, PhD); theory of computation (M Eng, PhD). *Faculty:* 74 full-time (10 women). *Students:* 209 full-time (46 women); includes 18 minority (1 African American, 16 Asian Americans or Pacific Islanders, 1 Hispanic American), 119 international. Average age 26. 897 applicants, 26% accepted, 109 enrolled. In 2009, 97 master's, 14 doctorates awarded. *Degree requirements:* For doctorate, comprehensive exam, thesis/dissertation. *Entrance requirements:* For master's, GRE General Test, 2 letters of recommendation; for doctorate, GRE General Test, GRE Subject Test (computer science or mathematics), 3 letters of recommendation. Additional exam requirements/recommendations for international students: Required—TOEFL (minimum score 505 paper-based; 213 computer-based; 77 iBT). *Application deadline:* For fall admission, 1/1 for domestic students. Application fee: $70. Electronic applications accepted. *Expenses:* Tuition: Full-time $29,500. Required fees: $70. Full-time tuition and fees vary according to degree level, program and student level. *Financial support:* In 2009–10, 100 students received support, including 10 fellowships with full tuition reimbursements available, 4 research assistantships with full tuition reimbursements available, 18 teaching assistantships with full tuition reimbursements available; institutionally sponsored loans, scholarships/grants, health care benefits, tuition waivers (full and partial), and unspecified assistantships also available. Financial award applicants required to submit FAFSA. *Faculty research:* Artificial intelligence, operating systems and databases, programming languages and security, scientific computing, theory of computing, computational biology and graphics. *Unit head:* Director of Graduate Studies, 607-255-8593, Fax: 607-255-4428. *Application contact:* Graduate Field Assistant, 607-255-8593, Fax: 607-255-4428, E-mail: phd@cs.cornell.edu.

Dalhousie University, Faculty of Computer Science, Halifax, NS B3H 1W5, Canada. Offers computational biology and bioinformatics (M Sc); computer science (PhD); computer science (project-based) (MA Sc); computer science (thesis-based) (MC Sc); electronic commerce (MEC); health informatics (MHI). *Degree requirements:* For master's, thesis (for some programs); for doctorate, thesis/dissertation. *Entrance requirements:* Additional exam requirements/recommendations for international students: Required—TOEFL, IELTS, 1 of the following 5 approved tests: TOEFL, IELTS, CANTEST, CAEL, Michigan English Language Assessment Battery. Electronic applications accepted.

Dartmouth College, Arts and Sciences Graduate Programs, Department of Computer Science, Hanover, NH 03755. Offers MS, PhD. *Faculty:* 16 full-time (1 woman), 10 part-time/adjunct (2 women). *Students:* 73 full-time (17 women); includes 5 minority (1 African American, 1 American Indian/Alaska Native, 3 Asian Americans or Pacific Islanders), 47 international. Average age 26. 300 applicants, 18% accepted, 33 enrolled. In 2009, 3 master's awarded. Terminal master's awarded for partial completion of doctoral program. *Degree requirements:* For master's, thesis; for doctorate, thesis/dissertation. *Entrance requirements:* For master's and doctorate, GRE General Test, GRE Subject Test. *Application deadline:* For fall admission, 2/1 priority date for domestic students. Application fee: $20. *Financial support:* In 2009–10, 35 students received support, including fellowships with full tuition reimbursements available (averaging $23,832 per year), research assistantships with full tuition reimbursements available (averaging $23,832 per year), teaching assistantships with full tuition reimbursements available (averaging $23,832 per year); career-related internships or fieldwork, institutionally sponsored loans, scholarships/grants, and tuition waivers (full and partial) also available. Support available to part-time students. Financial award application deadline: 2/1. *Faculty research:* Algorithms, computational geometry and learning, computer vision, information retrieval, robotics. *Unit head:* Dr. Thomas H. Cormen, Chair, 603-646-2206. *Application contact:* Joseph Elsener, Department Administrator, 603-646-2206.

DePaul University, College of Computing and Digital Media, Chicago, IL 60604. Offers business information technology (MS); computational finance (MS); computer and information sciences (PhD); computer game development (MS); computer graphics and motion technology (MS); computer science (MS); computer, information and network security (MS), including applied technology; digital cinema (MFA, MS), including information technology project management (MS); e-commerce technology (MS); human-computer interaction (MS); information systems (MS); information technology (MA); information technology project management (MS); software engineering (MS); telecommunications systems (MS); JD/MS. Part-time and evening/weekend programs available. Postbaccalaureate distance learning degree programs offered (no on-campus study). *Faculty:* 78 full-time (16 women), 191 part-time/adjunct (51 women). *Students:* 922 full-time (239 women), 887 part-time (209 women); includes 466 minority (193 African Americans, 3 American Indian/Alaska Native, 162 Asian Americans or Pacific Islanders, 108 Hispanic Americans), 276 international. Average age 31. 853 applicants, 67% accepted, 294 enrolled. In 2009, 444 master's, 4 doctorates awarded. *Degree requirements:* For master's, thesis (for some programs); for doctorate, comprehensive exam, thesis/dissertation. *Entrance requirements:* For master's, GRE or GMAT (MS in computational finance only), bachelor's degree; for doctorate, GRE, master's degree in computer science. Additional exam requirements/recommendations for international students: Required—TOEFL (minimum score 550 paper-based; 213 computer-based), IELTS (minimum score 6.5), Pearson Test of English (minimum score 53). *Application deadline:* For fall admission, 8/15 priority date for domestic students, 6/1 priority date for international students; for winter admission, 12/15 priority date for domestic students, 9/15 priority date for international students; for spring admission, 3/1 priority date for domestic students, 12/15 priority date for international students. Applications are processed on a rolling basis. Application fee: $25. Electronic applications accepted. *Expenses:* Contact institution. *Financial support:* In 2009–10, 69 students received support, including 6 fellowships with full tuition reimbursements available (averaging $25,858 per year), 75 teaching assistantships with full and partial tuition reimbursements available (averaging $5,780 per year); research assistantships, Federal Work-Study, scholarships/grants, tuition waivers (full and partial), and unspecified assistantships also available. Support available to part-time students. Financial award application deadline: 4/30; financial award applicants required to submit FAFSA. *Faculty research:* Bioinformatics, visual computing, graphics and animation, high performance and scientific computing, databases. Total annual research expenditures: $790,000. *Unit head:* Dr. David Miller, Dean, 312-362-8381, Fax: 312-362-5185. *Application contact:* Dr. Liz Friedman, Assistant Dean of Student Services, 312-362-5384, Fax: 312-362-5327, E-mail: efriedm2@cdm.depaul.edu.

DigiPen Institute of Technology, Master of Science in Computer Science Program, Redmond, WA 98052. Offers computer science (MS); computer science—part time program (MS). Part-time programs available. *Faculty:* 14 full-time (1 woman), 2 part-time/adjunct (0 women). *Students:* 28 full-time, 23 part-time; includes 1 African American, 5 Asian Americans or Pacific Islanders, 2 Hispanic Americans, 6 international. Average age 25. 55 applicants, 56% accepted, 21 enrolled. In 2009, 1 master's awarded. *Degree requirements:* For master's, comprehensive exam (for some programs), thesis (for some programs). *Entrance requirements:* For master's, GRE General Test, GRE Subject Test in computer science (for students with non-computer science degrees). Additional exam requirements/recommendations for international students: Required—TOEFL (minimum score 550 paper-based; 213 computer-based; 80 iBT). *Application deadline:* For fall admission, 2/1 priority date for domestic students; for spring admission, 7/1 for domestic students. Applications are processed on a rolling basis. Application fee: $35. Electronic applications accepted. *Expenses:* Tuition: Full-time $15,184; part-time $626 per credit hour. Required fees: $626 per credit hour. $80 per semester. One-time fee: $150. Tuition and fees vary according to course load and program. *Financial support:* In 2009–10, 2 students received support, including 1 fellowship with full and partial tuition reimbursement available (averaging $15,184 per year); career-related internships or fieldwork and scholarships/grants also available. Financial award application deadline: 5/1; financial award applicants required to submit FAFSA. *Faculty research:* Graphics, artificial intelligence, fuzzy sets and systems, animation algorithms, advanced rendering techniques, interpolation algorithms. *Unit head:* Dr. Xin Li, Dean of Faculty, 425-895-4425, E-mail: xli@digipen.edu. *Application contact:* Angela Kugler, Admissions Office, 425-558-0299, Fax: 425-558-0378, E-mail: admissions@digipen.edu.

Drexel University, College of Engineering, Department of Computer Science, Philadelphia, PA 19104-2875. Offers MS, PhD. *Entrance requirements:* For master's, GRE. Additional exam requirements/recommendations for international students: Required—TOEFL. Electronic applications accepted.

Duke University, Graduate School, Department of Computer Science, Durham, NC 27708. Offers MS, PhD. *Faculty:* 37 full-time. *Students:* 73 full-time (10 women); includes 4 minority (1 American Indian/Alaska Native, 2 Asian Americans or Pacific Islanders, 1 Hispanic American), 51 international. 296 applicants, 19% accepted, 17 enrolled. In 2009, 12 master's, 11 doctorates awarded. *Degree requirements:* For doctorate, thesis/dissertation. *Entrance requirements:* For master's, GRE General Test; for doctorate, GRE General Test, GRE Subject Test (recommended). Additional exam requirements/recommendations for international students: Required—TOEFL (minimum score 550 paper-based; 213 computer-based; 83 iBT), IELTS (minimum score 7). *Application deadline:* For fall admission, 12/8 priority date for domestic and international students. Application fee: $75. Electronic applications accepted. *Financial support:* Fellowships, research assistantships, teaching assistantships, Federal Work-Study available. Financial award application deadline: 12/31. *Unit head:* Jun Yang, Director of Graduate Studies, 919-660-6587, Fax: 919-660-6530, E-mail: junyang@cs.duke.edu. *Application contact:* Cynthia Robertson, Associate Dean for Academic Services, 919-684-3913, E-mail: grad-admissions@duke.edu.

East Carolina University, Graduate School, College of Technology and Computer Science, Department of Computer Science, Greenville, NC 27858-4353. Offers MS. Part-time and evening/weekend programs available. *Degree requirements:* For master's, comprehensive exam, thesis or alternative. *Entrance requirements:* For master's, GRE General Test. Additional exam requirements/recommendations for international students: Required—TOEFL. Electronic applications accepted. *Faculty research:* Software development, software engineering, artificial intelligence, bioinformatics, cryptography.

East Carolina University, Graduate School, College of Technology and Computer Science, Department of Technology Systems, Greenville, NC 27858-4353. Offers computer network professional (Certificate); industrial technology (MS), including computer networking management, digital communications, industrial distribution and logistics, information security, manufacturing, performance improvement, planning; information assurance (Certificate); occupational safety (MS); technology management (PhD); Website developer (Certificate). *Entrance requirements:* For master's and Certificate, GRE General Test or MAT, minimum GPA of 2.5; for doctorate, GRE General Test, related work experience.

Eastern Illinois University, Graduate School, College of Sciences, Department of Mathematics and Computer Science, Charleston, IL 61920-3099. Offers mathematics (MA); mathematics education (MA). *Faculty:* 30 full-time (6 women). In 2009, 9 master's awarded. *Entrance requirements:* For master's, GRE General Test. *Application deadline:* For fall admission, 3/31 priority date for domestic students. Applications are processed on a rolling basis. Application fee: $30. *Expenses:* Tuition, state resident: full-time $9434; part-time $239 per credit hour. Tuition, nonresident: full-time $23,774; part-time $717 per credit hour. Required fees: $802.63. *Financial support:* In 2009–10, research assistantships with tuition reimbursements (averaging $8,100 per year), 8 teaching assistantships with tuition reimbursements (averaging $8,100 per year) were awarded. *Unit head:* Dr. Peter Andrews, Chair, 217-581-6275, Fax: 217-581-6284, E-mail: pgandrews@eiu.edu. *Application contact:* Dr. Keith Wolcott, Coordinator, 217-581-6279, Fax: 217-581-6284, E-mail: kwolcott@eiu.edu.

Eastern Illinois University, Graduate School, Lumpkin College of Business and Applied Sciences, School of Technology, Charleston, IL 61920-3099. Offers computer technology (Certificate); quality systems (Certificate); technology (MS); technology security (Certificate); work performance improvement (Certificate). Part-time and evening/weekend programs available. *Faculty:* 14 full-time (2 women). In 2009, 39 master's, 14 other advanced degrees awarded. *Application deadline:* For fall admission, 3/31 priority date for domestic students. Applications are processed on a rolling basis. Application fee: $30. *Expenses:* Tuition, state resident: full-time $9434; part-time $239 per credit hour. Tuition, nonresident: full-time $23,774; part-time $717 per credit hour. Required fees: $802.63. *Financial support:* In 2009–10, 3 research assistantships with tuition reimbursements (averaging $8,100 per year), 3 teaching assistantships with tuition reimbursements (averaging $8,100 per year) were awarded. *Unit head:* Dr. Mahyar Izadi, Chairperson, 217-581-6269, Fax: 217-581-6607, E-mail: mizadi@eiu.edu. *Application contact:* Dr. Peter Ping Liu, Coordinator, 217-581-6267, Fax: 217-581-6607, E-mail: pliu@eiu.edu.

Eastern Michigan University, Graduate School, College of Arts and Sciences, Department of Computer Science, Ypsilanti, MI 48197. Offers artificial intelligence (Graduate Certificate); computer science (MS). Part-time and evening/weekend programs available. Postbaccalaureate distance learning degree programs offered (no on-campus study). *Faculty:* 15 full-time (5 women). *Students:* 16 full-time (6 women), 21 part-time (5 women); includes 6 minority (1 African American, 1 American Indian/Alaska Native, 4 Asian Americans or Pacific Islanders), 20 international. Average age 29. 88 applicants, 57% accepted, 10 enrolled. In 2009, 12 master's, 2 other advanced degrees awarded. *Degree requirements:* For master's, thesis or alternative. *Entrance requirements:* For master's, at least 18 credit hours of 200-level (or above) computer science courses including data structures, programming languages like java, C or C++, computer organization; courses in discrete mathematics, probability and statistics, linear algebra and calculus; minimum GPA of 2.75 in computer science. Additional exam requirements/recommendations for international students: Required—TOEFL. *Application deadline:* For fall admission, 8/1 for domestic students, 5/1 for international students; for winter admission, 12/1 for domestic students, 10/1 for international students; for spring admission, 4/1 for domestic students, 2/1 for international students. Application fee: $35. Tuition and fees vary according to course level. *Financial support:* Fellowships, research assistantships with full tuition reimbursements, teaching assistantships with full tuition reimbursements, career-related internships or fieldwork, Federal Work-Study, institutionally sponsored loans, scholarships/grants, tuition waivers (partial), and unspecified assistantships available. Support available to part-time students. Financial award applicants required to submit FAFSA. *Unit head:* Dr. William McMillan, Department Head, 734-487-1063, Fax: 734-487-6824, E-mail: wmcmillan@emich.edu. *Application contact:* Graduate Admissions, 734-487-3060, Fax: 734-487-6559, E-mail: graduate_admissions@emich.edu.

Eastern Michigan University, Graduate School, College of Arts and Sciences, Department of Mathematics, Ypsilanti, MI 48197. Offers applied statistics (MA); computer science (MA); mathematics (MA); mathematics education (MA). Part-time and evening/weekend programs available. Postbaccalaureate distance learning degree programs offered (minimal on-campus study). *Faculty:* 25 full-time (10 women). *Students:* 11 full-time (7 women), 39 part-time (17 women); includes 2 minority (1 African American, 1 Asian American or Pacific Islander), 11 international. Average age 35. 28 applicants, 75% accepted, 14 enrolled. In 2009, 15 master's awarded. *Degree requirements:* For master's, thesis optional. *Entrance requirements:* Additional exam requirements/recommendations for international students: Required—TOEFL. *Application deadline:* Applications are processed on a rolling basis. Application fee: $35. Tuition and fees vary according to course level. *Financial support:* Fellowships, research assistantships with full tuition reimbursements, teaching assistantships with full tuition reimbursements, career-related internships or fieldwork, Federal Work-Study, institutionally sponsored loans, scholarships/grants, tuition waivers (partial), and unspecified assistantships available. Support available to part-time students. Financial award applicants required to submit FAFSA. *Unit head:* Dr. Christopher Gardiner, Interim Department Head, 734-487-1444, Fax: 734-487-2489, E-mail: cgardiner@emich.edu. *Application contact:* Dr. Bingwu Wang, Graduate Coordinator, 734-487-5044, Fax: 734-487-2489, E-mail: bwang@emich.edu.

Eastern Washington University, Graduate Studies, College of Science, Health and Engineering, Department of Computer Science, Cheney, WA 99004-2431. Offers computer and technology-supported education (M Ed); computer science (MS). *Accreditation:* NCATE. Part-time programs available. *Degree requirements:* For master's, comprehensive exam, thesis or alternative. *Entrance requirements:* For master's, minimum GPA of 3.0. *Expenses:* Tuition, state resident: full-time $7476; part-time $249 per quarter hour. Tuition, nonresident: full-time $18,030; part-time $601 per quarter hour. Required fees: $3.50 per quarter hour. $142 per quarter.

East Stroudsburg University of Pennsylvania, Graduate School, College of Arts and Sciences, Department of Computer Science, East Stroudsburg, PA 18301-2999. Offers MS. Part-time and evening/weekend programs available. *Faculty:* 6 full-time (2 women). *Students:* 9 full-time (2 women), 6 part-time (1 woman); includes 1 minority (African American), 2 international. Average age 30. In 2009, 3 master's awarded. *Degree requirements:* For master's, comprehensive exam, thesis or alternative. *Entrance requirements:* For master's, bachelor's degree in computer science or related field. Additional exam requirements/recommendations for international students: Required—TOEFL (minimum score 560 paper-based; 220 computer-based; 83 iBT). *Application deadline:* For fall admission, 7/31 priority date for domestic students, 5/1 priority date for international students; for spring admission, 11/30 for domestic students, 10/1 for international students. Applications are processed on a rolling basis. Application fee: $50. *Financial support:* In 2009–10, 17 research assistantships with full and partial tuition reimbursements (averaging $2,502 per year) were awarded; career-related internships or fieldwork, Federal Work-Study, and institutionally sponsored loans also available. Financial award application deadline: 3/1; financial award applicants required to submit FAFSA. *Unit head:* Dr. Robert Marmelstein, Graduate Coordinator, 570-422-3666, Fax: 570-422-3490, E-mail: rmarmelstein@po-box.esu.edu. *Application contact:* Kevin Quintero, Graduate Admissions Coordinator, 570-422-3890, Fax: 570-422-3711, E-mail: kquintero@po-box.esu.edu.

East Tennessee State University, School of Graduate Studies, College of Business and Technology, Department of Computer and Information Sciences, Johnson City, TN 37614. Offers computer science (MS); information systems science (MS); software engineering (MS). Part-time and evening/weekend programs available. *Degree requirements:* For master's, comprehensive exam, thesis. *Entrance requirements:* For master's, GRE General Test, minimum GPA of 2.5. Additional exam requirements/recommendations for international students: Required—TOEFL (minimum score 550 paper-based; 213 computer-based). *Faculty research:* Operating systems, database design, artificial intelligence, simulation, parallel algorithms.

École Polytechnique de Montréal, Graduate Programs, Department of Electrical and Computer Engineering, Montréal, QC H3C 3A7, Canada. Offers automation (M Eng, M Sc A, PhD); computer science (M Eng, M Sc A, PhD); electrical engineering (DESS); electrotechnology (M Eng, M Sc A, PhD); microelectronics (M Eng, M Sc A, PhD); microwave technology (M Eng, M Sc A, PhD). Part-time and evening/weekend programs available. *Degree requirements:* For master's, one foreign language, thesis; for doctorate, one foreign language, thesis/dissertation. *Entrance requirements:* For master's, minimum GPA of 2.75; for doctorate, minimum GPA of 3.0. *Faculty research:* Microwaves, telecommunications, software engineering.

Elmhurst College, Graduate Programs, Program in Computer Network Systems, Elmhurst, IL 60126-3296. Offers MS. Part-time and evening/weekend programs available. Postbaccalaureate distance learning degree programs offered (minimal on-campus study). *Faculty:* 2 full-time (1 woman), 1 part-time/adjunct (0 women). *Students:* 19 part-time (5 women); includes 8 minority (3 African Americans, 1 Asian American or Pacific Islander, 4 Hispanic Americans). Average age 33. 18 applicants, 67% accepted, 10 enrolled. In 2009, 7 master's awarded. *Entrance requirements:* For master's, 3 recommendations. Additional exam requirements/recommendations for international students: Required—TOEFL (minimum score 550 paper-based; 213 computer-based). *Application deadline:* Applications are processed on a rolling basis. Application fee: $25. Electronic applications accepted. *Expenses:* Tuition: Part-time $700 per credit hour. Required fees: $60 per semester. Tuition and fees vary according to program. *Financial support:* In 2009–10, 1 student received support. Federal Work-Study and scholarships/grants available. Support available to part-time students. Financial award application deadline: 6/1; financial award applicants required to submit FAFSA. *Unit head:* Dr. Ted Lerud, Associate Dean of the Faculty, 630-617-3661, Fax: 630-617-6415, E-mail: gradadm@elmhurst.edu. *Application contact:* Elizabeth D. Kuebler, Director of Adult and Graduate Admission, 630-617-3069, Fax: 630-617-5501, E-mail: betsyk@elmhurst.edu.

Emory University, Graduate School of Arts and Sciences, Department of Mathematics and Computer Science, Atlanta, GA 30322-1100. Offers computer science (MS); mathematics (PhD). Terminal master's awarded for partial completion of doctoral program. *Degree requirements:* For master's, thesis; for doctorate, one foreign language, comprehensive exam, thesis/dissertation. *Entrance requirements:* For master's and doctorate, GRE General Test. Electronic applications accepted.

Fairleigh Dickinson University, Metropolitan Campus, University College: Arts, Sciences, and Professional Studies, School of Computer Sciences and Engineering, Program in Computer Science, Teaneck, NJ 07666-1914. Offers MS. *Students:* 62 full-time (28 women), 19 part-time (5 women), 66 international. Average age 25. 211 applicants, 61% accepted, 21 enrolled. In 2009, 54 master's awarded. *Application deadline:* Applications are processed on a rolling basis. Application fee: $40. *Application contact:* Susan Brooman, University Director of Graduate Admissions, 201-692-2554, Fax: 201-692-2560, E-mail: globaleducation@fdu.edu.

Ferris State University, College of Business, Big Rapids, MI 49307. Offers application development (MSISM); business intelligence and infomatics (MBA); database administration (MSISM); design and innovation management process (MBA); e-business (MSISM); networking (MSISM); quality management (MBA); security (MSISM). *Accreditation:* ACBSP. Part-time and evening/weekend programs available. *Faculty:* 10 full-time (3 women), 2 part-time/adjunct (both women). *Students:* 33 full-time (6 women), 134 part-time (65 women); includes 13 minority (8 African Americans, 2 American Indian/Alaska Native, 2 Asian Americans or Pacific Islanders, 1 Hispanic American), 33 international. Average age 30. 120 applicants, 31% accepted, 26 enrolled. In 2009, 66 master's awarded. *Entrance requirements:* For master's, GRE or GMAT (waived if GPA is 3.5 or better), minimum GPA of 3.0 in CIS and business core, 2.75 overall; writing sample; 3 letters of reference; resume. Additional exam requirements/recommendations for international students: Required—TOEFL (minimum score 500 paper-based; 173 computer-based; 64 iBT). *Application deadline:* For fall admission, 7/1 priority date for domestic students, 6/15 for international students; for winter admission, 11/1 priority date for domestic students, 10/15 for international students; for spring admission, 3/1 priority date for domestic students, 2/15 for international students. Applications are processed on a rolling basis. Application fee: $30 for international students. Electronic applications accepted. *Financial support:* In 2009–10, 14 teaching assistantships were awarded; career-related internships or fieldwork, Federal Work-Study, and unspecified assistantships also available. Support available to part-time students. Financial award applicants required to submit FAFSA. *Faculty research:* Quality improvement, client/server end-user computing, information management and policy, security, digital forensics. *Unit head:* Dr. David Steenstra, Department Chair, 231-591-2168, Fax: 231-591-2973, E-mail: yosts@ferris.edu. *Application contact:* Shannon Yost, Department Secretary, 231-591-2168, Fax: 231-591-2973, E-mail: yosts@ferris.edu.

Fitchburg State University, Division of Graduate and Continuing Education, Program in Computer Science, Fitchburg, MA 01420-2697. Offers MS. Part-time and evening/weekend programs available. *Students:* 43 full-time (16 women), 17 part-time (5 women); includes 3 minority (2 African Americans, 1 Asian American or Pacific Islander), 50 international. Average age 26. 31 applicants, 100% accepted, 23 enrolled. In 2009, 53 master's awarded. *Entrance requirements:* For master's, GRE General Test, appropriate bachelor's degree, letters of recommendation, resume. Additional exam requirements/recommendations for international students: Required—TOEFL (minimum score 550 paper-based; 213 computer-based; 79 iBT). *Application deadline:* Applications are processed on a rolling basis. Application fee: $25 ($50 for international students). *Expenses:* Tuition, area resident: Part-time $150 per credit. Tuition, state resident: part-time $150 per credit. Tuition, nonresident: part-time $150 per credit. Required fees: $120 per credit. *Financial support:* In 2009–10, research assistantships with partial tuition reimbursements (averaging $5,500 per year); Federal Work-Study, scholarships/grants, and unspecified assistantships also available. Support available to part-time students. Financial award application deadline: 3/1; financial award applicants required to submit FAFSA. *Unit head:* Dr. Nadimpalli Mahadev, Chair, 978-665-3270, Fax: 978-665-3658, E-mail: gce@fsc.edu. *Application contact:* Director of Admissions, 978-665-3144, Fax: 978-665-4540, E-mail: admissions@fsc.edu.

Florida Atlantic University, College of Engineering and Computer Science, Department of Computer Science and Engineering, Program in Computer Science, Boca Raton, FL 33431-0991. Offers MS, PhD. Part-time and evening/weekend programs available. *Students:* 37 full-time (9 women), 52 part-time (14 women); includes 30 minority (7 African Americans, 6 Asian Americans or Pacific Islanders, 17 Hispanic Americans), 26 international. Average age 33. 77 applicants, 56% accepted, 22 enrolled. In 2009, 35 master's, 3 doctorates awarded. *Degree requirements:* For master's, thesis optional; for doctorate, thesis/dissertation, qualifying exam. *Entrance requirements:* For master's, GRE General Test, minimum GPA of 3.0 in last 60 hours of undergraduate course work; for doctorate, minimum GPA of 3.5, master's degree. Additional exam requirements/recommendations for international students: Required—TOEFL. *Application deadline:* For fall admission, 7/1 priority date for domestic students, 2/15 for international students; for spring admission, 11/1 for domestic students, 7/15 for international students. Applications are processed on a rolling basis. Application fee: $30. *Expenses:* Tuition, state resident: full-time $7055; part-time $293.94 per credit hour. Tuition, nonresident: full-time $22,096; part-time $920.66 per credit hour. *Financial support:* Fellowships, research assistantships with partial tuition reimbursements, teaching assistantships with full tuition reimbursements, career-related internships or fieldwork, Federal Work-Study, and unspecified assistantships available. Support available to part-time students. Financial award application deadline: 4/1; financial award applicants required to submit FAFSA. *Faculty research:* Software engineering, artificial intelligence, performance evaluation, queuing theory, multimedia systems. *Unit head:* Dr. Borko Furht, Chairman, 561-297-3855, Fax: 561-297-2800. *Application contact:* Dr. Borko Furht, Chairman, 561-297-3855, Fax: 561-297-2800.

Florida Gulf Coast University, Lutgert College of Business, Program in Computer and Information Systems, Fort Myers, FL 33965-6565. Offers MS. *Entrance requirements:* For

Computer Science

Florida Gulf Coast University (continued)

master's, GMAT, minimum GPA of 3.0. Additional exam requirements/recommendations for international students: Required—TOEFL (minimum score 550 paper-based; 213 computer-based). Electronic applications accepted. *Faculty research:* Advanced distributed learning technologies, object-oriented systems analysis, database management systems, workgroup support systems, software engineering project management.

Florida Institute of Technology, Graduate Programs, College of Engineering, Computer Science Department, Melbourne, FL 32901-6975. Offers computer science (MS, PhD); software engineering (MS). Part-time and evening/weekend programs available. *Faculty:* 12 full-time (0 women). *Students:* 62 full-time (8 women), 70 part-time (12 women); includes 14 minority (7 African Americans, 3 Asian Americans or Pacific Islanders, 4 Hispanic Americans), 63 international. Average age 29. 218 applicants, 58% accepted, 31 enrolled. In 2009, 46 master's, 1 doctorate awarded. *Degree requirements:* For master's, comprehensive exam (for some programs), thesis (for some programs); for doctorate, comprehensive exam, thesis/dissertation, publication in journal, teaching experience (strongly encouraged), specialized research program. *Entrance requirements:* For master's, GRE General Test, minimum GPA of 3.0, 3 letters of recommendation; for doctorate, GRE General Test, GRE Subject Test in computer science (recommended), 3 letters of recommendation, minimum GPA of 3.5, resume, statement of objectives. Additional exam requirements/recommendations for international students: Required—TOEFL (minimum score 550 paper-based; 213 computer-based; 79 iBT). *Application deadline:* For fall admission, 4/1 for international students; for spring admission, 9/30 for international students. Applications are processed on a rolling basis. Application fee: $50. Electronic applications accepted. *Expenses:* Tuition: Part-time $1015 per credit. Tuition and fees vary according to campus/location and program. *Financial support:* In 2009–10, 22 students received support, including 8 research assistantships with full and partial tuition reimbursements available (averaging $5,001 per year), 14 teaching assistantships with full and partial tuition reimbursements available (averaging $9,917 per year); career-related internships or fieldwork, institutionally sponsored loans, tuition waivers (partial), unspecified assistantships, and tuition remissions also available. Support available to part-time students. Financial award application deadline: 3/1; financial award applicants required to submit FAFSA. *Faculty research:* Artificial intelligence, software engineering, management and processes, programming languages, database systems. Total annual research expenditures: $1.2 million. *Unit head:* Dr. William D. Shoaff, Department Head, 321-674-8066, Fax: 321-674-7046, E-mail: wds@cs.fit.edu. *Application contact:* Thomas M. Shea, Director of Graduate Admissions, 321-674-7577, Fax: 321-723-9468, E-mail: tshea@fit.edu.

See Close-Up on page 303.

Florida International University, College of Engineering and Computing, School of Computing and Information Sciences, Miami, FL 33199. Offers computer science (MS, PhD); computing and information sciences (MS, PhD); telecommunications and networking (MS). Part-time and evening/weekend programs available. *Faculty:* 30 full-time (3 women). *Students:* 76 full-time (24 women), 37 part-time (7 women); includes 39 minority (3 African Americans, 6 Asian Americans or Pacific Islanders, 30 Hispanic Americans), 63 international. Average age 30. 180 applicants, 14% accepted, 26 enrolled. In 2009, 29 master's, 5 doctorates awarded. *Degree requirements:* For master's, thesis or alternative; for doctorate, comprehensive exam, thesis/dissertation. *Entrance requirements:* For master's and doctorate, GRE General Test, 3 letters of recommendation, minimum GPA of 3.0. Additional exam requirements/recommendations for international students: Required—TOEFL (minimum score 550 paper-based; 80 iBT). *Application deadline:* For fall admission, 6/1 for domestic students, 4/1 for international students; for spring admission, 10/1 for domestic students, 9/1 for international students. Applications are processed on a rolling basis. Application fee: $30. Electronic applications accepted. *Expenses:* Tuition, state resident: full-time $8008; part-time $4004 per year. Tuition, nonresident: full-time $20,104; part-time $10,052 per year. Required fees: $298; $149 per term. *Financial support:* In 2009–10, 34 research assistantships (averaging $20,474 per year), 24 teaching assistantships (averaging $20,474 per year) were awarded; institutionally sponsored loans, scholarships/grants, and unspecified assistantships also available. Financial award application deadline: 3/1; financial award applicants required to submit FAFSA. *Faculty research:* Database systems, software engineering, operating systems, networks, bioinformatics and computational biology. Total annual research expenditures: $2.5 million. *Unit head:* Dr. Jainendra Navlakha, Interim Director, School of Computing and Information Sciences, 305-348-2023, Fax: 305-348-3549, E-mail: navlakha@cis.fiu.edu. *Application contact:* Maria Parrilla, Graduate Admissions Assistant, 305-348-1890, Fax: 305-348-6142, E-mail: grad_eng@fiu.edu.

Florida State University, The Graduate School, College of Arts and Sciences, Department of Computer Science, Tallahassee, FL 32306. Offers computer science (MS, PhD); information security (MS); software engineering (MS). Part-time programs available. *Faculty:* 17 full-time (1 woman), 2 part-time/adjunct (0 women). *Students:* 114 full-time (22 women), 16 part-time (3 women); includes 20 minority (4 African Americans, 1 American Indian/Alaska Native, 5 Asian Americans or Pacific Islanders, 10 Hispanic Americans), 66 international. Average age 28. 167 applicants, 72% accepted, 34 enrolled. In 2009, 29 master's, 2 doctorates awarded. Terminal master's awarded for partial completion of doctoral program. *Degree requirements:* For master's, thesis or alternative; for doctorate, comprehensive exam, thesis/dissertation. *Entrance requirements:* For master's, GRE General Test, minimum undergraduate GPA of 3.0; for doctorate, GRE General Test, minimum GPA of 3.5. Additional exam requirements/recommendations for international students: Required—TOEFL (minimum score 600 paper-based; 250 computer-based; 100 iBT). *Application deadline:* For fall admission, 3/1 priority date for domestic students, 3/1 for international students; for spring admission, 10/1 priority date for domestic students, 10/1 for international students. Application fee: $30. Electronic applications accepted. *Expenses:* Tuition, state resident: full-time $7413.36. Tuition, nonresident: full-time $22,567. *Financial support:* In 2009–10, 107 students received support, including 4 fellowships with full tuition reimbursements available (averaging $17,500 per year), 35 research assistantships with full tuition reimbursements available (averaging $17,000 per year), 62 teaching assistantships with full tuition reimbursements available (averaging $15,500 per year); career-related internships or fieldwork, scholarships/grants, health care benefits, and unspecified assistantships also available. Financial award application deadline: 3/1; financial award applicants required to submit FAFSA. *Faculty research:* Embedded systems, high performance computing, networking, operating systems, security. Total annual research expenditures: $1.4 million. *Unit head:* Dr. David Whalley, Chairman, 850-644-3506, Fax: 850-644-0058, E-mail: chair@cs.fsu.edu. *Application contact:* Matthew S. Claypool, Graduate Coordinator, 850-645-4975, Fax: 850-644-0058, E-mail: claypool@cs.fsu.edu.

Fordham University, Graduate School of Arts and Sciences, Department of Computer and Information Sciences, New York, NY 10458. Offers computer science (MS). Part-time and evening/weekend programs available. *Faculty:* 11 full-time (1 woman). *Students:* 5 full-time (2 women), 21 part-time (3 women); includes 5 minority (1 African American, 2 Asian Americans or Pacific Islanders, 2 Hispanic Americans), 10 international. Average age 32. 27 applicants, 70% accepted, 9 enrolled. In 2009, 13 master's awarded. *Degree requirements:* For master's, thesis optional. *Entrance requirements:* For master's, GRE General Test. Additional exam requirements/recommendations for international students: Required—TOEFL (minimum score 550 paper-based; 213 computer-based). *Application deadline:* For fall admission, 1/4 priority date for domestic students; for spring admission, 11/1 for domestic students. Application fee: $70. Electronic applications accepted. *Financial support:* In 2009–10, 5 students received support, including 1 fellowship with tuition reimbursement available (averaging $21,800 per year), 4 research assistantships with tuition reimbursements available (averaging $18,400 per year); career-related internships or fieldwork, institutionally sponsored loans, tuition waivers (full and partial), and unspecified assistantships also available. Financial award application deadline: 1/4; financial award applicants required to submit CSS PROFILE or FAFSA. *Faculty research:* Robotics and computer vision, data mining and informatics, information and networking, computation and algorithms, biomedical informatics. Total annual research expenditures: $50,000. *Unit head:* Dr. Damian Lyons, Chair, 718-817-4480, Fax: 718-817-4488. *Application contact:* Charlene Dundie, Director of Graduate Admissions, 718-817-4420, Fax: 718-817-3566, E-mail: dundie@fordham.edu.

Franklin University, Computer Science Program, Columbus, OH 43215-5399. Offers MS. Part-time and evening/weekend programs available. *Faculty:* 5 full-time (0 women), 8 part-time/adjunct (0 women). *Students:* 20 full-time (5 women), 27 part-time (8 women); includes 7 minority (2 African Americans, 5 Asian Americans or Pacific Islanders), 17 international. Average age 35. 7 applicants. In 2009, 32 master's awarded. *Degree requirements:* For master's, thesis or alternative. *Entrance requirements:* For master's, minimum undergraduate GPA of 2.75. Additional exam requirements/recommendations for international students: Required—TOEFL (minimum score 550 paper-based; 213 computer-based). *Application deadline:* For fall admission, 8/1 priority date for domestic students; for winter admission, 12/15 priority date for domestic students; for spring admission, 3/15 priority date for domestic students. Applications are processed on a rolling basis. Application fee: $30. Electronic applications accepted. *Expenses:* Contact institution. *Financial support:* Application deadline: 6/15; *Unit head:* Dr. Ron Hartung, Program Chair, 614-947-6139, Fax: 614-224-4025, E-mail: hartung@franklin.edu. *Application contact:* 614-797-4700, Fax: 614-221-7723, E-mail: gradschl@franklin.edu.

Frostburg State University, Graduate School, College of Liberal Arts and Sciences, Department of Computer Science, Program in Applied Computer Science, Frostburg, MD 21532-1099. Offers MS. *Faculty:* 5 full-time (1 woman), 1 (woman) part-time/adjunct. *Students:* 7 full-time (0 women), 1 international. Average age 24. 13 applicants, 62% accepted, 4 enrolled. In 2009, 4 master's awarded. *Entrance requirements:* Additional exam requirements/recommendations for international students: Required—TOEFL. *Application deadline:* Applications are processed on a rolling basis. Application fee: $30. Electronic applications accepted. *Expenses:* Tuition, state resident: full-time $5706; part-time $317 per credit hour. Tuition, nonresident: full-time $6948; part-time $386 per credit hour. Required fees: $1476; $82 per credit hour. $11 per term. One-time fee: $30 full-time. *Financial support:* In 2009–10, 5 research assistantships with full tuition reimbursements (averaging $5,000 per year) were awarded. Financial award application deadline: 3/1. *Unit head:* Dr. Mohsen Chitsaz, Program Coordinator, 301-687-4787, E-mail: mchitsaz@frostburg.edu. *Application contact:* Vickie Mazer, Director, Graduate Services, 301-687-7053, Fax: 301-687-4597, E-mail: vmmazer@frostburg.edu.

Gannon University, School of Graduate Studies, College of Engineering and Business, School of Engineering and Computer Science, Program in Computer and Information Science, Erie, PA 16541-0001. Offers MSCIS. Part-time and evening/weekend programs available. *Students:* 25 full-time (4 women), 18 part-time (8 women), 30 international. Average age 28. 282 applicants, 71% accepted, 18 enrolled. In 2009, 20 master's awarded. *Degree requirements:* For master's, research project or thesis. *Entrance requirements:* Additional exam requirements/recommendations for international students: Required—TOEFL (minimum score 79 iBT). *Application deadline:* Applications are processed on a rolling basis. Application fee: $25. Electronic applications accepted. *Expenses:* Tuition: Full-time $13,590; part-time $755 per credit. Required fees: $524; $17 per credit. Tuition and fees vary according to course load, degree level, campus/location and program. *Financial support:* Career-related internships or fieldwork, Federal Work-Study, scholarships/grants, traineeships, and unspecified assistantships available. Financial award application deadline: 7/1; financial award applicants required to submit FAFSA. *Unit head:* Dr. Steven Frezza, Chair, 814-871-7563, E-mail: frezza001@gannon.edu. *Application contact:* Kara Morgan, Assistant Director of Graduate Admissions, 814-871-5831, Fax: 814-871-5827, E-mail: graduate@gannon.edu.

George Mason University, Volgenau School of Information Technology and Engineering, Department of Computer Science, Fairfax, VA 22030. Offers biometrics (Certificate); computer games technology (Certificate); computer networking (Certificate); computer science (MS, PhD); data mining (Certificate); database management (Certificate); electronic commerce (Certificate); foundations of information systems (Certificate); information engineering (Certificate); information security and assurance (MS, Certificate); information systems (MS); intelligent agents (Certificate); software architecture (Certificate); software engineering (MS, Certificate); systems engineering (MS); Web-based software engineering (Certificate). Part-time and evening/weekend programs available. Postbaccalaureate distance learning degree programs offered. *Faculty:* 42 full-time (9 women), 18 part-time/adjunct (0 women). *Students:* 121 full-time (36 women), 489 part-time (118 women); includes 90 minority (11 African Americans, 70 Asian Americans or Pacific Islanders, 9 Hispanic Americans), 222 international. Average age 29. 882 applicants, 58% accepted, 147 enrolled. In 2009, 202 master's, 6 doctorates, 21 other advanced degrees awarded. *Degree requirements:* For master's, thesis optional; for doctorate, comprehensive exam, thesis/dissertation. *Entrance requirements:* For master's, GRE General Test, minimum GPA of 3.0 in last 60 hours, 3 letters of recommendation; for doctorate, GRE, 4-year BA degree, academic work in computer science, 3 letters of recommendation, statement of career goals and aspirations. Additional exam requirements/recommendations for international students: Required—TOEFL. *Application deadline:* For fall admission, 4/15 priority date for domestic students, 1/15 for international students; for spring admission, 11/15 for domestic students. Application fee: $75. Electronic applications accepted. *Expenses:* Tuition, state resident: full-time $7568; part-time $315.33 per credit hour. Tuition, nonresident: full-time $21,704; part-time $904.33 per credit hour. Required fees: $2184; $91 per credit hour. *Financial support:* In 2009–10, 106 students received support, including 3 fellowships (averaging $18,000 per year), 53 research assistantships (averaging $11,119 per year), 53 teaching assistantships (averaging $7,881 per year); unspecified assistantships and health care benefits (full-time research or teaching assistantship recipients) also available. Financial award application deadline: 3/1; financial award applicants required to submit FAFSA. *Faculty research:* Artificial intelligence, image processing/graphics, parallel/distributed systems, software engineering systems. Total annual research expenditures: $1.3 million. *Unit head:* Dr. Arun Sood, Director, 703-993-1524, Fax: 703-993-1710, E-mail: asood@gmu.edu. *Application contact:* Jay Shapiro, Professor, 703-993-1485, E-mail: jshapiro@gmu.edu.

Georgetown University, Graduate School of Arts and Sciences, Department of Computer Science, Washington, DC 20057. Offers MS. Part-time and evening/weekend programs available. *Degree requirements:* For master's, thesis optional. *Entrance requirements:* For master's, GRE, basic course work in data structures, advanced math, and programming; 3 letters of recommendation. Additional exam requirements/recommendations for international students: Required—TOEFL. Electronic applications accepted. *Faculty research:* Data mining, artificial intelligence, software engineering, security.

The George Washington University, School of Engineering and Applied Science, Department of Computer Science, Washington, DC 20052. Offers MS, D Sc. Part-time and evening/weekend programs available. *Faculty:* 15 full-time (3 women), 28 part-time/adjunct (4 women). *Students:* 117 full-time (34 women), 179 part-time (36 women); includes 60 minority (20 African Americans, 4 American Indian/Alaska Native, 33 Asian Americans or Pacific Islanders, 3 Hispanic Americans), 125 international. Average age 30. 331 applicants, 79% accepted, 79 enrolled. In 2009, 91 master's, 18 doctorates awarded. *Degree requirements:* For master's, thesis optional; for doctorate, thesis/dissertation, dissertation defense, qualifying exam. *Entrance requirements:* For master's, appropriate bachelor's degree, minimum GPA of 3.0; for doctorate, appropriate bachelor's or master's degree, minimum GPA of 3.3, GRE if highest earned degree is BS. Additional exam requirements/recommendations for international students: Required—TOEFL or George Washington University English as a Foreign Language Test. *Application deadline:* For fall admission, 3/1 priority date for domestic students; for spring admission, 10/1 for domestic students. Applications are processed on a rolling basis. Application fee: $60. *Financial support:* In 2009–10, 49 students received support; fellowships with tuition reimbursements available, research assistantships, teaching assistantships with tuition reimbursements available, career-related internships or fieldwork, institutionally sponsored loans, and tuition waivers available. Financial award application deadline: 3/1; financial award applicants required to submit FAFSA. *Faculty research:* Computer graphics, multimedia, VLSI, parallel processing. *Unit head:* Abdou Youssef, Chair, 202-994-7181, E-mail: ayoussef@

gwu.edu. *Application contact:* Adina Lav, Marketing, Recruiting and Admissions, 202-994-5827, Fax: 202-994-0909, E-mail: engineering@gwu.edu.

Georgia Institute of Technology, Graduate Studies and Research, College of Computing, Atlanta, GA 30332-0001. Offers algorithms, combinatorics, and optimization (PhD); computational science and engineering (MS, PhD); computer science (MS, MSCS, PhD); human computer interaction (MSHCI); human-centered computing (PhD); information security (MS). Part-time programs available. Postbaccalaureate distance learning degree programs offered. Terminal master's awarded for partial completion of doctoral program. *Degree requirements:* For master's, thesis optional; for doctorate, comprehensive exam, thesis/dissertation. *Entrance requirements:* For master's, GRE General Test, GRE Subject Test, minimum GPA of 3.0; for doctorate, GRE General Test, GRE Subject Test, minimum GPA of 3.3. Additional exam requirements/recommendations for international students: Required—TOEFL. *Faculty research:* Computer systems, graphics, intelligent systems and artificial intelligence, networks and telecommunications, software engineering.

Georgia Southwestern State University, Graduate Studies, School of Computer and Information Sciences, Americus, GA 31709-4693. Offers computer information systems (MS); computer science (MS). Part-time programs available. *Degree requirements:* For master's, thesis (for some programs). *Entrance requirements:* For master's, GRE General Test, minimum GPA of 3.0. Electronic applications accepted. *Faculty research:* Database, Internet technologies, computational complexity, encryption.

Georgia State University, College of Arts and Sciences, Department of Computer Science, Atlanta, GA 30302-3083. Offers MS, PhD. Part-time and evening/weekend programs available. Terminal master's awarded for partial completion of doctoral program. *Degree requirements:* For master's, comprehensive exam, thesis or alternative; for doctorate, thesis/dissertation, qualifying exam. *Entrance requirements:* For master's, GRE General Test, 3 letters of recommendation; for doctorate, 3 letters of recommendation. Additional exam requirements/recommendations for international students: Required—TOEFL. Electronic applications accepted. *Faculty research:* Computer networks, databases, artificial intelligence, bioinformatics, parallel and distributed computing, graphics and visualization.

Governors State University, College of Arts and Sciences, Program in Computer Science, University Park, IL 60466-0975. Offers MS. Part-time and evening/weekend programs available. *Degree requirements:* For master's, thesis or alternative. *Entrance requirements:* For master's, minimum GPA of 2.75.

Graduate School and University Center of the City University of New York, Graduate Studies, Program in Computer Science, New York, NY 10016-4039. Offers PhD. *Faculty:* 56 full-time (12 women). *Students:* 132 full-time (26 women), 1 part-time (0 women); includes 17 minority (4 African Americans, 9 Asian Americans or Pacific Islanders, 4 Hispanic Americans), 67 international. Average age 34. 47 applicants, 57% accepted, 17 enrolled. In 2009, 6 doctorates awarded. *Degree requirements:* For doctorate, one foreign language, thesis/dissertation. *Entrance requirements:* For doctorate, GRE General Test. Additional exam requirements/recommendations for international students: Required—TOEFL. *Application deadline:* For fall admission, 1/15 priority date for domestic students. Application fee: $125. Electronic applications accepted. *Financial support:* In 2009–10, 87 students received support, including 80 fellowships, 2 research assistantships, 6 teaching assistantships. Financial award application deadline: 2/1; financial award applicants required to submit FAFSA. *Unit head:* Dr. Ted Brown, Executive Officer, 212-817-8191, Fax: 212-817-1510, E-mail: tbrown@gc.cuny.edu. *Application contact:* Les Gribben, Director of Admissions, 212-817-7470, Fax: 212-817-1624, E-mail: lgribben@gc.cuny.edu.

Grand Valley State University, Padnos College of Engineering and Computing, School of Computing and Information Systems, Allendale, MI 49401-9403. Offers computer information systems (MS), including databases, distributed systems, management of information systems, object-oriented systems, software engineering. Part-time and evening/weekend programs available. *Faculty:* 11 full-time (0 women). *Students:* 10 full-time (3 women), 52 part-time (12 women); includes 8 minority (1 African American, 6 Asian Americans or Pacific Islanders, 1 Hispanic American), 11 international. Average age 33. 32 applicants, 81% accepted, 16 enrolled. In 2009, 22 master's awarded. *Degree requirements:* For master's, thesis or alternative. *Entrance requirements:* For master's, GMAT or GRE General Test. Additional exam requirements/recommendations for international students: Required—TOEFL. *Application deadline:* For fall admission, 6/1 for international students; for winter admission, 9/1 for international students. Applications are processed on a rolling basis. Application fee: $30. Electronic applications accepted. *Financial support:* In 2009–10, 9 students received support, including 5 fellowships (averaging $3,380 per year), 5 research assistantships with full and partial tuition reimbursements available (averaging $4,626 per year). *Faculty research:* Object technology, distributed computing, information systems management database, software engineering. *Unit head:* Paul Leidig, Director, 616-331-2038, Fax: 616-331-2106, E-mail: leidigp@gvsu.edu. *Application contact:* D. Robert Adams, CIS Graduate Program Chair, 616-331-3885, Fax: 616-331-2106, E-mail: adams@cis.gvsu.edu.

Hampton University, Graduate College, Department of Computer Science, Hampton, VA 23668. Offers MS. Part-time and evening/weekend programs available. *Degree requirements:* For master's, thesis or alternative. *Entrance requirements:* For master's, GRE General Test. *Faculty research:* Software testing, neural networks, parallel processing, computer graphics, natural language processing.

Harvard University, Graduate School of Arts and Sciences, School of Engineering and Applied Sciences, Cambridge, MA 02138. Offers applied mathematics (ME, SM, PhD); applied physics (ME, SM, PhD); computer science (ME, SM, PhD); engineering science (ME); engineering sciences (SM, PhD). Part-time programs available. *Faculty:* 57 full-time (9 women), 9 part-time/adjunct (1 woman). *Students:* 355 full-time (89 women), 3 part-time (0 women); includes 50 minority (4 African Americans, 40 Asian Americans or Pacific Islanders, 6 Hispanic Americans), 166 international. 1,617 applicants, 11% accepted, 88 enrolled. In 2009, 67 master's, 53 doctorates awarded. Terminal master's awarded for partial completion of doctoral program. *Degree requirements:* For master's, thesis optional; for doctorate, comprehensive exam, thesis/dissertation. *Entrance requirements:* For master's and doctorate, GRE General Test, GRE Subject Test (recommended), 3 letters of recommendation. Additional exam requirements/recommendations for international students: Required—TOEFL (minimum score 80 iBT). *Application deadline:* For fall admission, 12/31 priority date for domestic and international students. Application fee: $105. Electronic applications accepted. *Expenses:* Tuition: Full-time $33,696. Required fees: $1126. Full-time tuition and fees vary according to program. *Financial support:* In 2009–10, 115 fellowships with full tuition reimbursements (averaging $21,375 per year), 184 research assistantships with full and partial tuition reimbursements (averaging $28,500 per year), 76 teaching assistantships with full and partial tuition reimbursements (averaging $5,563 per year) were awarded; Federal Work-Study, institutionally sponsored loans, traineeships, and health care benefits also available. *Faculty research:* Applied mathematics, applied physics, computer science and electrical engineering, environmental engineering, mechanical and biomedical engineering. Total annual research expenditures: $43.8 million. *Unit head:* Cherry Murray, Dean, 617-495-5829, Fax: 617-495-5264, E-mail: dean@seas.harvard.edu. *Application contact:* Office of Admissions and Financial Aid, 617-495-5315, E-mail: admissions@seas.harvard.edu.

Hofstra University, College of Liberal Arts and Sciences, Department of Computer Science, Hempstead, NY 11549. Offers MA, MS. Part-time and evening/weekend programs available. Postbaccalaureate distance learning degree programs offered (no on-campus study). *Faculty:* 4 full-time (1 woman), 3 part-time/adjunct (0 women). *Students:* 2 full-time (0 women), 15 part-time (0 women), 1 international. Average age 36. 17 applicants, 94% accepted, 7 enrolled. In 2009, 7 master's awarded. *Degree requirements:* For master's, thesis optional. *Entrance requirements:* For master's, GRE, minimum GPA of 3.0. Additional exam requirements/recommendations for international students: Required—TOEFL (minimum score 550 paper-based; 213 computer-based; 80 iBT). *Application deadline:* Applications are processed on a rolling basis. Application fee: $60. Electronic applications accepted. *Expenses:* Tuition: Full-time $16,200; part-time $900 per credit hour. Required fees: $970; $145 per term. Tuition and fees vary according to program. *Financial support:* In 2009–10, 7 students received support, including 1 fellowship with full and partial tuition reimbursement available (averaging $2,410 per year); research assistantships with full and partial tuition reimbursements available, Federal Work-Study, institutionally sponsored loans, scholarships/grants, tuition waivers (full and partial), and unspecified assistantships also available. Support available to part-time students. Financial award applicants required to submit FAFSA. *Faculty research:* Computer vision; programming languages; data mining; software engineering; wireless sensor networks. Total annual research expenditures: $100,000. *Unit head:* Dr. Greda Kamberova, Chairperson, 516-463-5775, Fax: 516-463-5790, E-mail: cscglk@hofstra.edu. *Application contact:* Carol Drummer, Dean of Graduate Admissions, 516-463-4876, Fax: 516-463-4664, E-mail: gradstudent@hofstra.edu.

Hood College, Graduate School, Programs in Computer and Information Sciences, Frederick, MD 21701-8575. Offers computer and information sciences (MS); computer science (MS). Part-time and evening/weekend programs available. *Faculty:* 5 full-time (1 woman), 5 part-time/adjunct (1 woman). *Students:* 13 full-time (3 women), 65 part-time (14 women); includes 9 minority (3 African Americans, 3 Asian Americans or Pacific Islanders, 3 Hispanic Americans), 11 international. Average age 34. 33 applicants, 88% accepted, 23 enrolled. In 2009, 19 master's awarded. *Degree requirements:* For master's, thesis. *Entrance requirements:* For master's, minimum GPA of 2.75. Additional exam requirements/recommendations for international students: Required—TOEFL (minimum score 575 paper-based; 231 computer-based; 89 iBT). *Application deadline:* For fall admission, 7/15 for domestic and international students; for spring admission, 12/15 for domestic and international students. Applications are processed on a rolling basis. Application fee: $35. Electronic applications accepted. *Expenses:* Tuition: Full-time $6480; part-time $360 per credit. Required fees: $100; $50 per term. *Financial support:* Applicants required to submit FAFSA. *Faculty research:* Systems engineering, natural language, processing, database design, artificial intelligence and parallel distributed computing. *Unit head:* Dr. Xinlian Liu, Director, 301-696-3981, E-mail: liu@hood.edu. *Application contact:* Dr. Allen P. Flora, Dean of Graduate School, 301-696-3811, Fax: 301-696-3597, E-mail: gofurther@hood.edu.

Howard University, College of Engineering, Architecture, and Computer Sciences, School of Engineering and Computer Science, Department of Systems and Computer Science, Washington, DC 20059-0002. Offers MCS. Offered through the Graduate School of Arts and Sciences. Part-time programs available. *Degree requirements:* For master's, thesis. *Entrance requirements:* For master's, GRE General Test, minimum GPA of 3.0. Additional exam requirements/recommendations for international students: Required—TOEFL (minimum score 213 computer-based). Electronic applications accepted. *Faculty research:* Software engineering, software fault-tolerance, software reliability, artificial intelligence.

Illinois Institute of Technology, Graduate College, College of Science and Letters, Department of Computer Science, Chicago, IL 60616-3793. Offers computer science (MCS, MS, PhD); teaching (MST); telecommunications and software engineering (MTSE); MS/M Ch E. Part-time and evening/weekend programs available. Postbaccalaureate distance learning degree programs offered (no on-campus study). Terminal master's awarded for partial completion of doctoral program. *Degree requirements:* For master's, thesis (for some programs); for doctorate, comprehensive exam, thesis/dissertation. *Entrance requirements:* For master's and doctorate, GRE General Test, minimum undergraduate GPA of 3.0. Additional exam requirements/recommendations for international students: Required—TOEFL (minimum score 550 paper-based; 213 computer-based; 80 iBT). Electronic applications accepted. *Expenses:* Tuition: Full-time $17,550; part-time $888 per credit hour. Required fees: $850; $7.50 per credit hour. One-time fee: $50 full-time. Full-time tuition and fees vary according to program. *Faculty research:* Information retrieval, parallel and distributed computing, networking, algorithms, natural language processing.

Indiana State University, School of Graduate Studies, College of Arts and Sciences, Department of Mathematics and Computer Science, Terre Haute, IN 47809. Offers math teaching (MA, MS); mathematics and computer science (MA); mathematics and computer sciences (MS). Part-time programs available. *Degree requirements:* For master's, thesis or alternative. *Entrance requirements:* For master's, 24 semester hours of course work in undergraduate mathematics. Electronic applications accepted.

Indiana University Bloomington, School of Informatics, Program in Computer Science, Bloomington, IN 47405. Offers MS, PhD. *Faculty:* 33 full-time (6 women), 12 part-time/adjunct (1 woman). *Students:* 212 full-time (45 women), 14 part-time (3 women); includes 4 minority (all Asian Americans or Pacific Islanders), 166 international. Average age 26. 450 applicants, 52% accepted, 81 enrolled. In 2009, 35 master's, 18 doctorates awarded. Terminal master's awarded for partial completion of doctoral program. *Degree requirements:* For master's, thesis optional; for doctorate, comprehensive exam, thesis/dissertation, oral and written exams. *Entrance requirements:* For master's and doctorate, GRE General Test. Additional exam requirements/recommendations for international students: Required—TOEFL. *Application deadline:* For fall admission, 1/15 priority date for domestic students, 12/1 priority date for international students. Application fee: $55 ($65 for international students). Electronic applications accepted. *Financial support:* In 2009–10, 1 student received support, including 1 fellowship with full tuition reimbursement available (averaging $25,000 per year), 23 research assistantships with full tuition reimbursements available (averaging $14,000 per year), 43 teaching assistantships with full tuition reimbursements available (averaging $14,000 per year); health care benefits and unspecified assistantships also available. *Faculty research:* Artificial intelligence, database and information systems, distributed and parallel systems, foundations, programming languages and compilers. *Unit head:* Dr. Andrew Lumsdaine, Chairman, 812-855-7071, E-mail: lums@cs.indiana.edu. *Application contact:* Debbie Canada, Graduate Administrator, 812-855-6487, Fax: 812-855-4829, E-mail: gradvise@cs.indiana.edu.

Indiana University–Purdue University Fort Wayne, College of Engineering, Technology, and Computer Science, Department of Computer Science, Fort Wayne, IN 46805-1499. Offers applied computer science (MS). Part-time programs available. *Faculty:* 9 full-time (1 woman), 1 part-time/adjunct (0 women). *Students:* 6 full-time (2 women), 21 part-time (5 women); includes 4 minority (1 African American, 2 Asian Americans or Pacific Islanders, 1 Hispanic American), 1 international. Average age 34. 15 applicants, 87% accepted, 11 enrolled. In 2009, 6 master's awarded. *Entrance requirements:* For master's, GRE General Test, minimum GPA of 3.0. Additional exam requirements/recommendations for international students: Required—TOEFL (minimum score 550 paper-based; 213 computer-based; 77 iBT); Recommended—TWE. *Application deadline:* For fall admission, 7/15 for domestic students, 5/15 for international students; for spring admission, 12/1 for domestic students, 10/15 for international students. Applications are processed on a rolling basis. Application fee: $55 ($60 for international students). Electronic applications accepted. *Expenses:* Tuition, state resident: full-time $4595; part-time $255 per credit. Tuition, nonresident: full-time $10,963; part-time $609 per credit. Required fees: $528; $29.35 per credit. Tuition and fees vary according to course load. *Financial support:* In 2009–10, 3 teaching assistantships with partial tuition reimbursements (averaging $12,740 per year) were awarded; career-related internships or fieldwork, scholarships/grants, and unspecified assistantships also available. Support available to part-time students. Financial award application deadline: 3/1; financial award applicants required to submit FAFSA. *Unit head:* Dr. Peter Ng, Chair, 260-481-6237, Fax: 260-481-5734, E-mail: ngp@ipfw.edu. *Application contact:* Dr. David Liu, Graduate Program Director, 260-481-0182, Fax: 260-481-5734, E-mail: liud@ipfw.edu.

Indiana University–Purdue University Indianapolis, School of Science, Department of Computer and Information Science, Indianapolis, IN 46202-5132. Offers computer science (MS, PhD). Part-time and evening/weekend programs available. *Faculty:* 3 full-time (0 women). *Students:* 39 full-time (15 women), 52 part-time (19 women); includes 8 minority (4 African Americans, 3 Asian Americans or Pacific Islanders, 1 Hispanic American), 60 international.

Computer Science

Indiana University–Purdue University Indianapolis (continued)
Average age 27. In 2009, 23 master's awarded. *Degree requirements:* For master's, thesis optional. *Entrance requirements:* For master's, GRE, BS in computer science or the equivalent. *Application deadline:* For fall admission, 1/15 priority date for domestic students; for spring admission, 9/15 for domestic students. Applications are processed on a rolling basis. Application fee: $50 ($60 for international students). Electronic applications accepted. *Financial support:* In 2009–10, 4 fellowships (averaging $13,125 per year), 18 teaching assistantships with tuition reimbursements (averaging $6,915 per year) were awarded; research assistantships with tuition reimbursements, career-related internships or fieldwork, institutionally sponsored loans, and tuition waivers (full and partial) also available. Support available to part-time students. Financial award application deadline: 1/15; financial award applicants required to submit FAFSA. *Faculty research:* Artificial intelligence, graphics and visualization, computational geometry, database systems, distributed computing. *Unit head:* Mathew J. Palakal, Chair, 317-274-9727, Fax: 317-274-9742, E-mail: grad_advisor@cs.iupui.edu. *Application contact:* 317-274-9727, Fax: 317-274-9742, E-mail: admissions@cs.iupui.edu.

Indiana University South Bend, College of Liberal Arts and Sciences, South Bend, IN 46634-7111. Offers applied mathematics and computer science (MS); applied psychology (MA); English (MA); liberal studies (MLS). Part-time and evening/weekend programs available. *Faculty:* 79 full-time (33 women). *Students:* 27 full-time (10 women), 83 part-time (55 women); includes 17 minority (10 African Americans, 2 American Indian/Alaska Native, 2 Asian Americans or Pacific Islanders, 3 Hispanic Americans), 10 international. Average age 36. In 2009, 24 master's awarded. *Degree requirements:* For master's, thesis (for some programs). *Entrance requirements:* For master's, minimum GPA of 3.0. Additional exam requirements/recommendations for international students: Required—TOEFL. *Application deadline:* For fall admission, 7/31 priority date for domestic students, 7/1 priority date for international students; for spring admission, 3/31 priority date for domestic students, 11/1 priority date for international students. Applications are processed on a rolling basis. Application fee: $46 ($58 for international students). *Financial support:* In 2009–10, 5 students received support, including 5 teaching assistantships; Federal Work-Study also available. Support available to part-time students. *Faculty research:* Artificial intelligence, bioinformatics, English language and literature, creative writing, computer networks. Total annual research expenditures: $127,000. *Unit head:* Dr. Lynn R. Williams, Dean, 574-520-4322, Fax: 574-520-4528, E-mail: lwilliam@iusb.edu. *Application contact:* Dr. Lynn R. Williams, Dean, 574-520-4322, Fax: 574-520-4528, E-mail: lwilliam@iusb.edu.

Instituto Tecnológico y de Estudios Superiores de Monterrey, Campus Central de Veracruz, Graduate Programs, Córdoba, Mexico. Offers administration (MA); administration of information technologies (MTI); computer sciences (MCC); education (MEE); educational institution administration (MAD); educational technology (MTE); electronic commerce (MCE); finance (MAF); humanistic studies (MEH); international business for Latin America (MNL); marketing (MMT); science (MCP); technology management (MTT). Part-time and evening/weekend programs available. Postbaccalaureate distance learning degree programs offered (minimal on-campus study). *Degree requirements:* For master's, thesis (for some programs). *Entrance requirements:* For master's, PAEP College Board. Electronic applications accepted.

Instituto Tecnológico y de Estudios Superiores de Monterrey, Campus Ciudad de México, Virtual University Division, Ciudad de Mexico, Mexico. Offers administration of information technologies (MA); computer sciences (MA); education (MA, PhD); educational technology (MA); environmental engineering (MA); environmental systems (MA); humanistic studies (MA); industrial engineering (MA); international business for Latin America (MA); quality systems (MA); quality systems and productivity (MA). Part-time and evening/weekend programs available. Postbaccalaureate distance learning degree programs offered (minimal on-campus study). *Entrance requirements:* For master's and doctorate, Instituto entrance exam. Additional exam requirements/recommendations for international students: Required—TOEFL.

Instituto Tecnológico y de Estudios Superiores de Monterrey, Campus Cuernavaca, Programs in Information Science, Temixco, Mexico. Offers administration of information technology (MATI); computer science (MCC, DCC); information technology (MTI).

Instituto Tecnológico y de Estudios Superiores de Monterrey, Campus Estado de México, Professional and Graduate Division, Estado de Mexico, Mexico. Offers administration of information technologies (MITA); architecture (M Arch); business administration (GMBA, MBA); computer sciences (MCS, PhD); education (M Ed); educational institution administration (MAD); educational technology and innovation (PhD); electronic commerce (MEC); environmental systems (MS); finance (MAF); humanistic studies (MHS); information sciences and knowledge management (MISKM); information systems (MS); manufacturing systems (MS); marketing (MEM); quality systems and productivity (MS); science and materials engineering (PhD); telecommunications management (MTM). Part-time programs available. Postbaccalaureate distance learning degree programs offered (minimal on-campus study). *Degree requirements:* For master's, one foreign language, thesis (for some programs); for doctorate, one foreign language, thesis/dissertation. *Entrance requirements:* For master's, E-PAEP 500, interview; for doctorate, E-PAEP 500, research proposal. Additional exam requirements/recommendations for international students: Required—TOEFL (minimum score 550 paper-based). *Faculty research:* Surface treatments by plasmas, mechanical properties, robotics, graphical computing, mechatronics security protocols.

Instituto Tecnológico y de Estudios Superiores de Monterrey, Campus Irapuato, Graduate Programs, Irapuato, Mexico. Offers administration (MBA); administration of information technology (MAIT); administration of telecommunications (MAT); architecture (M Arch); computer science (MCS); education (M Ed); educational administration (MEA); educational innovation and technology (DEIT); educational technology (MET); electronic commerce (MBA); environmental administration and planning (MEAP); environmental systems (MES); finances (MBA); humanistic studies (MHS); international management for Latin American executives (MIMLAE); library and information science (MLIS); manufacturing quality management (MMQM); marketing research (MBA).

Instituto Tecnológico y de Estudios Superiores de Monterrey, Campus Monterrey, Graduate and Research Division, Program in Computer Science, Monterrey, Mexico. Offers artificial intelligence (PhD); computer science (MS); information systems (MS); information technology (MS). Part-time programs available. *Degree requirements:* For master's, one foreign language, thesis; for doctorate, one foreign language, thesis/dissertation. *Entrance requirements:* For master's, EXADEP; for doctorate, master's degree in related field. Additional exam requirements/recommendations for international students: Required—TOEFL. *Faculty research:* Distributed systems, software engineering, decision support systems.

Inter American University of Puerto Rico, Guayama Campus, Department of Natural and Applied Sciences, Guayama, PR 00785. Offers computer security and networks (MS).

Inter American University of Puerto Rico, Metropolitan Campus, Graduate Programs, Program in Open Information Systems, San Juan, PR 00919-1293. Offers MS. *Degree requirements:* For master's, 2 foreign languages.

International Technological University, Program in Computer Science, Santa Clara, CA 95050. Offers MS.

Iona College, School of Arts and Science, Program in Computer Science, New Rochelle, NY 10801-1890. Offers computer science (MS); telecommunications (MS). Part-time and evening/weekend programs available. *Faculty:* 10 full-time (4 women), 3 part-time/adjunct (0 women). *Students:* 25 part-time (5 women); includes 6 minority (3 African Americans, 3 Hispanic Americans), 1 international. Average age 36. 18 applicants, 72% accepted, 8 enrolled. In 2009, 7 master's awarded. *Degree requirements:* For master's, thesis or alternative. *Entrance requirements:* For master's, minimum GPA of 3.0. Additional exam requirements/recommendations for international students: Required—TOEFL (minimum score 550 paper-

based; 213 computer-based). *Application deadline:* Applications are processed on a rolling basis. Application fee: $50. Electronic applications accepted. *Expenses:* Contact institution. *Financial support:* Tuition waivers (partial) and unspecified assistantships available. Support available to part-time students. Financial award application deadline: 4/15; financial award applicants required to submit FAFSA. *Faculty research:* Telecommunications, expert systems, graph isomorphism, algorithms, formal verification of hardware. *Unit head:* Dr. Robert Schiaffino, Chair, 914-633-2338, E-mail: rschiaffino@iona.edu. *Application contact:* Veronica Jarek-Prinz, Director of Graduate Admissions, 914-633-2420, Fax: 914-633-2277, E-mail: vjarekprinz@iona.edu.

Iowa State University of Science and Technology, Graduate College, College of Liberal Arts and Sciences, Department of Computer Science, Ames, IA 50011. Offers MS, PhD. *Faculty:* 27 full-time (4 women), 1 part-time/adjunct (0 women). *Students:* 117 full-time (18 women), 23 part-time (7 women); includes 5 minority (1 African American, 3 Asian Americans or Pacific Islanders, 1 Hispanic American), 106 international. 344 applicants, 20% accepted, 20 enrolled. In 2009, 20 master's, 5 doctorates awarded. *Degree requirements:* For master's, thesis; for doctorate, thesis/dissertation. *Entrance requirements:* For master's and doctorate, GRE General Test. Additional exam requirements/recommendations for international students: Required—TOEFL (minimum score 550 paper-based; 79 iBT) or IELTS (minimum score 6.5). *Application deadline:* For fall admission, 1/1 priority date for domestic and international students; for spring admission, 9/1 priority date for domestic and international students. Application fee: $40 ($90 for international students). Electronic applications accepted. *Expenses:* Tuition, state resident: full-time $6716. Tuition, nonresident: full-time $8908. Tuition and fees vary according to course level, course load, program and student level. *Financial support:* In 2009–10, 64 research assistantships with full and partial tuition reimbursements (averaging $15,000 per year), 35 teaching assistantships with full and partial tuition reimbursements (averaging $15,000 per year) were awarded; fellowships, scholarships/grants, health care benefits, and unspecified assistantships also available. *Unit head:* Dr. Carl Chang, Chair, 515-294-4377, Fax: 515-294-0258, E-mail: grad_adm@cs.iastate.edu. *Application contact:* Samik Basu, Director of Graduate Education, 515-294-2987, E-mail: grad_adm@cs.iastate.edu.

Jackson State University, Graduate School, School of Science and Technology, Department of Computer Science, Jackson, MS 39217. Offers MS. Part-time and evening/weekend programs available. *Degree requirements:* For master's, comprehensive exam, thesis. *Entrance requirements:* For master's, GRE General Test. Additional exam requirements/recommendations for international students: Required—TOEFL.

Jacksonville State University, College of Graduate Studies and Continuing Education, College of Arts and Sciences, Program in Computer Systems and Software Design, Jacksonville, AL 36265-1602. Offers MS. Part-time and evening/weekend programs available. *Degree requirements:* For master's, comprehensive exam, thesis (for some programs). Electronic applications accepted.

James Madison University, The Graduate School, College of Integrated Science and Technology, Department of Computer Science, Harrisonburg, VA 22807. Offers MS. Post-baccalaureate distance learning degree programs offered. *Faculty:* 8 full-time (0 women). *Students:* 16 full-time (0 women), 49 part-time (2 women); includes 4 minority (2 African Americans, 1 American Indian/Alaska Native, 1 Asian American or Pacific Islander), 6 international. Average age 27. In 2009, 15 master's awarded. *Degree requirements:* For master's, thesis or alternative. *Entrance requirements:* For master's, GRE General Test. Additional exam requirements/recommendations for international students: Required—TOEFL. *Application deadline:* For fall admission, 5/1 priority date for domestic students; for spring admission, 9/1 priority date for domestic students. Applications are processed on a rolling basis. Application fee: $55. Electronic applications accepted. *Expenses:* Tuition, area resident: Part-time $305 per credit hour. Tuition, state resident: part-time $305 per credit hour. Tuition, nonresident: part-time $890 per credit hour. *Financial support:* In 2009–10, 10 students received support. Federal Work-Study available. Financial award application deadline: 3/1; financial award applicants required to submit FAFSA. *Unit head:* Dr. Malcolm G. Lane, Academic Unit Head, 540-568-2770. *Application contact:* Dr. Ralph Grove, Graduate Coordinator, 540-568-8772.

The Johns Hopkins University, Engineering for Professionals, Part-Time Program in Computer Science, Baltimore, MD 21218-2699. Offers bioinformatics (MS); computer science (MS, Post-Master's Certificate); telecommunications and networking (MS). Part-time and evening/weekend programs available. Postbaccalaureate distance learning degree programs offered (no on-campus study). *Faculty:* 58 part-time/adjunct (5 women). *Students:* 25 full-time (3 women), 411 part-time (65 women); includes 103 minority (27 African Americans, 65 Asian Americans or Pacific Islanders, 11 Hispanic Americans), 8 international. Average age 29. In 2009, 174 master's, 2 other advanced degrees awarded. *Application deadline:* Applications are processed on a rolling basis. Application fee: $75. Electronic applications accepted. *Financial support:* Institutionally sponsored loans available. *Unit head:* Dr. Ralph D. Semmel, Program Chair, 443-778-6179, E-mail: ralph.semmel@jhuapl.edu. *Application contact:* Priyanka Dwivedi, Admissions Manager, 410-516-2300, Fax: 410-579-8049, E-mail: pdwived1@jhu.edu.

The Johns Hopkins University, G. W. C. Whiting School of Engineering, Department of Computer Science, Baltimore, MD 21218-2699. Offers MSE, PhD. *Faculty:* 21 full-time (2 women), 16 part-time/adjunct (2 women). *Students:* 151 full-time (31 women), 6 part-time (0 women); includes 14 minority (2 African Americans, 9 Asian Americans or Pacific Islanders, 3 Hispanic Americans), 97 international. Average age 27. 498 applicants, 38% accepted, 57 enrolled. In 2009, 38 master's, 12 doctorates awarded. Terminal master's awarded for partial completion of doctoral program. *Degree requirements:* For master's, thesis optional; for doctorate, comprehensive exam, thesis/dissertation, oral exam. *Entrance requirements:* For master's and doctorate, GRE General Test. Additional exam requirements/recommendations for international students: Required—TOEFL (minimum score 600 paper-based; 250 computer-based). *Application deadline:* For fall admission, 12/19 for domestic and international students; for spring admission, 12/12 for domestic students, 9/26 for international students. Application fee: $25. Electronic applications accepted. *Financial support:* In 2009–10, 9 fellowships with full and partial tuition reimbursements (averaging $16,722 per year), 47 research assistantships with full tuition reimbursements (averaging $25,404 per year), 13 teaching assistantships with full tuition reimbursements (averaging $25,404 per year) were awarded; scholarships/grants, health care benefits, tuition waivers (partial), and unspecified assistantships also available. Financial award application deadline: 12/19. *Faculty research:* Computer medical systems, networks/distributed systems, algorithms, security, natural language processing. Total annual research expenditures: $1.1 million. *Unit head:* Dr. Gregory Hager, Chair, 410-516-5521, Fax: 410-516-6134, E-mail: hager@cs.jhu.edu. *Application contact:* Cathy Thornton, Sr. Academic Program Coordinator, 410-516-8775, Fax: 410-516-6134, E-mail: cthornton@jhu.edu.

The Johns Hopkins University, G. W. C. Whiting School of Engineering, Program in Engineering Management, Baltimore, MD 21218-2699. Offers biomaterials (MSEM); communications science (MSEM); computer science (MSEM); fluid mechanics (MSEM); materials science and engineering (MSEM); mechanical engineering (MSEM); mechanics and materials (MSEM); nano-biotechnology (MSEM); nanomaterials and nanotechnology (MSEM); probability and statistics (MSEM); smart product and device design (MSEM); systems analysis, management and environmental policy (MSEM). *Students:* 12 full-time (0 women), 3 international. Average age 23. 66 applicants, 67% accepted. *Entrance requirements:* For master's, GRE, 3 letters of recommendation, resume. Additional exam requirements/recommendations for international students: Required—TOEFL (minimum score 600 paper-based; 250 computer-based; 100 iBT) or IELTS (minimum score 7). *Application deadline:* For fall admission, 1/15 priority date for domestic students, 1/15 for international students; for spring admission, 9/15 priority date for domestic students, 9/15 for international students. Applications are processed on a rolling basis. Application fee: $75. Electronic applications accepted. *Financial support:* Fellowships, health care benefits available. *Unit head:* Dr. Edward R. Scheinerman, Interim Director/Vice

Dean for Education, School of Engineering/Professor, Applied Mathematics and Statistics, 410-516-7395, Fax: 410-516-4880, E-mail: ers@jhu.edu. *Application contact:* Dennis McIver, Coordinator of Graduate Admissions, 410-516-8174, Fax: 410-516-0780, E-mail: graduateadmissions@jhu.edu.

Kansas State University, Graduate School, College of Engineering, Department of Computing and Information Sciences, Manhattan, KS 66506. Offers computer science (MS, PhD); software engineering (MSE). Part-time programs available. Postbaccalaureate distance learning degree programs offered (minimal on-campus study). *Faculty:* 15 full-time (1 woman). *Students:* 74 full-time (14 women), 45 part-time (10 women); includes 3 minority (2 Asian Americans or Pacific Islanders, 1 Hispanic American), 86 international. Average age 26. 236 applicants, 49% accepted, 40 enrolled. In 2009, 27 master's, 5 doctorates awarded. Terminal master's awarded for partial completion of doctoral program. *Degree requirements:* For master's, thesis or alternative; for doctorate, thesis/dissertation, preliminary exams. *Entrance requirements:* For master's, GRE, bachelor's degree in computer science, minimum GPA of 3.0; for doctorate, GRE General Test, GRE Subject Test, master's degree in computer science or bachelor's degree and strong advanced computer knowledge. Additional exam requirements/recommendations for international students: Required—TOEFL (minimum score 575 paper-based; 233 computer-based). *Application deadline:* For fall admission, 2/1 priority date for domestic and international students; for spring admission, 8/1 priority date for domestic and international students. Applications are processed on a rolling basis. Application fee: $40 ($55 for international students). Electronic applications accepted. *Financial support:* In 2009–10, 27 research assistantships (averaging $16,260 per year), 24 teaching assistantships with full tuition reimbursements (averaging $14,294 per year) were awarded; career-related internships or fieldwork, institutionally sponsored loans, and scholarships/grants also available. Support available to part-time students. Financial award application deadline: 3/15; financial award applicants required to submit FAFSA. *Faculty research:* High-assurance software and programming languages, data mining, parallel and distributed computing, computer security, embedded systems. Total annual research expenditures: $1.5 million. *Unit head:* Gurdip E. Singh, Head, 785-532-7945, Fax: 785-532-7353, E-mail: gurdip@ksu.edu. *Application contact:* Dave Gustafson, Director, 785-532-6350, Fax: 785-532-7353, E-mail: dag@ksu.edu.

Kennesaw State University, College of Science and Mathematics, Program in Applied Computer Science, Kennesaw, GA 30144-5591. Offers MSaCS. Part-time programs available. Postbaccalaureate distance learning degree programs offered (minimal on-campus study). *Faculty:* 8 full-time (0 women). *Students:* 29 full-time (10 women), 14 part-time (2 women); includes 14 minority (11 African Americans, 3 Hispanic Americans), 15 international. Average age 32. 26 applicants, 73% accepted, 14 enrolled. In 2009, 11 master's awarded. *Entrance requirements:* For master's, GMAT or GRE, minimum GPA of 2.75. Additional exam requirements/recommendations for international students: Required—TOEFL (minimum score 550 paper-based; 213 computer-based; 80 iBT), IELTS (minimum score 6). *Application deadline:* For fall admission, 8/1 priority date for domestic students, 8/1 for international students; for spring admission, 12/1 priority date for domestic students, 12/1 for international students. Applications are processed on a rolling basis. Application fee: $60. Electronic applications accepted. *Expenses:* Contact institution. *Financial support:* In 2009–10, 2 research assistantships with full tuition reimbursements (averaging $15,000 per year) were awarded; Federal Work-Study and unspecified assistantships also available. Support available to part-time students. Financial award application deadline: 6/15; financial award applicants required to submit FAFSA. *Unit head:* Dr. Victor Clincy, Director, 770-420-4440, E-mail: vclincy@kennesaw.edu. *Application contact:* Vilma Marquez, Admissions Counselor, 770-420-4377, Fax: 770-423-6885, E-mail: ksugrad@kennesaw.edu.

Kent State University, College of Arts and Sciences, Department of Computer Science, Kent, OH 44242-0001. Offers MA, MS, PhD. Part-time and evening/weekend programs available. *Degree requirements:* For master's, thesis (for some programs); for doctorate, comprehensive exam, thesis/dissertation. *Entrance requirements:* Additional exam requirements/recommendations for international students: Required—TOEFL (minimum score 550 paper-based; 213 computer-based). Electronic applications accepted. *Faculty research:* Distributed and parallel processing, networking, computational science, graphics and visualization, database and data mining.

Kentucky State University, College of Mathematics, Sciences, Technology and Health, Frankfort, KY 40601. Offers aquaculture (MS); computer science (MS), including computer science theory, information assurance, information technology. Part-time and evening/weekend programs available. *Faculty:* 8 full-time (0 women), 1 part-time/adjunct (0 women). *Students:* 18 full-time (6 women), 18 part-time (4 women); includes 11 minority (8 African Americans, 1 Asian American or Pacific Islander, 2 Hispanic Americans), 7 international. Average age 35. 42 applicants, 55% accepted, 12 enrolled. In 2009, 8 master's awarded. *Degree requirements:* For master's, comprehensive exam, thesis optional. *Entrance requirements:* For master's, GRE, GMAT. Additional exam requirements/recommendations for international students: Required—TOEFL (minimum score 525 paper-based; 173 computer-based). *Application deadline:* For fall admission, 7/1 priority date for domestic students, 4/15 priority date for international students; for spring admission, 11/15 priority date for domestic students, 8/1 priority date for international students. Applications are processed on a rolling basis. Application fee: $30 ($100 for international students). Electronic applications accepted. *Expenses:* Tuition, state resident: full-time $5634; part-time $313 per credit hour. Tuition, nonresident: full-time $14,598; part-time $811 per credit hour. Required fees: $450; $25 per credit hour. *Financial support:* In 2009–10, 28 students received support, including 10 research assistantships (averaging $10,505 per year); career-related internships or fieldwork, scholarships/grants, tuition waivers (partial), and unspecified assistantships also available. Financial award application deadline: 4/15; financial award applicants required to submit FAFSA. *Unit head:* Dr. Charles Bennett, Dean, 502-597-6926, E-mail: charles.bennett@kysu.edu. *Application contact:* Cedric Cunningham, Administrative Assistant, Office of Graduate Studies, 502-597-6536, Fax: 502-597-6432, E-mail: cedric.cunningham@kysu.edu.

Knowledge Systems Institute, Program in Computer and Information Sciences, Skokie, IL 60076. Offers MS. Part-time and evening/weekend programs available. Postbaccalaureate distance learning degree programs offered (minimal on-campus study). *Degree requirements:* For master's, comprehensive exam, thesis. *Entrance requirements:* Additional exam requirements/recommendations for international students: Required—TOEFL (minimum score 550 paper-based; 213 computer-based; 79 iBT). Electronic applications accepted. *Faculty research:* Data mining, web development, database programming and administration.

Kutztown University of Pennsylvania, College of Liberal Arts and Sciences, Program in Computer Science, Kutztown, PA 19530-0730. Offers MS. Part-time and evening/weekend programs available. *Faculty:* 6 full-time (1 woman). *Students:* 9 full-time (2 women), 10 part-time (2 women); includes 3 minority (2 African Americans, 1 Hispanic American), 4 international. Average age 26. 21 applicants, 90% accepted, 6 enrolled. In 2009, 13 master's awarded. *Degree requirements:* For master's, comprehensive exam or thesis. *Entrance requirements:* For master's, GRE General Test. Additional exam requirements/recommendations for international students: Required—TOEFL. *Application deadline:* For fall admission, 8/15 priority date for domestic and international students; for spring admission, 12/15 priority date for domestic and international students. Applications are processed on a rolling basis. Application fee: $35. Electronic applications accepted. *Expenses:* Tuition, state resident: full-time $6666; part-time $370 per credit. Tuition, nonresident: full-time $10,666; part-time $593 per credit. Required fees: $62 per credit. $60 per semester. *Financial support:* Career-related internships or fieldwork, Federal Work-Study, scholarships/grants, and unspecified assistantships available. Financial award application deadline: 3/1; financial award applicants required to submit FAFSA. *Faculty research:* Artificial intelligence, expert systems, neural networks. *Unit head:* Linda L. Day, Chairperson, 610-683-4340, Fax: 610-683-4129, E-mail: day@kutztown.edu. *Application contact:* Kelly D. Burr, Associate Director, Graduate Admissions, 610-683-4200, Fax: 610-683-1393, E-mail: graduate@kutztown.edu.

Lakehead University, Graduate Studies, School of Mathematical Sciences, Thunder Bay, ON P7B 5E1, Canada. Offers computer science (M Sc); mathematical science (MA). Part-time and evening/weekend programs available. *Degree requirements:* For master's, thesis optional. *Entrance requirements:* For master's, minimum B average, honours degree in mathematics or computer science. Additional exam requirements/recommendations for international students: Required—TOEFL. *Faculty research:* Numerical analysis, classical analysis, theoretical computer science, abstract harmonic analysis, functional analysis.

Lamar University, College of Graduate Studies, College of Arts and Sciences, Department of Computer Science, Beaumont, TX 77710. Offers MS. Part-time programs available. *Faculty:* 6 full-time (2 women). *Students:* 59 full-time (15 women), 16 part-time (2 women); includes 2 minority (1 Asian American or Pacific Islander, 1 Hispanic American), 35 international. Average age 25. 162 applicants, 26% accepted, 33 enrolled. In 2009, 26 master's awarded. *Degree requirements:* For master's, comprehensive exams and project or thesis. *Entrance requirements:* For master's, GRE General Test, minimum GPA of 3.3 in last 60 hours of undergraduate course work or 3.0 overall. Additional exam requirements/recommendations for international students: Required—TOEFL (minimum score 550 paper-based; 213 computer-based). *Application deadline:* For fall admission, 5/15 priority date for domestic students; for spring admission, 10/1 priority date for domestic students. Applications are processed on a rolling basis. Application fee: $25 ($50 for international students). *Financial support:* In 2009–10, 2 research assistantships with partial tuition reimbursements (averaging $6,000 per year), 4 teaching assistantships with partial tuition reimbursements (averaging $6,000 per year) were awarded; institutionally sponsored loans, scholarships/grants, and tuition waivers (partial) also available. Financial award application deadline: 4/1. *Faculty research:* Computer architecture, network security. *Unit head:* Dr. Lawrence J. Osborne, Chair, 409-880-8775, Fax: 409-880-2364, E-mail: osborne@hal.lamar.edu. *Application contact:* Daisy Estrella, Coordinator of Graduate Admissions, 409-880-8349, Fax: 409-880-8414, E-mail: gradmissions@hal.lamar.edu.

La Salle University, School of Arts and Sciences, Program in Computer Information Science, Philadelphia, PA 19141-1199. Offers MS. Part-time and evening/weekend programs available. *Entrance requirements:* For master's, GRE or MAT, 18 undergraduate credits in computer science, professional experience. *Expenses:* Contact institution. *Faculty research:* Human-computer interaction, networks, technology trends, databases, groupware.

Lawrence Technological University, College of Arts and Sciences, Southfield, MI 48075-1058. Offers computer science (MS); educational technology (MET); science education (MSE); technical communication (MS). Part-time and evening/weekend programs available. *Faculty:* 14 full-time (6 women), 14 part-time/adjunct (4 women). *Students:* 6 full-time (3 women), 80 part-time (49 women); includes 19 minority (14 African Americans, 5 Asian Americans or Pacific Islanders), 12 international. Average age 35. 87 applicants, 57% accepted, 20 enrolled. In 2009, 34 master's awarded. *Degree requirements:* For master's, thesis (for some programs). *Entrance requirements:* For master's, GRE. Additional exam requirements/recommendations for international students: Required—TOEFL (minimum score 550 paper-based; 213 computer-based; 79 iBT). *Application deadline:* For fall admission, 8/1 priority date for domestic students, 6/1 for international students; for winter admission, 12/1 priority date for domestic students, 10/1 for international students; for spring admission, 5/1 priority date for domestic students, 3/1 for international students. Applications are processed on a rolling basis. Application fee: $50. Electronic applications accepted. *Expenses:* Tuition: Full-time $11,320; part-time $798 per credit hour. *Financial support:* Federal Work-Study available. Financial award application deadline: 4/1; financial award applicants required to submit FAFSA. *Unit head:* Dr. Hsiao-Ping Moore, Dean, 248-204-3500, Fax: 248-204-3518, E-mail: scidean@ltu.edu. *Application contact:* Jane Rohrback, Director of Admissions, 248-204-3160, Fax: 248-204-3188, E-mail: admissions@ltu.edu.

Lebanese American University, School of Arts and Sciences, Beirut, Lebanon. Offers computer science (MS); international affairs (MA).

Lehigh University, P.C. Rossin College of Engineering and Applied Science, Department of Computer Science and Engineering, Bethlehem, PA 18015. Offers computer engineering (M Eng, MS, PhD); computer science (M Eng, MS, PhD, MBA/E); MBA/E. Part-time programs available. *Faculty:* 16 full-time (2 women). *Students:* 59 full-time (12 women), 12 part-time (4 women); includes 2 minority (both Asian Americans or Pacific Islanders), 51 international. Average age 27. 177 applicants, 37% accepted, 16 enrolled. In 2009, 14 master's, 8 doctorates awarded. *Degree requirements:* For doctorate, thesis/dissertation, qualifying, general, and oral exams. *Entrance requirements:* For master's, GRE General Test, minimum GPA of 3.0; for doctorate, GRE General Test, minimum GPA of 3.5. Additional exam requirements/recommendations for international students: Required—TOEFL (minimum score 550 paper-based; 213 computer-based; 79 iBT). *Application deadline:* For fall admission, 4/1 for domestic and international students; for spring admission, 11/1 for domestic and international students. Applications are processed on a rolling basis. Application fee: $75. Electronic applications accepted. *Expenses:* Contact institution. *Financial support:* In 2009–10, 3 fellowships with full tuition reimbursements (averaging $16,530 per year), 7 research assistantships with full tuition reimbursements (averaging $15,000 per year), 4 teaching assistantships with full tuition reimbursements (averaging $15,795 per year) were awarded. Financial award application deadline: 1/15. *Faculty research:* Artificial intelligence, networking-pattern recognition, multimedia e-learning/data mining/Web search, mobile robotics, bioinformatics, computervision. Total annual research expenditures: $2.4 million. *Unit head:* Dr. Daniel P. Lopresti, Chairman, 610-758-5782, Fax: 610-758-4096, E-mail: dal9@lehigh.edu. *Application contact:* Judy Frenick, Graduate Coordinator, 610-758-3605, Fax: 610-758-4096, E-mail: jlf2@lehigh.edu.

Lehman College of the City University of New York, Division of Natural and Social Sciences, Department of Mathematics and Computer Science, Program in Computer Science, Bronx, NY 10468-1589. Offers MS. *Degree requirements:* For master's, one foreign language, thesis or alternative.

Long Island University, Brooklyn Campus, School of Business, Public Administration and Information Sciences, Department of Computer Science, Brooklyn, NY 11201-8423. Offers MS. *Entrance requirements:* For master's, GMAT or GRE General Test, 2 letters of recommendation. Additional exam requirements/recommendations for international students: Required—TOEFL (minimum score 500 paper-based; 173 computer-based). Electronic applications accepted.

Long Island University, C.W. Post Campus, College of Information and Computer Science, Department of Computer Science/Management Engineering, Brookville, NY 11548-1300. Offers information systems (MS); information technology education (MS); management engineering (MS). Part-time and evening/weekend programs available. *Degree requirements:* For master's, comprehensive exam, thesis or alternative. *Entrance requirements:* For master's, bachelor's degree in science, mathematics, or engineering; minimum GPA of 2.5. Additional exam requirements/recommendations for international students: Required—TOEFL (minimum score 500 paper-based; 173 computer-based). Electronic applications accepted. *Faculty research:* Inductive music learning, re-engineering business process, technology and ethics.

Louisiana State University and Agricultural and Mechanical College, Graduate School, College of Basic Sciences, Department of Computer Science, Baton Rouge, LA 70803. Offers computer science (MSSS, PhD); systems science (MSSS). Part-time programs available. *Faculty:* 19 full-time (3 women). *Students:* 78 full-time (18 women), 22 part-time (4 women); includes 11 minority (5 African Americans, 1 American Indian/Alaska Native, 5 Asian Americans or Pacific Islanders), 71 international. Average age 30. 157 applicants, 55% accepted, 11 enrolled. In 2009, 10 master's, 3 doctorates awarded. Terminal master's awarded for partial completion of doctoral program. *Degree requirements:* For master's, thesis; for doctorate, thesis/dissertation. *Entrance requirements:* For master's and doctorate, GRE General Test, minimum GPA of 3.0. Additional exam requirements/recommendations for international students: Required—TOEFL (minimum score 550 paper-based; 213 computer-based; 79 iBT) or IELTS (minimum score 6.5). *Application deadline:* For fall admission, 2/1 for domestic students, 5/15

Computer Science

Louisiana State University and Agricultural and Mechanical College (continued)
for international students; for spring admission, 10/1 for domestic students, 10/15 for international students. Applications are processed on a rolling basis. Application fee: $50 ($70 for international students). Electronic applications accepted. *Financial support:* In 2009–10, 84 students received support, including 9 fellowships with full tuition reimbursements available (averaging $28,150 per year), 38 research assistantships with full and partial tuition reimbursements available (averaging $16,409 per year), 23 teaching assistantships with full and partial tuition reimbursements available (averaging $15,990 per year); Federal Work-Study, institutionally sponsored loans, health care benefits, and unspecified assistantships also available. Financial award application deadline: 2/1; financial award applicants required to submit FAFSA. *Faculty research:* Robotics, artificial intelligence, algorithms, database software engineering, high-performance computing. Total annual research expenditures: $1.4 million. *Unit head:* Dr. Sitharama S. Iyengar, Chair, 225-578-1495, Fax: 225-578-1465, E-mail: iyengar@csc.lsu.edu. *Application contact:* Graduate Coordinator, 225-578-1495, Fax: 225-578-1465.

Louisiana State University in Shreveport, College of Sciences, Program in Computer Systems Technology, Shreveport, LA 71115-2399. Offers MS. *Students:* 6 full-time (0 women), 15 part-time (5 women); includes 3 minority (all African Americans), 3 international. Average age 33. 18 applicants, 94% accepted, 9 enrolled. In 2009, 5 master's awarded. *Degree requirements:* For master's, thesis or alternative. *Entrance requirements:* For master's, GRE, programming course in high-level language, interview. Additional exam requirements/recommendations for international students: Required—TOEFL (minimum score 500 paper-based; 173 computer-based; 61 iBT). *Application deadline:* For fall admission, 6/30 for domestic and international students; for spring admission, 11/30 for domestic and international students. Applications are processed on a rolling basis. Application fee: $10 ($20 for international students). *Financial support:* In 2009–10, 2 research assistantships with partial tuition reimbursements (averaging $20,000 per year) were awarded. *Unit head:* Dr. John Sigle, Program Director, 318-797-5093. *Application contact:* Dr. John Sigle, Program Director, 318-797-5093.

Louisiana Tech University, Graduate School, College of Engineering and Science, Department of Computer Science, Ruston, LA 71272. Offers MS. Part-time programs available. *Degree requirements:* For master's, thesis or alternative. *Entrance requirements:* For master's, GRE General Test, minimum GPA of 3.0 in last 60 hours. Additional exam requirements/recommendations for international students: Required—TOEFL. *Faculty research:* Computer systems organization, artificial intelligence, expert systems, graphics, program language.

Loyola Marymount University, College of Science and Engineering, Department of Electrical Engineering and Computer Science, Program in Computer Science, Los Angeles, CA 90045. Offers MS. Part-time and evening/weekend programs available. *Faculty:* 10 full-time (4 women), 1 part-time/adjunct (0 women). *Students:* 5 full-time (3 women), 2 part-time (0 women); includes 2 minority (1 African American, 1 Asian American or Pacific Islander), 2 international. Average age 35. 8 applicants, 13% accepted, 0 enrolled. In 2009, 3 master's awarded. *Degree requirements:* For master's, research seminar. *Entrance requirements:* Additional exam requirements/recommendations for international students: Required—TOEFL (minimum score 550 paper-based; 213 computer-based; 80 iBT). *Application deadline:* Applications are processed on a rolling basis. Application fee: $50. Electronic applications accepted. *Financial support:* In 2009–10, 3 students received support. Scholarships/grants available. Support available to part-time students. Financial award application deadline: 6/1; financial award applicants required to submit FAFSA. Total annual research expenditures: $19,443. *Unit head:* Dr. Ray Toal, Program Director, 310-338-2773, Fax: 310-338-2872, E-mail: rtoal@lmu.edu. *Application contact:* Chake H. Kouyoumjian, Associate Dean of Graduate Studies, 310-338-2721, Fax: 310-338-6086, E-mail: ckouyoum@lmu.edu.

Loyola University Chicago, Graduate School, Department of Computer Science, Chicago, IL 60660. Offers computer science (MS); information technology (MS); software technology (MS). Part-time and evening/weekend programs available. *Faculty:* 9 full-time (1 woman), 10 part-time/adjunct (2 women). *Students:* 49 full-time (18 women), 31 part-time (6 women); includes 17 minority (4 African Americans, 9 Asian Americans or Pacific Islanders, 4 Hispanic Americans), 30 international. Average age 27. 96 applicants, 57% accepted, 30 enrolled. In 2009, 32 master's awarded. *Entrance requirements:* For master's, 3 letters of recommendation, transcripts, statement of purpose. Additional exam requirements/recommendations for international students: Required—TOEFL (minimum score 550 paper-based; 213 computer-based; 79 iBT), IELTS (minimum score 6.5). *Application deadline:* For fall admission, 5/15 priority date for international students; for spring admission, 9/15 priority date for international students. Applications are processed on a rolling basis. Application fee: $0. Electronic applications accepted. *Expenses:* Tuition: Full-time $14,220; part-time $790 per credit hour. Required fees: $60 per semester hour. Tuition and fees vary according to program. *Financial support:* In 2009–10, 24 students received support, including 1 fellowship (averaging $3,000 per year), 16 teaching assistantships with partial tuition reimbursements available (averaging $2,900 per year); career-related internships or fieldwork, Federal Work-Study, scholarships/grants, tuition waivers (partial), and unspecified assistantships also available. Financial award application deadline: 3/15. *Faculty research:* Software engineering, high performance computing, algorithms and complexity. Total annual research expenditures: $22,000. *Unit head:* Dr. Chandra Sekharan, Chair, 312-915-7985, Fax: 312-915-7998, E-mail: csekhar@luc.edu. *Application contact:* Cecilia Murphy, Graduate Program Secretary, 312-915-7990, Fax: 312-915-7998, E-mail: gradinfo-cs@luc.edu.

Loyola University Maryland, Graduate Programs, College of Arts and Sciences, Department of Computer Science, Baltimore, MD 21210-2699. Offers computer science (MS); software engineering (MS). *Entrance requirements:* For master's, GRE General Test, GRE Subject Test (recommended). Additional exam requirements/recommendations for international students: Required—TOEFL (minimum score 550 paper-based; 213 computer-based).

Maharishi University of Management, Graduate Studies, Program in Computer Science, Fairfield, IA 52557. Offers MS. *Degree requirements:* For master's, thesis or alternative. *Entrance requirements:* For master's, GRE General Test, minimum GPA of 3.0. Additional exam requirements/recommendations for international students: Required—TOEFL. *Faculty research:* Parallel processing, computer systems in architecture.

Marist College, Graduate Programs, School of Computer Science and Mathematics, Poughkeepsie, NY 12601-1387. Offers information systems (MS, Adv C); software development (MS); technology management (MS). Part-time and evening/weekend programs available. Postbaccalaureate distance learning degree programs offered (minimal on-campus study). *Entrance requirements:* For master's, resume. Additional exam requirements/recommendations for international students: Required—TOEFL (minimum score 550 paper-based; 213 computer-based; 80 iBT); Recommended—IELTS (minimum score 6.5). Electronic applications accepted. *Expenses:* Tuition: Full-time $12,510; part-time $695 per credit hour. *Faculty research:* Data quality, artificial intelligence, imaging, analysis of algorithms, distributed systems and applications.

Marquette University, Graduate School, College of Arts and Sciences, Department of Mathematics, Statistics, and Computer Science, Milwaukee, WI 53201-1881. Offers bioinformatics (MS); computational sciences (PhD); computers (MS); mathematics education (MS). Part-time programs available. *Faculty:* 28 full-time (12 women), 7 part-time/adjunct (2 women). *Students:* 20 full-time (4 women), 25 part-time (4 women); includes 2 minority (both Asian Americans or Pacific Islanders), 20 international. Average age 31. 68 applicants, 47% accepted, 15 enrolled. In 2009, 16 master's, 1 doctorate awarded. Terminal master's awarded for partial completion of doctoral program. *Degree requirements:* For master's, comprehensive exam, thesis or alternative; for doctorate, 2 foreign languages, comprehensive exam, thesis/dissertation. *Entrance requirements:* For doctorate, sample of scholarly writing. Additional exam requirements/recommendations for international students: Required—TOEFL. Application fee: $40. *Financial support:* In 2009–10, 2 research assistantships, 20 teaching assistantships were awarded; Federal Work-Study, institutionally sponsored loans, scholarships/grants, and tuition waivers (full and partial) also available. Support available to part-time students. Financial award application deadline: 2/15. *Faculty research:* Models of physiological systems, mathematical immunology, computational group theory, mathematical logic, computational science. *Unit head:* Dr. Peter Jones, Chair, 414-288-3263, Fax: 414-288-1578. *Application contact:* Dr. Gary Krenz, Director of Graduate Studies, 414-288-6345.

Marquette University, Graduate School, College of Arts and Sciences, Program in Computing, Milwaukee, WI 53201-1881. Offers MS. *Students:* 2 full-time (0 women), 17 part-time (4 women); includes 3 minority (2 Asian Americans or Pacific Islanders, 1 Hispanic American), 4 international. Average age 30. 12 applicants, 75% accepted, 4 enrolled. In 2009, 9 master's awarded. *Application deadline:* Applications are processed on a rolling basis. Application fee: $40. Electronic applications accepted. *Unit head:* Dr. Doug Harris, Head, 414-288-3889, E-mail: douglas.harris@marquette.edu. *Application contact:* Erin Fox, Assistant Director for Recruitment, 414-288-5319, Fax: 414-288-1902, E-mail: erin.fox@marquette.edu.

Massachusetts Institute of Technology, School of Engineering, Department of Electrical Engineering and Computer Science, Cambridge, MA 02139-4307. Offers computer science (PhD, Sc D, ECS); electrical engineering (PhD, Sc D, EE); electrical engineering and computer science (M Eng, SM, PhD, Sc D); SM/MBA. *Faculty:* 123 full-time (16 women), 1 part-time/adjunct (0 women). *Students:* 764 full-time (171 women), 3 part-time (0 women); includes 161 minority (15 African Americans, 3 American Indian/Alaska Native, 116 Asian Americans or Pacific Islanders, 27 Hispanic Americans), 319 international. Average age 26. 2,692 applicants, 11% accepted, 233 enrolled. In 2009, 195 master's, 102 doctorates, 2 other advanced degrees awarded. Terminal master's awarded for partial completion of doctoral program. *Degree requirements:* For master's and other advanced degree, thesis; for doctorate, comprehensive exam, thesis/dissertation. *Entrance requirements:* Additional exam requirements/recommendations for international students: Required—TOEFL (minimum score 600 paper-based; 250 computer-based), IELTS (minimum score 7). *Application deadline:* For fall admission, 12/15 for domestic and international students. Application fee: $75. Electronic applications accepted. *Financial support:* In 2009–10, 757 students received support, including 133 fellowships with tuition reimbursements available (averaging $29,263 per year), 476 research assistantships with tuition reimbursements available (averaging $28,316 per year), 108 teaching assistantships with tuition reimbursements available (averaging $29,689 per year); career-related internships or fieldwork, Federal Work-Study, institutionally sponsored loans, scholarships/grants, health care benefits, and unspecified assistantships also available. *Faculty research:* Artificial intelligence and applications; robotics, computer architecture, communications, devices, bioelectrical engineering; computational biology, electronics, electrodynamics, photonics, control, signal processing, optimization, software, systems, networks; computation theory, cryptography, algorithms. Total annual research expenditures: $82.4 million. *Unit head:* Prof. W. Eric L. Grimson, Department Head, 617-253-4600, Fax: 617-258-7354, E-mail: hq@eecs.mit.edu. *Application contact:* Graduate Admissions, 617-253-4603, Fax: 617-258-7354, E-mail: grad-ap@eecs.mit.edu.

McGill University, Faculty of Graduate and Postdoctoral Studies, Faculty of Science, School of Computer Science, Montréal, QC H3A 2T5, Canada. Offers M Sc, PhD.

McMaster University, School of Graduate Studies, Faculty of Engineering, Department of Computing and Software, Hamilton, ON L8S 4M2, Canada. Offers computer science (M Sc, PhD); software engineering (M Eng, MA Sc, PhD). Part-time programs available. *Degree requirements:* For master's, thesis. *Entrance requirements:* Additional exam requirements/recommendations for international students: Required—TOEFL (minimum score 550 paper-based; 213 computer-based). *Faculty research:* Software engineering; theory of non-sequential systems; parallel and distributed computing; artificial intelligence; complexity, design, and analysis of algorithms; combinatorial computing, especially applications to molecular biology.

McNeese State University, Doré School of Graduate Studies, College of Science, Department of Mathematics, Computer Science, and Statistics, Lake Charles, LA 70609. Offers mathematical science (MS), including computer science, mathematics, statistics. Evening/weekend programs available. *Degree requirements:* For master's, comprehensive exam, thesis or alternative, written exam. *Entrance requirements:* For master's, GRE.

Memorial University of Newfoundland, School of Graduate Studies, Department of Computer Science, St. John's, NL A1C 5S7, Canada. Offers M Sc, PhD. Part-time programs available. *Degree requirements:* For master's, thesis; for doctorate, comprehensive exam, thesis/dissertation, oral thesis defense. *Entrance requirements:* For master's, GRE (strongly recommended), honors degree in computer science or related field; for doctorate, GRE (strongly recommended), master's degree in computer science. Additional exam requirements/recommendations for international students: Required—GRE. Electronic applications accepted. *Faculty research:* Theoretical computer science, parallel and distributed computing, scientific computing, software systems and artificial intelligence.

Metropolitan State University, College of Arts and Sciences, St. Paul, MN 55106-5000. Offers computer science (MS); liberal studies (MA); technical communication (MS). Part-time and evening/weekend programs available. *Entrance requirements:* For master's, minimum GPA of 2.75, resumè. Additional exam requirements/recommendations for international students: Required—TOEFL (minimum score 550 paper-based; 213 computer-based). *Expenses:* Tuition, state resident: full-time $5520; part-time $276 per credit hour. Tuition, nonresident: full-time $11,040; part-time $552 per credit hour. Required fees: $209; $10 per credit hour. Tuition and fees vary according to degree level. *Faculty research:* Computer security, software engineering, distributed systems, document design, diffusing of innovations, social issues and communication technology.

Michigan State University, The Graduate School, College of Engineering, Department of Computer Science and Engineering, East Lansing, MI 48824. Offers computer science (MS, PhD). *Entrance requirements:* Additional exam requirements/recommendations for international students: Required—TOEFL. Electronic applications accepted.

Michigan Technological University, Graduate School, College of Sciences and Arts, Department of Computer Science, Houghton, MI 49931. Offers computational science and engineering (PhD); computer science (MS, PhD). Part-time programs available. Terminal master's awarded for partial completion of doctoral program. *Degree requirements:* For master's, comprehensive exam, thesis optional; for doctorate, comprehensive exam, thesis/dissertation. *Entrance requirements:* Additional exam requirements/recommendations for international students: Required—TOEFL (minimum score 580 paper-based; 237 computer-based). Electronic applications accepted. *Expenses:* Contact institution. *Faculty research:* Artificial intelligence, graphics/visualization, software engineering, architecture and compiler optimization, human computing interaction.

Middle Tennessee State University, College of Graduate Studies, College of Basic and Applied Sciences, Department of Computer Science, Murfreesboro, TN 37132. Offers MS. Part-time and evening/weekend programs available. Postbaccalaureate distance learning degree programs offered. *Faculty:* 11 full-time (6 women). *Students:* 1 full-time (0 women), 32 part-time (11 women); includes 10 minority (1 African American, 9 Asian Americans or Pacific Islanders). Average age 26. 38 applicants, 26% accepted, 10 enrolled. In 2009, 6 master's awarded. *Degree requirements:* For master's, one foreign language, comprehensive exam, thesis. *Entrance requirements:* For master's, GRE. Additional exam requirements/recommendations for international students: Required—TOEFL (minimum score 525 paper-based; 195 computer-based; 71 iBT) or IELTS (minimum score 6). *Application deadline:* For fall admission, 6/1 for domestic and international students. Applications are processed on a rolling basis. Application fee: $25 ($30 for international students). Electronic applications accepted. *Expenses:* Tuition, state resident: full-time $4404. Tuition, nonresident: full-time $10,956. *Financial support:* In 2009–10, 10 students received support. Institutionally sponsored loans available. Support available to part-time students. Financial award application deadline: 5/1; financial award applicants required to submit FAFSA. *Unit head:* Dr. Richard Detmer, Chair, 615-898-2397,

Fax: 615-898-5567, E-mail: rdetmer@mtsu.edu. *Application contact:* Dr. Michael Allen, Dean and Vice Provost for Research, 615-898-2840, Fax: 615-904-8020, E-mail: mallen@mtsu.edu.

Midwestern State University, Graduate Studies, College of Science and Mathematics, Computer Science Program, Wichita Falls, TX 76308. Offers MS. Part-time and evening/weekend programs available. *Degree requirements:* For master's, comprehensive exam, thesis. *Entrance requirements:* For master's, GRE General Test. Additional exam requirements/recommendations for international students: Required—TOEFL (minimum score 573 paper-based; 230 computer-based). Electronic applications accepted. *Expenses:* Tuition, state resident: full-time $1620; part-time $90 per credit hour. Tuition, nonresident: full-time $2160; part-time $120 per credit hour. International tuition: $7506 full-time. Required fees: $3068.80; $145.60 per credit hour. $179 per semester. *Faculty research:* Efficient content delivery in wireless.

Mills College, Graduate Studies, Program in Computer Science, Oakland, CA 94613-1000. Offers computer science (Certificate); interdisciplinary computer science (MA). Part-time programs available. *Faculty:* 7 full-time (6 women), 2 part-time/adjunct (1 woman). *Students:* 5 full-time (4 women), 2 part-time (1 woman); includes 2 minority (1 African American, 1 Asian American or Pacific Islander). Average age 28. 11 applicants, 100% accepted, 6 enrolled. In 2009, 2 master's awarded. *Degree requirements:* For master's, thesis. *Entrance requirements:* Additional exam requirements/recommendations for international students: Required—TOEFL. *Application deadline:* For fall admission, 2/1 priority date for domestic students; for spring admission, 11/1 for domestic students. Applications are processed on a rolling basis. Application fee: $50. Electronic applications accepted. *Expenses:* Tuition: Full-time $26,326; part-time $6584 per course. Required fees: $896. One-time fee: $896 part-time. Tuition and fees vary according to program. *Financial support:* In 2009–10, 3 students received support. Career-related internships or fieldwork and residence awards available. Financial award application deadline: 2/1; financial award applicants required to submit FAFSA. *Faculty research:* Dynamical systems, linear programming, theory of computer viruses, interface design, intelligent tutoring systems. *Unit head:* Susan S. Wang, Department Head, 510-430-2138, E-mail: wang@mills.edu. *Application contact:* Jessica King, Graduate Admission Specialist, 510-430-3305, Fax: 510-430-2159, E-mail: rmcglaut@mills.edu.

Minnesota State University Mankato, College of Graduate Studies, College of Science, Engineering and Technology, Department of Computer Science, Mankato, MN 56001. Offers MS, Graduate Certificate. *Students:* 9 full-time (2 women), 14 part-time (8 women). *Degree requirements:* For master's, one foreign language, comprehensive exam, thesis or alternative. *Entrance requirements:* For master's, GRE General Test, GRE Subject Test (if GPA less than 2.75), minimum GPA of 3.0 during previous 2 years. Additional exam requirements/recommendations for international students: Required—TOEFL (minimum score 550 paper-based; 213 computer-based; 80 iBT). *Application deadline:* For fall admission, 7/1 priority date for domestic students; for spring admission, 11/1 for domestic students. Applications are processed on a rolling basis. Application fee: $40. Electronic applications accepted. *Expenses:* Tuition, state resident: full-time $5364. Tuition, nonresident: full-time $8314. *Financial support:* Fellowships with full tuition reimbursements, research assistantships with full tuition reimbursements, teaching assistantships with full tuition reimbursements, Federal Work-Study, institutionally sponsored loans, and unspecified assistantships available. Support available to part-time students. Financial award application deadline: 3/15; financial award applicants required to submit FAFSA. *Unit head:* Dr. Dean Kelley, Graduate Coordinator, 507-389-3238. *Application contact:* 507-389-2321, E-mail: grad@mnsu.edu.

Mississippi College, Graduate School, College of Arts and Sciences, School of Science and Mathematics, Department of Computer Science, Clinton, MS 39058. Offers M Ed, MS. Part-time programs available. *Faculty:* 3 full-time (1 woman). *Students:* 1 full-time (0 women), 11 part-time (1 woman), 10 international. Average age 27. In 2009, 9 master's awarded. *Degree requirements:* For master's, comprehensive exam, thesis or alternative. *Entrance requirements:* For master's, GRE. Additional exam requirements/recommendations for international students: Recommended—IELTS. *Application deadline:* For fall admission, 8/15 priority date for domestic students. Application fee: $30. *Expenses:* Tuition: Part-time $452 per credit hour. Required fees: $101 per semester. Tuition and fees vary according to degree level, campus/location, program and student level. *Financial support:* Federal Work-Study and unspecified assistantships available. Support available to part-time students. Financial award applicants required to submit FAFSA. *Unit head:* Dr. Stan Baldwin, Dean, 601-925-3321, E-mail: sbaldwin@mc.edu. *Application contact:* Elnora Lewis, Secretary, 601-925-3225, Fax: 601-925-3889, E-mail: lewis09@mc.edu.

Mississippi State University, Bagley College of Engineering, Department of Computer Science and Engineering, MS State, MS 39762. Offers computer science (MS, PhD). Part-time programs available. Postbaccalaureate distance learning degree programs offered (minimal on-campus study). *Faculty:* 18 full-time (3 women). *Students:* 53 full-time (10 women), 15 part-time (5 women); includes 12 minority (10 African Americans, 2 Asian Americans or Pacific Islanders), 30 international. Average age 28. 123 applicants, 26% accepted, 19 enrolled. In 2009, 15 master's, 8 doctorates awarded. *Degree requirements:* For master's, comprehensive exam, thesis, comprehensive oral or written exam; for doctorate, comprehensive exam, thesis/dissertation, comprehensive oral or written exam. *Entrance requirements:* For master's, GRE, minimum GPA of 2.75; for doctorate, GRE. Additional exam requirements/recommendations for international students: Required—TOEFL (minimum score 550 paper-based; 213 computer-based; 79 iBT); Recommended—IELTS (minimum score 6.5). *Application deadline:* For fall admission, 7/1 for domestic students, 5/1 for international students; for spring admission, 11/1 for domestic students, 9/1 for international students. Applications are processed on a rolling basis. Application fee: $40. Electronic applications accepted. *Expenses:* Tuition, state resident: full-time $2575.50; part-time $286.25 per credit hour. Tuition, nonresident: full-time $6510; part-time $723.50 per credit hour. Tuition and fees vary according to course load. *Financial support:* In 2009–10, 20 research assistantships with full tuition reimbursements (averaging $12,945 per year), 12 teaching assistantships with full tuition reimbursements (averaging $12,075 per year) were awarded; Federal Work-Study, institutionally sponsored loans, and unspecified assistantships also available. Financial award application deadline: 4/1; financial award applicants required to submit FAFSA. *Faculty research:* Artificial intelligence, software engineering, visualization, high performance computing. Total annual research expenditures: $12 million. *Unit head:* Dr. Ray Vaughn, Professor and Department Head, 662-325-2756, Fax: 662-325-8997, E-mail: office@cse.msstate.edu. *Application contact:* Dr. Edward B. Allen, Associate Professor and Graduate Coordinator, 662-325-7449, Fax: 662-325-8997, E-mail: allen@cse.msstate.edu.

Missouri State University, Graduate College, College of Natural and Applied Sciences, Department of Computer Science, Springfield, MO 65897. Offers MNAS. Part-time programs available. *Faculty:* 5 full-time (1 woman). *Students:* 4 full-time (1 woman), 1 international. Average age 26. 3 applicants, 100% accepted, 2 enrolled. In 2009, 1 master's awarded. *Degree requirements:* For master's, comprehensive exam, thesis or alternative. *Entrance requirements:* For master's, GRE, minimum GPA of 3.0. Additional exam requirements/recommendations for international students: Required—TOEFL (minimum score 550 paper-based; 213 computer-based; 79 iBT). *Application deadline:* For fall admission, 7/20 priority date for domestic students, 5/1 for international students; for spring admission, 12/20 priority date for domestic students, 9/1 for international students. Applications are processed on a rolling basis. Application fee: $35 ($50 for international students). Electronic applications accepted. *Expenses:* Tuition, state resident: full-time $3852; part-time $214 per credit hour. Tuition, nonresident: full-time $7524; part-time $418 per credit hour. Required fees: $696; $172 per semester. Tuition and fees vary according to course level, course load, degree level and program. *Financial support:* Federal Work-Study, institutionally sponsored loans, scholarships/grants, and unspecified assistantships available. Financial award application deadline: 3/31; financial award applicants required to submit FAFSA. *Faculty research:* Floating point numbers, data compression, graph theory. *Unit head:* Dr. Lloyd A. Smith, Head, 417-836-4157, Fax: 417-836-6659, E-mail: lloydsmith@missouristate.edu. *Application contact:* Eric

Eckert, Coordinator of Admissions and Recruitment, 417-836-5331, Fax: 417-836-6200, E-mail: ericeckert@missouristate.edu.

Missouri University of Science and Technology, Graduate School, Department of Computer Science, Rolla, MO 65409. Offers MS, PhD. Part-time programs available. Terminal master's awarded for partial completion of doctoral program. *Degree requirements:* For doctorate, thesis/dissertation, departmental qualifying exam. *Entrance requirements:* For master's, GRE General Test (minimum score 700 quantitative, 4 writing); for doctorate, GRE Subject Test (minimum score: quantitative 600, writing 3.5). Electronic applications accepted. *Faculty research:* Intelligent systems, artificial intelligence software engineering, distributed systems, database systems, computer systems.

Monmouth University, Graduate School, Department of Computer Science, West Long Branch, NJ 07764-1898. Offers computer science (MS); software design and development (Certificate). Part-time and evening/weekend programs available. *Faculty:* 5 full-time (2 women), 5 part-time/adjunct (0 women). *Students:* 16 full-time (5 women), 18 part-time (10 women); includes 1 minority (Asian American or Pacific Islander), 25 international. Average age 25. 31 applicants, 87% accepted, 5 enrolled. In 2009, 14 master's awarded. *Degree requirements:* For master's, thesis optional. *Entrance requirements:* For master's, minimum GPA of 3.0 in major, 2.75 overall. Additional exam requirements/recommendations for international students: Required—TOEFL (minimum score 550 paper-based; 213 computer-based; 79 iBT), IELTS (minimum score 5), Michigan English Language Assessment Battery (minimum score 77), Cambridge A, B, C. *Application deadline:* For fall admission, 7/15 priority date for domestic students, 6/1 for international students; for spring admission, 11/15 priority date for domestic students, 11/1 for international students. Applications are processed on a rolling basis. Application fee: $50. Electronic applications accepted. *Expenses:* Tuition: Part-time $773 per credit. Required fees: $157 per semester. *Financial support:* In 2009–10, 25 students received support, including 24 fellowships (averaging $1,411 per year), 15 research assistantships (averaging $5,912 per year); career-related internships or fieldwork, scholarships/grants, and unspecified assistantships also available. Support available to part-time students. Financial award application deadline: 3/1; financial award applicants required to submit FAFSA. *Faculty research:* Databases, natural language processing, protocols, performance analysis, communications networks (systems), telecommunications. *Unit head:* Dr. Cui Yu, Program Director, 732-571-4460, Fax: 732-263-5202, E-mail: cyu@monmouth.edu. *Application contact:* Kevin Roane, Director, Office of Graduate Admission, 732-571-3452, Fax: 732-263-5123, E-mail: gradadm@monmouth.edu.

Montana State University, College of Graduate Studies, College of Engineering, Department of Computer Science, Bozeman, MT 59717. Offers computer science (MS, PhD). Part-time programs available. *Faculty:* 11 full-time (1 woman), 1 part-time/adjunct (0 women). *Students:* 24 full-time (2 women), 62 part-time (8 women); includes 6 minority (1 American Indian/Alaska Native, 3 Asian Americans or Pacific Islanders, 2 Hispanic Americans), 28 international. Average age 27. 28 applicants, 61% accepted, 14 enrolled. In 2009, 5 master's awarded. *Degree requirements:* For master's, comprehensive exam; for doctorate, comprehensive exam, thesis/dissertation. *Entrance requirements:* For master's and doctorate, GRE General Test. Additional exam requirements/recommendations for international students: Required—TOEFL (minimum score 550 paper-based; 213 computer-based). *Application deadline:* For fall admission, 7/15 priority date for domestic students, 5/15 priority date for international students; for spring admission, 12/1 priority date for domestic students, 10/1 priority date for international students. Applications are processed on a rolling basis. Application fee: $30. Electronic applications accepted. *Expenses:* Tuition, state resident: full-time $5635; part-time $3492 per year. Tuition, nonresident: full-time $17,212; part-time $7865.10 per year. Required fees: $1441.05; $153.15 per credit. Tuition and fees vary according to course load and program. *Financial support:* In 2009–10, 24 students received support, including 1 fellowship (averaging $20,000 per year), 11 research assistantships with full and partial tuition reimbursements available (averaging $13,933 per year), 12 teaching assistantships with full and partial tuition reimbursements available (averaging $5,063 per year). Financial award application deadline: 3/1; financial award applicants required to submit FAFSA. *Faculty research:* Applied algorithms, artificial intelligence, data mining, software engineering, Web-based learning, wireless networking. Total annual research expenditures: $427,908. *Unit head:* Dr. John Paxton, Head, 406-994-4780, Fax: 406-994-4376, E-mail: paxton@cs.montana.edu. *Application contact:* Dr. Carl A. Fox, Vice Provost for Graduate Education, 406-994-4145, Fax: 406-994-7433, E-mail: gradstudy@montana.edu.

Montclair State University, The Graduate School, College of Science and Mathematics, Department of Computer Science, Montclair, NJ 07043-1624. Offers applied mathematics (MS); applied statistics (MS); CISCO (Certificate); informatics (MS); object oriented computing (Certificate). Part-time and evening/weekend programs available. *Faculty:* 14 full-time (3 women), 16 part-time/adjunct (6 women). *Students:* 10 full-time (6 women), 21 part-time (6 women). Average age 31. 15 applicants, 67% accepted, 6 enrolled. In 2009, 11 master's awarded. *Degree requirements:* For master's, comprehensive exam, thesis or alternative. *Entrance requirements:* For master's, GRE General Test, 2 letters of recommendation. Additional exam requirements/recommendations for international students: Required—TOEFL (minimum score 83 computer-based), or IELTS. *Application deadline:* For fall admission, 6/1 for international students; for spring admission, 10/1 for international students. Applications are processed on a rolling basis. Application fee: $60. Electronic applications accepted. *Expenses:* Tuition, area resident: part-time $486.74 per credit. Tuition, state resident: part-time $486.74 per credit. Tuition, nonresident: part-time $751.34 per credit. Tuition and fees vary according to degree level and program. *Financial support:* In 2009–10, 4 research assistantships with full tuition reimbursements (averaging $7,000 per year) were awarded; Federal Work-Study, scholarships/grants, and unspecified assistantships also available. Support available to part-time students. Financial award application deadline: 3/1; financial award applicants required to submit FAFSA. *Unit head:* Dr. Dorothy Deremer, Chairperson, 973-655-4166. *Application contact:* Amy Aiello, Director of Graduate Admissions and Operations, 973-655-5147, Fax: 973-655-7869, E-mail: graduate.school@montclair.edu.

Montclair State University, The Graduate School, College of Science and Mathematics, Department of Mathematics, Montclair, NJ 07043-1624. Offers math pedagogy (Ed D); mathematics (MS), including computer science, mathematics education, pure and applied mathematics, statistics; physical science (Certificate); teaching middle grades math (MS, Certificate). Part-time and evening/weekend programs available. *Faculty:* 30 full-time (10 women), 39 part-time/adjunct (19 women). *Students:* 15 full-time (7 women), 101 part-time (75 women). Average age 32. 55 applicants, 76% accepted, 31 enrolled. In 2009, 32 master's, 2 doctorates, 9 other advanced degrees awarded. *Degree requirements:* For master's, comprehensive exam. *Entrance requirements:* For master's, GRE General Test, 2 letters of recommendation. Additional exam requirements/recommendations for international students: Required—TOEFL (minimum score 83 computer-based), or IELTS. *Application deadline:* For fall admission, 6/1 for international students; for spring admission, 10/1 for international students. Applications are processed on a rolling basis. Application fee: $60. *Expenses:* Tuition, area resident: Part-time $486.74 per credit. Tuition, state resident: part-time $486.74 per credit. Tuition, nonresident: part-time $751.34 per credit. Tuition and fees vary according to degree level and program. *Financial support:* In 2009–10, 9 research assistantships with full tuition reimbursements (averaging $7,000 per year), 1 teaching assistantship with full tuition reimbursement (averaging $15,000 per year) were awarded; Federal Work-Study, scholarships/grants, and unspecified assistantships also available. Support available to part-time students. Financial award application deadline: 3/1; financial award applicants required to submit FAFSA. *Faculty research:* Infectious disease. *Unit head:* Dr. Helen Roberts, Chairperson, 973-655-5132. *Application contact:* Amy Aiello, Director of Graduate Admissions and Operations, 973-655-5147, Fax: 973-655-7869, E-mail: graduate.school@montclair.edu.

National University, Academic Affairs, School of Engineering and Technology, Department of Computer Science and Information Systems, La Jolla, CA 92037-1011. Offers computer science (MS); information systems (MS); software engineering (MS); technology management

Computer Science

National University (continued)
(MS). Part-time and evening/weekend programs available. Postbaccalaureate distance learning degree programs offered (no on-campus study). *Faculty:* 18 full-time (10 women), 30 part-time/adjunct (7 women). *Students:* 88 full-time (19 women), 163 part-time (31 women); includes 57 minority (24 African Americans, 24 Asian Americans or Pacific Islanders, 9 Hispanic Americans), 111 international. Average age 32. 146 applicants, 100% accepted, 89 enrolled. In 2009, 51 master's awarded. *Degree requirements:* For master's, thesis. *Entrance requirements:* For master's, interview, minimum GPA of 2.5. Additional exam requirements/recommendations for international students: Required—TOEFL (minimum score 550 paper-based; 213 computer-based; 79 iBT), IELTS (minimum score 6). *Application deadline:* Applications are processed on a rolling basis. Application fee: $60 ($65 for international students). Electronic applications accepted. *Expenses:* Tuition: Part-time $338 per quarter hour. *Financial support:* Career-related internships or fieldwork, institutionally sponsored loans, scholarships/grants, and tuition waivers (partial) available. Support available to part-time students. Financial award application deadline: 6/30; financial award applicants required to submit FAFSA. *Unit head:* Dr. Ron Uhlig, Interim Chair and Instructor, 858-309-3412, Fax: 858-309-3420, E-mail: ruhlig@nu.edu. *Application contact:* Dominick Giovanniello, Associate Regional Dean—San Diego, 800-NAT-UNIV, Fax: 858-541-7792, E-mail: dgiovann@nu.edu.

Naval Postgraduate School, Graduate Programs, Department of Computer Science, Monterey, CA 93943. Offers computer science (MS, PhD); modeling of virtual environments and simulations (MS, PhD); software engineering (MS, PhD). Program only open to commissioned officers of the United States and friendly nations and selected United States federal civilian employees. Part-time programs available. Postbaccalaureate distance learning degree programs offered (minimal on-campus study). *Degree requirements:* For master's, thesis; for doctorate, one foreign language, thesis/dissertation.

New Jersey Institute of Technology, Office of Graduate Studies, College of Computing Science, Department of Computer Science, Newark, NJ 07102. Offers bioinformatics (MS); computer science (MS, PhD); computing and business (MS); software engineering (MS). Part-time and evening/weekend programs available. Terminal master's awarded for partial completion of doctoral program. *Degree requirements:* For master's, thesis optional; for doctorate, thesis/dissertation. *Entrance requirements:* For master's, GRE General Test; for doctorate, GRE General Test, minimum graduate GPA of 3.5. Additional exam requirements/recommendations for international students: Required—TOEFL (minimum score 550 paper-based; 213 computer-based; 79 iBT). Electronic applications accepted.

New Mexico Highlands University, Graduate Studies, College of Arts and Sciences, Program in Media Arts and Computer Science, Las Vegas, NM 87701. Offers media arts and computer science (MS). *Degree requirements:* For master's, comprehensive exam, thesis. *Entrance requirements:* For master's, minimum undergraduate GPA of 3.0. Additional exam requirements/recommendations for international students: Required—TOEFL (minimum score 540 paper-based; 270 computer-based). *Faculty research:* Advanced digital compositing, photographic installations and exhibition design, pattern recognition, parallel and distributed computing, computer security education.

New Mexico Institute of Mining and Technology, Graduate Studies, Department of Computer Science, Socorro, NM 87801. Offers MS, PhD. Part-time programs available. *Degree requirements:* For master's, thesis optional; for doctorate, thesis/dissertation. *Entrance requirements:* For master's, GRE General Test; for doctorate, GRE General Test, GRE Subject Test. Additional exam requirements/recommendations for international students: Required—TOEFL. Electronic applications accepted.

New Mexico State University, Graduate School, College of Arts and Sciences, Department of Computer Science, Las Cruces, NM 88003-8001. Offers bioinformatics (MS); computer science (MS, PhD). Part-time programs available. *Faculty:* 9 full-time (2 women), 1 part-time/adjunct (0 women). *Students:* 97 full-time (20 women), 18 part-time (3 women); includes 7 minority (2 Asian Americans or Pacific Islanders, 5 Hispanic Americans), 92 international. Average age 27. 232 applicants, 82% accepted, 34 enrolled. In 2009, 16 master's, 2 doctorates awarded. Terminal master's awarded for partial completion of doctoral program. *Degree requirements:* For master's, comprehensive exam, thesis or alternative; for doctorate, comprehensive exam, thesis/dissertation, qualifying examination, thesis proposal. *Entrance requirements:* For master's and doctorate, BS in computer science. Additional exam requirements/recommendations for international students: Required—TOEFL. *Application deadline:* For fall admission, 3/1 priority date for domestic and international students; for spring admission, 11/1 priority date for domestic and international students. Applications are processed on a rolling basis. Application fee: $30 ($50 for international students). Electronic applications accepted. *Expenses:* Tuition, state resident: full-time $4080; part-time $223 per credit. Tuition, nonresident: full-time $14,256; part-time $647 per credit. Required fees: $1278; $639 per semester. *Financial support:* In 2009–10, 36 research assistantships (averaging $9,586 per year), 26 teaching assistantships (averaging $5,340 per year) were awarded; fellowships, career-related internships or fieldwork, Federal Work-Study, scholarships/grants, health care benefits, and unspecified assistantships also available. Support available to part-time students. Financial award application deadline: 3/1; financial award applicants required to submit FAFSA. *Faculty research:* Programming languages, artificial intelligence, software engineering, bioinformatics, data mining, computer networks. *Unit head:* Dr. Enrico Pontelli, Head, 575-646-3723, Fax: 575-646-1002, E-mail: epontell@cs.nmsu.edu. *Application contact:* Dr. Mingzhou Song, Chair, Admissions Committee, 575-646-4299, Fax: 575-646-1002, E-mail: joemsong@cs.nmsu.edu.

New York Institute of Technology, Graduate Division, School of Engineering and Computing Sciences, Program in Computer Science, Old Westbury, NY 11568-8000. Offers MS. Part-time and evening/weekend programs available. *Students:* 132 full-time (37 women), 65 part-time (17 women); includes 12 minority (5 African Americans, 5 Asian Americans or Pacific Islanders, 2 Hispanic Americans), 162 international. Average age 26. In 2009, 77 master's awarded. *Degree requirements:* For master's, project. *Entrance requirements:* For master's, GRE General Test (if QPA less than 2.85), minimum QPA of 2.85, BS in computer science or related field. Additional exam requirements/recommendations for international students: Required—TOEFL (minimum score 550 paper-based; 213 computer-based). *Application deadline:* For fall admission, 7/1 priority date for domestic students; for spring admission, 12/1 priority date for domestic students. Applications are processed on a rolling basis. Application fee: $50. Electronic applications accepted. *Expenses:* Tuition: Part-time $825 per credit. *Financial support:* Fellowships, research assistantships with partial tuition reimbursements, institutionally sponsored loans, tuition waivers (partial), and unspecified assistantships available. Support available to part-time students. Financial award applicants required to submit FAFSA. *Faculty research:* Image processing, multimedia CD-ROM, prototype modules of the DTV application environment. *Unit head:* Dr. Ayat Jafari, Chair, 516-686-7523, Fax: 516-686-7439, E-mail: ajafari@nyit.edu. *Application contact:* Dr. Jacquelyn Nealon, Vice President for Enrollment Services, 516-686-7925, Fax: 516-686-7597, E-mail: jnealon@nyit.edu.

New York University, Graduate School of Arts and Science, Courant Institute of Mathematical Sciences, Department of Computer Science, New York, NY 10012-1019. Offers computer science (MS, PhD); information systems (MS); scientific computing (MS). Part-time and evening/weekend programs available. *Faculty:* 30 full-time (1 woman). *Students:* 175 full-time (43 women), 99 part-time (20 women); includes 25 minority (1 African American, 20 Asian Americans or Pacific Islanders, 4 Hispanic Americans), 176 international. Average age 28. 716 applicants, 34% accepted, 72 enrolled. In 2009, 80 master's, 8 doctorates awarded. *Degree requirements:* For doctorate, thesis/dissertation, oral and written exams. *Entrance requirements:* For master's and doctorate, GRE General Test, GRE Subject Test. Additional exam requirements/recommendations for international students: Required—TOEFL. *Application deadline:* For fall admission, 1/4 for domestic students; for spring admission, 11/1 for domestic students. Application fee: $90. *Expenses:* Tuition: Full-time $30,528; part-time $1272 per credit. Required fees: $2177. *Financial support:* Fellowships with tuition reimbursements, research assistantships with tuition reimbursements, teaching assistantships with tuition reimbursements, Federal Work-Study, institutionally sponsored loans, scholarships/grants, health care benefits, and unspecified assistantships available. Financial award application deadline: 1/4; financial award applicants required to submit FAFSA. *Faculty research:* Distributed parallel and secure computing, computer graphics and vision, algorithmic and theory of computation, natural language processing, computational biology. *Unit head:* Margaret Wright, Director of Graduate Studies, Ph.D. program, 212-998-3011, Fax: 212-995-4124, E-mail: admissions@cs.nyu.edu. *Application contact:* Benjamin Goldberg, Director of Graduate Studies, M.A. program, 212-998-3011, Fax: 212-995-4124, E-mail: admissions@cs.nyu.edu.

Nicholls State University, Graduate Studies, College of Arts and Sciences, Department of Mathematics and Computer Science, Thibodaux, LA 70310. Offers community/technical college mathematics (MS). Part-time and evening/weekend programs available. *Degree requirements:* For master's, comprehensive exam. *Entrance requirements:* For master's, GRE General Test. Electronic applications accepted. *Faculty research:* Operations research, statistics, numerical analysis, algebra, topology.

Norfolk State University, School of Graduate Studies, School of Science and Technology, Department of Computer Science, Norfolk, VA 23504. Offers MS.

North Carolina Agricultural and Technical State University, Graduate School, College of Engineering, Department of Computer Science, Greensboro, NC 27411. Offers MSCS. Part-time programs available. *Degree requirements:* For master's, comprehensive exam, thesis (for some programs). *Faculty research:* Object-oriented analysis, artificial intelligence, distributed computing, societal implications of computing, testing.

North Carolina Agricultural and Technical State University, Graduate School, School of Technology, Department of Electronics, Computer, and Information Technology, Greensboro, NC 27411. Offers electronics and computer technology (MSIT).

North Carolina State University, Graduate School, College of Engineering, Department of Computer Science, Raleigh, NC 27695. Offers MC Sc, MS, PhD. Part-time programs available. Postbaccalaureate distance learning degree programs offered. *Degree requirements:* For master's, thesis optional; for doctorate, thesis/dissertation. *Entrance requirements:* For master's, GRE General Test, GRE Subject Test, minimum GPA of 3.0; for doctorate, GRE General Test, GRE Subject Test (recommended), minimum GPA of 3.5. Additional exam requirements/recommendations for international students: Required—TOEFL. Electronic applications accepted. *Faculty research:* Networking and performance analysis, theory and algorithms of computation, data mining, graphics and human computer interaction, software engineering and information security.

North Carolina State University, Graduate School, College of Engineering, Department of Electrical and Computer Engineering and Department of Computer Science, Program in Computer Networking, Raleigh, NC 27695. Offers MS. *Degree requirements:* For master's, thesis optional. *Entrance requirements:* For master's, GRE General Test, GRE Subject Test (recommended). Electronic applications accepted. *Faculty research:* High-speed networks, performance modelling, security, wireless and mobile.

North Central College, Graduate Programs, Department of Computer Science, Naperville, IL 60566-7063. Offers MS. Part-time and evening/weekend programs available. *Degree requirements:* For master's, project. *Entrance requirements:* For master's, interview. *Expenses:* Contact institution. *Faculty research:* Experimental broadband network.

North Dakota State University, College of Graduate and Interdisciplinary Studies, College of Science and Mathematics, Department of Computer Science, Fargo, ND 58108. Offers computer science (MS, PhD); operations research (MS); software engineering (MS, PhD, Certificate). Part-time programs available. *Faculty:* 14 full-time (1 woman). *Students:* 47 full-time (10 women), 118 part-time (20 women); includes 107 minority (2 African Americans, 104 Asian Americans or Pacific Islanders, 1 Hispanic American). Average age 24. 152 applicants, 63% accepted, 43 enrolled. In 2009, 24 master's, 5 doctorates awarded. *Degree requirements:* For master's, comprehensive exam, thesis optional; for doctorate, thesis/dissertation, qualifying exam. *Entrance requirements:* For master's, minimum GPA of 3.0, BS in computer science or related field; for doctorate, minimum GPA of 3.25, MS in computer science or related field. Additional exam requirements/recommendations for international students: Required—TOEFL (minimum score 550 paper-based; 213 computer-based; 79 iBT). *Application deadline:* For fall admission, 8/15 priority date for domestic students, 8/15 for international students; for spring admission, 12/15 priority date for domestic students, 12/15 for international students. Application fee: $45 ($60 for international students). *Financial support:* In 2009–10, 37 research assistantships with full tuition reimbursements (averaging $10,000 per year), 17 teaching assistantships with full tuition reimbursements (averaging $4,500 per year) were awarded; career-related internships or fieldwork, Federal Work-Study, institutionally sponsored loans, and tuition waivers (full) also available. Financial award application deadline: 4/15. *Faculty research:* Networking, software engineering, artificial intelligence, database, programming languages. Total annual research expenditures: $366,434. *Unit head:* Dr. Brian Slator, Head, 701-231-8562, Fax: 701-231-8255. *Application contact:* Dr. Ken R. Nygard, Graduate Coordinator, 701-231-9460, Fax: 701-231-8255, E-mail: kendall.nygard@ndsu.edu.

Northeastern Illinois University, Graduate College, College of Arts and Sciences, Department of Computer Science, Program in Computer Science, Chicago, IL 60625-4699. Offers MS. Part-time and evening/weekend programs available. *Degree requirements:* For master's, comprehensive exam, research project or thesis. *Entrance requirements:* For master's, minimum GPA of 2.75, proficiency in 2 higher-level computer languages, 1 course in discrete mathematics. Additional exam requirements/recommendations for international students: Required—TOEFL (minimum score 550 paper-based; 213 computer-based; 80 iBT). Electronic applications accepted. *Faculty research:* Telecommunications, database inference problems, decision making under uncertainty, belief networks, analysis of algorithms.

Northeastern University, College of Computer and Information Science, Boston, MA 02115-5096. Offers computer and information science (PhD); computer science (MS); health informatics (MS); information assurance (MS). Part-time and evening/weekend programs available. *Faculty:* 28 full-time (3 women), 3 part-time/adjunct (all women). *Students:* 180 full-time (48 women), 15 part-time (0 women); includes 4 minority (2 Asian Americans or Pacific Islanders, 2 Hispanic Americans), 154 international. 829 applicants, 52% accepted, 74 enrolled. In 2009, 97 master's, 5 doctorates awarded. Terminal master's awarded for partial completion of doctoral program. *Degree requirements:* For master's, thesis optional; for doctorate, comprehensive exam, thesis/dissertation. *Entrance requirements:* For master's and doctorate, GRE General Test. Additional exam requirements/recommendations for international students: Required—TOEFL or IELTS. *Application deadline:* For fall admission, 7/15 for domestic students, 5/1 for international students; for spring admission, 10/15 for domestic students, 9/1 for international students. Applications are processed on a rolling basis. Application fee: $50. Electronic applications accepted. *Expenses:* Contact institution. *Financial support:* In 2009–10, 59 students received support, including 1 fellowship, 35 research assistantships with full tuition reimbursements available (averaging $18,260 per year), 24 teaching assistantships with full tuition reimbursements available (averaging $18,260 per year); career-related internships or fieldwork, Federal Work-Study, institutionally sponsored loans, scholarships/grants, and unspecified assistantships also available. Financial award application deadline: 1/15. *Faculty research:* Programming languages, artificial intelligence, human-computer interaction, database management, network security. *Unit head:* Dr. Larry A. Finkelstein, Dean, 617-373-2462, Fax: 617-373-5121. *Application contact:* Dr. Agnes Chan, Associate Dean and Director of Graduate Program, 617-373-2462, Fax: 617-373-5121, E-mail: gradschool@ccs.neu.edu.

Northern Arizona University, Graduate College, College of Engineering, Forestry and Natural Sciences, Programs in Engineering, Flagstaff, AZ 86011. Offers civil engineering (MSE); computer science (MSE); electrical engineering (MSE); environmental engineering (MSE); mechanical engineering (MSE). Postbaccalaureate distance learning degree programs offered (no on-campus study). *Faculty:* 43 full-time (11 women). *Students:* 30 full-time (4 women), 9 part-time (0 women); includes 6 minority (4 American Indian/Alaska Native, 1 Asian American or Pacific Islander, 1 Hispanic American), 10 international. Average age 28. 42 applicants, 55% accepted, 12 enrolled. In 2009, 4 master's awarded. *Degree requirements:* For master's, thesis. *Entrance requirements:* Additional exam requirements/recommendations for international students: Required—TOEFL (minimum score 550 paper-based; 213 computer-based; 80 iBT), IELTS (minimum score 7). *Application deadline:* For fall admission, 3/1 priority date for domestic students, 9/1 priority date for international students; for spring admission, 9/15 priority date for domestic students. Applications are processed on a rolling basis. Application fee: $65. Electronic applications accepted. *Financial support:* In 2009–10, 9 research assistantships with partial tuition reimbursements, 9 teaching assistantships with partial tuition reimbursements were awarded; career-related internships or fieldwork, Federal Work-Study, scholarships/grants, health care benefits, and unspecified assistantships also available. Support available to part-time students. Financial award application deadline: 3/30; financial award applicants required to submit FAFSA. *Unit head:* Dr. Ernesto Penado, Chair, 928-523-9453, Fax: 928-523-2300, E-mail: ernesto.penado@nau.edu. *Application contact:* Dieter Otte, Coordinator, 928-523-0876, Fax: 928-523-2300, E-mail: dieter.otte@nau.edu.

Northern Illinois University, Graduate School, College of Liberal Arts and Sciences, Department of Computer Science, De Kalb, IL 60115-2854. Offers MS. Part-time and evening/weekend programs available. *Faculty:* 14 full-time (3 women). *Students:* 133 full-time (38 women), 44 part-time (17 women); includes 6 minority (1 African American, 3 Asian Americans or Pacific Islanders, 2 Hispanic Americans), 151 international. Average age 23. 261 applicants, 64% accepted, 79 enrolled. In 2009, 114 master's awarded. *Degree requirements:* For master's, comprehensive exam. *Entrance requirements:* For master's, GRE General Test, minimum GPA of 2.75. Additional exam requirements/recommendations for international students: Required—TOEFL (minimum score 550 paper-based; 213 computer-based). *Application deadline:* For fall admission, 6/1 for domestic students, 5/1 for international students; for spring admission, 11/1 for domestic students, 10/1 for international students. Applications are processed on a rolling basis. Application fee: $30. Electronic applications accepted. *Expenses:* Tuition, state resident: full-time $6576; part-time $274 per credit hour. Tuition, nonresident: full-time $13,152; part-time $548 per credit hour. Required fees: $1813; $75.53 per credit hour. Part-time tuition and fees vary according to course load. *Financial support:* In 2009–10, 2 research assistantships with full tuition reimbursements, 26 teaching assistantships with full tuition reimbursements were awarded; fellowships with full tuition reimbursements, career-related internships or fieldwork, Federal Work-Study, scholarships/grants, tuition waivers (full), and unspecified assistantships also available. Support available to part-time students. Financial award applicants required to submit FAFSA. *Faculty research:* Databases, theorem proving, artificial intelligence, neural networks, computer ethics. *Unit head:* Dr. Nicholas Karonis, Chair, 815-753-0349, Fax: 815-753-0342, E-mail: karonis@niu.edu. *Application contact:* Graduate School Office, 815-753-0395, E-mail: gradsch@niu.edu.

Northern Kentucky University, Office of Graduate Programs, College of Informatics, Department of Computer Science, Highland Heights, KY 41099. Offers computer information technology (MSCIT); computer science (MSCS); secure software engineering (Certificate). Part-time and evening/weekend programs available. *Students:* 2 full-time (0 women), 20 part-time (4 women), 2 international. Average age 32. 29 applicants, 24% accepted, 4 enrolled. In 2009, 5 master's, 2 Certificates awarded. *Degree requirements:* For master's, thesis optional. *Entrance requirements:* For master's, minimum GPA of 3.0, at least 4 semesters of undergraduate study in computer science including intermediate computer programming and data structures, one year of calculus and a course in discrete mathematics. Additional exam requirements/recommendations for international students: Required—TOEFL (minimum score 550 paper-based; 213 computer-based; 79 iBT); Recommended—IELTS (minimum score 6.5). *Application deadline:* For fall admission, 8/1 for domestic students, 6/1 for international students; for spring admission, 12/1 for domestic students, 10/1 for international students. Applications are processed on a rolling basis. Application fee: $40. Electronic applications accepted. *Expenses:* Tuition, state resident: full-time $6912; part-time $384 per credit hour. Tuition, nonresident: full-time $12,150; part-time $675 per credit hour. Tuition and fees vary according to course load, program and reciprocity agreements. *Financial support:* Scholarships/grants and unspecified assistantships available. Financial award applicants required to submit FAFSA. *Faculty research:* Data privacy, data mining, wireless security, secure software engineering, secure networking. *Unit head:* Dr. Maureen Doyle, Program Director, 859-572-5468, Fax: 859-572-6097, E-mail: doylem3@nku.edu. *Application contact:* Dr. Peg Griffin, Director of Graduate Programs, 859-572-6934, Fax: 859-572-6670, E-mail: griffinp@nku.edu.

Northwestern Polytechnic University, School of Engineering, Fremont, CA 94539-7482. Offers computer science (MS); computer systems engineering (MS); electrical engineering (MS). Part-time and evening/weekend programs available. *Degree requirements:* For master's, thesis optional. *Entrance requirements:* For master's, minimum GPA of 3.0. Additional exam requirements/recommendations for international students: Required—TOEFL (minimum score 550 paper-based; 213 computer-based; 79 iBT). *Faculty research:* Computer networking, database design, Internet technology, software engineering, digital signal processing.

Northwestern University, McCormick School of Engineering and Applied Science, Department of Electrical Engineering and Computer Science, Evanston, IL 60208. Offers computer science (MS, PhD); electrical and computer engineering (MS, PhD); electronic materials (MS, PhD, Certificate); information technology (MIT). MS and PhD admissions and degrees offered through The Graduate School. Part-time programs available. Terminal master's awarded for partial completion of doctoral program. *Degree requirements:* For master's, thesis or project; for doctorate, thesis/dissertation. *Faculty research:* Solid-state engineering networks and communications, photonics, parallel and distributed computing, VLSI design and computer-aided design.

Northwest Missouri State University, Graduate School, Melvin and Valorie Booth College of Business and Professional Studies, Department of Computer Science and Information Systems, Maryville, MO 64468-6001. Offers applied computer science (MS); instructional technology (Certificate); teaching instructional technology (MS Ed). Part-time programs available. *Faculty:* 11 full-time (5 women). *Students:* 105 full-time (26 women), 30 part-time (22 women); includes 1 minority (Asian American or Pacific Islander), 105 international. 198 applicants, 67% accepted, 43 enrolled. In 2009, 34 master's awarded. *Degree requirements:* For master's, comprehensive exam. *Entrance requirements:* For master's, GRE General Test, minimum GPA of 3.0. Additional exam requirements/recommendations for international students: Required—TOEFL (minimum score 550 paper-based; 213 computer-based). *Application deadline:* Applications are processed on a rolling basis. Application fee: $0 ($50 for international students). *Expenses:* Tuition, state resident: part-time $296.34 per credit hour. Tuition, nonresident: part-time $510.43 per credit hour. *Financial support:* In 2009–10, 3 research assistantships (averaging $6,000 per year), 7 teaching assistantships with full tuition reimbursements (averaging $6,000 per year) were awarded; unspecified assistantships also available. Financial award application deadline: 4/1; financial award applicants required to submit FAFSA. *Unit head:* Dr. Phillip Heeler, Chairperson, 660-562-1200. *Application contact:* Dr. Gregory Haddock, Dean of Graduate School, 660-562-1145, Fax: 660-562-1096, E-mail: gradsch@nwmissouri.edu.

Nova Southeastern University, Graduate School of Computer and Information Sciences, Fort Lauderdale, FL 33314-7796. Offers computer information systems (MS, PhD), including information security; computer science (MS, PhD); computing technology in education (PhD); information security (MS); information systems (MS, PhD); management information systems (MS), including information security (MS, PhD), management information systems; JD/MS. Part-time and evening/weekend programs available. Postbaccalaureate distance learning degree programs offered (no on-campus study). *Faculty:* 20 full-time (5 women), 21 part-time/adjunct (3 women). *Students:* 144 full-time (39 women), 1,004 part-time (305 women); includes 440 minority (219 African Americans, 9 American Indian/Alaska Native, 80 Asian Americans or Pacific Islanders, 132 Hispanic Americans), 42 international. Average age 41. In 2009, 1,152 master's, 38 doctorates awarded. Terminal master's awarded for partial completion of doctoral program. *Degree requirements:* For master's, thesis optional; for doctorate, thesis/dissertation. *Entrance requirements:* For master's, minimum undergraduate GPA of 2.5; for doctorate, master's degree, minimum graduate GPA of 3.25. *Application deadline:* Applications are processed on a rolling basis. Application fee: $50. Electronic applications accepted. *Expenses:* Contact institution. *Financial support:* Federal Work-Study, scholarships/grants, and unspecified assistantships available. Support available to part-time students. Financial award application deadline: 5/1. *Faculty research:* Artificial intelligence, database management, human-computer interaction, distance education, information security. *Unit head:* Dr. Amon Seagull, Interim Dean, 954-262-7300. *Application contact:* 954-262-2000, Fax: 954-262-2752, E-mail: scisinfo@nova.edu.

Oakland University, Graduate Study and Lifelong Learning, School of Engineering and Computer Science, Department of Computer Science and Engineering, Rochester, MI 48309-4401. Offers computer science (MS); embedded systems (MS); information systems engineering (MS); software engineering (MS). Part-time and evening/weekend programs available. *Entrance requirements:* For master's, minimum GPA of 3.0 for unconditional admission. Electronic applications accepted. *Expenses:* Contact institution. *Faculty research:* Cyber security, 3D imaging of neurochemicals in rat brains.

OGI School of Science & Engineering at Oregon Health & Science University, Graduate Studies, Department of Computer Science and Electrical Engineering, Beaverton, OR 97006-8921. Offers computer science (PhD); computer science and engineering (MS, PhD); electrical engineering (MS, PhD). Part-time and evening/weekend programs available. Terminal master's awarded for partial completion of doctoral program. *Degree requirements:* For master's, thesis optional; for doctorate, comprehensive exam, oral defense of dissertation. *Entrance requirements:* For master's and doctorate, GRE General Test. Additional exam requirements/recommendations for international students: Required—TOEFL (minimum score 650 paper-based; 280 computer-based). Electronic applications accepted. *Faculty research:* Computer systems architecture, intelligent and interactive systems, programming models and systems, theory of computation.

The Ohio State University, Graduate School, College of Engineering, Department of Computer Science and Engineering, Columbus, OH 43210. Offers computer and information science (MS, PhD); computer science and engineering (MS). *Faculty:* 40. *Students:* 231 full-time (49 women), 65 part-time (11 women); includes 7 minority (1 African American, 4 Asian Americans or Pacific Islanders, 2 Hispanic Americans), 223 international. Average age 27. In 2009, 41 master's, 23 doctorates awarded. *Degree requirements:* For master's, thesis optional; for doctorate, thesis/dissertation. *Entrance requirements:* Additional exam requirements/recommendations for international students: Recommended—TOEFL (minimum score 600 paper-based; 250 computer-based). *Application deadline:* For fall admission, 8/15 priority date for domestic students, 7/1 priority date for international students; for winter admission, 12/1 priority date for domestic students, 11/1 priority date for international students; for spring admission, 3/1 priority date for domestic students, 2/1 priority date for international students. Applications are processed on a rolling basis. Application fee: $40 ($50 for international students). Electronic applications accepted. *Expenses:* Tuition, state resident: full-time $10,683. Tuition, nonresident: full-time $25,923. Tuition and fees vary according to course load and program. *Financial support:* Fellowships, teaching assistantships, career-related internships or fieldwork, Federal Work-Study, institutionally sponsored loans, and administrative assistantships available. Support available to part-time students. Financial award application deadline: 1/15. *Application contact:* 614-292-9444, Fax: 614-292-3895, E-mail: domestic.grad@osu.edu.

Ohio University, Graduate College, Russ College of Engineering and Technology, School of Electrical Engineering and Computer Science, Athens, OH 45701-2979. Offers computer science (MS); electrical engineering (MS); electrical engineering and computer science (PhD). *Faculty:* 34 full-time (2 women), 9 part-time/adjunct (3 women). *Students:* 72 full-time (16 women), 26 part-time (3 women); includes 2 minority (1 African American, 1 Hispanic American), 70 international. 123 applicants, 67% accepted, 18 enrolled. In 2009, 21 master's, 4 doctorates awarded. *Degree requirements:* For master's, comprehensive exam (for some programs), thesis; for doctorate, comprehensive exam, thesis/dissertation, qualifying exams. *Entrance requirements:* For master's, GRE, BSEE or BSCS, minimum GPA of 3.0; for doctorate, GRE, MSEE or MSCS, minimum GPA of 3.0. Additional exam requirements/recommendations for international students: Required—TOEFL (minimum score 550 paper-based; 80 iBT) or IELTS Academic (minimum score 6.5). *Application deadline:* For fall admission, 2/1 priority date for domestic students, 1/1 priority date for international students; for winter admission, 6/1 priority date for domestic students, 5/1 priority date for international students; for spring admission, 8/15 priority date for domestic students, 7/15 priority date for international students. Applications are processed on a rolling basis. Application fee: $50 ($55 for international students). Electronic applications accepted. *Expenses:* Tuition, state resident: full-time $7839; part-time $323 per quarter hour. Tuition, nonresident: full-time $15,831; part-time $654 per quarter hour. Required fees: $2931. *Financial support:* In 2009–10, 54 research assistantships with full tuition reimbursements, 19 teaching assistantships with full tuition reimbursements were awarded; Federal Work-Study, institutionally sponsored loans, scholarships/grants, and unspecified assistantships also available. Financial award applicants required to submit FAFSA. *Faculty research:* Avionics, networking/communications, intelligent distribution, real-time computing, control systems, optical properties of semiconductors. Total annual research expenditures: $8.2 million. *Unit head:* Dr. Shawn D. Ostermann, Chair, 740-593-1566, Fax: 740-593-0007, E-mail: osterman@eecs.ohiou.edu. *Application contact:* Dr. David Matolak, Graduate Chair, 740-593-1241, Fax: 740-593-0007, E-mail: matolak@ohio.edu.

Oklahoma City University, Meinders School of Business, Division of Computer Science, Oklahoma City, OK 73106-1402. Offers). Part-time and evening/weekend programs available. *Faculty:* 5 full-time (0 women). *Students:* 47 full-time (36 women), 26 part-time (19 women); includes 2 minority (both Asian Americans or Pacific Islanders), 69 international. Average age 26. 195 applicants, 99% accepted. In 2009, 42 master's awarded. *Degree requirements:* For master's, comprehensive exam, thesis optional. *Entrance requirements:* For master's, minimum GPA of 3.0. Additional exam requirements/recommendations for international students: Required—TOEFL. *Application deadline:* For fall admission, 8/20 for domestic students; for spring admission, 1/6 for domestic students. Applications are processed on a rolling basis. Application fee: $50 ($70 for international students). *Expenses:* Contact institution. *Financial support:* Fellowships with partial tuition reimbursements, career-related internships or fieldwork, Federal Work-Study, and tuition waivers (partial) available. Support available to part-time students. Financial award application deadline: 8/1; financial award applicants required to submit FAFSA. *Faculty research:* Parallel processing, pedagogical techniques, databases, numerical analysis, gesture recognition. *Unit head:* Dr. Mahmood Shandiz, Interim Chair/Senior Associate Dean, 405-208-5130, Fax: 405-208-5098, E-mail: mshandiz@okcu.edu. *Application contact:* Michelle Lockhart, Director, Admissions, 800-633-7242, Fax: 405-208-5916, E-mail: gadmissions@okcu.edu.

Oklahoma State University, College of Arts and Sciences, Computer Science Department, Stillwater, OK 74078. Offers MS, PhD. *Faculty:* 14 full-time (0 women). *Students:* 52 full-time (15 women), 62 part-time (11 women); includes 6 minority (1 African American, 4 American Indian/Alaska Native, 1 Asian American or Pacific Islander), 79 international. Average age 30. 323 applicants, 46% accepted, 35 enrolled. In 2009, 17 master's, 1 doctorate awarded. *Degree requirements:* For master's, thesis optional; for doctorate, comprehensive exam, thesis/dissertation. *Entrance requirements:* For master's, GRE; for doctorate, GRE General Test, GRE Subject Test in computer science (recommended), 3 letters of recommendation. Additional exam requirements/recommendations for international students: Required—TOEFL (minimum score 550 paper-based; 79 iBT). *Application deadline:* For fall admission, 3/1 priority date for international students; for spring admission, 8/1 priority date for international students. Applications are processed on a rolling basis. Application fee: $40 ($75 for international students). Electronic applications accepted. *Expenses:* Tuition, state resident: full-time $3716; part-time $154.85 per credit hour. Tuition, nonresident: full-time $14,448; part-time $602 per credit hour. Required fees: $1772; $73.85 per credit hour. One-time fee: $50. Tuition and fees vary according to course load and campus/location. *Financial support:* In 2009–10, 3 research

Computer Science

Oklahoma State University (continued)
assistantships (averaging $9,080 per year), 23 teaching assistantships (averaging $12,634 per year) were awarded; career-related internships or fieldwork, Federal Work-Study, scholarships/grants, health care benefits, tuition waivers (partial), and unspecified assistantships also available. Support available to part-time students. Financial award application deadline: 3/1; financial award applicants required to submit FAFSA. *Unit head:* Dr. Subhash Kak, Head, 405-744-5668, Fax: 405-774-9097. *Application contact:* Dr. Gordon Emslie, Dean, 405-744-6368, Fax: 405-744-0355, E-mail: grad-i@okstate.edu.

Old Dominion University, College of Sciences, Program in Computer Science, Norfolk, VA 23529. Offers MS, PhD. Part-time programs available. *Faculty:* 16 full-time (5 women). *Students:* 51 full-time (12 women), 63 part-time (19 women); includes 3 minority (1 African American, 1 American Indian/Alaska Native, 1 Asian American or Pacific Islander), 86 international. Average age 28. 200 applicants, 60% accepted. In 2009, 42 master's, 4 doctorates awarded. Terminal master's awarded for partial completion of doctoral program. *Degree requirements:* For master's, thesis optional, comprehensive diagnostic exam; for doctorate, comprehensive exam, thesis/dissertation. *Entrance requirements:* For master's, GRE General Test, minimum GPA of 3.0; for doctorate, GRE General Test, MS in computer science. Additional exam requirements/recommendations for international students: Required—TOEFL. *Application deadline:* For fall admission, 7/1 for domestic students. Applications are processed on a rolling basis. Application fee: $40. *Expenses:* Tuition, state resident: full-time $8112; part-time $338 per credit. Tuition, nonresident: full-time $20,256; part-time $844 per credit. Required fees: $119 per semester. One-time fee: $50. *Financial support:* In 2009–10, 98 students received support, including 1 fellowship (averaging $2,021 per year), 27 research assistantships with tuition reimbursements available (averaging $8,736 per year), 28 teaching assistantships with tuition reimbursements available (averaging $7,926 per year); career-related internships or fieldwork, scholarships/grants, and tuition waivers (partial) also available. Support available to part-time students. Financial award application deadline: 2/15; financial award applicants required to submit FAFSA. *Faculty research:* Software engineering, foundations, high-performance computing, networking, mobile computer. Total annual research expenditures: $1.4 million. *Unit head:* Dr. Mohammed Zubair, Graduate Program Director, 757-683-3917, Fax: 757-683-4900, E-mail: csgpd@odu.edu. *Application contact:* Dr. Mohammed Zubair, Graduate Program Director, 757-683-3917, Fax: 757-683-4900, E-mail: csgpd@odu.edu.

Old Dominion University, Frank Batten College of Engineering and Technology, Program in Modeling and Simulation, Norfolk, VA 23529. Offers ME, MS, D Eng, PhD. Part-time and evening/weekend programs available. Postbaccalaureate distance learning degree programs offered (no on-campus study). *Faculty:* 11 full-time (1 woman), 7 part-time/adjunct (1 woman). *Students:* 12 full-time (3 women), 43 part-time (7 women); includes 11 minority (7 African Americans, 2 Asian Americans or Pacific Islanders, 2 Hispanic Americans), 7 international. Average age 38. 19 applicants, 89% accepted, 16 enrolled. In 2009, 18 master's, 2 doctorates awarded. Terminal master's awarded for partial completion of doctoral program. *Degree requirements:* For master's, comprehensive exam (for some programs), thesis (for some programs); for doctorate, comprehensive exam, thesis/dissertation, candidacy exam. *Entrance requirements:* For master's, GRE, proficiency in calculus, calculus-based statistics, and computer science; for doctorate, GRE, graduate-level proficiency in calculus, calculus-based statistics, and computer science. Additional exam requirements/recommendations for international students: Required—TOEFL (minimum score 600 paper-based). *Application deadline:* For fall admission, 6/1 for domestic students, 2/15 priority date for international students; for spring admission, 11/1 for domestic students, 10/1 for international students. Applications are processed on a rolling basis. Application fee: $40. Electronic applications accepted. *Expenses:* Tuition, state resident: full-time $8112; part-time $338 per credit. Tuition, nonresident: full-time $20,256; part-time $844 per credit. Required fees: $119 per semester. One-time fee: $50. *Financial support:* In 2009–10, 17 students received support, including 2 fellowships with full tuition reimbursements available (averaging $24,000 per year), 4 research assistantships with full tuition reimbursements available (averaging $21,000 per year), 5 teaching assistantships with full tuition reimbursements available (averaging $21,000 per year); career-related internships or fieldwork, scholarships/grants, and unspecified assistantships also available. Financial award application deadline: 4/15; financial award applicants required to submit FAFSA. *Faculty research:* Distributed simulation and interoperability, medical modeling and simulation, transportation modeling and simulation, human factors, discrete event systems. Total annual research expenditures: $5.7 million. *Unit head:* Dr. Roland Mielke, Graduate Program Director, 757-683-4570, Fax: 757-683-3220, E-mail: rmielke@odu.edu. *Application contact:* Dr. Roland Mielke, Graduate Program Director, 757-683-4570, Fax: 757-683-3220, E-mail: rmielke@odu.edu.

Oregon Health & Science University, OGI School of Science and Engineering, Department of Computer Science and Engineering, Portland, OR 97239-3098. Offers computer science and engineering (MS, PhD); electrical engineering (MS, PhD). Tuition and fees vary according to course level, course load, degree level, program and reciprocity agreements.

Oregon State University, Graduate School, College of Engineering, School of Electrical Engineering and Computer Science, Corvallis, OR 97331. Offers computer science (M Eng, MAIS, MS, PhD); electrical and computer engineering (M Eng, MS, PhD). *Faculty:* 38 full-time (6 women), 5 part-time/adjunct (3 women). *Students:* 216 full-time (41 women), 52 part-time (6 women); includes 24 minority (2 African Americans, 19 Asian Americans or Pacific Islanders, 3 Hispanic Americans), 149 international. Average age 29. In 2009, 48 master's, 15 doctorates awarded. *Degree requirements:* For doctorate, thesis/dissertation, qualifying exam, preliminary exam. *Entrance requirements:* For master's and doctorate, minimum GPA of 3.0 in last 90 hours of course work. Additional exam requirements/recommendations for international students: Required—TOEFL (minimum score 600 paper-based; 250 computer-based; 80 iBT). *Application deadline:* For fall admission, 1/15 for domestic and international students. Application fee: $50. Electronic applications accepted. *Expenses:* Tuition, state resident: full-time $9774; part-time $362 per credit. Tuition, nonresident: full-time $15,849; part-time $587 per credit. Required fees: $1639. Full-time tuition and fees vary according to course load and program. *Financial support:* Fellowships with full tuition reimbursements, research assistantships with full tuition reimbursements, teaching assistantships with full tuition reimbursements, career-related internships or fieldwork, Federal Work-Study, and institutionally sponsored loans available. Support available to part-time students. Financial award application deadline: 1/15. *Faculty research:* Optical materials and devices, data security and cryptography, analog and mixed-signal integrated circuit design, algorithms, computer graphics and vision. Total annual research expenditures: $7.5 million. *Unit head:* Dr. Theresa Shreeve Fiez, Director, 541-737-3118, Fax: 541-737-1300, E-mail: terri@eecs.oregonstate.edu. *Application contact:* Ferne Simendinger, Graduate Coordinator, 541-737-3617, Fax: 541-737-1300, E-mail: ferne@eecs.oregonstate.edu.

Pace University, Seidenberg School of Computer Science and Information Systems, New York, NY 10038. Offers computer communications and networks (Certificate); computer science (MS); computing studies (DPS); information systems (MS); Internet technologies for e-commerce (MS); Internet technology (MS); object-oriented programming (Certificate); security and information assurance (Certificate); software development and engineering (MS); telecommunications (MS, Certificate). Part-time and evening/weekend programs available. *Students:* 122 full-time (37 women), 424 part-time (131 women); includes 188 minority (76 African Americans, 1 American Indian/Alaska Native, 65 Asian Americans or Pacific Islanders, 46 Hispanic Americans), 110 international. Average age 35. 352 applicants, 89% accepted, 128 enrolled. In 2009, 137 master's, 11 doctorates, 3 other advanced degrees awarded. *Entrance requirements:* For master's, GRE General Test. Additional exam requirements/recommendations for international students: Required—TOEFL. *Application deadline:* For fall admission, 7/31 priority date for domestic students; for spring admission, 11/30 for domestic students. Applications are processed on a rolling basis. Application fee: $70. Electronic applications accepted. *Expenses:* Contact institution. *Financial support:* Research assistantships, career-related internships or fieldwork available. Support available to part-time students. Financial award applicants required to submit FAFSA. *Unit head:* Dr. Constance Knapp, Interim Dean, 914-773-3750, Fax: 914-773-3533, E-mail: cknapp@pace.edu. *Application contact:* Joanna Broda, Director of Graduate Admissions, 914-422-4283, Fax: 914-422-4287, E-mail: gradwp@pace.edu.

Pacific States University, College of Computer Science, Los Angeles, CA 90006. Offers computer science (MSCS); information systems (MSCS). Part-time and evening/weekend programs available. *Entrance requirements:* For master's, bachelor's degree in physics, engineering, computer science, or applied mathematics; minimum undergraduate GPA of 2.5 during last 90 hours of course work. Additional exam requirements/recommendations for international students: Required—TOEFL (minimum score 133 computer-based).

Penn State University Park, Graduate School, College of Engineering, Department of Computer Science and Engineering, State College, University Park, PA 16802-1503. Offers M Eng, MS, PhD.

See Close-Up on page 305.

Polytechnic Institute of NYU, Department of Computer Science and Engineering, Major in Computer Science, Brooklyn, NY 11201-2990. Offers MS, PhD. Part-time and evening/weekend programs available. *Students:* 225 full-time (58 women), 82 part-time (15 women); includes 35 minority (7 African Americans, 23 Asian Americans or Pacific Islanders, 5 Hispanic Americans), 226 international. 699 applicants, 66% accepted, 127 enrolled. In 2009, 76 master's, 2 doctorates awarded. *Degree requirements:* For master's, comprehensive exam (for some programs), thesis (for some programs); for doctorate, comprehensive exam, thesis/dissertation. *Entrance requirements:* For master's, BA or BS in computer science, mathematics, science, or engineering; working knowledge of a high-level program; for doctorate, GRE General Test, GRE Subject Test, qualifying exam, BA or BS in science, engineering, or management; MS or 1 year of graduate course work. Additional exam requirements/recommendations for international students: Required—TOEFL (minimum score 550 paper-based; 213 computer-based; 80 iBT); Recommended—IELTS (minimum score 6.5). *Application deadline:* For fall admission, 7/31 priority date for domestic students, 4/30 priority date for international students; for spring admission, 12/31 priority date for domestic students, 11/30 priority date for international students. Applications are processed on a rolling basis. Application fee: $75. Electronic applications accepted. *Expenses:* Tuition: Full-time $21,492; part-time $1194 per credit hour. Required fees: $1160; $204 per course. *Financial support:* Research assistantships, teaching assistantships, institutionally sponsored loans, scholarships/grants, and unspecified assistantships available. Support available to part-time students. Financial award applicants required to submit FAFSA. *Unit head:* Dr. Keith W. Ross, Head, 718-260-3859, Fax: 718-260-3609, E-mail: ross@poly.edu. *Application contact:* JeanCarlo Bonilla, Director of Graduate Enrollment Management, 718-260-3182, Fax: 718-260-3624, E-mail: gradinfo@poly.edu.

Polytechnic Institute of NYU, Long Island Graduate Center, Graduate Programs, Department of Computer Science and Engineering, Program in Computer Science, Melville, NY 11747. Offers MS. *Students:* 3 full-time (0 women), 23 part-time (3 women); includes 8 minority (all Asian Americans or Pacific Islanders), 1 international. 6 applicants, 100% accepted, 6 enrolled. In 2009, 13 master's awarded. *Degree requirements:* For master's, comprehensive exam (for some programs), thesis (for some programs). *Entrance requirements:* Additional exam requirements/recommendations for international students: Required—TOEFL (minimum score 550 paper-based; 213 computer-based; 80 iBT); Recommended—IELTS (minimum score 6.5). *Application deadline:* For fall admission, 7/31 priority date for domestic students, 4/30 priority date for international students; for spring admission, 12/31 priority date for domestic students, 11/30 priority date for international students. Applications are processed on a rolling basis. Application fee: $75. Electronic applications accepted. *Financial support:* Institutionally sponsored loans, scholarships/grants, and unspecified assistantships available. Support available to part-time students. Financial award applicants required to submit FAFSA. *Unit head:* Dr. Keith W. Ross, Department Head, 718-260-3859, E-mail: ross@poly.edu. *Application contact:* JeanCarlo Bonilla, Director of Graduate Enrollment Management, 718-260-3182, Fax: 718-260-3624, E-mail: gradinfo@poly.edu.

Polytechnic Institute of NYU, Westchester Graduate Center, Graduate Programs, Department of Computer Science and Engineering, Major in Computer Science, Hawthorne, NY 10532-1507. Offers MS. *Students:* 8 full-time (1 woman), 13 part-time (0 women); includes 3 minority (2 Asian Americans or Pacific Islanders, 1 Hispanic American), 6 international. 4 applicants, 100% accepted, 4 enrolled. In 2009, 3 master's awarded. *Degree requirements:* For master's, comprehensive exam (for some programs), thesis (for some programs). *Entrance requirements:* Additional exam requirements/recommendations for international students: Required—TOEFL (minimum score 550 paper-based; 213 computer-based; 80 iBT); Recommended—IELTS (minimum score 6.5). *Application deadline:* For fall admission, 7/31 priority date for domestic students, 4/30 priority date for international students; for spring admission, 12/31 priority date for domestic students, 11/30 priority date for international students. Applications are processed on a rolling basis. Application fee: $75. Electronic applications accepted. *Financial support:* Institutionally sponsored loans, scholarships/grants, and unspecified assistantships available. Support available to part-time students. *Unit head:* Dr. Keith W. Ross, Department Head, 718-260-3859, E-mail: ross@poly.edu. *Application contact:* JeanCarlo Bonilla, Director of Graduate Enrollment Management, 718-260-3182, Fax: 718-260-3624, E-mail: gradinfo@poly.edu.

Polytechnic University of Puerto Rico, Graduate School, Hato Rey, PR 00919. Offers business administration (MBA), including general studies, management of information systems, management of international enterprises; civil engineering (ME, MS); computer engineering (ME, MS); computer science (MS); electrical engineering (ME, MS); engineering management (MEM); environmental management (MEPM); landscape architecture (M Land Arch); manufacturing competitiveness (MMC, MS); manufacturing engineering (ME, MS). Part-time and evening/weekend programs available. *Entrance requirements:* For master's, 3 letters of recommendation.

Portland State University, Graduate Studies, Maseeh College of Engineering and Computer Science, Department of Computer Science, Portland, OR 97207-0751. Offers computer science (MS, PhD); software engineering (MSE). Part-time programs available. *Degree requirements:* For master's, thesis or alternative; for doctorate, thesis/dissertation. *Entrance requirements:* For master's, GRE General Test, minimum GPA of 3.0 in upper-division course work, 2 letters of recommendation, BS in computer science or allied field; for doctorate, MS in computer science or allied field. Additional exam requirements/recommendations for international students: Required—TOEFL (minimum score 550 paper-based; 213 computer-based). *Faculty research:* Formal methods, database systems, parallel programming environments, computer security, software tools.

Prairie View A&M University, College of Engineering, Prairie View, TX 77446-0519. Offers computer information systems (MSCIS); computer science (MSCS); electrical engineering (MSEE, PhDEE); engineering (MS Engr). Part-time and evening/weekend programs available. *Faculty:* 19 full-time (0 women). *Students:* 64 full-time (18 women), 47 part-time (14 women); includes 43 minority (36 African Americans, 4 Asian Americans or Pacific Islanders, 3 Hispanic Americans), 51 international. Average age 24. 50 applicants, 84% accepted, 33 enrolled. In 2009, 26 master's, 3 doctorates awarded. *Degree requirements:* For master's, thesis (for some programs); for doctorate, comprehensive exam, thesis/dissertation. *Entrance requirements:* For master's, GRE General Test, bachelor's degree in engineering from an ABET accredited institution; for doctorate, GRE. Additional exam requirements/recommendations for international students: Required—TOEFL (minimum score 550 paper-based). *Application deadline:* For fall admission, 7/1 priority date for domestic and international students; for spring admission, 11/1 priority date for domestic and international students. Application fee: $50. Electronic applications accepted. *Expenses:* Tuition, state resident: full-time $2200. Tuition, nonresident: full-time $5600. Required fees: $1720. Tuition and fees vary according to course load. *Financial support:* In 2009–10, 80 students received support, including 14 fellowships (averaging $1,050 per year), 16 research assistantships (averaging $16,150 per year), 13 teaching assistantships (averaging $14,000 per year); career-related internships or fieldwork, institutionally sponsored loans, scholarships/grants, health care benefits, tuition waivers (partial), and unspecified assistantships also available. Financial award application deadline: 3/1; financial award applicants required to submit FAFSA. *Faculty research:* Applied radiation research, thermal science, computational fluid dynamics, analog mixed signal, aerial space battlefield. Total annual research expenditures: $439,054. *Unit head:* Dr. Kendall T. Harris, Dean, 936-261-9956, Fax: 936-261-9869, E-mail: tharris@pvamu.edu. *Application contact:* Barbara A. Thompson, Administrative Assistant, 936-261-9896, Fax: 936-261-9869, E-mail: bathompson@pvamu.edu.

Princeton University, Graduate School, School of Engineering and Applied Science, Department of Computer Science, Princeton, NJ 08544-1019. Offers MSE, PhD. *Faculty:* 29 full-time (4 women). Terminal master's awarded for partial completion of doctoral program. *Degree requirements:* For master's, thesis; for doctorate, thesis/dissertation, general exam. *Entrance requirements:* For master's, GRE General Test, GRE Subject Test (recommended), 3 letters of recommendation; for doctorate, GRE General Test; GRE Subject Test recommended, official transcript(s), 3 letters of recommendation, personal statement. Additional exam requirements/recommendations for international students: Required—TOEFL. *Application deadline:* For fall admission, 12/15 for domestic and international students. Application fee: $90. Electronic applications accepted. *Financial support:* Fellowships with full tuition reimbursements, research assistantships with full tuition reimbursements, teaching assistantships with full tuition reimbursements, institutionally sponsored loans and health care benefits available. *Faculty research:* Computational biology and bioinformatics; computer and network systems; graphics, vision, and sound; machine learning, programming languages and security; theory. *Unit head:* Melissa Lawson, Graduate Program Administrator, 609-258-5387, Fax: 609-258-1771, E-mail: gradinfo@cs.princeton.edu. *Application contact:* Michelle Carman, Manager of Graduate Admissions, 609-258-3034, Fax: 609-258-7262, E-mail: gsadmit@princeton.edu.

Purdue University, Graduate School, College of Science, Department of Computer Sciences, West Lafayette, IN 47907. Offers MS, PhD. Part-time programs available. Terminal master's awarded for partial completion of doctoral program. *Degree requirements:* For master's, thesis optional; for doctorate, thesis/dissertation. *Entrance requirements:* For master's and doctorate, minimum GPA of 3.5. Additional exam requirements/recommendations for international students: Required—TOEFL (minimum score 600 paper-based; 250 computer-based), TWE (minimum score 5). Electronic applications accepted. *Faculty research:* Geometric modeling, information security, software systems, theory and algorithms, databases, networking.

Queens College of the City University of New York, Division of Graduate Studies, Mathematics and Natural Sciences Division, Department of Computer Science, Flushing, NY 11367-1597. Offers MA. Part-time and evening/weekend programs available. *Faculty:* 22 full-time (5 women). *Students:* 12 full-time (5 women), 63 part-time (16 women). 67 applicants, 64% accepted, 24 enrolled. In 2009, 14 master's awarded. *Degree requirements:* For master's, comprehensive exam, thesis optional. *Entrance requirements:* For master's, GRE, minimum GPA of 3.0. Additional exam requirements/recommendations for international students: Required—TOEFL. *Application deadline:* For fall admission, 4/1 for domestic students; for spring admission, 11/1 for domestic students. Applications are processed on a rolling basis. Application fee: $125. *Expenses:* Tuition, state resident: full-time $7360; part-time $310 per credit. Tuition, nonresident: part-time $575 per credit. One-time fee: $195.25 full-time; $145.25 part-time. *Financial support:* Career-related internships or fieldwork, Federal Work-Study, institutionally sponsored loans, tuition waivers (partial), and unspecified assistantships available. Support available to part-time students. Financial award application deadline: 4/1; financial award applicants required to submit FAFSA. *Faculty research:* Fifth-generation computing, hardware/software development, analysis of algorithms and theoretical computer science. *Unit head:* Dr. Zhigang Xiang, Chairperson, 718-997-3500. *Application contact:* Dr. Keitaro Yukawa, Graduate Adviser, 718-997-3500, E-mail: keitaro_yukawa@qc.edu.

Queen's University at Kingston, School of Graduate Studies and Research, Faculty of Arts and Sciences, School of Computing, Kingston, ON K7L 3N6, Canada. Offers M Sc, PhD. *Degree requirements:* For master's, thesis; for doctorate, comprehensive exam, thesis/dissertation. *Entrance requirements:* For master's, honours B Sc in computer science; for doctorate, M Sc in computer science. Additional exam requirements/recommendations for international students: Required—TOEFL, TWE. *Faculty research:* Software engineering, human computer interaction, data base, networks, computational geometry.

Regis University, College for Professional Studies, School of Computer and Information Sciences, Denver, CO 80221-1099. Offers database administration with IBM DB2 (Certificate); database administration with Oracle (Certificate); database development (Certificate); database technologies (MA); enterprise Java software development (Certificate); executive information technologies (Certificate); information assurance (MA, Certificate); information technology management (MA); software and information systems (M Sc); software engineering (MA, Certificate); storage area networks (Certificate); systems engineering (MA, Certificate). Offered at Boulder Campus, Northwest Denver Campus, Southeast Denver Campus, Fort Collins Campus, Colorado Springs Campus, and Broomfield Campus. Part-time and evening/weekend programs available. Postbaccalaureate distance learning degree programs offered (no on-campus study). *Degree requirements:* For master's, thesis, final research project. *Entrance requirements:* For master's, 2 years of related experience, resume, interview; for Certificate, 2 years of related experience, resumé. Additional exam requirements/recommendations for international students: Required—TOEFL (minimum score 213 computer-based), TWE (minimum score 5), TOEFL or university-based test. Electronic applications accepted. *Expenses:* Contact institution. *Faculty research:* Secure Virtual Laboratory Architecture, Joint IA project with W2C06 Institute, Information Policy, OLTP and OLAP Technologies, knowledge management, software architectures.

Rensselaer at Hartford, Department of Computer and Information Science, Hartford, CT 06120-2991. Offers computer science (MS); information technology (MS). Part-time and evening/weekend programs available. *Faculty:* 3 full-time (0 women), 6 part-time/adjunct (0 women). *Students:* 2 full-time (0 women), 50 part-time (6 women); includes 14 minority (2 African Americans, 6 Asian Americans or Pacific Islanders, 6 Hispanic Americans), 1 international. Average age 34. 17 applicants, 59% accepted, 10 enrolled. In 2009, 8 master's awarded. *Degree requirements:* For master's, thesis optional. *Entrance requirements:* For master's, GRE. Additional exam requirements/recommendations for international students: Required—TOEFL (minimum score 600 paper-based; 250 computer-based; 100 iBT). *Application deadline:* For fall admission, 8/30 priority date for domestic students, 8/1 priority date for international students. Applications are processed on a rolling basis. Application fee: $75. Electronic applications accepted. *Expenses:* Tuition: Full-time $31,800; part-time $1325 per credit hour. *Financial support:* Research assistantships, tuition waivers (full and partial) and unspecified assistantships available. Support available to part-time students. Financial award applicants required to submit FAFSA. *Unit head:* Dr. Houman Younessi, Assistant Dean for Academic Programs, 860-548-7880, E-mail: youneh@rpi.edu. *Application contact:* Kristin Galligan, Director, Enrollment Management and Marketing, 860-548-2480, Fax: 860-548-7823, E-mail: info@ewp.rpi.edu.

Rensselaer Polytechnic Institute, Graduate School, School of Science, Department of Computer Science, Troy, NY 12180-3590. Offers MS, PhD. Part-time programs available. *Faculty:* 19 full-time (4 women). *Students:* 74 full-time (10 women), 12 part-time (5 women); includes 14 Asian Americans or Pacific Islanders, 9 international. Average age 28. 332 applicants, 12% accepted, 24 enrolled. In 2009, 17 master's, 14 doctorates awarded. Terminal master's awarded for partial completion of doctoral program. *Degree requirements:* For master's, thesis; for doctorate, comprehensive exam, thesis/dissertation. *Entrance requirements:* For master's and doctorate, GRE General Test. Additional exam requirements/recommendations for international students: Required—TOEFL (minimum score 570 paper-based; 230 computer-based; 89 iBT). *Application deadline:* For fall admission, 1/1 priority date for domestic and international students; for spring admission, 8/15 priority date for domestic and international students. Applications are processed on a rolling basis. Application fee: $75. Electronic applications accepted. *Expenses:* Tuition: Full-time $38,100. *Financial support:* In 2009–10, 69 students received support, including 3 fellowships with full tuition reimbursements available (averaging $22,000 per year), 45 research assistantships with full tuition reimbursements available (averaging $16,500 per year), 21 teaching assistantships with full tuition reimbursements available (averaging $16,500 per year); unspecified assistantships also available. Financial award application deadline: 1/1. *Faculty research:* Computer vision and graphics, algorithms and theory, pervasive computing and networking, data mining and machine learning, semantic web. *Unit head:* Prof. Martin Hardwick, Acting Department Head, 518-276-8291, Fax: 518-276-4033, E-mail: hardwick@cs.rpi.edu. *Application contact:* Terry Hayden, Coordinator of Graduate Admissions, 518-276-8419, Fax: 518-276-4033, E-mail: grad-adm@cs.rpi.edu.

Rice University, Graduate Programs, George R. Brown School of Engineering, Department of Computer Science, Houston, TX 77251-1892. Offers MCS, MS, PhD. *Faculty:* 19 full-time (2 women), 3 part-time/adjunct (0 women). *Students:* 70 full-time (13 women), 1 part-time (0 women); includes 38 minority (1 African American, 36 Asian Americans or Pacific Islanders, 1 Hispanic American), 15 international. Average age 24. 315 applicants, 16% accepted, 23 enrolled. In 2009, 8 master's, 15 doctorates awarded. Terminal master's awarded for partial completion of doctoral program. *Degree requirements:* For master's, comprehensive exam; for doctorate, comprehensive exam, thesis/dissertation. *Entrance requirements:* For doctorate, Bachelor's Degree. Additional exam requirements/recommendations for international students: Required—TOEFL. *Application deadline:* For fall admission, 1/9 priority date for domestic students, 1/8 priority date for international students; for winter admission, 1/9 priority date for domestic and international students; for spring admission, 11/1 for domestic and international students. Application fee: $70. Electronic applications accepted. *Financial support:* In 2009–10, 6 fellowships (averaging $2,175 per year), 17 research assistantships (averaging $2,175 per year), teaching assistantships (averaging $2,175 per year) were awarded. Financial award applicants required to submit FAFSA. *Faculty research:* Programming languages and compiler construction; robotics, bioinformatics, algorithms—motion planning with emphasis on high-dimensional systems; network protocols, distributed systems, and operating systems—adaptive protocols for wireless; computer architecture, aperating systems—virtual machine monitors; computer graphics—application of computers to geometric problems and centered around general problem of representing geometric shapes. *Unit head:* Belia Martinez, Department Coordinator, 713-348-8213, Fax: 713-348-5930, E-mail: bellam@rice.edu. *Application contact:* Amanda Nokleby, Administrative Assistant, 713-348-2031, Fax: 713-348-5930, E-mail: akn3@rice.edu.

Rivier College, School of Graduate Studies, Department of Computer Science and Mathematics, Nashua, NH 03060. Offers computer science (MS); mathematics (MAT). Part-time and evening/weekend programs available. *Faculty:* 6 full-time (3 women), 4 part-time/adjunct (0 women). *Students:* 2 full-time (both women), 16 part-time (10 women); includes 1 minority (African American). Average age 36. In 2009, 10 master's awarded. *Entrance requirements:* For master's, GRE Subject Test. *Application deadline:* Applications are processed on a rolling basis. Application fee: $25. Electronic applications accepted. *Expenses:* Tuition: Part-time $447 per credit. *Financial support:* Available to part-time students. Application deadline: 2/1; *Unit head:* Dr. Paul Cunningham, Director, 603-897-8272, E-mail: pcunningham@rivier.edu. *Application contact:* Mathew Kittredge, Director of Graduate Admissions, 603-897-8129, Fax: 603-897-8810, E-mail: mkittredge@rivier.edu.

Rochester Institute of Technology, Graduate Enrollment Services, B. Thomas Golisano College of Computing and Information Sciences, Department of Computer Science, Rochester, NY 14623-5603. Offers MS. Part-time and evening/weekend programs available. *Students:* 180 full-time (30 women), 58 part-time (13 women); includes 9 minority (1 African American, 2 American Indian/Alaska Native, 4 Asian Americans or Pacific Islanders, 2 Hispanic Americans), 159 international. Average age 26. 424 applicants, 79% accepted, 73 enrolled. In 2009, 45 master's awarded. *Degree requirements:* For master's, thesis or project. *Entrance requirements:* For master's, GRE, minimum GPA of 3.0. Additional exam requirements/recommendations for international students: Required—TOEFL (minimum score 550 paper-based; 213 computer-based; 80 iBT), or IELTS (minimum score 6.5). *Application deadline:* For fall admission, 2/15 priority date for domestic and international students; for winter admission, 11/1 for domestic and international students. Applications are processed on a rolling basis. Application fee: $50. Electronic applications accepted. *Expenses:* Tuition: Full-time $31,533; part-time $876 per credit hour. Required fees: $210. *Financial support:* In 2009–10, 149 students received support; research assistantships with partial tuition reimbursements available, teaching assistantships with partial tuition reimbursements available, career-related internships or fieldwork, scholarships/grants, and unspecified assistantships available. Support available to part-time students. Financial award applicants required to submit FAFSA. *Faculty research:* Computational vision and acoustics, computer graphics and visualization, data management, distributed systems, intelligent systems, language design, security. *Unit head:* Prof. Paul Tymann, Department Chair, 585-475-2118, Fax: 585-475-4935, E-mail: ptt@cs.rit.edu. *Application contact:* Diane Ellison, Assistant Vice President, Graduate Enrollment Services, 585-475-2229, Fax: 585-475-7164, E-mail: gradinfo@rit.edu.

Rochester Institute of Technology, Graduate Enrollment Services, B. Thomas Golisano College of Computing and Information Sciences, Department of Networking, Security and Systems Administration, Program in Networking and Systems Administration, Rochester, NY 14623-5603. Offers network planning and design (AC); networking and systems administration (MS, AC). Part-time programs available. Postbaccalaureate distance learning degree programs offered (no on-campus study). *Students:* 36 full-time (3 women), 69 part-time (10 women); includes 5 African Americans, 1 Asian American or Pacific Islander, 24 international. Average age 29. 78 applicants, 54% accepted, 34 enrolled. In 2009, 5 master's awarded. *Degree requirements:* For master's, thesis (for some programs). *Entrance requirements:* For master's, GRE, minimum GPA of 3.0. Additional exam requirements/recommendations for international students: Required—TOEFL (minimum score 570 paper-based; 230 computer-based; 88 iBT), or IELTS (minimum score 6.5). *Application deadline:* For fall admission, 8/1 for domestic students, 7/1 for international students; for spring admission, 2/1 for domestic students. Applications are processed on a rolling basis. Application fee: $50. Electronic applications accepted. *Expenses:* Tuition: Full-time $31,533; part-time $876 per credit hour. Required fees: $210. *Financial support:* In 2009–10, 56 students received support; research assistantships with partial tuition reimbursements available, teaching assistantships with partial tuition reimbursements available, career-related internships or fieldwork, scholarships/grants, and unspecified assistantships available. Support available to part-time students. Financial award applicants required to submit FAFSA. *Unit head:* Prof. Dianne Bills, Graduate Coordinator, 585-475-2700, Fax: 585-475-6584, E-mail: informaticsgrad@rit.edu. *Application contact:* Diane Ellison, Assistant Vice President, Graduate Enrollment Services, 585-475-2229, Fax: 585-475-7164, E-mail: gradinfo@rit.edu.

Rochester Institute of Technology, Graduate Enrollment Services, B. Thomas Golisano College of Computing and Information Sciences, PhD Program in Computing and Information Sciences, Rochester, NY 14623-5603. Offers PhD. *Students:* 19 full-time (2 women), 6 part-time (1 woman); includes 2 Asian Americans or Pacific Islanders, 16 international. Average age 30. 43 applicants, 21% accepted, 6 enrolled. *Degree requirements:* For doctorate, thesis/dissertation. *Entrance requirements:* For doctorate, GRE, minimum GPA of 3.0. Additional exam requirements/recommendations for international students: Required—TOEFL (minimum score 570 paper-based; 230 computer-based; 88 iBT), or IELTS (minimum score 6.5). *Application deadline:* For fall admission, 1/15 priority date for domestic and international students. Applications are processed on a rolling basis. Application fee: $50. Electronic applications accepted. *Expenses:* Tuition: Full-time $31,533; part-time $876 per credit hour. Required fees: $210. *Financial support:* In 2009–10, 16 students received support; research assistantships with full and partial tuition reimbursements available, teaching assistantships with full and partial tuition reimbursements available, career-related internships or fieldwork, scholarships/grants, health care benefits, and unspecified assistantships available. Financial award applicants required to submit FAFSA. *Unit head:* Dr. Pengcheng Shi, Director, 585-475-6193, Fax: 585-475-5669, E-mail: phd@gccis.rit.edu. *Application contact:* Diane Ellison, Assistant Vice President, Graduate Enrollment Services, 585-475-2229, Fax: 585-475-7164, E-mail: gradinfo@rit.edu.

Computer Science

Roosevelt University, Graduate Division, College of Arts and Sciences, Department of Computer Science and Telecommunications, Program in Computer Science, Chicago, IL 60605. Offers MSC. Part-time and evening/weekend programs available. *Faculty research:* Artificial intelligence, software engineering, distributed databases, parallel processing.

Royal Military College of Canada, Division of Graduate Studies and Research, Science Division, Department of Mathematics and Computer Science, Kingston, ON K7K 7B4, Canada. Offers computer science (M Sc); mathematics (M Sc). *Degree requirements:* For master's, thesis. *Entrance requirements:* For master's, honours degree with second-class standing. Electronic applications accepted.

Rutgers, The State University of New Jersey, Camden, Graduate School of Arts and Sciences, Program in Computer Science, Camden, NJ 08102-1401. Offers MS. Part-time and evening/weekend programs available. *Degree requirements:* For master's, comprehensive exam, thesis (for some programs). *Entrance requirements:* For master's, GRE, 3 letters of recommendation. Additional exam requirements/recommendations for international students: Required—TOEFL, IELTS. Electronic applications accepted. *Faculty research:* Cryptography and computer security, approximation algorithms, optical networks and wireless communications, computational geometry, data compression and encoding.

Rutgers, The State University of New Jersey, New Brunswick, Graduate School-New Brunswick, Program in Computer Science, Piscataway, NJ 08854-8097. Offers MS, PhD. Part-time programs available. Terminal master's awarded for partial completion of doctoral program. *Degree requirements:* For master's, comprehensive exam, thesis; for doctorate, comprehensive exam, thesis/dissertation. *Entrance requirements:* For master's and doctorate, GRE General Test, GRE Subject Test. Additional exam requirements/recommendations for international students: Required—TOEFL. *Faculty research:* Artificial intelligence and machine learning, bioinformatics, algorithms and complexity, networking and operating systems, computational graphics and vision.

Sacred Heart University, Graduate Programs, College of Arts and Sciences, Department of Computer Science and Information Technology, Fairfield, CT 06825-1000. Offers computer science (MS); database (CPS); information technology (MS, CPS); information technology and network security (CPS); interactive multimedia (CPS); Web development (CPS). Part-time and evening/weekend programs available. *Faculty:* 7 full-time (4 women). *Students:* 20 full-time (6 women), 79 part-time (25 women); includes 10 minority (2 African Americans, 1 American Indian/Alaska Native, 5 Asian Americans or Pacific Islanders, 2 Hispanic Americans), 30 international. Average age 33. 66 applicants, 97% accepted, 26 enrolled. In 2009, 17 master's awarded. *Degree requirements:* For master's, thesis optional. *Entrance requirements:* Additional exam requirements/recommendations for international students: Required—TOEFL (minimum score 550 paper-based; 213 computer-based). *Application deadline:* Applications are processed on a rolling basis. Application fee: $50 ($100 for international students). Electronic applications accepted. *Expenses:* Tuition: Full-time $24,000; part-time $650 per credit. Required fees: $248. *Financial support:* Career-related internships or fieldwork, institutionally sponsored loans, and unspecified assistantships available. Support available to part-time students. Financial award applicants required to submit FAFSA. *Faculty research:* Contemporary market software. *Unit head:* Domenick Pinto, Academic Director and Chairperson, 203-371-7789, Fax: 203-371-0506, E-mail: pintod@sacredheart.edu. *Application contact:* Dean Alexis Haakonsen, Office of Graduate Admissions, 203-365-7619, Fax: 203-365-4732, E-mail: gradstudies@sacredheart.edu.

St. Cloud State University, School of Graduate Studies, College of Science and Engineering, Department of Computer Science, St. Cloud, MN 56301-4498. Offers MS. *Faculty:* 9 full-time (2 women). *Students:* 25 full-time (7 women), 23 part-time (5 women); includes 2 minority (1 African American, 1 Asian American or Pacific Islander), 42 international. 43 applicants, 33% accepted, 0 enrolled. In 2009, 10 master's awarded. *Degree requirements:* For master's, thesis or alternative. *Entrance requirements:* For master's, GRE General Test, minimum GPA of 2.75. Additional exam requirements/recommendations for international students: Required—Michigan English Language Assessment Battery; Recommended—TOEFL (minimum score 550 paper-based; 213 computer-based), IELTS (minimum score 6.5). *Application deadline:* For fall admission, 3/1 for domestic and international students; for spring admission, 10/1 for domestic students, 8/1 for international students. Application fee: $35. Electronic applications accepted. *Financial support:* Federal Work-Study, scholarships/grants, and unspecified assistantships available. Financial award application deadline: 3/1. *Unit head:* Dr. Ramnath Sarnath, Chairperson, 320-308-4966. *Application contact:* Linda Lou Krueger, School of Graduate Studies, 320-308-2113, Fax: 320-308-5371, E-mail: lekrueger@stcloudstate.edu.

St. Francis Xavier University, Graduate Studies, Department of Mathematics, Statistics and Computer Science, Antigonish, NS B2G 2W5, Canada. Offers computer science (M Sc). *Degree requirements:* For master's, thesis. *Entrance requirements:* For master's, bachelor's degree or equivalent in computer science with minimum B average, 2 letters of recommendation. Additional exam requirements/recommendations for international students: Required—TOEFL (minimum score 580 paper-based; 237 computer-based).

St. John's University, St. John's College of Liberal Arts and Sciences, Department of Mathematics and Computer Science, Queens, NY 11439. Offers algebra (MA); analysis (MA); applied mathematics (MA); computer science (MA); geometry-topology (MA); logic and foundations (MA); probability and statistics (MA). Part-time and evening/weekend programs available. *Students:* 3 full-time (0 women), 2 part-time (1 woman); includes 1 minority (Hispanic American), 1 international. Average age 25. 21 applicants, 67% accepted, 3 enrolled. In 2009, 2 master's awarded. *Degree requirements:* For master's, comprehensive exam, thesis optional. *Entrance requirements:* For master's, minimum GPA of 3.0. Additional exam requirements/recommendations for international students: Required—TOEFL (minimum score 500 paper-based; 173 computer-based; 61 iBT), IELTS (minimum score 5.5). *Application deadline:* For fall admission, 5/1 priority date for domestic and international students; for spring admission, 11/1 priority date for domestic and international students. Applications are processed on a rolling basis. Application fee: $70. Electronic applications accepted. *Expenses:* Tuition: Full-time $16,290; part-time $905 per credit. Required fees: $300; $150 per semester. Tuition and fees vary according to program. *Financial support:* Research assistantships, scholarships/grants available. Support available to part-time students. Financial award application deadline: 3/1; financial award applicants required to submit FAFSA. *Faculty research:* Functional analysis and operator theory, algebraic K-theory, applied mathematics, measure theory, differential geometry and mathematics education. *Unit head:* Dr. Charles Traina, Chair, 718-990-6166, E-mail: trainac@stjohns.edu. *Application contact:* Kathleen Davis, Director of Graduate Admission, 718-990-2790, Fax: 718-990-5686, E-mail: gradhelp@stjohns.edu.

Saint Joseph's University, College of Arts and Sciences, Department of Mathematics and Computer Science, Philadelphia, PA 19131-1395. Offers computer science (MS); mathematics and computer science (Post-Master's Certificate). Part-time and evening/weekend programs available. *Students:* 49 full-time (18 women), 20 part-time (4 women); includes 7 minority (5 African Americans, 2 Asian Americans or Pacific Islanders), 49 international. Average age 25. In 2009, 18 master's awarded. *Entrance requirements:* For master's, 2 letters of recommendation. Additional exam requirements/recommendations for international students: Required—or IELTS. *Application deadline:* For fall admission, 7/15 priority date for domestic students, 4/15 for international students; for winter admission, 4/15 for domestic students, 1/15 for international students; for spring admission, 11/15 priority date for domestic students, 10/15 for international students. Applications are processed on a rolling basis. Application fee: $35. Electronic applications accepted. *Expenses:* Tuition: Part-time $729 per credit hour. Tuition and fees vary according to degree level and program. *Financial support:* Teaching assistantships with partial tuition reimbursements, unspecified assistantships available. Financial award applicants required to submit FAFSA. *Faculty research:* Computer vision, pathways to careers. Total annual research expenditures: $175,000. *Unit head:* Dr. Jonathan Hodgson, Director, Graduate Computer Science, 610-660-1517, Fax: 610-660-3082, E-mail: jhodgson@sju.edu. *Application contact:* Kate McConnell, Director, Graduate College of Arts and Sciences Admissions and Retention, 610-660-3184, Fax: 610-660-3230, E-mail: kate.mcconnell@sju.edu.

St. Mary's University, Graduate School, Department of Computer Science, Program in Computer Information Systems, San Antonio, TX 78228-8507. Offers MS. Part-time programs available. *Degree requirements:* For master's, comprehensive exam. *Entrance requirements:* For master's, GMAT or GRE General Test. Additional exam requirements/recommendations for international students: Required—TOEFL (minimum score 530 paper-based; 213 computer-based; 80 iBT). Electronic applications accepted. *Expenses:* Tuition: Full-time $8004. Required fees: $536. One-time fee: $5 full-time. Full-time tuition and fees vary according to program. *Faculty research:* Artificial intelligence, database/knowledge base, software engineering, expert systems.

St. Mary's University, Graduate School, Department of Computer Science, Program in Computer Science, San Antonio, TX 78228-8507. Offers MS, JD/MS. Part-time programs available. *Degree requirements:* For master's, comprehensive exam, internship. *Entrance requirements:* For master's, GRE or GMAT. Additional exam requirements/recommendations for international students: Required—TOEFL (minimum score 550 paper-based; 213 computer-based; 80 iBT). Electronic applications accepted. *Expenses:* Tuition: Full-time $8004. Required fees: $536. One-time fee: $5 full-time. Full-time tuition and fees vary according to program.

Saint Xavier University, Graduate Studies, School of Arts and Sciences, Department of Mathematics and Computer Science, Chicago, IL 60655-3105. Offers applied computer science in Internet information systems (MS); mathematics and computer science (MA); MBA/MS. *Degree requirements:* For master's, thesis optional. *Expenses:* Tuition: Part-time $743 per credit hour. Required fees: $135 per semester.

Sam Houston State University, College of Arts and Sciences, Department of Computer Science, Huntsville, TX 77341. Offers computing and information science (MS). Part-time programs available. *Faculty:* 8 full-time (3 women). *Students:* 31 full-time (8 women), 24 part-time (6 women); includes 1 minority (African American), 31 international. Average age 29. 29 applicants, 83% accepted, 15 enrolled. In 2009, 9 master's awarded. *Entrance requirements:* For master's, GRE General Test. Additional exam requirements/recommendations for international students: Required—TOEFL (minimum score 550 paper-based; 213 computer-based; 79 iBT). *Application deadline:* For fall admission, 8/1 for domestic and international students; for spring admission, 12/1 for domestic and international students. Application fee: $20. *Expenses:* Tuition, state resident: full-time $3690; part-time $205 per credit hour. Tuition, nonresident: full-time $8676; part-time $482 per credit hour. Required fees: $1474. Tuition and fees vary according to course load and campus/location. *Financial support:* Research assistantships, teaching assistantships, Federal Work-Study, institutionally sponsored loans, and tuition waivers (partial) available. Support available to part-time students. Financial award application deadline: 5/31; financial award applicants required to submit FAFSA. *Unit head:* Dr. Peter Cooper, Chair, 936-294-1569, Fax: 936-294-4312, E-mail: css_pac@shsu.edu. *Application contact:* Dr. Jiuhung Ji, Advisor, 936-294-1579, E-mail: csc_jxj@shsu.edu.

San Diego State University, Graduate and Research Affairs, College of Sciences, Program in Computer Science, San Diego, CA 92182. Offers MS. Part-time programs available. *Degree requirements:* For master's, comprehensive exam or thesis. *Entrance requirements:* For master's, GRE General Test. Additional exam requirements/recommendations for international students: Required—TOEFL. Electronic applications accepted.

San Francisco State University, Division of Graduate Studies, College of Science and Engineering, Department of Computer Science, San Francisco, CA 94132-1722. Offers computer science (MS); computer science: computing and business (MS); computer science: computing for life sciences (MS); computer science: software and engineering (MS). Part-time programs available.

San Jose State University, Graduate Studies and Research, College of Science, Department of Computer Science, San Jose, CA 95192-0001. Offers MS. *Students:* 95 full-time (33 women), 66 part-time (14 women); includes 43 minority (1 African American, 37 Asian Americans or Pacific Islanders, 5 Hispanic Americans), 97 international. Average age 28. 410 applicants, 23% accepted, 44 enrolled. In 2009, 54 master's awarded. *Application deadline:* For fall admission, 6/29 for domestic students; for spring admission, 11/30 for domestic students. Applications are processed on a rolling basis. Application fee: $59. Electronic applications accepted. *Unit head:* Dr. Kenneth Louden, Chair, 408-924-5060, Fax: 408-924-5062. *Application contact:* Dr. Kenneth Louden, Chair, 408-924-5060, Fax: 408-924-5062.

Santa Clara University, School of Engineering, Department of Computer Science and Engineering, Santa Clara, CA 95053. Offers computer science and engineering (MS, PhD, Engineer); information assurance (Certificate); networking (Certificate); software engineering (MS, Certificate). Part-time and evening/weekend programs available. *Students:* 91 full-time (33 women), 98 part-time (26 women); includes 44 minority (3 African Americans, 39 Asian Americans or Pacific Islanders, 2 Hispanic Americans), 110 international. Average age 29. In 2009, 41 master's awarded. *Degree requirements:* For master's, thesis (for some programs); for doctorate, thesis/dissertation; for other advanced degree, thesis. *Entrance requirements:* For master's, GRE (waiver may be available); for doctorate, GRE, master's degree or equivalent; for other advanced degree, master's degree, published paper. Additional exam requirements/recommendations for international students: Required—TOEFL (minimum score 550 paper-based; 213 computer-based; 79 iBT). *Application deadline:* For fall admission, 8/13 for domestic students, 7/16 for international students; for winter admission, 10/29 for domestic students, 9/24 for international students; for spring admission, 2/25 for domestic students, 1/21 for international students. Applications are processed on a rolling basis. Application fee: $60. *Expenses:* Contact institution. *Financial support:* Research assistantships, teaching assistantships available. Financial award application deadline: 3/2; financial award applicants required to submit FAFSA. *Unit head:* Dr. Alex Zecevic, Chair, 408-554-2394, E-mail: azecevic@scu.edu. *Application contact:* Stacey Tinker, Director of Enrollment Management, 408-554-4748, Fax: 408-554-4323, E-mail: stinker@scu.edu.

Shippensburg University of Pennsylvania, School of Graduate Studies, College of Arts and Sciences, Department of Computer Science, Shippensburg, PA 17257-2299. Offers computer science (MS). Part-time and evening/weekend programs available. *Entrance requirements:* For master's, GRE (if GPA less than 2.75). Additional exam requirements/recommendations for international students: Required—TOEFL (minimum score 580 paper-based; 237 computer-based); Recommended—IELTS (minimum score 6). Electronic applications accepted.

Silicon Valley University, Graduate Programs, San Jose, CA 95131. Offers business administration (MBA); computer engineering (MSCE); computer science (MSCS). *Degree requirements:* For master's, project (MSCS).

Simon Fraser University, Graduate Studies, Faculty of Applied Sciences, School of Computing Science, Burnaby, BC V5A 1S6, Canada. Offers M Sc, PhD. *Degree requirements:* For master's, comprehensive exam, thesis or alternative; for doctorate, comprehensive exam, thesis/dissertation, qualifying exams. *Entrance requirements:* For master's, minimum GPA of 3.0; for doctorate, minimum GPA of 3.5. Additional exam requirements/recommendations for international students: Required—GRE General Test, GRE Subject Test, or IELTS. Electronic applications accepted. *Faculty research:* Artificial intelligence, computer hardware, computer systems, database systems, theory.

Simon Fraser University, Graduate Studies, Faculty of Applied Sciences, School of Interactive Arts and Technology, Surrey, BC V3T 2W1, Canada. Offers information technology (M Sc, PhD); interactive arts (M Sc, PhD). *Degree requirements:* For master's, thesis; for doctorate, comprehensive exam, thesis/dissertation. *Entrance requirements:* For master's, 2 references, curriculum vitae; for doctorate, 3 references, curriculm vitae, minimum GPA of 3.0. Additional exam requirements/recommendations for international students: Required—TOEFL (minimum score 570 paper-based; 230 computer-based), TWE (minimum score 5). Electronic applications accepted.

South Dakota School of Mines and Technology, Graduate Division, College of Science and Letters, Department of Mathematics and Computer Science, Rapid City, SD 57701-3995. Offers computer science (MS); robotics and intelligent autonomous systems (MS). Part-time programs available. *Faculty:* 8 full-time (1 woman), 3 part-time/adjunct (0 women). *Students:* 6 full-time (3 women), 6 part-time (1 woman); includes 2 minority (1 American Indian/Alaska Native, 1 Asian American or Pacific Islander), 3 international. Average age 34. 21 applicants, 48% accepted, 7 enrolled. In 2009, 7 master's awarded. *Entrance requirements:* Additional exam requirements/recommendations for international students: Required—TOEFL, TWE. *Application deadline:* For fall admission, 7/1 priority date for domestic students, 4/1 for international students; for spring admission, 11/1 for domestic students, 9/1 for international students. Applications are processed on a rolling basis. Application fee: $35. Electronic applications accepted. *Expenses:* Tuition, state resident: full-time $3340; part-time $139 per credit hour. Tuition, nonresident: full-time $7060; part-time $294 per credit hour. Required fees: $3270. *Financial support:* In 2009–10, 4 research assistantships with partial tuition reimbursements (averaging $13,139 per year), 6 teaching assistantships with partial tuition reimbursements (averaging $6,610 per year) were awarded; fellowships, Federal Work-Study and institutionally sponsored loans also available. Support available to part-time students. Financial award application deadline: 5/15. *Faculty research:* Database systems, remote sensing, numerical modeling, artificial intelligence, neural networks. *Unit head:* Dr. Kyle Riley, Chair, 605-394-6147, E-mail: kyle.riley@sdsmt.edu. *Application contact:* Jeannette R. Nilson, Administrative Support Coordinator, Graduate Education, 800-454-8162 Ext. 1206, Fax: 605-394-5360, E-mail: graduate_admissions@sdsmt.edu.

Southern Arkansas University–Magnolia, Graduate Programs, Magnolia, AR 71753. Offers agriculture (MS); business administration (MBA); computer and information sciences (MS); counseling (MS); education (M Ed), including counseling and development, curriculum and instruction emphasis, educational administration and supervision, elementary education, middle level emphasis, reading emphasis, secondary education, TESOL emphasis; kinesiology (MS); library media and information specialist (M Ed); mental health and clinical counseling (MS); public administration (EMPA); school counseling (M Ed); teaching (MAT). *Accreditation:* NCATE. Part-time and evening/weekend programs available. *Faculty:* 43 full-time (24 women), 12 part-time/adjunct (7 women). *Students:* 116 full-time (78 women); 333 part-time (255 women); includes 105 minority (98 African Americans, 3 American Indian/Alaska Native, 3 Asian Americans or Pacific Islanders, 1 Hispanic American), 11 international. Average age 33. In 2009, 88 master's awarded. *Degree requirements:* For master's, comprehensive exam, thesis optional. *Entrance requirements:* For master's, GRE, MAT or GMAT, minimum GPA of 2.75. *Application deadline:* For fall admission, 8/15 for domestic students; for winter admission, 1/8 for domestic students; for spring admission, 1/8 for domestic students. Applications are processed on a rolling basis. Application fee: $0. *Expenses:* Tuition, state resident: full-time $3798; part-time $211 per hour. Tuition, nonresident: full-time $5580; part-time $310 per hour. Required fees: $584. *Financial support:* Career-related internships or fieldwork, Federal Work-Study, scholarships/grants, tuition waivers (full), and unspecified assistantships available. Financial award applicants required to submit FAFSA. *Faculty research:* Alternative certification for teachers, supervision of instruction, instructional leadership, counseling. *Unit head:* Dr. Kim Bloss, Dean, Graduate Studies, 870-235-4150, Fax: 870-235-5227, E-mail: kkbloss@saumag.edu. *Application contact:* Dr. Kim Bloss, Dean, Graduate Studies, 870-235-4150, Fax: 870-235-5227, E-mail: kkbloss@saumag.edu.

Southern Connecticut State University, School of Graduate Studies, School of Communication, Information and Library Science, Department of Computer Science, New Haven, CT 06515-1355. Offers MS. *Faculty:* 6 full-time, 1 part-time/adjunct. *Students:* 6 full-time (1 woman), 21 part-time (10 women); includes 12 minority (2 African Americans, 9 Asian Americans or Pacific Islanders, 1 Hispanic American). 21 applicants, 33% accepted, 5 enrolled. In 2009, 6 master's awarded. *Entrance requirements:* For master's, GRE. *Application deadline:* Applications are processed on a rolling basis. Application fee: $50. Electronic applications accepted. Tuition and fees vary according to program. *Unit head:* Dr. Winnie Yu, Chairperson, 203-392-5812, Fax: 203-392-5898, E-mail: yuw1@southernct.edu. *Application contact:* Dr. Lisa Lancor, Coordinator, 203-392-5890, Fax: 203-392-5898, E-mail: lancorl1@southernct.edu.

Southern Illinois University Carbondale, Graduate School, College of Science, Department of Computer Science, Carbondale, IL 62901-4701. Offers MS, PhD. *Degree requirements:* For master's, thesis. *Entrance requirements:* For master's, previous undergraduate course work in computer science, minimum GPA of 2.7. Additional exam requirements/recommendations for international students: Required—TOEFL. *Faculty research:* Analysis of algorithms, VLSI testing, database systems, artificial intelligence, computer architecture.

Southern Illinois University Edwardsville, Graduate Studies and Research, School of Engineering, Department of Computer Science, Edwardsville, IL 62026-0001. Offers MS. Part-time programs available. *Faculty:* 11 full-time (0 women). *Students:* 12 full-time (6 women), 34 part-time (10 women); includes 2 minority (both Asian Americans or Pacific Islanders), 28 international. Average age 26. 150 applicants, 55% accepted. In 2009, 17 master's awarded. *Degree requirements:* For master's, thesis (for some programs), final exam. *Entrance requirements:* For master's, GRE. Additional exam requirements/recommendations for international students: Required—TOEFL (minimum score 550 paper-based; 213 computer-based; 79 iBT), IELTS (minimum score 6.5). *Application deadline:* For fall admission, 7/23 for domestic students, 6/1 for international students; for spring admission, 12/11 for domestic students, 10/1 for international students. Applications are processed on a rolling basis. Application fee: $30. Electronic applications accepted. *Expenses:* Tuition, state resident: part-time $1252.50 per semester. Tuition, nonresident: part-time $3131.25 per semester. Required fees: $586.85 per semester. Tuition and fees vary according to course load. *Financial support:* In 2009–10, 1 fellowship with full tuition reimbursement (averaging $8,370 per year), 4 research assistantships with full tuition reimbursements (averaging $8,064 per year), 10 teaching assistantships with full tuition reimbursements (averaging $8,064 per year) were awarded; career-related internships or fieldwork, Federal Work-Study, institutionally sponsored loans, scholarships/grants, traineeships, and unspecified assistantships also available. Support available to part-time students. Financial award application deadline: 3/1; financial award applicants required to submit FAFSA. *Unit head:* Dr. Jerry Weinberg, Chair, 618-650-2386. *Application contact:* Dr. Xudong Yu, Program Director, 618-650-2321, E-mail: xyu@siue.edu.

Southern Methodist University, Bobby B. Lyle School of Engineering, Department of Computer Science and Engineering, Dallas, TX 75275-0122. Offers computer engineering (MS Cp E, PhD); computer science (MS, PhD); security engineering (MS); software engineering (MS). Part-time and evening/weekend programs available. Postbaccalaureate distance learning degree programs offered (no on-campus study). *Faculty:* 13 full-time (2 women), 18 part-time/adjunct (1 woman). *Students:* 40 full-time (12 women), 167 part-time (22 women); includes 63 minority (18 African Americans, 28 Asian Americans or Pacific Islanders, 17 Hispanic Americans), 41 international. Average age 33. 180 applicants, 73% accepted, 69 enrolled. In 2009, 53 master's, 2 doctorates awarded. Terminal master's awarded for partial completion of doctoral program. *Degree requirements:* For master's, thesis optional; for doctorate, thesis/dissertation, oral and written qualifying exams, oral final exam (PhD). *Entrance requirements:* For master's, GRE General Test, minimum GPA of 3.0 in last 2 years; bachelor's degree in engineering, mathematics, or sciences; for doctorate, preliminary counseling exam (PhD), minimum GPA of 3.0, bachelor's degree in related field, MA (DE). Additional exam requirements/recommendations for international students: Required—TOEFL (minimum score 550 paper-based; 213 computer-based). *Application deadline:* For fall admission, 7/1 priority date for domestic students, 5/15 for international students; for spring admission, 11/15 for domestic students, 9/1 for international students. Applications are processed on a rolling basis. Application fee: $75. *Financial support:* In 2009–10, 20 students received support, including 6 research assistantships with full tuition reimbursements available (averaging $14,400 per year), 14 teaching assistantships with full tuition reimbursements available (averaging $14,400 per year). Financial award application deadline: 3/31; financial award applicants required to submit FAFSA. *Faculty research:* Trusted and high performance network computing, software engineering and management, knowledge engineering and management, computer arithmetic, computer architecture and CAD. Total annual research expenditures: $366,537. *Unit head:* Dr. Suku Nair, Chair, 214-768-2856, Fax: 214-768-3085, E-mail: nair@lyle.smu.edu. *Application contact:* Marc Valerin, Director of Graduate and Executive Admissions, 214-768-3042, E-mail: valerin@engr.smu.edu.

Southern Oregon University, Graduate Studies, College of Arts and Sciences, Department of Computer Science, Ashland, OR 97520. Offers applied computer science (PSM).

Southern Polytechnic State University, School of Computing and Software Engineering, Department of Computer Science and Software Engineering, Marietta, GA 30060-2896. Offers computer science (MS, Graduate Certificate, Graduate Transition Certificate); software engineering (MSSWE, Graduate Certificate). Part-time and evening/weekend programs available. Postbaccalaureate distance learning degree programs offered (no on-campus study). *Faculty:* 12 full-time (1 woman), 4 part-time/adjunct (0 women). *Students:* 54 full-time (20 women), 65 part-time (21 women); includes 16 African Americans, 13 Asian Americans or Pacific Islanders, 46 international. Average age 32. 72 applicants, 90% accepted, 35 enrolled. In 2009, 32 master's awarded. *Degree requirements:* For master's, thesis optional, capstone (software engineering). *Entrance requirements:* For master's, GRE (recommended). Additional exam requirements/recommendations for international students: Required—TOEFL (minimum score 550 paper-based; 213 computer-based; 79 iBT), IELTS (minimum score 6.5). *Application deadline:* For fall admission, 7/1 priority date for domestic students, 5/1 priority date for international students; for spring admission, 11/1 priority date for domestic students, 9/1 priority date for international students. Applications are processed on a rolling basis. Application fee: $20. Electronic applications accepted. *Expenses:* Tuition, state resident: full-time $2896; part-time $181 per credit hour. Tuition, nonresident: full-time $11,552; part-time $722 per credit hour. Required fees: $1096; $1096 per year. *Financial support:* In 2009–10, 3 research assistantships with full tuition reimbursements (averaging $1,500 per year), 11 teaching assistantships with full and partial tuition reimbursements (averaging $1,500 per year) were awarded; career-related internships or fieldwork, scholarships/grants, unspecified assistantships, and Coops also available. Financial award application deadline: 5/1; financial award applicants required to submit FAFSA. *Faculty research:* Image processing and artificial intelligence information retrieval, distributed computing, telemedicine applications, enterprise architectures, databases, software requirements engineering, software quality and metrics, usability, parallel and distributed computing, information security. *Unit head:* Dr. Venu Dasigi, Chair, 678-915-3571, Fax: 678-915-5511, E-mail: vdasigi@spsu.edu. *Application contact:* Nikki Palamiotis, Director of Graduate Studies, 678-915-4276, Fax: 678-915-7292, E-mail: npalamio@spsu.edu.

Southern University and Agricultural and Mechanical College, Graduate School, College of Sciences, Department of Computer Science, Baton Rouge, LA 70813. Offers information systems (MS); micro/minicomputer architecture (MS); operating systems (MS). Part-time programs available. Postbaccalaureate distance learning degree programs offered (minimal on-campus study). *Degree requirements:* For master's, thesis. *Entrance requirements:* For master's, GRE General Test, minimum GPA of 3.0, bachelor's degree in computer science or related field. Additional exam requirements/recommendations for international students: Required—TOEFL (minimum score 525 paper-based; 193 computer-based). *Faculty research:* Network theory, computational complexity, high speed computing, neural networking, data warehousing/mining.

Stanford University, School of Engineering, Department of Computer Science, Stanford, CA 94305-9991. Offers MS, PhD. Terminal master's awarded for partial completion of doctoral program. *Degree requirements:* For doctorate, thesis/dissertation. *Entrance requirements:* For master's, GRE General Test; for doctorate, GRE General Test, GRE Computer Science Subject Test. Additional exam requirements/recommendations for international students: Required—TOEFL. Electronic applications accepted. *Expenses:* Tuition: Full-time $37,380; part-time $2760 per quarter. Required fees: $501.

Stanford University, School of Engineering, Program in Scientific Computing and Computational Mathematics, Stanford, CA 94305-9991. Offers MS, PhD. Terminal master's awarded for partial completion of doctoral program. *Degree requirements:* For doctorate, thesis/dissertation, qualifying exam. *Entrance requirements:* For master's, GRE General Test; for doctorate, GRE General Test, GRE Subject Test. Additional exam requirements/recommendations for international students: Required—TOEFL. Electronic applications accepted. *Expenses:* Tuition: Full-time $37,380; part-time $2760 per quarter. Required fees: $501.

State University of New York at Binghamton, Graduate School, School of Arts and Sciences, Department of Mathematical Sciences, Binghamton, NY 13902-6000. Offers computer science (MA, PhD); probability and statistics (MA, PhD). Part-time programs available. *Faculty:* 24 full-time (4 women), 11 part-time/adjunct (6 women). *Students:* 43 full-time (14 women), 25 part-time (10 women); includes 8 minority (4 African Americans, 1 Asian American or Pacific Islander, 3 Hispanic Americans), 29 international. Average age 27. 79 applicants, 47% accepted, 19 enrolled. In 2009, 8 master's, 3 doctorates awarded. Terminal master's awarded for partial completion of doctoral program. *Degree requirements:* For master's, thesis or alternative; for doctorate, 2 foreign languages, thesis/dissertation. *Entrance requirements:* For master's and doctorate, GRE General Test, GRE Subject Test. Additional exam requirements/recommendations for international students: Required—TOEFL (minimum score 550 paper-based; 213 computer-based; 80 iBT). *Application deadline:* For fall admission, 4/15 priority date for domestic and international students; for spring admission, 11/30 priority date for domestic and international students. Applications are processed on a rolling basis. Application fee: $60. Electronic applications accepted. *Financial support:* In 2009–10, 60 students received support, including 3 fellowships with full tuition reimbursements available (averaging $16,500 per year), 5 research assistantships with full tuition reimbursements available (averaging $16,500 per year), 48 teaching assistantships with full tuition reimbursements available (averaging $16,500 per year); career-related internships or fieldwork, Federal Work-Study, institutionally sponsored loans, scholarships/grants, health care benefits, and unspecified assistantships also available. Financial award application deadline: 2/15; financial award applicants required to submit FAFSA. *Unit head:* Dr. Fernando Guzman, Chairperson, 607-777-2148, E-mail: fer@math.binghamton.edu. *Application contact:* Victoria Williams, Recruiting and Admissions Coordinator, 607-777-2151, Fax: 607-777-2501, E-mail: vwilliam@binghamton.edu.

State University of New York at Binghamton, Graduate School, Thomas J. Watson School of Engineering and Applied Science, Department of Computer Science, Binghamton, NY 13902-6000. Offers M Eng, MS, PhD. Part-time programs available. *Faculty:* 16 full-time (2 women), 15 part-time/adjunct (6 women). *Students:* 151 full-time (36 women), 125 part-time (22 women); includes 13 minority (10 Asian Americans or Pacific Islanders, 3 Hispanic Americans), 210 international. Average age 26. 382 applicants, 75% accepted, 72 enrolled. In 2009, 54 master's, 7 doctorates awarded. *Degree requirements:* For master's, thesis or alternative; for doctorate, thesis/dissertation. *Entrance requirements:* For master's and doctorate, GRE General Test, GRE Subject Test. Additional exam requirements/recommendations for international students: Required—TOEFL. *Application deadline:* For fall admission, 4/15 priority date for domestic students, 1/15 priority date for international students; for spring admission, 11/1 for domestic students, 10/1 priority date for international students. Applications are processed on a rolling basis. Application fee: $60. Electronic applications accepted. *Financial support:* In 2009–10, 69 students received support, including 1 fellowship with full tuition reimbursement available (averaging $16,500 per year), 22 research assistantships with full tuition reimbursements available (averaging $16,500 per year), 29 teaching assistantships with full tuition reimbursements available (averaging $16,500 per year); career-related internships or fieldwork, Federal Work-Study, institutionally sponsored loans, scholarships/grants, health care benefits, and unspecified assistantships also available. Financial award application deadline: 2/15; financial award applicants required to submit FAFSA. *Unit head:* Dr. Kanad Ghose, Chair, 607-777-4803, E-mail: ghose@cs.binghamton.edu. *Application contact:* Victoria Williams, Recruiting and Admissions Coordinator, 607-777-2151, Fax: 607-777-2501, E-mail: vwilliam@binghamton.edu.

Computer Science

State University of New York at New Paltz, Graduate School, School of Science and Engineering, Department of Computer Science, New Paltz, NY 12561. Offers MS. Part-time and evening/weekend programs available. *Faculty:* 4 full-time (0 women), 1 part-time/adjunct (0 women). *Students:* 27 full-time (8 women), 21 part-time (3 women); includes 7 minority (3 African Americans, 3 Asian Americans or Pacific Islanders, 1 Hispanic American), 35 international. Average age 25. 84 applicants, 71% accepted, 14 enrolled. In 2009, 24 master's awarded. *Degree requirements:* For master's, comprehensive exam, thesis. *Entrance requirements:* For master's, minimum GPA of 3.0, proficiency in program assembly. Additional exam requirements/recommendations for international students: Required—TOEFL (minimum score 550 paper-based; 213 computer-based; 80 iBT), IELTS (minimum score 6.5). *Application deadline:* For fall admission, 5/15 priority date for domestic students, 5/15 for international students; for spring admission, 11/15 for domestic and international students. Applications are processed on a rolling basis. Application fee: $50. Electronic applications accepted. *Financial support:* In 2009–10, 3 students received support, including 3 teaching assistantships with partial tuition reimbursements available (averaging $5,000 per year); unspecified assistantships also available. Financial award application deadline: 8/1; financial award applicants required to submit FAFSA. *Unit head:* Dr. Andrew Pletch, Chair, 845-257-3990, Fax: 845-257-3996, E-mail: pletcha@newpaltz.edu. *Application contact:* Dr. Paul Zuckerman, Coordinator, 845-257-3516, E-mail: zuckerpr@newpaltz.edu.

State University of New York Institute of Technology, School of Information Systems and Engineering Technology, Program in Computer and Information Science, Utica, NY 13504-3050. Offers MS. Part-time and evening/weekend programs available. *Degree requirements:* For master's, thesis or project. *Entrance requirements:* For master's, GRE General Test, minimum GPA of 3.0, letter of recommendation. Additional exam requirements/recommendations for international students: Required—TOEFL (minimum score 550 paper-based; 213 computer-based). *Faculty research:* Cryptography, distributed systems, computer-aided system theory, reasoning with uncertainty, grid computing.

Stephen F. Austin State University, Graduate School, College of Business, Department of Computer Science, Nacogdoches, TX 75962. Offers MS. Part-time programs available. *Degree requirements:* For master's, comprehensive exam, thesis optional. *Entrance requirements:* For master's, GRE General Test. Additional exam requirements/recommendations for international students: Required—TOEFL.

Stevens Institute of Technology, Graduate School, Charles V. Schaefer Jr. School of Engineering, Department of Computer Science, Program in Computer Science, Hoboken, NJ 07030. Offers MS, PhD. *Expenses:* Tuition: Full-time $9900; part-time $1100 per credit. Required fees: $286 per semester.

Stevens Institute of Technology, Graduate School, Wesley J. Howe School of Technology Management, Program in Information Systems, Hoboken, NJ 07030. Offers computer science (MS); e-commerce (MS); enterprise systems (MS); entrepreneurial information technology (MS); information architecture (MS); information management (MS, Certificate); information security (MS); information technology in financial services industry (MS); information technology in the pharmaceutical industry (MS); information technology outsourcing management (MS); project management (MS, Certificate); software engineering (MS); telecommunications (MS). *Degree requirements:* For master's, thesis optional. *Entrance requirements:* For master's, GMAT, GRE General Test. Additional exam requirements/recommendations for international students: Required—TOEFL. Electronic applications accepted. *Expenses:* Tuition: Full-time $9900; part-time $1100 per credit. Required fees: $286 per semester.

Stony Brook University, State University of New York, Graduate School, College of Engineering and Applied Sciences, Department of Computer Science, Stony Brook, NY 11794. Offers computer science (MS, PhD); information systems (Certificate); information systems engineering (MS); software engineering (Certificate). *Faculty:* 34 full-time (6 women), 1 part-time/adjunct (0 women). *Students:* 239 full-time (61 women), 33 part-time (9 women); includes 16 minority (1 African American, 14 Asian Americans or Pacific Islanders, 1 Hispanic American), 221 international. Average age 25. 1,139 applicants, 25% accepted. In 2009, 84 master's, 20 doctorates awarded. *Degree requirements:* For master's, thesis or alternative; for doctorate, comprehensive exam, thesis/dissertation. *Entrance requirements:* For master's and doctorate, GRE General Test. Additional exam requirements/recommendations for international students: Required—TOEFL. *Application deadline:* For fall admission, 1/15 for domestic students. Application fee: $60. *Expenses:* Tuition, state resident: full-time $8370; part-time $349 per credit. Tuition, nonresident: full-time $13,250; part-time $552 per credit. Required fees: $933. *Financial support:* In 2009–10, 81 research assistantships, 30 teaching assistantships were awarded; fellowships also available. *Faculty research:* Artificial intelligence, computer architecture, database management systems, VLSI, operating systems. Total annual research expenditures: $5.1 million. *Unit head:* Prof. Arie Kauffman, Chairman, 631-632-8428. *Application contact:* Graduate Director, 631-632-8462, Fax: 631-632-8334.

Suffolk University, College of Arts and Sciences, Department of Mathematics and Computer Science, Boston, MA 02108-2770. Offers software engineering and databases (MSCS). Part-time and evening/weekend programs available. *Faculty:* 13 full-time (2 women). *Students:* 21 full-time (8 women), 14 part-time (8 women); includes 1 minority (Asian American or Pacific Islander), 21 international. Average age 27. 45 applicants, 71% accepted, 10 enrolled. In 2009, 6 master's awarded. *Degree requirements:* For master's, thesis optional. *Entrance requirements:* For master's, statement of professional goals, official transcripts, 2 letters of recommendation, resume. Additional exam requirements/recommendations for international students: Required—TOEFL (minimum score 550 paper-based; 213 computer-based; 80 iBT). *Application deadline:* For fall admission, 6/15 priority date for domestic students, 6/15 for international students; for spring admission, 11/1 priority date for domestic students, 11/1 for international students. Applications are processed on a rolling basis. Application fee: $50. Electronic applications accepted. *Expenses:* Contact institution. *Financial support:* In 2009–10, 22 students received support, including 19 fellowships with full and partial tuition reimbursements available (averaging $8,776 per year); career-related internships or fieldwork, Federal Work-Study, and institutionally sponsored loans also available. Financial award application deadline: 4/1; financial award applicants required to submit FAFSA. *Faculty research:* Peer-to-peer systems, grid cluster computing, human-computer interaction, large scale, IP networks, distributed load balancing. *Unit head:* Dr. Paul Ezust, Chairperson, 617-573-8251, Fax: 617-573-8591, E-mail: ezust@mcs.suffolk.edu. *Application contact:* Judith Reynolds, Director of Graduate Admissions, 617-573-8302, Fax: 617-305-1733, E-mail: grad.admission@suffolk.edu.

Syracuse University, L. C. Smith College of Engineering and Computer Science, Program in Computer Science, Syracuse, NY 13244. Offers MS. Part-time programs available. *Students:* 83 full-time (16 women), 14 part-time (2 women); includes 2 minority (both Asian Americans or Pacific Islanders), 89 international. Average age 24. 439 applicants, 46% accepted, 41 enrolled. In 2009, 63 master's awarded. *Entrance requirements:* For master's, GRE General Test. Additional exam requirements/recommendations for international students: Required—TOEFL (minimum score 100 iBT). *Application deadline:* For fall admission, 6/1 priority date for domestic and international students. Applications are processed on a rolling basis. Application fee: $75. Electronic applications accepted. *Expenses:* Tuition: Full-time $26,808; part-time $1117 per credit. Required fees: $1024. *Financial support:* Fellowships with full tuition reimbursements, research assistantships with full and partial tuition reimbursements, teaching assistantships with full and partial tuition reimbursements, tuition waivers (partial) available. Financial award application deadline: 1/1; financial award applicants required to submit FAFSA. *Unit head:* Dr. Jae Oh, Program Director, 315-443-4740, Fax: 315-443-2583, E-mail: jcoh@syr.edu. *Application contact:* Heather Paris, Information Contact, 315-443-2368, E-mail: hdparis@syr.edu.

Télé-université, Graduate Programs, Québec, QC G1K 9H5, Canada. Offers computer science (PhD); corporate finance (MS); distance learning (MS). Part-time programs available.

Temple University, Graduate School, College of Science and Technology, Department of Computer and Information Sciences, Philadelphia, PA 19122-6096. Offers MS, PhD. Part-time and evening/weekend programs available. Terminal master's awarded for partial completion of doctoral program. *Degree requirements:* For doctorate, thesis/dissertation. *Entrance requirements:* For master's and doctorate, GRE General Test, minimum GPA of 3.0. Additional exam requirements/recommendations for international students: Required—TOEFL (minimum score 550 paper-based; 213 computer-based; 79 iBT). Electronic applications accepted. *Faculty research:* Artificial intelligence, information systems, software engineering, network-distributed systems.

Tennessee Technological University, Graduate School, College of Arts and Sciences, Department of Computer Science, Cookeville, TN 38505. Offers MS. *Students:* 7 full-time (0 women), 7 part-time (1 woman); includes 3 minority (2 Asian Americans or Pacific Islanders, 1 Hispanic American). 26 applicants, 27% accepted, 5 enrolled. In 2009, 2 master's awarded. *Degree requirements:* For master's, thesis or alternative. *Entrance requirements:* For master's, GRE. Additional exam requirements/recommendations for international students: Required—TOEFL (minimum score 550 paper-based; 79 iBT), IELTS (minimum score 5.5). *Application deadline:* For fall admission, 8/1 for domestic students, 5/1 for international students; for spring admission, 12/1 for domestic and international students. Application fee: $25 ($30 for international students). *Expenses:* Tuition, state resident: full-time $7034; part-time $368 per credit hour. *Financial support:* In 2009–10, 4 research assistantships (averaging $7,500 per year), 3 teaching assistantships (averaging $7,500 per year) were awarded. Financial award application deadline: 4/1. *Unit head:* Dr. Doug Talbert, Interim Chairperson, 931-372-3691, Fax: 931-372-3686. *Application contact:* Shelia K. Kendrick, Coordinator of Graduate Studies, 931-372-3808, Fax: 931-372-3497, E-mail: skendrick@tntech.edu.

Texas A&M University, College of Engineering, Department of Computer Science, College Station, TX 77843. Offers computer engineering (M En, MS, PhD); computer science (MCS, MS, PhD). Part-time programs available. *Faculty:* 42. *Students:* 267 full-time (43 women), 43 part-time (8 women); includes 25 minority (6 African Americans, 2 American Indian/Alaska Native, 9 Asian Americans or Pacific Islanders, 8 Hispanic Americans), 211 international. Average age 28. In 2009, 30 master's, 20 doctorates awarded. *Degree requirements:* For master's, thesis (for some programs); for doctorate, thesis/dissertation. *Entrance requirements:* For master's and doctorate, GRE General Test. Additional exam requirements/recommendations for international students: Required—TOEFL (minimum score 213 computer-based). *Application deadline:* For fall admission, 3/1 priority date for domestic and international students; for spring admission, 8/1 priority date for domestic and international students. Applications are processed on a rolling basis. Application fee: $50 ($75 for international students). Electronic applications accepted. *Expenses:* Tuition, state resident: full-time $3991.32; part-time $221.74 per credit hour. Tuition, nonresident: full-time $9049; part-time $502.74 per credit hour. *Financial support:* In 2009–10, research assistantships with tuition reimbursements (averaging $15,478 per year), teaching assistantships (averaging $15,913 per year) were awarded; fellowships with full tuition reimbursements also available. Financial award application deadline: 3/1. *Faculty research:* Software, systems, informatics, human-centered systems, theory. *Unit head:* Dr. Hank Walker, Head, 979-845-5534, Fax: 979-847-8578, E-mail: walker@cse.tamu.edu. *Application contact:* Dr. Jianer Chen, Graduate Adviser, 979-845-8981, Fax: 979-862-3684, E-mail: grad-advisor@cs.tamu.edu.

Texas A&M University–Commerce, Graduate School, College of Arts and Sciences, Department of Computer Science and Information Systems, Commerce, TX 75429-3011. Offers computer science (MS). Part-time programs available. *Degree requirements:* For master's, comprehensive exam, thesis (for some programs). *Entrance requirements:* For master's, GMAT or GRE General Test. Electronic applications accepted. *Faculty research:* Programming.

Texas A&M University–Corpus Christi, Graduate Studies and Research, College of Science and Technology, Program in Computer Science, Corpus Christi, TX 78412-5503. Offers MS. Part-time and evening/weekend programs available. *Degree requirements:* For master's, comprehensive exam, thesis (for some programs). *Entrance requirements:* For master's, GRE General Test. Additional exam requirements/recommendations for international students: Required—TOEFL. Electronic applications accepted.

Texas A&M University–Kingsville, College of Graduate Studies, College of Engineering, Department of Electrical Engineering and Computer Science, Program in Computer Science, Kingsville, TX 78363. Offers MS. *Degree requirements:* For master's, comprehensive exam, thesis or alternative. *Entrance requirements:* For master's, GRE General Test, minimum GPA of 3.0. Additional exam requirements/recommendations for international students: Required—TOEFL. *Faculty research:* Operating systems, programming languages, database systems, computer architecture, artificial intelligence.

Texas Southern University, School of Science and Technology, Department of Computer Science, Houston, TX 77004-4584. Offers MS. *Faculty:* 2 full-time (1 woman). *Students:* 6 full-time (4 women), 8 part-time (4 women); all minorities (11 African Americans, 3 Asian Americans or Pacific Islanders). Average age 37. 6 applicants, 100% accepted, 3 enrolled. In 2009, 9 master's awarded. *Application deadline:* For fall admission, 7/1 for domestic and international students; for spring admission, 11/1 for domestic and international students. Applications are processed on a rolling basis. Application fee: $50 ($75 for international students). Electronic applications accepted. *Expenses:* Tuition, state resident: full-time $1805; part-time $100 per credit hour. Tuition, nonresident: full-time $6470; part-time $343 per credit hour. Tuition and fees vary according to course level, course load and degree level. *Financial support:* In 2009–10, 1 research assistantship (averaging $1,500 per year), 5 teaching assistantships (averaging $4,608 per year) were awarded; fellowships, scholarships/grants and unspecified assistantships also available. *Unit head:* Dr. Khaled Kamel, Chair, 713-313-7582, E-mail: kamel_ka@tsu.edu. *Application contact:* Lulueua Nasser, Administrative Secretary, 713-313-7679, E-mail: nasser_la@tsu.edu.

Texas State University–San Marcos, Graduate School, College of Science, Department of Computer Science, San Marcos, TX 78666. Offers computer science (MA, MS); software engineering (MS). Part-time programs available. *Faculty:* 17 full-time (3 women). *Students:* 73 full-time (25 women), 52 part-time (11 women); includes 57 minority (5 African Americans, 1 American Indian/Alaska Native, 39 Asian Americans or Pacific Islanders, 12 Hispanic Americans), 40 international. Average age 28. 67 applicants, 96% accepted, 31 enrolled. In 2009, 38 master's awarded. *Degree requirements:* For master's, comprehensive exam, thesis (for some programs). *Entrance requirements:* For master's, GRE General Test, minimum GPA of 2.75 in last 60 hours of course work. Additional exam requirements/recommendations for international students: Required—TOEFL (minimum score 550 paper-based; 213 computer-based). *Application deadline:* For fall admission, 6/15 priority date for domestic students, 6/1 priority date for international students; for spring admission, 10/15 priority date for domestic students, 10/1 priority date for international students. Applications are processed on a rolling basis. Application fee: $40 ($90 for international students). Electronic applications accepted. *Expenses:* Tuition, state resident: full-time $5784; part-time $241 per credit hour. Tuition, nonresident: part-time $551 per credit hour. Required fees: $1728; $48 per credit hour. $306. Tuition and fees vary according to course load. *Financial support:* In 2009–10, 73 students received support, including 22 research assistantships (averaging $5,257 per year), 21 teaching assistantships (averaging $4,973 per year); career-related internships or fieldwork, Federal Work-Study, and institutionally sponsored loans also available. Support available to part-time students. Financial award application deadline: 4/1; financial award applicants required to submit FAFSA. *Faculty research:* Software engineering, artificial intelligence, multimedia, distributed/parallel computing, database systems, operating systems. Total annual research expenditures: $63,204. *Unit head:* Dr. Hongchi Shi, Chair, 512-245-3409, Fax: 512-245-8750. *Application contact:* Dr. Khosrow Kaikhah, Head, 512-245-3409, Fax: 512-245-8750, E-mail: kk02@txstate.edu.

Texas Tech University, Graduate School, College of Engineering, Department of Computer Science, Lubbock, TX 79409. Offers computer science (MS, PhD); software engineering (MS). Part-time programs available. *Faculty:* 12 full-time (3 women). *Students:* 100 full-time (25 women), 35 part-time (6 women); includes 2 minority (both Hispanic Americans), 110 international. Average age 26. 320 applicants, 48% accepted, 37 enrolled. In 2009, 29 master's,

2 doctorates awarded. *Degree requirements:* For master's, thesis or alternative; for doctorate, thesis/dissertation. *Entrance requirements:* For master's and doctorate, GRE General Test, minimum GPA of 3.0. Additional exam requirements/recommendations for international students: Required—TOEFL (minimum score 550 paper-based; 213 computer-based). *Application deadline:* For fall admission, 3/1 priority date for international students; for spring admission, 11/1 priority date for international students. Applications are processed on a rolling basis. Application fee: $50 ($75 for international students). Electronic applications accepted. *Expenses:* Tuition, state resident: full-time $5100; part-time $213 per credit hour. Tuition, nonresident: full-time $11,748; part-time $490 per credit hour. Required fees: $2298; $50 per credit hour. $555 per semester. *Financial support:* In 2009–10, 24 research assistantships with partial tuition reimbursements (averaging $18,542 per year), 17 teaching assistantships with partial tuition reimbursements (averaging $12,567 per year) were awarded; Federal Work-Study and institutionally sponsored loans also available. Support available to part-time students. Financial award application deadline: 4/15; financial award applicants required to submit FAFSA. *Faculty research:* Artificial intelligence, software engineering and languages, high performance computing, logic programming, image processing. Total annual research expenditures: $683,303. *Unit head:* Dr. Joseph Urban, Chair, 806-742-3527, Fax: 806-742-3519, E-mail: joseph.urban@ttu.edu. *Application contact:* Dr. Susan Mengel, Graduate Advisor, 806-742-3527, Fax: 806-742-3519, E-mail: graduate_programs@cs.ttu.edu.

Towson University, College of Graduate Studies and Research, Program in Computer Science, Towson, MD 21252-0001. Offers MS. Part-time and evening/weekend programs available. *Degree requirements:* For master's, thesis optional, exam. *Entrance requirements:* For master's, minimum GPA of 3.0, bachelor's degree in computer science or completion of 1-3 preparatory courses. Additional exam requirements/recommendations for international students: Required—TOEFL (minimum score 550 paper-based). Electronic applications accepted. *Faculty research:* Deductive databases, neural nets, software engineering, data communications and networks.

Trent University, Graduate Studies, Program in Applications of Modeling in the Natural and Social Sciences, Department of Computer Studies, Peterborough, ON K9J 7B8, Canada. Offers M Sc. *Degree requirements:* For master's, thesis. *Entrance requirements:* For master's, honours degree.

Troy University, Graduate School, College of Arts and Sciences, Program in Computer and Information Science, Troy, AL 36082. Offers computer science (MS). Part-time and evening/weekend programs available. *Students:* 3 full-time (1 woman), 23 part-time (8 women); includes 16 minority (13 African Americans, 3 Asian Americans or Pacific Islanders). Average age 35. 36 applicants, 42% accepted. In 2009, 1 master's awarded. *Degree requirements:* For master's, comprehensive exam, thesis or research project. *Entrance requirements:* For master's, GRE, BS in computer science. Additional exam requirements/recommendations for international students: Required—TOEFL (minimum score 523 paper-based; 193 computer-based; 70 iBT), IELTS (minimum score 6). *Application deadline:* For fall admission, 6/1 for international students; for spring admission, 10/15 for international students. Applications are processed on a rolling basis. Application fee: $50. Electronic applications accepted. *Unit head:* Dr. Emrah Orhun, Associate Professor, 334-273-9923, Fax: 334-241-9734, E-mail: corhun@troy.edu. *Application contact:* Brenda K. Campbell, Director of Graduate Admissions, 334-670-3178, Fax: 334-670-3733, E-mail: bcamp@troy.edu.

Tufts University, Graduate School of Arts and Sciences, Graduate Certificate Programs, Computer Science Program, Medford, MA 02155. Offers Certificate. Part-time and evening/weekend programs available. Electronic applications accepted. *Expenses:* Tuition: Full-time $38,096; part-time $3962 per credit. Required fees: $686; $40 per year. Tuition and fees vary according to course level, course load, degree level, program and student level.

Tufts University, Graduate School of Arts and Sciences, Graduate Certificate Programs, Post-Baccalaureate Minor Program in Computer Science, Medford, MA 02155. Offers Certificate. Part-time and evening/weekend programs available. Electronic applications accepted. *Expenses:* Tuition: Full-time $38,096; part-time $3962 per credit. Required fees: $686; $40 per year. Tuition and fees vary according to course level, course load, degree level, program and student level.

Tufts University, School of Engineering, Department of Computer Science, Medford, MA 02155. Offers MS, PhD. Part-time programs available. *Faculty:* 16 full-time, 1 part-time/adjunct. *Students:* 56 (15 women); includes 6 minority (1 African American, 4 Asian Americans or Pacific Islanders, 1 Hispanic American), 16 international. Average age 27. 109 applicants, 31% accepted, 12 enrolled. In 2009, 9 master's, 6 doctorates awarded. Terminal master's awarded for partial completion of doctoral program. *Degree requirements:* For master's, thesis (for some programs); for doctorate, thesis/dissertation. *Entrance requirements:* For master's and doctorate, GRE. Additional exam requirements/recommendations for international students: Required—TOEFL (minimum score 550 paper-based; 213 computer-based; 80 iBT). *Application deadline:* For fall admission, 1/15 for domestic students, 12/15 for international students; for spring admission, 9/15 for domestic and international students. Applications are processed on a rolling basis. Application fee: $75. Electronic applications accepted. *Expenses:* Tuition: Full-time $38,096; part-time $3962 per credit. Required fees: $686; $40 per year. Tuition and fees vary according to course level, course load, degree level, program and student level. *Financial support:* Fellowships with full tuition reimbursements, research assistantships with full and partial tuition reimbursements, teaching assistantships with full and partial tuition reimbursements, Federal Work-Study, scholarships/grants, tuition waivers (partial), and unspecified assistantships available. Financial award application deadline: 1/15; financial award applicants required to submit FAFSA. *Unit head:* Diane Souvaine, Chair, 617-627-3217, Fax: 617-627-3220. *Application contact:* Lenore Cowen, Information Contact, 617-623-3217, Fax: 617-627-3220.

Union Graduate College, School of Engineering and Computer Science, Schenectady, NY 12308-3107. Offers computer science (MS); electrical engineering (MS); engineering and management systems (MS); mechanical engineering (MS). Part-time and evening/weekend programs available. *Faculty:* 24 part-time/adjunct (1 woman). *Students:* 10 full-time (0 women), 60 part-time (7 women); includes 5 minority (1 African American, 1 American Indian/Alaska Native, 2 Asian Americans or Pacific Islanders, 1 Hispanic American), 5 international. Average age 27. 47 applicants, 55% accepted, 25 enrolled. In 2009, 28 master's awarded. *Degree requirements:* For master's, capstone course. *Entrance requirements:* For master's, minimum GPA of 3.0, letters of recommendation. Additional exam requirements/recommendations for international students: Required—TOEFL (minimum score 550 paper-based; 213 computer-based). *Application deadline:* Applications are processed on a rolling basis. Application fee: $60. Electronic applications accepted. *Expenses:* Contact institution. *Financial support:* Research assistantships, Federal Work-Study, scholarships/grants, health care benefits, and tuition waivers (full and partial) available. Support available to part-time students. Financial award applicants required to submit FAFSA. *Unit head:* Robert Kozik, Dean, 515-631-9881, Fax: 518-631-9902, E-mail: kozikr@union.edu. *Application contact:* Diane Trzaskos, Coordinator, Admissions, 518-631-9837, Fax: 518-631-9901, E-mail: trzaskod@uniongraduatecollege.edu.

Universidad Autonoma de Guadalajara, Graduate Programs, Guadalajara, Mexico. Offers administrative law and justice (LL M); advertising and corporate communications (MA); architecture (M Arch); business (MBA); computational science (MCC); education (Ed M, Ed D); English-Spanish translation (MA); fiscal law (MA); integrated management of digital animation (MA); international business (MIB); international corporate law (LL M); internet technologies (MS); labor health (MS); manufacturing systems (MMS); philosophy (MA, PhD); power electronics (MS); quality systems (MQS); renewable energy (MS); social evaluation of projects (MBA); strategic market research (MBA); teaching mathematics (MA).

Universidad de las Américas–Puebla, Division of Graduate Studies, School of Engineering, Program in Computer Engineering, Puebla, Mexico. Offers computer science (MS). Part-time and evening/weekend programs available. *Degree requirements:* For master's, one foreign language, thesis. *Faculty research:* Computers in education, robotics, artificial intelligence.

Universidad de las Américas–Puebla, Division of Graduate Studies, School of Engineering, Program in Computer Science, Puebla, Mexico. Offers PhD.

Université de Moncton, Faculty of Science, Information Technology Programs, Moncton, NB E1A 3E9, Canada. Offers M Sc, Certificate, Diploma. Part-time programs available. *Degree requirements:* For master's, thesis. Electronic applications accepted. *Faculty research:* Programming, databases, networks.

Université de Montréal, Faculty of Arts and Sciences, Department of Computer Science and Operational Research, Montréal, QC H3C 3J7, Canada. Offers computer systems (M Sc, PhD). Part-time programs available. Terminal master's awarded for partial completion of doctoral program. *Degree requirements:* For master's, one foreign language, thesis; for doctorate, one foreign language, thesis/dissertation, general exam. *Entrance requirements:* For master's, B Sc in related field; for doctorate, MA or M Sc in related field. Electronic applications accepted. *Faculty research:* Optimization statistics, programming languages, telecommunications, theoretical computer science, artificial intelligence.

Université du Québec à Trois-Rivières, Graduate Programs, Program in Mathematics and Computer Science, Trois-Rivières, QC G9A 5H7, Canada. Offers M Sc. *Faculty research:* Probability, statistics.

Université du Québec en Outaouais, Graduate Programs, Program in Computer Network, Gatineau, QC J8X 3X7, Canada. Offers computer science (M Sc, PhD).

Université Laval, Faculty of Sciences and Engineering, Department of Computer Science, Programs in Computer Science, Québec, QC G1K 7P4, Canada. Offers M Sc, PhD. Terminal master's awarded for partial completion of doctoral program. *Degree requirements:* For master's, thesis; for doctorate, thesis/dissertation. *Entrance requirements:* For master's and doctorate, knowledge of French and English. Electronic applications accepted.

University at Albany, State University of New York, College of Computing and Information, Department of Computer Science, Albany, NY 12222-0001. Offers MS, PhD. *Degree requirements:* For master's, comprehensive exam, project or thesis; for doctorate, comprehensive exam, thesis/dissertation, area exams. *Entrance requirements:* For master's and doctorate, GRE General Test. Additional exam requirements/recommendations for international students: Required—TOEFL (minimum score 550 paper-based; 213 computer-based). Electronic applications accepted. *Faculty research:* Algorithm design and analysis, artificial intelligence, computational logic, databases, numerical analysis.

University at Buffalo, the State University of New York, Graduate School, School of Engineering and Applied Sciences, Department of Computer Science and Engineering, Buffalo, NY 14260. Offers MS, PhD. Part-time programs available. *Faculty:* 32 full-time (4 women). *Students:* 279 full-time (55 women), 18 part-time (1 woman); includes 3 minority (1 African American, 2 Asian Americans or Pacific Islanders), 249 international. Average age 27. 1,489 applicants, 34% accepted, 120 enrolled. In 2009, 77 master's, 18 doctorates awarded. Terminal master's awarded for partial completion of doctoral program. *Degree requirements:* For master's, thesis or alternative; for doctorate, thesis/dissertation, comprehensive qualifying exam. *Entrance requirements:* For master's and doctorate, GRE General Test. Additional exam requirements/recommendations for international students: Required—TOEFL (minimum score 550 paper-based; 213 computer-based; 79 iBT). *Application deadline:* For fall admission, 8/15 for domestic and international students. Application fee: $50. Electronic applications accepted. *Financial support:* In 2009–10, 105 students received support, including 9 fellowships with full tuition reimbursements available (averaging $28,900 per year), 39 research assistantships with full tuition reimbursements available (averaging $20,900 per year), 34 teaching assistantships with full tuition reimbursements available (averaging $24,000 per year); career-related internships or fieldwork, Federal Work-Study, institutionally sponsored loans, health care benefits, tuition waivers (partial), and unspecified assistantships also available. Financial award application deadline: 12/15; financial award applicants required to submit FAFSA. *Faculty research:* Bioinformatics, pattern recognition, computer networks and security, theory and algorithms, databases and data mining. Total annual research expenditures: $5 million. *Unit head:* Dr. Aidong Zhang, Chairman, 716-645-3180, Fax: 716-645-3464, E-mail: azhang@buffalo.edu. *Application contact:* Dr. Jan Chomicki, Director of Graduate Studies, 716-645-4735, Fax: 716-645-3464, E-mail: chomicki@buffalo.edu.

University of Advancing Technology, Master of Science Program in Technology, Tempe, AZ 85283-1042. Offers advancing computer science (MS); emerging technologies (MS); game production and management (MS); information assurance (MS); technology leadership (MS). *Degree requirements:* For master's, project or thesis. *Entrance requirements:* Additional exam requirements/recommendations for international students: Required—TOEFL (minimum score 550 paper-based). Electronic applications accepted. *Faculty research:* Artificial intelligence, fractals, organizational management.

The University of Akron, Graduate School, Buchtel College of Arts and Sciences, Department of Computer Science, Akron, OH 44325. Offers MS. *Faculty:* 7 full-time (1 woman), 1 part-time/adjunct (0 women). *Students:* 54 full-time (17 women), 6 part-time (1 woman); includes 1 minority (Hispanic American), 53 international. Average age 24. 83 applicants, 65% accepted, 7 enrolled. In 2009, 16 master's awarded. *Degree requirements:* For master's, seminar and comprehensive exam or thesis. *Entrance requirements:* For master's, GRE, baccalaureate degree in chemistry, biochemistry, or a related field, minimum GPA of 2.75, 3 letters of recommendation. Additional exam requirements/recommendations for international students: Required—TOEFL (minimum score 550 paper-based; 213 computer-based; 79 iBT). *Application deadline:* For fall admission, 2/15 for domestic and international students; for spring admission, 10/1 for domestic and international students. Application fee: $30 ($40 for international students). *Expenses:* Tuition, state resident: full-time $6570; part-time $365 per credit hour. Tuition, nonresident: full-time $11,250; part-time $625 per credit hour. *Financial support:* In 2009–10, 4 research assistantships with full and partial tuition reimbursements, 18 teaching assistantships with full and partial tuition reimbursements were awarded. *Faculty research:* Bioinformatics, database/data mining, networking, parallel computing, visualization. Total annual research expenditures: $3,249. *Unit head:* Dr. Chien-Chung Chan, Chair, 330-972-8805, E-mail: chan@uakron.edu. *Application contact:* Dr. Chien-Chung Chan, Chair, 330-972-8805, E-mail: chan@uakron.edu.

The University of Alabama, Graduate School, College of Engineering, Department of Computer Science, Tuscaloosa, AL 35487-0290. Offers MS, PhD. *Faculty:* 14 full-time (2 women). *Students:* 55 full-time (10 women), 2 part-time (0 women); includes 4 minority (all African Americans), 35 international. Average age 51. 111 applicants, 29% accepted, 20 enrolled. In 2009, 9 master's, 3 doctorates awarded. Terminal master's awarded for partial completion of doctoral program. *Degree requirements:* For master's, comprehensive exam, thesis (for some programs); for doctorate, comprehensive exam, thesis/dissertation. *Entrance requirements:* For master's and doctorate, GRE, minimum undergraduate GPA of 3.0 from ABET-accredited program. Additional exam requirements/recommendations for international students: Required—TOEFL. *Application deadline:* For fall admission, 7/1 priority date for domestic students, 3/15 for international students; for spring admission, 11/1 priority date for domestic students, 7/1 for international students. Applications are processed on a rolling basis. Application fee: $50 ($60 for international students). Electronic applications accepted. *Expenses:* Tuition, state resident: full-time $7000. Tuition, nonresident: full-time $19,200. *Financial support:* In 2009–10, 28 students received support, including 2 fellowships with tuition reimbursements available (averaging $15,000 per year), 10 research assistantships with full tuition reimbursements available (averaging $14,400 per year), 18 teaching assistantships with full tuition reimbursements available (averaging $14,400 per year); health care benefits and unspecified assistantships also available. Financial award application deadline: 4/1. *Faculty research:* Software engineering, networking, database management, robotics, algorithms. Total annual research expenditures: $5.6 million. *Unit head:* Dr. David Cordes, Professor and Department Head, 205-348-6363, Fax: 205-348-0219, E-mail: david.cordes@ua.edu. *Application contact:* Dr.

Computer Science

The University of Alabama (continued)

Susan Vrbsky, Associate Professor and Graduate Program Director, 205-348-6363, Fax: 205-348-0219, E-mail: vrbsky@cs.ua.edu.

The University of Alabama at Birmingham, College of Arts and Sciences, Program in Computer and Information Sciences, Birmingham, AL 35294. Offers MS, PhD. Terminal master's awarded for partial completion of doctoral program. *Degree requirements:* For master's, thesis optional; for doctorate, thesis/dissertation. *Entrance requirements:* For master's and doctorate, GRE General Test. Additional exam requirements/recommendations for international students: Required—TOEFL. Electronic applications accepted. *Faculty research:* Theory and software systems, intelligent systems, systems architecture, high performance computing, computer architecture, computer graphics, data mining, software engineering.

The University of Alabama in Huntsville, School of Graduate Studies, College of Science, Department of Computer Science, Huntsville, AL 35899. Offers computer science (MS, PhD); software engineering (MSSE, Certificate). Part-time and evening/weekend programs available. *Faculty:* 11 full-time (3 women), 2 part-time/adjunct (1 woman). *Students:* 40 full-time (10 women), 73 part-time (18 women); includes 11 minority (5 African Americans, 6 Asian Americans or Pacific Islanders), 46 international. Average age 30. 142 applicants, 54% accepted, 38 enrolled. In 2009, 54 master's, 6 doctorates, 2 other advanced degrees awarded. *Degree requirements:* For master's, comprehensive exam, thesis or alternative, oral and written exams; for doctorate, comprehensive exam, thesis/dissertation, oral and written exams. *Entrance requirements:* For master's, doctorate, and Certificate, GRE General Test, minimum GPA of 3.0. Additional exam requirements/recommendations for international students: Required—TOEFL (minimum score 550 paper-based; 213 computer-based; 62 iBT). *Application deadline:* For fall admission, 7/15 for domestic students, 4/1 for international students; for spring admission, 11/30 for domestic students, 9/1 for international students. Applications are processed on a rolling basis. Application fee: $40 ($50 for international students). Electronic applications accepted. *Expenses:* Tuition, state resident: part-time $355.75 per credit hour. Tuition, nonresident: part-time $847.10 per credit hour. Required fees: $210.80 per semester. Tuition and fees vary according to course load and program. *Financial support:* In 2009–10, 34 students received support, including 10 research assistantships with full and partial tuition reimbursements available (averaging $10,321 per year), 24 teaching assistantships with full and partial tuition reimbursements available (averaging $9,073 per year); career-related internships or fieldwork, Federal Work-Study, institutionally sponsored loans, scholarships/grants, health care benefits, and unspecified assistantships also available. Support available to part-time students. Financial award application deadline: 4/1; financial award applicants required to submit FAFSA. *Faculty research:* Software engineering and systems, computer graphics and visualization, computer networking, artificial intelligence, modeling and simulation. Total annual research expenditures: $4.3 million. *Unit head:* Dr. Heggere Ranganath, Chair, 256-824-6088, Fax: 256-824-6239, E-mail: ranganat@uah.edu. *Application contact:* Kathy Biggs, Graduate Studies Admissions Manager, 256-824-6199, Fax: 256-824-6405, E-mail: deangrad@uah.edu.

University of Alaska Fairbanks, College of Natural Sciences and Mathematics, Department of Computer Science, Fairbanks, AK 99775-6670. Offers computer science (MS); software engineering (MSE). Part-time programs available. *Faculty:* 6 full-time (1 woman), 1 part-time/adjunct (0 women). *Students:* 7 full-time (1 woman), 5 part-time (2 women); includes 1 minority (Asian American or Pacific Islander). Average age 38. 15 applicants, 40% accepted, 6 enrolled. In 2009, 2 master's awarded. *Degree requirements:* For master's, comprehensive exam, thesis or alternative. *Entrance requirements:* For master's, GRE General Test. Additional exam requirements/recommendations for international students: Required—TOEFL (minimum score 550 paper-based; 213 computer-based; 80 iBT). *Application deadline:* For fall admission, 6/1 for domestic students, 3/1 for international students; for spring admission, 10/15 for domestic students, 9/1 for international students. Application fee: $60. *Expenses:* Tuition, state resident: full-time $7584; part-time $316 per credit. Tuition, nonresident: full-time $15,504; part-time $646 per credit. Required fees: $23 per credit. $135 per semester. Tuition and fees vary according to course level, course load and reciprocity agreements. *Financial support:* In 2009–10, 1 research assistantship (averaging $11,880 per year), 1 teaching assistantship (averaging $15,284 per year) were awarded; fellowships, career-related internships or fieldwork, Federal Work-Study, scholarships/grants, health care benefits, and unspecified assistantships also available. Support available to part-time students. Financial award application deadline: 7/1; financial award applicants required to submit FAFSA. *Faculty research:* Interaction with a virtual reality environment, synthetic aperture radar interferometry software. *Unit head:* Dr. Kara Nance, Department Chair, 907-474-2777, Fax: 907-474-5030, E-mail: fycsci@uaf.edu. *Application contact:* Dr. Kara Nance, Department Chair, 907-474-2777, Fax: 907-474-5030, E-mail: fycsci@uaf.edu.

University of Alberta, Faculty of Graduate Studies and Research, Department of Computing Science, Edmonton, AB T6G 2E1, Canada. Offers M Sc, PhD. Part-time programs available. *Faculty:* 48 full-time (4 women), 10 part-time/adjunct (1 woman). *Students:* 170 full-time (22 women), 30 part-time (4 women). 700 applicants, 9% accepted, 45 enrolled. In 2009, 46 master's, 9 doctorates awarded. Terminal master's awarded for partial completion of doctoral program. *Degree requirements:* For master's, thesis (for some programs), oral exam, seminar; for doctorate, thesis/dissertation, oral exam, seminar. *Entrance requirements:* For master's and doctorate, GRE General Test. Additional exam requirements/recommendations for international students: Required—TOEFL. *Application deadline:* For fall admission, 2/1 priority date for domestic students, 2/1 for international students. Applications are processed on a rolling basis. Application fee: $100 Canadian dollars. Tuition and fees charges are reported in Canadian dollars. *Expenses:* Tuition, area resident: Full-time $4626.24 Canadian dollars; part-time $99.72 Canadian dollars per unit. International tuition: $8216 Canadian dollars full-time. Required fees: $3589.92 Canadian dollars; $99.72 Canadian dollars per unit. $215 Canadian dollars per term. *Financial support:* In 2009–10, 110 students received support, including 30 research assistantships (averaging $19,000 per year), 80 teaching assistantships (averaging $19,000 per year); career-related internships or fieldwork and scholarships/grants also available. Support available to part-time students. Financial award application deadline: 2/1. *Faculty research:* Artificial intelligence, multimedia, distributed computing, theory, software engineering. *Unit head:* Dr. J. Nelson Amaral, Associate Chair, 780-492-4194, Fax: 780-492-6393. *Application contact:* Edith Drummond, Information Contact, 780-492-4194, Fax: 780-492-6393, E-mail: gradinfo@cs.ualberta.ca.

The University of Arizona, Graduate College, College of Science, Department of Computer Science, Tucson, AZ 85721. Offers MS, PhD. Part-time programs available. *Faculty:* 15 full-time (0 women). *Students:* 69 full-time (16 women), 6 part-time (0 women); includes 6 minority (1 African American, 1 American Indian/Alaska Native, 4 Asian Americans or Pacific Islanders), 44 international. Average age 27. 307 applicants, 12% accepted, 16 enrolled. In 2009, 18 master's, 5 doctorates awarded. Terminal master's awarded for partial completion of doctoral program. *Degree requirements:* For master's, thesis optional; for doctorate, comprehensive exam, thesis/dissertation. *Entrance requirements:* For master's, GRE General Test, minimum GPA of 3.2; for doctorate, GRE General Test, minimum undergraduate GPA of 3.5. Additional exam requirements/recommendations for international students: Required—TOEFL (minimum score 600 paper-based; 250 computer-based; 100 iBT). *Application deadline:* For fall admission, 6/1 for domestic students, 1/15 for international students. Application fee: $75. Electronic applications accepted. *Expenses:* Tuition, state resident: full-time $9028. Tuition, nonresident: full-time $24,890. *Financial support:* In 2009–10, 54 students received support, including 6 fellowships with full tuition reimbursements available (averaging $25,000 per year), 28 research assistantships with full tuition reimbursements available (averaging $16,597 per year), 11 teaching assistantships with full tuition reimbursements available (averaging $14,858 per year); scholarships/grants, health care benefits, tuition waivers (full and partial), and unspecified assistantships also available. Financial award application deadline: 1/15. *Faculty research:* Operating systems, theory of computation, programming languages, databases, algorithms, networks. Total annual research expenditures: $2.9 million. *Unit head:* Dr. Paul Cohen, Department Head, 520-626-2818, Fax: 520-626-5997. *Application contact:*

Rhonda L. Leiva, Senior Program Coordinator, 520-621-4049, Fax: 520-626-5997, E-mail: gradadmissions@cs.arizona.edu.

University of Arkansas, Graduate School, College of Engineering, Department of Computer Science and Computer Engineering, Program in Computer Science, Fayetteville, AR 72701-1201. Offers MS, PhD. *Students:* 12 full-time (1 woman), 23 part-time (2 women); includes 1 minority (Asian American or Pacific Islander), 20 international. In 2009, 8 master's, 2 doctorates awarded. *Degree requirements:* For doctorate, thesis/dissertation. Application fee: $40 ($50 for international students). *Expenses:* Tuition, state resident: full-time $7355; part-time $356.58 per hour. Tuition, nonresident: full-time $17,401; part-time $775.17 per hour. Required fees: $1203. *Financial support:* In 2009–10, 3 fellowships with tuition reimbursements, 18 research assistantships, 3 teaching assistantships were awarded; career-related internships or fieldwork and Federal Work-Study also available. Support available to part-time students. Financial award application deadline: 4/1; financial award applicants required to submit FAFSA. *Unit head:* Dr. Susan Gauch, Departmental Chair, 479-575-6197, Fax: 479-575-5339, E-mail: sgauch@uark.edu. *Application contact:* Dr. Gordon Beavers, Graduate Coordinator, 479-575-6040, Fax: 479-575-5339, E-mail: gordonb@uark.edu.

University of Arkansas at Little Rock, Graduate School, George W. Donughey College of Engineering and Information Technology, Department of Computer Science, Little Rock, AR 72204-1099. Offers computer and information science (MS). Part-time and evening/weekend programs available. *Degree requirements:* For master's, thesis optional. *Entrance requirements:* For master's, GRE General Test, minimum GPA of 3.0; bachelor's degree in computer science, mathematics, or appropriate alternative.

University of Atlanta, Graduate Programs, Atlanta, GA 30360. Offers business (MS); business administration (Exec MBA, MBA, DBA); computer science (MS); educational leadership (MS, Ed D); health administration (MS); healthcare administration (D Sc, Graduate Certificate); information technology for management (Graduate Certificate); international project management (Graduate Certificate); law (JD); project management (Graduate Certificate); social science (MS). Postbaccalaureate distance learning degree programs offered.

University of Bridgeport, School of Engineering, Departments of Computer Science and Computer Engineering, Bridgeport, CT 06604. Offers computer engineering (MS); computer science (MS); computer science and engineering (PhD). *Degree requirements:* For master's, thesis optional; for doctorate, comprehensive exam, thesis/dissertation. *Entrance requirements:* Additional exam requirements/recommendations for international students: Recommended—TOEFL (minimum score 550 paper-based; 213 computer-based; 80 iBT), IELTS (minimum score 6.5). Electronic applications accepted.

The University of British Columbia, Faculty of Science, Department of Computer Science, Vancouver, BC V6T 1Z4, Canada. Offers M Sc, PhD. Part-time programs available. *Degree requirements:* For doctorate, comprehensive exam, thesis/dissertation. *Entrance requirements:* For master's and doctorate, GRE. Additional exam requirements/recommendations for international students: Required—TOEFL (minimum score 600 paper-based; 250 computer-based; 100 iBT). Electronic applications accepted. *Faculty research:* Computational intelligence, data management and mining, theory, graphics, network security and systems.

University of Calgary, Faculty of Graduate Studies, Faculty of Science, Department of Computer Science, Calgary, AB T2N 1N4, Canada. Offers computer science (M Sc, PhD); software engineering (M Sc). Part-time programs available. *Degree requirements:* For master's, comprehensive exam (for some programs), thesis (for some programs); for doctorate, thesis/dissertation, oral and written departmental exam. *Entrance requirements:* For master's, bachelor's degree in computer science; for doctorate, M Sc in computer science. Additional exam requirements/recommendations for international students: Required—TOEFL (minimum score 600 paper-based; 250 computer-based), GRE General Test recommended; Recommended—TWE. Electronic applications accepted. *Faculty research:* Visual and interactive computing, quantum computing and cryptography, evolutionary software engineering, distributed systems and algorithms.

University of California, Berkeley, Graduate Division, College of Engineering, Department of Electrical Engineering and Computer Sciences, Berkeley, CA 94720-1500. Offers computer science (MS, PhD); electrical engineering (MS, PhD). *Students:* 534 full-time (68 women). Average age 27. 2,789 applicants, 94 enrolled. In 2009, 60 master's, 70 doctorates awarded. *Degree requirements:* For master's, comprehensive exam or thesis; for doctorate, thesis/dissertation, qualifying exam. *Entrance requirements:* For master's and doctorate, GRE General Test, minimum GPA of 3.0, 3 letters of recommendation. Additional exam requirements/recommendations for international students: Required—TOEFL. *Application deadline:* For fall admission, 12/15 for domestic students. Application fee: $70 ($90 for international students). Electronic applications accepted. *Financial support:* Fellowships, research assistantships, teaching assistantships, scholarships/grants and unspecified assistantships available. *Unit head:* Prof. Stuart Russell, Chair, 510-642-3214, E-mail: eecs-chair@eecs.berkeley.edu. *Application contact:* Admission Assistant, 510-642-3068, Fax: 510-642-7644, E-mail: gradadmissions@eecs.berkeley.edu.

University of California, Davis, College of Engineering, Graduate Group in Computer Science, Davis, CA 95616. Offers MS, PhD. Terminal master's awarded for partial completion of doctoral program. *Degree requirements:* For master's, comprehensive exam (for some programs), thesis optional; for doctorate, comprehensive exam, thesis/dissertation. *Entrance requirements:* For master's and doctorate, GRE General Test, GRE Subject Test, minimum GPA of 3.0. Additional exam requirements/recommendations for international students: Required—TOEFL (minimum score 550 paper-based; 213 computer-based). Electronic applications accepted. *Faculty research:* Intrusion detection, malicious code detection, next generation light wave computer networks, biological algorithms, parallel processing.

University of California, Irvine, Office of Graduate Studies, Donald Bren School of Information and Computer Sciences, Irvine, CA 92697. Offers information and computer science (MS, PhD); networked systems (MS, PhD). *Students:* 316 full-time (78 women), 31 part-time (5 women); includes 52 minority (3 African Americans, 41 Asian Americans or Pacific Islanders, 8 Hispanic Americans), 194 international. Average age 27. 1,448 applicants, 23% accepted, 111 enrolled. In 2009, 86 master's, 43 doctorates awarded. Terminal master's awarded for partial completion of doctoral program. *Degree requirements:* For master's, thesis; for doctorate, thesis/dissertation. *Entrance requirements:* For master's and doctorate, GRE General Test, GRE Subject Test, minimum GPA of 3.0. Additional exam requirements/recommendations for international students: Required—TOEFL (minimum score 550 paper-based; 213 computer-based). *Application deadline:* For fall admission, 1/15 priority date for domestic students, 1/15 for international students. Applications are processed on a rolling basis. Application fee: $70 ($90 for international students). Electronic applications accepted. *Financial support:* Fellowships, research assistantships with full tuition reimbursements, teaching assistantships, institutionally sponsored loans, traineeships, health care benefits, and unspecified assistantships available. Financial award application deadline: 3/1; financial award applicants required to submit FAFSA. *Faculty research:* Artificial intelligence, computer system design, software, biomedical computing, theory. *Unit head:* Debra J. Richardson, Interim Dean, 949-824-7405, Fax: 949-824-3976, E-mail: djr@uci.edu. *Application contact:* Kris Bolcer, Assistant Director, Graduate Affairs, 949-824-2277, Fax: 949-824-3976, E-mail: kris@ics.uci.edu.

University of California, Irvine, Office of Graduate Studies, School of Engineering, Department of Electrical Engineering and Computer Science, Irvine, CA 92697. Offers electrical engineering and computer science (MS, PhD); networked systems (MS, PhD). Part-time programs available. *Students:* 224 full-time (34 women), 28 part-time (3 women); includes 42 minority (1 African American, 40 Asian Americans or Pacific Islanders, 1 Hispanic American), 168 international. Average age 29. 1,116 applicants, 16% accepted, 67 enrolled. In 2009, 47 master's, 18 doctorates awarded. Terminal master's awarded for partial completion of doctoral program. *Degree requirements:* For doctorate, thesis/dissertation. *Entrance requirements:* For master's and doctorate, GRE General Test, minimum GPA of 3.0, 3 letters of recommendation. Additional exam requirements/recommendations for international students: Required—TOEFL (minimum score 550 paper-based; 213 computer-based). *Application deadline:* For fall admission, 1/15 priority date for domestic students, 1/15 for international students. Applications are processed on a rolling basis. Application fee: $70 ($90 for international students). Electronic applications accepted. *Financial support:* In 2009–10, fellowships (averaging $14,656 per year); research assistantships with full tuition reimbursements, teaching assistantships, institutionally sponsored loans, traineeships, health care benefits, and unspecified assistantships also available. Financial award application deadline: 3/1; financial award applicants required to submit FAFSA. *Faculty research:* Optics and electronic devices and circuits, signal processing, communications, machine vision, power electronics. *Unit head:* Dr. Jean-Luc Gaudiot, Chair, 949-824-5689, Fax: 949-824-3779, E-mail: gaudiot@uci.edu. *Application contact:* Ronnie A. Gran, Graduate Admissions Coordinator, 949-824-5489, Fax: 949-824-1853, E-mail: ragran@uci.edu.

University of California, Los Angeles, Graduate Division, Henry Samueli School of Engineering and Applied Science, Department of Computer Science, Los Angeles, CA 90095-1596. Offers MS, PhD, MBA/MS. *Faculty:* 33 full-time (3 women). *Students:* 337 full-time (43 women); includes 92 minority (3 African Americans, 81 Asian Americans or Pacific Islanders, 8 Hispanic Americans), 151 international. 790 applicants, 36% accepted, 102 enrolled. In 2009, 80 master's, 27 doctorates awarded. *Degree requirements:* For master's, comprehensive exam or thesis; for doctorate, thesis/dissertation, qualifying exams. *Entrance requirements:* For master's, GRE General Test, GRE Subject Test, minimum GPA of 3.0; for doctorate, GRE General Test, GRE Subject Test, minimum GPA of 3.25. Additional exam requirements/recommendations for international students: Required—TOEFL (minimum score 560 paper-based; 220 computer-based). *Application deadline:* For fall admission, 12/15 for domestic and international students. Application fee: $70 ($90 for international students). Electronic applications accepted. *Financial support:* In 2009–10, 53 fellowships, 256 research assistantships, 101 teaching assistantships were awarded; Federal Work-Study, institutionally sponsored loans, and tuition waivers (full and partial) also available. Financial award application deadline: 1/15; financial award applicants required to submit FAFSA. Total annual research expenditures: $9 million. *Unit head:* Dr. Jason Cong, Chair, 310-825-8145. *Application contact:* Wenona Colinco, Student Affairs Officer, 310-825-0060, Fax: 310-825-2273, E-mail: wcolinco@cs.ucla.edu.

University of California, Merced, Division of Graduate Studies, School of Engineering, Merced, CA 95343. Offers electrical engineering and computer science (MS, PhD). *Expenses:* Tuition, nonresident: full-time $15,102. Required fees: $10,919.

University of California, Riverside, Graduate Division, Department of Computer Science and Engineering, Riverside, CA 92521-0102. Offers computer science (MS, PhD). Part-time programs available. *Faculty:* 20 full-time (0 women), 2 part-time/adjunct (0 women). *Students:* 143 full-time (24 women), 6 part-time (0 women); includes 67 minority (7 African Americans, 57 Asian Americans or Pacific Islanders, 3 Hispanic Americans), 45 international. Average age 28. 497 applicants, 24% accepted, 40 enrolled. In 2009, 13 master's, 11 doctorates awarded. Terminal master's awarded for partial completion of doctoral program. *Degree requirements:* For master's, thesis or project; for doctorate, thesis/dissertation, qualifying exams. *Entrance requirements:* For master's, GRE General Test (minimum score 1100), minimum GPA of 3.2; competence in CS 150, CS 152, CS 153, CS 161/161L at UCR (or equivalent elsewhere); for doctorate, GRE General Test (minimum score of 1100), minimum GPA of 3.2; competence in CS 150, CS 152, CS 153, CS 161/161L at UCR (or equivalent elsewhere). Additional exam requirements/recommendations for international students: Required—TOEFL (minimum score 550 paper-based; 213 computer-based; 80 iBT). *Application deadline:* For fall admission, 5/1 for domestic students, 2/1 for international students. Application fee: $85 ($100 for international students). Electronic applications accepted. *Financial support:* In 2009–10, 76 students received support, including 34 fellowships with partial tuition reimbursements available (averaging $16,000 per year), 51 research assistantships with partial tuition reimbursements available (averaging $14,240 per year), 29 teaching assistantships with partial tuition reimbursements available (averaging $16,000 per year); career-related internships or fieldwork, institutionally sponsored loans, health care benefits, and unspecified assistantships also available. Financial award application deadline: 2/1; financial award applicants required to submit FAFSA. *Faculty research:* Algorithms, bioinformatics, logic; architecture, compilers, embedded systems, verification; databases, data mining, A.I., graphics; systems, networks. Total annual research expenditures: $2.2 million. *Unit head:* Dr. Laxmi Bhuyan, Chair, 951-827-5639, Fax: 951-827-4643, E-mail: gradadmission@ucr.edu. *Application contact:* Amy S. Ricks, Graduate Student Affairs Officer, 951-827-5639, Fax: 951-827-4643, E-mail: gradadmission@cs.ucr.edu.

See Close-Up on page 307.

University of California, San Diego, Office of Graduate Studies, Department of Computer Science and Engineering, La Jolla, CA 92093. Offers computer engineering (MS, PhD); computer science (MS, PhD). *Degree requirements:* For doctorate, thesis/dissertation. *Entrance requirements:* For master's and doctorate, GRE General Test. Electronic applications accepted. *Faculty research:* Analysis of algorithms, combinatorial algorithms, discrete optimization.

See Close-Up on page 311.

University of California, San Diego, Office of Graduate Studies, Interdisciplinary Program in Cognitive Science, La Jolla, CA 92093. Offers cognitive science/anthropology (PhD); cognitive science/communication (PhD); cognitive science/computer science and engineering (PhD); cognitive science/linguistics (PhD); cognitive science/neuroscience (PhD); cognitive science/philosophy (PhD); cognitive science/psychology (PhD); cognitive science/sociology (PhD). Admissions offered through affiliated departments. *Degree requirements:* For doctorate, thesis/dissertation. *Entrance requirements:* For doctorate, GRE General Test, acceptance into one of the eight participating departments. *Faculty research:* Language and cognition, philosophy of mind, visual perception, biological anthropology, sociolinguistics.

University of California, Santa Barbara, Graduate Division, College of Engineering, Department of Computer Science, Santa Barbara, CA 93106-5110. Offers computational science and engineering (PhD); computer science (MS, PhD). *Faculty:* 33 full-time (5 women), 4 part-time/adjunct (0 women). *Students:* 147 full-time (30 women). Average age 27. 559 applicants, 23% accepted, 45 enrolled. In 2009, 26 master's, 19 doctorates awarded. Terminal master's awarded for partial completion of doctoral program. *Degree requirements:* For master's, comprehensive exam (for some programs), thesis (for some programs), project (for some programs); for doctorate, thesis/dissertation. *Entrance requirements:* For master's, GRE, 3 letters of recommendation, resume/curriculum vitae; for doctorate, GRE, 3 letters of recommendation, statement of purpose, personal achievements/contributions statement, resume/curriculum vitae, transcripts for post-secondary institutions attended. Additional exam requirements/recommendations for international students: Required—TOEFL (minimum score 600 paper-based; 250 computer-based; 100 iBT) or IELTS (minimum score 7). *Application deadline:* For fall admission, 12/15 for domestic and international students. Application fee: $70 ($90 for international students). Electronic applications accepted. *Financial support:* In 2009–10, 115 students received support, including 18 fellowships with full and partial tuition reimbursements available (averaging $17,300 per year), 73 research assistantships with full and partial tuition reimbursements available (averaging $9,600 per year), 54 teaching assistantships with partial tuition reimbursements available (averaging $7,200 per year); career-related internships or fieldwork, Federal Work-Study, institutionally sponsored loans, scholarships/grants, traineeships, health care benefits, tuition waivers (full and partial), and unspecified assistantships also available. Financial award application deadline: 12/15; financial award applicants required to submit FAFSA. *Faculty research:* Networking and security, database systems, computational science and engineering, programming languages and software engineering, human computer interaction. Total annual research expenditures: $5.8 million. *Unit head:* Prof. Amr El Abbadi, Chair, 805-893-5334, Fax: 805-893-8553, E-mail: amr@cs.ucsb.edu. *Application contact:* Amanda Hoagland, Graduate Program Assistant, 805-893-4322, Fax: 805-893-8553, E-mail: gradhelp@cs.ucsb.edu.

University of California, Santa Cruz, Division of Graduate Studies, Jack Baskin School of Engineering, Department of Computer Science, Santa Cruz, CA 95064. Offers MS, PhD. *Degree requirements:* For master's, thesis; for doctorate, one foreign language, thesis/dissertation, qualifying exam. *Entrance requirements:* For master's and doctorate, GRE General Test, GRE Subject Test. *Faculty research:* Algorithm analysis, artificial intelligence, computer graphics, information and communication theory, problem-solving techniques.

University of Central Arkansas, Graduate School, College of Natural Sciences and Math, Department of Applied Computing, Conway, AR 72035-0001. Offers MS. *Faculty:* 5 full-time (0 women). *Students:* 10 full-time (0 women), 1 part-time (0 women); includes 2 minority (1 American Indian/Alaska Native, 1 Asian American or Pacific Islander), 7 international. Average age 27. 7 applicants, 100% accepted, 1 enrolled. In 2009, 4 master's awarded. *Entrance requirements:* For master's, GRE, minimum GPA of 2.7. Additional exam requirements/recommendations for international students: Required—TOEFL (minimum score 550 paper-based; 213 computer-based). *Application deadline:* For fall admission, 3/1 for domestic students. Application fee: $25 ($50 for international students). *Expenses:* Tuition, state resident: full-time $5136; part-time $214 per credit hour. Required fees: $379.50; $127 per term. Tuition and fees vary according to course level, course load and campus/location. *Financial support:* Federal Work-Study, scholarships/grants, and unspecified assistantships available. Financial award applicants required to submit FAFSA. *Unit head:* Chenyi Hu, Department Chair, 501-450-3401, Fax: 501-450-5615, E-mail: chu@uca.edu. *Application contact:* Brenda Herring, Admissions Assistant, 501-450-5065, Fax: 501-450-5678, E-mail: bherring@uca.edu.

University of Central Florida, College of Engineering and Computer Science, School of Electrical Engineering and Computer Science, Program in Computer Science, Orlando, FL 32816. Offers MS, PhD. Part-time and evening/weekend programs available. *Students:* 124 full-time (27 women), 157 part-time (26 women); includes 41 minority (9 African Americans, 1 American Indian/Alaska Native, 18 Asian Americans or Pacific Islanders, 13 Hispanic Americans), 71 international. Average age 30. 298 applicants, 59% accepted, 3 enrolled. In 2009, 39 master's, 8 doctorates awarded. *Degree requirements:* For master's, thesis or alternative; for doctorate, thesis/dissertation, candidacy exam, departmental qualifying exam. *Entrance requirements:* For master's, GRE General Test, GRE Subject Test, minimum GPA of 3.0 in last 60 hours; for doctorate, GRE Subject Test, minimum GPA of 3.0 in last 60 hours. Additional exam requirements/recommendations for international students: Required—TOEFL. *Application deadline:* For fall admission, 7/15 priority date for domestic students; for spring admission, 12/1 priority date for domestic students. Application fee: $30. Electronic applications accepted. *Expenses:* Tuition, state resident: part-time $306.31 per credit hour. Tuition, nonresident: part-time $1099.01 per credit hour. Part-time tuition and fees vary according to degree level and program. *Financial support:* In 2009–10, 70 students received support, including 18 fellowships with partial tuition reimbursements available (averaging $7,100 per year), 51 research assistantships with partial tuition reimbursements available (averaging $10,200 per year), 21 teaching assistantships with partial tuition reimbursements available (averaging $9,600 per year); career-related internships or fieldwork, Federal Work-Study, institutionally sponsored loans, tuition waivers (partial), and unspecified assistantships also available. Financial award application deadline: 3/1; financial award applicants required to submit FAFSA. *Faculty research:* Parallel processing, databases, algorithms, virtual reality. *Application contact:* Graduate Program Coordinator.

University of Central Missouri, The Graduate School, College of Science and Technology, Warrensburg, MO 64093. Offers applied mathematics (MS); aviation safety (MS); biology (MS); computer science (MS); environmental studies (MA); industrial management (MS); mathematics (MS); technology (MS); technology management (PhD). Part-time programs available. Postbaccalaureate distance learning degree programs offered. *Faculty:* 59. *Students:* 99 full-time (31 women), 85 part-time (37 women). Average age 33. 45 applicants, 96% accepted, 42 enrolled. In 2009, 68 master's awarded. *Entrance requirements:* Additional exam requirements/recommendations for international students: Required—TOEFL (minimum score 550 paper-based; 79 computer-based). *Application deadline:* For fall admission, 6/1 priority date for domestic students, 5/1 for international students; for spring admission, 10/1 priority date for domestic students, 10/1 for international students. Applications are processed on a rolling basis. Application fee: $30 ($75 for international students). Electronic applications accepted. *Expenses:* Tuition, area resident: Part-time $245.80 per credit hour. Tuition, nonresident: part-time $491.60 per credit hour. Required fees: $24.20 per credit hour. Full-time tuition and fees vary according to course load, degree level, campus/location and reciprocity agreements. *Financial support:* In 2009–10, 15 students received support; fellowships with full and partial tuition reimbursements available, research assistantships with full and partial tuition reimbursements available, teaching assistantships with full and partial tuition reimbursements available, career-related internships or fieldwork, Federal Work-Study, scholarships/grants, and administrative and laboratory assistantships available. Support available to part-time students. Financial award application deadline: 3/1; financial award applicants required to submit FAFSA. *Unit head:* Dr. Alice Greife, Dean, 660-543-4450, Fax: 660-543-8031, E-mail: greife@ucmo.edu. *Application contact:* Laurie Delap, Admissions Coordinator, 660-543-4621, Fax: 660-543-4778, E-mail: gradinfo@ucmo.edu.

University of Central Oklahoma, College of Graduate Studies and Research, College of Mathematics and Science, Department of Mathematics and Statistics, Edmond, OK 73034-5209. Offers applied mathematical sciences (MS), including computer science, mathematics, mathematics/computer science teaching, statistics. Part-time programs available. *Degree requirements:* For master's, thesis. *Entrance requirements:* Additional exam requirements/recommendations for international students: Required—TOEFL (minimum score 550 paper-based; 213 computer-based). Electronic applications accepted. *Faculty research:* Curvature, FAA, math education.

University of Chicago, Division of the Physical Sciences, Department of Computer Science, Professional Master's Program in Computer Science, Chicago, IL 60637-1513. Offers SM. Part-time and evening/weekend programs available. *Entrance requirements:* For master's, GRE. Additional exam requirements/recommendations for international students: Required—TOEFL. Electronic applications accepted.

University of Cincinnati, Graduate School, College of Engineering, Department of Electrical and Computer Engineering and Computer Science, Program in Computer Science, Cincinnati, OH 45221. Offers MS. *Degree requirements:* For master's, thesis. *Entrance requirements:* For master's, GRE General Test, GRE Subject Test or BS in computer science. Additional exam requirements/recommendations for international students: Required—TOEFL (minimum score 550 paper-based; 213 computer-based).

University of Cincinnati, Graduate School, College of Engineering, Department of Electrical and Computer Engineering and Computer Science, Program in Computer Science and Engineering, Cincinnati, OH 45221. Offers PhD. *Degree requirements:* For doctorate, thesis/dissertation. *Entrance requirements:* For doctorate, GRE General Test. Additional exam requirements/recommendations for international students: Required—TOEFL.

University of Colorado at Boulder, Graduate School, College of Engineering and Applied Science, Department of Computer Science, Boulder, CO 80309. Offers ME, MS, PhD. *Faculty:* 29 full-time (7 women). *Students:* 112 full-time (16 women), 76 part-time (9 women); includes 21 minority (4 African Americans, 1 American Indian/Alaska Native, 12 Asian Americans or Pacific Islanders, 4 Hispanic Americans), 43 international. Average age 30. 271 applicants, 21% accepted, 25 enrolled. In 2009, 50 master's, 11 doctorates awarded. *Degree requirements:* For master's, comprehensive exam, thesis or alternative; for doctorate, one foreign language, thesis/dissertation. *Entrance requirements:* For master's, minimum undergraduate GPA of 3.0. *Application deadline:* For fall admission, 2/28 priority date for domestic students, 12/1 for international students; for spring admission, 10/15 for domestic students, 9/1 for international students. Applications are processed on a rolling basis. Application fee: $50 ($60 for international students). *Financial support:* In 2009–10, 31 fellowships (averaging $14,694 per year), 48 research assistantships (averaging $17,046 per year), 5 teaching assistantships

Computer Science

University of Colorado at Boulder (continued)

(averaging $15,703 per year) were awarded; tuition waivers (full) also available. *Faculty research:* Artificial intelligence, databases, hardware systems, hypermedia, machine learning, networks, numerical analysis, parallel computation, program analysis, programming languages. Total annual research expenditures: $4 million.

University of Colorado at Colorado Springs, Graduate School, College of Engineering and Applied Science, Department of Computer Science, Colorado Springs, CO 80933-7150. Offers computer science (MS); engineering (PhD). Part-time programs available. *Faculty:* 11 full-time (1 woman). *Students:* 24 full-time (4 women), 30 part-time (3 women); includes 12 minority (1 American Indian/Alaska Native, 7 Asian Americans or Pacific Islanders, 4 Hispanic Americans), 6 international. Average age 31. 28 applicants, 82% accepted, 19 enrolled. In 2009, 11 master's, 1 doctorate awarded. *Degree requirements:* For master's, thesis optional, oral final exam; for doctorate, comprehensive exam, thesis/dissertation, oral final exam. *Entrance requirements:* For master's, GRE General Test, minimum GPA of 3.0, 2 semesters of course work in calculus, 1 other math course, course work in computer science; for doctorate, GRE General Test, GRE Subject Test (computer science), bachelor's or master's degree in computer science; minimum GPA of 3.3 in all previous course work; 2 semesters of calculus and one course in discrete math, statistics, and linear algebra. Additional exam requirements/recommendations for international students: Required—TOEFL. *Application deadline:* For fall admission, 6/15 priority date for domestic students; for spring admission, 11/14 for domestic students. Applications are processed on a rolling basis. Application fee: $60 ($75 for international students). *Expenses:* Tuition, state resident: full-time $8922; part-time $639 per credit hour. Tuition, nonresident: full-time $19,372; part-time $1154 per credit hour. Tuition and fees vary according to course level, course load, degree level, program, reciprocity agreements and student level. *Financial support:* Teaching assistantships, Federal Work-Study and scholarships/grants available. Financial award application deadline: 3/1; financial award applicants required to submit FAFSA. *Unit head:* Dr. Richard Wiener, Chair, 719-255-3325, Fax: 719-255-3369, E-mail: rsw@runbox.com. *Application contact:* Dr. Richard Wiener, Chair, 719-255-3325, Fax: 719-255-3369, E-mail: rsw@runbox.com.

University of Colorado Denver, Business School, Program in Computer Science and Information Systems, Denver, CO 80217-3364. Offers PhD. *Students:* 3 full-time (1 woman), 13 part-time (2 women); includes 2 minority (1 Asian American or Pacific Islander, 1 Hispanic American), 6 international. 39 applicants, 100% accepted, 0 enrolled. In 2009, 1 doctorate awarded. *Degree requirements:* For doctorate, comprehensive exam, thesis/dissertation. *Entrance requirements:* For doctorate, GMAT or GRE General Test, minimum undergraduate GPA of 3.0, graduate 3.5; resume. Additional exam requirements/recommendations for international students: Required—TOEFL (minimum score 525 paper-based; 197 computer-based). *Application deadline:* For fall admission, 6/1 for domestic students, 3/15 for international students; for spring admission, 11/1 for domestic students, 10/1 for international students. Application fee: $50 ($75 for international students). Electronic applications accepted. *Financial support:* Federal Work-Study, institutionally sponsored loans, and scholarships/grants available. Support available to part-time students. Financial award application deadline: 4/1; financial award applicants required to submit FAFSA. *Unit head:* Dr. Jahangir Karimi, Head, 303-556-5881, E-mail: jahangir.karimi@ucdenver.edu. *Application contact:* Shelly Townley, Admissions Coordinator, 303-556-5956, Fax: 303-556-5904, E-mail: shelly.townley@ucdenver.edu.

University of Colorado Denver, College of Engineering and Applied Science, Department of Computer Science and Engineering, Program in Computer Science and Information Systems, Denver, CO 80217-3364. Offers PhD. *Students:* 1 (woman) full-time, 7 part-time (3 women); includes 1 minority (Asian American or Pacific Islander), 4 international. 13 applicants, 23% accepted, 3 enrolled. In 2009, 2 doctorates awarded. *Degree requirements:* For doctorate, comprehensive exam, thesis/dissertation. *Entrance requirements:* For doctorate, GRE General Test or GMAT, portfolio. Additional exam requirements/recommendations for international students: Required—TOEFL (minimum score 525 paper-based; 197 computer-based). *Application deadline:* For fall admission, 6/1 for domestic students. Application fee: $50 ($75 for international students). *Financial support:* Federal Work-Study and scholarships/grants available. Financial award application deadline: 4/1; financial award applicants required to submit FAFSA. *Unit head:* Gita Alaghband, Co-Director, 303-556-2940, Fax: 303-556-8369, E-mail: gita.alaghband@ucdenver.edu. *Application contact:* Frances Moore, Program Assistant, 303-556-4083, Fax: 303-556-8369, E-mail: frances.moore@ucdenver.edu.

University of Colorado Denver, College of Liberal Arts and Sciences, Program in Integrated Sciences, Denver, CO 80217-3364. Offers applied science (MIS); computer science (MIS); mathematics (MIS). *Students:* 3 part-time (1 woman); includes 1 minority (African American). 1 applicant, 0% accepted, 0 enrolled. In 2009, 4 master's awarded. *Financial support:* Research assistantships, teaching assistantships available. Financial award application deadline: 4/1; financial award applicants required to submit FAFSA. *Application contact:* Tammy Stone, Associate Dean, Curriculum and Student Affairs, 303-556-3063, Fax: 303-556-4861.

University of Connecticut, Graduate School, School of Engineering, Department of Computer Science and Engineering, Storrs, CT 06269. Offers computer science (MS, PhD), including artificial intelligence, computer architecture, computer science, operating systems, robotics, software engineering. *Faculty:* 27 full-time (4 women). *Students:* 86 full-time (16 women), 20 part-time (0 women); includes 6 minority (3 African Americans, 1 Asian American or Pacific Islander, 2 Hispanic Americans), 64 international. Average age 30. 154 applicants, 16% accepted, 14 enrolled. In 2009, 17 master's, 6 doctorates awarded. Terminal master's awarded for partial completion of doctoral program. *Degree requirements:* For master's, comprehensive exam, thesis or alternative; for doctorate, thesis/dissertation. *Entrance requirements:* For master's and doctorate, GRE General Test. Additional exam requirements/recommendations for international students: Required—TOEFL (minimum score 550 paper-based; 213 computer-based). *Application deadline:* For fall admission, 2/1 priority date for domestic and international students; for spring admission, 11/1 for domestic students, 10/1 for international students. Applications are processed on a rolling basis. Application fee: $55. Electronic applications accepted. *Expenses:* Tuition, state resident: full-time $4725; part-time $525 per credit. Tuition, nonresident: full-time $12,267; part-time $1363 per credit. Required fees: $346 per semester. Tuition and fees vary according to course load. *Financial support:* In 2009–10, 59 research assistantships with full tuition reimbursements, 17 teaching assistantships with full tuition reimbursements were awarded; fellowships, Federal Work-Study, scholarships/grants, health care benefits, and unspecified assistantships also available. Financial award application deadline: 2/1; financial award applicants required to submit FAFSA. *Unit head:* Reda Ammar, Head, 860-486-5285, Fax: 860-486-4817, E-mail: reda@engr.uconn.edu. *Application contact:* Steven Demurjian, Chairperson, 860-486-4818, E-mail: steven.demurjian@uconn.edu.

University of Dayton, Graduate School, College of Arts and Sciences, Department of Computer Science, Dayton, OH 45469-1300. Offers MCS. Part-time and evening/weekend programs available. *Faculty:* 7 full-time (2 women), 1 part-time/adjunct (0 women). *Students:* 19 full-time (7 women), 9 part-time (1 woman); includes 2 minority (1 African American, 1 Hispanic American), 17 international. Average age 27. 85 applicants, 33% accepted, 6 enrolled. In 2009, 2 master's awarded. *Degree requirements:* For master's, software project, additional coursework, or thesis. *Entrance requirements:* For master's, GRE General Test, 3 specified undergraduate courses in computer science, minimum undergraduate GPA of 3.0, or performance on placement exam. Additional exam requirements/recommendations for international students: Required—TOEFL (minimum score 550 paper-based; 213 computer-based; 80 iBT), IELTS (minimum score 6.5). *Application deadline:* For fall admission, 8/1 for domestic students, 3/1 priority date for international students; for winter admission, 7/1 priority date for international students; for spring admission, 1/1 priority date for international students. Applications are processed on a rolling basis. Application fee: $0. Electronic applications accepted. *Expenses:* Tuition: Full-time $8412; part-time $701 per credit hour. Required fees: $325; $65 per course. $25 per semester. Tuition and fees vary according to course load, degree level and program. *Financial support:* In 2009–10, 4 students received support, including 4 teaching

assistantships with tuition reimbursements available (averaging $9,900 per year); institutionally sponsored loans, health care benefits, and unspecified assistantships also available. Financial award applicants required to submit FAFSA. Total annual research expenditures: $250,000. *Unit head:* Dr. Dale Courte, Chair, Computer Science Department, 937-229-3831, E-mail: dale.courte@notes.udayton.edu. *Application contact:* Graduate Admissions, 937-229-4411, Fax: 937-229-4729, E-mail: gradadmission@udayton.edu.

University of Delaware, College of Engineering, Department of Computer and Information Sciences, Newark, DE 19716. Offers MS, PhD. Part-time programs available. Terminal master's awarded for partial completion of doctoral program. *Degree requirements:* For master's, thesis optional; for doctorate, comprehensive exam, thesis/dissertation. *Entrance requirements:* For master's and doctorate, GRE General Test. Additional exam requirements/recommendations for international students: Required—TOEFL (minimum score 550 paper-based; 213 computer-based). Electronic applications accepted. *Faculty research:* Artificial intelligence, computational theory, graphics and computer vision, networks, systems.

See Close-Up on page 313.

University of Denver, Faculty of Natural Sciences and Mathematics, Department of Mathematics, Denver, CO 80208. Offers applied mathematics (MA, MS); computer science (MS); mathematics (PhD). Part-time programs available. *Faculty:* 14 full-time (5 women), 1 part-time/adjunct (0 women). *Students:* 4 full-time (1 woman), 9 part-time (4 women); includes 2 minority (both Hispanic Americans), 4 international. Average age 27. 33 applicants, 82% accepted, 8 enrolled. In 2009, 4 master's awarded. Terminal master's awarded for partial completion of doctoral program. *Degree requirements:* For master's, computer language, foreign language, or laboratory experience; for doctorate, one foreign language, thesis/dissertation, oral and written exams. *Entrance requirements:* For master's and doctorate, GRE General Test. Additional exam requirements/recommendations for international students: Required—TOEFL. *Application deadline:* Applications are processed on a rolling basis. Application fee: $50. Electronic applications accepted. *Expenses:* Tuition: Full-time $34,596; part-time $961 per quarter hour. Required fees: $4 per quarter hour. Tuition and fees vary according to course load, campus/location and program. *Financial support:* In 2009–10, 1 research assistantship with full and partial tuition reimbursement (averaging $17,000 per year), 11 teaching assistantships with full and partial tuition reimbursements (averaging $17,000 per year) were awarded; career-related internships or fieldwork, Federal Work-Study, institutionally sponsored loans, and scholarships/grants also available. Support available to part-time students. Financial award application deadline: 3/1; financial award applicants required to submit FAFSA. *Faculty research:* Real-time software, convex bodies, multidimensional data, parallel computer clusters. *Unit head:* Dr. Alvaro Arias, Chairperson, 303-871-3559. *Application contact:* Information Contact, 303-871-2911, E-mail: info@math.du.edu.

University of Denver, School of Engineering and Computer Science, Department of Computer Science, Denver, CO 80208. Offers MS, PhD. Part-time programs available. *Faculty:* 8 full-time (2 women), 5 part-time/adjunct (1 woman). *Students:* 3 full-time (0 women), 80 part-time (13 women); includes 11 minority (3 African Americans, 4 Asian Americans or Pacific Islanders, 4 Hispanic Americans), 14 international. Average age 33. 71 applicants, 85% accepted, 33 enrolled. In 2009, 10 master's, 3 doctorates awarded. *Degree requirements:* For doctorate, comprehensive exam, thesis/dissertation. *Entrance requirements:* For master's and doctorate, GRE General Test. Additional exam requirements/recommendations for international students: Required—TOEFL (minimum score 550 paper-based; 213 computer-based). *Application deadline:* Applications are processed on a rolling basis. Application fee: $50. Electronic applications accepted. *Expenses:* Tuition: Full-time $34,596; part-time $961 per quarter hour. Required fees: $4 per quarter hour. Tuition and fees vary according to course load, campus/location and program. *Financial support:* In 2009–10, 1 research assistantship with full and partial tuition reimbursement (averaging $17,000 per year), 10 teaching assistantships with full and partial tuition reimbursements (averaging $17,000 per year) were awarded; fellowships with full and partial tuition reimbursements, career-related internships or fieldwork, Federal Work-Study, institutionally sponsored loans, and scholarships/grants also available. Financial award application deadline: 3/1; financial award applicants required to submit FAFSA. *Faculty research:* Gaming, UML designs, STAMP. Total annual research expenditures: $545,000. *Unit head:* Dr. Anneliese Andrews, Chair, 303-871-2458, Fax: 303-871-3010. *Application contact:* Information Contact, 303-871-2458, E-mail: info@cs.du.edu.

University of Denver, School of Engineering and Computer Science, Department of Electrical and Computer Engineering, Denver, CO 80208. Offers computer engineering (MS); computer science and engineering (MS); electrical engineering (MS). Part-time and evening/weekend programs available. *Faculty:* 1 full-time (0 women). *Students:* 3 full-time (0 women), 122 part-time (17 women); includes 21 minority (1 African American, 11 Asian Americans or Pacific Islanders, 9 Hispanic Americans), 24 international. Average age 31. 112 applicants, 88% accepted, 56 enrolled. In 2009, 28 master's awarded. Terminal master's awarded for partial completion of doctoral program. *Degree requirements:* For master's, thesis (for some programs). *Entrance requirements:* For master's, GRE General Test, letters of reference. Additional exam requirements/recommendations for international students: Required—TOEFL (minimum score 570 paper-based; 230 computer-based). *Application deadline:* Applications are processed on a rolling basis. Application fee: $50. Electronic applications accepted. *Expenses:* Tuition: Full-time $34,596; part-time $961 per quarter hour. Required fees: $4 per quarter hour. Tuition and fees vary according to course load, campus/location and program. *Financial support:* In 2009–10, 14 research assistantships with full and partial tuition reimbursements (averaging $17,000 per year), 6 teaching assistantships with full and partial tuition reimbursements (averaging $10,000 per year) were awarded. Financial award application deadline: 3/1; financial award applicants required to submit FAFSA. *Unit head:* Dr. Kimon Valavanis, Chair, 303-871-2586. *Application contact:* Information Contact, 303-871-6618, E-mail: dgilmore@du.edu.

University of Denver, University College, Denver, CO 80208. Offers applied communication (MAS, MPS, Certificate); computer information systems (MAS, Certificate); environmental policy and management (MAS, Certificate); geographic information systems (MAS, Certificate); human resource administration (MPS, Certificate); knowledge and information technologies (MAS); liberal studies (MLS, Certificate); modern languages (MLS, Certificate); organizational leadership (MPS, Certificate); security management (Certificate); technology management (MAS, Certificate), including 21st century strategic management (MAS), international markets (MAS), project management (MAS), research and development management (MAS); telecommunications (MAS, Certificate), including broadband (MAS), telecommunications management and policy (MAS), telecommunications technology (MAS), wireless networks (MAS). Part-time and evening/weekend programs available. Postbaccalaureate distance learning degree programs offered (no on-campus study). *Faculty:* 160 part-time/adjunct (64 women). *Students:* 53 full-time (25 women), 984 part-time (551 women); includes 171 minority (72 African Americans, 10 American Indian/Alaska Native, 33 Asian Americans or Pacific Islanders, 56 Hispanic Americans), 75 international. Average age 36. 537 applicants, 96% accepted, 494 enrolled. In 2009, 229 master's, 109 Certificates awarded. *Entrance requirements:* Additional exam requirements/recommendations for international students: Required—TOEFL (minimum score 550 paper-based; 213 computer-based). *Application deadline:* Applications are processed on a rolling basis. Application fee: $75. Electronic applications accepted. *Expenses:* Contact institution. *Financial support:* Applicants required to submit FAFSA. *Unit head:* Dr. James Davis, Dean, 303-871-2291, Fax: 303-871-4047, E-mail: jdavis@du.edu. *Application contact:* Information Contact, 303-871-3155.

University of Detroit Mercy, College of Engineering and Science, Department of Mathematics and Computer Science, Program in Computer Science, Detroit, MI 48221. Offers computer systems applications (MSCS); software engineering (MSCS). Evening/weekend programs available. *Entrance requirements:* For master's, minimum GPA of 3.0.

University of Evansville, College of Engineering and Computer Science, Department of Electrical Engineering and Computer Science, Evansville, IN 47722. Offers MS. Part-time programs available. *Faculty:* 2 full-time (1 woman). *Students:* 2 part-time (1 woman). Average

age 30. In 2009, 1 master's awarded. *Degree requirements:* For master's, thesis. *Entrance requirements:* For master's, GRE, minimum undergraduate GPA of 2.8, 2 letters of recommendation, BS in electrical engineering or computer science. Additional exam requirements/recommendations for international students: Required—TOEFL (minimum score 530 paper-based; 71 iBT), IELTS (minimum score 6). *Application deadline:* For fall admission, 5/1 priority date for domestic and international students. Applications are processed on a rolling basis. Application fee: $25 ($50 for international students). *Expenses:* Contact institution. *Financial support:* In 2009–10, 1 student received support. Scholarships/grants available. Financial award application deadline: 6/1; financial award applicants required to submit FAFSA. *Faculty research:* Digital signal processing, computer algorithms, distributed systems, microcontrollers. *Unit head:* Dr. Dick Blandford, Department Chair, 812-488-2570, Fax: 812-488-2662, E-mail: blandford@evansville.edu. *Application contact:* Dr. Dick Blandford, Department Chair, 812-488-2570, Fax: 812-488-2662, E-mail: blandford@evansville.edu.

University of Florida, Graduate School, College of Engineering and College of Liberal Arts and Sciences, Department of Computer and Information Science and Engineering, Gainesville, FL 32611. Offers computer engineering (ME, MS, PhD); computer science (MS); digital arts and sciences (MS). Part-time programs available. *Degree requirements:* For master's, thesis (for some programs); for doctorate, thesis/dissertation. *Entrance requirements:* For master's and doctorate, GRE General Test, minimum GPA of 3.0. Additional exam requirements/recommendations for international students: Required—TOEFL (minimum score 550 paper-based; 213 computer-based). Electronic applications accepted. *Faculty research:* Artificial intelligence, networks security, distributed computing, parallel processing system, vision and visualization, database systems.

University of Georgia, Graduate School, College of Arts and Sciences, Department of Computer Science, Athens, GA 30602. Offers applied mathematical science (MAMS); computer science (MS, PhD). *Faculty:* 20 full-time (3 women). *Students:* 100 full-time (23 women), 21 part-time (2 women); includes 4 minority (1 African American, 3 Asian Americans or Pacific Islanders), 87 international. 121 applicants. In 2009, 18 master's, 4 doctorates awarded. *Degree requirements:* For doctorate, thesis/dissertation. *Entrance requirements:* For master's and doctorate, GRE General Test. *Application deadline:* For fall admission, 7/1 priority date for domestic students, 4/15 for international students; for spring admission, 11/15 for domestic and international students. Applications are processed on a rolling basis. Application fee: $50. Electronic applications accepted. *Expenses:* Tuition, state resident: full-time $6000; part-time $250 per credit hour. Tuition, nonresident: full-time $20,904; part-time $871 per credit hour. Required fees: $730 per semester. *Financial support:* In 2009–10, 55 students received support, including 20 research assistantships, 31 teaching assistantships; fellowships, tuition waivers (full) and unspecified assistantships also available. *Unit head:* Dr. Eileen T. Kraemer, Head, 706-542-5799, Fax: 706-542-5799, E-mail: eileen@cs.uga.edu. *Application contact:* Dr. Hamid R. Arabnia, Graduate Coordinator, 706-542-2911, Fax: 706-542-2966, E-mail: hra@cs.uga.edu.

University of Guelph, Graduate Program Services, College of Physical and Engineering Science, Department of Computing and Information Science, Guelph, ON N1G 2W1, Canada. Offers applied computer science (M Sc); computer science (PhD). *Degree requirements:* For master's, thesis; for doctorate, comprehensive exam, thesis/dissertation. *Entrance requirements:* For master's, major or minor in computer science, honors degree; for doctorate, M Sc in computer science or related discipline. Additional exam requirements/recommendations for international students: Required—TOEFL (minimum score 600 paper-based; 250 computer-based; 89 iBT), IELTS (minimum score 6.5). Electronic applications accepted. *Faculty research:* Modeling and theory, distributed computing, soft computing, software and information systems, data and knowledge management.

University of Hawaii at Manoa, Graduate Division, College of Natural Sciences, Department of Information and Computer Sciences, Honolulu, HI 96822. Offers computer science (MS, PhD); library and information science (MLI Sc, Graduate Certificate), including advanced library and information science (Graduate Certificate), library and information science (MLI Sc). Part-time programs available. *Faculty:* 22 full-time (8 women), 1 part-time/adjunct (0 women). *Students:* 32 full-time (5 women), 22 part-time (2 women); includes 20 minority (18 Asian Americans or Pacific Islanders, 2 Hispanic Americans), 11 international. Average age 31. 40 applicants, 63% accepted, 11 enrolled. In 2009, 6 master's, 2 doctorates awarded. *Degree requirements:* For master's, thesis optional; for doctorate, comprehensive exam, thesis/dissertation. *Entrance requirements:* For master's and doctorate, GRE. Additional exam requirements/recommendations for international students: Required—TOEFL (minimum score 580 paper-based; 237 computer-based; 92 iBT), IELTS (minimum score 5). *Application deadline:* For fall admission, 3/15 for domestic students, 1/15 for international students; for spring admission, 9/1 for domestic students, 8/1 for international students. Application fee: $60. *Expenses:* Tuition, state resident: full-time $8900; part-time $372 per credit. Tuition, nonresident: full-time $21,400; part-time $898 per credit. Required fees: $207 per semester. *Financial support:* In 2009–10, 1 student received support, including 2 fellowships (averaging $2,375 per year), 14 research assistantships (averaging $19,455 per year), 9 teaching assistantships (averaging $15,849 per year); tuition waivers (full and partial) also available. *Faculty research:* Software engineering, telecommunications, artificial intelligence, multimedia. Total annual research expenditures: $235,000. *Application contact:* Henri Casanova, Graduate Chair, 808-956-5428, Fax: 808-956-3548, E-mail: henric@hawaii.edu.

University of Houston, College of Natural Sciences and Mathematics, Department of Computer Science, Houston, TX 77204. Offers MA, MS, PhD. Part-time programs available. *Faculty:* 22 full-time (2 women), 6 part-time/adjunct (3 women). *Students:* 227 full-time (59 women), 49 part-time (11 women); includes 29 minority (4 African Americans, 1 American Indian/Alaska Native, 19 Asian Americans or Pacific Islanders, 5 Hispanic Americans), 231 international. Average age 26. 353 applicants, 82% accepted, 55 enrolled. In 2009, 70 master's, 4 doctorates awarded. Terminal master's awarded for partial completion of doctoral program. *Degree requirements:* For master's, thesis or alternative; for doctorate, comprehensive exam, thesis/dissertation. *Entrance requirements:* For master's and doctorate, GRE. Additional exam requirements/recommendations for international students: Required—TOEFL (minimum score 550 paper-based; 213 computer-based; 79 iBT). *Application deadline:* For fall admission, 4/1 for domestic and international students; for spring admission, 10/1 for domestic and international students. Applications are processed on a rolling basis. Application fee: $0 ($75 for international students). Electronic applications accepted. *Expenses:* Tuition, state resident: full-time $7676; part-time $320 per credit hour. Tuition, nonresident: full-time $14,324; part-time $597 per credit hour. Required fees: $3034. *Financial support:* In 2009–10, 42 fellowships with full tuition reimbursements (averaging $17,200 per year), 50 research assistantships with full tuition reimbursements (averaging $9,600 per year), 88 teaching assistantships with full tuition reimbursements (averaging $9,600 per year) were awarded; career-related internships or fieldwork, Federal Work-Study, institutionally sponsored loans, scholarships/grants, health care benefits, and unspecified assistantships also available. Support available to part-time students. Financial award application deadline: 2/1; financial award applicants required to submit FAFSA. *Faculty research:* Databases, networks, image analysis, security, animation. *Unit head:* Dr. Jaspal Subhlok, Chairperson (Interim), 713-743-3340, Fax: 713-743-3335, E-mail: jaspal@uh.edu. *Application contact:* Elizabeth Faig, Academic Advisor, 713-743-3407, E-mail: gradinfo@cs.uh.edu.

See Close-Up on page 315.

University of Houston–Clear Lake, School of Science and Computer Engineering, Program in Computer Science, Houston, TX 77058-1098. Offers MS. Part-time and evening/weekend programs available. *Entrance requirements:* For master's, GRE General Test. Additional exam requirements/recommendations for international students: Required—TOEFL (minimum score 550 paper-based; 213 computer-based).

University of Houston–Victoria, School of Arts and Sciences, Program in Computer Science, Victoria, TX 77901-4450. Offers MS. Part-time and evening/weekend programs available.

Postbaccalaureate distance learning degree programs offered (no on-campus study). *Degree requirements:* For master's, comprehensive exam (for some programs), thesis (for some programs). *Entrance requirements:* For master's, GRE. Additional exam requirements/recommendations for international students: Required—TOEFL (minimum score 550 paper-based; 213 computer-based).

University of Idaho, College of Graduate Studies, College of Engineering, Department of Computer Science, Moscow, ID 83844-2282. Offers MS, PhD. *Faculty:* 9 full-time, 1 part-time/adjunct. *Students:* 24 full-time, 17 part-time. In 2009, 3 master's, 6 doctorates awarded. *Degree requirements:* For master's, thesis; for doctorate, thesis/dissertation. *Entrance requirements:* For master's, GRE General Test, minimum GPA of 3.0; for doctorate, minimum undergraduate GPA of 2.8, 3.0 graduate. Additional exam requirements/recommendations for international students: Required—TOEFL. *Application deadline:* For fall admission, 8/1 for domestic students; for spring admission, 12/15 for domestic students. Application fee: $55 ($60 for international students). *Expenses:* Tuition, state resident: full-time $6120. Tuition, nonresident: full-time $17,712. *Financial support:* Research assistantships, teaching assistantships, career-related internships or fieldwork available. Financial award application deadline: 2/15. *Faculty research:* Artificial intelligence, computer and network security, software engineering. *Unit head:* Dr. Greg Donahoe, Acting Chair, 208-885-6589. *Application contact:* Dr. Greg Donahoe, Acting Chair, 208-885-6589.

University of Illinois at Chicago, Graduate College, College of Engineering, Department of Computer Science, Chicago, IL 60607-7128. Offers MS, PhD. Part-time programs available. *Degree requirements:* For master's, thesis or alternative; for doctorate, thesis/dissertation, departmental qualifying exam. *Entrance requirements:* For master's, BS in related field, minimum GPA of 2.75; for doctorate, GRE General Test, minimum GPA of 2.75, MS in related field. Additional exam requirements/recommendations for international students: Required—TOEFL.

University of Illinois at Chicago, Graduate College, College of Liberal Arts and Sciences, Department of Mathematics, Statistics, and Computer Science, Chicago, IL 60607-7128. Offers applied mathematics (MS, PhD); computational finance (MS, PhD); computer science (MS, PhD); mathematics (DA); mathematics and information sciences for industry (MS); probability and statistics (PhD); pure mathematics (MS, PhD); statistics (MS); teaching of mathematics (MST), including elementary, secondary. Part-time programs available. *Degree requirements:* For master's, comprehensive exam; for doctorate, one foreign language, thesis/dissertation. *Entrance requirements:* For master's and doctorate, GRE General Test, minimum GPA of 2.75. Additional exam requirements/recommendations for international students: Required—TOEFL. Electronic applications accepted.

University of Illinois at Springfield, Graduate Programs, College of Liberal Arts and Sciences, Program in Computer Science, Springfield, IL 62703-5407. Offers MS. Part-time and evening/weekend programs available. Postbaccalaureate distance learning degree programs offered (no on-campus study). *Faculty:* 8 full-time (1 woman), 13 part-time/adjunct (3 women). *Students:* 70 full-time (16 women), 114 part-time (25 women); includes 8 minority (4 African Americans, 3 Asian Americans or Pacific Islanders, 1 Hispanic American), 103 international. Average age 29. 280 applicants, 70% accepted, 55 enrolled. In 2009, 111 master's awarded. *Degree requirements:* For master's, research seminar. *Entrance requirements:* For master's, GRE General Test, minimum undergraduate GPA of 2.7. Additional exam requirements/recommendations for international students: Required—TOEFL (minimum score 550 paper-based; 213 computer-based; 79 iBT). *Application deadline:* Applications are processed on a rolling basis. Application fee: $50 ($60 for international students). Electronic applications accepted. *Expenses:* Tuition, state resident: full-time $6390; part-time $266.25 per credit hour. Tuition, nonresident: full-time $14,226; part-time $592.75 per credit hour. Required fees: $2044; $14.36 per credit hour. $722.50 per term. *Financial support:* In 2009–10, research assistantships with full tuition reimbursements (averaging $8,109 per year), teaching assistantships with full tuition reimbursements (averaging $8,109 per year) were awarded; career-related internships or fieldwork, Federal Work-Study, scholarships/grants, health care benefits, and unspecified assistantships also available. Support available to part-time students. Financial award application deadline: 11/15; financial award applicants required to submit FAFSA. *Unit head:* Ted Mims, Program Administrator, 217-206-7326, Fax: 217-206-6217, E-mail: mims.ted@uis.edu. *Application contact:* Dr. Lynn Pardie, Office of Graduate Studies, 800-252-8533, Fax: 217-206-7623, E-mail: pardie.lynn@uis.edu.

University of Illinois at Urbana–Champaign, Graduate College, College of Engineering, Department of Computer Science, Champaign, IL 61820. Offers bioinformatics (MS); computer science (MCS, MS, PhD); MCS/JD; MCS/M Arch; MCS/MBA. Part-time programs available. Postbaccalaureate distance learning degree programs offered (no on-campus study). *Faculty:* 51 full-time (5 women), 1 part-time/adjunct (0 women). *Students:* 284 full-time (49 women), 174 part-time (23 women); includes 40 minority (4 African Americans, 35 Asian Americans or Pacific Islanders, 1 Hispanic American), 279 international. 1,288 applicants, 8% accepted, 87 enrolled. In 2009, 56 master's, 42 doctorates awarded. *Entrance requirements:* For master's and doctorate, minimum GPA of 3.0. Additional exam requirements/recommendations for international students: Required—TOEFL (minimum score 600 paper-based; 250 computer-based; 100 iBT), or IELTS (minimum score 6.5). *Application deadline:* Applications are processed on a rolling basis. Application fee: $60 ($75 for international students). Electronic applications accepted. *Financial support:* In 2009–10, 36 fellowships, 266 research assistantships, 100 teaching assistantships were awarded; tuition waivers (full and partial) also available. *Unit head:* Robin A. Rutenbar, Head, 217-333-3373, Fax: 217-333-3501, E-mail: rutenbar@illinois.edu. *Application contact:* Rhonda McElroy, Coordinator of Graduate Programs, 217-244-2745, Fax: 217-244-6073, E-mail: rmcelroy@illinois.edu.

The University of Iowa, Graduate College, College of Liberal Arts and Sciences, Department of Computer Science, Iowa City, IA 52242-1316. Offers MCS, MS, PhD. *Degree requirements:* For master's, thesis optional, exam; for doctorate, comprehensive exam, thesis/dissertation. *Entrance requirements:* For master's, minimum GPA of 3.0; for doctorate, GRE General Test, minimum GPA of 3.0. Additional exam requirements/recommendations for international students: Required—TOEFL (minimum score 550 paper-based; 213 computer-based; 81 iBT). Electronic applications accepted.

The University of Kansas, Graduate Studies, School of Engineering, Department of Electrical Engineering and Computer Science, Program in Computer Science, Lawrence, KS 66045. Offers MS, PhD. Part-time and evening/weekend programs available. *Students:* 48 full-time (12 women), 28 part-time (3 women); includes 9 minority (2 African Americans, 1 American Indian/Alaska Native, 5 Asian Americans or Pacific Islanders, 1 Hispanic American), 27 international. Average age 28. 101 applicants, 31% accepted, 11 enrolled. In 2009, 19 master's, 5 doctorates awarded. Terminal master's awarded for partial completion of doctoral program. *Degree requirements:* For master's, thesis optional, exam; for doctorate, one foreign language, comprehensive exam, thesis/dissertation, qualifying exams. *Entrance requirements:* For master's, GRE, minimum GPA of 3.0; for doctorate, GRE, minimum GPA of 3.5. Additional exam requirements/recommendations for international students: Required—TOEFL (minimum score 600 paper-based; 250 computer-based; 100 iBT). *Application deadline:* For fall admission, 3/1 priority date for domestic students, 3/1 for international students; for spring admission, 10/1 priority date for domestic students, 10/1 for international students. Applications are processed on a rolling basis. Application fee: $45 ($55 for international students). Electronic applications accepted. *Expenses:* Tuition, state resident: full-time $6492; part-time $270.50 per credit hour. Tuition, nonresident: full-time $15,510; part-time $646.25 per credit hour. Required fees: $847; $70.56 per credit hour. Tuition and fees vary according to course load and program. *Financial support:* Fellowships with full and partial tuition reimbursements, research assistantships with full and partial tuition reimbursements, teaching assistantships with full and partial tuition reimbursements, career-related internships or fieldwork, scholarships/grants, and unspecified assistantships available. Financial award application deadline: 1/1. *Faculty research:* Communication systems and networking, computer systems design, interactive intelligent systems, bioinformatics. *Unit head:* Glenn Prescott, Chairperson, 785-864-4620, Fax: 785-864-3226.

Computer Science

The University of Kansas (continued)

Application contact: Pam Shadoin, Assistant to Graduate Director, 785-864-4487, Fax: 785-864-3226, E-mail: graduate@eecs.ku.edu.

University of Kentucky, Graduate School, College of Engineering, Program in Computer Science, Lexington, KY 40506-0032. Offers MS, PhD. *Degree requirements:* For master's, comprehensive exam, thesis optional; for doctorate, one foreign language, comprehensive exam, thesis/dissertation. *Entrance requirements:* For master's, GRE General Test, minimum undergraduate GPA of 2.75; for doctorate, GRE General Test, minimum undergraduate GPA of 3.0. Additional exam requirements/recommendations for international students: Required—TOEFL (minimum score 550 paper-based; 213 computer-based). Electronic applications accepted. *Faculty research:* Artificial intelligence and databases, communication networks and operating systems, graphics and vision, numerical analysis, theory.

University of Lethbridge, School of Graduate Studies, Lethbridge, AB T1K 3M4, Canada. Offers accounting (MScM); addictions counseling (M Sc); agricultural biotechnology (M Sc); agricultural studies (M Sc, MA); anthropology (MA); archaeology (MA); art (MA, MFA); biochemistry (M Sc); biological sciences (M Sc); biomolecular science (PhD); biosystems and biodiversity (PhD); Canadian studies (MA); chemistry (M Sc); computer science (M Sc); computer science and geographical information science (M Sc); counseling psychology (M Ed); dramatic arts (MA); earth, space, and physical science (PhD); economics (MA); educational leadership (M Ed); English (MA); environmental science (M Sc); evolution and behavior (PhD); exercise science (M Sc); finance (MScM); French (MA); French/German (MA); French/Spanish (MA); general education (M Ed); general management (MScM); geography (M Sc, MA); German (MA); health science (M Sc); health sciences (MA); history (MA); human resource management and labour relations (MScM); individualized multidisciplinary (M Sc, MA); information systems (MScM); international management (MScM); kinesiology (M Sc, MA); management (M Sc, MA); marketing (MScM); mathematics (M Sc); music (M Mus, MA); Native American studies (MA); neuroscience (M Sc, PhD); new media (MA); nursing (M Sc); philosophy (MA); physics (M Sc); policy and strategy (MScM); political science (MA); psychology (M Sc, MA); religious studies (MA); social sciences (MA); sociology (MA); theatre and dramatic arts (MFA); theoretical and computational science (PhD); urban and regional studies (MA); women's studies (MA). Part-time and evening/weekend programs available. *Degree requirements:* For doctorate, comprehensive exam, thesis/dissertation. *Entrance requirements:* For master's, GMAT (M Sc in management), bachelor's degree in related field, minimum GPA of 3.0 during previous 20 graded semester courses, 2 years teaching or related experience (M Ed); for doctorate, master's degree, minimum graduate GPA of 3.5. Additional exam requirements/recommendations for international students: Required—TOEFL. *Faculty research:* Movement and brain plasticity, gibberellin physiology, photosynthesis, carbon cycling, molecular properties of main-group ring components.

University of Louisiana at Lafayette, College of Engineering, Center for Advanced Computer Studies, Lafayette, LA 70504. Offers computer engineering (MS, PhD); computer science (MS, PhD). Part-time programs available. Terminal master's awarded for partial completion of doctoral program. *Degree requirements:* For master's, thesis or alternative; for doctorate, comprehensive exam, thesis/dissertation, final oral exam. *Entrance requirements:* For master's, GRE General Test, minimum GPA of 2.75; for doctorate, GRE General Test, minimum GPA of 3.0. Additional exam requirements/recommendations for international students: Required—TOEFL. Electronic applications accepted.

University of Louisville, J.B. Speed School of Engineering, Department of Computer Engineering and Computer Science, Louisville, KY 40292-0001. Offers computer engineering and computer science (M Eng, MS); computer science (MS); computer science and engineering (PhD); data mining (Certificate); network and information security (Certificate). *Accreditation:* ABET (one or more programs are accredited). Part-time programs available. Postbaccalaureate distance learning degree programs offered (no on-campus study). *Faculty:* 15 full-time (0 women). *Students:* 75 full-time (10 women), 42 part-time (10 women); includes 10 minority (7 African Americans, 2 Asian Americans or Pacific Islanders, 1 Hispanic American), 46 international. Average age 30. 66 applicants, 59% accepted, 21 enrolled. In 2009, 26 master's, 9 doctorates, 1 other advanced degree awarded. Terminal master's awarded for partial completion of doctoral program. *Degree requirements:* For master's, comprehensive exam (for some programs), thesis or alternative; for doctorate, comprehensive exam, thesis/dissertation, minimum GPA of 3.0. *Entrance requirements:* For master's, doctorate, and Certificate, GRE General Test. Additional exam requirements/recommendations for international students: Required—TOEFL (minimum score 550 paper-based; 213 computer-based; 80 iBT). *Application deadline:* For fall admission, 7/12 priority date for domestic and international students; for winter admission, 11/29 priority date for domestic and international students; for spring admission, 3/28 priority date for domestic and international students. Applications are processed on a rolling basis. Application fee: $50. Electronic applications accepted. *Financial support:* In 2009–10, 38 students received support, including 8 fellowships with full tuition reimbursements available (averaging $20,000 per year), 20 research assistantships with full tuition reimbursements available (averaging $20,700 per year), 6 teaching assistantships with full tuition reimbursements available (averaging $20,000 per year). Financial award application deadline: 1/25; financial award applicants required to submit FAFSA. *Faculty research:* Software systems engineering, information security and forensics, multimedia and vision, mobile and distributed computing, intelligent systems. Total annual research expenditures: $1.4 million. *Unit head:* Dr. Adel S. Elmaghraby, Chair, 502-852-6304, Fax: 502-852-4713, E-mail: adel@louisville.edu. *Application contact:* Dr. Michael Day, Associate Dean, 502-852-6195, Fax: 502-852-6294, E-mail: day@louisville.edu.

University of Maine, Graduate School, College of Liberal Arts and Sciences, Department of Computer Science, Orono, ME 04469. Offers MS, PhD. Part-time programs available. *Faculty:* 7 full-time (1 woman). *Students:* 8 full-time (1 woman), 5 part-time (1 woman); includes 1 minority (Asian American or Pacific Islander), 3 international. Average age 33. 15 applicants, 33% accepted, 2 enrolled. In 2009, 1 doctorate awarded. *Degree requirements:* For master's, thesis optional; for doctorate, thesis/dissertation. *Entrance requirements:* For master's and doctorate, GRE General Test, GRE Subject Test. Additional exam requirements/recommendations for international students: Required—TOEFL. *Application deadline:* For fall admission, 2/1 priority date for domestic students. Applications are processed on a rolling basis. Application fee: $65. Electronic applications accepted. *Financial support:* In 2009–10, 2 research assistantships with tuition reimbursements (averaging $22,554 per year), 9 teaching assistantships with tuition reimbursements (averaging $19,554 per year) were awarded; career-related internships or fieldwork, Federal Work-Study, institutionally sponsored loans, and tuition waivers (full) also available. Financial award application deadline: 3/1. *Faculty research:* Theory, software engineering, graphics, applications, artificial intelligence. *Unit head:* Dr. George Markowsky, Chair, 207-581-3912, Fax: 207-581-4977. *Application contact:* Scott G. Delcourt, Associate Dean of the Graduate School, 207-581-3291, Fax: 207-581-3232, E-mail: graduate@maine.edu.

University of Management and Technology, Program in Computer Science and Information Technology, Arlington, VA 22209. Offers computer science (MS); information technology (AC); information technology project management (MS); management information systems (MS); project management (AC); software engineering (MS). Part-time and evening/weekend programs available. Postbaccalaureate distance learning degree programs offered (no on-campus study). *Entrance requirements:* For master's, 3 recommendations, resume. Additional exam requirements/recommendations for international students: Required—TOEFL (minimum score 550 paper-based; 213 computer-based). Electronic applications accepted.

University of Manitoba, Faculty of Graduate Studies, Faculty of Science, Department of Computer Science, Winnipeg, MB R3T 2N2, Canada. Offers M Sc, PhD. *Degree requirements:* For master's, thesis or alternative; for doctorate, thesis/dissertation.

University of Maryland, Baltimore County, Graduate School, College of Engineering and Information Technology, Department of Computer Science and Electrical Engineering, Program in Computer Science, Baltimore, MD 21250. Offers MS, PhD. Part-time programs available. *Students:* 103 full-time (26 women), 56 part-time (7 women); includes 24 minority (9 African Americans, 1 American Indian/Alaska Native, 9 Asian Americans or Pacific Islanders, 5 Hispanic Americans), 54 international. Average age 29. 314 applicants, 55% accepted, 45 enrolled. In 2009, 19 master's, 2 doctorates awarded. *Degree requirements:* For master's, comprehensive exam (for some programs), thesis (for some programs); for doctorate, comprehensive exam, thesis/dissertation. *Entrance requirements:* For master's, GRE General Test, strong background in computer science and math courses; for doctorate, GRE General Test, MS in computer science (strongly recommended). Additional exam requirements/recommendations for international students: Required—TOEFL (minimum score 550 paper-based; 213 computer-based; 80 iBT). *Application deadline:* For fall admission, 6/1 for domestic students, 1/1 for international students; for spring admission, 11/1 for domestic students, 6/1 for international students. Applications are processed on a rolling basis. Application fee: $50. Electronic applications accepted. *Financial support:* In 2009–10, 2 fellowships with full tuition reimbursements (averaging $24,000 per year), 37 research assistantships with full tuition reimbursements (averaging $17,000 per year), 26 teaching assistantships with full tuition reimbursements (averaging $17,000 per year) were awarded; career-related internships or fieldwork, Federal Work-Study, scholarships/grants, health care benefits, tuition waivers (partial), and unspecified assistantships also available. Support available to part-time students. Financial award application deadline: 6/30; financial award applicants required to submit FAFSA. *Faculty research:* Security and information assurance, intelligent agents and semantic web, wireless networking. *Unit head:* Dr. Charles K. Nicholas, Professor and Chair, 410-455-3500, Fax: 410-455-3969, E-mail: nicholas@cs.umbc.edu. *Application contact:* Dr. Yun Peng, Professor and Graduate Program Coordinator, 410-455-3816, Fax: 410-455-3969, E-mail: ypeng@cs.umbc.edu.

University of Maryland, Baltimore County, Graduate School, College of Engineering and Information Technology, Department of Information Systems, Program in Human-Centered Computing, Baltimore, MD 21250. Offers MS, PhD. Part-time and evening/weekend programs available. *Students:* 8 full-time (4 women), 20 part-time (11 women); includes 4 minority (3 African Americans, 1 Asian American or Pacific Islander), 2 international. Average age 30. 29 applicants, 59% accepted, 7 enrolled. In 2009, 2 master's awarded. Terminal master's awarded for partial completion of doctoral program. *Degree requirements:* For master's, comprehensive exam (for some programs), thesis optional; for doctorate, comprehensive exam, thesis/dissertation. *Entrance requirements:* For master's, minimum GPA of 3.0; for doctorate, GRE General Test or GMAT, minimum GPA of 3.0, competence in statistical analysis and experimental design (recommended). Additional exam requirements/recommendations for international students: Required—TOEFL (minimum score 550 paper-based; 213 computer-based; 80 iBT). *Application deadline:* For fall admission, 6/1 for domestic students, 1/1 for international students; for spring admission, 11/1 for domestic students, 6/1 for international students. Applications are processed on a rolling basis. Application fee: $50. Electronic applications accepted. *Financial support:* Career-related internships or fieldwork, Federal Work-Study, scholarships/grants, health care benefits, tuition waivers (partial), and unspecified assistantships available. Support available to part-time students. Financial award application deadline: 6/30; financial award applicants required to submit FAFSA. *Faculty research:* Human-centered computing, artificial intelligence, database/data mining, decision-making support systems, software engineering/systems analysis and design. *Unit head:* Dr. Andrew L. Sears, Professor and Chair, 410-455-3883, Fax: 410-455-1217, E-mail: asears@umbc.edu. *Application contact:* Dr. Aryya Gangopadhyay, Associate Professor and Graduate Program Director, 410-455-2620, Fax: 410-455-1217, E-mail: gangopad@umbc.edu.

University of Maryland, College Park, Academic Affairs, College of Computer, Mathematical and Physical Sciences, Department of Computer Science, College Park, MD 20742. Offers MS, PhD. Part-time and evening/weekend programs available. *Faculty:* 72 full-time (10 women), 2 part-time/adjunct (1 woman). *Students:* 203 full-time (35 women), 18 part-time (2 women); includes 21 minority (2 African Americans, 17 Asian Americans or Pacific Islanders, 2 Hispanic Americans), 106 international. 981 applicants, 12% accepted, 37 enrolled. In 2009, 30 master's, 20 doctorates awarded. Terminal master's awarded for partial completion of doctoral program. *Degree requirements:* For master's, thesis or scholarly paper and exam; for doctorate, thesis/dissertation. *Entrance requirements:* For master's and doctorate, GRE General Test, GRE Subject Test (recommended), minimum GPA of 3.0, 3 letters of recommendation. Additional exam requirements/recommendations for international students: Required—TOEFL; Recommended—TWE. *Application deadline:* For fall admission, 12/15 for domestic and international students; for spring admission, 10/15 for domestic students, 6/1 for international students. Applications are processed on a rolling basis. Application fee: $60. Electronic applications accepted. *Expenses:* Tuition, area resident: Part-time $471 per credit hour. Tuition, state resident: part-time $471 per credit hour. Tuition, nonresident: part-time $1016 per credit hour. Required fees: $337.04 per term. *Financial support:* In 2009–10, 3 fellowships with full and partial tuition reimbursements (averaging $16,802 per year), 120 research assistantships with tuition reimbursements (averaging $19,577 per year), 64 teaching assistantships with tuition reimbursements (averaging $18,509 per year) were awarded; career-related internships or fieldwork, Federal Work-Study, and scholarships/grants also available. Support available to part-time students. Financial award applicants required to submit FAFSA. *Faculty research:* Artificial intelligence, computer applications, information processing, bioinformatics and computational biology, human computer interaction. Total annual research expenditures: $5.3 million. *Unit head:* Dr. Larry S. Davis, Chairperson, 301-405-2662, Fax: 301-314-1353, E-mail: lsdavis@umd.edu. *Application contact:* Dean of Graduate School, 301-405-0358.

University of Maryland Eastern Shore, Graduate Programs, Department of Mathematics and Computer Sciences, Princess Anne, MD 21853-1299. Offers applied computer science (MS). Part-time and evening/weekend programs available. *Degree requirements:* For master's, thesis or alternative, research project. *Entrance requirements:* For master's, GRE General Test, minimum GPA of 3.0. Additional exam requirements/recommendations for international students: Required—TOEFL (minimum score 213 computer-based; 80 iBT). Electronic applications accepted.

University of Massachusetts Amherst, Graduate School, College of Natural Sciences, Department of Computer Science, Amherst, MA 01003. Offers MS, PhD. Part-time programs available. *Faculty:* 45 full-time (6 women). *Students:* 132 full-time (23 women), 50 part-time (7 women); includes 5 minority (2 African Americans, 3 Asian Americans or Pacific Islanders), 93 international. Average age 28. 692 applicants, 10% accepted, 32 enrolled. In 2009, 30 master's, 8 doctorates awarded. Terminal master's awarded for partial completion of doctoral program. *Degree requirements:* For master's, thesis or alternative; for doctorate, comprehensive exam, thesis/dissertation. *Entrance requirements:* For master's and doctorate, GRE General Test. Additional exam requirements/recommendations for international students: Required—TOEFL (minimum score 550 paper-based; 213 computer-based; 80 iBT), IELTS (minimum score 6.5), TWE. *Application deadline:* For fall admission, 12/15 for domestic and international students. Applications are processed on a rolling basis. Application fee: $50 ($65 for international students). Electronic applications accepted. *Expenses:* Tuition, state resident: full-time $2640; part-time $110 per credit. Tuition, nonresident: full-time $9936; part-time $414 per credit. Tuition and fees vary according to course load. *Financial support:* In 2009–10, 9 fellowships with full tuition reimbursements (averaging $6,270 per year), 169 research assistantships with full tuition reimbursements (averaging $16,607 per year), 57 teaching assistantships with full tuition reimbursements (averaging $8,361 per year) were awarded; career-related internships or fieldwork, Federal Work-Study, institutionally sponsored loans, scholarships/grants, traineeships, health care benefits, tuition waivers (full), and unspecified assistantships also available. *Faculty research:* Artificial intelligence, robotics, computer vision, and wearable computing; autonomous and multiagent systems; information retrieval, data mining and machine learning; networking, distributed systems and security. *Unit head:* Dr. James Allan, Graduate Program Director, 413-545-3640, Fax: 413-545-1249. *Application contact:* Jean M. Ames, Supervisor of Admissions, 413-545-0721, Fax: 413-577-0010, E-mail: gradadm@grad.umass.edu.

University of Massachusetts Boston, Office of Graduate Studies, College of Science and Mathematics, Program in Computer Science, Boston, MA 02125-3393. Offers MS, PhD. Part-time and evening/weekend programs available. *Degree requirements:* For master's, comprehensive exam, thesis optional, capstone final project; for doctorate, comprehensive exam, thesis/dissertation, oral exams. *Entrance requirements:* For master's and doctorate, GRE General Test, minimum GPA of 2.75. *Faculty research:* Queuing theory, database design theory, computer networks, theory of database query languages, real-time systems.

University of Massachusetts Dartmouth, Graduate School, College of Engineering, Program in Computer Science, North Dartmouth, MA 02747-2300. Offers computer networks and distributed systems (Postbaccalaureate Certificate); computer science (MS); computer systems (Postbaccalaureate Certificate); software development and design (Postbaccalaureate Certificate). Part-time programs available. Postbaccalaureate distance learning degree programs offered. *Faculty:* 10 full-time (2 women), 1 part-time/adjunct (0 women). *Students:* 29 full-time (7 women), 36 part-time (8 women), 48 international. Average age 25. 81 applicants, 89% accepted, 20 enrolled. In 2009, 25 master's awarded. *Degree requirements:* For master's, thesis or alternative. *Entrance requirements:* For master's, GRE General Test, 3 letters of recommendation. Additional exam requirements/recommendations for international students: Required—TOEFL (minimum score 500 paper-based). *Application deadline:* For fall admission, 6/30 priority date for domestic students, 4/30 priority date for international students; for spring admission, 11/15 priority date for domestic students, 9/15 priority date for international students. Applications are processed on a rolling basis. Application fee: $35 ($55 for international students). Electronic applications accepted. *Expenses:* Tuition, state resident: full-time $2071; part-time $86.29 per credit. Tuition, nonresident: full-time $8099; part-time $337.46 per credit. Required fees: $9446. Tuition and fees vary according to class time, course load and reciprocity agreements. *Financial support:* In 2009–10, 5 research assistantships with full tuition reimbursements (averaging $9,246 per year), 6 teaching assistantships with full tuition reimbursements (averaging $4,896 per year) were awarded; Federal Work-Study and unspecified assistantships also available. Support available to part-time students. Financial award application deadline: 3/1; financial award applicants required to submit FAFSA. *Faculty research:* Tracking of mesoscale features, modeling and analysis of workflow management, brain modeling, software engineering, multi-agent systems. Total annual research expenditures: $518,000. *Unit head:* Dr. Jan Bergandy, Director, 508-999-8293, Fax: 508-999-9144, E-mail: jbergandy@umassd.edu. *Application contact:* Elan Turcotte-Shamski, Graduate Admissions Officer, 508-999-8604, Fax: 508-999-8183, E-mail: graduate@umassd.edu.

University of Massachusetts Lowell, College of Arts and Sciences, Department of Computer Science, Lowell, MA 01854-2881. Offers MS, PhD, Sc D. Part-time programs available. *Degree requirements:* For master's, thesis optional; for doctorate, thesis/dissertation. *Entrance requirements:* For master's and doctorate, GRE General Test. *Faculty research:* Networks, multimedia systems, human-computer interaction, graphics and visualization databases.

University of Memphis, Graduate School, College of Arts and Sciences, Department of Computer Science, Memphis, TN 38152. Offers applied computer science (MS); computer science (MS, PhD). *Faculty:* 15 full-time (3 women), 1 part-time/adjunct (0 women). *Students:* 58 full-time (22 women), 27 part-time (4 women); includes 9 minority (7 African Americans, 2 Asian Americans or Pacific Islanders), 63 international. Average age 28. 56 applicants, 80% accepted, 32 enrolled. In 2009, 10 master's, 1 doctorate awarded. *Degree requirements:* For master's, comprehensive exam, thesis; for doctorate, comprehensive exam, thesis/dissertation. *Entrance requirements:* For master's and doctorate, GRE, letters of recommendation. Additional exam requirements/recommendations for international students: Required—TOEFL (minimum score 550 paper-based; 210 computer-based; 80 iBT). Application fee: $35 ($60 for international students). *Expenses:* Tuition, state resident: full-time $6246; part-time $347 per credit hour. Tuition, nonresident: full-time $15,894; part-time $883 per credit hour. Required fees: $1160. Full-time tuition and fees vary according to course load, degree level and program. *Financial support:* In 2009–10, 9 students received support; research assistantships with full tuition reimbursements available, teaching assistantships with full tuition reimbursements available, Federal Work-Study, scholarships/grants, and unspecified assistantships available. Financial award application deadline: 2/15; financial award applicants required to submit FAFSA. *Faculty research:* Network security, biomolecular and distributed computing, wireless sensor networks, artificial intelligence. *Unit head:* Dr. Sajjan Shiva, Chair, 901-678-5667, Fax: 901-678-2480, E-mail: info@cs.memphis.edu. *Application contact:* Dr. David Lin, Graduate Studies Coordinator, 901-678-3135, E-mail: davidlin@memphis.edu.

University of Memphis, Graduate School, College of Arts and Sciences, Department of Mathematical Sciences, Memphis, TN 38152. Offers applied mathematics (MS); applied statistics (PhD); bioinformatics (MS); computer science (PhD); computer sciences (MS); mathematics (MS, PhD); statistics (MS, PhD). Part-time programs available. *Faculty:* 19 full-time (4 women), 3 part-time/adjunct (0 women). *Students:* 38 full-time (19 women), 25 part-time (9 women); includes 4 minority (2 African Americans, 2 Asian Americans or Pacific Islanders), 29 international. Average age 34. 26 applicants, 96% accepted, 11 enrolled. In 2009, 6 master's, 5 doctorates awarded. Terminal master's awarded for partial completion of doctoral program. *Degree requirements:* For master's, comprehensive exam; for doctorate, one foreign language, thesis/dissertation, oral exams. *Entrance requirements:* For master's and doctorate, GRE General Test, minimum GPA of 2.5. Additional exam requirements/recommendations for international students: Required—TOEFL (minimum score 550 paper-based; 210 computer-based). *Application deadline:* For fall admission, 8/1 for domestic students, 5/1 priority date for international students; for spring admission, 12/1 for domestic students, 9/1 priority date for international students. Applications are processed on a rolling basis. Application fee: $35 ($60 for international students). Electronic applications accepted. *Expenses:* Tuition, state resident: full-time $6246; part-time $347 per credit hour. Tuition, nonresident: full-time $15,894; part-time $883 per credit hour. Required fees: $1160. Full-time tuition and fees vary according to course load, degree level and program. *Financial support:* In 2009–10, 22 students received support; fellowships with full tuition reimbursements available, research assistantships with full tuition reimbursements available, teaching assistantships with full tuition reimbursements available, career-related internships or fieldwork, Federal Work-Study, scholarships/grants, and unspecified assistantships available. Financial award application deadline: 2/15; financial award applicants required to submit FAFSA. *Faculty research:* Combinatorics, ergodic theory, graph theory, Ramsey theory, applied statistics. *Unit head:* Dr. James E. Jamison, Chairman, 901-678-2482, Fax: 901-678-2480, E-mail: jjamison@memphis.edu. *Application contact:* Dr. Anna Kaminska, Coordinator of Graduate Studies, 901-678-2494, Fax: 901-678-2480.

University of Miami, Graduate School, College of Arts and Sciences, Department of Computer Science, Coral Gables, FL 33124. Offers MS, PhD. Part-time programs available. Postbaccalaureate distance learning degree programs offered (no on-campus study). *Degree requirements:* For master's, comprehensive exam (for some programs), thesis. *Entrance requirements:* For master's, GRE. Additional exam requirements/recommendations for international students: Required—TOEFL. Electronic applications accepted. *Faculty research:* Algorithm engineering, automated reasoning, computer graphics, cryptography, security network.

University of Michigan, Horace H. Rackham School of Graduate Studies, College of Engineering, Department of Computer Science and Engineering, Ann Arbor, MI 48109. Offers MS, MSE, PhD. *Faculty:* 43 full-time (4 women). *Students:* 210 full-time (27 women), 2 part-time (0 women); includes 23 minority (4 African Americans, 15 Asian Americans or Pacific Islanders, 4 Hispanic Americans), 123 international. 841 applicants, 22% accepted, 64 enrolled. In 2009, 35 master's, 35 doctorates awarded. *Expenses:* Tuition, state resident: full-time $17,286; part-time $1099 per credit hour. Tuition, nonresident: full-time $34,944; part-time $2080 per credit hour. Required fees: $95 per semester. Tuition and fees vary according to course load, degree level and program. *Faculty research:* Solid state electronics and optics; communications, control, signal process; sensors and integrated circuitry, others; software systems; artificial intelligence; hardware systems. *Unit head:* Prof. Farnam Jahanian, Department Chair, 734-647-1807, Fax: 734-763-1503, E-mail: farnam@umich.edu. *Application contact:* Dawn Freysinger, Graduate Programs Coordinator, 734-647-1807, Fax: 734-763-1503, E-mail: dawnf@umich.edu.

University of Michigan, Horace H. Rackham School of Graduate Studies, College of Engineering, Department of Electrical Engineering and Computer Science, Ann Arbor, MI 48109. Offers MS, MSE, PhD. ECE Department offers degrees in both Electrical Engineering and Electrical Engineering: Systems. *Faculty:* 61 full-time (6 women). *Students:* 396 full-time (44 women), 8 part-time (0 women); includes 49 minority (9 African Americans, 34 Asian Americans or Pacific Islanders, 6 Hispanic Americans), 280 international. 1,289 applicants, 27% accepted, 127 enrolled. In 2009, 91 master's, 56 doctorates awarded. *Expenses:* Tuition, state resident: full-time $17,286; part-time $1099 per credit hour. Tuition, nonresident: full-time $34,944; part-time $2080 per credit hour. Required fees: $95 per semester. Tuition and fees vary according to course load, degree level and program. *Faculty research:* Solid state electronics and optics; communications, control, signal process; sensors and integrated circuitry, others; software systems; artificial intelligence; hardware systems. *Unit head:* Prof. Khalil Najafi, Chair, 734-647-7010, Fax: 734-647-7009, E-mail: najafi@umich.edu. *Application contact:* Beth Stalnaker, Graduate Coordinator, 734- 647-1758, Fax: 734-763-1503, E-mail: beths@umich.edu.

University of Michigan–Dearborn, College of Engineering and Computer Science, Department of Computer and Information Science, Dearborn, MI 48128-1491. Offers MS. Part-time and evening/weekend programs available. Postbaccalaureate distance learning degree programs offered (minimal on-campus study). *Faculty:* 13 full-time (1 woman), 4 part-time/adjunct (0 women). *Students:* 4 full-time (0 women), 55 part-time (10 women); includes 10 minority (2 African Americans, 6 Asian Americans or Pacific Islanders, 2 Hispanic Americans), 13 international. Average age 33. 25 applicants, 48% accepted, 12 enrolled. In 2009, 22 master's awarded. *Degree requirements:* For master's, thesis optional. *Entrance requirements:* For master's, bachelor's degree in mathematics, computer science, or engineering; minimum GPA of 3.0. Additional exam requirements/recommendations for international students: Required—TOEFL (minimum score 560 paper-based; 220 computer-based; 84 iBT). *Application deadline:* For fall admission, 6/15 priority date for domestic students, 4/1 for international students; for winter admission, 10/15 priority date for domestic students, 8/1 for international students; for spring admission, 2/15 priority date for domestic students, 12/1 for international students. Application fee: $60 ($75 for international students). *Expenses:* Tuition, area resident: Part-time $504.10 per credit hour. Tuition, state resident: part-time $504.10 per credit hour. Tuition, nonresident: part-time $957.90 per credit hour. *Financial support:* In 2009–10, 2 research assistantships with full and partial tuition reimbursements (averaging $7,700 per year) were awarded; career-related internships or fieldwork also available. Financial award application deadline: 4/1; financial award applicants required to submit FAFSA. *Faculty research:* Information systems, geometric modeling, networks, databases. Total annual research expenditures: $54,056. *Unit head:* Dr. William I. Grosky, Chair, 313-583-6424, Fax: 313-593-4256, E-mail: wgrosky@umich.edu. *Application contact:* Katherine R. Markotan, Intermediate Academic Records Assistant, 313-436-9145, Fax: 313-593-4256, E-mail: tabatha@umd.umich.edu.

University of Michigan–Flint, College of Arts and Sciences, Program in Computer and Information Systems, Flint, MI 48502-1950. Offers computer science and information systems (MS). Part-time programs available. *Faculty:* 2 full-time (1 woman). *Students:* 6 full-time (0 women), 54 part-time (10 women); includes 8 minority (4 African Americans, 4 Asian Americans or Pacific Islanders), 18 international. Average age 31. 55 applicants, 73% accepted, 15 enrolled. In 2009, 14 master's awarded. *Degree requirements:* For master's, thesis or alternative. *Entrance requirements:* For master's, minimum undergraduate GPA of 3.0. Additional exam requirements/recommendations for international students: Required—TOEFL (minimum score 560 paper-based; 220 computer-based; 84 iBT), IELTS (minimum score 6.5). *Application deadline:* For fall admission, 8/1 priority date for domestic students, 5/1 priority date for international students; for winter admission, 11/15 priority date for domestic students, 9/1 priority date for international students; for spring admission, 3/15 priority date for domestic students, 1/1 priority date for international students. Application fee: $55. *Expenses:* Contact institution. *Financial support:* Federal Work-Study, scholarships/grants, and unspecified assistantships available. Support available to part-time students. Financial award application deadline: 6/1; financial award applicants required to submit FAFSA. *Unit head:* Dr. Michael Farmer, Director, 810-762-3131, Fax: 810-766-6780. *Application contact:* Bradley T. Maki, Director of Graduate Admissions, 810-762-3171, Fax: 810-766-6789, E-mail: bmaki@umflint.edu.

University of Minnesota, Duluth, Graduate School, Swenson College of Science and Engineering, Department of Computer Science, Duluth, MN 55812-2496. Offers MS. Part-time programs available. *Faculty:* 9 full-time (1 woman). *Students:* 23 full-time (10 women), 1 part-time (0 women), 20 international. Average age 24. 37 applicants, 62% accepted, 12 enrolled. In 2009, 10 master's awarded. *Entrance requirements:* For master's, GRE General Test, minimum GPA of 3.0. Additional exam requirements/recommendations for international students: Required—TOEFL (minimum score 550 paper-based; 213 computer-based). *Application deadline:* For fall admission, 4/15 for domestic and international students. Applications are processed on a rolling basis. Application fee: $75 ($95 for international students). Electronic applications accepted. *Financial support:* In 2009–10, 1 fellowship with partial tuition reimbursement, 4 research assistantships with full and partial tuition reimbursements (averaging $13,120 per year), 18 teaching assistantships with full and partial tuition reimbursements (averaging $13,120 per year) were awarded; institutionally sponsored loans, scholarships/grants, and unspecified assistantships also available. Support available to part-time students. Financial award application deadline: 3/15. *Faculty research:* Information retrieval, artificial intelligence, machine learning, parallel/distributed computing, graphics. *Unit head:* Dr. Carolyn J. Crouch, Director of Graduate Studies, 218-726-7607, Fax: 218-726-8240, E-mail: cs@d.umn.edu. *Application contact:* Tami Vatalaro, Executive Administrative Specialist, 218-726-7523, Fax: 218-726-6970, E-mail: grad@d.umn.edu.

University of Minnesota, Twin Cities Campus, Graduate School, Scientific Computation Program, Minneapolis, MN 55455-0213. Offers MS, PhD. Part-time programs available. *Degree requirements:* For master's, thesis; for doctorate, thesis/dissertation. *Entrance requirements:* For doctorate, GRE General Test. Additional exam requirements/recommendations for international students: Required—TOEFL (minimum score 550 paper-based; 213 computer-based; 79 iBT), IELTS (minimum score 6.5). Electronic applications accepted. *Faculty research:* Parallel computations, quantum mechanical dynamics, computational materials science, computational fluid dynamics, computational neuroscience.

University of Minnesota, Twin Cities Campus, Institute of Technology, Department of Computer Science and Engineering, Minneapolis, MN 55455-0213. Offers computer and information sciences (MCIS, MS, PhD). Part-time programs available. Terminal master's awarded for partial completion of doctoral program. *Degree requirements:* For doctorate, thesis/dissertation. *Entrance requirements:* For master's and doctorate, GRE General Test. *Faculty research:* Software systems, numerical analysis, theory, artificial intelligence.

University of Missouri, Graduate School, College of Engineering, Department of Computer Science, Columbia, MO 65211. Offers MS, PhD. Part-time programs available. *Degree requirements:* For doctorate, thesis/dissertation. *Entrance requirements:* For master's, GRE General Test, minimum GPA of 3.0; for doctorate, GRE General Test. Additional exam requirements/recommendations for international students: Required—TOEFL (minimum score 577 paper-based; 233 computer-based; 90 iBT).

University of Missouri–Kansas City, School of Computing and Engineering, Kansas City, MO 64110-2499. Offers civil engineering (MS); computer and electrical engineering (PhD); computer science (MS), including bioinformatics, software engineering, telecommunications networking; computer science and informatics (PhD); computing (PhD); electrical engineering (MS); engineering (PhD); mechanical engineering (MS); telecommunications (PhD). PhD (interdisciplinary) offered through the School of Graduate Studies. Part-time programs available. *Faculty:* 40 full-time (5 women), 28 part-time/adjunct (0 women). *Students:* 230 full-time (46 women), 158 part-time (31 women); includes 20 minority (5 African Americans, 12 Asian

Computer Science

University of Missouri–Kansas City (continued)
Americans or Pacific Islanders, 3 Hispanic Americans), 313 international. Average age 24. 484 applicants, 64% accepted, 106 enrolled. In 2009, 144 master's awarded. *Degree requirements:* For doctorate, thesis/dissertation. *Entrance requirements:* For master's, GRE General Test, minimum GPA of 3.0, 3 letters of recommendations from professors; for doctorate, GRE General Test, minimum GPA of 3.5. Additional exam requirements/recommendations for international students: Required—TOEFL (minimum score 550 paper-based; 213 computer-based; 80 iBT). *Application deadline:* For fall admission, 1/15 priority date for domestic students, 1/15 for international students. Applications are processed on a rolling basis. Application fee: $45 ($50 for international students). *Expenses:* Tuition, state resident: full-time $5378; part-time $299 per credit hour. Tuition, nonresident: full-time $13,881; part-time $771 per credit hour. Required fees: $641; $71 per credit hour. Tuition and fees vary according to course load and program. *Financial support:* In 2009–10, 29 research assistantships with partial tuition reimbursements (averaging $15,040 per year), 10 teaching assistantships with partial tuition reimbursements (averaging $12,118 per year) were awarded; career-related internships or fieldwork, Federal Work-Study, scholarships/grants, tuition waivers (partial), and unspecified assistantships also available. Support available to part-time students. Financial award application deadline: 3/1; financial award applicants required to submit FAFSA. *Faculty research:* Algorithms, bioinformatics and medical informatics, biomechanics/biomaterials, civil engineering materials, networking and telecommunications, thermal science. Total annual research expenditures: $1.4 million. *Unit head:* Dr. Kevin Z. Truman, Dean, 816-235-2399, Fax: 816-235-5159. *Application contact:* Dr. Kevin Z. Truman, Dean, 816-235-2399, Fax: 816-235-5159.

University of Missouri–St. Louis, College of Arts and Sciences, Department of Mathematics and Computer Science, St. Louis, MO 63121. Offers applied mathematics (PhD), including computer science; computer science (MS); mathematics (MA). Part-time and evening/weekend programs available. *Faculty:* 16 full-time (2 women), 1 part-time/adjunct (0 women). *Students:* 24 full-time (11 women), 47 part-time (11 women); includes 7 minority (5 African Americans, 1 American Indian/Alaska Native, 1 Asian American or Pacific Islander), 27 international. Average age 30. 88 applicants, 53% accepted, 20 enrolled. In 2009, 23 master's, 1 doctorate awarded. *Degree requirements:* For master's, thesis optional; for doctorate, thesis/dissertation. *Entrance requirements:* For master's, 2 letters of recommendation; for doctorate, GRE General Test, 3 letters of recommendation. Additional exam requirements/recommendations for international students: Required—TOEFL (minimum score 550 paper-based; 213 computer-based). *Application deadline:* For fall admission, 7/1 priority date for domestic and international students; for spring admission, 12/1 priority date for domestic and international students. Applications are processed on a rolling basis. Application fee: $35 ($40 for international students). Electronic applications accepted. *Expenses:* Tuition, state resident: full-time $5377; part-time $297.70 per credit hour. Tuition, nonresident: full-time $13,882; part-time $771.20 per credit hour. Required fees: $220; $12.20 per credit hour. One-time fee: $12. Tuition and fees vary according to course level, campus/location and program. *Financial support:* In 2009–10, 3 research assistantships with full and partial tuition reimbursements (averaging $9,563 per year), 5 teaching assistantships with full and partial tuition reimbursements (averaging $13,500 per year) were awarded; fellowships with full tuition reimbursements also available. Financial award applicants required to submit FAFSA. *Faculty research:* Statistics, algebra, analysis. *Unit head:* Dr. Shiying Zhao, Director of Graduate Studies, 314-516-5741, Fax: 314-516-5400, E-mail: zhao@arch.cs.umsl.edu. *Application contact:* 314-516-5458, Fax: 314-516-6996, E-mail: gradadm@umsl.edu.

The University of Montana, Graduate School, College of Arts and Sciences, Department of Computer Science, Missoula, MT 59812-0002. Offers MS. Part-time programs available. *Degree requirements:* For master's, project or thesis. *Entrance requirements:* For master's, GRE General Test. Additional exam requirements/recommendations for international students: Required—TOEFL (minimum score 525 paper-based; 197 computer-based). *Faculty research:* Parallel and distributed systems, neural networks, genetic algorithms, machine learning, data visualization, artificial intelligence.

University of Nebraska at Omaha, Graduate Studies, College of Information Science and Technology, Department of Computer Science, Omaha, NE 68182. Offers MA, MS. Part-time and evening/weekend programs available. *Faculty:* 18 full-time (2 women). *Students:* 22 full-time (3 women), 58 part-time (9 women); includes 3 minority (1 African American, 2 Asian Americans or Pacific Islanders), 28 international. Average age 38. 106 applicants, 45% accepted, 24 enrolled. In 2009, 19 master's awarded. *Degree requirements:* For master's, comprehensive exam, thesis (for some programs). *Entrance requirements:* For master's, GRE General Test, minimum GPA of 3.0, course work in computer science. Additional exam requirements/recommendations for international students: Required—TOEFL (minimum score 500 paper-based; 173 computer-based; 61 iBT). *Application deadline:* For fall admission, 7/1 priority date for domestic students; for spring admission, 11/15 priority date for domestic students. Applications are processed on a rolling basis. Application fee: $45. Electronic applications accepted. *Financial support:* In 2009–10, 22 students received support; research assistantships, teaching assistantships, Federal Work-Study, institutionally sponsored loans, scholarships/grants, tuition waivers (full), and unspecified assistantships available. Support available to part-time students. Financial award application deadline: 3/1; financial award applicants required to submit FAFSA. *Unit head:* Dr. Qiuming Zhu, Chairperson, 402-554-2423. *Application contact:* Carla Frakes, Information Contact, 402-554-2423.

University of Nebraska–Lincoln, Graduate College, College of Arts and Sciences and College of Engineering, Department of Computer Science and Engineering, Lincoln, NE 68588. Offers bioinformatics (MS, PhD); computer engineering (MS, PhD); computer science (MS, PhD); information technology (PhD). *Degree requirements:* For master's, thesis optional; for doctorate, comprehensive exam, thesis/dissertation. *Entrance requirements:* For master's and doctorate, GRE General Test. Additional exam requirements/recommendations for international students: Required—TOEFL (minimum score 600 paper-based; 250 computer-based). Electronic applications accepted. *Faculty research:* Software engineering, geo- and bio-informatics, scientific computation, secure communication.

University of Nevada, Las Vegas, Graduate College, Howard R. Hughes College of Engineering, School of Computer Science, Las Vegas, NV 89154-4019. Offers MS, PhD. Part-time programs available. *Faculty:* 13 full-time (2 women). *Students:* 23 full-time (8 women), 15 part-time (2 women); includes 3 minority (all Asian Americans or Pacific Islanders), 20 international. Average age 30. 43 applicants, 81% accepted, 17 enrolled. In 2009, 10 master's awarded. *Degree requirements:* For master's, comprehensive exam, thesis optional, project; for doctorate, comprehensive exam, thesis/dissertation. *Entrance requirements:* For master's, GRE General Test; for doctorate, GRE General Test, GRE Subject Test (computer science). Additional exam requirements/recommendations for international students: Required—TOEFL (minimum score 550 paper-based; 213 computer-based; 80 iBT), IELTS (minimum score 7). *Application deadline:* For fall admission, 2/1 priority date for domestic and international students; for spring admission, 10/1 priority date for domestic and international students. Applications are processed on a rolling basis. Application fee: $60 ($95 for international students). Electronic applications accepted. *Financial support:* In 2009–10, 15 students received support, including 15 teaching assistantships with partial tuition reimbursements available (averaging $10,000 per year); institutionally sponsored loans, scholarships/grants, health care benefits, and unspecified assistantships also available. Financial award application deadline: 3/1. *Unit head:* Dr. John Minor, Director/ Associate Professor, 702-895-3715, Fax: 702-895-2639, E-mail: minor@cs.unlv.edu. *Application contact:* Graduate College Admissions Evaluator, 702-895-3320, Fax: 702-895-4180, E-mail: gradcollege@unlv.edu.

University of Nevada, Reno, Graduate School, College of Engineering, Department of Computer Science and Engineering, Program in Computer Science, Reno, NV 89557. Offers MS. *Degree requirements:* For master's, thesis optional. *Entrance requirements:* For master's, GRE General Test, minimum GPA of 2.75. Additional exam requirements/recommendations for international students: Required—TOEFL (minimum score 500 paper-based; 173 computer-based; 61 iBT), IELTS (minimum score 6). Electronic applications accepted. *Faculty research:* Evolutionary computing systems, computer vision/virtual reality, software engineering.

University of Nevada, Reno, Graduate School, College of Engineering, Department of Computer Science and Engineering, Program in Computer Science and Engineering, Reno, NV 89557. Offers PhD. *Degree requirements:* For doctorate, thesis/dissertation. *Entrance requirements:* For doctorate, GRE General Test, minimum GPA of 3.0. Additional exam requirements/recommendations for international students: Required—TOEFL (minimum score 500 paper-based; 173 computer-based; 61 iBT), IELTS (minimum score 6). Electronic applications accepted. *Faculty research:* Evolutionary computing systems, computer vision/virtual reality, software engineering.

University of New Brunswick Fredericton, School of Graduate Studies, Faculty of Computer Science, Fredericton, NB E3B 5A3, Canada. Offers M Sc CS, PhD. Part-time programs available. *Faculty:* 22 full-time (4 women). *Students:* 60 full-time (18 women), 16 part-time (4 women). In 2009, 22 master's, 3 doctorates awarded. *Degree requirements:* For master's, thesis; for doctorate, comprehensive exam, thesis/dissertation, qualifying exam. *Entrance requirements:* For master's, Minimum GPA of 3.0; undergraduate degree with sufficient Computer Science background.; for doctorate, Research-based Master's degree in Computer Science or related area; student must have a supervisor before being accepted. Additional exam requirements/recommendations for international students: Required—TOEFL (minimum score 580 paper-based; 237 computer-based), TWE (minimum score 4), or IELTS (minimum score 7). *Application deadline:* For fall admission, 3/1 priority date for domestic students. Application fee: $50 Canadian dollars. Electronic applications accepted. Tuition and fees charges are reported in Canadian dollars. *Expenses:* Tuition, area resident: Full-time $5562 Canadian dollars; part-time $2781 Canadian dollars per year. Required fees: $49.75 Canadian dollars per term. *Financial support:* In 2009–10, 3 fellowships, 40 research assistantships (averaging $40,000 per year), 45 teaching assistantships (averaging $5,000 per year) were awarded. *Faculty research:* Artificial intelligence, data communications and wireless computing, high performance computing, network and information security, software engineering. *Unit head:* Dr. Eric Aubanel, Director of Graduate Studies, 506-458-7268, Fax: 506-453-3566, E-mail: aubanel@unb.ca. *Application contact:* Linda Sales, Graduate Secretary, 506-458-7285, Fax: 506-453-3566, E-mail: lsales@unb.ca.

University of New Hampshire, Graduate School, College of Engineering and Physical Sciences, Department of Computer Science, Durham, NH 03824. Offers MS, PhD. Part-time and evening/weekend programs available. *Faculty:* 10 full-time (2 women). *Students:* 42 full-time (10 women), 25 part-time (5 women); includes 3 minority (all Asian Americans or Pacific Islanders), 29 international. Average age 31. 60 applicants, 77% accepted, 22 enrolled. In 2009, 6 master's awarded. *Degree requirements:* For master's, thesis or alternative; for doctorate, thesis/dissertation. *Entrance requirements:* For master's and doctorate, GRE General Test. Additional exam requirements/recommendations for international students: Required—TOEFL (minimum score 550 paper-based; 213 computer-based; 80 iBT). *Application deadline:* For fall admission, 4/1 priority date for domestic students, 4/1 for international students; for spring admission, 12/1 for domestic students. Applications are processed on a rolling basis. Application fee: $65. Electronic applications accepted. *Expenses:* Tuition, state resident: full-time $10,380; part-time $577 per credit hour. Tuition, nonresident: full-time $24,350; part-time $1002 per credit hour. Required fees: $1550; $387.50 per semester. Tuition and fees vary according to course load and program. *Financial support:* In 2009–10, 44 students received support, including 2 fellowships, 11 research assistantships, 11 teaching assistantships; career-related internships or fieldwork, Federal Work-Study, scholarships/grants, and tuition waivers (full and partial) also available. Support available to part-time students. *Faculty research:* Programming languages, compiler design, parallel algorithms, computer graphics, artificial intelligence. *Unit head:* Dr. Philip J. Hatcher, Chairperson, 603-862-2678. *Application contact:* Carolyn Kirkpatrick, Administrative Assistant, 603-862-3778, E-mail: office@cs.unh.edu.

University of New Haven, Graduate School, Henry C. Lee College of Criminal Justice and Forensic Sciences, Program in Criminal Justice, West Haven, CT 06516-1916. Offers crime analysis (MS); criminal justice management (MS); forensic computer investigation (MS, Certificate); forensic psychology (MS); victim advocacy and services management (Certificate); victimology (MS). Part-time and evening/weekend programs available. *Faculty:* 8 full-time (2 women), 10 part-time/adjunct (4 women). *Students:* 25 full-time (17 women), 37 part-time (26 women); includes 20 minority (12 African Americans, 1 Asian American or Pacific Islander, 7 Hispanic Americans), 1 international. Average age 25. 62 applicants, 85% accepted, 28 enrolled. In 2009, 30 master's awarded. *Degree requirements:* For master's, thesis or alternative. *Entrance requirements:* Additional exam requirements/recommendations for international students: Required—TOEFL (minimum score 520 paper-based; 190 computer-based; 70 iBT), IELTS (minimum score 5.5). *Application deadline:* For fall admission, 5/31 for international students; for winter admission, 10/15 for international students; for spring admission, 1/15 for international students. Applications are processed on a rolling basis. Application fee: $50. Electronic applications accepted. *Expenses:* Tuition: Part-time $700 per credit. Required fees: $45 per term. One-time fee: $390 part-time. *Financial support:* Research assistantships with partial tuition reimbursements, teaching assistantships with partial tuition reimbursements, career-related internships or fieldwork, Federal Work-Study, scholarships/grants, tuition waivers, and unspecified assistantships available. Support available to part-time students. Financial award applicants required to submit FAFSA. *Unit head:* Dr. James J. Cassidy, Coordinator, 203-932-7374. *Application contact:* Eloise Gormley, Director of Graduate Admissions, 203-932-7449, Fax: 203-932-7137, E-mail: gradinfo@newhaven.edu.

University of New Haven, Graduate School, Tagliatela College of Engineering, Program in Computer and Information Science, West Haven, CT 06516-1916. Offers computer science (MS, Certificate), including advanced applications (MS), computer applications (Certificate), computer programming (Certificate), computer systems (MS), computing (Certificate), database and information systems (MS), network administration (Certificate), network systems (MS), software engineering and development (MS). Part-time and evening/weekend programs available. *Faculty:* 9 full-time (2 women), 5 part-time/adjunct (0 women). *Students:* 21 full-time (8 women), 32 part-time (8 women); includes 5 minority (2 African Americans, 1 Asian American or Pacific Islander, 2 Hispanic Americans), 26 international. Average age 30. 163 applicants, 88% accepted, 18 enrolled. In 2009, 24 master's awarded. *Degree requirements:* For master's, thesis or alternative. *Entrance requirements:* Additional exam requirements/recommendations for international students: Required—TOEFL (minimum score 520 paper-based; 190 computer-based; 70 iBT); Recommended—IELTS (minimum score 5.5). *Application deadline:* For fall admission, 5/31 for international students; for winter admission, 10/15 for international students; for spring admission, 1/15 for international students. Applications are processed on a rolling basis. Application fee: $50. Electronic applications accepted. *Expenses:* Tuition: Part-time $700 per credit. Required fees: $45 per term. One-time fee: $390 part-time. *Financial support:* Research assistantships with partial tuition reimbursements, teaching assistantships with partial tuition reimbursements, career-related internships or fieldwork, Federal Work-Study, scholarships/grants, tuition waivers, and unspecified assistantships available. Support available to part-time students. Financial award applicants required to submit FAFSA. *Unit head:* Dr. Tahany Fergany, Coordinator, 203-932-7067. *Application contact:* Eloise Gormley, Director of Graduate Admissions, 203-932-7449, Fax: 203-932-7137, E-mail: gradinfo@newhaven.edu.

University of New Mexico, Graduate School, School of Engineering, Department of Computer Science, Albuquerque, NM 87131-2039. Offers MS, PhD. Part-time programs available. *Faculty:* 20 full-time (3 women), 4 part-time/adjunct (2 women). *Students:* 87 full-time (16 women), 39 part-time (5 women); includes 5 minority (1 Asian American or Pacific Islander, 4 Hispanic Americans), 67 international. Average age 30. 167 applicants, 34% accepted, 21 enrolled. In 2009, 18 master's, 6 doctorates awarded. Terminal master's awarded for partial completion of doctoral program. *Degree requirements:* For master's, thesis or alternative; for doctorate, comprehensive exam, thesis/dissertation. *Entrance requirements:* For master's and doctorate, GRE General Test, minimum GPA of 3.0. Additional exam requirements/recommendations for international students: Required—TOEFL (minimum score 520 paper-based; 190 computer-based; 68 iBT) or IELTS (minimum score 7). *Application deadline:* For fall admission, 1/15 for domestic students, 3/1 for international students; for spring admission, 8/1 for domestic and international students. Applications are processed on a rolling basis. Application fee: $50. Electronic applications accepted. *Expenses:* Tuition, state resident: full-time $2098.80; part-time $233.20 per credit hour. Tuition, nonresident: full-time $6650. Required fees: $25 per semester. Tuition and fees vary according to course load, program and reciprocity agreements. *Financial support:* In 2009–10, 13 students received support, including 1 fellowship with tuition reimbursement available (averaging $14,000 per year), 42 research assistantships with tuition reimbursements available (averaging $13,500 per year), 6 teaching assistantships with tuition reimbursements available (averaging $12,650 per year); career-related internships or fieldwork, scholarships/grants, and health care benefits also available. Financial award application deadline: 1/15; financial award applicants required to submit FAFSA. *Faculty research:* Artificial life, genetic algorithms, computer security, complexity theory, interactive computer graphics, operating systems and networking, biology and computation, machine learning, automated reasoning, quantum computation. Total annual research expenditures: $2.4 million. *Unit head:* Dr. Stephanie Forrest, Chairperson, 505-277-3112, Fax: 505-277-6927, E-mail: forrest@cs.unm.edu. *Application contact:* Lynne Jacobsen, Coordinator Program Advisement, 505-277-3122, Fax: 505-277-6927, E-mail: ljake@cs.unm.edu.

University of New Orleans, Graduate School, College of Sciences, Department of Computer Science, New Orleans, LA 70148. Offers MS. *Entrance requirements:* For master's, GRE General Test. Additional exam requirements/recommendations for international students: Required—TOEFL (minimum score 550 paper-based; 213 computer-based; 79 iBT). Electronic applications accepted.

The University of North Carolina at Chapel Hill, Graduate School, College of Arts and Sciences, Department of Computer Science, Chapel Hill, NC 27599. Offers MS, PhD. Part-time programs available. Postbaccalaureate distance learning degree programs offered. Terminal master's awarded for partial completion of doctoral program. *Degree requirements:* For master's, comprehensive exam, thesis or alternative, programming product; for doctorate, comprehensive exam, thesis/dissertation, programming product, teaching requirement. *Entrance requirements:* For master's and doctorate, GRE General Test, minimum GPA of 3.0. Additional exam requirements/recommendations for international students: Required—TOEFL (minimum score 575 paper-based; 233 computer-based). Electronic applications accepted. *Faculty research:* Bioinformatics, graphics, hardware, systems, theory.

See Close-Up on page 317.

The University of North Carolina at Charlotte, Graduate School, College of Computing and Informatics, Department of Computer Science, Charlotte, NC 28223-0001. Offers MS. *Faculty:* 22 full-time (6 women), 2 part-time/adjunct (0 women). *Students:* 94 full-time (24 women), 28 part-time (7 women); includes 2 African Americans, 4 Asian Americans or Pacific Islanders, 90 international. Average age 25. 315 applicants, 73% accepted, 53 enrolled. In 2009, 70 master's awarded. *Degree requirements:* For master's, thesis optional. *Entrance requirements:* For master's, GRE General Test, minimum GPA of 3.0 during previous 2 years, 2.8 overall. Additional exam requirements/recommendations for international students: Required—TOEFL (minimum score 557 paper-based; 220 computer-based; 83 iBT). *Application deadline:* For fall admission, 7/1 for domestic students, 5/1 for international students; for spring admission, 11/1 for domestic students, 10/1 for international students. Applications are processed on a rolling basis. Application fee: $55. Electronic applications accepted. *Financial support:* In 2009–10, 48 students received support, including 2 fellowships (averaging $31,075 per year), 14 research assistantships (averaging $11,083 per year), 32 teaching assistantships (averaging $10,823 per year); career-related internships or fieldwork, Federal Work-Study, institutionally sponsored loans, scholarships/grants, and unspecified assistantships also available. Support available to part-time students. Financial award application deadline: 4/1; financial award applicants required to submit FAFSA. *Faculty research:* Visualization; visual analytics and computer graphics; intelligent and interactive systems; data mining theory, systems, and application; networked systems; computer game design. *Unit head:* Dr. Larry F. Hodges, Chair, 704-687-8552, Fax: 704-687-3516, E-mail: lfhodges@uncc.edu. *Application contact:* Kathy B. Giddings, Director of Graduate Admissions, 704-687-3366, Fax: 704-687-3279, E-mail: gradadm@uncc.edu.

The University of North Carolina at Greensboro, Graduate School, College of Arts and Sciences, Department of Computer Science, Greensboro, NC 27412-5001. Offers MS.

The University of North Carolina Wilmington, College of Arts and Sciences, Program in Computer Science and Information Systems, Wilmington, NC 28403-3297. Offers MS. *Entrance requirements:* For master's, GMAT or GRE, 3 letters of recommendation, resume.

University of North Dakota, Graduate School, John D. Odegard School of Aerospace Sciences, Department of Computer Science, Grand Forks, ND 58202. Offers MS. Part-time programs available. *Degree requirements:* For master's, comprehensive exam, thesis or alternative. *Entrance requirements:* For master's, GRE General Test, minimum GPA of 3.0. Additional exam requirements/recommendations for international students: Required—TOEFL (minimum score 550 paper-based; 213 computer-based; 79 iBT), IELTS (minimum score 6.5). Electronic applications accepted. *Faculty research:* Operating systems, simulation, parallel computation, hypermedia, graph theory.

University of Northern British Columbia, Office of Graduate Studies, Prince George, BC V2N 4Z9, Canada. Offers business administration (Diploma); community health science (M Sc); disability management (MA); education (M Ed); first nations studies (MA); gender studies (MA); history (MA); interdisciplinary studies (MA); international studies (MA); mathematical, computer and physical sciences (M Sc); natural resources and environmental studies (M Sc, MA, MNRES, PhD); political science (MA); psychology (M Sc, PhD); social work (MSW). Part-time and evening/weekend programs available. Postbaccalaureate distance learning degree programs offered (no on-campus study). *Degree requirements:* For master's, thesis; for doctorate, thesis/dissertation. *Entrance requirements:* For master's, GRE, minimum B average in undergraduate course work; for doctorate, candidacy exam, minimum A average in graduate course work.

University of Northern Iowa, Graduate College, College of Natural Sciences, Department of Computer Science, Cedar Falls, IA 50614. Offers MA, MS. *Students:* 6 full-time (0 women), 7 part-time (2 women), 11 international. 31 applicants, 45% accepted, 5 enrolled. In 2009, 4 master's awarded. *Degree requirements:* For master's, comprehensive exam (for some programs), thesis (for some programs). *Entrance requirements:* For master's, GRE, minimum GPA of 3.0. Additional exam requirements/recommendations for international students: Required—TOEFL (minimum score 600 paper-based; 250 computer-based; 100 iBT). *Application deadline:* For fall admission, 8/1 priority date for domestic students. Applications are processed on a rolling basis. Application fee: $30 ($50 for international students). Electronic applications accepted. *Financial support:* Application deadline: 2/1. *Unit head:* Dr. Eugene Wallingford, Head, 319-273-2618, Fax: 319-273-7123, E-mail: wallingf@cs.uni.edu. *Application contact:* Laurie S. Russell, Record Analyst, 319-273-2623, Fax: 319-273-6792, E-mail: laurie.russell@uni.edu.

University of North Florida, College of Computing, Engineering, and Construction, Jacksonville, FL 32224. Offers civil engineering (MSCE); computer and information sciences (MS); electrical engineering (MSEE); mechanical engineering (MSME). Part-time programs available. *Faculty:* 35 full-time (6 women). *Students:* 21 full-time (4 women), 64 part-time (11 women); includes 22 minority (6 African Americans, 9 Asian Americans or Pacific Islanders, 7 Hispanic Americans), 10 international. Average age 31. 82 applicants, 45% accepted, 14 enrolled. In 2009, 6 master's awarded. *Degree requirements:* For master's, thesis optional. *Entrance requirements:* For master's, GRE General Test, minimum GPA of 3.0 in last 60 hours of course work. Additional exam requirements/recommendations for international students: Required—TOEFL (minimum score 500 paper-based; 173 computer-based). *Application deadline:* For fall admission, 7/1 priority date for domestic students, 5/1 for international students; for spring admission, 11/1 priority date for domestic students, 10/1 for international students. Applications are processed on a rolling basis. Application fee: $30. Electronic applications accepted. *Expenses:* Tuition, state resident: full-time $6649.20; part-time $277.05 per credit hour. Tuition, nonresident: full-time $22,970; part-time $957.08 per credit hour. Required fees: $985; $41.03 per credit hour. *Financial support:* In 2009–10, 20 students received support, including 5 research assistantships (averaging $5,009 per year), 3 teaching assistantships (averaging $2,844 per year); Federal Work-Study and tuition waivers (partial) also available. Support available to part-time students. Financial award application deadline: 4/1; financial award applicants required to submit FAFSA. *Faculty research:* Parallel and distributed computing, networks, generic programming, algorithms, artificial intelligence. Total annual research expenditures: $2.2 million. *Unit head:* Dr. Neal Coulter, Dean, 904-620-1350, E-mail: ncoulter@unf.edu. *Application contact:* Dr. Roger Eggen, Director of Graduate Studies for Computer Science, 904-320-2985, Fax: 904-620-2988, E-mail: ree@unf.edu.

University of North Texas, Robert B. Toulouse School of Graduate Studies, College of Engineering, Department of Computer Science and Engineering, Denton, TX 76203-5017. Offers computer science (MS); computer science and engineering (PhD). Terminal master's awarded for partial completion of doctoral program. *Degree requirements:* For master's, comprehensive exam (for some programs), thesis (for some programs); for doctorate, comprehensive exam, thesis/dissertation. *Entrance requirements:* For master's, GRE General Test (minimum score 400 verbal, 700 quantitative, 600 analytical or 4.0), minimum GPA of 3.0; for doctorate, GRE General Test (minimum scores: Verbal 50th percentile, Quantitative 700, Analytical 600 or 4.5), minimum GPA of 3.5, 3 letters of recommendation. Additional exam requirements/recommendations for international students: Required—TOEFL (minimum score 550 paper-based; 213 computer-based; 79 iBT), proof of English language proficiency required for non-native English speakers; Recommended—IELTS (minimum score 6.5). Application fee: $50 ($75 for international students). Electronic applications accepted. *Expenses:* Tuition, state resident: full-time $4298; part-time $239 per contact hour. Tuition, nonresident: full-time $9878; part-time $549 per contact hour. Required fees: $265 per contact hour. *Financial support:* Fellowships with tuition reimbursements, research assistantships with tuition reimbursements, teaching assistantships with tuition reimbursements, career-related internships or fieldwork, Federal Work-Study, and institutionally sponsored loans available. Financial award application deadline: 4/1; financial award applicants required to submit FAFSA. *Faculty research:* Databases and data mining, computer architecture, cryptography, agent-oriented software engineering, graph theory, low power synthesis. *Application contact:* Graduate Program Coordinator, 940-565-2767, Fax: 940-565-2799, E-mail: armin.mikler@unt.edu.

University of Notre Dame, Graduate School, College of Engineering, Department of Computer Science and Engineering, Notre Dame, IN 46556. Offers MSCSE, PhD. Terminal master's awarded for partial completion of doctoral program. *Degree requirements:* For master's, comprehensive exam; for doctorate, thesis/dissertation, candidacy exam. *Entrance requirements:* For master's and doctorate, GRE General Test. Additional exam requirements/recommendations for international students: Required—TOEFL (minimum score 600 paper-based; 250 computer-based; 80 iBT). Electronic applications accepted. *Faculty research:* Algorithms and theory of computer science, artificial intelligence, behavior-based robotics, biometrics, computer vision.

University of Oklahoma, Graduate College, College of Engineering, School of Computer Science, Norman, OK 73019. Offers MS, PhD. *Faculty:* 18 full-time (3 women). *Students:* 62 full-time (11 women), 30 part-time (1 woman); includes 6 minority (1 African American, 1 American Indian/Alaska Native, 3 Asian Americans or Pacific Islanders, 1 Hispanic American), 51 international. 87 applicants, 92% accepted, 19 enrolled. In 2009, 17 master's, 4 doctorates awarded. Terminal master's awarded for partial completion of doctoral program. *Degree requirements:* For master's, thesis optional, oral exams, qualifying exam; for doctorate, thesis/dissertation, general exam, qualifying exam. *Entrance requirements:* For master's and doctorate, GRE General Test. Additional exam requirements/recommendations for international students: Required—TOEFL (minimum score 550 paper-based; 250 computer-based). *Application deadline:* For fall admission, 1/15 priority date for domestic students, 4/1 for international students; for spring admission, 11/1 for domestic students, 9/1 for international students. Applications are processed on a rolling basis. Application fee: $40 ($90 for international students). Electronic applications accepted. *Expenses:* Tuition, state resident: full-time $3744; part-time $156 per credit hour. Tuition, nonresident: full-time $13,577; part-time $565.70 per credit hour. Required fees: $2415; $90.10 per credit hour. *Financial support:* In 2009–10, 71 students received support, including 3 fellowships (averaging $4,167 per year), 16 research assistantships with partial tuition reimbursements available (averaging $13,378 per year), 16 teaching assistantships with partial tuition reimbursements available (averaging $12,956 per year); unspecified assistantships also available. Financial award application deadline: 3/1; financial award applicants required to submit FAFSA. *Faculty research:* Artificial intelligence and robotics, scientific computing, computer architecture, computer networks, database management, high performance computing, visual analytics, cryptography. Total annual research expenditures: $2.4 million. *Unit head:* Sridhar Radhakrishnan, Interim Director, 405-325-1867, Fax: 405-325-4044, E-mail: sridhar@ou.edu. *Application contact:* Sridhar Radhakrishnan, Interim Director, 405-325-1867, Fax: 405-325-4044, E-mail: sridhar@ou.edu.

University of Oregon, Graduate School, College of Arts and Sciences, Department of Computer and Information Science, Eugene, OR 97403. Offers MA, MS, PhD. Part-time programs available. Terminal master's awarded for partial completion of doctoral program. *Degree requirements:* For doctorate, thesis/dissertation. *Entrance requirements:* For master's and doctorate, GRE General Test, minimum GPA of 3.0. Additional exam requirements/recommendations for international students: Required—TOEFL. *Faculty research:* Artificial intelligence, graphics, natural-language processing, expert systems, operating systems.

University of Ottawa, Faculty of Graduate and Postdoctoral Studies, Faculty of Engineering, Ottawa-Carleton Institute for Computer Science, Ottawa, ON K1N 6N5, Canada. Offers MCS, PhD. *Degree requirements:* For master's, thesis or alternative; for doctorate, comprehensive exam, thesis/dissertation, two seminars. *Entrance requirements:* For master's, honors degree or equivalent, minimum B average; for doctorate, minimum B+ average. Electronic applications accepted. *Faculty research:* Knowledge-based and intelligent systems, algorithms, parallel and distributed systems.

University of Pennsylvania, School of Engineering and Applied Science, Department of Computer and Information Science, Philadelphia, PA 19104. Offers MCIT, MSE, PhD. Part-time programs available. *Faculty:* 41 full-time (5 women), 9 part-time/adjunct (2 women). *Students:* 194 full-time (35 women), 55 part-time (13 women); includes 19 minority (3 African Americans, 15 Asian Americans or Pacific Islanders, 1 Hispanic American), 131 international. 977 applicants, 22% accepted, 109 enrolled. In 2009, 86 master's, 18 doctorates awarded. Terminal master's awarded for partial completion of doctoral program. *Degree requirements:* For master's, thesis optional; for doctorate, thesis/dissertation. *Entrance requirements:* For master's and doctorate, GRE General Test. Additional exam requirements/recommendations for international students: Required—TOEFL. *Application deadline:* For fall admission, 6/1 priority date for domestic students, 5/1 priority date for international students. Applications are processed on a rolling basis. Application fee: $70. Electronic applications accepted. *Expenses:* Tuition: Full-time $25,660; part-time $4758 per course. Required fees: $2152; $270 per course. Tuition and fees vary according to course load, degree level and program. *Financial support:* Fellowships with full tuition reimbursements, research assistantships with full tuition reimbursements, teaching assistantships, institutionally sponsored loans, scholarships/grants, traineeships, health care benefits, and unspecified assistantships available. *Faculty research:* AI, computer systems graphics, information management, robotics, software systems theory.

University of Pittsburgh, School of Arts and Sciences, Department of Computer Science, Pittsburgh, PA 15260. Offers MS, PhD. Part-time programs available. *Faculty:* 17 full-time (4 women). *Students:* 93 full-time (16 women), 3 part-time (0 women); includes 26 minority (1 African American, 22 Asian Americans or Pacific Islanders, 3 Hispanic Americans), 32 international. Average age 26. 352 applicants, 15% accepted, 17 enrolled. In 2009, 5 master's,

Computer Science

University of Pittsburgh (continued)

7 doctorates awarded. Terminal master's awarded for partial completion of doctoral program. *Degree requirements:* For master's, thesis or alternative; for doctorate, comprehensive exam, thesis/dissertation, preliminary exams. *Entrance requirements:* For master's and doctorate, GRE General Test. Additional exam requirements/recommendations for international students: Required—TOEFL (minimum score 600 paper-based; 250 computer-based; 90 iBT). *Application deadline:* For fall admission, 1/15 for domestic and international students; for winter admission, 9/15 for domestic and international students. Applications are processed on a rolling basis. Application fee: $50. Electronic applications accepted. *Expenses:* Tuition, state resident: full-time $16,402; part-time $665 per credit. Tuition, nonresident: full-time $28,694; part-time $1175 per credit. Required fees: $690; $175 per term. Tuition and fees vary according to program. *Financial support:* In 2009–10, 58 students received support, including 8 fellowships with full tuition reimbursements available (averaging $17,822 per year), 20 research assistantships with full tuition reimbursements available (averaging $16,811 per year), 29 teaching assistantships with full tuition reimbursements available (averaging $15,065 per year); career-related internships or fieldwork, Federal Work-Study, scholarships/grants, health care benefits, and tuition waivers (partial) also available. Financial award application deadline: 1/15. *Faculty research:* Algorithms and theory, artificial intelligence, parallel and distributed systems, software systems and interfaces. Total annual research expenditures: $3.6 million. *Unit head:* Dr. Daniel Mosse, Chairman, 412-624-8493, Fax: 412-624-8854, E-mail: mosse@cs.pitt.edu. *Application contact:* Keena Walker, Graduate Secretary, 412-624-5755, Fax: 412-624-8561, E-mail: keena@cs.pitt.edu.

University of Regina, Faculty of Graduate Studies and Research, Faculty of Science, Department of Computer Science, Regina, SK S4S 0A2, Canada. Offers M Sc, PhD. *Faculty:* 19 full-time (2 women), 3 part-time/adjunct (0 women). *Students:* 42 full-time (14 women), 13 part-time (2 women). 73 applicants, 37% accepted. In 2009, 13 master's awarded. *Degree requirements:* For master's, thesis (for some programs); for doctorate, thesis/dissertation. *Entrance requirements:* Additional exam requirements/recommendations for international students: Required—TOEFL (minimum score 580 paper-based; 237 computer-based; 80 iBT). *Application deadline:* For fall admission, 3/15 for domestic students; for spring admission, 9/15 for domestic students. Applications are processed on a rolling basis. Application fee: $90 ($100 for international students). *Financial support:* In 2009–10, 16 fellowships (averaging $19,000 per year), 4 research assistantships (averaging $16,910 per year), 15 teaching assistantships (averaging $6,650 per year) were awarded; career-related internships or fieldwork and scholarships/grants also available. Financial award application deadline: 6/15. *Faculty research:* Expert systems, image processing, artificial intelligence, data mining, data and knowledge bases. *Unit head:* Dr. Xue Dong Yang, Head, 306-585-4692, Fax: 306-585-4745, E-mail: xue-dong.yang@uregina.ca. *Application contact:* Dr. Malek Mouhoub, Graduate Program Coordinator, 306-585-4700, E-mail: mouhoubm@cs.uregina.ca.

University of Rhode Island, Graduate School, College of Arts and Sciences, Department of Computer Science and Statistics, Kingston, RI 02881. Offers applied mathematics (PhD), including computer science, statistics; computer science (MS, PhD); digital forensics (Graduate Certificate); statistics (MS). Part-time programs available. *Faculty:* 10 full-time (3 women), 3 part-time/adjunct (1 woman). *Students:* 18 full-time (5 women), 20 part-time (6 women); includes 4 minority (2 Asian Americans or Pacific Islanders, 2 Hispanic Americans), 7 international. In 2009, 7 master's awarded. *Degree requirements:* For master's, comprehensive exam (for some programs), thesis optional; for doctorate, comprehensive exam, thesis/dissertation. *Entrance requirements:* For master's and doctorate, GRE, 2 letters of recommendation. Additional exam requirements/recommendations for international students: Required—TOEFL (minimum score 550 paper-based; 213 computer-based). *Application deadline:* For fall admission, 7/15 for domestic students, 2/1 for international students; for spring admission, 11/15 for domestic students, 7/15 for international students. Application fee: $65. Electronic applications accepted. *Expenses:* Tuition, state resident: full-time $8828; part-time $490 per credit hour. Tuition, nonresident: full-time $22,100; part-time $1228 per credit hour. Required fees: $1118; $57 per semester. Tuition and fees vary according to program. *Financial support:* In 2009–10, 10 teaching assistantships with full and partial tuition reimbursements (averaging $11,094 per year) were awarded. Financial award application deadline: 2/1; financial award applicants required to submit FAFSA. *Faculty research:* Bioinformatics, computer and digital forensics, behavioral model of pedestrian dynamics, real-time distributed object computing, cryptography. Total annual research expenditures: $694,026. *Unit head:* Dr. James G. Kowalski, Chair, 401-874-2510, Fax: 401-874-4617, E-mail: kowalski@cs.uri.edu. *Application contact:* Dr. Victor Fay-Wolfe, Director of Graduate Studies, 401-874-2701, Fax: 401-874-4617, E-mail: wolfe@cs.uri.edu.

University of Rochester, The College, Arts and Sciences, Department of Computer Science, Rochester, NY 14627. Offers MS, PhD. Terminal master's awarded for partial completion of doctoral program. *Degree requirements:* For doctorate, thesis/dissertation, qualifying exam. *Entrance requirements:* For master's and doctorate, GRE General Test. Additional exam requirements/recommendations for international students: Required—TOEFL.

See Close-Up on page 319.

University of San Francisco, College of Arts and Sciences, Department of Computer Science, San Francisco, CA 94117-1080. Offers computer science (MS); Web science (MS). Part-time programs available. *Faculty:* 5 full-time (1 woman). *Students:* 46 full-time (7 women), 11 part-time (2 women); includes 2 minority (1 Asian American or Pacific Islander, 1 Hispanic American), 38 international. Average age 28. 102 applicants, 69% accepted, 22 enrolled. In 2009, 20 master's awarded. *Degree requirements:* For master's, thesis optional. *Entrance requirements:* For master's, GRE General Test, GRE Subject Test, BS in computer science or related field. Additional exam requirements/recommendations for international students: Required—TOEFL. *Application deadline:* For fall admission, 7/1 priority date for domestic students; for spring admission, 12/1 for domestic students. Applications are processed on a rolling basis. Application fee: $55 ($65 for international students). *Expenses:* Tuition: Full-time $19,710; part-time $1095 per unit. Part-time tuition and fees vary according to degree level, campus/location and program. *Financial support:* In 2009–10, 25 students received support; fellowships, teaching assistantships, career-related internships or fieldwork and Federal Work-Study available. Financial award application deadline: 3/2; financial award applicants required to submit FAFSA. *Faculty research:* Software engineering, computer graphics, computer networks. *Unit head:* Dr. Terence Parr, Chairman, 415-422-6530. *Application contact:* Mark Landerghini, Graduate Adviser, 415-422-5135, E-mail: asgraduate@usfca.edu.

University of Saskatchewan, College of Graduate Studies and Research, College of Arts and Sciences, Department of Computer Science, Saskatoon, SK S7N 5A2, Canada. Offers M Sc, PhD. *Faculty:* 34. *Students:* 104. In 2009, 20 master's, 1 doctorate awarded. *Degree requirements:* For master's, thesis; for doctorate, comprehensive exam (for some programs), thesis/dissertation. *Entrance requirements:* For master's and doctorate, GRE. Additional exam requirements/recommendations for international students: Required—TOEFL (minimum score 80 iBT); Recommended—IELTS (minimum score 6.5). *Application deadline:* For fall admission, 7/1 priority date for domestic students. Applications are processed on a rolling basis. Application fee: $75. Electronic applications accepted. Tuition and fees charges are reported in Canadian dollars. *Expenses:* Tuition, area resident: Full-time $3000 Canadian dollars; part-time $500 Canadian dollars per term. Required fees: $700 Canadian dollars; $100 Canadian dollars per term. *Financial support:* Fellowships, research assistantships, teaching assistantships available. Financial award application deadline: 1/31. *Unit head:* Dr. Eric Neufeld, Head, 306-966-4887, Fax: 306-966-4884, E-mail: eric.neufeld@usask.ca. *Application contact:* Dr. Anthony Kusalik, Graduate Chair, 306-966-4897, Fax: 306-966-4884, E-mail: kusalik@cs.usask.ca.

University of South Alabama, Graduate School, School of Computer and Information Sciences, Mobile, AL 36688-0002. Offers computer science (MS); information systems (MS). Part-time and evening/weekend programs available. *Degree requirements:* For master's, thesis optional, project. *Entrance requirements:* For master's, GRE General Test. *Expenses:* Tuition, state resident: part-time $218 per contact hour. Required fees: $1102 per year. *Faculty research:* Numerical analysis, artificial intelligence, simulation, medical applications, software engineering.

University of South Carolina, The Graduate School, College of Engineering and Computing, Department of Computer Science and Engineering, Columbia, SC 29208. Offers computer science and engineering (ME, MS, PhD); software engineering (MS). Part-time and evening/weekend programs available. Postbaccalaureate distance learning degree programs offered (minimal on-campus study). *Degree requirements:* For master's, comprehensive exam, thesis (for some programs); for doctorate, comprehensive exam, thesis/dissertation. *Entrance requirements:* For master's and doctorate, GRE General Test. Additional exam requirements/recommendations for international students: Required—TOEFL (minimum score 570 paper-based; 230 computer-based). Electronic applications accepted. *Faculty research:* Computer security, computer vision, artificial intelligence, multiagent systems, bioinformatics.

The University of South Dakota, Graduate School, College of Arts and Sciences, Department of Computer Science, Vermillion, SD 57069-2390. Offers computational sciences and statistics (PhD); computer science (MS). Part-time programs available. *Degree requirements:* For master's, thesis optional. *Entrance requirements:* For master's, GRE General Test, GRE Subject Test (recommended), minimum GPA of 2.7. Additional exam requirements/recommendations for international students: Required—TOEFL (minimum score 550 paper-based; 213 computer-based; 79 iBT). Electronic applications accepted.

University of Southern California, Graduate School, Viterbi School of Engineering, Department of Computer Science, Programs in Computer Science, Los Angeles, CA 90089. Offers MS, PhD. *Degree requirements:* For master's, thesis optional; for doctorate, thesis/dissertation. *Entrance requirements:* For master's and doctorate, GRE General Test. *Application deadline:* For fall admission, 5/1 for domestic students. Applications are processed on a rolling basis. Application fee: $85. *Expenses:* Tuition: Full-time $25,980; part-time $1315 per unit. Required fees: $554. One-time fee: $35 full-time. Full-time tuition and fees vary according to degree level and program. *Financial support:* Fellowships, research assistantships, teaching assistantships available. Financial award application deadline: 2/15; financial award applicants required to submit FAFSA. *Faculty research:* Multi-media and virtual reality, databases. *Application contact:* Steve Schrader, Director of Student Affairs, 213-740-4779, E-mail: steve.schrader@usc.edu.

University of Southern Maine, School of Applied Science, Engineering, and Technology, Department of Computer Science, Portland, ME 04104-9300. Offers MS. Part-time programs available. *Degree requirements:* For master's, thesis. *Entrance requirements:* For master's, GRE General Test, minimum GPA of 3.0. Additional exam requirements/recommendations for international students: Required—TOEFL. Electronic applications accepted. *Faculty research:* Computer networks, database systems, software engineering, theory of computability, human factors.

University of Southern Mississippi, Graduate School, College of Science and Technology, School of Computing, Hattiesburg, MS 39406-0001. Offers computational science (MS, PhD); computer science (MS, PhD); engineering technology (MS). *Faculty:* 18 full-time (3 women), 1 (woman) part-time/adjunct. *Students:* 72 full-time (20 women), 21 part-time (6 women); includes 7 minority (5 African Americans, 2 Hispanic Americans), 51 international. Average age 29. 101 applicants, 61% accepted, 24 enrolled. In 2009, 15 master's awarded. *Degree requirements:* For master's, comprehensive exam, thesis; for doctorate, comprehensive exam, thesis/dissertation. *Entrance requirements:* For master's, GRE General Test, minimum GPA of 2.75 in last 60 hours. Additional exam requirements/recommendations for international students: Required—TOEFL. *Application deadline:* For fall admission, 3/15 priority date for domestic students, 3/15 for international students. Applications are processed on a rolling basis. Application fee: $35. *Expenses:* Tuition, state resident: full-time $5096; part-time $284 per hour. Tuition, nonresident: full-time $13,052; part-time $726 per hour. Required fees: $402. Tuition and fees vary according to course level and course load. *Financial support:* In 2009–10, 29 research assistantships with full tuition reimbursements (averaging $8,750 per year), 7 teaching assistantships with full tuition reimbursements (averaging $9,944 per year) were awarded; Federal Work-Study and institutionally sponsored loans also available. Financial award application deadline: 3/15; financial award applicants required to submit FAFSA. *Faculty research:* Satellite telecommunications, advanced life-support systems, artificial intelligence. *Unit head:* Dr. Adel Ali, Chair, 601-266-4949, Fax: 601-266-6452. *Application contact:* Shonna Breland, Manager of Graduate Admissions, 601-266-6563, Fax: 601-266-5138.

University of South Florida, Graduate School, College of Engineering, Department of Computer Science and Engineering, Tampa, FL 33620-9951. Offers computer science (MSCS); computer science and engineering (PhD); comuter science (MSCP). Part-time programs available. *Faculty:* 18 full-time (1 woman). *Students:* 57 full-time (8 women), 39 part-time (10 women); includes 12 minority (5 African Americans, 1 Asian American or Pacific Islander, 6 Hispanic Americans), 48 international. Average age 32. 146 applicants, 43% accepted, 21 enrolled. In 2009, 15 master's, 9 doctorates awarded. Terminal master's awarded for partial completion of doctoral program. *Degree requirements:* For master's, comprehensive exam, thesis; for doctorate, comprehensive exam, thesis/dissertation, teaching of undergraduate computer science and engineering course. *Entrance requirements:* For master's, GRE General Test (minimum score 500 verbal, 700 quantitative), minimum GPA of 3.3 in last 60 hours of coursework; for doctorate, GRE General Test (minimum score: 500 Verbal, 700 Quantitative), minimum GPA of 3.3 in last 60 hours of coursework, MS (recommended). Additional exam requirements/recommendations for international students: Required—TOEFL (minimum score 550 paper-based; 213 computer-based). *Application deadline:* For fall admission, 2/15 for domestic students, 1/2 for international students; for spring admission, 10/15 for domestic students, 6/1 for international students. Application fee: $30. Electronic applications accepted. *Financial support:* In 2009–10, 67 students received support, including teaching assistantships with tuition reimbursements available (averaging $28,565 per year); unspecified assistantships also available. Financial award application deadline: 1/2; financial award applicants required to submit FAFSA. *Faculty research:* Computer vision, networks, artificial intelligence, computer architecture, software security. Total annual research expenditures: $1.2 million. *Unit head:* Sudeep Sarkar, Director, Fax: 813-974-5094, E-mail: sarkar@cse.usf.edu. *Application contact:* Sudeep Sarkar, Director, Fax: 813-974-5094, E-mail: sarkar@cse.usf.edu.

The University of Tennessee, Graduate School, College of Arts and Sciences, Department of Computer Science, Knoxville, TN 37996. Offers MS, PhD. Part-time programs available. *Degree requirements:* For master's, thesis or alternative; for doctorate, thesis/dissertation. *Entrance requirements:* For master's and doctorate, GRE General Test, minimum GPA of 2.7. Additional exam requirements/recommendations for international students: Required—TOEFL. Electronic applications accepted. *Expenses:* Tuition, state resident: full-time $6826; part-time $380 per semester hour. Tuition, nonresident: full-time $21,844; part-time $1147 per semester hour. Tuition and fees vary according to program.

The University of Tennessee, Graduate School, College of Engineering, Department of Electrical Engineering and Computer Science, Knoxville, TN 37996. Offers computer engineering (MS, PhD); computer science (MS, PhD); electrical engineering (MS, PhD); reliability and maintainability engineering (MS); MS/MBA. Part-time programs available. *Faculty:* 40 full-time (4 women), 13 part-time/adjunct (2 women). *Students:* 141 full-time (25 women), 62 part-time (11 women); includes 11 minority (4 African Americans, 5 Asian Americans or Pacific Islanders, 2 Hispanic Americans), 109 international. Average age 30. 603 applicants, 12% accepted, 45 enrolled. In 2009, 55 master's, 24 doctorates awarded. *Degree requirements:* For master's, thesis or alternative; for doctorate, comprehensive exam, thesis/dissertation. *Entrance requirements:* For master's, GRE, minimum GPA of 3.0; for doctorate, GRE General Test, minimum GPA of 3.0. Additional exam requirements/recommendations for international students: Required—TOEFL (minimum score 550 paper-based; 213 computer-based). *Application deadline:* For fall admission, 2/1 priority date for domestic and international students; for spring admission, 6/15 priority date for international students. Applications are processed on a rolling basis. Application fee: $35. Electronic applications accepted. *Expenses:* Tuition, state resident: full-time $6826; part-time $380 per semester hour. Tuition, nonresident: full-time $21,844; part-time $1147 per semester hour. Tuition and fees vary according to program. *Financial support:* In 2009–10, 139 students received support, including 32 fellowships with full tuition reimbursements available (averaging $5,448 per year), 118 research assistantships with full tuition reimbursements available (averaging $16,800 per year), 68 teaching assistantships with full tuition reimbursements available (averaging $12,996 per year); career-related internships or fieldwork, Federal Work-Study, institutionally sponsored loans, health care benefits, and unspecified assistantships also available. Financial award application deadline: 2/1; financial award applicants required to submit FAFSA. *Faculty research:* Artificial intelligence and visualization; microelectronics, mixed-signal electronics, VLSI, embedded systems; scientific and distributed computing; computer vision, robotics, and image processing; power electronics, power systems, communications. Total annual research expenditures: $9.1 million. *Unit head:* Dr. Kevin Tomsovic, Head, 865-974-3461, Fax: 865-974-3461, E-mail: tomsovic@eecs.utk.edu. *Application contact:* Dr. Masood Parang, Associate Dean of Student Affairs, 865-974-2454, Fax: 865-974-9871, E-mail: mparang@utk.edu.

The University of Tennessee at Chattanooga, Graduate School, College of Engineering and Computer Science, Program in Computer Science, Chattanooga, TN 37403. Offers MS, Graduate Certificate. Part-time and evening/weekend programs available. *Faculty:* 4 full-time (2 women), 2 part-time/adjunct (both women). *Students:* 11 full-time (4 women), 13 part-time (5 women); includes 1 minority (African American), 7 international. Average age 32. 37 applicants, 51% accepted, 4 enrolled. In 2009, 3 master's awarded. *Degree requirements:* For master's, comprehensive exam, thesis. *Entrance requirements:* For master's, GRE General Test. Additional exam requirements/recommendations for international students: Required—TOEFL (minimum score 550 paper-based; 213 computer-based; 79 iBT), IELTS (minimum score 6). *Application deadline:* For fall admission, 8/1 priority date for domestic students, 6/1 for international students; for spring admission, 12/1 priority date for domestic students, 10/1 for international students. Applications are processed on a rolling basis. Application fee: $35. Electronic applications accepted. *Expenses:* Tuition, state resident: full-time $5404; part-time $300 per credit hour. Tuition, nonresident: full-time $16,702; part-time $928 per credit hour. Required fees: $1150; $130 per credit hour. *Financial support:* In 2009–10, 3 research assistantships with full and partial tuition reimbursements (averaging $5,500 per year), 1 teaching assistantship with full and partial tuition reimbursement (averaging $5,500 per year) were awarded; career-related internships or fieldwork, scholarships/grants, and unspecified assistantships also available. Support available to part-time students. *Faculty research:* Power systems, computer architecture, pattern recognition, artificial intelligence, statistical data analysis. Total annual research expenditures: $107,279. *Unit head:* Dr. Joseph Kizza, Department Head, 423-425-4349, Fax: 423-425-5442, E-mail: joseph-kizza@utc.edu. *Application contact:* Dr. Stephanie Bellar, Dean of Graduate Studies, 423-425-4666, Fax: 423-425-5223, E-mail: stephanie-bellar@utc.edu.

The University of Tennessee Space Institute, Graduate Programs, Program in Electrical Engineering and Computer Science, Tullahoma, TN 37388-9700. Offers MS, PhD. *Faculty:* 2 full-time (0 women). *Students:* 1 full-time (0 women). 1 applicant, 0% accepted, 0 enrolled. *Degree requirements:* For master's, thesis (for some programs); for doctorate, one foreign language, thesis/dissertation. *Entrance requirements:* Additional exam requirements/recommendations for international students: Required—TOEFL (minimum score 550 paper-based; 213 computer-based), IELTS (minimum score 6.5). *Application deadline:* For fall admission, 2/1 for international students; for spring admission, 6/15 for international students. Applications are processed on a rolling basis. Application fee: $35. Electronic applications accepted. *Expenses:* Tuition, state resident: full-time $6826; part-time $380 per hour. Tuition, nonresident: full-time $20,622; part-time $1147 per hour. Required fees: $10 per hour. One-time fee: $90 full-time. *Financial support:* Fellowships, research assistantships with full tuition reimbursements, career-related internships or fieldwork, Federal Work-Study, institutionally sponsored loans, health care benefits, tuition waivers (full and partial), and unspecified assistantships available. Financial award applicants required to submit FAFSA. *Unit head:* Dr. Monty Smith, Degree Program Chairman, 931-393-7480, Fax: 931-393-7530, E-mail: msmith@utsi.edu. *Application contact:* Dee Merriman, Coordinator III, 931-393-7293, Fax: 931-393-7201, E-mail: dmerrima@utsi.edu.

The University of Texas at Arlington, Graduate School, College of Engineering, Department of Computer Science and Engineering, Arlington, TX 76019. Offers M Engr, M Sw En, MS, PhD. Part-time and evening/weekend programs available. Postbaccalaureate distance learning degree programs offered (minimal on-campus study). *Faculty:* 28 full-time (2 women). *Students:* 167 full-time (42 women), 93 part-time (23 women); includes 11 minority (4 African Americans, 6 Asian Americans or Pacific Islanders, 1 Hispanic American), 211 international. 524 applicants, 98% accepted, 59 enrolled. In 2009, 120 master's, 11 doctorates awarded. Terminal master's awarded for partial completion of doctoral program. *Degree requirements:* For master's, comprehensive exam (for some programs), thesis optional; for doctorate, comprehensive exam, thesis/dissertation. *Entrance requirements:* For master's, GRE General Test, minimum GPA of 3.0 (3.2 in computer science-related classes); for doctorate, GRE General Test, minimum GPA of 3.5. Additional exam requirements/recommendations for international students: Required—TOEFL (minimum score 550 paper-based; 230 computer-based; 92 iBT). *Application deadline:* For fall admission, 6/6 for domestic students, 4/4 for international students; for spring admission, 10/17 for domestic students, 9/5 for international students. Applications are processed on a rolling basis. Application fee: $35 ($50 for international students). *Financial support:* In 2009–10, 20 fellowships (averaging $1,000 per year), research assistantships (averaging $13,500 per year), 75 teaching assistantships (averaging $13,500 per year) were awarded; career-related internships or fieldwork and scholarships/grants also available. Financial award application deadline: 6/1; financial award applicants required to submit FAFSA. *Faculty research:* Algorithms, homeland security, mobile pervasive computing, high performance computing bioinformation. *Unit head:* Dr. Fillia Makedon, Chairman, 817-272-3680. *Application contact:* Dr. Bahram Khalili, Graduate Advisor, 817-272-5407, Fax: 817-272-3784, E-mail: khalili@uta.edu.

The University of Texas at Austin, Graduate School, College of Natural Sciences, Department of Computer Sciences, Austin, TX 78712-1111. Offers MA, MSCS, PhD. *Degree requirements:* For master's, thesis optional; for doctorate, thesis/dissertation, oral proposal, final defense. *Entrance requirements:* For master's and doctorate, GRE General Test, GRE Subject Test, bachelor's degree in computer sciences preferred. Additional exam requirements/recommendations for international students: Required—TOEFL. Electronic applications accepted. *Faculty research:* Artificial intelligence, distributed computing, networks, algorithms, experimental systems.

The University of Texas at Dallas, Erik Jonsson School of Engineering and Computer Science, Program in Computer Science, Richardson, TX 75080. Offers computer science (MS, PhD); software engineering (MS, PhD). Part-time and evening/weekend programs available. *Faculty:* 43 full-time (6 women), 2 part-time/adjunct (1 woman). *Students:* 424 full-time (117 women), 187 part-time (39 women); includes 47 minority (3 African Americans, 1 American Indian/Alaska Native, 36 Asian Americans or Pacific Islanders, 7 Hispanic Americans), 454 international. Average age 27. 863 applicants, 52% accepted, 135 enrolled. In 2009, 218 master's, 15 doctorates awarded. *Degree requirements:* For master's, thesis optional; for doctorate, thesis/dissertation. *Entrance requirements:* For master's, GRE General Test, minimum GPA of 3.0 in undergraduate course work, 3.3 in quantitative course work; for doctorate, GRE General Test, minimum GPA of 3.5. Additional exam requirements/recommendations for international students: Required—TOEFL (minimum score 550 paper-based; 213 computer-based). *Application deadline:* For fall admission, 7/15 for domestic students, 5/1 priority date for international students; for spring admission, 11/15 for domestic students, 9/1 priority date for international students. Applications are processed on a rolling basis. Application fee: $50 ($100 for international students). Electronic applications accepted. *Expenses:* Tuition, state resident: full-time $11,068; part-time $461 per credit hour. Tuition, nonresident: full-time $21,178; part-time $882 per credit hour. Tuition and fees vary according to course load. *Financial support:* In 2009–10, 11 fellowships with full tuition reimbursements (averaging $18,900 per year), 67 research assistantships with full tuition reimbursements (averaging $18,406 per year), 42 teaching assistantships with full tuition reimbursements (averaging $17,869 per year) were awarded; career-related internships or fieldwork, Federal Work-Study, institutionally sponsored loans, and scholarships/grants also available. Support available to part-time students. Financial award application deadline: 4/30; financial award applicants required to submit FAFSA. *Faculty research:* Telecommunication networks, parallel processing, nanotechnology, artificial intelligence, software engineering. *Unit head:* Dr. Dung T. Huynh, Head, 972-883-2169, Fax: 972-883-2349, E-mail: huynh@utdallas.edu. *Application contact:* Eric Moden, Evaluator, 972-883-4228, Fax: 972-883-2813, E-mail: gradecs@utdallas.edu.

The University of Texas at El Paso, Graduate School, College of Engineering, Department of Computer Science, El Paso, TX 79968-0001. Offers computer science (MS, PhD); information technology (MSIT). Part-time and evening/weekend programs available. *Students:* 59 (15 women); includes 25 minority (2 Asian Americans or Pacific Islanders, 23 Hispanic Americans), 30 international. Average age 34. In 2009, 17 master's, 3 doctorates awarded. *Degree requirements:* For master's, thesis optional; for doctorate, thesis/dissertation. *Entrance requirements:* For master's, GRE, minimum GPA of 3.0; for doctorate, GRE, Statement of Purpose, Letters of Reference. Additional exam requirements/recommendations for international students: Required—TOEFL; Recommended—IELTS. *Application deadline:* For fall admission, 8/1 priority date for domestic students, 3/1 for international students; for spring admission, 11/1 priority date for domestic students, 9/1 for international students. Applications are processed on a rolling basis. Application fee: $45 ($80 for international students). Electronic applications accepted. *Financial support:* In 2009–10, research assistantships with partial tuition reimbursements (averaging $21,125 per year), teaching assistantships with partial tuition reimbursements (averaging $16,900 per year) were awarded; fellowships with partial tuition reimbursements, institutionally sponsored loans, scholarships/grants, health care benefits, tuition waivers (partial), and unspecified assistantships also available. Support available to part-time students. Financial award application deadline: 3/15; financial award applicants required to submit FAFSA. *Unit head:* Dr. Eunice E. Santos, Chair, 915-747-5480 Ext. 5480, Fax: 915-747-5030, E-mail: eesantos@utep.edu. *Application contact:* Dr. Patricia D. Witherspoon, Dean of the Graduate School, 915-747-5491, Fax: 915-747-5788, E-mail: withersp@utep.edu.

The University of Texas at San Antonio, College of Sciences, Department of Computer Science, San Antonio, TX 78249-0617. Offers MS, PhD. Part-time programs available. *Faculty:* 17 full-time (4 women), 2 part-time/adjunct (0 women). *Students:* 69 full-time (18 women), 47 part-time (6 women); includes 15 minority (1 African American, 5 Asian Americans or Pacific Islanders, 9 Hispanic Americans), 65 international. Average age 29. 153 applicants, 56% accepted, 41 enrolled. In 2009, 10 master's, 5 doctorates awarded. *Degree requirements:* For master's, comprehensive exam, thesis (for some programs); for doctorate, comprehensive exam, thesis/dissertation. *Entrance requirements:* For master's, GRE General Test, minimum GPA of 3.0 in last 60 hours; for doctorate, GRE General Test, minimum GPA of 3.0. Additional exam requirements/recommendations for international students: Required—TOEFL (minimum score 500 paper-based; 173 computer-based; 61 iBT), IELTS (minimum score 5). *Application deadline:* For fall admission, 7/1 for domestic students, 4/1 for international students; for spring admission, 11/1 for domestic students, 9/1 for international students. Applications are processed on a rolling basis. Application fee: $45 ($80 for international students). Electronic applications accepted. *Expenses:* Tuition, state resident: full-time $3975; part-time $221 per contact hour. Tuition, nonresident: full-time $13,947; part-time $775 per contact hour. Required fees: $1853. *Financial support:* In 2009–10, 69 students received support, including 5 fellowships (averaging $25,000 per year), 40 research assistantships (averaging $18,547 per year), 36 teaching assistantships (averaging $13,500 per year); career-related internships or fieldwork, scholarships/grants, tuition waivers, and unspecified assistantships also available. Support available to part-time students. *Faculty research:* Computer and information security, high performance computing, bioinfomatics and computational biology, programming languages and compilers. Total annual research expenditures: $1.4 million. *Unit head:* Dr. Kleanthis Psarris, Chair, 210-458-4434, Fax: 210-458-4437, E-mail: kleanthis.psarris@utsa.edu. *Application contact:* Dr. Weining Zhang, Graduate Advisor, 210-458-5557, E-mail: wzhang@cs.utsa.edu.

The University of Texas at Tyler, College of Engineering and Computer Science, Department of Computer Science, Tyler, TX 75799-0001. Offers computer science (MS); interdisciplinary studies (MSIS). *Faculty:* 7 full-time (0 women). *Students:* 15 full-time (4 women), 15 part-time (5 women), 23 international. Average age 25. 28 applicants, 68% accepted, 5 enrolled. In 2009, 10 master's awarded. *Degree requirements:* For master's, comprehensive exam, thesis optional. *Entrance requirements:* For master's, GRE General Test, previous course work in data structures and computer organization, 6 hours of course work in calculus and statistics. Additional exam requirements/recommendations for international students: Required—TOEFL (minimum score 79 computer-based). *Application deadline:* For fall admission, 6/15 priority date for domestic students, 7/1 priority date for international students; for spring admission, 10/15 priority date for domestic students, 11/1 priority date for international students. Applications are processed on a rolling basis. Application fee: $25 ($50 for international students). Electronic applications accepted. *Expenses:* Tuition, state resident: part-time $665 per semester hour. Tuition, nonresident: part-time $942 per semester hour. Part-time tuition and fees vary according to degree level and program. *Financial support:* In 2009–10, 5 research assistantships (averaging $2,590 per year), 5 teaching assistantships (averaging $3,090 per year) were awarded; scholarships/grants also available. Financial award application deadline: 7/1; financial award applicants required to submit FAFSA. *Faculty research:* Database design, software engineering, client-server architecture, visual programming, data mining, computer security, digital image processing, simulation and modeling, computer science education. Total annual research expenditures: $20,000. *Unit head:* Dr. Stephen Rainwater, Acting Chair, 903-566-7235, Fax: 903-565-5607, E-mail: srainwater@uttyler.edu. *Application contact:* Dr. Stephen Rainwater.

The University of Texas of the Permian Basin, Office of Graduate Studies, College of Arts and Sciences, Department of Math and Computer Science, Odessa, TX 79762-0001. Offers computer science (MS). Part-time and evening/weekend programs available. *Degree requirements:* For master's, comprehensive exam, thesis or alternative. *Entrance requirements:* For master's, GRE General Test. Additional exam requirements/recommendations for international students: Required—TOEFL (minimum score 550 paper-based; 213 computer-based).

The University of Texas–Pan American, College of Science and Engineering, Department of Computer Science, Edinburg, TX 78539. Offers MS. Part-time and evening/weekend programs available. Postbaccalaureate distance learning degree programs offered (minimal on-campus study). *Degree requirements:* For master's, final written exam, project. *Entrance requirements:* For master's, GRE General Test, minimum GPA of 3.0 in last 60 hours. Additional exam requirements/recommendations for international students: Required—TOEFL. *Expenses:* Tuition, state resident: full-time $3630.60; part-time $201.70 per credit hour. Tuition, nonresident: full-time $8617; part-time $478.70 per credit hour. Required fees: $806.50. *Faculty research:* Artificial intelligence, distributed systems internet computing, theoretical computer sciences, information visualization.

University of the District of Columbia, School of Engineering and Applied Science, Department of Computer Science and Information Technology, Program in Computer Science, Washington, DC 20008-1175. Offers MS. *Students:* 2 full-time (1 woman), 3 part-time (0 women); includes 3 minority (1 Asian American or Pacific Islander, 2 Hispanic Americans). Average age 29. *Degree requirements:* For master's, thesis optional. *Expenses:* Tuition, state resident: full-time $7580. Tuition, nonresident: full-time $14,580. Required fees: $620. *Unit head:* Dr. Byunggu Yu, Chair, 202-274-6289, E-mail: byu@udc.edu. *Application contact:* Ann Marie Waterman, Associate Vice President of Admission, Recruitment and Admission, 202-274-6069.

The University of Toledo, College of Graduate Studies, College of Engineering, Department of Electrical Engineering and Computer Science, Toledo, OH 43606-3390. Offers computer

Computer Science

The University of Toledo (continued)
science (MS, PhD); electrical engineering (MS, PhD). Part-time and evening/weekend programs available. *Degree requirements:* For master's, thesis or alternative; for doctorate, thesis/dissertation, qualifying exam. *Entrance requirements:* For master's, GRE General Test, minimum GPA of 3.0; for doctorate, GRE General Test, minimum GPA of 3.3. Additional exam requirements/recommendations for international students: Required—TOEFL (minimum score 550 paper-based; 213 computer-based; 80 iBT). Electronic applications accepted. *Faculty research:* Communication and signal processing, high performance computing systems, intelligent systems, power electronics and energy systems, RF and microwave systems, sensors and medical devices, solid state devices.

University of Toronto, School of Graduate Studies, Physical Sciences Division, Department of Computer Science, Toronto, ON M5S 1A1, Canada. Offers M Sc, PhD. Part-time programs available. *Degree requirements:* For master's, thesis; for doctorate, thesis/dissertation, thesis defense/oral exam. *Entrance requirements:* For master's, GRE (recommended), minimum B+ average overall and in final year; resume; 3 letters of reference; background in computer science and mathematics preferred; for doctorate, minimum B+ average overall and in final year; resumé; 3 letters of reference; background in computer science and mathematics preferred. Additional exam requirements/recommendations for international students: Required—TOEFL (minimum score 580 paper-based; 237 computer-based), TWE (minimum score 5).

University of Tulsa, Graduate School, College of Engineering and Natural Sciences, Department of Mathematical and Computer Sciences, Program in Computer Science, Tulsa, OK 74104-3189. Offers MS, PhD, JD/MS, MBA/MS. Part-time programs available. *Faculty:* 9 full-time (1 woman). *Students:* 50 full-time (6 women), 17 part-time (3 women); includes 8 minority (2 African Americans, 2 American Indian/Alaska Native, 2 Asian Americans or Pacific Islanders, 2 Hispanic Americans), 14 international. Average age 25. 80 applicants, 69% accepted, 32 enrolled. In 2009, 37 master's, 2 doctorates awarded. *Degree requirements:* For master's, thesis (for some programs); for doctorate, comprehensive exam, thesis/dissertation. *Entrance requirements:* For master's and doctorate, GRE General Test. Additional exam requirements/recommendations for international students: Required—TOEFL (minimum score 550 paper-based; 213 computer-based; 80 iBT), IELTS (minimum score 6). *Application deadline:* Applications are processed on a rolling basis. Application fee: $40. Electronic applications accepted. *Expenses:* Tuition: Full-time $16,182; part-time $899 per credit hour. Required fees: $4 per credit hour. Tuition and fees vary according to course load. *Financial support:* In 2009–10, 24 students received support, including 2 fellowships with full and partial tuition reimbursements available (averaging $14,500 per year), 11 research assistantships with full and partial tuition reimbursements available (averaging $12,190 per year), 11 teaching assistantships with full and partial tuition reimbursements available (averaging $11,068 per year); Federal Work-Study, scholarships/grants, health care benefits, tuition waivers (full and partial), and unspecified assistantships also available. Support available to part-time students. Financial award application deadline: 2/1; financial award applicants required to submit FAFSA. *Faculty research:* Robotics, human-computer interaction, systems security, information assurance, machine learning, intelligent systems, software engineering, distributed systems, evolutionary computation, computational biology, bioinformatics. Total annual research expenditures: $9.9 million. *Application contact:* Dr. Rosanne Gamble, Advisor, 918-631-2988, Fax: 918-631-3077, E-mail: gamble@utulsa.edu.

University of Tulsa, Graduate School, Collins College of Business, Business Administration/Computer Science Program, Tulsa, OK 74104-3189. Offers MBA/MS. Part-time programs available. *Students:* 2 full-time (0 women). Average age 27. 2 applicants, 100% accepted, 2 enrolled. *Entrance requirements:* Additional exam requirements/recommendations for international students: Required—TOEFL (minimum score 575 paper-based; 231 computer-based; 79 iBT), IELTS (minimum score 6.5). *Application deadline:* Applications are processed on a rolling basis. Application fee: $40. Electronic applications accepted. *Expenses:* Tuition: Full-time $16,182; part-time $899 per credit hour. Required fees: $4 per credit hour. Tuition and fees vary according to course load. *Financial support:* In 2009–10, 2 students received support, including 1 fellowship with full and partial tuition reimbursement available (averaging $2,175 per year), 1 teaching assistantship with full and partial tuition reimbursement available (averaging $11,594 per year); research assistantships with full and partial tuition reimbursements available, career-related internships or fieldwork, Federal Work-Study, institutionally sponsored loans, scholarships/grants, health care benefits, tuition waivers, and unspecified assistantships also available. Support available to part-time students. Financial award application deadline: 2/1; financial award applicants required to submit FAFSA. *Unit head:* Dr. Markham Collins, Associate Dean, 918-631-2783, Fax: 918-631-2142, E-mail: mark-collins@utulsa.edu. *Application contact:* Information Contact, E-mail: graduate-business@utulsa.edu.

University of Utah, The Graduate School, College of Engineering, School of Computing, Salt Lake City, UT 84112-9205. Offers computational engineering and science (MS); computer science (M Phil, MS, PhD); computing (MS, PhD). *Faculty:* 27 full-time (3 women). *Students:* 165 full-time (21 women), 58 part-time (7 women); includes 5 minority (1 African American, 3 Asian Americans or Pacific Islanders, 1 Hispanic American), 133 international. Average age 28. 101 applicants, 95% accepted, 70 enrolled. In 2009, 40 master's, 13 doctorates awarded. Terminal master's awarded for partial completion of doctoral program. *Degree requirements:* For master's, comprehensive exam (for some programs), thesis (for some programs); for doctorate, comprehensive exam, thesis/dissertation. *Entrance requirements:* For master's and doctorate, GRE General Test, minimum GPA of 3.0. Additional exam requirements/recommendations for international students: Required—TOEFL (minimum score 500 paper-based; 173 computer-based; 61 iBT). *Application deadline:* For fall admission, 12/15 for domestic and international students. Application fee: $55 ($65 for international students). Electronic applications accepted. *Expenses:* Tuition, state resident: full-time $4004; part-time $1674 per semester. Tuition, nonresident: full-time $14,134; part-time $5915 per semester. Required fees: $324 per semester. Tuition and fees vary according to course load, degree level and program. *Financial support:* In 2009–10, 1 student received support, including 2 fellowships with full tuition reimbursements available (averaging $20,000 per year), 100 research assistantships with full tuition reimbursements available (averaging $18,000 per year), 35 teaching assistantships with full tuition reimbursements available (averaging $11,000 per year); scholarships/grants, traineeships, health care benefits, and unspecified assistantships also available. Financial award application deadline: 12/15; financial award applicants required to submit FAFSA. *Faculty research:* Computer-aided graphic design, VLSI, information retrieval, portable artificial intelligence systems, functional programming. Total annual research expenditures: $5.4 million. *Unit head:* Dr. Martin Berzins, Director, 801-581-8224, Fax: 801-581-5843, E-mail: mb@cs.utah.edu. *Application contact:* Dr. Suresh Venkatasubramanian, Director of Graduate Studies, 801-581-8224, Fax: 801-581-5843, E-mail: suresh@cs.utah.edu.

University of Vermont, Graduate College, College of Engineering and Mathematics, Program in Computer Science, Burlington, VT 05405. Offers MS, PhD. *Students:* 27 (5 women), 10 international. 62 applicants, 39% accepted, 5 enrolled. In 2009, 5 master's awarded. *Degree requirements:* For master's, thesis or alternative. *Entrance requirements:* For master's, GRE General Test. Additional exam requirements/recommendations for international students: Required—TOEFL (minimum score 550 paper-based; 213 computer-based; 80 iBT). *Application deadline:* For fall admission, 4/1 priority date for domestic students. Applications are processed on a rolling basis. Application fee: $40. Electronic applications accepted. *Expenses:* Tuition, area resident: Part-time $508 per credit hour. Tuition, state resident: part-time $508 per credit hour. Tuition, nonresident: part-time $1281 per credit hour. *Financial support:* Research assistantships, teaching assistantships available. Financial award application deadline: 3/1. *Unit head:* Dr. Xindong Wu, Chair, 802-656-3330. *Application contact:* Prof. B. Lee, Coordinator, 802-656-3330.

University of Victoria, Faculty of Graduate Studies, Faculty of Engineering, Department of Computer Science, Victoria, BC V8W 2Y2, Canada. Offers M Sc, PhD. Part-time programs available. Terminal master's awarded for partial completion of doctoral program. *Degree*

requirements: For master's, thesis or alternative; for doctorate, thesis/dissertation, candidacy exam. *Entrance requirements:* For master's, GRE (recommended), B Sc in computer science/software engineering or the equivalent or bachelor's degree in mathematics with emphasis on computer science (recommended); for doctorate, GRE (recommended), MS in computer science or equivalent (recommended). Additional exam requirements/recommendations for international students: Required—TOEFL (minimum score 575 paper-based; 233 computer-based), IELTS (minimum score 7). Electronic applications accepted. *Faculty research:* Functional and logic programming, numerical analysis, parallel and distributed computing, software systems, theoretical computer science, VLSI design and testing.

University of Virginia, School of Engineering and Applied Science, Department of Computer Science, Charlottesville, VA 22903. Offers MCS, MS, PhD. *Faculty:* 27 full-time (3 women). *Students:* 78 full-time (14 women), 2 part-time (1 woman); includes 4 minority (1 African American, 3 Asian Americans or Pacific Islanders), 41 international. Average age 27. 349 applicants, 9% accepted, 12 enrolled. In 2009, 19 master's, 7 doctorates awarded. *Degree requirements:* For master's, thesis (for some programs); for doctorate, comprehensive exam, thesis/dissertation. *Entrance requirements:* For master's, GRE General Test, 3 letters of recommendation; for doctorate, GRE General Test, 3 letters of recommendation; essay. Additional exam requirements/recommendations for international students: Required—TOEFL (minimum score 650 paper-based; 250 computer-based; 90 iBT), IELTS (minimum score 7). *Application deadline:* For fall admission, 8/1 for domestic students, 4/1 for international students; for winter admission, 12/1 for domestic students, 8/1 for international students; for spring admission, 5/1 for domestic students, 1/1 for international students. Applications are processed on a rolling basis. Application fee: $60. Electronic applications accepted. *Financial support:* Fellowships available. Financial award application deadline: 10/15; financial award applicants required to submit FAFSA. *Faculty research:* Systems programming, operating systems, analysis of programs and computation theory, programming languages, software engineering. *Unit head:* Mary Lou Soffa, Chair, 434-982-2200, Fax: 434-982-2214, E-mail: inquiry@cs.virginia.edu. *Application contact:* Kathryn C. Thornton, Assistant Dean for Graduate Programs, 434-924-3897, Fax: 434-982-2214, E-mail: seas-grad-admission@cs.virginia.edu.

University of Washington, Graduate School, College of Engineering, Department of Computer Science and Engineering, Seattle, WA 98195-2350. Offers computer science (MS, PhD). *Faculty:* 44 full-time (5 women), 27 part-time/adjunct (7 women). *Students:* 194 full-time (47 women), 10 part-time (2 women); includes 22 minority (20 Asian Americans or Pacific Islanders, 2 Hispanic Americans), 62 international. Average age 28. 1,129 applicants, 13% accepted, 90 enrolled. In 2009, 79 master's, 16 doctorates awarded. *Degree requirements:* For doctorate, thesis/dissertation, research project. *Entrance requirements:* For doctorate, GRE General Test, minimum GPA of 3.0. Additional exam requirements/recommendations for international students: Required—TOEFL (minimum score 600 paper-based; 250 computer-based; 100 iBT), IELTS (minimum score 7). *Application deadline:* For fall admission, 12/15 for domestic and international students. Application fee: $65. Electronic applications accepted. *Financial support:* In 2009–10, 5 students received support, including 39 fellowships with full tuition reimbursements available (averaging $20,286 per year), 97 research assistantships with full tuition reimbursements available (averaging $19,845 per year), 22 teaching assistantships with full tuition reimbursements available (averaging $19,845 per year); career-related internships or fieldwork, traineeships, and health care benefits also available. Financial award application deadline: 12/15. *Faculty research:* Theory, systems, artificial intelligence, graphics, databases. Total annual research expenditures: $14.9 million. *Unit head:* Dr. Henry M. Levy, Professor and Chair, 206-543-9204, Fax: 206-543-2969, E-mail: levy@cs.washington.edu. *Application contact:* Lindsay Michimoto, Graduate Admissions Information Contact, 206-543-1695, Fax: 206-543-2969, E-mail: lindsaym@cs.washington.edu.

University of Waterloo, Graduate Studies, Faculty of Mathematics, David R. Cheriton School of Computer Science, Waterloo, ON N2L 3G1, Canada. Offers computer science (M Math, PhD); software engineering (M Math); statistics and computing (M Math). Part-time programs available. *Degree requirements:* For master's, research paper or thesis; for doctorate, comprehensive exam, thesis/dissertation. *Entrance requirements:* For master's, honors degree in field, minimum B+ average; for doctorate, master's degree, minimum B+ average. *Faculty research:* Computer graphics, artificial intelligence, algorithms and complexity, distributed computing and networks, software engineering.

The University of Western Ontario, Faculty of Graduate Studies, Physical Sciences Division, Department of Computer Science, London, ON N6A 5B8, Canada. Offers M Sc, PhD. Part-time programs available. *Degree requirements:* For master's, thesis, project, or course work; for doctorate, thesis/dissertation. *Entrance requirements:* For master's, B Sc in computer science or comparable academic qualifications; for doctorate, M Sc in computer science or comparable academic qualifications. Additional exam requirements/recommendations for international students: Required—TOEFL. *Faculty research:* Artificial intelligence and logic programming, graphics and image processing, software and systems, theory of computing, symbolic mathematical computation.

University of West Florida, College of Arts and Sciences: Sciences, Department of Computer Science, Pensacola, FL 32514-5750. Offers computer science (MS); software engineering (MS). Part-time and evening/weekend programs available. *Faculty:* 8 full-time (3 women), 2 part-time/adjunct (both women). *Students:* 41 full-time (16 women), 87 part-time (25 women); includes 33 minority (8 African Americans, 1 American Indian/Alaska Native, 16 Asian Americans or Pacific Islanders, 8 Hispanic Americans), 5 international. Average age 36. 46 applicants, 96% accepted, 38 enrolled. In 2009, 14 master's awarded. *Degree requirements:* For master's, thesis optional. *Entrance requirements:* For master's, GRE General Test. Additional exam requirements/recommendations for international students: Required—TOEFL (minimum score 550 paper-based; 213 computer-based). *Application deadline:* For fall admission, 6/1 for domestic students, 5/15 for international students; for spring admission, 11/1 for domestic students, 10/1 for international students. Applications are processed on a rolling basis. Application fee: $30. *Expenses:* Tuition, state resident: full-time $4982; part-time $260 per credit hour. Tuition, nonresident: full-time $20,059; part-time $919 per credit hour. Required fees: $1247; $52 per credit hour. *Financial support:* In 2009–10, 3 teaching assistantships with partial tuition reimbursements (averaging $3,760 per year) were awarded; unspecified assistantships also available. Financial award application deadline: 4/15; financial award applicants required to submit FAFSA. *Unit head:* Dr. Leo Ter Haar, Chairperson, 850-474-2542. *Application contact:* Terry McCray, Assistant Director of Graduate Admissions, 850-473-7718, Fax: 850-473-7714, E-mail: gradadmissions@uwf.edu.

University of West Georgia, Graduate School, College of Arts and Sciences, Department of Computer Science, Carrollton, GA 30118. Offers applied computer science (MS); human centered computing (Certificate); software development (Certificate); system and network administration (Certificate); Web technologies (Certificate). Part-time and evening/weekend programs available. *Faculty:* 8 full-time (3 women). *Students:* 14 full-time (6 women), 14 part-time (6 women); includes 5 minority (4 African Americans, 1 Hispanic American), 6 international. Average age 35. 13 applicants, 92% accepted, 5 enrolled. In 2009, 2 master's awarded. *Degree requirements:* For master's, comprehensive exam, thesis optional. *Entrance requirements:* For master's, GRE, bachelor's degree, minimum overall undergraduate GPA of 2.5; for Certificate, bachelor's degree, minimum overall undergraduate GPA of 2.5. *Application deadline:* For fall admission, 7/17 priority date for domestic students; for spring admission, 11/20 for domestic students. Applications are processed on a rolling basis. Application fee: $30. Electronic applications accepted. *Expenses:* Tuition, state resident: full-time $2952; part-time $164 per semester hour. Tuition, nonresident: full-time $11,808; part-time $656 per semester hour. Required fees: $42.90 per semester hour. $307 per semester. Tuition and fees vary according to course load. *Financial support:* In 2009–10, 10 research assistantships with full tuition reimbursements (averaging $6,000 per year) were awarded; unspecified assistantships also available. Financial award application deadline: 7/1; financial award applicants required to submit FAFSA. *Faculty research:* Artificial intelligence, software engineering, web technologies, database, networks. *Unit head:* Dr. Adel M. Abunawass, Chair, 678-839-6485,

Fax: 678-839-6486, E-mail: adel@westga.edu. *Application contact:* Dr. Charles W. Clark, Dean, 678-839-6508, E-mail: cclark@westga.edu.

University of Windsor, Faculty of Graduate Studies, Faculty of Science, School of Computer Science, Windsor, ON N9B 3P4, Canada. Offers M Sc, PhD. Part-time programs available. *Degree requirements:* For master's, thesis; for doctorate, comprehensive exam, thesis/dissertation. *Entrance requirements:* For master's, GRE, minimum B average; for doctorate, master's degree in computer science, minimum B+ average. Additional exam requirements/recommendations for international students: Required—TOEFL (minimum score 580 paper-based; 237 computer-based). Electronic applications accepted. *Faculty research:* Data mining, distributed query optimization, distributed object based systems, grid computing, querying multimedia database systems.

University of Wisconsin–Madison, Graduate School, College of Letters and Science, Department of Computer Sciences, Madison, WI 53706-1380. Offers MS, PhD. Part-time programs available. Terminal master's awarded for partial completion of doctoral program. *Degree requirements:* For doctorate, thesis/dissertation. *Entrance requirements:* For master's and doctorate, GRE General Test, GRE Subject Test. Electronic applications accepted. *Expenses:* Tuition, state resident: part-time $594 per credit. Tuition, nonresident: part-time $1504 per credit. Required fees: $65 per credit. Tuition and fees vary according to course load, program and reciprocity agreements.

University of Wisconsin–Milwaukee, Graduate School, College of Engineering and Applied Science, Program in Computer Science, Milwaukee, WI 53201-0413. Offers computer science (MS, PhD). Part-time programs available. *Faculty:* 31 full-time (4 women). *Students:* 16 full-time (4 women), 23 part-time (3 women); includes 4 minority (3 Asian Americans or Pacific Islanders, 1 Hispanic American), 11 international. Average age 32. 60 applicants, 55% accepted, 4 enrolled. In 2009, 17 master's awarded. *Degree requirements:* For master's, comprehensive exam (for some programs), thesis or alternative; for doctorate, comprehensive exam, thesis/dissertation, internship. *Entrance requirements:* For master's, GRE, minimum GPA of 2.75; for doctorate, GRE, minimum GPA of 3.5. Additional exam requirements/recommendations for international students: Required—TOEFL (minimum score 550 paper-based; 79 iBT), IELTS (minimum score 6.5). *Application deadline:* For fall admission, 1/1 priority date for domestic students; for spring admission, 9/1 for domestic students. Applications are processed on a rolling basis. Application fee: $45 ($75 for international students). *Expenses:* Tuition, state resident: full-time $8800. Tuition, nonresident: full-time $20,760. Tuition and fees vary according to program and reciprocity agreements. *Financial support:* In 2009–10, 3 research assistantships, 14 teaching assistantships were awarded; fellowships, career-related internships or fieldwork and unspecified assistantships also available. Support available to part-time students. Financial award application deadline: 4/15. Total annual research expenditures: $194,236. *Unit head:* John Boyland, Representative, 414-229-4677, Fax: 414-229-6958, E-mail: csgpr@uwm.edu. *Application contact:* General Information Contact, 414-229-4982, Fax: 414-229-6967, E-mail: gradschool@uwm.edu.

University of Wisconsin–Parkside, School of Business and Technology, Program in Computer and Information Systems, Kenosha, WI 53141-2000. Offers MSCIS. *Entrance requirements:* For master's, GRE General Test or GMAT, 3 letters of recommendation, minimum GPA of 3.0. *Faculty research:* Distributed systems, data bases, natural language processing, event-driven systems.

University of Wisconsin–Platteville, School of Graduate Studies, College of Engineering, Mathematics and Science, Program in Computer Science, Platteville, WI 53818-3099. Offers MS. Part-time programs available. *Students:* 8 full-time (0 women), 2 part-time (0 women), 5 international. 10 applicants, 60% accepted, 6 enrolled. In 2009, 1 master's awarded. *Degree requirements:* For master's, comprehensive exam, thesis or alternative. *Entrance requirements:* Additional exam requirements/recommendations for international students: Required—TOEFL (minimum score 500 paper-based; 173 computer-based; 61 iBT). *Application deadline:* For fall admission, 7/1 priority date for domestic students; for spring admission, 11/1 for domestic students. Applications are processed on a rolling basis. Application fee: $56. Electronic applications accepted. *Expenses:* Tuition, state resident: full-time $6706. Tuition, nonresident: full-time $16,772. *Financial support:* Research assistantships with partial tuition reimbursements available. *Unit head:* Dr. Robert Hasker, Coordinator, 608-342-1561, Fax: 608-342-1965, E-mail: csse@uwplatt.edu. *Application contact:* Lisa Popp, School of Graduate Studies, 608-342-1322, Fax: 608-342-1389, E-mail: poppl@uwplatt.edu.

University of Wyoming, College of Engineering and Applied Sciences, Department of Computer Science, Laramie, WY 82070. Offers MS, PhD. Part-time programs available. Terminal master's awarded for partial completion of doctoral program. *Degree requirements:* For master's, thesis; for doctorate, thesis/dissertation. *Entrance requirements:* For master's and doctorate, GRE General Test, minimum GPA of 3.0. Additional exam requirements/recommendations for international students: Required—TOEFL (minimum score 550 paper-based; 213 computer-based), IELTS (minimum score 6). Electronic applications accepted. *Faculty research:* Fault-tolerant computing, distributed systems, knowledge representation, automated reasoning, parallel database access, formal methods.

Utah State University, School of Graduate Studies, College of Science, Department of Computer Science, Logan, UT 84322. Offers MCS, MS, PhD. Part-time and evening/weekend programs available. Postbaccalaureate distance learning degree programs offered. *Degree requirements:* For master's, thesis (for some programs), research project; for doctorate, thesis/dissertation. *Entrance requirements:* For master's, GRE General Test, GRE Subject Test, minimum GPA of 3.25, prerequisite coursework in math, 3 recommendation letters; for doctorate, GRE General Test, minimum GPA of 3.25, BS or MS. Additional exam requirements/recommendations for international students: Required—TOEFL. Electronic applications accepted. *Faculty research:* Artificial intelligence, software engineering, parallelism.

Vanderbilt University, School of Engineering, Department of Electrical Engineering and Computer Science, Program in Computer Science, Nashville, TN 37240-1001. Offers M Eng, MS, PhD. MS and PhD offered through the Graduate School. Part-time programs available. *Faculty:* 14 full-time (2 women). *Students:* 60 full-time (9 women); includes 2 minority (both Asian Americans or Pacific Islanders), 32 international. Average age 26. 229 applicants, 13% accepted, 14 enrolled. In 2009, 13 master's, 7 doctorates awarded. Terminal master's awarded for partial completion of doctoral program. *Degree requirements:* For master's, thesis (for some programs); for doctorate, comprehensive exam, thesis/dissertation. *Entrance requirements:* For master's and doctorate, GRE General Test, 3 letters of recommendation. Additional exam requirements/recommendations for international students: Required—TOEFL. *Application deadline:* For fall admission, 1/15 for domestic and international students; for spring admission, 11/1 for domestic and international students. Application fee: $0. Electronic applications accepted. *Financial support:* In 2009–10, fellowships with full tuition reimbursements (averaging $30,000 per year), research assistantships with full tuition reimbursements (averaging $21,600 per year), teaching assistantships with full tuition reimbursements (averaging $18,000 per year) were awarded; career-related internships or fieldwork, institutionally sponsored loans, scholarships/grants, health care benefits, tuition waivers (full and partial), and unspecified assistantships also available. Support available to part-time students. Financial award application deadline: 1/15. *Faculty research:* Artificial intelligence, performance evaluation, databases, software engineering, computational science. *Unit head:* Dr. Daniel M. Fleetwood, Chair, 615-322-2771, Fax: 615-343-6702, E-mail: dan.fleetwood@vanderbilt.edu. *Application contact:* Dr. Jerry Spinrad, Director of Graduate Studies, 615-343-7549, Fax: 615-322-0677, E-mail: eecsinfo@eecsmail.vuse.vanderbilt.edu.

Villanova University, College of Engineering, Department of Electrical and Computer Engineering, Program in Computer Engineering, Villanova, PA 19085-1699. Offers computer architectures (Certificate); computer engineering (MSCPE). Part-time and evening/weekend programs available. *Degree requirements:* For master's, thesis optional. *Entrance requirements:* For master's, GRE General Test (for applicants with degrees from foreign universities), BEE,

minimum GPA of 3.0. Additional exam requirements/recommendations for international students: Required—TOEFL (minimum score 600 paper-based; 250 computer-based; 100 iBT). Electronic applications accepted. *Expenses:* Tuition: Part-time $630 per credit. Required fees: $60 per credit. Part-time tuition and fees vary according to degree level and program. *Faculty research:* Expert systems, computer vision, neural networks, image processing, computer architectures.

Villanova University, Graduate School of Liberal Arts and Sciences, Department of Computing Sciences, Villanova, PA 19085-1699. Offers computer science (MS); software engineering (MS). Part-time and evening/weekend programs available. *Faculty:* 7 full-time (1 woman), 6 part-time/adjunct (2 women). *Students:* 60 full-time (21 women), 32 part-time (6 women); includes 9 minority (1 African American, 8 Asian Americans or Pacific Islanders), 54 international. Average age 28. 73 applicants, 88% accepted, 27 enrolled. In 2009, 17 master's awarded. *Degree requirements:* For master's, thesis optional, independent study project. *Entrance requirements:* For master's, GRE, minimum GPA of 3.0. Additional exam requirements/recommendations for international students: Required—TOEFL. *Application deadline:* For fall admission, 3/1 priority date for domestic and international students; for spring admission, 11/15 priority date for domestic and international students. Applications are processed on a rolling basis. Application fee: $50. Electronic applications accepted. *Expenses:* Contact institution. *Financial support:* Research assistantships, Federal Work-Study and scholarships/grants available. Financial award applicants required to submit FAFSA. *Unit head:* Dr. Robert Beck, Chair, 610-519-7310. *Application contact:* Dr. Robert Beck, Chair, 610-519-7310.

See Close-Up on page 321.

Virginia Commonwealth University, Graduate School, School of Engineering, Department of Computer Science, Richmond, VA 23284-9005. Offers computer science (MS, PhD, Certificate); engineering (PhD). *Degree requirements:* For master's, thesis optional. *Entrance requirements:* For master's, GRE General Test.

Virginia International University, Computer Programs Department, Fairfax, VA 22030. Offers computer science (MS); information systems (MS). Part-time programs available. *Faculty:* 2 full-time (both women), 4 part-time/adjunct (0 women). *Students:* 62 full-time (30 women), all international. Average age 26. 175 applicants, 26% accepted, 9 enrolled. In 2009, 26 master's awarded. *Entrance requirements:* For master's, bachelor's degree. Additional exam requirements/recommendations for international students: Required—TOEFL (minimum score 550 paper-based; 213 computer-based; 80 iBT), IELTS. *Application deadline:* For fall admission, 7/31 for domestic students, 7/3 for international students; for spring admission, 12/18 for domestic students, 11/20 for international students. Applications are processed on a rolling basis. Application fee: $100. Electronic applications accepted. *Expenses:* Tuition: Full-time $10,044; part-time $569 per credit. One-time fee: $75. Tuition and fees vary according to degree level. *Financial support:* In 2009–10, 9 students received support. Scholarships/grants available. Financial award application deadline: 7/1. *Unit head:* Emilia Butu, Chair, 703-591-7042 Ext. 307, Fax: 703-591-7046, E-mail: emilia@viu.edu. *Application contact:* Emily L. Kraus, Director of Admissions, 703-591-7042 Ext. 309, Fax: 703-591-7048, E-mail: admissions@viu.edu.

Virginia Polytechnic Institute and State University, Graduate School, College of Engineering, Department of Computer Science, Blacksburg, VA 24061. Offers computer science (MS, PhD); information systems (MIS). *Entrance requirements:* For master's and doctorate, GRE General Test. Additional exam requirements/recommendations for international students: Required—TOEFL (minimum score 550 paper-based; 213 computer-based). Electronic applications accepted. *Faculty research:* Bioinformatics, human-computer interaction, problem-solving environments, high performance computing, software engineering.

Virginia Polytechnic Institute and State University, VT Online, Blacksburg, VA 24061. Offers aerospace engineering (MS); business information systems (Graduate Certificate); career and technical education (MS); computer engineering (M Eng, MS); decision support systems (Graduate Certificate); eLearning leadership (MA); electrical engineering (M Eng, MS); engineering administration (MEA); environmental politics and policy (Graduate Certificate); foundations of political analysis (Graduate Certificate); health product risk management (Graduate Certificate); information policy and society (Graduate Certificate); information security (Graduate Certificate); instructional technology (MA); liberal arts (Graduate Certificate); life sciences: health product risk management (MS); natural resources (MNR, Graduate Certificate); networking (Graduate Certificate); nonprofit and nongovernmental organization management (Graduate Certificate); ocean engineering (MS); political science (MA); security studies (Graduate Certificate); software development (Graduate Certificate).

Virginia State University, School of Graduate Studies, Research, and Outreach, School of Engineering, Science and Technology, Department of Mathematics and Computer Science, Petersburg, VA 23806-0001. Offers computer science (MS); mathematics (MS); mathematics education (M Ed). *Degree requirements:* For master's, thesis (for some programs).

Wake Forest University, Graduate School of Arts and Sciences, Department of Computer Science, Winston-Salem, NC 27109. Offers MS. Part-time programs available. *Degree requirements:* For master's, one foreign language, thesis optional. *Entrance requirements:* For master's, GRE General Test. Additional exam requirements/recommendations for international students: Required—TOEFL (minimum score 213 computer-based; 79 iBT). Electronic applications accepted.

Washington State University, Graduate School, College of Engineering and Architecture, School of Electrical Engineering and Computer Science, Program in Computer Science, Pullman, WA 99164. Offers MS, PhD. *Faculty:* 30. *Students:* 47 full-time (11 women), 13 part-time (5 women); includes 3 minority (2 Asian Americans or Pacific Islanders, 1 Hispanic American), 35 international. Average age 29. 270 applicants, 16% accepted, 22 enrolled. In 2009, 14 master's, 5 doctorates awarded. *Degree requirements:* For master's, comprehensive exam (for some programs), thesis optional, oral exam; for doctorate, comprehensive exam, thesis/dissertation, oral exam, qualifying exam. *Entrance requirements:* For master's and doctorate, GRE General Test, GRE Subject Test, Applications should include a statement of purpose giving qualifications, research interests, and goals; official college transcripts; GRE scores, and three letters of recommendation. Additional exam requirements/recommendations for international students: Required—TOEFL (minimum score 520 paper-based; 190 computer-based), IELTS. *Application deadline:* For fall admission, 1/10 priority date for domestic students, 1/10 for international students; for spring admission, 7/1 for domestic and international students. Applications are processed on a rolling basis. Application fee: $50. *Financial support:* In 2009–10, 28 students received support, including 2 fellowships (averaging $2,500 per year), 4 research assistantships with full and partial tuition reimbursements available (averaging $13,917 per year), 17 teaching assistantships with full and partial tuition reimbursements available (averaging $13,056 per year); career-related internships or fieldwork, Federal Work-Study, institutionally sponsored loans, tuition waivers (partial), and teaching associateships also available. Financial award application deadline: 2/10; financial award applicants required to submit FAFSA. *Faculty research:* Networks, software engineering, database systems, computer graphics, algorithmics. *Unit head:* Dr. Ali Saberi, Chair, 509-335-6636, Fax: 509-335-3818, E-mail: sidra@eecs.wsu.edu. *Application contact:* Graduate School Admissions, 800-GRADWSU, Fax: 509-335-1949, E-mail: gradsch@wsu.edu.

Washington State University Tri-Cities, Graduate Programs, College of Engineering and Computer Science, Richland, WA 99352. Offers computer science (MS, PhD); electrical and computer engineering (PhD); electrical engineering (MS); mechanical engineering (MS, PhD). Part-time programs available. *Faculty:* 28. *Students:* 4 full-time (0 women), 25 part-time (8 women); includes 2 minority (both African Americans), 1 international. *Degree requirements:* For master's, comprehensive exam, thesis (for some programs); for doctorate, comprehensive exam, thesis/dissertation, oral exam. *Entrance requirements:* For master's and doctorate, GRE, minimum GPA of 3.0, 3 letters of recommendation. Additional exam requirements/recommendations for international students: Required—TOEFL (minimum score 550 paper-based; 213 computer-based). *Application deadline:* For fall admission, 1/10 priority date for

Computer Science

Washington State University Tri-Cities (continued)
domestic students, 1/10 for international students; for spring admission, 7/1 priority date for domestic students, 7/1 for international students. Application fee: $50. *Expenses:* Tuition, state resident: part-time $423 per credit. Tuition, nonresident: part-time $1032 per credit. *Financial support:* Application deadline: 3/1. *Faculty research:* Positive ion track structure, biological systems computer simulations. *Unit head:* Dr. Ali Saberi, Chair, 509-372-7178, E-mail: sidra@eecs.wsu.edu. *Application contact:* Dr. Scott Hudson, Associate Director, 509-372-7254, Fax: 509-335-1949, E-mail: hudson@tricity.wsu.edu.

Washington State University Vancouver, Graduate Programs, School of Engineering and Computer Science, Vancouver, WA 98686. Offers computer science (MS); mechanical engineering (MS). Part-time programs available. *Faculty:* 9. *Students:* 14 full-time (1 woman), 5 part-time (1 woman); includes 1 minority (Asian American or Pacific Islander), 5 international. In 2009, 4 master's awarded. *Degree requirements:* For master's, comprehensive exam (for some programs), thesis, research project. *Entrance requirements:* For master's, minimum GPA of 3.0, 3 letters of recommendation with evaluation forms, resume. Additional exam requirements/recommendations for international students: Required—TOEFL (minimum score 550 paper-based). *Application deadline:* For fall admission, 1/10 priority date for domestic students, 1/10 for international students; for spring admission, 7/1 priority date for domestic students, 7/1 for international students. Applications are processed on a rolling basis. Application fee: $50. *Expenses:* Tuition, state resident: full-time $4228; part-time $423 per credit. Tuition, nonresident: full-time $10,322; part-time $1032 per credit. *Financial support:* In 2009–10, research assistantships with full tuition reimbursements (averaging $14,634 per year), teaching assistantships with full tuition reimbursements (averaging $13,383 per year) were awarded; health care benefits and unspecified assistantships also available. Financial award application deadline: 2/15. *Faculty research:* Software design, artificial intelligence, sensor networks, robotics, nanotechnology. Total annual research expenditures: $3.4 million. *Unit head:* Dr. Hakan Gurocak, Director, 360-546-9637, Fax: 360-546-9438, E-mail: hgurocak@vancouver.wsu.edu. *Application contact:* Peggy Moore, Academic Coordinator, 360-546-9638, Fax: 360-546-9438, E-mail: moorep@vancouver.wsu.edu.

Washington University in St. Louis, Henry Edwin Sever Graduate School of Engineering and Applied Science, Department of Computer Science and Engineering, St. Louis, MO 63130-4899. Offers computer engineering (MS, PhD); computer science (MS, PhD); computer science and engineering (M Eng). Part-time programs available. *Faculty:* 21 full-time (3 women), 6 part-time/adjunct (0 women). *Students:* 99 full-time (11 women), 68 part-time (11 women); includes 15 minority (4 African Americans, 9 Asian Americans or Pacific Islanders, 2 Hispanic Americans), 50 international. Average age 26. 351 applicants, 19% accepted, 47 enrolled. In 2009, 38 master's, 9 doctorates awarded. Terminal master's awarded for partial completion of doctoral program. *Degree requirements:* For master's, thesis optional; for doctorate, thesis/dissertation. *Entrance requirements:* For doctorate, GRE General Test. Additional exam requirements/recommendations for international students: Required—TOEFL. *Application deadline:* For fall admission, 1/15 for domestic and international students; for spring admission, 9/15 for domestic and international students. Applications are processed on a rolling basis. Application fee: $60. Electronic applications accepted. *Financial support:* In 2009–10, 4 fellowships with full tuition reimbursements (averaging $26,950 per year), 59 research assistantships with full tuition reimbursements (averaging $26,950 per year) were awarded; health care benefits, tuition waivers (partial), and unspecified assistantships also available. Financial award application deadline: 1/30. *Faculty research:* Artificial intelligence, computational genomics, computer and systems architecture, media and machines, networking and communication, software systems. Total annual research expenditures: $6 million. *Unit head:* Dr. Gruia-Catalin Roman, Chair, 314-935-6132, Fax: 314-935-7302, E-mail: roman@cse.wustl.edu. *Application contact:* Madeline Hawkins, Project Specialist, 314-935-6132, Fax: 314-935-7302, E-mail: admissions@cse.wustl.edu.

Wayne State University, College of Liberal Arts and Sciences, Department of Computer Science, Detroit, MI 48202. Offers computer science (MA, MS, PhD); scientific computing (Certificate). *Degree requirements:* For master's, thesis (for some programs); for doctorate, thesis/dissertation. *Entrance requirements:* For master's, GRE General Test, minimum GPA of 3.0, letters of recommendation; for doctorate, GRE General Test, minimum GPA of 3.3; letters of recommendation; personal statement. Additional exam requirements/recommendations for international students: Required—TOEFL (minimum score 550 paper-based; 213 computer-based); Recommended—TWE (minimum score 6). Electronic applications accepted. *Faculty research:* Software engineering; databases; bioinformatics; artificial intelligence; networking; distributes and parallel computing; security; graphics; visualizations.

Webster University, George Herbert Walker School of Business and Technology, Department of Mathematics and Computer Science, St. Louis, MO 63119-3194. Offers computer science/distributed systems (MS, Certificate); decision support systems (Certificate); web services (Certificate). Part-time and evening/weekend programs available. Postbaccalaureate distance learning degree programs offered (no on-campus study). *Faculty:* 7 full-time, 8 part-time/adjunct. *Students:* 2 full-time (1 woman), 64 part-time (22 women); includes 20 minority (13 African Americans, 1 American Indian/Alaska Native, 5 Asian Americans or Pacific Islanders, 1 Hispanic American). Average age 39. In 2009, 4 master's, 6 other advanced degrees awarded. *Entrance requirements:* For master's, 36 hours of graduate course work. Additional exam requirements/recommendations for international students: Required—TOEFL. *Application deadline:* Applications are processed on a rolling basis. Application fee: $25 ($50 for international students). *Expenses:* Tuition: Part-time $565 per credit hour. Tuition and fees vary according to degree level, campus/location and program. *Financial support:* Federal Work-Study available. Support available to part-time students. Financial award application deadline: 4/1; financial award applicants required to submit FAFSA. *Faculty research:* Databases, computer information systems networks, operating systems, computer architecture. *Unit head:* Al Cawns, Chair, 314-968-7127, Fax: 314-963-6050, E-mail: cawnsae@webster.edu. *Application contact:* Matt Nolan, Assoc. V.P.—Enrollment Management / Dean of Admissions, Fax: 314-968-7116, E-mail: gadmit@webster.edu.

West Chester University of Pennsylvania, Office of Graduate Studies, College of Arts and Sciences, Department of Computer Science, West Chester, PA 19383. Offers computer science (MS, Certificate); computer security (Certificate); information systems (Certificate); Web technology (Certificate). Part-time and evening/weekend programs available. *Students:* 4 full-time (3 women), 15 part-time (5 women); includes 3 minority (1 African American, 2 Asian Americans or Pacific Islanders), 8 international. Average age 26. 20 applicants, 85% accepted, 9 enrolled. In 2009, 11 master's awarded. *Degree requirements:* For master's, thesis optional. *Entrance requirements:* For master's, GRE, three letters of recommendation; for Certificate, GRE General Test. Additional exam requirements/recommendations for international students: Required—TOEFL (minimum score 550 paper-based; 213 computer-based; 80 iBT). *Application deadline:* For fall admission, 4/15 priority date for domestic students, 3/15 for international students; for spring admission, 10/15 for domestic students, 9/1 for international students. Applications are processed on a rolling basis. Application fee: $35. Electronic applications accepted. *Expenses:* Tuition, state resident: full-time $6666; part-time $370 per credit. Tuition, nonresident: full-time $10,666; part-time $593 per credit. Required fees: $122.56 per credit. *Financial support:* In 2009–10, 6 research assistantships with full and partial tuition reimbursements (averaging $5,000 per year) were awarded; unspecified assistantships also available. Support available to part-time students. Financial award application deadline: 2/15; financial award applicants required to submit FAFSA. *Faculty research:* Automata theory, compilers, non well-founded sets. *Unit head:* Dr. James Fabrey, Chair, 610-436-2204, E-mail: jfabrey@wcupa.edu. *Application contact:* Dr. Afrand Agah, Graduate Coordinator, 610-436-4419, E-mail: aagah@wcupa.edu.

Western Carolina University, Graduate School, College of Arts and Sciences, Department of Mathematics and Computer Science, Cullowhee, NC 28723. Offers applied mathematics (MS). Part-time and evening/weekend programs available. *Students:* 10 full-time (4 women). Average age 28. 6 applicants, 67% accepted, 3 enrolled. In 2009, 9 master's awarded. *Degree requirements:* For master's, thesis or alternative. *Entrance requirements:* For master's, GRE General Test, appropriate undergraduate degree, 3 letters of recommendation. Additional exam requirements/recommendations for international students: Required—TOEFL (minimum score 550 paper-based; 270 computer-based; 79 iBT). *Application deadline:* For fall admission, 5/1 priority date for domestic students; for spring admission, 9/1 priority date for domestic students. Applications are processed on a rolling basis. Application fee: $45. *Financial support:* In 2009–10, 7 students received support, including 7 teaching assistantships with full and partial tuition reimbursements available (averaging $9,000 per year); fellowships, research assistantships with full and partial tuition reimbursements available, career-related internships or fieldwork, institutionally sponsored loans, scholarships/grants, and unspecified assistantships also available. Financial award application deadline: 3/31; financial award applicants required to submit FAFSA. *Unit head:* Dr. Mark Holliday, Head, 828-227-7245, Fax: 828-227-7240, E-mail: holliday@email.wcu.edu. *Application contact:* Admissions Specialist for Applied Mathematics, 828-227-7398, Fax: 828-227-7480, E-mail: gradsch@email.wcu.edu.

Western Illinois University, School of Graduate Studies, College of Business and Technology, Department of Computer Science, Macomb, IL 61455-1390. Offers MS. Part-time programs available. *Students:* 64 full-time (22 women), 35 part-time (7 women); includes 2 minority (1 African American, 1 Hispanic American), 84 international. Average age 24. 70 applicants, 76% accepted. In 2009, 30 master's awarded. *Degree requirements:* For master's, thesis or alternative. *Entrance requirements:* For master's, proficiency in Java. Additional exam requirements/recommendations for international students: Required—TOEFL (minimum score 550 paper-based; 213 computer-based; 80 iBT). *Application deadline:* Applications are processed on a rolling basis. Application fee: $30. Electronic applications accepted. *Expenses:* Tuition, state resident: full-time $4486; part-time $249.21 per credit hour. Tuition, nonresident: full-time $8972; part-time $498.42 per credit hour. Required fees: $72.62 per credit hour. *Financial support:* In 2009–10, 21 students received support, including 11 research assistantships with full tuition reimbursements available (averaging $7,280 per year), 10 teaching assistantships with full tuition reimbursements available (averaging $8,400 per year). Financial award applicants required to submit FAFSA. *Unit head:* Dr. Kathleen Neumann, Chairperson, 309-298-1452. *Application contact:* Evelyn Hoing, Assistant Director of Graduate Studies, 309-298-1806, Fax: 309-298-2345, E-mail: grad-office@wiu.edu.

Western Kentucky University, Graduate Studies, Ogden College of Science and Engineering, Department of Computer Science, Bowling Green, KY 42101. Offers MS. *Degree requirements:* For master's, comprehensive exam, thesis optional. *Entrance requirements:* For master's, GRE General Test, minimum GPA of 2.75. Additional exam requirements/recommendations for international students: Required—TOEFL (minimum score 555 paper-based; 213 computer-based; 79 iBT). *Expenses:* Tuition, state resident: full-time $4160; part-time $416 per credit hour. Tuition, nonresident: full-time $9550; part-time $506 per credit hour. Tuition and fees vary according to campus/location and reciprocity agreements. *Faculty research:* Visual studio, assessment.

Western Michigan University, Graduate College, College of Engineering and Applied Sciences, Department of Computer Science, Kalamazoo, MI 49008. Offers MS, PhD. *Degree requirements:* For master's, thesis optional, oral exams; for doctorate, 2 foreign languages, thesis/dissertation. *Entrance requirements:* For master's and doctorate, GRE General Test.

Western Washington University, Graduate School, College of Sciences and Technology, Department of Computer Science, Bellingham, WA 98225-5996. Offers MS. Part-time programs available. *Degree requirements:* For master's, thesis optional, project. *Entrance requirements:* For master's, GRE General Test, minimum GPA of 3.0 in last 60 semester hours or last 90 quarter hours. Additional exam requirements/recommendations for international students: Required—TOEFL (minimum score 567 paper-based; 227 computer-based). Electronic applications accepted. *Faculty research:* Distributed operating systems, data mining, machine learning, robotics, information retrieval, graphics and visualization, parallel and distributed computing.

West Virginia University, College of Engineering and Mineral Resources, Lane Department of Computer Science and Electrical Engineering, Program in Computer Science, Morgantown, WV 26506. Offers MSCS, PhD. Part-time programs available. *Degree requirements:* For master's, thesis; for doctorate, comprehensive exam, thesis/dissertation. *Entrance requirements:* For master's, GRE General Test, letters of recommendation; for doctorate, GRE General Test, GRE Subject Test, MS in computer science, letters of recommendation. Additional exam requirements/recommendations for international students: Required—TOEFL. *Faculty research:* Artificial intelligence, knowledge-based simulation, data communications, mathematical computations, software engineering.

Wichita State University, Graduate School, College of Engineering, Department of Electrical Engineering and Computer Science, Wichita, KS 67260. Offers computer networking (MS); computer science (MS); electrical engineering (MS, PhD). Part-time and evening/weekend programs available. *Expenses:* Tuition, state resident: full-time $4247; part-time $235.95 per credit hour. Tuition, nonresident: full-time $11,171; part-time $620.60 per credit hour. Required fees: $34; $3.60 per credit hour. $17 per term. Tuition and fees vary according to campus/location and program. *Unit head:* Dr. John Watkins, Chair, 316-978-3156, Fax: 316-978-5408, E-mail: john.watkins@wichita.edu. *Application contact:* Dr. John Watkins, Chair, 316-978-3156, Fax: 316-978-5408, E-mail: john.watkins@wichita.edu.

Winston-Salem State University, Program in Computer Science and Information Technology, Winston-Salem, NC 27110-0003. Offers MS. Part-time programs available. *Degree requirements:* For master's, thesis optional. *Entrance requirements:* For master's, GRE, resume. Electronic applications accepted. *Faculty research:* Artificial intelligence, network protocols, software engineering.

Worcester Polytechnic Institute, Graduate Studies and Research, Department of Computer Science, Worcester, MA 01609-2280. Offers computer and communications networks (MS); computer science (MS, PhD, Advanced Certificate, Graduate Certificate). Part-time and evening/weekend programs available. *Faculty:* 18 full-time (3 women), 3 part-time/adjunct (0 women). *Students:* 57 full-time (16 women), 47 part-time (6 women). 228 applicants, 66% accepted, 39 enrolled. In 2009, 35 master's, 2 doctorates awarded. Terminal master's awarded for partial completion of doctoral program. *Degree requirements:* For master's, thesis optional; for doctorate, comprehensive exam, thesis/dissertation. *Entrance requirements:* For master's, GRE General Test, GRE Subject Test in computer science (recommended), 3 letters of recommendation; for doctorate, GRE General Test, GRE Subject Test in computer science (recommended), 3 letters of recommendation, statement of purpose. Additional exam requirements/recommendations for international students: Required—TOEFL (minimum score 550 paper-based; 213 computer-based; 79 iBT), IELTS (minimum score 6.5). *Application deadline:* For fall admission, 1/15 priority date for domestic and international students; for spring admission, 10/15 priority date for domestic and international students. Applications are processed on a rolling basis. Application fee: $70. Electronic applications accepted. *Financial support:* Career-related internships or fieldwork, institutionally sponsored loans, scholarships/grants, and unspecified assistantships available. Financial award application deadline: 1/15. *Faculty research:* Computer networks and distributed systems, databases and data mining, artificial intelligence, computer graphics and visualization, applied logic and security. *Application contact:* Dr. Carolina Ruiz, Graduate Coordinator, 508-831-5357, Fax: 508-831-5776, E-mail: ruiz@wpi.edu.

Wright State University, School of Graduate Studies, College of Engineering and Computer Science, Department of Computer Science and Engineering, Computer Science Program, Dayton, OH 45435. Offers MS. *Degree requirements:* For master's, thesis optional. *Entrance requirements:* For master's, GRE General Test, minimum GPA of 3.0 in major, 2.7 overall. Additional exam requirements/recommendations for international students: Required—TOEFL.

Wright State University, School of Graduate Studies, College of Engineering and Computer Science, Department of Computer Science and Engineering, Program in Computer Science and Engineering, Dayton, OH 45435. Offers PhD. *Degree requirements:* For doctorate, thesis/dissertation, candidacy and general exams. *Entrance requirements:* For doctorate, GRE General Test, minimum GPA of 3.3. Additional exam requirements/recommendations for international students: Required—TOEFL.

Yale University, Graduate School of Arts and Sciences, Department of Computer Science, New Haven, CT 06520. Offers MS, PhD. *Degree requirements:* For doctorate, thesis/dissertation. *Entrance requirements:* For doctorate, GRE General Test, GRE Subject Test.

York University, Faculty of Graduate Studies, Faculty of Science and Engineering, Program in Computer Science, Toronto, ON M3J 1P3, Canada. Offers M Sc, PhD. *Degree requirements:* For master's, thesis or alternative; for doctorate, comprehensive exam, thesis/dissertation, internship or practicum. Electronic applications accepted.

Youngstown State University, Graduate School, College of Science, Technology, Engineering and Mathematics, Department of Computer Science and Information Systems, Youngstown, OH 44555-0001. Offers computing and information systems (MCIS). Part-time programs available. *Degree requirements:* For master's, thesis or capstone project. *Entrance requirements:* For master's, GRE or GMAT. Additional exam requirements/recommendations for international students: Required—TOEFL (minimum score 550 paper-based; 213 computer-based). *Faculty research:* Networking, computational science, graphics and visualization, database and data mining, biometrics, artificial intelligence, online learning environments.

Youngstown State University, Graduate School, College of Science, Technology, Engineering and Mathematics, Department of Mathematics and Statistics, Youngstown, OH 44555-0001. Offers applied mathematics (MS); computer science (MS); secondary mathematics (MS); statistics (MS). Part-time programs available. *Degree requirements:* For master's, comprehensive exam, thesis optional. *Entrance requirements:* For master's, minimum GPA of 2.7 in computer science and mathematics. Additional exam requirements/recommendations for international students: Required—TOEFL. *Faculty research:* Regression analysis, numerical analysis, statistics, Markov chain, topology and fuzzy sets.

Database Systems

Colorado Technical University Colorado Springs, Graduate Studies, Program in Computer Science, Colorado Springs, CO 80907-3896. Offers computer science (DCS); computer systems security (MSCS); database systems (MSCS); software engineering (MSCS). Part-time and evening/weekend programs available. Postbaccalaureate distance learning degree programs offered. *Degree requirements:* For master's, thesis or alternative; for doctorate, thesis/dissertation. *Entrance requirements:* For doctorate, minimum graduate GPA of 3.0, 5 years of related work experience. *Faculty research:* Software engineering, systems engineering.

Colorado Technical University Denver, Program in Computer Science, Greenwood Village, CO 80111. Offers computer systems security (MSCS); database systems (MSCS); software engineering (MSCS). Part-time and evening/weekend programs available. *Degree requirements:* For master's, thesis or alternative. *Entrance requirements:* For master's, minimum undergraduate GPA of 3.0, resume.

Ferris State University, College of Business, Big Rapids, MI 49307. Offers application development (MSISM); business intelligence and infomatics (MBA); database administration (MSISM); design and innovation management process (MBA); e-business (MSISM); networking (MSISM); quality management (MBA); security (MSISM). *Accreditation:* ACBSP. Part-time and evening/weekend programs available. *Faculty:* 10 full-time (3 women), 2 part-time/adjunct (both women). *Students:* 33 full-time (6 women), 134 part-time (65 women); includes 13 minority (8 African Americans, 2 American Indian/Alaska Native, 2 Asian Americans or Pacific Islanders, 1 Hispanic American), 33 international. Average age 30. 120 applicants, 31% accepted, 26 enrolled. In 2009, 66 master's awarded. *Entrance requirements:* For master's, GRE or GMAT (waived if GPA is 3.5 or better), minimum GPA of 3.0 in CIS and business core, 2.75 overall; writing sample; 3 letters of reference; resume. Additional exam requirements/recommendations for international students: Required—TOEFL (minimum score 500 paper-based; 173 computer-based; 64 iBT). *Application deadline:* For fall admission, 7/1 priority date for domestic students, 6/15 for international students; for winter admission, 11/1 priority date for domestic students, 10/15 for international students; for spring admission, 3/1 priority date for domestic students, 2/15 for international students. Applications are processed on a rolling basis. Application fee: $30 for international students. Electronic applications accepted. *Financial support:* In 2009–10, 14 teaching assistantships were awarded; career-related internships or fieldwork, Federal Work-Study, and unspecified assistantships also available. Support available to part-time students. Financial award applicants required to submit FAFSA. *Faculty research:* Quality improvement, client/server end-user computing, information management and policy, security, digital forensics. *Unit head:* Dr. David Steenstra, Department Chair, 231-591-2168, Fax: 231-591-2973, E-mail: yosts@ferris.edu. *Application contact:* Shannon Yost, Department Secretary, 231-591-2168, Fax: 231-591-2973, E-mail: yosts@ferris.edu.

George Mason University, Volgenau School of Information Technology and Engineering, Department of Computer Science, Fairfax, VA 22030. Offers biometrics (Certificate); computer games technology (Certificate); computer networking (Certificate); computer science (MS, PhD); data mining (Certificate); database management (Certificate); electronic commerce (Certificate); foundations of information systems (Certificate); information engineering (Certificate); information security and assurance (MS, Certificate); information systems (MS); intelligent agents (Certificate); software architecture (Certificate); software engineering (MS, Certificate); systems engineering (MS); Web-based software engineering (Certificate). Part-time and evening/weekend programs available. Postbaccalaureate distance learning degree programs offered. *Faculty:* 42 full-time (9 women), 18 part-time/adjunct (0 women). *Students:* 121 full-time (36 women), 489 part-time (118 women); includes 90 minority (11 African Americans, 70 Asian Americans or Pacific Islanders, 9 Hispanic Americans), 222 international. Average age 29. 882 applicants, 58% accepted, 147 enrolled. In 2009, 202 master's, 6 doctorates, 21 other advanced degrees awarded. *Degree requirements:* For master's, thesis optional; for doctorate, comprehensive exam, thesis/dissertation. *Entrance requirements:* For master's, GRE General Test, minimum GPA of 3.0 in last 60 hours, 3 letters of recommendation; for doctorate, GRE, 4-year BA degree, academic work in computer science, 3 letters of recommendation, statement of career goals and aspirations. Additional exam requirements/recommendations for international students: Required—TOEFL. *Application deadline:* For fall admission, 4/15 priority date for domestic students, 1/15 for international students; for spring admission, 11/15 for domestic students. Application fee: $75. Electronic applications accepted. *Expenses:* Tuition, state resident: full-time $7568; part-time $315.33 per credit hour. Tuition, nonresident: full-time $21,704; part-time $904.33 per credit hour. Required fees: $2184; $91 per credit hour. *Financial support:* In 2009–10, 106 students received support, including 3 fellowships (averaging $18,000 per year), 53 research assistantships (averaging $11,119 per year), 53 teaching assistantships (averaging $7,881 per year); unspecified assistantships and health care benefits (full-time research or teaching assistantship recipients) also available. Financial award application deadline: 3/1; financial award applicants required to submit FAFSA. *Faculty research:* Artificial intelligence, image processing/graphics, parallel/distributed systems, software engineering systems. Total annual research expenditures: $1.3 million. *Unit head:* Dr. Arun Sood, Director, 703-993-1524, Fax: 703-993-1710, E-mail: asood@gmu.edu. *Application contact:* Jay Shapiro, Professor, 703-993-1485, E-mail: jshapiro@gmu.edu.

Minnesota State University Mankato, College of Graduate Studies, College of Science, Engineering and Technology, Department of Information Systems and Technology, Mankato, MN 56001. Offers database technologies (Certificate); information technology (MS). *Students:* 3 full-time (0 women), 2 part-time (both women). *Degree requirements:* For master's, comprehensive exam, thesis or alternative. *Entrance requirements:* For master's, GRE General Test, minimum GPA of 3.0 during previous 2 years. Additional exam requirements/recommendations for international students: Required—TOEFL (minimum score 550 paper-based; 213 computer-based; 80 iBT). *Application deadline:* For fall admission, 7/1 priority date for domestic students; for spring admission, 11/1 for domestic students. Applications are processed on a rolling basis. Electronic applications accepted. *Expenses:* Tuition, state resident: full-time $5364. Tuition, nonresident: full-time $8314. *Financial support:* Research assistantships with full tuition reimbursements, teaching assistantships with full tuition reimbursements, unspecified assistantships available. Financial award application deadline: 3/15; financial award applicants required to submit FAFSA. *Unit head:* Dr. Leon Tietz, Chairperson, 507-389-1412. *Application contact:* 507-389-2321, E-mail: grad@mnsu.edu.

National University, Academic Affairs, School of Engineering and Technology, Department of Applied Engineering, La Jolla, CA 92037-1011. Offers database administration (MS); engineering management (MS); environmental engineering (MS); homeland security and safety engineering (MS); system engineering (MS); wireless communications (MS). Part-time and evening/weekend programs available. Postbaccalaureate distance learning degree programs offered (no on-campus study). *Faculty:* 6 full-time (1 woman), 7 part-time/adjunct (1 woman). *Students:* 61 full-time (16 women), 176 part-time (35 women); includes 54 minority (11 African Americans, 1 American Indian/Alaska Native, 23 Asian Americans or Pacific Islanders, 19 Hispanic Americans), 117 international. Average age 31. 133 applicants, 100% accepted, 83 enrolled. In 2009, 34 master's awarded. *Degree requirements:* For master's, thesis. *Entrance requirements:* For master's, interview, minimum GPA of 2.5. Additional exam requirements/recommendations for international students: Required—TOEFL (minimum score 550 paper-based; 213 computer-based; 79 iBT), IELTS (minimum score 6). *Application deadline:* Applications are processed on a rolling basis. Application fee: $60 ($65 for international students). Electronic applications accepted. *Expenses:* Tuition: Part-time $338 per quarter hour. *Financial support:* Career-related internships or fieldwork, institutionally sponsored loans, scholarships/grants, and tuition waivers (partial) available. Support available to part-time students. Financial award application deadline: 6/30; financial award applicants required to submit FAFSA. *Unit head:* Dr. Shekar Viswanathan, Chair and Associate Professor, 858-309-8416, Fax: 858-309-3420, E-mail: sviswana@nu.edu. *Application contact:* Dominick Giovanniello, Associate Regional Dean—San Diego, 800-NAT-UNIV, Fax: 858-541-7792, E-mail: dgiovann@nu.edu.

New York University, School of Continuing and Professional Studies, Division of Programs in Business, Graduate Programs in Management and Systems, New York, NY 10012-1019. Offers core business competencies (Advanced Certificate); database technologies (MS); enterprise and risk management (Advanced Certificate); enterprise risk management (MS); information technologies (Advanced Certificate); strategy and leadership (MS, Advanced Certificate); systems management (MS). Part-time and evening/weekend programs available. Postbaccalaureate distance learning degree programs offered (no on-campus study). *Faculty:* 2 full-time (0 women), 21 part-time/adjunct (6 women). *Students:* 32 full-time (18 women), 197 part-time (78 women). Average age 34. 168 applicants, 80% accepted, 69 enrolled. In 2009, 51 master's, 7 other advanced degrees awarded. *Degree requirements:* For master's, thesis, capstone project. *Entrance requirements:* For master's, GMAT or GRE General Test (for recent graduates), resume, 2 letters of recommendation, essay. Additional exam requirements/recommendations for international students: Required—TOEFL (minimum score 600 paper-based; 250 computer-based; 100 iBT), TWE. *Application deadline:* For fall admission, 2/1 priority date for domestic and international students; for spring admission, 10/15 priority date for domestic students, 8/15 priority date for international students. Applications are processed on a rolling basis. Application fee: $75. Electronic applications accepted. *Expenses:* Tuition: Full-time $30,528; part-time $1272 per credit. Required fees: $2177. *Financial support:* In 2009–10, 61 students received support, including 61 fellowships (averaging $2,300 per year); scholarships/grants also available. Support available to part-time students. Financial award application deadline: 3/1; financial award applicants required to submit FAFSA. *Unit head:* Israel Moskowitz, Director, 212-992-3600, Fax: 212-992-3650, E-mail: im36@nyu.edu. *Application contact:* Helen Sapp, Assistant Director, 212-992-3600, Fax: 212-992-3650, E-mail: helen.sapp@nyu.edu.

Northwestern University, School of Continuing Studies, Program in Information Systems, Evanston, IL 60208. Offers database and Internet technologies (MS); information systems management (MS); information systems security (MS); software project management and development (MS).

Regis University, College for Professional Studies, School of Computer and Information Sciences, Denver, CO 80221-1099. Offers database administration with IBM DB2 (Certificate); database administration with Oracle (Certificate); database development (Certificate); database technologies (MA); enterprise Java software development (Certificate); executive information technologies (Certificate); information assurance (MA, Certificate); information technology management (MA); software and information systems (M Sc); software engineering (MA, Certificate); storage area networks (Certificate); systems engineering (MA, Certificate). Offered at Boulder Campus, Northwest Denver Campus, Southeast Denver Campus, Fort Collins Campus, Colorado Springs Campus, and Broomfield Campus. Part-time and evening/weekend programs available. Postbaccalaureate distance learning degree programs offered (no on-campus study). *Degree requirements:* For master's, thesis, final research project. *Entrance requirements:* For master's, 2 years of related experience, resume, interview; for Certificate, 2 years of related experience, resumé. Additional exam requirements/recommendations for international students: Required—TOEFL (minimum score 213 computer-based), TWE (minimum score 5), TOEFL or university-based test. Electronic applications accepted. *Expenses:* Contact institution. *Faculty research:* Secure Virtual Laboratory Architecture, Joint IA project with W2C06 Institute, Information Policy, OLTP and OLAP Technologies, knowledge management, software architectures.

Rochester Institute of Technology, Graduate Enrollment Services, B. Thomas Golisano College of Computing and Information Sciences, Department of Information Technology, Rochester, NY 14623-5603. Offers database administration (AC); human computer interaction (MS); information assurance (AC); information technology (MS); interactive multimedia development (AC); software development and management (MS). Part-time and evening/weekend programs available. Postbaccalaureate distance learning degree programs offered (minimal on-campus study). *Students:* 95 full-time (32 women), 107 part-time (26 women); includes 16 minority (7 African Americans, 1 American Indian/Alaska Native, 5 Asian Americans or Pacific Islanders, 3 Hispanic Americans), 81 international. Average age 30. 162 applicants, 64% accepted, 52 enrolled. In 2009, 66 master's, 6 other advanced degrees awarded. *Degree requirements:* For master's, thesis or project. *Entrance requirements:* For master's, GRE, minimum GPA of 3.0. Additional exam requirements/recommendations for international students: Required—TOEFL (minimum score 570 paper-based; 230 computer-based; 99 iBT), or IELTS (minimum score 6.5). *Application deadline:* For fall admission, 8/1 for domestic students, 7/1

Database Systems

Rochester Institute of Technology (continued)
for international students; for spring admission, 2/1 for domestic students. Applications are processed on a rolling basis. Application fee: $50. Electronic applications accepted. *Expenses:* Tuition: Full-time $31,533; part-time $876 per credit hour. Required fees: $210. *Financial support:* In 2009–10, 137 students received support; research assistantships with partial tuition reimbursements available, teaching assistantships with partial tuition reimbursements available, career-related internships or fieldwork, scholarships/grants, and unspecified assistantships available. Support available to part-time students. Financial award applicants required to submit FAFSA. *Faculty research:* Human computer interaction: eye tracking, usability engineering, usability testing, ubiquitous computing, interface design and development; platform-independent Multiuser Online Virtual Environments (MOVEs); simulation; service computing, query optimization, data mining and integration; applications programming, interface designs, needs assessment, data modeling, database administration. *Unit head:* Prof. Jeffrey Lasky, Department Chair, 585-475-2284, Fax: 585-475-6584, E-mail: jalics@rit.edu. *Application contact:* Diane Ellison, Assistant Vice President, Graduate Enrollment Services, 585-475-2229, Fax: 585-475-7164, E-mail: gradinfo@rit.edu.

Sacred Heart University, Graduate Programs, College of Arts and Sciences, Department of Computer Science and Information Technology, Fairfield, CT 06825-1000. Offers computer science (MS); database (CPS); information technology (MS, CPS); information technology and network security (CPS); interactive multimedia (CPS); Web development (CPS). Part-time and evening/weekend programs available. *Faculty:* 7 full-time (4 women). *Students:* 20 full-time (6 women), 79 part-time (25 women); includes 10 minority (2 African Americans, 1 American Indian/Alaska Native, 5 Asian Americans or Pacific Islanders, 2 Hispanic Americans), 30 international. Average age 33. 66 applicants, 97% accepted, 26 enrolled. In 2009, 17 master's awarded. *Degree requirements:* For master's, thesis optional. *Entrance requirements:* Additional exam requirements/recommendations for international students: Required—TOEFL (minimum score 550 paper-based; 213 computer-based). *Application deadline:* Applications are processed on a rolling basis. Application fee: $50 ($100 for international students). Electronic applications accepted. *Expenses:* Tuition: Full-time $24,000; part-time $650 per credit. Required fees: $248. *Financial support:* Career-related internships or fieldwork, institutionally sponsored loans, and unspecified assistantships available. Support available to part-time students. Financial award applicants required to submit FAFSA. *Faculty research:* Contemporary market software. *Unit head:* Domenick Pinto, Academic Director and Chairperson, 203-371-7789, Fax: 203-371-0506, E-mail: pintod@sacredheart.edu. *Application contact:* Dean Alexis Haakonsen, Office of Graduate Admissions, 203-365-7619, Fax: 203-365-4732, E-mail: gradstudies@sacredheart.edu.

Stevens Institute of Technology, Graduate School, Charles V. Schaefer Jr. School of Engineering, Department of Computer Science, Hoboken, NJ 07030. Offers computer graphics (Certificate); computer science (MS, PhD); computer systems (Certificate); database management systems (Certificate); distributed systems (Certificate); elements of computer science (Certificate); enterprise computing (Certificate); enterprise security and information assurance (Certificate); health informatics (Certificate); multimedia experience and management (Certificate); networks and systems administration (Certificate); security and privacy (Certificate); service oriented computing (Certificate); software design (Certificate); theoretical computer science (Certificate). Part-time and evening/weekend programs available. Terminal master's awarded for partial completion of doctoral program. *Degree requirements:* For master's, thesis optional; for doctorate, variable foreign language requirement, comprehensive exam, thesis/dissertation. *Entrance requirements:* For master's and doctorate, GRE, minimum GPA of 3.0. Additional exam requirements/recommendations for international students: Required—TOEFL. Electronic applications accepted. *Expenses:* Tuition: Full-time $9900; part-time $1100 per credit. Required fees: $286 per semester. *Faculty research:* Semantics, reliability theory, programming language, cyber security.

Towson University, College of Graduate Studies and Research, Program in Applied Information Technology, Towson, MD 21252-0001. Offers applied information technology (D Sc); database management (Certificate); information security and assurance (Certificate); information systems management (Certificate); Internet application development (Certificate); networking technologies (Certificate); software engineering (Certificate). *Entrance requirements:* For doctorate, minimum GPA 3.0, letter of intent, resumè, 2 letters of recommendation, personal assessment forms, official transcripts. Additional exam requirements/recommendations for international students: Required—TOEFL (minimum score 550 paper-based). Electronic applications accepted.

University of New Haven, Graduate School, Tagliatela College of Engineering, Program in Computer and Information Science, West Haven, CT 06516-1916. Offers computer science (MS, Certificate), including advanced applications (MS), computer applications (Certificate), computer programming (Certificate), computer systems (MS), computing (Certificate), database and information systems (MS), network administration (Certificate), network systems (MS), software engineering and development (MS). Part-time and evening/weekend programs available. *Faculty:* 9 full-time (2 women), 5 part-time/adjunct (0 women). *Students:* 21 full-time (8 women), 32 part-time (8 women); includes 5 minority (2 African Americans, 1 Asian American or Pacific Islander, 2 Hispanic Americans), 26 international. Average age 30. 163 applicants, 88% accepted, 18 enrolled. In 2009, 24 master's awarded. *Degree requirements:* For master's, thesis or alternative. *Entrance requirements:* Additional exam requirements/recommendations for international students: Required—TOEFL (minimum score 520 paper-based; 190 computer-based; 70 iBT); Recommended—IELTS (minimum score 5.5). *Application deadline:* For fall admission, 5/31 for international students; for winter admission, 10/15 for international students; for spring admission, 1/15 for international students. Applications are processed on a rolling basis. Application fee: $50. Electronic applications accepted. *Expenses:* Tuition: Part-time $700 per credit. Required fees: $45 per term. One-time fee: $390 part-time. *Financial support:* Research assistantships with partial tuition reimbursements, teaching assistantships with partial tuition reimbursements, career-related internships or fieldwork, Federal Work-Study, scholarships/grants, tuition waivers, and unspecified assistantships available. Support available to part-time students. Financial award applicants required to submit FAFSA. *Unit head:* Dr. Tahany Fergany, Coordinator, 203-932-7067. *Application contact:* Eloise Gormley, Director of Graduate Admissions, 203-932-7449, Fax: 203-932-7137, E-mail: gradinfo@newhaven.edu.

University of West Florida, College of Professional Studies, Department of Professional and Community Leadership, Program in Administration, Pensacola, FL 32514-5750. Offers acquisition and contract administration (MSA); biomedical/pharmaceutical (MSA); criminal justice administration (MSA); database administration (MSA); education leadership (MSA); healthcare administration (MSA); human performance technology (MSA); leadership (MSA); nursing administration (MSA); public administration (MSA); software engineering administration (MSA). Part-time and evening/weekend programs available. Postbaccalaureate distance learning degree programs offered (no on-campus study). *Students:* 33 full-time (21 women), 168 part-time (97 women); includes 53 minority (32 African Americans, 2 American Indian/Alaska Native, 5 Asian Americans or Pacific Islanders, 14 Hispanic Americans), 1 international. Average age 34. 103 applicants, 74% accepted, 64 enrolled. In 2009, 47 master's awarded. *Entrance requirements:* For master's, GRE General Test, letter of intent, names of references. Additional exam requirements/recommendations for international students: Required—TOEFL (minimum score 550 paper-based; 213 computer-based). *Application deadline:* For fall admission, 6/1 for domestic students, 5/15 for international students; for spring admission, 11/1 for domestic students, 10/1 for international students. Applications are processed on a rolling basis. Application fee: $30. *Expenses:* Tuition, state resident: full-time $4982; part-time $260 per credit hour. Tuition, nonresident: full-time $20,059; part-time $919 per credit hour. Required fees: $1247; $52 per credit hour. *Financial support:* Unspecified assistantships available. Financial award application deadline: 4/15; financial award applicants required to submit FAFSA. *Unit head:* Dr. Karen Rasmussen, Chairperson, 850-474-2301, Fax: 850-474-2804. *Application contact:* Terry McCray, Assistant Director of Graduate Admissions, 850-473-7718, Fax: 850-473-7714, E-mail: gradadmissions@uwf.edu.

Financial Engineering

Claremont Graduate University, Graduate Programs, Financial Engineering Program, Claremont, CA 91711-6160. Offers MSFE, MS/EMBA, MS/MBA, MS/PhD. *Students:* 47 full-time (11 women), 11 part-time (5 women); includes 6 minority (5 Asian Americans or Pacific Islanders, 1 Hispanic American), 37 international. Average age 27. In 2009, 38 master's awarded. *Entrance requirements:* For master's, GRE General Test or GMAT. Additional exam requirements/recommendations for international students: Required—TOEFL (minimum score 550 paper-based; 213 computer-based; 80 iBT). *Application deadline:* For fall admission, 2/1 priority date for domestic students. Applications are processed on a rolling basis. Application fee: $60. Electronic applications accepted. *Expenses:* Tuition: Full-time $35,046; part-time $1524 per credit. Required fees: $161 per semester. *Financial support:* Fellowships, Federal Work-Study, institutionally sponsored loans, and scholarships/grants available. Support available to part-time students. Financial award application deadline: 2/15; financial award applicants required to submit FAFSA. *Unit head:* Jim Mills, Co-Director, 909-607-3310, E-mail: jim.mills@cgu.edu. *Application contact:* Christina Wassanaar, Administrative Director, 909-607-7812, E-mail: christina.wassenaar@cgu.edu.

See Close-Up on page 295.

Columbia University, Fu Foundation School of Engineering and Applied Science, Department of Industrial Engineering and Operations Research, New York, NY 10027. Offers engineering management systems (MS); financial engineering (MS); industrial engineering (Engr); industrial engineering and operations research (MS, Eng Sc D, PhD); MS/MBA. Part-time and evening/weekend programs available. Postbaccalaureate distance learning degree programs offered (no on-campus study). *Faculty:* 13 full-time (1 woman), 3 part-time/adjunct (1 woman). *Students:* 260 full-time (69 women), 173 part-time (50 women); includes 27 minority (1 African American, 24 Asian Americans or Pacific Islanders, 2 Hispanic Americans), 348 international. Average age 25. 1,262 applicants, 35% accepted, 193 enrolled. In 2009, 211 master's, 7 doctorates awarded. *Degree requirements:* For doctorate, thesis/dissertation, oral and written qualifying exams. *Entrance requirements:* For master's, doctorate, and Engr, GRE General Test. Additional exam requirements/recommendations for international students: Required—TOEFL. *Application deadline:* For fall admission, 12/1 priority date for domestic and international students; for spring admission, 10/1 priority date for domestic and international students. Application fee: $70. Electronic applications accepted. *Financial support:* In 2009–10, 49 students received support, including 6 fellowships (averaging $2,500 per year), 23 research assistantships with full tuition reimbursements available (averaging $22,500 per year), 20 teaching assistantships with full tuition reimbursements available (averaging $22,500 per year); career-related internships or fieldwork, health care benefits, and unspecified assistantships also available. Financial award application deadline: 12/1; financial award applicants required to submit FAFSA. *Faculty research:* Combinatorial optimization and mathematical programming; financial engineering; supply chain management and inventory theory; applied probability; queuing theory; scheduling, and simulation. *Unit head:* Dr. Cliff S. Stein, Department Chair; Professor, 212-854-5238, Fax: 212-854-8103, E-mail: cliff@ieor.columbia.edu. *Application contact:* Adina Berrios Brooks, Student Affairs Manager, 212-854-1934, Fax: 212-854-8103, E-mail: admit@ieor.columbia.edu.

HEC Montreal, School of Business Administration, Master of Science Programs in Administration, Program in Financial Engineering, Montréal, QC H3T 2A7, Canada. Offers M Sc. All courses are given in French. Part-time programs available. *Students:* 42 full-time (11 women), 4 part-time (0 women). 56 applicants, 52% accepted, 10 enrolled. In 2009, 12 master's awarded. *Degree requirements:* For master's, one foreign language, thesis. *Application deadline:* For fall admission, 3/15 for domestic and international students; for winter admission, 9/15 for domestic and international students. Application fee: $77 Canadian dollars. Electronic applications accepted. Tuition and fees charges are reported in Canadian dollars. *Expenses:* Tuition, area resident: Part-time $65.60 Canadian dollars per credit. Tuition, state resident: full-time $2361.60 Canadian dollars; part-time $183.36 Canadian dollars per credit. Tuition, nonresident: full-time $6601 Canadian dollars; part-time $448.13 Canadian dollars per credit. International tuition: $16,132.68 Canadian dollars full-time. Required fees: $1254.15 Canadian dollars; $28.99 Canadian dollars per course. $91.68 Canadian dollars per term. Tuition and fees vary according to degree level and program. *Financial support:* Fellowships, research assistantships, teaching assistantships, scholarships/grants available. Financial award application deadline: 10/2. *Unit head:* Dr. Claude Laurin, Director, 514-340-6485, Fax: 514-340-5690, E-mail: claude.laurin@hec.ca. *Application contact:* Francine Blais, Administrative Director, 514-340-6112, Fax: 514-340-6411, E-mail: francine.blais@hec.ca.

The International University of Monaco, Graduate Programs, Monte Carlo, Monaco. Offers entrepreneurship (EMBA, MBA); financial engineering (M Sc); hedge fund and private equity (M Sc); international marketing (EMBA, MBA); international wealth management (M Sc); luxury goods and services (EMBA, M Sc, MBA); wealth and asset management (EMBA, MBA). Part-time programs available. *Degree requirements:* For master's, comprehensive exam (for some programs), applied research project. *Entrance requirements:* Additional exam requirements/recommendations for international students: Required—TOEFL (minimum score 550 paper-based; 213 computer-based), IELTS. Electronic applications accepted. *Faculty research:* Gaming, leadership, disintermediation.

Kent State University, Graduate School of Management, Program in Financial Engineering, Kent, OH 44242-0001. Offers MSFE. *Faculty:* 6 full-time (2 women). *Students:* 48 full-time (23 women); includes 2 minority (1 African American, 1 Asian American or Pacific Islander), 41 international. Average age 26. 170 applicants, 85% accepted, 48 enrolled. In 2009, 15 master's awarded. *Degree requirements:* For master's, capstone project. *Entrance requirements:* For master's, GMAT or GRE. Additional exam requirements/recommendations for international students: Required—TOEFL (minimum score 525 paper-based; 196 computer-based; 71 iBT). *Application deadline:* For fall admission, 2/1 priority date for domestic students, 2/1 for international students. Application fee: $30 ($60 for international students). Electronic applications accepted. *Financial support:* In 2009–10, 2 students received support, including 2 research assistantships with full tuition reimbursements available (averaging $12,000 per year); Federal Work-Study also available. Financial award application deadline: 2/1. *Faculty research:* Stochastic models, financial derivatives. *Unit head:* Dr. Mark E. Holder, Associate Professor, 330-672-2426, Fax: 330-672-9806, E-mail: mholder@kent.edu. *Application contact:* Rebecca Evans, Program Administrator, 330-672-0190, Fax: 330-672-9806, E-mail: msfe@kent.edu.

North Carolina State University, Graduate School, College of Agriculture and Life Sciences and College of Engineering and College of Physical and Mathematical Sciences, Program in Financial Mathematics, Raleigh, NC 27695. Offers MFM. Part-time programs available. *Degree requirements:* For master's, thesis optional, project/internship. *Entrance requirements:* For master's, GRE General Test. Additional exam requirements/recommendations for international students: Required—TOEFL (minimum score 550 paper-based; 213 computer-based). Electronic applications accepted. *Faculty research:* Financial mathematics modeling and computation, futures, options and commodities markets, real options, credit risk, portfolio optimization.

Polytechnic Institute of NYU, Department of Finance and Risk Engineering, Brooklyn, NY 11201-2990. Offers financial engineering (MS, Advanced Certificate), including capital markets (MS), computational finance (MS), financial technology (MS); financial technology management (Advanced Certificate); organizational behavior (Advanced Certificate); risk management (Advanced Certificate); technology management (Advanced Certificate). Part-time and evening/weekend programs available. *Faculty:* 6 full-time (1 woman), 20 part-time/adjunct (4 women). *Students:* 196 full-time (71 women), 79 part-time (15 women); includes 28 minority (5 African Americans, 23 Asian Americans or Pacific Islanders), 202 international. Average age 26. 497 applicants, 45% accepted, 85 enrolled. In 2009, 102 master's awarded. *Degree requirements:* For master's, comprehensive exam (for some programs), thesis (for some programs). *Entrance requirements:* For master's, GMAT, minimum B average in undergraduate course work. Additional exam requirements/recommendations for international students: Required—TOEFL (minimum score 550 paper-based; 213 computer-based; 80 iBT); Recommended—IELTS (minimum score 6.5). *Application deadline:* For fall admission, 7/31 priority date for domestic students, 4/30 priority date for international students; for spring admission, 12/31 priority date for domestic students, 11/30 priority date for international students. Applications are processed on a rolling basis. Application fee: $75. Electronic applications accepted. *Expenses:* Tuition: Full-time $21,492; part-time $1194 per credit hour. Required fees: $1160; $204 per course. *Financial support:* Institutionally sponsored loans, scholarships/grants, and unspecified assistantships available. Support available to part-time students. Financial award applicants required to submit FAFSA. *Unit head:* Prof. Charles S. Tapiero, Academic Director, 718-260-3653, Fax: 718-260-3874, E-mail: ctapiero@poly.edu. *Application contact:* JeanCarlo Bonilla, Director of Graduate Enrollment Management, 718-260-3182, Fax: 718-260-3624.

Polytechnic Institute of NYU, Long Island Graduate Center, Graduate Programs, Department of Finance and Risk Engineering, Major in Financial Engineering, Melville, NY 11747. Offers MS, AC. Part-time and evening/weekend programs available. *Entrance requirements:* Additional exam requirements/recommendations for international students: Required—TOEFL (minimum score 550 paper-based; 213 computer-based; 80 iBT); Recommended—IELTS (minimum score 6.5). *Application deadline:* For fall admission, 7/31 priority date for domestic students, 4/30 priority date for international students; for spring admission, 12/31 priority date for domestic students, 11/30 priority date for international students. Applications are processed on a rolling basis. Application fee: $75. Electronic applications accepted. *Financial support:* Institutionally sponsored loans, scholarships/grants, and unspecified assistantships available. Support available to part-time students. *Unit head:* Dr. Charles S. Tapiero, Department Head, 718-260-3653, E-mail: ctapiero@poly.edu. *Application contact:* JeanCarlo Bonilla, Director of Graduate Enrollment Management, 718-260-3182, Fax: 718-260-3624, E-mail: gradinfo@poly.edu.

Polytechnic Institute of NYU, Westchester Graduate Center, Graduate Programs, Department of Finance and Risk Engineering, Major in Financial Engineering, Hawthorne, NY 10532-1507. Offers capital markets (MS); computational finance (MS); financial engineering (AC); financial technology (MS); financial technology management (AC); information management (AC). *Students:* 9 full-time (6 women), 8 international. *Degree requirements:* For master's, comprehensive exam (for some programs), thesis (for some programs). *Entrance requirements:* Additional exam requirements/recommendations for international students: Required—TOEFL (minimum score 550 paper-based; 213 computer-based; 80 iBT); Recommended—IELTS (minimum score 6.5). *Application deadline:* For fall admission, 7/31 priority date for domestic students, 4/30 priority date for international students; for spring admission, 12/31 priority date for domestic students, 11/30 priority date for international students. Applications are processed on a rolling basis. Application fee: $75. Electronic applications accepted. *Financial support:* Institutionally sponsored loans, scholarships/grants, and unspecified assistantships available. Support available to part-time students. *Unit head:* Dr. Charles S. Tapiero, Department Head, 718-260-3653, E-mail: ctapiero@poly.edu. *Application contact:* JeanCarlo Bonilla, Director of Graduate Enrollment Management, 718-260-3182, Fax: 718-260-3624, E-mail: gradinfo@poly.edu.

Princeton University, Graduate School, School of Engineering and Applied Science, Department of Operations Research and Financial Engineering, Princeton, NJ 08544-1019. Offers M Eng, MSE, PhD. *Faculty:* 14 full-time (1 woman). Terminal master's awarded for partial completion of doctoral program. *Degree requirements:* For master's, thesis (for some programs), thesis required for M.S.E. degree; no thesis required for M.Eng. degree; for doctorate, thesis/dissertation, general exam. *Entrance requirements:* For master's and doctorate, GRE General Test, official transcript(s), 3 letters of recommendation, personal statement. Additional exam requirements/recommendations for international students: Required—TOEFL. *Application deadline:* For fall admission, 12/31 for domestic and international students. Electronic applications accepted. *Financial support:* Fellowships with full tuition reimbursements, research assistantships with full tuition reimbursements, teaching assistantships with full tuition reimbursements, institutionally sponsored loans and health care benefits available. Financial award application deadline: 1/2. *Faculty research:* Applied and computational mathematics; financial mathematics; optimization, queuing theory, and machine learning; statistics and stochastic analysis; transportation and logistics. *Unit head:* Kimberly Lupinacci, Graduate Program Administrator, 609-258-4018, Fax: 609-258-4363, E-mail: orfgrad@princeton.edu. *Application contact:* Michelle Carman, Manager, Graduate Admissions, 609-258-3034, Fax: 609-258-7262, E-mail: gsadmit@princeton.edu.

Rensselaer Polytechnic Institute, Graduate School, Lally School of Management and Technology, Program in Financial Engineering and Risk Analysis, Troy, NY 12180-3590. *Expenses:* Tuition: Full-time $38,100.

Stevens Institute of Technology, Graduate School, School of Systems and Enterprises, Program in Financial Engineering, Hoboken, NJ 07030. Offers MS. *Expenses:* Tuition: Full-time $9900; part-time $1100 per credit. Required fees: $286 per semester.

Temple University, Graduate School, Fox School of Business, Specialized Master's Programs, Philadelphia, PA 19122-6096. Offers accounting and financial management (MS); actuarial science (MS); finance (MS); financial engineering (MS); healthcare financial management (MS); healthcare management (MHM); human resource management (MS); management information systems (MS); marketing (MS); statistics (MS). *Accreditation:* AACSB. Part-time programs available. *Entrance requirements:* For master's, GRE General Test or GMAT, minimum undergraduate GPA of 3.0. Additional exam requirements/recommendations for international students: Required—TOEFL (minimum score 600 paper-based; 250 computer-based; 100 iBT), IELTS (minimum score 7.5).

University at Buffalo, the State University of New York, Graduate School, School of Management, Buffalo, NY 14260. Offers accounting (MS); business administration (MBA); finance (MS), including financial engineering, financial management; information assurance (Certificate); management (PhD); management information systems (MS); supply chains and operations management (MS); Au D/MBA; JD/MBA; M Arch/MBA; MA/MBA; MD/MBA; MPH/MBA; MSW/MBA; Pharm D/MBA. *Accreditation:* AACSB. Part-time and evening/weekend programs available. *Faculty:* 66 full-time (19 women), 21 part-time/adjunct (4 women). *Students:* 502 full-time (176 women), 199 part-time (54 women); includes 29 minority (10 African Americans, 16 Asian Americans or Pacific Islanders, 3 Hispanic Americans), 306 international. Average age 27. 1,944 applicants, 31% accepted, 324 enrolled. In 2009, 363 master's, 7 doctorates, 3 other advanced degrees awarded. *Degree requirements:* For master's, thesis (for some programs); for doctorate, comprehensive exam, thesis/dissertation. *Entrance requirements:* For master's, GMAT (MBA, MS in accounting), GRE General Test (for all other MS degrees); for doctorate, GMAT or GRE. Additional exam requirements/recommendations for international students: Required—TOEFL (minimum score 230 computer-based; 95 iBT). *Application deadline:* For fall admission, 6/2 priority date for domestic students, 3/1 priority date for international students. Applications are processed on a rolling basis. Application fee: $100. Electronic applications accepted. *Expenses:* Contact institution. *Financial support:* In 2009–10, 91 students received support, including 5 fellowships with full and partial tuition reimbursements available (averaging $4,000 per year), 41 research assistantships with full and partial tuition reimbursements available (averaging $16,000 per year), 28 teaching assistantships with full and partial tuition reimbursements available (averaging $15,000 per year); career-related internships or fieldwork, Federal Work-Study, institutionally sponsored loans, scholarships/grants, health care benefits, and unspecified assistantships also available. Financial award application deadline: 2/15; financial award applicants required to submit FAFSA. *Faculty research:* Earnings management and electronic information assurance, supply chains and operations management, corporate financing and asset pricing, consumer behavior and quantitative modeling of marketing behavior, leadership and politics in organizations. Total annual research expenditures: $230,000. *Unit head:* David W. Frasier, Assistant Dean, 716-645-3204, Fax: 716-645-2341, E-mail: davidf@buffalo.edu. *Application contact:* David W. Frasier, Assistant Dean, 716-645-3204, Fax: 716-645-2341, E-mail: davidf@buffalo.edu.

University of California, Berkeley, Graduate Division, Haas School of Business, Master of Financial Engineering Program, Berkeley, CA 94720-1500. Offers MFE. *Students:* 63 full-time (9 women); includes 8 minority (1 African American, 7 Asian Americans or Pacific Islanders), 41 international. Average age 28. 401 applicants, 25% accepted. In 2009, 64 master's awarded. *Degree requirements:* For master's, comprehensive exam, internship/applied finance project. *Entrance requirements:* For master's, GMAT or GRE (waived if candidate holds PhD), bachelor's degree with minimum GPA of 3.0 or equivalent; two recommendation letters. Additional exam requirements/recommendations for international students: Required—TOEFL (minimum score 570 paper-based; 230 computer-based; 68 iBT). *Application deadline:* For winter admission, 12/1 for domestic students; for spring admission, 9/1 for international students. Applications are processed on a rolling basis. Application fee: $250. Electronic applications accepted. *Expenses:* Contact institution. *Financial support:* Teaching assistantships, scholarships/grants available. Financial award applicants required to submit FAFSA. *Faculty research:* Financial economics, modern portfolio theory, valuation of exotic options, mortgage markets. *Unit head:* Linda Kreitzman, Executive Director, 510-643-4345, Fax: 415-298-0990, E-mail: lindak@haas.berkeley.edu. *Application contact:* Christina Henri, Assistant Director, 510-642-4417, Fax: 510-643-4345, E-mail: mfe@haas.berkeley.edu.

University of Hawaii at Manoa, Graduate Division, Shidler College of Business, Program in Financial Engineering, Honolulu, HI 96822. Offers MS. Part-time programs available. *Faculty:* 8 full-time (1 woman), 2 part-time/adjunct (0 women). *Students:* 29 full-time (4 women); includes 8 minority (1 American Indian/Alaska Native, 7 Asian Americans or Pacific Islanders), 16 international. Average age 27. 61 applicants, 66% accepted. *Degree requirements:* For master's, thesis optional. *Entrance requirements:* For master's, GRE General Test. Additional exam requirements/recommendations for international students: Required—TOEFL (minimum score 600 paper-based; 250 computer-based; 100 iBT), IELTS (minimum score 7). *Application deadline:* For fall admission, 5/1 for domestic students. Application fee: $60. *Expenses:* Tuition, state resident: full-time $8900; part-time $372 per credit. Tuition, nonresident: full-time $21,400; part-time $898 per credit. Required fees: $207 per semester. *Financial support:* In 2009–10, 8 fellowships (averaging $2,869 per year), 2 research assistantships (averaging $18,210 per year), 1 teaching assistantship (averaging $15,558 per year) were awarded. Total annual research expenditures: $20,000. *Unit head:* Gunter Eric Meissner, Gradiate Chair, Director, 808-956-2535, Fax: 808-956-9887, E-mail: meissner@hawaii.edu. *Application contact:* V. Vance Roley, Dean, 808-956-8377.

University of Illinois at Urbana–Champaign, Graduate College, College of Engineering, Department of Industrial and Enterprise Systems Engineering, Champaign, IL 61820. Offers financial engineering (MS); industrial engineering (MS, PhD); systems and entrepreneurial engineering (MS, PhD); MBA/MS. *Faculty:* 21 full-time (5 women), 1 part-time/adjunct (0 women). *Students:* 56 full-time (18 women), 17 part-time (7 women); includes 1 minority (African American), 54 international. 255 applicants, 9% accepted, 16 enrolled. In 2009, 13 master's, 7 doctorates awarded. *Entrance requirements:* For master's and doctorate, GRE, minimum GPA of 3.25. Additional exam requirements/recommendations for international students: Required—TOEFL (minimum score 613 paper-based; 257 computer-based; 103 iBT), or IELTS (minimum score 7). *Application deadline:* Applications are processed on a rolling basis. Application fee: $60 ($75 for international students). Electronic applications accepted. *Financial support:* In 2009–10, 7 fellowships, 37 research assistantships, 44 teaching assistantships were awarded; tuition waivers (full and partial) also available. *Unit head:* Jong-Shi Pang, Head, 217-244-5703, Fax: 217-244-5705, E-mail: jspang@illinois.edu. *Application contact:* Donna J. Eiskamp, Coordinator of Graduate Programs, 217-333-2730, Fax: 217-244-5705, E-mail: deiskamp@illinois.edu.

University of Tulsa, Graduate School, Collins College of Business, Program in Finance, Tulsa, OK 74104-3189. Offers corporate finance (MS); investments and portfolio management (MS); risk management (MS); JD/MSF; MBA/MSF; MSF/MSAM. Part-time and evening/weekend programs available. *Faculty:* 10 full-time (1 woman). *Students:* 21 full-time (10 women), 7 part-time (5 women); includes 1 minority (Hispanic American), 10 international. Average age 25. 62 applicants, 52% accepted, 8 enrolled. In 2009, 11 master's awarded. *Degree requirements:* For master's, thesis optional. *Entrance requirements:* For master's, GMAT or GRE. Additional exam requirements/recommendations for international students: Required—TOEFL (minimum score 575 paper-based; 231 computer-based), IELTS (minimum score 6.5). *Application deadline:* Applications are processed on a rolling basis. Application fee: $40. Electronic applications accepted. *Expenses:* Tuition: Full-time $16,182; part-time $899 per credit hour. Required fees: $4 per credit hour. Tuition and fees vary according to course load. *Financial support:* In 2009–10, 8 students received support, including 1 research assistantship with full and partial tuition reimbursement available (averaging $12,088 per year), 7 teaching assistantships with full and partial tuition reimbursements available (averaging $9,506 per year); fellowships with full and partial tuition reimbursements available, career-related internships or fieldwork, Federal Work-Study, institutionally sponsored loans, scholarships/grants, health care benefits, tuition waivers (full and partial), and unspecified assistantships also available. Support available to part-time students. Financial award application deadline: 2/1; financial award applicants required to submit FAFSA. *Unit head:* Dr. Markham Collins, Associate Dean of the Collins College of Business, 918-631-2783, Fax: 918-631-2142, E-mail: markham-collins@utulsa.edu. *Application contact:* Dr. Markham Collins, Associate Dean of the Collins College of Business, 918-631-2783, Fax: 918-631-2142, E-mail: markham-collins@utulsa.edu.

Game Design and Development

Academy of Art University, Graduate Program, School of Animation and Visual Effects, San Francisco, CA 94105-3410. Offers 2D animation (MFA); 3D animation (MFA); 3D modeling (MFA); games (MFA); visual effects (MFA). Part-time programs available. Postbaccalaureate distance learning degree programs offered (no on-campus study). *Degree requirements:* For master's, final review. *Entrance requirements:* For master's, portfolio. Electronic applications accepted.

Concordia University, School of Graduate Studies, Faculty of Engineering and Computer Science, Concordia Institute for Information Systems Engineering (CIISE), Montréal, QC H3G 1M8, Canada. Offers 3D graphics and game development (Certificate); information systems security (M Eng, MA Sc); quality systems engineering (M Eng, MA Sc); service engineering and network management (Certificate).

DePaul University, College of Computing and Digital Media, Chicago, IL 60604. Offers business information technology (MS); computational finance (MS); computer and information sciences (PhD); computer game development (MS); computer graphics and motion technology (MS); computer science (MS); computer, information and network security (MS), including applied technology; digital cinema (MFA, MS), including information technology project management (MS); e-commerce technology (MS); human-computer interaction (MS); information systems (MS); information technology (MA); information technology project management (MS); software engineering (MS); telecommunications systems (MS); JD/MS. Part-time and evening/weekend programs available. Postbaccalaureate distance learning degree programs offered (no on-campus study). *Faculty:* 78 full-time (16 women), 191 part-time/adjunct (51 women). *Students:* 922 full-time (239 women), 887 part-time (209 women); includes 466 minority (193 African Americans, 3 American Indian/Alaska Native, 162 Asian Americans or Pacific Islanders, 108 Hispanic Americans), 276 international. Average age 31. 853 applicants, 67% accepted, 294 enrolled. In 2009, 444 master's, 4 doctorates awarded. *Degree requirements:* For master's, thesis (for some programs); for doctorate, comprehensive exam, thesis/dissertation. *Entrance requirements:* For master's, GRE or GMAT (MS in computational finance only), bachelor's degree; for doctorate, GRE, master's degree in computer science. Additional exam requirements/recommendations for international students: Required—TOEFL (minimum score 550 paper-based; 213 computer-based), IELTS (minimum score 6.5), Pearson Test of English (minimum score 53). *Application deadline:* For fall admission, 8/15 priority date for domestic students, 6/1 priority date for international students; for winter admission, 12/15 priority date for domestic students, 9/15 priority date for international students; for spring admission, 3/1 priority date for domestic students, 12/15 priority date for international students. Applications are processed on a rolling basis. Application fee: $25. Electronic applications accepted. *Expenses:* Contact institution. *Financial support:* In 2009–10, 69 students received support, including 6 fellowships with full tuition reimbursements available (averaging $25,858 per year), 75 teaching assistantships with full and partial tuition reimbursements available (averaging $5,780 per year); research assistantships, Federal Work-Study, scholarships/grants, tuition waivers (full and partial), and unspecified assistantships also available. Support available to part-time students. Financial award application deadline: 4/30; financial award applicants required to submit FAFSA. *Faculty research:* Bioinformatics, visual computing, graphics and animation, high performance and scientific computing, databases. Total annual research expenditures: $790,000. *Unit head:* Dr. David Miller, Dean, 312-362-8381, Fax: 312-362-5185. *Application contact:* Dr. Liz Friedman, Assistant Dean of Student Services, 312-362-5384, Fax: 312-362-5327, E-mail: efriedm2@cdm.depaul.edu.

Full Sail University, Game Design Master of Science Program—Campus, Winter Park, FL 32792-7437. Offers MS.

George Mason University, Volgenau School of Information Technology and Engineering, Department of Computer Science, Fairfax, VA 22030. Offers biometrics (Certificate); computer games technology (Certificate); computer networking (Certificate); computer science (MS, PhD); data mining (Certificate); database management (Certificate); electronic commerce (Certificate); foundations of information systems (Certificate); information engineering (Certificate); information security and assurance (MS, Certificate); information systems (MS); intelligent agents (Certificate); software architecture (Certificate); software engineering (MS, Certificate); systems engineering (MS); Web-based software engineering (Certificate). Part-time and evening/weekend programs available. Postbaccalaureate distance learning degree programs offered. *Faculty:* 42 full-time (9 women), 18 part-time/adjunct (0 women). *Students:* 121 full-time (36 women), 489 part-time (118 women); includes 90 minority (11 African Americans, 70 Asian Americans or Pacific Islanders, 9 Hispanic Americans), 222 international. Average age 29. 882 applicants, 58% accepted, 147 enrolled. In 2009, 202 master's, 6 doctorates, 21 other advanced degrees awarded. *Degree requirements:* For master's, thesis optional; for doctorate, comprehensive exam, thesis/dissertation. *Entrance requirements:* For master's, GRE General Test, minimum GPA of 3.0 in last 60 hours, 3 letters of recommendation; for doctorate, GRE, 4-year BA degree, academic work in computer science, 3 letters of recommendation, statement of career goals and aspirations. Additional exam requirements/recommendations for international students: Required—TOEFL. *Application deadline:* For fall admission, 4/15 priority date for domestic students, 1/15 for international students; for spring admission, 11/15 for domestic students. Application fee: $75. Electronic applications accepted. *Expenses:* Tuition, state resident: full-time $7568; part-time $315.33 per credit hour. Tuition, nonresident: full-time $21,704; part-time $904.33 per credit hour. Required fees: $2184; $91 per credit hour. *Financial support:* In 2009–10, 106 students received support, including 3 fellowships (averaging $18,000 per year), 53 research assistantships (averaging $11,119 per year), 53 teaching assistantships (averaging $7,881 per year); unspecified assistantships and health care benefits (full-time research or teaching assistantship recipients) also available. Financial award application deadline: 3/1; financial award applicants required to submit FAFSA. *Faculty research:* Artificial intelligence, image processing/graphics, parallel/distributed systems, software engineering systems. Total annual research expenditures: $1.3 million. *Unit head:* Dr. Arun Sood, Director, 703-993-1524, Fax: 703-993-1710, E-mail: asood@gmu.edu. *Application contact:* Jay Shapiro, Professor, 703-993-1485, E-mail: jshapiro@gmu.edu.

Michigan State University, The Graduate School, College of Communication Arts and Sciences, Department of Telecommunication, Information Studies, and Media, East Lansing, MI 48824. Offers digital media arts and technology (MA); information and telecommunication management (MA); information, policy and society (MA); serious game design (MA). *Entrance requirements:* Additional exam requirements/recommendations for international students: Required—TOEFL. Electronic applications accepted.

National University, Academic Affairs, School of Media and Communication, Department of Media, La Jolla, CA 92037-1011. Offers digital cinema (MFA); educational and instructional technology (MS); video game production and design (MFA). Part-time and evening/weekend programs available. Postbaccalaureate distance learning degree programs offered (no on-campus study). *Faculty:* 9 full-time (4 women), 13 part-time/adjunct (4 women). *Students:* 68 full-time (26 women), 118 part-time (45 women); includes 64 minority (29 African Americans, 10 Asian Americans or Pacific Islanders, 25 Hispanic Americans), 1 international. Average age 39. 118 applicants, 100% accepted, 70 enrolled. In 2009, 58 master's awarded. *Degree requirements:* For master's, thesis. *Entrance requirements:* For master's, interview, minimum GPA of 2.5. Additional exam requirements/recommendations for international students: Required—TOEFL (minimum score 550 paper-based; 213 computer-based; 79 iBT), IELTS (minimum score 6). *Application deadline:* Applications are processed on a rolling basis. Application fee: $60 ($65 for international students). Electronic applications accepted. *Expenses:* Tuition: Part-time $338 per quarter hour. *Financial support:* Career-related internships or fieldwork, institutionally sponsored loans, scholarships/grants, and tuition waivers (partial) available. Support available to part-time students. Financial award application deadline: 6/30; financial award applicants required to submit FAFSA. *Unit head:* Dr. Timothy Langdell, Department Chair, 310-662-2149, Fax: 858-309-3450, E-mail: tlangdell@nu.edu. *Application contact:* Dominick Giovanniello, Associate Regional Dean—San Diego, 800-NAT-UNIV, Fax: 858-541-7792, E-mail: dgiovann@nu.edu.

Rochester Institute of Technology, Graduate Enrollment Services, B. Thomas Golisano College of Computing and Information Sciences, Department of Interactive Games and Media, Rochester, NY 14623-5603. Offers game design and development (MS). Part-time programs available. *Students:* 19 full-time (3 women), 2 part-time (0 women); includes 1 minority (Hispanic American), 2 international. Average age 26. 24 applicants, 54% accepted, 8 enrolled. In 2009, 3 master's awarded. *Degree requirements:* For master's, thesis. *Entrance requirements:* For master's, GRE, minimum GPA of 3.25. Additional exam requirements/recommendations for international students: Required—TOEFL (minimum score 570 paper-based; 230 computer-based; 88 iBT), or IELTS (minimum score 6.5). *Application deadline:* For fall admission, 1/15 priority date for domestic students, 1/1 priority date for international students. Applications are processed on a rolling basis. Application fee: $50. Electronic applications accepted. *Expenses:* Tuition: Full-time $31,533; part-time $876 per credit hour. Required fees: $210. *Financial support:* In 2009–10, 19 students received support; research assistantships with partial tuition reimbursements available, teaching assistantships with partial tuition reimbursements available, career-related internships or fieldwork, scholarships/grants, and unspecified assistantships available. Support available to part-time students. Financial award applicants required to submit FAFSA. *Faculty research:* Experimental game design and development, exploratory research in visualization environments and integrated media frameworks, outreach efforts that surround games and underlying technologies, support of STEM learning through games and interactive entertainment, the application of games and game technology to non-entertainment domains (Serious Games), small, discrete play experiences (Casual Games). *Unit head:* Andrew Phelps, Chair, 585-475-6464, Fax: 585-475-2181, E-mail: informaticsgrad@rit.edu. *Application contact:* Diane Ellison, Assistant Vice President, Graduate Enrollment Services, 585-475-2229, Fax: 585-475-7164, E-mail: gradinfo@rit.edu.

Savannah College of Art and Design, Graduate School, Program in Interactive Design and Game Development, Savannah, GA 31402-3146. Offers MA, MFA. Part-time programs available. *Degree requirements:* For master's, thesis, internships. *Entrance requirements:* For master's, interview, portfolio. Additional exam requirements/recommendations for international students: Required—TOEFL (minimum score 450 paper-based; 133 computer-based). Electronic applications accepted. *Expenses:* Tuition: Full-time $28,515; part-time $627 per credit hour. One-time fee: $500. Tuition and fees vary according to course load.

University of Advancing Technology, Master of Science Program in Technology, Tempe, AZ 85283-1042. Offers advancing computer science (MS); emerging technologies (MS); game production and management (MS); information assurance (MS); technology leadership (MS). *Degree requirements:* For master's, project or thesis. *Entrance requirements:* Additional exam requirements/recommendations for international students: Required—TOEFL (minimum score 550 paper-based). Electronic applications accepted. *Faculty research:* Artificial intelligence, fractals, organizational management.

University of Southern California, Graduate School, Viterbi School of Engineering, Department of Computer Science, Los Angeles, CA 90089. Offers computer networks (MS); computer science (MS, PhD); computer security (MS); game development (MS); high performance computing and simulations (MS); human language technology (MS); intelligent robotics (MS); multimedia and creative technologies (MS); software engineering (MS). Part-time programs available. Postbaccalaureate distance learning degree programs offered (no on-campus study). *Faculty:* 26 full-time (2 women), 56 part-time/adjunct (7 women). *Students:* 711 full-time (148 women), 304 part-time (55 women); includes 76 minority (5 African Americans, 59 Asian Americans or Pacific Islanders, 12 Hispanic Americans), 816 international. 2,017 applicants, 39% accepted, 382 enrolled. In 2009, 332 master's, 32 doctorates awarded. Terminal master's awarded for partial completion of doctoral program. *Degree requirements:* For doctorate, comprehensive exam, thesis/dissertation. *Entrance requirements:* For master's, GRE General Test; for doctorate, General GRE. *Application deadline:* For fall admission, 3/1 priority date for domestic and international students; for spring admission, 10/1 priority date for domestic and international students. Applications are processed on a rolling basis. Application fee: $85. Electronic applications accepted. *Expenses:* Tuition: Full-time $25,980; part-time $1315 per unit. Required fees: $554. One-time fee: $35 full-time. Full-time tuition and fees vary according to degree level and program. *Financial support:* In 2009–10, fellowships with full tuition reimbursements (averaging $30,000 per year), research assistantships with full tuition reimbursements (averaging $19,250 per year), teaching assistantships with full tuition reimbursements (averaging $19,250 per year) were awarded; career-related internships or fieldwork, scholarships/grants, health care benefits, and unspecified assistantships also available. Financial award application deadline: 12/1; financial award applicants required to submit CSS PROFILE or FAFSA. *Faculty research:* Databases, computer graphics and computer vision, software engineering, networks and security, robotics, multimedia and virtual reality. Total annual research expenditures: $10 million. *Unit head:* Dr. Shanghua Teng, Seeley G. Mudd Professor of Engineering and Department Chair, 213-740-4498, E-mail: shanghua@ usc.edu. *Application contact:* Steve Schrader, Director of Student Affairs, 213-740-4779, E-mail: steve.schrader@usc.edu.

Health Informatics

American Sentinel University, Graduate Programs, Englewood, CO 80112. Offers business administration (MBA); business intelligence (MS); computer science (MSCS); health information management (MS); healthcare (MBA); information systems (MSIS); nursing (MSN). Part-time and evening/weekend programs available. Postbaccalaureate distance learning degree programs offered (no on-campus study). *Entrance requirements:* Additional exam requirements/recommendations for international students: Required—TOEFL (minimum score 600 paper-based; 215 computer-based). Electronic applications accepted.

Arkansas Tech University, Graduate College, College of Natural and Health Sciences, Russellville, AR 72801. Offers fisheries and wildlife biology (MS); health informatics (MS); nursing (MSN). *Students:* 6 full-time (5 women), 12 part-time (6 women). Average age 31. In 2009, 1 master's awarded. *Degree requirements:* For master's, thesis, project. *Entrance requirements:* For master's, GRE General Test. Additional exam requirements/recommendations for international students: Required—TOEFL (minimum score 550 paper-based; 213 computer-based; 79 iBT), IELTS (minimum score 6). *Application deadline:* For fall admission, 3/1 priority date for domestic students, 5/1 priority date for international students; for spring admission, 10/1 priority date for domestic and international students. Applications are processed on a rolling basis. Application fee: $0 ($30 for international students). Electronic applications accepted. *Expenses:* Tuition, state resident: full-time $3438; part-time $191 per hour. Tuition, nonresident: full-time $6876; part-time $382 per hour. Required fees: $482; $9 per credit hour. $140 per semester. Tuition and fees vary according to course load. *Financial support:* In 2009–10, teaching assistantships with full tuition reimbursements (averaging $4,000 per year); research assistantships, career-related internships or fieldwork, Federal Work-Study, scholarships/ grants, health care benefits, and unspecified assistantships also available. Support available to part-time students. Financial award application deadline: 4/15; financial award applicants required to submit FAFSA. *Faculty research:* Fisheries, warblers, fish movement, darter populations, bob white studies. *Unit head:* Dr. Richard Cohoon, Dean, 479-964-0816, E-mail: richard. cohoon@atu.edu. *Application contact:* Dr. Mary B. Gunter, Dean of Graduate College, 479-968-0398, Fax: 479-964-0542, E-mail: graduate.school@atu.edu.

Barry University, College of Health Sciences, Graduate Certificate Programs, Miami Shores, FL 33161-6695. Offers health care leadership (Certificate); health care planning and informatics (Certificate); histotechnology (Certificate); long term care management (Certificate); medical group practice management (Certificate); quality improvement and outcomes management (Certificate).

Benedictine University, Graduate Programs, Program in Public Health, Lisle, IL 60532-0900. Offers administration of health care institutions (MPH); dietetics (MPH); disaster management (MPH); health education (MPH); health information systems (MPH); MBA/MPH; MPH/MS. Part-time and evening/weekend programs available. Postbaccalaureate distance learning degree programs offered. *Entrance requirements:* For master's, MAT, GRE, or GMAT. Additional exam requirements/recommendations for international students: Required—TOEFL (minimum score 550 paper-based; 213 computer-based).

Claremont Graduate University, Graduate Programs, School of Information Systems and Technology, Claremont, CA 91711-6160. Offers electronic commerce (MS, PhD); health information management (MS); information systems (Certificate); knowledge management (MS, PhD); systems development (MS, PhD); telecommunications and networking (MS, PhD); MBA/MS. Part-time programs available. *Faculty:* 6 full-time (1 woman), 1 part-time/adjunct (0 women). *Students:* 78 full-time (28 women), 35 part-time (11 women); includes 32 minority (8 African Americans, 1 American Indian/Alaska Native, 16 Asian Americans or Pacific Islanders, 7 Hispanic Americans), 32 international. Average age 38. In 2009, 31 master's, 11 doctorates, 1 other advanced degree awarded. *Degree requirements:* For doctorate, comprehensive exam, thesis/dissertation, portfolio. *Entrance requirements:* For master's and doctorate, GMAT, GRE General Test. Additional exam requirements/recommendations for international students: Required—TOEFL (minimum score 550 paper-based; 213 computer-based; 80 iBT). *Application deadline:* For fall admission, 2/1 priority date for domestic students. Applications are processed on a rolling basis. Application fee: $60. Electronic applications accepted. *Expenses:* Tuition: Full-time $35,046; part-time $1524 per credit. Required fees: $161 per semester. *Financial support:* Fellowships, research assistantships, teaching assistantships, Federal Work-Study, institutionally sponsored loans, and scholarships/grants available. Support available to part-time students. Financial award application deadline: 2/15; financial award applicants required to submit FAFSA. *Faculty research:* GPSS, man-machine interaction, organizational aspects of computing, implementation of information systems, information systems practice. *Unit head:* Terry Ryan, Dean, 909-607-9591, Fax: 909-621-8564, E-mail: terry.ryan@cgu.edu. *Application contact:* Matt Hutter, Director of External Affairs, 909-621-3180, Fax: 909-621-8564, E-mail: matt.hutter@cgu.edu.

The College of St. Scholastica, Graduate Studies, Department of Health Information Management, Duluth, MN 55811-4199. Offers MA, Certificate. Part-time programs available. Postbaccalaureate distance learning degree programs offered (minimal on-campus study). *Degree requirements:* For master's, thesis. *Entrance requirements:* For master's, minimum GPA of 3.0. Additional exam requirements/recommendations for international students: Required—TOEFL (minimum score 550 paper-based; 213 computer-based; 79 iBT). Electronic applications accepted. *Expenses:* Contact institution. *Faculty research:* Electronic health record implementation, personal health records, Athens project.

Emory University, Graduate School of Arts and Sciences, Department of Biostatistics, Atlanta, GA 30322-1100. Offers biostatistics (MPH, MSPH, PhD); public health informatics (MSPH). *Degree requirements:* For doctorate, comprehensive exam, thesis/dissertation. *Entrance requirements:* For doctorate, GRE General Test. Additional exam requirements/recommendations for international students: Required—TOEFL (minimum score 550 paper-based; 220 computer-based). Electronic applications accepted. *Faculty research:* Vaccine efficacy, clinical trials, spatial statistics, statistical genetics, neuroimaging.

Emory University, Rollins School of Public Health, Program in Public Health Informatics, Atlanta, GA 30322-1100. Offers MSPH. Part-time programs available. *Degree requirements:* For master's, thesis, practicum. *Entrance requirements:* For master's, GRE General Test. Additional exam requirements/recommendations for international students: Required—TOEFL (minimum score 550 paper-based; 213 computer-based; 80 iBT). Electronic applications accepted. *Expenses:* Contact institution.

George Mason University, College of Health and Human Services, Department of Health Administration and Policy, Fairfax, VA 22030. Offers assisted living/senior housing administration (Certificate); health and medical policy (MS); health care security and privacy (Certificate); health information systems (Certificate); health systems management (MS); quality improvement and outcomes management in health care (Certificate); risk management and patient safety (Certificate); senior housing administration (MS). *Faculty:* 13 full-time (3 women), 10 part-time/ adjunct (6 women). *Students:* 26 full-time (15 women), 95 part-time (75 women); includes 30 minority (13 African Americans, 12 Asian Americans or Pacific Islanders, 5 Hispanic Americans), 9 international. Average age 33. 74 applicants, 59% accepted, 31 enrolled. In 2009, 19 master's, 5 other advanced degrees awarded. *Degree requirements:* For master's, comprehensive exam, internship. *Entrance requirements:* For master's, GRE, curriculum vitae, 2 letters of recommendation. Additional exam requirements/recommendations for international students: Required—TOEFL. *Application deadline:* For fall admission, 3/1 priority date for domestic students; for spring admission, 11/1 for domestic students. Applications are processed on a rolling basis. Application fee: $75. Electronic applications accepted. *Expenses:* Tuition, state resident: full-time $7568; part-time $315.33 per credit hour. Tuition, nonresident: full-time $21,704; part-time $904.33 per credit hour. Required fees: $2184; $91 per credit hour. *Financial support:* In 2009–10, 1 student received support, including 1 research assistantship with full and partial tuition reimbursement available (averaging $4,440 per year); Federal Work-Study, scholarships/grants, unspecified assistantships, and health care benefits (full-time research or teaching assistantship recipients) also available. Support available to part-time students. *Faculty research:* Universal health care, publications, relationships between malpractice pressure and rates of cesarean section and VBAC, seniors and Wii gaming, relationships between changes in physician's incomes and practice settings and their care to Medicaid and charity patients. Total annual research expenditures: $838,668. *Unit head:* Dr. P. J. Maddox, Chair, 703-993-1982, E-mail: pmaddox@gmu.edu. *Application contact:* Adam McCutcheon, Office Manager, 703-993-1929, E-mail: amccutch@gmu.edu.

Indiana University Bloomington, School of Informatics, Bloomington, IN 47408. Offers bioinformatics (MS); chemical informatics (MS); computer science (MS, PhD); health informatics (MS); human computer interaction (MS); informatics (PhD); laboratory informatics (MS); media arts and science (MS); music informatics (MS); security informatics (MS); MS/PhD. PhD offered through University Graduate School. Part-time programs available. Postbaccalaureate distance learning degree programs offered (no on-campus study). *Faculty:* 63 full-time (12 women). *Students:* 367 full-time (93 women), 32 part-time (11 women); includes 18 minority (4 African Americans, 1 American Indian/Alaska Native, 11 Asian Americans or Pacific Islanders, 2 Hispanic Americans), 254 international. Average age 27. 676 applicants, 52% accepted, 146

enrolled. In 2009, 82 master's, 18 doctorates awarded. Terminal master's awarded for partial completion of doctoral program. *Degree requirements:* For master's, thesis optional; for doctorate, comprehensive exam, thesis/dissertation, oral and written exams. *Entrance requirements:* For master's and doctorate, GRE, letters of reference. Additional exam requirements/ recommendations for international students: Required—TOEFL. *Application deadline:* For fall admission, 1/15 for domestic students, 12/1 for international students. Application fee: $55 ($65 for international students). Electronic applications accepted. *Financial support:* In 2009–10, 2 fellowships with full and partial tuition reimbursements (averaging $20,000 per year), 41 research assistantships (averaging $14,000 per year), 84 teaching assistantships (averaging $13,000 per year) were awarded; Federal Work-Study, institutionally sponsored loans, scholarships/grants, health care benefits, tuition waivers (full and partial), and unspecified assistantships also available. Support available to part-time students. Total annual research expenditures: $2 million. *Unit head:* Dr. David Leake, Associate Dean for Graduate Studies, 812-855-9756, E-mail: leake@cs.indiana.edu. *Application contact:* Rachel Lawmaster, Manager of Graduate Admissions and Studies, 812-856-3622, Fax: 812-856-3825, E-mail: raclee@indiana.edu.

The Johns Hopkins University, School of Medicine, Division of Health Sciences Informatics, Baltimore, MD 21218-2699. Offers applied health sciences informatics (MS); health sciences informatics research (MS). *Faculty:* 40 part-time/adjunct (10 women). *Students:* 7 full-time (3 women); includes 2 minority (both Asian Americans or Pacific Islanders), 2 international. 20 applicants, 15% accepted, 1 enrolled. In 2009, 3 master's awarded. *Degree requirements:* For master's, thesis, publications, practica. *Application deadline:* For spring admission, 2/15 priority date for domestic students, 2/15 for international students. Application fee: $85. Electronic applications accepted. *Financial support:* In 2009–10, 3 fellowships with full tuition reimbursements (averaging $42,750 per year) were awarded; career-related internships or fieldwork and health care benefits also available. *Faculty research:* Decision modeling, consumer health informatics, digital libraries, data standards, patient safety. Total annual research expenditures: $963,103. *Unit head:* Dr. Harold P. Lehmann, Director, Training Program, 410-502-2569, Fax: 410-614-2064, E-mail: lehmann@jhmi.edu. *Application contact:* Kersti Winny, Academic Program Administrator, 410-502-3768, Fax: 410-614-2064, E-mail: kwinny@jhmi.edu.

Medical College of Georgia, School of Graduate Studies, Program in Public Health–Informatics, Augusta, GA 30912. Offers MPH. Part-time programs available. *Degree requirements:* For master's, thesis (for some programs). *Entrance requirements:* For master's, GRE General Test. Additional exam requirements/recommendations for international students: Required—TOEFL. Electronic applications accepted. Full-time tuition and fees vary according to campus/location, program and student level.

Northeastern University, College of Computer and Information Science, Boston, MA 02115-5096. Offers computer and information science (PhD); computer science (MS); health informatics (MS); information assurance (MS). Part-time and evening/weekend programs available. *Faculty:* 28 full-time (3 women), 3 part-time/adjunct (all women). *Students:* 180 full-time (48 women), 15 part-time (0 women); includes 4 minority (2 Asian Americans or Pacific Islanders, 2 Hispanic Americans), 154 international. 829 applicants, 52% accepted, 74 enrolled. In 2009, 97 master's, 5 doctorates awarded. Terminal master's awarded for partial completion of doctoral program. *Degree requirements:* For master's, thesis optional; for doctorate, comprehensive exam, thesis/dissertation. *Entrance requirements:* For master's and doctorate, GRE General Test. Additional exam requirements/recommendations for international students: Required—TOEFL or IELTS. *Application deadline:* For fall admission, 7/15 for domestic students, 5/1 for international students; for spring admission, 10/15 for domestic students, 9/1 for international students. Applications are processed on a rolling basis. Application fee: $50. Electronic applications accepted. *Expenses:* Contact institution. *Financial support:* In 2009–10, 59 students received support, including 1 fellowship, 35 research assistantships with full tuition reimbursements available (averaging $18,260 per year), 24 teaching assistantships with full tuition reimbursements available (averaging $18,260 per year); career-related internships or fieldwork, Federal Work-Study, institutionally sponsored loans, scholarships/grants, and unspecified assistantships also available. Financial award application deadline: 1/15. *Faculty research:* Programming languages, artificial intelligence, human-computer interaction, database management, network security. *Unit head:* Dr. Larry A. Finkelstein, Dean, 617-373-2462, Fax: 617-373-5121. *Application contact:* Dr. Agnes Chan, Associate Dean and Director of Graduate Program, 617-373-2462, Fax: 617-373-5121, E-mail: gradschool@ccs.neu.edu.

Northern Kentucky University, Office of Graduate Programs, College of Informatics, Program in Health Informatics, Highland Heights, KY 41099. Offers MS, Certificate. Part-time and evening/weekend programs available. *Students:* 7 full-time (6 women), 41 part-time (25 women); includes 5 minority (all African Americans), 3 international. Average age 40. 35 applicants, 54% accepted, 16 enrolled. In 2009, 1 master's, 7 other advanced degrees awarded. *Degree requirements:* For master's, capstone. *Entrance requirements:* For master's, MAT, GRE, or GMAT, minimum GPA 3.0. Additional exam requirements/recommendations for international students: Required—TOEFL (minimum score 550 paper-based; 213 computer-based; 79 iBT); Recommended—IELTS (minimum score 6.5). *Application deadline:* For fall admission, 8/1 for domestic students, 6/1 for international students; for spring admission, 12/1 for domestic students, 10/1 for international students. Applications are processed on a rolling basis. Application fee: $40. Electronic applications accepted. *Expenses:* Tuition, state resident: full-time $6912; part-time $384 per credit hour. Tuition, nonresident: full-time $12,150; part-time $675 per credit hour. Tuition and fees vary according to course load, program and reciprocity agreements. *Financial support:* Unspecified assistantships available. Financial award applicants required to submit FAFSA. *Unit head:* Dr. Gary Ozanich, Director, 859-572-1397, E-mail: ozanichg1@nku.edu. *Application contact:* Dr. Peg Griffin, Director of Graduate Programs, 859-572-6934, Fax: 859-572-6670, E-mail: griffinp@nku.edu.

Nova Southeastern University, Health Professions Division, College of Osteopathic Medicine, Program in Biomedical Informatics, Fort Lauderdale, FL 33314-7796. Offers biomedical informatics (MS); clinical informatics (Graduate Certificate); public health informatics (Graduate Certificate). *Unit head:* Dr. Jennie Q. Lou, Director, 954-262-1619, E-mail: jlou@nova.edu. *Application contact:* Ellen Rondino, College of Osteopathic Medicine Admissions Counselor, 866-817-4068.

Saint Joseph's University, College of Arts and Sciences, Department of Health Services, Philadelphia, PA 19131-1395. Offers health administration (MS, Post-Master's Certificate); health care ethics (Post-Master's Certificate); health education (MS, Post-Master's Certificate); health informatics (Post-Master's Certificate); healthcare ethics (MS); nurse anesthesia (MS); school nurse certification (MS). Part-time and evening/weekend programs available. *Students:* 10 full-time (5 women), 180 part-time (135 women); includes 67 minority (50 African Americans, 11 Asian Americans or Pacific Islanders, 6 Hispanic Americans), 8 international. Average age 36. In 2009, 72 master's awarded. *Entrance requirements:* For master's, GRE (if GPA less than 2.75), 2 letters of recommendation, minimum GPA of 2.75, resume. Additional exam requirements/recommendations for international students: Required—TOEFL (minimum score 550 paper-based; 213 computer-based; 79 iBT). *Application deadline:* For fall admission, 7/15 priority date for domestic students, 4/15 for international students; for winter admission, 1/15 for international students; for spring admission, 11/15 priority date for domestic students, 10/15 for international students. Applications are processed on a rolling basis. Application fee: $35. Electronic applications accepted. *Expenses:* Tuition: Part-time $729 per credit hour. Tuition and fees vary according to degree level and program. *Financial support:* Career-related internships or fieldwork and unspecified assistantships available. Financial award applicants required to submit FAFSA. *Unit head:* Nakia Henderson, Director, 610-660-2952, E-mail: nakia.henderson@sju.edu. *Application contact:* Kate McConnell, Director, Graduate College of Arts and Sciences Admissions and Retention, 610-660-3184, Fax: 610-660-3230, E-mail: kate.mcconnell@sju.edu.

Stephens College, Division of Graduate and Continuing Studies, Columbia, MO 65215-0002. Offers business (MBA, MSL); counseling (M Ed), including counseling; curriculum and instruction

Health Informatics

Stephens College (continued)

(M Ed); health information administration (Postbaccalaureate Certificate). Part-time and evening/weekend programs available. Postbaccalaureate distance learning degree programs offered (minimal on-campus study). *Faculty:* 5 full-time (all women), 41 part-time/adjunct (31 women). *Students:* 208 full-time (178 women), 66 part-time (56 women); includes 36 minority (24 African Americans, 6 Asian Americans or Pacific Islanders, 6 Hispanic Americans). Average age 34. 91 applicants, 62% accepted, 51 enrolled. In 2009, 62 master's awarded. *Entrance requirements:* For master's, minimum GPA of 3.0 in last 60 hours. Additional exam requirements/recommendations for international students: Required—TOEFL (minimum score 213 computer-based). *Application deadline:* For fall admission, 7/25 priority date for domestic and international students; for winter admission, 12/1 priority date for domestic and international students; for spring admission, 4/25 priority date for domestic and international students. Applications are processed on a rolling basis. Application fee: $40. Electronic applications accepted. *Expenses:* Tuition: Part-time $350 per credit. Required fees: $25 per credit. *Financial support:* In 2009–10, 174 students received support, including 6 fellowships with full tuition reimbursements available (averaging $6,805 per year); scholarships/grants and unspecified assistantships also available. Financial award applicants required to submit FAFSA. *Faculty research:* Educational psychology, outcomes assessment. *Unit head:* Dean Suzanne Sharp, Dean of Graduate and Continuing Studies, 573-876-7123, Fax: 573-876-7237, E-mail: online@stephens.edu. *Application contact:* Jennifer Deaver, Director of Marketing and Recruitment, 800-388-7579, E-mail: online@stephens.edu.

Stevens Institute of Technology, Graduate School, Charles V. Schaefer Jr. School of Engineering, Department of Computer Science, Hoboken, NJ 07030. Offers computer graphics (Certificate); computer science (MS, PhD); computer systems (Certificate); database management systems (Certificate); distributed systems (Certificate); elements of computer science (Certificate); enterprise computing (Certificate); enterprise security and information assurance (Certificate); health informatics (Certificate); multimedia experience and management (Certificate); networks and systems administration (Certificate); security and privacy (Certificate); service oriented computing (Certificate); software design (Certificate); theoretical computer science (Certificate). Part-time and evening/weekend programs available. Terminal master's awarded for partial completion of doctoral program. *Degree requirements:* For master's, thesis optional; for doctorate, variable foreign language requirement, comprehensive exam, thesis/dissertation. *Entrance requirements:* For master's and doctorate, GRE, minimum GPA of 3.0. Additional exam requirements/recommendations for international students: Required—TOEFL. Electronic applications accepted. *Expenses:* Tuition: Full-time $9900; part-time $1100 per credit. Required fees: $286 per semester. *Faculty research:* Semantics, reliability theory, programming language, cyber security.

TUI University, College of Health Sciences, Program in Health Sciences, Cypress, CA 90630. Offers clinical research administration (MS, Certificate); emergency and disaster management (MS, Certificate); environmental health science (Certificate); health care administration (PhD); health care management (MS), including health informatics; health education (MS, Certificate); health informatics (Certificate); health sciences (PhD); international health (MS); international health: educator or researcher option (PhD); international health: practitioner option (PhD); law and expert witness studies (MS, Certificate); public health (MS); quality assurance (Certificate). Part-time and evening/weekend programs available. Postbaccalaureate distance learning degree programs offered (no on-campus study). *Degree requirements:* For doctorate, comprehensive exam, thesis/dissertation, defense of dissertation. *Entrance requirements:* For master's, minimum GPA of 2.5 (students with GPA 3.0 or greater may transfer up to 30% of graduate level credits); for doctorate, minimum GPA of 3.4, curriculum vitae, course work in research methods or statistics. Additional exam requirements/recommendations for international students: Required—TOEFL. Electronic applications accepted.

The University of Alabama at Birmingham, School of Health Professions, Department of Health Services Administration, Program in Health Informatics, Birmingham, AL 35294. Offers MS. *Degree requirements:* For master's, thesis or alternative. *Entrance requirements:* For master's, GRE General Test, MAT, minimum GPA of 3.0, course work in computing fundamentals and programming. Electronic applications accepted. *Faculty research:* Healthcare/medical informatics, natural language processing, application of expert systems, graphical user interface design.

University of Illinois at Chicago, Graduate College, College of Applied Health Sciences, Program in Health Informatics, Chicago, IL 60607-7128. Offers MS. Postbaccalaureate distance learning degree programs offered (no on-campus study).

University of Illinois at Urbana–Champaign, Graduate College, Graduate School of Library and Information Science, Champaign, IL 61820. Offers bioinformatics: library and information science (MS); library and information science (MS, PhD, CAS); library and information science: digital libraries (CAS). *Accreditation:* ALA (one or more programs are accredited). Postbaccalaureate distance learning degree programs offered. *Faculty:* 26 full-time (13 women), 9 part-time/adjunct (6 women). *Students:* 321 full-time (229 women), 310 part-time (230 women); includes 101 minority (34 African Americans, 4 American Indian/Alaska Native, 36 Asian Americans or Pacific Islanders, 27 Hispanic Americans), 35 international. 747 applicants, 53% accepted, 217 enrolled. In 2009, 240 master's, 7 doctorates, 6 other advanced degrees awarded. *Entrance requirements:* For master's, GRE General Test, minimum GPA of 3.0; for doctorate, minimum GPA of 3.0; for CAS, master's degree in library and information science or related field with minimum GPA of 3.0. Additional exam requirements/recommendations for international students: Required—TOEFL (minimum score 620 paper-based; 260 computer-based; 105 iBT), or IELTS (minimum score 7). *Application deadline:* Applications are processed on a rolling basis. Application fee: $60 ($75 for international students). Electronic applications accepted. *Financial support:* In 2009–10, 52 fellowships, 41 research assistantships, 27 teaching assistantships were awarded; tuition waivers (full and partial) also available. *Unit head:* John Unsworth, Dean, 217-333-3281, Fax: 217-244-3302, E-mail: unsworth@illinois.edu. *Application contact:* Valerie Youngen, Admissions and Records Representative, 217-333-0734, Fax: 217-244-3302, E-mail: vyoungen@llinois.edu.

The University of Iowa, Graduate College, Program in Informatics, Iowa City, IA 52242-1316. Offers bioinformatics and computational biology (Certificate); health informatics (MS, PhD, Certificate); information science (MS, PhD, Certificate). *Degree requirements:* For master's, thesis optional; for doctorate, comprehensive exam, thesis/dissertation. *Entrance requirements:* For master's and doctorate, GRE General Test, minimum GPA of 3.0. Additional exam requirements/recommendations for international students: Required—TOEFL (minimum score 550 paper-based; 213 computer-based; 81 iBT). Electronic applications accepted.

University of La Verne, College of Business and Public Management, Program in Health Administration, La Verne, CA 91750-4443. Offers financial management (MHA); health administration (MHA); human resources (MHA); information management (MHA); leadership and management (MHA); managed care (MHA); marketing and business development (MHA). Part-time programs available. *Faculty:* 22 full-time (11 women), 41 part-time/adjunct (8 women). *Students:* 32 full-time (19 women), 21 part-time (16 women); includes 25 minority (9 African Americans, 10 Asian Americans or Pacific Islanders, 6 Hispanic Americans). Average age 34. In 2009, 19 master's awarded. *Entrance requirements:* For master's, minimum undergraduate GPA of 2.5, 3 letters of reference, curriculum vitae or resume, writing sample. Additional exam requirements/recommendations for international students: Required—TOEFL (minimum score 550 paper-based; 213 computer-based). *Application deadline:* Applications are processed on a rolling basis. Application fee: $50. *Expenses:* Contact institution. *Financial support:* Application deadline: 3/2; *Unit head:* Joan Branin, Chairperson, 909-593-3511 Ext. 4247, E-mail: jbranin@laverne.edu. *Application contact:* Barbara Cox, Program and Admissions Specialist, 909-593-3511 Ext. 4004, Fax: 909-392-2761, E-mail: bcox@laverne.edu.

University of Maryland University College, Graduate School of Management and Technology, Program in Health Administration Informatics, Adelphi, MD 20783. Offers MS, Certificate. Part-time and evening/weekend programs available. Postbaccalaureate distance learning degree programs offered (no on-campus study). *Students:* 6 full-time (4 women), 122 part-time (83 women); includes 73 minority (59 African Americans, 11 Asian Americans or Pacific Islanders, 3 Hispanic Americans). Average age 40. 73 applicants, 100% accepted, 37 enrolled. In 2009, 7 master's, 4 other advanced degrees awarded. *Degree requirements:* For master's, thesis or alternative. *Application deadline:* Applications are processed on a rolling basis. Application fee: $40. Electronic applications accepted. *Expenses:* Tuition, state resident: full-time $7704; part-time $428 per credit hour. Tuition, nonresident: full-time $11,862; part-time $659 per credit hour. *Financial support:* Federal Work-Study and scholarships/grants available. Support available to part-time students. Financial award application deadline: 6/1; financial award applicants required to submit FAFSA. *Unit head:* Dr. Katherine Marconi, Director, 240-684-2400, Fax: 240-684-2401, E-mail: kmarconi@umuc.edu. *Application contact:* Coordinator, Graduate Admissions, 800-888-UMUC, Fax: 240-684-2151, E-mail: newgrad@umuc.edu.

University of Massachusetts Lowell, School of Health and Environment, Department of Community Health and Sustainability, Lowell, MA 01854-2881. Offers health management and policy (MS, Graduate Certificate). Part-time programs available. *Degree requirements:* For master's, thesis optional. *Entrance requirements:* For master's, GRE General Test. *Faculty research:* Alzheimer's disease, total quality management systems, information systems, market analysis.

University of Minnesota, Twin Cities Campus, Graduate School, Program in Health Informatics, Minneapolis, MN 55455-0213. Offers MHI, MS, PhD, MD/MHI. Part-time programs available. *Faculty:* 20 full-time (6 women), 8 part-time/adjunct (2 women). *Students:* 36 full-time (15 women), 17 part-time (7 women); includes 27 minority (4 African Americans, 23 Asian Americans or Pacific Islanders). Average age 34. 24 applicants, 58% accepted, 9 enrolled. In 2009, 4 master's, 3 doctorates awarded. *Degree requirements:* For master's, thesis or alternative; for doctorate, thesis/dissertation. *Entrance requirements:* For master's and doctorate, GRE General Test, previous course work in life sciences, programming, calculus. Additional exam requirements/recommendations for international students: Required—TOEFL (minimum score 550 paper-based; 237 computer-based). *Application deadline:* For fall admission, 6/15 for domestic and international students; for winter admission, 10/15 for domestic and international students; for spring admission, 3/15 for domestic and international students. Applications are processed on a rolling basis. Application fee: $75. Electronic applications accepted. *Financial support:* In 2009–10, 18 students received support, including 8 fellowships with full tuition reimbursements available (averaging $40,905 per year), 9 research assistantships with full and partial tuition reimbursements available (averaging $16,868 per year), 1 teaching assistantship with full and partial tuition reimbursement available (averaging $16,868 per year); Federal Work-Study, scholarships/grants, traineeships, and tuition waivers (full and partial) also available. Financial award application deadline: 1/15. *Faculty research:* Medical decision making, physiological control systems, population studies, clinical information systems, telemedicine. Total annual research expenditures: $1.4 million. *Unit head:* Dr. Terrence Adam, Director of Graduate Studies, 612-625-5825, Fax: 612-625-7166, E-mail: adamx004@umn.edu. *Application contact:* Jessica Whitcombe-Trance, Executive Administrative Specialist, 612-626-3348, Fax: 612-626-7227, E-mail: jwhitcom@umn.edu.

University of Missouri, Graduate School, Department of Health Management and Informatics, Columbia, MO 65211. Offers health administration (MHA); health informatics (MHA); health services management (MHA). *Accreditation:* CAHME. Part-time programs available. *Entrance requirements:* For master's, GRE General Test or GMAT, minimum GPA of 3.0. Additional exam requirements/recommendations for international students: Required—TOEFL (minimum score 500 paper-based; 173 computer-based; 61 iBT).

The University of North Carolina at Charlotte, Graduate School, College of Computing and Informatics, Department of Bioinformatics and Genomics, Charlotte, NC 28223-0001. Offers bioinformatics (PMS). Part-time programs available. *Faculty:* 12 full-time (6 women). *Students:* 11 full-time (3 women), 5 part-time (3 women); includes 1 African American, 1 Asian American or Pacific Islander, 4 international. Average age 29. 35 applicants, 51% accepted, 9 enrolled. Terminal master's awarded for partial completion of doctoral program. *Degree requirements:* For master's, internship, research project, or thesis. *Entrance requirements:* For master's, GRE, minimum undergraduate GPA of 3.0, overall and in undergraduate major. Additional exam requirements/recommendations for international students: Required—TOEFL (minimum score 557 paper-based; 220 computer-based; 83 iBT). *Application deadline:* For fall admission, 7/15 for domestic students, 5/1 for international students; for spring admission, 11/15 for domestic students, 10/1 for international students. Applications are processed on a rolling basis. Application fee: $55. Electronic applications accepted. *Financial support:* In 2009–10, 9 fellowships (averaging $36,391 per year), 12 research assistantships (averaging $10,433 per year), 5 teaching assistantships (averaging $17,385 per year) were awarded; career-related internships or fieldwork, institutionally sponsored loans, scholarships/grants, and unspecified assistantships also available. Support available to part-time students. *Faculty research:* High-throughput studies, computational biophysics, structural bioinformatics, metagenomics, computational mass spectrometry. Total annual research expenditures: $13,917. *Unit head:* Dr. Larry Mays, Chairman, 704-687-8555, E-mail: lemays@uncc.edu. *Application contact:* Kathy B. Giddings, Director of Graduate Admissions, 704-687-5503, Fax: 704-687-3279, E-mail: gradadm@uncc.edu.

University of Phoenix, The Artemis School, College of Health and Human Services, Phoenix, AZ 85034-7209. Offers administration of justice and security (MS); community counseling (MSC); education (MHA); family nurse practitioner (MSN); gerontology (MHA); health administration (MHA); health care education (MSN); health care management (MBA, MSN); informatics (MHA); marriage, family, and child therapy (MSC); nursing (MSN); nursing for nurse practitioners (MSN); psychology (MS); MSN/MBA; MSN/MHA. *Accreditation:* AACN. Evening/weekend programs available. Postbaccalaureate distance learning degree programs offered. *Degree requirements:* For master's, thesis (for some programs). *Entrance requirements:* For master's, 3 years of work experience, minimum undergraduate GPA of 2.5, RN license. Additional exam requirements/recommendations for international students: Required—TOEFL (minimum score 550 paper-based; 213 computer-based; 79 iBT). Electronic applications accepted.

University of Phoenix–Birmingham Campus, College of Health and Human Services, Birmingham, AL 35244. Offers education (MHA); gerontology (MHA); health administration (MHA); health care management (MBA); informatics (MHA); nursing (MSN); nursing/health care education (MSN); MSN/MBA; MSN/MHA.

University of Phoenix–Phoenix Campus, The Artemis School, College of Health and Human Services, Phoenix, AZ 85040-1958. Offers community counseling (MSC); education (MHA); family nurse practitioner (MSN); gerontology (MHA); health administration (MHA); health care education (MSN); health care management (MBA); informatics (MHA); marriage, family, and child therapy (MSC); nurse practitioner (Certificate); nursing (MSN); nursing health care education (Certificate); psychology (MS); MSN/MBA; MSN/MHA. Evening/weekend programs available. *Degree requirements:* For master's, thesis (for some programs). *Entrance requirements:* For master's, 3 years of work experience in field, minimum undergraduate GPA of 2.5, RN license. Additional exam requirements/recommendations for international students: Required—TOEFL (minimum score 550 paper-based; 213 computer-based; 79 iBT). Electronic applications accepted.

University of Pittsburgh, School of Health and Rehabilitation Sciences, Master's Programs in Health and Rehabilitation Sciences, Pittsburgh, PA 15260. Offers health and rehabilitation sciences (MS), including clinical dietetics and nutrition, health care supervision and management, health information systems, occupational therapy, physical therapy, rehabilitation counseling, rehabilitation science and technology, sports medicine, wellness and human performance. *Accreditation:* APTA. Part-time and evening/weekend programs available. *Faculty:* 30 full-time (14 women), 4 part-time/adjunct (3 women). *Students:* 81 full-time (47 women), 54 part-time (27 women); includes 10 minority (6 African Americans, 4 Asian Americans or Pacific Islanders),

44 international. Average age 29. 326 applicants, 65% accepted, 130 enrolled. In 2009, 93 master's awarded. *Degree requirements:* For master's, comprehensive exam (for some programs), thesis optional. *Entrance requirements:* For master's, minimum GPA of 3.0. Additional exam requirements/recommendations for international students: Required—TOEFL, IELTS. *Application deadline:* For fall admission, 1/31 for international students; for spring admission, 7/31 for international students. Applications are processed on a rolling basis. Application fee: $50. Electronic applications accepted. *Expenses:* Contact institution. *Financial support:* In 2009–10, 3 research assistantships with full tuition reimbursements (averaging $18,450 per year) were awarded; teaching assistantships, Federal Work-Study, institutionally sponsored loans, traineeships, and unspecified assistantships also available. Financial award applicants required to submit FAFSA. *Faculty research:* Assistive technology, seating and wheeled mobility, cellular neurophysiology, low back syndrome, augmentative communication. Total annual research expenditures: $6.5 million. *Unit head:* Dr. Clifford E. Brubaker, Dean, 412-383-6560, Fax: 412-383-6535, E-mail: cliffb@pitt.edu. *Application contact:* Shameem Gangjee, Director of Admissions, 412-383-6558, Fax: 412-383-6535, E-mail: admissions@shrs.pitt.edu.

University of Puerto Rico, Medical Sciences Campus, School of Health Professions, Program in Health Information Administration, San Juan, PR 00936-5067. Offers MS. Part-time programs available. *Degree requirements:* For master's, one foreign language, thesis or alternative, internship. *Entrance requirements:* For master's, EXADEP or GRE General Test, minimum GPA of 2.5, interview, fluency in Spanish. *Faculty research:* Quality of medical records, health information data.

The University of Texas Health Science Center at Houston, School of Health Information Sciences, Houston, TX 77225-0036. Offers health informatics (MS, PhD, Certificate); MPH/MS; MPH/PhD. Part-time programs available. Postbaccalaureate distance learning degree programs offered (no on-campus study). *Degree requirements:* For master's, thesis; for doctorate, thesis/dissertation. *Entrance requirements:* For master's and doctorate, GRE or MAT. Additional exam requirements/recommendations for international students: Required—TOEFL (minimum score 550 paper-based; 213 computer-based; 87 iBT). Electronic applications accepted. *Faculty research:* Patient safety, human computer interface, artificial intelligence, decision support tools, 3-D visualization, biomedical engineering.

University of Victoria, Faculty of Graduate Studies, Faculty of Human and Social Development, School of Health Information Science, Victoria, BC V8W 2Y2, Canada. Offers M Sc. *Degree requirements:* For master's, thesis or research project. *Entrance requirements:* Additional exam requirements/recommendations for international students: Required—TOEFL (minimum score 575 paper-based).

University of Virginia, School of Medicine, Department of Public Health Sciences, Program in Clinical Research, Charlottesville, VA 22903. Offers clinical investigation and patient-oriented research (MS); informatics in medicine (MS). Part-time programs available. *Students:* 4 full-time (2 women), 14 part-time (7 women); includes 4 minority (3 Asian Americans or Pacific Islanders, 1 Hispanic American). Average age 35. 4 applicants, 100% accepted, 3 enrolled. In 2009, 13 master's awarded. *Degree requirements:* For master's, thesis (for some programs). *Entrance requirements:* For master's, 2 letters of recommendation. Additional exam requirements/recommendations for international students: Required—TOEFL (minimum score 600 paper-based; 250 computer-based; 90 iBT). *Application deadline:* For fall admission, 3/1 priority date for domestic and international students. Application fee: $60. Electronic applications accepted. *Financial support:* Career-related internships or fieldwork available. Financial award applicants required to submit FAFSA. *Unit head:* Dr. William A. Knaus, Chair, 434-924-8430, Fax: 434-924-8437. *Application contact:* Tracey L. Brookman, Academic Programs Administrator, 434-924-8430, Fax: 434-924-8437, E-mail: ms-hes@virginia.edu.

University of Washington, Graduate School, School of Medicine and Graduate School, Graduate Programs in Medicine, Department of Medical Education and Biomedical Informatics, Division of Biomedical and Health Informatics, Seattle, WA 98195. Offers MS, PhD. *Entrance requirements:* For master's and doctorate, GRE General Test, minimum GPA of 3.0; previous undergraduate course work in biology, computer programming, and mathematics. Additional exam requirements/recommendations for international students: Required—TOEFL (minimum score 580 paper-based; 237 computer-based; 70 iBT). Electronic applications accepted. *Faculty research:* Bio-clinical informatics, information retrieval, human-computer interaction, knowledge-based systems, telehealth.

University of Wisconsin–Milwaukee, Graduate School, College of Health Sciences, Interdepartmental Program in Healthcare Informatics, Milwaukee, WI 53201-0413. Offers MS, Certificate. *Faculty:* 6 full-time (3 women). *Students:* 7 full-time (2 women), 7 part-time (5 women); includes 1 minority (African American), 2 international. Average age 34. 16 applicants, 63% accepted, 6 enrolled. In 2009, 5 master's awarded. *Degree requirements:* For master's, comprehensive exam, thesis optional. *Entrance requirements:* For master's, GRE General Test. Additional exam requirements/recommendations for international students: Required—TOEFL (minimum score 550 paper-based; 79 iBT), IELTS (minimum score 6.5). *Expenses:* Tuition, state resident: full-time $8800. Tuition, nonresident: full-time $20,760. Tuition and fees vary according to program and reciprocity agreements. *Financial support:* In 2009–10, 2 research assistantships, 1 teaching assistantship were awarded; fellowships also available. Total annual research expenditures: $562,516. *Unit head:* Timothy Patrick, Representative, 414-229-6849, Fax: 414-229-2619, E-mail: tp5@uwm.edu. *Application contact:* General Information Contact, 414-229-4982, Fax: 414-229-6967, E-mail: gradschool@uwm.edu.

Walden University, Graduate Programs, School of Health Sciences, Minneapolis, MN 55401. Offers clinical research administration (MS); health informatics (MS); health services (PhD), including community health promotion and education, general program, health management and policy; healthcare administration (MHA); public health (MPH, PhD), including community health promotion and education (PhD), epidemiology (PhD). Part-time and evening/weekend programs available. Postbaccalaureate distance learning degree programs offered (minimal on-campus study). *Faculty:* 14 full-time, 136 part-time/adjunct. *Students:* 2,121 full-time (1,670 women), 724 part-time (568 women); includes 1,370 minority (1,149 African Americans, 20 American Indian/Alaska Native, 95 Asian Americans or Pacific Islanders, 106 Hispanic Americans), 134 international. Average age 40. In 2009, 232 master's, 24 doctorates awarded. *Degree requirements:* For doctorate, thesis/dissertation, residency. *Entrance requirements:* For master's, bachelor's degree or equivalent in related field, minimum GPA of 2.5; for doctorate, master's degree or equivalent in related field; minimum GPA of 3.0; official transcripts; three years of related professional/academic experience (preferred); access to computer and Internet. Additional exam requirements/recommendations for international students: Required—TOEFL (minimum score 550 paper-based; 213 computer-based), IELTS (minimum score 6.5), or Michigan English Language Assessment Battery (minimum score 82). *Application deadline:* Applications are processed on a rolling basis. Application fee: $50. Electronic applications accepted. *Expenses:* Tuition: Full-time $13,665; part-time $560 per credit. Required fees: $1375. Tuition and fees vary according to course load, degree level and program. *Financial support:* In 2009–10, 152 students received support; fellowships, Federal Work-Study, scholarships/grants, unspecified assistantships, and family tuition reduction, active duty/veteran tuition reduction, group tuition reduction, interest-free payment plans available. Support available to part-time students. Financial award applicants required to submit FAFSA. *Unit head:* Dr. Jorg Westermann, Interim Associate Dean, 800-925-3368. *Application contact:* Jennifer Hall, Director of Enrollment, 866-4-WALDEN, E-mail: info@waldenu.edu.

Human-Computer Interaction

Carnegie Mellon University, School of Computer Science, Department of Human-Computer Interaction, Pittsburgh, PA 15213-3891. Offers MHCI, PhD. *Entrance requirements:* For master's, GRE General Test, GRE Subject Test.

Cornell University, Graduate School, Graduate Fields of Arts and Sciences, Field of Information Science, Ithaca, NY 14853-0001. Offers cognition (PhD); human computer interaction (PhD); information systems (PhD); social aspects of information (PhD). *Faculty:* 35 full-time (10 women). *Students:* 14 full-time (4 women); includes 1 minority (Asian American or Pacific Islander), 6 international. Average age 31. 53 applicants, 9% accepted, 5 enrolled. In 2009, 3 doctorates awarded. *Degree requirements:* For doctorate, comprehensive exam, thesis/dissertation. *Entrance requirements:* For doctorate, GRE General Test, 3 letters of recommendation. Additional exam requirements/recommendations for international students: Required—TOEFL (minimum score 550 paper-based; 213 computer-based; 77 iBT). *Application deadline:* For fall admission, 1/1 for domestic students. Application fee: $70. Electronic applications accepted. *Expenses:* Tuition: Full-time $29,500. Required fees: $70. Full-time tuition and fees vary according to degree level, program and student level. *Financial support:* In 2009–10, 10 students received support, including 1 fellowship with full tuition reimbursement available, 2 research assistantships with full tuition reimbursements available, 2 teaching assistantships with full tuition reimbursements available; institutionally sponsored loans, scholarships/grants, tuition waivers (full and partial), and unspecified assistantships also available. Financial award applicants required to submit FAFSA. *Faculty research:* Digital libraries, game theory, data mining, human-computer interaction, computational linguistics. *Unit head:* Director of Graduate Studies, 607-255-5925. *Application contact:* Graduate Field Assistant, 607-255-5925, E-mail: info@infosci.cornell.edu.

Dalhousie University, Faculty of Engineering, Department of Internetworking, Halifax, NS B3J 1Z1, Canada. Offers M Eng. *Students:* 24 full-time (0 women), 5 part-time (0 women). 56 applicants, 82% accepted. In 2009, 3 master's awarded. *Entrance requirements:* Additional exam requirements/recommendations for international students: Required—TOEFL, IELTS, CANTEST, CAEL, or Michigan English Language Assessment Battery. *Application deadline:* For fall admission, 6/1 for domestic students, 4/1 for international students; for winter admission, 11/15 for domestic students, 8/31 for international students; for spring admission, 2/28 for domestic students, 12/31 for international students. Application fee: $70. Electronic applications accepted. *Unit head:* Dr. William Robertson, Director, 902-494-1114, Fax: 902-494-2057, E-mail: bill.robertson@dal.ca. *Application contact:* Shelley Caines, Program Administrator, 902-494-1114, Fax: 902-494-2057, E-mail: shelley.caines@dal.ca.

DePaul University, College of Computing and Digital Media, Chicago, IL 60604. Offers business information technology (MS); computational finance (MS); computer and information sciences (PhD); computer game development (MS); computer graphics and motion technology (MS); computer science (MS); computer, information and network security (MS), including applied technology; digital cinema (MFA, MS), including information technology project management (MS); e-commerce technology (MS); human-computer interaction (MS); information systems (MS); information technology (MA); information technology project management (MS); software engineering (MS); telecommunications systems (MS); JD/MS. Part-time and evening/weekend programs available. Postbaccalaureate distance learning degree programs offered (no on-campus study). *Faculty:* 78 full-time (16 women), 191 part-time/adjunct (51 women). *Students:* 922 full-time (239 women), 887 part-time (209 women); includes 466 minority (193 African Americans, 3 American Indian/Alaska Native, 162 Asian Americans or Pacific Islanders, 108 Hispanic Americans), 276 international. Average age 31. 853 applicants, 67% accepted, 294 enrolled. In 2009, 444 master's, 4 doctorates awarded. *Degree requirements:* For master's, thesis (for some programs); for doctorate, comprehensive exam, thesis/dissertation. *Entrance requirements:* For master's, GRE or GMAT (MS in computational finance only), bachelor's degree; for doctorate, GRE, master's degree in computer science. Additional exam requirements/recommendations for international students: Required—TOEFL (minimum score 550 paper-based; 213 computer-based), IELTS (minimum score 6.5), Pearson Test of English (minimum score 53). *Application deadline:* For fall admission, 8/15 priority date for domestic students, 6/1 priority date for international students; for winter admission, 12/15 priority date for domestic students, 9/15 priority date for international students; for spring admission, 3/1 priority date for domestic students, 12/15 priority date for international students. Applications are processed on a rolling basis. Application fee: $25. Electronic applications accepted. *Expenses:* Contact institution. *Financial support:* In 2009–10, 69 students received support, including 6 fellowships with full tuition reimbursements available (averaging $25,858 per year), 75 teaching assistantships with full and partial tuition reimbursements available (averaging $5,780 per year); research assistantships, Federal Work-Study, scholarships/grants, tuition waivers (full and partial), and unspecified assistantships also available. Support available to part-time students. Financial award application deadline: 4/30; financial award applicants required to submit FAFSA. *Faculty research:* Bioinformatics, visual computing, graphics and animation, high performance and scientific computing, databases. Total annual research expenditures: $790,000. *Unit head:* Dr. David Miller, Dean, 312-362-8381, Fax: 312-362-5185. *Application contact:* Dr. Liz Friedman, Assistant Dean of Student Services, 312-362-5384, Fax: 312-362-5327, E-mail: efriedm2@cdm.depaul.edu.

Georgia Institute of Technology, Graduate Studies and Research, College of Computing, Multidisciplinary Program in Human Computer Interaction, Atlanta, GA 30332-0001. Offers MSHCI. Part-time programs available. *Degree requirements:* For master's, project. *Entrance requirements:* For master's, GRE General Test. Additional exam requirements/recommendations for international students: Required—TOEFL (minimum score 600 paper-based; 250 computer-based). Electronic applications accepted.

Indiana University Bloomington, School of Informatics, Bloomington, IN 47408. Offers bioinformatics (MS); chemical informatics (MS); computer science (MS, PhD); health informatics (MS); human-computer interaction (MS); informatics (PhD); laboratory informatics (MS); media arts and science (MS); music informatics (MS); security informatics (MS); MS/PhD. PhD offered through University Graduate School. Part-time programs available. Postbaccalaureate distance learning degree programs offered (no on-campus study). *Faculty:* 63 full-time (12 women). *Students:* 367 full-time (93 women), 32 part-time (11 women); includes 18 minority (4 African Americans, 1 American Indian/Alaska Native, 11 Asian Americans or Pacific Islanders, 2 Hispanic Americans), 254 international. Average age 27. 676 applicants, 52% accepted, 146 enrolled. In 2009, 82 master's, 18 doctorates awarded. Terminal master's awarded for partial completion of doctoral program. *Degree requirements:* For master's, thesis optional; for doctorate, comprehensive exam, thesis/dissertation, oral and written exams. *Entrance requirements:* For master's and doctorate, GRE, letters of reference. Additional exam requirements/recommendations for international students: Required—TOEFL. *Application deadline:* For fall admission, 1/15 for domestic students, 12/1 for international students. Application fee: $55 ($65 for international students). Electronic applications accepted. *Financial support:* In 2009–10, 2 fellowships with full and partial tuition reimbursements (averaging $20,000 per year), 41 research assistantships (averaging $14,000 per year), 84 teaching assistantships (averaging

Human-Computer Interaction

Indiana University Bloomington (continued)
$13,000 per year) were awarded; Federal Work-Study, institutionally sponsored loans, scholarships/grants, health care benefits, tuition waivers (full and partial), and unspecified assistantships also available. Support available to part-time students. Total annual research expenditures: $2 million. *Unit head:* Dr. David Leake, Associate Dean for Graduate Studies, 812-855-9756, E-mail: leake@cs.indiana.edu. *Application contact:* Rachel Lawmaster, Manager of Graduate Admissions and Studies, 812-856-3622, Fax: 812-856-3825, E-mail: raclee@indiana.edu.

Iowa State University of Science and Technology, Graduate College, Interdisciplinary Programs, Program in Human-Computer Interaction, Ames, IA 50011. Offers MS, PhD. *Students:* 36 full-time (8 women), 34 part-time (16 women); includes 8 minority (4 African Americans, 2 Asian Americans or Pacific Islanders, 2 Hispanic Americans), 7 international. In 2009, 6 master's, 4 doctorates awarded. *Degree requirements:* For master's, thesis; for doctorate, thesis/dissertation. *Entrance requirements:* For master's, GRE General Test; for doctorate, GRE General Test, e-portfolio of research. Additional exam requirements/recommendations for international students: Required—TOEFL (minimum score 580 paper-based; 95 iBT) or IELTS (minimum score 7). *Application deadline:* For fall admission, 1/15 priority date for domestic and international students. Application fee: $40 ($90 for international students). *Expenses:* Tuition, state resident: full-time $6716. Tuition, nonresident: full-time $8908. Tuition and fees vary according to course level, course load, program and student level. *Financial support:* In 2009–10, 25 research assistantships with full and partial tuition reimbursements (averaging $16,000 per year), 1 teaching assistantship with full and partial tuition reimbursement (averaging $15,000 per year) were awarded. *Unit head:* Dr. James Oliver, Chair, Supervising Committee, 515-294-2089, E-mail: info@hci.iastate.edu. *Application contact:* Pam Shill, Information Contact, 515-294-5836, Fax: 515-294-2592, E-mail: grad_admissions@iastate.edu.

Naval Postgraduate School, Graduate Programs, Department of Computer Science, Program in Modeling of Virtual Environments and Simulations, Monterey, CA 93943. Offers MS, PhD. Program only open to commissioned officers of the United States and friendly nations and selected United States federal civilian employees. Part-time programs available. *Degree requirements:* For master's, thesis; for doctorate, one foreign language, thesis/dissertation.

Old Dominion University, College of Arts and Letters, Graduate Programs in International Studies, Norfolk, VA 23529. Offers conflict and cooperation (PhD), including women's studies certificate; U.S. foreign policy (MA), including modeling and simulation certificate. Part-time programs available. *Faculty:* 14 full-time (3 women). *Students:* 53 full-time (26 women), 44 part-time (17 women); includes 6 minority (3 African Americans, 3 Hispanic Americans), 29 international. Average age 32. 99 applicants, 54% accepted, 30 enrolled. In 2009, 18 master's, 5 doctorates awarded. Terminal master's awarded for partial completion of doctoral program. *Degree requirements:* For master's, one foreign language, comprehensive exam, thesis optional; for doctorate, one foreign language, comprehensive exam, thesis/dissertation. *Entrance requirements:* For master's, GRE General Test, sample of written work, 2 letters of recommendation; for doctorate, GRE General Test, sample of written work, 3 letters of recommendation. Additional exam requirements/recommendations for international students: Required—TOEFL (minimum score 570 paper-based; 230 computer-based). *Application deadline:* For fall admission, 3/15 for domestic students, 2/15 for international students; for spring admission, 10/15 for domestic and international students. Application fee: $40. Electronic applications accepted. *Expenses:* Tuition, state resident: full-time $8112; part-time $338 per credit. Tuition, nonresident: full-time $20,256; part-time $844 per credit. Required fees: $119 per semester. One-time fee: $50. *Financial support:* In 2009–10, 20 students received support, including 2 fellowships (averaging $13,000 per year), 9 research assistantships with tuition reimbursements available (averaging $11,000 per year), 9 teaching assistantships with tuition reimbursements available (averaging $11,000 per year); career-related internships or fieldwork, institutionally sponsored loans, scholarships/grants, and unspecified assistantships also available. Support available to part-time students. Financial award application deadline: 2/15; financial award applicants required to submit FAFSA. *Faculty research:* U. S. foreign policy, international security, transatlantic and transpacific relations, transnational issues, IPE and development. Total annual research expenditures: $330,391. *Unit head:* Dr. Regina Karp, Graduate Program Director, 757-683-5700, Fax: 757-683-5701, E-mail: rkarp@odu.edu. *Application contact:* Dr. Angelica Huizar, 757-683-3988, Fax: 757-683-5701, E-mail: ahuizar@odu.edu.

Rensselaer Polytechnic Institute, Graduate School, School of Humanities and Social Sciences, Department of Language, Literature, and Communication, Program in Human-Computer Interaction, Troy, NY 12180-3590. Offers MS. Part-time programs available. *Faculty:* 14 full-time (8 women). *Students:* 6 full-time (1 woman), 21 part-time (13 women); includes 3 minority (2 African Americans, 1 Asian American or Pacific Islander), 1 international. 34 applicants, 59% accepted, 14 enrolled. In 2009, 12 master's awarded. *Degree requirements:* For master's, thesis optional. *Entrance requirements:* For master's, GRE General Test, resume. Additional exam requirements/recommendations for international students: Required—TOEFL. *Application deadline:* For fall admission, 1/15 priority date for domestic students; for spring admission, 10/15 priority date for domestic students. Applications are processed on a rolling basis. Application fee: $75. Electronic applications accepted. *Expenses:* Tuition: Full-time $38,100. *Financial support:* Career-related internships or fieldwork and institutionally sponsored loans available. *Faculty research:* Usability, games research, HCI interfaces for impaired users, web and interface design, information architecture. *Unit head:* Prof. James P. Zappen, Acting Department Head, 518-276-6468, Fax: 518-276-4092, E-mail: zappenj@rpi.edu.

Application contact: Kathy A. Colman, Recruitment Coordinator, 518-276-6469, Fax: 518-276-4092, E-mail: colmak@rpi.edu.

Rochester Institute of Technology, Graduate Enrollment Services, B. Thomas Golisano College of Computing and Information Sciences, Department of Information Technology, Program in Human Computer Interaction, Rochester, NY 14623-5603. Offers MS. Part-time programs available. Postbaccalaureate distance learning degree programs offered (minimal on-campus study). *Students:* 14 full-time (8 women), 6 part-time (1 woman); includes 2 African Americans, 1 Asian American or Pacific Islander, 5 international. Average age 29. 25 applicants, 64% accepted, 9 enrolled. *Degree requirements:* For master's, thesis or project. *Entrance requirements:* For master's, GRE, minimum GPA of 3.0. Additional exam requirements/recommendations for international students: Required—TOEFL (minimum score 570 paper-based; 230 computer-based; 88 iBT), or IELTS (minimum score 6.5). *Application deadline:* For fall admission, 8/1 for domestic students, 7/1 for international students; for spring admission, 2/1 for domestic students. Applications are processed on a rolling basis. Application fee: $50. Electronic applications accepted. *Expenses:* Tuition: Full-time $31,533; part-time $876 per credit hour. Required fees: $210. *Financial support:* In 2009–10, 17 students received support; research assistantships with partial tuition reimbursements available, teaching assistantships with partial tuition reimbursements available, career-related internships or fieldwork, scholarships/grants, and unspecified assistantships available. Support available to part-time students. Financial award applicants required to submit FAFSA. *Unit head:* Prof. Dianne Bills, Graduate Program Coordinator, 585-475-2700, Fax: 585-475-6584, E-mail: informaticsgrad@rit.edu. *Application contact:* Diane Ellison, Assistant Vice President, Graduate Enrollment Services, 585-475-2229, Fax: 585-475-7164, E-mail: gradinfo@rit.edu.

State University of New York at Oswego, Graduate Studies, College of Arts and Sciences, Interdisciplinary Program in Human Computer Interaction, Oswego, NY 13126. Offers MA. Part-time programs available. *Entrance requirements:* For master's, GRE, minimum GPA of 3.0. Additional exam requirements/recommendations for international students: Required—TOEFL (minimum score 560 paper-based; 220 computer-based).

Tufts University, Graduate School of Arts and Sciences, Graduate Certificate Programs, Human-Computer Interaction Program, Medford, MA 02155. Offers Certificate. Part-time and evening/weekend programs available. Electronic applications accepted. *Expenses:* Tuition: Full-time $38,096; part-time $3962 per credit. Required fees: $686; $40 per year. Tuition and fees vary according to course level, course load, degree level, program and student level.

University of Baltimore, Graduate School, The Yale Gordon College of Liberal Arts, School of Information Arts and Technologies, Baltimore, MD 21201-5779. Offers communications design (DCD); human-computer interaction (MS); interaction design and information technology (MS). Part-time and evening/weekend programs available. *Entrance requirements:* For master's, GRE or MAT, minimum undergraduate GPA of 3.0. Additional exam requirements/recommendations for international students: Required—TOEFL (minimum score 550 paper-based; 213 computer-based).

University of Illinois at Urbana–Champaign, Graduate College, Graduate School of Library and Information Science, Champaign, IL 61820. Offers bioinformatics: library and information science (MS); library and information science (MS, PhD, CAS); library and information science: digital libraries (CAS). *Accreditation:* ALA (one or more programs are accredited). Postbaccalaureate distance learning degree programs offered. *Faculty:* 26 full-time (13 women), 9 part-time/adjunct (6 women). *Students:* 321 full-time (229 women), 310 part-time (230 women); includes 101 minority (34 African Americans, 4 American Indian/Alaska Native, 36 Asian Americans or Pacific Islanders, 27 Hispanic Americans), 35 international. 747 applicants, 53% accepted, 217 enrolled. In 2009, 240 master's, 7 doctorates, 6 other advanced degrees awarded. *Entrance requirements:* For master's, GRE General Test, minimum GPA of 3.0; for doctorate, minimum GPA of 3.0; for CAS, master's degree in library and information science or related field with minimum GPA of 3.0. Additional exam requirements/recommendations for international students: Required—TOEFL (minimum score 620 paper-based; 260 computer-based; 105 iBT), or IELTS (minimum score 7). *Application deadline:* Applications are processed on a rolling basis. Application fee: $60 ($75 for international students). Electronic applications accepted. *Financial support:* In 2009–10, 52 fellowships, 41 research assistantships, 27 teaching assistantships were awarded; tuition waivers (full and partial) also available. *Unit head:* John Unsworth, Dean, 217-333-3281, Fax: 217-244-3302, E-mail: unsworth@illinois.edu. *Application contact:* Valerie Youngen, Admissions and Records Representative, 217-333-0734, Fax: 217-244-3302, E-mail: vyoungen@llinois.edu.

University of Michigan, Horace H. Rackham School of Graduate Studies, School of Information, Ann Arbor, MI 48109-1107. Offers archives and records management (MS); human-computer interaction (MS); information (MS, PhD); information economics, management and policy (MS); library and information services (MS). *Accreditation:* ALA (one or more programs are accredited). Part-time programs available. *Degree requirements:* For master's, variable foreign language requirement, thesis optional; for doctorate, one foreign language, thesis/dissertation, oral defense of dissertation, preliminary exam. *Entrance requirements:* For master's and doctorate, GRE General Test. Additional exam requirements/recommendations for international students: Required—TOEFL (minimum score 600 paper-based; 250 computer-based). Electronic applications accepted. *Expenses:* Tuition, state resident: full-time $17,286; part-time $1099 per credit hour. Tuition, nonresident: full-time $34,944; part-time $2080 per credit hour. Required fees: $95 per semester. Tuition and fees vary according to course load, degree level and program.

Information Science

Alcorn State University, School of Graduate Studies, School of Arts and Sciences, Department of Mathematical Sciences, Alcorn State, MS 39096-7500. Offers computer and information sciences (MS).

American InterContinental University Dunwoody Campus, Program in Information Technology, Atlanta, GA 30328. Offers MIT. Part-time and evening/weekend programs available. *Degree requirements:* For master's, technical proficiency demonstration. *Entrance requirements:* For master's, Computer Programmer Aptitude Battery Exam, interview. Electronic applications accepted. *Faculty research:* Operating systems, security issues, networks and routing, computer hardware.

American InterContinental University Online, Program in Information Technology, Hoffman Estates, IL 60192. Offers Internet security (MIT); IT project management (MIT). Evening/weekend programs available. Postbaccalaureate distance learning degree programs offered (no on-campus study). *Entrance requirements:* Additional exam requirements/recommendations for international students: Required—TOEFL (minimum score 550 paper-based; 213 computer-based). Electronic applications accepted.

American InterContinental University South Florida, Program in Information Technology, Weston, FL 33326. Offers Internet security (MIT); wireless computer forensics (MIT). Part-time and evening/weekend programs available. *Entrance requirements:* Additional exam requirements/recommendations for international students: Required—TOEFL (minimum score 670 paper-based). Electronic applications accepted.

Arizona State University, Graduate College, College of Technology and Innovation, Department of Technology Management, Tempe, AZ 85287. Offers MS. Part-time and evening/weekend

programs available. *Degree requirements:* For master's, thesis or applied project and oral defense. *Entrance requirements:* For master's, GRE, 30 semester hours in technology or high school equivalent; 16 semester hours of physical science and math; adequate technical preparation in a selected technology; resume; industrial experience (strongly recommended); minimum GPA of 3.0. Additional exam requirements/recommendations for international students: Required—TOEFL (minimum score 550 paper-based; 213 computer-based; 83 iBT); Recommended—TWE. Electronic applications accepted. *Faculty research:* Digital imaging, digital publishing, Internet development/e-commerce, information databases, multimedia, commercial digital photography, digital workflow, computer graphics modeling and animation, information design, sociotechnology, visual and technical literacy, environmental management, quality mgmt, project mgmt, international environmental, industrial ethics, hazardous materials, environmental chemistry.

Arkansas Tech University, Graduate College, College of Applied Sciences, Russellville, AR 72801. Offers emergency management (MS); engineering (M Engr); information technology (MS). Part-time programs available. *Students:* 73 full-time (17 women), 50 part-time (22 women); includes 8 minority (4 African Americans, 1 American Indian/Alaska Native, 1 Asian American or Pacific Islander, 2 Hispanic Americans), 55 international. Average age 29. In 2009, 38 master's awarded. *Degree requirements:* For master's, comprehensive exam (for some programs), thesis (for some programs), internship. *Entrance requirements:* For master's, GRE General Test. Additional exam requirements/recommendations for international students: Required—TOEFL (minimum score 550 paper-based; 213 computer-based; 79 iBT), IELTS (minimum score 6). *Application deadline:* For fall admission, 3/1 priority date for domestic students, 5/1 priority date for international students; for spring admission, 10/1 priority date for domestic and international students. Applications are processed on a rolling basis. Application fee: $0 ($30 for international students). Electronic applications accepted. *Expenses:* Tuition, state resident: full-time $3438; part-time $191 per hour. Tuition, nonresident: full-time $6876; part-time $382 per hour. Required fees: $482; $9 per credit hour. $140 per semester. Tuition and fees vary according to course load. *Financial support:* In 2009–10, teaching assistantships with full tuition reimbursements (averaging $4,000 per year); research assistantships, career-related internships or fieldwork, Federal Work-Study, scholarships/grants, health care benefits, and unspecified assistantships also available. Support available to part-time students. Financial award application deadline: 4/15; financial award applicants required to submit FAFSA. *Unit head:* Dr. William Hoefler, Dean, 479-968-0353 Ext. 501, E-mail: whoeflerjr@atu.edu. *Application contact:* Dr. Mary B. Gunter, Dean of Graduate College, 479-968-0398, Fax: 479-964-0542, E-mail: graduate.school@atu.edu.

Aspen University, Program in Information Technology, Denver, CO 80246. Offers MS, Certificate. Part-time and evening/weekend programs available. Postbaccalaureate distance learning degree programs offered (no on-campus study). Electronic applications accepted.

Athabasca University, School of Computing and Information Systems, Athabasca, AB T9S 3A3, Canada. Offers information systems (M Sc). Part-time programs available. Postbaccalaureate distance learning degree programs offered (no on-campus study). *Faculty:* 11 full-time (1 woman), 2 part-time/adjunct (0 women). *Students:* 217 part-time. Average age 36. 28 applicants, 4 enrolled. In 2009, 34 master's awarded. *Degree requirements:* For master's, thesis optional. *Entrance requirements:* For master's, B Sc in computing or other bachelor's degree and IT experience. *Application deadline:* For fall admission, 3/1 for domestic students, 2/1 for international students. Application fee: $80. Electronic applications accepted. *Expenses:* Contact institution. *Faculty research:* Distributed systems multimedia, computer science education, e-services. *Unit head:* Dr. Kinshuk Kinshuk, Director, 780-675-6812, Fax: 780-675-6973, E-mail: kinshuk@athabascau.ca. *Application contact:* Karie Chambers, Student Support and Program Advisor, 780-675-6789, Fax: 780-675-6148, E-mail: karie-lynnc@athabascau.ca.

Ball State University, Graduate School, College of Communication, Information, and Media, Center for Information and Communication Sciences, Muncie, IN 47306-1099. Offers MS.

Barry University, School of Adult and Continuing Education, Program in Information Technology, Miami Shores, FL 33161-6695. Offers MS. Part-time and evening/weekend programs available. *Entrance requirements:* For master's, GMAT, GRE or MAT, bachelor's degree in information technology, related area or professional experience. Electronic applications accepted.

Bellevue University, Graduate School, Program in Computer Information Systems, Bellevue, NE 68005-3098. Offers MS.

Bentley University, McCallum Graduate School of Business, Program in Information Technology, Waltham, MA 02452-4705. Offers MSIT. Part-time and evening/weekend programs available. *Faculty:* 65 full-time (24 women), 16 part-time/adjunct (6 women). *Students:* 17 full-time (3 women), 27 part-time (7 women); includes 3 minority (2 Asian Americans or Pacific Islanders, 1 Hispanic American), 15 international. Average age 28. 71 applicants, 61% accepted, 13 enrolled. *Entrance requirements:* For master's, GMAT or GRE General Test. Additional exam requirements/recommendations for international students: Required—TOEFL (minimum score 600 paper-based; 250 computer-based; 100 iBT) or IELTS (minimum score 7). *Application deadline:* For fall admission, 12/1 priority date for domestic and international students. Application fee: $50. Electronic applications accepted. *Expenses:* Tuition: Full-time $26,208; part-time $1092 per credit. Required fees: $404. *Financial support:* Application deadline: 6/1; *Faculty research:* Information search, information technology ethics, IT governance, ERP usability, information visualization. *Unit head:* William Schiano, MSIT Director, 781-891-2555, E-mail: wschiano@bentley.edu. *Application contact:* Sharon Hill, Director of Graduate Admissions, 781-891-2108, Fax: 781-891-2464, E-mail: bentleygraduateadmissions@bentley.edu.

Bradley University, Graduate School, College of Liberal Arts and Sciences, Department of Computer Science and Information Systems, Peoria, IL 61625-0002. Offers computer information systems (MS); computer science (MS). Part-time and evening/weekend programs available. *Degree requirements:* For master's, comprehensive exam, thesis or alternative, programming test. *Entrance requirements:* For master's, 2 letters of recommendation. Additional exam requirements/recommendations for international students: Required—TOEFL (minimum score 550 paper-based; 213 computer-based; 79 iBT).

Brigham Young University, Graduate Studies, Ira A. Fulton College of Engineering and Technology, School of Technology, Provo, UT 84602-1001. Offers construction management (MS); information technology (MS); manufacturing systems (MS); technology and engineering education (MS). *Faculty:* 25 full-time (0 women). *Students:* 23 full-time (3 women); includes 3 minority (2 Asian Americans or Pacific Islanders, 1 Hispanic American). Average age 25. 14 applicants, 71% accepted, 6 enrolled. In 2009, 13 master's awarded. *Degree requirements:* For master's, thesis. *Entrance requirements:* For master's, GRE General Test, GMAT (construction management), minimum GPA of 3.0 in last 60 hours of course work. Additional exam requirements/recommendations for international students: Required—TOEFL (minimum score 580 paper-based; 237 computer-based; 85 iBT). *Application deadline:* For fall admission, 2/15 for domestic and international students; for winter admission, 9/15 for domestic and international students; for spring admission, 2/15 for domestic and international students. Application fee: $50. Electronic applications accepted. *Expenses:* Tuition: Full-time $5580; part-time $301 per credit hour. Tuition and fees vary according to student's religious affiliation. *Financial support:* In 2009–10, 9 research assistantships (averaging $4,774 per year), 7 teaching assistantships (averaging $4,481 per year) were awarded; fellowships, career-related internships or fieldwork also available. Financial award application deadline: 2/1. *Faculty research:* Real time process control in IT, electronic physical design, processing and non-linear systems, networking, computerized systems in CM. Total annual research expenditures: $52,000. *Unit head:* Val D. Hawks, Director, 801-422-6300, Fax: 801-422-0490, E-mail: hawksv@byu.edu. *Application contact:* Ronald E. Terry, Graduate Coordinator, 801-422-4297, Fax: 801-422-0490, E-mail: ralowe@byu.edu.

Brooklyn College of the City University of New York, Division of Graduate Studies, Department of Computer and Information Science, Brooklyn, NY 11210-2889. Offers computer science (MA, PhD); computer science and health science (MS); information systems (MS); parallel and distributed computing (Advanced Certificate). The department offers courses at Brooklyn College that are creditable toward the CUNY doctoral degree. Part-time and evening/weekend programs available. *Degree requirements:* For master's, comprehensive exam, thesis or alternative. *Entrance requirements:* For master's, previous course work in computer science, 2 letters of recommendation. Additional exam requirements/recommendations for international students: Required—TOEFL (minimum score 525 paper-based; 195 computer-based; 70 iBT). Electronic applications accepted. *Faculty research:* Networks and distributed systems, programming languages, modeling and computer applications, algorithms, artificial intelligence, theoretical computer science.

California State University, Fullerton, Graduate Studies, College of Business and Economics, Department of Information Systems and Decision Sciences, Fullerton, CA 92834-9480. Offers information systems (MS); information systems (decision sciences) (MS); information systems (e-commerce) (MS); information technology (MS); management science (MBA). Part-time programs available. *Students:* 9 full-time (3 women), 72 part-time (13 women); includes 32 minority (3 African Americans, 22 Asian Americans or Pacific Islanders, 7 Hispanic Americans), 16 international. Average age 33. 105 applicants, 50% accepted, 38 enrolled. In 2009, 29 master's awarded. *Degree requirements:* For master's, project or thesis. *Entrance requirements:* For master's, GMAT, minimum AACSB index of 950. Application fee: $55. *Expenses:* Tuition, nonresident: full-time $11,160; part-time $373 per credit. Required fees: $1440 per term. Tuition and fees vary according to course load, degree level and program. *Financial support:* Career-related internships or fieldwork, Federal Work-Study, institutionally sponsored loans, and scholarships/grants available. Support available to part-time students. Financial award application deadline: 3/1; financial award applicants required to submit FAFSA. *Unit head:* Dr. Bhushan Kapoor, Chair, 657-278-2221. *Application contact:* Admissions/Applications, 657-278-2371.

Capitol College, Graduate Programs, Laurel, MD 20708-9759. Offers business administration (MBA); computer science (MS); electrical engineering (MS); information and telecommunications systems management (MS); information architecture (MS); network security (MS). Part-time and evening/weekend programs available. Postbaccalaureate distance learning degree programs offered (no on-campus study). *Entrance requirements:* For master's, minimum GPA of 3.0. Electronic applications accepted.

Carleton University, Faculty of Graduate Studies, Faculty of Engineering and Design, Ottawa-Carleton Institute for Electrical Engineering, Department of Systems and Computer Engineering, Program in Information and Systems Science, Ottawa, ON K1S 5B6, Canada. Offers M Sc.

Carleton University, Faculty of Graduate Studies, Faculty of Science, Information and Systems Science Program, Ottawa, ON K1S 5B6, Canada. Offers M Sc. *Degree requirements:* For master's, thesis optional. *Entrance requirements:* For master's, honors degree. Additional exam requirements/recommendations for international students: Required—TOEFL. *Faculty research:* Software engineering, real-time and microprocessor programming, computer communications.

Carleton University, Faculty of Graduate Studies, Faculty of Science, School of Computer Science, Ottawa, ON K1S 5B6, Canada. Offers computer science (MCS, PhD); information and system science (M Sc). Part-time programs available. *Degree requirements:* For master's, thesis optional, project; for doctorate, comprehensive exam, thesis/dissertation. *Entrance requirements:* For master's, honors degree. Additional exam requirements/recommendations for international students: Required—TOEFL. *Faculty research:* Programming systems, theory of computing, computer applications, computer systems.

Carnegie Mellon University, H. John Heinz III College, School of Information Systems and Management, Program in Information Systems Management, Pittsburgh, PA 15213-3891. Offers MISM.

Carnegie Mellon University, H. John Heinz III College, School of Information Systems and Management, Program in Information Technology–Australia, Adelaide, PA 5000, Australia. Offers MSIT.

Carnegie Mellon University, School of Computer Science, Language Technologies Institute, Pittsburgh, PA 15213-3891. Offers MLT, PhD. Terminal master's awarded for partial completion of doctoral program. *Degree requirements:* For doctorate, thesis/dissertation. *Entrance requirements:* For master's and doctorate, GRE General Test, GRE Subject Test. Additional exam requirements/recommendations for international students: Required—TOEFL. *Faculty research:* Machine translation, natural language processing, speech and information retrieval, literacy.

Case Western Reserve University, School of Graduate Studies, The Case School of Engineering, Department of Electrical Engineering and Computer Science, Cleveland, OH 44106. Offers computer engineering (MS, PhD); computing and information sciences (MS, PhD); electrical engineering (MS, PhD); systems and control engineering (MS, PhD). Part-time and evening/weekend programs available. Postbaccalaureate distance learning degree programs offered (minimal on-campus study). *Faculty:* 32 full-time (2 women). *Students:* 175 full-time (26 women), 28 part-time (6 women); includes 9 minority (3 African Americans, 6 Asian Americans or Pacific Islanders), 107 international. In 2009, 29 master's, 15 doctorates awarded. Terminal master's awarded for partial completion of doctoral program. *Degree requirements:* For master's, thesis; for doctorate, thesis/dissertation, qualifying exam, teaching experience. *Entrance requirements:* For master's and doctorate, GRE General Test. Additional exam requirements/recommendations for international students: Required—TOEFL. *Application deadline:* For fall admission, 2/1 for domestic students; for spring admission, 11/1 for domestic students. Applications are processed on a rolling basis. Application fee: $50. *Financial support:* Fellowships with full and partial tuition reimbursements, research assistantships with full and partial tuition reimbursements, teaching assistantships, career-related internships or fieldwork, Federal Work-Study, and institutionally sponsored loans available. Support available to part-time students. Financial award application deadline: 3/1; financial award applicants required to submit FAFSA. *Faculty research:* Applied artificial intelligence, automation, computer-aided design and testing of digital systems. Total annual research expenditures: $5.5 million. *Unit head:* Dwight Davy, Department Chair, 216-368-2802, E-mail: dtd@case.edu. *Application contact:* David Easler, Student Affairs Coordinator, 216-368-4080, Fax: 216-368-2801, E-mail: david.easler@case.edu.

The Citadel, The Military College of South Carolina, Citadel Graduate College, Department of Mathematics and Computer Science, Charleston, SC 29409. Offers computer and information science (MS); mathematics education (MAE). *Accreditation:* NCATE (one or more programs are accredited). Part-time and evening/weekend programs available. *Faculty:* 3 full-time (0 women), 1 part-time/adjunct (0 women). *Students:* 1 (woman) full-time, 18 part-time (8 women); includes 1 minority (Asian American or Pacific Islander). Average age 35. In 2009, 3 master's awarded. *Degree requirements:* For master's, comprehensive exam (for some programs), thesis (for some programs). *Entrance requirements:* For master's, GRE (minimum score 1000 for MS; minimum score 900 verbal and quantitative for MAT, raw score of 396), minimum undergraduate GPA of 3.0 (MS) or 2.5 (MAT); competency, demonstrated through coursework, approved work experience, or a program-administrated competency exam, in the areas of basic computer architecture, object-oriented programming, discrete mathematics, and data structures (MS); successful completion of 7 courses (MAT). Additional exam requirements/recommendations for international students: Required—TOEFL (minimum score 550 paper-based; 213 computer-based; 79 iBT). *Application deadline:* Applications are processed on a rolling basis. Application fee: $30. Electronic applications accepted. *Expenses:* Tuition, state resident: part-time $400 per credit hour. Tuition, nonresident: part-time $657 per credit hour. Required fees: $40 per term. *Financial support:* Health care benefits and unspecified assistantships available. Support available to part-time students. Financial award application deadline: 7/1; financial award applicants required to submit FAFSA. *Unit head:* Dr. John I. Moore, Department Head, 843-953-5048, Fax: 843-953-7391, E-mail: john.moore@citadel.edu. *Application contact:* Dr. George L. Rudolph, Computer and Information Science Program Director, 843-953-5032, Fax: 843-953-7391, E-mail: george.rudolph@citadel.edu.

Claremont Graduate University, Graduate Programs, School of Information Systems and Technology, Claremont, CA 91711-6160. Offers electronic commerce (MS, PhD); health information management (MS); information systems (Certificate); knowledge management (MS, PhD); systems development (MS, PhD); telecommunications and networking (MS, PhD); MBA/MS. Part-time programs available. *Faculty:* 6 full-time (1 woman), 1 part-time/adjunct (0 women). *Students:* 78 full-time (28 women), 35 part-time (11 women); includes 32 minority (8 African Americans, 1 American Indian/Alaska Native, 16 Asian Americans or Pacific Islanders, 7 Hispanic Americans), 32 international. Average age 38. In 2009, 31 master's, 11 doctorates, 1 other advanced degree awarded. *Degree requirements:* For doctorate, comprehensive exam, thesis/dissertation, portfolio. *Entrance requirements:* For master's and doctorate, GMAT, GRE General Test. Additional exam requirements/recommendations for international students: Required—TOEFL (minimum score 550 paper-based; 213 computer-based; 80 iBT). *Application deadline:* For fall admission, 2/1 priority date for domestic students. Applications are processed on a rolling basis. Application fee: $60. Electronic applications accepted. *Expenses:* Tuition: Full-time $35,046; part-time $1524 per credit. Required fees: $161 per semester. *Financial support:* Fellowships, research assistantships, teaching assistantships, Federal Work-Study, institutionally sponsored loans, and scholarships/grants available. Support available to part-time students. Financial award application deadline: 2/15; financial award applicants required to submit FAFSA. *Faculty research:* GPSS, man-machine interaction, organizational aspects of computing, implementation of information systems, information systems practice. *Unit head:* Terry Ryan, Dean, 909-607-9591, Fax: 909-621-8564, E-mail: terry.ryan@cgu.edu. *Application*

Information Science

Claremont Graduate University (continued)
contact: Matt Hutter, Director of External Affairs, 909-621-3180, Fax: 909-621-8564, E-mail: matt.hutter@cgu.edu.

Clark Atlanta University, School of Arts and Sciences, Department of Computer and Information Science, Atlanta, GA 30314. Offers MS. Part-time programs available. *Faculty:* 5 full-time (1 woman). *Students:* 5 full-time (1 woman), 5 part-time (3 women); includes 9 minority (all African Americans), 1 international. Average age 31. 7 applicants, 100% accepted, 3 enrolled. In 2009, 3 master's awarded. *Degree requirements:* For master's, one foreign language, thesis. *Entrance requirements:* For master's, GRE General Test, minimum GPA of 2.5. Additional exam requirements/recommendations for international students: Required—TOEFL (minimum score 550 paper-based; 173 computer-based). *Application deadline:* For fall admission, 4/1 for domestic and international students; for spring admission, 11/1 for domestic and international students. Applications are processed on a rolling basis. Application fee: $40 ($55 for international students). *Expenses:* Tuition: Full-time $12,240; part-time $680 per credit hour. Required fees: $710; $355 per semester. *Financial support:* In 2009–10, 1 research assistantship, 3 teaching assistantships were awarded; career-related internships or fieldwork, Federal Work-Study, scholarships/grants, and unspecified assistantships also available. Support available to part-time students. Financial award application deadline: 4/30; financial award applicants required to submit FAFSA. *Unit head:* Dr. Roy George, Chairperson, 404-880-6945, E-mail: rgeorge@cau.edu. *Application contact:* Michelle Clark-Davis, Graduate Program Admissions, 404-880-6605, E-mail: cauadmissions@cau.edu.

Clarkson University, Graduate School, School of Arts and Sciences, Program in Information Technology, Potsdam, NY 13699. Offers MS. Part-time programs available. *Students:* 8 full-time (1 woman), 3 part-time (1 woman); includes 1 minority (American Indian/Alaska Native), 5 international. Average age 30. 24 applicants, 54% accepted, 4 enrolled. In 2009, 4 master's awarded. *Entrance requirements:* For master's, GRE, 3 letters of recommendation; resume (recommended). Additional exam requirements/recommendations for international students: Required—TOEFL, TSE (recommended). *Application deadline:* For fall admission, 1/30 priority date for domestic and international students; for spring admission, 9/1 priority date for domestic and international students. Applications are processed on a rolling basis. Application fee: $25 ($35 for international students). Electronic applications accepted. *Expenses:* Tuition: Part-time $1074 per credit hour. *Financial support:* In 2009–10, 7 students received support. *Faculty research:* Information networks, technical communications, networking management information systems. Total annual research expenditures: $23,353. *Unit head:* Dr. William D. Horn, Director, 315-268-6420, Fax: 315-268-7994, E-mail: horn@clarkson.edu. *Application contact:* Jennifer E. Reed, Graduate School Coordinator for School of Arts and Sciences, 315-268-3802, Fax: 315-268-3989, E-mail: jreed@clarkson.edu.

See Close-Up on page 297.

Clark University, Graduate School, College of Professional and Continuing Education, Program in Information Technology, Worcester, MA 01610-1477. Offers MSIT. *Students:* 7 full-time (3 women), 26 part-time (6 women); includes 5 minority (3 African Americans, 2 Asian Americans or Pacific Islanders), 7 international. Average age 35. 8 applicants, 100% accepted, 8 enrolled. In 2009, 7 master's awarded. *Degree requirements:* For master's, thesis or alternative. *Application deadline:* Applications are processed on a rolling basis. Application fee: $50. Electronic applications accepted. *Expenses:* Tuition: Full-time $34,900; part-time $4362.50 per course. *Financial support:* Tuition waivers (partial) available. *Unit head:* Max E. Hess, Director of Graduate Studies, 508-793-7217, Fax: 508-793-7232. *Application contact:* Julia Parent, Director of Marketing, Communications, and Admissions, 508-793-7217, Fax: 508-793-7232, E-mail: jparent@clarku.edu.

Cleveland State University, College of Graduate Studies, Nance College of Business Administration, Department of Computer and Information Science, Cleveland, OH 44115. Offers computer and information science (MCIS); information systems (DBA). Part-time and evening/weekend programs available. Terminal master's awarded for partial completion of doctoral program. *Degree requirements:* For master's, thesis optional; for doctorate, comprehensive exam, thesis/dissertation. *Entrance requirements:* For master's, GRE or GMAT, minimum GPA of 2.75; for doctorate, GRE or GMAT, MBA, MCIS or equivalent. Additional exam requirements/recommendations for international students: Required—TOEFL (minimum score 525 paper-based; 197 computer-based; 78 iBT). Electronic applications accepted. *Faculty research:* Artificial intelligence, object oriented analysis, database design, software efficiency, distributed system, geographical information systems.

Coleman University, Program in Information Technology, San Diego, CA 92123. Offers MSIT. Evening/weekend programs available. *Entrance requirements:* For master's, bachelor's degree in computer field, minimum GPA of 3.0. Additional exam requirements/recommendations for international students: Required—TOEFL (minimum score 500 paper-based).

The College of Saint Rose, Graduate Studies, School of Mathematics and Sciences, Program in Computer Information Systems, Albany, NY 12203-1419. Offers MS. Part-time and evening/weekend programs available. *Degree requirements:* For master's, comprehensive exam, research component. *Entrance requirements:* For master's, minimum GPA of 3.0, 9 undergraduate credits in math. Additional exam requirements/recommendations for international students: Required—TOEFL (minimum score 550 paper-based; 213 computer-based). Electronic applications accepted.

Cornell University, Graduate School, Graduate Fields of Arts and Sciences, Field of Information Science, Ithaca, NY 14853-0001. Offers cognition (PhD); human computer interaction (PhD); information systems (PhD); social aspects of information (PhD). *Faculty:* 35 full-time (10 women). *Students:* 14 full-time (4 women); includes 1 minority (Asian American or Pacific Islander), 6 international. Average age 31. 53 applicants, 9% accepted, 5 enrolled. In 2009, 3 doctorates awarded. *Degree requirements:* For doctorate, comprehensive exam, thesis/dissertation. *Entrance requirements:* For doctorate, GRE General Test, 3 letters of recommendation. Additional exam requirements/recommendations for international students: Required—TOEFL (minimum score 550 paper-based; 213 computer-based; 77 iBT). *Application deadline:* For fall admission, 1/1 for domestic students. Application fee: $70. Electronic applications accepted. *Expenses:* Tuition: Full-time $29,500. Required fees: $70. Full-time tuition and fees vary according to degree level, program and student level. *Financial support:* In 2009–10, 10 students received support, including 1 fellowship with full tuition reimbursement available, 2 research assistantships with full tuition reimbursements available, 2 teaching assistantships with full tuition reimbursements available; institutionally sponsored loans, scholarships/grants, tuition waivers (full and partial), and unspecified assistantships also available. Financial award applicants required to submit FAFSA. *Faculty research:* Digital libraries, game theory, data mining, human-computer interaction, computational linguistics. *Unit head:* Director of Graduate Studies, 607-255-5925. *Application contact:* Graduate Field Assistant, 607-255-5925, E-mail: info@infosci.cornell.edu.

Dakota State University, College of Business and Information Systems, Madison, SD 57042-1799. Offers MSHI, MSIA, MSIS, D Sc IS. *Accreditation:* ACBSP. Part-time and evening/weekend programs available. Postbaccalaureate distance learning degree programs offered (minimal on-campus study). *Faculty:* 23 full-time (3 women), 1 part-time/adjunct (0 women). *Students:* 51 full-time (7 women), 148 part-time (34 women); includes 18 minority (4 African Americans, 3 American Indian/Alaska Native, 7 Asian Americans or Pacific Islanders, 4 Hispanic Americans), 59 international. Average age 35. 112 applicants, 58% accepted, 59 enrolled. In 2009, 38 master's awarded. *Degree requirements:* For master's, comprehensive exam, examination, integrative project; for doctorate, comprehensive exam, thesis/dissertation, portfolio. *Entrance requirements:* For master's, GRE General Test, demonstration of information systems skills, minimum GPA of 2.75 (MSIS); for doctorate, GRE General Test, demonstration of information systems skills. Additional exam requirements/recommendations for international students: Required—TOEFL (minimum score 550 paper-based; 213 computer-based). *Application deadline:* For fall admission, 8/1 for domestic students, 6/1 for international students; for spring admission, 12/1 for domestic students, 10/1 for international students. Applications are processed on a rolling basis. Application fee: $35 ($85 for international students). Electronic applications accepted. *Financial support:* In 2009–10, 55 students received support, including 7 fellowships with partial tuition reimbursements available (averaging $31,837 per year), 15 research assistantships with partial tuition reimbursements available (averaging $11,116 per year), 4 teaching assistantships with partial tuition reimbursements available (averaging $31,837 per year); Federal Work-Study, scholarships/grants, and administrative assistantships also available. Support available to part-time students. Financial award applicants required to submit FAFSA. *Faculty research:* E-commerce, data mining and data warehousing, effectiveness of hybrid learning environments, biometrics and information assurance, decision support systems. *Unit head:* Dr. Tom Halverson, Dean, 605-256-5165, Fax: 605-256-5060, E-mail: tom.halverson@dsu.edu. *Application contact:* Annette Miller, Secretary, Office of Graduate Studies and Research, 605-256-5799, Fax: 605-256-5093, E-mail: annette.miller@dsu.edu.

See Close-Up on page 301.

DePaul University, College of Computing and Digital Media, Chicago, IL 60604. Offers business information technology (MS); computational finance (MS); computer and information sciences (PhD); computer game development (MS); computer graphics and motion technology (MS); computer science (MS); computer, information and network security (MS), including applied technology; digital cinema (MFA, MS), including information technology project management (MS); e-commerce technology (MS); human-computer interaction (MS); information systems (MS); information technology (MA); information technology project management (MS); software engineering (MS); telecommunications systems (MS); JD/MS. Part-time and evening/weekend programs available. Postbaccalaureate distance learning degree programs offered (no on-campus study). *Faculty:* 78 full-time (16 women), 191 part-time/adjunct (51 women). *Students:* 922 full-time (239 women), 887 part-time (209 women); includes 466 minority (193 African Americans, 3 American Indian/Alaska Native, 162 Asian Americans or Pacific Islanders, 108 Hispanic Americans), 276 international. Average age 31. 853 applicants, 67% accepted, 294 enrolled. In 2009, 444 master's, 4 doctorates awarded. *Degree requirements:* For master's, thesis (for some programs); for doctorate, comprehensive exam, thesis/dissertation. *Entrance requirements:* For master's, GRE or GMAT (MS in computational finance only), bachelor's degree; for doctorate, GRE, master's degree in computer science. Additional exam requirements/recommendations for international students: Required—TOEFL (minimum score 550 paper-based; 213 computer-based), IELTS (minimum score 6.5), Pearson Test of English (minimum score 53). *Application deadline:* For fall admission, 8/15 priority date for domestic students, 6/1 priority date for international students; for winter admission, 12/15 priority date for domestic students, 9/15 priority date for international students; for spring admission, 3/1 priority date for domestic students, 12/15 priority date for international students. Applications are processed on a rolling basis. Application fee: $25. Electronic applications accepted. *Expenses:* Contact institution. *Financial support:* In 2009–10, 69 students received support, including 6 fellowships with full tuition reimbursements available (averaging $25,858 per year), 75 teaching assistantships with full and partial tuition reimbursements available (averaging $5,780 per year); research assistantships, Federal Work-Study, scholarships/grants, tuition waivers (full and partial), and unspecified assistantships also available. Support available to part-time students. Financial award application deadline: 4/30; financial award applicants required to submit FAFSA. *Faculty research:* Bioinformatics, visual computing, graphics and animation, high performance and scientific computing, databases. Total annual research expenditures: $790,000. *Unit head:* Dr. David Miller, Dean, 312-362-8381, Fax: 312-362-5185. *Application contact:* Dr. Liz Friedman, Assistant Dean of Student Services, 312-362-5384, Fax: 312-362-5327, E-mail: efriedm2@cdm.depaul.edu.

DeSales University, Graduate Division, Program in Information Systems, Center Valley, PA 18034-9568. Offers MSIS. Part-time programs available. *Students:* 14 part-time. In 2009, 218 master's awarded. *Degree requirements:* For master's, comprehensive exam, thesis optional. *Entrance requirements:* Additional exam requirements/recommendations for international students: Required—TOEFL. *Application deadline:* Applications are processed on a rolling basis. Application fee: $35. Electronic applications accepted. *Expenses:* Tuition: Full-time $17,500; part-time $665 per credit. Full-time tuition and fees vary according to program. Part-time tuition and fees vary according to course load. *Financial support:* Applicants required to submit FAFSA. *Faculty research:* Digital communication, numerical analysis, database design. *Unit head:* Bonita Moyer, Director, 610-282-1100 Ext. 1392, Fax: 610-282-2254, E-mail: bonita.moyer@desales.edu. *Application contact:* Caryn Stopper, Director of Graduate Admissions, 610-282-1100 Ext. 1768, Fax: 610-282-2254, E-mail: caryn.stopper@desales.edu.

Drexel University, The iSchool at Drexel, College of Information Science and Technology, Master of Science (Library and Information Science) Program, Philadelphia, PA 19104-2875. Offers archival studies (MS); competitive intelligence and knowledge management (MS); digital libraries (MS); library and information services (MS); school library media (MS); youth services (MS). Part-time and evening/weekend programs available. Postbaccalaureate distance learning degree programs offered (no on-campus study). *Faculty:* 34 full-time (19 women), 24 part-time/adjunct (9 women). *Students:* 248 full-time (187 women), 363 part-time (289 women); includes 47 minority (16 African Americans, 1 American Indian/Alaska Native, 17 Asian Americans or Pacific Islanders, 13 Hispanic Americans), 9 international. Average age 34. 465 applicants, 50% accepted, 224 enrolled. In 2009, 272 master's awarded. *Entrance requirements:* For master's, GRE General Test. Additional exam requirements/recommendations for international students: Required—TOEFL (minimum score 600 paper-based; 250 computer-based; 100 iBT). *Application deadline:* For fall admission, 8/1 for domestic and international students; for spring admission, 2/1 for domestic and international students. Applications are processed on a rolling basis. Electronic applications accepted. *Expenses:* Contact institution. *Financial support:* In 2009–10, 217 students received support, including 213 fellowships with partial tuition reimbursements available (averaging $225 per year); institutionally sponsored loans, scholarships/grants, and fellowships also available. Support available to part-time students. Financial award applicants required to submit FAFSA. *Faculty research:* Library and information resources and services, knowledge organization and representation, information retrieval/information visualization/bibliometrics, information needs and behaviors, digital libraries. Total annual research expenditures: $2 million. *Unit head:* Dr. David E. Fenske, Dean and Isaac L. Auerbach Professor of Information Science, 215-895-2475, Fax: 215-895-6378, E-mail: fenske@drexel.edu. *Application contact:* Matthew Lechtenberg, Graduate Admissions Manager, 215-895-1951, Fax: 215-895-2303, E-mail: ml333@drexel.edu.

Drexel University, The iSchool at Drexel, College of Information Science and Technology, PhD in Information Studies Program, Philadelphia, PA 19104-2875. Offers PhD. Part-time and evening/weekend programs available. *Faculty:* 43 full-time (23 women). *Students:* 42 full-time (21 women), 10 part-time (2 women); includes 13 minority (4 African Americans, 8 Asian Americans or Pacific Islanders, 1 Hispanic American), 18 international. Average age 36. 66 applicants, 23% accepted, 9 enrolled. In 2009, 12 doctorates awarded. *Degree requirements:* For doctorate, thesis/dissertation. *Entrance requirements:* For doctorate, GRE General Test. Additional exam requirements/recommendations for international students: Required—TOEFL (minimum score 600 paper-based; 250 computer-based; 100 iBT). *Application deadline:* For fall admission, 2/1 for domestic and international students. Applications are processed on a rolling basis. Electronic applications accepted. *Financial support:* In 2009–10, 8 students received support, including 18 research assistantships with full tuition reimbursements available (averaging $25,000 per year), 2 teaching assistantships with full tuition reimbursements available (averaging $19,500 per year); career-related internships or fieldwork, institutionally sponsored loans, scholarships/grants, traineeships, health care benefits, tuition waivers (partial), and unspecified assistantships also available. Financial award application deadline: 2/1. *Faculty research:* Information retrieval/information visualization/bibliometrics, human-computer interaction, digital libraries, databases, text/data mining, healthcare informatics, school library media. Total annual research expenditures: $2 million. *Unit head:* Dr. David E. Fenske, Dean and Isaac L. Auerbach Professor of Information Science, 215-895-2475, Fax: 215-895-6378, E-mail: fenske@drexel.edu. *Application contact:* Matthew Lechtenberg, Graduate Admissions Manager, 215-895-1951, Fax: 215-895-2303, E-mail: ml333@drexel.edu.

East Carolina University, Graduate School, College of Education, Department of Business, Career, and Technical Education, Greenville, NC 27858-4353. Offers information technologies (MS); vocation education (MA Ed). *Accreditation:* NCATE. Part-time and evening/weekend programs available. Postbaccalaureate distance learning degree programs offered (no on-campus study). *Degree requirements:* For master's, comprehensive exam, thesis optional. *Entrance requirements:* For master's, GRE or MAT, minimum GPA of 2.5, bachelor's degree in related field, teaching license (MA Ed). Additional exam requirements/recommendations for international students: Required—TOEFL.

East Tennessee State University, School of Graduate Studies, College of Business and Technology, Department of Computer and Information Sciences, Johnson City, TN 37614. Offers computer science (MS); information systems science (MS); software engineering (MS). Part-time and evening/weekend programs available. *Degree requirements:* For master's, comprehensive exam, thesis. *Entrance requirements:* For master's, GRE General Test, minimum GPA of 2.5. Additional exam requirements/recommendations for international students: Required—TOEFL (minimum score 550 paper-based; 213 computer-based). *Faculty research:* Operating systems, database design, artificial intelligence, simulation, parallel algorithms.

Everglades University, Graduate Programs, Program in Information Technology, Boca Raton, FL 33431. Offers MIT. *Entrance requirements:* Additional exam requirements/recommendations for international students: Recommended—TOEFL (minimum score 500 paper-based; 173 computer-based). Electronic applications accepted.

Florida Gulf Coast University, Lutgert College of Business, Program in Computer and Information Systems, Fort Myers, FL 33965-6565. Offers MS. *Entrance requirements:* For master's, GMAT, minimum GPA of 3.0. Additional exam requirements/recommendations for international students: Required—TOEFL (minimum score 550 paper-based; 213 computer-based). Electronic applications accepted. *Faculty research:* Advanced distributed learning technologies, object-oriented systems analysis, database management systems, workgroup support systems, software engineering project management.

Florida International University, College of Engineering and Computing, School of Computing and Information Sciences, Miami, FL 33199. Offers computer science (MS, PhD); computing and information sciences (MS, PhD); telecommunications and networking (MS). Part-time and evening/weekend programs available. *Faculty:* 30 full-time (3 women). *Students:* 76 full-time (24 women), 37 part-time (7 women); includes 39 minority (3 African Americans, 6 Asian Americans or Pacific Islanders, 30 Hispanic Americans), 63 international. Average age 30. 180 applicants, 14% accepted, 26 enrolled. In 2009, 29 master's, 5 doctorates awarded. *Degree requirements:* For master's, thesis or alternative; for doctorate, comprehensive exam, thesis/dissertation. *Entrance requirements:* For master's and doctorate, GRE General Test, 3 letters of recommendation, minimum GPA of 3.0. Additional exam requirements/recommendations for international students: Required—TOEFL (minimum score 550 paper-based; 80 iBT). *Application deadline:* For fall admission, 6/1 for domestic students, 4/1 for international students; for spring admission, 10/1 for domestic students, 9/1 for international students. Applications are processed on a rolling basis. Application fee: $30. Electronic applications accepted. *Expenses:* Tuition, state resident: full-time $8008; part-time $4004 per year. Tuition, nonresident: full-time $20,104; part-time $10,052 per year. Required fees: $298; $149 per term. *Financial support:* In 2009–10, 34 research assistantships (averaging $20,474 per year), 24 teaching assistantships (averaging $20,474 per year) were awarded; institutionally sponsored loans, scholarships/grants, and unspecified assistantships also available. Financial award application deadline: 3/1; financial award applicants required to submit FAFSA. *Faculty research:* Database systems, software engineering, operating systems, networks, bioinformatics and computational biology. Total annual research expenditures: $2.5 million. *Unit head:* Dr. Jainendra Navlakha, Interim Director, School of Computing and Information Sciences, 305-348-2023, Fax: 305-348-3549, E-mail: navlakha@cis.fiu.edu. *Application contact:* Maria Parrilla, Graduate Admissions Assistant, 305-348-1890, Fax: 305-348-6142, E-mail: grad_eng@fiu.edu.

Gannon University, School of Graduate Studies, College of Engineering and Business, School of Engineering and Computer Science, Program in Computer and Information Science, Erie, PA 16541-0001. Offers MSCIS. Part-time and evening/weekend programs available. *Students:* 25 full-time (4 women), 18 part-time (8 women), 30 international. Average age 28. 282 applicants, 71% accepted, 18 enrolled. In 2009, 20 master's awarded. *Degree requirements:* For master's, research project or thesis. *Entrance requirements:* Additional exam requirements/recommendations for international students: Required—TOEFL (minimum score 79 iBT). *Application deadline:* Applications are processed on a rolling basis. Application fee: $25. Electronic applications accepted. *Expenses:* Tuition: Full-time $13,590; part-time $755 per credit. Required fees: $524; $17 per credit. Tuition and fees vary according to course load, degree level, campus/location and program. *Financial support:* Career-related internships or fieldwork, Federal Work-Study, scholarships/grants, traineeships, and unspecified assistantships available. Financial award application deadline: 7/1; financial award applicants required to submit FAFSA. *Unit head:* Dr. Steven Frezza, Chair, 814-871-7563, E-mail: frezza001@gannon.edu. *Application contact:* Kara Morgan, Assistant Director of Graduate Admissions, 814-871-5831, Fax: 814-871-5827, E-mail: graduate@gannon.edu.

George Mason University, Volgenau School of Information Technology and Engineering, Department of Applied Information Technology, Fairfax, VA 22030. Offers MS. *Faculty:* 15 full-time (6 women), 40 part-time/adjunct (10 women). *Students:* 30 full-time (6 women), 47 part-time (11 women); includes 25 minority (3 African Americans, 18 Asian Americans or Pacific Islanders, 4 Hispanic Americans), 6 international. Average age 29. 46 applicants, 74% accepted, 31 enrolled. *Degree requirements:* For master's, capstone course. *Entrance requirements:* Additional exam requirements/recommendations for international students: Required—TOEFL. *Application deadline:* For fall admission, 3/1 priority date for domestic students; for spring admission, 10/15 for domestic students. Application fee: $75. *Expenses:* Tuition, state resident: full-time $7568; part-time $315.33 per credit hour. Tuition, nonresident: full-time $21,704; part-time $904.33 per credit hour. Required fees: $2184; $91 per credit hour. *Financial support:* In 2009–10, 3 students received support, including 3 teaching assistantships (averaging $5,330 per year); Federal Work-Study, institutionally sponsored loans, unspecified assistantships, and health care benefits (full-time research or teaching assistantship recipients) also available. Financial award application deadline: 3/1. Total annual research expenditures: $986,428. *Unit head:* Lloyd Griffiths, Dean, 703-993-1500, Fax: 703-993-1734, E-mail: lgriffiths@gmu.edu. *Application contact:* Nicole Sealey, Graduate Admission & Enrollment Services Director, 703-993-3932, E-mail: nsealey@gmu.edu.

George Mason University, Volgenau School of Information Technology and Engineering, Program in Information Technology, Fairfax, VA 22030. Offers PhD, Engr. *Faculty:* 15 full-time (6 women), 40 part-time/adjunct (10 women). *Students:* 20 full-time (3 women), 169 part-time (28 women); includes 29 minority (12 African Americans, 2 American Indian/Alaska Native, 15 Asian Americans or Pacific Islanders), 54 international. Average age 39. 82 applicants, 56% accepted, 19 enrolled. In 2009, 14 doctorates awarded. *Degree requirements:* For doctorate, comprehensive exam, thesis/dissertation, internship. *Entrance requirements:* For doctorate, GRE, 3 letters of recommendation, resume. Additional exam requirements/recommendations for international students: Required—TOEFL (minimum score 575 paper-based; 230 computer-based). *Application deadline:* For fall admission, 2/1 priority date for domestic students; for spring admission, 11/1 for domestic students. Application fee: $75. Electronic applications accepted. *Expenses:* Tuition, state resident: full-time $7568; part-time $315.33 per credit hour. Tuition, nonresident: full-time $21,704; part-time $904.33 per credit hour. Required fees: $2184; $91 per credit hour. *Financial support:* In 2009–10, 32 students received support, including 1 fellowship with full tuition reimbursement available (averaging $18,000 per year), 12 research assistantships with full and partial tuition reimbursements available (averaging $12,315 per year), 19 teaching assistantships with full and partial tuition reimbursements available (averaging $10,589 per year); Federal Work-Study, scholarships/grants, unspecified assistantships, and health care benefits (full-time research or teaching assistantship recipients) also available. Support available to part-time students. Financial award application deadline: 3/1; financial award applicants required to submit FAFSA. *Faculty research:* Rapid pace of technological innovation, need for efficient and effective technology development, unwavering interoperability challenges, the scope and complexity of major system design requirements. *Unit head:* Dr. Donald Gantz, Professor and Chair, 703-993-3565, E-mail: dgantz@gmu.edu. *Application contact:* Stephanie Katavolos, Program Administrator, 703-993-2972, E-mail: skatavol@gmu.edu.

Georgia Southwestern State University, Graduate Studies, School of Computer and Information Sciences, Americus, GA 31709-4693. Offers computer information systems (MS); computer science (MS). Part-time programs available. *Degree requirements:* For master's, thesis (for some programs). *Entrance requirements:* For master's, GRE General Test, minimum GPA of 3.0. Electronic applications accepted. *Faculty research:* Database, Internet technologies, computational complexity, encryption.

Georgia State University, J. Mack Robinson College of Business, Program in General Business Administration, Atlanta, GA 30302-3083. Offers accounting/information systems (MBA); economics (MBA, MS); enterprise risk management (MBA); general business (MBA); general business administration (EMBA, PMBA); information systems consulting (MBA); information systems risk management (MBA); international business and information technology (MBA); international entrepreneurship (MBA); MBA/JD. *Accreditation:* AACSB. Part-time and evening/weekend programs available. *Entrance requirements:* For master's, GMAT. Additional exam requirements/recommendations for international students: Required—TOEFL (minimum score 610 paper-based; 255 computer-based; 101 iBT). Electronic applications accepted.

Grand Valley State University, Padnos College of Engineering and Computing, School of Computing and Information Systems, Allendale, MI 49401-9403. Offers computer information systems (MS), including databases, distributed systems, management of information systems, object-oriented systems, software engineering. Part-time and evening/weekend programs available. *Faculty:* 11 full-time (0 women). *Students:* 10 full-time (3 women), 52 part-time (12 women); includes 8 minority (1 African American, 6 Asian Americans or Pacific Islanders, 1 Hispanic American), 11 international. Average age 33. 32 applicants, 81% accepted, 16 enrolled. In 2009, 22 master's awarded. *Degree requirements:* For master's, thesis or alternative. *Entrance requirements:* For master's, GMAT or GRE General Test. Additional exam requirements/recommendations for international students: Required—TOEFL. *Application deadline:* For fall admission, 6/1 for international students; for winter admission, 9/1 for international students. Applications are processed on a rolling basis. Application fee: $30. Electronic applications accepted. *Financial support:* In 2009–10, 9 students received support, including 5 fellowships (averaging $3,380 per year), 5 research assistantships with full and partial tuition reimbursements available (averaging $4,626 per year). *Faculty research:* Object technology, distributed computing, information systems management database, software engineering. *Unit head:* Paul Leidig, Director, 616-331-2038, Fax: 616-331-2106, E-mail: leidigp@gvsu.edu. *Application contact:* D. Robert Adams, CIS Graduate Program Chair, 616-331-3885, Fax: 616-331-2106, E-mail: adams@cis.gvsu.edu.

Harvard University, Extension School, Cambridge, MA 02138-3722. Offers applied sciences (CAS); biotechnology (ALM); educational technologies (ALM); educational technology (CET); English for graduate and professional studies (DGP); environmental management (ALM, CEM); information technology (ALM); journalism (ALM); liberal arts (ALM); management (ALM, CM); mathematics for teaching (ALM); museum studies (ALM); premedical studies (Diploma); publication and communication (CPC). Part-time and evening/weekend programs available. *Degree requirements:* For master's, thesis. *Entrance requirements:* For master's, 3 completed graduate courses with grade of B or higher. Additional exam requirements/recommendations for international students: Required—TOEFL (minimum score 600 paper-based; 250 computer-based), TWE (minimum score 5). *Expenses:* Contact institution.

Harvard University, Graduate School of Arts and Sciences, Program in Information, Technology and Management, Cambridge, MA 02138. Offers PhD. *Expenses:* Tuition: Full-time $33,696. Required fees: $1126. Full-time tuition and fees vary according to program.

Hood College, Graduate School, Program in Management of Information Technology, Frederick, MD 21701-8575. Offers MS. Part-time and evening/weekend programs available. *Faculty:* 1 (woman) full-time, 2 part-time/adjunct (1 woman). *Students:* 4 full-time (2 women), 13 part-time (4 women); includes 3 minority (2 African Americans, 1 Asian American or Pacific Islander), 2 international. Average age 37. 9 applicants, 78% accepted, 3 enrolled. In 2009, 2 master's awarded. *Degree requirements:* For master's, thesis. *Entrance requirements:* For master's, minimum GPA of 2.75. Additional exam requirements/recommendations for international students: Required—TOEFL (minimum score 575 paper-based; 231 computer-based; 89 iBT). *Application deadline:* For fall admission, 7/15 for domestic and international students; for spring admission, 12/15 for domestic and international students. Applications are processed on a rolling basis. Application fee: $35. Electronic applications accepted. *Expenses:* Tuition: Full-time $6480; part-time $360 per credit. Required fees: $100; $50 per term. *Financial support:* Applicants required to submit FAFSA. *Faculty research:* Systems engineering, parallel distributed computing, strategy, business ethics, entrepreneurship. *Unit head:* Raymond Myers, Director, 301-696-3724, E-mail: myers@hood.edu. *Application contact:* Dr. Allen P. Flora, Dean of Graduate School, 301-696-3811, Fax: 301-696-3597, E-mail: gofurther@hood.edu.

Hood College, Graduate School, Programs in Computer and Information Sciences, Frederick, MD 21701-8575. Offers computer and information sciences (MS); computer science (MS). Part-time and evening/weekend programs available. *Faculty:* 5 full-time (1 woman), 5 part-time/adjunct (1 woman). *Students:* 13 full-time (3 women), 65 part-time (14 women); includes 9 minority (3 African Americans, 3 Asian Americans or Pacific Islanders, 3 Hispanic Americans), 11 international. Average age 34. 33 applicants, 88% accepted, 23 enrolled. In 2009, 19 master's awarded. *Degree requirements:* For master's, thesis. *Entrance requirements:* For master's, minimum GPA of 2.75. Additional exam requirements/recommendations for international students: Required—TOEFL (minimum score 575 paper-based; 231 computer-based; 89 iBT). *Application deadline:* For fall admission, 7/15 for domestic and international students; for spring admission, 12/15 for domestic and international students. Applications are processed on a rolling basis. Application fee: $35. Electronic applications accepted. *Expenses:* Tuition: Full-time $6480; part-time $360 per credit. Required fees: $100; $50 per term. *Financial support:* Applicants required to submit FAFSA. *Faculty research:* Systems engineering, natural language, processing, database design, artificial intelligence and parallel distributed computing. *Unit head:* Dr. Xinlian Liu, Director, 301-696-3981, E-mail: liu@hood.edu. *Application contact:* Dr. Allen P. Flora, Dean of Graduate School, 301-696-3811, Fax: 301-696-3597, E-mail: gofurther@hood.edu.

Indiana University Bloomington, School of Informatics, Bloomington, IN 47408. Offers bioinformatics (MS); chemical informatics (MS); computer science (MS, PhD); health informatics (MS); human computer interaction (MS); informatics (PhD); laboratory informatics (MS); media arts and science (MS); music informatics (MS); security informatics (MS); MS/PhD. PhD offered through University Graduate School. Part-time programs available. Postbaccalaureate distance learning degree programs offered (no on-campus study). *Faculty:* 63 full-time (12 women). *Students:* 367 full-time (93 women), 32 part-time (11 women); includes 18 minority (4 African Americans, 1 American Indian/Alaska Native, 11 Asian Americans or Pacific Islanders, 2 Hispanic Americans), 254 international. Average age 27. 676 applicants, 52% accepted, 146 enrolled. In 2009, 82 master's, 18 doctorates awarded. Terminal master's awarded for partial completion of doctoral program. *Degree requirements:* For master's, thesis optional; for doctorate, comprehensive exam, thesis/dissertation, oral and written exams. *Entrance requirements:* For master's and doctorate, GRE, letters of reference. Additional exam requirements/recommendations for international students: Required—TOEFL. *Application deadline:* For fall admission, 1/15 for domestic students, 12/1 for international students. Application fee: $55 ($65 for international students). Electronic applications accepted. *Financial support:* In 2009–10, 2 fellowships with full and partial tuition reimbursements (averaging $20,000 per year), 41 research assistantships (averaging $14,000 per year), 84 teaching assistantships (averaging $13,000 per year) were awarded; Federal Work-Study, institutionally sponsored loans,

Information Science

Indiana University Bloomington (continued)
scholarships/grants, health care benefits, tuition waivers (full and partial), and unspecified assistantships also available. Support available to part-time students. Total annual research expenditures: $2 million. *Unit head:* Dr. David Leake, Associate Dean for Graduate Studies, 812-855-9756, E-mail: leake@cs.indiana.edu. *Application contact:* Rachel Lawmaster, Manager of Graduate Admissions and Studies, 812-856-3622, Fax: 812-856-3825, E-mail: raclee@indiana.edu.

Indiana University Bloomington, School of Library and Information Science, Bloomington, IN 47405-3907. Offers MIS, MLS, PhD, Sp LIS, JD/MLS, MIS/MA, MLS/MA, MPA/MIS, MPA/MLS. *Accreditation:* ALA (one or more programs are accredited). Part-time programs available. *Faculty:* 16 full-time (7 women). *Students:* 263 full-time (189 women), 82 part-time (49 women); includes 24 minority (8 African Americans, 1 American Indian/Alaska Native, 8 Asian Americans or Pacific Islanders, 7 Hispanic Americans), 38 international. Average age 29. 305 applicants, 84% accepted, 117 enrolled. In 2009, 162 master's, 1 doctorate, 3 other advanced degrees awarded. *Degree requirements:* For doctorate, thesis/dissertation. *Entrance requirements:* For master's and doctorate, GRE General Test, 3 letters of reference. Additional exam requirements/recommendations for international students: Required—TOEFL (minimum score 600 paper-based; 250 computer-based; 100 iBT). *Application deadline:* For fall admission, 5/15 priority date for domestic students, 12/1 priority date for international students; for spring admission, 10/15 priority date for domestic students, 9/1 priority date for international students. Applications are processed on a rolling basis. Application fee: $55 ($65 for international students). Electronic applications accepted. *Expenses:* Contact institution. *Financial support:* Fellowships with full and partial tuition reimbursements, research assistantships with full and partial tuition reimbursements, career-related internships or fieldwork, Federal Work-Study, institutionally sponsored loans, scholarships/grants, tuition waivers (partial), and unspecified assistantships available. Support available to part-time students. Financial award application deadline: 1/15. *Faculty research:* Scholarly communication, interface design, library and management policy, computer-mediated communication, information retrieval. *Unit head:* Dr. Blaise Cronin, Dean, 812-855-2848, Fax: 812-855-6166, E-mail: bcronin@indiana.edu. *Application contact:* Rhonda Spencer, Director of Admissions, 812-855-2018, Fax: 812-855-6166, E-mail: slis@indiana.edu.

Indiana University–Purdue University Fort Wayne, College of Engineering, Technology, and Computer Science, Program in Technology, Fort Wayne, IN 46805-1499. Offers facilities and construction management (MS); industrial technology/manufacturing (MS); information technology/advanced computer applications (MS). Part-time programs available. *Faculty:* 10 full-time (6 women), 2 part-time/adjunct (0 women). *Students:* 6 full-time (3 women), 18 part-time (1 woman); includes 4 minority (3 Asian Americans or Pacific Islanders, 1 Hispanic American), 3 international. Average age 33. 13 applicants, 100% accepted, 12 enrolled. *Entrance requirements:* For master's, minimum GPA of 3.0. Additional exam requirements/recommendations for international students: Required—TOEFL (minimum score 550 paper-based; 213 computer-based; 77 iBT), TWE. *Application deadline:* For fall admission, 7/15 for domestic students, 5/15 for international students; for spring admission, 12/1 for domestic students, 10/15 for international students. Applications are processed on a rolling basis. Application fee: $55 ($60 for international students). Electronic applications accepted. *Expenses:* Tuition, state resident: full-time $4595; part-time $255 per credit. Tuition, nonresident: full-time $10,963; part-time $609 per credit. Required fees: $528; $29.35 per credit. Tuition and fees vary according to course load. *Financial support:* Career-related internships or fieldwork, scholarships/grants, and unspecified assistantships available. Support available to part-time students. Financial award application deadline: 3/1; financial award applicants required to submit FAFSA. *Unit head:* Dr. Gerard Voland, Dean, 260-481-6839, Fax: 260-481-5734, E-mail: volandg@ipfw.edu. *Application contact:* Dr. Paul Lin, Graduate Program Director, 260-481-6339, Fax: 260-481-5734, E-mail: lin@ipfw.edu.

Indiana University–Purdue University Indianapolis, School of Informatics, Indianapolis, IN 46202-2896. Offers informatics (PhD); media arts and science (MS). Part-time and evening/weekend programs available. *Faculty:* 3 full-time (0 women). *Students:* 36 full-time (11 women), 76 part-time (29 women); includes 19 minority (12 African Americans, 5 Asian Americans or Pacific Islanders, 2 Hispanic Americans), 29 international. Average age 34. 70 applicants, 71% accepted, 33 enrolled. In 2009, 39 master's awarded. *Degree requirements:* For master's, multimedia project. *Entrance requirements:* For master's, minimum undergraduate GPA of 3.0, graduate 3.2; interview; portfolio; BA with demonstrated media arts skills. Additional exam requirements/recommendations for international students: Required—TOEFL. *Application deadline:* For fall admission, 3/15 for domestic students; for spring admission, 11/15 for domestic students. Application fee: $55 ($65 for international students). *Financial support:* In 2009–10, 6 fellowships (averaging $17,447 per year), 13 teaching assistantships (averaging $9,392 per year) were awarded; career-related internships or fieldwork, Federal Work-Study, institutionally sponsored loans, and scholarships/grants also available. Support available to part-time students. *Unit head:* Darrell L. Bailey, Executive Associate Dean, 317-278-4636, Fax: 317-278-7769. *Application contact:* Dr. Sherry Queener, Director, Graduate Studies and Associate Dean, 317-274-1577, Fax: 317-278-2380.

Indiana University–Purdue University Indianapolis, School of Library and Information Science, Indianapolis, IN 46202-2896. Offers MLS. Part-time and evening/weekend programs available. *Faculty:* 3 full-time (2 women). *Students:* 78 full-time (56 women), 232 part-time (190 women); includes 30 minority (20 African Americans, 1 American Indian/Alaska Native, 5 Asian Americans or Pacific Islanders, 4 Hispanic Americans). Average age 34. 95 applicants, 95% accepted, 79 enrolled. In 2009, 97 master's awarded. *Entrance requirements:* For master's, GRE General Test. Additional exam requirements/recommendations for international students: Required—TOEFL (minimum score 600 paper-based). *Application deadline:* For fall admission, 7/15 priority date for domestic students; for spring admission, 11/15 priority date for domestic students. Applications are processed on a rolling basis. Application fee: $55 ($65 for international students). *Financial support:* In 2009–10, 2 teaching assistantships (averaging $9,500 per year) were awarded; career-related internships or fieldwork, Federal Work-Study, institutionally sponsored loans, and scholarships/grants also available. Support available to part-time students. *Unit head:* Dr. Daniel Collison, Executive Associate Dean, 317-278-2375, Fax: 317-278-1807, E-mail: slisindy@iupui.edu. *Application contact:* Dr. Daniel Collison, Executive Associate Dean, 317-278-2375, Fax: 317-278-1807, E-mail: slisindy@iupui.edu.

Instituto Tecnológico y de Estudios Superiores de Monterrey, Campus Cuernavaca, Programs in Information Science, Temixco, Mexico. Offers administration of information technology (MATI); computer science (MCC, DCC); information technology (MTI).

Instituto Tecnológico y de Estudios Superiores de Monterrey, Campus Estado de México, Professional and Graduate Division, Estado de Mexico, Mexico. Offers administration of information technologies (MITA); architecture (M Arch); business administration (GMBA, MBA); computer sciences (MCS, PhD); education (M Ed); educational institution administration (MAD); educational technology and innovation (PhD); electronic commerce (MEC); environmental systems (MS); finance (MAF); humanistic studies (MHS); information sciences and knowledge management (MISKM); information systems (MS); manufacturing systems (MS); marketing (MEM); quality systems and productivity (MS); science and materials engineering (PhD); telecommunications management (MTM). Part-time programs available. Postbaccalaureate distance learning degree programs offered (minimal on-campus study). *Degree requirements:* For master's, one foreign language, thesis (for some programs); for doctorate, one foreign language, thesis/dissertation. *Entrance requirements:* For master's, E-PAEP 500, interview; for doctorate, E-PAEP 500, research proposal. Additional exam requirements/recommendations for international students: Required—TOEFL (minimum score 550 paper-based). *Faculty research:* Surface treatments by plasmas, mechanical properties, robotics, graphical computing, mechatronics security protocols.

Instituto Tecnológico y de Estudios Superiores de Monterrey, Campus Irapuato, Graduate Programs, Irapuato, Mexico. Offers administration (MBA); administration of information

technology (MAIT); administration of telecommunications (MAT); architecture (M Arch); computer science (MCS); education (M Ed); educational administration (MEA); educational innovation and technology (DEIT); educational technology (MET); electronic commerce (MBA); environmental administration and planning (MEAP); environmental systems (MES); finances (MBA); humanistic studies (MHS); international management for Latin American executives (MIMLAE); library and information science (MLIS); manufacturing quality management (MMQM); marketing research (MBA).

Instituto Tecnológico y de Estudios Superiores de Monterrey, Campus Monterrey, Graduate and Research Division, Program in Computer Science, Monterrey, Mexico. Offers artificial intelligence (PhD); computer science (MS); information systems (MS); information technology (MS). Part-time programs available. *Degree requirements:* For master's, one foreign language, thesis; for doctorate, one foreign language, thesis/dissertation. *Entrance requirements:* For master's, EXADEP; for doctorate, master's degree in related field. Additional exam requirements/recommendations for international students: Required—TOEFL. *Faculty research:* Distributed systems, software engineering, decision support systems.

Instituto Tecnológico y de Estudios Superiores de Monterrey, Campus Monterrey, Graduate and Research Division, Program in Informatics, Monterrey, Mexico. Offers PhD. Part-time programs available. *Degree requirements:* For doctorate, one foreign language, thesis/dissertation, technological project, arbitrated publication of articles. *Entrance requirements:* For doctorate, GRE General Test, GRE Subject Test, master's degree in related field. Additional exam requirements/recommendations for international students: Required—TOEFL. *Faculty research:* Artificial intelligence, distributed systems, software engineering, decision support systems.

Instituto Tecnológico y de Estudios Superiores de Monterrey, Campus Sonora Norte, Program in Technological Information Management, Hermosillo, Mexico. Offers MA.

Iowa State University of Science and Technology, Graduate College, Interdisciplinary Programs, Program in Information Assurance, Ames, IA 50011. Offers MS. *Students:* 5 full-time (1 woman), 34 part-time (6 women); includes 5 minority (2 African Americans, 2 Asian Americans or Pacific Islanders, 1 Hispanic American), 3 international. In 2009, 13 master's awarded. *Degree requirements:* For master's, thesis or alternative. *Entrance requirements:* For master's, GRE General Test. Additional exam requirements/recommendations for international students: Required—TOEFL (minimum score 570 paper-based; 79 iBT) or IELTS (minimum score 6.5). *Application deadline:* For fall admission, 5/1 priority date for domestic and international students; for spring admission, 11/1 priority date for domestic and international students. Application fee: $40 ($90 for international students). *Expenses:* Tuition, state resident: full-time $6716. Tuition, nonresident: full-time $8908. Tuition and fees vary according to course level, course load, program and student level. *Financial support:* In 2009–10, 5 research assistantships with full and partial tuition reimbursements (averaging $13,500 per year) were awarded; teaching assistantships with full and partial tuition reimbursements, health care benefits and unspecified assistantships also available. *Unit head:* Dr. Doug Jacobson, Chair of Supervising Committee, 515-294-8307, E-mail: infas@iac.iastate.edu. *Application contact:* Information Contact, 515-294-5836, Fax: 515-294-2592, E-mail: grad_admissions@iastate.edu.

The Johns Hopkins University, G. W. C. Whiting School of Engineering, Information Security Institute, Baltimore, MD 21218-2699. Offers MSSI. Part-time programs available. *Faculty:* 6 part-time/adjunct (0 women). *Students:* 23 full-time (2 women), 20 part-time (1 woman); includes 4 minority (2 African Americans, 1 Asian American or Pacific Islander, 1 Hispanic American), 24 international. Average age 25. 70 applicants, 93% accepted, 16 enrolled. In 2009, 13 master's awarded. *Degree requirements:* For master's, project. *Entrance requirements:* For master's, GRE, minimum GPA of 3.0. Additional exam requirements/recommendations for international students: Required—TOEFL (minimum score 600 paper-based; 250 computer-based). *Application deadline:* For fall admission, 6/15 priority date for domestic students, 3/15 for international students; for spring admission, 11/15 for domestic students, 11/1 for international students. Applications are processed on a rolling basis. Application fee: $25. Electronic applications accepted. *Financial support:* In 2009–10, 28 students received support, including 3 teaching assistantships with tuition reimbursements available (averaging $3,000 per year); fellowships with full tuition reimbursements available, career-related internships or fieldwork, Federal Work-Study, institutionally sponsored loans, scholarships/grants, traineeships, health care benefits, tuition waivers (partial), and unspecified assistantships also available. *Faculty research:* Critical infrastructure protection, insider/outsider cryptography and encryption methodologies, international policy protocols, web based intellectual property rights. Total annual research expenditures: $675,000. *Unit head:* Dr. Gerald M. Masson, Director, 410-516-7013, Fax: 410-516-3301, E-mail: masson@jhu.edu. *Application contact:* Deborah K. Higgins, Graduate Coordinator, 410-516-8521, Fax: 410-516-3301, E-mail: dhiggins@jhu.edu.

Kansas State University, Graduate School, College of Engineering, Department of Computing and Information Sciences, Manhattan, KS 66506. Offers computer science (MS, PhD); software engineering (MSE). Part-time programs available. Postbaccalaureate distance learning degree programs offered (minimal on-campus study). *Faculty:* 15 full-time (1 woman). *Students:* 74 full-time (14 women), 45 part-time (10 women); includes 3 minority (2 Asian Americans or Pacific Islanders, 1 Hispanic American), 86 international. Average age 26. 236 applicants, 49% accepted, 40 enrolled. In 2009, 27 master's, 5 doctorates awarded. Terminal master's awarded for partial completion of doctoral program. *Degree requirements:* For master's, thesis or alternative; for doctorate, thesis/dissertation, preliminary exams. *Entrance requirements:* For master's, GRE, bachelor's degree in computer science, minimum GPA of 3.0; for doctorate, GRE General Test, GRE Subject Test, master's degree in computer science or bachelor's degree and strong advanced computer knowledge. Additional exam requirements/recommendations for international students: Required—TOEFL (minimum score 575 paper-based; 233 computer-based). *Application deadline:* For fall admission, 2/1 priority date for domestic and international students; for spring admission, 8/1 priority date for domestic and international students. Applications are processed on a rolling basis. Application fee: $40 ($55 for international students). Electronic applications accepted. *Financial support:* In 2009–10, 27 research assistantships (averaging $16,260 per year), 24 teaching assistantships with full tuition reimbursements (averaging $14,294 per year) were awarded; career-related internships or fieldwork, institutionally sponsored loans, and scholarships/grants also available. Support available to part-time students. Financial award application deadline: 3/15; financial award applicants required to submit FAFSA. *Faculty research:* High-assurance software and programming languages, data mining, parallel and distributed computing, computer security, embedded systems. Total annual research expenditures: $1.5 million. *Unit head:* Gurdip E. Singh, Head, 785-532-7945, Fax: 785-532-7353, E-mail: gurdip@ksu.edu. *Application contact:* Dave Gustafson, Director, 785-532-6350, Fax: 785-532-7353, E-mail: dag@ksu.edu.

Kennesaw State University, College of Science and Mathematics, Program in Information Systems, Kennesaw, GA 30144-5591. Offers MSIS. Part-time programs available. *Faculty:* 14 full-time (3 women), 1 (woman) part-time/adjunct. *Students:* 30 full-time (8 women), 43 part-time (12 women); includes 21 minority (17 African Americans, 2 Asian Americans or Pacific Islanders, 2 Hispanic Americans), 9 international. Average age 34. 42 applicants, 74% accepted, 22 enrolled. In 2009, 24 master's awarded. *Entrance requirements:* For master's, GMAT or GRE General Test, minimum GPA of 2.75. Additional exam requirements/recommendations for international students: Required—TOEFL (minimum score 550 paper-based; 213 computer-based; 80 iBT), IELTS (minimum score 6). *Application deadline:* For fall admission, 8/1 for domestic and international students; for spring admission, 11/1 for domestic and international students. Applications are processed on a rolling basis. Application fee: $60. Electronic applications accepted. *Expenses:* Tuition, state resident: full-time $2341; part-time $196 per credit hour. Tuition, nonresident: full-time $9396; part-time $783 per credit hour. Required fees: $573 per semester. *Financial support:* In 2009–10, 2 research assistantships with full tuition reimbursements (averaging $15,000 per year) were awarded; Federal Work-Study and unspecified assistantships also available. Support available to part-time students. Financial award application deadline: 6/15; financial award applicants required to submit FAFSA. *Unit head:* Dr. Amy

Woszczynski, Director, 770-423-6005, Fax: 770-423-6731, E-mail: awoszczy@kennesaw.edu. *Application contact:* Vilma Marquez, Admissions Counselor, 770-420-4377, Fax: 770-423-6885, E-mail: ksugrad@kennesaw.edu.

Kent State University, College of Communication and Information, Interdisciplinary Program in Information Architecture and Knowledge Management, Kent, OH 44242-0001. Offers MS. Part-time and evening/weekend programs available. *Degree requirements:* For master's, capstone or thesis. *Entrance requirements:* For master's, GRE (recommended). *Faculty research:* Information architecture, knowledge management, usability, organizational memory management, information design, user interface design.

Kentucky State University, College of Mathematics, Sciences, Technology and Health, Frankfort, KY 40601. Offers aquaculture (MS); computer science (MS), including computer science theory, information assurance, information technology. Part-time and evening/weekend programs available. *Faculty:* 8 full-time (0 women), 1 part-time/adjunct (0 women). *Students:* 18 full-time (6 women), 18 part-time (4 women); includes 11 minority (8 African Americans, 1 Asian American or Pacific Islander, 2 Hispanic Americans), 7 international. Average age 35. 42 applicants, 55% accepted, 12 enrolled. In 2009, 8 master's awarded. *Degree requirements:* For master's, comprehensive exam, thesis optional. *Entrance requirements:* For master's, GRE, GMAT. Additional exam requirements/recommendations for international students: Required—TOEFL (minimum score 525 paper-based; 173 computer-based). *Application deadline:* For fall admission, 7/1 priority date for domestic students, 4/15 priority date for international students; for spring admission, 11/15 priority date for domestic students, 8/1 priority date for international students. Applications are processed on a rolling basis. Application fee: $30 ($100 for international students). Electronic applications accepted. *Expenses:* Tuition, state resident: full-time $5634; part-time $313 per credit hour. Tuition, nonresident: full-time $14,598; part-time $811 per credit hour. Required fees: $450; $25 per credit hour. *Financial support:* In 2009–10, 28 students received support, including 10 research assistantships (averaging $10,505 per year); career-related internships or fieldwork, scholarships/grants, tuition waivers (partial), and unspecified assistantships also available. Financial award application deadline: 4/15; financial award applicants required to submit FAFSA. *Unit head:* Dr. Charles Bennett, Dean, 502-597-6926, E-mail: charles.bennett@kysu.edu. *Application contact:* Cedric Cunningham, Administrative Assistant, Office of Graduate Studies, 502-597-6536, Fax: 502-597-6432, E-mail: cedric.cunningham@kysu.edu.

Kettering University, Graduate School, Department of Business, Flint, MI 48504. Offers business administration (MBA); engineering management (MSEM); information technology (MSIT); manufacturing management (MSMM); manufacturing operations (MSMO); operations management (MSOM). *Accreditation:* ACBSP. Part-time and evening/weekend programs available. Postbaccalaureate distance learning degree programs offered (no on-campus study). *Faculty:* 9 full-time (3 women), 4 part-time/adjunct (0 women). *Students:* 12 full-time (5 women), 251 part-time (79 women); includes 42 minority (27 African Americans, 1 American Indian/Alaska Native, 9 Asian Americans or Pacific Islanders, 5 Hispanic Americans), 15 international. Average age 32. 74 applicants, 78% accepted, 31 enrolled. In 2009, 123 master's awarded. *Entrance requirements:* Additional exam requirements/recommendations for international students: Required—TOEFL (minimum score 550 paper-based; 213 computer-based; 79 iBT). *Application deadline:* For fall admission, 9/15 for domestic students, 6/15 for international students; for winter admission, 12/15 for domestic students, 9/15 for international students; for spring admission, 3/15 for domestic students, 12/15 for international students. Applications are processed on a rolling basis. Electronic applications accepted. *Expenses:* Tuition: Full-time $11,120; part-time $695 per credit hour. *Financial support:* In 2009–10, 101 students received support, including fellowships with full tuition reimbursements available (averaging $13,000 per year), research assistantships with full tuition reimbursements available (averaging $13,000 per year), teaching assistantships with full tuition reimbursements available (averaging $13,000 per year); Federal Work-Study, scholarships/grants, and tuition waivers (partial) also available. Support available to part-time students. Financial award application deadline: 7/15. *Unit head:* Dr. Tony Hain, Vice President of Graduate Studies and Corporate Connections, 810-762-9616, Fax: 810-762-9935, E-mail: thain@kettering.edu. *Application contact:* Bonnie Switzer, Admissions Representative, 810-762-7953, Fax: 810-762-9935, E-mail: bswitzer@kettering.edu.

Knowledge Systems Institute, Program in Computer and Information Sciences, Skokie, IL 60076. Offers MS. Part-time and evening/weekend programs available. Postbaccalaureate distance learning degree programs offered (minimal on-campus study). *Degree requirements:* For master's, comprehensive exam, thesis. *Entrance requirements:* Additional exam requirements/recommendations for international students: Required—TOEFL (minimum score 550 paper-based; 213 computer-based; 79 iBT). Electronic applications accepted. *Faculty research:* Data mining, web development, database programming and administration.

Lamar University, College of Graduate Studies, College of Business, Beaumont, TX 77710. Offers accounting (MBA); experiential business and entrepreneurship (MBA); financial management (MBA); healthcare administration (MBA); information systems (MBA); management (MBA). *Accreditation:* AACSB. Part-time and evening/weekend programs available. *Faculty:* 18 full-time (4 women), 4 part-time/adjunct (0 women). *Students:* 62 full-time (27 women), 59 part-time (16 women); includes 19 minority (8 African Americans, 6 Asian Americans or Pacific Islanders, 5 Hispanic Americans), 19 international. Average age 29. 210 applicants, 34% accepted, 33 enrolled. In 2009, 41 master's awarded. *Degree requirements:* For master's, comprehensive exam (for some programs), thesis optional. *Entrance requirements:* For master's, GMAT. Additional exam requirements/recommendations for international students: Required—TOEFL (minimum score 525 paper-based; 197 computer-based). *Application deadline:* For fall admission, 3/15 priority date for domestic students; for spring admission, 10/1 priority date for domestic students. Applications are processed on a rolling basis. Application fee: $25 ($50 for international students). *Financial support:* In 2009–10, 12 students received support, including 4 research assistantships with partial tuition reimbursements available; fellowships with tuition reimbursements available, career-related internships or fieldwork, Federal Work-Study, institutionally sponsored loans, scholarships/grants, and tuition waivers (partial) also available. Support available to part-time students. Financial award application deadline: 4/1; financial award applicants required to submit FAFSA. *Faculty research:* Marketing, finance, quantitative methods, management information systems, legal, environmental. *Unit head:* Dr. Enrique R. Venta, Dean, 409-880-8604, Fax: 409-880-8088, E-mail: henry.venta@lamar.edu. *Application contact:* Dr. Brad Mayer, Professor and Associate Dean, 409-880-2383, Fax: 409-880-8605, E-mail: bradley.mayer@lamar.edu.

Lehigh University, College of Business and Economics, Department of Accounting, Bethlehem, PA 18015. Offers accounting and information analysis (MS). *Accreditation:* AACSB. *Faculty:* 7 full-time (0 women), 2 part-time/adjunct (0 women). *Students:* 28 full-time (11 women), 5 part-time (4 women), 6 international. Average age 26. 157 applicants, 33% accepted, 14 enrolled. In 2009, 22 master's awarded. *Entrance requirements:* For master's, GMAT. Additional exam requirements/recommendations for international students: Required—TOEFL (minimum score 105 iBT). *Application deadline:* For fall admission, 5/1 for domestic and international students. Applications are processed on a rolling basis. Application fee: $100. Electronic applications accepted. *Expenses:* Contact institution. *Financial support:* In 2009–10, 6 research assistantships with partial tuition reimbursements (averaging $1,000 per year) were awarded; scholarships/grants and tuition waivers (partial) also available. Financial award application deadline: 1/15. *Faculty research:* Behavioral accounting, internal control, information systems, supply chain management, financial accounting. *Unit head:* Dr. James A. Largay, Director, 610-758-3409, Fax: 610-758-6429, E-mail: jal3@lehigh.edu. *Application contact:* Corinn McBride, Director of Recruitment and Admissions, 610-758-3418, Fax: 610-758-5283, E-mail: com207@lehigh.edu.

Long Island University, C.W. Post Campus, College of Information and Computer Science, Department of Computer Science/Management Engineering, Brookville, NY 11548-1300. Offers information systems (MS); information technology education (MS); management engineering

(MS). Part-time and evening/weekend programs available. *Degree requirements:* For master's, comprehensive exam, thesis or alternative. *Entrance requirements:* For master's, bachelor's degree in science, mathematics, or engineering; minimum GPA of 2.5. Additional exam requirements/recommendations for international students: Required—TOEFL (minimum score 500 paper-based; 173 computer-based). Electronic applications accepted. *Faculty research:* Inductive music learning, re-engineering business process, technology and ethics.

Loyola University Chicago, Graduate School, Department of Computer Science, Chicago, IL 60660. Offers computer science (MS); information technology (MS); software technology (MS). Part-time and evening/weekend programs available. *Faculty:* 9 full-time (1 woman), 10 part-time/adjunct (2 women). *Students:* 49 full-time (18 women), 31 part-time (6 women); includes 17 minority (4 African Americans, 9 Asian Americans or Pacific Islanders, 4 Hispanic Americans), 30 international. Average age 27. 96 applicants, 57% accepted, 30 enrolled. In 2009, 32 master's awarded. *Entrance requirements:* For master's, 3 letters of recommendation, transcripts, statement of purpose. Additional exam requirements/recommendations for international students: Required—TOEFL (minimum score 550 paper-based; 213 computer-based; 79 iBT), IELTS (minimum score 6.5). *Application deadline:* For fall admission, 5/15 priority date for international students; for spring admission, 9/15 priority date for international students. Applications are processed on a rolling basis. Application fee: $0. Electronic applications accepted. *Expenses:* Tuition: Full-time $14,220; part-time $790 per credit hour. Required fees: $60 per semester hour. Tuition and fees vary according to program. *Financial support:* In 2009–10, 24 students received support, including 1 fellowship (averaging $3,000 per year), 16 teaching assistantships with partial tuition reimbursements available (averaging $2,900 per year); career-related internships or fieldwork, Federal Work-Study, scholarships/grants, tuition waivers (partial), and unspecified assistantships also available. Financial award application deadline: 3/15. *Faculty research:* Software engineering, high performance computing, algorithms and complexity. Total annual research expenditures: $22,000. *Unit head:* Dr. Chandra Sekharan, Chair, 312-915-7985, Fax: 312-915-7998, E-mail: csekhar@luc.edu. *Application contact:* Cecilia Murphy, Graduate Program Secretary, 312-915-7990, Fax: 312-915-7998, E-mail: gradinfo-cs@luc.edu.

Marlboro College, Graduate School, Program in Information Technologies, Marlboro, VT 05344. Offers MS. Part-time and evening/weekend programs available. Postbaccalaureate distance learning degree programs offered (minimal on-campus study). *Faculty:* 9 part-time/adjunct (6 women). *Students:* 4 full-time (2 women), 11 part-time (6 women). Average age 40. 2 applicants, 100% accepted, 2 enrolled. In 2009, 3 master's awarded. *Degree requirements:* For master's, capstone project. *Entrance requirements:* For master's, 2 letters of recommendation. *Application deadline:* For fall admission, 3/1 priority date for domestic students. Applications are processed on a rolling basis. Application fee: $0. Electronic applications accepted. *Expenses:* Tuition: Full-time $9520; part-time $680 per credit. Tuition and fees vary according to course load and program. *Financial support:* Available to part-time students. Applicants required to submit FAFSA. *Application contact:* Joe Heslin, Associate Director of Admissions, 802-258-9209, Fax: 802-258-9201, E-mail: jheslin@gradcenter.marlboro.edu.

Marshall University, Academic Affairs Division, College of Information Technology and Engineering, Weisberg Division of Engineering and Computer Science, Program in Information Systems, Huntington, WV 25755. Offers MS. Part-time and evening/weekend programs available. *Faculty:* 9 full-time (1 woman), 2 part-time/adjunct (0 women). *Students:* 14 full-time (5 women), 17 part-time (3 women); includes 2 minority (both African Americans), 9 international. Average age 30. In 2009, 9 master's awarded. *Degree requirements:* For master's, final project, oral exam. *Entrance requirements:* For master's, GRE General Test or MAT, minimum undergraduate GPA of 2.5. *Application fee:* $40. *Financial support:* Tuition waivers (full) available. Support available to part-time students. Financial award application deadline: 8/1; financial award applicants required to submit FAFSA. *Unit head:* Dr. Thomas D. Hankins, Professor, 304-746-2044, E-mail: hankins@marshall.edu. *Application contact:* Information Contact, 304-746-1900, Fax: 304-746-1902, E-mail: services@marshall.edu.

Marywood University, Academic Affairs, Insalaco College of Creative and Performing Arts, Department of Communication Arts, Program in Information Sciences, Scranton, PA 18509-1598. Offers corporate communication (Certificate); e-business (Certificate); health communication (Certificate); information sciences (MS), including library science/information specialist; instructional technology (Certificate). *Students:* 1 full-time (0 women), 4 part-time (3 women). Average age 32. In 2009, 3 master's awarded. *Entrance requirements:* Additional exam requirements/recommendations for international students: Required—TOEFL (minimum score 550 paper-based; 213 computer-based; 79 iBT). *Application deadline:* For fall admission, 4/1 priority date for domestic students, 3/31 priority date for international students; for spring admission, 11/1 priority date for domestic students, 8/31 priority date for international students. Applications are processed on a rolling basis. Application fee: $35. Electronic applications accepted. *Expenses:* Tuition: Part-time $715 per credit. Required fees: $270 per semester. Tuition and fees vary according to degree level, campus/location and program. *Financial support:* Career-related internships or fieldwork, scholarships/grants, and unspecified assistantships available. Support available to part-time students. Financial award application deadline: 6/30; financial award applicants required to submit FAFSA. *Application contact:* Tammy Manka, Assistant Director of Graduate Admissions, 866-279-9663, E-mail: tmanka@marywood.edu.

Massachusetts Institute of Technology, School of Engineering, Department of Civil and Environmental Engineering, Cambridge, MA 02139-4307. Offers biological oceanography (PhD, Sc D); chemical oceanography (PhD, Sc D); civil and environmental engineering (M Eng, SM, PhD, Sc D); civil and environmental systems (PhD, Sc D); civil engineering (PhD, Sc D, CE); coastal engineering (PhD, Sc D); construction engineering and management (PhD, Sc D); environmental biology (PhD, Sc D); environmental chemistry (PhD, Sc D); environmental engineering (PhD, Sc D); environmental fluid mechanics (PhD, Sc D); geotechnical and geoenvironmental engineering (PhD, Sc D); hydrology (PhD, Sc D); information technology (PhD, Sc D); oceanographic engineering (PhD, Sc D); structures and materials (PhD, Sc D); transportation (PhD, Sc D); SM/MBA. *Faculty:* 36 full-time (5 women). *Students:* 190 full-time (59 women); includes 22 minority (2 African Americans, 14 Asian Americans or Pacific Islanders, 6 Hispanic Americans), 103 international. Average age 26. 478 applicants, 25% accepted, 76 enrolled. In 2009, 72 master's, 14 doctorates awarded. *Degree requirements:* For master's and CE, thesis; for doctorate, comprehensive exam, thesis/dissertation. *Entrance requirements:* For master's and doctorate, GRE General Test. Additional exam requirements/recommendations for international students: Required—TOEFL (minimum score 577 paper-based; 233 computer-based; 90 iBT), IELTS (minimum score 7). *Application deadline:* For fall admission, 1/2 for domestic and international students. Application fee: $75. Electronic applications accepted. *Financial support:* In 2009–10, 185 students received support, including 40 fellowships with tuition reimbursements available (averaging $27,725 per year), 97 research assistantships with tuition reimbursements available (averaging $28,035 per year), 21 teaching assistantships with tuition reimbursements available (averaging $24,802 per year); career-related internships or fieldwork, Federal Work-Study, institutionally sponsored loans, scholarships/grants, health care benefits, and unspecified assistantships also available. *Faculty research:* Environmental chemistry, environmental microbiology, environmental fluid mechanics and coastal engineering, geotechnical engineering and geomechanics, hydrology and hydroclimatology, mechanics of materials and structures, operations research/supply chain, transportation. Total annual research expenditures: $16.6 million. *Unit head:* Prof. Andrew Whittle, Department Head, 617-253-7101. *Application contact:* Patricia Glidden, Graduate Admissions Coordinator, 617-253-7119, Fax: 617-258-6775, E-mail: cee-admissions@mit.edu.

Missouri University of Science and Technology, Graduate School, Department of Business and Information Technology, Rolla, MO 65409. Offers business and information technology (MBA); information science and technology (MS). *Degree requirements:* For master's, thesis or alternative. *Entrance requirements:* Additional exam requirements/recommendations for international students: Required—TOEFL (minimum score 600 paper-based; 250 computer-based).

Information Science

Montclair State University, The Graduate School, College of Science and Mathematics, Department of Computer Science, Montclair, NJ 07043-1624. Offers applied mathematics (MS); applied statistics (MS); CISCO (Certificate); informatics (MS); object oriented computing (Certificate). Part-time and evening/weekend programs available. *Faculty:* 14 full-time (3 women), 16 part-time/adjunct (6 women). *Students:* 10 full-time (6 women), 21 part-time (6 women). Average age 31. 15 applicants, 67% accepted, 6 enrolled. In 2009, 11 master's awarded. *Degree requirements:* For master's, comprehensive exam, thesis or alternative. *Entrance requirements:* For master's, GRE General Test, 2 letters of recommendation. Additional exam requirements/recommendations for international students: Required—TOEFL (minimum score 83 computer-based), or IELTS. *Application deadline:* For fall admission, 6/1 for international students; for spring admission, 10/1 for international students. Applications are processed on a rolling basis. Application fee: $60. Electronic applications accepted. *Expenses:* Tuition, area resident: Part-time $486.74 per credit. Tuition, state resident: part-time $486.74 per credit. Tuition, nonresident: part-time $751.34 per credit. Tuition and fees vary according to degree level and program. *Financial support:* In 2009–10, 4 research assistantships with full tuition reimbursements (averaging $7,000 per year) were awarded; Federal Work-Study, scholarships/grants, and unspecified assistantships also available. Support available to part-time students. Financial award application deadline: 3/1; financial award applicants required to submit FAFSA. *Unit head:* Dr. Dorothy Deremer, Chairperson, 973-655-4166. *Application contact:* Amy Aiello, Director of Graduate Admissions and Operations, 973-655-5147, Fax: 973-655-7869, E-mail: graduate.school@montclair.edu.

National University, Academic Affairs, School of Engineering and Technology, Department of Computer Science and Information Systems, La Jolla, CA 92037-1011. Offers computer science (MS); information systems (MS); software engineering (MS); technology management (MS). Part-time and evening/weekend programs available. Postbaccalaureate distance learning degree programs offered (no on-campus study). *Faculty:* 18 full-time (10 women), 30 part-time/adjunct (7 women). *Students:* 88 full-time (19 women), 163 part-time (31 women); includes 57 minority (24 African Americans, 24 Asian Americans or Pacific Islanders, 9 Hispanic Americans), 111 international. Average age 32. 146 applicants, 100% accepted, 89 enrolled. In 2009, 51 master's awarded. *Degree requirements:* For master's, thesis. *Entrance requirements:* For master's, interview, minimum GPA of 2.5. Additional exam requirements/recommendations for international students: Required—TOEFL (minimum score 550 paper-based; 213 computer-based; 79 iBT), IELTS (minimum score 6). *Application deadline:* Applications are processed on a rolling basis. Application fee: $60 ($65 for international students). Electronic applications accepted. *Expenses:* Tuition: Part-time $338 per quarter hour. *Financial support:* Career-related internships or fieldwork, institutionally sponsored loans, scholarships/grants, and tuition waivers (partial) available. Support available to part-time students. Financial award application deadline: 6/30; financial award applicants required to submit FAFSA. *Unit head:* Dr. Ron Uhlig, Interim Chair and Instructor, 858-309-3412, Fax: 858-309-3420, E-mail: ruhlig@nu.edu. *Application contact:* Dominick Giovanniello, Associate Regional Dean—San Diego, 800-NAT-UNIV, Fax: 858-541-7792, E-mail: dgiovann@nu.edu.

Naval Postgraduate School, Graduate Programs, Department of Information Sciences, Monterey, CA 93943. Offers information sciences (MS); knowledge superiority (MS, Certificate). Program open only to commissioned officers of the United States and friendly nations and selected United States federal civilian employees. Part-time programs available. *Degree requirements:* For master's, thesis.

New Jersey Institute of Technology, Office of Graduate Studies, College of Computing Science, Program in Information Systems, Newark, NJ 07102. Offers business and information systems (MS); emergency management and business continuity (MS); information systems (MS, PhD). Part-time and evening/weekend programs available. Terminal master's awarded for partial completion of doctoral program. *Degree requirements:* For master's, thesis optional; for doctorate, thesis/dissertation. *Entrance requirements:* For master's, GRE General Test; for doctorate, GRE General Test, minimum graduate GPA of 3.5. Additional exam requirements/recommendations for international students: Required—TOEFL (minimum score 550 paper-based; 213 computer-based; 79 iBT). Electronic applications accepted.

Northeastern University, College of Computer and Information Science, Boston, MA 02115-5096. Offers computer and information science (PhD); computer science (MS); health informatics (MS); information assurance (MS). Part-time and evening/weekend programs available. *Faculty:* 28 full-time (3 women), 3 part-time/adjunct (all women). *Students:* 180 full-time (48 women), 15 part-time (0 women); includes 4 minority (2 Asian Americans or Pacific Islanders, 2 Hispanic Americans), 154 international. 829 applicants, 52% accepted, 74 enrolled. In 2009, 97 master's, 5 doctorates awarded. Terminal master's awarded for partial completion of doctoral program. *Degree requirements:* For master's, thesis optional; for doctorate, comprehensive exam, thesis/dissertation. *Entrance requirements:* For master's and doctorate, GRE General Test. Additional exam requirements/recommendations for international students: Required—TOEFL or IELTS. *Application deadline:* For fall admission, 7/15 for domestic students, 5/1 for international students; for spring admission, 10/15 for domestic students, 9/1 for international students. Applications are processed on a rolling basis. Application fee: $50. Electronic applications accepted. *Expenses:* Contact institution. *Financial support:* In 2009–10, 59 students received support, including 1 fellowship, 35 research assistantships with full tuition reimbursements available (averaging $18,260 per year), 24 teaching assistantships with full tuition reimbursements available (averaging $18,260 per year); career-related internships or fieldwork, Federal Work-Study, institutionally sponsored loans, scholarships/grants, and unspecified assistantships also available. Financial award application deadline: 1/15. *Faculty research:* Programming languages, artificial intelligence, human-computer interaction, database management, network security. *Unit head:* Dr. Larry A. Finkelstein, Dean, 617-373-2462, Fax: 617-373-5121. *Application contact:* Dr. Agnes Chan, Associate Dean and Director of Graduate Program, 617-373-2462, Fax: 617-373-5121, E-mail: gradschool@ccs.neu.edu.

Northeastern University, College of Engineering, Information Systems Program, Boston, MA 02115-5096. Offers MS, Certificate. Part-time programs available. Postbaccalaureate distance learning degree programs offered (no on-campus study). *Faculty:* 8 part-time/adjunct (2 women). *Students:* 117 full-time (44 women), 6 part-time (0 women); includes 2 minority (1 African American, 1 Hispanic American), 113 international. Average age 26. 163 applicants, 86% accepted, 37 enrolled. In 2009, 53 master's awarded. *Degree requirements:* For master's, thesis optional. *Entrance requirements:* For master's, GRE General Test. Additional exam requirements/recommendations for international students: Required—TOEFL (minimum score 600 paper-based; 250 computer-based; 80 iBT). *Application deadline:* For fall admission, 1/15 priority date for domestic and international students. Applications are processed on a rolling basis. Application fee: $50. Electronic applications accepted. *Financial support:* In 2009–10, 18 students received support, including 1 fellowship with full tuition reimbursement available (averaging $18,320 per year), 1 research assistantship with full tuition reimbursement available, 12 teaching assistantships with full tuition reimbursements available; career-related internships or fieldwork, Federal Work-Study, scholarships/grants, tuition waivers (full), and unspecified assistantships also available. Support available to part-time students. Financial award application deadline: 1/15; financial award applicants required to submit FAFSA. *Faculty research:* Simulation analysis, software architecture. *Unit head:* Dr. Khaled Bugrara, Director, 617-373-3699. *Application contact:* Stephen L. Gibson, Associate Director, 617-373-2711, Fax: 617-373-2501, E-mail: grad-eng@coe.neu.edu.

Northern Kentucky University, Office of Graduate Programs, College of Informatics, Department of Business Informatics, Highland Heights, KY 41099. Offers business informatics (MS, Certificate); corporate information security (Certificate); enterprise resource planning (Certificate). Part-time and evening/weekend programs available. Postbaccalaureate distance learning degree programs offered (no on-campus study). *Students:* 5 full-time (2 women), 30 part-time (13 women); includes 5 minority (3 African Americans, 2 Asian Americans or Pacific Islanders), 4 international. Average age 32. 23 applicants, 57% accepted, 7 enrolled. In 2009, 15 master's, 6 other advanced degrees awarded. *Degree requirements:* For master's, capstone and portfolio (some programs), internship. *Entrance requirements:* For master's, GMAT (minimum score 450), GRE General Test (minimum combined score 1000), resume, min 3.0 GPA, 3 letters of recommendation. Additional exam requirements/recommendations for international students: Required—TOEFL (minimum score 550 paper-based; 213 computer-based; 79 iBT); Recommended—IELTS (minimum score 6.5). *Application deadline:* For fall admission, 8/1 priority date for domestic students, 6/1 for international students; for spring admission, 12/1 priority date for domestic students, 10/1 for international students. Applications are processed on a rolling basis. Application fee: $40. Electronic applications accepted. *Expenses:* Tuition, state resident: full-time $6912; part-time $384 per credit hour. Tuition, nonresident: full-time $12,150; part-time $675 per credit hour. Tuition and fees vary according to course load, program and reciprocity agreements. *Financial support:* Unspecified assistantships available. Financial award applicants required to submit FAFSA. *Faculty research:* Information systems implementation, information systems security, business analytics, healthcare informatics. Total annual research expenditures: $50,000. *Unit head:* Dr. Vijay Raghavan, Director, 859-572-6358, E-mail: raghavan@nku.edu. *Application contact:* Dr. Peg Griffin, Director of Graduate Programs, 859-572-6934, Fax: 859-572-6670, E-mail: griffinp@nku.edu.

Northwestern University, McCormick School of Engineering and Applied Science, Department of Electrical Engineering and Computer Science, Program in Information Technology, Evanston, IL 60208. Offers MIT. *Entrance requirements:* For master's, GRE General Test, 2 years of professional experience.

Nova Southeastern University, Graduate School of Computer and Information Sciences, Fort Lauderdale, FL 33314-7796. Offers computer information systems (MS, PhD), including information security; computer science (MS, PhD); computing technology in education (PhD); information security (MS); information systems (MS, PhD); management information systems (MS), including information security (MS, PhD), management information systems; JD/MS. Part-time and evening/weekend programs available. Postbaccalaureate distance learning degree programs offered (no on-campus study). *Faculty:* 20 full-time (5 women), 21 part-time/adjunct (3 women). *Students:* 144 full-time (39 women), 1,004 part-time (305 women); includes 440 minority (219 African Americans, 9 American Indian/Alaska Native, 80 Asian Americans or Pacific Islanders, 132 Hispanic Americans), 42 international. Average age 41. In 2009, 1,152 master's, 38 doctorates awarded. Terminal master's awarded for partial completion of doctoral program. *Degree requirements:* For master's, thesis optional; for doctorate, thesis/dissertation. *Entrance requirements:* For master's, minimum undergraduate GPA of 2.5; for doctorate, master's degree, minimum graduate GPA of 3.25. *Application deadline:* Applications are processed on a rolling basis. Application fee: $50. Electronic applications accepted. *Expenses:* Contact institution. *Financial support:* Federal Work-Study, scholarships/grants, and unspecified assistantships available. Support available to part-time students. Financial award application deadline: 5/1. *Faculty research:* Artificial intelligence, database management, human-computer interaction, distance education, information security. *Unit head:* Dr. Amon Seagull, Interim Dean, 954-262-7300. *Application contact:* 954-262-2000, Fax: 954-262-2752, E-mail: scisinfo@nova.edu.

The Ohio State University, Graduate School, College of Engineering, Department of Computer Science and Engineering, Columbus, OH 43210. Offers computer and information science (MS, PhD); computer science and engineering (MS). *Faculty:* 40. *Students:* 231 full-time (49 women), 65 part-time (11 women); includes 7 minority (1 African American, 4 Asian Americans or Pacific Islanders, 2 Hispanic Americans), 223 international. Average age 27. In 2009, 41 master's, 23 doctorates awarded. *Degree requirements:* For master's, thesis optional; for doctorate, thesis/dissertation. *Entrance requirements:* Additional exam requirements/recommendations for international students: Recommended—TOEFL (minimum score 600 paper-based; 250 computer-based). *Application deadline:* For fall admission, 8/15 priority date for domestic students, 7/1 priority date for international students; for winter admission, 12/1 priority date for domestic students, 11/1 priority date for international students; for spring admission, 3/1 priority date for domestic students, 2/1 priority date for international students. Applications are processed on a rolling basis. Application fee: $40 ($50 for international students). Electronic applications accepted. *Expenses:* Tuition, state resident: full-time $10,683. Tuition, nonresident: full-time $25,923. Tuition and fees vary according to course load and program. *Financial support:* Fellowships, teaching assistantships, career-related internships or fieldwork, Federal Work-Study, institutionally sponsored loans, and administrative assistantships available. Support available to part-time students. Financial award application deadline: 1/15. *Application contact:* 614-292-9444, Fax: 614-292-3895, E-mail: domestic.grad@osu.edu.

Oklahoma State University, William S. Spears School of Business, Department of Management Science and Information Systems, Stillwater, OK 74078. Offers management information systems (MS); management science and information systems (PhD); telecommunications management (MS). Part-time programs available. Postbaccalaureate distance learning degree programs offered. *Faculty:* 15 full-time (2 women), 1 part-time/adjunct (0 women). *Students:* 75 full-time (25 women), 80 part-time (17 women); includes 7 minority (1 African American, 4 American Indian/Alaska Native, 2 Asian Americans or Pacific Islanders), 100 international. Average age 29. 251 applicants, 38% accepted, 41 enrolled. In 2009, 58 master's awarded. *Degree requirements:* For master's, thesis or alternative; for doctorate, comprehensive exam, thesis/dissertation. *Entrance requirements:* For master's and doctorate, GRE or GMAT. Additional exam requirements/recommendations for international students: Required—TOEFL (minimum score 550 paper-based; 79 iBT). *Application deadline:* For fall admission, 3/1 priority date for international students; for spring admission, 8/1 priority date for international students. Applications are processed on a rolling basis. Application fee: $40 ($75 for international students). Electronic applications accepted. *Expenses:* Tuition, state resident: full-time $3716; part-time $154.85 per credit hour. Tuition, nonresident: full-time $14,448; part-time $602 per credit hour. Required fees: $1772; $73.85 per credit hour. One-time fee: $50. Tuition and fees vary according to course load and campus/location. *Financial support:* In 2009–10, 2 research assistantships (averaging $6,720 per year), 14 teaching assistantships (averaging $13,962 per year) were awarded; career-related internships or fieldwork, Federal Work-Study, scholarships/grants, health care benefits, tuition waivers (partial), and unspecified assistantships also available. Support available to part-time students. Financial award application deadline: 3/1; financial award applicants required to submit FAFSA. *Unit head:* Dr. Rick Wilson, Head, 405-744-3551, Fax: 405-744-5180. *Application contact:* Dr. Gordon Emslie, Dean, 405-744-6368, Fax: 405-744-0355, E-mail: grad-i@okstate.edu.

Old Dominion University, College of Business and Public Administration, Doctoral Program in Business Administration, Norfolk, VA 23529. Offers finance (PhD); information technology (PhD); marketing (PhD); strategic management (PhD). *Accreditation:* AACSB. *Faculty:* 21 full-time (2 women). *Students:* 28 full-time (12 women), 14 part-time (6 women); includes 5 minority (3 African Americans, 2 Asian Americans or Pacific Islanders), 25 international. Average age 35. 31 applicants, 65% accepted, 8 enrolled. In 2009, 6 doctorates awarded. *Degree requirements:* For doctorate, comprehensive exam, thesis/dissertation. *Entrance requirements:* For doctorate, GMAT. Additional exam requirements/recommendations for international students: Required—TOEFL (minimum score 550 paper-based; 213 computer-based; 79 iBT). *Application deadline:* For fall admission, 4/1 priority date for domestic and international students. Application fee: $50. Electronic applications accepted. *Expenses:* Tuition, state resident: full-time $8112; part-time $338 per credit. Tuition, nonresident: full-time $20,256; part-time $844 per credit. Required fees: $119 per semester. One-time fee: $50. *Financial support:* In 2009–10, 23 students received support, including 4 fellowships with full tuition reimbursements available (averaging $15,000 per year), 13 research assistantships with full tuition reimbursements available (averaging $15,000 per year), 6 teaching assistantships with full tuition reimbursements available (averaging $15,000 per year); career-related internships or fieldwork and scholarships/grants also available. Financial award application deadline: 4/1; financial award applicants required to submit FAFSA. *Faculty research:* International business, buyer behavior, financial markets, strategy, operations research. *Unit head:* Dr. Sylvia C. Hudgins, Graduate Program Director, 757-683-3551, Fax: 757-683-4076, E-mail: shudgins@odu.edu. *Application contact:* Dr. Sylvia C. Hudgins, Graduate Program Director, 757-683-3551, Fax: 757-683-4076, E-mail: shudgins@odu.edu.

Pace University, Seidenberg School of Computer Science and Information Systems, New York, NY 10038. Offers computer communications and networks (Certificate); computer science (MS); computing studies (DPS); information systems (MS); Internet technologies for e-commerce (MS); Internet technology (MS); object-oriented programming (Certificate); security and information assurance (Certificate); software development and engineering (MS); telecommunications (MS, Certificate). Part-time and evening/weekend programs available. *Students:* 122 full-time (37 women), 424 part-time (131 women); includes 188 minority (76 African Americans, 1 American Indian/Alaska Native, 65 Asian Americans or Pacific Islanders, 46 Hispanic Americans), 110 international. Average age 35. 352 applicants, 89% accepted, 128 enrolled. In 2009, 137 master's, 11 doctorates, 3 other advanced degrees awarded. *Entrance requirements:* For master's, GRE General Test. Additional exam requirements/recommendations for international students: Required—TOEFL. *Application deadline:* For fall admission, 7/31 priority date for domestic students; for spring admission, 11/30 for domestic students. Applications are processed on a rolling basis. Application fee: $70. Electronic applications accepted. *Expenses:* Contact institution. *Financial support:* Research assistantships, career-related internships or fieldwork available. Support available to part-time students. Financial award applicants required to submit FAFSA. *Unit head:* Dr. Constance Knapp, Interim Dean, 914-773-3750, Fax: 914-773-3533, E-mail: cknapp@pace.edu. *Application contact:* Joanna Broda, Director of Graduate Admissions, 914-422-4283, Fax: 914-422-4287, E-mail: gradwp@pace.edu.

Polytechnic Institute of NYU, Westchester Graduate Center, Graduate Programs, Department of Computer Science and Engineering, Major in Information Systems Engineering, Hawthorne, NY 10532-1507. Offers MS. Evening/weekend programs available. *Students:* 7 full-time (4 women), 5 part-time (1 woman), 5 international. 6 applicants, 100% accepted, 6 enrolled. In 2009, 2 master's awarded. *Degree requirements:* For master's, comprehensive exam (for some programs), thesis (for some programs). *Entrance requirements:* Additional exam requirements/recommendations for international students: Required—TOEFL (minimum score 550 paper-based; 213 computer-based; 80 iBT); Recommended—IELTS (minimum score 6.5). *Application deadline:* For fall admission, 7/31 priority date for domestic students, 4/30 priority date for international students; for spring admission, 12/31 priority date for domestic students, 11/30 priority date for international students. Applications are processed on a rolling basis. Application fee: $75. Electronic applications accepted. *Financial support:* Institutionally sponsored loans, scholarships/grants, and unspecified assistantships available. Support available to part-time students. *Unit head:* Dr. Keith W. Ross, Department Head, 718-260-3859, E-mail: ross@poly.edu. *Application contact:* JeanCarlo Bonilla, Director of Graduate Enrollment Management, 718-260-3182, Fax: 718-260-3624, E-mail: gradinfo@poly.edu.

Regis University, College for Professional Studies, School of Computer and Information Sciences, Denver, CO 80221-1099. Offers database administration with IBM DB2 (Certificate); database administration with Oracle (Certificate); database development (Certificate); database technologies (MA); enterprise Java software development (Certificate); executive information technologies (Certificate); information assurance (MA, Certificate); information technology management (MA); software and information systems (M Sc); software engineering (MA, Certificate); storage area networks (Certificate); systems engineering (MA, Certificate). Offered at Boulder Campus, Northwest Denver Campus, Southeast Denver Campus, Fort Collins Campus, Colorado Springs Campus, and Broomfield Campus. Part-time and evening/weekend programs available. Postbaccalaureate distance learning degree programs offered (no on-campus study). *Degree requirements:* For master's, thesis, final research project. *Entrance requirements:* For master's, 2 years of related experience, resume, interview; for Certificate, 2 years of related experience, resumé. Additional exam requirements/recommendations for international students: Required—TOEFL (minimum score 213 computer-based), TWE (minimum score 5), TOEFL or university-based test. Electronic applications accepted. *Expenses:* Contact institution. *Faculty research:* Secure Virtual Laboratory Architecture, Joint IA project with W2C06 Institute, Information Policy, OLTP and OLAP Technologies, knowledge management, software architectures.

Rensselaer at Hartford, Department of Computer and Information Science, Program in Information Technology, Hartford, CT 06120-2991. Offers MS. Part-time and evening/weekend programs available. *Faculty:* 2 full-time (0 women). *Students:* 15 part-time (6 women); includes 4 minority (2 African Americans, 1 Asian American or Pacific Islander, 1 Hispanic American). Average age 34. 10 applicants, 40% accepted, 4 enrolled. In 2009, 6 master's awarded. *Entrance requirements:* For master's, GRE. Additional exam requirements/recommendations for international students: Required—TOEFL (minimum score 600 paper-based; 250 computer-based; 100 iBT). *Application deadline:* For fall admission, 8/30 priority date for domestic students, 8/1 priority date for international students. Applications are processed on a rolling basis. Application fee: $75. Electronic applications accepted. *Expenses:* Tuition: Full-time $31,800; part-time $1325 per credit hour. *Financial support:* Research assistantships, career-related internships or fieldwork, tuition waivers (full and partial), and unspecified assistantships available. Support available to part-time students. Financial award applicants required to submit FAFSA. *Unit head:* Dr. Houman Younessi, Chair, 860-548-7880, E-mail: youneh@rpi.edu. *Application contact:* Kristin Galligan, Director, Enrollment Management and Marketing, 860-548-2480, Fax: 860-548-7823, E-mail: info@ewp.rpi.edu.

Rensselaer Polytechnic Institute, Graduate School, School of Science, Interdisciplinary Program in Information Technology, Troy, NY 12180-3590. Offers MS. Part-time programs available. *Faculty:* 82 full-time (11 women). *Students:* 34 full-time (11 women), 16 part-time (7 women); includes 5 minority (all Asian Americans or Pacific Islanders). 125 applicants, 62% accepted, 22 enrolled. In 2009, 27 master's awarded. *Degree requirements:* For master's, capstone course. *Entrance requirements:* For master's, GRE. Additional exam requirements/recommendations for international students: Required—TOEFL. *Application deadline:* For fall admission, 1/15 priority date for domestic and international students; for spring admission, 8/15 priority date for domestic students, 8/15 for international students. Applications are processed on a rolling basis. Application fee: $75. Electronic applications accepted. *Expenses:* Tuition: Full-time $38,100. *Financial support:* In 2009–10, 5 students received support, including 5 teaching assistantships with full tuition reimbursements available (averaging $16,500 per year); career-related internships or fieldwork, institutionally sponsored loans, scholarships/grants, health care benefits, tuition waivers (partial), and unspecified assistantships also available. Financial award application deadline: 3/15. *Faculty research:* Web science, database systems, software design, human-computer interaction, networking, information technology, financial engineering. *Unit head:* Dr. James Hendler, Associate Dean, 518-276-2660, Fax: 518-276-6687, E-mail: hendler@cs.rpi.edu. *Application contact:* Linda Kramarchyk, Program Manager, 518-276-6304, Fax: 518-276-6687, E-mail: kramal@rpi.edu.

Robert Morris University, Graduate Studies, School of Communications and Information Systems, Moon Township, PA 15108-1189. Offers communication and information systems (MS); competitive intelligence systems (MS); information security and assurance (MS); information systems and communications (D Sc); information systems management (MS); information technology project management (MS); Internet information systems (MS); organizational studies (MS). Part-time and evening/weekend programs available. *Faculty:* 28 full-time (9 women), 9 part-time/adjunct (3 women). *Students:* 257 part-time (76 women); includes 41 minority (31 African Americans, 8 Asian Americans or Pacific Islanders, 2 Hispanic Americans), 16 international. Average age 33. 106 applicants, 100% accepted, 106 enrolled. In 2009, 84 master's, 8 doctorates awarded. *Degree requirements:* For doctorate, thesis/dissertation. *Entrance requirements:* For doctorate, employer letter of endorsement, interview. Additional exam requirements/recommendations for international students: Required—TOEFL (minimum score 550 paper-based; 213 computer-based; 79 iBT). *Application deadline:* For fall admission, 7/1 priority date for domestic and international students; for spring admission, 11/1 priority date for domestic and international students. Applications are processed on a rolling basis. Application fee: $35. Electronic applications accepted. *Expenses:* Contact institution. *Financial support:* Research assistantships with partial tuition reimbursements, institutionally sponsored loans and unspecified assistantships available. Support available to part-time students. Financial award application deadline: 5/1. *Unit head:* Dr. Barbara J. Levine, Dean, 412-397-2591, Fax: 412-397-2481, E-mail: levine@rmu.edu. *Application contact:* Deborah Roach, Assistant Dean, Graduate Admissions, 412-397-5200, Fax: 412-397-2425, E-mail: graduateadmissions@rmu.edu.

Rochester Institute of Technology, Graduate Enrollment Services, B. Thomas Golisano College of Computing and Information Sciences, Department of Information Technology, Program in Information Technology, Rochester, NY 14623-5603. Offers MS. Part-time and evening/weekend programs available. *Students:* 78 full-time (22 women), 62 part-time (17 women); includes 9 minority (4 African Americans, 1 American Indian/Alaska Native, 3 Asian Americans or Pacific Islanders, 1 Hispanic American), 76 international. Average age 29. 122 applicants, 63% accepted, 33 enrolled. In 2009, 53 master's awarded. *Degree requirements:* For master's, thesis or project. *Entrance requirements:* For master's, GRE, minimum GPA of 3.0. Additional exam requirements/recommendations for international students: Required—TOEFL (minimum score 570 paper-based; 230 computer-based; 88 iBT), or IELTS (minimum score 6.5). *Application deadline:* For fall admission, 8/1 for domestic students, 7/1 for international students; for spring admission, 2/1 for domestic students. Applications are processed on a rolling basis. Application fee: $50. Electronic applications accepted. *Expenses:* Tuition: Full-time $31,533; part-time $876 per credit hour. Required fees: $210. *Financial support:* In 2009–10, 101 students received support; research assistantships with partial tuition reimbursements available, teaching assistantships with partial tuition reimbursements available, career-related internships or fieldwork, scholarships/grants, and unspecified assistantships available. Support available to part-time students. Financial award applicants required to submit FAFSA. *Unit head:* Prof. Dianne Bills, Graduate Program Coordinator, 585-475-2700, Fax: 585-475-6584, E-mail: informaticsgrad@rit.edu. *Application contact:* Diane Ellison, Assistant Vice President, Graduate Enrollment Services, 585-475-2229, Fax: 585-475-7164, E-mail: gradinfo@rit.edu.

Rochester Institute of Technology, Graduate Enrollment Services, B. Thomas Golisano College of Computing and Information Sciences, PhD Program in Computing and Information Sciences, Rochester, NY 14623-5603. Offers PhD. *Students:* 19 full-time (2 women), 6 part-time (1 woman); includes 2 Asian Americans or Pacific Islanders, 16 international. Average age 30. 43 applicants, 21% accepted, 6 enrolled. *Degree requirements:* For doctorate, thesis/dissertation. *Entrance requirements:* For doctorate, GRE, minimum GPA of 3.0. Additional exam requirements/recommendations for international students: Required—TOEFL (minimum score 570 paper-based; 230 computer-based; 88 iBT), or IELTS (minimum score 6.5). *Application deadline:* For fall admission, 1/15 priority date for domestic and international students. Applications are processed on a rolling basis. Application fee: $50. Electronic applications accepted. *Expenses:* Tuition: Full-time $31,533; part-time $876 per credit hour. Required fees: $210. *Financial support:* In 2009–10, 16 students received support; research assistantships with full and partial tuition reimbursements available, teaching assistantships with full and partial tuition reimbursements available, career-related internships or fieldwork, scholarships/grants, health care benefits, and unspecified assistantships available. Financial award applicants required to submit FAFSA. *Unit head:* Dr. Pengcheng Shi, Director, 585-475-6193, Fax: 585-475-5669, E-mail: phd@gccis.rit.edu. *Application contact:* Diane Ellison, Assistant Vice President, Graduate Enrollment Services, 585-475-2229, Fax: 585-475-7164, E-mail: gradinfo@rit.edu.

Sacred Heart University, Graduate Programs, College of Arts and Sciences, Department of Computer Science and Information Technology, Fairfield, CT 06825-1000. Offers computer science (MS); database (CPS); information technology (MS, CPS); information technology and network security (CPS); interactive multimedia (CPS); Web development (CPS). Part-time and evening/weekend programs available. *Faculty:* 7 full-time (4 women). *Students:* 20 full-time (6 women), 79 part-time (25 women); includes 10 minority (2 African Americans, 1 American Indian/Alaska Native, 5 Asian Americans or Pacific Islanders, 2 Hispanic Americans), 30 international. Average age 33. 66 applicants, 97% accepted, 26 enrolled. In 2009, 17 master's awarded. *Degree requirements:* For master's, thesis optional. *Entrance requirements:* Additional exam requirements/recommendations for international students: Required—TOEFL (minimum score 550 paper-based; 213 computer-based). *Application deadline:* Applications are processed on a rolling basis. Application fee: $50 ($100 for international students). Electronic applications accepted. *Expenses:* Tuition: Full-time $24,000; part-time $650 per credit. Required fees: $248. *Financial support:* Career-related internships or fieldwork, institutionally sponsored loans, and unspecified assistantships available. Support available to part-time students. Financial award applicants required to submit FAFSA. *Faculty research:* Contemporary market software. *Unit head:* Domenick Pinto, Academic Director and Chairperson, 203-371-7789, Fax: 203-371-0506, E-mail: pintod@sacredheart.edu. *Application contact:* Dean Alexis Haakonsen, Office of Graduate Admissions, 203-365-7619, Fax: 203-365-4732, E-mail: gradstudies@sacredheart.edu.

St. Mary's University, Graduate School, Department of Computer Science, Program in Computer Information Systems, San Antonio, TX 78228-8507. Offers MS. Part-time programs available. *Degree requirements:* For master's, comprehensive exam. *Entrance requirements:* For master's, GMAT or GRE General Test. Additional exam requirements/recommendations for international students: Required—TOEFL (minimum score 530 paper-based; 213 computer-based; 80 iBT). Electronic applications accepted. *Expenses:* Tuition: Full-time $8004. Required fees: $536. One-time fee: $5 full-time. Full-time tuition and fees vary according to program. *Faculty research:* Artificial intelligence, database/knowledge base, software engineering, expert systems.

Saint Xavier University, Graduate Studies, School of Arts and Sciences, Department of Mathematics and Computer Science, Chicago, IL 60655-3105. Offers applied computer science in Internet information systems (MS); mathematics and computer science (MA); MBA/MS. *Degree requirements:* For master's, thesis optional. *Expenses:* Tuition: Part-time $743 per credit hour. Required fees: $135 per semester.

Sam Houston State University, College of Arts and Sciences, Department of Computer Science, Huntsville, TX 77341. Offers computing and information science (MS). Part-time programs available. *Faculty:* 8 full-time (3 women). *Students:* 31 full-time (8 women), 24 part-time (6 women); includes 1 minority (African American), 31 international. Average age 29. 29 applicants, 83% accepted, 15 enrolled. In 2009, 9 master's awarded. *Entrance requirements:* For master's, GRE General Test. Additional exam requirements/recommendations for international students: Required—TOEFL (minimum score 550 paper-based; 213 computer-based; 79 iBT). *Application deadline:* For fall admission, 8/1 for domestic and international students; for spring admission, 12/1 for domestic and international students. Application fee: $20. *Expenses:* Tuition, state resident: full-time $3690; part-time $205 per credit hour. Tuition, nonresident: full-time $8676; part-time $482 per credit hour. Required fees: $1474. Tuition and fees vary according to course load and campus/location. *Financial support:* Research assistantships, teaching assistantships, Federal Work-Study, institutionally sponsored loans, and tuition waivers (partial) available. Support available to part-time students. Financial award application deadline: 5/31; financial award applicants required to submit FAFSA. *Unit head:* Dr. Peter Cooper, Chair, 936-294-1569, Fax: 936-294-4312, E-mail: css_pac@shsu.edu. *Application contact:* Dr. Jiuhung Ji, Advisor, 936-294-1579, E-mail: csc_jxj@shsu.edu.

Simon Fraser University, Graduate Studies, Faculty of Applied Sciences, School of Interactive Arts and Technology, Surrey, BC V3T 2W1, Canada. Offers information technology (M Sc, PhD); interactive arts (M Sc, PhD). *Degree requirements:* For master's, thesis; for doctorate, comprehensive exam, thesis/dissertation. *Entrance requirements:* For master's, 2 references, curriculum vitae; for doctorate, 3 references, curriculm vitae, minimum GPA of 3.0. Additional exam requirements/recommendations for international students: Required—TOEFL (minimum score 570 paper-based; 230 computer-based), TWE (minimum score 5). Electronic applications accepted.

Southern Methodist University, Bobby B. Lyle School of Engineering, Department of Engineering Management, Information, and Systems, Dallas, TX 75275. Offers applied science (MS); engineering management (MSEM, DE); information engineering and management (MSIEM); operations research (MS, PhD); systems engineering (MS, PhD). Part-time and evening/weekend programs available. Postbaccalaureate distance learning degree programs offered. *Faculty:* 10 full-time (3 women), 22 part-time/adjunct (2 women). *Students:* 54 full-time

Information Science

Southern Methodist University (continued)
(24 women), 288 part-time (68 women); includes 96 minority (30 African Americans, 2 American Indian/Alaska Native, 35 Asian Americans or Pacific Islanders, 29 Hispanic Americans), 38 international. Average age 33. 125 applicants, 74% accepted, 60 enrolled. In 2009, 128 master's, 3 doctorates awarded. Terminal master's awarded for partial completion of doctoral program. *Degree requirements:* For master's, thesis optional; for doctorate, thesis/dissertation, oral and written qualifying exams. *Entrance requirements:* For master's, minimum GPA of 3.0 in last 2 years; bachelor's degree in engineering, mathematics, sciences, or technical area; for doctorate, GRE General Test (operations research, engineering management), bachelor's degree in related field. Additional exam requirements/recommendations for international students: Required—TOEFL. *Application deadline:* For fall admission, 7/1 for domestic students, 5/15 for international students; for spring admission, 11/15 for domestic students, 9/1 for international students. Applications are processed on a rolling basis. Application fee: $75. *Financial support:* In 2009–10, 8 students received support, including 3 research assistantships with full tuition reimbursements available (averaging $18,000 per year), 9 teaching assistantships with full tuition reimbursements available (averaging $18,000 per year); tuition waivers (full) also available. *Faculty research:* Telecommunications, decision systems, information engineering, operations research, software. Total annual research expenditures: $172,823. *Unit head:* Dr. Richard S. Barr, Chair, 214-768-1772, Fax: 214-768-1112, E-mail: emis@lyle.smu.edu. *Application contact:* Marc Valerin, Director of Graduate and Executive Admissions, 214-768-3042, E-mail: valerin@lyle.smu.edu.

Southern Polytechnic State University, School of Arts and Sciences, Department of English, Technical Communication, and Media Arts, Marietta, GA 30060-2896. Offers communications management (Graduate Certificate); content development (Graduate Certificate); information and instructional design (MSIID); information design and communication (MS); instructional design (Graduate Certificate); technical and professional communication (Graduate Certificate); visual communication and graphics (Graduate Certificate). Part-time and evening/weekend programs available. Postbaccalaureate distance learning degree programs offered (no on-campus study). *Faculty:* 4 full-time (3 women), 1 part-time/adjunct (0 women). *Students:* 5 full-time (all women), 50 part-time (32 women); includes 18 African Americans, 2 international. Average age 38. 32 applicants, 94% accepted, 26 enrolled. In 2009, 8 master's awarded. *Degree requirements:* For master's, thesis or internship; for Graduate Certificate, thesis optional, 18 hours completed through thesis option (6 hours), internship option (6 hours) or advanced coursework option (6 hours). *Entrance requirements:* For master's, GRE, statement of purpose, writing sample, professional recommendations, timed essay; for Graduate Certificate, writing sample, professional recommendations. Additional exam requirements/recommendations for international students: Required—TOEFL (minimum score 550 paper-based; 213 computer-based; 79 iBT), IELTS (minimum score 6.5). *Application deadline:* For fall admission, 5/1 priority date for domestic students, 7/1 priority date for international students; for spring admission, 9/1 priority date for domestic students, 11/1 priority date for international students. Applications are processed on a rolling basis. Application fee: $20. Electronic applications accepted. *Expenses:* Tuition, state resident: full-time $2896; part-time $181 per credit hour. Tuition, nonresident: full-time $11,552; part-time $722 per credit hour. Required fees: $1096; $1096 per year. *Financial support:* In 2009–10, 1 research assistantship with full tuition reimbursement (averaging $4,000 per year), 1 teaching assistantship with partial tuition reimbursement (averaging $4,000 per year) were awarded; career-related internships or fieldwork, Federal Work-Study, scholarships/grants, and unspecified assistantships also available. Support available to part-time students. Financial award application deadline: 5/1; financial award applicants required to submit FAFSA. *Faculty research:* Usability, user-centered design, instructional design, information architecture, information design. *Unit head:* Dr. Mark Nunes, Chair, 678-915-7202, Fax: 678-915-7425, E-mail: mnunes@spsu.edu. *Application contact:* Nikki Palamiotis, Director of Graduate Studies, 678-915-4276, Fax: 678-915-7292, E-mail: npalamio@spsu.edu.

Southern Polytechnic State University, School of Computing and Software Engineering, Department of Information Technology, Marietta, GA 30060-2896. Offers business continuity (Graduate Certificate); information security and assurance (Graduate Certificate); information technology (MSIT, Graduate Certificate); information technology fundamentals (Graduate Certificate). Part-time and evening/weekend programs available. Postbaccalaureate distance learning degree programs offered (minimal on-campus study). *Faculty:* 9 full-time (4 women), 3 part-time/adjunct (1 woman). *Students:* 32 full-time (10 women), 62 part-time (21 women); includes 32 African Americans, 9 Asian Americans or Pacific Islanders, 2 Hispanic Americans, 14 international. Average age 34. 53 applicants, 89% accepted, 36 enrolled. In 2009, 21 master's awarded. *Degree requirements:* For master's, thesis or alternative. *Entrance requirements:* For master's, minimum GPA of 2.75; for Graduate Certificate, bachelor's degree. Additional exam requirements/recommendations for international students: Required—TOEFL (minimum score 550 paper-based; 213 computer-based; 79 iBT), IELTS (minimum score 6.5). *Application deadline:* For fall admission, 7/1 priority date for domestic students, 5/1 priority date for international students; for spring admission, 11/1 priority date for domestic students, 9/1 priority date for international students. Applications are processed on a rolling basis. Application fee: $20. Electronic applications accepted. *Expenses:* Tuition, state resident: full-time $2896; part-time $181 per credit hour. Tuition, nonresident: full-time $11,552; part-time $722 per credit hour. Required fees: $1096; $1096 per year. *Financial support:* In 2009–10, 12 students received support, including 12 research assistantships with tuition reimbursements available (averaging $1,500 per year); career-related internships or fieldwork, scholarships/grants, and unspecified assistantships also available. Support available to part-time students. Financial award application deadline: 5/1; financial award applicants required to submit FAFSA. *Faculty research:* IT ethics, user interface design, IT security, IT integration, IT management. *Unit head:* Dr. Ju Au Wang, Chair, 678-915-3718, Fax: 678-915-5511, E-mail: jwang@spsu.edu. *Application contact:* Nikki Palamiotis, Director of Graduate Studies, 678-915-4276, Fax: 678-915-7292, E-mail: npalamio@spsu.edu.

State University of New York Institute of Technology, School of Arts and Sciences, Program in Information Design and Technology, Utica, NY 13504-3050. Offers MS. Part-time and evening/weekend programs available. *Degree requirements:* For master's, thesis or project. *Entrance requirements:* For master's, minimum GPA of 3.0; 2 letters of recommendation; portfolio; bachelor's degree in communication, rhetoric, journalism, English, or computer science, or 15 hours of communication. Additional exam requirements/recommendations for international students: Required—TOEFL (minimum score 550 paper-based; 213 computer-based). *Faculty research:* Textual-visualization, ethics and technology, behavioral information security.

State University of New York Institute of Technology, School of Information Systems and Engineering Technology, Program in Computer and Information Science, Utica, NY 13504-3050. Offers MS. Part-time and evening/weekend programs available. *Degree requirements:* For master's, thesis or project. *Entrance requirements:* For master's, GRE General Test, minimum GPA of 3.0, letter of recommendation. Additional exam requirements/recommendations for international students: Required—TOEFL (minimum score 550 paper-based; 213 computer-based). *Faculty research:* Cryptography, distributed systems, computer-aided system theory, reasoning with uncertainty, grid computing.

Stevens Institute of Technology, Graduate School, Wesley J. Howe School of Technology Management, Program in Information Systems, Hoboken, NJ 07030. Offers computer science (MS); e-commerce (MS); enterprise systems (MS); entrepreneurial information technology (MS); information architecture (MS); information management (MS, Certificate); information security (MS); information technology in financial services industry (MS); information technology in the pharmaceutical industry (MS); information technology outsourcing management (MS); project management (MS, Certificate); software engineering (MS); telecommunications (MS). *Degree requirements:* For master's, thesis optional. *Entrance requirements:* For master's, GMAT, GRE General Test. Additional exam requirements/recommendations for international students: Required—TOEFL. Electronic applications accepted. *Expenses:* Tuition: Full-time $9900; part-time $1100 per credit. Required fees: $286 per semester.

Stevenson University, Graduate and Professional Studies Programs, Program in Advanced Information Technologies, Stevenson, MD 21153. Offers MS. *Degree requirements:* For master's, capstone course.

Strayer University, Graduate Studies, Washington, DC 20005-2603. Offers accounting (MS); acquisition (MBA); business administration (MBA); communications technology (MS); educational management (M Ed); finance (MBA); health services administration (MHSA); hospitality and tourism management (MBA); human resource management (MBA); information systems (MS), including computer security management, decision support system management, enterprise resource management, network management, software engineering management, systems development management; management (MBA); management information systems (MS); marketing (MBA); professional accounting (MS), including accounting information systems, controllership, taxation; public administration (MPA); supply chain management (MBA); technology in education (M Ed). Programs also offered at campus locations in Birmingham, AL; Chamblee, GA; Cobb County, GA; Morrow, GA; White Marsh, MD; Charleston, SC; Columbia, SC; Greensboro, NC; Greenville, SC; Lexington, KY; Louisville, KY; Nashville, TN; North Raleigh, NC; Washington, DC. Part-time and evening/weekend programs available. Postbaccalaureate distance learning degree programs offered (minimal on-campus study). *Degree requirements:* For master's, thesis. *Entrance requirements:* For master's, GMAT, GRE General Test, bachelor's degree from an accredited college or university, minimum undergraduate GPA of 2.75. Electronic applications accepted.

Syracuse University, L. C. Smith College of Engineering and Computer Science, Program in Computer and Information Science and Engineering, Syracuse, NY 13244. Offers PhD. *Students:* 18 full-time (5 women), 11 part-time (1 woman); includes 2 minority (both Asian Americans or Pacific Islanders), 17 international. Average age 34. 53 applicants, 19% accepted, 7 enrolled. In 2009, 1 doctorate awarded. *Degree requirements:* For doctorate, thesis/dissertation. *Entrance requirements:* For doctorate, GRE General Test and subject test in computer science). Additional exam requirements/recommendations for international students: Required—TOEFL (minimum score 100 iBT). *Application deadline:* For fall admission, 5/1 priority date for domestic and international students. Applications are processed on a rolling basis. Application fee: $75. Electronic applications accepted. *Expenses:* Tuition: Full-time $26,808; part-time $1117 per credit. Required fees: $1024. *Financial support:* Fellowships with full tuition reimbursements, research assistantships with full and partial tuition reimbursements, teaching assistantships with full and partial tuition reimbursements, tuition waivers (partial) available. *Unit head:* Dr. Chilukuri Mohan, Dept. Chair, 315-443-2322, Fax: 315-443-2583, E-mail: ckmohan@syr.edu. *Application contact:* Heather Paris, Information Contact, 315-443-2368, Fax: 315-443-2583, E-mail: hdparis@syr.edu.

Syracuse University, School of Information Studies, Program in Information Science and Technology, Syracuse, NY 13244. Offers PhD. *Students:* 40 full-time (21 women), 7 part-time (4 women); includes 8 minority (5 African Americans, 3 Asian Americans or Pacific Islanders), 23 international. Average age 36. 4,667 applicants, 0% accepted, 7 enrolled. In 2009, 4 doctorates awarded. *Degree requirements:* For doctorate, thesis/dissertation. *Entrance requirements:* For doctorate, GRE General Test (recommended), interview. Additional exam requirements/recommendations for international students: Required—TOEFL (minimum score 100 iBT). *Application deadline:* For fall admission, 1/8 priority date for domestic and international students. Application fee: $75. Electronic applications accepted. *Expenses:* Tuition: Full-time $26,808; part-time $1117 per credit. Required fees: $1024. *Financial support:* Fellowships with tuition reimbursements, research assistantships with tuition reimbursements, teaching assistantships with tuition reimbursements, tuition waivers (partial) available. Financial award application deadline: 1/1; financial award applicants required to submit FAFSA. *Unit head:* Ping Zang, Director, 315-443-5617, Fax: 315-443-6886, E-mail: pzhang@syr.edu. *Application contact:* Susan Corieri, Director of Enrollment Management, 315-443-2575, E-mail: ist@syr.edu.

Temple University, Graduate School, College of Science and Technology, Department of Computer and Information Sciences, Philadelphia, PA 19122-6096. Offers MS, PhD. Part-time and evening/weekend programs available. Terminal master's awarded for partial completion of doctoral program. *Degree requirements:* For doctorate, thesis/dissertation. *Entrance requirements:* For master's and doctorate, GRE General Test, minimum GPA of 3.0. Additional exam requirements/recommendations for international students: Required—TOEFL (minimum score 550 paper-based; 213 computer-based; 79 iBT). Electronic applications accepted. *Faculty research:* Artificial intelligence, information systems, software engineering, network-distributed systems.

Towson University, College of Graduate Studies and Research, Master's Program in Applied Information Technology, Towson, MD 21252-0001. Offers MS.

Towson University, College of Graduate Studies and Research, Program in Applied Information Technology, Towson, MD 21252-0001. Offers applied information technology (D Sc); database management (Certificate); information security and assurance (Certificate); information systems management (Certificate); Internet application development (Certificate); networking technologies (Certificate); software engineering (Certificate). *Entrance requirements:* For doctorate, minimum GPA 3.0, letter of intent, resumé, 2 letters of recommendation, personal assessment forms, official transcripts. Additional exam requirements/recommendations for international students: Required—TOEFL (minimum score 550 paper-based). Electronic applications accepted.

Towson University, College of Graduate Studies and Research, Program in Internet Application Development, Towson, MD 21252-0001. Offers Certificate. Part-time and evening/weekend programs available. Electronic applications accepted.

Towson University, College of Graduate Studies and Research, Program in Networking Technologies, Towson, MD 21252-0001. Offers Certificate. Part-time and evening/weekend programs available.

Trevecca Nazarene University, Graduate Division, School of Education, Major in Library and Information Science, Nashville, TN 37210-2877. Offers MLI Sc. Evening/weekend programs available. *Students:* 36 full-time (all women). Average age 39. In 2009, 15 master's awarded. *Degree requirements:* For master's, exit assessment. *Entrance requirements:* For master's, GRE General Test, MAT, technology pre-assessment, minimum GPA of 2.7, 2 reference forms. Additional exam requirements/recommendations for international students: Required—TOEFL (minimum score 550 paper-based; 213 computer-based). *Application deadline:* Applications are processed on a rolling basis. Application fee: $25. *Expenses:* Contact institution. *Financial support:* Applicants required to submit FAFSA. *Unit head:* Dr. Esther Swink, Dean, School of Education/Director of Graduate Education Program, 615-248-1201, Fax: 615-248-1597, E-mail: admissions_ged@trevecca.edu. *Application contact:* Admissions Office, 615-248-1201, Fax: 615-248-1597, E-mail: admissions_ged@trevecca.edu.

Université de Sherbrooke, Faculty of Sciences, Department of Informatics, Sherbrooke, QC J1K 2R1, Canada. Offers M Sc, PhD. *Degree requirements:* For master's, thesis. Electronic applications accepted.

University at Albany, State University of New York, College of Computing and Information, Albany, NY 12222-0001. Offers computer science (MS, PhD); information science (PhD); information studies (MS, CAS), including information science. *Accreditation:* ALA (one or more programs are accredited). Part-time programs available. *Degree requirements:* For doctorate, thesis/dissertation. *Entrance requirements:* For doctorate, GRE General Test. Additional exam requirements/recommendations for international students: Required—TOEFL (minimum score 550 paper-based; 213 computer-based). Electronic applications accepted. *Faculty research:* Human-computer interaction, government information management, library information science, web development, social implications of technology.

The University of Alabama at Birmingham, College of Arts and Sciences, Program in Computer and Information Sciences, Birmingham, AL 35294. Offers MS, PhD. Terminal master's awarded for partial completion of doctoral program. *Degree requirements:* For master's, thesis optional; for doctorate, thesis/dissertation. *Entrance requirements:* For master's and doctorate, GRE General Test. Additional exam requirements/recommendations for international students: Required—TOEFL. Electronic applications accepted. *Faculty research:* Theory and software systems, intelligent systems, systems architecture, high performance computing, computer architecture, computer graphics, data mining, software engineering.

University of Arkansas at Little Rock, Graduate School, George W. Donughey College of Engineering and Information Technology, Program in Information Quality, Little Rock, AR 72204-1099. Offers MS.

University of Baltimore, Graduate School, The Yale Gordon College of Liberal Arts, School of Information Arts and Technologies, Baltimore, MD 21201-5779. Offers communications design (DCD); human-computer interaction (MS); interaction design and information technology (MS). Part-time and evening/weekend programs available. *Entrance requirements:* For master's, GRE or MAT, minimum undergraduate GPA of 3.0. Additional exam requirements/ recommendations for international students: Required—TOEFL (minimum score 550 paper-based; 213 computer-based).

University of California, Irvine, Office of Graduate Studies, Donald Bren School of Information and Computer Sciences, Irvine, CA 92697. Offers information and computer science (MS, PhD); networked systems (MS, PhD). *Students:* 316 full-time (78 women), 31 part-time (5 women); includes 52 minority (3 African Americans, 41 Asian Americans or Pacific Islanders, 8 Hispanic Americans), 194 international. Average age 27. 1,448 applicants, 23% accepted, 111 enrolled. In 2009, 86 master's, 43 doctorates awarded. Terminal master's awarded for partial completion of doctoral program. *Degree requirements:* For master's, thesis; for doctorate, thesis/dissertation. *Entrance requirements:* For master's and doctorate, GRE General Test, GRE Subject Test, minimum GPA of 3.0. Additional exam requirements/recommendations for international students: Required—TOEFL (minimum score 550 paper-based; 213 computer-based). *Application deadline:* For fall admission, 1/15 priority date for domestic students, 1/15 for international students. Applications are processed on a rolling basis. Application fee: $70 ($90 for international students). Electronic applications accepted. *Financial support:* Fellowships, research assistantships with full tuition reimbursements, teaching assistantships, institutionally sponsored loans, traineeships, health care benefits, and unspecified assistantships available. Financial award application deadline: 3/1; financial award applicants required to submit FAFSA. *Faculty research:* Artificial intelligence, computer system design, software, biomedical computing, theory. *Unit head:* Debra J. Richardson, Interim Dean, 949-824-7405, Fax: 949-824-3976, E-mail: djr@uci.edu. *Application contact:* Kris Bolcer, Assistant Director, Graduate Affairs, 949-824-2277, Fax: 949-824-3976, E-mail: kris@ics.uci.edu.

University of Central Missouri, The Graduate School, College of Education, Warrensburg, MO 64093. Offers career and technical education administration (MS); career and technical education industry training (MS); career and technical education leadership/teaching (MS); college student personnel administration (MS); counseling (MS); curriculum and instruction (Ed S); educational leadership (Ed D); educational technology (MS); elementary education/ educational foundations and literacy (MSE); elementary school administration (MSE); elementary school principalship (Ed S); human services/learning resources (Ed S); human services/ professional counseling (Ed S); human services/special education (Ed S); human services/ technology and occupational education (Ed S); K-12 education/educational foundations and literacy (MSE); K-12 special education (MSE); library science and information services (MS); literacy education (MSE); secondary education/educational foundations & literacy (MSE); secondary school administration (MSE); secondary school principalship (Ed S); superintendency (Ed S); teaching (MAT). Part-time programs available. Postbaccalaureate distance learning degree programs offered. *Faculty:* 42. *Students:* 123 full-time (82 women), 721 part-time (552 women); includes 58 minority (38 African Americans, 3 American Indian/Alaska Native, 6 Asian Americans or Pacific Islanders, 11 Hispanic Americans), 6 international. Average age 34. 229 applicants, 88% accepted, 190 enrolled. In 2009, 212 master's, 47 other advanced degrees awarded. *Entrance requirements:* Additional exam requirements/recommendations for international students: Required—TOEFL (minimum score 550 paper-based; 79 computer-based). *Application deadline:* For fall admission, 6/1 priority date for domestic students, 5/1 for international students; for spring admission, 10/1 priority date for domestic students, 10/1 for international students. Applications are processed on a rolling basis. Application fee: $30 ($75 for international students). Electronic applications accepted. *Expenses:* Tuition, area resident: Part-time $245.80 per credit hour. Tuition, nonresident: part-time $491.60 per credit hour. Required fees: $24.20 per credit hour. Full-time tuition and fees vary according to course load, degree level, campus/location and reciprocity agreements. *Financial support:* Research assistantships with full and partial tuition reimbursements, teaching assistantships with full and partial tuition reimbursements, career-related internships or fieldwork, Federal Work-Study, scholarships/ grants, and administrative and laboratory assistantships available. Support available to part-time students. Financial award application deadline: 3/1; financial award applicants required to submit FAFSA. *Unit head:* Dr. Michael Wright, Dean, 660-543-4272, Fax: 660-543-8753, E-mail: mwright@ucmo.edu. *Application contact:* Laurie Delap, Admissions Coordinator, 660-543-4621, Fax: 660-543-4778, E-mail: gradinfo@ucmo.edu.

University of Colorado at Colorado Springs, Graduate School, College of Engineering and Applied Science, Department of Mechanical and Aerospace Engineering, Colorado Springs, CO 80933-7150. Offers engineering management (ME); information operations (ME); manufacturing (ME); mechanical engineering (MS); software engineering (ME); space operations (ME); space systems (MS). Part-time and evening/weekend programs available. *Faculty:* 10 full-time (2 women). *Students:* 14 full-time (4 women), 13 part-time (2 women); includes 3 minority (2 Asian Americans or Pacific Islanders, 1 Hispanic American). Average age 30. 39 applicants, 82% accepted, 16 enrolled. In 2009, 6 master's awarded. *Degree requirements:* For master's, thesis optional. *Entrance requirements:* For master's, GRE General Test, bachelor's degree in engineering or related degree, minimum GPA of 3.0. Additional exam requirements/ recommendations for international students: Required—TOEFL. *Application deadline:* For fall admission, 5/1 for domestic students; for spring admission, 10/1 for domestic students. Applications are processed on a rolling basis. Application fee: $60 ($75 for international students). *Expenses:* Tuition, state resident: full-time $8922; part-time $639 per credit hour. Tuition, nonresident: full-time $19,372; part-time $1154 per credit hour. Tuition and fees vary according to course level, course load, degree level, program, reciprocity agreements and student level. *Financial support:* Federal Work-Study and scholarships/grants available. Support available to part-time students. Financial award application deadline: 3/1; financial award applicants required to submit FAFSA. *Faculty research:* Neural networks, artificial intelligence, robust control, space operations, space propulsion. *Unit head:* Dr. T. S. Kalkur, Chair, 719-255-3147, Fax: 719-255-3042, E-mail: kalkur@eas.uccs.edu. *Application contact:* Siew Nylund, Academic Adviser, 719-255-3243, Fax: 719-255-3589, E-mail: snylund@eas.uccs.edu.

University of Colorado Denver, College of Engineering and Applied Science, Department of Computer Science and Engineering, Program in Computer Science and Information Systems, Denver, CO 80217-3364. Offers PhD. *Students:* 1 (woman) full-time, 7 part-time (3 women); includes 1 minority (Asian American or Pacific Islander), 4 international. 13 applicants, 23% accepted, 3 enrolled. In 2009, 2 doctorates awarded. *Degree requirements:* For doctorate, comprehensive exam, thesis/dissertation. *Entrance requirements:* For doctorate, GRE General Test or GMAT, portfolio. Additional exam requirements/recommendations for international students: Required—TOEFL (minimum score 525 paper-based; 197 computer-based). *Application deadline:* For fall admission, 6/1 for domestic students. Application fee: $50 ($75 for international students). *Financial support:* Federal Work-Study and scholarships/grants available. Financial award application deadline: 4/1; financial award applicants required to submit FAFSA. *Unit head:* Gita Alaghband, Co-Director, 303-556-2940, Fax: 303-556-8369, E-mail: gita.alaghband@ucdenver.edu. *Application contact:* Frances Moore, Program Assistant, 303-556-4083, Fax: 303-556-8369, E-mail: frances.moore@ucdenver.edu.

University of Delaware, College of Engineering, Department of Computer and Information Sciences, Newark, DE 19716. Offers MS, PhD. Part-time programs available. Terminal master's awarded for partial completion of doctoral program. *Degree requirements:* For master's, thesis optional; for doctorate, comprehensive exam, thesis/dissertation. *Entrance requirements:* For master's and doctorate, GRE General Test. Additional exam requirements/recommendations for international students: Required—TOEFL (minimum score 550 paper-based; 213 computer-based). Electronic applications accepted. *Faculty research:* Artificial intelligence, computational theory, graphics and computer vision, networks, systems.

See Close-Up on page 313.

University of Detroit Mercy, College of Business Administration, Program in Information Assurance, Detroit, MI 48221. Offers MS.

University of Florida, Graduate School, College of Engineering and College of Liberal Arts and Sciences, Department of Computer and Information Science and Engineering, Gainesville, FL 32611. Offers computer engineering (ME, MS, PhD); computer science (MS); digital arts and sciences (MS). Part-time programs available. *Degree requirements:* For master's, thesis (for some programs); for doctorate, thesis/dissertation. *Entrance requirements:* For master's and doctorate, GRE General Test, minimum GPA of 3.0. Additional exam requirements/ recommendations for international students: Required—TOEFL (minimum score 550 paper-based; 213 computer-based). Electronic applications accepted. *Faculty research:* Artificial intelligence, networks security, distributed computing, parallel processing system, vision and visualization, database systems.

University of Hawaii at Manoa, Graduate Division, Interdisciplinary Program in Communication and Information Sciences, Honolulu, HI 96822. Offers PhD. Part-time programs available. *Faculty:* 40 full-time (13 women), 15 part-time/adjunct (3 women). *Students:* 21 full-time (11 women), 10 part-time (7 women); includes 5 minority (4 Asian Americans or Pacific Islanders, 1 Hispanic American), 10 international. Average age 39. 14 applicants, 29% accepted, 2 enrolled. In 2009, 7 doctorates awarded. *Degree requirements:* For doctorate, comprehensive exam, thesis/dissertation. *Entrance requirements:* For doctorate, GRE or GMAT. Additional exam requirements/recommendations for international students: Required—TOEFL (minimum score 600 paper-based; 250 computer-based; 100 iBT), IELTS (minimum score 7). *Application deadline:* For fall admission, 3/1 for domestic students, 1/15 for international students. Application fee: $60. *Expenses:* Tuition, state resident: full-time $8900; part-time $372 per credit. Tuition, nonresident: full-time $21,400; part-time $898 per credit. Required fees: $207 per semester. *Financial support:* In 2009–10, 2 fellowships (averaging $2,125 per year), 5 research assistantships (averaging $18,096 per year), 6 teaching assistantships (averaging $15,980 per year) were awarded. *Application contact:* Daniel Suthers, Graduate Chair, 808-956-3493, Fax: 808-956-3548, E-mail: cischair@hawaii.edu.

University of Hawaii at Manoa, Graduate Division, Shidler College of Business, Program in Business Administration, Honolulu, HI 96822. Offers Asian business studies (MBA); Chinese business studies (MBA); decision sciences (MBA); entrepreneurship (MBA); finance (MBA); finance and banking (MBA); human resources management (MBA); information management (MBA); information technology (MBA); international business (MBA); Japanese business studies (MBA); marketing (MBA); organizational behavior (MBA); organizational management (MBA); real estate (MBA); student-designed track (MBA). *Accreditation:* AACSB. Part-time and evening/ weekend programs available. *Faculty:* 46 full-time (8 women), 9 part-time/adjunct (4 women). *Students:* 259 full-time (90 women), 105 part-time (43 women); includes 123 minority (118 Asian Americans or Pacific Islanders, 5 Hispanic Americans), 119 international. Average age 32. 336 applicants, 52% accepted, 150 enrolled. In 2009, 113 master's awarded. *Degree requirements:* For master's, thesis optional. *Entrance requirements:* For master's, GMAT, minimum GPA of 3.0. Additional exam requirements/recommendations for international students: Required—TOEFL (minimum score 600 paper-based; 250 computer-based; 100 iBT), IELTS (minimum score 7). *Application deadline:* For fall admission, 5/1 for domestic students, 3/1 for international students. Application fee: $60. *Expenses:* Contact institution. *Financial support:* In 2009–10, 24 students received support, including 98 fellowships (averaging $3,481 per year), 3 research assistantships (averaging $16,626 per year). Total annual research expenditures: $427,000. *Application contact:* Tung Bui, Graduate Chair, 808-956-5565, Fax: 808-956-9889, E-mail: tung.bui@hawaii.edu.

University of Houston, Bauer College of Business, Decision and Information Sciences Program, Houston, TX 77204. Offers management information systems (MBA, PhD). Part-time and evening/weekend programs available. *Faculty:* 12 full-time (1 woman), 9 part-time/adjunct (0 women). *Expenses:* Tuition, state resident: full-time $7676; part-time $320 per credit hour. Tuition, nonresident: full-time $14,324; part-time $597 per credit hour. Required fees: $3034. *Financial support:* In 2009–10, 6 teaching assistantships with full tuition reimbursements (averaging $7,100 per year) were awarded; fellowships with full tuition reimbursements, research assistantships with full tuition reimbursements, career-related internships or fieldwork, Federal Work-Study, institutionally sponsored loans, scholarships/grants, health care benefits, and unspecified assistantships also available. Support available to part-time students. Financial award application deadline: 2/1; financial award applicants required to submit FAFSA. *Unit head:* Dr. Basheer Khumawala, Chair, 713-743-4747, E-mail: bkhumawala@uh.edu. *Application contact:* 713-743-4900, Fax: 713-743-4942, E-mail: oss@uh.edu.

University of Houston, College of Technology, Department of Information and Logistics Technology, Houston, TX 77204. Offers technology project management (MS), including information systems security, logistics. Part-time and evening/weekend programs available. *Faculty:* 6 full-time (3 women), 6 part-time/adjunct (2 women). *Students:* 59 full-time (18 women), 47 part-time (15 women); includes 18 minority (6 African Americans, 5 Asian Americans or Pacific Islanders, 7 Hispanic Americans), 58 international. Average age 29. 69 applicants, 87% accepted, 33 enrolled. In 2009, 25 master's awarded. *Degree requirements:* For master's, project or thesis (most programs). *Entrance requirements:* For master's, GMAT. Additional exam requirements/recommendations for international students: Required—TOEFL (minimum score 550 paper-based; 79 iBT). *Application deadline:* For fall admission, 7/1 for domestic students, 4/1 for international students; for spring admission, 12/1 for domestic students, 10/1 for international students. Applications are processed on a rolling basis. Application fee: $75 ($150 for international students). Electronic applications accepted. *Expenses:* Tuition, state resident: full-time $7676; part-time $320 per credit hour. Tuition, nonresident: full-time $14,324; part-time $597 per credit hour. Required fees: $3034. *Financial support:* In 2009–10, 11 fellowships with full tuition reimbursements (averaging $10,500 per year), 1 research assistantship with full tuition reimbursement (averaging $10,500 per year), 4 teaching assistantships with full tuition reimbursements (averaging $10,500 per year) were awarded. *Unit head:* Michael Gibson, Chairperson, 713-743-5116, E-mail: mlgibson@uh.edu. *Application contact:* Tiffany Roosa, Graduate Advisor, 713-743-2987, Fax: 713-743-4151, E-mail: troosa@uh.edu.

University of Houston–Clear Lake, School of Science and Computer Engineering, Program in Computer Information Systems, Houston, TX 77058-1098. Offers MS. Part-time and evening/ weekend programs available. *Entrance requirements:* For master's, GRE General Test. Additional exam requirements/recommendations for international students: Required—TOEFL (minimum score 550 paper-based; 213 computer-based).

University of Illinois at Urbana–Champaign, Graduate College, Graduate School of Library and Information Science, Champaign, IL 61820. Offers bioinformatics: library and information science (MS); library and information science (MS, PhD, CAS); library and information science: digital libraries (CAS). *Accreditation:* ALA (one or more programs are accredited). Postbaccalaureate distance learning degree programs offered. *Faculty:* 26 full-time (13 women), 9 part-time/adjunct (6 women). *Students:* 321 full-time (229 women), 310 part-time (230 women); includes 101 minority (34 African Americans, 4 American Indian/Alaska Native, 36 Asian Americans or Pacific Islanders, 27 Hispanic Americans), 35 international. 747 applicants, 53% accepted, 217 enrolled. In 2009, 240 master's, 7 doctorates, 6 other advanced degrees awarded. *Entrance requirements:* For master's, GRE General Test, minimum GPA of 3.0; for

Information Science

University of Illinois at Urbana–Champaign (continued)

doctorate, minimum GPA of 3.0; for CAS, master's degree in library and information science or related field with minimum GPA of 3.0. Additional exam requirements/recommendations for international students: Required—TOEFL (minimum score 620 paper-based; 260 computer-based; 105 iBT), or IELTS (minimum score 7). *Application deadline:* Applications are processed on a rolling basis. Application fee: $60 ($75 for international students). Electronic applications accepted. *Financial support:* In 2009–10, 52 fellowships, 41 research assistantships, 27 teaching assistantships were awarded; tuition waivers (full and partial) also available. *Unit head:* John Unsworth, Dean, 217-333-3281, Fax: 217-244-3302, E-mail: unsworth@illinois.edu. *Application contact:* Valerie Youngen, Admissions and Records Representative, 217-333-0734, Fax: 217-244-3302, E-mail: vyoungen@llinois.edu.

The University of Iowa, Graduate College, Program in Informatics, Iowa City, IA 52242-1316. Offers bioinformatics and computational biology (Certificate); health informatics (MS, PhD, Certificate); information science (MS, PhD, Certificate). *Degree requirements:* For master's, thesis optional; for doctorate, comprehensive exam, thesis/dissertation. *Entrance requirements:* For master's and doctorate, GRE General Test, minimum GPA of 3.0. Additional exam requirements/recommendations for international students: Required—TOEFL (minimum score 550 paper-based; 213 computer-based; 81 iBT). Electronic applications accepted.

University of Management and Technology, Program in Computer Science and Information Technology, Arlington, VA 22209. Offers computer science (MS); information technology (AC); information technology project management (MS); management information systems (MS); project management (AC); software engineering (MS). Part-time and evening/weekend programs available. Postbaccalaureate distance learning degree programs offered (no on-campus study). *Entrance requirements:* For master's, 3 recommendations, resume. Additional exam requirements/recommendations for international students: Required—TOEFL (minimum score 550 paper-based; 213 computer-based). Electronic applications accepted.

University of Maryland, Baltimore County, Graduate School, College of Engineering and Information Technology, Department of Information Systems, Program in Information Systems, Baltimore, MD 21250. Offers MS, PhD. Part-time programs available. Postbaccalaureate distance learning degree programs offered (no on-campus study). *Students:* 84 full-time (38 women), 377 part-time (119 women); includes 136 minority (75 African Americans, 1 American Indian/Alaska Native, 55 Asian Americans or Pacific Islanders, 5 Hispanic Americans), 73 international. Average age 33. 264 applicants, 80% accepted, 103 enrolled. In 2009, 87 master's, 4 doctorates awarded. *Degree requirements:* For master's, comprehensive exam (for some programs), thesis optional; for doctorate, comprehensive exam, thesis/dissertation. *Entrance requirements:* For master's, minimum GPA of 3.0; for doctorate, GRE General Test or GMAT, minimum GPA of 3.0, competence in statistical analysis and experimental design (recommended). Additional exam requirements/recommendations for international students: Required—TOEFL (minimum score 550 paper-based; 213 computer-based; 80 iBT). *Application deadline:* For fall admission, 6/1 for domestic students, 1/1 for international students; for spring admission, 11/1 for domestic students, 6/1 for international students. Applications are processed on a rolling basis. Application fee: $50. Electronic applications accepted. *Financial support:* In 2009–10, 1 fellowship with full tuition reimbursement (averaging $30,000 per year), 11 research assistantships with full tuition reimbursements (averaging $20,000 per year), 15 teaching assistantships with full tuition reimbursements (averaging $19,000 per year) were awarded; career-related internships or fieldwork, Federal Work-Study, scholarships/grants, health care benefits, tuition waivers (partial), and unspecified assistantships also available. Support available to part-time students. Financial award application deadline: 6/30; financial award applicants required to submit FAFSA. *Faculty research:* Human-centered computing, artificial intelligence, database/data mining, decision-making support systems, software engineering/systems analysis and design. *Unit head:* Dr. Andrew L. Sears, Professor and Chair, 410-455-3883, Fax: 410-455-1217, E-mail: asears@umbc.edu. *Application contact:* Dr. Aryya Gangopadhyay, Associate Professor and Graduate Program Director, 410-455-2620, Fax: 410-455-1217, E-mail: gangopad@umbc.edu.

University of Maryland University College, Graduate School of Management and Technology, Program in Accounting and Information Technology, Adelphi, MD 20783. Offers MS, Certificate. Part-time and evening/weekend programs available. Postbaccalaureate distance learning degree programs offered (no on-campus study). *Students:* 3 full-time (1 woman), 204 part-time (117 women); includes 113 minority (88 African Americans, 18 Asian Americans or Pacific Islanders, 7 Hispanic Americans), 2 international. Average age 37. 92 applicants, 100% accepted, 40 enrolled. In 2009, 35 master's, 2 other advanced degrees awarded. *Degree requirements:* For master's, thesis or alternative. *Application deadline:* Applications are processed on a rolling basis. Application fee: $50. Electronic applications accepted. *Expenses:* Tuition, state resident: full-time $7704; part-time $428 per credit hour. Tuition, nonresident: full-time $11,862; part-time $659 per credit hour. *Financial support:* Federal Work-Study and scholarships/grants available. Support available to part-time students. Financial award application deadline: 6/1; financial award applicants required to submit FAFSA. *Unit head:* Dr. Kathryn Klose, Program Director, Financial Management and Accounting, 240-684-2400, Fax: 301-684-2401, E-mail: kklose@umuc.edu. *Application contact:* Coordinator, Graduate Admissions, 800-888-UMUC, Fax: 240-684-2151, E-mail: newgrad@umuc.edu.

University of Maryland University College, Graduate School of Management and Technology, Program in Information Technology, Adelphi, MD 20783. Offers MS, Certificate. Part-time and evening/weekend programs available. Postbaccalaureate distance learning degree programs offered (no on-campus study). *Students:* 26 full-time (8 women), 1,762 part-time (582 women); includes 805 minority (577 African Americans, 7 American Indian/Alaska Native, 136 Asian Americans or Pacific Islanders, 85 Hispanic Americans), 40 international. Average age 36. 431 applicants, 100% accepted, 342 enrolled. In 2009, 177 master's, 12 other advanced degrees awarded. *Degree requirements:* For master's, thesis or alternative. *Application deadline:* Applications are processed on a rolling basis. Application fee: $50. Electronic applications accepted. *Expenses:* Tuition, state resident: full-time $7704; part-time $428 per credit hour. Tuition, nonresident: full-time $11,862; part-time $659 per credit hour. *Financial support:* Federal Work-Study and scholarships/grants available. Support available to part-time students. Financial award application deadline: 6/1; financial award applicants required to submit FAFSA. *Unit head:* Dr. Garth MacKenzie, Associate Chair and Program Director, ITEC Core, 240-684-2400, Fax: 240-684-2401, E-mail: gmackenzie@umuc.edu. *Application contact:* Coordinator, Graduate Admissions, 800-888-UMUC, Fax: 240-684-2151, E-mail: newgrad@umuc.edu.

University of Michigan, Horace H. Rackham School of Graduate Studies, School of Information, Ann Arbor, MI 48109-1107. Offers archives and records management (MS); human-computer interaction (MS); information (MS, PhD); information economics, management and policy (MS); library and information services (MS). *Accreditation:* ALA (one or more programs are accredited). Part-time programs available. *Degree requirements:* For master's, variable foreign language requirement, thesis optional; for doctorate, one foreign language, thesis/dissertation, oral defense of dissertation, preliminary exam. *Entrance requirements:* For master's and doctorate, GRE General Test. Additional exam requirements/recommendations for international students: Required—TOEFL (minimum score 600 paper-based; 250 computer-based). Electronic applications accepted. *Expenses:* Tuition, state resident: full-time $17,286; part-time $1099 per credit hour. Tuition, nonresident: full-time $34,944; part-time $2080 per credit hour. Required fees: $95 per semester. Tuition and fees vary according to course load, degree level and program.

University of Michigan–Dearborn, College of Engineering and Computer Science, Department of Computer and Information Science, Program in Computer and Information Science, Dearborn, MI 48128-1491. Offers MS. Part-time and evening/weekend programs available. Postbaccalaureate distance learning degree programs offered (minimal on-campus study). *Faculty:* 13 full-time (1 woman), 4 part-time/adjunct (0 women). *Students:* 4 full-time (0 women), 55 part-time (10 women); includes 10 minority (2 African Americans, 6 Asian Americans or Pacific Islanders, 2 Hispanic Americans), 13 international. Average age 33. 25 applicants, 48% accepted, 12 enrolled. In 2009, 22 master's awarded. *Degree requirements:* For master's, thesis optional. *Entrance requirements:* For master's, bachelor's degree in mathematics, computer science or engineering; minimum GPA of 3.0. Additional exam requirements/recommendations for international students: Required—TOEFL (minimum score 560 paper-based; 220 computer-based; 84 iBT). *Application deadline:* For fall admission, 6/15 priority date for domestic students, 4/1 for international students; for winter admission, 10/15 priority date for domestic students, 8/1 for international students; for spring admission, 2/15 priority date for domestic students, 12/1 for international students. Application fee: $60 ($75 for international students). *Expenses:* Tuition, area resident: Part-time $504.10 per credit hour. Tuition, state resident: part-time $504.10 per credit hour. Tuition, nonresident: part-time $957.90 per credit hour. *Financial support:* In 2009–10, 2 research assistantships with full and partial tuition reimbursements (averaging $7,700 per year) were awarded; career-related internships or fieldwork also available. Financial award application deadline: 4/1; financial award applicants required to submit FAFSA. *Faculty research:* Information systems, geometric modeling, networks, databases. Total annual research expenditures: $54,056. *Unit head:* Dr. William I. Grosky, Chair, 313-583-6424, Fax: 313-593-4256, E-mail: wgrosky@umich.edu. *Application contact:* Katherine R. Markotan, Intermediate Academic Records Assistant, 313-436-9145, Fax: 313-593-4256, E-mail: tabatha@umd.umich.edu.

University of Michigan–Dearborn, College of Engineering and Computer Science, Department of Industrial and Manufacturing Systems Engineering, Dearborn, MI 48128-1491. Offers engineering management (MS); industrial and systems engineering (MSE); information systems and technology (MS); information systems engineering (PhD); MBA/MSE. Part-time and evening/weekend programs available. *Faculty:* 14 full-time (0 women), 5 part-time/adjunct (0 women). *Students:* 16 full-time (5 women), 179 part-time (56 women); includes 45 minority (6 African Americans, 26 Asian Americans or Pacific Islanders, 13 Hispanic Americans). Average age 31. 63 applicants, 62% accepted, 37 enrolled. In 2009, 67 master's awarded. *Degree requirements:* For master's, thesis optional. *Entrance requirements:* For master's, bachelor's degree in applied mathematics, computer science, engineering, or physical science; minimum GPA of 3.0. Additional exam requirements/recommendations for international students: Required—TOEFL (minimum score 560 paper-based; 220 computer-based; 84 iBT). *Application deadline:* For fall admission, 8/1 priority date for domestic students, 4/1 for international students; for winter admission, 12/1 priority date for domestic students, 8/1 for international students; for spring admission, 4/1 for domestic students, 12/1 for international students. Applications are processed on a rolling basis. Application fee: $60 ($75 for international students). *Expenses:* Tuition, area resident: Part-time $504.10 per credit hour. Tuition, state resident: part-time $504.10 per credit hour. Tuition, nonresident: part-time $957.90 per credit hour. *Financial support:* Fellowships, research assistantships, teaching assistantships, Federal Work-Study available. Financial award application deadline: 4/1; financial award applicants required to submit FAFSA. *Faculty research:* Health care systems, data and knowledge management, human factors engineering, machine diagnostics, precision machining. *Unit head:* Dr. Armen Zakarian, Chair, 313-593-5361, Fax: 313-593-3692, E-mail: zakarian@umd.umich.edu. *Application contact:* Joey W. Woods, Graduate Program Assistant, 313-593-5361, Fax: 313-593-3692, E-mail: jwwoods@umd.umich.edu.

University of Michigan–Flint, College of Arts and Sciences, Program in Computer and Information Systems, Flint, MI 48502-1950. Offers computer science and information systems (MS). Part-time programs available. *Faculty:* 2 full-time (1 woman). *Students:* 6 full-time (0 women), 54 part-time (10 women); includes 8 minority (4 African Americans, 4 Asian Americans or Pacific Islanders), 18 international. Average age 31. 55 applicants, 73% accepted, 15 enrolled. In 2009, 14 master's awarded. *Degree requirements:* For master's, thesis or alternative. *Entrance requirements:* For master's, minimum undergraduate GPA of 3.0. Additional exam requirements/recommendations for international students: Required—TOEFL (minimum score 560 paper-based; 220 computer-based; 84 iBT), IELTS (minimum score 6.5). *Application deadline:* For fall admission, 8/1 priority date for domestic students, 5/1 priority date for international students; for winter admission, 11/15 priority date for domestic students, 9/1 priority date for international students; for spring admission, 3/15 priority date for domestic students, 1/1 priority date for international students. Application fee: $55. *Expenses:* Contact institution. *Financial support:* Federal Work-Study, scholarships/grants, and unspecified assistantships available. Support available to part-time students. Financial award application deadline: 6/1; financial award applicants required to submit FAFSA. *Unit head:* Dr. Michael Farmer, Director, 810-762-3131, Fax: 810-766-6780. *Application contact:* Bradley T. Maki, Director of Graduate Admissions, 810-762-3171, Fax: 810-766-6789, E-mail: bmaki@umflint.edu.

University of Minnesota, Twin Cities Campus, Institute of Technology, Department of Computer Science and Engineering, Minneapolis, MN 55455-0213. Offers computer and information sciences (MCIS, MS, PhD). Part-time programs available. Terminal master's awarded for partial completion of doctoral program. *Degree requirements:* For doctorate, thesis/dissertation. *Entrance requirements:* For master's and doctorate, GRE General Test. *Faculty research:* Software systems, numerical analysis, theory, artificial intelligence.

University of Nebraska at Omaha, Graduate Studies, College of Information Science and Technology, Department of Information Systems and Quantitative Analysis, Omaha, NE 68182. Offers information systems and quantitative analysis (Certificate); information technology (PhD); management information systems (MS). Part-time and evening/weekend programs available. *Faculty:* 18 full-time (10 women). *Students:* 65 full-time (29 women), 100 part-time (31 women); includes 9 minority (4 African Americans, 4 Asian Americans or Pacific Islanders, 1 Hispanic American), 70 international. Average age 37. 173 applicants, 42% accepted, 39 enrolled. In 2009, 42 master's, 1 doctorate, 23 other advanced degrees awarded. *Degree requirements:* For master's, comprehensive exam, thesis (for some programs); for doctorate, comprehensive exam, thesis/dissertation. *Entrance requirements:* For master's, GMAT or GRE General Test; for doctorate, GMAT or GRE General Test, letters of recommendation. Additional exam requirements/recommendations for international students: Required—TOEFL (minimum score 575 paper-based; 230 computer-based; 89 iBT). *Application deadline:* For fall admission, 3/15 for domestic students; for spring admission, 10/1 for domestic students. Applications are processed on a rolling basis. Application fee: $45. Electronic applications accepted. *Financial support:* In 2009–10, 67 students received support; fellowships, research assistantships with tuition reimbursements available, teaching assistantships with tuition reimbursements available, career-related internships or fieldwork, Federal Work-Study, scholarships/grants, tuition waivers (partial), and unspecified assistantships available. Financial award application deadline: 3/1; financial award applicants required to submit FAFSA. *Unit head:* Dr. Ilze Zigurs, Chairperson, 402-554-3770. *Application contact:* Carla Frakes, Information Contact, 402-554-2423.

University of Nebraska–Lincoln, Graduate College, College of Arts and Sciences and College of Engineering, Department of Computer Science and Engineering, Lincoln, NE 68588. Offers bioinformatics (MS, PhD); computer engineering (MS, PhD); computer science (MS, PhD); information technology (PhD). *Degree requirements:* For master's, thesis optional; for doctorate, comprehensive exam, thesis/dissertation. *Entrance requirements:* For master's and doctorate, GRE General Test. Additional exam requirements/recommendations for international students: Required—TOEFL (minimum score 600 paper-based; 250 computer-based). Electronic applications accepted. *Faculty research:* Software engineering, geo- and bio-informatics, scientific computation, secure communication.

University of Nevada, Las Vegas, Graduate College, Howard R. Hughes College of Engineering, School of Informatics, Las Vegas, NV 89154-4054. Offers MS, PhD. *Faculty:* 5 full-time (3 women), 1 part-time/adjunct (0 women). *Students:* 5 full-time (0 women), 4 part-time (1 woman); includes 4 minority (all Asian Americans or Pacific Islanders), 4 international. Average age 37. 18 applicants, 50% accepted, 5 enrolled. In 2009, 1 master's awarded. *Degree requirements:* For master's, project; for doctorate, comprehensive exam, thesis/dissertation. *Entrance requirements:* For master's, GRE General Test (verbal and quantitative), GMAT; for doctorate, GRE General Test (Verbal and Quantitative), GMAT. Additional exam requirements/recommendations for international students: Required—TOEFL (minimum score 550 paper-based; 213 computer-based; 80 iBT), IELTS (minimum score 7). *Application deadline:*

For fall admission, 3/15 priority date for domestic and international students; for spring admission, 10/1 priority date for domestic and international students. Applications are processed on a rolling basis. Application fee: $60 ($95 for international students). Electronic applications accepted. *Financial support:* In 2009–10, 3 students received support, including 1 research assistantship with partial tuition reimbursement available (averaging $10,000 per year), 2 teaching assistantships with partial tuition reimbursements available (averaging $12,000 per year); institutionally sponsored loans, scholarships/grants, health care benefits, and unspecified assistantships also available. Financial award application deadline: 3/1. *Faculty research:* Digital security, healthcare informatics, human computer interaction, ecology informatics, hospitality, gaming informatics. *Unit head:* Dr. Hal Berghel, Director/ Associate Dean, 702-895-2441, Fax: 702-895-0577, E-mail: hlb@berghel.net. *Application contact:* Graduate College Admissions Evaluator, 702-895-3320, Fax: 702-895-4180, E-mail: gradcollege@univ.edu.

University of New Haven, Graduate School, Tagliatela College of Engineering, Program in Computer and Information Science, West Haven, CT 06516-1916. Offers computer science (MS, Certificate, including advanced applications (MS), computer applications (Certificate), computer programming (Certificate), computer systems (MS), computing (Certificate), database and information systems (MS), network administration (Certificate), network systems (MS), software engineering and development (MS). Part-time and evening/weekend programs available. *Faculty:* 9 full-time (2 women), 5 part-time/adjunct (0 women). *Students:* 21 full-time (8 women), 32 part-time (8 women); includes 5 minority (2 African Americans, 1 Asian American or Pacific Islander, 2 Hispanic Americans), 26 international. Average age 30. 163 applicants, 88% accepted, 18 enrolled. In 2009, 24 master's awarded. *Degree requirements:* For master's, thesis or alternative. *Entrance requirements:* Additional exam requirements/recommendations for international students: Required—TOEFL (minimum score 520 paper-based; 190 computer-based; 70 iBT); Recommended—IELTS (minimum score 5.5). *Application deadline:* For fall admission, 5/31 for international students; for winter admission, 10/15 for international students; for spring admission, 1/15 for international students. Applications are processed on a rolling basis. Application fee: $50. Electronic applications accepted. *Expenses:* Tuition: Part-time $700 per credit. Required fees: $45 per term. One-time fee: $390 part-time. *Financial support:* Research assistantships with partial tuition reimbursements, teaching assistantships with partial tuition reimbursements, career-related internships or fieldwork, Federal Work-Study, scholarships/grants, tuition waivers, and unspecified assistantships available. Support available to part-time students. Financial award applicants required to submit FAFSA. *Unit head:* Dr. Tahany Fergany, Coordinator, 203-932-7067. *Application contact:* Eloise Gormley, Director of Graduate Admissions, 203-932-7449, Fax: 203-932-7137, E-mail: gradinfo@newhaven.edu.

The University of North Carolina at Charlotte, Graduate School, College of Computing and Informatics, Department of Information Technology, Charlotte, NC 28223-0001. Offers information technology (MS, PhD). *Faculty:* 15 full-time (3 women), 3 part-time/adjunct (0 women). *Students:* 146 full-time (39 women), 61 part-time (15 women); includes 27 minority (14 African Americans, 2 American Indian/Alaska Native, 7 Asian Americans or Pacific Islanders, 4 Hispanic Americans), 90 international. Average age 29. 162 applicants, 69% accepted, 59 enrolled. In 2009, 35 master's, 5 doctorates awarded. *Degree requirements:* For master's, thesis optional; for doctorate, comprehensive exam, thesis/dissertation. *Entrance requirements:* For master's, GRE or GMAT, minimum undergraduate GPA of 2.8 overall, 2.0 in last 2 years; for doctorate, GRE or GMAT, working knowledge of 2 high-level programming languages. Additional exam requirements/recommendations for international students: Required—TOEFL (minimum score 557 paper-based; 220 computer-based; 83 iBT). *Application deadline:* For fall admission, 7/1 for domestic students, 5/1 for international students; for spring admission, 11/1 for domestic students, 10/1 for international students. Applications are processed on a rolling basis. Application fee: $55. Electronic applications accepted. *Financial support:* In 2009–10, 21 students received support, including 7 research assistantships (averaging $12,800 per year), 14 teaching assistantships (averaging $10,600 per year); career-related internships or fieldwork, Federal Work-Study, institutionally sponsored loans, scholarships/grants, and unspecified assistantships also available. Support available to part-time students. Financial award application deadline: 4/1; financial award applicants required to submit FAFSA. *Faculty research:* Information security, information privacy, information assurance, cryptography, software engineering, enterprise integration, intelligent information systems, human computer interaction. Total annual research expenditures: $2.2 million. *Unit head:* Dr. Ken Chen, Program Director, 704-687-8545, Fax: 704-687-6065, E-mail: chen@uncc.edu. *Application contact:* Kathy B. Giddings, Director of Graduate Admissions, 704-687-5503, Fax: 704-687-3279, E-mail: gradadm@uncc.edu.

University of North Florida, College of Computing, Engineering, and Construction, Jacksonville, FL 32224. Offers civil engineering (MSCE); computer and information sciences (MS); electrical engineering (MSEE); mechanical engineering (MSME). Part-time programs available. *Faculty:* 35 full-time (6 women). *Students:* 21 full-time (4 women), 64 part-time (11 women); includes 22 minority (6 African Americans, 9 Asian Americans or Pacific Islanders, 7 Hispanic Americans), 10 international. Average age 31. 82 applicants, 45% accepted, 14 enrolled. In 2009, 6 master's awarded. *Degree requirements:* For master's, thesis optional. *Entrance requirements:* For master's, GRE General Test, minimum GPA of 3.0 in last 60 hours of course work. Additional exam requirements/recommendations for international students: Required—TOEFL (minimum score 500 paper-based; 173 computer-based). *Application deadline:* For fall admission, 7/1 priority date for domestic students, 5/1 for international students; for spring admission, 11/1 priority date for domestic students, 10/1 for international students. Applications are processed on a rolling basis. Application fee: $30. Electronic applications accepted. *Expenses:* Tuition, state resident: full-time $6649.20; part-time $277.05 per credit hour. Tuition, nonresident: full-time $22,970; part-time $957.08 per credit hour. Required fees: $985; $41.03 per credit hour. *Financial support:* In 2009–10, 20 students received support, including 5 research assistantships (averaging $5,009 per year), 3 teaching assistantships (averaging $2,844 per year); Federal Work-Study and tuition waivers (partial) also available. Support available to part-time students. Financial award application deadline: 4/1; financial award applicants required to submit FAFSA. *Faculty research:* Parallel and distributed computing, networks, generic programming, algorithms, artificial intelligence. Total annual research expenditures: $2.2 million. *Unit head:* Dr. Neal Coulter, Dean, 904-620-1350, E-mail: ncoulter@unf.edu. *Application contact:* Dr. Roger Eggen, Director of Graduate Studies for Computer Science, 904-320-2985, Fax: 904-620-2988, E-mail: ree@unf.edu.

University of Oregon, Graduate School, College of Arts and Sciences, Department of Computer and Information Science, Eugene, OR 97403. Offers MA, MS, PhD. Part-time programs available. Terminal master's awarded for partial completion of doctoral program. *Degree requirements:* For doctorate, thesis/dissertation. *Entrance requirements:* For master's and doctorate, GRE General Test, minimum GPA of 3.0. Additional exam requirements/recommendations for international students: Required—TOEFL. *Faculty research:* Artificial intelligence, graphics, natural-language processing, expert systems, operating systems.

University of Ottawa, Faculty of Graduate and Postdoctoral Studies, Faculty of Engineering, Engineering Management Program, Ottawa, ON K1N 6N5, Canada. Offers engineering management (M Eng); information technology (Certificate); project management (Certificate). *Degree requirements:* For master's, thesis or alternative. *Entrance requirements:* For master's and Certificate, honors degree or equivalent, minimum B average. Electronic applications accepted.

University of Pennsylvania, School of Engineering and Applied Science, Department of Computer and Information Science, Philadelphia, PA 19104. Offers MCIT, MSE, PhD. Part-time programs available. *Faculty:* 41 full-time (5 women), 9 part-time/adjunct (2 women). *Students:* 194 full-time (35 women), 55 part-time (13 women); includes 19 minority (3 African Americans, 15 Asian Americans or Pacific Islanders, 1 Hispanic American), 131 international. 977 applicants, 22% accepted, 109 enrolled. In 2009, 86 master's, 18 doctorates awarded. Terminal master's awarded for partial completion of doctoral program. *Degree requirements:* For master's, thesis optional; for doctorate, thesis/dissertation. *Entrance requirements:* For master's and doctorate, GRE General Test. Additional exam requirements/recommendations for international students: Required—TOEFL. *Application deadline:* For fall admission, 6/1 priority date for domestic

students, 5/1 priority date for international students. Applications are processed on a rolling basis. Application fee: $70. Electronic applications accepted. *Expenses:* Tuition: Full-time $25,660; part-time $4758 per course. Required fees: $2152; $270 per course. Tuition and fees vary according to course load, degree level and program. *Financial support:* Fellowships with full tuition reimbursements, research assistantships with full tuition reimbursements, teaching assistantships, institutionally sponsored loans, scholarships/grants, traineeships, health care benefits, and unspecified assistantships available. *Faculty research:* AI, computer systems graphics, information management, robotics, software systems theory.

University of Phoenix–Cincinnati Campus, John Sperling School of Business, College of Information Systems and Technology, West Chester, OH 45069-4875. Offers electronic business (MBA); information systems (MIS); technology management (MBA). Evening/weekend programs available. Postbaccalaureate distance learning degree programs offered. *Degree requirements:* For master's, thesis (for some programs). *Entrance requirements:* For master's, minimum undergraduate GPA of 2.5, 3 years of work experience. Additional exam requirements/recommendations for international students: Required—TOEFL (minimum score 550 paper-based; 213 computer-based; 79 iBT). Electronic applications accepted.

University of Phoenix–Phoenix Campus, The John Sperling School of Business, College of Information Systems and Technology, Phoenix, AZ 85040-1958. Offers management (MIS); technology management (MBA). Evening/weekend programs available. *Degree requirements:* For master's, thesis (for some programs). *Entrance requirements:* For master's, 3 years of work experience, minimum undergraduate GPA of 3.0. Additional exam requirements/recommendations for international students: Required—TOEFL (minimum score 550 paper-based; 213 computer-based; 79 iBT). Electronic applications accepted.

University of Pittsburgh, School of Arts and Sciences, Intelligent Systems Program, Pittsburgh, PA 15260. Offers MS, PhD. *Faculty:* 25 full-time (7 women). *Students:* 21 full-time (4 women), 12 international. Average age 30. 31 applicants, 16% accepted, 3 enrolled. In 2009, 1 master's, 5 doctorates awarded. Terminal master's awarded for partial completion of doctoral program. *Degree requirements:* For master's, thesis; for doctorate, comprehensive exam, thesis/dissertation. *Entrance requirements:* For master's and doctorate, GRE General Test. Additional exam requirements/recommendations for international students: Required—TOEFL. *Application deadline:* For fall admission, 2/1 priority date for domestic and international students. Applications are processed on a rolling basis. Application fee: $50. Electronic applications accepted. *Expenses:* Tuition, state resident: full-time $16,402; part-time $665 per credit. Tuition, nonresident: full-time $28,694; part-time $1175 per credit. Required fees: $690; $175 per term. Tuition and fees vary according to program. *Financial support:* In 2009–10, 17 students received support, including 8 fellowships with full tuition reimbursements available (averaging $17,972 per year), 6 research assistantships with full tuition reimbursements available (averaging $24,648 per year); Federal Work-Study, institutionally sponsored loans, scholarships/grants, traineeships, health care benefits, and unspecified assistantships also available. Financial award application deadline: 2/1. *Faculty research:* Medical artificial intelligence, expert systems, clinical decision support, plan generation and recognition, special cognition. *Unit head:* Janyce Wiebe, Director, 412-624-9590, Fax: 412-624-8561, E-mail: wiebe@cs.pitt.edu. *Application contact:* Wendy Bergstein, Administrator, 412-624-5755, Fax: 412-624-8561, E-mail: wab23@pitt.edu.

University of Pittsburgh, School of Information Sciences, Information Science and Technology Program, Pittsburgh, PA 15260. Offers information science (MSIS, PhD, Certificate). Part-time and evening/weekend programs available. *Faculty:* 11 full-time (0 women), 1 part-time/adjunct (0 women). *Students:* 112 full-time (35 women), 44 part-time (11 women); includes 11 minority (3 African Americans, 7 Asian Americans or Pacific Islanders, 1 Hispanic American), 88 international. 175 applicants, 71% accepted, 45 enrolled. In 2009, 34 master's, 1 other advanced degree awarded. *Degree requirements:* For master's, thesis optional; for doctorate, comprehensive exam, thesis/dissertation. *Entrance requirements:* For master's, GRE General Test, bachelor's degree with minimum GPA of 3.0; course work in structured programming language, statistics, mathematics; for doctorate, GRE General Test, master's degree; minimum QPA of 3.3; course work in statistics, mathematics, programming, cognitive psychology, systems analysis & design; for Certificate, Master's in IS, Telecom, or related field. Additional exam requirements/recommendations for international students: Required—TOEFL (minimum score 550 paper-based; 213 computer-based; 80 iBT). *Application deadline:* For fall admission, 7/15 priority date for domestic students, 1/15 for international students; for winter admission, 11/1 priority date for domestic students, 6/15 for international students; for spring admission, 3/15 priority date for domestic students, 12/15 for international students. Applications are processed on a rolling basis. Application fee: $50. Electronic applications accepted. *Expenses:* Contact institution. *Financial support:* Fellowships with full and partial tuition reimbursements, research assistantships with full and partial tuition reimbursements, teaching assistantships with full and partial tuition reimbursements, career-related internships or fieldwork, scholarships/grants, health care benefits, tuition waivers (full and partial), and unspecified assistantships available. Financial award application deadline: 1/15; financial award applicants required to submit FAFSA. *Faculty research:* Adaptive web systems, systems analysis and design, geoinformatics, database and web systems, information assurance and security. *Unit head:* Dr. Paul Munro, Program Chair, 412-624-4427, Fax: 421-624-2788, E-mail: pmunro@sis.pitt.edu. *Application contact:* Shabana Reza, Student Recruiting Coordinator, 412-624-3988, Fax: 412-624-5231, E-mail: isinq@sis.pitt.edu.

University of Puerto Rico, Mayagüez Campus, Graduate Studies, College of Engineering, Program in Computing Information Science and Engineering, Mayagüez, PR 00681-9000. Offers PhD. Part-time programs available. *Degree requirements:* For doctorate, comprehensive exam, thesis/dissertation. *Entrance requirements:* For doctorate, GRE, BS degree in engineering or science; the equivalent of undergraduate courses in data structures, programming language, calculus III and linear algebra. *Faculty research:* Algorithms, computer architectures.

University of South Africa, College of Human Sciences, Pretoria, South Africa. Offers adult education (M Ed); African languages (MA, PhD); African politics (MA, PhD); Afrikaans (MA, PhD); ancient history (MA, PhD); ancient Near Eastern studies (MA, PhD); anthropology (MA, PhD); applied linguistics (MA); Arabic (MA, PhD); archaeology (MA); art history (MA); Biblical archaeology (MA); Biblical studies (M Th, D Th, PhD); Christian spirituality (M Th, D Th); church history (M Th, D Th); classical studies (MA, PhD); clinical psychology (MA); communication (MA, PhD); comparative education (M Ed, Ed D); consulting psychology (D Admin, D Com, PhD); curriculum studies (M Ed, Ed D); development studies (M Admin, MA, D Admin, PhD); didactics (M Ed, Ed D); education (M Tech); education management (M Ed, Ed D); educational psychology (M Ed); English (MA); environmental education (M Ed); French (MA, PhD); German (MA, PhD); Greek (MA); guidance and counseling (M Ed); health studies (MA, PhD), including health sciences education (MA), health services management (MA), medical and surgical nursing science (critical care general) (MA), midwifery and neonatal nursing science (MA), trauma and emergency care (MA); history (MA, PhD); history of education (Ed D); inclusive education (M Ed, Ed D); information and communications technology policy and regulation (MA); information science (MA, MIS, PhD); international politics (MA, PhD); Islamic studies (MA, PhD); Italian (MA, PhD); Judaica (MA, PhD); linguistics (MA, PhD); mathematical education (M Ed); mathematics education (MA); missiology (M Th, D Th); modern Hebrew (MA, PhD); musicology (MA, MMus, D Mus, PhD); natural science education (M Ed); New Testament (M Th, D Th); Old Testament (D Th); pastoral therapy (M Th, D Th); philosophy (MA); philosophy of education (M Ed, Ed D); politics (MA, PhD); Portuguese (MA, PhD); practical theology (M Th, D Th); psychology (MA, MS, PhD); psychology of education (M Ed, Ed D); public health (MA); religious studies (MA, D Th, PhD); Romance languages (MA); Russian (MA, PhD); Semitic languages (MA, PhD); social behavior studies in HIV/AIDS (MA); social science (mental health) (MA); social science in development studies (MA); social science in psychology (MA); social science in social work (MA); social science in sociology (MA); social work (MSW, DSW, PhD); socio-education (M Ed, Ed D); sociolinguistics (MA); sociology (MA, PhD); Spanish (MA, PhD); systematic theology (M Th, D Th); TESOL (teaching

Information Science

University of South Africa (continued)

English to speakers of other languages) (MA); theological ethics (M Th, D Th); theory of literature (MA, PhD); urban ministries (D Th); urban ministry (M Th).

University of South Alabama, Graduate School, School of Computer and Information Sciences, Mobile, AL 36688-0002. Offers computer science (MS); information systems (MS). Part-time and evening/weekend programs available. *Degree requirements:* For master's, thesis optional, project. *Entrance requirements:* For master's, GRE General Test. *Expenses:* Tuition, state resident: part-time $218 per contact hour. Required fees: $1102 per year. *Faculty research:* Numerical analysis, artificial intelligence, simulation, medical applications, software engineering.

The University of Tennessee, Graduate School, College of Communication and Information, School of Information Sciences, Knoxville, TN 37996. Offers MS, PhD. *Accreditation:* ALA (one or more programs are accredited). Part-time programs available. Postbaccalaureate distance learning degree programs offered (no on-campus study). *Degree requirements:* For master's, thesis or alternative. *Entrance requirements:* For master's, GRE General Test, minimum GPA of 2.7. Additional exam requirements/recommendations for international students: Required—TOEFL. Electronic applications accepted. *Expenses:* Tuition, state resident: full-time $6826; part-time $380 per semester hour. Tuition, nonresident: full-time $21,844; part-time $1147 per semester hour. Tuition and fees vary according to program.

The University of Texas at El Paso, Graduate School, College of Engineering, Department of Computer Science, El Paso, TX 79968-0001. Offers computer science (MS, PhD); information technology (MSIT). Part-time and evening/weekend programs available. *Students:* 59 (15 women); includes 25 minority (2 Asian Americans or Pacific Islanders, 23 Hispanic Americans), 30 international. Average age 34. In 2009, 17 master's, 3 doctorates awarded. *Degree requirements:* For master's, thesis optional; for doctorate, thesis/dissertation. *Entrance requirements:* For master's, GRE, minimum GPA of 3.0; for doctorate, GRE, Statement of Purpose, Letters of Reference. Additional exam requirements/recommendations for international students: Required—TOEFL; Recommended—IELTS. *Application deadline:* For fall admission, 8/1 priority date for domestic students, 3/1 for international students; for spring admission, 11/1 priority date for domestic students, 9/1 for international students. Applications are processed on a rolling basis. Application fee: $45 ($80 for international students). Electronic applications accepted. *Financial support:* In 2009–10, research assistantships with partial tuition reimbursements (averaging $21,125 per year), teaching assistantships with partial tuition reimbursements (averaging $16,900 per year) were awarded; fellowships with partial tuition reimbursements, institutionally sponsored loans, scholarships/grants, health care benefits, tuition waivers (partial), and unspecified assistantships also available. Support available to part-time students. Financial award application deadline: 3/15; financial award applicants required to submit FAFSA. *Unit head:* Dr. Eunice E. Santos, Chair, 915-747-5480 Ext. 5480, Fax: 915-747-5030, E-mail: eesantos@utep.edu. *Application contact:* Dr. Patricia D. Witherspoon, Dean of the Graduate School, 915-747-5491, Fax: 915-747-5788, E-mail: withersp@utep.edu.

The University of Texas at San Antonio, College of Business, Department of Information Systems and Technology Management, San Antonio, TX 78249-0617. Offers business administration-information technology (PhD); information systems (MBA); information technology (MSIT); management technology (MSMOT). *Faculty:* 10 full-time (3 women), 1 part-time/adjunct (0 women). *Students:* 16 full-time (5 women), 88 part-time (22 women); includes 33 minority (4 African Americans, 1 American Indian/Alaska Native, 6 Asian Americans or Pacific Islanders, 22 Hispanic Americans), 8 international. Average age 34. 51 applicants, 61% accepted, 22 enrolled. In 2009, 45 master's awarded. *Degree requirements:* For master's, comprehensive exam (for some programs), thesis (for some programs). *Entrance requirements:* For master's, GMAT, minimum GPA of 3.0. Additional exam requirements/recommendations for international students: Required—TOEFL (minimum score 500 paper-based; 173 computer-based; 61 iBT), IELTS (minimum score 5). *Application deadline:* For fall admission, 7/1 for domestic students, 4/1 for international students; for spring admission, 11/1 for domestic students, 9/1 for international students. Applications are processed on a rolling basis. Application fee: $45 ($80 for international students). Electronic applications accepted. *Expenses:* Tuition, state resident: full-time $3975; part-time $221 per contact hour. Tuition, nonresident: full-time $13,947; part-time $775 per contact hour. Required fees: $1853. *Financial support:* In 2009–10, 7 students received support, including 7 research assistantships (averaging $10,400 per year), 8 teaching assistantships (averaging $7,800 per year); scholarships/grants, tuition waivers (partial), and unspecified assistantships also available. Support available to part-time students. *Faculty research:* Infrastructure assurance, digitalforensics, management of technology, e-commerce, technology transfer. Total annual research expenditures: $162,886. *Unit head:* Dr. Glenn Dietrich, Chair, 210-458-5354, Fax: 210-458-6305, E-mail: gdietrich@utsa.edu. *Application contact:* Jan Clark, Graduate Advisor, 210-458-5244, E-mail: jan.clark@utsa.edu.

University of the Sacred Heart, Graduate Programs, Department of Business Administration, Program in Information Technology, San Juan, PR 00914-0383. Offers Certificate.

University of Washington, Graduate School, The Information School, Seattle, WA 98195. Offers information management (MSIM); information science (PhD); library and information science (MLIS). *Accreditation:* ALA (one or more programs are accredited). Part-time and evening/weekend programs available. Postbaccalaureate distance learning degree programs offered (minimal on-campus study). *Faculty:* 39 full-time (16 women), 14 part-time/adjunct (11 women). *Students:* 258 full-time (169 women), 277 part-time (191 women); includes 77 minority (13 African Americans, 7 American Indian/Alaska Native, 41 Asian Americans or Pacific Islanders, 16 Hispanic Americans), 68 international. Average age 33. 733 applicants, 53% accepted, 219 enrolled. In 2009, 164 master's, 4 doctorates awarded. Terminal master's awarded for partial completion of doctoral program. *Degree requirements:* For master's, comprehensive exam (for some programs), culminating experience project (thesis, capstone or portfolio), internship; for doctorate, comprehensive exam, thesis/dissertation. *Entrance requirements:* For master's, GRE General Test, GMAT, minimum GPA of 3.0; for doctorate, GRE General Test, minimum GPA of 3.0. Additional exam requirements/recommendations for international students: Required—TOEFL (minimum score 580 paper-based; 237 computer-based; 92 iBT), IELTS (minimum score 7), MLT (minimum score 90). *Application deadline:* For fall admission, 12/15 for domestic students, 11/1 for international students. Application fee: $65. Electronic applications accepted. *Expenses:* Contact institution. *Financial support:* In 2009–10, 98 students received support, including 5 fellowships with full tuition reimbursements available (averaging $15,204 per year), 15 research assistantships with full and partial tuition reimbursements available (averaging $16,608 per year), 13 teaching assistantships with full tuition reimbursements available (averaging $17,350 per year); career-related internships or fieldwork, Federal Work-Study, institutionally sponsored loans, scholarships/grants, health care benefits, tuition waivers (full and partial), and unspecified assistantships also available. Support available to part-time students. Financial award application deadline: 2/28; financial award applicants required to submit FAFSA. *Faculty research:* Human computer interaction, information policy and ethics, knowledge organization, information literacy and access, information assurance and cyber security. Total annual research expenditures: $4.7 million. *Unit head:* Dr. Harry Bruce, Dean. *Application contact:* Kari Brothers, Admissions Counselor, 206-616-5541, Fax: 206-616-3152, E-mail: kari683@uw.edu.

University of Waterloo, Graduate Studies, Faculty of Engineering, Department of Management Sciences, Waterloo, ON N2L 3G1, Canada. Offers applied operations research (MA Sc, MMS, PhD); information systems (MA Sc, MMS, PhD); management of technology (MA Sc, MMS, PhD). Part-time programs available. Postbaccalaureate distance learning degree programs offered (no on-campus study). *Degree requirements:* For master's, research paper or thesis; for doctorate, comprehensive exam, thesis/dissertation. *Entrance requirements:* For master's, GMAT or GRE, honors degree, minimum B average, resume; for doctorate, GMAT or GRE, master's degree, minimum A- average, resumé. Additional exam requirements/recommendations for international students: Required—TOEFL, TWE. *Faculty research:* Operations research, manufacturing systems, scheduling, information systems.

University of Wisconsin–Parkside, School of Business and Technology, Program in Computer and Information Systems, Kenosha, WI 53141-2000. Offers MSCIS. *Entrance requirements:* For master's, GRE General Test or GMAT, 3 letters of recommendation, minimum GPA of 3.0. *Faculty research:* Distributed systems, data bases, natural language processing, event-driven systems.

University of Wisconsin–Stout, Graduate School, College of Technology, Engineering, and Management, Program in Information and Communication Technologies, Menomonie, WI 54751. Offers MS. Part-time programs available. Postbaccalaureate distance learning degree programs offered (minimal on-campus study). *Degree requirements:* For master's, thesis. *Entrance requirements:* For master's, minimum GPA of 2.75. Additional exam requirements/recommendations for international students: Required—TOEFL (minimum score 500 paper-based; 173 computer-based; 61 iBT). Electronic applications accepted.

Virginia Polytechnic Institute and State University, Graduate School, College of Engineering, Department of Computer Science, Program in Information Systems, Blacksburg, VA 24061. Offers MIS. *Entrance requirements:* For master's, GRE General Test. Additional exam requirements/recommendations for international students: Required—TOEFL. Electronic applications accepted.

Youngstown State University, Graduate School, College of Science, Technology, Engineering and Mathematics, Department of Computer Science and Information Systems, Youngstown, OH 44555-0001. Offers computing and information systems (MCIS). Part-time programs available. *Degree requirements:* For master's, thesis or capstone project. *Entrance requirements:* For master's, GRE or GMAT. Additional exam requirements/recommendations for international students: Required—TOEFL (minimum score 550 paper-based; 213 computer-based). *Faculty research:* Networking, computational science, graphics and visualization, database and data mining, biometrics, artificial intelligence, online learning environments.

Internet Engineering

New Jersey Institute of Technology, Office of Graduate Studies, Newark College of Engineering, Department of Electrical and Computer Engineering, Program in Internet Engineering, Newark, NJ 07102. Offers MS. Part-time and evening/weekend programs available. *Degree requirements:* For master's, thesis optional. *Entrance requirements:* For master's, GRE General Test. Additional exam requirements/recommendations for international students: Required—TOEFL (minimum score 550 paper-based; 213 computer-based; 79 iBT). Electronic applications accepted.

University of Georgia, Graduate School, Terry College of Business, Program in Internet Technology, Athens, GA 30602. Offers MIT. *Students:* 51 applicants, 61% accepted. *Application deadline:* For fall admission, 7/1 priority date for domestic students; for spring admission, 11/15 for domestic students. Application fee: $50. *Expenses:* Tuition, state resident: full-time $6000; part-time $250 per credit hour. Tuition, nonresident: full-time $20,904; part-time $871 per credit hour. Required fees: $730 per semester. *Unit head:* Dr. Craig A. Piercy, Director, 706-542-3589, Fax: 706-583-0037, E-mail: cpiercy@terry.uga.edu. *Application contact:* Dr. Craig A. Piercy, Director, 706-542-3589, Fax: 706-583-0037, E-mail: cpiercy@terry.uga.edu.

University of San Francisco, College of Arts and Sciences, Department of Computer Science, Program in Web Science, San Francisco, CA 94117-1080. Offers MS. *Faculty:* 5 full-time (1 woman). *Students:* 18 full-time (2 women), 3 part-time (0 women), 13 international. Average age 29. 28 applicants, 71% accepted, 8 enrolled. In 2009, 4 master's awarded. *Expenses:* Tuition: Full-time $19,710; part-time $1095 per unit. Part-time tuition and fees vary according to degree level, campus/location and program. *Financial support:* In 2009–10, 12 students received support. *Unit head:* Terence Parr, Graduate Director, 415-422-6530, Fax: 415-422-5800. *Application contact:* Mark Landerghini, Graduate Adviser, 415-422-5135, E-mail: asgraduate@usfca.edu.

Wilmington University, College of Technology, New Castle, DE 19720-6491. Offers corporate training (MS); information assurance (MS); information systems technologies (MS); Internet web design (MS); management information systems (MS). Part-time and evening/weekend programs available. *Entrance requirements:* Additional exam requirements/recommendations for international students: Required—TOEFL (minimum score 500 paper-based; 173 computer-based). Electronic applications accepted.

Medical Informatics

Arizona State University, Graduate College, Ira A. Fulton School of Engineering, Department of Biomedical Informatics, Tempe, AZ 85287. Offers MS, PhD.

Cambridge College, School of Management, Cambridge, MA 02138-5304. Offers business negotiation and conflict resolution (M Mgt); general business (M Mgt); health care informatics (M Mgt); health care management (M Mgt); leadership in human and organizational dynamics (M Mgt); non-profit and public organization management (M Mgt); small business development (M Mgt); technology management (M Mgt). Part-time and evening/weekend programs available. *Faculty:* 4 full-time (3 women), 65 part-time/adjunct (32 women). *Students:* 297 full-time (178 women), 234 part-time (155 women); includes 217 minority (122 African Americans, 53 Asian Americans or Pacific Islanders, 42 Hispanic Americans), 135 international. Average age 39. In 2009, 259 master's awarded. *Degree requirements:* For master's, thesis, seminars. *Entrance requirements:* For master's, resume, 2 professional references. Additional exam requirements/recommendations for international students: Required—TOEFL (minimum score 550 paper-based; 213 computer-based; 79 iBT); Recommended—IELTS (minimum score 6). *Application deadline:* Applications are processed on a rolling basis. Application fee: $30. Electronic applications accepted. *Expenses:* Contact institution. *Financial support:* In 2009–10, 170 students received support. Career-related internships or fieldwork, Federal Work-Study, and scholarships/grants available. Financial award applicants required to submit FAFSA. *Faculty research:* Negotiation, mediation and conflict resolution; leadership; management of diverse organizations; case studies and simulation methodologies for management education, digital as a second language: social networking for digital immigrants. *Unit head:* Dr. Mary Ann Joseph, Acting Dean, 617-873-0227, E-mail: maryann.joseph@cambridgecollege.edu. *Application contact:* Stephen Lyons, Director of Enrollment, Graduate and N.I.T.E. Programs, 617-868-1000, Fax: 617-349-3561, E-mail: stephen.lyons@cambridgecollege.edu.

Columbia University, College of Dental Medicine and Graduate School of Arts and Sciences, Programs in Dental Specialties, New York, NY 10027. Offers advanced education in general dentistry (Certificate); biomedical informatics (MA, PhD); endodontics (Certificate); orthodontics (MS, Certificate); periodontics (MS, Certificate); prosthodontics (MS, Certificate); science education (MA). *Degree requirements:* For master's, thesis, presentation of seminar. *Entrance requirements:* For master's, GRE General Test, DDS or equivalent. *Expenses:* Contact institution. *Faculty research:* Analysis of growth/form, pulpal microcirculation, implants, microbiology of oral environment, calcified tissues.

Columbia University, College of Physicians and Surgeons, Department of Biomedical Informatics, New York, NY 10032. Offers M Phil, MA, PhD, MD/PhD. *Degree requirements:* For doctorate, thesis/dissertation. *Entrance requirements:* For master's and doctorate, GRE General Test, knowledge of computational techniques. Additional exam requirements/recommendations for international students: Required—TOEFL. Electronic applications accepted. *Faculty research:* Bioinformatics, bioimaging, clinical informatics, public health informatics.

Dalhousie University, Faculty of Computer Science, Halifax, NS B3H 1W5, Canada. Offers computational biology and bioinformatics (M Sc); computer science (PhD); computer science (project-based) (MA Sc); computer science (thesis-based) (MC Sc); electronic commerce (MEC); health informatics (MHI). *Degree requirements:* For master's, thesis (for some programs); for doctorate, thesis/dissertation. *Entrance requirements:* Additional exam requirements/recommendations for international students: Required—TOEFL, IELTS, 1 of the following 5 approved tests: TOEFL, IELTS, CANTEST, CAEL, Michigan English Language Assessment Battery. Electronic applications accepted.

Drexel University, The iSchool at Drexel, College of Information Science and Technology, Philadelphia, PA 19104-2875. Offers healthcare informatics (Certificate); information science and technology (PMC); information studies (PhD); information studies and technology (Advanced Certificate); information systems (MSIS); library and information science (MS), including archival studies, competitive intelligence and knowledge management, digital libraries, library and information services, school library media, youth services; software engineering (MSSE). *Accreditation:* ALA (one or more programs are accredited). Part-time and evening/weekend programs available. Postbaccalaureate distance learning degree programs offered (no on-campus study). *Faculty:* 34 full-time (19 women), 24 part-time/adjunct (9 women). *Students:* 279 full-time (192 women), 571 part-time (372 women); includes 96 minority (36 African Americans, 1 American Indian/Alaska Native, 36 Asian Americans or Pacific Islanders, 23 Hispanic Americans), 48 international. Average age 34. 644 applicants, 68% accepted, 289 enrolled. In 2009, 318 master's, 12 doctorates, 15 other advanced degrees awarded. *Degree requirements:* For doctorate, thesis/dissertation. *Entrance requirements:* For master's and doctorate, GRE General Test. Additional exam requirements/recommendations for international students: Required—TOEFL (minimum score 600 paper-based; 250 computer-based; 100 iBT). *Application deadline:* For fall admission, 8/1 for domestic and international students; for spring admission, 2/1 for domestic and international students. Applications are processed on a rolling basis. Electronic applications accepted. *Expenses:* Contact institution. *Financial support:* In 2009–10, 250 students received support, including 235 fellowships with partial tuition reimbursements available (averaging $225 per year), 18 research assistantships with full tuition reimbursements available (averaging $25,000 per year), 2 teaching assistantships with full tuition reimbursements available (averaging $25,000 per year); institutionally sponsored loans, scholarships/grants, health care benefits, tuition waivers (partial), unspecified assistantships, and fellowships also available. Support available to part-time students. Financial award applicants required to submit FAFSA. *Faculty research:* Information retrieval/information visualization/bibliometrics, human-computer interaction, digital libraries, databases, text/data mining. Total annual research expenditures: $2 million. *Unit head:* Dr. David E. Fenske, Dean and Isaac L. Auerbach Professor of Information Science, 215-895-2475, Fax: 215-895-6378, E-mail: fenske@drexel.edu. *Application contact:* Matthew Lechtenberg, Graduate Admissions Manager, 215-895-1951, Fax: 215-895-2303, E-mail: ml333@drexel.edu.

Excelsior College, School of Health Sciences, Albany, NY 12203-5159. Offers healthcare informatics (Certificate); hospice and palliative care (Certificate); nursing management (Certificate). Part-time and evening/weekend programs available. Postbaccalaureate distance learning degree programs offered (no on-campus study). *Entrance requirements:* For degree, bachelor's degree in applicable field. Electronic applications accepted. *Faculty research:* Use of technology in online learning.

Grand Valley State University, Padnos College of Engineering and Computing, Medical and Bioinformatics Program, Allendale, MI 49401-9403. Offers MS. Part-time and evening/weekend programs available. *Faculty:* 4 full-time (0 women). *Students:* 12 full-time (3 women), 7 part-time (4 women); includes 1 minority (Asian American or Pacific Islander), 12 international. Average age 28. 18 applicants, 72% accepted, 1 enrolled. In 2009, 6 master's awarded. *Degree requirements:* For master's, thesis or alternative. Application fee: $30. *Financial support:* In 2009–10, 9 students received support, including 1 fellowship (averaging $1,575 per year), 9 research assistantships with full and partial tuition reimbursements available (averaging $7,208 per year); career-related internships or fieldwork, tuition waivers (full), and unspecified assistantships also available. *Faculty research:* Biomedical informatics, information visualization, data mining, high-performance computing, computational biology. *Unit head:* Dr. Paul Leidig, Director, 616-331-2308, Fax: 616-331-2106, E-mail: leidigp@gvsu.edu. *Application contact:* Dr. David Elrod, PSM Coordinator, 616-331-8643, E-mail: elrod@gvsu.edu.

Harvard University, Harvard Medical School and Graduate School of Arts and Sciences, Division of Health Sciences and Technology, Program in Biomedical Informatics, Cambridge, MA 02138. Offers SM. *Students:* 5 full-time (1 woman); includes 4 minority (1 American Indian/Alaska Native, 2 Asian Americans or Pacific Islanders, 1 Hispanic American). Average age 36. 12 applicants, 25% accepted, 2 enrolled. In 2009, 5 master's awarded. *Degree requirements:* For master's, thesis. *Entrance requirements:* For master's, MD or other doctoral degree in a medically relevant field. Additional exam requirements/recommendations for inter-

national students: Required—TOEFL. *Application deadline:* For fall admission, 12/15 for domestic and international students; for spring admission, 11/1 for domestic and international students. Application fee: $70. *Expenses:* Contact institution. *Financial support:* In 2009–10, 2 students received support, including 1 fellowship with full tuition reimbursement available (averaging $18,755 per year), 1 research assistantship with full tuition reimbursement available (averaging $58,498 per year); career-related internships or fieldwork, institutionally sponsored loans, traineeships, and unspecified assistantships also available. Financial award application deadline: 12/15; financial award applicants required to submit FAFSA. *Faculty research:* Bioinformatics, machine learning and predictive modeling, patents safety personal monitoring, clinical decision making, disaster response and public health. *Unit head:* Dr. Alexa McCray, Program Director, 617-432-2144, E-mail: alexa_mccray@hms.harvard.edu. *Application contact:* Traci Anderson, Academic Programs Administrator, 617-258-7470, E-mail: tanderso@mit.edu.

Marymount University, School of Business Administration, Program in Information Technology, Arlington, VA 22207-4299. Offers computer security and information assurance (Certificate); health care informatics (Certificate); information technology (MS, Certificate); information technology project management: technology leadership (Certificate). Part-time and evening/weekend programs available. *Faculty:* 6 full-time (3 women), 4 part-time/adjunct (0 women). *Students:* 28 full-time (11 women), 23 part-time (6 women); includes 15 minority (9 African Americans, 1 American Indian/Alaska Native, 4 Asian Americans or Pacific Islanders, 1 Hispanic American), 21 international. Average age 31. 45 applicants, 100% accepted, 26 enrolled. In 2009, 19 master's, 1 other advanced degree awarded. *Degree requirements:* For master's, thesis or alternative. *Entrance requirements:* For master's, GMAT or GRE General Test, interview, resume, bachelor's degree in computer-related field or degree in another subject with a post-baccalaureate certificate in a computer-related field; for Certificate, resume. Additional exam requirements/recommendations for international students: Required—TOEFL (minimum score 600 paper-based; 250 computer-based; 96 iBT), IELTS (minimum score 6.5). *Application deadline:* For fall admission, 7/15 for domestic students, 7/1 for international students; for spring admission, 11/15 for domestic students, 10/15 for international students. Applications are processed on a rolling basis. Application fee: $40. Electronic applications accepted. *Expenses:* Tuition: Full-time $13,050; part-time $725 per credit hour. Required fees: $135; $7.50 per credit hour. *Financial support:* In 2009–10, 5 students received support; research assistantships with full tuition reimbursements available, career-related internships or fieldwork, Federal Work-Study, scholarships/grants, and unspecified assistantships available. Support available to part-time students. Financial award applicants required to submit FAFSA. *Unit head:* Dr. Diane Murphy, Chair, 703-284-5958, Fax: 703-527-3830, E-mail: diane.murphy@marymount.edu. *Application contact:* Francesca Reed, Director, Graduate Admissions, 703-284-5901, Fax: 703-527-3815, E-mail: grad.admissions@marymount.edu.

Massachusetts Institute of Technology, Harvard-MIT Division of Health Sciences and Technology, Program in Biomedical Informatics, Cambridge, MA 02139-4307. Offers SM. *Students:* 5 full-time (1 woman); includes 4 minority (1 American Indian/Alaska Native, 2 Asian Americans or Pacific Islanders, 1 Hispanic American). Average age 36. 12 applicants, 25% accepted, 2 enrolled. In 2009, 5 master's awarded. *Degree requirements:* For master's, thesis. *Entrance requirements:* For master's, MD or current enrollment in an MD program or other doctoral degree in medically relevant field. Additional exam requirements/recommendations for international students: Required—TOEFL. *Application deadline:* For fall admission, 12/15 for domestic and international students; for spring admission, 11/1 for domestic and international students. Application fee: $70. Electronic applications accepted. *Financial support:* In 2009–10, 2 students received support, including 1 fellowship with full tuition reimbursement available (averaging $18,755 per year), 1 research assistantship with full tuition reimbursement available (averaging $58,498 per year); career-related internships or fieldwork, institutionally sponsored loans, traineeships, and unspecified assistantships also available. Financial award application deadline: 12/15. *Faculty research:* Bioinformatics, clinical decision-making, machine learning and predictive modeling, national safety, personal monitoring. *Unit head:* Dr. Alexa McCray, Program Director, 617-432-2144, E-mail: alexa_mccray@hms.harvard.edu. *Application contact:* Traci Anderson, Academic Programs Administrator, 617-253-7470, E-mail: tanderso@mit.edu.

Medical College of Wisconsin, Graduate School of Biomedical Sciences, Program in Medical Informatics, Milwaukee, WI 53226-0509. Offers MS. Part-time and evening/weekend programs available. *Degree requirements:* For master's, thesis or alternative. *Entrance requirements:* For master's, GMAT or GRE General Test. Additional exam requirements/recommendations for international students: Required—TOEFL. *Faculty research:* Computer science.

Middle Tennessee State University, College of Graduate Studies, College of Basic and Applied Sciences, Program in Professional Science, Murfreesboro, TN 37132. Offers biostatistics (MS); health care informatics (MS). Part-time and evening/weekend programs available. Postbaccalaureate distance learning degree programs offered. *Students:* 5 full-time (2 women), 52 part-time (32 women); includes 27 minority (11 African Americans, 14 Asian Americans or Pacific Islanders, 2 Hispanic Americans). Average age 28. 40 applicants, 55% accepted, 22 enrolled. In 2009, 21 master's awarded. *Degree requirements:* For master's, comprehensive exam. *Entrance requirements:* For master's, GRE. Additional exam requirements/recommendations for international students: Required—TOEFL (minimum score 525 paper-based; 195 computer-based; 71 iBT) or IELTS (minimum score 6). *Application deadline:* For fall admission, 6/1 for domestic and international students. Applications are processed on a rolling basis. Application fee: $25 ($30 for international students). *Expenses:* Tuition, state resident: full-time $4404. Tuition, nonresident: full-time $10,956. *Financial support:* In 2009–10, 7 students received support. Institutionally sponsored loans available. Support available to part-time students. Financial award application deadline: 5/1. *Unit head:* Dr. Thomas Cheatham, Dean, 615-898-5508, Fax: 615-898-2615. *Application contact:* Dr. Michael Allen, Dean and Vice Provost for Research, 615-898-2840, Fax: 615-904-8020, E-mail: mallen@mtsu.edu.

Milwaukee School of Engineering, Rader School of Business, Program in Medical Informatics, Milwaukee, WI 53202-3109. Offers MS. Part-time and evening/weekend programs available. *Faculty:* 1 full-time (0 women), 5 part-time/adjunct (1 woman). *Students:* 1 (woman) full-time, 12 part-time (8 women); includes 1 minority (African American). Average age 25. 12 applicants, 50% accepted, 4 enrolled. In 2009, 8 master's awarded. *Degree requirements:* For master's, thesis or alternative, capstone course, research project. *Entrance requirements:* For master's, GRE General Test or GMAT, 2 letters of recommendation. Additional exam requirements/recommendations for international students: Required—TOEFL (minimum score 79 iBT). *Application deadline:* Applications are processed on a rolling basis. Application fee: $30. Electronic applications accepted. *Expenses:* Tuition: Part-time $603 per credit. *Financial support:* In 2009–10, 8 students received support. Career-related internships or fieldwork available. Support available to part-time students. Financial award applicants required to submit FAFSA. *Faculty research:* Information technology, data bases. *Unit head:* Dr. John Traxler, Director, 414-277-2218, Fax: 414-277-7279, E-mail: traxler@msoe.edu. *Application contact:* David E. Tietyen, Graduate Admissions Director, 800-332-6763, Fax: 414-277-7475, E-mail: wp@msoe.edu.

Northwestern University, School of Continuing Studies, Program in Medical Informatics, Evanston, IL 60208. Offers MS. Postbaccalaureate distance learning degree programs offered.

Nova Southeastern University, Health Professions Division, College of Osteopathic Medicine, Program in Biomedical Informatics, Fort Lauderdale, FL 33314-7796. Offers biomedical informatics (MS); clinical informatics (Graduate Certificate); public health informatics (Graduate Certificate). *Unit head:* Dr. Jennie Q. Lou, Director, 954-262-1619, E-mail: jlou@nova.edu. *Application contact:* Ellen Rondino, College of Osteopathic Medicine Admissions Counselor, 866-817-4068.

Oregon Health & Science University, School of Medicine, Graduate Programs in Medicine, Department of Medical Informatics and Clinical Epidemiology, Portland, OR 97239-3098.

Medical Informatics

Oregon Health & Science University (continued)

Offers biomedical informatics (MS, PhD, Certificate). Part-time programs available. Postbaccalaureate distance learning degree programs offered (minimal on-campus study). *Degree requirements:* For master's, thesis; for doctorate, comprehensive exam, thesis/dissertation. *Entrance requirements:* For master's and doctorate, GRE General Test, coursework in computer programming, human anatomy and physiology. Additional exam requirements/recommendations for international students: Required—TOEFL. Electronic applications accepted. *Expenses:* Contact institution. *Faculty research:* Information retrieval, telemedicine, consumer health informatics, information needs assessment, healthcare quality.

Stanford University, School of Medicine, Graduate Programs in Medicine, Biomedical Informatics Program, Stanford, CA 94305-9991. Offers MS, PhD. Terminal master's awarded for partial completion of doctoral program. *Degree requirements:* For master's, thesis; for doctorate, thesis/dissertation. *Entrance requirements:* For doctorate, GRE or MCAT. Additional exam requirements/recommendations for international students: Required—TOEFL. Electronic applications accepted. *Expenses:* Tuition: Full-time $37,380; part-time $2760 per quarter. Required fees: $501.

The University of Arizona, College of Nursing, Tucson, AZ 85721. Offers health care informatics (Certificate); nurse practitioner (MS, Certificate); nursing (DNP, PhD); rural health (Certificate). *Accreditation:* AACN. Part-time programs available. Postbaccalaureate distance learning degree programs offered (minimal on-campus study). *Faculty:* 19. *Students:* 63 full-time (58 women), 81 part-time (71 women); includes 3 minority (all Hispanic Americans), 9 international. Average age 41. In 2009, 25 master's, 19 doctorates awarded. Terminal master's awarded for partial completion of doctoral program. *Degree requirements:* For master's, thesis optional; for doctorate, comprehensive exam, thesis/dissertation. *Entrance requirements:* For master's, BSN, eligibility for RN license; for doctorate, BSN; for Certificate, GRE General Test, Arizona RN license, BSN, minimum GPA of 3.0. Additional exam requirements/recommendations for international students: Required—TOEFL (minimum score 550 paper-based; 213 computer-based; 79 iBT). *Application deadline:* For fall admission, 1/15 for domestic and international students. Applications are processed on a rolling basis. Application fee: $75. Electronic applications accepted. *Expenses:* Contact institution. *Financial support:* In 2009–10, 6 research assistantships with full tuition reimbursements (averaging $15,552 per year) were awarded; teaching assistantships, career-related internships or fieldwork, institutionally sponsored loans, scholarships/grants, traineeships, health care benefits, tuition waivers (full), and unspecified assistantships also available. Financial award application deadline: 6/1. *Faculty research:* Vulnerable populations, injury mechanisms and biobehavioral responses, health care systems, informatics, rural health. Total annual research expenditures: $4.9 million. *Unit head:* Dr. Carolyn Murdaugh, Associate Dean, 520-626-7124, Fax: 520-626-6424, E-mail: cmurdaugh@nursing.arizona.edu. *Application contact:* Sally J. Reel, Assistant Dean, Student Affairs, 520-626-6767, Fax: 520-626-6424, E-mail: sreel@nursing.arizona.edu.

University of California, Davis, Graduate Studies, Graduate Group in Health Informatics, Davis, CA 95616. Offers MS. *Entrance requirements:* Additional exam requirements/recommendations for international students: Required—TOEFL (minimum score 550 paper-based; 213 computer-based).

University of California, San Francisco, School of Pharmacy and Graduate Division, Graduate Program in Biological and Medical Informatics, San Francisco, CA 94158-2517. Offers PhD. *Faculty:* 28 full-time (6 women). *Students:* 30 full-time (7 women); includes 7 minority (3 Asian Americans or Pacific Islanders, 4 Hispanic Americans), 1 international. Average age 28. 126 applicants, 29% accepted, 12 enrolled. In 2009, 3 doctorates awarded. Terminal master's awarded for partial completion of doctoral program. *Degree requirements:* For doctorate, thesis/dissertation, cumulative qualifying exams, proposal defense. *Entrance requirements:* For doctorate, GRE General Test, minimum GPA of 3.0. Additional exam requirements/recommendations for international students: Required—TOEFL (minimum score 550 paper-based; 213 computer-based; 80 iBT). *Application deadline:* For fall admission, 12/1 for domestic and international students. Application fee: $70 ($90 for international students). *Financial support:* In 2009–10, 3 fellowships with full tuition reimbursements (averaging $27,000 per year), 26 research assistantships with full tuition reimbursements (averaging $27,000 per year) were awarded; career-related internships or fieldwork, scholarships/grants, traineeships, health care benefits, tuition waivers (full), and stipends also available. *Faculty research:* Bioinformatics, biomedical computing, decision science and engineering, imaging informatics, knowledge management/telehealth/health services research. *Unit head:* Thomas E. Ferrin, Director, 415-476-2299, Fax: 415-502-1755, E-mail: tef@cgl.ucsf.edu. *Application contact:* Julia Molla, Program Administrator, 415-514-0249, Fax: 415-514-0502, E-mail: jmolla@cgl.ucsf.edu.

University of Illinois at Urbana–Champaign, Graduate College, Graduate School of Library and Information Science, Champaign, IL 61820. Offers bioinformatics: library and information science (MS); library and information science (MS, PhD, CAS); library and information science: digital libraries (CAS). *Accreditation:* ALA (one or more programs are accredited). Postbaccalaureate distance learning degree programs offered. *Faculty:* 26 full-time (13 women), 9 part-time/adjunct (6 women). *Students:* 321 full-time (229 women), 310 part-time (230 women); includes 101 minority (34 African Americans, 4 American Indian/Alaska Native, 36 Asian Americans or Pacific Islanders, 27 Hispanic Americans), 35 international. 747 applicants, 53% accepted, 217 enrolled. In 2009, 240 master's, 7 doctorates, 6 other advanced degrees awarded. *Entrance requirements:* For master's, GRE General Test, minimum GPA of 3.0; for doctorate, minimum GPA of 3.0; for CAS, master's degree in library and information science or related field with minimum GPA of 3.0. Additional exam requirements/recommendations for international students: Required—TOEFL (minimum score 620 paper-based; 260 computer-based; 105 iBT), or IELTS (minimum score 7). *Application deadline:* Applications are processed on a rolling basis. Application fee: $60 ($75 for international students). Electronic applications accepted. *Financial support:* In 2009–10, 52 fellowships, 41 research assistantships, 27 teaching assistantships were awarded; tuition waivers (full and partial) also available. *Unit head:* John Unsworth, Dean, 217-333-3281, Fax: 217-244-3302, E-mail: unsworth@illinois.edu. *Application contact:* Valerie Youngen, Admissions and Records Representative, 217-333-0734, Fax: 217-244-3302, E-mail: vyoungen@llinois.edu.

The University of Kansas, University of Kansas Medical Center, School of Nursing, Kansas City, KS 66160. Offers clinical research management (PMC); family nurse practitioner (PMC); health care informatics (PMC); health professions educator (PMC); nurse midwife (PMC); nursing (MS, DNP, PhD); organizational leadership (PMC); psychiatric/mental health nurse practitioner (PMC); public health nursing (PMC). *Accreditation:* AACN; ACNM/DOA. Part-time programs available. Postbaccalaureate distance learning degree programs offered (minimal on-campus study). *Faculty:* 65. *Students:* 59 full-time (56 women), 309 part-time (285 women); includes 37 minority (17 African Americans, 4 American Indian/Alaska Native, 7 Asian Americans or Pacific Islanders, 9 Hispanic Americans), 10 international. Average age 38. 138 applicants, 59% accepted, 82 enrolled. In 2009, 78 master's, 3 doctorates awarded. Terminal master's awarded for partial completion of doctoral program. *Degree requirements:* For master's, thesis optional, general oral exam; for doctorate, one foreign language, thesis/dissertation, comprehensive oral and written exam. *Entrance requirements:* For master's, bachelor's degree in nursing, minimum GPA of 3.0, RN license, 1 year of clinical experience; for doctorate, GRE General Test, master's degree in nursing, minimum GPA of 3.5. Additional exam requirements/recommendations for international students: Required—TOEFL. *Application deadline:* For fall admission, 4/1 for domestic students; for spring admission, 9/1 for domestic students. Application fee: $60. Electronic applications accepted. *Expenses:* Tuition, state resident: full-time $6492; part-time $270.50 per credit hour. Tuition, nonresident: full-time $15,510; part-time $646.25 per credit hour. Required fees: $847; $70.56 per credit hour. Tuition and fees vary according to course load and program. *Financial support:* In 2009–10, 93 students received support, including 7 research assistantships (averaging $24,000 per year), 23 teaching assistantships with full and partial tuition reimbursements available (averaging $24,000 per year); traineeships also available. Financial award application deadline: 2/14; financial award applicants required to submit FAFSA. *Faculty research:* Breastfeeding practices of teen mothers, national database of nursing quality indicators, caregiving of families of patients using technology in the home, self care talk intervention partnership between caregivers of stroke survivors and nurses, smoking cessation. Total annual research expenditures: $5 million. *Unit head:* Dr. Karen L. Miller, Dean, 913-588-1601, Fax: 913-588-1660, E-mail: kmiller@kumc.edu. *Application contact:* Dr. Rita K. Clifford, Associate Dean, Student Affairs, 913-588-1619, Fax: 913-588-1615, E-mail: rcliffor@kumc.edu.

University of Medicine and Dentistry of New Jersey, School of Health Related Professions, Department of Health Informatics, Program in Biomedical Informatics, Newark, NJ 07107-1709. Offers MS, PhD, DMD/MS, MD/MS. *Entrance requirements:* Additional exam requirements/recommendations for international students: Required—TOEFL. Electronic applications accepted.

University of Medicine and Dentistry of New Jersey, School of Health Related Professions, Department of Health Informatics, Program in Health Care Informatics, Newark, NJ 07107-1709. Offers Certificate. *Entrance requirements:* Additional exam requirements/recommendations for international students: Required—TOEFL. Electronic applications accepted.

The University of Tennessee at Chattanooga, Graduate School, College of Health, Education and Professional Studies, School of Nursing, Chattanooga, TN 37403. Offers administration (MSN); certified nurse anesthetist (Post-Master's Certificate); education (MSN); family nurse practitioner (MSN, Post-Master's Certificate); health care informatics (Post-Master's Certificate); nurse anesthesia (MSN); nurse education (Post-Master's Certificate). *Accreditation:* AACN; AANA/CANAEP (one or more programs are accredited). *Faculty:* 4 full-time (all women). *Students:* 42 full-time (33 women), 53 part-time (38 women); includes 10 minority (5 African Americans, 1 American Indian/Alaska Native, 2 Asian Americans or Pacific Islanders, 2 Hispanic Americans). Average age 35. 13 applicants, 31% accepted, 3 enrolled. In 2009, 36 master's, 5 other advanced degrees awarded. *Degree requirements:* For master's, thesis optional, qualifying exams, professional project; for Post-Master's Certificate, thesis or alternative, practicum, seminar. *Entrance requirements:* For master's, GRE General Test, MAT, BSN, minimum GPA of 3.0, eligibility for Tennessee RN license, 1 year direct patient care experience; for Post-Master's Certificate, GRE General Test, MAT, MSN, minimum GPA of 3.0, eligibility for Tennessee RN license, one year of direct patient care experience. Additional exam requirements/recommendations for international students: Required—TOEFL (minimum score 550 paper-based; 213 computer-based; 79 iBT), IELTS (minimum score 6). *Application deadline:* For fall admission, 8/1 priority date for domestic students, 6/1 for international students; for spring admission, 12/1 priority date for domestic students, 10/1 for international students. Applications are processed on a rolling basis. Application fee: $35. Electronic applications accepted. *Expenses:* Tuition, state resident: full-time $5404; part-time $300 per credit hour. Tuition, nonresident: full-time $16,702; part-time $928 per credit hour. Required fees: $1150; $130 per credit hour. *Financial support:* Career-related internships or fieldwork and scholarships/grants available. Support available to part-time students. *Faculty research:* Diabetes in women, health care for elderly, alternative medicine, hypertension, nurse anesthesia. Total annual research expenditures: $1.5 million. *Unit head:* Dr. Kay R. Lindgren, Head, 423-425-4646, Fax: 423-425-4668, E-mail: kay-lindgren@utc.edu. *Application contact:* Dr. Stephanie Bellar, Dean of Graduate Studies, 423-425-4666, Fax: 423-425-5223, E-mail: stephanie-bellar@utc.edu.

University of Washington, Graduate School, School of Medicine and Graduate School, Graduate Programs in Medicine, Department of Medical Education and Biomedical Informatics, Division of Biomedical and Health Informatics, Seattle, WA 98195. Offers MS, PhD. *Entrance requirements:* For master's and doctorate, GRE General Test, minimum GPA of 3.0; previous undergraduate course work in biology, computer programming, and mathematics. Additional exam requirements/recommendations for international students: Required—TOEFL (minimum score 580 paper-based; 237 computer-based; 70 iBT). Electronic applications accepted. *Faculty research:* Bio-clinical informatics, information retrieval, human-computer interaction, knowledge-based systems, telehealth.

University of Wisconsin–Milwaukee, Graduate School, College of Engineering and Applied Science, Program in Medical Informatics, Milwaukee, WI 53201-0413. Offers PhD. *Students:* 7 full-time (2 women), 5 part-time (1 woman); includes 2 minority (1 African American, 1 Asian American or Pacific Islander), 5 international. Average age 37. 14 applicants, 57% accepted, 2 enrolled. *Degree requirements:* For doctorate, comprehensive exam, thesis/dissertation. *Entrance requirements:* For doctorate, GRE, GMAT or MCAT. Additional exam requirements/recommendations for international students: Required—TOEFL (minimum score 600 paper-based; 250 computer-based; 79 iBT), IELTS (minimum score 6.5). *Expenses:* Tuition, state resident: full-time $8800. Tuition, nonresident: full-time $20,760. Tuition and fees vary according to program and reciprocity agreements. *Unit head:* Susan McRoy, Representative, 414-229-4677, Fax: 414-229-4677, E-mail: mcroy@uwm.edu. *Application contact:* General Information Contact, 414-229-4982, Fax: 414-229-6967, E-mail: gradschool@uwm.edu.

Software Engineering

Andrews University, School of Graduate Studies, College of Technology, Department of Engineering, Computer Science, and Engineering Technology, Berrien Springs, MI 49104. Offers software engineering (MS). *Faculty:* 6 full-time (1 woman). *Students:* 7 full-time (1 woman), 2 part-time (0 women); includes 1 minority (African American), 6 international. Average age 31. 9 applicants, 56% accepted, 4 enrolled. In 2009, 3 master's awarded. *Entrance requirements:* For master's, GRE, minimum GPA of 2.6. Additional exam requirements/recommendations for international students: Required—TOEFL. *Application deadline:* Applications are processed on a rolling basis. Application fee: $40. *Unit head:* Dr. George Agoki, Chairman, 269-471-3420. *Application contact:* Carolyn Hurst, Supervisor of Graduate Admission, 800-253-2874, Fax: 269-471-6321, E-mail: graduate@andrews.edu.

Arizona State University, Graduate College, Ira A. Fulton School of Engineering, ASU Engineering Online Programs, Tempe, AZ 85287. Offers construction (MS); embedded systems (M Eng); enterprise systems innovation and management (MSE); modeling and simulation (M Eng); quality and reliability engineering (M Eng); software engineering (MSE); systems engineering (M Eng).

Auburn University, Graduate School, Ginn College of Engineering, Department of Computer Science and Software Engineering, Auburn University, AL 36849. Offers MS, MSWE, PhD. Part-time programs available. *Faculty:* 19 full-time (3 women). *Students:* 58 full-time (15 women), 65 part-time (17 women); includes 19 minority (16 African Americans, 1 Asian American or Pacific Islander, 2 Hispanic Americans), 59 international. Average age 30. 214

applicants, 33% accepted, 19 enrolled. In 2009, 21 master's, 11 doctorates awarded. *Degree requirements:* For master's, thesis (for some programs); for doctorate, thesis/dissertation. *Entrance requirements:* For master's and doctorate, GRE General Test, GRE Subject Test. *Application deadline:* For fall admission, 7/7 for domestic students; for spring admission, 11/24 for domestic students. Applications are processed on a rolling basis. Application fee: $50 ($60 for international students). Electronic applications accepted. *Expenses:* Tuition, state resident: full-time $6240. Tuition, nonresident: full-time $18,720. International tuition: $18,938 full-time. Required fees: $492. Tuition and fees vary according to course load, program and reciprocity agreements. *Financial support:* Research assistantships, teaching assistantships, Federal Work-Study available. Support available to part-time students. Financial award application deadline: 3/15; financial award applicants required to submit FAFSA. *Faculty research:* Parallelizable, scalable software translations; graphical representations of algorithms, structures, and processes; graph drawing. Total annual research expenditures: $400,000. *Unit head:* Dr. Kai Chang, Chair, 334-844-6310. *Application contact:* Dr. George Flowers, Dean of the Graduate School, 334-844-2125.

Bowling Green State University, Graduate College, College of Arts and Sciences, Department of Computer Science, Bowling Green, OH 43403. Offers computer science (MS), including operations research, parallel and distributed computing, software engineering. Part-time programs available. *Degree requirements:* For master's, thesis or alternative. *Entrance requirements:* For master's, GRE General Test. Additional exam requirements/recommendations for international students: Required—TOEFL. Electronic applications accepted. *Faculty research:* Artificial intelligence, real time and concurrent programming languages, behavioral aspects of computing, network protocols.

Brandeis University, Rabb School of Continuing Studies, Division of Graduate Professional Studies, Software Engineering Program, Waltham, MA 02454-9110. Offers MSE, Graduate Certificate. Part-time and evening/weekend programs available. Postbaccalaureate distance learning degree programs offered (no on-campus study). *Faculty:* 2 full-time (both women), 32 part-time/adjunct (8 women). *Students:* 1 (woman) full-time, 116 part-time (18 women); includes 21 minority (3 African Americans, 10 Asian Americans or Pacific Islanders, 8 Hispanic Americans). Average age 35. 22 applicants, 95% accepted, 21 enrolled. In 2009, 54 master's, 5 other advanced degrees awarded. *Entrance requirements:* For master's, resume, letter of recommendation; for Graduate Certificate, resume, official transcripts, recommendations. Additional exam requirements/recommendations for international students: Recommended—TOEFL (minimum score 600 paper-based; 250 computer-based; 100 iBT). *Application deadline:* For fall admission, 6/15 priority date for domestic students; for winter admission, 10/15 priority date for domestic students; for spring admission, 2/15 priority date for domestic students. Application fee: $50. *Unit head:* Erik Hemdal, Program Chair, 781-736-8787, Fax: 781-736-3420, E-mail: ehemdal@brandeis.edu. *Application contact:* Frances Stearns, Associate Director of Admissions and Student Services, 781-736-8785, Fax: 781-736-3420, E-mail: fstearns@brandeis.edu.

California State University, Fullerton, Graduate Studies, College of Engineering and Computer Science, Department of Computer Science, Fullerton, CA 92834-9480. Offers computer science (MS); software engineering (MS). Part-time programs available. Postbaccalaureate distance learning degree programs offered. *Students:* 71 full-time (28 women), 268 part-time (58 women); includes 120 minority (9 African Americans, 96 Asian Americans or Pacific Islanders, 15 Hispanic Americans), 134 international. Average age 30. 390 applicants, 60% accepted, 102 enrolled. In 2009, 126 master's awarded. *Degree requirements:* For master's, comprehensive exam, project or thesis. *Entrance requirements:* For master's, GRE General Test, minimum undergraduate GPA of 2.5. *Application fee:* $55. *Expenses:* Tuition, nonresident: full-time $11,160; part-time $373 per credit. Required fees: $1440 per term. Tuition and fees vary according to course load, degree level and program. *Financial support:* Career-related internships or fieldwork, Federal Work-Study, institutionally sponsored loans, and scholarships/grants available. Support available to part-time students. Financial award application deadline: 3/1; financial award applicants required to submit FAFSA. *Faculty research:* Software engineering, development of computer networks. *Unit head:* Dr. James Choi, Chair, 657-278-3700. *Application contact:* Admissions/Applications, 657-278-2371.

California State University, Northridge, Graduate Studies, College of Engineering and Computer Science, Department of Computer Science, Northridge, CA 91330. Offers computer science (MS); software engineering (MS). Part-time and evening/weekend programs available. *Faculty:* 17 full-time (2 women), 11 part-time/adjunct (3 women). *Students:* 28 full-time (7 women), 45 part-time (6 women); includes 1 African American, 14 Asian Americans or Pacific Islanders, 4 Hispanic Americans, 18 international. Average age 31. 257 applicants, 23% accepted, 32 enrolled. In 2009, 11 master's awarded. *Degree requirements:* For master's, thesis. *Entrance requirements:* For master's, GRE General Test, minimum GPA of 2.5. Additional exam requirements/recommendations for international students: Required—TOEFL. *Application deadline:* For fall admission, 11/30 for domestic students. Application fee: $55. *Financial support:* Application deadline: 3/1. *Faculty research:* Radar data processing. *Unit head:* Prof. Steven G. Stepanek, Chair, 818-677-3398. *Application contact:* Prof. Steven G. Stepanek, Chair, 818-677-3398.

California State University, Sacramento, Graduate Studies, College of Engineering and Computer Science, Department of Computer Science, Sacramento, CA 95819. Offers computer systems (MS); software engineering (MS). Part-time and evening/weekend programs available. *Degree requirements:* For master's, thesis or alternative, writing proficiency exam. *Entrance requirements:* Additional exam requirements/recommendations for international students: Required—TOEFL. Electronic applications accepted.

Carnegie Mellon University, Carnegie Institute of Technology, Information Networking Institute, Pittsburgh, PA 15213. Offers information networking (MS); information security technology and management (MS); information technology—information security (MS); information technology—mobility (MS); information technology—software management (MS). *Degree requirements:* For master's, thesis optional. *Entrance requirements:* For master's, GRE General Test, bachelor's degree in computer science, computer engineering, or electrical engineering, or related technology degree; programming skills (C/C++ fluency for some programs). Additional exam requirements/recommendations for international students: Required—TOEFL. *Faculty research:* Computer forensics and incident response; dependable systems, embedded systems, mobile systems, and sensor networks; computer and information networks, network and information security, human and socio-economic factors in secure system design; wireless sensor networks, survivable embedded systems, signal processing/compression; strategic management, international strategic management, group dynamics and decision-making structures, simulated competitive environments.

Carnegie Mellon University, School of Computer Science, Software Engineering Program, Pittsburgh, PA 15213-3891. Offers MSE, PhD. *Entrance requirements:* For master's, GRE General Test, GRE Subject Test (computer science), 2 years of experience in large-scale software development project.

Carnegie Mellon University, Tepper School of Business, Pittsburgh, PA 15213-3891. Offers accounting (PhD); algorithms, combinatorics, and optimization (MS, PhD); business management and software engineering (MBMSE); civil engineering and industrial management (MS); computational finance (MSCF); economics (MS, PhD); electronic commerce (MS); environmental engineering and management (MEEM); finance (PhD); financial economics (PhD); industrial administration (MBA), including administration and public management; information systems (PhD); management of manufacturing and automation (PhD); marketing (PhD); mathematical finance (PhD); operations research (PhD); organizational behavior and theory (PhD); political economy (PhD); production and operations management (PhD); public policy and management (MS, MSED); software engineering and business management (MS); JD/MS; JD/MSIA; M Div/MS; MOM/MSIA; MSCF/MSIA. Part-time programs available. Terminal master's awarded for partial completion of doctoral program. *Degree requirements:* For doctorate, thesis/dissertation. *Entrance requirements:* For master's, GMAT. Additional exam requirements/recommendations for international students: Required—TOEFL. *Expenses:* Contact institution.

Carroll University, Program in Software Engineering, Waukesha, WI 53186-5593. Offers MSE. Part-time and evening/weekend programs available. *Faculty:* 4 full-time (1 woman). *Students:* 1 full-time (0 women), 26 part-time (5 women); includes 3 minority (1 African American, 1 Asian American or Pacific Islander, 1 Hispanic American), 3 international. Average age 34. 15 applicants, 53% accepted, 2 enrolled. In 2009, 5 master's awarded. *Degree requirements:* For master's, professional experience, capstone project. *Entrance requirements:* For master's, BA or BS, 2 years professional experience. Additional exam requirements/recommendations for international students: Required—TOEFL. *Application deadline:* For fall admission, 9/15 priority date for domestic students. Applications are processed on a rolling basis. Application fee: $0. Electronic applications accepted. *Expenses:* Tuition: Part-time $505 per credit. *Financial support:* In 2009–10, 2 students received support. Institutionally sponsored loans available. Support available to part-time students. *Faculty research:* Networking, artificial intelligence, virtual reality, effective teaching of software design, computer science pedagogy. *Unit head:* Dr. Chenglie Hu, Associate Professor of Computer Science and Program Director, 262-524-7170, E-mail: chu@carrollu.edu. *Application contact:* Tami Bartunek, Graduate Admission Counselor, 262-524-7643, E-mail: tbartune@carrollu.edu.

Cleveland State University, College of Graduate Studies, Fenn College of Engineering, Department of Electrical and Computer Engineering, Cleveland, OH 44115. Offers electrical engineering (MS, D Eng); software engineering (MS). Part-time programs available. *Degree requirements:* For master's, thesis optional; for doctorate, thesis/dissertation, qualifying and candidacy exams. *Entrance requirements:* For master's, GRE General Test (minimum score 650 quantitative), minimum GPA of 2.75; for doctorate, GRE General Test (quantitative score in 80th percentile), minimum GPA of 3.25. Additional exam requirements/recommendations for international students: Required—TOEFL (minimum score 535 paper-based; 197 computer-based; 65 iBT). *Faculty research:* Computer networks, knowledge-based control systems, artificial intelligence, digital communications, MEMS, sensors, power systems, power electronics.

Colorado Technical University Colorado Springs, Graduate Studies, Program in Computer Science, Colorado Springs, CO 80907-3896. Offers computer science (DCS); computer systems security (MSCS); database systems (MSCS); software engineering (MSCS). Part-time and evening/weekend programs available. Postbaccalaureate distance learning degree programs offered. *Degree requirements:* For master's, thesis or alternative; for doctorate, thesis/dissertation. *Entrance requirements:* For doctorate, minimum graduate GPA of 3.0, 5 years of related work experience. *Faculty research:* Software engineering, systems engineering.

Colorado Technical University Denver, Program in Computer Science, Greenwood Village, CO 80111. Offers computer systems security (MSCS); database systems (MSCS); software engineering (MSCS). Part-time and evening/weekend programs available. *Degree requirements:* For master's, thesis or alternative. *Entrance requirements:* For master's, minimum undergraduate GPA of 3.0, resume.

Colorado Technical University Sioux Falls, Program in Computing, Sioux Falls, SD 57108. Offers computer systems security (MSCS); software engineering (MSCS).

Concordia University, School of Graduate Studies, Faculty of Engineering and Computer Science, Department of Computer Science and Software Engineering, Montréal, QC H3G 1M8, Canada. Offers computer science (M App Comp Sc, M Comp Sc, PhD, Diploma); software engineering (MA Sc). *Degree requirements:* For master's, one foreign language, thesis optional; for doctorate, one foreign language, comprehensive exam, thesis/dissertation. *Faculty research:* Computer systems and applications, mathematics of computation, pattern recognition, artificial intelligence and robotics.

Concordia University, School of Graduate Studies, Faculty of Engineering and Computer Science, Department of Mechanical and Industrial Engineering, Montréal, QC H3G 1M8, Canada. Offers composites (M Eng); industrial engineering (M Eng, MA Sc); mechanical engineering (M Eng, MA Sc, PhD, Certificate); software systems for industrial engineering (Certificate). *Degree requirements:* For master's, variable foreign language requirement, thesis or alternative; for doctorate, comprehensive exam, thesis/dissertation. *Faculty research:* Mechanical systems, fluid control systems, thermofluids engineering and robotics, industrial control systems.

DePaul University, College of Computing and Digital Media, Chicago, IL 60604. Offers business information technology (MS); computational finance (MS); computer and information sciences (PhD); computer game development (MS); computer graphics and motion technology (MS); computer science (MS); computer, information and network security (MS), including applied technology; digital cinema (MFA, MS), including information technology project management (MS); e-commerce technology (MS); human-computer interaction (MS); information systems (MS); information technology (MA); information technology project management (MS); software engineering (MS); telecommunications systems (MS); JD/MS. Part-time and evening/weekend programs available. Postbaccalaureate distance learning degree programs offered (no on-campus study). *Faculty:* 78 full-time (16 women), 191 part-time/adjunct (51 women). *Students:* 922 full-time (239 women), 887 part-time (209 women); includes 466 minority (193 African Americans, 3 American Indian/Alaska Native, 162 Asian Americans or Pacific Islanders, 108 Hispanic Americans), 276 international. Average age 31. 853 applicants, 67% accepted, 294 enrolled. In 2009, 444 master's, 4 doctorates awarded. *Degree requirements:* For master's, thesis (for some programs); for doctorate, comprehensive exam, thesis/dissertation. *Entrance requirements:* For master's, GRE or GMAT (MS in computational finance only), bachelor's degree; for doctorate, GRE, master's degree in computer science. Additional exam requirements/recommendations for international students: Required—TOEFL (minimum score 550 paper-based; 213 computer-based), IELTS (minimum score 6.5), Pearson Test of English (minimum score 53). *Application deadline:* For fall admission, 8/15 priority date for domestic students, 6/1 priority date for international students; for winter admission, 12/15 priority date for domestic students, 9/15 priority date for international students; for spring admission, 3/1 priority date for domestic students, 12/15 priority date for international students. Applications are processed on a rolling basis. Application fee: $25. Electronic applications accepted. *Expenses:* Contact institution. *Financial support:* In 2009–10, 69 students received support, including 6 fellowships with full tuition reimbursements available (averaging $25,858 per year), 75 teaching assistantships with full and partial tuition reimbursements available (averaging $5,780 per year); research assistantships, Federal Work-Study, scholarships/grants, tuition waivers (full and partial), and unspecified assistantships also available. Support available to part-time students. Financial award application deadline: 4/30; financial award applicants required to submit FAFSA. *Faculty research:* Bioinformatics, visual computing, graphics and animation, high performance and scientific computing, databases. Total annual research expenditures: $790,000. *Unit head:* Dr. David Miller, Dean, 312-362-8381, Fax: 312-362-5185. *Application contact:* Dr. Liz Friedman, Assistant Dean of Student Services, 312-362-5384, Fax: 312-362-5327, E-mail: efriedm2@cdm.depaul.edu.

Drexel University, College of Engineering, Department of Electrical and Computer Engineering, Program in Software Engineering, Philadelphia, PA 19104-2875. Offers MSSE. *Entrance requirements:* For master's, GRE. Additional exam requirements/recommendations for international students: Required—TOEFL. Electronic applications accepted.

Drexel University, The iSchool at Drexel, College of Information Science and Technology, Philadelphia, PA 19104-2875. Offers healthcare informatics (Certificate); information science and technology (PMC); information studies (PhD); information studies and technology (Advanced Certificate); information systems (MSIS); library and information science (MS), including archival studies, competitive intelligence and knowledge management, digital libraries, library and information services, school library media, youth services; software engineering (MSSE). *Accreditation:* ALA (one or more programs are accredited). Part-time and evening/weekend programs available. Postbaccalaureate distance learning degree programs offered (no on-campus study). *Faculty:* 34 full-time (19 women), 24 part-time/adjunct (9 women). *Students:* 279 full-time (192 women), 571 part-time (372 women); includes 96 minority (36 African Americans, 1 American Indian/Alaska Native, 36 Asian Americans or Pacific Islanders, 23

Software Engineering

Drexel University (continued)

Hispanic Americans), 48 international. Average age 34. 644 applicants, 68% accepted, 289 enrolled. In 2009, 318 master's, 12 doctorates, 15 other advanced degrees awarded. *Degree requirements:* For doctorate, thesis/dissertation. *Entrance requirements:* For master's and doctorate, GRE General Test. Additional exam requirements/recommendations for international students: Required—TOEFL (minimum score 600 paper-based; 250 computer-based; 100 iBT). *Application deadline:* For fall admission, 8/1 for domestic and international students; for spring admission, 2/1 for domestic and international students. Applications are processed on a rolling basis. Electronic applications accepted. *Expenses:* Contact institution. *Financial support:* In 2009–10, 250 students received support, including 235 fellowships with partial tuition reimbursements available (averaging $225 per year), 18 research assistantships with full tuition reimbursements available (averaging $25,000 per year), 2 teaching assistantships with full tuition reimbursements available (averaging $25,000 per year); institutionally sponsored loans, scholarships/grants, health care benefits, tuition waivers (partial), unspecified assistantships, and fellowships also available. Support available to part-time students. Financial award applicants required to submit FAFSA. *Faculty research:* Information retrieval/information visualization/bibliometrics, human-computer interaction, digital libraries, databases, text/data mining. Total annual research expenditures: $2 million. *Unit head:* Dr. David E. Fenske, Dean and Isaac L. Auerbach Professor of Information Science, 215-895-2475, Fax: 215-895-6378, E-mail: fenske@drexel.edu. *Application contact:* Matthew Lechtenberg, Graduate Admissions Manager, 215-895-1951, Fax: 215-895-2303, E-mail: ml333@drexel.edu.

East Tennessee State University, School of Graduate Studies, College of Business and Technology, Department of Computer and Information Sciences, Johnson City, TN 37614. Offers computer science (MS); information systems science (MS); software engineering (MS). Part-time and evening/weekend programs available. *Degree requirements:* For master's, comprehensive exam, thesis. *Entrance requirements:* For master's, GRE General Test, minimum GPA of 2.5. Additional exam requirements/recommendations for international students: Required—TOEFL (minimum score 550 paper-based; 213 computer-based). *Faculty research:* Operating systems, database design, artificial intelligence, simulation, parallel algorithms.

Embry-Riddle Aeronautical University, Daytona Beach Campus Graduate Program, Department of Computer and Software Engineering, Daytona Beach, FL 32114-3900. Offers software engineering (MSE). Part-time and evening/weekend programs available. *Faculty:* 3 full-time (0 women), 1 part-time/adjunct (0 women). *Students:* 29 full-time (6 women), 3 part-time (0 women); includes 2 minority (both African Americans), 14 international. Average age 24. 24 applicants, 54% accepted, 6 enrolled. In 2009, 8 master's awarded. *Degree requirements:* For master's, thesis or alternative. *Entrance requirements:* For master's, minimum GPA of 3.0 in senior year, 2.5 overall; course work in computer science. Additional exam requirements/recommendations for international students: Required—TOEFL (minimum score 550 paper-based; 213 computer-based; 79 iBT). *Application deadline:* For fall admission, 8/1 priority date for domestic students; for spring admission, 12/1 priority date for domestic students. Applications are processed on a rolling basis. Application fee: $50. *Expenses:* Tuition: Full-time $13,740; part-time $1145 per credit hour. *Financial support:* In 2009–10, 18 students received support, including 1 research assistantship with full and partial tuition reimbursement available (averaging $5,248 per year), 6 teaching assistantships with full and partial tuition reimbursements available (averaging $5,248 per year); career-related internships or fieldwork, Federal Work-Study, and unspecified assistantships also available. Financial award application deadline: 4/15; financial award applicants required to submit FAFSA. *Unit head:* Dr. Massood Towhidnejad, Program Coordinator, 386-226-6891, Fax: 386-226-6678, E-mail: towhid@erau.edu. *Application contact:* Keith Deaton, Director, International and Graduate Admissions, 800-388-3728, Fax: 386-226-7070, E-mail: graduate.admissions@erau.edu.

Fairfield University, School of Engineering, Fairfield, CT 06824-5195. Offers electrical and computer engineering (MS); management of technology (MS); mechanical engineering (MS); software engineering (MS). Part-time and evening/weekend programs available. *Degree requirements:* For master's, thesis, capstone course. *Entrance requirements:* For master's, interview, minimum GPA of 2.8, resume, 2 recommendations. Additional exam requirements/recommendations for international students: Required—TOEFL (minimum score 550 paper-based; 213 computer-based; 80 iBT). Electronic applications accepted. *Expenses:* Contact institution. *Faculty research:* Vehicle dynamics, image processing, multimedia in instruction, thermal packaging, character recognition, photovoltaics and nanotechnology, Web technology.

Florida Agricultural and Mechanical University, Division of Graduate Studies, Research, and Continuing Education, College of Arts and Sciences, Department of Computer Information Sciences, Tallahassee, FL 32307-3200. Offers software engineering (MS). *Faculty:* 11 full-time (3 women). *Students:* 20 full-time (7 women), 4 part-time (1 woman); includes 18 minority (all African Americans), 6 international. In 2009, 4 master's awarded. *Entrance requirements:* Additional exam requirements/recommendations for international students: Required—TOEFL. *Application deadline:* For fall admission, 5/18 for domestic students, 12/18 for international students; for spring admission, 11/12 for domestic students, 5/12 for international students. Application fee: $20. *Unit head:* Dr. Edward Jones, Chairperson, 850-599-3042, Fax: 850-599-3221. *Application contact:* Dr. Bobby C. Granville, Graduate Coordinator, 850-599-3022, Fax: 850-599-3221.

Florida Institute of Technology, Graduate Programs, College of Engineering, Computer Science Department, Melbourne, FL 32901-6975. Offers computer science (MS, PhD); software engineering (MS). Part-time and evening/weekend programs available. *Faculty:* 12 full-time (0 women). *Students:* 62 full-time (8 women), 70 part-time (12 women); includes 14 minority (7 African Americans, 3 Asian Americans or Pacific Islanders, 4 Hispanic Americans), 63 international. Average age 29. 218 applicants, 58% accepted, 31 enrolled. In 2009, 46 master's, 1 doctorate awarded. *Degree requirements:* For master's, comprehensive exam (for some programs), thesis (for some programs); for doctorate, comprehensive exam, thesis/dissertation, publication in journal, teaching experience (strongly encouraged), specialized research program. *Entrance requirements:* For master's, GRE General Test, minimum GPA of 3.0, 3 letters of recommendation; for doctorate, GRE General Test, GRE Subject Test in computer science (recommended), 3 letters of recommendation, minimum GPA of 3.5, resume, statement of objectives. Additional exam requirements/recommendations for international students: Required—TOEFL (minimum score 550 paper-based; 213 computer-based; 79 iBT). *Application deadline:* For fall admission, 4/1 for international students; for spring admission, 9/30 for international students. Applications are processed on a rolling basis. Application fee: $50. Electronic applications accepted. *Expenses:* Tuition: Part-time $1015 per credit. Tuition and fees vary according to campus/location and program. *Financial support:* In 2009–10, 22 students received support, including 8 research assistantships with full and partial tuition reimbursements available (averaging $5,001 per year), 14 teaching assistantships with full and partial tuition reimbursements available (averaging $9,917 per year); career-related internships or fieldwork, institutionally sponsored loans, tuition waivers (partial), unspecified assistantships, and tuition remissions also available. Support available to part-time students. Financial award application deadline: 3/1; financial award applicants required to submit FAFSA. *Faculty research:* Artificial intelligence, software engineering, management and processes, programming languages, database systems. Total annual research expenditures: $1.2 million. *Unit head:* Dr. William D. Shoaff, Department Head, 321-674-8066, Fax: 321-674-7046, E-mail: wds@cs.fit.edu. *Application contact:* Thomas M. Shea, Director of Graduate Admissions, 321-674-7577, Fax: 321-723-9468, E-mail: tshea@fit.edu.

See Close-Up on page 303.

Florida State University, The Graduate School, College of Arts and Sciences, Department of Computer Science, Tallahassee, FL 32306. Offers computer science (MS, PhD); information security (MS); software engineering (MS). Part-time programs available. *Faculty:* 17 full-time (1 woman), 2 part-time/adjunct (0 women). *Students:* 114 full-time (22 women), 16 part-time (3 women); includes 20 minority (4 African Americans, 1 American Indian/Alaska Native, 5 Asian Americans or Pacific Islanders, 10 Hispanic Americans), 66 international. Average age 28. 167 applicants, 72% accepted, 34 enrolled. In 2009, 29 master's, 2 doctorates awarded. Terminal master's awarded for partial completion of doctoral program. *Degree requirements:* For master's, thesis or alternative; for doctorate, comprehensive exam, thesis/dissertation. *Entrance requirements:* For master's, GRE General Test, minimum undergraduate GPA of 3.0; for doctorate, GRE General Test, minimum GPA of 3.5. Additional exam requirements/recommendations for international students: Required—TOEFL (minimum score 600 paper-based; 250 computer-based; 100 iBT). *Application deadline:* For fall admission, 3/1 priority date for domestic students, 3/1 for international students; for spring admission, 10/1 priority date for domestic students, 10/1 for international students. Application fee: $30. Electronic applications accepted. *Expenses:* Tuition, state resident: full-time $7413.36. Tuition, nonresident: full-time $22,567. *Financial support:* In 2009–10, 107 students received support, including 4 fellowships with full tuition reimbursements available (averaging $17,500 per year), 35 research assistantships with full tuition reimbursements available (averaging $17,000 per year), 62 teaching assistantships with full tuition reimbursements available (averaging $15,500 per year); career-related internships or fieldwork, scholarships/grants, health care benefits, and unspecified assistantships also available. Financial award application deadline: 3/1; financial award applicants required to submit FAFSA. *Faculty research:* Embedded systems, high performance computing, networking, operating systems, security. Total annual research expenditures: $1.4 million. *Unit head:* Dr. David Whalley, Chairman, 850-644-3506, Fax: 850-644-0058, E-mail: chair@cs.fsu.edu. *Application contact:* Matthew S. Claypool, Graduate Coordinator, 850-645-4975, Fax: 850-644-0058, E-mail: claypool@cs.fsu.edu.

Gannon University, School of Graduate Studies, College of Engineering and Business, School of Engineering and Computer Science, Program in Embedded Software Engineering, Erie, PA 16541-0001. Offers MSES. Part-time and evening/weekend programs available. *Students:* 7 full-time (1 woman), 13 part-time (3 women), 16 international. Average age 25. 24 applicants, 79% accepted, 2 enrolled. In 2009, 18 master's awarded. *Degree requirements:* For master's, thesis or project. *Entrance requirements:* For master's, bachelor's degree in engineering, minimum QPA of 2.5. Additional exam requirements/recommendations for international students: Required—TOEFL (minimum score 79 iBT). *Application deadline:* Applications are processed on a rolling basis. Application fee: $25. Electronic applications accepted. *Expenses:* Tuition: Full-time $13,590; part-time $755 per credit. Required fees: $524; $17 per credit. Tuition and fees vary according to course load, degree level, campus/location and program. *Financial support:* Career-related internships or fieldwork, Federal Work-Study, scholarships/grants, traineeships, and unspecified assistantships available. Financial award application deadline: 7/1; financial award applicants required to submit FAFSA. *Unit head:* Dr. Fong Mak, Chair, 814-871-7625, E-mail: mak001@gannon.edu. *Application contact:* Kara Morgan, Assistant Director of Graduate Admissions, 814-871-5831, Fax: 814-871-5827, E-mail: graduate@gannon.edu.

George Mason University, Volgenau School of Information Technology and Engineering, Department of Computer Science, Fairfax, VA 22030. Offers biometrics (Certificate); computer games technology (Certificate); computer networking (Certificate); computer science (MS, PhD); data mining (Certificate); database management (Certificate); electronic commerce (Certificate); foundations of information systems (Certificate); information engineering (Certificate); information security and assurance (MS, Certificate); information systems (MS); intelligent agents (Certificate); software architecture (Certificate); software engineering (MS, Certificate); systems engineering (MS); Web-based software engineering (Certificate). Part-time and evening/weekend programs available. Postbaccalaureate distance learning degree programs offered. *Faculty:* 42 full-time (9 women), 18 part-time/adjunct (0 women). *Students:* 121 full-time (36 women), 489 part-time (118 women); includes 90 minority (11 African Americans, 70 Asian Americans or Pacific Islanders, 9 Hispanic Americans), 222 international. Average age 29. 882 applicants, 58% accepted, 147 enrolled. In 2009, 202 master's, 6 doctorates, 21 other advanced degrees awarded. *Degree requirements:* For master's, thesis optional; for doctorate, comprehensive exam, thesis/dissertation. *Entrance requirements:* For master's, GRE General Test, minimum GPA of 3.0 in last 60 hours, 3 letters of recommendation; for doctorate, GRE, 4-year BA degree, academic work in computer science, 3 letters of recommendation, statement of career goals and aspirations. Additional exam requirements/recommendations for international students: Required—TOEFL. *Application deadline:* For fall admission, 4/15 priority date for domestic students, 1/15 for international students; for spring admission, 11/15 for domestic students. Application fee: $75. Electronic applications accepted. *Expenses:* Tuition, state resident: full-time $7568; part-time $315.33 per credit hour. Tuition, nonresident: full-time $21,704; part-time $904.33 per credit hour. Required fees: $2184; $91 per credit hour. *Financial support:* In 2009–10, 106 students received support, including 3 fellowships (averaging $18,000 per year), 53 research assistantships (averaging $11,119 per year), 53 teaching assistantships (averaging $7,881 per year); unspecified assistantships and health care benefits (full-time research or teaching assistantship recipients) also available. Financial award application deadline: 3/1; financial award applicants required to submit FAFSA. *Faculty research:* Artificial intelligence, image processing/graphics, parallel/distributed systems, software engineering systems. Total annual research expenditures: $1.3 million. *Unit head:* Dr. Arun Sood, Director, 703-993-1524, Fax: 703-993-1710, E-mail: asood@gmu.edu. *Application contact:* Jay Shapiro, Professor, 703-993-1485, E-mail: jshapiro@gmu.edu.

Grand Valley State University, Padnos College of Engineering and Computing, School of Computing and Information Systems, Allendale, MI 49401-9403. Offers computer information systems (MS), including databases, distributed systems, management of information systems, object-oriented systems, software engineering. Part-time and evening/weekend programs available. *Faculty:* 11 full-time (0 women). *Students:* 10 full-time (3 women), 52 part-time (12 women); includes 8 minority (1 African American, 6 Asian Americans or Pacific Islanders, 1 Hispanic American), 11 international. Average age 33. 32 applicants, 81% accepted, 16 enrolled. In 2009, 22 master's awarded. *Degree requirements:* For master's, thesis or alternative. *Entrance requirements:* For master's, GMAT or GRE General Test. Additional exam requirements/recommendations for international students: Required—TOEFL. *Application deadline:* For fall admission, 6/1 for international students; for winter admission, 9/1 for international students. Applications are processed on a rolling basis. Application fee: $30. Electronic applications accepted. *Financial support:* In 2009–10, 9 students received support, including 5 fellowships (averaging $3,380 per year), 5 research assistantships with full and partial tuition reimbursements available (averaging $4,626 per year). *Faculty research:* Object technology, distributed computing, information systems management database, software engineering. *Unit head:* Paul Leidig, Director, 616-331-2038, Fax: 616-331-2106, E-mail: leidigp@gvsu.edu. *Application contact:* D. Robert Adams, CIS Graduate Program Chair, 616-331-3885, Fax: 616-331-2106, E-mail: adams@cis.gvsu.edu.

Hawai'i Pacific University, College of Business Administration, Program in Information Systems, Honolulu, HI 96813. Offers knowledge management (MSIS); software engineering (MSIS); telecommunications security (MSIS). *Faculty:* 9 full-time (2 women), 3 part-time/adjunct (1 woman). *Students:* 54 full-time (14 women), 60 part-time (17 women); includes 50 minority (4 African Americans, 40 Asian Americans or Pacific Islanders, 6 Hispanic Americans), 49 international. Average age 32. In 2009, 52 master's awarded. *Expenses:* Tuition: Full-time $12,600; part-time $700 per credit hour. Tuition and fees vary according to program. *Unit head:* Dr. Gordon Jones, Dean, 808-544-1181, Fax: 808-544-0247, E-mail: gjones@hpu.edu. *Application contact:* Danny Lam, Assistant Director of Graduate Admissions, 808-544-1135, Fax: 808-544-0280, E-mail: graduate@hpu.edu.

Illinois Institute of Technology, Graduate College, Armour College of Engineering, Department of Electrical and Computer Engineering, Chicago, IL 60616-3793. Offers biomedical imaging and signals (MBMI); computer engineering (MS, PhD); electrical and computer engineering (MECE); electrical engineering (MS, PhD); electricity markets (MEM); manufacturing engineering (MME, MS); network engineering (MNE); power engineering (MPE); telecommunications and software engineering (MTSE); VLSI and microelectronics (MVM). Part-time and evening/weekend programs available. Terminal master's awarded for partial completion of doctoral program. *Degree requirements:* For master's, comprehensive exam, thesis (for some programs); for doctorate, comprehensive exam, thesis/dissertation. *Entrance requirements:* For master's and doctorate, GRE General Test, minimum undergraduate GPA of 3.0. Additional exam requirements/recommendations for international students: Required—TOEFL (minimum score 550 paper-based; 213 computer-based; 80 iBT). Electronic applications accepted. *Expenses:* Tuition: Full-time $17,550; part-time $888 per credit hour. Required fees: $850; $7.50 per credit hour. One-time fee: $50 full-time. Full-time tuition and fees vary according to program. *Faculty research:* Communications and signal processing, computers and digital systems, electronics and electromagnetics, power and control systems.

Illinois Institute of Technology, Graduate College, College of Science and Letters, Department of Computer Science, Chicago, IL 60616-3793. Offers computer science (MCS, MS, PhD); teaching (MST); telecommunications and software engineering (MTSE); MS/M Ch E. Part-time and evening/weekend programs available. Postbaccalaureate distance learning degree programs offered (no on-campus study). Terminal master's awarded for partial completion of doctoral program. *Degree requirements:* For master's, thesis (for some programs); for doctorate, comprehensive exam, thesis/dissertation. *Entrance requirements:* For master's and doctorate, GRE General Test, minimum undergraduate GPA of 3.0. Additional exam requirements/recommendations for international students: Required—TOEFL (minimum score 550 paper-based; 213 computer-based; 80 iBT). Electronic applications accepted. *Expenses:* Tuition: Full-time $17,550; part-time $888 per credit hour. Required fees: $850; $7.50 per credit hour. One-time fee: $50 full-time. Full-time tuition and fees vary according to program. *Faculty research:* Information retrieval, parallel and distributed computing, networking, algorithms, natural language processing.

International Technological University, Program in Software Engineering, Santa Clara, CA 95050. Offers MSSE, PhD. *Degree requirements:* For master's, thesis or alternative. *Entrance requirements:* For master's, 3 semesters of calculus, minimum GPA of 2.5. Additional exam requirements/recommendations for international students: Required—TOEFL. *Faculty research:* Software testing, web management, client service and the Internet.

Jacksonville State University, College of Graduate Studies and Continuing Education, College of Arts and Sciences, Program in Computer Systems and Software Design, Jacksonville, AL 36265-1602. Offers MS. Part-time and evening/weekend programs available. *Degree requirements:* For master's, comprehensive exam, thesis (for some programs). Electronic applications accepted.

Kansas State University, Graduate School, College of Engineering, Department of Computing and Information Sciences, Manhattan, KS 66506. Offers computer science (MS, PhD); software engineering (MSE). Part-time programs available. Postbaccalaureate distance learning degree programs offered (minimal on-campus study). *Faculty:* 15 full-time (1 woman). *Students:* 74 full-time (14 women), 45 part-time (10 women); includes 3 minority (2 Asian Americans or Pacific Islanders, 1 Hispanic American), 86 international. Average age 26. 236 applicants, 49% accepted, 40 enrolled. In 2009, 27 master's, 5 doctorates awarded. Terminal master's awarded for partial completion of doctoral program. *Degree requirements:* For master's, thesis or alternative; for doctorate, thesis/dissertation, preliminary exams. *Entrance requirements:* For master's, GRE, bachelor's degree in computer science, minimum GPA of 3.0; for doctorate, GRE General Test, GRE Subject Test, master's degree in computer science or bachelor's degree and strong advanced computer knowledge. Additional exam requirements/recommendations for international students: Required—TOEFL (minimum score 575 paper-based; 233 computer-based). *Application deadline:* For fall admission, 2/1 priority date for domestic and international students; for spring admission, 8/1 priority date for domestic and international students. Applications are processed on a rolling basis. Application fee: $40 ($55 for international students). Electronic applications accepted. *Financial support:* In 2009–10, 27 research assistantships (averaging $16,260 per year), 24 teaching assistantships with full tuition reimbursements (averaging $14,294 per year) were awarded; career-related internships or fieldwork, institutionally sponsored loans, and scholarships/grants also available. Support available to part-time students. Financial award application deadline: 3/15; financial award applicants required to submit FAFSA. *Faculty research:* High-assurance software and programming languages, data mining, parallel and distributed computing, computer security, embedded systems. Total annual research expenditures: $1.5 million. *Unit head:* Gurdip E. Singh, Head, 785-532-7945, Fax: 785-532-7353, E-mail: gurdip@ksu.edu. *Application contact:* Dave Gustafson, Director, 785-532-6350, Fax: 785-532-7353, E-mail: dag@ksu.edu.

Loyola University Chicago, Graduate School, Department of Computer Science, Chicago, IL 60660. Offers computer science (MS); information technology (MS); software technology (MS). Part-time and evening/weekend programs available. *Faculty:* 9 full-time (1 woman), 10 part-time/adjunct (2 women). *Students:* 49 full-time (18 women), 31 part-time (6 women); includes 17 minority (4 African Americans, 9 Asian Americans or Pacific Islanders, 4 Hispanic Americans), 30 international. Average age 27. 96 applicants, 57% accepted, 30 enrolled. In 2009, 32 master's awarded. *Entrance requirements:* For master's, 3 letters of recommendation, transcripts, statement of purpose. Additional exam requirements/recommendations for international students: Required—TOEFL (minimum score 550 paper-based; 213 computer-based; 79 iBT), IELTS (minimum score 6.5). *Application deadline:* For fall admission, 5/15 priority date for international students; for spring admission, 9/15 priority date for international students. Applications are processed on a rolling basis. Application fee: $0. Electronic applications accepted. *Expenses:* Tuition: Full-time $14,220; part-time $790 per credit hour. Required fees: $60 per semester hour. Tuition and fees vary according to program. *Financial support:* In 2009–10, 24 students received support, including 1 fellowship (averaging $3,000 per year), 16 teaching assistantships with partial tuition reimbursements available (averaging $2,900 per year); career-related internships or fieldwork, Federal Work-Study, scholarships/grants, tuition waivers (partial), and unspecified assistantships also available. Financial award application deadline: 3/15. *Faculty research:* Software engineering, high performance computing, algorithms and complexity. Total annual research expenditures: $22,000. *Unit head:* Dr. Chandra Sekharan, Chair, 312-915-7985, Fax: 312-915-7998, E-mail: csekhar@luc.edu. *Application contact:* Cecilia Murphy, Graduate Program Secretary, 312-915-7990, Fax: 312-915-7998, E-mail: gradinfo-cs@luc.edu.

Loyola University Maryland, Graduate Programs, College of Arts and Sciences, Department of Computer Science, Baltimore, MD 21210-2699. Offers computer science (MS); software engineering (MS). *Entrance requirements:* For master's, GRE General Test, GRE Subject Test (recommended). Additional exam requirements/recommendations for international students: Required—TOEFL (minimum score 550 paper-based; 213 computer-based).

Marist College, Graduate Programs, School of Computer Science and Mathematics, Poughkeepsie, NY 12601-1387. Offers information systems (MS, Adv C); software development (MS); technology management (MS). Part-time and evening/weekend programs available. Postbaccalaureate distance learning degree programs offered (minimal on-campus study). *Entrance requirements:* For master's, resume. Additional exam requirements/recommendations for international students: Required—TOEFL (minimum score 550 paper-based; 213 computer-based; 80 iBT); Recommended—IELTS (minimum score 6.5). Electronic applications accepted. *Expenses:* Tuition: Full-time $12,510; part-time $695 per credit hour. *Faculty research:* Data quality, artificial intelligence, imaging, analysis of algorithms, distributed systems and applications.

McMaster University, School of Graduate Studies, Faculty of Engineering, Department of Computing and Software, Hamilton, ON L8S 4M2, Canada. Offers computer science (M Sc, PhD); software engineering (M Eng, MA Sc, PhD). Part-time programs available. *Degree requirements:* For master's, thesis. *Entrance requirements:* Additional exam requirements/recommendations for international students: Required—TOEFL (minimum score 550 paper-based; 213 computer-based). *Faculty research:* Software engineering; theory of non-sequential systems; parallel and distributed computing; artificial intelligence; complexity, design, and analysis of algorithms; combinatorial computing, especially applications to molecular biology.

Mercer University, Graduate Studies, Macon Campus, School of Engineering, Macon, GA 31207-0003. Offers biomedical engineering (MSE); computer engineering (MSE); electrical engineering (MSE); engineering management (MSE); environmental engineering (MSE); environmental systems (MS); mechanical engineering (MSE); software engineering (MSE); software systems (MS); technical communications management (MS); technical management (MS). Part-time and evening/weekend programs available. Postbaccalaureate distance learning degree programs offered (no on-campus study). *Faculty:* 19 full-time (4 women), 1 part-time/adjunct (0 women). *Students:* 6 full-time (1 woman), 95 part-time (22 women); includes 22 minority (5 African Americans, 13 Asian Americans or Pacific Islanders, 4 Hispanic Americans), 3 international. Average age 33. In 2009, 42 master's awarded. *Degree requirements:* For master's, thesis or alternative. *Entrance requirements:* For master's, minimum undergraduate GPA of 3.0. Additional exam requirements/recommendations for international students: Required—TOEFL. *Application deadline:* For fall admission, 7/1 for domestic students; for spring admission, 11/15 for domestic students. Applications are processed on a rolling basis. Application fee: $35 ($50 for international students). Electronic applications accepted. *Expenses:* Contact institution. *Financial support:* Federal Work-Study available. *Unit head:* Dr. Wade H. Shaw, Dean, 478-301-2459, Fax: 478-301-5593, E-mail: shaw_wh@mercer.edu. *Application contact:* Greg Lofton, Graduate Program Coordinator, 478-301-5480, Fax: 478-301-5434, E-mail: lofton_g@mercer.edu.

Miami University, Graduate School, School of Engineering and Applied Science, Oxford, OH 45056. Offers computational science and engineering (MS); computer science and software engineering (MCS), including computer science; paper and chemical engineering (MS); software development (Certificate). *Students:* 35 full-time (14 women), 9 part-time (2 women); includes 4 minority (all Asian Americans or Pacific Islanders), 25 international. *Entrance requirements:* For master's, GRE, minimum undergraduate GPA of 3.0 during previous 2 years or 2.75 overall. Additional exam requirements/recommendations for international students: Required—TOEFL. Application fee: $50. *Expenses:* Tuition, state resident: full-time $11,280. Tuition, nonresident: full-time $24,912. Required fees: $516. *Financial support:* Fellowships with full tuition reimbursements, research assistantships, teaching assistantships, Federal Work-Study, health care benefits, tuition waivers (full), and unspecified assistantships available. Financial award application deadline: 3/1. *Unit head:* Dr. Marek Dollar, Dean, 513-529-0700, E-mail: seasfyi@muohio.edu. *Application contact:* Mary York, Domestic Graduate Admission Coordinator or Janet Miller, International Graduate Admission Coordinator, 513-529-3734, Fax: 513-529-3734, E-mail: gradschool@muohio.edu.

Monmouth University, Graduate School, Department of Computer Science, West Long Branch, NJ 07764-1898. Offers computer science (MS); software design and development (Certificate). Part-time and evening/weekend programs available. *Faculty:* 5 full-time (2 women), 5 part-time/adjunct (0 women). *Students:* 16 full-time (5 women), 18 part-time (10 women); includes 1 minority (Asian American or Pacific Islander), 25 international. Average age 25. 31 applicants, 87% accepted, 5 enrolled. In 2009, 14 master's awarded. *Degree requirements:* For master's, thesis optional. *Entrance requirements:* For master's, minimum GPA of 3.0 in major, 2.75 overall. Additional exam requirements/recommendations for international students: Required—TOEFL (minimum score 550 paper-based; 213 computer-based; 79 iBT), IELTS (minimum score 5), Michigan English Language Assessment Battery (minimum score 77), Cambridge A, B, C. *Application deadline:* For fall admission, 7/15 priority date for domestic students, 6/1 for international students; for spring admission, 11/15 priority date for domestic students, 11/1 for international students. Applications are processed on a rolling basis. Application fee: $50. Electronic applications accepted. *Expenses:* Tuition: Part-time $773 per credit. Required fees: $157 per semester. *Financial support:* In 2009–10, 25 students received support, including 24 fellowships (averaging $1,411 per year), 15 research assistantships (averaging $5,912 per year); career-related internships or fieldwork, scholarships/grants, and unspecified assistantships also available. Support available to part-time students. Financial award application deadline: 3/1; financial award applicants required to submit FAFSA. *Faculty research:* Databases, natural language processing, protocols, performance analysis, communications networks (systems), telecommunications. *Unit head:* Dr. Cui Yu, Program Director, 732-571-4460, Fax: 732-263-5202, E-mail: cyu@monmouth.edu. *Application contact:* Kevin Roane, Director, Office of Graduate Admission, 732-571-3452, Fax: 732-263-5123, E-mail: gradadm@monmouth.edu.

Monmouth University, Graduate School, Department of Computer Science and Software Engineering, West Long Branch, NJ 07764-1898. Offers software development (Certificate); software engineering (MS, Certificate). Part-time and evening/weekend programs available. *Faculty:* 5 full-time (1 woman), 4 part-time/adjunct (1 woman). *Students:* 25 full-time (2 women), 40 part-time (8 women); includes 23 minority (6 African Americans, 13 Asian Americans or Pacific Islanders, 4 Hispanic Americans), 6 international. Average age 27. 20 applicants, 100% accepted, 8 enrolled. In 2009, 26 master's awarded. *Degree requirements:* For master's, thesis or alternative, practicum. *Entrance requirements:* For master's, bachelor's degree in computer science, engineering, mathematics, or physics; minimum GPA of 3.0; 1 year of software development experience. Additional exam requirements/recommendations for international students: Required—TOEFL (minimum score 550 paper-based; 213 computer-based; 79 iBT), IELTS (minimum score 5), Michigan English Language Assessment Battery (minimum score 77), Cambridge A, B, C. *Application deadline:* For fall admission, 7/15 priority date for domestic students, 6/1 for international students; for spring admission, 11/15 priority date for domestic students, 11/1 for international students. Applications are processed on a rolling basis. Application fee: $50. Electronic applications accepted. *Expenses:* Contact institution. *Financial support:* In 2009–10, 9 students received support, including 6 fellowships (averaging $1,104 per year), 3 research assistantships (averaging $7,112 per year); career-related internships or fieldwork, scholarships/grants, and unspecified assistantships also available. Support available to part-time students. Financial award applicants required to submit FAFSA. *Faculty research:* Conceptual structures, real time software, business rules, project management, software related to homeland security. *Unit head:* Dr. Daniela Rosca, Program Director, 732-571-4459, Fax: 732-263-5253, E-mail: drosca@monmouth.edu. *Application contact:* Kevin Roane, Director, Office of Graduate Admission, 732-571-3452, Fax: 732-263-5123, E-mail: gradadm@monmouth.edu.

National University, Academic Affairs, School of Engineering and Technology, Department of Computer Science and Information Systems, La Jolla, CA 92037-1011. Offers computer science (MS); information systems (MS); software engineering (MS); technology management (MS). Part-time and evening/weekend programs available. Postbaccalaureate distance learning degree programs offered (no on-campus study). *Faculty:* 18 full-time (10 women), 30 part-time/adjunct (7 women). *Students:* 88 full-time (19 women), 163 part-time (31 women); includes 57 minority (24 African Americans, 24 Asian Americans or Pacific Islanders, 9 Hispanic Americans), 111 international. Average age 32. 146 applicants, 100% accepted, 89 enrolled. In 2009, 51 master's awarded. *Degree requirements:* For master's, thesis. *Entrance requirements:* For master's, interview, minimum GPA of 2.5. Additional exam requirements/recommendations for international students: Required—TOEFL (minimum score 550 paper-based; 213 computer-based; 79 iBT), IELTS (minimum score 6). *Application deadline:* Applications are processed on a rolling basis. Application fee: $60 ($65 for international students). Electronic applications accepted. *Expenses:* Tuition: Part-time $338 per quarter hour. *Financial support:* Career-related internships or fieldwork, institutionally sponsored loans, scholarships/grants, and tuition waivers (partial) available. Support available to part-time students. Financial award application deadline: 6/30; financial award applicants required to submit FAFSA. *Unit head:* Dr. Ron Uhlig, Interim Chair and Instructor, 858-309-3412, Fax: 858-309-3420, E-mail: ruhlig@nu.edu. *Application contact:* Dominick Giovanniello, Associate Regional Dean—San Diego, 800-NAT-UNIV, Fax: 858-541-7792, E-mail: dgiovann@nu.edu.

Naval Postgraduate School, Graduate Programs, Department of Computer Science, Monterey, CA 93943. Offers computer science (MS, PhD); modeling of virtual environments and simulations (MS, PhD); software engineering (MS, PhD). Program only open to commissioned officers of the United States and friendly nations and selected United States federal civilian employees. Part-time programs available. Postbaccalaureate distance learning degree programs offered (minimal on-campus study). *Degree requirements:* For master's, thesis; for doctorate, one foreign language, thesis/dissertation.

Software Engineering

New Jersey Institute of Technology, Office of Graduate Studies, College of Computing Science, Department of Computer Science, Newark, NJ 07102. Offers bioinformatics (MS); computer science (MS, PhD); computing and business (MS); software engineering (MS). Part-time and evening/weekend programs available. Terminal master's awarded for partial completion of doctoral program. *Degree requirements:* For master's, thesis optional; for doctorate, thesis/dissertation. *Entrance requirements:* For master's, GRE General Test; for doctorate, GRE General Test, minimum graduate GPA of 3.5. Additional exam requirements/ recommendations for international students: Required—TOEFL (minimum score 550 paper-based; 213 computer-based; 79 iBT). Electronic applications accepted.

North Dakota State University, College of Graduate and Interdisciplinary Studies, College of Science and Mathematics, Department of Computer Science, Program in Software Engineering, Fargo, ND 58108. Offers MS, PhD, Certificate. Part-time programs available. Postbaccalaureate distance learning degree programs offered (minimal on-campus study). *Students:* 15 full-time (5 women), 32 part-time (6 women); includes 1 American Indian/Alaska Native, 2 Asian Americans or Pacific Islanders, 1 Hispanic American, 24 international. In 2009, 3 master's, 2 doctorates awarded. Terminal master's awarded for partial completion of doctoral program. *Degree requirements:* For master's, comprehensive exam, thesis optional; for doctorate, thesis/dissertation, qualifying exam. *Entrance requirements:* For master's and doctorate, minimum GPA of 3.0 in software engineering or related field. Additional exam requirements/ recommendations for international students: Required—TOEFL (minimum score 550 paper-based; 213 computer-based; 79 iBT). *Application deadline:* For fall admission, 8/15 priority date for domestic and international students; for spring admission, 12/15 priority date for domestic and international students. Application fee: $45 ($60 for international students). *Financial support:* Research assistantships with full tuition reimbursements, teaching assistantships with full tuition reimbursements, career-related internships or fieldwork, Federal Work-Study, institutionally sponsored loans, and tuition waivers (full) available. Financial award application deadline: 4/15. *Faculty research:* Data knowledge and engineering requirements, formal methods for software, software measurement and mobile agents, software development process. *Unit head:* Dr. Brian Slator, Head, 701-231-8562, Fax: 701-231-8255. *Application contact:* Dr. Ken R. Nygard, Graduate Coordinator, 701-231-9460, Fax: 701-231-8255, E-mail: kendall.nygard@ndsu.edu.

Northern Kentucky University, Office of Graduate Programs, College of Informatics, Department of Computer Science, Highland Heights, KY 41099. Offers computer information technology (MSCIT); computer science (MSCS); secure software engineering (Certificate). Part-time and evening/weekend programs available. *Students:* 2 full-time (0 women), 20 part-time (4 women), 2 international. Average age 32. 29 applicants, 24% accepted, 4 enrolled. In 2009, 5 master's, 2 Certificates awarded. *Degree requirements:* For master's, thesis optional. *Entrance requirements:* For master's, minimum GPA of 3.0, at least 4 semesters of undergraduate study in computer science including intermediate computer programming and data structures, one year of calculus and a course in discrete mathematics. Additional exam requirements/recommendations for international students: Required—TOEFL (minimum score 550 paper-based; 213 computer-based; 79 iBT); Recommended—IELTS (minimum score 6.5). *Application deadline:* For fall admission, 8/1 for domestic students, 6/1 for international students; for spring admission, 12/1 for domestic students, 10/1 for international students. Applications are processed on a rolling basis. Application fee: $40. Electronic applications accepted. *Expenses:* Tuition, state resident: full-time $6912; part-time $384 per credit hour. Tuition, nonresident: full-time $12,150; part-time $675 per credit hour. Tuition and fees vary according to course load, program and reciprocity agreements. *Financial support:* Scholarships/ grants and unspecified assistantships available. Financial award applicants required to submit FAFSA. *Faculty research:* Data privacy, data mining, wireless security, secure software engineering, secure networking. *Unit head:* Dr. Maureen Doyle, Program Director, 859-572-5468, Fax: 859-572-6097, E-mail: doylem3@nku.edu. *Application contact:* Dr. Peg Griffin, Director of Graduate Programs, 859-572-6934, Fax: 859-572-6670, E-mail: griffinp@nku.edu.

Northwestern University, School of Continuing Studies, Program in Information Systems, Evanston, IL 60208. Offers database and Internet technologies (MS); information systems management (MS); information systems security (MS); software project management and development (MS).

Oakland University, Graduate Study and Lifelong Learning, School of Engineering and Computer Science, Department of Computer Science and Engineering, Rochester, MI 48309-4401. Offers computer science (MS); embedded systems (MS); information systems engineering (MS); software engineering (MS). Part-time and evening/weekend programs available. *Entrance requirements:* For master's, minimum GPA of 3.0 for unconditional admission. Electronic applications accepted. *Expenses:* Contact institution. *Faculty research:* Cyber security, 3D imaging of neurochemicals in rat brains.

Pace University, Seidenberg School of Computer Science and Information Systems, New York, NY 10038. Offers computer communications and networks (Certificate); computer science (MS); computing studies (DPS); information systems (MS); Internet technologies for e-commerce (MS); Internet technology (MS); object-oriented programming (Certificate); security and information assurance (Certificate); software development and engineering (MS); telecommunications (MS, Certificate). Part-time and evening/weekend programs available. *Students:* 122 full-time (37 women), 424 part-time (131 women); includes 188 minority (76 African Americans, 1 American Indian/Alaska Native, 65 Asian Americans or Pacific Islanders, 46 Hispanic Americans), 110 international. Average age 35. 352 applicants, 89% accepted, 128 enrolled. In 2009, 137 master's, 11 doctorates, 3 other advanced degrees awarded. *Entrance requirements:* For master's, GRE General Test. Additional exam requirements/recommendations for international students: Required—TOEFL. *Application deadline:* For fall admission, 7/31 priority date for domestic students; for spring admission, 11/30 for domestic students. Applications are processed on a rolling basis. Application fee: $70. Electronic applications accepted. *Expenses:* Contact institution. *Financial support:* Research assistantships, career-related internships or fieldwork available. Support available to part-time students. Financial award applicants required to submit FAFSA. *Unit head:* Dr. Constance Knapp, Interim Dean, 914-773-3750, Fax: 914-773-3533, E-mail: cknapp@pace.edu. *Application contact:* Joanna Broda, Director of Graduate Admissions, 914-422-4283, Fax: 914-422-4287, E-mail: gradwp@pace.edu.

Polytechnic Institute of NYU, Department of Computer Science and Engineering, Major in Software Engineering, Brooklyn, NY 11201-2990. Offers Graduate Certificate. *Students:* 1 applicant, 100% accepted. *Application deadline:* For fall admission, 7/31 priority date for domestic students, 4/30 priority date for international students; for spring admission, 12/31 priority date for domestic students, 11/30 priority date for international students. Applications are processed on a rolling basis. Application fee: $75. Electronic applications accepted. *Expenses:* Tuition: Full-time $21,492; part-time $1194 per credit hour. Required fees: $1160; $204 per course. *Unit head:* Dr. Keith W. Ross, Head, 718-260-3859, Fax: 718-260-3609, E-mail: ross@poly.edu. *Application contact:* JeanCarlo Bonilla, Director of Graduate Enrollment Management, 718-260-3182, Fax: 718-260-3624, E-mail: gradinfo@poly.edu.

Polytechnic Institute of NYU, Long Island Graduate Center, Graduate Programs, Department of Computer Science and Engineering, Program in Software Engineering, Melville, NY 11747. Offers MS. *Entrance requirements:* Additional exam requirements/recommendations for international students: Required—TOEFL (minimum score 550 paper-based; 213 computer-based; 80 iBT); Recommended—IELTS (minimum score 6.5). *Application deadline:* For fall admission, 7/31 priority date for domestic students, 4/30 priority date for international students; for spring admission, 12/31 priority date for domestic students, 11/30 priority date for international students. Applications are processed on a rolling basis. Application fee: $75. Electronic applications accepted. *Financial support:* Institutionally sponsored loans, scholarships/grants, and unspecified assistantships available. Support available to part-time students. *Unit head:* Dr. Keith W. Ross, Department Head, 718-260-3859, E-mail: ross@poly.edu. *Application contact:* JeanCarlo Bonilla, Director of Graduate Enrollment Management, 718-260-3182, Fax: 718-260-3624, E-mail: gradinfo@poly.edu.

Portland State University, Graduate Studies, Maseeh College of Engineering and Computer Science, Department of Computer Science, Portland, OR 97207-0751. Offers computer science (MS, PhD); software engineering (MSE). Part-time programs available. *Degree requirements:* For master's, thesis or alternative; for doctorate, thesis/dissertation. *Entrance requirements:* For master's, GRE General Test, minimum GPA of 3.0 in upper-division course work, 2 letters of recommendation, BS in computer science or allied field; for doctorate, MS in computer science or allied field. Additional exam requirements/recommendations for international students: Required—TOEFL (minimum score 550 paper-based; 213 computer-based). *Faculty research:* Formal methods, database systems, parallel programming environments, computer security, software tools.

Regis University, College for Professional Studies, School of Computer and Information Sciences, Denver, CO 80221-1099. Offers database administration with IBM DB2 (Certificate); database administration with Oracle (Certificate); database development (Certificate); database technologies (MA); enterprise Java software development (Certificate); executive information technologies (Certificate); information assurance (MA, Certificate); information technology management (MA); software and information systems (M Sc); software engineering (MA, Certificate); storage area networks (Certificate); systems engineering (MA, Certificate). Offered at Boulder Campus, Northwest Denver Campus, Southeast Denver Campus, Fort Collins Campus, Colorado Springs Campus, and Broomfield Campus. Part-time and evening/ weekend programs available. Postbaccalaureate distance learning degree programs offered (no on-campus study). *Degree requirements:* For master's, thesis, final research project. *Entrance requirements:* For master's, 2 years of related experience, resume, interview; for Certificate, 2 years of related experience, resumé. Additional exam requirements/ recommendations for international students: Required—TOEFL (minimum score 213 computer-based), TWE (minimum score 5), TOEFL or university-based test. Electronic applications accepted. *Expenses:* Contact institution. *Faculty research:* Secure Virtual Laboratory Architecture, Joint IA project with W2C06 Institute, Information Policy, OLTP and OLAP Technologies, knowledge management, software architectures.

Rochester Institute of Technology, Graduate Enrollment Services, B. Thomas Golisano College of Computing and Information Sciences, Department of Information Technology, Program in Software Development and Management, Rochester, NY 14623-5603. Offers MS. Part-time and evening/weekend programs available. Postbaccalaureate distance learning degree programs offered (no on-campus study). *Students:* 33 part-time (5 women); includes 1 Asian American or Pacific Islander, 1 Hispanic American. Average age 35. 9 applicants, 67% accepted, 6 enrolled. In 2009, 10 master's awarded. *Degree requirements:* For master's, thesis or alternative, project. *Entrance requirements:* For master's, minimum GPA of 3.0. Additional exam requirements/recommendations for international students: Required—TOEFL (minimum score 570 paper-based; 230 computer-based; 88 iBT), or IELTS (minimum score 6.5). *Application deadline:* For fall admission, 8/1 for domestic students, 7/1 for international students; for spring admission, 2/1 for domestic students. Applications are processed on a rolling basis. Application fee: $50. Electronic applications accepted. *Expenses:* Tuition: Full-time $31,533; part-time $876 per credit hour. Required fees: $210. *Financial support:* In 2009–10, 13 students received support; research assistantships with partial tuition reimbursements available, teaching assistantships with partial tuition reimbursements available, career-related internships or fieldwork, scholarships/grants, and unspecified assistantships available. Support available to part-time students. Financial award applicants required to submit FAFSA. *Unit head:* Prof. Dianne Bills, Graduate Program Coordinator, 585-475-2700, Fax: 585-475-6584, E-mail: informaticsgrad@rit.edu. *Application contact:* Diane Ellison, Assistant Vice President, Graduate Enrollment Services, 585-475-2229, Fax: 585-475-7164, E-mail: gradinfo@rit.edu.

Rochester Institute of Technology, Graduate Enrollment Services, B. Thomas Golisano College of Computing and Information Sciences, Department of Software Engineering, Rochester, NY 14623-5603. Offers MS. Part-time programs available. *Students:* 12 full-time (1 woman), 4 part-time (2 women); includes 1 minority (Asian American or Pacific Islander), 8 international. Average age 29. 29 applicants, 55% accepted, 9 enrolled. In 2009, 6 master's awarded. *Degree requirements:* For master's, thesis or project. *Entrance requirements:* For master's, GRE, minimum GPA of 3.0. Additional exam requirements/recommendations for international students: Required—TOEFL (minimum score 570 paper-based; 230 computer-based; 88 iBT), or IELTS (minimum score 6.5). *Application deadline:* For fall admission, 2/15 priority date for domestic and international students; for winter admission, 11/1 for domestic and international students; for spring admission, 2/1 for domestic and international students. Applications are processed on a rolling basis. Application fee: $50. Electronic applications accepted. *Expenses:* Tuition: Full-time $31,533; part-time $876 per credit hour. Required fees: $210. *Financial support:* In 2009–10, 15 students received support; research assistantships with partial tuition reimbursements available, teaching assistantships with partial tuition reimbursements available, career-related internships or fieldwork, scholarships/grants, and unspecified assistantships available. Support available to part-time students. Financial award applicants required to submit FAFSA. *Faculty research:* Software engineering education, software architecture and design, architectural styles and design patterns, mathematical foundations of software engineering, object-oriented software development, augmented and virtual reality systems, engineering of real-time and embedded software systems, concurrent systems, distributed systems, data communications and networking, programming environments and tools, computer graphics, computer vision. *Unit head:* Dr. Fernando J. Naveda, Department Chair, 585-475-5461, E-mail: jfn@se.rit.edu. *Application contact:* Diane Ellison, Assistant Vice President, Graduate Enrollment Services, 585-475-2229, Fax: 585-475-7164, E-mail: gradinfo@rit.edu.

Royal Military College of Canada, Division of Graduate Studies and Research, Engineering Division, Department of Electrical and Computer Engineering, Kingston, ON K7K 7B4, Canada. Offers computer engineering (M Eng, PhD); electrical engineering (M Eng, PhD); software engineering (M Eng, PhD). *Degree requirements:* For master's, thesis; for doctorate, comprehensive exam, thesis/dissertation. *Entrance requirements:* For master's, honours degree with second-class standing in the appropriate field; for doctorate, master's degree. Electronic applications accepted.

St. Mary's University, Graduate School, Department of Engineering, Program in Software Engineering, San Antonio, TX 78228-8507. Offers MS. Part-time programs available. *Degree requirements:* For master's, comprehensive exam. *Entrance requirements:* For master's, GRE. Additional exam requirements/recommendations for international students: Required—TOEFL (minimum score 550 paper-based; 213 computer-based; 80 iBT). Electronic applications accepted. *Expenses:* Tuition: Full-time $8004. Required fees: $536. One-time fee: $5 full-time. Full-time tuition and fees vary according to program.

San Francisco State University, Division of Graduate Studies, College of Science and Engineering, Department of Computer Science, San Francisco, CA 94132-1722. Offers computer science (MS); computer science: computing and business (MS); computer science: computing for life sciences (MS); computer science: software and engineering (MS). Part-time programs available.

San Jose State University, Graduate Studies and Research, Charles W. Davidson College of Engineering, Department of Computer Engineering, San Jose, CA 95192-0001. Offers computer engineering (MS); software engineering (MS). *Students:* 357 full-time (112 women), 320 part-time (143 women); includes 102 minority (3 African Americans, 94 Asian Americans or Pacific Islanders, 5 Hispanic Americans), 542 international. Average age 27. 688 applicants, 56% accepted, 185 enrolled. In 2009, 474 master's awarded. *Degree requirements:* For master's, comprehensive exam, thesis. *Entrance requirements:* For master's, GRE General Test. *Application deadline:* For fall admission, 6/29 for domestic students; for spring admission, 11/30 for domestic students. Applications are processed on a rolling basis. Application fee: $59. Electronic applications accepted. *Financial support:* Teaching assistantships, career-related internships or fieldwork, Federal Work-Study, and institutionally sponsored loans available. Support available to part-time students. Financial award application deadline: 5/1; financial award applicants required to submit FAFSA. *Faculty research:* Robotics, database management systems, computer networks. *Unit head:* Dr. Sigurd Meldal, Chair, 408-924-4150. *Application contact:* Dr. Sigurd Meldal, Chair, 408-924-4150.

Santa Clara University, School of Engineering, Department of Computer Science and Engineering, Santa Clara, CA 95053. Offers computer science and engineering (MS, PhD, Engineer); information assurance (Certificate); networking (Certificate); software engineering (MS, Certificate). Part-time and evening/weekend programs available. *Students:* 91 full-time (33 women), 98 part-time (26 women); includes 44 minority (3 African Americans, 39 Asian Americans or Pacific Islanders, 2 Hispanic Americans), 110 international. Average age 29. In 2009, 41 master's awarded. *Degree requirements:* For master's, thesis (for some programs); for doctorate, thesis/dissertation; for other advanced degree, thesis. *Entrance requirements:* For master's, GRE (waiver may be available); for doctorate, GRE, master's degree or equivalent; for other advanced degree, master's degree, published paper. Additional exam requirements/recommendations for international students: Required—TOEFL (minimum score 550 paper-based; 213 computer-based; 79 iBT). *Application deadline:* For fall admission, 8/13 for domestic students, 7/16 for international students; for winter admission, 10/29 for domestic students, 9/24 for international students; for spring admission, 2/25 for domestic students, 1/21 for international students. Applications are processed on a rolling basis. Application fee: $60. *Expenses:* Contact institution. *Financial support:* Research assistantships, teaching assistantships available. Financial award application deadline: 3/2; financial award applicants required to submit FAFSA. *Unit head:* Dr. Alex Zecevic, Chair, 408-554-2394, E-mail: azecevic@scu.edu. *Application contact:* Stacey Tinker, Director of Enrollment Management, 408-554-4748, Fax: 408-554-4323, E-mail: stinker@scu.edu.

Seattle University, College of Science and Engineering, Program in Software Engineering, Seattle, WA 98122-1090. Offers MSE. Part-time and evening/weekend programs available. *Degree requirements:* For master's, thesis. *Entrance requirements:* For master's, GRE General Test, 2 years of related work experience.

Southern Methodist University, Bobby B. Lyle School of Engineering, Department of Computer Science and Engineering, Dallas, TX 75275-0122. Offers computer engineering (MS Cp E, PhD); computer science (MS, PhD); security engineering (MS); software engineering (MS). Part-time and evening/weekend programs available. Postbaccalaureate distance learning degree programs offered (no on-campus study). *Faculty:* 13 full-time (2 women), 18 part-time/adjunct (1 woman). *Students:* 40 full-time (12 women), 167 part-time (22 women); includes 63 minority (18 African Americans, 28 Asian Americans or Pacific Islanders, 17 Hispanic Americans), 41 international. Average age 33. 180 applicants, 73% accepted, 69 enrolled. In 2009, 53 master's, 2 doctorates awarded. Terminal master's awarded for partial completion of doctoral program. *Degree requirements:* For master's, thesis optional; for doctorate, thesis/dissertation, oral and written qualifying exams, oral final exam (PhD). *Entrance requirements:* For master's, GRE General Test, minimum GPA of 3.0 in last 2 years; bachelor's degree in engineering, mathematics, or sciences; for doctorate, preliminary counseling exam (PhD), minimum GPA of 3.0, bachelor's degree in related field, MA (DE). Additional exam requirements/recommendations for international students: Required—TOEFL (minimum score 550 paper-based; 213 computer-based). *Application deadline:* For fall admission, 7/1 priority date for domestic students, 5/15 for international students; for spring admission, 11/15 for domestic students, 9/1 for international students. Applications are processed on a rolling basis. Application fee: $75. *Financial support:* In 2009–10, 20 students received support, including 6 research assistantships with full tuition reimbursements available (averaging $14,400 per year), 14 teaching assistantships with full tuition reimbursements available (averaging $14,400 per year). Financial award application deadline: 3/31; financial award applicants required to submit FAFSA. *Faculty research:* Trusted and high performance network computing, software engineering and management, knowledge engineering and management, computer arithmetic, computer architecture and CAD. Total annual research expenditures: $366,537. *Unit head:* Dr. Suku Nair, Chair, 214-768-2856, Fax: 214-768-3085, E-mail: nair@lyle.smu.edu. *Application contact:* Marc Valerin, Director of Graduate and Executive Admissions, 214-768-3042, E-mail: valerin@engr.smu.edu.

Southern Polytechnic State University, School of Computing and Software Engineering, Department of Computer Science and Software Engineering, Marietta, GA 30060-2896. Offers computer science (MS, Graduate Certificate, Graduate Transition Certificate); software engineering (MSSWE, Graduate Certificate). Part-time and evening/weekend programs available. Postbaccalaureate distance learning degree programs offered (no on-campus study). *Faculty:* 12 full-time (1 woman), 4 part-time/adjunct (0 women). *Students:* 54 full-time (20 women), 65 part-time (21 women); includes 16 African Americans, 13 Asian Americans or Pacific Islanders, 46 international. Average age 32. 72 applicants, 90% accepted, 35 enrolled. In 2009, 32 master's awarded. *Degree requirements:* For master's, thesis optional, capstone (software engineering). *Entrance requirements:* For master's, GRE (recommended). Additional exam requirements/recommendations for international students: Required—TOEFL (minimum score 550 paper-based; 213 computer-based; 79 iBT), IELTS (minimum score 6.5). *Application deadline:* For fall admission, 7/1 priority date for domestic students, 5/1 priority date for international students; for spring admission, 11/1 priority date for domestic students, 9/1 priority date for international students. Applications are processed on a rolling basis. Application fee: $20. Electronic applications accepted. *Expenses:* Tuition, state resident: full-time $2896; part-time $181 per credit hour. Tuition, nonresident: full-time $11,552; part-time $722 per credit hour. Required fees: $1096; $1096 per year. *Financial support:* In 2009–10, 3 research assistantships with full tuition reimbursements (averaging $1,500 per year), 11 teaching assistantships with full and partial tuition reimbursements (averaging $1,500 per year) were awarded; career-related internships or fieldwork, scholarships/grants, unspecified assistantships, and Coops also available. Financial award application deadline: 5/1; financial award applicants required to submit FAFSA. *Faculty research:* Image processing and artificial intelligence information retrieval, distributed computing, telemedicine applications, enterprise architectures, databases, software requirements engineering, software quality and metrics, usability, parallel and distributed computing, information security. *Unit head:* Dr. Venu Dasigi, Chair, 678-915-3571, Fax: 678-915-5511, E-mail: vdasigi@spsu.edu. *Application contact:* Nikki Palamiotis, Director of Graduate Studies, 678-915-4276, Fax: 678-915-7292, E-mail: npalamio@spsu.edu.

Stevens Institute of Technology, Graduate School, Charles V. Schaefer Jr. School of Engineering, Department of Computer Science, Hoboken, NJ 07030. Offers computer graphics (Certificate); computer science (MS, PhD); computer systems (Certificate); database management systems (Certificate); distributed systems (Certificate); elements of computer science (Certificate); enterprise computing (Certificate); enterprise security and information assurance (Certificate); health informatics (Certificate); multimedia experience and management (Certificate); networks and systems administration (Certificate); security and privacy (Certificate); service oriented computing (Certificate); software design (Certificate); theoretical computer science (Certificate). Part-time and evening/weekend programs available. Terminal master's awarded for partial completion of doctoral program. *Degree requirements:* For master's, thesis optional; for doctorate, variable foreign language requirement, comprehensive exam, thesis/dissertation. *Entrance requirements:* For master's and doctorate, GRE, minimum GPA of 3.0. Additional exam requirements/recommendations for international students: Required—TOEFL. Electronic applications accepted. *Expenses:* Tuition: Full-time $9900; part-time $1100 per credit. Required fees: $286 per semester. *Faculty research:* Semantics, reliability theory, programming language, cyber security.

Stevens Institute of Technology, Graduate School, School of Systems and Enterprises, Program in Software Engineering, Hoboken, NJ 07030. Offers MS. *Entrance requirements:* Additional exam requirements/recommendations for international students: Required—TOEFL. *Expenses:* Tuition: Full-time $9900; part-time $1100 per credit. Required fees: $286 per semester.

Stony Brook University, State University of New York, Graduate School, College of Engineering and Applied Sciences, Department of Computer Science, Stony Brook, NY 11794. Offers computer science (MS, PhD); information systems (Certificate); information systems engineering (MS); software engineering (Certificate). *Faculty:* 34 full-time (6 women), 1 part-time/adjunct (0 women). *Students:* 239 full-time (61 women), 33 part-time (9 women); includes 16 minority (1 African American, 14 Asian Americans or Pacific Islanders, 1 Hispanic American), 221 international. Average age 25. 1,139 applicants, 25% accepted. In 2009, 84 master's, 20 doctorates awarded. *Degree requirements:* For master's, thesis or alternative; for doctorate, comprehensive exam, thesis/dissertation. *Entrance requirements:* For master's and doctorate, GRE General Test. Additional exam requirements/recommendations for international students: Required—TOEFL. *Application deadline:* For fall admission, 1/15 for domestic students. Application fee: $60. *Expenses:* Tuition, state resident: full-time $8370; part-time $349 per credit. Tuition, nonresident: full-time $13,250; part-time $552 per credit. Required fees: $933. *Financial support:* In 2009–10, 81 research assistantships, 30 teaching assistantships were awarded; fellowships also available. *Faculty research:* Artificial intelligence, computer architecture, database management systems, VLSI, operating systems. Total annual research expenditures: $5.1 million. *Unit head:* Prof. Arie Kauffman, Chairman, 631-632-8428. *Application contact:* Graduate Director, 631-632-8462, Fax: 631-632-8334.

Stratford University, School of Graduate Studies, Falls Church, VA 22043. Offers accounting (MS); business administration (IMBA, MBA); enterprise business management (MS); entrepreneurial management (MS); information assurance (MS); information systems (MS); software engineering (MS); telecommunications (MS). Part-time and evening/weekend programs available. Postbaccalaureate distance learning degree programs offered (no on-campus study). *Faculty:* 35 full-time (15 women), 115 part-time/adjunct (25 women). *Students:* 944 full-time (430 women), 15 part-time (5 women). Average age 26. 950 applicants, 45% accepted, 415 enrolled. In 2009, 412 master's awarded. *Degree requirements:* For master's, comprehensive exam, capstone project. *Entrance requirements:* For master's, baccalaureate degree. Additional exam requirements/recommendations for international students: Required—TOEFL (minimum score 500 paper-based; 173 computer-based; 61 iBT). *Application deadline:* Applications are processed on a rolling basis. Application fee: $50. Electronic applications accepted. *Expenses:* Tuition: Full-time $10,530; part-time $390 per credit. Tuition and fees vary according to course load. *Financial support:* Federal Work-Study available. Financial award applicants required to submit FAFSA. *Unit head:* Dr. Habib Khan, Chief Academic Officer, 703-821-8570 Ext. 3305, Fax: 703-734-5335, E-mail: hkhan@stratford.edu. *Application contact:* James Ray, Director of Admissions, 703-821-8570 Ext. 3021, Fax: 703-734-5339, E-mail: jray@stratford.edu.

Strayer University, Graduate Studies, Washington, DC 20005-2603. Offers accounting (MS); acquisition (MBA); business administration (MBA); communications technology (MS); educational management (M Ed); finance (MBA); health services administration (MHSA); hospitality and tourism management (MBA); human resource management (MBA); information systems (MS), including computer security management, decision support system management, enterprise resource management, network management, software engineering management, systems development management; management (MBA); management information systems (MS); marketing (MBA); professional accounting (MS), including accounting information systems, controllership, taxation; public administration (MPA); supply chain management (MBA); technology in education (M Ed). Programs also offered at campus locations in Birmingham, AL; Chamblee, GA; Cobb County, GA; Morrow, GA; White Marsh, MD; Charleston, SC; Columbia, SC; Greensboro, NC; Greenville, SC; Lexington, KY; Louisville, KY; Nashville, TN; North Raleigh, NC; Washington, DC. Part-time and evening/weekend programs available. Postbaccalaureate distance learning degree programs offered (minimal on-campus study). *Degree requirements:* For master's, thesis. *Entrance requirements:* For master's, GMAT, GRE General Test, bachelor's degree from an accredited college or university, minimum undergraduate GPA of 2.75. Electronic applications accepted.

Texas State University–San Marcos, Graduate School, College of Science, Department of Computer Science, Program in Software Engineering, San Marcos, TX 78666. Offers MS. *Faculty:* 7 full-time (3 women). *Students:* 12 full-time (5 women), 10 part-time (1 woman); includes 10 minority (3 African Americans, 5 Asian Americans or Pacific Islanders, 2 Hispanic Americans), 4 international. Average age 30. 13 applicants, 100% accepted, 6 enrolled. In 2009, 3 master's awarded. *Degree requirements:* For master's, comprehensive exam, thesis (for some programs). *Entrance requirements:* For master's, GRE General Test, minimum GPA of 2.75 in last 60 hours of course work. Additional exam requirements/recommendations for international students: Required—TOEFL (minimum score 550 paper-based; 213 computer-based). *Application deadline:* For fall admission, 6/15 priority date for domestic students, 6/1 priority date for international students; for spring admission, 10/15 priority date for domestic students, 10/1 priority date for international students. Applications are processed on a rolling basis. Application fee: $40 ($90 for international students). Electronic applications accepted. *Expenses:* Tuition, state resident: full-time $5784; part-time $241 per credit hour. Tuition, nonresident: part-time $551 per credit hour. Required fees: $1728; $48 per credit hour. $306. Tuition and fees vary according to course load. *Financial support:* In 2009–10, 13 students received support, including 4 research assistantships (averaging $5,974 per year), 4 teaching assistantships (averaging $5,245 per year). Financial award application deadline: 4/1; financial award applicants required to submit FAFSA. *Unit head:* Dr. Khosrow Kaikhah, Head, 512-245-3409, Fax: 512-245-8750, E-mail: kk02@txstate.edu. *Application contact:* Dr. Khosrow Kaikhah, Head, 512-245-3409, Fax: 512-245-8750, E-mail: kk02@txstate.edu.

Texas Tech University, Graduate School, College of Engineering, Department of Computer Science, Lubbock, TX 79409. Offers computer science (MS, PhD); software engineering (MS). Part-time programs available. *Faculty:* 12 full-time (3 women). *Students:* 100 full-time (25 women), 35 part-time (6 women); includes 2 minority (both Hispanic Americans), 110 international. Average age 26. 320 applicants, 48% accepted, 37 enrolled. In 2009, 29 master's, 2 doctorates awarded. *Degree requirements:* For master's, thesis or alternative; for doctorate, thesis/dissertation. *Entrance requirements:* For master's and doctorate, GRE General Test, minimum GPA of 3.0. Additional exam requirements/recommendations for international students: Required—TOEFL (minimum score 550 paper-based; 213 computer-based). *Application deadline:* For fall admission, 3/1 priority date for international students; for spring admission, 11/1 priority date for international students. Applications are processed on a rolling basis. Application fee: $50 ($75 for international students). Electronic applications accepted. *Expenses:* Tuition, state resident: full-time $5100; part-time $213 per credit hour. Tuition, nonresident: full-time $11,748; part-time $490 per credit hour. Required fees: $2298; $50 per credit hour. $555 per semester. *Financial support:* In 2009–10, 24 research assistantships with partial tuition reimbursements (averaging $18,542 per year), 17 teaching assistantships with partial tuition reimbursements (averaging $12,567 per year) were awarded; Federal Work-Study and institutionally sponsored loans also available. Support available to part-time students. Financial award application deadline: 4/15; financial award applicants required to submit FAFSA. *Faculty research:* Artificial intelligence, software engineering and languages, high performance computing, logic programming, image processing. Total annual research expenditures: $683,303. *Unit head:* Dr. Joseph Urban, Chair, 806-742-3527, Fax: 806-742-3519, E-mail: joseph.urban@ttu.edu. *Application contact:* Dr. Susan Mengel, Graduate Advisor, 806-742-3527, Fax: 806-742-3519, E-mail: graduate_programs@cs.ttu.edu.

Towson University, College of Graduate Studies and Research, Program in Applied Information Technology, Towson, MD 21252-0001. Offers applied information technology (D Sc); database management (Certificate); information security and assurance (Certificate); information systems management (Certificate); Internet application development (Certificate); networking technologies (Certificate); software engineering (Certificate). *Entrance requirements:* For doctorate, minimum GPA 3.0, letter of intent, resumé, 2 letters of recommendation, personal assessment forms, official transcripts. Additional exam requirements/recommendations for international students: Required—TOEFL (minimum score 550 paper-based). Electronic applications accepted.

Towson University, College of Graduate Studies and Research, Program in Software Engineering, Towson, MD 21252-0001. Offers Certificate. Part-time and evening/weekend programs available. Electronic applications accepted.

Software Engineering

Université du Québec en Outaouais, Graduate Programs, Department of Language Studies, Gatineau, QC J8X 3X7, Canada. Offers localisation (DESS).

Université Laval, Faculty of Sciences and Engineering, Program in Software Engineering, Québec, QC G1K 7P4, Canada. Offers Diploma. Part-time programs available. *Entrance requirements:* For degree, knowledge of French. Electronic applications accepted.

The University of Alabama in Huntsville, School of Graduate Studies, College of Engineering, Department of Electrical and Computer Engineering, Huntsville, AL 35899. Offers computer engineering (MSE, PhD); electrical engineering (MSE, PhD); optical science and engineering (PhD); optics and photonics (MSE); software engineering (MSSE). Part-time and evening/weekend programs available. *Faculty:* 22 full-time (2 women), 3 part-time/adjunct (0 women). *Students:* 42 full-time (10 women), 147 part-time (18 women); includes 16 minority (7 African Americans, 6 Asian Americans or Pacific Islanders, 3 Hispanic Americans), 28 international. Average age 31. 205 applicants, 53% accepted, 58 enrolled. In 2009, 53 master's, 4 doctorates awarded. *Degree requirements:* For master's, comprehensive exam, thesis or alternative, oral and written exams; for doctorate, comprehensive exam, thesis/dissertation, oral and written exams. *Entrance requirements:* For master's, GRE General Test, appropriate bachelor's degree, minimum GPA of 3.0; for doctorate, GRE General Test, minimum GPA of 3.0. Additional exam requirements/recommendations for international students: Required—TOEFL (minimum score 500 paper-based; 173 computer-based; 62 iBT). *Application deadline:* For fall admission, 7/15 for domestic students, 4/1 for international students; for spring admission, 11/30 for domestic students, 9/1 for international students. Applications are processed on a rolling basis. Application fee: $40 ($50 for international students). Electronic applications accepted. *Expenses:* Tuition, state resident: part-time $355.75 per credit hour. Tuition, nonresident: part-time $847.10 per credit hour. Required fees: $210.80 per semester. Tuition and fees vary according to course load and program. *Financial support:* In 2009–10, 28 students received support, including 11 research assistantships with full and partial tuition reimbursements available (averaging $11,113 per year), 16 teaching assistantships with full and partial tuition reimbursements available (averaging $10,479 per year); career-related internships or fieldwork, Federal Work-Study, institutionally sponsored loans, scholarships/grants, health care benefits, tuition waivers, and unspecified assistantships also available. Support available to part-time students. Financial award application deadline: 4/1; financial award applicants required to submit FAFSA. *Faculty research:* Optical signal processing, electromagnetics, photonics, nonlinear waves, computer architecture. Total annual research expenditures: $3.4 million. *Unit head:* Dr. Reza Adhami, Chair, 256-824-6316, Fax: 256-824-6803, E-mail: adhami@ece.uah.edu. *Application contact:* Kathy Biggs, Graduate Studies Admissions Manager, 256-824-6199, Fax: 256-824-6405, E-mail: deangrad@uah.edu.

The University of Alabama in Huntsville, School of Graduate Studies, College of Science, Department of Computer Science, Huntsville, AL 35899. Offers computer science (MS, PhD); software engineering (MSSE, Certificate). Part-time and evening/weekend programs available. *Faculty:* 11 full-time (3 women), 2 part-time/adjunct (1 woman). *Students:* 40 full-time (10 women), 73 part-time (18 women); includes 11 minority (5 African Americans, 6 Asian Americans or Pacific Islanders), 46 international. Average age 30. 142 applicants, 54% accepted, 38 enrolled. In 2009, 54 master's, 6 doctorates, 2 other advanced degrees awarded. *Degree requirements:* For master's, comprehensive exam, thesis or alternative, oral and written exams; for doctorate, comprehensive exam, thesis/dissertation, oral and written exams. *Entrance requirements:* For master's, doctorate, and Certificate, GRE General Test, minimum GPA of 3.0. Additional exam requirements/recommendations for international students: Required—TOEFL (minimum score 550 paper-based; 213 computer-based; 62 iBT). *Application deadline:* For fall admission, 7/15 for domestic students, 4/1 for international students; for spring admission, 11/30 for domestic students, 9/1 for international students. Applications are processed on a rolling basis. Application fee: $40 ($50 for international students). Electronic applications accepted. *Expenses:* Tuition, state resident: part-time $355.75 per credit hour. Tuition, nonresident: part-time $847.10 per credit hour. Required fees: $210.80 per semester. Tuition and fees vary according to course load and program. *Financial support:* In 2009–10, 34 students received support, including 10 research assistantships with full and partial tuition reimbursements available (averaging $10,321 per year), 24 teaching assistantships with full and partial tuition reimbursements available (averaging $9,073 per year); career-related internships or fieldwork, Federal Work-Study, institutionally sponsored loans, scholarships/grants, health care benefits, and unspecified assistantships also available. Support available to part-time students. Financial award application deadline: 4/1; financial award applicants required to submit FAFSA. *Faculty research:* Software engineering and systems, computer graphics and visualization, computer networking, artificial intelligence, modeling and simulation. Total annual research expenditures: $4.3 million. *Unit head:* Dr. Heggere Ranganath, Chair, 256-824-6088, Fax: 256-824-6239, E-mail: ranganat@uah.edu. *Application contact:* Kathy Biggs, Graduate Studies Admissions Manager, 256-824-6199, Fax: 256-824-6405, E-mail: deangrad@uah.edu.

University of Alaska Fairbanks, College of Natural Sciences and Mathematics, Department of Computer Science, Fairbanks, AK 99775-6670. Offers computer science (MS); software engineering (MSE). Part-time programs available. *Faculty:* 6 full-time (1 woman), 1 part-time/adjunct (0 women). *Students:* 7 full-time (1 woman), 5 part-time (2 women); includes 1 minority (Asian American or Pacific Islander). Average age 38. 15 applicants, 40% accepted, 6 enrolled. In 2009, 2 master's awarded. *Degree requirements:* For master's, comprehensive exam, thesis or alternative. *Entrance requirements:* For master's, GRE General Test. Additional exam requirements/recommendations for international students: Required—TOEFL (minimum score 550 paper-based; 213 computer-based; 80 iBT). *Application deadline:* For fall admission, 6/1 for domestic students, 3/1 for international students; for spring admission, 10/15 for domestic students, 9/1 for international students. Application fee: $60. *Expenses:* Tuition, state resident: full-time $7584; part-time $316 per credit. Tuition, nonresident: full-time $15,504; part-time $646 per credit. Required fees: $23 per credit. $135 per semester. Tuition and fees vary according to course level, course load and reciprocity agreements. *Financial support:* In 2009–10, 1 research assistantship (averaging $11,880 per year), 1 teaching assistantship (averaging $15,284 per year) were awarded; fellowships, career-related internships or fieldwork, Federal Work-Study, scholarships/grants, health care benefits, and unspecified assistantships also available. Support available to part-time students. Financial award application deadline: 7/1; financial award applicants required to submit FAFSA. *Faculty research:* Interaction with a virtual reality environment, synthetic aperture radar interferometry software. *Unit head:* Dr. Kara Nance, Department Chair, 907-474-2777, Fax: 907-474-5030, E-mail: fycsci@uaf.edu. *Application contact:* Dr. Kara Nance, Department Chair, 907-474-2777, Fax: 907-474-5030, E-mail: fycsci@uaf.edu.

The University of British Columbia, Faculty of Applied Science, Program in Software Systems, Vancouver, BC V6T 1Z1, Canada. Offers MSS. *Degree requirements:* For master's, internship. *Entrance requirements:* For master's, bachelor's degree in science, engineering, business or technology (non-computer science). Additional exam requirements/recommendations for international students: Required—TOEFL (minimum score 600 paper-based; 250 computer-based; 100 iBT), IELTS (minimum score 6.5). Electronic applications accepted. *Expenses:* Contact institution.

University of Calgary, Faculty of Graduate Studies, Faculty of Science, Department of Computer Science, Calgary, AB T2N 1N4, Canada. Offers computer science (M Sc, PhD); software engineering (M Sc). Part-time programs available. *Degree requirements:* For master's, comprehensive exam (for some programs), thesis (for some programs); for doctorate, thesis/dissertation, oral and written departmental exam. *Entrance requirements:* For master's, bachelor's degree in computer science; for doctorate, M Sc in computer science. Additional exam requirements/recommendations for international students: Required—TOEFL (minimum score 600 paper-based; 250 computer-based), GRE General Test recommended; Recommended—TWE. Electronic applications accepted. *Faculty research:* Visual and interactive computing, quantum computing and cryptography, evolutionary software engineering, distributed systems and algorithms.

University of Colorado at Colorado Springs, Graduate School, College of Engineering and Applied Science, Department of Mechanical and Aerospace Engineering, Colorado Springs, CO 80933-7150. Offers engineering management (ME); information operations (ME); manufacturing (ME); mechanical engineering (MS); software engineering (ME); space operations (ME); space systems (MS). Part-time and evening/weekend programs available. *Faculty:* 10 full-time (2 women). *Students:* 14 full-time (4 women), 13 part-time (2 women); includes 3 minority (2 Asian Americans or Pacific Islanders, 1 Hispanic American). Average age 30. 39 applicants, 82% accepted, 16 enrolled. In 2009, 6 master's awarded. *Degree requirements:* For master's, thesis optional. *Entrance requirements:* For master's, GRE General Test, bachelor's degree in engineering or related degree, minimum GPA of 3.0. Additional exam requirements/recommendations for international students: Required—TOEFL. *Application deadline:* For fall admission, 5/1 for domestic students; for spring admission, 10/1 for domestic students. Applications are processed on a rolling basis. Application fee: $60 ($75 for international students). *Expenses:* Tuition, state resident: full-time $8922; part-time $639 per credit hour. Tuition, nonresident: full-time $19,372; part-time $1154 per credit hour. Tuition and fees vary according to course level, course load, degree level, program, reciprocity agreements and student level. *Financial support:* Federal Work-Study and scholarships/grants available. Support available to part-time students. Financial award application deadline: 3/1; financial award applicants required to submit FAFSA. *Faculty research:* Neural networks, artificial intelligence, robust control, space operations, space propulsion. *Unit head:* Dr. T. S. Kalkur, Chair, 719-255-3147, Fax: 719-255-3042, E-mail: kalkur@eas.uccs.edu. *Application contact:* Siew Nylund, Academic Adviser, 719-255-3243, Fax: 719-255-3589, E-mail: snylund@eas.uccs.edu.

University of Connecticut, Graduate School, School of Engineering, Department of Computer Science and Engineering, Storrs, CT 06269. Offers computer science (MS, PhD), including artificial intelligence, computer architecture, computer science, operating systems, robotics, software engineering. *Faculty:* 27 full-time (4 women). *Students:* 86 full-time (16 women), 20 part-time (0 women); includes 6 minority (3 African Americans, 1 Asian American or Pacific Islander, 2 Hispanic Americans), 64 international. Average age 30. 154 applicants, 16% accepted, 14 enrolled. In 2009, 17 master's, 6 doctorates awarded. Terminal master's awarded for partial completion of doctoral program. *Degree requirements:* For master's, comprehensive exam, thesis or alternative; for doctorate, thesis/dissertation. *Entrance requirements:* For master's and doctorate, GRE General Test. Additional exam requirements/recommendations for international students: Required—TOEFL (minimum score 550 paper-based; 213 computer-based). *Application deadline:* For fall admission, 2/1 priority date for domestic and international students; for spring admission, 11/1 for domestic students, 10/1 for international students. Applications are processed on a rolling basis. Application fee: $55. Electronic applications accepted. *Expenses:* Tuition, state resident: full-time $4725; part-time $525 per credit. Tuition, nonresident: full-time $12,267; part-time $1363 per credit. Required fees: $346 per semester. Tuition and fees vary according to course load. *Financial support:* In 2009–10, 59 research assistantships with full tuition reimbursements, 17 teaching assistantships with full tuition reimbursements were awarded; fellowships, Federal Work-Study, scholarships/grants, health care benefits, and unspecified assistantships also available. Financial award application deadline: 2/1; financial award applicants required to submit FAFSA. *Unit head:* Reda Ammar, Head, 860-486-5285, Fax: 860-486-4817, E-mail: reda@engr.uconn.edu. *Application contact:* Steven Demurjian, Chairperson, 860-486-4818, E-mail: steven.demurjian@uconn.edu.

University of Detroit Mercy, College of Engineering and Science, Department of Mathematics and Computer Science, Program in Computer Science, Detroit, MI 48221. Offers computer systems applications (MSCS); software engineering (MSCS). Evening/weekend programs available. *Entrance requirements:* For master's, minimum GPA of 3.0.

University of Houston–Clear Lake, School of Science and Computer Engineering, Program in Software Engineering, Houston, TX 77058-1098. Offers MS. Part-time and evening/weekend programs available. *Entrance requirements:* For master's, GRE General Test. Additional exam requirements/recommendations for international students: Required—TOEFL (minimum score 550 paper-based; 213 computer-based).

University of Management and Technology, Program in Computer Science and Information Technology, Arlington, VA 22209. Offers computer science (MS); information technology (AC); information technology project management (MS); management information systems (MS); project management (AC); software engineering (MS). Part-time and evening/weekend programs available. Postbaccalaureate distance learning degree programs offered (no on-campus study). *Entrance requirements:* For master's, 3 recommendations, resume. Additional exam requirements/recommendations for international students: Required—TOEFL (minimum score 550 paper-based; 213 computer-based). Electronic applications accepted.

University of Massachusetts Dartmouth, Graduate School, College of Engineering, Program in Computer Science, North Dartmouth, MA 02747-2300. Offers computer networks and distributed systems (Postbaccalaureate Certificate); computer science (MS); computer systems (Postbaccalaureate Certificate); software development and design (Postbaccalaureate Certificate). Part-time programs available. Postbaccalaureate distance learning degree programs offered. *Faculty:* 10 full-time (2 women), 1 part-time/adjunct (0 women). *Students:* 29 full-time (7 women), 36 part-time (8 women), 48 international. Average age 25. 81 applicants, 89% accepted, 20 enrolled. In 2009, 25 master's awarded. *Degree requirements:* For master's, thesis or alternative. *Entrance requirements:* For master's, GRE General Test, 3 letters of recommendation. Additional exam requirements/recommendations for international students: Required—TOEFL (minimum score 500 paper-based). *Application deadline:* For fall admission, 6/30 priority date for domestic students, 4/30 priority date for international students; for spring admission, 11/15 priority date for domestic students, 9/15 priority date for international students. Applications are processed on a rolling basis. Application fee: $35 ($55 for international students). Electronic applications accepted. *Expenses:* Tuition, state resident: full-time $2071; part-time $86.29 per credit. Tuition, nonresident: full-time $8099; part-time $337.46 per credit. Required fees: $9446. Tuition and fees vary according to class time, course load and reciprocity agreements. *Financial support:* In 2009–10, 5 research assistantships with full tuition reimbursements (averaging $9,246 per year), 6 teaching assistantships with full tuition reimbursements (averaging $4,896 per year) were awarded; Federal Work-Study and unspecified assistantships also available. Support available to part-time students. Financial award application deadline: 3/1; financial award applicants required to submit FAFSA. *Faculty research:* Tracking of mesoscale features, modeling and analysis of workflow management, brain modeling, software engineering, multi-agent systems. Total annual research expenditures: $518,000. *Unit head:* Dr. Jan Bergandy, Director, 508-999-8293, Fax: 508-999-9144, E-mail: jbergandy@umassd.edu. *Application contact:* Elan Turcotte-Shamski, Graduate Admissions Officer, 508-999-8604, Fax: 508-999-8183, E-mail: graduate@umassd.edu.

University of Michigan–Dearborn, College of Engineering and Computer Science, Department of Electrical and Computer Engineering, Program in Software Engineering, Dearborn, MI 48128-1491. Offers MS. Part-time and evening/weekend programs available. *Faculty:* 14 full-time (0 women), 2 part-time/adjunct (1 woman). *Students:* 1 full-time (0 women), 29 part-time (5 women); includes 8 minority (3 African Americans, 4 Asian Americans or Pacific Islanders, 1 Hispanic American), 2 international. Average age 34. 19 applicants, 79% accepted, 12 enrolled. In 2009, 8 master's awarded. *Degree requirements:* For master's, thesis optional. *Entrance requirements:* For master's, bachelor's degree in mathematics, computer science or engineering, minimum GPA of 3.0. Additional exam requirements/recommendations for international students: Required—TOEFL (minimum score 560 paper-based; 220 computer-based; 84 iBT). *Application deadline:* For fall admission, 6/15 for domestic students, 4/1 for international students; for winter admission, 10/15 for domestic students, 8/1 for international students; for spring admission, 2/15 for domestic students, 12/1 for international students. Application fee: $60 ($75 for international students). *Expenses:* Tuition, area resident: Part-time $504.10 per credit hour. Tuition, state resident: part-time $504.10 per credit hour. Tuition, nonresident: part-time $957.90 per credit hour. *Financial support:* Research assistantships with full tuition reimbursements, career-related internships or fieldwork available. Financial award application deadline: 4/1; financial award applicants required to submit FAFSA. *Faculty* *research:* Information systems, geometric modeling, networks, databases. Total annual research expenditures: $54,056. *Unit head:* Dr. YiLu Murphey, Chair, 313-593-5028, Fax: 313-583-6336, E-mail: yilu@umich.edu. *Application contact:* Sandra Krzyskowski.

University of Missouri–Kansas City, School of Computing and Engineering, Kansas City, MO 64110-2499. Offers civil engineering (MS); computer and electrical engineering (PhD); computer science (MS), including bioinformatics, software engineering, telecommunications networking; computer science and informatics (PhD); computing (PhD); electrical engineering (MS); engineering (PhD); mechanical engineering (MS); telecommunications (PhD). PhD (interdisciplinary) offered through the School of Graduate Studies. Part-time programs available. *Faculty:* 40 full-time (5 women), 28 part-time/adjunct (0 women). *Students:* 230 full-time (46 women), 158 part-time (31 women); includes 20 minority (5 African Americans, 12 Asian Americans or Pacific Islanders, 3 Hispanic Americans), 313 international. Average age 24. 484 applicants, 64% accepted, 106 enrolled. In 2009, 144 master's awarded. *Degree requirements:* For doctorate, thesis/dissertation. *Entrance requirements:* For master's, GRE General Test, minimum GPA of 3.0, 3 letters of recommendations from professors; for doctorate, GRE General Test, minimum GPA of 3.5. Additional exam requirements/recommendations for international students: Required—TOEFL (minimum score 550 paper-based; 213 computer-based; 80 iBT). *Application deadline:* For fall admission, 1/15 priority date for domestic students, 1/15 for international students. Applications are processed on a rolling basis. Application fee: $45 ($50 for international students). *Expenses:* Tuition, state resident: full-time $5378; part-time $299 per credit hour. Tuition, nonresident: full-time $13,881; part-time $771 per credit hour. Required fees: $641; $71 per credit hour. Tuition and fees vary according to course load and program. *Financial support:* In 2009–10, 29 research assistantships with partial tuition reimbursements (averaging $15,040 per year), 10 teaching assistantships with partial tuition reimbursements (averaging $12,118 per year) were awarded; career-related internships or fieldwork, Federal Work-Study, scholarships/grants, tuition waivers (partial), and unspecified assistantships also available. Support available to part-time students. Financial award application deadline: 3/1; financial award applicants required to submit FAFSA. *Faculty research:* Algorithms, bioinformatics and medical informatics, biomechanics/biomaterials, civil engineering materials, networking and telecommunications, thermal science. Total annual research expenditures: $1.4 million. *Unit head:* Dr. Kevin Z. Truman, Dean, 816-235-2399, Fax: 816-235-5159. *Application contact:* Dr. Kevin Z. Truman, Dean, 816-235-2399, Fax: 816-235-5159.

University of New Haven, Graduate School, Tagliatela College of Engineering, Program in Computer and Information Science, West Haven, CT 06516-1916. Offers computer science (MS, Certificate), including advanced applications (MS), computer applications (Certificate), computer programming (Certificate), computer systems (MS), computing (Certificate), database and information systems (MS), network administration (Certificate), network systems (MS), software engineering and development (MS). Part-time and evening/weekend programs available. *Faculty:* 9 full-time (2 women), 5 part-time/adjunct (0 women). *Students:* 21 full-time (8 women), 32 part-time (8 women); includes 5 minority (2 African Americans, 1 Asian American or Pacific Islander, 2 Hispanic Americans), 26 international. Average age 30. 163 applicants, 88% accepted, 18 enrolled. In 2009, 24 master's awarded. *Degree requirements:* For master's, thesis or alternative. *Entrance requirements:* Additional exam requirements/recommendations for international students: Required—TOEFL (minimum score 520 paper-based; 190 computer-based; 70 iBT); Recommended—IELTS (minimum score 5.5). *Application deadline:* For fall admission, 5/31 for international students; for winter admission, 10/15 for international students; for spring admission, 1/15 for international students. Applications are processed on a rolling basis. Application fee: $50. Electronic applications accepted. *Expenses:* Tuition: Part-time $700 per credit. Required fees: $45 per term. One-time fee: $390 part-time. *Financial support:* Research assistantships with partial tuition reimbursements, teaching assistantships with partial tuition reimbursements, career-related internships or fieldwork, Federal Work-Study, scholarships/grants, tuition waivers, and unspecified assistantships available. Support available to part-time students. Financial award applicants required to submit FAFSA. *Unit head:* Dr. Tahany Fergany, Coordinator, 203-932-7067. *Application contact:* Eloise Gormley, Director of Graduate Admissions, 203-932-7449, Fax: 203-932-7137, E-mail: gradinfo@newhaven.edu.

University of St. Thomas, Graduate Studies, Graduate Programs in Software, Saint Paul, MN 55105. Offers advanced studies in business analysis (Certificate); computer security (Certificate); information systems (Certificate); software design and development (Certificate); software engineering (MS); software management (MS); software systems (MSS); MS/MBA. Part-time and evening/weekend programs available. *Degree requirements:* For master's, thesis optional. *Entrance requirements:* Additional exam requirements/recommendations for international students: Required—TOEFL. *Application deadline:* For fall admission, 8/1 priority date for domestic students, 5/1 priority date for international students; for spring admission, 1/1 priority date for domestic students, 10/1 priority date for international students. Applications are processed on a rolling basis. Application fee: $30. *Expenses:* Contact institution. *Financial support:* Federal Work-Study, institutionally sponsored loans, and scholarships/grants available. Financial award application deadline: 4/1. *Faculty research:* Data mining, distributed databases, bioinformatics, computer security. *Unit head:* Dr. Bhabani Misra, Director, 651-962-5508, Fax: 651-962-5543, E-mail: bsmisra@stthomas.edu. *Application contact:* Douglas J. Stubeda, Assistant Director, 651-962-5503, Fax: 651-962-5543, E-mail: djstubeda@stthomas.edu.

The University of Scranton, College of Graduate and Continuing Education, Program in Software Engineering, Scranton, PA 18510. Offers MS. Part-time and evening/weekend programs available. *Faculty:* 8 full-time (0 women). *Students:* 11 full-time (3 women), 8 part-time (1 woman), 4 international. Average age 27. 29 applicants, 72% accepted. In 2009, 5 master's awarded. *Degree requirements:* For master's, thesis, capstone experience. *Entrance requirements:* For master's, GMAT or GRE, minimum GPA of 3.0. Additional exam requirements/recommendations for international students: Required—TOEFL (minimum score 500 paper-based; 173 computer-based), IELTS (minimum score 5.5). *Application deadline:* For fall admission, 3/1 priority date for domestic students. Applications are processed on a rolling basis. Application fee: $0. *Financial support:* In 2009–10, 6 students received support, including 6 teaching assistantships with full tuition reimbursements available (averaging $8,800 per year); fellowships, career-related internships or fieldwork, Federal Work-Study, and unspecified assistantships also available. Support available to part-time students. Financial award application deadline: 3/1. *Faculty research:* Database, parallel and distributed systems, computer network, real time systems. *Unit head:* Dr. Yaodong Bi, Director, 570-941-6108, Fax: 570-941-4250, E-mail: biy1@scranton.edu. *Application contact:* Joseph M. Roback, Director of Admissions, 570-941-4385, Fax: 570-941-5928, E-mail: robackj2@scranton.edu.

University of South Carolina, The Graduate School, College of Engineering and Computing, Department of Computer Science and Engineering, Columbia, SC 29208. Offers computer science and engineering (ME, MS, PhD); software engineering (MS). Part-time and evening/weekend programs available. Postbaccalaureate distance learning degree programs offered (minimal on-campus study). *Degree requirements:* For master's, comprehensive exam, thesis (for some programs); for doctorate, comprehensive exam, thesis/dissertation. *Entrance requirements:* For master's and doctorate, GRE General Test. Additional exam requirements/recommendations for international students: Required—TOEFL (minimum score 570 paper-based; 230 computer-based). Electronic applications accepted. *Faculty research:* Computer security, computer vision, artificial intelligence, multiagent systems, bioinformatics.

University of Southern California, Graduate School, Viterbi School of Engineering, Department of Computer Science, Los Angeles, CA 90089. Offers computer networks (MS); computer science (MS, PhD); computer security (MS); game development (MS); high performance computing and simulations (MS); human language technology (MS); intelligent robotics (MS); multimedia and creative technologies (MS); software engineering (MS). Part-time programs available. Postbaccalaureate distance learning degree programs offered (no on-campus study). *Faculty:* 26 full-time (2 women), 56 part-time/adjunct (7 women). *Students:* 711 full-time (148 women), 304 part-time (55 women); includes 76 minority (5 African Americans, 59 Asian Americans or Pacific Islanders, 12 Hispanic Americans), 816 international. 2,017 applicants, 39% accepted, 382 enrolled. In 2009, 332 master's, 32 doctorates awarded. Terminal master's awarded for partial completion of doctoral program. *Degree requirements:* For doctorate, comprehensive exam, thesis/dissertation. *Entrance requirements:* For master's, GRE General Test; for doctorate, General GRE. *Application deadline:* For fall admission, 3/1 priority date for domestic and international students; for spring admission, 10/1 priority date for domestic and international students. Applications are processed on a rolling basis. Application fee: $85. Electronic applications accepted. *Expenses:* Tuition: Full-time $25,980; part-time $1315 per unit. Required fees: $554. One-time fee: $35 full-time. Full-time tuition and fees vary according to degree level and program. *Financial support:* In 2009–10, fellowships with full tuition reimbursements (averaging $30,000 per year), research assistantships with full tuition reimbursements (averaging $19,250 per year), teaching assistantships with full tuition reimbursements (averaging $19,250 per year) were awarded; career-related internships or fieldwork, scholarships/grants, health care benefits, and unspecified assistantships also available. Financial award application deadline: 12/1; financial award applicants required to submit CSS PROFILE or FAFSA. *Faculty research:* Databases, computer graphics and computer vision, software engineering, networks and security, robotics, multimedia and virtual reality. Total annual research expenditures: $10 million. *Unit head:* Dr. Shanghua Teng, Seeley G. Mudd Professor of Engineering and Department Chair, 213-740-4498, E-mail: shanghua@ usc.edu. *Application contact:* Steve Schrader, Director of Student Affairs, 213-740-4779, E-mail: steve.schrader@usc.edu.

The University of Texas at Arlington, Graduate School, College of Engineering, Department of Computer Science and Engineering, Arlington, TX 76019. Offers M Engr, M Sw En, MS, PhD. Part-time and evening/weekend programs available. Postbaccalaureate distance learning degree programs offered (minimal on-campus study). *Faculty:* 28 full-time (2 women). *Students:* 167 full-time (42 women), 93 part-time (23 women); includes 11 minority (4 African Americans, 6 Asian Americans or Pacific Islanders, 1 Hispanic American), 211 international. 524 applicants, 98% accepted, 59 enrolled. In 2009, 120 master's, 11 doctorates awarded. Terminal master's awarded for partial completion of doctoral program. *Degree requirements:* For master's, comprehensive exam (for some programs), thesis optional; for doctorate, comprehensive exam, thesis/dissertation. *Entrance requirements:* For master's, GRE General Test, minimum GPA of 3.0 (3.2 in computer science-related classes); for doctorate, GRE General Test, minimum GPA of 3.5. Additional exam requirements/recommendations for international students: Required—TOEFL (minimum score 550 paper-based; 230 computer-based; 92 iBT). *Application deadline:* For fall admission, 6/6 for domestic students, 4/4 for international students; for spring admission, 10/17 for domestic students, 9/5 for international students. Applications are processed on a rolling basis. Application fee: $35 ($50 for international students). *Financial support:* In 2009–10, 20 fellowships (averaging $1,000 per year), research assistantships (averaging $13,500 per year), 75 teaching assistantships (averaging $13,500 per year) were awarded; career-related internships or fieldwork and scholarships/grants also available. Financial award application deadline: 6/1; financial award applicants required to submit FAFSA. *Faculty research:* Algorithms, homeland security, mobile pervasive computing, high performance computing bioinformation. *Unit head:* Dr. Fillia Makedon, Chairman, 817-272-3680. *Application contact:* Dr. Bahram Khalili, Graduate Advisor, 817-272-5407, Fax: 817-272-3784, E-mail: khalili@uta.edu.

The University of Texas at Dallas, Erik Jonsson School of Engineering and Computer Science, Program in Computer Science, Richardson, TX 75080. Offers computer science (MS, PhD); software engineering (MS, PhD). Part-time and evening/weekend programs available. *Faculty:* 43 full-time (6 women), 2 part-time/adjunct (1 woman). *Students:* 424 full-time (117 women), 187 part-time (39 women); includes 47 minority (3 African Americans, 1 American Indian/Alaska Native, 36 Asian Americans or Pacific Islanders, 7 Hispanic Americans), 454 international. Average age 27. 863 applicants, 52% accepted, 135 enrolled. In 2009, 218 master's, 15 doctorates awarded. *Degree requirements:* For master's, thesis optional; for doctorate, thesis/dissertation. *Entrance requirements:* For master's, GRE General Test, minimum GPA of 3.0 in undergraduate course work, 3.3 in quantitative course work; for doctorate, GRE General Test, minimum GPA of 3.5. Additional exam requirements/recommendations for international students: Required—TOEFL (minimum score 550 paper-based; 213 computer-based). *Application deadline:* For fall admission, 7/15 for domestic students, 5/1 priority date for international students; for spring admission, 11/15 for domestic students, 9/1 priority date for international students. Applications are processed on a rolling basis. Application fee: $50 ($100 for international students). Electronic applications accepted. *Expenses:* Tuition, state resident: full-time $11,068; part-time $461 per credit hour. Tuition, nonresident: full-time $21,178; part-time $882 per credit hour. Tuition and fees vary according to course load. *Financial support:* In 2009–10, 11 fellowships with full tuition reimbursements (averaging $18,900 per year), 67 research assistantships with full tuition reimbursements (averaging $18,406 per year), 42 teaching assistantships with full tuition reimbursements (averaging $17,869 per year) were awarded; career-related internships or fieldwork, Federal Work-Study, institutionally sponsored loans, and scholarships/grants also available. Support available to part-time students. Financial award application deadline: 4/30; financial award applicants required to submit FAFSA. *Faculty research:* Telecommunication networks, parallel processing, nanotechnology, artificial intelligence, software engineering. *Unit head:* Dr. Dung T. Huynh, Head, 972-883-2169, Fax: 972-883-2349, E-mail: huynh@utdallas.edu. *Application contact:* Eric Moden, Evaluator, 972-883-4228, Fax: 972-883-2813, E-mail: gradecs@utdallas.edu.

University of Washington, Bothell, Program in Computing and Software Systems, Bothell, WA 98011-8246. Offers MS. Part-time and evening/weekend programs available. *Faculty:* 8 full-time (1 woman). *Students:* 1 full-time (0 women), 27 part-time (3 women); includes 13 minority (1 African American, 11 Asian Americans or Pacific Islanders, 1 Hispanic American), 1 international. Average age 33. 42 applicants, 76% accepted, 27 enrolled. *Entrance requirements:* For master's, GRE. Additional exam requirements/recommendations for international students: Required—TOEFL (minimum score 580 paper-based; 237 computer-based; 92 iBT). *Application deadline:* For fall admission, 7/1 for domestic students. Application fee: $65. Electronic applications accepted. *Expenses:* Contact institution. *Financial support:* Applicants required to submit FAFSA. *Faculty research:* Computer vision, artificial intelligence, software engineering, computer graphics, parallel and distributed systems. *Unit head:* Dr. Michael Stiber. *Application contact:* Megan Jewell, Graduate Advisor, E-mail: mjewell@uwb.edu.

University of Washington, Tacoma, Graduate Programs, Program in Computing and Software Systems, Tacoma, WA 98402-3100. Offers MS. Part-time programs available. *Faculty:* 15 full-time (4 women), 6 part-time/adjunct (1 woman). *Students:* 15 full-time (7 women), 20 part-time (1 woman); includes 8 minority (6 Asian Americans or Pacific Islanders, 2 Hispanic Americans), 7 international. Average age 30. 30 applicants, 73% accepted, 15 enrolled. In 2009, 11 master's awarded. *Degree requirements:* For master's, capstone project/thesis or 15 credits elective coursework. *Entrance requirements:* For master's, GRE, All: UW Graduate Application, MS CSS Graduate Application, Personal Statement, Resume, Transcripts, Recommendations (3) International: Statement of Financial Ability, 1-20 Form, OFFICIAL transcripts and degree statements from all institutions attended with certified translations in English. Additional exam requirements/recommendations for international students: Required—TOEFL (minimum score 580 paper-based; 237 computer-based; 92 iBT), IELTS (minimum score 7), MLT (minimum score 90). *Application deadline:* For fall admission, 4/15 priority date for domestic students; for winter admission, 10/15 priority date for domestic students; for spring admission, 1/15 priority date for domestic students. Applications are processed on a rolling basis. Application fee: $65. Electronic applications accepted. *Expenses:* Tuition, state resident: full-time $10,660; part-time $484 per credit. Tuition, nonresident: full-time $24,000; part-time $1119 per credit. Required fees: $150 per term. Tuition and fees vary according to course load and program. *Faculty research:* Formal methods, software engineering, data streaming and data mining, computer engineering and science education, information assurance and computer security. *Unit head:* Dr. Orlando Baiocchi, Director, 253-692-5860, Fax: 253-692-5862, E-mail: uwtech@u.washington.edu. *Application contact:* Dr. Kim Davenport, Program Administrator and Graduate Advisor, 253-692-5860, Fax: 253-692-5862, E-mail: uwtech@u.washington.edu.

University of Waterloo, Graduate Studies, Faculty of Engineering, Department of Electrical and Computer Engineering, Waterloo, ON N2L 3G1, Canada. Offers electrical and computer

Software Engineering

University of Waterloo (continued)

engineering (M Eng, MA Sc, PhD); electrical and computer engineering (software engineering) (MA Sc). Part-time programs available. *Degree requirements:* For master's, research paper or thesis; for doctorate, comprehensive exam, thesis/dissertation. *Entrance requirements:* For master's, honors degree, minimum B+ average; for doctorate, master's degree, minimum A-average. Additional exam requirements/recommendations for international students: Required—TOEFL (minimum score 550 paper-based; 213 computer-based), TWE (minimum score 4). Electronic applications accepted. *Faculty research:* Communications, computers, systems and control, silicon devices, power engineering.

University of Waterloo, Graduate Studies, Faculty of Mathematics, David R. Cheriton School of Computer Science, Waterloo, ON N2L 3G1, Canada. Offers computer science (M Math, PhD); software engineering (M Math); statistics and computing (M Math). Part-time programs available. *Degree requirements:* For master's, research paper or thesis; for doctorate, comprehensive exam, thesis/dissertation. *Entrance requirements:* For master's, honors degree in field, minimum B+ average; for doctorate, master's degree, minimum B+ average. *Faculty research:* Computer graphics, artificial intelligence, algorithms and complexity, distributed computing and networks, software engineering.

University of West Florida, College of Arts and Sciences: Sciences, Department of Computer Science, Pensacola, FL 32514-5750. Offers computer science (MS); software engineering (MS). Part-time and evening/weekend programs available. *Faculty:* 8 full-time (3 women), 2 part-time/adjunct (both women). *Students:* 41 full-time (16 women), 87 part-time (25 women); includes 33 minority (8 African Americans, 1 American Indian/Alaska Native, 16 Asian Americans or Pacific Islanders, 8 Hispanic Americans), 5 international. Average age 36. 46 applicants, 96% accepted, 38 enrolled. In 2009, 14 master's awarded. *Degree requirements:* For master's, thesis optional. *Entrance requirements:* For master's, GRE General Test. Additional exam requirements/recommendations for international students: Required—TOEFL (minimum score 550 paper-based; 213 computer-based). *Application deadline:* For fall admission, 6/1 for domestic students, 5/15 for international students; for spring admission, 11/1 for domestic students, 10/1 for international students. Applications are processed on a rolling basis. Application fee: $30. *Expenses:* Tuition, state resident: full-time $4982; part-time $260 per credit hour. Tuition, nonresident: full-time $20,059; part-time $919 per credit hour. Required fees: $1247; $52 per credit hour. *Financial support:* In 2009–10, 3 teaching assistantships with partial tuition reimbursements (averaging $3,760 per year) were awarded; unspecified assistantships also available. Financial award application deadline: 4/15; financial award applicants required to submit FAFSA. *Unit head:* Dr. Leo Ter Haar, Chairperson, 850-474-2542. *Application contact:* Terry McCray, Assistant Director of Graduate Admissions, 850-473-7718, Fax: 850-473-7714, E-mail: gradadmissions@uwf.edu.

University of West Florida, College of Professional Studies, Department of Professional and Community Leadership, Program in Administration, Pensacola, FL 32514-5750. Offers acquisition and contract administration (MSA); biomedical/pharmaceutical (MSA); criminal justice administration (MSA); database administration (MSA); education leadership (MSA); healthcare administration (MSA); human performance technology (MSA); leadership (MSA); nursing administration (MSA); public administration (MSA); software engineering administration (MSA). Part-time and evening/weekend programs available. Postbaccalaureate distance learning degree programs offered (no on-campus study). *Students:* 33 full-time (21 women), 168 part-time (97 women); includes 53 minority (32 African Americans, 2 American Indian/Alaska Native, 5 Asian Americans or Pacific Islanders, 14 Hispanic Americans), 1 international. Average age 34. 103 applicants, 74% accepted, 64 enrolled. In 2009, 47 master's awarded. *Entrance requirements:* For master's, GRE General Test, letter of intent, names of references. Additional exam requirements/recommendations for international students: Required—TOEFL (minimum score 550 paper-based; 213 computer-based). *Application deadline:* For fall admission, 6/1 for domestic students, 5/15 for international students; for spring admission, 11/1 for domestic students, 10/1 for international students. Applications are processed on a rolling basis. Application fee: $30. *Expenses:* Tuition, state resident: full-time $4982; part-time $260 per credit hour. Tuition, nonresident: full-time $20,059; part-time $919 per credit hour. Required fees: $1247; $52 per credit hour. *Financial support:* Unspecified assistantships available. Financial award application deadline: 4/15; financial award applicants required to submit FAFSA. *Unit head:* Dr. Karen Rasmussen, Chairperson, 850-474-2301, Fax: 850-474-2804. *Application contact:* Terry McCray, Assistant Director of Graduate Admissions, 850-473-7718, Fax: 850-473-7714, E-mail: gradadmissions@uwf.edu.

University of West Georgia, Graduate School, College of Arts and Sciences, Department of Computer Science, Carrollton, GA 30118. Offers applied computer science (MS); human centered computing (Certificate); software development (Certificate); system and network administration (Certificate); Web technologies (Certificate). Part-time and evening/weekend programs available. *Faculty:* 8 full-time (3 women). *Students:* 14 full-time (6 women), 14 part-time (6 women); includes 5 minority (4 African Americans, 1 Hispanic American), 6 international. Average age 35. 13 applicants, 92% accepted, 5 enrolled. In 2009, 2 master's awarded. *Degree requirements:* For master's, comprehensive exam, thesis optional. *Entrance requirements:* For master's, GRE, bachelor's degree, minimum overall undergraduate GPA of 2.5; for Certificate, bachelor's degree, minimum overall undergraduate GPA of 2.5. *Application deadline:* For fall admission, 7/17 priority date for domestic students; for spring admission, 11/20 for domestic students. Applications are processed on a rolling basis. Application fee: $30. Electronic applications accepted. *Expenses:* Tuition, state resident: full-time $2952; part-time $164 per semester hour. Tuition, nonresident: full-time $11,808; part-time $656 per semester hour. Required fees: $42.90 per semester hour. $307 per semester. Tuition and fees vary according to course load. *Financial support:* In 2009–10, 10 research assistantships with full tuition reimbursements (averaging $6,000 per year) were awarded; unspecified assistantships also available. Financial award application deadline: 7/1; financial award applicants required to submit FAFSA. *Faculty research:* Artificial intelligence, software engineering, web technologies, database, networks. *Unit head:* Dr. Adel M. Abunawass, Chair, 678-839-6485, Fax: 678-839-6486, E-mail: adel@westga.edu. *Application contact:* Dr. Charles W. Clark, Dean, 678-839-6508, E-mail: cclark@westga.edu.

University of Wisconsin–La Crosse, Office of University Graduate Studies, College of Science and Health, Department of Computer Science, La Crosse, WI 54601-3742. Offers

software engineering (MSE). *Faculty:* 7 full-time (1 woman). *Students:* 36 full-time (10 women), 21 part-time (2 women); includes 1 minority (Asian American or Pacific Islander), 33 international. Average age 27. 38 applicants, 82% accepted, 10 enrolled. In 2009, 11 master's awarded. *Degree requirements:* For master's, thesis. *Entrance requirements:* Additional exam requirements/recommendations for international students: Required—TOEFL (minimum score 550 paper-based; 213 computer-based; 79 iBT). *Application deadline:* For fall admission, 5/1 priority date for domestic students; for spring admission, 11/1 priority date for domestic students. Applications are processed on a rolling basis. Application fee: $56. Electronic applications accepted. *Financial support:* In 2009–10, 4 research assistantships (averaging $10,124 per year) were awarded. *Unit head:* Dr. Kasi Periyasamy, Software Engineering Program Director, 608-785-6823, E-mail: periyasa.kas2@uwlax.edu. *Application contact:* Kathryn Kiefer, Associate Director of Admissions, 608-785-8939, E-mail: admissions@uwlax.edu.

Villanova University, Graduate School of Liberal Arts and Sciences, Department of Computing Sciences, Villanova, PA 19085-1699. Offers computer science (MS); software engineering (MS). Part-time and evening/weekend programs available. *Faculty:* 7 full-time (1 woman), 6 part-time/adjunct (2 women). *Students:* 60 full-time (21 women), 32 part-time (6 women); includes 9 minority (1 African American, 8 Asian Americans or Pacific Islanders), 54 international. Average age 28. 73 applicants, 88% accepted, 27 enrolled. In 2009, 17 master's awarded. *Degree requirements:* For master's, thesis optional, independent study project. *Entrance requirements:* For master's, GRE, minimum GPA of 3.0. Additional exam requirements/recommendations for international students: Required—TOEFL. *Application deadline:* For fall admission, 3/1 priority date for domestic and international students; for spring admission, 11/15 priority date for domestic and international students. Applications are processed on a rolling basis. Application fee: $50. Electronic applications accepted. *Expenses:* Contact institution. *Financial support:* Research assistantships, Federal Work-Study and scholarships/grants available. Financial award applicants required to submit FAFSA. *Unit head:* Dr. Robert Beck, Chair, 610-519-7310. *Application contact:* Dr. Robert Beck, Chair, 610-519-7310.

See Close-Up on page 321.

Virginia Polytechnic Institute and State University, VT Online, Blacksburg, VA 24061. Offers aerospace engineering (MS); business information systems (Graduate Certificate); career and technical education (MS); computer engineering (M Eng, MS); decision support systems (Graduate Certificate); eLearning leadership (MA); electrical engineering (M Eng, MS); engineering administration (MEA); environmental politics and policy (Graduate Certificate); foundations of political analysis (Graduate Certificate); health product risk management (Graduate Certificate); information policy and society (Graduate Certificate); information security (Graduate Certificate); instructional technology (MA); liberal arts (Graduate Certificate); life sciences: health product risk management (MS); natural resources (MNR, Graduate Certificate); networking (Graduate Certificate); nonprofit and nongovernmental organization management (Graduate Certificate); ocean engineering (MS); political science (MA); security studies (Graduate Certificate); software development (Graduate Certificate).

Walden University, Graduate Programs, NTU School of Engineering and Applied Science, Minneapolis, MN 55401. Offers competitive product management (Postbaccalaureate Certificate); engineering management (Postbaccalaureate Certificate); software engineering (MS); software project management (Postbaccalaureate Certificate); software testing (Postbaccalaureate Certificate); systems engineering (MS, Postbaccalaureate Certificate); technical project management (Postbaccalaureate Certificate). Part-time and evening/weekend programs available. Postbaccalaureate distance learning degree programs offered (no on-campus study). *Faculty:* 31 part-time/adjunct. *Students:* 22 full-time (6 women), 120 part-time (14 women); includes 26 minority (19 African Americans, 7 Asian Americans or Pacific Islanders). Average age 38. In 2009, 41 master's awarded. *Degree requirements:* For master's, thesis optional. *Entrance requirements:* For master's, bachelor's degree or equivalent in related field, minimum GPA of 2.5. Additional exam requirements/recommendations for international students: Required—TOEFL (minimum score 550 paper-based; 213 computer-based), IELTS (minimum score 6.5), or Michigan English Language Assessment Battery (minimum score 82). *Application deadline:* Applications are processed on a rolling basis. Application fee: $50. Electronic applications accepted. *Expenses:* Tuition: Full-time $13,665; part-time $560 per credit. Required fees: $1375. Tuition and fees vary according to course load, degree level and program. *Financial support:* Fellowships, Federal Work-Study, scholarships/grants, unspecified assistantships, and family tuition reduction, active duty/veteran tuition reduction, group tuition reduction, interest-free payment plans available. Support available to part-time students. Financial award applicants required to submit FAFSA. *Unit head:* Colin Wightman, Interim Associate Dean, 800-925-3368. *Application contact:* Jennifer Hall, Director of Enrollment, 866-4-WALDEN, E-mail: info@walden.edu.

West Virginia University, College of Engineering and Mineral Resources, Lane Department of Computer Science and Electrical Engineering, Program in Software Engineering, Morgantown, WV 26506. Offers MSSE. *Entrance requirements:* For master's, GRE or work experience.

Widener University, Graduate Programs in Engineering, Program in Computer and Software Engineering, Chester, PA 19013-5792. Offers M Eng. Part-time and evening/weekend programs available. *Students:* 2 full-time (1 woman), 2 part-time (0 women), 2 international. Average age 28. In 2009, 5 master's awarded. *Degree requirements:* For master's, thesis optional. *Application deadline:* For fall admission, 8/1 priority date for domestic students; for spring admission, 12/1 for domestic students. Applications are processed on a rolling basis. Application fee: $25 ($300 for international students). *Financial support:* Research assistantships with full tuition reimbursements, unspecified assistantships available. Financial award application deadline: 3/15. *Faculty research:* Computer and software engineering, computer network fault-tolerant computing, optical computing. *Unit head:* Dr. Bryen E. Lorenz, Chairman, Department of Electrical/Telecommunication Engineering, 610-499-4064, Fax: 610-499-4059, E-mail: bryen.f.lorenz@widener.edu. *Application contact:* Dr. Bryen E. Lorenz, Chairman, Department of Electrical/Telecommunication Engineering, 610-499-4064, Fax: 610-499-4059, E-mail: bryen.f.lorenz@widener.edu.

Winthrop University, College of Business Administration, Program in Software Project Management, Rock Hill, SC 29733. Offers software development (MS); software project management (Certificate). *Entrance requirements:* For master's, GMAT.

Systems Science

Arizona State University, Graduate College, Ira A. Fulton School of Engineering, ASU Engineering Online Programs, Tempe, AZ 85287. Offers construction (MS); embedded systems (M Eng); enterprise systems innovation and management (MSE); modeling and simulation (M Eng); quality and reliability engineering (M Eng); software engineering (MSE); systems engineering (M Eng).

Carleton University, Faculty of Graduate Studies, Faculty of Engineering and Design, Ottawa-Carleton Institute for Electrical Engineering, Department of Systems and Computer Engineering, Program in Information and Systems Science, Ottawa, ON K1S 5B6, Canada. Offers M Sc.

Carleton University, Faculty of Graduate Studies, Faculty of Science, Information and Systems Science Program, Ottawa, ON K1S 5B6, Canada. Offers M Sc. *Degree requirements:* For master's, thesis optional. *Entrance requirements:* For master's, honors degree. Additional

exam requirements/recommendations for international students: Required—TOEFL. *Faculty research:* Software engineering, real-time and microprocessor programming, computer communications.

Carleton University, Faculty of Graduate Studies, Faculty of Science, School of Computer Science, Ottawa, ON K1S 5B6, Canada. Offers computer science (MCS, PhD); information and system science (M Sc). Part-time programs available. *Degree requirements:* For master's, thesis optional, project; for doctorate, comprehensive exam, thesis/dissertation. *Entrance requirements:* For master's, honors degree. Additional exam requirements/recommendations for international students: Required—TOEFL. *Faculty research:* Programming systems, theory of computing, computer applications, computer systems.

Claremont Graduate University, Graduate Programs, School of Information Systems and Technology, Claremont, CA 91711-6160. Offers electronic commerce (MS, PhD); health information management (MS); information systems (Certificate); knowledge management (MS, PhD); systems development (MS, PhD); telecommunications and networking (MS, PhD); MBA/MS. Part-time programs available. *Faculty:* 6 full-time (1 woman), 1 part-time/adjunct (0 women). *Students:* 78 full-time (28 women), 35 part-time (11 women); includes 32 minority (8 African Americans, 1 American Indian/Alaska Native, 16 Asian Americans or Pacific Islanders, 7 Hispanic Americans), 32 international. Average age 38. In 2009, 31 master's, 11 doctorates, 1 other advanced degree awarded. *Degree requirements:* For doctorate, comprehensive exam, thesis/dissertation, portfolio. *Entrance requirements:* For master's and doctorate, GMAT, GRE General Test. Additional exam requirements/recommendations for international students: Required—TOEFL (minimum score 550 paper-based; 213 computer-based; 80 iBT). *Application deadline:* For fall admission, 2/1 priority date for domestic students. Applications are processed on a rolling basis. Application fee: $60. Electronic applications accepted. *Expenses:* Tuition: Full-time $35,046; part-time $1524 per credit. Required fees: $161 per semester. *Financial support:* Fellowships, research assistantships, teaching assistantships, Federal Work-Study, institutionally sponsored loans, and scholarships/grants available. Support available to part-time students. Financial award application deadline: 2/15; financial award applicants required to submit FAFSA. *Faculty research:* GPSS, man-machine interaction, organizational aspects of computing, implementation of information systems, information systems practice. *Unit head:* Terry Ryan, Dean, 909-607-9591, Fax: 909-621-8564, E-mail: terry.ryan@cgu.edu. *Application contact:* Matt Hutter, Director of External Affairs, 909-621-3180, Fax: 909-621-8564, E-mail: matt.hutter@cgu.edu.

Eastern Illinois University, Graduate School, Lumpkin College of Business and Applied Sciences, School of Technology, Charleston, IL 61920-3099. Offers computer technology (Certificate); quality systems (Certificate); technology (MS); technology security (Certificate); work performance improvement (Certificate). Part-time and evening/weekend programs available. *Faculty:* 14 full-time (2 women). In 2009, 39 master's, 14 other advanced degrees awarded. *Application deadline:* For fall admission, 3/31 priority date for domestic students. Applications are processed on a rolling basis. Application fee: $30. *Expenses:* Tuition, state resident: full-time $9434; part-time $239 per credit hour. Tuition, nonresident: full-time $23,774; part-time $717 per credit hour. Required fees: $802.63. *Financial support:* In 2009–10, 3 research assistantships with tuition reimbursements (averaging $8,100 per year), 3 teaching assistantships with tuition reimbursements (averaging $8,100 per year) were awarded. *Unit head:* Dr. Mahyar Izadi, Chairperson, 217-581-6269, Fax: 217-581-6607, E-mail: mizadi@eiu.edu. *Application contact:* Dr. Peter Ping Liu, Coordinator, 217-581-6267, Fax: 217-581-6607, E-mail: pliu@eiu.edu.

Fairleigh Dickinson University, Metropolitan Campus, University College: Arts, Sciences, and Professional Studies, Program in Systems Science, Teaneck, NJ 07666-1914. Offers MS. *Students:* 1 (woman) full-time, all international. Average age 23. 2 applicants, 100% accepted, 1 enrolled. In 2009, 2 master's awarded. *Entrance requirements:* For master's, GRE General Test. *Application deadline:* Applications are processed on a rolling basis. Application fee: $40. *Application contact:* Susan Brooman, University Director of Graduate Admissions, 201-692-2554, Fax: 201-692-2560, E-mail: globaleducation@fdu.edu.

Hood College, Graduate School, Program in Management of Information Technology, Frederick, MD 21701-8575. Offers MS. Part-time and evening/weekend programs available. *Faculty:* 1 (woman) full-time, 2 part-time/adjunct (1 woman). *Students:* 4 full-time (2 women), 13 part-time (4 women); includes 3 minority (2 African Americans, 1 Asian American or Pacific Islander), 2 international. Average age 37. 9 applicants, 78% accepted, 3 enrolled. In 2009, 2 master's awarded. *Degree requirements:* For master's, thesis. *Entrance requirements:* For master's, minimum GPA of 2.75. Additional exam requirements/recommendations for international students: Required—TOEFL (minimum score 575 paper-based; 231 computer-based; 89 iBT). *Application deadline:* For fall admission, 7/15 for domestic and international students; for spring admission, 12/15 for domestic and international students. Applications are processed on a rolling basis. Application fee: $35. Electronic applications accepted. *Expenses:* Tuition: Full-time $6480; part-time $360 per credit. Required fees: $100; $50 per term. *Financial support:* Applicants required to submit FAFSA. *Faculty research:* Systems engineering, parallel distributed computing, strategy, business ethics, entrepreneurship. *Unit head:* Raymond Myers, Director, 301-696-3724, E-mail: myers@hood.edu. *Application contact:* Dr. Allen P. Flora, Dean of Graduate School, 301-696-3811, Fax: 301-696-3597, E-mail: gofurther@hood.edu.

Louisiana State University and Agricultural and Mechanical College, Graduate School, College of Basic Sciences, Department of Computer Science, Baton Rouge, LA 70803. Offers computer science (MSSS, PhD); systems science (MSSS). Part-time programs available. *Faculty:* 19 full-time (3 women). *Students:* 78 full-time (18 women), 22 part-time (4 women); includes 11 minority (5 African Americans, 1 American Indian/Alaska Native, 5 Asian Americans or Pacific Islanders), 71 international. Average age 30. 157 applicants, 55% accepted, 11 enrolled. In 2009, 10 master's, 3 doctorates awarded. Terminal master's awarded for partial completion of doctoral program. *Degree requirements:* For master's, thesis; for doctorate, thesis/dissertation. *Entrance requirements:* For master's and doctorate, GRE General Test, minimum GPA of 3.0. Additional exam requirements/recommendations for international students: Required—TOEFL (minimum score 550 paper-based; 213 computer-based; 79 iBT) or IELTS (minimum score 6.5). *Application deadline:* For fall admission, 2/1 for domestic students, 5/15 for international students; for spring admission, 10/1 for domestic students, 10/15 for international students. Applications are processed on a rolling basis. Application fee: $50 ($70 for international students). Electronic applications accepted. *Financial support:* In 2009–10, 84 students received support, including 9 fellowships with full tuition reimbursements available (averaging $28,150 per year), 38 research assistantships with full and partial tuition reimbursements available (averaging $16,409 per year), 23 teaching assistantships with full and partial tuition reimbursements available (averaging $15,990 per year); Federal Work-Study, institutionally sponsored loans, health care benefits, and unspecified assistantships also available. Financial award application deadline: 2/1; financial award applicants required to submit FAFSA. *Faculty research:* Robotics, artificial intelligence, algorithms, database software engineering, high-performance computing. Total annual research expenditures: $1.4 million. *Unit head:* Dr. Sitharama S. Iyengar, Chair, 225-578-1495, Fax: 225-578-1465, E-mail: iyengar@csc.lsu.edu. *Application contact:* Graduate Coordinator, 225-578-1495, Fax: 225-578-1465.

Louisiana State University in Shreveport, College of Sciences, Program in Computer Systems Technology, Shreveport, LA 71115-2399. Offers MS. *Students:* 6 full-time (0 women), 15 part-time (5 women); includes 3 minority (all African Americans), 3 international. Average age 33. 18 applicants, 94% accepted, 9 enrolled. In 2009, 5 master's awarded. *Degree requirements:* For master's, thesis or alternative. *Entrance requirements:* For master's, GRE, programming course in high-level language, interview. Additional exam requirements/recommendations for international students: Required—TOEFL (minimum score 500 paper-based; 173 computer-based; 61 iBT). *Application deadline:* For fall admission, 6/30 for domestic and international students; for spring admission, 11/30 for domestic and international students. Applications are processed on a rolling basis. Application fee: $10 ($20 for international students). *Financial support:* In 2009–10, 2 research assistantships with partial tuition reimbursements (averaging $20,000 per year) were awarded. *Unit head:* Dr. John Sigle, Program Director, 318-797-5093. *Application contact:* Dr. John Sigle, Program Director, 318-797-5093.

Miami University, Graduate School, School of Engineering and Applied Science, Department of Computer Science and Software Engineering, Oxford, OH 45056. Offers computer science (MCS). *Students:* 18 full-time (9 women), 7 part-time (1 woman); includes 3 minority (all Asian Americans or Pacific Islanders), 14 international. *Entrance requirements:* For master's, GRE, minimum cumulative undergraduate GPA of 3.0. Additional exam requirements/recommendations for international students: Required—TOEFL (minimum score 500 paper-based; 250 computer-based). *Application deadline:* For fall admission, 2/1 for domestic and international students. Application fee: $50. *Expenses:* Tuition, state resident: full-time $11,280. Tuition, nonresident: full-time $24,912. Required fees: $516. *Financial support:* Fellowships, research assistantships, teaching assistantships, Federal Work-Study, health care benefits, tuition waivers (full), and unspecified assistantships available. Financial award application deadline: 3/1. *Unit head:* Dr. Doug Troy, Chair, 513-529-0340, E-mail: troyda@muohio.edu. *Application contact:* Dr. Doug Troy, Chair, 513-529-0340, E-mail: troyda@muohio.edu.

Oakland University, Graduate Study and Lifelong Learning, School of Engineering and Computer Science, Department of Computer Science and Engineering, Rochester, MI 48309-4401. Offers computer science (MS); embedded systems (MS); information systems engineering (MS); software engineering (MS). Part-time and evening/weekend programs available. *Entrance requirements:* For master's, minimum GPA of 3.0 for unconditional admission. Electronic applications accepted. *Expenses:* Contact institution. *Faculty research:* Cyber security, 3D imaging of neurochemicals in rat brains.

Portland State University, Graduate Studies, Maseeh College of Engineering and Computer Science, Department of Engineering and Technology Management, Portland, OR 97207-0751. Offers engineering and technology management (M Eng); engineering management (MS); manufacturing engineering (ME); manufacturing management (M Eng); systems science/engineering management (PhD); MS/MBA; MS/MS. Part-time and evening/weekend programs available. *Degree requirements:* For master's, thesis optional; for doctorate, one foreign language, thesis/dissertation, oral and written exams. *Entrance requirements:* For master's, minimum GPA of 3.0 in upper-division course work, BS degree in civil engineering; for doctorate, GRE General Test, GRE Subject Test, minimum GPA of 3.0 in upper-division course work. Additional exam requirements/recommendations for international students: Required—TOEFL (minimum score 550 paper-based; 213 computer-based). *Faculty research:* Scheduling, hierarchical decision modeling, operations research, knowledge-based information systems.

Portland State University, Graduate Studies, Systems Science Program, Portland, OR 97207-0751. Offers computational intelligence (Certificate); computer modeling and simulation (Certificate); systems science (MS); systems science/anthropology (PhD); systems science/business administration (PhD); systems science/civil engineering (PhD); systems science/economics (PhD); systems science/engineering management (PhD); systems science/general (PhD); systems science/mathematical sciences (PhD); systems science/mechanical engineering (PhD); systems science/psychology (PhD); systems science/sociology (PhD). *Degree requirements:* For doctorate, variable foreign language requirement, thesis/dissertation. *Entrance requirements:* For master's, 2 letters of recommendation; for doctorate, GMAT, GRE General Test, minimum undergraduate GPA of 3.0. Additional exam requirements/recommendations for international students: Required—TOEFL. *Faculty research:* Systems theory and methodology, artificial intelligence neural networks, information theory, nonlinear dynamics/chaos, modeling and simulation.

Rensselaer at Hartford, Department of Engineering, Program in Computer and Systems Engineering, Hartford, CT 06120-2991. Offers ME. *Faculty:* 2 full-time (0 women), 2 part-time/adjunct (0 women). *Students:* 21 part-time (3 women); includes 6 minority (1 African American, 1 Asian American or Pacific Islander, 4 Hispanic Americans). Average age 34. 8 applicants, 75% accepted, 6 enrolled. In 2009, 5 master's awarded. *Entrance requirements:* For master's, GRE. *Application deadline:* For fall admission, 8/30 priority date for domestic students, 8/1 for international students. Application fee: $75. *Expenses:* Tuition: Full-time $31,800; part-time $1325 per credit hour. *Unit head:* Dr. Ernesto Gutierrez-Miravete, 860-548-2464, E-mail: gutiee@rpi.edu. *Application contact:* Kristin Galligan, Director, Enrollment Management and Marketing, 860-548-2480, Fax: 860-548-7823, E-mail: info@ewp.rpi.edu.

Southern Methodist University, Bobby B. Lyle School of Engineering, Department of Engineering Management, Information, and Systems, Dallas, TX 75275. Offers applied science (MS); engineering management (MSEM, DE); information engineering and management (MSIEM); operations research (MS, PhD); systems engineering (MS, PhD). Part-time and evening/weekend programs available. Postbaccalaureate distance learning degree programs offered. *Faculty:* 10 full-time (3 women), 22 part-time/adjunct (2 women). *Students:* 54 full-time (24 women), 288 part-time (68 women); includes 96 minority (30 African Americans, 2 American Indian/Alaska Native, 35 Asian Americans or Pacific Islanders, 29 Hispanic Americans), 38 international. Average age 33. 125 applicants, 74% accepted, 60 enrolled. In 2009, 128 master's, 3 doctorates awarded. Terminal master's awarded for partial completion of doctoral program. *Degree requirements:* For master's, thesis optional; for doctorate, thesis/dissertation, oral and written qualifying exams. *Entrance requirements:* For master's, minimum GPA of 3.0 in last 2 years; bachelor's degree in engineering, mathematics, sciences, or technical area; for doctorate, GRE General Test (operations research, engineering management), bachelor's degree in related field. Additional exam requirements/recommendations for international students: Required—TOEFL. *Application deadline:* For fall admission, 7/1 for domestic students, 5/15 for international students; for spring admission, 11/15 for domestic students, 9/1 for international students. Applications are processed on a rolling basis. Application fee: $75. *Financial support:* In 2009–10, 8 students received support, including 3 research assistantships with full tuition reimbursements available (averaging $18,000 per year), 9 teaching assistantships with full tuition reimbursements available (averaging $18,000 per year); tuition waivers (full) also available. *Faculty research:* Telecommunications, decision systems, information engineering, operations research, software. Total annual research expenditures: $172,823. *Unit head:* Dr. Richard S. Barr, Chair, 214-768-1772, Fax: 214-768-1112, E-mail: emis@lyle.smu.edu. *Application contact:* Marc Valerin, Director of Graduate and Executive Admissions, 214-768-3042, E-mail: valerin@lyle.smu.edu.

State University of New York at Binghamton, Graduate School, Thomas J. Watson School of Engineering and Applied Science, Department of Systems Science and Industrial Engineering, Binghamton, NY 13902-6000. Offers M Eng, MS, MSAT, PhD. Part-time and evening/weekend programs available. *Faculty:* 10 full-time (3 women), 4 part-time/adjunct (0 women). *Students:* 97 full-time (20 women), 74 part-time (13 women); includes 20 minority (7 African Americans, 2 American Indian/Alaska Native, 7 Asian Americans or Pacific Islanders, 4 Hispanic Americans), 116 international. Average age 29. 149 applicants, 71% accepted, 47 enrolled. In 2009, 29 master's, 10 doctorates awarded. Terminal master's awarded for partial completion of doctoral program. *Degree requirements:* For master's, thesis or alternative; for doctorate, thesis/dissertation. *Entrance requirements:* For master's and doctorate, GRE General Test, GRE Subject Test. Additional exam requirements/recommendations for international students: Required—TOEFL. *Application deadline:* For fall admission, 4/15 priority date for domestic students, 1/15 priority date for international students; for spring admission, 11/1 for domestic students, 10/1 priority date for international students. Applications are processed on a rolling basis. Application fee: $60. Electronic applications accepted. *Financial support:* In 2009–10, 76 students received support, including 58 research assistantships with full tuition reimbursements available (averaging $16,500 per year), 12 teaching assistantships with full tuition reimbursements available (averaging $16,500 per year); career-related internships or fieldwork, Federal Work-Study, institutionally sponsored loans, scholarships/grants, health care benefits, tuition waivers (full and partial), and unspecified assistantships also available. Financial award application deadline: 2/15; financial award applicants required to submit FAFSA. *Faculty research:* Problem restructuring, protein modeling. *Unit head:* Dr. Nagen Nagarur, Chair, 607-777-3027, E-mail: nnagarur@binghamton.edu. *Application contact:* Victoria Williams, Recruiting and Admissions Coordinator, 607-777-2151, Fax: 607-777-2501, E-mail: vwilliam@binghamton.edu.

Stevens Institute of Technology, Graduate School, Charles V. Schaefer Jr. School of Engineering, Department of Mechanical Engineering, Program in Integrated Product Development, Hoboken, NJ 07030. Offers armament engineering (M Eng); computer and electrical engineering (M Eng); manufacturing technologies (M Eng); systems reliability and design (M Eng). *Expenses:* Tuition: Full-time $9900; part-time $1100 per credit. Required fees: $286 per semester.

Stevens Institute of Technology, Graduate School, School of Systems and Enterprises, Program in Enterprise Systems, Hoboken, NJ 07030. Offers MS, PhD. *Expenses:* Tuition: Full-time $9900; part-time $1100 per credit. Required fees: $286 per semester.

Strayer University, Graduate Studies, Washington, DC 20005-2603. Offers accounting (MS); acquisition (MBA); business administration (MBA); communications technology (MS); educational

Systems Science

Strayer University *(continued)*
management (M Ed); finance (MBA); health services administration (MHSA); hospitality and tourism management (MBA); human resource management (MBA); information systems (MS), including computer security management, decision support system management, enterprise resource management, network management, software engineering management, systems development management; management (MBA); management information systems (MS); marketing (MBA); professional accounting (MS), including accounting information systems, controllership, taxation; public administration (MPA); supply chain management (MBA); technology in education (M Ed). Programs also offered at campus locations in Birmingham, AL; Chamblee, GA; Cobb County, GA; Morrow, GA; White Marsh, MD; Charleston, SC; Columbia, SC; Greensboro, NC; Greenville, SC; Lexington, KY; Louisville, KY; Nashville, TN; North Raleigh, NC; Washington, DC. Part-time and evening/weekend programs available. Postbaccalaureate distance learning degree programs offered (minimal on-campus study). *Degree requirements:* For master's, thesis. *Entrance requirements:* For master's, GMAT, GRE General Test, bachelor's degree from an accredited college or university, minimum undergraduate GPA of 2.75. Electronic applications accepted.

Universidad Autonoma de Guadalajara, Graduate Programs, Guadalajara, Mexico. Offers administrative law and justice (LL M); advertising and corporate communications (MA); architecture (M Arch); business (MBA); computational science (MCC); education (Ed M, Ed D); English-Spanish translation (MA); fiscal law (MA); integrated management of digital animation (MA); international business (MIB); international corporate law (LL M); internet technologies (MS); labor health (MS); manufacturing systems (MMS); philosophy (MA, PhD); power electronics (MS); quality systems (MQS); renewable energy (MS); social evaluation of projects (MBA); strategic market research (MBA); teaching mathematics (MA).

University of Michigan–Dearborn, College of Engineering and Computer Science, Department of Industrial and Manufacturing Systems Engineering, Dearborn, MI 48128-1491. Offers engineering management (MS); industrial and systems engineering (MSE); information systems and technology (MS); information systems engineering (PhD); MBA/MSE. Part-time and evening/weekend programs available. *Faculty:* 14 full-time (0 women), 5 part-time/adjunct (0 women). *Students:* 16 full-time (5 women), 179 part-time (56 women); includes 45 minority (6 African Americans, 26 Asian Americans or Pacific Islanders, 13 Hispanic Americans). Average age 31. 63 applicants, 62% accepted, 37 enrolled. In 2009, 67 master's awarded. *Degree requirements:* For master's, thesis optional. *Entrance requirements:* For master's, bachelor's degree in applied mathematics, computer science, engineering, or physical science; minimum GPA of 3.0. Additional exam requirements/recommendations for international students: Required—TOEFL (minimum score 560 paper-based; 220 computer-based; 84 iBT). *Application deadline:* For fall admission, 8/1 priority date for domestic students, 4/1 for international students; for winter admission, 12/1 priority date for domestic students, 8/1 for international students; for spring admission, 4/1 for domestic students, 12/1 for international students. Applications are processed on a rolling basis. Application fee: $60 ($75 for international students). *Expenses:* Tuition, area resident: Part-time $504.10 per credit hour. Tuition, state resident: part-time $504.10 per credit hour. Tuition, nonresident: part-time $957.90 per credit hour. *Financial support:* Fellowships, research assistantships, teaching assistantships, Federal Work-Study available. Financial award application deadline: 4/1; financial award applicants required to submit FAFSA. *Faculty research:* Health care systems, data and knowledge management, human factors engineering, machine diagnostics, precision machining. *Unit head:* Dr. Armen Zakarian, Chair, 313-593-5361, Fax: 313-593-3692, E-mail: zakarian@umd.umich.edu. *Application contact:* Joey W. Woods, Graduate Program Assistant, 313-593-5361, Fax: 313-593-3692, E-mail: jwwoods@umd.umich.edu.

The University of North Carolina Wilmington, College of Arts and Sciences, Program in Computer Science and Information Systems, Wilmington, NC 28403-3297. Offers MS. *Entrance requirements:* For master's, GMAT or GRE, 3 letters of recommendation, resume.

University of Ottawa, Faculty of Graduate and Postdoctoral Studies, Interdisciplinary Programs, Ottawa, ON K1N 6N5, Canada. Offers e-business (Certificate); e-commerce (Certificate); finance (Certificate); health services and policies research (Diploma); population health (PhD); population health risk assessment and management (Certificate); public management and governance (Certificate); systems science (Certificate).

University of Ottawa, Faculty of Graduate and Postdoctoral Studies, Systems Science Program, Ottawa, ON K1N 6N5, Canada. Offers M Sc, M Sys Sc, Certificate. Part-time and evening/weekend programs available. *Degree requirements:* For master's and Certificate, thesis optional. *Entrance requirements:* For master's, bachelor's degree or equivalent, minimum B average; for Certificate, honors degree or equivalent, minimum B average. Additional exam requirements/recommendations for international students: Recommended—TOEFL (minimum score 237 computer-based). Electronic applications accepted. *Faculty research:* Software engineering, communication systems, information systems, production management, corporate managerial modeling.

Washington University in St. Louis, Henry Edwin Sever Graduate School of Engineering and Applied Science, Department of Electrical and Systems Engineering, St. Louis, MO 63130-4899. Offers electrical engineering (MS, D Sc, PhD); systems science and mathematics (MS, D Sc, PhD). Part-time programs available. *Faculty:* 17 full-time (2 women), 5 part-time/adjunct (1 woman). *Students:* 75 full-time (33 women), 21 part-time (2 women); includes 10 minority (1 African American, 8 Asian Americans or Pacific Islanders, 1 Hispanic American), 45 international. Average age 23. 281 applicants, 29% accepted, 25 enrolled. In 2009, 16 master's, 4 doctorates awarded. Terminal master's awarded for partial completion of doctoral program. *Degree requirements:* For master's, thesis or alternative; for doctorate, comprehensive exam, thesis/dissertation. *Entrance requirements:* For master's, minimum GPA of 3.0 in the last 2 years of undergraduate course work; for doctorate, GRE. Additional exam requirements/recommendations for international students: Required—TOEFL (minimum score 550 paper-based; 213 computer-based; 80 iBT). *Application deadline:* For fall admission, 1/15 for domestic and international students. Applications are processed on a rolling basis. Application fee: $60. Electronic applications accepted. *Financial support:* In 2009–10, 8 fellowships with full tuition reimbursements (averaging $20,000 per year), 29 research assistantships with full tuition reimbursements (averaging $26,950 per year) were awarded; teaching assistantships with full tuition reimbursements, career-related internships or fieldwork, Federal Work-Study, institutionally sponsored loans, scholarships/grants, and unspecified assistantships also available. Financial award application deadline: 1/15; financial award applicants required to submit FAFSA. *Faculty research:* Applied physics and electronics, signal and image processing, systems analysis, biomedicine, and energy. Total annual research expenditures: $1 million. *Unit head:* Dr. Arye Nehorai, Chair, 314-935-5565, Fax: 314-935-7500, E-mail: nehorai@ese.wustl.edu. *Application contact:* Shauna Dollison, Director of Graduate Programs, 314-935-4830, Fax: 314-935-7500.

Worcester Polytechnic Institute, Graduate Studies and Research, Department of Social Science and Policy Studies, Worcester, MA 01609-2280. Offers interdisciplinary social science (PhD); system dynamics (MS, Graduate Certificate). Part-time and evening/weekend programs available. Postbaccalaureate distance learning degree programs offered (no on-campus study). *Faculty:* 3 full-time (0 women), 2 part-time/adjunct (0 women). *Students:* 12 part-time (11 women). 13 applicants, 85% accepted, 5 enrolled. In 2009, 2 master's awarded. *Entrance requirements:* For master's, GRE General Test, 3 letters of recommendation. Additional exam requirements/recommendations for international students: Required—TOEFL (minimum score 550 paper-based; 213 computer-based; 79 iBT), IELTS (minimum score 6.5). *Application deadline:* For fall admission, 1/15 priority date for domestic students, 1/15 for international students; for spring admission, 10/15 priority date for domestic students, 10/15 for international students. Applications are processed on a rolling basis. Application fee: $70. Electronic applications accepted. *Financial support:* Career-related internships or fieldwork, institutionally sponsored loans, scholarships/grants, and unspecified assistantships available. Financial award application deadline: 1/15. *Faculty research:* Sustainable development, information economics, judgment and decision making, learning science, system dynamics, social simulation, political economies. *Unit head:* Dr. James K. Doyle, Head, 508-831-5296, Fax: 508-831-5896, E-mail: doyle@wpi.edu. *Application contact:* Dr. Oleg Pavlov, Graduate Coordinator, 508-831-5296, Fax: 508-831-5896, E-mail: opavlov@wpi.edu.

Carnegie Mellon

CARNEGIE MELLON UNIVERSITY

School of Computer Science
Doctoral Program in Computer Science

Program of Study

The Department of Computer Science offers the degree of Doctor of Philosophy. Requirements for the Ph.D. are successful completion of course requirements and submission of a thesis describing original, independent research. An initial acculturation program (the Immigration Course) involves students in all the activities of the department. Participation in one or more of the ongoing research projects is a key factor in a student's education. Visitors come to Carnegie Mellon in a steady stream from universities and laboratories throughout the world for various lengths of time, joining the faculty members and students in an active colloquium program.

Research Facilities

The Carnegie Mellon University (CMU) School of Computer Science (SCS) research facility has a large number and wide variety of computers available for faculty and graduate student use—approximately 4,000 machines. About one third are Linux/UNIX on Intel and AMD platforms, 60 percent are Windows systems, and Macintosh computers make up the remainder. Every incoming graduate student is provided with a new, high-powered personal computer; some receive a dual-boot configuration to provide both Windows and Linux. SCS facilities include a rich variety of computing infrastructure services of very high quality, including e-mail, shared file service (AFS), authentication, remote-access services (vpn, iPass), backup, printing, software licensing, and hardware repair. The SCS environment also includes a growing number of high-performance computer clusters; support services are available for the entire life cycle of the cluster, including help for specification and purchasing. For all aspects of computing, there is a dedicated support (help) staff within the facility which provides full support for users, applications, machines, and services via a menu of premium support services.

Beyond these college resources, the University maintains computation facilities of various kinds for general use. The Pittsburgh Supercomputing Center (PSC) is a joint effort of Carnegie Mellon and the University of Pittsburgh, together with Westinghouse Corporation. It is supported by several federal agencies, the commonwealth of Pennsylvania, and private industry. It is a leading partner in the TeraGrid, the National Science Foundation's cyberinfrastructure program. It operates several supercomputing-class machines, including a Cray XT3 MPP machine with 2,068 compute nodes and 4,136 processors.

Carnegie Mellon operates a fully interconnected, multimedia, multiprotocol campus network. The system incorporates state-of-the-art commercial technology and spans multiple segments to all campus buildings in a redundant backbone infrastructure that enables unfettered access among all campus systems, including the PSC supercomputers. The University currently provides wireless data communication campuswide.

SCS has two 1Gbps links to the Carnegie Mellon campus network. The University has two redundant 1Gbps links to the PSC, and through PSC the University connects to the commodity Internet and the Abilene research network. This connection is shared with the University of Pittsburgh, Penn State University, and West Virginia University.

Financial Aid

Most students in the department are supported by graduate research fellowships during the academic year. In 2010–11, each student will receive full tuition plus a stipend of $2310 per month for the academic year. Dependency allowances are available; students who receive external fellowships may be given supplementary stipends.

Summer support is normally available for many students, particularly those working on their dissertations. However, since the University believes that it is also good for students to gain experience in industry for one or two summers during their careers at Carnegie Mellon, faculty and staff members are able to provide valuable help in finding suitable summer employment.

Cost of Study

Tuition and fees for full-time graduate students in 2010–11 are $36,430 for the academic year. This figure is subject to change.

Living and Housing Costs

Limited University housing is available for graduate students, but a wide variety of accommodations are available in the surrounding community.

Student Group

Carnegie Mellon has a total enrollment of approximately 10,000 students, of whom approximately 4,600 are graduate students. About 150 full-time students are enrolled in the Doctoral Program in Computer Science, which makes the student-faculty member ratio lower than 2:1. Admission to the program is highly competitive; about 25 students enroll each year.

Student Outcomes

Carnegie Mellon's computer science doctoral program aims to produce well-educated researchers and future leaders in computer science. Approximately 25 students graduate each year, with more than half accepting positions in industrial research laboratories. Those preferring academic careers accept both tenure- and research-track positions at many of the top universities in the country.

Location

Carnegie Mellon is located in Oakland, the cultural center of Pittsburgh, on a 90-acre campus adjacent to Schenley Park, the largest city park. The campus is close to the many cultural and sports activities of the city and is only 4 miles from the downtown business district. Pittsburgh is the headquarters for many of the nation's biggest corporations. There is a large concentration of research laboratories in the area.

The University

Founded in 1900 by Andrew Carnegie, the Carnegie Institute of Technology joined with Mellon Institute (now the Carnegie Mellon Research Institute) in 1967 to become Carnegie Mellon University. With this merger, one of the leading research and education institutions in the country was established.

Applying

Each prospective student's application, test scores, transcripts, and reference letters must be received by December 15. Notification of acceptance is made by March 1. Minimum preparation normally includes an undergraduate program in mathematics, physics, electrical engineering, or computer science and some experience in computer programming. Excellence and promise may balance a lack of formal preparation. Applications must be accompanied by GRE General Test scores. The TOEFL is required for all nonnative English speakers.

Correspondence and Information

Graduate Admissions
Department of Computer Science
Carnegie Mellon University
5000 Forbes Avenue
Pittsburgh, Pennsylvania 15213
Phone: 412-268-3863
E-mail: grad-adm@cs.cmu.edu
Web site: http://www.csd.cs.cmu.edu/education/phd/

Carnegie Mellon University

THE FACULTY AND THEIR RESEARCH

V. Adamchik, Associate Teaching Professor: computational mathematics, special functions, computer algebra.

J. Aldrich, Associate Professor (ISR): programming languages, program analysis, type systems, formal methods, and software engineering.

D. Andersen, Assistant Professor: networks, distributed systems, resilient networked systems, wireless and overlay networks.

Z. Bar-Joseph, Associate Professor (CS/ML): computational biology, systems biology, time-series analysis, applied machine learning.

G. Blelloch, Professor: compilers, parallel architectures, parallel languages, parallel algorithms.

A. Blum, Professor: machine-learning theory, online algorithms, approximation algorithms, algorithmic game theory.

L. Blum, Distinguished Career Professor: complexity and real computation.

M. Blum, Nelson University Professor: theoretical computer science.

S. Brookes, Professor: mathematical theory of computation, theory and semantics of programming languages.

R. Bryant, Dean and University Professor (CS): formal verification of hardware and embedded systems, data structures and algorithms for representing and reasoning about different classes of logic.

P. Capell, Senior Technical Staff (SEI): software engineering.

J. Carbonell, Professor (LTI/CS) and Director (LTI): artificial intelligence, natural-language processing, machine learning, machine translation.

J. Carrasquel, Associate Teaching Professor: programming in C++.

M. Christel, Senior Systems Scientist (ETC): digital video interfaces, information visualization, digital libraries.

E. Clarke, FORE Systems University Professor: hardware and software verification, automatic theorem proving, symbolic computation, parallel algorithms and programming, applications of logic to problems in computer science.

T. Cortina, Associate Teaching Professor: program design and analysis, Java programming language.

K. Crary, Associate Professor: programming languages and compilers, type theory, certified code, grid computing.

W. Dann, Associate Teaching Professor: visualization in programming and programming languages, innovative approaches to introductory programming.

R. Dannenberg, Associate Research Professor (CS/Art): computer music, interactive real-time systems.

A. Datta, Research Scientist (CyLab): computer and network security, privacy, cryptography, programming languages, specification and verification, applications of mathematical logic in computer science.

D. Durand, Associate Professor (Biological Sciences/CS): computational molecular biology and genomics, evolution of genomic organization and function.

D. Eckhardt, Associate Teaching Professor: operating systems, networking, wireless networks.

A. Efros, Associate Professor (CS/RI): computer graphics, computer vision.

M. Erdmann, Professor (CS/RI): robotics: mechanics of manipulation, mobile manipulation, shape sensing, uncertainty; computational molecular biology: protein structure, protein knot theory.

S. Fahlman, Research Professor: artificial intelligence, knowledge representation, machine learning.

C. Faloutsos, Professor: multimedia and text databases, indexing, data mining, fractals, database performance.

D. Feinberg, Assistant Teaching Professor: object-oriented programming.

E. Fink, Senior Systems Scientist (LTI/CS): artificial intelligence, machine learning, computational geometry.

A. Frieze, Professor (Mathematics): algorithms, random structures, combinatorics.

G. Ganger, Professor (ECE): operating systems; storage/file systems; security, networking, and distributed systems.

D. Garlan, Professor (CS/ISR): software engineering, software architecture, pervasive computing, formal methods, self-healing systems.

G. Gibson, Professor: computer systems, computer architecture, operating systems, file systems, storage systems, networking.

S. Goldstein, Associate Professor: compilers and architectures for electronic nanotechnology, reconfigurable computing, programmable matter and claytronics.

C. Guestrin, Associate Professor (ML/CS): machine learning, sensor networks, distributed systems, computer vision, planning under uncertainty.

A. Gunawardena, Associate Teaching Professor: adaptive e-learning systems.

A. Gupta, Associate Professor: approximation algorithms, metric embeddings, network algorithms.

M. Harchol-Balter, Associate Professor: distributed computing, performance analysis, scheduling and resource allocation, workload characterization.

R. Harper, Professor: programming languages, type theory, logical framework, certifying compilers, mechanized reasoning, verification.

A. Hauptmann, Senior Systems Scientist: multimedia digital libraries, information retrieval from speech and video.

J. Hodgins, Professor (CS/RI): computer graphics, computer animation, motion capture, dynamic simulation, humanoid robotics.

J. Hoe, Professor (ECE): computer architecture, high-level hardware description and synthesis.

T. Hoffmann, Assistant Teaching Professor: object-based programming.

T. Kanade, University Professor (CS/RI): computer vision, virtualized reality, autonomous mobile robots, medical robotics, sensors.

T. Keating, Assistant Teaching Professor: technical communication for computer scientists.

G. Kesden, Associate Teaching Professor: programming, distributed systems, competitive programming.

J. Lafferty, Professor (CS/LTI/ML): machine learning, algorithms for probabilistic inference, text processing and information retrieval.

C. Langmead, Associate Professor (CS/Biological Sciences): computational molecular biology, structural biology, systems biology.

P. Lee, Professor: compilers for advanced programming languages, semantics-based analysis and optimization, application of advanced languages to systems programming, functional programming, formal semantics.

T. Lee, Associate Professor (CS/CNBC): biological and computer vision, neural code, neural computation and modeling.

G. Levin, Associate Professor (Art): electronic time-based art, nonverbal communications protocols in cybernetic systems, computer vision, software design.

J. Lopez, Systems Scientist: data-intensive computing at large scale, computational databases, parallel and distributed systems, scalable I/O and indexing techniques for large multidimensional spatial datasets, data compression and visualization.

M. Mason, Professor (RI/CS) and Director (RI): robotics, mobile manipulators, mechanics of manipulation, manufacturing automation.

R. Maxion, Research Professor: computer dependability and security, information warfare, intrusion detection, system diagnosis.

G. Miller, Professor: parallel computation; sparse matrix, graph, and number-theoretic algorithms.

T. Mitchell, E. Fredkin University Professor (ML/CS) and Head (ML): machine learning, brain imaging, intelligent Web agents, data mining, artificial intelligence.

A. Moore, Professor (RI/CS): data mining.

J. Morris, Professor and Dean, SV Campus: distributed personal computer systems, software engineering, functional programming, user interfaces.

T. Mowry, Professor: computer architecture, compilers, operating systems, parallel processing, database performance.

S. Narasimhan, Associate Professor: computer vision, computer graphics.

R. O'Donnell, Assistant Professor: learning theory, complexity theory, discrete Fourier analysis, combinatorics, probability, Gaussian space.

D. O'Hallaron, Professor (CS/ECE): computer systems, scientific computing, computational database systems, virtualization.

A. Perrig, Professor (CS/ECE/EPP): computer and network security, applied cryptography, security policy, sensor networks.

F. Pfenning, Professor and Director of Graduate Programs: logic and computation, type theory, functional programming, automated deduction, trustworthy computing.

A. Platzer, Assistant Professor: verification of hybrid systems, automated theorem proving, model checking, dynamic logic, hybrid logic, decision procedures, computer algebra and symbolic computation, model theory, verification of object-oriented systems, verification algorithms.

N. Pollard, Associate Professor (RI/CS): computer graphics, humanoid robotics, physically based character animation, manipulation planning and control.

R. Ravi, Professor (TSB/CS): approximation algorithms, combinatorial optimization, computational biology.

R. Reddy, University Professor (ISR/CS): artificial intelligence, speech recognition and understanding, mobile autonomous robots, learning by doing.

M. Reid-Miller, Assistant Teaching Professor: pipelining.

J. Reynolds, Professor: programming language design, specification and verification of programs, mathematical semantics.

J. Roberts, Teaching Professor: programming in C++.

S. Rudich, Professor: complexity theory, cryptography, combinatorics, probability.

A. Rudnicky, Principal Systems Scientist (CS/LTI): speech recognition, spoken language interaction, interface design, dialog systems.

T. Sandholm, Professor: e-commerce, game theory, artificial intelligence, auctions, automated negotiation, combinatorial optimization, bounded rationality.

M. Satyanarayanan, Carnegie Group Professor of Computer Science: mobile and pervasive computing, distributed file systems, measurement and evaluation, security.

B. Schmerl, Senior Systems Scientist: software engineering, software architectures, programming environments, pervasive computing, dynamic reconfiguration.

R. Schwartz, Associate Professor (Biological Sciences/CS): computational molecular biology, biological modeling and simulation, computational genetics/genomics.

D. Scott, University Professor (Emeritus): semantics of computer languages, computer algebra.

S. Seshan, Associate Professor: network protocols/services/applications, distributed systems, mobile computing, wireless networks.

M. Shaw, Perlis Professor (ISR/CS): software architecture, software engineering, programming systems and methodologies.

D. Siewiorek, Buhl University Professor: computer architecture, fault-tolerant computing, design automation, parallel processing, mobile computing, rapid prototyping.

R. Simmons, Research Professor (RI/CS): autonomous mobile robots, robot architectures, multirobot coordination, human-robot social interaction, planning and task execution, diagnosis.

D. Slater, Assistant Teaching Professor: programming in C++.

D. Sleator, Professor: data structures, graph algorithms, online algorithms, parsing natural languages.

P. Steenkiste, Professor (CS/ECE): networking, network services, ubiquitous computing, distributed systems.

M. Stehlik, Teaching Professor and Assistant Dean for Undergraduate Education: programming systems, human-computer interaction.

R. Stern, Professor (ECE): acoustics of speech production.

K. Sutner, Teaching Professor and Associate Dean for Undergraduate Education: automata theory, computer algebra.

D. Touretzky, Research Professor (CS/CNBC): computational neuroscience, spatial representations in the brain, cognitive robotics.

A. Treuille, Assistant Professor (CS/RI): computer graphics, numerical computing, scientific discovery games.

M. Veloso, Professor: artificial intelligence; planning, execution, and learning in autonomous agents; multiagent and multirobot systems; robot soccer.

L. Von Ahn, Assistant Professor: novel techniques for utilizing computational abilities of humans, human-computer interaction, AI, theoretical cryptography and security.

H. Wactlar, Research Professor: information systems, digital libraries, distributed operating systems, networking.

J. Wing, Professor and Department Head: formal specification and verification, software security, trustworthy systems, distributed systems, programming methodology.

E. Xing, Associate Professor (ML): machine learning, computational biology, statistical genetics, algorithms for probabilistic inference/learning, evolutionary genomics and information retrieval.

Y. Yang, Professor (LTI/CS): machine learning applied to text classification, information retrieval, computational biology.

H. Zhang, Professor: computer networks, Internet, quality of service, distributed systems.

CLAREMONT GRADUATE UNIVERSITY

Financial Engineering Program

Financial Engineering
Claremont Graduate University

Program of Study

The Financial Engineering Program at Claremont Graduate University (CGU) is a joint program between the School of Mathematical Sciences and the Peter F. Drucker and Masatoshi Ito Graduate School of Management, based on the belief that the integration of a rigorous mathematics curriculum enables students to develop analytical skills and simulation techniques needed to analyze and evaluate financial products and other risk exposures. The use of case studies and field-based internships develops the methods and insights students must have to interpret organizational needs and goals in the design of appropriate financial, organizational, and product-market risks. With this unique structure, students receive a focused yet practical multidisciplinary education in financial engineering that is both critically important to management and quantitatively extensive.

Students who pursue the M.S. in Financial Engineering on a full-time basis (16 units per semester) complete the program in three semesters. Students who pursue the M.S. degree on a part-time basis generally take one or two courses per semester and typically complete the degree in about six semesters.

The course schedule for the three-semester completion track is as follows: the first semester (fall), probability, financial accounting, corporate finance, and an elective; second semester (spring), stochastic processes, statistics, financial derivatives, and an elective; and the third semester (fall), math finance, asset management, and two electives.

This intensive and highly focused program prepares graduates for careers in a broad range of specialties that include risk management, valuations, fixed income, financial analysis, asset management, hedging analysis, credit risk analysis, actuarial sciences, and structured products.

Research Facilities

Faculty members are actively engaged in research in the areas of strategy development and execution, leadership models, organizational development and revitalization, new-venture finance, venture capital models for emerging economies, and quality-of-life measurement and tools. There are several research institutes and centers that provide opportunities for funded research, the organization of research colloquiums on a national and international scale, and the integration of the Ph.D. program.

The program has a Bloomberg terminal available for student use. The libraries' collections include more than 2 million volumes: books, journals, magazines, and newspapers as well as a variety of media resources. Currently, the libraries provide electronic access to articles in more than 35,000 journals and receive more than 3,500 journals in print. This large collection of electronic resources provides ready access to a wide variety of materials: bibliographic, full-text, multimedia, data, sound, and images.

Financial Aid

Merit-based fellowships are available to those who qualify. Domestic students are also eligible to apply for federal student loans. A large portion of admitted students receive some form of financial aid.

Cost of Study

For the 2010–11 year, the cost of tuition for the Master of Science in Financial Engineering is $1554 per unit. This amount does not include room and board. For a more detailed breakdown of tuition and fees, students should visit http://www.cgu.edu/pages/7631. asp.

Living and Housing Costs

For details about housing and pricing structure, students should visit http://www.cgu.edu/pages/1156.asp.

Student Group

CGU prides itself on its diverse, talented, and proactive student population. Drawn from a pool of exceptional candidates, students in the Financial Engineering Program have a wide range of interests.

Student Outcomes

Recent graduates have been hired by the following companies: Goldman Sachs, Deutsche Bank, Moodys KMV, Trust Company of the West, Wilshire Associates, Markit, Bank of America, Southern California Edison, Western Asset, Moore Capital Management, Primus, Axioma, and Credit Agricole Asset Management. The starting salaries range from $60,000 to $80,000 plus bonus, depending on work experience and location.

Location

Claremont residents enjoy both a small-town atmosphere and easy access to one of the nation's most metropolitan and diverse cities. Sometimes called "the city of trees and PhDs," Claremont is located 35 miles east of downtown Los Angeles. It is a residential community of 36,000 situated in the foothills of the San Gabriel Mountains, ideally located for those who enjoy skiing, hiking, swimming, and camping. Mountains, deserts, and beaches are all within an hour's drive, and the climate is sunny most of the year. In 2007, *Money* magazine ranked Claremont fifth out of 100 best places to live in the United States.

The University

Claremont Graduate University is like no other graduate-level university in the nation. Founded in 1925, CGU is an independent institution devoted entirely to graduate study. As a member of the Claremont Colleges, a consortium of seven independent institutions, CGU is able to offer a greater breadth of faculty and campus resources than is typical of other universities with 2,000 students. Students are encouraged to pursue personal academic interests and research agendas even when they transcend the boundaries between individual departments.

Applying

To apply, please visit the school Web site for priority application deadlines and additional application information. Students applying to the M.S.F.E. degree program must have had completed multivariate calculus and linear algebra with a grade of B or better, and be familiar with one of the following programming languages: C, C++, Java, VB, or Matlab. The Financial Engineering program is currently accepting application for the fall semesters only. Spring entry is open only to students pursuing a dual F.E./M.B.A. or F.E./math degree. For more information on dual degrees, please visit http://www.cgu.edu/pages/5714.asp.

Correspondence and Information

Financial Engineering Program
Claremont Graduate University
1021 North Dartmouth Avenue
Claremont, California 91711-6160
Phone: 909-607-7811
        800-944-4312 (toll-free)
Fax: 909-621-8551
E-mail: drucker@cgu.edu
Web site: http://www.cgu.edu/fineng

Claremont Graduate University

THE FACULTY AND THEIR RESEARCH

Management and Finance

Murat Binay, Assistant Professor of Finance; Ph.D. (finance), Texas at Austin. Initial public offerings, payout policy, corporate governance.

James Mills, Visiting Professor of Finance and Co-Academic Director of the Financial Engineering Program; Ph.D., Oregon. Financial derivatives, risk management.

Jay Prag, Clinical Associate Professor; Ph.D. (finance), Rochester. Not-for-profit finance, corporate culture and valuation.

Vijay Sathe, Professor of Management; Ph.D. (management), Ohio State. Corporate entrepreneurship, managing for global advantage.

James Wallace, Associate Professor of Accounting; Ph.D., Washington (Seattle). Alternate performance metrics, corporate social responsibility.

Hideki Yamawaki, Professor of Management and Associate Dean; Ph.D. (economics), Harvard. International business strategy, multinational corporate management.

Mathematics and Statistics

John Angus, Dean of the School of Mathematical; Ph.D. (applied statistics), California, Riverside. Mathematical finance and stochastic calculus, reliability theory and fault tolerant design, Global Positioning System/satellite navigation.

Ellis Cumberbatch, Professor of Mathematics and Program Director of the Joint Ph.D. Program in Engineering and Industrial Applied Mathematics; Ph.D. (mathematics), Manchester (England). Applied mathematics, industrial modeling, differential equations, fluid mechanics, semiconductors.

Andrew Nguyen, Adjunct Professor; Ph.D. (mathematics), California, Irvine. Probability, statistics, stochastic processes.

Henry Schellhorn, Assistant Professor of Mathematics and Program Co-Academic Director; Ph.D. (operations research), UCLA. Credit risk, interest-rate models, queuing theory.

CLARKSON UNIVERSITY

Information Technology

Programs of Study	The Master of Science in information technology (IT) program offers an interdisciplinary, broad-based curriculum for this professional degree. Students take courses from a range of disciplines that include math and computer science, electrical and computer engineering, technical communications, and management information systems. The one-year program has a practical orientation that emphasizes hands-on learning and real-world experience in collaborative projects.
	The master's degree in IT program comprises a minimum of 30 credit hours, which include one course treating modern object-oriented design in a language such as C++, one course treating the principles of computing and telecommunication systems, one course in the management of technology, three courses in application of information technology, and 6 credits of project work. Additional credits can include course or project work. Through course selection and project work, students can focus on areas in IT they find compelling.
	Students in this program develop a broad base of competencies in hardware, operating systems, computer applications, and the management of technology. At the same time, they can choose to explore specific application areas through elective classes and project work. Projects focus on real-world problems that provide experience directly applicable to IT in an organizational setting.
	Clarkson provides access to some of the latest equipment and software. Individuals can install and run multiple operating systems (UNIX/Linux, Microsoft Windows, VMware), manage Web servers, create storefront CGIs, and administer databases.
	The academic year consists of two semesters of fifteen weeks each. There is no formal summer session for graduate classes, but many students complete their projects during this time.
	Students can also opt to complete their degree in 1½ years, taking 10 credits each semester.
Financial Aid	Partial-tuition assistantships are available for all full-time students who are accepted. This includes up to 30 percent off the cost of tuition until degree requirements are met. This assistantship is merit-based.
Cost of Study	Tuition for graduate work is $1136 per credit hour for 2010–11. Fees are about $440 per year.
Living and Housing Costs	Estimated living expenses off campus are approximately $11,000 a year, which includes rent, food, books, clothing, recreation, and miscellaneous expenses. Most graduate students live off campus, as on-campus housing is very limited.
Student Group	There are approximately 400 total graduate students and 2,700 undergraduates.
Location	Clarkson is located in Potsdam, a quintessential college town, nestled in the foothills of the northern Adirondack region of New York. The beautiful northeast corner of the state is the home of the 6-million-acre Adirondack Park. Within 2 hours of the campus are Lake Placid and the cosmopolitan Canadian cities of Montreal and Ottawa.
The University	Founded in 1896, Clarkson stands out among America's private nationally ranked research institutions because of its dynamic collaborative learning environment, innovative degree and research programs, and unmatched track record for producing leaders and innovators.
	Clarkson is New York State's highest-ranked small research institution. The University attracts 3,000 enterprising students from diverse backgrounds (including some 400 graduate students) who thrive in rigorous programs in engineering, arts, sciences, business, and health sciences.
Applying	Although there is a rolling admission policy, the recommended application deadlines are May 15 for the fall semester and October 15 for the spring semester for U.S. applicants. International applicants are encouraged to apply by April 15 for the fall semester and October 1 for the spring semester. Students who apply by January 31 for the fall semester receive priority for assistantships and other financial aid. Prospective students may submit an online application using a credit card. Study may begin in August or January. Scores on the General Test of the GRE are required for all applications. TOEFL scores must be submitted by all applicants for whom English is a second language.
Correspondence and Information	Information Technology Graduate School Box 5802 Clarkson University Potsdam, New York 13699-5802 Phone: 315-268-3802 Fax: 315-268-3989 E-mail: sciencegrad@clarkson.edu horn@clarkson.edu Web site: http://www.clarkson.edu/graduate

Clarkson University

THE FACULTY

Fifteen full-time regular faculty members and 2 full-time regular instructors from the four departments participate in the graduate information technology program. The disciplines that compose the IT program include math and computer science, electrical and computer engineering, technical communications, and management information systems.

SAMPLE INFORMATION TECHNOLOGY PROJECTS

Web-Based System for Teaching Controller Performance Assessment
Fall 2005

Adviser: Dr. Raghunathan Rengasamy

This project includes the development of a C++ interface for communicating, with an experiment for controlling the level of liquid in multiple tanks. Matlab is used to control the liquid level by opening and closing valves that regulate the flow into the various tanks. A module written in C++ is integrated with a Web server for displaying real time on the Web data from the experiment. The system allows for a two-way communication so that commands from the Web can be directly fed to the experimental system. The complete site contains a calendar, software for user registration, authentication, and other resources.

Automatic Web Survey Generator and Administrator
Fall 2005

Adviser: Dr. Wm. Dennis Horn

This system automates the process of creating surveys. The survey administrator enters questions for the survey. Multiple choices for the answers are generated by the software based on a predefined value. The survey generator is password protected to prevent unwanted people from creating or modifying surveys. When users take the survey, results are stored in a flat database. Additional software analyzes the data and presents results on the Web behind authentication. PHP is used for the survey generation and analytical processing. JavaScript is used for validation. HTML/CSS is used for the basic HTML page design.

HPC Cluster
Summer 2004

Adviser: Professor Wm. Dennis Horn

The purpose of this project was to create a computational cluster to be used by the mechanical and aeronautical engineering faculty members and select graduate students. The hardware for this project consists of:

(1) IBM xSeries 345 with dual hyperthreaded 2.8-GHz Xeon processors (four logical processors), 2.5 GB of RAM, and two 36-GB Ultra-360 SCSI disks in Raid 0. This box serves as the management node.

(2) IBM 1350 Blade Centers fully populated with fourteen blades each. Each blade contains two hyperthreaded 2.8-GHz Xeon processors, 2.5 GB of RAM, and a 40-GB laptop hard drive. The blades and the management node are connected with each other using both gigabit Ethernet and Myrinet (a high-speed, low-latency, fiber-optic connection). Each node runs a version of SuSE Linux Professional Edition Version 9.1 and IBM's cluster services manager.

Documentation of Cisco Routers and Switches
Spring 2004

Adviser: Professor Jeanna Matthews

This project documents the configuration of Cisco Routers and Switches in Clarkson University's Cisco-ITL laboratory. The document includes basic router configuration, password recovery, Cisco switches in the ITL, IOS commands, upgrading router IOSes, making network cables and so forth. The document enables future students to maintain the equipment, set up experiments and classes, and update the hardware and software.

E-mail Gateway
Spring 2004

Adviser: Professor Wm. Dennis Horn

This project created an e-mail gateway to handle all incoming and outgoing e-mail from Clarkson's campus. This gateway sits between the Internet and Clarkson's internal mail system and runs antivirus and antispam measures against all SMTP messages that it receives. The hardware for this project consists of an IBM xSeries 345 with dual hyperthreaded 3.2-GHz Xeon processors (four logical processors), 2 GB of RAM, and two 36-GB Ultra-360 SCSI disks in Raid 0. The software running on this box consists of a patched qmail (MTA), spamassassin (antispam), uvscan (antivirus), and a collection of custom Perl scripts to prevent blatant spam attacks. When fully operational, this box handles upwards of 100,000 messages per day and contains approximately 13,000 messages in its queue. The majority of these queued messages are bounces generated as the result of undeliverable mail.

Windmill Research Project
Fall 2002

Adviser: Professor Kenneth Visser

Every 10 seconds, sensors at the Windmill Site (Potsdam, New York, Airport) record data on wind speed at 18 meters, 12 meters, and 6 meters; wind direction at 18 meters and 6 meters; and the temperature, relative humidity, and pressure. This project reduces the massive amount of raw data to human-interpretable form by creating an HTML interface that allows researchers to select time intervals of minutes, hours, days, weeks, and months and graph changes over periods of days, months, and years. Perl/CGI is used to crunch the data in less than a second and graph it, using the Perl GD.pm module, in PNG format. Graphs are scaled to fit on the screen, and multiple graphs can be placed in a single display for comparison.

COLUMBIA UNIVERSITY

Department of Computer Science

Programs of Study

The doctoral program of the Department of Computer Science is geared toward the exceptional student. The faculty believes that the best way to learn how to do research is by doing it; therefore, starting in their first semester, students conduct joint research with faculty members. In addition to conducting research they also prepare themselves for the Ph.D. comprehensive examinations, which test breadth in computer science. The primary educational goal is to prepare students for research and teaching careers either in universities or in industry. The Department enjoys a low doctoral student–faculty ratio (about 4:1).

Current research areas include artificial intelligence, collaborative work, computational biology, computational complexity, computational learning theory, computer architecture, computer-aided design of digital systems, databases, digital libraries, distributed computing, graphics, HCI, logic synthesis, mobile and wearable computing, multimedia, natural-language processing, networking, network management, operating systems, parallel processing, robotics, security, software engineering, user interfaces, virtual and augmented reality, vision, and Web technologies.

The Department also offers the Master of Science degree in computer science. This program can be completed within three semesters of full-time classwork. Completing the optional thesis generally stretches the program to two years. The M.S. degree can also be earned through part-time study.

Research Facilities

The Department has well-equipped lab areas for research in computer graphics, computer-aided digital design, computer vision, databases and digital libraries, data mining and knowledge discovery, distributed systems, mobile and wearable computing, natural-language processing, networking, operating systems, programming systems, robotics, user interfaces, and real-time multimedia.

The computer facilities include a shared infrastructure of Sun and Linux multiprocessor file servers, NetApp file servers, a large disk backup server, a student interactive teaching and research lab of high-end multimedia workstations, a large VMware system for teaching, a programming laboratory with 18 Windows workstations and 63 Linux workstations, a large cluster of Linux servers for computational work, a cluster of Sun servers, and a compute cluster consisting of a Linux cloud that can support approximately 5000 VMware instances. The research infrastructure includes hundreds of workstations and PCs running Solaris, Windows, Linux, and Mac OSX; 7 terabytes of disk space are backed up by a Sun StorEdge LT02 with a 100-tape library unit.

Research labs contain several large Linux and Solaris clusters, Puma 500 and IBM robotic arms, a UTAH-MIT dexterous hand, an Adept-1 robot, mobile research robots, a real-time defocus range sensor, interactive 3-D graphics workstations with 3-D position and orientation trackers, prototype wearable computers, wall-sized stereo projection systems, see-through head-mounted displays, a networking testbed with three Cisco 7500 backbone routers, traffic generators, Ethernet switches, and a 17-node (34CPU) IBM Netfinity cluster. The Department uses a 3COM SIP IP phone system. The protocol was developed in the Department.

The servers are connected on a gigabit network; all have remote consoles and remote power for easy maintenance after hours. The rest of the Department's computers are connected via a switched 100 Mb/s Ethernet network, which has direct connectivity to the campus OC-3 Internet and Internet2 gateways. The campus has 802.11 a/b wireless LAN coverage.

The research facility is supported by a full-time staff of professional system administrators and programmers aided by a number of part-time student system administrators.

Financial Aid

Most doctoral students and a few master's students receive graduate research assistantships. The stipend for 2009–10 was $2708 per month for the academic year. In addition, graduate research assistants receive full tuition exemption. A limited number of teaching assistantships are available to both doctoral and master's students.

Cost of Study

Tuition and fees totaled approximately $32,000 for the M.S. program and $36,000 for the Ph.D. program for the 2009–10 academic year.

Living and Housing Costs

In 2009–10, apartments in University-owned buildings cost $1293 and up per month. Rooms are also available at International House; these cost $8217 and up per academic year.

Student Group

There are 120 Ph.D. students in the Department. A large proportion of Columbia University's student body is at the graduate level; of the 25,459 students, 15,819 are in the graduate or professional schools.

Location

New York City is the intellectual, artistic, cultural, gastronomic, corporate, financial, and media center of the United States, and perhaps of the world. The city is renowned for its theaters, museums, libraries, restaurants, opera, and music. Inexpensive student tickets for cultural and sporting events are frequently available, and the museums are open to students at very modest cost or are free. The ethnic variety of the city adds to its appeal. The city is bordered by uncongested areas of great beauty that provide varied types of recreation, such as hiking, camping, skiing, and ocean and lake swimming. There are superb beaches on Long Island and in New Jersey, while to the north lie the Catskill, Green, Berkshire, and Adirondack mountains. Close at hand is the beautiful Hudson River valley.

The University

Columbia University was established as King's College in 1754. Today it consists of sixteen schools and faculties and is one of the leading universities in the world. The University draws students from many countries. The high caliber of the students and faculty makes it an intellectually stimulating place to be. Columbia University is located on Morningside Heights, close to Lincoln Center for the Performing Arts, Greenwich Village, Central Park, and midtown Manhattan. Columbia athletic teams compete in the Ivy League.

Applying

For maximum consideration for admission to the doctoral program, students should submit the required application materials before December 1 for the fall term and before October 1 for the spring term. Applicants must submit official applications, transcripts, at least three recommendation letters, and a $70 application fee. The General and Subject Tests of the Graduate Record Examinations are required for all computer science graduate applicants. The deadlines for applications to the master's program are February 15 for fall admission and October 1 for spring admission.

Program information can be found at http://www.cs.columbia.edu. Further details on admission and online application for the M.S. program are on the Web at http://www.cs.columbia.edu/education/admissions#msadmissions and for the Ph.D. program at http://www.cs.columbia.edu/education/admissions#phd.

Correspondence and Information

Fu Foundation School of Engineering and Applied Science
Department of Computer Science
450 Computer Science Building
Mail Code 0401
Columbia University
1214 Amsterdam Avenue
New York, New York 10027-7003
Phone: 212-939-7000
Web site: http://www.cs.columbia.edu/education/admissions

Columbia University

THE FACULTY AND THEIR RESEARCH

Alfred V. Aho, Lawrence Gussman Professor. Programming languages, compilers, software, quantum computing.

Peter K. Allen, Professor. Robotics, computer vision, 3-D modeling.

Peter Belhumeur, Professor. Computer vision, biometrics, face recognition, computational photography, computer graphics, biological species identification.

Steven M. Bellovin, Professor. Internet security, computer security, privacy, information technology policy.

Adam H. Cannon, Assistant Professor. Machine learning, statistical pattern recognition, computer science education.

Luca Carloni, Associate Professor. Computer-aided design, embedded systems, multi-core platform architectures, cyber-physical systems.

Stephen A. Edwards, Associate Professor. Embedded systems, domain-specific languages, compilers, hardware-software codesign, computer-aided design.

Steven K. Feiner, Professor. Computer graphics and user interfaces, augmented reality and virtual environments, mobile and wearable computing, knowledge-based design of graphics and multimedia, computer games, information visualization, hypermedia.

Luis Gravano, Associate Professor. Databases, digital libraries, distributed search over text databases, Web search, "top-k" query processing, information extraction, text mining.

Eitan Grinspun, Associate Professor. Computer graphics, scientific computing: computational mechanics, mathematical foundations of graphics, discrete differential geometry.

Jonathan L. Gross, Professor of Computer Science, Mathematics, and Mathematical Statistics. Computational aspects of topological graph theory and knot theory, enumerative analysis, and combinatorial models; applications to network layouts on higher-order surfaces and to interactive computer graphics of weaves and links.

Julia Hirschberg, Professor. Natural-language processing.

Tony Jebara, Associate Professor. Machine learning: vision, graphs, and spatio-temporal modeling.

Gail E. Kaiser, Professor. Software testing, collaborative work, computer and network security, parallel computing and distributed systems, self-managing systems, Web technologies, information management, software development environments and tools.

John R. Kender, Professor. Computer vision, video understanding, visual user interfaces, medical imaging processing, artificial intelligence.

Angelos D. Keromytis, Associate Professor. Computer and network security.

Martha Kim, Associate Professor. Computer architecture, hardware systems, hardware/software interaction, parallel hardware and software systems.

Tal G. Malkin, Associate Professor. Cryptography, information and network security, foundations of computer science, computational complexity, distributed computation, randomness in computation, approximation algorithms.

Kathleen R. McKeown, Henry and Gertrude Rothschild Professor. Artificial intelligence, natural-language processing, language generation, multimedia explanation, text summarization, user interfaces, user modeling, digital libraries.

Vishal Misra, Associate Professor. Networking, modeling and performance evaluation, information theory.

Shree K. Nayar, T. C. Chang Professor. Computer vision, computational imaging, computer graphics, robotics, human-computer interfaces.

Jason Nieh, Associate Professor. Operating systems, distributed systems, mobile computing, thin-client computing, performance evaluation.

Steven M. Nowick, Associate Professor. Asynchronous and mixed timing circuits, computer-aided digital design, low-power and high-performance digital systems.

Itsik Pe'er, Assistant Professor. Computational biology, genomics, medical and population genetics, isolated and admixed populations, analysis of heritable variation in cancer.

Kenneth A. Ross, Professor. Databases, query optimization, declarative languages for database systems, logic programming, architecture-sensitive software design.

Daniel Rubenstein, Associate Professor. Computer networks, network robustness and security, multimedia networking, performance evaluation, algorithms, low-power networking.

Henning G. Schulzrinne, Professor. Computer networks, multimedia systems, mobile and wireless systems, ubiquitous and pervasive computing.

Rocco A. Servedio, Associate Professor. Computational learning theory, computational complexity theory, randomized algorithms, machine-learning quantum computation, cryptography, combinatorics.

Simha Sethumadhavan, Assistant Professor. Computer architecture, hardware security.

Salvatore J. Stolfo, Professor. Computer security, intrusion detection systems, parallel computing, artificial intelligence, machine learning.

Joseph F. Traub, Edwin Howard Armstrong Professor. Quantum computing, computational complexity, information-based complexity, financial computations.

Henryk Woźniakowski, Professor. Computational complexity, information-based complexity, quantum computing, algorithmic analysis, numerical mathematics.

Junfeng Yang, Assistant Professor. Operating systems, software reliability, security, storage systems.

Mihalis Yannakakis, Percy K. and Vida L. W. Hudson Professor. Algorithms, complexity theory, combinatorial optimization, databases, testing and verification.

Yechiam Yemini, Professor. Computer networks.

Associated Faculty/Research Scientists

Mona T. Diab, Associate Research Scientist, Center for Computational Learning Systems. Computational linguistics, statistical natural language processing, machine learning, computational lexical semantics, multilinguality, social communication, Arabic natural language processing.

Haimonti Dutta, Associate Research Scientist, Center for Computational Learning Systems. Data mining and machine learning, data intensive computing, distributed data mining and optimization.

Nizar Habash, Research Scientist, Center for Computational Learning Systems. Natural-language processing, machine translation, multilingual processing, natural-language generation.

Claire Monteleoni, Associate Research Scientist, Center for Computational Learning Systems. Machine learning: theory and algorithms for active learning, online learning, and privacy- preserving machine learning; climate science.

Rebecca J. Passonneau, Research Scientist, Center for Computational Learning Systems. Natural language processing, spoken dialogue systems, text classification for real world problems, discourse and dialogue structure, reference and temporal reference, corpus design and annotation, evaluation.

Dana Pe'er, Assistant Professor (Biological Sciences). Computational biology, machine learning, biological networks, genomics and systems biology.

Owen Rambow, Research Scientist, Center for Computational Learning Systems. Natural-language processing, language in social networks, natural-language syntax, multilingual processing, natural-language generation.

Ansaf Salleb-Aouissi, Associate Research Scientist, Center for Computational Learning Systems. Machine learning, data mining: rule induction, frequent patterns, ranking, multi-relational learning, applications.

Clifford Stein, Professor. Algorithms, combinatorial optimization, scheduling, network algorithms.

Stephen H. Unger, Professor Emeritus of Computer Science and Electrical Engineering. Logic circuits theory, digital systems, self-timed systems, parallel processing, technology-society interface, engineering ethics.

Vladimir Vapnik, Professor, Computer Science and Center for Computational Learning Systems. Empirical inference, support vector machines, kernel methods, transductive inference.

David L. Waltz, Director, Center for Computational Learning Systems. Machine learning, cognitive modeling.

Arthur G. Werschulz, Adjunct Senior Research Scientist. Information-based complexity, especially that of partial differential equations, integral equations, and ill-posed problems.

DAKOTA STATE UNIVERSITY

Department of Information Systems and Technology

Programs of Study

Dakota State University (DSU) offers graduate degree programs in educational technology (M.S.E.T.), information assurance (M.S.I.A.), health informatics (M.S.H.I.), and information systems (M.S.I.S. and D.Sc.). The programs are available online or on campus. Educational technology requires a one-week residency on campus. There are no other required graduate program residencies.

The Master of Science in Educational Technology program (M.S.E.T) empowers educators and trainers to meet the increasing demands of integrating technology in curriculum and instruction. Specializations include distance education, technology systems, and a K–12 educational technology endorsement. Students take 36 credits in common core courses, which are shared between DSU and the University of South Dakota. GetEducated.com rates the program a best buy. For more information, students should visit http://www.dsu.edu/mset/index.aspx.

The Master of Science in Information Assurance program (M.S.I.A.) prepares graduates to protect an organization's information assets. Both the National Security Agency and the Department of Homeland Security have designated DSU as a National Center of Academic Excellence in Information Assurance Education (CAEIAE). The program requires 36 hours beyond the baccalaureate, including eight core courses (24 credit hours) and a four-course sequence (12 credit hours) in a specialization. Specializations include banking and financial security, wireless and networking security, and Internet and e-commerce. GetEducated.com rates the program a best buy. For more information, students should visit http://www.dsu.edu/msia/index.aspx.

The Master of Science in Health Informatics (M.S.H.I.) is intended to produce graduates who are expected to play a key role in the design, development, and management of health information systems in health-care related facilities, agencies, and organizations, in integrated delivery systems, and in interconnected, community-wide health data exchanges and regional networks. The program is intended to attract students with a variety of educational backgrounds and disciplines. The program requires 33 hours beyond the baccalaureate, including seven core courses (21 credit hours), three elective courses (9 credit hours), and a three-credit capstone experience. For more information, students should visit http://www.dsu.edu/mshi/index.aspx.

The Master of Science in Information Systems program (M.S.I.S.) focuses on the integration of information technology with business problems and opportunities. Specializations include data management, electronic commerce, network administration and security, and health-care information systems. GetEducated.com rates it a best buy. For more information, students should visit http://www.dsu.edu/msis/index.aspx.

The Doctor of Science (D.Sc.) in information systems program prepares students for careers in teaching, research, consulting, and corporate employment. Specializations include decision support, knowledge and data management, information assurance and computer security, and health-care information systems. The D.Sc. requires 88 semester credit hours. Students take 63 credit hours of graduate course work: 27 credit hours of master's-level information systems, which may be waived for students who have completed the M.S.I.S. program or equivalent; 9 credit hours of research methods; and 27 credit hours of research specialization, including research seminars and core and elective courses. D.Sc. students must also complete a screening examination, a qualifying portfolio, and 25 credit hours of dissertation. For more information, students should visit http://www.dsu.edu/doctor-of-science/index.aspx.

Research Facilities

The Karl E. Mundt Library provides access to an extensive collection of materials through its online library catalog, which includes more than 4.5 million holdings of more than seventy libraries in the South Dakota Library Network (SDLN). In addition to being an online catalog of library holdings, the SDLN has been enriched by the addition of a number of external databases, most notably, EBSCO's Academic Search Premier, Lexis-Nexis Academic, ProQuest Research Library, and ABI-Inform. Many of these databases provide the full text and images of articles and books. Web-based access to the information services provides students with access to databases critical to their disciplines. Materials held by other libraries are readily available through the electronic interlibrary loan system or full text. The library also provides online access to tutorials and other research aides.

DSU also offers an Advanced Informatics Research Lab (AIRL) which is a state-of-the-art computing lab supporting applied information systems research in the areas of decision support data and knowledge management, information assurance, and health care. It supports the information systems faculty, graduate assistants, and students (online and on-campus) involved in the D.Sc. in information systems program. The lab includes infrastructure to support development and deployment of prototypes and other research results and computing capacity for conducting statistical analysis and running and solving models. It allows distance students access to computing resources and specialized workstations and software. The AIRL also has a variety of decision support tools and technologies for building and deploying DSS. Its servers run Windows and Linux operating systems and the lab provides support for .NET, JAVA and other development environment/technologies, e.g., MS SQL, Visual Studio 2005, etc.

An excellent computer environment is found at DSU. Computer laboratories are available in every academic building on campus. To provide ample facilities for both instruction and outside course work, labs are used directly in teaching and for general access. For the convenience of students, microcomputers are located in the dorms, in the Trojan Center (student union), and the library. In addition to cabled connections, a wireless network also supports mobile computing devices in each academic building, the Trojan Center, and the library.

Financial Aid

Graduate students apply for federal financial aid with the Free Application for Federal Student Aid (FAFSA), either online or with a paper form. Graduate students may be eligible to receive Federal Stafford Loans and Federal Perkins Loans but not Federal Pell Grants or Federal Supplemental Education Opportunity Grants. In addition, graduate assistantships are available to qualified graduate students, based on need and/or merit and available funds. Recipients of an assistantship receive a reduced tuition rate (student pays one third the state-support tuition rate) and a stipend as established by the Board of Regents. More information is available online at http://www.dsu.edu/gradoffice/grad-assistantships.aspx or by telephone at 605-256-5799.

Cost of Study

For the academic year 2009–10, tuition per credit hour ranged from $139 to $337 depending on residency and delivery of the courses. Online courses were $338 per credit for both in-state and out-of-state students. Fees totaled around $114 per credit hour for all students in classes on the DSU campus. More information is available at http://www.dsu.edu/gradoffice/grad-tuition-fees.aspx.

Living and Housing Costs

On-campus housing is available. Local telephone service, cable TV, and Internet access are included in the semester room fee. Students are expected to provide their own phone. Each hall has one or more kitchens, TV lounges, and card/coin-operated washers and dryers. Residence hall rates range between $1319 and $1732 per semester, whereas apartments are $1597 per person per semester. Meal plans range from $987 to $1125 per semester. The Madison community has several apartment complexes and off-campus housing.

Location

DSU is in Madison, South Dakota, less than an hour northwest of Sioux Falls. Madison is in the state's southern lakes region, which offers great outdoor recreation. The University is minutes from Lake Herman State Park and Walker's Point Recreation Area. Madison offers a variety of options for dining, shopping, and entertainment. For fitness and other recreation, students can easily walk to Madison's excellent Community Center. Madison is a safe town, with little traffic and a high quality of life as well as job opportunities for students and spouses.

The University

Dakota State University (DSU) strives to be one of the best technological universities in the Midwest. *U.S. News & World Report* ranked DSU the number 1 Top Public Baccalaureate College in the Midwest in 2007, 2008, 2009, and again in 2010. DSU is accredited by the North Central Association of Colleges and Schools, and GetEducated.com rates its online master's degree programs as best buys.

Applying

In general, students should have earned a baccalaureate degree from a regionally accredited college or university. Each applicant must provide a completed application form, the $35 application fee ($85 for international students), one official transcript for all college work, three forms of recommendation, and official scores on the standardized graduate admission test (GRE). All international applicants must take the Test of English as a Foreign Language (TOEFL) and score at least 550 on the PBT (213 on the CBT or 79 on the iBT). Students should check online for program-specific requirements and deadlines.

Correspondence and Information

Dr. Omar El-Gayar, Dean
Office of Graduate Studies & Research
Dakota State University
Madison, South Dakota 57042-1799

Phone: 605-256-5799
Fax: 605-256-5093
E-mail: omar.el-gayar@dsu.edu
Web site: http://www.dsu.edu/gradoffice/index.aspx

Dakota State University

THE FACULTY

Richard Avery, Associate Professor of Mathematics; Ph.D., Nebraska–Lincoln.
Richard Christoph, Professor of Computer Information Systems; Ph.D., Clemson.
Amit Deokar, Assistant Professor of Information Systems; Ph.D., Arizona.
Omar El-Gayar, Associate Professor and Dean of Graduate Studies and Research; Ph.D., Hawaii at Manoa.
William Figg, Associate Professor of Computer Information Systems; Ph.D., Capella.
Mark Geary, Assistant Professor of Education, Ph.D.
Steve Graham, Assistant Professor of Computer Science; Ph.D., Kansas.
Tom Halverson, Associate Professor of Computer Science and Dean of the College of Business and Information Systems; Ph.D., Iowa.
Mark Hawkes, Associate Professor of Instructional Technology and Program Coordinator of the Master of Science in Educational Technology; Ph.D., Syracuse.
Stephen Krebsbach, Associate Professor of Computer Science; Ph.D., North Dakota State.
Sreekanth Malladi, Assistant Professor of Information Assurance; Ph.D., Idaho.
Mark Moran, Assistant Professor of Information Systems; M.B.A., South Dakota; Ph.D., Capella.
Jeff Palmer, Professor of Mathematics; Ph.D., Washington State.
Josh Pauli, Assistant Professor of Information Systems; Ph.D., North Dakota State.
Wayne Pauli, Assistant Professor of Information Systems and Director of Center of Excellence in Computer Information Systems; Ph.D., Capella.
Ronghua Shan, Associate Professor of Computer Science/Information Systems; Ph.D., Nebraska–Lincoln.
Kevin Streff, Assistant Professor of Information Assurance, Director of Center of Excellence in Information Assurance, and MSIA Program Coordinator; Ph.D., Capella.
Daniel Talley, Associate Professor of Economics; Ph.D., Oregon.
Haomin Wang, Associate Professor of Instructional Technology and Webmaster; Ed.D., Northern Arizona.
Robert Warren, Professor of Science Education; Ph.D., Utah.
Don Wiken, Associate Professor of Education; Ed.D., South Dakota.

FLORIDA INSTITUTE OF TECHNOLOGY

College of Engineering
Department of Computer Sciences

Programs of Study

The Department of Computer Sciences offers programs of graduate study leading to the degrees of Master of Science in Computer Science, Master of Science in Software Engineering, and Doctor of Philosophy in Computer Science. Major areas of study include artificial intelligence, computer networks, computer security, data mining and machine learning, database systems, information assurance, programming languages, software engineering, and software testing.

The master's degree in computer science offers students the opportunity to pursue advanced studies in various areas of computer science. The program is designed for students with baccalaureate degrees in computer science and provides a solid preparation for those who may pursue a doctorate. All students must complete and defend a thesis or pass a final program examination during their last semester.

The master's degree in software engineering offers the student the opportunity to advance their skills in software development and software project management. The program is designed for students with baccalaureate degrees in computer science or closely related fields. Software testing and computer security are fields of emphasis within the Department. All students must complete and defend a thesis or pass a final program examination during their last semester.

The doctoral program is designed to provide research in the disciplines of computer science. The program requires broad knowledge of computer science fundamentals, mastery of a specialized subject, and the creativity to produce a dissertation based on original research.

Research Facilities

The computer science program occupies approximately 2,500 square feet of laboratory space and 2,000 square feet of office space in the Harris Center for Science and Engineering, a state-of-the-art research facility that houses the Harris Institute for Assured Information. Computer laboratories support active research programs in artificial intelligence, computer networks, computer security, database systems, programming languages, software engineering, and software testing. The program provides graduate students with a wide range of computing resources for course work and research. The College of Engineering and the University provide additional computer laboratories for student use. Computer resources include Unix and Windows servers and clients. All machines are connected on a 1-Gb internal network and externally to Internet2.

Financial Aid

Graduate teaching and research assistantships are available to qualified students. For 2010–11, stipends range from $12,500 to $14,000 for nine months. All assistantships include tuition remission. Computer-based information on scholarships, loan funds, and other student assistance may be obtained from the Financial Aid Office and the Department's Web site at http://cs.fit.edu.

Cost of Study

In 2010–11, tuition is $1040 per semester credit hour for all graduate students. Tuition is remitted for students awarded assistantships.

Living and Housing Costs

The cost of living in central Florida is approximately 15 percent lower than the national average. Housing for single students is available in on-campus dormitories. Efficiency apartments as well as one-, two-, or three-bedroom apartments for single and married students can be obtained in the area surrounding the Institute. Average monthly rental rates range from $325 to $550.

Student Group

The Department currently has an enrollment of 160 graduate students from colleges throughout the world. Approximately 25 percent of the graduate students are women, and 59 percent are international students.

Student Outcomes

Graduates of the College of Engineering have found employment with such firms as IBM, Microsoft, Texas Instruments, Oracle, Cadence, NASA, Harris Corp., AT&T, General Electric, Northrop Grumman, Lockheed Martin, McDonnell Douglas, Rockwell International, Advanced Micro Devices, USF&G, United Technologies, Honeywell, Computer Sciences Raytheon, ITT Aerospace, U.S. Patent Office, CIA, Los Alamos National Laboratory, Hewlett-Packard, Intel, Naval Air Systems Command, Naval Undersea Warfare Center, and Rational Software.

Location

Florida Tech's main campus is located in Melbourne, a residential community on Florida's Space Coast. Melbourne is the key city in south Brevard County, which also encompasses nine other smaller communities on the mainland and beachside. The Kennedy Space Center and Disney World are within a 90-minute drive of the Institute. The area's economy is a well-balanced mix of electronics, aviation, light manufacturing, opticals, communications, agriculture, and tourism.

The Institute

Florida Tech was founded in 1958 and has developed rapidly into a university that provides both undergraduate and graduate education in the sciences and engineering for selected students from throughout the United States and many countries. Current enrollment on the Melbourne campus is about 4,000. In addition to computer sciences, Florida Tech offers graduate programs in aerospace engineering, airport development management, applied mathematics, aquaculture, aviation science, biotechnology, business administration, cell and molecular biology, chemical engineering, chemistry, civil engineering, computer education, computer engineering, ecology, electrical engineering, engineering management, environmental management, environmental resource management, environmental science, industrial/organizational psychology, managerial communication, marine biology, mathematics education, mechanical engineering, ocean engineering, oceanography, operations research, physics, science education, space sciences, and technical and professional communication.

Applying

Further information and application forms for admission may be obtained from the Graduate Admissions Office. Students are required to take the GRE General Test and encouraged to take the Subject Test in Computer Science and submit scores for consideration. Separate application for financial aid must be made on forms available from the Department's Web site at http://cs.fit.edu and must be submitted by March 15.

Correspondence and Information

Office of Graduate Admissions
Florida Institute of Technology
150 West University Boulevard
Melbourne, Florida 32901-6975
Phone: 321-674-8027
Fax: 407-723-9468
E-mail: grad-admissions@fit.edu
Web site: http://www.fit.edu

Dr. W. D. Shoaff, Head
Department of Computer Sciences
Florida Institute of Technology
150 West University Boulevard
Melbourne, Florida 32901-6975
Phone: 321-674-8763
E-mail: wds@cs.fit.edu
Web site: http://cs.fit.edu

Florida Institute of Technology

THE FACULTY AND THEIR RESEARCH

William Allen, Associate Professor; Ph.D., Central Florida, 2003. Network security. Generic danger detection for mission continuity. In *Proceedings: Eighth International Symposium on Network Computing and Application,* 2009 (with R. Ford et al). The ISDF framework: Integrating security patterns and best practices. In *Proceedings: Third International Conference on Information Security and Assurance,* 2009 (with A. Alkussayer). (E-mail: wallen@cs.fit.edu)

Phil Bernhard, Associate Professor; Ph.D., SUNY at Albany, 1988. Databases, database performance tuning and optimization, software engineering. Extracting data models from legacy database systems: A case study in reverse engineering. *Proceedings of the 2005 International Conference on Information and Knowledge Engineering,* Las Vegas, Nevada, June 20–23, 2005, CSREA Press, 2005 *(with E. Wilson, A. Hebert, and K. L. Fox).* (E-mail: pbernhar@cs.fit.edu)

Pat Bond, Adjunct Professor; Ph.D., Georgia, 1976. Software architecture, software systems. Better prediction of software failure times using order statistics. *Journal of Chinese International Industrial Engineering,* in press (with N. Abosaq). Improvement of software reliability modeling predictions by the detection and removal of test outliers. In *ACM-SE 47: Proceedings of the Forty-Seventh Annual Southeast Regional Conference,* New York, New York, 2009 (with N. Abosaq). Better prediction of software failure times using robust statistical techniques. In *Asian International Workshop on Advanced Reliability Modeling,* 2008 (with N. Abosaq). (E-mail: pbond@cs.fit.edu)

Philip K. Chan, Associate Professor; Ph.D., Columbia, 1996. Scalable and adaptive systems, machine learning, data mining, parallel and distributed computing. Increasing coverage to improve detection of network and host anomalies. *Mach. Learn.,* in press (with G. Tandon). Learning implicit user interest hierarchy for context in personalization. *Appl. Intell.* 28(2):153–66, 2008 (with H. R. Kim). (E-mail: pkc@cs.fit.edu)

Richard Ford, Professor and Director of the Harris Institute for Assured Information; D.Phil., Oxford, 1992. Information assurance, network security. Probabilistic suffix models for API sequence analysis of Windows XP applications. *Pattern Recogn.* 41(1):90–101, 2008 (with G. Mazeroff, J. Gregor, and M. Thomason). How not to be seen ii: The defenders fight back. *IEEE Security and Privacy Magazine* 5(6):65–8, 2007 (with W. H. Allen). (E-mail: rford@cs.fit.edu)

Keith Gallagher, Associate Professor; Ph.D., Maryland, Baltimore, 1990. Dependence clusters in source code. *ACM Trans. Program. Lang. Syst.,* 32(1):1–33, 2009 (with M. Harmon, D. Binkley, N. Gold, and J. Krinke). Program slicing. *IEEE Frontiers of Software Maintenance,* IEEE Press, 2008 (with D. Binkley). (E-mail: kgallagher@cs.fit.edu)

Cem Kaner, Professor; Ph.D., McMaster, 1984; J.D., Golden Gate, 1993. Building a free courseware community around an online software testing curriculum. *Eighth Annual MERLOT International Conference,* August, 2008 (with R. L. Fiedler and S. Barber). A cautionary note on checking software engineering papers for plagiarism. *IEEE Transactions on Education* 51(2):184–8, 2008 (with R. L. Fiedler). Good enough V and V for simulations: Some possibly helpful thoughts from the law and ethics of commercial software. In *Simulation Interoperability Workshop,* Providence, Rhode Island, April, 2008 (with S. J. Swenson). (E-mail: ckaner@cs.fit.edu)

Gerald Marin, Professor; Ph.D., North Carolina State, 1970. Computer networks, network security. A three-tier damage-driven security infrastructure for mission continuity. In *Proceedings, IEEE Military Communications Conference (MILCOM),* 2008 (with M. Carvalho, R. Ford, and W. Allen). Towards the detection of emulated environments via analysis of the stochastic nature of system calls. *Proceedings, Twentieth International Conference on Software Engineering and Knowledge Engineering,* 2008 (with T. Praveen et al). (E-mail: gmarin@cs.fit.edu)

Ronaldo Menezes, Associate Professor; Ph.D., York (England), 1999. Coordination and distributed systems, parallel models of computing. Handling dynamic networks using evolution in ant-colony optimization. In *IEA/AIE '08: Proceedings of the Twenty-First International Conference on Industrial, Engineering and Other Applications of Applied Intelligent Systems,* Berlin, Heidelberg, Springer-Verlag, pp. 795–804, 2008 (with C. Roach). An adaptive in-network aggregation operator for query processing in wireless sensor networks. *J. Syst. Software* 81(3):328–42, 2008 (with A. Brayner et al). A study of terrain coverage models. *Proceedings of the ACM Symposium on Applied Computing,* New York, New York, pp. 1964–8, 2008. (E-mail: rmenezes@cs.fit.edu)

Debasis Mitra, Professor; Ph.D., Indian Institute of Technology (Kharagpur), 1984; Ph.D., Louisiana at Lafayette, 1994. Artificial intelligence, medical imaging, spatio-temporal reasoning. Geant4 simulation of a cosmic ray muon tomography system with micro pattern gas detectors for the detection of high-z materials. *IEEE Transactions on Nuclear Science,* June 2009 (with J. Helsby et al). (E-mail: dmitra@cs.fit.edu)

J. Richard Newman, Professor and Director of the School of Computing; Ph.D., Southwestern Louisiana, 1976. Software engineering, information systems management, CASE tools for clean-room software engineering, legal issues, program specification tools. An undergraduate curriculum in software engineering. *Proc. Fourth Annu. Conf. Software Eng. Educ., SEI.* April 1990 (with Mills and Engle). Performance issues for an expert system written in Ada. *Fifty-Fourth Annual Meeting of the Florida Academy of Sciences.* Melbourne, Florida, March 23, 1990 (with Buoni and Baggs). (E-mail: newman@cs.fit.edu)

Eraldo Ribeiro, Associate Professor; Ph.D., York (England), 2000. Computer vision and animation. Learning structural models in multiple projection spaces. In *ICIAR '09 Proceedings of the Sixth International Conference on Image Analysis and Recognition,* 2009 (with R. Filipovych). Discovering constrained substructures in bayesian trees using the e.m. algorithm. In *ICIAR '08: Proceedings of the 5th International Conference on Image Analysis and Recognition,* Berlin, Heidelberg, Springer-Verlag, 2008. (E-mail: eribeiro@cs.fit.edu)

William D. Shoaff, Associate Professor; Ph.D., Southern Illinois, 1981. Mathematical programming, parallel algorithms, parallel processing, supercomputers, computer modeling in genetics, computer graphics. Texture mapping with wavelet transforms. *IASTED Comput. Graphics Imaging,* pp. 289–93, 1999. Integrating literate programming and cleanroom software engineering. *Second Australasian Conf. Comput. Sci. Educ.,* 1997. Domain independent temporal reasoning with recurring events. *Comput. Intelligence,* 1996. (E-mail: wds@cs.fit.edu)

Marius Silaghi, Assistant Professor; Ph.D., Swiss Federal Institute of Technology, 2002. Artificial intelligence, distributed problem solving, asynchronous algorithms. Maintaining consistency for ABT. Directed soft arc consistency in pseudo-trees. In *Proceedings of Autonomous Agents and Mulitiagent Systems,* 2009 (with T. Matsui et al). ADOPT-ing: Unifying asynchronous distributed optimization with asynchronous backtracking. *Journal of Autonomous Agents and Multi-Agent Systems (JAAMAS),* November 2008. (E-mail: msilaghi@cs.fit.edu)

Ryan Stansifer, Associate Professor; Ph.D., Cornell, 1985. Programming languages, compilers, information systems, internationalization. Implementations of bidirectional reordering algorithms. Higher-order functional programming and wildcards in Java. In *ACM-SE 45: Proceedings of the Forty-Fifth Annual Southeast Regional Conference.,* New York, New York, 2007 (with N. Sridranop). (E-mail: ryan@cs.fit.edu)

Scott Tilley, Professor and Director of Software Engineering; Ph.D., Victoria (Canada), 1995. Software engineering and evolution; computer security; software testing. Toward an evaluation framework of SOA security testing tools. *Proceedings of the Third IEEE International Systems Conference.* Managing legal risks associated with intellectual property on the Web. *Int. J. Bus. Inf. Syst.,* 3(1): 86–106, 2008 (with H. Kienle, D. German, and H. Muller). (E-mail: stilley@cs.fit.edu)

PENN STATE UNIVERSITY PARK

College of Engineering
Department of Computer Science and Engineering

Programs of Study

The Department of Computer Science and Engineering (CSE) offers Master of Engineering (30 credits), Master of Science (30 credits), and doctoral degree (48 credits) programs in computer science and engineering at the University Park Campus. Doctoral candidates must take a 1-credit CSE research experience course within the first two semesters, and a written, two-part candidacy examination must be completed during the first three regular semesters after entering the Ph.D. program. Students must pass a comprehensive examination and English competency and communication requirements. A thesis must be defended. Detailed regulations are in the Department's graduate brochure, which is available through the Department or online at the University's Web site.

Research Facilities

The Department of Computer Science and Engineering maintains computer system laboratories at the Information Sciences and Technology Building. The Department currently supports 3,500 user accounts on 425 UNIX workstations and servers. A number of computer vendors are represented in the Department's collection of systems, including Sun Microsystems, Apple, Dell, Compaq, Silicon Graphics, HP, and others. Operating systems include Solaris, MS Windows XP, OS X, Linux, and IRIX. The computer systems are connected to one or more of the thirty currently running subnets in CSE's Class B Internet address allocation. A gigabit connection to the campus backbone network allows any user to easily communicate with other research facilities around the world. The University has connections to the VbNS and commercial ISPs for access to other sites. Programming languages available to the users in the Department include C, C++, Pascal, FORTRAN, Scheme, Java, PROLOG, ML, Common LISP C#, and VB. StarOffice, MS Office, TeX, Troff, and Framemaker are available for typesetting and document preparation. There is a large collection of VLSI/CAD tools, including design system software from Cadence, Synopsys, and MicroMagic, Inc. The MathWorks MATLAB package and a number of its toolboxes are also available. Several classroom/labs in CSE are equipped with high-quality audiovisual configurations to foster interactive learning.

Financial Aid

Graduate students can be supported by a variety of fellowships and research or teaching assistantships. In 2009–10, stipends for half-time research or teaching assistantships ranged from $14,625 to $15,705. Grants-in-aid that cover tuition accompany these stipends. About half of the graduate students in the Department now receive financial assistance. A half-time assistant is expected to work 20 hours per week and must schedule 9–12 credits per semester.

Cost of Study

Tuition in 2009–10 is $8161 for Pennsylvania residents and $14,213 for nonresidents. Tuition fees; information technology ($230), activity ($76), student facilities fee ($100), and surcharge ($750) fees; and 80 percent of the mandatory health insurance coverage are included with a teaching/research assistantship. The above fees are for 9 or more credits.

Living and Housing Costs

University and private housing is available. The University's facilities range from dormitory rooms for single students to two-bedroom units for families. In 2009–10, dormitory rooms cost $2535 or more per semester, room and full board are approximately $4715 per semester, shared apartments are $2600 or more per semester, and family housing starts at $880 per month. Privately owned apartments are available and average from $500 to $950 per month for a shared apartment to $625 to $800 per month for single occupancy.

Student Group

Overall Penn State enrollment includes approximately 87,163 students, with 44,832 students at University Park (the main campus). There are more than 6,200 graduate students enrolled at University Park, 1,329 of whom are in the College of Engineering. Currently, there are 195 graduate students enrolled in the Department of Computer Science and Engineering. Students come from all parts of the United States. Penn State also has a diverse international population.

Student Outcomes

The demand for computer science and engineering graduates with master's and doctoral degrees is high. Starting salaries for doctoral graduates range from $90,000 to $100,000 per year in industrial positions. Recruiting for academic positions that begin in 2010–11 is strong, and candidates can expect annual salary offers ranging from $70,000 to $85,000. Almost all employers in today's economy utilize the expertise of computer science and engineering professionals. This demand for CSE graduates will continue for the foreseeable future.

Location

The University Park campus is located at the center of the state in the borough of State College. The town and its surrounding area, with a population of about 79,400, are located in low, rolling-mountain country and offer a variety of recreational activities. The community and the University present a wide array of cultural and athletic events.

The University and The Department

Penn State, founded in 1855, is a land-grant institution that offers undergraduate and graduate programs. The Department of Computer Science and Engineering was formed in 1993 and combines the strengths of the former Department of Computer Science and the Computer Engineering Program. The Department at Penn State consists of more than 40 faculty members, all of whom are graduate research faculty members. Research labs that are set up by both individuals and faculty groups enhance graduate education in the Department and provide opportunities for real-world projects that prepare students for future employment.

Applying

Applicants should hold a baccalaureate degree in computer science/engineering or a related field, with a minimum junior/senior GPA of 3.0. All applicants must provide a one-page statement of purpose, three letters of recommendation, and scores from the general aptitude test of the Graduate Record Examination (GRE). Electronic versions of these forms can be found online at http://www.cse.psu.edu/prospective/graduate/apply. The GRE Subject Test in computer science is also recommended. International students whose native language is not English must submit a TOEFL score unless they have received a degree from a U.S. institution. A minimum TOEFL score of 550 on the paper-based test, 213 on the computer-based test, or 80 with a 19 on the speaking section for the Internet-based test (iBT) is required. The minimum composite score for the IELTS is 6.5. To be considered for financial aid, international applicants must present a score from the Test of Spoken English (TSE); a score of less than 55 requires remedial course work in English as a second language. If the applicant has taken the TOEFL iBT, they are not required to take the TSE, since the TOEFL iBT has a speaking component; an iBT score of less than 26 requires remedial course work in English as a second language. Fall applicants who wish to be considered for financial aid should have completed applications on file before January 1.

Correspondence and Information

CSE Graduate Office
Department of Computer Science and Engineering
Penn State University Park
111 Information Sciences and Technology Building
University Park, Pennsylvania 16802-6822

Phone: 814-865-9505
Fax: 814-865-3176
E-mail: corl@cse.psu.edu
Web site: http://www.cse.psu.edu/

Penn State University Park

THE FACULTY AND THEIR RESEARCH

R. Acharya, Professor and Department Head; Ph.D., Mayo, 1984. Bioinformatics, data mining, netcentric computing, information fusion.

Jesse Barlow, Professor; Ph.D., Northwestern, 1981. Numerical linear algebra, scientific computing, linear algebra in signal and image processing.

Piotr Berman, Associate Professor; Ph.D., MIT, 1985. Computational complexity, approximation algorithms, theory of distributed systems, computational molecular biology.

Guohong Cao, Professor; Ph.D., Ohio State, 1999. Mobile computing, wireless networks, sensor networks, wireless network security.

Swarat Chaudhuri, Assistant Professor; Ph.D., Pennsylvania, 2007. Program analysis, formal methods in software engineering, and applications of logic, automata, and concurrency theory.

Kyusun Choi, Assistant Professor; Ph.D., Penn State, 1993. Mixed-signal VLSI circuit design, RF ASICs, DSP architecture for RF signal, 4G wireless wrist PDA, embedded microcomputer.

Robert T. Collins, Associate Professor; Ph.D., Massachusetts, 1993. Computer vision, with current emphasis on video scene understanding, automated surveillance, human activity modeling, and real-time tracking.

Lee D. Coraor, Associate Professor; Ph.D., Iowa, 1978. Digital systems, field-programmable gate arrays, microprocessor systems, computer architecture.

Chita R. Das, Distinguished Professor; Ph.D., Southwestern Louisiana, 1986. Computer architecture, parallel and distributed computing, cluster systems, network-on-chip (NoC) architectures, Internet QoS, mobile computing, performance evaluation, fault-tolerant computing, multimedia systems.

Dennis F. Dunn, Associate Professor and Director of Academic Affairs; Ph.D., Penn State, 1992. Medical imaging, image processing, texture analysis, document image analysis, human-vision modeling, robotics.

Martin Fürer, Professor; Ph.D., ETH-Zurich (Switzerland), 1978. Efficient discrete algorithms, approximation algorithms, computational complexity, the graph isomorphism problem.

Sean Hallgren, Assistant Professor; Ph.D., Berkeley, 2000. Theoretical computer science, quantum computing.

John Hannan, Associate Professor; Ph.D., Pennsylvania, 1990. Programming language semantics and implementation, program analysis and verification, logic and computation, type theory, functional programming.

Mary Jane Irwin, Evan Pugh Professor and A. Robert Noll Chair of Engineering; Ph.D., Illinois at Urbana-Champaign, 1977. Computer architecture, embedded and mobile computing systems design, power aware design, emerging technologies in computing systems.

Trent Jaeger, Associate Professor; Ph.D., Michigan, 1997. Computer security analysis, operating systems, security policies, source code analysis.

Mahmut Kandemir, Professor; Ph.D., Syracuse, 1999. Embedded systems, programming languages, compilers, power-aware computing, dependable computing, input/output systems.

George Kesidis, Professor of CSE and EE; Ph.D., Berkeley, 1992. Modeling and performance evaluation of communication/computer networking mechanisms, scheduling and routing, Internet security, network economics, games.

Daniel Kifer, Assistant Professor of CSE; Ph.D., Cornell, 2008. Privacy, data mining, machine learning with background knowledge, management of uncertain data.

Thomas F. La Porta, Distinguished Professor of CSE; Ph.D., Columbia, 1992. Mobility management; mobile data systems, including networks, protocols, and applications; signaling and control for telecommunication networks; security for wireless networks.

Wang-Chien Lee, Associate Professor; Ph.D., Ohio State, 1996. Database systems, pervasive and mobile computing, location-based services, peer-to-peer networks, wireless sensor networks, security, Internet technologies.

Yanxi Liu, Associate Professor of CSE and EE; Ph.D., Massachusetts Amherst, 1990. Computational symmetry, group theory and applications, machine learning (particularly low-dimensional subspace learning from very large, multi-modality feature set), computer-aided diagnosis, computer vision, computer graphics, biomedical image analysis/indexing/retrieval, robotics.

Patrick McDaniel, Associate Professor; Ph.D., Michigan, 2001. Systems and network security, security policy, networking, distributed systems, public policy, network management, applied cryptography, privacy.

John J. Metzner, Professor; Eng.Sc.D., NYU, 1958. Reliable data communications, including multicasting, error-correcting codes, multi-access wireless network protocols, efficient replicated file comparison, information theory.

Webb C. Miller, Professor of Biology and CSE; Ph.D., Washington (Seattle), 1969. Algorithms and software for molecular biology.

Vijaykrishnan Narayanan, Professor; Ph.D., South Florida, 1998. Energy-aware and reliable systems, embedded systems, nano/VLSI systems, computer architecture.

Padma Raghavan, Professor; Ph.D., Penn State, 1991. Scientific computing, parallel sparse computations, energy-aware high-performance computing, computational modeling and simulation.

Sofya Raskhodnikova, Assistant Professor; Ph.D., MIT, 2003. Randomized algorithms, computational complexity, private data analysis.

Suzanne Shontz, Assistant Professor; Ph.D., Cornell, 2004. Parallel scientific computing, mesh generation, numerical optimization, computational materials science, computational medicine.

Anand Sivasubramaniam, Professor; Ph.D., Georgia Tech, 1995. Operating systems, computer architecture, databases, mobile computing, performance evaluation.

Adam Smith, Assistant Professor; Ph.D., MIT, 2004. Cryptography, database privacy, information theory, quantum computing.

Bhuvan Urgaonkar, Assistant Professor; Ph.D., Massachusetts, 2005. Distributed systems, operating systems, computer networks.

Yuan Xie, Associate Professor; Ph.D., Princeton, 2002. VLSI design, computer architecture, embedded systems design, electronics design automation.

Sencun Zhu, Assistant Professor of CSE and of the College of IST; Ph.D., George Mason, 2004. Network and systems security, software security, wireless security, Internet privacy.

UNIVERSITY OF CALIFORNIA, RIVERSIDE

Department of Computer Science and Engineering

Programs of Study

The Department of Computer Science and Engineering (CSE) at the University of California, Riverside (UCR) offers the Master of Science (M.S.) and Doctor of Philosophy (Ph.D.) degrees in computer science. The Department also has a new five-year joint B.S./M.S. degree in computer science and computer engineering. Although relatively young, CSE has quickly become a well-established and well-known research department, with 116 Ph.D. and 34 M.S. students enrolled in the 2009–10 academic year. CSE had 14 M.S. and 15 Ph.D. graduates in 2008–09; all went on to highly regarded university and industry positions. The Department has 5 full-time lecturers and 20 tenure-track faculty members, including 3 ACM fellows, 3 IEEE fellows, 4 AAAS fellows, 1 NSF Presidential Young Investigator, 1 AFOSR Young Investigator, and 7 NSF CAREER award holders. The Department receives around $3.5 million in external research funding each year.

The M.S. program is ideal for professionals seeking greater depth in several subject areas. The program requires 48 quarter units and is typically completed in five quarters of full-time study. M.S. students may choose between a thesis option (which combines 36 quarter units of course work with 12 quarter units of thesis research) and a nonthesis option (which requires 44 quarter units of course work and a 4-credit capstone project).

The Ph.D. program is heavily integrated with the Department's research activities and is intended for well-qualified individuals who wish to pursue careers in academic or industrial research. The program requires 48 quarter units and is typically completed in five years of full-time study. In addition to satisfying the same course work requirements as the M.S. thesis option, Ph.D. students must successfully pass a rigorous set of qualifying examinations and complete an original research project under the supervision of a faculty adviser who is familiar with the candidate's chosen field of specialization. At the conclusion of the candidate's research, a faculty committee evaluates the work on the basis of both a written dissertation and a final oral defense.

The Department has active research programs in many areas, including algorithm design, artificial intelligence, computational biology, computer architecture, computer networks, distributed systems, operating systems, databases, compilers, software engineering, multimedia systems, VLSI/CAD, embedded systems design, and theory of computation.

Research Facilities

The Department is located in the new Engineering Building Unit II, within the Bourns College of Engineering. For the general campus community, the UCR's Computing and Communications Services Organization maintains a variety of fully serviced networked computing facilities and research access to the Supercomputer Center at the University of California, San Diego. While these services are available to the campus at large, the Department operates additional facilities for its own use.

The Department maintains seven centrally managed instructional labs equipped with personal computers which run on a CentOS Linux base operating system. Windows access is provided by use of terminal server clients that access the Department's bank of Windows terminal servers. VMware, VirtualBox, and User Mode Linux are used in upper-division classes, such as operating systems and UNIX system administration, where students carry out kernel programming projects. Special hardware and software are provided for classes, including Synopsys software packages for embedded systems design and Xilinx FPGAs. The Department is also home to dedicated research laboratories, including the Algorithms and Computational Biology Lab, Computer Architecture and Embedded Systems Lab (CARES), Distributed Systems Lab, Logic and Stochastic Verification Lab, Networks and Communications Lab, Riverside Graphics Lab (RGL), and Systems and Security Research Lab (SSRL). An SGI Altix 4700 supercomputer with 64 Itanium processors and an RASC blade containing Xilinx FPGA are used to support research in algorithms and computational biology, and architecture and embedded systems.

UCR opened a state-of-the-art four-story 106,000-square-foot science library in 1998. The engineering collection is housed in the new library, which is located next to Engineering Building Unit II. The library has 1,500 reader and computer stations with over 1 million volumes in science and engineering and hundreds of database and online information sources. The library has a dedicated engineering librarian with special training in information technology to assist the engineering faculty members and students.

Financial Aid

Several forms of financial assistance are available, including multiple fellowships (some specifically geared towards diversity and exceptional achievers), teaching assistant (TA) or graduate student researcher (GSR) appointments, tuition, and fee grants. The Department awards TAs, GSRs, and tuition and fee grants and nominates students for fellowships to the campus Graduate Division on a competitive basis. Offers of financial assistance may be multiyear and may incorporate a combination of fellowship and TA and/or GSR appointments. Other forms of support are need-based and administered through the Office of Financial Aid.

Cost of Study

In 2009–10, the cost of study is approximately $3714 per quarter for California residents and $8726 per quarter for nonresidents. Fees are subject to change and may be covered as part of a fellowship or TA or GSR appointment.

Living and Housing Costs

UCR offers a number of housing options, both on campus and off campus. On-campus housing monthly rents start at $250 for single students and $460 for married students and families. Housing for students living off campus is available at a competitive rate. For more information on housing, students should visit http://housing.ucr.edu.

Student Group

CSE celebrates the diversity of the graduate student population and values the different life experiences that each student brings to the Department. Not only is UCR recognized as one of the most diverse research universities in the nation, the campus is also in the midst of a tremendous growth spurt with many new and remodeled facilities in various stages of development. CSE is a young graduate program, offering research and educational opportunities with an established tradition of close collegial relations between graduate students and faculty that is rare at other universities. UCR also offers active student chapters of many professional engineering organizations including the Association for Computing Machinery (ACM), the American Indian Science and Engineering Society (AISES), the Biomedical Engineering Society (BMES), the Institute of Electrical and Electronics Engineers (IEEE), the Linux Users Group, the National Society of Black Engineers (NSBE), the Society of Hispanic Professional Engineers (SHPE), the Society of Women Engineers (SWE), and the Tau Beta Pi Honor Society.

Location

UCR has a beautifully scenic and parklike campus of 1,200 acres at the foot of the Box Springs Mountains, within a short driving distance of all Southern California attractions and the metropolitan areas of Los Angeles, Orange County, and San Diego. UCR's unique setting allows the potential for residents to go surfing in the morning, mountain hiking (or skiing in winter) in the afternoon, and enjoy a winery or Broadway play in the evening. Riverside is also noted for its palm-lined avenues and relatively low cost of living. CSE students at UCR can choose to be involved in a variety of community and campus activities and organizations. The smaller campus provides a relaxed and personal atmosphere with specialized attention and guidance from faculty. As a part of the prestigious UC system, students can also take advantage of the innovative research, first-rate professors, and worldwide networking that the system offers.

The University

UCR began in 1907 as the Citrus Experiment Station to support the state's emerging citrus industry and became a campus of the University of California in 1954. Academic divisions at UCR include the College of Natural and Agricultural Sciences; the College of Humanities, Arts, and Social Sciences; the Marlan and Rosemary Bourns College of Engineering; the Graduate School of Education; the A. Gary Anderson Graduate School of Management; the Division of Biomedical Sciences; and the Graduate Division. The campus features the Citrus Research Center-Agricultural Experiment Station, Air Pollution Research Center, UCR/California Museum of Photography, Center for Ideas and Society, Center for Social and Behavioral Science Research, Institute of Geophysics and Planetary Physics, Centers for Water and Wildland Resources, and eight sites in the UC Natural Reserve System, including the Philip L. Boyd Deep Canyon Desert Research Center. An overall view of UCR can be found at http://collegeportrait.ucr.edu/pdf/ucr_college_portrait.pdf.

Applying

All domestic application fees for the 2011–12 academic year will be waived by the Department. Applicants should have a degree in computer science, computer engineering, or a closely related field; a satisfactory overall GPA from their undergraduate studies; three strong letters of recommendation; and a minimum score of 1100 on the GRE General Test. International students, permanent residents, and U.S. citizens whose native language is not English and who do not have a bachelor's or postgraduate degree from an institution where English is the exclusive language of instruction must complete the Test of English as a Foreign Language (TOEFL). Information about individual graduate degree programs can be accessed through the Bourns College of Engineering Web site at http://www.engr.ucr.edu. Information regarding admission criteria and online applications are obtainable through the department Web site and the Graduate Division Web site at http://www.graddiv.ucr.edu. To find out about research opportunities available through the College, students should explore the various department and research center Web sites in the College. The deadline for admission and financial support consideration is January 5. All applications must be submitted online at http://gradis.ucr.edu.

Correspondence and Information

Graduate Admissions Advisor
Department of Computer Science and Engineering
University of California, Riverside
Riverside, California 92521
Phone: 951-827-5639
Fax: 951-827-4643
E-mail: gradadmission@cs.ucr.edu
Web site: http://www.cs.ucr.edu

University of California, Riverside

THE FACULTY AND THEIR RESEARCH

Laxmi Bhuyan, Professor and Chair; Ph.D., Wayne State, 1982. Computer architecture, multiprocessor cache memories, interconnection networks, parallel and distributed computing, fault-tolerant computing, performance and reliability.

Philip Brisk, Assistant Professor; Ph.D., UCLA, 2006. Reconfigurable computing, application-specific and customizable processors, computer architecture, compilers.

Marek Chrobak, Professor; Ph.D., Warsaw, 1985. Algorithms, data structures, theory of computation.

Gianfranco Ciardo, Professor; Ph.D., Duke, 1989. Logic, performance, reliability modeling and tools, model checking and verification of finite-state systems.

Michalis Faloutsos, Professor; Ph.D., Toronto, 1998. Computer networks, routing algorithms, multicasting, Internet protocols.

Rajiv Gupta, Professor; Ph.D., Pittsburgh, 1987. Compilers and architectures for embedded systems; software tools for profiling, slicing, and debugging; program analysis: static, dynamic, and profile-based.

Tao Jiang, Professor; Ph.D., Minnesota, Twin Cities, 1988. Computational molecular biology, design and analysis of algorithms.

Eamonn Keogh, Professor; Ph.D., California, Irvine, 2001. Information retrieval, specializing in techniques for solving similarity and indexing problems in time-series datasets.

Srikanth Krishnamurthy, Professor; Ph.D., California, San Diego, 1997. Wireless networks, Internet technology, broadband networks, multimedia systems, satellite systems.

Stefano Lonardi, Associate Professor; Ph.D., Purdue, 2001. Computational molecular biology, data compression, data mining.

Mart Molle, Professor; Ph.D., UCLA, 1981. Computer networking, performance evaluation, distributed algorithms.

Walid Najjar, Professor; Ph.D., USC, 1988. Design of computer systems, emphasis on parallel, reconfigurable, and custom-design systems.

Iulian Neamtiu, Assistant Professor; Ph.D.; Maryland, College Park, 2008. Programming languages, operating systems, software engineering.

Teodor Przymusinski, Professor; Ph.D., Polish Academy of Science, Warsaw, 1974. Artificial intelligence, knowledge representation, logic programming.

Chinya Ravishankar, Professor and Associate Dean; Ph.D., Wisconsin–Madison, 1987. Databases, distributed systems, networking, programming languages.

Christian Shelton, Assistant Professor; Ph.D., MIT, 2001. Algorithms, sequential decision making, computational game theory.

Vassilis Tsotras, Professor; Ph.D., Columbia, 1991. Database management, access methods, temporal and spatiotemporal databases, parallel databases.

Frank Vahid, Professor; Ph.D., California, Irvine, 1994. Embedded computing systems, system-on-a-chip design, hardware/software codesign.

Neal Young, Associate Professor; Ph.D., Princeton, 1991. Design and analysis of algorithms and data structures.

Victor Zordan, Associate Professor; Ph.D., Georgia Tech, 2002. Computer animation, human body simulation, physically based modeling, motor control, robotics.

UNIVERSITY OF CALIFORNIA, SAN DIEGO

Bioinformatics and Systems Biology Graduate Program

Programs of Study	The University of California, San Diego (UC San Diego) offers a graduate program leading to the Doctor of Philosophy (Ph.D.) in bioinformatics and systems biology. Bioinformatics has been defined as computer-assisted analyses of large data sets pertinent to biological processes. The Bioinformatics and Systems Biology Graduate Program draws upon the expertise of affiliated faculty members from the Division of Biological Sciences; the Departments of Bioengineering, Chemistry and Biochemistry, Computer Science and Engineering, Mathematics, Physics, and the Biomedical Sciences Graduate program.
	The program is organized around a formal course requirement. There are four compulsory core courses and four courses to be chosen from a list of electives approved by the Curriculum Committee. One 4-unit course in the winter and spring quarters as well as the summer sessions will be a research rotation in the laboratory of a program faculty member. The electives are intended to maximize the flexibility of the program, but at least one course must be chosen from the biology field and one from the computer science and engineering field. It is general program policy to be as adaptive as possible to the needs of the individual student. Upon completion of formal course requirements, students are required to take a qualifying examination that tests their capabilities and ascertains their potential for independent study and research. The degree requires the completion of a dissertation and defense of the research. The normal time for completion of a Ph.D. in the Bioinformatics and Systems Biology Graduate Program is five years.
	There is enormous demand from industry for trained professionals in bioinformatics. The pharmaceutical industry, agribusiness, and biotechnology companies often draw people with the appropriate interdisciplinary skills from academia. A new era in biology is underway; the ability to decipher the genetic code of living organisms is dramatically changing the understanding of the natural world and promises to substantially improve the quality of human life. The accelerated growth of modern biology warrants revolutionary changes in academic curricula and the need for academic faculty members who have broad interdisciplinary training. The Bioinformatics and Systems Biology Graduate Program is designed to prepare students for a career in industry and/or academia.
Research Facilities	UC San Diego is a premier research institution with state-of-the-art research facilities. In addition to all the standard experimental facilities, there are several fully equipped computer laboratories connected by high-speed networks to the San Diego Supercomputer Center, the School of Medicine, and the Division of Natural and Physical Sciences, and the California Institute for Telecommunication and Information Technology (CalIT2). In addition, a Bioinformatics Computer Library is available for students in the program.
Financial Aid	The program supports full-time graduate students at the Ph.D. level. Financial support is available in the form of fellowships, traineeships, teaching assistantships, and research assistantships. Awarding of financial support is competitive, and stipends average $25,000 for the academic year, plus tuition and fees. Sources of funding include University fellowships and traineeships from an NIH training grant. Funds for support of international students are extremely limited, and the selection process is highly competitive.
Cost of Study	Projected graduate student fees and tuition for 2010–11 are $4162.50 for full-time students who are California residents; nonresidents pay $9196.50 per quarter. Fees are subject to change.
Living and Housing Costs	UC San Diego provides Associated Residential Community Housing (ARCH) which offers housing to eligible graduate and professional students in four residential communities. Current monthly rates range from $438 for a single student to $1074 for a family. More details are available at http://hdh.ucsd.edu/arch/gradhousing.html. In fall 2010, UC San Diego ARCH is scheduled to open Rita L. Atkinson Residences, with housing for an additional 450 graduate students; more information can be found at http://hdh.ucsd.edu/rlar.
	There is also a variety of off-campus housing in the surrounding community. Prevailing rents range from $613 per month for a room in a private home to $1361 or more per month for a two-bedroom apartment. Information may be obtained at http://www.ucsd.edu/current-students/student-life/housing/offcampus/search.html.
Student Group	The 2009–10 campus enrollment was 26,500 students, of whom 22,500 are undergraduates and 4,000 are graduate students. Currently, the Bioinformatics and Systems Biology Graduate Program has an enrollment of 51 graduate students.
Location	The 2,040-acre campus spreads from the coastline, where the Scripps Institution of Oceanography is located, across a large wooded portion of the Torrey Pines Mesa overlooking the Pacific Ocean. To the east and north lie mountains, and to the south are Mexico and the almost uninhabited seacoast of Baja California.
The University	The University of California System has ten campuses. UC San Diego comprises the General Campus, the School of Medicine, and the Scripps Institute of Oceanography. Established in La Jolla in 1960, it is one of the newer campuses, but in this short time it has become one of the major universities in the country.
Applying	Admissions criteria are in accordance with the general requirements of the Office of Graduate Studies (OGS). Candidates ought to have an interdisciplinary track record and persuasion to work across biology, medicine, computational sciences, and engineering. The most competitive applicants have an undergraduate degree in any of the disciplines in the biological sciences, the physical sciences, computer science, mathematics, or engineering with a strong background in the complementary disciplines.
	Admission review will be on a competitive basis, based on the applicant's undergraduate track record, Graduate Record Examination (GRE) General Test scores, and other scholastic achievements. Special attention will be given to the quantitative and analytical section scores of the GRE. Attention will also be given to the motivation and career plans of applicants. The applicants will be screened and evaluated by the program's admissions committee with input from faculty in all participating departments. In addition, applicants must submit a completed UC San Diego Application for Graduate Admission found at https://graduateapp.ucsd.edu (use major code BF76). Official transcripts (English translation must accompany official transcript when written in other languages), TOFEL scores (required only for international applicants whose native language is not English and whose undergraduate education was conducted in a language other than English), and three letters of recommendation from individuals who can attest to the academic competence and to the depth of the applicant's interest in pursuing graduate study must also be submitted for consideration. The deadline for filing a fall 2011 application for both international and U.S. residents is January 7, 2011. Applications are considered for admission for the fall quarter only. UCSD's institutional ETS code is 4836, the program/department code is 1603, and the TOEFL code is 69.
Correspondence and Information	Bioinformatics and Systems Biology Graduate Program Powell Focht Bioengineering Hall, Room 228 University of California, San Diego La Jolla, California 92093-0419
	Phone: 858-822-4948 E-mail: bioinfo@ucsd.edu Web site: http://bioinformatics.ucsd.edu

University of California, San Diego

THE FACULTY AND THEIR RESEARCH

Department of Bioengineering

Gaurav Arya, Ph.D., Assistant Professor. Gene regulation ranging from chromatin structure regulation to protein-DNA recognition; optimization of the design of short peptides and siRNAs that can bind to genes and mRNAs with maximum efficiency; development of new, computationally efficient multi-scale simulation methods to allow the systematic study of such complex biological systems.

Xiaohua Huang, Ph.D., Assistant Professor. Genomics, molecular biotechnology, and bioinformatics including chemistry and biophysics of protein and DNA molecules and technologies to uncover greater information regarding the human genome and genetics.

Andrew D. McCulloch, Ph.D., Professor. In-vivo, in vitro, and computational models to investigate the relationships between the cellular and extracellular structure of cardiac and electrical and mechanical function of the normal and diseased heart; tissue engineering for cardiac regeneration; systems biology approaches to cardiac genotype-phenotype relationships.

Bernhard Palsson, Ph.D., Professor. Reconstruction of genome scale networks (metabolic, regulatory, and signaling); mathematical assessment of their properties and experimental determination of their functions; systems biology.

Shankar Subramaniam, Ph.D., Professor. Bioinformatics and systems biology; networks and phenotypes for mammalian biology.

Kun Zhang, Ph.D., Assistant Professor. Development and application of new genome technologies, with emphasis on stem cell research and personalized medicine.

Division of Biological Sciences

Steven Briggs, Ph.D., Professor. Molecular mechanisms by which mechanical forces induce a signal transduction and modulate gene expression results in cellular function, such as proliferation functions, such as proliferation migration and apoptosis.

Joseph R. Ecker, Ph.D., Adjunct Professor. Molecular biology and genetics of plants.

Terry Gaasterland, Ph.D., Professor and Director of Scripps Genome Center. Computation and analysis to interpret each microbial genome in its environmental, ecological, and evolutionary context.

Jeff Hasty, Ph.D., Associate Professor. Computational genomics and the dynamics of gene regulatory networks.

Trey Ideker, Ph.D., Associate Professor. Developing large-scale, computer-aided models of biological signaling and regulatory pathways.

Steve Kay, Ph.D., Professor and Dean. Construction and evolution of complex genetic networks that underlie circadian rhythms in animals and plants; development and use of cutting-edge technologies for measuring transcription in live cells, tissues and intact organisms.

Amy Kiger, Ph.D., Assistant Professor. Functional genomics of cellular morphogenesis.

Eduardo Macagno, Ph.D., Professor. Neurobiological research: molecular pathways underlying the regulation of neuronal growth cone dynamics and interactions leading to neuronal arbor formation, studies of the roles of gap junctions in the early differentiation of the central nervous system, application of imaging mass spectrometry to the mapping of peptides and proteins in leech embryos and adult nervous system sections.

James Posakony, Ph.D., Professor. Computational and biological approaches to elucidate the structure and operation of gene regulatory networks that direct animal development.

Scott Rifkin, Ph.D., Assistant Professor. Evolutionary biology, patterns of gene expression.

Milton H. Saier Jr., Ph.D., Professor. Transcriptional and metabolic regulation in bacteria, transport-protein evolution.

Julian I. Schroeder, Ph.D., Professor. Molecular and cell biological elucidation of signal-transduction cascades in higher plant cells.

Inder Verma, Ph.D., Adjunct Professor. Understanding the molecular mechanism of the function of proto-oncogenes and suppressor genes, gene therapy.

School of Medicine

Ruben Abagyan, Ph.D., Professor. Protein-protein docking and interface prediction interaction, ligand docking and drug discovery, molecular modeling and bioinformatics, force field development.

Philip E. Bourne, Ph.D., Professor. Structural bioinformatics, structural genomics, protein structure classification, protein structure prediction, protein-protein interactions, protein evolution, cell signaling, apoptosis.

Pieter Dorrestein, Ph.D., Assistant Professor. Biosynthesis and functional roles of post-translational modifications that may be involved in antibiotic resistance.

Joseph Gleeson, M.D., Associate Professor. Neurosciences, brain development, cell proliferation, neurogenetics, seizures.

Christopher Glass, M.D., Ph.D., Professor. Molecular mechanisms by which sequence-specific transcription factors regulate the development and function of macrophages.

Lawrence S. B. Goldstein, Ph.D., Professor. Understanding the molecular mechanisms of organelle and vesicle movement and the role of transport dysfunction in neurodegenerative diseases.

Vivian Hook, Ph.D., Professor. Protease mechanisms in peptide neurotransmitters and in neurodegenerative diseases.

Richard Kolodner, Ph.D. Professor. Genetic and biochemical mechanisms of genetic recombination, DNA repair and suppression of spontaneous mutations using *Saccharomyces cerevisiae*, mouse and human systems.

Sanjay Nigam, M.D., Professor. Molecular and cellular mechanisms of branching morphogenesis as they relate to organ development.

Lucila Ohno-Machado, M.D., Ph.D., Professor. Biomedical informatics, prognostic modeling using parsimonious machine learning algorithms.

Sergei Kosakovsky Pond, Ph.D., Assistant Adjunct Professor. Algorithms and software for statistical analysis, inference and hypothesis testing on molecular sequence data, particularly in challenges posed by studying the evolution of HIV, with its extreme mutation and recombination rates, multiple adaptive mechanisms, and computational challenges involved in the analysis of very large molecular datasets.

Bing Ren, Ph.D., Professor. Understanding how the complex gene regulatory networks in mammalian cells control cellular proliferation and differentiation.

Douglas Richman, M.D., Professor In Residence. Natural history and molecular pathogenesis of HIV in a cohort of actually infected patients; studies include cell-mediated and neutralizing antibody immune responses to HIV and the viral escape and evolution in response to these.

Michael Rosenfeld, M.D., Professor. Molecular mechanisms by which diverse signaling pathways regulate gene expression to control development and homeostasis.

Dorothy Sears, Ph.D., Assistant Adjunct Professor. Insulin resistance, type 2 diabetes, obesity, PPARgamma, inflammation.

Palmer W. Taylor, Ph.D., Professor and Dean. Structure and function of receptors, enzymes, and adhesion molecules involved in neurotransmission.

Christopher Woelk, Ph.D., Assistant Adjunct Professor. Cellular modulation of protein coding and non-coding gene expression resulting from HIV-1 infection, infectious diseases, pathogen evolution, evolution and regulation of immunomodulatory gene families, disease diagnosis, and predicting outcomes with gene expression classifiers, identification of interferon-induced antiviral host factors, identification of putative vaccine candidates in the *Coccidioides posadadii* genome using reverse vaccinology approaches.

Ronghui (Lily) Xu, Ph.D., Associate Professor. Statistical methods applicable to the study of cancer.

Gene Yeo, Ph.D., Assistant Professor. Understand the impact of RNA processing and regulation in human normal and cancer stem cell biology and neural differentiation.

Department of Chemistry and Biochemistry

Alexander Hoffmann, Ph.D., Professor and Program Associate Director, Bioinformatics and Systems Biology Graduate Program. Signaling, computational network, transcription stress and immune and inflammatory responses, apoptosis, proliferation.

Patricia A. Jennings, Ph.D., Professor. Biophysical chemistry: Protein structure, dynamics and folding: 2, 3, and 4D NMR spectroscopy; PCR; equilibrium and kinetic-fluorescence, absorbance and circular dichroism spectroscopies.

Simpson Joseph, Ph.D., Professor. Mechanism of translation, process of initiation in eukaryotes.

J. Andrew McCammon, Ph.D., Professor. Computer simulation studies of proteins and subcellular structures, computer-aided drug discovery.

Susan S. Taylor, Ph.D., Professor. Relation of structure to function in cAMP-dependent protein kinase.

Roger Tsien, Ph.D., Professor. Engineering and use of new molecules to measure and perturb these messengers; cellular mechanisms of synaptic plasticity, especially in the cerebellum; stimulus–transcription coupling via cAMP-dependent protein kinase.

Wei Wang, Ph.D., Associate Professor. Inference of gene regulatory networks and determination of protein specificity.

Leor Weinberger, Ph.D., Assistant Professor. Dynamical systems biology; stochastic noise and feedback in gene circuits, single-cell biology, computational modeling and experiment.

Peter Wolynes, Ph.D., Professor. Theoretical chemistry/biochemistry, statistical mechanics of biomolecules and condensed matter, protein folding and function.

John C. Wooley, Ph.D., Adjunct Professor. Pharmacogenomics, structural genomics, computational biology.

Department of Computer Science and Engineering

Scott B. Baden, Ph.D., Professor. New models of execution that would allow one to express self-optimizing programs.

Vineet Bafna, Ph.D., Professor. Computational proteomics.

Nuno Bandeira, Ph.D., Assistant Professor. Bioinformatics, computational mass spectrometry.

Richard K. Belew, Ph.D., Professor. HIV drug resistance co-evolution, science publication models.

Sanjoy Dasgupta, Ph.D., Associate Professor. Development of algorithms for the statistical analysis of high-dimensional data, machine learning.

Charles P. Elkan, Ph.D., Professor. Artificial intelligence with applications to biological problems.

Yoav Freund, Ph.D., Professor. Computational learning theory and the related areas in probability theory, information theory, statistics, and pattern recognition; applications of machine learning algorithms in bioinformatics, computer vision, network routing, and high-performance computing.

Pavel Pevzner, Ph.D., Professor, Ronald R. Taylor Chair, and Program Director. Bioinformatics and Systems Biology Graduate Program. Computational molecular biology.

Department of Mathematics

Michael J. Holst, Ph.D., Professor. Numerical analysis, scientific computation, protein electrostatics.

Glenn Tesler, Ph.D., Assistant Professor. Genome analysis and combinatorial mathematics.

Ruth J. Williams, Ph.D., Professor. Probability theory, stochastic processes.

Department of Physics

Terence Hwa, Ph.D., Professor. Structure and function of receptors and enzymes involved in neurotransmission, biological sequence analysis.

Jose N. Onuchic, Ph.D., Professor. Theoretical and computational methods for molecular biophysics and chemical reactions in condensed matter.

UNIVERSITY OF CALIFORNIA, SAN DIEGO

Department of Computer Science and Engineering

Programs of Study

The Department of Computer Science and Engineering (CSE) at the University of California, San Diego (UCSD), offers programs leading to the M.S. and Ph.D. degrees in computer science and computer engineering. The M.S. program typically takes two years to complete and prepares students for positions in the computer and communications industries. The Ph.D. program typically takes less than six years to complete and prepares students for leading positions in technology industries, research labs, and academia. The core of these educational programs is built on the research activities of the Department. The Department has significant strengths in most major fields of computer science and engineering, with particular specializations in algorithms and complexity, artificial intelligence, bioinformatics, computer architecture and compilers, computer graphics and vision, cryptography and security, databases and information management, embedded systems and software, high-performance computing, programming systems, systems and networking, and VLSI/CAD.

Research Facilities

The true force behind the Department's research is its students, who are regarded as colleagues and partners. The Department of Computer Science and Engineering provides extensive computing resources for research and education. This includes more than 300 high-performance UNIX/Linux and Windows-based workstations, a large number of laptop systems, and several hundred wireless personal digital assistants. In addition to general-purpose file, e-mail, Web, and computer servers, the Department maintains two network-attached terabyte disk arrays and four separate high-performance computer clusters. Through the San Diego Supercomputer Center (SDSC), which is a unique national facility, members have direct access to a variety of vector, multithreaded, and parallel supercomputers as well as a state-of-the-art high-performance visualization laboratory. Department network communications include a gigabit Ethernet backbone, offering connectivity to both the commodity Internet and high-performance research networks such as Internet2. The Department has wireless Internet connectivity via a campuswide 802.11b network and an experimental broadband wireless system in concert with Qualcomm. The Department supports specialized equipment for individual research efforts in computer vision, computer graphics and computer architecture, networking, security, mobile systems, and distributed computing.

Financial Aid

A variety of fellowships were available to Ph.D. students in 2009–10, providing stipends of $18,000 to $25,000. In lieu of a fellowship, Ph.D. students (and occasionally M.S. students) may be appointed to either a research or a teaching assistantship that provides a monthly stipend of $1848 or $2102, respectively. Tuition and fees, including health insurance coverage, are included in fellowship and assistantship awards.

Cost of Study

For the 2009–10 academic year, California resident fees were $11,044.50 (residents are tuition-exempt). Tuition and fees for nonresidents were $26,086.50. U.S. citizens and permanent residents can typically become California state residents after residing in the state for twelve months.

Living and Housing Costs

UCSD maintains apartments for couples, families, and single graduate students, with costs ranging from $468 to $1311 per month. For further information, students should contact Affiliated Housing at ahoinfo@ucsd.edu or visit http://hds.ucsd.edu/arch/gradhousing.html.

Student Group

In the fall of 2009, there were 325 graduate students in the CSE department. Of these, 68 were new students (37 M.S.; 31 Ph.D.). The University's current graduate and professional student population is approximately 4,800.

Location

UCSD is located in La Jolla, a suburban seaside resort in San Diego. Consistently rated as one of the top ten places to live in the U.S., San Diego offers an ideal climate, averaging 70°F/21°C degrees with mostly sunny days and a wide variety of cultural activities. The campus overlooks the Pacific Ocean and miles of sandy beaches, where sports, including surfing, snorkeling, and hang gliding, can be enjoyed year-round. The mountains to the east provide opportunities for hiking, rock climbing, and skiing. San Diego is just north of the U.S.-Mexico border, offering richly diverse cultural experiences that are unique to this international city. San Diego is a renowned high-tech and biotech community supported by University research and entrepreneurialism. San Diego is regarded as the wireless capital of the world, providing limitless opportunities for current students and future graduates.

The University

Established in 1964, UCSD is one of ten campuses of the University of California System. Despite its youth, UCSD is regarded as one of the premiere research institutions in the U.S., either public or private. The National Research Council has ranked it tenth for graduate program excellence, and the National Science Foundation ranked UCSD sixth in the nation and first in the UC System in federal research and development funding. CSE partner programs and institutes include the San Diego Supercomputer Center, Center for Wireless Communications, Center for Networked Systems, Institute for Neural Computation, Department of Electrical and Computer Engineering, California Institute for Telecommunications and Information Technology, the interdisciplinary Bioinformatics Graduate Program, and the Rady School of Management.

Applying

The application deadline for fall 2011 admission is December 15, 2010. Applicants must hold a bachelor's degree or its equivalent. Suggested undergraduate training should be in one of the following disciplines: computer science, mathematics, electrical engineering, biology (bioinformatics), or physics. Applicants with degrees in other disciplines are considered if there is demonstrated preparation through appropriate course work in computer science. The General Test of the Graduate Record Examinations (GRE) is required, and the Subject Test in computer science is recommended. Most international applicants whose native language is not English are required to take the Test of English as a Foreign Language (TOEFL). The University of California does not discriminate on the basis of race, color, national origin, religion, sex, disability, age, or sexual orientation in any of its policies, procedures, or practices, including, but not limited to, academic admission, financial aid, education services, and student employment.

Correspondence and Information

Graduate Affairs
Department of Computer Science and Engineering, 0443
University of California, San Diego
La Jolla, California 92093-0443

Phone: 858-822-5978
Fax: 858-822-3319
E-mail: gradinfo@cs.ucsd.edu
Web site: http://www.cse.ucsd.edu

University of California, San Diego

THE FACULTY AND THEIR RESEARCH

Scott B. Baden, Professor; Ph.D., Berkeley. High-performance and large-scale scientific computation.

Vineet Bafna, Assistant Professor; Ph.D., Penn State. Computational molecular biology, bioinformatics, proteomics, approximational algorithms, human genome, human proteome, protein identification, expressed sequence tags (EST) analysis.

Mihir Bellare, Professor; Ph.D., MIT. Computer security focusing on authentication, encryption, and electronic payment standards that have helped secure transactions over the Internet and advance e-commerce standards.

Serge Belongie, Assistant Professor; Ph.D., Berkeley. Emerging fields of computer vision and object recognition, biometrics (fingerprint recognition), video segmentation.

Francine Berman, Professor and Director, San Diego Supercomputer Center (SDSC) and National Partnership for Advanced Computational Infrastructure (NPACI); Ph.D., Washington (Seattle). High-performance and grid computing: programming environments, adaptive middleware, scheduling, and performance predication.

Walter A. Burkhard, Professor; Ph.D., Berkeley. Storage system algorithms expert with interest in data layouts, disk arrays, RAID, video servers, replicated file systems.

Samuel R. Buss, Adjunct Professor; Ph.D., Princeton. Bounded arithmetic, proof theory and complexity, mathematical logic and behavioral logic.

J. Lawrence Carter, Professor Emeritus; Ph.D., Berkeley. Scientific computation, performance programming, parallel computation, machine and system architecture for high performance.

Chung-Kuan Cheng, Professor; Ph.D., Berkeley. Computer-aided design, VLSI layout automation, circuit partitioning, network flow optimization, physical design of multichip modules for hybrid package.

Garrison W. Cottrell, Professor; Ph.D., Rochester. Facial recognition, neural networks, human cognition, cognitive science, computational philosophy, artificial intelligence (AI).

Sanjoy Dasgupta, Assistant Professor; Ph.D., Berkeley. High-dimensional statistics, clustering, algorithms for finding underlying patterns in high-dimensional data, machine learning.

Alin Deutsch, Assistant Professor; Ph.D., Pennsylvania. Semistructured and XML data, data security, adaptive distributed query design, design and optimization of query languages.

Charles Elkan, Professor; Ph.D., Cornell. Automated reasoning, artificial intelligence, machine learning, database systems, expert systems, computational biology, data mining.

Jeanne Ferrante, Professor; Ph.D., MIT. Compiling techniques for large-scale computing.

Yoav Freund, Professor; Ph.D., California, Santa Cruz. Computational learning theory and related areas in probability theory, information theory, statistics, pattern recognition.

Fan Chung Graham, Professor; Ph.D., Pennsylvania. Algorithmic design, parallel computing, communications networks, Internet computing, discrete geometry, active compilers for the grid.

Ronald Graham, Irwin and Joan Jacobs Endowed Chair of Computer and Information Sciences; Ph.D., Berkeley. Computer science; Internet routing; mathematics, including combinatorics, number theory, graph theory, and discrete and computational geometry.

William G. Griswold, Professor; Ph.D., Washington (Seattle). Software engineering and ubiquitous computing, specializing in location-based systems, aspect-oriented programming, software design, and educational technology.

Rajesh K. Gupta, Professor and Qualcomm Endowed Chair in Embedded Microsystems; Ph.D., Stanford. Embedded systems and mobile computing, including the integration of software and hardware to make computers more portable and energy efficient (power-aware computing).

William E. Howden, Professor; Ph.D., California, Irvine. Software testing and analysis, error modeling and prevention, software design, embedded systems.

T. C. Hu, Professor Emeritus; Ph.D., Brown. Combinatorial algorithms, mathematical programming, networks and graphs, VLSI circuit layout.

Russell Impagliazzo, Professor; Ph.D., Berkeley. Computational complexity, cryptography, circuit complexity, computational randomness.

Henrik Wann Jensen, Associate Professor; Ph.D., Denmark Technical. Computer graphics, specializing in the rendering of realistic images of natural phenomena, global illumination, and appearance modeling.

Ranjit Jhala, Assistant Professor; Ph.D., Berkeley. Techniques for building reliable systems: model checking, automated deduction, program analysis, type systems, programming languages, software engineering, and logic.

Andrew B. Kahng, Professor; Ph.D., California, San Diego. Physical design of very large scale integrated circuits (VLSI); international technology roadmap for semiconductors (ITRS), the technology developments needed to keep pace with Moore's Law.

Sidney Karin, Professor; Ph.D., Michigan. Computational science and engineering, high-performance computing, data-intensive computing, scientific visualization and interaction environments, computer and network security, networking.

David Kriegman, Professor; Ph.D., Stanford. Computer vision, computer graphics, face recognition, vision-guided robotics.

Ingolf H. Krueger, Assistant Professor in Residence; Ph.D., Munich Technical. Service-oriented software and systems engineering; programming methodology; design, implementation, and verification of distributed reactive systems.

Sorin Lerner, Assistant Professor; Ph.D., Washington (Seattle). Programming language and analysis, including domain-specific languages, compilation, formal methods, and automated theorem proving.

Keith Marzullo, Professor; Ph.D., Stanford. Fault-tolerant computing with focus on Internet, grid computing, and other distributed networks that have radically changed the challenges of assuring reliability.

Daniele Micciancio, Assistant Professor; Ph.D., MIT. Cryptography, complexity, and the relation of the two; developing, testing, and validating algorithms for securing e-commerce and other computer transactions.

Alex Orailoglu, Professor; Ph.D., Illinois at Urbana-Champaign. Electronic design automation, VLSI testing, synthesis of fault-tolerant integrated circuits (ICs).

Alon Orlitsky, Adjunct Professor; Ph.D., Stanford. Communications and information theory, with particular interests in signal processing, data compression, speech recognition, and learning theory.

Yannis G. Papakonstantinou, Associate Professor; Ph.D., Stanford. Database systems and Internet technologies, specifically data integration applications that require search, querying and interaction with the information of multiple distributed sources, such as multiple Web sites.

Joseph Pasquale, Beyster Professor; Ph.D., Berkeley. Operating systems and networks, focusing on improving performance and reliability of Internet-scale systems.

Ramamohan Paturi, Professor and Department Chair; Ph.D., Penn State. Algorithms, complexity theory, satisfiability, lower bounds, digital libraries, data mining, machine learning, information technology (IT) education.

Pavel Pevzner, Professor and Taylor Chair; Ph.D., Moscow Institute of Physics and Technology. Computational molecular biology and bioinformatics.

Tajana Rosing, Assistant Professor; Ph.D., Stanford. Embedded system design, resource management at the system level, hardware management and embedded software optimization, power management algorithms.

Laurence Saul, Associate Professor; Ph.D., M.I.T. Machine learning, pattern recognition, voice processing, auditory computation, methods for high-dimensional data analysis.

Stefan Savage, Assistant Professor; Ph.D., Washington (Seattle). Computer security issues (especially worms, viruses, bonnets, intrusion detection, and denial-of-service attacks), wireless networking, operating system kernel design.

Walter J. Savitch, Professor Emeritus; Ph.D., Berkeley. Complexity theory, formal language theory, computational linguistics, development of computer science education materials.

Larry Smarr, Professor; Ph.D., Texas at Austin. Internet, information technology, telecommunications, supercomputing, interdisciplinary research, networking, the wireless Web.

Allan Snavely, Adjunct Professor; Ph.D., California, San Diego. High-performance computing, architecture, performance modeling and prediction, computer grid economics.

Alex C. Snoeren, Assistant Professor; Ph.D., MIT. Computer systems, including operating systems and networking, particularly protocols to support secure and robust wide area mobile computing.

Steven Swanson, Assistant Professor; Ph.D., Washington (Seattle). Unconventional processor architectures that require novel approaches to problems such as performance, power, and programmability.

Michael Taylor, Assistant Professor; Ph.D., MIT. Computer architecture, parallel computing, microprocessor and VLSI circuit design, on-chip interconnection networks.

Dean Tullsen, Associate Professor; Ph.D., Washington (Seattle). Processor architecture for high-end computing, innovation to double the performance of a new generation of microprocessors.

Amin Vahdat, Associate Professor; Ph.D., Berkeley. Computer networks, distributed systems, operating systems, Internet security, mobile/wireless systems.

Alexander Vardy, Adjunct Professor; Ph.D., Tel-Aviv. Information theory specializing in error-correcting codes for data transmission and storage.

George Varghese, Professor; Ph.D., MIT. Very-high-speed communications in computer networks and the Internet, making the Internet as fast and reliable as electric and telephone utilities.

Victor Vianu, Professor; Ph.D., USC. Databases in the age of the World Wide Web.

Geoffrey M. Voelker, Assistant Professor; Ph.D., Washington (Seattle). Computer systems research in operating systems, distributed systems, networking, mobile and wireless computing.

Matthias Zwicker, Assistant Professor; Ph.D., Zurich. Computer graphics.

UNIVERSITY OF DELAWARE

Department of Computer and Information Sciences

Programs of Study	The Department of Computer and Information Sciences (CIS) offers programs leading to the Master of Science and Doctor of Philosophy degrees. The M.S. program, which is normally completed in four semesters of full-time study, prepares students for doctoral studies or for professional employment. The doctoral program consists of additional course work and supervised research leading to a dissertation. There is no foreign language requirement.
	Departmental research areas include artificial intelligence (machine learning, multiagent systems, planning and problem solving), bioinformatics, compiler optimization and compilation for parallel machines, computational theory (computational learning theory, design and analysis of algorithms, computability theory), graphics and computer vision, natural-language processing (discourse and dialogue, generation, information extraction, summarization), networks (transport layer protocols, mobile and wireless networks, network management, security, performance modeling, simulation), rehabilitation engineering (augmentative communication, speech recognition and enhancement), robotics, software engineering (program analysis and testing), symbolic mathematical computation (algebraic algorithms, parallelization), and systems (parallel and distributed computing, grid and volunteer computing, algorithm and architecture design for massive parallelism).
	The Department's faculty members are recognized internationally for their research expertise. Their research is supported by numerous research grants from NSF, NIH, ARL, DOE, DARPA, and other federal agencies and private corporations. They are editors or associate editors of scientific journals, serve as program committee chairs and members of the program committees for major conferences, and are officers in international professional organizations. Despite their extensive research and professional commitments, Departmental faculty members pride themselves on close, personal interaction with students in both their research groups and the courses they teach. Seven CIS faculty members have won the University of Delaware Excellence-in-Teaching Award (an award given annually to only 4 out of 1,200 faculty members University-wide) and 1 has received the University's Excellence-in-Advising Award.
Research Facilities	The Department operates a joint research lab with the Department of Electrical and Computer Engineering that connects an extensive network of approximately 300 PC/UNIX-based workstations distributed among several general graduate student labs and several specialized research labs, such as Global Computing, Distributed and Metasystems, Verified Software, Computer Graphics, Dynamic Vision, Vims Vision, Software Analysis and Compilation, DEGAS Networking, Network Management and Optimization, LinBox, Bioinformatics, Computational Learning, Multi Agent Systems, Natural Language Processing, and Protocol Engineering.
	All machines are connected via fast Ethernet, several wireless networks, and a Gigabit Ethernet switch that provides high performance, security, and monitoring. The Department makes substantial use of University-wide facilities in its research and instructional programs. Almost all undergraduate instructional computing is done on University-wide facilities, though the Department also maintains a separate network of Sun systems for specialized instruction. The University of Delaware has two major connections to the Internet: an OC-3 (155 Mb/s) as a member of the nationwide network research Abilene (Internet2) project and a 1Gb/s fiber link to a local ISP. The recently expanded University library system contains more than 2.5 million bound volumes and is a government depository library, housing more than 400,000 government publications, including U.S. patents. The library subscribes to more than 20,000 periodicals, including a wide variety of computer science publications. The library also has electronic subscriptions to more than 32,000 journals. Full access to all IEEE journals and conference proceedings is available through the IEEE Xplore digital library.
Financial Aid	Fellowships and teaching research assistantships are available. For 2009–10, fellowship stipends were $15,000 and up, and assistantships ranged from $16,000 to $25,000; all included waiver of tuition. More than 50 percent of the full-time computer and information sciences graduate students receive fellowships or assistantships. Fellowships and traineeships are also available under a number of federal programs. Some summer stipends are available.
Cost of Study	For 2009–10, course fees for full-time students were $8540 per academic year for residents of Delaware and $22,240 per academic year for nonresidents. Tuition is waived for funded students.
Living and Housing Costs	The University has a limited number of one- and two-bedroom apartments for single and married graduate students who are enrolled in a full-time program of study. Campus housing prices range from $580 for an efficiency, to $930 for a one bedroom, and $1085 for a two bedroom. The Campus Housing Office maintains a listing of available off-campus accommodations near the University.
Student Group	There are currently about 110 graduate students in the Department. Approximately 95 percent are full-time students, and three fourths of these are supported by assistantships, fellowships, or external business organizations. The total campus enrollment is approximately 21,000, including 3,400 graduate students. The University of Delaware operates on a two-semester system, with additional summer sessions and a one-month winter session. Few graduate courses are offered during the summer and winter sessions; graduate students have opportunities to teach and do research during these sessions.
Location	Newark (pronounced "new ark"), Delaware, is a pleasant university community of 28,500 people. Located 1 hour from Philadelphia and Baltimore and about 2 hours from Washington, D.C. and New York, Newark offers the advantages of a small community but is still within easy traveling distance of major cities along the East Coast. Newark is also close to many recreational and scenic areas including the Chesapeake Bay, Atlantic beaches, and state parks and ski areas in Pennsylvania.
The University	The University of Delaware developed from a small private academy founded in 1743 and is today a state-assisted, privately controlled, coeducational land-grant and sea-grant university. The beautifully landscaped Newark campus consists of 2,041 acres, with 446 buildings in a predominately Georgian architectural style.
Applying	The general application deadlines are July 1 and December 1 for the fall and spring semesters, respectively. Deadlines for applications to be considered for financial aid (fellowships, assistantships, and tuition scholarships) are February 1 and October 1 for the fall and spring semesters, respectively; late applications are considered if positions exist. Notification of the admissions decision is provided promptly upon receipt of credentials. In addition to the completed application form and the application fee of $60, applicants must forward official transcripts of their previous academic records, including at least three letters of recommendation (preferably from past professors), a statement of rank in class, GRE General Test scores, and a TOEFL score if English is not their first language and they have not received a degree from a U.S. institution. Students normally enter with undergraduate preparation in computer science and mathematics. However, well-qualified students with varied backgrounds are encouraged to apply; minor deficiencies can be made up after matriculation.
Correspondence and Information	Professor Christopher Rasmussen Chair, Graduate Recruiting and Admissions Committee Department of Computer and Information Sciences University of Delaware Newark, Delaware 19716-2586 Phone: 302-831-2712 Fax: 302-831-8458 E-mail: gradprgm@cis.udel.edu Web site: http://www.udel.edu (University home page) http://www.cis.udel.edu (CIS home page index)

University of Delaware

THE FACULTY AND THEIR RESEARCH

Paul D. Amer, Alumni Distinguished Professor; Ph.D., Ohio State, 1979. Computer networks, transport layer services and protocols, data compression in multimedia.

James S. Atlas, Assistant Professor; Ph.D., Delaware, 2009. Constraint optimization, multi-agent systems, artificial intelligence, grid and parallel computing.

M. Sandra Carberry, Professor; Ph.D., Delaware, 1985. Natural language processing, user modeling, artificial intelligence.

Benjamin A. Carterette, Assistant Professor; Ph.D., Massachusetts, 2008. Information retrieval and organization, retrieval performance evaluation, search and full-text indexing, empirical methods, statistical methods.

John Case, Professor; Ph.D., Illinois, 1969. Computational learning theory, bioinformatics.

John Cavazos, Assistant Professor; Ph.D., Massachusetts, 2004. Compilers, programming languages, run-time systems, virtual machines, computer architecture, machine learning, statistical methods.

Daniel L. Chester, Associate Professor; Ph.D., Berkeley, 1973. Artificial intelligence, natural language processing, theorem proving, knowledge representation, computer vision.

James Clause, Assistant Professor; Ph.D., Georgia Tech, 2010. Software engineering.

Keith Decker, Associate Professor; Ph.D., Massachusetts, 1995. Distributed problem solving, multiagent systems, real-time problem solving, computational organization design, parallel and distributed planning and scheduling, distributed information gathering, bioinformatics.

Terry Harvey, Assistant Professor; Ph.D., Delaware, 2006. Natural language generation, multi-agent systems, artificial intelligence.

Chandra Kambhamettu, Professor; Ph.D., South Florida, 1994. Computer vision, computer graphics, image processing, bioinformatics and multimedia.

Li Liao, Associate Professor; Ph.D., Peking (China), 1992. Bioinformatics, statistical inference, machine learning, artificial intelligence.

Errol L. Lloyd, Professor; Ph.D., MIT, 1980. Design and analysis of algorithms.

Kathleen F. McCoy, Professor; Ph.D., Pennsylvania, 1985. Artificial intelligence, natural language generation and understanding, discourse phenomena, rehabilitation engineering, augmentative communication, assistive technology.

Lori L. Pollock, Professor; Ph.D., Pittsburgh, 1986. Organizing compilers, software testing, program analysis for software tools, mobile code security, parallel and distributive systems.

Christopher E. Rasmussen, Associate Professor; Ph.D., Yale, 2000. Computer vision, mobile robotics, artificial intelligence.

B. David Saunders, Professor and Department Chair; Ph.D., Wisconsin, 1975. Computer algebra, exact linear algebra, parallel computation.

Adarshpal S. Sethi, Professor; Ph.D., Indian Institute of Technology (Kanpur), 1978. Computer networks, network management, fault management, quality-of-service and resource management, management of wireless networks.

Vijay K. Shanker, Professor; Ph.D., Pennsylvania, 1987. Artificial intelligence, natural language processing, unification-based grammatical systems, knowledge-representation languages.

Chien-Chung Shen, Associate Professor; Ph.D., UCLA, 1992. Ad hoc, sensor, and satellite networks; network and service management; distributed object and peer-to-peer computing; simulation.

Stephen F. Siegel, Assistant Professor; Ph.D., Chicago, 1993. Concurrent and distributed software systems, linear programming and group theory, parallel computation.

D. Martin Swany, Associate Professor; Ph.D., California, Santa Barbara, 2003. Grid computing, clustering, performance modeling.

M. Taufer, Assistant Professor; Ph.D., Swiss Federal Institute of Technology, 2002. Distributed and parallel systems, adaptive and distributed scientific applications, grid and volunteer computing, distributed databases, workload characterizations and performance prediction in HPC systems and applications.

Cathy H. Wu, Edward G. Jefferson Professor; Director, Center for Bioinformatics and Computational Biology; and Director, Protein Information Resource; Ph.D., Purdue, 1984. Biological text mining, biological ontology, computational systems biology, protein structure-function-network analysis, bioinformatics cyberinfrastructure.

Jungyi Yu, Associate Professor; Ph.D., MIT, 2005. Computer graphics, computer vision, medical imaging, optics and camera design, multimedia.

Joint, Adjunct, and Research Faculty

Cecelia Arighi, Research Assistant Professor; Ph.D., Buenos Aires, 2001. Protein-centric database curation, biological text mining, biological ontology.

Stephan Bohacek, Assistant Professor (joint with Electrical and Computer Engineering); Ph.D., USC, 1999. Congestion control, routing, Internet security and pricing, ad hoc networks, control theory, biomedical modeling.

Charles G. Boncelet, Professor (joint with Electrical and Computer Engineering); Ph.D., Princeton, 1984. Signal processing, algorithms, networking.

H. Timothy Bunnell, Research Associate Professor (A. I. DuPont Hospital for Children); Ph.D., Penn State, 1983. Speech perception, speech synthesis and speech recognition, speech aids for people with disabilities.

Chuming Chen, Research Assistant Professor; Ph. D., South Carolina, 2008. Bioinformatics, data integration, proteomics informatics, Semantic Web, description logics, ontology engineering, high-performance computing, network security.

Hui Fang, Assistant Professor (joint with Electrical and Computer Engineering); Ph.D., Illinois at Urbana-Champaign, 2007. Information retrieval, bioinformatics, data mining, databases.

Guang Gao, Professor (joint with Electrical and Computer Engineering); Ph.D., MIT, 1996. Computer architecture and systems, parallel and distributed systems.

Jeffrey Heinz, Assistant Professor (joint with Linguistics and Cognitive Sciences); Ph.D., UCLA, 2007. Phonology, learning theory, computational linguistics, Austronesian languages.

Hongzhan Huang, Research Associate Professor; Ph.D., California, Davis, 1993. Bioinformatics, protein-centric database, computational system biology.

Mihailo Kaplarevic, Research Assistant Professor; Ph.D., Delaware, 2007. Application of high-performance computing in computational biology and bioinformatics, distributed informational system design, optimization of bioinformatics applications for cluster computing.

Xiaoming Li, Assistant Professor (joint with Electrical and Computer Engineering); Ph.D., Illinois at Urbana-Champaign, 2006. Code generation and optimization, compilers, and interaction between hardware and software.

Lisa Marvel, Research Assistant Professor; Ph.D., Delaware, 1999. United States Army Research Lab, steganography and mobile code security.

Blake Meyers, Assistant Professor (joint with Plant and Soil Sciences); Ph.D., California, Davis, 1998. Transcriptional analysis in *Arabidopsis*.

David Mills, Professor (joint with Electrical and Computer Engineering); Ph.D., Michigan, 1971. Computer networks and security.

Beth Mineo, Associate Professor (Director, joint with Center for Disabilities Studies); Ph.D. Assistive technology, speech and language therapy, early childhood education.

Natalia Petrova, Research Assistant Professor; Ph.D., Georgetown, 2008. Bioinformatics, machine learning, protein function prediction.

David Wood, Research Professor; Ph.D., Rhode Island, 1972. DNA computing, analysis of algorithms, computer algebra, linear algebra.

Professional Staff

Yongxing Chen, Computer Information Technology Associate IV, Computer and Information Sciences.

Michael Davis, Director, EE/CIS Research Laboratory.

Linda Magner, Assistant to the Chair.

Ben Miller, Assistant Director, EE/CIS Research Laboratory.

Andrew Roosen, Computer Information Technology Associate III, EE/CIS Research Laboratory.

UNIVERSITY OF HOUSTON

Department of Computer Science
M.S. and Ph.D. Degree Programs

Programs of Study

The Department of Computer Science at the University of Houston (UH) offers programs leading to the Master of Science (M.S.) and Doctor of Philosophy (Ph.D.) degrees in computer science. Fields of specialization include artificial intelligence (AI), biomedical informatics and robotics, computer graphics, computer networks, computer vision, database management systems, parallel and distributed computing, scientific computing, software engineering, and theory.

The M.S. degree requires 24 hours of course work and a thesis. A nonthesis M.S. degree is also available. Requirements for the Ph.D. degree include a dissertation and 36 hours of course work after the B.S.

Research Facilities

The Department maintains UNIX servers running Solaris and Linux that serve e-mail, Web pages, and file shares. Students have access to more than 140 workstations that include Linux and Windows within the Department labs, and remote access to most Department resources is also provided. High-performance computing resources include an Apple XServe Cluster and several 8-way AMD Opteron SMPs. A regional ATM OC3-12 system linking UH facilities with Rice University and Baylor College of Medicine is operational. UH is on the Internet backbone and is part of the experimental Internet2.

Financial Aid

Graduate students with teaching or research assistantships are provided a stipend of between $1200 and $1400 per month, depending on the student's qualifications. Application for the assistantship should be made directly to the Department. The deadlines are February 1 (for fall) and October 1 (for spring). Many graduate students are employed by the University of Houston and work as research or teaching assistants for the Department of Computer Science or other departments. Other students hold part-time or full-time jobs working for companies in the Houston metropolitan area.

Cost of Study

Tuition and fees for Texas residents were approximately $3250 per semester in 2009–10; nonresidents, including international students, paid about $6250 per semester. Students receiving financial assistance qualify for resident status and for Graduate Assistant Tuition Fellowships.

Living and Housing Costs

On-campus housing costs approximately $2500 per semester. For students in off-campus housing, apartments begin at about $550 per month.

Student Group

There are approximately 250 graduate students in the Department, 70 of whom are Ph.D. students. These students come from all over the world, including Asia, Europe, the Middle East, and the Americas. The Department maintains exchange student agreements with universities in China, France, Germany, Mexico, Sweden, Taiwan, and others.

Student Outcomes

The Ph.D. graduates find employment in both academic institutions and industry, such as GTE labs, nationwide. The demand for graduates who earn a master's degree is great, and most M.S. students find positions prior to graduation.

Location

Houston is the fourth-largest city in the U.S. and maintains a high rate of economic growth. Many large companies have their headquarters located in Houston, and the Texas Medical Center in Houston is the second-largest in the United States. The weather in Houston is rarely cold, and, compared to other U.S. cities, the living expenses are quite low. Moreover, Houston has restaurants and grocery stores offering food from all over the world and gives residents access to theaters and concerts, the Houston opera and symphony, many outdoor festivals, and college and professional sports events, including the Astros, the Rockets, the Texans, and its soccer team, the Dynamo. Houston is only 50 miles from the Gulf of Mexico, which offers beaches and opportunities for fishing, crabbing, windsurfing, and other water-related activities.

The University and The Department

The Department of Computer Science is committed to high-quality, state-of-the-art education and research in the highly diverse and cosmopolitan environment that the University of Houston and the city of Houston provide. The University of Houston is the only doctoral degree–granting component and the largest campus of the state-supported UH System and serves as a strong research and intellectual base for the city of Houston, the state of Texas, and the United States. Serving 37,000 students in thirteen colleges, UH ranks among the top eighty research universities in the country. Research grants and awards to UH exceeded $110 million in 2009.

The Department, one of six departments in the College of Natural Sciences and Mathematics, maintains strong ties with several research institutes on campus, including the High Performance Computing Center, the Texas Learning and Computation Center, and the Institute of Molecular Design as well as Methodist Hospital in the Texas Medical Center.

Applying

Applicants must have a bachelor's degree and are evaluated based on both their scores from the Graduate Record Examinations (GRE) and their GPA over the last 60 credit hours of undergraduate study. Moreover, the education background in mathematics and computer science, the quality of schools and programs where past degrees were obtained, letters of recommendation, and other accomplishments of the applicant are also considered. Students with degrees in fields other than computer science may be admitted; they may have to complete additional course work. The admission process for the graduate programs is competitive.

Correspondence and Information

Dr. Ernst L. Leiss
Director of Graduate Studies
Department of Computer Science
University of Houston
501 PGH
Houston, Texas 77204-3010
Phone: 713-743-3350
Fax: 713-743-3335
E-mail: gradinfo@cs.uh.edu
Web site: http://www.cs.uh.edu

University of Houston

THE FACULTY AND THEIR RESEARCH

Barbara Chapman, Professor; Ph.D., Trinity (Dublin). Compiler technology, parallel programming languages, tool support for application development, parallel computing and high-performance computing, computational grids.

Albert M. K. Cheng, Associate Professor; Ph.D., Texas at Austin. Real-time systems, distributed systems, AI, software engineering, computer security, computer networks.

Kam-Hoi Cheng, Associate Professor; Ph.D., Minnesota. Artificial intelligence, object-oriented analysis and design, VLSI, parallel and distributed processing, networks, architecture, algorithm and complexity.

Zhigang Deng, Assistant Professor; Ph.D., USC. Computer graphics, computer animation, interactive media and gaming, human-computer interaction.

Christoph F. Eick, Associate Professor; Ph.D., Karlsruhe (West Germany). Artificial intelligence, knowledge-based systems, evolutionary computing, data mining, databases.

Yuriy Fofanov, Associate Professor; Ph.D., Kuibyshev (Samara) State (USSR). Bioinformatics, applied statistics, mathematical modeling and information theory.

Edgar Gabriel, Assistant Professor; Ph.D., Stuttgart (Germany). Message-passing systems, high-performance computing, parallel computing on distributed memory machines, grid computing.

Marc Garbey, Professor; Ph.D., Ecole Centrale de Lyon (France). Algorithms, numerical analysis, parallel computation, scientific computing.

Victoria Hilford, Instructional Assistant Professor; Ph.D., Houston. Programming languages, object-oriented analysis and design, database management, software engineering, Web programming.

J. C. Huang, Professor Emeritus; Ph.D., Pennsylvania. Software engineering, real-time computer systems, program analysis and testing.

S.-H. Stephen Huang, Professor; Ph.D., Texas at Austin. Data structures, design and analysis of algorithms, parallel and distributed processing, data security.

Olin G. Johnson, Professor; Ph.D., Berkeley. Numerical analysis, high-performance computing.

S. Lennart Johnsson, Cullen Professor of Computer Science; Ph.D., Chalmers (Sweden). Parallel computing, scientific computation.

Ioannis A. Kakadiaris, Eckhard Pfeiffer Professor; Ph.D., Pennsylvania. Computer vision, medical imaging, computer graphics, physics-based modeling, estimation and synthesis of the shape and motion of articulated objects.

Willis K. King, Professor Emeritus; Ph.D., Pennsylvania. Computer architecture, distributed systems.

Ernst L. Leiss, Professor and Director of Graduate Studies; Dr. Techn., TU Wien (Vienna). Vector and parallel computing, data security, formal and programming languages, geophysical data processing.

Carlos Ordonez, Assistant Professor; Ph.D., Georgia Tech. Relational database systems, data mining, machine learning.

Jehan-François Pâris, Professor; Ph.D., Berkeley. Distributed systems, file systems, fault-tolerant computing, performance evaluation.

Ioannis Pavlidis, Eckhard Pfeiffer Professor; Ph.D., Minnesota. Computer vision, pattern recognition, bioinformatics, medical imaging, software engineering.

B. Montgomery Pettitt, Cullen Professor of Chemistry, Computer Science, and Biochemical and Biophysical Sciences and Director, Institute for Molecular Design; Ph.D., Houston. High-performance computing, parallel processing, numerical analysis, visualization.

Shishir Shah, Assistant Professor; Ph.D., Texas at Austin. Quantitative microscopy, computational biology, image analysis, computer vision, pattern recognition, image instrumentation.

Jaspal Subhlok, Professor and Department Chair; Ph.D., Rice. Parallel and distributed systems, adaptive and network-aware computing, compilers.

Nikolaos Tsekos, Associate Professor: Ph.D., Minnesota. Robotics and physiology, magnetic resonance imaging.

Rakesh M. Verma, Professor; Ph.D., SUNY at Stony Brook. Symbolic computation, declarative programming languages, automated deduction, parallel computing, temporal and spatial databases.

Ricardo Vilalta, Associate Professor; Ph.D., Illinois at Urbana-Champaign. Machine learning, computational and statistical learning theory, neural networks, data mining, artificial intelligence.

Rong Zheng, Assistant Professor; Ph.D., Illinois at Urbana-Champaign. Wireless networking, distributed systems, network simulation, performance modeling.

CURRENT RESEARCH PROJECTS
Data security in object-oriented and in multimedia systems.
Fast and efficient rewriting methods for verification and equational programming.
Efficient sequential and parallel storage and access methods for temporal and spatial databases.
Techniques, tools, and algorithms for video-on-demand.
Distributed network cashing.
Tools for network-aware parallel and distributed computing.
Tools and software technologies for OpenMP.
Grid computing.
Efficient metacomputing in combustion.
Program transformation for high-performance parallel computing.
Input/output management in high-performance computing, including parallel I/O.
Parallel and distributed algorithms.
Biomedical image analysis.
Functional brain mapping.
Automatic segmentation of the left ventricle from MR data.
Visualization tools for biomedical applications.
DNA microarray data analysis.
Rigorous reliability assessment of embedded safety-critical systems.
Self-stabilizing safety-critical applications over wide-area networks.
Timing analysis and verification of real-time systems.
Tools for data mining.
Meta-learning and self-adaptive classifiers.
Supervised clustering.
Machine learning applied to physics and astronomy.
Cooperative camera network.
Human identification at a distance.
Detection of events for threat evaluation and recognition.
Information assurance.

UNIVERSITY OF NORTH CAROLINA AT CHAPEL HILL

Department of Computer Science

Programs of Study	The Department offers the Ph.D. and a professional M.S. degree. Study for the M.S. degree includes algorithms, programming languages, and hardware as well as important areas of application. The Ph.D. program includes courses in specialized areas and preparation for teaching and advanced research. Students pursue particular areas of their choice and are actively involved in research. The curricula emphasize the design and application of real computer systems and the portion of theory that guides and supports practice. The Department's orientation is experimental, with clusters of research in algorithms and complexity theory, bioinformatics and computational biology, computer architectures, computer graphics and image analysis, computer-supported cooperative work, computer security, computer vision, distributed systems, geometric modeling and computation, hardware systems and design, high-performance and parallel computing, human-machine interaction, hypermedia and digital libraries, mechanical theorem proving, Monte Carlo methods, multimedia systems, networking, physically-based modeling, real-time systems, robotics, and software engineering and environments. Students holding an assistantship can typically expect to earn the M.S. degree in two academic years and the Ph.D. in four or five years.
Research Facilities	All of the Department's computing facilities are housed in two adjoining four-story computer science buildings that feature specialized research laboratories for graphics and image processing, telepresence and computer vision, computer building and design, and collaborative, distributed, and parallel systems. Completed in summer 2008, the newly constructed addition to the building allows for additional office and research space, including an updated graphics lab and new computer security and robotics labs. The labs, offices, conference areas, and classrooms are bound together by the Department's fully integrated distributed computing environment, which includes more than 1,000 computers, ranging from older systems used for generating network traffic for simulated Internet experiments to state-of-the-art workstations and clusters for graphics- and compute-intensive research. These systems are integrated by high-speed networks and by software that is consistent at the user level over the many architectural platforms. Each student is assigned a computer, with computer assignments based on the students' research or teaching responsibilities and their seniority within the Department. In addition to the Departmental servers and office systems, the research laboratories contain a wide variety of specialized equipment and facilities. The nearby Brauer Library has extensive holdings in mathematics, physics, statistics, operations research, and computer science.
Financial Aid	During the academic year, most students are supported by assistantships and fellowships. The stipend for research and teaching assistantships for the nine-month academic year in 2010–11 is $17,000 (20 hours per week). Full-time summer employment on a research project is normally available to students who would like to receive support. The rate for summer 2010 was $850 (40 hours per week) for ten to twelve weeks. This produces a combined annual financial package for graduate assistants of approximately $27,200. Students with assistantships qualify for a Graduate Student Tuition Grant and pay no tuition; they are responsible for paying student fees of $875 per semester. Graduate Student Tuition Grants typically cover M.S. students for four semesters of study and Ph.D. students for ten semesters of study. At no additional cost to them, students are also covered by a comprehensive major medical insurance program, underwritten by Blue Cross/Blue Shield of North Carolina. Each semester, the Department provides a $500 educational fund to any student who receives a competitive fellowship that is not granted by the University of North Carolina at Chapel Hill (UNC–Chapel Hill). The fund may be used for education-related expenses, including books, journals, travel, computer supplies and accessories, and professional memberships. The Department also awards a $1500 supplement each semester to nonservice fellowship holders who join a research team. To apply for an assistantship, the applicant should check the appropriate item on the admission application form. Applicants for assistantships are automatically considered for all available fellowships. Students can expect continued support, contingent upon satisfactory work performance and academic progress. Students are not assigned to specific research projects or teaching assistant positions immediately upon being admitted to the department. Assignments are made just prior to the start of each semester, after faculty members and students have had an opportunity to meet and to discuss their interests. Students are encouraged to gain professional experience through summer internships with companies in the Research Triangle area or in other parts of the country.
Cost of Study	For the 2009–10 academic year, tuition and fees for graduate students at the University of North Carolina at Chapel Hill were $7162 for state residents and $21,560 for nonresidents. Virtually all graduate students in computer science pay no tuition, as mentioned in the Financial Aid section.
Living and Housing Costs	Annual living costs for single graduate students in the Chapel Hill area are estimated by University staff members to be $18,000 or higher. On-campus housing is available for both married and single students attending the University.
Student Group	The Department of Computer Science enrolls approximately 140 graduate students, most of whom attend full-time.
Student Outcomes	A majority of the Department's master's graduates work in industry, in companies ranging from small start-up operations to government research labs and large research and development corporations. Ph.D. graduates work in both academia and industry. Academic employment ranges from positions in four-year colleges, where teaching is the primary focus, to positions at major research universities. Some graduates take postdoctoral positions at research laboratories prior to continuing in industry or joining academia.
Location	Chapel Hill (population 49,900) is a scenic college town located in the heart of North Carolina, where small-town charm mixes with a cosmopolitan atmosphere to provide students with a rich and varied living experience. The town and the surrounding area offer many cultural advantages, including excellent theater and music, museums, and a planetarium. There are also many opportunities to watch and to participate in sports. The Carolina beaches, the Outer Banks, Great Smoky Mountains National Park, and the Blue Ridge Mountains are only a few hours' drive away. The Research Triangle of North Carolina is formed by the University of North Carolina at Chapel Hill, Duke University in Durham, and North Carolina State University in Raleigh. The universities have a combined enrollment of more than 74,000 students, have libraries with more than 14 million volumes with interconnected catalogs and have national prominence in a variety of disciplines. Collectively, they conduct more than $1.5 billion in research each year.
The University and The Department	The 729-acre central campus of UNC–Chapel Hill is among the most beautiful in the country. Of the approximately 28,500 students enrolled, nearly 11,000 are graduate and professional students. The Department's primary missions are research and graduate and undergraduate teaching. It offers the B.S., M.S., and Ph.D. degrees. The Computer Science Students' Association sponsors both professional and social events and represents the students in Departmental matters. Its president is a voting member at faculty meetings. There is much interaction between students and faculty members, and students contribute to nearly every aspect of the Department's operation.
Applying	Applications for fall admission, complete with a personal statement, all transcripts, three letters of recommendation, and official GRE and/or TOEFL scores should be received by the Graduate School no later than January 1. Early submission is encouraged. International applicants should consider completing their applications earlier to allow time for processing financial and visa documents. Applicants should check the Department Web site for the latest information regarding application deadlines.
Correspondence and Information	For written information about graduate study: Admissions and Graduate Studies Department of Computer Science Campus Box 3175, Brooks Computer Science Building University of North Carolina Chapel Hill, North Carolina 27599-3175 Phone: 919-962-1900 Fax: 919-962-1799 E-mail: admit@cs.unc.edu Web site: http://www.cs.unc.edu For applications and admissions information: The Graduate School Campus Box 4010, 200 Bynum Hall University of North Carolina Chapel Hill, North Carolina 27599-4010 Phone: 919-966-2611 E-mail: gradinfo@unc.edu Web site: http://gradschool.unc.edu/

University of North Carolina at Chapel Hill

THE FACULTY AND THEIR RESEARCH

Stan Ahalt, Professor and Director of the Renaissance Computing Institute (RENCI); Ph.D., Clemson, 1986. Signal, image, and video processing; high-performance scientific and industrial computing; pattern recognition applied to national security problems; high-productivity, domain-specific languages.

Ron Alterovitz, Assistant Professor; Ph.D., Berkeley, 2006. Medical robotics, motion planning, physically-based simulation, optimization, medical image analysis.

James Anderson, Professor; Ph.D., Texas at Austin, 1990. Distributed and concurrent algorithms, real-time systems, fault-tolerant computing, formal methods.

Sanjoy K. Baruah, Professor; Ph.D., Texas at Austin, 1993. Scheduling theory, real-time and safety-critical system design, computer networks, resource allocation and sharing in distributed computing environments.

Gary Bishop, Professor; Ph.D., North Carolina at Chapel Hill, 1984. Hardware and software for man-machine interaction, 3-D interactive computer graphics, virtual environments, tracking technologies, image-based rendering.

Frederick P. Brooks Jr., Kenan Professor; Ph.D., Harvard, 1956. 3-D interactive computer graphics, human-computer interaction, virtual worlds, computer architecture, the design process.

Peter Calingaert, Professor Emeritus; Ph.D., Harvard, 1955.

Prasun Dewan, Professor; Ph.D., Wisconsin–Madison, 1986. User interfaces, distributed collaboration, software engineering environments, object-oriented databases, mobile computing.

Jan-Michael Frahm, Research Assistant Professor; Ph.D., Kiel (Germany), 2005. Computer vision, image-based modeling, image and video analysis, multiview geometry, geometric and photometric camera calibration, markerless augmented reality.

Henry Fuchs, Federico Gil Professor; Ph.D., Utah, 1975. High-performance graphics hardware, 3-D medical imaging, head-mounted displays, virtual environments.

John H. Halton, Professor Emeritus; D.Phil., Oxford, 1960.

Kye S. Hedlund, Associate Professor; Ph.D., Purdue, 1982. Computer-aided design, computer architecture, algorithm design and analysis, parallel processing.

Kevin Jeffay, Gillian Cell Distinguished Professor and Associate Chairman for Academic Affairs; Ph.D., Washington (Seattle), 1989. Real-time systems, operating systems, distributed systems, multimedia networking, computer-supported cooperative work, performance evaluation.

Jasleen Kaur, Associate Professor; Ph.D., Texas at Austin, 2002. Design of networks and operating systems, specifically resource management for providing service guarantees, Internet measurements, overlay and peer-to-peer networks, and router architectures.

Anselmo A. Lastra, Professor and Chairman; Ph.D., Duke, 1988. Interactive 3-D computer graphics, hardware architectures for computer graphics.

Svetlana Lazebnik, Assistant Professor; Ph.D., Illinois at Urbana-Champaign, 2006. Computer vision, object recognition and scene interpretation, Internet photo collections, machine learning.

Ming C. Lin, John R. and Louise S. Parker Distinguished Professor; Ph.D., Berkeley, 1993. Physically based and geometric modeling, applied computational geometry, robotics, distributed interactive simulation, virtual environments, algorithm analysis.

Gyula A. Magó, Professor Emeritus; Ph.D., Cambridge, 1970.

Dinesh Manocha, Phi Delta Theta/Matthew Mason Distinguished Professor; Ph.D., Berkeley, 1992. Geometric and solid modeling, physically based modeling, computer graphics, simulation-based design, symbolic and scientific computation, computational geometry.

Ketan Mayer-Patel, Associate Professor and Director of Graduate Admissions; Ph.D., Berkeley, 1999. Multimedia systems, networking, multicast applications.

Leonard McMillan, Associate Professor; Ph.D., North Carolina at Chapel Hill, 1997. Computer graphics, image processing, computer vision, multimedia, microelectronics, computer organization.

Fabian Monrose, Associate Professor; Ph.D., NYU, 1999. Computer and network security, biometrics, user authentification.

Tessa Joseph Nicholas, Lecturer; Ph.D., North Carolina at Chapel Hill, 2008. New media arts and poetics, digital communities, digital-age ethics.

Marc Niethammer, Assistant Professor; Ph.D., Georgia Tech, 2004. Quantitative image analysis, shape analysis, diffusion-weighted magnetic resonance imaging, cellular imaging, visual tracking and estimation theory, structural health monitoring.

Stephen M. Pizer, Kenan Professor; Ph.D., Harvard, 1967. Image analysis and display, human and computer vision, graphics, numerical computing, medical imaging.

David A. Plaisted, Professor; Ph.D., Stanford, 1976. Mechanical theorem proving, term rewriting systems, logic programming, algorithms.

Marc Pollefeys, Associate Professor; Ph.D., Leuven (Belgium), 1999. Computer vision, image-based modeling and rendering, image and video analysis, multiview geometry.

Jan F. Prins, Professor and Director of Graduate Studies; Ph.D., Cornell, 1987. Parallel algorithms, languages and architectures, high-level programming languages, compilers, formal techniques in program development, algorithms for structural biology and bioinformatics.

Timothy L. Quigg, Lecturer and Associate Chairman for Administration and Finance; M.P.A., North Carolina State, 1979. Intellectual property rights, industrial relations, contract management, research administration.

Michael K. Reiter, Lawrence M. Slifkin Distinguished Professor; Ph.D., Cornell, 1993. Computer and network security, distributed systems, applied cryptography.

Montek Singh, Associate Professor; Ph.D., Columbia, 2002. High-performance and low-power digital systems, asynchronous circuits and systems, VLSI CAD, graphics hardware.

F. Donelson Smith, Research Professor; Ph.D., North Carolina at Chapel Hill, 1978. Computer networks, operating systems, distributed systems, multimedia, computer-supported cooperative work.

John B. Smith, Professor; Ph.D., North Carolina at Chapel Hill, 1970. Computer-supported cooperative work, hypermedia systems, World Wide Web architecture and programming, Java object storage and access.

Jack S. Snoeyink, Professor; Ph.D., Stanford, 1990. Computational geometry, algorithms for geographical information systems and structural biology, geometric modeling and computation, algorithms and data structures, theory of computation.

Donald F. Stanat, Professor Emeritus; Ph.D., Michigan, 1966.

David Stotts, Professor; Ph.D., Virginia, 1985. Computer-supported cooperative work, hypermedia, software engineering and formal methods, programming languages and concurrency, interoperable distributed systems.

Martin Styner, Research Assistant Professor; Ph.D., North Carolina at Chapel Hill, 2001. Medical image analysis, 3-D object shape representation and quantitative shape analysis, image processing.

Russell M. Taylor II, Research Professor; Ph.D., North Carolina at Chapel Hill, 1994. 3-D interactive computer graphics, virtual worlds, distributed computing, scientific visualization, human-computer interaction.

Leandra Vicci, Lecturer and Director, Applied Engineering Laboratory; B.S., Antioch (Ohio), 1964. Information processing hardware: theory, practice, systems, and applications.

Jeannie M. Walsh, Lecturer Emeritus; M.S., Oklahoma State, 1984.

Wei Wang, Associate Professor; Ph.D., UCLA, 1999. Data mining, database systems, bioinformatics.

Stephen F. Weiss, Professor Emeritus; Ph.D., Cornell, 1970.

Gregory F. Welch, Research Professor; Ph.D., North Carolina at Chapel Hill, 1997. Human-machine interaction, 3-D interactive computer graphics, virtual/augmented environment tracking systems, shared virtual environments and telecollaboration.

Mary C. Whitton, Research Associate Professor; M.S., North Carolina State, 1984. Virtual and augmented reality systems for data visualization, computer graphics system architectures.

William V. Wright, Research Professor Emeritus; Ph.D., North Carolina at Chapel Hill, 1972. Interactive systems for supporting scientific research, molecular graphics, architecture and implementation of computing systems.

Adjunct Faculty

Stephen Aylward, Adjunct Associate Professor; Ph.D., North Carolina at Chapel Hill, 1997.

Larry Conrad, Professor of the Practice, Vice Chancellor for Information Technology, and Chief Information Officer; M.S., Arizona State.

Brad Davis, Adjunct Assistant Professor; Ph.D., North Carolina at Chapel Hill, 2008. Image analysis, shape analysis, image processing, statistical methods in nonlinear spaces, medical applications, visualization, software engineering.

Nick England, Adjunct Research Professor; E.E., North Carolina State, 1974. Systems architectures for graphics and imaging, scientific visualization, volume rendering, interactive surface modeling.

Mark Foskey, Adjunct Research Assistant Professor; Ph.D., California, San Diego, 1994. Computer-aided surgical planning, computer-aided diagnosis, geometric computation.

Rob Fowler, Adjunct Professor; Ph.D., Washington (Seattle), 1985. Effectiveness of high-end systems in serving the needs of scientists, developing software tools that enhance the performance of grid-enabled applications.

Guido Gerig, Adjunct Professor; Ph.D., Swiss Federal Institute of Technology, 1987. Image analysis, shape-based object recognition, 3-D object representation and quantitative analysis, medical image processing.

Morgan Giddings, Adjunct Assistant Professor; Ph.D., Wisconsin, 1997.

Shawn Gomez, Adjunct Assistant Professor; Eng.Sc.D., Columbia. Bioinformatics, computational biology, systems biology.

Chris Healey, Adjunct Associate Professor; Ph.D., British Columbia, 1996. Computer graphics, scientific visualization, perception and cognitive vision, color, texture, databases, computational geometry.

M. Gail Jones, Adjunct Professor; Ph.D., North Carolina State, 1987. Science education, gender and science, high-stakes assessment nanotechnology education, haptics and learning.

Sarang Joshi, Adjunct Associate Professor; D.Sc., Washington (St. Louis), 1997.

Hye-Chung (Monica) Kum, Adjunct Assistant Professor; Ph.D., North Carolina at Chapel Hill, 2004. Program evaluation, management of human services agencies, social welfare policy and program analysis using KDD (Knowledge Discovery in Databases), technology on social welfare administrative data, research methods.

J. Stephen Marron, Adjunct Professor; Ph.D., UCLA, 1982. Smoothing methods for curve estimation.

Steven E. Molnar, Adjunct Associate Professor; Ph.D., North Carolina at Chapel Hill, 1991. Architectures for real-time computer graphics, VLSI-based system design, parallel rendering algorithms.

Frank Mueller, Adjunct Associate Professor; Ph.D., Florida State, 1994.

Andrew B. Nobel, Adjunct Professor; Ph.D., Stanford, 1992. Statistical analysis of microarrays, analysis of Internet traffic, nonparametric interference, pattern recognition: clustering and clarification.

Lars S. Nyland, Adjunct Associate Professor; Ph.D., Duke, 1991. High-performance computing, hardware systems, computer graphics and image analysis, geometric modeling and computation, parallel algorithms, parallel computer architecture, programming languages, program transformation and optimization techniques, scientific computing, real-time systems, distributed systems.

John Poulton, Adjunct Research Professor; Ph.D., North Carolina at Chapel Hill, 1980. Graphics architectures, VLSI-based system design, design tools, rapid system prototyping.

Diane Pozefsky, Adjunct Professor; Ph.D., North Carolina at Chapel Hill, 1979. Software engineering and environments; computer education; serious games design and development; social, legal, and ethical issues concerning information technology.

Julian Rosenman, Adjunct Professor; Ph.D., Texas at Austin 1971; M.D., Texas Health Science Center at Dallas, 1977. Computer graphics for treatment of cancer patients, contrast enhancement of poor-quality X rays.

Dinggang Shen, Adjunct Associate Professor; Ph.D., Shanghai Jiao Tong (China), 1995.

Diane H. Sonnenwald, Adjunct Professor; Ph.D., Rutgers, 1993. Collaboration among multidisciplinary, cross-organizational teams, collaboration across distances, collaboration technology, human information behavior, digital libraries.

Richard Superfine, Adjunct Professor; Ph.D., Berkeley, 1991. Condensed-matter physics, biophysics, microscopy.

Alexander Tropsha, Adjunct Professor; Ph.D., Moscow State (Russia), 1986.

Sean Washburn, Adjunct Professor; Ph.D., Duke, 1982. Condensed-matter physics, materials science.

UNIVERSITY OF ROCHESTER

Department of Computer Science

Program of Study	The Department of Computer Science at the University of Rochester offers an intensive research-oriented program leading to the degree of Doctor of Philosophy. Emphasis is currently being placed on the areas of natural language understanding; vision, virtual reality, and machine perception; systems software for parallel and distributed computing; and the theory of computation. A number of joint faculty appointments and programs with other departments (including the Departments of Linguistics, Mathematics, Philosophy, Electrical and Computer Engineering, Psychology, Cognitive Science, Dermatology, and Neuroscience) add breadth to the program. Additional enrichment is gained from an extensive program of seminar presentations and the participation of visiting professors.

Milestones in the doctoral program include a broad comprehensive exam at the end of the first year, a deeper area exam in the student's chosen subfield at the end of the second year—at which point the master's degree is generally awarded—and a thesis proposal at the end of the third year. Completion of a doctoral dissertation typically requires one to two more years, with formal feedback from the student's thesis committee twice a year.

The Department is entering its thirty-fifth year of operation and has a young, energetic faculty, and a student-faculty ratio of 3.5:1. Students receive individual attention in the shaping of their graduate programs and have an active role in the design of laboratory facilities and software.

Research Facilities
The department maintains a high-speed local network of computers that its faculty, staff, and students can use for research. As of spring 2008, the computers on the network include approximately 90 high-end PCs running Linux, and another 30 workstations of other kinds (Suns, SGI machines, Macintoshes, and PCs running Windows), with an extensive collection of file and computer servers. Almost all machines are connected by switched Gigabit Ethernet; the remainder is on 100Mb switched Ethernet. A pair of 802.11a/b/g wireless networks, one inside and the other outside the department firewall also covers all department space. Resources for the Computer Systems and Engineering Group include a 32-processor IBM p690 Regatta multiprocessor, with 1.3GHz Power4 processors, 32GB of physical memory, and 128MB of cache; 16- and 8-processor SunFire multiprocessors; three 8-core, 32-thread Sun T1000 (Niagara) multiprocessors; a 72-node, 144-processor IBM-branded Linux cluster; and miscellaneous other 2-, 4-, and 8-processor machines. Other facilities include several high-end Pentium servers and high-end lab equipment for power measurement in mobile systems. The department is an active participant in the PlanetLab global network testbed, and has access to machines at the University's Center for Research Computing (CRC), the Laboratory for Laser Energetics, and the Pittsburgh Supercomputing Center. CRC resources include an 84-node, 672-core IBM Linux cluster with 8TF peak performance; researchers in Computer Science are among the leading users of this cluster. The Vision and Robotics Laboratory is equipped with two Unimation Puma 700 series robot arms, a Utah four-fingered anthropomorphic hand, two ActivMedia mobile robots, about a dozen computational vision sensors (computer and pair of pan-tilt-zoom camera), real-time image-processing hardware, and a Vivid 900 3-D laser-scanning range and image sensor. The Laboratory for Assisted Cognition Environments (LACE) contains a heavily instrumented simulated living space that is used for experiments in human behavior recognition. Activities performed in the kitchen or living room area are measured with environment-based sensors, such as motion sensors and cameras, as well as wearable sensors, such as the Mobile Sensing Platform (MSP) and iBracelet RFID reader from Intel Research. The MSP has sensors that measure 3-D acceleration, audio, barometric pressure, infrared and visible light, and temperature, while the iBracelet detects RFID tags that are placed on objects of interest throughout the lab. Assistive technologies developed in the lab can communicate with users through WiFi enabled PDAs or a 52-inch wall-mounted Sony LCD screen. The Speech Lab contains equipment for digitizing, storing, and analyzing audio signals. Undergraduate majors and those taking upper level computer science courses are given accounts in two computing labs reserved solely for undergraduate use. All workstations in these labs were replaced in the summer of 2006 with high-end Pentium 4 PCs and cycle servers running Fedora Core 5 Linux. RAID-equipped Sun servers provide file service. One of the labs, reserved for majors only, doubles as undergraduate lounge and library space. Each of the department's faculty, staff, and student desks is equipped with a workstation, and additional workstations are maintained in public areas. The department makes every effort to provide the latest facilities in hardware and software to enhance the productivity and impact of its research.

Financial Aid
The Department works to ensure that all doctoral students are fully supported by graduate assistantships or fellowships. In return, students are expected to participate in the Department's research activities from the outset of their graduate career and to assist with teaching duties during two or three semesters over the course of the graduate program. The appointment in 2010–11 provides an assistantship stipend of $1850 per month as well as full tuition remission. Many students accept summer research support from the Department (a twelve-month total of $22,200); most others take summer jobs in industry.

Cost of Study
Full-time graduate tuition for the 2010–11 academic year is $39,488 for 32 credit hours but is waived for supported students. Mandatory health fees ($552 for 2010–11) are paid by the Department; required medical insurance is available from the University for $1560 per year.

Living and Housing Costs
University-owned graduate housing facilities include more than 800 apartments. Rents range from $475 per month for a single furnished room to $785 per month for a furnished two-bedroom apartment. The Housing Office maintains a listing of accommodations near the University. A comprehensive board plan is available.

Student Group
The current full-time population at the University of Rochester is approximately 7,300 students, including more than 2,700 graduate students. There are full-time graduate students in the Department of Computer Science, all of whom are supported by assistantships, fellowships, or tuition grants.

Student Outcomes
Many of the Department's graduates have gone on to academic appointments at top schools, including Carnegie Mellon, Stanford, Maryland, Illinois, Pennsylvania, North Carolina, Wisconsin, Northwestern, Rice, Boston, Virginia, Princeton, Chicago, MIT, Utah, Oregon, Rose-Hulman, Lehigh, and Johns Hopkins. Those accepting nonacademic positions have gone to top research labs, including Bell Labs, IBM, Xerox, Olivetti Research Center, Philips Laboratories, Lockheed Martin, Matsushita, the International Computer Science Institute, Microsoft, Martin Marietta, David Sarnoff Research Center, Siemens, Digital Equipment Corporation, Google, Intel, and Silicon Graphics.

Location
Located on the south shore of Lake Ontario, a short drive from the Finger Lakes region, Rochester is a cultural center of upstate New York and has a metropolitan area population of just over a million. Opportunities for cultural activities are offered the year round by the Strasenburgh Planetarium, the University's Memorial Art Gallery, the International Museum of Photography, the Rochester Museum and Science Center, the Rochester City Ballet, and the Eastman Theatre. Rochester and the surrounding area have many lovely parks, and in the winter, there are many ski areas within an hour's drive. Known as the photographic and optical capital of the world, Rochester is the home of Eastman Kodak, the Xerox Corporation, Bausch & Lomb, and many other high-tech companies.

The University
The University of Rochester is an independent university that offers more than forty-five doctoral programs and ninety master's degree programs in the following schools and colleges: the College that is made up of Arts and Sciences and the School of Engineering and Applied Sciences, the Eastman School of Music, the School of Medicine and Dentistry, the School of Nursing, the William E. Simon Graduate School of Business Administration, and the Margaret Warner Graduate School of Education and Human Development. The River Campus, where the Department of Computer Science is located, is situated on the east bank of the Genesee River, about 2 miles south of downtown Rochester.

Applying
Applicants must apply electronically. For maximum consideration for the fall term, applications, personal statements, transcripts, recommendations, and scores on the Graduate Record Examinations (GRE) must be submitted no later than January 15. The GRE should be taken no later than December. The General Test is required, and the Subject Test in computer science, math, or physics is highly recommended. International students should also submit their scores on the Test of English as a Foreign Language (TOEFL).

Correspondence and Information
Admissions Committee
Department of Computer Science
734 Computer Studies Building
University of Rochester
Rochester, New York 14627-0226

Phone: 585-275-7737
E-mail: admissions@cs.rochester.edu
Web site: http://www.cs.rochester.edu

University of Rochester

THE FACULTY AND THEIR RESEARCH

James F. Allen, John H. Dessauer Professor of Computer Science; Ph.D., Toronto, 1979. Artificial intelligence; natural language processing; dialog systems; planning; representation of plans, goals, time, and action.

Jeffrey Bigham, Assistant Professor of Computer Science; Ph.D. Washington (Seattle), 2009. Human-computer interaction with a focus on Web applications and making computers accessible by the blind.

Christopher M. Brown, Professor of Computer Science; Ph.D., Chicago, 1972. Artificial intelligence, computer vision, graphics, robotics.

Chen Ding, Associate Professor of Computer Science; Ph.D., Rice, 2000. Advanced compilation, static, and runtime program analysis and transformation, memory hierarchy management, programming issues in parallel and distributed computing.

Sandhya Dwarkadas, Professor of Computer Science; Ph.D., Rice, 1992. Parallel and distributed computing, compiler and run-time support for parallelism, computer architecture, networks, simulation methodology, performance evaluation, parallel applications research.

George Ferguson, Scientist, Computer Science; Ph.D., Rochester, 1995. Intelligent systems, planning, knowledge representation, agents and architectures, collaboration.

Daniel Gildea, Assistant Professor of Computer Science; Ph.D., Berkeley, 2001. Natural language processing and machine learning, statistical machine translation and language understanding.

Wendi Heinzelman, Associate Professor of Electrical and Computer Engineering; Ph.D., MIT, 2000. Wireless communications, mobile systems, signal and image processing, multimedia systems.

Lane A. Hemaspaandra, Professor of Computer Science; Ph.D., Cornell, 1987. Computational complexity theory, algorithms from complexity, probabilistic and unambiguous computation, approximate computation, fault-tolerant computation, semi-feasible algorithms, cryptography, complexity-theoretic aspects of voting systems.

Engin Ipek, Assistant Professor of Computer Science; Ph.D. Cornell, 2008. Computer architecture, with an emphasis on multicore architectures, hardware-software interaction, and the application of machine learning to computer systems.

Robert A. Jacobs, Professor of Brain and Cognitive Sciences and of Computer Science; Ph.D., Massachusetts, 1990. Machine learning, reasoning under uncertainty, artificial intelligence, computational cognitive science.

Henry A. Kautz, Professor of Computer Science; Ph.D., Rochester, 1987. User modeling, sensor-based ubiquitous computing, and automated reasoning.

Randal C. Nelson, Associate Professor of Computer Science; Ph.D., Maryland, 1988. Artificial intelligence, computer vision with an emphasis on the use of visual information for control of systems in real-world environments, robotics.

Thaddeus F. Pawlicki, Instructor/Undergraduate Advisor; Ph.D., Buffalo, 1989. Computer vision, medical image processing.

Lenhart K. Schubert, Professor of Computer Science; Ph.D., Toronto, 1970. Knowledge representation and organization, general and specialized inference methods, natural language understanding, planning and acting.

Michael L. Scott, Professor of Computer Science; Ph.D., Wisconsin, 1985. Parallel and distributed systems software, operating systems, programming languages, program development tools.

Joel I. Seiferas, Associate Professor of Computer Science; Ph.D., MIT, 1974. Computational, descriptive, and combinatorial complexity; lower bound techniques.

Kai Shen, Assistant Professor of Computer Science; Ph.D., California, Santa Barbara, 2002. Parallel and distributed software systems, operating systems, computer networks.

Daniel Stefankovic, Assistant Professor of Computer Science; Ph.D., Chicago, 2005. Theoretical computer science: algorithmic problems on curves on surfaces, Markov chain sampling, algorithmic game theory, graph drawing, and applications of discrete and continuous Fourier transforms.

VILLANOVA UNIVERSITY

Department of Computing Sciences

Programs of Study
The Department of Computing Sciences supports education and research across the broad spectrum of computing. The Department offers the Master of Science (M.S.) in computer science program, the Master of Science in software engineering program, the Bachelor of Science/Master of Science integrated program, and graduate certificate programs.

The Master of Science in computer science program provides expertise in applied and basic computing through its course offerings in computer systems, software engineering, languages, and algorithms. It is designed to prepare students for a career as a computing professional, although some students go on to pursue a Ph.D. degree at another university. Students entering the program are required to be proficient in computer programming and have a background in computer architecture and in mathematics. While an undergraduate degree in computing is ideal, students who have completed related courses or have work experience in these areas may be considered.

The M.S. degree in computer science requires the student to complete ten 3-credit courses, including core courses in algorithms and data structures, computer systems, design and analysis of algorithms, linguistics of programming languages, and theory of computability; electives; and an independent study project.

The M.S. degree in software engineering requires the student to complete ten 3-credit courses, including courses in algorithms and data structures, computer systems, software engineering, requirements engineering, software design and evolution, and database concepts; electives; and an independent study project.

In both the M.S. in computer science and the M.S. in software engineering programs, the thesis-option elective helps students transition to a Ph.D. program. The independent study course enables the student to explore a computing topic under the guidance of a faculty adviser. Students may choose to participate in a graduate computing practicum that adds 1 credit to the requirements; this track requires work experience in a related field. In both programs, the distribution of requirements between core courses and electives depends on the student's background. Both programs include entry points for students with a variety of backgrounds.

The Department also offers graduate certificates in knowledge-based systems, networks, systems programming, and Web technologies. Each certificate requires five courses, including an independent study in the topic area. Students enrolled in the Department's B.S./M.S. integrated program are able to graduate with a bachelor's and master's degree in five years.

Research Facilities
The Falvey Memorial Library houses more than 107,000 books and 1 million microform items and subscribes to approximately 3,000 print journals and fifty newspapers. In addition, an extensive collection of nonprint media includes more than 6,000 videotapes, audiotapes, and CDs. The Special Collections area houses approximately 15,000 items; some of these items are rare or unique, and most require special handling and preservation.

The Office for University Information Technologies (UNIT) maintains all central and distributed computers throughout the University and manages two public student labs with more than 170 workstations. In addition, the Department maintains research laboratories in areas of artificial intelligence, software engineering, multimedia systems, and information retrieval/digital libraries. The University is an institutional member of the ACM Digital Library, providing full-text access to all publications of the ACM.

Financial Aid
Graduate assistantships provide tuition remission and stipends of $13,100 per academic year in exchange for working 20 hours per week in the Department as teaching or research assistants or as systems support or office support staff members. Tuition scholarships award full remission of tuition and academic fees in exchange for 7 hours of work per week. The Villanova Computing Scholars Program awards $3125 per year to undergraduate students who are accepted into the program. These students participate in enrichment seminars and work on research projects with faculty members.

Cost of Study
Graduate tuition is $700 per academic credit, plus an additional $60 in general fees. Students also pay $50 per year in parking fees.

Living and Housing Costs
No on-campus housing is available to graduate students, but there are many apartment complexes in the area where graduate students find housing. Off-campus housing generally costs $600 to $1400 per month, depending on the apartment's size and location.

Student Group
There are approximately 60 full-time and 160 part-time students in the graduate program. The majority of students work in high-tech fields, but they come from a wide range of backgrounds. Most hold undergraduate degrees in computer science or computer engineering, but some enter the program with relevant work experience.

Student Outcomes
Some graduates of the program enter a Ph.D. in computer science program, while others go straight into the business world, working in a number of capacities, including software engineering, Web programming, network security, user interface design, data warehousing, corporate information management, database management, expert and knowledge systems, and search engine development.

Location
Villanova University provides a tranquil setting for study and reflection. Situated on the historic Main Line, a western suburb of Philadelphia, Villanova is located on Lancaster Avenue (Route 30), 2 minutes from the Blue Route (Route 476) and 5 minutes from the Pennsylvania Turnpike, Schuylkill Expressway, and Route 202. Philadelphia's revitalized Center City is 25 minutes away by train, and historic Valley Forge and the Brandywine Valley are easily accessible by car. Villanova is within easy driving distance of several other premier institutions of higher learning, including Bryn Mawr, Haverford, and Swarthmore Colleges; Drexel and Temple Universities; and the University of Pennsylvania. With ample parking and mass transit stops right on University grounds, the campus allows for easy travel by car, bus, or train.

The University
Villanova University is an independent coeducational institution of higher learning founded by the Augustinian Order of the Roman Catholic Church. Founded in 1842, it is the oldest and largest Catholic university in Pennsylvania and one of only eighteen Catholic universities to have a Phi Beta Kappa chapter. The University consists of five colleges that enroll more than 10,000 students and is consistently ranked by *U.S. News and World Report* as having one of the top master's degree programs in the northern region.

Applying
Prospective students are required to submit an application for admission, official transcripts of all previous college work, official GRE scores (if planning full-time study), three letters of recommendation, and a $50 nonrefundable application fee. The deadline to apply is August 1 for fall admission, December 1 for spring admission, and May 1 for summer admission. Those applying for assistantships should apply before April 15. Applications must be sent to the Graduate Studies Office, College of Liberal Arts and Sciences, Villanova University, 800 Lancaster Avenue, Villanova, Pennsylvania 19085-1699. An online application is available at the University's Web site at http://www.gradartsci.villanova.edu.

Correspondence and Information
Department of Computing Sciences
161 Mendel Science Center
Villanova University
800 Lancaster Avenue
Villanova, Pennsylvania 19085-1699

Phone: 610-519-7310
Fax: 610-519-7889
E-mail: gradcomputing@villanova.edu
Web site: http://csc.villanova.edu/

Villanova University

THE FACULTY AND THEIR RESEARCH

The full-time faculty members in the Department of Computing Sciences are deeply committed to the mission of excellence in pedagogy and research. Their diversity and experience provide a rich environment for growth and learning. Most of the adjunct faculty members are computing professionals from the high-tech corridor surrounding Villanova. Their contributions in teaching and their collaboration with full-time faculty members on various projects bring additional insight from the commercial world into the classrooms.

Full-Time Faculty
Robert Beck, Professor and Chair; Ph.D. (mathematics), Pennsylvania. Evaluation techniques and metrics for user interfaces; models for computational biology; symbolic computation, especially for linear algebra and Lie algebras; algorithms for operations research.

Lillian Cassel, Professor; Ph.D. (computer science), Delaware. Digital libraries and information retrieval on the Web.

Mirela Damian, Assistant Professor; Ph.D. (computer science), Iowa. Computational geometry, graph theory, mobile computing.

William Fleischman, Professor; Ph.D. (mathematics), Lehigh. Parallel computing, biological systems monitoring.

Vijay Gehlot, Assistant Professor and Graduate Program Director; Ph.D. (computer and information science), Pennsylvania. Systems modeling and analysis, petri nets, formal methods and specification/verification, programming languages, compilation techniques.

Don Goelman, Associate Professor; Ph.D. (mathematics), Pennsylvania. Database systems, data modeling, algorithms.

Catherine Helwig, Instructor; M.S. (computer science), Villanova. Object-oriented software, algorithms, data structures.

Giorgi Japaridze, Associate Professor; Ph.D. (computer science), Pennsylvania. Modal-logical means of studying provability, logic of resources and tasks.

Dan Joyce, Associate Professor and Graduate Independent Study Coordinator; Ph.D. (computer science), Temple. Software engineering, software requirements identification, software engineering education within a computer science department.

Frank Klassner, Associate Professor; Ph.D. (computer science), Massachusetts. Artificial intelligence, Web-based software systems, signal processing.

Anany Levitin, Professor; Ph.D. (mathematics), Hebrew (Jerusalem). Algorithm design techniques, data and information.

Mary-Angela Papalaskari, Assistant Professor; Ph.D. (artificial intelligence), Edinburgh (Scotland). Artificial intelligence, computational theory.

Tom Way, Assistant Professor; Ph.D. (computer science), Delaware. Distributed and parallel computing, human-computer interaction, nanotechnology and nanocomputers, convergence of technology and entertainment industries.

Barbara Zimmerman, Instructor; M.S. (computer science), Maryland. Object-oriented software, algorithms, database systems.

Adjunct Faculty
Robert Arakelian, Adjunct Instructor. Information security.

Tim Ay, Adjunct Instructor; M.S. (computer science), Villanova. Artificial intelligence, software project management.

Nancy Bercich, Adjunct Instructor. Object-oriented software, database management.

Chris Connolly, Adjunct Instructor; M.S. (computer engineering), Villanova. Java/J2EE, enterprise computing, LDAP.

James Dullea, Adjunct Instructor; Ph.D. (information science and technology), Drexel. Information management, data modeling, information metrics, data warehousing.

Brian Ellis, Adjunct Instructor.

Nancy Hagelgans, Adjunct Instructor.

Arthur Mansky, Adjunct Instructor; M.S. (computer science), Delaware. Software project management, systems programming.

Paula Matuszek, Adjunct Instructor; Ph.D. (school psychology), Texas at Austin. Software engineering, text mining, knowledge-based systems.

David McGrath, Adjunct Instructor. Object-oriented software.

Marc Meketon, Adjunct Instructor; Ph.D. (operations research), Cornell. Object-oriented software, software engineering, algorithms.

Sue Metzger, Adjunct Instructor; M.S.E., M.O.T., Pennsylvania. Information systems, enterprise computing.

Najib Nadi, Adjunct Instructor and Systems Administrator; M.S. (computer science), Villanova. Systems programming, systems administration.

Robin Qiu, Adjunct Instructor; Ph.D. (industrial engineering and computer science), Penn State. Information system modeling, control of manufacturing systems, XML-oriented technologies and applications, distributed computing systems, component-based software design and development, enterprise integration, networking and connectivity.

Paul Schragger, Adjunct Instructor; Ph.D. (electrical engineering), Delaware. Networks, distributed computing, software engineering.

Jill Tilney, Adjunct Instructor.

Sydney Weinstein, Adjunct Instructor; M.S. (electrical and computer engineering), Massachusetts Amherst. Networks, computer security, data warehousing, e-commerce.

Bruce Weir, Adjunct Instructor; M.S. (computer science), Villanova. Software project management, software process improvement, software engineering.

Section 9
Electrical and Computer Engineering

This section contains a directory of institutions offering graduate work in electrical and computer engineering, followed by in-depth entries submitted by institutions that chose to prepare detailed program descriptions. Additional information about programs listed in the directory but not augmented by an in-depth entry may be obtained by writing directly to the dean of a graduate school or chair of a department at the address given in the directory.

For programs offering related work, see also in this book *Computer Science and Information Technology, Energy and Power Engineering, Engineering and Applied Sciences, Industrial Engineering,* and *Mechanical Engineering and Mechanics.* In another guide in this series: **Graduate Programs in the Physical Sciences, Mathematics, Agricultural Sciences, the Environment & Natural Resources**
See *Mathematical Sciences* and *Physics*

CONTENTS

Close-Ups and Display

Computer Engineering

Air Force Institute of Technology, Graduate School of Engineering and Management, Department of Electrical and Computer Engineering, Dayton, OH 45433-7765. Offers computer engineering (MS, PhD); computer systems/science (MS); electrical engineering (MS, PhD); electro-optics (MS, PhD). *Accreditation:* ABET (one or more programs are accredited). Part-time programs available. *Degree requirements:* For master's, thesis; for doctorate, thesis/dissertation. *Entrance requirements:* For master's and doctorate, GRE General Test, minimum GPA of 3.0, U.S. citizenship. *Faculty research:* Remote sensing, information survivability, microelectronics, computer networks, artificial intelligence.

American University of Beirut, Graduate Programs, Faculty of Engineering and Architecture, Beirut, Lebanon. Offers civil engineering (ME, PhD); electrical and computer engineering (ME, PhD); engineering management (MEM); environmental and water resources (ME); environmental and water resources engineering (PhD); environmental technology (MSES); mechanical engineering (ME, PhD); urban design (MUD); urban planning and policy (MUP). Part-time programs available. *Degree requirements:* For master's, one foreign language, comprehensive exam, thesis (for some programs); for doctorate, one foreign language, comprehensive exam, thesis/dissertation, publications. *Entrance requirements:* For master's, letters of recommendation; for doctorate, letters of recommendation, master's degree, transcripts, curriculum vitae, interview. Additional exam requirements/recommendations for international students: Required—TOEFL (minimum score 600 paper-based; 250 computer-based; 100 iBT), IELTS (minimum score 7.5). Electronic applications accepted.

American University of Sharjah, Graduate Programs, Sharjah, United Arab Emirates. Offers business (EMBA, GEMPA, MBA); chemical engineering (MS Ch E); civil engineering (MSCE); computer engineering (MS); electrical engineering (MSEE); mechanical engineering (MSME); mechatronics engineering (MS); public administration (MPA); teaching English to speakers of other languages (MA); translation and interpreting (MA); urban planning (MUP). Part-time and evening/weekend programs available. *Faculty:* 59 full-time (4 women), 5 part-time/adjunct (1 woman). *Students:* 101 full-time (44 women), 218 part-time (95 women). Average age 27. 184 applicants, 83% accepted, 92 enrolled. In 2009, 97 master's awarded. *Entrance requirements:* For master's, GMAT (MBA). Additional exam requirements/recommendations for international students: Required—TOEFL (minimum score 550 paper-based; 213 computer-based; 80 iBT), TWE (minimum score 5). *Application deadline:* For fall admission, 7/30 priority date for domestic students, 7/15 priority date for international students; for spring admission, 12/31 priority date for domestic students, 12/16 for international students. Applications are processed on a rolling basis. Application fee: $300. Electronic applications accepted. Tuition charges are reported in United Arab Emirates dirhams. *Expenses:* Tuition: Part-time 3250 United Arab Emirates dirhams per credit hour. *Financial support:* In 2009–10, 63 students received support, including 28 research assistantships with tuition reimbursements available, 35 teaching assistantships with tuition reimbursements available. *Faculty research:* Chemical engineering, civil engineering, computer engineering, electrical engineering, linguistics, translation. *Unit head:* Ghada S. Sami, Admissions Manager, 971-65151006 Ext. 1006, Fax: 971-65151020, E-mail: graduateadmission@aus.edu. *Application contact:* Ghada S. Sami, Admissions Manager, 971-65151006 Ext. 1006, Fax: 971-65151020, E-mail: graduateadmission@aus.edu.

Arizona State University, Graduate College, College of Technology and Innovation, Division of Computing Studies, Tempe, AZ 85287. Offers computing studies (MCST); technology (MS). Part-time programs available. *Degree requirements:* For master's, thesis or applied project. *Entrance requirements:* For master's, 30 semester hours or equivalent in technology, including course work applicable to computer systems; minimum of 16 semester hours in science and math. Additional exam requirements/recommendations for international students: Required—TOEFL (minimum score 550 paper-based; 213 computer-based; 83 iBT); Recommended—TWE. *Faculty research:* Software process and automated workflow, software architecture, dotal technologies, relational database systems, embedded systems.

Arizona State University, Graduate College, College of Technology and Innovation, Electronic Systems Department, Tempe, AZ 85287. Offers MS. Part-time and evening/weekend programs available. *Degree requirements:* For master's, comprehensive exam, thesis optional. *Entrance requirements:* For master's, GRE, 30 semester hours or equivalent in area of study, minimum of 16 hours of mathematics and science. Additional exam requirements/recommendations for international students: Required—TOEFL (minimum score 550 paper-based; 213 computer-based; 83 iBT); Recommended—TWE. Electronic applications accepted. *Faculty research:* IC packaging, semiconductor processing, surface characterization of thin films, solar cells failure analysis, fatigue life prediction for soldier joints.

Auburn University, Graduate School, Ginn College of Engineering, Department of Electrical and Computer Engineering, Auburn University, AL 36849. Offers MEE, MS, PhD. Part-time programs available. *Faculty:* 27 full-time (2 women), 3 part-time/adjunct (1 woman). *Students:* 69 full-time (10 women), 48 part-time (10 women); includes 7 minority (2 African Americans, 1 American Indian/Alaska Native, 3 Asian Americans or Pacific Islanders, 1 Hispanic American), 72 international. Average age 27. 355 applicants, 57% accepted, 16 enrolled. In 2009, 27 master's, 7 doctorates awarded. *Degree requirements:* For master's, comprehensive exam, thesis (for some programs); for doctorate, thesis/dissertation. *Entrance requirements:* For master's and doctorate, GRE General Test, GRE Subject Test. *Application deadline:* For fall admission, 7/7 for domestic students; for spring admission, 11/24 for domestic students. Applications are processed on a rolling basis. Application fee: $50 ($60 for international students). Electronic applications accepted. *Expenses:* Tuition, state resident: full-time $6240. Tuition, nonresident: full-time $18,720. International tuition: $18,938 full-time. Required fees: $492. Tuition and fees vary according to course load, program and reciprocity agreements. *Financial support:* Fellowships, research assistantships, teaching assistantships, Federal Work-Study available. Support available to part-time students. Financial award application deadline: 3/15; financial award applicants required to submit FAFSA. *Faculty research:* Power systems, energy conversion, electronics, electromagnetics, digital systems. *Unit head:* Dr. J. David Irwin, Head, 334-844-1800. *Application contact:* Dr. George Flowers, Dean of the Graduate School, 334-844-2125.

Baylor University, Graduate School, School of Engineering and Computer Science, Department of Engineering, Waco, TX 76798. Offers biomedical engineering (MSBE); electrical and computer engineering (MSECE); engineering (ME); mechanical engineering (MSME). *Faculty:* 14 full-time (1 woman). *Students:* 19 full-time (1 woman), 5 part-time (1 woman); includes 4 minority (1 African American, 1 Asian American or Pacific Islander, 2 Hispanic Americans), 8 international. In 2009, 8 master's awarded. *Unit head:* Dr. Mike Thompson, Graduate Director, 254-710-4188. *Application contact:* Linda Keer, Administrative Assistant, 254-710-4188, Fax: 254-710-3870, E-mail: linda_kerr@baylor.edu.

Boise State University, Graduate College, College of Engineering, Department of Electrical and Computer Engineering, Boise, ID 83725-0399. Offers computer engineering (M Engr, MS); electrical and computer engineering (PhD); electrical engineering (M Engr, MS). Part-time and evening/weekend programs available. *Degree requirements:* For master's, thesis. *Entrance requirements:* For master's, GRE General Test, minimum GPA of 3.0. Additional exam requirements/recommendations for international students: Required—TOEFL. Electronic applications accepted. *Expenses:* Tuition, state resident: full-time $3106; part-time $209 per credit. Tuition, nonresident: part-time $284 per credit.

Boston University, College of Engineering, Department of Electrical and Computer Engineering, Boston, MA 02215. Offers computer engineering (MS, PhD); electrical engineering (MS, PhD); photonics (MS). Part-time programs available. *Faculty:* 41 full-time (3 women). *Students:* 182 full-time (40 women), 16 part-time (2 women); includes 21 minority (4 African Americans, 15 Asian Americans or Pacific Islanders, 2 Hispanic Americans), 118 international. Average age 24. 592 applicants, 30% accepted, 66 enrolled. In 2009, 62 master's, 19 doctorates awarded. Terminal master's awarded for partial completion of doctoral program. *Degree requirements:* For master's, thesis optional; for doctorate, comprehensive exam, thesis/dissertation. *Entrance requirements:* For master's and doctorate, GRE General Test. Additional exam requirements/recommendations for international students: Required—TOEFL (minimum score 550 paper-based; 213 computer-based; 84 iBT), IELTS (minimum score 6). *Application deadline:* For fall admission, 4/1 for domestic and international students; for spring admission, 10/1 for domestic and international students. Applications are processed on a rolling basis. Application fee: $70. Electronic applications accepted. *Expenses:* Tuition: Full-time $37,910; part-time $1184 per credit hour. Required fees: $386; $40 per semester. Part-time tuition and fees vary according to class time, course level, degree level and program. *Financial support:* In 2009–10, 134 students received support, including 11 fellowships with full tuition reimbursements available (averaging $27,600 per year), 88 research assistantships with full tuition reimbursements available (averaging $18,400 per year), 18 teaching assistantships with full tuition reimbursements available (averaging $18,400 per year); career-related internships or fieldwork, Federal Work-Study, institutionally sponsored loans, scholarships/grants, traineeships, and health care benefits also available. Financial award application deadline: 1/15; financial award applicants required to submit FAFSA. *Faculty research:* Communications and computer networks; signal, image, video, and multimedia processing; solid-state materials, devices, and photonics; systems, control, and reliable computing; VLSI, computer engineering and high-performance computing. *Unit head:* Dr. Francesco Cerrina, Chairman, 617-353-7175, Fax: 617-353-6440, E-mail: fcerrina@bu.edu. *Application contact:* Cheryl Kelley, Director of Graduate Programs, 617-353-9760, Fax: 617-353-0259, E-mail: enggrad@bu.edu.

Brigham Young University, Graduate Studies, Ira A. Fulton College of Engineering and Technology, Department of Electrical and Computer Engineering, Provo, UT 84602. Offers MS, PhD. *Faculty:* 24 full-time (0 women). *Students:* 91 full-time (6 women), 24 international. Average age 28. 43 applicants, 72% accepted, 22 enrolled. In 2009, 13 master's, 10 doctorates awarded. *Degree requirements:* For master's, thesis optional; for doctorate, comprehensive exam, thesis/dissertation. *Entrance requirements:* For master's and doctorate, GRE General Test, minimum GPA of 3.2 in last 60 hours of course work. Additional exam requirements/recommendations for international students: Required—TOEFL (minimum score 580 paper-based; 237 computer-based; 85 iBT). *Application deadline:* For fall admission, 1/15 for domestic and international students; for winter admission, 9/15 for domestic and international students. Application fee: $50. Electronic applications accepted. *Expenses:* Tuition: Full-time $5580; part-time $301 per credit hour. Tuition and fees vary according to student's religious affiliation. *Financial support:* In 2009–10, 65 students received support, including 2 fellowships with full tuition reimbursements available (averaging $19,500 per year), 53 research assistantships with full tuition reimbursements available (averaging $19,500 per year), 10 teaching assistantships with full tuition reimbursements available (averaging $19,500 per year); scholarships/grants also available. Financial award application deadline: 5/15; financial award applicants required to submit FAFSA. *Faculty research:* Microwave remote sensing, reconfigurable computing, microelectronics circuit design and fabrication, array and image processing, wireless communications, computer architecture. Total annual research expenditures: $3.1 million. *Unit head:* Dr. Michael A. Jensen, Chair, 801-422-4012, Fax: 801-422-0201, E-mail: jensen@ee.byu.edu. *Application contact:* Janalyn L. Mergist, Graduate Secretary, 801-422-4013, Fax: 801-422-0201, E-mail: janalyn@ee.byu.edu.

Brown University, Graduate School, Division of Engineering, Program in Electrical Sciences and Computer Engineering, Providence, RI 02912. Offers Sc M, PhD. *Degree requirements:* For doctorate, thesis/dissertation, preliminary exam.

California State University, Chico, Graduate School, College of Engineering, Computer Science, and Technology, Department of Electrical and Computer Engineering, Option in Computer Engineering, Chico, CA 95929-0722. Offers MS. *Students:* 3 full-time (0 women), 1 part-time (0 women); includes 1 Asian American or Pacific Islander. Average age 26. 6 applicants, 67% accepted, 1 enrolled. In 2009, 6 master's awarded. *Degree requirements:* For master's, thesis or alternative. *Entrance requirements:* For master's, GRE General Test, 2 letters of recommendation. Additional exam requirements/recommendations for international students: Required—TOEFL (minimum score 550 paper-based; 213 computer-based; 80 iBT), IELTS (minimum score 6.8). *Application deadline:* For fall admission, 3/1 priority date for domestic students, 3/1 for international students; for spring admission, 9/15 priority date for domestic students, 9/15 for international students. Applications are processed on a rolling basis. Application fee: $55. Electronic applications accepted. *Unit head:* Dr. Adel Ghandakly, Graduate Coordinator, 530-898-5343. *Application contact:* Dr. Adel Ghandakly, Graduate Coordinator, 530-898-5343.

California State University, Long Beach, Graduate Studies, College of Engineering, Department of Computer Engineering and Computer Science, Long Beach, CA 90840. Offers computer engineering (MSCS); computer science (MSCS). Part-time programs available. *Faculty:* 17 full-time (9 women), 2 part-time/adjunct (0 women). *Students:* 104 full-time (20 women), 97 part-time (20 women); includes 48 minority (3 African Americans, 36 Asian Americans or Pacific Islanders, 9 Hispanic Americans), 99 international. Average age 28. 294 applicants, 69% accepted, 50 enrolled. *Degree requirements:* For master's, thesis or alternative. *Entrance requirements:* Additional exam requirements/recommendations for international students: Required—TOEFL. *Application deadline:* For fall admission, 3/1 for domestic students. Application fee: $55. Electronic applications accepted. *Expenses:* Required fees: $1802 per semester. Part-time tuition and fees vary according to course load. *Financial support:* Teaching assistantships, Federal Work-Study, institutionally sponsored loans, scholarships/grants, and unspecified assistantships available. Financial award application deadline: 3/2. *Faculty research:* Artificial intelligence, software engineering, computer simulation and modeling, user-interface design, networking. *Unit head:* Dr. Kenneth James, Chair, 562-985-5105, Fax: 562-985-7823, E-mail: james@csulb.edu. *Application contact:* Dr. Burkhard Englert, Graduate Advisor, 562-985-7987, Fax: 562-985-7823, E-mail: benglert@.csulb.edu.

Carnegie Mellon University, Carnegie Institute of Technology, Department of Electrical and Computer Engineering, Pittsburgh, PA 15213-3891. Offers biomedical engineering (MS); electrical and computer engineering (MS, PhD). Part-time programs available. *Degree requirements:* For master's, thesis; for doctorate, thesis/dissertation, qualifying exam, teaching experience. *Entrance requirements:* For master's and doctorate, GRE General Test. Additional exam requirements/recommendations for international students: Required—TOEFL. *Faculty research:* Computer-aided design, solid-state devices, VLSI, processing, robotics and controls, signal processing, data systems storage.

See Close-Up on page 363.

Carnegie Mellon University, Carnegie Institute of Technology, Information Networking Institute, Pittsburgh, PA 15213. Offers information networking (MS); information security technology and management (MS); information technology—information security (MS); information technology—mobility (MS); information technology—software management (MS). *Degree requirements:* For master's, thesis optional. *Entrance requirements:* For master's, GRE General Test, bachelor's degree in computer science, computer engineering, or electrical engineering, or related technology degree; programming skills (C/C++ fluency for some programs). Additional exam requirements/recommendations for international students: Required—TOEFL. *Faculty research:* Computer forensics and incident response; dependable systems, embedded systems, mobile systems, and sensor networks; computer and information networks, network and information security, human and socio-economic factors in secure system design; wireless sensor networks, survivable embedded systems, signal processing/compression; strategic management, international strategic management, group dynamics and decision-making structures, simulated competitive environments.

Case Western Reserve University, School of Graduate Studies, The Case School of Engineering, Department of Electrical Engineering and Computer Science, Cleveland, OH

44106. Offers computer engineering (MS, PhD); computing and information sciences (MS, PhD); electrical engineering (MS, PhD); systems and control engineering (MS, PhD). Part-time and evening/weekend programs available. Postbaccalaureate distance learning degree programs offered (minimal on-campus study). *Faculty:* 32 full-time (2 women). *Students:* 175 full-time (26 women), 28 part-time (6 women); includes 9 minority (3 African Americans, 6 Asian Americans or Pacific Islanders), 107 international. In 2009, 29 master's, 15 doctorates awarded. Terminal master's awarded for partial completion of doctoral program. *Degree requirements:* For master's, thesis; for doctorate, thesis/dissertation, qualifying exam, teaching experience. *Entrance requirements:* For master's and doctorate, GRE General Test. Additional exam requirements/recommendations for international students: Required—TOEFL. *Application deadline:* For fall admission, 2/1 for domestic students; for spring admission, 11/1 for domestic students. Applications are processed on a rolling basis. Application fee: $50. *Financial support:* Fellowships with full and partial tuition reimbursements, research assistantships with full and partial tuition reimbursements, teaching assistantships, career-related internships or fieldwork, Federal Work-Study, and institutionally sponsored loans available. Support available to part-time students. Financial award application deadline: 3/1; financial award applicants required to submit FAFSA. *Faculty research:* Applied artificial intelligence, automation, computer-aided design and testing of digital systems. Total annual research expenditures: $5.5 million. *Unit head:* Dwight Davy, Department Chair, 216-368-2802, E-mail: dtd@case.edu. *Application contact:* David Easler, Student Affairs Coordinator, 216-368-4080, Fax: 216-368-2801, E-mail: david.easler@case.edu.

Clarkson University, Graduate School, Wallace H. Coulter School of Engineering, Department of Electrical and Computer Engineering, Potsdam, NY 13699. Offers electrical and computer engineering (PhD); electrical engineering (ME, MS). Part-time programs available. *Faculty:* 20 full-time (5 women), 2 part-time/adjunct (both women). *Students:* 44 full-time (11 women), 1 (woman) part-time; includes 1 minority (American Indian/Alaska Native), 22 international. Average age 28. 95 applicants, 51% accepted, 10 enrolled. In 2009, 9 master's, 5 doctorates awarded. Terminal master's awarded for partial completion of doctoral program. *Degree requirements:* For master's, thesis; for doctorate, comprehensive exam, thesis/dissertation, departmental qualifying exam. *Entrance requirements:* For master's, GRE, resume, 3 letters of recommendation; for doctorate, GRE, transcripts of all college coursework, resume, personal statement, three letters of recommendation. Additional exam requirements/recommendations for international students: Required—TOEFL (minimum score 550 paper-based; 213 computer-based; 80 iBT), IELTS (minimum score 6.5). *Application deadline:* For fall admission, 1/30 priority date for domestic and international students; for spring admission, 9/1 priority date for domestic and international students. Applications are processed on a rolling basis. Application fee: $25 ($35 for international students). Electronic applications accepted. *Expenses:* Tuition: Part-time $1074 per credit hour. *Financial support:* In 2009–10, 30 students received support, including 4 fellowships (averaging $30,000 per year), 8 research assistantships (averaging $20,190 per year), 7 teaching assistantships (averaging $20,190 per year); scholarships/grants, tuition waivers (partial), and unspecified assistantships also available. *Faculty research:* Robotics, electrical machines, power systems, thermo-elastic wave propagation, fingerprint vitality. Total annual research expenditures: $1.3 million. *Unit head:* Dr. Thomas H. Ortmeyer, Department Chair, 315-268-6511, Fax: 315-268-7994. *Application contact:* Kelly Sharlow, Assistant to the Dean, 315-268-7929, Fax: 315-268-4494, E-mail: ksharlow@clarkson.edu.

Clemson University, Graduate School, College of Engineering and Science, Department of Electrical and Computer Engineering, Program in Computer Engineering, Clemson, SC 29634. Offers MS, PhD. *Students:* 31 full-time (6 women), 5 part-time (1 woman); includes 3 minority (2 African Americans, 1 Asian American or Pacific Islander), 18 international. Average age 36. 95 applicants, 40% accepted, 11 enrolled. In 2009, 13 master's, 2 doctorates awarded. *Degree requirements:* For master's, thesis or alternative; for doctorate, thesis/dissertation, departmental qualifying exam. *Entrance requirements:* For master's and doctorate, GRE General Test. Additional exam requirements/recommendations for international students: Required—TOEFL. *Application deadline:* Applications are processed on a rolling basis. Application fee: $70 ($80 for international students). Electronic applications accepted. *Expenses:* Tuition, state resident: full-time $8684; part-time $528 per credit hour. Tuition, nonresident: full-time $15,330; part-time $1078 per credit hour. Required fees: $736; $37 per semester. Part-time tuition and fees vary according to course load and program. *Financial support:* In 2009–10, 23 students received support, including 5 fellowships with full and partial tuition reimbursements available (averaging $15,304 per year), 11 research assistantships with partial tuition reimbursements available (averaging $17,729 per year), 7 teaching assistantships with partial tuition reimbursements available (averaging $12,796 per year); career-related internships or fieldwork, institutionally sponsored loans, scholarships/grants, health care benefits, and unspecified assistantships also available. Support available to part-time students. Financial award applicants required to submit FAFSA. *Faculty research:* Interface applications, software development, multisystem communications, artificial intelligence, robotics. *Unit head:* Dr. Darren Dawson, Chair, 864-656-5249, Fax: 864-656-5917, E-mail: ddarren@clemson.edu. *Application contact:* Dr. Daniel Noneaker, 864-656-0100, Fax: 864-656-5917, E-mail: ece-grad-program@ces.clemson.edu.

Colorado Technical University Colorado Springs, Graduate Studies, Program in Computer Engineering, Colorado Springs, CO 80907-3896. Offers MSCE. Part-time and evening/weekend programs available. Postbaccalaureate distance learning degree programs offered. *Degree requirements:* For master's, thesis or alternative.

Colorado Technical University Denver, Program in Computer Engineering, Greenwood Village, CO 80111. Offers MS.

Columbia University, Fu Foundation School of Engineering and Applied Science, Department of Electrical Engineering, New York, NY 10027. Offers computer engineering (MS); electrical engineering (MS, Eng Sc D, PhD, Engr); solid state science and engineering (MS, Eng Sc D, PhD). PhD offered through the Graduate School of Arts and Sciences. Part-time programs available. Postbaccalaureate distance learning degree programs offered (no on-campus study). *Faculty:* 17 full-time (1 woman), 4 part-time/adjunct (0 women). *Students:* 223 full-time (39 women), 108 part-time (11 women); includes 34 minority (2 African Americans, 29 Asian Americans or Pacific Islanders, 3 Hispanic Americans), 226 international. Average age 26. 787 applicants, 32% accepted, 129 enrolled. In 2009, 87 master's, 14 doctorates awarded. *Degree requirements:* For doctorate, thesis/dissertation, qualifying exam. *Entrance requirements:* For master's, doctorate, and Engr, GRE General Test. Additional exam requirements/recommendations for international students: Required—TOEFL. *Application deadline:* For fall admission, 12/1 priority date for domestic and international students; for spring admission, 10/1 priority date for domestic and international students. Application fee: $70. Electronic applications accepted. *Financial support:* In 2009–10, 88 students received support, including 8 fellowships with full tuition reimbursements available (averaging $33,570 per year), 57 research assistantships with full tuition reimbursements available (averaging $30,000 per year), 23 teaching assistantships with full tuition reimbursements available (averaging $30,000 per year); health care benefits and unspecified assistantships also available. Financial award application deadline: 12/1; financial award applicants required to submit FAFSA. *Faculty research:* Signal and information processing, networking and communications, integrated circuits and systems, systems biology, micro devices, electromagnetics, plasma physics, photonics, computer engineering. *Unit head:* Dr. Shih-Fu Chang, Professor and Department Chair, 212-854-6894, Fax: 212-854-0300, E-mail: sfchang@ee.columbia.edu. *Application contact:* Elsa Sanchez, Academic Program Officer, 212-854-3104, Fax: 212-932-9421, E-mail: elsa@ee.columbia.edu.

See Close-Up on page 365.

Concordia University, School of Graduate Studies, Faculty of Engineering and Computer Science, Department of Electrical and Computer Engineering, Montréal, QC H3G 1M8, Canada. Offers M Eng, MA Sc, PhD. *Degree requirements:* For master's, thesis optional; for doctorate, comprehensive exam, thesis/dissertation. *Faculty research:* Computer communications and protocols, circuits and systems, graph theory, VLSI systems, microelectronics.

Cornell University, Graduate School, Graduate Fields of Engineering, Field of Electrical and Computer Engineering, Ithaca, NY 14853-0001. Offers computer engineering (M Eng, PhD); electrical engineering (M Eng, PhD); electrical systems (M Eng, PhD); electrophysics (M Eng, PhD). *Faculty:* 71 full-time (5 women). *Students:* 252 full-time (42 women); includes 33 minority (1 African American, 28 Asian Americans or Pacific Islanders, 4 Hispanic Americans), 139 international. Average age 26. 807 applicants, 29% accepted, 106 enrolled. In 2009, 84 master's, 18 doctorates awarded. *Degree requirements:* For doctorate, comprehensive exam, thesis/dissertation. *Entrance requirements:* For master's, GRE General Test, 2 letters of recommendation; for doctorate, GRE General Test, 3 letters of recommendation. Additional exam requirements/recommendations for international students: Required—TOEFL (minimum score 600 paper-based; 250 computer-based; 77 iBT). *Application deadline:* For fall admission, 1/15 priority date for domestic students. Application fee: $70. Electronic applications accepted. *Expenses:* Tuition: Full-time $29,500. Required fees: $70. Full-time tuition and fees vary according to degree level, program and student level. *Financial support:* In 2009–10, 150 students received support, including 26 fellowships with full tuition reimbursements available, 7 research assistantships with full tuition reimbursements available, 1 teaching assistantship with full tuition reimbursement available; institutionally sponsored loans, scholarships/grants, health care benefits, tuition waivers (full and partial), and unspecified assistantships also available. Financial award applicants required to submit FAFSA. *Faculty research:* Communications; information theory; signal processing, and power control; computer engineering; microelectromechanical systems and nanotechnology. *Unit head:* Director of Graduate Studies, 607-255-4304. *Application contact:* Graduate Field Assistant, 607-255-4304, E-mail: meng@ece.cornell.edu.

Dalhousie University, Faculty of Engineering, Department of Electrical and Computer Engineering, Halifax, NS B3J 1Z1, Canada. Offers M Eng, MA Sc, PhD. *Faculty:* 9 full-time (0 women), 4 part-time/adjunct (0 women). *Students:* 40 full-time (8 women), 6 part-time (0 women). Average age 27. 113 applicants, 50% accepted. In 2009, 12 master's, 2 doctorates awarded. *Degree requirements:* For master's, thesis; for doctorate, thesis/dissertation. *Entrance requirements:* Additional exam requirements/recommendations for international students: Required—TOEFL, IELTS, CANTEST, CAEL, or Michigan English Language Assessment Battery. *Application deadline:* For fall admission, 6/1 for domestic students, 4/1 for international students; for winter admission, 11/15 for domestic students, 8/31 for international students; for spring admission, 2/28 for domestic students, 12/31 for international students. Applications are processed on a rolling basis. Application fee: $70. Electronic applications accepted. *Financial support:* Fellowships, research assistantships, teaching assistantships, scholarships/grants and unspecified assistantships available. *Faculty research:* Communications, computer engineering, power engineering, electronics, systems engineering. *Unit head:* Dr. Ezz El-Masry, Head, 902-494-3106, Fax: 902-422-7535, E-mail: ece.admin@dal.ca. *Application contact:* Dr. Jacek Ilow, Graduate Coordinator, 902-494-3981, Fax: 902-422-7535, E-mail: j.ilow@dal.ca.

Dartmouth College, Thayer School of Engineering, Program in Computer Engineering, Hanover, NH 03755. Offers MS, PhD. *Degree requirements:* For master's, thesis; for doctorate, thesis/dissertation, candidacy oral exam. *Entrance requirements:* For master's and doctorate, GRE General Test. *Application deadline:* For fall admission, 1/1 priority date for domestic students. Application fee: $45. *Financial support:* Fellowships, research assistantships, teaching assistantships, career-related internships or fieldwork, Federal Work-Study, institutionally sponsored loans, and tuition waivers (full and partial) available. Financial award application deadline: 1/15. *Faculty research:* Analog VLSI, electromagnetic fields and waves, electronic instrumentation, microelectromechanical systems, optics, lasers and non-linear optics, power electronics and integrated power converters, networking, parallel and distributed computing, simulation, VLSI design and testing, wireless networking. Total annual research expenditures: $4.9 million. *Unit head:* Dr. Joseph J. Helbie, Dean, 603-646-2238, Fax: 603-646-2580, E-mail: joseph.j.helbie@dartmouth.edu. *Application contact:* Candace S. Potter, Graduate Admissions Administrator, 603-646-3844, Fax: 603-646-1620, E-mail: candace.potter@dartmouth.edu.

Drexel University, College of Engineering, Department of Electrical and Computer Engineering, Program in Computer Engineering, Philadelphia, PA 19104-2875. Offers MS. Part-time and evening/weekend programs available. *Degree requirements:* For master's, thesis (for some programs). Electronic applications accepted.

See Close-Up on page 367.

Duke University, Graduate School, Pratt School of Engineering, Department of Electrical and Computer Engineering, Durham, NC 27708. Offers MS, PhD. Part-time programs available. *Faculty:* 36 full-time. *Students:* 156 full-time (37 women); includes 13 minority (5 African Americans, 5 Asian Americans or Pacific Islanders, 3 Hispanic Americans), 103 international. 451 applicants, 34% accepted, 63 enrolled. In 2009, 38 master's, 15 doctorates awarded. Terminal master's awarded for partial completion of doctoral program. *Degree requirements:* For doctorate, thesis/dissertation. *Entrance requirements:* For master's and doctorate, GRE General Test. Additional exam requirements/recommendations for international students: Required—TOEFL (minimum score 550 paper-based; 213 computer-based; 83 iBT), IELTS (minimum score 7). *Application deadline:* For fall admission, 12/8 priority date for domestic and international students; for spring admission, 11/1 for domestic students. Application fee: $75. Electronic applications accepted. *Financial support:* Fellowships, research assistantships, Federal Work-Study available. Financial award application deadline: 12/31. *Unit head:* Steve Cummer, Director of Graduate Studies, 919-660-5256, Fax: 919-660-5293, E-mail: samantha@ee.duke.edu. *Application contact:* Cynthia Robertson, Associate Dean for Enrollment Services, 919-684-3913, E-mail: grad-admissions@duke.edu.

See Close-Up on page 369.

École Polytechnique de Montréal, Graduate Programs, Department of Electrical and Computer Engineering, Montréal, QC H3C 3A7, Canada. Offers automation (M Eng, M Sc A, PhD); computer science (M Eng, M Sc A, PhD); electrical engineering (DESS); electrotechnology (M Eng, M Sc A, PhD); microelectronics (M Eng, M Sc A, PhD); microwave technology (M Eng, M Sc A, PhD). Part-time and evening/weekend programs available. *Degree requirements:* For master's, one foreign language, thesis; for doctorate, one foreign language, thesis/dissertation. *Entrance requirements:* For master's, minimum GPA of 2.75; for doctorate, minimum GPA of 3.0. *Faculty research:* Microwaves, telecommunications, software engineering.

Fairfield University, School of Engineering, Fairfield, CT 06824-5195. Offers electrical and computer engineering (MS); management of technology (MS); mechanical engineering (MS); software engineering (MS). Part-time and evening/weekend programs available. *Degree requirements:* For master's, thesis, capstone course. *Entrance requirements:* For master's, interview, minimum GPA of 2.8, resume, 2 recommendations. Additional exam requirements/recommendations for international students: Required—TOEFL (minimum score 550 paper-based; 213 computer-based; 80 iBT). Electronic applications accepted. *Expenses:* Contact institution. *Faculty research:* Vehicle dynamics, image processing, multimedia in instruction, thermal packaging, character recognition, photovoltaics and nanotechnology, Web technology.

Fairleigh Dickinson University, Metropolitan Campus, University College: Arts, Sciences, and Professional Studies, School of Computer Sciences and Engineering, Program in Computer Engineering, Teaneck, NJ 07666-1914. Offers MS. *Students:* 4 full-time (1 woman), 2 part-time (0 women), 5 international. Average age 23. 17 applicants, 41% accepted, 1 enrolled. In 2009, 6 master's awarded. *Application deadline:* Applications are processed on a rolling basis. Application fee: $40. *Application contact:* Susan Brooman, University Director of Graduate Admissions, 201-692-2554, Fax: 201-692-2560, E-mail: globaleducation@fdu.edu.

Florida Atlantic University, College of Engineering and Computer Science, Department of Computer Science and Engineering, Program in Computer Engineering, Boca Raton, FL 33431-0991. Offers MS, PhD. Part-time and evening/weekend programs available. *Students:* 30 full-time (8 women), 27 part-time (6 women); includes 19 minority (2 African Americans, 12 Asian Americans or Pacific Islanders, 5 Hispanic Americans), 26 international. Average age 31. 35 applicants, 60% accepted, 11 enrolled. In 2009, 16 master's, 1 doctorate awarded.

Computer Engineering

Florida Atlantic University (continued)

Terminal master's awarded for partial completion of doctoral program. *Degree requirements:* For master's, thesis optional; for doctorate, thesis/dissertation, qualifying exam. *Entrance requirements:* For master's, GRE General Test, minimum GPA of 3.0; for doctorate, minimum GPA of 3.5, master's degree. Additional exam requirements/recommendations for international students: Required—TOEFL. *Application deadline:* For fall admission, 7/1 priority date for domestic students, 2/15 for international students; for spring admission, 11/1 for domestic students, 7/15 for international students. Applications are processed on a rolling basis. Application fee: $30. *Expenses:* Tuition, state resident: full-time $7055; part-time $293.94 per credit hour. Tuition, nonresident: full-time $22,096; part-time $920.66 per credit hour. *Financial support:* Fellowships, research assistantships with partial tuition reimbursements, teaching assistantships with full tuition reimbursements, career-related internships or fieldwork, Federal Work-Study, and unspecified assistantships available. Support available to part-time students. Financial award application deadline: 4/1; financial award applicants required to submit FAFSA. *Faculty research:* VLSI and neural networks, data communications, fault tolerance, data security, parallel systems. *Unit head:* Dr. Borko Furht, Chairman, 561-297-3855, Fax: 561-297-2800. *Application contact:* Dr. Borko Furht, Chairman, 561-297-3855, Fax: 561-297-2800.

Florida Institute of Technology, Graduate Programs, College of Engineering, Electrical and Computer Engineering Department, Melbourne, FL 32901-6975. Offers computer engineering (MS, PhD); electrical engineering (MS, PhD). Part-time and evening/weekend programs available. *Faculty:* 9 full-time (1 woman), 1 part-time/adjunct (0 women). *Students:* 80 full-time (14 women), 38 part-time (7 women); includes 10 minority (1 African American, 3 Asian Americans or Pacific Islanders, 6 Hispanic Americans), 73 international. Average age 28. 276 applicants, 65% accepted, 32 enrolled. In 2009, 37 master's, 6 doctorates awarded. *Degree requirements:* For master's, comprehensive exam (for some programs), thesis (for some programs), final program exam, faculty-supervised specialized research; for doctorate, comprehensive exam, thesis/dissertation, complete program of significant original research. *Entrance requirements:* For master's, GRE, minimum GPA of 3.0, bachelor's degree from an ABET-accredited program; for doctorate, 3 letters of recommendation, resume, minimum GPA of 3.2, statement of objectives, on campus interview (highly recommended). Additional exam requirements/recommendations for international students: Required—TOEFL (minimum score 550 paper-based; 213 computer-based; 79 iBT). *Application deadline:* For fall admission, 4/1 for international students; for spring admission, 9/30 for international students. Applications are processed on a rolling basis. Application fee: $50. Electronic applications accepted. *Expenses:* Tuition: Part-time $1015 per credit. Tuition and fees vary according to campus/location and program. *Financial support:* In 2009–10, 16 students received support, including 4 research assistantships with full and partial tuition reimbursements available (averaging $4,952 per year), 12 teaching assistantships with full and partial tuition reimbursements available (averaging $3,467 per year); career-related internships or fieldwork, institutionally sponsored loans, tuition waivers (partial), unspecified assistantships, and tuition remissions also available. Support available to part-time students. Financial award application deadline: 3/1; financial award applicants required to submit FAFSA. *Faculty research:* Electro-optics, electromagnetics, microelectronics, communications, computer architecture, neural networks. Total annual research expenditures: $380,187. *Unit head:* Dr. Samuel P. Kozaitis, Department Head, 321-674-8060, Fax: 321-674-8192, E-mail: kozaitis@fit.edu. *Application contact:* Thomas M. Shea, Director of Graduate Admissions, 321-674-7577, Fax: 321-723-9468, E-mail: tshea@fit.edu.

See Close-Up on page 371.

Florida International University, College of Engineering and Computing, Department of Electrical and Computer Engineering, Program in Computer Engineering, Miami, FL 33175. Offers MS. Part-time and evening/weekend programs available. *Students:* 4 full-time (1 woman), 5 part-time (0 women); includes 5 minority (1 African American, 1 Asian American or Pacific Islander, 3 Hispanic Americans), 3 international. Average age 26. 26 applicants, 19% accepted, 5 enrolled. In 2009, 5 master's awarded. *Degree requirements:* For master's, thesis optional. *Entrance requirements:* For master's, minimum GPA of 3.0, resume, 3 letters of recommendation, letter of intent. Additional exam requirements/recommendations for international students: Required—TOEFL (minimum score 550 paper-based; 80 iBT). *Application deadline:* For fall admission, 6/1 for domestic students, 4/1 for international students; for spring admission, 10/1 for domestic students, 9/1 for international students. Applications are processed on a rolling basis. Application fee: $30. Electronic applications accepted. *Expenses:* Tuition, state resident: full-time $8008; part-time $4004 per year. Tuition, nonresident: full-time $20,104; part-time $10,052 per year. Required fees: $298; $149 per term. *Financial support:* Institutionally sponsored loans and scholarships/grants available. Financial award application deadline: 3/1; financial award applicants required to submit FAFSA. *Unit head:* Dr. Kang Yen, Chair, Electrical and Computer Engineering Department, 305-348-3037, Fax: 305-348-3707, E-mail: yenk@fiu.edu. *Application contact:* Maria Parrilla, Graduate Admissions Assistant, 305-348-1890, Fax: 305-348-6142, E-mail: grad_eng@fiu.edu.

George Mason University, Volgenau School of Information Technology and Engineering, Department of Electrical and Computer Engineering, Fairfax, VA 22030. Offers advanced networking protocols for telecommunications (Certificate); communications and networking (Certificate); computer engineering (MS); computer forensics (MS); electrical and computer engineering (PhD); electrical engineering (MS); network technology and applications (Certificate); networks, system integration and testing (Certificate); signal processing (Certificate); telecom systems modeling (Certificate); telecommunications (MS); telecommunications forensics and security (Certificate); VLSI design/manufacturing (Certificate); wireless communication (Certificate). Part-time and evening/weekend programs available. *Faculty:* 29 full-time (4 women), 37 part-time/adjunct (5 women). *Students:* 115 full-time (18 women), 308 part-time (46 women); includes 84 minority (17 African Americans, 51 Asian Americans or Pacific Islanders, 16 Hispanic Americans), 179 international. Average age 29. 461 applicants, 67% accepted, 105 enrolled. In 2009, 157 master's, 6 doctorates, 61 other advanced degrees awarded. *Degree requirements:* For master's, thesis optional; for doctorate, comprehensive exam, thesis or scholarly paper. *Entrance requirements:* For master's, GMAT or GRE General Test, letters of recommendation, resume; for doctorate, GRE/GMAT, personal goal statement, 2 transcripts, letter of recommendation. Additional exam requirements/recommendations for international students: Required—TOEFL. *Application deadline:* For fall admission, 7/15 priority date for domestic and international students; for spring admission, 12/2 for domestic students, 12/1 for international students. Applications are processed on a rolling basis. Application fee: $75. Electronic applications accepted. *Expenses:* Tuition, state resident: full-time $7568; part-time $315.33 per credit hour. Tuition, nonresident: full-time $21,704; part-time $904.33 per credit hour. Required fees: $2184; $91 per credit hour. *Financial support:* In 2009–10, 64 students received support, including 2 fellowships with full tuition reimbursements available (averaging $18,000 per year), 22 research assistantships with full and partial tuition reimbursements available (averaging $8,469 per year), 42 teaching assistantships with full and partial tuition reimbursements available (averaging $6,291 per year); career-related internships or fieldwork, Federal Work-Study, scholarships/grants, unspecified assistantships, and health care benefits (full-time research or teaching assistantship recipients) also available. Support available to part-time students. Financial award application deadline: 3/1; financial award applicants required to submit FAFSA. *Faculty research:* Communication networks, signal processing, system failure diagnosis, multiprocessors, material processing using microwave energy. Total annual research expenditures: $3 million. *Unit head:* Dr. Andre Manitius, Chairperson, 703-993-1569, Fax: 703-993-1601, E-mail: ece@gmu.edu. *Application contact:* Jessica Skinner, Associate Dean, 703-993-1569, E-mail: jskinne6@gmu.edu.

The George Washington University, School of Engineering and Applied Science, Department of Electrical and Computer Engineering, Washington, DC 20052. Offers electrical and computer engineering (MS, D Sc); telecommunication and computers (MS). Part-time and evening/weekend programs available. *Faculty:* 23 full-time (2 women), 6 part-time/adjunct (0 women). *Students:* 98 full-time (19 women), 132 part-time (14 women); includes 33 minority (12 African Americans, 1 American Indian/Alaska Native, 18 Asian Americans or Pacific Islanders, 2 Hispanic Americans), 126 international. Average age 30. 293 applicants, 88% accepted, 64 enrolled. In 2009, 54 master's, 5 doctorates awarded. *Degree requirements:* For master's, thesis optional; for doctorate, comprehensive exam, thesis/dissertation, dissertation defense, qualifying exam. *Entrance requirements:* For master's, appropriate bachelor's degree, minimum GPA of 3.0; for doctorate, appropriate bachelor's or master's degree, minimum GPA of 3.3, GRE if highest earned degree is BS. Additional exam requirements/recommendations for international students: Required—TOEFL or George Washington University English as a Foreign Language Test. *Application deadline:* For fall admission, 3/1 priority date for domestic students; for spring admission, 10/1 for domestic students. Applications are processed on a rolling basis. Application fee: $60. *Financial support:* In 2009–10, 39 students received support; fellowships with tuition reimbursements available, research assistantships, teaching assistantships with tuition reimbursements available, career-related internships or fieldwork and institutionally sponsored loans available. Financial award application deadline: 3/1; financial award applicants required to submit FAFSA. *Faculty research:* Computer graphics, multimedia systems. *Unit head:* Can E. Korman, Chair, 202-994-4952, E-mail: korman@gwu.edu. *Application contact:* Adina Lav, Marketing, Recruiting and Admissions, 202-994-5827, Fax: 202-994-0909, E-mail: engineering@gwu.edu.

Georgia Institute of Technology, Graduate Studies and Research, College of Computing, Atlanta, GA 30332-0001. Offers algorithms, combinatorics, and optimization (PhD); computational science and engineering (MS, PhD); computer science (MS, MSCS, PhD); human computer interaction (MSHCI); human-centered computing (PhD); information security (MS). Part-time programs available. Postbaccalaureate distance learning degree programs offered. Terminal master's awarded for partial completion of doctoral program. *Degree requirements:* For master's, thesis optional; for doctorate, comprehensive exam, thesis/dissertation. *Entrance requirements:* For master's, GRE General Test, GRE Subject Test, minimum GPA of 3.0; for doctorate, GRE General Test, GRE Subject Test, minimum GPA of 3.3. Additional exam requirements/recommendations for international students: Required—TOEFL. *Faculty research:* Computer systems, graphics, intelligent systems and artificial intelligence, networks and telecommunications, software engineering.

Georgia Institute of Technology, Graduate Studies and Research, College of Engineering, School of Electrical and Computer Engineering, Atlanta, GA 30332-0001. Offers MS, MSEE, PhD. Part-time programs available. Postbaccalaureate distance learning degree programs offered (minimal on-campus study). Terminal master's awarded for partial completion of doctoral program. *Degree requirements:* For master's, thesis optional; for doctorate, thesis/dissertation. *Entrance requirements:* For master's, GRE General Test, minimum GPA of 3.0; for doctorate, GRE General Test, minimum GPA of 3.5. Additional exam requirements/recommendations for international students: Required—TOEFL. *Faculty research:* Telecommunications, computer systems, microelectronics, optical engineering, digital signal processing.

Grand Valley State University, Padnos College of Engineering and Computing, School of Engineering, Allendale, MI 49401-9403. Offers electrical and computer engineering (MSE); manufacturing operations (MSE); mechanical engineering (MSE); product design and manufacturing engineering (MSE). Part-time and evening/weekend programs available. *Faculty:* 6 full-time (0 women). *Students:* 8 full-time (1 woman), 37 part-time (4 women), 4 international. Average age 30. 21 applicants, 86% accepted, 10 enrolled. In 2009, 12 master's awarded. *Degree requirements:* For master's, project or thesis. *Entrance requirements:* For master's, engineering degree, minimum GPA of 3.0. Additional exam requirements/recommendations for international students: Required—TOEFL. *Application deadline:* Applications are processed on a rolling basis. Application fee: $30. Electronic applications accepted. *Financial support:* In 2009–10, 11 students received support, including 3 fellowships (averaging $1,083 per year), 9 research assistantships with full tuition reimbursements available (averaging $7,304 per year); career-related internships or fieldwork, Federal Work-Study, institutionally sponsored loans, scholarships/grants, and unspecified assistantships also available. *Faculty research:* Digital signal processing, computer aided design, computer aided manufacturing, manufacturing simulation, biomechanics, product design. Total annual research expenditures: $300,000. *Unit head:* Dr. Charles Standridge, Acting Director, 616-331-6750, Fax: 616-331-7215, E-mail: standric@gvsu.edu. *Application contact:* Dr. Pranod Chaphalkar, Graduate Director, 616-331-6843, Fax: 616-331-7215, E-mail: chaphalp@gvsu.edu.

Illinois Institute of Technology, Graduate College, Armour College of Engineering, Department of Electrical and Computer Engineering, Chicago, IL 60616-3793. Offers biomedical imaging and signals (MBMI); computer engineering (MS, PhD); electrical and computer engineering (MECE); electrical engineering (MS, PhD); electricity markets (MEM); manufacturing engineering (MME, MS); network engineering (MNE); power engineering (MPE); telecommunications and software engineering (MTSE); VLSI and microelectronics (MVM). Part-time and evening/weekend programs available. Terminal master's awarded for partial completion of doctoral program. *Degree requirements:* For master's, comprehensive exam, thesis (for some programs); for doctorate, comprehensive exam, thesis/dissertation. *Entrance requirements:* For master's and doctorate, GRE General Test, minimum undergraduate GPA of 3.0. Additional exam requirements/recommendations for international students: Required—TOEFL (minimum score 550 paper-based; 213 computer-based; 80 iBT). Electronic applications accepted. *Expenses:* Tuition: Full-time $17,550; part-time $888 per credit hour. Required fees: $850; $7.50 per credit hour. One-time fee: $50 full-time. Full-time tuition and fees vary according to program. *Faculty research:* Communications and signal processing, computers and digital systems, electronics and electromagnetics, power and control systems.

Indiana State University, School of Graduate Studies, College of Technology, Department of Electronics and Computer Technology, Terre Haute, IN 47809. Offers MS. *Degree requirements:* For master's, thesis or alternative. *Entrance requirements:* For master's, bachelor's degree in industrial technology or related field. Additional exam requirements/recommendations for international students: Required—TOEFL. Electronic applications accepted.

Indiana University–Purdue University Fort Wayne, College of Engineering, Technology, and Computer Science, Department of Engineering, Fort Wayne, IN 46805-1499. Offers computer engineering (MS); electrical engineering (MS); mechanical engineering (MS); systems engineering (MS). Part-time programs available. *Faculty:* 15 full-time (3 women). *Students:* 4 full-time (0 women), 29 part-time (5 women); includes 2 minority (1 African American, 1 Asian American or Pacific Islander), 5 international. Average age 29. 13 applicants, 92% accepted, 7 enrolled. In 2009, 1 master's awarded. *Entrance requirements:* For master's, minimum GPA of 3.0. Additional exam requirements/recommendations for international students: Required—TOEFL (minimum score 550 paper-based; 213 computer-based; 77 iBT); Recommended—TWE. *Application deadline:* For fall admission, 7/15 priority date for domestic students, 3/1 priority date for international students; for spring admission, 12/1 priority date for domestic students, 9/1 priority date for international students. Applications are processed on a rolling basis. Application fee: $55 ($60 for international students). Electronic applications accepted. *Expenses:* Tuition, state resident: full-time $4595; part-time $255 per credit. Tuition, nonresident: full-time $10,963; part-time $609 per credit. Required fees: $528; $29.35 per credit. Tuition and fees vary according to course load. *Financial support:* In 2009–10, 1 research assistantship with partial tuition reimbursement (averaging $12,740 per year), 3 teaching assistantships with partial tuition reimbursements (averaging $12,740 per year) were awarded. Financial award application deadline: 3/1; financial award applicants required to submit FAFSA. *Faculty research:* Synthesis technique, Markov parameters. Total annual research expenditures: $57,918. *Unit head:* Dr. Donald Mueller, Chair, 260-481-5707, Fax: 260-481-6281, E-mail: mueller@engr.ipfw.edu. *Application contact:* Dr. Donald Mueller, Chair, 260-481-5707, Fax: 260-481-6281, E-mail: mueller@engr.ipfw.edu.

Indiana University–Purdue University Indianapolis, School of Engineering and Technology, Department of Electrical Engineering, Indianapolis, IN 46202-2896. Offers biomedical engineering (MS, PhD); electrical and computer engineering (MS, MSECE, PhD), including biomedical engineering (MSECE), control and automation (MSECE), signal processing (MSECE); engineering (interdisciplinary) (MSE). *Students:* 41 full-time (10 women), 27 part-time (2 women); includes 11 minority (5 African Americans, 4 Asian Americans or Pacific Islanders, 2 Hispanic Americans), 38 international. Average age 27. 178 applicants, 56% accepted, 54 enrolled. In 2009, 28 master's awarded. Application fee: $55 ($65 for international students). *Unit head:* Yaobin Chen, Unit Head, 317-274-4032, Fax: 317-274-4493. *Application contact:* Valerie Diemer, Graduate Program, 317-278-4960, Fax: 317-278-1671, E-mail: grad@engr.iupui.edu.

Instituto Tecnológico y de Estudios Superiores de Monterrey, Campus Chihuahua, Graduate Programs, Chihuahua, Mexico. Offers computer systems engineering (Ingeniero); electrical engineering (Ingeniero); electromechanical engineering (Ingeniero); electronic engineering (Ingeniero); engineering administration (MEA); industrial engineering (MIE, Ingeniero); international trade (MIT); mechanical engineering (Ingeniero).

International Technological University, Program in Computer Engineering, Santa Clara, CA 95050. Offers MSCE. *Degree requirements:* For master's, thesis or alternative. *Entrance requirements:* For master's, 3 semesters of calculus, minimum GPA of 2.5. Additional exam requirements/recommendations for international students: Required—TOEFL. *Faculty research:* Computer networking management, digital systems, embedded system design.

Iowa State University of Science and Technology, Graduate College, College of Engineering, Department of Electrical and Computer Engineering, Ames, IA 50011. Offers computer engineering (M Eng, MS, PhD); electrical engineering (M Eng, MS, PhD). *Faculty:* 52 full-time (3 women), 5 part-time/adjunct (2 women). *Students:* 223 full-time (39 women), 109 part-time (16 women); includes 13 minority (2 African Americans, 8 Asian Americans or Pacific Islanders, 3 Hispanic Americans), 214 international. 1,103 applicants, 11% accepted, 69 enrolled. In 2009, 30 master's, 27 doctorates awarded. *Degree requirements:* For master's, thesis or alternative; for doctorate, thesis/dissertation. *Entrance requirements:* For master's and doctorate, GRE General Test. Additional exam requirements/recommendations for international students: Required—TOEFL (minimum score 550 paper-based; 79 iBT) or IELTS (minimum score 6.5). *Application deadline:* For fall admission, 1/15 priority date for domestic and international students; for spring admission, 9/15 for domestic and international students. Application fee: $40 ($90 for international students). Electronic applications accepted. *Expenses:* Tuition, state resident: full-time $6716. Tuition, nonresident: full-time $8908. Tuition and fees vary according to course level, course load, program and student level. *Financial support:* In 2009–10, 137 research assistantships with full and partial tuition reimbursements (averaging $15,000 per year), 40 teaching assistantships with full and partial tuition reimbursements (averaging $14,500 per year) were awarded; fellowships, scholarships/grants, health care benefits, and unspecified assistantships also available. *Unit head:* Dr. Arun Somani, Chair, 515-294-2664, E-mail: ecegrad@ee.iastate.edu. *Application contact:* Dr. Akhilesh Tyagi, Director of Graduate Education, 515-294-2667, E-mail: ecegrad@iastate.edu.

The Johns Hopkins University, Engineering for Professionals, Part-time Program in Electrical and Computer Engineering, Baltimore, MD 21218-2699. Offers MS, Post-Master's Certificate. Part-time and evening/weekend programs available. *Faculty:* 40 part-time/adjunct (1 woman). *Students:* 25 full-time (7 women), 303 part-time (47 women); includes 88 minority (23 African Americans, 47 Asian Americans or Pacific Islanders, 18 Hispanic Americans), 5 international. Average age 29. In 2009, 127 master's, 4 other advanced degrees awarded. *Application deadline:* Applications are processed on a rolling basis. Application fee: $75. Electronic applications accepted. *Financial support:* Institutionally sponsored loans available. *Unit head:* Dr. Dexter G. Smith, Program Chair, 443-778-5879, E-mail: dexter.smith@jhuapl.edu. *Application contact:* Priyanka Dwivedi, Admissions Manager, 410-516-2300, Fax: 410-579-8049, E-mail: pdwived1@jhu.edu.

The Johns Hopkins University, G. W. C. Whiting School of Engineering, Department of Electrical and Computer Engineering, Baltimore, MD 21218-2699. Offers MSE, PhD. *Faculty:* 21 full-time (2 women), 13 part-time/adjunct (0 women). *Students:* 125 full-time (21 women), 5 part-time (0 women); includes 9 minority (3 African Americans, 5 Asian Americans or Pacific Islanders, 1 Hispanic American), 90 international. Average age 27. 275 applicants, 43% accepted, 38 enrolled. In 2009, 23 master's, 15 doctorates awarded. Terminal master's awarded for partial completion of doctoral program. *Degree requirements:* For master's, thesis optional; for doctorate, thesis/dissertation, Qualifying Exam, Oral Exam, Seminar. *Entrance requirements:* For master's, GRE General Test, 3 letters of recommendation, SOP; for doctorate, GRE General Test, Transcripts, 3 Letters of Recommendation, SOP. Additional exam requirements/recommendations for international students: Required—TOEFL (minimum score 600 paper-based; 250 computer-based; 100 iBT). *Application deadline:* For fall admission, 1/15 for domestic and international students. Application fee: $75. Electronic applications accepted. *Financial support:* In 2009–10, 7 fellowships with full tuition reimbursements (averaging $20,000 per year), 49 research assistantships with full tuition reimbursements (averaging $20,000 per year), 14 teaching assistantships with full tuition reimbursements (averaging $20,000 per year) were awarded; career-related internships or fieldwork, Federal Work-Study, institutionally sponsored loans, scholarships/grants, health care benefits, tuition waivers (partial), and unspecified assistantships also available. Financial award application deadline: 1/15. *Faculty research:* Computer engineering, systems and control, language and speech processing, photonics and optoelectronics, signals. Total annual research expenditures: $2.2 million. *Unit head:* Dr. Jin U. Kang, Chair, 410-516-7031, Fax: 410-516-5566, E-mail: jkang@jhu.edu. *Application contact:* Felicia C. Roane, Academic Coordinator II, 410-516-4808, Fax: 410-516-5566, E-mail: eceinfo@jhu.edu.

Lakehead University, Graduate Studies, Faculty of Engineering, Thunder Bay, ON P7B 5E1, Canada. Offers control engineering (M Sc Engr); electrical/computer engineering (M Sc Engr); environmental engineering (M Sc Engr). Part-time programs available. *Degree requirements:* For master's, thesis. *Entrance requirements:* For master's, bachelor's degree in chemical, electrical or mechanical engineering, minimum B average. Additional exam requirements/recommendations for international students: Required—TOEFL. *Faculty research:* Pulp and paper, adaptive/process control, robust/interactive learning control, vibration control.

Lawrence Technological University, College of Engineering, Southfield, MI 48075-1058. Offers automotive engineering (MAE); civil engineering (MCE); construction engineering management (MS); electrical and computer engineering (MS); engineering management (ME); industrial engineering (MSIE); manufacturing systems (MEMS, DE); mechanical engineering (MS); mechatronic systems engineering (MS). Part-time and evening/weekend programs available. *Faculty:* 20 full-time (4 women), 12 part-time/adjunct (0 women). *Students:* 15 full-time (4 women), 389 part-time (50 women); includes 57 minority (22 African Americans, 1 American Indian/Alaska Native, 30 Asian Americans or Pacific Islanders, 4 Hispanic Americans), 137 international. Average age 31. 361 applicants, 52% accepted, 108 enrolled. In 2009, 161 master's, 1 doctorate awarded. *Degree requirements:* For master's, thesis (for some programs). *Entrance requirements:* Additional exam requirements/recommendations for international students: Required—TOEFL (minimum score 550 paper-based; 213 computer-based; 79 iBT). *Application deadline:* For fall admission, 8/1 priority date for domestic students, 6/1 for international students; for winter admission, 12/1 priority date for domestic students, 10/1 for international students; for spring admission, 5/1 priority date for domestic students, 3/1 for international students. Applications are processed on a rolling basis. Application fee: $50. Electronic applications accepted. *Expenses:* Tuition: Full-time $11,320; part-time $798 per credit hour. *Financial support:* Federal Work-Study and institutionally sponsored loans available. Support available to part-time students. Financial award application deadline: 4/1; financial award applicants required to submit FAFSA. *Faculty research:* Advanced composite materials in bridges, strengthening existing bridges with carbon and glass fiber sheets, development of drive shafts using composite materials. *Unit head:* Dr. Nabil Grace, Interim Dean, 248-204-2500, Fax: 248-204-2509, E-mail: engrdean@ltu.edu. *Application contact:* Jane Rohrback, Director of Admissions, 248-204-3160, Fax: 248-204-3188, E-mail: admissions@ltu.edu.

Lehigh University, P.C. Rossin College of Engineering and Applied Science, Department of Computer Science and Engineering, Bethlehem, PA 18015. Offers computer engineering (M Eng, MS, PhD); computer science (M Eng, MS, PhD, MBA/E); MBA/E. Part-time programs

available. *Faculty:* 16 full-time (2 women). *Students:* 59 full-time (12 women), 12 part-time (4 women); includes 2 minority (both Asian Americans or Pacific Islanders), 51 international. Average age 27. 177 applicants, 37% accepted, 16 enrolled. In 2009, 14 master's, 8 doctorates awarded. *Degree requirements:* For doctorate, thesis/dissertation, qualifying, general, and oral exams. *Entrance requirements:* For master's, GRE General Test, minimum GPA of 3.0; for doctorate, GRE General Test, minimum GPA of 3.5. Additional exam requirements/recommendations for international students: Required—TOEFL (minimum score 550 paper-based; 213 computer-based; 79 iBT). *Application deadline:* For fall admission, 4/1 for domestic and international students; for spring admission, 11/1 for domestic and international students. Applications are processed on a rolling basis. Application fee: $75. Electronic applications accepted. *Expenses:* Contact institution. *Financial support:* In 2009–10, 3 fellowships with full tuition reimbursements (averaging $16,530 per year), 7 research assistantships with full tuition reimbursements (averaging $15,000 per year), 4 teaching assistantships with full tuition reimbursements (averaging $15,795 per year) were awarded. Financial award application deadline: 1/15. *Faculty research:* Artificial intelligence, networking-pattern recognition, multimedia e-learning/data mining/Web search, mobile robotics, bioinformatics, computervision. Total annual research expenditures: $2.4 million. *Unit head:* Dr. Daniel P. Lopresti, Chairman, 610-758-5782, Fax: 610-758-4096, E-mail: dal9@lehigh.edu. *Application contact:* Judy Frenick, Graduate Coordinator, 610-758-3605, Fax: 610-758-4096, E-mail: jlf2@lehigh.edu.

Louisiana State University and Agricultural and Mechanical College, Graduate School, College of Engineering, Department of Electrical and Computer Engineering, Baton Rouge, LA 70803. Offers MSEE, PhD. *Faculty:* 27 full-time (1 woman). *Students:* 108 full-time (23 women), 6 part-time (2 women); includes 9 minority (3 African Americans, 2 Asian Americans or Pacific Islanders, 4 Hispanic Americans), 98 international. Average age 26. 229 applicants, 75% accepted, 27 enrolled. In 2009, 9 master's, 6 doctorates awarded. Terminal master's awarded for partial completion of doctoral program. *Degree requirements:* For master's, thesis optional; for doctorate, thesis/dissertation. *Entrance requirements:* For master's, GRE General Test, minimum GPA of 3.0; for doctorate, GRE General Test, minimum GPA of 3.5. Additional exam requirements/recommendations for international students: Required—TOEFL (minimum score 550 paper-based; 213 computer-based; 79 iBT) or IELTS (minimum score 6.5). *Application deadline:* For fall admission, 1/25 priority date for domestic students, 5/15 for international students; for spring admission, 10/15 for international students. Applications are processed on a rolling basis. Application fee: $50 ($70 for international students). Electronic applications accepted. *Financial support:* In 2009–10, 91 students received support, including 6 fellowships with full and partial tuition reimbursements available (averaging $22,476 per year), 40 research assistantships with full and partial tuition reimbursements available (averaging $13,185 per year), 31 teaching assistantships with full and partial tuition reimbursements available (averaging $13,270 per year); Federal Work-Study, institutionally sponsored loans, health care benefits, tuition waivers (full and partial), and unspecified assistantships also available. Financial award application deadline: 2/28; financial award applicants required to submit FAFSA. *Faculty research:* Computer engineering, electronics, control systems and signal processing, communications. Total annual research expenditures: $1 million. *Unit head:* Dr. Jorge Aravena, Interim Chair, 225-578-5243, Fax: 225-578-5200, E-mail: aravena@ece.lsu.edu. *Application contact:* Dr. Ramachanran Vaidyanathan, Graduate Adviser, 225-578-5551, Fax: 225-578-5200, E-mail: vaidy@ece.lsu.edu.

Manhattan College, Graduate Division, School of Engineering, Program in Computer Engineering, Riverdale, NY 10471. Offers MS. Part-time and evening/weekend programs available. *Degree requirements:* For master's, thesis or alternative. *Entrance requirements:* For master's, GRE (recommended), minimum GPA of 3.0. Additional exam requirements/recommendations for international students: Required—TOEFL (minimum score 550 paper-based; 213 computer-based).

Marquette University, Graduate School, College of Engineering, Department of Electrical and Computer Engineering, Milwaukee, WI 53201-1881. Offers computing (MS); electrical engineering (MS, PhD). Part-time and evening/weekend programs available. *Faculty:* 14 full-time (2 women), 2 part-time/adjunct (0 women). *Students:* 27 full-time (6 women), 25 part-time (4 women); includes 4 minority (3 African Americans, 1 Asian American or Pacific Islander), 25 international. Average age 29. 62 applicants, 69% accepted, 14 enrolled. In 2009, 14 master's, 6 doctorates awarded. Terminal master's awarded for partial completion of doctoral program. *Degree requirements:* For master's, thesis optional; for doctorate, thesis/dissertation, dissertation defense, qualifying exam. *Entrance requirements:* For master's, GRE General Test; for doctorate, GRE General Test, minimum GPA of 3.0. Additional exam requirements/recommendations for international students: Required—TOEFL. *Application deadline:* For fall admission, 7/15 priority date for domestic students; for spring admission, 11/15 for domestic students. Applications are processed on a rolling basis. Application fee: $40. Electronic applications accepted. *Financial support:* In 2009–10, 33 students received support, including 11 fellowships with full tuition reimbursements available (averaging $17,100 per year), 10 research assistantships with full tuition reimbursements available (averaging $15,200 per year), 12 teaching assistantships with full tuition reimbursements available (averaging $11,600 per year); Federal Work-Study, institutionally sponsored loans, and scholarships/grants also available. Support available to part-time students. Financial award application deadline: 2/15. *Faculty research:* Electric machines, drives, and controls; applied solid-state electronics; computers and signal processing; microwaves and antennas; solid state devices and acoustic wave sensors. Total annual research expenditures: $1.2 million. *Unit head:* Dr. Edwin E. Yaz, Chair, 414-288-6820, Fax: 414-288-5579, E-mail: edwin.yaz@marquette.edu. *Application contact:* Dr. Fabien J. Josse, Director of Graduate Studies, 414-288-6789, Fax: 414-288-5579, E-mail: fabien.josse@marquette.edu.

McGill University, Faculty of Graduate and Postdoctoral Studies, Faculty of Engineering, Department of Electrical and Computer Engineering, Montréal, QC H3A 2T5, Canada. Offers M Eng, PhD.

Memorial University of Newfoundland, School of Graduate Studies, Faculty of Engineering and Applied Science, St. John's, NL A1C 5S7, Canada. Offers civil engineering (M Eng, PhD); electrical and computer engineering (M Eng, PhD); mechanical engineering (M Eng, PhD); ocean and naval architecture engineering (M Eng, PhD). Part-time programs available. *Degree requirements:* For master's, thesis; for doctorate, comprehensive exam, thesis/dissertation, oral thesis defense. *Entrance requirements:* For master's, 2nd class degree; for doctorate, master's degree in engineering. Electronic applications accepted. *Faculty research:* Engineering analysis, environmental and hydrotechnical studies, manufacturing and robotics, mechanics, structures and materials.

Memorial University of Newfoundland, School of Graduate Studies, Interdisciplinary Program in Computer Engineering, St. John's, NL A1C 5S7, Canada. Offers MA Sc. *Degree requirements:* For master's, project course. *Entrance requirements:* For master's, 2nd class engineering degree.

Mercer University, Graduate Studies, Macon Campus, School of Engineering, Macon, GA 31207-0003. Offers biomedical engineering (MSE); computer engineering (MSE); electrical engineering (MSE); engineering management (MSE); environmental engineering (MSE); environmental systems (MS); mechanical engineering (MSE); software engineering (MSE); software systems (MS); technical communications management (MS); technical management (MS). Part-time and evening/weekend programs available. Postbaccalaureate distance learning degree programs offered (no on-campus study). *Faculty:* 19 full-time (4 women), 1 part-time/adjunct (0 women). *Students:* 6 full-time (1 woman), 95 part-time (22 women); includes 22 minority (5 African Americans, 13 Asian Americans or Pacific Islanders, 4 Hispanic Americans), 3 international. Average age 33. In 2009, 42 master's awarded. *Degree requirements:* For master's, thesis or alternative. *Entrance requirements:* For master's, minimum undergraduate GPA of 3.0. Additional exam requirements/recommendations for international students: Required—TOEFL. *Application deadline:* For fall admission, 7/1 for domestic students; for spring admission, 11/15 for domestic students. Applications are processed on a rolling basis.

Computer Engineering

Mercer University (continued)

Application fee: $35 ($50 for international students). Electronic applications accepted. *Expenses:* Contact institution. *Financial support:* Federal Work-Study available. *Unit head:* Dr. Wade H. Shaw, Dean, 478-301-2459, Fax: 478-301-5593, E-mail: shaw_wh@mercer.edu. *Application contact:* Greg Lofton, Graduate Program Coordinator, 478-301-5480, Fax: 478-301-5434, E-mail: lofton_g@mercer.edu.

Michigan Technological University, Graduate School, College of Engineering, Program in Computational Science and Engineering, Houghton, MI 49931. Offers PhD. Part-time programs available. *Degree requirements:* For doctorate, comprehensive exam, thesis/dissertation. *Entrance requirements:* For doctorate, MS in relevant discipline. Additional exam requirements/recommendations for international students: Required—TOEFL (minimum score 550 paper-based; 213 computer-based). Electronic applications accepted. *Expenses:* Contact institution.

Mississippi State University, Bagley College of Engineering, Department of Electrical and Computer Engineering, MS State, MS 39762. Offers computer engineering (MS, PhD); electrical engineering (MS, PhD). Part-time programs available. Postbaccalaureate distance learning degree programs offered (minimal on-campus study). *Faculty:* 21 full-time (1 woman). *Students:* 88 full-time (11 women), 40 part-time (11 women); includes 6 minority (2 African Americans, 2 Asian Americans or Pacific Islanders, 2 Hispanic Americans), 90 international. Average age 28. 207 applicants, 37% accepted, 36 enrolled. In 2009, 30 master's, 9 doctorates awarded. Terminal master's awarded for partial completion of doctoral program. *Degree requirements:* For master's, comprehensive exam, thesis optional; for doctorate, comprehensive exam, thesis/dissertation, written exam. *Entrance requirements:* For master's, GRE General Test, minimum undergraduate GPA of 3.0; for doctorate, GRE, minimum graduate GPA of 3.5. Additional exam requirements/recommendations for international students: Required—TOEFL (minimum score 550 paper-based; 213 computer-based; 79 iBT); Recommended—IELTS (minimum score 6.5). *Application deadline:* For fall admission, 7/1 for domestic students, 5/1 for international students; for spring admission, 11/1 for domestic students, 9/1 for international students. Applications are processed on a rolling basis. Application fee: $40. Electronic applications accepted. *Expenses:* Tuition, state resident: full-time $2575.50; part-time $286.25 per credit hour. Tuition, nonresident: full-time $6510; part-time $723.50 per credit hour. Tuition and fees vary according to course load. *Financial support:* In 2009–10, 115 research assistantships with full tuition reimbursements (averaging $12,585 per year), 19 teaching assistantships with full tuition reimbursements (averaging $14,016 per year) were awarded; Federal Work-Study, institutionally sponsored loans, scholarships/grants, and unspecified assistantships also available. Financial award application deadline: 4/1; financial award applicants required to submit FAFSA. *Faculty research:* Digital computing, power, controls, communication systems, microelectronics. Total annual research expenditures: $14 million. *Unit head:* Dr. Nicholas H. Younan, Professor and Interim Department Head, 662-325-3721, Fax: 662-325-2298, E-mail: ece-head@ece.msstate.edu. *Application contact:* Dr. James E. Fowler, Professor and Interim Graduate Program Director, 662-325-3640, Fax: 662-325-2298, E-mail: fowler@ece.msstate.edu.

Missouri University of Science and Technology, Graduate School, School of Engineering, Department of Electrical and Computer Engineering, Rolla, MO 65409. Offers computer engineering (MS, DE, PhD); electrical engineering (MS, DE, PhD). Part-time and evening/weekend programs available. Terminal master's awarded for partial completion of doctoral program. *Degree requirements:* For master's, thesis optional; for doctorate, comprehensive exam, thesis/dissertation, departmental qualifying exam. *Entrance requirements:* For master's, GRE General Test (minimum score 1100 verbal and quantitative, writing 4.5); for doctorate, GRE General Test (minimum score: verbal and quantitative 1100, writing 3.5). Additional exam requirements/recommendations for international students: Required—TOEFL. Electronic applications accepted. *Faculty research:* Power systems, computer/communication networks, intelligent control/robotics, robust control, nanotechnologies.

Montana State University, College of Graduate Studies, College of Engineering, Department of Electrical and Computer Engineering, Bozeman, MT 59717. Offers electrical engineering (MS); engineering (PhD), including electrical and computer engineering option. Part-time programs available. *Faculty:* 13 full-time (0 women), 5 part-time/adjunct (1 woman). *Students:* 14 full-time (1 woman), 30 part-time (6 women); includes 2 minority (1 Asian American or Pacific Islander, 1 Hispanic American), 14 international. Average age 25. 28 applicants. In 2009, 17 master's, 1 doctorate awarded. *Degree requirements:* For master's, comprehensive exam, thesis (for some programs); for doctorate, comprehensive exam, thesis/dissertation. *Entrance requirements:* For master's, GRE General Test; for doctorate, GRE General Test, MS Degree. Additional exam requirements/recommendations for international students: Required—TOEFL (minimum score 550 paper-based; 213 computer-based). *Application deadline:* For fall admission, 7/15 priority date for domestic students, 5/15 priority date for international students; for spring admission, 12/1 priority date for domestic students, 10/1 priority date for international students. Applications are processed on a rolling basis. Application fee: $30. Electronic applications accepted. *Expenses:* Tuition, state resident: full-time $5635; part-time $3492 per year. Tuition, nonresident: full-time $17,212; part-time $7865.10 per year. Required fees: $1441.05; $153.15 per credit. Tuition and fees vary according to course load and program. *Financial support:* In 2009–10, 33 students received support, including 26 research assistantships with tuition reimbursements available (averaging $19,000 per year), 7 teaching assistantships with tuition reimbursements available (averaging $12,600 per year). Financial award application deadline: 3/1; financial award applicants required to submit FAFSA. *Faculty research:* Wireless and optical networks, micro-electrical mechanical systems, optics and optical electronics, power systems, signal processing. Total annual research expenditures: $2.7 million. *Unit head:* Dr. Robert Maher, Head, 406-994-2505, Fax: 406-994-5958, E-mail: rmaher@ece.montana.edu. *Application contact:* Dr. Carl A. Fox, Vice Provost for Graduate Education, 406-994-4145, Fax: 406-994-7433, E-mail: gradstudy@montana.edu.

Naval Postgraduate School, Graduate Programs, Department of Electrical and Computer Engineering, Monterey, CA 93943. Offers MS, PhD, Eng. Program only open to commissioned officers of the United States and friendly nations and selected United States federal civilian employees. *Accreditation:* ABET (one or more programs are accredited). Part-time programs available. Postbaccalaureate distance learning degree programs offered (minimal on-campus study). *Degree requirements:* For master's and Eng, thesis; for doctorate, one foreign language, thesis/dissertation.

New Jersey Institute of Technology, Office of Graduate Studies, Newark College of Engineering, Department of Electrical and Computer Engineering, Program in Computer Engineering, Newark, NJ 07102. Offers MS, PhD. Part-time and evening/weekend programs available. Terminal master's awarded for partial completion of doctoral program. *Degree requirements:* For master's, thesis optional; for doctorate, thesis/dissertation, residency. *Entrance requirements:* For master's, GRE General Test; for doctorate, GRE General Test, minimum graduate GPA of 3.5. Additional exam requirements/recommendations for international students: Required—TOEFL (minimum score 550 paper-based; 213 computer-based; 79 iBT). Electronic applications accepted.

New Mexico State University, Graduate School, College of Engineering, Klipsch School of Electrical and Computer Engineering, Las Cruces, NM 88003-8001. Offers MSEE, PhD. Part-time and evening/weekend programs available. Postbaccalaureate distance learning degree programs offered (no on-campus study). *Faculty:* 18 full-time (1 woman). *Students:* 100 full-time (18 women), 46 part-time (2 women); includes 24 minority (1 African American, 1 American Indian/Alaska Native, 2 Asian Americans or Pacific Islanders, 20 Hispanic Americans), 87 international. Average age 28. 240 applicants, 67% accepted, 39 enrolled. In 2009, 32 master's, 6 doctorates awarded. Terminal master's awarded for partial completion of doctoral program. *Degree requirements:* For master's, thesis (for some programs), final oral or written exam; for doctorate, comprehensive exam, thesis/dissertation. *Entrance requirements:* For master's, GRE, minimum GPA of 3.0; for doctorate, departmental qualifying exam, minimum GPA of 3.0. Additional exam requirements/recommendations for international students: Required—TOEFL. *Application deadline:* For fall admission, 3/1 priority date for domestic and international students; for spring admission, 8/1 priority date for domestic and international students. Applications are processed on a rolling basis. Application fee: $30 ($50 for international students). Electronic applications accepted. *Expenses:* Tuition, state resident: full-time $4080; part-time $223 per credit. Tuition, nonresident: full-time $14,256; part-time $647 per credit. Required fees: $1278; $639 per semester. *Financial support:* In 2009–10, 75 students received support, including 33 research assistantships (averaging $6,921 per year), 33 teaching assistantships (averaging $5,224 per year); fellowships, career-related internships or fieldwork, Federal Work-Study, health care benefits, and unspecified assistantships also available. Support available to part-time students. Financial award application deadline: 3/1. *Faculty research:* Image and digital signal processing, energy systems, wireless communication, analog VLSI design, electro-optics. *Unit head:* Dr. Paul Furth, Interim Head, 575-646-3117, Fax: 575-646-1435, E-mail: pfurth@nmsu.edu. *Application contact:* Sue Kord, Records Technician I, 575-646-6440, Fax: 575-646-1435, E-mail: kkord@nmsu.edu.

New York Institute of Technology, Graduate Division, School of Engineering and Computing Sciences, Program in Electrical Engineering and Computer Engineering, Old Westbury, NY 11568-8000. Offers MS. Part-time and evening/weekend programs available. *Students:* 104 full-time (27 women), 71 part-time (9 women); includes 17 minority (5 African Americans, 9 Asian Americans or Pacific Islanders, 3 Hispanic Americans), 121 international. Average age 26. In 2009, 73 master's awarded. *Degree requirements:* For master's, project. *Entrance requirements:* For master's, GRE General Test (if QPA less than 2.85), BS in electrical engineering or related field, minimum QPA of 2.85. Additional exam requirements/recommendations for international students: Required—TOEFL (minimum score 550 paper-based; 213 computer-based). *Application deadline:* For fall admission, 7/1 priority date for domestic students; for spring admission, 12/1 priority date for domestic students. Applications are processed on a rolling basis. Application fee: $50. Electronic applications accepted. *Expenses:* Tuition: Part-time $825 per credit. *Financial support:* Fellowships, research assistantships with partial tuition reimbursements, institutionally sponsored loans, tuition waivers (full and partial), and unspecified assistantships available. Support available to part-time students. Financial award applicants required to submit FAFSA. *Faculty research:* Computer networks, control theory, light waves and optics, robotics, signal processing. *Unit head:* Dr. Ayat Jafari, Chair, 516-686-7523, Fax: 516-686-7439, E-mail: ajafari@nyit.edu. *Application contact:* Dr. Jacquelyn Nealon, Vice President for Enrollment Services, 516-686-7925, Fax: 516-686-7597, E-mail: jnealon@nyit.edu.

Norfolk State University, School of Graduate Studies, School of Science and Technology, Program in Electronics Engineering, Norfolk, VA 23504. Offers MS.

North Carolina Agricultural and Technical State University, Graduate School, College of Engineering, Department of Electrical and Computer Engineering, Greensboro, NC 27411. Offers electrical engineering (MSEE, PhD), including communications and signal processing (MSEE), computer engineering (MSEE), electronic and optical materials and devices (MSEE), power systems and controls (MSEE). Part-time programs available. *Degree requirements:* For master's, project, thesis defense; for doctorate, thesis/dissertation. *Entrance requirements:* For master's, GRE General Test, GRE Subject Test, minimum GPA of 2.8; for doctorate, GRE General Test, minimum GPA of 3.0. *Faculty research:* Semiconductor compounds, VLSI design, image processing, optical systems and devices, fault-tolerant computing.

North Carolina State University, Graduate School, College of Engineering, Department of Electrical and Computer Engineering, Program in Computer Engineering, Raleigh, NC 27695. Offers MS, PhD. *Degree requirements:* For master's, thesis (for some programs); for doctorate, thesis/dissertation. *Entrance requirements:* For master's and doctorate, GRE. Additional exam requirements/recommendations for international students: Required—TOEFL (minimum score 575 paper-based). Electronic applications accepted. *Faculty research:* Computer architecture, parallel processing, embedded computer systems, VLSI design, computer networking performance and control.

North Dakota State University, College of Graduate and Interdisciplinary Studies, College of Engineering and Architecture, Department of Electrical and Computer Engineering, Fargo, ND 58108. Offers MS, PhD. Part-time programs available. *Faculty:* 15. *Students:* 27 full-time (7 women), 16 part-time (2 women); includes 1 Asian American or Pacific Islander, 26 international. Average age 28. 110 applicants, 20% accepted, 8 enrolled. In 2009, 8 master's, 1 doctorate awarded. Terminal master's awarded for partial completion of doctoral program. *Degree requirements:* For master's, comprehensive exam, thesis; for doctorate, comprehensive exam, thesis/dissertation. *Entrance requirements:* Additional exam requirements/recommendations for international students: Required—TOEFL (minimum score 525 paper-based; 197 computer-based; 71 iBT). *Application deadline:* For fall admission, 3/1 priority date for domestic and international students. Application fee: $45 ($60 for international students). Electronic applications accepted. *Financial support:* In 2009–10, 30 students received support, including 2 fellowships with full tuition reimbursements available (averaging $25,000 per year), 6 research assistantships with full tuition reimbursements available (averaging $8,100 per year), 10 teaching assistantships with full tuition reimbursements available (averaging $8,100 per year); career-related internships or fieldwork, Federal Work-Study, institutionally sponsored loans, and tuition waivers (full) also available. Financial award application deadline: 3/1. *Faculty research:* Computers, power and control systems, microwaves, communications and signal processing, bioengineering. Total annual research expenditures: $599,000. *Unit head:* Dr. Daniel L. Ewert, Chair, 701-231-7019, Fax: 701-231-8677, E-mail: dan.ewert@ndsu.nodak.edu. *Application contact:* Dr. Jacob Glower, Associate Professor, 701-231-8068, E-mail: jacob.glower@ndsu.edu.

Northeastern University, College of Engineering, Department of Electrical and Computer Engineering, Boston, MA 02115-5096. Offers computer engineering (PhD); electrical engineering (MS, PhD); engineering leadership (MS). *Faculty:* 45 full-time (6 women), 2 part-time/adjunct (both women). *Students:* 267 full-time (53 women), 117 part-time (19 women); includes 1 Hispanic American, 180 international. 921 applicants, 49% accepted, 96 enrolled. In 2009, 71 master's, 18 doctorates awarded. *Degree requirements:* For master's, thesis optional; for doctorate, thesis/dissertation, departmental qualifying exam. *Entrance requirements:* For master's and doctorate, GRE General Test. Additional exam requirements/recommendations for international students: Required—TOEFL (minimum score 550 paper-based; 213 computer-based). *Application deadline:* For fall admission, 1/15 priority date for domestic and international students. Applications are processed on a rolling basis. Application fee: $50. Electronic applications accepted. *Financial support:* In 2009–10, 136 students received support, including 1 fellowship with full tuition reimbursement available, 86 research assistantships with full tuition reimbursements available (averaging $18,320 per year), 49 teaching assistantships with full tuition reimbursements available (averaging $18,320 per year); career-related internships or fieldwork, Federal Work-Study, scholarships/grants, tuition waivers (full), and unspecified assistantships also available. Support available to part-time students. Financial award application deadline: 1/15; financial award applicants required to submit FAFSA. *Faculty research:* Signal processing and sensor data fusion, plasma science, sensing and imaging, power electronics, computer engineering. *Unit head:* Dr. Ali Abur, Chairman, 617-373-4159, Fax: 617-373-8970. *Application contact:* Stephen L. Gibson, Associate Director, 617-373-2711, Fax: 617-373-2501, E-mail: grad-eng@coe.neu.edu.

Northwestern Polytechnic University, School of Engineering, Fremont, CA 94539-7482. Offers computer science (MS); computer systems engineering (MS); electrical engineering (MS). Part-time and evening/weekend programs available. *Degree requirements:* For master's, thesis optional. *Entrance requirements:* For master's, minimum GPA of 3.0. Additional exam requirements/recommendations for international students: Required—TOEFL (minimum score 550 paper-based; 213 computer-based; 79 iBT). *Faculty research:* Computer networking, database design, Internet technology, software engineering, digital signal processing.

Northwestern University, McCormick School of Engineering and Applied Science, Department of Electrical Engineering and Computer Science, Evanston, IL 60208. Offers computer science (MS, PhD); electrical and computer engineering (MS, PhD); electronic materials (MS, PhD,

Certificate); information technology (MIT). MS and PhD admissions and degrees offered through The Graduate School. Part-time programs available. Terminal master's awarded for partial completion of doctoral program. *Degree requirements:* For master's, thesis or project; for doctorate, thesis/dissertation. *Faculty research:* Solid-state engineering networks and communications, photonics, parallel and distributed computing, VLSI design and computer-aided design.

Oakland University, Graduate Study and Lifelong Learning, School of Engineering and Computer Science, Department of Computer Science and Engineering, Rochester, MI 48309-4401. Offers computer science (MS); embedded systems (MS); information systems engineering (MS); software engineering (MS). Part-time and evening/weekend programs available. *Entrance requirements:* For master's, minimum GPA of 3.0 for unconditional admission. Electronic applications accepted. *Expenses:* Contact institution. *Faculty research:* Cyber security, 3D imaging of neurochemicals in rat brains.

Oakland University, Graduate Study and Lifelong Learning, School of Engineering and Computer Science, Department of Electrical and Systems Engineering, Program in Electrical and Computer Engineering, Rochester, MI 48309-4401. Offers MS. Part-time and evening/weekend programs available. *Entrance requirements:* For master's, minimum GPA of 3.0 for unconditional admission. Additional exam requirements/recommendations for international students: Required—TOEFL (minimum score 550 paper-based; 213 computer-based). Electronic applications accepted. *Expenses:* Contact institution.

OGI School of Science & Engineering at Oregon Health & Science University, Graduate Studies, Department of Computer Science and Electrical Engineering, Beaverton, OR 97006-8921. Offers computer science (PhD); computer science and engineering (MS, PhD); electrical engineering (MS, PhD). Part-time and evening/weekend programs available. Terminal master's awarded for partial completion of doctoral program. *Degree requirements:* For master's, thesis optional; for doctorate, comprehensive exam, oral defense of dissertation. *Entrance requirements:* For master's and doctorate, GRE General Test. Additional exam requirements/recommendations for international students: Required—TOEFL (minimum score 650 paper-based; 280 computer-based). Electronic applications accepted. *Faculty research:* Computer systems architecture, intelligent and interactive systems, programming models and systems, theory of computation.

The Ohio State University, Graduate School, College of Engineering, Department of Computer Science and Engineering, Columbus, OH 43210. Offers computer and information science (MS, PhD); computer science and engineering (MS). *Faculty:* 40. *Students:* 231 full-time (49 women), 65 part-time (11 women); includes 7 minority (1 African American, 4 Asian Americans or Pacific Islanders, 2 Hispanic Americans), 223 international. Average age 27. In 2009, 41 master's, 23 doctorates awarded. *Degree requirements:* For master's, thesis optional; for doctorate, thesis/dissertation. *Entrance requirements:* Additional exam requirements/recommendations for international students: Recommended—TOEFL (minimum score 600 paper-based; 250 computer-based). *Application deadline:* For fall admission, 8/15 priority date for domestic students, 7/1 priority date for international students; for winter admission, 12/1 priority date for domestic students, 11/1 priority date for international students; for spring admission, 3/1 priority date for domestic students, 2/1 priority date for international students. Applications are processed on a rolling basis. Application fee: $40 ($50 for international students). Electronic applications accepted. *Expenses:* Tuition, state resident: full-time $10,683. Tuition, nonresident: full-time $25,923. Tuition and fees vary according to course load and program. *Financial support:* Fellowships, teaching assistantships, career-related internships or fieldwork, Federal Work-Study, institutionally sponsored loans, and administrative assistantships available. Support available to part-time students. Financial award application deadline: 1/15. *Application contact:* 614-292-9444, Fax: 614-292-3895, E-mail: domestic.grad@osu.edu.

Oklahoma State University, College of Engineering, Architecture and Technology, School of Electrical and Computer Engineering, Stillwater, OK 74078. Offers MS, PhD. Postbaccalaureate distance learning degree programs offered. *Faculty:* 25 full-time (2 women), 2 part-time/adjunct (0 women). *Students:* 92 full-time (17 women), 95 part-time (13 women); includes 14 minority (2 African Americans, 3 American Indian/Alaska Native, 6 Asian Americans or Pacific Islanders, 3 Hispanic Americans), 129 international. Average age 28. 455 applicants, 29% accepted, 43 enrolled. In 2009, 42 master's, 5 doctorates awarded. *Degree requirements:* For master's, thesis or alternative; for doctorate, comprehensive exam, thesis/dissertation. *Entrance requirements:* For master's and doctorate, GRE or GMAT. Additional exam requirements/recommendations for international students: Required—TOEFL (minimum score 550 paper-based; 79 iBT). *Application deadline:* For fall admission, 3/1 priority date for international students; for spring admission, 8/1 priority date for international students. Applications are processed on a rolling basis. Application fee: $40 ($75 for international students). Electronic applications accepted. *Expenses:* Tuition, state resident: full-time $3716; part-time $154.85 per credit hour. Tuition, nonresident: full-time $14,448; part-time $602 per credit hour. Required fees: $1772; $73.85 per credit hour. One-time fee: $50. Tuition and fees vary according to course load and campus/location. *Financial support:* In 2009–10, 53 research assistantships (averaging $9,883 per year), 33 teaching assistantships (averaging $8,112 per year) were awarded; career-related internships or fieldwork, Federal Work-Study, scholarships/grants, health care benefits, tuition waivers (partial), and unspecified assistantships also available. Support available to part-time students. Financial award application deadline: 3/1; financial award applicants required to submit FAFSA. *Unit head:* Dr. Keith Teague, Head, 405-744-5151, Fax: 405-744-9198. *Application contact:* Dr. Gordon Emslie, Dean, 405-744-6368, Fax: 405-744-0355, E-mail: grad-i@okstate.edu.

Old Dominion University, Frank Batten College of Engineering and Technology, Program in Electrical and Computer Engineering, Norfolk, VA 23529. Offers ME, MS, PhD. Part-time programs available. Postbaccalaureate distance learning degree programs offered (minimal on-campus study). *Faculty:* 25 full-time (1 woman), 2 part-time/adjunct (1 woman). *Students:* 65 full-time (13 women), 64 part-time (20 women); includes 12 minority (3 African Americans, 1 American Indian/Alaska Native, 8 Asian Americans or Pacific Islanders), 86 international. Average age 29. 15 applicants, 73% accepted, 4 enrolled. In 2009, 39 master's, 5 doctorates awarded. *Degree requirements:* For doctorate, thesis/dissertation, candidacy exam, diagnostic exam. *Entrance requirements:* For doctorate, GRE. Additional exam requirements/recommendations for international students: Required—TOEFL. *Application deadline:* For fall admission, 6/1 for domestic students, 4/15 for international students; for spring admission, 11/1 for domestic students, 10/1 for international students. Applications are processed on a rolling basis. Application fee: $40. Electronic applications accepted. *Expenses:* Tuition, state resident: full-time $8112; part-time $338 per credit. Tuition, nonresident: full-time $20,256; part-time $844 per credit. Required fees: $119 per semester. One-time fee: $50. *Financial support:* In 2009–10, 3 fellowships with full tuition reimbursements (averaging $15,000 per year), 38 research assistantships with full and partial tuition reimbursements (averaging $15,000 per year), 41 teaching assistantships with full and partial tuition reimbursements (averaging $15,000 per year) were awarded; career-related internships or fieldwork, Federal Work-Study, scholarships/grants, tuition waivers (partial), and unspecified assistantships also available. Support available to part-time students. Financial award application deadline: 2/15; financial award applicants required to submit FAFSA. *Faculty research:* Digital signal processing, control engineering, gaseous electronics, ultrafast (femtosecom) laser applications, interaction of fields with living organisms. Total annual research expenditures: $3 million. *Unit head:* Dr. Sach Albin, Graduate Program Director, 757-683-4967, Fax: 757-683-3220, E-mail: ecegpd@odu.edu. *Application contact:* Dr. Linda Vahala, Associate Dean, 757-683-3789, Fax: 757-683-4898, E-mail: lvahala@odu.edu.

Oregon Health & Science University, OGI School of Science and Engineering, Department of Computer Science and Engineering, Portland, OR 97239-3098. Offers computer science and engineering (MS, PhD); electrical engineering (MS, PhD). Tuition and fees vary according to course level, course load, degree level, program and reciprocity agreements.

Oregon State University, Graduate School, College of Engineering, School of Electrical Engineering and Computer Science, Corvallis, OR 97331. Offers computer science (M Eng, MAIS, MS, PhD); electrical and computer engineering (M Eng, MS, PhD). *Faculty:* 38 full-time (6 women), 5 part-time/adjunct (3 women). *Students:* 216 full-time (41 women), 52 part-time (6 women); includes 24 minority (2 African Americans, 19 Asian Americans or Pacific Islanders, 3 Hispanic Americans), 149 international. Average age 29. In 2009, 48 master's, 15 doctorates awarded. *Degree requirements:* For doctorate, thesis/dissertation, qualifying exam, preliminary exam. *Entrance requirements:* For master's and doctorate, minimum GPA of 3.0 in last 90 hours of course work. Additional exam requirements/recommendations for international students: Required—TOEFL (minimum score 600 paper-based; 250 computer-based; 80 iBT). *Application deadline:* For fall admission, 1/15 for domestic and international students. Application fee: $50. Electronic applications accepted. *Expenses:* Tuition, state resident: full-time $9774; part-time $362 per credit. Tuition, nonresident: full-time $15,849; part-time $587 per credit. Required fees: $1639. Full-time tuition and fees vary according to course load and program. *Financial support:* Fellowships with full tuition reimbursements, research assistantships with full tuition reimbursements, teaching assistantships with full tuition reimbursements, career-related internships or fieldwork, Federal Work-Study, and institutionally sponsored loans available. Support available to part-time students. Financial award application deadline: 1/15. *Faculty research:* Optical materials and devices, data security and cryptography, analog and mixed-signal integrated circuit design, algorithms, computer graphics and vision. Total annual research expenditures: $7.5 million. *Unit head:* Dr. Theresa Shreeve Fiez, Director, 541-737-3118, Fax: 541-737-1300, E-mail: terri@eecs.oregonstate.edu. *Application contact:* Ferne Simendinger, Graduate Coordinator, 541-737-3617, Fax: 541-737-1300, E-mail: ferne@eecs.oregonstate.edu.

Penn State University Park, Graduate School, College of Engineering, Department of Computer Science and Engineering, State College, University Park, PA 16802-1503. Offers M Eng, MS, PhD.

See Close-Up on page 305.

Polytechnic Institute of NYU, Department of Electrical and Computer Engineering, Major in Computer Engineering, Brooklyn, NY 11201-2990. Offers MS, Certificate. *Students:* 25 full-time (2 women), 20 part-time (2 women); includes 9 minority (1 African American, 8 Asian Americans or Pacific Islanders), 28 international. 88 applicants, 74% accepted, 17 enrolled. In 2009, 19 master's awarded. *Degree requirements:* For master's, comprehensive exam (for some programs), thesis (for some programs). *Entrance requirements:* For master's, BS in electrical engineering. Additional exam requirements/recommendations for international students: Required—TOEFL (minimum score 550 paper-based; 213 computer-based; 80 iBT); Recommended—IELTS (minimum score 6.5). *Application deadline:* For fall admission, 7/31 priority date for domestic students, 4/30 priority date for international students; for spring admission, 12/31 priority date for domestic students, 11/30 priority date for international students. Applications are processed on a rolling basis. Application fee: $75. Electronic applications accepted. *Expenses:* Tuition: Full-time $21,492; part-time $1194 per credit hour. Required fees: $1160; $204 per course. *Financial support:* Applicants required to submit FAFSA. *Unit head:* Dr. Jonathan Chao, Head, 718-860-3478, Fax: 718-260-3302, E-mail: chao@poly.edu. *Application contact:* JeanCarlo Bonilla, Director of Graduate Enrollment Management, 718-260-3182, Fax: 718-260-3624.

Polytechnic Institute of NYU, Long Island Graduate Center, Graduate Programs, Department of Electrical and Computer Engineering, Major in Computer Engineering, Melville, NY 11747. Offers MS. *Students:* 2 full-time (1 woman), 4 part-time (1 woman); includes 1 minority (African American), 2 international. In 2009, 1 master's awarded. *Degree requirements:* For master's, comprehensive exam (for some programs), thesis (for some programs). *Entrance requirements:* Additional exam requirements/recommendations for international students: Required—TOEFL (minimum score 550 paper-based; 213 computer-based; 80 iBT); Recommended—IELTS (minimum score 6.5). *Application deadline:* For fall admission, 7/31 priority date for domestic students, 4/30 priority date for international students; for spring admission, 12/31 priority date for domestic students, 11/30 priority date for international students. Applications are processed on a rolling basis. Application fee: $75. Electronic applications accepted. *Financial support:* Institutionally sponsored loans, scholarships/grants, and unspecified assistantships available. Support available to part-time students. *Unit head:* Dr. Jonathan Chao, Department Head, 718-260-3302, E-mail: chao@poly.edu. *Application contact:* JeanCarlo Bonilla, Director of Graduate Enrollment Management, 718-260-3182, Fax: 718-260-3624, E-mail: gradinfo@poly.edu.

Polytechnic Institute of NYU, Westchester Graduate Center, Graduate Programs, Department of Electrical and Computer Engineering, Major in Computer Engineering, Hawthorne, NY 10532-1507. Offers MS. *Degree requirements:* For master's, comprehensive exam (for some programs), thesis (for some programs). *Entrance requirements:* Additional exam requirements/recommendations for international students: Required—TOEFL (minimum score 550 paper-based; 213 computer-based; 80 iBT); Recommended—IELTS (minimum score 6.5). *Application deadline:* For fall admission, 7/31 priority date for domestic students, 4/30 priority date for international students; for spring admission, 12/31 priority date for domestic students, 11/30 priority date for international students. Applications are processed on a rolling basis. Application fee: $75. Electronic applications accepted. *Financial support:* Institutionally sponsored loans, scholarships/grants, and unspecified assistantships available. Support available to part-time students. Financial award applicants required to submit FAFSA. *Unit head:* Dr. Jonathan Chao, Department Head, 718-260-3302, E-mail: chao@poly.edu. *Application contact:* JeanCarlo Bonilla, Director of Graduate Enrollment Management, 718-260-3182, Fax: 718-260-3624, E-mail: gradinfo@poly.edu.

Polytechnic University of Puerto Rico, Graduate School, Hato Rey, PR 00919. Offers business administration (MBA), including general studies, management of information systems, management of international enterprises; civil engineering (ME, MS); computer engineering (ME, MS); computer science (MS); electrical engineering (ME, MS); engineering management (MEM); environmental management (MEPM); landscape architecture (M Land Arch); manufacturing competitiveness (MMC, MS); manufacturing engineering (ME, MS). Part-time and evening/weekend programs available. *Entrance requirements:* For master's, 3 letters of recommendation.

Polytechnic University of the Americas–Orlando Campus, Graduate School, Winter Park, FL 32792. Offers business administration (MBA); civil engineering (MS); computer engineering (MS); electrical engineering (MS); engineering management (MEM). Part-time and evening/weekend programs available. Postbaccalaureate distance learning degree programs offered (no on-campus study). *Entrance requirements:* For master's, minimum GPA of 3.0. Electronic applications accepted.

Portland State University, Graduate Studies, Maseeh College of Engineering and Computer Science, Department of Electrical and Computer Engineering, Portland, OR 97207-0751. Offers M Eng, MS, PhD. Part-time and evening/weekend programs available. *Degree requirements:* For master's, variable foreign language requirement, oral exam; for doctorate, one foreign language, comprehensive exam, thesis/dissertation, oral and written exams. *Entrance requirements:* For master's, minimum GPA of 3.0 in upper-division course work or 2.75 overall, BS in electrical or computer engineering or allied field; for doctorate, GRE General Test, GRE Subject Test, minimum GPA of 3.0 in upper-division course work, MS in electrical engineering or allied field. Additional exam requirements/recommendations for international students: Required—TOEFL (minimum score 550 paper-based; 213 computer-based). *Faculty research:* Optics and laser systems, design automation, VLSI design, computer systems, power electronics.

Purdue University, College of Engineering, School of Electrical and Computer Engineering, West Lafayette, IN 47907-2035. Offers MS, MSE, MSECE, PhD. MS and PhD degree programs in biomedical engineering offered jointly with School of Mechanical Engineering and School of Chemical Engineering. Part-time programs available. Postbaccalaureate distance learning degree programs offered (no on-campus study). Terminal master's awarded for partial completion of doctoral program. *Entrance requirements:* For master's and doctorate, GRE General Test,

Computer Engineering

Purdue University (continued)
minimum GPA of 3.25. Additional exam requirements/recommendations for international students: Required—TOEFL (minimum score 550 paper-based; 213 computer-based; 77 iBT). Electronic applications accepted. *Faculty research:* Automatic controls; biomedical imaging; computer engineering; communications, networking signal and image processing; fields and optics.

Purdue University Calumet, Graduate School, School of Engineering, Mathematics, and Science, Department of Engineering, Hammond, IN 46323-2094. Offers computer engineering (MSE); electrical engineering (MSE); engineering (MS); mechanical engineering (MSE). Evening/weekend programs available. *Entrance requirements:* Additional exam requirements/recommendations for international students: Required—TOEFL.

Queen's University at Kingston, School of Graduate Studies and Research, Faculty of Applied Science, Department of Electrical and Computer Engineering, Kingston, ON K7L 3N6, Canada. Offers M Eng, M Sc, M Sc Eng, PhD. Part-time programs available. *Degree requirements:* For master's, thesis optional; for doctorate, comprehensive exam, thesis/dissertation. *Entrance requirements:* Additional exam requirements/recommendations for international students: Required—TOEFL (minimum score 580 paper-based; 237 computer-based). *Faculty research:* Communications and signal processing systems, computer engineering systems.

Rensselaer at Hartford, Department of Engineering, Program in Computer and Systems Engineering, Hartford, CT 06120-2991. Offers ME. *Faculty:* 2 full-time (0 women), 2 part-time/adjunct (0 women). *Students:* 21 part-time (3 women); includes 6 minority (1 African American, 1 Asian American or Pacific Islander, 4 Hispanic Americans). Average age 34. 8 applicants, 75% accepted, 6 enrolled. In 2009, 5 master's awarded. *Entrance requirements:* For master's, GRE. *Application deadline:* For fall admission, 8/30 priority date for domestic students, 8/1 for international students. Application fee: $75. *Expenses:* Tuition: Full-time $31,800; part-time $1325 per credit hour. *Unit head:* Dr. Ernesto Gutierrez-Miravete, 860-548-2464, E-mail: gutiee@rpi.edu. *Application contact:* Kristin Galligan, Director, Enrollment Management and Marketing, 860-548-2480, Fax: 860-548-7823, E-mail: info@ewp.rpi.edu.

Rensselaer Polytechnic Institute, Graduate School, School of Engineering, Department of Electrical, Computer, and Systems Engineering, Program in Computer and Systems Engineering, Troy, NY 12180-3590. Offers M Eng, MS, PhD. Part-time programs available. *Faculty:* 48 full-time (5 women), 7 part-time/adjunct (1 woman). *Students:* 10 full-time (0 women), 2 part-time (1 woman); includes 1 Hispanic American. 84 applicants, 26% accepted, 12 enrolled. In 2009, 18 master's, 3 doctorates awarded. Terminal master's awarded for partial completion of doctoral program. *Degree requirements:* For master's, thesis (for some programs); for doctorate, thesis/dissertation. *Entrance requirements:* For master's, GRE; for doctorate, GRE, qualifying exam, candidacy exam. Additional exam requirements/recommendations for international students: Required—TOEFL (minimum score 570 paper-based; 89 iBT). *Application deadline:* For fall admission, 1/15 priority date for domestic and international students; for spring admission, 8/15 priority date for domestic and international students. Applications are processed on a rolling basis. Application fee: $75. Electronic applications accepted. *Expenses:* Tuition: Full-time $38,100. *Financial support:* In 2009–10, 7 fellowships with full tuition reimbursements (averaging $21,000 per year), 88 research assistantships with full tuition reimbursements (averaging $20,000 per year), 41 teaching assistantships (averaging $16,500 per year) were awarded; career-related internships or fieldwork, institutionally sponsored loans, and unspecified assistantships also available. Financial award application deadline: 1/15. *Faculty research:* Multimedia via ATM, mobile robotics, thermophotovoltaic devices, microelectronic interconnections, agile manufacturing. Total annual research expenditures: $3.7 million. *Unit head:* Dr. Kim L. Boyer, Head, 518-276-2150, Fax: 518-276-6261, E-mail: kim@ecse.rpi.edu. *Application contact:* Ann Bruno, Manager of Student Services and Graduate Enrollment, 518-276-2554, Fax: 518-276-4403, E-mail: ann@ecse.rpi.edu.

Rice University, Graduate Programs, George R. Brown School of Engineering, Department of Electrical and Computer Engineering, Houston, TX 77251-1892. Offers bioengineering (MS, PhD); circuits, controls, and communication systems (MS, PhD); computer science and engineering (MS, PhD); electrical engineering (MEE); lasers, microwaves, and solid-state electronics (MS, PhD); MBA/MEE. Part-time programs available. *Degree requirements:* For master's, thesis (for some programs); for doctorate, thesis/dissertation. *Entrance requirements:* For master's and doctorate, GRE General Test, GRE Subject Test, minimum GPA of 3.0. Additional exam requirements/recommendations for international students: Required—TOEFL (minimum score 600 paper-based; 250 computer-based; 90 iBT). Electronic applications accepted. *Faculty research:* Physical electronics, systems, computer engineering, bioengineering.

Rice University, Graduate Programs, George R. Brown School of Engineering, Program in Computational Science and Engineering, Houston, TX 77251-1892. Offers MCSE.

Rochester Institute of Technology, Graduate Enrollment Services, Kate Gleason College of Engineering, Department of Computer Engineering, Rochester, NY 14623-5603. Offers MS. Part-time programs available. *Students:* 29 full-time (4 women), 11 part-time (0 women); includes 4 minority (all Asian Americans or Pacific Islanders), 10 international. Average age 24. 92 applicants, 45% accepted, 10 enrolled. In 2009, 25 master's awarded. *Degree requirements:* For master's, thesis. *Entrance requirements:* For master's, GRE, minimum GPA of 3.0. Additional exam requirements/recommendations for international students: Required—TOEFL (minimum score 570 paper-based; 230 computer-based; 88 iBT), or IELTS (minimum score 6.5). *Application deadline:* For fall admission, 2/15 priority date for domestic and international students; for winter admission, 10/15 for domestic students, 10/15 priority date for international students. Applications are processed on a rolling basis. Application fee: $50. *Expenses:* Tuition: Full-time $31,533; part-time $876 per credit hour. Required fees: $210. *Financial support:* In 2009–10, 36 students received support; fellowships with partial tuition reimbursements available, research assistantships with partial tuition reimbursements available, teaching assistantships with partial tuition reimbursements available, career-related internships or fieldwork, institutionally sponsored loans, scholarships/grants, and unspecified assistantships available. Support available to part-time students. Financial award applicants required to submit FAFSA. *Faculty research:* Object detection and tracking using multiple cameras; face detection and recognition; pose and gaze estimation; activity recognition; power constrained processing; lossless image compression; color forms processing; adaptive thresholding; automatic albuming; MPEG-7 color, shape and motion descriptors, Web printing. *Unit head:* Dr. Andreas Savakis, Department Head, 585-475-2987, Fax: 585-475-4084, E-mail: andreas.savakis@rit.edu. *Application contact:* Diane Ellison, Assistant Vice President, Graduate Enrollment Services, 585-475-2229, Fax: 585-475-7164, E-mail: gradinfo@rit.edu.

Rose-Hulman Institute of Technology, Faculty of Engineering and Applied Sciences, Department of Electrical and Computer Engineering, Terre Haute, IN 47803-3999. Offers electrical and computer engineering (M Eng); electrical engineering (MS). Part-time programs available. Postbaccalaureate distance learning degree programs offered (minimal on-campus study). *Faculty:* 18 full-time (4 women), 1 (woman) part-time/adjunct. *Students:* 16 full-time (4 women), 2 part-time (0 women); includes 1 minority (Hispanic American), 8 international. Average age 24. 25 applicants, 88% accepted, 12 enrolled. In 2009, 5 master's awarded. *Degree requirements:* For master's, thesis (for some programs). *Entrance requirements:* For master's, GRE, minimum GPA of 3.0. Additional exam requirements/recommendations for international students: Required—TOEFL (minimum score 580 paper-based; 237 computer-based; 92 iBT). *Application deadline:* For fall admission, 2/1 priority date for domestic students. Applications are processed on a rolling basis. Application fee: $0. *Expenses:* Tuition: Full-time $33,900; part-time $987 per credit hour. *Financial support:* In 2009–10, 8 students received support; fellowships with full and partial tuition reimbursements available, research assistantships with full and partial tuition reimbursements available, institutionally sponsored loans, scholarships/grants, and tuition waivers (full and partial) available. *Faculty research:* Wireless systems, VLSI design, aerial robotics, power system dynamics and control, image and speech processing. Total annual research expenditures: $430,205. *Unit head:* Dr. Frederick Berry, Chairman, 812-877-8105, Fax: 812-877-8895, E-mail: frederick.berry@rose-hulman.edu. *Application contact:* Dr. Daniel J. Moore, Associate Dean of the Faculty, 812-877-8110, Fax: 812-877-8061, E-mail: daniel.j.moore@rose-hulman.edu.

Royal Military College of Canada, Division of Graduate Studies and Research, Engineering Division, Department of Electrical and Computer Engineering, Kingston, ON K7K 7B4, Canada. Offers computer engineering (M Eng, PhD); electrical engineering (M Eng, PhD); software engineering (M Eng, PhD). *Degree requirements:* For master's, thesis; for doctorate, comprehensive exam, thesis/dissertation. *Entrance requirements:* For master's, honours degree with second-class standing in the appropriate field; for doctorate, master's degree. Electronic applications accepted.

Rutgers, The State University of New Jersey, New Brunswick, Graduate School-New Brunswick, Program in Electrical and Computer Engineering, Piscataway, NJ 08854-8097. Offers communications and solid-state electronics (MS, PhD); computer engineering (MS, PhD); control systems (MS, PhD); digital signal processing (MS, PhD). Part-time programs available. Terminal master's awarded for partial completion of doctoral program. *Degree requirements:* For master's, thesis or alternative; for doctorate, thesis/dissertation. *Entrance requirements:* For master's and doctorate, GRE General Test. Additional exam requirements/recommendations for international students: Required—TOEFL. Electronic applications accepted. *Faculty research:* Communication and information processing, wireless information networks, micro-vacuum devices, machine vision, VLSI design.

See Close-Up on page 373.

St. Mary's University, Graduate School, Department of Engineering, Program in Electrical Engineering, San Antonio, TX 78228-8507. Offers electrical engineering (MS); electrical/computer engineering (MS). Part-time programs available. *Degree requirements:* For master's, comprehensive exam. *Entrance requirements:* For master's, GRE General Test. Additional exam requirements/recommendations for international students: Required—TOEFL (minimum score 550 paper-based; 213 computer-based; 80 iBT). Electronic applications accepted. *Expenses:* Tuition: Full-time $8004. Required fees: $536. One-time fee: $5 full-time. Full-time tuition and fees vary according to program. *Faculty research:* Image processing, control, communication, artificial intelligence, robotics.

San Jose State University, Graduate Studies and Research, Charles W. Davidson College of Engineering, Department of Computer Engineering, San Jose, CA 95192-0001. Offers computer engineering (MS); software engineering (MS). *Students:* 357 full-time (112 women), 320 part-time (143 women); includes 102 minority (3 African Americans, 94 Asian Americans or Pacific Islanders, 5 Hispanic Americans), 542 international. Average age 27. 688 applicants, 56% accepted, 185 enrolled. In 2009, 474 master's awarded. *Degree requirements:* For master's, comprehensive exam, thesis. *Entrance requirements:* For master's, GRE General Test. *Application deadline:* For fall admission, 6/29 for domestic students; for spring admission, 11/30 for domestic students. Applications are processed on a rolling basis. Application fee: $59. Electronic applications accepted. *Financial support:* Teaching assistantships, career-related internships or fieldwork, Federal Work-Study, and institutionally sponsored loans available. Support available to part-time students. Financial award application deadline: 5/1; financial award applicants required to submit FAFSA. *Faculty research:* Robotics, database management systems, computer networks. *Unit head:* Dr. Sigurd Meldal, Chair, 408-924-4150. *Application contact:* Dr. Sigurd Meldal, Chair, 408-924-4150.

Santa Clara University, School of Engineering, Department of Computer Science and Engineering, Santa Clara, CA 95053. Offers computer science and engineering (MS, PhD, Engineer); information assurance (Certificate); networking (Certificate); software engineering (MS, Certificate). Part-time and evening/weekend programs available. *Students:* 91 full-time (33 women), 98 part-time (26 women); includes 44 minority (3 African Americans, 39 Asian Americans or Pacific Islanders, 2 Hispanic Americans), 110 international. Average age 29. In 2009, 41 master's awarded. *Degree requirements:* For master's, thesis (for some programs); for doctorate, thesis/dissertation; for other advanced degree, thesis. *Entrance requirements:* For master's, GRE (waiver may be available); for doctorate, GRE, master's degree or equivalent; for other advanced degree, master's degree, published paper. Additional exam requirements/recommendations for international students: Required—TOEFL (minimum score 550 paper-based; 213 computer-based; 79 iBT). *Application deadline:* For fall admission, 8/13 for domestic students, 7/16 for international students; for winter admission, 10/29 for domestic students, 9/24 for international students; for spring admission, 2/25 for domestic students, 1/21 for international students. Applications are processed on a rolling basis. Application fee: $60. *Expenses:* Contact institution. *Financial support:* Research assistantships, teaching assistantships available. Financial award application deadline: 3/2; financial award applicants required to submit FAFSA. *Unit head:* Dr. Alex Zecevic, Chair, 408-554-2394, E-mail: azecevic@scu.edu. *Application contact:* Stacey Tinker, Director of Enrollment Management, 408-554-4748, Fax: 408-554-4323, E-mail: stinker@scu.edu.

Silicon Valley University, Graduate Programs, San Jose, CA 95131. Offers business administration (MBA); computer engineering (MSCE); computer science (MSCS). *Degree requirements:* For master's, project (MSCS).

Southern Illinois University Carbondale, Graduate School, College of Engineering, Department of Electrical and Computer Engineering, Carbondale, IL 62901-4701. Offers MS, PhD. *Degree requirements:* For master's, comprehensive exam, thesis. *Entrance requirements:* For master's, minimum GPA of 2.7. Additional exam requirements/recommendations for international students: Required—TOEFL. *Faculty research:* Circuits and power systems, communications and signal processing, controls and systems, electromagnetics and optics, electronics instrumentation and bioengineering.

Southern Methodist University, Bobby B. Lyle School of Engineering, Department of Computer Science and Engineering, Dallas, TX 75275-0122. Offers computer engineering (MS Cp E, PhD); computer science (MS, PhD); security engineering (MS); software engineering (MS). Part-time and evening/weekend programs available. Postbaccalaureate distance learning degree programs offered (no on-campus study). *Faculty:* 13 full-time (2 women), 18 part-time/adjunct (1 woman). *Students:* 40 full-time (12 women), 167 part-time (22 women); includes 63 minority (18 African Americans, 28 Asian Americans or Pacific Islanders, 17 Hispanic Americans), 41 international. Average age 33. 180 applicants, 73% accepted, 69 enrolled. In 2009, 53 master's, 2 doctorates awarded. Terminal master's awarded for partial completion of doctoral program. *Degree requirements:* For master's, thesis optional; for doctorate, thesis/dissertation, oral and written qualifying exams, oral final exam (PhD). *Entrance requirements:* For master's, GRE General Test, minimum GPA of 3.0 in last 2 years; bachelor's degree in engineering, mathematics, or sciences; for doctorate, preliminary counseling exam (PhD), minimum GPA of 3.0, bachelor's degree in related field, MA (DE). Additional exam requirements/recommendations for international students: Required—TOEFL (minimum score 550 paper-based; 213 computer-based). *Application deadline:* For fall admission, 7/1 priority date for domestic students, 5/15 for international students; for spring admission, 11/15 for domestic students, 9/1 for international students. Applications are processed on a rolling basis. Application fee: $75. *Financial support:* In 2009–10, 20 students received support, including 6 research assistantships with full tuition reimbursements available (averaging $14,400 per year), 14 teaching assistantships with full tuition reimbursements available (averaging $14,400 per year). Financial award application deadline: 3/31; financial award applicants required to submit FAFSA. *Faculty research:* Trusted and high performance network computing, software engineering and management, knowledge engineering and management, computer arithmetic, computer architecture and CAD. Total annual research expenditures: $366,537. *Unit head:* Dr. Suku Nair, Chair, 214-768-2856, Fax: 214-768-3085, E-mail: nair@lyle.smu.edu. *Application contact:* Marc Valerin, Director of Graduate and Executive Admissions, 214-768-3042, E-mail: valerin@engr.smu.edu.

Southern Polytechnic State University, School of Engineering Technology and Management, Department of Electrical and Computer Engineering Technology, Marietta, GA 30060-2896. Offers engineering technology/electrical (MS). Part-time and evening/weekend programs available. *Faculty:* 7 full-time (1 woman), 2 part-time/adjunct (0 women). *Students:* 24 full-time (3 women), 6 part-time (1 woman); includes 11 minority (4 African Americans, 1 American Indian/Alaska Native, 5 Asian Americans or Pacific Islanders, 1 Hispanic American), 12 international. Average age 29. 19 applicants, 84% accepted, 12 enrolled. In 2009, 10 master's awarded. *Degree requirements:* For master's, thesis. *Entrance requirements:* For master's, GRE (minimum score 500 quantitative/verbal/analytical), minimum GPA of 2.75. Additional exam requirements/recommendations for international students: Required—TOEFL (minimum score 550 paper-based; 213 computer-based; 79 iBT), IELTS (minimum score 6.5). *Application deadline:* For fall admission, 7/1 priority date for domestic students, 5/1 priority date for international students; for spring admission, 11/1 priority date for domestic students, 9/1 priority date for international students. Applications are processed on a rolling basis. Application fee: $20. Electronic applications accepted. *Expenses:* Tuition, state resident: full-time $2896; part-time $181 per credit hour. Tuition, nonresident: full-time $11,552; part-time $722 per credit hour. Required fees: $1096; $1096 per year. *Financial support:* In 2009–10, 5 students received support, including 4 teaching assistantships with partial tuition reimbursements available (averaging $3,000 per year); career-related internships or fieldwork, scholarships/grants, and unspecified assistantships also available. Support available to part-time students. Financial award application deadline: 5/1; financial award applicants required to submit FAFSA. *Faculty research:* Analog and digital communications, computer networking, analog and low power electronics design, control systems and digital signal processing, instrumentation (medical and industrial). *Unit head:* Dr. Austin Asgill, Chair, 678-915-7796, Fax: 678-915-7285, E-mail: aasgill@spsu.edu. *Application contact:* Nikki A. Palamiotis, Director of Graduate Studies, 678-915-4276, Fax: 678-915-7292, E-mail: npalamio@spsu.edu.

State University of New York at New Paltz, Graduate School, School of Science and Engineering, Department of Electrical and Computer Engineering, New Paltz, NY 12561. Offers electrical engineering (MS). Part-time and evening/weekend programs available. *Faculty:* 9 full-time (2 women), 3 part-time/adjunct (1 woman). *Students:* 88 full-time (20 women), 29 part-time (4 women); includes 3 minority (all Asian Americans or Pacific Islanders), 104 international. Average age 24. 115 applicants, 63% accepted, 24 enrolled. In 2009, 67 master's awarded. *Degree requirements:* For master's, comprehensive exam, thesis optional. *Entrance requirements:* For master's, GRE General Test, minimum GPA of 3.0. Additional exam requirements/recommendations for international students: Required—TOEFL (minimum score 550 paper-based; 213 computer-based; 80 iBT), IELTS (minimum score 6.5). *Application deadline:* For fall admission, 5/15 priority date for domestic students, 5/15 for international students; for spring admission, 11/15 for domestic and international students. Applications are processed on a rolling basis. Application fee: $50. Electronic applications accepted. *Financial support:* In 2009–10, 11 students received support. Tuition waivers (partial) available. *Unit head:* Dr. Baback Izadi, Chair, 845-257-3823, E-mail: bai@eng.newpaltz.edu. *Application contact:* Caroline Murphy, Graduate Admissions Advisor, 845-257-3285, Fax: 845-257-3284, E-mail: gradschool@newpaltz.edu.

Stevens Institute of Technology, Graduate School, Charles V. Schaefer Jr. School of Engineering, Department of Electrical and Computer Engineering, Program in Computer Engineering, Hoboken, NJ 07030. Offers computer engineering (PhD); computer systems (M Eng); data communications and networks (M Eng); digital signal processing (Certificate); digital systems design (M Eng); engineered software systems (M Eng); image processing and multimedia (M Eng); information system security (M Eng); information systems (M Eng); real-time and embedded systems (Certificate). Part-time and evening/weekend programs available. Terminal master's awarded for partial completion of doctoral program. *Degree requirements:* For doctorate, thesis/dissertation. *Entrance requirements:* For master's, doctorate, and Certificate, GRE. Additional exam requirements/recommendations for international students: Required—TOEFL. Electronic applications accepted. *Expenses:* Tuition: Full-time $9900; part-time $1100 per credit. Required fees: $286 per semester.

Stevens Institute of Technology, Graduate School, Charles V. Schaefer Jr. School of Engineering, Department of Mechanical Engineering, Program in Integrated Product Development, Hoboken, NJ 07030. Offers armament engineering (M Eng); computer and electrical engineering (M Eng); manufacturing technologies (M Eng); systems reliability and design (M Eng). *Expenses:* Tuition: Full-time $9900; part-time $1100 per credit. Required fees: $286 per semester.

Stony Brook University, State University of New York, Graduate School, College of Engineering and Applied Sciences, Department of Electrical and Computer Engineering, Program in Computer Engineering, Stony Brook, NY 11794. Offers MS, PhD. *Expenses:* Tuition, state resident: full-time $8370; part-time $349 per credit. Tuition, nonresident: full-time $13,250; part-time $552 per credit. Required fees: $933.

Stony Brook University, State University of New York, School of Professional Development, Stony Brook, NY 11794. Offers biology-grade 7-12 (MAT); chemistry-grade 7-12 (MAT); coaching (Graduate Certificate); computer integrated engineering (Graduate Certificate); earth science-grade 7-12 (MAT); educational computing (Graduate Certificate); educational leadership (Advanced Certificate); English-grade 7-12 (MAT); environmental management (Graduate Certificate); environmental/occupational health and safety (Graduate Certificate); French-grade 7-12 (MAT); German-grade 7-12 (MAT); human resource management (Graduate Certificate); information systems management (Graduate Certificate); Italian-grade 7-12 (MAT); liberal studies (MA); mathematics-grade 7-12 (MAT); operation research (Graduate Certificate); physics-grade 7-12 (MAT); school administration and supervision (Graduate Certificate); school building leadership (Graduate Certificate); school district administration (Graduate Certificate); school district business leadership (Advanced Certificate); school district leadership (Graduate Certificate); social science and the professions (MPS), including environmental waste management, human resource management; social studies-grade 7-12 (MAT); Spanish-grade 7-12 (MAT); waste management (Graduate Certificate). Part-time and evening/weekend programs available. Postbaccalaureate distance learning degree programs offered. *Faculty:* 5 full-time (3 women), 131 part-time/adjunct (53 women). *Students:* 317 full-time (187 women), 1,200 part-time (773 women); includes 187 minority (77 African Americans, 2 American Indian/Alaska Native, 22 Asian Americans or Pacific Islanders, 86 Hispanic Americans), 11 international. Average age 28. In 2009, 597 master's, 234 other advanced degrees awarded. *Degree requirements:* For master's, one foreign language, thesis or alternative. *Application deadline:* Applications are processed on a rolling basis. Application fee: $62. *Expenses:* Tuition, state resident: full-time $8370; part-time $349 per credit. Tuition, nonresident: full-time $13,250; part-time $552 per credit. Required fees: $933. *Financial support:* Fellowships, research assistantships, teaching assistantships, career-related internships or fieldwork available. Support available to part-time students. *Unit head:* Dr. Paul J. Edelson, Dean, 631-632-7052, Fax: 631-632-9046, E-mail: paul.edelson@stonybrook.edu. *Application contact:* Dr. Paul J. Edelson, Dean, 631-632-7052, Fax: 631-632-9046, E-mail: paul.edelson@stonybrook.edu.

Syracuse University, L. C. Smith College of Engineering and Computer Science, Program in Computer Engineering, Syracuse, NY 13244. Offers MS, CE. Part-time and evening/weekend programs available. *Students:* 119 full-time (18 women), 31 part-time (4 women); includes 3 minority (2 African Americans, 1 Asian American or Pacific Islander), 130 international. Average age 25. 93 applicants, 70% accepted, 17 enrolled. In 2009, 79 master's awarded. *Degree requirements:* For CE, thesis. *Entrance requirements:* For master's and CE, GRE General Test. Additional exam requirements/recommendations for international students: Required—TOEFL (minimum score 100 iBT). *Application deadline:* For fall admission, 6/1 priority date for domestic and international students. Applications are processed on a rolling basis. Application fee: $75. Electronic applications accepted. *Expenses:* Tuition: Full-time $26,808; part-time $1117 per credit. Required fees: $1024. *Financial support:* Fellowships with full tuition reimbursements, research assistantships with full tuition reimbursements, teaching assistantships with full tuition reimbursements, tuition waivers (partial) available. Financial award application deadline: 1/1. *Faculty research:* Hardware, software, computer applications. *Unit head:* Dr. Roger Chen, Program Director, 315-443-4179, E-mail: crchen@syr.edu. *Application contact:* Heather Paris, 315-443-2655, Fax: 315-443-2583, E-mail: hdparis@syr.edu.

Syracuse University, L. C. Smith College of Engineering and Computer Science, Program in Electrical and Computer Engineering, Syracuse, NY 13244. Offers PhD. *Students:* 38 full-time (11 women), 8 part-time (1 woman), 39 international. Average age 27. 122 applicants, 12% accepted, 10 enrolled. In 2009, 1 doctorate awarded. *Entrance requirements:* For doctorate, GRE General Test. Additional exam requirements/recommendations for international students: Required—TOEFL (minimum score 100 iBT). *Application deadline:* For fall admission, 6/1 priority date for domestic and international students. Application fee: $75. Electronic applications accepted. *Expenses:* Tuition: Full-time $26,808; part-time $1117 per credit. Required fees: $1024. *Financial support:* Fellowships with full tuition reimbursements, research assistantships with full and partial tuition reimbursements, teaching assistantships with full and partial tuition reimbursements, tuition waivers (partial) available. Financial award application deadline: 1/1. *Application contact:* Heather Paris, Information Contact, 315-443-2368, Fax: 315-443-2583, E-mail: hdparis@syr.edu.

Temple University, Graduate School, College of Engineering, Department of Electrical and Computer Engineering, Philadelphia, PA 19122-6096. Offers electrical engineering (MSE). Part-time and evening/weekend programs available. *Degree requirements:* For master's, thesis optional. *Entrance requirements:* For master's, GRE General Test, minimum GPA of 3.0. Additional exam requirements/recommendations for international students: Required—TOEFL (minimum score 550 paper-based; 213 computer-based; 79 iBT). Electronic applications accepted. *Faculty research:* Computer engineering, intelligent control, microprocessors, digital processing, neutral networks.

Texas A&M University, College of Engineering, Department of Computer Science, College Station, TX 77843. Offers computer engineering (M En, MS, PhD); computer science (MCS, MS, PhD). Part-time programs available. *Faculty:* 42. *Students:* 267 full-time (43 women), 43 part-time (8 women); includes 25 minority (6 African Americans, 2 American Indian/Alaska Native, 9 Asian Americans or Pacific Islanders, 8 Hispanic Americans), 211 international. Average age 28. In 2009, 30 master's, 20 doctorates awarded. *Degree requirements:* For master's, thesis (for some programs); for doctorate, thesis/dissertation. *Entrance requirements:* For master's and doctorate, GRE General Test. Additional exam requirements/recommendations for international students: Required—TOEFL (minimum score 213 computer-based). *Application deadline:* For fall admission, 3/1 priority date for domestic and international students; for spring admission, 8/1 priority date for domestic and international students. Applications are processed on a rolling basis. Application fee: $50 ($75 for international students). Electronic applications accepted. *Expenses:* Tuition, state resident: full-time $3991.32; part-time $221.74 per credit hour. Tuition, nonresident: full-time $9049; part-time $502.74 per credit hour. *Financial support:* In 2009–10, research assistantships with tuition reimbursements (averaging $15,478 per year), teaching assistantships (averaging $15,913 per year) were awarded; fellowships with full tuition reimbursements also available. Financial award application deadline: 3/1. *Faculty research:* Software, systems, informatics, human-centered systems, theory. *Unit head:* Dr. Hank Walker, Head, 979-845-5534, Fax: 979-847-8578, E-mail: walker@cse.tamu.edu. *Application contact:* Dr. Jianer Chen, Graduate Adviser, 979-845-8981, Fax: 979-862-3684, E-mail: grad-advisor@cs.tamu.edu.

Texas A&M University, College of Engineering, Department of Electrical and Computer Engineering, College Station, TX 77843. Offers computer engineering (M Eng, MS, PhD); electrical engineering (MS, PhD). *Faculty:* 64. *Students:* 484 full-time (65 women), 45 part-time (7 women); includes 42 minority (4 African Americans, 1 American Indian/Alaska Native, 19 Asian Americans or Pacific Islanders, 18 Hispanic Americans), 419 international. Average age 28. In 2009, 83 master's, 26 doctorates awarded. *Degree requirements:* For master's, thesis (MS); for doctorate, thesis/dissertation. *Entrance requirements:* For master's and doctorate, GRE General Test. Additional exam requirements/recommendations for international students: Required—TOEFL. Application fee: $50 ($75 for international students). *Expenses:* Tuition, state resident: full-time $3991.32; part-time $221.74 per credit hour. Tuition, nonresident: full-time $9049; part-time $502.74 per credit hour. *Financial support:* Fellowships, research assistantships, teaching assistantships, career-related internships or fieldwork available. Financial award application deadline: 4/1; financial award applicants required to submit FAFSA. *Faculty research:* Solid-state, electric power systems, and communications engineering. *Unit head:* Dr. Scott Miller, Head, 979-845-7441, E-mail: smiller@ece.tamu.edu. *Application contact:* Graduate Advisor, 979-845-7441.

The University of Akron, Graduate School, College of Engineering, Department of Electrical and Computer Engineering, Akron, OH 44325. Offers MS, PhD. Evening/weekend programs available. *Faculty:* 16 full-time (1 woman), 4 part-time/adjunct (0 women). *Students:* 44 full-time (9 women), 10 part-time (3 women); includes 1 minority (Asian American or Pacific Islander), 39 international. Average age 25. 148 applicants, 27% accepted, 21 enrolled. In 2009, 4 master's, 4 doctorates awarded. *Degree requirements:* For master's, oral comprehensive exam or thesis; for doctorate, one foreign language, thesis/dissertation, candidacy exam, qualifying exam. *Entrance requirements:* For master's, GRE, minimum GPA of 2.75, letters of recommendation; for doctorate, GRE, minimum GPA of 3.0 with bachelor's degree, 3.5 with master's degree; letters of recommendation; personal statement. Additional exam requirements/recommendations for international students: Required—TOEFL (minimum score 550 paper-based; 213 computer-based; 79 iBT). *Application deadline:* Applications are processed on a rolling basis. Application fee: $30 ($40 for international students). Electronic applications accepted. *Expenses:* Tuition, state resident: full-time $6570; part-time $365 per credit hour. Tuition, nonresident: full-time $11,250; part-time $625 per credit hour. *Financial support:* In 2009–10, 8 research assistantships with full tuition reimbursements, 34 teaching assistantships with full tuition reimbursements were awarded; career-related internships or fieldwork also available. *Faculty research:* Computational electromagnetics and nondestructive testing, control systems, sensors and actuators applications and networks, alternative energy systems and hybrid vehicles, analog IC design embedded systems. Total annual research expenditures: $446,688. *Unit head:* Dr. Jose De Abreu-Garcia, Chair, 330-972-6709, E-mail: jdeabreu-garcia@uakron.edu. *Application contact:* Dr. Jose De Abreu-Garcia, Chair, 330-972-6709, E-mail: jdeabreu-garcia@uakron.edu.

The University of Alabama, Graduate School, College of Engineering, Department of Electrical and Computer Engineering, Tuscaloosa, AL 35487-0286. Offers electrical engineering (MS, PhD). Part-time programs available. Postbaccalaureate distance learning degree programs offered (minimal on-campus study). *Faculty:* 14 full-time (4 women). *Students:* 39 full-time (6 women), 6 part-time (4 women); includes 1 minority (Asian American or Pacific Islander), 30 international. Average age 26. 81 applicants, 27% accepted, 8 enrolled. In 2009, 12 master's, 2 doctorates awarded. *Median time to degree:* Of those who began their doctoral program in fall 2001, 80% received their degree in 8 years or less. *Degree requirements:* For master's, thesis or alternative; for doctorate, one foreign language, comprehensive exam, thesis/dissertation. *Entrance requirements:* For master's, GRE (for students from non ABET accredited schools), minimum GPA of 3.0 in last 60 hours of course work or overall; for doctorate, GRE (for students from non ABET-accredited schools), minimum GPA of 3.0 overall. Additional exam requirements/recommendations for international students: Required—TOEFL (minimum score 550 paper-based; 213 computer-based). *Application deadline:* For fall admission, 7/1 priority date for domestic students, 1/15 priority date for international students; for spring admission, 11/1 priority date for domestic students, 6/1 priority date for international students. Applications are processed on a rolling basis. Application fee: $50 ($60 for international students). Electronic applications accepted. *Expenses:* Tuition, state resident: full-time $7000. Tuition, nonresident: full-time $19,200. *Financial support:* In 2009–10, 1 fellowship with full tuition reimbursement (averaging $15,000 per year), 14 research assistantships with full tuition reimbursements (averaging $14,000 per year), 6 teaching assistantships with full tuition reimbursements (averaging $11,025 per year) were awarded; health care benefits and unspecified assistantships also available. *Faculty research:* Devices and materials, electromechanical systems, embedded systems. Total annual research expenditures: $783,506.

Computer Engineering

The University of Alabama (continued)
Unit head: Dr. D. Jeff Jackson, Department Head, 205-348-2919, Fax: 205-348-6959, E-mail: jjackson@eng.ua.edu. *Application contact:* Dr. Tim Haskew, Graduate Program Director, 205-348-1766, Fax: 205-348-6959, E-mail: thaskew@eng.ua.edu.

The University of Alabama at Birmingham, School of Engineering, Program in Computer Engineering, Birmingham, AL 35294. Offers PhD.

The University of Alabama in Huntsville, School of Graduate Studies, College of Engineering, Department of Electrical and Computer Engineering, Huntsville, AL 35899. Offers computer engineering (MSE, PhD); electrical engineering (MSE, PhD); optical science and engineering (PhD); optics and photonics (MSE); software engineering (MSSE). Part-time and evening/weekend programs available. *Faculty:* 22 full-time (2 women), 3 part-time/adjunct (0 women). *Students:* 42 full-time (10 women), 147 part-time (18 women); includes 16 minority (7 African Americans, 6 Asian Americans or Pacific Islanders, 3 Hispanic Americans), 28 international. Average age 31. 205 applicants, 53% accepted, 58 enrolled. In 2009, 53 master's, 4 doctorates awarded. *Degree requirements:* For master's, comprehensive exam, thesis or alternative, oral and written exams; for doctorate, comprehensive exam, thesis/dissertation, oral and written exams. *Entrance requirements:* For master's, GRE General Test, appropriate bachelor's degree, minimum GPA of 3.0; for doctorate, GRE General Test, minimum GPA of 3.0. Additional exam requirements/recommendations for international students: Required—TOEFL (minimum score 500 paper-based; 173 computer-based; 62 iBT). *Application deadline:* For fall admission, 7/15 for domestic students, 4/1 for international students; for spring admission, 11/30 for domestic students, 9/1 for international students. Applications are processed on a rolling basis. Application fee: $40 ($50 for international students). Electronic applications accepted. *Expenses:* Tuition, state resident: part-time $355.75 per credit hour. Tuition, nonresident: part-time $847.10 per credit hour. Required fees: $210.80 per semester. Tuition and fees vary according to course load and program. *Financial support:* In 2009–10, 28 students received support, including 11 research assistantships with full and partial tuition reimbursements available (averaging $11,113 per year), 16 teaching assistantships with full and partial tuition reimbursements available (averaging $10,479 per year); career-related internships or fieldwork, Federal Work-Study, institutionally sponsored loans, scholarships/grants, health care benefits, tuition waivers, and unspecified assistantships also available. Support available to part-time students. Financial award application deadline: 4/1; financial award applicants required to submit FAFSA. *Faculty research:* Optical signal processing, electromagnetics, photonics, nonlinear waves, computer architecture. Total annual research expenditures: $3.4 million. *Unit head:* Dr. Reza Adhami, Chair, 256-824-6316, Fax: 256-824-6803, E-mail: adhami@ece.uah.edu. *Application contact:* Kathy Biggs, Graduate Studies Admissions Manager, 256-824-6199, Fax: 256-824-6405, E-mail: deangrad@uah.edu.

University of Alaska Fairbanks, College of Engineering and Mines, Department of Electrical and Computer Engineering, Fairbanks, AK 99775-5915. Offers electrical engineering (MEE, MS, PhD); engineering (PhD). Part-time programs available. *Faculty:* 7 full-time (2 women). *Students:* 14 full-time (3 women), 2 part-time (1 woman), 10 international. Average age 29. 11 applicants, 36% accepted, 4 enrolled. In 2009, 5 master's awarded. Terminal master's awarded for partial completion of doctoral program. *Degree requirements:* For master's, comprehensive exam, thesis or alternative; for doctorate, comprehensive exam, thesis/dissertation, oral exam, oral defense. *Entrance requirements:* For master's and doctorate, GRE General Test. Additional exam requirements/recommendations for international students: Required—TOEFL (minimum score 550 paper-based; 213 computer-based; 80 iBT). *Application deadline:* For fall admission, 6/1 for domestic students, 3/1 for international students; for spring admission, 10/15 for domestic students, 9/1 for international students. Applications are processed on a rolling basis. Application fee: $60. Electronic applications accepted. *Expenses:* Tuition, state resident: full-time $7584; part-time $316 per credit. Tuition, nonresident: full-time $15,504; part-time $646 per credit. Required fees: $23 per credit. $135 per semester. Tuition and fees vary according to course level, course load and reciprocity agreements. *Financial support:* In 2009–10, 2 fellowships (averaging $6,749 per year), 6 research assistantships (averaging $15,656 per year), 2 teaching assistantships (averaging $8,087 per year) were awarded; career-related internships or fieldwork, Federal Work-Study, scholarships/grants, health care benefits, and unspecified assistantships also available. Support available to part-time students. Financial award application deadline: 7/1; financial award applicants required to submit FAFSA. *Faculty research:* Geomagnetically-induced currents in power lines, electromagnetic wave propagation, laser radar systems, bioinformatics, distributed sensor networks. *Unit head:* Dr. Charles Mayer, Chair, 907-474-7137, Fax: 907-474-5135, E-mail: fyee@uaf.edu. *Application contact:* Dr. Charles Mayer, Chair, 907-474-7137, Fax: 907-474-5135, E-mail: fyee@uaf.edu.

University of Alberta, Faculty of Graduate Studies and Research, Department of Electrical and Computer Engineering, Edmonton, AB T6G 2E1, Canada. Offers communications (M Eng, M Sc, PhD); computer engineering (M Eng, M Sc, PhD); electromagnetics (M Eng, M Sc, PhD); nanotechnology and microdevices (M Eng, M Sc, PhD); power/power electronics (M Eng, M Sc, PhD); systems (M Eng, M Sc, PhD). *Faculty:* 42 full-time (3 women), 12 part-time/adjunct (0 women). *Students:* 252 full-time (28 women), 65 part-time (10 women). Average age 26. 1,500 applicants, 5% accepted. Terminal master's awarded for partial completion of doctoral program. *Degree requirements:* For master's, thesis; for doctorate, thesis/dissertation. *Entrance requirements:* Additional exam requirements/recommendations for international students: Required—TOEFL. *Application deadline:* For fall admission, 4/30 for domestic students; for winter admission, 8/30 for domestic students. Applications are processed on a rolling basis. Application fee: $0 Canadian dollars. Electronic applications accepted. Tuition and fees charges are reported in Canadian dollars. *Expenses:* Tuition, area resident: Full-time $4626.24 Canadian dollars; part-time $99.72 Canadian dollars per unit. International tuition: $8216 Canadian dollars full-time. Required fees: $3589.92 Canadian dollars; $99.72 Canadian dollars per unit. $215 Canadian dollars per term. *Financial support:* In 2009–10, 80 students received support; fellowships, research assistantships, teaching assistantships, scholarships/grants available. *Faculty research:* Controls, communications, microelectronics, electromagnetics. Total annual research expenditures: $3 million Canadian dollars. *Unit head:* Dr. H. J. Marquez, Chair, 780-492-0161, Fax: 780-492-1811. *Application contact:* Michelle Vaage, Graduate Student Advisor, 780-492-0161, Fax: 780-492-1811, E-mail: gradinfo@ece.ualberta.ca.

The University of Arizona, Graduate College, College of Engineering, Department of Electrical and Computer Engineering, Tucson, AZ 85721. Offers M Eng, MS, PhD. Part-time programs available. *Faculty:* 34. *Students:* 114 full-time (20 women), 59 part-time (10 women); includes 11 minority (8 Asian Americans or Pacific Islanders, 3 Hispanic Americans), 126 international. Average age 30. 514 applicants, 23% accepted, 38 enrolled. In 2009, 19 master's, 16 doctorates awarded. *Degree requirements:* For master's, thesis (for some programs); for doctorate, thesis/dissertation. *Entrance requirements:* For master's, GRE General Test, 3 letters of recommendation, statement of purpose; for doctorate, GRE General Test, master's degree in related field, 3 letters of recommendation, statement of purpose. Additional exam requirements/recommendations for international students: Required—TOEFL (minimum score 550 paper-based; 213 computer-based; 79 iBT). *Application deadline:* For fall admission, 12/15 for domestic and international students; for spring admission, 7/15 for domestic and international students. Applications are processed on a rolling basis. Application fee: $75. Electronic applications accepted. *Expenses:* Tuition, state resident: full-time $9028. Tuition, nonresident: full-time $24,890. *Financial support:* In 2009–10, 48 research assistantships with full tuition reimbursements (averaging $18,695 per year), 12 teaching assistantships with full tuition reimbursements (averaging $17,970 per year) were awarded; institutionally sponsored loans, scholarships/grants, health care benefits, and unspecified assistantships also available. Financial award application deadline: 3/15. *Faculty research:* Communication systems, control systems, signal processing, computer-aided logic. Total annual research expenditures: $7.1 million. *Unit head:* Dr. Jerzy W. Rozenblit, Head, 520-621-6193, E-mail: head@ece.arizona.edu. *Application contact:* Tami J. Whelan, Senior Graduate Academic Adviser, 520-621-6195, Fax: 520-621-8076, E-mail: whelan@ece.arizona.edu.

University of Arkansas, Graduate School, College of Engineering, Department of Computer Science and Computer Engineering, Program in Computer Engineering, Fayetteville, AR 72701-1201. Offers MS Cmp E, MSE, PhD. *Students:* 2 full-time (0 women), 22 part-time (1 woman); includes 2 minority (1 African American, 1 Hispanic American), 7 international. In 2009, 4 master's, 1 doctorate awarded. *Degree requirements:* For master's, thesis optional; for doctorate, one foreign language, thesis/dissertation. Application fee: $40 ($50 for international students). *Expenses:* Tuition, state resident: full-time $7355; part-time $356.58 per hour. Tuition, nonresident: full-time $17,401; part-time $775.17 per hour. Required fees: $1203. *Financial support:* In 2009–10, 2 fellowships with tuition reimbursements, 9 research assistantships, 9 teaching assistantships were awarded; career-related internships or fieldwork and Federal Work-Study also available. Support available to part-time students. Financial award application deadline: 4/1; financial award applicants required to submit FAFSA. *Unit head:* Dr. Susan Gauch, Departmental Chair, 479-575-6197, Fax: 479-575-5339, E-mail: sgauch@uark.edu. *Application contact:* Dr. Gordon Beavers, Graduate Coordinator, 479-575-6040, Fax: 479-575-5339, E-mail: gordonb@uark.edu.

University of Bridgeport, School of Engineering, Departments of Computer Science and Computer Engineering, Bridgeport, CT 06604. Offers computer engineering (MS); computer science (MS); computer science and engineering (PhD). *Degree requirements:* For master's, thesis optional; for doctorate, comprehensive exam, thesis/dissertation. *Entrance requirements:* Additional exam requirements/recommendations for international students: Recommended—TOEFL (minimum score 550 paper-based; 213 computer-based; 80 iBT), IELTS (minimum score 6.5). Electronic applications accepted.

The University of British Columbia, Faculty of Applied Science, Program in Electrical and Computer Engineering, Vancouver, BC V6T 1Z1, Canada. Offers M Eng, MA Sc, PhD. Part-time programs available. *Degree requirements:* For master's, thesis (for some programs); for doctorate, thesis/dissertation. *Entrance requirements:* Additional exam requirements/recommendations for international students: Required—TOEFL (minimum score 600 paper-based; 250 computer-based; 100 iBT), TWE. Electronic applications accepted. *Faculty research:* Applied electromagnetics, biomedical engineering, communications and signal processing, computer and software engineering, power engineering, robotics, solid-state, systems and control.

University of Calgary, Faculty of Graduate Studies, Schulich School of Engineering, Department of Electrical and Computer Engineering, Calgary, AB T2N 1N4, Canada. Offers M Eng, M Sc, PhD. Part-time programs available. *Degree requirements:* For master's, thesis (M Sc); for doctorate, thesis/dissertation, candidacy exam. *Entrance requirements:* For master's and doctorate, minimum GPA of 3.0. Additional exam requirements/recommendations for international students: Required—TOEFL (minimum score 550 paper-based; 213 computer-based), IELTS (minimum score 7), TOEFL or IELTS. Electronic applications accepted. *Faculty research:* Biomedical and bioelectrics, telecommunications and signal processing, software and computer engineering, power and control, microelectronics and instrumentation.

University of California, Davis, College of Engineering, Program in Electrical and Computer Engineering, Davis, CA 95616. Offers MS, PhD. Terminal master's awarded for partial completion of doctoral program. *Degree requirements:* For master's, comprehensive exam (for some programs), thesis (for some programs); for doctorate, thesis/dissertation, preliminary and qualifying exams, thesis defense. *Entrance requirements:* For master's, GRE General Test, minimum GPA of 3.2; for doctorate, GRE, minimum graduate GPA of 3.5. Additional exam requirements/recommendations for international students: Required—TOEFL (minimum score 550 paper-based; 213 computer-based). Electronic applications accepted.

University of California, Riverside, Graduate Division, Department of Electrical Engineering, Riverside, CA 92521-0102. Offers electrical engineering (MS, PhD), including computer engineering, control and robotics, intelligent systems, nano-materials, devices and circuits, signal processing and communications. Terminal master's awarded for partial completion of doctoral program. *Degree requirements:* For master's, thesis optional; for doctorate, thesis/dissertation, qualifying exams. *Entrance requirements:* For master's and doctorate, GRE General Test, minimum GPA of 3.25. Additional exam requirements/recommendations for international students: Required—TOEFL (minimum score 550 paper-based; 213 computer-based; 80 iBT). Electronic applications accepted. *Faculty research:* Solid state devices, integrated circuits, signal processing.

See Close-Up on page 375.

University of California, San Diego, Office of Graduate Studies, Department of Computer Science and Engineering, La Jolla, CA 92093. Offers computer engineering (MS, PhD); computer science (MS, PhD). *Degree requirements:* For doctorate, thesis/dissertation. *Entrance requirements:* For master's and doctorate, GRE General Test. Electronic applications accepted. *Faculty research:* Analysis of algorithms, combinatorial algorithms, discrete optimization.

See Close-Up on page 311.

University of California, San Diego, Office of Graduate Studies, Department of Electrical and Computer Engineering, La Jolla, CA 92093. Offers applied ocean science (MS, PhD); applied physics (MS, PhD); communication theory and systems (MS, PhD); computer engineering (MS, PhD); electrical engineering (M Eng); electronic circuits and systems (MS, PhD); intelligent systems, robotics and control (MS, PhD); photonics (MS, PhD); signal and image processing (MS, PhD). MS only offered to students who have been admitted to the PhD program. *Entrance requirements:* For master's and doctorate, GRE General Test. Electronic applications accepted.

University of California, San Diego, Office of Graduate Studies, Interdisciplinary Program in Cognitive Science, La Jolla, CA 92093. Offers cognitive science/anthropology (PhD); cognitive science/communication (PhD); cognitive science/computer science and engineering (PhD); cognitive science/linguistics (PhD); cognitive science/neuroscience (PhD); cognitive science/philosophy (PhD); cognitive science/psychology (PhD); cognitive science/sociology (PhD). Admissions offered through affiliated departments. *Degree requirements:* For doctorate, thesis/dissertation. *Entrance requirements:* For doctorate, GRE General Test, acceptance into one of the eight participating departments. *Faculty research:* Language and cognition, philosophy of mind, visual perception, biological anthropology, sociolinguistics.

University of California, Santa Barbara, Graduate Division, College of Engineering, Department of Chemical Engineering, Santa Barbara, CA 93106-5080. Offers chemical engineering (MS, PhD); computational science and engineering (PhD). *Faculty:* 21 full-time (1 woman). *Students:* 69 full-time (18 women). Average age 25. 285 applicants, 23% accepted, 16 enrolled. In 2009, 2 master's, 15 doctorates awarded. Terminal master's awarded for partial completion of doctoral program. *Degree requirements:* For master's, thesis or comprehensive exam; for doctorate, thesis/dissertation, candidacy exam, dissertation defense, defense exam, seminar presentation. *Entrance requirements:* For master's, GRE General Test, 3 letters of recommendation, resume/curriculum vitae; for doctorate, GRE General Test, 3 letters of recommendation, statement of purpose, personal achievements/contributions statement, resume/curriculum vitae, transcripts for post-secondary institutions attended. Additional exam requirements/recommendations for international students: Required—TOEFL (minimum score 560 paper-based; 220 computer-based; 83 iBT) or IELTS (minimum score 7). *Application deadline:* For fall admission, 1/15 priority date for domestic and international students. Application fee: $70 ($90 for international students). Electronic applications accepted. *Financial support:* In 2009–10, 68 students received support, including 32 fellowships with full and partial tuition reimbursements available (averaging $8,200 per year), 63 research assistantships with full and partial tuition reimbursements available (averaging $10,800 per year), 41 teaching assistantships with partial tuition reimbursements available (averaging $3,400 per year); Federal Work-Study, institutionally sponsored loans, scholarships/grants, health care benefits, tuition waivers (full and partial), and unspecified assistantships also available. Financial award application deadline: 1/15; financial award applicants required to submit FAFSA. *Faculty research:* Fluid transport, complex fluid and polymers, biomaterials/bioengineering, catalysis and reaction engineering, systems process design and control. Total annual research expenditures: $7.4 million. *Unit head:* Prof. Michael Doherty, Chair, 805-893-5309, Fax: 805-893-4731, E-mail: mfd@engineering.ucsb.edu. *Application contact:* Laura Crownover, Student Affairs Officer, 805-893-8671, Fax: 805-893-4731, E-mail: laura@engineering.ucsb.edu.

University of California, Santa Barbara, Graduate Division, College of Engineering, Department of Computer Science, Santa Barbara, CA 93106-5110. Offers computational science and engineering (PhD); computer science (MS, PhD). *Faculty:* 33 full-time (5 women), 4 part-time/adjunct (0 women). *Students:* 147 full-time (30 women). Average age 27. 559 applicants, 23% accepted, 45 enrolled. In 2009, 26 master's, 19 doctorates awarded. Terminal master's awarded for partial completion of doctoral program. *Degree requirements:* For master's, comprehensive exam (for some programs), thesis (for some programs), project (for some programs); for doctorate, thesis/dissertation. *Entrance requirements:* For master's, GRE, 3 letters of recommendation, resume/curriculum vitae; for doctorate, GRE, 3 letters of recommendation, statement of purpose, personal achievements/contributions statement, resume/curriculum vitae, transcripts for post-secondary institutions attended. Additional exam requirements/recommendations for international students: Required—TOEFL (minimum score 600 paper-based; 250 computer-based; 100 iBT) or IELTS (minimum score 7). *Application deadline:* For fall admission, 12/15 for domestic and international students. Application fee: $70 ($90 for international students). Electronic applications accepted. *Financial support:* In 2009–10, 115 students received support, including 18 fellowships with full and partial tuition reimbursements available (averaging $17,300 per year), 73 research assistantships with full and partial tuition reimbursements available (averaging $9,600 per year), 54 teaching assistantships with partial tuition reimbursements available (averaging $7,200 per year); career-related internships or fieldwork, Federal Work-Study, institutionally sponsored loans, scholarships/grants, traineeships, health care benefits, tuition waivers (full and partial), and unspecified assistantships also available. Financial award application deadline: 12/15; financial award applicants required to submit FAFSA. *Faculty research:* Networking and security, database systems, computational science and engineering, programming languages and software engineering, human computer interaction. Total annual research expenditures: $5.8 million. *Unit head:* Prof. Amr El Abbadi, Chair, 805-893-5334, Fax: 805-893-8553, E-mail: amr@cs.ucsb.edu. *Application contact:* Amanda Hoagland, Graduate Program Assistant, 805-893-4322, Fax: 805-893-8553, E-mail: gradhelp@cs.ucsb.edu.

University of California, Santa Barbara, Graduate Division, College of Engineering, Department of Electrical and Computer Engineering, Santa Barbara, CA 93106-9560. Offers computational science and engineering (PhD); electrical and computer engineering (PhD); MS/PhD. *Faculty:* 39 full-time (3 women), 1 part-time/adjunct (0 women). *Students:* 277 full-time (52 women). Average age 26. 1,135 applicants, 19% accepted, 50 enrolled. In 2009, 58 master's, 26 doctorates awarded. Terminal master's awarded for partial completion of doctoral program. *Degree requirements:* For master's, comprehensive exam, thesis; for doctorate, thesis/dissertation, screening exam, qualifying exam, dissertation defense exam. *Entrance requirements:* For master's, GRE General Test, 3 letters of recommendation, resume/curriculum vitae; for doctorate, GRE General Test, 3 letters of recommendation, statement of purpose, personal achievements/contributions statement, resume/curriculum vitae, transcripts for post-secondary institutions attended. Additional exam requirements/recommendations for international students: Required—TOEFL (minimum score 550 paper-based; 213 computer-based; 80 iBT) or IELTS (minimum score 7). *Application deadline:* For fall admission, 12/15 for domestic and international students; for winter admission, 11/1 for domestic and international students; for spring admission, 1/1 for domestic and international students. Application fee: $70 ($90 for international students). Electronic applications accepted. *Financial support:* In 2009–10, 209 students received support, including 52 fellowships with full and partial tuition reimbursements available (averaging $8,600 per year), 163 research assistantships with full and partial tuition reimbursements available (averaging $12,100 per year), 54 teaching assistantships with partial tuition reimbursements available (averaging $7,400 per year); career-related internships or fieldwork, Federal Work-Study, institutionally sponsored loans, scholarships/grants, traineeships, health care benefits, tuition waivers (full and partial), and unspecified assistantships also available. Financial award application deadline: 12/15; financial award applicants required to submit FAFSA. *Faculty research:* Communications, signal processing, computer engineering, control, electronics and photonics. Total annual research expenditures: $21.6 million. *Unit head:* Prof. Jerry Gibson, Chair, 805-893-3821, Fax: 805-893-3262, E-mail: gibson@ece.ucsb.edu. *Application contact:* Erika Raquel Klukovich, Graduate Admissions Coordinator, 805-893-3114, Fax: 805-893-5402, E-mail: erika@ece.ucsb.edu.

University of California, Santa Barbara, Graduate Division, College of Engineering, Department of Mechanical Engineering, Santa Barbara, CA 93106-5070. Offers computational science and engineering (PhD); mechanical engineering (MS, PhD); MS/PhD. *Faculty:* 33 full-time (4 women), 5 part-time/adjunct (0 women). *Students:* 74 full-time (15 women). Average age 27. 204 applicants, 21% accepted, 15 enrolled. In 2009, 2 master's, 15 doctorates awarded. *Degree requirements:* For master's, thesis; for doctorate, comprehensive exam, thesis/dissertation. *Entrance requirements:* For master's, GRE, 3 letters of recommendation, statement of purpose, personal achievements/contributions statement, resume/curriculum vitae, transcripts for post-secondary institutions attended; for doctorate, GRE General Test, 3 letters of recommendation, resume/curriculum vitae. Additional exam requirements/recommendations for international students: Required—TOEFL (minimum score 550 paper-based; 213 computer-based; 80 iBT) or IELTS (minimum score 7). *Application deadline:* For fall admission, 1/1 for domestic and international students. Application fee: $70 ($90 for international students). Electronic applications accepted. *Financial support:* In 2009–10, 72 students received support, including 29 fellowships with full and partial tuition reimbursements available (averaging $11,500 per year), 55 research assistantships with full and partial tuition reimbursements available (averaging $10,800 per year), 40 teaching assistantships with partial tuition reimbursements available (averaging $7,100 per year); Federal Work-Study, institutionally sponsored loans, scholarships/grants, health care benefits, tuition waivers (full and partial), and unspecified assistantships also available. Financial award application deadline: 1/1; financial award applicants required to submit FAFSA. *Faculty research:* Micro/nanoscale technology; computational science and engineering; dynamics, controls and robotics; thermofluid sciences, solid mechanics, materials, and structures. Total annual research expenditures: $4.9 million. *Unit head:* Prof. Kimberly Turner, Chair, 805-893-5106, Fax: 805-893-8486, E-mail: turner@engineering.ucsb.edu. *Application contact:* Laura Reynolds, Staff Graduate Program Advisor, 805-893-2239, Fax: 805-893-8651, E-mail: meegrad@engineering.ucsb.edu.

University of California, Santa Barbara, Graduate Division, College of Letters and Sciences, Division of Mathematics, Life, and Physical Sciences, Department of Earth Science, Santa Barbara, CA 93106-9620. Offers geological sciences (MS, PhD), including computational science and engineering (MS), geological sciences; geophysics (MS), including computational science and engineering, geophysics. *Faculty:* 20 full-time (4 women). *Students:* 35 full-time (15 women). Average age 27. 90 applicants, 27% accepted, 9 enrolled. In 2009, 3 master's, 4 doctorates awarded. *Degree requirements:* For master's, comprehensive exam, thesis; for doctorate, comprehensive exam, thesis/dissertation. *Entrance requirements:* For master's, GRE General Test, 3 letters of recommendation, resume/curriculum vitae; for doctorate, GRE General Test, 3 letters of recommendation, statement of purpose, personal achievements/contributions statement, resume/curriculum vitae, transcripts for post-secondary institutions attended. Additional exam requirements/recommendations for international students: Required—TOEFL (minimum score 550 paper-based; 213 computer-based; 80 iBT) or IELTS (minimum score 7). *Application deadline:* For fall admission, 2/1 for domestic students, 1/1 for international students. Application fee: $70 ($90 for international students). Electronic applications accepted. *Financial support:* In 2009–10, 35 students received support, including 21 fellowships with full and partial tuition reimbursements available (averaging $6,200 per year), 17 research assistantships with full and partial tuition reimbursements available (averaging $6,000 per year), 28 teaching assistantships with partial tuition reimbursements available (averaging $7,600 per year); career-related internships or fieldwork, Federal Work-Study, institutionally

sponsored loans, scholarships/grants, traineeships, health care benefits, and unspecified assistantships also available. Financial award applicants required to submit FAFSA. *Faculty research:* Tectonics, geochronology, paleontology, volcanology, geomorphology. *Unit head:* Dr. Ralph Archuleta, Chair, 805-893-8441, E-mail: ralph@crustal.ucsb.edu. *Application contact:* Samuel C. Rifkin, Graduate Program Assistant, 805-893-3329, Fax: 805-893-2314, E-mail: rifkin@geol.ucsb.edu.

University of California, Santa Barbara, Graduate Division, College of Letters and Sciences, Division of Mathematics, Life, and Physical Sciences, Department of Ecology, Evolution, and Marine Biology, Santa Barbara, CA 93106-9620. Offers computational science and engineering (PhD); MA/PhD. *Faculty:* 39 full-time (8 women). *Students:* 56 full-time (35 women). Average age 30. 135 applicants, 13% accepted, 7 enrolled. In 2009, 7 master's, 15 doctorates awarded. Terminal master's awarded for partial completion of doctoral program. *Degree requirements:* For master's, comprehensive exam (for some programs), thesis (for some programs); for doctorate, comprehensive exam, thesis/dissertation. *Entrance requirements:* For master's, GRE General Test, 3 letters of recommendation, resume/curriculum vitae; for doctorate, GRE General Test, 3 letters of recommendation, statement of purpose, personal achievements/contributions statement, resume/curriculum vitae, transcripts for post-secondary institutions attended. Additional exam requirements/recommendations for international students: Required—TOEFL (minimum score 550 paper-based; 213 computer-based; 80 iBT) or IELTS. *Application deadline:* For fall admission, 12/15 for domestic and international students. Application fee: $70 ($90 for international students). Electronic applications accepted. *Financial support:* In 2009–10, 54 students received support, including 26 fellowships with full and partial tuition reimbursements available (averaging $17,900 per year), 16 research assistantships with full and partial tuition reimbursements available (averaging $7,300 per year), 35 teaching assistantships with partial tuition reimbursements available (averaging $9,100 per year); Federal Work-Study, institutionally sponsored loans, scholarships/grants, traineeships, health care benefits, tuition waivers (full and partial), and unspecified assistantships also available. Financial award applicants required to submit FAFSA. *Faculty research:* Ecology, population genetics, stream ecology, evolution, marine biology. *Unit head:* Robert Warner, Chair, 805-893-2415, Fax: 805-893-4724, E-mail: eembchair@lifesci.ucsb.edu. *Application contact:* Alina Haas, Staff Graduate Advisor, 805-893-3023, Fax: 805-893-5885, E-mail: haas@lifesci.ucsb.edu.

University of California, Santa Barbara, Graduate Division, College of Letters and Sciences, Division of Mathematics, Life, and Physical Sciences, Department of Mathematics, Santa Barbara, CA 93106-3080. Offers applied mathematics (MA); computational science and engineering (PhD); mathematics (MA, PhD); MA/PhD. *Faculty:* 31 full-time (3 women). *Students:* 54 full-time (14 women). Average age 26. 151 applicants, 26% accepted, 14 enrolled. In 2009, 5 master's, 14 doctorates awarded. Terminal master's awarded for partial completion of doctoral program. *Degree requirements:* For master's, comprehensive exam (for some programs), thesis (for some programs); for doctorate, comprehensive exam, thesis/dissertation. *Entrance requirements:* For master's, GRE General Test, GRE Subject Test (mathematics), 3 letters of recommendation, resume/curriculum vitae; for doctorate, GRE General Test, GRE Subject Test (math), 3 letters of recommendation, statement of purpose, personal achievements/contributions statement, resume/curriculum vitae, transcripts for post-secondary institutions attended. Additional exam requirements/recommendations for international students: Required—TOEFL (minimum score 575 paper-based; 231 computer-based; 80 iBT) or IELTS (7). *Application deadline:* For fall admission, 1/1 for domestic and international students. Application fee: $70 ($90 for international students). Electronic applications accepted. *Financial support:* In 2009–10, 54 students received support, including 13 fellowships with full and partial tuition reimbursements available (averaging $13,200 per year), 13 research assistantships with full and partial tuition reimbursements available (averaging $6,500 per year), 48 teaching assistantships with partial tuition reimbursements available (averaging $10,600 per year); Federal Work-Study, institutionally sponsored loans, scholarships/grants, health care benefits, and unspecified assistantships also available. Financial award applicants required to submit FAFSA. *Faculty research:* Topology, differential geometry, algebra, applied mathematics, partial differential equations. Total annual research expenditures: $204,214. *Unit head:* Prof. Jeffrey Stopple, Chair, 805-893-8330, Fax: 805-893-2385, E-mail: stopple@math.ucsb.edu. *Application contact:* Medina Price, Graduate Advisor, 805-893-8192, Fax: 805-893-2385, E-mail: price@math.ucsb.edu.

University of California, Santa Cruz, Division of Graduate Studies, Jack Baskin School of Engineering, Program in Computer Engineering, Santa Cruz, CA 95064. Offers computer engineering (MS, PhD); network engineering (MS). *Degree requirements:* For doctorate, one foreign language, comprehensive exam, thesis/dissertation, oral exams. *Entrance requirements:* For master's and doctorate, GRE General Test, GRE Subject Test. *Faculty research:* Computer-aided design of digital systems.

University of Central Florida, College of Engineering and Computer Science, School of Electrical Engineering and Computer Science, Program in Computer Engineering, Orlando, FL 32816. Offers computer engineering (MS Cp E, PhD). Part-time and evening/weekend programs available. *Students:* 67 full-time (7 women), 52 part-time (9 women); includes 27 minority (3 African Americans, 9 Asian Americans or Pacific Islanders, 15 Hispanic Americans), 46 international. Average age 29. 83 applicants, 66% accepted, 34 enrolled. In 2009, 24 master's, 6 doctorates awarded. *Degree requirements:* For master's, thesis or alternative; for doctorate, thesis/dissertation, departmental qualifying exam, candidacy exam. *Entrance requirements:* For master's, GRE General Test, minimum GPA of 3.0 in last 60 hours; for doctorate, GRE General Test, minimum GPA of 3.5 in last 60 hours. Additional exam requirements/recommendations for international students: Required—TOEFL. *Application deadline:* For fall admission, 7/15 priority date for domestic students; for spring admission, 12/1 priority date for domestic students. Electronic applications accepted. *Expenses:* Tuition, state resident: part-time $306.31 per credit hour. Tuition, nonresident: part-time $1099.01 per credit hour. Part-time tuition and fees vary according to degree level and program. *Financial support:* In 2009–10, 35 students received support, including 6 fellowships (averaging $11,700 per year), 29 research assistantships (averaging $9,300 per year), 10 teaching assistantships (averaging $8,200 per year); tuition waivers (partial) also available.

University of Cincinnati, Graduate School, College of Engineering, Department of Electrical and Computer Engineering and Computer Science, Program in Computer Engineering, Cincinnati, OH 45221. Offers MS. *Degree requirements:* For master's, thesis. *Entrance requirements:* For master's, GRE General Test. Additional exam requirements/recommendations for international students: Required—TOEFL (minimum score 550 paper-based; 213 computer-based). Electronic applications accepted. *Faculty research:* Digital signal processing, large-scale systems, picture processing.

University of Cincinnati, Graduate School, College of Engineering, Department of Electrical and Computer Engineering and Computer Science, Program in Computer Science and Engineering, Cincinnati, OH 45221. Offers PhD. *Degree requirements:* For doctorate, thesis/dissertation. *Entrance requirements:* For doctorate, GRE General Test. Additional exam requirements/recommendations for international students: Required—TOEFL.

University of Colorado at Boulder, Graduate School, College of Engineering and Applied Science, Department of Electrical, Computer and Energy Engineering, Boulder, CO 80309. Offers ME, MS, PhD. Part-time programs available. Postbaccalaureate distance learning degree programs offered (no on-campus study). *Faculty:* 36 full-time (5 women). *Students:* 196 full-time (30 women), 94 part-time (21 women); includes 15 minority (1 African American, 12 Asian Americans or Pacific Islanders, 2 Hispanic Americans), 132 international. Average age 28. 654 applicants, 29% accepted, 66 enrolled. In 2009, 66 master's, 14 doctorates awarded. Terminal master's awarded for partial completion of doctoral program. *Degree requirements:* For master's, thesis or alternative; for doctorate, one foreign language, thesis/dissertation, departmental qualifying exam. *Entrance requirements:* For master's, GRE General Test, minimum undergraduate GPA of 3.0; for doctorate, GRE General Test, minimum undergraduate GPA of 3.5. *Application deadline:* For fall admission, 1/15 priority date for

Computer Engineering

University of Colorado at Boulder (continued)
domestic students, 12/1 for international students; for spring admission, 10/1 for domestic and international students. Applications are processed on a rolling basis. Application fee: $50 ($60 for international students). *Financial support:* In 2009–10, 31 fellowships (averaging $8,965 per year), 107 research assistantships (averaging $14,806 per year) were awarded; career-related internships or fieldwork, scholarships/grants, and tuition waivers (full) also available. Financial award application deadline: 1/15. *Faculty research:* Biomedical engineering and cognitive disabilities, computer engineering VLSI CAD, dynamics and control systems, digital signal processing communications, electromagnetics, RF and microwaves, nonostructures and devices, optics and optoelectronics, power electronics and renewable energy systems. Total annual research expenditures: $7.4 million.

University of Colorado Denver, College of Engineering and Applied Science, Department of Computer Science and Engineering, Denver, CO 80217-3364. Offers computer science and engineering (MS); computer science and information systems (PhD). Part-time and evening/weekend programs available. *Students:* 17 full-time (11 women), 48 part-time (16 women); includes 9 minority (1 African American, 7 Asian Americans or Pacific Islanders, 1 Hispanic American), 34 international. 86 applicants, 44% accepted, 15 enrolled. In 2009, 22 master's awarded. *Degree requirements:* For master's, thesis or alternative; for doctorate, comprehensive exam, thesis/dissertation. *Entrance requirements:* For master's, GRE; for doctorate, GRE or GMAT, portfolio. Additional exam requirements/recommendations for international students: Required—TOEFL (minimum score 500 paper-based; 172 computer-based). *Application deadline:* For fall admission, 4/1 for domestic students; for spring admission, 10/1 for domestic students. Applications are processed on a rolling basis. Application fee: $50 ($75 for international students). Electronic applications accepted. *Financial support:* Research assistantships, teaching assistantships, career-related internships or fieldwork and Federal Work-Study available. Financial award application deadline: 4/1; financial award applicants required to submit FAFSA. *Unit head:* Bogdan Chlebus, Chair, 303-556-8537, Fax: 303-556-8369, E-mail: bogdan.chlebus@ucdenver.edu. *Application contact:* Frances Moore, Program Assistant, 303-556-4083, Fax: 303-556-8369, E-mail: frances.moore@ucdenver.edu.

University of Dayton, Graduate School, School of Engineering, Department of Electrical and Computer Engineering, Dayton, OH 45469-1300. Offers MSEE, DE, PhD. Part-time and evening/weekend programs available. *Faculty:* 9 full-time (0 women), 3 part-time/adjunct (1 woman). *Students:* 59 full-time (13 women), 31 part-time (3 women); includes 8 minority (4 African Americans, 3 Asian Americans or Pacific Islanders, 1 Hispanic American), 56 international. Average age 27. 198 applicants, 44% accepted, 28 enrolled. In 2009, 18 master's, 3 doctorates awarded. *Degree requirements:* For master's, thesis optional; for doctorate, variable foreign language requirement, thesis/dissertation, departmental qualifying exam. *Entrance requirements:* Additional exam requirements/recommendations for international students: Required—TOEFL (minimum score 550 paper-based; 213 computer-based; 80 iBT). *Application deadline:* For fall admission, 8/1 for domestic students, 3/1 priority date for international students; for winter admission, 7/1 priority date for international students; for spring admission, 1/1 priority date for international students. Applications are processed on a rolling basis. Application fee: $0 ($50 for international students). Electronic applications accepted. *Expenses:* Tuition: Full-time $8412; part-time $701 per credit hour. Required fees: $325; $65 per course. $25 per semester. Tuition and fees vary according to course load, degree level and program. *Financial support:* In 2009–10, 1 fellowship (averaging $27,500 per year), 15 research assistantships with full tuition reimbursements (averaging $15,000 per year), 5 teaching assistantships with full tuition reimbursements (averaging $9,000 per year) were awarded. Financial award application deadline: 5/1; financial award applicants required to submit FAFSA. *Faculty research:* Electrical engineering, video processing, leaky wave antenna. Total annual research expenditures: $1.1 million. *Unit head:* Dr. Guru Subramanyam, Chair, 937-229-3611. *Application contact:* Graduate Admissions, 937-229-4411, Fax: 937-229-4729, E-mail: gradadmission@udayton.edu.

University of Delaware, College of Engineering, Department of Electrical and Computer Engineering, Newark, DE 19716. Offers MSECE, PhD. Part-time programs available. Post-baccalaureate distance learning degree programs offered (no on-campus study). Terminal master's awarded for partial completion of doctoral program. *Degree requirements:* For master's, thesis optional; for doctorate, thesis/dissertation. *Entrance requirements:* For master's, GRE General Test; for doctorate, GRE General Test, qualifying exam. Additional exam requirements/recommendations for international students: Required—TOEFL. Electronic applications accepted. *Faculty research:* HIV Evolution During Dynamic Therapy, compressive sensing in imaging, sensor, networks, and UWB radios, computer network time synchronization, silicon spintronics, devices and imaging in the high-terahertz band.

University of Denver, School of Engineering and Computer Science, Department of Electrical and Computer Engineering, Denver, CO 80208. Offers computer engineering (MS); computer science and engineering (MS); electrical engineering (MS). Part-time and evening/weekend programs available. *Faculty:* 1 full-time (0 women). *Students:* 3 full-time (0 women), 122 part-time (17 women); includes 21 minority (1 African American, 11 Asian Americans or Pacific Islanders, 9 Hispanic Americans), 24 international. Average age 31. 112 applicants, 88% accepted, 56 enrolled. In 2009, 28 master's awarded. Terminal master's awarded for partial completion of doctoral program. *Degree requirements:* For master's, thesis (for some programs). *Entrance requirements:* For master's, GRE General Test, letters of reference. Additional exam requirements/recommendations for international students: Required—TOEFL (minimum score 570 paper-based; 230 computer-based). *Application deadline:* Applications are processed on a rolling basis. Application fee: $50. Electronic applications accepted. *Expenses:* Tuition: Full-time $34,596; part-time $961 per quarter hour. Required fees: $4 per quarter hour. Tuition and fees vary according to course load, campus/location and program. *Financial support:* In 2009–10, 14 research assistantships with full and partial tuition reimbursements (averaging $17,000 per year), 6 teaching assistantships with full and partial tuition reimbursements (averaging $10,000 per year) were awarded. Financial award application deadline: 3/1; financial award applicants required to submit FAFSA. *Unit head:* Dr. Kimon Valavanis, Chair, 303-871-2586. *Application contact:* Information Contact, 303-871-6618, E-mail: dgilmore@du.edu.

University of Detroit Mercy, College of Engineering and Science, Department of Electrical and Computer Engineering, Detroit, MI 48221. Offers computer engineering (ME, DE); mechatronics systems (ME, DE); signals and systems (ME, DE). Evening/weekend programs available. *Degree requirements:* For doctorate, thesis/dissertation. *Faculty research:* Electromagnetics, computer architecture, systems.

University of Florida, Graduate School, College of Engineering and College of Liberal Arts and Sciences, Department of Computer and Information Science and Engineering, Gainesville, FL 32611. Offers computer engineering (ME, MS, PhD); computer science (MS); digital arts and sciences (MS). Part-time programs available. *Degree requirements:* For master's, thesis (for some programs); for doctorate, thesis/dissertation. *Entrance requirements:* For master's and doctorate, GRE General Test, minimum GPA of 3.0. Additional exam requirements/recommendations for international students: Required—TOEFL (minimum score 550 paper-based; 213 computer-based). Electronic applications accepted. *Faculty research:* Artificial intelligence, networks security, distributed computing, parallel processing system, vision and visualization, database systems.

University of Florida, Graduate School, College of Engineering, Department of Electrical and Computer Engineering, Gainesville, FL 32611. Offers ME, MS, PhD, Engr. Part-time programs available. Terminal master's awarded for partial completion of doctoral program. *Degree requirements:* For master's, comprehensive exam (for some programs), thesis optional; for doctorate, comprehensive exam, thesis/dissertation; for Engr, thesis. *Entrance requirements:* For master's, GRE General Test, minimum GPA of 3.0; for doctorate, GRE General Test, minimum GPA of 3.5; for Engr, GRE General Test. Additional exam requirements/recommendations for international students: Required—TOEFL (minimum score 550 paper-based; 213 computer-based). Electronic applications accepted. *Faculty research:* Communications, electronics, digital signal processing, computer engineering.

University of Houston, Cullen College of Engineering, Department of Electrical and Computer Engineering, Houston, TX 77204. Offers MEE, MSEE, PhD. Part-time and evening/weekend programs available. *Faculty:* 25 full-time (2 women), 3 part-time/adjunct (1 woman). *Students:* 207 full-time (54 women), 39 part-time (6 women); includes 21 minority (2 African Americans, 17 Asian Americans or Pacific Islanders, 2 Hispanic Americans), 203 international. Average age 25. 387 applicants, 60% accepted, 83 enrolled. In 2009, 42 master's, 7 doctorates awarded. Terminal master's awarded for partial completion of doctoral program. *Degree requirements:* For master's, thesis (for some programs); for doctorate, comprehensive exam, thesis/dissertation. *Entrance requirements:* For master's and doctorate, GRE General Test. Additional exam requirements/recommendations for international students: Required—TOEFL (minimum score 580 paper-based; 237 computer-based; 92 iBT). *Application deadline:* For fall admission, 2/1 for domestic and international students; for spring admission, 8/1 for domestic and international students. Application fee: $25 ($75 for international students). Electronic applications accepted. *Expenses:* Tuition, state resident: full-time $7676; part-time $320 per credit hour. Tuition, nonresident: full-time $14,324; part-time $597 per credit hour. Required fees: $3034. *Financial support:* In 2009–10, 9 fellowships with full tuition reimbursements (averaging $15,500 per year), 43 research assistantships with full tuition reimbursements (averaging $12,500 per year), 48 teaching assistantships with full tuition reimbursements (averaging $12,550 per year) were awarded; career-related internships or fieldwork, Federal Work-Study, institutionally sponsored loans, scholarships/grants, health care benefits, and unspecified assistantships also available. Support available to part-time students. Financial award application deadline: 2/1. *Faculty research:* Applied electromagnetics and microelectronics, signal and image processing, biomedical engineering, geophysical applications, control engineering. *Unit head:* Dr. John Wolfe, Interim Chairman, 713-743-4449, E-mail: wolfe@uh.edu. *Application contact:* MyTrang Baccam, Graduate Academic Advisor, 713-743-4403, E-mail: ece_grad_admit@uh.edu.

University of Houston–Clear Lake, School of Science and Computer Engineering, Program in Computer Engineering, Houston, TX 77058-1098. Offers MS. Part-time and evening/weekend programs available. *Entrance requirements:* For master's, GRE General Test. Additional exam requirements/recommendations for international students: Required—TOEFL (minimum score 550 paper-based; 213 computer-based).

University of Idaho, College of Graduate Studies, College of Engineering, Department of Electrical and Computer Engineering, Program in Computer Engineering, Moscow, ID 83844-2282. Offers M Engr, MS. *Students:* 4 full-time, 1 part-time. In 2009, 3 master's awarded. *Degree requirements:* For master's, thesis. *Entrance requirements:* For master's, minimum GPA of 2.8. *Application deadline:* For fall admission, 8/1 for domestic students; for spring admission, 12/15 for domestic students. Application fee: $55 ($60 for international students). *Expenses:* Tuition, state resident: full-time $6120. Tuition, nonresident: full-time $17,712. *Financial support:* Federal Work-Study available. Financial award application deadline: 2/15. *Unit head:* Dr. Brian Johnson, Chair, 208-885-6902. *Application contact:* Dr. Brian Johnson, Chair, 208-885-6902.

University of Illinois at Chicago, Graduate College, College of Engineering, Department of Electrical and Computer Engineering, Program in Electrical and Computer Engineering, Chicago, IL 60607-7128. Offers MS, PhD. Part-time programs available. *Degree requirements:* For master's, thesis or alternative; for doctorate, thesis/dissertation, departmental qualifying exam. *Entrance requirements:* For master's, minimum GPA of 2.75, BS in related field; for doctorate, GRE General Test, minimum GPA of 2.75, MS in related field. Additional exam requirements/recommendations for international students: Required—TOEFL.

University of Illinois at Urbana–Champaign, Graduate College, College of Engineering, Department of Electrical and Computer Engineering, Champaign, IL 61820. Offers electrical and computer engineering (MS, PhD); MS/MBA. *Faculty:* 87 full-time (6 women), 4 part-time/adjunct (0 women). *Students:* 478 full-time (65 women), 38 part-time (3 women); includes 58 minority (9 African Americans, 39 Asian Americans or Pacific Islanders, 10 Hispanic Americans), 293 international. 1,446 applicants, 16% accepted, 107 enrolled. In 2009, 98 master's, 56 doctorates awarded. *Entrance requirements:* For master's, GRE, minimum GPA of 3.0; for doctorate, GRE. Additional exam requirements/recommendations for international students: Required—TOEFL (minimum score 590 paper-based; 243 computer-based; 96 iBT), or IELTS (minimum score 6.5). *Application deadline:* Applications are processed on a rolling basis. Application fee: $60 ($75 for international students). Electronic applications accepted. *Financial support:* In 2009–10, 52 fellowships, 404 research assistantships, 172 teaching assistantships were awarded; tuition waivers (full and partial) also available. *Unit head:* Andreas C. Cangellaris, Head, 217-333-6037, Fax: 217-244-7075, E-mail: cangella@illinois.edu. *Application contact:* Laurie A. Fisher, Administrative Aide, 217-333-9709, Fax: 217-333-8582, E-mail: fisher2@illinois.edu.

The University of Iowa, Graduate College, College of Engineering, Department of Electrical and Computer Engineering, Iowa City, IA 52242-1316. Offers MS, PhD. Part-time programs available. *Faculty:* 19 full-time (1 woman), 1 part-time/adjunct (0 women). *Students:* 64 full-time (15 women); includes 6 minority (3 African Americans, 2 Asian Americans or Pacific Islanders, 1 Hispanic American), 36 international. Average age 29. 126 applicants, 24% accepted, 13 enrolled. In 2009, 12 master's, 2 doctorates awarded. *Degree requirements:* For master's, comprehensive exam, thesis optional; for doctorate, comprehensive exam, thesis/dissertation, PhD qualifying exam. *Entrance requirements:* For master's and doctorate, GRE. Additional exam requirements/recommendations for international students: Required—TOEFL (minimum score 550 paper-based; 213 computer-based; 81 iBT). *Application deadline:* For fall admission, 2/1 priority date for domestic students, 2/1 for international students. Applications are processed on a rolling basis. Application fee: $60 ($100 for international students). Electronic applications accepted. *Financial support:* In 2009–10, 3 fellowships with partial tuition reimbursements (averaging $19,146 per year), 49 research assistantships with partial tuition reimbursements (averaging $18,073 per year), 13 teaching assistantships with partial tuition reimbursements (averaging $17,324 per year) were awarded; scholarships/grants and unspecified assistantships also available. Financial award application deadline: 2/1; financial award applicants required to submit FAFSA. *Faculty research:* Applied optics and nanotechnology; computational genomics; large-scale intelligent and control systems; medical image processing; VLSI design and test. Total annual research expenditures: $7.1 million. *Unit head:* Dr. Milan Sonka, Departmental Executive Officer, 319-335-6052, Fax: 319-335-6028, E-mail: milan-sonka@uiowa.edu. *Application contact:* Cathy Kern, Secretary, 319-335-5197, Fax: 319-335-6028, E-mail: ece@engineering.uiowa.edu.

The University of Kansas, Graduate Studies, School of Engineering, Department of Electrical Engineering and Computer Science, Program in Computer Engineering, Lawrence, KS 66045. Offers MS. Part-time programs available. *Students:* 11 full-time (2 women), 4 part-time (2 women), 11 international. Average age 24. 13 applicants, 23% accepted, 1 enrolled. In 2009, 5 master's awarded. *Degree requirements:* For master's, thesis optional, exam. *Entrance requirements:* For master's, GRE, minimum GPA of 3.0. Additional exam requirements/recommendations for international students: Required—TOEFL (minimum score 600 paper-based; 250 computer-based; 100 iBT). *Application deadline:* For fall admission, 3/1 priority date for domestic students, 3/1 for international students; for spring admission, 10/1 priority date for domestic students, 10/1 for international students. Applications are processed on a rolling basis. Application fee: $45 ($55 for international students). Electronic applications accepted. *Expenses:* Tuition, state resident: full-time $6492; part-time $270.50 per credit hour. Tuition, nonresident: full-time $15,510; part-time $646.25 per credit hour. Required fees: $847; $70.56 per credit hour. Tuition and fees vary according to course load and program. *Financial support:* Fellowships with full and partial tuition reimbursements, research assistantships with full and partial tuition reimbursements, teaching assistantships with full and partial tuition reimbursements, career-related internships or fieldwork, scholarships/grants, and unspecified assistantships available. Financial award application deadline: 1/1. *Faculty research:* Communication systems and networking, computer systems design, interactive intelligent systems, radar systems and remote sensing, bioinformatics. *Unit head:* Glenn Prescott, Chairperson,

785-864-4620, Fax: 785-864-3226. *Application contact:* Pam Shadoin, Assistant to Graduate Director, 785-864-4487, Fax: 785-864-3226, E-mail: graduate@eecs.ku.edu.

University of Louisiana at Lafayette, College of Engineering, Center for Advanced Computer Studies, Lafayette, LA 70504. Offers computer engineering (MS, PhD); computer science (MS, PhD). Part-time programs available. Terminal master's awarded for partial completion of doctoral program. *Degree requirements:* For master's, thesis or alternative; for doctorate, comprehensive exam, thesis/dissertation, final oral exam. *Entrance requirements:* For master's, GRE General Test, minimum GPA of 2.75; for doctorate, GRE General Test, minimum GPA of 3.0. Additional exam requirements/recommendations for international students: Required—TOEFL. Electronic applications accepted.

University of Louisiana at Lafayette, College of Engineering, Department of Electrical and Computer Engineering, Lafayette, LA 70504. Offers computer engineering (MS, PhD); telecommunications (MSTC). *Degree requirements:* For master's, thesis or alternative; for doctorate, comprehensive exam, thesis/dissertation, final oral exam. *Entrance requirements:* For master's, GRE General Test, minimum GPA of 2.75. Additional exam requirements/recommendations for international students: Required—TOEFL (minimum score 550 paper-based; 213 computer-based). Electronic applications accepted.

University of Louisville, J.B. Speed School of Engineering, Department of Computer Engineering and Computer Science, Louisville, KY 40292-0001. Offers computer engineering and computer science (M Eng, MS); computer science (MS); computer science and engineering (PhD); data mining (Certificate); network and information security (Certificate). *Accreditation:* ABET (one or more programs are accredited). Part-time programs available. Postbaccalaureate distance learning degree programs offered (no on-campus study). *Faculty:* 15 full-time (0 women). *Students:* 75 full-time (10 women), 42 part-time (10 women); includes 10 minority (7 African Americans, 2 Asian Americans or Pacific Islanders, 1 Hispanic American), 46 international. Average age 30. 66 applicants, 59% accepted, 21 enrolled. In 2009, 26 master's, 9 doctorates, 1 other advanced degree awarded. Terminal master's awarded for partial completion of doctoral program. *Degree requirements:* For master's, comprehensive exam (for some programs), thesis or alternative; for doctorate, comprehensive exam, thesis/dissertation, minimum GPA of 3.0. *Entrance requirements:* For master's, doctorate, and Certificate, GRE General Test. Additional exam requirements/recommendations for international students: Required—TOEFL (minimum score 550 paper-based; 213 computer-based; 80 iBT). *Application deadline:* For fall admission, 7/12 priority date for domestic and international students; for winter admission, 11/29 priority date for domestic and international students; for spring admission, 3/28 priority date for domestic and international students. Applications are processed on a rolling basis. Application fee: $50. Electronic applications accepted. *Financial support:* In 2009–10, 38 students received support, including 8 fellowships with full tuition reimbursements available (averaging $20,000 per year), 20 research assistantships with full tuition reimbursements available (averaging $20,700 per year), 6 teaching assistantships with full tuition reimbursements available (averaging $20,000 per year). Financial award application deadline: 1/25; financial award applicants required to submit FAFSA. *Faculty research:* Software systems engineering, information security and forensics, multimedia and vision, mobile and distributed computing, intelligent systems. Total annual research expenditures: $1.4 million. *Unit head:* Dr. Adel S. Elmaghraby, Chair, 502-852-6304, Fax: 502-852-4713, E-mail: adel@louisville.edu. *Application contact:* Dr. Michael Day, Associate Dean, 502-852-6195, Fax: 502-852-6294, E-mail: day@louisville.edu.

University of Louisville, J.B. Speed School of Engineering, Department of Electrical and Computer Engineering, Louisville, KY 40292-0001. Offers M Eng, MS, PhD. *Accreditation:* ABET (one or more programs are accredited). Part-time programs available. *Faculty:* 21 full-time (4 women), 1 part-time/adjunct (0 women). *Students:* 69 full-time (12 women), 23 part-time (3 women); includes 15 minority (7 African Americans, 8 Asian Americans or Pacific Islanders), 39 international. Average age 28. 53 applicants, 40% accepted, 12 enrolled. In 2009, 32 master's, 6 doctorates awarded. Terminal master's awarded for partial completion of doctoral program. *Degree requirements:* For master's, comprehensive exam (for some programs), thesis or alternative; for doctorate, comprehensive exam, thesis/dissertation, minimum GPA of 3.0. *Entrance requirements:* For master's and doctorate, GRE General Test. Additional exam requirements/recommendations for international students: Required—TOEFL (minimum score 550 paper-based; 213 computer-based; 80 iBT). *Application deadline:* For fall admission, 7/12 priority date for domestic and international students; for winter admission, 11/29 priority date for domestic and international students; for spring admission, 3/28 priority date for domestic and international students. Applications are processed on a rolling basis. Application fee: $50. Electronic applications accepted. *Financial support:* In 2009–10, 24 students received support, including 6 fellowships with full tuition reimbursements available (averaging $20,000 per year), 8 research assistantships with full tuition reimbursements available (averaging $19,300 per year), 8 teaching assistantships with full tuition reimbursements available (averaging $20,000 per year). Financial award application deadline: 1/25; financial award applicants required to submit FAFSA. *Faculty research:* Nanotechnology; microfabrication; computer engineering; control, communication and signal processing; electronic devices and systems. Total annual research expenditures: $3.5 million. *Unit head:* James H. Graham, Acting Chair, 502-852-6289, Fax: 502-852-6807, E-mail: jhgrah01@louisville.edu. *Application contact:* Dr. Michael Day, Associate Dean, 502-852-6195, Fax: 502-852-7294, E-mail: day@louisville.edu.

University of Maine, Graduate School, College of Engineering, Department of Electrical and Computer Engineering, Orono, ME 04469. Offers computer engineering (MS); electrical engineering (MS, PhD). Part-time programs available. *Faculty:* 12 full-time (1 woman), 1 part-time/adjunct (0 women). *Students:* 29 full-time (4 women), 13 part-time (2 women); includes 4 minority (all Asian Americans or Pacific Islanders), 16 international. Average age 27. 28 applicants, 43% accepted, 10 enrolled. In 2009, 4 master's awarded. *Degree requirements:* For master's, thesis (for some programs); for doctorate, thesis/dissertation. *Entrance requirements:* For master's and doctorate, GRE General Test. Additional exam requirements/recommendations for international students: Required—TOEFL. *Application deadline:* For fall admission, 2/1 priority date for domestic students. Applications are processed on a rolling basis. Application fee: $65. Electronic applications accepted. *Financial support:* In 2009–10, 21 research assistantships with tuition reimbursements (averaging $21,737 per year), 2 teaching assistantships with tuition reimbursements (averaging $12,790 per year) were awarded; Federal Work-Study, institutionally sponsored loans, and tuition waivers (full and partial) also available. Financial award application deadline: 3/1. *Unit head:* Dr. Monamad Musavi, Chair, 207-581-2243. *Application contact:* Scott G. Delcourt, Associate Dean of the Graduate School, 207-581-3291, Fax: 207-581-3232, E-mail: graduate@maine.edu.

University of Manitoba, Faculty of Graduate Studies, Faculty of Engineering, Department of Electrical and Computer Engineering, Winnipeg, MB R3T 2N2, Canada. Offers M Eng, M Sc, PhD. *Degree requirements:* For master's, thesis; for doctorate, thesis/dissertation.

University of Maryland, Baltimore County, Graduate School, College of Engineering and Information Technology, Department of Computer Science and Electrical Engineering, Program in Computer Engineering, Baltimore, MD 21250. Offers MS, PhD. Part-time programs available. *Students:* 16 full-time (3 women), 10 part-time (1 woman); includes 4 minority (1 African American, 2 Asian Americans or Pacific Islanders, 1 Hispanic American), 10 international. Average age 29. 24 applicants, 71% accepted, 5 enrolled. In 2009, 8 master's, 3 doctorates awarded. *Degree requirements:* For master's, comprehensive exam (for some programs), thesis or alternative; for doctorate, comprehensive exam, thesis/dissertation. *Entrance requirements:* For master's, GRE General Test, strong background in computer engineering, computer science, and math courses; for doctorate, GRE General Test, MS in computer science (strongly recommended). Additional exam requirements/recommendations for international students: Required—TOEFL (minimum score 550 paper-based; 213 computer-based; 80 iBT). *Application deadline:* For fall admission, 6/1 for domestic students, 1/1 for international students; for spring admission, 11/1 for domestic students, 6/1 for international students. Applications are processed on a rolling basis. Application fee: $50. Electronic applications accepted. *Financial support:* In 2009–10, 1 research assistantship with partial tuition reimbursement (averaging $17,000 per year), 6 teaching assistantships with partial tuition reimbursements (averaging $17,000 per year) were awarded; career-related internships or fieldwork, Federal Work-Study, scholarships/grants, health care benefits, tuition waivers (partial), and unspecified assistantships also available. Support available to part-time students. Financial award application deadline: 6/30; financial award applicants required to submit FAFSA. *Faculty research:* VLSI, signal processing and communication. *Unit head:* Dr. Charles K. Nicholas, Professor and Chair, 410-455-3500, Fax: 410-455-3969, E-mail: nicholas@cs.umbc.edu. *Application contact:* Dr. John Pinkston, Professor and Graduate Program Coordinator, 410-455-1338, Fax: 410-455-3969, E-mail: pinkston@cs.umbc.edu.

University of Maryland, College Park, Academic Affairs, A. James Clark School of Engineering, Department of Electrical and Computer Engineering, College Park, MD 20742. Offers electrical and computer engineering (M Eng, MS, PhD); electrical engineering (MS, PhD); telecommunications (MS). Part-time and evening/weekend programs available. Postbaccalaureate distance learning degree programs offered. *Faculty:* 104 full-time (10 women), 21 part-time/adjunct (3 women). *Students:* 394 full-time (89 women), 56 part-time (11 women); includes 53 minority (10 African Americans, 38 Asian Americans or Pacific Islanders, 5 Hispanic Americans), 318 international. 1,515 applicants, 19% accepted, 109 enrolled. In 2009, 88 master's, 44 doctorates awarded. *Degree requirements:* For master's, thesis optional; for doctorate, thesis/dissertation, oral exam, qualifying exam. *Entrance requirements:* For master's and doctorate, GRE General Test, 3 letters of recommendation. *Application deadline:* For fall admission, 5/1 for domestic students, 2/1 for international students; for spring admission, 6/1 for international students. Applications are processed on a rolling basis. Application fee: $60. Electronic applications accepted. *Expenses:* Tuition, area resident: Part-time $471 per credit hour. Tuition, state resident: part-time $471 per credit hour. Tuition, nonresident: part-time $1016 per credit hour. Required fees: $337.04 per term. *Financial support:* In 2009–10, 9 fellowships with full and partial tuition reimbursements (averaging $15,387 per year), 169 research assistantships with tuition reimbursements (averaging $17,751 per year), 81 teaching assistantships with tuition reimbursements (averaging $16,896 per year) were awarded; career-related internships or fieldwork also available. Financial award applicants required to submit FAFSA. *Faculty research:* Communications and control, electrophysics, micro-electronics, robotics, computer engineering. Total annual research expenditures: $10.7 million. *Unit head:* Dr. Pat Gerard O'Shea, Chairman, 301-405-3683, E-mail: poshea@umd.edu. *Application contact:* Dean of Graduate School, 301-405-0376, Fax: 301-314-9305.

University of Massachusetts Amherst, Graduate School, College of Engineering, Department of Electrical and Computer Engineering, Amherst, MA 01003. Offers MS, PhD. Part-time programs available. *Faculty:* 38 full-time (2 women). *Students:* 162 full-time (31 women), 18 part-time (3 women); includes 13 minority (5 African Americans, 4 Asian Americans or Pacific Islanders, 4 Hispanic Americans), 135 international. Average age 26. 640 applicants, 29% accepted, 74 enrolled. In 2009, 36 master's, 3 doctorates awarded. Terminal master's awarded for partial completion of doctoral program. *Degree requirements:* For master's, thesis or alternative; for doctorate, comprehensive exam, thesis/dissertation. *Entrance requirements:* For master's and doctorate, GRE General Test. Additional exam requirements/recommendations for international students: Required—TOEFL (minimum score 550 paper-based; 213 computer-based; 80 iBT), IELTS (minimum score 6.5). *Application deadline:* For fall admission, 1/15 for domestic and international students; for spring admission, 10/1 for domestic and international students. Applications are processed on a rolling basis. Application fee: $50 ($65 for international students). Electronic applications accepted. *Expenses:* Tuition, state resident: full-time $2640; part-time $110 per credit. Tuition, nonresident: full-time $9936; part-time $414 per credit. Tuition and fees vary according to course load. *Financial support:* In 2009–10, 3 fellowships with full tuition reimbursements (averaging $11,111 per year), 114 research assistantships with full tuition reimbursements (averaging $12,785 per year), 32 teaching assistantships with full tuition reimbursements (averaging $5,161 per year) were awarded; career-related internships or fieldwork, Federal Work-Study, scholarships/grants, traineeships, health care benefits, tuition waivers, and unspecified assistantships also available. Support available to part-time students. Financial award application deadline: 1/15; financial award applicants required to submit FAFSA. *Unit head:* Dr. C. Mani Krishna, Graduate Program Director, 413-545-4583, Fax: 413-545-4611, E-mail: ecegrad@ecs.umass.edu. *Application contact:* Jean M. Ames, Supervisor of Admissions, 413-545-0722, Fax: 413-577-0010, E-mail: gradadm@grad.umass.edu.

University of Massachusetts Dartmouth, Graduate School, College of Engineering, Department of Electrical and Computer Engineering, North Dartmouth, MA 02747-2300. Offers acoustics (Postbaccalaureate Certificate); communications (Postbaccalaureate Certificate); computer engineering (MS, PhD); computer systems engineering (Postbaccalaureate Certificate); digital signal processing (Postbaccalaureate Certificate); electrical engineering (MS, PhD); electrical engineering systems (Postbaccalaureate Certificate). Part-time programs available. *Faculty:* 18 full-time (3 women), 4 part-time/adjunct (0 women). *Students:* 39 full-time (11 women), 42 part-time (8 women); includes 8 minority (2 African Americans, 5 Asian Americans or Pacific Islanders, 1 Hispanic American), 46 international. Average age 28. 99 applicants, 80% accepted, 26 enrolled. In 2009, 34 master's, 1 doctorate, 3 other advanced degrees awarded. *Degree requirements:* For master's, culminating project or thesis; for doctorate, comprehensive exam, thesis/dissertation. *Entrance requirements:* For master's, GRE General Test, minimum undergraduate GPA of 3.0, 3 letters or recommendation; for doctorate, GRE. Additional exam requirements/recommendations for international students: Required—TOEFL (minimum score 550 paper-based; 213 computer-based). *Application deadline:* For fall admission, 2/1 priority date for domestic students, 12/1 for international students; for spring admission, 11/1 priority date for domestic students, 9/1 for international students. Applications are processed on a rolling basis. Application fee: $40 ($60 for international students). Electronic applications accepted. *Expenses:* Tuition, state resident: full-time $2071; part-time $86.29 per credit. Tuition, nonresident: full-time $8099; part-time $337.46 per credit. Required fees: $9446. Tuition and fees vary according to class time, course load and reciprocity agreements. *Financial support:* In 2009–10, 2 fellowships with full tuition reimbursements (averaging $16,000 per year), 14 research assistantships with full tuition reimbursements (averaging $11,096 per year), 9 teaching assistantships with full tuition reimbursements (averaging $12,500 per year) were awarded; Federal Work-Study and unspecified assistantships also available. Support available to part-time students. Financial award application deadline: 3/1; financial award applicants required to submit FAFSA. *Faculty research:* Speech acoustics, marine applications, signals and systems, applies electromagnetics, intelligent agency. Total annual research expenditures: $935,000. *Unit head:* Dr. Karen Payton, Director, 508-999-8434, Fax: 508-999-8489, E-mail: kpayton@umassd.edu. *Application contact:* Elan Turcotte-Shamski, Graduate Admissions Officer, 508-999-8604, Fax: 508-999-8183, E-mail: graduate@umassd.edu.

University of Massachusetts Lowell, James B. Francis College of Engineering, Department of Electrical and Computer Engineering, Program in Computer Engineering, Lowell, MA 01854-2881. Offers MS Eng. *Degree requirements:* For master's, thesis optional.

University of Memphis, Graduate School, Herff College of Engineering, Department of Electrical and Computer Engineering, Memphis, TN 38152. Offers automatic control systems (MS); biomedical systems (MS); communications and propagation systems (MS); computer engineering (PhD); electrical engineering (PhD); engineering computer systems (MS). *Faculty:* 8 full-time (1 woman), 2 part-time/adjunct (0 women). *Students:* 32 full-time (6 women), 4 part-time (1 woman); includes 3 African Americans, 1 Asian American or Pacific Islander, 25 international. Average age 26. 30 applicants, 87% accepted, 21 enrolled. In 2009, 10 master's awarded. *Degree requirements:* For master's, comprehensive exam, thesis or alternative. *Entrance requirements:* For master's, GRE General Test or MAT, minimum undergraduate GPA of 2.5. *Application deadline:* For fall admission, 8/1 for domestic students; for spring admission, 12/1 for domestic students. Application fee: $35 ($60 for international students). *Expenses:* Tuition, state resident: full-time $6246; part-time $347 per credit hour. Tuition, nonresident: full-time $15,894; part-time $883 per credit hour. Required fees: $1160. Full-time tuition and fees vary according to course load, degree level and program. *Financial support:* In

Computer Engineering

University of Memphis (continued)
2009–10, 4 students received support; research assistantships, teaching assistantships, career-related internships or fieldwork, Federal Work-Study, scholarships/grants, and unspecified assistantships available. Financial award application deadline: 2/15; financial award applicants required to submit FAFSA. *Faculty research:* Image processing, imaging sensors, biomedical systems, intelligent systems. *Unit head:* Dr. David J. Russomanno, Chair and Ballard Professor, 901-678-2175, Fax: 901-678-5469, E-mail: russmnn@memphis.edu. *Application contact:* Dr. Steven T. Griffin, Coordinator of Graduate Studies, 901-678-5268, Fax: 901-678-5469, E-mail: stgriffn@memphis.edu.

University of Memphis, Graduate School, Herff College of Engineering, Department of Engineering Technology, Memphis, TN 38152. Offers computer engineering technology (MS); electronics engineering technology (MS); manufacturing engineering technology (MS). Part-time and evening/weekend programs available. *Faculty:* 5 full-time (0 women). *Students:* 4 full-time (1 woman), 6 part-time (1 woman); includes 4 minority (all African Americans), 2 international. Average age 38. 2 applicants, 50% accepted, 1 enrolled. *Degree requirements:* For master's, comprehensive exam, thesis optional. *Entrance requirements:* For master's, GRE General Test, minimum undergraduate GPA of 2.5. *Application deadline:* For fall admission, 8/1 for domestic students; for spring admission, 12/1 for domestic students. Applications are processed on a rolling basis. Application fee: $25 ($50 for international students). Electronic applications accepted. *Expenses:* Tuition, state resident: full-time $6246; part-time $347 per credit hour. Tuition, nonresident: full-time $15,894; part-time $883 per credit hour. Required fees: $1160. Full-time tuition and fees vary according to course load, degree level and program. *Financial support:* In 2009–10, 5 students received support; research assistantships with full tuition reimbursements available, career-related internships or fieldwork, Federal Work-Study, scholarships/grants, and unspecified assistantships available. Financial award application deadline: 2/15; financial award applicants required to submit FAFSA. *Faculty research:* Teacher education services-technology education; flexible manufacturing control systems; embedded, dedicated, and real-time computer systems; network, Internet, and web-based programming; analog and digital electronic communication systems. *Unit head:* Deborah J. Hochstein, Chairman, 901-678-2225, Fax: 901-678-5145, E-mail: dhochstn@memphis.edu. *Application contact:* Carl R. Williams, Coordinator of Graduate Studies, 901-678-3296, Fax: 901-678-5145, E-mail: crwillia@memphis.edu.

University of Miami, Graduate School, College of Engineering, Department of Electrical and Computer Engineering, Coral Gables, FL 33124. Offers MSECE, PhD. Part-time programs available. *Degree requirements:* For master's, thesis (for some programs); for doctorate, comprehensive exam, thesis/dissertation, dissertation proposal defense. *Entrance requirements:* For master's, GRE General Test, minimum GPA of 3.0; for doctorate, GRE General Test, minimum undergraduate GPA of 3.3, graduate 3.5. Additional exam requirements/recommendations for international students: Required—TOEFL (minimum score 550 paper-based; 213 computer-based; 59 iBT), IELTS (minimum score 7). Electronic applications accepted. *Faculty research:* Computer network, image processing, database systems, digital signal processing, machine intelligence.

University of Michigan, Horace H. Rackham School of Graduate Studies, College of Engineering, Department of Computer Science and Engineering, Ann Arbor, MI 48109. Offers MS, MSE, PhD. *Faculty:* 43 full-time (4 women). *Students:* 210 full-time (27 women), 2 part-time (0 women); includes 23 minority (4 African Americans, 15 Asian Americans or Pacific Islanders, 4 Hispanic Americans), 123 international. 841 applicants, 22% accepted, 64 enrolled. In 2009, 35 master's, 35 doctorates awarded. *Expenses:* Tuition, state resident: full-time $17,286; part-time $1099 per credit hour. Tuition, nonresident: full-time $34,944; part-time $2080 per credit hour. Required fees: $95 per semester. Tuition and fees vary according to course load, degree level and program. *Faculty research:* Solid state electronics and optics; communications, control, signal process; sensors and integrated circuitry, others; software systems; artificial intelligence; hardware systems. *Unit head:* Prof. Farnam Jahanian, Department Chair, 734-647-1807, Fax: 734-763-1503, E-mail: farnam@umich.edu. *Application contact:* Dawn Freysinger, Graduate Programs Coordinator, 734-647-1807, Fax: 734-763-1503, E-mail: dawnf@umich.edu.

University of Michigan–Dearborn, College of Engineering and Computer Science, Department of Electrical and Computer Engineering, Dearborn, MI 48128-1491. Offers computer engineering (MSE); electrical engineering (MSE); software engineering (MS). Part-time programs available. *Faculty:* 8 full-time (1 woman). *Students:* 22 full-time (4 women), 124 part-time (22 women); includes 34 minority (5 African Americans, 27 Asian Americans or Pacific Islanders, 2 Hispanic Americans). Average age 29. 51 applicants, 35% accepted, 24 enrolled. In 2009, 11 master's awarded. *Degree requirements:* For master's, thesis optional. *Entrance requirements:* For master's, GRE (recommended), bachelor's degree in electrical and computer engineering or equivalent, minimum GPA of 3.0. Additional exam requirements/recommendations for international students: Required—TOEFL (minimum score 560 paper-based; 220 computer-based; 84 iBT). *Application deadline:* For fall admission, 8/1 priority date for domestic students, 5/1 for international students; for winter admission, 12/1 priority date for domestic students, 11/1 for international students; for spring admission, 4/1 priority date for domestic students, 3/1 for international students. Applications are processed on a rolling basis. Application fee: $60 ($75 for international students). *Expenses:* Tuition, area resident: Part-time $504.10 per credit hour. Tuition, state resident: part-time $504.10 per credit hour. Tuition, nonresident: part-time $957.90 per credit hour. *Financial support:* In 2009–10, 7 fellowships (averaging $18,331 per year), 12 research assistantships with full tuition reimbursements (averaging $15,494 per year) were awarded; teaching assistantships, Federal Work-Study also available. Financial award application deadline: 4/1; financial award applicants required to submit FAFSA. *Faculty research:* Fuzzy systems and applications, machine vision, pattern recognition and machine intelligence, vehicle electronics, wireless communications. *Unit head:* Dr. Lu Murphey, Chair, 313-593-5028, Fax: 313-583-6336, E-mail: yilu@umich.edu. *Application contact:* Sandra Marie Krzyskowski, Intermediate Academic Records Assistant, 313-593-5420, Fax: 313-583-6336, E-mail: ece-grad@umd.umich.edu.

University of Minnesota, Duluth, Graduate School, Swenson College of Science and Engineering, Department of Electrical and Computer Engineering, Duluth, MN 55812-2496. Offers MSECE. Part-time programs available. *Faculty:* 7 full-time (1 woman). *Students:* 11 full-time (1 woman), 7 international. Average age 26. 21 applicants, 86% accepted, 4 enrolled. In 2009, 5 master's awarded. *Degree requirements:* For master's, thesis. *Entrance requirements:* Additional exam requirements/recommendations for international students: Recommended—IELTS, TWE. *Application deadline:* For fall admission, 7/15 for domestic and international students; for spring admission, 11/1 for domestic and international students. Applications are processed on a rolling basis. Application fee: $75 ($95 for international students). *Financial support:* In 2009–10, 11 students received support, including 9 research assistantships with partial tuition reimbursements available (averaging $6,449 per year), 11 teaching assistantships with partial tuition reimbursements available (averaging $6,449 per year); health care benefits and unspecified assistantships also available. Financial award application deadline: 9/1. *Faculty research:* Biomedical instrumentation, transportation systems, computer hardware and software, signal processing, optical communications. Total annual research expenditures: $200,000. *Unit head:* Dr. Imran Hayee, Director of Graduate Studies, 218-726-6743, Fax: 218-726-7267, E-mail: ihayee@d.umn.edu. *Application contact:* Tami Vatalaro, Executive Administration Specialist, 218-726-7523, Fax: 218-726-6970, E-mail: grad@d.umn.edu.

University of Minnesota, Twin Cities Campus, Institute of Technology, Department of Electrical Engineering, Minneapolis, MN 55455-0213. Offers MEE, MSEE, PhD. Part-time programs available. *Degree requirements:* For master's, thesis or alternative; for doctorate, thesis/dissertation. *Entrance requirements:* Additional exam requirements/recommendations for international students: Required—TOEFL (minimum score 550 paper-based; 213 computer-based), GRE. *Faculty research:* Signal processing, microelectronics, computers, controls, power electronics.

University of Minnesota, Twin Cities Campus, Institute of Technology, Program in Computer Engineering, Minneapolis, MN 55455-0213. Offers M Comp E, MS. Part-time programs available. Postbaccalaureate distance learning degree programs offered (no on-campus study). *Degree requirements:* For master's, thesis or alternative. *Entrance requirements:* Additional exam requirements/recommendations for international students: Required—TOEFL. *Faculty research:* Computer networks, parallel computing, software engineering, VLSI and CAI, databases.

University of Missouri–Kansas City, School of Computing and Engineering, Kansas City, MO 64110-2499. Offers civil engineering (MS); computer and electrical engineering (PhD); computer science (MS), including bioinformatics, software engineering, telecommunications networking; computer science and informatics (PhD); computing (PhD); electrical engineering (MS); engineering (PhD); mechanical engineering (MS); telecommunications (PhD). PhD (interdisciplinary) offered through the School of Graduate Studies. Part-time programs available. *Faculty:* 40 full-time (5 women), 28 part-time/adjunct (0 women). *Students:* 230 full-time (46 women), 158 part-time (31 women); includes 20 minority (5 African Americans, 12 Asian Americans or Pacific Islanders, 3 Hispanic Americans), 313 international. Average age 24. 484 applicants, 64% accepted, 106 enrolled. In 2009, 144 master's awarded. *Degree requirements:* For doctorate, thesis/dissertation. *Entrance requirements:* For master's, GRE General Test, minimum GPA of 3.0, 3 letters of recommendations from professors; for doctorate, GRE General Test, minimum GPA of 3.5. Additional exam requirements/recommendations for international students: Required—TOEFL (minimum score 550 paper-based; 213 computer-based; 80 iBT). *Application deadline:* For fall admission, 1/15 priority date for domestic students, 1/15 for international students. Applications are processed on a rolling basis. Application fee: $45 ($50 for international students). *Expenses:* Tuition, state resident: full-time $5378; part-time $299 per credit hour. Tuition, nonresident: full-time $13,881; part-time $771 per credit hour. Required fees: $641; $71 per credit hour. Tuition and fees vary according to course load and program. *Financial support:* In 2009–10, 29 research assistantships with partial tuition reimbursements (averaging $15,040 per year), 10 teaching assistantships with partial tuition reimbursements (averaging $12,118 per year) were awarded; career-related internships or fieldwork, Federal Work-Study, scholarships/grants, tuition waivers (partial), and unspecified assistantships also available. Support available to part-time students. Financial award application deadline: 3/1; financial award applicants required to submit FAFSA. *Faculty research:* Algorithms, bioinformatics and medical informatics, biomechanics/biomaterials, civil engineering materials, networking and telecommunications, thermal science. Total annual research expenditures: $1.4 million. *Unit head:* Dr. Kevin Z. Truman, Dean, 816-235-2399, Fax: 816-235-5159. *Application contact:* Dr. Kevin Z. Truman, Dean, 816-235-2399, Fax: 816-235-5159.

University of Nebraska–Lincoln, Graduate College, College of Arts and Sciences and College of Engineering, Department of Computer Science and Engineering, Lincoln, NE 68588. Offers bioinformatics (MS, PhD); computer engineering (MS, PhD); computer science (MS, PhD); information technology (PhD). *Degree requirements:* For master's, thesis optional; for doctorate, comprehensive exam, thesis/dissertation. *Entrance requirements:* For master's and doctorate, GRE General Test. Additional exam requirements/recommendations for international students: Required—TOEFL (minimum score 600 paper-based; 250 computer-based). Electronic applications accepted. *Faculty research:* Software engineering, geo- and bio-informatics, scientific computation, secure communication.

University of Nevada, Las Vegas, Graduate College, Howard R. Hughes College of Engineering, Department of Electrical and Computer Engineering, Las Vegas, NV 89154-4026. Offers MSE, PhD. Part-time programs available. *Faculty:* 14 full-time (1 woman), 3 part-time/adjunct (0 women). *Students:* 33 full-time (5 women), 17 part-time (3 women); includes 7 minority (2 African Americans, 5 Asian Americans or Pacific Islanders), 33 international. Average age 29. 54 applicants, 74% accepted, 20 enrolled. In 2009, 22 master's, 1 doctorate awarded. *Degree requirements:* For master's, comprehensive exam, thesis (for some programs), project; for doctorate, comprehensive exam, thesis/dissertation. *Entrance requirements:* Additional exam requirements/recommendations for international students: Required—TOEFL (minimum score 550 paper-based; 213 computer-based; 80 iBT), IELTS (minimum score 7). *Application deadline:* For fall admission, 2/1 priority date for domestic and international students; for spring admission, 10/1 priority date for domestic and international students. Applications are processed on a rolling basis. Application fee: $60 ($95 for international students). Electronic applications accepted. *Financial support:* In 2009–10, 25 students received support, including 12 research assistantships with partial tuition reimbursements available (averaging $12,220 per year), 13 teaching assistantships with partial tuition reimbursements available (averaging $10,307 per year); institutionally sponsored loans, scholarships/grants, health care benefits, tuition waivers (full), and unspecified assistantships also available. Financial award application deadline: 3/1. *Unit head:* Dr. Henry Selvaraj, Chair/ Professor, 702-895-4183, Fax: 702-895-4075, E-mail: ece.chair@unlv.edu. *Application contact:* Graduate College Admissions Evaluator, 702-895-3320, Fax: 702-895-4180, E-mail: gradcollege@unlv.edu.

University of Nevada, Reno, Graduate School, College of Engineering, Department of Computer Science and Engineering, Program in Computer Engineering, Reno, NV 89557. Offers MS. *Degree requirements:* For master's, thesis optional. *Entrance requirements:* For master's, GRE General Test, minimum GPA of 2.75. Additional exam requirements/recommendations for international students: Required—TOEFL (minimum score 500 paper-based; 173 computer-based; 61 iBT), IELTS (minimum score 6). Electronic applications accepted. *Faculty research:* Evolutionary computing systems, computer vision/virtual reality, software engineering.

University of Nevada, Reno, Graduate School, College of Engineering, Department of Computer Science and Engineering, Program in Computer Science and Engineering, Reno, NV 89557. Offers PhD. *Degree requirements:* For doctorate, thesis/dissertation. *Entrance requirements:* For doctorate, GRE General Test, minimum GPA of 3.0. Additional exam requirements/recommendations for international students: Required—TOEFL (minimum score 500 paper-based; 173 computer-based; 61 iBT), IELTS (minimum score 6). Electronic applications accepted. *Faculty research:* Evolutionary computing systems, computer vision/virtual reality, software engineering.

University of New Brunswick Fredericton, School of Graduate Studies, Faculty of Engineering, Department of Electrical and Computer Engineering, Fredericton, NB E3B 5A3, Canada. Offers M Eng, M Sc E, PhD. Part-time programs available. *Faculty:* 16 full-time (3 women), 1 part-time/adjunct (0 women). *Students:* 54 full-time (3 women), 8 part-time (1 woman). 45 applicants, 44% accepted. In 2009, 14 master's, 5 doctorates awarded. *Degree requirements:* For master's, thesis, Research Proposal; for Master's in Engineering: 10 Graduate Courses required; for doctorate, comprehensive exam, thesis/dissertation, research proposal. *Entrance requirements:* For master's, minimum GPA of 3.0 or B; acceptable English score; references; for doctorate, MSc 80%, minimum GPA of 3.0 or B; previous transcripts; acceptable English score; and references. Additional exam requirements/recommendations for international students: Required—TOEFL (minimum score 580 paper-based; 237 computer-based), TWE, or IELTS (minimum score 7). *Application deadline:* Applications are processed on a rolling basis. Application fee: $50 Canadian dollars. Tuition and fees charges are reported in Canadian dollars. *Expenses:* Tuition, area resident: Full-time $5562 Canadian dollars; part-time $2781 Canadian dollars per year. Required fees: $49.75 Canadian dollars per term. *Financial support:* In 2009–10, 26 research assistantships (averaging $14,400 per year), 25 teaching assistantships were awarded; fellowships also available. *Faculty research:* Biomedical engineering, communications, controls, electromagnetic systems, embedded systems, optical fiber systems, sustainable energy signal processing, software systems. *Unit head:* Dr. Maryhelen Stevenson, Director of Graduate Studies, 504-447-3147, Fax: 504-453-3589, E-mail: stevenso@unb.ca. *Application contact:* Shelley Cormier, Graduate Secretary, 506-452-6142, Fax: 506-453-3589, E-mail: scormier@unb.ca.

University of New Haven, Graduate School, Tagliatela College of Engineering, Program in Electrical Engineering, West Haven, CT 06516-1916. Offers communications/dsp (MS); control system (MS); electrical and computer engineering (MS); electrical engineering (MS). Part-time and evening/weekend programs available. *Faculty:* 9 full-time (2 women), 5 part-time/adjunct (0 women). *Students:* 38 full-time (10 women), 11 part-time (3 women); includes 3 minority (all African Americans), 39 international. Average age 25. 185 applicants, 92% accepted, 22 enrolled. In 2009, 40 master's awarded. *Degree requirements:* For master's, thesis or alternative. *Entrance requirements:* For master's, bachelor's degree in electrical engineering. Additional exam requirements/recommendations for international students: Required—TOEFL (minimum score 520 paper-based; 190 computer-based; 70 iBT); Recommended—IELTS (minimum score 5.5). *Application deadline:* For fall admission, 5/31 for international students; for winter admission, 10/15 for international students; for spring admission, 1/15 for international students. Applications are processed on a rolling basis. Application fee: $50. Electronic applications accepted. *Expenses:* Tuition: Part-time $700 per credit. Required fees: $45 per term. One-time fee: $390 part-time. *Financial support:* Research assistantships with partial tuition reimbursements, teaching assistantships with partial tuition reimbursements, career-related internships or fieldwork, Federal Work-Study, scholarships/grants, tuition waivers, and unspecified assistantships available. Support available to part-time students. Financial award applicants required to submit FAFSA. *Unit head:* Dr. Ali Golbazi, Professor and Chair, 203-932-7164. *Application contact:* Eloise Gormley, Director of Graduate Admissions, 203-932-7449, Fax: 203-932-7137, E-mail: gradinfo@newhaven.edu.

University of New Mexico, Graduate School, School of Engineering, Department of Electrical and Computer Engineering, Albuquerque, NM 87131-2039. Offers computer engineering (MS, PhD); electrical engineering (MS, PhD). Part-time and evening/weekend programs available. Postbaccalaureate distance learning degree programs offered (no on-campus study). *Faculty:* 49 full-time (6 women), 5 part-time/adjunct (0 women). *Students:* 163 full-time (31 women), 64 part-time (9 women); includes 29 minority (1 African American, 1 American Indian/Alaska Native, 6 Asian Americans or Pacific Islanders, 21 Hispanic Americans), 123 international. Average age 30. 273 applicants, 37% accepted, 61 enrolled. In 2009, 28 master's, 15 doctorates awarded. Terminal master's awarded for partial completion of doctoral program. *Degree requirements:* For master's, thesis; for doctorate, comprehensive exam, thesis/dissertation. *Entrance requirements:* For master's, GRE General Test, minimum GPA of 3.0; for doctorate, GRE General Test, minimum GPA of 3.5. Additional exam requirements/recommendations for international students: Required—TOEFL (minimum score 550 paper-based; 213 computer-based; 79 iBT). *Application deadline:* For fall admission, 2/15 for domestic students, 2/15 for international students; for spring admission, 11/1 for domestic students, 6/15 for international students. Application fee: $50. Electronic applications accepted. *Expenses:* Tuition, state resident: full-time $2098.80; part-time $233.20 per credit hour. Tuition, nonresident: full-time $6650. Required fees: $25 per semester. Tuition and fees vary according to course load, program and reciprocity agreements. *Financial support:* In 2009–10, 22 students received support, including 2 fellowships with tuition reimbursements available (averaging $12,500 per year), 85 research assistantships with tuition reimbursements available (averaging $13,000 per year), 16 teaching assistantships with tuition reimbursements available (averaging $13,715 per year); scholarships/grants, health care benefits, and unspecified assistantships also available. Financial award application deadline: 2/15; financial award applicants required to submit FAFSA. *Faculty research:* Advanced graphics and visualization, biomedical engineering, communications and networking, networked control systems, photonics and microelectronics, pulsed power and high-power electromagnetics, reconfigurable systems. Total annual research expenditures: $3.2 million. *Unit head:* Dr. Chaouki T. Abdallah, Chair, 505-277-0298, Fax: 505-277-1439, E-mail: chaouki@ece.unm.edu. *Application contact:* Elmyra Grelle, Coordinator—Graduate Programs, 505-277-2600, Fax: 505-277-1439, E-mail: egrelle@ece.unm.edu.

See Close-Up on page 377.

The University of North Carolina at Charlotte, Graduate School, The William States Lee College of Engineering, Department of Electrical and Computer Engineering, Charlotte, NC 28223-0001. Offers electrical engineering (MSEE, PhD). Part-time and evening/weekend programs available. *Faculty:* 26 full-time (1 woman). *Students:* 103 full-time (19 women), 59 part-time (8 women); includes 4 African Americans, 4 Asian Americans or Pacific Islanders, 3 Hispanic Americans, 117 international. Average age 26. 410 applicants, 46% accepted, 40 enrolled. In 2009, 43 master's, 3 doctorates awarded. Terminal master's awarded for partial completion of doctoral program. *Degree requirements:* For master's, thesis optional, thesis or project; for doctorate, thesis/dissertation. *Entrance requirements:* For master's, GRE General Test, minimum GPA of 3.0 in undergraduate major, 2.75 overall; for doctorate, GRE General Test, 3 letters of reference. Additional exam requirements/recommendations for international students: Required—TOEFL (minimum score 557 paper-based; 220 computer-based; 83 iBT). *Application deadline:* For fall admission, 7/1 for domestic students, 5/1 for international students; for spring admission, 11/1 for domestic students, 10/1 for international students. Applications are processed on a rolling basis. Application fee: $55. Electronic applications accepted. *Financial support:* In 2009–10, 55 students received support, including 1 fellowship (averaging $45,000 per year), 8 research assistantships (averaging $7,186 per year), 46 teaching assistantships (averaging $8,303 per year); career-related internships or fieldwork, institutionally sponsored loans, scholarships/grants, and unspecified assistantships also available. Support available to part-time students. Financial award application deadline: 4/1; financial award applicants required to submit FAFSA. *Faculty research:* Integrated circuits self test, control systems, optoelectronics/microelectronics devices and systems, communications, computer engineering. Total annual research expenditures: $1.2 million. *Unit head:* Dr. Ian Ferguson, Chair, 704-687-8404, Fax: 704-687-4762, E-mail: ianf@uncc.edu. *Application contact:* Kathy B. Giddings, Director of Graduate Admissions, 704-687-5503, Fax: 704-687-3279, E-mail: gradadm@uncc.edu.

University of North Texas, Robert B. Toulouse School of Graduate Studies, College of Engineering, Department of Computer Science and Engineering, Denton, TX 76203-5017. Offers computer science (MS); computer science and engineering (PhD). Terminal master's awarded for partial completion of doctoral program. *Degree requirements:* For master's, comprehensive exam (for some programs), thesis (for some programs); for doctorate, comprehensive exam, thesis/dissertation. *Entrance requirements:* For master's, GRE General Test (minimum score 400 verbal, 700 quantitative, 600 analytical or 4.0), minimum GPA of 3.0; for doctorate, GRE General Test (minimum scores: Verbal 50th percentile, Quantitative 700, Analytical 600 or 4.5), minimum GPA of 3.5, 3 letters of recommendation. Additional exam requirements/recommendations for international students: Required—TOEFL (minimum score 550 paper-based; 213 computer-based; 79 iBT), proof of English language proficiency required for non-native English speakers; Recommended—IELTS (minimum score 6.5). Application fee: $50 ($75 for international students). Electronic applications accepted. *Expenses:* Tuition, state resident: full-time $4298; part-time $239 per contact hour. Tuition, nonresident: full-time $9878; part-time $549 per contact hour. Required fees: $265 per contact hour. *Financial support:* Fellowships with tuition reimbursements, research assistantships with tuition reimbursements, teaching assistantships with tuition reimbursements, career-related internships or fieldwork, Federal Work-Study, and institutionally sponsored loans available. Financial award application deadline: 4/1; financial award applicants required to submit FAFSA. *Faculty research:* Databases and data mining, computer architecture, cryptography, agent-oriented software engineering, graph theory, low power synthesis. *Application contact:* Graduate Program Coordinator, 940-565-2767, Fax: 940-565-2799, E-mail: armin.mikler@unt.edu.

University of Notre Dame, Graduate School, College of Engineering, Department of Computer Science and Engineering, Notre Dame, IN 46556. Offers MSCSE, PhD. Terminal master's awarded for partial completion of doctoral program. *Degree requirements:* For master's, comprehensive exam; for doctorate, thesis/dissertation, candidacy exam. *Entrance requirements:* For master's and doctorate, GRE General Test. Additional exam requirements/recommendations for international students: Required—TOEFL (minimum score 600 paper-based; 250 computer-based; 80 iBT). Electronic applications accepted. *Faculty research:* Algorithms and theory of computer science, artificial intelligence, behavior-based robotics, biometrics, computer vision.

See Display on this page.

University of Oklahoma, Graduate College, College of Engineering, Department of Electrical and Computer Engineering, Norman, OK 73019. Offers electrical and computer engineering

Computer Engineering

University of Oklahoma (continued)

(MS, PhD); telecommunication systems engineering (MS). Part-time programs available. *Faculty:* 37 full-time (1 woman), 3 part-time/adjunct (0 women). *Students:* 118 full-time (30 women), 24 part-time (2 women); includes 16 minority (3 African Americans, 3 American Indian/Alaska Native, 8 Asian Americans or Pacific Islanders, 2 Hispanic Americans), 82 international. 76 applicants, 70% accepted, 25 enrolled. In 2009, 40 master's, 10 doctorates awarded. Terminal master's awarded for partial completion of doctoral program. *Degree requirements:* For master's, thesis, oral exam; for doctorate, thesis/dissertation, general exam, oral exam, qualifying exam. *Entrance requirements:* For master's and doctorate, GRE General Test. Additional exam requirements/recommendations for international students: Required—TOEFL (minimum score 550 paper-based; 213 computer-based). *Application deadline:* For fall admission, 5/15 for domestic students, 4/1 for international students; for spring admission, 9/1 for domestic and international students. Applications are processed on a rolling basis. Application fee: $40 ($90 for international students). Electronic applications accepted. *Expenses:* Tuition, state resident: full-time $3744; part-time $156 per credit hour. Tuition, nonresident: full-time $13,577; part-time $565.70 per credit hour. Required fees: $2415; $90.10 per credit hour. *Financial support:* In 2009–10, 108 students received support, including 66 research assistantships with partial tuition reimbursements available (averaging $12,776 per year), 21 teaching assistantships with partial tuition reimbursements available (averaging $12,448 per year); career-related internships or fieldwork, scholarships/grants, health care benefits, and unspecified assistantships also available. Financial award application deadline: 4/15; financial award applicants required to submit FAFSA. *Faculty research:* Signal and image processing, weather radar, solid state electronics, biomedical computer hardware design, power/electrical energy. Total annual research expenditures: $5.1 million. *Unit head:* Dr. James Sluss, Director, 405-325-4721, Fax: 405-325-7066, E-mail: sluss@ou.edu. *Application contact:* Samuel C. Lee, Graduate Liaison, 405-325-8131, Fax: 405-325-7066, E-mail: ecegrad@ou.edu.

University of Ottawa, Faculty of Graduate and Postdoctoral Studies, Faculty of Engineering, Ottawa-Carleton Institute for Electrical and Computer Engineering, Ottawa, ON K1N 6N5, Canada. Offers M Eng, MA Sc, PhD. *Degree requirements:* For master's, thesis or alternative, project; for doctorate, comprehensive exam, thesis/dissertation. *Entrance requirements:* For master's, honors degree or equivalent, minimum B average; for doctorate, minimum A- average. Electronic applications accepted. *Faculty research:* CAD, CSE, distributed systems and BISDN, CCN, DOC.

University of Puerto Rico, Mayagüez Campus, Graduate Studies, College of Engineering, Department of Electrical and Computer Engineering, Mayagüez, PR 00681-9000. Offers computer engineering (ME, MS); electrical engineering (ME, MS). Part-time programs available. *Degree requirements:* For master's, comprehensive exam, thesis. *Entrance requirements:* For master's, proficiency in English and Spanish, BS degree in electrical or computer engineering or equivalent, minimum GPA of 3.0. Additional exam requirements/recommendations for international students: Required—TOEFL (minimum score 450 paper-based). *Faculty research:* Microcomputer interfacing, control systems, power systems, electronics.

University of Regina, Faculty of Graduate Studies and Research, Faculty of Engineering and Applied Science, Program in Electronic Systems Engineering, Regina, SK S4S 0A2, Canada. Offers M Eng, MA Sc, PhD. *Faculty:* 5 full-time (0 women). *Students:* 19 full-time (3 women), 5 part-time (0 women). 36 applicants, 44% accepted. In 2009, 7 master's, 1 doctorate awarded. *Degree requirements:* For master's, thesis (for some programs). *Entrance requirements:* For doctorate, master's degree. Additional exam requirements/recommendations for international students: Required—TOEFL (minimum score 550 paper-based; 213 computer-based; 80 iBT). *Application deadline:* Applications are processed on a rolling basis. Application fee: $90 ($100 for international students). Electronic applications accepted. *Financial support:* In 2009–10, 8 fellowships (averaging $19,000 per year), 3 research assistantships (averaging $16,910 per year), 12 teaching assistantships (averaging $6,650 per year) were awarded; career-related internships or fieldwork and scholarships/grants also available. Financial award application deadline: 6/15. *Faculty research:* Signal image processing, fiber optic network, analog/digital VLSI, expert system communication network. *Unit head:* Dr. Raman Paranjape, Graduate Program Coordinator, 306-585-5290, Fax: 306-585-4855, E-mail: raman.paranjape@uregina.ca. *Application contact:* Crystal Pick, Information Contact, 306-337-2603, E-mail: crystal.pick@uregina.ca.

University of Rhode Island, Graduate School, College of Engineering, Department of Electrical, Computer and Biomedical Engineering, Kingston, RI 02881. Offers MS, PhD, Graduate Certificate. Part-time programs available. *Faculty:* 18 full-time (3 women), 2 part-time/adjunct (0 women). *Students:* 27 full-time (7 women), 17 part-time (2 women); includes 7 minority (2 African Americans, 2 Asian Americans or Pacific Islanders, 3 Hispanic Americans), 13 international. In 2009, 13 master's, 3 doctorates awarded. *Degree requirements:* For master's, comprehensive exam (for some programs), thesis optional; for doctorate, comprehensive exam, thesis/dissertation. *Entrance requirements:* For master's and doctorate, 2 letters of recommendation. Additional exam requirements/recommendations for international students: Required—TOEFL (minimum score 550 paper-based; 213 computer-based). *Application deadline:* For fall admission, 7/15 for domestic students, 2/1 for international students; for spring admission, 11/15 for domestic students, 7/15 for international students. Application fee: $65. Electronic applications accepted. *Expenses:* Tuition, state resident: full-time $8828; part-time $490 per credit hour. Tuition, nonresident: full-time $22,100; part-time $1228 per credit hour. Required fees: $1118; $57 per semester. Tuition and fees vary according to program. *Financial support:* In 2009–10, 5 research assistantships with full and partial tuition reimbursements (averaging $4,888 per year), 4 teaching assistantships with full and partial tuition reimbursements (averaging $6,726 per year) were awarded. Financial award application deadline: 7/15; financial award applicants required to submit FAFSA. *Faculty research:* Biomedical Instrumentation, cardiac physiology and computational modeling, analog/digital CMOS circuits, neural-machine interface, digital circuit design and VLSI testing. Total annual research expenditures: $744,413. *Unit head:* Dr. G. Faye Boudreaux-Bartels, Chair, 401-874-5805, Fax: 401-782-6422, E-mail: boud@ele.uri.edu. *Application contact:* Dr. Godi Fischer, Director of Graduate Studies, 401-874-5879, Fax: 401-782-6422, E-mail: fischer@ele.uri.edu.

University of Rochester, The College, School of Engineering and Applied Sciences, Department of Electrical and Computer Engineering, Rochester, NY 14627. Offers MS, PhD. Terminal master's awarded for partial completion of doctoral program. *Degree requirements:* For master's, comprehensive exam; for doctorate, thesis/dissertation, preliminary and oral exams. *Entrance requirements:* For master's and doctorate, GRE. Additional exam requirements/recommendations for international students: Required—TOEFL.

University of South Carolina, The Graduate School, College of Engineering and Computing, Department of Computer Science and Engineering, Columbia, SC 29208. Offers computer science and engineering (ME, MS, PhD); software engineering (MS). Part-time and evening/weekend programs available. Postbaccalaureate distance learning degree programs offered (minimal on-campus study). *Degree requirements:* For master's, comprehensive exam, thesis (for some programs); for doctorate, comprehensive exam, thesis/dissertation. *Entrance requirements:* For master's and doctorate, GRE General Test. Additional exam requirements/recommendations for international students: Required—TOEFL (minimum score 570 paper-based; 230 computer-based). Electronic applications accepted. *Faculty research:* Computer security, computer vision, artificial intelligence, multiagent systems, bioinformatics.

University of Southern California, Graduate School, Viterbi School of Engineering, Department of Computer Science, Los Angeles, CA 90089. Offers computer networks (MS); computer science (MS, PhD); computer security (MS); game development (MS); high performance computing and simulations (MS); human language technology (MS); intelligent robotics (MS); multimedia and creative technologies (MS); software engineering (MS). Part-time programs available. Postbaccalaureate distance learning degree programs offered (no on-campus study). *Faculty:* 26 full-time (2 women), 56 part-time/adjunct (7 women). *Students:* 711 full-time (148 women), 304 part-time (55 women); includes 76 minority (5 African Americans, 59 Asian Americans or Pacific Islanders, 12 Hispanic Americans), 816 international. 2,017 applicants, 39% accepted, 382 enrolled. In 2009, 332 master's, 32 doctorates awarded. Terminal master's awarded for partial completion of doctoral program. *Degree requirements:* For doctorate, comprehensive exam, thesis/dissertation. *Entrance requirements:* For master's, GRE General Test; for doctorate, General GRE. *Application deadline:* For fall admission, 3/1 priority date for domestic and international students; for spring admission, 10/1 priority date for domestic and international students. Applications are processed on a rolling basis. Application fee: $85. Electronic applications accepted. *Expenses:* Tuition: Full-time $25,980; part-time $1315 per unit. Required fees: $554. One-time fee: $35 full-time. Full-time tuition and fees vary according to degree level and program. *Financial support:* In 2009–10, fellowships with full tuition reimbursements (averaging $30,000 per year), research assistantships with full tuition reimbursements (averaging $19,250 per year), teaching assistantships with full tuition reimbursements (averaging $19,250 per year) were awarded; career-related internships or fieldwork, scholarships/grants, health care benefits, and unspecified assistantships also available. Financial award application deadline: 12/1; financial award applicants required to submit CSS PROFILE or FAFSA. *Faculty research:* Databases, computer graphics and computer vision, software engineering, networks and security, robotics, multimedia and virtual reality. Total annual research expenditures: $10 million. *Unit head:* Dr. Shanghua Teng, Seeley G. Mudd Professor of Engineering and Department Chair, 213-740-4498, E-mail: shanghua@ usc.edu. *Application contact:* Steve Schrader, Director of Student Affairs, 213-740-4779, E-mail: steve.schrader@usc.edu.

University of Southern California, Graduate School, Viterbi School of Engineering, Ming Hsieh Department of Electrical Engineering, Los Angeles, CA 90089. Offers computer engineering (MS, PhD); computer networks (MS), including electrical engineering; computer-aided engineering (MS); electrical engineering (PhD, Engr); engineering technology commercialization (Graduate Certificate); systems architecting and engineering (MS). Part-time programs available. Postbaccalaureate distance learning degree programs offered. *Faculty:* 59 full-time (3 women), 31 part-time/adjunct (1 woman). *Students:* 883 full-time (146 women), 451 part-time (65 women); includes 197 minority (16 African Americans, 159 Asian Americans or Pacific Islanders, 22 Hispanic Americans), 957 international. 2,377 applicants, 45% accepted, 514 enrolled. In 2009, 351 master's, 41 doctorates, 2 other advanced degrees awarded. Terminal master's awarded for partial completion of doctoral program. *Degree requirements:* For doctorate, thesis/dissertation. *Entrance requirements:* For master's, GRE General Test; for doctorate, General GRE. *Application deadline:* For fall admission, 3/1 priority date for domestic and international students; for spring admission, 10/1 priority date for domestic and international students. Applications are processed on a rolling basis. Application fee: $85. Electronic applications accepted. *Expenses:* Tuition: Full-time $25,980; part-time $1315 per unit. Required fees: $554. One-time fee: $35 full-time. Full-time tuition and fees vary according to degree level and program. *Financial support:* Career-related internships or fieldwork, scholarships/grants, health care benefits, and unspecified assistantships available. Financial award application deadline: 12/1; financial award applicants required to submit CSS PROFILE or FAFSA. *Faculty research:* Communications, computer engineering and networks, control systems, integrated circuits and systems, electromagnetics and energy conversion, micro electro-mechanical systems and nanotechnology, photonics and quantum electronics, plasma research, signal and image processing. Total annual research expenditures: $16.2 million. *Unit head:* Dr. Alexander A. Sawchuk, Chair, 213-740-4622, Fax: 213-740-4651, E-mail: sawchuk@sipi.usc.edu. *Application contact:* Diane Demetras, Student Affairs Coordinator, 213-740-4485, E-mail: eesystem@usc.edu.

University of South Florida, Graduate School, College of Engineering, Department of Computer Science and Engineering, Tampa, FL 33620-9951. Offers computer science (MSCS); computer science and engineering (PhD); comuter science (MSCP). Part-time programs available. *Faculty:* 18 full-time (1 woman). *Students:* 57 full-time (8 women), 39 part-time (10 women); includes 12 minority (5 African Americans, 1 Asian American or Pacific Islander, 6 Hispanic Americans), 48 international. Average age 32. 146 applicants, 43% accepted, 21 enrolled. In 2009, 15 master's, 9 doctorates awarded. Terminal master's awarded for partial completion of doctoral program. *Degree requirements:* For master's, comprehensive exam, thesis; for doctorate, comprehensive exam, thesis/dissertation, teaching of undergraduate computer science and engineering course. *Entrance requirements:* For master's, GRE General Test (minimum score 500 verbal, 700 quantitative), minimum GPA of 3.3 in last 60 hours of coursework; for doctorate, GRE General Test (minimum score: 500 Verbal, 700 Quantitative), minimum GPA of 3.3 in last 60 hours of coursework, MS (recommended). Additional exam requirements/recommendations for international students: Required—TOEFL (minimum score 550 paper-based; 213 computer-based). *Application deadline:* For fall admission, 2/15 for domestic students, 1/2 for international students; for spring admission, 10/15 for domestic students, 6/1 for international students. Application fee: $30. Electronic applications accepted. *Financial support:* In 2009–10, 67 students received support, including teaching assistantships with tuition reimbursements available (averaging $28,565 per year); unspecified assistantships also available. Financial award application deadline: 1/2; financial award applicants required to submit FAFSA. *Faculty research:* Computer vision, networks, artificial intelligence, computer architecture, software security. Total annual research expenditures: $1.2 million. *Unit head:* Sudeep Sarkar, Director, Fax: 813-974-5094, E-mail: sarkar@cse.usf.edu. *Application contact:* Sudeep Sarkar, Director, Fax: 813-974-5094, E-mail: sarkar@cse.usf.edu.

The University of Tennessee, Graduate School, College of Engineering, Department of Electrical Engineering and Computer Science, Knoxville, TN 37996. Offers computer engineering (MS, PhD); computer science (MS, PhD); electrical engineering (MS, PhD); reliability and maintainability engineering (MS); MS/MBA. Part-time programs available. *Faculty:* 40 full-time (4 women), 13 part-time/adjunct (2 women). *Students:* 141 full-time (25 women), 62 part-time (11 women); includes 11 minority (4 African Americans, 5 Asian Americans or Pacific Islanders, 2 Hispanic Americans), 109 international. Average age 30. 603 applicants, 12% accepted, 45 enrolled. In 2009, 55 master's, 24 doctorates awarded. *Degree requirements:* For master's, thesis or alternative; for doctorate, comprehensive exam, thesis/dissertation. *Entrance requirements:* For master's, GRE, minimum GPA of 3.0; for doctorate, GRE General Test, minimum GPA of 3.0. Additional exam requirements/recommendations for international students: Required—TOEFL (minimum score 550 paper-based; 213 computer-based). *Application deadline:* For fall admission, 2/1 priority date for domestic and international students; for spring admission, 6/15 priority date for international students. Applications are processed on a rolling basis. Application fee: $35. Electronic applications accepted. *Expenses:* Tuition, state resident: full-time $6826; part-time $380 per semester hour. Tuition, nonresident: full-time $21,844; part-time $1147 per semester hour. Tuition and fees vary according to program. *Financial support:* In 2009–10, 139 students received support, including 32 fellowships with full tuition reimbursements available (averaging $5,448 per year), 118 research assistantships with full tuition reimbursements available (averaging $16,800 per year), 68 teaching assistantships with full tuition reimbursements available (averaging $12,996 per year); career-related internships or fieldwork, Federal Work-Study, institutionally sponsored loans, health care benefits, and unspecified assistantships also available. Financial award application deadline: 2/1; financial award applicants required to submit FAFSA. *Faculty research:* Artificial intelligence and visualization; microelectronics, mixed-signal electronics, VLSI, embedded systems; scientific and distributed computing; computer vision, robotics, and image processing; power electronics, power systems, communications. Total annual research expenditures: $9.1 million. *Unit head:* Dr. Kevin Tomsovic, Head, 865-974-3461, Fax: 865-974-3461, E-mail: tomsovic@eecs.utk.edu. *Application contact:* Dr. Masood Parang, Associate Dean of Student Affairs, 865-974-2454, Fax: 865-974-9871, E-mail: mparang@utk.edu.

The University of Texas at Arlington, Graduate School, College of Engineering, Department of Computer Science and Engineering, Arlington, TX 76019. Offers M Engr, M Sw En, MS, PhD. Part-time and evening/weekend programs available. Postbaccalaureate distance learning degree programs offered (minimal on-campus study). *Faculty:* 28 full-time (2 women). *Students:* 167 full-time (42 women), 93 part-time (23 women); includes 11 minority (4 African Americans, 6 Asian Americans or Pacific Islanders, 1 Hispanic American), 211 international. 524 applicants,

98% accepted, 59 enrolled. In 2009, 120 master's, 11 doctorates awarded. Terminal master's awarded for partial completion of doctoral program. *Degree requirements:* For master's, comprehensive exam (for some programs), thesis optional; for doctorate, comprehensive exam, thesis/dissertation. *Entrance requirements:* For master's, GRE General Test, minimum GPA of 3.0 (3.2 in computer science-related classes); for doctorate, GRE General Test, minimum GPA of 3.5. Additional exam requirements/recommendations for international students: Required—TOEFL (minimum score 550 paper-based; 230 computer-based; 92 iBT). *Application deadline:* For fall admission, 6/6 for domestic students, 4/4 for international students; for spring admission, 10/17 for domestic students, 9/5 for international students. Applications are processed on a rolling basis. Application fee: $35 ($50 for international students). *Financial support:* In 2009–10, 20 fellowships (averaging $1,000 per year), research assistantships (averaging $13,500 per year), 75 teaching assistantships (averaging $13,500 per year) were awarded; career-related internships or fieldwork and scholarships/grants also available. Financial award application deadline: 6/1; financial award applicants required to submit FAFSA. *Faculty research:* Algorithms, homeland security, mobile pervasive computing, high performance computing bioinformation. *Unit head:* Dr. Fillia Makedon, Chairman, 817-272-3680. *Application contact:* Dr. Bahram Khalili, Graduate Advisor, 817-272-5407, Fax: 817-272-3784, E-mail: khalili@uta.edu.

The University of Texas at Austin, Graduate School, Cockrell School of Engineering, Department of Electrical and Computer Engineering, Austin, TX 78712-1111. Offers MSE, PhD. Part-time programs available. *Entrance requirements:* For master's, GRE General Test, minimum GPA of 3.3 in upper-division course work; for doctorate, GRE General Test. Electronic applications accepted.

The University of Texas at Dallas, Erik Jonsson School of Engineering and Computer Science, Programs in Electrical Engineering, Richardson, TX 75080. Offers computer engineering (MS, PhD); electrical engineering (MSEE, PhD); microelectronics (MSEE, PhD); telecommunications (MSEE, MSTE, PhD). Part-time and evening/weekend programs available. *Faculty:* 43 full-time (3 women), 3 part-time/adjunct (0 women). *Students:* 391 full-time (78 women), 160 part-time (23 women); includes 86 minority (14 African Americans, 59 Asian Americans or Pacific Islanders, 13 Hispanic Americans), 383 international. Average age 27. 1,292 applicants, 31% accepted, 168 enrolled. In 2009, 149 master's, 14 doctorates awarded. *Degree requirements:* For master's, thesis or major design project; for doctorate, thesis/dissertation. *Entrance requirements:* For master's, GRE General Test, minimum GPA of 3.0 in related bachelor's degree; for doctorate, GRE General Test, minimum GPA of 3.5. Additional exam requirements/recommendations for international students: Required—TOEFL (minimum score 550 paper-based; 213 computer-based). *Application deadline:* For fall admission, 7/15 for domestic students, 5/1 priority date for international students; for spring admission, 11/15 for domestic students, 9/1 priority date for international students. Applications are processed on a rolling basis. Application fee: $50 ($100 for international students). Electronic applications accepted. *Expenses:* Tuition, state resident: full-time $11,068; part-time $461 per credit hour. Tuition, nonresident: full-time $21,178; part-time $882 per credit hour. Tuition and fees vary according to course load. *Financial support:* In 2009–10, 1 fellowship with full tuition reimbursement (averaging $18,000 per year), 116 research assistantships with full tuition reimbursements (averaging $17,579 per year), 41 teaching assistantships with full tuition reimbursements (averaging $17,516 per year) were awarded; Federal Work-Study, institutionally sponsored loans, scholarships/grants, unspecified assistantships, and co-op positions also available. Support available to part-time students. Financial award application deadline: 4/30; financial award applicants required to submit FAFSA. *Faculty research:* Communications and signal processing, solid-state devices and circuits, digital systems, optical devices, materials and systems, lasers and photonics. *Unit head:* Dr. John H. L. Hansen, Head, 972-883-2910, Fax: 972-883-2710, E-mail: john.hansen@utdallas.edu. *Application contact:* Kathy Gribble, Coordinator, 972-883-2649, Fax: 972-883-2813, E-mail: gradecs@utdallas.edu.

The University of Texas at El Paso, Graduate School, College of Engineering, Department of Electrical and Computer Engineering, El Paso, TX 79968-0001. Offers computer engineering (MS); electrical and computer engineering (PhD); electrical engineering (MS). Part-time and evening/weekend programs available. *Degree requirements:* For master's, thesis optional; for doctorate, thesis/dissertation. *Entrance requirements:* For master's, GRE General Test, minimum GPA of 3.0; for doctorate, GRE General Test, qualifying exam, minimum graduate GPA of 3.0. Additional exam requirements/recommendations for international students: Required—TOEFL. Electronic applications accepted. *Faculty research:* Signal and image processing, computer architecture, fiber optics, computational electromagnetics, electronic displays and thin films.

The University of Texas at San Antonio, College of Engineering, Department of Electrical and Computer Engineering, San Antonio, TX 78249-0617. Offers computer engineering (MS); electrical engineering (MSEE, PhD). Part-time and evening/weekend programs available. *Faculty:* 20 full-time (3 women), 1 part-time/adjunct (0 women). *Students:* 99 full-time (25 women), 59 part-time (8 women); includes 26 minority (4 African Americans, 7 Asian Americans or Pacific Islanders, 15 Hispanic Americans), 104 international. Average age 28. 206 applicants, 80% accepted, 48 enrolled. In 2009, 43 master's, 4 doctorates awarded. *Degree requirements:* For master's, comprehensive exam (for some programs), thesis (for some programs); for doctorate, comprehensive exam, thesis/dissertation. *Entrance requirements:* For master's, GRE General Test, minimum GPA of 3.0 in last 60 hours of undergraduate degree; for doctorate, GRE General Test. Additional exam requirements/recommendations for international students: Required—TOEFL (minimum score 500 paper-based; 173 computer-based). *Application deadline:* For fall admission, 7/1 for domestic students, 4/1 for international students; for spring admission, 11/1 for domestic students, 9/1 for international students. Applications are processed on a rolling basis. Application fee: $45 ($80 for international students). Electronic applications accepted. *Expenses:* Tuition, state resident: full-time $3975; part-time $221 per contact hour. Tuition, nonresident: full-time $13,947; part-time $775 per contact hour. Required fees: $1853. *Financial support:* In 2009–10, 60 students received support, including 10 fellowships (averaging $34,425 per year), 62 research assistantships (averaging $11,312 per year), 41 teaching assistantships (averaging $11,244 per year); career-related internships or fieldwork, scholarships/grants, and unspecified assistantships also available. Support available to part-time students. Financial award application deadline: 3/31. Total annual research expenditures: $873,745. *Unit head:* Dr. Mehdi Shadaram, Chair, 210-458-4431, Fax: 210-458-5947, E-mail: mshadaram@utsa.edu. *Application contact:* Chunjiang Qian, Graduate Advisor, 210-458-5587, E-mail: chunjiang.qian@utsa.edu.

University of Toronto, School of Graduate Studies, Physical Sciences Division, Faculty of Applied Science and Engineering, Department of Electrical and Computer Engineering, Toronto, ON M5S 1A1, Canada. Offers M Eng, MA Sc, PhD. Part-time programs available. *Degree requirements:* For master's, thesis (for some programs), oral thesis defense (MA Sc); for doctorate, thesis/dissertation, qualifying exam, thesis defense. *Entrance requirements:* For master's, four-year degree in electrical or computer engineering, minimum B average, 2 letters of reference; for doctorate, minimum B+ average, MA Sc in electrical or computer engineering, 2 letters of reference.

University of Victoria, Faculty of Graduate Studies, Faculty of Engineering, Department of Electrical and Computer Engineering, Victoria, BC V8W 2Y2, Canada. Offers M Eng, MA Sc, PhD. *Degree requirements:* For master's, thesis; for doctorate, thesis/dissertation, candidacy exam. *Entrance requirements:* For master's, GRE (recommended), bachelor's degree in engineering; for doctorate, GRE (recommended), master's degree. Additional exam requirements/recommendations for international students: Required—TOEFL (minimum score 575 paper-based; 233 computer-based), IELTS (minimum score 7). Electronic applications accepted. *Faculty research:* Communications and computers; electromagnetics, microwaves, and optics; electronics; power systems, signal processing, and control.

University of Virginia, School of Engineering and Applied Science, Department of Electrical and Computer Engineering, Program in Computer Engineering, Charlottesville, VA 22903. Offers ME, MS, PhD. Postbaccalaureate distance learning degree programs offered (no on-campus study). *Students:* 26 full-time (5 women), 1 part-time (0 women), 23 international. Average age 26. 58 applicants, 9% accepted, 5 enrolled. In 2009, 5 master's, 1 doctorate awarded. Terminal master's awarded for partial completion of doctoral program. *Degree requirements:* For master's, thesis (for some programs); for doctorate, comprehensive exam, thesis/dissertation. *Entrance requirements:* For master's, GRE General Test, 3 letters of recommendation; for doctorate, GRE General Test, 3 letters of recommendation; essay. Additional exam requirements/recommendations for international students: Required—TOEFL (minimum score 650 paper-based; 250 computer-based; 90 iBT), IELTS (minimum score 7). *Application deadline:* For fall admission, 8/1 for domestic students, 4/1 for international students; for winter admission, 12/1 for domestic students, 8/1 for international students; for spring admission, 5/1 for domestic students, 1/1 for international students. Applications are processed on a rolling basis. Application fee: $60. Electronic applications accepted. *Financial support:* Fellowships, research assistantships, teaching assistantships available. Financial award application deadline: 1/15; financial award applicants required to submit FAFSA. *Faculty research:* Computer architecture, VLSI, switching theory, operating systems, real-time and embedded systems, compiler, software systems and software engineering, fault-tolerant computing and reliability engineering. *Unit head:* Joanne B. Dugan, Director, 434-924-3198, Fax: 434-924-8818, E-mail: compe@virginia.edu. *Application contact:* Joanne B. Dugan, Director, 434-924-3198, Fax: 434-924-8818, E-mail: compe@virginia.edu.

University of Washington, Bothell, Program in Computing and Software Systems, Bothell, WA 98011-8246. Offers MS. Part-time and evening/weekend programs available. *Faculty:* 8 full-time (1 woman). *Students:* 1 full-time (0 women), 27 part-time (3 women); includes 13 minority (1 African American, 11 Asian Americans or Pacific Islanders, 1 Hispanic American), 1 international. Average age 33. 42 applicants, 76% accepted, 27 enrolled. *Entrance requirements:* For master's, GRE. Additional exam requirements/recommendations for international students: Required—TOEFL (minimum score 580 paper-based; 237 computer-based; 92 iBT). *Application deadline:* For fall admission, 7/1 for domestic students. Application fee: $65. Electronic applications accepted. *Expenses:* Contact institution. *Financial support:* Applicants required to submit FAFSA. *Faculty research:* Computer vision, artificial intelligence, software engineering, computer graphics, parallel and distributed systems. *Unit head:* Dr. Michael Stiber. *Application contact:* Megan Jewell, Graduate Advisor, E-mail: mjewell@uwb.edu.

University of Washington, Tacoma, Graduate Programs, Program in Computing and Software Systems, Tacoma, WA 98402-3100. Offers MS. Part-time programs available. *Faculty:* 15 full-time (4 women), 6 part-time/adjunct (1 woman). *Students:* 15 full-time (7 women), 20 part-time (1 woman); includes 8 minority (6 Asian Americans or Pacific Islanders, 2 Hispanic Americans), 7 international. Average age 30. 30 applicants, 73% accepted, 15 enrolled. In 2009, 11 master's awarded. *Degree requirements:* For master's, capstone project/thesis or 15 credits elective coursework. *Entrance requirements:* For master's, GRE, All: UW Graduate Application, MS CSS Graduate Application, Personal Statement, Resume, Transcripts, Recommendations (3) International: Statement of Financial Ability, 1-20 Form, OFFICIAL transcripts and degree statements from all institutions attended with certified translations in English. Additional exam requirements/recommendations for international students: Required—TOEFL (minimum score 580 paper-based; 237 computer-based; 92 iBT), IELTS (minimum score 7), MLT (minimum score 90). *Application deadline:* For fall admission, 4/15 priority date for domestic students; for winter admission, 10/15 priority date for domestic students; for spring admission, 1/15 priority date for domestic students. Applications are processed on a rolling basis. Application fee: $65. Electronic applications accepted. *Expenses:* Tuition, state resident: full-time $10,660; part-time $484 per credit. Tuition, nonresident: full-time $24,000; part-time $1119 per credit. Required fees: $150 per term. Tuition and fees vary according to course load and program. *Faculty research:* Formal methods, software engineering, data streaming and data mining, computer engineering and science education, information assurance and computer security. *Unit head:* Dr. Orlando Baiocchi, Director, 253-692-5860, Fax: 253-692-5862, E-mail: uwtech@u.washington.edu. *Application contact:* Dr. Kim Davenport, Program Administrator and Graduate Advisor, 253-692-5860, Fax: 253-692-5862, E-mail: uwtech@u.washington.edu.

University of Waterloo, Graduate Studies, Faculty of Engineering, Department of Electrical and Computer Engineering, Waterloo, ON N2L 3G1, Canada. Offers electrical and computer engineering (M Eng, MA Sc, PhD); electrical and computer engineering (software engineering) (MA Sc). Part-time programs available. *Degree requirements:* For master's, research paper or thesis; for doctorate, comprehensive exam, thesis/dissertation. *Entrance requirements:* For master's, honors degree, minimum B+ average; for doctorate, master's degree, minimum A- average. Additional exam requirements/recommendations for international students: Required—TOEFL (minimum score 550 paper-based; 213 computer-based), TWE (minimum score 4). Electronic applications accepted. *Faculty research:* Communications, computers, systems and control, silicon devices, power engineering.

The University of Western Ontario, Faculty of Graduate Studies, Physical Sciences Division, Faculty of Engineering, London, ON N6A 5B8, Canada. Offers chemical and biochemical engineering (ME Sc, PhD); civil and environmental engineering (M Eng, ME Sc, PhD); electrical and computer engineering (M Eng, ME Sc, PhD); mechanical and materials engineering (M Eng, ME Sc, PhD). Part-time programs available. Terminal master's awarded for partial completion of doctoral program. *Degree requirements:* For master's, thesis; for doctorate, thesis/dissertation. *Entrance requirements:* For master's, minimum B average; for doctorate, minimum B+ average. *Faculty research:* Wind, geotechnical, chemical reactor engineering, applied electrostatics, biochemical engineering.

University of Wisconsin–Milwaukee, Graduate School, College of Engineering and Applied Science, Program in Engineering, Milwaukee, WI 53201-0413. Offers civil engineering (MS); electrical and computer engineering (MS); energy engineering (Certificate); engineering (PhD); engineering management (MS); engineering mechanics (MS); ergonomics (Certificate); industrial and management engineering (MS); manufacturing engineering (MS); materials engineering (MS); mechanical engineering (MS); MUP/MS. Part-time programs available. *Faculty:* 44 full-time (6 women). *Students:* 119 full-time (22 women), 130 part-time (22 women); includes 23 minority (2 African Americans, 14 Asian Americans or Pacific Islanders, 7 Hispanic Americans), 126 international. Average age 32. 231 applicants, 67% accepted, 33 enrolled. In 2009, 29 master's, 14 doctorates awarded. *Degree requirements:* For master's, comprehensive exam (for some programs), thesis or alternative; for doctorate, comprehensive exam, thesis/dissertation, internship. *Entrance requirements:* For master's, GRE, minimum GPA of 2.75; for doctorate, GRE, minimum GPA of 3.5. Additional exam requirements/recommendations for international students: Required—TOEFL (minimum score 550 paper-based; 79 iBT), IELTS (minimum score 6.5). *Application deadline:* For fall admission, 1/1 priority date for domestic students; for spring admission, 9/1 for domestic students. Applications are processed on a rolling basis. Application fee: $45 ($75 for international students). *Expenses:* Tuition, state resident: full-time $8800. Tuition, nonresident: full-time $20,760. Tuition and fees vary according to program and reciprocity agreements. *Financial support:* In 2009–10, 18 research assistantships, 51 teaching assistantships were awarded; fellowships, career-related internships or fieldwork, Federal Work-Study, and unspecified assistantships also available. Support available to part-time students. Financial award application deadline: 4/15. Total annual research expenditures: $2.9 million. *Unit head:* David Yu, Head, 414-229-6169, E-mail: yu@uwm.edu. *Application contact:* Betty Warras, General Information Contact, 414-229-4982, Fax: 414-229-6967, E-mail: bwarras@uwm.edu.

Villanova University, College of Engineering, Department of Electrical and Computer Engineering, Program in Computer Engineering, Villanova, PA 19085-1699. Offers computer architectures (Certificate); computer engineering (MSCPE). Part-time and evening/weekend programs available. *Degree requirements:* For master's, thesis optional. *Entrance requirements:* For master's, GRE General Test (for applicants with degrees from foreign universities), BEE, minimum GPA of 3.0. Additional exam requirements/recommendations for international students: Required—TOEFL (minimum score 600 paper-based; 250 computer-based; 100 iBT). Electronic applications accepted. *Expenses:* Tuition: Part-time $630 per credit. Required fees: $60 per

Computer Engineering

Villanova University (continued)
credit. Part-time tuition and fees vary according to degree level and program. *Faculty research:* Expert systems, computer vision, neural networks, image processing, computer architectures.

Virginia Polytechnic Institute and State University, Graduate School, College of Engineering, Department of Electrical and Computer Engineering, Blacksburg, VA 24061. Offers computer engineering (M Eng, MS, PhD); electrical engineering (M Eng, MS, PhD). *Entrance requirements:* For master's and doctorate, GRE General Test. Additional exam requirements/recommendations for international students: Required—TOEFL (minimum score 590 paper-based; 243 computer-based). Electronic applications accepted. *Faculty research:* Electromagnetics, controls, electronics, power, communications.

Virginia Polytechnic Institute and State University, VT Online, Blacksburg, VA 24061. Offers aerospace engineering (MS); business information systems (Graduate Certificate); career and technical education (MS); computer engineering (M Eng, MS); decision support systems (Graduate Certificate); eLearning leadership (MA); electrical engineering (M Eng, MS); engineering administration (MEA); environmental politics and policy (Graduate Certificate); foundations of political analysis (Graduate Certificate); health product risk management (Graduate Certificate); information policy and society (Graduate Certificate); information security (Graduate Certificate); instructional technology (MA); liberal arts (Graduate Certificate); life sciences: health product risk management (MS); natural resources (MNR, Graduate Certificate); networking (Graduate Certificate); nonprofit and nongovernmental organization management (Graduate Certificate); ocean engineering (MS); political science (MA); security studies (Graduate Certificate); software development (Graduate Certificate).

Washington State University, Graduate School, College of Engineering and Architecture, School of Electrical Engineering and Computer Science, Program in Computer Engineering, Pullman, WA 99164. Offers MS, PhD. *Degree requirements:* For master's, comprehensive exam (for some programs), thesis optional, research project; for doctorate, comprehensive exam, thesis/dissertation. *Entrance requirements:* For master's, GRE, 3 letters of recommendation; for doctorate, 3 letters of recommendation. Additional exam requirements/recommendations for international students: Required—TOEFL.

Washington State University Tri-Cities, Graduate Programs, College of Engineering and Computer Science, Richland, WA 99352. Offers computer science (MS, PhD); electrical and computer engineering (PhD); electrical engineering (MS); mechanical engineering (MS, PhD). Part-time programs available. *Faculty:* 28. *Students:* 4 full-time (0 women), 25 part-time (8 women); includes 2 minority (both African Americans), 1 international. *Degree requirements:* For master's, comprehensive exam, thesis (for some programs); for doctorate, comprehensive exam, thesis/dissertation, oral exam. *Entrance requirements:* For master's and doctorate, GRE, minimum GPA of 3.0, 3 letters of recommendation. Additional exam requirements/recommendations for international students: Required—TOEFL (minimum score 550 paper-based; 213 computer-based). *Application deadline:* For fall admission, 1/10 priority date for domestic students, 1/10 for international students; for spring admission, 7/1 priority date for domestic students, 7/1 for international students. Application fee: $50. *Expenses:* Tuition, state resident: part-time $423 per credit. Tuition, nonresident: part-time $1032 per credit. *Financial support:* Application deadline: 3/1. *Faculty research:* Positive ion track structure, biological systems computer simulations. *Unit head:* Dr. Ali Saberi, Chair, 509-372-7178, E-mail: sidra@eecs.wsu.edu. *Application contact:* Dr. Scott Hudson, Associate Director, 509-372-7254, Fax: 509-335-1949, E-mail: hudson@tricity.wsu.edu.

Washington University in St. Louis, Henry Edwin Sever Graduate School of Engineering and Applied Science, Department of Computer Science and Engineering, St. Louis, MO 63130-4899. Offers computer engineering (MS, PhD); computer science (MS, PhD); computer science and engineering (M Eng). Part-time programs available. *Faculty:* 21 full-time (3 women), 6 part-time/adjunct (0 women). *Students:* 99 full-time (11 women), 68 part-time (11 women); includes 15 minority (4 African Americans, 9 Asian Americans or Pacific Islanders, 2 Hispanic Americans), 50 international. Average age 26. 351 applicants, 19% accepted, 47 enrolled. In 2009, 38 master's, 9 doctorates awarded. Terminal master's awarded for partial completion of doctoral program. *Degree requirements:* For master's, thesis optional; for doctorate, thesis/dissertation. *Entrance requirements:* For doctorate, GRE General Test. Additional exam requirements/recommendations for international students: Required—TOEFL. *Application deadline:* For fall admission, 1/15 for domestic and international students; for spring admission, 9/15 for domestic and international students. Applications are processed on a rolling basis. Application fee: $60. Electronic applications accepted. *Financial support:* In 2009–10, 4 fellowships with full tuition reimbursements (averaging $26,950 per year), 59 research assistantships with full tuition reimbursements (averaging $26,950 per year) were awarded; health care benefits, tuition waivers (partial), and unspecified assistantships also available. Financial award application deadline: 1/30. *Faculty research:* Artificial intelligence, computational genomics, computer and systems architecture, media and machines, networking and communication, software systems. Total annual research expenditures: $6 million. *Unit head:* Dr. Gruia-Catalin Roman, Chair, 314-935-6132, Fax: 314-935-7302, E-mail: roman@cse.wustl.edu. *Application contact:* Madeline Hawkins, Project Specialist, 314-935-6132, Fax: 314-935-7302, E-mail: admissions@cse.wustl.edu.

Wayne State University, College of Engineering, Department of Electrical and Computer Engineering, Program in Computer Engineering, Detroit, MI 48202. Offers MS, PhD. *Degree requirements:* For master's, thesis optional; for doctorate, thesis/dissertation. *Entrance requirements:* Additional exam requirements/recommendations for international students: Required—TOEFL (minimum score 550 paper-based; 213 computer-based), Michigan English Language Assessment Battery (minimum score: 85); Recommended—TWE (minimum score 6). Electronic applications accepted. *Faculty research:* Neural networks, parallel processing, pattern recognition, VLSI, computer architecture.

Western Michigan University, Graduate College, College of Engineering and Applied Sciences, Department of Electrical and Computer Engineering, Kalamazoo, MI 49008. Offers computer engineering (MSE, PhD); electrical and computer engineering (PhD); electrical engineering (MSE). Part-time programs available. *Degree requirements:* For master's, thesis optional. *Entrance requirements:* For master's, minimum GPA of 3.0. *Faculty research:* Fiber optics, computer architecture, bioelectromagnetics, acoustics.

West Virginia University, College of Engineering and Mineral Resources, Lane Department of Computer Science and Electrical Engineering, Program in Computer Engineering, Morgantown, WV 26506. Offers PhD. *Degree requirements:* For doctorate, comprehensive exam, thesis/dissertation. *Entrance requirements:* For doctorate, GRE General Test, minimum GPA of 3.0, letters of recommendation. Additional exam requirements/recommendations for international students: Required—TOEFL. *Faculty research:* Software engineering, microprocessor applications, microelectronic systems, fault tolerance, advanced computer architectures and networks.

Wichita State University, Graduate School, College of Engineering, Department of Electrical Engineering and Computer Science, Wichita, KS 67260. Offers computer networking (MS); computer science (MS); electrical engineering (MS, PhD). Part-time and evening/weekend programs available. *Expenses:* Tuition, state resident: full-time $4247; part-time $235.95 per credit hour. Tuition, nonresident: full-time $11,171; part-time $620.60 per credit hour. Required fees: $34; $3.60 per credit hour. $17 per term. Tuition and fees vary according to campus/location and program. *Unit head:* Dr. John Watkins, Chair, 316-978-3156, Fax: 316-978-5408, E-mail: john.watkins@wichita.edu. *Application contact:* Dr. John Watkins, Chair, 316-978-3156, Fax: 316-978-5408, E-mail: john.watkins@wichita.edu.

Widener University, Graduate Programs in Engineering, Program in Computer and Software Engineering, Chester, PA 19013-5792. Offers M Eng. Part-time and evening/weekend programs available. *Students:* 2 full-time (1 woman), 2 part-time (0 women), 2 international. Average age 28. In 2009, 5 master's awarded. *Degree requirements:* For master's, thesis optional. *Application deadline:* For fall admission, 8/1 priority date for domestic students; for spring admission, 12/1 for domestic students. Applications are processed on a rolling basis. Application fee: $25 ($300 for international students). *Financial support:* Research assistantships with full tuition reimbursements, unspecified assistantships available. Financial award application deadline: 3/15. *Faculty research:* Computer and software engineering, computer network fault-tolerant computing, optical computing. *Unit head:* Dr. Bryen E. Lorenz, Chairman, Department of Electrical/Telecommunication Engineering, 610-499-4064, Fax: 610-499-4059, E-mail: bryen.f.lorenz@widener.edu. *Application contact:* Dr. Bryen E. Lorenz, Chairman, Department of Electrical/Telecommunication Engineering, 610-499-4064, Fax: 610-499-4059, E-mail: bryen.f.lorenz@widener.edu.

Worcester Polytechnic Institute, Graduate Studies and Research, Department of Electrical and Computer Engineering, Worcester, MA 01609-2280. Offers electrical and computer engineering (Advanced Certificate, Graduate Certificate); electrical engineering (MS, PhD). Part-time and evening/weekend programs available. *Faculty:* 16 full-time (1 woman), 2 part-time/adjunct (0 women). *Students:* 54 full-time (8 women), 98 part-time (13 women). 418 applicants, 58% accepted, 80 enrolled. In 2009, 49 master's, 5 doctorates awarded. Terminal master's awarded for partial completion of doctoral program. *Degree requirements:* For master's, thesis optional; for doctorate, comprehensive exam, thesis/dissertation. *Entrance requirements:* For master's, 3 letters of recommendation; for doctorate, 3 letters of recommendation, statement of purpose. Additional exam requirements/recommendations for international students: Required—TOEFL (minimum score 550 paper-based; 213 computer-based; 79 iBT), IELTS (minimum score 6.5). *Application deadline:* For fall admission, 1/15 priority date for domestic students, 1/15 for international students; for spring admission, 10/15 priority date for domestic students, 10/15 for international students. Applications are processed on a rolling basis. Application fee: $70. Electronic applications accepted. *Financial support:* Career-related internships or fieldwork, institutionally sponsored loans, scholarships/grants, and unspecified assistantships available. Financial award application deadline: 1/15. *Faculty research:* Analog and mixed signal IC design, cryptography and data security, communication systems and networking, biomedical signal processing, image processing and visualization. *Unit head:* Dr. Fred Looft, Department Head, 508-831-5231, Fax: 508-831-5491, E-mail: fjlooft@wpi.edu. *Application contact:* Dr. Peder Pedersen, Graduate Coordinator, 508-831-5351, Fax: 508-831-5491, E-mail: pedersen@wpi.edu.

Wright State University, School of Graduate Studies, College of Engineering and Computer Science, Department of Computer Science and Engineering, Computer Engineering Program, Dayton, OH 45435. Offers MSCE. *Degree requirements:* For master's, thesis optional. *Entrance requirements:* For master's, GRE General Test, minimum GPA of 3.0 in major, 2.7 overall. Additional exam requirements/recommendations for international students: Required—TOEFL. *Faculty research:* Networking and digital communications, parallel and concurrent computing, robotics and control, computer vision, optical computing.

Wright State University, School of Graduate Studies, College of Engineering and Computer Science, Department of Computer Science and Engineering, Program in Computer Science and Engineering, Dayton, OH 45435. Offers PhD. *Degree requirements:* For doctorate, thesis/dissertation, candidacy and general exams. *Entrance requirements:* For doctorate, GRE General Test, minimum GPA of 3.3. Additional exam requirements/recommendations for international students: Required—TOEFL.

Youngstown State University, Graduate School, College of Science, Technology, Engineering and Mathematics, Department of Electrical and Computer Engineering, Youngstown, OH 44555-0001. Offers computer engineering (MSE); electrical engineering (MSE). Part-time and evening/weekend programs available. *Degree requirements:* For master's, thesis optional. *Entrance requirements:* For master's, minimum GPA of 2.75 in field. Additional exam requirements/recommendations for international students: Required—TOEFL. *Faculty research:* Computer-aided design, power systems, electromagnetic energy conversion, sensors, control systems.

Electrical Engineering

Air Force Institute of Technology, Graduate School of Engineering and Management, Department of Electrical and Computer Engineering, Dayton, OH 45433-7765. Offers computer engineering (MS, PhD); computer systems/science (MS); electrical engineering (MS, PhD); electro-optics (MS, PhD). *Accreditation:* ABET (one or more programs are accredited). Part-time programs available. *Degree requirements:* For master's, thesis; for doctorate, thesis/dissertation. *Entrance requirements:* For master's and doctorate, GRE General Test, minimum GPA of 3.0, U.S. citizenship. *Faculty research:* Remote sensing, information survivability, microelectronics, computer networks, artificial intelligence.

Alfred University, Graduate School, New York State College of Ceramics, School of Engineering, Alfred, NY 14802-1205. Offers biomedical materials engineering science (MS); ceramic engineering (MS); ceramics (PhD); electrical engineering (MS); glass science (MS, PhD); materials science and engineering (MS, PhD); mechanical engineering (MS). *Degree requirements:* For master's, thesis; for doctorate, thesis/dissertation. *Entrance requirements:* Additional exam requirements/recommendations for international students: Required—TOEFL (minimum score 590 paper-based; 243 computer-based). Electronic applications accepted. *Expenses:* Contact institution. *Faculty research:* Fine-particle technology, x-ray diffraction, superconductivity, electronic materials.

American University of Beirut, Graduate Programs, Faculty of Engineering and Architecture, Beirut, Lebanon. Offers civil engineering (ME, PhD); electrical and computer engineering (ME, PhD); engineering management (MEM); environmental and water resources (ME); environmental and water resources engineering (PhD); environmental technology (MSES); mechanical engineering (ME, PhD); urban design (MUD); urban planning and policy (MUP). Part-time programs available. *Degree requirements:* For master's, one foreign language, comprehensive exam, thesis (for some programs); for doctorate, one foreign language, comprehensive exam, thesis/dissertation, publications. *Entrance requirements:* For master's, letters of recommendation; for doctorate, letters of recommendation, master's degree, transcripts, curriculum vitae, interview. Additional exam requirements/recommendations for international students: Required—TOEFL (minimum score 600 paper-based; 250 computer-based; 100 iBT), IELTS (minimum score 7.5). Electronic applications accepted.

American University of Sharjah, Graduate Programs, Sharjah, United Arab Emirates. Offers business (EMBA, GEMPA, MBA); chemical engineering (MS Ch E); civil engineering (MSCE); computer engineering (MS); electrical engineering (MSEE); mechanical engineering (MSME); mechatronics engineering (MS); public administration (MPA); teaching English to speakers of other languages (MA); translation and interpreting (MA); urban planning (MUP). Part-time and evening/weekend programs available. *Faculty:* 59 full-time (4 women), 5 part-time/adjunct (1 woman). *Students:* 101 full-time (44 women), 218 part-time (95 women). Average age 27. 184 applicants, 83% accepted, 92 enrolled. In 2009, 97 master's awarded. *Entrance requirements:* For master's, GMAT (MBA). Additional exam requirements/recommendations for international students: Required—TOEFL (minimum score 550 paper-based; 213 computer-based; 80 iBT), TWE (minimum score 5). *Application deadline:* For fall admission, 7/30 priority date for domestic students, 7/15 priority date for international students; for spring admission, 12/31 priority date for domestic students, 12/16 for international students. Applications are processed on a rolling basis. Application fee: $300. Electronic applications accepted. Tuition charges are reported in United Arab Emirates dirhams. *Expenses:* Tuition: Part-time 3250 United Arab Emirates dirhams per credit hour. *Financial support:* In 2009–10, 63 students received support, including 28 research assistantships with tuition reimbursements available, 35 teaching assistantships with tuition reimbursements available. *Faculty research:* Chemical engineering, civil engineering, computer engineering, electrical engineering, linguistics, translation. *Unit head:* Ghada S. Sami, Admissions Manager, 971-65151006 Ext. 1006, Fax: 971-65151020, E-mail: graduateadmission@aus.edu. *Application contact:* Ghada S. Sami, Admissions Manager, 971-65151006 Ext. 1006, Fax: 971-65151020, E-mail: graduateadmission@aus.edu.

Arizona State University, Graduate College, College of Technology and Innovation, Electronic Systems Department, Tempe, AZ 85287. Offers MS. Part-time and evening/weekend programs available. *Degree requirements:* For master's, comprehensive exam, thesis optional. *Entrance requirements:* For master's, GRE, 30 semester hours or equivalent in area of study, minimum of 16 hours of mathematics and science. Additional exam requirements/recommendations for international students: Required—TOEFL (minimum score 550 paper-based; 213 computer-based; 83 iBT); Recommended—TWE. Electronic applications accepted. *Faculty research:* IC packaging, semiconductor processing, surface characterization of thin films, solar cells failure analysis, fatigue life prediction for soldier joints.

Arizona State University, Graduate College, Ira A. Fulton School of Engineering, Department of Electrical Engineering, Tempe, AZ 85287. Offers MS, MSE, PhD. *Degree requirements:* For master's, thesis or alternative; for doctorate, thesis/dissertation. *Entrance requirements:* For master's and doctorate, GRE General Test (recommended). Additional exam requirements/recommendations for international students: Required—TOEFL.

Auburn University, Graduate School, Ginn College of Engineering, Department of Electrical and Computer Engineering, Auburn University, AL 36849. Offers MEE, MS, PhD. Part-time programs available. *Faculty:* 27 full-time (2 women), 3 part-time/adjunct (1 woman). *Students:* 69 full-time (10 women), 48 part-time (10 women); includes 7 minority (2 African Americans, 1 American Indian/Alaska Native, 3 Asian Americans or Pacific Islanders, 1 Hispanic American), 72 international. Average age 27. 355 applicants, 57% accepted, 16 enrolled. In 2009, 27 master's, 7 doctorates awarded. *Degree requirements:* For master's, comprehensive exam, thesis (for some programs); for doctorate, thesis/dissertation. *Entrance requirements:* For master's and doctorate, GRE General Test, GRE Subject Test. *Application deadline:* For fall admission, 7/7 for domestic students; for spring admission, 11/24 for domestic students. Applications are processed on a rolling basis. Application fee: $50 ($60 for international students). Electronic applications accepted. *Expenses:* Tuition, state resident: full-time $6240. Tuition, nonresident: full-time $18,720. International tuition: $18,938 full-time. Required fees: $492. Tuition and fees vary according to course load, program and reciprocity agreements. *Financial support:* Fellowships, research assistantships, teaching assistantships, Federal Work-Study available. Support available to part-time students. Financial award application deadline: 3/15; financial award applicants required to submit FAFSA. *Faculty research:* Power systems, energy conversion, electronics, electromagnetics, digital systems. *Unit head:* Dr. J. David Irwin, Head, 334-844-1800. *Application contact:* Dr. George Flowers, Dean of the Graduate School, 334-844-2125.

Baylor University, Graduate School, School of Engineering and Computer Science, Waco, TX 76798. Offers computer science (MS); engineering (ME, MSBE, MSECE, MSME), including biomedical engineering (MSBE), electrical and computer engineering (MSECE), engineering (ME), mechanical engineering (MSME). Part-time programs available. *Students:* 40 full-time (6 women), 6 part-time (1 woman); includes 7 minority (1 African American, 1 Asian American or Pacific Islander, 5 Hispanic Americans), 19 international. In 2009, 18 master's awarded. *Degree requirements:* For master's, thesis optional. *Entrance requirements:* For master's, GRE General Test. *Application deadline:* For fall admission, 8/1 for domestic students; for spring admission, 12/1 for domestic students. Applications are processed on a rolling basis. Application fee: $25. *Financial support:* Teaching assistantships available. Financial award application deadline: 3/15. *Faculty research:* Database systems, advanced architecture, operations research. *Unit head:* Dr. Greg Speegle, Graduate Program Director, 254-710-3876, Fax: 254-710-3839, E-mail: greg_speegle@baylor.edu. *Application contact:* Suzanne Keener, Administrative Assistant, 254-710-3588, Fax: 254-710-3870.

Boise State University, Graduate College, College of Engineering, Department of Electrical and Computer Engineering, Boise, ID 83725-0399. Offers computer engineering (M Engr, MS); electrical and computer engineering (PhD); electrical engineering (M Engr, MS). Part-time and evening/weekend programs available. *Degree requirements:* For master's, thesis. *Entrance requirements:* For master's, GRE General Test, minimum GPA of 3.0. Additional exam requirements/recommendations for international students: Required—TOEFL. Electronic applications accepted. *Expenses:* Tuition, state resident: full-time $3106; part-time $209 per credit. Tuition, nonresident: part-time $284 per credit.

Boston University, College of Engineering, Department of Electrical and Computer Engineering, Boston, MA 02215. Offers computer engineering (MS, PhD); electrical engineering (MS, PhD); photonics (MS). Part-time programs available. *Faculty:* 41 full-time (3 women). *Students:* 182 full-time (40 women), 16 part-time (2 women); includes 21 minority (4 African Americans, 15 Asian Americans or Pacific Islanders, 2 Hispanic Americans), 118 international. Average age 24. 592 applicants, 30% accepted, 66 enrolled. In 2009, 62 master's, 19 doctorates awarded. Terminal master's awarded for partial completion of doctoral program. *Degree requirements:* For master's, thesis optional; for doctorate, comprehensive exam, thesis/dissertation. *Entrance requirements:* For master's and doctorate, GRE General Test. Additional exam requirements/recommendations for international students: Required—TOEFL (minimum score 550 paper-based; 213 computer-based; 84 iBT), IELTS (minimum score 6). *Application deadline:* For fall admission, 4/1 for domestic and international students; for spring admission, 10/1 for domestic and international students. Applications are processed on a rolling basis. Application fee: $70. Electronic applications accepted. *Expenses:* Tuition: Full-time $37,910; part-time $1184 per credit hour. Required fees: $386; $40 per semester. Part-time tuition and fees vary according to class time, course level, degree level and program. *Financial support:* In 2009–10, 134 students received support, including 11 fellowships with full tuition reimbursements available (averaging $27,600 per year), 88 research assistantships with full tuition reimbursements available (averaging $18,400 per year), 18 teaching assistantships with full tuition reimbursements available (averaging $18,400 per year); career-related internships or fieldwork, Federal Work-Study, institutionally sponsored loans, scholarships/grants, traineeships, and health care benefits also available. Financial award application deadline: 1/15; financial award applicants required to submit FAFSA. *Faculty research:* Communications and computer networks; signal, image, video, and multimedia processing; solid-state materials, devices, and photonics; systems, control, and reliable computing; VLSI, computer engineering and high-performance computing. *Unit head:* Dr. Francesco Cerrina, Chairman, 617-353-7175, Fax: 617-353-6440, E-mail: fcerrina@bu.edu. *Application contact:* Cheryl Kelley, Director of Graduate Programs, 617-353-9760, Fax: 617-353-0259, E-mail: enggrad@bu.edu.

Bradley University, Graduate School, College of Engineering and Technology, Department of Electrical Engineering, Peoria, IL 61625-0002. Offers MSEE. Part-time and evening/weekend programs available. *Degree requirements:* For master's, comprehensive exam. *Entrance requirements:* For master's, GRE, minimum GPA of 3.0. Additional exam requirements/recommendations for international students: Required—TOEFL (minimum score 550 paper-based; 213 computer-based; 79 iBT).

Brigham Young University, Graduate Studies, Ira A. Fulton College of Engineering and Technology, Department of Electrical and Computer Engineering, Provo, UT 84602. Offers MS, PhD. *Faculty:* 24 full-time (0 women). *Students:* 91 full-time (6 women), 24 international. Average age 28. 43 applicants, 72% accepted, 22 enrolled. In 2009, 13 master's, 10 doctorates awarded. *Degree requirements:* For master's, thesis optional; for doctorate, comprehensive exam, thesis/dissertation. *Entrance requirements:* For master's and doctorate, GRE General Test, minimum GPA of 3.2 in last 60 hours of course work. Additional exam requirements/recommendations for international students: Required—TOEFL (minimum score 580 paper-based; 237 computer-based; 85 iBT). *Application deadline:* For fall admission, 1/15 for domestic and international students; for winter admission, 9/15 for domestic and international students. Application fee: $50. Electronic applications accepted. *Expenses:* Tuition: Full-time $5580; part-time $301 per credit hour. Tuition and fees vary according to student's religious affiliation. *Financial support:* In 2009–10, 65 students received support, including 2 fellowships with full tuition reimbursements available (averaging $19,500 per year), 53 research assistantships with full tuition reimbursements available (averaging $19,500 per year), 10 teaching assistantships with full tuition reimbursements available (averaging $19,500 per year); scholarships/grants also available. Financial award application deadline: 5/15; financial award applicants required to submit FAFSA. *Faculty research:* Microwave remote sensing, reconfigurable computing, microelectronics circuit design and fabrication, array and image processing, wireless communications, computer architecture. Total annual research expenditures: $3.1 million. *Unit head:* Dr. Michael A. Jensen, Chair, 801-422-4012, Fax: 801-422-0201, E-mail: jensen@ee.byu.edu. *Application contact:* Janalyn L. Mergist, Graduate Secretary, 801-422-4013, Fax: 801-422-0201, E-mail: janalyn@ee.byu.edu.

Brown University, Graduate School, Division of Engineering, Program in Electrical Sciences and Computer Engineering, Providence, RI 02912. Offers Sc M, PhD. *Degree requirements:* For doctorate, thesis/dissertation, preliminary exam.

Bucknell University, Graduate Studies, College of Engineering, Department of Electrical Engineering, Lewisburg, PA 17837. Offers MS, MSEE. Part-time programs available. *Degree requirements:* For master's, thesis. *Entrance requirements:* For master's, GRE General Test, GRE Subject Test, minimum GPA of 2.8. Additional exam requirements/recommendations for international students: Required—TOEFL.

California Institute of Technology, Division of Engineering and Applied Science, Option in Electrical Engineering, Pasadena, CA 91125-0001. Offers MS, PhD, Engr. *Faculty:* 12 full-time (3 women). *Students:* 104 full-time (15 women). 681 applicants, 7% accepted, 32 enrolled. In 2009, 21 master's, 14 doctorates awarded. *Degree requirements:* For doctorate, thesis/dissertation. *Application deadline:* For fall admission, 1/15 for domestic students. Application fee: $0. Electronic applications accepted. *Financial support:* In 2009–10, 17 fellowships, 65 research assistantships, 28 teaching assistantships were awarded. *Faculty research:* Solid-state electronics, power electronics, communications, controls, submillimeter-wave integrated circuits. *Unit head:* Dr. Babak Hassibi, Executive Officer, 626-395-4810, E-mail: hassibi@caltech.edu. *Application contact:* Natalie Gilmore, Assistant Dean of Graduate Studies, 626-395-3812, Fax: 626-577-9246, E-mail: ngilmore@caltech.edu.

California Polytechnic State University, San Luis Obispo, College of Engineering, Department of Electrical Engineering, San Luis Obispo, CA 93407. Offers MS. Part-time programs available. *Faculty:* 13 full-time (3 women), 1 part-time/adjunct (0 women). *Students:* 34 full-time (0 women), 10 part-time (3 women); includes 13 minority (10 Asian Americans or Pacific Islanders, 3 Hispanic Americans), 4 international. Average age 26. 33 applicants, 55% accepted, 15 enrolled. In 2009, 20 master's awarded. *Degree requirements:* For master's, thesis. *Entrance requirements:* For master's, GRE General Test, minimum GPA of 3.0 in last 90 quarter units. Additional exam requirements/recommendations for international students: Required—TOEFL (minimum score 550 paper-based; 213 computer-based), or IELTS (minimum score 6). *Application deadline:* For fall admission, 7/1 for domestic students, 11/30 for international students; for winter admission, 11/1 for domestic students, 6/30 for international students; for spring admission, 2/1 for domestic students. Applications are processed on a rolling basis. Application fee: $55. Electronic applications accepted. *Expenses:* Tuition, nonresident: full-time $11,160; part-time $248 per unit. Required fees: $7134; $1553 per quarter. *Financial support:* Fellowships, research assistantships, teaching assistantships, career-related internships or fieldwork, Federal Work-Study, scholarships/grants, and unspecified assistantships available. Support available to part-time students. Financial award application deadline: 3/2; financial award applicants required to submit FAFSA. *Faculty research:* Communications, systems analysis, control systems, electronic devices, microprocessors. *Unit head:* Dr. Dennis Derickson, Graduate Coordinator, 805-756-7584, Fax: 805-756-1456, E-mail: ddericks@calpoly.edu. *Application contact:* Dr. Dennis Derickson, Graduate Coordinator, 805-756-7584, Fax: 805-756-1456, E-mail: ddericks@calpoly.edu.

California State Polytechnic University, Pomona, Academic Affairs, College of Engineering, Pomona, CA 91768-2557. Offers civil engineering (MS); electrical engineering (MSEE); engineering (MSE); engineering management (MS); mechanical engineering (MS). Part-time programs available. *Faculty:* 95 full-time (17 women), 71 part-time/adjunct (6 women). *Students:* 36 full-time (3 women), 198 part-time (33 women); includes 104 minority (1 African American, 2 American Indian/Alaska Native, 69 Asian Americans or Pacific Islanders, 32 Hispanic Americans), 42 international. Average age 28. 237 applicants, 49% accepted, 73 enrolled. In 2009, 46 master's awarded. *Degree requirements:* For master's, thesis or comprehensive exam. *Entrance requirements:* For master's, GRE General Test or minimum GPA of 3.0 in upper-level course work. Additional exam requirements/recommendations for international students: Required—TOEFL. *Application deadline:* For fall admission, 5/1 priority date for domestic students; for winter admission, 10/15 priority date for domestic students; for spring admission, 1/2 priority date for domestic students. Applications are processed on a rolling basis. Application fee: $55. Electronic applications accepted. *Expenses:* Tuition, nonresident: full-time $6696; part-time $248 per credit. Required fees: $5487; $3237 per term. Tuition and fees vary according to course load, degree level and program. *Financial support:* In 2009–10, 1 fellowship, 6 research assistantships, 5 teaching assistantships were awarded; career-related internships or fieldwork, Federal Work-Study, institutionally sponsored loans, and unspecified assistantships also available. Support available to part-time students. Financial award application deadline: 3/2; financial award applicants required to submit FAFSA. *Faculty research:* Aerospace; alternative vehicles; communications, computers, and controls; engineering management. Total annual research expenditures: $650,000. *Unit head:* Dr. Edward Hohmann, Dean, 909-869-2472, Fax: 909-869-4370, E-mail: echohmann@csupomona.edu. *Application contact:* Dr. Edward Hohmann, Dean, 909-869-2472, Fax: 909-869-4370, E-mail: echohmann@csupomona.edu.

California State University, Chico, Graduate School, College of Engineering, Computer Science, and Technology, Department of Electrical and Computer Engineering, Option in Electronics Engineering, Chico, CA 95929-0722. Offers MS. *Students:* 1 full-time (0 women), 16 part-time (3 women); includes 2 minority (both Asian Americans or Pacific Islanders), 12 international. Average age 25. 46 applicants, 80% accepted, 6 enrolled. In 2009, 8 master's awarded. *Degree requirements:* For master's, thesis or alternative. *Entrance requirements:* For master's, GRE General Test, 2 letters of recommendation. Additional exam requirements/recommendations for international students: Required—TOEFL (minimum score 550 paper-based; 213 computer-based; 80 iBT), IELTS (minimum score 6.5). *Application deadline:* For fall admission, 3/1 priority date for domestic students, 3/1 for international students; for spring admission, 9/15 priority date for domestic students, 9/15 for international students. Applica-

Electrical Engineering

California State University, Chico (continued)
tions are processed on a rolling basis. Application fee: $55. Electronic applications accepted. *Unit head:* Dr. Adel Ghandakly, Graduate Coordinator, 530-898-5343. *Application contact:* Dr. Adel Ghandakly, Graduate Coordinator, 530-898-5343.

California State University, Fresno, Division of Graduate Studies, College of Engineering and Computer Science, Program in Electrical Engineering, Fresno, CA 93740-8027. Offers MS. Offered at Edwards Air Force Base. Part-time and evening/weekend programs available. *Degree requirements:* For master's, thesis or alternative. *Entrance requirements:* For master's, GRE General Test, minimum GPA of 2.7. Additional exam requirements/recommendations for international students: Required—TOEFL. Electronic applications accepted. *Faculty research:* Research in electromagnetic devices.

California State University, Fullerton, Graduate Studies, College of Engineering and Computer Science, Department of Electrical Engineering, Fullerton, CA 92834-9480. Offers electrical engineering (MS); systems engineering (MS). Part-time programs available. *Students:* 53 full-time (9 women), 120 part-time (25 women); includes 35 minority (31 Asian Americans or Pacific Islanders, 4 Hispanic Americans), 108 international. Average age 26. 207 applicants, 63% accepted, 55 enrolled. In 2009, 51 master's awarded. *Degree requirements:* For master's, comprehensive exam, project or thesis. *Entrance requirements:* For master's, GRE General Test, GRE Subject Test, minimum undergraduate GPA of 2.5, 3.0 graduate. Application fee: $55. *Expenses:* Tuition, nonresident: full-time $11,160; part-time $373 per credit. Required fees: $1440 per term. Tuition and fees vary according to course load, degree level and program. *Financial support:* Career-related internships or fieldwork, Federal Work-Study, institutionally sponsored loans, and scholarships/grants available. Support available to part-time students. Financial award application deadline: 3/1; financial award applicants required to submit FAFSA. *Unit head:* Dr. Mostafa Shiva, Chair, 657-278-3013. *Application contact:* Admissions/Applications, 657-278-2371.

California State University, Long Beach, Graduate Studies, College of Engineering, Department of Electrical Engineering, Long Beach, CA 90840. Offers MSEE. Part-time programs available. *Faculty:* 16 full-time (1 woman), 7 part-time/adjunct (0 women). *Students:* 124 full-time (16 women), 81 part-time (7 women); includes 63 minority (8 African Americans, 1 American Indian/Alaska Native, 44 Asian Americans or Pacific Islanders, 10 Hispanic Americans), 122 international. Average age 27. 267 applicants, 72% accepted, 65 enrolled. *Degree requirements:* For master's, comprehensive exam or thesis. *Entrance requirements:* Additional exam requirements/recommendations for international students: Required—TOEFL. *Application deadline:* For fall admission, 3/1 for domestic students. Application fee: $55. Electronic applications accepted. *Expenses:* Required fees: $1802 per semester. Part-time tuition and fees vary according to course load. *Financial support:* Teaching assistantships, career-related internships or fieldwork, Federal Work-Study, institutionally sponsored loans, scholarships/grants, and unspecified assistantships available. Financial award application deadline: 3/2. *Faculty research:* Health care systems, VLSI, communications, CAD/CAM. *Unit head:* Dr. Bahram Shahian, Chair, 562-985-8041, Fax: 562-985-5327, E-mail: shahian@csulb.edu. *Application contact:* Dr. Fumio Hamano, Graduate Adviser, 562-985-7580, Fax: 562-985-5327, E-mail: fhamano@csulb.edu.

California State University, Los Angeles, Graduate Studies, College of Engineering, Computer Science, and Technology, Department of Electrical and Computer Engineering, Los Angeles, CA 90032-8530. Offers electrical engineering (MS). Part-time and evening/weekend programs available. *Faculty:* 5 full-time (2 women), 3 part-time/adjunct (2 women). *Students:* 64 full-time (13 women), 159 part-time (23 women); includes 52 minority (9 African Americans, 24 Asian Americans or Pacific Islanders, 19 Hispanic Americans), 158 international. Average age 27. 74 applicants, 100% accepted, 29 enrolled. In 2009, 56 master's awarded. *Degree requirements:* For master's, comprehensive exam or thesis. *Entrance requirements:* For master's, GRE General Test, GRE Subject Test. Additional exam requirements/recommendations for international students: Required—TOEFL (minimum score 550 paper-based). *Application deadline:* For fall admission, 5/1 for domestic and international students. Applications are processed on a rolling basis. Application fee: $55. Electronic applications accepted. *Financial support:* Federal Work-Study available. Support available to part-time students. Financial award application deadline: 3/1. *Unit head:* Dr. Fred Daneshgaran, Chair, 323-343-4470, Fax: 323-343-4547, E-mail: fdanesh@calstatela.edu. *Application contact:* Dr. Cheryl L. Ney, Associate Vice President for Academic Affairs and Dean of Graduate Studies, 323-343-3820, Fax: 323-343-5653, E-mail: cney@cslanet.calstatela.edu.

California State University, Northridge, Graduate Studies, College of Engineering and Computer Science, Department of Electrical and Computer Engineering, Northridge, CA 91330. Offers electrical engineering (MS). Part-time and evening/weekend programs available. *Faculty:* 14 full-time (4 women), 15 part-time/adjunct (3 women). *Students:* 106 full-time (11 women), 136 part-time (23 women); includes 1 African American, 19 Asian Americans or Pacific Islanders, 15 Hispanic Americans, 152 international. Average age 27. 431 applicants, 69% accepted, 74 enrolled. In 2009, 47 master's awarded. *Degree requirements:* For master's, thesis or alternative. *Entrance requirements:* For master's, GRE General Test, minimum GPA of 2.75. Additional exam requirements/recommendations for international students: Required—TOEFL. *Application deadline:* For fall admission, 11/30 for domestic students. Application fee: $55. *Financial support:* Application deadline: 3/1. *Faculty research:* Reflector antenna study. *Unit head:* Dr. Ali Amini, Chair, 818-677-2190, E-mail: ece@csun.edu. *Application contact:* Dr. Ali Amini, Graduate Coordinator, 818-677-2190, E-mail: ece@csun.edu.

California State University, Sacramento, Graduate Studies, College of Engineering and Computer Science, Department of Electrical and Electronic Engineering, Sacramento, CA 95819. Offers electrical engineering (MS). Part-time and evening/weekend programs available. *Degree requirements:* For master's, writing proficiency exam. *Entrance requirements:* Additional exam requirements/recommendations for international students: Required—TOEFL. Electronic applications accepted.

Capitol College, Graduate Programs, Laurel, MD 20708-9759. Offers business administration (MBA); computer science (MS); electrical engineering (MS); information and telecommunications systems management (MS); information architecture (MS); network security (MS). Part-time and evening/weekend programs available. Postbaccalaureate distance learning degree programs offered (no on-campus study). *Entrance requirements:* For master's, minimum GPA of 3.0. Electronic applications accepted.

Carleton University, Faculty of Graduate Studies, Faculty of Engineering and Design, Ottawa-Carleton Institute for Electrical Engineering, Department of Electronics, Ottawa, ON K1S 5B6, Canada. Offers electrical engineering (M Eng, MA Sc, PhD). *Degree requirements:* For master's, thesis optional; for doctorate, comprehensive exam, thesis/dissertation. *Entrance requirements:* For master's, honors degree; for doctorate, MA Sc or M Eng. Additional exam requirements/recommendations for international students: Required—TOEFL.

Carleton University, Faculty of Graduate Studies, Faculty of Engineering and Design, Ottawa-Carleton Institute for Electrical Engineering, Department of Systems and Computer Engineering, Ottawa, ON K1S 5B6, Canada. Offers electrical engineering (MA Sc, PhD); information and systems science (M Sc); technology innovation management (M Eng, MA Sc). *Degree requirements:* For master's, thesis optional. *Entrance requirements:* For master's, honors degree. Additional exam requirements/recommendations for international students: Required—TOEFL. *Faculty research:* Design manufacturing management; network design, protocols, and performance; software engineering; wireless and satellite communications.

Carnegie Mellon University, Carnegie Institute of Technology, Department of Electrical and Computer Engineering, Pittsburgh, PA 15213-3891. Offers biomedical engineering (MS); electrical and computer engineering (MS, PhD). Part-time programs available. *Degree requirements:* For master's, thesis; for doctorate, thesis/dissertation, qualifying exam, teaching experience. *Entrance requirements:* For master's and doctorate, GRE General Test. Additional exam requirements/recommendations for international students: Required—TOEFL. *Faculty research:* Computer-aided design, solid-state devices, VLSI, processing, robotics and controls, signal processing, data systems storage.

See Close-Up on page 363.

Case Western Reserve University, School of Graduate Studies, The Case School of Engineering, Department of Electrical Engineering and Computer Science, Cleveland, OH 44106. Offers computer engineering (MS, PhD); computing and information sciences (MS, PhD); electrical engineering (MS, PhD); systems and control engineering (MS, PhD). Part-time and evening/weekend programs available. Postbaccalaureate distance learning degree programs offered (minimal on-campus study). *Faculty:* 32 full-time (2 women). *Students:* 175 full-time (26 women), 28 part-time (6 women); includes 9 minority (3 African Americans, 6 Asian Americans or Pacific Islanders), 107 international. In 2009, 29 master's, 15 doctorates awarded. Terminal master's awarded for partial completion of doctoral program. *Degree requirements:* For master's, thesis; for doctorate, thesis/dissertation, qualifying exam, teaching experience. *Entrance requirements:* For master's and doctorate, GRE General Test. Additional exam requirements/recommendations for international students: Required—TOEFL. *Application deadline:* For fall admission, 2/1 for domestic students; for spring admission, 11/1 for domestic students. Applications are processed on a rolling basis. Application fee: $50. *Financial support:* Fellowships with full and partial tuition reimbursements, research assistantships with full and partial tuition reimbursements, teaching assistantships, career-related internships or fieldwork, Federal Work-Study, and institutionally sponsored loans available. Support available to part-time students. Financial award application deadline: 3/1; financial award applicants required to submit FAFSA. *Faculty research:* Applied artificial intelligence, automation, computer-aided design and testing of digital systems. Total annual research expenditures: $5.5 million. *Unit head:* Dwight Davy, Department Chair, 216-368-2802, E-mail: dtd@case.edu. *Application contact:* David Easler, Student Affairs Coordinator, 216-368-4080, Fax: 216-368-2801, E-mail: david.easler@case.edu.

The Catholic University of America, School of Engineering, Department of Electrical Engineering and Computer Science, Washington, DC 20064. Offers antennas and electromagnetic propagation (MEE, MSCS, D Engr); bioimaging (MEE, MSCS, PhD); bioinformatics and intelligent information systems (MEE, D Engr, PhD); distributed and real-time systems (MEE, MSCS, D Engr, PhD); high speed communications and networking (MSCS, D Engr, PhD); information security (MEE, MSCS, PhD); micro-optics (MEE, MSCS, D Engr, PhD); signal and image processing (MEE, MSCS, D Engr). Part-time programs available. *Faculty:* 7 full-time (2 women), 6 part-time/adjunct (0 women). *Students:* 10 full-time (4 women), 50 part-time (7 women); includes 10 minority (3 African Americans, 4 Asian Americans or Pacific Islanders, 3 Hispanic Americans), 12 international. Average age 34. 50 applicants, 54% accepted, 11 enrolled. In 2009, 10 master's awarded. *Degree requirements:* For master's, thesis or alternative; for doctorate, comprehensive exam, thesis/dissertation, qualifying exam, oral exams. *Entrance requirements:* For master's, statement of purpose, official copies of academic transcripts, three letters of recommendation; for doctorate, 3 letters of recommendation. Additional exam requirements/recommendations for international students: Required—TOEFL (minimum score 580 paper-based; 237 computer-based). *Application deadline:* For fall admission, 8/1 priority date for domestic students, 7/15 for international students; for spring admission, 12/1 priority date for domestic students, 10/15 for international students. Applications are processed on a rolling basis. Application fee: $55. Electronic applications accepted. *Expenses:* Contact institution. *Financial support:* Fellowships, research assistantships, teaching assistantships, Federal Work-Study, scholarships/grants, tuition waivers (full and partial), and unspecified assistantships available. Financial award application deadline: 2/1; financial award applicants required to submit FAFSA. *Faculty research:* Signal and image processing, computer communications, robotics, intelligent controls, bioelectromagnetics. Total annual research expenditures: $1.2 million. *Unit head:* Dr. Phillip Regalia, Chair, 202-319-5879, Fax: 202-319-5195, E-mail: regalia@cua.edu. *Application contact:* Julie Schwing, Director of Graduate Admissions, 202-319-5057, Fax: 202-319-6533, E-mail: cua-admissions@cua.edu.

City College of the City University of New York, Graduate School, Grove School of Engineering, Department of Electrical Engineering, New York, NY 10031-9198. Offers ME, MS, PhD. Part-time programs available. *Degree requirements:* For master's, thesis optional; for doctorate, one foreign language, comprehensive exam, thesis/dissertation. *Entrance requirements:* For master's and doctorate, GRE General Test. Additional exam requirements/recommendations for international students: Required—TOEFL (minimum score 500 paper-based; 173 computer-based; 61 iBT). *Faculty research:* Optical electronics, microwaves, communication, signal processing, control systems.

Clarkson University, Graduate School, Wallace H. Coulter School of Engineering, Department of Electrical and Computer Engineering, Potsdam, NY 13699. Offers electrical and computer engineering (PhD); electrical engineering (ME, MS). Part-time programs available. *Faculty:* 20 full-time (5 women), 2 part-time/adjunct (both women). *Students:* 44 full-time (11 women), 1 (woman) part-time; includes 1 minority (American Indian/Alaska Native), 22 international. Average age 28. 95 applicants, 51% accepted, 10 enrolled. In 2009, 9 master's, 5 doctorates awarded. Terminal master's awarded for partial completion of doctoral program. *Degree requirements:* For master's, thesis; for doctorate, comprehensive exam, thesis/dissertation, departmental qualifying exam. *Entrance requirements:* For master's, GRE, resume, 3 letters of recommendation; for doctorate, GRE, transcripts of all college coursework, resume, personal statement, three letters of recommendation. Additional exam requirements/recommendations for international students: Required—TOEFL (minimum score 550 paper-based; 213 computer-based; 80 iBT), IELTS (minimum score 6.5). *Application deadline:* For fall admission, 1/30 priority date for domestic and international students; for spring admission, 9/1 priority date for domestic and international students. Applications are processed on a rolling basis. Application fee: $25 ($35 for international students). Electronic applications accepted. *Expenses:* Tuition: Part-time $1074 per credit hour. *Financial support:* In 2009–10, 30 students received support, including 4 fellowships (averaging $30,000 per year), 8 research assistantships (averaging $20,190 per year), 7 teaching assistantships (averaging $20,190 per year); scholarships/grants, tuition waivers (partial), and unspecified assistantships also available. *Faculty research:* Robotics, electrical machines, power systems, thermo-elastic wave propagation, fingerprint vitality. Total annual research expenditures: $1.3 million. *Unit head:* Dr. Thomas H. Ortmeyer, Department Chair, 315-268-6511, Fax: 315-268-7994. *Application contact:* Kelly Sharlow, Assistant to the Dean, 315-268-7929, Fax: 315-268-4494, E-mail: ksharlow@clarkson.edu.

Clemson University, Graduate School, College of Engineering and Science, Department of Electrical and Computer Engineering, Program in Electrical Engineering, Clemson, SC 29634. Offers M Engr, MS, PhD. *Students:* 93 full-time (17 women), 19 part-time (2 women); includes 7 minority (5 African Americans, 2 Asian Americans or Pacific Islanders), 81 international. Average age 26. 519 applicants, 27% accepted, 40 enrolled. In 2009, 28 master's, 4 doctorates awarded. *Degree requirements:* For master's, thesis or alternative; for doctorate, thesis/dissertation, departmental qualifying exam. *Entrance requirements:* For master's, GRE General Test (MS); for doctorate, GRE General Test. Additional exam requirements/recommendations for international students: Required—TOEFL. *Application deadline:* For fall admission, 6/1 for domestic students, 4/15 for international students; for spring admission, 9/15 for international students. Applications are processed on a rolling basis. Application fee: $70 ($80 for international students). Electronic applications accepted. *Expenses:* Tuition, state resident: full-time $8684; part-time $528 per credit hour. Tuition, nonresident: full-time $15,330; part-time $1078 per credit hour. Required fees: $736; $37 per semester. Part-time tuition and fees vary according to course load and program. *Financial support:* In 2009–10, 67 students received support, including 8 fellowships with full and partial tuition reimbursements available (averaging $4,938 per year), 31 research assistantships with partial tuition reimbursements available (averaging $16,651 per year), 18 teaching assistantships with partial tuition reimbursements available (averaging $13,056 per year); career-related internships or fieldwork, institutionally sponsored loans, scholarships/grants, health care benefits, and unspecified assistantships also available. Support available to part-time students. Financial award applicants required to submit FAFSA. *Faculty research:* Microelectronics, robotics, signal processing/communications, power systems, control. *Unit head:* Dr. Darren Dawson, Chair, 864-656-5249, Fax: 864-656-5917, E-mail: ddarren@clemson.edu. *Application contact:* Dr. Daniel Noneaker, 864-656-0100, Fax: 864-656-5917, E-mail: ece-grad-program@ces.clemson.edu.

Cleveland State University, College of Graduate Studies, Fenn College of Engineering, Department of Electrical and Computer Engineering, Cleveland, OH 44115. Offers electrical engineering (MS, D Eng); software engineering (MS). Part-time programs available. *Degree requirements:* For master's, thesis optional; for doctorate, thesis/dissertation, qualifying and candidacy exams. *Entrance requirements:* For master's, GRE General Test (minimum score 650 quantitative), minimum GPA of 2.75; for doctorate, GRE General Test (quantitative score in 80th percentile), minimum GPA of 3.25. Additional exam requirements/recommendations for international students: Required—TOEFL (minimum score 535 paper-based; 197 computer-based; 65 iBT). *Faculty research:* Computer networks, knowledge-based control systems, artificial intelligence, digital communications, MEMS, sensors, power systems, power electronics.

Colorado State University, Graduate School, College of Engineering, Department of Electrical and Computer Engineering, Fort Collins, CO 80523-1373. Offers electrical engineering (MEE, MS, PhD). Part-time programs available. Postbaccalaureate distance learning degree programs offered (no on-campus study). *Faculty:* 20 full-time (1 woman), 2 part-time/adjunct (0 women). *Students:* 42 full-time (5 women), 65 part-time (8 women); includes 8 minority (2 American Indian/Alaska Native, 2 Asian Americans or Pacific Islanders, 4 Hispanic Americans), 55 international. Average age 28. 365 applicants, 22% accepted, 28 enrolled. In 2009, 12 master's, 11 doctorates awarded. *Degree requirements:* For master's, comprehensive exam (for some programs), thesis (for some programs), final exam; for doctorate, comprehensive exam, thesis/dissertation, qualifying, preliminary, and final exams. *Entrance requirements:* For master's, GRE General Test, minimum GPA of 3.5, BA/BS from ABET-accredited institution, 3 letters of recommendation; for doctorate, GRE General Test, minimum GPA of 3.5, transcripts, 3 letters of recommendation, statement of purpose. Additional exam requirements/recommendations for international students: Required—TOEFL (minimum score 550 paper-based; 213 computer-based; 80 iBT), IELTS. *Application deadline:* For fall admission, 2/1 priority date for domestic and international students; for spring admission, 9/1 priority date for domestic and international students. Applications are processed on a rolling basis. Application fee: $50. Electronic applications accepted. *Expenses:* Tuition, state resident: full-time $6434; part-time $359.10 per credit. Tuition, nonresident: full-time $18,116; part-time $1006.45 per credit. Required fees: $1496; $83 per credit. *Financial support:* In 2009–10, 70 students received support, including 5 fellowships with tuition reimbursements available (averaging $40,554 per year), 61 research assistantships with tuition reimbursements available (averaging $16,548 per year), 4 teaching assistantships with tuition reimbursements available (averaging $7,659 per year); Federal Work-Study and scholarships/grants also available. Financial award application deadline: 2/1; financial award applicants required to submit FAFSA. *Faculty research:* Communications, optoelectronics, controls and robotics, computer engineering, radar remote sensing. Total annual research expenditures: $10 million. *Unit head:* Dr. Anthony A. Maciejewski, Head, 970-491-6600, Fax: 970-491-2249, E-mail: aam@engr.colostate.edu. *Application contact:* Elisabeth L. Wadman, Academic Advisor, 970-491-6706, Fax: 970-491-2249, E-mail: elisabeth.wadman@colostate.edu.

Colorado Technical University Colorado Springs, Graduate Studies, Program in Electrical Engineering, Colorado Springs, CO 80907-3896. Offers MSEE. Part-time and evening/weekend programs available. Postbaccalaureate distance learning degree programs offered. *Degree requirements:* For master's, thesis or alternative. *Faculty research:* Electronic systems design, communication systems design.

Colorado Technical University Denver, Program in Electrical Engineering, Greenwood Village, CO 80111. Offers MS.

Columbia University, Fu Foundation School of Engineering and Applied Science, Department of Electrical Engineering, New York, NY 10027. Offers computer engineering (MS); electrical engineering (MS, Eng Sc D, PhD, Engr); solid state science and engineering (MS, Eng Sc D, PhD). PhD offered through the Graduate School of Arts and Sciences. Part-time programs available. Postbaccalaureate distance learning degree programs offered (no on-campus study). *Faculty:* 17 full-time (1 woman), 4 part-time/adjunct (0 women). *Students:* 223 full-time (39 women), 108 part-time (11 women); includes 34 minority (2 African Americans, 29 Asian Americans or Pacific Islanders, 3 Hispanic Americans), 226 international. Average age 26. 787 applicants, 32% accepted, 129 enrolled. In 2009, 87 master's, 14 doctorates awarded. *Degree requirements:* For doctorate, thesis/dissertation, qualifying exam. *Entrance requirements:* For master's, doctorate, and Engr, GRE General Test. Additional exam requirements/recommendations for international students: Required—TOEFL. *Application deadline:* For fall admission, 12/1 priority date for domestic and international students; for spring admission, 10/1 priority date for domestic and international students. Application fee: $70. Electronic applications accepted. *Financial support:* In 2009–10, 88 students received support, including 8 fellowships with full tuition reimbursements available (averaging $33,570 per year), 57 research assistantships with full tuition reimbursements available (averaging $30,000 per year), 23 teaching assistantships with full tuition reimbursements available (averaging $30,000 per year); health care benefits and unspecified assistantships also available. Financial award application deadline: 12/1; financial award applicants required to submit FAFSA. *Faculty research:* Signal and information processing, networking and communications, integrated circuits and systems, systems biology, micro devices, electromagnetics, plasma physics, photonics, computer engineering. *Unit head:* Dr. Shih-Fu Chang, Professor and Department Chair, 212-854-6894, Fax: 212-854-0300, E-mail: sfchang@ee.columbia.edu. *Application contact:* Elsa Sanchez, Academic Program Officer, 212-854-3104, Fax: 212-932-9421, E-mail: elsa@ee.columbia.edu.

See Close-Up on page 365.

Concordia University, School of Graduate Studies, Faculty of Engineering and Computer Science, Department of Electrical and Computer Engineering, Montréal, QC H3G 1M8, Canada. Offers M Eng, MA Sc, PhD. *Degree requirements:* For master's, thesis optional; for doctorate, comprehensive exam, thesis/dissertation. *Faculty research:* Computer communications and protocols, circuits and systems, graph theory, VLSI systems, microelectronics.

Cooper Union for the Advancement of Science and Art, Albert Nerken School of Engineering, New York, NY 10003-7120. Offers chemical engineering (ME); civil engineering (ME); electrical engineering (ME); mechanical engineering (ME). Part-time programs available. *Faculty:* 27 full-time (1 woman), 15 part-time/adjunct (2 women). *Students:* 66 full-time (8 women), 20 part-time (1 woman); includes 30 minority (2 African Americans, 1 American Indian/Alaska Native, 19 Asian Americans or Pacific Islanders, 8 Hispanic Americans), 10 international. Average age 24. 80 applicants, 90% accepted, 56 enrolled. In 2009, 18 master's awarded. *Degree requirements:* For master's, thesis. *Entrance requirements:* For master's, GRE, BE, minimum GPA of 3.5. Additional exam requirements/recommendations for international students: Required—TOEFL (minimum score 600 paper-based; 250 computer-based; 100 iBT). *Application deadline:* For fall admission, 5/1 for domestic and international students. Applications are processed on a rolling basis. Application fee: $65. *Expenses:* Tuition: Full-time $35,000. Required fees: $1650. *Financial support:* Fellowships with tuition reimbursements, career-related internships or fieldwork, Federal Work-Study, tuition waivers (full), and all admitted students receive full-tuition scholarships available. Support available to part-time students. Financial award application deadline: 5/1; financial award applicants required to submit CSS PROFILE or FAFSA. *Faculty research:* Civil infrastructure, imaging and sensing technology, biomedical engineering, encryption technology, process engineering. *Unit head:* Dr. Simon Ben-Avi, Dean, 212-353-4285, E-mail: benavi@cooper.edu. *Application contact:* Student Contact, 212-353-4120, E-mail: admissions@cooper.edu.

Cornell University, Graduate School, Graduate Fields of Engineering, Field of Electrical and Computer Engineering, Ithaca, NY 14853-0001. Offers computer engineering (M Eng, PhD); electrical engineering (M Eng, PhD); electrical systems (M Eng, PhD); electrophysics (M Eng, PhD). *Faculty:* 71 full-time (5 women). *Students:* 252 full-time (42 women); includes 33 minority (1 African American, 28 Asian Americans or Pacific Islanders, 4 Hispanic Americans), 139 international. Average age 26. 807 applicants, 29% accepted, 106 enrolled. In 2009, 84 master's, 18 doctorates awarded. *Degree requirements:* For doctorate, comprehensive exam, thesis/dissertation. *Entrance requirements:* For master's, GRE General Test, 2 letters of recommendation; for doctorate, GRE General Test, 3 letters of recommendation. Additional exam requirements/recommendations for international students: Required—TOEFL (minimum score 600 paper-based; 250 computer-based; 77 iBT). *Application deadline:* For fall admission, 1/15 priority date for domestic students. Application fee: $70. Electronic applications accepted. *Expenses:* Tuition: Full-time $29,500. Required fees: $70. Full-time tuition and fees vary according to degree level, program and student level. *Financial support:* In 2009–10, 150 students received support, including 26 fellowships with full tuition reimbursements available, 7 research assistantships with full tuition reimbursements available, 1 teaching assistantship with full tuition reimbursement available; institutionally sponsored loans, scholarships/grants, health care benefits, tuition waivers (full and partial), and unspecified assistantships also available. Financial award applicants required to submit FAFSA. *Faculty research:* Communications; information theory; signal processing, and power control; computer engineering; microelectromechanical systems and nanotechnology. *Unit head:* Director of Graduate Studies, 607-255-4304. *Application contact:* Graduate Field Assistant, 607-255-4304, E-mail: meng@ece.cornell.edu.

Dalhousie University, Faculty of Engineering, Department of Electrical and Computer Engineering, Halifax, NS B3J 1Z1, Canada. Offers M Eng, MA Sc, PhD. *Faculty:* 9 full-time (0 women), 4 part-time/adjunct (0 women). *Students:* 40 full-time (8 women), 6 part-time (0 women). Average age 27. 113 applicants, 50% accepted. In 2009, 12 master's, 2 doctorates awarded. *Degree requirements:* For master's, thesis; for doctorate, thesis/dissertation. *Entrance requirements:* Additional exam requirements/recommendations for international students: Required—TOEFL, IELTS, CANTEST, CAEL, or Michigan English Language Assessment Battery. *Application deadline:* For fall admission, 6/1 for domestic students, 4/1 for international students; for winter admission, 11/15 for domestic students, 8/31 for international students; for spring admission, 2/28 for domestic students, 12/31 for international students. Applications are processed on a rolling basis. Application fee: $70. Electronic applications accepted. *Financial support:* Fellowships, research assistantships, teaching assistantships, scholarships/grants and unspecified assistantships available. *Faculty research:* Communications, computer engineering, power engineering, electronics, systems engineering. *Unit head:* Dr. Ezz El-Masry, Head, 902-494-3106, Fax: 902-422-7535, E-mail: ece.admin@dal.ca. *Application contact:* Dr. Jacek Ilow, Graduate Coordinator, 902-494-3981, Fax: 902-422-7535, E-mail: j.ilow@dal.ca.

Dartmouth College, Thayer School of Engineering, Program in Electrical Engineering, Hanover, NH 03755. Offers MS, PhD. *Degree requirements:* For master's, thesis; for doctorate, thesis/dissertation, candidacy oral exam. *Entrance requirements:* For master's and doctorate, GRE General Test. *Application deadline:* For fall admission, 1/1 priority date for domestic students. Application fee: $40 ($50 for international students). *Financial support:* Career-related internships or fieldwork, Federal Work-Study, institutionally sponsored loans, and tuition waivers (full and partial) available. Financial award application deadline: 1/15. *Faculty research:* Power electronics and microengineering, signal/image processing and communications, optics, lasers and optoelectronics, electromagnetic fields and waves. *Unit head:* Dr. Joseph J. Helbie, Dean, 603-646-2238, Fax: 603-646-2580, E-mail: joseph.j.helbie@dartmouth.edu. *Application contact:* Candace S. Potter, Graduate Admissions Administrator, 603-646-3844, Fax: 603-646-1620, E-mail: candace.potter@dartmouth.edu.

Drexel University, College of Engineering, Department of Electrical and Computer Engineering, Program in Electrical Engineering, Philadelphia, PA 19104-2875. Offers MSEE. Part-time and evening/weekend programs available. Terminal master's awarded for partial completion of doctoral program. *Degree requirements:* For master's, thesis (for some programs). Electronic applications accepted.

See Close-Up on page 367.

Duke University, Graduate School, Pratt School of Engineering, Department of Electrical and Computer Engineering, Durham, NC 27708. Offers MS, PhD. Part-time programs available. *Faculty:* 36 full-time. *Students:* 156 full-time (37 women); includes 13 minority (5 African Americans, 5 Asian Americans or Pacific Islanders, 3 Hispanic Americans), 103 international. 451 applicants, 34% accepted, 63 enrolled. In 2009, 38 master's, 15 doctorates awarded. Terminal master's awarded for partial completion of doctoral program. *Degree requirements:* For doctorate, thesis/dissertation. *Entrance requirements:* For master's and doctorate, GRE General Test. Additional exam requirements/recommendations for international students: Required—TOEFL (minimum score 550 paper-based; 213 computer-based; 83 iBT), IELTS (minimum score 7). *Application deadline:* For fall admission, 12/8 priority date for domestic and international students; for spring admission, 11/1 for domestic students. Application fee: $75. Electronic applications accepted. *Financial support:* Fellowships, research assistantships, Federal Work-Study available. Financial award application deadline: 12/31. *Unit head:* Steve Cummer, Director of Graduate Studies, 919-660-5256, Fax: 919-660-5293, E-mail: samantha@ee.duke.edu. *Application contact:* Cynthia Robertson, Associate Dean for Enrollment Services, 919-684-3913, E-mail: grad-admissions@duke.edu.

See Close-Up on page 369.

École Polytechnique de Montréal, Graduate Programs, Department of Electrical and Computer Engineering, Montréal, QC H3C 3A7, Canada. Offers automation (M Eng, M Sc A, PhD); computer science (M Eng, M Sc A, PhD); electrical engineering (DESS); electrotechnology (M Eng, M Sc A, PhD); microelectronics (M Eng, M Sc A, PhD); microwave technology (M Eng, M Sc A, PhD). Part-time and evening/weekend programs available. *Degree requirements:* For master's, one foreign language, thesis; for doctorate, one foreign language, thesis/dissertation. *Entrance requirements:* For master's, minimum GPA of 2.75; for doctorate, minimum GPA of 3.0. *Faculty research:* Microwaves, telecommunications, software engineering.

Fairfield University, School of Engineering, Fairfield, CT 06824-5195. Offers electrical and computer engineering (MS); management of technology (MS); mechanical engineering (MS); software engineering (MS). Part-time and evening/weekend programs available. *Degree requirements:* For master's, thesis, capstone course. *Entrance requirements:* For master's, interview, minimum GPA of 2.8, resume, 2 recommendations. Additional exam requirements/recommendations for international students: Required—TOEFL (minimum score 550 paper-based; 213 computer-based; 80 iBT). Electronic applications accepted. *Expenses:* Contact institution. *Faculty research:* Vehicle dynamics, image processing, multimedia in instruction, thermal packaging, character recognition, photovoltaics and nanotechnology, Web technology.

Fairleigh Dickinson University, Metropolitan Campus, University College: Arts, Sciences, and Professional Studies, School of Computer Sciences and Engineering, Program in Electrical Engineering, Teaneck, NJ 07666-1914. Offers MSEE. *Students:* 53 full-time (12 women), 18 part-time (3 women), 63 international. Average age 24. 193 applicants, 68% accepted, 21 enrolled. In 2009, 40 master's awarded. *Entrance requirements:* For master's, GRE General Test. *Application deadline:* Applications are processed on a rolling basis. Application fee: $40. *Application contact:* Susan Brooman, University Director of Graduate Admissions, 201-692-2554, Fax: 201-692-2560, E-mail: globaleducation@fdu.edu.

Florida Agricultural and Mechanical University, Division of Graduate Studies, Research, and Continuing Education, FAMU-FSU College of Engineering, Department of Electrical Engineering, Tallahassee, FL 32307-3200. Offers MS, PhD. *Faculty:* 18 full-time (4 women). *Students:* 24 full-time (10 women), 14 part-time (2 women); includes 32 minority (31 African Americans, 1 Asian American or Pacific Islander), 6 international. In 2009, 1 doctorate awarded. *Degree requirements:* For master's, comprehensive exam, thesis, conference paper; for doctorate, comprehensive exam, thesis/dissertation, publishable paper. *Entrance requirements:* For master's, GRE General Test, minimum GPA of 3.0; for doctorate, minimum GPA of 3.3. Additional exam requirements/recommendations for international students: Required—TOEFL

Electrical Engineering

Florida Agricultural and Mechanical University (continued)
(minimum score 550 paper-based; 213 computer-based). *Application deadline:* For fall admission, 7/1 for domestic students, 3/1 for international students. Application fee: $20. *Faculty research:* Electromagnetics, computer security, advanced power systems, sensor systems. *Unit head:* Dr. Reginald Perry, Chairperson, 850-410-6100. *Application contact:* Dr. Chanta M. Haywood, Dean of Graduate Studies, Research, and Continuing Education, 850-599-3315, Fax: 850-599-3727.

Florida Atlantic University, College of Engineering and Computer Science, Department of Electrical Engineering, Boca Raton, FL 33431-0991. Offers MS, PhD. Part-time and evening/weekend programs available. Postbaccalaureate distance learning degree programs offered (minimal on-campus study). *Faculty:* 12 full-time (3 women). *Students:* 14 full-time (3 women), 29 part-time (6 women); includes 19 minority (5 African Americans, 4 Asian Americans or Pacific Islanders, 10 Hispanic Americans), 13 international. Average age 33. 42 applicants, 52% accepted, 9 enrolled. In 2009, 9 master's, 2 doctorates awarded. Terminal master's awarded for partial completion of doctoral program. *Degree requirements:* For master's, thesis optional; for doctorate, thesis/dissertation, qualifying exam. *Entrance requirements:* For master's and doctorate, GRE General Test, minimum GPA of 3.0. Additional exam requirements/recommendations for international students: Required—TOEFL. *Application deadline:* For fall admission, 7/1 priority date for domestic students, 2/15 for international students; for spring admission, 11/1 for domestic students, 7/15 for international students. Applications are processed on a rolling basis. Application fee: $30. *Expenses:* Tuition, state resident: full-time $7055; part-time $293.94 per credit hour. Tuition, nonresident: full-time $22,096; part-time $920.66 per credit hour. *Financial support:* Fellowships, research assistantships with full and partial tuition reimbursements, teaching assistantships with full and partial tuition reimbursements, career-related internships or fieldwork, Federal Work-Study, and unspecified assistantships available. Support available to part-time students. Financial award application deadline: 4/1; financial award applicants required to submit FAFSA. *Faculty research:* Telecommunications, signal processing, imaging systems, electromagnetics, controls. *Unit head:* Dr. Borko Furht, Interim Chair, 561-297-3412, Fax: 561-297-2336. *Application contact:* Marilyn Russo, Senior Secretary, 561-297-3412, Fax: 561-297-2659, E-mail: mrusso@fau.edu.

Florida Institute of Technology, Graduate Programs, College of Engineering, Electrical and Computer Engineering Department, Melbourne, FL 32901-6975. Offers computer engineering (MS, PhD); electrical engineering (MS, PhD). Part-time and evening/weekend programs available. *Faculty:* 9 full-time (1 woman), 1 part-time/adjunct (0 women). *Students:* 80 full-time (14 women), 38 part-time (7 women); includes 10 minority (1 African American, 3 Asian Americans or Pacific Islanders, 6 Hispanic Americans), 73 international. Average age 28. 276 applicants, 65% accepted, 32 enrolled. In 2009, 37 master's, 6 doctorates awarded. *Degree requirements:* For master's, comprehensive exam (for some programs), thesis (for some programs), final program exam, faculty-supervised specialized research; for doctorate, comprehensive exam, thesis/dissertation, complete program of significant original research. *Entrance requirements:* For master's, GRE, minimum GPA of 3.0, bachelor's degree from an ABET-accredited program; for doctorate, 3 letters of recommendation, resume, minimum GPA of 3.2, statement of objectives, on campus interview (highly recommended). Additional exam requirements/recommendations for international students: Required—TOEFL (minimum score 550 paper-based; 213 computer-based; 79 iBT). *Application deadline:* For fall admission, 4/1 for international students; for spring admission, 9/30 for international students. Applications are processed on a rolling basis. Application fee: $50. Electronic applications accepted. *Expenses:* Tuition: Part-time $1015 per credit. Tuition and fees vary according to campus/location and program. *Financial support:* In 2009–10, 16 students received support, including 4 research assistantships with full and partial tuition reimbursements available (averaging $4,952 per year), 12 teaching assistantships with full and partial tuition reimbursements available (averaging $3,467 per year); career-related internships or fieldwork, institutionally sponsored loans, tuition waivers (partial), unspecified assistantships, and tuition remissions also available. Support available to part-time students. Financial award application deadline: 3/1; financial award applicants required to submit FAFSA. *Faculty research:* Electro-optics, electromagnetics, microelectronics, communications, computer architecture, neural networks. Total annual research expenditures: $380,187. *Unit head:* Dr. Samuel P. Kozaitis, Department Head, 321-674-8060, Fax: 321-674-8192, E-mail: kozaitis@fit.edu. *Application contact:* Thomas M. Shea, Director of Graduate Admissions, 321-674-7577, Fax: 321-723-9468, E-mail: tshea@fit.edu.

See Close-Up on page 371.

Florida International University, College of Engineering and Computing, Department of Electrical and Computer Engineering, Program in Electrical Engineering, Miami, FL 33175. Offers MS, PhD. Part-time and evening/weekend programs available. *Students:* 19 full-time (8 women), 9 part-time (4 women); includes 22 minority (6 Asian Americans or Pacific Islanders, 16 Hispanic Americans). Average age 29. 205 applicants, 13% accepted, 26 enrolled. In 2009, 53 master's, 6 doctorates awarded. Terminal master's awarded for partial completion of doctoral program. *Degree requirements:* For master's, thesis optional; for doctorate, comprehensive exam, thesis/dissertation. *Entrance requirements:* For master's, minimum undergraduate GPA of 3.0 in upper-level coursework, resume, letters of recommendation, letter of intent; for doctorate, GRE General Test, minimum graduate GPA of 3.3, resume, master's degree, letters of recommendation, letter of intent. Additional exam requirements/recommendations for international students: Required—TOEFL (minimum score 550 paper-based; 80 iBT). *Application deadline:* For fall admission, 6/1 for domestic students, 4/1 for international students; for spring admission, 10/1 for domestic students, 9/1 for international students. Applications are processed on a rolling basis. Application fee: $30. Electronic applications accepted. *Expenses:* Tuition, state resident: full-time $8008; part-time $4004 per year. Tuition, nonresident: full-time $20,104; part-time $10,052 per year. Required fees: $298; $149 per term. *Financial support:* Institutionally sponsored loans and scholarships/grants available. Financial award application deadline: 3/1; financial award applicants required to submit FAFSA. *Unit head:* Dr. Kang Yen, Chair, Electrical and Computer Engineering Department, 305-348-3037, Fax: 305-348-3707, E-mail: yenk@fiu.edu. *Application contact:* Maria Parrilla, Graduate Admissions Assistant, 305-348-1890, Fax: 305-348-6142, E-mail: grad_eng@fiu.edu.

Florida State University, The Graduate School, FAMU-FSU College of Engineering, Department of Electrical and Computer Engineering, Tallahassee, FL 32306. Offers electrical engineering (MS, PhD). Part-time programs available. *Faculty:* 18 full-time (2 women), 1 part-time/adjunct (0 women). *Students:* 96 full-time (17 women); includes 74 minority (21 African Americans, 46 Asian Americans or Pacific Islanders, 7 Hispanic Americans). Average age 26. 161 applicants, 61% accepted, 19 enrolled. In 2009, 11 master's, 8 doctorates awarded. *Degree requirements:* For master's, thesis; for doctorate, comprehensive exam, thesis/dissertation, preliminary exam, qualifying exam. *Entrance requirements:* For master's, GRE General Test, minimum GPA of 3.0, BS in electrical engineering; for doctorate, GRE General Test, minimum graduate GPA of 3.3, MS in electrical engineering. Additional exam requirements/recommendations for international students: Required—TOEFL (minimum score 550 paper-based; 213 computer-based). *Application deadline:* For fall admission, 7/1 for domestic and international students; for spring admission, 11/1 for domestic and international students. Applications are processed on a rolling basis. Application fee: $30. *Expenses:* Tuition, state resident: full-time $7413.36. Tuition, nonresident: full-time $22,567. *Financial support:* In 2009–10, 53 students received support, including fellowships with full tuition reimbursements available (averaging $12,000 per year), 23 research assistantships with full tuition reimbursements available (averaging $15,800 per year), 13 teaching assistantships with full tuition reimbursements available (averaging $15,800 per year); career-related internships or fieldwork, institutionally sponsored loans, scholarships/grants, and tuition waivers (full) also available. Financial award application deadline: 6/15. *Faculty research:* Electromagnetics, digital signal processing, computer systems, image processing, laser optics. Total annual research expenditures: $829,000. *Unit head:* Dr. Victor DeBrunner, Chair and Professor, 850-410-6476, Fax: 850-410-6479, E-mail: victor.debrunner@eng.fsu.edu. *Application contact:* Melissa Jackson, Coordinator of Academic Programs, 850-410-6454, Fax: 850-410-6479, E-mail: ecegrad@eng.fsu.edu.

Gannon University, School of Graduate Studies, College of Engineering and Business, School of Engineering and Computer Science, Program in Electrical Engineering, Erie, PA 16541-0001. Offers MSEE. Part-time and evening/weekend programs available. *Students:* 65 full-time (8 women), 31 part-time (3 women); includes 2 minority (1 American Indian/Alaska Native, 1 Asian American or Pacific Islander), 89 international. Average age 24. 307 applicants, 95% accepted, 36 enrolled. In 2009, 101 master's awarded. *Degree requirements:* For master's, thesis or project. *Entrance requirements:* For master's, bachelor's degree in engineering, minimum QPA of 2.5. Additional exam requirements/recommendations for international students: Required—TOEFL (minimum score 79 iBT). *Application deadline:* Applications are processed on a rolling basis. Application fee: $25. Electronic applications accepted. *Expenses:* Tuition: Full-time $13,590; part-time $755 per credit. Required fees: $524; $17 per credit. Tuition and fees vary according to course load, degree level, campus/location and program. *Financial support:* Career-related internships or fieldwork, scholarships/grants, traineeships, and unspecified assistantships available. Financial award application deadline: 7/1; financial award applicants required to submit FAFSA. *Unit head:* Dr. Fong Mak, Chair, 814-871-7625, E-mail: mak001@gannon.edu. *Application contact:* Kara Morgan, Assistant Director of Graduate Admissions, 814-871-5831, Fax: 814-871-5827, E-mail: graduate@gannon.edu.

George Mason University, Volgenau School of Information Technology and Engineering, Department of Electrical and Computer Engineering, Fairfax, VA 22030. Offers advanced networking protocols for telecommunications (Certificate); communications and networking (Certificate); computer engineering (MS); computer forensics (MS); electrical and computer engineering (PhD); electrical engineering (MS); network technology and applications (Certificate); networks, system integration and testing (Certificate); signal processing (Certificate); telecom systems modeling (Certificate); telecommunications (MS); telecommunications forensics and security (Certificate); VLSI design/manufacturing (Certificate); wireless communication (Certificate). Part-time and evening/weekend programs available. *Faculty:* 29 full-time (4 women), 37 part-time/adjunct (5 women). *Students:* 115 full-time (18 women), 308 part-time (46 women); includes 84 minority (17 African Americans, 51 Asian Americans or Pacific Islanders, 16 Hispanic Americans), 179 international. Average age 29. 461 applicants, 67% accepted, 105 enrolled. In 2009, 157 master's, 6 doctorates, 61 other advanced degrees awarded. *Degree requirements:* For master's, thesis optional; for doctorate, comprehensive exam, thesis or scholarly paper. *Entrance requirements:* For master's, GMAT or GRE General Test, letters of recommendation, resume; for doctorate, GRE/GMAT, personal goal statement, 2 transcripts, letter of recommendation. Additional exam requirements/recommendations for international students: Required—TOEFL. *Application deadline:* For fall admission, 7/15 priority date for domestic and international students; for spring admission, 12/2 for domestic students, 12/1 for international students. Applications are processed on a rolling basis. Application fee: $75. Electronic applications accepted. *Expenses:* Tuition, state resident: full-time $7568; part-time $315.33 per credit hour. Tuition, nonresident: full-time $21,704; part-time $904.33 per credit hour. Required fees: $2184; $91 per credit hour. *Financial support:* In 2009–10, 64 students received support, including 2 fellowships with full tuition reimbursements available (averaging $18,000 per year), 22 research assistantships with full and partial tuition reimbursements available (averaging $8,469 per year), 42 teaching assistantships with full and partial tuition reimbursements available (averaging $6,291 per year); career-related internships or fieldwork, Federal Work-Study, scholarships/grants, unspecified assistantships, and health care benefits (full-time research or teaching assistantship recipients) also available. Support available to part-time students. Financial award application deadline: 3/1; financial award applicants required to submit FAFSA. *Faculty research:* Communication networks, signal processing, system failure diagnosis, multiprocessors, material processing using microwave energy. Total annual research expenditures: $3 million. *Unit head:* Dr. Andre Manitius, Chairperson, 703-993-1569, Fax: 703-993-1601, E-mail: ece@gmu.edu. *Application contact:* Jessica Skinner, Associate Dean, 703-993-1569, E-mail: jskinne6@gmu.edu.

The George Washington University, School of Engineering and Applied Science, Department of Electrical and Computer Engineering, Washington, DC 20052. Offers electrical and computer engineering (MS, D Sc); telecommunication and computers (MS). Part-time and evening/weekend programs available. *Faculty:* 23 full-time (2 women), 6 part-time/adjunct (0 women). *Students:* 98 full-time (19 women), 132 part-time (14 women); includes 33 minority (12 African Americans, 1 American Indian/Alaska Native, 18 Asian Americans or Pacific Islanders, 2 Hispanic Americans), 126 international. Average age 30. 293 applicants, 88% accepted, 64 enrolled. In 2009, 54 master's, 5 doctorates awarded. *Degree requirements:* For master's, thesis optional; for doctorate, comprehensive exam, thesis/dissertation, dissertation defense, qualifying exam. *Entrance requirements:* For master's, appropriate bachelor's degree, minimum GPA of 3.0; for doctorate, appropriate bachelor's or master's degree, minimum GPA of 3.3, GRE if highest earned degree is BS. Additional exam requirements/recommendations for international students: Required—TOEFL or George Washington University English as a Foreign Language Test. *Application deadline:* For fall admission, 3/1 priority date for domestic students; for spring admission, 10/1 for domestic students. Applications are processed on a rolling basis. Application fee: $60. *Financial support:* In 2009–10, 39 students received support; fellowships with tuition reimbursements available, research assistantships, teaching assistantships with tuition reimbursements available, career-related internships or fieldwork and institutionally sponsored loans available. Financial award application deadline: 3/1; financial award applicants required to submit FAFSA. *Faculty research:* Computer graphics, multimedia systems. *Unit head:* Can E. Korman, Chair, 202-994-4952, E-mail: korman@gwu.edu. *Application contact:* Adina Lav, Marketing, Recruiting and Admissions, 202-994-5827, Fax: 202-994-0909, E-mail: engineering@gwu.edu.

Georgia Institute of Technology, Graduate Studies and Research, College of Engineering, School of Electrical and Computer Engineering, Atlanta, GA 30332-0001. Offers MS, MSEE, PhD. Part-time programs available. Postbaccalaureate distance learning degree programs offered (minimal on-campus study). Terminal master's awarded for partial completion of doctoral program. *Degree requirements:* For master's, thesis optional; for doctorate, thesis/dissertation. *Entrance requirements:* For master's, GRE General Test, minimum GPA of 3.0; for doctorate, GRE General Test, minimum GPA of 3.5. Additional exam requirements/recommendations for international students: Required—TOEFL. *Faculty research:* Telecommunications, computer systems, microelectronics, optical engineering, digital signal processing.

Georgia Southern University, Jack N. Averitt College of Graduate Studies, Allen E. Paulson College of Science and Technology, Department of Mechanical and Electrical Engineering Technology, Statesboro, GA 30460. Offers M Tech, MSAE. Part-time and evening/weekend programs available. *Students:* 31 full-time (6 women), 17 part-time (4 women); includes 15 minority (13 African Americans, 2 Hispanic Americans), 5 international. Average age 27. 25 applicants, 100% accepted, 25 enrolled. In 2009, 3 master's awarded. *Degree requirements:* For master's, comprehensive exam, thesis optional. *Entrance requirements:* For master's, GRE. Additional exam requirements/recommendations for international students: Required—TOEFL (minimum score 550 paper-based; 213 computer-based; 80 iBT). *Application deadline:* For fall admission, 3/1 priority date for domestic and international students; for spring admission, 10/1 priority date for domestic students, 10/1 for international students. Applications are processed on a rolling basis. Application fee: $50. Electronic applications accepted. *Expenses:* Tuition, state resident: full-time $5040; part-time $210 per credit hour. Tuition, nonresident: full-time $20,136; part-time $839 per credit hour. Required fees: $1644. *Financial support:* In 2009–10, 28 students received support, including 4 research assistantships with partial tuition reimbursements available (averaging $7,200 per year); tuition waivers (partial) and unspecified assistantships also available. Financial award application deadline: 4/15; financial award applicants required to submit FAFSA. *Faculty research:* Interdisciplinary research in computational mechanics, experimental and computational biofuel combustion and tribology, mechatronics and control, thermomechanical and thermofluid finite element modeling, information technology. *Unit head:* Dr. Mohammad S. Davoud, Director, 912-478-0540, Fax: 912-478-1455, E-mail: mdavoud@georgiasouthern.edu. *Application contact:* Dr. Charles Ziglar, Coordinator for Graduate Student Recruitment, 912-478-5384, Fax: 912-478-0740, E-mail: gradadmissions@georgiasouthern.edu.

Graduate School and University Center of the City University of New York, Graduate Studies, Program in Engineering, New York, NY 10016-4039. Offers biomedical engineering (PhD); chemical engineering (PhD); civil engineering (PhD); electrical engineering (PhD); mechanical engineering (PhD). *Faculty:* 68 full-time (1 woman). *Students:* 115 full-time (33 women), 8 part-time (2 women); includes 17 minority (5 African Americans, 8 Asian Americans or Pacific Islanders, 4 Hispanic Americans), 68 international. Average age 34. 119 applicants, 48% accepted, 26 enrolled. In 2009, 30 doctorates awarded. *Degree requirements:* For doctorate, thesis/dissertation. *Entrance requirements:* For doctorate, GRE General Test. Additional exam requirements/recommendations for international students: Required—TOEFL. Application fee: $125. Electronic applications accepted. *Financial support:* In 2009–10, 61 fellowships, 10 teaching assistantships were awarded; research assistantships, Federal Work-Study, institutionally sponsored loans, and tuition waivers (full and partial) also available. Financial award application deadline: 2/1; financial award applicants required to submit FAFSA. *Unit head:* Dr. Mumtaz Kassir, Executive Officer, 212-650-8031, Fax: 212-650-8029, E-mail: kassir@ce-mail.engr.ccny.cuny.edu. *Application contact:* Les Gribben, Director of Admissions, 212-817-7470, Fax: 212-817-1624, E-mail: lgribben@gc.cuny.edu.

See Close-Up on page 69.

Grand Valley State University, Padnos College of Engineering and Computing, School of Engineering, Allendale, MI 49401-9403. Offers electrical and computer engineering (MSE); manufacturing operations (MSE); mechanical engineering (MSE); product design and manufacturing engineering (MSE). Part-time and evening/weekend programs available. *Faculty:* 6 full-time (0 women). *Students:* 8 full-time (1 woman), 37 part-time (4 women), 4 international. Average age 30. 21 applicants, 86% accepted, 10 enrolled. In 2009, 12 master's awarded. *Degree requirements:* For master's, project or thesis. *Entrance requirements:* For master's, engineering degree, minimum GPA of 3.0. Additional exam requirements/recommendations for international students: Required—TOEFL. *Application deadline:* Applications are processed on a rolling basis. Application fee: $30. Electronic applications accepted. *Financial support:* In 2009–10, 11 students received support, including 3 fellowships (averaging $1,083 per year), 9 research assistantships with full tuition reimbursements available (averaging $7,304 per year); career-related internships or fieldwork, Federal Work-Study, institutionally sponsored loans, scholarships/grants, and unspecified assistantships also available. *Faculty research:* Digital signal processing, computer aided design, computer aided manufacturing, manufacturing simulation, biomechanics, product design. Total annual research expenditures: $300,000. *Unit head:* Dr. Charles Standridge, Acting Director, 616-331-6750, Fax: 616-331-7215, E-mail: standric@gvsu.edu. *Application contact:* Dr. Pranod Chaphalkar, Graduate Director, 616-331-6843, Fax: 616-331-7215, E-mail: chaphalp@gvsu.edu.

Howard University, College of Engineering, Architecture, and Computer Sciences, School of Engineering and Computer Science, Department of Electrical Engineering, Washington, DC 20059-0002. Offers M Eng, PhD. Offered through the Graduate School of Arts and Sciences. Part-time programs available. *Degree requirements:* For master's, thesis (for some programs), qualifying exam; for doctorate, thesis/dissertation, preliminary exam. *Entrance requirements:* For master's, GRE General Test, bachelor's degree in electrical engineering, minimum GPA of 3.0; for doctorate, GRE General Test, minimum GPA of 3.0. Additional exam requirements/recommendations for international students: Required—TOEFL. Electronic applications accepted. *Faculty research:* Solid-state electronics, antennas and microwaves, communications and signal processing, controls and power systems, nanotechnology.

Illinois Institute of Technology, Graduate College, Armour College of Engineering, Department of Electrical and Computer Engineering, Chicago, IL 60616-3793. Offers biomedical imaging and signals (MBMI); computer engineering (MS, PhD); electrical and computer engineering (MECE); electrical engineering (MS, PhD); electricity markets (MEM); manufacturing engineering (MME, MS); network engineering (MNE); power engineering (MPE); telecommunications and software engineering (MTSE); VLSI and microelectronics (MVM). Part-time and evening/weekend programs available. Terminal master's awarded for partial completion of doctoral program. *Degree requirements:* For master's, comprehensive exam, thesis (for some programs); for doctorate, comprehensive exam, thesis/dissertation. *Entrance requirements:* For master's and doctorate, GRE General Test, minimum undergraduate GPA of 3.0. Additional exam requirements/recommendations for international students: Required—TOEFL (minimum score 550 paper-based; 213 computer-based; 80 iBT). Electronic applications accepted. *Expenses:* Tuition: Full-time $17,550; part-time $888 per credit hour. Required fees: $850; $7.50 per credit hour. One-time fee: $50 full-time. Full-time tuition and fees vary according to program. *Faculty research:* Communications and signal processing, computers and digital systems, electronics and electromagnetics, power and control systems.

Indiana University–Purdue University Fort Wayne, College of Engineering, Technology, and Computer Science, Department of Engineering, Fort Wayne, IN 46805-1499. Offers computer engineering (MS); electrical engineering (MS); mechanical engineering (MS); systems engineering (MS). Part-time programs available. *Faculty:* 15 full-time (3 women). *Students:* 4 full-time (0 women), 29 part-time (5 women); includes 2 minority (1 African American, 1 Asian American or Pacific Islander), 5 international. Average age 29. 13 applicants, 92% accepted, 7 enrolled. In 2009, 1 master's awarded. *Entrance requirements:* For master's, minimum GPA of 3.0. Additional exam requirements/recommendations for international students: Required—TOEFL (minimum score 550 paper-based; 213 computer-based; 77 iBT); Recommended—TWE. *Application deadline:* For fall admission, 7/15 priority date for domestic students, 3/1 priority date for international students; for spring admission, 12/1 priority date for domestic students, 9/1 priority date for international students. Applications are processed on a rolling basis. Application fee: $55 ($60 for international students). Electronic applications accepted. *Expenses:* Tuition, state resident: full-time $4595; part-time $255 per credit. Tuition, nonresident: full-time $10,963; part-time $609 per credit. Required fees: $528; $29.35 per credit. Tuition and fees vary according to course load. *Financial support:* In 2009–10, 1 research assistantship with partial tuition reimbursement (averaging $12,740 per year), 3 teaching assistantships with partial tuition reimbursements (averaging $12,740 per year) were awarded. Financial award application deadline: 3/1; financial award applicants required to submit FAFSA. *Faculty research:* Synthesis technique, Markov parameters. Total annual research expenditures: $57,918. *Unit head:* Dr. Donald Mueller, Chair, 260-481-5707, Fax: 260-481-6281, E-mail: mueller@engr.ipfw.edu. *Application contact:* Dr. Donald Mueller, Chair, 260-481-5707, Fax: 260-481-6281, E-mail: mueller@engr.ipfw.edu.

Indiana University–Purdue University Indianapolis, School of Engineering and Technology, Department of Electrical Engineering, Indianapolis, IN 46202-2896. Offers biomedical engineering (MS, PhD); electrical and computer engineering (MS, MSECE, PhD), including biomedical engineering (MSECE), control and automation (MSECE), signal processing (MSECE); engineering (interdisciplinary) (MSE). *Students:* 41 full-time (10 women), 27 part-time (2 women); includes 11 minority (5 African Americans, 4 Asian Americans or Pacific Islanders, 2 Hispanic Americans), 38 international. Average age 27. 178 applicants, 56% accepted, 54 enrolled. In 2009, 28 master's awarded. Application fee: $55 ($65 for international students). *Unit head:* Yaobin Chen, Unit Head, 317-274-4032, Fax: 317-274-4493. *Application contact:* Valerie Diemer, Graduate Program, 317-278-4960, Fax: 317-278-1671, E-mail: grad@engr.iupui.edu.

Instituto Tecnológico y de Estudios Superiores de Monterrey, Campus Chihuahua, Graduate Programs, Chihuahua, Mexico. Offers computer systems engineering (Ingeniero); electrical engineering (Ingeniero); electromechanical engineering (Ingeniero); electronic engineering (Ingeniero); engineering administration (MEA); industrial engineering (MIE, Ingeniero); international trade (MIT); mechanical engineering (Ingeniero).

Instituto Tecnológico y de Estudios Superiores de Monterrey, Campus Monterrey, Graduate and Research Division, Programs in Engineering, Monterrey, Mexico. Offers applied statistics (M Eng); artificial intelligence (PhD); automation engineering (M Eng); chemical engineering (M Eng); civil engineering (M Eng); electrical engineering (M Eng); electronic engineering (M Eng); environmental engineering (M Eng); industrial engineering (M Eng, PhD);

manufacturing engineering (M Eng); mechanical engineering (M Eng); systems and quality engineering (M Eng). Part-time and evening/weekend programs available. Terminal master's awarded for partial completion of doctoral program. *Degree requirements:* For master's, one foreign language, thesis; for doctorate, one foreign language, thesis/dissertation. *Entrance requirements:* For master's, EXADEP; for doctorate, GRE, master's degree in related field. Additional exam requirements/recommendations for international students: Required—TOEFL. *Faculty research:* Flexible manufacturing cells, materials, statistical methods, environmental prevention, control and evaluation.

International Technological University, Program in Electrical Engineering, Santa Clara, CA 95050. Offers MSEE, PhD. Part-time and evening/weekend programs available. *Degree requirements:* For master's, thesis or alternative. *Entrance requirements:* For master's, 3 semesters of calculus, minimum GPA of 2.5. Additional exam requirements/recommendations for international students: Required—TOEFL. *Faculty research:* VLSI design, digital systems, routing and optimization theory.

Iowa State University of Science and Technology, Graduate College, College of Engineering, Department of Electrical and Computer Engineering, Ames, IA 50011. Offers computer engineering (M Eng, MS, PhD); electrical engineering (M Eng, MS, PhD). *Faculty:* 52 full-time (3 women), 5 part-time/adjunct (2 women). *Students:* 223 full-time (39 women), 109 part-time (16 women); includes 13 minority (2 African Americans, 8 Asian Americans or Pacific Islanders, 3 Hispanic Americans), 214 international. 1,103 applicants, 11% accepted, 69 enrolled. In 2009, 30 master's, 27 doctorates awarded. *Degree requirements:* For master's, thesis or alternative; for doctorate, thesis/dissertation. *Entrance requirements:* For master's and doctorate, GRE General Test. Additional exam requirements/recommendations for international students: Required—TOEFL (minimum score 550 paper-based; 79 iBT) or IELTS (minimum score 6.5). *Application deadline:* For fall admission, 1/15 priority date for domestic and international students; for spring admission, 9/15 for domestic and international students. Application fee: $40 ($90 for international students). Electronic applications accepted. *Expenses:* Tuition, state resident: full-time $6716. Tuition, nonresident: full-time $8908. Tuition and fees vary according to course level, course load, program and student level. *Financial support:* In 2009–10, 137 research assistantships with full and partial tuition reimbursements (averaging $15,000 per year), 40 teaching assistantships with full and partial tuition reimbursements (averaging $14,500 per year) were awarded; fellowships, scholarships/grants, health care benefits, and unspecified assistantships also available. *Unit head:* Dr. Arun Somani, Chair, 515-294-2664, E-mail: ecegrad@ee.iastate.edu. *Application contact:* Dr. Akhilesh Tyagi, Director of Graduate Education, 515-294-2667, E-mail: ecegrad@iastate.edu.

The Johns Hopkins University, Engineering for Professionals, Part-time Program in Electrical and Computer Engineering, Baltimore, MD 21218-2699. Offers MS, Post-Master's Certificate. Part-time and evening/weekend programs available. *Faculty:* 40 part-time/adjunct (1 woman). *Students:* 25 full-time (7 women), 303 part-time (47 women); includes 88 minority (23 African Americans, 47 Asian Americans or Pacific Islanders, 18 Hispanic Americans), 5 international. Average age 29. In 2009, 127 master's, 4 other advanced degrees awarded. *Application deadline:* Applications are processed on a rolling basis. Application fee: $75. Electronic applications accepted. *Financial support:* Institutionally sponsored loans available. *Unit head:* Dr. Dexter G. Smith, Program Chair, 443-778-5879, E-mail: dexter.smith@jhuapl.edu. *Application contact:* Priyanka Dwivedi, Admissions Manager, 410-516-2300, Fax: 410-579-8049, E-mail: pdwived1@jhu.edu.

The Johns Hopkins University, G. W. C. Whiting School of Engineering, Department of Electrical and Computer Engineering, Baltimore, MD 21218-2699. Offers MSE, PhD. *Faculty:* 21 full-time (2 women), 13 part-time/adjunct (0 women). *Students:* 125 full-time (21 women), 5 part-time (0 women); includes 9 minority (3 African Americans, 5 Asian Americans or Pacific Islanders, 1 Hispanic American), 90 international. Average age 27. 275 applicants, 43% accepted, 38 enrolled. In 2009, 23 master's, 15 doctorates awarded. Terminal master's awarded for partial completion of doctoral program. *Degree requirements:* For master's, thesis optional; for doctorate, thesis/dissertation, Qualifying Exam, Oral Exam, Seminar. *Entrance requirements:* For master's, GRE General Test, 3 letters of recommendation, SOP; for doctorate, GRE General Test, Transcripts, 3 Letters of Recommendation, SOP. Additional exam requirements/recommendations for international students: Required—TOEFL (minimum score 600 paper-based; 250 computer-based; 100 iBT). *Application deadline:* For fall admission, 1/15 for domestic and international students. Application fee: $75. Electronic applications accepted. *Financial support:* In 2009–10, 7 fellowships with full tuition reimbursements (averaging $20,000 per year), 49 research assistantships with full tuition reimbursements (averaging $20,000 per year), 14 teaching assistantships with full tuition reimbursements (averaging $20,000 per year) were awarded; career-related internships or fieldwork, Federal Work-Study, institutionally sponsored loans, scholarships/grants, health care benefits, tuition waivers (partial), and unspecified assistantships also available. Financial award application deadline: 1/15. *Faculty research:* Computer engineering, systems and control, language and speech processing, photonics and optoelectronics, signals. Total annual research expenditures: $2.2 million. *Unit head:* Dr. Jin U. Kang, Chair, 410-516-7031, Fax: 410-516-5566, E-mail: jkang@jhu.edu. *Application contact:* Felicia C. Roane, Academic Coordinator II, 410-516-4808, Fax: 410-516-5566, E-mail: eceinfo@jhu.edu.

Kansas State University, Graduate School, College of Engineering, Department of Electrical and Computer Engineering, Manhattan, KS 66506. Offers electrical engineering (MS, PhD). Postbaccalaureate distance learning degree programs offered (no on-campus study). *Faculty:* 18 full-time (3 women), 3 part-time/adjunct (1 woman). *Students:* 34 full-time (3 women), 65 part-time (18 women); includes 9 minority (2 African Americans, 1 American Indian/Alaska Native, 4 Asian Americans or Pacific Islanders, 2 Hispanic Americans), 38 international. Average age 28. 199 applicants, 19% accepted, 34 enrolled. In 2009, 34 master's, 5 doctorates awarded. *Degree requirements:* For master's, thesis or alternative, final exam; for doctorate, thesis/dissertation, preliminary exams. *Entrance requirements:* For master's, GRE General Test, bachelor's degree in electrical engineering or computer science, minimum GPA of 3.0; for doctorate, GRE General Test. Additional exam requirements/recommendations for international students: Required—TOEFL (minimum score 600 paper-based). *Application deadline:* For fall admission, 2/1 priority date for domestic and international students; for spring admission, 8/1 priority date for domestic and international students. Applications are processed on a rolling basis. Application fee: $40 ($55 for international students). Electronic applications accepted. *Financial support:* In 2009–10, 29 research assistantships (averaging $16,581 per year), 1 teaching assistantship with full tuition reimbursement (averaging $16,600 per year) were awarded; career-related internships or fieldwork, institutionally sponsored loans, and scholarships/grants also available. Support available to part-time students. Financial award application deadline: 3/1; financial award applicants required to submit FAFSA. *Faculty research:* Energy systems and renewable energy, computer systems and real time embedded systems, communication systems and signal processing, integrated circuits and devices, bioengineering. Total annual research expenditures: $784,366. *Unit head:* Don Gruenbacher, Head, 785-532-4692, Fax: 785-532-1188, E-mail: grue@ksu.edu. *Application contact:* Andrew Rys, Director, 785-532-4665, Fax: 785-532-1188, E-mail: andrys@ksu.edu.

Kettering University, Graduate School, Electrical and Computer Engineering Department, Flint, MI 48504. Offers electrical engineering (MS Eng). Part-time and evening/weekend programs available. Postbaccalaureate distance learning degree programs offered (no on-campus study). *Faculty:* 2 full-time (0 women), 1 part-time/adjunct (0 women). *Students:* 8 part-time (1 woman); includes 1 minority (Hispanic American), 1 international. Average age 28. 2 applicants, 50% accepted, 0 enrolled. *Degree requirements:* For master's, thesis optional. *Entrance requirements:* Additional exam requirements/recommendations for international students: Required—TOEFL (minimum score 550 paper-based; 213 computer-based; 79 iBT). *Application deadline:* For fall admission, 9/15 for domestic students, 6/15 for international students; for winter admission, 12/15 for domestic students, 9/15 for international students; for spring admission, 3/15 for domestic students, 12/15 for international students. Applications are processed on a rolling basis. Application fee: $0. Electronic applications accepted. *Expenses:*

Electrical Engineering

Kettering University (continued)

Tuition: Full-time $11,120; part-time $695 per credit hour. *Financial support:* In 2009–10, 3 students received support, including fellowships with full tuition reimbursements available (averaging $13,000 per year), research assistantships with full tuition reimbursements available (averaging $13,000 per year), teaching assistantships with full tuition reimbursements available (averaging $13,000 per year); Federal Work-Study, scholarships/grants, and tuition waivers (partial) also available. Support available to part-time students. Financial award application deadline: 7/15; financial award applicants required to submit CSS PROFILE or FAFSA. *Unit head:* Dr. James McDonald, Interim Head, 810-762-9500 Ext. 5690, Fax: 810-762-9830, E-mail: jmcdonal@kettering.edu. *Application contact:* Bonnie Switzer, Admissions Representative, 810-762-7953, Fax: 810-762-9935, E-mail: bswitzer@kettering.edu.

Lakehead University, Graduate Studies, Faculty of Engineering, Thunder Bay, ON P7B 5E1, Canada. Offers control engineering (M Sc Engr); electrical/computer engineering (M Sc Engr); environmental engineering (M Sc Engr). Part-time programs available. *Degree requirements:* For master's, thesis. *Entrance requirements:* For master's, bachelor's degree in chemical, electrical or mechanical engineering, minimum B average. Additional exam requirements/recommendations for international students: Required—TOEFL. *Faculty research:* Pulp and paper, adaptive/process control, robust/interactive learning control, vibration control.

Lamar University, College of Graduate Studies, College of Engineering, Department of Electrical Engineering, Beaumont, TX 77710. Offers ME, MES, DE. Part-time programs available. *Faculty:* 6 full-time (0 women). *Students:* 143 full-time (24 women), 51 part-time (9 women); includes 1 minority (Asian American or Pacific Islander), 134 international. Average age 23. 311 applicants, 23% accepted, 56 enrolled. In 2009, 75 master's, 1 doctorate awarded. *Degree requirements:* For master's, thesis (for some programs); for doctorate, thesis/dissertation. *Entrance requirements:* For master's and doctorate, GRE General Test. Additional exam requirements/recommendations for international students: Required—TOEFL. *Application deadline:* For fall admission, 5/15 priority date for domestic students; for spring admission, 10/1 priority date for domestic students. Applications are processed on a rolling basis. Application fee: $25 ($50 for international students). *Financial support:* In 2009–10, 2 fellowships with partial tuition reimbursements (averaging $6,000 per year), 20 research assistantships with partial tuition reimbursements (averaging $6,000 per year), 2 teaching assistantships with partial tuition reimbursements (averaging $4,500 per year) were awarded; tuition waivers (partial) also available. Financial award application deadline: 4/1. *Faculty research:* Video processing, photonics, VLSI design, computer networking. *Unit head:* Dr. Harley Ross Myler, Chair, 409-880-8746, Fax: 409-880-8121, E-mail: mylerhr@hal.lamar.edu. *Application contact:* Jane Stanley McCabe, Information Contact, 409-880-8746, Fax: 409-880-8121, E-mail: eece@hal.lamar.edu.

Lawrence Technological University, College of Engineering, Southfield, MI 48075-1058. Offers automotive engineering (MAE); civil engineering (MCE); construction engineering management (MS); electrical and computer engineering (MS); engineering management (ME); industrial engineering (MSIE); manufacturing systems (MEMS, DE); mechanical engineering (MS); mechatronic systems engineering (MS). Part-time and evening/weekend programs available. *Faculty:* 20 full-time (4 women), 12 part-time/adjunct (0 women). *Students:* 15 full-time (4 women), 389 part-time (50 women); includes 57 minority (22 African Americans, 1 American Indian/Alaska Native, 30 Asian Americans or Pacific Islanders, 4 Hispanic Americans), 137 international. Average age 31. 361 applicants, 52% accepted, 108 enrolled. In 2009, 161 master's, 1 doctorate awarded. *Degree requirements:* For master's, thesis (for some programs). *Entrance requirements:* Additional exam requirements/recommendations for international students: Required—TOEFL (minimum score 550 paper-based; 213 computer-based; 79 iBT). *Application deadline:* For fall admission, 8/1 priority date for domestic students, 6/1 for international students; for winter admission, 12/1 priority date for domestic students, 10/1 for international students; for spring admission, 5/1 priority date for domestic students, 3/1 for international students. Applications are processed on a rolling basis. Application fee: $50. Electronic applications accepted. *Expenses:* Tuition: Full-time $11,320; part-time $798 per credit hour. *Financial support:* Federal Work-Study and institutionally sponsored loans available. Support available to part-time students. Financial award application deadline: 4/1; financial award applicants required to submit FAFSA. *Faculty research:* Advanced composite materials in bridges, strengthening existing bridges with carbon and glass fiber sheets, development of drive shafts using composite materials. *Unit head:* Dr. Nabil Grace, Interim Dean, 248-204-2500, Fax: 248-204-2509, E-mail: engrdean@ltu.edu. *Application contact:* Jane Rohrback, Director of Admissions, 248-204-3160, Fax: 248-204-3188, E-mail: admissions@ltu.edu.

Lehigh University, P.C. Rossin College of Engineering and Applied Science, Department of Electrical and Computer Engineering, Bethlehem, PA 18015. Offers electrical engineering (M Eng, MS, PhD); photonics (MS); wireless network engineering (MS). Part-time programs available. *Faculty:* 19 full-time (3 women). *Students:* 68 full-time (15 women), 16 part-time (5 women), 66 international. Average age 27. 215 applicants, 23% accepted, 22 enrolled. In 2009, 13 master's, 6 doctorates awarded. Terminal master's awarded for partial completion of doctoral program. *Degree requirements:* For master's, thesis optional; for doctorate, thesis/dissertation, qualifying or comprehensive exam for all 1st year PhD's; general exam 7 months or more prior to completion/dissertation defense. *Entrance requirements:* For master's and doctorate, GRE General Test, BS in field or related field. Additional exam requirements/recommendations for international students: Required—TOEFL (minimum score 79 iBT). *Application deadline:* For fall admission, 1/15 priority date for domestic and international students; for spring admission, 11/1 for domestic and international students. Application fee: $70. Electronic applications accepted. *Financial support:* In 2009–10, 67 students received support, including 4 fellowships with full tuition reimbursements available (averaging $15,300 per year), 42 research assistantships with full tuition reimbursements available (averaging $20,000 per year), 6 teaching assistantships with full tuition reimbursements available (averaging $15,300 per year); career-related internships or fieldwork, Federal Work-Study, institutionally sponsored loans, scholarships/grants, tuition waivers (full and partial), and unspecified assistantships also available. Support available to part-time students. Financial award application deadline: 1/15. *Faculty research:* Nanostructures/nanodevices, Terahertz generation, analog devices, mixed mode design and signal circuits, optoelectronic sensors, micro-fabrication technology and design, packaging/reliability of microsensors, coding and networking information theory, radio frequency, wireless and optical wireless communication, wireless networks. Total annual research expenditures: $3.6 million. *Unit head:* Dr. Filbert J. Bartoli, Chair, 610-758-4069, Fax: 610-758-6279, E-mail: dmb4@lehigh.edu. *Application contact:* Tammy Shellock, Graduate Coordinator, 610-758-4072, Fax: 610-758-6279, E-mail: tjs7@lehigh.edu.

Louisiana State University and Agricultural and Mechanical College, Graduate School, College of Engineering, Department of Electrical and Computer Engineering, Baton Rouge, LA 70803. Offers MSEE, PhD. *Faculty:* 27 full-time (1 woman). *Students:* 108 full-time (23 women), 6 part-time (2 women); includes 9 minority (3 African Americans, 2 Asian Americans or Pacific Islanders, 4 Hispanic Americans), 98 international. Average age 26. 229 applicants, 75% accepted, 27 enrolled. In 2009, 9 master's, 6 doctorates awarded. Terminal master's awarded for partial completion of doctoral program. *Degree requirements:* For master's, thesis optional; for doctorate, thesis/dissertation. *Entrance requirements:* For master's, GRE General Test, minimum GPA of 3.0; for doctorate, GRE General Test, minimum GPA of 3.5. Additional exam requirements/recommendations for international students: Required—TOEFL (minimum score 550 paper-based; 213 computer-based; 79 iBT) or IELTS (minimum score 6.5). *Application deadline:* For fall admission, 1/25 priority date for domestic students, 5/15 for international students; for spring admission, 10/15 for international students. Applications are processed on a rolling basis. Application fee: $50 ($70 for international students). Electronic applications accepted. *Financial support:* In 2009–10, 91 students received support, including 6 fellowships with full and partial tuition reimbursements available (averaging $22,476 per year), 40 research assistantships with full and partial tuition reimbursements available (averaging $13,185 per year), 31 teaching assistantships with full and partial tuition reimbursements available (averaging $13,270 per year); Federal Work-Study, institutionally sponsored loans, health care benefits, tuition waivers (full and partial), and unspecified assistantships also available. Financial award application deadline: 2/28; financial award applicants required to submit FAFSA. *Faculty research:* Computer engineering, electronics, control systems and signal processing, communications. Total annual research expenditures: $1 million. *Unit head:* Dr. Jorge Aravena, Interim Chair, 225-578-5243, Fax: 225-578-5200, E-mail: aravena@ece.lsu.edu. *Application contact:* Dr. Ramachanran Vaidyanathan, Graduate Adviser, 225-578-5551, Fax: 225-578-5200, E-mail: vaidy@ece.lsu.edu.

Louisiana Tech University, Graduate School, College of Engineering and Science, Department of Electrical Engineering, Ruston, LA 71272. Offers MS, PhD. Part-time programs available. Terminal master's awarded for partial completion of doctoral program. *Degree requirements:* For master's, thesis; for doctorate, thesis/dissertation. *Entrance requirements:* For master's, GRE General Test, minimum GPA of 3.0 in last 60 hours; for doctorate, minimum graduate GPA of 3.25 (with MS) or GRE General Test. Additional exam requirements/recommendations for international students: Required—TOEFL. *Faculty research:* Communications, computers and microprocessors, electrical and power systems, pattern recognition, robotics.

Loyola Marymount University, College of Science and Engineering, Department of Electrical Engineering and Computer Science, Program in Electrical Engineering, Los Angeles, CA 90045. Offers MSE. Part-time and evening/weekend programs available. *Faculty:* 10 full-time (4 women), 1 part-time/adjunct (0 women). *Students:* 2 part-time (0 women); includes 1 minority (Asian American or Pacific Islander), 1 international. Average age 33. 7 applicants, 0% accepted, 0 enrolled. In 2009, 2 master's awarded. *Degree requirements:* For master's, research seminar. *Entrance requirements:* Additional exam requirements/recommendations for international students: Required—TOEFL (minimum score 550 paper-based; 213 computer-based; 80 iBT). *Application deadline:* Applications are processed on a rolling basis. Application fee: $50. Electronic applications accepted. *Financial support:* In 2009–10, 2 students received support. Scholarships/grants available. Support available to part-time students. Financial award application deadline: 6/1; financial award applicants required to submit FAFSA. Total annual research expenditures: $19,443. *Unit head:* Dr. Stephanie August, Graduate Director, 310-338-5973, Fax: 310-338-2872, E-mail: saugust@lmu.edu. *Application contact:* Chake H. Kouyoumjian, Associate Dean of Graduate Admissions, 310-338-2721, Fax: 310-338-6086, E-mail: ckouyoum@lmu.edu.

Manhattan College, Graduate Division, School of Engineering, Program in Electrical Engineering, Riverdale, NY 10471. Offers MS. Part-time and evening/weekend programs available. *Degree requirements:* For master's, thesis or alternative. *Entrance requirements:* For master's, GRE (recommended), minimum GPA of 3.0. Additional exam requirements/recommendations for international students: Required—TOEFL (minimum score 550 paper-based; 213 computer-based). *Faculty research:* Multimedia tools, neural networks, robotic control systems, magnetic resonance imaging, telemedicine, computer-based instruction.

Marquette University, Graduate School, College of Engineering, Department of Electrical and Computer Engineering, Milwaukee, WI 53201-1881. Offers computing (MS); electrical engineering (MS, PhD). Part-time and evening/weekend programs available. *Faculty:* 14 full-time (2 women), 2 part-time/adjunct (0 women). *Students:* 27 full-time (6 women), 25 part-time (4 women); includes 4 minority (3 African Americans, 1 Asian American or Pacific Islander), 25 international. Average age 29. 62 applicants, 69% accepted, 14 enrolled. In 2009, 14 master's, 6 doctorates awarded. Terminal master's awarded for partial completion of doctoral program. *Degree requirements:* For master's, thesis optional; for doctorate, thesis/dissertation, dissertation defense, qualifying exam. *Entrance requirements:* For master's, GRE General Test; for doctorate, GRE General Test, minimum GPA of 3.0. Additional exam requirements/recommendations for international students: Required—TOEFL. *Application deadline:* For fall admission, 7/15 priority date for domestic students; for spring admission, 11/15 for domestic students. Applications are processed on a rolling basis. Application fee: $40. Electronic applications accepted. *Financial support:* In 2009–10, 33 students received support, including 11 fellowships with full tuition reimbursements available (averaging $17,100 per year), 10 research assistantships with full tuition reimbursements available (averaging $15,200 per year), 12 teaching assistantships with full tuition reimbursements available (averaging $11,600 per year); Federal Work-Study, institutionally sponsored loans, and scholarships/grants also available. Support available to part-time students. Financial award application deadline: 2/15. *Faculty research:* Electric machines, drives, and controls; applied solid-state electronics; computers and signal processing; microwaves and antennas; solid state devices and acoustic wave sensors. Total annual research expenditures: $1.2 million. *Unit head:* Dr. Edwin E. Yaz, Chair, 414-288-6820, Fax: 414-288-5579, E-mail: edwin.yaz@marquette.edu. *Application contact:* Dr. Fabien J. Josse, Director of Graduate Studies, 414-288-6789, Fax: 414-288-5579, E-mail: fabien.josse@marquette.edu.

Massachusetts Institute of Technology, School of Engineering, Department of Electrical Engineering and Computer Science, Cambridge, MA 02139-4307. Offers computer science (PhD, Sc D, ECS); electrical engineering (PhD, Sc D, EE); electrical engineering and computer science (M Eng, SM, PhD, Sc D); SM/MBA. *Faculty:* 123 full-time (16 women), 1 part-time/adjunct (0 women). *Students:* 764 full-time (171 women), 3 part-time (0 women); includes 161 minority (15 African Americans, 3 American Indian/Alaska Native, 116 Asian Americans or Pacific Islanders, 27 Hispanic Americans), 319 international. Average age 26. 2,692 applicants, 11% accepted, 233 enrolled. In 2009, 195 master's, 102 doctorates, 2 other advanced degrees awarded. Terminal master's awarded for partial completion of doctoral program. *Degree requirements:* For master's and other advanced degree, thesis; for doctorate, comprehensive exam, thesis/dissertation. *Entrance requirements:* Additional exam requirements/recommendations for international students: Required—TOEFL (minimum score 600 paper-based; 250 computer-based), IELTS (minimum score 7). *Application deadline:* For fall admission, 12/15 for domestic and international students. Application fee: $75. Electronic applications accepted. *Financial support:* In 2009–10, 757 students received support, including 133 fellowships with tuition reimbursements available (averaging $29,263 per year), 476 research assistantships with tuition reimbursements available (averaging $28,316 per year), 108 teaching assistantships with tuition reimbursements available (averaging $29,689 per year); career-related internships or fieldwork, Federal Work-Study, institutionally sponsored loans, scholarships/grants, health care benefits, and unspecified assistantships also available. *Faculty research:* Artificial intelligence and applications; robotics, computer architecture, communications, devices, bioelectrical engineering; computational biology, electronics, electrodynamics, photonics, control, signal processing, optimization, software, systems, networks; computation theory, cryptography, algorithms. Total annual research expenditures: $82.4 million. *Unit head:* Prof. W. Eric L. Grimson, Department Head, 617-253-4600, Fax: 617-258-7354, E-mail: hq@eecs.mit.edu. *Application contact:* Graduate Admissions, 617-253-4603, Fax: 617-258-7354, E-mail: grad-ap@eecs.mit.edu.

McGill University, Faculty of Graduate and Postdoctoral Studies, Faculty of Engineering, Department of Electrical and Computer Engineering, Montréal, QC H3A 2T5, Canada. Offers M Eng, PhD.

McMaster University, School of Graduate Studies, Faculty of Engineering, Department of Electrical and Computer Engineering, Hamilton, ON L8S 4M2, Canada. Offers electrical engineering (M Eng, MA Sc, PhD). *Degree requirements:* For master's, thesis; for doctorate, comprehensive exam, thesis/dissertation. *Entrance requirements:* Additional exam requirements/recommendations for international students: Required—TOEFL (minimum score 550 paper-based; 213 computer-based). *Faculty research:* Robust and blind adaptive filtering, topics in statistical signal processing, local and metropolitan area networks, smart antennas, embedded wireless communications.

McNeese State University, Doré School of Graduate Studies, College of Engineering and Engineering Technology, Lake Charles, LA 70609. Offers chemical engineering (M Eng); civil engineering (M Eng); electrical engineering (M Eng); engineering management (M Eng); mechanical engineering (M Eng). Part-time and evening/weekend programs available. *Degree requirements:* For master's, thesis or alternative. *Entrance requirements:* For master's, GRE, minimum undergraduate GPA of 3.0. Additional exam requirements/recommendations for international students: Required—TOEFL.

Memorial University of Newfoundland, School of Graduate Studies, Faculty of Engineering and Applied Science, St. John's, NL A1C 5S7, Canada. Offers civil engineering (M Eng, PhD); electrical and computer engineering (M Eng, PhD); mechanical engineering (M Eng, PhD); ocean and naval architecture engineering (M Eng, PhD). Part-time programs available. *Degree requirements:* For master's, thesis; for doctorate, comprehensive exam, thesis/dissertation, oral thesis defense. *Entrance requirements:* For master's, 2nd class degree; for doctorate, master's degree in engineering. Electronic applications accepted. *Faculty research:* Engineering analysis, environmental and hydrotechnical studies, manufacturing and robotics, mechanics, structures and materials.

Mercer University, Graduate Studies, Macon Campus, School of Engineering, Macon, GA 31207-0003. Offers biomedical engineering (MSE); computer engineering (MSE); electrical engineering (MSE); engineering management (MSE); environmental engineering (MSE); environmental systems (MS); mechanical engineering (MSE); software engineering (MSE); software systems (MS); technical communications management (MS); technical management (MS). Part-time and evening/weekend programs available. Postbaccalaureate distance learning degree programs offered (no on-campus study). *Faculty:* 19 full-time (4 women), 1 part-time/adjunct (0 women). *Students:* 6 full-time (1 woman), 95 part-time (22 women); includes 22 minority (5 African Americans, 13 Asian Americans or Pacific Islanders, 4 Hispanic Americans), 3 international. Average age 33. In 2009, 42 master's awarded. *Degree requirements:* For master's, thesis or alternative. *Entrance requirements:* For master's, minimum undergraduate GPA of 3.0. Additional exam requirements/recommendations for international students: Required—TOEFL. *Application deadline:* For fall admission, 7/1 for domestic students; for spring admission, 11/15 for domestic students. Applications are processed on a rolling basis. Application fee: $35 ($50 for international students). Electronic applications accepted. *Expenses:* Contact institution. *Financial support:* Federal Work-Study available. *Unit head:* Dr. Wade H. Shaw, Dean, 478-301-2459, Fax: 478-301-5593, E-mail: shaw_wh@mercer.edu. *Application contact:* Greg Lofton, Graduate Program Coordinator, 478-301-5480, Fax: 478-301-5434, E-mail: lofton_g@mercer.edu.

Michigan State University, The Graduate School, College of Engineering, Department of Electrical and Computer Engineering, East Lansing, MI 48824. Offers electrical engineering (MS, PhD). *Entrance requirements:* Additional exam requirements/recommendations for international students: Required—TOEFL. Electronic applications accepted.

Michigan Technological University, Graduate School, College of Engineering, Department of Electrical and Computer Engineering, Houghton, MI 49931. Offers electrical engineering (MS, PhD). Part-time programs available. Postbaccalaureate distance learning degree programs offered (minimal on-campus study). Terminal master's awarded for partial completion of doctoral program. *Degree requirements:* For master's, comprehensive exam, thesis (for some programs); for doctorate, comprehensive exam, thesis/dissertation. *Entrance requirements:* Additional exam requirements/recommendations for international students: Required—TOEFL (minimum score 550 paper-based; 213 computer-based). Electronic applications accepted. *Expenses:* Contact institution. *Faculty research:* Information systems (signal processing and communications), solid-state electronics, power and energy systems, computer engineering.

Minnesota State University Mankato, College of Graduate Studies, College of Science, Engineering and Technology, Department of Electrical and Computer Engineering and Technology, Mankato, MN 56001. Offers MSE. *Students:* 8 full-time (0 women), 27 part-time (3 women). *Degree requirements:* For master's, comprehensive exam, thesis. *Entrance requirements:* For master's, GRE General Test, minimum GPA of 3.0 during previous 2 years. Additional exam requirements/recommendations for international students: Required—TOEFL (minimum score 550 paper-based; 213 computer-based; 80 iBT). *Application deadline:* For fall admission, 7/1 priority date for domestic students; for spring admission, 11/1 for domestic students. Applications are processed on a rolling basis. Application fee: $40. Electronic applications accepted. *Expenses:* Tuition, state resident: full-time $5364. Tuition, nonresident: full-time $8314. *Financial support:* Research assistantships with full tuition reimbursements, teaching assistantships with full tuition reimbursements, unspecified assistantships available. Financial award application deadline: 3/15. *Unit head:* Dr. William Hudson, Chairperson, 507-389-5747. *Application contact:* 507-389-2321, E-mail: grad@mnsu.edu.

Mississippi State University, Bagley College of Engineering, Department of Electrical and Computer Engineering, MS State, MS 39762. Offers computer engineering (MS, PhD); electrical engineering (MS, PhD). Part-time programs available. Postbaccalaureate distance learning degree programs offered (minimal on-campus study). *Faculty:* 21 full-time (1 woman). *Students:* 88 full-time (11 women), 40 part-time (11 women); includes 6 minority (2 African Americans, 2 Asian Americans or Pacific Islanders, 2 Hispanic Americans), 90 international. Average age 28. 207 applicants, 37% accepted, 36 enrolled. In 2009, 30 master's, 9 doctorates awarded. Terminal master's awarded for partial completion of doctoral program. *Degree requirements:* For master's, comprehensive exam, thesis optional; for doctorate, comprehensive exam, thesis/dissertation, written exam. *Entrance requirements:* For master's, GRE General Test, minimum undergraduate GPA of 3.0; for doctorate, GRE, minimum graduate GPA of 3.5. Additional exam requirements/recommendations for international students: Required—TOEFL (minimum score 550 paper-based; 213 computer-based; 79 iBT); Recommended—IELTS (minimum score 6.5). *Application deadline:* For fall admission, 7/1 for domestic students, 5/1 for international students; for spring admission, 11/1 for domestic students, 9/1 for international students. Applications are processed on a rolling basis. Application fee: $40. Electronic applications accepted. *Expenses:* Tuition, state resident: full-time $2575.50; part-time $286.25 per credit hour. Tuition, nonresident: full-time $6510; part-time $723.50 per credit hour. Tuition and fees vary according to course load. *Financial support:* In 2009–10, 115 research assistantships with full tuition reimbursements (averaging $12,585 per year), 19 teaching assistantships with full tuition reimbursements (averaging $14,016 per year) were awarded; Federal Work-Study, institutionally sponsored loans, scholarships/grants, and unspecified assistantships also available. Financial award application deadline: 4/1; financial award applicants required to submit FAFSA. *Faculty research:* Digital computing, power, controls, communication systems, microelectronics. Total annual research expenditures: $14 million. *Unit head:* Dr. Nicholas H. Younan, Professor and Interim Department Head, 662-325-3721, Fax: 662-325-2298, E-mail: ece-head@ece.msstate.edu. *Application contact:* Dr. James E. Fowler, Professor and Interim Graduate Program Director, 662-325-3640, Fax: 662-325-2298, E-mail: fowler@ece.msstate.edu.

Missouri University of Science and Technology, Graduate School, School of Engineering, Department of Electrical and Computer Engineering, Rolla, MO 65409. Offers computer engineering (MS, DE, PhD); electrical engineering (MS, DE, PhD). Part-time and evening/weekend programs available. Terminal master's awarded for partial completion of doctoral program. *Degree requirements:* For master's, thesis optional; for doctorate, comprehensive exam, thesis/dissertation, departmental qualifying exam. *Entrance requirements:* For master's, GRE General Test (minimum score 1100 verbal and quantitative, writing 4.5); for doctorate, GRE General Test (minimum score: verbal and quantitative 1100, writing 3.5). Additional exam requirements/recommendations for international students: Required—TOEFL. Electronic applications accepted. *Faculty research:* Power systems, computer/communication networks, intelligent control/robotics, robust control, nanotechnologies.

Montana State University, College of Graduate Studies, College of Engineering, Department of Electrical and Computer Engineering, Bozeman, MT 59717. Offers electrical engineering (MS); engineering (PhD), including electrical and computer engineering option. Part-time programs available. *Faculty:* 13 full-time (0 women), 5 part-time/adjunct (1 woman). *Students:* 14 full-time (1 woman), 30 part-time (6 women); includes 2 minority (1 Asian American or Pacific Islander, 1 Hispanic American), 14 international. Average age 25. 28 applicants. In 2009, 17 master's, 1 doctorate awarded. *Degree requirements:* For master's, comprehensive exam, thesis (for some programs); for doctorate, comprehensive exam, thesis/dissertation. *Entrance requirements:* For master's, GRE General Test; for doctorate, GRE General Test, MS

Degree. Additional exam requirements/recommendations for international students: Required—TOEFL (minimum score 550 paper-based; 213 computer-based). *Application deadline:* For fall admission, 7/15 priority date for domestic students, 5/15 priority date for international students; for spring admission, 12/1 priority date for domestic students, 10/1 priority date for international students. Applications are processed on a rolling basis. Application fee: $30. Electronic applications accepted. *Expenses:* Tuition, state resident: full-time $5635; part-time $3492 per year. Tuition, nonresident: full-time $17,212; part-time $7865.10 per year. Required fees: $1441.05; $153.15 per credit. Tuition and fees vary according to course load and program. *Financial support:* In 2009–10, 33 students received support, including 26 research assistantships with tuition reimbursements available (averaging $19,000 per year), 7 teaching assistantships with tuition reimbursements available (averaging $12,600 per year). Financial award application deadline: 3/1; financial award applicants required to submit FAFSA. *Faculty research:* Wireless and optical networks, micro-electrical mechanical systems, optics and optical electronics, power systems, signal processing. Total annual research expenditures: $2.7 million. *Unit head:* Dr. Robert Maher, Head, 406-994-2505, Fax: 406-994-5958, E-mail: rmaher@ece.montana.edu. *Application contact:* Dr. Carl A. Fox, Vice Provost for Graduate Education, 406-994-4145, Fax: 406-994-7433, E-mail: gradstudy@montana.edu.

Montana Tech of The University of Montana, Graduate School, Electrical Engineering Program, Butte, MT 59701-8997. Offers MS. Part-time programs available. *Faculty:* 4 full-time (0 women). *Students:* 5 full-time (2 women), 4 part-time (1 woman), 1 international. 10 applicants, 40% accepted, 0 enrolled. In 2009, 2 master's awarded. *Degree requirements:* For master's, comprehensive exam (for some programs), thesis optional. *Entrance requirements:* For master's, minimum GPA of 3.0. Additional exam requirements/recommendations for international students: Required—TOEFL (minimum score 525 paper-based; 195 computer-based; 71 iBT). *Application deadline:* For fall admission, 4/1 priority date for domestic students, 3/1 priority date for international students; for spring admission, 10/1 priority date for domestic students, 7/1 priority date for international students. Applications are processed on a rolling basis. Application fee: $30. Electronic applications accepted. *Expenses:* Tuition, state resident: full-time $5068; part-time $319 per credit. Tuition, nonresident: full-time $14,815; part-time $875 per credit. Tuition and fees vary according to course load and campus/location. *Financial support:* In 2009–10, 3 students received support, including 3 teaching assistantships with partial tuition reimbursements available (averaging $8,000 per year); research assistantships with full tuition reimbursements available, career-related internships or fieldwork, tuition waivers (full and partial), and unspecified assistantships also available. Financial award application deadline: 4/1. *Faculty research:* Energy grid modernization, battery diagnostics instrumentation, wind turbine research, improving energy efficiency. *Unit head:* Dr. Daniel Trudnowski, Professor, 406-496-4681, Fax: 406-496-4849, E-mail: dtrudnowski@mtech.edu. *Application contact:* Cindy Dunstan, Administrator, Graduate School, 406-496-4304, Fax: 406-496-4710, E-mail: cdunstan@mtech.edu.

Morgan State University, School of Graduate Studies, Clarence M. Mitchell, Jr. School of Engineering, Baltimore, MD 21251. Offers civil engineering (M Eng, D Eng); electrical engineering (M Eng, D Eng); industrial engineering (M Eng, D Eng); transportation (MS). Part-time and evening/weekend programs available. *Degree requirements:* For master's, thesis, comprehensive exam or equivalent; for doctorate, thesis/dissertation, comprehensive exam or equivalent. *Entrance requirements:* For master's, GRE, minimum undergraduate GPA of 2.5; for doctorate, GRE, minimum GPA of 3.0. Additional exam requirements/recommendations for international students: Required—TOEFL (minimum score 550 paper-based; 213 computer-based).

Naval Postgraduate School, Graduate Programs, Department of Electrical and Computer Engineering, Monterey, CA 93943. Offers MS, PhD, Eng. Program only open to commissioned officers of the United States and friendly nations and selected United States federal civilian employees. *Accreditation:* ABET (one or more programs are accredited). Part-time programs available. Postbaccalaureate distance learning degree programs offered (minimal on-campus study). *Degree requirements:* For master's and Eng, thesis; for doctorate, one foreign language, thesis/dissertation.

Naval Postgraduate School, Graduate Programs, Program in Undersea Warfare, Monterey, CA 93943. Offers applied science (MS); electrical engineering (MS); engineering acoustics (MS); operations research (MS); physical oceanography (MS). Program only open to commissioned officers of the United States and friendly nations and selected United States federal civilian employees. Part-time programs available. *Degree requirements:* For master's, thesis.

New Jersey Institute of Technology, Office of Graduate Studies, Newark College of Engineering, Department of Electrical and Computer Engineering, Program in Electrical Engineering, Newark, NJ 07102. Offers MS, PhD. Part-time and evening/weekend programs available. Terminal master's awarded for partial completion of doctoral program. *Degree requirements:* For master's, thesis optional; for doctorate, thesis/dissertation, residency. *Entrance requirements:* For master's, GRE General Test; for doctorate, GRE General Test, minimum graduate GPA of 3.5. Additional exam requirements/recommendations for international students: Required—TOEFL (minimum score 550 paper-based; 213 computer-based; 79 iBT). Electronic applications accepted.

New Mexico Institute of Mining and Technology, Graduate Studies, Department of Electrical Engineering, Socorro, NM 87801. Offers MS. *Entrance requirements:* Additional exam requirements/recommendations for international students: Required—TOEFL (minimum score 540 paper-based; 207 computer-based). Electronic applications accepted.

New Mexico State University, Graduate School, College of Engineering, Klipsch School of Electrical and Computer Engineering, Las Cruces, NM 88003-8001. Offers MSEE, PhD. Part-time and evening/weekend programs available. Postbaccalaureate distance learning degree programs offered (no on-campus study). *Faculty:* 18 full-time (1 woman). *Students:* 100 full-time (18 women), 46 part-time (2 women); includes 24 minority (1 African American, 1 American Indian/Alaska Native, 2 Asian Americans or Pacific Islanders, 20 Hispanic Americans), 87 international. Average age 28. 240 applicants, 67% accepted, 39 enrolled. In 2009, 32 master's, 6 doctorates awarded. Terminal master's awarded for partial completion of doctoral program. *Degree requirements:* For master's, thesis (for some programs), final oral or written exam; for doctorate, comprehensive exam, thesis/dissertation. *Entrance requirements:* For master's, GRE, minimum GPA of 3.0; for doctorate, departmental qualifying exam, minimum GPA of 3.0. Additional exam requirements/recommendations for international students: Required—TOEFL. *Application deadline:* For fall admission, 3/1 priority date for domestic and international students; for spring admission, 8/1 priority date for domestic and international students. Applications are processed on a rolling basis. Application fee: $30 ($50 for international students). Electronic applications accepted. *Expenses:* Tuition, state resident: full-time $4080; part-time $223 per credit. Tuition, nonresident: full-time $14,256; part-time $647 per credit. Required fees: $1278; $639 per semester. *Financial support:* In 2009–10, 75 students received support, including 33 research assistantships (averaging $6,921 per year), 33 teaching assistantships (averaging $5,224 per year); fellowships, career-related internships or fieldwork, Federal Work-Study, health care benefits, and unspecified assistantships also available. Support available to part-time students. Financial award application deadline: 3/1. *Faculty research:* Image and digital signal processing, energy systems, wireless communication, analog VLSI design, electro-optics. *Unit head:* Dr. Paul Furth, Interim Head, 575-646-3117, Fax: 575-646-1435, E-mail: pfurth@nmsu.edu. *Application contact:* Sue Kord, Records Technician I, 575-646-6440, Fax: 575-646-1435, E-mail: kkord@nmsu.edu.

New York Institute of Technology, Graduate Division, School of Engineering and Computing Sciences, Program in Electrical Engineering and Computer Engineering, Old Westbury, NY 11568-8000. Offers MS. Part-time and evening/weekend programs available. *Students:* 104 full-time (27 women), 71 part-time (9 women); includes 17 minority (5 African Americans, 9 Asian Americans or Pacific Islanders, 3 Hispanic Americans), 121 international. Average age 26. In 2009, 73 master's awarded. *Degree requirements:* For master's, project. *Entrance requirements:* For master's, GRE General Test (if QPA less than 2.85), BS in electrical engineering or related field, minimum QPA of 2.85. Additional exam requirements/

Electrical Engineering

New York Institute of Technology (continued)
recommendations for international students: Required—TOEFL (minimum score 550 paper-based; 213 computer-based). *Application deadline:* For fall admission, 7/1 priority date for domestic students; for spring admission, 12/1 priority date for domestic students. Applications are processed on a rolling basis. Application fee: $50. Electronic applications accepted. *Expenses:* Tuition: Part-time $825 per credit. *Financial support:* Fellowships, research assistantships with partial tuition reimbursements, institutionally sponsored loans, tuition waivers (full and partial), and unspecified assistantships available. Support available to part-time students. Financial award applicants required to submit FAFSA. *Faculty research:* Computer networks, control theory, light waves and optics, robotics, signal processing. *Unit head:* Dr. Ayat Jafari, Chair, 516-686-7523, Fax: 516-686-7439, E-mail: ajafari@nyit.edu. *Application contact:* Dr. Jacquelyn Nealon, Vice President for Enrollment Services, 516-686-7925, Fax: 516-686-7597, E-mail: jnealon@nyit.edu.

Norfolk State University, School of Graduate Studies, School of Science and Technology, Program in Electronics Engineering, Norfolk, VA 23504. Offers MS.

North Carolina Agricultural and Technical State University, Graduate School, College of Engineering, Department of Electrical and Computer Engineering, Greensboro, NC 27411. Offers electrical engineering (MSEE, PhD), including communications and signal processing (MSEE), computer engineering (MSEE), electronic and optical materials and devices (MSEE), power systems and controls (MSEE). Part-time programs available. *Degree requirements:* For master's, project, thesis defense; for doctorate, thesis/dissertation. *Entrance requirements:* For master's, GRE General Test, GRE Subject Test, minimum GPA of 2.8; for doctorate, GRE General Test, minimum GPA of 3.0. *Faculty research:* Semiconductor compounds, VLSI design, image processing, optical systems and devices, fault-tolerant computing.

North Carolina Agricultural and Technical State University, Graduate School, School of Technology, Department of Electronics, Computer, and Information Technology, Greensboro, NC 27411. Offers electronics and computer technology (MSIT).

North Carolina State University, Graduate School, College of Engineering, Department of Electrical and Computer Engineering, Program in Electrical Engineering, Raleigh, NC 27695. Offers MS, PhD. *Degree requirements:* For master's, thesis (for some programs); for doctorate, thesis/dissertation. *Entrance requirements:* For master's and doctorate, GRE. Additional exam requirements/recommendations for international students: Required—TOEFL (minimum score 575 paper-based). Electronic applications accepted. *Faculty research:* Microwave devices, wireless communications, nanoelectronics and photonics, robotic and mechatronics, power electronics.

North Dakota State University, College of Graduate and Interdisciplinary Studies, College of Engineering and Architecture, Department of Electrical and Computer Engineering, Fargo, ND 58108. Offers MS, PhD. Part-time programs available. *Faculty:* 15. *Students:* 27 full-time (7 women), 16 part-time (2 women); includes 1 Asian American or Pacific Islander, 26 international. Average age 28. 110 applicants, 20% accepted, 8 enrolled. In 2009, 8 master's, 1 doctorate awarded. Terminal master's awarded for partial completion of doctoral program. *Degree requirements:* For master's, comprehensive exam, thesis; for doctorate, comprehensive exam, thesis/dissertation. *Entrance requirements:* Additional exam requirements/recommendations for international students: Required—TOEFL (minimum score 525 paper-based; 197 computer-based; 71 iBT). *Application deadline:* For fall admission, 3/1 priority date for domestic and international students. Application fee: $45 ($60 for international students). Electronic applications accepted. *Financial support:* In 2009–10, 30 students received support, including 2 fellowships with full tuition reimbursements available (averaging $25,000 per year), 6 research assistantships with full tuition reimbursements available (averaging $8,100 per year), 10 teaching assistantships with full tuition reimbursements available (averaging $8,100 per year); career-related internships or fieldwork, Federal Work-Study, institutionally sponsored loans, and tuition waivers (full) also available. Financial award application deadline: 3/1. *Faculty research:* Computers, power and control systems, microwaves, communications and signal processing, bioengineering. Total annual research expenditures: $599,000. *Unit head:* Dr. Daniel L. Ewert, Chair, 701-231-7019, Fax: 701-231-8677, E-mail: dan.ewert@ndsu.nodak.edu. *Application contact:* Dr. Jacob Glower, Associate Professor, 701-231-8068, E-mail: jacob.glower@ndsu.edu.

Northeastern University, College of Engineering, Department of Electrical and Computer Engineering, Boston, MA 02115-5096. Offers computer engineering (PhD); electrical engineering (MS, PhD); engineering leadership (MS). *Faculty:* 45 full-time (6 women), 2 part-time/adjunct (both women). *Students:* 267 full-time (53 women), 117 part-time (19 women); includes 1 Hispanic American, 180 international. 921 applicants, 49% accepted, 96 enrolled. In 2009, 71 master's, 18 doctorates awarded. *Degree requirements:* For master's, thesis optional; for doctorate, thesis/dissertation, departmental qualifying exam. *Entrance requirements:* For master's and doctorate, GRE General Test. Additional exam requirements/recommendations for international students: Required—TOEFL (minimum score 550 paper-based; 213 computer-based). *Application deadline:* For fall admission, 1/15 priority date for domestic and international students. Applications are processed on a rolling basis. Application fee: $50. Electronic applications accepted. *Financial support:* In 2009–10, 136 students received support, including 1 fellowship with full tuition reimbursement available, 86 research assistantships with full tuition reimbursements available (averaging $18,320 per year), 49 teaching assistantships with full tuition reimbursements available (averaging $18,320 per year); career-related internships or fieldwork, Federal Work-Study, scholarships/grants, tuition waivers (full), and unspecified assistantships also available. Support available to part-time students. Financial award application deadline: 1/15; financial award applicants required to submit FAFSA. *Faculty research:* Signal processing and sensor data fusion, plasma science, sensing and imaging, power electronics, computer engineering. *Unit head:* Dr. Ali Abur, Chairman, 617-373-4159, Fax: 617-373-8970. *Application contact:* Stephen L. Gibson, Associate Director, 617-373-2711, Fax: 617-373-2501, E-mail: grad-eng@coe.neu.edu.

Northern Arizona University, Graduate College, College of Engineering, Forestry and Natural Sciences, Programs in Engineering, Flagstaff, AZ 86011. Offers civil engineering (MSE); computer science (MSE); electrical engineering (MSE); environmental engineering (MSE); mechanical engineering (MSE). Postbaccalaureate distance learning degree programs offered (no on-campus study). *Faculty:* 43 full-time (11 women). *Students:* 30 full-time (4 women), 9 part-time (0 women); includes 6 minority (4 American Indian/Alaska Native, 1 Asian American or Pacific Islander, 1 Hispanic American), 10 international. Average age 28. 42 applicants, 55% accepted, 12 enrolled. In 2009, 4 master's awarded. *Degree requirements:* For master's, thesis. *Entrance requirements:* Additional exam requirements/recommendations for international students: Required—TOEFL (minimum score 550 paper-based; 213 computer-based; 80 iBT), IELTS (minimum score 7). *Application deadline:* For fall admission, 3/1 priority date for domestic students, 9/1 priority date for international students; for spring admission, 9/15 priority date for domestic students. Applications are processed on a rolling basis. Application fee: $65. Electronic applications accepted. *Financial support:* In 2009–10, 9 research assistantships with partial tuition reimbursements, 9 teaching assistantships with partial tuition reimbursements were awarded; career-related internships or fieldwork, Federal Work-Study, scholarships/grants, health care benefits, and unspecified assistantships also available. Support available to part-time students. Financial award application deadline: 3/30; financial award applicants required to submit FAFSA. *Unit head:* Dr. Ernesto Penado, Chair, 928-523-9453, Fax: 928-523-2300, E-mail: ernesto.penado@nau.edu. *Application contact:* Dieter Otte, Coordinator, 928-523-0876, Fax: 928-523-2300, E-mail: dieter.otte@nau.edu.

Northern Illinois University, Graduate School, College of Engineering and Engineering Technology, Department of Electrical Engineering, De Kalb, IL 60115-2854. Offers MS. Part-time and evening/weekend programs available. *Faculty:* 9 full-time (0 women). *Students:* 51 full-time (14 women), 27 part-time (5 women); includes 2 minority (1 Asian American or Pacific Islander, 1 Hispanic American), 63 international. Average age 24. 225 applicants, 33% accepted, 31

enrolled. In 2009, 26 master's awarded. *Degree requirements:* For master's, comprehensive exam, thesis optional. *Entrance requirements:* For master's, GRE General Test, minimum GPA of 2.75. Additional exam requirements/recommendations for international students: Required—TOEFL (minimum score 550 paper-based; 213 computer-based). *Application deadline:* For fall admission, 6/1 for domestic students, 5/1 for international students; for spring admission, 11/1 for domestic students, 10/1 for international students. Applications are processed on a rolling basis. Application fee: $30. Electronic applications accepted. *Expenses:* Tuition, state resident: full-time $6576; part-time $274 per credit hour. Tuition, nonresident: full-time $13,152; part-time $548 per credit hour. Required fees: $1813; $75.53 per credit hour. Part-time tuition and fees vary according to course load. *Financial support:* In 2009–10, 1 research assistantship with full tuition reimbursement, 15 teaching assistantships with full tuition reimbursements were awarded; fellowships with full tuition reimbursements, career-related internships or fieldwork, Federal Work-Study, scholarships/grants, tuition waivers (full), and staff assistantships also available. Support available to part-time students. Financial award applicants required to submit FAFSA. *Faculty research:* Digital signal processing, optics, nano-electronic devices, physion electronics, VLSI. *Unit head:* Dr. Ibrahim Abdel-motaleb, Chair, 815-753-1290, Fax: 815-753-1289, E-mail: ibrahim@niu.edu. *Application contact:* Graduate School Office, 815-753-0395, E-mail: gradsch@niu.edu.

Northwestern Polytechnic University, School of Engineering, Fremont, CA 94539-7482. Offers computer science (MS); computer systems engineering (MS); electrical engineering (MS). Part-time and evening/weekend programs available. *Degree requirements:* For master's, thesis optional. *Entrance requirements:* For master's, minimum GPA of 3.0. Additional exam requirements/recommendations for international students: Required—TOEFL (minimum score 550 paper-based; 213 computer-based; 79 iBT). *Faculty research:* Computer networking, database design, Internet technology, software engineering, digital signal processing.

Northwestern University, McCormick School of Engineering and Applied Science, Department of Electrical Engineering and Computer Science, Evanston, IL 60208. Offers computer science (MS, PhD); electrical and computer engineering (MS, PhD); electronic materials (MS, PhD, Certificate); information technology (MIT). MS and PhD admissions and degrees offered through The Graduate School. Part-time programs available. Terminal master's awarded for partial completion of doctoral program. *Degree requirements:* For master's, thesis or project; for doctorate, thesis/dissertation. *Faculty research:* Solid-state engineering networks and communications, photonics, parallel and distributed computing, VLSI design and computer-aided design.

Oakland University, Graduate Study and Lifelong Learning, School of Engineering and Computer Science, Department of Electrical and Systems Engineering, Program in Electrical and Computer Engineering, Rochester, MI 48309-4401. Offers MS. Part-time and evening/weekend programs available. *Entrance requirements:* For master's, minimum GPA of 3.0 for unconditional admission. Additional exam requirements/recommendations for international students: Required—TOEFL (minimum score 550 paper-based; 213 computer-based). Electronic applications accepted. *Expenses:* Contact institution.

OGI School of Science & Engineering at Oregon Health & Science University, Graduate Studies, Department of Computer Science and Electrical Engineering, Beaverton, OR 97006-8921. Offers computer science (PhD); computer science and engineering (MS, PhD); electrical engineering (MS, PhD). Part-time and evening/weekend programs available. Terminal master's awarded for partial completion of doctoral program. *Degree requirements:* For master's, thesis optional; for doctorate, comprehensive exam, oral defense of dissertation. *Entrance requirements:* For master's and doctorate, GRE General Test. Additional exam requirements/recommendations for international students: Required—TOEFL (minimum score 650 paper-based; 280 computer-based). Electronic applications accepted. *Faculty research:* Computer systems architecture, intelligent and interactive systems, programming models and systems, theory of computation.

The Ohio State University, Graduate School, College of Engineering, Department of Electrical and Computer Engineering, Columbus, OH 43210. Offers electrical engineering (MS, PhD). Part-time programs available. *Faculty:* 68. *Students:* 226 full-time (34 women), 65 part-time (14 women); includes 15 minority (3 African Americans, 1 American Indian/Alaska Native, 8 Asian Americans or Pacific Islanders, 3 Hispanic Americans), 188 international. Average age 27. In 2009, 62 master's, 19 doctorates awarded. Terminal master's awarded for partial completion of doctoral program. *Degree requirements:* For master's, thesis optional; for doctorate, thesis/dissertation. *Entrance requirements:* Additional exam requirements/recommendations for international students: Required—TOEFL (minimum score 580 paper-based; 237 computer-based). *Application deadline:* For fall admission, 8/15 priority date for domestic students, 7/1 priority date for international students; for winter admission, 12/1 priority date for domestic students, 11/1 priority date for international students; for spring admission, 3/1 priority date for domestic students, 2/1 priority date for international students. Applications are processed on a rolling basis. Application fee: $40 ($50 for international students). Electronic applications accepted. *Expenses:* Tuition, state resident: full-time $10,683. Tuition, nonresident: full-time $25,923. Tuition and fees vary according to course load and program. *Financial support:* In 2009–10, 25 fellowships with full tuition reimbursements (averaging $18,000 per year), 100 research assistantships with full tuition reimbursements (averaging $18,000 per year), 30 teaching assistantships with full tuition reimbursements (averaging $15,000 per year) were awarded; career-related internships or fieldwork, Federal Work-Study, institutionally sponsored loans, scholarships/grants, traineeships, health care benefits, and unspecified assistantships also available. Support available to part-time students. Total annual research expenditures: $13 million. *Unit head:* Roberto Rojas-Teran, Graduate Studies Committee Chair, 614-292-2571, Fax: 614-292-7596, E-mail: rojas-teran.1@osu.edu. *Application contact:* 614-292-9444, Fax: 614-292-3895, E-mail: domestic.grad@osu.edu.

Ohio University, Graduate College, Russ College of Engineering and Technology, School of Electrical Engineering and Computer Science, Athens, OH 45701-2979. Offers computer science (MS); electrical engineering (MS); electrical engineering and computer science (PhD). *Faculty:* 34 full-time (2 women), 9 part-time/adjunct (3 women). *Students:* 72 full-time (16 women), 26 part-time (3 women); includes 2 minority (1 African American, 1 Hispanic American), 70 international. 123 applicants, 67% accepted, 18 enrolled. In 2009, 21 master's, 4 doctorates awarded. *Degree requirements:* For master's, comprehensive exam (for some programs), thesis; for doctorate, comprehensive exam, thesis/dissertation, qualifying exams. *Entrance requirements:* For master's, GRE, BSEE or BSCS, minimum GPA of 3.0; for doctorate, GRE, MSEE or MSCS, minimum GPA of 3.0. Additional exam requirements/recommendations for international students: Required—TOEFL (minimum score 550 paper-based; 80 iBT) or IELTS Academic (minimum score 6.5). *Application deadline:* For fall admission, 2/1 priority date for domestic students, 1/1 priority date for international students; for winter admission, 6/1 priority date for domestic students, 5/1 priority date for international students; for spring admission, 8/15 priority date for domestic students, 7/15 priority date for international students. Applications are processed on a rolling basis. Application fee: $50 ($55 for international students). Electronic applications accepted. *Expenses:* Tuition, state resident: full-time $7839; part-time $323 per quarter hour. Tuition, nonresident: full-time $15,831; part-time $654 per quarter hour. Required fees: $2931. *Financial support:* In 2009–10, 54 research assistantships with full tuition reimbursements, 19 teaching assistantships with full tuition reimbursements were awarded; Federal Work-Study, institutionally sponsored loans, scholarships/grants, and unspecified assistantships also available. Financial award applicants required to submit FAFSA. *Faculty research:* Avionics, networking/communications, intelligent distribution, real-time computing, control systems, optical properties of semiconductors. Total annual research expenditures: $8.2 million. *Unit head:* Dr. Shawn D. Ostermann, Chair, 740-593-1566, Fax: 740-593-0007, E-mail: osterman@eecs.ohiou.edu. *Application contact:* Dr. David Matolak, Graduate Chair, 740-593-1241, Fax: 740-593-0007, E-mail: matolak@ohio.edu.

Oklahoma State University, College of Engineering, Architecture and Technology, School of Electrical and Computer Engineering, Stillwater, OK 74078. Offers MS, PhD. Postbaccalaureate distance learning degree programs offered. *Faculty:* 25 full-time (2 women), 2 part-time/adjunct (0 women). *Students:* 92 full-time (17 women), 95 part-time (13 women); includes 14 minority (2 African Americans, 3 American Indian/Alaska Native, 6 Asian Americans or Pacific Islanders, 3 Hispanic Americans), 129 international. Average age 28. 455 applicants, 29% accepted, 43 enrolled. In 2009, 42 master's, 5 doctorates awarded. *Degree requirements:* For master's, thesis or alternative; for doctorate, comprehensive exam, thesis/dissertation. *Entrance requirements:* For master's and doctorate, GRE or GMAT. Additional exam requirements/recommendations for international students: Required—TOEFL (minimum score 550 paper-based; 79 iBT). *Application deadline:* For fall admission, 3/1 priority date for international students; for spring admission, 8/1 priority date for international students. Applications are processed on a rolling basis. Application fee: $40 ($75 for international students). Electronic applications accepted. *Expenses:* Tuition, state resident: full-time $3716; part-time $154.85 per credit hour. Tuition, nonresident: full-time $14,448; part-time $602 per credit hour. Required fees: $1772; $73.85 per credit hour. One-time fee: $50. Tuition and fees vary according to course load and campus/location. *Financial support:* In 2009–10, 53 research assistantships (averaging $9,883 per year), 33 teaching assistantships (averaging $8,112 per year) were awarded; career-related internships or fieldwork, Federal Work-Study, scholarships/grants, health care benefits, tuition waivers (partial), and unspecified assistantships also available. Support available to part-time students. Financial award application deadline: 3/1; financial award applicants required to submit FAFSA. *Unit head:* Dr. Keith Teague, Head, 405-744-5151, Fax: 405-744-9198. *Application contact:* Dr. Gordon Emslie, Dean, 405-744-6368, Fax: 405-744-0355, E-mail: grad-i@okstate.edu.

Old Dominion University, Frank Batten College of Engineering and Technology, Program in Electrical and Computer Engineering, Norfolk, VA 23529. Offers ME, MS, PhD. Part-time programs available. Postbaccalaureate distance learning degree programs offered (minimal on-campus study). *Faculty:* 25 full-time (1 woman), 2 part-time/adjunct (1 woman). *Students:* 65 full-time (13 women), 64 part-time (20 women); includes 12 minority (3 African Americans, 1 American Indian/Alaska Native, 8 Asian Americans or Pacific Islanders), 86 international. Average age 29. 15 applicants, 73% accepted, 4 enrolled. In 2009, 39 master's, 5 doctorates awarded. *Degree requirements:* For doctorate, thesis/dissertation, candidacy exam, diagnostic exam. *Entrance requirements:* For doctorate, GRE. Additional exam requirements/recommendations for international students: Required—TOEFL. *Application deadline:* For fall admission, 6/1 for domestic students, 4/15 for international students; for spring admission, 11/1 for domestic students, 10/1 for international students. Applications are processed on a rolling basis. Application fee: $40. Electronic applications accepted. *Expenses:* Tuition, state resident: full-time $8112; part-time $338 per credit. Tuition, nonresident: full-time $20,256; part-time $844 per credit. Required fees: $119 per semester. One-time fee: $50. *Financial support:* In 2009–10, 3 fellowships with full tuition reimbursements (averaging $15,000 per year), 38 research assistantships with full and partial tuition reimbursements (averaging $15,000 per year), 41 teaching assistantships with full and partial tuition reimbursements (averaging $15,000 per year) were awarded; career-related internships or fieldwork, Federal Work-Study, scholarships/grants, tuition waivers (partial), and unspecified assistantships also available. Support available to part-time students. Financial award application deadline: 2/15; financial award applicants required to submit FAFSA. *Faculty research:* Digital signal processing, control engineering, gaseous electronics, ultrafast (femtosecom) laser applications, interaction of fields with living organisms. Total annual research expenditures: $3 million. *Unit head:* Dr. Sach Albin, Graduate Program Director, 757-683-4967, Fax: 757-683-3220, E-mail: ecegpd@odu.edu. *Application contact:* Dr. Linda Vahala, Associate Dean, 757-683-3789, Fax: 757-683-4898, E-mail: lvahala@odu.edu.

Oregon Health & Science University, OGI School of Science and Engineering, Department of Computer Science and Engineering, Portland, OR 97239-3098. Offers computer science and engineering (MS, PhD); electrical engineering (MS, PhD). Tuition and fees vary according to course level, course load, degree level, program and reciprocity agreements.

Oregon State University, Graduate School, College of Engineering, School of Electrical Engineering and Computer Science, Corvallis, OR 97331. Offers computer science (M Eng, MAIS, MS, PhD); electrical and computer engineering (M Eng, MS, PhD). *Faculty:* 38 full-time (6 women), 5 part-time/adjunct (3 women). *Students:* 216 full-time (41 women), 52 part-time (6 women); includes 24 minority (2 African Americans, 19 Asian Americans or Pacific Islanders, 3 Hispanic Americans), 149 international. Average age 29. In 2009, 48 master's, 15 doctorates awarded. *Degree requirements:* For doctorate, thesis/dissertation, qualifying exam, preliminary exam. *Entrance requirements:* For master's and doctorate, minimum GPA of 3.0 in last 90 hours of course work. Additional exam requirements/recommendations for international students: Required—TOEFL (minimum score 600 paper-based; 250 computer-based; 80 iBT). *Application deadline:* For fall admission, 1/15 for domestic and international students. Application fee: $50. Electronic applications accepted. *Expenses:* Tuition, state resident: full-time $9774; part-time $362 per credit. Tuition, nonresident: full-time $15,849; part-time $587 per credit. Required fees: $1639. Full-time tuition and fees vary according to course load and program. *Financial support:* Fellowships with full tuition reimbursements, research assistantships with full tuition reimbursements, teaching assistantships with full tuition reimbursements, career-related internships or fieldwork, Federal Work-Study, and institutionally sponsored loans available. Support available to part-time students. Financial award application deadline: 1/15. *Faculty research:* Optical materials and devices, data security and cryptography, analog and mixed-signal integrated circuit design, algorithms, computer graphics and vision. Total annual research expenditures: $7.5 million. *Unit head:* Dr. Theresa Shreeve Fiez, Director, 541-737-3118, Fax: 541-737-1300, E-mail: terri@eecs.oregonstate.edu. *Application contact:* Ferne Simendinger, Graduate Coordinator, 541-737-3617, Fax: 541-737-1300, E-mail: ferne@eecs.oregonstate.edu.

Penn State University Park, Graduate School, College of Engineering, Department of Electrical Engineering, State College, University Park, PA 16802-1503. Offers MS, PhD.

Polytechnic Institute of NYU, Department of Electrical and Computer Engineering, Major in Electrical Engineering, Brooklyn, NY 11201-2990. Offers MS, PhD. Part-time and evening/weekend programs available. *Students:* 356 full-time (91 women), 184 part-time (20 women); includes 62 minority (14 African Americans, 41 Asian Americans or Pacific Islanders, 7 Hispanic Americans), 408 international. 1,098 applicants, 67% accepted, 234 enrolled. In 2009, 165 master's, 10 doctorates awarded. *Degree requirements:* For master's, comprehensive exam (for some programs), thesis (for some programs); for doctorate, comprehensive exam, thesis/dissertation. *Entrance requirements:* For master's, BS in electrical engineering; for doctorate, qualifying exam, MS in electrical engineering. Additional exam requirements/recommendations for international students: Required—TOEFL (minimum score 550 paper-based; 213 computer-based; 80 iBT); Recommended—IELTS (minimum score 6.5). *Application deadline:* For fall admission, 7/31 priority date for domestic students, 4/30 priority date for international students; for spring admission, 12/31 priority date for domestic students, 11/30 priority date for international students. Applications are processed on a rolling basis. Application fee: $75. Electronic applications accepted. *Expenses:* Tuition: Full-time $21,492; part-time $1194 per credit hour. Required fees: $1160; $204 per course. *Financial support:* Fellowships, research assistantships, teaching assistantships, institutionally sponsored loans, scholarships/grants, and unspecified assistantships available. Support available to part-time students. Financial award applicants required to submit FAFSA. *Unit head:* Dr. Jonathan Chao, Head, 718-860-3478, Fax: 718-260-3302, E-mail: chao@poly.edu. *Application contact:* JeanCarlo Bonilla, Director of Graduate Enrollment Management, 718-260-3182, Fax: 718-260-3624, E-mail: gradinfo@poly.edu.

Polytechnic Institute of NYU, Long Island Graduate Center, Graduate Programs, Department of Electrical and Computer Engineering, Major in Electrical Engineering, Melville, NY 11747. Offers MS. Part-time and evening/weekend programs available. *Students:* 8 full-time (1 woman), 43 part-time (3 women); includes 7 minority (3 African Americans, 4 Asian Americans or Pacific Islanders), 12 international. 13 applicants, 100% accepted, 13 enrolled. In 2009, 15 master's awarded. *Degree requirements:* For master's, comprehensive exam (for some programs), thesis (for some programs). *Entrance requirements:* Additional exam requirements/recommendations for international students: Required—TOEFL (minimum score 550 paper-based; 213 computer-based; 80 iBT); Recommended—IELTS (minimum score 6.5). *Application deadline:* For fall admission, 7/31 priority date for domestic students, 4/30 priority date for international students; for spring admission, 12/31 priority date for domestic students, 11/30 priority date for international students. Applications are processed on a rolling basis. Application fee: $75. Electronic applications accepted. *Financial support:* Institutionally sponsored loans, scholarships/grants, and unspecified assistantships available. Support available to part-time students. Financial award applicants required to submit FAFSA. *Unit head:* Dr. Jonathan Chao, Department Head, 718-260-3302, E-mail: chao@poly.edu. *Application contact:* JeanCarlo Bonilla, Director of Graduate Enrollment Management, 718-260-3182, Fax: 718-260-3624, E-mail: gradinfo@poly.edu.

Polytechnic Institute of NYU, Westchester Graduate Center, Graduate Programs, Department of Electrical and Computer Engineering, Major in Electrical Engineering, Hawthorne, NY 10532-1507. Offers MS. *Students:* 15 full-time (2 women), 33 part-time (7 women); includes 10 minority (7 African Americans, 3 Asian Americans or Pacific Islanders), 15 international. 10 applicants, 100% accepted, 10 enrolled. In 2009, 1 master's awarded. *Degree requirements:* For master's, comprehensive exam (for some programs), thesis (for some programs). *Entrance requirements:* Additional exam requirements/recommendations for international students: Required—TOEFL (minimum score 550 paper-based; 213 computer-based; 80 iBT); Recommended—IELTS (minimum score 6.5). *Application deadline:* For fall admission, 7/31 priority date for domestic students, 4/30 priority date for international students; for spring admission, 12/31 priority date for domestic students, 11/30 priority date for international students. Applications are processed on a rolling basis. Application fee: $75. Electronic applications accepted. *Financial support:* Institutionally sponsored loans, scholarships/grants, and unspecified assistantships available. Support available to part-time students. *Unit head:* Dr. Jonathan Chao, Department Head, 718-260-3302, E-mail: chao@poly.edu. *Application contact:* JeanCarlo Bonilla, Director of Graduate Enrollment Management, 718-260-3182, Fax: 718-260-3624, E-mail: gradinfo@poly.edu.

Polytechnic University of Puerto Rico, Graduate School, Hato Rey, PR 00919. Offers business administration (MBA), including general studies, management of information systems, management of international enterprises; civil engineering (ME, MS); computer engineering (ME, MS); computer science (MS); electrical engineering (ME, MS); engineering management (MEM); environmental management (MEPM); landscape architecture (M Land Arch); manufacturing competitiveness (MMC, MS); manufacturing engineering (ME, MS). Part-time and evening/weekend programs available. *Entrance requirements:* For master's, 3 letters of recommendation.

Polytechnic University of the Americas–Orlando Campus, Graduate School, Winter Park, FL 32792. Offers business administration (MBA); civil engineering (MS); computer engineering (MS); electrical engineering (MS); engineering management (MEM). Part-time and evening/weekend programs available. Postbaccalaureate distance learning degree programs offered (no on-campus study). *Entrance requirements:* For master's, minimum GPA of 3.0. Electronic applications accepted.

Portland State University, Graduate Studies, Maseeh College of Engineering and Computer Science, Department of Electrical and Computer Engineering, Portland, OR 97207-0751. Offers M Eng, MS, PhD. Part-time and evening/weekend programs available. *Degree requirements:* For master's, variable foreign language requirement, oral exam; for doctorate, one foreign language, comprehensive exam, thesis/dissertation, oral and written exams. *Entrance requirements:* For master's, minimum GPA of 3.0 in upper-division course work or 2.75 overall, BS in electrical or computer engineering or allied field; for doctorate, GRE General Test, GRE Subject Test, minimum GPA of 3.0 in upper-division course work, MS in electrical engineering or allied field. Additional exam requirements/recommendations for international students: Required—TOEFL (minimum score 550 paper-based; 213 computer-based). *Faculty research:* Optics and laser systems, design automation, VLSI design, computer systems, power electronics.

Prairie View A&M University, College of Engineering, Prairie View, TX 77446-0519. Offers computer information systems (MSCIS); computer science (MSCS); electrical engineering (MSEE, PhDEE); engineering (MS Engr). Part-time and evening/weekend programs available. *Faculty:* 19 full-time (0 women). *Students:* 64 full-time (18 women), 47 part-time (14 women); includes 43 minority (36 African Americans, 4 Asian Americans or Pacific Islanders, 3 Hispanic Americans), 51 international. Average age 24. 50 applicants, 84% accepted, 33 enrolled. In 2009, 26 master's, 3 doctorates awarded. *Degree requirements:* For master's, thesis (for some programs); for doctorate, comprehensive exam, thesis/dissertation. *Entrance requirements:* For master's, GRE General Test, bachelor's degree in engineering from an ABET accredited institution; for doctorate, GRE. Additional exam requirements/recommendations for international students: Required—TOEFL (minimum score 550 paper-based). *Application deadline:* For fall admission, 7/1 priority date for domestic and international students; for spring admission, 11/1 priority date for domestic and international students. Application fee: $50. Electronic applications accepted. *Expenses:* Tuition, state resident: full-time $2200. Tuition, nonresident: full-time $5600. Required fees: $1720. Tuition and fees vary according to course load. *Financial support:* In 2009–10, 80 students received support, including 14 fellowships (averaging $1,050 per year), 16 research assistantships (averaging $16,150 per year), 13 teaching assistantships (averaging $14,000 per year); career-related internships or fieldwork, institutionally sponsored loans, scholarships/grants, health care benefits, tuition waivers (partial), and unspecified assistantships also available. Financial award application deadline: 3/1; financial award applicants required to submit FAFSA. *Faculty research:* Applied radiation research, thermal science, computational fluid dynamics, analog mixed signal, aerial space battlefield. Total annual research expenditures: $439,054. *Unit head:* Dr. Kendall T. Harris, Dean, 936-261-9956, Fax: 936-261-9869, E-mail: tharris@pvamu.edu. *Application contact:* Barbara A. Thompson, Administrative Assistant, 936-261-9896, Fax: 936-261-9869, E-mail: bathompson@pvamu.edu.

Princeton University, Graduate School, School of Engineering and Applied Science, Department of Electrical Engineering, Princeton, NJ 08544-1019. Offers M Eng, PhD. *Faculty:* 28 full-time (3 women). Terminal master's awarded for partial completion of doctoral program. *Degree requirements:* For doctorate, thesis/dissertation, general exam. *Entrance requirements:* For master's, GRE General Test, 3 letters of recommendation; for doctorate, GRE General Test, official transcript(s), 3 letters of recommendation, personal statement. Additional exam requirements/recommendations for international students: Required—TOEFL. *Application deadline:* For fall admission, 12/31 for domestic and international students. Application fee: $90. Electronic applications accepted. *Financial support:* Fellowships with full tuition reimbursements, research assistantships with full tuition reimbursements, teaching assistantships with full tuition reimbursements, institutionally sponsored loans and health care benefits available. *Faculty research:* Computer engineering, electronic materials and devices, information sciences and systems, optics and optical electronics. *Unit head:* Sarah Braude, Graduate Program Administrator, 609-258-6728, Fax: 609-258-8259, E-mail: ee-gradadmin@princeton.edu. *Application contact:* Michelle Carman, Manager of Graduate Admission, 609-258-3034, Fax: 609-258-7262, E-mail: gsadmit@princeton.edu.

Purdue University, College of Engineering, School of Electrical and Computer Engineering, West Lafayette, IN 47907-2035. Offers MS, MSE, MSECE, PhD. MS and PhD degree programs in biomedical engineering offered jointly with School of Mechanical Engineering and School of Chemical Engineering. Part-time programs available. Postbaccalaureate distance learning degree programs offered (no on-campus study). Terminal master's awarded for partial completion of doctoral program. *Entrance requirements:* For master's and doctorate, GRE General Test, minimum GPA of 3.25. Additional exam requirements/recommendations for international students: Required—TOEFL (minimum score 550 paper-based; 213 computer-based; 77 iBT). Electronic applications accepted. *Faculty research:* Automatic controls; biomedical imaging; computer engineering; communications, networking signal and image processing; fields and optics.

Purdue University Calumet, Graduate School, School of Engineering, Mathematics, and Science, Department of Engineering, Hammond, IN 46323-2094. Offers computer engineering

Electrical Engineering

Purdue University Calumet (continued)
(MSE); electrical engineering (MSE); engineering (MS); mechanical engineering (MSE). Evening/weekend programs available. *Entrance requirements:* Additional exam requirements/recommendations for international students: Required—TOEFL.

Queen's University at Kingston, School of Graduate Studies and Research, Faculty of Applied Science, Department of Electrical and Computer Engineering, Kingston, ON K7L 3N6, Canada. Offers M Eng, M Sc, M Sc Eng, PhD. Part-time programs available. *Degree requirements:* For master's, thesis optional; for doctorate, comprehensive exam, thesis/dissertation. *Entrance requirements:* Additional exam requirements/recommendations for international students: Required—TOEFL (minimum score 580 paper-based; 237 computer-based). *Faculty research:* Communications and signal processing systems, computer engineering systems.

Rensselaer at Hartford, Department of Engineering, Program in Electrical Engineering, Hartford, CT 06120-2991. Offers ME, MS. Part-time and evening/weekend programs available. *Faculty:* 3 full-time (0 women), 3 part-time/adjunct (0 women). *Students:* 1 full-time (0 women), 44 part-time (5 women); includes 13 minority (1 African American, 7 Asian Americans or Pacific Islanders, 5 Hispanic Americans). Average age 34. 12 applicants, 58% accepted, 7 enrolled. In 2009, 7 master's awarded. *Degree requirements:* For master's, thesis optional. *Entrance requirements:* For master's, GRE. Additional exam requirements/recommendations for international students: Required—TOEFL (minimum score 600 paper-based; 250 computer-based; 100 iBT). *Application deadline:* For fall admission, 8/6 priority date for domestic students. Applications are processed on a rolling basis. Application fee: $75. *Expenses:* Tuition: Full-time $31,800; part-time $1325 per credit hour. *Financial support:* Research assistantships, tuition waivers (full and partial) and unspecified assistantships available. Support available to part-time students. Financial award applicants required to submit FAFSA. *Unit head:* Dr. Ernesto Gutierrez-Miravete, 860-548-2464, E-mail: gutiee@rpi.edu. *Application contact:* Kristin Galligan, Director, Enrollment Management and Marketing, 860-548-2480, Fax: 860-548-7823, E-mail: info@ewp.rpi.edu.

Rensselaer Polytechnic Institute, Graduate School, School of Engineering, Department of Electrical, Computer, and Systems Engineering, Program in Electrical Engineering, Troy, NY 12180-3590. Offers M Eng, MS, PhD. Part-time programs available. Postbaccalaureate distance learning degree programs offered (no on-campus study). *Faculty:* 46 full-time (3 women), 7 part-time/adjunct (1 woman). *Students:* 116 full-time (22 women), 4 part-time (1 woman); includes 5 Asian Americans or Pacific Islanders, 4 Hispanic Americans, 79 international. 506 applicants, 18% accepted, 23 enrolled. In 2009, 30 master's, 16 doctorates awarded. Terminal master's awarded for partial completion of doctoral program. *Degree requirements:* For master's, thesis (for some programs); for doctorate, thesis/dissertation. *Entrance requirements:* For master's, GRE; for doctorate, GRE, qualifying exam, candidacy exam. Additional exam requirements/recommendations for international students: Required—TOEFL (minimum score 570 paper-based; 89 iBT). *Application deadline:* For fall admission, 1/15 priority date for domestic and international students; for spring admission, 8/15 priority date for domestic and international students. Applications are processed on a rolling basis. Application fee: $75. Electronic applications accepted. *Expenses:* Tuition: Full-time $38,100. *Financial support:* In 2009–10, 4 fellowships, 64 research assistantships, 20 teaching assistantships were awarded; career-related internships or fieldwork, institutionally sponsored loans, and unspecified assistantships also available. Financial award application deadline: 1/15. *Faculty research:* Networking and multimedia via ATM, thermophotovoltaic devices, microelectronic interconnections, agile manufacturing, mobile robotics. Total annual research expenditures: $3.7 million. *Unit head:* Dr. Kim L. Boyer, Head, 518-276-2150, Fax: 518-276-6261, E-mail: kim@ecse.rpi.edu. *Application contact:* Ann Bruno, Manager of Student Services and Graduate Enrollment, 518-276-2554, Fax: 518-276-4403, E-mail: ann@ecse.rpi.edu.

Rice University, Graduate Programs, George R. Brown School of Engineering, Department of Electrical and Computer Engineering, Houston, TX 77251-1892. Offers bioengineering (MS, PhD); circuits, controls, and communication systems (MS, PhD); computer science and engineering (MS, PhD); electrical engineering (MEE); lasers, microwaves, and solid-state electronics (MS, PhD); MBA/MEE. Part-time programs available. *Degree requirements:* For master's, thesis (for some programs); for doctorate, thesis/dissertation. *Entrance requirements:* For master's and doctorate, GRE General Test, GRE Subject Test, minimum GPA of 3.0. Additional exam requirements/recommendations for international students: Required—TOEFL (minimum score 600 paper-based; 250 computer-based; 90 iBT). Electronic applications accepted. *Faculty research:* Physical electronics, systems, computer engineering, bioengineering.

Rochester Institute of Technology, Graduate Enrollment Services, Kate Gleason College of Engineering, Department of Electrical Engineering, Rochester, NY 14623-5603. Offers MSEE. Part-time programs available. *Students:* 80 full-time (11 women), 34 part-time (5 women); includes 9 minority (3 African Americans, 4 Asian Americans or Pacific Islanders, 2 Hispanic Americans), 60 international. Average age 26. 268 applicants, 57% accepted, 38 enrolled. In 2009, 32 master's awarded. *Degree requirements:* For master's, thesis optional. *Entrance requirements:* For master's, GRE, minimum GPA of 3.0. Additional exam requirements/recommendations for international students: Required—TOEFL (minimum score 570 paper-based; 230 computer-based; 88 iBT), or IELTS (minimum score 6.5). *Application deadline:* For fall admission, 2/15 priority date for domestic and international students; for winter admission, 10/15 for domestic and international students. Applications are processed on a rolling basis. Application fee: $50. Electronic applications accepted. *Expenses:* Tuition: Full-time $31,533; part-time $876 per credit hour. Required fees: $210. *Financial support:* In 2009–10, 64 students received support; research assistantships with partial tuition reimbursements available, teaching assistantships with partial tuition reimbursements available, career-related internships or fieldwork, institutionally sponsored loans, scholarships/grants, and unspecified assistantships available. Support available to part-time students. Financial award applicants required to submit FAFSA. *Faculty research:* Integrated optics, control systems, digital signal processing, robotic vision. *Unit head:* Dr. Sohail Dianat, Interim Department Head, 585-475-6740, Fax: 585-475-5845, E-mail: ee@rit.edu. *Application contact:* Diane Ellison, Assistant Vice President, Graduate Enrollment Services, 585-475-2229, Fax: 585-475-7164, E-mail: gradinfo@rit.edu.

Rochester Institute of Technology, Graduate Enrollment Services, Kate Gleason College of Engineering, Department of Microelectronic Engineering, Program in Microelectronic Engineering, Rochester, NY 14623-5603. Offers MS. Part-time programs available. *Students:* 14 full-time (4 women), 6 part-time (1 woman); includes 1 Asian American or Pacific Islander, 1 Hispanic American, 7 international. Average age 27. 22 applicants, 73% accepted, 10 enrolled. In 2009, 9 master's awarded. *Degree requirements:* For master's, thesis. *Entrance requirements:* Additional exam requirements/recommendations for international students: Required—TOEFL (minimum score 570 paper-based; 230 computer-based; 88 iBT), or IELTS (minimum score 6.5). *Application deadline:* For fall admission, 2/15 priority date for domestic and international students; for winter admission, 10/15 for domestic and international students. Applications are processed on a rolling basis. Application fee: $50. Electronic applications accepted. *Expenses:* Tuition: Full-time $31,533; part-time $876 per credit hour. Required fees: $210. *Financial support:* In 2009–10, 16 students received support; research assistantships with partial tuition reimbursements available, teaching assistantships with partial tuition reimbursements available, career-related internships or fieldwork, institutionally sponsored loans, scholarships/grants, and unspecified assistantships available. Support available to part-time students. Financial award applicants required to submit FAFSA. *Unit head:* Dr. Robert Pearson, Director, 585-475-2165, Fax: 585-475-5845, E-mail: eme@rit.edu. *Application contact:* Diane Ellison, Assistant Vice President, Graduate Enrollment Services, 585-475-2229, Fax: 585-475-7164, E-mail: gradinfo@rit.edu.

Rose-Hulman Institute of Technology, Faculty of Engineering and Applied Sciences, Department of Electrical and Computer Engineering, Terre Haute, IN 47803-3999. Offers electrical and computer engineering (M Eng); electrical engineering (MS). Part-time programs available. Postbaccalaureate distance learning degree programs offered (minimal on-campus study). *Faculty:* 18 full-time (4 women), 1 (woman) part-time/adjunct. *Students:* 16 full-time (4 women), 2 part-time (0 women); includes 1 minority (Hispanic American), 8 international. Average age 24. 25 applicants, 88% accepted, 12 enrolled. In 2009, 5 master's awarded. *Degree requirements:* For master's, thesis (for some programs). *Entrance requirements:* For master's, GRE, minimum GPA of 3.0. Additional exam requirements/recommendations for international students: Required—TOEFL (minimum score 580 paper-based; 237 computer-based; 92 iBT). *Application deadline:* For fall admission, 2/1 priority date for domestic students. Applications are processed on a rolling basis. Application fee: $0. *Expenses:* Tuition: Full-time $33,900; part-time $987 per credit hour. *Financial support:* In 2009–10, 8 students received support; fellowships with full and partial tuition reimbursements available, research assistantships with full and partial tuition reimbursements available, institutionally sponsored loans, scholarships/grants, and tuition waivers (full and partial) available. *Faculty research:* Wireless systems, VLSI design, aerial robotics, power system dynamics and control, image and speech processing. Total annual research expenditures: $430,205. *Unit head:* Dr. Frederick Berry, Chairman, 812-877-8105, Fax: 812-877-8895, E-mail: frederick.berry@rose-hulman.edu. *Application contact:* Dr. Daniel J. Moore, Associate Dean of the Faculty, 812-877-8110, Fax: 812-877-8061, E-mail: daniel.j.moore@rose-hulman.edu.

Rowan University, Graduate School, College of Engineering, Department of Electrical Engineering, Glassboro, NJ 08028-1701. Offers MS. Part-time and evening/weekend programs available. *Faculty:* 3 full-time (0 women). *Students:* 5 full-time (0 women), 6 part-time (1 woman); includes 4 minority (1 African American, 3 Asian Americans or Pacific Islanders). Average age 26. 4 applicants, 100% accepted, 3 enrolled. In 2009, 5 master's awarded. *Degree requirements:* For master's, thesis. *Entrance requirements:* For master's, GRE General Test. Additional exam requirements/recommendations for international students: Required—TOEFL. *Application deadline:* Applications are processed on a rolling basis. Application fee: $50. Electronic applications accepted. *Expenses:* Tuition, state resident: full-time $10,624; part-time $590 per semester hour. Tuition, nonresident: full-time $10,624; part-time $590 per semester hour. Required fees: $2320; $125 per semester hour. *Financial support:* Research assistantships available. *Unit head:* Dr. Shreekanth Mandayam, Graduate Studies Coordinator, 856-256-5333, Fax: 856-256-5241, E-mail: shreek@rowan.edu. *Application contact:* Dr. Ralph Dusseau, Program Adviser, 856-256-5332.

Royal Military College of Canada, Division of Graduate Studies and Research, Engineering Division, Department of Electrical and Computer Engineering, Kingston, ON K7K 7B4, Canada. Offers computer engineering (M Eng, PhD); electrical engineering (M Eng, PhD); software engineering (M Eng, PhD). *Degree requirements:* For master's, thesis; for doctorate, comprehensive exam, thesis/dissertation. *Entrance requirements:* For master's, honours degree with second-class standing in the appropriate field; for doctorate, master's degree. Electronic applications accepted.

Rutgers, The State University of New Jersey, New Brunswick, Graduate School-New Brunswick, Program in Electrical and Computer Engineering, Piscataway, NJ 08854-8097. Offers communications and solid-state electronics (MS, PhD); computer engineering (MS, PhD); control systems (MS, PhD); digital signal processing (MS, PhD). Part-time programs available. Terminal master's awarded for partial completion of doctoral program. *Degree requirements:* For master's, thesis or alternative; for doctorate, thesis/dissertation. *Entrance requirements:* For master's and doctorate, GRE General Test. Additional exam requirements/recommendations for international students: Required—TOEFL. Electronic applications accepted. *Faculty research:* Communication and information processing, wireless information networks, micro-vacuum devices, machine vision, VLSI design.

See Close-Up on page 373.

St. Cloud State University, School of Graduate Studies, College of Science and Engineering, Department of Electrical and Computer Engineering, St. Cloud, MN 56301-4498. Offers electrical engineering (MS). *Faculty:* 11 full-time (2 women). *Students:* 6 full-time (1 woman), 19 part-time (5 women); includes 1 minority (Asian American or Pacific Islander), 22 international. 28 applicants, 43% accepted, 0 enrolled. In 2009, 1 master's awarded. *Degree requirements:* For master's, thesis or alternative. *Entrance requirements:* For master's, GRE General Test, minimum GPA of 2.75. Additional exam requirements/recommendations for international students: Required—Michigan English Language Assessment Battery; Recommended—TOEFL (minimum score 550 paper-based; 213 computer-based), IELTS (minimum score 6.5). *Application deadline:* For fall admission, 6/1 priority date for domestic students, 4/1 for international students; for spring admission, 10/1 priority date for domestic students, 8/1 for international students. Applications are processed on a rolling basis. Application fee: $35. Electronic applications accepted. *Financial support:* Federal Work-Study, scholarships/grants, and unspecified assistantships available. *Unit head:* Dr. Timothy Vogt, Chairperson, 320-308-2997, Fax: 320-308-5127, E-mail: ece@stcloudstate.edu. *Application contact:* Linda Lou Krueger, School of Graduate Studies, 320-308-2113, Fax: 320-308-5371, E-mail: lekrueger@stcloudstate.edu.

St. Mary's University, Graduate School, Department of Engineering, Program in Electrical Engineering, San Antonio, TX 78228-8507. Offers electrical engineering (MS); electrical/computer engineering (MS). Part-time programs available. *Degree requirements:* For master's, comprehensive exam. *Entrance requirements:* For master's, GRE General Test. Additional exam requirements/recommendations for international students: Required—TOEFL (minimum score 550 paper-based; 213 computer-based; 80 iBT). Electronic applications accepted. *Expenses:* Tuition: Full-time $8004. Required fees: $536. One-time fee: $5 full-time. Full-time tuition and fees vary according to program. *Faculty research:* Image processing, control, communication, artificial intelligence, robotics.

San Diego State University, Graduate and Research Affairs, College of Engineering, Department of Electrical and Computer Engineering, San Diego, CA 92182. Offers electrical engineering (MS). Evening/weekend programs available. *Entrance requirements:* For master's, GRE General Test. Additional exam requirements/recommendations for international students: Required—TOEFL. Electronic applications accepted. *Faculty research:* Ultra-high speed integral circuits and systems, naval command control and ocean surveillance, signal processing and analysis.

San Jose State University, Graduate Studies and Research, Charles W. Davidson College of Engineering, Department of Electrical Engineering, San Jose, CA 95192-0001. Offers MS. *Students:* 315 full-time (57 women), 245 part-time (43 women); includes 89 minority (5 African Americans, 1 American Indian/Alaska Native, 76 Asian Americans or Pacific Islanders, 7 Hispanic Americans), 420 international. Average age 26. 548 applicants, 60% accepted, 168 enrolled. In 2009, 211 master's awarded. *Degree requirements:* For master's, thesis. *Entrance requirements:* For master's, GRE General Test. *Application deadline:* For fall admission, 6/29 for domestic students; for spring admission, 11/30 for domestic students. Applications are processed on a rolling basis. Application fee: $59. Electronic applications accepted. *Financial support:* Applicants required to submit FAFSA. *Unit head:* Dr. Avtar Singh, Chair, 408-924-3924, Fax: 408-924-3925. *Application contact:* Dr. Avtar Singh, Chair, 408-924-3924, Fax: 408-924-3925.

Santa Clara University, School of Engineering, Department of Electrical Engineering, Santa Clara, CA 95053. Offers analog circuit design (Certificate); ASIC design and test (Certificate); data storage technologies (Certificate); digital signal processing (Certificate); electrical engineering (MS, PhD, Engineer); fundamentals of electrical engineering (Certificate); microwave and antennas (Certificate); telecommunications management (Certificate). Part-time and evening/weekend programs available. *Degree requirements:* For master's, thesis or alternative; for doctorate, thesis/dissertation; for other advanced degree, thesis. *Entrance requirements:* For master's, GRE General Test, minimum GPA of 2.75; for doctorate, GRE General Test, GRE Subject Test, master's degree or equivalent; for other advanced degree, master's degree, published paper. Additional exam requirements/recommendations for international students: Required—TOEFL. Electronic applications accepted. *Expenses:* Contact institution.

South Dakota School of Mines and Technology, Graduate Division, College of Engineering, Department of Electrical and Computer Engineering, Rapid City, SD 57701-3995. Offers electrical engineering (MS). Part-time programs available. *Faculty:* 10 full-time (1 woman), 2 part-time/adjunct (1 woman). *Students:* 9 full-time (1 woman), 4 part-time (0 women), 6 international. Average age 27. 16 applicants, 50% accepted, 2 enrolled. In 2009, 20 master's awarded. *Degree requirements:* For master's, thesis. *Entrance requirements:* Additional exam requirements/recommendations for international students: Required—TOEFL, TWE. *Application deadline:* For fall admission, 7/1 priority date for domestic students, 4/1 for international students; for spring admission, 11/1 for domestic students, 9/1 for international students. Applications are processed on a rolling basis. Application fee: $35. Electronic applications accepted. *Expenses:* Tuition, state resident: full-time $3340; part-time $139 per credit hour. Tuition, nonresident: full-time $7060; part-time $294 per credit hour. Required fees: $3270. *Financial support:* In 2009–10, 2 fellowships (averaging $2,450 per year), 7 research assistantships with partial tuition reimbursements (averaging $13,840 per year), 6 teaching assistantships with partial tuition reimbursements (averaging $4,698 per year) were awarded; Federal Work-Study and institutionally sponsored loans also available. Support available to part-time students. Financial award application deadline: 5/15. *Faculty research:* Semiconductors, systems, digital systems, computers, superconductivity. Total annual research expenditures: $49,294. *Unit head:* Dr. Brian Hemmelman, Chair, 605-394-1219, E-mail: brian.hemmelman@sdsmt.edu. *Application contact:* Jeannette R. Nilson, Administrative Support Coordinator, Graduate Education, 800-454-8162 Ext. 1206, Fax: 605-394-5360, E-mail: graduate_admissions@sdsmt.edu.

South Dakota State University, Graduate School, College of Engineering, Department of Electrical Engineering and Computer Science, Brookings, SD 57007. Offers electrical engineering (PhD); engineering (MS). Part-time programs available. *Degree requirements:* For master's, thesis (for some programs), oral exam; for doctorate, comprehensive exam, thesis/dissertation, oral exam. *Entrance requirements:* For master's and doctorate, GRE. Additional exam requirements/recommendations for international students: Required—TOEFL (minimum score 575 paper-based). *Faculty research:* Image processing, communications, power systems, electronic materials and devices, nanotechnology, photovoltaics.

Southern Illinois University Carbondale, Graduate School, College of Engineering, Department of Electrical and Computer Engineering, Carbondale, IL 62901-4701. Offers MS, PhD. *Degree requirements:* For master's, comprehensive exam, thesis. *Entrance requirements:* For master's, minimum GPA of 2.7. Additional exam requirements/recommendations for international students: Required—TOEFL. *Faculty research:* Circuits and power systems, communications and signal processing, controls and systems, electromagnetics and optics, electronics instrumentation and bioengineering.

Southern Illinois University Carbondale, Graduate School, College of Engineering, Program in Engineering Science, Carbondale, IL 62901-4701. Offers electrical systems (PhD); fossil energy (PhD); mechanics (PhD). *Degree requirements:* For doctorate, thesis/dissertation. *Entrance requirements:* For doctorate, GRE General Test, minimum GPA of 3.5. Additional exam requirements/recommendations for international students: Required—TOEFL.

Southern Illinois University Edwardsville, Graduate Studies and Research, School of Engineering, Department of Electrical and Computer Engineering, Edwardsville, IL 62026-0001. Offers electrical engineering (MS). Part-time and evening/weekend programs available. *Faculty:* 10 full-time (0 women). *Students:* 41 full-time (7 women), 57 part-time (13 women); includes 3 minority (all African Americans), 76 international. Average age 26. 196 applicants, 42% accepted. In 2009, 27 master's awarded. *Degree requirements:* For master's, thesis or research paper, final exam. *Entrance requirements:* For master's, minimum undergraduate GPA of 2.75 in engineering, mathematics, and science courses. Additional exam requirements/recommendations for international students: Required—TOEFL (minimum score 550 paper-based; 213 computer-based; 79 iBT), IELTS (minimum score 6.5). *Application deadline:* For fall admission, 7/23 for domestic students, 6/1 for international students; for spring admission, 12/11 for domestic students, 10/1 for international students. Applications are processed on a rolling basis. Application fee: $30. Electronic applications accepted. *Expenses:* Tuition, state resident: part-time $1252.50 per semester. Tuition, nonresident: part-time $3131.25 per semester. Required fees: $586.85 per semester. Tuition and fees vary according to course load. *Financial support:* In 2009–10, 2 fellowships with full tuition reimbursements (averaging $8,370 per year), 6 research assistantships with full tuition reimbursements (averaging $8,064 per year), 37 teaching assistantships with full tuition reimbursements (averaging $8,064 per year) were awarded; career-related internships or fieldwork, Federal Work-Study, institutionally sponsored loans, scholarships/grants, traineeships, and unspecified assistantships also available. Support available to part-time students. Financial award application deadline: 3/1; financial award applicants required to submit FAFSA. *Unit head:* Dr. Luis Youn, Chair, 618-650-2524, E-mail: lyoun@siue.edu. *Application contact:* Dr. Scott Umbaugh, Program Director, 618-650-2948, E-mail: sumbaug@siue.edu.

Southern Methodist University, Bobby B. Lyle School of Engineering, Department of Electrical Engineering, Dallas, TX 75275-0338. Offers electrical engineering (MSEE, PhD); telecommunications (MS). Part-time and evening/weekend programs available. Postbaccalaureate distance learning degree programs offered (no on-campus study). *Faculty:* 14 full-time (1 woman), 7 part-time/adjunct (1 woman). *Students:* 71 full-time (15 women), 94 part-time (21 women); includes 28 minority (7 African Americans, 15 Asian Americans or Pacific Islanders, 6 Hispanic Americans), 101 international. Average age 28. 270 applicants, 49% accepted, 46 enrolled. In 2009, 52 master's, 5 doctorates awarded. Terminal master's awarded for partial completion of doctoral program. *Degree requirements:* For master's, thesis optional; for doctorate, thesis/dissertation, oral and written qualifying exams, oral final exam. *Entrance requirements:* For master's, GRE General Test, minimum GPA of 3.0 in last 2 years; bachelor's degree in engineering, mathematics, or sciences; for doctorate, preliminary counseling exam, minimum GPA of 3.0, bachelor's degree in related field. Additional exam requirements/recommendations for international students: Required—TOEFL. *Application deadline:* For fall admission, 7/1 priority date for domestic students, 5/15 for international students; for spring admission, 11/15 for domestic students, 9/1 for international students. Applications are processed on a rolling basis. Application fee: $75. Electronic applications accepted. *Financial support:* In 2009–10, 38 students received support, including 22 research assistantships with full tuition reimbursements available (averaging $19,200 per year), 16 teaching assistantships with full tuition reimbursements available (averaging $14,400 per year); unspecified assistantships also available. Financial award application deadline: 5/15; financial award applicants required to submit FAFSA. *Faculty research:* Mobile communications, optical communications, digital signal processing, photonics. *Unit head:* Dr. Marc P. Christensen, Chair, 214-768-3113, Fax: 214-768-3573, E-mail: mpc@lyle.smu.edu. *Application contact:* Marc Valerin, Director of Graduate and Executive Admissions, 214-768-3042, Fax: 214-768-3778, E-mail: valerin@lyle.smu.edu.

Southern Polytechnic State University, School of Engineering Technology and Management, Department of Electrical and Computer Engineering Technology, Marietta, GA 30060-2896. Offers engineering technology/electrical (MS). Part-time and evening/weekend programs available. *Faculty:* 7 full-time (1 woman), 2 part-time/adjunct (0 women). *Students:* 24 full-time (3 women), 6 part-time (1 woman); includes 11 minority (4 African Americans, 1 American Indian/Alaska Native, 5 Asian Americans or Pacific Islanders, 1 Hispanic American), 12 international. Average age 29. 19 applicants, 84% accepted, 12 enrolled. In 2009, 10 master's awarded. *Degree requirements:* For master's, thesis. *Entrance requirements:* For master's, GRE (minimum score 500 quantitative/verbal/analytical), minimum GPA of 2.75. Additional exam requirements/recommendations for international students: Required—TOEFL (minimum score 550 paper-based; 213 computer-based; 79 iBT), IELTS (minimum score 6.5). *Application deadline:* For fall admission, 7/1 priority date for domestic students, 5/1 priority date for international students; for spring admission, 11/1 priority date for domestic students, 9/1 priority date for international students. Applications are processed on a rolling basis. Application fee: $20. Electronic applications accepted. *Expenses:* Tuition, state resident: full-time $2896; part-time $181 per credit hour. Tuition, nonresident: full-time $11,552; part-time $722 per credit hour. Required fees: $1096; $1096 per year. *Financial support:* In 2009–10, 5 students received support, including 4 teaching assistantships with partial tuition reimbursements available (averaging $3,000 per year); career-related internships or fieldwork, scholarships/grants, and unspecified assistantships also available. Support available to part-time students. Financial award application deadline: 5/1; financial award applicants required to submit FAFSA. *Faculty research:* Analog and digital communications, computer networking, analog and low power electronics design, control systems and digital signal processing, instrumentation (medical and industrial). *Unit head:* Dr. Austin Asgill, Chair, 678-915-7796, Fax: 678-915-7285, E-mail: aasgill@spsu.edu. *Application contact:* Nikki A. Palamiotis, Director of Graduate Studies, 678-915-4276, Fax: 678-915-7292, E-mail: npalamio@spsu.edu.

Stanford University, School of Engineering, Department of Electrical Engineering, Stanford, CA 94305-9991. Offers MS, PhD, Eng. Terminal master's awarded for partial completion of doctoral program. *Degree requirements:* For doctorate, thesis/dissertation; for Eng, thesis. *Entrance requirements:* For master's, doctorate, and Eng, GRE General Test. Additional exam requirements/recommendations for international students: Required—TOEFL. Electronic applications accepted. *Expenses:* Tuition: Full-time $37,380; part-time $2760 per quarter. Required fees: $501.

State University of New York at Binghamton, Graduate School, Thomas J. Watson School of Engineering and Applied Science, Department of Electrical and Computer Engineering, Binghamton, NY 13902-6000. Offers M Eng, MS, PhD. Part-time and evening/weekend programs available. *Faculty:* 11 full-time (1 woman), 3 part-time/adjunct (0 women). *Students:* 53 full-time (4 women), 119 part-time (16 women); includes 24 minority (4 African Americans, 14 Asian Americans or Pacific Islanders, 6 Hispanic Americans), 93 international. Average age 27. 230 applicants, 54% accepted, 36 enrolled. In 2009, 36 master's, 3 doctorates awarded. *Degree requirements:* For master's, thesis or alternative; for doctorate, thesis/dissertation. *Entrance requirements:* For master's and doctorate, GRE General Test, GRE Subject Test. Additional exam requirements/recommendations for international students: Required—TOEFL. *Application deadline:* For fall admission, 4/15 priority date for domestic students, 1/15 priority date for international students; for spring admission, 11/1 for domestic students, 10/1 priority date for international students. Applications are processed on a rolling basis. Application fee: $60. Electronic applications accepted. *Financial support:* In 2009–10, 39 students received support, including 1 fellowship with full tuition reimbursement available (averaging $16,500 per year), 18 research assistantships with full tuition reimbursements available (averaging $16,500 per year), 15 teaching assistantships with full tuition reimbursements available (averaging $16,500 per year); career-related internships or fieldwork, Federal Work-Study, institutionally sponsored loans, scholarships/grants, health care benefits, and unspecified assistantships also available. Financial award application deadline: 2/15; financial award applicants required to submit FAFSA. *Unit head:* Dr. Stephen Zahorian, Chairperson, 607-777-4846, E-mail: zahorian@binghamton.edu. *Application contact:* Victoria Williams, Recruiting and Admissions Coordinator, 607-777-2151, Fax: 607-777-2501, E-mail: vwilliam@binghamton.edu.

State University of New York at New Paltz, Graduate School, School of Science and Engineering, Department of Electrical and Computer Engineering, New Paltz, NY 12561. Offers electrical engineering (MS). Part-time and evening/weekend programs available. *Faculty:* 9 full-time (2 women), 3 part-time/adjunct (1 woman). *Students:* 88 full-time (20 women), 29 part-time (4 women); includes 3 minority (all Asian Americans or Pacific Islanders), 104 international. Average age 24. 115 applicants, 63% accepted, 24 enrolled. In 2009, 67 master's awarded. *Degree requirements:* For master's, comprehensive exam, thesis optional. *Entrance requirements:* For master's, GRE General Test, minimum GPA of 3.0. Additional exam requirements/recommendations for international students: Required—TOEFL (minimum score 550 paper-based; 213 computer-based; 80 iBT), IELTS (minimum score 6.5). *Application deadline:* For fall admission, 5/15 priority date for domestic students, 5/15 for international students; for spring admission, 11/15 for domestic and international students. Applications are processed on a rolling basis. Application fee: $50. Electronic applications accepted. *Financial support:* In 2009–10, 11 students received support. Tuition waivers (partial) available. *Unit head:* Dr. Baback Izadi, Chair, 845-257-3823, E-mail: bai@eng.newpaltz.edu. *Application contact:* Caroline Murphy, Graduate Admissions Advisor, 845-257-3285, Fax: 845-257-3284, E-mail: gradschool@newpaltz.edu.

Stevens Institute of Technology, Graduate School, Charles V. Schaefer Jr. School of Engineering, Department of Electrical and Computer Engineering, Program in Electrical Engineering, Hoboken, NJ 07030. Offers computer architecture and digital system design (M Eng); electrical engineering (PhD); microelectronics and photonics science and technology (M Eng); signal processing for communications (M Eng); telecommunications systems engineering (M Eng); wireless communications (M Eng, Certificate). *Degree requirements:* For master's, thesis optional; for doctorate, variable foreign language requirement, thesis/dissertation. *Entrance requirements:* For master's, doctorate, and Certificate, GRE. Additional exam requirements/recommendations for international students: Required—TOEFL. Electronic applications accepted. *Expenses:* Tuition: Full-time $9900; part-time $1100 per credit. Required fees: $286 per semester.

Stevens Institute of Technology, Graduate School, Charles V. Schaefer Jr. School of Engineering, Department of Mechanical Engineering, Program in Integrated Product Development, Hoboken, NJ 07030. Offers armament engineering (M Eng); computer and electrical engineering (M Eng); manufacturing technologies (M Eng); systems reliability and design (M Eng). *Expenses:* Tuition: Full-time $9900; part-time $1100 per credit. Required fees: $286 per semester.

Stevens Institute of Technology, Graduate School, Charles V. Schaefer Jr. School of Engineering, Interdisciplinary Program in Microelectronics and Photonics, Hoboken, NJ 07030. Offers Certificate. *Expenses:* Tuition: Full-time $9900; part-time $1100 per credit. Required fees: $286 per semester.

Stony Brook University, State University of New York, Graduate School, College of Engineering and Applied Sciences, Department of Electrical and Computer Engineering, Program in Electrical Engineering, Stony Brook, NY 11794. Offers MS, PhD. *Expenses:* Tuition, state resident: full-time $8370; part-time $349 per credit. Tuition, nonresident: full-time $13,250; part-time $552 per credit. Required fees: $933.

Syracuse University, L. C. Smith College of Engineering and Computer Science, Program in Electrical and Computer Engineering, Syracuse, NY 13244. Offers PhD. *Students:* 38 full-time (11 women), 8 part-time (1 woman), 39 international. Average age 27. 122 applicants, 12% accepted, 10 enrolled. In 2009, 1 doctorate awarded. *Entrance requirements:* For doctorate, GRE General Test. Additional exam requirements/recommendations for international students: Required—TOEFL (minimum score 100 iBT). *Application deadline:* For fall admission, 6/1 priority date for domestic and international students. Application fee: $75. Electronic applications accepted. *Expenses:* Tuition: Full-time $26,808; part-time $1117 per credit. Required fees: $1024. *Financial support:* Fellowships with full tuition reimbursements, research assistantships with full and partial tuition reimbursements, teaching assistantships with full and partial tuition reimbursements, tuition waivers (partial) available. Financial award application deadline: 1/1. *Application contact:* Heather Paris, Information Contact, 315-443-2368, Fax: 315-443-2583, E-mail: hdparis@syr.edu.

Syracuse University, L. C. Smith College of Engineering and Computer Science, Program in Electrical Engineering, Syracuse, NY 13244. Offers MS, EE. Part-time programs available. *Students:* 68 full-time (15 women), 51 part-time (6 women); includes 6 minority (3 African Americans, 3 Asian Americans or Pacific Islanders), 77 international. Average age 26. 322 applicants, 58% accepted, 34 enrolled. In 2009, 60 master's awarded. *Entrance requirements:* For master's, GRE General Test. Additional exam requirements/recommendations for international students: Required—TOEFL (minimum score 100 iBT). *Application deadline:* For fall admission, 6/1 priority date for domestic and international students. Applications are processed on a rolling basis. Application fee: $75. Electronic applications accepted. *Expenses:* Tuition:

Electrical Engineering

Syracuse University (continued)

Full-time $26,808; part-time $1117 per credit. Required fees: $1024. *Financial support:* Fellowships with full tuition reimbursements, research assistantships with full and partial tuition reimbursements, teaching assistantships with full and partial tuition reimbursements, scholarships/grants and tuition waivers (partial) available. Financial award application deadline: 1/1. *Faculty research:* Electromagnetics, electronic devices, systems. *Unit head:* Dr. Qi Wang Song, Program Director, 315-443-4395, Fax: 315-443-2583, E-mail: qwsong@syr.edu. *Application contact:* Heather Paris, 315-443-2368, Fax: 315-443-2583, E-mail: hdparis@syr.edu.

Syracuse University, L. C. Smith College of Engineering and Computer Science, Program in Microwave Engineering, Syracuse, NY 13244. Offers CAS. Part-time programs available. In 2009, 2 CASs awarded. *Degree requirements:* For CAS, thesis. *Entrance requirements:* For degree, GRE General Test. Additional exam requirements/recommendations for international students: Required—TOEFL (minimum score 100 iBT). *Application deadline:* For fall admission, 6/1 priority date for domestic and international students. Applications are processed on a rolling basis. Application fee: $75. Electronic applications accepted. *Expenses:* Tuition: Full-time $26,808; part-time $1117 per credit. Required fees: $1024. *Financial support:* Fellowships with full tuition reimbursements, research assistantships with full and partial tuition reimbursements, teaching assistantships with full and partial tuition reimbursements, tuition waivers (partial) available. *Faculty research:* Software engineering, parallel and high-performance computing, computer aided design and architectures, coding theory, neural networks. *Unit head:* Chair, 315-443-5807. *Application contact:* Heather Paris, Information Contact, 315-443-2655, Fax: 315-443-2583, E-mail: hdparis@syr.edu.

Temple University, Graduate School, College of Engineering, Department of Electrical and Computer Engineering, Philadelphia, PA 19122-6096. Offers electrical engineering (MSE). Part-time and evening/weekend programs available. *Degree requirements:* For master's, thesis optional. *Entrance requirements:* For master's, GRE General Test, minimum GPA of 3.0. Additional exam requirements/recommendations for international students: Required—TOEFL (minimum score 550 paper-based; 213 computer-based; 79 iBT). Electronic applications accepted. *Faculty research:* Computer engineering, intelligent control, microprocessors, digital processing, neutral networks.

Tennessee Technological University, Graduate School, College of Engineering, Department of Electrical Engineering, Cookeville, TN 38505. Offers MS, PhD. Part-time programs available. *Faculty:* 19 full-time (0 women). *Students:* 35 full-time (10 women), 9 part-time (2 women); includes 34 minority (3 African Americans, 31 Asian Americans or Pacific Islanders). Average age 27. 107 applicants, 59% accepted, 16 enrolled. In 2009, 22 master's awarded. *Degree requirements:* For master's, thesis. *Entrance requirements:* For master's, GRE. Additional exam requirements/recommendations for international students: Required—TOEFL (minimum score 550 paper-based; 79 iBT), IELTS (minimum score 5.5). *Application deadline:* For fall admission, 8/1 for domestic students, 5/1 for international students; for spring admission, 12/1 for domestic students, 10/1 for international students. Application fee: $25 ($30 for international students). Electronic applications accepted. *Expenses:* Tuition, state resident: full-time $7034; part-time $368 per credit hour. *Financial support:* In 2009–10, 1 fellowship (averaging $8,000 per year), 9 research assistantships (averaging $7,650 per year), 15 teaching assistantships (averaging $7,500 per year) were awarded; career-related internships or fieldwork also available. Financial award application deadline: 4/1. *Faculty research:* Control, digital, and power systems. *Unit head:* Dr. Stephen Parke, Chairperson, 931-372-3397, Fax: 931-372-3436. *Application contact:* Shelia K. Kendrick, Coordinator of Graduate Studies, 931-372-3808, Fax: 931-372-3497, E-mail: skendrick@tntech.edu.

Texas A&M University, College of Engineering, Department of Electrical and Computer Engineering, College Station, TX 77843. Offers computer engineering (M Eng, MS, PhD); electrical engineering (MS, PhD). *Faculty:* 64. *Students:* 484 full-time (65 women), 45 part-time (7 women); includes 42 minority (4 African Americans, 1 American Indian/Alaska Native, 19 Asian Americans or Pacific Islanders, 18 Hispanic Americans), 419 international. Average age 28. In 2009, 83 master's, 26 doctorates awarded. *Degree requirements:* For master's, thesis (MS); for doctorate, thesis/dissertation. *Entrance requirements:* For master's and doctorate, GRE General Test. Additional exam requirements/recommendations for international students: Required—TOEFL. Application fee: $50 ($75 for international students). *Expenses:* Tuition, state resident: full-time $3991.32; part-time $221.74 per credit hour. Tuition, nonresident: full-time $9049; part-time $502.74 per credit hour. *Financial support:* Fellowships, research assistantships, teaching assistantships, career-related internships or fieldwork available. Financial award application deadline: 4/1; financial award applicants required to submit FAFSA. *Faculty research:* Solid-state, electric power systems, and communications engineering. *Unit head:* Dr. Scott Miller, Head, 979-845-7441, E-mail: smiller@ece.tamu.edu. *Application contact:* Graduate Advisor, 979-845-7441.

Texas A&M University–Kingsville, College of Graduate Studies, College of Engineering, Department of Electrical Engineering and Computer Science, Program in Electrical Engineering, Kingsville, TX 78363. Offers ME, MS. *Degree requirements:* For master's, comprehensive exam, thesis or alternative. *Entrance requirements:* For master's, GRE General Test, minimum GPA of 3.0. Additional exam requirements/recommendations for international students: Required—TOEFL.

Texas Tech University, Graduate School, College of Engineering, Department of Electrical and Computer Engineering, Lubbock, TX 79409. Offers electrical engineering (MSEE, PhD). Part-time programs available. *Faculty:* 18 full-time (4 women), 3 part-time/adjunct (0 women). *Students:* 142 full-time (29 women), 25 part-time (7 women); includes 8 minority (2 African Americans, 1 Asian American or Pacific Islander, 5 Hispanic Americans), 109 international. Average age 24. 562 applicants, 27% accepted, 39 enrolled. In 2009, 47 master's, 5 doctorates awarded. *Degree requirements:* For master's, thesis or alternative; for doctorate, thesis/dissertation. *Entrance requirements:* For master's and doctorate, GRE General Test, minimum GPA of 3.0. Additional exam requirements/recommendations for international students: Required—TOEFL (minimum score 550 paper-based; 213 computer-based). *Application deadline:* For fall admission, 3/1 priority date for international students; for spring admission, 11/1 priority date for international students. Applications are processed on a rolling basis. Application fee: $50 ($75 for international students). Electronic applications accepted. *Expenses:* Tuition, state resident: full-time $5100; part-time $213 per credit hour. Tuition, nonresident: full-time $11,748; part-time $490 per credit hour. Required fees: $2298; $50 per credit hour. $555 per semester. *Financial support:* In 2009–10, 72 research assistantships with partial tuition reimbursements (averaging $26,944 per year), 27 teaching assistantships with partial tuition reimbursements (averaging $12,170 per year) were awarded; Federal Work-Study and institutionally sponsored loans also available. Support available to part-time students. Financial award application deadline: 4/15; financial award applicants required to submit FAFSA. *Faculty research:* Computer vision in image processing, pulsed power, power electronics, nanotechnology, advanced vehicle engineering. Total annual research expenditures: $592,183. *Unit head:* Dr. Vittal Rao, Chair, 806-742-3533, Fax: 806-742-1245, E-mail: vittal.rao@ttu.edu. *Application contact:* Dr. Vittal Rao, Chair, 806-742-3533, Fax: 806-742-1245, E-mail: vittal.rao@ttu.edu.

Tufts University, Graduate School of Arts and Sciences, Graduate Certificate Programs, Microwave and Wireless Engineering Program, Medford, MA 02155. Offers Certificate. Part-time and evening/weekend programs available. Electronic applications accepted. *Expenses:* Tuition: Full-time $38,096; part-time $3962 per credit. Required fees: $686; $40 per year. Tuition and fees vary according to course level, course load, degree level, program and student level.

Tufts University, School of Engineering, Department of Electrical and Computer Engineering, Medford, MA 02155. Offers electrical engineering (MS, PhD). Part-time programs available. *Faculty:* 13 full-time, 3 part-time/adjunct. *Students:* 56 (15 women); includes 6 minority (1 African American, 4 Asian Americans or Pacific Islanders, 1 Hispanic American), 16 international. Average age 27. 109 applicants, 31% accepted, 12 enrolled. In 2009, 9 master's, 6 doctorates awarded. Terminal master's awarded for partial completion of doctoral program. *Degree requirements:* For master's, thesis or alternative; for doctorate, thesis/dissertation. *Entrance requirements:* For master's and doctorate, GRE General Test. Additional exam requirements/recommendations for international students: Required—TOEFL (minimum score 550 paper-based; 213 computer-based; 80 iBT). *Application deadline:* For fall admission, 1/15 priority date for domestic students, 12/15 for international students; for spring admission, 10/15 for domestic students, 9/15 for international students. Applications are processed on a rolling basis. Application fee: $75. Electronic applications accepted. *Expenses:* Tuition: Full-time $38,096; part-time $3962 per credit. Required fees: $686; $40 per year. Tuition and fees vary according to course level, course load, degree level, program and student level. *Financial support:* Fellowships with full tuition reimbursements, research assistantships with full and partial tuition reimbursements, teaching assistantships with full and partial tuition reimbursements, Federal Work-Study, scholarships/grants, tuition waivers (partial), and unspecified assistantships available. Financial award application deadline: 2/1; financial award applicants required to submit FAFSA. *Unit head:* Jeffrey Hopwood, Chair, 617-627-3217, Fax: 617-627-3220. *Application contact:* Eric Miller, Graduate Advisor, 617-627-3217.

Tuskegee University, Graduate Programs, College of Engineering, Architecture and Physical Sciences, Department of Electrical Engineering, Tuskegee, AL 36088. Offers MSEE. *Faculty:* 8 full-time (0 women). *Students:* 36 full-time (12 women), 1 part-time (0 women); includes 20 minority (19 African Americans, 1 Asian American or Pacific Islander), 13 international. Average age 26. In 2009, 4 master's awarded. *Degree requirements:* For master's, thesis or alternative. *Entrance requirements:* For master's, GRE General Test, GRE Subject Test. Additional exam requirements/recommendations for international students: Required—TOEFL (minimum score 500 paper-based; 69 computer-based). *Application deadline:* For fall admission, 7/15 for domestic students. Applications are processed on a rolling basis. Application fee: $25 ($35 for international students). *Expenses:* Tuition: Full-time $15,630; part-time $940 per credit hour. Required fees: $650. *Financial support:* Fellowships, research assistantships, teaching assistantships, career-related internships or fieldwork, Federal Work-Study, and institutionally sponsored loans available. Support available to part-time students. Financial award application deadline: 4/15. *Faculty research:* Photovoltaic insulation, automatic guidance and control, wind energy. *Unit head:* Dr. Sammie Giles, Director, 334-727-8298. *Application contact:* Dr. Robert L. Laney, Vice President/Director of Admissions and Enrollment Management, 334-727-8580, Fax: 334-727-5750, E-mail: planey@tuskegee.edu.

Union Graduate College, School of Engineering and Computer Science, Schenectady, NY 12308-3107. Offers computer science (MS); electrical engineering (MS); engineering and management systems (MS); mechanical engineering (MS). Part-time and evening/weekend programs available. *Faculty:* 24 part-time/adjunct (1 woman). *Students:* 10 full-time (0 women), 60 part-time (7 women); includes 5 minority (1 African American, 1 American Indian/Alaska Native, 2 Asian Americans or Pacific Islanders, 1 Hispanic American), 5 international. Average age 27. 47 applicants, 55% accepted, 25 enrolled. In 2009, 28 master's awarded. *Degree requirements:* For master's, capstone course. *Entrance requirements:* For master's, minimum GPA of 3.0, letters of recommendation. Additional exam requirements/recommendations for international students: Required—TOEFL (minimum score 550 paper-based; 213 computer-based). *Application deadline:* Applications are processed on a rolling basis. Application fee: $60. Electronic applications accepted. *Expenses:* Contact institution. *Financial support:* Research assistantships, Federal Work-Study, scholarships/grants, health care benefits, and tuition waivers (full and partial) available. Support available to part-time students. Financial award applicants required to submit FAFSA. *Unit head:* Robert Kozik, Dean, 515-631-9881, Fax: 518-631-9902, E-mail: kozikr@union.edu. *Application contact:* Diane Trzaskos, Coordinator, Admissions, 518-631-9837, Fax: 518-631-9901, E-mail: trzaskod@uniongraduatecollege.edu.

Universidad de las Américas–Puebla, Division of Graduate Studies, School of Engineering, Program in Electronic Engineering, Puebla, Mexico. Offers MS. Part-time and evening/weekend programs available. *Faculty research:* Telecommunications, data processing, digital systems.

Université de Moncton, Faculty of Engineering, Program in Electrical Engineering, Moncton, NB E1A 3E9, Canada. Offers M Sc A. *Degree requirements:* For master's, thesis, proficiency in French. *Faculty research:* Telecommunications, electronics and instrumentation, analog and digital electronics, electronic control of machines, energy systems, electronic design.

Université de Sherbrooke, Faculty of Engineering, Department of Electrical Engineering and Computer Engineering, Sherbrooke, QC J1K 2R1, Canada. Offers electrical engineering (M Sc A, PhD). *Degree requirements:* For master's, one foreign language, thesis; for doctorate, comprehensive exam, thesis/dissertation. *Entrance requirements:* For master's, bachelor's degree in engineering or equivalent. Electronic applications accepted. *Faculty research:* Minielectronics, biomedical engineering, digital signal prolonging and telecommunications, software engineering and artificial intelligence.

Université du Québec à Trois-Rivières, Graduate Programs, Program in Electrical Engineering, Trois-Rivières, QC G9A 5H7, Canada. Offers M Sc A, PhD. Part-time programs available. *Degree requirements:* For master's, thesis; for doctorate, thesis/dissertation. *Entrance requirements:* For master's, appropriate bachelor's degree, proficiency in French; for doctorate, appropriate master's degree, proficiency in French. *Faculty research:* Industrial electronics.

Université Laval, Faculty of Sciences and Engineering, Department of Electrical and Computer Engineering, Programs in Electrical Engineering, Québec, QC G1K 7P4, Canada. Offers M Sc, PhD. Terminal master's awarded for partial completion of doctoral program. *Degree requirements:* For master's, thesis (for some programs); for doctorate, thesis/dissertation. *Entrance requirements:* For master's and doctorate, knowledge of French and English. Electronic applications accepted.

University at Buffalo, the State University of New York, Graduate School, School of Engineering and Applied Sciences, Department of Electrical Engineering, Buffalo, NY 14260. Offers M Eng, MS, PhD. Part-time programs available. *Faculty:* 26 full-time (4 women), 3 part-time/adjunct (1 woman). *Students:* 233 full-time (50 women), 24 part-time (2 women); includes 16 minority (7 African Americans, 8 Asian Americans or Pacific Islanders, 1 Hispanic American), 207 international. Average age 27. 1,107 applicants, 28% accepted, 113 enrolled. In 2009, 55 master's, 6 doctorates awarded. Terminal master's awarded for partial completion of doctoral program. *Degree requirements:* For master's, comprehensive exam (for some programs), thesis or exam; for doctorate, comprehensive exam, thesis/dissertation. *Entrance requirements:* For master's and doctorate, GRE General Test. Additional exam requirements/recommendations for international students: Required—TOEFL (minimum score 550 paper-based; 213 computer-based; 79 iBT). *Application deadline:* For fall admission, 12/31 for domestic and international students; for spring admission, 8/31 for domestic and international students. Applications are processed on a rolling basis. Application fee: $50. Electronic applications accepted. *Financial support:* In 2009–10, 57 students received support, including 9 fellowships with full tuition reimbursements available (averaging $28,900 per year), 25 research assistantships with full tuition reimbursements available (averaging $24,000 per year), 26 teaching assistantships with full tuition reimbursements available (averaging $20,900 per year); career-related internships or fieldwork, Federal Work-Study, institutionally sponsored loans, tuition waivers (full and partial), and unspecified assistantships also available. Financial award application deadline: 2/1; financial award applicants required to submit FAFSA. *Faculty research:* High power electronics and plasmas, electronic materials signal and image processing, photonics and communications, optics, nanoelectronics. Total annual research expenditures: $3.2 million. *Unit head:* Dr. Alexander N. Cartwright, Chairman, 716-645-3115, Fax: 716-645-3656, E-mail: anc@buffalo.edu. *Application contact:* Dr. Wayne A. Anderson, Director of Graduate Admissions, 716-645-1031, Fax: 716-645-3656, E-mail: eegradapply@buffalo.edu.

The University of Akron, Graduate School, College of Engineering, Department of Electrical and Computer Engineering, Akron, OH 44325. Offers MS, PhD. Evening/weekend programs available. *Faculty:* 16 full-time (1 woman), 4 part-time/adjunct (0 women). *Students:* 44 full-time

(9 women), 10 part-time (3 women); includes 1 minority (Asian American or Pacific Islander), 39 international. Average age 25. 148 applicants, 27% accepted, 21 enrolled. In 2009, 4 master's, 4 doctorates awarded. *Degree requirements:* For master's, oral comprehensive exam or thesis; for doctorate, one foreign language, thesis/dissertation, candidacy exam, qualifying exam. *Entrance requirements:* For master's, GRE, minimum GPA of 2.75, letters of recommendation; for doctorate, GRE, minimum GPA of 3.0 with bachelor's degree, 3.5 with master's degree; letters of recommendation; personal statement. Additional exam requirements/recommendations for international students: Required—TOEFL (minimum score 550 paper-based; 213 computer-based; 79 iBT). *Application deadline:* Applications are processed on a rolling basis. Application fee: $30 ($40 for international students). Electronic applications accepted. *Expenses:* Tuition, state resident: full-time $6570; part-time $365 per credit hour. Tuition, nonresident: full-time $11,250; part-time $625 per credit hour. *Financial support:* In 2009–10, 8 research assistantships with full tuition reimbursements, 34 teaching assistantships with full tuition reimbursements were awarded; career-related internships or fieldwork also available. *Faculty research:* Computational electromagnetics and nondestructive testing, control systems, sensors and actuators applications and networks, alternative energy systems and hybrid vehicles, analog IC design embedded systems. Total annual research expenditures: $446,688. *Unit head:* Dr. Jose De Abreu-Garcia, Chair, 330-972-6709, E-mail: jdeabreu-garcia@uakron.edu. *Application contact:* Dr. Jose De Abreu-Garcia, Chair, 330-972-6709, E-mail: jdeabreu-garcia@uakron.edu.

The University of Alabama, Graduate School, College of Engineering, Department of Electrical and Computer Engineering, Tuscaloosa, AL 35487-0286. Offers electrical engineering (MS, PhD). Part-time programs available. Postbaccalaureate distance learning degree programs offered (minimal on-campus study). *Faculty:* 14 full-time (4 women). *Students:* 39 full-time (6 women), 6 part-time (4 women); includes 1 minority (Asian American or Pacific Islander), 30 international. Average age 26. 81 applicants, 27% accepted, 8 enrolled. In 2009, 12 master's, 2 doctorates awarded. *Median time to degree:* Of those who began their doctoral program in fall 2001, 80% received their degree in 8 years or less. *Degree requirements:* For master's, thesis or alternative; for doctorate, one foreign language, comprehensive exam, thesis/dissertation. *Entrance requirements:* For master's, GRE (for students from non ABET accredited schools), minimum GPA of 3.0 in last 60 hours of course work or overall; for doctorate, GRE (for students from non ABET-accredited schools), minimum GPA of 3.0 overall. Additional exam requirements/recommendations for international students: Required—TOEFL (minimum score 550 paper-based; 213 computer-based). *Application deadline:* For fall admission, 7/1 priority date for domestic students, 1/15 priority date for international students; for spring admission, 11/1 priority date for domestic students, 6/1 priority date for international students. Applications are processed on a rolling basis. Application fee: $50 ($60 for international students). Electronic applications accepted. *Expenses:* Tuition, state resident: full-time $7000. Tuition, nonresident: full-time $19,200. *Financial support:* In 2009–10, 1 fellowship with full tuition reimbursement (averaging $15,000 per year), 14 research assistantships with full tuition reimbursements (averaging $14,000 per year), 6 teaching assistantships with full tuition reimbursements (averaging $11,025 per year) were awarded; health care benefits and unspecified assistantships also available. *Faculty research:* Devices and materials, electromechanical systems, embedded systems. Total annual research expenditures: $783,506. *Unit head:* Dr. D. Jeff Jackson, Department Head, 205-348-2919, Fax: 205-348-6959, E-mail: jjackson@eng.ua.edu. *Application contact:* Dr. Tim Haskew, Graduate Program Director, 205-348-1766, Fax: 205-348-6959, E-mail: thaskew@eng.ua.edu.

The University of Alabama at Birmingham, School of Engineering, Program in Electrical Engineering, Birmingham, AL 35294. Offers MSEE.

The University of Alabama in Huntsville, School of Graduate Studies, College of Engineering, Department of Electrical and Computer Engineering, Huntsville, AL 35899. Offers computer engineering (MSE, PhD); electrical engineering (MSE, PhD); optical science and engineering (PhD); optics and photonics (MSE); software engineering (MSSE). Part-time and evening/weekend programs available. *Faculty:* 22 full-time (2 women), 3 part-time/adjunct (0 women). *Students:* 42 full-time (10 women), 147 part-time (18 women); includes 16 minority (7 African Americans, 6 Asian Americans or Pacific Islanders, 3 Hispanic Americans), 28 international. Average age 31. 205 applicants, 53% accepted, 58 enrolled. In 2009, 53 master's, 4 doctorates awarded. *Degree requirements:* For master's, comprehensive exam, thesis or alternative, oral and written exams; for doctorate, comprehensive exam, thesis/dissertation, oral and written exams. *Entrance requirements:* For master's, GRE General Test, appropriate bachelor's degree, minimum GPA of 3.0; for doctorate, GRE General Test, minimum GPA of 3.0. Additional exam requirements/recommendations for international students: Required—TOEFL (minimum score 500 paper-based; 173 computer-based; 62 iBT). *Application deadline:* For fall admission, 7/15 for domestic students, 4/1 for international students; for spring admission, 11/30 for domestic students, 9/1 for international students. Applications are processed on a rolling basis. Application fee: $40 ($50 for international students). Electronic applications accepted. *Expenses:* Tuition, state resident: part-time $355.75 per credit hour. Tuition, nonresident: part-time $847.10 per credit hour. Required fees: $210.80 per semester. Tuition and fees vary according to course load and program. *Financial support:* In 2009–10, 28 students received support, including 11 research assistantships with full and partial tuition reimbursements available (averaging $11,113 per year), 16 teaching assistantships with full and partial tuition reimbursements available (averaging $10,479 per year); career-related internships or fieldwork, Federal Work-Study, institutionally sponsored loans, scholarships/grants, health care benefits, tuition waivers, and unspecified assistantships also available. Support available to part-time students. Financial award application deadline: 4/1; financial award applicants required to submit FAFSA. *Faculty research:* Optical signal processing, electromagnetics, photonics, nonlinear waves, computer architecture. Total annual research expenditures: $3.4 million. *Unit head:* Dr. Reza Adhami, Chair, 256-824-6316, Fax: 256-824-6803, E-mail: adhami@ece.uah.edu. *Application contact:* Kathy Biggs, Graduate Studies Admissions Manager, 256-824-6199, Fax: 256-824-6405, E-mail: deangrad@uah.edu.

University of Alaska Fairbanks, College of Engineering and Mines, Department of Electrical and Computer Engineering, Fairbanks, AK 99775-5915. Offers electrical engineering (MEE, MS, PhD); engineering (PhD). Part-time programs available. *Faculty:* 7 full-time (2 women). *Students:* 14 full-time (3 women), 2 part-time (1 woman), 10 international. Average age 29. 11 applicants, 36% accepted, 4 enrolled. In 2009, 5 master's awarded. Terminal master's awarded for partial completion of doctoral program. *Degree requirements:* For master's, comprehensive exam, thesis or alternative; for doctorate, comprehensive exam, thesis/dissertation, oral exam, oral defense. *Entrance requirements:* For master's and doctorate, GRE General Test. Additional exam requirements/recommendations for international students: Required—TOEFL (minimum score 550 paper-based; 213 computer-based; 80 iBT). *Application deadline:* For fall admission, 6/1 for domestic students, 3/1 for international students; for spring admission, 10/15 for domestic students, 9/1 for international students. Applications are processed on a rolling basis. Application fee: $60. Electronic applications accepted. *Expenses:* Tuition, state resident: full-time $7584; part-time $316 per credit. Tuition, nonresident: full-time $15,504; part-time $646 per credit. Required fees: $23 per credit. $135 per semester. Tuition and fees vary according to course level, course load and reciprocity agreements. *Financial support:* In 2009–10, 2 fellowships (averaging $6,749 per year), 6 research assistantships (averaging $15,656 per year), 2 teaching assistantships (averaging $8,087 per year) were awarded; career-related internships or fieldwork, Federal Work-Study, scholarships/grants, health care benefits, and unspecified assistantships also available. Support available to part-time students. Financial award application deadline: 7/1; financial award applicants required to submit FAFSA. *Faculty research:* Geomagnetically-induced currents in power lines, electromagnetic wave propagation, laser radar systems, bioinformatics, distributed sensor networks. *Unit head:* Dr. Charles Mayer, Chair, 907-474-7137, Fax: 907-474-5135, E-mail: fyee@uaf.edu. *Application contact:* Dr. Charles Mayer, Chair, 907-474-7137, Fax: 907-474-5135, E-mail: fyee@uaf.edu.

University of Alberta, Faculty of Graduate Studies and Research, Department of Electrical and Computer Engineering, Edmonton, AB T6G 2E1, Canada. Offers communications (M Eng, M Sc, PhD); computer engineering (M Eng, M Sc, PhD); electromagnetics (M Eng, M Sc, PhD); nanotechnology and microdevices (M Eng, M Sc, PhD); power/power electronics (M Eng, M Sc, PhD); systems (M Eng, M Sc, PhD). *Faculty:* 42 full-time (3 women), 12 part-time/adjunct (0 women). *Students:* 252 full-time (28 women), 65 part-time (10 women). Average age 26. 1,500 applicants, 5% accepted.Terminal master's awarded for partial completion of doctoral program. *Degree requirements:* For master's, thesis; for doctorate, thesis/dissertation. *Entrance requirements:* Additional exam requirements/recommendations for international students: Required—TOEFL. *Application deadline:* For fall admission, 4/30 for domestic students; for winter admission, 8/30 for domestic students. Applications are processed on a rolling basis. Application fee: $0 Canadian dollars. Electronic applications accepted. Tuition and fees charges are reported in Canadian dollars. *Expenses:* Tuition, area resident: Full-time $4626.24 Canadian dollars; part-time $99.72 Canadian dollars per unit. International tuition: $8216 Canadian dollars full-time. Required fees: $3589.92 Canadian dollars; $99.72 Canadian dollars per unit. $215 Canadian dollars per term. *Financial support:* In 2009–10, 80 students received support; fellowships, research assistantships, teaching assistantships, scholarships/grants available. *Faculty research:* Controls, communications, microelectronics, electromagnetics. Total annual research expenditures: $3 million Canadian dollars. *Unit head:* Dr. H. J. Marquez, Chair, 780-492-0161, Fax: 780-492-1811. *Application contact:* Michelle Vaage, Graduate Student Advisor, 780-492-0161, Fax: 780-492-1811, E-mail: gradinfo@ece.ualberta.ca.

The University of Arizona, Graduate College, College of Engineering, Department of Electrical and Computer Engineering, Tucson, AZ 85721. Offers M Eng, MS, PhD. Part-time programs available. *Faculty:* 34. *Students:* 114 full-time (20 women), 59 part-time (10 women); includes 11 minority (8 Asian Americans or Pacific Islanders, 3 Hispanic Americans), 126 international. Average age 30. 514 applicants, 23% accepted, 38 enrolled. In 2009, 19 master's, 16 doctorates awarded. *Degree requirements:* For master's, thesis (for some programs); for doctorate, thesis/dissertation. *Entrance requirements:* For master's, GRE General Test, 3 letters of recommendation, statement of purpose; for doctorate, GRE General Test, master's degree in related field, 3 letters of recommendation, statement of purpose. Additional exam requirements/recommendations for international students: Required—TOEFL (minimum score 550 paper-based; 213 computer-based; 79 iBT). *Application deadline:* For fall admission, 12/15 for domestic and international students; for spring admission, 7/15 for domestic and international students. Applications are processed on a rolling basis. Application fee: $75. Electronic applications accepted. *Expenses:* Tuition, state resident: full-time $9028. Tuition, nonresident: full-time $24,890. *Financial support:* In 2009–10, 48 research assistantships with full tuition reimbursements (averaging $18,695 per year), 12 teaching assistantships with full tuition reimbursements (averaging $17,970 per year) were awarded; institutionally sponsored loans, scholarships/grants, health care benefits, and unspecified assistantships also available. Financial award application deadline: 3/15. *Faculty research:* Communication systems, control systems, signal processing, computer-aided logic. Total annual research expenditures: $7.1 million. *Unit head:* Dr. Jerzy W. Rozenblit, Head, 520-621-6193, E-mail: head@ece.arizona.edu. *Application contact:* Tami J. Whelan, Senior Graduate Academic Adviser, 520-621-6195, Fax: 520-621-8076, E-mail: whelan@ece.arizona.edu.

University of Arkansas, Graduate School, College of Engineering, Department of Electrical Engineering, Program in Electrical Engineering, Fayetteville, AR 72701-1201. Offers MSEE, PhD. *Students:* 24 full-time (0 women), 58 part-time (5 women); includes 2 minority (both African Americans), 56 international. In 2009, 15 master's, 5 doctorates awarded. *Entrance requirements:* For master's and doctorate, GRE General Test. Application fee: $40 ($50 for international students). *Expenses:* Tuition, state resident: full-time $7355; part-time $356.58 per hour. Tuition, nonresident: full-time $17,401; part-time $775.17 per hour. Required fees: $1203. *Financial support:* In 2009–10, 10 fellowships with tuition reimbursements, 52 research assistantships, 4 teaching assistantships were awarded. Financial award application deadline: 4/1. *Unit head:* Dr. Juan Balda, Department Chair, 479-575-3005, E-mail: jbalda@uark.edu. *Application contact:* Dr. Randy Brown, Graduate Coordinator, 479-575-6581, E-mail: rlb02@uark.edu.

University of Bridgeport, School of Engineering, Department of Electrical Engineering, Bridgeport, CT 06604. Offers MS. Part-time and evening/weekend programs available. *Degree requirements:* For master's, thesis optional. *Entrance requirements:* Additional exam requirements/recommendations for international students: Recommended—TOEFL (minimum score 550 paper-based; 213 computer-based; 80 iBT), IELTS (minimum score 6.5). Electronic applications accepted.

The University of British Columbia, Faculty of Applied Science, Program in Electrical and Computer Engineering, Vancouver, BC V6T 1Z1, Canada. Offers M Eng, MA Sc, PhD. Part-time programs available. *Degree requirements:* For master's, thesis (for some programs); for doctorate, thesis/dissertation. *Entrance requirements:* Additional exam requirements/recommendations for international students: Required—TOEFL (minimum score 600 paper-based; 250 computer-based; 100 iBT), TWE. Electronic applications accepted. *Faculty research:* Applied electromagnetics, biomedical engineering, communications and signal processing, computer and software engineering, power engineering, robotics, solid-state, systems and control.

University of Calgary, Faculty of Graduate Studies, Schulich School of Engineering, Department of Electrical and Computer Engineering, Calgary, AB T2N 1N4, Canada. Offers M Eng, M Sc, PhD. Part-time programs available. *Degree requirements:* For master's, thesis (M Sc); for doctorate, thesis/dissertation, candidacy exam. *Entrance requirements:* For master's and doctorate, minimum GPA of 3.0. Additional exam requirements/recommendations for international students: Required—TOEFL (minimum score 550 paper-based; 213 computer-based), IELTS (minimum score 7), TOEFL or IELTS. Electronic applications accepted. *Faculty research:* Biomedical and bioelectrics, telecommunications and signal processing, software and computer engineering, power and control, microelectronics and instrumentation.

University of California, Berkeley, Graduate Division, College of Engineering, Department of Electrical Engineering and Computer Sciences, Berkeley, CA 94720-1500. Offers computer science (MS, PhD); electrical engineering (MS, PhD). *Students:* 534 full-time (68 women). Average age 27. 2,789 applicants, 94 enrolled. In 2009, 60 master's, 70 doctorates awarded. *Degree requirements:* For master's, comprehensive exam or thesis; for doctorate, thesis/dissertation, qualifying exam. *Entrance requirements:* For master's and doctorate, GRE General Test, minimum GPA of 3.0, 3 letters of recommendation. Additional exam requirements/recommendations for international students: Required—TOEFL. *Application deadline:* For fall admission, 12/15 for domestic students. Application fee: $70 ($90 for international students). Electronic applications accepted. *Financial support:* Fellowships, research assistantships, teaching assistantships, scholarships/grants and unspecified assistantships available. *Unit head:* Prof. Stuart Russell, Chair, 510-642-3214, E-mail: eecs-chair@eecs.berkeley.edu. *Application contact:* Admission Assistant, 510-642-3068, Fax: 510-642-7644, E-mail: gradadmissions@eecs.berkeley.edu.

University of California, Davis, College of Engineering, Program in Electrical and Computer Engineering, Davis, CA 95616. Offers MS, PhD. Terminal master's awarded for partial completion of doctoral program. *Degree requirements:* For master's, comprehensive exam (for some programs), thesis (for some programs); for doctorate, thesis/dissertation, preliminary and qualifying exams, thesis defense. *Entrance requirements:* For master's, GRE General Test, minimum GPA of 3.2; for doctorate, GRE, minimum graduate GPA of 3.5. Additional exam requirements/recommendations for international students: Required—TOEFL (minimum score 550 paper-based; 213 computer-based). Electronic applications accepted.

University of California, Irvine, Office of Graduate Studies, School of Engineering, Department of Electrical Engineering and Computer Science, Irvine, CA 92697. Offers electrical engineering and computer science (MS, PhD); networked systems (MS, PhD). Part-time programs available. *Students:* 224 full-time (34 women), 28 part-time (3 women); includes 42 minority (1 African American, 40 Asian Americans or Pacific Islanders, 1 Hispanic American), 168 international. Average age 29. 1,116 applicants, 16% accepted, 67 enrolled. In 2009, 47 master's, 18 doctorates awarded. Terminal master's awarded for partial completion of doctoral program.

Electrical Engineering

University of California, Irvine (continued)

Degree requirements: For doctorate, thesis/dissertation. *Entrance requirements:* For master's and doctorate, GRE General Test, minimum GPA of 3.0, 3 letters of recommendation. Additional exam requirements/recommendations for international students: Required—TOEFL (minimum score 550 paper-based; 213 computer-based). *Application deadline:* For fall admission, 1/15 priority date for domestic students, 1/15 for international students. Applications are processed on a rolling basis. Application fee: $70 ($90 for international students). Electronic applications accepted. *Financial support:* In 2009–10, fellowships (averaging $14,656 per year); research assistantships with full tuition reimbursements, teaching assistantships, institutionally sponsored loans, traineeships, health care benefits, and unspecified assistantships also available. Financial award application deadline:-3/1; financial award applicants required to submit FAFSA. *Faculty research:* Optics and electronic devices and circuits, signal processing, communications, machine vision, power electronics. *Unit head:* Dr. Jean-Luc Gaudiot, Chair, 949-824-5689, Fax: 949-824-3779, E-mail: gaudiot@uci.edu. *Application contact:* Ronnie A. Gran, Graduate Admissions Coordinator, 949-824-5489, Fax: 949-824-1853, E-mail: ragran@uci.edu.

University of California, Los Angeles, Graduate Division, Henry Samueli School of Engineering and Applied Science, Department of Electrical Engineering, Los Angeles, CA 90095-1594. Offers electrical engineering (MS, PhD). *Faculty:* 47 full-time (4 women). *Students:* 371 full-time (38 women); includes 96 minority (2 African Americans, 88 Asian Americans or Pacific Islanders, 6 Hispanic Americans), 210 international. 1,147 applicants, 29% accepted, 103 enrolled. In 2009, 70 master's, 39 doctorates awarded. *Degree requirements:* For master's, comprehensive exam or thesis; for doctorate, thesis/dissertation, qualifying exams. *Entrance requirements:* For master's, GRE General Test, minimum GPA of 3.0; for doctorate, GRE General Test, minimum GPA of 3.25. Additional exam requirements/recommendations for international students: Required—TOEFL (minimum score 560 paper-based; 220 computer-based). *Application deadline:* For fall admission, 12/15 for domestic and international students. Application fee: $70 ($90 for international students). Electronic applications accepted. *Financial support:* In 2009–10, 151 fellowships, 414 research assistantships, 104 teaching assistantships were awarded; career-related internships or fieldwork, Federal Work-Study, institutionally sponsored loans, and tuition waivers (full and partial) also available. Financial award application deadline: 1/15; financial award applicants required to submit FAFSA. Total annual research expenditures: $20.1 million. *Unit head:* Dr. Ali Sayed, Chair, 310-206-1655. *Application contact:* Deeona Columbia, Student Affairs Officer, 310-825-7574, E-mail: deeona@ea.ucla.edu.

University of California, Merced, Division of Graduate Studies, School of Engineering, Merced, CA 95343. Offers electrical engineering and computer science (MS, PhD). *Expenses:* Tuition, nonresident: full-time $15,102. Required fees: $10,919.

University of California, Riverside, Graduate Division, Department of Electrical Engineering, Riverside, CA 92521-0102. Offers electrical engineering (MS, PhD), including computer engineering, control and robotics, intelligent systems, nano-materials, devices and circuits, signal processing and communications. Terminal master's awarded for partial completion of doctoral program. *Degree requirements:* For master's, thesis optional; for doctorate, thesis/dissertation, qualifying exams. *Entrance requirements:* For master's and doctorate, GRE General Test, minimum GPA of 3.25. Additional exam requirements/recommendations for international students: Required—TOEFL (minimum score 550 paper-based; 213 computer-based; 80 iBT). Electronic applications accepted. *Faculty research:* Solid state devices, integrated circuits, signal processing.

See Close-Up on page 375.

University of California, San Diego, Office of Graduate Studies, Department of Electrical and Computer Engineering, La Jolla, CA 92093. Offers applied ocean science (MS, PhD); applied physics (MS, PhD); communication theory and systems (MS, PhD); computer engineering (MS, PhD); electrical engineering (M Eng); electronic circuits and systems (MS, PhD); intelligent systems, robotics and control (MS, PhD); photonics (MS, PhD); signal and image processing (MS, PhD). MS only offered to students who have been admitted to the PhD program. *Entrance requirements:* For master's and doctorate, GRE General Test. Electronic applications accepted.

University of California, Santa Barbara, Graduate Division, College of Engineering, Department of Electrical and Computer Engineering, Santa Barbara, CA 93106-9560. Offers computational science and engineering (PhD); electrical and computer engineering (PhD); MS/PhD. *Faculty:* 39 full-time (3 women), 1 part-time/adjunct (0 women). *Students:* 277 full-time (52 women). Average age 26. 1,135 applicants, 19% accepted, 50 enrolled. In 2009, 58 master's, 26 doctorates awarded. Terminal master's awarded for partial completion of doctoral program. *Degree requirements:* For master's, comprehensive exam, thesis; for doctorate, thesis/dissertation, screening exam, qualifying exam, dissertation defense exam. *Entrance requirements:* For master's, GRE General Test, 3 letters of recommendation, resume/curriculum vitae; for doctorate, GRE General Test, 3 letters of recommendation, statement of purpose, personal achievements/contributions statement, resume/curriculum vitae, transcripts for post-secondary institutions attended. Additional exam requirements/recommendations for international students: Required—TOEFL (minimum score 550 paper-based; 213 computer-based; 80 iBT) or IELTS (minimum score 7). *Application deadline:* For fall admission, 12/15 for domestic and international students; for winter admission, 11/1 for domestic and international students; for spring admission, 1/1 for domestic and international students. Application fee: $70 ($90 for international students). Electronic applications accepted. *Financial support:* In 2009–10, 209 students received support, including 52 fellowships with full and partial tuition reimbursements available (averaging $8,600 per year), 163 research assistantships with full and partial tuition reimbursements available (averaging $12,100 per year), 54 teaching assistantships with partial tuition reimbursements available (averaging $7,400 per year); career-related internships or fieldwork, Federal Work-Study, institutionally sponsored loans, scholarships/grants, traineeships, health care benefits, tuition waivers (full and partial), and unspecified assistantships also available. Financial award application deadline: 12/15; financial award applicants required to submit FAFSA. *Faculty research:* Communications, signal processing, computer engineering, control, electronics and photonics. Total annual research expenditures: $21.6 million. *Unit head:* Prof. Jerry Gibson, Chair, 805-893-3821, Fax: 805-893-3262, E-mail: gibson@ece.ucsb.edu. *Application contact:* Erika Raquel Klukovich, Graduate Admissions Coordinator, 805-893-3114, Fax: 805-893-5402, E-mail: erika@ece.ucsb.edu.

University of California, Santa Cruz, Division of Graduate Studies, Jack Baskin School of Engineering, Department of Electrical Engineering, Santa Cruz, CA 95064. Offers MS, PhD. *Entrance requirements:* For master's and doctorate, GRE General Test. Additional exam requirements/recommendations for international students: Required—TOEFL. Electronic applications accepted.

University of Central Florida, College of Engineering and Computer Science, School of Electrical Engineering and Computer Science, Program in Electrical Engineering, Orlando, FL 32816. Offers electrical engineering (MSEE, PhD); electronic circuits (Certificate). Part-time and evening/weekend programs available. *Students:* 123 full-time (26 women), 93 part-time (12 women); includes 50 minority (12 African Americans, 1 American Indian/Alaska Native, 13 Asian Americans or Pacific Islanders, 24 Hispanic Americans), 85 international. Average age 28. 276 applicants, 52% accepted, 56 enrolled. In 2009, 3 master's, 11 doctorates awarded. *Degree requirements:* For master's, thesis or alternative; for doctorate, thesis/dissertation, departmental qualifying exam, candidacy exam. *Entrance requirements:* For master's, GRE General Test, minimum GPA of 3.0 in last 60 hours; for doctorate, GRE General Test, minimum GPA of 3.5 in last 60 hours. Additional exam requirements/recommendations for international students: Required—TOEFL. *Application deadline:* For fall admission, 7/15 priority date for domestic students; for spring admission, 12/1 priority date for domestic students. Application fee: $30. Electronic applications accepted. *Expenses:* Tuition, state resident: part-time $306.31 per credit hour. Tuition, nonresident: part-time $1099.01 per credit hour. Part-time tuition and fees vary according to degree level and program. *Financial support:* In 2009–10, 70 students

received support, including 17 fellowships (averaging $9,700 per year), 73 research assistantships (averaging $9,450 per year), 2 teaching assistantships (averaging $7,400 per year); tuition waivers (partial) also available.

University of Cincinnati, Graduate School, College of Engineering, Department of Electrical and Computer Engineering and Computer Science, Program in Electrical Engineering, Cincinnati, OH 45221. Offers MS, PhD. *Degree requirements:* For master's, thesis; for doctorate, thesis/dissertation. *Entrance requirements:* For master's and doctorate, GRE General Test. Additional exam requirements/recommendations for international students: Required—TOEFL (minimum score 550 paper-based; 213 computer-based). *Faculty research:* Integrated circuits and optical devices, charge-coupled devices, photosensitive devices.

University of Colorado at Boulder, Graduate School, College of Engineering and Applied Science, Department of Electrical, Computer and Energy Engineering, Boulder, CO 80309. Offers ME, MS, PhD. Part-time programs available. Postbaccalaureate distance learning degree programs offered (no on-campus study). *Faculty:* 36 full-time (5 women). *Students:* 196 full-time (30 women), 94 part-time (21 women); includes 15 minority (1 African American, 12 Asian Americans or Pacific Islanders, 2 Hispanic Americans), 132 international. Average age 28. 654 applicants, 29% accepted, 66 enrolled. In 2009, 66 master's, 14 doctorates awarded. Terminal master's awarded for partial completion of doctoral program. *Degree requirements:* For master's, thesis or alternative; for doctorate, one foreign language, thesis/dissertation, departmental qualifying exam. *Entrance requirements:* For master's, GRE General Test, minimum undergraduate GPA of 3.0; for doctorate, GRE General Test, minimum undergraduate GPA of 3.5. *Application deadline:* For fall admission, 1/15 priority date for domestic students, 12/1 for international students; for spring admission, 10/1 for domestic and international students. Applications are processed on a rolling basis. Application fee: $50 ($60 for international students). *Financial support:* In 2009–10, 31 fellowships (averaging $8,965 per year), 107 research assistantships (averaging $14,806 per year) were awarded; career-related internships or fieldwork, scholarships/grants, and tuition waivers (full) also available. Financial award application deadline: 1/15. *Faculty research:* Biomedical engineering and cognitive disabilities, computer engineering VLSI CAD, dynamics and control systems, digital signal processing communications, electromagnetics, RF and microwaves, nonostructures and devices, optics and optoelectronics, power electronics and renewable energy systems. Total annual research expenditures: $7.4 million.

University of Colorado at Colorado Springs, Graduate School, College of Engineering and Applied Science, Department of Electrical and Computer Engineering, Colorado Springs, CO 80933-7150. Offers electrical engineering (ME, MS, PhD). Part-time and evening/weekend programs available. *Faculty:* 7 full-time (2 women), 2 part-time/adjunct (0 women). *Students:* 10 full-time (1 woman), 21 part-time (1 woman); includes 6 minority (1 African American, 2 Asian Americans or Pacific Islanders, 3 Hispanic Americans), 3 international. Average age 33. 29 applicants, 79% accepted, 13 enrolled. In 2009, 11 master's awarded. *Degree requirements:* For master's, thesis (for some programs), final oral exam (for non-thesis option); for doctorate, comprehensive exam, thesis/dissertation, preliminary exam. *Entrance requirements:* For master's, GRE General Test, minimum GPA of 3.0, BS or course work in electrical engineering; for doctorate, GRE General Test, minimum GPA of 3.3. Additional exam requirements/recommendations for international students: Required—TOEFL. Application fee: $60 ($75 for international students). *Expenses:* Tuition, state resident: full-time $8922; part-time $639 per credit hour. Tuition, nonresident: full-time $19,372; part-time $1154 per credit hour. Tuition and fees vary according to course level, course load, degree level, program, reciprocity agreements and student level. *Financial support:* Fellowships, research assistantships, teaching assistantships, career-related internships or fieldwork, Federal Work-Study, and scholarships/grants available. Support available to part-time students. Financial award application deadline: 3/1; financial award applicants required to submit FAFSA. *Faculty research:* Integrated ferroelectric devices; applied electromagnetics; digital/mixed-signal circuit design, test and design for testability; signal processing for communications and controls. *Unit head:* Dr. T. S. Kalkur, Chair, 719-255-3147, Fax: 719-255-3589. *Application contact:* Laura Baur, Academic Adviser, 719-255-3351, Fax: 719-255-3589, E-mail: lbaur@uccs.edu.

University of Colorado Denver, College of Engineering and Applied Science, Department of Electrical Engineering, Denver, CO 80217-3364. Offers M Eng, MS. Part-time and evening/weekend programs available. *Students:* 14 full-time (2 women), 64 part-time (8 women); includes 15 minority (4 African Americans, 9 Asian Americans or Pacific Islanders, 2 Hispanic Americans), 40 international. 123 applicants, 42% accepted, 18 enrolled. In 2009, 17 master's awarded. *Degree requirements:* For master's, thesis or alternative. *Entrance requirements:* For master's, GRE. Additional exam requirements/recommendations for international students: Required—TOEFL (minimum score 525 paper-based; 193 computer-based). *Application deadline:* For fall admission, 4/1 for domestic students; for spring admission, 10/1 for domestic students. Applications are processed on a rolling basis. Application fee: $50 ($75 for international students). Electronic applications accepted. *Financial support:* Research assistantships, teaching assistantships, career-related internships or fieldwork and Federal Work-Study available. Financial award application deadline: 4/1; financial award applicants required to submit FAFSA. *Unit head:* Dr. Renjeng Su, Chair, 303-352-3609, Fax: 303-556-2383, E-mail: renjeng.su@ucdenver.edu. *Application contact:* Janiece Hockaday, Administrative Assistant, 303-556-2872, Fax: 303-556-2383, E-mail: janiece.hockaday@ucdenver.edu.

University of Connecticut, Graduate School, School of Engineering, Department of Electrical and Computer Engineering, Field of Electrical Engineering, Storrs, CT 06269. Offers MS, PhD. *Faculty:* 28 full-time (2 women). *Students:* 101 full-time (29 women), 27 part-time (7 women); includes 12 minority (1 African American, 7 Asian Americans or Pacific Islanders, 4 Hispanic Americans), 79 international. Average age 29. 335 applicants, 8% accepted, 12 enrolled. In 2009, 11 master's, 6 doctorates awarded. Terminal master's awarded for partial completion of doctoral program. *Degree requirements:* For master's, comprehensive exam; for doctorate, thesis/dissertation. *Entrance requirements:* For master's and doctorate, GRE General Test. Additional exam requirements/recommendations for international students: Required—TOEFL (minimum score 550 paper-based; 213 computer-based). *Application deadline:* For fall admission, 2/1 priority date for domestic and international students; for spring admission, 11/1 for domestic students, 10/1 for international students. Applications are processed on a rolling basis. Application fee: $55. Electronic applications accepted. *Expenses:* Tuition, state resident: full-time $4725; part-time $525 per credit. Tuition, nonresident: full-time $12,267; part-time $1363 per credit. Required fees: $346 per semester. Tuition and fees vary according to course load. *Financial support:* In 2009–10, 84 research assistantships with full tuition reimbursements, 4 teaching assistantships with full tuition reimbursements were awarded; fellowships, Federal Work-Study, scholarships/grants, health care benefits, and unspecified assistantships also available. Financial award application deadline: 2/1; financial award applicants required to submit FAFSA. *Unit head:* Eric Donkor, Chairperson, 860-486-3018, E-mail: eric.donkor@uconn.edu. *Application contact:* Dee Stolstrom, Administrative Assistant, 860-486-4816, E-mail: denise@engr.uconn.edu.

University of Dayton, Graduate School, School of Engineering, Department of Electrical and Computer Engineering, Dayton, OH 45469-1300. Offers MSEE, DE, PhD. Part-time and evening/weekend programs available. *Faculty:* 9 full-time (0 women), 3 part-time/adjunct (1 woman). *Students:* 59 full-time (13 women), 31 part-time (3 women); includes 8 minority (4 African Americans, 3 Asian Americans or Pacific Islanders, 1 Hispanic American), 56 international. Average age 27. 198 applicants, 44% accepted, 28 enrolled. In 2009, 18 master's, 3 doctorates awarded. *Degree requirements:* For master's, thesis optional; for doctorate, variable foreign language requirement, thesis/dissertation, departmental qualifying exam. *Entrance requirements:* Additional exam requirements/recommendations for international students: Required—TOEFL (minimum score 550 paper-based; 213 computer-based; 80 iBT). *Application deadline:* For fall admission, 8/1 for domestic students, 3/1 priority date for international students; for winter admission, 7/1 priority date for international students; for spring admission, 1/1 priority date for international students. Applications are processed on a rolling basis. Application fee: $0 ($50 for international students). Electronic applications accepted. *Expenses:* Tuition: Full-time $8412; part-time $701 per credit hour. Required fees: $325; $65 per course. $25 per semester. Tuition and fees vary according to course load, degree level and program. *Financial support:* In 2009–10, 1 fellowship (averaging $27,500 per year), 15 research assistantships with full tuition reimbursements (averaging $15,000 per year), 5 teaching assistantships with full tuition reimbursements (averaging $9,000 per year) were awarded. Financial award application deadline: 5/1; financial award applicants required to submit FAFSA. *Faculty research:* Electrical engineering, video processing, leaky wave antenna. Total annual research expenditures: $1.1 million. *Unit head:* Dr. Guru Subramanyam, Chair, 937-229-3611. *Application contact:* Graduate Admissions, 937-229-4411, Fax: 937-229-4729, E-mail: gradadmission@udayton.edu.

University of Delaware, College of Engineering, Department of Electrical and Computer Engineering, Newark, DE 19716. Offers MSECE, PhD. Part-time programs available. Post-baccalaureate distance learning degree programs offered (no on-campus study). Terminal master's awarded for partial completion of doctoral program. *Degree requirements:* For master's, thesis optional; for doctorate, thesis/dissertation. *Entrance requirements:* For master's, GRE General Test; for doctorate, GRE General Test, qualifying exam. Additional exam requirements/recommendations for international students: Required—TOEFL. Electronic applications accepted. *Faculty research:* HIV Evolution During Dynamic Therapy, compressive sensing in imaging, sensor, networks, and UWB radios, computer network time synchronization, silicon spintronics, devices and imaging in the high-terahertz band.

University of Denver, School of Engineering and Computer Science, Department of Electrical and Computer Engineering, Denver, CO 80208. Offers computer engineering (MS); computer science and engineering (MS); electrical engineering (MS). Part-time and evening/weekend programs available. *Faculty:* 1 full-time (0 women). *Students:* 3 full-time (0 women), 122 part-time (17 women); includes 21 minority (1 African American, 11 Asian Americans or Pacific Islanders, 9 Hispanic Americans), 24 international. Average age 31. 112 applicants, 88% accepted, 56 enrolled. In 2009, 28 master's awarded. Terminal master's awarded for partial completion of doctoral program. *Degree requirements:* For master's, thesis (for some programs). *Entrance requirements:* For master's, GRE General Test, letters of reference. Additional exam requirements/recommendations for international students: Required—TOEFL (minimum score 570 paper-based; 230 computer-based). *Application deadline:* Applications are processed on a rolling basis. Application fee: $50. Electronic applications accepted. *Expenses:* Tuition: Full-time $34,596; part-time $961 per quarter hour. Required fees: $4 per quarter hour. Tuition and fees vary according to course load, campus/location and program. *Financial support:* In 2009–10, 14 research assistantships with full and partial tuition reimbursements (averaging $17,000 per year), 6 teaching assistantships with full and partial tuition reimbursements (averaging $10,000 per year) were awarded. Financial award application deadline: 3/1; financial award applicants required to submit FAFSA. *Unit head:* Dr. Kimon Valavanis, Chair, 303-871-2586. *Application contact:* Information Contact, 303-871-6618, E-mail: dgilmore@du.edu.

University of Detroit Mercy, College of Engineering and Science, Department of Electrical and Computer Engineering, Detroit, MI 48221. Offers computer engineering (ME, DE); mechatronics systems (ME, DE); signals and systems (ME, DE). Evening/weekend programs available. *Degree requirements:* For doctorate, thesis/dissertation. *Faculty research:* Electromagnetics, computer architecture, systems.

University of Evansville, College of Engineering and Computer Science, Department of Electrical Engineering and Computer Science, Evansville, IN 47722. Offers MS. Part-time programs available. *Faculty:* 2 full-time (1 woman). *Students:* 2 part-time (1 woman). Average age 30. In 2009, 1 master's awarded. *Degree requirements:* For master's, thesis. *Entrance requirements:* For master's, GRE, minimum undergraduate GPA of 2.8, 2 letters of recommendation, BS in electrical engineering or computer science. Additional exam requirements/recommendations for international students: Required—TOEFL (minimum score 530 paper-based; 71 iBT), IELTS (minimum score 6). *Application deadline:* For fall admission, 5/1 priority date for domestic and international students. Applications are processed on a rolling basis. Application fee: $25 ($50 for international students). *Expenses:* Contact institution. *Financial support:* In 2009–10, 1 student received support. Scholarships/grants available. Financial award application deadline: 6/1; financial award applicants required to submit FAFSA. *Faculty research:* Digital signal processing, computer algorithms, distributed systems, microcontrollers. *Unit head:* Dr. Dick Blandford, Department Chair, 812-488-2570, Fax: 812-488-2662, E-mail: blandford@evansville.edu. *Application contact:* Dr. Dick Blandford, Department Chair, 812-488-2570, Fax: 812-488-2662, E-mail: blandford@evansville.edu.

University of Florida, Graduate School, College of Engineering, Department of Electrical and Computer Engineering, Gainesville, FL 32611. Offers ME, MS, PhD, Engr. Part-time programs available. Terminal master's awarded for partial completion of doctoral program. *Degree requirements:* For master's, comprehensive exam (for some programs), thesis optional; for doctorate, comprehensive exam, thesis/dissertation; for Engr, thesis. *Entrance requirements:* For master's, GRE General Test, minimum GPA of 3.0; for doctorate, GRE General Test, minimum GPA of 3.5; for Engr, GRE General Test. Additional exam requirements/recommendations for international students: Required—TOEFL (minimum score 550 paper-based; 213 computer-based). Electronic applications accepted. *Faculty research:* Communications, electronics, digital signal processing, computer engineering.

University of Hawaii at Manoa, Graduate Division, College of Engineering, Department of Electrical Engineering, Honolulu, HI 96822. Offers MS, PhD. Part-time programs available. *Faculty:* 19 full-time (1 woman), 12 part-time/adjunct (1 woman). *Students:* 58 full-time (17 women), 12 part-time (3 women); includes 26 minority (all Asian Americans or Pacific Islanders), 28 international. Average age 28. 42 applicants, 81% accepted, 15 enrolled. In 2009, 8 master's, 3 doctorates awarded. *Degree requirements:* For master's, comprehensive exam, thesis; for doctorate, comprehensive exam, thesis/dissertation. *Entrance requirements:* For master's and doctorate, GRE General Test. Additional exam requirements/recommendations for international students: Required—TOEFL (minimum score 540 paper-based; 207 computer-based; 76 iBT), IELTS (minimum score 5). *Application deadline:* For fall admission, 3/1 for domestic students, 1/15 for international students; for spring admission, 9/1 for domestic students, 8/1 for international students. Applications are processed on a rolling basis. Application fee: $50. *Expenses:* Tuition, state resident: full-time $8900; part-time $372 per credit. Tuition, nonresident: full-time $21,400; part-time $898 per credit. Required fees: $207 per semester. *Financial support:* In 2009–10, 1 fellowship (averaging $1,000 per year), 38 research assistantships (averaging $18,081 per year), 9 teaching assistantships (averaging $14,705 per year) were awarded; tuition waivers (full and partial) also available. *Faculty research:* Computers and artificial intelligence, communication and networking, control theory, physical electronics, VLSI design, micromillimeter waves. Total annual research expenditures: $735,000. *Application contact:* N. Thomas Gaarder, Chairperson, 808-956-7586, Fax: 808-956-3427, E-mail: gaarder@hawaii.edu.

University of Houston, Cullen College of Engineering, Department of Electrical and Computer Engineering, Houston, TX 77204. Offers MEE, MSEE, PhD. Part-time and evening/weekend programs available. *Faculty:* 25 full-time (2 women), 3 part-time/adjunct (1 woman). *Students:* 207 full-time (54 women), 39 part-time (6 women); includes 21 minority (2 African Americans, 17 Asian Americans or Pacific Islanders, 2 Hispanic Americans), 203 international. Average age 25. 387 applicants, 60% accepted, 83 enrolled. In 2009, 42 master's, 7 doctorates awarded. Terminal master's awarded for partial completion of doctoral program. *Degree requirements:* For master's, thesis (for some programs); for doctorate, comprehensive exam, thesis/dissertation. *Entrance requirements:* For master's and doctorate, GRE General Test. Additional exam requirements/recommendations for international students: Required—TOEFL (minimum score 580 paper-based; 237 computer-based; 92 iBT). *Application deadline:* For fall admission, 2/1 for domestic and international students; for spring admission, 8/1 for domestic and international students. Application fee: $25 ($75 for international students). Electronic applications accepted. *Expenses:* Tuition, state resident: full-time $7676; part-time $320 per credit hour. Tuition, nonresident: full-time $14,324; part-time $597 per credit hour. Required fees: $3034. *Financial support:* In 2009–10, 9 fellowships with full tuition reimbursements (averaging $15,500 per year), 43 research assistantships with full tuition reimbursements (averaging $12,500 per year), 48 teaching assistantships with full tuition reimbursements (averaging $12,550 per year) were awarded; career-related internships or fieldwork, Federal Work-Study, institutionally sponsored loans, scholarships/grants, health care benefits, and unspecified assistantships also available. Support available to part-time students. Financial award application deadline: 2/1. *Faculty research:* Applied electromagnetics and microelectronics, signal and image processing, biomedical engineering, geophysical applications, control engineering. *Unit head:* Dr. John Wolfe, Interim Chairman, 713-743-4449, E-mail: wolfe@uh.edu. *Application contact:* MyTrang Baccam, Graduate Academic Advisor, 713-743-4403, E-mail: ece_grad_admit@uh.edu.

University of Idaho, College of Graduate Studies, College of Engineering, Department of Electrical and Computer Engineering, Program in Electrical Engineering, Moscow, ID 83844-2282. Offers M Engr, MS, PhD. *Students:* 40 full-time, 85 part-time. In 2009, 25 master's awarded. Application fee: $55 ($60 for international students). *Expenses:* Tuition, state resident: full-time $6120. Tuition, nonresident: full-time $17,712. *Unit head:* Dr. Brian Johnson, Chair, 208-885-6902. *Application contact:* Dr. Brian Johnson, Chair, 208-885-6902.

University of Illinois at Chicago, Graduate College, College of Engineering, Department of Electrical and Computer Engineering, Program in Electrical and Computer Engineering, Chicago, IL 60607-7128. Offers MS, PhD. Part-time programs available. *Degree requirements:* For master's, thesis or alternative; for doctorate, thesis/dissertation, departmental qualifying exam. *Entrance requirements:* For master's, minimum GPA of 2.75, BS in related field; for doctorate, GRE General Test, minimum GPA of 2.75, MS in related field. Additional exam requirements/recommendations for international students: Required—TOEFL.

University of Illinois at Urbana–Champaign, Graduate College, College of Engineering, Department of Electrical and Computer Engineering, Champaign, IL 61820. Offers electrical and computer engineering (MS, PhD); MS/MBA. *Faculty:* 87 full-time (6 women), 4 part-time/adjunct (0 women). *Students:* 478 full-time (65 women), 38 part-time (3 women); includes 58 minority (9 African Americans, 39 Asian Americans or Pacific Islanders, 10 Hispanic Americans), 293 international. 1,446 applicants, 16% accepted, 107 enrolled. In 2009, 98 master's, 56 doctorates awarded. *Entrance requirements:* For master's, GRE, minimum GPA of 3.0; for doctorate, GRE. Additional exam requirements/recommendations for international students: Required—TOEFL (minimum score 590 paper-based; 243 computer-based; 96 iBT), or IELTS (minimum score 6.5). *Application deadline:* Applications are processed on a rolling basis. Application fee: $60 ($75 for international students). Electronic applications accepted. *Financial support:* In 2009–10, 52 fellowships, 404 research assistantships, 172 teaching assistantships were awarded; tuition waivers (full and partial) also available. *Unit head:* Andreas C. Cangellaris, Head, 217-333-6037, Fax: 217-244-7075, E-mail: cangella@illinois.edu. *Application contact:* Laurie A. Fisher, Administrative Aide, 217-333-9709, Fax: 217-333-8582, E-mail: fisher2@illinois.edu.

The University of Iowa, Graduate College, College of Engineering, Department of Electrical and Computer Engineering, Iowa City, IA 52242-1316. Offers MS, PhD. Part-time programs available. *Faculty:* 19 full-time (1 woman), 1 part-time/adjunct (0 women). *Students:* 64 full-time (15 women); includes 6 minority (3 African Americans, 2 Asian Americans or Pacific Islanders, 1 Hispanic American), 36 international. Average age 29. 126 applicants, 24% accepted, 13 enrolled. In 2009, 12 master's, 2 doctorates awarded. *Degree requirements:* For master's, comprehensive exam, thesis optional; for doctorate, comprehensive exam, thesis/dissertation, PhD qualifying exam. *Entrance requirements:* For master's and doctorate, GRE. Additional exam requirements/recommendations for international students: Required—TOEFL (minimum score 550 paper-based; 213 computer-based; 81 iBT). *Application deadline:* For fall admission, 2/1 priority date for domestic students, 2/1 for international students. Applications are processed on a rolling basis. Application fee: $60 ($100 for international students). Electronic applications accepted. *Financial support:* In 2009–10, 3 fellowships with partial tuition reimbursements (averaging $19,146 per year), 49 research assistantships with partial tuition reimbursements (averaging $18,073 per year), 13 teaching assistantships with partial tuition reimbursements (averaging $17,324 per year) were awarded; scholarships/grants and unspecified assistantships also available. Financial award application deadline: 2/1; financial award applicants required to submit FAFSA. *Faculty research:* Applied optics and nanotechnology; computational genomics; large-scale intelligent and control systems; medical image processing; VLSI design and test. Total annual research expenditures: $7.1 million. *Unit head:* Dr. Milan Sonka, Departmental Executive Officer, 319-335-6052, Fax: 319-335-6028, E-mail: milan-sonka@uiowa.edu. *Application contact:* Cathy Kern, Secretary, 319-335-5197, Fax: 319-335-6028, E-mail: ece@engineering.uiowa.edu.

The University of Kansas, Graduate Studies, School of Engineering, Department of Electrical Engineering and Computer Science, Program in Electrical Engineering, Lawrence, KS 66045. Offers MS, DE, PhD. Part-time programs available. *Students:* 61 full-time (14 women), 16 part-time (3 women); includes 2 minority (1 African American, 1 Asian American or Pacific Islander), 45 international. Average age 27. 139 applicants, 35% accepted, 15 enrolled. In 2009, 21 master's, 2 doctorates awarded. Terminal master's awarded for partial completion of doctoral program. *Degree requirements:* For master's, thesis optional, exam; for doctorate, one foreign language, comprehensive exam, thesis/dissertation, qualifying exams. *Entrance requirements:* For master's, GRE, minimum GPA of 3.0; for doctorate, GRE, minimum GPA of 3.5. Additional exam requirements/recommendations for international students: Required—TOEFL (minimum score 600 paper-based; 250 computer-based; 100 iBT). *Application deadline:* For fall admission, 3/1 priority date for domestic students, 3/1 for international students; for spring admission, 10/1 priority date for domestic students, 10/1 for international students. Applications are processed on a rolling basis. Application fee: $45 ($55 for international students). Electronic applications accepted. *Expenses:* Tuition, state resident: full-time $6492; part-time $270.50 per credit hour. Tuition, nonresident: full-time $15,510; part-time $646.25 per credit hour. Required fees: $847; $70.56 per credit hour. Tuition and fees vary according to course load and program. *Financial support:* Fellowships with full and partial tuition reimbursements, research assistantships with full and partial tuition reimbursements, teaching assistantships with full and partial tuition reimbursements, career-related internships or fieldwork, scholarships/grants, and unspecified assistantships available. Financial award application deadline: 1/1. *Faculty research:* Communication systems and networking, computer systems design, radar systems and remote sensing. *Unit head:* Glenn Prescott, Chairperson, 785-864-4620, Fax: 785-864-3226. *Application contact:* Pam Shadoin, Assistant to Graduate Director, 785-864-4487, Fax: 785-864-3226, E-mail: graduate@eecs.ku.edu.

University of Kentucky, Graduate School, College of Engineering, Program in Electrical Engineering, Lexington, KY 40506-0032. Offers MSEE, PhD. *Degree requirements:* For master's, comprehensive exam, thesis optional; for doctorate, one foreign language, comprehensive exam, thesis/dissertation. *Entrance requirements:* For master's, GRE General Test, minimum undergraduate GPA of 2.75; for doctorate, GRE General Test, minimum undergraduate GPA of 3.0. Additional exam requirements/recommendations for international students: Required—TOEFL (minimum score 550 paper-based; 213 computer-based). Electronic applications accepted. *Faculty research:* Signal processing, systems, and control; electromagnetic field theory; power electronics and machines; computer engineering and VLSI; materials and devices.

University of Louisville, J.B. Speed School of Engineering, Department of Electrical and Computer Engineering, Louisville, KY 40292-0001. Offers M Eng, MS, PhD. *Accreditation:* ABET (one or more programs are accredited). Part-time programs available. *Faculty:* 21 full-time (4 women), 1 part-time/adjunct (0 women). *Students:* 69 full-time (12 women), 23 part-time (3 women); includes 15 minority (7 African Americans, 8 Asian Americans or Pacific Islanders), 39 international. Average age 28. 53 applicants, 40% accepted, 12 enrolled. In 2009, 32 master's, 6 doctorates awarded. Terminal master's awarded for partial completion of doctoral program. *Degree requirements:* For master's, comprehensive exam (for some programs), thesis or alternative; for doctorate, comprehensive exam, thesis/dissertation, minimum GPA of 3.0. *Entrance requirements:* For master's and doctorate, GRE General Test. Additional

Electrical Engineering

University of Louisville (continued)
exam requirements/recommendations for international students: Required—TOEFL (minimum score 550 paper-based; 213 computer-based; 80 iBT). *Application deadline:* For fall admission, 7/12 priority date for domestic and international students; for winter admission, 11/29 priority date for domestic and international students; for spring admission, 3/28 priority date for domestic and international students. Applications are processed on a rolling basis. Application fee: $50. Electronic applications accepted. *Financial support:* In 2009–10, 24 students received support, including 6 fellowships with full tuition reimbursements available (averaging $20,000 per year), 8 research assistantships with full tuition reimbursements available (averaging $19,300 per year), 8 teaching assistantships with full tuition reimbursements available (averaging $20,000 per year). Financial award application deadline: 1/25; financial award applicants required to submit FAFSA. *Faculty research:* Nanotechnology; microfabrication; computer engineering; control, communication and signal processing; electronic devices and systems. Total annual research expenditures: $3.5 million. *Unit head:* James H. Graham, Acting Chair, 502-852-6289, Fax: 502-852-6807, E-mail: jhgrah01@louisville.edu. *Application contact:* Dr. Michael Day, Associate Dean, 502-852-6195, Fax: 502-852-7294, E-mail: day@louisville.edu.

University of Maine, Graduate School, College of Engineering, Department of Electrical and Computer Engineering, Orono, ME 04469. Offers computer engineering (MS); electrical engineering (MS, PhD). Part-time programs available. *Faculty:* 12 full-time (1 woman), 1 part-time/adjunct (0 women). *Students:* 29 full-time (4 women), 13 part-time (2 women); includes 4 minority (all Asian Americans or Pacific Islanders), 16 international. Average age 27. 28 applicants, 43% accepted, 10 enrolled. In 2009, 4 master's awarded. *Degree requirements:* For master's, thesis (for some programs); for doctorate, thesis/dissertation. *Entrance requirements:* For master's and doctorate, GRE General Test. Additional exam requirements/recommendations for international students: Required—TOEFL. *Application deadline:* For fall admission, 2/1 priority date for domestic students. Applications are processed on a rolling basis. Application fee: $65. Electronic applications accepted. *Financial support:* In 2009–10, 21 research assistantships with tuition reimbursements (averaging $21,737 per year), 2 teaching assistantships with tuition reimbursements (averaging $12,790 per year) were awarded; Federal Work-Study, institutionally sponsored loans, and tuition waivers (full and partial) also available. Financial award application deadline: 3/1. *Unit head:* Dr. Monamad Musavi, Chair, 207-581-2243. *Application contact:* Scott G. Delcourt, Associate Dean of the Graduate School, 207-581-3291, Fax: 207-581-3232, E-mail: graduate@maine.edu.

University of Manitoba, Faculty of Graduate Studies, Faculty of Engineering, Department of Electrical and Computer Engineering, Winnipeg, MB R3T 2N2, Canada. Offers M Eng, M Sc, PhD. *Degree requirements:* For master's, thesis; for doctorate, thesis/dissertation.

University of Maryland, Baltimore County, Graduate School, College of Engineering and Information Technology, Department of Computer Science and Electrical Engineering, Program in Electrical Engineering, Baltimore, MD 21250. Offers MS, PhD. Part-time programs available. *Students:* 31 full-time (6 women), 22 part-time (3 women); includes 15 minority (6 African Americans, 7 Asian Americans or Pacific Islanders, 2 Hispanic Americans), 21 international. Average age 31. 75 applicants, 56% accepted, 7 enrolled. In 2009, 11 master's, 9 doctorates awarded. *Degree requirements:* For master's, thesis optional; for doctorate, comprehensive exam, thesis/dissertation. *Entrance requirements:* For master's, GRE General Test, BS from ABET-accredited undergraduate program in electrical engineering or strong background in computer science, math, physics, or other engineering science; for doctorate, GRE General Test, BS from ABET-accredited undergraduate program in electrical engineering or strong background in computer science. Additional exam requirements/recommendations for international students: Required—TOEFL (minimum score 550 paper-based; 213 computer-based; 80 iBT). *Application deadline:* For fall admission, 6/1 for domestic students, 1/1 for international students; for spring admission, 11/1 for domestic students, 6/1 for international students. Applications are processed on a rolling basis. Application fee: $50. Electronic applications accepted. *Financial support:* In 2009–10, 3 research assistantships with partial tuition reimbursements (averaging $17,000 per year), 6 teaching assistantships with partial tuition reimbursements (averaging $17,000 per year) were awarded; fellowships with partial tuition reimbursements, career-related internships or fieldwork, Federal Work-Study, scholarships/grants, health care benefits, tuition waivers (partial), and unspecified assistantships also available. Support available to part-time students. Financial award application deadline: 6/30; financial award applicants required to submit FAFSA. *Unit head:* Dr. Charles K. Nicholas, Professor and Chair, 410-455-3500, Fax: 410-455-3969, E-mail: nicholas@cs.umbc.edu. *Application contact:* Dr. Li Yan, Professor and Graduate Program Coordinator, 410-455-3558, Fax: 410-455-3969, E-mail: liyan@cs.umbc.edu.

University of Maryland, College Park, Academic Affairs, A. James Clark School of Engineering, Department of Continuing and Distance Learning in Engineering, Professional Program in Engineering, College Park, MD 20742. Offers aerospace engineering (M Eng); chemical engineering (M Eng); civil engineering (M Eng); electrical engineering (M Eng); engineering (Certificate); fire protection engineering (M Eng); materials science and engineering (M Eng); mechanical engineering (M Eng); reliability engineering (M Eng); systems engineering (M Eng). Part-time and evening/weekend programs available. Postbaccalaureate distance learning degree programs offered. *Students:* 50 full-time (15 women), 234 part-time (41 women); includes 91 minority (36 African Americans, 39 Asian Americans or Pacific Islanders, 16 Hispanic Americans), 45 international. 137 applicants, 69% accepted, 77 enrolled. In 2009, 103 master's awarded. *Entrance requirements:* For master's, 3 letters of recommendation. *Application deadline:* For fall admission, 8/15 for domestic students, 1/10 for international students; for spring admission, 12/15 for domestic students, 6/1 for international students. Applications are processed on a rolling basis. Application fee: $60. Electronic applications accepted. *Expenses:* Tuition, area resident: Part-time $471 per credit hour. Tuition, state resident: part-time $471 per credit hour. Tuition, nonresident: part-time $1016 per credit hour. Required fees: $337.04 per term. *Financial support:* In 2009–10, 2 research assistantships with tuition reimbursements (averaging $19,561 per year), 9 teaching assistantships with tuition reimbursements (averaging $16,849 per year) were awarded; fellowships, Federal Work-Study and scholarships/grants also available. Support available to part-time students. Financial award applicants required to submit FAFSA. *Unit head:* Dr. George Syrmos, Director, 301-405-3633, Fax: 301-314-3305, E-mail: syrmos@umd.edu. *Application contact:* Dean of Graduate School, 301-405-0376, Fax: 301-314-9305.

University of Maryland, College Park, Academic Affairs, A. James Clark School of Engineering, Department of Electrical and Computer Engineering, College Park, MD 20742. Offers electrical and computer engineering (M Eng, MS, PhD); electrical engineering (MS, PhD); telecommunications (MS). Part-time and evening/weekend programs available. Postbaccalaureate distance learning degree programs offered. *Faculty:* 104 full-time (10 women), 21 part-time/adjunct (3 women). *Students:* 394 full-time (89 women), 56 part-time (11 women); includes 53 minority (10 African Americans, 38 Asian Americans or Pacific Islanders, 5 Hispanic Americans), 318 international. 1,515 applicants, 19% accepted, 109 enrolled. In 2009, 88 master's, 44 doctorates awarded. *Degree requirements:* For master's, thesis optional; for doctorate, thesis/dissertation, oral exam, qualifying exam. *Entrance requirements:* For master's and doctorate, GRE General Test, 3 letters of recommendation. *Application deadline:* For fall admission, 5/1 for domestic students, 2/1 for international students; for spring admission, 6/1 for international students. Applications are processed on a rolling basis. Application fee: $60. Electronic applications accepted. *Expenses:* Tuition, area resident: Part-time $471 per credit hour. Tuition, state resident: part-time $471 per credit hour. Tuition, nonresident: part-time $1016 per credit hour. Required fees: $337.04 per term. *Financial support:* In 2009–10, 9 fellowships with full and partial tuition reimbursements (averaging $15,387 per year), 169 research assistantships with tuition reimbursements (averaging $17,751 per year), 81 teaching assistantships with tuition reimbursements (averaging $16,896 per year) were awarded; career-related internships or fieldwork also available. Financial award applicants required to submit FAFSA. *Faculty research:* Communications and control, electrophysics, micro-electronics, robotics, computer engineering. Total annual research expenditures: $10.7 million. *Unit head:* Dr. Pat Gerard O'Shea, Chairman, 301-405-3683, E-mail: poshea@umd.edu. *Application contact:* Dean of Graduate School, 301-405-0376, Fax: 301-314-9305.

University of Massachusetts Amherst, Graduate School, College of Engineering, Department of Electrical and Computer Engineering, Amherst, MA 01003. Offers MS, PhD. Part-time programs available. *Faculty:* 38 full-time (2 women). *Students:* 162 full-time (31 women), 18 part-time (3 women); includes 13 minority (5 African Americans, 4 Asian Americans or Pacific Islanders, 4 Hispanic Americans), 135 international. Average age 26. 640 applicants, 29% accepted, 74 enrolled. In 2009, 36 master's, 3 doctorates awarded. Terminal master's awarded for partial completion of doctoral program. *Degree requirements:* For master's, thesis or alternative; for doctorate, comprehensive exam, thesis/dissertation. *Entrance requirements:* For master's and doctorate, GRE General Test. Additional exam requirements/recommendations for international students: Required—TOEFL (minimum score 550 paper-based; 213 computer-based; 80 iBT), IELTS (minimum score 6.5). *Application deadline:* For fall admission, 1/15 for domestic and international students; for spring admission, 10/1 for domestic and international students. Applications are processed on a rolling basis. Application fee: $50 ($65 for international students). Electronic applications accepted. *Expenses:* Tuition, state resident: full-time $2640; part-time $110 per credit. Tuition, nonresident: full-time $9936; part-time $414 per credit. Tuition and fees vary according to course load. *Financial support:* In 2009–10, 3 fellowships with full tuition reimbursements (averaging $11,111 per year), 114 research assistantships with full tuition reimbursements (averaging $12,785 per year), 32 teaching assistantships with full tuition reimbursements (averaging $5,161 per year) were awarded; career-related internships or fieldwork, Federal Work-Study, scholarships/grants, traineeships, health care benefits, tuition waivers, and unspecified assistantships also available. Support available to part-time students. Financial award application deadline: 1/15; financial award applicants required to submit FAFSA. *Unit head:* Dr. C. Mani Krishna, Graduate Program Director, 413-545-4583, Fax: 413-545-4611, E-mail: ecegrad@ecs.umass.edu. *Application contact:* Jean M. Ames, Supervisor of Admissions, 413-545-0722, Fax: 413-577-0010, E-mail: gradadm@grad.umass.edu.

University of Massachusetts Dartmouth, Graduate School, College of Engineering, Department of Electrical and Computer Engineering, North Dartmouth, MA 02747-2300. Offers acoustics (Postbaccalaureate Certificate); communications (Postbaccalaureate Certificate); computer engineering (MS, PhD); computer systems engineering (Postbaccalaureate Certificate); digital signal processing (Postbaccalaureate Certificate); electrical engineering (MS, PhD); electrical engineering systems (Postbaccalaureate Certificate). Part-time programs available. *Faculty:* 18 full-time (3 women), 4 part-time/adjunct (0 women). *Students:* 39 full-time (11 women), 42 part-time (8 women); includes 8 minority (2 African Americans, 5 Asian Americans or Pacific Islanders, 1 Hispanic American), 46 international. Average age 28. 99 applicants, 80% accepted, 26 enrolled. In 2009, 34 master's, 1 doctorate, 3 other advanced degrees awarded. *Degree requirements:* For master's, culminating project or thesis; for doctorate, comprehensive exam, thesis/dissertation. *Entrance requirements:* For master's, GRE General Test, minimum undergraduate GPA of 3.0, 3 letters or recommendation; for doctorate, GRE. Additional exam requirements/recommendations for international students: Required—TOEFL (minimum score 550 paper-based; 213 computer-based). *Application deadline:* For fall admission, 2/1 priority date for domestic students, 12/1 for international students; for spring admission, 11/1 priority date for domestic students, 9/1 for international students. Applications are processed on a rolling basis. Application fee: $40 ($60 for international students). Electronic applications accepted. *Expenses:* Tuition, state resident: full-time $2071; part-time $86.29 per credit. Tuition, nonresident: full-time $8099; part-time $337.46 per credit. Required fees: $9446. Tuition and fees vary according to class time, course load and reciprocity agreements. *Financial support:* In 2009–10, 2 fellowships with full tuition reimbursements (averaging $16,000 per year), 14 research assistantships with full tuition reimbursements (averaging $11,096 per year), 9 teaching assistantships with full tuition reimbursements (averaging $12,500 per year) were awarded; Federal Work-Study and unspecified assistantships also available. Support available to part-time students. Financial award application deadline: 3/1; financial award applicants required to submit FAFSA. *Faculty research:* Speech acoustics, marine applications, signals and systems, applies electromagnetics, intelligent agency. Total annual research expenditures: $935,000. *Unit head:* Dr. Karen Payton, Director, 508-999-8434, Fax: 508-999-8489, E-mail: kpayton@umassd.edu. *Application contact:* Elan Turcotte-Shamski, Graduate Admissions Officer, 508-999-8604, Fax: 508-999-8183, E-mail: graduate@umassd.edu.

University of Massachusetts Lowell, James B. Francis College of Engineering, Department of Electrical and Computer Engineering, Program in Electrical Engineering, Lowell, MA 01854-2881. Offers MS Eng, D Eng. Part-time and evening/weekend programs available. Terminal master's awarded for partial completion of doctoral program. *Degree requirements:* For master's, thesis; for doctorate, 2 foreign languages, thesis/dissertation. *Entrance requirements:* For master's and doctorate, GRE General Test.

University of Memphis, Graduate School, Herff College of Engineering, Department of Electrical and Computer Engineering, Memphis, TN 38152. Offers automatic control systems (MS); biomedical systems (MS); communications and propagation systems (MS); computer engineering (PhD); electrical engineering (PhD); engineering computer systems (MS). *Faculty:* 8 full-time (1 woman), 2 part-time/adjunct (0 women). *Students:* 32 full-time (6 women), 4 part-time (1 woman); includes 3 African Americans, 1 Asian American or Pacific Islander, 25 international. Average age 26. 30 applicants, 87% accepted, 21 enrolled. In 2009, 10 master's awarded. *Degree requirements:* For master's, comprehensive exam, thesis or alternative. *Entrance requirements:* For master's, GRE General Test or MAT, minimum undergraduate GPA of 2.5. *Application deadline:* For fall admission, 8/1 for domestic students; for spring admission, 12/1 for domestic students. Application fee: $35 ($60 for international students). *Expenses:* Tuition, state resident: full-time $6246; part-time $347 per credit hour. Tuition, nonresident: full-time $15,894; part-time $883 per credit hour. Required fees: $1160. Full-time tuition and fees vary according to course load, degree level and program. *Financial support:* In 2009–10, 4 students received support; research assistantships, teaching assistantships, career-related internships or fieldwork, Federal Work-Study, scholarships/grants, and unspecified assistantships available. Financial award application deadline: 2/15; financial award applicants required to submit FAFSA. *Faculty research:* Image processing, imaging sensors, biomedical systems, intelligent systems. *Unit head:* Dr. David J. Russomanno, Chair and Ballard Professor, 901-678-2175, Fax: 901-678-5469, E-mail: russmnn@memphis.edu. *Application contact:* Dr. Steven T. Griffin, Coordinator of Graduate Studies, 901-678-5268, Fax: 901-678-5469, E-mail: stgriffn@memphis.edu.

University of Miami, Graduate School, College of Engineering, Department of Electrical and Computer Engineering, Coral Gables, FL 33124. Offers MSECE, PhD. Part-time programs available. *Degree requirements:* For master's, thesis (for some programs); for doctorate, comprehensive exam, thesis/dissertation, dissertation proposal defense. *Entrance requirements:* For master's, GRE General Test, minimum GPA of 3.0; for doctorate, GRE General Test, minimum undergraduate GPA of 3.3, graduate 3.5. Additional exam requirements/recommendations for international students: Required—TOEFL (minimum score 550 paper-based; 213 computer-based; 59 iBT), IELTS (minimum score 7). Electronic applications accepted. *Faculty research:* Computer network, image processing, database systems, digital signal processing, machine intelligence.

University of Michigan, Horace H. Rackham School of Graduate Studies, College of Engineering, Department of Electrical Engineering and Computer Science, Ann Arbor, MI 48109. Offers MS, MSE, PhD. ECE Department offers degrees in both Electrical Engineering and Electrical Engineering: Systems. *Faculty:* 61 full-time (6 women). *Students:* 396 full-time (44 women), 8 part-time (0 women); includes 49 minority (9 African Americans, 34 Asian Americans or Pacific Islanders, 6 Hispanic Americans), 280 international. 1,289 applicants, 27% accepted, 127 enrolled. In 2009, 91 master's, 56 doctorates awarded. *Expenses:* Tuition, state resident: full-time $17,286; part-time $1099 per credit hour. Tuition, nonresident: full-time $34,944; part-time $2080 per credit hour. Required fees: $95 per semester. Tuition and fees vary according to course load, degree level and program. *Faculty research:* Solid state electronics and optics; communications, control, signal process; sensors and integrated circuitry, others; software systems; artificial intelligence; hardware systems. *Unit head:* Prof. Khalil Najafi, Chair, 734-647-7010, Fax: 734-647-7009, E-mail: najafi@umich.edu. *Application contact:* Beth Stalnaker, Graduate Coordinator, 734- 647-1758, Fax: 734-763-1503, E-mail: beths@umich.edu.

University of Michigan–Dearborn, College of Engineering and Computer Science, Department of Electrical and Computer Engineering, Dearborn, MI 48128-1491. Offers computer engineering (MSE); electrical engineering (MSE); software engineering (MS). Part-time programs available. *Faculty:* 8 full-time (1 woman). *Students:* 22 full-time (4 women), 124 part-time (22 women); includes 34 minority (5 African Americans, 27 Asian Americans or Pacific Islanders, 2 Hispanic Americans). Average age 29. 51 applicants, 35% accepted, 24 enrolled. In 2009, 11 master's awarded. *Degree requirements:* For master's, thesis optional. *Entrance requirements:* For master's, GRE (recommended), bachelor's degree in electrical and computer engineering or equivalent, minimum GPA of 3.0. Additional exam requirements/recommendations for international students: Required—TOEFL (minimum score 560 paper-based; 220 computer-based; 84 iBT). *Application deadline:* For fall admission, 8/1 priority date for domestic students, 5/1 for international students; for winter admission, 12/1 priority date for domestic students, 11/1 for international students; for spring admission, 4/1 priority date for domestic students, 3/1 for international students. Applications are processed on a rolling basis. Application fee: $60 ($75 for international students). *Expenses:* Tuition, area resident: Part-time $504.10 per credit hour. Tuition, state resident: part-time $504.10 per credit hour. Tuition, nonresident: part-time $957.90 per credit hour. *Financial support:* In 2009–10, 7 fellowships (averaging $18,331 per year), 12 research assistantships with full tuition reimbursements (averaging $15,494 per year) were awarded; teaching assistantships, Federal Work-Study also available. Financial award application deadline: 4/1; financial award applicants required to submit FAFSA. *Faculty research:* Fuzzy systems and applications, machine vision, pattern recognition and machine intelligence, vehicle electronics, wireless communications. *Unit head:* Dr. Lu Murphey, Chair, 313-593-5028, Fax: 313-583-6336, E-mail: yilu@umich.edu. *Application contact:* Sandra Marie Krzyskowski, Intermediate Academic Records Assistant, 313-593-5420, Fax: 313-583-6336, E-mail: ece-grad@umd.umich.edu.

University of Minnesota, Duluth, Graduate School, Swenson College of Science and Engineering, Department of Electrical and Computer Engineering, Duluth, MN 55812-2496. Offers MSECE. Part-time programs available. *Faculty:* 7 full-time (1 woman). *Students:* 11 full-time (1 woman), 7 international. Average age 26. 21 applicants, 86% accepted, 4 enrolled. In 2009, 5 master's awarded. *Degree requirements:* For master's, thesis. *Entrance requirements:* Additional exam requirements/recommendations for international students: Recommended—IELTS, TWE. *Application deadline:* For fall admission, 7/15 for domestic and international students; for spring admission, 11/1 for domestic and international students. Applications are processed on a rolling basis. Application fee: $75 ($95 for international students). *Financial support:* In 2009–10, 11 students received support, including 9 research assistantships with partial tuition reimbursements available (averaging $6,449 per year), 11 teaching assistantships with partial tuition reimbursements available (averaging $6,449 per year); health care benefits and unspecified assistantships also available. Financial award application deadline: 9/1. *Faculty research:* Biomedical instrumentation, transportation systems, computer hardware and software, signal processing, optical communications. Total annual research expenditures: $200,000. *Unit head:* Dr. Imran Hayee, Director of Graduate Studies, 218-726-6743, Fax: 218-726-7267, E-mail: ihayee@d.umn.edu. *Application contact:* Tami Vatalaro, Executive Administration Specialist, 218-726-7523, Fax: 218-726-6970, E-mail: grad@d.umn.edu.

University of Minnesota, Twin Cities Campus, Institute of Technology, Department of Electrical Engineering, Minneapolis, MN 55455-0213. Offers MEE, MSEE, PhD. Part-time programs available. *Degree requirements:* For master's, thesis or alternative; for doctorate, thesis/dissertation. *Entrance requirements:* Additional exam requirements/recommendations for international students: Required—TOEFL (minimum score 550 paper-based; 213 computer-based), GRE. *Faculty research:* Signal processing, microelectronics, computers, controls, power electronics.

University of Missouri, Graduate School, College of Engineering, Department of Electrical and Computer Engineering, Columbia, MO 65211. Offers MS, PhD. *Degree requirements:* For master's, thesis or alternative; for doctorate, thesis/dissertation. *Entrance requirements:* For master's, GRE General Test, minimum GPA of 3.0; for doctorate, GRE General Test, GRE Subject Test, minimum GPA of 3.0. Additional exam requirements/recommendations for international students: Required—TOEFL (minimum score 550 paper-based; 213 computer-based; 80 iBT).

University of Missouri–Kansas City, School of Computing and Engineering, Kansas City, MO 64110-2499. Offers civil engineering (MS); computer and electrical engineering (PhD); computer science (MS), including bioinformatics, software engineering, telecommunications networking; computer science and informatics (PhD); computing (PhD); electrical engineering (MS); engineering (PhD); mechanical engineering (MS); telecommunications (PhD). PhD (interdisciplinary) offered through the School of Graduate Studies. Part-time programs available. *Faculty:* 40 full-time (5 women), 28 part-time/adjunct (0 women). *Students:* 230 full-time (46 women), 158 part-time (31 women); includes 20 minority (5 African Americans, 12 Asian Americans or Pacific Islanders, 3 Hispanic Americans), 313 international. Average age 24. 484 applicants, 64% accepted, 106 enrolled. In 2009, 144 master's awarded. *Degree requirements:* For doctorate, thesis/dissertation. *Entrance requirements:* For master's, GRE General Test, minimum GPA of 3.0, 3 letters of recommendations from professors; for doctorate, GRE General Test, minimum GPA of 3.5. Additional exam requirements/recommendations for international students: Required—TOEFL (minimum score 550 paper-based; 213 computer-based; 80 iBT). *Application deadline:* For fall admission, 1/15 priority date for domestic students, 1/15 for international students. Applications are processed on a rolling basis. Application fee: $45 ($50 for international students). *Expenses:* Tuition, state resident: full-time $5378; part-time $299 per credit hour. Tuition, nonresident: full-time $13,881; part-time $771 per credit hour. Required fees: $641; $71 per credit hour. Tuition and fees vary according to course load and program. *Financial support:* In 2009–10, 29 research assistantships with partial tuition reimbursements (averaging $15,040 per year), 10 teaching assistantships with partial tuition reimbursements (averaging $12,118 per year) were awarded; career-related internships or fieldwork, Federal Work-Study, scholarships/grants, tuition waivers (partial), and unspecified assistantships also available. Support available to part-time students. Financial award application deadline: 3/1; financial award applicants required to submit FAFSA. *Faculty research:* Algorithms, bioinformatics and medical informatics, biomechanics/biomaterials, civil engineering materials, networking and telecommunications, thermal science. Total annual research expenditures: $1.4 million. *Unit head:* Dr. Kevin Z. Truman, Dean, 816-235-2399, Fax: 816-235-5159. *Application contact:* Dr. Kevin Z. Truman, Dean, 816-235-2399, Fax: 816-235-5159.

University of Nebraska–Lincoln, Graduate College, College of Engineering, Department of Electrical Engineering, Lincoln, NE 68588. Offers MS, PhD. *Degree requirements:* For master's, thesis optional; for doctorate, comprehensive exam, thesis/dissertation. *Entrance requirements:* For master's and doctorate, GRE General Test. Additional exam requirements/recommendations for international students: Required—TOEFL (minimum score 550 paper-based; 213 computer-based). Electronic applications accepted. *Faculty research:* Electromagnetics, communications, biomedical digital signal processing, electrical breakdown of gases, optical properties of microelectronic materials.

University of Nevada, Las Vegas, Graduate College, Howard R. Hughes College of Engineering, Department of Electrical and Computer Engineering, Las Vegas, NV 89154-4026. Offers MSE, PhD. Part-time programs available. *Faculty:* 14 full-time (1 woman), 3 part-time/adjunct (0 women). *Students:* 33 full-time (5 women), 17 part-time (3 women); includes 7 minority (2 African Americans, 5 Asian Americans or Pacific Islanders), 33 international. Average age 29. 54 applicants, 74% accepted, 20 enrolled. In 2009, 22 master's, 1 doctorate awarded. *Degree requirements:* For master's, comprehensive exam, thesis (for some programs), project; for doctorate, comprehensive exam, thesis/dissertation. *Entrance requirements:* Additional exam requirements/recommendations for international students: Required—TOEFL (minimum score 550 paper-based; 213 computer-based; 80 iBT), IELTS (minimum score 7). *Application deadline:* For fall admission, 2/1 priority date for domestic and international students; for spring admission, 10/1 priority date for domestic and international students. Applications are processed on a rolling basis. Application fee: $60 ($95 for international students). Electronic applications accepted. *Financial support:* In 2009–10, 25 students received support, including 12 research assistantships with partial tuition reimbursements available (averaging $12,220 per year), 13 teaching assistantships with partial tuition reimbursements available (averaging $10,307 per year); institutionally sponsored loans, scholarships/grants, health care benefits, tuition waivers (full), and unspecified assistantships also available. Financial award application deadline: 3/1. *Unit head:* Dr. Henry Selvaraj, Chair/ Professor, 702-895-4183, Fax: 702-895-4075, E-mail: ece.chair@unlv.edu. *Application contact:* Graduate College Admissions Evaluator, 702-895-3320, Fax: 702-895-4180, E-mail: gradcollege@unlv.edu.

University of Nevada, Reno, Graduate School, College of Engineering, Department of Electrical Engineering, Reno, NV 89557. Offers MS, PhD. Terminal master's awarded for partial completion of doctoral program. *Degree requirements:* For master's, thesis optional; for doctorate, thesis/dissertation. *Entrance requirements:* For master's, GRE General Test, minimum GPA of 2.75; for doctorate, GRE General Test, minimum GPA of 3.0. Additional exam requirements/recommendations for international students: Required—TOEFL (minimum score 500 paper-based; 173 computer-based; 61 iBT), IELTS (minimum score 6). Electronic applications accepted. *Faculty research:* Acoustics, neural networking, synthetic aperture radar simulation, optical fiber communications and sensors.

University of New Brunswick Fredericton, School of Graduate Studies, Faculty of Engineering, Department of Electrical and Computer Engineering, Fredericton, NB E3B 5A3, Canada. Offers M Eng, M Sc E, PhD. Part-time programs available. *Faculty:* 16 full-time (3 women), 1 part-time/adjunct (0 women). *Students:* 54 full-time (3 women), 8 part-time (1 woman). 45 applicants, 44% accepted. In 2009, 14 master's, 5 doctorates awarded. *Degree requirements:* For master's, thesis, Research Proposal; for Master's in Engineering: 10 Graduate Courses required; for doctorate, comprehensive exam, thesis/dissertation, research proposal. *Entrance requirements:* For master's, minimum GPA of 3.0 or B; acceptable English score; references; for doctorate, MSc 80%, minimum GPA of 3.0 or B; previous transcripts; acceptable English score; and references. Additional exam requirements/recommendations for international students: Required—TOEFL (minimum score 580 paper-based; 237 computer-based), TWE, or IELTS (minimum score 7). *Application deadline:* Applications are processed on a rolling basis. Application fee: $50 Canadian dollars. Tuition and fees charges are reported in Canadian dollars. *Expenses:* Tuition, area resident: Full-time $5562 Canadian dollars; part-time $2781 Canadian dollars per year. Required fees: $49.75 Canadian dollars per term. *Financial support:* In 2009–10, 26 research assistantships (averaging $14,400 per year), 25 teaching assistantships were awarded; fellowships also available. *Faculty research:* Biomedical engineering, communications, controls, electromagnetic systems, embedded systems, optical fiber systems, sustainable energy signal processing, software systems. *Unit head:* Dr. Maryhelen Stevenson, Director of Graduate Studies, 504-447-3147, Fax: 504-453-3589, E-mail: stevenso@unb.ca. *Application contact:* Shelley Cormier, Graduate Secretary, 506-452-6142, Fax: 506-453-3589, E-mail: scormier@unb.ca.

University of New Hampshire, Graduate School, College of Engineering and Physical Sciences, Department of Electrical and Computer Engineering, Durham, NH 03824. Offers electrical engineering (MS, PhD). Part-time and evening/weekend programs available. *Faculty:* 11 full-time (0 women). *Students:* 19 full-time (1 woman), 22 part-time (4 women); includes 1 minority (Asian American or Pacific Islander), 10 international. Average age 31. 65 applicants, 57% accepted, 11 enrolled. In 2009, 16 master's, 2 doctorates awarded. *Degree requirements:* For master's, thesis or alternative; for doctorate, thesis/dissertation. *Entrance requirements:* For master's, GRE (for non-U. S. university bachelor's degree holders); for doctorate, GRE (for non-US university bachelor's degree holders). Additional exam requirements/recommendations for international students: Required—TOEFL (minimum score 550 paper-based; 213 computer-based; 80 iBT). *Application deadline:* For fall admission, 4/1 priority date for domestic students, 4/1 for international students; for spring admission, 12/1 for domestic students. Applications are processed on a rolling basis. Application fee: $65. Electronic applications accepted. *Expenses:* Tuition, state resident: full-time $10,380; part-time $577 per credit hour. Tuition, nonresident: full-time $24,350; part-time $1002 per credit hour. Required fees: $1550; $387.50 per semester. Tuition and fees vary according to course load and program. *Financial support:* In 2009–10, 18 students received support, including 2 fellowships, 8 research assistantships, 7 teaching assistantships; Federal Work-Study, scholarships/grants, and tuition waivers (full and partial) also available. Support available to part-time students. Financial award application deadline: 2/15. *Faculty research:* Biomedical engineering, communications systems and information theory, digital systems, illumination engineering. *Unit head:* John LaCourse, Chairperson, 603-862-1324. *Application contact:* Kathryn Reynolds, Administrative Assistant, 603-862-1358, E-mail: ece.dept@unh.edu.

University of New Haven, Graduate School, Tagliatela College of Engineering, Program in Electrical Engineering, West Haven, CT 06516-1916. Offers communications/dsp (MS); control system (MS); electrical and computer engineering (MS); electrical engineering (MS). Part-time and evening/weekend programs available. *Faculty:* 9 full-time (2 women), 5 part-time/adjunct (0 women). *Students:* 38 full-time (10 women), 11 part-time (3 women); includes 3 minority (all African Americans), 39 international. Average age 25. 185 applicants, 92% accepted, 22 enrolled. In 2009, 40 master's awarded. *Degree requirements:* For master's, thesis or alternative. *Entrance requirements:* For master's, bachelor's degree in electrical engineering. Additional exam requirements/recommendations for international students: Required—TOEFL (minimum score 520 paper-based; 190 computer-based; 70 iBT); Recommended—IELTS (minimum score 5.5). *Application deadline:* For fall admission, 5/31 for international students; for winter admission, 10/15 for international students; for spring admission, 1/15 for international students. Applications are processed on a rolling basis. Application fee: $50. Electronic applications accepted. *Expenses:* Tuition: Part-time $700 per credit. Required fees: $45 per term. One-time fee: $390 part-time. *Financial support:* Research assistantships with partial tuition reimbursements, teaching assistantships with partial tuition reimbursements, career-related internships or fieldwork, Federal Work-Study, scholarships/grants, tuition waivers, and unspecified assistantships available. Support available to part-time students. Financial award applicants required to submit FAFSA. *Unit head:* Dr. Ali Golbazi, Professor and Chair, 203-932-7164. *Application contact:* Eloise Gormley, Director of Graduate Admissions, 203-932-7449, Fax: 203-932-7137, E-mail: gradinfo@newhaven.edu.

University of New Mexico, Graduate School, School of Engineering, Department of Electrical and Computer Engineering, Albuquerque, NM 87131-2039. Offers computer engineering (MS, PhD); electrical engineering (MS, PhD). Part-time and evening/weekend programs available. Postbaccalaureate distance learning degree programs offered (no on-campus study). *Faculty:* 49 full-time (6 women), 5 part-time/adjunct (0 women). *Students:* 163 full-time (31 women), 64 part-time (9 women); includes 29 minority (1 African American, 1 American Indian/Alaska Native, 6 Asian Americans or Pacific Islanders, 21 Hispanic Americans), 123 international. Average age 30. 273 applicants, 37% accepted, 61 enrolled. In 2009, 28 master's, 15 doctorates awarded. Terminal master's awarded for partial completion of doctoral program. *Degree requirements:* For master's, thesis; for doctorate, comprehensive exam, thesis/dissertation. *Entrance requirements:* For master's, GRE General Test, minimum GPA of 3.0; for doctorate, GRE General Test, minimum GPA of 3.5. Additional exam requirements/recommendations for international students: Required—TOEFL (minimum score 550 paper-based; 213 computer-based; 79 iBT). *Application deadline:* For fall admission, 7/15 for domestic students, 2/15 for international students; for spring admission, 11/1 for domestic students, 6/15 for international students. Application fee: $50. Electronic applications accepted. *Expenses:* Tuition, state resident: full-time $2098.80; part-time $233.20 per credit hour. Tuition, nonresident: full-time $6650. Required fees: $25 per semester. Tuition and fees vary according to course load, program and reciprocity agreements. *Financial support:* In 2009–10, 22 students received

Electrical Engineering

University of New Mexico (continued)

support, including 2 fellowships with tuition reimbursements available (averaging $12,500 per year), 85 research assistantships with tuition reimbursements available (averaging $13,000 per year), 16 teaching assistantships with tuition reimbursements available (averaging $13,715 per year); scholarships/grants, health care benefits, and unspecified assistantships also available. Financial award application deadline: 2/15; financial award applicants required to submit FAFSA. *Faculty research:* Advanced graphics and visualization, biomedical engineering, communications and networking, networked control systems, photonics and microelectronics, pulsed power and high-power electromagnetics, reconfigurable systems. Total annual research expenditures: $3.2 million. *Unit head:* Dr. Chaouki T. Abdallah, Chair, 505-277-0298, Fax: 505-277-1439, E-mail: chaouki@ece.unm.edu. *Application contact:* Elmyra Grelle, Coordinator—Graduate Programs, 505-277-2600, Fax: 505-277-1439, E-mail: egrelle@ece.unm.edu.

See Close-Up on page 377.

The University of North Carolina at Charlotte, Graduate School, The William States Lee College of Engineering, Department of Electrical and Computer Engineering, Charlotte, NC 28223-0001. Offers electrical engineering (MSEE, PhD). Part-time and evening/weekend programs available. *Faculty:* 26 full-time (1 woman). *Students:* 103 full-time (19 women), 59 part-time (8 women); includes 4 African Americans, 4 Asian Americans or Pacific Islanders, 3 Hispanic Americans, 117 international. Average age 26. 410 applicants, 46% accepted, 40 enrolled. In 2009, 43 master's, 3 doctorates awarded. Terminal master's awarded for partial completion of doctoral program. *Degree requirements:* For master's, thesis optional, thesis or project; for doctorate, thesis/dissertation. *Entrance requirements:* For master's, GRE General Test, minimum GPA of 3.0 in undergraduate major, 2.75 overall; for doctorate, GRE General Test, 3 letters of reference. Additional exam requirements/recommendations for international students: Required—TOEFL (minimum score 557 paper-based; 220 computer-based; 83 iBT). *Application deadline:* For fall admission, 7/1 for domestic students, 5/1 for international students; for spring admission, 11/1 for domestic students, 10/1 for international students. Applications are processed on a rolling basis. Application fee: $55. Electronic applications accepted. *Financial support:* In 2009–10, 55 students received support, including 1 fellowship (averaging $45,000 per year), 8 research assistantships (averaging $7,186 per year), 46 teaching assistantships (averaging $8,303 per year); career-related internships or fieldwork, institutionally sponsored loans, scholarships/grants, and unspecified assistantships also available. Support available to part-time students. Financial award application deadline: 4/1; financial award applicants required to submit FAFSA. *Faculty research:* Integrated circuits self test, control systems, optoelectronics/microelectronics devices and systems, communications, computer engineering. Total annual research expenditures: $1.2 million. *Unit head:* Dr. Ian Ferguson, Chair, 704-687-8404, Fax: 704-687-4762, E-mail: ianf@uncc.edu. *Application contact:* Kathy B. Giddings, Director of Graduate Admissions, 704-687-5503, Fax: 704-687-3279, E-mail: gradadm@uncc.edu.

University of North Dakota, Graduate School, School of Engineering and Mines, Department of Electrical Engineering, Grand Forks, ND 58202. Offers M Engr, MS. Part-time programs available. *Degree requirements:* For master's, comprehensive exam, thesis or alternative. *Entrance requirements:* For master's, GRE General Test, minimum GPA of 3.0 (MS), minimum GPA of 2.5 (M Engr). Additional exam requirements/recommendations for international students: Required—TOEFL (minimum score 550 paper-based; 213 computer-based; 79 iBT), IELTS (minimum score 6.5). Electronic applications accepted. *Faculty research:* Controls and robotics, signal processing, energy conversion, microwaves, computer engineering.

University of North Florida, College of Computing, Engineering, and Construction, Jacksonville, FL 32224. Offers civil engineering (MSCE); computer and information sciences (MS); electrical engineering (MSEE); mechanical engineering (MSME). Part-time programs available. *Faculty:* 35 full-time (6 women). *Students:* 21 full-time (4 women), 64 part-time (11 women); includes 22 minority (6 African Americans, 9 Asian Americans or Pacific Islanders, 7 Hispanic Americans), 10 international. Average age 31. 82 applicants, 45% accepted, 14 enrolled. In 2009, 6 master's awarded. *Degree requirements:* For master's, thesis optional. *Entrance requirements:* For master's, GRE General Test, minimum GPA of 3.0 in last 60 hours of course work. Additional exam requirements/recommendations for international students: Required—TOEFL (minimum score 500 paper-based; 173 computer-based). *Application deadline:* For fall admission, 7/1 priority date for domestic students, 5/1 for international students; for spring admission, 11/1 priority date for domestic students, 10/1 for international students. Applications are processed on a rolling basis. Application fee: $30. Electronic applications accepted. *Expenses:* Tuition, state resident: full-time $6649.20; part-time $277.05 per credit hour. Tuition, nonresident: full-time $22,970; part-time $957.08 per credit hour. Required fees: $985; $41.03 per credit hour. *Financial support:* In 2009–10, 20 students received support, including 5 research assistantships (averaging $5,009 per year), 3 teaching assistantships (averaging $2,844 per year); Federal Work-Study and tuition waivers (partial) also available. Support available to part-time students. Financial award application deadline: 4/1; financial award applicants required to submit FAFSA. *Faculty research:* Parallel and distributed computing, networks, generic programming, algorithms, artificial intelligence. Total annual research expenditures: $2.2 million. *Unit head:* Dr. Neal Coulter, Dean, 904-620-1350, E-mail: ncoulter@unf.edu. *Application contact:* Dr. Roger Eggen, Director of Graduate Studies for Computer Science, 904-320-2985, Fax: 904-620-2988, E-mail: ree@unf.edu.

University of North Texas, Robert B. Toulouse School of Graduate Studies, College of Engineering, Department of Electrical Engineering, Denton, TX 76203. Offers MS. Part-time programs available. *Degree requirements:* For master's, thesis optional. *Entrance requirements:* For master's, GRE, minimum GPA of 3.0. Additional exam requirements/recommendations for international students: Required—TOEFL (minimum score 550 paper-based; 213 computer-based; 79 iBT), proof of English language proficiency required for non-native English speakers. Application fee: $50 ($75 for international students). *Expenses:* Tuition, state resident: full-time $4298; part-time $239 per contact hour. Tuition, nonresident: full-time $9878; part-time $549 per contact hour. Required fees: $265 per contact hour. *Financial support:* Fellowships with tuition reimbursements, research assistantships with tuition reimbursements, teaching assistantships with tuition reimbursements, career-related internships or fieldwork, scholarships/grants, health care benefits, tuition waivers (full), and unspecified assistantships available. Financial award application deadline: 4/1. *Faculty research:* Ecological and environmental modeling, radar systems, wireless communication, human-computer interaction, computer vision, signal processing, information assurance, VISI design. *Application contact:* Graduate Advisor, 940-891-6942, Fax: 940-891-6881, E-mail: fu@unt.edu.

University of Notre Dame, Graduate School, College of Engineering, Department of Electrical Engineering, Notre Dame, IN 46556. Offers MSEE, PhD. Terminal master's awarded for partial completion of doctoral program. *Degree requirements:* For master's, comprehensive exam; for doctorate, thesis/dissertation, candidacy exam. *Entrance requirements:* For master's and doctorate, GRE General Test. Additional exam requirements/recommendations for international students: Required—TOEFL (minimum score 600 paper-based; 250 computer-based; 80 iBT). Electronic applications accepted. *Faculty research:* Electronic properties of materials and devices, signal and imaging processing, communication theory, control theory and applications, optoelectronics.

See Display on page 337 and Close-Up on page 379.

University of Oklahoma, Graduate College, College of Engineering, Department of Electrical and Computer Engineering, Program in Electrical and Computer Engineering, Norman, OK 73019. Offers MS, PhD. Part-time programs available. *Students:* 115 full-time (28 women), 24 part-time (2 women); includes 16 minority (3 African Americans, 3 American Indian/Alaska Native, 8 Asian Americans or Pacific Islanders, 2 Hispanic Americans), 79 international. 68 applicants, 68% accepted, 24 enrolled. In 2009, 33 master's, 10 doctorates awarded. Terminal master's awarded for partial completion of doctoral program. *Degree requirements:* For master's, thesis, oral exam; for doctorate, thesis/dissertation, general exam, oral exam, qualifying exam. *Entrance requirements:* For master's and doctorate, GRE General Test. Additional exam requirements/recommendations for international students: Required—TOEFL (minimum score 550 paper-based; 213 computer-based). *Application deadline:* For fall admission, 5/15 for domestic students, 4/1 for international students; for spring admission, 9/1 for domestic and international students. Applications are processed on a rolling basis. Application fee: $40 ($90 for international students). Electronic applications accepted. *Expenses:* Tuition, state resident: full-time $3744; part-time $156 per credit hour. Tuition, nonresident: full-time $13,577; part-time $565.70 per credit hour. Required fees: $2415; $90.10 per credit hour. *Financial support:* In 2009–10, 108 students received support. Career-related internships or fieldwork, scholarships/grants, health care benefits, and unspecified assistantships available. Financial award application deadline: 4/15; financial award applicants required to submit FAFSA. *Faculty research:* Signal and image processing, biomedical imaging, weather radar, solid state electronics, intelligent transportation systems, navigation systems, power/electrical energy, control systems, communications computer hardware design. *Unit head:* Dr. James Sluss, Director, 405-325-4721, Fax: 405-325-7066, E-mail: sluss@ou.edu. *Application contact:* Lynn Hall, Graduate Program Assistant, 405-325-4285, Fax: 405-325-7066, E-mail: lynnhall@ou.edu.

University of Ottawa, Faculty of Graduate and Postdoctoral Studies, Faculty of Engineering, Ottawa-Carleton Institute for Electrical and Computer Engineering, Ottawa, ON K1N 6N5, Canada. Offers M Eng, MA Sc, PhD. *Degree requirements:* For master's, thesis or alternative, project; for doctorate, comprehensive exam, thesis/dissertation. *Entrance requirements:* For master's, honors degree or equivalent, minimum B average; for doctorate, minimum A- average. Electronic applications accepted. *Faculty research:* CAD, CSE, distributed systems and BISDN, CCN, DOC.

University of Pennsylvania, School of Engineering and Applied Science, Department of Electrical and Systems Engineering, Philadelphia, PA 19104. Offers MSE, PhD. Part-time programs available. *Faculty:* 27 full-time (2 women), 8 part-time/adjunct (0 women). *Students:* 121 full-time (29 women), 44 part-time (7 women); includes 22 minority (4 African Americans, 17 Asian Americans or Pacific Islanders, 1 Hispanic American), 101 international. 574 applicants, 32% accepted, 105 enrolled. In 2009, 61 master's, 8 doctorates awarded. Terminal master's awarded for partial completion of doctoral program. *Degree requirements:* For master's, thesis optional; for doctorate, comprehensive exam, thesis/dissertation. *Entrance requirements:* For master's and doctorate, GRE General Test. Additional exam requirements/recommendations for international students: Required—TOEFL. *Application deadline:* For fall admission, 6/1 priority date for domestic students, 5/1 priority date for international students; for spring admission, 11/1 priority date for domestic students, 10/1 priority date for international students. Applications are processed on a rolling basis. Application fee: $70. Electronic applications accepted. *Expenses:* Tuition: Full-time $25,660; part-time $4758 per course. Required fees: $2152; $270 per course. Tuition and fees vary according to course load, degree level and program. *Financial support:* Fellowships, research assistantships, teaching assistantships, institutionally sponsored loans, scholarships/grants, traineeships, health care benefits, and unspecified assistantships available. *Faculty research:* Electro-optics, microwave and millimeter-wave optics, solid-state and chemical electronics, electromagnetic propagation, telecommunications.

University of Pittsburgh, School of Engineering, Department of Electrical Engineering, Pittsburgh, PA 15260. Offers MSEE, PhD. Part-time programs available. Postbaccalaureate distance learning degree programs offered. *Faculty:* 14 full-time (1 woman), 14 part-time/adjunct (1 woman). *Students:* 79 full-time (14 women), 52 part-time (1 woman); includes 9 minority (4 African Americans, 4 Asian Americans or Pacific Islanders, 1 Hispanic American), 51 international. 418 applicants, 28% accepted, 37 enrolled. In 2009, 14 master's, 9 doctorates awarded. Terminal master's awarded for partial completion of doctoral program. *Degree requirements:* For master's, thesis optional; for doctorate, comprehensive exam, thesis/dissertation, final oral exams. *Entrance requirements:* For master's and doctorate, GRE General Test, minimum QPA of 3.0. Additional exam requirements/recommendations for international students: Required—TOEFL (minimum score 550 paper-based; 213 computer-based; 80 iBT). *Application deadline:* For fall admission, 3/1 priority date for domestic students; for spring admission, 7/1 priority date for domestic students. Applications are processed on a rolling basis. Application fee: $50. Electronic applications accepted. *Expenses:* Tuition, state resident: full-time $16,402; part-time $665 per credit. Tuition, nonresident: full-time $28,694; part-time $1175 per credit. Required fees: $690; $175 per term. Tuition and fees vary according to program. *Financial support:* In 2009–10, 53 students received support, including 4 fellowships with full tuition reimbursements available (averaging $20,772 per year), 31 research assistantships with full tuition reimbursements available (averaging $22,000 per year), 26 teaching assistantships with full tuition reimbursements available (averaging $21,000 per year); scholarships/grants and tuition waivers (full and partial) also available. Financial award application deadline: 4/15. *Faculty research:* Computer engineering, image processing, signal processing, electro-optic devices, controls/power. Total annual research expenditures: $1.5 million. *Unit head:* Dr. William Stanchina, Chairman, 412-624-8000, Fax: 412-624-8003, E-mail: wstanchina@engr.bitt.edu. *Application contact:* Steven Levitan, Graduate Coordinator, 412-624-8001, Fax: 412-624-8003, E-mail: levitan@engr.pitt.edu.

University of Puerto Rico, Mayagüez Campus, Graduate Studies, College of Engineering, Department of Electrical and Computer Engineering, Mayagüez, PR 00681-9000. Offers computer engineering (ME, MS); electrical engineering (ME, MS). Part-time programs available. *Degree requirements:* For master's, comprehensive exam, thesis. *Entrance requirements:* For master's, proficiency in English and Spanish, BS degree in electrical or computer engineering or equivalent, minimum GPA of 3.0. Additional exam requirements/recommendations for international students: Required—TOEFL (minimum score 450 paper-based). *Faculty research:* Microcomputer interfacing, control systems, power systems, electronics.

University of Rhode Island, Graduate School, College of Engineering, Department of Electrical, Computer and Biomedical Engineering, Kingston, RI 02881. Offers MS, PhD, Graduate Certificate. Part-time programs available. *Faculty:* 18 full-time (3 women), 2 part-time/adjunct (0 women). *Students:* 27 full-time (7 women), 17 part-time (2 women); includes 7 minority (2 African Americans, 2 Asian Americans or Pacific Islanders, 3 Hispanic Americans), 13 international. In 2009, 13 master's, 3 doctorates awarded. *Degree requirements:* For master's, comprehensive exam (for some programs), thesis optional; for doctorate, comprehensive exam, thesis/dissertation. *Entrance requirements:* For master's and doctorate, 2 letters of recommendation. Additional exam requirements/recommendations for international students: Required—TOEFL (minimum score 550 paper-based; 213 computer-based). *Application deadline:* For fall admission, 7/15 for domestic students, 2/1 for international students; for spring admission, 11/15 for domestic students, 7/15 for international students. Application fee: $65. Electronic applications accepted. *Expenses:* Tuition, state resident: full-time $8828; part-time $490 per credit hour. Tuition, nonresident: full-time $22,100; part-time $1228 per credit hour. Required fees: $1118; $57 per semester. Tuition and fees vary according to program. *Financial support:* In 2009–10, 5 research assistantships with full and partial tuition reimbursements (averaging $4,888 per year), 4 teaching assistantships with full and partial tuition reimbursements (averaging $6,726 per year) were awarded. Financial award application deadline: 7/15; financial award applicants required to submit FAFSA. *Faculty research:* Biomedical Instrumentation, cardiac physiology and computational modeling, analog/digital CMOS circuits, neural-machine interface, digital circuit design and VLSI testing. Total annual research expenditures: $744,413. *Unit head:* Dr. G. Faye Boudreaux-Bartels, Chair, 401-874-5805, Fax: 401-782-6422, E-mail: boud@ele.uri.edu. *Application contact:* Dr. Godi Fischer, Director of Graduate Studies, 401-874-5879, Fax: 401-782-6422, E-mail: fischer@ele.uri.edu.

University of Rochester, The College, School of Engineering and Applied Sciences, Department of Electrical and Computer Engineering, Rochester, NY 14627. Offers MS, PhD. Terminal master's awarded for partial completion of doctoral program. *Degree requirements:* For master's, comprehensive exam; for doctorate, thesis/dissertation, preliminary and oral exams. *Entrance requirements:* For master's and doctorate, GRE. Additional exam requirements/recommendations for international students: Required—TOEFL.

University of Saskatchewan, College of Graduate Studies and Research, College of Engineering, Department of Electrical Engineering, Saskatoon, SK S7N 5A2, Canada. Offers M Eng, M Sc, PhD. *Degree requirements:* For master's, thesis (for some programs); for doctorate, thesis/dissertation. *Entrance requirements:* For master's and doctorate, GRE. Additional exam requirements/recommendations for international students: Required—TOEFL. Tuition and fees charges are reported in Canadian dollars. *Expenses:* Tuition, area resident: Full-time $3000 Canadian dollars; part-time $500 Canadian dollars per term. Required fees: $700 Canadian dollars; $100 Canadian dollars per term.

University of South Alabama, Graduate School, College of Engineering, Department of Electrical and Computer Engineering, Mobile, AL 36688-0002. Offers electrical engineering (MSEE). Part-time programs available. *Degree requirements:* For master's, project or thesis. *Entrance requirements:* For master's, GRE General Test, BS in engineering, minimum GPA of 3.0. *Expenses:* Tuition, state resident: part-time $218 per contact hour. Required fees: $1102 per year.

University of South Carolina, The Graduate School, College of Engineering and Computing, Department of Electrical Engineering, Columbia, SC 29208. Offers ME, MS, PhD. Part-time and evening/weekend programs available. Postbaccalaureate distance learning degree programs offered (minimal on-campus study). *Degree requirements:* For master's, comprehensive exam, thesis (for some programs); for doctorate, comprehensive exam, thesis/dissertation, qualifying exam. *Entrance requirements:* For master's and doctorate, GRE General Test. Additional exam requirements/recommendations for international students: Required—TOEFL (minimum score 570 paper-based; 230 computer-based; 88 iBT). Electronic applications accepted. *Faculty research:* Microelectronics, photonics, wireless communications, signal integrity, energy and control systems.

University of Southern California, Graduate School, Viterbi School of Engineering, Ming Hsieh Department of Electrical Engineering, Los Angeles, CA 90089. Offers computer engineering (MS, PhD); computer networks (MS), including electrical engineering; computer-aided engineering (MS); electrical engineering (PhD, Engr); engineering technology commercialization (Graduate Certificate); systems architeching and engineering (MS). Part-time programs available. Postbaccalaureate distance learning degree programs offered. *Faculty:* 59 full-time (3 women), 31 part-time/adjunct (1 woman). *Students:* 883 full-time (146 women), 451 part-time (65 women); includes 197 minority (16 African Americans, 159 Asian Americans or Pacific Islanders, 22 Hispanic Americans), 957 international. 2,377 applicants, 45% accepted, 514 enrolled. In 2009, 351 master's, 41 doctorates, 2 other advanced degrees awarded. Terminal master's awarded for partial completion of doctoral program. *Degree requirements:* For doctorate, thesis/dissertation. *Entrance requirements:* For master's, GRE General Test; for doctorate, General GRE. *Application deadline:* For fall admission, 3/1 priority date for domestic and international students; for spring admission, 10/1 priority date for domestic and international students. Applications are processed on a rolling basis. Application fee: $85. Electronic applications accepted. *Expenses:* Tuition: Full-time $25,980; part-time $1315 per unit. Required fees: $554. One-time fee: $35 full-time. Full-time tuition and fees vary according to degree level and program. *Financial support:* Career-related internships or fieldwork, scholarships/grants, health care benefits, and unspecified assistantships available. Financial award application deadline: 12/1; financial award applicants required to submit CSS PROFILE or FAFSA. *Faculty research:* Communications, computer engineering and networks, control systems, integrated circuits and systems, electromagnetics and energy conversion, micro electro-mechanical systems and nanotechnology, photonics and quantum electronics, plasma research, signal and image processing. Total annual research expenditures: $16.2 million. *Unit head:* Dr. Alexander A. Sawchuk, Chair, 213-740-4622, Fax: 213-740-4651, E-mail: sawchuk@sipi.usc.edu. *Application contact:* Diane Demetras, Student Affairs Coordinator, 213-740-4485, E-mail: eesystem@usc.edu.

University of South Florida, Graduate School, College of Engineering, Department of Electrical Engineering, Tampa, FL 33620-9951. Offers ME, MSEE, MSES, PhD. Part-time programs available. Postbaccalaureate distance learning degree programs offered (no on-campus study). *Faculty:* 20 full-time (3 women), 3 part-time/adjunct (0 women). *Students:* 125 full-time (31 women), 88 part-time (12 women); includes 57 minority (19 African Americans, 1 American Indian/Alaska Native, 16 Asian Americans or Pacific Islanders, 21 Hispanic Americans), 97 international. Average age 32. 191 applicants, 63% accepted, 57 enrolled. In 2009, 59 master's, 11 doctorates awarded. Terminal master's awarded for partial completion of doctoral program. *Degree requirements:* For master's, comprehensive exam, thesis or alternative; for doctorate, comprehensive exam, thesis/dissertation. *Entrance requirements:* For master's, GRE General Test (minimum score 1000 verbal and quantitative, 700 quantitative), minimum GPA of 3.0 in last 60 hours of coursework; for doctorate, GRE General Test (Quantitative 700, combined Verbal and Quantitative 1100). Additional exam requirements/recommendations for international students: Required—TOEFL (minimum score 550 paper-based; 213 computer-based; 79 iBT). *Application deadline:* For fall admission, 2/15 for domestic students, 1/2 for international students; for spring admission, 10/15 for domestic students, 6/1 for international students. Application fee: $30. Electronic applications accepted. *Financial support:* In 2009–10, teaching assistantships with tuition reimbursements (averaging $19,107 per year). Financial award applicants required to submit FAFSA. *Faculty research:* Silicon processing, micro/millimeter waves, communication and signal processing, clean energy and sustainability, bioengineering. Total annual research expenditures: $2.4 million. *Unit head:* Dr. Sal Morgera, Department Chair, 813-974-1004, E-mail: morgera@usf.edu. *Application contact:* Dr. Kenneth A. Buckle, Director, 813-974-4772, Fax: 813-974-5250, E-mail: buckle@usf.edu.

The University of Tennessee, Graduate School, College of Engineering, Department of Electrical Engineering and Computer Science, Knoxville, TN 37996. Offers computer engineering (MS, PhD); computer science (MS, PhD); electrical engineering (MS, PhD); reliability and maintainability engineering (MS); MS/MBA. Part-time programs available. *Faculty:* 40 full-time (4 women), 13 part-time/adjunct (2 women). *Students:* 141 full-time (25 women), 62 part-time (11 women); includes 11 minority (4 African Americans, 5 Asian Americans or Pacific Islanders, 2 Hispanic Americans), 109 international. Average age 30. 603 applicants, 12% accepted, 45 enrolled. In 2009, 55 master's, 24 doctorates awarded. *Degree requirements:* For master's, thesis or alternative; for doctorate, comprehensive exam, thesis/dissertation. *Entrance requirements:* For master's, GRE, minimum GPA of 3.0; for doctorate, GRE General Test, minimum GPA of 3.0. Additional exam requirements/recommendations for international students: Required—TOEFL (minimum score 550 paper-based; 213 computer-based). *Application deadline:* For fall admission, 2/1 priority date for domestic and international students; for spring admission, 6/15 priority date for international students. Applications are processed on a rolling basis. Application fee: $35. Electronic applications accepted. *Expenses:* Tuition, state resident: full-time $6826; part-time $380 per semester hour. Tuition, nonresident: full-time $21,844; part-time $1147 per semester hour. Tuition and fees vary according to program. *Financial support:* In 2009–10, 139 students received support, including 32 fellowships with full tuition reimbursements available (averaging $5,448 per year), 118 research assistantships with full tuition reimbursements available (averaging $16,800 per year), 68 teaching assistantships with full tuition reimbursements available (averaging $12,996 per year); career-related internships or fieldwork, Federal Work-Study, institutionally sponsored loans, health care benefits, and unspecified assistantships also available. Financial award application deadline: 2/1; financial award applicants required to submit FAFSA. *Faculty research:* Artificial intelligence and visualization; microelectronics, mixed-signal electronics, VLSI, embedded systems; scientific and distributed computing; computer vision, robotics, and image processing; power electronics, power systems, communications. Total annual research expenditures: $9.1 million. *Unit head:* Dr. Kevin Tomsovic, Head, 865-974-3461, Fax: 865-974-3461, E-mail: tomsovic@eecs.utk.edu. *Application contact:* Dr. Masood Parang, Associate Dean of Student Affairs, 865-974-2454, Fax: 865-974-9871, E-mail: mparang@utk.edu.

The University of Tennessee at Chattanooga, Graduate School, College of Engineering and Computer Science, Program in Engineering, Chattanooga, TN 37403. Offers chemical (MS Engr); civil (MS Engr); computational (MS Engr); electrical (MS Engr); industrial (MS Engr); mechanical (MS Engr). Part-time and evening/weekend programs available. *Faculty:* 8 full-time (0 women). *Students:* 22 full-time (7 women), 30 part-time (3 women); includes 9 minority (4 African Americans, 4 Asian Americans or Pacific Islanders, 1 Hispanic American), 9 international. Average age 29. 59 applicants, 59% accepted, 19 enrolled. In 2009, 9 master's awarded. *Degree requirements:* For master's, comprehensive exam, thesis or alternative, engineering project. *Entrance requirements:* For master's, GRE General Test, minimum undergraduate GPA of 2.5 or 3.0 in last 30 hours of coursework. Additional exam requirements/recommendations for international students: Required—TOEFL (minimum score 550 paper-based; 213 computer-based; 79 iBT), IELTS (minimum score 6). *Application deadline:* For fall admission, 8/1 priority date for domestic students, 6/1 for international students; for spring admission, 12/1 priority date for domestic students, 10/1 for international students. Applications are processed on a rolling basis. Application fee: $35. Electronic applications accepted. *Expenses:* Tuition, state resident: full-time $5404; part-time $300 per credit hour. Tuition, nonresident: full-time $16,702; part-time $928 per credit hour. Required fees: $1150; $130 per credit hour. *Financial support:* In 2009–10, 23 research assistantships with full and partial tuition reimbursements (averaging $5,500 per year) were awarded; career-related internships or fieldwork, scholarships/grants, and unspecified assistantships also available. Support available to part-time students. *Faculty research:* Quality control and reliability engineering, financial management, thermal science, energy conservation, structural analysis. Total annual research expenditures: $2.6 million. *Unit head:* Dr. Neslihan Alp, Director, 423-425-4032, Fax: 423-425-5229, E-mail: neslihan-alp@utc.edu. *Application contact:* Dr. Stephanie Bellar, Dean of Graduate Studies, 423-425-4666, Fax: 423-425-5223, E-mail: stephanie-bellar@utc.edu.

The University of Tennessee Space Institute, Graduate Programs, Program in Electrical Engineering and Computer Science, Tullahoma, TN 37388-9700. Offers MS, PhD. *Faculty:* 2 full-time (0 women). *Students:* 1 full-time (0 women). 1 applicant, 0% accepted, 0 enrolled. *Degree requirements:* For master's, thesis (for some programs); for doctorate, one foreign language, thesis/dissertation. *Entrance requirements:* Additional exam requirements/recommendations for international students: Required—TOEFL (minimum score 550 paper-based; 213 computer-based), IELTS (minimum score 6.5). *Application deadline:* For fall admission, 2/1 for international students; for spring admission, 6/15 for international students. Applications are processed on a rolling basis. Application fee: $35. Electronic applications accepted. *Expenses:* Tuition, state resident: full-time $6826; part-time $380 per hour. Tuition, nonresident: full-time $20,622; part-time $1147 per hour. Required fees: $10 per hour. One-time fee: $90 full-time. *Financial support:* Fellowships, research assistantships with full tuition reimbursements, career-related internships or fieldwork, Federal Work-Study, institutionally sponsored loans, health care benefits, tuition waivers (full and partial), and unspecified assistantships available. Financial award applicants required to submit FAFSA. *Unit head:* Dr. Monty Smith, Degree Program Chairman, 931-393-7480, Fax: 931-393-7530, E-mail: msmith@utsi.edu. *Application contact:* Dee Merriman, Coordinator III, 931-393-7293, Fax: 931-393-7201, E-mail: dmerrima@utsi.edu.

The University of Texas at Arlington, Graduate School, College of Engineering, Department of Electrical Engineering, Arlington, TX 76019. Offers M Engr, MS, PhD. Part-time and evening/weekend programs available. Postbaccalaureate distance learning degree programs offered (no on-campus study). *Faculty:* 23 full-time (0 women), 3 part-time/adjunct (1 woman). *Students:* 293 full-time (51 women), 150 part-time (17 women); includes 17 minority (6 African Americans, 1 American Indian/Alaska Native, 8 Asian Americans or Pacific Islanders, 2 Hispanic Americans), 379 international. 507 applicants, 99% accepted, 113 enrolled. In 2009, 100 master's, 11 doctorates awarded. Terminal master's awarded for partial completion of doctoral program. *Degree requirements:* For master's, thesis optional; for doctorate, comprehensive exam, thesis/dissertation, research potential assessment. *Entrance requirements:* For master's, GRE General Test, minimum GPA of 3.25; for doctorate, GRE General Test, minimum GPA of 3.5. Additional exam requirements/recommendations for international students: Required—TOEFL (minimum score 550 paper-based; 220 computer-based); Recommended—TWE (minimum score 4). *Application deadline:* For fall admission, 6/16 for domestic students, 4/4 for international students; for spring admission, 10/17 for domestic students, 9/5 for international students. Applications are processed on a rolling basis. Application fee: $35 ($50 for international students). *Financial support:* In 2009–10, 202 students received support, including 23 fellowships (averaging $1,000 per year), 60 research assistantships (averaging $14,400 per year), 1 teaching assistantship (averaging $9,600 per year); Federal Work-Study, institutionally sponsored loans, scholarships/grants, and unspecified assistantships also available. Financial award application deadline: 6/1; financial award applicants required to submit FAFSA. *Faculty research:* Nanotech and MEMS, digital image processing, telecommunications and optics, energy systems and power electronics, VLSI and semiconductors. Total annual research expenditures: $1 million. *Unit head:* Dr. Jonathan Bredow, Chair, 817-272-3497, Fax: 817-272-2253, E-mail: jbredow@uta.edu. *Application contact:* Dr. William E. Dillon, Graduate Adviser, 817-272-2671, Fax: 817-272-1509, E-mail: eedept@uta.edu.

The University of Texas at Austin, Graduate School, Cockrell School of Engineering, Department of Electrical and Computer Engineering, Austin, TX 78712-1111. Offers MSE, PhD. Part-time programs available. *Entrance requirements:* For master's, GRE General Test, minimum GPA of 3.3 in upper-division course work; for doctorate, GRE General Test. Electronic applications accepted.

The University of Texas at Dallas, Erik Jonsson School of Engineering and Computer Science, Programs in Electrical Engineering, Richardson, TX 75080. Offers computer engineering (MS, PhD); electrical engineering (MSEE, PhD); microelectronics (MSEE, PhD); telecommunications (MSEE, MSTE, PhD). Part-time and evening/weekend programs available. *Faculty:* 43 full-time (3 women), 3 part-time/adjunct (0 women). *Students:* 391 full-time (78 women), 160 part-time (23 women); includes 86 minority (14 African Americans, 59 Asian Americans or Pacific Islanders, 13 Hispanic Americans), 383 international. Average age 27. 1,292 applicants, 31% accepted, 168 enrolled. In 2009, 149 master's, 14 doctorates awarded. *Degree requirements:* For master's, thesis or major design project; for doctorate, thesis/dissertation. *Entrance requirements:* For master's, GRE General Test, minimum GPA of 3.0 in related bachelor's degree; for doctorate, GRE General Test, minimum GPA of 3.5. Additional exam requirements/recommendations for international students: Required—TOEFL (minimum score 550 paper-based; 213 computer-based). *Application deadline:* For fall admission, 7/15 for domestic students, 5/1 priority date for international students; for spring admission, 11/15 for domestic students, 9/1 priority date for international students. Applications are processed on a rolling basis. Application fee: $50 ($100 for international students). Electronic applications accepted. *Expenses:* Tuition, state resident: full-time $11,068; part-time $461 per credit hour. Tuition, nonresident: full-time $21,178; part-time $882 per credit hour. Tuition and fees vary according to course load. *Financial support:* In 2009–10, 1 fellowship with full tuition reimbursement (averaging $18,000 per year), 116 research assistantships with full tuition reimbursements (averaging $17,579 per year), 41 teaching assistantships with full tuition reimbursements (averaging $17,516 per year) were awarded; Federal Work-Study, institutionally sponsored loans, scholarships/grants, unspecified assistantships, and co-op positions also available. Support available to part-time students. Financial award application deadline: 4/30; financial award applicants required to submit FAFSA. *Faculty research:* Communications and signal processing, solid-state devices and circuits, digital systems, optical devices, materials and systems, lasers and photonics. *Unit head:* Dr. John H. L. Hansen, Head, 972-883-2910, Fax: 972-883-2710, E-mail: john.hansen@utdallas.edu. *Application contact:* Kathy Gribble, Coordinator, 972-883-2649, Fax: 972-883-2813, E-mail: gradecs@utdallas.edu.

The University of Texas at El Paso, Graduate School, College of Engineering, Department of Electrical and Computer Engineering, El Paso, TX 79968-0001. Offers computer engineering (MS); electrical and computer engineering (PhD); electrical engineering (MS). Part-time and evening/weekend programs available. *Degree requirements:* For master's, thesis optional; for doctorate, thesis/dissertation. *Entrance requirements:* For master's, GRE General Test, minimum GPA of 3.0; for doctorate, GRE General Test, qualifying exam, minimum graduate GPA of 3.0. Additional exam requirements/recommendations for international students: Required—TOEFL.

Electrical Engineering

The University of Texas at El Paso *(continued)*
Electronic applications accepted. *Faculty research:* Signal and image processing, computer architecture, fiber optics, computational electromagnetics, electronic displays and thin films.

The University of Texas at San Antonio, College of Engineering, Department of Electrical and Computer Engineering, San Antonio, TX 78249-0617. Offers computer engineering (MS); electrical engineering (MSEE, PhD). Part-time and evening/weekend programs available. *Faculty:* 20 full-time (3 women), 1 part-time/adjunct (0 women). *Students:* 99 full-time (25 women), 59 part-time (8 women); includes 26 minority (4 African Americans, 7 Asian Americans or Pacific Islanders, 15 Hispanic Americans), 104 international. Average age 28. 206 applicants, 80% accepted, 48 enrolled. In 2009, 43 master's, 4 doctorates awarded. *Degree requirements:* For master's, comprehensive exam (for some programs), thesis (for some programs); for doctorate, comprehensive exam, thesis/dissertation. *Entrance requirements:* For master's, GRE General Test, minimum GPA of 3.0 in last 60 hours of undergraduate degree; for doctorate, GRE General Test. Additional exam requirements/recommendations for international students: Required—TOEFL (minimum score 500 paper-based; 173 computer-based). *Application deadline:* For fall admission, 7/1 for domestic students, 4/1 for international students; for spring admission, 11/1 for domestic students, 9/1 for international students. Applications are processed on a rolling basis. Application fee: $45 ($80 for international students). Electronic applications accepted. *Expenses:* Tuition, state resident: full-time $3975; part-time $221 per contact hour. Tuition, nonresident: full-time $13,947; part-time $775 per contact hour. Required fees: $1853. *Financial support:* In 2009–10, 60 students received support, including 10 fellowships (averaging $34,425 per year), 62 research assistantships (averaging $11,312 per year), 41 teaching assistantships (averaging $11,244 per year); career-related internships or fieldwork, scholarships/grants, and unspecified assistantships also available. Support available to part-time students. Financial award application deadline: 3/31. Total annual research expenditures: $873,745. *Unit head:* Dr. Mehdi Shadaram, Chair, 210-458-4431, Fax: 210-458-5947, E-mail: mshadaram@utsa.edu. *Application contact:* Chunjiang Qian, Graduate Advisor, 210-458-5587, E-mail: chunjiang.qian@utsa.edu.

The University of Texas at Tyler, College of Engineering and Computer Science, Department of Electrical Engineering, Tyler, TX 75799-0001. Offers MS. Part-time and evening/weekend programs available. *Faculty:* 6 full-time (0 women). *Students:* 16 full-time (2 women), 11 part-time (2 women); includes 4 minority (1 African American, 3 Asian Americans or Pacific Islanders), 17 international. Average age 26. 27 applicants, 100% accepted, 3 enrolled. In 2009, 3 master's awarded. *Degree requirements:* For master's, comprehensive exam (for some programs). *Entrance requirements:* For master's, GRE General Test, bachelor's degree in electrical engineering. Additional exam requirements/recommendations for international students: Required—TOEFL (minimum score 79 computer-based). *Application deadline:* For fall admission, 8/17 priority date for domestic students, 7/1 priority date for international students; for spring admission, 12/21 priority date for domestic students, 11/1 priority date for international students. Application fee: $25 ($50 for international students). *Expenses:* Tuition, state resident: part-time $665 per semester hour. Tuition, nonresident: part-time $942 per semester hour. Part-time tuition and fees vary according to degree level and program. *Financial support:* In 2009–10, 4 research assistantships (averaging $6,000 per year), 6 teaching assistantships (averaging $6,000 per year) were awarded. Financial award application deadline: 7/1. *Faculty research:* Electronics, digital sign processing, real time systems electromagnetic fields, semiconductor modeling. Total annual research expenditures: $1 million. *Unit head:* Dr. Mukul Shirvaikar, Chair, 903-565-5620, Fax: 903-566-7148, E-mail: mshirvaik@uttyler.edu. *Application contact:* Dr. Mikul Shirvaikar.

The University of Texas–Pan American, College of Science and Engineering, Department of Electrical Engineering, Edinburg, TX 78539. Offers MS. *Expenses:* Tuition, state resident: full-time $3630.60; part-time $201.70 per credit hour. Tuition, nonresident: full-time $8617; part-time $478.70 per credit hour. Required fees: $806.50.

The University of Toledo, College of Graduate Studies, College of Engineering, Department of Electrical Engineering and Computer Science, Toledo, OH 43606-3390. Offers computer science (MS, PhD); electrical engineering (MS, PhD). Part-time and evening/weekend programs available. *Degree requirements:* For master's, thesis or alternative; for doctorate, thesis/dissertation, qualifying exam. *Entrance requirements:* For master's, GRE General Test, minimum GPA of 3.0; for doctorate, GRE General Test, minimum GPA of 3.3. Additional exam requirements/recommendations for international students: Required—TOEFL (minimum score 550 paper-based; 213 computer-based; 80 iBT). Electronic applications accepted. *Faculty research:* Communication and signal processing, high performance computing systems, intelligent systems, power electronics and energy systems, RF and microwave systems, sensors and medical devices, solid state devices.

University of Toronto, School of Graduate Studies, Physical Sciences Division, Faculty of Applied Science and Engineering, Department of Electrical and Computer Engineering, Toronto, ON M5S 1A1, Canada. Offers M Eng, MA Sc, PhD. Part-time programs available. *Degree requirements:* For master's, thesis (for some programs), oral thesis defense (MA Sc); for doctorate, thesis/dissertation, qualifying exam, thesis defense. *Entrance requirements:* For master's, four-year degree in electrical or computer engineering, minimum B average, 2 letters of reference; for doctorate, minimum B+ average, MA Sc in electrical or computer engineering, 2 letters of reference.

University of Tulsa, Graduate School, College of Engineering and Natural Sciences, Department of Electrical Engineering, Tulsa, OK 74104-3189. Offers ME, MSE. Part-time programs available. *Faculty:* 8 full-time (0 women). *Students:* 15 full-time (2 women), 2 part-time (0 women), 9 international. Average age 26. 29 applicants, 62% accepted, 6 enrolled. In 2009, 11 master's awarded. *Degree requirements:* For master's, comprehensive exam (for some programs), design report (ME), thesis (MS). *Entrance requirements:* For master's, GRE General Test. Additional exam requirements/recommendations for international students: Required—TOEFL (minimum score 550 paper-based; 213 computer-based; 80 iBT), IELTS (minimum score 6). *Application deadline:* Applications are processed on a rolling basis. Application fee: $40. Electronic applications accepted. *Expenses:* Tuition: Full-time $16,182; part-time $899 per credit hour. Required fees: $4 per credit hour. Tuition and fees vary according to course load. *Financial support:* In 2009–10, 10 students received support, including 3 research assistantships with full and partial tuition reimbursements available (averaging $6,689 per year), 7 teaching assistantships with full and partial tuition reimbursements available (averaging $9,938 per year); fellowships with full and partial tuition reimbursements available, career-related internships or fieldwork, Federal Work-Study, scholarships/grants, health care benefits, tuition waivers (full and partial), and unspecified assistantships also available. Support available to part-time students. Financial award application deadline: 2/1; financial award applicants required to submit FAFSA. *Faculty research:* VLSI microprocessors, intelligent systems, electromagnetics, intrusion detection systems, digital electronics. Total annual research expenditures: $2 million. *Unit head:* Dr. Gerald R. Kane, Chairperson, 918-631-3280. *Application contact:* Dr. Heng-Ming Tai, Adviser, 918-631-3271, Fax: 918-631-3344, E-mail: tai@utulsa.edu.

University of Utah, The Graduate School, College of Engineering, Department of Electrical and Computer Engineering, Salt Lake City, UT 84112. Offers electrical engineering (M Phil, ME, MS, PhD, EE). Part-time programs available. *Faculty:* 27 full-time (2 women), 1 part-time/adjunct (0 women). *Students:* 87 full-time (9 women), 47 part-time (2 women); includes 8 minority (1 African American, 5 Asian Americans or Pacific Islanders, 2 Hispanic Americans), 65 international. Average age 28. 194 applicants, 62% accepted, 38 enrolled. In 2009, 28 master's, 7 doctorates awarded. Terminal master's awarded for partial completion of doctoral program. *Degree requirements:* For master's, comprehensive exam (for some programs), thesis (for some programs); for doctorate, comprehensive exam, thesis/dissertation. *Entrance requirements:* For master's, GRE General Test, minimum GPA of 3.2; for doctorate, GRE General Test, minimum GPA of 3.5. Additional exam requirements/recommendations for international students: Required—TOEFL (minimum score 600 paper-based; 250 computer-based; 100 iBT). *Application deadline:* For fall admission, 4/1 priority date for domestic students, 1/15

for international students; for spring admission, 10/1 for domestic students. Applications are processed on a rolling basis. Application fee: $55 ($65 for international students). Electronic applications accepted. *Expenses:* Tuition, state resident: full-time $4004; part-time $1674 per semester. Tuition, nonresident: full-time $14,134; part-time $5915 per semester. Required fees: $324 per semester. Tuition and fees vary according to course load, degree level and program. *Financial support:* In 2009–10, 2 students received support, including 4 fellowships with full tuition reimbursements available (averaging $20,000 per year), 45 research assistantships with full tuition reimbursements available (averaging $13,900 per year), 11 teaching assistantships with full tuition reimbursements available (averaging $11,000 per year); Federal Work-Study, institutionally sponsored loans, health care benefits, and unspecified assistantships also available. Financial award application deadline: 2/15; financial award applicants required to submit FAFSA. *Faculty research:* Semiconductors, VLSI design, control systems, electromagnetics and applied optics, communication theory and digital signal processing. Total annual research expenditures: $6.1 million. *Unit head:* Dr. Gianluca Lazzi, Chair, 801-581-6941, Fax: 801-581-5281, E-mail: lazzi@utah.edu. *Application contact:* Lori S. Walk, Graduate Coordinator, 801-581-6943, Fax: 801-581-5281, E-mail: lwalk@ece.utah.edu.

University of Vermont, Graduate College, College of Engineering and Mathematics, Department of Electrical Engineering, Burlington, VT 05405. Offers MS, PhD. *Students:* 34 (4 women); includes 2 minority (both Asian Americans or Pacific Islanders), 12 international. 41 applicants, 73% accepted, 11 enrolled. In 2009, 7 master's, 1 doctorate awarded. *Degree requirements:* For master's, thesis or alternative; for doctorate, one foreign language, thesis/dissertation. *Entrance requirements:* For master's, GRE General Test. Additional exam requirements/recommendations for international students: Required—TOEFL (minimum score 550 paper-based; 213 computer-based; 80 iBT). *Application deadline:* For fall admission, 2/1 priority date for domestic students. Applications are processed on a rolling basis. Application fee: $40. Electronic applications accepted. *Expenses:* Tuition, area resident: Part-time $508 per credit hour. Tuition, state resident: part-time $508 per credit hour. Tuition, nonresident: part-time $1281 per credit hour. *Financial support:* Fellowships, research assistantships, teaching assistantships available. Financial award application deadline: 3/1. *Unit head:* Dr. Jeff Marshall, Director, 802-656-3331. *Application contact:* Prof. Kurt Oughstun, Coordinator, 802-656-3331.

University of Victoria, Faculty of Graduate Studies, Faculty of Engineering, Department of Electrical and Computer Engineering, Victoria, BC V8W 2Y2, Canada. Offers M Eng, MA Sc, PhD. *Degree requirements:* For master's, thesis; for doctorate, thesis/dissertation, candidacy exam. *Entrance requirements:* For master's, GRE (recommended), bachelor's degree in engineering; for doctorate, GRE (recommended), master's degree. Additional exam requirements/recommendations for international students: Required—TOEFL (minimum score 575 paper-based; 233 computer-based), IELTS (minimum score 7). Electronic applications accepted. *Faculty research:* Communications and computers; electromagnetics, microwaves, and optics; electronics; power systems, signal processing, and control.

University of Virginia, School of Engineering and Applied Science, Department of Electrical and Computer Engineering, Program in Electrical Engineering, Charlottesville, VA 22903. Offers ME, MS, PhD. *Students:* 117 full-time (28 women), 4 part-time (2 women); includes 10 minority (4 African Americans, 6 Asian Americans or Pacific Islanders), 66 international. Average age 27. 261 applicants, 16% accepted, 25 enrolled. In 2009, 20 master's, 6 doctorates awarded. *Degree requirements:* For doctorate, thesis/dissertation. *Entrance requirements:* For master's, GRE General Test, 3 letters of recommendation; for doctorate, GRE General Test, 3 letters of recommendation; essay. Additional exam requirements/recommendations for international students: Required—TOEFL (minimum score 650 paper-based; 250 computer-based; 100 iBT), IELTS (minimum score 7). *Application deadline:* For fall admission, 8/1 for domestic students, 1/15 for international students; for winter admission, 12/1 for domestic students, 8/1 for international students; for spring admission, 5/1 for domestic students. Applications are processed on a rolling basis. Application fee: $60. Electronic applications accepted. *Financial support:* Fellowships, research assistantships, teaching assistantships available. Financial award application deadline: 1/15; financial award applicants required to submit FAFSA. *Unit head:* Chair. *Application contact:* Nathan Swami, Graduate Program Director, 434-924-3960, Fax: 434-924-8818, E-mail: nathanswami@virginia.edu.

University of Washington, Graduate School, College of Engineering, Department of Electrical Engineering, Seattle, WA 98195-2500. Offers MSEE, PhD. *Faculty:* 42 full-time (7 women), 30 part-time/adjunct (5 women). *Students:* 214 full-time (38 women), 32 part-time (4 women); includes 34 minority (28 Asian Americans or Pacific Islanders, 6 Hispanic Americans), 107 international. 593 applicants, 39% accepted, 110 enrolled. In 2009, 39 master's, 29 doctorates awarded. *Degree requirements:* For master's, thesis optional; for doctorate, thesis/dissertation. *Entrance requirements:* For master's, GRE General Test, minimum GPA of 3.0; for doctorate, GRE General Test, MS, minimum GPA of 3.0. Additional exam requirements/recommendations for international students: Required—TOEFL (minimum score 580 paper-based; 237 computer-based; 70 iBT). *Application deadline:* For fall admission, 1/1 for domestic students, 12/15 for international students. Application fee: $65. Electronic applications accepted. *Financial support:* In 2009–10, 7 students received support, including 11 fellowships with full tuition reimbursements available (averaging $22,500 per year), 128 research assistantships with partial tuition reimbursements available (averaging $18,900 per year), 44 teaching assistantships with partial tuition reimbursements available (averaging $14,400 per year); career-related internships or fieldwork, Federal Work-Study, and institutionally sponsored loans also available. Financial award application deadline: 2/1. *Faculty research:* Controls and robotics, communications and signal processing, electromagnetics, optics and acoustics, electronic devices and photonics. Total annual research expenditures: $14.2 million. *Unit head:* Dr. Leung Tsang, Professor and Chair, 206-221-5270, Fax: 206-543-3842, E-mail: tsang@ee.washington.edu. *Application contact:* Frankye Jones, EE Graduate Program Advisor, 206-221-7913, Fax: 206-543-3842, E-mail: frankye@u.washington.edu.

University of Waterloo, Graduate Studies, Faculty of Engineering, Department of Electrical and Computer Engineering, Waterloo, ON N2L 3G1, Canada. Offers electrical and computer engineering (M Eng, MA Sc, PhD); electrical and computer engineering (software engineering) (MA Sc). Part-time programs available. *Degree requirements:* For master's, research paper or thesis; for doctorate, comprehensive exam, thesis/dissertation. *Entrance requirements:* For master's, honors degree, minimum B+ average; for doctorate, master's degree, minimum A-average. Additional exam requirements/recommendations for international students: Required—TOEFL (minimum score 550 paper-based; 213 computer-based), TWE (minimum score 4). Electronic applications accepted. *Faculty research:* Communications, computers, systems and control, silicon devices, power engineering.

The University of Western Ontario, Faculty of Graduate Studies, Physical Sciences Division, Faculty of Engineering, London, ON N6A 5B8, Canada. Offers chemical and biochemical engineering (ME Sc, PhD); civil and environmental engineering (M Eng, ME Sc, PhD); electrical and computer engineering (M Eng, ME Sc, PhD); mechanical and materials engineering (M Eng, ME Sc, PhD). Part-time programs available. Terminal master's awarded for partial completion of doctoral program. *Degree requirements:* For master's, thesis; for doctorate, thesis/dissertation. *Entrance requirements:* For master's, minimum B average; for doctorate, minimum B+ average. *Faculty research:* Wind, geotechnical, chemical reactor engineering, applied electrostatics, biochemical engineering.

University of Windsor, Faculty of Graduate Studies, Faculty of Engineering, Department of Electrical and Computer Engineering, Windsor, ON N9B 3P4, Canada. Offers electrical engineering (M Eng, MA Sc, PhD). Part-time programs available. *Degree requirements:* For master's, thesis; for doctorate, comprehensive exam, thesis/dissertation. *Entrance requirements:* For master's, minimum B average; for doctorate, master's degree, minimum B+ average. Additional exam requirements/recommendations for international students: Required—TOEFL (minimum score 600 paper-based; 250 computer-based). Electronic applications accepted. *Faculty research:* Systems, signals, power.

University of Wisconsin–Madison, Graduate School, College of Engineering, Department of Electrical and Computer Engineering, Madison, WI 53706-1380. Offers electrical engineering (MS, PhD). Part-time programs available. Postbaccalaureate distance learning degree programs offered (minimal on-campus study). *Faculty:* 38 full-time (5 women), 2 part-time/adjunct (0 women). *Students:* 333 full-time (47 women); includes 28 minority (3 African Americans, 20 Asian Americans or Pacific Islanders, 5 Hispanic Americans). Average age 27. 946 applicants, 35% accepted, 85 enrolled. In 2009, 40 master's, 26 doctorates awarded. Terminal master's awarded for partial completion of doctoral program. *Degree requirements:* For master's, thesis or alternative; for doctorate, thesis/dissertation, exam. *Entrance requirements:* For master's and doctorate, GRE General Test. Additional exam requirements/recommendations for international students: Required—TOEFL (minimum score 580 paper-based; 237 computer-based; 92 iBT). *Application deadline:* For fall admission, 3/1 for domestic students, 11/15 for international students; for spring admission, 9/30 for domestic and international students. Applications are processed on a rolling basis. Application fee: $56. Electronic applications accepted. *Expenses:* Tuition, state resident: part-time $594 per credit. Tuition, nonresident: part-time $1504 per credit. Required fees: $65 per credit. Tuition and fees vary according to course load, program and reciprocity agreements. *Financial support:* In 2009–10, 202 students received support, including 26 fellowships with full tuition reimbursements available (averaging $13,000 per year), 151 research assistantships with full tuition reimbursements available (averaging $20,184 per year), 94 teaching assistantships with full tuition reimbursements available (averaging $9,392 per year); career-related internships or fieldwork, Federal Work-Study, institutionally sponsored loans, health care benefits, and unspecified assistantships also available. Support available to part-time students. Financial award application deadline: 1/5. *Faculty research:* Microelectronics, computer architecture, power electronics and systems, communications, signal processing. Total annual research expenditures: $13.8 million. *Unit head:* John Booske, Chair, 608-262-8548, Fax: 608-262-1267, E-mail: ecechair@ece.wisc.edu. *Application contact:* Marc Nowak, Student Status Examiner, 608-265-5570, Fax: 608-890-1174, E-mail: gradscty@cae.wisc.edu.

University of Wisconsin–Milwaukee, Graduate School, College of Engineering and Applied Science, Program in Engineering, Milwaukee, WI 53201-0413. Offers civil engineering (MS); electrical and computer engineering (MS); energy engineering (Certificate); engineering (PhD); engineering management (MS); engineering mechanics (MS); ergonomics (Certificate); industrial and management engineering (MS); manufacturing engineering (MS); materials engineering (MS); mechanical engineering (MS); MUP/MS. Part-time programs available. *Faculty:* 44 full-time (6 women). *Students:* 119 full-time (22 women), 130 part-time (22 women); includes 23 minority (2 African Americans, 14 Asian Americans or Pacific Islanders, 7 Hispanic Americans), 126 international. Average age 32. 231 applicants, 67% accepted, 33 enrolled. In 2009, 29 master's, 14 doctorates awarded. *Degree requirements:* For master's, comprehensive exam (for some programs), thesis or alternative; for doctorate, comprehensive exam, thesis/dissertation, internship. *Entrance requirements:* For master's, GRE, minimum GPA of 2.75; for doctorate, GRE, minimum GPA of 3.5. Additional exam requirements/recommendations for international students: Required—TOEFL (minimum score 550 paper-based; 79 iBT), IELTS (minimum score 6.5). *Application deadline:* For fall admission, 1/1 priority date for domestic students; for spring admission, 9/1 for domestic students. Applications are processed on a rolling basis. Application fee: $45 ($75 for international students). *Expenses:* Tuition, state resident: full-time $8800. Tuition, nonresident: full-time $20,760. Tuition and fees vary according to program and reciprocity agreements. *Financial support:* In 2009–10, 18 research assistantships, 51 teaching assistantships were awarded; fellowships, career-related internships or fieldwork, Federal Work-Study, and unspecified assistantships also available. Support available to part-time students. Financial award application deadline: 4/15. Total annual research expenditures: $2.9 million. *Unit head:* David Yu, Head, 414-229-6169, E-mail: yu@uwm.edu. *Application contact:* Betty Warras, General Information Contact, 414-229-4982, Fax: 414-229-6967, E-mail: bwarras@uwm.edu.

University of Wyoming, College of Engineering and Applied Sciences, Department of Electrical and Computer Engineering, Laramie, WY 82070. Offers electrical engineering (MS, PhD). Part-time programs available. *Degree requirements:* For master's, thesis (for some programs); for doctorate, comprehensive exam, thesis/dissertation, dissertation proposal/presentation. *Entrance requirements:* For master's, GRE General Test, minimum undergraduate GPA of 3.0; for doctorate, GRE General Test, minimum GPA of 3.0. Additional exam requirements/recommendations for international students: Required—TOEFL (minimum score 550 paper-based; 213 computer-based; 79 iBT). Electronic applications accepted. *Faculty research:* Robotics and controls, signal and image processing, power electronics, power systems, computer networks, wind energy.

Utah State University, School of Graduate Studies, College of Engineering, Department of Electrical and Computer Engineering, Logan, UT 84322. Offers electrical engineering (ME, MS, PhD). Part-time programs available. *Degree requirements:* For master's, thesis (for some programs); for doctorate, comprehensive exam, thesis/dissertation. *Entrance requirements:* For master's, GRE General Test, minimum GPA of 3.0, BS in electrical engineering, 3 recommendation letters; for doctorate, GRE General Test, minimum GPA of 3.0, MS in electrical engineering, 3 recommendation letters. Additional exam requirements/recommendations for international students: Required—TOEFL. Electronic applications accepted. *Faculty research:* Parallel processing, networking, control systems, digital signal processing, communications.

Vanderbilt University, School of Engineering, Department of Electrical Engineering and Computer Science, Program in Electrical Engineering, Nashville, TN 37240-1001. Offers M Eng, MS, PhD. MS and PhD offered through Graduate School. Part-time programs available. *Faculty:* 22 full-time (1 woman). *Students:* 88 full-time (28 women); includes 7 minority (5 African Americans, 1 Asian American or Pacific Islander, 1 Hispanic American), 45 international. Average age 27. 270 applicants, 11% accepted, 21 enrolled. In 2009, 20 master's, 22 doctorates awarded. Terminal master's awarded for partial completion of doctoral program. *Degree requirements:* For master's, thesis; for doctorate, comprehensive exam, thesis/dissertation. *Entrance requirements:* For master's and doctorate, GRE General Test, 3 letters of recommendation. Additional exam requirements/recommendations for international students: Required—TOEFL. *Application deadline:* For fall admission, 1/15 for domestic and international students; for spring admission, 11/1 for domestic and international students. Application fee: $0. Electronic applications accepted. *Financial support:* In 2009–10, 85 students received support, including fellowships with full and partial tuition reimbursements available (averaging $30,000 per year), research assistantships with full tuition reimbursements available (averaging $21,600 per year), teaching assistantships with full tuition reimbursements available (averaging $18,000 per year); career-related internships or fieldwork, institutionally sponsored loans, scholarships/grants, health care benefits, tuition waivers (full and partial), and unspecified assistantships also available. Support available to part-time students. Financial award application deadline: 1/15. *Faculty research:* Robotics, microelectronics, signal and image processing, VLSI, solid-state sensors, radiation effects and reliability. *Unit head:* Dr. Daniel M. Fleetwood, Chair, 615-322-2771, Fax: 615-343-6702, E-mail: dan.fleetwood@vanderbilt.edu. *Application contact:* Dr. Bharat Bhuva, Director of Graduate Studies, 615-343-3184, Fax: 615-343-6614, E-mail: bharat.bhuva@vanderbilt.edu.

Villanova University, College of Engineering, Department of Electrical and Computer Engineering, Program in Electrical Engineering, Villanova, PA 19085-1699. Offers communication systems engineering (Certificate); electric power systems (Certificate); electrical engineering (MSEE); electro mechanical systems (Certificate); high frequency systems (Certificate); intelligent systems (Certificate); wireless and digital communications (Certificate). Part-time and evening/weekend programs available. *Degree requirements:* For master's, thesis optional. *Entrance requirements:* For master's, GRE General Test (for applicants with degrees from foreign universities), BEE, minimum GPA of 3.0. Additional exam requirements/recommendations for international students: Required—TOEFL (minimum score 600 paper-based; 250 computer-based; 100 iBT). *Expenses:* Tuition: Part-time $630 per credit. Required fees: $60 per credit. Part-time tuition and fees vary according to degree level and program. *Faculty research:* Signal processing, communications, antennas, devices.

Virginia Commonwealth University, Graduate School, School of Engineering, Department of Electrical and Computer Engineering, Richmond, VA 23284-9005. Offers electrical engineering (MS, PhD).

Virginia Polytechnic Institute and State University, Graduate School, College of Engineering, Department of Electrical and Computer Engineering, Blacksburg, VA 24061. Offers computer engineering (M Eng, MS, PhD); electrical engineering (M Eng, MS, PhD). *Entrance requirements:* For master's and doctorate, GRE General Test. Additional exam requirements/recommendations for international students: Required—TOEFL (minimum score 590 paper-based; 243 computer-based). Electronic applications accepted. *Faculty research:* Electromagnetics, controls, electronics, power, communications.

Virginia Polytechnic Institute and State University, VT Online, Blacksburg, VA 24061. Offers aerospace engineering (MS); business information systems (Graduate Certificate); career and technical education (MS); computer engineering (M Eng, MS); decision support systems (Graduate Certificate); eLearning leadership (MA); electrical engineering (M Eng, MS); engineering administration (MEA); environmental politics and policy (Graduate Certificate); foundations of political analysis (Graduate Certificate); health product risk management (Graduate Certificate); information policy and society (Graduate Certificate); information security (Graduate Certificate); instructional technology (MA); liberal arts (Graduate Certificate); life sciences: health product risk management (MS); natural resources (MNR, Graduate Certificate); networking (Graduate Certificate); nonprofit and nongovernmental organization management (Graduate Certificate); ocean engineering (MS); political science (MA); security studies (Graduate Certificate); software development (Graduate Certificate).

Washington State University, Graduate School, College of Engineering and Architecture, School of Electrical Engineering and Computer Science, Program in Electrical Engineering, Pullman, WA 99164. Offers MS, PhD. *Faculty:* 30. *Students:* 61 full-time (5 women), 12 part-time (2 women); includes 1 minority (African American), 51 international. Average age 29. 307 applicants, 12% accepted, 17 enrolled. In 2009, 5 master's, 5 doctorates awarded. *Degree requirements:* For master's, comprehensive exam (for some programs), thesis, oral exam; for doctorate, comprehensive exam, thesis/dissertation, oral exam, qualifying exam, preliminary exam, oral defense of dissertation. *Entrance requirements:* For master's and doctorate, GRE General Test, Students considering graduate study in electrical engineering and computer science should major in computer engineering, electrical engineering, or computer science. Applications should include a statement of purpose giving qualifications, research interests, and goals; official college transcripts; GRE scores, and three letters of recommendation. Additional exam requirements/recommendations for international students: Required—TOEFL (minimum score 520 paper-based; 190 computer-based), IELTS. *Application deadline:* For fall admission, 1/10 priority date for domestic students, 1/10 for international students; for spring admission, 7/1 for domestic and international students. Applications are processed on a rolling basis. Application fee: $50. *Financial support:* In 2009–10, 3 fellowships with full tuition reimbursements (averaging $2,500 per year), 18 research assistantships with full tuition reimbursements (averaging $13,917 per year), 24 teaching assistantships with full tuition reimbursements (averaging $13,056 per year) were awarded; career-related internships or fieldwork, Federal Work-Study, and institutionally sponsored loans also available. Financial award application deadline: 2/10; financial award applicants required to submit FAFSA. *Faculty research:* Energy and power systems, microelectronics, electrophysics controls, systems telecommunications. *Unit head:* Dr. Ali Saberi, Chair, 509-335-6636, Fax: 509-335-3818, E-mail: sidra@eecs.wsu.edu. *Application contact:* Graduate School Admissions, 800-GRADWSU, Fax: 509-335-1949, E-mail: gradsch@wsu.edu.

Washington State University Tri-Cities, Graduate Programs, College of Engineering and Computer Science, Richland, WA 99352. Offers computer science (MS, PhD); electrical and computer engineering (PhD); electrical engineering (MS); mechanical engineering (MS, PhD). Part-time programs available. *Faculty:* 28. *Students:* 4 full-time (0 women), 25 part-time (8 women); includes 2 minority (both African Americans), 1 international. *Degree requirements:* For master's, comprehensive exam, thesis (for some programs); for doctorate, comprehensive exam, thesis/dissertation, oral exam. *Entrance requirements:* For master's and doctorate, GRE, minimum GPA of 3.0, 3 letters of recommendation. Additional exam requirements/recommendations for international students: Required—TOEFL (minimum score 550 paper-based; 213 computer-based). *Application deadline:* For fall admission, 1/10 priority date for domestic students, 1/10 for international students; for spring admission, 7/1 priority date for domestic students, 7/1 for international students. Application fee: $50. *Expenses:* Tuition, state resident: part-time $423 per credit. Tuition, nonresident: part-time $1032 per credit. *Financial support:* Application deadline: 3/1. *Faculty research:* Positive ion track structure, biological systems computer simulations. *Unit head:* Dr. Ali Saberi, Chair, 509-372-7178, E-mail: sidra@eecs.wsu.edu. *Application contact:* Dr. Scott Hudson, Associate Director, 509-372-7254, Fax: 509-335-1949, E-mail: hudson@tricity.wsu.edu.

Washington University in St. Louis, Henry Edwin Sever Graduate School of Engineering and Applied Science, Department of Electrical and Systems Engineering, St. Louis, MO 63130-4899. Offers electrical engineering (MS, D Sc, PhD); systems science and mathematics (MS, D Sc, PhD). Part-time programs available. *Faculty:* 17 full-time (2 women), 5 part-time/adjunct (1 woman). *Students:* 75 full-time (33 women), 21 part-time (2 women); includes 10 minority (1 African American, 8 Asian Americans or Pacific Islanders, 1 Hispanic American), 45 international. Average age 23. 281 applicants, 29% accepted, 25 enrolled. In 2009, 16 master's, 4 doctorates awarded. Terminal master's awarded for partial completion of doctoral program. *Degree requirements:* For master's, thesis or alternative; for doctorate, comprehensive exam, thesis/dissertation. *Entrance requirements:* For master's, minimum GPA of 3.0 in the last 2 years of undergraduate course work; for doctorate, GRE. Additional exam requirements/recommendations for international students: Required—TOEFL (minimum score 550 paper-based; 213 computer-based; 80 iBT). *Application deadline:* For fall admission, 1/15 for domestic and international students. Applications are processed on a rolling basis. Application fee: $60. Electronic applications accepted. *Financial support:* In 2009–10, 8 fellowships with full tuition reimbursements (averaging $20,000 per year), 29 research assistantships with full tuition reimbursements (averaging $26,950 per year) were awarded; teaching assistantships with full tuition reimbursements, career-related internships or fieldwork, Federal Work-Study, institutionally sponsored loans, scholarships/grants, and unspecified assistantships also available. Financial award application deadline: 1/15; financial award applicants required to submit FAFSA. *Faculty research:* Applied physics and electronics, signal and image processing, systems analysis, biomedicine, and energy. Total annual research expenditures: $1 million. *Unit head:* Dr. Arye Nehorai, Chair, 314-935-5565, Fax: 314-935-7500, E-mail: nehorai@ese.wustl.edu. *Application contact:* Shauna Dollison, Director of Graduate Programs, 314-935-4830, Fax: 314-935-7500.

Wayne State University, College of Engineering, Department of Electrical and Computer Engineering, Program in Electrical Engineering, Detroit, MI 48202. Offers MS, PhD. *Degree requirements:* For master's, thesis optional; for doctorate, thesis/dissertation. *Entrance requirements:* Additional exam requirements/recommendations for international students: Required—TOEFL (minimum score 550 paper-based; 213 computer-based), Michigan English Language Assessment Battery (minimum score: 85); Recommended—TWE (minimum score 6). Electronic applications accepted. *Faculty research:* Biomedical systems, control systems, solid state materials, optical materials, hybrid vehicle.

Western Michigan University, Graduate College, College of Engineering and Applied Sciences, Department of Electrical and Computer Engineering, Kalamazoo, MI 49008. Offers computer engineering (MSE, PhD); electrical and computer engineering (PhD); electrical engineering (MSE). Part-time programs available. *Degree requirements:* For master's, thesis optional. *Entrance requirements:* For master's, minimum GPA of 3.0. *Faculty research:* Fiber optics, computer architecture, bioelectromagnetics, acoustics.

Western New England College, School of Engineering, Department of Electrical Engineering, Springfield, MA 01119. Offers MSE. Part-time and evening/weekend programs available. *Students:* 8 part-time (2 women); includes 2 Asian Americans or Pacific Islanders, 1 Hispanic

Electrical Engineering

Western New England College (continued)
American. Average age 29. In 2009, 3 master's awarded. *Degree requirements:* For master's, comprehensive exam, thesis optional. *Entrance requirements:* For master's, GRE, bachelor's degree in engineering or related field, Two recommendations, Resume. *Application deadline:* Applications are processed on a rolling basis. Application fee: $30. *Expenses:* Tuition: Part-time $552 per credit hour. Part-time tuition and fees vary according to program. *Financial support:* Available to part-time students. Applicants required to submit FAFSA. *Faculty research:* Superconductors, microwave cooking, computer voice output, digital filters, computer engineering. *Unit head:* Dr. James J. Moriarty, Chair, 413-782-1272, E-mail: jmoriart@wnec.edu. *Application contact:* Matt Fox, Director of Recruiting and Marketing for Adult Learners, 413-782-1249, Fax: 413-782-1779, E-mail: study@wnec.edu.

West Virginia University, College of Engineering and Mineral Resources, Lane Department of Computer Science and Electrical Engineering, Program in Electrical Engineering, Morgantown, WV 26506. Offers MSEE, PhD. Terminal master's awarded for partial completion of doctoral program. *Degree requirements:* For master's, thesis or alternative; for doctorate, comprehensive exam, thesis/dissertation. *Entrance requirements:* For master's and doctorate, GRE General Test, minimum GPA of 3.0, letters of recommendation. Additional exam requirements/recommendations for international students: Required—TOEFL. *Faculty research:* Power and control systems, communications and signal processing, electromechanical systems, microelectronics and photonics.

Wichita State University, Graduate School, College of Engineering, Department of Electrical Engineering and Computer Science, Wichita, KS 67260. Offers computer networking (MS); computer science (MS); electrical engineering (MS, PhD). Part-time and evening/weekend programs available. *Expenses:* Tuition, state resident: full-time $4247; part-time $235.95 per credit hour. Tuition, nonresident: full-time $11,171; part-time $620.60 per credit hour. Required fees: $34; $3.60 per credit hour. $17 per term. Tuition and fees vary according to campus/location and program. *Unit head:* Dr. John Watkins, Chair, 316-978-3156, Fax: 316-978-5408, E-mail: john.watkins@wichita.edu. *Application contact:* Dr. John Watkins, Chair, 316-978-3156, Fax: 316-978-5408, E-mail: john.watkins@wichita.edu.

Wilkes University, College of Graduate and Professional Studies, College of Science and Engineering, Division of Engineering and Physics, Wilkes-Barre, PA 18766-0002. Offers electrical engineering (MSEE); engineering operations and strategy (MS). Part-time programs available. *Students:* 15 full-time (2 women), 19 part-time (2 women), 25 international. Average age 26. In 2009, 26 master's awarded. *Entrance requirements:* For master's, GRE General Test. Additional exam requirements/recommendations for international students: Required—TOEFL (minimum score 500 paper-based; 173 computer-based; 79 iBT). *Application deadline:* Applications are processed on a rolling basis. Application fee: $45. *Financial support:* Federal Work-Study and unspecified assistantships available. Financial award application deadline: 3/1; financial award applicants required to submit FAFSA. *Unit head:* Dr. Rodney Ridley, Director, 570-408-4824, Fax: 570-408-7846, E-mail: rodney.ridley@wilkes.edu. *Application contact:* Kathleen Houlihan, Director of Graduate Studies, 570-408-3235, Fax: 570-408-7846, E-mail: kathleen.houlihan@wilkes.edu.

Woods Hole Oceanographic Institution, MIT/WHOI Joint Program in Oceanography/Applied Ocean Science and Engineering, Woods Hole, MA 02543-1541. Offers applied ocean sciences (PhD); biological oceanography (PhD, Sc D); chemical oceanography (PhD, Sc D); civil and environmental and oceanographic engineering (PhD); electrical and oceanographic engineering (PhD); geochemistry (PhD); geophysics (PhD); marine biology (PhD); marine geochemistry (PhD, Sc D); marine geology (PhD, Sc D); marine geophysics (PhD); mechanical and oceanographic engineering (PhD); ocean engineering (PhD); oceanographic engineering (M Eng, MS, PhD, Sc D, Eng); paleoceanography (PhD); physical oceanography (PhD, Sc D). Terminal master's awarded for partial completion of doctoral program. *Degree requirements:* For master's and Eng, thesis (for some programs); for doctorate, thesis/dissertation. *Entrance requirements:* For master's, GRE General Test; for doctorate, GRE General Test, GRE Subject Test. Additional exam requirements/recommendations for international students: Required—TOEFL. Electronic applications accepted.

Worcester Polytechnic Institute, Graduate Studies and Research, Department of Electrical and Computer Engineering, Worcester, MA 01609-2280. Offers electrical and computer engineering (Advanced Certificate, Graduate Certificate); electrical engineering (MS, PhD). Part-time and evening/weekend programs available. *Faculty:* 16 full-time (1 woman), 2 part-time/adjunct (0 women). *Students:* 54 full-time (8 women), 98 part-time (13 women). 418 applicants, 58% accepted, 80 enrolled. In 2009, 49 master's, 5 doctorates awarded. Terminal master's awarded for partial completion of doctoral program. *Degree requirements:* For master's, thesis optional; for doctorate, comprehensive exam, thesis/dissertation. *Entrance requirements:* For master's, 3 letters of recommendation; for doctorate, 3 letters of recommendation, statement of purpose. Additional exam requirements/recommendations for international students: Required—TOEFL (minimum score 550 paper-based; 213 computer-based; 79 iBT), IELTS (minimum score 6.5). *Application deadline:* For fall admission, 1/15 priority date for domestic students, 1/15 for international students; for spring admission, 10/15 priority date for domestic students, 10/15 for international students. Applications are processed on a rolling basis. Application fee: $70. Electronic applications accepted. *Financial support:* Career-related internships or fieldwork, institutionally sponsored loans, scholarships/grants, and unspecified assistantships available. Financial award application deadline: 1/15. *Faculty research:* Analog and mixed signal IC design, cryptography and data security, communication systems and networking, biomedical signal processing, image processing and visualization. *Unit head:* Dr. Fred Looft, Department Head, 508-831-5231, Fax: 508-831-5491, E-mail: fjlooft@wpi.edu. *Application contact:* Dr. Peder Pedersen, Graduate Coordinator, 508-831-5351, Fax: 508-831-5491, E-mail: pedersen@wpi.edu.

Wright State University, School of Graduate Studies, College of Engineering and Computer Science, Programs in Engineering, Program in Electrical Engineering, Dayton, OH 45435. Offers MSE. Part-time and evening/weekend programs available. *Degree requirements:* For master's, thesis or course option alternative. *Entrance requirements:* Additional exam requirements/recommendations for international students: Required—TOEFL. *Faculty research:* Robotics, circuit design, power electronics, image processing, communication systems.

Yale University, Graduate School of Arts and Sciences, School of Engineering and Applied Science, Department of Electrical Engineering, New Haven, CT 06520. Offers MS, PhD. Terminal master's awarded for partial completion of doctoral program. *Degree requirements:* For doctorate, thesis/dissertation, exam. *Entrance requirements:* For master's and doctorate, GRE General Test. Additional exam requirements/recommendations for international students: Required—TOEFL. *Faculty research:* Signal processing, control, and communications; digital systems and computer engineering; microelectronics and photonics; nanotechnology; computers, sensors, and networking.

Youngstown State University, Graduate School, College of Science, Technology, Engineering and Mathematics, Department of Electrical and Computer Engineering, Youngstown, OH 44555-0001. Offers computer engineering (MSE); electrical engineering (MSE). Part-time and evening/weekend programs available. *Degree requirements:* For master's, thesis optional. *Entrance requirements:* For master's, minimum GPA of 2.75 in field. Additional exam requirements/recommendations for international students: Required—TOEFL. *Faculty research:* Computer-aided design, power systems, electromagnetic energy conversion, sensors, control systems.

Carnegie Mellon

CARNEGIE MELLON UNIVERSITY

Department of Electrical and Computer Engineering

Programs of Study

Graduate study in the Department of Electrical and Computer Engineering (ECE) prepares students for roles in research, development, design, and leadership positions. The Department offers two graduate degree programs that lead to an M.S. or a Ph.D. degree in electrical and computer engineering.

Students who have earned a B.S. or M.S. and whose intention is to obtain a Ph.D. degree may apply to the Ph.D. program. The Ph.D. program is a research-oriented degree. Those students in the Ph.D. program who do not already have an M.S. degree are required to complete an academic course of study that usually results in the awarding of an M.S. degree prior to the Ph.D.

The Professional M.S. program is more course intensive than the research-oriented Ph.D. program. This program is for students who have a B.S. degree and are interested in further professional development. Students in this program study the fundamentals of electrical and computer engineering and have the opportunity for in-depth specialization in a particular aspect of this field. Upon enrollment in the Department, students are given the opportunity, with the help of a faculty adviser, to choose an educational program that is consistent with their background and is best suited to their own academic goals.

Fulfillment of the Ph.D. requirements takes three to four years beyond an M.S. degree and requires passing a qualifying examination, completing two internships in university teaching, writing a thesis that describes the results of independent research, and passing an oral defense of the research.

The Department is home to several internationally recognized research centers and laboratories, including the Data Storage Systems Center (DSSC), Center for Silicon Systems Implementation (CSSI), Center for Circuit and System Solutions (C2S2), Computer Architecture Laboratory at Carnegie Mellon (CALCM), Advanced Mechatronics Laboratory (AML), Micro Electro-Mechanical Systems (MEMS) Laboratory, Parallel Data Laboratory (PDL), Multimedia Laboratory, General Motors Collaborative Laboratory at Carnegie Mellon, and Center for Memory Intensive Self Configuring ICs.

Faculty members hold joint appointments with other departments, and most of them also have close ties with various interdisciplinary research centers in the University, such as the Institute for Complex Engineered Systems (ICES), Robotics Institute (RI), Information Networking Institute (INI), Institute for Software Research (ISRI), Human Computer Interaction Institute (HCII), Center for Nano-Enabled Devices and Energy Technology, and Carnegie Mellon CyLab in Network and Computer Security, including CyLabs Mobility Research Center at Carnegie Mellon's West Coast campus.

Major areas of research include agent-based systems; communications, wireless, and broadband networking; biomedical engineering; communications/information systems and engineering; computer system and network architecture; computer-aided design of VLSI circuits, systems, and technology, including synthesis, verification, simulation, test, manufacturing, custom analog and digital IC design, and semiconductor fabrication; information storage technology and systems, including magnetic and optical recording; design, fabrication, and characterization of microelectromechanical systems; design optimization; distributed and real-time/multimedia systems; distributed computer systems; electronic, magnetic, and optical materials and processing; embedded systems; fault tolerance and affordable dependable computing; high-performance I/O systems; high-speed processor architectures and design; information security; intelligent and hybrid control; intelligent robotics; manufacturing systems and automatic assembly; mobile and wireless computing; nanotechnology; neural networks; operating systems; parallel processing; rapid prototyping; sensory-based and supervisory control; signal processing in optical, video, image, speech, storage, and mobility systems; and technology and public policy.

Research Facilities

The Department has extensive computational facilities that include more than 2,000 networked workstations supporting research and education. Many of these are deployed in a cluster configuration to accommodate large and/or time-intensive batch computations. Research projects also make frequent use of supercomputers, which are available to the Department through the Pittsburgh Supercomputing Center. These systems are all connected to the CMU campuswide computer network via gigabit or faster Ethernet networking as well as via the Andrew Wireless Network. The centers and laboratories within the Department use advanced hardware and software infrastructure and experimental facilities that are conducive to building systems in all areas of research within the Department. A fully equipped 4,000-square-foot, class 100 clean room supports research in MEMS, nanotechnology, semiconductors, and magnetic and optical device research and can be used to produce state-of-the-art solid-state and recording devices.

Since most of the research is multidisciplinary and collaborative, students and faculty members have access to experimental and laboratory facilities housed in several multidisciplinary institutes.

Financial Aid

Graduate research assistantships are available to U.S. and international students admitted to the graduate Ph.D. program and include a typical stipend of about $2240 per month plus tuition. In the award of financial aid, consideration is given to the student's undergraduate and graduate academic records, GRE and TOEFL scores, and letters of reference indicating outstanding academic potential.

Virtually all students in the research-intensive Ph.D. program receive financial aid, which covers tuition, fees, and reasonable living expenses for the entire year. All applicants are considered for financial aid, and no special form is required.

Students in the Professional M.S. program are ineligible to receive Departmental fellowships that cover tuition and living expenses. Students in this program are self-supported and must complete at least two academic semesters before they are eligible to apply to the Ph.D. program, if they so choose.

Cost of Study

Tuition for graduate students enrolled in the Department of Electrical and Computer Engineering is set at $36,700 for the academic year 2010–11. Books and supplies cost about $2300 per year.

Living and Housing Costs

Graduate accommodations are not provided, although there are various board plans available in nearby rooms or apartments. Approximate living expenses, including room and board, insurance, transportation, and miscellaneous expenses, average $22,000 per academic year, exclusive of tuition.

Student Group

The campus enrollment averages 10,402 students; 4,644 are graduate students. The University has 1,426 full-time faculty members. Within the Department of Electrical and Computer Engineering, there are 341 full-time graduate students in the master's program and in the Ph.D. program

Location

The greater Pittsburgh metropolitan area has more than 2 million residents. The Carnegie Mellon campus encompasses approximately 100 acres and adjoins a 500-acre city park and quiet residential communities with abundant student housing.

The University

The University is composed of the Carnegie Institute of Technology (the Engineering School), Mellon College of Science, the College of Fine Arts, the Graduate School of Industrial Administration, the Heinz School, the College of Humanities and Social Sciences, and the School of Computer Sciences.

Applying

All applicants are required to take the GRE (General Test) at least six weeks prior to the application deadline. All students whose native language is not English are required to take the Test of English as a Foreign Language (TOEFL). Applications for the fall semester must be received by December 31, 2008. Official transcripts, three letters of recommendation, and official GRE and TOEFL scores must be provided. Additional information about the graduate programs, faculty and research initiatives, and application procedures are located on the ECE Web site listed in the Correspondence and Information section.

Correspondence and Information

Graduate Admissions Office, HH B204
Department of Electrical and Computer Engineering
Carnegie Mellon University
Pittsburgh, Pennsylvania 15213
Phone: 412-268-6327
Fax: 412-268-3155
E-mail: apps@ece.cmu.edu
Web site: http://www.ece.cmu.edu

Carnegie Mellon University

THE FACULTY AND THEIR RESEARCH

J. Bain, Professor and Associate Director, DSSC; Ph.D., Stanford, 1993: magnetic materials, thin-film magnetic devices, magnetic disk and tape recording. V. Bhagavatula, Professor; Ph.D., Carnegie Mellon, 1980: coding and signal processing for data storage, biometrics, pattern recognition. R. Blanton, Professor and Director, CSSI; Ph.D., Michigan, 1985: test and verification of VLSI circuits and systems. D. J. Brumley, Professor. L. R. Carley, ST Microelectronics Professor; Ph.D., MIT, 1984: CAD and design of analog signal processing circuits and MEMS systems. D. P. Casasent, George Westinghouse Professor and Director, Optics Lab; Ph.D., Illinois, 1969: pattern recognition, neural nets, ATR image processing and product inspection. S. H. Charap, Professor Emeritus; Ph.D., Rutgers, 1959: applied magnetism, with particular emphasis on magnetic recording. T. Chen, Professor; Ph.D., Caltech, 1993: multimedia coding and streaming, computer vision, pattern recognition, computer graphics, multimodal biometrics. A. Davidson, Senior Systems Scientist; Ph.D., Harvard, 1976: device physics, nonlinear dynamics, MEMS-based mass storage. G. K. Fedder, Howard M. Wilkoff Professor of ECE and Robotics and Director, Institute for Complex Engineered Systems; Ph.D., Berkeley, 1994: MEMS, MEMS CAD, microrobotics. F. Franchetti, Systems Scientist; Ph.D., Vienna Technical, 2003: automatic performance tuning, digital signal-processing transforms, advanced architectures. R. Gandhi, Systems Engineer; Ph.D., California, Santa Barbara, 2000: wireless systems and signal/video compression. G. Ganger, Professor of ECE and CS and Director, Parallel Data Lab; Ph.D., Michigan, 1995: operating systems, security, distributed systems, storage/file systems, networking. V. Gligor, Professor; Ph.D., Berkeley, 1976. D. W. Greve, Professor; Ph.D., Lehigh, 1979: semiconductor device physics, semiconductor process technology, sensors. J. F. Hoburg, Professor; Ph.D., MIT, 1975: electromagnetics, electromechanics, magnetic shielding, applied electrostatics, electrohydrodynamics, microfluidics. J. C. Hoe, Associate Professor of ECE and CS; Ph.D., MIT, 2000: computer architecture, high-level hardware description and synthesis. M. Ilic, Professor of ECE and EPP; Ph.D., Washington (St. Louis), 1980: large-scale systems modeling and simulation, power systems control and pricing algorithms, critical infrastructures/interdependencies. A. G. Jordan, Keithley University Professor Emeritus of ECE and Robotics; Ph.D., Carnegie Tech, 1959: advanced video systems, robotics. P. K. Khosla, Dowd Professor of Engineering and Robotics; Dean, Carnegie Institute of Technology; and Director, Carnegie Mellon CyLab; Ph.D., Carnegie Mellon, 1986. H. S. Kim, Drew D. Perkins Professor and Director, CyLab Korea; Ph.D., Toronto, 1990: advanced switch and network architectures, fault-tolerant network architectures, network management and control. P. J. Koopman, Associate Professor of ECE and CS; Ph.D., Carnegie Mellon, 1989: distributed embedded systems, survivable system architecture, dependability. B. H. Krogh, Professor; Ph.D., Illinois at Urbana-Champaign, 1982: Synthesis and verification of embedded control software, distributed control strategies, distributed supervisory control, information and control in wireless sensor networks, discrete event and hybrid dynamic systems. M. H. Kryder, University Professor; Ph.D., Caltech, 1970: magnetic recording, optical recording, ferroelectric materials. D. N. Lambeth, Professor of ECE and MSE; Ph.D., MIT, 1973: physical and chemical sensors, transducers, MEMS, magnetism, materials, thin films, data storage, RF devices. X. Li, Systems Scientist; Ph.D., Carnegie Mellon, 2005: integrated circuits, computer-aided design. Y. Luo, Assistant Professor; Ph.D., Columbia, 2000: nanoelectronic devices, molecular electronics, nanoscale materials and fabrication techniques. K. Mai, Assistant Professor; Ph.D., Stanford, 2005: digital circuit design, computer architecture, memory design, reconfigurable computing. W. Maly, U. A. and Helen Whitaker Professor; Ph.D., Polish Academy of Sciences, 1975: computer-aided design and manufacturing of VLSICs. D. Marculescu, Associate Professor; Ph.D., USC, 1998: VLSI/computer architecture, energy-aware computing. R. Marculescu, Professor; Ph.D., USC, 1998: computer-aided design of digital systems, low-power design, embedded systems. M. G. Morgan, Lord Professor of ECE and EPP and Department Head, EPP; Ph.D., California, San Diego, 1969: technology and policy, including climate change and electric power. J. M. F. Moura, Professor; D.Sc., MIT, 1975: communications; statistical signal/image, video, and multimedia processing; wavelet transforms. T. Mukherjee, Professor; Ph.D., Carnegie Mellon, 1995: methodologies for microelectromechanical systems (MEMS) and biofluidic microsystems. O. Mutulu, Professor. W. Nace, Lecturer. P. Narasimhan, Associate Professor of ECE and CS; Ph.D., California, Santa Barbara, 1999: fault tolerance, survivability, real time, distributed systems, middleware. R. Negi, Associate Professor; Ph.D., Stanford, 2000: wireless systems, networking, signal processing, coding for communications, information theory. C. P. Neuman, Professor; Ph.D., Harvard, 1968: control engineering and robotics. D. O'Hallaron, Associate Professor of ECE and CS; Ph.D., Virginia, 1986: scientific computing, parallel computing, computational database systems, virtualization. J. Paramesh, Assistant Professor; Ph.D., Washington (Seattle), 2006. A. Perrig, Associate Professor of ECE, EPP, and CS and Director of CyLab; Ph.D., Carnegie Mellon, 2001: information systems security, focusing on network security (Internet, mobile computing, and sensor networks) and trusted computing. L. T. Pileggi, Tanoto Professor; Ph.D., Carnegie Mellon, 1989: design, implementation, and modeling of integrated circuits and systems. M. Püschel, Associate Research Professor; Ph.D., Karlsruhe (Germany), 1998: signal processing (theory, algorithms, implementations), scientific computing, compilers, applied mathematics. R. Rajkumar, Professor and Director, GM Collaborative Laboratory; Ph.D., Carnegie Mellon, 1989: multimedia and real-time systems. D. Ricketts, Assistant Professor; Ph.D., Harvard, 2006: nanoscale electronics, nanoscale devices, nonlinear dynamics, analog circuits. R. A. Rohrer, Professor Emeritus; Ph.D., Berkeley, 1963: electronic circuits, systems design automation. R. A. Rutenbar, Jatras Professor of ECE and CS; Ph.D., Michigan, 1984: VLSI CAD, algorithms, analog and digital circuits, automatic speech recognition. T. E. Schlesinger, Professor and Head of ECE; Ph.D., Caltech, 1985: optoelectronics, information storage, nanotechnology. D. P. Siewiorek, Buhl University Professor of ECE and CS and Director, HCI Institute; Ph.D., Stanford, 1972: computer architecture, reliability, context-aware mobile computing. B. Sinopoli, Assistant Professor; Ph.D., Berkeley, 2005: networked embedded control systems, sensory/actuator networks, control theory. D. D. Stancil, Professor; Ph.D., MIT, 1981: wireless communication, nanophotonics, spin-wave devices. P. A. Steenkiste, Professor of ECE and CS; Ph.D., Stanford, 1987: computer networks, distributed systems, pervasive computing. R. M. Stern Jr., Professor of ECE, CS, and BME; Ph.D., MIT, 1976: automatic speech recognition, auditory perception, signal processing. A. J. Strojwas, Keithley Professor; Ph.D., Carnegie Mellon, 1982: statistically based CAD/CAM of VLSI circuits. T. Sullivan, AssociateTeaching Professor; Ph.D., Carnegie Mellon, 1996: audio signal processing, music and sound recording applications. S. N. Talukdar, Professor Emeritus; Ph.D., Purdue, 1970: agent-based systems, distributed problem solving, power systems, organization design. D. E. Thomas Jr., Professor; Ph.D., Carnegie Mellon, 1977: computer-aided design of single-chip heterogeneous multiprocessing systems. O. Tonguz, Professor; Ph.D., Rutgers, 1990: optical networks, wireless communications and high-speed networking. E. Towe, Grobstein Professor of ECE and MSE; Ph.D., MIT, 1997: photonics, optical networks, biophotonics, sensors, quantum phenomena in optical materials. R. M. White, University Professor Emeritus; Ph.D., Stanford, 1964: magnetic device phenomena, technology policy. J. G. Zhu, ABB Professor and Director, DSSC; Ph.D., California, San Diego, 1989: micromagnetics, magnetoelectronic devices, magnetic recording.

COLUMBIA UNIVERSITY

Department of Electrical Engineering

Programs of Study	The Department of Electrical Engineering offers programs of study leading to the degrees of Master of Science (M.S.), Electrical Engineer (E.E.), Doctor of Engineering Science (Eng.Sc.D.), and Doctor of Philosophy (Ph.D.). Registration as a nondegree candidate (special student) is also permitted.
	There are no prescribed course requirements for these degrees. Students, in consultation with their faculty advisers, design their own programs, focusing on particular fields. Among them are semiconductor physics materials and devices; telecommunication systems and computer networks; high-speed analog, RF analog, and mixed analog/digital integrated circuits and systems; image, video, audio, and speech processing; electromagnetic theory and applications; plasma physics; quantum electronics; photonics; sensory perception; genomics and bio-EE; and medical electronics.
	Graduate studies are closely associated with research. Faculty members are engaged in theoretical and experimental research in various areas of their disciplines.
	Access also exists to a number of interdisciplinary programs, such as Computer Engineering, Solid-State Science and Engineering, and Bioengineering. In addition, substantial research interactions occur with the Departments of Applied Physics, Computer Science, and Industrial Engineering and Operations Research and with the College of Physicians and Surgeons.
	The requirements for the Ph.D. and Eng.Sc.D. degrees are identical. Both require a dissertation based on the candidate's original research, conducted under the supervision of a faculty member. The work may be theoretical or experimental or both. The E.E. professional degree program does not require a thesis. It provides specialization beyond the M.S. degree in a field chosen by the student and is particularly suited to those who wish to advance their professional development after a period of industrial employment.
Research Facilities	Every phase of current research activities is fully supported and carried out in one of more than a dozen well-equipped research laboratories run by the Department. Specifically, laboratory research is conducted in the following laboratories: Multimedia Networking Laboratory, Ultrafast Opto-Electronics Laboratory, Photonics Laboratory, Microelectronics Device Fabrication Laboratory, Digital Video and Multimedia Laboratory, Molecular Beam Epitaxy Laboratory, Laser Processing and Quantum Physics Laboratory, Integrated Systems Laboratory, Laboratory for Recognition and Organization of Speech and Audio, Lightwave Communications Laboratory, Bioelectronic Systems Laboratory, Columbia Laboratory for Unconventional Electronics, and Plasma Physics Laboratory (in conjunction with the Department of Applied Physics).
Financial Aid	Teaching assistantships and graduate research assistantships are available. For the 2010–11 academic year, stipends were $2555 per month plus tuition exemption.
Cost of Study	The annual tuition for 2010–11 was about $41,580, plus fees.
Living and Housing Costs	The University provides limited housing for graduate men and women who are registered either for an approved program of full-time academic study or for doctoral dissertation research. University residence halls include traditional dormitory facilities as well as suites and apartments for single and married students; furnishings and utilities may be included. An estimated minimum of $20,000 should be allowed for board, room, and personal expenses for the academic year.
	University Real Estate properties include apartments owned and managed by the University in the immediate vicinity of the Morningside Heights campus. These are leased yearly, as they become available, to single and married students at rates that reflect the size and location of each apartment as well as whether furnishings or utilities are included.
	Requests for additional information and application forms should be directed to the Assignments Office, 111 Wallach Hall, Columbia University, New York, New York 10027.
Student Group	In 2010–11, enrollment in the Department of Electrical Engineering totaled 594 students and included 90 undergraduates (71 electrical engineering juniors and seniors and 19 computer engineering juniors and seniors), 302 electrical engineering master's degree candidates, 41 computer engineering master's candidates, 150 doctoral candidates with master's degrees, and 11 professional candidates. The student population has a diverse and international character.
Location	The proximity of many local industries provides strong student-industry contact and excellent job opportunities. Cooperative research projects are available in neighboring industrial laboratories, which are engaged in research and development in computers, telecommunications, electronics, defense, and health care. Adjunct faculty members from industry provide courses in areas of current professional interest. Frequent colloquia are given on current research by distinguished speakers from industry and neighboring universities.
The University	Since its founding in 1754, Columbia University has attracted students interested in the issues of their times. Opened as King's College under charter of King George II to "prevent the growth of republican principles which prevail already too much in the colonies," it instead educated founders of a new and powerful nation: Alexander Hamilton, John Jay, Robert Livingston, and Gouverneur Morris. Since then such notable figures as Michael Pupin, Edwin Armstrong, and Jacob Millman have served as professors of electrical engineering at Columbia.
Applying	The Department of Electrical Engineering uses an online application that can be found at http://www.engineering.columbia.edu/admissions/grad/application/. October 1 is the priority deadline for all spring applicants. December 1 is the priority deadline for fall doctoral applicants. February 15 is the priority deadline for fall M.S. and professional degree applicants. Notification of admission decisions are mailed beginning March 1.
Correspondence and Information	Office of Engineering Admissions Department of Electrical Engineering 524 S.W. Mudd, Mail Code 4708 Columbia University 500 West 120th Street New York, New York 10027 Phone: 212-854-6438 E-mail: seasgradmit@columbia.edu Web site: http://www.engineering.columbia.edu/admissions (admissions home page) http://www.ee.columbia.edu (Department home page)

Columbia University

THE FACULTY AND THEIR RESEARCH

Dimitris Anastassiou, Professor; Ph.D., Berkeley, 1979. Computational biology, with emphasis on systems-based gene expression analysis and comparative genomics. (phone: 212-854-3113; e-mail: anastas@ee.columbia.edu)

Keren Bergman, Professor; Ph.D., MIT, 1994. Optical interconnection networks for high-performance computing, photonic networks-on-chip, silicon photonics for high-speed interconnects, WDM optical networking, high-capacity optical packet switching, ultrafast lasers and devices, quantum noise in optical systems. (phone: 212-854-2280; e-mail: bergman@ee.columbia.edu)

Shih-Fu Chang, Professor; Ph.D., Berkeley, 1993. Multimedia search, digital video analysis, statistical pattern recognition, machine learning, multimedia forensics and security. (phone: 212-854-6894; e-mail: sfchang@ee.columbia.edu)

Edward Coffman, Professor; Ph.D., UCLA, 1966. Performance evaluation and optimization of computer communication systems and networks, scheduling theory, bin-packing theory, probabilistic analysis of algorithms, random structures in nanotechnology. (phone: 212-854-2152; e-mail: egc@ee.columbia.edu)

Paul Diament, Professor; Ph.D., Columbia, 1963. Antennas for satellite communications, fiber optics, waveguiding in VLSI chips, electromagnetics and free-electron lasers. (phone: 212-854-3111; e-mail: diament@ee.columbia.edu)

Dan Ellis, Associate Professor; Ph.D., MIT, 1996. Audio information extraction, speech recognition, source separation, music informat retrieval, computational hearing, sound visualization. (phone: 212-854-8928; e-mail: dpwe@ee.columbia.edu)

Dirk Englund, Assistant Professor; Ph.D., Stanford, 2008. Quantum information and metrology, nanophotonics, advanced optoelectronic devices, nuclear spin dynamics in semiconductors. (phone: 212 851-5958; email: englund@columbia.edu)

Tony F. Heinz, David M. Rickey Professor; Ph.D., Berkeley, 1982. Ultrafast optics and spectroscopy, nonlinear optics, properties of nanostructures and interfaces. (phone: 212-854-6564; e-mail: tony.heinz@columbia.edu)

Predrag Jelenkovic, Associate Professor; Ph.D., Columbia, 1996. Mathematical modeling and analysis of resource control and management in multimedia communication networks. (phone: 212-854-8174; e-mail: predrag@ee.columbia.edu)

Peter Kinget, Associate Professor; Ph.D., Leuven (Belgium), 1996. Design and analysis of analog, mixed-mode, and RF integrated circuits; analog and RF signal processing; device mismatch; ultra-low voltage; low power circuits in nanoscale CMOS. (e-mail: kinget@ee.columbia.edu)

Harish Krishnaswamy, Assistant Professor, Ph. D., USC, 2009. Radio-frequency (RF), millimeter-wave (mm-Wave) and sub-mmWave integrated circuits, with an emphasis on multiple-antenna systems, efficient, high-power transmitters, sub-mmWave signal sources, and low-phase-noise oscillators. (phone: 212-854-8196; email: harish@ee.columbia.edu)

Ioannis Kymissis, Assistant Professor; Ph.D., MIT, 2003. Organic semiconductors, OFETs, photodetectors, OLEDs, large-area thin-film electronics, hybrid device integration. (phone: 212-854-4023; e-mail: johnkym@ee.columbia.edu)

Aurel A. Lazar, Professor; Ph.D., Princeton, 1980. Time encoding and information representation in sensory systems, spike processing and neural computation in the cortex. (phone: 212-854-1747; e-mail: aurel@ee.columbia.edu)

Nicholas Maxemchuk, Professor; Ph.D., Pennsylvania, 1975. Communications networks: protocols, topological design, applications. (phone: 212-854-0580; e-mail: nick@ee.columbia.edu)

Vishal Misra, Associate Professor; Ph.D., Massachusetts Amherst, 2000. Networking, modeling and performance evaluation, information theory. (phone: 212-939-7061; e-mail: misra@cs.columbia.edu)

Steven M. Nowick, Associate Professor; Ph.D., Stanford, 1993. Asynchronous and mixed-timing circuits, computer-aided digital design, low-power and high-performance digital systems. (phone: 212-939-7056; e-mail: nowick@cs.columbia.edu)

Richard M. Osgood Jr., Higgins Professor; Ph.D., MIT, 1973. Integrated and guided-wave SI and other optoelectronic devices and their design, semiconductor and nanoscale surface physics and chemistry, ultrafast laser sources, quantum size studies. (phone: 212-854-4462; e-mail: osgood@columbia.edu)

Dan Rubenstein, Associate Professor; Ph.D., Massachusetts Amherst, 2000. Networking, network algorithms, protocols, performance evaluation, network security. (phone: 212-854-0050; e-mail: danr@ee.columbia.edu)

Henning Schulzrinne, Professor; Ph.D., Massachusetts Amherst. Internet real-time and multimedia services and protocols, wireless networks, modeling and analysis of computer communication networks, network security. (phone: 212-939-7004; e-mail: hgs@cs.columbia.edu)

Amiya K. Sen, Professor; Ph.D., Columbia, 1963. Plasma instabilities and their feedback control, plasma turbulence and anomalous transport. (phone: 212-854-3124; e-mail: amiya@ee.columbia.edu)

Kenneth Shepard, Associate Professor; Ph.D., Stanford, 1992. Design and analysis of mixed-signal CMOS integrated circuits, bioelectronics, application of CMOS circuit design tobiological applications, carbon-based electronics integrated with CMOS. (phone: 212-854-2529; e-mail: shepard@ee.columbia.edu)

Yannis Tsividis, Charles Batchelor Professor; Ph.D., Berkeley, 1976. Analog and mixed-signal integrated circuits, RF integrated circuits, circuit theory, analog and mixed signal processing. (phone: 212-854-4229; e-mail: tsividis@ee.columbia.edu)

Wen I. Wang, Thayer Lindsley Professor; Ph.D., Cornell, 1981. Quantum and heterostructure optoelectronics, materials and devices, photovoltaics, molecular bean epitaxy. (phone: 212-854-1748; e-mail: wen@ee.columbia.edu)

Xiaodong Wang, Associate Professor; Ph.D., Princeton, 1998. Statistical signal processing, multiuser communication theory, wireless communications. (phone: 212-854-6592; e-mail: wangx@ee.columbia.edu)

Charles A. Zukowski, Professor; Ph.D., MIT, 1985. Design and analysis of digital VLSI circuits, simulation of circuits and biological networks, communication circuits. (phone: 212-854-2073; e-mail: caz@columbia.edu)

Gil Zussman, Assistant Professor; Ph.D., Technion–Israel Institute of Technology, 2004. Wireless and mobile networks, including ad hoc, mesh, sensor, vehicular, and cognitive radio networks. (phone: 212-854-8670; e-mail: gil@ee.columbia.edu)

DREXEL UNIVERSITY

College of Engineering
Department of Electrical and Computer Engineering

Programs of Study

The Department of Electrical and Computer Engineering offers graduate studies leading to the Master of Science (M.S.) and Doctor of Philosophy (Ph.D.) degrees. Several Master of Science programs are available, leading to degrees in computer engineering (MSCPE), electrical engineering (MSEE), software engineering (MSSE), and telecommunications engineering (MSEET).

The Department's research and education activities can be divided broadly into six areas: computer engineering; control, robotics, and intelligent systems; electrophysics; image and signal processing and interpretation; power and energy engineering; and telecommunications and networking. Individualized plans of study within and across these areas are developed by students and their advisers to suit the student's educational and research needs.

The Master of Science degree typically requires 45 quarter credits selected from relevant classes offered by the Department, as well as pertinent classes offered by other departments within the College of Engineering and the Departments of Mathematics and Physics. A six-month internship in industry is a popular option. Both thesis and non-thesis options are available. Students who plan to continue their studies toward the Ph.D. degree are encouraged to select the thesis option.

Students who pursue computer engineering are offered specializations such as high performance, distributed, and fault tolerant computing; parallel algorithms and architectures; security and information assurance; networking; algorithms; computer architecture and organization; operating systems; advanced programming techniques; embedded systems; and VLSI design and fabrication.

In the area of software engineering, available specializations include advanced data structures, computer systems specifications, database systems, human computer interaction, software reliability and testing, advanced operating systems, and networking.

Among the specializations offered to students who pursue telecommunications engineering are modulation, coding and cryptography; information theory; terrestrial, satellite, cellular, and mobile communication systems; networking and information assurance; microwaves, antennas, and electromagnetics; optical communications; communication policy and law; and the business and economics of telecommunications.

The Ph.D. degree follows an individual plan of study (typically 90 quarter credits beyond the B.S. degree or 45 credits beyond the M.S. degree) and the development of an original thesis. Entry into the program requires a candidacy examination. Intermediate steps include a thesis proposal and presentation of progress reports in Departmental seminars. Ph.D. candidates are expected to develop original manuscripts for presentation and publication in conferences and refereed journals and are prepared for careers in research and development and in higher education.

Research Facilities

Research facilities for engineering students include the Antenna Laboratory and an anechoic chamber, the Center for Electric Power Engineering, the Center for Microwave/Lightwave Engineering, the Center for Telecommunications and Information Networking, the Data Fusion Laboratory (which engages in robotics), the Digital Signal Processing Laboratory, the Diagnostic Ultrasonic Signal Processing Laboratory, the Fiberoptics and Photonics Laboratory, the Imaging and Computer Vision Center, the Microwave-Photonics Device Laboratories, the Microelectronics Clean Room, the Multimedia Signal Processing Laboratory, the Scaled Signals and Systems Laboratory, the Thin Film and Ion Beam Laboratory, a VLSI Design Facility, an Ultrasound Transducer Research Facility, and the Wireless Systems Laboratory. The W. W. Hagerty Library offers a comprehensive online selection of journals, research databases, and digital books and houses nearly 500,000 books, periodicals, and microforms. The Electronic Learning Center provides access to well-equipped state-of-the-art computing facilities and software as well as electronic resources, CDs, and DVDs.

Financial Aid

Departmental teaching and research assistantships, which include full tuition and monthly stipends (starting at $2100 per month) are available based on instructional and research needs. Ph.D. candidates are eligible for consideration for the Koerner Family and the George Hill Jr. Endowed Fellowships.

Cost of Study

The tuition rate for the 2010–11 academic year is $960 per credit hour plus general student fees. Tuition and fees are waived (in part or in full) for students who receive Departmental assistantships.

Living and Housing Costs

On-campus housing is available. One-, two- and three- bedroom suites are available. Ample off-campus housing is also available.

Student Group

There are 237 graduate students in the ECE Department, of whom 33 are women and 88 are international students.

Location

The campus is located in Philadelphia, a major North American city and a major commercial, educational, and cultural center for the nation. Philadelphia is home to Independence Hall and the Liberty Bell, Fairmount Park, the Philadelphia Museum of Art, the Barnes Collection, the Franklin Institute, the Philadelphia Orchestra, the Academy of Music, the Curtis Institute, the Academy of Vocal Arts, Walnut Street Theater, the Forrest Theater, the Annenberg Center for the Performing Arts, the Reading Terminal Market, and the Italian Market. Sports teams include the Phillies, Eagles, Flyers, and 76ers.

The University

Drexel University was founded in 1891 by Philadelphia financier and philanthropist Anthony J. Drexel as the Drexel Institute of Art, Science and Industry. Today, this privately controlled, nonsectarian, and coeducational institution has more than 13,000 undergraduate and 7,000 graduate and professional students, attending eight colleges and three schools. These include the College of Engineering, the College of Law, and the College of Medicine. As one of the first schools to adopt mandatory cooperative education programs, Drexel now provides educational and internship opportunities through 1,500 business, industrial, governmental, and other institutions located in twenty-seven states and eleven other countries. A major attribute of Drexel is its strong connections and cooperation with industry and government organizations in the greater-Philadelphia area, and its significant impact on business and commerce as well as industrial, research, and development activities in Pennsylvania, New Jersey, and the Mid-Atlantic region.

Applying

Prospective students should have an undergraduate degree in one of the following areas: engineering, computer science, mathematics, and physics. Students who hold degrees in other engineering and science disciplines are also considered. Graduate Admissions can be contacted via e-mail at admissions@drexel.edu.

Correspondence and Information

Dr. Kapil Dandekar
Assistant Department Head for Graduate Affairs
Department of Electrical and Computer Engineering
Drexel University
3141 Chestnut Street
Philadelphia, Pennsylvania 19104-2875

Phone: 215-571-3579
E-mail: advising@ece.drexel.edu
Web site: http://www.ece.drexel.edu

Drexel University

THE FACULTY AND THEIR RESEARCH

S. Basavaiah, Auxiliary Professor; Ph.D., Pennsylvania. VLSI design, VLSI technology, low-power CMOS circuits, thin-film technology, interconnect technology. (basu@cbis.ece.drexel.edu)

Fernand Cohen, Professor; Ph.D., Brown. Computer vision, image processing, texture. (fscohen@coe.drexel.edu)

Kapil Dandekar, Associate Professor; Ph.D., Texas at Austin. Application of computational electromagnetics and signal processing to the study of next-generation wireless communication systems. (dandekar@ece.drexel.edu)

Afshin Daryoush, Professor; Ph.D., Drexel. Electrophysics: telecommunications, electromagnetic fields, antennas, microwave and millimeter wave solid-state devices and circuits, microwave photonics, fiber optics, microwave spectroscopy. (daryoush@ece.drexel.edu)

Jaudelice Cavalcante de Oliveira, Assistant Professor; Ph.D., Georgia Tech. Next-generation Internet, quality of service (QoS) in computer communication networks, QoS routing and traffic engineering, wireless networks (ad-hoc and sensor networks), network management and control. (jau@ece.drexel.edu)

Bruce A. Eisenstein, Arthur J. Rowland Professor and Associate Dean of the College of Engineering; Ph.D., Pennsylvania. Systems and biomedical: digital signal processing, pattern recognition, communication theory. (eisenstein@coe.drexel.edu)

Adam K. Fontecchio, Associate Professor and Assistant Department Head for Undergraduate Studies; Ph.D., Brown. Electrooptics, liquid crystals, polymer-dispersed liquid crystals, holography, remote sensing, color filtration, electrically switchable Bragg gratings. (fontecchio@ece.drexel.edu)

Gennady Friedman, Professor; Ph.D., Maryland. Nanoscale magnetic systems and their biological and biomedical applications, miniature nuclear magnetic resonance sensors and systems, liquid microdrop–based microelectromechanical systems (MEMS). (gary@ece.drexel.edu)

Eli Fromm, Roy A. Brothers University Professor; Ph.D., Thomas Jefferson. Biotelemetry, bioinstrumentation, professional society activities, engineering education/research. (fromme@drexel.edu)

Edwin L. Gerber, Professor and Assistant Head of the Department for Evening Programs; Ph.D., Pennsylvania. Electrophysics: physical electronics, electronic devices, computerized instrumentation. (gerber@ece.drexel.edu)

Allon Guez, Professor; Ph.D., Florida. Robotics, control dynamic systems, intelligent control, linear systems, nonlinear systems, optimal control. (guezal@drexel.edu)

Mark Hempstead, Assistant Professor; Ph.D., Harvard. Computer engineering, power-aware computer architecture, low-power VLSI design, wireless sensor networks. (mhempstead@coe.drexel.edu)

Peter Herczfeld, Lester A. Kraus Professor; Ph.D., Minnesota. Microwaves and millimeter waves, lightwave engineering, fiber optics, solar energy, solid-state electronics. (herczfeld@ece.drexel.edu)

Leonid Hrebien, Professor and Assistant Department Head for Graduate Studies; Ph.D., Drexel. Systems and biomedical: bioinformatics, acceleration effects on cardiovascular and cerebrovascular functions. (lhrebien@coe.drexel.edu)

Paul R. Kalata, Associate Professor; Ph.D., IIT. Systems: estimation, identification and control theory, adaptive control and filtering, computer control systems. (kalata@ece.drexel.edu)

Moshe Kam, Robert Quinn Professor and Department Head; Ph.D., Drexel. Detection and estimation, decision theory, decision fusion, information assurance, robot navigation, forensic pattern recognition. (kam@minerva.ece.drexel.edu)

Nagarajan Kandasamy, Assistant Professor; Ph.D., Michigan. Embedded systems, self-managing systems, reliable and fault-tolerant computing, distributed systems, computer architecture, testing and verification of digital systems. (kandasamy@ece.drexel.edu)

Youngmoo Kim, Assistant Professor; Ph.D., MIT. Music and audio analysis and synthesis, machine understanding of audio for information retrieval, entertainment media technologies, MPEG standards. (youngmoo@coe.drexel.edu)

Timothy P. Kurzweg, Associate Professor; Ph.D., Pittsburgh. Mixed-signal multidomain modeling and simulation, optical interconnects, optical MEMS, optical microsystems, system-level simulation, free-space optics, computer architecture, system on a chip (SOC). (kurzweg@ece.drexel.edu)

Peter A. Lewin, Richard Beard Professor and Director, Biomedical Ultrasound Research and Education Center; Ph.D., Denmark. Biomedical ultrasonics, biological effects of ultrasound, physical acoustics. (lewin@ece.drexel.edu)

Karen Nan Miu Miller, Associate Professor; Ph.D., Cornell. Power systems: power distribution system planning and operation, distribution automation, optimization techniques. (miu@ece.drexel.edu)

Bahram Nabet, Professor and Associate Dean of the College of Engineering, Special Projects; Ph.D., Washington (Seattle). Electrophysics: compound semiconductor devices and circuits, fabrication and modeling, photonics, neural networks, vision. (nabet@ece.drexel.edu)

Prawat Nagvajara, Associate Professor; Ph.D., Boston University. Design and testing of computer hardware, fault-tolerant computing, error-correcting codes. (prawat_nagvajara@ece.drexel.edu)

Dagmar Niebur, Associate Professor and Assistant Department Head, Planning and Development; Ph.D., Swiss Federal Institute of Technology (Lausanne). Intelligent information processing techniques for power system monitoring and control. (niebur@ece.drexel.edu)

Chikaodinaka O. D. Nwankpa, Professor; Ph.D., IIT. Power: power systems planning and operation; systems: modeling and control of nonlinear systems, stochastic systems theory. (nwankpa@ece.drexel.edu)

Banu Onaral, H. H. Sun Professor and Director of the School of Biomedical Engineering, Science, and Health Systems; Ph.D., Pennsylvania. Biomedical signal processing, complexity and scaling in biomedical signals and systems. (onaral@ece.drexel.edu)

Kambiz Pourrezaei, Professor; Ph.D., Rensselaer. Applications of microelectronics to biomedicine, biomaterials. (pourrezaei@coe.drexel.edu)

Karkal G. Prabhu, Auxiliary Professor; Ph.D., Harvard. Software reliability, real-time systems, neural networks, pattern recognition. (karkal.s.prabhu@drexel.edu)

Arye Rosen, Academy Professor of Biomedical Engineering and Electrical Engineering; Ph.D., Drexel. Biomedical applications of electromagnetic waves, microwave interaction with tissue, biosensors. (arye.rosen@drexel.edu)

Gail Rosen, Assistant Professor; Ph.D., Georgia Tech. Signal processing, signal processing for biological analysis and modeling, bioinspired designs, source localization and tracking. (gailr@ece.drexel.edu)

Kevin J. Scoles, Associate Professor and Associate Dean for Undergraduate Affairs; Ph.D., Dartmouth. Electrophysics: device fabrication, photovoltaics, solid-state physics, digital circuit design, computer-aided design. (kscoles@ece.drexel.edu)

Harish Sethu, Associate Professor; Ph.D., Lehigh. Computer networks, parallel computer architectures, parallel and distributed computing, switching networks and topologies, logic devices, computer arithmetic. (sethu@ece.drexel.edu)

P. Mohana Shankar, Allen Rothwarf Professor; Ph.D., Indian Institute of Technology (Delhi). Telecommunications, mobile systems, fiber optics, biomedical ultrasonics. (shankar@ece.drexel.edu)

Baris Taskin, Assistant Professor; Ph.D., Pittsburgh, Electronic design automation, advanced timing and synchronization methodologies for high-performance digital VLSI circuits, mixed-signal system design and optimization methodologies. (taskin@coe.drexel.edu)

Lazar Trachtenberg, Professor; D.Sc., Technion (Israel). Design and testing of hardware (multilevel gate arrays), fault-tolerant computing, design of reliable suboptimal digital filters. (trachtenberg@ece.drexel.edu)

Oleh J. Tretiak, Robert C. Disque Professor; Sc.D., MIT. Computers and image processing: microcomputer image processing workstation, computer tomography, pattern recognition computer systems. (tretiak@ece.drexel.edu)

John Walsh, Assistant Professor; Ph.D., Cornell. Performance and convergence of belief, expectation propagation and turbo decoding/equalization/synchronization, permeation models for ion channels, composite adaptive systems theory. (jwalsh@ece.drexel.edu)

Steven Weber, Assistant Professor; Ph.D., Texas at Austin. Streaming multimedia, rate-adaptation mechanisms for networks, distributed algorithms on networks. (sweber@ece.drexel.edu)

DUKE UNIVERSITY

Department of Electrical and Computer Engineering

Programs of Study

Graduate study in the Department of Electrical and Computer Engineering (ECE) is intended to prepare students for leadership roles in academia, industry, and government that require creative technical problem-solving skills. The Department offers both Ph.D. and M.S. degree programs, with opportunities for study in a broad spectrum of areas within the disciplines of electrical and computer engineering. Research and course offerings in the Department are organized into five areas of specialization: computer engineering, microsystems and nanosystems, photonics, sensing and waves, and signal processing and communications. Interdisciplinary programs are also available that connect the above programs with those in other engineering departments and computer science, the natural sciences, and the Medical School. Students in the Department may also be involved in research conducted in one of the Duke centers, e.g., the Fitzpatrick Center for Photonics and Communications. Under a reciprocal agreement with neighboring universities, a student may include some courses offered at the University of North Carolina at Chapel Hill and North Carolina State University in Raleigh. Since an important criterion for admitting new students is the match between student and faculty research interests, prospective students are encouraged to indicate which Departmental specialization areas they are interested in when applying.

Research Facilities

The ECE department currently occupies approximately 47,000 square feet in two buildings: the Fitzpatrick Center for Interdisciplinary Engineering, Medicine and Applied Sciences (CIEMAS) and Hudson Hall. CIEMAS houses cross-disciplinary activities involving the Pratt School and its partners in the fields of bioengineering, photonics, microsystems integration, sensing and simulation, and materials science and materials engineering. This comprehensive facility provides extensive fabrication and test laboratories, Departmental offices, teaching labs, and other lab support spaces as well as direct access to a café. In addition, a state-of-the-art clean room for nanotechnology research is currently under development on its main floor. Hudson Hall is the oldest of the buildings in the engineering complex. It was built in 1948 when the Engineering School moved to Duke's West Campus and was known as Old Red. An annex was built onto the back of the building in 1972, and in 1992, the building was expanded again and renamed Hudson Hall to honor Fitzgerald S. (Jerry) Hudson E'46. Hudson Hall is home to all four departments in the Pratt School of Engineering, as well as the school's laboratories, computing facilities, offices, and classrooms.

Financial Aid

Financial support is available for the majority of Ph.D. students. Graduate fellowships for the first two semesters of study cover full stipend, registration fees, and tuition. Beyond this initial period, students may receive research assistantships funded by faculty research grants, which together with financial aid, cover their full registration fees, tuition, and stipend until completion of a degree.

Cost of Study

For the 2010–11 year, tuition for doctoral students is $39,150; for master's students it is approximately $10,125 per semester (9 units at $1125 per unit). In addition, a registration fee of $2755 is required each semester.

Living and Housing Costs

Duke has residential apartment facilities available to graduate students through an application process. These furnished apartments are available for continuous occupancy throughout the calendar year. Academic-year rates in central campus apartments range from $5800 per occupant for 3 students in a three-bedroom apartment to $8710 for an efficiency apartment. Several apartment complexes are close to the campus.

Student Group

In the academic year 2010–11, a total of 155 students are enrolled, of whom 122 are doctoral students and 33 are M.S. students.

Location

Located in the rolling central Piedmont area of North Carolina, the Duke University campus is widely regarded as one of the most beautiful in the nation. The four-season climate is mild, but good winter skiing is available in the North Carolina mountains a few hours' drive to the west, and ocean recreation is a similar distance away to the east. Duke is readily accessible by Interstates 85 and 40 and from Raleigh-Durham International Airport, which is about a 20-minute drive from the campus via Interstate 40 and the Durham expressway.

The University and The Department

Trinity College, founded in 1859, was selected by James B. Duke as the major recipient of a 1924 endowment that enabled a university to be organized around the college and to be named for Washington B. Duke, the family patriarch. A department of engineering was established at Trinity College in 1910, and the Department of Electrical Engineering was formed in 1920. Its name changed to the Department of Electrical and Computer Engineering in 1996. Duke University remains a privately supported university, with more than 11,000 students in degree programs.

Applying

Admission to the Department is based on a review of previous education and experience, the applicant's statement of intent, letters of evaluation, standardized test scores (GRE and TOEFL), and grade point average. The application deadline for spring admission is October 15. December 8 is the priority deadline for submission of Ph.D. applications for admission and financial award for the fall semester. January 30 is the priority deadline for submission of M.S. applications for admission.

Correspondence and Information

Steven A. Cummer
Professor and Director of Graduate Studies
Department of Electrical and Computer Engineering
Pratt School of Engineering, Box 90291
Duke University
Durham, North Carolina 27708-0291
Phone: 919-660-5245
E-mail: dgs@ee.duke.edu
Web site: http://www.ee.duke.edu

Duke University

THE FACULTY AND THEIR RESEARCH

John A. Board, Associate Professor of ECE and Computer Science; D.Phil., Oxford. High performance scientific computing and simulation, novel computer architectures, cluster computing and parallel processing, ubiquitous computing.

David J. Brady, Professor; Ph.D., Caltech. Computational optical sensor systems, hyperspectral microscopy, Raman spectroscopy for tissue chemometrics, optical coherence sensors and infrared spectral filters.

Martin A. Brooke, Associate Professor; Ph.D., USC. Integrated analog CMOS circuit design, integrated nanoscale systems, mixed signal VLSI design, sensing and sensor systems, optical imaging and communications, analog and power electronics, electronic circuit assembly and testing.

April S. Brown, John Cocke Professor and Sr. Associate Dean for Research; D.Sc., Cornell. Nanomaterial manufacturing and characterization, sensing and sensor systems, nanoscale/microscale computing systems, integrated nanoscale systems.

Lawrence Carin, William H. Younger Professor; Ph.D., Maryland, College Park, Homeland security, sensing and sensor systems, signal processing, land mine detection.

Krishnendu Chakrabarty, Professor; Ph.D., Michigan. Computer engineering, nanoscale/microscale computing systems, self-assembled computer architecture, micro-electronic mechanical machines, failure analysis, integrated nanoscale systems, microsystems.

Leslie M. Collins, Professor and Chair; Ph.D., Michigan. Sensing and sensor systems, homeland security, land mine detection, neural prosthesis, geophysics, signal processing.

Steven A. Cummer, Jeffrey N. Vinik Associate Professor and Director of Graduate Studies; Ph.D., Stanford. Geophysics, photonics, atmospheric science, metamaterials, electromagnetics.

Chris Dwyer, Assistant Professor; Ph.D., North Carolina at Chapel Hill. Self-assembled computer architecture, nanoscale/microscale computing systems, nanomaterial manufacturing and characterization, computer engineering, biological computing, computer architecture, nanoscience, materials.

Richard B. Fair, Lord-Chandran Professor; Ph.D., Duke. Computer engineering, sensing and sensor systems, electronic devices, integrated nanoscale systems, medical diagnostics, microsystems, semiconductors.

Jeffrey T. Glass, Professor and Hogg Family Director, Engineering Management and Entrepreneurship; Ph.D., Virginia. Micro-electronic mechanical machines, engineering management, entrepreneurship, social entrepreneurship, sensing and sensor systems, materials.

Michael R. Gustafson, Assistant Professor of the Practice; Ph.D., Duke. Engineering education, electronic circuit assembly and testing, electronic devices.

Lisa G. Huettel, Associate Professor of the Practice and Director of Undergraduate Studies; Ph.D., Duke. Sensing and sensor systems, engineering education, signal processing, distributed systems.

William T. Joines, Professor; Ph.D., Duke. Photonics and electromagnetics.

Nan M. Jokerst, J. A. Jones Professor; Ph.D., USC. Photonics, sensing and sensor systems, nanomaterial manufacturing and characterization, semiconductors, integrated nanoscale systems, microsystems.

Tom Katsouleas, Professor and Dean; Ph.D., Physics, UCLA. Use of plasmas as novel particle accelerators and light sources.

Jungsang Kim, Associate Professor; Ph.D., Stanford. Photonics, micro-electronic mechanical machines, sensing and sensor systems, semiconductors, quantum information, integrated nanoscale systems.

Jeffrey L. Krolik, Professor; Ph.D., Toronto (Canada). Sensing and sensor systems, signal processing, acoustics, medical imaging, homeland security, electromagnetics, antennas.

Xuejun Liao, Assistant Research Professor; Ph.D., China. Pattern recognition and machine learning, bioinformatics, signal processing.

Qing H. Liu, Professor; Ph.D., Illinois at Urbana-Champaign. Electromagnetics, antennas, medical imaging, photonics, acoustics, computational electromagnetics.

Daniel L. Marks, Assistant Research Professor; Ph.D., Illinois at Urbana-Champaign. Imaging and spectroscopy.

Hisham Z. Massoud, Professor; Ph.D., Stanford. Nanomaterial manufacturing and characterization, nanoscale/microscale computing systems, computer engineering, engineering education, electronic devices, manufacturing, semiconductors, microsystems.

James Morizio, Assistant Research Professor; Ph.D., Duke. Computer engineering, nanoscale/microscale computing systems, biological computing, mixed signal VLSI design, integrated analog CMOS circuit design.

Kenneth D. Morton Jr., Assistant Research Professor; Ph.D., Duke. Statistical signal processing, sensing and sensor systems, machine learning, land mine detection, acoustics.

Loren W. Nolte, Professor; Ph.D., Michigan. Sensing and sensor systems, medical imaging, signal processing.

Douglas P. Nowacek, Repass-Rodgers University Associate Professor of Conservation Technology and Associate Professor of ECE; Ph.D., MIT/Woods Hole Oceanographic Institution. Acoustics, micro-electronic mechanical machines.

Maxim Raginsky, Assistant Research Professor; Ph.D., Northwestern. Signal processing, sensing and sensor systems, information theory, statistical learning theory, optimization and games, stochastic adaptive control.

Matthew S. Reynolds, Assistant Professor; Ph.D., MIT. RFID and its applications to robotics and human-computer interaction, ultra-low power sensing and computation, parasitic power and smart materials, surfaces, spaces.

Romit Roy Choudhury, Assistant Professor; Ph.D., Illinois at Urbana-Champaign. Computer engineering, antennas, electronic devices, wireless networking, mobile computing, distributed systems.

David R. Smith, William Bevan Professor; Ph.D., California, San Diego. Photonics, metamaterials, electromagnetic, plasmonics.

Daniel J. Sorin, Associate Professor; Ph.D., Wisconsin–Madison. Computer engineering, computer architecture, fault tolerance, reliability.

Adrienne D. Stiff-Roberts, Assistant Professor; Ph.D., Michigan. Nanomaterial manufacturing and characterization, semiconductor photonic devices, photonics, nanoscience.

Peter A. Torrione; Assistant Research Professor; Ph.D., Duke. Statistical signal processing, machine learning, pattern recognition, buried threat detection.

Kishor S. Trivedi; Hudson Professor (joint with Computer Science); Ph.D., Illinois at Urbana-Champaign. Computer engineering, failure analysis, fault tolerance, reliability, computer architecture.

Rebecca Willett, Assistant Professor; Ph.D., Rice. Sensing and sensor systems, homeland security, medical imaging, K–12 education in science and mathematics, signal processing, photonics, distributed systems.

Gary A. Ybarra, Professor of the Practice; Ph.D., North Carolina State. Engineering education, K–12 education in science and mathematics, medical imaging.

Tomoyuki Yoshie, Assistant Professor; Ph.D., Caltech. Photonics, semiconductor photonic devices, nanoscale/microscale computing systems, quantum information, integrated nanoscale systems.

FLORIDA INSTITUTE OF TECHNOLOGY

College of Engineering
Department of Electrical and Computer Engineering

Programs of Study

Florida Institute of Technology offers programs of study leading to the Master of Science and Doctor of Philosophy degrees in electrical engineering and computer engineering. These programs are designed to provide opportunities for students' development of professional engineering competence and scholarly achievement.

Research Facilities

There are more than 12,000 square feet of well-equipped laboratory facilities available for use by students, faculty members, and researchers. Computing facilities include many PCs running both Linux and Windows-based operating systems that are networked via Ethernet and a WAN. Research facilities support basic and applied research in communications, photonics, and signal processing. Agencies of the federal and state governments, as well as major corporations, support research efforts in these and other technical areas.

Financial Aid

Graduate teaching and research assistantships are available to qualified students. For 2010–11, typical stipends range upward from $9600 for twelve months for approximately half-time duties. Some assistantships include tuition.

Cost of Study

For 2010–11, tuition is $1040 per semester credit hour for all students. Tuition is included with some graduate assistantships.

Living and Housing Costs

Room and board on campus cost approximately $4500 per semester. On-campus housing (dormitories and apartments) is available for full-time single and married graduate students, but priority for dormitory rooms is given to undergraduate students. Many apartment complexes and rental houses are available near the campus.

Student Outcomes

Graduates of the programs in electrical and computer engineering are employed by such companies as IBM, Texas Instruments, NASA, Harris Corporation, AT&T, General Electric, Northrop Grumman, Lockheed Martin, McDonnell Douglas, Rockwell International, United Technologies, Honeywell, Computer Sciences Raytheon, ITT Aerospace, Los Alamos National Lab, Hewlett-Packard, Intel, Naval Air Systems Command, Naval Undersea Warfare Center, Computer Task Group, and the Boeing Company.

Location

The campus is located in Melbourne, on Florida's east coast. It is an area 3 miles from Atlantic Ocean beaches, with a year-round subtropical climate. The area's economy is supported by a well-balanced mix of industries in electronics, aviation, light manufacturing, optics, communications, agriculture, and tourism. Many companies support activities at the Kennedy Space Center.

The Institute

Florida Institute of Technology, founded in 1958, has developed into a distinctive independent university that provides undergraduate and graduate education in engineering and sciences for students from throughout the United States and many other countries. Florida Tech is supported by local industry and is the recipient of many research grants and contracts.

Applying

Applicants for graduate study in electrical engineering should have an undergraduate degree in electrical engineering, while those applying for graduate study in computer engineering should have an undergraduate degree in computer engineering. An applicant whose degree is in another field of engineering or in the applied sciences will be reviewed; however, undergraduate course work in the field of study is generally required prior to starting the Master of Science program.

Forms and instructions for applying for admission and assistantships are sent upon request. Doctoral applicants are asked to submit three letters of recommendation from academic references and a statement of purpose giving their reason for graduate study. Although the GRE is not required, it is considered for students with marginal undergraduate academic performance. International students applying for assistantships must have a TOEFL score greater than 600 and a TSE score of at least 45. International students without English proficiency and with a TOEFL score of less than 550 may need to enroll in language courses before beginning their graduate studies. Separate application for an assistantship should be made on forms available from the Graduate School.

Correspondence and Information

Office of Graduate Admissions
Florida Institute of Technology
150 West University Boulevard
Melbourne, Florida 32901-6988
Phone: 321-674-8027
       800-944-4348 (toll-free in the U.S.)
Fax: 321-723-9468
E-mail: grad-admissions@fit.edu
Web site: http://www.fit.edu

Dr. S. Kozaitis
Electrical and Computer Engineering
Florida Institute of Technology
150 West University Boulevard
Melbourne, Florida 32901-6988
Phone: 321-674-8060
Fax: 321-674-8192
E-mail: kozaitis@fit.edu
Web site: http://coe.fit.edu/ee

Florida Institute of Technology

THE FACULTY AND THEIR RESEARCH

Georgios C. Anagnostopoulos: Machine learning, pattern recognition.
Susan Earles: Semiconductor modeling, processing, and fabrication.
Barry G. Grossman: Fiber-optic sensor systems and smart structures.
John Hadjilogiou: Computer organization and architecture.
Fredric M. Ham, Harris Professor: Digital signal processing, neural networks.
Veton Z. Këpuska: Human-machine interaction and communication, speech processing and recognition.
Ivica Kostanic: Telecommunications, wireless telecommunications.
Samuel P. Kozaitis: Automated feature extraction, image fusion.
Brian A. Lail: Antenna-coupled sensors, computational and applied electromagnetics, EMI, EMC.
Syed H. Murshid: Photonics, fiber-optic sensors, instrumentation.
Robert Sullivan: Power systems, power electronics.

RESEARCH AREAS

Physical Electronics

The research in this area primarily deals with photonics research, as performed in fiber-optic sensors and communications systems. Research includes unique fiber-optic devices and techniques using modal multiplexing, allowing communications channels to operate with expanded bit rates and optical encryption and switching devices. Fiber-optic sensors are developed for 2-D and 3-D structural health monitoring of strain and material failure; environmental applications, such as hydrogen detection; and homeland security applications. Instrumentation includes a wide variety of equipment used in developing fiber-optic systems. S. Earles, B. Grossman, S. Murshid.

Information Processing

Much of the research contributes to the solution of major national problems in signal and image processing. These include automated object detection, image fusion, noise reduction, and speech processing and recognition. Techniques being used include neural networks, wavelets, higher-order statistics, and statistical pattern recognition. New neural network architectures and robust learning rules have been developed. Algorithms have been developed for near-real-time detection and classification of nuclear explosions for purposes of monitoring nuclear testing. Other work has used wavelet analysis for image fusion and noise reduction. In addition, a voice-activated PowerPoint presentation and elevator simulator have been developed. G. Anagnostopoulos, F. Ham, V. Këpuska, S. Kozaitis.

Communications

The abundance of computational power and communications requires a robust infrastructure, providing security, multimedia capabilities, and location-dependent services. The work in this area primarily involves topics related to high-performance computers and communications, multimedia over the Internet, and firewall design issues, with emphasis on computer security. Experimental work is also being performed on antennas. I. Kostanic, B. Lail.

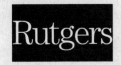

RUTGERS, THE STATE UNIVERSITY OF NEW JERSEY, NEW BRUNSWICK

Department of Electrical and Computer Engineering

Programs of Study

The graduate program in electrical and computer engineering, which leads to the M.S. and Ph.D. degrees, has facilities for education and research in communications, computer engineering, control systems, digital signal processing, and solid-state electronics. Computer engineering involves the architecture and design of computing machines, information processing, computer vision, virtual reality, VLSI design and testing, and software engineering. Control systems is concerned with the design, analysis, simulation, and mathematical modeling of systems to ensure that an automatic process, such as that of a robot or spacecraft, meets and maintains certain criteria. Digital signal processing deals with discrete-time information processing, digital filter design, spectral analysis, and special-purpose signal processors. Electrical communications systems analysis and design is concentrated in the areas of wireless communications, ad-hoc networks, network security, source and channel encoding, analog and digital modulation methods, information theory, and telecommunication networks. Solid-state electronics encompasses the areas of silicon carbide devices, semiconductor lasers, electro-optical modulation, solar cells, integrated circuits, characterization of semiconductor materials and devices, and nanotechnology.

Master of Science degree candidates may elect either a thesis or nonthesis option. The thesis option consists of 24 credits of course work, 6 credits of research leading to a master's thesis, and a final thesis presentation. In the nonthesis option, a candidate must complete 30 credits of course work with a minimum GPA of 3.0 and write a technical paper that must be presented in public as a seminar. Requirements for the M.S. degree may be satisfied for all options in a part-time evening program for students employed in industry and other students whose obligations preclude full-time study.

Admission into the Ph.D. program requires an M.S. in electrical and/or computer engineering. Applicants having an M.S. in a closely related discipline may be admitted into the program provided their preparation has no significant deficiencies. A student is considered to be a Ph.D. candidate after satisfactory completion of the Ph.D. qualifying exam. A Ph.D. candidate, in conjunction with an adviser, is required to select a dissertation committee, submit a plan of study, and orally present a dissertation proposal. Minimum requirements for the Ph.D. degree include 36 credits beyond the baccalaureate in courses approved by the dissertation adviser, 12 credits of either course work or research, and 24 credits of research leading to the Ph.D. dissertation. A public defense serves as the final Ph.D. dissertation exam. There is no foreign language requirement.

Research Facilities

The research centers within the Department include the Wireless Information Networks Laboratory (WINLAB), with a focus on wireless communications technologies, and the Microelectronics Research Laboratory (MERL), a semiconductor device fabrication clean room. Additional research is conducted with various Rutgers research centers established by the New Jersey Commission of Science and Technology, particularly the Center for Advanced Information Processing (CAIP). In addition to the extensive facilities available at these centers, the Department maintains the Digital Communications and Image Transmission Laboratory, Digital Signal Processing Systems Laboratory, Local Area Network Laboratory, Machine Vision Laboratory, Robotics and Sensorics Laboratory, VLSI CAD Laboratory, Laboratory for Engineering Information Systems, and solid-state experimental facilities for crystal growth and preparation, electrical characterization, design and fabrication, optical measurements, structure and composition analysis, and thin-film deposition measurements. For detailed information on these and other facilities available to graduate students, students should contact the Graduate Director or visit the Web site at http://www.ece.rutgers.edu.

Financial Aid

Assistantships and fellowships are available. For 2009–10, a typical assistantship or fellowship academic-year stipend totaled about $23,112 plus tuition. Assistantships also include health benefits and a full tuition waiver. In the award of financial aid, consideration is given to the student's undergraduate academic record, performance on the GRE, and letters of reference indicating outstanding ability.

Cost of Study

Tuition was $577 per credit for state residents and $875 per credit for out-of-state residents for the academic year 2009–10.

Living and Housing Costs

Graduate housing is available. Graduate students in the Department of Electrical and Computer Engineering may also reside in nearby off-campus apartments. Various meal plans are available.

Student Group

The Department has about 220 graduate students.

Location

New Brunswick (population 42,000), is in central New Jersey off Exit 9 of the New Jersey Turnpike and along the New York–Philadelphia railroad line. It is about 33 miles from New York City; frequent express bus service is available from a station near the College Avenue campus to terminals in central Manhattan. Princeton is 16 miles south, Philadelphia about 60 miles south, and Washington, D.C., within 200 miles.

The University

Rutgers, The State University of New Jersey, with more than 50,000 students on three campuses in Camden, Newark, and New Brunswick, is one of the nation's major public institutions of higher education. With twenty-seven schools and colleges, Rutgers offers over 100 undergraduate majors and more than 100 graduate and professional degree programs. Rutgers has a unique history as a Colonial college, a land-grant institution, and a state university. Chartered in 1766 as Queen's College, the eighth institution of higher learning to be founded in the colonies before the Revolution, the school opened its doors in New Brunswick in 1771 with one instructor, one sophomore, and a handful of freshmen. In 1825, the name of the college was changed to Rutgers to honor a former trustee and revolutionary war veteran, Colonel Henry Rutgers.

Applying

Admission materials are available online and from the Office of Graduate and Professional Admissions, Rutgers, The State University of New Jersey, 18 Bishop Place, New Brunswick, New Jersey 08901 (732-932-7711). A complete application consists of the application form, letters of recommendation, the application fee, official transcripts of previous academic work, a personal statement or essay, and scores on the GRE General Test. Detailed procedures and instructions accompany the application forms. The online application is available at http://gradstudy.rutgers.edu.

Correspondence and Information

Graduate Director
Department of Electrical and Computer Engineering
Rutgers University
94 Brett Road
Piscataway, New Jersey 08854-8058
Phone: 732-445-2578
E-mail: ece_grad@ece.rutgers.edu
Web site: http://www.ece.rutgers.edu

Rutgers, The State University of New Jersey, New Brunswick

THE FACULTY AND THEIR RESEARCH

Grigore Burdea, Professor; Ph.D., NYU. Virtual reality systems and applications, force feedback interfaces, virtual rehabilitation, telerehabilitation.

Michael L. Bushnell, Professor; Ph.D., Carnegie Mellon. Computer-aided design of VLSI integrated circuits, silicon compilers, artificial intelligence techniques.

Kristin Dana, Associate Professor; Ph.D., Columbia. Computer vision and computer graphics, surface modeling and texture analysis.

David G. Daut, Professor; Ph.D., Rensselaer. Communications and information processing: digital communication system design and analysis, image coding and transmission.

Zoran R. Gajic, Professor; Ph.D., Michigan State. Singular perturbation methods in control system analysis, linear stochastic estimation.

Marco Gruteser, Associate Professor; Ph.D., Colorado at Boulder. Pervasive computing architectures, location-aware systems, mobile networking, privacy and security, sensor networks.

Wei Jiang, Assistant Professor; Ph.D., Texas at Austin. Optoelectronics, photonic crystals, silicone photonics, nanophotonics, nanoimprint, optical interconnects.

Yicheng Lu, Professor; Ph.D., Colorado at Boulder. Solid-state materials and devices, wide band gap semiconductors, nanotechnology, multifunctional sensors.

Richard Mammone, Professor; Ph.D., CUNY Graduate Center. Image restoration, speech recognition, medical imaging.

Narayan B. Mandayam, Professor; Ph.D., Rice. Wireless communications, radio resource management, cognitive radios and protocols for spectrum sharing.

Ivan Marsic, Professor; Ph.D., Rutgers. Software engineering, computer networks, mobile and distributed computing, groupware, user interfaces.

Sigrid R. McAfee, Associate Professor; Ph.D., Polytechnic of New York. Electrical properties and deep levels in semiconductors, quantum theory of heterostructures, transmission line and waveguide theory.

Peter Meer, Professor; D.Sc., Technion (Israel). Computer vision, pattern recognition, applied robust estimation, probabilistic algorithms for machine-vision problems.

Sophocles J. Orfanidis, Associate Professor; Ph.D., Yale. Signal estimation and modeling methods, adaptive signal processing and spectrum estimation.

Paul Panayotatos, Professor; Eng.Sc.D., Columbia. Organic semiconductor solar cells, optical interconnects, microelectromechanical devices.

Manish Parashar, Professor; Ph.D., Syracuse. Parallel and distributed computing, scientific computing, and software engineering.

Dario Pompili, Assistant Professor; Ph.D., Georgia Tech. Ad hoc and sensor networks, underwater acoustic communications, traffic engineering and overlay networks, network optimization and control.

Lawrence Rabiner, Professor; Ph.D., MIT. Digital signal and speech processing, communications, networking.

Dipankar Raychaudhuri, Professor and Director, WINLAB; Ph.D., SUNY at Stony Brook. Network architecture and protocols, wireless communications, pervasive computing, experimental system prototyping.

Christopher Rose, Professor; Ph.D., MIT. Wireless communications theory and systems, opportunistic communications, spectrum sharing, interstellar communication and communications as a fundamental physical property.

Peddapullaiah Sannuti, Professor; Ph.D., Illinois at Urbana-Champaign. Internal and external stabilization of linear systems with constraints.

Kuang Sheng, Associate Professor; Ph.D., Heriot-Watt (Scotland). Solid-state power ICs, electronics, novel devices, SOI technology.

Deborah Silver, Professor; Ph.D., Princeton. Scientific visualization, volume graphics, medical visualization, information visualization, and multimedia systems.

Pedrag Spasojevic, Associate Professor; Ph.D., Texas A&M. Wireless and wired digital communications, adaptive and statistical signal processing.

Moncef B. Tayahi, Assistant Professor; Ph.D., Connecticut. Carbon, graphite, and diamond nanostructured power electronic devices; sensors and wireless sensor networks.

Wade Trappe, Associate Professor; Ph.D., Maryland, College Park. Multimedia and multicast information security, signal, image, and video processing.

Joseph Wilder, Research Professor; Ph.D., Pennsylvania. Image processing, pattern recognition, machine vision.

Roy Yates, Professor; Ph.D., MIT. Routing and flow control for integrated broadband networks, reversible queuing systems, wireless cellular communication systems.

Yanyong Zhang, Assistant Professor; Ph.D., Penn State. Operating systems, parallel and distributed systems, networking.

Jian Zhao, Professor; Ph.D., Carnegie Mellon. Wide bandgap (SiC, GaN) semiconductor power electronic and photonic devices, smart power ICs, high-temperature packaging.

UCRIVERSIDE
UNIVERSITY OF CALIFORNIA

UNIVERSITY OF CALIFORNIA, RIVERSIDE

Bourns College of Engineering
Department of Electrical Engineering

Programs of Study

The Department of Electrical Engineering (EE) at the University of California, Riverside (UCR), offers programs leading to M.S. and Ph.D. degrees. Research focus areas currently include communications, computer vision, control, detection and estimation, distributed systems, electronic and hybrid bioinorganic materials, error-correcting codes, image processing, information theory, intelligent sensors, intelligent systems, machine learning, modeling and simulation, molecular electronics, multimedia, nanostructures and nanodevices, navigation, neural networks, pattern recognition, robotics and automation, quantum computing, single-electronics, signal processing, solid-state devices and circuits, spintronics, system identification, and transportation systems. The Master of Science degree requires a minimum of 36 quarter credits and may be completed in three to four academic quarters of full-time study. Both thesis and nonthesis options are offered for the M.S. degree program. The Ph.D. program requires approximately three years of full-time study beyond the master's degree. In consultation with a faculty adviser, Ph.D. students plan their program of study. The doctoral dissertation is based on original research in the field of specialization. Students with teaching or research appointments should expect to take longer than full-time students to complete their degrees.

Research Facilities

In 2005, the Department relocated to a new building, Engineering Building Unit II, within the Bourns College of Engineering. For the general campus community, the UC Riverside systems group for Computing and Communications maintains a variety of fully serviced networked computing facilities and research access to the UC supercomputer. While these services are available to the campus at large, the Department of Electrical Engineering operates additional facilities using its own computer and computing systems. All of the College's students and faculty and staff members have individual account access to one or more of these systems, as do all students in service courses offered by the College.

The College of Engineering houses a new, fully equipped 2,000-square-foot Nanofabrication Cleanroom Facility, which was opened in 2005. Adjacent to the cleanroom is another user facility, the Analytical Microscopy Laboratory, which features transmission electron microscopes (TEM), scanning electron microscopes (SEM), and X-ray and other relevant equipment. Among other facilities and equipment available in the Department of Electrical Engineering are molecular beam epitaxial (MBE) chambers, atomic force microscopes (AFM), micro-Raman and photoluminescence spectroscopy, and electrical, optical, and thermal characterization systems. Excellent facilities for synthesis and characterization of nanomaterials are also available at the University Center for Nanoscale Science and Engineering.

UCR opened a four-story, 106,000-square-foot science library in 1998. The engineering collection is housed in the library, which is located next to Bourns Hall. The library has 1,500 reader and computer stations, with more than 1 million volumes in science and engineering, and hundreds of database and online information sources. The library has a dedicated engineering librarian with special training in information technology to assist the engineering faculty and students.

Financial Aid

Several forms of financial assistance are available, including fellowships, teaching assistant (TA) or graduate student researcher (GSR) appointments, and tuition and fee grants. The Department awards TAs, GSRs, and tuition and fee grants and nominates students for fellowships on a competitive basis to the campus Graduate Division. Offers of financial assistance may be multiyear, combining fellowship and TA and/or GSR appointments. Other forms of support are need-based and administered through the Office of Financial Aid.

Cost of Study

In 2010–11, the cost of study is estimated at $4274 per quarter for California residents and $9308 per quarter for nonresidents. Fees are subject to change and may be covered as part of a fellowship, TA, or GSR appointment.

Living and Housing Costs

UCR offers a number of housing options, both on campus and off campus. On-campus monthly rents range start at $250 for single students and $460 for married students and families. Housing for students living off campus is available at a competitive rate. For more information on housing, students should call 951-827-6350 or visit http://housing.ucr.edu.

Student Group

Campus enrollment in fall 2009 was 19,439. The Bourns College of Engineering enrolled 1,714 undergraduate and 437 graduate students.

Location

The University of California, Riverside, is set on a beautiful parklike campus of 1,200 acres at the foot of the Box Springs Mountains. One of ten campuses of the renowned University of California system, UCR offers the unique advantages of a large research institution along with opportunities for personal faculty attention. Located in Southern California's rapidly growing Inland Empire, the historic city of Riverside is noted for its palm-lined avenues, mild climate, and lower cost of living. Riverside is centrally located, offering easy access to the best geographical features of Southern California, including mountain resorts, ocean beaches, and desert playgrounds. The metropolitan areas of Los Angeles, Orange County, and San Diego are all within a short distance.

The University

UC Riverside began in 1907 as the Citrus Experiment Station to support the state's emerging citrus industry and became a campus of the University of California in 1954. Academic divisions at UCR include the College of Natural and Agricultural Sciences; the College of Humanities, Arts, and Social Sciences; the Marlan and Rosemary Bourns College of Engineering; the Graduate School of Education; the A. Gary Anderson Graduate School of Management; the Division of Biomedical Sciences; and the Graduate Division. The campus features the Citrus Research Center–Agricultural Experiment Station, Air Pollution Research Center, UCR/California Museum of Photography, Center for Ideas and Society, Center for Social and Behavioral Science Research, Institute of Geophysics and Planetary Physics, Centers for Water and Wildland Resources, and eight sites in the UC Natural Reserve System, including the Philip L. Boyd Deep Canyon Desert Research Center.

Applying

Applicants should have a degree in engineering or closely related fields, have a satisfactory overall GPA from their undergraduate studies, good letters of recommendation, and high scores on the GRE General Test. International students, permanent residents, and U.S. citizens whose native language is not English and who do not have a bachelor's or postgraduate degree from an institution where English is the exclusive language of instruction must complete the Test of English as a Foreign Language (TOEFL). Information about individual graduate degree programs can be accessed through the Bourns College of Engineering Web site at http://www.engr.ucr.edu. Information regarding admission criteria and online applications are obtainable through the Graduate Division Web site at http://www.graddiv.ucr.edu. To find out about research opportunities available through the College, students should explore the various department and research center Web sites in the College. The deadline for admission and financial support consideration is January 5, but applications after that date are welcomed.

Correspondence and Information

Graduate Advisor
Department of Electrical Engineering
University of California, Riverside
Riverside, California 92521
Phone: 951-827-2484
Fax: 951-827-2425
E-mail: grad-adm@ee.ucr.edu
Web site: http://www.engr.ucr.edu (Bourns College of Engineering)
http://www.graddiv.ucr.edu (Graduate Division)

University of California, Riverside

THE FACULTY AND THEIR RESEARCH

Afshin Abdollahi, Assistant Professor; Ph.D., USC, 2006. Computer-aided design methodologies and techniques, low-power design, logic synthesis and verification, quantum computation and quantum circuit synthesis, nanocircuit and nanotechnology.

Alexander A. Balandin, Professor; Ph.D., Notre Dame, 1996. Electronic materials and nanostructures, nanoelectronic and optoelectronic devices, nanophononics, hybrid bioinorganic nanosystems, thermal management of nanoscale devices, noise phenomena, wide band gap materials and devices, thermoelectric and photovoltaic devices.

Matthew Barth, Professor; Ph.D., California, Santa Barbara, 1990. Intelligent transportation systems (ITS), transportation and emissions modeling, vehicle activity analysis, electric and hybrid electric vehicles, mobile robot navigation, active computer vision, panoramic sensing techniques, distributed vision.

Gerardo Beni, Professor; Ph.D., UCLA, 1974. Swarm intelligence, multimedia for educational technology, financial engineering.

Bir Bhanu, Distinguished Professor; Ph.D., USC, 1981. Computer vision, machine learning, pattern recognition, artificial intelligence, multimedia and spatial databases, image processing, graphics and visualization, robotics and intelligent systems.

Jie Chen, Professor; Ph.D., Michigan, 1990. System identification, robust and robust-adaptive control, linear multivariable system theory, nonlinear control, optimization and complexity theory, active control of noise and vibration, magnetic bearing systems.

Ilya Dumer, Professor; Ph.D., Russian Academy of Sciences, 1981. Error-correcting coding for data transmission and storage, decoding algorithms, nonbinary codes, concatenated design, defect-correcting codes.

Jay A. Farrell, Professor; Ph.D., Notre Dame, 1989. Learning control systems, autonomous vehicles and intelligent transportation systems, global positioning systems.

Elaine Haberer, Assistant Professor; Ph.D., California, Santa Barbara, 2005. Biologically-mediated assembly of materials for electronic, optoelectronic, and energy applications; nano-structured hybrid materials; novel top-down and bottom-up assembly techniques.

Susan Hackwood, Professor; Ph.D., Leicester Polytechnic (England), 1979. Science and technology policy, distributed asynchronous signal processing and cellular robot systems.

Yingbo Hua, Professor; Ph.D., Syracuse, 1988. High-resolution signal processing, sensor array processing, wireless communications, channel identification and equalization, principal component analysis, blind system identification.

Sakhrat Khizroev, Professor; Ph.D., Carnegie Mellon, 1999. Nanomagnetic devices, spintronics, magnetic memory, protein-based memory devices, nanomagnetic resonance–based systems.

Alexander Korotkov, Professor; Ph.D., Moscow State, 1991. Single-electronics (physics and device applications, including single-electron logic and memory), electron transport in nanostructures, noise analysis, quantum measurements in quantum computing, quantum feedback.

Roger K. Lake, Professor; Ph.D., Purdue, 1992. Theory of electron transport through nanostructured, disordered, and amorphous materials; modeling semiconductor devices from the atomistic, to the device, through the circuit level; theoretical and computational electronics and optoelectronics; ultra-scaled devices and device physics; high-frequency and transient quantum device simulation; novel materials, devices, and architectures.

Ping Liang, Associate Professor; Ph.D., Pittsburgh, 1987. Image processing and analysis, medical image processing, pattern recognition, artificial neural networks, signal processing pattern formation in distributed systems, multimedia and human-machine interface.

Jianlin Liu, Associate Professor; Ph.D., UCLA, 2003. Semiconductor materials and devices, molecular beam epitaxial (MBE) growth of semiconductor materials and nanostructures, nanostructure and nanodevice fabrication via self-assembly and advanced lithography, flash memory and single-electron memory, spintronics, low-dimensional thermoelectrics and devices, solid-state lighting and sensing.

Anastasios Mourikis, Assistant Professor; Ph.D., Minnesota, 2008. Vision-aided inertial navigation, multi-robot systems, distributed estimation in mobile sensor networks, simultaneous localization and mapping, structure from motion, analytically predicting estimation accuracy of localization algorithms and developing methodologies for optimal resource utilization in localization systems with limited resources.

Ilya Lyubomirsky, Assistant Professor; Ph.D., MIT, 1999. Fiber-optic and free-space optical communications, optical satellite systems, coherent optical receivers, optical propagation through atmospheric turbulence, DSP-based equalization techniques.

Mihri Ozkan, Professor; Ph.D., California, San Diego, 2001. Design of multifunctional, smart, and complex systems, such as lab-on-a-chip platforms that require the integration of optical, electrical, chemical, biological, and fluidic (mechanical) components constructed from dissimilar materials.

Amit K. Roy-Chowdhury, Associate Professor; Ph.D., Maryland, 2002. Computer vision; signal, image, and video processing; pattern recognition.

Sheldon Tan, Associate Professor; Ph.D., Iowa, 1999. Automation for VLSI integrated circuits: high-performance power/ground distribution network design and optimization, simulation and synthesis of mixed-signal/RF/analog circuits, embedded system design based on FPGA platforms and signal integrity issues in VLSI physical design (cross-talk analysis, substrate noise analysis, and optimization).

Ertem Tuncel, Associate Professor; Ph.D., California, Santa Barbara, 2002. Information theory; multiterminal source and channel coding, with emphasis on multiresolution and sensor networks; data compression for efficient content-based retrieval from high-dimensional static and streaming databases; fundamental limits of content-based retrieval performance.

Albert Z. Wang, Professor; Ph.D., Buffalo, SUNY, 1996. RF/analog/mixed-signal integrated circuits; reliability and electrostatic-discharge protection design for IC, SoC (system-on-a-chip), IC CAD, and modeling; emerging semiconductor and nano devices.

Zhengyuan (Daniel) Xu, Professor; Ph.D., Stevens, 1999. Channel estimation and equalization, multiuser detection for wireless CDMA systems, space-time and multirate signal processing for communications, diversity combining, time-varying system identification and optimization, miscellaneous problems in CDMA systems.

UNIVERSITY OF NEW MEXICO

Department of Electrical and Computer Engineering

The University of New Mexico

Programs of Study

Graduate work leading to the M.S. and Ph.D. degrees is offered by the Department in the areas of bioengineering, communications, computational intelligence, computer architecture, computer networks and systems, control systems, electromagnetics, image processing, microelectronics and optoelectronics, plasma science, and signal processing. The M.S. degree is also offered in optical science and engineering. The master's degree program requires 30 semester credit hours for a thesis option and 33 semester credit hours for a nonthesis option. The Ph.D. program requires that a minimum of 24 graduate credit hours beyond the master's degree be completed at the University of New Mexico (UNM). Additional course work and research leading to the dissertation are geared to the individual student's needs and interests. As a potential candidate for the Ph.D. program, each student must pass the Ph.D. qualifying examination to establish levels and areas of scholastic competence.

Research Facilities

The Department maintains state-of-the-art laboratories for computer vision and image processing, wireless communications, high-performance computing and networking, laser and electrooptics, microprocessors (including advanced DSP platforms and emerging architectures), microwaves and antennas, pulsed power and plasma science, real-time computing and embedded systems (including a number of mobile robots and advanced real-time development systems), solid-state fabrication, and virtual reality/advanced human-computer interfaces. In addition, the Department has a close affiliation with excellent research laboratories and terascale supercomputing platforms at the Albuquerque Center for High Performance Computing, the Sandia National Laboratories, the Air Force Research Laboratory, and the Los Alamos National Laboratory. Sponsored research expenditures for the past three years were approximately $13 million each year.

Financial Aid

Support is available in the form of teaching, graduate, and research assistantships. Graduate internship programs are conducted with local industries, such as Sandia National Laboratories and the Air Force Research Laboratories. Annual stipends for full-time assistantships require no more than 20 hours of service per week for the academic year and include a tuition waiver of up to 12 credit hours per semester. Assistants are paid on a scale of $1200 to $2400 per month.

Cost of Study

In 2010–11, tuition for students carrying 12 or more credit hours was $2995 for state residents and $9579 for nonresidents per semester. All residents carrying 11 or fewer credit hours paid $252 per semester credit hour. Nonresidents paid $252 per semester credit hour for up to 6 credit hours and $800 per semester credit hour for 7 semester credit hours and above. Domestic students can meet the requirements for resident status by living continuously in New Mexico for at least one year prior to registration for the following semester and by providing satisfactory evidence of their intent to retain residency in New Mexico. International students must provide proof of financial support prior to admission to UNM.

Living and Housing Costs

Living costs in Albuquerque are somewhat lower than those in other cities of comparable size. In addition to tuition and fees, a single domestic student's expenses are estimated at $16,000 per year; expenses for a single international student are approximately $24,000 per year, including tuition and fees.

Student Group

Students come from all parts of the United States as well as from many other countries around the world. The graduate enrollment in the Department, including part-time students, is about 275, of whom 150 are post-M.S. or Ph.D. candidates. During the past two years, the Department has awarded ninety master's degrees and thirty-five Ph.D. degrees.

Student Outcomes

The current demand for graduate engineers is excellent, and the employment rate for electrical engineering and computer engineering graduates has been almost 100 percent. Graduates of the Department have been employed in various positions, such as senior engineer, vice president, manufacturing, electronics engineer, and systems engineer. Examples of companies that hire the Department's graduates include Intel, Motorola, IBM, Ford, Agilent, Xilinx, Northrop Grumman, Boeing, ATK Mission Research, Microsoft, and Honeywell in addition to small entrepreneurial companies and the National Labs (Sandia, Los Alamos, etc.).

Location

Albuquerque's metropolitan population is more than 670,000 and is the largest city in New Mexico. The city offers a delightful and interesting blend of several cultures; a wide variety of cultural, artistic, and aesthetic events are available year-round. Many of these take place on the campus, while others are located in the city and neighboring pueblos. The Indian Pueblo Cultural Center, the National Atomic Museum, and the UNM Maxwell Museum of Anthropology are facilities of particular interest. Albuquerque lies between the low land of the Rio Grande and the towering 11,000-foot Sandia Mountains. In this "Land of Enchantment" environment, the climate is dry and warm, and sunny days are followed by cool nights. Hiking, fishing, ballooning, mountain climbing, and skiing are only a few of the recreational activities that are readily available.

The University and The Department

The University of New Mexico was established in 1889 and is situated on 600 acres in the center of metropolitan Albuquerque. It is the largest university in the state, with more than 30,000 students. UNM is a Carnegie-designated Doctoral/Research-Extensive University, one of only three in the U.S. In the most recent *U.S. News & World Report*, the electrical engineering program was ranked fifty-third in the nation and twenty-eighth among all public universities, while the computer engineering program was ranked seventy-second in the nation and forty-eighth among all public universities.

The resources of the University and its proximity to Sandia National Laboratories, Kirtland Air Force Base, and the Los Alamos National Laboratory provide an excellent environment for advanced studies and research.

Applying

Prospective domestic applicants should contact the Office of Graduate Studies as well as the Department of Electrical and Computer Engineering for the latest information and dates. The GRE General Test is required for admission to both the M.S. and Ph.D. programs. Applications, fees, and transcripts should be on file with the Office of Graduate Studies by July 1 for domestic students and February 15 for international students for the fall semester, by November 1 for domestic students and June 15 for international students for the spring semester, and by April 30 for the summer session.

Correspondence and Information

Graduate Office
Department of Electrical and Computer Engineering
MSC01 1100
1 University of New Mexico
Albuquerque, New Mexico 87131-0001

Phone: 505-277-2600
Fax: 505-277-1439
E-mail: gradinfo@ece.unm.edu
Web site: http://www.ece.unm.edu

University of New Mexico

THE FACULTY AND THEIR RESEARCH

Chaouki T. Abdallah, Professor and Chair; Ph.D., Georgia Tech. Control systems, control of computing systems, reconfigurable systems and networks.

Ganesh Balakrishnan, Assistant Professor; Ph.D., New Mexico. Semiconductor device development including epitaxy and characterization, high-power vertical-external-cavity surface-emitting lasers, novel semiconductor material development for mid-infrared lasers.

Steven R. J. Brueck, Distinguished Professor and Director, Center for High Technology Materials (CHTM); Ph.D., MIT. Nanoscale lithography and nanofabrication with applications to nanophotonics, nanofluidics, and nanoscale epitaxial growth and sources/detectors; tunable infrared lasers; ultrahigh resolution optical microscopy.

Vincent D. Calhoun, Professor and Chief Technology Officer, The Mind Research Network; Ph.D., Maryland, Baltimore County. Biomedical engineering, psychiatric neuroimaging, functional and structural magnetic resonance imaging (MRI), multimodal data fusion, medical image analysis.

Thomas P. Caudell, Professor; Ph.D., Arizona. Computational cognitive neurosciences, neural networks theory and simulation, virtual reality and visualization, art/science collaborations, evolutionary computation, high-performance computing, autonomous robotics.

Christos G. Christodoulou, Professor; Ph.D., North Carolina State. Modeling of electromagnetic systems, smart antennas, reconfigurable antennas, machine learning applications in electromagnetics.

Rafael Fierro, Associate Professor; Ph.D., Texas at Arlington. Cooperative control of multi-agent systems, cyber-physical systems, mobile sensor and robotic networks, motion planning under sensing/communication constraints, optimization-based multivehicle coordination.

Charles B. Fleddermann, Professor; Associate Dean (Academic Affairs), School of Engineering; Ph.D., Illinois at Urbana-Champaign. Plasma processing, physical electronics, photovoltaics.

Nasir Ghani, Associate Professor; Ph.D., Waterloo. High-speed networking, cyber-infrastructures, protocols and architectures, traffic engineering, routing, network virtualization, optical and access networks, TCP/IP enhancements, performance evaluation, survivability, network simulation, stochastic modeling.

Mark A. Gilmore, Associate Professor; Ph.D., UCLA. Plasma physics, plasma diagnostics, magnetic confinement fusion, microwave engineering.

Majeed M. Hayat, Professor; Ph.D., Wisconsin–Madison. Statistical communication theory, signal and image processing, algorithms for infrared spectral sensors and imagers, novel avalanche photodiodes, optical communication, cooperative distributed sensing and computing, algorithms for synthetic aperture radar, applied probability and stochastic processes.

Gregory L. Heileman, Professor, Associate Chair, and Director, Undergraduate Program; Ph.D., Central Florida. Data structures and algorithmic analysis; theory of information, security and computing; machine learning and pattern recognition.

Stephen D. Hersee, Professor; Ph.D., Brighton Polytechnic (England). GaN-based nanowire devices and nanostructures, advanced semiconductor materials and devices.

Mani Hossein-Zadeh, Assistant Professor; Ph.D., USC. Electrooptics, microwave-photonic devices and systems, ultra-high-Q optical microresonators, optomechanical interaction in UH-Q optical resonators, optical communication, photonic sensors, optofluidics and plasmonics.

Ravinder K. Jain, Professor; Ph.D., Berkeley. Quantum electronics, optoelectronics, electrooptics, experimental solid-state physics.

Sudharman K. Jayaweera, Assistant Professor; Ph.D., Princeton. Wireless communications, statistical signal processing, network information theory, wireless sensor networks, cognitive radios, cooperative communications, information theoretic aspects of networked control systems, game theory, distributed signal processing.

Ramiro Jordan, Associate Professor, Founder and Executive VP, Ibero American Science and Technology Consortium (ISTEC); Ph.D., Kansas State. Communications, wireless sensor networks, multidimensional signal processing and embedded systems.

Sanjay Krishna, Professor and Associate Director, CHTM; Ph.D., Michigan. Investigation of nanostructured semiconductor materials for mid infrared lasers, detectors, and thermophotovoltaic cells; nanoscale materials consisting of self-assembled quantum dots, strain-layer superlattices for next generation bio-inspired sensors.

Luke F. Lester, Professor and General Chair, Optical Science in Engineering; Ph.D., Cornell. RF photonics, solar cells, semiconductor lasers, and quantum dot devices.

Yasamin Mostofi, Assistant Professor; Ph.D., Stanford. Cooperative/sensor networks, wireless communication networks, networked control systems, control and dynamical systems.

Marek Osinski, Professor; Ph.D., Institute of Physics, Polish Academy of Sciences. Magnetic nanoparticles, nanotechnology, colloidal nanocrystals, nuclear radiation detectors, semiconductor lasers, optoelectronic devices and materials, integrated optoelectronic circuits, group-III nitrides, degradation mechanisms and reliability, computer simulation, biomedical applications of nanocrystals.

Marios S. Pattichis, Associate Professor; Ph.D., Texas at Austin. Biomedical image and video processing and communications, medical imaging, dynamically reconfigurable systems, general methods for image and video analysis.

Fernando Perez-Gonzalez, Professor, Prince of Asturias Endowed Chair; Ph.D., Vigo (Spain). Information forensics and security, digital watermarking, cognitive radio, digital communications, adaptive algorithms.

James F. Plusquellic, Associate Professor; Ph.D., Pittsburgh. IC Trust, design for manufacturability, defect-based and data-driven VLSI test, small delay faulty test, model-to-hardware correlation and IC fabrication process monitors.

L. Howard Pollard, Assistant Professor; Ph.D., Illinois at Urbana-Champaign. Computer architecture, digital design, fault tolerance, microprocessors, FPGA systems, space electronics.

Balu Santhanam, Associate Professor; Ph.D., Georgia Tech. Digital signal processing, statistical communication theory, adaptive filtering, time-frequency analysis and representations, multicomponent AM-FM signal modeling, SAR-based vibrometry and related nonstationary signal analysis, ICA-related signal separation and classification.

Edl Schamiloglu, Professor; Ph.D., Cornell. Physics and technology of charged particle beam generation and propagation, high-power microwave sources and effects, pulsed-power science and technologies, plasma physics and diagnostics, electromagnetics and wave propagation, neurosystems engineering.

Pradeep Sen, Assistant Professor; Ph.D., Stanford. Computer graphics, real-time rendering, computational photography, computer vision, image processing.

Wei Wennie Shu, Associate Professor, Associate Chair, and Director, Graduate Program; Ph.D., Illinois at Urbana-Champaign. Distributed systems, multimedia networking, mobile ad-hoc and sensor networks, overlay network services, biomed modeling and simulation.

Jamesina J. Simpson, Assistant Professor; Ph.D., Northwestern. Computational electromagnetics theory and applications, especially finite-difference time-domain (FDTD) solutions of Maxwell's equations; research topics range from near-DC to light and include wave propagation in the Earth-ionosphere system and optical interactions with living tissues.

Payman Zarkesh-Ha, Assistant Professor; Ph.D., Georgia Tech. Statistical modeling of VLSI systems, design for manufacturability, low-power and high-performance VLSI design.

Joint Appointees

Edward S. Angel, Professor; Ph.D., USC. Computer graphics, scientific visualization.

Jean-Claude M. Diels, Professor; Ph.D., Brussels (Belgium). Laser physics and nonlinear optics, ultrafast phenomena.

Frank L. Gilfeather, Professor; Ph.D., California, Irvine. High-performance computing applications and functional analysis.

Sang M. Han, Associate Professor; Ph.D., California, Santa Barbara. Chemical and nuclear engineering.

Terran D. R. Lane, Assistant Professor; Ph.D., Purdue. Machine learning, including applications to bioinformatics, information security, user and cognitive modeling, and neuroimaging; reinforcement learning, behavior, and control; artificial intelligence in general.

Zayd Chad Leseman, Assistant Professor; Ph.D., Illinois at Urbana-Champaign. MEMS, NEMS, photonic crystals, and carbon nanostructures.

Ronald Lumia, Professor; Ph.D., Virginia. Robotics, automation, image processing.

Stefan Posse, Associate Professor; Ph.D., Düsseldorf (Germany). MR imaging and spectroscopy.

Timothy J. Ross, Professor; Ph.D., Stanford. Structural system reliability, structural dynamics, autonomous control, fuzzy logic, fuzzy set theory, risk assessment.

Wolfgang G. Rudolph, Professor; Ph.D., Jena (Germany). Laser physics, ultrashort light pulses, time-resolved spectroscopy and imaging.

Monsoor Sheik-Bahae, Associate Professor; Ph.D., SUNY at Buffalo. Lasers and photonics, coherent and ultrafast processes in semiconductors, laser cooling of solids, nonlinear optics.

Gregory P. Starr, Professor; Ph.D., Stanford. Robotics and dynamic systems and controls.

Mahmoud Reda Taha, Assistant Professor; Ph.D., Calgary (Canada). Structural health monitoring, application of artificial intelligence in structural engineering and biomechanics.

Research Professors

Ladan Arissian, Research Assistant Professor; Ph.D., New Mexico.
Simon Barriga, Research Assistant Professor; Ph.D., New Mexico.
Carl E. Baum, Distinguished Adjunct Professor and IEEE Fellow; Ph.D., Caltech.
Jerald C. Buchenauer, Research Professor; Ph.D., Cornell.
Joseph Costantine, Post-Doctoral Fellow; Ph.D., New Mexico.
Larry Ralph Dawson, Research Professor; Ph.D., USC.
David Dietz, Research Professor; Ph.D., Indiana.
Peter Dorato, Professor Emeritus; D.E.E., Polytechnic of Brooklyn.
Abdel-Rahman A. El-Emawy, Research Associate Professor; Ph.D., Colorado State.
Ihab El-Kady, Research Associate Professor; Ph.D., Iowa State.
Mikhail Isaakovich Fuks, Research Professor; Ph.D., Gorky State (Russia).
John A. Gaudet, Research Professor; Ph.D., Air Force Tech.
Edward D. Graham, Lecturer and Research Professor; Ph.D., North Carolina State.
Michael John Healy, Research Scholar; M.S., Idaho.
Sameer D. Hemmady, Research Assistant Professor; Ph.D., Maryland, College Park.
Craig Kief, Research Scholar; M.S., New Mexico.
Olga Lavrova, Lecturer and Research Assistant Professor; Ph.D., California, Santa Barbara.
Alan G. Lynn, Research Assistant Professor; Ph.D., Texas at Austin.
Victor Murray Herrera, Research Assistant Professor; Ph.D., New Mexico.
Mikhail N. Naydenkov, Post-Doctoral Fellow; Ph.D., Academy of Sciences (Russia).
Matthew P. Pepin, Post-Doctoral Fellow; Ph.D., Air Force Tech.
Andrew C. Pineda, Senior Research Scientist; Ph.D., Harvard.
Elena A. Plis, Research Assistant Professor; Ph.D., New Mexico.
John Rasure, Research Associate Professor; Ph.D., Kansas State.
Thomas J. Rotter, Research Assistant Professor; Ph.D., New Mexico.
Yagyadeva D. Sharma, Research Assistant Professor; Ph.D., New Delhi (India).
Gennady Smolyakov, Research Assistant Professor; Ph.D., Saratov State (Russia).
Samuel D. Stearns, Research Professor; D.Sc., New Mexico.
Mehmet F. Su, Research Assistant Professor; Ph.D., New Mexico.
Steven C. Suddarth, Research Professor; Ph.D., Washington (Seattle).
Victor M. Vergara, Research Assistant Professor; Ph.D., New Mexico.
Li Wang, Post-Doctoral Fellow; Ph.D., New Mexico.
Christopher Watts, Research Professor; Ph.D., Wisconsin–Madison.
Honggang Yu, Research Assistant Professor; Ph.D., New Mexico.

RESEARCH CENTERS ASSOCIATED WITH THE DEPARTMENT

Center for High Technology Materials (CHTM). Creating a leading optoelectronics and nanotechnology research center is the primary goal of the CHTM, an interdisciplinary organization that sponsors and encourages research efforts in the Departments of Electrical and Computer Engineering, Physics and Astronomy, Chemistry, and Chemical and Nuclear Engineering. CHTM's multilateral mission involves both research and education. It is dedicated to encouraging and strengthening interactions and the flow of technology among the University, government laboratories, and private industry, while promoting economic development in the state.

UNIVERSITY OF NOTRE DAME

College of Engineering
Department of Electrical Engineering

Programs of Study

The Department offers programs leading to the M.S. and Ph.D. degrees in electrical engineering. Research areas include communications systems, control systems, signal and image processing, solid-state nanoelectronics, microwave electronics, optoelectronic materials and devices, and ultrahigh-speed and microwave-integrated circuits. A research M.S. degree requires 30 credit hours beyond the B.S., with at least 6 credit hours coming from thesis research. A research M.S. also requires the completion and defense of an M.S. thesis. A nonresearch M.S. degree requires 30 course credit hours of course work. All students must take a qualifying examination at the end of their second semester of graduate study; successful completion of the exam is required to receive an M.S. degree and to continue to the Ph.D. program. Doctoral students must accumulate a minimum of 36 course credits beyond the B.S. degree, pass the qualifying and candidacy examinations at the Ph.D. level, spend at least two years in resident study, and write and defend a Ph.D. dissertation.

Research Facilities

There are several major research laboratories in the Department to support the study of electronic and photonic materials and devices and the analysis and design of communication systems, control systems, and signal and image processing algorithms.

The Notre Dame Nanofabrication Facility allows fabrication of ICs and devices with geometries as small as 6 nm. The 9,000-square-foot cleanroom is divided into areas of class 100, 1,000 and 10,000 cleanliness areas. The facility contains a broad range of fabrication equipment for processing a variety of materials for circuits and devices. Lithography tools include an i-line stepper; two contact lithography systems; and Elionix 7700 and Vistec EPG500 plus electron-beam lithography systems. Etching systems include a Oerlikon Shuttlelock ICP, Alcatel ICP deep RIE, MemStar XeF2 etcher, and PlasmaTherm 790 RIE, and two plasma etchers. Deposition systems include a FirstNano LPCVD, Unaxis PECVD, atmospheric CVD, six evaporators, and three sputtering systems. Thermal processing capabilities include eight furnace tubes and two rapid thermal processing systems. Inspection systems include ISI and Elionix SEMs, Hitachi FESEM, a prism coupler, an interferometer, an ellipsometer, a variable-angle spectroscopic ellipsometer, two surface profilers, a four-point probe, and two Zeiss optical microscopes. Postprocessing equipment includes a wafer-dicing saw, two wire bonders, and a die bonder. In addition, the clean room houses facilities for molecular-beam epitaxial (MBE) growth of III-V nitride materials and growth of graphene.

The Low-Temperature Nanoelectronics Lab houses equipment such as a ^{3}He cryostat capable of 300 mK and magnetic fields of 8T, a ^{3}He system for RF measurements, and a dilution refrigerator capable of 10mK, with fields up to 8T.

The High-Speed Circuits and Devices Laboratory houses a state-of-the-art microwave and high-speed digital device and circuits characterization facility. Full on-wafer testing capability, including analog characterization to 220 GHz and digital testing to 12.5 Gb/s, allow for comprehensive characterization of both analog and digital high-speed microelectronic circuits. In addition, facilities for high-speed optoelectronic characterization of detectors and photoreceiver subsystems for fiber-optic telecommunications are available. State-of-the-art microwave CAD, data collection, and data analysis facilities are also in place for rapid circuit design and characterization.

The Semiconductor Optics Lab includes a 15-watt Argon-ion laser, a tunable, mode-locked Ti:sapphire laser delivering femtosecond pulses, an He-Cd laser, and He cryostats with high spatial resolution and magnetic fields up to 12 Tesla.

The Laboratory for Image and Signal Analysis (LISA) features state-of-the-art workstations for the development and analysis of digital signal, image, and video processing algorithms in addition to equipment for the acquisition, processing, and real-time display of HDTV sequences; cameras; frame grabbers; several high-definition 24-bit color monitors; and specialized printers.

The Control Systems Research Laboratory contains several workstations networked to a set of dSpace miniboxes (microcontrollers) and a network of personal computers (PCs) running QNX (a real-time version of UNIX).

The Wireless Institute and the associated Wireless At Notre Dame (WAND) Lab have a full complement of RF measurement equipment, wide-band digitizers, and connections to roof antennas as well as a full complement of supporting workstations. WAND also offers an environment for software radio development and testing.

The Network Communications and Information Processing (NCIP) Lab provides a test bed for sensor network technology, network protocol design, and distributed signal processing.

The Department has its own electronics shop run by a full-time technician, and the solid-state laboratories are overseen by a full-time professional specialist and two full-time technicians; similarly, the WAND lab has a full-time engineer available for hardware prototype design and development. Another full-time professional specialist manages the Department's undergraduate laboratories.

Financial Aid

Several prestigious fellowships are available to highly qualified first-time applicants, women, and students from groups that are underrepresented in engineering. Also available are about twenty-five teaching assistantships and several research assistantships that provide stipends of at least $2100 per month. All appointments include full remission of academic-year tuition.

Cost of Study

Tuition in 2010–11 for graduate students is $19,855 per semester for full-time study. Tuition is waived for fellowship and assistantship recipients.

Living and Housing Costs

Two large modern apartment complexes are available on campus for single graduate students. Married student housing and apartments adjacent to the campus in South Bend are also available, renting for $470 to $600 per month. The cost of living is below the national average. More information is available at http://www.nd.edu/~orlh.

Student Group

The Department has 80 undergraduates and 110 graduate students. It awards about nineteen M.S. degrees and fifteen Ph.D. degrees per year.

Location

The University is the cultural center of the northern Indiana–southwestern Michigan area and offers extensive cultural, social, and sports events throughout the year. Its 2,150-acre campus is just north of South Bend, a city of about 130,000 people, and approximately 90 miles east of Chicago (a 2-hour trip by car or train). South Bend's Morris Civic Auditorium hosts performances of Broadway plays and is the home of a first-rate symphony orchestra.

The University and The College

The University was founded in 1842 by the Reverend Edward Frederick Sorin and 6 brothers of the Congregation of Holy Cross. It was chartered as a university in 1844, and engineering studies were begun in 1873. The campus's twin lakes and many wooded areas provide a setting of natural beauty for more than 102 University buildings. The engineering buildings, Cushing and Fitzpatrick Halls, were erected in 1931 and 1979, respectively, and a new building, Stinson-Remick Hall was completed in 2010.

Applying

GRE General Test scores, TOEFL scores for international students, two transcripts showing academic credits and degrees, and letters of recommendation from 3 or 4 college faculty members are required. The application process is carried out online, starting at the Web site http://graduateschool.nd.edu. The GRE should be taken no later than January preceding the academic year of enrollment, particularly if financial aid is desired. The application deadline is February 1 for fall admission and November 1 for spring. The application fee for fall admission is $35 for applications submitted by December 1 and $50 for applications submitted after this date.

Correspondence and Information

Graduate Admissions
Department of Electrical Engineering
University of Notre Dame
Notre Dame, Indiana 46556-5637

Phone: 574-631-8264
E-mail: eegrad@nd.edu
Web site: http://ee.nd.edu

University of Notre Dame

THE FACULTY AND THEIR RESEARCH

Panos J. Antsaklis, H. C. and E. A. Brosey Professor of Electrical Engineering; Ph.D., Brown, 1977. Distributed sensor/actuator networks, network congestion control, networked control systems, system theory, digital signal processing, stability theory, multidimensional systems.

Peter H. Bauer, Professor; Ph.D., Miami (Florida), 1988. Digital filters, multidimensional systems and filtering, robust stability.

Gary H. Bernstein, Frank M. Freimann Professor of Electrical Engineering; Ph.D., Arizona State, 1987. Nanostructure fabrication, electron beam lithography, high-speed circuits.

William B. Berry, Professor Emeritus; Ph.D., Purdue, 1964. Solid-state energy conversion, thermoelectrics, photovoltaics.

Kevin W. Bowyer, Concurrent Professor; Ph.D., Duke, 1980. Computer vision and image processing, pattern recognition, medical image analysis.

Jay B. Brockman, Concurrent Associate Professor; Ph.D., Carnegie Mellon, 1992. Computer architecture, VLSI, processing-in-memory architecture, multidisciplinary design methodologies.

Daniel J. Costello, Leonard Bettex Professor of Electrical Engineering, Emeritus; Ph.D., Notre Dame, 1969. Information theory, channel coding, digital communications, wireless communications.

Patrick J. Fay, Professor; Ph.D., Illinois at Urbana-Champaign, 1996. Microwave device characterization; monolithic microwave integrated circuit (MMIC) and optoelectronic integrated circuit (OEIC) design, fabrication, and characterization; device technologies for ultrahigh-speed digital circuits.

Thomas E. Fuja, Professor and Chair; Ph.D., Cornell, 1987. Digital communications, error control coding, joint source-channel coding, information theory.

Vijay Gupta, Assistant Professor; Ph.D., Caltech, 2007. Cyberphysical systems, sensor-actuator networks, distributed estimation and control, networked and embedded control.

Martin Haenggi, Associate Professor; Ph.D., Swiss Federal Institute of Technology, 1999. Wireless communications and networks, nonlinear dynamics.

Douglas C. Hall, Associate Professor; Ph.D., Illinois at Urbana-Champaign, 1991. Optoelectronics device characterization, fabrication, semi-conductor lasers, materials studies.

Yih-Fang Huang, Professor; Ph.D., Princeton, 1982. Statistical signal processing and communications image source coding, adaptive systems, neural networks.

Debdeep Jena, Assistant Professor; Ph.D., California, Santa Barbara, 2003. Semiconductor growth, physics and device applications, epitaxial nanostructures, charge, heat and spin transport.

Thomas H. Kosel, Associate Professor; Ph.D., Berkeley, 1975. Wear, erosion, electron microscopy, abrasion, tribology, crystal defects.

J. Nicholas Laneman, Associate Professor; Ph.D., MIT, 2002. Multiuser and wireless communications, signal processing, information theory.

Michael D. Lemmon, Professor; Ph.D., Carnegie Mellon, 1990. Real-time embedded control systems, networked control systems, sensor networks, mathematical systems theory.

Craig S. Lent, Frank M. Freimann Professor of Electrical Engineering; Ph.D., Minnesota, 1984. Solid-state physics and devices, quantum transport, quantum cellular automata.

Christine M. Maziar, Professor, Vice President, and Associate Provost of the University; Ph.D., Purdue, 1986. Device modeling and simulation for transport in ultrasmall semiconductor materials and structures.

James L. Merz, Frank M. Freimann Professor of Electrical Engineering, Emeritus; Ph.D., Harvard, 1967. Optical properties of nanostructures; quantum wells, wires and dots; optoelectronic materials.

Anthony N. Michel, Frank M. Freimann Professor of Electrical Engineering, Emeritus; Ph.D., Marquette, 1968; D.Sc., Graz (Austria), 1973. Circuit and system theory, large-scale systems.

Paolo Minero, Assistant Professor; Ph.D., California, San Diego, 2011. Communication networks.

Alexander Mintairov, Research Professor; Ph.D., Ioffe (Russia), 1987. Nanophotonics and nanoplasmonics, near-field optical spectroscopy, solid-state optoelectronic devices and materials, physics of nanostructures.

Alexei Orlov, Research Professor; Ph.D., Russian Academy of Science (Moscow), 1990. Design fabrication and testing on nanoelectronic and cryoelectronic devices.

Wolfgang Porod, Frank M. Freimann Professor of Electrical Engineering; Ph.D., Graz (Austria), 1981. Solid-state devices, computational electronics, nanoelectronics.

Thomas G. Pratt, Research Associate Professor; Ph.D., Georgia Tech, 1999. Communications and signal processing.

Ken D. Sauer, Associate Professor and Associate Chair for Undergraduate Studies; Ph.D., Princeton, 1989. Tomographic imaging, multivariate detection and estimation, image compression.

R. Michael Schafer, Professional Specialist; Ph.D., Notre Dame, 1980 (1996). Data networks, quality of service in data networks, multiprotocol label switching (MPLS).

Alan C. Seabaugh, Professor; Ph.D., Virginia, 1985. High-speed devices and circuits, nanoelectronics, nanofabrication, electromechanical devices, bioagent detection.

Gregory L. Snider, Professor and Associate Chair for Graduate Studies; Ph.D., California, Santa Barbara, 1991. Design and fabrication of nanoelectronic devices.

Robert L. Stevenson, Professor; Ph.D., Purdue, 1990. Statistical and multidimensional signal and image processing, computer vision.

Greg Timp, Keough-Hesburgh Chair in Electrical Engineering and Biological Sciences; Ph.D., MIT, 1984. Nanobiotechnology and cell biology.

Mark Wistey, Assistant Professor; Ph.D., Stanford, 2005. Group IV photonics, III-V devices, molecular beam epitaxy.

Grace Xing, Assistant Professor; Ph.D., California, Santa Barbara, 2003. Semiconductor growth, physics, processing and devices, nanostructures and nanotechnologies.

RESEARCH AREAS

Electronic Circuits and Systems. Approximately half of the faculty members have research interests in this area, which includes communications, systems and control, and signal and image processing. Ongoing projects include work in these areas: communications (sensor networks, graph-based channel coding and iterative decoding, software radio, network analysis via random graphs, capacity-approaching performance on fading channels, cooperative communications, and novel transceiver architectures), systems and control (networked control systems, design and scaling of cyber-physical systems, statistical control, and supervisory control of hybrid systems), and signal and image processing (tomographic image reconstruction, restoration, and enhancement, detection, and estimation and their applications).

Electronic Materials and Devices. The other half of the faculty members have research interests in the area that includes solid-state, nanoelectronic, and optoelectronic materials and devices. Ongoing projects include work in these areas: materials and nanostructures (Si/Ge, III-V, and II-VI semiconductors, including nitride-based semiconductors; complex oxides; molecular beam epitaxy; nanomagnetics; nanowires and tubes; quantum dots; molecular and magnetic quantum-dot cellular automata; and grapheme), nanoelectronics and energy-efficient electronics (quantum devices, quantum-dot cellular automata, silicon-based single-electron devices, and integrated CMOS and nanoelectronics), photonics and optoelectronics (semiconductor lasers; photonic integration; photodetectors, ranging from the IR to the UV; Er-doped waveguide amplifiers; and high-speed optoelectronics), nanobioelectronics (nanofabrication and sensor technologies, cell-semiconductor communication, and fluidics), advanced electronics (high-performance compound-semiconductor electronic devices, microwave/millimeter-wave integrated circuit (MMIC) design and fabrication, millimeter-wave detectors and imaging, wafer bonding, and advanced packaging and interconnects), and energy harvesting (thermal and photovoltaic energy converters, acoustic and rf energy extraction technology, and autonomous micro/nanosystems).

Section 10
Energy and Power Engineering

This section contains a directory of institutions offering graduate work in energy and power engineering, followed by an in-depth entry submitted by an institution that chose to prepare a detailed program description. Additional information about programs listed in the directory but not augmented by an in-depth entry may be obtained by writing directly to the dean of a graduate school or chair of a department at the address given in the directory.

For programs offering related work, see also in this book *Computer Science and Information Technology, Engineering and Applied Sciences, Industrial Engineering,* and *Mechanical Engineering and Mechanics.* In another guide in this series:
Graduate Programs in the Physical Sciences, Mathematics, Agricultural Sciences, the Environment & Natural Resources
See *Physics* and *Mathematical Sciences*

CONTENTS

Energy and Power Engineering

Kettering University, Graduate School, Mechanical Engineering Department, Flint, MI 48504. Offers automotive systems (MS Eng); computer aided engineering simulation (MS Eng); mechanical cognate (MS Eng); mechanical design (MS Eng); sustainable energy and hybrid technology (MS Eng). Part-time and evening/weekend programs available. Postbaccalaureate distance learning degree programs offered (no on-campus study). *Faculty:* 14 full-time (1 woman). *Students:* 8 full-time (0 women), 35 part-time (7 women); includes 2 minority (1 Asian American or Pacific Islander, 1 Hispanic American), 8 international. Average age 26. 6 applicants, 67% accepted, 2 enrolled. In 2009, 20 master's awarded. *Degree requirements:* For master's, thesis optional. *Entrance requirements:* Additional exam requirements/recommendations for international students: Required—TOEFL (minimum score 550 paper-based; 213 computer-based; 79 iBT). *Application deadline:* For fall admission, 9/15 for domestic students, 6/15 for international students; for winter admission, 12/15 for domestic students, 9/15 for international students; for spring admission, 3/15 for domestic students, 12/15 for international students. Applications are processed on a rolling basis. Application fee: $0. Electronic applications accepted. *Expenses:* Tuition: Full-time $11,120; part-time $695 per credit hour. *Financial support:* In 2009–10, 24 students received support, including fellowships with full tuition reimbursements available (averaging $13,000 per year), research assistantships with full tuition reimbursements available (averaging $13,000 per year), teaching assistantships with full tuition reimbursements available (averaging $13,000 per year); Federal Work-Study, scholarships/grants, and tuition waivers (partial) also available. Support available to part-time students. Financial award application deadline: 7/15; financial award applicants required to submit CSS PROFILE or FAFSA. *Faculty research:* Fuel cells, chemical agents, crash safety, bio-gas, sustainable energy. Total annual research expenditures: $3.9 million. *Unit head:* Dr. K. Joel Berry, Head, 810-762-7833, Fax: 810-762-7860, E-mail: jberry@kettering.edu. *Application contact:* Bonnie Switzer, Graduate Admissions Officer, 810-762-7953, Fax: 810-762-9935, E-mail: bswitzer@kettering.edu.

Lehigh University, P.C. Rossin College of Engineering and Applied Science, Program in Energy Systems Engineering, Bethlehem, PA 18015. Offers M Eng. *Faculty:* 1 part-time/adjunct (0 women). *Students:* 25 full-time (6 women); includes 1 minority (Asian American or Pacific Islander), 4 international. Average age 23. 154 applicants, 23% accepted, 25 enrolled. *Entrance requirements:* For master's, GRE. Additional exam requirements/recommendations for international students: Required—TOEFL (minimum score 79 iBT). *Application deadline:* For fall admission, 5/15 for domestic students. Applications are processed on a rolling basis. Application fee: $75. Electronic applications accepted. *Financial support:* Scholarships/grants available. *Unit head:* Dr. Andrew Coleman, Director, 610-758-6311, E-mail: andrew.coleman@lehigh.edu. *Application contact:* Shaku Jain-Cocks, Graduate Coordinator, 610-758-6311, Fax: 610-758-5623, E-mail: shj208@lehigh.edu.

Marylhurst University, Department of Business Administration, Marylhurst, OR 97036-0261. Offers finance (MBA); general management (MBA); government policy and administration (MBA); green development (MBA); health care management (MBA); marketing (MBA); natural and organic resources (MBA); nonprofit management (MBA); organizational behavior (MBA); real estate (MBA); renewable energy (MBA); sustainable business (MBA). Part-time and evening/weekend programs available. Postbaccalaureate distance learning degree programs offered (no on-campus study). *Faculty:* 2 full-time (1 woman), 28 part-time/adjunct (5 women). *Students:* 30 full-time (12 women), 627 part-time (323 women); includes 79 minority (28 African Americans, 3 American Indian/Alaska Native, 17 Asian Americans or Pacific Islanders, 31 Hispanic Americans), 9 international. Average age 37. 299 applicants, 80% accepted, 209 enrolled. In 2009, 193 master's awarded. *Degree requirements:* For master's, comprehensive exam, capstone course. *Entrance requirements:* For master's, GMAT (if GPA less than 3.0 and fewer than 5 years of work experience), interview, resume, 2 letters of recommendation. Additional exam requirements/recommendations for international students: Recommended—TOEFL (minimum score 550 paper-based; 213 computer-based; 80 iBT). *Application deadline:* For fall admission, 9/11 priority date for domestic and international students; for winter admission, 12/15 priority date for domestic and international students; for spring admission, 3/17 priority date for domestic and international students. Applications are processed on a rolling basis. Application fee: $40 ($50 for international students). Electronic applications accepted. *Financial support:* Scholarships/grants available. Support available to part-time students. Financial award applicants required to submit FAFSA. *Unit head:* Bob Hanks, Director of Business and Real Estate Programs, 503-636-8141, Fax: 503-697-5597, E-mail: mba@marylhurst.edu. *Application contact:* Kathleen Schneff, Admissions Specialist, 800-634-9982 Ext. 3322, Fax: 503-635-6585, E-mail: admissions@marylhurst.edu.

New Jersey Institute of Technology, Office of Graduate Studies, Newark College of Engineering, Department of Electrical and Computer Engineering, Program in Power and Energy Systems, Newark, NJ 07102. Offers MS. Part-time and evening/weekend programs available. Postbaccalaureate distance learning degree programs offered. *Degree requirements:* For master's, thesis optional. *Entrance requirements:* For master's, GRE General Test. Additional exam requirements/recommendations for international students: Required—TOEFL (minimum score 550 paper-based; 213 computer-based; 79 iBT). Electronic applications accepted.

New York Institute of Technology, Graduate Division, School of Engineering and Computing Sciences, Program in Energy Management, Old Westbury, NY 11568-8000. Offers energy management (MS); energy technology (Advanced Certificate); environmental management (Advanced Certificate); facilities management (Advanced Certificate). Part-time and evening/weekend programs available. Postbaccalaureate distance learning degree programs offered. *Students:* 53 full-time (8 women), 105 part-time (14 women); includes 38 minority (13 African Americans, 1 American Indian/Alaska Native, 9 Asian Americans or Pacific Islanders, 15 Hispanic Americans), 33 international. Average age 33. In 2009, 25 master's, 15 other advanced degrees awarded. *Degree requirements:* For master's, comprehensive exam, thesis or alternative. *Entrance requirements:* For master's, minimum QPA of 2.85. Additional exam requirements/recommendations for international students: Required—TOEFL (minimum score 550 paper-based; 213 computer-based). *Application deadline:* For fall admission, 7/1 priority date for domestic students; for spring admission, 12/1 priority date for domestic students. Applications are processed on a rolling basis. Application fee: $50. Electronic applications accepted. *Expenses:* Tuition: Part-time $825 per credit. *Financial support:* Fellowships, research assistantships with partial tuition reimbursements, institutionally sponsored loans, tuition waivers (full and partial), and unspecified assistantships available. Support available to part-time students. Financial award applicants required to submit FAFSA. *Unit head:* Dr. Frank Zeman, Director, 212-261-1656, Fax: 212-261-1748, E-mail: fzeman@nyit.edu. *Application contact:* Dr. Jacquelyn Nealon, Vice President for Enrollment Services, 516-686-7925, Fax: 516-686-7597, E-mail: jnealon@nyit.edu.

North Carolina Agricultural and Technical State University, Graduate School, College of Engineering, Department of Electrical and Computer Engineering, Greensboro, NC 27411. Offers electrical engineering (MSEE, PhD), including communications and signal processing (MSEE), computer engineering (MSEE), electronic and optical materials and devices (MSEE), power systems and controls (MSEE). Part-time programs available. *Degree requirements:* For master's, project, thesis defense; for doctorate, thesis/dissertation. *Entrance requirements:* For master's, GRE General Test, GRE Subject Test, minimum GPA of 2.8; for doctorate, GRE General Test, minimum GPA of 3.0. *Faculty research:* Semiconductor compounds, VLSI design, image processing, optical systems and devices, fault-tolerant computing.

Northeastern University, College of Engineering, Program in Energy Systems, Boston, MA 02115-5096. Offers MS. Part-time programs available. *Students:* 10 full-time (3 women), 1 part-time (0 women); includes 3 minority (2 African Americans, 1 Asian American or Pacific Islander), 1 international. Average age 25. 12 applicants, 92% accepted, 11 enrolled. *Entrance requirements:* For master's, GRE General Test. Additional exam requirements/recommendations for international students: Required—TOEFL (minimum score 550 paper-based; 213 computer-based). *Application deadline:* For fall admission, 1/15 for domestic and international students. Applications are processed on a rolling basis. Application fee: $50. Electronic applications accepted. *Financial support:* Career-related internships or fieldwork, Federal Work-Study, scholarships/grants, tuition waivers (full), and unspecified assistantships available. Support available to part-time students. Financial award application deadline: 1/15; financial award applicants required to submit FAFSA. *Unit head:* Dr. Yaman Yener, Associate Dean of Engineering for Research and Graduate Studies, 617-373-2711, Fax: 617-373-2501. *Application contact:* Stephen L. Gibson, Associate Director, 617-373-2711, Fax: 617-373-2501, E-mail: grad-eng@coe.neu.edu.

Pontificia Universidad Catolica Madre y Maestra, Graduate School, Santiago, Dominican Republic. Offers administration (M Adm); architecture of interiors (M Arch); architecture of tourist lodgings (M Arch); banking and financial management (M Mgmt); civil law (LL M); construction administration (ME); corporate business law (LL M); criminal procedure law (LL M); environmental engineering (ME, MEE); finance (M Mgmt); history applied to education (M Ed); human resources (EMBA); insurance (M Mgmt); international business (M Mgmt); labor law and Social Security (LL M); logistics management (ME); marketing (M Mgmt); renewable energy (ME); strategic cost management (M Mgmt). *Entrance requirements:* For master's, curriculum vitae, interview.

Rensselaer Polytechnic Institute, Graduate School, School of Engineering, Department of Electrical, Computer, and Systems Engineering, Troy, NY 12180-3590. Offers computer and systems engineering (M Eng, MS, PhD); electrical engineering (M Eng, MS, PhD). Part-time programs available. *Faculty:* 37 full-time (5 women), 3 part-time/adjunct (0 women). *Students:* 126 full-time (22 women), 6 part-time (2 women); includes 5 Asian Americans or Pacific Islanders, 5 Hispanic Americans, 79 international. 652 applicants, 19% accepted, 38 enrolled. In 2009, 40 master's, 20 doctorates awarded. Terminal master's awarded for partial completion of doctoral program. *Degree requirements:* For master's, thesis (for some programs); for doctorate, thesis/dissertation, qualifying exam, candidacy exam. *Entrance requirements:* For master's and doctorate, GRE. Additional exam requirements/recommendations for international students: Required—TOEFL (minimum score 570 paper-based; 89 iBT). *Application deadline:* For fall admission, 1/15 priority date for domestic and international students; for spring admission, 8/15 priority date for domestic and international students. Applications are processed on a rolling basis. Application fee: $75. Electronic applications accepted. *Expenses:* Tuition: Full-time $38,100. *Financial support:* In 2009–10, 7 fellowships with full tuition reimbursements (averaging $21,000 per year), 88 research assistantships with full tuition reimbursements (averaging $20,000 per year), 41 teaching assistantships with full tuition reimbursements (averaging $16,500 per year) were awarded; career-related internships or fieldwork, institutionally sponsored loans, and unspecified assistantships also available. Financial award application deadline: 1/15. *Faculty research:* Networking, microelectronics, controls, robotics, power, ULSE and computer architecture, computer vision and image processing. Total annual research expenditures: $3.7 million. *Unit head:* Dr. Kim L. Boyer, Head, 518-276-2150, Fax: 518-276-6261, E-mail: kim@ecse.rpi.edu. *Application contact:* Ann Bruno, Manager of Student Services and Graduate Enrollment, 518-276-2554, Fax: 518-276-4403, E-mail: ann@ecse.rpi.edu.

Southern Illinois University Carbondale, Graduate School, College of Engineering, Program in Engineering Science, Carbondale, IL 62901-4701. Offers electrical systems (PhD); fossil energy (PhD); mechanics (PhD). *Degree requirements:* For doctorate, thesis/dissertation. *Entrance requirements:* For doctorate, GRE General Test, minimum GPA of 3.5. Additional exam requirements/recommendations for international students: Required—TOEFL.

Universidad Autonoma de Guadalajara, Graduate Programs, Guadalajara, Mexico. Offers administrative law and justice (LL M); advertising and corporate communications (MA); architecture (M Arch); business (MBA); computational science (MCC); education (Ed M, Ed D); English-Spanish translation (MA); fiscal law (MA); integrated management of digital animation (MA); international business (MIB); international corporate law (LL M); internet technologies (MS); labor health (MS); manufacturing systems (MMS); philosophy (MA, PhD); power electronics (MS); quality systems (MQS); renewable energy (MS); social evaluation of projects (MBA); strategic market research (MBA); teaching mathematics (MA).

University of Alberta, Faculty of Graduate Studies and Research, Department of Electrical and Computer Engineering, Edmonton, AB T6G 2E1, Canada. Offers communications (M Eng, M Sc, PhD); computer engineering (M Eng, M Sc, PhD); electromagnetics (M Eng, M Sc, PhD); nanotechnology and microdevices (M Eng, M Sc, PhD); power/power electronics (M Eng, M Sc, PhD); systems (M Eng, M Sc, PhD). *Faculty:* 42 full-time (3 women), 12 part-time/adjunct (0 women). *Students:* 252 full-time (28 women), 65 part-time (10 women). Average age 26. 1,500 applicants, 5% accepted. Terminal master's awarded for partial completion of doctoral program. *Degree requirements:* For master's, thesis; for doctorate, thesis/dissertation. *Entrance requirements:* Additional exam requirements/recommendations for international students: Required—TOEFL. *Application deadline:* For fall admission, 4/30 for domestic students; for winter admission, 8/30 for domestic students. Applications are processed on a rolling basis. Application fee: $0 Canadian dollars. Electronic applications accepted. Tuition and fees charges are reported in Canadian dollars. *Expenses:* Tuition, area resident: Full-time $4626.24 Canadian dollars; part-time $99.72 Canadian dollars per unit. International tuition: $8216 Canadian dollars full-time. Required fees: $3589.92 Canadian dollars; $99.72 Canadian dollars per unit. $215 Canadian dollars per term. *Financial support:* In 2009–10, 80 students received support; fellowships, research assistantships, teaching assistantships, scholarships/grants available. *Faculty research:* Controls, communications, microelectronics, electromagnetics. Total annual research expenditures: $3 million Canadian dollars. *Unit head:* Dr. H. J. Marquez, Chair, 780-492-0161, Fax: 780-492-1811. *Application contact:* Michelle Vaage, Graduate Student Advisor, 780-492-0161, Fax: 780-492-1811, E-mail: gradinfo@ece.ualberta.ca.

University of Massachusetts Lowell, James B. Francis College of Engineering, Program in Energy Engineering, Lowell, MA 01854-2881. Offers MS Eng, D Eng, PhD. *Degree requirements:* For master's, thesis optional. *Entrance requirements:* For master's, GRE General Test. Additional exam requirements/recommendations for international students: Required—TOEFL.

University of Memphis, Graduate School, Herff College of Engineering, Department of Mechanical Engineering, Memphis, TN 38152. Offers design and mechanical engineering (MS); energy systems (MS); industrial engineering (MS); mechanical engineering (PhD); mechanical systems (MS); power systems (MS). Part-time programs available. *Faculty:* 8 full-time (0 women). *Students:* 3 full-time (1 woman), 8 part-time (0 women); includes 2 minority (both African Americans), 5 international. Average age 30. 11 applicants, 64% accepted, 3 enrolled. In 2009, 5 master's awarded. Terminal master's awarded for partial completion of doctoral program. *Degree requirements:* For master's, comprehensive exam, thesis; for doctorate, comprehensive exam, thesis/dissertation. *Entrance requirements:* For master's, GRE General Test, BS in mechanical engineering, minimum undergraduate GPA of 3.0. *Application deadline:* For fall admission, 8/1 for domestic students; for spring admission, 12/1 for domestic students. Application fee: $35 ($60 for international students). *Expenses:* Tuition, state resident: full-time $6246; part-time $347 per credit hour. Tuition, nonresident: full-time $15,894; part-time $883 per credit hour. Required fees: $1160. Full-time tuition and fees vary according to course load, degree level and program. *Financial support:* In 2009–10, 6 students received support; fellowships with full tuition reimbursements available, research assistantships with full tuition reimbursements available, teaching assistantships with full tuition reimbursements available, career-related internships or fieldwork, Federal Work-Study, scholarships/grants, and unspecified assistantships available. Financial award application deadline: 2/15; financial award applicants required to submit FAFSA. *Faculty research:* Computational fluid dynamics, computational mechanics, integrated design, nondestructive testing, operations research. *Unit head:* Dr. John I. Hochstein, Chair, 901-678-2173, Fax: 901-678-5459, E-mail:

jhochste@memphis.edu. *Application contact:* Dr. Teong Tan, Graduate Studies Coordinator, 901-678-3264, Fax: 901-678-5459, E-mail: ttan@memphis.edu.

The University of Tennessee at Chattanooga, Graduate School, College of Engineering and Computer Science, Program in Engineering Management, Chattanooga, TN 37403. Offers engineering management (MS); fundamentals of engineering management (Graduate Certificate); power systems management (Graduate Certificate); project and value management (Graduate Certificate); quality management (Graduate Certificate). Postbaccalaureate distance learning degree programs offered (no on-campus study). *Faculty:* 4 full-time (1 woman). *Students:* 22 full-time (7 women), 69 part-time (11 women); includes 25 minority (12 African Americans, 9 Asian Americans or Pacific Islanders, 4 Hispanic Americans), 12 international. Average age 33. 46 applicants, 67% accepted, 24 enrolled. In 2009, 25 master's, 8 other advanced degrees awarded. *Degree requirements:* For master's, thesis. *Entrance requirements:* For master's, GRE General Test, letters of recommendation; minimum undergraduate GPA of 2.5 overall or 3.0 in senior year. Additional exam requirements/recommendations for international students: Required—TOEFL (minimum score 550 paper-based; 213 computer-based; 79 iBT), IELTS (minimum score 6). *Application deadline:* For fall admission, 8/1 priority date for domestic students, 6/1 for international students; for spring admission, 12/1 priority date for domestic students, 10/1 for international students. Applications are processed on a rolling basis. Application fee: $35. Electronic applications accepted. *Expenses:* Tuition, state resident: full-time $5404; part-time $300 per credit hour. Tuition, nonresident: full-time $16,702; part-time $928 per credit hour. Required fees: $1150; $130 per credit hour. *Financial support:* In 2009–10, 5 research assistantships with full and partial tuition reimbursements (averaging $5,500 per year) were awarded; career-related internships or fieldwork, scholarships/grants, and unspecified assistantships also available. Support available to part-time students. *Faculty research:* Plant layout design, lean manufacturing, six sigma, value management, product development. *Unit head:* Dr. Neslihan Alp, Director, 423-425-4032, Fax: 423-425-5229, E-mail: neslihan-alp@utc.edu. *Application contact:* Dr. Stephanie Bellar, Dean of Graduate Studies, 423-425-4666, Fax: 423-425-5223, E-mail: stephanie-bellar@utc.edu.

University of Wisconsin–Madison, Graduate School, College of Engineering, Department of Mechanical Engineering, Madison, WI 53706-1380. Offers energy systems (ME); engine systems (ME); mechanical engineering (MS, PhD); polymers (ME). Part-time programs available. Postbaccalaureate distance learning degree programs offered (no on-campus study). *Faculty:* 33 full-time (3 women), 1 part-time/adjunct (0 women). *Students:* 178 full-time (20 women), 27 part-time (2 women); includes 19 minority (3 African Americans, 9 Asian Americans or Pacific Islanders, 7 Hispanic Americans). Average age 25. 613 applicants, 29% accepted, 72 enrolled. In 2009, 36 master's, 22 doctorates awarded. Terminal master's awarded for partial completion of doctoral program. *Degree requirements:* For master's, thesis optional; for doctorate, thesis/dissertation, qualifying exam, preliminary exam. *Entrance requirements:* For master's, GRE, BS in mechanical engineering or related field, minimum GPA of 3.0 in last 60 hours of course work; for doctorate, GRE, BS in mechanical engineering or related field, minimum undergraduate GPA of 3.0 in last 60 hours of course work. Additional exam requirements/recommendations for international students: Required—TOEFL (minimum score 550 paper-based; 213 computer-based; 80 iBT). *Application deadline:* For fall admission, 5/1 for domestic students, 6/1 for international students; for spring admission, 11/30 for domestic students, 10/1 for international students. Applications are processed on a rolling basis. Application fee: $56. Electronic applications accepted. *Expenses:* Tuition, state resident: part-time $594 per credit. Tuition, nonresident: part-time $1504 per credit. Required fees: $65 per credit. Tuition and fees vary according to course load, program and reciprocity agreements. *Financial support:* In 2009–10, 12 fellowships with full tuition reimbursements (averaging $22,224 per year), 138 research assistantships with full tuition reimbursements (averaging $19,596 per year), 36 teaching assistantships with full tuition reimbursements (averaging $8,595 per year) were awarded; career-related internships or fieldwork, institutionally sponsored loans, scholarships/grants, traineeships, health care benefits, and unspecified assistantships also available. *Faculty research:* Design and manufacturing, materials processing, combustion, energy systems nanotechnology. Total annual research expenditures: $10 million. *Unit head:* Roxann L. Engelstad, Chair, 608-262-5745, Fax: 608-265-2316, E-mail: engelsta@engr.wisc.edu. *Application contact:* Roxann L. Engelstad, Chair, 608-262-5745, Fax: 608-265-2316, E-mail: engelsta@engr.wisc.edu.

Worcester Polytechnic Institute, Graduate Studies and Research, Programs in Interdisciplinary Studies, Worcester, MA 01609-2280. Offers bioscience administration (MS); impact engineering (MS); manufacturing engineering management (MS); power systems management (MS); social science (PhD); systems modeling (MS). Part-time and evening/weekend programs available. *Faculty:* 1 part-time/adjunct (0 women). *Students:* 3 full-time (1 woman), 126 part-time (24 women). 184 applicants, 68% accepted, 100 enrolled. In 2009, 19 master's awarded. *Degree requirements:* For master's, thesis; for doctorate, comprehensive exam, thesis/dissertation. *Entrance requirements:* For master's and doctorate, 3 letters of recommendation. Additional exam requirements/recommendations for international students: Required—TOEFL (minimum score 550 paper-based; 213 computer-based; 79 iBT), IELTS (minimum score 6.5). *Application deadline:* For fall admission, 1/15 priority date for domestic students; for spring admission, 10/15 priority date for domestic students. Application fee: $70. *Financial support:* Institutionally sponsored loans, scholarships/grants, and unspecified assistantships available. Financial award application deadline: 1/15. *Unit head:* Dr. Fred J. Looft, Head, 508-831-5231, Fax: 508-831-5491, E-mail: fjlooft@wpi.edu. *Application contact:* Lynne Dougherty, Administrative Assistant, 508-831-5301, Fax: 508-831-5717, E-mail: grad@wpi.edu.

Nuclear Engineering

Air Force Institute of Technology, Graduate School of Engineering and Management, Department of Engineering Physics, Dayton, OH 45433-7765. Offers applied physics (MS, PhD); electro-optics (MS, PhD); materials science (PhD); nuclear engineering (MS, PhD); space physics (MS). Part-time programs available. *Degree requirements:* For master's, thesis; for doctorate, thesis/dissertation. *Entrance requirements:* For master's and doctorate, GRE General Test, minimum GPA of 3.0, U.S. citizenship. *Faculty research:* High-energy lasers, space physics, nuclear weapon effects, semiconductor physics.

Colorado School of Mines, Graduate School, Program in Nuclear Engineering, Golden, CO 80401. Offers MS, PhD. Part-time programs available. *Students:* 12 full-time (1 woman); includes 1 minority (Hispanic American). Average age 31. 11 applicants, 82% accepted, 4 enrolled. In 2009, 1 master's awarded. *Degree requirements:* For master's, thesis (for some programs); for doctorate, comprehensive exam, thesis/dissertation. *Entrance requirements:* For master's and doctorate, GRE General Test. Additional exam requirements/recommendations for international students: Required—TOEFL (minimum score 550 paper-based; 213 computer-based; 80 iBT). *Application deadline:* For fall admission, 1/15 priority date for domestic and international students; for spring admission, 9/1 priority date for domestic and international students. Electronic applications accepted. *Expenses:* Tuition, state resident: full-time $10,584; part-time $588 per credit hour. Tuition, nonresident: full-time $24,750; part-time $1375 per credit hour. Required fees: $1654; $827.10 per semester. *Financial support:* In 2009–10, 8 students received support, including 1 fellowship with full tuition reimbursement available (averaging $20,000 per year), 4 research assistantships with full tuition reimbursements available (averaging $20,000 per year), 3 teaching assistantships with full tuition reimbursements available (averaging $20,000 per year); career-related internships or fieldwork, Federal Work-Study, institutionally sponsored loans, scholarships/grants, health care benefits, and unspecified assistantships also available. Financial award application deadline: 1/15. *Faculty research:* Nuclear materials and nuclear fuel cycle. *Unit head:* Dr. Uwe Greife, Interim Academic Program Director, 303-273-3618, Fax: 303-279-3919, E-mail: ugreife@mines.edu. *Application contact:* Dr. Uwe Greife, Interim Academic Program Director, 303-273-3618, Fax: 303-273-3919, E-mail: ugreife@mines.edu.

École Polytechnique de Montréal, Graduate Programs, Institute of Nuclear Engineering, Montréal, QC H3C 3A7, Canada. Offers nuclear engineering (M Eng, PhD, DESS); nuclear engineering, socio-economics of energy (M Sc A). *Degree requirements:* For master's, one foreign language, thesis; for doctorate, one foreign language, thesis/dissertation. *Entrance requirements:* For master's, minimum GPA of 2.75; for doctorate, minimum GPA of 3.0. *Faculty research:* Nuclear technology, thermohydraulics.

Georgia Institute of Technology, Graduate Studies and Research, College of Engineering, George W. Woodruff School of Mechanical Engineering, Nuclear and Radiological Engineering and Medical Physics Programs, Atlanta, GA 30332-0001. Offers medical physics (MS); nuclear and radiological engineering (MSNE, PhD). Part-time programs available. Postbaccalaureate distance learning degree programs offered (no on-campus study). Terminal master's awarded for partial completion of doctoral program. *Degree requirements:* For master's, thesis optional; for doctorate, comprehensive exam, thesis/dissertation. *Entrance requirements:* For master's and doctorate, GRE General Test, minimum GPA of 3.0. Additional exam requirements/recommendations for international students: Required—TOEFL (minimum score 580 paper-based; 240 computer-based). *Faculty research:* Reactor physics, nuclear materials, plasma physics, radiation detection, radiological assessment.

Idaho State University, Office of Graduate Studies, College of Engineering, Nuclear Engineering Department, Pocatello, ID 83209. Offers engineering and applied science (PhD); nuclear science and engineering (MS, PhD, Postbaccalaureate Certificate). Part-time programs available. *Faculty:* 1 full-time (0 women). *Students:* 25 full-time (6 women), 19 part-time (2 women); includes 2 minority (both Asian Americans or Pacific Islanders), 9 international. Average age 35. In 2009, 5 master's, 3 doctorates, 1 other advanced degree awarded. *Degree requirements:* For master's, comprehensive exam (for some programs), thesis, seminar; for doctorate, comprehensive exam, thesis/dissertation, oral and written exams at the end of 1st year; for Postbaccalaureate Certificate, comprehensive exam (for some programs), thesis optional, seminar. *Entrance requirements:* For master's, GRE; for doctorate, master's degree in engineering, physics, geosciences, math, etc.; 3 letters of recommendation; for Postbaccalaureate Certificate, GRE if GPA is between 2.0 and 3.0, bachelor's degree, minimum GPA of 3.0 in upper division courses. Additional exam requirements/recommendations for international students: Required—TOEFL (minimum score 550 paper-based; 213 computer-based; 80 iBT). *Application deadline:* For fall admission, 7/1 for domestic students, 6/1 for international students; for spring admission, 12/1 for domestic students, 11/1 for international students. Applications are processed on a rolling basis. Application fee: $55. Electronic applications accepted. *Expenses:* Tuition, state resident: full-time $3318; part-time $297 per credit hour. Tuition, nonresident: full-time $13,120; part-time $437 per credit hour. Required fees: $2530. Tuition and fees vary according to program. *Financial support:* In 2009–10, 11 research assistantships with full and partial tuition reimbursements (averaging $6,800 per year), teaching assistantships with full and partial tuition reimbursements (averaging $9,401 per year) were awarded; career-related internships or fieldwork, Federal Work-Study, institutionally sponsored loans, scholarships/grants, traineeships, health care benefits, tuition waivers (full and partial), and unspecified assistantships also available. Support available to part-time students. Financial award application deadline: 1/1; financial award applicants required to submit FAFSA. *Unit head:* Dr. George Imel, Chair, 208-282-3732, Fax: 208-282-4538, E-mail: gimel@isu.edu. *Application contact:* Ellen Combs, Graduate School Technical Records Specialist, 208-282-2150, Fax: 208-282-4847, E-mail: combelle@isu.edu.

Kansas State University, Graduate School, College of Engineering, Department of Mechanical and Nuclear Engineering, Manhattan, KS 66506. Offers mechanical engineering (MS, PhD); nuclear engineering (MS, PhD). *Faculty:* 21 full-time (1 woman), 3 part-time/adjunct (0 women). *Students:* 35 full-time (11 women), 51 part-time (4 women); includes 5 minority (1 African American, 1 American Indian/Alaska Native, 2 Asian Americans or Pacific Islanders, 1 Hispanic American), 32 international. Average age 28. 68 applicants, 38% accepted, 22 enrolled. In 2009, 11 master's, 2 doctorates awarded. *Degree requirements:* For master's, thesis or alternative; for doctorate, comprehensive exam, thesis/dissertation. *Entrance requirements:* For master's, GRE General Test, minimum GPA of 3.0 in physics, mathematics, and chemistry; for doctorate, GRE General Test, master's degree in mechanical engineering. Additional exam requirements/recommendations for international students: Required—TOEFL. *Application deadline:* For fall admission, 2/1 priority date for domestic and international students; for spring admission, 7/1 priority date for domestic students, 8/1 priority date for international students. Applications are processed on a rolling basis. Application fee: $40 ($55 for international students). Electronic applications accepted. *Financial support:* In 2009–10, 44 research assistantships (averaging $15,984 per year), 4 teaching assistantships with full and partial tuition reimbursements (averaging $14,916 per year) were awarded; career-related internships or fieldwork, Federal Work-Study, institutionally sponsored loans, and scholarships/grants also available. Support available to part-time students. Financial award application deadline: 3/1; financial award applicants required to submit FAFSA. *Faculty research:* Radiation detection and protection, heat and mass transfer, machine design, control systems, nuclear reactor physics and engineering. Total annual research expenditures: $2.3 million. *Unit head:* Donald Fenton, Head, 785-532-2321, Fax: 785-532-7057, E-mail: fenton@ksu.edu. *Application contact:* Steve Eckels, Director, 785-532-2283, Fax: 785-532-7057, E-mail: grad@mne.ksu.edu.

Massachusetts Institute of Technology, School of Engineering, Department of Nuclear Science and Engineering, Cambridge, MA 02139-4307. Offers SM, PhD, Sc D, NE. *Faculty:* 15 full-time (4 women). *Students:* 108 full-time (15 women); includes 10 minority (2 African Americans, 1 American Indian/Alaska Native, 5 Asian Americans or Pacific Islanders, 2 Hispanic Americans), 41 international. Average age 26. 148 applicants, 32% accepted, 30 enrolled. In 2009, 24 master's, 15 doctorates awarded. Terminal master's awarded for partial completion of doctoral program. *Degree requirements:* For master's and NE, thesis; for doctorate, comprehensive exam, thesis/dissertation. *Entrance requirements:* For master's, doctorate, and NE, GRE General Test. Additional exam requirements/recommendations for international students: Required—TOEFL (minimum score 577 paper-based; 233 computer-based; 90 iBT) or IELTS (minimum score 7). *Application deadline:* For fall admission, 1/7 for domestic and international students; for spring admission, 10/15 for domestic and international students. Application fee: $75. Electronic applications accepted. *Financial support:* In 2009–10, 103 students received support, including 33 fellowships with tuition reimbursements available (averaging $29,198 per year), 61 research assistantships with tuition reimbursements available (averaging $28,474 per year), 4 teaching assistantships with tuition reimbursements available (averaging $29,020 per year); career-related internships or fieldwork, Federal Work-Study, institutionally sponsored loans, scholarships/grants, health care benefits, and unspecified assistantships also available. *Faculty research:* Nuclear systems management and policy, fission reactor systems design, risk assessment and management engineering, plasma physics and fusion engineering, radiation science, nuclear imaging and quantum information. Total annual research expenditures: $12.8 million. *Unit head:* Prof. Richard Lester, Department

Nuclear Engineering

Massachusetts Institute of Technology (continued)
Head, 617-253-5456, E-mail: nse-info@mit.edu. *Application contact:* Academic Programs Administrator, 617-253-3814, Fax: 617-258-7437, E-mail: applynse@mit.edu.

McMaster University, School of Graduate Studies, Faculty of Engineering, Department of Engineering Physics, Hamilton, ON L8S 4M2, Canada. Offers engineering physics (M Eng, MA Sc, PhD); nuclear engineering (PhD). *Degree requirements:* For master's, thesis or alternative; for doctorate, comprehensive exam, thesis/dissertation. *Entrance requirements:* For master's, minimum B average in engineering, mathematics, or physical sciences. Additional exam requirements/recommendations for international students: Required—TOEFL (minimum score 550 paper-based; 213 computer-based). *Faculty research:* Non-thermal plasmas for pollution control and electrostatic precipitation, bulk and thin film luminescent materials, devices and systems for optical fiber communications, physics and applications of III-V materials and devices, defect spectroscopy in semiconductors.

Missouri University of Science and Technology, Graduate School, Department of Mining and Nuclear Engineering, Rolla, MO 65409. Offers mining engineering (MS, DE, PhD); nuclear engineering (MS, DE, PhD). *Degree requirements:* For master's, thesis optional; for doctorate, comprehensive exam. *Entrance requirements:* For master's, GRE (minimum score 600 quantitative, 3 writing); for doctorate, GRE (minimum score: quantitative 600, writing 3.5). Additional exam requirements/recommendations for international students: Required—TOEFL (minimum score 550 paper-based; 213 computer-based). *Faculty research:* Mine health and safety, nuclear radiation transport, modeling of mining operations, radiation effects, blasting.

North Carolina State University, Graduate School, College of Engineering, Department of Nuclear Engineering, Raleigh, NC 27695. Offers MNE, MS, PhD. *Degree requirements:* For master's, thesis (for some programs); for doctorate, thesis/dissertation. *Entrance requirements:* For master's, bachelor's degree in engineering or GRE; for doctorate, engineering degree or GRE. Electronic applications accepted. *Faculty research:* Computational reactor engineering, plasma applications, waste management, materials, radiation applications and measurement.

The Ohio State University, Graduate School, College of Engineering, Department of Mechanical Engineering, Program in Nuclear Engineering, Columbus, OH 43210. Offers MS, PhD. *Faculty:* 12. *Students:* 20 full-time (4 women), 9 part-time (1 woman); includes 2 minority (1 African American, 1 Hispanic American), 6 international. Average age 29. In 2009, 8 master's awarded. *Degree requirements:* For master's, thesis optional; for doctorate, thesis/dissertation. *Entrance requirements:* Additional exam requirements/recommendations for international students: Recommended—TOEFL (minimum score 600 paper-based; 250 computer-based). *Application deadline:* For fall admission, 8/15 priority date for domestic students, 7/1 priority date for international students; for winter admission, 12/1 priority date for domestic students, 11/1 priority date for international students; for spring admission, 3/1 priority date for domestic students, 2/1 priority date for international students. Applications are processed on a rolling basis. Application fee: $40 ($50 for international students). Electronic applications accepted. *Expenses:* Tuition, state resident: full-time $10,683. Tuition, nonresident: full-time $25,923. Tuition and fees vary according to course load and program. *Financial support:* Fellowships, research assistantships, teaching assistantships, career-related internships or fieldwork, Federal Work-Study, and institutionally sponsored loans available. Support available to part-time students. *Unit head:* Tunc Aldemir, Graduate Studies Committee Chair, 614-292-7930, Fax: 614-292-3163, E-mail: aldemir.1@osu.edu. *Application contact:* 614-292-9444, Fax: 614-292-3895, E-mail: domestic.grad@osu.edu.

Oregon State University, Graduate School, College of Engineering, Department of Nuclear Engineering and Radiation Health Physics, Corvallis, OR 97331. Offers nuclear engineering (M Eng, MS, PhD); radiation health physics (MA, MHP, MS, PhD). Part-time programs available. *Faculty:* 11 full-time (2 women). *Students:* 89 full-time (34 women), 27 part-time (16 women); includes 13 minority (1 African American, 7 Asian Americans or Pacific Islanders, 5 Hispanic Americans), 8 international. Average age 33. 51 applicants, 61% accepted, 12 enrolled. In 2009, 7 master's, 1 doctorate awarded. Terminal master's awarded for partial completion of doctoral program. *Degree requirements:* For master's, thesis; for doctorate, thesis/dissertation. *Entrance requirements:* For master's and doctorate, GRE General Test, minimum GPA of 3.0 in last 90 hours. Additional exam requirements/recommendations for international students: Required—TOEFL (minimum score 550 paper-based; 213 computer-based). *Application deadline:* For fall admission, 6/15 for domestic students. Applications are processed on a rolling basis. Application fee: $50. *Expenses:* Tuition, state resident: full-time $9774; part-time $362 per credit. Tuition, nonresident: full-time $15,849; part-time $587 per credit. Required fees: $1639. Full-time tuition and fees vary according to course load and program. *Financial support:* In 2009–10, 3 fellowships with full tuition reimbursements (averaging $16,650 per year), 14 research assistantships with partial tuition reimbursements (averaging $12,627 per year), 6 teaching assistantships with full tuition reimbursements (averaging $12,627 per year) were awarded; institutionally sponsored loans also available. Support available to part-time students. Financial award application deadline: 2/1. *Faculty research:* Reactor thermal hydraulics and safety, applications of radiation and nuclear techniques, computational methods development, environmental transport of radioactive materials. Total annual research expenditures: $2.5 million. *Unit head:* Dr. Jose N. Reyes, Head, 541-737-2343, Fax: 541-737-0480, E-mail: nuc_engr@engr.orst.edu. *Application contact:* Dr. Kristie Marsh, Academic Program Assistant, 541-737-7066, Fax: 541-737-0480, E-mail: nuc_engr@engr.orst.edu.

Penn State University Park, Graduate School, College of Engineering, Department of Mechanical and Nuclear Engineering, State College, University Park, PA 16802-1503. Offers M Eng, MS, PhD. *Faculty research:* Reactor safety, radiation damage, advanced controls, radiation instrumentation, computational methods.

Purdue University, College of Engineering, School of Nuclear Engineering, West Lafayette, IN 47907-2017. Offers MS, MSNE, PhD. Part-time programs available. Terminal master's awarded for partial completion of doctoral program. *Entrance requirements:* For master's and doctorate, GRE General Test, minimum GPA of 3.0. Additional exam requirements/recommendations for international students: Required—TOEFL (minimum score 550 paper-based; 213 computer-based; 77 iBT); Recommended—TWE. Electronic applications accepted. *Faculty research:* Nuclear reactor safety, thermal hydraulics, fusion technology, reactor materials, reactor physics.

Rensselaer Polytechnic Institute, Graduate School, School of Engineering, Department of Mechanical, Aerospace, and Nuclear Engineering, Program in Nuclear Engineering, Troy, NY 12180-3590. Offers nuclear engineering (M Eng, MS); nuclear engineering and science (PhD). Part-time programs available. *Faculty:* 7 full-time (1 woman), 2 part-time/adjunct (0 women). *Students:* 23 full-time (3 women), 1 part-time (0 women), 12 international. Average age 27. 22 applicants, 36% accepted, 2 enrolled. In 2009, 1 master's, 2 doctorates awarded. *Degree requirements:* For master's, thesis (for some programs); for doctorate, thesis/dissertation. *Entrance requirements:* For master's and doctorate, GRE. Additional exam requirements/recommendations for international students: Required—TOEFL (minimum score 600 paper-based; 250 computer-based; 100 iBT). *Application deadline:* For fall admission, 1/15 priority date for domestic students, 1/15 for international students; for spring admission, 1/15 priority date for domestic students, 1/15 for international students. Applications are processed on a rolling basis. Application fee: $75. Electronic applications accepted. *Expenses:* Tuition: Full-time $38,100. *Financial support:* In 2009–10, 17 students received support, including 5 fellowships with full tuition reimbursements available (averaging $22,000 per year), 10 research assistantships with full tuition reimbursements available (averaging $16,500 per year), 7 teaching assistantships with full tuition reimbursements available (averaging $16,500 per year); career-related internships or fieldwork and unspecified assistantships also available. Financial award application deadline: 2/1. *Faculty research:* Nuclear data measurement, multiphase flow and heat transfer, environmental and operational health physics, fusion reactor engineering and safety. *Unit head:* Dr. Timothy Wei, Head, 518-276-6351, Fax: 518-276-6025, E-mail: weit@rpi.edu. *Application contact:* Prof. Thierry A. Blanchet, Associate Chair of Graduate Studies, 518-276-8697, Fax: 518-276-2623, E-mail: blanct@rpi.edu.

Royal Military College of Canada, Division of Graduate Studies and Research, Engineering Division, Program in Nuclear Engineering, Kingston, ON K7K 7B4, Canada. Offers M Eng, MA Sc, PhD. *Degree requirements:* For master's, thesis; for doctorate, comprehensive exam, thesis/dissertation. *Entrance requirements:* For master's, honours degree with second-class standing; for doctorate, master's degree. Electronic applications accepted.

Royal Military College of Canada, Division of Graduate Studies and Research, Engineering Division, Program in Nuclear Science, Kingston, ON K7K 7B4, Canada. Offers M Sc, PhD. *Degree requirements:* For master's, thesis; for doctorate, comprehensive exam, thesis/dissertation. *Entrance requirements:* For master's, honour's degree with second-class standing; for doctorate, master's degree. Electronic applications accepted.

Texas A&M University, College of Engineering, Department of Nuclear Engineering, College Station, TX 77843. Offers health physics (MS); nuclear engineering (M Eng, MS, PhD). *Faculty:* 19. *Students:* 93 full-time (14 women), 18 part-time (4 women); includes 13 minority (2 African Americans, 6 Asian Americans or Pacific Islanders, 5 Hispanic Americans), 24 international. Average age 28. In 2009, 13 master's, 8 doctorates awarded. *Degree requirements:* For master's, thesis or alternative; for doctorate, thesis/dissertation, departmental qualifying exams. *Entrance requirements:* For master's and doctorate, GRE General Test, 3 letters of recommendation. Additional exam requirements/recommendations for international students: Required—TOEFL. *Application deadline:* For fall admission, 3/1 for domestic and international students; for spring admission, 8/1 for domestic and international students. Applications are processed on a rolling basis. Application fee: $50 ($75 for international students). Electronic applications accepted. *Expenses:* Tuition, state resident: full-time $3991.32; part-time $221.74 per credit hour. Tuition, nonresident: full-time $9049; part-time $502.74 per credit hour. *Financial support:* Fellowships, research assistantships, career-related internships or fieldwork, scholarships/grants, and unspecified assistantships available. Financial award application deadline: 4/1; financial award applicants required to submit FAFSA. *Faculty research:* Accelerators, aerosols, computational transport, fission, fusion. Total annual research expenditures: $4.2 million. *Unit head:* Dr. Yassin Hassan, Head, 979-845-1956, E-mail: y-hassan@tamu.edu. *Application contact:* Graduate Coordinator, 979-845-7090.

University of California, Berkeley, Graduate Division, College of Engineering, Department of Nuclear Engineering, Berkeley, CA 94720-1730. Offers M Eng, MS, D Eng, PhD. *Students:* 63 full-time (14 women). Average age 27. 113 applicants, 18 enrolled. In 2009, 16 master's, 4 doctorates awarded. *Degree requirements:* For master's, project or thesis; for doctorate, thesis/dissertation, oral exam. *Entrance requirements:* For master's and doctorate, GRE General Test, minimum GPA of 3.0, 3 letters of recommendation. Additional exam requirements/recommendations for international students: Required—TOEFL. *Application deadline:* For fall admission, 12/15 for domestic students. Application fee: $70 ($90 for international students). *Financial support:* Fellowships, research assistantships, teaching assistantships, unspecified assistantships available. *Faculty research:* Applied nuclear reactions and instrumentation, fission reactor engineering, fusion reactor technology, nuclear waste and materials management, radiation protection and environmental effects. *Unit head:* Prof. Per Peterson, Chair, 510-642-4077, Fax: 510-643-9685. *Application contact:* Lisa Zemelman, Student Affairs Officer, 510-642-5760, Fax: 510-643-9685, E-mail: gradinfo@nuc.berkeley.edu.

University of Cincinnati, Graduate School, College of Engineering, Department of Mechanical, Industrial and Nuclear Engineering, Program in Nuclear Engineering, Cincinnati, OH 45221. Offers MS, PhD. Part-time programs available. Terminal master's awarded for partial completion of doctoral program. *Degree requirements:* For master's, project or thesis; for doctorate, thesis/dissertation. *Entrance requirements:* For master's and doctorate, GRE General Test. Additional exam requirements/recommendations for international students: Required—TOEFL (minimum score 575 paper-based; 233 computer-based). Electronic applications accepted. *Faculty research:* Nuclear fission reactor engineering, reduction and fusion effects, health and medical physics, radiological assessment.

University of Florida, Graduate School, College of Engineering, Department of Nuclear and Radiological Engineering, Gainesville, FL 32611. Offers nuclear engineering sciences (ME, MS, PhD, Engr). *Degree requirements:* For master's, one foreign language, thesis; for doctorate, one foreign language, thesis/dissertation; for Engr, thesis optional. *Entrance requirements:* For master's and doctorate, GRE General Test, minimum GPA of 3.0; for Engr, GRE General Test. Additional exam requirements/recommendations for international students: Required—TOEFL (minimum score 550 paper-based; 213 computer-based). Electronic applications accepted. *Faculty research:* Robotics, Florida radon mitigation, nuclear space power, radioactive waste management, internal dosimetry.

University of Idaho, College of Graduate Studies, College of Engineering, Department of Engineering, Program in Nuclear Engineering, Moscow, ID 83844-2282. Offers M Engr, MS, PhD. *Faculty:* 1 full-time, 1 part-time/adjunct. *Students:* 13 full-time, 17 part-time. In 2009, 4 master's, 1 doctorate awarded. *Degree requirements:* For master's, thesis or alternative; for doctorate, thesis/dissertation. *Entrance requirements:* For master's, minimum GPA of 2.8; for doctorate, minimum undergraduate GPA of 2.8, 3.0 graduate. Additional exam requirements/recommendations for international students: Required—TOEFL. *Application deadline:* For fall admission, 8/1 for domestic students; for spring admission, 12/15 for domestic students. Application fee: $55 ($60 for international students). *Expenses:* Tuition, state resident: full-time $6120. Tuition, nonresident: full-time $17,712. *Financial support:* Application deadline: 2/15. *Unit head:* Dr. Wudneh Admassu, Director, 208-282-7962, E-mail: wadmassu@uidaho.edu. *Application contact:* Dr. Wudneh Admassu, Director, 208-282-7962, E-mail: wadmassu@uidaho.edu.

University of Illinois at Urbana–Champaign, Graduate College, College of Engineering, Department of Nuclear, Plasma, and Radiological Engineering, Champaign, IL 61820. Offers nuclear engineering (MS, PhD). *Faculty:* 10 full-time (0 women), 2 part-time/adjunct (0 women). *Students:* 61 full-time (9 women), 3 part-time (0 women); includes 3 minority (1 African American, 1 Asian American or Pacific Islander, 1 Hispanic American), 43 international. 72 applicants, 47% accepted, 14 enrolled. In 2009, 3 master's, 4 doctorates awarded. *Entrance requirements:* For master's and doctorate, minimum GPA of 3.0. Additional exam requirements/recommendations for international students: Required—TOEFL (minimum score 550 paper-based; 213 computer-based; 79 iBT), or IELTS. *Application deadline:* Applications are processed on a rolling basis. Application fee: $60 ($75 for international students). Electronic applications accepted. *Financial support:* In 2009–10, 8 fellowships, 37 research assistantships, 22 teaching assistantships were awarded; tuition waivers (full and partial) also available. *Unit head:* James F. Stubbins, Head, 217-333-6474, Fax: 217-333-3906, E-mail: jstubbin@illinois.edu. *Application contact:* Becky Meline, Admissions and Records Officer, 217-333-3598, Fax: 217-333-3906, E-mail: bmeline@illinois.edu.

See Close-Up on page 387.

University of Maryland, College Park, Academic Affairs, A. James Clark School of Engineering, Department of Materials and Nuclear Engineering, Nuclear Engineering Program, College Park, MD 20742. Offers ME, MS, PhD. Part-time and evening/weekend programs available. Postbaccalaureate distance learning degree programs offered. *Students:* 15 full-time (5 women), 2 part-time (1 woman); includes 6 minority (1 African American, 1 Asian American or Pacific Islander, 4 Hispanic Americans), 1 international. 29 applicants, 28% accepted, 5 enrolled. In 2009, 2 master's awarded. *Degree requirements:* For master's, thesis optional; for doctorate, variable foreign language requirement, thesis/dissertation, oral exam. *Entrance requirements:* For master's and doctorate, GRE General Test, minimum GPA of 3.0. Additional exam requirements/recommendations for international students: Required—TOEFL. *Application deadline:* For fall admission, 2/1 for domestic and international students; for spring admission, 8/1 for domestic students, 6/1 for international students. Applications are processed on a rolling basis. Application fee: $60. Electronic applications accepted. *Expenses:* Tuition, area resident: Part-time $471 per credit hour. Tuition, state resident: part-time $471 per credit hour. Tuition, nonresident: part-time $1016 per credit hour. Required fees: $337.04 per term. *Financial support:* In 2009–10, 4 research assistantships (averaging $22,413 per year) were awarded; fellowships, teaching assistantships, tuition waivers (full) also available. Financial award applicants required to submit FAFSA. *Faculty research:* Reliability and risk assessment, heat transfer and two-phase flow, reactor safety analysis, nuclear reactor, radiation/polymers. *Unit head:* Dr. Mohammad Modarres, Head, 301-405-5226, Fax: 301-314-9601, E-mail: modarres@umd.edu. *Application contact:* Dean of Graduate School, 301-405-0358, Fax: 301-314-9305.

University of Massachusetts Lowell, James B. Francis College of Engineering, Program in Energy Engineering, Lowell, MA 01854-2881. Offers MS Eng, D Eng, PhD. *Degree requirements:* For master's, thesis optional. *Entrance requirements:* For master's, GRE General Test. Additional exam requirements/recommendations for international students: Required—TOEFL.

University of Michigan, Horace H. Rackham School of Graduate Studies, College of Engineering, Department of Nuclear Engineering and Radiological Sciences, Ann Arbor, MI 48109. Offers nuclear engineering (Nuc E); nuclear engineering and radiological sciences (MSE, PhD); nuclear science (MS, PhD). *Faculty:* 20 full-time (2 women). *Students:* 106 full-time (16 women), 3 part-time (1 woman); includes 11 minority (6 Asian Americans or Pacific Islanders, 5 Hispanic Americans), 22 international. 140 applicants, 49% accepted, 31 enrolled. In 2009, 21 master's, 5 doctorates awarded. Terminal master's awarded for partial completion of doctoral program. *Degree requirements:* For master's, thesis optional; for doctorate, thesis/dissertation, oral defense of dissertation, preliminary exams. *Entrance requirements:* For master's and doctorate, GRE General Test. Additional exam requirements/recommendations for international students: Required—TOEFL (minimum score 560 paper-based; 220 computer-based). *Application deadline:* Applications are processed on a rolling basis. Application fee: $60 ($75 for international students). Electronic applications accepted. *Expenses:* Tuition, state resident: full-time $17,286; part-time $1099 per credit hour. Tuition, nonresident: full-time $34,944; part-time $2080 per credit hour. Required fees: $95 per semester. Tuition and fees vary according to course load, degree level and program. *Financial support:* Fellowships, research assistantships, teaching assistantships, career-related internships or fieldwork, institutionally sponsored loans, scholarships/grants, traineeships, health care benefits, and unspecified assistantships available. *Faculty research:* Radiation safety, environmental sciences, medical physics, fission systems and radiation transport, materials, plasmas and fusion, radiation measurements and imaging. *Unit head:* Dr. William R. Martin, Chair, 734-764-4260, Fax: 734-763-4540, E-mail: wrm@umich.edu. *Application contact:* Peggy Jo Gramer, Graduate Program Coordinator, 734-615-8810, Fax: 734-763-4540, E-mail: pjgramer@umich.edu.

University of Missouri, Graduate School, Nuclear Science and Engineering Institute, Columbia, MO 65211. Offers nuclear power engineering (MS, PhD), including health physics (MS), medical physics (MS), nuclear power engineering (MS). *Degree requirements:* For master's, research project; for doctorate, thesis/dissertation. *Entrance requirements:* For master's and doctorate, GRE General Test. Additional exam requirements/recommendations for international students: Required—TOEFL (minimum score 500 paper-based; 173 computer-based; 61 iBT).

University of Nevada, Las Vegas, Graduate College, Howard R. Hughes College of Engineering, Department of Mechanical Engineering, Las Vegas, NV 89154-4027. Offers aerospace engineering (MS); biomedical engineering (MS); materials and nuclear engineering (MS); mechanical engineering (MS, PhD). Part-time programs available. *Faculty:* 17 full-time (0 women), 10 part-time/adjunct (0 women). *Students:* 39 full-time (4 women), 28 part-time (6 women); includes 10 minority (1 African American, 8 Asian Americans or Pacific Islanders, 1 Hispanic American), 28 international. Average age 30. 64 applicants, 83% accepted, 22 enrolled. In 2009, 13 master's, 7 doctorates awarded. *Degree requirements:* For master's, comprehensive exam, thesis (for some programs), project; for doctorate, comprehensive exam, thesis/dissertation. *Entrance requirements:* For master's and doctorate, GRE General Test. Additional exam requirements/recommendations for international students: Required—TOEFL (minimum score 550 paper-based; 213 computer-based; 80 iBT), IELTS (minimum score 7). *Application deadline:* For fall admission, 5/1 priority date for domestic and international students; for spring admission, 10/1 priority date for domestic and international students. Applications are processed on a rolling basis. Application fee: $60 ($95 for international students). Electronic applications accepted. *Financial support:* In 2009–10, 37 students received support, including 21 research assistantships with partial tuition reimbursements available (averaging $13,335 per year), 16 teaching assistantships with partial tuition reimbursements available (averaging $11,000 per year); institutionally sponsored loans, scholarships/grants, health care benefits, and unspecified assistantships also available. Financial award application deadline: 3/1. *Unit head:* Dr. Woosoon Yim, Chair/Professor, 702-895-0956, Fax: 702-895-3936, E-mail: wy@me.unlv.edu. *Application contact:* Graduate College Admissions Evaluator, 702-895-3320, Fax: 702-895-4180, E-mail: gradcollege@unlv.edu.

University of New Mexico, Graduate School, School of Engineering, Department of Chemical and Nuclear Engineering, Program in Nuclear Engineering, Albuquerque, NM 87131-2039. Offers MS, PhD. Part-time programs available. Postbaccalaureate distance learning degree programs offered (no on-campus study). *Faculty:* 33 full-time (8 women), 4 part-time/adjunct (0 women). *Students:* 19 full-time (3 women), 18 part-time (3 women); includes 9 minority (1 African American, 1 American Indian/Alaska Native, 1 Asian American or Pacific Islander, 6 Hispanic Americans), 1 international. Average age 34. 27 applicants, 41% accepted, 5 enrolled. In 2009, 8 master's, 2 doctorates awarded. Terminal master's awarded for partial completion of doctoral program. *Degree requirements:* For master's, thesis (for some programs); for doctorate, comprehensive exam, thesis/dissertation. *Entrance requirements:* For master's, GRE General Test, minimum GPA of 3.0, 3 letters of recommendation, letter of intent; for doctorate, GRE General Test, 3 letters of recommendation, letter of intent. Additional exam requirements/recommendations for international students: Required—TOEFL. *Application deadline:* For fall admission, 1/15 priority date for domestic students, 3/1 for international students; for spring admission, 7/15 priority date for domestic students, 8/1 for international students. Application fee: $50. Electronic applications accepted. *Expenses:* Tuition, state resident: full-time $2098.80; part-time $233.20 per credit hour. Tuition, nonresident: full-time $6650. Required fees: $25 per semester. Tuition and fees vary according to course load, program and reciprocity agreements. *Financial support:* In 2009–10, 6 students received support, including 10 research assistantships with full tuition reimbursements available (averaging $21,600 per year); fellowships, teaching assistantships, scholarships/grants, health care benefits, and tuition waivers (full) also available. Financial award application deadline: 3/1; financial award applicants required to submit FAFSA. *Faculty research:* Plasma science, space power, thermal hydraulics, radiation measurement and protection, fusion plasma measurements, medical physics, nuclear criticality safety, radiation measurements and protection, radiation transport modeling and simulation, Monte Carlo methods. Total annual research expenditures: $1 million. *Unit head:* Dr. Timothy Ward, Chair, 505-277-5431, Fax: 505-277-5433, E-mail: tward@unm.edu. *Application contact:* Jocelyn White, Coordinator, Program Advisor, 505-277-5606, Fax: 505-277-5433, E-mail: jowhite@unm.edu.

University of South Carolina, The Graduate School, College of Engineering and Computing, Department of Nuclear Engineering, Columbia, SC 29208. Offers ME, MS, PhD. Part-time and evening/weekend programs available. Postbaccalaureate distance learning degree programs offered. *Degree requirements:* For master's, thesis (for some programs); for doctorate, thesis/dissertation. *Entrance requirements:* For master's and doctorate, GRE General Test. Additional exam requirements/recommendations for international students: Required—TOEFL (minimum score 600 paper-based; 250 computer-based; 100 iBT). Electronic applications accepted.

The University of Tennessee, Graduate School, College of Engineering, Department of Nuclear and Radiological Engineering, Knoxville, TN 37996. Offers nuclear engineering (MS, PhD); reliability and maintainability engineering (MS); MS/MBA. Part-time programs available. *Faculty:* 17 full-time (0 women), 16 part-time/adjunct (1 woman). *Students:* 48 full-time (6 women), 30 part-time (3 women); includes 3 minority (2 African Americans, 1 Asian American or Pacific Islander), 10 international. Average age 24. 123 applicants, 46% accepted, 31 enrolled. In 2009, 15 master's, 4 doctorates awarded. *Degree requirements:* For master's, thesis or alternative; for doctorate, comprehensive exam, thesis/dissertation. *Entrance requirements:* For master's and doctorate, GRE General Test, minimum GPA of 2.7. Additional exam requirements/recommendations for international students: Required—TOEFL (minimum score 213 computer-based). *Application deadline:* For fall admission, 2/1 priority date for domestic students. Applications are processed on a rolling basis. Application fee: $35. Electronic applications accepted. *Expenses:* Tuition, state resident: full-time $6826; part-time $380 per semester hour. Tuition, nonresident: full-time $21,844; part-time $1147 per semester hour. Tuition and fees vary according to program. *Financial support:* In 2009–10, 48 students received support, including 12 fellowships with full tuition reimbursements available (averaging $19,800 per year), 45 research assistantships with full tuition reimbursements available (averaging $17,916 per year), 4 teaching assistantships with full tuition reimbursements available (averaging $9,756 per year); career-related internships or fieldwork, Federal Work-Study, institutionally sponsored loans, and unspecified assistantships also available. Financial award application deadline: 2/1; financial award applicants required to submit FAFSA. *Faculty research:* Heat transfer and fluid dynamics; instrumentation, sensors and controls; maintenance and reliability; radiological engineering; reactor system design and safety. Total annual research expenditures: $3.3 million. *Unit head:* Dr. Harold L. Dodds, Head, 865-974-2525, Fax: 865-974-0668, E-mail: hdj@utk.edu. *Application contact:* Dr. Masood Parang, Associate Dean of Student Affairs, 865-974-2454, Fax: 865-974-9871, E-mail: mparang@utk.edu.

University of Utah, The Graduate School, College of Engineering, Department of Civil and Environmental Engineering, Program in Nuclear Engineering, Salt Lake City, UT 84112. Offers ME, MS, PhD. Part-time programs available. *Students:* 6 full-time (0 women), 2 part-time (0 women), 1 international. Average age 34. 10 applicants, 60% accepted, 1 enrolled. In 2009, 2 master's awarded. Terminal master's awarded for partial completion of doctoral program. *Degree requirements:* For master's, comprehensive exam, thesis (for some programs), special project (ME), thesis (MS); for doctorate, comprehensive exam, thesis/dissertation, qualifying exam. *Entrance requirements:* For master's and doctorate, GRE General Test, minimum GPA of 3.0. Additional exam requirements/recommendations for international students: Required—TOEFL (minimum score 580 paper-based; 173 computer-based; 93 iBT). *Application deadline:* For fall admission, 4/1 for domestic and international students; for spring admission, 11/1 for domestic and international students. Applications are processed on a rolling basis. Application fee: $55 ($65 for international students). Electronic applications accepted. *Expenses:* Tuition, state resident: full-time $4004; part-time $1674 per semester. Tuition, nonresident: full-time $14,134; part-time $5915 per semester. Required fees: $324 per semester. Tuition and fees vary according to course load, degree level and program. *Financial support:* In 2009–10, 2 students received support, including 1 research assistantship with full tuition reimbursement available (averaging $20,016 per year), 1 teaching assistantship with full tuition reimbursement available (averaging $19,200 per year); fellowships, career-related internships or fieldwork, institutionally sponsored loans, scholarships/grants, traineeships, health care benefits, and unspecified assistantships also available. Support available to part-time students. Financial award application deadline: 2/15; financial award applicants required to submit FAFSA. *Faculty research:* Dosimetry, material damage, energy. Total annual research expenditures: $350,542. *Unit head:* Dr. Paul J. Tikalsky, Advisor, 801-581-6931, Fax: 801-585-5477, E-mail: tikalsky@civil.utah.edu. *Application contact:* Amanda May, Academic Program Specialist, 801-581-6931, Fax: 801-585-5477, E-mail: amandam@civil.utah.edu.

University of Wisconsin–Madison, Graduate School, College of Engineering, Department of Engineering Physics, Madison, WI 53706-1380. Offers engineering mechanics (MS, PhD); nuclear engineering and engineering physics (MS, PhD). Part-time programs available. Postbaccalaureate distance learning degree programs offered (minimal on-campus study). *Faculty:* 21 full-time (1 woman), 8 part-time/adjunct (2 women). *Students:* 88 full-time (8 women), 4 part-time (0 women); includes 5 minority (1 African American, 2 Asian Americans or Pacific Islanders, 2 Hispanic Americans). Average age 25. 152 applicants, 54% accepted, 19 enrolled. In 2009, 18 master's, 8 doctorates awarded. Terminal master's awarded for partial completion of doctoral program. *Degree requirements:* For master's, thesis optional; for doctorate, thesis/dissertation. *Entrance requirements:* For master's and doctorate, GRE General Test, minimum GPA of 3.0 in last 60 hours, appropriate bachelor's degree. Additional exam requirements/recommendations for international students: Required—TOEFL (minimum score 600 paper-based; 245 computer-based). *Application deadline:* For fall admission, 1/15 priority date for domestic students. Applications are processed on a rolling basis. Application fee: $56. Electronic applications accepted. *Expenses:* Tuition, state resident: part-time $594 per credit. Tuition, nonresident: part-time $1504 per credit. Required fees: $65 per credit. Tuition and fees vary according to course load, program and reciprocity agreements. *Financial support:* In 2009–10, 78 students received support, including 7 fellowships with full tuition reimbursements available (averaging $20,760 per year), 71 research assistantships with full tuition reimbursements available (averaging $19,596 per year), 10 teaching assistantships with full tuition reimbursements available (averaging $12,894 per year); career-related internships or fieldwork, Federal Work-Study, and institutionally sponsored loans also available. Support available to part-time students. Financial award application deadline: 1/15. *Faculty research:* Fission reactor engineering and safety, plasma physics and fusion technology, plasma processing and ion implantation, nanotechnology, engineering mechanics and astronautics. Total annual research expenditures: $12.4 million. *Unit head:* Dr. Michael L. Corradini, Chair, 608-263-1646, Fax: 608-263-7451, E-mail: corradini@engr.wisc.edu. *Application contact:* Dr. Michael L. Corradini, Chair, 608-263-1646, Fax: 608-263-7451, E-mail: corradini@engr.wisc.edu.

Virginia Commonwealth University, Graduate School, School of Engineering, Program in Nuclear Engineering, Richmond, VA 23284-9005. Offers MS. *Entrance requirements:* For master's, BS in nuclear or mechanical engineering or a closely related discipline.

UNIVERSITY OF ILLINOIS AT URBANA–CHAMPAIGN

Department of Nuclear, Plasma, and Radiological Engineering

Programs of Study

The Department offers curricula leading to the M.S. and Ph.D. degrees in nuclear, plasma, and radiological engineering (NPRE). The M.S. program requires 32 semester hours of approved graduate credit, including a required thesis. A student must spend a minimum of two semesters in residence. The Ph.D. degree program can be divided into three stages, the last two of which must be completed in residence: a master's degree or the equivalent of 32 semester hours; 32 semester hours of course work beyond the M.S.; and 32 semester hours of dissertation research, a dissertation, and a final examination. Areas of research include fission and fusion engineering and technology; plasma engineering and processing; shielding and radiation effects; thermal hydraulics and reactor safety; nuclear materials, corrosion, and irradiation damage; neutron scattering; neutron activation analysis; nuclear nonproliferation and public policy issues; waste management and site remediation; and biomedical imaging and health physics.

Research Facilities

A wide range of major research resources are available for NPRE research. A dense plasma focus fusion-related device for high-temperature plasma studies and an ultrahigh-vacuum laboratory for plasma-material interaction studies are available. Graduate students often perform interdisciplinary research work in the Materials Research Laboratory, Microelectronics Laboratory, Coordinated Science Laboratory, National Center for Supercomputing Applications, and Beckman Institute for Advanced Science and Technology. Faculty members in these laboratories hold affiliate appointments in the degree-granting departments. The mechanical behavior program provides a variety of facilities for studies of nuclear materials. Other radiological laboratories are also available for environmental studies and nuclear spectroscopy, health physics and radiation studies, nuclear-waste management, thermal hydraulics and reactor safety, reactor physics and reactor kinetics, controlled nuclear fusion, direct energy conversion, and lasers and plasma physics. The Department of Nuclear, Plasma, and Radiological Engineering also has a direct link to the National Magnetic Fusion Computer Center in Livermore, California, and is a participant in the Computational Science and Engineering Program on campus. In addition, a wide array of microcomputers and workstations are available for student use.

Financial Aid

Most graduate students receive some form of financial aid through fellowships or research, teaching, or general assistantships. Financial support sources include federally sponsored traineeships and fellowships and University and industrial fellowships. The University is approved for several fellowships, including those from the Department of Energy, the Nuclear Regulatory Commission, the National Academy for Nuclear Training Institute for Nuclear Power Operations, the National Science Foundation, and Hertz. Part- and full-time research, teaching, and general assistantships, which include exemption from tuition and partial fees, are also available. For 2009–10, stipends started at $17,604 for entering students and the highest level was $19,827; stipends are for the nine-month academic year for half-time work (approximately 20 hours per week). The normal course load for a student working half-time is about three courses per semester.

Cost of Study

Tuition and fees vary according to the number of semester hours taken. For students who have fellowships or assistantships, tuition and some fees are waived, but remaining health insurance and other miscellaneous fees are the responsibility of the student. For incoming graduate students on an average program of 12 hours, tuition for the nine-month academic year in 2009–10 was $13,636 for Illinois residents and $26,902 for nonresidents.

Living and Housing Costs

University graduate residence halls are available with and without board contracts. Privately owned rooms and apartments are also available at comparable rates.

Student Group

On-campus enrollment at the Illinois campus in 2009–10 was 41,918 students: 31,209 undergraduates and 10,709 graduate and professional students. In 2009–10, the College of Engineering enrolled 9,138 students: 6,475 undergraduates and 2,663 graduate students. In 2009–10, there were 69 graduate students in the nuclear engineering graduate programs.

Student Outcomes

Graduates from the Department of Nuclear, Plasma, and Radiological Engineering are targeted for employment by power utility companies and their contractors and suppliers, regulatory agencies, research laboratories, semiconductor processing companies, and medical centers. They are also sought out by other universities for faculty positions. A sampling of recent employers includes Exelon; Westinghouse, General Electric, Sargent & Lundy, and Fauske and Associates; the Nuclear Regulatory Commission; General Atomics; Department of Energy Laboratories including Argonne, Fermilab, Idaho, and Los Alamos national laboratories; Novellus; and Provena medical centers. Starting salaries are among the highest in the engineering field.

Location

The University is located 150 miles south of Chicago in the twin cities of Urbana and Champaign (population 119,030). The area is primarily a university community, with excellent schools, parks, and shopping facilities. Willard Airport, major rail service, and three interstate highways provide rapid and accessible transportation. Many cultural and recreational facilities normally found only in a large city are available.

The University and The Department

The University of Illinois at Urbana-Champaign is in its second century of operation and is recognized as a national center of excellence in graduate education. The College of Engineering, founded in 1868, has grown and prospered with the University, establishing itself as a productive center of engineering research and education. Nuclear engineering was established in 1958 as an interdisciplinary program and was granted departmental status in 1986. The unit's name was changed to the Department of Nuclear, Plasma, and Radiological Engineering in 1999 to reflect the three paths typically followed by students and the wide variety of courses available. In fall 2008, the degree names were changed from nuclear engineering to nuclear, plasma, and radiological engineering. Fall 2008 also marked the Department's fiftieth anniversary as a degree-granting entity. Because of its original interdisciplinary nature, its research is carried out in several facilities. The affiliated Center for Plasma Material Interactions is housed in the Nuclear Radiation Laboratory. Fusion research is coordinated through the Fusion Studies Laboratory. A Thin Film Laboratory is used for running sputtering experiments. Administrative offices and most classes are in Talbot Laboratory or on the engineering campus. Further experimental facilities for thermal hydraulics, imaging with ionizing radiation, and a variety of materials research are also available.

Applying

Students must have a strong background in mathematics, science, and/or engineering. An average of B (3.0/4.0) or better is required. Official GRE scores for the general test are required. Students from non-English-speaking countries must demonstrate proficiency in English, which is measured by TOEFL or IELTS scores. The required minimum score on the TOEFL iBT is 79; on the IELTS it is 6.5, with a score of 6 or higher in all sub-sections. If admitted, additional English study may be necessary following a campus-administered English Placement Test (EPT). The application deadline for fall admission consideration is January 15. Applications submitted after this deadline may still be considered, upon discretion of the Graduate Admissions Committee. Early application is strongly advised, especially if the applicant is requesting financial assistance. Students interested in spring- or summer-semester entry should contact the Department before applying. Generally, spring or summer semester entry is not encouraged. The application deadline for spring admission consideration is September 15 and for summer, January 15.

Correspondence and Information

Becky Meline, Admissions and Records Officer
Department of Nuclear, Plasma, and Radiological Engineering
216 Talbot Laboratory
University of Illinois at Urbana-Champaign
104 South Wright Street
Urbana, Illinois 61801-2984
Phone: 217-333-3598
Fax: 217-333-2906
E-mail: nuclear@illinois.edu
Web site: http://www.npre.illinois.edu

University of Illinois at Urbana–Champaign

THE FACULTY AND THEIR RESEARCH

Professors

R. A. Axford, Ph.D. Application of the Lie theory of local transformation groups to the solution of linear and nonlinear systems of differential equations that arise in engineering science, theoretical physics, applied mathematics, computational physics of nuclear energy systems.

B. G. Jones, Ph.D. Thermal hydraulics, reactor safety, multiphase flow, boiling heat transfer, turbulence measurement and modeling, flow-induced vibrations and hydroacoustics, human-machine interfaces for reactor control and simulation, food irradiation safety.

G. H. Miley, Ph.D. Fusion systems, plasma engineering, reactor kinetics, high-voltage technology, nuclear-pumped lasers, direct energy conversion, hydrogen energy production and fuel cells, low-energy nuclear reactions in solids.

D. N. Ruzic, Ph.D. Experimental fusion research, modeling of edge-plasma atomic physics, atomic properties of potential first-wall materials, plasma-material interaction, plasma processing of semiconductors, extreme ultraviolet (EUV) sources for lithography, physical and chemical vapor deposition.

C. E. Singer, Ph.D. Energy economics, energy and security, advanced propulsion systems, nuclear proliferation, South Asian nuclear programs.

J. F. Stubbins, Ph.D. Development, analysis, and application of materials, primarily for energy-related applications; nuclear systems design and analysis; nuclear materials, irradiation damage, and effects; mechanical properties; high-temperature corrosion and stress corrosion cracking; electron microscopy.

R. Uddin, Ph.D. Advanced computational methods, theoretical and CFD, radiation transport and reactor physics, reactor engineering, multiphase flow, reliability and risk analysis, virtual reactor simulation.

Associate Professors

B. J. Heuser, Ph.D. Hydrogen/metal systems, defects in materials, thin-film structures, numerical simulations of spallation source systems, neutron scattering techniques.

M. H. Ragheb, Ph.D. Computational methods, reactor theory, Monte Carlo methods, radiation protection and shielding, probabilistic risk assessment, applied artificial intelligence, supercomputing.

Assistant Professor

L. J. Meng, Ph.D. Ultrahigh-resolution imaging systems for biomedical/molecular imaging applications, novel imaging sensor based on room-temperature semiconductor detectors.

Adjunct and Affiliate Faculty

In addition to the full-time faculty members, professors and professionals in a broad range of engineering disciplines are formally affiliated with the Department of Nuclear Engineering. They provide a breadth of expertise that broadens opportunities for research activities.

M. Aref, M.D., Ph.D., Department of Nuclear, Plasma, and Radiological Engineering.

R. S. Averback, Ph.D., Department of Materials Science and Engineering.

S. A. Boppart, Ph.D., Department of Electrical and Computer Engineering.

T. J. Dolan, Ph.D., Department of Nuclear, Plasma, and Radiological Engineering.

M. H. Garada, Ph.D., Provena Covenant Medical Center, Champaign, Illinois.

B. E. Jurczyk, Ph.D., Starfire Industries LLC.

K. K. Kim, Ph.D., Department of Electrical and Computer Engineering.

S. M. Larson, Ph.D., Department of Civil and Environmental Engineering.

C. P. Marsh, Ph.D., Construction Engineering Research Laboratory, Champaign, Illinois.

D. W. Miller, Ph.D., Department of Nuclear, Plasma, and Radiological Engineering.

R. F. Nelson, Ph.D., Radiation Oncology Department, Carle Clinic, Urbana, Illinois.

M. J. Neumann, Ph.D., Soladigm, San Jose, California.

S. L. Rohde, Ph.D., University of Nebraska–Lincoln.

W. R. Roy, Ph.D., Illinois State Geological Survey, Champaign, Illinois.

R. A. Stubbers, Ph.D., Starfire Industries, LLC.

B. G. Thomas, Ph.D., Department of Mechanical and Industrial Engineering.

D. R. Trinkle, Ph.D., Department of Materials Science and Engineering.

S. P. Vanka, Ph.D., Department of Mechanical Science and Engineering.

Section 11
Engineering Design

This section contains a directory of institutions offering graduate work in engineering design. Additional information about programs listed in the directory but not augmented by an in-depth entry may be obtained by writing directly to the dean of a graduate school or chair of a department at the address given in the directory.

For programs offering related work, see also in this book *Aerospace/ Aeronautical Engineering; Agricultural Engineering and Bioengineering; Biomedical Engineering and Biotechnology; Computer Science and Information Technology; Electrical and Computer Engineering; Energy and Power Engineering; Engineering and Applied Sciences; Industrial Engineering; Management of Engineering and Technology;* and *Mechanical Engineering and Mechanics.* In another guide in this series:
Graduate Programs in the Biological Sciences
See *Biological and Biomedical Sciences*

CONTENTS

Program Directory

Close-Up

See:

Engineering Design

Kettering University, Graduate School, Mechanical Engineering Department, Flint, MI 48504. Offers automotive systems (MS Eng); computer aided engineering simulation (MS Eng); mechanical cognate (MS Eng); mechanical design (MS Eng); sustainable energy and hybrid technology (MS Eng). Part-time and evening/weekend programs available. Postbaccalaureate distance learning degree programs offered (no on-campus study). *Faculty:* 14 full-time (1 woman). *Students:* 8 full-time (0 women), 35 part-time (7 women); includes 2 minority (1 Asian American or Pacific Islander, 1 Hispanic American), 8 international. Average age 26. 6 applicants, 67% accepted, 2 enrolled. In 2009, 20 master's awarded. *Degree requirements:* For master's, thesis optional. *Entrance requirements:* Additional exam requirements/recommendations for international students: Required—TOEFL (minimum score 550 paper-based; 213 computer-based; 79 iBT). *Application deadline:* For fall admission, 9/15 for domestic students, 6/15 for international students; for winter admission, 12/15 for domestic students, 9/15 for international students; for spring admission, 3/15 for domestic students, 12/15 for international students. Applications are processed on a rolling basis. Application fee: $0. Electronic applications accepted. *Expenses:* Tuition: Full-time $11,120; part-time $695 per credit hour. *Financial support:* In 2009–10, 24 students received support, including fellowships with full tuition reimbursements available (averaging $13,000 per year), research assistantships with full tuition reimbursements available (averaging $13,000 per year), teaching assistantships with full tuition reimbursements available (averaging $13,000 per year); Federal Work-Study, scholarships/grants, and tuition waivers (partial) also available. Support available to part-time students. Financial award application deadline: 7/15; financial award applicants required to submit CSS PROFILE or FAFSA. *Faculty research:* Fuel cells, chemical agents, crash safety, bio-gas, sustainable energy. Total annual research expenditures: $3.9 million. *Unit head:* Dr. K. Joel Berry, Head, 810-762-7833, Fax: 810-762-7860, E-mail: jberry@kettering.edu. *Application contact:* Bonnie Switzer, Graduate Admissions Officer, 810-762-7953, Fax: 810-762-9935, E-mail: bswitzer@kettering.edu.

Northwestern University, McCormick School of Engineering and Applied Science, Segal Design Institute, Program in Engineering Design and Innovation, Evanston, IL 60208. Offers MS. *Entrance requirements:* For master's, GRE, 2 letters of recommendation. Additional exam requirements/recommendations for international students: Required—TOEFL or IELTS. Electronic applications accepted.

Polytechnic Institute of NYU, Long Island Graduate Center, Graduate Programs, Department of Electrical and Computer Engineering, Interdisciplinary Major in Wireless Innovations, Melville, NY 11747. Offers M Engr. Part-time and evening/weekend programs available. *Students:* 10 full-time (2 women), 10 part-time (4 women); includes 3 minority (1 African American, 1 Asian American or Pacific Islander, 1 Hispanic American), 12 international. 100 applicants, 51% accepted, 6 enrolled. *Degree requirements:* For master's, comprehensive exam (for some programs), thesis (for some programs). *Entrance requirements:* Additional exam requirements/recommendations for international students: Required—TOEFL (minimum score 550 paper-based; 213 computer-based; 80 iBT); Recommended—IELTS (minimum score 6.5). *Application deadline:* For fall admission, 7/31 priority date for domestic students, 4/30 priority date for international students; for spring admission, 12/31 priority date for domestic students, 11/30 priority date for international students. Applications are processed on a rolling basis. Application fee: $75. Electronic applications accepted. *Financial support:* Institutionally sponsored loans, scholarships/grants, and unspecified assistantships available. Support available to part-time students. *Unit head:* Dr. Jonathan Chao, Department Head, 718-260-3302, Fax: 718-260-3906, E-mail: chao@poly.edu. *Application contact:* JeanCarlo Bonilla, Director of Graduate Enrollment Management, 718-260-3182, Fax: 718-260-3624, E-mail: gradinfo@poly.edu.

Rochester Institute of Technology, Graduate Enrollment Services, Kate Gleason College of Engineering, Department of Design, Development and Manufacturing, Rochester, NY 14623-5603. Offers manufacturing leadership (MS); product development (MS). Part-time and evening/weekend programs available. *Students:* 5 full-time (2 women), 50 part-time (7 women); includes 4 minority (2 African Americans, 2 Hispanic Americans), 6 international. Average age 38. 30 applicants, 33% accepted, 9 enrolled. In 2009, 22 master's awarded. *Degree requirements:* For master's, capstone. *Entrance requirements:* For master's, minimum GPA of 2.5. Additional exam requirements/recommendations for international students: Required—TOEFL (minimum score 570 paper-based; 230 computer-based; 88 iBT), or IELTS (minimum score 6.5). *Application deadline:* For fall admission, 2/15 priority date for domestic and international students. Applications are processed on a rolling basis. Application fee: $50. Electronic applications accepted. *Expenses:* Tuition: Full-time $31,533; part-time $876 per credit hour. Required fees: $210. *Financial support:* In 2009–10, 7 students received support. *Faculty research:* Computer-integrated manufacturing, industrial ergonomics, optics and photonics, micromachines, electrochemical heating, signal and image processing, cardiovascular biomechanics, robotics and control, VLSI design, electron beam lithography, computer architecture, multimedia information systems, object-oriented software development. *Unit head:* Mark Smith, Director, 585-475-7971, Fax: 585-475-7955, E-mail: mpdmail@rit.edu. *Application contact:* Diane Ellison, Assistant Vice President, Graduate Enrollment Services, 585-475-2229, Fax: 585-475-7164, E-mail: gradinfo@rit.edu.

San Diego State University, Graduate and Research Affairs, College of Engineering, Department of Mechanical Engineering, San Diego, CA 92182. Offers engineering sciences and applied mechanics (PhD); manufacture and design (MS); mechanical engineering (MS). Evening/weekend programs available. *Degree requirements:* For master's, comprehensive exam (for some programs), thesis (for some programs); for doctorate, thesis/dissertation. *Entrance requirements:* For master's, GRE General Test; for doctorate, GRE, 3 letters of recommendation. Additional exam requirements/recommendations for international students: Required—TOEFL. Electronic applications accepted. *Faculty research:* Energy analysis and diagnosis, seawater pump design, space-related research.

Santa Clara University, School of Engineering, Department of Mechanical Engineering, Santa Clara, CA 95053. Offers controls (Certificate); dynamics (Certificate); materials engineering (Certificate); mechanical design analysis (Certificate); mechanical engineering (MS, PhD, Engineer); mechatronics systems engineering (Certificate); technology jump-start (Certificate); thermofluids (Certificate). Part-time and evening/weekend programs available. *Students:* 36 full-time (5 women), 61 part-time (10 women); includes 27 minority (1 American Indian/Alaska Native, 22 Asian Americans or Pacific Islanders, 4 Hispanic Americans), 15 international. Average age 28. In 2009, 17 master's awarded. *Degree requirements:* For master's, thesis (for some programs); for doctorate, thesis/dissertation; for other advanced degree, thesis. *Entrance requirements:* For master's, GRE (waiver may be available); for doctorate, GRE, master's degree or equivalent; for other advanced degree, master's degree, published paper. Additional exam requirements/recommendations for international students: Required—TOEFL (minimum score 550 paper-based; 213 computer-based; 79 iBT). *Application deadline:* For fall admission, 8/13 for domestic students, 7/16 for international students; for winter admission, 10/29 for domestic students, 9/24 for international students; for spring admission, 2/25 for domestic students, 1/21 for international students. Applications are processed on a rolling basis. Application fee: $60. *Expenses:* Contact institution. *Financial support:* Research assistantships, teaching assistantships available. Financial award application deadline: 3/2; financial award applicants required to submit FAFSA. *Faculty research:* Development of Small Satellite Design, Tests and Operations Technology. Total annual research expenditures: $585,448. *Unit head:* Dr. Alex Zecevic, Associate Dean for Graduate Studies, 408-554-2394, E-mail: azecevic@scu.edu. *Application contact:* Stacey Tinker, 408-554-4748, Fax: 408-554-4323, E-mail: stinker@scu.edu.

Stanford University, School of Engineering, Department of Mechanical Engineering, Program in Product Design, Stanford, CA 94305-9991. Offers MS. *Entrance requirements:* For master's, GRE General Test, undergraduate degree in engineering, math or sciences. Additional exam requirements/recommendations for international students: Required—TOEFL. *Expenses:* Tuition: Full-time $37,380; part-time $2760 per quarter. Required fees: $501.

See Close-Up on page 525.

Stevens Institute of Technology, Graduate School, Charles V. Schaefer Jr. School of Engineering, Department of Mechanical Engineering, Program in Product Architecture and Engineering, Hoboken, NJ 07030. Offers M Eng. *Expenses:* Tuition: Full-time $9900; part-time $1100 per credit. Required fees: $286 per semester.

University of Central Florida, College of Engineering and Computer Science, Department of Industrial Engineering and Management Systems, Orlando, FL 32816. Offers applied operations research (Certificate); design for usability (Certificate); industrial engineering (MSIE, PhD); industrial ergonomics and safety (Certificate); project engineering (Certificate); quality assurance (Certificate); systems engineering (Certificate); systems simulation for engineers (Certificate); training simulation (Certificate). Part-time and evening/weekend programs available. *Faculty:* 14 full-time (2 women), 9 part-time/adjunct (6 women). *Students:* 108 full-time (22 women), 143 part-time (54 women); includes 76 minority (21 African Americans, 1 American Indian/Alaska Native, 14 Asian Americans or Pacific Islanders, 40 Hispanic Americans), 64 international. Average age 32. 204 applicants, 66% accepted, 88 enrolled. In 2009, 59 master's, 17 doctorates, 14 other advanced degrees awarded. *Degree requirements:* For master's, thesis; for doctorate, thesis/dissertation, departmental qualifying exam, candidacy exam. *Entrance requirements:* For master's, GRE General Test, minimum GPA of 3.0 in last 60 hours of course work; for doctorate, minimum GPA of 3.5 in last 60 hours of course work. Additional exam requirements/recommendations for international students: Required—TOEFL. *Application deadline:* For fall admission, 7/15 priority date for domestic students; for spring admission, 12/1 priority date for domestic students. Application fee: $30. Electronic applications accepted. *Expenses:* Tuition, state resident: part-time $306.31 per credit hour. Tuition, nonresident: part-time $1099.01 per credit hour. Part-time tuition and fees vary according to degree level and program. *Financial support:* In 2009–10, 20 students received support, including 8 fellowships with partial tuition reimbursements available (averaging $7,600 per year), 9 research assistantships with partial tuition reimbursements available (averaging $12,400 per year), 5 teaching assistantships with partial tuition reimbursements available (averaging $13,000 per year); career-related internships or fieldwork, Federal Work-Study, institutionally sponsored loans, tuition waivers (partial), and unspecified assistantships also available. Financial award application deadline: 3/1; financial award applicants required to submit FAFSA. *Unit head:* Dr. Waldemar Karwowski, Chair, E-mail: wkar@mail.ucf.edu. *Application contact:* Dr. Waldemar Karwowski, Chair, E-mail: wkar@mail.ucf.edu.

Worcester Polytechnic Institute, Graduate Studies and Research, School of Business, Worcester, MA 01609-2280. Offers information technology (MS), including information security management; management (Graduate Certificate); marketing and technological innovation (MS); operations design and leadership (MS); technology (MBA). *Accreditation:* AACSB. Part-time and evening/weekend programs available. Postbaccalaureate distance learning degree programs offered (no on-campus study). *Faculty:* 25 full-time (12 women), 6 part-time/adjunct (2 women). *Students:* 89 full-time (44 women), 198 part-time (47 women). Average age 32. 229 applicants, 70% accepted, 71 enrolled. In 2009, 69 master's awarded. *Degree requirements:* For master's, thesis optional. *Entrance requirements:* For master's, GMAT (MBA), GMAT or GRE General Test (MS), resume; for Graduate Certificate, GMAT or GRE General Test, statement of purpose, 3 letters of recommendation. Additional exam requirements/recommendations for international students: Required—TOEFL (minimum score 550 paper-based; 213 computer-based; 79 iBT), IELTS (minimum score 6.5). *Application deadline:* For fall admission, 7/1 priority date for domestic students, 6/1 priority date for international students; for spring admission, 11/1 priority date for domestic students, 10/1 priority date for international students. Applications are processed on a rolling basis. Application fee: $70. Electronic applications accepted. *Financial support:* Career-related internships or fieldwork, institutionally sponsored loans, scholarships/grants, and unspecified assistantships available. Financial award application deadline: 6/1. *Faculty research:* Organizational aesthetics, resistance in organizations, dynamics of product innovation, economic approaches to productivity, corporate earnings forecasts and value relevance, ERP implementation, improving Web accessibility, information quality assessment, measuring strategic and transactional IT, website quality, service operations modeling, health care operations and performance analysis, loan process design. *Unit head:* Dr. Mark Rice, Dean, 508-831-5218, Fax: 508-831-5720, E-mail: rice@wpi.edu. *Application contact:* Norm Wilkinson, Director, Graduate Management Programs, 508-831-5957, Fax: 508-831-5720, E-mail: nwilkins@wpi.edu.

Section 12
Engineering Physics

This section contains a directory of institutions offering graduate work in engineering physics. Additional information about programs listed in the directory but not augmented by an in-depth entry may be obtained by writing directly to the dean of a graduate school or chair of a department at the address given in the directory.

For programs offering related work, see also in this book *Electrical and Computer Engineering, Energy and Power Engineering (Nuclear Engineering), Engineering and Applied Sciences,* and *Materials Sciences and Engineering.* In the other guides in this series:

Graduate Programs in the Biological Sciences
See *Biophysics*
Graduate Programs in the Physical Sciences, Mathematics, Agricultural Sciences, the Environment & Natural Resources

See *Physics*
Graduate Programs in Business, Education, Health, Information Studies, Law & Social Work
See *Health Sciences (Medical Physics)*

CONTENTS

Program Directory

Engineering Physics

Air Force Institute of Technology, Graduate School of Engineering and Management, Department of Engineering Physics, Dayton, OH 45433-7765. Offers applied physics (MS, PhD); electro-optics (MS, PhD); materials science (PhD); nuclear engineering (MS, PhD); space physics (MS). Part-time programs available. *Degree requirements:* For master's, thesis; for doctorate, thesis/dissertation. *Entrance requirements:* For master's and doctorate, GRE General Test, minimum GPA of 3.0, U.S. citizenship. *Faculty research:* High-energy lasers, space physics, nuclear weapon effects, semiconductor physics.

Appalachian State University, Cratis D. Williams Graduate School, Department of Physics and Astronomy, Boone, NC 28608. Offers engineering physics (MS). Part-time programs available. *Faculty:* 14 full-time (2 women). *Students:* 17 full-time (8 women), 3 part-time (1 woman). 13 applicants, 100% accepted, 9 enrolled. In 2009, 10 master's awarded. *Degree requirements:* For master's, comprehensive exam, thesis optional. *Entrance requirements:* For master's, GRE General Test, 3 letters of recommendation. Additional exam requirements/recommendations for international students: Required—TOEFL (minimum score 570 paper-based; 230 computer-based; 79 iBT), IELTS (minimum score 6.5). *Application deadline:* For fall admission, 7/1 for domestic students, 2/1 for international students; for spring admission, 11/1 for domestic students, 7/1 for international students. Applications are processed on a rolling basis. Application fee: $50. Electronic applications accepted. *Expenses:* Tuition, state resident: full-time $2960. Tuition, nonresident: full-time $14,051. Required fees: $2320. *Financial support:* In 2009–10, 1 research assistantship with tuition reimbursement (averaging $10,000 per year), 7 teaching assistantships with tuition reimbursements (averaging $9,500 per year) were awarded; fellowships, career-related internships or fieldwork, Federal Work-Study, scholarships/grants, and unspecified assistantships also available. Financial award application deadline: 4/1. *Faculty research:* Raman spectroscopy, applied electrostatics, scanning tunneling microscope/atomic force microscope (STM/AFM), stellar spectroscopy and photometry, surface physics, remote sensing. Total annual research expenditures: $430,000. *Unit head:* Dr. Leon Ginsberg, Chairperson, 828-262-3090, E-mail: ginsberglh@appstate.edu. *Application contact:* Dr. Sid Clements, Director, 828-262-2447, E-mail: clementsjs@appstate.edu.

Cornell University, Graduate School, Graduate Fields of Engineering, Field of Applied Physics, Ithaca, NY 14853-0001. Offers applied physics (PhD); engineering physics (M Eng). *Faculty:* 48 full-time (5 women). *Students:* 72 full-time (10 women); includes 10 minority (8 Asian Americans or Pacific Islanders, 2 Hispanic Americans), 30 international. Average age 26. 153 applicants, 37% accepted, 18 enrolled. In 2009, 15 master's, 16 doctorates awarded. *Degree requirements:* For doctorate, comprehensive exam, thesis/dissertation, written exams. *Entrance requirements:* For master's, GRE General Test, 3 letters of recommendation; for doctorate, GRE General Test, GRE Subject Test (physics), GRE Writing Assessment, 3 letters of recommendation. Additional exam requirements/recommendations for international students: Required—TOEFL (minimum score 600 paper-based; 250 computer-based; 77 iBT). *Application deadline:* For fall admission, 1/15 for domestic students. Application fee: $70. Electronic applications accepted. *Expenses:* Tuition: Full-time $29,500. Required fees: $70. Full-time tuition and fees vary according to degree level, program and student level. *Financial support:* In 2009–10, 70 students received support, including 1 fellowship with full tuition reimbursement available, 3 research assistantships with full tuition reimbursements available, 8 teaching assistantships with full tuition reimbursements available; institutionally sponsored loans, scholarships/grants, health care benefits, tuition waivers (full and partial), and unspecified assistantships also available. *Faculty research:* Quantum and nonlinear optics, plasma physics, solid state physics, condensed matter physics and nanotechnology, electron and x-ray spectroscopy. *Unit head:* Graduate Faculty Representative, 607-255-0638. *Application contact:* Graduate Field Assistant, 607-255-0638, E-mail: aep_info@cornell.edu.

Dartmouth College, Thayer School of Engineering, Program in Engineering Physics, Hanover, NH 03755. Offers MS, PhD. Application fee: $45. *Faculty research:* Computational physics, medical physics, radiation physics, plasma science and magneto hydro-dynamics, magnetospheric and ionospheric physics. *Unit head:* Dr. Joseph J. Helbie, Dean, 603-646-2238, Fax: 603-646-2580, E-mail: joseph.j.helbie@dartmouth.edu. *Application contact:* Candace S. Potter, Graduate Admissions Administrator, 603-646-3844, Fax: 603-646-1620, E-mail: candace.potter@dartmouth.edu.

École Polytechnique de Montréal, Graduate Programs, Department of Engineering Physics, Montréal, QC H3C 3A7, Canada. Offers optical engineering (M Eng, M Sc A, PhD); solid-state physics and engineering (M Eng, M Sc A, PhD). Part-time programs available. *Degree requirements:* For master's, one foreign language, thesis; for doctorate, one foreign language, thesis/dissertation. *Entrance requirements:* For master's, minimum GPA of 2.75; for doctorate, minimum GPA of 3.0. *Faculty research:* Optics, thin-film physics, laser spectroscopy, plasmas, photonic devices.

George Mason University, College of Science, Department of Physics and Astronomy, Fairfax, VA 22030. Offers applied and engineering physics (MS). *Degree requirements:* For master's, thesis optional. *Entrance requirements:* For master's, minimum GPA of 2.75 in last 60 hours of course work. Electronic applications accepted. *Expenses:* Tuition, state resident: full-time $7568; part-time $315.33 per credit hour. Tuition, nonresident: full-time $21,704; part-time $904.33 per credit hour. Required fees: $2184; $91 per credit hour.

McMaster University, School of Graduate Studies, Faculty of Engineering, Department of Engineering Physics, Hamilton, ON L8S 4M2, Canada. Offers engineering physics (M Eng, MA Sc, PhD); nuclear engineering (PhD). *Degree requirements:* For master's, thesis or alternative; for doctorate, comprehensive exam, thesis/dissertation. *Entrance requirements:* For master's, minimum B average in engineering, mathematics, or physical sciences. Additional exam requirements/recommendations for international students: Required—TOEFL (minimum score 550 paper-based; 213 computer-based). *Faculty research:* Non-thermal plasmas for pollution control and electrostatic precipitation, bulk and thin film luminescent materials, devices and systems for optical fiber communications, physics and applications of III-V materials and devices, defect spectroscopy in semiconductors.

Michigan Technological University, Graduate School, College of Sciences and Arts, Department of Physics, Program in Engineering Physics, Houghton, MI 49931. Offers PhD. Part-time programs available. *Degree requirements:* For doctorate, comprehensive exam, thesis/dissertation. *Entrance requirements:* For doctorate, BS in physics or related discipline. Additional exam requirements/recommendations for international students: Required—TOEFL (minimum score 570 paper-based; 230 computer-based). Electronic applications accepted.

The Ohio State University, Graduate School, College of Engineering, Department of Engineering Physics, Columbus, OH 43210. Offers MS, PhD. Electronic applications accepted. *Expenses:* Tuition, state resident: full-time $10,683. Tuition, nonresident: full-time $25,923. Tuition and fees vary according to course load and program.

Polytechnic Institute of NYU, Department of Electrical and Computer Engineering, Major in Electrophysics, Brooklyn, NY 11201-2990. Offers MS. Part-time and evening/weekend programs available. *Students:* 9 full-time (2 women), 2 part-time (1 woman); includes 2 minority (both Asian Americans or Pacific Islanders), 9 international. 16 applicants, 56% accepted, 5 enrolled. *Degree requirements:* For master's, comprehensive exam (for some programs), thesis (for some programs). *Entrance requirements:* For master's, BS in electrical engineering. Additional exam requirements/recommendations for international students: Required—TOEFL (minimum score 550 paper-based; 213 computer-based; 80 iBT); Recommended—IELTS (minimum score 6.5). *Application deadline:* For fall admission, 7/31 priority date for domestic students, 4/30 priority date for international students; for spring admission, 12/31 priority date for domestic students, 11/30 priority date for international students. Applications are processed on a rolling basis. Application fee: $75. Electronic applications accepted. *Expenses:* Tuition: Full-time $21,492; part-time $1194 per credit hour. Required fees: $1160; $204 per course. *Financial support:* Fellowships, research assistantships, teaching assistantships, institutionally sponsored loans, scholarships/grants, and unspecified assistantships available. Support available to part-time students. Financial award applicants required to submit FAFSA. *Unit head:* Dr. Jonathan Chao, Head, 718-860-3478, Fax: 718-260-3302, E-mail: chao@poly.edu. *Application contact:* JeanCarlo Bonilla, Director of Graduate Enrollment Management, 718-260-3182, Fax: 718-260-3624.

Polytechnic Institute of NYU, Long Island Graduate Center, Graduate Programs, Department of Electrical and Computer Engineering, Major in Electrophysics, Melville, NY 11747. Offers MS. Part-time and evening/weekend programs available. *Students:* 1 part-time (0 women). *Degree requirements:* For master's, comprehensive exam (for some programs), thesis (for some programs). *Entrance requirements:* Additional exam requirements/recommendations for international students: Required—TOEFL (minimum score 550 paper-based; 213 computer-based; 80 iBT); Recommended—IELTS (minimum score 6.5). *Application deadline:* For fall admission, 7/31 priority date for domestic students, 4/30 priority date for international students; for spring admission, 12/31 priority date for domestic students, 11/30 priority date for international students. Applications are processed on a rolling basis. Application fee: $75. Electronic applications accepted. *Financial support:* Institutionally sponsored loans, scholarships/grants, and unspecified assistantships available. Support available to part-time students. Financial award applicants required to submit FAFSA. *Unit head:* Dr. Jonathan Chao, Department Head, 718-260-3302, E-mail: chao@poly.edu. *Application contact:* JeanCarlo Bonilla, Director of Graduate Enrollment Management, 718-260-3182, Fax: 718-260-3624, E-mail: gradinfo@poly.edu.

Rensselaer Polytechnic Institute, Graduate School, School of Engineering, Department of Mechanical, Aerospace, and Nuclear Engineering, Program in Engineering Physics, Troy, NY 12180-3590. Offers MS, PhD. Part-time programs available. *Faculty:* 1 full-time (0 women). *Students:* 1 full-time (0 women). Average age 27. 3 applicants, 67% accepted, 1 enrolled. In 2009, 1 doctorate awarded. Terminal master's awarded for partial completion of doctoral program. *Degree requirements:* For master's, thesis (for some programs); for doctorate, thesis/dissertation. *Entrance requirements:* For master's and doctorate, GRE. Additional exam requirements/recommendations for international students: Required—TOEFL (minimum score 600 paper-based; 250 computer-based; 100 iBT). *Application deadline:* For fall admission, 1/15 priority date for domestic students, 1/15 for international students; for spring admission, 10/15 priority date for domestic students, 1/15 for international students. Applications are processed on a rolling basis. Application fee: $75. Electronic applications accepted. *Expenses:* Tuition: Full-time $38,100. *Financial support:* In 2009–10, 1 research assistantship (averaging $16,500 per year) was awarded; fellowships, teaching assistantships, career-related internships or fieldwork, tuition waivers, and unspecified assistantships also available. Financial award application deadline: 2/1. *Faculty research:* Nuclear data management, multiphase flow and heat transfer, environmental and operational health physics, fusion reactor engineering and safety, radiation destruction of hazardous chemicals. *Unit head:* Dr. Timothy Wei, Head, 518-276-6351, Fax: 518-276-6025, E-mail: weit@rpi.edu. *Application contact:* Dr. Thierry A. Blanchet, Associate Chair of Graduate Studies, 518-276-8697, Fax: 518-276-2623, E-mail: blanct@rpi.edu.

Stevens Institute of Technology, Graduate School, Charles V. Schaefer Jr. School of Engineering, Department of Physics and Engineering Physics, Hoboken, NJ 07030. Offers applied optics (Certificate); engineering physics (M Eng); microdevices and microsystems (Certificate); physics (MS, PhD); plasma and surface physics (Certificate). Part-time and evening/weekend programs available. Terminal master's awarded for partial completion of doctoral program. *Degree requirements:* For master's, thesis optional; for doctorate, thesis/dissertation. *Entrance requirements:* For master's and doctorate, GRE. Additional exam requirements/recommendations for international students: Required—TOEFL. Electronic applications accepted. *Expenses:* Tuition: Full-time $9900; part-time $1100 per credit. Required fees: $286 per semester. *Faculty research:* Laser spectroscopy, physical kinetics, semiconductor-device physics, condensed-matter theory.

The University of British Columbia, Faculty of Science, Program in Physics, Program in Engineering Physics, Vancouver, BC V6T 1Z1, Canada. Offers MA Sc. *Degree requirements:* For master's, thesis. *Entrance requirements:* For master's, honors degree. Additional exam requirements/recommendations for international students: Required—TOEFL. *Faculty research:* Solid-state, nuclear, solar, and plasma physics; applied and nonlinear optics.

University of California, San Diego, Office of Graduate Studies, Department of Mechanical and Aerospace Engineering, Program in Engineering Physics, La Jolla, CA 92093. Offers MS, PhD. Part-time programs available. *Degree requirements:* For master's, comprehensive exam or thesis; for doctorate, thesis/dissertation, qualifying exam. *Entrance requirements:* For master's and doctorate, GRE General Test, minimum GPA of 3.0. Additional exam requirements/recommendations for international students: Required—TOEFL. Electronic applications accepted. *Faculty research:* Combustion engineering, environmental mechanics, magnetic recording, materials processing, computational fluid dynamics.

University of Maine, Graduate School, College of Liberal Arts and Sciences, Department of Physics and Astronomy, Program in Engineering Physics, Orono, ME 04469. Offers M Eng. *Students:* 2 applicants, 50% accepted, 1 enrolled. *Degree requirements:* For master's, thesis or alternative. *Entrance requirements:* For master's, GRE General Test, GRE Subject Test. Additional exam requirements/recommendations for international students: Required—TOEFL. *Application deadline:* For fall admission, 2/1 priority date for domestic students; for spring admission, 10/15 for domestic students. Applications are processed on a rolling basis. Application fee: $65. *Financial support:* In 2009–10, 1 teaching assistantship with tuition reimbursement (averaging $12,790 per year) was awarded. Financial award application deadline: 3/1. *Unit head:* Dr. Susan McKay, Chair, 207-581-1015, Fax: 207-581-3410. *Application contact:* Scott G. Delcourt, Associate Dean of the Graduate School, 207-581-3291, Fax: 207-581-3232, E-mail: graduate@maine.edu.

University of Oklahoma, Graduate College, College of Engineering, Program in Engineering Physics, Norman, OK 73019-0390. Offers MS, PhD. *Students:* 1 part-time (0 women); minority (Asian American or Pacific Islander). In 2009, 3 master's awarded. Terminal master's awarded for partial completion of doctoral program. *Degree requirements:* For master's, thesis or alternative, departmental qualifying exam; for doctorate, thesis/dissertation, comprehensive, departmental qualifying, oral, and written exams. *Entrance requirements:* For master's and doctorate, GRE General Test, GRE Subject Test (physics), previous course work in physics. Additional exam requirements/recommendations for international students: Required—TOEFL (minimum score 550 paper-based; 213 computer-based). *Application deadline:* For fall admission, 3/1 priority date for domestic students, 4/1 for international students; for spring admission, 10/1 for domestic students, 9/1 for international students. Applications are processed on a rolling basis. Application fee: $40 ($90 for international students). Electronic applications accepted. *Expenses:* Tuition, state resident: full-time $3744; part-time $156 per credit hour. Tuition, nonresident: full-time $13,577; part-time $565.70 per credit hour. Required fees: $2415; $90.10 per credit hour. *Financial support:* Scholarships/grants, health care benefits, tuition waivers (full), and unspecified assistantships available. Financial award application deadline: 3/1; financial award applicants required to submit FAFSA. *Faculty research:* Nanoscience, ulta cold atoms, high energy physics. *Unit head:* Mike Santos, Director, 405-325-3961, Fax: 405-325-7557, E-mail: msantos@ou.edu. *Application contact:* Mike Santos, Director, 405-325-3961, Fax: 405-325-7557, E-mail: msantos@ou.edu.

University of Saskatchewan, College of Graduate Studies and Research, College of Arts and Sciences, Department of Physics and Engineering Physics, Saskatoon, SK S7N 5A2, Canada. Offers M Sc, PhD. *Faculty:* 40. *Students:* 46. In 2009, 6 master's, 3 doctorates awarded. *Degree requirements:* For master's, thesis; for doctorate, comprehensive exam (for some

Engineering Physics

programs), thesis/dissertation. *Entrance requirements:* Additional exam requirements/recommendations for international students: Required—TOEFL (minimum score 80 iBT); Recommended—IELTS (minimum score 6.5). *Application deadline:* For fall admission, 7/1 priority date for domestic students. Applications are processed on a rolling basis. Application fee: $75. Electronic applications accepted. Tuition and fees charges are reported in Canadian dollars. *Expenses:* Tuition, area resident: Full-time $3000 Canadian dollars; part-time $500 Canadian dollars per term. Required fees: $700 Canadian dollars; $100 Canadian dollars per term. *Financial support:* Fellowships, research assistantships, teaching assistantships available. Financial award application deadline: 1/31. *Unit head:* Dr. Cary Rangacharyulu, Head, 306-966-6393, Fax: 306-966-6400, E-mail: cary@sask.usask.ca. *Application contact:* Dr. Chijin Xiao, Graduate Chair, 306-966-6409, Fax: 306-966-6400, E-mail: chijin.xiao@usask.ca.

University of Tulsa, Graduate School, College of Engineering and Natural Sciences, Department of Physics and Engineering Physics, Program in Engineering Physics, Tulsa, OK 74104-3189. Offers MS. Part-time programs available. *Students:* 2 full-time (both women), both international. Average age 23. 2 applicants, 0% accepted, 0 enrolled. *Degree requirements:* For master's, thesis. *Entrance requirements:* For master's, GRE General Test. Additional exam requirements/recommendations for international students: Required—TOEFL (minimum score 550 paper-based; 213 computer-based; 80 iBT), IELTS (minimum score 6). *Application deadline:* Applications are processed on a rolling basis. Application fee: $40. Electronic applications accepted. *Expenses:* Tuition: Full-time $16,182; part-time $899 per credit hour. Required fees: $4 per credit hour. Tuition and fees vary according to course load. *Financial support:* In 2009–10, 2 students received support, including 2 research assistantships (averaging $11,592 per year); fellowships, teaching assistantships, career-related internships or fieldwork, Federal Work-Study, scholarships/grants, health care benefits, tuition waivers (full and partial), and unspecified assistantships also available. Support available to part-time students. *Faculty research:* Nanotechnology, theoretical plasma physics/fusion, condensed matter, laser spectroscopy, optics and optical applications for environmental applications. *Unit head:* Dr. George Miller, Advisor and Program Chair, 918-631-3021, Fax: 918-631-2995, E-mail: george-miller@utulsa.edu. *Application contact:* Dr. George Miller, Advisor and Program Chair, 918-631-3021, Fax: 918-631-2995, E-mail: george-miller@utulsa.edu.

University of Virginia, School of Engineering and Applied Science, Program in Engineering Physics, Charlottesville, VA 22903. Offers MEP, MS, PhD. Postbaccalaureate distance learning degree programs offered (no on-campus study). *Students:* 27 full-time (6 women); includes 4 minority (2 African Americans, 2 Asian Americans or Pacific Islanders), 6 international. Average age 27. 32 applicants, 19% accepted, 2 enrolled. In 2009, 2 master's, 8 doctorates awarded. *Degree requirements:* For master's, comprehensive exam; for doctorate, comprehensive exam, thesis/dissertation. *Entrance requirements:* For master's and doctorate, GRE General Test, 3 recommendations. Additional exam requirements/recommendations for international students: Required—TOEFL. *Application deadline:* For fall admission, 1/15 for domestic and international students. Applications are processed on a rolling basis. Application fee: $60. Electronic applications accepted. *Financial support:* Fellowships, research assistantships, teaching assistantships available. Financial award application deadline: 2/1; financial award applicants required to submit FAFSA. *Faculty research:* Continuum and rarefied gas dynamics, ultracentrifuge isotope enrichment, solid-state physics, atmospheric physics, atomic collisions. *Unit head:* Petra Reinke, Co-Chair, 434-924-7237, Fax: 434-982-5660, E-mail: pr6e@virginia.edu. *Application contact:* Kathryn C. Thornton, Assistant Dean for Graduate Programs, 434-924-3897, Fax: 434-982-2214, E-mail: seas-grad-admission@cs.virginia.edu.

University of Wisconsin–Madison, Graduate School, College of Engineering, Department of Engineering Physics, Madison, WI 53706-1380. Offers engineering mechanics (MS, PhD); nuclear engineering and engineering physics (MS, PhD). Part-time programs available. Postbaccalaureate distance learning degree programs offered (minimal on-campus study). *Faculty:* 21 full-time (1 woman), 8 part-time/adjunct (2 women). *Students:* 88 full-time (8 women), 4 part-time (0 women); includes 5 minority (1 African American, 2 Asian Americans or Pacific Islanders, 2 Hispanic Americans). Average age 25. 152 applicants, 54% accepted, 19 enrolled. In 2009, 18 master's, 8 doctorates awarded. Terminal master's awarded for partial completion of doctoral program. *Degree requirements:* For master's, thesis optional; for doctorate, thesis/dissertation. *Entrance requirements:* For master's and doctorate, GRE General Test, minimum GPA of 3.0 in last 60 hours, appropriate bachelor's degree. Additional exam requirements/recommendations for international students: Required—TOEFL (minimum score 600 paper-based; 245 computer-based). *Application deadline:* For fall admission, 1/15 priority date for domestic students. Applications are processed on a rolling basis. Application fee: $56. Electronic applications accepted. *Expenses:* Tuition, state resident: part-time $594 per credit. Tuition, nonresident: part-time $1504 per credit. Required fees: $65 per credit. Tuition and fees vary according to course load, program and reciprocity agreements. *Financial support:* In 2009–10, 78 students received support, including 7 fellowships with full tuition reimbursements available (averaging $20,760 per year), 71 research assistantships with full tuition reimbursements available (averaging $19,596 per year), 10 teaching assistantships with full tuition reimbursements available (averaging $12,894 per year); career-related internships or fieldwork, Federal Work-Study, and institutionally sponsored loans also available. Support available to part-time students. Financial award application deadline: 1/15. *Faculty research:* Fission reactor engineering and safety, plasma physics and fusion technology, plasma processing and ion implantation, nanotechnology, engineering mechanics and astronautics. Total annual research expenditures: $12.4 million. *Unit head:* Dr. Michael L. Corradini, Chair, 608-263-1646, Fax: 608-263-7451, E-mail: corradini@engr.wisc.edu. *Application contact:* Dr. Michael L. Corradini, Chair, 608-263-1646, Fax: 608-263-7451, E-mail: corradini@engr.wisc.edu.

Yale University, Graduate School of Arts and Sciences, School of Engineering and Applied Science, Department of Applied Physics, New Haven, CT 06520. Offers MS, PhD. Terminal master's awarded for partial completion of doctoral program. *Degree requirements:* For doctorate, thesis/dissertation, area exam. *Entrance requirements:* For master's and doctorate, GRE General Test. Additional exam requirements/recommendations for international students: Required—TOEFL. *Faculty research:* Condensed-matter physics, optical physics, materials science.

Section 13
Geological, Mineral/Mining, and Petroleum Engineering

This section contains a directory of institutions offering graduate work in geological, mineral/mining, and petroleum engineering. Additional information about programs listed in the directory but not augmented by an in-depth entry may be obtained by writing directly to the dean of a graduate school or chair of a department at the address given in the directory.

For programs offering related work, see also in this book *Chemical Engineering, Civil and Environmental Engineering, Electrical and Computer Engineering, Energy and Power Engineering, Engineering and Applied Sciences, Management of Engineering and Technology,* and *Materials Sciences and Engineering.* In another guide in this series:

Graduate Programs in the Physical Sciences, Mathematics, Agricultural Sciences, the Environment & Natural Resources
See *Geosciences* and *Marine Sciences and Oceanography*

CONTENTS

Program Directories

Geological Engineering

Arizona State University, Graduate College, College of Liberal Arts and Sciences, Division of Natural Sciences, School of Earth and Space Exploration, Tempe, AZ 85287. Offers astrophysics (MS, PhD); geological sciences (MS, PhD). *Degree requirements:* For master's, thesis or alternative; for doctorate, thesis/dissertation. *Entrance requirements:* For master's and doctorate, GRE.

Colorado School of Mines, Graduate School, Department of Geology and Geological Engineering, Golden, CO 80401. Offers geochemistry (MS, PMS, PhD); geological engineering (ME, MS, PhD); geology (MS, PhD). Part-time programs available. *Faculty:* 26 full-time (7 women), 4 part-time/adjunct (2 women). *Students:* 101 full-time (38 women), 24 part-time (10 women); includes 8 minority (1 African American, 2 American Indian/Alaska Native, 2 Asian Americans or Pacific Islanders, 3 Hispanic Americans), 19 international. Average age 29. 175 applicants, 65% accepted, 40 enrolled. In 2009, 28 master's, 3 doctorates awarded. *Degree requirements:* For master's, thesis (for some programs); for doctorate, comprehensive exam, thesis/dissertation. *Entrance requirements:* For master's and doctorate, GRE General Test. Additional exam requirements/recommendations for international students: Required—TOEFL (minimum score 550 paper-based; 213 computer-based; 80 iBT). *Application deadline:* For fall admission, 1/15 for domestic and international students; for spring admission, 9/1 for domestic and international students. Application fee: $50 ($70 for international students). Electronic applications accepted. *Expenses:* Tuition, state resident: full-time $10,584; part-time $588 per credit hour. Tuition, nonresident: full-time $24,750; part-time $1375 per credit hour. Required fees: $1654; $827.10 per semester. *Financial support:* In 2009–10, 65 students received support, including 7 fellowships with full tuition reimbursements available (averaging $20,000 per year), 40 research assistantships with full tuition reimbursements available (averaging $20,000 per year), 18 teaching assistantships with full tuition reimbursements available (averaging $20,000 per year); scholarships/grants, health care benefits, and unspecified assistantships also available. Financial award application deadline: 1/15; financial award applicants required to submit FAFSA. *Faculty research:* Predictive sediment modeling, petrophysics, aquifer-contaminant flow modeling, water-rock interactions, geotechnical engineering. Total annual research expenditures: $2.6 million. *Unit head:* Dr. John Humphrey, Department Head, 303-273-3819, Fax: 303-273-3859, E-mail: jhumphre@mines.edu. *Application contact:* Marilyn Schwinger, Administrative Assistant, 303-273-3800, Fax: 303-273-3859, E-mail: mschwing@mines.edu.

Colorado School of Mines, Graduate School, Department of Geophysics, Golden, CO 80401. Offers geophysical engineering (ME, MS, PhD); geophysics (MS, PhD); mineral exploration and mining geosciences (PMS). Part-time programs available. *Faculty:* 15 full-time (1 woman), 4 part-time/adjunct (0 women). *Students:* 67 full-time (15 women), 6 part-time (1 woman); includes 5 minority (1 American Indian/Alaska Native, 2 Asian Americans or Pacific Islanders, 2 Hispanic Americans), 40 international. Average age 30. 130 applicants, 40% accepted, 20 enrolled. In 2009, 9 master's, 6 doctorates awarded. *Degree requirements:* For master's, thesis (for some programs); for doctorate, one foreign language, comprehensive exam, thesis/dissertation, oral exams. *Entrance requirements:* For master's and doctorate, GRE General Test. Additional exam requirements/recommendations for international students: Required—TOEFL (minimum score 550 paper-based; 213 computer-based; 80 iBT). *Application deadline:* For fall admission, 1/15 for domestic and international students; for spring admission, 9/1 for domestic and international students. Application fee: $50 ($70 for international students). Electronic applications accepted. *Expenses:* Tuition, state resident: full-time $10,584; part-time $588 per credit hour. Tuition, nonresident: full-time $24,750; part-time $1375 per credit hour. Required fees: $1654; $827.10 per semester. *Financial support:* In 2009–10, 58 students received support, including 6 fellowships with full tuition reimbursements available (averaging $20,000 per year), 47 research assistantships with full tuition reimbursements available (averaging $20,000 per year), 5 teaching assistantships with full tuition reimbursements available (averaging $20,000 per year); scholarships/grants, health care benefits, and unspecified assistantships also available. Financial award application deadline: 1/15; financial award applicants required to submit FAFSA. *Faculty research:* Seismic exploration, gravity and geomagnetic fields, electrical mapping and sounding, bore hole measurements, environmental physics. Total annual research expenditures: $3.8 million. *Unit head:* Dr. Terence K. Young, Department Head, 303-273-3454, Fax: 303-273-3478, E-mail: tkyoung@mines.edu. *Application contact:* Michelle Szobody, Office Manager, 303-273-3935, Fax: 303-273-3478, E-mail: mszobody@mines.edu.

Michigan Technological University, Graduate School, College of Engineering, Department of Geological and Mining Engineering and Sciences, Program in Geological Engineering, Houghton, MI 49931. Offers MS, PhD. Part-time programs available. Terminal master's awarded for partial completion of doctoral program. *Degree requirements:* For master's, comprehensive exam; for doctorate, comprehensive exam, thesis/dissertation. *Entrance requirements:* Additional exam requirements/recommendations for international students: Required—TOEFL (minimum score 550 paper-based; 213 computer-based). Electronic applications accepted. *Expenses:* Contact institution.

Missouri University of Science and Technology, Graduate School, Department of Geological Sciences and Engineering, Rolla, MO 65409. Offers geological engineering (MS, DE, PhD); geology and geophysics (MS, PhD), including geochemistry, geology, geophysics, groundwater and environmental geology; petroleum engineering (MS, DE, PhD). Part-time programs available. *Degree requirements:* For master's, thesis optional; for doctorate, comprehensive exam, thesis/dissertation. *Entrance requirements:* For master's, GRE General Test (minimum score 600 quantitative, writing 3.5), minimum GPA of 3.0 in last 4 semesters; for doctorate, GRE General Test (minimum: Q 600, GRE WR 3.5). Additional exam requirements/recommendations for international students: Required—TOEFL. Electronic applications accepted. *Faculty research:* Digital image processing and geographic information systems, mineralogy, igneous and sedimentary petrology-geochemistry, sedimentology groundwater hydrology and contaminant transport.

Montana Tech of The University of Montana, Graduate School, Geosciences Programs, Butte, MT 59701-8997. Offers geochemistry (MS); geological engineering (MS); geology (MS); geophysical engineering (MS); hydrogeological engineering (MS); hydrogeology (MS). Part-time programs available. *Faculty:* 18 full-time (4 women), 3 part-time/adjunct (2 women). *Students:* 16 full-time (8 women), 6 part-time (4 women); includes 1 minority (African American), 1 international. 6 applicants, 67% accepted, 4 enrolled. In 2009, 7 degrees awarded. *Degree requirements:* For master's, comprehensive exam (for some programs), thesis (for some programs). *Entrance requirements:* For master's, GRE General Test, minimum GPA of 3.0. Additional exam requirements/recommendations for international students: Required—TOEFL (minimum score 525 paper-based; 195 computer-based; 71 iBT). *Application deadline:* For fall admission, 4/1 priority date for domestic students, 3/1 priority date for international students; for spring admission, 10/1 priority date for domestic students, 7/1 priority date for international students. Applications are processed on a rolling basis. Application fee: $30. Electronic applications accepted. *Expenses:* Tuition, state resident: full-time $5068; part-time $319 per credit. Tuition, nonresident: full-time $14,815; part-time $875 per credit. Tuition and fees vary according to course load and campus/location. *Financial support:* In 2009–10, 11 students received support, including 5 teaching assistantships with partial tuition reimbursements available (averaging $8,000 per year); research assistantships with partial tuition reimbursements available, career-related internships or fieldwork, tuition waivers (full and partial), and unspecified assistantships also available. Financial award application deadline: 4/1; financial award applicants required to submit FAFSA. *Faculty research:* Water resource development, seismic processing, petroleum reservoir characterization, environmental geochemistry, geologic mapping. *Unit head:* Dr. Diane Wolfgram, Department Head, 406-496-4353, Fax: 406-496-4260, E-mail: dwolfgram@mtech.edu. *Application contact:* Cindy Dunstan, Administrator, Graduate School, 406-496-4304, Fax: 406-496-4710, E-mail: cdunstan@mtech.edu.

South Dakota School of Mines and Technology, Graduate Division, College of Engineering, Department of Geology and Geological Engineering, Rapid City, SD 57701-3995. Offers geology and geological engineering (MS, PhD); paleontology (MS). Part-time programs available. *Faculty:* 7 full-time (0 women). *Students:* 19 full-time (2 women), 10 part-time (3 women); includes 2 minority (1 African American, 1 American Indian/Alaska Native), 6 international. Average age 31. 23 applicants, 70% accepted, 6 enrolled. In 2009, 10 master's awarded. *Degree requirements:* For master's, thesis; for doctorate, thesis/dissertation. *Entrance requirements:* For master's and doctorate, GRE General Test, GRE Subject Test. Additional exam requirements/recommendations for international students: Required—TOEFL, TWE. *Application deadline:* For fall admission, 7/1 priority date for domestic students, 4/1 for international students; for spring admission, 11/1 for domestic students, 9/1 for international students. Applications are processed on a rolling basis. Application fee: $35. Electronic applications accepted. *Expenses:* Tuition, state resident: full-time $3340; part-time $139 per credit hour. Tuition, nonresident: full-time $7060; part-time $294 per credit hour. Required fees: $3270. *Financial support:* In 2009–10, 4 fellowships (averaging $1,800 per year), 4 research assistantships with partial tuition reimbursements (averaging $7,047 per year), 8 teaching assistantships with partial tuition reimbursements (averaging $5,286 per year) were awarded; Federal Work-Study and institutionally sponsored loans also available. Support available to part-time students. Financial award application deadline: 5/15. *Faculty research:* Contaminants in soil, nitrate leaching, environmental changes, fracture formations, greenhouse effect. Total annual research expenditures: $18,865. *Unit head:* Dr. Maribeth Price, Chair, 605-394-1290, E-mail: maribeth.price@sdsmt.edu. *Application contact:* Jeannette R. Nilson, Administrative Support Coordinator, Graduate Education, 800-454-8162 Ext. 1206, Fax: 605-394-5360, E-mail: graduate_admissions@sdsmt.edu.

University of Alaska Anchorage, School of Engineering, Program in Arctic Engineering, Anchorage, AK 99508. Offers MS. Part-time and evening/weekend programs available. *Degree requirements:* For master's, thesis or alternative, engineering project report. *Entrance requirements:* For master's, bachelor's degree in engineering. Additional exam requirements/recommendations for international students: Required—TOEFL (minimum score 550 paper-based; 213 computer-based). *Faculty research:* Load-bearing ice, control of drifting snow, permafrost and foundations, frozen ground engineering.

University of Alaska Fairbanks, College of Engineering and Mines, Department of Mining and Geological Engineering, Fairbanks, AK 99775-5800. Offers geological engineering (MS, PhD); mineral preparation engineering (MS); mining engineering (MS, PhD). Part-time programs available. *Students:* 8 full-time (1 woman), 5 part-time (2 women), 8 international. Average age 33. 11 applicants, 64% accepted, 4 enrolled. In 2009, 4 master's, 1 doctorate awarded. *Degree requirements:* For master's, comprehensive exam, thesis or alternative; for doctorate, comprehensive exam, thesis/dissertation, oral exam, oral defense. *Entrance requirements:* For doctorate, GRE General Test. Additional exam requirements/recommendations for international students: Required—TOEFL (minimum score 550 paper-based; 213 computer-based; 80 iBT). *Application deadline:* For fall admission, 6/1 for domestic students, 3/1 for international students; for spring admission, 10/15 for domestic students, 9/1 for international students. Applications are processed on a rolling basis. Application fee: $60. Electronic applications accepted. *Expenses:* Tuition, state resident: full-time $7584; part-time $316 per credit. Tuition, nonresident: full-time $15,504; part-time $646 per credit. Required fees: $23 per credit. $135 per semester. Tuition and fees vary according to course level, course load and reciprocity agreements. *Financial support:* In 2009–10, 1 research assistantship (averaging $4,612 per year), 3 teaching assistantships (averaging $7,088 per year) were awarded; fellowships, career-related internships or fieldwork, Federal Work-Study, scholarships/grants, health care benefits, and unspecified assistantships also available. Support available to part-time students. Financial award application deadline: 7/1; financial award applicants required to submit FAFSA. *Faculty research:* Underground mining in permafrost, testing of ultra clean diesel, slope stability, fractal and mathematical morphology, soil and rock mechanics. *Unit head:* Dr. Rajive Ganguli, Chair, 907-474-7388, Fax: 907-474-6635, E-mail: fyminge@uaf.edu. *Application contact:* Dr. Rajive Ganguli, Chair, 907-474-7388, Fax: 907-474-6635, E-mail: fyminge@uaf.edu.

The University of Arizona, Graduate College, College of Engineering, Department of Mining, Geological and Geophysical Engineering, Tucson, AZ 85721. Offers geological engineering (MS, PhD); mining engineering (M Eng, Certificate), including mine health and safety (Certificate), mine information and production technology (Certificate), mining engineering (M Eng), rock mechanics (Certificate). Part-time programs available. Postbaccalaureate distance learning degree programs offered (minimal on-campus study). *Faculty:* 7. *Students:* 9 full-time (0 women), 12 part-time (1 woman); includes 1 minority (Hispanic American), 10 international. Average age 38. 28 applicants, 32% accepted, 4 enrolled. In 2009, 5 master's, 2 doctorates awarded. *Degree requirements:* For master's, thesis; for doctorate, thesis/dissertation. *Entrance requirements:* For master's, GRE General Test, 3 letters of recommendation; for doctorate, GRE General Test, 3 letters of recommendation, statements of purpose. Additional exam requirements/recommendations for international students: Required—TOEFL (minimum score 550 paper-based; 213 computer-based; 79 iBT). *Application deadline:* For fall admission, 6/1 for domestic students, 12/1 for international students; for spring admission, 10/1 for domestic students, 6/1 for international students. Applications are processed on a rolling basis. Application fee: $75. *Expenses:* Tuition, state resident: full-time $9028. Tuition, nonresident: full-time $24,890. *Financial support:* In 2009–10, 4 research assistantships with full tuition reimbursements (averaging $18,074 per year), 2 teaching assistantships with full tuition reimbursements (averaging $20,526 per year) were awarded; institutionally sponsored loans, scholarships/grants, health care benefits, tuition waivers (partial), and unspecified assistantships also available. Financial award application deadline: 4/1. *Faculty research:* Geomechanics, mineral processing, information technology, automation, geosensing. Total annual research expenditures: $420,172. *Unit head:* Dr. Mary M. Poulton, Head, 520-621-6063, Fax: 520-621-8330, E-mail: mpoulton@u.arizona.edu. *Application contact:* Olivia Hanson, Graduate Advisor, 520-621-6063, Fax: 520-621-8330, E-mail: ohanson@engr.arizona.edu.

The University of British Columbia, Faculty of Science, Department of Earth and Ocean Sciences, Vancouver, BC V6T 1Z4, Canada. Offers atmospheric science (M Sc, PhD); geological engineering (M Eng, MA Sc, PhD); geological sciences (M Sc, PhD); geophysics (M Sc, MA Sc, PhD); oceanography (M Sc, PhD). *Degree requirements:* For master's, thesis (for some programs); for doctorate, comprehensive exam, thesis/dissertation. *Entrance requirements:* Additional exam requirements/recommendations for international students: Required—TOEFL (minimum score 600 paper-based; 250 computer-based; 100 iBT). Electronic applications accepted. *Faculty research:* Oceans and atmosphere, environmental earth science, hydro geology, mineral deposits, geophysics.

University of Hawaii at Manoa, Graduate Division, School of Ocean and Earth Science and Technology, Department of Geology and Geophysics, Honolulu, HI 96822. Offers high-pressure geophysics and geochemistry (MS, PhD); hydrogeology and engineering geology (MS, PhD); marine geology and geophysics (MS, PhD); planetary geosciences and remote sensing (MS, PhD); seismology and solid-earth geophysics (MS, PhD); volcanology, petrology, and geochemistry (MS, PhD). Part-time programs available. *Faculty:* 73 full-time (16 women), 15 part-time/adjunct (3 women). *Students:* 42 full-time (20 women), 8 part-time (5 women); includes 7 minority (1 African American, 4 Asian Americans or Pacific Islanders, 2 Hispanic Americans), 6 international. Average age 29. 56 applicants, 25% accepted, 6 enrolled. In 2009, 4 master's, 7 doctorates awarded. Terminal master's awarded for partial completion of doctoral program. *Degree requirements:* For master's, thesis optional; for doctorate, comprehensive exam, thesis/dissertation. *Entrance requirements:* For master's and doctorate, GRE General Test, minimum GPA of 3.0. Additional exam requirements/recommendations for international students: Required—TOEFL (minimum score 580 paper-based; 237 computer-based; 92 iBT), IELTS (minimum score 5). *Application deadline:* For fall admission, 1/15 for domestic students, 1/1 for international students; for spring admission, 9/1 for domestic students, 8/15 for international students. Application fee: $60. *Expenses:* Tuition, state resident: full-time $8900; part-time $372 per credit. Tuition, nonresident: full-time $21,400; part-time $898 per credit. Required fees: $207 per semester. *Financial support:* In 2009–10, 1 student received support, including 4 fellowships (averaging $9,338 per year), 31 research assistantships (averaging $23,877 per year), 5 teaching assistantships (averaging $20,466 per year). Total annual research expenditures: $3.8 million. *Application contact:* Dr. Charles Fletcher, Chair, 808-956-7640, Fax: 808-956-5512, E-mail: gg-grad-chair@hawaii.edu.

University of Idaho, College of Graduate Studies, College of Engineering, Department of Civil Engineering, Program in Geological Engineering, Moscow, ID 83844-2282. Offers MS. *Students:* 7 part-time. In 2009, 5 master's awarded. *Degree requirements:* For master's, one foreign language, thesis. *Entrance requirements:* For master's, minimum GPA of 2.8. *Application deadline:* For fall admission, 8/1 for domestic students; for spring admission, 12/15 for domestic students. Application fee: $55 ($60 for international students). *Expenses:* Tuition, state resident: full-time $6120. Tuition, nonresident: full-time $17,712. *Financial support:* Application deadline: 2/15. *Faculty research:* Slope stability and landslide mitigation, erosion and sediment control for construction sites, rock engineering and rock reinforcement, underground natural gas storage. *Unit head:* Dr. Richard Nielsen, Chair, 208-885-6782. *Application contact:* Dr. Richard Nielsen, Chair, 208-885-6782.

University of Minnesota, Twin Cities Campus, Institute of Technology, Department of Civil Engineering, Minneapolis, MN 55455-0213. Offers civil engineering (MCE, MS, PhD); geological engineering (M Geo E, MS, PhD). Part-time programs available. *Degree requirements:* For master's, thesis optional; for doctorate, thesis/dissertation. *Entrance requirements:* For master's and doctorate, GRE General Test. Additional exam requirements/recommendations for international students: Required—TOEFL. *Faculty research:* Environmental engineering, rock mechanics, water resources, structural engineering, transportation.

University of Nevada, Reno, Graduate School, College of Science, Mackay School of Earth Sciences and Engineering, Department of Geological Sciences, Program in Geological Engineering, Reno, NV 89557. Offers MS, PhD. Terminal master's awarded for partial completion of doctoral program. *Degree requirements:* For master's, thesis optional; for doctorate, thesis/dissertation. *Entrance requirements:* For master's and doctorate, GRE General Test, minimum GPA of 2.75. Additional exam requirements/recommendations for international students: Required—TOEFL (minimum score 500 paper-based; 173 computer-based; 61 iBT), IELTS (minimum score 6). Electronic applications accepted. *Faculty research:* Reclamation, remediation, restoration.

University of North Dakota, Graduate School, School of Engineering and Mines, Department of Geological Engineering, Grand Forks, ND 58202. Offers M Engr, MS. *Degree requirements:* For master's, thesis. *Entrance requirements:* For master's, GRE General Test. Additional exam requirements/recommendations for international students: Required—TOEFL (minimum score 550 paper-based; 213 computer-based; 79 iBT), IELTS (minimum score 6.5). Electronic applications accepted.

University of Oklahoma, Graduate College, College of Earth and Energy, School of Petroleum and Geological Engineering, Program in Geological Engineering, Norman, OK 73019-0390. Offers MS, PhD. Part-time programs available. Postbaccalaureate distance learning degree programs offered (no on-campus study). *Students:* 3 full-time (1 woman), 1 part-time (0 women); includes 1 minority (American Indian/Alaska Native), 3 international. 5 applicants, 40% accepted, 2 enrolled. *Entrance requirements:* Additional exam requirements/recommendations for international students: Required—TOEFL (minimum score 550 paper-based; 213 computer-based). *Application deadline:* For fall admission, 6/1 for domestic students, 4/1 for international students; for spring admission, 11/1 for domestic students, 9/1 for international students. Applications are processed on a rolling basis. Application fee: $40 ($90 for international students). Electronic applications accepted. *Expenses:* Tuition, state resident: full-time $3744; part-time $156 per credit hour. Tuition, nonresident: full-time $13,577; part-time $565.70 per credit hour. Required fees: $2415; $90.10 per credit hour. *Financial support:* In 2009–10, 1 student received support. Unspecified assistantships available. *Unit head:* Dr. Chandra Rai, Director, 405-325-2921, Fax: 405-325-7477, E-mail: crai@ou.edu. *Application contact:* Dr. Dean Oliver, Professor, 405-325-0189, Fax: 405-325-7477, E-mail: dsoliver@ou.edu.

University of Utah, The Graduate School, College of Mines and Earth Sciences, Department of Geology and Geophysics, Salt Lake City, UT 84112. Offers environmental engineering (ME, MS, PhD); geological engineering (ME, MS, PhD); geology (MS, PhD); geophysics (MS, PhD). *Faculty:* 20 full-time (3 women), 5 part-time/adjunct (1 woman). *Students:* 40 full-time (16 women), 27 part-time (9 women); includes 1 minority (Hispanic American), 17 international. Average age 32. 109 applicants, 23% accepted, 17 enrolled. In 2009, 18 master's, 5 doctorates awarded. Terminal master's awarded for partial completion of doctoral program. *Degree requirements:* For master's, comprehensive exam, thesis; for doctorate, thesis/dissertation, qualifying exam (written and oral). *Entrance requirements:* For master's and doctorate, GRE General Test, minimum GPA of 3.25. Additional exam requirements/recommendations for international students: Required—TOEFL (minimum score 500 paper-based; 173 computer-based). *Application deadline:* For fall admission, 1/15 priority date for domestic and international students. Applications are processed on a rolling basis. Application fee: $55 ($65 for international students). Electronic applications accepted. *Expenses:* Tuition, state resident: full-time $4004; part-time $1674 per semester. Tuition, nonresident: full-time $14,134; part-time $5915 per semester. Required fees: $324 per semester. Tuition and fees vary according to course load, degree level and program. *Financial support:* In 2009–10, 22 students received support, including 11 fellowships with full tuition reimbursements available (averaging $13,450 per year), 45 research assistantships with full tuition reimbursements available (averaging $21,858 per year), 11 teaching assistantships with full tuition reimbursements available (averaging $13,450 per year); career-related internships or fieldwork, institutionally sponsored loans, scholarships/grants, unspecified assistantships, and stipends also available. Financial award application deadline: 1/15; financial award applicants required to submit FAFSA. *Faculty research:* Igneous, metamorphic, and sedimentary petrology; ore deposits; aqueous geochemistry; isotope geochemistry; heat flow. Total annual research expenditures: $2.2 million. *Unit head:* Dr. Marjorie A. Chan, Chair, 801-581-7162, Fax: 801-581-7065, E-mail: marjorie.chan@utah.edu. *Application contact:* Dr. Allan A. Ekdale, Director of Graduate Studies, 801-581-7266, Fax: 801-581-7065, E-mail: a.ekdale@utah.edu.

University of Wisconsin–Madison, Graduate School, College of Engineering, Geological Engineering Program, Madison, WI 53706-1380. Offers MS, PhD. Part-time programs available. *Faculty:* 17 full-time (3 women). *Students:* 5 full-time (1 woman), 4 part-time (0 women); includes 1 minority (Hispanic American), 1 international. Average age 25. 27 applicants, 74% accepted, 3 enrolled. In 2009, 2 master's awarded. *Degree requirements:* For doctorate, thesis/dissertation. *Entrance requirements:* For master's and doctorate, GRE. Additional exam requirements/recommendations for international students: Required—TOEFL (minimum score 550 paper-based; 213 computer-based; 80 iBT). *Application deadline:* For fall admission, 3/5 priority date for domestic and international students; for spring admission, 9/30 priority date for domestic and international students. Applications are processed on a rolling basis. Application fee: $56. Electronic applications accepted. *Expenses:* Tuition, state resident: part-time $594 per credit. Tuition, nonresident: part-time $1504 per credit. Required fees: $65 per credit. Tuition and fees vary according to course load, program and reciprocity agreements. *Financial support:* In 2009–10, 9 students received support, including fellowships with full tuition reimbursements available (averaging $22,224 per year), 12 research assistantships with full tuition reimbursements available (averaging $40,368 per year), 1 teaching assistantship with full tuition reimbursement available (averaging $28,175 per year); Federal Work-Study, scholarships/grants, and unspecified assistantships also available. Support available to part-time students. Financial award application deadline: 1/2. *Faculty research:* Constitute models for geomaterials, rock fracture, in situ stress determination, environmental geotechnics, site remediation. Total annual research expenditures: $1.2 million. *Unit head:* Craig H. Benson, Chair, 608-262-3491, Fax: 608-263-2453, E-mail: benson@engr.wisc.edu. *Application contact:* Marc D. Nowak, Program Coordinator, 608-265-5570, Fax: 608-890-1174, E-mail: mrnowak@wisc.edu.

Mineral/Mining Engineering

Colorado School of Mines, Graduate School, Department of Geophysics, Golden, CO 80401. Offers geophysical engineering (ME, MS, PhD); geophysics (MS, PhD); mineral exploration and mining geosciences (PMS). Part-time programs available. *Faculty:* 15 full-time (1 woman), 4 part-time/adjunct (0 women). *Students:* 67 full-time (15 women), 6 part-time (1 woman); includes 5 minority (1 American Indian/Alaska Native, 2 Asian Americans or Pacific Islanders, 2 Hispanic Americans), 40 international. Average age 30. 130 applicants, 40% accepted, 20 enrolled. In 2009, 9 master's, 6 doctorates awarded. *Degree requirements:* For master's, thesis (for some programs); for doctorate, one foreign language, comprehensive exam, thesis/dissertation, oral exams. *Entrance requirements:* For master's and doctorate, GRE General Test. Additional exam requirements/recommendations for international students: Required—TOEFL (minimum score 550 paper-based; 213 computer-based; 80 iBT). *Application deadline:* For fall admission, 1/15 for domestic and international students; for spring admission, 9/1 for domestic and international students. Application fee: $50 ($70 for international students). Electronic applications accepted. *Expenses:* Tuition, state resident: full-time $10,584; part-time $588 per credit hour. Tuition, nonresident: full-time $24,750; part-time $1375 per credit hour. Required fees: $1654; $827.10 per semester. *Financial support:* In 2009–10, 58 students received support, including 6 fellowships with full tuition reimbursements available (averaging $20,000 per year), 47 research assistantships with full tuition reimbursements available (averaging $20,000 per year), 5 teaching assistantships with full tuition reimbursements available (averaging $20,000 per year); scholarships/grants, health care benefits, and unspecified assistantships also available. Financial award application deadline: 1/15; financial award applicants required to submit FAFSA. *Faculty research:* Seismic exploration, gravity and geomagnetic fields, electrical mapping and sounding, bore hole measurements, environmental physics. Total annual research expenditures: $3.8 million. *Unit head:* Dr. Terence K. Young, Department Head, 303-273-3454, Fax: 303-273-3478, E-mail: tkyoung@mines.edu. *Application contact:* Michelle Szobody, Office Manager, 303-273-3935, Fax: 303-273-3478, E-mail: mszobody@mines.edu.

Colorado School of Mines, Graduate School, Department of Mining Engineering, Golden, CO 80401. Offers engineer of mines (ME); mining and earth systems engineering (MS). Part-time programs available. *Faculty:* 6 full-time (0 women), 6 part-time/adjunct (1 woman). *Students:* 24 full-time (4 women), 6 part-time (1 woman); includes 3 minority (1 African American, 1 Asian American or Pacific Islander, 1 Hispanic American), 14 international. Average age 27. 36 applicants, 100% accepted, 9 enrolled. In 2009, 13 master's awarded. *Degree requirements:* For master's, thesis (for some programs); for doctorate, one foreign language, comprehensive exam, thesis/dissertation. *Entrance requirements:* For master's and doctorate, GRE General Test. Additional exam requirements/recommendations for international students: Required—TOEFL (minimum score 550 paper-based; 213 computer-based; 80 iBT). *Application deadline:* For fall admission, 1/15 priority date for domestic and international students; for spring admission, 9/1 priority date for domestic and international students. Application fee: $50 ($70 for international students). Electronic applications accepted. *Expenses:* Tuition, state resident: full-time $10,584; part-time $588 per credit hour. Tuition, nonresident: full-time $24,750; part-time $1375 per credit hour. Required fees: $1654; $827.10 per semester. *Financial support:* In 2009–10, 7 students received support, including fellowships with full tuition reimbursements available (averaging $20,000 per year), 2 research assistantships with full tuition reimbursements available (averaging $20,000 per year), 5 teaching assistantships with full tuition reimbursements available (averaging $20,000 per year); scholarships/grants, health care benefits, and unspecified assistantships also available. Financial award application deadline: 1/15; financial award applicants required to submit FAFSA. *Faculty research:* Mine evaluation and planning, geostatistics, mining robotics, water jet cutting, rock mechanics. Total annual research expenditures: $528,619. *Unit head:* Dr. Kadri Dagdelen, Department Head, 303-273-3711, Fax: 303-273-3719, E-mail: kdagdele@mines.edu. *Application contact:* Christine Monroe, Administrative Assistant, 303-273-3992, Fax: 303-273-3719, E-mail: cmonroe@mines.edu.

Columbia University, Fu Foundation School of Engineering and Applied Science, Department of Earth and Environmental Engineering, New York, NY 10027. Offers earth and environmental engineering (MS, Eng Sc D, PhD); metallurgical engineering (Engr); mining engineering (Engr); MS/MBA. Part-time programs available. Postbaccalaureate distance learning degree programs offered (minimal on-campus study). *Faculty:* 7 full-time (0 women), 4 part-time/adjunct (1 woman). *Students:* 50 full-time (19 women), 20 part-time (7 women); includes 3 minority (1 African American, 1 American Indian/Alaska Native, 1 Asian American or Pacific Islander), 33 international. Average age 28. 149 applicants, 25% accepted, 18 enrolled. In 2009, 12 master's, 4 doctorates awarded. Terminal master's awarded for partial completion of doctoral program. *Degree requirements:* For master's, thesis; for doctorate, thesis/dissertation, qualifying exam. *Entrance requirements:* For master's, doctorate, and Engr, GRE General Test. Additional exam requirements/recommendations for international students: Required—TOEFL. *Application deadline:* For fall admission, 12/1 priority date for domestic and international students; for spring admission, 10/1 priority date for domestic and international students. Application fee: $70. Electronic applications accepted. *Financial support:* In 2009–10, 39 students received support, including 6 fellowships with full and partial tuition reimbursements available (averaging $16,478 per year), 26 research assistantships with full tuition reimbursements available (averaging $27,733 per year), 7 teaching assistantships with full tuition reimbursements available (averaging $22,500 per year); health care benefits and unspecified assistantships also available. Financial award application deadline: 12/1; financial award applicants required to submit FAFSA. *Faculty research:* Sustainable energy and materials, waste to energy, water resources and climate risks, environmental health engineering, life cycle analysis. *Unit head:* Dr. Klaus S. Lackner, Department Chair; Maurice Ewing and J. Lamar Worzel Professor of Geophysics, 212-854-0304, Fax: 212-854-7081, E-mail: kl2010@columbia.edu. *Application contact:* Peter Rennee, Department Administrator, 212-854-7065, Fax: 212-854-7081, E-mail: pr99@columbia.edu.

Dalhousie University, Faculty of Engineering, Department of Mineral Resource Engineering, Halifax, NS B3J 1Z1, Canada. Offers mineral resource engineering (M Eng, MA Sc, PhD). *Faculty:* 4 full-time (1 woman), 3 part-time/adjunct (0 women). *Students:* Average age 35. *Degree requirements:* For master's, thesis; for doctorate, thesis/dissertation. *Entrance requirements:* Additional exam requirements/recommendations for international students: Required—TOEFL, IELTS, CANTEST, CAEL, or Michigan English Language Assessment

Mineral/Mining Engineering

Dalhousie University (continued)

Battery. *Application deadline:* For fall admission, 6/1 for domestic students, 4/1 for international students; for winter admission, 11/30 for domestic students, 8/31 for international students; for spring admission, 2/28 for domestic students, 12/31 for international students. Applications are processed on a rolling basis. Application fee: $70. Electronic applications accepted. *Financial support:* Fellowships, research assistantships, teaching assistantships, scholarships/grants and unspecified assistantships available. *Faculty research:* Mining technology, environmental impact, petroleum engineering, mine waste management, rock mechanics. *Unit head:* Dr. Steve Zou, Head, 902-494-3954, Fax: 902-494-3108, E-mail: steve.zou@dal.ca. *Application contact:* Dr. Margaret Walsh, Graduate Coordinator, 902-494-8430, Fax: 902-494-3108, E-mail: mwalsh2@dal.ca.

Laurentian University, School of Graduate Studies and Research, Programme in Geology (Earth Sciences), Sudbury, ON P3E 2C6, Canada. Offers geology (M Sc); mineral deposits and precambrian geology (PhD); mineral exploration (M Sc). Part-time programs available. *Degree requirements:* For master's, thesis. *Entrance requirements:* For master's, honors degree with second class or better. *Faculty research:* Localization and metallogenesis of Ni-Cu-(PGE) sulfide mineralization in the Thompson Nickel Belt, mapping lithology and ore-grade and monitoring dissolved organic carbon in lakes using remote sensing, global reefs, volcanic effects on VMS deposits.

Laurentian University, School of Graduate Studies and Research, School of Engineering, Sudbury, ON P3E 2C6, Canada. Offers mineral resources engineering (M Eng, MA Sc); natural resources engineering (PhD). Part-time programs available. *Faculty research:* Mining engineering, rock mechanics (tunneling, rockbursts, rock support), metallurgy (mineral processing, hydro and pyrometallurgy), simulations and remote mining, simulations and scheduling.

McGill University, Faculty of Graduate and Postdoctoral Studies, Faculty of Engineering, Department of Mining and Materials Engineering, Montréal, QC H3A 2T5, Canada. Offers materials engineering (M Eng, PhD); mining engineering (M Eng, M Sc, PhD, Diploma).

Michigan Technological University, Graduate School, College of Engineering, Department of Geological and Mining Engineering and Sciences, Program in Mining Engineering, Houghton, MI 49931. Offers MS, PhD. Part-time programs available. Terminal master's awarded for partial completion of doctoral program. *Degree requirements:* For master's, comprehensive exam; for doctorate, comprehensive exam, thesis/dissertation. *Entrance requirements:* Additional exam requirements/recommendations for international students: Required—TOEFL (minimum score 550 paper-based; 213 computer-based). Electronic applications accepted. *Expenses:* Contact institution.

Missouri University of Science and Technology, Graduate School, Department of Mining and Nuclear Engineering, Rolla, MO 65409. Offers mining engineering (MS, DE, PhD); nuclear engineering (MS, DE, PhD). *Degree requirements:* For master's, thesis optional; for doctorate, comprehensive exam. *Entrance requirements:* For master's, GRE (minimum score 600 quantitative, 3 writing); for doctorate, GRE (minimum score: quantitative 600, writing 3.5). Additional exam requirements/recommendations for international students: Required—TOEFL (minimum score 550 paper-based; 213 computer-based). *Faculty research:* Mine health and safety, nuclear radiation transport, modeling of mining operations, radiation effects, blasting.

Montana Tech of The University of Montana, Graduate School, Metallurgical/Mineral Processing Engineering Programs, Butte, MT 59701-8997. Offers MS. Part-time programs available. *Faculty:* 5 full-time (0 women). *Students:* 6 full-time (2 women), 2 part-time (1 woman); includes 1 minority (American Indian/Alaska Native). 6 applicants, 67% accepted, 1 enrolled. In 2009, 1 master's awarded. *Degree requirements:* For master's, comprehensive exam (for some programs), thesis optional. *Entrance requirements:* For master's, GRE General Test, minimum GPA of 3.0. Additional exam requirements/recommendations for international students: Required—TOEFL (minimum score 525 paper-based; 195 computer-based; 71 iBT). *Application deadline:* For fall admission, 4/1 priority date for domestic students, 3/1 priority date for international students; for spring admission, 10/1 priority date for domestic students, 7/1 priority date for international students. Applications are processed on a rolling basis. Application fee: $30. Electronic applications accepted. *Expenses:* Tuition, state resident: full-time $5068; part-time $319 per credit. Tuition, nonresident: full-time $14,815; part-time $875 per credit. Tuition and fees vary according to course load and campus/location. *Financial support:* In 2009–10, 5 students received support, including 5 teaching assistantships with partial tuition reimbursements available (averaging $6,000 per year); research assistantships with partial tuition reimbursements available, career-related internships or fieldwork, tuition waivers (full and partial), and unspecified assistantships also available. Financial award application deadline: 4/1; financial award applicants required to submit FAFSA. *Faculty research:* Stabilizing hazardous waste, decontamination of metals by melt refining, ultraviolet enhancement of stabilization reactions, extractive metallurgy, fuel cells. *Unit head:* Dr. Courtney Young, Department Head, 406-496-4158, Fax: 406-496-4664, E-mail: cyoung@mtech.edu. *Application contact:* Cindy Dunstan, Administrator, Graduate School, 406-496-4304, Fax: 406-496-4710, E-mail: cdunstan@mtech.edu.

Montana Tech of The University of Montana, Graduate School, Mining Engineering Program, Butte, MT 59701-8997. Offers MS. Part-time programs available. *Faculty:* 6 full-time (1 woman). *Students:* 2 applicants, 50% accepted, 0 enrolled. In 2009, 1 master's awarded. *Degree requirements:* For master's, thesis optional. *Entrance requirements:* For master's, minimum GPA of 3.0. Additional exam requirements/recommendations for international students: Required—TOEFL (minimum score 525 paper-based; 195 computer-based; 71 iBT). *Application deadline:* For fall admission, 4/1 priority date for domestic students, 3/1 priority date for international students; for spring admission, 10/1 priority date for domestic students, 7/1 priority date for international students. Applications are processed on a rolling basis. Application fee: $30. Electronic applications accepted. *Expenses:* Tuition, state resident: full-time $5068; part-time $319 per credit. Tuition, nonresident: full-time $14,815; part-time $875 per credit. Tuition and fees vary according to course load and campus/location. *Financial support:* Research assistantships, teaching assistantships with partial tuition reimbursements, career-related internships or fieldwork, tuition waivers (full and partial), and unspecified assistantships available. Financial award application deadline: 4/1; financial award applicants required to submit FAFSA. *Faculty research:* Geostatistics, geomechanics, mine planning, economic models, equipment selection. *Unit head:* Dr. Diane Wolfgram, Department Head, 406-496-4353, Fax: 406-496-4260, E-mail: dwolfgram@mtech.edu. *Application contact:* Cindy Dunstan, Administrator, Graduate School, 406-496-4304, Fax: 406-496-4710, E-mail: cdunstan@mtech.edu.

New Mexico Institute of Mining and Technology, Graduate Studies, Department of Mining and Mineral Engineering, Socorro, NM 87801. Offers MS. *Degree requirements:* For master's, thesis. *Entrance requirements:* Additional exam requirements/recommendations for international students: Required—TOEFL (minimum score 540 paper-based; 207 computer-based). *Faculty research:* Drilling and blasting, geological engineering, mine design, applied mineral exploration, rock mechanics.

Queen's University at Kingston, School of Graduate Studies and Research, Faculty of Applied Science, Department of Mining Engineering, Kingston, ON K7L 3N6, Canada. Offers M Eng, M Sc, M Sc Eng, PhD. Part-time programs available. *Degree requirements:* For master's, thesis optional; for doctorate, comprehensive exam, thesis/dissertation. *Entrance requirements:* Additional exam requirements/recommendations for international students: Required—TOEFL (minimum score 550 paper-based; 213 computer-based). Electronic applications accepted. *Faculty research:* Rock mechanics, drilling, ventilation/environmental control, gold extraction.

Southern Illinois University Carbondale, Graduate School, College of Engineering, Department of Mining and Mineral Resources Engineering, Carbondale, IL 62901-4701. Offers mining engineering (MS). *Degree requirements:* For master's, comprehensive exam, thesis. *Entrance requirements:* For master's, minimum GPA of 2.7. Additional exam requirements/

recommendations for international students: Required—TOEFL. *Faculty research:* Rock mechanics and ground control, mine subsidence, mine systems analysis, fine coal cleaning, surface mine reclamation.

Université du Québec en Abitibi-Témiscamingue, Graduate Programs, Program in Engineering, Rouyn-Noranda, QC J9X 5E4, Canada. Offers engineering (ME); mineral engineering (ME); mining engineering (DESS).

Université Laval, Faculty of Sciences and Engineering, Department of Mining, Metallurgical and Materials Engineering, Programs in Mining Engineering, Québec, QC G1K 7P4, Canada. Offers M Sc, PhD. Terminal master's awarded for partial completion of doctoral program. *Degree requirements:* For master's, thesis; for doctorate, comprehensive exam, thesis/dissertation. *Entrance requirements:* For master's and doctorate, knowledge of French and English. Electronic applications accepted.

University of Alaska Fairbanks, College of Engineering and Mines, Department of Mining and Geological Engineering, Program in Mineral Preparation Engineering, Fairbanks, AK 99775. Offers MS. Part-time programs available. *Students:* 1 part-time (0 women). Average age 39. *Degree requirements:* For master's, comprehensive exam, thesis or alternative. *Entrance requirements:* For master's, GRE General Test. Additional exam requirements/recommendations for international students: Required—TOEFL (minimum score 550 paper-based; 213 computer-based; 80 iBT). *Application deadline:* For fall admission, 6/1 for domestic students, 3/1 for international students; for spring admission, 10/15 for domestic students, 9/1 for international students. Applications are processed on a rolling basis. Application fee: $60. Electronic applications accepted. *Expenses:* Tuition, state resident: full-time $7584; part-time $316 per credit. Tuition, nonresident: full-time $15,504; part-time $646 per credit. Required fees: $23 per credit. $135 per semester. Tuition and fees vary according to course level, course load and reciprocity agreements. *Financial support:* Fellowships, research assistantships, teaching assistantships, career-related internships or fieldwork, Federal Work-Study, scholarships/grants, health care benefits, and unspecified assistantships available. Support available to part-time students. Financial award application deadline: 7/1; financial award applicants required to submit FAFSA. *Faculty research:* Washability of coal, microbial mining, mineral leaching, pollution control technology, concentration of target minerals. *Unit head:* Dr. Rajive Ganguli, Department Chair, 907-474-7388, Fax: 907-474-6635, E-mail: fyminge@uaf.edu. *Application contact:* Dr. Rajive Ganguli, Department Chair, 907-474-7388, Fax: 907-474-6635, E-mail: fyminge@uaf.edu.

University of Alberta, Faculty of Graduate Studies and Research, Department of Civil and Environmental Engineering, Edmonton, AB T6G 2E1, Canada. Offers construction engineering and management (M Eng, M Sc, PhD); environmental engineering (M Eng, M Sc, PhD); environmental science (M Sc, PhD); geoenvironmental engineering (M Eng, M Sc, PhD); geotechnical engineering (M Eng, M Sc, PhD); mining engineering (M Eng, M Sc, PhD); petroleum engineering (M Eng, M Sc, PhD); structural engineering (M Eng, M Sc, PhD); water resources (M Eng, M Sc, PhD). Part-time programs available. Postbaccalaureate distance learning degree programs offered (minimal on-campus study). *Faculty:* 44 full-time (3 women), 2 part-time/adjunct (0 women). *Students:* 215 full-time (49 women), 99 part-time (19 women). 1,428 applicants, 15% accepted, 123 enrolled. In 2009, 124 master's, 34 doctorates awarded. *Degree requirements:* For master's, thesis (for some programs); for doctorate, thesis/dissertation. *Entrance requirements:* For master's, minimum GPA of 3.0 in last 2 years of undergraduate studies; for doctorate, minimum GPA of 3.0. Additional exam requirements/recommendations for international students: Required—TOEFL (minimum score 550 paper-based; 213 computer-based). *Application deadline:* For fall admission, 6/1 priority date for domestic students, 6/1 for international students; for winter admission, 11/1 for domestic students, 9/15 for international students. Applications are processed on a rolling basis. Application fee: $0 Canadian dollars. Electronic applications accepted. Tuition and fees charges are reported in Canadian dollars. *Expenses:* Tuition, area resident: Full-time $4626.24 Canadian dollars; part-time $99.72 Canadian dollars per unit. International tuition: $8216 Canadian dollars full-time. Required fees: $3589.92 Canadian dollars; $99.72 Canadian dollars per unit. $215 Canadian dollars per term. *Financial support:* In 2009–10, 88 research assistantships with full and partial tuition reimbursements, 134 teaching assistantships with full and partial tuition reimbursements were awarded; scholarships/grants and tuition waivers (full and partial) also available. Financial award application deadline: 4/1. *Faculty research:* Mining. Total annual research expenditures: $6,791 Canadian dollars. *Unit head:* Dr. David Zhu, Associate Chair, Graduate Studies, 780-492-1198, Fax: 403-492-8198. *Application contact:* Gwen Mendoza, Student Services Officer, 403-492-1539, Fax: 403-492-0249, E-mail: civegrad@ualberta.ca.

The University of Arizona, Graduate College, College of Engineering, Department of Mining, Geological and Geophysical Engineering, Program in Mining Engineering, Tucson, AZ 85721. Offers mine health and safety (Certificate); mine information and production technology (Certificate); mining engineering (M Eng); rock mechanics (Certificate). Part-time programs available. Postbaccalaureate distance learning degree programs offered (minimal on-campus study). *Students:* 1 part-time (0 women), all international. Average age 40. *Degree requirements:* For master's, thesis. *Entrance requirements:* For master's, GRE General Test, 3 letters of recommendation, statement of purpose. Additional exam requirements/recommendations for international students: Required—TOEFL (minimum score 550 paper-based; 213 computer-based; 79 iBT). *Application deadline:* For fall admission, 6/1 for domestic students, 12/1 for international students; for spring admission, 10/1 for domestic students, 6/1 for international students. Applications are processed on a rolling basis. Application fee: $75. Electronic applications accepted. *Expenses:* Tuition, state resident: full-time $9028. Tuition, nonresident: full-time $24,890. *Financial support:* Institutionally sponsored loans, scholarships/grants, health care benefits, tuition waivers (partial), and unspecified assistantships available. Financial award application deadline: 4/1. *Faculty research:* Mine system design, in-site leaching, fluid flow in rocks, geostatistics, rock mechanics. *Unit head:* Dr. Mary M. Poulton, Head, 520-621-6063, Fax: 520-621-8330, E-mail: mpoulton@u.arizona.edu. *Application contact:* Olivia Hanson, Graduate Advisor, 520-621-6063, Fax: 520-621-8330, E-mail: ohanson@engr.arizona.edu.

The University of British Columbia, Faculty of Applied Science, Program in Mining Engineering, Vancouver, BC V6T 1Z4, Canada. Offers M Eng, MA Sc, PhD. *Degree requirements:* For master's, thesis; for doctorate, thesis/dissertation. *Entrance requirements:* Additional exam requirements/recommendations for international students: Required—TOEFL (minimum score 213 computer-based; 80 iBT), IELTS. *Faculty research:* Advanced mining methods and automation, rock mechanics, mine economics, operations research, mine waste management, environmental aspects of mining, process control, fine particle processing, surface chemistry.

University of Idaho, College of Graduate Studies, College of Engineering, Department of Materials Science and Engineering, Program in Materials Science and Engineering, Moscow, ID 83844-2282. Offers materials science and engineering (PhD), including mining engineering; metallurgical engineering (MS). *Students:* 6 full-time, 1 part-time. In 2009, 5 master's, 1 doctorate awarded. *Expenses:* Tuition, state resident: full-time $6120. Tuition, nonresident: full-time $17,712. *Unit head:* Dr. Wudneh Admassu, Chair, 208-885-6376. *Application contact:* Dr. Wudneh Admassu, Chair, 208-885-6376.

University of Kentucky, Graduate School, College of Engineering, Program in Mining Engineering, Lexington, KY 40506-0032. Offers MME, MS Min, PhD. *Degree requirements:* For master's, comprehensive exam, thesis optional; for doctorate, one foreign language, comprehensive exam, thesis/dissertation. *Entrance requirements:* For master's, GRE General Test, minimum undergraduate GPA of 2.75; for doctorate, GRE General Test, minimum undergraduate GPA of 3.0. Additional exam requirements/recommendations for international students: Required—TOEFL (minimum score 550 paper-based; 213 computer-based). Electronic applications accepted. *Faculty research:* Benefication of fine and ultrafine particles, operation research in mining and mineral processing, land reclamation.

University of Nevada, Reno, Graduate School, College of Science, Mackay School of Earth Sciences and Engineering, Department of Mining Engineering, Reno, NV 89557. Offers MS. *Degree requirements:* For master's, thesis optional. *Entrance requirements:* For master's, GRE, minimum GPA of 2.75. Additional exam requirements/recommendations for international students: Required—TOEFL (minimum score 500 paper-based; 173 computer-based; 61 iBT), IELTS (minimum score 6). Electronic applications accepted. *Faculty research:* Mine ventilation, rock mechanics, mine design.

University of North Dakota, Graduate School, School of Engineering and Mines, Department of Civil Engineering, Grand Forks, ND 58202. Offers civil engineering (M Engr); sanitary engineering (M Engr), including soils and structures engineering, surface mining engineering. Part-time programs available. *Degree requirements:* For master's, comprehensive exam, thesis or alternative. *Entrance requirements:* For master's, GRE General Test, minimum GPA of 2.5. Additional exam requirements/recommendations for international students: Required—TOEFL (minimum score 550 paper-based; 213 computer-based; 79 iBT), IELTS (minimum score 6.5). Electronic applications accepted. *Faculty research:* Soil-structures, environmental-water resources.

The University of Texas at Austin, Graduate School, Cockrell School of Engineering, Department of Petroleum and Geosystems Engineering, Program in Energy and Earth Resources, Austin, TX 78712-1111. Offers MA. *Degree requirements:* For master's, thesis, seminar. *Entrance requirements:* For master's, GRE General Test. Additional exam requirements/recommendations for international students: Required—TOEFL. Electronic applications accepted.

University of Utah, The Graduate School, College of Mines and Earth Sciences, Department of Mining Engineering, Salt Lake City, UT 84112. Offers ME, MS, PhD. Part-time programs available. *Faculty:* 5 full-time (0 women). *Students:* 4 full-time (0 women), 3 part-time (0 women); includes 1 minority (Asian American or Pacific Islander), 3 international. Average age 36. 12 applicants, 25% accepted, 1 enrolled. In 2009, 2 master's awarded. *Degree requirements:* For master's, comprehensive exam (ME), thesis (MS); for doctorate, one foreign language, thesis/dissertation. *Entrance requirements:* For master's, GRE General Test (nonresidents only), minimum undergraduate GPA of 3.0; for doctorate, GRE General Test. Additional exam

requirements/recommendations for international students: Required—TOEFL (minimum score 550 paper-based; 173 computer-based; 60 iBT). *Application deadline:* For fall admission, 4/1 for domestic and international students; for spring admission, 11/1 priority date for domestic students, 11/1 for international students. Application fee: $55 ($65 for international students). Electronic applications accepted. *Expenses:* Tuition, state resident: full-time $4004; part-time $1674 per semester. Tuition, nonresident: full-time $14,134; part-time $5915 per semester. Required fees: $324 per semester. Tuition and fees vary according to course load, degree level and program. *Financial support:* In 2009–10, 3 students received support, including fellowships with tuition reimbursements available (averaging $16,000 per year), research assistantships with tuition reimbursements available (averaging $17,000 per year); teaching assistantships, career-related internships or fieldwork and institutionally sponsored loans also available. Support available to part-time students. Financial award application deadline: 2/15. *Faculty research:* Blasting, underground coal mine design and operations, rock mechanics, mine ventilation, 2-D and 3-D visualization, mine automation, mine safety. Total annual research expenditures: $477,156. *Unit head:* Dr. Michael Gordon Nelson, Chair, 801-585-3064, Fax: 801-585-5410, E-mail: nelsonelson@aol.com. *Application contact:* Pam Hofmann, Administrative Assistant, 801-581-7198, Fax: 801-585-5410, E-mail: pamhofmann@utah.edu.

Virginia Polytechnic Institute and State University, Graduate School, College of Engineering, Department of Mining and Minerals Engineering, Blacksburg, VA 24061. Offers M Eng, MS, PhD. *Entrance requirements:* For master's and doctorate, GRE. Additional exam requirements/recommendations for international students: Required—TOEFL (minimum score 550 paper-based; 213 computer-based). Electronic applications accepted. *Faculty research:* Sensor development, slope stability, rock fracture, mechanics, ground control, environmental remediation.

West Virginia University, College of Engineering and Mineral Resources, Department of Mining Engineering, Morgantown, WV 26506. Offers MS Min E, PhD. Part-time programs available. *Degree requirements:* For master's, thesis; for doctorate, comprehensive exam, thesis/dissertation. *Entrance requirements:* For master's, minimum GPA of 3.0; for doctorate, GRE General Test, MS in mineral engineering, minimum GPA of 3.5. Additional exam requirements/recommendations for international students: Required—TOEFL. *Faculty research:* Mine safety.

Petroleum Engineering

Colorado School of Mines, Graduate School, Department of Petroleum Engineering, Golden, CO 80401. Offers petroleum engineering (ME, MS, PhD); petroleum reservoir systems (PMS). Part-time programs available. *Faculty:* 13 full-time (4 women), 4 part-time/adjunct (1 woman). *Students:* 70 full-time (18 women), 4 part-time (0 women); includes 1 minority (African American), 53 international. Average age 29. 184 applicants, 45% accepted, 15 enrolled. In 2009, 23 master's, 1 doctorate awarded. *Degree requirements:* For master's, thesis (for some programs); for doctorate, one foreign language, comprehensive exam, thesis/dissertation. *Entrance requirements:* For master's and doctorate, GRE General Test. Additional exam requirements/recommendations for international students: Required—TOEFL (minimum score 550 paper-based; 213 computer-based; 80 iBT). *Application deadline:* For fall admission, 1/15 priority date for domestic and international students; for spring admission, 9/1 priority date for domestic and international students. Application fee: $50 ($70 for international students). Electronic applications accepted. *Expenses:* Tuition, state resident: full-time $10,584; part-time $588 per credit hour. Tuition, nonresident: full-time $24,750; part-time $1375 per credit hour. Required fees: $1654; $827.10 per semester. *Financial support:* In 2009–10, 36 students received support, including 3 fellowships with full tuition reimbursements available (averaging $20,000 per year), 19 research assistantships with full tuition reimbursements available (averaging $20,000 per year), 14 teaching assistantships with full tuition reimbursements available (averaging $20,000 per year); career-related internships or fieldwork, scholarships/grants, health care benefits, and unspecified assistantships also available. Financial award application deadline: 1/15; financial award applicants required to submit FAFSA. *Faculty research:* Dynamic rock mechanics, deflagration theory, geostatistics, geochemistry, petrophysics. Total annual research expenditures: $1 million. *Unit head:* Dr. Ramona Graves, Department Head, 303-273-3746, Fax: 303-273-3189, E-mail: rgraves@mines.edu. *Application contact:* Denise Winn-Bower, Administrative Assistant, 303-273-3740, Fax: 303-273-3189, E-mail: dwinnbow@mines.edu.

Louisiana State University and Agricultural and Mechanical College, Graduate School, College of Engineering, Department of Petroleum Engineering, Baton Rouge, LA 70803. Offers MS Pet E, PhD. *Faculty:* 9 full-time (1 woman). *Students:* 36 full-time (7 women), 5 part-time (1 woman); includes 1 minority (African American), 37 international. Average age 28. 224 applicants, 7% accepted, 9 enrolled. In 2009, 8 master's, 1 doctorate awarded. *Degree requirements:* For master's, thesis or alternative; for doctorate, thesis/dissertation, exam. *Entrance requirements:* For master's and doctorate, GRE General Test, minimum GPA of 3.0. Additional exam requirements/recommendations for international students: Required—TOEFL (minimum score 550 paper-based; 213 computer-based; 79 iBT) or IELTS (minimum score 6.5). *Application deadline:* For fall admission, 1/25 priority date for domestic students, 5/15 for international students; for spring admission, 10/15 for international students. Applications are processed on a rolling basis. Application fee: $50 ($70 for international students). Electronic applications accepted. *Financial support:* In 2009–10, 33 students received support, including 29 research assistantships with full and partial tuition reimbursements available (averaging $13,327 per year), 1 teaching assistantship with full and partial tuition reimbursement available (averaging $5,750 per year); fellowships, Federal Work-Study, institutionally sponsored loans, health care benefits, and unspecified assistantships also available. Financial award applicants required to submit FAFSA. *Faculty research:* Rock properties, well logging, production engineering, drilling, reservoir engineering. Total annual research expenditures: $945,635. *Unit head:* Dr. Stephen O. Sears, Chair, 225-578-6055, Fax: 225-578-6039, E-mail: sosears@lsu.edu. *Application contact:* Dr. Andrew Wojtanowicz, Graduate Adviser, 225-578-6049, Fax: 225-578-6039, E-mail: awojtan@lsu.edu.

Missouri University of Science and Technology, Graduate School, Department of Geological Sciences and Engineering, Rolla, MO 65409. Offers geological engineering (MS, DE, PhD); geology and geophysics (MS, PhD), including geochemistry, geology, geophysics, groundwater and environmental geology; petroleum engineering (MS, DE, PhD). Part-time programs available. *Degree requirements:* For master's, thesis optional; for doctorate, comprehensive exam, thesis/dissertation. *Entrance requirements:* For master's, GRE General Test (minimum score 600 quantitative, writing 3.5), minimum GPA of 3.0 in last 4 semesters; for doctorate, GRE General Test (minimum: Q 600, GRE WR 3.5). Additional exam requirements/recommendations for international students: Required—TOEFL. Electronic applications accepted. *Faculty research:* Digital image processing and geographic information systems, mineralogy, igneous and sedimentary petrology-geochemistry, sedimentology groundwater hydrology and contaminant transport.

Montana Tech of The University of Montana, Graduate School, Department of Petroleum Engineering, Butte, MT 59701-8997. Offers MS. Part-time and evening/weekend programs available. *Faculty:* 6 full-time (2 women), 1 part-time/adjunct (0 women). *Students:* 5 full-time (0 women), 1 part-time (0 women); includes 2 minority (both African Americans), 1 international. 34 applicants, 3% accepted, 0 enrolled. In 2009, 6 master's awarded. *Degree requirements:* For master's, thesis optional. *Entrance requirements:* For master's, minimum GPA of 3.0. Additional exam requirements/recommendations for international students: Required—TOEFL

(minimum score 525 paper-based; 195 computer-based; 71 iBT). *Application deadline:* For fall admission, 4/1 priority date for domestic students, 3/1 priority date for international students; for spring admission, 10/1 priority date for domestic students, 7/1 priority date for international students. Applications are processed on a rolling basis. Application fee: $30. Electronic applications accepted. *Expenses:* Tuition, state resident: full-time $5068; part-time $319 per credit. Tuition, nonresident: full-time $14,815; part-time $875 per credit. Tuition and fees vary according to course load and campus/location. *Financial support:* In 2009–10, 6 students received support, including 5 teaching assistantships with partial tuition reimbursements available (averaging $6,000 per year); research assistantships, career-related internships or fieldwork, institutionally sponsored loans, and tuition waivers (full and partial) also available. Financial award application deadline: 4/1; financial award applicants required to submit FAFSA. *Faculty research:* Reservoir characterization, simulations, near well bore problems, PVT, environmental waste. *Unit head:* Leo Heath, Head, 406-496-4507, Fax: 406-496-4417, E-mail: lheath@mtech.edu. *Application contact:* Cindy Dunstan, Administrator, Graduate School, 406-496-4304, Fax: 406-496-4710, E-mail: cdunstan@mtech.edu.

New Mexico Institute of Mining and Technology, Graduate Studies, Program in Petroleum Engineering, Socorro, NM 87801. Offers MS, PhD. *Degree requirements:* For master's, thesis optional; for doctorate, thesis/dissertation. *Entrance requirements:* For master's, GRE General Test; for doctorate, GRE General Test, GRE Subject Test. Additional exam requirements/recommendations for international students: Required—TOEFL (minimum score 540 paper-based; 207 computer-based). *Faculty research:* Enhanced recovery processes, drilling and production, reservoir evaluation, produced water management, wettability and phase behavior.

Stanford University, School of Earth Sciences, Department of Petroleum Engineering, Stanford, CA 94305-9991. Offers MS, PhD, Eng. Terminal master's awarded for partial completion of doctoral program. *Degree requirements:* For doctorate, thesis/dissertation; for Eng, thesis. *Entrance requirements:* For master's, doctorate, and Eng, GRE General Test. Additional exam requirements/recommendations for international students: Required—TOEFL. Electronic applications accepted. *Expenses:* Tuition: Full-time $37,380; part-time $2760 per quarter. Required fees: $501.

Texas A&M University, College of Engineering, Harold Vance Department of Petroleum Engineering, College Station, TX 77843. Offers M Eng, MS, PhD. Part-time programs available. Postbaccalaureate distance learning degree programs offered (no on-campus study). *Faculty:* 26. *Students:* 220 full-time (39 women), 73 part-time (16 women); includes 29 minority (7 African Americans, 12 Asian Americans or Pacific Islanders, 10 Hispanic Americans), 213 international. Average age 25. In 2009, 50 master's, 18 doctorates awarded. *Degree requirements:* For master's, comprehensive exam, thesis (MS); for doctorate, comprehensive exam, thesis/dissertation. *Entrance requirements:* For master's and doctorate, GRE General Test. Additional exam requirements/recommendations for international students: Required—TOEFL (minimum score 550 paper-based; 213 computer-based). *Application deadline:* Applications are processed on a rolling basis. Application fee: $50 ($75 for international students). Electronic applications accepted. *Expenses:* Tuition, state resident: full-time $3991.32; part-time $221.74 per credit hour. Tuition, nonresident: full-time $9049; part-time $502.74 per credit hour. *Financial support:* In 2009–10, fellowships (averaging $1,000 per year), research assistantships (averaging $15,000 per year), teaching assistantships (averaging $15,000 per year) were awarded; career-related internships or fieldwork and tuition waivers (partial) also available. Financial award application deadline: 3/1; financial award applicants required to submit FAFSA. *Faculty research:* Drilling and well stimulation, well completions and well performance, reservoir modeling and reservoir description, reservoir simulation, improved/enhanced recovery. *Unit head:* Dr. Daulat Mamora, Head, 979-845-2255, E-mail: daulat.mamora@pe.tamu.edu. *Application contact:* Dr. Thomas A. Blasingame, Graduate Advisor, 979-847-9095, Fax: 979-845-1307, E-mail: t-blasingame@tamu.edu.

Texas A&M University–Kingsville, College of Graduate Studies, College of Engineering, Department of Chemical Engineering and Natural Gas Engineering, Program in Natural Gas Engineering, Kingsville, TX 78363. Offers ME, MS. *Degree requirements:* For master's, comprehensive exam, thesis or alternative. *Entrance requirements:* For master's, GRE General Test, minimum GPA of 3.0. Additional exam requirements/recommendations for international students: Required—TOEFL. *Faculty research:* Gas processing, coal gasification and liquefaction, enhanced oil recovery, gas measurement, unconventional gas recovery.

Texas Tech University, Graduate School, College of Engineering, Department of Petroleum Engineering, Lubbock, TX 79409. Offers MSPE, PhD. Part-time programs available. *Faculty:* 5 full-time (1 woman). *Students:* 25 full-time (1 woman), 4 part-time (1 woman), 26 international. Average age 30. 198 applicants, 21% accepted, 8 enrolled. In 2009, 3 master's awarded. *Degree requirements:* For master's, thesis or alternative; for doctorate, thesis/dissertation. *Entrance requirements:* For master's, GRE General Test, minimum GPA of 3.0. Additional exam requirements/recommendations for international students: Required—TOEFL (minimum

Petroleum Engineering

Texas Tech University (continued)
score 550 paper-based; 213 computer-based). *Application deadline:* For fall admission, 3/1 priority date for international students; for spring admission, 11/1 priority date for international students. Applications are processed on a rolling basis. Application fee: $50 ($75 for international students). Electronic applications accepted. *Expenses:* Tuition, state resident: full-time $5100; part-time $213 per credit hour. Tuition, nonresident: full-time $11,748; part-time $490 per credit hour. Required fees: $2298; $50 per credit hour. $555 per semester. *Financial support:* In 2009–10, 4 teaching assistantships with partial tuition reimbursements (averaging $12,000 per year) were awarded; research assistantships with partial tuition reimbursements, career-related internships or fieldwork, Federal Work-Study, and institutionally sponsored loans also available. Support available to part-time students. Financial award application deadline: 4/15; financial award applicants required to submit FAFSA. *Faculty research:* New artificial lift optimization, fatigue failure in tubular, pore to reservoir scale porous media model, transport and thermodynamic fluid property measurements, geologic carbon dioxide storage in gas hydrate and reservoir. Total annual research expenditures: $119,412. *Unit head:* Dr. Lloyd R. Heinze, Chair, 806-742-3573, Fax: 806-742-3502, E-mail: lloyd.heinze@ttu.edu. *Application contact:* Jamie L. Perez, Advisor, 806-742-3573 Ext. 223, Fax: 806-742-3502, E-mail: jamie.l.perez@ttu.edu.

University of Alaska Fairbanks, College of Engineering and Mines, Department of Petroleum Engineering, Fairbanks, AK 99775. Offers MS, PhD. Part-time programs available. *Students:* 20 full-time (3 women), 8 part-time (3 women); includes 1 minority (Asian American or Pacific Islander), 18 international. Average age 28. 45 applicants, 38% accepted, 10 enrolled. In 2009, 10 master's awarded. *Degree requirements:* For master's, comprehensive exam, thesis or alternative; for doctorate, comprehensive exam, thesis/dissertation, oral exam, oral defense. *Entrance requirements:* For doctorate, GRE General Test. Additional exam requirements/recommendations for international students: Required—TOEFL (minimum score 550 paper-based; 213 computer-based; 80 iBT). *Application deadline:* For fall admission, 6/1 for domestic students, 3/1 for international students; for spring admission, 10/15 for domestic students, 9/1 for international students. Applications are processed on a rolling basis. Application fee: $60. Electronic applications accepted. *Expenses:* Tuition, state resident: full-time $7584; part-time $316 per credit. Tuition, nonresident: full-time $15,504; part-time $646 per credit. Required fees: $23 per credit. $135 per semester. Tuition and fees vary according to course level, course load and reciprocity agreements. *Financial support:* In 2009–10, 1 fellowship (averaging $13,500 per year), 8 research assistantships (averaging $9,281 per year), 5 teaching assistantships (averaging $8,487 per year) were awarded; career-related internships or fieldwork, Federal Work-Study, scholarships/grants, health care benefits, and unspecified assistantships also available. Support available to part-time students. Financial award application deadline: 7/1; financial award applicants required to submit FAFSA. *Faculty research:* Gas-to-liquid transportation hydraulics and issues, carbon sequestration, enhanced oil recovery, reservoir engineering, coalbed methane. *Unit head:* Dr. Catherine Hanks, Chair, 907-474-7734, Fax: 907-474-5912, E-mail: fyipete@uaf.edu. *Application contact:* Dr. Catherine Hanks, Chair, 907-474-7734, Fax: 907-474-5912, E-mail: fyipete@uaf.edu.

University of Alberta, Faculty of Graduate Studies and Research, Department of Civil and Environmental Engineering, Edmonton, AB T6G 2E1, Canada. Offers construction engineering and management (M Eng, M Sc, PhD); environmental engineering (M Eng, M Sc, PhD); environmental science (M Sc, PhD); geoenvironmental engineering (M Eng, M Sc, PhD); geotechnical engineering (M Eng, M Sc, PhD); mining engineering (M Eng, M Sc, PhD); petroleum engineering (M Eng, M Sc, PhD); structural engineering (M Eng, M Sc, PhD); water resources (M Eng, M Sc, PhD). Part-time programs available. Postbaccalaureate distance learning degree programs offered (minimal on-campus study). *Faculty:* 44 full-time (3 women), 2 part-time/adjunct (0 women). *Students:* 215 full-time (49 women), 99 part-time (19 women). 1,428 applicants, 15% accepted, 123 enrolled. In 2009, 124 master's, 34 doctorates awarded. *Degree requirements:* For master's, thesis (for some programs); for doctorate, thesis/dissertation. *Entrance requirements:* For master's, minimum GPA of 3.0 in last 2 years of undergraduate studies; for doctorate, minimum GPA of 3.0. Additional exam requirements/recommendations for international students: Required—TOEFL (minimum score 550 paper-based; 213 computer-based). *Application deadline:* For fall admission, 6/1 priority date for domestic students, 6/1 for international students; for winter admission, 11/1 for domestic students, 9/15 for international students. Applications are processed on a rolling basis. Application fee: $0 Canadian dollars. Electronic applications accepted. Tuition and fees charges are reported in Canadian dollars. *Expenses:* Tuition, area resident: Full-time $4626.24 Canadian dollars; part-time $99.72 Canadian dollars per unit. International tuition: $8216 Canadian dollars full-time. Required fees: $3589.92 Canadian dollars; $99.72 Canadian dollars per unit. $215 Canadian dollars per term. *Financial support:* In 2009–10, 88 research assistantships with full and partial tuition reimbursements, 134 teaching assistantships with full and partial tuition reimbursements were awarded; scholarships/grants and tuition waivers (full and partial) also available. Financial award application deadline: 4/1. *Faculty research:* Mining. Total annual research expenditures: $6,791 Canadian dollars. *Unit head:* Dr. David Zhu, Associate Chair, Graduate Studies, 780-492-1198, Fax: 403-492-8198. *Application contact:* Gwen Mendoza, Student Services Officer, 403-492-1539, Fax: 403-492-0249, E-mail: civegrad@ualberta.ca.

University of Calgary, Faculty of Graduate Studies, Schulich School of Engineering, Department of Chemical and Petroleum Engineering, Calgary, AB T2N 1N4, Canada. Offers M Eng, M Sc, PhD. Part-time programs available. *Degree requirements:* For master's, thesis (for some programs); for doctorate, comprehensive exam, thesis/dissertation, candidacy exam. *Entrance requirements:* For master's, minimum GPA of 3.0; for doctorate, minimum GPA of 3.5. Additional exam requirements/recommendations for international students: Required—TOEFL (minimum score 550 paper-based; 213 computer-based; 80 iBT), IELTS (minimum score 7). Electronic applications accepted. *Faculty research:* Environmental engineering, biomedical engineering modeling, simulation and control, petroleum recovery and reservoir engineering, phase equilibria and transport properties.

The University of Kansas, Graduate Studies, School of Engineering, Department of Chemical and Petroleum Engineering, Lawrence, KS 66045. Offers chemical engineering (MS); chemical/petroleum engineering (PhD); petroleum engineering (MS). Part-time programs available. *Faculty:* 15 full-time (3 women). *Students:* 55 full-time (25 women); includes 2 minority (1 Asian American or Pacific Islander, 1 Hispanic American), 41 international. Average age 28. 70 applicants, 30% accepted, 16 enrolled. In 2009, 6 master's, 7 doctorates awarded. *Degree requirements:* For master's, thesis (for some programs), exam; for doctorate, comprehensive exam, thesis/dissertation, qualifying exams. *Entrance requirements:* For master's, GRE General Test, minimum GPA of 3.0; for doctorate, GRE General Test, minimum GPA of 3.5. Additional exam requirements/recommendations for international students: Required—TOEFL. *Application deadline:* For fall admission, 1/10 priority date for domestic students, 1/10 for international students; for spring admission, 6/10 priority date for domestic students, 6/10 for international students. Applications are processed on a rolling basis. Application fee: $45 ($55 for international students). Electronic applications accepted. *Expenses:* Tuition, state resident: full-time $6492; part-time $270.50 per credit hour. Tuition, nonresident: full-time $15,510; part-time $646.25 per credit hour. Required fees: $847; $70.56 per credit hour. Tuition and fees vary according to course load and program. *Financial support:* Fellowships, research assistantships with full and partial tuition reimbursements, teaching assistantships with full and partial tuition reimbursements, career-related internships or fieldwork, Federal Work-Study, scholarships/grants, traineeships, and unspecified assistantships available. Financial award application deadline: 1/31; financial award applicants required to submit FAFSA. *Faculty research:* Enhanced oil recovery, catalysis and kinetics, electrochemical engineering, biomedical engineering, semiconductor materials processing. *Unit head:* Prof. Laurence Weatherley, Chairperson, 785-864-4965, Fax: 785-864-4967, E-mail: lweather@ku.edu. *Application contact:* Prof. Marylee Southard, Graduate Recruiting Officer, 785-864-4965, Fax: 785-864-4967, E-mail: marylee@ku.edu.

University of Louisiana at Lafayette, College of Engineering, Department of Petroleum Engineering, Lafayette, LA 70504. Offers MSE. Evening/weekend programs available. *Degree requirements:* For master's, comprehensive exam, thesis or alternative. *Entrance requirements:* For master's, GRE General Test, minimum GPA of 2.85. Electronic applications accepted.

University of Oklahoma, Graduate College, College of Earth and Energy, School of Petroleum and Geological Engineering, Program in Petroleum Engineering, Norman, OK 73019-0390. Offers natural gas engineering (MS); petroleum engineering (MS, PhD). Part-time programs available. Postbaccalaureate distance learning degree programs offered (minimal on-campus study). *Students:* 74 full-time (15 women), 13 part-time (1 woman); includes 4 minority (1 African American, 2 Asian Americans or Pacific Islanders, 1 Hispanic American), 73 international. 103 applicants, 25% accepted, 19 enrolled. In 2009, 11 master's, 2 doctorates awarded. Terminal master's awarded for partial completion of doctoral program. *Degree requirements:* For master's, thesis optional, industrial team project or thesis; for doctorate, thesis/dissertation. *Entrance requirements:* For master's, GRE General Test, bachelor's degree in engineering, 3 letters of recommendation, minimum GPA of 3.0 during final 60 hours of undergraduate course work; for doctorate, GRE General Test, minimum GPA of 3.0, 3 letters of recommendation. Additional exam requirements/recommendations for international students: Required—TOEFL (minimum score 550 paper-based; 213 computer-based). *Application deadline:* For fall admission, 6/1 priority date for domestic students, 4/1 for international students; for spring admission, 11/1 for domestic students, 9/1 for international students. Applications are processed on a rolling basis. Application fee: $40 ($90 for international students). Electronic applications accepted. *Expenses:* Tuition, state resident: full-time $3744; part-time $156 per credit hour. Tuition, nonresident: full-time $13,577; part-time $565.70 per credit hour. Required fees: $2415; $90.10 per credit hour. *Financial support:* In 2009–10, 67 students received support. Career-related internships or fieldwork, health care benefits, and unspecified assistantships available. Financial award application deadline: 4/15; financial award applicants required to submit FAFSA. *Faculty research:* Petrophysics, history watching, well-bore stimulation, unconventional reservoirs. *Unit head:* Dr. Chandra Rai, Director, 405-325-2921, Fax: 405-325-7477, E-mail: crai@ou.edu. *Application contact:* Dr. Dean Oliver, Professor, 405-325-0189, Fax: 405-325-7477, E-mail: dsoliver@ou.edu.

University of Pittsburgh, School of Engineering, Department of Chemical and Petroleum Engineering, Pittsburgh, PA 15260. Offers chemical engineering (MS Ch E, PhD); petroleum engineering (MSPE); MS Ch E/MSPE. Part-time programs available. Postbaccalaureate distance learning degree programs offered. *Faculty:* 16 full-time (2 women), 25 part-time/adjunct (4 women). *Students:* 41 full-time (9 women), 6 part-time (2 women); includes 4 minority (2 Asian Americans or Pacific Islanders, 2 Hispanic Americans), 25 international. 171 applicants, 12% accepted, 5 enrolled. In 2009, 2 master's, 4 doctorates awarded. *Degree requirements:* For master's, thesis; for doctorate, comprehensive exam, thesis/dissertation, final oral exams. *Entrance requirements:* For master's and doctorate, GRE General Test, minimum QPA of 3.2. Additional exam requirements/recommendations for international students: Required—TOEFL (minimum score 550 paper-based; 213 computer-based; 80 iBT). *Application deadline:* For fall admission, 3/1 priority date for domestic students; for spring admission, 7/1 priority date for domestic students. Applications are processed on a rolling basis. Application fee: $50. Electronic applications accepted. *Expenses:* Tuition, state resident: full-time $16,402; part-time $665 per credit. Tuition, nonresident: full-time $28,694; part-time $1175 per credit. Required fees: $690; $175 per term. Tuition and fees vary according to program. *Financial support:* In 2009–10, 38 students received support, including 1 fellowship with full tuition reimbursement available (averaging $20,772 per year), 26 research assistantships with full tuition reimbursements available (averaging $24,000 per year), 6 teaching assistantships with full tuition reimbursements available (averaging $22,000 per year); scholarships/grants, traineeships, and tuition waivers (full and partial) also available. Financial award application deadline: 4/15. *Faculty research:* Biotechnology, polymers, catalysis, energy and environment, computational modeling. Total annual research expenditures: $5.1 million. *Unit head:* Dr. J. Karl Johnson, Chairman, 412-624-5644, Fax: 412-624-9639, E-mail: johnson@engr.pitt.edu. *Application contact:* William Federspiel, Associate Professor and Graduate Coordinator, 412-624-9499, Fax: 412-624-9639, E-mail: federspiel@engrng.pitt.edu.

University of Regina, Faculty of Graduate Studies and Research, Faculty of Engineering and Applied Science, Program in Petroleum Systems Engineering, Regina, SK S4S 0A2, Canada. Offers M Eng, MA Sc, PhD. *Faculty:* 5 full-time (0 women). *Students:* 27 full-time (3 women), 4 part-time (1 woman). 84 applicants, 35% accepted. In 2009, 2 master's, 2 doctorates awarded. *Entrance requirements:* Additional exam requirements/recommendations for international students: Required—TOEFL (minimum score 580 paper-based; 237 computer-based; 80 iBT). Application fee: $90 ($100 for international students). *Financial support:* In 2009–10, 6 fellowships (averaging $19,000 per year), 3 research assistantships (averaging $16,910 per year), 9 teaching assistantships (averaging $6,650 per year) were awarded. *Unit head:* Dr. Farshid Torabi, Graduate Program Coordinator, 306-337-3287, E-mail: farshid.torabi@uregina.ca. *Application contact:* Crystal Pick, Graduate Program Coordinator, 306-337-3603, E-mail: crystal.pick@uregina.ca.

University of Southern California, Graduate School, Viterbi School of Engineering, Mork Family Department of Chemical Engineering and Materials Science, Los Angeles, CA 90089. Offers chemical engineering (MS, PhD, Engr); materials science (MS, PhD, Engr); petroleum engineering (MS, PhD, Engr); smart oilifield technologies (MS, Graduate Certificate). Part-time programs available. Postbaccalaureate distance learning degree programs offered (no on-campus study). *Faculty:* 17 full-time (3 women), 14 part-time/adjunct (1 woman). *Students:* 182 full-time (63 women), 70 part-time (23 women); includes 33 minority (8 African Americans, 18 Asian Americans or Pacific Islanders, 7 Hispanic Americans), 170 international. 443 applicants, 37% accepted, 72 enrolled. In 2009, 37 master's, 19 doctorates, 4 other advanced degrees awarded. Terminal master's awarded for partial completion of doctoral program. *Degree requirements:* For doctorate, thesis/dissertation. *Entrance requirements:* For master's, GRE General Test; for doctorate, General GRE. *Application deadline:* For fall admission, 3/1 priority date for domestic and international students; for spring admission, 10/1 priority date for domestic and international students. Applications are processed on a rolling basis. Application fee: $85. Electronic applications accepted. *Expenses:* Contact institution. *Financial support:* In 2009–10, 12 fellowships with full tuition reimbursements (averaging $30,000 per year), 70 research assistantships with full tuition reimbursements (averaging $19,250 per year), 29 teaching assistantships with full tuition reimbursements (averaging $19,250 per year) were awarded; career-related internships or fieldwork, scholarships/grants, health care benefits, and unspecified assistantships also available. Financial award application deadline: 12/1; financial award applicants required to submit CSS PROFILE or FAFSA. *Faculty research:* Heterogeneous materials and porous media, statistical mechanics, molecular simulation, polymer science and engineering, advanced materials, reaction engineering and catalysis, membrane processes and separation, biochemical engineering, cell culture, bioreactor modeling, petroleum engineering. Total annual research expenditures: $8.8 million. *Unit head:* Dr. Theodore Tsotsis, Chair, 213-740-2069, Fax: 213-740-8053, E-mail: tsotsis@usc.edu. *Application contact:* Petra P. Sapir, Student Service Advisor, 213-740-6011, Fax: 213-740-7797, E-mail: ppearce@usc.edu.

The University of Texas at Austin, Graduate School, Cockrell School of Engineering, Department of Petroleum and Geosystems Engineering, Austin, TX 78712-1111. Offers energy and earth resources (MA); petroleum engineering (MS, PhD). Evening/weekend programs available. Postbaccalaureate distance learning degree programs offered (no on-campus study). *Entrance requirements:* For master's and doctorate, GRE General Test. Electronic applications accepted.

University of Tulsa, Graduate School, College of Engineering and Natural Sciences, Department of Petroleum Engineering, Tulsa, OK 74104-3189. Offers ME, MSE, PhD. Part-time programs available. *Faculty:* 11 full-time (0 women). *Students:* 71 full-time (11 women), 14 part-time (2 women), 81 international. Average age 27. 252 applicants, 25% accepted, 22 enrolled. In 2009, 10 master's, 4 doctorates awarded. *Degree requirements:* For master's, thesis (MSE); for doctorate, one foreign language, comprehensive exam, thesis/dissertation. *Entrance requirements:* For master's and doctorate, GRE General Test. Additional exam requirements/

recommendations for international students: Required—TOEFL (minimum score 550 paper-based; 213 computer-based; 80 iBT), IELTS (minimum score 6). *Application deadline:* Applications are processed on a rolling basis. Application fee: $40. Electronic applications accepted. *Expenses:* Tuition: Full-time $16,182; part-time $899 per credit hour. Required fees: $4 per credit hour. Tuition and fees vary according to course load. *Financial support:* In 2009–10, 55 students received support, including 8 fellowships with partial tuition reimbursements available (averaging $4,526 per year), 45 research assistantships with full and partial tuition reimbursements available (averaging $11,948 per year), 8 teaching assistantships with full and partial tuition reimbursements available (averaging $11,126 per year); career-related internships or fieldwork, Federal Work-Study, scholarships/grants, health care benefits, tuition waivers (full and partial), and unspecified assistantships also available. Support available to part-time students. Financial award application deadline: 2/1; financial award applicants required to submit FAFSA. *Faculty research:* Artificial lift, drilling, multiphase flow in pipes, separation technology, horizontal well technology, reservoir characterization, well testing, reservoir simulation, and unconventional natural gas. Total annual research expenditures: $7.2 million. *Unit head:* Dr. Mohan Kelkar, Chairperson, 918-631-3036, Fax: 915-631-2059, E-mail: mohan@utulsa.edu. *Application contact:* Dr. Jagan Mahadevan, Adviser, 918-631-3906, Fax: 918-631-5142, E-mail: jmahadevan@utulsa.edu.

University of Wyoming, College of Engineering and Applied Sciences, Department of Chemical and Petroleum Engineering, Program in Petroleum Engineering, Laramie, WY 82070. Offers MS, PhD. Part-time programs available. Terminal master's awarded for partial completion of doctoral program. *Degree requirements:* For master's, thesis; for doctorate, thesis/dissertation. *Entrance requirements:* For master's and doctorate, GRE General Test, minimum GPA of 3.0. Additional exam requirements/recommendations for international students: Required—TOEFL (minimum score 600 paper-based; 250 computer-based). Electronic applications accepted. *Faculty research:* Oil recovery methods, oil production, coal bed methane.

West Virginia University, College of Engineering and Mineral Resources, Department of Petroleum and Natural Gas Engineering, Morgantown, WV 26506. Offers MSPNGE, PhD. Part-time programs available. *Degree requirements:* For master's, thesis; for doctorate, thesis/dissertation. *Entrance requirements:* For master's, minimum GPA of 3.0, BS or equivalent in petroleum or natural gas engineering; for doctorate, minimum GPA of 3.0, BS or MS in petroleum engineering from an ABET accredited or an internationally recognized petroleum engineering program or equivalent. Additional exam requirements/recommendations for international students: Required—TOEFL. *Faculty research:* Gas reservoir engineering, well logging, environment artificial intelligence.

Section 14
Industrial Engineering

This section contains a directory of institutions offering graduate work in industrial engineering, followed by an in-depth entry submitted by an institution that chose to prepare a detailed program description. Additional information about programs listed in the directory but not augmented by an in-depth entry may be obtained by writing directly to the dean of a graduate school or chair of a department at the address given in the directory.

For programs offering related work, see also in this book *Computer Science and Information Technology, Electrical and Computer Engineering, Energy and Power Engineering, Engineering and Applied Sciences,* and *Management of Engineering and Technology.* In the other guides in this series:

Graduate Programs in the Physical Sciences, Mathematics, Agricultural Sciences, the Environment & Natural Resources
See *Mathematical Sciences*
Graduate Programs in Business, Education, Health, Information Studies, Law & Social Work
See *Business Administration and Management*

CONTENTS

Program Directories

Automotive Engineering

Central Michigan University, Central Michigan University Off-Campus Programs, Program in Administration, Mount Pleasant, MI 48859. Offers acquisitions administration (MSA, Certificate); general administration (MSA, Certificate); health services administration (MSA, Certificate); human resources administration (MSA, Certificate); information resource management (MSA, Certificate); international administration (MSA, Certificate); leadership (MSA, Certificate); public administration (MSA, Certificate); vehicle design and manufacturing administration (MSA, Certificate). Part-time and evening/weekend programs available. Postbaccalaureate distance learning degree programs offered (no on-campus study). *Students:* Average age 38. *Entrance requirements:* For master's, minimum GPA of 2.7 in major. *Application deadline:* Applications are processed on a rolling basis. Application fee: $50. Electronic applications accepted. *Financial support:* Scholarships/grants available. Support available to part-time students. Financial award applicants required to submit FAFSA. *Unit head:* Dr. Nana Korsah, Director, MSA Programs, 989-774-6525, E-mail: korsa1na@cmich.edu. *Application contact:* 877-268-4636, E-mail: cmuoffcampus@cmich.edu.

Clemson University, Graduate School, College of Engineering and Science, Department of Mechanical Engineering, Program in Automotive Engineering, Clemson, SC 29634. Offers MS, PhD. *Students:* 70 full-time (5 women), 4 part-time (0 women); includes 2 minority (both African Americans), 43 international. Average age 26. 114 applicants, 82% accepted, 30 enrolled. In 2009, 8 master's awarded. *Degree requirements:* For master's, one foreign language, industrial internship; for doctorate, one foreign language, thesis/dissertation. *Entrance requirements:* For master's, GRE; for doctorate, GRE, MS or 2 years post-bachelor's experience. Additional exam requirements/recommendations for international students: Required—TOEFL. *Application deadline:* Applications are processed on a rolling basis. Application fee: $70 ($80 for international students). Electronic applications accepted. *Expenses:* Contact institution. *Financial support:* In 2009–10, 29 students received support, including 3 fellowships with partial tuition reimbursements available (averaging $14,500 per year), 24 research assistantships with partial tuition reimbursements available (averaging $18,277 per year); career-related internships or fieldwork, institutionally sponsored loans, scholarships/grants, traineeships, health care benefits, and unspecified assistantships also available. Support available to part-time students. Financial award application deadline: 2/1. *Faculty research:* Systems integration, manufacturing product design/development/vehicle electronics. *Unit head:* Dr. Donald Beasley, Mechanical Engineering Department Chair, 864-656-5622, Fax: 864-656-4435, E-mail: debsl@exchange.clemson.edu. *Application contact:* Dr. Mohammed Omar, Coordinator, 864-656-5537, Fax: 864-656-4435, E-mail: momar@clemson.edu.

Kettering University, Graduate School, Mechanical Engineering Department, Flint, MI 48504. Offers automotive systems (MS Eng); computer aided engineering simulation (MS Eng); mechanical cognate (MS Eng); mechanical design (MS Eng); sustainable energy and hybrid technology (MS Eng). Part-time and evening/weekend programs available. Postbaccalaureate distance learning degree programs offered (no on-campus study). *Faculty:* 14 full-time (1 woman). *Students:* 8 full-time (0 women), 35 part-time (7 women); includes 2 minority (1 Asian American or Pacific Islander, 1 Hispanic American), 8 international. Average age 26. 6 applicants, 67% accepted, 2 enrolled. In 2009, 20 master's awarded. *Degree requirements:* For master's, thesis optional. *Entrance requirements:* Additional exam requirements/recommendations for international students: Required—TOEFL (minimum score 550 paper-based; 213 computer-based; 79 iBT). *Application deadline:* For fall admission, 9/15 for domestic students, 6/15 for international students; for winter admission, 12/15 for domestic students, 9/15 for international students; for spring admission, 3/15 for domestic students, 12/15 for international students. Applications are processed on a rolling basis. Application fee: $0. Electronic applications accepted. *Expenses:* Tuition: Full-time $11,120; part-time $695 per credit hour. *Financial support:* In 2009–10, 24 students received support, including fellowships with full tuition reimbursements available (averaging $13,000 per year), research assistantships with full tuition reimbursements available (averaging $13,000 per year), teaching assistantships with full tuition reimbursements available (averaging $13,000 per year); Federal Work-Study, scholarships/grants, and tuition waivers (partial) also available. Support available to part-time students. Financial award application deadline: 7/15; financial award applicants required to submit CSS PROFILE or FAFSA. *Faculty research:* Fuel cells, chemical agents, crash safety, bio-gas, sustainable energy. Total annual research expenditures: $3.9 million. *Unit head:* Dr. K. Joel Berry, Head, 810-762-7833, Fax: 810-762-7860, E-mail: jberry@kettering.edu. *Application contact:* Bonnie Switzer, Graduate Admissions Officer, 810-762-7953, Fax: 810-762-9935, E-mail: bswitzer@kettering.edu.

Lawrence Technological University, College of Engineering, Southfield, MI 48075-1058. Offers automotive engineering (MAE); civil engineering (MCE); construction engineering management (MS); electrical and computer engineering (MS); engineering management (ME); industrial engineering (MSIE); manufacturing systems (MEMS, DE); mechanical engineering (MS); mechatronic systems engineering (MS). Part-time and evening/weekend programs available. *Faculty:* 20 full-time (4 women), 12 part-time/adjunct (0 women). *Students:* 15 full-time (4 women), 389 part-time (50 women); includes 57 minority (22 African Americans, 1 American Indian/Alaska Native, 30 Asian Americans or Pacific Islanders, 4 Hispanic Americans), 137 international. Average age 31. 361 applicants, 52% accepted, 108 enrolled. In 2009, 161 master's, 1 doctorate awarded. *Degree requirements:* For master's, thesis (for some programs). *Entrance requirements:* Additional exam requirements/recommendations for international students: Required—TOEFL (minimum score 550 paper-based; 213 computer-based; 79 iBT). *Application deadline:* For fall admission, 8/1 priority date for domestic students, 6/1 for international students; for winter admission, 12/1 priority date for domestic students, 10/1 for international students; for spring admission, 5/1 priority date for domestic students, 3/1 for international students. Applications are processed on a rolling basis. Application fee: $50. Electronic applications accepted. *Expenses:* Tuition: Full-time $11,320; part-time $798 per credit hour. *Financial support:* Federal Work-Study and institutionally sponsored loans available. Support available to part-time students. Financial award application deadline: 4/1; financial award applicants required to submit FAFSA. *Faculty research:* Advanced composite materials in bridges, strengthening existing bridges with carbon and glass fiber sheets, development of drive shafts using composite materials. *Unit head:* Dr. Nabil Grace, Interim Dean, 248-204-2500, Fax: 248-204-2509, E-mail: engrdean@ltu.edu. *Application contact:* Jane Rohrback, Director of Admissions, 248-204-3160, Fax: 248-204-3188, E-mail: admissions@ltu.edu.

Minnesota State University Mankato, College of Graduate Studies, College of Science, Engineering and Technology, Department of Automotive and Manufacturing Engineering Technology, Mankato, MN 56001. Offers manufacturing engineering technology (MS). *Students:* 4 full-time (0 women), 8 part-time (0 women). *Degree requirements:* For master's, comprehensive exam, thesis. *Entrance requirements:* For master's, GRE General Test (if GPA less than 3.0), minimum GPA of 3.0 during previous 2 years. Additional exam requirements/recommendations for international students: Required—TOEFL. *Application deadline:* For fall admission, 7/1 priority date for domestic students; for spring admission, 11/1 for domestic students. Applications are processed on a rolling basis. Application fee: $40. Electronic applications accepted. *Expenses:* Tuition, state resident: full-time $5364. Tuition, nonresident: full-time $8314. *Financial support:* Research assistantships with full tuition reimbursements, teaching assistantships with full tuition reimbursements, unspecified assistantships available. Financial award application deadline: 3/15; financial award applicants required to submit FAFSA. *Unit head:* Dr. William Peterson, Chairperson, 507-389-6157. *Application contact:* 507-389-2321, E-mail: grad@mnsu.edu.

Old Dominion University, Frank Batten College of Engineering and Technology, Program in Motorsports, Norfolk, VA 23529. Offers ME. Part-time programs available. Postbaccalaureate distance learning degree programs offered (minimal on-campus study). *Faculty:* 5 full-time (0 women), 2 part-time/adjunct (0 women). *Students:* 5 applicants, 80% accepted. *Degree requirements:* For master's, comprehensive exam, exam/project. *Entrance requirements:* For master's, GRE, minimum GPA of 3.0. Additional exam requirements/recommendations for international students: Required—TOEFL (minimum score 550 paper-based; 230 computer-based; 79 iBT). *Application deadline:* For fall admission, 7/1 priority date for domestic students, 5/1 priority date for international students; for spring admission, 10/1 priority date for domestic students, 9/1 priority date for international students. Applications are processed on a rolling basis. Application fee: $40. Electronic applications accepted. *Expenses:* Tuition, state resident: full-time $8112; part-time $338 per credit. Tuition, nonresident: full-time $20,256; part-time $844 per credit. Required fees: $119 per semester. One-time fee: $50. *Financial support:* Research assistantships with partial tuition reimbursements, career-related internships or fieldwork, scholarships/grants, and unspecified assistantships available. Financial award application deadline: 2/15; financial award applicants required to submit FAFSA. *Unit head:* Dr. Colin Britcher, Chair, 757-683-4916, Fax: 757-683-3200, E-mail: britcher@aero.odu.edu. *Application contact:* Dr. Brett Newman, Graduate Program Director, 757-683-5860, Fax: 757-683-3200, E-mail: aeroinfo@odu.edu.

University of Michigan–Dearborn, College of Engineering and Computer Science, Interdisciplinary Programs, MSE Program in Automotive Systems Engineering, Dearborn, MI 48128-1491. Offers MSE. Part-time and evening/weekend programs available. Postbaccalaureate distance learning degree programs offered. *Faculty:* 1 full-time (0 women). *Students:* 9 full-time (0 women), 26 part-time (2 women); includes 7 minority (1 African American, 6 Hispanic Americans), 15 international. Average age 30. 37 applicants, 73% accepted, 9 enrolled. In 2009, 21 master's awarded. *Degree requirements:* For master's, thesis optional. *Entrance requirements:* For master's, bachelor's degree in applied mathematics, computer science, engineering, or physical science; minimum GPA of 3.0. Additional exam requirements/recommendations for international students: Required—TOEFL (minimum score 560 paper-based; 220 computer-based; 84 iBT). *Application deadline:* For fall admission, 8/1 priority date for domestic students, 4/1 for international students; for winter admission, 12/1 priority date for domestic students, 8/1 for international students; for spring admission, 4/1 priority date for domestic students, 12/1 for international students. Applications are processed on a rolling basis. Application fee: $60 ($75 for international students). Electronic applications accepted. *Expenses:* Tuition, area resident: Part-time $504.10 per credit hour. Tuition, state resident: part-time $504.10 per credit hour. Tuition, nonresident: part-time $957.90 per credit hour. *Financial support:* Scholarships/grants and unspecified assistantships available. Financial award application deadline: 4/1; financial award applicants required to submit FAFSA. *Faculty research:* Performance of lightweight automotive materials, stamping, hydroforming, tailor-welded blanking, automotive composites processing and design, thermoplastic matrix composites, injection molding. *Unit head:* Dr. Pankaj K. Mallick, Director/Professor, 313-593-5119, Fax: 313-593-5386, E-mail: pkm@umich.edu. *Application contact:* Sherry Boyd, Intermediate Administrative Assistant, 313-593-5582, Fax: 313-593-5386, E-mail: idpgrad@umd.umich.edu.

University of Michigan–Dearborn, College of Engineering and Computer Science, Interdisciplinary Programs, PhD Program in Automotive Systems Engineering, Dearborn, MI 48128-1491. Offers PhD. Part-time and evening/weekend programs available. *Faculty:* 1 full-time (0 women). *Students:* 2 full-time (0 women), 8 part-time (0 women); includes 1 minority (Hispanic American), 7 international. Average age 29. 12 applicants, 83% accepted, 10 enrolled. *Degree requirements:* For doctorate, thesis/dissertation. *Entrance requirements:* For doctorate, GRE. Additional exam requirements/recommendations for international students: Required—TOEFL (minimum score 560 paper-based; 220 computer-based; 84 iBT). *Application deadline:* For fall admission, 8/1 priority date for domestic students, 4/1 for international students; for winter admission, 12/1 priority date for domestic students, 8/1 for international students; for spring admission, 4/1 priority date for domestic students, 12/1 for international students. Applications are processed on a rolling basis. Application fee: $60. Electronic applications accepted. *Expenses:* Tuition, area resident: Part-time $504.10 per credit hour. Tuition, state resident: part-time $504.10 per credit hour. Tuition, nonresident: part-time $957.90 per credit hour. *Financial support:* Scholarships/grants and unspecified assistantships available. Financial award applicants required to submit FAFSA. *Unit head:* Dr. Pankaj K. Mallick, Director/Professor, 313-593-5119, Fax: 313-593-5386, E-mail: pkm@umich.edu. *Application contact:* Sherry Boyd, Intermediate Administrative Assistant, 313-593-5582, Fax: 313-593-5386, E-mail: idpgrad@umd.umich.edu.

See Close-Up on page 431.

Industrial/Management Engineering

Arizona State University, Graduate College, Ira A. Fulton School of Engineering, Department of Industrial Engineering, Tempe, AZ 85287. Offers MS, MSE, PhD, MSE/MIMOT. *Degree requirements:* For master's, thesis or alternative; for doctorate, thesis/dissertation. *Entrance requirements:* For master's, GRE General Test (recommended), minimum GPA of 3.0; for doctorate, GRE General Test (recommended), minimum GPA of 3.5.

Auburn University, Graduate School, Ginn College of Engineering, Department of Industrial and Systems Engineering, Auburn University, AL 36849. Offers MISE, MS, PhD. Part-time programs available. *Faculty:* 10 full-time (1 woman), 4 part-time/adjunct (0 women). *Students:* 89 full-time (21 women), 49 part-time (13 women); includes 16 minority (12 African Americans, 3 Asian Americans or Pacific Islanders, 1 Hispanic American), 66 international. Average age 29. 252 applicants, 62% accepted, 50 enrolled. In 2009, 20 master's, 7 doctorates awarded. *Degree requirements:* For master's, thesis (MS); for doctorate, thesis/dissertation. *Entrance requirements:* For master's and doctorate, GRE General Test. *Application deadline:* For fall admission, 7/7 for domestic students; for spring admission, 11/24 for domestic students. Applications are processed on a rolling basis. Application fee: $50 ($60 for international students). *Expenses:* Tuition, state resident: full-time $6240. Tuition, nonresident: full-time $18,720. International tuition: $18,938 full-time. Required fees: $492. Tuition and fees vary according to course load, program and reciprocity agreements. *Financial support:* Fellowships, research assistantships, teaching assistantships, Federal Work-Study available. Support available to part-time students. Financial award application deadline: 3/15; financial award applicants required to submit FAFSA. *Unit head:* Dr. Alice E. Smith, Chair, 334-844-1401. *Application contact:* Dr. George Flowers, Dean of the Graduate School, 334-844-2125.

Bradley University, Graduate School, College of Engineering and Technology, Department of Industrial and Manufacturing Engineering and Technology, Peoria, IL 61625-0002. Offers industrial engineering (MSIE); manufacturing engineering (MSIE). Part-time and evening/weekend programs available. *Degree requirements:* For master's, comprehensive exam, project. *Entrance requirements:* For master's, minimum GPA of 3.0. Additional exam requirements/

recommendations for international students: Required—TOEFL (minimum score 550 paper-based; 213 computer-based; 79 iBT).

Buffalo State College, State University of New York, The Graduate School, Faculty of Applied Science and Education, Department of Technology, Program in Industrial Technology, Buffalo, NY 14222-1095. Offers MS. *Degree requirements:* For master's, thesis or project. *Entrance requirements:* For master's, minimum GPA of 2.5. Additional exam requirements/recommendations for international students: Required—TOEFL (minimum score 550 paper-based; 213 computer-based).

California Polytechnic State University, San Luis Obispo, College of Engineering, Department of Industrial Engineering, San Luis Obispo, CA 93407. Offers MS. Part-time programs available. *Faculty:* 5 full-time (2 women). *Students:* 14 full-time (2 women), 3 part-time (1 woman); includes 5 minority (1 Asian American or Pacific Islander, 4 Hispanic Americans). Average age 24. 11 applicants, 91% accepted, 8 enrolled. In 2009, 2 master's awarded. *Degree requirements:* For master's, comprehensive exam (for some programs), thesis (for some programs). *Entrance requirements:* For master's, GRE General Test, minimum GPA of 3.0 in last 90 quarter units of course work. Additional exam requirements/recommendations for international students: Required—TOEFL (minimum score 550 paper-based; 213 computer-based), or IELTS (minimum score 6). *Application deadline:* For fall admission, 7/1 for domestic students, 11/30 for international students; for winter admission, 11/1 for domestic students, 6/30 for international students; for spring admission, 2/1 for domestic students. Applications are processed on a rolling basis. Application fee: $55. Electronic applications accepted. *Expenses:* Tuition, nonresident: full-time $11,160; part-time $248 per unit. Required fees: $7134; $1553 per quarter. *Financial support:* Fellowships, research assistantships, teaching assistantships, career-related internships or fieldwork, Federal Work-Study, institutionally sponsored loans, and scholarships/grants available. Support available to part-time students. Financial award application deadline: 3/2; financial award applicants required to submit FAFSA. *Faculty research:* Operations research, simulation, project management, supply chain and logistics, quality engineering. *Unit head:* Dr. Liz Schlemer, Graduate Coordinator, 805-756-2183, Fax: 805-756-5439, E-mail: lschleme@calpoly.edu. *Application contact:* Dr. Liz Schlemer, Graduate Coordinator, 805-756-2183, Fax: 805-756-5439, E-mail: lschleme@calpoly.edu.

California State University, Fresno, Division of Graduate Studies, College of Agricultural Sciences and Technology, Department of Industrial Technology, Fresno, CA 93740-8027. Offers MS. Part-time and evening/weekend programs available. *Degree requirements:* For master's, comprehensive exam (for some programs), thesis (for some programs). *Entrance requirements:* For master's, GRE General Test, minimum GPA of 2.5. Additional exam requirements/recommendations for international students: Required—TOEFL. Electronic applications accepted. *Faculty research:* Fuels/pollution, energy, outdoor storage methods.

California State University, Northridge, Graduate Studies, College of Engineering and Computer Science, Department of Manufacturing Systems Engineering and Management, Northridge, CA 91330. Offers engineering automation (MS); engineering management (MS); manufacturing systems engineering (MS); materials engineering (MS). Postbaccalaureate distance learning degree programs offered. *Faculty:* 6 full-time (1 woman), 33 part-time/adjunct (12 women). *Students:* 137 full-time (18 women), 115 part-time (20 women); includes 4 African Americans, 22 Asian Americans or Pacific Islanders, 19 Hispanic Americans, 149 international. Average age 27. 210 applicants, 68% accepted, 69 enrolled. In 2009, 78 master's awarded. *Entrance requirements:* For master's, GRE (if cumulative undergraduate GPA less than 3.0). *Application deadline:* For fall admission, 3/30 for domestic students; for spring admission, 9/30 for domestic students. Application fee: $55. *Unit head:* Prof. Behzad Bavarian, Acting Chair, 818-677-2167. *Application contact:* Prof. Behzad Bavarian, Acting Chair, 818-677-2167.

Central Washington University, Graduate Studies and Research, College of Education and Professional Studies, Department of Industrial and Engineering Technology, Ellensburg, WA 98926. Offers engineering technology (MS). Part-time programs available. *Faculty:* 15 full-time (0 women). *Students:* 6 full-time (2 women), 14 part-time (0 women); includes 3 minority (1 African American, 2 Asian Americans or Pacific Islanders). 10 applicants, 90% accepted, 9 enrolled. In 2009, 11 master's awarded. *Degree requirements:* For master's, thesis or alternative. *Entrance requirements:* For master's, minimum GPA of 3.0. Additional exam requirements/recommendations for international students: Required—TOEFL (minimum score 550 paper-based; 213 computer-based; 79 iBT). *Application deadline:* For fall admission, 2/1 priority date for domestic students; for winter admission, 10/1 for domestic students; for spring admission, 1/1 for domestic students. Applications are processed on a rolling basis. Application fee: $50. Electronic applications accepted. *Expenses:* Tuition, state resident: full-time $7353; part-time $245 per credit. Tuition, nonresident: full-time $16,383; part-time $546 per credit. Required fees: $882. Tuition and fees vary according to degree level. *Financial support:* In 2009–10, 3 teaching assistantships with full and partial tuition reimbursements (averaging $9,145 per year) were awarded; career-related internships or fieldwork, Federal Work-Study, and health care benefits also available. *Unit head:* Dr. Michael Whelan, Chair, 509-963-1756. *Application contact:* Justine Eason, Admissions Program Coordinator, 509-963-3103, Fax: 509-963-1799, E-mail: masters@cwu.edu.

Clemson University, Graduate School, College of Engineering and Science, Department of Industrial Engineering, Clemson, SC 29634. Offers MS, PhD. Part-time programs available. *Faculty:* 10 full-time (3 women), 1 (woman) part-time/adjunct. *Students:* 58 full-time (20 women), 95 part-time (34 women); includes 18 minority (6 African Americans, 1 American Indian/Alaska Native, 8 Asian Americans or Pacific Islanders, 3 Hispanic Americans), 63 international. Average age 30. 213 applicants, 80% accepted, 63 enrolled. In 2009, 20 master's, 2 doctorates awarded. Terminal master's awarded for partial completion of doctoral program. *Degree requirements:* For master's, thesis or alternative; for doctorate, thesis/dissertation. *Entrance requirements:* For master's and doctorate, GRE General Test. Additional exam requirements/recommendations for international students: Required—TOEFL. *Application deadline:* For fall admission, 6/1 for domestic students, 4/15 for international students; for spring admission, 9/15 for international students. Applications are processed on a rolling basis. Application fee: $70 ($80 for international students). Electronic applications accepted. *Expenses:* Tuition, state resident: full-time $8684; part-time $528 per credit hour. Tuition, nonresident: full-time $15,330; part-time $1078 per credit hour. Required fees: $736; $37 per semester. Part-time tuition and fees vary according to course load and program. *Financial support:* In 2009–10, 34 students received support, including 17 research assistantships with partial tuition reimbursements available (averaging $18,891 per year), 16 teaching assistantships with partial tuition reimbursements available (averaging $16,916 per year); fellowships with full and partial tuition reimbursements available, career-related internships or fieldwork, institutionally sponsored loans, scholarships/grants, health care benefits, and unspecified assistantships also available. Support available to part-time students. Financial award applicants required to submit FAFSA. *Faculty research:* Computer-integrated manufacturing, human-computer interaction, ergonomics, quality engineering. Total annual research expenditures: $714,166. *Unit head:* Dr. Anand Gramopadhye, Head, 864-656-4716, E-mail: agramop@ces.clemson.edu. *Application contact:* William G. Ferrell, Coordinator, 864-656-2724, E-mail: fwillia@clemson.edu.

Cleveland State University, College of Graduate Studies, Fenn College of Engineering, Department of Industrial and Manufacturing Engineering, Cleveland, OH 44115. Offers industrial engineering (MS, D Eng). Part-time programs available. Terminal master's awarded for partial completion of doctoral program. *Degree requirements:* For master's, thesis or alternative; for doctorate, thesis/dissertation, candidacy and qualifying exams. *Entrance requirements:* For master's, GRE General Test, minimum GPA of 2.75; for doctorate, GRE General Test, minimum GPA of 3.25. Additional exam requirements/recommendations for international students: Required—TOEFL (minimum score 525 paper-based; 197 computer-based). *Faculty research:* Modeling of manufacturing systems, statistical process control, computerized production planning and facilities design, cellular manufacturing, artificial intelligence and sensors.

Colorado State University–Pueblo, College of Education, Engineering and Professional Studies, Department of Engineering, Pueblo, CO 81001-4901. Offers industrial and systems engineering (MS). *Degree requirements:* For master's, thesis optional. *Entrance requirements:* For master's, GRE General Test. Additional exam requirements/recommendations for international students: Required—TOEFL (minimum score 500 paper-based). *Faculty research:* Nanotechnology, applied operations, research transportation, decision analysis.

Columbia University, Fu Foundation School of Engineering and Applied Science, Department of Industrial Engineering and Operations Research, New York, NY 10027. Offers engineering management systems (MS); financial engineering (MS); industrial engineering (Engr); industrial engineering and operations research (MS, Eng Sc D, PhD); MS/MBA. Part-time and evening/weekend programs available. Postbaccalaureate distance learning degree programs offered (no on-campus study). *Faculty:* 13 full-time (1 woman), 3 part-time/adjunct (1 woman). *Students:* 260 full-time (69 women), 173 part-time (50 women); includes 27 minority (1 African American, 24 Asian Americans or Pacific Islanders, 2 Hispanic Americans), 348 international. Average age 25. 1,262 applicants, 35% accepted, 193 enrolled. In 2009, 211 master's, 7 doctorates awarded. *Degree requirements:* For doctorate, thesis/dissertation, oral and written qualifying exams. *Entrance requirements:* For master's, doctorate, and Engr, GRE General Test. Additional exam requirements/recommendations for international students: Required—TOEFL. *Application deadline:* For fall admission, 12/1 priority date for domestic and international students; for spring admission, 10/1 priority date for domestic and international students. Application fee: $70. Electronic applications accepted. *Financial support:* In 2009–10, 49 students received support, including 6 fellowships (averaging $2,500 per year), 23 research assistantships with full tuition reimbursements available (averaging $22,500 per year), 20 teaching assistantships with full tuition reimbursements available (averaging $22,500 per year); career-related internships or fieldwork, health care benefits, and unspecified assistantships also available. Financial award application deadline: 12/1; financial award applicants required to submit FAFSA. *Faculty research:* Combinatorial optimization and mathematical programming; financial engineering; supply chain management and inventory theory; applied probability; queuing theory; scheduling, and simulation. *Unit head:* Dr. Cliff S. Stein, Department Chair; Professor, 212-854-5238, Fax: 212-854-8103, E-mail: cliff@ieor.columbia.edu. *Application contact:* Adina Berrios Brooks, Student Affairs Manager, 212-854-1934, Fax: 212-854-8103, E-mail: admit@ieor.columbia.edu.

Concordia University, School of Graduate Studies, Faculty of Engineering and Computer Science, Department of Mechanical and Industrial Engineering, Montréal, QC H3G 1M8, Canada. Offers composites (M Eng); industrial engineering (M Eng, MA Sc); mechanical engineering (M Eng, MA Sc, PhD, Certificate); software systems for industrial engineering (Certificate). *Degree requirements:* For master's, variable foreign language requirement, thesis or alternative; for doctorate, comprehensive exam, thesis/dissertation. *Faculty research:* Mechanical systems, fluid control systems, thermofluids engineering and robotics, industrial control systems.

Cornell University, Graduate School, Graduate Fields of Engineering, Field of Operations Research and Information Engineering, Ithaca, NY 14853-0001. Offers applied probability and statistics (PhD); manufacturing systems engineering (PhD); mathematical programming (PhD); operations research and industrial engineering (M Eng). *Faculty:* 46 full-time (9 women). *Students:* 163 full-time (46 women); includes 20 minority (2 African Americans, 12 Asian Americans or Pacific Islanders, 6 Hispanic Americans), 103 international. Average age 25. 774 applicants, 29% accepted, 91 enrolled. In 2009, 85 master's, 6 doctorates awarded. *Degree requirements:* For doctorate, comprehensive exam, thesis/dissertation. *Entrance requirements:* For master's and doctorate, GRE General Test, 3 letters of recommendation. Additional exam requirements/recommendations for international students: Required—TOEFL (minimum score 600 paper-based; 250 computer-based; 77 iBT). *Application deadline:* For fall admission, 1/15 for domestic students. Application fee: $70. Electronic applications accepted. *Expenses:* Tuition: Full-time $29,500. Required fees: $70. Full-time tuition and fees vary according to degree level, program and student level. *Financial support:* In 2009–10, 44 students received support, including 6 fellowships with full tuition reimbursements available, 5 teaching assistantships with full tuition reimbursements available; research assistantships with full tuition reimbursements available, institutionally sponsored loans, scholarships/grants, health care benefits, tuition waivers (full and partial), and unspecified assistantships also available. Financial award applicants required to submit FAFSA. *Faculty research:* Mathematical programming and combinatorial optimization, statistics, stochastic processes, mathematical finance, simulation, manufacturing, e-commerce. *Unit head:* Director of Graduate Studies, 607-255-9128, Fax: 607-255-9129. *Application contact:* Graduate Field Assistant, 607-255-9128, Fax: 607-255-9129, E-mail: orie@cornell.edu.

Dalhousie University, Faculty of Engineering, Department of Industrial Engineering, Halifax, NS B3J 2X4, Canada. Offers M Eng, MA Sc, PhD. *Faculty:* 8 full-time (0 women), 2 part-time/adjunct (1 woman). *Students:* 8 full-time (3 women), 4 part-time (1 woman), 7 international. 22 applicants, 55% accepted. In 2009, 2 master's awarded. *Degree requirements:* For master's, thesis; for doctorate, thesis/dissertation. *Entrance requirements:* Additional exam requirements/recommendations for international students: Required—TOEFL, IELTS, CANTEST, CAEL, or Michigan English Language Assessment Battery. *Application deadline:* For fall admission, 6/1 for domestic students, 4/1 for international students; for winter admission, 11/15 for domestic students, 8/31 for international students; for spring admission, 2/28 for domestic students, 12/31 for international students. Applications are processed on a rolling basis. Application fee: $70. Electronic applications accepted. *Financial support:* Fellowships, research assistantships, teaching assistantships, scholarships/grants and unspecified assistantships available. *Faculty research:* Industrial ergonomics, operations research, production manufacturing systems, scheduling stochastic models. *Unit head:* Dr. Claver Diallo, Head, 902-494-3281, Fax: 902-420-7858, E-mail: eldon.gunn@dal.ca. *Application contact:* Dr. Qi-Ming He, 902-494-6141, Fax: 902-494-7858, E-mail: qi-ming.he@dal.ca.

East Carolina University, Graduate School, College of Technology and Computer Science, Department of Technology Systems, Greenville, NC 27858-4353. Offers computer network professional (Certificate); industrial technology (MS), including computer networking management, digital communications, industrial distribution and logistics, information security, manufacturing, performance improvement, planning; information assurance (Certificate); occupational safety (MS); technology management (PhD); Website developer (Certificate). *Entrance requirements:* For master's and Certificate, GRE General Test or MAT, minimum GPA of 2.5; for doctorate, GRE General Test, related work experience.

Eastern Kentucky University, The Graduate School, College of Business and Technology, Department of Technology, Program in Industrial Technology, Richmond, KY 40475-3102. Offers MS. Part-time programs available. *Entrance requirements:* For master's, GRE General Test, minimum GPA of 2.5. *Faculty research:* Quality control, dental implants, manufacturing technology.

École Polytechnique de Montréal, Graduate Programs, Department of Mathematics and Industrial Engineering, Montréal, QC H3C 3A7, Canada. Offers ergonomy (M Eng, M Sc A, DESS); mathematical method in CA engineering (M Eng, M Sc A, PhD); operational research (M Eng, M Sc A, PhD); production (M Eng, M Sc A); technology management (M Eng, M Sc A). Part-time programs available. *Degree requirements:* For master's, one foreign language, thesis. *Entrance requirements:* For master's, minimum GPA of 2.75. *Faculty research:* Use of computers in organizations.

Florida Agricultural and Mechanical University, Division of Graduate Studies, Research, and Continuing Education, FAMU-FSU College of Engineering, Department of Industrial Engineering, Tallahassee, FL 32307-3200. Offers MS, PhD. *Faculty:* 15 full-time (1 woman). *Students:* 24 full-time (10 women), 14 part-time (2 women); includes 32 minority (31 African Americans, 1 Asian American or Pacific Islander), 6 international. In 2009, 3 master's awarded. *Degree requirements:* For master's, thesis optional. *Entrance requirements:* For master's, GRE General Test, minimum GPA of 3.0. Additional exam requirements/recommendations for international students: Required—TOEFL (minimum score 550 paper-based; 213 computer-

Industrial/Management Engineering

Florida Agricultural and Mechanical University (continued)

based). *Application deadline:* For fall admission, 7/1 for domestic students, 3/1 for international students. Application fee: $20. *Faculty research:* Design for environmentally conscious manufacturing, affordable composite manufacturing, integrated product and process design, precision machining research. *Unit head:* Dr. Ben Wang, Chairperson, 850-410-6100. *Application contact:* Dr. Chanta M. Haywood, Dean of Graduate Studies, Research, and Continuing Education, 850-599-3315, Fax: 850-599-3727.

Florida State University, The Graduate School, FAMU-FSU College of Engineering, Department of Industrial and Manufacturing Engineering, Tallahassee, FL 32306. Offers industrial engineering (MS, PhD). *Faculty:* 10 full-time (1 woman), 1 (woman) part-time/adjunct. *Students:* 55 full-time (10 women); includes 42 minority (16 African Americans, 22 Asian Americans or Pacific Islanders, 4 Hispanic Americans). Average age 24. 84 applicants, 54% accepted, 13 enrolled. In 2009, 13 master's, 3 doctorates awarded. *Degree requirements:* For master's, thesis; for doctorate, thesis/dissertation, preliminary exam, qualifying exam. *Entrance requirements:* For master's, GRE General Test, minimum GPA of 3.0; for doctorate, GRE General Test, minimum GPA of 3.0 (without MS in industrial engineering), 3.4 (with MS in industrial engineering). Additional exam requirements/recommendations for international students: Required—TOEFL (minimum score 550 paper-based; 213 computer-based; 80 iBT). *Application deadline:* For fall admission, 7/1 for domestic and international students; for spring admission, 11/1 for domestic and international students. Applications are processed on a rolling basis. Application fee: $30. *Expenses:* Tuition, state resident: full-time $7413.36. Tuition, nonresident: full-time $22,567. *Financial support:* In 2009–10, 31 students received support, including 1 fellowship with full tuition reimbursement available (averaging $18,000 per year), 22 research assistantships with full tuition reimbursements available (averaging $15,000 per year), 1 teaching assistantship with full tuition reimbursement available (averaging $15,000 per year); tuition waivers (full) also available. Financial award application deadline: 6/15. *Faculty research:* Precision manufacturing, composite manufacturing, green manufacturing, applied optimization, simulation. Total annual research expenditures: $3.7 million. *Unit head:* Dr. Chun (Chuck) Zhang, Chair and Professor, 850-410-6355, Fax: 850-410-6342, E-mail: chzhang@eng.fsu.edu. *Application contact:* Stephanie Salters, Office Manager, 850-410-6345, Fax: 850-410-6342, E-mail: salters@eng.fsu.edu.

Georgia Institute of Technology, Graduate Studies and Research, College of Engineering, School of Industrial and Systems Engineering, Program in Industrial and Systems Engineering, Atlanta, GA 30332-0001. Offers algorithms, combinatorics, and optimization (PhD); industrial and systems engineering (PhD); industrial engineering (MS, MSIE); statistics (MS Stat). Part-time programs available. Terminal master's awarded for partial completion of doctoral program. *Degree requirements:* For master's, thesis optional; for doctorate, thesis/dissertation. *Entrance requirements:* For master's and doctorate, GRE General Test, minimum GPA of 3.0. Additional exam requirements/recommendations for international students: Required—TOEFL. Electronic applications accepted. *Faculty research:* Computer-integrated manufacturing systems, materials handling systems, production and distribution.

Illinois State University, Graduate School, College of Applied Science and Technology, Department of Technology, Normal, IL 61790-2200. Offers MS. *Degree requirements:* For master's, thesis or alternative. *Entrance requirements:* For master's, GRE General Test, minimum GPA of 2.8. *Faculty research:* National Center for Engineering and Technology Education, Illinois Manufacturing Extension Center Field Office hosting, model for the professional development of K-12 technology education teachers, Illinois State University Illinois Mathermatics and Science Partnership, Illinois University council for career and technical education.

Indiana State University, School of Graduate Studies, College of Technology, Program in Industrial Technology, Terre Haute, IN 47809. Offers MS. *Entrance requirements:* For master's, bachelor's degree in industrial technology or related field. Additional exam requirements/recommendations for international students: Required—TOEFL. Electronic applications accepted.

Indiana University–Purdue University Fort Wayne, College of Engineering, Technology, and Computer Science, Program in Technology, Fort Wayne, IN 46805-1499. Offers facilities and construction management (MS); industrial technology/manufacturing (MS); information technology/advanced computer applications (MS). Part-time programs available. *Faculty:* 10 full-time (6 women), 2 part-time/adjunct (0 women). *Students:* 6 full-time (3 women), 18 part-time (1 woman); includes 4 minority (3 Asian Americans or Pacific Islanders, 1 Hispanic American), 3 international. Average age 33. 13 applicants, 100% accepted, 12 enrolled. *Entrance requirements:* For master's, minimum GPA of 3.0. Additional exam requirements/recommendations for international students: Required—TOEFL (minimum score 550 paper-based; 213 computer-based; 77 iBT), TWE. *Application deadline:* For fall admission, 7/15 for domestic students, 5/15 for international students; for spring admission, 12/1 for domestic students, 10/15 for international students. Applications are processed on a rolling basis. Application fee: $55 ($60 for international students). Electronic applications accepted. *Expenses:* Tuition, state resident: full-time $4595; part-time $255 per credit. Tuition, nonresident: full-time $10,963; part-time $609 per credit. Required fees: $528; $29.35 per credit. Tuition and fees vary according to course load. *Financial support:* Career-related internships or fieldwork, scholarships/grants, and unspecified assistantships available. Support available to part-time students. Financial award application deadline: 3/1; financial award applicants required to submit FAFSA. *Unit head:* Dr. Gerard Voland, Dean, 260-481-6839, Fax: 260-481-5734, E-mail: volandg@ipfw.edu. *Application contact:* Dr. Paul Lin, Graduate Program Director, 260-481-6339, Fax: 260-481-5734, E-mail: lin@ipfw.edu.

Instituto Tecnologico de Santo Domingo, Graduate School, Santo Domingo, Dominican Republic. Offers applied linguistics (MA); construction administration (M Mgmt); corporate finance (M Mgmt); education (M Ed); engineering (M Eng), including data telecommunications, industrial engineering, logistics and supply chain, maintenance engineering, sanitary and environmental engineering, structural engineering; environmental science (M En S), including environmental education, environmental management, marine and coastal ecosystems, natural resources management; family therapy (MA); food science and technology (MS); human development (MA); human resources administration (M Mgmt); international business (M Mgmt); labor risks (M Mgmt); management (M Mgmt); marketing (M Mgmt); mathematics (MS); organizational development (M Mgmt); planning and taxation (M Mgmt); psychology (MA); social science (M Ed); upper management (M Mgmt). *Entrance requirements:* For master's, birth certificate, minimum GPA of 2.0.

Instituto Tecnológico y de Estudios Superiores de Monterrey, Campus Chihuahua, Graduate Programs, Chihuahua, Mexico. Offers computer systems engineering (Ingeniero); electrical engineering (Ingeniero); electromechanical engineering (Ingeniero); electronic engineering (Ingeniero); engineering administration (MEA); industrial engineering (MIE, Ingeniero); international trade (MIT); mechanical engineering (Ingeniero).

Instituto Tecnológico y de Estudios Superiores de Monterrey, Campus Ciudad de México, Virtual University Division, Ciudad de Mexico, Mexico. Offers administration of information technologies (MA); computer sciences (MA); education (MA, PhD); educational technology (MA); environmental engineering (MA); environmental systems (MA); humanistic studies (MA); industrial engineering (MA); international business for Latin America (MA); quality systems (MA); quality systems and productivity (MA). Part-time and evening/weekend programs available. Postbaccalaureate distance learning degree programs offered (minimal on-campus study). *Entrance requirements:* For master's and doctorate, Instituto entrance exam. Additional exam requirements/recommendations for international students: Required—TOEFL.

Instituto Tecnológico y de Estudios Superiores de Monterrey, Campus Laguna, Graduate School, Torreón, Mexico. Offers business administration (MBA); industrial engineering (MIE); management information systems (MS). Part-time programs available. *Entrance requirements:* For master's, GMAT. *Faculty research:* Computer communications from home to the University.

Instituto Tecnológico y de Estudios Superiores de Monterrey, Campus Monterrey, Graduate and Research Division, Programs in Engineering, Monterrey, Mexico. Offers applied statistics (M Eng); artificial intelligence (PhD); automation engineering (M Eng); chemical engineering (M Eng); civil engineering (M Eng); electrical engineering (M Eng); electronic engineering (M Eng); environmental engineering (M Eng); industrial engineering (M Eng, PhD); manufacturing engineering (M Eng); mechanical engineering (M Eng); systems and quality engineering (M Eng). Part-time and evening/weekend programs available. Terminal master's awarded for partial completion of doctoral program. *Degree requirements:* For master's, one foreign language, thesis; for doctorate, one foreign language, thesis/dissertation. *Entrance requirements:* For master's, EXADEP; for doctorate, GRE, master's degree in related field. Additional exam requirements/recommendations for international students: Required—TOEFL. *Faculty research:* Flexible manufacturing cells, materials, statistical methods, environmental prevention, control and evaluation.

Iowa State University of Science and Technology, Graduate College, College of Engineering, Department of Industrial and Manufacturing Systems Engineering, Ames, IA 50011. Offers industrial engineering (M Eng, MS, PhD); operations research (MS); systems engineering (M Eng). *Faculty:* 12 full-time (2 women). *Students:* 36 full-time (13 women), 39 part-time (7 women); includes 6 minority (3 African Americans, 1 Asian American or Pacific Islander, 2 Hispanic Americans), 34 international. 169 applicants, 21% accepted, 16 enrolled. In 2009, 11 master's, 5 doctorates awarded. *Degree requirements:* For master's, thesis or alternative; for doctorate, thesis/dissertation. *Entrance requirements:* For master's and doctorate, GRE General Test. Additional exam requirements/recommendations for international students: Required—TOEFL (minimum score 550 paper-based; 213 computer-based; 79 iBT) or IELTS (minimum score 6.5). *Application deadline:* For fall admission, 1/15 priority date for international students; for spring admission, 7/15 priority date for international students. Application fee: $40 ($90 for international students). Electronic applications accepted. *Expenses:* Tuition, state resident: full-time $6716. Tuition, nonresident: full-time $8908. Tuition and fees vary according to course level, course load, program and student level. *Financial support:* In 2009–10, 26 research assistantships with full and partial tuition reimbursements (averaging $17,000 per year), 4 teaching assistantships with full and partial tuition reimbursements (averaging $16,000 per year) were awarded; fellowships, scholarships/grants, health care benefits, and unspecified assistantships also available. *Faculty research:* Economic modeling, valuation techniques, robotics, digital controls, systems reliability. *Unit head:* Dr. Gary Mirka, Chair, 515-294-8661, Fax: 515-294-3524. *Application contact:* Dr. Sarah Ryan, Director of Graduate Studies, 515-294-4347, E-mail: smryan@iastate.edu.

Kansas State University, Graduate School, College of Engineering, Department of Industrial and Manufacturing Systems Engineering, Manhattan, KS 66506. Offers engineering management (MEM); industrial engineering (MS, PhD); operations research (MS). Part-time programs available. Postbaccalaureate distance learning degree programs offered. *Faculty:* 9 full-time (1 woman), 2 part-time/adjunct (1 woman). *Students:* 38 full-time (12 women), 48 part-time (14 women); includes 4 minority (1 African American, 1 Asian American or Pacific Islander, 2 Hispanic Americans), 27 international. Average age 30. 85 applicants, 60% accepted, 41 enrolled. In 2009, 20 master's, 1 doctorate awarded. *Degree requirements:* For master's, thesis or alternative; for doctorate, thesis/dissertation. *Entrance requirements:* For master's, GRE General Test, bachelor's degree in engineering, mathematics, or physical science; for doctorate, GRE General Test, master's degree in engineering or industrial manufacturing. Additional exam requirements/recommendations for international students: Required—TOEFL. *Application deadline:* For fall admission, 2/1 priority date for domestic and international students; for spring admission, 8/1 priority date for domestic and international students. Applications are processed on a rolling basis. Application fee: $40 ($55 for international students). Electronic applications accepted. *Financial support:* In 2009–10, 19 research assistantships (averaging $10,372 per year), 1 teaching assistantship with full tuition reimbursement (averaging $12,450 per year) were awarded; Federal Work-Study, institutionally sponsored loans, and scholarships/grants also available. Support available to part-time students. Financial award application deadline: 3/1; financial award applicants required to submit FAFSA. *Faculty research:* Ergonomics, healthcare systems engineering, manufacturing processes, operations research, engineering management. Total annual research expenditures: $484,594. *Unit head:* Bradley Kramer, Head, 785-532-5606, Fax: 785-532-7810, E-mail: bradleyk@ksu.edu. *Application contact:* E. Stanley Lee, Director, 785-532-3730, Fax: 785-532-7810, E-mail: eslee@ksu.edu.

Lamar University, College of Graduate Studies, College of Engineering, Department of Industrial Engineering, Beaumont, TX 77710. Offers engineering management (MEM); industrial engineering (ME, MES, DE). *Faculty:* 7 full-time (0 women). *Students:* 34 full-time (4 women), 8 part-time (1 woman); includes 6 minority (2 African Americans, 3 Asian Americans or Pacific Islanders, 1 Hispanic American), 25 international. Average age 26. 89 applicants, 39% accepted, 9 enrolled. In 2009, 16 master's awarded. *Degree requirements:* For doctorate, thesis/dissertation. *Entrance requirements:* For master's and doctorate, GRE General Test. Additional exam requirements/recommendations for international students: Required—TOEFL. *Application deadline:* For fall admission, 5/15 priority date for domestic students; for spring admission, 10/1 priority date for domestic students. Applications are processed on a rolling basis. Application fee: $25 ($50 for international students). *Financial support:* In 2009–10, 2 fellowships (averaging $6,000 per year), 4 research assistantships (averaging $1,000 per year), 2 teaching assistantships (averaging $4,500 per year) were awarded. Financial award application deadline: 4/1. *Faculty research:* Process simulation, total quality management, ergonomics and safety, scheduling. *Unit head:* Dr. Victor Zaloom, Chair, 409-880-8804, Fax: 409-880-8121. *Application contact:* Dr. Hsing-Wei Chu, Professor, 409-880-8804, Fax: 409-880-8121.

Lawrence Technological University, College of Engineering, Southfield, MI 48075-1058. Offers automotive engineering (MAE); civil engineering (MCE); construction engineering management (MS); electrical and computer engineering (MS); engineering management (ME); industrial engineering (MSIE); manufacturing systems (MEMS, DE); mechanical engineering (MS); mechatronic systems engineering (MS). Part-time and evening/weekend programs available. *Faculty:* 20 full-time (4 women), 12 part-time/adjunct (0 women). *Students:* 15 full-time (4 women), 389 part-time (50 women); includes 57 minority (22 African Americans, 1 American Indian/Alaska Native, 30 Asian Americans or Pacific Islanders, 4 Hispanic Americans), 137 international. Average age 31. 361 applicants, 52% accepted, 108 enrolled. In 2009, 161 master's, 1 doctorate awarded. *Degree requirements:* For master's, thesis (for some programs). *Entrance requirements:* Additional exam requirements/recommendations for international students: Required—TOEFL (minimum score 550 paper-based; 213 computer-based; 79 iBT). *Application deadline:* For fall admission, 8/1 priority date for domestic students, 6/1 for international students; for winter admission, 12/1 priority date for domestic students, 10/1 for international students; for spring admission, 5/1 priority date for domestic students, 3/1 for international students. Applications are processed on a rolling basis. Application fee: $50. Electronic applications accepted. *Expenses:* Tuition: Full-time $11,320; part-time $798 per credit hour. *Financial support:* Federal Work-Study and institutionally sponsored loans available. Support available to part-time students. Financial award application deadline: 4/1; financial award applicants required to submit FAFSA. *Faculty research:* Advanced composite materials in bridges, strengthening existing bridges with carbon and glass fiber sheets, development of drive shafts using composite materials. *Unit head:* Dr. Nabil Grace, Interim Dean, 248-204-2500, Fax: 248-204-2509, E-mail: engrdean@ltu.edu. *Application contact:* Jane Rohrback, Director of Admissions, 248-204-3160, Fax: 248-204-3188, E-mail: admissions@ltu.edu.

Lehigh University, P.C. Rossin College of Engineering and Applied Science, Department of Industrial and Systems Engineering, Bethlehem, PA 18015. Offers analytical finance (MS); industrial engineering (M Eng, MS, PhD); information and systems engineering (M Eng, MS); management science (MS); quality engineering (MS); MBA/E. Part-time programs available. Postbaccalaureate distance learning degree programs offered (no on-campus study). *Faculty:* 12 full-time (1 woman), 1 part-time/adjunct (0 women). *Students:* 60 full-time (25 women), 20 part-time (5 women); includes 3 minority (all Asian Americans or Pacific Islanders), 51 international. Average age 28. 445 applicants, 9% accepted, 24 enrolled. In 2009, 26 master's, 8 doctorates awarded. *Degree requirements:* For master's, thesis (MS); project (M Eng); for doctorate, comprehensive exam, thesis/dissertation. *Entrance requirements:* For master's and doctorate, GRE General Test. Additional exam requirements/recommendations for international students: Required—TOEFL (minimum score 550 paper-based; 213 computer-based; 79 iBT). *Application deadline:* For fall admission, 7/15 for domestic and international students; for spring admission, 12/1 for domestic and international students. Applications are processed on a rolling basis. Application fee: $75. Electronic applications accepted. *Financial support:* In 2009–10, 26 students received support, including 9 fellowships with full tuition reimbursements available (averaging $19,265 per year), 10 research assistantships with full tuition reimbursements available (averaging $14,700 per year), 5 teaching assistantships with full tuition reimbursements available (averaging $16,020 per year); career-related internships or fieldwork, Federal Work-Study, institutionally sponsored loans, scholarships/grants, tuition waivers, and unspecified assistantships also available. Financial award application deadline: 1/15. *Faculty research:* Optimization, mathematical programming, logistics and supply chain, stochastic processes, large-scale computing, financial engineering. Total annual research expenditures: $2.1 million. *Unit head:* Dr. Tamas Terlaky, Chair, 610-758-4050, Fax: 610-758-4886, E-mail: terlaky@lehigh.edu. *Application contact:* Rita R. Frey, Graduate Coordinator, 610-758-4051, Fax: 610-758-4886, E-mail: ise@lehigh.edu.

Louisiana State University and Agricultural and Mechanical College, Graduate School, College of Engineering, Department of Construction Management and Industrial Engineering, Baton Rouge, LA 70803. Offers engineering science (PhD); industrial engineering (MSIE). *Faculty:* 13 full-time (5 women). *Students:* 14 full-time (1 woman), 9 part-time (2 women), 19 international. Average age 27. 30 applicants, 73% accepted, 6 enrolled. In 2009, 5 master's awarded. Terminal master's awarded for partial completion of doctoral program. *Degree requirements:* For master's, thesis; for doctorate, thesis/dissertation. *Entrance requirements:* For master's and doctorate, GRE General Test, minimum GPA of 3.0. Additional exam requirements/recommendations for international students: Required—TOEFL (minimum score 550 paper-based; 213 computer-based; 79 iBT) or IELTS (minimum score 6.5). *Application deadline:* For fall admission, 1/25 priority date for domestic students, 5/15 for international students; for spring admission, 10/15 for international students. Applications are processed on a rolling basis. Application fee: $50 ($70 for international students). Electronic applications accepted. *Financial support:* In 2009–10, 17 students received support, including 9 research assistantships with partial tuition reimbursements available (averaging $11,242 per year), 4 teaching assistantships with partial tuition reimbursements available (averaging $8,380 per year); fellowships, Federal Work-Study, institutionally sponsored loans, health care benefits, and unspecified assistantships also available. Financial award application deadline: 5/1; financial award applicants required to submit FAFSA. *Faculty research:* Ergonomics and occupational health, information technology, production systems, supply management, construction safety and methods. Total annual research expenditures: $178,060. *Unit head:* Dr. Thomas Ray, Chair, 225-578-5369, Fax: 225-578-5109, E-mail: tray@lsu.edu. *Application contact:* Dr. Fereydoun Aghazadeh, Graduate Adviser, 225-578-5112, Fax: 225-578-5109, E-mail: aghazadeh@lsu.edu.

Louisiana Tech University, Graduate School, College of Engineering and Science, Department of Industrial Engineering, Ruston, LA 71272. Offers MS.

Mississippi State University, Bagley College of Engineering, Department of Industrial and Systems Engineering, MS State, MS 39762. Offers engineering (PhD), including industrial engineering; industrial engineering (MS). Part-time programs available. Postbaccalaureate distance learning degree programs offered (no on-campus study). *Faculty:* 9 full-time (3 women), 1 part-time/adjunct (0 women). *Students:* 50 full-time (16 women), 48 part-time (5 women); includes 18 minority (11 African Americans, 6 Asian Americans or Pacific Islanders, 1 Hispanic American), 37 international. Average age 33. 71 applicants, 44% accepted, 21 enrolled. In 2009, 11 master's, 3 doctorates awarded. *Degree requirements:* For master's, comprehensive exam (for some programs), thesis (for some programs), comprehensive oral or written exam; for doctorate, thesis/dissertation, candidacy exam. *Entrance requirements:* For master's, GRE General Test, minimum GPA of 3.0; for doctorate, GRE General Test, minimum GPA of 3.3. Additional exam requirements/recommendations for international students: Required—TOEFL (minimum score 550 paper-based; 213 computer-based; 79 iBT); Recommended—IELTS (minimum score 6.5). *Application deadline:* For fall admission, 7/1 for domestic students, 5/1 for international students; for spring admission, 11/1 for domestic students, 9/1 for international students. Applications are processed on a rolling basis. Application fee: $40. *Expenses:* Tuition, state resident: full-time $2575.50; part-time $286.25 per credit hour. Tuition, nonresident: full-time $6510; part-time $723.50 per credit hour. Tuition and fees vary according to course load. *Financial support:* In 2009–10, 25 research assistantships with full tuition reimbursements (averaging $11,579 per year), 4 teaching assistantships with full tuition reimbursements (averaging $8,632 per year) were awarded; Federal Work-Study, institutionally sponsored loans, and unspecified assistantships also available. Financial award application deadline: 4/1; financial award applicants required to submit FAFSA. *Faculty research:* Operations research, ergonomics, production systems, management systems, transportation. *Unit head:* Dr. Royce Bowden, Professor and Head, 662-325-3865, Fax: 662-325-7618, E-mail: bowden@ise.msstate.edu. *Application contact:* Dr. John Usher, Professor, 662-325-7624, Fax: 662-325-7618, E-mail: usher@ise.msstate.edu.

Montana State University, College of Graduate Studies, College of Engineering, Department of Mechanical and Industrial Engineering, Bozeman, MT 59717. Offers engineering (PhD), including industrial engineering option, mechanical engineering option; industrial and management engineering (MS); mechanical engineering (MS). Part-time programs available. *Faculty:* 18 full-time (2 women), 4 part-time/adjunct (1 woman). *Students:* 20 full-time (3 women), 21 part-time (1 woman); includes 2 minority (1 American Indian/Alaska Native, 1 Asian American or Pacific Islander), 9 international. Average age 26. 44 applicants, 48% accepted, 8 enrolled. In 2009, 13 master's awarded. *Degree requirements:* For master's, comprehensive exam, thesis, oral exams; for doctorate, comprehensive exam, thesis/dissertation, qualifying exam. *Entrance requirements:* For master's and doctorate, GRE General Test. Additional exam requirements/recommendations for international students: Required—TOEFL (minimum score 550 paper-based; 213 computer-based). *Application deadline:* For fall admission, 7/15 priority date for domestic students, 5/15 priority date for international students; for spring admission, 12/1 priority date for domestic students, 10/1 priority date for international students. Applications are processed on a rolling basis. Application fee: $30. Electronic applications accepted. *Expenses:* Tuition, state resident: full-time $5635; part-time $3492 per year. Tuition, nonresident: full-time $17,212; part-time $7865.10 per year. Required fees: $1441.05; $153.15 per credit. Tuition and fees vary according to course load and program. *Financial support:* In 2009–10, 30 students received support, including 2 fellowships with full tuition reimbursements available (averaging $18,000 per year), 14 research assistantships with full and partial tuition reimbursements available (averaging $9,493 per year), 22 teaching assistantships with full and partial tuition reimbursements available (averaging $4,782 per year); scholarships/grants and unspecified assistantships also available. Financial award application deadline: 3/1; financial award applicants required to submit FAFSA. *Faculty research:* Design and manufacture; energy systems, materials and structures, measurement systems, systems modeling. Total annual research expenditures: $1.3 million. *Unit head:* Dr. Chris Jenkins, Head, 406-994-2203, Fax: 406-994-6292, E-mail: cjenkins@me.montana.edu. *Application contact:* Dr. Carl A. Fox, Vice Provost for Graduate Education, 406-994-4145, Fax: 406-994-7433, E-mail: gradstudy@montana.edu.

Montana Tech of The University of Montana, Graduate School, Project Engineering and Management Program, Butte, MT 59701-8997. Offers MPEM. Part-time and evening/weekend programs available. Postbaccalaureate distance learning degree programs offered (no on-campus study). *Faculty:* 1 full-time (0 women), 7 part-time/adjunct (1 woman). *Students:* 15 part-time (6 women); includes 2 minority (both American Indian/Alaska Native). 10 applicants, 50% accepted, 3 enrolled. In 2009, 3 master's awarded. *Degree requirements:* For master's, comprehensive exam, final project presentation. *Entrance requirements:* For master's, minimum GPA of 3.0. Additional exam requirements/recommendations for international students: Required—TOEFL (minimum score 550 paper-based; 213 computer-based; 71 iBT). *Application deadline:* For fall admission, 4/1 priority date for domestic students, 3/1 priority date for international students; for spring admission, 10/1 priority date for domestic students, 7/1 priority date for international students. Applications are processed on a rolling basis. Application fee: $30. Electronic applications accepted. *Expenses:* Tuition, state resident: full-time $5068; part-time $319 per credit. Tuition, nonresident: full-time $14,815; part-time $875 per credit. Tuition and fees vary according to course load and campus/location. *Financial support:* Application deadline: 4/1. *Unit head:* Dr. Kumar Ganesan, Director, 406-496-4239, Fax: 406-496-4650, E-mail: kganesan@mtech.edu. *Application contact:* Cindy Dunstan, Administrator, Graduate School, 406-496-4304, Fax: 406-496-4710, E-mail: cdunstan@mtech.edu.

Morehead State University, Graduate Programs, College of Science and Technology, Department of Industrial and Engineering Technology, Morehead, KY 40351. Offers career and technical education (MS); engineering technology (MS). Part-time and evening/weekend programs available. *Faculty:* 6 full-time (2 women). *Students:* 11 full-time (2 women), 14 part-time (5 women); includes 1 minority (African American), 3 international. Average age 33. 17 applicants, 41% accepted, 6 enrolled. In 2009, 18 master's awarded. *Degree requirements:* For master's, completion and defense of thesis or written and oral comprehensive exit exams. *Entrance requirements:* For master's, GRE, minimum undergraduate GPA of 3.0 in major. Additional exam requirements/recommendations for international students: Required—TOEFL (minimum score 500 paper-based; 173 computer-based). *Application deadline:* For fall admission, 8/1 priority date for domestic and international students; for spring admission, 12/1 priority date for domestic and international students. Applications are processed on a rolling basis. Application fee: $30. Electronic applications accepted. *Expenses:* Tuition, state resident: full-time $6318; part-time $351 per credit hour. Tuition, nonresident: full-time $15,804; part-time $878 per credit hour. *Financial support:* In 2009–10, 1 research assistantship (averaging $10,000 per year), 3 teaching assistantships (averaging $10,000 per year) were awarded; unspecified assistantships also available. Financial award application deadline: 3/15; financial award applicants required to submit FAFSA. *Unit head:* Dr. Ahmad Zargari, Chair and Professor, 606-783-2425, Fax: 606-783-5030, E-mail: a.zargar@moreheadstate.edu. *Application contact:* Michelle Barber, Graduate Recruitment and Retention Assistant Director, 606-783-5127, Fax: 606-783-5061, E-mail: b.cowsert@moreheadstate.edu.

Morgan State University, School of Graduate Studies, Clarence M. Mitchell, Jr. School of Engineering, Baltimore, MD 21251. Offers civil engineering (M Eng, D Eng); electrical engineering (M Eng, D Eng); industrial engineering (M Eng, D Eng); transportation (MS). Part-time and evening/weekend programs available. *Degree requirements:* For master's, thesis, comprehensive exam or equivalent; for doctorate, thesis/dissertation, comprehensive exam or equivalent. *Entrance requirements:* For master's, GRE, minimum undergraduate GPA of 2.5; for doctorate, GRE, minimum GPA of 3.0. Additional exam requirements/recommendations for international students: Required—TOEFL (minimum score 550 paper-based; 213 computer-based).

New Jersey Institute of Technology, Office of Graduate Studies, Newark College of Engineering, Department of Industrial and Manufacturing Engineering, Program in Industrial Engineering, Newark, NJ 07102. Offers MS, PhD. Part-time and evening/weekend programs available. Terminal master's awarded for partial completion of doctoral program. *Degree requirements:* For master's, thesis or alternative; for doctorate, thesis/dissertation. *Entrance requirements:* For master's, GRE General Test; for doctorate, GRE General Test, minimum graduate GPA of 3.5. Additional exam requirements/recommendations for international students: Required—TOEFL (minimum score 550 paper-based; 213 computer-based; 79 iBT). Electronic applications accepted. *Faculty research:* Knowledge-based systems, CAS/CAM simulation and interface, expert system.

New Mexico State University, Graduate School, College of Engineering, Department of Industrial Engineering, Las Cruces, NM 88003-8001. Offers MSIE, PhD. Part-time and evening/weekend programs available. Postbaccalaureate distance learning degree programs offered (no on-campus study). *Faculty:* 5 full-time (1 woman). *Students:* 45 full-time (21 women), 77 part-time (25 women); includes 46 minority (8 African Americans, 1 American Indian/Alaska Native, 4 Asian Americans or Pacific Islanders, 33 Hispanic Americans), 25 international. Average age 31. 79 applicants, 86% accepted, 38 enrolled. In 2009, 37 master's, 3 doctorates awarded. *Degree requirements:* For master's, thesis optional; for doctorate, comprehensive exam, thesis/dissertation. *Entrance requirements:* For doctorate, qualifying exam. Additional exam requirements/recommendations for international students: Required—TOEFL. *Application deadline:* For fall admission, 7/1 priority date for domestic students, 3/1 for international students; for spring admission, 11/1 for domestic students, 10/1 for international students. Applications are processed on a rolling basis. Application fee: $30 ($50 for international students). Electronic applications accepted. *Expenses:* Tuition, state resident: full-time $4080; part-time $223 per credit. Tuition, nonresident: full-time $14,256; part-time $647 per credit. Required fees: $1278; $639 per semester. *Financial support:* In 2009–10, 5 research assistantships (averaging $11,030 per year), 16 teaching assistantships (averaging $7,705 per year) were awarded; fellowships, career-related internships or fieldwork, Federal Work-Study, health care benefits, and unspecified assistantships also available. Financial award application deadline: 3/1. *Faculty research:* Simulation, stochastic modeling, optimization, systems engineering. *Unit head:* Dr. Edward Pines, Head, 575-646-4923, Fax: 575-646-2976, E-mail: epines@nmsu.edu. *Application contact:* Sarah Deyoe, Departmental Secretary, 575-646-4923, Fax: 575-646-2976, E-mail: sdeyoe@nmsu.edu.

North Carolina Agricultural and Technical State University, Graduate School, College of Engineering, Department of Industrial and Systems Engineering, Greensboro, NC 27411. Offers industrial engineering (MSIE, PhD). Part-time programs available. *Degree requirements:* For master's, thesis, project; for doctorate, thesis/dissertation. *Entrance requirements:* For master's, GRE General Test (recommended); for doctorate, GRE General Test. *Faculty research:* Human-machine systems engineering, management systems engineering, operations research and systems analysis, production systems engineering.

North Carolina State University, Graduate School, College of Engineering, Edward P. Fitts Department of Industrial and Systems Engineering, Raleigh, NC 27695. Offers industrial engineering (MIE, MS, PhD). Part-time programs available. Terminal master's awarded for partial completion of doctoral program. *Degree requirements:* For master's, thesis optional; for doctorate, thesis/dissertation. *Entrance requirements:* For master's, GRE General Test, minimum GPA of 3.0; for doctorate, GRE General Test. Additional exam requirements/recommendations for international students: Required—TOEFL. Electronic applications accepted.

North Dakota State University, College of Graduate and Interdisciplinary Studies, College of Engineering and Architecture, Department of Industrial and Manufacturing Engineering, Fargo, ND 58108. Offers industrial and manufacturing engineering (PhD); industrial engineering and management (MS); manufacturing engineering (MS). Part-time programs available. *Faculty:* 13 full-time (2 women), 1 part-time/adjunct (0 women). *Students:* 16 full-time (4 women), 10 part-time (3 women), 25 international. Average age 26. 25 applicants, 88% accepted, 9 enrolled. In 2009, 7 master's awarded. *Degree requirements:* For doctorate, comprehensive exam, thesis/dissertation. *Entrance requirements:* For master's, GRE General Test, bachelor's degree in engineering; for doctorate, GRE General Test, master's degree in engineering. Additional exam requirements/recommendations for international students: Required—TOEFL (minimum score 550 paper-based; 213 computer-based; 79 iBT), TWE (minimum score 4). *Application deadline:* For fall admission, 3/1 priority date for domestic students, 3/1 for international students; for spring admission, 11/1 priority date for domestic students, 11/1 for international students. Applications are processed on a rolling basis. Application fee: $45 ($60 for international students). Electronic applications accepted. *Financial support:* In 2009–10, 2 fellowships with full tuition reimbursements (averaging $15,000 per year), 9 research assistantships with full tuition reimbursements (averaging $12,000 per year), 16 teaching assistantships with full tuition reimbursements (averaging $12,000 per year) were awarded; Federal Work-Study, institutionally sponsored loans, scholarships/grants, and unspecified assistantships also available. Financial award application deadline: 4/1. *Faculty research:* Electronics manufacturing, quality engineering, manufacturing process science, healthcare, lean manufacturing.

Industrial/Management Engineering

North Dakota State University (continued)

Total annual research expenditures: $60,000. *Unit head:* Prof. Kambiz Farahmand, Chair, 701-231-7287, Fax: 701-231-7195, E-mail: kambiz.farahmand@ndsu.edu. *Application contact:* Dr. David A. Wittrock, Dean, 701-231-7033, Fax: 701-231-6524.

Northeastern University, College of Engineering, Department of Mechanical, Industrial, and Manufacturing Engineering, Boston, MA 02115-5096. Offers engineering management (MS); industrial engineering (MS, PhD); mechanical engineering (MS, PhD); operations research (MS). Part-time programs available. *Faculty:* 34 full-time (2 women), 7 part-time/adjunct (0 women). *Students:* 270 full-time (56 women), 137 part-time (27 women); includes 4 African Americans, 9 Asian Americans or Pacific Islanders, 3 Hispanic Americans, 182 international. 573 applicants, 75% accepted, 142 enrolled. In 2009, 94 master's, 9 doctorates awarded. *Degree requirements:* For master's, thesis (for some programs); for doctorate, thesis/dissertation, departmental qualifying exam. *Entrance requirements:* For master's and doctorate, GRE General Test. Additional exam requirements/recommendations for international students: Required—TOEFL (minimum score 550 paper-based; 213 computer-based; 80 iBT). *Application deadline:* For fall admission, 1/15 priority date for domestic and international students; for spring admission, 11/1 priority date for domestic students. Applications are processed on a rolling basis. Application fee: $50. Electronic applications accepted. *Financial support:* In 2009–10, 79 students received support, including 42 research assistantships with full tuition reimbursements available (averaging $18,320 per year), 37 teaching assistantships with full tuition reimbursements available; fellowships with full tuition reimbursements available, career-related internships or fieldwork, Federal Work-Study, scholarships/grants, health care benefits, and unspecified assistantships also available. Support available to part-time students. Financial award application deadline: 1/15; financial award applicants required to submit FAFSA. *Faculty research:* Dry sliding instabilities, droplet deposition, combustion, manufacturing systems, nano-manufacturing, advanced materials processing, bio-nano robotics, burning speed measurement, virtual environments. *Unit head:* Dr. Hameed Metghalchi, Chairman, 617-373-2973, Fax: 617-373-2921. *Application contact:* Stephen L. Gibson, Associate Director, 617-373-2711, Fax: 617-373-2501, E-mail: grad-eng@coe.neu.edu.

Northern Illinois University, Graduate School, College of Engineering and Engineering Technology, Department of Industrial Engineering, De Kalb, IL 60115-2854. Offers MS. Part-time programs available. *Faculty:* 4 full-time (1 woman), 1 part-time/adjunct (0 women). *Students:* 33 full-time (9 women), 33 part-time (6 women); includes 6 minority (2 Asian Americans or Pacific Islanders, 4 Hispanic Americans), 51 international. Average age 25. 101 applicants, 68% accepted, 21 enrolled. In 2009, 28 master's awarded. *Degree requirements:* For master's, comprehensive exam, thesis optional. *Entrance requirements:* For master's, GRE General Test, minimum GPA of 2.75. Additional exam requirements/recommendations for international students: Required—TOEFL (minimum score 550 paper-based; 213 computer-based). *Application deadline:* For fall admission, 6/1 for domestic students, 5/1 for international students; for spring admission, 11/1 for domestic students, 10/1 for international students. Applications are processed on a rolling basis. Application fee: $30. Electronic applications accepted. *Expenses:* Tuition, state resident: full-time $6576; part-time $274 per credit hour. Tuition, nonresident: full-time $13,152; part-time $548 per credit hour. Required fees: $1813; $75.53 per credit hour. Part-time tuition and fees vary according to course load. *Financial support:* In 2009–10, 4 research assistantships, 6 teaching assistantships were awarded; fellowships, Federal Work-Study, scholarships/grants, tuition waivers (full), and staff assistantships also available. Support available to part-time students. Financial award applicants required to submit FAFSA. *Faculty research:* Assembly robots, engineering ethics, quality cost models, data mining. *Unit head:* Dr. Omar Ghrayeb, Chair, 815-753-1349, Fax: 815-753-0823. *Application contact:* Graduate School Office, 815-753-0395, E-mail: gradsch@niu.edu.

Northwestern University, McCormick School of Engineering and Applied Science, Department of Industrial Engineering and Management Sciences, Evanston, IL 60208. Offers engineering management (MEM); industrial engineering and management science (MS, PhD); operations research (MS, PhD). MS and PhD admissions and degrees offered through The Graduate School. Terminal master's awarded for partial completion of doctoral program. *Degree requirements:* For master's, comprehensive exam; for doctorate, comprehensive exam, thesis/dissertation. Electronic applications accepted. *Faculty research:* Production, logistics, optimization, simulation, statistics.

The Ohio State University, Graduate School, College of Engineering, Program in Industrial and Systems Engineering, Columbus, OH 43210. Offers MS, PhD. *Faculty:* 39. *Students:* 52 full-time (16 women), 39 part-time (5 women); includes 7 minority (1 African American, 3 Asian Americans or Pacific Islanders, 3 Hispanic Americans), 57 international. Average age 29. In 2009, 23 master's, 11 doctorates awarded. *Degree requirements:* For master's, thesis optional; for doctorate, thesis/dissertation. *Entrance requirements:* For master's and doctorate, GRE General Test. Additional exam requirements/recommendations for international students: Recommended—TOEFL (minimum score 600 paper-based; 250 computer-based). *Application deadline:* For fall admission, 8/15 priority date for domestic students, 11/1 priority date for international students; for winter admission, 12/1 priority date for domestic students, 7/1 priority date for international students; for spring admission, 3/1 priority date for domestic students, 2/1 priority date for international students. Applications are processed on a rolling basis. Application fee: $40 ($50 for international students). Electronic applications accepted. *Expenses:* Tuition, state resident: full-time $10,683. Tuition, nonresident: full-time $25,923. Tuition and fees vary according to course load and program. *Financial support:* Fellowships, research assistantships, teaching assistantships, career-related internships or fieldwork, Federal Work-Study, institutionally sponsored loans, and unspecified assistantships available. Support available to part-time students. *Unit head:* Jerald Brevick, Graduate Studies Committee Chair, E-mail: brevick.1@osu.edu. *Application contact:* 614-292-9444, Fax: 614-292-3895, E-mail: domestic.grad@osu.edu.

Ohio University, Graduate College, Russ College of Engineering and Technology, Department of Industrial and Systems Engineering, Athens, OH 45701-2979. Offers M Eng Mgt, MS. Part-time and evening/weekend programs available. *Faculty:* 8 full-time (0 women), 1 part-time/adjunct (0 women). *Students:* 22 full-time (7 women), 26 part-time (4 women); includes 2 minority (both African Americans), 22 international. 53 applicants, 66% accepted, 13 enrolled. In 2009, 16 master's awarded. *Degree requirements:* For master's, comprehensive exam (for some programs), thesis optional, research project. *Entrance requirements:* For master's, GRE General Test. Additional exam requirements/recommendations for international students: Required—TOEFL (minimum score 550 paper-based; 80 iBT) or IELTS Academic (minimum score 6.5). *Application deadline:* For fall admission, 3/1 priority date for domestic and international students; for winter admission, 9/1 priority date for domestic and international students; for spring admission, 1/1 priority date for domestic and international students. Applications are processed on a rolling basis. Application fee: $50 ($55 for international students). Electronic applications accepted. *Expenses:* Tuition, state resident: full-time $7839; part-time $323 per quarter hour. Tuition, nonresident: full-time $15,831; part-time $654 per quarter hour. Required fees: $2931. *Financial support:* In 2009–10, research assistantships with full tuition reimbursements (averaging $9,000 per year); Federal Work-Study, institutionally sponsored loans, tuition waivers (full), and unspecified assistantships also available. Financial award application deadline: 2/15; financial award applicants required to submit FAFSA. *Faculty research:* Software systems integration, human factors and ergonomics. Total annual research expenditures: $350,000. *Unit head:* Dr. Robert P. Judd, Chairman, 740-593-0106, Fax: 740-593-0778, E-mail: judd@ohio.edu. *Application contact:* Dr. Gursel Suer, Graduate Chairman, 740-593-1542, Fax: 740-593-0778, E-mail: suer@ohio.edu.

Ohio University, Graduate College, Russ College of Engineering and Technology, Program in Mechanical and Systems Engineering, Athens, OH 45701-2979. Offers industrial (PhD); mechanical (PhD). *Faculty:* 40 full-time (1 woman), 1 part-time/adjunct (0 women). *Students:* 15 full-time (2 women), 4 part-time (0 women), 13 international. 13 applicants, 54% accepted, 1 enrolled. In 2009, 4 doctorates awarded. *Degree requirements:* For doctorate, comprehensive

exam, thesis/dissertation. *Entrance requirements:* For doctorate, GRE General Test, MS in engineering or related field. Additional exam requirements/recommendations for international students: Required—TOEFL (minimum score 550 paper-based; 80 iBT) or IELTS Academic (minimum score 6.5). *Application deadline:* For fall admission, 3/15 priority date for domestic and international students. Applications are processed on a rolling basis. Application fee: $50 ($55 for international students). Electronic applications accepted. *Expenses:* Tuition, state resident: full-time $7839; part-time $323 per quarter hour. Tuition, nonresident: full-time $15,831; part-time $654 per quarter hour. Required fees: $2931. *Financial support:* In 2009–10, 4 research assistantships with full tuition reimbursements (averaging $14,000 per year) were awarded; Federal Work-Study, institutionally sponsored loans, and unspecified assistantships also available. Financial award application deadline: 3/15; financial award applicants required to submit FAFSA. *Faculty research:* Material processing, expert systems, environmental geo-technical manufacturing, thermal systems, robotics. Total annual research expenditures: $1.8 million. *Unit head:* Dr. James Rankin, Associate Dean for Research and Graduate Studies, 740-593-1482, Fax: 740-593-0659, E-mail: rankinj@ohio.edu. *Application contact:* Dr. James Rankin, Associate Dean for Research and Graduate Studies, 740-593-1482, Fax: 740-593-0659, E-mail: rankin@ohio.edu.

Oklahoma State University, College of Engineering, Architecture and Technology, School of Industrial Engineering and Management, Stillwater, OK 74078. Offers MS, PhD. Post-baccalaureate distance learning degree programs offered. *Faculty:* 12 full-time (1 woman), 2 part-time/adjunct (1 woman). *Students:* 86 full-time (10 women), 173 part-time (30 women); includes 22 minority (5 African Americans, 4 American Indian/Alaska Native, 9 Asian Americans or Pacific Islanders, 4 Hispanic Americans), 111 international. Average age 31. 321 applicants, 48% accepted, 70 enrolled. In 2009, 76 master's, 4 doctorates awarded. *Degree requirements:* For master's, creative component or thesis; for doctorate, comprehensive exam, thesis/dissertation. *Entrance requirements:* For master's and doctorate, GRE or GMAT. Additional exam requirements/recommendations for international students: Required—TOEFL (minimum score 550 paper-based; 79 iBT). *Application deadline:* For fall admission, 3/1 priority date for international students; for spring admission, 8/1 priority date for international students. Applications are processed on a rolling basis. Application fee: $40 ($75 for international students). Electronic applications accepted. *Expenses:* Tuition, state resident: full-time $3716; part-time $154.85 per credit hour. Tuition, nonresident: full-time $14,448; part-time $602 per credit hour. Required fees: $1772; $73.85 per credit hour. One-time fee: $50. Tuition and fees vary according to course load and campus/location. *Financial support:* In 2009–10, 36 research assistantships (averaging $10,270 per year), 26 teaching assistantships (averaging $6,531 per year) were awarded; career-related internships or fieldwork, Federal Work-Study, scholarships/grants, health care benefits, tuition waivers (partial), and unspecified assistantships also available. Support available to part-time students. Financial award application deadline: 3/1; financial award applicants required to submit FAFSA. *Unit head:* Dr. William J. Kolarik, Head, 405-744-6055, Fax: 405-744-4654. *Application contact:* Dr. Gordon Emslie, Dean, 405-744-6368, Fax: 405-744-0355, E-mail: grad-i@okstate.edu.

Oregon State University, Graduate School, College of Engineering, School of Mechanical, Industrial, and Manufacturing Engineering, Corvallis, OR 97331. Offers human systems engineering (MS, PhD); industrial engineering (MS, PhD); information systems engineering (MS, PhD); manufacturing engineering (M Engr); manufacturing systems engineering (MS, PhD); materials science (MAIS, MS, PhD); mechanical engineering (MS, PhD); nano/micro fabrication (MS, PhD). Part-time programs available. Postbaccalaureate distance learning degree programs offered (minimal on-campus study). *Faculty:* 26 full-time (2 women), 2 part-time/adjunct (1 woman). *Students:* 136 full-time (25 women), 12 part-time (2 women); includes 11 minority (3 African Americans, 4 Asian Americans or Pacific Islanders, 4 Hispanic Americans), 46 international. Average age 29. 53 applicants, 42% accepted, 13 enrolled. In 2009, 26 master's, 10 doctorates awarded. *Degree requirements:* For master's, thesis or alternative; for doctorate, thesis/dissertation. *Entrance requirements:* For master's, placement exam, minimum GPA of 3.0 in last 90 hours of course work; for doctorate, GRE, placement exam, minimum GPA of 3.0 in last 90 hours of course work. Additional exam requirements/recommendations for international students: Required—TOEFL (minimum score 550 paper-based; 213 computer-based). *Application deadline:* For fall admission, 3/1 for domestic students. Applications are processed on a rolling basis. Application fee: $50. *Expenses:* Tuition, state resident: full-time $9774; part-time $362 per credit. Tuition, nonresident: full-time $15,849; part-time $587 per credit. Required fees: $1639. Full-time tuition and fees vary according to course load and program. *Financial support:* In 2009–10, 10 research assistantships with full tuition reimbursements (averaging $11,124 per year), 8 teaching assistantships with full tuition reimbursements (averaging $7,020 per year) were awarded; fellowships with full tuition reimbursements, institutionally sponsored loans and instructorships also available. Support available to part-time students. Financial award application deadline: 2/1. *Faculty research:* Computer-integrated manufacturing, human factors, robotics, decision support systems, simulation modeling and analysis. Total annual research expenditures: $1.3 million. *Unit head:* Dr. Belinda A. Batten, Head, 541-737-3441, Fax: 541-737-2600, E-mail: info-mime@oregonstate.edu. *Application contact:* Jean Robinson, Graduate Records Specialist, 541-737-7009, Fax: 541-737-2600, E-mail: jean.robinson@oregonstate.edu.

Penn State University Park, Graduate School, College of Engineering, Department of Industrial and Manufacturing Engineering, State College, University Park, PA 16802-1503. Offers M Eng, MS, PhD.

Polytechnic Institute of NYU, Department of Interdisciplinary Studies, Major in Industrial Engineering, Brooklyn, NY 11201-2990. Offers MS. Part-time and evening/weekend programs available. *Students:* 26 full-time (5 women), 6 part-time (2 women); includes 4 minority (1 Asian American or Pacific Islander, 3 Hispanic Americans), 25 international. Average age 30. 65 applicants, 77% accepted, 13 enrolled. In 2009, 12 master's awarded. *Degree requirements:* For master's, comprehensive exam (for some programs), thesis (for some programs). *Entrance requirements:* For master's, BE or BS in engineering, physics, chemistry, mathematical sciences, or biological sciences or MBA. Additional exam requirements/recommendations for international students: Required—TOEFL (minimum score 550 paper-based; 213 computer-based; 80 iBT); Recommended—IELTS (minimum score 6.5). *Application deadline:* For fall admission, 7/31 priority date for domestic students, 4/30 priority date for international students; for spring admission, 12/31 priority date for domestic students, 11/30 priority date for international students. Applications are processed on a rolling basis. Application fee: $75. Electronic applications accepted. *Expenses:* Tuition: Full-time $21,492; part-time $1194 per credit hour. Required fees: $1160; $204 per course. *Financial support:* Institutionally sponsored loans, scholarships/grants, and unspecified assistantships available. Support available to part-time students. Financial award applicants required to submit FAFSA. *Application contact:* JeanCarlo Bonilla, Director of Graduate Enrollment Management, 718-260-3182, Fax: 718-260-3624, E-mail: gradinfo@poly.edu.

Polytechnic Institute of NYU, Long Island Graduate Center, Graduate Programs, Department of Interdisciplinary Studies, Major in Industrial Engineering, Melville, NY 11747. Offers MS. Part-time and evening/weekend programs available. *Students:* 1 full-time (0 women), all international. *Entrance requirements:* Additional exam requirements/recommendations for international students: Required—TOEFL (minimum score 550 paper-based; 213 computer-based; 80 iBT); Recommended—IELTS (minimum score 6.5). *Application deadline:* For fall admission, 7/31 priority date for domestic students, 4/30 priority date for international students; for spring admission, 12/31 priority date for domestic students, 11/30 priority date for international students. Applications are processed on a rolling basis. Application fee: $75. Electronic applications accepted. *Financial support:* Institutionally sponsored loans, scholarships/grants, and unspecified assistantships available. Support available to part-time students. *Application contact:* JeanCarlo Bonilla, Director of Graduate Enrollment Management, 718-260-3182, Fax: 718-260-3624, E-mail: gradinfo@poly.edu.

Polytechnic Institute of NYU, Long Island Graduate Center, Graduate Programs, Department of Mechanical and Aerospace Engineering, Melville, NY 11747. Offers aeronautics and astronautics (MS); industrial engineering (MS); manufacturing engineering (MS); mechanical engineering (MS). Part-time and evening/weekend programs available. *Students:* 1 (woman) part-time. Average age 25. In 2009, 2 master's awarded. *Degree requirements:* For master's, comprehensive exam (for some programs), thesis (for some programs). *Entrance requirements:* Additional exam requirements/recommendations for international students: Required—TOEFL (minimum score 550 paper-based; 213 computer-based; 80 iBT); Recommended—IELTS (minimum score 6.5). *Application deadline:* For fall admission, 7/31 priority date for domestic students, 4/30 priority date for international students; for spring admission, 12/31 priority date for domestic students, 11/30 priority date for international students. Applications are processed on a rolling basis. Application fee: $75. Electronic applications accepted. *Financial support:* In 2009–10, 16 fellowships with tuition reimbursements (averaging $1,394 per year) were awarded; research assistantships with tuition reimbursements, institutionally sponsored loans, scholarships/grants, and unspecified assistantships also available. Support available to part-time students. Financial award applicants required to submit FAFSA. *Faculty research:* UV filter, fuel efficient hydrodynamic containment for gas core fission, turbulent boundary layer research. *Unit head:* Dr. George Vradis, Department Head, 718-260-3875, E-mail: gvradis@duke.poly.edu. *Application contact:* JeanCarlo Bonilla, Director of Graduate Enrollment Management, 718-260-3182, Fax: 718-260-3624, E-mail: gradinfo@poly.edu.

Polytechnic Institute of NYU, Westchester Graduate Center, Graduate Programs, Department of Interdisciplinary Studies, Major in Industrial Engineering, Hawthorne, NY 10532-1507. Offers MS. *Students:* 1 full-time (0 women), 1 part-time (0 women), both international. *Entrance requirements:* Additional exam requirements/recommendations for international students: Required—TOEFL (minimum score 550 paper-based; 213 computer-based; 80 iBT); Recommended—IELTS (minimum score 6.5). *Application deadline:* For fall admission, 7/31 priority date for domestic students, 4/30 priority date for international students; for spring admission, 12/31 priority date for domestic students, 11/30 priority date for international students. Applications are processed on a rolling basis. Application fee: $75. Electronic applications accepted. *Financial support:* Institutionally sponsored loans, scholarships/grants, and unspecified assistantships available. Support available to part-time students. *Application contact:* JeanCarlo Bonilla, Director of Graduate Enrollment Management, 718-260-3182, Fax: 718-260-3624, E-mail: gradinfo@poly.edu.

Purdue University, College of Engineering, School of Industrial Engineering, West Lafayette, IN 47907-2023. Offers MS, MSIE, PhD. Part-time programs available. Postbaccalaureate distance learning degree programs offered (no on-campus study). Terminal master's awarded for partial completion of doctoral program. *Entrance requirements:* For master's and doctorate, GRE General Test, minimum GPA of 3.0. Additional exam requirements/recommendations for international students: Required—TOEFL (minimum score 570 paper-based; 220 computer-based); Recommended—TWE. Electronic applications accepted. *Faculty research:* Precision manufacturing process, computer-aided manufacturing, computer-aided process planning, knowledge-based systems, combinatorics.

Rensselaer Polytechnic Institute, Graduate School, School of Engineering, Department of Industrial and Systems Engineering, Program in Decision Sciences and Engineering Systems, Troy, NY 12180-3590. Offers industrial and systems engineering (PhD). Part-time programs available. *Faculty:* 10 full-time (2 women). *Students:* 21 full-time (7 women), 1 part-time (0 women); includes 2 minority (both Asian Americans or Pacific Islanders), 15 international. Average age 28. 60 applicants, 7% accepted, 4 enrolled. In 2009, 6 doctorates awarded. Terminal master's awarded for partial completion of doctoral program. *Degree requirements:* For doctorate, thesis/dissertation. *Entrance requirements:* For doctorate, GRE General Test (minimum score 550 verbal). Additional exam requirements/recommendations for international students: Required—TOEFL (minimum score 570 paper-based). *Application deadline:* For fall admission, 1/1 priority date for domestic students, 1/1 for international students; for spring admission, 8/15 for domestic and international students. Applications are processed on a rolling basis. Application fee: $75. Electronic applications accepted. *Expenses:* Tuition: Full-time $38,100. *Financial support:* In 2009–10, 20 students received support, including 1 fellowship with full tuition reimbursement available (averaging $22,000 per year), 12 research assistantships with full tuition reimbursements available (averaging $22,000 per year), 7 teaching assistantships with full tuition reimbursements available (averaging $16,500 per year); career-related internships or fieldwork and institutionally sponsored loans also available. Financial award application deadline: 1/1. *Faculty research:* Decision support systems, simulation and modeling, statistical methods/computing, operations research, supply chain logistics. Total annual research expenditures: $1.3 million. *Unit head:* Dr. Charles J. Malmborg, Department Head, 518-276-2773, Fax: 518-276-8227, E-mail: malmbc@rpi.edu. *Application contact:* Mary Wagner, Graduate Coordinator, 518-276-2895, Fax: 518-276-8227, E-mail: wagnem@rpi.edu.

Rensselaer Polytechnic Institute, Graduate School, School of Engineering, Department of Industrial and Systems Engineering, Program in Industrial and Management Engineering, Troy, NY 12180-3590. Offers M Eng, MS. Part-time programs available. *Faculty:* 9 full-time (1 woman). *Students:* 6 full-time (2 women), 3 part-time (0 women); includes 1 minority (Hispanic American), 1 international. 64 applicants, 16% accepted, 7 enrolled. In 2009, 15 master's awarded. *Degree requirements:* For master's, thesis (for some programs). *Entrance requirements:* For master's, GRE General Test (minimum score 550 verbal). Additional exam requirements/recommendations for international students: Required—TOEFL (minimum score 570 paper-based). *Application deadline:* For fall admission, 1/1 priority date for domestic students, 1/1 for international students; for spring admission, 8/15 for domestic and international students. Applications are processed on a rolling basis. Application fee: $75. Electronic applications accepted. *Expenses:* Tuition: Full-time $38,100. *Financial support:* Fellowships, research assistantships with full tuition reimbursements, teaching assistantships with full tuition reimbursements, career-related internships or fieldwork and institutionally sponsored loans available. Financial award application deadline: 1/1. *Faculty research:* Decision support systems, simulation and modeling, statistical methods/computing, operations research, supply chain logistics. Total annual research expenditures: $1.3 million. *Unit head:* Dr. Charles J. Malmborg, Department Head, 518-276-2895, Fax: 518-276-8227, E-mail: malmbc@rpi.edu. *Application contact:* Mary Wagner, Graduate Coordinator, 518-276-2895, Fax: 518-276-8227, E-mail: wagnem@rpi.edu.

Rochester Institute of Technology, Graduate Enrollment Services, Kate Gleason College of Engineering, Department of Industrial and Systems Engineering, Rochester, NY 14623-5603. Offers engineering management (ME); industrial engineering (ME, MS); manufacturing engineering (ME, MS); systems engineering (ME). Part-time programs available. *Students:* 62 full-time (17 women), 10 part-time (5 women); includes 5 minority (2 African Americans, 2 Asian Americans or Pacific Islanders, 1 Hispanic American), 55 international. Average age 25. 186 applicants, 50% accepted, 40 enrolled. In 2009, 53 master's awarded. *Degree requirements:* For master's, internship. *Entrance requirements:* For master's, GRE, minimum GPA of 3.0. Additional exam requirements/recommendations for international students: Required—TOEFL (minimum score 570 paper-based; 230 computer-based; 88 iBT), or IELTS (minimum score 6.5). *Application deadline:* For fall admission, 2/15 priority date for domestic and international students. Applications are processed on a rolling basis. Application fee: $50. *Expenses:* Tuition: Full-time $31,533; part-time $876 per credit hour. Required fees: $210. *Financial support:* In 2009–10, 63 students received support; research assistantships with partial tuition reimbursements available, teaching assistantships with partial tuition reimbursements available, career-related internships or fieldwork, institutionally sponsored loans, scholarships/grants, tuition waivers (partial), and unspecified assistantships available. Support available to part-time students. Financial award applicants required to submit FAFSA. *Faculty research:* Safety, manufacturing (CAM), simulation. *Unit head:* Dr. Jacqueline Mozrall, Department Head, 585-475-2598, E-mail: ise@rit.edu. *Application contact:* Diane Ellison, Assistant Vice President, Graduate Enrollment Services, 585-475-2229, Fax: 585-475-7164, E-mail: gradinfo@rit.edu.

Rutgers, The State University of New Jersey, New Brunswick, Graduate School-New Brunswick, Program in Industrial and Systems Engineering, Piscataway, NJ 08854-8097. Offers industrial and systems engineering (MS, PhD); information technology (MS); manufacturing systems engineering (MS); quality and reliability engineering (MS). Part-time and evening/weekend programs available. Terminal master's awarded for partial completion of doctoral program. *Degree requirements:* For master's, thesis or alternative, seminar; for doctorate, comprehensive exam, thesis/dissertation. *Entrance requirements:* For master's and doctorate, GRE General Test. Additional exam requirements/recommendations for international students: Required—TOEFL. *Faculty research:* Production and manufacturing systems, quality and reliability engineering, systems engineering and aviation safety.

St. Mary's University, Graduate School, Department of Engineering, Program in Industrial Engineering, San Antonio, TX 78228-8507. Offers engineering computer applications (MS); engineering management (MS); industrial engineering (MS); operations research (MS); JD/MS. Part-time programs available. *Degree requirements:* For master's, comprehensive exam. *Entrance requirements:* For master's, GRE General Test, BS in science or engineering, minimum GPA of 3.0. Additional exam requirements/recommendations for international students: Required—TOEFL (minimum score 550 paper-based; 213 computer-based; 80 iBT). Electronic applications accepted. *Expenses:* Tuition: Full-time $8004. Required fees: $536. One-time fee: $5 full-time. Full-time tuition and fees vary according to program. *Faculty research:* Robotics, artificial intelligence, manufacturing engineering.

Sam Houston State University, College of Arts and Sciences, Department of Agricultural Sciences, Huntsville, TX 77341. Offers agriculture (MS); industrial technology (MA). Part-time and evening/weekend programs available. *Faculty:* 8 full-time (1 woman), 2 part-time/adjunct (0 women). *Students:* 26 full-time (13 women), 16 part-time (5 women); includes 1 minority (Hispanic American), 1 international. Average age 27. 18 applicants, 100% accepted, 17 enrolled. In 2009, 12 master's awarded. *Degree requirements:* For master's, thesis optional. *Entrance requirements:* For master's, GRE General Test, minimum GPA of 2.5. Additional exam requirements/recommendations for international students: Required—TOEFL (minimum score 550 paper-based; 213 computer-based; 79 iBT). *Application deadline:* For fall admission, 8/1 for domestic and international students; for spring admission, 12/1 for domestic and international students. Application fee: $20. Electronic applications accepted. *Expenses:* Tuition, state resident: full-time $3690; part-time $205 per credit hour. Tuition, nonresident: full-time $8676; part-time $482 per credit hour. Required fees: $1474. Tuition and fees vary according to course load and campus/location. *Financial support:* Teaching assistantships, career-related internships or fieldwork available. Financial award application deadline: 5/31; financial award applicants required to submit FAFSA. *Unit head:* Dr. Stanley F. Kelley, Chair, 936-294-1189, Fax: 936-294-1232, E-mail: sfkelley@shsu.edu. *Application contact:* Tammy Gray, Advisor, 936-294-1230, E-mail: dca_tag@shsu.edu.

San Jose State University, Graduate Studies and Research, Charles W. Davidson College of Engineering, Department of Industrial and Systems Engineering, San Jose, CA 95192-0001. Offers industrial and systems engineering (MS). Part-time programs available. *Students:* 64 full-time (22 women), 61 part-time (33 women); includes 27 minority (1 African American, 1 American Indian/Alaska Native, 20 Asian Americans or Pacific Islanders, 5 Hispanic Americans), 63 international. Average age 29. 129 applicants, 60% accepted, 40 enrolled. In 2009, 53 master's awarded. *Degree requirements:* For master's, comprehensive exam. *Application deadline:* For fall admission, 6/29 for domestic students; for spring admission, 11/30 for domestic students. Applications are processed on a rolling basis. Application fee: $59. Electronic applications accepted. *Financial support:* Federal Work-Study available. Financial award applicants required to submit FAFSA. *Unit head:* Dr. Yasser Dessouky, Chair, 408-924-4133. *Application contact:* Dr. Louis Freund, Graduate Program Coordinator, 408-924-3890.

South Dakota State University, Graduate School, College of Engineering, Department of Engineering Technology and Management, Brookings, SD 57007. Offers industrial management (MS). *Degree requirements:* For master's, comprehensive exam, thesis (for some programs), oral exam. *Entrance requirements:* Additional exam requirements/recommendations for international students: Required—TOEFL (minimum score 575 paper-based). *Faculty research:* Query, economic development, statistical process control, foreign business plans, operations management.

Southern Illinois University Edwardsville, Graduate Studies and Research, School of Engineering, Department of Mechanical and Industrial Engineering, Program in Industrial Engineering, Edwardsville, IL 62026-0001. Offers MS. Part-time programs available. *Students:* 5 full-time (0 women), 3 part-time (0 women). Average age 26. 19 applicants, 74% accepted. In 2009, 1 master's awarded. *Degree requirements:* For master's, thesis or final exam. *Entrance requirements:* For master's, GRE (for applicants whose degree is from non-ABET accredited institution). Additional exam requirements/recommendations for international students: Required—TOEFL (minimum score 550 paper-based; 213 computer-based; 79 iBT), IELTS (minimum score 6.5). *Application deadline:* For fall admission, 7/23 for domestic students, 6/1 for international students; for spring admission, 12/11 for domestic students, 10/1 for international students. Applications are processed on a rolling basis. Electronic applications accepted. *Expenses:* Tuition, state resident: part-time $1252.50 per semester. Tuition, nonresident: part-time $3131.25 per semester. Required fees: $586.85 per semester. Tuition and fees vary according to course load. *Financial support:* In 2009–10, 1 research assistantship with full tuition reimbursement (averaging $8,064 per year), 3 teaching assistantships with full tuition reimbursements (averaging $8,064 per year) were awarded; career-related internships or fieldwork, Federal Work-Study, institutionally sponsored loans, scholarships/grants, traineeships, and unspecified assistantships also available. Support available to part-time students. Financial award application deadline: 3/1; financial award applicants required to submit FAFSA. *Unit head:* Dr. S. Cem Karacal, Director, 618-650-2435, E-mail: skaraca@siue.edu. *Application contact:* Dr. S. Cem Karacal, Director, 618-650-2435, E-mail: skaraca@siue.edu.

Southern Polytechnic State University, School of Engineering Technology and Management, Department of Industrial Engineering Technology, Marietta, GA 30060-2896. Offers quality assurance (MS, Graduate Certificate). Part-time and evening/weekend programs available. Postbaccalaureate distance learning degree programs offered (minimal on-campus study). *Faculty:* 3 full-time (2 women), 4 part-time/adjunct (3 women). *Students:* 4 full-time (1 woman), 80 part-time (23 women); includes 15 African Americans, 5 Asian Americans or Pacific Islanders, 3 Hispanic Americans, 6 international. Average age 42. 30 applicants, 97% accepted, 18 enrolled. In 2009, 29 master's awarded. *Degree requirements:* For master's and Graduate Certificate, comprehensive exam (for some programs). *Entrance requirements:* For master's, 2 years full-time work experience in industrial engineering field, 3 reference forms, minimum GPA of 2.7; for Graduate Certificate, 2 years full-time work experience, minimum GPA of 2.7. Additional exam requirements/recommendations for international students: Required—TOEFL (minimum score 550 paper-based; 213 computer-based; 79 iBT), IELTS (minimum score 6.5). *Application deadline:* For fall admission, 7/1 priority date for domestic students, 5/1 priority date for international students; for spring admission, 11/1 priority date for domestic students, 9/1 priority date for international students. Applications are processed on a rolling basis. Application fee: $20. Electronic applications accepted. *Expenses:* Tuition, state resident: full-time $2896; part-time $181 per credit hour. Tuition, nonresident: full-time $11,552; part-time $722 per credit hour. Required fees: $1096; $1096 per year. *Financial support:* In 2009–10, 1 research assistantship with partial tuition reimbursement (averaging $1,500 per year) was awarded; career-related internships or fieldwork, scholarships/grants, and unspecified assistantships also available. Support available to part-time students. Financial award application deadline: 5/1; financial award applicants required to submit FAFSA. *Faculty research:* Application on industrial engineering to public sector, investigation of the response model method in robust design, effectiveness of on-line education, learning community, physical and mechanical properties of shape-wear garments to their functional performance, the advantage of tablet computer technology in a distance learning format, NSF grant for research in the field of Health Care, BRIGE: Optimization Models for Public Health Policy. *Unit head:* Tom Ball, Chair, 678-915-7162, Fax: 678-915-4991, E-mail: tball@spsu.edu. *Application contact:* Nikki Palamiotis, Director of Graduate Studies, 678-915-4276, Fax: 678-915-7292, E-mail: npalamio@spsu.edu.

Stanford University, School of Engineering, Department of Management Science and Engineering, Stanford, CA 94305-9991. Offers management science and engineering (MS,

Industrial/Management Engineering

Stanford University (continued)

PhD). Terminal master's awarded for partial completion of doctoral program. *Degree requirements:* For doctorate, thesis/dissertation, qualification procedure. *Entrance requirements:* For master's and doctorate, GRE General Test. Additional exam requirements/recommendations for international students: Required—TOEFL. Electronic applications accepted. *Expenses:* Tuition: Full-time $37,380; part-time $2760 per quarter. Required fees: $501.

State University of New York at Binghamton, Graduate School, Thomas J. Watson School of Engineering and Applied Science, Department of Systems Science and Industrial Engineering, Binghamton, NY 13902-6000. Offers M Eng, MS, MSAT, PhD. Part-time and evening/weekend programs available. *Faculty:* 10 full-time (3 women), 4 part-time/adjunct (0 women). *Students:* 97 full-time (20 women), 74 part-time (13 women); includes 20 minority (7 African Americans, 2 American Indian/Alaska Native, 7 Asian Americans or Pacific Islanders, 4 Hispanic Americans), 116 international. Average age 29. 149 applicants, 71% accepted, 47 enrolled. In 2009, 29 master's, 10 doctorates awarded. Terminal master's awarded for partial completion of doctoral program. *Degree requirements:* For master's, thesis or alternative; for doctorate, thesis/dissertation. *Entrance requirements:* For master's and doctorate, GRE General Test, GRE Subject Test. Additional exam requirements/recommendations for international students: Required—TOEFL. *Application deadline:* For fall admission, 4/15 priority date for domestic students, 1/15 priority date for international students; for spring admission, 11/1 for domestic students, 10/1 priority date for international students. Applications are processed on a rolling basis. Application fee: $60. Electronic applications accepted. *Financial support:* In 2009–10, 76 students received support, including 58 research assistantships with full tuition reimbursements available (averaging $16,500 per year), 12 teaching assistantships with full tuition reimbursements available (averaging $16,500 per year); career-related internships or fieldwork, Federal Work-Study, institutionally sponsored loans, scholarships/grants, health care benefits, tuition waivers (full and partial), and unspecified assistantships also available. Financial award application deadline: 2/15; financial award applicants required to submit FAFSA. *Faculty research:* Problem restructuring, protein modeling. *Unit head:* Dr. Nagen Nagarur, Chair, 607-777-3027, E-mail: nnagarur@binghamton.edu. *Application contact:* Victoria Williams, Recruiting and Admissions Coordinator, 607-777-2151, Fax: 607-777-2501, E-mail: vwilliam@binghamton.edu.

Texas A&M University, College of Engineering, Department of Industrial and Systems Engineering, College Station, TX 77843. Offers industrial and systems engineering (M Eng, MS); industrial engineering (D Eng, PhD). Part-time programs available. Postbaccalaureate distance learning degree programs offered (no on-campus study). *Faculty:* 22. *Students:* 258 full-time (61 women), 28 part-time (9 women); includes 24 minority (6 African Americans, 3 Asian Americans or Pacific Islanders, 15 Hispanic Americans), 225 international. Average age 28. In 2009, 85 master's, 11 doctorates awarded. *Degree requirements:* For master's, comprehensive exam (for some programs), thesis optional; for doctorate, comprehensive exam, dissertation (PhD). *Entrance requirements:* For master's and doctorate, GRE General Test. Additional exam requirements/recommendations for international students: Required—TOEFL. *Application deadline:* For fall admission, 3/1 priority date for domestic and international students; for spring admission, 8/1 priority date for domestic and international students. Applications are processed on a rolling basis. Application fee: $50 ($75 for international students). Electronic applications accepted. *Expenses:* Tuition, state resident: full-time $3991.32; part-time $221.74 per credit hour. Tuition, nonresident: full-time $9049; part-time $502.74 per credit hour. *Financial support:* In 2009–10, fellowships with partial tuition reimbursements (averaging $25,000 per year), research assistantships with partial tuition reimbursements (averaging $12,000 per year), teaching assistantships with partial tuition reimbursements (averaging $12,000 per year) were awarded; career-related internships or fieldwork, scholarships/grants, and unspecified assistantships also available. Financial award application deadline: 2/1. *Faculty research:* Manufacturing systems, computer integration, operations research, logistics, simulation. *Unit head:* Dr. Guy Curry, Head, 979-845-5535, Fax: 979-847-9005, E-mail: g-curry@tamu.edu. *Application contact:* Graduate Advisor, 979-845-5536, Fax: 979-458-4299.

Texas A&M University–Commerce, Graduate School, College of Business and Technology, Department of Industrial Engineering and Technology, Commerce, TX 75429-3011. Offers industrial technology (MS); technology management (MS). Part-time programs available. *Degree requirements:* For master's, comprehensive exam, thesis (for some programs). *Entrance requirements:* For master's, GMAT, GRE General Test. Electronic applications accepted. *Faculty research:* Environmental science, engineering microelectronics, natural sciences.

Texas A&M University–Kingsville, College of Graduate Studies, College of Engineering, Department of Mechanical and Industrial Engineering, Program in Industrial Engineering, Kingsville, TX 78363. Offers ME, MS. *Degree requirements:* For master's, comprehensive exam, thesis or alternative. *Entrance requirements:* For master's, GRE General Test, minimum GPA of 3.0. Additional exam requirements/recommendations for international students: Required—TOEFL. *Faculty research:* Robotics and automation, neural networks and fuzzy logic, systems engineering/simulation modeling, integrated manufacturing and production systems.

Texas Southern University, School of Science and Technology, Department of Industrial Technology, Houston, TX 77004-4584. Offers MS. *Faculty:* 6 full-time (0 women). *Students:* 5 full-time (2 women), 1 part-time (0 women); includes 5 minority (4 African Americans, 1 Hispanic American), 1 international. Average age 32. 4 applicants, 100% accepted, 2 enrolled. In 2009, 2 master's awarded. *Degree requirements:* For master's, comprehensive exam. *Entrance requirements:* For master's, GRE General Test, minimum GPA of 2.5. Additional exam requirements/recommendations for international students: Required—TOEFL. *Application deadline:* For fall admission, 7/1 for domestic and international students; for spring admission, 11/1 for domestic and international students. Applications are processed on a rolling basis. Application fee: $50 ($75 for international students). Electronic applications accepted. *Expenses:* Tuition, state resident: full-time $1805; part-time $100 per credit hour. Tuition, nonresident: full-time $6470; part-time $343 per credit hour. Tuition and fees vary according to course level, course load and degree level. *Financial support:* In 2009–10, 1 teaching assistantship (averaging $13,500 per year) was awarded; scholarships/grants and unspecified assistantships also available. Financial award application deadline: 5/1. Total annual research expenditures: $500,000. *Unit head:* Dr. Jesse Horner, Chair, 713-313-7144, E-mail: horner_je@tsu.edu. *Application contact:* Lulueua Nasser, Administrative Secretary, 713-313-7679, E-mail: nasser_la@tsu.edu.

Texas State University–San Marcos, Graduate School, College of Science, Department of Engineering Technology, Program in Industrial Technology, San Marcos, TX 78666. Offers MST. Part-time and evening/weekend programs available. *Faculty:* 8 full-time (0 women), 2 part-time/adjunct (0 women). *Students:* 20 full-time (4 women), 18 part-time (3 women); includes 12 minority (2 African Americans, 3 Asian Americans or Pacific Islanders, 7 Hispanic Americans). Average age 29. 14 applicants, 100% accepted, 9 enrolled. In 2009, 7 master's awarded. *Degree requirements:* For master's, comprehensive exam, thesis optional. *Entrance requirements:* For master's, minimum GPA of 2.75 in last 60 hours of undergraduate work. Additional exam requirements/recommendations for international students: Required—TOEFL (minimum score 550 paper-based; 213 computer-based). *Application deadline:* For fall admission, 6/15 priority date for domestic students, 6/1 priority date for international students; for spring admission, 10/15 priority date for domestic students, 10/1 priority date for international students. Applications are processed on a rolling basis. Application fee: $40 ($90 for international students). *Expenses:* Tuition, state resident: full-time $5784; part-time $241 per credit hour. Tuition, nonresident: part-time $551 per credit hour. Required fees: $1728; $48 per credit hour. $306. Tuition and fees vary according to course load. *Financial support:* In 2009–10, 25 students received support, including 1 research assistantship (averaging $4,928 per year), 4 teaching assistantships (averaging $5,076 per year); career-related internships or fieldwork, Federal Work-Study, and institutionally sponsored loans also available. Support available to part-time students. Financial award application deadline: 4/1; financial award applicants required to submit FAFSA. *Unit head:* Dr. Andy Batey, Graduate Adviser, 512-245-2137, Fax: 512-245-3052, E-mail: ab08@txstate.edu. *Application contact:* Dr. Andy Batey, Graduate Adviser, 512-245-2137, Fax: 512-245-3052, E-mail: ab08@txstate.edu.

Texas Tech University, Graduate School, College of Engineering, Department of Industrial Engineering, Lubbock, TX 79409. Offers industrial engineering (MSIE, PhD); manufacturing systems engineering (MSMSE); systems and engineering management (MSSEM, PhD). Part-time programs available. *Faculty:* 11 full-time (2 women). *Students:* 85 full-time (19 women), 48 part-time (8 women); includes 9 minority (4 African Americans, 2 Asian Americans or Pacific Islanders, 3 Hispanic Americans), 80 international. Average age 29. 298 applicants, 61% accepted, 24 enrolled. In 2009, 21 master's, 7 doctorates awarded. *Degree requirements:* For master's, thesis or alternative; for doctorate, thesis/dissertation. *Entrance requirements:* For master's and doctorate, GRE General Test, minimum GPA of 3.0. Additional exam requirements/recommendations for international students: Required—TOEFL (minimum score 550 paper-based; 213 computer-based). *Application deadline:* For fall admission, 3/1 priority date for international students; for spring admission, 11/1 priority date for international students. Applications are processed on a rolling basis. Application fee: $50 ($75 for international students). Electronic applications accepted. *Expenses:* Tuition, state resident: full-time $5100; part-time $213 per credit hour. Tuition, nonresident: full-time $11,748; part-time $490 per credit hour. Required fees: $2298; $50 per credit hour. $555 per semester. *Financial support:* In 2009–10, 14 research assistantships with partial tuition reimbursements (averaging $14,979 per year), 10 teaching assistantships with partial tuition reimbursements (averaging $13,050 per year) were awarded; Federal Work-Study and institutionally sponsored loans also available. Support available to part-time students. Financial award application deadline: 4/15; financial award applicants required to submit FAFSA. *Faculty research:* Knowledge and engineering management, environmentally conscious manufacturing, biomechanical simulation, aviation security, supply chain management. Total annual research expenditures: $476,488. *Unit head:* Dr. Pat Patterson, Chair, 806-742-3543, Fax: 806-742-3411, E-mail: pat.patterson@ttu.edu. *Application contact:* Dr. Mario Beruvides, Professor, 806-742-3543, Fax: 806-742-3411, E-mail: mario.beruvides@ttu.edu.

Universidad de las Américas–Puebla, Division of Graduate Studies, School of Engineering, Program in Industrial Engineering, Puebla, Mexico. Offers industrial engineering (MS); production management (M Adm). Part-time and evening/weekend programs available. *Degree requirements:* For master's, one foreign language, thesis. *Faculty research:* Textile industry, quality control.

Université de Moncton, Faculty of Engineering, Program in Industrial Engineering, Moncton, NB E1A 3E9, Canada. Offers M Sc A. *Degree requirements:* For master's, thesis, proficiency in French. *Faculty research:* Production systems, optimization, simulation and expert systems, modeling and warehousing systems, quality control.

Université du Québec à Trois-Rivières, Graduate Programs, Program in Industrial Engineering, Trois-Rivières, QC G9A 5H7, Canada. Offers M Sc, DESS. *Entrance requirements:* For degree, appropriate bachelor's degree, proficiency in French. *Faculty research:* Production.

Université Laval, Faculty of Sciences and Engineering, Programs in Industrial Engineering, Québec, QC G1K 7P4, Canada. Offers Diploma. Part-time programs available. *Entrance requirements:* For degree, knowledge of French. Electronic applications accepted.

University at Buffalo, the State University of New York, Graduate School, School of Engineering and Applied Sciences, Department of Industrial and Systems Engineering, Buffalo, NY 14260. Offers M Eng, MS, PhD. Part-time programs available. Postbaccalaureate distance learning degree programs offered (minimal on-campus study). *Faculty:* 11 full-time (1 woman), 3 part-time/adjunct (0 women). *Students:* 136 full-time (30 women), 22 part-time (4 women); includes 5 minority (2 African Americans, 2 Asian Americans or Pacific Islanders, 1 Hispanic American), 114 international. Average age 28. 679 applicants, 33% accepted, 50 enrolled. In 2009, 33 master's, 7 doctorates awarded. Terminal master's awarded for partial completion of doctoral program. *Degree requirements:* For master's, comprehensive exam (for some programs), thesis or alternative; for doctorate, thesis/dissertation. *Entrance requirements:* For master's and doctorate, GRE General Test. Additional exam requirements/recommendations for international students: Required—TOEFL (minimum score 550 paper-based; 213 computer-based; 79 iBT). *Application deadline:* For fall admission, 2/1 priority date for domestic students; for spring admission, 8/1 for domestic students. Applications are processed on a rolling basis. Application fee: $50. Electronic applications accepted. *Financial support:* In 2009–10, 47 students received support, including 14 fellowships with full tuition reimbursements available (averaging $28,900 per year), 25 research assistantships with full and partial tuition reimbursements available (averaging $24,000 per year), 20 teaching assistantships with partial tuition reimbursements available (averaging $20,900 per year); Federal Work-Study, institutionally sponsored loans, tuition waivers (full and partial), and unspecified assistantships also available. Financial award application deadline: 2/1; financial award applicants required to submit FAFSA. *Faculty research:* Ergonomics, operations research, production systems, human factors. Total annual research expenditures: $13.2 million. *Unit head:* Dr. Rakesh Nagi, Chairman, 716-645-2357, Fax: 716-645-3302, E-mail: iegrad@buffalo.edu. *Application contact:* Dr. Victor Paquet, Director of Graduate Studies, 716-645-4712, Fax: 716-645-3302, E-mail: iegrad@buffalo.edu.

The University of Alabama in Huntsville, School of Graduate Studies, College of Engineering, Department of Industrial and Systems Engineering/Engineering Management, Huntsville, AL 35899. Offers industrial and systems engineering (PhD), including engineering management (MSE, PhD), industrial engineering, systems engineering (MSE, PhD); industrial engineering (MSE), including engineering management (MSE, PhD), missile systems engineering, modeling and simulation, rotorcraft systems engineering, systems engineering (MSE, PhD); operations research (MSOR). Part-time and evening/weekend programs available. Postbaccalaureate distance learning degree programs offered (minimal on-campus study). *Faculty:* 6 full-time (2 women). *Students:* 6 full-time (0 women), 138 part-time (37 women); includes 17 minority (14 African Americans, 1 American Indian/Alaska Native, 2 Hispanic Americans), 9 international. Average age 36. 75 applicants, 53% accepted, 29 enrolled. In 2009, 38 master's, 6 doctorates awarded. *Degree requirements:* For master's, comprehensive exam, thesis or alternative, oral and written exams; for doctorate, comprehensive exam, thesis/dissertation, oral and written exams. *Entrance requirements:* For master's and doctorate, GRE General Test, minimum GPA of 3.0. Additional exam requirements/recommendations for international students: Required—TOEFL (minimum score 500 paper-based; 173 computer-based; 62 iBT). *Application deadline:* For fall admission, 7/15 for domestic students, 4/1 for international students; for spring admission, 11/30 for domestic students, 9/1 for international students. Applications are processed on a rolling basis. Application fee: $40 ($50 for international students). Electronic applications accepted. *Expenses:* Tuition, state resident: part-time $355.75 per credit hour. Tuition, nonresident: part-time $847.10 per credit hour. Required fees: $210.80 per semester. Tuition and fees vary according to course load and program. *Financial support:* In 2009–10, 4 students received support, including 4 teaching assistantships with full and partial tuition reimbursements available (averaging $11,733 per year); career-related internships or fieldwork, Federal Work-Study, institutionally sponsored loans, scholarships/grants, health care benefits, and unspecified assistantships also available. Support available to part-time students. Financial award application deadline: 4/1; financial award applicants required to submit FAFSA. *Faculty research:* Engineering management, systems engineering, manufacturing, logistics, simulation. Total annual research expenditures: $19.6 million. *Unit head:* Dr. James Swain, Chair, 256-824-6749, Fax: 256-824-6733, E-mail: jswain@ise.uah.edu. *Application contact:* Kathy Biggs, Graduate Studies Admissions Manager, 256-824-6199, Fax: 256-824-6405, E-mail: deangrad@uah.edu.

The University of Arizona, Graduate College, College of Engineering, Department of Systems and Industrial Engineering, Program in Industrial Engineering, Tucson, AZ 85721. Offers MS. Part-time programs available. Postbaccalaureate distance learning degree programs offered. *Students:* 3 full-time (1 woman), 2 international. Average age 24. 25 applicants, 40% accepted. In 2009, 4 master's awarded. *Entrance requirements:* Additional exam requirements/

recommendations for international students: Required—TOEFL (minimum score 575 paper-based; 233 computer-based; 80 iBT). *Application deadline:* For fall admission, 6/1 for domestic students, 12/1 for international students; for spring admission, 9/1 for domestic students, 6/1 for international students. Applications are processed on a rolling basis. Application fee: $75. Electronic applications accepted. *Expenses:* Tuition, state resident: full-time $9028. Tuition, nonresident: full-time $24,890. *Financial support:* Institutionally sponsored loans, scholarships/grants, and unspecified assistantships available. *Faculty research:* Operations research, manufacturing systems, quality and reliability, statistical/engineering design. *Unit head:* Dr. K. Larry Head, Head, 520-621-6551, E-mail: larry@sie.arizona.edu. *Application contact:* Linda Cramer, Graduate Secretary, 520-626-4644, Fax: 520-621-6555, E-mail: gradapp@sie.arizona.edu.

The University of Arizona, Graduate College, College of Engineering, Department of Systems and Industrial Engineering, Program in Systems and Industrial Engineering, Tucson, AZ 85721. Offers MS, PhD. Postbaccalaureate distance learning degree programs offered. *Students:* 16 full-time (5 women), 8 part-time (1 woman), 21 international. Average age 30. 24 applicants, 75% accepted, 6 enrolled. In 2009, 2 doctorates awarded. *Degree requirements:* For doctorate, thesis/dissertation. *Entrance requirements:* For master's, GRE General Test (500 Verbal, 700 Quantitative, 650 Analytical), 3 letters of recommendation, letter of intent; for doctorate, GRE General Test (500 Verbal, 750 Quantitative, 700 Analytical), 3 letters of recommendation, letter of intent. Additional exam requirements/recommendations for international students: Required—TOEFL (minimum score 575 paper-based; 233 computer-based; 80 iBT). *Application deadline:* For fall admission, 6/1 for domestic students, 12/1 for international students; for spring admission, 9/1 for domestic students, 6/1 for international students. Applications are processed on a rolling basis. Application fee: $75. Electronic applications accepted. *Expenses:* Tuition, state resident: full-time $9028. Tuition, nonresident: full-time $24,890. *Financial support:* Tuition waivers (full) and unspecified assistantships available. *Faculty research:* Optimization, systems theory, logistics, transportation, embedded systems. *Unit head:* Dr. K. Larry Head, Head, 520-621-6551, E-mail: larry@sie.arizona.edu. *Application contact:* Linda Cramer, Graduate Secretary, 520-626-4644, Fax: 520-621-6555, E-mail: gradapp@sie.arizona.edu.

University of Arkansas, Graduate School, College of Engineering, Department of Industrial Engineering, Program in Industrial Engineering, Fayetteville, AR 72701-1201. Offers MSE, MSIE, PhD. *Students:* 25 full-time (9 women), 17 part-time (6 women); includes 1 minority (Hispanic American), 23 international. In 2009, 14 master's, 7 doctorates awarded. *Degree requirements:* For master's, thesis optional; for doctorate, one foreign language, thesis/dissertation. Application fee: $40 ($50 for international students). *Expenses:* Tuition, state resident: full-time $7355; part-time $356.58 per hour. Tuition, nonresident: full-time $17,401; part-time $775.17 per hour. Required fees: $1203. *Financial support:* In 2009–10, 3 fellowships, 32 research assistantships were awarded; teaching assistantships, career-related internships or fieldwork and Federal Work-Study also available. Support available to part-time students. Financial award application deadline: 4/1; financial award applicants required to submit FAFSA. *Unit head:* Dr. Kim Needy, Departmental Chairperson, 479-575-3157, Fax: 479-575-8431, E-mail: kneedy@uark.edu. *Application contact:* Dr. Manuel D. Rossetti, Graduate Coordinator, 479-575-6756, E-mail: rossetti@uark.edu.

University of California, Berkeley, Graduate Division, College of Engineering, Department of Industrial Engineering and Operations Research, Berkeley, CA 94720-1500. Offers M Eng, MS, D Eng, PhD. *Students:* 70 full-time (19 women). Average age 27. 415 applicants, 18 enrolled. In 2009, 28 master's, 6 doctorates awarded. *Degree requirements:* For master's, comprehensive exam or thesis (MS); for doctorate, thesis/dissertation, qualifying exam. *Entrance requirements:* For master's and doctorate, GRE General Test, minimum GPA of 3.0, 3 letters of recommendation. *Application deadline:* For fall admission, 1/5 for domestic students. Application fee: $70 ($90 for international students). *Financial support:* Fellowships, research assistantships, teaching assistantships, career-related internships or fieldwork, Federal Work-Study, tuition waivers (full and partial), and unspecified assistantships available. *Faculty research:* Mathematical programming, robotics and manufacturing, linear and nonlinear optimization, production planning and scheduling, queuing theory. *Unit head:* Prof. Rhonda Righter, Chair, 510-642-5485, Fax: 510-642-1403, E-mail: gradadm@ieor.berkeley.edu. *Application contact:* Anayancy Paz, Student Affairs Officer, 510-642-5485, Fax: 510-642-1403, E-mail: gradadm@ieor.berkeley.edu.

University of Central Florida, College of Engineering and Computer Science, Department of Industrial Engineering and Management Systems, Orlando, FL 32816. Offers applied operations research (Certificate); design for usability (Certificate); industrial engineering (MSIE, PhD); industrial ergonomics and safety (Certificate); project engineering (Certificate); quality assurance (Certificate); systems engineering (Certificate); systems simulation for engineers (Certificate); training simulation (Certificate). Part-time and evening/weekend programs available. *Faculty:* 14 full-time (2 women), 9 part-time/adjunct (6 women). *Students:* 108 full-time (22 women), 143 part-time (54 women); includes 76 minority (21 African Americans, 1 American Indian/Alaska Native, 14 Asian Americans or Pacific Islanders, 40 Hispanic Americans), 64 international. Average age 32. 204 applicants, 66% accepted, 88 enrolled. In 2009, 59 master's, 17 doctorates, 14 other advanced degrees awarded. *Degree requirements:* For master's, thesis; for doctorate, thesis/dissertation, departmental qualifying exam, candidacy exam. *Entrance requirements:* For master's, GRE General Test, minimum GPA of 3.0 in last 60 hours of course work; for doctorate, minimum GPA of 3.5 in last 60 hours of course work. Additional exam requirements/recommendations for international students: Required—TOEFL. *Application deadline:* For fall admission, 7/15 priority date for domestic students; for spring admission, 12/1 priority date for domestic students. Application fee: $30. Electronic applications accepted. *Expenses:* Tuition, state resident: part-time $306.31 per credit hour. Tuition, nonresident: part-time $1099.01 per credit hour. Part-time tuition and fees vary according to degree level and program. *Financial support:* In 2009–10, 20 students received support, including 8 fellowships with partial tuition reimbursements available (averaging $7,600 per year), 9 research assistantships with partial tuition reimbursements available (averaging $12,400 per year), 5 teaching assistantships with partial tuition reimbursements available (averaging $13,000 per year); career-related internships or fieldwork, Federal Work-Study, institutionally sponsored loans, tuition waivers (partial), and unspecified assistantships also available. Financial award application deadline: 3/1; financial award applicants required to submit FAFSA. *Unit head:* Dr. Waldemar Karwowski, Chair, E-mail: wkar@mail.ucf.edu. *Application contact:* Dr. Waldemar Karwowski, Chair, E-mail: wkar@mail.ucf.edu.

University of Cincinnati, Graduate School, College of Engineering, Department of Mechanical, Industrial and Nuclear Engineering, Program in Industrial Engineering, Cincinnati, OH 45221. Offers MS, PhD, MBA/MS. Part-time and evening/weekend programs available. *Degree requirements:* For master's, oral exam, thesis defense; for doctorate, variable foreign language requirement, thesis/dissertation, oral exam. *Entrance requirements:* For master's and doctorate, GRE General Test. Additional exam requirements/recommendations for international students: Required—TOEFL (minimum score 575 paper-based; 233 computer-based). Electronic applications accepted. *Faculty research:* Operations research, engineering administration, safety.

University of Florida, Graduate School, College of Engineering, Department of Industrial and Systems Engineering, Gainesville, FL 32611. Offers ME, MS, PhD, Engr. *Degree requirements:* For master's, thesis optional, core exam; for doctorate, comprehensive exam, thesis/dissertation; for Engr, thesis. *Entrance requirements:* For master's and doctorate, GRE General Test, minimum GPA of 3.0; for Engr, GRE General Test. Additional exam requirements/recommendations for international students: Required—TOEFL (minimum score 550 paper-based; 213 computer-based). Electronic applications accepted.

University of Houston, Cullen College of Engineering, Department of Industrial Engineering, Houston, TX 77204. Offers MIE, MSIE, PhD. Part-time and evening/weekend programs available. *Faculty:* 7 full-time (1 woman), 8 part-time/adjunct (0 women). *Students:* 99 full-time (24 women), 36 part-time (1 woman); includes 8 minority (4 African Americans, 1 Asian American or Pacific Islander, 3 Hispanic Americans), 119 international. Average age 26. 188 applicants, 77% accepted, 34 enrolled. In 2009, 44 master's, 2 doctorates awarded. Terminal master's awarded for partial completion of doctoral program. *Degree requirements:* For master's, thesis (for some programs); for doctorate, thesis/dissertation, departmental qualifying exam. *Entrance requirements:* For master's and doctorate, GRE General Test. Additional exam requirements/recommendations for international students: Required—TOEFL; Recommended—IELTS. *Application deadline:* For fall admission, 5/1 for domestic and international students; for spring admission, 11/1 for domestic and international students. Application fee: $25 ($75 for international students). Electronic applications accepted. *Expenses:* Tuition, state resident: full-time $7676; part-time $320 per credit hour. Tuition, nonresident: full-time $14,324; part-time $597 per credit hour. Required fees: $3034. *Financial support:* In 2009–10, 19 fellowships with full tuition reimbursements (averaging $10,500 per year), 11 research assistantships with full tuition reimbursements (averaging $10,500 per year), 26 teaching assistantships with full tuition reimbursements (averaging $10,500 per year) were awarded; career-related internships or fieldwork, Federal Work-Study, institutionally sponsored loans, scholarships/grants, health care benefits, and unspecified assistantships also available. Support available to part-time students. Financial award application deadline: 2/1. *Unit head:* Dr. Hamid R. Parsaei, Chairman, 713-743-6041, Fax: 713-743-4190, E-mail: parsaei@uh.edu. *Application contact:* Betty Garrett, Advising Assistant, 713-743-4188, Fax: 713-743-4190, E-mail: bgarrett@central.uh.edu.

University of Illinois at Chicago, Graduate College, College of Engineering, Department of Mechanical and Industrial Engineering, Program in Industrial Engineering, Chicago, IL 60607-7128. Offers MS. Part-time programs available. *Degree requirements:* For master's, thesis. *Entrance requirements:* For master's, GRE General Test, minimum GPA of 2.75. Additional exam requirements/recommendations for international students: Required—TOEFL. Electronic applications accepted. *Faculty research:* Systems modeling.

University of Illinois at Chicago, Graduate College, College of Engineering, Department of Mechanical and Industrial Engineering, Program in Industrial Engineering and Operations Research, Chicago, IL 60607-7128. Offers PhD. Part-time programs available. *Degree requirements:* For doctorate, thesis/dissertation. *Entrance requirements:* For doctorate, GRE General Test, minimum GPA of 2.75. Additional exam requirements/recommendations for international students: Required—TOEFL. Electronic applications accepted.

University of Illinois at Urbana–Champaign, Graduate College, College of Engineering, Department of Industrial and Enterprise Systems Engineering, Champaign, IL 61820. Offers financial engineering (MS); industrial engineering (MS, PhD); systems and entrepreneurial engineering (MS, PhD); MBA/MS. *Faculty:* 21 full-time (5 women), 1 part-time/adjunct (0 women). *Students:* 56 full-time (18 women), 17 part-time (7 women); includes 1 minority (African American), 54 international. 255 applicants, 9% accepted, 16 enrolled. In 2009, 13 master's, 7 doctorates awarded. *Entrance requirements:* For master's and doctorate, GRE, minimum GPA of 3.25. Additional exam requirements/recommendations for international students: Required—TOEFL (minimum score 613 paper-based; 257 computer-based; 103 iBT), or IELTS (minimum score 7). *Application deadline:* Applications are processed on a rolling basis. Application fee: $60 ($75 for international students). Electronic applications accepted. *Financial support:* In 2009–10, 7 fellowships, 37 research assistantships, 44 teaching assistantships were awarded; tuition waivers (full and partial) also available. *Unit head:* Jong-Shi Pang, Head, 217-244-5703, Fax: 217-244-5705, E-mail: jspang@illinois.edu. *Application contact:* Donna J. Eiskamp, Coordinator of Graduate Programs, 217-333-2730, Fax: 217-244-5705, E-mail: deiskamp@illinois.edu.

University of Illinois at Urbana–Champaign, Graduate College, College of Engineering, Department of Mechanical Science and Engineering, Champaign, IL 61820. Offers mechanical engineering (MS, PhD); theoretical and applied mechanics (MS, PhD); MS/MBA. *Faculty:* 54 full-time (4 women), 2 part-time/adjunct (0 women). *Students:* 331 full-time (38 women), 34 part-time (5 women); includes 28 minority (1 African American, 18 Asian Americans or Pacific Islanders, 9 Hispanic Americans), 189 international. 488 applicants, 39% accepted, 95 enrolled. In 2009, 48 master's, 32 doctorates awarded. Terminal master's awarded for partial completion of doctoral program. *Entrance requirements:* For master's, GRE General Test, minimum GPA of 3.25; for doctorate, GRE General Test, minimum GPA of 3.5. Additional exam requirements/recommendations for international students: Required—TOEFL (minimum score 613 paper-based; 257 computer-based; 103 iBT), v. *Application deadline:* Applications are processed on a rolling basis. Application fee: $60 ($75 for international students). Electronic applications accepted. *Financial support:* In 2009–10, 37 fellowships, 271 research assistantships, 90 teaching assistantships were awarded; tuition waivers (full and partial) also available. *Faculty research:* Combustion and propulsion, design methodology, dynamic systems and controls, energy transfer, materials behavior and processing, manufacturing systems operations, management. *Unit head:* Placid Mathew Ferreira, Head, 217-333-0639, Fax: 217-244-6534, E-mail: pferreir@illinois.edu. *Application contact:* Kathy A. Smith, Admissions and Records Officer, 217-244-4539, Fax: 217-244-6534, E-mail: smith15@illinois.edu.

The University of Iowa, Graduate College, College of Engineering, Department of Industrial Engineering, Iowa City, IA 52242-1316. Offers engineering design and manufacturing (MS, PhD); ergonomics (MS, PhD); information and engineering management (MS, PhD); operations research (MS, PhD); quality engineering (MS, PhD). *Faculty:* 6 full-time (0 women). *Students:* 37 full-time (11 women); includes 3 minority (1 African American, 1 Asian American or Pacific Islander, 1 Hispanic American), 11 international. Average age 28. 65 applicants, 18% accepted, 7 enrolled. In 2009, 7 master's, 3 doctorates awarded. *Degree requirements:* For master's, thesis optional, exam; for doctorate, comprehensive exam, thesis/dissertation, final defense exam. *Entrance requirements:* For master's and doctorate, GRE General Test. Additional exam requirements/recommendations for international students: Required—TOEFL (minimum score 550 paper-based; 213 computer-based; 81 iBT). *Application deadline:* For fall admission, 7/15 for domestic students, 4/15 for international students; for spring admission, 12/1 for domestic students, 10/1 for international students. Applications are processed on a rolling basis. Application fee: $60 ($100 for international students). Electronic applications accepted. *Financial support:* In 2009–10, 2 fellowships with partial tuition reimbursements (averaging $30,450 per year), 22 research assistantships with partial tuition reimbursements (averaging $20,000 per year), 5 teaching assistantships with partial tuition reimbursements (averaging $16,630 per year) were awarded; career-related internships or fieldwork, scholarships/grants, and unspecified assistantships also available. Support available to part-time students. Financial award applicants required to submit FAFSA. *Faculty research:* Operations research; informatics; human factors engineering; manufacturing systems; human-machine interaction. Total annual research expenditures: $4.1 million. *Unit head:* Dr. Lea-Der Chen, Departmental Executive Officer, 319-335-5674, Fax: 319-335-5669, E-mail: lea-der-chen@uiowa.edu. *Application contact:* Jennifer Rumping, Secretary, 319-335-5939, Fax: 319-335-5669, E-mail: indeng@engineering.uiowa.edu.

University of Louisville, J.B. Speed School of Engineering, Department of Industrial Engineering, Louisville, KY 40292-0001. Offers engineering management (M Eng); industrial engineering (M Eng, MS, PhD); logistics and distribution (Certificate). *Accreditation:* ABET (one or more programs are accredited). Part-time programs available. *Faculty:* 9 full-time (1 woman). *Students:* 37 full-time (13 women), 35 part-time (7 women); includes 11 minority (6 African Americans, 5 Asian Americans or Pacific Islanders), 19 international. Average age 29. 62 applicants, 61% accepted, 23 enrolled. In 2009, 27 master's, 2 doctorates awarded. Terminal master's awarded for partial completion of doctoral program. *Degree requirements:* For master's, comprehensive exam (for some programs), thesis or alternative; for doctorate, comprehensive exam, thesis/dissertation, minimum GPA of 3.0. *Entrance requirements:* For master's and doctorate, GRE General Test. Additional exam requirements/recommendations for international students: Required—TOEFL (minimum score 550 paper-based; 213 computer-based; 80 iBT). *Application deadline:* For fall admission, 7/12 priority date for domestic and international students; for winter admission, 11/29 priority date for domestic and international students; for spring admission, 3/28 priority date for domestic and international students. Applications are processed on a rolling basis. Application fee: $50. Electronic applications accepted. *Financial support:* In 2009–10, 16 students received support, including 8 fellowships

Industrial/Management Engineering

University of Louisville (continued)

with full tuition reimbursements available (averaging $20,000 per year), 1 research assistantship with full tuition reimbursement available (averaging $20,000 per year), 6 teaching assistantships with full tuition reimbursements available (averaging $20,000 per year). Financial award application deadline: 1/25; financial award applicants required to submit FAFSA. *Faculty research:* Optimization,computer simulation, logistics and distribution, ergonomics and human factors, advanced manufacturing process. Total annual research expenditures: $359,000. *Unit head:* Dr. John S. Usher, Chair, 502-852-6342, Fax: 502-852-5633, E-mail: usher@louisville.edu. *Application contact:* Dr. Michael Day, Associate Dean, 502-852-6195, Fax: 502-852-7294, E-mail: day@louisville.edu.

University of Manitoba, Faculty of Graduate Studies, Faculty of Engineering, Department of Mechanical and Manufacturing Engineering, Winnipeg, MB R3T 2N2, Canada. Offers M Eng, M Sc, PhD. *Degree requirements:* For master's, thesis; for doctorate, thesis/dissertation.

University of Massachusetts Amherst, Graduate School, College of Engineering, Department of Mechanical and Industrial Engineering, Program in Industrial Engineering and Operations Research, Amherst, MA 01003. Offers MS, PhD. Part-time programs available. *Students:* 11 full-time (3 women), 9 part-time (3 women); includes 1 minority (Asian American or Pacific Islander), 12 international. Average age 30. 105 applicants, 38% accepted, 6 enrolled. In 2009, 4 master's, 4 doctorates awarded. Terminal master's awarded for partial completion of doctoral program. *Degree requirements:* For master's, thesis or alternative, project; for doctorate, comprehensive exam, thesis/dissertation. *Entrance requirements:* For master's and doctorate, GRE General Test. Additional exam requirements/recommendations for international students: Required—TOEFL (minimum score 550 paper-based; 213 computer-based; 80 iBT), IELTS (minimum score 6.5). *Application deadline:* For fall admission, 1/15 for domestic and international students; for spring admission, 10/1 for domestic and international students. Applications are processed on a rolling basis. Application fee: $50 ($65 for international students). Electronic applications accepted. *Expenses:* Tuition, state resident: full-time $2640; part-time $110 per credit. Tuition, nonresident: full-time $9936; part-time $414 per credit. Tuition and fees vary according to course load. *Financial support:* Fellowships with full tuition reimbursements, research assistantships with full tuition reimbursements, teaching assistantships with full tuition reimbursements, career-related internships or fieldwork, Federal Work-Study, scholarships/grants, traineeships, health care benefits, tuition waivers, and unspecified assistantships available. Support available to part-time students. Financial award application deadline: 1/15; financial award applicants required to submit FAFSA. *Unit head:* Dr. David P. Schmidt, Graduate Program Director, 413-545-3827, Fax: 413-545-1027. *Application contact:* Jean M. Ames, Supervisor of Admissions, 413-545-0722, Fax: 413-577-0100, E-mail: gradadm@grad.umass.edu.

University of Massachusetts Amherst, Graduate School, Interdisciplinary Programs, Program in Industrial Engineering and Business Administration, Amherst, MA 01003. Offers MBA/MSIE. Part-time programs available. *Students:* 4 applicants, 0% accepted, 0 enrolled. *Entrance requirements:* Additional exam requirements/recommendations for international students: Required—TOEFL (minimum score 600 paper-based; 250 computer-based; 100 iBT), IELTS (minimum score 7). *Application deadline:* For fall admission, 1/15 for domestic and international students. Applications are processed on a rolling basis. Application fee: $50 ($65 for international students). Electronic applications accepted. *Expenses:* Tuition, state resident: full-time $2640; part-time $110 per credit. Tuition, nonresident: full-time $9936; part-time $414 per credit. Tuition and fees vary according to course load. *Financial support:* Career-related internships or fieldwork, Federal Work-Study, scholarships/grants, traineeships, health care benefits, tuition waivers (full), and unspecified assistantships available. Support available to part-time students. *Unit head:* Dr. David P. Schmidt, Graduate Program Director, 413-545-3827, Fax: 413-545-1027. *Application contact:* Jean M. Ames, Supervisor of Admissions, 413-545-0722, Fax: 413-577-0010, E-mail: gradadm@grad.umass.edu.

University of Massachusetts Lowell, School of Health and Environment, Department of Work Environment, Lowell, MA 01854-2881. Offers cleaner production and pollution prevention (MS, Sc D); environmental risk assessment (Certificate); epidemiology (MS, Sc D); ergonomics and safety (MS, Sc D); identification and control of ergonomic hazards (Certificate); job stress and healthy job redesign (Certificate); occupational and environmental hygiene (MS, Sc D); radiological health physics and general work environment protection (Certificate); work environment policy (MS, Sc D). *Accreditation:* ABET (one or more programs are accredited). Part-time programs available. Terminal master's awarded for partial completion of doctoral program. *Degree requirements:* For master's, thesis optional; for doctorate, thesis/dissertation. *Entrance requirements:* For master's and doctorate, GRE General Test. Additional exam requirements/recommendations for international students: Required—TOEFL.

University of Memphis, Graduate School, Herff College of Engineering, Department of Mechanical Engineering, Memphis, TN 38152. Offers design and mechanical engineering (MS); energy systems (MS); industrial engineering (MS); mechanical engineering (PhD); mechanical systems (MS); power systems (MS). Part-time programs available. *Faculty:* 8 full-time (0 women). *Students:* 3 full-time (1 woman), 8 part-time (0 women); includes 2 minority (both African Americans), 5 international. Average age 30. 11 applicants, 64% accepted, 3 enrolled. In 2009, 5 master's awarded. Terminal master's awarded for partial completion of doctoral program. *Degree requirements:* For master's, comprehensive exam, thesis; for doctorate, comprehensive exam, thesis/dissertation. *Entrance requirements:* For master's, GRE General Test, BS in mechanical engineering, minimum undergraduate GPA of 3.0. *Application deadline:* For fall admission, 8/1 for domestic students; for spring admission, 12/1 for domestic students. Application fee: $35 ($60 for international students). *Expenses:* Tuition, state resident: full-time $6246; part-time $347 per credit hour. Tuition, nonresident: full-time $15,894; part-time $883 per credit hour. Required fees: $1160. Full-time tuition and fees vary according to course load, degree level and program. *Financial support:* In 2009–10, 6 students received support; fellowships with full tuition reimbursements available, research assistantships with full tuition reimbursements available, teaching assistantships with full tuition reimbursements available, career-related internships or fieldwork, Federal Work-Study, scholarships/grants, and unspecified assistantships available. Financial award application deadline: 2/15; financial award applicants required to submit FAFSA. *Faculty research:* Computational fluid dynamics, computational mechanics, integrated design, nondestructive testing, operations research. *Unit head:* Dr. John I. Hochstein, Chair, 901-678-2173, Fax: 901-678-5459, E-mail: jhochste@memphis.edu. *Application contact:* Dr. Teong Tan, Graduate Studies Coordinator, 901-678-3264, Fax: 901-678-5459, E-mail: ttan@memphis.edu.

University of Miami, Graduate School, College of Engineering, Department of Industrial Engineering, Coral Gables, FL 33124. Offers ergonomics (PhD); industrial engineering (MSIE, PhD); management of technology (MS); occupational ergonomics and safety (MS, MSOES), including environmental health and safety (MS), occupational ergonomics and safety (MSOES); MBA/MSIE. Part-time programs available. *Degree requirements:* For master's, thesis (for some programs); for doctorate, comprehensive exam, thesis/dissertation. *Entrance requirements:* For master's and doctorate, GRE General Test, minimum GPA of 3.0. Additional exam requirements/recommendations for international students: Required—TOEFL (minimum score 550 paper-based; 213 computer-based). *Faculty research:* Logistics, supply chain management, industrial applications of biomechanics and ergonomics, technology management, back pain, aging, operations research, manufacturing, safety, human reliability, energy assessment.

University of Michigan, Horace H. Rackham School of Graduate Studies, College of Engineering, Department of Industrial and Operations Engineering, Ann Arbor, MI 48109. Offers MS, MSE, PhD, MBA/MS, MBA/MSE. Part-time programs available. *Faculty:* 21 full-time (4 women). *Students:* 178 full-time (46 women), 23 part-time (5 women); includes 22 minority (2 African Americans, 15 Asian Americans or Pacific Islanders, 5 Hispanic Americans), 122 international. 481 applicants, 31% accepted, 73 enrolled. In 2009, 96 master's, 6 doctorates awarded. Terminal master's awarded for partial completion of doctoral program. *Degree requirements:* For doctorate, oral defense of dissertation, preliminary exams, qualifying exam.

Entrance requirements: For master's, GRE General Test, minimum GPA of 3.2; for doctorate, GRE General Test, minimum GPA of 3.5. Additional exam requirements/recommendations for international students: Required—TOEFL. *Application deadline:* Applications are processed on a rolling basis. Application fee: $60 ($75 for international students). Electronic applications accepted. *Expenses:* Tuition, state resident: full-time $17,286; part-time $1099 per credit hour. Tuition, nonresident: full-time $34,944; part-time $2080 per credit hour. Required fees: $95 per semester. Tuition and fees vary according to course load, degree level and program. *Financial support:* In 2009–10, 71 students received support; fellowships, research assistantships, teaching assistantships, Federal Work-Study, institutionally sponsored loans, scholarships/grants, traineeships, health care benefits, and unspecified assistantships available. Financial award applicants required to submit FAFSA. *Faculty research:* Production/distribution/logistics, financial engineering and enterprise systems, ergonomics (physical and cognitive), stochastic processes, linear and nonlinear optimization, operations research. *Unit head:* Mark Daskin, Chair, 734-764-9422, Fax: 734-764-3451, E-mail: msdaskin@umich.edu. *Application contact:* Matt Irelan, Graduate Student Advisor/Program Coordinator, 734-764-6480, Fax: 734-764-3451, E-mail: mirelan@umich.edu.

University of Michigan–Dearborn, College of Engineering and Computer Science, Department of Industrial and Manufacturing Systems Engineering, Dearborn, MI 48128-1491. Offers engineering management (MS); industrial and systems engineering (MSE); information systems and technology (MS); information systems engineering (PhD); MBA/MSE. Part-time and evening/weekend programs available. *Faculty:* 14 full-time (0 women), 5 part-time/adjunct (0 women). *Students:* 16 full-time (5 women), 179 part-time (56 women); includes 45 minority (6 African Americans, 26 Asian Americans or Pacific Islanders, 13 Hispanic Americans). Average age 31. 63 applicants, 62% accepted, 37 enrolled. In 2009, 67 master's awarded. *Degree requirements:* For master's, thesis optional. *Entrance requirements:* For master's, bachelor's degree in applied mathematics, computer science, engineering, or physical science; minimum GPA of 3.0. Additional exam requirements/recommendations for international students: Required—TOEFL (minimum score 560 paper-based; 220 computer-based; 84 iBT). *Application deadline:* For fall admission, 8/1 priority date for domestic students, 4/1 for international students; for winter admission, 12/1 priority date for domestic students, 8/1 for international students; for spring admission, 4/1 for domestic students, 12/1 for international students. Applications are processed on a rolling basis. Application fee: $60 ($75 for international students). *Expenses:* Tuition, area resident: Part-time $504.10 per credit hour. Tuition, state resident: part-time $504.10 per credit hour. Tuition, nonresident: part-time $957.90 per credit hour. *Financial support:* Fellowships, research assistantships, teaching assistantships, Federal Work-Study available. Financial award application deadline: 4/1; financial award applicants required to submit FAFSA. *Faculty research:* Health care systems, data and knowledge management, human factors engineering, machine diagnostics, precision machining. *Unit head:* Dr. Armen Zakarian, Chair, 313-593-5361, Fax: 313-593-3692, E-mail: zakarian@umd.umich.edu. *Application contact:* Joey W. Woods, Graduate Program Assistant, 313-593-5361, Fax: 313-593-3692, E-mail: jwwoods@umd.umich.edu.

See Close-Up on page 431.

University of Minnesota, Twin Cities Campus, Institute of Technology, Department of Mechanical Engineering, Program in Industrial Engineering, Minneapolis, MN 55455-0213. Offers MSIE, PhD. Part-time programs available. *Degree requirements:* For doctorate, thesis/dissertation. *Entrance requirements:* For master's, GRE General Test, minimum GPA of 3.0; for doctorate, GRE General Test.

University of Missouri, Graduate School, College of Engineering, Department of Industrial and Manufacturing Systems Engineering, Columbia, MO 65211. Offers MS, PhD. *Degree requirements:* For master's, thesis or alternative; for doctorate, thesis/dissertation. *Entrance requirements:* For master's and doctorate, GRE General Test, minimum GPA of 3.0. Additional exam requirements/recommendations for international students: Required—TOEFL (minimum score 550 paper-based; 213 computer-based; 80 iBT).

University of Nebraska–Lincoln, Graduate College, College of Engineering, Department of Industrial and Management Systems Engineering, Lincoln, NE 68588. Offers engineering management (M Eng); industrial and management systems engineering (MS, PhD); manufacturing systems engineering (MS). Postbaccalaureate distance learning degree programs offered. *Degree requirements:* For master's, thesis optional; for doctorate, comprehensive exam, thesis/dissertation. *Entrance requirements:* For master's and doctorate, GRE. Additional exam requirements/recommendations for international students: Required—TOEFL (minimum score 525 paper-based; 195 computer-based). Electronic applications accepted. *Faculty research:* Ergonomics, occupational safety, quality control, industrial packaging, facility design.

University of New Haven, Graduate School, Tagliatela College of Engineering, Program in Industrial Engineering, West Haven, CT 06516-1916. Offers industrial engineering (MSIE); lean-six sigma (Certificate); quality engineering (Certificate). Part-time and evening/weekend programs available. *Faculty:* 3 full-time (1 woman), 2 part-time/adjunct (1 woman). *Students:* 13 full-time (1 woman), 19 part-time (1 woman); includes 6 minority (2 African Americans, 2 Asian Americans or Pacific Islanders, 2 Hispanic Americans), 14 international. Average age 28. 39 applicants, 87% accepted, 8 enrolled. In 2009, 24 master's, 11 Certificates awarded. *Degree requirements:* For master's, thesis or alternative. *Entrance requirements:* For master's, bachelor's degree in engineering. Additional exam requirements/recommendations for international students: Required—TOEFL (minimum score 520 paper-based; 190 computer-based; 70 iBT); Recommended—IELTS (minimum score 5.5). *Application deadline:* For fall admission, 5/31 for international students; for winter admission, 10/15 for international students; for spring admission, 1/15 for international students. Applications are processed on a rolling basis. Application fee: $50. Electronic applications accepted. *Expenses:* Tuition: Part-time $700 per credit. Required fees: $45 per term. One-time fee: $390 part-time. *Financial support:* Research assistantships with partial tuition reimbursements, teaching assistantships with partial tuition reimbursements, career-related internships or fieldwork, Federal Work-Study, scholarships/grants, tuition waivers, and unspecified assistantships available. Support available to part-time students. Financial award applicants required to submit FAFSA. *Unit head:* Dr. Alexis Sommes, Coordinator, 203-932-7434. *Application contact:* Eloise Gormley, Director of Graduate Admissions, 203-932-7449, Fax: 203-932-7137, E-mail: gradinfo@newhaven.edu.

University of Oklahoma, Graduate College, College of Engineering, School of Industrial Engineering, Norman, OK 73019. Offers MS, PhD. Part-time programs available. *Faculty:* 15 full-time (5 women). *Students:* 43 full-time (14 women), 22 part-time (5 women); includes 7 minority (1 African American, 1 American Indian/Alaska Native, 4 Asian Americans or Pacific Islanders, 1 Hispanic American), 35 international. 60 applicants, 87% accepted, 16 enrolled. In 2009, 13 master's, 2 doctorates awarded. *Degree requirements:* For master's, comprehensive exam, thesis (for some programs); for doctorate, thesis/dissertation, qualifying exam. *Entrance requirements:* For master's and doctorate, GRE, minimum GPA of 3.0, 3 letters of reference, resume or curriculum vitae. Additional exam requirements/recommendations for international students: Required—TOEFL (minimum score 550 paper-based; 213 computer-based). *Application deadline:* For fall admission, 6/1 priority date for domestic students, 4/1 for international students; for spring admission, 11/1 for domestic students, 9/1 for international students. Applications are processed on a rolling basis. Application fee: $40 ($90 for international students). Electronic applications accepted. *Expenses:* Tuition, state resident: full-time $3744; part-time $156 per credit hour. Tuition, nonresident: full-time $13,577; part-time $565.70 per credit hour. Required fees: $2415; $90.10 per credit hour. *Financial support:* In 2009–10, 33 students received support, including 15 research assistantships with partial tuition reimbursements available (averaging $13,288 per year), 10 teaching assistantships with partial tuition reimbursements available (averaging $10,575 per year); scholarships/grants and unspecified assistantships also available. Financial award application deadline: 5/1; financial award applicants required to submit FAFSA. *Faculty research:* Logistics and supply chain management, computational optimization, human factors, manufacturing, simulation and stochastic modeling. Total annual research expenditures: $2.6 million. *Unit head:* Dr. Randa Shehab, Director, 405-325-3721, Fax: 405-325-7555, E-mail: rlshehab@ou.edu. *Application contact:* Amy J. Piper, Student Services Coordinator, 405-325-3721, Fax: 405-325-7555, E-mail: ajpiper@ou.edu.

University of Pittsburgh, School of Engineering, Department of Industrial Engineering, Pittsburgh, PA 15260. Offers MSIE, PhD. Part-time programs available. Postbaccalaureate distance learning degree programs offered. *Faculty:* 10 full-time (2 women), 14 part-time/adjunct (2 women). *Students:* 53 full-time (20 women), 42 part-time (10 women); includes 10 minority (5 African Americans, 1 Asian American or Pacific Islander, 4 Hispanic Americans), 46 international. 418 applicants, 28% accepted, 37 enrolled. In 2009, 18 master's, 5 doctorates awarded. Terminal master's awarded for partial completion of doctoral program. *Degree requirements:* For master's, thesis optional; for doctorate, comprehensive exam, thesis/dissertation, final oral exams. *Entrance requirements:* For master's and doctorate, GRE General Test, minimum QPA of 3.0. Additional exam requirements/recommendations for international students: Required—TOEFL (minimum score 550 paper-based; 213 computer-based; 80 iBT). *Application deadline:* For fall admission, 3/1 priority date for domestic students; for spring admission, 7/1 priority date for domestic students. Applications are processed on a rolling basis. Application fee: $50. Electronic applications accepted. *Expenses:* Tuition, state resident: full-time $16,402; part-time $665 per credit. Tuition, nonresident: full-time $28,694; part-time $1175 per credit. Required fees: $690; $175 per term. Tuition and fees vary according to program. *Financial support:* In 2009–10, 19 students received support, including 3 fellowships with full tuition reimbursements available (averaging $20,772 per year), 29 research assistantships with full tuition reimbursements available (averaging $22,000 per year), 5 teaching assistantships with full tuition reimbursements available (averaging $21,000 per year); scholarships/grants and tuition waivers (full and partial) also available. Financial award application deadline: 4/15. *Faculty research:* Operations research, engineering management, computational intelligence, manufacturing, information systems. Total annual research expenditures: $1.1 million. *Unit head:* Dr. Bopaya Bidanda, Chairman, 412-624-9830, Fax: 412-624-9831. *Application contact:* Dr. Jayant Rajgopal, Graduate Coordinator, 412-624-9840, Fax: 412-624-9831, E-mail: rajgopal@engrng.pitt.edu.

University of Puerto Rico, Mayagüez Campus, Graduate Studies, College of Engineering, Department of Industrial Engineering, Mayagüez, PR 00681-9000. Offers industrial engineering (MS); management systems (MS). Part-time programs available. *Degree requirements:* For master's, comprehensive exam, thesis, project. *Entrance requirements:* For master's, minimum GPA of 2.5; proficiency in English and Spanish; rank in relation to other members of graduating class; BS degree in engineering. Additional exam requirements/recommendations for international students: Required—TOEFL.

University of Regina, Faculty of Graduate Studies and Research, Faculty of Engineering and Applied Science, Program in Industrial Systems Engineering, Regina, SK S4S 0A2, Canada. Offers M Eng, MA Sc, PhD. *Faculty:* 10 full-time (0 women). *Students:* 27 full-time (3 women), 3 part-time (1 woman). 71 applicants, 55% accepted. In 2009, 6 master's, 3 doctorates awarded. *Degree requirements:* For master's, thesis (for some programs). *Entrance requirements:* For doctorate, master's degree. Additional exam requirements/recommendations for international students: Required—TOEFL (minimum score 550 paper-based; 213 computer-based; 80 iBT). *Application deadline:* Applications are processed on a rolling basis. Application fee: $90 ($100 for international students). *Financial support:* In 2009–10, 6 fellowships (averaging $19,000 per year), 3 research assistantships (averaging $16,910 per year), 10 teaching assistantships (averaging $6,650 per year) were awarded; career-related internships or fieldwork and scholarships/grants also available. Financial award application deadline: 6/15. *Faculty research:* Gas separation and purification, welding. *Unit head:* Dr. Denise Stilling, Graduate Program Coordinator, 306-337-2696, E-mail: denise.stilling@uregina.ca. *Application contact:* Crystal Pick, 306-337-2603, E-mail: crystal.pick@uregina.ca.

University of Southern California, Graduate School, Viterbi School of Engineering, Department of Industrial and Systems Engineering, Los Angeles, CA 90089. Offers digital supply chain management (MS); engineering management (MS); engineering technology communication (Graduate Certificate); health systems operations (Graduate Certificate); industrial and systems engineering (MS, PhD, Engr); manufacturing engineering (MS); operations research engineering (MS); optimization and supply chain management (Graduate Certificate); product development engineering (MS); safety systems and security (MS); systems architecting and engineering (MS, Graduate Certificate); systems safety and security (Graduate Certificate); transportation systems (Graduate Certificate); MS/MBA. Part-time programs available. Postbaccalaureate distance learning degree programs offered (minimal on-campus study). *Faculty:* 11 full-time (2 women), 39 part-time/adjunct (7 women). *Students:* 250 full-time (71 women), 145 part-time (37 women); includes 67 minority (6 African Americans, 2 American Indian/Alaska Native, 39 Asian Americans or Pacific Islanders, 20 Hispanic Americans), 253 international. 679 applicants, 58% accepted, 206 enrolled. In 2009, 98 master's, 7 doctorates awarded. Terminal master's awarded for partial completion of doctoral program. *Degree requirements:* For doctorate, thesis/dissertation. *Entrance requirements:* For master's, GRE General Test; for doctorate, General GRE. *Application deadline:* For fall admission, 3/1 priority date for domestic and international students; for spring admission, 10/1 for domestic students, 10/1 priority date for international students. Applications are processed on a rolling basis. Application fee: $85. Electronic applications accepted. *Expenses:* Tuition: Full-time $25,980; part-time $1315 per unit. Required fees: $554. One-time fee: $35 full-time. Full-time tuition and fees vary according to degree level and program. *Financial support:* In 2009–10, fellowships with full tuition reimbursements (averaging $30,000 per year), research assistantships with full tuition reimbursements (averaging $19,250 per year), teaching assistantships with full tuition reimbursements (averaging $19,250 per year) were awarded; career-related internships or fieldwork, scholarships/grants, health care benefits, and unspecified assistantships also available. Financial award application deadline: 12/1; financial award applicants required to submit CSS PROFILE or FAFSA. *Faculty research:* Health systems, music cognition and retrieval, transportation andlogistics, manufacturing and automation, engineering systems design, risk and economic analysis. Total annual research expenditures: $1.2 million. *Unit head:* Dr. James E. Moore, Chair, 213-740-4885, Fax: 213-740-1120, E-mail: jmoore@usc.edu. *Application contact:* Mary Ordaz, Student Service Advisor, 213-740-4886, Fax: 213-740-1120, E-mail: isedept@usc.edu.

University of South Florida, Graduate School, College of Engineering, Department of Industrial and Management Systems Engineering, Tampa, FL 33620-9951. Offers engineering management (MSEM, MSIE); engineering science (PhD); industrial engineering (MIE, MSIE, PhD). Part-time programs available. Postbaccalaureate distance learning degree programs offered (minimal on-campus study). *Faculty:* 10 full-time (2 women), 6 part-time/adjunct (1 woman). *Students:* 68 full-time (24 women), 67 part-time (12 women); includes 31 minority (10 African Americans, 6 Asian Americans or Pacific Islanders, 15 Hispanic Americans), 49 international. Average age 32. 112 applicants, 63% accepted, 37 enrolled. In 2009, 42 master's, 2 doctorates awarded. Terminal master's awarded for partial completion of doctoral program. *Degree requirements:* For master's, comprehensive exam, thesis (for some programs); for doctorate, comprehensive exam, thesis/dissertation, 2 tools of research as specified by dissertation committee. *Entrance requirements:* For master's, GRE General Test, minimum GPA of 3.0 in last 60 hours of coursework; for doctorate, GRE General Test, minimum GPA of 3.0 in last 60 hours of coursework or in master's program. Additional exam requirements/recommendations for international students: Required—TOEFL (minimum score 550 paper-based; 213 computer-based; 80 iBT). *Application deadline:* For fall admission, 2/15 for domestic students, 1/2 for international students; for spring admission, 10/15 for domestic students, 6/1 for international students. Application fee: $30. Electronic applications accepted. *Financial support:* In 2009–10, teaching assistantships with partial tuition reimbursements (averaging $28,163 per year); tuition waivers (partial) also available. Financial award applicants required to submit FAFSA. *Faculty research:* Bio-Health engineering, engineering health care systems, energy markets, nanotechnology and nanomanufacturing, transportation and logistics, innovation in education. Total annual research expenditures: $1 million. *Unit head:* Dr. Jose Zayas-Castro, Department Chair, 813-974-2269, Fax: 813-974-5953, E-mail: josezaya@usf.edu. *Application contact:* Dr. Michael Weng, Program Coordinator, 813-974-5575, Fax: 813-974-5953, E-mail: mxweng@usf.edu.

The University of Tennessee, Graduate School, College of Engineering, Department of Industrial and Information Engineering, Knoxville, TN 37996. Offers engineering management (MS, PhD); industrial engineering (MS, PhD); reliability and maintainability engineering (MS); MS/MBA. Part-time programs available. Postbaccalaureate distance learning degree programs offered (no on-campus study). *Faculty:* 7 full-time (1 woman), 5 part-time/adjunct (0 women). *Students:* 30 full-time (8 women), 53 part-time (11 women); includes 14 minority (9 African Americans, 2 American Indian/Alaska Native, 3 Asian Americans or Pacific Islanders), 26 international. Average age 25. 77 applicants, 78% accepted, 20 enrolled. In 2009, 13 master's, 4 doctorates awarded. *Degree requirements:* For master's, thesis; for doctorate, comprehensive exam, thesis/dissertation. *Entrance requirements:* For master's, GRE General Test, minimum GPA of 2.7, 3 letters of recommendation; for doctorate, MS, 3 letters of recommendation. Additional exam requirements/recommendations for international students: Required—TOEFL (minimum score 550 paper-based; 213 computer-based). *Application deadline:* For fall admission, 2/1 priority date for domestic and international students; for spring admission, 6/15 priority date for international students. Applications are processed on a rolling basis. Application fee: $35. Electronic applications accepted. *Expenses:* Tuition, state resident: full-time $6826; part-time $380 per semester hour. Tuition, nonresident: full-time $21,844; part-time $1147 per semester hour. Tuition and fees vary according to program. *Financial support:* In 2009–10, 11 research assistantships with full tuition reimbursements (averaging $12,792 per year), 8 teaching assistantships with full tuition reimbursements (averaging $7,044 per year) were awarded; career-related internships or fieldwork, Federal Work-Study, institutionally sponsored loans, health care benefits, and unspecified assistantships also available. Financial award application deadline: 2/1; financial award applicants required to submit FAFSA. *Faculty research:* Dependability and reliability of large computer networks; design of lean, reliable systems; operations research in the automotive industry; sports equipment testing; defense-oriented supply chain modeling. Total annual research expenditures: $488,000. *Unit head:* Dr. R. Bruce Robinson, Interim Head, 865-974-3333, Fax: 865-974-0588, E-mail: rbr@utk.edu. *Application contact:* Dr. Denise Jackson, Graduate Representative, E-mail: djackson@utk.edu.

The University of Tennessee, Graduate School, College of Engineering, Department of Mechanical, Aerospace and Biomedical Engineering, Program in Engineering Science, Knoxville, TN 37996. Offers applied artificial intelligence (MS); composite materials (MS, PhD); computational mechanics (MS, PhD); engineering science (MS, PhD); fluid mechanics (MS, PhD); industrial engineering (PhD); optical engineering (MS, PhD); solid mechanics (MS, PhD); MS/MBA. Part-time programs available. *Students:* 9 full-time (0 women), 4 part-time (1 woman); includes 2 minority (both African Americans), 2 international. Average age 34. 5 applicants, 60% accepted, 1 enrolled. In 2009, 2 master's awarded. *Degree requirements:* For master's, thesis or alternative; for doctorate, comprehensive exam, thesis/dissertation. *Entrance requirements:* For master's and doctorate, GRE, minimum GPA of 2.7. Additional exam requirements/recommendations for international students: Required—TOEFL (minimum score 550 paper-based; 213 computer-based). *Application deadline:* For fall admission, 2/1 priority date for domestic and international students; for spring admission, 6/15 priority date for international students. Applications are processed on a rolling basis. Application fee: $35. Electronic applications accepted. *Expenses:* Tuition, state resident: full-time $6826; part-time $380 per semester hour. Tuition, nonresident: full-time $21,844; part-time $1147 per semester hour. Tuition and fees vary according to program. *Financial support:* In 2009–10, 1 student received support, including 5 research assistantships with full tuition reimbursements available (averaging $14,628 per year), 2 teaching assistantships with full tuition reimbursements available (averaging $10,104 per year); fellowships, career-related internships or fieldwork, Federal Work-Study, institutionally sponsored loans, health care benefits, and unspecified assistantships also available. Financial award application deadline: 2/1; financial award applicants required to submit FAFSA. *Faculty research:* Thermal science, computational mechanics, computational fluid dynamics, micro/nano-scale science and engineering for bio-systems. *Unit head:* Dr. William Hamel, Head, 865-974-5115, Fax: 865-974-5274, E-mail: whamel@utk.edu. *Application contact:* Dr. Gary V. Smith, Chair, Graduate Programs Committee, 865-974-5271, E-mail: gvsmith@utk.edu.

The University of Tennessee at Chattanooga, Graduate School, College of Engineering and Computer Science, Program in Engineering, Chattanooga, TN 37403. Offers chemical (MS Engr); civil (MS Engr); computational (MS Engr); electrical (MS Engr); industrial (MS Engr); mechanical (MS Engr). Part-time and evening/weekend programs available. *Faculty:* 8 full-time (0 women). *Students:* 22 full-time (7 women), 30 part-time (3 women); includes 9 minority (4 African Americans, 4 Asian Americans or Pacific Islanders, 1 Hispanic American), 9 international. Average age 29. 59 applicants, 59% accepted, 19 enrolled. In 2009, 9 master's awarded. *Degree requirements:* For master's, comprehensive exam, thesis or alternative, engineering project. *Entrance requirements:* For master's, GRE General Test, minimum undergraduate GPA of 2.5 or 3.0 in last 30 hours of coursework. Additional exam requirements/recommendations for international students: Required—TOEFL (minimum score 550 paper-based; 213 computer-based; 79 iBT), IELTS (minimum score 6). *Application deadline:* For fall admission, 8/1 priority date for domestic students, 6/1 for international students; for spring admission, 12/1 priority date for domestic students, 10/1 for international students. Applications are processed on a rolling basis. Application fee: $35. Electronic applications accepted. *Expenses:* Tuition, state resident: full-time $5404; part-time $300 per credit hour. Tuition, nonresident: full-time $16,702; part-time $928 per credit hour. Required fees: $1150; $130 per credit hour. *Financial support:* In 2009–10, 23 research assistantships with full and partial tuition reimbursements (averaging $5,500 per year) were awarded; career-related internships or fieldwork, scholarships/grants, and unspecified assistantships also available. Support available to part-time students. *Faculty research:* Quality control and reliability engineering, financial management, thermal science, energy conservation, structural analysis. Total annual research expenditures: $2.6 million. *Unit head:* Dr. Neslihan Alp, Director, 423-425-4032, Fax: 423-425-5229, E-mail: neslihan-alp@utc.edu. *Application contact:* Dr. Stephanie Bellar, Dean of Graduate Studies, 423-425-4666, Fax: 423-425-5223, E-mail: stephanie-bellar@utc.edu.

The University of Texas at Arlington, Graduate School, College of Engineering, Department of Industrial and Manufacturing Systems Engineering, Program in Engineering Management, Arlington, TX 76019. Offers MS. Part-time and evening/weekend programs available. Postbaccalaureate distance learning degree programs offered (minimal on-campus study). *Students:* 29 full-time (8 women), 13 part-time (2 women); includes 5 minority (3 African Americans, 1 Asian American or Pacific Islander, 1 Hispanic American), 25 international. 64 applicants, 98% accepted, 14 enrolled. In 2009, 100 degrees awarded. *Degree requirements:* For master's, comprehensive exam, thesis optional. *Entrance requirements:* For master's, GRE, 3 years of full-time work experience, minimum GPA of 3.0. Additional exam requirements/recommendations for international students: Required—TOEFL (minimum score 550 paper-based; 213 computer-based). *Application deadline:* For fall admission, 6/6 for domestic students, 4/4 for international students; for spring admission, 10/17 for domestic students, 9/5 for international students. Application fee: $35 ($50 for international students). *Financial support:* Fellowships, research assistantships, teaching assistantships, career-related internships or fieldwork, Federal Work-Study, institutionally sponsored loans, scholarships/grants, and unspecified assistantships available. Financial award application deadline: 6/1; financial award applicants required to submit FAFSA. *Unit head:* Dr. Donald H. Liles, Chair, 817-272-3092, Fax: 817-272-3406, E-mail: dliles@uta.edu. *Application contact:* Dr. Donald H. Liles, Chair, 817-272-3092, Fax: 817-272-3092, E-mail: dliles@uta.edu.

The University of Texas at Austin, Graduate School, Cockrell School of Engineering, Department of Mechanical Engineering, Program in Operations Research and Industrial Engineering, Austin, TX 78712-1111. Offers MS, PhD. *Entrance requirements:* For master's and doctorate, GRE General Test. Additional exam requirements/recommendations for international students: Required—TOEFL.

The University of Texas at El Paso, Graduate School, College of Engineering, Department of Industrial Engineering, El Paso, TX 79968-0001. Offers industrial engineering (MS); manufacturing engineering (MS); systems engineering (MS, Certificate). Part-time and evening/weekend programs available. *Degree requirements:* For master's, thesis optional. *Entrance requirements:* For master's, GRE General Test, minimum GPA of 3.0 in major. Additional exam

Industrial/Management Engineering

The University of Texas at El Paso (continued)
requirements/recommendations for international students: Required—TOEFL. Electronic applications accepted. *Faculty research:* Computer vision, automated inspection, simulation and modeling.

The University of Toledo, College of Graduate Studies, College of Engineering, Department of Mechanical, Industrial, and Manufacturing Engineering, Toledo, OH 43606-3390. Offers industrial engineering (MS, PhD); mechanical engineering (MS, PhD). Part-time programs available. Postbaccalaureate distance learning degree programs offered (minimal on-campus study). *Degree requirements:* For master's, thesis optional; for doctorate, thesis/dissertation, qualifying exam. *Entrance requirements:* For master's, GRE General Test, minimum GPA of 3.0; for doctorate, GRE General Test, minimum GPA of 3.3. Additional exam requirements/recommendations for international students: Required—TOEFL (minimum score 550 paper-based; 213 computer-based; 80 iBT). Electronic applications accepted. *Faculty research:* Computational and experimental thermal sciences, manufacturing process and systems, mechanics, materials, design, quality and management engineering systems.

University of Toronto, School of Graduate Studies, Physical Sciences Division, Faculty of Applied Science and Engineering, Department of Mechanical and Industrial Engineering, Toronto, ON M5S 1A1, Canada. Offers M Eng, MA Sc, PhD. Part-time programs available. *Degree requirements:* For master's, thesis (for some programs), oral exam/thesis defense (MA Sc); for doctorate, thesis/dissertation, thesis defense, qualifying examination. *Entrance requirements:* For master's, GRE (recommended), minimum B+ average in last 2 years of undergraduate study, 2 letters of reference, resume, must be a Canadian citizen or a permanent resident (M Eng); for doctorate, GRE (recommended), minimum B+ average, 2 letters of reference, resumé. Additional exam requirements/recommendations for international students: Required—TOEFL (580 paper-based, 237 computer-based), Michigan English Language Assessment Battery (85), IELTS (7) or COPE (4).

University of Washington, Graduate School, College of Engineering, Department of Industrial and Systems Engineering, Seattle, WA 98195-2650. Offers MSIE, PhD. Part-time programs available. Postbaccalaureate distance learning degree programs offered (minimal on-campus study). *Faculty:* 8 full-time (4 women), 13 part-time/adjunct (2 women). *Students:* 34 full-time (13 women), 13 part-time (4 women); includes 10 minority (7 Asian Americans or Pacific Islanders, 3 Hispanic Americans), 24 international. Average age 29. 167 applicants, 51% accepted, 23 enrolled. In 2009, 12 master's, 2 doctorates awarded. Terminal master's awarded for partial completion of doctoral program. *Degree requirements:* For master's, thesis optional; for doctorate, comprehensive exam, thesis/dissertation. *Entrance requirements:* For master's and doctorate, GRE General Test, minimum GPA of 3.0. Additional exam requirements/recommendations for international students: Required—TOEFL (minimum score 580 paper-based; 237 computer-based; 70 iBT). *Application deadline:* For fall admission, 2/1 priority date for domestic students, 2/1 for international students. Applications are processed on a rolling basis. Application fee: $65. Electronic applications accepted. *Financial support:* In 2009–10, 1 student received support, including 1 fellowship (averaging $12,492 per year), 22 research assistantships with full tuition reimbursements available (averaging $14,751 per year), 10 teaching assistantships with full tuition reimbursements available (averaging $14,751 per year); career-related internships or fieldwork, scholarships/grants, traineeships, and tuition waivers (full) also available. Financial award application deadline: 2/1. *Faculty research:* Manufacturing, operations research, supply chain systems, human interface technology, quality control, logistics systems, bio-industrial systems. Total annual research expenditures: $182,000. *Unit head:* Dr. Richard Lee Storch, Professor and Chair, 206-543-1427, Fax: 206-685-3072, E-mail: rlstorch@u.washington.edu. *Application contact:* Jennifer W. Tsai, Academic Counselor, 206-543-5041, Fax: 206-685-3072, E-mail: ieadvise@u.washington.edu.

University of Windsor, Faculty of Graduate Studies, Faculty of Engineering, Department of Industrial and Manufacturing Systems Engineering, Windsor, ON N9B 3P4, Canada. Offers industrial engineering (M Eng, MA Sc); manufacturing systems engineering (PhD). Part-time programs available. *Degree requirements:* For master's, thesis; for doctorate, comprehensive exam, thesis/dissertation. *Entrance requirements:* For master's, minimum B average; for doctorate, master's degree, minimum B average. Additional exam requirements/recommendations for international students: Required—TOEFL (minimum score 560 paper-based; 220 computer-based). Electronic applications accepted. *Faculty research:* Human factors, operations research.

University of Wisconsin–Madison, Graduate School, College of Engineering, Department of Industrial and Systems Engineering, Madison, WI 53706. Offers MS, PhD. Part-time programs available. *Faculty:* 20 full-time (6 women), 11 part-time/adjunct (4 women). *Students:* 164 full-time (48 women), 18 part-time (3 women); includes 13 minority (3 African Americans, 3 American Indian/Alaska Native, 5 Asian Americans or Pacific Islanders, 2 Hispanic Americans), 131 international. Average age 27. 349 applicants, 56% accepted, 78 enrolled. In 2009, 38 master's, 14 doctorates awarded. Terminal master's awarded for partial completion of doctoral program. *Degree requirements:* For master's, thesis optional; for doctorate, comprehensive exam, thesis/dissertation. *Entrance requirements:* For master's, GRE General Test, min GPA of 3.0 (3.00 in last 60 crs) BS in engineering or equivalent course in Computer Programming, course in Stats, 2 intro ISYE courses; for doctorate, GRE General Test, minimum GPA of 3.0 (3.00 in last 60 credits). Additional exam requirements/recommendations for international students: Recommended—TOEFL (minimum score 600 paper-based; 250 computer-based; 104 iBT). *Application deadline:* For fall admission, 4/1 priority date for domestic and international students; for spring admission, 10/1 priority date for domestic and international students. Application fee: $56. Electronic applications accepted. *Expenses:* Tuition, state resident: part-time $594 per credit. Tuition, nonresident: part-time $1504 per credit. Required fees: $65 per credit. Tuition and fees vary according to course load, program and reciprocity agreements. *Financial support:* In 2009–10, 70 students received support, including 1 fellowship with full tuition reimbursement available (averaging $21,760 per year), 47 research assistantships with full tuition reimbursements available (averaging $40,368 per year), 22 teaching assistantships with full tuition reimbursements available (averaging $28,175 per year); career-related internships or fieldwork, Federal Work-Study, institutionally sponsored loans, scholarships/grants, traineeships, health care benefits, and unspecified assistantships also available. *Faculty research:* Human factors and ergonomics, manufacturing and production systems, health systems engineering, decision science/operations research, quality engineering. Total annual research expenditures: $12.2 million. *Unit head:* Dr. Patricia F. Brennan, Chair, 608-262-9227, Fax: 608-262-8454, E-mail: pbrennan@engr.wisc.edu. *Application contact:* Anne Duchek, Graduate Admissions Coordinator, 608-890-2765, Fax: 608-890-2204, E-mail: amduchek@engr.wisc.edu.

University of Wisconsin–Milwaukee, Graduate School, College of Engineering and Applied Science, Program in Engineering, Milwaukee, WI 53201-0413. Offers civil engineering (MS); electrical and computer engineering (MS); energy engineering (Certificate); engineering (PhD); engineering management (MS); engineering mechanics (MS); ergonomics (Certificate); industrial and management engineering (MS); manufacturing engineering (MS); materials engineering (MS); mechanical engineering (MS); MUP/MS. Part-time programs available. *Faculty:* 44 full-time (6 women). *Students:* 119 full-time (22 women), 130 part-time (22 women); includes 23 minority (2 African Americans, 14 Asian Americans or Pacific Islanders, 7 Hispanic Americans), 126 international. Average age 32. 231 applicants, 67% accepted, 33 enrolled. In 2009, 29 master's, 14 doctorates awarded. *Degree requirements:* For master's, comprehensive exam (for some programs), thesis or alternative; for doctorate, comprehensive exam, thesis/

dissertation, internship. *Entrance requirements:* For master's, GRE, minimum GPA of 2.75; for doctorate, GRE, minimum GPA of 3.5. Additional exam requirements/recommendations for international students: Required—TOEFL (minimum score 550 paper-based; 79 iBT), IELTS (minimum score 6.5). *Application deadline:* For fall admission, 1/1 priority date for domestic students; for spring admission, 9/1 for domestic students. Applications are processed on a rolling basis. Application fee: $45 ($75 for international students). *Expenses:* Tuition, state resident: full-time $8800. Tuition, nonresident: full-time $20,760. Tuition and fees vary according to program and reciprocity agreements. *Financial support:* In 2009–10, 18 research assistantships, 51 teaching assistantships were awarded; fellowships, career-related internships or fieldwork, Federal Work-Study, and unspecified assistantships also available. Support available to part-time students. Financial award application deadline: 4/15. Total annual research expenditures: $2.9 million. *Unit head:* David Yu, Head, 414-229-6169, E-mail: yu@uwm.edu. *Application contact:* Betty Warras, General Information Contact, 414-229-4982, Fax: 414-229-6967, E-mail: bwarras@uwm.edu.

University of Wisconsin–Stout, Graduate School, College of Technology, Engineering, and Management, MS Program in Risk Control, Menomonie, WI 54751. Offers MS. Part-time programs available. *Degree requirements:* For master's, thesis. *Entrance requirements:* For master's, minimum GPA of 3.0. Additional exam requirements/recommendations for international students: Required—TOEFL (minimum score 500 paper-based; 173 computer-based; 61 iBT). Electronic applications accepted. *Faculty research:* Environmental microbiology, water supply safety, facilities planning, industrial ventilation, bioterrorist.

Virginia Polytechnic Institute and State University, Graduate School, College of Engineering, Department of Industrial and Systems Engineering, Blacksburg, VA 24061. Offers engineering administration (MEA); industrial engineering (M Eng, MS, PhD); operations research (M Eng, MS, PhD); systems engineering (M Eng, MS). *Entrance requirements:* For master's and doctorate, GRE. Additional exam requirements/recommendations for international students: Required—TOEFL (minimum score 550 paper-based; 213 computer-based). Electronic applications accepted.

Wayne State University, College of Engineering, Department of Industrial and Manufacturing Engineering, Program in Industrial Engineering, Detroit, MI 48202. Offers MS, PhD. *Degree requirements:* For master's, thesis optional; for doctorate, thesis/dissertation. *Entrance requirements:* For master's, baccalaureate degree in enginnering from an ABET institution, minimum undergraduate GPA of 2.8; for doctorate, minimum graduate GPA of 3.5. Additional exam requirements/recommendations for international students: Required—TOEFL (minimum score 550 paper-based; 213 computer-based), GRE; Recommended—TWE (minimum score 6). Electronic applications accepted. *Faculty research:* Reliability and quality, technology management, manufacturing systems, operations research, concurrent engineering.

Western Carolina University, Graduate School, Kimmel School of Construction Management and Technology, Department of Engineering and Technology, Cullowhee, NC 28723. Offers MS. Part-time programs available. *Students:* 18 full-time (1 woman), 5 part-time (2 women). Average age 23. 31 applicants, 94% accepted, 19 enrolled. In 2009, 7 master's awarded. *Degree requirements:* For master's, comprehensive exam. *Entrance requirements:* For master's, GRE, appropriate undergraduate degree with minimum GPA of 3.0, 3 letters of recommendation. Additional exam requirements/recommendations for international students: Required—TOEFL (minimum score 550 paper-based; 270 computer-based; 79 iBT). *Application deadline:* For fall admission, 5/1 priority date for domestic students; for spring admission, 9/1 priority date for domestic students. Applications are processed on a rolling basis. Application fee: $45. *Financial support:* In 2009–10, 14 students received support, including 12 research assistantships with full and partial tuition reimbursements available (averaging $7,333 per year), 2 teaching assistantships with full and partial tuition reimbursements available (averaging $8,000 per year); fellowships, institutionally sponsored loans, scholarships/grants, and unspecified assistantships also available. Financial award application deadline: 3/31; financial award applicants required to submit FAFSA. *Faculty research:* Electrophysiology, 3D graphics, digital signal processing, CAM and advanced machining, fluid power, polymer science, wireless communication. *Unit head:* Dr. Ken Burbank, Head, 828-227-7368, Fax: 828-227-7838, E-mail: kburbank@email.wcu.edu. *Application contact:* Admissions Specialist for Engineering and Technology, 828-227-7398, Fax: 828-227-7480, E-mail: gradsch@email.wcu.edu.

Western Michigan University, Graduate College, College of Engineering and Applied Sciences, Department of Industrial and Manufacturing Engineering, Program in Industrial Engineering, Kalamazoo, MI 49008. Offers MSE. *Entrance requirements:* For master's, minimum GPA of 3.0.

Western New England College, School of Engineering, Department of Industrial and Manufacturing Engineering, Springfield, MA 01119. Offers production management (MSEM). Part-time and evening/weekend programs available. *Students:* 30 part-time (6 women); includes 2 African Americans, 2 Asian Americans or Pacific Islanders, 1 Hispanic American. In 2009, 8 master's awarded. *Degree requirements:* For master's, comprehensive exam, thesis optional. *Entrance requirements:* For master's, GRE, bachelor's degree in engineering or related field, Two Letters of Recommendation, and Resume. *Application deadline:* Applications are processed on a rolling basis. Application fee: $30. *Expenses:* Tuition: Part-time $552 per credit hour. Part-time tuition and fees vary according to program. *Financial support:* Available to part-time students. Applicants required to submit FAFSA. *Faculty research:* Project scheduling, flexible manufacturing systems, facility layout, energy management. *Unit head:* Dr. Eric W. Haffner, Chair, 413-782-1272, E-mail: ehaffner@wnec.edu. *Application contact:* Matt Fox, Director of Recruiting and Marketing for Adult Learners, 413-782-1249, Fax: 413-782-1779, E-mail: ce@wnec.edu.

West Virginia University, College of Engineering and Mineral Resources, Department of Industrial and Management Systems Engineering, Program in Industrial Engineering, Morgantown, WV 26506. Offers engineering (MSE); industrial engineering (MSIE, PhD). Part-time programs available. *Degree requirements:* For master's, thesis or alternative; for doctorate, comprehensive exam, thesis/dissertation. *Entrance requirements:* For master's, GRE General Test, minimum GPA of 3.0 Regular; 2.75 Provisional; for doctorate, GRE General Test, minimum GPA of 3.5. Additional exam requirements/recommendations for international students: Required—TOEFL (minimum score 550 paper-based; 213 computer-based; 80 iBT). Electronic applications accepted. *Faculty research:* Production planning and control, quality control, robotics and CIMS, ergonomics, castings.

Wichita State University, Graduate School, College of Engineering, Department of Industrial and Manufacturing Engineering, Wichita, KS 67260. Offers MEM, MS, PhD. Part-time programs available. In 2009, 37 master's, 3 doctorates awarded. *Entrance requirements:* Additional exam requirements/recommendations for international students: Required—TOEFL. *Expenses:* Tuition, state resident: full-time $4247; part-time $235.95 per credit hour. Tuition, nonresident: full-time $11,171; part-time $620.60 per credit hour. Required fees: $34; $3.60 per credit hour. $17 per term. Tuition and fees vary according to campus/location and program. *Financial support:* Teaching assistantships available. *Unit head:* Dr. Krishna Krishnan, Chair, 316-978-3425, Fax: 316-978-3742, E-mail: krishna.krishnan@wichita.edu. *Application contact:* Dr. Krishna Krishnan, Chair, 316-978-3425, Fax: 316-978-3742, E-mail: krishna.krishnan@wichita.edu.

Youngstown State University, Graduate School, College of Science, Technology, Engineering and Mathematics, Department of Industrial and Systems Engineering, Youngstown, OH 44555-0001. Offers MSE.

Manufacturing Engineering

Arizona State University, Graduate College, College of Technology and Innovation, Department of Mechanical and Manufacturing Engineering Technology, Tempe, AZ 85287. Offers MS. Part-time and evening/weekend programs available. *Degree requirements:* For master's, thesis or applied project and oral defense, final examination. *Entrance requirements:* For master's, resume, industrial experience beyond bachelor degree (recommended). Additional exam requirements/recommendations for international students: Required—TOEFL (minimum score 550 paper-based; 213 computer-based; 83 iBT); Recommended—TWE. Electronic applications accepted. *Faculty research:* Manufacturing modeling and simulation 'smart' and composite materials, optimization of turbine engines, machinability and manufacturing processes design, fuel cells and other alternative energy sources.

Arizona State University, Graduate College, Ira A. Fulton School of Engineering, School of Materials, Tempe, AZ 85287. Offers materials science and engineering (MS, MSE, PhD); semiconductor processing and packaging (MSE). *Degree requirements:* For doctorate, thesis/dissertation. *Entrance requirements:* For doctorate, GRE.

Bowling Green State University, Graduate College, College of Technology, Department of Technology Systems, Bowling Green, OH 43403. Offers construction management (MIT); manufacturing technology (MIT). Part-time programs available. *Degree requirements:* For master's, thesis or alternative. *Entrance requirements:* For master's, GRE General Test. Additional exam requirements/recommendations for international students: Required—TOEFL. Electronic applications accepted.

Bradley University, Graduate School, College of Engineering and Technology, Department of Industrial and Manufacturing Engineering and Technology, Peoria, IL 61625-0002. Offers industrial engineering (MSIE); manufacturing engineering (MSIE). Part-time and evening/weekend programs available. *Degree requirements:* For master's, comprehensive exam, project. *Entrance requirements:* For master's, minimum GPA of 3.0. Additional exam requirements/recommendations for international students: Required—TOEFL (minimum score 550 paper-based; 213 computer-based; 79 iBT).

California State University, Northridge, Graduate Studies, College of Engineering and Computer Science, Department of Manufacturing Systems Engineering and Management, Northridge, CA 91330. Offers engineering automation (MS); engineering management (MS); manufacturing systems engineering (MS); materials engineering (MS). Postbaccalaureate distance learning degree programs offered. *Faculty:* 6 full-time (1 woman), 33 part-time/adjunct (12 women). *Students:* 137 full-time (18 women), 115 part-time (20 women); includes 4 African Americans, 22 Asian Americans or Pacific Islanders, 19 Hispanic Americans, 149 international. Average age 27. 210 applicants, 68% accepted, 69 enrolled. In 2009, 78 master's awarded. *Entrance requirements:* For master's, GRE (if cumulative undergraduate GPA less than 3.0). *Application deadline:* For fall admission, 3/30 for domestic students; for spring admission, 9/30 for domestic students. Application fee: $55. *Unit head:* Prof. Behzad Bavarian, Acting Chair, 818-677-2167. *Application contact:* Prof. Behzad Bavarian, Acting Chair, 818-677-2167.

Clemson University, Graduate School, College of Agriculture, Forestry and Life Sciences, Department of Packaging Science, Clemson, SC 29634. Offers MS. *Faculty:* 7 full-time (2 women), 1 part-time/adjunct (0 women). *Students:* 7 full-time (4 women), 1 part-time (0 women), 2 international. Average age 26. 12 applicants, 42% accepted, 2 enrolled. In 2009, 7 master's awarded. *Entrance requirements:* For master's, GRE General Test. *Application deadline:* For fall admission, 4/15 for international students; for spring admission, 9/15 for international students. Applications are processed on a rolling basis. Application fee: $70 ($80 for international students). Electronic applications accepted. *Expenses:* Contact institution. *Financial support:* In 2009–10, 7 students received support, including 1 fellowship with full and partial tuition reimbursement available (averaging $4,666 per year), 7 teaching assistantships with partial tuition reimbursements available (averaging $13,656 per year); research assistantships with partial tuition reimbursements available, career-related internships or fieldwork, institutionally sponsored loans, scholarships/grants, health care benefits, and unspecified assistantships also available. Support available to part-time students. Total annual research expenditures: $189,211. *Unit head:* Dr. Bob Kimmel, Department Chair, 864-656-5691, Fax: 864-656-4395, E-mail: rthms@clemson.edu. *Application contact:* Dr. Ron Thomas, Coordinator, 864-656-5697, Fax: 864-656-4395, E-mail: rthms@clemson.edu.

Cornell University, Graduate School, Graduate Fields of Engineering, Field of Operations Research and Information Engineering, Ithaca, NY 14853-0001. Offers applied probability and statistics (PhD); manufacturing systems engineering (PhD); mathematical programming (PhD); operations research and industrial engineering (M Eng). *Faculty:* 46 full-time (9 women). *Students:* 163 full-time (46 women); includes 20 minority (2 African Americans, 12 Asian Americans or Pacific Islanders, 6 Hispanic Americans), 103 international. Average age 25. 774 applicants, 29% accepted, 91 enrolled. In 2009, 85 master's, 6 doctorates awarded. *Degree requirements:* For doctorate, comprehensive exam, thesis/dissertation. *Entrance requirements:* For master's and doctorate, GRE General Test, 3 letters of recommendation. Additional exam requirements/recommendations for international students: Required—TOEFL (minimum score 600 paper-based; 250 computer-based; 77 iBT). *Application deadline:* For fall admission, 1/15 for domestic students. Application fee: $70. Electronic applications accepted. *Expenses:* Tuition: Full-time $29,500. Required fees: $70. Full-time tuition and fees vary according to degree level, program and student level. *Financial support:* In 2009–10, 44 students received support, including 6 fellowships with full tuition reimbursements available, 5 teaching assistantships with full tuition reimbursements available; research assistantships with full tuition reimbursements available, institutionally sponsored loans, scholarships/grants, health care benefits, tuition waivers (full and partial), and unspecified assistantships also available. Financial award applicants required to submit FAFSA. *Faculty research:* Mathematical programming and combinatorial optimization, statistics, stochastic processes, mathematical finance, simulation, manufacturing, e-commerce. *Unit head:* Director of Graduate Studies, 607-255-9128, Fax: 607-255-9129. *Application contact:* Graduate Field Assistant, 607-255-9128, Fax: 607-255-9129, E-mail: orie@cornell.edu.

Dartmouth College, Thayer School of Engineering, Program in Manufacturing Systems, Hanover, NH 03755. Offers MS, PhD. Application fee: $45. *Faculty research:* Scheduling, production planning and control, facilities planning, project management, design for assembly and manufacturing. *Unit head:* Dr. Joseph J. Helbie, Dean, 603-646-2238, Fax: 603-646-2580, E-mail: joseph.j.helbie@dartmouth.edu. *Application contact:* Candace S. Potter, Graduate Admissions Administrator, 603-646-3844, Fax: 603-646-1620, E-mail: candace.potter@dartmouth.edu.

East Carolina University, Graduate School, College of Technology and Computer Science, Department of Technology Systems, Greenville, NC 27858-4353. Offers computer network professional (Certificate); industrial technology (MS), including computer networking management, digital communications, industrial distribution and logistics, information security, manufacturing, performance improvement, planning; information assurance (Certificate); occupational safety (MS); technology management (PhD); Website developer (Certificate). *Entrance requirements:* For master's and Certificate, GRE General Test or MAT, minimum GPA of 2.5; for doctorate, GRE General Test, related work experience.

Eastern Kentucky University, The Graduate School, College of Business and Technology, Department of Technology, Richmond, KY 40475-3102. Offers industrial education (MS), including occupational training and development, technical administration, technology education; industrial technology (MS). Part-time and evening/weekend programs available. *Entrance requirements:* For master's, GRE General Test, minimum GPA of 2.5. *Faculty research:* Lunar excavation, computer networking, integrating academic and vocational education.

East Tennessee State University, School of Graduate Studies, College of Business and Technology, Department of Technology and Geomatics, Johnson City, TN 37614. Offers digital media (MS); engineering technology (MS); industrial arts/technology education (MS). Part-time programs available. *Degree requirements:* For master's, thesis or alternative, final oral exam. *Entrance requirements:* For master's, bachelor's degree in technical or related area, minimum GPA of 3.0. Additional exam requirements/recommendations for international students: Required—TOEFL (minimum score 550 paper-based; 213 computer-based). *Faculty research:* Computer-integrated manufacturing, technology education, CAD/CAM, organizational change.

Florida State University, The Graduate School, FAMU-FSU College of Engineering, Department of Industrial and Manufacturing Engineering, Tallahassee, FL 32306. Offers industrial engineering (MS, PhD). *Faculty:* 10 full-time (1 woman), 1 (woman) part-time/adjunct. *Students:* 55 full-time (10 women); includes 42 minority (16 African Americans, 22 Asian Americans or Pacific Islanders, 4 Hispanic Americans). Average age 24. 84 applicants, 54% accepted, 13 enrolled. In 2009, 13 master's, 3 doctorates awarded. *Degree requirements:* For master's, thesis; for doctorate, thesis/dissertation, preliminary exam, qualifying exam. *Entrance requirements:* For master's, GRE General Test, minimum GPA of 3.0; for doctorate, GRE General Test, minimum GPA of 3.0 (without MS in industrial engineering), 3.4 (with MS in industrial engineering). Additional exam requirements/recommendations for international students: Required—TOEFL (minimum score 550 paper-based; 213 computer-based; 80 iBT). *Application deadline:* For fall admission, 7/1 for domestic and international students; for spring admission, 11/1 for domestic and international students. Applications are processed on a rolling basis. Application fee: $30. *Expenses:* Tuition, state resident: full-time $7413.36. Tuition, nonresident: full-time $22,567. *Financial support:* In 2009–10, 31 students received support, including 1 fellowship with full tuition reimbursement available (averaging $18,000 per year), 22 research assistantships with full tuition reimbursements available (averaging $15,000 per year), 1 teaching assistantship with full tuition reimbursement available (averaging $15,000 per year); tuition waivers (full) also available. Financial award application deadline: 6/15. *Faculty research:* Precision manufacturing, composite manufacturing, green manufacturing, applied optimization, simulation. Total annual research expenditures: $3.7 million. *Unit head:* Dr. Chun (Chuck) Zhang, Chair and Professor, 850-410-6355, Fax: 850-410-6342, E-mail: chzhang@eng.fsu.edu. *Application contact:* Stephanie Salters, Office Manager, 850-410-6345, Fax: 850-410-6342, E-mail: salters@eng.fsu.edu.

Grand Valley State University, Padnos College of Engineering and Computing, School of Engineering, Allendale, MI 49401-9403. Offers electrical and computer engineering (MSE); manufacturing operations (MSE); mechanical engineering (MSE); product design and manufacturing engineering (MSE). Part-time and evening/weekend programs available. *Faculty:* 6 full-time (0 women). *Students:* 8 full-time (1 woman), 37 part-time (4 women), 4 international. Average age 30. 21 applicants, 86% accepted, 10 enrolled. In 2009, 12 master's awarded. *Degree requirements:* For master's, project or thesis. *Entrance requirements:* For master's, engineering degree, minimum GPA of 3.0. Additional exam requirements/recommendations for international students: Required—TOEFL. *Application deadline:* Applications are processed on a rolling basis. Application fee: $30. Electronic applications accepted. *Financial support:* In 2009–10, 11 students received support, including 3 fellowships (averaging $1,083 per year), 9 research assistantships with full tuition reimbursements available (averaging $7,304 per year); career-related internships or fieldwork, Federal Work-Study, institutionally sponsored loans, scholarships/grants, and unspecified assistantships also available. *Faculty research:* Digital signal processing, computer aided design, computer aided manufacturing, manufacturing simulation, biomechanics, product design. Total annual research expenditures: $300,000. *Unit head:* Dr. Charles Standridge, Acting Director, 616-331-6750, Fax: 616-331-7215, E-mail: standric@gvsu.edu. *Application contact:* Dr. Pranod Chaphalkar, Graduate Director, 616-331-6843, Fax: 616-331-7215, E-mail: chaphalp@gvsu.edu.

Illinois Institute of Technology, Graduate College, Armour College of Engineering, Department of Chemical and Biological Engineering, Chicago, IL 60616-3793. Offers biological engineering (MBE); chemical engineering (M Ch E, MS, PhD); food process engineering (MFPE); food processing engineering (MS); gas engineering (MGE); manufacturing engineering (MME, MS); MS/M Ch E. Part-time and evening/weekend programs available. Postbaccalaureate distance learning degree programs offered. Terminal master's awarded for partial completion of doctoral program. *Degree requirements:* For master's, comprehensive exam, thesis (for some programs); for doctorate, comprehensive exam, thesis/dissertation. *Entrance requirements:* For master's and doctorate, GRE General Test, minimum undergraduate GPA of 3.0. Additional exam requirements/recommendations for international students: Required—TOEFL (minimum score 550 paper-based; 213 computer-based; 80 iBT). Electronic applications accepted. *Expenses:* Tuition: Full-time $17,550; part-time $888 per credit hour. Required fees: $850; $7.50 per credit hour. One-time fee: $50 full-time. Full-time tuition and fees vary according to program. *Faculty research:* Biochemical, bioenergy, biosensors, tissue engineering, fuel cells, batteries, renewable energy, gas cleaning, particle technology, fluidization, colloid and interfacial engineering complex fluids, polymers, complex systems and dynamics.

Illinois Institute of Technology, Graduate College, Armour College of Engineering, Department of Electrical and Computer Engineering, Chicago, IL 60616-3793. Offers biomedical imaging and signals (MBMI); computer engineering (MS, PhD); electrical and computer engineering (MECE); electrical engineering (MS, PhD); electricity markets (MEM); manufacturing engineering (MME, MS); network engineering (MNE); power engineering (MPE); telecommunications and software engineering (MTSE); VLSI and microelectronics (MVM). Part-time and evening/weekend programs available. Terminal master's awarded for partial completion of doctoral program. *Degree requirements:* For master's, comprehensive exam, thesis (for some programs); for doctorate, comprehensive exam, thesis/dissertation. *Entrance requirements:* For master's and doctorate, GRE General Test, minimum undergraduate GPA of 3.0. Additional exam requirements/recommendations for international students: Required—TOEFL (minimum score 550 paper-based; 213 computer-based; 80 iBT). Electronic applications accepted. *Expenses:* Tuition: Full-time $17,550; part-time $888 per credit hour. Required fees: $850; $7.50 per credit hour. One-time fee: $50 full-time. Full-time tuition and fees vary according to program. *Faculty research:* Communications and signal processing, computers and digital systems, electronics and electromagnetics, power and control systems.

Illinois Institute of Technology, Graduate College, Armour College of Engineering, Department of Mechanical, Materials and Aerospace Engineering, Chicago, IL 60616-3793. Offers manufacturing engineering (MME, MS); materials science and engineering (MMME, MS, PhD); mechanical and aerospace engineering (MMAE, MS, PhD). Part-time programs available. Terminal master's awarded for partial completion of doctoral program. *Degree requirements:* For master's, comprehensive exam (for some programs), thesis (for some programs); for doctorate, comprehensive exam, thesis/dissertation. *Entrance requirements:* For master's and doctorate, GRE General Test, minimum undergraduate GPA of 3.0. Additional exam requirements/recommendations for international students: Required—TOEFL (minimum score 550 paper-based; 213 computer-based; 80 iBT). Electronic applications accepted. *Expenses:* Tuition: Full-time $17,550; part-time $888 per credit hour. Required fees: $850; $7.50 per credit hour. One-time fee: $50 full-time. Full-time tuition and fees vary according to program. *Faculty research:* Active flow control, bio-fluid dynamics, acoustics and separated flows, digital design and manufacturing and high performance materials, two-phase flows in micro scales and combustion-driven MEMS, global positioning systems, experimental and computational solid mechanics.

Instituto Tecnológico y de Estudios Superiores de Monterrey, Campus Monterrey, Graduate and Research Division, Programs in Engineering, Monterrey, Mexico. Offers applied statistics (M Eng); artificial intelligence (PhD); automation engineering (M Eng); chemical engineering (M Eng); civil engineering (M Eng); electrical engineering (M Eng); electronic engineering (M Eng); environmental engineering (M Eng); industrial engineering (M Eng, PhD);

Manufacturing Engineering

Instituto Tecnológico y de Estudios Superiores de Monterrey, Campus Monterrey (continued)
manufacturing engineering (M Eng); mechanical engineering (M Eng); systems and quality engineering (M Eng). Part-time and evening/weekend programs available. Terminal master's awarded for partial completion of doctoral program. *Degree requirements:* For master's, one foreign language, thesis; for doctorate, one foreign language, thesis/dissertation. *Entrance requirements:* For master's, EXADEP; for doctorate, GRE, master's degree in related field. Additional exam requirements/recommendations for international students: Required—TOEFL. *Faculty research:* Flexible manufacturing cells, materials, statistical methods, environmental prevention, control and evaluation.

Kansas State University, Graduate School, College of Engineering, Department of Industrial and Manufacturing Systems Engineering, Manhattan, KS 66506. Offers engineering management (MEM); industrial engineering (MS, PhD); operations research (MS). Part-time programs available. Postbaccalaureate distance learning degree programs offered. *Faculty:* 9 full-time (1 woman), 2 part-time/adjunct (1 woman). *Students:* 38 full-time (12 women), 48 part-time (14 women); includes 4 minority (1 African American, 1 Asian American or Pacific Islander, 2 Hispanic Americans), 27 international. Average age 30. 85 applicants, 60% accepted, 41 enrolled. In 2009, 20 master's, 1 doctorate awarded. *Degree requirements:* For master's, thesis or alternative; for doctorate, thesis/dissertation. *Entrance requirements:* For master's, GRE General Test, bachelor's degree in engineering, mathematics, or physical science; for doctorate, GRE General Test, master's degree in engineering or industrial manufacturing. Additional exam requirements/recommendations for international students: Required—TOEFL. *Application deadline:* For fall admission, 2/1 priority date for domestic and international students; for spring admission, 8/1 priority date for domestic and international students. Applications are processed on a rolling basis. Application fee: $40 ($55 for international students). Electronic applications accepted. *Financial support:* In 2009–10, 19 research assistantships (averaging $10,372 per year), 1 teaching assistantship with full tuition reimbursement (averaging $12,450 per year) were awarded; Federal Work-Study, institutionally sponsored loans, and scholarships/grants also available. Support available to part-time students. Financial award application deadline: 3/1; financial award applicants required to submit FAFSA. *Faculty research:* Ergonomics, healthcare systems engineering, manufacturing processes, operations research, engineering management. Total annual research expenditures: $484,594. *Unit head:* Bradley Kramer, Head, 785-532-5606, Fax: 785-532-7810, E-mail: bradleyk@ksu.edu. *Application contact:* E. Stanley Lee, Director, 785-532-3730, Fax: 785-532-7810, E-mail: eslee@ksu.edu.

Kettering University, Graduate School, Department of Business, Flint, MI 48504. Offers business administration (MBA); engineering management (MSEM); information technology (MSIT); manufacturing management (MSMM); manufacturing operations (MSMO); operations management (MSOM). *Accreditation:* ACBSP. Part-time and evening/weekend programs available. Postbaccalaureate distance learning degree programs offered (no on-campus study). *Faculty:* 9 full-time (3 women), 4 part-time/adjunct (0 women). *Students:* 12 full-time (5 women), 251 part-time (79 women); includes 42 minority (27 African Americans, 1 American Indian/Alaska Native, 9 Asian Americans or Pacific Islanders, 5 Hispanic Americans), 15 international. Average age 32. 74 applicants, 78% accepted, 31 enrolled. In 2009, 123 master's awarded. *Entrance requirements:* Additional exam requirements/recommendations for international students: Required—TOEFL (minimum score 550 paper-based; 213 computer-based; 79 iBT). *Application deadline:* For fall admission, 9/15 for domestic students, 6/15 for international students; for winter admission, 12/15 for domestic students, 9/15 for international students; for spring admission, 3/15 for domestic students, 12/15 for international students. Applications are processed on a rolling basis. Electronic applications accepted. *Expenses:* Tuition: Full-time $11,120; part-time $695 per credit hour. *Financial support:* In 2009–10, 101 students received support, including fellowships with full tuition reimbursements available (averaging $13,000 per year), research assistantships with full tuition reimbursements available (averaging $13,000 per year), teaching assistantships with full tuition reimbursements available (averaging $13,000 per year); Federal Work-Study, scholarships/grants, and tuition waivers (partial) also available. Support available to part-time students. Financial award application deadline: 7/15. *Unit head:* Dr. Tony Hain, Vice President of Graduate Studies and Corporate Connections, 810-762-9616, Fax: 810-762-9935, E-mail: thain@kettering.edu. *Application contact:* Bonnie Switzer, Admissions Representative, 810-762-7953, Fax: 810-762-9935, E-mail: bswitzer@kettering.edu.

Kettering University, Graduate School, Department of Industrial and Manufacturing Engineering, Flint, MI 48504. Offers manufacturing systems engineering (MS Eng). Part-time and evening/weekend programs available. Postbaccalaureate distance learning degree programs offered (no on-campus study). *Faculty:* 6 full-time (2 women), 1 part-time/adjunct (0 women). *Students:* 10 part-time (2 women); includes 1 minority (African American), 1 international. Average age 30. 33 applicants, 64% accepted, 10 enrolled. In 2009, 4 master's awarded. *Degree requirements:* For master's, thesis optional. *Entrance requirements:* Additional exam requirements/recommendations for international students: Required—TOEFL (minimum score 550 paper-based; 213 computer-based; 79 iBT). *Application deadline:* For fall admission, 9/15 for domestic students, 6/15 for international students; for winter admission, 12/15 for domestic students, 9/5 for international students; for spring admission, 3/15 for domestic students, 12/5 for international students. Applications are processed on a rolling basis. Application fee: $0. Electronic applications accepted. *Expenses:* Tuition: Full-time $11,120; part-time $695 per credit hour. *Financial support:* In 2009–10, 4 students received support, including fellowships with full tuition reimbursements available (averaging $13,000 per year), research assistantships with full tuition reimbursements available (averaging $13,000 per year), teaching assistantships with full tuition reimbursements available (averaging $13,000 per year); Federal Work-Study, scholarships/grants, and tuition waivers (partial) also available. Support available to part-time students. Financial award application deadline: 7/15; financial award applicants required to submit CSS PROFILE or FAFSA. *Faculty research:* Machine part testing, geothermal system study, office procedure study. Total annual research expenditures: $28,072. *Unit head:* Dr. W. L. Scheller, Head, 810-762-7974, E-mail: wschelle@kettering.edu. *Application contact:* Bonnie Switzer, Admissions Representative, 810-762-7953, Fax: 810-762-9935, E-mail: bswitzer@kettering.edu.

Lawrence Technological University, College of Engineering, Southfield, MI 48075-1058. Offers automotive engineering (MAE); civil engineering (MCE); construction engineering management (MS); electrical and computer engineering (MS); engineering management (ME); industrial engineering (MSIE); manufacturing systems (MEMS, DE); mechanical engineering (MS); mechatronic systems engineering (MS). Part-time and evening/weekend programs available. *Faculty:* 20 full-time (4 women), 12 part-time/adjunct (0 women). *Students:* 15 full-time (4 women), 389 part-time (50 women); includes 57 minority (22 African Americans, 1 American Indian/Alaska Native, 30 Asian Americans or Pacific Islanders, 4 Hispanic Americans), 137 international. Average age 31. 361 applicants, 52% accepted, 108 enrolled. In 2009, 161 master's, 1 doctorate awarded. *Degree requirements:* For master's, thesis (for some programs). *Entrance requirements:* Additional exam requirements/recommendations for international students: Required—TOEFL (minimum score 550 paper-based; 213 computer-based; 79 iBT). *Application deadline:* For fall admission, 8/1 priority date for domestic students, 6/1 for international students; for winter admission, 12/1 priority date for domestic students, 10/1 for international students; for spring admission, 5/1 priority date for domestic students, 3/1 for international students. Applications are processed on a rolling basis. Application fee: $50. Electronic applications accepted. *Expenses:* Tuition: Full-time $11,320; part-time $798 per credit hour. *Financial support:* Federal Work-Study and institutionally sponsored loans available. Support available to part-time students. Financial award application deadline: 4/1; financial award applicants required to submit FAFSA. *Faculty research:* Advanced composite materials in bridges, strengthening existing bridges with carbon and glass fiber sheets, development of drive shafts using composite materials. *Unit head:* Dr. Nabil Grace, Interim Dean, 248-204-2500, Fax: 248-204-2509, E-mail: engrdean@ltu.edu. *Application contact:* Jane Rohrback, Director of Admissions, 248-204-3160, Fax: 248-204-3188, E-mail: admissions@ltu.edu.

Lehigh University, P.C. Rossin College of Engineering and Applied Science, Program in Manufacturing Systems Engineering, Bethlehem, PA 18015. Offers MS, MBA/E. Part-time and evening/weekend programs available. Postbaccalaureate distance learning degree programs offered (no on-campus study). *Students:* 2 full-time (0 women), 30 part-time (6 women); includes 3 minority (1 African American, 2 Asian Americans or Pacific Islanders), 1 international. Average age 33. 68 applicants, 19% accepted, 9 enrolled. In 2009, 6 master's awarded. *Degree requirements:* For master's, comprehensive exam, project or thesis. *Entrance requirements:* For master's, GRE General Test, minimum GPA of 2.75. Additional exam requirements/recommendations for international students: Required—TOEFL (minimum score 620 paper-based; 260 computer-based; 85 iBT). *Application deadline:* For fall admission, 7/15 for domestic and international students; for spring admission, 12/1 for domestic and international students. Applications are processed on a rolling basis. Application fee: $65. Electronic applications accepted. *Faculty research:* Manufacturing systems design, development, and implementation; accounting and management; agile/lean systems; supply chain issues; sustainable systems design; product design. *Unit head:* Dr. Keith M. Gardiner, Director, 610-758-5070, Fax: 610-758-6527, E-mail: kg03@lehigh.edu. *Application contact:* Carolyn C. Jones, Graduate Coordinator, 610-758-5157, Fax: 610-758-6527, E-mail: ccj1@lehigh.edu.

Marquette University, Graduate School, College of Engineering, Department of Mechanical and Industrial Engineering, Milwaukee, WI 53201-1881. Offers engineering management (MS); mechanical engineering (MS, PhD), including manufacturing systems engineering. Part-time and evening/weekend programs available. *Faculty:* 16 full-time (0 women), 3 part-time/adjunct (0 women). *Students:* 26 full-time (4 women), 49 part-time (7 women); includes 3 minority (2 African Americans, 1 Asian American or Pacific Islander), 11 international. Average age 28. 60 applicants, 73% accepted, 16 enrolled. In 2009, 21 master's, 1 doctorate awarded. Terminal master's awarded for partial completion of doctoral program. *Degree requirements:* For master's, thesis; for doctorate, comprehensive exam, thesis/dissertation, qualifying exam. *Entrance requirements:* For master's and doctorate, GRE General Test, minimum GPA of 3.0. Additional exam requirements/recommendations for international students: Required—TOEFL. *Application deadline:* For fall admission, 8/1 priority date for domestic students; for spring admission, 1/1 priority date for domestic students. Applications are processed on a rolling basis. Application fee: $40. Electronic applications accepted. *Financial support:* In 2009–10, 19 students received support, including 5 fellowships with tuition reimbursements available (averaging $11,600 per year), 6 research assistantships with tuition reimbursements available (averaging $11,490 per year), 8 teaching assistantships with tuition reimbursements available (averaging $11,490 per year); Federal Work-Study, institutionally sponsored loans, scholarships/grants, and tuition waivers (full and partial) also available. Support available to part-time students. Financial award application deadline: 2/15. *Faculty research:* Computer-integrated manufacturing, energy conversion, simulation modeling and optimization, applied mechanics, metallurgy. *Unit head:* Dr. Kyle Kim, Chair, 414-288-7259, Fax: 414-288-7790, E-mail: kyle.kim@marquette.edu. *Application contact:* Dr. Nicholas J. Nigro, Director of Graduate Studies, 414-288-3518, Fax: 414-288-7790, E-mail: nicholas.nigro@marquette.edu.

Massachusetts Institute of Technology, School of Engineering, Department of Mechanical Engineering, Cambridge, MA 02139-4307. Offers manufacturing (M Eng); mechanical engineering (SM, PhD, Sc D, Mech E); naval architecture and marine engineering (SM, PhD, Sc D); naval engineering (Naval E); ocean engineering (SM, PhD, Sc D), including); oceanographic engineering (SM, PhD, Sc D); SM/MBA. *Faculty:* 68 full-time (8 women). *Students:* 489 full-time (80 women); includes 58 minority (7 African Americans, 3 American Indian/Alaska Native, 30 Asian Americans or Pacific Islanders, 18 Hispanic Americans), 211 international. Average age 27. 966 applicants, 24% accepted, 144 enrolled. In 2009, 110 master's, 45 doctorates, 9 other advanced degrees awarded. Terminal master's awarded for partial completion of doctoral program. *Degree requirements:* For master's and other advanced degree, thesis; for doctorate, comprehensive exam, thesis/dissertation. *Entrance requirements:* For master's, doctorate, and other advanced degree, GRE General Test. Additional exam requirements/recommendations for international students: Required—TOEFL (minimum score 577 paper-based; 233 computer-based; 91 iBT), IELTS (minimum score 7), IELTS preferred. *Application deadline:* For fall admission, 12/15 for domestic and international students. Application fee: $75. Electronic applications accepted. *Financial support:* In 2009–10, 453 students received support, including 76 fellowships with tuition reimbursements available (averaging $22,340 per year), 312 research assistantships with tuition reimbursements available (averaging $26,967 per year), 35 teaching assistantships with tuition reimbursements available (averaging $29,932 per year); career-related internships or fieldwork, Federal Work-Study, institutionally sponsored loans, scholarships/grants, health care benefits, and unspecified assistantships also available. *Faculty research:* Mechanics: modeling, experimentation and computation, design, manufacturing, product development, controls, instrumentation, robotics, energy science and engineering, ocean science and engineering, bioengineering, micro and nano engineering. Total annual research expenditures: $39 million. *Unit head:* Prof. Mary C. Boyce, Department Head, 617-253-2201, Fax: 617-258-6156, E-mail: mehq@mit.edu. *Application contact:* Graduate Office, 617-253-2291, Fax: 617-258-5802, E-mail: megradoffice@mit.edu.

Michigan State University, The Graduate School, College of Agriculture and Natural Resources, School of Packaging, East Lansing, MI 48824. Offers MS, PhD. *Entrance requirements:* Additional exam requirements/recommendations for international students: Required—TOEFL. Electronic applications accepted.

Minnesota State University Mankato, College of Graduate Studies, College of Science, Engineering and Technology, Department of Automotive and Manufacturing Engineering Technology, Mankato, MN 56001. Offers manufacturing engineering technology (MS). *Students:* 4 full-time (0 women), 8 part-time (0 women). *Degree requirements:* For master's, comprehensive exam, thesis. *Entrance requirements:* For master's, GRE General Test (if GPA less than 3.0), minimum GPA of 3.0 during previous 2 years. Additional exam requirements/recommendations for international students: Required—TOEFL. *Application deadline:* For fall admission, 7/1 priority date for domestic students; for spring admission, 11/1 for domestic students. Applications are processed on a rolling basis. Application fee: $40. Electronic applications accepted. *Expenses:* Tuition, state resident: full-time $5364. Tuition, nonresident: full-time $8314. *Financial support:* Research assistantships with full tuition reimbursements, teaching assistantships with full tuition reimbursements, unspecified assistantships available. Financial award application deadline: 3/15; financial award applicants required to submit FAFSA. *Unit head:* Dr. William Peterson, Chairperson, 507-389-6157. *Application contact:* 507-389-2321, E-mail: grad@mnsu.edu.

Missouri University of Science and Technology, Graduate School, Department of Engineering Management and Systems Engineering, Rolla, MO 65409. Offers engineering management (MS, DE, PhD); manufacturing engineering (M Eng, MS); systems engineering (MS, PhD). *Degree requirements:* For master's, thesis optional; for doctorate, comprehensive exam. *Entrance requirements:* For master's, GRE (minimum score 1150 verbal and quantitative, 4.5 writing); for doctorate, GRE (minimum score: 1100 verbal and quantitative, 3.5 writing). Additional exam requirements/recommendations for international students: Required—TOEFL (minimum score 580 paper-based; 213 computer-based). *Faculty research:* Management of technology, industrial engineering, manufacturing engineering, packaging engineering, quality engineering.

New Jersey Institute of Technology, Office of Graduate Studies, Newark College of Engineering, Department of Industrial and Manufacturing Engineering, Program in Manufacturing Engineering, Newark, NJ 07102. Offers MS. Part-time and evening/weekend programs available. *Degree requirements:* For master's, thesis or alternative. *Entrance requirements:* For master's, GRE General Test. Additional exam requirements/recommendations for international students: Required—TOEFL (minimum score 550 paper-based; 213 computer-based; 79 iBT). Electronic applications accepted. *Faculty research:* Knowledge-based systems, CAS/CAM simulation and interface, expert system.

North Carolina State University, Graduate School, College of Engineering, Integrated Manufacturing Systems Engineering Institute, Raleigh, NC 27695. Offers MIMS. Part-time programs available. *Degree requirements:* For master's, thesis optional. *Entrance requirements:* For master's, GRE. Additional exam requirements/recommendations for international students: Required—TOEFL. Electronic applications accepted. *Faculty research:* Mechatronics, manufacturing systems modeling, systems integration product and process engineering, logistics.

North Dakota State University, College of Graduate and Interdisciplinary Studies, College of Engineering and Architecture, Department of Industrial and Manufacturing Engineering, Fargo, ND 58108. Offers industrial and manufacturing engineering (PhD); industrial engineering and management (MS); manufacturing engineering (MS). Part-time programs available. *Faculty:* 13 full-time (2 women), 1 part-time/adjunct (0 women). *Students:* 16 full-time (4 women), 10 part-time (3 women), 25 international. Average age 26. 25 applicants, 88% accepted, 9 enrolled. In 2009, 7 master's awarded. *Degree requirements:* For doctorate, comprehensive exam, thesis/dissertation. *Entrance requirements:* For master's, GRE General Test, bachelor's degree in engineering; for doctorate, GRE General Test, master's degree in engineering. Additional exam requirements/recommendations for international students: Required—TOEFL (minimum score 550 paper-based; 213 computer-based; 79 iBT), TWE (minimum score 4). *Application deadline:* For fall admission, 3/1 priority date for domestic students, 3/1 for international students; for spring admission, 11/1 priority date for domestic students, 11/1 for international students. Applications are processed on a rolling basis. Application fee: $45 ($60 for international students). Electronic applications accepted. *Financial support:* In 2009–10, 2 fellowships with full tuition reimbursements (averaging $15,000 per year), 9 research assistantships with full tuition reimbursements (averaging $12,000 per year), 16 teaching assistantships with full tuition reimbursements (averaging $12,000 per year) were awarded; Federal Work-Study, institutionally sponsored loans, scholarships/grants, and unspecified assistantships also available. Financial award application deadline: 4/1. *Faculty research:* Electronics manufacturing, quality engineering, manufacturing process science, healthcare, lean manufacturing. Total annual research expenditures: $60,000. *Unit head:* Prof. Kambiz Farahmand, Chair, 701-231-7287, Fax: 701-231-7195, E-mail: kambiz.farahmand@ndsu.edu. *Application contact:* Dr. David A. Wittrock, Dean, 701-231-7033, Fax: 701-231-6524.

Northeastern University, College of Engineering, Department of Mechanical, Industrial, and Manufacturing Engineering, Boston, MA 02115-5096. Offers engineering management (MS); industrial engineering (MS, PhD); mechanical engineering (MS, PhD); operations research (MS). Part-time programs available. *Faculty:* 34 full-time (2 women), 7 part-time/adjunct (0 women). *Students:* 270 full-time (56 women), 137 part-time (27 women); includes 4 African Americans, 9 Asian Americans or Pacific Islanders, 3 Hispanic Americans, 182 international. 573 applicants, 75% accepted, 142 enrolled. In 2009, 94 master's, 9 doctorates awarded. *Degree requirements:* For master's, thesis (for some programs); for doctorate, thesis/dissertation, departmental qualifying exam. *Entrance requirements:* For master's and doctorate, GRE General Test. Additional exam requirements/recommendations for international students: Required—TOEFL (minimum score 550 paper-based; 213 computer-based; 80 iBT). *Application deadline:* For fall admission, 1/15 priority date for domestic and international students; for spring admission, 11/1 priority date for domestic students. Applications are processed on a rolling basis. Application fee: $50. Electronic applications accepted. *Financial support:* In 2009–10, 79 students received support, including 42 research assistantships with full tuition reimbursements available (averaging $18,320 per year), 37 teaching assistantships with full tuition reimbursements available; fellowships with full tuition reimbursements available, career-related internships or fieldwork, Federal Work-Study, scholarships/grants, health care benefits, and unspecified assistantships also available. Support available to part-time students. Financial award application deadline: 1/15; financial award applicants required to submit FAFSA. *Faculty research:* Dry sliding instabilities, droplet deposition, combustion, manufacturing systems, nano-manufacturing, advanced materials processing, bio-nano robotics, burning speed measurement, virtual environments. *Unit head:* Dr. Hameed Metghalchi, Chairman, 617-373-2973, Fax: 617-373-2921. *Application contact:* Stephen L. Gibson, Associate Director, 617-373-2711, Fax: 617-373-2501, E-mail: grad-eng@coe.neu.edu.

Northwestern University, McCormick School of Engineering and Applied Science, Department of Mechanical Engineering, Program in Manufacturing Engineering, Evanston, IL 60208. Offers MME. Part-time programs available.

Old Dominion University, Frank Batten College of Engineering and Technology, Program in Mechanical Engineering, Norfolk, VA 23529. Offers design and manufacturing (ME); mechanical engineering (ME, MS, D Eng, PhD). Part-time and evening/weekend programs available. Postbaccalaureate distance learning degree programs offered (no on-campus study). *Faculty:* 15 full-time (2 women). *Students:* 30 full-time (5 women), 44 part-time (11 women); includes 12 minority (2 African Americans, 7 Asian Americans or Pacific Islanders, 3 Hispanic Americans), 31 international. Average age 29. 59 applicants, 44% accepted, 18 enrolled. In 2009, 17 master's, 1 doctorate awarded. *Degree requirements:* For master's, comprehensive exam, thesis optional; for doctorate, thesis/dissertation, candidacy exam. *Entrance requirements:* For master's, GRE, minimum GPA of 3.0; for doctorate, GRE, minimum GPA of 3.5. Additional exam requirements/recommendations for international students: Required—TOEFL (minimum score 550 paper-based; 213 computer-based). *Application deadline:* For fall admission, 6/1 for domestic students, 2/15 priority date for international students; for spring admission, 11/1 for domestic students, 10/1 for international students. Applications are processed on a rolling basis. Application fee: $40 ($50 for international students). Electronic applications accepted. *Expenses:* Tuition, state resident: full-time $8112; part-time $338 per credit. Tuition, nonresident: full-time $20,256; part-time $844 per credit. Required fees: $119 per semester. One-time fee: $50. *Financial support:* In 2009–10, 31 students received support, including 5 fellowships with partial tuition reimbursements available (averaging $16,000 per year), 11 research assistantships with partial tuition reimbursements available (averaging $15,000 per year), 15 teaching assistantships with partial tuition reimbursements available (averaging $6,400 per year); career-related internships or fieldwork, institutionally sponsored loans, scholarships/grants, and unspecified assistantships also available. Financial award application deadline: 2/15; financial award applicants required to submit FAFSA. *Faculty research:* Computational applied mechanics, manufacturing, experimental stress analysis, systems dynamics and control, mechanical design. Total annual research expenditures: $975,887. *Unit head:* Dr. Jen-Kuang Huang, Chair, 757-683-3734, Fax: 757-683-5344, E-mail: jhuang@odu.edu. *Application contact:* Dr. Gene Hou, Graduate Program Director, 757-683-3728, Fax: 757-683-5344, E-mail: megpd@odu.edu.

Oregon State University, Graduate School, College of Engineering, School of Mechanical, Industrial, and Manufacturing Engineering, Corvallis, OR 97331. Offers human systems engineering (MS, PhD); industrial engineering (MS, PhD); information systems engineering (MS, PhD); manufacturing engineering (M Engr); manufacturing systems engineering (MS, PhD); materials science (MAIS, MS, PhD); mechanical engineering (MS, PhD); nano/micro fabrication (MS, PhD). Part-time programs available. Postbaccalaureate distance learning degree programs offered (minimal on-campus study). *Faculty:* 26 full-time (2 women), 2 part-time/adjunct (1 woman). *Students:* 136 full-time (25 women), 12 part-time (2 women); includes 11 minority (3 African Americans, 4 Asian Americans or Pacific Islanders, 4 Hispanic Americans), 46 international. Average age 29. 53 applicants, 42% accepted, 13 enrolled. In 2009, 26 master's, 10 doctorates awarded. *Degree requirements:* For master's, thesis or alternative; for doctorate, thesis/dissertation. *Entrance requirements:* For master's, placement exam, minimum GPA of 3.0 in last 90 hours of course work; for doctorate, GRE, placement exam, minimum GPA of 3.0 in last 90 hours of course work. Additional exam requirements/recommendations for international students: Required—TOEFL (minimum score 550 paper-based; 213 computer-based). *Application deadline:* For fall admission, 3/1 for domestic students. Applications are processed on a rolling basis. Application fee: $50. *Expenses:* Tuition, state resident: full-time $9774; part-time $362 per credit. Tuition, nonresident: full-time $15,849; part-time $587 per credit. Required fees: $1639. Full-time tuition and fees vary according to course load and program. *Financial support:* In 2009–10, 10 research assistantships with full tuition reimbursements (averaging $11,124 per year), 8 teaching assistantships with full tuition reimbursements (averaging $7,020 per year) were awarded; fellowships with full tuition reimbursements, institutionally sponsored loans and instructorships also available. Support available to part-time students. Financial award application deadline: 2/1. *Faculty research:* Computer-integrated manufacturing, human factors, robotics, decision support systems, simulation modeling and analysis. Total annual research expenditures: $1.3 million. *Unit head:* Dr. Belinda A. Batten, Head, 541-737-3441, Fax: 541-737-2600, E-mail: info-mime@oregonstate.edu. *Application contact:* Jean Robinson, Graduate Records Specialist, 541-737-7009, Fax: 541-737-2600, E-mail: jean.robinson@oregonstate.edu.

Penn State University Park, Graduate School, College of Engineering, Department of Industrial and Manufacturing Engineering, State College, University Park, PA 16802-1503. Offers M Eng, MS, PhD.

Polytechnic Institute of NYU, Department of Interdisciplinary Studies, Major in Manufacturing Engineering, Brooklyn, NY 11201-2990. Offers MS. Part-time and evening/weekend programs available. *Students:* 9 full-time (2 women), 9 part-time (4 women); includes 3 minority (1 African American, 2 Hispanic Americans), 6 international. 20 applicants, 55% accepted, 5 enrolled. In 2009, 7 master's awarded. *Degree requirements:* For master's, comprehensive exam (for some programs), thesis (for some programs). *Entrance requirements:* For master's, BE or BS in engineering, physics, chemistry, mathematical sciences, or biological sciences or MBA. Additional exam requirements/recommendations for international students: Required—TOEFL (minimum score 550 paper-based; 213 computer-based; 80 iBT); Recommended—IELTS (minimum score 6.5). *Application deadline:* For fall admission, 7/31 priority date for domestic students, 4/30 priority date for international students; for spring admission, 12/31 priority date for domestic students, 11/30 priority date for international students. Applications are processed on a rolling basis. Application fee: $75. Electronic applications accepted. *Expenses:* Tuition: Full-time $21,492; part-time $1194 per credit hour. Required fees: $1160; $204 per course. *Financial support:* Institutionally sponsored loans, scholarships/grants, and unspecified assistantships available. Support available to part-time students. Financial award applicants required to submit FAFSA. *Application contact:* JeanCarlo Bonilla, Director of Graduate Enrollment Management, 718-260-3182, Fax: 718-260-3624, E-mail: gradinfo@poly.edu.

Polytechnic Institute of NYU, Long Island Graduate Center, Graduate Programs, Department of Interdisciplinary Studies, Major in Manufacturing Engineering, Melville, NY 11747. Offers MS. Part-time and evening/weekend programs available. *Entrance requirements:* Additional exam requirements/recommendations for international students: Required—TOEFL (minimum score 550 paper-based; 213 computer-based; 80 iBT); Recommended—IELTS (minimum score 6.5). *Application deadline:* For fall admission, 7/31 priority date for domestic students, 4/30 priority date for international students; for spring admission, 12/31 priority date for domestic students, 11/30 priority date for international students. Applications are processed on a rolling basis. Application fee: $75. Electronic applications accepted. *Financial support:* Institutionally sponsored loans, scholarships/grants, and unspecified assistantships available. Support available to part-time students. *Application contact:* JeanCarlo Bonilla, Director of Graduate Enrollment Management, 718-260-3182, Fax: 718-260-3624, E-mail: gradinfo@poly.edu.

Polytechnic Institute of NYU, Long Island Graduate Center, Graduate Programs, Department of Mechanical and Aerospace Engineering, Melville, NY 11747. Offers aeronautics and astronautics (MS); industrial engineering (MS); manufacturing engineering (MS); mechanical engineering (MS). Part-time and evening/weekend programs available. *Students:* 1 (woman) part-time. Average age 25. In 2009, 2 master's awarded. *Degree requirements:* For master's, comprehensive exam (for some programs), thesis (for some programs). *Entrance requirements:* Additional exam requirements/recommendations for international students: Required—TOEFL (minimum score 550 paper-based; 213 computer-based; 80 iBT); Recommended—IELTS (minimum score 6.5). *Application deadline:* For fall admission, 7/31 priority date for domestic students, 4/30 priority date for international students; for spring admission, 12/31 priority date for domestic students, 11/30 priority date for international students. Applications are processed on a rolling basis. Application fee: $75. Electronic applications accepted. *Financial support:* In 2009–10, 16 fellowships with tuition reimbursements (averaging $1,394 per year) were awarded; research assistantships with tuition reimbursements, institutionally sponsored loans, scholarships/grants, and unspecified assistantships also available. Support available to part-time students. Financial award applicants required to submit FAFSA. *Faculty research:* UV filter, fuel efficient hydrodynamic containment for gas core fission, turbulent boundary layer research. *Unit head:* Dr. George Vradis, Department Head, 718-260-3875, E-mail: gvradis@duke.poly.edu. *Application contact:* JeanCarlo Bonilla, Director of Graduate Enrollment Management, 718-260-3182, Fax: 718-260-3624, E-mail: gradinfo@poly.edu.

Polytechnic Institute of NYU, Westchester Graduate Center, Graduate Programs, Department of Interdisciplinary Studies, Major in Manufacturing Engineering, Hawthorne, NY 10532-1507. Offers MS. *Entrance requirements:* Additional exam requirements/recommendations for international students: Required—TOEFL (minimum score 550 paper-based; 213 computer-based; 80 iBT); Recommended—IELTS (minimum score 6.5). *Application deadline:* For fall admission, 7/31 priority date for domestic students, 4/30 priority date for international students; for spring admission, 12/31 priority date for domestic students, 11/30 priority date for international students. Applications are processed on a rolling basis. Application fee: $75. Electronic applications accepted. *Financial support:* Institutionally sponsored loans, scholarships/grants, and unspecified assistantships available. Support available to part-time students. *Application contact:* JeanCarlo Bonilla, Director of Graduate Enrollment Management, 718-260-3182, Fax: 718-260-3624, E-mail: gradinfo@poly.edu.

Polytechnic University of Puerto Rico, Graduate School, Hato Rey, PR 00919. Offers business administration (MBA), including general studies, management of information systems, management of international enterprises; civil engineering (ME, MS); computer engineering (ME, MS); computer science (MS); electrical engineering (ME, MS); engineering management (MEM); environmental management (MEPM); landscape architecture (M Land Arch); manufacturing competitiveness (MMC, MS); manufacturing engineering (ME, MS). Part-time and evening/weekend programs available. *Entrance requirements:* For master's, 3 letters of recommendation.

Portland State University, Graduate Studies, Maseeh College of Engineering and Computer Science, Department of Engineering and Technology Management, Program in Manufacturing Engineering, Portland, OR 97207-0751. Offers ME. Part-time and evening/weekend programs available. *Degree requirements:* For master's, comprehensive exam. *Entrance requirements:* For master's, minimum GPA of 3.0 in upper-division course work, BS in engineering or allied field. Additional exam requirements/recommendations for international students: Required—TOEFL (minimum score 550 paper-based; 213 computer-based). *Faculty research:* Quality assurance, concurrent engineering, production scheduling and control, manufacturing automation.

Rochester Institute of Technology, Graduate Enrollment Services, College of Applied Science and Technology, Department of Electrical, Computer and Telecommunications Engineering Technology, Program in Manufacturing and Mechanical Systems Integration, Rochester, NY 14623-5603. Offers MS. Part-time and evening/weekend programs available. *Students:* 17 full-time (2 women), 14 part-time (0 women); includes 2 Hispanic Americans, 11 international. Average age 30. 18 applicants, 78% accepted, 12 enrolled. In 2009, 9 master's awarded. *Degree requirements:* For master's, thesis. *Entrance requirements:* For master's, GRE, minimum GPA of 3.0. Additional exam requirements/recommendations for international students: Required—TOEFL (minimum score 550 paper-based; 213 computer-based; 79 iBT), or IELTS (minimum score 6.5). *Application deadline:* For fall admission, 2/15 priority date for domestic and international students; for winter admission, 11/1 for domestic and international students; for spring admission, 2/1 for domestic and international students. Applications are processed on a rolling basis. Application fee: $50. *Expenses:* Tuition: Full-time $31,533; part-time $876 per credit hour. Required fees: $210. *Financial support:* In 2009–10, 26 students received support; research assistantships with partial tuition reimbursements available, teaching assistantships with partial tuition reimbursements available, career-related internships or fieldwork, scholarships/grants, and unspecified assistantships available. Support available to part-time students. Financial award application deadline: 2/15; financial award applicants required to

Manufacturing Engineering

Rochester Institute of Technology (continued)
submit FAFSA. *Unit head:* Dr. S. Manian Ramkumar, Program Chair, 585-475-6081, Fax: 585-475-5227, E-mail: smrmet@rit.edu. *Application contact:* Diane Ellison, Assistant Vice President, Graduate Enrollment Services, 585-475-2229, Fax: 585-475-7164, E-mail: gradinfo@rit.edu.

Rochester Institute of Technology, Graduate Enrollment Services, College of Applied Science and Technology, Department of Manufacturing and Mechanical Engineering Technology/Packaging Science, Rochester, NY 14623-5603. Offers MS. Part-time programs available. *Students:* 17 full-time (13 women), 9 part-time (2 women); includes 4 minority (2 African Americans, 2 Asian Americans or Pacific Islanders), 9 international. Average age 29. 17 applicants, 65% accepted, 7 enrolled. In 2009, 10 master's awarded. *Degree requirements:* For master's, thesis or alternative. *Entrance requirements:* For master's, minimum GPA of 3.0. Additional exam requirements/recommendations for international students: Required—TOEFL (minimum score 550 paper-based; 213 computer-based; 79 iBT), or IELTS (minimum score 6.5). *Application deadline:* For fall admission, 2/15 priority date for domestic and international students; for winter admission, 11/1 for domestic and international students; for spring admission, 2/1 for domestic and international students. Applications are processed on a rolling basis. Application fee: $50. *Expenses:* Tuition: Full-time $31,533; part-time $876 per credit hour. Required fees: $210. *Financial support:* In 2009–10, 22 students received support; research assistantships with partial tuition reimbursements available, teaching assistantships with partial tuition reimbursements available, career-related internships or fieldwork, scholarships/grants, and unspecified assistantships available. Support available to part-time students. Financial award application deadline: 2/15; financial award applicants required to submit FAFSA. *Faculty research:* Dynamics involved in logistics and the performance features of different materials; design, sustainability, mathematics, and marketing. *Unit head:* Deanna Jacobs, Program Chair, 585-475-6801, Fax: 585-475-5227, E-mail: dmjipk@rit.edu. *Application contact:* Diane Ellison, Assistant Vice President, Graduate Enrollment Services, 585-475-2229, Fax: 585-475-7164, E-mail: gradinfo@rit.edu.

Rochester Institute of Technology, Graduate Enrollment Services, Kate Gleason College of Engineering, Department of Design, Development and Manufacturing, Rochester, NY 14623-5603. Offers manufacturing leadership (MS); product development (MS). Part-time and evening/weekend programs available. *Students:* 5 full-time (2 women), 50 part-time (7 women); includes 4 minority (2 African Americans, 2 Hispanic Americans), 6 international. Average age 38. 30 applicants, 33% accepted, 9 enrolled. In 2009, 22 master's awarded. *Degree requirements:* For master's, capstone. *Entrance requirements:* For master's, minimum GPA of 2.5. Additional exam requirements/recommendations for international students: Required—TOEFL (minimum score 570 paper-based; 230 computer-based; 88 iBT), or IELTS (minimum score 6.5). *Application deadline:* For fall admission, 2/15 priority date for domestic and international students. Applications are processed on a rolling basis. Application fee: $50. Electronic applications accepted. *Expenses:* Tuition: Full-time $31,533; part-time $876 per credit hour. Required fees: $210. *Financial support:* In 2009–10, 7 students received support. *Faculty research:* Computer-integrated manufacturing, industrial ergonomics, optics and photonics, micromachines, electrochemical heating, signal and image processing, cardiovascular biomechanics, robotics and control, VLSI design, electron beam lithography, computer architecture, multimedia information systems, object-oriented software development. *Unit head:* Mark Smith, Director, 585-475-7971, Fax: 585-475-7955, E-mail: mpdmail@rit.edu. *Application contact:* Diane Ellison, Assistant Vice President, Graduate Enrollment Services, 585-475-2229, Fax: 585-475-7164, E-mail: gradinfo@rit.edu.

Rochester Institute of Technology, Graduate Enrollment Services, Kate Gleason College of Engineering, Department of Industrial and Systems Engineering, Rochester, NY 14623-5603. Offers engineering management (ME); industrial engineering (ME, MS); manufacturing engineering (ME, MS); systems engineering (ME). Part-time programs available. *Students:* 62 full-time (17 women), 10 part-time (5 women); includes 5 minority (2 African Americans, 2 Asian Americans or Pacific Islanders, 1 Hispanic American), 55 international. Average age 25. 186 applicants, 50% accepted, 40 enrolled. In 2009, 53 master's awarded. *Degree requirements:* For master's, internship. *Entrance requirements:* For master's, GRE, minimum GPA of 3.0. Additional exam requirements/recommendations for international students: Required—TOEFL (minimum score 570 paper-based; 230 computer-based; 88 iBT), or IELTS (minimum score 6.5). *Application deadline:* For fall admission, 2/15 priority date for domestic and international students. Applications are processed on a rolling basis. Application fee: $50. *Expenses:* Tuition: Full-time $31,533; part-time $876 per credit hour. Required fees: $210. *Financial support:* In 2009–10, 63 students received support; research assistantships with partial tuition reimbursements available, teaching assistantships with partial tuition reimbursements available, career-related internships or fieldwork, institutionally sponsored loans, scholarships/grants, tuition waivers (partial), and unspecified assistantships available. Support available to part-time students. Financial award applicants required to submit FAFSA. *Faculty research:* Safety, manufacturing (CAM), simulation. *Unit head:* Dr. Jacqueline Mozrall, Department Head, 585-475-2598, E-mail: ise@rit.edu. *Application contact:* Diane Ellison, Assistant Vice President, Graduate Enrollment Services, 585-475-2229, Fax: 585-475-7164, E-mail: gradinfo@rit.edu.

Rochester Institute of Technology, Graduate Enrollment Services, Kate Gleason College of Engineering, Department of Microelectronic Engineering, Program in Microelectronic Manufacturing Engineering, Rochester, NY 14623-5603. Offers ME. Part-time programs available. *Students:* 2 full-time (0 women), 4 part-time (0 women); includes 1 Asian American or Pacific Islander, 3 international. Average age 37. 7 applicants, 43% accepted, 2 enrolled. In 2009, 2 master's awarded. *Entrance requirements:* Additional exam requirements/recommendations for international students: Required—TOEFL (minimum score 570 paper-based; 230 computer-based; 88 iBT), or IELTS (minimum score 6.5). *Application deadline:* For fall admission, 2/15 for domestic students, 2/15 priority date for international students. *Expenses:* Tuition: Full-time $31,533; part-time $876 per credit hour. Required fees: $210. *Financial support:* In 2009–10, 1 student received support. Available to part-time students. Applicants required to submit FAFSA. *Unit head:* Dr. Robert Pearson, Director, 585-475-2165, Fax: 585-475-5845, E-mail: eme@rit.edu. *Application contact:* Diane Ellison, Assistant Vice President, Graduate Enrollment Services, 585-475-2229, Fax: 585-475-7164, E-mail: gradinfo@rit.edu.

Southern Illinois University Carbondale, Graduate School, College of Engineering, Program in Manufacturing Systems, Carbondale, IL 62901-4701. Offers MS. *Degree requirements:* For master's, comprehensive exam, thesis. *Entrance requirements:* For master's, minimum GPA of 2.7. Additional exam requirements/recommendations for international students: Required—TOEFL. *Faculty research:* Computer-aided manufacturing, robotics, quality assurance.

Southern Methodist University, Bobby B. Lyle School of Engineering, Department of Mechanical Engineering, Dallas, TX 75205. Offers electronic and optical packaging (MS); manufacturing systems management (MS); mechanical engineering (MSME, PhD). Part-time and evening/weekend programs available. Postbaccalaureate distance learning degree programs offered (no on-campus study). *Faculty:* 13 full-time (2 women), 6 part-time/adjunct (0 women). *Students:* 30 full-time (9 women), 42 part-time (6 women); includes 10 minority (1 African American, 3 Asian Americans or Pacific Islanders, 6 Hispanic Americans), 22 international. Average age 30. 53 applicants, 98% accepted, 52 enrolled. In 2009, 15 master's, 6 doctorates awarded. Terminal master's awarded for partial completion of doctoral program. *Degree requirements:* For master's, thesis optional; for doctorate, thesis/dissertation, oral and written qualifying exams, oral final exam. *Entrance requirements:* For master's, GRE General Test, minimum GPA of 3.0 in last 2 years; bachelor's degree in engineering, mathematics, or sciences; for doctorate, preliminary counseling exam, minimum graduate GPA of 3.0, bachelor's degree in related field. Additional exam requirements/recommendations for international students: Required—TOEFL. *Application deadline:* For fall admission, 7/1 for domestic students, 5/15 for international students; for spring admission, 11/15 for domestic students, 9/1 for international students. Applications are processed on a rolling basis. Application fee: $75. *Financial support:* In 2009–10, 17 students received support, including 10 research assistantships with full and partial tuition reimbursements available (averaging $16,000 per year), 7 teaching assistantships with full and partial tuition reimbursements available (averaging $16,000 per year); Federal Work-Study, institutionally sponsored loans, and tuition waivers (full and partial) also available. Financial award applicants required to submit FAFSA. *Faculty research:* Design, systems, and controls; thermal and fluid sciences. Total annual research expenditures: $774,564. *Unit head:* Dr. Volkan Otugen, Chairman, 214-768-3200, Fax: 214-768-1473, E-mail: otugen@engr.smu.edu. *Application contact:* Marc Valerin, Director of Graduate and Executive Admissions, 214-768-3042, E-mail: valerin@engr.smu.edu.

Stevens Institute of Technology, Graduate School, Charles V. Schaefer Jr. School of Engineering, Department of Mechanical Engineering, Program in Integrated Product Development, Hoboken, NJ 07030. Offers armament engineering (M Eng); computer and electrical engineering (M Eng); manufacturing technologies (M Eng); systems reliability and design (M Eng). *Expenses:* Tuition: Full-time $9900; part-time $1100 per credit. Required fees: $286 per semester.

Texas A&M University, College of Engineering, Department of Engineering Technology and Industrial Distribution, College Station, TX 77843. Offers MID. *Faculty:* 9. *Students:* 17 full-time (5 women); includes 4 minority (1 African American, 3 Hispanic Americans). In 2009, 13 master's awarded. *Entrance requirements:* Additional exam requirements/recommendations for international students: Required—TOEFL. *Application deadline:* For fall admission, 3/1 priority date for domestic and international students; for spring admission, 8/1 priority date for domestic and international students. Applications are processed on a rolling basis. Application fee: $50 ($75 for international students). Electronic applications accepted. *Expenses:* Tuition, state resident: full-time $3991.32; part-time $221.74 per credit hour. Tuition, nonresident: full-time $9049; part-time $502.74 per credit hour. *Financial support:* Application deadline: 2/1. *Unit head:* Dr. Dan Jennings, Head, 979-845-4951, E-mail: djennings@tamu.edu. *Application contact:* Karen Butler-Purry, Assistant Dean, 979-845-7200, Fax: 979-847-8654, E-mail: eapo@tamu.edu.

Texas Tech University, Graduate School, College of Engineering, Department of Industrial Engineering, Lubbock, TX 79409. Offers industrial engineering (MSIE, PhD); manufacturing systems engineering (MSMSE); systems and engineering management (MSSEM, PhD). Part-time programs available. *Faculty:* 11 full-time (2 women). *Students:* 85 full-time (19 women), 48 part-time (8 women); includes 9 minority (4 African Americans, 2 Asian Americans or Pacific Islanders, 3 Hispanic Americans), 80 international. Average age 29. 298 applicants, 61% accepted, 24 enrolled. In 2009, 21 master's, 7 doctorates awarded. *Degree requirements:* For master's, thesis or alternative; for doctorate, thesis/dissertation. *Entrance requirements:* For master's and doctorate, GRE General Test, minimum GPA of 3.0. Additional exam requirements/recommendations for international students: Required—TOEFL (minimum score 550 paper-based; 213 computer-based). *Application deadline:* For fall admission, 3/1 priority date for international students; for spring admission, 11/1 priority date for international students. Applications are processed on a rolling basis. Application fee: $50 ($75 for international students). Electronic applications accepted. *Expenses:* Tuition, state resident: full-time $5100; part-time $213 per credit hour. Tuition, nonresident: full-time $11,748; part-time $490 per credit hour. Required fees: $2298; $50 per credit hour. $555 per semester. *Financial support:* In 2009–10, 14 research assistantships with partial tuition reimbursements (averaging $14,979 per year), 10 teaching assistantships with partial tuition reimbursements (averaging $13,050 per year) were awarded; Federal Work-Study and institutionally sponsored loans also available. Support available to part-time students. Financial award application deadline: 4/15; financial award applicants required to submit FAFSA. *Faculty research:* Knowledge and engineering management, environmentally conscious manufacturing, biomechanical simulation, aviation security, supply chain management. Total annual research expenditures: $476,488. *Unit head:* Dr. Pat Patterson, Chair, 806-742-3543, Fax: 806-742-3411, E-mail: pat.patterson@ttu.edu. *Application contact:* Dr. Mario Beruvides, Professor, 806-742-3543, Fax: 806-742-3411, E-mail: mario.beruvides@ttu.edu.

Tufts University, Graduate School of Arts and Sciences, Graduate Certificate Programs, Manufacturing Engineering Program, Medford, MA 02155. Offers Certificate. Part-time and evening/weekend programs available. Electronic applications accepted. *Expenses:* Tuition: Full-time $38,096; part-time $3962 per credit. Required fees: $686; $40 per year. Tuition and fees vary according to course level, course load, degree level, program and student level.

Universidad Autonoma de Guadalajara, Graduate Programs, Guadalajara, Mexico. Offers administrative law and justice (LL M); advertising and corporate communications (MA); architecture (M Arch); business (MBA); computational science (MCC); education (Ed M, Ed D); English-Spanish translation (MA); fiscal law (MA); integrated management of digital animation (MA); international business (MIB); international corporate law (LL M); internet technologies (MS); labor health (MS); manufacturing systems (MMS); philosophy (MA, PhD); power electronics (MS); quality systems (MQS); renewable energy (MS); social evaluation of projects (MBA); strategic market research (MBA); teaching mathematics (MA).

Universidad de las Américas–Puebla, Division of Graduate Studies, School of Engineering, Program in Manufacturing Administration, Puebla, Mexico. Offers MS. *Faculty research:* Operations research, construction.

University of Calgary, Faculty of Graduate Studies, Schulich School of Engineering, Department of Mechanical and Manufacturing Engineering, Calgary, AB T2N 1N4, Canada. Offers M Eng, M Sc, PhD. *Degree requirements:* For master's, thesis (for some programs); for doctorate, thesis/dissertation, candidacy exam. *Entrance requirements:* For master's, minimum GPA of 3.0; for doctorate, minimum GPA of 3.3. Additional exam requirements/recommendations for international students: Required—TOEFL (minimum score 550 paper-based; 213 computer-based), IELTS (minimum score 7). *Faculty research:* Thermofluids, solid mechanics, materials, biomechanics, manufacturing.

University of California, Los Angeles, Graduate Division, Henry Samueli School of Engineering and Applied Science, Department of Mechanical and Aerospace Engineering, Program in Manufacturing Engineering, Los Angeles, CA 90095-1597. Offers MS. *Students:* 7 applicants, 29% accepted, 0 enrolled. In 2009, 3 master's awarded. *Degree requirements:* For master's, comprehensive exam or thesis. *Entrance requirements:* For master's, GRE General Test, minimum GPA of 3.0. Additional exam requirements/recommendations for international students: Required—TOEFL (minimum score 560 paper-based; 220 computer-based). *Application deadline:* For fall admission, 1/5 for domestic and international students; for winter admission, 10/1 for domestic students; for spring admission, 12/31 for domestic students. Application fee: $70 ($90 for international students). Electronic applications accepted. *Financial support:* Fellowships, research assistantships, teaching assistantships, Federal Work-Study, institutionally sponsored loans, and tuition waivers (full and partial) available. Financial award application deadline: 1/5; financial award applicants required to submit FAFSA. *Unit head:* Dr. Adrienne Lavine, Chair, 310-825-7468. *Application contact:* Angie Castillo, Student Affairs Officer, 310-825-7793, Fax: 310-206-4830, E-mail: angie@ea.ucla.edu.

University of Colorado at Colorado Springs, Graduate School, College of Engineering and Applied Science, Department of Mechanical and Aerospace Engineering, Colorado Springs, CO 80933-7150. Offers engineering management (ME); information operations (ME); manufacturing (ME); mechanical engineering (MS); software engineering (ME); space operations (ME); space systems (MS). Part-time and evening/weekend programs available. *Faculty:* 10 full-time (2 women). *Students:* 14 full-time (4 women), 13 part-time (2 women); includes 3 minority (2 Asian Americans or Pacific Islanders, 1 Hispanic American). Average age 30. 39 applicants, 82% accepted, 16 enrolled. In 2009, 6 master's awarded. *Degree requirements:* For master's, thesis optional. *Entrance requirements:* For master's, GRE General Test, bachelor's degree in engineering or related degree, minimum GPA of 3.0. Additional exam requirements/recommendations for international students: Required—TOEFL. *Application deadline:* For fall admission, 5/1 for domestic students; for spring admission, 10/1 for domestic students. Applications are processed on a rolling basis. Application fee: $60 ($75 for international students). *Expenses:* Tuition, state resident: full-time $8922; part-time $639 per credit hour. Tuition, nonresident: full-time $19,372; part-time $1154 per credit hour. Tuition and fees vary according to course level, course load, degree level, program, reciprocity agreements and student level. *Financial support:* Federal Work-Study and scholarships/grants available. Support available to part-time students. Financial award application deadline: 3/1; financial award applicants required to submit FAFSA. *Faculty research:* Neural networks, artificial intelligence, robust control, space operations, space propulsion. *Unit head:* Dr. T. S. Kalkur, Chair, 719-255-3147, Fax: 719-255-3042, E-mail: kalkur@eas.uccs.edu. *Application contact:* Siew Nylund, Academic Adviser, 719-255-3243, Fax: 719-255-3589, E-mail: snylund@eas.uccs.edu.

The University of Iowa, Graduate College, College of Engineering, Department of Industrial Engineering, Iowa City, IA 52242-1316. Offers engineering design and manufacturing (MS, PhD); ergonomics (MS, PhD); information and engineering management (MS, PhD); operations research (MS, PhD); quality engineering (MS, PhD). *Faculty:* 6 full-time (0 women). *Students:* 37 full-time (11 women); includes 3 minority (1 African American, 1 Asian American or Pacific Islander, 1 Hispanic American), 11 international. Average age 28. 65 applicants, 18% accepted, 7 enrolled. In 2009, 7 master's, 3 doctorates awarded. *Degree requirements:* For master's, thesis optional, exam; for doctorate, comprehensive exam, thesis/dissertation, final defense exam. *Entrance requirements:* For master's and doctorate, GRE General Test. Additional exam requirements/recommendations for international students: Required—TOEFL (minimum score 550 paper-based; 213 computer-based; 81 iBT). *Application deadline:* For fall admission, 7/15 for domestic students, 4/15 for international students; for spring admission, 12/1 for domestic students, 10/1 for international students. Applications are processed on a rolling basis. Application fee: $60 ($100 for international students). Electronic applications accepted. *Financial support:* In 2009–10, 2 fellowships with partial tuition reimbursements (averaging $30,450 per year), 22 research assistantships with partial tuition reimbursements (averaging $20,000 per year), 5 teaching assistantships with partial tuition reimbursements (averaging $16,630 per year) were awarded; career-related internships or fieldwork, scholarships/grants, and unspecified assistantships also available. Support available to part-time students. Financial award applicants required to submit FAFSA. *Faculty research:* Operations research; informatics; human factors engineering; manufacturing systems; human-machine interaction. Total annual research expenditures: $4.1 million. *Unit head:* Dr. Lea-Der Chen, Departmental Executive Officer, 319-335-5674, Fax: 319-335-5669, E-mail: lea-der-chen@uiowa.edu. *Application contact:* Jennifer Rumping, Secretary, 319-335-5939, Fax: 319-335-5669, E-mail: indeng@engineering.uiowa.edu.

University of Kentucky, Graduate School, College of Engineering, Program in Manufacturing Systems Engineering, Lexington, KY 40506-0032. Offers MSMSE. *Degree requirements:* For master's, comprehensive exam. *Entrance requirements:* For master's, GRE General Test, minimum undergraduate GPA of 2.75. Additional exam requirements/recommendations for international students: Required—TOEFL (minimum score 550 paper-based; 213 computer-based). Electronic applications accepted. *Faculty research:* Manufacturing processes and equipment, manufacturing systems and control, computer-aided design and manufacturing, automation in manufacturing, electric manufacturing and packaging.

University of Manitoba, Faculty of Graduate Studies, Faculty of Engineering, Department of Mechanical and Manufacturing Engineering, Winnipeg, MB R3T 2N2, Canada. Offers M Eng, M Sc, PhD. *Degree requirements:* For master's, thesis; for doctorate, thesis/dissertation.

University of Maryland, College Park, Academic Affairs, A. James Clark School of Engineering, Department of Mechanical Engineering, College Park, MD 20742. Offers electronic packaging and reliability (MS, PhD); manufacturing and design (MS, PhD); mechanics and materials (MS, PhD); reliability engineering (M Eng, MS, PhD); thermal and fluid sciences (MS, PhD). Part-time and evening/weekend programs available. Postbaccalaureate distance learning degree programs offered. *Faculty:* 84 full-time (5 women), 14 part-time/adjunct (1 woman). *Students:* 217 full-time (37 women), 76 part-time (13 women); includes 39 minority (11 African Americans, 2 American Indian/Alaska Native, 18 Asian Americans or Pacific Islanders, 8 Hispanic Americans), 140 international. 420 applicants, 21% accepted, 64 enrolled. In 2009, 40 master's, 33 doctorates awarded. *Degree requirements:* For master's, thesis optional; for doctorate, thesis/dissertation, qualifying exam. *Entrance requirements:* For master's, GRE General Test, 3 letters of recommendation; for doctorate, GRE General Test, minimum GPA of 3.0. Additional exam requirements/recommendations for international students: Required—TOEFL. *Application deadline:* For fall admission, 5/15 for domestic students, 2/1 for international students; for spring admission, 10/1 for domestic students, 6/1 for international students. Applications are processed on a rolling basis. Application fee: $60. Electronic applications accepted. *Expenses:* Tuition, area resident: Part-time $471 per credit hour. Tuition, state resident: part-time $471 per credit hour. Tuition, nonresident: part-time $1016 per credit hour. Required fees: $337.04 per term. *Financial support:* In 2009–10, 7 fellowships with full and partial tuition reimbursements (averaging $13,060 per year), 168 research assistantships with tuition reimbursements (averaging $23,703 per year), 10 teaching assistantships with tuition reimbursements (averaging $18,884 per year) were awarded; Federal Work-Study and scholarships/grants also available. Support available to part-time students. Financial award applicants required to submit FAFSA. *Faculty research:* Injection molding, electronic packaging, fluid mechanics, product engineering. Total annual research expenditures: $15 million. *Unit head:* Dr. Avram Bar-Cohen, Chairman, 301-405-3173, Fax: 301-314-9477, E-mail: abc@umd.edu. *Application contact:* Dr., Graduate Director, 301-405-0376.

University of Memphis, Graduate School, Herff College of Engineering, Department of Engineering Technology, Memphis, TN 38152. Offers computer engineering technology (MS); electronics engineering technology (MS); manufacturing engineering technology (MS). Part-time and evening/weekend programs available. *Faculty:* 5 full-time (0 women). *Students:* 4 full-time (1 woman), 6 part-time (1 woman); includes 4 minority (all African Americans), 2 international. Average age 38. 2 applicants, 50% accepted, 1 enrolled. *Degree requirements:* For master's, comprehensive exam, thesis optional. *Entrance requirements:* For master's, GRE General Test, minimum undergraduate GPA of 2.5. *Application deadline:* For fall admission, 8/1 for domestic students; for spring admission, 12/1 for domestic students. Applications are processed on a rolling basis. Application fee: $25 ($50 for international students). Electronic applications accepted. *Expenses:* Tuition, state resident: full-time $6246; part-time $347 per credit hour. Tuition, nonresident: full-time $15,894; part-time $883 per credit hour. Required fees: $1160. Full-time tuition and fees vary according to course load, degree level and program. *Financial support:* In 2009–10, 5 students received support; research assistantships with full tuition reimbursements available, career-related internships or fieldwork, Federal Work-Study, scholarships/grants, and unspecified assistantships available. Financial award application deadline: 2/15; financial award applicants required to submit FAFSA. *Faculty research:* Teacher education services-technology education; flexible manufacturing control systems; embedded, dedicated, and real-time computer systems; network, Internet, and web-based programming; analog and digital electronic communication systems. *Unit head:* Deborah J. Hochstein, Chairman, 901-678-2225, Fax: 901-678-5145, E-mail: dhochstn@memphis.edu. *Application contact:* Carl R. Williams, Coordinator of Graduate Studies, 901-678-3296, Fax: 901-678-5145, E-mail: crwillia@memphis.edu.

University of Michigan–Dearborn, College of Engineering and Computer Science, Interdisciplinary Programs, Program in Manufacturing Systems Engineering, Dearborn, MI 48128-1491. Offers MSE. Part-time and evening/weekend programs available. *Faculty:* 1 full-time (0 women). *Students:* 5 full-time (0 women), 13 part-time (3 women); includes 3 minority (2 African Americans, 1 Asian American or Pacific Islander), 7 international. Average age 30. 5 applicants, 100% accepted, 2 enrolled. In 2009, 3 master's awarded. *Degree requirements:* For master's, thesis optional. *Entrance requirements:* For master's, bachelor's degree in applied mathematics, computer science, engineering, or physical science; minimum GPA of 3.0. Additional exam requirements/recommendations for international students: Required—TOEFL (minimum score 560 paper-based; 220 computer-based; 84 iBT). *Application deadline:* For fall admission, 8/1 priority date for domestic students, 4/1 for international students; for winter admission, 12/1 priority date for domestic students, 8/1 for international students; for spring admission, 4/1 priority date for domestic students, 12/1 for international students. Applications are processed

on a rolling basis. Application fee: $60 ($75 for international students). Electronic applications accepted. *Expenses:* Tuition, area resident: Part-time $504.10 per credit hour. Tuition, state resident: part-time $504.10 per credit hour. Tuition, nonresident: part-time $957.90 per credit hour. *Financial support:* Scholarships/grants and unspecified assistantships available. Financial award application deadline: 4/1; financial award applicants required to submit FAFSA. *Faculty research:* Toolwear metrology, paper handling, grinding wheel imbalance, machine mission. *Unit head:* Dr. Pankaj K. Mallick, Director/Professor, 313-593-5119, Fax: 313-593-5386, E-mail: pkm@umich.edu. *Application contact:* Sherry Boyd, Intermediate Administrative Assistant, 313-593-5582, Fax: 313-593-5386, E-mail: idpgrad@umd.umich.edu.

University of Missouri, Graduate School, College of Engineering, Department of Industrial and Manufacturing Systems Engineering, Columbia, MO 65211. Offers MS, PhD. *Degree requirements:* For master's, thesis or alternative; for doctorate, thesis/dissertation. *Entrance requirements:* For master's and doctorate, GRE General Test, minimum GPA of 3.0. Additional exam requirements/recommendations for international students: Required—TOEFL (minimum score 550 paper-based; 213 computer-based; 80 iBT).

University of Nebraska–Lincoln, Graduate College, College of Engineering, Department of Industrial and Management Systems Engineering, Lincoln, NE 68588. Offers engineering management (M Eng); industrial and management systems engineering (MS, PhD); manufacturing systems engineering (MS). Postbaccalaureate distance learning degree programs offered. *Degree requirements:* For master's, thesis optional; for doctorate, comprehensive exam, thesis/dissertation. *Entrance requirements:* For master's and doctorate, GRE. Additional exam requirements/recommendations for international students: Required—TOEFL (minimum score 525 paper-based; 195 computer-based). Electronic applications accepted. *Faculty research:* Ergonomics, occupational safety, quality control, industrial packaging, facility design.

University of New Mexico, Graduate School, School of Engineering, Manufacturing Engineering Program, Albuquerque, NM 87131-2039. Offers MEME, MBA/MEME. Part-time programs available. *Faculty:* 1 part-time/adjunct (0 women). *Students:* 1 full-time (0 women), 7 part-time (1 woman); includes 1 minority (American Indian/Alaska Native), 4 international. Average age 33. 8 applicants, 50% accepted, 1 enrolled. In 2009, 3 master's awarded. *Degree requirements:* For master's, 500 hours relevant industry experience, paid or unpaid. *Entrance requirements:* For master's, GRE General Test (minimum score: 400 verbal, 600 quantitative, 3.5 analytical writing), minimum GPA of 3.0. Additional exam requirements/recommendations for international students: Required—TOEFL (minimum score 550 paper-based; 213 computer-based; 79 iBT). *Application deadline:* For fall admission, 7/30 priority date for domestic students, 3/1 for international students; for spring admission, 11/30 priority date for domestic students, 8/1 for international students. Application fee: $50. Electronic applications accepted. *Expenses:* Tuition, state resident: full-time $2098.80; part-time $233.20 per credit hour. Tuition, nonresident: full-time $6650. Required fees: $25 per semester. Tuition and fees vary according to course load, program and reciprocity agreements. *Financial support:* In 2009–10, 5 students received support, including 8 research assistantships with partial tuition reimbursements available (averaging $27,000 per year); career-related internships or fieldwork and health care benefits also available. Support available to part-time students. Financial award application deadline: 3/1; financial award applicants required to submit FAFSA. *Faculty research:* Robotics, automation control and machine vision, microsystems and microgrippers, semiconductor manufacturing and metrology, cross training and operations of technicians and engineers. Total annual research expenditures: $1.1 million. *Unit head:* Dr. John E. Wood, Director, 505-272-7150, Fax: 505-272-7152, E-mail: jw@unm.edu. *Application contact:* Arden L. Ballantine, Information Contact, 505-272-7150, Fax: 505-272-7152, E-mail: aballant@unm.edu.

University of Regina, Faculty of Graduate Studies and Research, Faculty of Engineering and Applied Science, Program in Advanced Manufacturing and Processing, Regina, SK S4S 0A2, Canada. Offers MA Sc. *Faculty:* 1 full-time (0 women). *Students:* 3 full-time (1 woman). *Degree requirements:* For master's, thesis. *Entrance requirements:* Additional exam requirements/recommendations for international students: Required—TOEFL (minimum score 550 paper-based; 213 computer-based; 80 iBT). *Application deadline:* Applications are processed on a rolling basis. Application fee: $90 ($100 for international students). *Financial support:* Fellowships, research assistantships, teaching assistantships, scholarships/grants available. Financial award application deadline: 6/15.

University of Regina, Faculty of Graduate Studies and Research, Faculty of Engineering and Applied Science, Program in Process Systems Engineering, Regina, SK S4S 0A2, Canada. Offers M Eng, MA Sc. *Faculty:* 12 full-time (2 women). *Students:* 8 full-time (3 women). 23 applicants, 52% accepted. In 2009, 1 master's awarded. *Entrance requirements:* Additional exam requirements/recommendations for international students: Required—TOEFL (minimum score 550 paper-based; 213 computer-based; 80 iBT). *Application fee:* $90 ($100 for international students). *Financial support:* In 2009–10, 1 research assistantship (averaging $16,910 per year), 1 teaching assistantship (averaging $6,650 per year) were awarded; fellowships also available. *Unit head:* Dr. David deMontigny, Graduate Program Coordinator, 306-585-4490, E-mail: david.demontigny@uregina.ca. *Application contact:* Crystal Pick, Information Contact, 306-337-2603, E-mail: crystal.pick@uregina.ca.

University of St. Thomas, Graduate Studies, School of Engineering, St. Paul, MN 55105-1096. Offers engineering and technology management (Certificate); manufacturing systems (MS); manufacturing systems engineering (MMSE); systems engineering (MS); technology management (MS). *Accreditation:* ABET (one or more programs are accredited). Electronic applications accepted. *Expenses:* Contact institution.

University of Southern California, Graduate School, Viterbi School of Engineering, Department of Industrial and Systems Engineering, Los Angeles, CA 90089. Offers digital supply chain management (MS); engineering management (MS); engineering technology communication (Graduate Certificate); health systems operations (Graduate Certificate); industrial and systems engineering (MS, PhD, Engr); manufacturing engineering (MS); operations research engineering (MS); optimization and supply chain management (Graduate Certificate); product development engineering (MS); safety systems and security (MS); systems architecting and engineering (MS, Graduate Certificate); systems safety and security (Graduate Certificate); transportation systems (Graduate Certificate); MS/MBA. Part-time programs available. Postbaccalaureate distance learning degree programs offered (minimal on-campus study). *Faculty:* 11 full-time (2 women), 39 part-time/adjunct (7 women). *Students:* 250 full-time (71 women), 145 part-time (37 women); includes 67 minority (6 African Americans, 2 American Indian/Alaska Native, 39 Asian Americans or Pacific Islanders, 20 Hispanic Americans), 253 international. 679 applicants, 58% accepted, 206 enrolled. In 2009, 98 master's, 7 doctorates awarded. Terminal master's awarded for partial completion of doctoral program. *Degree requirements:* For doctorate, thesis/dissertation. *Entrance requirements:* For master's, GRE General Test; for doctorate, General GRE. *Application deadline:* For fall admission, 3/1 priority date for domestic and international students; for spring admission, 10/1 for domestic students, 10/1 priority date for international students. Applications are processed on a rolling basis. Application fee: $85. Electronic applications accepted. *Expenses:* Tuition: full-time $25,980; part-time $1315 per unit. Required fees: $554. One-time fee: $35 full-time. Full-time tuition and fees vary according to degree level and program. *Financial support:* In 2009–10, fellowships with full tuition reimbursements (averaging $30,000 per year), research assistantships with full tuition reimbursements (averaging $19,250 per year), teaching assistantships with full tuition reimbursements (averaging $19,250 per year) were awarded; career-related internships or fieldwork, scholarships/grants, health care benefits, and unspecified assistantships also available. Financial award application deadline: 12/1; financial award applicants required to submit CSS PROFILE or FAFSA. *Faculty research:* Health systems, music cognition and retrieval, transportation andlogistics, manufacturing and automation, engineering systems design, risk and economic analysis. Total annual research expenditures: $1.2 million. *Unit head:* Dr. James E. Moore, Chair, 213-740-4885, Fax: 213-740-1120, E-mail: jmoore@usc.edu. *Application contact:* Mary Ordaz, Student Service Advisor, 213-740-4886, Fax: 213-740-1120, E-mail: isedept@usc.edu.

Manufacturing Engineering

University of Southern Maine, School of Applied Science, Engineering, and Technology, Department of Technology, Portland, ME 04104-9300. Offers manufacturing systems (MS). *Entrance requirements:* Additional exam requirements/recommendations for international students: Required—TOEFL. Electronic applications accepted.

The University of Texas at El Paso, Graduate School, College of Engineering, Department of Industrial Engineering, El Paso, TX 79968-0001. Offers industrial engineering (MS); manufacturing engineering (MS); systems engineering (MS, Certificate). Part-time and evening/weekend programs available. *Degree requirements:* For master's, thesis optional. *Entrance requirements:* For master's, GRE General Test, minimum GPA of 3.0 in major. Additional exam requirements/recommendations for international students: Required—TOEFL. Electronic applications accepted. *Faculty research:* Computer vision, automated inspection, simulation and modeling.

The University of Texas–Pan American, College of Science and Engineering, Department of Manufacturing Engineering, Edinburg, TX 78539. Offers MS. *Expenses:* Tuition, state resident: full-time $3630.60; part-time $201.70 per credit hour. Tuition, nonresident: full-time $8617; part-time $478.70 per credit hour. Required fees: $806.50.

University of Windsor, Faculty of Graduate Studies, Faculty of Engineering, Department of Industrial and Manufacturing Systems Engineering, Windsor, ON N9B 3P4, Canada. Offers industrial engineering (M Eng, MA Sc); manufacturing systems engineering (PhD). Part-time programs available. *Degree requirements:* For master's, thesis; for doctorate, comprehensive exam, thesis/dissertation. *Entrance requirements:* For master's, minimum B average; for doctorate, master's degree, minimum B average. Additional exam requirements/recommendations for international students: Required—TOEFL (minimum score 560 paper-based; 220 computer-based). Electronic applications accepted. *Faculty research:* Human factors, operations research.

University of Wisconsin–Madison, Graduate School, College of Engineering, Manufacturing Systems Engineering Program, Madison, WI 53706. Offers MS. Part-time programs available. Postbaccalaureate distance learning degree programs offered (minimal on-campus study). *Faculty:* 32 part-time/adjunct (6 women). *Students:* 30 full-time (4 women), 6 part-time (0 women); includes 3 minority (2 Asian Americans or Pacific Islanders, 1 Hispanic American), 26 international. Average age 27. 40 applicants, 38% accepted. In 2009, 7 master's awarded. *Degree requirements:* For master's, thesis (for some programs), independent research projects. *Entrance requirements:* For master's, GRE General Test. Additional exam requirements/recommendations for international students: Required—TOEFL. *Application deadline:* For fall admission, 6/15 priority date for domestic students; for spring admission, 10/31 priority date for domestic students. Applications are processed on a rolling basis. Application fee: $45. Electronic applications accepted. *Expenses:* Tuition, state resident: part-time $594 per credit. Tuition, nonresident: part-time $1504 per credit. Required fees: $65 per credit. Tuition and fees vary according to course load, program and reciprocity agreements. *Financial support:* In 2009–10, 10 students received support, including 8 fellowships with tuition reimbursements available (averaging $16,500 per year), 2 research assistantships with tuition reimbursements available (averaging $19,000 per year); career-related internships or fieldwork, Federal Work-Study, institutionally sponsored loans, and unspecified assistantships also available. *Faculty research:* CAD/CAM, rapid prototyping, lead time reduction, quick response manufacturing. Total annual research expenditures: $250,000. *Unit head:* Ananth Krishnamurthy, Director, 608-262-0921, Fax: 608-265-4017, E-mail: ananth@engr.wisc.edu. *Application contact:* John Loeffelholz, Administrative Assistant, 608-262-0921, Fax: 608-265-4017, E-mail: mse@engr.wisc.edu.

University of Wisconsin–Milwaukee, Graduate School, College of Engineering and Applied Science, Program in Engineering, Milwaukee, WI 53201-0413. Offers civil engineering (MS); electrical and computer engineering (MS); energy engineering (Certificate); engineering (PhD); engineering management (MS); engineering mechanics (MS); ergonomics (Certificate); industrial and management engineering (MS); manufacturing engineering (MS); materials engineering (MS); mechanical engineering (MS); MUP/MS. Part-time programs available. *Faculty:* 44 full-time (6 women). *Students:* 119 full-time (22 women), 130 part-time (22 women); includes 23 minority (2 African Americans, 14 Asian Americans or Pacific Islanders, 7 Hispanic Americans), 126 international. Average age 32. 231 applicants, 67% accepted, 33 enrolled. In 2009, 29 master's, 14 doctorates awarded. *Degree requirements:* For master's, comprehensive exam (for some programs), thesis or alternative; for doctorate, comprehensive exam, thesis/dissertation, internship. *Entrance requirements:* For master's, GRE, minimum GPA of 2.75; for doctorate, GRE, minimum GPA of 3.5. Additional exam requirements/recommendations for international students: Required—TOEFL (minimum score 550 paper-based; 79 iBT), IELTS (minimum score 6.5). *Application deadline:* For fall admission, 1/1 priority date for domestic students; for spring admission, 9/1 for domestic students. Applications are processed on a rolling basis. Application fee: $45 ($75 for international students). *Expenses:* Tuition, state resident: full-time $8800. Tuition, nonresident: full-time $20,760. Tuition and fees vary according to program and reciprocity agreements. *Financial support:* In 2009–10, 18 research assistantships, 51 teaching assistantships were awarded; fellowships, career-related internships or fieldwork, Federal Work-Study, and unspecified assistantships also available. Support available to part-time students. Financial award application deadline: 4/15. Total annual research expenditures: $2.9 million. *Unit head:* David Yu, Head, 414-229-6169, E-mail: yu@uwm.edu. *Application contact:* Betty Warras, General Information Contact, 414-229-4982, Fax: 414-229-6967, E-mail: bwarras@uwm.edu.

University of Wisconsin–Stout, Graduate School, College of Technology, Engineering, and Management, Program in Manufacturing Engineering, Menomonie, WI 54751. Offers MS. Postbaccalaureate distance learning degree programs offered (minimal on-campus study). *Degree requirements:* For master's, thesis. *Entrance requirements:* For master's, minimum GPA of 3.0. Additional exam requirements/recommendations for international students: Required—TOEFL (minimum score 500 paper-based; 173 computer-based; 61 iBT). Electronic applications accepted. *Faculty research:* General ceramics patents, metal matrix composites, solidification processing, high temperature processing.

Villanova University, College of Engineering, Department of Mechanical Engineering, Villanova, PA 19085-1699. Offers electro-mechanical systems (Certificate); machinery dynamics (Certificate); mechanical engineering (MSME); thermofluid systems (Certificate). Part-time and evening/weekend programs available. Postbaccalaureate distance learning degree programs offered (no on-campus study). *Entrance requirements:* For master's, GRE General Test (for applicants with degrees from foreign universities), BME, minimum GPA of 3.0. Additional exam requirements/recommendations for international students: Required—TOEFL (minimum score 600 paper-based; 250 computer-based; 100 iBT). Electronic applications accepted. *Expenses:* Tuition: Part-time $630 per credit. Required fees: $60 per credit. Part-time tuition and fees vary according to degree level and program. *Faculty research:* Composite materials, power plant systems, fluid mechanics, automated manufacturing, dynamic analysis.

Wayne State University, College of Engineering, Department of Industrial and Manufacturing Engineering, Program in Manufacturing Engineering, Detroit, MI 48202. Offers MS. *Degree requirements:* For master's, thesis optional. *Entrance requirements:* For master's, minimum undergraduate GPA of 2.8, Baccalaureate degree in engineering from an ABET institution. Additional exam requirements/recommendations for international students: Required—TOEFL (minimum score 550 paper-based; 213 computer-based), GRE; Recommended—TWE (minimum score 6). *Faculty research:* Design for manufacturing, machine tools, manufacturing processes, material selection for manufacturing, manufacturing systems.

Western Illinois University, School of Graduate Studies, College of Business and Technology, Department of Engineering Technology, Macomb, IL 61455-1390. Offers manufacturing engineering systems (MS). Part-time programs available. *Students:* 14 full-time (1 woman), 7 part-time (0 women); includes 1 minority (African American), 10 international. Average age 25. 20 applicants, 75% accepted. In 2009, 10 master's awarded. *Degree requirements:* For master's, thesis or alternative. *Entrance requirements:* Additional exam requirements/recommendations for international students: Required—TOEFL (minimum score 550 paper-based; 213 computer-based; 80 iBT). *Application deadline:* Applications are processed on a rolling basis. Application fee: $30. Electronic applications accepted. *Expenses:* Tuition, state resident: full-time $4486; part-time $249.21 per credit hour. Tuition, nonresident: full-time $8972; part-time $498.42 per credit hour. Required fees: $72.62 per credit hour. *Financial support:* In 2009–10, 9 students received support, including 9 research assistantships with full tuition reimbursements available (averaging $7,280 per year). Financial award applicants required to submit FAFSA. *Unit head:* Dr. Ray Diez, Chairperson, 309-298-1091. *Application contact:* Evelyn Hoing, Assistant Director of Graduate Studies, 309-298-1806, Fax: 309-298-2345, E-mail: grad-office@wiu.edu.

Western Michigan University, Graduate College, College of Engineering and Applied Sciences, Department of Industrial and Manufacturing Engineering, Program in Manufacturing Engineering, Kalamazoo, MI 49008. Offers MS. *Entrance requirements:* For master's, GRE General Test, minimum GPA of 3.0.

Western New England College, School of Engineering, Department of Industrial and Manufacturing Engineering, Springfield, MA 01119. Offers production management (MSEM). Part-time and evening/weekend programs available. *Students:* 30 part-time (6 women); includes 2 African Americans, 2 Asian Americans or Pacific Islanders, 1 Hispanic American. In 2009, 8 master's awarded. *Degree requirements:* For master's, comprehensive exam, thesis optional. *Entrance requirements:* For master's, GRE, bachelor's degree in engineering or related field, Two Letters of Recommendation, and Resume. *Application deadline:* Applications are processed on a rolling basis. Application fee: $30. *Expenses:* Tuition: Part-time $552 per credit hour. Part-time tuition and fees vary according to program. *Financial support:* Available to part-time students. Applicants required to submit FAFSA. *Faculty research:* Project scheduling, flexible manufacturing systems, facility layout, energy management. *Unit head:* Dr. Eric W. Haffner, Chair, 413-782-1272, E-mail: ehaffner@wnec.edu. *Application contact:* Matt Fox, Director of Recruiting and Marketing for Adult Learners, 413-782-1249, Fax: 413-782-1779, E-mail: ce@wnec.edu.

Wichita State University, Graduate School, College of Engineering, Department of Industrial and Manufacturing Engineering, Wichita, KS 67260. Offers MEM, MS, PhD. Part-time programs available. In 2009, 37 master's, 3 doctorates awarded. *Entrance requirements:* Additional exam requirements/recommendations for international students: Required—TOEFL. *Expenses:* Tuition, state resident: full-time $4247; part-time $235.95 per credit hour. Tuition, nonresident: full-time $11,171; part-time $620.60 per credit hour. Required fees: $34; $3.60 per credit hour. $17 per term. Tuition and fees vary according to campus/location and program. *Financial support:* Teaching assistantships available. *Unit head:* Dr. Krishna Krishnan, Chair, 316-978-3425, Fax: 316-978-3742, E-mail: krishna.krishnan@wichita.edu. *Application contact:* Dr. Krishna Krishnan, Chair, 316-978-3425, Fax: 316-978-3742, E-mail: krishna.krishnan@wichita.edu.

Worcester Polytechnic Institute, Graduate Studies and Research, Department of Mechanical Engineering, Program in Manufacturing Engineering, Worcester, MA 01609-2280. Offers MS, PhD. Part-time and evening/weekend programs available. *Faculty:* 3 full-time (0 women), 1 part-time/adjunct (0 women). *Students:* 15 full-time (2 women), 30 part-time (11 women). 47 applicants, 47% accepted, 22 enrolled. In 2009, 13 master's, 1 doctorate awarded. *Degree requirements:* For master's, thesis optional; for doctorate, comprehensive exam, thesis/dissertation, research proposal. *Entrance requirements:* For master's and doctorate, 3 letters of recommendation. Additional exam requirements/recommendations for international students: Required—TOEFL (minimum score 550 paper-based; 213 computer-based; 79 iBT), IELTS (minimum score 6.5). *Application deadline:* For fall admission, 1/15 priority date for domestic and international students; for spring admission, 10/15 priority date for domestic and international students. Applications are processed on a rolling basis. Application fee: $70. Electronic applications accepted. *Financial support:* Career-related internships or fieldwork, institutionally sponsored loans, scholarships/grants, and unspecified assistantships available. Financial award application deadline: 1/15. *Faculty research:* Manufacturing processes and systems, design for manufacturability, CAD/CAM applications, surface metrology, materials processing. *Unit head:* Dr. Kevin Rong, Director, 508-831-6088, Fax: 508-831-5673, E-mail: rong@wpi.edu. *Application contact:* Susan Milkman, Graduate Secretary, 508-831-6088, Fax: 508-831-5673, E-mail: smilkman@wpi.edu.

Worcester Polytechnic Institute, Graduate Studies and Research, Programs in Interdisciplinary Studies, Worcester, MA 01609-2280. Offers bioscience administration (MS); impact engineering (MS); manufacturing engineering management (MS); power systems management (MS); social science (PhD); systems modeling (MS). Part-time and evening/weekend programs available. *Faculty:* 1 part-time/adjunct (0 women). *Students:* 3 full-time (1 woman), 126 part-time (24 women). 184 applicants, 68% accepted, 100 enrolled. In 2009, 19 master's awarded. *Degree requirements:* For master's, thesis; for doctorate, comprehensive exam, thesis/dissertation. *Entrance requirements:* For master's and doctorate, 3 letters of recommendation. Additional exam requirements/recommendations for international students: Required—TOEFL (minimum score 550 paper-based; 213 computer-based; 79 iBT), IELTS (minimum score 6.5). *Application deadline:* For fall admission, 1/15 priority date for domestic students; for spring admission, 10/15 priority date for domestic students. Application fee: $70. *Financial support:* Institutionally sponsored loans, scholarships/grants, and unspecified assistantships available. Financial award application deadline: 1/15. *Unit head:* Dr. Fred J. Looft, Head, 508-831-5231, Fax: 508-831-5491, E-mail: fjlooft@wpi.edu. *Application contact:* Lynne Dougherty, Administrative Assistant, 508-831-5301, Fax: 508-831-5717, E-mail: grad@wpi.edu.

Pharmaceutical Engineering

New Jersey Institute of Technology, Office of Graduate Studies, Newark College of Engineering, Department of Chemical Engineering, Interdisciplinary Program in Pharmaceutical Engineering, Newark, NJ 07102. Offers MS. Part-time and evening/weekend programs available. *Degree requirements:* For master's, thesis optional. *Entrance requirements:* For master's,

GRE General Test. Additional exam requirements/recommendations for international students: Required—TOEFL (minimum score 550 paper-based; 213 computer-based; 79 iBT). Electronic applications accepted.

Reliability Engineering

Arizona State University, Graduate College, Ira A. Fulton School of Engineering, ASU Engineering Online Programs, Tempe, AZ 85287. Offers construction (MS); embedded systems (M Eng); enterprise systems innovation and management (MSE); modeling and simulation (M Eng); quality and reliability engineering (M Eng); software engineering (MSE); systems engineering (M Eng).

The University of Arizona, Graduate College, College of Engineering, Department of Systems and Industrial Engineering, Program in Reliability and Quality Engineering, Tucson, AZ 85721. Offers MS. Part-time programs available. Postbaccalaureate distance learning degree programs offered. *Students:* 1 (woman) full-time, all international. Average age 27. 1 applicant, 0% accepted, 0 enrolled. *Entrance requirements:* Additional exam requirements/recommendations for international students: Required—TOEFL (minimum score 550 paper-based; 213 computer-based; 79 iBT). *Application deadline:* Applications are processed on a rolling basis. Application fee: $75. Electronic applications accepted. *Expenses:* Tuition, state resident: full-time $9028. Tuition, nonresident: full-time $24,890. *Financial support:* Unspecified assistantships available. *Unit head:* Dr. K. Larry Head, Head, 520-621-6551, E-mail: larry@sie.arizona.edu. *Application contact:* Graduate Secretary, 520-626-4644, Fax: 520-621-6555, E-mail: gradapp@sie.arizona.edu.

University of Maryland, College Park, Academic Affairs, A. James Clark School of Engineering, Department of Continuing and Distance Learning in Engineering, Professional Program in Engineering, College Park, MD 20742. Offers aerospace engineering (M Eng); chemical engineering (M Eng); civil engineering (M Eng); electrical engineering (M Eng); engineering (Certificate); fire protection engineering (M Eng); materials science and engineering (M Eng); mechanical engineering (M Eng); reliability engineering (M Eng); systems engineering (M Eng). Part-time and evening/weekend programs available. Postbaccalaureate distance learning degree programs offered. *Students:* 50 full-time (15 women), 234 part-time (41 women); includes 91 minority (36 African Americans, 39 Asian Americans or Pacific Islanders, 16 Hispanic Americans), 45 international. 137 applicants, 69% accepted, 77 enrolled. In 2009, 103 master's awarded. *Entrance requirements:* For master's, 3 letters of recommendation. *Application deadline:* For fall admission, 8/15 for domestic students, 1/10 for international students; for spring admission, 12/15 for domestic students, 6/1 for international students. Applications are processed on a rolling basis. Application fee: $60. Electronic applications accepted. *Expenses:* Tuition, area resident: Part-time $471 per credit hour. Tuition, state resident: part-time $471 per credit hour. Tuition, nonresident: part-time $1016 per credit hour. Required fees: $337.04 per term. *Financial support:* In 2009–10, 2 research assistantships with tuition reimbursements (averaging $19,561 per year), 9 teaching assistantships with tuition reimbursements (averaging $16,849 per year) were awarded; fellowships, Federal Work-Study and scholarships/grants also available. Support available to part-time students. Financial award applicants required to submit FAFSA. *Unit head:* Dr. George Syrmos, Director, 301-405-3633, Fax: 301-314-3305, E-mail: syrmos@umd.edu. *Application contact:* Dean of Graduate School, 301-405-0376, Fax: 301-314-9305.

University of Maryland, College Park, Academic Affairs, A. James Clark School of Engineering, Department of Mechanical Engineering, Reliability Engineering Program, College Park, MD 20742. Offers M Eng, MS, PhD. Part-time and evening/weekend programs available. Postbaccalaureate distance learning degree programs offered. *Students:* 31 full-time (10 women), 28 part-time (7 women); includes 8 minority (3 African Americans, 1 Asian American or Pacific Islander, 4 Hispanic Americans), 22 international. 23 applicants, 43% accepted, 8 enrolled. In 2009, 11 master's, 7 doctorates awarded. *Degree requirements:* For master's, thesis optional; for doctorate, thesis/dissertation. *Entrance requirements:* For master's, GRE General Test, 3 letters of recommendation; for doctorate, GRE General Test, minimum GPA of 3.0. Additional exam requirements/recommendations for international students: Required—TOEFL. *Application deadline:* For fall admission, 5/1 for domestic students, 2/1 for international students; for spring admission, 10/1 for domestic students, 6/1 for international students. Applications are processed on a rolling basis. Application fee: $60. Electronic applications accepted. *Expenses:* Tuition, area resident: Part-time $471 per credit hour. Tuition, state resident: part-time $471 per credit hour. Tuition, nonresident: part-time $1016 per credit hour. Required fees: $337.04 per term. *Financial support:* In 2009–10, 14 research assistantships (averaging $23,776 per year), 1 teaching assistantship (averaging $17,544 per year) were awarded; fellowships, career-related internships or fieldwork also available. Financial award applicants required to submit FAFSA. *Faculty research:* Electron linear acceleration, x-ray and imaging. *Unit head:* Dr. Aristos Christou, Professor and Chair, 301-405-5208, Fax: 301-314-9601, E-mail: christou@eng.umd.edu. *Application contact:* Information Contact, 301-405-0376.

The University of Tennessee, Graduate School, College of Engineering, Department of Chemical Engineering, Knoxville, TN 37996. Offers chemical engineering (MS, PhD); reliability and maintainability engineering (MS); MS/MBA. *Faculty:* 12 full-time (1 woman), 12 part-time/adjunct (0 women). *Students:* 25 full-time (7 women), 10 part-time (3 women); includes 3 minority (1 American Indian/Alaska Native, 2 Asian Americans or Pacific Islanders), 24 international. Average age 23. 73 applicants, 23% accepted, 8 enrolled. In 2009, 4 master's, 1 doctorate awarded. *Degree requirements:* For master's, thesis or alternative; for doctorate, comprehensive exam, thesis/dissertation. *Entrance requirements:* For master's and doctorate, GRE General Test, minimum GPA of 2.7, 2 reference forms. Additional exam requirements/recommendations for international students: Required—TOEFL (minimum score 550 paper-based; 213 computer-based). *Application deadline:* For fall admission, 2/1 priority date for domestic and international students; for spring admission, 6/15 priority date for international students. Applications are processed on a rolling basis. Application fee: $35. Electronic applications accepted. *Expenses:* Tuition, state resident: full-time $6826; part-time $380 per semester hour. Tuition, nonresident: full-time $21,844; part-time $1147 per semester hour. Tuition and fees vary according to program. *Financial support:* In 2009–10, 10 students received support, including 26 research assistantships with full tuition reimbursements available (averaging $21,612 per year), 9 teaching assistantships with full tuition reimbursements available (averaging $17,520 per year); career-related internships or fieldwork, Federal Work-Study, institutionally sponsored loans, health care benefits, and unspecified assistantships also available. Financial award application deadline: 2/1; financial award applicants required to submit FAFSA. *Faculty research:* Molecular and cellular bioengineering; engineering of soft, functional and structural materials; bio-fuels; molecular modeling and simulations; fuel cells and energy storage devices. Total annual research expenditures: $2.3 million. *Unit head:* Dr. Bamin Khomami, Head, 865-974-2421, Fax: 865-974-7076, E-mail: bkhomami@utk.edu. *Application contact:* Dr. Paul Frymier, Graduate Program Coordinator, 865-974-4961, Fax: 865-974-7076, E-mail: pdf@utk.edu.

The University of Tennessee, Graduate School, College of Engineering, Department of Electrical Engineering and Computer Science, Knoxville, TN 37996. Offers computer engineering (MS, PhD); computer science (MS, PhD); electrical engineering (MS, PhD); reliability and

maintainability engineering (MS); MS/MBA. Part-time programs available. *Faculty:* 40 full-time (4 women), 13 part-time/adjunct (2 women). *Students:* 141 full-time (25 women), 62 part-time (11 women); includes 11 minority (4 African Americans, 5 Asian Americans or Pacific Islanders, 2 Hispanic Americans), 109 international. Average age 30. 603 applicants, 12% accepted, 45 enrolled. In 2009, 55 master's, 24 doctorates awarded. *Degree requirements:* For master's, thesis or alternative; for doctorate, comprehensive exam, thesis/dissertation. *Entrance requirements:* For master's, GRE, minimum GPA of 3.0; for doctorate, GRE General Test, minimum GPA of 3.0. Additional exam requirements/recommendations for international students: Required—TOEFL (minimum score 550 paper-based; 213 computer-based). *Application deadline:* For fall admission, 2/1 priority date for domestic and international students; for spring admission, 6/15 priority date for international students. Applications are processed on a rolling basis. Application fee: $35. Electronic applications accepted. *Expenses:* Tuition, state resident: full-time $6826; part-time $380 per semester hour. Tuition, nonresident: full-time $21,844; part-time $1147 per semester hour. Tuition and fees vary according to program. *Financial support:* In 2009–10, 139 students received support, including 32 fellowships with full tuition reimbursements available (averaging $5,448 per year), 118 research assistantships with full tuition reimbursements available (averaging $16,800 per year), 68 teaching assistantships with full tuition reimbursements available (averaging $12,996 per year); career-related internships or fieldwork, Federal Work-Study, institutionally sponsored loans, health care benefits, and unspecified assistantships also available. Financial award application deadline: 2/1; financial award applicants required to submit FAFSA. *Faculty research:* Artificial intelligence and visualization; microelectronics, mixed-signal electronics, VLSI, embedded systems; scientific and distributed computing; computer vision, robotics, and image processing; power electronics, power systems, communications. Total annual research expenditures: $9.1 million. *Unit head:* Dr. Kevin Tomsovic, Head, 865-974-3461, Fax: 865-974-3461, E-mail: tomsovic@eecs.utk.edu. *Application contact:* Dr. Masood Parang, Associate Dean of Student Affairs, 865-974-2454, Fax: 865-974-9871, E-mail: mparang@utk.edu.

The University of Tennessee, Graduate School, College of Engineering, Department of Industrial and Information Engineering, Knoxville, TN 37996. Offers engineering management (MS, PhD); industrial engineering (MS, PhD); reliability and maintainability engineering (MS); MS/MBA. Part-time programs available. Postbaccalaureate distance learning degree programs offered (no on-campus study). *Faculty:* 7 full-time (1 woman), 5 part-time/adjunct (0 women). *Students:* 30 full-time (8 women), 53 part-time (11 women); includes 14 minority (9 African Americans, 2 American Indian/Alaska Native, 3 Asian Americans or Pacific Islanders), 26 international. Average age 25. 77 applicants, 78% accepted, 20 enrolled. In 2009, 13 master's, 4 doctorates awarded. *Degree requirements:* For master's, thesis; for doctorate, comprehensive exam, thesis/dissertation. *Entrance requirements:* For master's, GRE General Test, minimum GPA of 2.7, 3 letters of recommendation; for doctorate, MS, 3 letters of recommendation. Additional exam requirements/recommendations for international students: Required—TOEFL (minimum score 550 paper-based; 213 computer-based). *Application deadline:* For fall admission, 2/1 priority date for domestic and international students; for spring admission, 6/15 priority date for international students. Applications are processed on a rolling basis. Application fee: $35. Electronic applications accepted. *Expenses:* Tuition, state resident: full-time $6826; part-time $380 per semester hour. Tuition, nonresident: full-time $21,844; part-time $1147 per semester hour. Tuition and fees vary according to program. *Financial support:* In 2009–10, 11 research assistantships with full tuition reimbursements (averaging $12,792 per year), 8 teaching assistantships with full tuition reimbursements (averaging $7,044 per year) were awarded; career-related internships or fieldwork, Federal Work-Study, institutionally sponsored loans, health care benefits, and unspecified assistantships also available. Financial award application deadline: 2/1; financial award applicants required to submit FAFSA. *Faculty research:* Dependability and reliability of large computer networks; design of lean, reliable systems; operations research in the automotive industry; sports equipment testing; defense-oriented supply chain modeling. Total annual research expenditures: $488,000. *Unit head:* Dr. R. Bruce Robinson, Interim Head, 865-974-3333, Fax: 865-974-0588, E-mail: rbr@utk.edu. *Application contact:* Dr. Denise Jackson, Graduate Representative, E-mail: djackson@utk.edu.

The University of Tennessee, Graduate School, College of Engineering, Department of Materials Science and Engineering, Knoxville, TN 37996. Offers materials science and engineering (MS, PhD); polymer engineering (MS, PhD); reliability and maintainability engineering (MS); MS/MBA. Part-time programs available. *Faculty:* 19 full-time (2 women), 7 part-time/adjunct (1 woman). *Students:* 71 full-time (14 women), 7 part-time (1 woman); includes 5 minority (4 African Americans, 1 Asian American or Pacific Islander), 51 international. Average age 24. 141 applicants, 20% accepted, 14 enrolled. In 2009, 11 master's, 13 doctorates awarded. *Degree requirements:* For master's, thesis or alternative; for doctorate, comprehensive exam, thesis/dissertation. *Entrance requirements:* For master's and doctorate, minimum GPA of 3.0. Additional exam requirements/recommendations for international students: Required—TOEFL (minimum score 550 paper-based; 213 computer-based). *Application deadline:* For fall admission, 2/1 priority date for domestic and international students; for spring admission, 6/15 priority date for international students. Applications are processed on a rolling basis. Application fee: $35. Electronic applications accepted. *Expenses:* Tuition, state resident: full-time $6826; part-time $380 per semester hour. Tuition, nonresident: full-time $21,844; part-time $1147 per semester hour. Tuition and fees vary according to program. *Financial support:* In 2009–10, 4 students received support, including 3 fellowships with full tuition reimbursements available (averaging $8,892 per year), 72 research assistantships with full tuition reimbursements available (averaging $19,812 per year), 14 teaching assistantships with full tuition reimbursements available (averaging $17,580 per year); career-related internships or fieldwork, Federal Work-Study, institutionally sponsored loans, health care benefits, and unspecified assistantships also available. Financial award application deadline: 2/1; financial award applicants required to submit FAFSA. *Faculty research:* Polymer chemistry, processing, and characterization; advanced structural materials; functional materials (electronic, magnetic and optical); mechanical behavior of materials; neutron materials science. Total annual research expenditures: $6.1 million. *Unit head:* Dr. George Pharr, Head, 865-974-5336, Fax: 865-974-4115, E-mail: pharr@utk.edu. *Application contact:* Dr. Masood Parang, Associate Dean of Student Affairs, 865-974-2454, Fax: 865-974-9871, E-mail: mparang@utk.edu.

The University of Tennessee, Graduate School, College of Engineering, Department of Nuclear and Radiological Engineering, Knoxville, TN 37996. Offers nuclear engineering (MS, PhD); reliability and maintainability engineering (MS); MS/MBA. Part-time programs available. *Faculty:* 17 full-time (0 women), 16 part-time/adjunct (1 woman). *Students:* 48 full-time (6 women), 30 part-time (3 women); includes 3 minority (2 African Americans, 1 Asian American or Pacific Islander), 10 international. Average age 24. 123 applicants, 46% accepted, 31 enrolled. In 2009, 15 master's, 4 doctorates awarded. *Degree requirements:* For master's, thesis or alternative; for doctorate, comprehensive exam, thesis/dissertation. *Entrance*

Reliability Engineering

The University of Tennessee (continued)

requirements: For master's and doctorate, GRE General Test, minimum GPA of 2.7. Additional exam requirements/recommendations for international students: Required—TOEFL (minimum score 213 computer-based). *Application deadline:* For fall admission, 2/1 priority date for domestic students. Applications are processed on a rolling basis. Application fee: $35. Electronic applications accepted. *Expenses:* Tuition, state resident: full-time $6826; part-time $380 per semester hour. Tuition, nonresident: full-time $21,844; part-time $1147 per semester hour. Tuition and fees vary according to program. *Financial support:* In 2009–10, 48 students received support, including 12 fellowships with full tuition reimbursements available (averaging $19,800 per year), 45 research assistantships with full tuition reimbursements available (averaging $17,916 per year), 4 teaching assistantships with full tuition reimbursements available (averaging $9,756 per year); career-related internships or fieldwork, Federal Work-Study, institutionally sponsored loans, and unspecified assistantships also available. Financial award application deadline: 2/1; financial award applicants required to submit FAFSA. *Faculty research:* Heat transfer and fluid dynamics; instrumentation, sensors and controls; maintenance and reliability; radiological engineering; reactor system design and safety. Total annual research expenditures: $3.3 million. *Unit head:* Dr. Harold L. Dodds, Head, 865-974-2525, Fax: 865-974-0668, E-mail: hdj@utk.edu. *Application contact:* Dr. Masood Parang, Associate Dean of Student Affairs, 865-974-2454, Fax: 865-974-9871, E-mail: mparang@utk.edu.

Safety Engineering

Embry-Riddle Aeronautical University, Program in Safety Science, Prescott, AZ 86301-3720. Offers MSSS. *Faculty:* 4 full-time (1 woman). *Students:* 41 full-time (12 women), 4 part-time (2 women); includes 3 minority (2 African Americans, 1 Hispanic American), 7 international. Average age 27. 27 applicants, 93% accepted, 21 enrolled. In 2009, 9 master's awarded. *Degree requirements:* For master's, thesis (for some programs). *Entrance requirements:* Additional exam requirements/recommendations for international students: Required—TOEFL (minimum score 550 paper-based; 213 computer-based; 79 iBT). *Application deadline:* For fall admission, 8/1 priority date for domestic students; for spring admission, 12/1 priority date for domestic students. Applications are processed on a rolling basis. Application fee: $50. Electronic applications accepted. *Expenses:* Tuition: Full-time $13,740; part-time $1145 per credit hour. *Financial support:* In 2009–10, 34 students received support, including 13 research assistantships with full tuition reimbursements available (averaging $2,400 per year); career-related internships or fieldwork, Federal Work-Study, and unspecified assistantships also available. Support available to part-time students. Financial award application deadline: 4/15; financial award applicants required to submit FAFSA. *Unit head:* Dr. Gary Northam, Chair, 928-777-3964, Fax: 928-777-6958. *Application contact:* Debra Cates-Foster, Graduate Admissions Coordinator, 928-777-6697, Fax: 928-777-6958, E-mail: deborahipfingston@erau.edu.

Indiana University Bloomington, School of Health, Physical Education and Recreation, Department of Applied Health Science, Bloomington, IN 47405-7000. Offers health behavior (PhD); health promotion (MS); human development/family studies (MS); nutrition science (MS); public health (MPH); safety management (MS); school and college health programs (MS). *Accreditation:* CEPH (one or more programs are accredited). *Faculty:* 24 full-time (12 women). *Students:* 131 full-time (92 women), 22 part-time (20 women); includes 35 minority (22 African Americans, 1 American Indian/Alaska Native, 5 Asian Americans or Pacific Islanders, 7 Hispanic Americans), 29 international. Average age 31. 118 applicants, 71% accepted, 52 enrolled. In 2009, 43 master's, 6 doctorates awarded. *Degree requirements:* For master's, thesis optional; for doctorate, thesis/dissertation. *Entrance requirements:* For master's, GRE (MS in nutrition science), 3 recommendations; for doctorate, GRE, 3 recommendations. Additional exam requirements/recommendations for international students: Required—TOEFL (minimum score 550 paper-based; 213 computer-based; 79 iBT). *Application deadline:* For fall admission, 4/30 priority date for domestic students, 12/1 priority date for international students; for spring admission, 11/15 priority date for domestic students, 9/1 priority date for international students. Application fee: $55 ($65 for international students). *Financial support:* In 2009–10, 80 students received support, including 12 fellowships (averaging $2,316 per year), 50 research assistantships with full and partial tuition reimbursements available (averaging $6,973 per year), 27 teaching assistantships with full and partial tuition reimbursements available (averaging $11,067 per year); career-related internships or fieldwork, Federal Work-Study, institutionally sponsored loans, scholarships/grants, tuition waivers (partial), and fee remissions also available. Financial award application deadline: 3/1. *Faculty research:* Cancer education, HIV/AIDS and drug education, public health, parent-child interactions, safety education. Total annual research expenditures: $2.8 million. *Unit head:* Dr. Mohammad R. Torabi, Chair, 812-855-4808, Fax: 812-855-3936, E-mail: torabi@indiana.edu. *Application contact:* Dr. Mohammad R. Torabi, Chair, 812-855-4808, Fax: 812-855-3936, E-mail: torabi@indiana.edu.

Murray State University, College of Health Sciences and Human Services, Program in Occupational Safety and Health, Murray, KY 42071. Offers environmental science (MS); industrial hygiene (MS); safety management (MS). *Accreditation:* ABET. Part-time programs available. *Degree requirements:* For master's, comprehensive exam, thesis optional, professional internship. Electronic applications accepted. *Faculty research:* Light effects on plant growth, ergonomics, toxic effects of pets' pesticides, traffic safety.

National University, Academic Affairs, School of Engineering and Technology, Department of Applied Engineering, La Jolla, CA 92037-1011. Offers database administration (MS); engineering management (MS); environmental engineering (MS); homeland security and safety engineering (MS); system engineering (MS); wireless communications (MS). Part-time and evening/weekend programs available. Postbaccalaureate distance learning degree programs offered (no on-campus study). *Faculty:* 6 full-time (1 woman), 7 part-time/adjunct (1 woman). *Students:* 61 full-time (16 women), 176 part-time (35 women); includes 54 minority (11 African Americans, 1 American Indian/Alaska Native, 23 Asian Americans or Pacific Islanders, 19 Hispanic Americans), 117 international. Average age 31. 133 applicants, 100% accepted, 83 enrolled. In 2009, 34 master's awarded. *Degree requirements:* For master's, thesis. *Entrance requirements:* For master's, interview, minimum GPA of 2.5. Additional exam requirements/recommendations for international students: Required—TOEFL (minimum score 550 paper-based; 213 computer-based; 79 iBT), IELTS (minimum score 6). *Application deadline:* Applications are processed on a rolling basis. Application fee: $60 ($65 for international students). Electronic applications accepted. *Expenses:* Tuition: Part-time $338 per quarter hour. *Financial support:* Career-related internships or fieldwork, institutionally sponsored loans, scholarships/grants, and tuition waivers (partial) available. Support available to part-time students. Financial award application deadline: 6/30; financial award applicants required to submit FAFSA. *Unit head:* Dr. Shekar Viswanathan, Chair and Associate Professor, 858-309-8416, Fax: 858-309-3420, E-mail: sviswana@nu.edu. *Application contact:* Dominick Giovanniello, Associate Regional Dean—San Diego, 800-NAT-UNIV, Fax: 858-541-7792, E-mail: dgiovann@nu.edu.

New Jersey Institute of Technology, Office of Graduate Studies, Newark College of Engineering, Department of Industrial and Manufacturing Engineering, Program in Occupational Safety and Health Engineering, Newark, NJ 07102. Offers MS. Part-time and evening/weekend programs available. *Degree requirements:* For master's, thesis or alternative. *Entrance requirements:* For master's, GRE General Test. Additional exam requirements/recommendations for international students: Required—TOEFL (minimum score 550 paper-based; 213 computer-based; 79 iBT). Electronic applications accepted. *Faculty research:* Human factors engineering, manufacturing systems, materials, manufacturing automation and computer integration.

University of Minnesota, Duluth, Graduate School, Swenson College of Science and Engineering, Department of Mechanical and Industrial Engineering, Duluth, MN 55812-2496. Offers engineering management (MSEM); environmental health and safety (MEHS). Part-time and evening/weekend programs available. Postbaccalaureate distance learning degree programs offered (no on-campus study). *Degree requirements:* For master's, comprehensive exam, thesis or alternative, capstone design project (MSEM), field project (MEHS). *Entrance requirements:* For master's, GRE (MEHS), interview (MEHS), letters of recommendation. Additional exam requirements/recommendations for international students: Required—TOEFL (minimum score 550 paper-based; 213 computer-based). *Faculty research:* Transportation, ergonomics, toxicology, supply chain management, automation and robotics.

University of Southern California, Graduate School, Viterbi School of Engineering, Department of Industrial and Systems Engineering, Los Angeles, CA 90089. Offers digital supply chain management (MS); engineering management (MS); engineering technology communication (Graduate Certificate); health systems operations (Graduate Certificate); industrial and systems engineering (MS, PhD, Engr); manufacturing engineering (MS); operations research engineering (MS); optimization and supply chain management (Graduate Certificate); product development engineering (MS); safety systems and security (MS); systems architecting and engineering (MS, Graduate Certificate); systems safety and security (Graduate Certificate); transportation systems (Graduate Certificate); MS/MBA. Part-time programs available. Postbaccalaureate distance learning degree programs offered (minimal on-campus study). *Faculty:* 11 full-time (2 women), 39 part-time/adjunct (7 women). *Students:* 250 full-time (71 women), 145 part-time (37 women); includes 67 minority (6 African Americans, 2 American Indian/Alaska Native, 39 Asian Americans or Pacific Islanders, 20 Hispanic Americans), 253 international. 679 applicants, 58% accepted, 206 enrolled. In 2009, 98 master's, 7 doctorates awarded. Terminal master's awarded for partial completion of doctoral program. *Degree requirements:* For doctorate, thesis/dissertation. *Entrance requirements:* For master's, GRE General Test; for doctorate, General GRE. *Application deadline:* For fall admission, 3/1 priority date for domestic and international students; for spring admission, 10/1 for domestic students, 10/1 priority date for international students. Applications are processed on a rolling basis. Application fee: $85. Electronic applications accepted. *Expenses:* Tuition: Full-time $25,980; part-time $1315 per unit. Required fees: $554. One-time fee: $35 full-time. Full-time tuition and fees vary according to degree level and program. *Financial support:* In 2009–10, fellowships with full tuition reimbursements (averaging $30,000 per year), research assistantships with full tuition reimbursements (averaging $19,250 per year), teaching assistantships with full tuition reimbursements (averaging $19,250 per year) were awarded; career-related internships or fieldwork, scholarships/grants, health care benefits, and unspecified assistantships also available. Financial award application deadline: 12/1; financial award applicants required to submit CSS PROFILE or FAFSA. *Faculty research:* Health systems, music cognition and retrieval, transportation andlogistics, manufacturing and automation, engineering systems design, risk and economic analysis. Total annual research expenditures: $1.2 million. *Unit head:* Dr. James E. Moore, Chair, 213-740-4885, Fax: 213-740-1120, E-mail: jmoore@usc.edu. *Application contact:* Mary Ordaz, Student Service Advisor, 213-740-4886, Fax: 213-740-1120, E-mail: isedept@usc.edu.

West Virginia University, College of Engineering and Mineral Resources, Department of Industrial and Management Systems Engineering, Program in Safety Management, Morgantown, WV 26506. Offers MS. *Accreditation:* ABET. *Degree requirements:* For master's, comprehensive exam, thesis optional. *Entrance requirements:* For master's, minimum GPA of 3.0 for regular admission; 2.75 for provisional. Additional exam requirements/recommendations for international students: Required—TOEFL (minimum score 550 paper-based; 213 computer-based; 80 iBT). Electronic applications accepted.

Systems Engineering

Air Force Institute of Technology, Graduate School of Engineering and Management, Department of Aeronautics and Astronautics, Dayton, OH 45433-7765. Offers aeronautical engineering (MS, PhD); astronautical engineering (MS, PhD); materials science (MS, PhD); space operations (MS); systems engineering (MS, PhD). *Accreditation:* ABET (one or more programs are accredited). Part-time programs available. *Degree requirements:* For master's, thesis; for doctorate, thesis/dissertation. *Entrance requirements:* For master's and doctorate, GRE General Test, minimum GPA of 3.0, U.S. citizenship. *Faculty research:* Computational fluid dynamics, experimental aerodynamics, computational structural mechanics, experimental structural mechanics, aircraft and spacecraft stability and control.

The American University of Athens, The School of Graduate Studies, Athens, Greece. Offers biomedical sciences (MS); business (MBA); business communication (MA); computer sciences (MS); engineering and applied sciences (MS); politics and policy making (MA); systems engineering (MS); telecommunications (MS). *Entrance requirements:* For master's, resum&e, 2 recommendation letters. Additional exam requirements/recommendations for international students: Required—TOEFL (minimum score 550 paper-based; 213 computer-based). *Faculty research:* Nanotechnology, environmental sciences, rock mechanics, human skin studies, Monte Carlo algorithms and software.

Arizona State University, Graduate College, Ira A. Fulton School of Engineering, ASU Engineering Online Programs, Tempe, AZ 85287. Offers construction (MS); embedded systems (M Eng); enterprise systems innovation and management (MSE); modeling and simulation (M Eng); quality and reliability engineering (M Eng); software engineering (MSE); systems engineering (M Eng).

Systems Engineering

Auburn University, Graduate School, Ginn College of Engineering, Department of Industrial and Systems Engineering, Auburn University, AL 36849. Offers MISE, MS, PhD. Part-time programs available. *Faculty:* 10 full-time (1 woman), 4 part-time/adjunct (0 women). *Students:* 89 full-time (21 women), 49 part-time (13 women); includes 16 minority (12 African Americans, 3 Asian Americans or Pacific Islanders, 1 Hispanic American), 66 international. Average age 29. 252 applicants, 62% accepted, 50 enrolled. In 2009, 20 master's, 7 doctorates awarded. *Degree requirements:* For master's, thesis (MS); for doctorate, thesis/dissertation. *Entrance requirements:* For master's and doctorate, GRE General Test. *Application deadline:* For fall admission, 7/7 for domestic students; for spring admission, 11/24 for domestic students. Applications are processed on a rolling basis. Application fee: $50 ($60 for international students). *Expenses:* Tuition, state resident: full-time $6240. Tuition, nonresident: full-time $18,720. International tuition: $18,938 full-time. Required fees: $492. Tuition and fees vary according to course load, program and reciprocity agreements. *Financial support:* Fellowships, research assistantships, teaching assistantships, Federal Work-Study available. Support available to part-time students. Financial award application deadline: 3/15; financial award applicants required to submit FAFSA. *Unit head:* Dr. Alice E. Smith, Chair, 334-844-1401. *Application contact:* Dr. George Flowers, Dean of the Graduate School, 334-844-2125.

Boston University, College of Engineering, Division of Systems Engineering, Boston, MA 02215. Offers M Eng, MS, PhD. Part-time programs available. *Students:* 30 full-time (5 women), 2 part-time (both women); includes 2 minority (both Asian Americans or Pacific Islanders), 24 international. Average age 27. 154 applicants, 17% accepted, 11 enrolled. In 2009, 4 master's, 5 doctorates awarded. Terminal master's awarded for partial completion of doctoral program. *Degree requirements:* For master's, thesis optional; for doctorate, comprehensive exam, thesis/dissertation. *Entrance requirements:* For master's and doctorate, GRE General Test. Additional exam requirements/recommendations for international students: Required—TOEFL (minimum score 550 paper-based; 213 computer-based; 84 iBT), IELTS (minimum score 6). *Application deadline:* For fall admission, 4/1 for domestic and international students; for spring admission, 10/1 for domestic and international students. Applications are processed on a rolling basis. Application fee: $70. Electronic applications accepted. *Expenses:* Tuition: Full-time $37,910; part-time $1184 per credit hour. Required fees: $386; $40 per semester. Part-time tuition and fees vary according to class time, course level, degree level and program. *Financial support:* In 2009–10, 27 students received support, including 4 fellowships with full tuition reimbursements available (averaging $27,600 per year), 20 research assistantships with full tuition reimbursements available (averaging $18,400 per year), 3 teaching assistantships with full tuition reimbursements available (averaging $18,400 per year); career-related internships or fieldwork, Federal Work-Study, institutionally sponsored loans, scholarships/grants, traineeships, and health care benefits also available. Financial award application deadline: 1/15; financial award applicants required to submit FAFSA. *Faculty research:* Communication, network, sensing, and information systems; control systems, automation, and robotics; discrete event, queuing, hybrid, and complex systems; optimization and algorithms; production, service, distribution, and energy systems. *Unit head:* Dr. Christos Cassandras, Division Head, 617-353-7154, Fax: 617-353-5548, E-mail: cgc@bu.edu. *Application contact:* Cheryl Kelley, Director of Graduate Programs, 617-353-9760, Fax: 617-353-0259, E-mail: enggrad@bu.edu.

California Institute of Technology, Division of Engineering and Applied Science, Option in Control and Dynamical Systems, Pasadena, CA 91125-0001. Offers MS, PhD. *Faculty:* 3 full-time (0 women). *Students:* 21 full-time (8 women). 72 applicants, 10% accepted, 3 enrolled. In 2009, 1 doctorate awarded. *Degree requirements:* For doctorate, thesis/dissertation. *Application deadline:* For fall admission, 1/15 for domestic students. Application fee: $0. *Financial support:* In 2009–10, 6 fellowships, 15 research assistantships, 4 teaching assistantships were awarded. *Faculty research:* Robustness, multivariable and nonlinear systems, optimal control, decentralized control, modeling and system identification for robust control. *Unit head:* Dr. Jerrold Marsden, Option Representative, 626-395-4176, E-mail: jmarsden@caltech.edu. *Application contact:* Natalie Gilmore, Assistant Dean of Graduate Studies, 626-395-3812, Fax: 626-577-9246, E-mail: ngilmore@caltech.edu.

California State University, Fullerton, Graduate Studies, College of Engineering and Computer Science, Department of Electrical Engineering, Fullerton, CA 92834-9480. Offers electrical engineering (MS); systems engineering (MS). Part-time programs available. *Students:* 53 full-time (9 women), 120 part-time (25 women); includes 35 minority (31 Asian Americans or Pacific Islanders, 4 Hispanic Americans), 108 international. Average age 26. 207 applicants, 63% accepted, 55 enrolled. In 2009, 51 master's awarded. *Degree requirements:* For master's, comprehensive exam, project or thesis. *Entrance requirements:* For master's, GRE General Test, GRE Subject Test, minimum undergraduate GPA of 2.5, 3.0 graduate. Application fee: $55. *Expenses:* Tuition, nonresident: full-time $11,160; part-time $373 per credit. Required fees: $1440 per term. Tuition and fees vary according to course load, degree level and program. *Financial support:* Career-related internships or fieldwork, Federal Work-Study, institutionally sponsored loans, and scholarships/grants available. Support available to part-time students. Financial award application deadline: 3/1; financial award applicants required to submit FAFSA. *Unit head:* Dr. Mostafa Shiva, Chair, 657-278-3013. *Application contact:* Admissions/Applications, 657-278-2371.

California State University, Northridge, Graduate Studies, College of Engineering and Computer Science, Department of Manufacturing Systems Engineering and Management, Northridge, CA 91330. Offers engineering automation (MS); engineering management (MS); manufacturing systems engineering (MS); materials engineering (MS). Postbaccalaureate distance learning degree programs offered. *Faculty:* 6 full-time (1 woman), 33 part-time/adjunct (12 women). *Students:* 137 full-time (18 women), 115 part-time (20 women); includes 4 African Americans, 22 Asian Americans or Pacific Islanders, 19 Hispanic Americans, 149 international. Average age 27. 210 applicants, 68% accepted, 69 enrolled. In 2009, 78 master's awarded. *Entrance requirements:* For master's, GRE (if cumulative undergraduate GPA less than 3.0). *Application deadline:* For fall admission, 3/30 for domestic students; for spring admission, 9/30 for domestic students. Application fee: $55. *Unit head:* Prof. Behzad Bavarian, Acting Chair, 818-677-2167. *Application contact:* Prof. Behzad Bavarian, Acting Chair, 818-677-2167.

Carleton University, Faculty of Graduate Studies, Faculty of Engineering and Design, Ottawa-Carleton Institute for Electrical Engineering, Department of Systems and Computer Engineering, Ottawa, ON K1S 5B6, Canada. Offers electrical engineering (MA Sc, PhD); information and systems science (M Sc); technology innovation management (M Eng, MA Sc). *Degree requirements:* For master's, thesis optional. *Entrance requirements:* For master's, honors degree. Additional exam requirements/recommendations for international students: Required—TOEFL. *Faculty research:* Design manufacturing management; network design, protocols, and performance; software engineering; wireless and satellite communications.

Carnegie Mellon University, Carnegie Institute of Technology, Information Networking Institute, Pittsburgh, PA 15213. Offers information networking (MS); information security technology and management (MS); information technology—information security (MS); information technology—mobility (MS); information technology—software management (MS). *Degree requirements:* For master's, thesis optional. *Entrance requirements:* For master's, GRE General Test, bachelor's degree in computer science, computer engineering, or electrical engineering, or related technology degree; programming skills (C/C++ fluency for some programs). Additional exam requirements/recommendations for international students: Required—TOEFL. *Faculty research:* Computer forensics and incident response; dependable systems, embedded systems, mobile systems, and sensor networks; computer and information networks, network and information security, human and socio-economic factors in secure system design; wireless sensor networks, survivable embedded systems, signal processing/compression; strategic management, international strategic management, group dynamics and decision-making structures, simulated competitive environments.

Case Western Reserve University, School of Graduate Studies, The Case School of Engineering, Department of Electrical Engineering and Computer Science, Cleveland, OH 44106. Offers computer engineering (MS, PhD); computing and information sciences (MS, PhD); electrical engineering (MS, PhD); systems and control engineering (MS, PhD). Part-time and evening/weekend programs available. Postbaccalaureate distance learning degree programs offered (minimal on-campus study). *Faculty:* 32 full-time (2 women). *Students:* 175 full-time (26 women), 28 part-time (6 women); includes 9 minority (3 African Americans, 6 Asian Americans or Pacific Islanders), 107 international. In 2009, 29 master's, 15 doctorates awarded. Terminal master's awarded for partial completion of doctoral program. *Degree requirements:* For master's, thesis; for doctorate, thesis/dissertation, qualifying exam, teaching experience. *Entrance requirements:* For master's and doctorate, GRE General Test. Additional exam requirements/recommendations for international students: Required—TOEFL. *Application deadline:* For fall admission, 2/1 for domestic students; for spring admission, 11/1 for domestic students. Applications are processed on a rolling basis. Application fee: $50. *Financial support:* Fellowships with full and partial tuition reimbursements, research assistantships with full and partial tuition reimbursements, teaching assistantships, career-related internships or fieldwork, Federal Work-Study, and institutionally sponsored loans available. Support available to part-time students. Financial award application deadline: 3/1; financial award applicants required to submit FAFSA. *Faculty research:* Applied artificial intelligence, automation, computer-aided design and testing of digital systems. Total annual research expenditures: $5.5 million. *Unit head:* Dwight Davy, Department Chair, 216-368-2802, E-mail: dtd@case.edu. *Application contact:* David Easler, Student Affairs Coordinator, 216-368-4080, Fax: 216-368-2801, E-mail: david.easler@case.edu.

The Catholic University of America, School of Engineering, Department of Civil Engineering, Washington, DC 20064. Offers environmental engineering (MCE, MSE, D Engr, PhD, Certificate); environmental engineering and management (MCE, MSE, PhD, Certificate); environmental engineering and management (D Engr); fluid and solid mechanics (MCE, MSE, PhD, Certificate); geotechnical engineering (MCE, MSE, PhD, Certificate); management of construction (MCE, MSE, D Engr, PhD); structural engineering (MSE, D Engr, PhD); systems engineering (MSE, D Engr, PhD, Certificate). Part-time programs available. *Faculty:* 5 full-time (0 women), 7 part-time/adjunct (1 woman). *Students:* 7 full-time (3 women), 18 part-time (5 women); includes 6 minority (3 African Americans, 3 Hispanic Americans), 11 international. Average age 32. 36 applicants, 47% accepted, 9 enrolled. In 2009, 8 master's, 2 doctorates awarded. *Degree requirements:* For master's, thesis optional; for doctorate, comprehensive exam, thesis/dissertation. *Entrance requirements:* For master's and doctorate, statement of purpose, official copies of academic transcripts, three letters of recommendation. Additional exam requirements/recommendations for international students: Required—TOEFL (minimum score 580 paper-based; 237 computer-based). *Application deadline:* For fall admission, 8/1 priority date for domestic students, 7/15 for international students; for spring admission, 12/1 priority date for domestic students, 10/15 for international students. Applications are processed on a rolling basis. Application fee: $55. Electronic applications accepted. *Expenses:* Contact institution. *Financial support:* Fellowships, research assistantships, teaching assistantships, Federal Work-Study, scholarships/grants, tuition waivers (full and partial), and unspecified assistantships available. Financial award application deadline: 2/1; financial award applicants required to submit FAFSA. *Faculty research:* Geotechnical engineering, solid mechanics, construction engineering and management, environmental engineering, structural engineering. Total annual research expenditures: $438,834. *Unit head:* Dr. Lu Sun, Chair, 202-319-5164, Fax: 202-319-6677, E-mail: sunl@cua.edu. *Application contact:* Julie Schwing, Director of Graduate Admissions, 202-319-5057, Fax: 202-319-6533, E-mail: cua-admissions@cua.edu.

Colorado School of Mines, Graduate School, Division of Engineering, Golden, CO 80401. Offers engineering systems (ME, MS, PhD). Part-time programs available. *Faculty:* 47 full-time (8 women), 14 part-time/adjunct (3 women). *Students:* 156 full-time (29 women), 49 part-time (10 women); includes 19 minority (3 African Americans, 9 Asian Americans or Pacific Islanders, 7 Hispanic Americans), 33 international. Average age 30. 227 applicants, 90% accepted, 85 enrolled. In 2009, 56 master's, 4 doctorates awarded. *Degree requirements:* For master's, thesis (for some programs); for doctorate, one foreign language, comprehensive exam, thesis/dissertation. *Entrance requirements:* For master's and doctorate, GRE General Test. Additional exam requirements/recommendations for international students: Required—TOEFL (minimum score 550 paper-based; 213 computer-based; 80 iBT). *Application deadline:* For fall admission, 1/15 priority date for domestic and international students; for spring admission, 9/1 priority date for domestic and international students. Application fee: $50 ($70 for international students). Electronic applications accepted. *Expenses:* Tuition, state resident: full-time $10,584; part-time $588 per credit hour. Tuition, nonresident: full-time $24,750; part-time $1375 per credit hour. Required fees: $1654; $827.10 per semester. *Financial support:* In 2009–10, 58 students received support, including 6 fellowships with full tuition reimbursements available (averaging $20,000 per year), 47 research assistantships with full tuition reimbursements available (averaging $20,000 per year), 5 teaching assistantships with full tuition reimbursements available (averaging $20,000 per year); scholarships/grants, health care benefits, and unspecified assistantships also available. Financial award application deadline: 1/15; financial award applicants required to submit FAFSA. *Faculty research:* Geotechnical engineering, offshore mechanics, analytical design, process simulation, health monitoring. Total annual research expenditures: $1.7 million. *Unit head:* Dr. Terence Parker, Division Director, 303-273-3657, Fax: 303-273-3602, E-mail: tparker@mines.edu. *Application contact:* Kathy Burris, Administrative Assistant, 303-384-2394, Fax: 303-273-3602, E-mail: kburris@mines.edu.

Colorado State University–Pueblo, College of Education, Engineering and Professional Studies, Department of Engineering, Pueblo, CO 81001-4901. Offers industrial and systems engineering (MS). *Degree requirements:* For master's, thesis optional. *Entrance requirements:* For master's, GRE General Test. Additional exam requirements/recommendations for international students: Required—TOEFL (minimum score 500 paper-based). *Faculty research:* Nanotechnology, applied operations, research transportation, decision analysis.

Colorado Technical University Colorado Springs, Graduate Studies, Program in Systems Engineering, Colorado Springs, CO 80907-3896. Offers MS.

Colorado Technical University Denver, Program in Systems Engineering, Greenwood Village, CO 80111. Offers MS.

Concordia University, School of Graduate Studies, Faculty of Engineering and Computer Science, Concordia Institute for Information Systems Engineering (CIISE), Montréal, QC H3G 1M8, Canada. Offers 3D graphics and game development (Certificate); information systems security (M Eng, MA Sc); quality systems engineering (M Eng, MA Sc); service engineering and network management (Certificate).

Cornell University, Graduate School, Graduate Fields of Engineering, Field of Systems Engineering, Ithaca, NY 14853-0001. Offers M Eng. *Faculty:* 21 full-time (2 women). *Students:* 89 full-time (14 women); includes 21 minority (3 African Americans, 13 Asian Americans or Pacific Islanders, 5 Hispanic Americans), 5 international. Average age 27. 54 applicants, 83% accepted, 33 enrolled. In 2009, 38 master's awarded. *Degree requirements:* For master's, thesis. *Entrance requirements:* For master's, GRE General Test. Additional exam requirements/recommendations for international students: Required—TOEFL (minimum score 600 paper-based; 250 computer-based; 77 iBT). *Application deadline:* For fall admission, 2/1 priority date for domestic students. Application fee: $70. *Expenses:* Tuition: Full-time $29,500. Required fees: $70. Full-time tuition and fees vary according to degree level, program and student level. *Financial support:* Fellowships with full and partial tuition reimbursements, research assistantships with full and partial tuition reimbursements, teaching assistantships with full and partial tuition reimbursements, institutionally sponsored loans, scholarships/grants, health care benefits, tuition waivers (full and partial), and unspecified assistantships available. Financial award applicants required to submit FAFSA. *Faculty research:* Space systems, systems engineering of mechanical and aerospace systems, multi-echelon inventory theory, math modeling of complex systems, chain supply integration. *Unit head:* Director of Graduate Studies, 607-255-8998, Fax: 607-255-9004, E-mail: systemseng@cornell.edu. *Application contact:* Graduate Field Assistant, 607-255-8998, Fax: 607-255-9004, E-mail: systemseng@cornell.edu.

Systems Engineering

Embry-Riddle Aeronautical University, Daytona Beach Campus Graduate Program, Department of Human Factors and Systems, Daytona Beach, FL 32114-3900. Offers human factors engineering (MSHFS); systems engineering (MSHFS). Part-time and evening/weekend programs available. *Faculty:* 5 full-time (2 women). *Students:* 35 full-time (18 women), 13 part-time (7 women); includes 8 minority (3 African Americans, 5 Hispanic Americans). Average age 25. 25 applicants, 68% accepted, 14 enrolled. In 2009, 5 master's awarded. *Degree requirements:* For master's, thesis, practicum, qualifying oral exam. *Entrance requirements:* For master's, minimum GPA of 2.5. Additional exam requirements/recommendations for international students: Required—TOEFL (minimum score 550 paper-based; 213 computer-based; 79 iBT). *Application deadline:* For fall admission, 8/1 priority date for domestic students; for spring admission, 12/1 priority date for domestic students. Applications are processed on a rolling basis. Application fee: $50. *Expenses:* Tuition: Full-time $13,740; part-time $1145 per credit hour. *Financial support:* In 2009–10, 21 students received support, including 3 research assistantships with full and partial tuition reimbursements available (averaging $5,400 per year); teaching assistantships with full and partial tuition reimbursements available, career-related internships or fieldwork and unspecified assistantships also available. Financial award application deadline: 4/15; financial award applicants required to submit FAFSA. *Unit head:* Dr. Shawn Doherty, Program Coordinator, 386-226-6249, Fax: 386-226-7050, E-mail: dohertsh@erau.edu. *Application contact:* Keith Deaton, Director, International and Graduate Admissions, 800-388-3728, Fax: 386-226-7070, E-mail: graduate.admissions@erau.edu.

Florida Institute of Technology, Graduate Programs, College of Engineering, Engineering Systems Department, Melbourne, FL 32901-6975. Offers engineering management (MS); systems engineering (MS). Part-time and evening/weekend programs available. *Faculty:* 4 full-time (0 women), 2 part-time/adjunct (0 women). *Students:* 14 full-time (2 women), 129 part-time (31 women); includes 21 minority (7 African Americans, 6 Asian Americans or Pacific Islanders, 8 Hispanic Americans), 16 international. Average age 36. 103 applicants, 69% accepted, 24 enrolled. In 2009, 108 master's awarded. *Degree requirements:* For master's, comprehensive exam (for some programs), thesis optional, portfolio of competencies and summary of career relevance. *Entrance requirements:* For master's, GRE General Test (if GPA less than 3.0), BS in engineering, minimum GPA of 3.0, 2 letters of recommendation, resume, bachelor's degree from ABET-accredited program. Additional exam requirements/recommendations for international students: Required—TOEFL (minimum score 550 paper-based; 213 computer-based; 79 iBT). *Application deadline:* For fall admission, 4/1 for international students; for spring admission, 9/30 for international students. Applications are processed on a rolling basis. Application fee: $50. Electronic applications accepted. *Expenses:* Tuition: Part-time $1015 per credit. Tuition and fees vary according to campus/location and program. *Financial support:* In 2009–10, 1 student received support, including 1 research assistantship with full and partial tuition reimbursement available (averaging $5,000 per year); career-related internships or fieldwork, institutionally sponsored loans, unspecified assistantships, and tuition remissions also available. Support available to part-time students. Financial award application deadline: 3/1; financial award applicants required to submit FAFSA. *Faculty research:* System/software engineering, simulation and analytical modeling, project management, multimedia tools, quality. *Unit head:* Dr. Muzaffar A. Shaikh, Department Head, 321-674-7345, Fax: 321-674-7136, E-mail: mshaikh@fit.edu. *Application contact:* Thomas M. Shea, Director of Graduate Admissions, 321-674-7577, Fax: 321-723-9468, E-mail: tshea@fit.edu.

See Close-Up on page 467.

George Mason University, Volgenau School of Information Technology and Engineering, Department of Civil, Environmental, and Infrastructure Engineering, Fairfax, VA 22030. Offers civil and infrastructure engineering (MS, PhD); civil infrastructure and security engineering (Certificate); leading technical enterprises (Certificate); sustainability and the environment (Certificate); water resources engineering (Certificate). Part-time and evening/weekend programs available. *Faculty:* 9 full-time (3 women), 15 part-time/adjunct (0 women). *Students:* 19 full-time (3 women), 61 part-time (18 women); includes 16 minority (5 African Americans, 7 Asian Americans or Pacific Islanders, 4 Hispanic Americans), 8 international. Average age 33. 102 applicants, 58% accepted, 43 enrolled. In 2009, 13 master's, 2 other advanced degrees awarded. *Degree requirements:* For master's, thesis (for some programs), 30 credits, departmental seminars; for doctorate, thesis/dissertation, qualifying exams. *Entrance requirements:* For master's, GRE or GMAT. Additional exam requirements/recommendations for international students: Required—TOEFL (minimum score 575 paper-based; 230 computer-based; 88 iBT). *Application deadline:* For fall admission, 3/15 priority date for domestic students, 3/15 for international students; for spring admission, 11/1 for domestic students, 10/1 for international students. Application fee: $75. Electronic applications accepted. *Expenses:* Tuition, state resident: full-time $7568; part-time $315.33 per credit hour. Tuition, nonresident: full-time $21,704; part-time $904.33 per credit hour. Required fees: $2184; $91 per credit hour. *Financial support:* In 2009–10, 12 students received support, including 2 research assistantships with full and partial tuition reimbursements available (averaging $15,000 per year), 10 teaching assistantships with full and partial tuition reimbursements available (averaging $4,557 per year); career-related internships or fieldwork, scholarships/grants, unspecified assistantships, and health care benefits (full-time research or teaching assistantship recipients) also available. Support available to part-time students. Financial award application deadline: 3/1; financial award applicants required to submit FAFSA. *Faculty research:* Evolutionary design, infrastructure security, intelligent transportation systems, national transportation networks, water quality modeling. Total annual research expenditures: $67,461. *Unit head:* Dr. Michael Bronzini, Chair, 703-993-1504, Fax: 703-993-1521. *Application contact:* Lisa Nolder, Graduate Student Services Director, 703-993-1499, E-mail: snolder@gmu.edu.

George Mason University, Volgenau School of Information Technology and Engineering, Department of Computer Science, Fairfax, VA 22030. Offers biometrics (Certificate); computer games technology (Certificate); computer networking (Certificate); computer science (MS, PhD); data mining (Certificate); database management (Certificate); electronic commerce (Certificate); foundations of information systems (Certificate); information engineering (Certificate); information security and assurance (MS, Certificate); information systems (MS); intelligent agents (Certificate); software architecture (Certificate); software engineering (MS, Certificate); systems engineering (MS); Web-based software engineering (Certificate). Part-time and evening/weekend programs available. Postbaccalaureate distance learning degree programs offered. *Faculty:* 42 full-time (9 women), 18 part-time/adjunct (0 women). *Students:* 121 full-time (36 women), 489 part-time (118 women); includes 90 minority (11 African Americans, 70 Asian Americans or Pacific Islanders, 9 Hispanic Americans), 222 international. Average age 29. 882 applicants, 58% accepted, 147 enrolled. In 2009, 202 master's, 6 doctorates, 21 other advanced degrees awarded. *Degree requirements:* For master's, thesis optional; for doctorate, comprehensive exam, thesis/dissertation. *Entrance requirements:* For master's, GRE General Test, minimum GPA of 3.0 in last 60 hours, 3 letters of recommendation; for doctorate, GRE, 4-year BA degree, academic work in computer science, 3 letters of recommendation, statement of career goals and aspirations. Additional exam requirements/recommendations for international students: Required—TOEFL. *Application deadline:* For fall admission, 4/15 priority date for domestic students, 1/15 for international students; for spring admission, 11/15 for domestic students. Application fee: $75. Electronic applications accepted. *Expenses:* Tuition, state resident: full-time $7568; part-time $315.33 per credit hour. Tuition, nonresident: full-time $21,704; part-time $904.33 per credit hour. Required fees: $2184; $91 per credit hour. *Financial support:* In 2009–10, 106 students received support, including 3 fellowships (averaging $18,000 per year), 53 research assistantships (averaging $11,119 per year), 53 teaching assistantships (averaging $7,881 per year); unspecified assistantships and health care benefits (full-time research or teaching assistantship recipients) also available. Financial award application deadline: 3/1; financial award applicants required to submit FAFSA. *Faculty research:* Artificial intelligence, image processing/graphics, parallel/distributed systems, software engineering systems. Total annual research expenditures: $1.3 million. *Unit head:* Dr. Arun Sood, Director, 703-993-1524, Fax: 703-993-1710, E-mail: asood@gmu.edu. *Application contact:* Jay Shapiro, Professor, 703-993-1485, E-mail: jshapiro@gmu.edu.

George Mason University, Volgenau School of Information Technology and Engineering, Department of Systems Engineering and Operations Research, Fairfax, VA 22030. Offers

architecture-based systems integration (Certificate); command, control, communication, computing and intelligence (Certificate); computational modeling (Certificate); discovery, design and innovation (Certificate); military operations research (Certificate); operations research (MS); systems engineering (MS); systems engineering analysis and architecture (Certificate); systems engineering and operations research (PhD); systems engineering of software intensive systems (Certificate). Part-time and evening/weekend programs available. *Faculty:* 17 full-time (4 women), 12 part-time/adjunct (5 women). *Students:* 23 full-time (3 women), 191 part-time (43 women); includes 42 minority (11 African Americans, 2 American Indian/Alaska Native, 17 Asian Americans or Pacific Islanders, 12 Hispanic Americans), 13 international. Average age 37. 156 applicants, 68% accepted, 55 enrolled. In 2009, 41 master's, 1 doctorate, 8 other advanced degrees awarded. *Degree requirements:* For master's, thesis optional; for doctorate, comprehensive exam, thesis/dissertation, qualifying exams. *Entrance requirements:* For master's, GRE General Test, 3 letters of recommendation, resume; for doctorate, GRE, undergraduate and graduate transcripts, 3 letters of reference, resume, statement of career goals and aspirations, self assessment of background. Additional exam requirements/recommendations for international students: Required—TOEFL. *Application deadline:* For fall admission, 3/15 priority date for domestic students, 2/15 priority date for international students; for spring admission, 10/1 for domestic and international students. Application fee: $75. Electronic applications accepted. *Expenses:* Tuition, state resident: full-time $7568; part-time $315.33 per credit hour. Tuition, nonresident: full-time $21,704; part-time $904.33 per credit hour. Required fees: $2184; $91 per credit hour. *Financial support:* In 2009–10, 8 students received support, including 5 research assistantships with full and partial tuition reimbursements available (averaging $9,113 per year), 3 teaching assistantships with full and partial tuition reimbursements available (averaging $10,997 per year); career-related internships or fieldwork, Federal Work-Study, scholarships/grants, unspecified assistantships, and health care benefits (full-time research or teaching assistantship recipients) also available. Support available to part-time students. Financial award application deadline: 3/1; financial award applicants required to submit FAFSA. *Faculty research:* Requirements engineering, signal processing, systems architecture, data fusion. Total annual research expenditures: $1.1 million. *Unit head:* Dr. Ariela Sofer, Chairman, 703-993-1692, Fax: 703-993-1521, E-mail: asofer@gmu.edu. *Application contact:* Dr. K. C. Chang, Graduate Coordinator, 703-993-1639, E-mail: kchang@gmu.edu.

The George Washington University, School of Engineering and Applied Science, Department of Engineering Management and Systems Engineering, Washington, DC 20052. Offers MS, D Sc, App Sc, Engr, Graduate Certificate. Part-time and evening/weekend programs available. *Faculty:* 17 full-time (1 woman), 18 part-time/adjunct (2 women). *Students:* 116 full-time (28 women), 1,181 part-time (290 women); includes 348 minority (152 African Americans, 7 American Indian/Alaska Native, 128 Asian Americans or Pacific Islanders, 61 Hispanic Americans), 121 international. Average age 35. 574 applicants, 93% accepted, 333 enrolled. In 2009, 431 master's, 26 doctorates, 321 other advanced degrees awarded. *Degree requirements:* For master's, thesis optional; for doctorate, one foreign language, thesis/dissertation, final and qualifying exams, submission of articles; for other advanced degree, professional project. *Entrance requirements:* For master's, appropriate bachelor's degree, minimum GPA of 2.7, second semester calculus; for doctorate, appropriate master's degree, minimum GPA of 3.5, 2 letters of recommendation; for other advanced degree, appropriate master's degree, minimum GPA of 3.4. Additional exam requirements/recommendations for international students: Required—TOEFL or George Washington University English as a Foreign Language Test. *Application deadline:* For fall admission, 3/1 for domestic students; for spring admission, 10/1 for domestic students. Applications are processed on a rolling basis. Application fee: $60. *Financial support:* In 2009–10, 35 students received support; fellowships with tuition reimbursements available, research assistantships, teaching assistantships with tuition reimbursements available, career-related internships or fieldwork and institutionally sponsored loans available. Financial award application deadline: 3/1; financial award applicants required to submit FAFSA. *Faculty research:* Artificial intelligence and expert systems, human factors engineering and systems analysis. Total annual research expenditures: $421,800. *Unit head:* Dr. Thomas Mazzuchi, Chair, 202-994-7424, Fax: 202-994-0245, E-mail: mazzu@gwu.edu. *Application contact:* Adina Lav, Marketing, Recruiting and Admissions, 202-994-5827, Fax: 202-994-0909, E-mail: engineering@gwu.edu.

Georgia Institute of Technology, Graduate Studies and Research, College of Engineering, School of Industrial and Systems Engineering, Program in Industrial and Systems Engineering, Atlanta, GA 30332-0001. Offers algorithms, combinatorics, and optimization (PhD); industrial and systems engineering (PhD); industrial engineering (MS, MSIE); statistics (MS Stat). Part-time programs available. Terminal master's awarded for partial completion of doctoral program. *Degree requirements:* For master's, thesis optional; for doctorate, thesis/dissertation. *Entrance requirements:* For master's and doctorate, GRE General Test, minimum GPA of 3.0. Additional exam requirements/recommendations for international students: Required—TOEFL. Electronic applications accepted. *Faculty research:* Computer-integrated manufacturing systems, materials handling systems, production and distribution.

Harrisburg University of Science and Technology, Program in Information Systems Engineering and Management, Harrisburg, PA 17101. Offers digital government specialization (MS); digital health specialization (MS); entrepreneurship specialization (MS). Part-time programs available. *Faculty:* 1 full-time (0 women), 2 part-time/adjunct (0 women). *Degree requirements:* For master's, comprehensive exam, thesis optional. *Entrance requirements:* Additional exam requirements/recommendations for international students: Required—TOEFL (minimum score 520 paper-based; 200 computer-based; 80 iBT). *Application deadline:* For fall admission, 8/1 priority date for domestic students, 7/1 priority date for international students. Applications are processed on a rolling basis. Application fee: $0. Electronic applications accepted. *Expenses:* Tuition: Full-time $18,000; part-time $650 per semester hour. *Financial support:* Scholarships/grants available. Financial award applicants required to submit FAFSA. *Unit head:* Dr. Amjad Umar, Director and Professor, 717-901-5141, Fax: 717-901-3141, E-mail: aumar@harrisburgu.edu. *Application contact:* Julie Cullings, Information Contact, 717-901-5163, Fax: 717-901-3163, E-mail: admissions@harrisburgu.edu.

Indiana University–Purdue University Fort Wayne, College of Engineering, Technology, and Computer Science, Department of Engineering, Fort Wayne, IN 46805-1499. Offers computer engineering (MS); electrical engineering (MS); mechanical engineering (MS); systems engineering (MS). Part-time programs available. *Faculty:* 15 full-time (3 women). *Students:* 4 full-time (0 women), 29 part-time (5 women); includes 2 minority (1 African American, 1 Asian American or Pacific Islander), 5 international. Average age 29. 13 applicants, 92% accepted, 7 enrolled. In 2009, 1 master's awarded. *Entrance requirements:* For master's, minimum GPA of 3.0. Additional exam requirements/recommendations for international students: Required—TOEFL (minimum score 550 paper-based; 213 computer-based; 77 iBT); Recommended—TWE. *Application deadline:* For fall admission, 7/15 priority date for domestic students, 3/1 priority date for international students; for spring admission, 12/1 priority date for domestic students, 9/1 priority date for international students. Applications are processed on a rolling basis. Application fee: $55 ($60 for international students). Electronic applications accepted. *Expenses:* Tuition, state resident: full-time $4595; part-time $255 per credit. Tuition, nonresident: full-time $10,963; part-time $609 per credit. Required fees: $528; $29.35 per credit. Tuition and fees vary according to course load. *Financial support:* In 2009–10, 1 research assistantship with partial tuition reimbursement (averaging $12,740 per year), 3 teaching assistantships with partial tuition reimbursements (averaging $12,740 per year) were awarded. Financial award application deadline: 3/1; financial award applicants required to submit FAFSA. *Faculty research:* Synthesis technique, Markov parameters. Total annual research expenditures: $57,918. *Unit head:* Dr. Donald Mueller, Chair, 260-481-5707, Fax: 260-481-6281, E-mail: mueller@engr.ipfw.edu. *Application contact:* Dr. Donald Mueller, Chair, 260-481-5707, Fax: 260-481-6281, E-mail: mueller@engr.ipfw.edu.

Instituto Tecnológico y de Estudios Superiores de Monterrey, Campus Chihuahua, Graduate Programs, Chihuahua, Mexico. Offers computer systems engineering (Ingeniero); electrical engineering (Ingeniero); electromechanical engineering (Ingeniero); electronic engineering (Ingeniero); engineering administration (MEA); industrial engineering (MIE, Ingeniero); international trade (MIT); mechanical engineering (Ingeniero).

Instituto Tecnológico y de Estudios Superiores de Monterrey, Campus Monterrey, Graduate and Research Division, Programs in Engineering, Monterrey, Mexico. Offers applied statistics (M Eng); artificial intelligence (PhD); automation engineering (M Eng); chemical engineering (M Eng); civil engineering (M Eng); electrical engineering (M Eng); electronic engineering (M Eng); environmental engineering (M Eng); industrial engineering (M Eng, PhD); manufacturing engineering (M Eng); mechanical engineering (M Eng); systems and quality engineering (M Eng). Part-time and evening/weekend programs available. Terminal master's awarded for partial completion of doctoral program. *Degree requirements:* For master's, one foreign language, thesis; for doctorate, one foreign language, thesis/dissertation. *Entrance requirements:* For master's, EXADEP; for doctorate, GRE, master's degree in related field. Additional exam requirements/recommendations for international students: Required—TOEFL. *Faculty research:* Flexible manufacturing cells, materials, statistical methods, environmental prevention, control and evaluation.

Iowa State University of Science and Technology, Graduate College, College of Engineering, Program in Systems Engineering, Ames, IA 50011. Offers M Eng. *Students:* 40 part-time (10 women); includes 9 minority (5 African Americans, 2 Asian Americans or Pacific Islanders, 2 Hispanic Americans), 3 international. 26 applicants, 77% accepted, 18 enrolled. In 2009, 65 master's awarded. *Entrance requirements:* Additional exam requirements/recommendations for international students: Required—TOEFL (minimum score 550 paper-based; 79 iBT) or IELTS (minimum score 6.5). *Application deadline:* Applications are processed on a rolling basis. Application fee: $40 ($90 for international students). Electronic applications accepted. *Expenses:* Tuition, state resident: full-time $6716. Tuition, nonresident: full-time $8908. Tuition and fees vary according to course level, course load, program and student level. *Financial support:* Research assistantships with full and partial tuition reimbursements, teaching assistantships with full and partial tuition reimbursements, scholarships/grants, health care benefits, and unspecified assistantships available. *Unit head:* Dr. Douglas D. Gemmill, Supervisory Committee Chair, 515-294-8731, Fax: 515-294-3524, E-mail: syseng@iastate.edu. *Application contact:* Dr. Douglas D. Gemmill, Supervisory Committee Chair, 515-294-8731, Fax: 515-294-3524, E-mail: syseng@iastate.edu.

The Johns Hopkins University, Engineering for Professionals, Part-time Program in Systems Engineering, Baltimore, MD 21218-2699. Offers MS, Graduate Certificate, Post-Master's Certificate. Part-time and evening/weekend programs available. Postbaccalaureate distance learning degree programs offered (no on-campus study). *Faculty:* 33 part-time/adjunct (3 women). *Students:* 2 full-time (0 women), 420 part-time (97 women); includes 132 minority (54 African Americans, 1 American Indian/Alaska Native, 58 Asian Americans or Pacific Islanders, 19 Hispanic Americans), 4 international. Average age 34. In 2009, 134 master's, 3 other advanced degrees awarded. *Application deadline:* Applications are processed on a rolling basis. Application fee: $75. Electronic applications accepted. *Unit head:* Dr. Ronald R. Luman, Program Chair, 443-778-5239, E-mail: ronald.luman@jhuapl.edu. *Application contact:* Priyanka Dwivedi, Admissions Manager, 410-516-2300, Fax: 410-579-8049, E-mail: pdwived1@jhu.edu.

Lehigh University, P.C. Rossin College of Engineering and Applied Science, Department of Industrial and Systems Engineering, Bethlehem, PA 18015. Offers analytical finance (MS); industrial engineering (M Eng, MS, PhD); information and systems engineering (M Eng, MS); management science (MS); quality engineering (MS); MBA/E. Part-time programs available. Postbaccalaureate distance learning degree programs offered (no on-campus study). *Faculty:* 12 full-time (1 woman), 1 part-time/adjunct (0 women). *Students:* 60 full-time (25 women), 20 part-time (5 women); includes 3 minority (all Asian Americans or Pacific Islanders), 51 international. Average age 28. 445 applicants, 9% accepted, 24 enrolled. In 2009, 26 master's, 8 doctorates awarded. *Degree requirements:* For master's, thesis (MS); project (M Eng); for doctorate, comprehensive exam, thesis/dissertation. *Entrance requirements:* For master's and doctorate, GRE General Test. Additional exam requirements/recommendations for international students: Required—TOEFL (minimum score 550 paper-based; 213 computer-based; 79 iBT). *Application deadline:* For fall admission, 7/15 for domestic and international students; for spring admission, 12/1 for domestic and international students. Applications are processed on a rolling basis. Application fee: $75. Electronic applications accepted. *Financial support:* In 2009–10, 26 students received support, including 9 fellowships with full tuition reimbursements available (averaging $19,265 per year), 10 research assistantships with full tuition reimbursements available (averaging $14,700 per year), 5 teaching assistantships with full tuition reimbursements available (averaging $16,020 per year); career-related internships or fieldwork, Federal Work-Study, institutionally sponsored loans, scholarships/grants, tuition waivers, and unspecified assistantships also available. Financial award application deadline: 1/15. *Faculty research:* Optimization, mathematical programming, logistics and supply chain, stochastic processes, large-scale computing, financial engineering. Total annual research expenditures: $2.1 million. *Unit head:* Dr. Tamas Terlaky, Chair, 610-758-4050, Fax: 610-758-4886, E-mail: terlaky@lehigh.edu. *Application contact:* Rita R. Frey, Graduate Coordinator, 610-758-4051, Fax: 610-758-4886, E-mail: ise@lehigh.edu.

Lehigh University, P.C. Rossin College of Engineering and Applied Science, Program in Manufacturing Systems Engineering, Bethlehem, PA 18015. Offers MS, MBA/E. Part-time and evening/weekend programs available. Postbaccalaureate distance learning degree programs offered (no on-campus study). *Students:* 2 full-time (0 women), 30 part-time (6 women); includes 3 minority (1 African American, 2 Asian Americans or Pacific Islanders), 1 international. Average age 33. 68 applicants, 19% accepted, 9 enrolled. In 2009, 6 master's awarded. *Degree requirements:* For master's, comprehensive exam, project or thesis. *Entrance requirements:* For master's, GRE General Test, minimum GPA of 2.75. Additional exam requirements/recommendations for international students: Required—TOEFL (minimum score 620 paper-based; 260 computer-based; 85 iBT). *Application deadline:* For fall admission, 7/15 for domestic and international students; for spring admission, 12/1 for domestic and international students. Applications are processed on a rolling basis. Application fee: $65. Electronic applications accepted. *Faculty research:* Manufacturing systems design, development, and implementation; accounting and management; agile/lean systems; supply chain issues; sustainable systems design; product design. *Unit head:* Dr. Keith M. Gardiner, Director, 610-758-5070, Fax: 610-758-6527, E-mail: kg03@lehigh.edu. *Application contact:* Carolyn C. Jones, Graduate Coordinator, 610-758-5157, Fax: 610-758-6527, E-mail: ccj1@lehigh.edu.

Loyola Marymount University, College of Business Administration, MBA/MS Program in Systems Engineering, Los Angeles, CA 90045. Offers MBA/MS. Part-time programs available. *Faculty:* 56 full-time (15 women), 11 part-time/adjunct (1 woman). *Students:* 12 full-time (6 women), 4 part-time (1 woman); includes 3 Asian Americans or Pacific Islanders, 4 Hispanic Americans. Average age 29. 6 applicants, 67% accepted, 3 enrolled. *Entrance requirements:* Additional exam requirements/recommendations for international students: Required—TOEFL (minimum score 600 paper-based; 250 computer-based; 100 iBT). *Application deadline:* For fall admission, 7/15 for domestic students; for spring admission, 12/15 for domestic students. Application fee: $50. Electronic applications accepted. *Expenses:* Contact institution. *Financial support:* In 2009–10, 2 students received support. Career-related internships or fieldwork, institutionally sponsored loans, scholarships/grants, and unspecified assistantships available. Financial award application deadline: 7/15; financial award applicants required to submit FAFSA. *Unit head:* Dr. Donald Draper, Dean, 310-338-7504, Fax: 310-338-2899, E-mail: ddraper@lmu.edu. *Application contact:* Dr. Rachelle Katz, Associate Dean and Director of MBA Program, 310-338-2848, E-mail: rkatz@lmu.edu.

Loyola Marymount University, College of Science and Engineering, Department of Systems Engineering and Engineering Management, Program in System Engineering Leadership, Los Angeles, CA 90045-2659. Offers MS, MS/MBA. *Faculty:* 1 full-time (0 women), 5 part-time/adjunct (1 woman). *Students:* 12 full-time (6 women), 4 part-time (1 woman); includes 7 minority (3 Asian Americans or Pacific Islanders, 4 Hispanic Americans). Average age 29. 6 applicants, 67% accepted, 3 enrolled. In 2009, 5 master's awarded. *Degree requirements:* For master's, thesis. *Entrance requirements:* For master's, GMAT, letters of recommendation. Additional exam requirements/recommendations for international students: Required—TOEFL (minimum score 550 paper-based; 213 computer-based; 80 iBT). *Application deadline:* For fall admission, 7/15 for domestic students; for spring admission, 12/15 for domestic students. Applications are processed on a rolling basis. Application fee: $50. Electronic applications accepted. *Financial support:* In 2009–10, 2 students received support. Scholarships/grants and unspecified assistantships available. Support available to part-time students. Financial award application deadline: 6/1; financial award applicants required to submit FAFSA. *Unit head:* Dr. Bohdan W. Oppenheim, Program Director, 310-338-2825, Fax: 310-338-6028, E-mail: boppenheim@lmu.edu. *Application contact:* Chake Kouyoumjian, Associate Dean for Graduate Studies, 310-338-2721, Fax: 310-338-6086, E-mail: chake.kouyoumjian@lmu.edu.

Loyola Marymount University, College of Science and Engineering, Department of Systems Engineering and Engineering Management, Program in Systems Engineering, Los Angeles, CA 90045. Offers MS. *Faculty:* 1 full-time (0 women), 5 part-time/adjunct (1 woman). *Students:* 17 full-time (6 women), 12 part-time (3 women); includes 5 African Americans, 8 Asian Americans or Pacific Islanders, 3 Hispanic Americans, 3 international. Average age 31. 22 applicants, 86% accepted, 13 enrolled. In 2009, 10 master's awarded. *Entrance requirements:* For master's, Personal Statement, Resume, Letters of Recommendation. Additional exam requirements/recommendations for international students: Required—TOEFL (minimum score 550 paper-based; 213 computer-based; 80 iBT). *Application deadline:* For fall admission, 4/15 for domestic students; for spring admission, 12/15 for domestic students. Application fee: $50. Electronic applications accepted. *Financial support:* In 2009–10, 5 students received support. Scholarships/grants and unspecified assistantships available. Support available to part-time students. Financial award applicants required to submit FAFSA. Total annual research expenditures: $78,981. *Unit head:* Dr. Fred Brown, Program Director, 310-338-7878, Fax: 310-338-5249, E-mail: fbrown@lmu.edu. *Application contact:* Chake Kouyoumjian, Associate Dean of Graduate Studies, 310-338-2721, Fax: 310-338-6086, E-mail: graduate@lmu.edu.

Massachusetts Institute of Technology, School of Engineering, Engineering Systems Division, Cambridge, MA 02139-4307. Offers engineering and management (SM); engineering systems (SM, PhD); logistics (M Eng); technology and policy (SM); technology, management and policy (PhD); SM/MBA. *Faculty:* 8 full-time (0 women). *Students:* 285 full-time (72 women), 1 part-time (0 women); includes 36 minority (8 African Americans, 19 Asian Americans or Pacific Islanders, 9 Hispanic Americans), 116 international. Average age 31. 874 applicants, 28% accepted, 188 enrolled. In 2009, 143 master's, 11 doctorates awarded. *Degree requirements:* For master's, thesis; for doctorate, comprehensive exam, thesis/dissertation. *Entrance requirements:* For master's and doctorate, GRE General Test or GMAT (for some programs). Additional exam requirements/recommendations for international students: Required—IELTS (minimum score 7.5); Recommended—TOEFL (minimum score 610 paper-based; 255 computer-based; 103 iBT). Application fee: $75. *Expenses:* Contact institution. *Financial support:* In 2009–10, 224 students received support, including 41 fellowships with tuition reimbursements available (averaging $26,522 per year), 95 research assistantships with tuition reimbursements available (averaging $26,506 per year), 17 teaching assistantships with tuition reimbursements available (averaging $21,300 per year); career-related internships or fieldwork, Federal Work-Study, institutionally sponsored loans, scholarships/grants, health care benefits, and unspecified assistantships also available. *Faculty research:* Critical infrastructures, extended enterprises, energy and sustainability, health care delivery, humans and technology, uncertainty and dynamics, design and implementation, networks and flows, policy and standards. Total annual research expenditures: $10.7 million. *Unit head:* Prof. Yossi Sheffi, Director, 617-253-1764, E-mail: esdinquiries@mit.edu. *Application contact:* Graduate Admissions, 617-253-1182, E-mail: esdgrad@mit.edu.

Mississippi State University, Bagley College of Engineering, Department of Industrial and Systems Engineering, MS State, MS 39762. Offers engineering (PhD), including industrial engineering; industrial engineering (MS). Part-time programs available. Postbaccalaureate distance learning degree programs offered (no on-campus study). *Faculty:* 9 full-time (3 women), 1 part-time/adjunct (0 women). *Students:* 50 full-time (16 women), 48 part-time (5 women); includes 18 minority (11 African Americans, 6 Asian Americans or Pacific Islanders, 1 Hispanic American), 37 international. Average age 33. 71 applicants, 44% accepted, 21 enrolled. In 2009, 11 master's, 3 doctorates awarded. *Degree requirements:* For master's, comprehensive exam (for some programs), thesis (for some programs), comprehensive oral or written exam; for doctorate, thesis/dissertation, candidacy exam. *Entrance requirements:* For master's, GRE General Test, minimum GPA of 3.0; for doctorate, GRE General Test, minimum GPA of 3.3. Additional exam requirements/recommendations for international students: Required—TOEFL (minimum score 550 paper-based; 213 computer-based; 79 iBT); Recommended—IELTS (minimum score 6.5). *Application deadline:* For fall admission, 7/1 for domestic students, 5/1 for international students; for spring admission, 11/1 for domestic students, 9/1 for international students. Applications are processed on a rolling basis. Application fee: $40. *Expenses:* Tuition, state resident: full-time $2575.50; part-time $286.25 per credit hour. Tuition, nonresident: full-time $6510; part-time $723.50 per credit hour. Tuition and fees vary according to course load. *Financial support:* In 2009–10, 25 research assistantships with full tuition reimbursements (averaging $11,579 per year), 4 teaching assistantships with full tuition reimbursements (averaging $8,632 per year) were awarded; Federal Work-Study, institutionally sponsored loans, and unspecified assistantships also available. Financial award application deadline: 4/1; financial award applicants required to submit FAFSA. *Faculty research:* Operations research, ergonomics, production systems, management systems, transportation. *Unit head:* Dr. Royce Bowden, Professor and Head, 662-325-3865, Fax: 662-325-7618, E-mail: bowden@ise.msstate.edu. *Application contact:* Dr. John Usher, Professor, 662-325-7624, Fax: 662-325-7618, E-mail: usher@ise.msstate.edu.

Missouri University of Science and Technology, Graduate School, Department of Engineering Management and Systems Engineering, Rolla, MO 65409. Offers engineering management (MS, DE, PhD); manufacturing engineering (M Eng, MS); systems engineering (MS, PhD). *Degree requirements:* For master's, thesis optional; for doctorate, comprehensive exam. *Entrance requirements:* For master's, GRE (minimum score 1150 verbal and quantitative, 4.5 writing); for doctorate, GRE (minimum score: 1100 verbal and quantitative, 3.5 writing). Additional exam requirements/recommendations for international students: Required—TOEFL (minimum score 580 paper-based; 213 computer-based). *Faculty research:* Management of technology, industrial engineering, manufacturing engineering, packaging engineering, quality engineering.

National University, Academic Affairs, School of Engineering and Technology, Department of Applied Engineering, La Jolla, CA 92037-1011. Offers database administration (MS); engineering management (MS); environmental engineering (MS); homeland security and safety engineering (MS); system engineering (MS); wireless communications (MS). Part-time and evening/weekend programs available. Postbaccalaureate distance learning degree programs offered (no on-campus study). *Faculty:* 6 full-time (1 woman), 7 part-time/adjunct (1 woman). *Students:* 61 full-time (16 women), 176 part-time (35 women); includes 54 minority (11 African Americans, 1 American Indian/Alaska Native, 23 Asian Americans or Pacific Islanders, 19 Hispanic Americans), 117 international. Average age 31. 133 applicants, 100% accepted, 83 enrolled. In 2009, 34 master's awarded. *Degree requirements:* For master's, thesis. *Entrance requirements:* For master's, interview, minimum GPA of 2.5. Additional exam requirements/recommendations for international students: Required—TOEFL (minimum score 550 paper-based; 213 computer-based; 79 iBT), IELTS (minimum score 6). *Application deadline:* Applications are processed on a rolling basis. Application fee: $60 ($65 for international students). Electronic applications accepted. *Expenses:* Tuition: Part-time $338 per quarter hour. *Financial support:* Career-related internships or fieldwork, institutionally sponsored loans, scholarships/grants, and tuition waivers (partial) available. Support available to part-time students. Financial award application deadline: 6/30; financial award applicants required to submit FAFSA. *Unit head:* Dr. Shekar Viswanathan, Chair and Associate Professor, 858-309-8416, Fax: 858-309-3420, E-mail: sviswana@nu.edu. *Application contact:* Dominick Giovanniello, Associate Regional Dean—San Diego, 800-NAT-UNIV, Fax: 858-541-7792, E-mail: dgiovann@nu.edu.

Systems Engineering

Naval Postgraduate School, Graduate Programs, Department of Systems Engineering, Monterey, CA 93943. Offers systems engineering (MS, PhD, Certificate); systems engineering and analysis (MS); systems engineering management (MS). Program only open to commissioned officers of the United States and friendly nations and selected United States federal civilian employees. Part-time programs available. *Degree requirements:* For master's, thesis.

North Carolina Agricultural and Technical State University, Graduate School, College of Engineering, Department of Industrial and Systems Engineering, Greensboro, NC 27411. Offers industrial engineering (MSIE, PhD). Part-time programs available. *Degree requirements:* For master's, thesis, project; for doctorate, thesis/dissertation. *Entrance requirements:* For master's, GRE General Test (recommended); for doctorate, GRE General Test. *Faculty research:* Human-machine systems engineering, management systems engineering, operations research and systems analysis, production systems engineering.

Oakland University, Graduate Study and Lifelong Learning, School of Engineering and Computer Science, Department of Computer Science and Engineering, Rochester, MI 48309-4401. Offers computer science (MS); embedded systems (MS); information systems engineering (MS); software engineering (MS). Part-time and evening/weekend programs available. *Entrance requirements:* For master's, minimum GPA of 3.0 for unconditional admission. Electronic applications accepted. *Expenses:* Contact institution. *Faculty research:* Cyber security, 3D imaging of neurochemicals in rat brains.

Oakland University, Graduate Study and Lifelong Learning, School of Engineering and Computer Science, Department of Industrial and Systems Engineering, Program in Systems Engineering, Rochester, MI 48309-4401. Offers MS, PhD. *Degree requirements:* For doctorate, thesis/dissertation. *Entrance requirements:* For master's and doctorate, minimum GPA of 3.0 for unconditional admission. Additional exam requirements/recommendations for international students: Required—TOEFL (minimum score 550 paper-based; 213 computer-based). Electronic applications accepted. *Expenses:* Contact institution.

The Ohio State University, Graduate School, College of Engineering, Program in Industrial and Systems Engineering, Columbus, OH 43210. Offers MS, PhD. *Faculty:* 39. *Students:* 52 full-time (16 women), 39 part-time (5 women); includes 7 minority (1 African American, 3 Asian Americans or Pacific Islanders, 3 Hispanic Americans), 57 international. Average age 29. In 2009, 23 master's, 11 doctorates awarded. *Degree requirements:* For master's, thesis optional; for doctorate, thesis/dissertation. *Entrance requirements:* For master's and doctorate, GRE General Test. Additional exam requirements/recommendations for international students: Recommended—TOEFL (minimum score 600 paper-based; 250 computer-based). *Application deadline:* For fall admission, 8/15 priority date for domestic students, 11/1 priority date for international students; for winter admission, 12/1 priority date for domestic students, 7/1 priority date for international students; for spring admission, 3/1 priority date for domestic students, 2/1 priority date for international students. Applications are processed on a rolling basis. Application fee: $40 ($50 for international students). Electronic applications accepted. *Expenses:* Tuition, state resident: full-time $10,683. Tuition, nonresident: full-time $25,923. Tuition and fees vary according to course load and program. *Financial support:* Fellowships, research assistantships, teaching assistantships, career-related internships or fieldwork, Federal Work-Study, institutionally sponsored loans, and unspecified assistantships available. Support available to part-time students. *Unit head:* Jerald Brevick, Graduate Studies Committee Chair, E-mail: brevick.1@osu.edu. *Application contact:* 614-292-9444, Fax: 614-292-3895, E-mail: domestic.grad@osu.edu.

Ohio University, Graduate College, Russ College of Engineering and Technology, Department of Industrial and Systems Engineering, Athens, OH 45701-2979. Offers M Eng Mgt, MS. Part-time and evening/weekend programs available. *Faculty:* 8 full-time (0 women), 1 part-time/adjunct (0 women). *Students:* 22 full-time (7 women), 26 part-time (4 women); includes 2 minority (both African Americans), 22 international. 53 applicants, 66% accepted, 13 enrolled. In 2009, 16 master's awarded. *Degree requirements:* For master's, comprehensive exam (for some programs), thesis optional, research project. *Entrance requirements:* For master's, GRE General Test. Additional exam requirements/recommendations for international students: Required—TOEFL (minimum score 550 paper-based; 80 iBT) or IELTS Academic (minimum score 6.5). *Application deadline:* For fall admission, 3/1 priority date for domestic and international students; for winter admission, 9/1 priority date for domestic and international students; for spring admission, 1/1 priority date for domestic and international students. Applications are processed on a rolling basis. Application fee: $50 ($55 for international students). Electronic applications accepted. *Expenses:* Tuition, state resident: full-time $7839; part-time $323 per quarter hour. Tuition, nonresident: full-time $15,831; part-time $654 per quarter hour. Required fees: $2931. *Financial support:* In 2009–10, research assistantships with full tuition reimbursements (averaging $9,000 per year); Federal Work-Study, institutionally sponsored loans, tuition waivers (full), and unspecified assistantships also available. Financial award application deadline: 2/15; financial award applicants required to submit FAFSA. *Faculty research:* Software systems integration, human factors and ergonomics. Total annual research expenditures: $350,000. *Unit head:* Dr. Robert P. Judd, Chairman, 740-593-0106, Fax: 740-593-0778, E-mail: judd@ohio.edu. *Application contact:* Dr. Gursel Suer, Graduate Chairman, 740-593-1542, Fax: 740-593-0778, E-mail: suer@ohio.edu.

Old Dominion University, Frank Batten College of Engineering and Technology, Program in Engineering Management and Systems Engineering, Norfolk, VA 23529. Offers D Eng. Part-time and evening/weekend programs available. Postbaccalaureate distance learning degree programs offered (no on-campus study). *Faculty:* 15 full-time (2 women), 3 part-time/adjunct (0 women). *Students:* 1 full-time (0 women), 8 part-time (2 women); includes 1 minority (African American). Average age 45. *Degree requirements:* For doctorate, thesis/dissertation, candidacy exam. *Entrance requirements:* For doctorate, GRE, resume, letters of recommendation, minimum GPA of 3.0, interview. Additional exam requirements/recommendations for international students: Required—TOEFL (minimum score 550 paper-based; 213 computer-based; 79 iBT). *Application deadline:* For fall admission, 6/1 priority date for domestic students, 4/15 for international students; for spring admission, 11/1 priority date for domestic students, 2/1 for international students. Applications are processed on a rolling basis. Application fee: $40. Electronic applications accepted. *Expenses:* Tuition, state resident: full-time $8112; part-time $338 per credit. Tuition, nonresident: full-time $20,256; part-time $844 per credit. Required fees: $119 per semester. One-time fee: $50. *Financial support:* In 2009–10, research assistantships with full and partial tuition reimbursements (averaging $20,000 per year), teaching assistantships with full and partial tuition reimbursements (averaging $20,000 per year) were awarded; fellowships, career-related internships or fieldwork and tuition waivers also available. Support available to part-time students. Financial award application deadline: 2/15; financial award applicants required to submit FAFSA. *Faculty research:* Project management, systems engineering, modeling and simulation, virtual collaboration environments, multidisciplinary designs. Total annual research expenditures: $3.2 million. *Unit head:* Dr. Resit Unal, Department Chair, 757-683-4558, Fax: 757-683-5640, E-mail: enmagpd@odu.edu. *Application contact:* Dr. Ghaith Rabadi, Graduate Program Director, 757-683-4558, Fax: 757-683-5640, E-mail: enmagpd@odu.edu.

Old Dominion University, Frank Batten College of Engineering and Technology, Program in Systems Engineering, Norfolk, VA 23529. Offers ME. Part-time and evening/weekend programs available. Postbaccalaureate distance learning degree programs offered (no on-campus study). *Faculty:* 15 full-time (2 women), 3 part-time/adjunct (0 women). *Students:* 7 full-time (1 woman), 13 part-time (3 women); includes 7 minority (5 African Americans, 1 American Indian/Alaska Native, 1 Asian American or Pacific Islander), 2 international. Average age 33. 5 applicants, 100% accepted, 4 enrolled. In 2009, 9 master's awarded. *Degree requirements:* For master's, comprehensive exam, project. *Entrance requirements:* For master's, GRE, minimum GPA of 3.0. Additional exam requirements/recommendations for international students: Required—TOEFL (minimum score 550 paper-based; 213 computer-based; 79 iBT). *Application deadline:* For fall admission, 6/1 priority date for domestic students, 4/15 for international students; for spring admission, 11/1 priority date for domestic students, 2/1 for international students. Applications are processed on a rolling basis. Application fee: $40. Electronic applications accepted. *Expenses:* Tuition, state resident: full-time $8112; part-time $338 per credit. Tuition, nonresident: full-time $20,256; part-time $844 per credit. Required fees: $119 per semester. One-time fee: $50. *Financial support:* In 2009–10, research assistantships with partial tuition reimbursements (averaging $20,000 per year), teaching assistantships with partial tuition reimbursements (averaging $20,000 per year) were awarded; fellowships, career-related internships or fieldwork, scholarships/grants, and tuition waivers (partial) also available. Support available to part-time students. Financial award application deadline: 2/15; financial award applicants required to submit FAFSA. *Faculty research:* System of systems engineering, complex systems, optimization. Total annual research expenditures: $3.2 million. *Unit head:* Dr. Resit Unal, Chair, 757-683-4558, Fax: 757-683-5640, E-mail: enmagpd@odu.edu. *Application contact:* Dr. Ghaith Rabadi, Graduate Program Director, 757-683-4558, Fax: 757-683-5640, E-mail: enmagpd@odu.edu.

Oregon State University, Graduate School, College of Engineering, School of Mechanical, Industrial, and Manufacturing Engineering, Corvallis, OR 97331. Offers human systems engineering (MS, PhD); industrial engineering (MS, PhD); information systems engineering (MS, PhD); manufacturing engineering (M Engr); manufacturing systems engineering (MS, PhD); materials science (MAIS, MS, PhD); mechanical engineering (MS, PhD); nano/micro fabrication (MS, PhD). Part-time programs available. Postbaccalaureate distance learning degree programs offered (minimal on-campus study). *Faculty:* 26 full-time (2 women), 2 part-time/adjunct (1 woman). *Students:* 136 full-time (25 women), 12 part-time (2 women); includes 11 minority (3 African Americans, 4 Asian Americans or Pacific Islanders, 4 Hispanic Americans), 46 international. Average age 29. 53 applicants, 42% accepted, 13 enrolled. In 2009, 26 master's, 10 doctorates awarded. *Degree requirements:* For master's, thesis or alternative; for doctorate, thesis/dissertation. *Entrance requirements:* For master's, placement exam, minimum GPA of 3.0 in last 90 hours of course work; for doctorate, GRE, placement exam, minimum GPA of 3.0 in last 90 hours of course work. Additional exam requirements/recommendations for international students: Required—TOEFL (minimum score 550 paper-based; 213 computer-based). *Application deadline:* For fall admission, 3/1 for domestic students. Applications are processed on a rolling basis. Application fee: $50. *Expenses:* Tuition, state resident: full-time $9774; part-time $362 per credit. Tuition, nonresident: full-time $15,849; part-time $587 per credit. Required fees: $1639. Full-time tuition and fees vary according to course load and program. *Financial support:* In 2009–10, 10 research assistantships with full tuition reimbursements (averaging $11,124 per year), 8 teaching assistantships with full tuition reimbursements (averaging $7,020 per year) were awarded; fellowships with full tuition reimbursements, institutionally sponsored loans and instructorships also available. Support available to part-time students. Financial award application deadline: 2/1. *Faculty research:* Computer-integrated manufacturing, human factors, robotics, decision support systems, simulation modeling and analysis. Total annual research expenditures: $1.3 million. *Unit head:* Dr. Belinda A. Batten, Head, 541-737-3441, Fax: 541-737-2600, E-mail: info-mime@oregonstate.edu. *Application contact:* Jean Robinson, Graduate Records Specialist, 541-737-7009, Fax: 541-737-2600, E-mail: jean.robinson@oregonstate.edu.

Polytechnic Institute of NYU, Department of Electrical and Computer Engineering, Major in Systems Engineering, Brooklyn, NY 11201-2990. Offers MS. Part-time and evening/weekend programs available. *Students:* 3 full-time (2 women), 4 part-time (1 woman); includes 1 minority (Asian American or Pacific Islander), 2 international. 12 applicants, 67% accepted, 2 enrolled. *Degree requirements:* For master's, comprehensive exam (for some programs), thesis (for some programs). *Entrance requirements:* For master's, BS in electrical engineering. Additional exam requirements/recommendations for international students: Required—TOEFL (minimum score 550 paper-based; 213 computer-based; 80 iBT); Recommended—IELTS (minimum score 6.5). *Application deadline:* For fall admission, 7/31 priority date for domestic students, 4/30 priority date for international students; for spring admission, 12/31 priority date for domestic students, 11/30 priority date for international students. Applications are processed on a rolling basis. Application fee: $75. Electronic applications accepted. *Expenses:* Tuition: Full-time $21,492; part-time $1194 per credit hour. Required fees: $1160; $204 per course. *Financial support:* Fellowships, research assistantships, teaching assistantships, institutionally sponsored loans, scholarships/grants, and unspecified assistantships available. Support available to part-time students. Financial award applicants required to submit FAFSA. *Unit head:* Dr. Jonathan Chao, Head, 718-860-3478, Fax: 718-260-3302, E-mail: chao@poly.edu. *Application contact:* JeanCarlo Bonilla, Director of Graduate Enrollment Management, 718-260-3182, Fax: 718-260-3624.

Polytechnic Institute of NYU, Long Island Graduate Center, Graduate Programs, Department of Computer Science and Engineering, Program in Distributed Information Systems Engineering, Melville, NY 11747. Offers MS. *Students:* 1 part-time (0 women). *Degree requirements:* For master's, comprehensive exam (for some programs), thesis (for some programs). *Entrance requirements:* Additional exam requirements/recommendations for international students: Required—TOEFL (minimum score 550 paper-based; 213 computer-based; 80 iBT); Recommended—IELTS (minimum score 6.5). *Application deadline:* For fall admission, 7/31 priority date for domestic students, 4/30 priority date for international students; for spring admission, 12/31 priority date for domestic students, 11/30 priority date for international students. Applications are processed on a rolling basis. Application fee: $75. Electronic applications accepted. *Financial support:* Institutionally sponsored loans, scholarships/grants, and unspecified assistantships available. Support available to part-time students. *Unit head:* Dr. Keith W. Ross, Department Head, 718-260-3859, E-mail: ross@poly.edu. *Application contact:* JeanCarlo Bonilla, Director of Graduate Enrollment Management, 718-260-3182, Fax: 718-260-3624, E-mail: gradinfo@poly.edu.

Polytechnic Institute of NYU, Long Island Graduate Center, Graduate Programs, Department of Electrical and Computer Engineering, Program in Systems Engineering, Melville, NY 11747. Offers MS. Part-time and evening/weekend programs available. *Students:* 8 part-time (1 woman); includes 2 minority (1 Asian American or Pacific Islander, 1 Hispanic American). 4 applicants, 100% accepted, 4 enrolled. *Degree requirements:* For master's, comprehensive exam (for some programs), thesis (for some programs). *Entrance requirements:* Additional exam requirements/recommendations for international students: Required—TOEFL (minimum score 550 paper-based; 213 computer-based; 80 iBT); Recommended—IELTS (minimum score 6.5). *Application deadline:* For fall admission, 7/31 priority date for domestic students, 4/30 priority date for international students; for spring admission, 12/31 priority date for domestic students, 11/30 priority date for international students. Applications are processed on a rolling basis. Application fee: $75. Electronic applications accepted. *Financial support:* Institutionally sponsored loans, scholarships/grants, and unspecified assistantships available. Support available to part-time students. *Unit head:* Dr. Jonathan Chao, Department Head, 718-260-3302, E-mail: chao@poly.edu. *Application contact:* JeanCarlo Bonilla, Director of Graduate Enrollment Management, 718-260-3182, Fax: 718-260-3624, E-mail: gradinfo@poly.edu.

Portland State University, Graduate Studies, Maseeh College of Engineering and Computer Science, Program in Systems Engineering, Portland, OR 97207-0751. Offers systems engineering (M Eng); systems engineering fundamentals (Certificate). Postbaccalaureate distance learning degree programs offered (no on-campus study). *Degree requirements:* For master's, internship/project. *Entrance requirements:* For master's, 3 years of engineering experience, bachelor's degree in engineering, minimum undergraduate GPA of 3.0 in upper division courses. Additional exam requirements/recommendations for international students: Required—TOEFL (minimum score 550 paper-based; 213 computer-based).

Regis University, College for Professional Studies, School of Computer and Information Sciences, Denver, CO 80221-1099. Offers database administration with IBM DB2 (Certificate); database administration with Oracle (Certificate); database development (Certificate); database technologies (MA); enterprise Java software development (Certificate); executive information technologies (Certificate); information assurance (MA, Certificate); information technology management (MA); software and information systems (M Sc); software engineering (MA,

Certificate); storage area networks (Certificate); systems engineering (MA, Certificate). Offered at Boulder Campus, Northwest Denver Campus, Southeast Denver Campus, Fort Collins Campus, Colorado Springs Campus, and Broomfield Campus. Part-time and evening/weekend programs available. Postbaccalaureate distance learning degree programs offered (no on-campus study). *Degree requirements:* For master's, thesis, final research project. *Entrance requirements:* For master's, 2 years of related experience, resume, interview; for Certificate, 2 years of related experience, resumé. Additional exam requirements/recommendations for international students: Required—TOEFL (minimum score 213 computer-based), TWE (minimum score 5), TOEFL or university-based test. Electronic applications accepted. *Expenses:* Contact institution. *Faculty research:* Secure Virtual Laboratory Architecture, Joint IA project with W2C06 Institute, Information Policy, OLTP and OLAP Technologies, knowledge management, software architectures.

Rensselaer Polytechnic Institute, Graduate School, School of Engineering, Department of Electrical, Computer, and Systems Engineering, Program in Computer and Systems Engineering, Troy, NY 12180-3590. Offers M Eng, MS, PhD. Part-time programs available. *Faculty:* 48 full-time (5 women), 7 part-time/adjunct (1 woman). *Students:* 10 full-time (0 women), 2 part-time (1 woman); includes 1 Hispanic American. 84 applicants, 26% accepted, 12 enrolled. In 2009, 18 master's, 3 doctorates awarded. Terminal master's awarded for partial completion of doctoral program. *Degree requirements:* For master's, thesis (for some programs); for doctorate, thesis/dissertation. *Entrance requirements:* For master's, GRE; for doctorate, GRE, qualifying exam, candidacy exam. Additional exam requirements/recommendations for international students: Required—TOEFL (minimum score 570 paper-based; 89 iBT). *Application deadline:* For fall admission, 1/15 priority date for domestic and international students; for spring admission, 8/15 priority date for domestic and international students. Applications are processed on a rolling basis. Application fee: $75. Electronic applications accepted. *Expenses:* Tuition: Full-time $38,100. *Financial support:* In 2009–10, 7 fellowships with full tuition reimbursements (averaging $21,000 per year), 88 research assistantships with full tuition reimbursements (averaging $20,000 per year), 41 teaching assistantships (averaging $16,500 per year) were awarded; career-related internships or fieldwork, institutionally sponsored loans, and unspecified assistantships also available. Financial award application deadline: 1/15. *Faculty research:* Multimedia via ATM, mobile robotics, thermophotovoltaic devices, microelectronic interconnections, agile manufacturing. Total annual research expenditures: $3.7 million. *Unit head:* Dr. Kim L. Boyer, Head, 518-276-2150, Fax: 518-276-6261, E-mail: kim@ecse.rpi.edu. *Application contact:* Ann Bruno, Manager of Student Services and Graduate Enrollment, 518-276-2554, Fax: 518-276-4403, E-mail: ann@ecse.rpi.edu.

Rensselaer Polytechnic Institute, Graduate School, School of Engineering, Department of Industrial and Systems Engineering, Program in Decision Sciences and Engineering Systems, Troy, NY 12180-3590. Offers industrial and systems engineering (PhD). Part-time programs available. *Faculty:* 10 full-time (2 women). *Students:* 21 full-time (7 women), 1 part-time (0 women); includes 2 minority (both Asian Americans or Pacific Islanders), 15 international. Average age 28. 60 applicants, 7% accepted, 4 enrolled. In 2009, 6 doctorates awarded. Terminal master's awarded for partial completion of doctoral program. *Degree requirements:* For doctorate, thesis/dissertation. *Entrance requirements:* For doctorate, GRE General Test (minimum score 550 verbal). Additional exam requirements/recommendations for international students: Required—TOEFL (minimum score 570 paper-based). *Application deadline:* For fall admission, 1/1 priority date for domestic students, 1/1 for international students; for spring admission, 8/15 for domestic and international students. Applications are processed on a rolling basis. Application fee: $75. Electronic applications accepted. *Expenses:* Tuition: Full-time $38,100. *Financial support:* In 2009–10, 20 students received support, including 1 fellowship with full tuition reimbursement available (averaging $22,000 per year), 12 research assistantships with full tuition reimbursements available (averaging $22,000 per year), 7 teaching assistantships with full tuition reimbursements available (averaging $16,500 per year); career-related internships or fieldwork and institutionally sponsored loans also available. Financial award application deadline: 1/1. *Faculty research:* Decision support systems, simulation and modeling, statistical methods/computing, operations research, supply chain logistics. Total annual research expenditures: $1.3 million. *Unit head:* Dr. Charles J. Malmborg, Department Head, 518-276-2773, Fax: 518-276-8227, E-mail: malmbc@rpi.edu. *Application contact:* Mary Wagner, Graduate Coordinator, 518-276-2895, Fax: 518-276-8227, E-mail: wagnem@rpi.edu.

Rensselaer Polytechnic Institute, Graduate School, School of Engineering, Department of Industrial and Systems Engineering, Program in Systems Engineering and Technology Management, Troy, NY 12180-3590. Offers M Eng. Part-time programs available. *Faculty:* 9 full-time (1 woman). *Students:* 3 full-time (0 women). 3 applicants, 100% accepted, 3 enrolled. *Degree requirements:* For master's, thesis (for some programs). *Entrance requirements:* For master's, GRE General Test (minimum 550 Verbal). Additional exam requirements/recommendations for international students: Required—TOEFL (minimum score 570 paper-based). *Application deadline:* For fall admission, 1/1 priority date for domestic students, 1/1 for international students; for spring admission, 8/15 for domestic and international students. Applications are processed on a rolling basis. Application fee: $75. Electronic applications accepted. *Expenses:* Tuition: Full-time $38,100. *Financial support:* Fellowships, research assistantships, teaching assistantships, career-related internships or fieldwork and institutionally sponsored loans available. Financial award application deadline: 1/1. *Faculty research:* Decision support systems, simulation and modeling, statistical methods/computing, operations research, supply chain logistics. Total annual research expenditures: $1.3 million. *Unit head:* Dr. Charles J. Malmborg, Department Head, 518-276-2895, Fax: 518-276-8227, E-mail: malmbc@rpi.edu. *Application contact:* Mary Wagner, Graduate Coordinator, 518-276-2895, Fax: 518-276-8227, E-mail: wagnem@rpi.edu.

Rochester Institute of Technology, Graduate Enrollment Services, Kate Gleason College of Engineering, Department of Design, Development and Manufacturing, Program in Product Development, Rochester, NY 14623-5603. Offers MS. Part-time and evening/weekend programs available. *Students:* 37 part-time (3 women); includes 1 Hispanic American, 1 international. Average age 38. 2 applicants, 50% accepted, 1 enrolled. In 2009, 14 master's awarded. *Entrance requirements:* For master's, undergraduate degree in engineering or related field, minimum GPA of 3.0, 5 years experience in product development. Additional exam requirements/recommendations for international students: Required—TOEFL (minimum score 570 paper-based; 230 computer-based; 88 iBT), or IELTS (minimum score 6.5). *Application deadline:* For fall admission, 2/15 priority date for domestic and international students. Application fee: $50. *Expenses:* Contact institution. *Financial support:* Applicants required to submit FAFSA. *Unit head:* Mark Smith, Director, 585-475-7971, Fax: 585-475-7955, E-mail: mpdmail@rit.edu. *Application contact:* Diane Ellison, Assistant Vice President, Graduate Enrollment Services, 585-475-2229, Fax: 585-475-7164, E-mail: gradinfo@rit.edu.

Rochester Institute of Technology, Graduate Enrollment Services, Kate Gleason College of Engineering, Department of Industrial and Systems Engineering, Rochester, NY 14623-5603. Offers engineering management (ME); industrial engineering (ME, MS); manufacturing engineering (ME, MS); systems engineering (ME). Part-time programs available. *Students:* 62 full-time (17 women), 10 part-time (5 women); includes 5 minority (2 African Americans, 2 Asian Americans or Pacific Islanders, 1 Hispanic American), 55 international. Average age 25. 186 applicants, 50% accepted, 40 enrolled. In 2009, 53 master's awarded. *Degree requirements:* For master's, internship. *Entrance requirements:* For master's, GRE, minimum GPA of 3.0. Additional exam requirements/recommendations for international students: Required—TOEFL (minimum score 570 paper-based; 230 computer-based; 88 iBT), or IELTS (minimum score 6.5). *Application deadline:* For fall admission, 2/15 priority date for domestic and international students. Applications are processed on a rolling basis. Application fee: $50. *Expenses:* Tuition: Full-time $31,533; part-time $876 per credit hour. Required fees: $210. *Financial support:* In 2009–10, 63 students received support; research assistantships with partial tuition reimbursements available, teaching assistantships with partial tuition reimbursements available, career-related internships or fieldwork, institutionally sponsored loans, scholarships/grants, tuition waivers (partial), and unspecified assistantships available. Support available to part-time students. Financial award applicants required to submit FAFSA. *Faculty research:* Safety,

manufacturing (CAM), simulation. *Unit head:* Dr. Jacqueline Mozrall, Department Head, 585-475-2598, E-mail: ise@rit.edu. *Application contact:* Diane Ellison, Assistant Vice President, Graduate Enrollment Services, 585-475-2229, Fax: 585-475-7164, E-mail: gradinfo@rit.edu.

Rochester Institute of Technology, Graduate Enrollment Services, Kate Gleason College of Engineering, Department of Microsystems Engineering, Rochester, NY 14623-5603. Offers PhD. Part-time programs available. *Students:* 34 full-time (5 women), 2 part-time (0 women); includes 2 minority (1 African American, 1 Hispanic American), 14 international. Average age 31. 43 applicants, 23% accepted, 9 enrolled. *Degree requirements:* For doctorate, comprehensive exam, thesis/dissertation. *Entrance requirements:* For doctorate, GRE. Additional exam requirements/recommendations for international students: Required—TOEFL (minimum score 570 paper-based; 230 computer-based; 88 iBT), or IELTS (minimum score 6.5). *Application deadline:* For fall admission, 2/15 priority date for domestic and international students. Application fee: $50. *Expenses:* Tuition: Full-time $31,533; part-time $876 per credit hour. Required fees: $210. *Financial support:* In 2009–10, 35 students received support; fellowships with full tuition reimbursements available, research assistantships with partial tuition reimbursements available, teaching assistantships with partial tuition reimbursements available, career-related internships or fieldwork, institutionally sponsored loans, scholarships/grants, health care benefits, and unspecified assistantships available. Support available to part-time students. Financial award applicants required to submit FAFSA. *Faculty research:* Scaling-driven nanoelectronics, MEMS (micro-electro-mechanical systems), Photonics and nanophotonics imaging, communications, and sensing research, photovoltaics research in silicon, organic, and stacked solar cells and thrmovoltaics, microfluids research on the behavior, control, and manipulation of fluids at the micro-scale. *Unit head:* Dr. Bruce Smith, Director, 585-475-2145, Fax: 585-475-6879, E-mail: bwsemc@rit.edu. *Application contact:* Diane Ellison, Assistant Vice President, Graduate Enrollment Services, 585-475-2229, Fax: 585-475-7164, E-mail: gradinfo@rit.edu.

Rutgers, The State University of New Jersey, New Brunswick, Graduate School-New Brunswick, Program in Industrial and Systems Engineering, Piscataway, NJ 08854-8097. Offers industrial and systems engineering (MS, PhD); information technology (MS); manufacturing systems engineering (MS); quality and reliability engineering (MS). Part-time and evening/weekend programs available. Terminal master's awarded for partial completion of doctoral program. *Degree requirements:* For master's, thesis or alternative, seminar; for doctorate, comprehensive exam, thesis/dissertation. *Entrance requirements:* For master's and doctorate, GRE General Test. Additional exam requirements/recommendations for international students: Required—TOEFL. *Faculty research:* Production and manufacturing systems, quality and reliability engineering, systems engineering and aviation safety.

San Jose State University, Graduate Studies and Research, Charles W. Davidson College of Engineering, Department of Industrial and Systems Engineering, San Jose, CA 95192-0001. Offers industrial and systems engineering (MS). Part-time programs available. *Students:* 64 full-time (22 women), 61 part-time (33 women); includes 27 minority (1 African American, 1 American Indian/Alaska Native, 20 Asian Americans or Pacific Islanders, 5 Hispanic Americans), 63 international. Average age 29. 129 applicants, 60% accepted, 40 enrolled. In 2009, 53 master's awarded. *Degree requirements:* For master's, comprehensive exam. *Application deadline:* For fall admission, 6/29 for domestic students; for spring admission, 11/30 for domestic students. Applications are processed on a rolling basis. Application fee: $59. Electronic applications accepted. *Financial support:* Federal Work-Study available. Financial award applicants required to submit FAFSA. *Unit head:* Dr. Yasser Dessouky, Chair, 408-924-4133. *Application contact:* Dr. Louis Freund, Graduate Program Coordinator, 408-924-3890.

Southern Methodist University, Bobby B. Lyle School of Engineering, Department of Engineering Management, Information, and Systems, Dallas, TX 75275. Offers applied science (MS); engineering management (MSEM, DE); information engineering and management (MSIEM); operations research (MS, PhD); systems engineering (MS, PhD). Part-time and evening/weekend programs available. Postbaccalaureate distance learning degree programs offered. *Faculty:* 10 full-time (3 women), 22 part-time/adjunct (2 women). *Students:* 54 full-time (24 women), 288 part-time (68 women); includes 96 minority (30 African Americans, 2 American Indian/Alaska Native, 35 Asian Americans or Pacific Islanders, 29 Hispanic Americans), 38 international. Average age 33. 125 applicants, 74% accepted, 60 enrolled. In 2009, 128 master's, 3 doctorates awarded. Terminal master's awarded for partial completion of doctoral program. *Degree requirements:* For master's, thesis optional; for doctorate, thesis/dissertation, oral and written qualifying exams. *Entrance requirements:* For master's, minimum GPA of 3.0 in last 2 years; bachelor's degree in engineering, mathematics, sciences, or technical area; for doctorate, GRE General Test (operations research, engineering management), bachelor's degree in related field. Additional exam requirements/recommendations for international students: Required—TOEFL. *Application deadline:* For fall admission, 7/1 for domestic students, 5/15 for international students; for spring admission, 11/15 for domestic students, 9/1 for international students. Applications are processed on a rolling basis. Application fee: $75. *Financial support:* In 2009–10, 8 students received support, including 3 research assistantships with full tuition reimbursements available (averaging $18,000 per year), 9 teaching assistantships with full tuition reimbursements available (averaging $18,000 per year); tuition waivers (full) also available. *Faculty research:* Telecommunications, decision systems, information engineering, operations research, software. Total annual research expenditures: $172,823. *Unit head:* Dr. Richard S. Barr, Chair, 214-768-1772, Fax: 214-768-1112, E-mail: emis@lyle.smu.edu. *Application contact:* Marc Valerin, Director of Graduate and Executive Admissions, 214-768-3042, E-mail: valerin@lyle.smu.edu.

Southern Polytechnic State University, Division of Engineering, Marietta, GA 30060-2896. Offers systems engineering (MS, Advanced Certificate, Graduate Certificate). Part-time and evening/weekend programs available. *Faculty:* 3 full-time (2 women), 2 part-time/adjunct (0 women). *Students:* 6 full-time (2 women), 44 part-time (10 women); includes 12 African Americans, 1 Asian American or Pacific Islander, 5 Hispanic Americans, 1 international. Average age 37. 24 applicants, 92% accepted, 18 enrolled. In 2009, 4 master's awarded. *Entrance requirements:* Additional exam requirements/recommendations for international students: Required—TOEFL (minimum score 550 paper-based; 213 computer-based; 79 iBT), IELTS (minimum score 6.5). *Application deadline:* For fall admission, 7/1 priority date for domestic students, 5/1 priority date for international students; for spring admission, 11/1 priority date for domestic students, 9/1 priority date for international students. Applications are processed on a rolling basis. Application fee: $20. Electronic applications accepted. *Expenses:* Tuition, state resident: full-time $2896; part-time $181 per credit hour. Tuition, nonresident: full-time $11,552; part-time $722 per credit hour. Required fees: $1096; $1096 per year. *Financial support:* In 2009–10, 6 students received support. *Unit head:* Dr. Tom Currin, Associate Dean, 678-915-7482, Fax: 678-915-5527, E-mail: tcurrin@spsu.edu. *Application contact:* Nikki Palamiotis, Director of Graduate Studies, 678-915-4276, Fax: 678-915-7292, E-mail: npalamio@spsu.edu.

Stevens Institute of Technology, Graduate School, School of Systems and Enterprises, Program in Systems Engineering, Hoboken, NJ 07030. Offers agile systems and enterprises (Certificate); systems and supportability engineering (Certificate); systems engineering (M Eng, PhD); systems engineering management (Certificate). *Expenses:* Tuition: Full-time $9900; part-time $1100 per credit. Required fees: $286 per semester.

Stony Brook University, State University of New York, Graduate School, College of Engineering and Applied Sciences, Department of Computer Science, Program in Information Systems Engineering, Stony Brook, NY 11794. Offers MS. *Expenses:* Tuition, state resident: full-time $8370; part-time $349 per credit. Tuition, nonresident: full-time $13,250; part-time $552 per credit. Required fees: $933.

Texas Tech University, Graduate School, College of Engineering, Department of Industrial Engineering, Lubbock, TX 79409. Offers industrial engineering (MSIE, PhD); manufacturing systems engineering (MSMSE); systems and engineering management (MSSEM, PhD). Part-time programs available. *Faculty:* 11 full-time (2 women). *Students:* 85 full-time (19 women), 48 part-time (8 women); includes 9 minority (4 African Americans, 2 Asian Americans

Systems Engineering

Texas Tech University *(continued)*

or Pacific Islanders, 3 Hispanic Americans), 80 international. Average age 29. 298 applicants, 61% accepted, 24 enrolled. In 2009, 21 master's, 7 doctorates awarded. *Degree requirements:* For master's, thesis or alternative; for doctorate, thesis/dissertation. *Entrance requirements:* For master's and doctorate, GRE General Test, minimum GPA of 3.0. Additional exam requirements/recommendations for international students: Required—TOEFL (minimum score 550 paper-based; 213 computer-based). *Application deadline:* For fall admission, 3/1 priority date for international students; for spring admission, 11/1 priority date for international students. Applications are processed on a rolling basis. Application fee: $50 ($75 for international students). Electronic applications accepted. *Expenses:* Tuition, state resident: full-time $5100; part-time $213 per credit hour. Tuition, nonresident: full-time $11,748; part-time $490 per credit hour. Required fees: $2298; $50 per credit hour. $555 per semester. *Financial support:* In 2009–10, 14 research assistantships with partial tuition reimbursements (averaging $14,979 per year), 10 teaching assistantships with partial tuition reimbursements (averaging $13,050 per year) were awarded; Federal Work-Study and institutionally sponsored loans also available. Support available to part-time students. Financial award application deadline: 4/15; financial award applicants required to submit FAFSA. *Faculty research:* Knowledge and engineering management, environmentally conscious manufacturing, biomechanical simulation, aviation security, supply chain management. Total annual research expenditures: $476,488. *Unit head:* Dr. Pat Patterson, Chair, 806-742-3543, Fax: 806-742-3411, E-mail: pat.patterson@ttu.edu. *Application contact:* Dr. Mario Beruvides, Professor, 806-742-3543, Fax: 806-742-3411, E-mail: mario.beruvides@ttu.edu.

The University of Alabama in Huntsville, School of Graduate Studies, College of Engineering, Department of Industrial and Systems Engineering/Engineering Management, Huntsville, AL 35899. Offers industrial and systems engineering (PhD), including engineering management (MSE, PhD), industrial engineering, systems engineering (MSE, PhD); industrial engineering (MSE), including engineering management (MSE, PhD), missile systems engineering, modeling and simulation, rotorcraft systems engineering, systems engineering (MSE, PhD); operations research (MSOR). Part-time and evening/weekend programs available. Postbaccalaureate distance learning degree programs offered (minimal on-campus study). *Faculty:* 6 full-time (2 women). *Students:* 6 full-time (0 women), 138 part-time (37 women); includes 17 minority (14 African Americans, 1 American Indian/Alaska Native, 2 Hispanic Americans), 9 international. Average age 36. 75 applicants, 53% accepted, 29 enrolled. In 2009, 38 master's, 6 doctorates awarded. *Degree requirements:* For master's, comprehensive exam, thesis or alternative, oral and written exams; for doctorate, comprehensive exam, thesis/dissertation, oral and written exams. *Entrance requirements:* For master's and doctorate, GRE General Test, minimum GPA of 3.0. Additional exam requirements/recommendations for international students: Required—TOEFL (minimum score 500 paper-based; 173 computer-based; 62 iBT). *Application deadline:* For fall admission, 7/15 for domestic students, 4/1 for international students; for spring admission, 11/30 for domestic students, 9/1 for international students. Applications are processed on a rolling basis. Application fee: $40 ($50 for international students). Electronic applications accepted. *Expenses:* Tuition, state resident: part-time $355.75 per credit hour. Tuition, nonresident: part-time $847.10 per credit hour. Required fees: $210.80 per semester. Tuition and fees vary according to course load and program. *Financial support:* In 2009–10, 4 students received support, including 4 teaching assistantships with full and partial tuition reimbursements available (averaging $11,733 per year); career-related internships or fieldwork, Federal Work-Study, institutionally sponsored loans, scholarships/grants, health care benefits, and unspecified assistantships also available. Support available to part-time students. Financial award application deadline: 4/1; financial award applicants required to submit FAFSA. *Faculty research:* Engineering management, systems engineering, manufacturing, logistics, simulation. Total annual research expenditures: $19.6 million. *Unit head:* Dr. James Swain, Chair, 256-824-6749, Fax: 256-824-6733, E-mail: jswain@ise.uah.edu. *Application contact:* Kathy Biggs, Graduate Studies Admissions Manager, 256-824-6199, Fax: 256-824-6405, E-mail: deangrad@uah.edu.

University of Alberta, Faculty of Graduate Studies and Research, Department of Electrical and Computer Engineering, Edmonton, AB T6G 2E1, Canada. Offers communications (M Eng, M Sc, PhD); computer engineering (M Eng, M Sc, PhD); electromagnetics (M Eng, M Sc, PhD); nanotechnology and microdevices (M Eng, M Sc, PhD); power/power electronics (M Eng, M Sc, PhD); systems (M Eng, M Sc, PhD). *Faculty:* 42 full-time (3 women), 12 part-time/adjunct (0 women). *Students:* 252 full-time (28 women), 65 part-time (10 women). Average age 26. 1,500 applicants, 5% accepted.Terminal master's awarded for partial completion of doctoral program. *Degree requirements:* For master's, thesis; for doctorate, thesis/dissertation. *Entrance requirements:* Additional exam requirements/recommendations for international students: Required—TOEFL. *Application deadline:* For fall admission, 4/30 for domestic students; for winter admission, 8/30 for domestic students. Applications are processed on a rolling basis. Application fee: $0 Canadian dollars. Electronic applications accepted. Tuition and fees charges are reported in Canadian dollars. *Expenses:* Tuition, area resident: Full-time $4626.24 Canadian dollars; part-time $99.72 Canadian dollars per unit. International tuition: $8216 Canadian dollars full-time. Required fees: $3589.92 Canadian dollars; $99.72 Canadian dollars per unit. $215 Canadian dollars per term. *Financial support:* In 2009–10, 80 students received support; fellowships, research assistantships, teaching assistantships, scholarships/grants available. *Faculty research:* Controls, communications, microelectronics, electromagnetics. Total annual research expenditures: $3 million Canadian dollars. *Unit head:* Dr. H. J. Marquez, Chair, 780-492-0161, Fax: 780-492-1811. *Application contact:* Michelle Vaage, Graduate Student Advisor, 780-492-0161, Fax: 780-492-1811, E-mail: gradinfo@ece.ualberta.ca.

The University of Arizona, Graduate College, College of Engineering, Department of Systems and Industrial Engineering, Program in Systems and Industrial Engineering, Tucson, AZ 85721. Offers MS, PhD. Postbaccalaureate distance learning degree programs offered. *Students:* 16 full-time (5 women), 8 part-time (1 woman), 21 international. Average age 30. 24 applicants, 75% accepted, 6 enrolled. In 2009, 2 doctorates awarded. *Degree requirements:* For doctorate, thesis/dissertation. *Entrance requirements:* For master's, GRE General Test (500 Verbal, 700 Quantitative, 650 Analytical), 3 letters of recommendation, letter of intent; for doctorate, GRE General Test (500 Verbal, 750 Quantitative, 700 Analytical), 3 letters of recommendation, letter of intent. Additional exam requirements/recommendations for international students: Required—TOEFL (minimum score 575 paper-based; 233 computer-based; 80 iBT). *Application deadline:* For fall admission, 6/1 for domestic students, 12/1 for international students; for spring admission, 9/1 for domestic students, 6/1 for international students. Applications are processed on a rolling basis. Application fee: $75. Electronic applications accepted. *Expenses:* Tuition, state resident: full-time $9028. Tuition, nonresident: full-time $24,890. *Financial support:* Tuition waivers (full) and unspecified assistantships available. *Faculty research:* Optimization, systems theory, logistics, transportation, embedded systems. *Unit head:* Dr. K. Larry Head, Head, 520-621-6551, E-mail: larry@sie.arizona.edu. *Application contact:* Linda Cramer, Graduate Secretary, 520-626-4644, Fax: 520-621-6555, E-mail: gradapp@sie.arizona.edu.

The University of Arizona, Graduate College, College of Engineering, Department of Systems and Industrial Engineering, Program in Systems Engineering, Tucson, AZ 85721. Offers MS, PhD. Part-time programs available. *Students:* 8 full-time (1 woman), 11 part-time (5 women), 1 international. Average age 28. 20 applicants, 60% accepted, 9 enrolled. In 2009, 7 master's awarded. *Entrance requirements:* For master's, GRE General Test (500 Verbal, 700 Quantitative, 650 Analytical), 3 letters of recommendation, letter of intent; for doctorate, GRE General Test (500 Verbal, 750 Quantitative, 700 Analytical), minimum GPA of 3.5, 3 letters of recommendation, letter of intent. Additional exam requirements/recommendations for international students: Required—TOEFL (minimum score 575 paper-based; 233 computer-based; 80 iBT). *Application deadline:* For fall admission, 6/1 for domestic students, 12/1 for international students; for spring admission, 10/1 for domestic students, 6/1 for international students. Applications are processed on a rolling basis. Application fee: $75. Electronic applications accepted. *Expenses:* Tuition, state resident: full-time $9028. Tuition, nonresident: full-time $24,890. *Financial support:* Institutionally sponsored loans, scholarships/grants, and unspecified assistantships available. *Faculty research:* Man/machine systems, optimal control, algorithmic

probability. *Unit head:* Dr. K. Larry Head, Head, 520-621-6551, E-mail: larry@sie.arizona.edu. *Application contact:* Linda Cramer, Graduate Secretary, 520-626-4644, Fax: 520-621-6555, E-mail: gradapp@sie.arizona.edu.

University of Arkansas at Little Rock, Graduate School, George W. Donaghey College of Engineering and Information Technology, Department of Systems Engineering, Little Rock, AR 72204-1099. Offers Graduate Certificate.

University of Central Florida, College of Engineering and Computer Science, Department of Industrial Engineering and Management Systems, Orlando, FL 32816. Offers applied operations research (Certificate); design for usability (Certificate); industrial engineering (MSIE, PhD); industrial ergonomics and safety (Certificate); project engineering (Certificate); quality assurance (Certificate); systems engineering (Certificate); systems simulation for engineers (Certificate); training simulation (Certificate). Part-time and evening/weekend programs available. *Faculty:* 14 full-time (2 women), 9 part-time/adjunct (6 women). *Students:* 108 full-time (22 women), 143 part-time (54 women); includes 76 minority (21 African Americans, 1 American Indian/Alaska Native, 14 Asian Americans or Pacific Islanders, 40 Hispanic Americans), 64 international. Average age 32. 204 applicants, 66% accepted, 88 enrolled. In 2009, 59 master's, 17 doctorates, 14 other advanced degrees awarded. *Degree requirements:* For master's, thesis; for doctorate, thesis/dissertation, departmental qualifying exam, candidacy exam. *Entrance requirements:* For master's, GRE General Test, minimum GPA of 3.0 in last 60 hours of course work; for doctorate, minimum GPA of 3.5 in last 60 hours of course work. Additional exam requirements/recommendations for international students: Required—TOEFL. *Application deadline:* For fall admission, 7/15 priority date for domestic students; for spring admission, 12/1 priority date for domestic students. Application fee: $30. Electronic applications accepted. *Expenses:* Tuition, state resident: part-time $306.31 per credit hour. Tuition, nonresident: part-time $1099.01 per credit hour. Part-time tuition and fees vary according to degree level and program. *Financial support:* In 2009–10, 20 students received support, including 8 fellowships with partial tuition reimbursements available (averaging $7,600 per year), 9 research assistantships with partial tuition reimbursements available (averaging $12,400 per year), 5 teaching assistantships with partial tuition reimbursements available (averaging $13,000 per year); career-related internships or fieldwork, Federal Work-Study, institutionally sponsored loans, tuition waivers (partial), and unspecified assistantships also available. Financial award application deadline: 3/1; financial award applicants required to submit FAFSA. *Unit head:* Dr. Waldemar Karwowski, Chair, E-mail: wkar@mail.ucf.edu. *Application contact:* Dr. Waldemar Karwowski, Chair, E-mail: wkar@mail.ucf.edu.

University of Florida, Graduate School, College of Engineering, Department of Industrial and Systems Engineering, Gainesville, FL 32611. Offers ME, MS, PhD, Engr. *Degree requirements:* For master's, thesis optional, core exam; for doctorate, comprehensive exam, thesis/dissertation; for Engr, thesis. *Entrance requirements:* For master's and doctorate, GRE General Test, minimum GPA of 3.0; for Engr, GRE General Test. Additional exam requirements/recommendations for international students: Required—TOEFL (minimum score 550 paper-based; 213 computer-based). Electronic applications accepted.

University of Houston–Clear Lake, School of Science and Computer Engineering, Program in System Engineering, Houston, TX 77058-1098. Offers MS. *Entrance requirements:* Additional exam requirements/recommendations for international students: Required—TOEFL (minimum score 550 paper-based; 213 computer-based).

University of Illinois at Urbana–Champaign, Graduate College, College of Engineering, Department of Industrial and Enterprise Systems Engineering, Champaign, IL 61820. Offers financial engineering (MS); industrial engineering (MS, PhD); systems and entrepreneurial engineering (MS, PhD); MBA/MS. *Faculty:* 21 full-time (5 women), 1 part-time/adjunct (0 women). *Students:* 56 full-time (18 women), 17 part-time (7 women); includes 1 minority (African American), 54 international. 255 applicants, 9% accepted, 16 enrolled. In 2009, 13 master's, 7 doctorates awarded. *Entrance requirements:* For master's and doctorate, GRE, minimum GPA of 3.25. Additional exam requirements/recommendations for international students: Required—TOEFL (minimum score 613 paper-based; 257 computer-based; 103 iBT), or IELTS (minimum score 7). *Application deadline:* Applications are processed on a rolling basis. Application fee: $60 ($75 for international students). Electronic applications accepted. *Financial support:* In 2009–10, 7 fellowships, 37 research assistantships, 44 teaching assistantships were awarded; tuition waivers (full and partial) also available. *Unit head:* Jong-Shi Pang, Head, 217-244-5703, Fax: 217-244-5705, E-mail: jspang@illinois.edu. *Application contact:* Donna J. Eiskamp, Coordinator of Graduate Programs, 217-333-2730, Fax: 217-244-5705, E-mail: deiskamp@illinois.edu.

University of Maryland, Baltimore County, Graduate School, College of Engineering and Information Technology, Department of Computer Science and Electrical Engineering, Program in Systems Engineering, Baltimore, MD 21250. Offers MS, Postbaccalaureate Certificate. Part-time programs available. *Students:* 3 full-time (0 women), 21 part-time (5 women); includes 12 minority (8 African Americans, 4 Asian Americans or Pacific Islanders), 2 international. Average age 33. 13 applicants, 77% accepted, 9 enrolled. In 2009, 2 master's, 10 other advanced degrees awarded. *Degree requirements:* For master's, comprehensive exam (for some programs), thesis optional. *Entrance requirements:* For master's, BS in engineering or information technology with minimum GPA of 3.0. Additional exam requirements/recommendations for international students: Required—TOEFL (minimum score 550 paper-based; 213 computer-based; 80 iBT). *Application deadline:* For fall admission, 7/1 for domestic and international students; for spring admission, 12/1 for domestic and international students. Applications are processed on a rolling basis. Application fee: $50. Electronic applications accepted. *Financial support:* Career-related internships or fieldwork, Federal Work-Study, scholarships/grants, health care benefits, tuition waivers (partial), and unspecified assistantships available. Support available to part-time students. Financial award application deadline: 6/30; financial award applicants required to submit FAFSA. *Faculty research:* Systems architecture design, modeling and simulation, design and risk analysis, system integrations test, management and engineering projects. *Unit head:* Dr. Charles K. Nicholas, Professor and Chair, 410-455-3500, Fax: 410-455-3969, E-mail: nicholas@cs.umbc.edu. *Application contact:* Dr. Ted M. Foster, Professor of Practice and Assistant Dean, COEIT, 410-455-1564, Fax: 410-455-3559, E-mail: tfoster@umbc.edu.

University of Maryland, College Park, Academic Affairs, A. James Clark School of Engineering, Department of Continuing and Distance Learning in Engineering, Professional Program in Engineering, College Park, MD 20742. Offers aerospace engineering (M Eng); chemical engineering (M Eng); civil engineering (M Eng); electrical engineering (M Eng); engineering (Certificate); fire protection engineering (M Eng); materials science and engineering (M Eng); mechanical engineering (M Eng); reliability engineering (M Eng); systems engineering (M Eng). Part-time and evening/weekend programs available. Postbaccalaureate distance learning degree programs offered. *Students:* 50 full-time (15 women), 234 part-time (41 women); includes 91 minority (36 African Americans, 39 Asian Americans or Pacific Islanders, 16 Hispanic Americans), 45 international. 137 applicants, 69% accepted, 77 enrolled. In 2009, 103 master's awarded. *Entrance requirements:* For master's, 3 letters of recommendation. *Application deadline:* For fall admission, 8/15 for domestic students, 1/10 for international students; for spring admission, 12/15 for domestic students, 6/1 for international students. Applications are processed on a rolling basis. Application fee: $60. Electronic applications accepted. *Expenses:* Tuition, area resident: Part-time $471 per credit hour. Tuition, state resident: part-time $471 per credit hour. Tuition, nonresident: part-time $1016 per credit hour. Required fees: $337.04 per term. *Financial support:* In 2009–10, 2 research assistantships with tuition reimbursements (averaging $19,561 per year), 9 teaching assistantships with tuition reimbursements (averaging $16,849 per year) were awarded; fellowships, Federal Work-Study and scholarships/grants also available. Support available to part-time students. Financial award applicants required to submit FAFSA. *Unit head:* Dr. George Syrmos, Director, 301-405-3633, Fax: 301-314-3305, E-mail: syrmos@umd.edu. *Application contact:* Dean of Graduate School, 301-405-0376, Fax: 301-314-9305.

University of Maryland, College Park, Academic Affairs, A. James Clark School of Engineering, Systems Engineering Program, College Park, MD 20742. Offers M Eng, MS. Part-time and evening/weekend programs available. *Students:* 2 full-time (both women), 1 part-time (0 women); includes 1 minority (Asian American or Pacific Islander). 39 applicants, 26% accepted, 2 enrolled. *Degree requirements:* For master's, thesis optional. *Entrance requirements:* For master's, GRE General Test, minimum GPA of 3.0. *Application deadline:* For fall admission, 5/31 for domestic students, 2/1 for international students. Applications are processed on a rolling basis. Application fee: $60. Electronic applications accepted. *Expenses:* Tuition, area resident: Part-time $471 per credit hour. Tuition, state resident: part-time $471 per credit hour. Tuition, nonresident: part-time $1016 per credit hour. Required fees: $337.04 per term. *Financial support:* In 2009–10, 1 research assistantship with tuition reimbursement (averaging $16,551 per year) was awarded; fellowships with tuition reimbursements, teaching assistantships with tuition reimbursements, Federal Work-Study and scholarships/grants also available. Support available to part-time students. Financial award applicants required to submit FAFSA. *Faculty research:* Automation, computer, information, manufacturing, and process systems. *Unit head:* Dr. Eyad Abed, Professor and Director, 301-405-6615, E-mail: abed@isrmail.isr.umd.edu. *Application contact:* Dean of Graduate School, 301-405-0358, Fax: 301-314-9305.

University of Michigan–Dearborn, College of Engineering and Computer Science, Department of Industrial and Manufacturing Systems Engineering, Dearborn, MI 48128-1491. Offers engineering management (MS); industrial and systems engineering (MSE); information systems and technology (MS); information systems engineering (PhD); MBA/MSE. Part-time and evening/weekend programs available. *Faculty:* 14 full-time (0 women), 5 part-time/adjunct (0 women). *Students:* 16 full-time (5 women), 179 part-time (56 women); includes 45 minority (6 African Americans, 26 Asian Americans or Pacific Islanders, 13 Hispanic Americans). Average age 31. 63 applicants, 62% accepted, 37 enrolled. In 2009, 67 master's awarded. *Degree requirements:* For master's, thesis optional. *Entrance requirements:* For master's, bachelor's degree in applied mathematics, computer science, engineering, or physical science; minimum GPA of 3.0. Additional exam requirements/recommendations for international students: Required—TOEFL (minimum score 560 paper-based; 220 computer-based; 84 iBT). *Application deadline:* For fall admission, 8/1 priority date for domestic students, 4/1 for international students; for winter admission, 12/1 priority date for domestic students, 8/1 for international students; for spring admission, 4/1 for domestic students, 12/1 for international students. Applications are processed on a rolling basis. Application fee: $60 ($75 for international students). *Expenses:* Tuition, area resident: Part-time $504.10 per credit hour. Tuition, state resident: part-time $504.10 per credit hour. Tuition, nonresident: part-time $957.90 per credit hour. *Financial support:* Fellowships, research assistantships, teaching assistantships, Federal Work-Study available. Financial award application deadline: 4/1; financial award applicants required to submit FAFSA. *Faculty research:* Health care systems, data and knowledge management, human factors engineering, machine diagnostics, precision machining. *Unit head:* Dr. Armen Zakarian, Chair, 313-593-5361, Fax: 313-593-3692, E-mail: zakarian@umd.umich.edu. *Application contact:* Joey W. Woods, Graduate Program Assistant, 313-593-5361, Fax: 313-593-3692, E-mail: jwwoods@umd.umich.edu.

See Close-Up on page 431.

University of Michigan–Dearborn, College of Engineering and Computer Science, Interdisciplinary Programs, Program in Information Systems Engineering, Dearborn, MI 48128-1491. Offers PhD. Part-time and evening/weekend programs available. *Faculty:* 1 full-time (0 women). *Students:* 9 part-time (1 woman); includes 1 Asian American or Pacific Islander, 6 international. Average age 32. 13 applicants, 69% accepted, 9 enrolled. *Degree requirements:* For doctorate, thesis/dissertation. *Entrance requirements:* For doctorate, GRE. Additional exam requirements/recommendations for international students: Required—TOEFL (minimum score 560 paper-based; 220 computer-based; 84 iBT). *Application deadline:* For fall admission, 8/1 priority date for domestic students, 4/1 priority date for international students; for winter admission, 12/1 priority date for domestic students, 8/1 priority date for international students; for spring admission, 4/1 priority date for domestic students, 12/1 priority date for international students. Applications are processed on a rolling basis. Application fee: $60. Electronic applications accepted. *Expenses:* Tuition, area resident: Part-time $504.10 per credit hour. Tuition, state resident: part-time $504.10 per credit hour. Tuition, nonresident: part-time $957.90 per credit hour. *Financial support:* In 2009–10, 6 research assistantships (averaging $19,000 per year) were awarded; scholarships/grants and unspecified assistantships also available. Financial award applicants required to submit FAFSA. *Unit head:* Dr. Pankaj K. Mallick, Director/Professor, 313-593-5119, Fax: 313-593-5386, E-mail: pkm@umich.edu. *Application contact:* Sherry Boyd, Intermediate Administrative Assistant, 313-593-5582, Fax: 313-593-5386, E-mail: idpgrad@umd.umich.edu.

See Close-Up on page 431.

University of Minnesota, Twin Cities Campus, Institute of Technology, Technological Leadership Institute, Program in Infrastructure Systems Engineering, Minneapolis, MN 55455-0213. Offers MSISE. Evening/weekend programs available. *Faculty:* 3 full-time (0 women), 5 part-time/adjunct (0 women). *Students:* 15 full-time (5 women); includes 2 Asian Americans or Pacific Islanders. Average age 36. 12 applicants, 83% accepted, 10 enrolled. In 2009, 7 master's awarded. *Degree requirements:* For master's, capstone project. *Entrance requirements:* For master's, minimum of one year of work experience in related field, undergraduate degree in civil engineering or related field, minimum GPA of 3.0. Additional exam requirements/recommendations for international students: Required—TOEFL (minimum score 580 paper-based; 240 computer-based; 90 iBT). *Application deadline:* For spring admission, 10/15 priority date for domestic students. Applications are processed on a rolling basis. Application fee: $75 ($95 for international students). Electronic applications accepted. *Expenses:* Contact institution. *Financial support:* In 2009–10, 3 students received support, including 3 fellowships with partial tuition reimbursements available (averaging $4,800 per year); institutionally sponsored loans and scholarships/grants also available. Financial award application deadline: 11/15; financial award applicants required to submit FAFSA. *Faculty research:* Water distribution, pavement maintenance and management, traffic management systems, infrastructure systems maintenance and management. *Unit head:* Dr. Vaughan Voller, Director of Graduate Studies, 612-625-0764, Fax: 612-626-7750, E-mail: volle001@tc.umn.edu. *Application contact:* Jenna Egan, Student Services and Admissions, 612-624-4380, Fax: 612-624-7510, E-mail: tliss@umn.edu.

University of New Haven, Graduate School, Tagliatela College of Engineering, Program in Computer and Information Science, West Haven, CT 06516-1916. Offers computer science (MS, Certificate), including advanced applications (MS), computer applications (Certificate), computer programming (Certificate), computer systems (MS), computing (Certificate), database and information systems (MS), network administration (Certificate), network systems (MS), software engineering and development (MS). Part-time and evening/weekend programs available. *Faculty:* 9 full-time (2 women), 5 part-time/adjunct (0 women). *Students:* 21 full-time (8 women), 32 part-time (8 women); includes 5 minority (2 African Americans, 1 Asian American or Pacific Islander, 2 Hispanic Americans), 26 international. Average age 30. 163 applicants, 88% accepted, 18 enrolled. In 2009, 24 master's awarded. *Degree requirements:* For master's, thesis or alternative. *Entrance requirements:* Additional exam requirements/recommendations for international students: Required—TOEFL (minimum score 520 paper-based; 190 computer-based; 70 iBT); Recommended—IELTS (minimum score 5.5). *Application deadline:* For fall admission, 5/31 for international students; for winter admission, 10/15 for international students; for spring admission, 1/15 for international students. Applications are processed on a rolling basis. Application fee: $50. Electronic applications accepted. *Expenses:* Tuition: Part-time $700 per credit. Required fees: $45 per term. One-time fee: $390 part-time. *Financial support:* Research assistantships with partial tuition reimbursements, teaching assistantships with partial tuition reimbursements, career-related internships or fieldwork, Federal Work-Study, scholarships/grants, tuition waivers, and unspecified assistantships available. Support available to part-time students. Financial award applicants required to submit FAFSA. *Unit head:* Dr. Tahany Fergany, Coordinator, 203-932-7067. *Application contact:* Eloise Gormley, Director of Graduate Admissions, 203-932-7449, Fax: 203-932-7137, E-mail: gradinfo@newhaven.edu.

The University of North Carolina at Charlotte, Graduate School, The William States Lee College of Engineering, Department of Civil and Environmental Engineering, Program in Infrastructure and Environmental Systems (INES), Charlotte, NC 28223-0001. Offers infrastructure and environmental systems design (PhD); infrastructure and environmental systems management (PhD). *Faculty:* 17 full-time (2 women), 1 part-time/adjunct (0 women). *Students:* 26 full-time (9 women), 9 part-time (2 women); includes 2 minority (both African Americans), 17 international. Average age 32. 13 applicants, 62% accepted, 6 enrolled. In 2009, 3 doctorates awarded. *Degree requirements:* For doctorate, thesis/dissertation, dissertation defense, qualifying exam. *Entrance requirements:* Additional exam requirements/recommendations for international students: Required—TOEFL (minimum score 557 paper-based; 220 computer-based; 83 iBT). *Application deadline:* For fall admission, 7/1 for domestic students, 5/1 for international students; for spring admission, 11/1 for domestic students, 10/1 for international students. Applications are processed on a rolling basis. Application fee: $55. Electronic applications accepted. *Financial support:* Research assistantships, teaching assistantships, career-related internships or fieldwork, Federal Work-Study, institutionally sponsored loans, scholarships/grants, and unspecified assistantships available. Support available to part-time students. Financial award application deadline: 4/1; financial award applicants required to submit FAFSA. Total annual research expenditures: $968,217. *Unit head:* Dr. David T. Young, Chair, Civil Engineering, 704-687-4178, Fax: 704-687-6953, E-mail: dyoung@uncc.edu. *Application contact:* Kathy B. Giddings, Director of Graduate Admissions, 704-687-5503, Fax: 704-687-3279, E-mail: gradadm@uncc.edu.

University of Pennsylvania, School of Engineering and Applied Science, Department of Electrical and Systems Engineering, Philadelphia, PA 19104. Offers MSE, PhD. Part-time programs available. *Faculty:* 27 full-time (2 women), 8 part-time/adjunct (0 women). *Students:* 121 full-time (29 women), 44 part-time (7 women); includes 22 minority (4 African Americans, 17 Asian Americans or Pacific Islanders, 1 Hispanic American), 101 international. 574 applicants, 32% accepted, 105 enrolled. In 2009, 61 master's, 8 doctorates awarded. Terminal master's awarded for partial completion of doctoral program. *Degree requirements:* For master's, thesis optional; for doctorate, comprehensive exam, thesis/dissertation. *Entrance requirements:* For master's and doctorate, GRE General Test. Additional exam requirements/recommendations for international students: Required—TOEFL. *Application deadline:* For fall admission, 6/1 priority date for domestic students, 5/1 priority date for international students; for spring admission, 11/1 priority date for domestic students, 10/1 priority date for international students. Applications are processed on a rolling basis. Application fee: $70. Electronic applications accepted. *Expenses:* Tuition: Full-time $25,660; part-time $4758 per course. Required fees: $2152; $270 per course. Tuition and fees vary according to course load, degree level and program. *Financial support:* Fellowships, research assistantships, teaching assistantships, institutionally sponsored loans, scholarships/grants, traineeships, health care benefits, and unspecified assistantships available. *Faculty research:* Electro-optics, microwave and millimeter-wave optics, solid-state and chemical electronics, electromagnetic propagation, telecommunications.

University of Regina, Faculty of Graduate Studies and Research, Faculty of Engineering and Applied Science, Program in Industrial Systems Engineering, Regina, SK S4S 0A2, Canada. Offers M Eng, MA Sc, PhD. *Faculty:* 10 full-time (0 women). *Students:* 27 full-time (3 women), 3 part-time (1 woman). 71 applicants, 55% accepted. In 2009, 6 master's, 3 doctorates awarded. *Degree requirements:* For master's, thesis (for some programs). *Entrance requirements:* For doctorate, master's degree. Additional exam requirements/recommendations for international students: Required—TOEFL (minimum score 550 paper-based; 213 computer-based; 80 iBT). *Application deadline:* Applications are processed on a rolling basis. Application fee: $90 ($100 for international students). *Financial support:* In 2009–10, 6 fellowships (averaging $19,000 per year), 3 research assistantships (averaging $16,910 per year), 10 teaching assistantships (averaging $6,650 per year) were awarded; career-related internships or fieldwork and scholarships/grants also available. Financial award application deadline: 6/15. *Faculty research:* Gas separation and purification, welding. *Unit head:* Dr. Denise Stilling, Graduate Program Coordinator, 306-337-2696, E-mail: denise.stilling@uregina.ca. *Application contact:* Crystal Pick, 306-337-2603, E-mail: crystal.pick@uregina.ca.

University of Regina, Faculty of Graduate Studies and Research, Faculty of Engineering and Applied Science, Program in Petroleum Systems Engineering, Regina, SK S4S 0A2, Canada. Offers M Eng, MA Sc, PhD. *Faculty:* 5 full-time (0 women). *Students:* 27 full-time (3 women), 4 part-time (1 woman). 84 applicants, 35% accepted. In 2009, 2 master's, 2 doctorates awarded. *Entrance requirements:* Additional exam requirements/recommendations for international students: Required—TOEFL (minimum score 580 paper-based; 237 computer-based; 80 iBT). Application fee: $90 ($100 for international students). *Financial support:* In 2009–10, 6 fellowships (averaging $19,000 per year), 3 research assistantships (averaging $16,910 per year), 9 teaching assistantships (averaging $6,650 per year) were awarded. *Unit head:* Dr. Farshid Torabi, Graduate Program Coordinator, 306-337-3287, E-mail: farshid.torabi@uregina.ca. *Application contact:* Crystal Pick, Graduate Program Coordinator, 306-337-3603, E-mail: crystal.pick@uregina.ca.

University of St. Thomas, Graduate Studies, School of Engineering, St. Paul, MN 55105-1096. Offers engineering and technology management (Certificate); manufacturing systems (MS); manufacturing systems engineering (MMSE); systems engineering (MS); technology management (MS). *Accreditation:* ABET (one or more programs are accredited). Electronic applications accepted. *Expenses:* Contact institution.

University of Southern California, Graduate School, Viterbi School of Engineering, Department of Industrial and Systems Engineering, Program in Systems Architecting and Engineering, Los Angeles, CA 90089. Offers MS. Postbaccalaureate distance learning degree programs offered (no on-campus study). *Students:* 3 full-time (0 women), 177 part-time (30 women); includes 61 minority (10 African Americans, 3 American Indian/Alaska Native, 31 Asian Americans or Pacific Islanders, 17 Hispanic Americans), 1 international. In 2009, 82 master's awarded. Application fee: $85. Electronic applications accepted. *Expenses:* Tuition: Full-time $25,980; part-time $1315 per unit. Required fees: $554. One-time fee: $35 full-time. Full-time tuition and fees vary according to degree level and program. *Unit head:* Dr. James E. Moore, Chair, 213-740-4885, Fax: 213-740-1120, E-mail: jmoore@usc.edu. *Application contact:* Mary Ordaz, Student Service Advisor, 213-740-4886, Fax: 213-740-1120, E-mail: isedept@usc.edu.

University of Southern California, Graduate School, Viterbi School of Engineering, Ming Hsieh Department of Electrical Engineering, Los Angeles, CA 90089. Offers computer engineering (MS, PhD); computer networks (MS), including electrical engineering; computer-aided engineering (MS); electrical engineering (PhD, Engr); engineering technology commercialization (Graduate Certificate); systems architeching and engineering (MS). Part-time programs available. Postbaccalaureate distance learning degree programs offered. *Faculty:* 59 full-time (3 women), 31 part-time/adjunct (1 woman). *Students:* 883 full-time (146 women), 451 part-time (65 women); includes 197 minority (16 African Americans, 159 Asian Americans or Pacific Islanders, 22 Hispanic Americans), 957 international. 2,377 applicants, 45% accepted, 514 enrolled. In 2009, 351 master's, 41 doctorates, 2 other advanced degrees awarded. Terminal master's awarded for partial completion of doctoral program. *Degree requirements:* For doctorate, thesis/dissertation. *Entrance requirements:* For master's, GRE General Test; for doctorate, General GRE. *Application deadline:* For fall admission, 3/1 priority date for domestic and international students; for spring admission, 10/1 priority date for domestic and international students. Applications are processed on a rolling basis. Application fee: $85. Electronic applications accepted. *Expenses:* Tuition: Full-time $25,980; part-time $1315 per unit. Required fees: $554. One-time fee: $35 full-time. Full-time tuition and fees vary according to degree level and program. *Financial support:* Career-related internships or fieldwork, scholarships/grants, health care benefits, and unspecified assistantships available. Financial award application deadline: 12/1; financial award applicants required to submit CSS PROFILE or FAFSA. *Faculty research:* Communications, computer engineering and networks, control systems, integrated circuits and systems, electromagnetics and energy conversion, micro electro-mechanical systems and nanotechnology, photonics and quantum electronics, plasma research, signal and image

Systems Engineering

University of Southern California (continued)

processing. Total annual research expenditures: $16.2 million. *Unit head:* Dr. Alexander A. Sawchuk, Chair, 213-740-4622, Fax: 213-740-4651, E-mail: sawchuk@sipi.usc.edu. *Application contact:* Diane Demetras, Student Affairs Coordinator, 213-740-4485, E-mail: eesystem@usc.edu.

The University of Texas at Arlington, Graduate School, College of Engineering, Department of Industrial and Manufacturing Systems Engineering, Program in Systems Engineering, Arlington, TX 76019. Offers MS. *Students:* 1 (woman) full-time, 16 part-time (4 women); includes 3 minority (1 African American, 1 Asian American or Pacific Islander, 1 Hispanic American), 1 international. 7 applicants, 100% accepted, 3 enrolled. In 2009, 5 master's awarded. *Unit head:* Dr. Donald H. Liles, Chair, 817-272-3092, Fax: 817-272-3406, E-mail: dliles@uta.edu. *Application contact:* Dr. Sheik Imrhan, Graduate Advisor, 817-272-3167, Fax: 817-272-3406, E-mail: imrhan@uta.edu.

The University of Texas at El Paso, Graduate School, College of Engineering, Department of Industrial Engineering, El Paso, TX 79968-0001. Offers industrial engineering (MS); manufacturing engineering (MS); systems engineering (MS, Certificate). Part-time and evening/weekend programs available. *Degree requirements:* For master's, thesis optional. *Entrance requirements:* For master's, GRE General Test, minimum GPA of 3.0 in major. Additional exam requirements/recommendations for international students: Required—TOEFL. Electronic applications accepted. *Faculty research:* Computer vision, automated inspection, simulation and modeling.

University of Virginia, School of Engineering and Applied Science, Department of Systems and Information Engineering, Charlottesville, VA 22903. Offers ME, MS, PhD, ME/MBA. Post-baccalaureate distance learning degree programs offered (no on-campus study). *Faculty:* 19 full-time (2 women). *Students:* 82 full-time (25 women), 5 part-time (1 woman); includes 17 minority (1 African American, 11 Asian Americans or Pacific Islanders, 5 Hispanic Americans), 32 international. Average age 27. 124 applicants, 33% accepted, 24 enrolled. In 2009, 47 master's, 2 doctorates awarded. *Degree requirements:* For master's, comprehensive exam (for some programs); for doctorate, comprehensive exam, thesis/dissertation. *Entrance requirements:* For master's, GRE General Test, 3 letters of recommendation; for doctorate, GRE General Test, 3 letters of recommendation; essay. Additional exam requirements/recommendations for international students: Required—TOEFL (minimum score 650 paper-based; 250 computer-based; 90 iBT), IELTS (minimum score 7). *Application deadline:* For fall admission, 8/1 for domestic students, 4/1 for international students; for winter admission, 12/1 for domestic students, 8/1 for international students; for spring admission, 5/1 for domestic students, 1/1 for international students. Applications are processed on a rolling basis. Application fee: $60. Electronic applications accepted. *Financial support:* Fellowships, research assistantships, teaching assistantships available. Financial award application deadline: 1/15; financial award applicants required to submit FAFSA. *Faculty research:* Systems integration, human factors, computational statistics and simulation, risk and decision analysis, optimization and control. *Unit head:* Barry Horowitz, Chair, 434-924-5393, Fax: 434-982-2972. *Application contact:* Departmental Office, 434-924-5393, Fax: 434-982-2972, E-mail: siegradadministration@virginia.edu.

University of Waterloo, Graduate Studies, Faculty of Engineering, Department of Systems Design Engineering, Waterloo, ON N2L 3G1, Canada. Offers M Eng, MA Sc, PhD. Part-time programs available. *Degree requirements:* For master's, research project or thesis; for doctorate, comprehensive exam, thesis/dissertation. *Entrance requirements:* For master's, honors degree, minimum B average, resumé; for doctorate, master's degree, minimum A- average. Additional exam requirements/recommendations for international students: Required—TOEFL, TWE. Electronic applications accepted. *Faculty research:* Ergonomics, human factors and biomedical engineering, modeling and simulation, pattern analysis, machine intelligence and robotics.

University of Wisconsin–Madison, Graduate School, College of Engineering, Department of Industrial and Systems Engineering, Madison, WI 53706. Offers MS, PhD. Part-time programs available. *Faculty:* 20 full-time (6 women), 11 part-time/adjunct (4 women). *Students:* 164 full-time (48 women), 18 part-time (3 women); includes 13 minority (3 African Americans, 3 American Indian/Alaska Native, 5 Asian Americans or Pacific Islanders, 2 Hispanic Americans), 131 international. Average age 27. 349 applicants, 56% accepted, 78 enrolled. In 2009, 38 master's, 14 doctorates awarded. Terminal master's awarded for partial completion of doctoral program. *Degree requirements:* For master's, thesis optional; for doctorate, comprehensive exam, thesis/dissertation. *Entrance requirements:* For master's, GRE General Test, min GPA of 3.0 (3.00 in last 60 crs) BS in engineering or equivalent course in Computer Programming, course in Stats, 2 intro ISYE courses; for doctorate, GRE General Test, minimum GPA of 3.0 (3.00 in last 60 credits). Additional exam requirements/recommendations for international students: Recommended—TOEFL (minimum score 600 paper-based; 250 computer-based;

104 iBT). *Application deadline:* For fall admission, 4/1 priority date for domestic and international students; for spring admission, 10/1 priority date for domestic and international students. Application fee: $56. Electronic applications accepted. *Expenses:* Tuition, state resident: part-time $594 per credit. Tuition, nonresident: part-time $1504 per credit. Required fees: $65 per credit. Tuition and fees vary according to course load, program and reciprocity agreements. *Financial support:* In 2009–10, 70 students received support, including 1 fellowship with full tuition reimbursement available (averaging $21,760 per year), 47 research assistantships with full tuition reimbursements available (averaging $40,368 per year), 22 teaching assistantships with full tuition reimbursements available (averaging $28,175 per year); career-related internships or fieldwork, Federal Work-Study, institutionally sponsored loans, scholarships/grants, traineeships, health care benefits, and unspecified assistantships also available. *Faculty research:* Human factors and ergonomics, manufacturing and production systems, health systems engineering, decision science/operations research, quality engineering. Total annual research expenditures: $12.2 million. *Unit head:* Dr. Patricia F. Brennan, Chair, 608-262-9227, Fax: 608-262-8454, E-mail: pbrennan@engr.wisc.edu. *Application contact:* Anne Duchek, Graduate Admissions Coordinator, 608-890-2765, Fax: 608-890-2204, E-mail: amduchek@engr.wisc.edu.

Virginia Polytechnic Institute and State University, Graduate School, College of Engineering, Department of Industrial and Systems Engineering, Program in Systems Engineering, Blacksburg, VA 24061. Offers M Eng, MS. *Entrance requirements:* For master's, GRE. Additional exam requirements/recommendations for international students: Required—TOEFL (minimum score 550 paper-based; 213 computer-based). Electronic applications accepted.

Walden University, Graduate Programs, NTU School of Engineering and Applied Science, Minneapolis, MN 55401. Offers competitive product management (Postbaccalaureate Certificate); engineering management (Postbaccalaureate Certificate); software engineering (MS); software project management (Postbaccalaureate Certificate); software testing (Postbaccalaureate Certificate); systems engineering (MS, Postbaccalaureate Certificate); technical project management (Postbaccalaureate Certificate). Part-time and evening/weekend programs available. Postbaccalaureate distance learning degree programs offered (no on-campus study). *Faculty:* 31 part-time/adjunct. *Students:* 22 full-time (6 women), 120 part-time (14 women); includes 26 minority (19 African Americans, 7 Asian Americans or Pacific Islanders). Average age 38. In 2009, 41 master's awarded. *Degree requirements:* For master's, thesis optional. *Entrance requirements:* For master's, bachelor's degree or equivalent in related field, minimum GPA of 2.5. Additional exam requirements/recommendations for international students: Required—TOEFL (minimum score 550 paper-based; 213 computer-based), IELTS (minimum score 6.5), or Michigan English Language Assessment Battery (minimum score 82). *Application deadline:* Applications are processed on a rolling basis. Application fee: $50. Electronic applications accepted. *Expenses:* Tuition: Full-time $13,665; part-time $560 per credit. Required fees: $1375. Tuition and fees vary according to course load, degree level and program. *Financial support:* Fellowships, Federal Work-Study, scholarships/grants, unspecified assistantships, and family tuition reduction, active duty/veteran tuition reduction, group tuition reduction, interest-free payment plans available. Support available to part-time students. Financial award applicants required to submit FAFSA. *Unit head:* Colin Wightman, Interim Associate Dean, 800-925-3368. *Application contact:* Jennifer Hall, Director of Enrollment, 866-4-WALDEN, E-mail: info@walden.edu.

Western International University, Graduate Programs in Business, Master of Science Program in Information System Engineering, Phoenix, AZ 85021-2718. Offers MS. Part-time and evening/weekend programs available. Postbaccalaureate distance learning degree programs offered (no on-campus study). *Faculty:* 14 part-time/adjunct (2 women). *Students:* 89 full-time (24 women); includes 21 minority (5 African Americans, 1 American Indian/Alaska Native, 5 Asian Americans or Pacific Islanders, 10 Hispanic Americans), 5 international. Average age 39. In 2009, 17 master's awarded. *Entrance requirements:* For master's, minimum GPA of 2.75. Additional exam requirements/recommendations for international students: Required—TOEFL (minimum score 550 paper-based; 213 computer-based; 79 iBT), TWE (minimum score 5), IELTS. *Application deadline:* Applications are processed on a rolling basis. Application fee: $25. Electronic applications accepted. *Expenses:* Tuition: Full-time $12,600. One-time fee: $25 full-time. *Financial support:* Applicants required to submit FAFSA. *Unit head:* Dr. Deborah DeSimone, Chief Academic Officer, 602-429-1135, E-mail: deborah.desimone@west.edu. *Application contact:* Melissa Machuca, Director of Enrollment, 602-943-2311, Fax: 602-371-8637.

West Virginia University Institute of Technology, College of Engineering, Program in Control Systems Engineering, Montgomery, WV 25136. Offers MS. Part-time programs available. *Degree requirements:* For master's, thesis or alternative, fieldwork. *Entrance requirements:* For master's, GRE General Test, minimum GPA of 3.0. Additional exam requirements/recommendations for international students: Required—TOEFL. *Faculty research:* Process control.

DEARBORN

UNIVERSITY OF MICHIGAN–DEARBORN

College of Engineering and Computer Science
Ph.D. Programs

Programs of Study	The University of Michigan–Dearborn offers two Ph.D. degrees through the College of Engineering and Computer Science.
	The Ph.D. in information systems engineering is an interdisciplinary collaboration between three departments: computer and information science, electrical and computer engineering, and industrial and manufacturing systems engineering. The program is designed to meet the need of engineers who want to be the technology leaders of the future. It is a 50-credit-hour postgraduate program and can be pursued on either a full- or part-time basis. The classes are held in the evening for the convenience of working engineers. The areas of specialization include information management and knowledge engineering, computer networks and computer architecture, intelligent systems and human/computer interaction, graphics and visualization, supply chain informatics, and Web services and security.
	The Ph.D. program in automotive systems engineering is designed to meet the needs of engineers who intend to pursue a career as technical specialists and serve as technical leaders, innovators, and research mentors. It is a 50-credit-hour postgraduate program and can be pursued on either a full- or part-time basis. The classes are held in the evening for the convenience of working engineers. The areas of specialization include materials and materials processing, energy systems and thermal management, dynamics and controls, power electronics, vehicle design, manufacturing and systems integration, and vehicle informatics and communication.
Research Facilities	The College of Engineering and Computer Science built the Engineering Complex in 1997, adding 53,000 square feet of laboratory, classroom, office, and study space. The complex houses a rapid prototype laboratory, a human factors laboratory, a design studio, a hypermedia laboratory, and CAD, PC, Macintosh, networking, and Sun computer laboratories. The Manufacturing Systems Engineering Laboratory building is equipped with laboratories that include metrology, machine dynamics and diagnostics, precision machining, and computer-integrated manufacturing. This component of manufacturing research is supplemented by an extensive array of computers dedicated to the engineering disciplines. In addition, the College has several other experimental laboratories available for research: machine vision and intelligence, design and fatigue, acoustics and vibrations, combustion engines and fuels, vehicle electronics, plastics and composites, circuits, electronic control systems, energy conversion, manufacturing simulation, 3-D imaging, applied thermodynamics, fluid mechanics, heat transfer, computer automation, robotics, data communications, and digital systems. Combined, the College's facilities provide effective and comprehensive areas for teaching, student projects, research, and faculty projects that affect curriculum and build strong partnerships with industry, government, and the community.
	The College also features several centers and institutes—the Institute for Advanced Vehicle Systems, the Center for Lightweight Automotive Materials and Processing, the Henry W. Patton Center for Engineering Education & Practice, and the Vetronics Institute—to further facilitate advanced research objectives.
Cost of Study	Pre-candidate engineering students who are residents of Michigan are assessed $504.10 per credit hour for 1–8 credits and $287.25 per credit hour for 9 or more credits. Nonresident tuition for doctorate pre-candidate students is $957.90 per credit hour for 1–8 credits and $622.15 per credit hour for 9 or more credits. Both residents and nonresidents pay a $163.25 registration fee.
	Doctorate engineering students are assessed $504.10 per credit hour for 1–8 credits and $287.25 per credit hour for 9 or more credits, with a $163.25 registration fee. There is also a doctorate candidacy maintenance assessment of $823.55.
	Engineering courses at the 300–499 level carry an additional upper division course premium tuition assessment of $47.35 per credit hour. Engineering courses at the 500 and above level are assessed an additional $77.25 per credit hour.
	The technology assessment for all engineering students is $78.95 (6 or fewer credit hours) or $157.95 (7 or more credit hours).
Living and Housing Costs	The local living costs are somewhat dependent upon the availability of housing. An estimation of living costs beyond the cost of study is $1400 per month.
Student Group	Enrollment at the University of Michigan–Dearborn is 8,700 students. Of this figure, 2,500 students are enrolled in the College of Engineering and Computer Science.
Location	The University of Michigan–Dearborn is located in the heart of Michigan's largest urban area, just 10 miles from downtown Detroit and a wide variety of cultural, athletic, and recreational opportunities. Many outdoor recreation facilities, including rivers, lakes, beaches, and ski areas are within a short driving distance.
The University	The University of Michigan–Dearborn is one of three campuses governed by the University of Michigan Board of Regents. As a regional campus of the University of Michigan system, it shares in the tradition of excellence in teaching, research, and service. The campus, which is located on 202 acres of the former estate of the late Henry Ford, is primarily a commuter campus. It was founded in 1959 as a senior-level institution offering only junior, senior, and graduate courses. Since 1971, the Dearborn campus has offered full four-year degree programs and expanded its graduate offerings. As part of the University of Michigan System, U of M–Dearborn enjoys the resources of a large multiuniversity and the advantages of moderate size.
Applying	Applications for Ph.D. admission, accompanied by a nonrefundable fee of $60, transcripts, and letters of recommendation should reach the department by May 15 for the fall term and September 15 for the winter term. Application materials can be downloaded via the College's Web site at http://www.engin.umd.umich.edu/pros_students/phd_forms.php.
Correspondence and Information	For information about the Ph.D. programs at the University please contact:

College of Engineering and Computer Science
Director of Doctoral Program
Room 116 MSEL
University of Michigan–Dearborn
4901 Evergreen Road
Dearborn, Michigan 48128-1491

Phone: 313-593-5582
Fax: 313-593-5386
E-mail: idpgrad@umd.umich.edu
Web site: http://www.engin.umd.umich.edu/phd

University of Michigan–Dearborn

THE FACULTY AND THEIR RESEARCH

Alan Argento, Professor of Mechanical Engineering; Ph.D., Michigan, 1989. Structural dynamics, vibration.

Vivek Bhise, Professor of Industrial and Manufacturing Systems Engineering; Ph.D., Ohio State, 1971. Human factors engineering, vehicle ergonomics, total quality management.

Charu Chandra, Associate Professor of Industrial and Manufacturing Systems Engineering; Ph.D., Arizona State, 1994. Supply chain management, enterprise resource planning systems.

Yubao Chen, Professor of Industrial and Manufacturing Systems Engineering; Ph.D., Wisconsin–Madison, 1986. Knowledge-based systems, intelligent diagnosis and monitoring, reliability engineering.

Chi L. Chow, Professor of Mechanical Engineering; Ph.D., London, 1965. Fatigue, fracture mechanics, damage mechanics.

Jinhua Guo, Assistant Professor of Computer and Information Science; Ph.D., Georgia, 2002. Networking, wireless networks, vehicular networks, security and privacy.

Dohoy Jung, Assistant Professor of Mechanical Engineering; Ph.D., Michigan–Dearborn, 2001. Advanced energy conversion in automotive systems including internal combustion engine processes, hybrid powertrain, PEM fuel cell, vehicle thermal management, system integration.

HongTae Kang, Assistant Professor of Mechanical Engineering; Ph.D., Alabama, 1999. Fatigue, finite element analysis.

Taehyung Kim, Assistant Professor of Electrical and Computer Engineering; Ph.D., Texas A&M, 2003. Power electronics, vehicle control systems.

Ghassan Kridli, Associate Professor of Industrial and Manufacturing Systems Engineering; Ph.D., Missouri–Columbia, 1997. Materials processing, metal forming.

Cheol Lee, Assistant Professor of Industrial and Manufacturing Systems Engineering; Ph.D., Purdue, 2000. Dynamic systems, machining.

Ben Q. Li, Professor, Mechanical Engineering; Ph.D., Berkeley, 1989. Heat and mass transfer.

Xiangyang (Sean) Li, Assistant Professor of Industrial and Manufacturing Systems Engineering; Ph.D., Arizona State, 2001. Information systems, intelligent systems, knowledge management.

Yung-wen Liu, Assistant Professor of Industrial and Manufacturing Systems Engineering; Ph.D., Washington (Seattle), 2006. Reliability and quality engineering.

P. K. Mallick, Professor of Mechanical Engineering; Ph.D., IIT, 1973. Composite materials, polymers, light metals, joining, materials processing, design.

Carole Mei, Associate Professor of Mechanical Engineering; Ph.D., Auckland (New Zealand), 1999. Vibration and acoustics, controls.

Chris Mi, Assistant Professor of Electrical and Computer Engineering; Ph.D., Toronto, 2000. Power electronics, electrical machines, vehicle electronics, alternative energy.

Pravansu Mohanty, Associate Professor of Mechanical Engineering; Ph.D., McGill, 1994. Nanostructures, casting, thermal spray technology, rapid prototyping.

Yi Lu Murphey, Professor of Electrical and Computer Engineering; Ph.D., Michigan, 1989. Intelligent systems, machine learning.

Elsayed A. Orady, Professor of Industrial and Manufacturing Systems Engineering; Ph.D., McMaster, 1982. Manufacturing processes, machine tool and tool design, metrology.

Eric Ratts, Associate Professor of Mechanical Engineering; Ph.D., MIT, 1993. Refrigeration, heat transfer.

Paul C. Richardson, Associate Professor of Electrical and Computer Engineering; Ph.D., Oakland, 1999. Wireless communications, target tracking.

Tariq Shamim, Associate Professor of Mechanical Engineering; Ph.D., Michigan, 1997. Combustion and advanced energy systems, emissions control, CFD.

Taehyun Shim, Associate Professor of Mechanical Engineering; Ph.D., California, Davis, 2000. Vehicle dynamics, multibody dynamics, controls.

Keshav S. Varde, Professor of Mechanical Engineering; Ph.D., Rochester, 1971. Powertrain, emissions, alternative fuels.

Weidong Xiang, Assistant Professor of Electrical and Computer Engineering; Ph.D., Tsinghua (China), 1999. Wireless and broadband communications.

Armen Zakarian, Associate Professor, Department of Industrial and Manufacturing Systems Engineering; Ph.D., Iowa, 1997. Modeling and analysis of manufacturing systems, system/product engineering and architecting.

Yi Zhang, Professor of Mechanical Engineering; Ph.D., Illinois, 1989. Kinematics and mechanical design, powertrains.

Dongming Zhao, Associate Professor of Electrical and Computer Engineering; Ph.D., Rutgers, 1990. Digital image processing, financial data processing.

Oleg Zikanov, Associate Professor of Mechanical Engineering; Ph.D., Moscow State (Russia), 1993. Computational fluid mechanics.

Section 15
Management of Engineering and Technology

This section contains a directory of institutions offering graduate work in management of engineering and technology, followed by in-depth entries submitted by institutions that chose to prepare detailed program descriptions. Additional information about programs listed in the directory but not augmented by an in-depth entry may be obtained by writing directly to the dean of a graduate school or chair of a department at the address given in the directory.

For programs offering related work, in the other guides in this series:

Graduate Programs in the Humanities, Arts & Social Sciences
See *Applied Arts and Design, Architecture, Economics,* and *Sociology, Anthropology, and Archaeology*

Graduate Programs in the Biological Sciences
See *Ecology, Environmental Biology,* and *Evolutionary Biology* and *Biophysics (Radiation Biology)*

Graduate Programs in Business, Education, Health, Information Studies, Law & Social Work
See *Business Administration and Management, Health Services (Health Services Management and Hospital Administration), Law,* and *Public Health*

CONTENTS

Program Directories

Close-Ups

See also:

Construction Management

The American University in Dubai, Master in Business Administration Program, Dubai, United Arab Emirates. Offers general (MBA); healthcare management (MBA); international finance (MBA); international marketing (MBA); management of construction enterprises (MBA). Part-time and evening/weekend programs available. *Degree requirements:* For master's, thesis optional. *Entrance requirements:* For master's, GMAT, Interview. Additional exam requirements/recommendations for international students: Required—TOEFL (minimum score 550 paper-based; 213 computer-based; 79 iBT). Electronic applications accepted.

Arizona State University, Graduate College, Ira A. Fulton School of Engineering, ASU Engineering Online Programs, Tempe, AZ 85287. Offers construction (MS); embedded systems (M Eng); enterprise systems innovation and management (MSE); modeling and simulation (M Eng); quality and reliability engineering (M Eng); software engineering (MSE); systems engineering (M Eng).

Auburn University, Graduate School, College of Architecture, Design, and Construction, Department of Building Science, Auburn University, AL 36849. Offers building science (MBS); construction management (MBS). *Faculty:* 18 full-time (1 woman), 3 part-time/adjunct (1 woman). *Students:* 23 full-time (6 women), 25 part-time (3 women); includes 3 minority (1 African American, 2 Hispanic Americans), 4 international. Average age 27. 83 applicants, 60% accepted, 42 enrolled. In 2009, 7 master's awarded. *Entrance requirements:* For master's, GRE General Test. *Application deadline:* For fall admission, 7/17 for domestic students; for spring admission, 11/24 for domestic students. Applications are processed on a rolling basis. Application fee: $50 ($60 for international students). Electronic applications accepted. *Expenses:* Tuition, state resident: full-time $6240. Tuition, nonresident: full-time $18,720. International tuition: $18,938 full-time. Required fees: $492. Tuition and fees vary according to course load, program and reciprocity agreements. *Financial support:* Application deadline: 3/15; *Unit head:* John D. Murphy, Head, 334-844-4518. *Application contact:* Dr. George Flowers, Dean of the Graduate School, 334-844-2125.

Bowling Green State University, Graduate College, College of Technology, Department of Technology Systems, Bowling Green, OH 43403. Offers construction management (MIT); manufacturing technology (MIT). Part-time programs available. *Degree requirements:* For master's, thesis or alternative. *Entrance requirements:* For master's, GRE General Test. Additional exam requirements/recommendations for international students: Required—TOEFL. Electronic applications accepted.

Brigham Young University, Graduate Studies, Ira A. Fulton College of Engineering and Technology, School of Technology, Provo, UT 84602-1001. Offers construction management (MS); information technology (MS); manufacturing systems (MS); technology and engineering education (MS). *Faculty:* 25 full-time (0 women). *Students:* 23 full-time (3 women); includes 3 minority (2 Asian Americans or Pacific Islanders, 1 Hispanic American). Average age 25. 14 applicants, 71% accepted, 6 enrolled. In 2009, 13 master's awarded. *Degree requirements:* For master's, thesis. *Entrance requirements:* For master's, GRE General Test, GMAT (construction management), minimum GPA of 3.0 in last 60 hours of course work. Additional exam requirements/recommendations for international students: Required—TOEFL (minimum score 580 paper-based; 237 computer-based; 85 iBT). *Application deadline:* For fall admission, 2/15 for domestic and international students; for winter admission, 9/15 for domestic and international students; for spring admission, 2/15 for domestic and international students. Application fee: $50. Electronic applications accepted. *Expenses:* Tuition: Full-time $5580; part-time $301 per credit hour. Tuition and fees vary according to student's religious affiliation. *Financial support:* In 2009–10, 9 research assistantships (averaging $4,774 per year), 7 teaching assistantships (averaging $4,481 per year) were awarded; fellowships, career-related internships or fieldwork also available. Financial award application deadline: 2/1. *Faculty research:* Real time process control in IT, electronic physical design, processing and non-linear systems, networking, computerized systems in CM. Total annual research expenditures: $52,000. *Unit head:* Val D. Hawks, Director, 801-422-6300, Fax: 801-422-0490, E-mail: hawksv@byu.edu. *Application contact:* Ronald E. Terry, Graduate Coordinator, 801-422-4297, Fax: 801-422-0490, E-mail: ralowe@byu.edu.

California State University, East Bay, Academic Programs and Graduate Studies, College of Science, Engineering Department, Hayward, CA 94542-3000. Offers construction management (MS); engineering management (MS). *Faculty:* 4 full-time (2 women). *Students:* 24 full-time (9 women), 61 part-time (17 women); includes 27 minority (6 African Americans, 14 Asian Americans or Pacific Islanders, 7 Hispanic Americans), 33 international. Average age 31. 124 applicants, 59% accepted, 36 enrolled. In 2009, 5 master's awarded. *Entrance requirements:* For master's, GRE or GMAT, minimum GPA of 2.5. Additional exam requirements/recommendations for international students: Required—TOEFL (minimum score 550 paper-based; 213 computer-based). *Application deadline:* For fall admission, 6/30 for domestic and international students. Application fee: $55. Electronic applications accepted. *Financial support:* Federal Work-Study and institutionally sponsored loans available. Support available to part-time students. *Unit head:* Dr. Saeid Motavalli, Chair, 510-885-2654, Fax: 510-885-2678, E-mail: saeid.motavalli@csueastbay.edu. *Application contact:* Donna Wiley, Interim Associate Director, 510-885-2928, Fax: 510-885-4777, E-mail: donna.wiley@csueastbay.edu.

Carnegie Mellon University, College of Fine Arts, School of Architecture, Pittsburgh, PA 15213-3891. Offers architectural engineering construction management (M Sc); architecture (MSA); architecture, engineering, and construction management (PhD); building performance and diagnostics (M Sc, PhD); computational design (M Sc, PhD); sustainable design (M Sc); urban design (M Sc). Terminal master's awarded for partial completion of doctoral program. *Degree requirements:* For doctorate, thesis/dissertation. *Entrance requirements:* For master's and doctorate, GRE General Test. Additional exam requirements/recommendations for international students: Required—TOEFL.

The Catholic University of America, School of Engineering, Department of Civil Engineering, Washington, DC 20064. Offers environmental engineering (MCE, MSE, D Engr, PhD, Certificate); environmental engineering and management (MCE, MSE, PhD, Certificate); environmental engineering and management (D Engr); fluid and solid mechanics (MCE, MSE, PhD, Certificate); geotechnical engineering (MCE, MSE, PhD, Certificate); management of construction (MCE, MSE, D Engr, PhD); structural engineering (MSE, D Engr, PhD); systems engineering (MSE, D Engr, PhD, Certificate). Part-time programs available. *Faculty:* 5 full-time (0 women), 7 part-time/adjunct (1 woman). *Students:* 7 full-time (3 women), 18 part-time (5 women); includes 6 minority (3 African Americans, 3 Hispanic Americans), 11 international. Average age 32. 36 applicants, 47% accepted, 9 enrolled. In 2009, 8 master's, 2 doctorates awarded. *Degree requirements:* For master's, thesis optional; for doctorate, comprehensive exam, thesis/dissertation. *Entrance requirements:* For master's and doctorate, statement of purpose, official copies of academic transcripts, three letters of recommendation. Additional exam requirements/recommendations for international students: Required—TOEFL (minimum score 580 paper-based; 237 computer-based). *Application deadline:* For fall admission, 8/1 priority date for domestic students, 7/15 for international students; for spring admission, 12/1 priority date for domestic students, 10/15 for international students. Applications are processed on a rolling basis. Application fee: $55. Electronic applications accepted. *Expenses:* Contact institution. *Financial support:* Fellowships, research assistantships, teaching assistantships, Federal Work-Study, scholarships/grants, tuition waivers (full and partial), and unspecified assistantships available. Financial award application deadline: 2/1; financial award applicants required to submit FAFSA. *Faculty research:* Geotechnical engineering, solid mechanics, construction engineering and management, environmental engineering, structural engineering. Total annual research expenditures: $438,834. *Unit head:* Dr. Lu Sun, Chair, 202-319-5164, Fax: 202-319-6677, E-mail: sunl@cua.edu. *Application contact:* Julie Schwing, Director of Graduate Admissions, 202-319-5057, Fax: 202-319-6533, E-mail: cua-admissions@cua.edu.

Central Connecticut State University, School of Graduate Studies, School of Technology, Department of Manufacturing and Construction Management, New Britain, CT 06050-4010. Offers construction management (MS, Certificate); lean manufacturing and six sigma (Certificate); supply chain and logistics (Certificate); technology management (MS). Part-time and evening/weekend programs available. *Faculty:* 17 full-time (5 women), 25 part-time/adjunct (1 woman). *Students:* 13 full-time (4 women), 66 part-time (9 women); includes 11 minority (4 African Americans, 4 Asian Americans or Pacific Islanders, 3 Hispanic Americans), 4 international. Average age 33. 46 applicants, 50% accepted, 17 enrolled. In 2009, 27 master's, 1 other advanced degree awarded. *Degree requirements:* For master's, comprehensive exam, thesis or alternative; for Certificate, qualifying exam. *Entrance requirements:* For master's, minimum undergraduate GPA of 2.7. Additional exam requirements/recommendations for international students: Required—TOEFL. *Application deadline:* For fall admission, 7/1 for domestic students; for spring admission, 12/1 for domestic students. Applications are processed on a rolling basis. Application fee: $50. Electronic applications accepted. *Expenses:* Tuition, area resident: Full-time $4662; part-time $440 per credit. Tuition, state resident: full-time $6994; part-time $440 per credit. Tuition, nonresident: full-time $12,988; part-time $440 per credit. Required fees: $3606. One-time fee: $62 part-time. *Financial support:* In 2009–10, 5 students received support, including 3 research assistantships; career-related internships or fieldwork, Federal Work-Study, scholarships/grants, and unspecified assistantships also available. Support available to part-time students. Financial award application deadline: 3/1; financial award applicants required to submit FAFSA. *Faculty research:* All aspects of middle management, technical supervision in the workplace. *Unit head:* Dr. Jacob Kovel, Chair, 860-832-1830. *Application contact:* Dr. Jacob Kovel, Chair, 860-832-1830.

Clemson University, Graduate School, College of Architecture, Arts, and Humanities, Department of Construction Science and Management, Clemson, SC 29634. Offers MCSM. Part-time programs available. *Faculty:* 5 full-time (2 women). *Students:* 16 full-time (3 women), 8 part-time (1 woman); includes 1 minority (Hispanic American), 8 international. Average age 27. 24 applicants, 67% accepted, 4 enrolled. In 2009, 2 master's awarded. *Degree requirements:* For master's, thesis optional. *Entrance requirements:* For master's, GRE General Test, one year of construction experience, current resume. Additional exam requirements/recommendations for international students: Required—TOEFL. *Application deadline:* For fall admission, 1/1 for domestic students, 4/15 for international students; for spring admission, 9/1 for domestic students, 9/15 for international students. Application fee: $70 ($80 for international students). Electronic applications accepted. *Expenses:* Tuition, state resident: full-time $8684; part-time $528 per credit hour. Tuition, nonresident: full-time $15,330; part-time $1078 per credit hour. Required fees: $736; $37 per semester. Part-time tuition and fees vary according to course load and program. *Financial support:* In 2009–10, 11 students received support; research assistantships with partial tuition reimbursements available, teaching assistantships with partial tuition reimbursements available, career-related internships or fieldwork, institutionally sponsored loans, scholarships/grants, health care benefits, and unspecified assistantships available. Support available to part-time students. Financial award applicants required to submit FAFSA. *Faculty research:* Computer applications, employer incentive programs, artificial intelligence, productivity improvement, financial management. Total annual research expenditures: $51,788. *Unit head:* Roger Liska, Chair, 864-656-0181, Fax: 864-656-0204, E-mail: riggor@clemson.edu. *Application contact:* Roger Liska, 864-656-0181, Fax: 864-656-0204, E-mail: riggor@clemson.edu.

Colorado State University, Graduate School, College of Applied Human Sciences, Department of Construction Management, Fort Collins, CO 80523-1584. Offers MS. Part-time and evening/weekend programs available. *Faculty:* 11 full-time (4 women), 1 part-time/adjunct (0 women). *Students:* 25 full-time (5 women), 34 part-time (8 women), 5 international. Average age 34. 88 applicants, 35% accepted, 19 enrolled. In 2009, 10 master's awarded. *Degree requirements:* For master's, thesis. *Entrance requirements:* For master's, BA/BS from accredited institution, minimum GPA of 3.0. Additional exam requirements/recommendations for international students: Required—TOEFL (minimum score 550 paper-based; 217 computer-based). *Application deadline:* For fall admission, 2/15 priority date for domestic students, 4/1 priority date for international students; for spring admission, 9/1 priority date for domestic and international students. Applications are processed on a rolling basis. Application fee: $50. Electronic applications accepted. *Expenses:* Tuition, state resident: full-time $6434; part-time $359.10 per credit. Tuition, nonresident: full-time $18,116; part-time $1006.45 per credit. Required fees: $1496; $83 per credit. *Financial support:* In 2009–10, 12 students received support, including 5 research assistantships (averaging $9,186 per year), 7 teaching assistantships with full tuition reimbursements available (averaging $15,320 per year); fellowships, career-related internships or fieldwork, Federal Work-Study, scholarships/grants, and unspecified assistantships also available. Financial award applicants required to submit FAFSA. *Faculty research:* Sustainable construction management, construction materials science, information technology and transfer, renewable energy systems, Internet project management. Total annual research expenditures: $179,089. *Unit head:* Dr. Mostafa M. Khattab, Interim Head, 970-491-6808, Fax: 970-491-2473, E-mail: mostafa.khattab@colostate.edu. *Application contact:* Deanne Douglas, Graduate Liaison, 970-491-0435, Fax: 970-491-2473, E-mail: deanne.douglas@colostate.edu.

Columbia University, Fu Foundation School of Engineering and Applied Science, Department of Civil Engineering and Engineering Mechanics, New York, NY 10027. Offers civil engineering (MS, Eng Sc D, PhD, Engr); construction engineering and management (MS); engineering mechanics (MS, Eng Sc D, PhD, Engr). Part-time programs available. Postbaccalaureate distance learning degree programs offered (no on-campus study). *Faculty:* 10 full-time (1 woman), 4 part-time/adjunct (0 women). *Students:* 89 full-time (24 women), 48 part-time (16 women); includes 17 minority (2 African Americans, 8 Asian Americans or Pacific Islanders, 7 Hispanic Americans), 72 international. Average age 27. 221 applicants, 54% accepted, 48 enrolled. In 2009, 38 master's, 1 doctorate awarded. Terminal master's awarded for partial completion of doctoral program. *Degree requirements:* For doctorate, thesis/dissertation, qualifying exam. *Entrance requirements:* For master's, doctorate, and Engr, GRE General Test. Additional exam requirements/recommendations for international students: Required—TOEFL. *Application deadline:* For fall admission, 12/1 priority date for domestic and international students; for spring admission, 10/1 priority date for domestic and international students. Application fee: $70. Electronic applications accepted. *Financial support:* In 2009–10, 29 students received support, including 5 fellowships with full tuition reimbursements available (averaging $33,518 per year), 12 research assistantships with full tuition reimbursements available (averaging $32,761 per year), 12 teaching assistantships with full tuition reimbursements available (averaging $32,761 per year); health care benefits also available. Financial award application deadline: 12/1; financial award applicants required to submit FAFSA. *Faculty research:* Motion monitoring of Manhattan Bridge, lightweight concrete panels, simulation of life of well sealant, intercultural knowledge system dynamics, corrosion monitoring of New York City bridges. *Unit head:* Dr. Upmanu Lall, Interim Chairman and Professor, 212-854-8905, Fax: 212-854-7081, E-mail: lall@civil.columbia.edu. *Application contact:* Rene B. Testa, Professor, 212-854-3143, Fax: 212-854-6267, E-mail: testa@civil.columbia.edu.

Columbia University, School of Continuing Education, Program in Construction Administration, New York, NY 10027. Offers MS. Part-time and evening/weekend programs available. *Faculty:* 22 part-time/adjunct (3 women). *Students:* 2 full-time (0 women), 81 part-time (14 women); includes 25 minority (12 African Americans, 8 Asian Americans or Pacific Islanders, 5 Hispanic Americans), 5 international. Average age 35. 31 applicants, 81% accepted, 21 enrolled. *Degree requirements:* For master's, minimum GPA of 3.0 or internship. *Entrance requirements:* For master's, bachelor's degree, minimum GPA of 3.0. *Application deadline:* For fall admission, 4/15 for domestic students. Application fee: $50. Electronic applications accepted. *Financial support:* Institutionally sponsored loans available. *Unit head:* Dennis Green, Program Director, 212-854-7436, E-mail: dg30@columbia.edu. *Application contact:* Bryce Weinert, Admissions Adviser, 212-854-9666, E-mail: sce-apply@columbia.edu.

Drexel University, School of Technology and Professional Studies, Philadelphia, PA 19104-2875. Offers construction management (MS); engineering technology (MS); food science (MS); hospitality management (MS); professional studies: creativity studies (MS); professional studies: e-learning leadership (MS); professional studies: homeland security management (MS); project management (MS); property management (MS); sport management (MS). Post-baccalaureate distance learning degree programs offered.

Eastern Michigan University, Graduate School, College of Technology, School of Engineering Technology, Program in Construction Management, Ypsilanti, MI 48197. Offers MS. Part-time and evening/weekend programs available. Postbaccalaureate distance learning degree programs offered (minimal on-campus study). *Students:* 5 full-time (0 women), 24 part-time (8 women); includes 4 minority (3 African Americans, 1 Hispanic American), 8 international. Average age 34. In 2009, 17 master's awarded. *Entrance requirements:* Additional exam requirements/recommendations for international students: Required—TOEFL. *Application deadline:* Applications are processed on a rolling basis. Application fee: $35. Tuition and fees vary according to course level. *Financial support:* Fellowships, research assistantships with full tuition reimbursements, teaching assistantships with full tuition reimbursements, career-related internships or fieldwork, Federal Work-Study, institutionally sponsored loans, scholarships/grants, tuition waivers (partial), and unspecified assistantships available. Support available to part-time students. Financial award applicants required to submit FAFSA. *Unit head:* Dr. William Moylan, Program Coordinator, 734-487-2721, Fax: 734-487-8755, E-mail: wmoylan@emich.edu. *Application contact:* Dr. William Moylan, Program Coordinator, 734-487-2721, Fax: 734-487-8755, E-mail: wmoylan@emich.edu.

Florida International University, College of Engineering and Computing, Department of Construction Management, Miami, FL 33175. Offers MS. Part-time and evening/weekend programs available. *Faculty:* 6 full-time (0 women). *Students:* 88 full-time (23 women), 104 part-time (30 women); includes 95 minority (19 African Americans, 4 Asian Americans or Pacific Islanders, 72 Hispanic Americans), 35 international. Average age 32. 142 applicants, 37% accepted, 49 enrolled. In 2009, 92 master's awarded. *Degree requirements:* For master's, thesis optional. *Entrance requirements:* For master's, minimum GPA of 3.0 in upper-level course work; If GPA is below 3.0, GRE or GMAT will be taken into consideration. Additional exam requirements/recommendations for international students: Required—TOEFL (minimum score 550 paper-based; 80 iBT). *Application deadline:* For fall admission, 6/1 for domestic students, 4/1 for international students; for spring admission, 10/1 for domestic students, 9/1 for international students. Applications are processed on a rolling basis. Application fee: $30. Electronic applications accepted. *Expenses:* Tuition, state resident: full-time $8008; part-time $4004 per year. Tuition, nonresident: full-time $20,104; part-time $10,052 per year. Required fees: $298; $149 per term. *Financial support:* In 2009–10, 5 students received support. Institutionally sponsored loans, scholarships/grants, and unspecified assistantships available. Financial award application deadline: 3/1; financial award applicants required to submit FAFSA. *Faculty research:* Information technology, construction organizations, contracts and partnerships in construction, construction education, concrete technology. *Unit head:* Dr. Irtishad Ahmad, Chair, Construction Management Department, 305-348-3045, Fax: 305-348-6255, E-mail: irtishad.ahmad@fiu.edu. *Application contact:* Maria Parrilla, Graduate Admissions Assistant, 305-348-1890, Fax: 305-348-6142, E-mail: grad_eng@fiu.edu.

Harrisburg University of Science and Technology, Program in Project Management, Harrisburg, PA 17101. Offers construction services specialization (MS); governmental services specialization (MS); information technology specialization (MS). Part-time and evening/weekend programs available. *Faculty:* 1 full-time (0 women), 3 part-time/adjunct (0 women). *Students:* 1 full-time (0 women), 21 part-time (4 women); includes 5 minority (2 African Americans, 3 Asian Americans or Pacific Islanders), 2 international. Average age 30. 26 applicants, 92% accepted, 22 enrolled. In 2009, 3 master's awarded. *Entrance requirements:* For master's, BS, BBA. Additional exam requirements/recommendations for international students: Required—TOEFL (minimum score 520 paper-based; 200 computer-based; 80 iBT). *Application deadline:* For fall admission, 8/1 priority date for domestic students, 7/1 priority date for international students. Applications are processed on a rolling basis. Application fee: $0. Electronic applications accepted. *Expenses:* Tuition: Full-time $18,000; part-time $650 per semester hour. *Financial support:* In 2009–10, 7 students received support. Scholarships/grants available. Financial award applicants required to submit FAFSA. *Unit head:* Dr. Amjad Umar, Director and Professor, 717-901-5141, Fax: 717-901-3141, E-mail: aumar@harrisburgu.edu. *Application contact:* Julie Cullings, Information Contact, 717-901-5163, Fax: 717-901-3163, E-mail: admissions@harrisburgu.edu.

Indiana University–Purdue University Fort Wayne, College of Engineering, Technology, and Computer Science, Program in Technology, Fort Wayne, IN 46805-1499. Offers facilities and construction management (MS); industrial technology/manufacturing (MS); information technology/advanced computer applications (MS). Part-time programs available. *Faculty:* 10 full-time (6 women), 2 part-time/adjunct (0 women). *Students:* 6 full-time (3 women), 18 part-time (1 woman); includes 4 minority (3 Asian Americans or Pacific Islanders, 1 Hispanic American), 3 international. Average age 33. 13 applicants, 100% accepted, 12 enrolled. *Entrance requirements:* For master's, minimum GPA of 3.0. Additional exam requirements/recommendations for international students: Required—TOEFL (minimum score 550 paper-based; 213 computer-based; 77 iBT), TWE. *Application deadline:* For fall admission, 7/15 for domestic students, 5/15 for international students; for spring admission, 12/1 for domestic students, 10/15 for international students. Applications are processed on a rolling basis. Application fee: $55 ($60 for international students). Electronic applications accepted. *Expenses:* Tuition, state resident: full-time $4595; part-time $255 per credit. Tuition, nonresident: full-time $10,963; part-time $609 per credit. Required fees: $528; $29.35 per credit. Tuition and fees vary according to course load. *Financial support:* Career-related internships or fieldwork, scholarships/grants, and unspecified assistantships available. Support available to part-time students. Financial award application deadline: 3/1; financial award applicants required to submit FAFSA. *Unit head:* Dr. Gerard Voland, Dean, 260-481-6839, Fax: 260-481-5734, E-mail: volandg@ipfw.edu. *Application contact:* Dr. Paul Lin, Graduate Program Director, 260-481-6339, Fax: 260-481-5734, E-mail: lin@ipfw.edu.

Instituto Tecnologico de Santo Domingo, Graduate School, Santo Domingo, Dominican Republic. Offers applied linguistics (MA); construction administration (M Mgmt); corporate finance (M Mgmt); education (M Ed); engineering (M Eng), including data telecommunications, industrial engineering, logistics and supply chain, maintenance engineering, sanitary and environmental engineering, structural engineering; environmental science (M En S), including environmental education, environmental management, marine and coastal ecosystems, natural resources management; family therapy (MA); food science and technology (MS); human development (MA); human resources administration (M Mgmt); international business (M Mgmt); labor risks (M Mgmt); management (M Mgmt); marketing (M Mgmt); mathematics (MS); organizational development (M Mgmt); planning and taxation (M Mgmt); psychology (MA); social science (M Ed); upper management (M Mgmt). *Entrance requirements:* For master's, birth certificate, minimum GPA of 2.0.

Marquette University, Graduate School, College of Engineering, Department of Civil and Environmental Engineering, Milwaukee, WI 53201-1881. Offers construction and public works management (MS, PhD); environmental/water resources engineering (MS, PhD); structural/geotechnical engineering (MS, PhD); transportation planning and engineering (MS, PhD). Part-time and evening/weekend programs available. *Faculty:* 13 full-time (0 women), 2 part-time/adjunct (1 woman). *Students:* 16 full-time (4 women), 17 part-time (2 women); includes 2 minority (1 Asian American or Pacific Islander, 1 Hispanic American), 13 international. Average age 27. 47 applicants, 85% accepted, 11 enrolled. In 2009, 8 master's, 1 doctorate awarded. Terminal master's awarded for partial completion of doctoral program. *Degree requirements:* For master's, comprehensive exam, thesis or alternative; for doctorate, thesis/dissertation. *Entrance requirements:* For master's and doctorate, GRE General Test, minimum GPA of 3.0. Additional exam requirements/recommendations for international students: Required—TOEFL. *Application deadline:* For fall admission, 6/1 priority date for domestic students. Applications are processed on a rolling basis. Application fee: $40. Electronic applications accepted. *Financial support:* In 2009–10, 13 students received support, including 5 fellowships with tuition reimbursements available (averaging $7,697 per year), 3 research assistantships with tuition reimbursements available (averaging $24,570 per year), 5 teaching assistantships with tuition reimbursements available (averaging $24,804 per year); Federal Work-Study, institutionally sponsored loans, scholarships/grants, and tuition waivers (full and partial) also available. Support available to part-time students. Financial award application deadline: 2/15. *Faculty research:* Highway safety, highway performance, and intelligent transportation systems; surface mount technology; watershed management. Total annual research expenditures: $138,209. *Unit head:* Dr. Michael S. Switzenbaum, Chair, 414-288-7030, Fax: 414-288-7521, E-mail: michael.switzenbaum@marquette.edu. *Application contact:* Dr. Stephen M. Heinrich, Director of Graduate Studies, 414-288-5466, E-mail: stephen.heinrich@marquette.edu.

Michigan State University, The Graduate School, College of Agriculture and Natural Resources and College of Social Science, School of Planning, Design and Construction, East Lansing, MI 48824. Offers construction management (MS, PhD); environmental design (MA); interior design and facilities management (MA); international planning studies (MIPS); urban and regional planning (MURP). *Degree requirements:* For master's, thesis or alternative. *Entrance requirements:* Additional exam requirements/recommendations for international students: Required—TOEFL. Electronic applications accepted.

Missouri State University, Graduate College, College of Business Administration, Department of Technology and Construction Management, Springfield, MO 65897. Offers MS. Part-time programs available. *Faculty:* 5 full-time (0 women). *Students:* 14 full-time (3 women), 36 part-time (12 women); includes 7 minority (2 African Americans, 2 American Indian/Alaska Native, 1 Asian American or Pacific Islander, 2 Hispanic Americans), 2 international. Average age 34. 18 applicants, 83% accepted, 10 enrolled. In 2009, 9 master's awarded. *Degree requirements:* For master's, thesis or alternative. *Entrance requirements:* For master's, GRE or GMAT, minimum GPA of 2.75. Additional exam requirements/recommendations for international students: Required—TOEFL (minimum score 550 paper-based; 213 computer-based; 79 iBT). *Application deadline:* For fall admission, 7/20 for domestic students, 5/1 for international students; for spring admission, 12/20 for domestic students, 9/1 for international students. Applications are processed on a rolling basis. Application fee: $35 ($50 for international students). Electronic applications accepted. *Expenses:* Tuition, state resident: full-time $3852; part-time $214 per credit hour. Tuition, nonresident: full-time $7524; part-time $418 per credit hour. Required fees: $696; $172 per semester. Tuition and fees vary according to course level, course load, degree level and program. *Financial support:* Federal Work-Study, institutionally sponsored loans, scholarships/grants, and unspecified assistantships available. Financial award application deadline: 3/31; financial award applicants required to submit FAFSA. *Unit head:* Dr. Shawn Strong, Head, 417-836-5121, Fax: 417-836-8556, E-mail: indmgt@missouristate.edu. *Application contact:* Dr. R. Neal Callahan, Director, 417-836-5160, Fax: 417-836-8556, E-mail: nealcallahan@missouristate.edu.

New York University, School of Continuing and Professional Studies, Schack Institute of Real Estate, Program in Construction Management, New York, NY 10012-1019. Offers construction management (Advanced Certificate); construction management for the development process (MS); project management (MS). Part-time and evening/weekend programs available. *Faculty:* 4 full-time (0 women), 18 part-time/adjunct (2 women). *Students:* 9 full-time (4 women), 91 part-time (19 women); includes 12 minority (3 African Americans, 1 American Indian/Alaska Native, 6 Asian Americans or Pacific Islanders, 2 Hispanic Americans). Average age 32. 61 applicants, 74% accepted, 24 enrolled. In 2009, 42 master's, 27 other advanced degrees awarded. *Degree requirements:* For master's, capstone project. *Entrance requirements:* For master's, GRE General Test or GMAT (for recent graduates), resume, 2 letters of recommendation. Additional exam requirements/recommendations for international students: Required—TOEFL (minimum score 600 paper-based; 250 computer-based; 100 iBT), TWE. *Application deadline:* For fall admission, 2/1 priority date for domestic and international students; for spring admission, 10/15 priority date for domestic students, 8/15 priority date for international students. Applications are processed on a rolling basis. Application fee: $75. Electronic applications accepted. *Expenses:* Tuition: Full-time $30,528; part-time $1272 per credit. Required fees: $2177. *Financial support:* In 2009–10, 30 students received support, including 30 fellowships (averaging $2,006 per year); scholarships/grants also available. Support available to part-time students. Financial award application deadline: 3/1; financial award applicants required to submit FAFSA. *Unit head:* James Stuckey, Divisional Dean, 212-992-3335, Fax: 212-992-3686, E-mail: james.stuckey@nyu.edu. *Application contact:* Jennifer Monahan, Assistant Director, 212-992-3335, Fax: 212-992-3686, E-mail: jm189@nyu.edu.

North Carolina Agricultural and Technical State University, Graduate School, School of Technology, Department of Construction Management and Occupational Safety and Health, Greensboro, NC 27411. Offers construction management (MSIT); occupational safety and health (MSIT).

North Dakota State University, College of Graduate and Interdisciplinary Studies, College of Engineering and Architecture, Department of Construction Management and Engineering, Fargo, ND 58108. Offers construction management (MS). *Students:* 9 full-time (1 woman), 3 part-time (0 women), 9 international. *Entrance requirements:* Additional exam requirements/recommendations for international students: Required—TOEFL (minimum score 525 paper-based; 197 computer-based; 71 iBT). *Application deadline:* Applications are processed on a rolling basis. Application fee: $45 ($60 for international students). Electronic applications accepted. *Unit head:* Dr. Charles McIntyre, Chair, 701-231-7879, Fax: 701-231-7431, E-mail: charles.mcintyre@ndsu.edu. *Application contact:* Dr. David A. Wittrock, Dean, 701-231-7033, Fax: 701-231-6524.

Philadelphia University, School of Architecture, Program in Construction Management, Philadelphia, PA 19144. Offers MS.

Polytechnic Institute of NYU, Department of Civil Engineering, Major in Construction Management, Brooklyn, NY 11201-2990. Offers MS. *Students:* 39 full-time (7 women), 48 part-time (11 women); includes 25 minority (11 African Americans, 7 Asian Americans or Pacific Islanders, 7 Hispanic Americans), 26 international. 100 applicants, 83% accepted, 30 enrolled. In 2009, 18 master's awarded. *Degree requirements:* For master's, comprehensive exam (for some programs), thesis (for some programs). *Entrance requirements:* Additional exam requirements/recommendations for international students: Required—TOEFL (minimum score 550 paper-based; 213 computer-based; 80 iBT); Recommended—IELTS (minimum score 6.5). *Application deadline:* For fall admission, 7/31 priority date for domestic students, 4/30 priority date for international students; for spring admission, 12/31 priority date for domestic students, 10/30 priority date for international students. Applications are processed on a rolling basis. Application fee: $75. Electronic applications accepted. *Expenses:* Tuition: Full-time $21,492; part-time $1194 per credit hour. Required fees: $1160; $204 per course. *Financial support:* Institutionally sponsored loans, scholarships/grants, and unspecified assistantships available. Support available to part-time students. *Unit head:* Dr. Lawrence Chiarelli, Head, 718-260-4040, Fax: 718-260-3433, E-mail: lchiarel@poly.edu. *Application contact:* JeanCarlo Bonilla, Director of Graduate Enrollment Management, 718-260-3182, Fax: 718-260-3624, E-mail: gradinfo@poly.edu.

Polytechnic Institute of NYU, Department of Technology Management, Brooklyn, NY 11201-2990. Offers construction management (Advanced Certificate); electronic business management (Advanced Certificate); entrepreneurship (Advanced Certificate); human resources management (Advanced Certificate); information management (Advanced Certificate); management (MS); management of technology (MS); organizational behavior (MS, Advanced Certificate); project management (Advanced Certificate); technology management (MBA, PhD, Advanced Certificate); telecommunications and information management (MS); telecommunications management (Advanced Certificate). Part-time and evening/weekend programs available. *Faculty:* 5 full-time (1 woman), 26 part-time/adjunct (3 women). *Students:* 272 full-time (111 women), 103 part-time (41 women); includes 64 minority (20 African Americans, 1 American Indian/Alaska Native, 34 Asian Americans or Pacific Islanders, 9 Hispanic Americans), 193

Construction Management

Polytechnic Institute of NYU (continued)

international. Average age 30. 518 applicants, 57% accepted, 135 enrolled. In 2009, 148 master's awarded. *Degree requirements:* For master's, comprehensive exam (for some programs), thesis (for some programs); for doctorate, comprehensive exam, thesis/dissertation. *Entrance requirements:* For master's, GMAT, minimum B average in undergraduate course work. Additional exam requirements/recommendations for international students: Required—TOEFL (minimum score 550 paper-based; 213 computer-based; 80 iBT); Recommended—IELTS (minimum score 6.5). *Application deadline:* For fall admission, 7/31 priority date for domestic students, 4/30 priority date for international students; for spring admission, 12/31 priority date for domestic students, 11/30 priority date for international students. Applications are processed on a rolling basis. Application fee: $75. Electronic applications accepted. *Expenses:* Tuition: Full-time $21,492; part-time $1194 per credit hour. Required fees: $1160; $204 per course. *Financial support:* In 2009–10, 1 fellowship (averaging $26,400 per year) was awarded; research assistantships, teaching assistantships, institutionally sponsored loans, scholarships/grants, and unspecified assistantships also available. Support available to part-time students. *Unit head:* Prof. Bharadwaj Rao, Head, 718-260-3617, Fax: 718-260-3874, E-mail: brao@poly.edu. *Application contact:* JeanCarlo Bonilla, Director of Graduate Enrollment Management, 718-260-3182, Fax: 718-260-3624, E-mail: gradinfo@poly.edu.

Polytechnic Institute of NYU, Long Island Graduate Center, Graduate Programs, Department of Civil Engineering, Major in Construction Management, Melville, NY 11747. Offers MS. Part-time and evening/weekend programs available. *Students:* 3 part-time (0 women). *Entrance requirements:* Additional exam requirements/recommendations for international students: Required—TOEFL (minimum score 550 paper-based; 213 computer-based; 80 iBT); Recommended—IELTS (minimum score 6.5). *Application deadline:* For fall admission, 7/31 priority date for domestic students, 4/30 priority date for international students; for spring admission, 12/31 priority date for domestic students, 11/30 priority date for international students. Applications are processed on a rolling basis. Application fee: $75. Electronic applications accepted. *Financial support:* Institutionally sponsored loans, scholarships/grants, and unspecified assistantships available. Support available to part-time students. *Unit head:* Dr. Lawrence Chiarelli, Department Head, 718-260-4040, E-mail: lchiarel@duke.poly.edu. *Application contact:* JeanCarlo Bonilla, Director of Graduate Enrollment Management, 718-260-3182, Fax: 718-260-3624, E-mail: gradinfo@poly.edu.

Roger Williams University, School of Engineering, Computing and Construction Management, Bristol, RI 02809. Offers construction management (MSCM).

Rowan University, Graduate School, College of Engineering, Department of Civil and Environmental Engineering, Program in Construction Management, Glassboro, NJ 08028-1701. Offers MS. *Students:* 3 part-time (0 women). Average age 28. *Entrance requirements:* For master's, GRE General Test. Additional exam requirements/recommendations for international students: Required—TOEFL. *Application deadline:* Applications are processed on a rolling basis. Application fee: $50. Electronic applications accepted. *Expenses:* Tuition, state resident: full-time $10,624; part-time $590 per semester hour. Tuition, nonresident: full-time $10,624; part-time $590 per semester hour. Required fees: $2320; $125 per semester hour. *Unit head:* Kauser Jahan, Chair, 856-256-5323, E-mail: jahan@rowan.edu. *Application contact:* Dr. Ralph Dusseau, Program Adviser, 856-256-5332.

South Dakota School of Mines and Technology, Graduate Division, College of Engineering, Department of Civil and Environmental Engineering, Rapid City, SD 57701-3995. Offers civil engineering (MS); construction management (MS). Part-time programs available. *Faculty:* 12 full-time (2 women), 1 (woman) part-time/adjunct. *Students:* 26 full-time (6 women), 6 part-time (5 women), 8 international. Average age 25. 28 applicants, 89% accepted, 15 enrolled. In 2009, 26 master's awarded. *Entrance requirements:* Additional exam requirements/recommendations for international students: Required—TOEFL, TWE. *Application deadline:* For fall admission, 7/1 priority date for domestic students, 4/1 for international students; for spring admission, 11/1 for domestic students, 9/1 for international students. Applications are processed on a rolling basis. Application fee: $35. Electronic applications accepted. *Expenses:* Tuition, state resident: full-time $3340; part-time $139 per credit hour. Tuition, nonresident: full-time $7060; part-time $294 per credit hour. Required fees: $3270. *Financial support:* In 2009–10, 5 fellowships (averaging $4,050 per year), 9 research assistantships with partial tuition reimbursements (averaging $12,388 per year), 21 teaching assistantships with partial tuition reimbursements (averaging $4,520 per year) were awarded; Federal Work-Study and institutionally sponsored loans also available. Support available to part-time students. Financial award application deadline: 5/15. *Faculty research:* Concrete technology, environmental and sanitation engineering, water resources engineering, composite materials, geotechnical engineering. Total annual research expenditures: $356,502. *Unit head:* Dr. Henry Mott, Chair, 605-394-5170, E-mail: henry.mott@sdsmt.edu. *Application contact:* Jeannette R. Nilson, Administrative Support Coordinator, Graduate Education, 800-454-8162 Ext. 1206, Fax: 605-394-5360, E-mail: graduate_admissions@sdsmt.edu.

Southern Polytechnic State University, School of Architecture, Civil Engineering Technology and Construction, Department of Construction Management, Marietta, GA 30060-2896. Offers MS. Part-time and evening/weekend programs available. *Faculty:* 6 full-time (0 women), 1 part-time/adjunct (0 women). *Students:* 25 full-time (7 women), 7 part-time (1 woman); includes 7 African Americans, 3 Asian Americans or Pacific Islanders, 8 international. Average age 36. 15 applicants, 87% accepted, 5 enrolled. In 2009, 12 master's awarded. *Degree requirements:* For master's, thesis or alternative. *Entrance requirements:* For master's, GMAT or GRE, 3 reference forms, minimum GPA of 2.75. Additional exam requirements/recommendations for international students: Required—TOEFL (minimum score 550 paper-based; 213 computer-based; 79 iBT), IELTS (minimum score 6.5). *Application deadline:* For fall admission, 7/1 priority date for domestic students, 5/1 priority date for international students; for spring admission, 11/1 priority date for domestic students, 9/1 priority date for international students. Applications are processed on a rolling basis. Application fee: $20. Electronic applications accepted. *Expenses:* Tuition, state resident: full-time $2896; part-time $181 per credit hour. Tuition, nonresident: full-time $11,552; part-time $722 per credit hour. Required fees: $1096; $1096 per year. *Financial support:* In 2009–10, 16 students received support, including 12 research assistantships with tuition reimbursements available (averaging $1,500 per year); career-related internships or fieldwork, scholarships/grants, and unspecified assistantships also available. Support available to part-time students. Financial award application deadline: 5/1; financial award applicants required to submit FAFSA. *Faculty research:* Environmental construction and green building techniques, risk management, bidding strategies in construction, construction worker safety, building automation and performance measurements. Total annual research expenditures: $115,000. *Unit head:* Dr. Khalid M. Siddiqi, Chair, 678-915-7221, Fax: 678-915-4966, E-mail: ksiddiqi@spsu.edu. *Application contact:* Nikki Palamiotis, Director of Graduate Studies, 678-915-4276, Fax: 678-915-7292, E-mail: npalamio@spsu.edu.

State University of New York College of Environmental Science and Forestry, Department of Construction Management and Wood Products Engineering, Syracuse, NY 13210-2779. Offers environmental and resources engineering (MPS, MS, PhD). *Degree requirements:* For master's, thesis (for some programs); for doctorate, comprehensive exam, thesis/dissertation. *Entrance requirements:* For master's and doctorate, GRE General Test, minimum GPA of 3.0. Additional exam requirements/recommendations for international students: Required—TOEFL (minimum score 550 paper-based; 213 computer-based; 80 iBT), IELTS (minimum score 6).

Stevens Institute of Technology, Graduate School, Charles V. Schaefer Jr. School of Engineering, Department of Civil, Environmental, and Ocean Engineering, Program in Construction Management, Hoboken, NJ 07030. Offers construction accounting/estimating (Certificate); construction engineering (Certificate); construction law/disputes (Certificate); construction management (MS); construction/quality management (Certificate). *Degree requirements:* For master's, thesis optional. *Entrance requirements:* For master's, GMAT, GRE General Test. Additional exam requirements/recommendations for international students:

Required—TOEFL. Electronic applications accepted. *Expenses:* Tuition: Full-time $9900; part-time $1100 per credit. Required fees: $286 per semester.

Texas A&M University, College of Architecture, Department of Construction Science, College Station, TX 77843. Offers construction management (MS). *Faculty:* 15. *Students:* 85 full-time (26 women), 5 part-time (1 woman); includes 2 minority (both Asian Americans or Pacific Islanders), 76 international. Average age 30. In 2009, 42 master's awarded. *Degree requirements:* For master's, comprehensive exam. *Entrance requirements:* For master's, GRE General Test. Additional exam requirements/recommendations for international students: Required—TOEFL. *Application deadline:* For fall admission, 4/1 priority date for domestic students; for winter admission, 1/1 priority date for domestic students; for spring admission, 9/1 priority date for domestic students. Applications are processed on a rolling basis. Application fee: $50 ($75 for international students). Electronic applications accepted. *Expenses:* Tuition, state resident: full-time $3991.32; part-time $221.74 per credit hour. Tuition, nonresident: full-time $9049; part-time $502.74 per credit hour. *Financial support:* In 2009–10, fellowships with partial tuition reimbursements (averaging $1,000 per year), research assistantships with partial tuition reimbursements (averaging $9,000 per year), teaching assistantships with partial tuition reimbursements (averaging $9,000 per year) were awarded. Financial award application deadline: 4/1; financial award applicants required to submit FAFSA. *Faculty research:* Fire safety, housing foundations, construction project management, quality management.

Texas A&M University, College of Engineering, Zachry Department of Civil Engineering, College Station, TX 77843. Offers construction engineering and management (M Eng, MS, D Eng, PhD); environmental engineering (M Eng, MS, D Eng, PhD); geotechnical engineering (M Eng, MS, D Eng, PhD); materials engineering (M Eng, MS, D Eng, PhD); ocean engineering (M Eng, MS, D Eng, PhD); structural engineering (M Eng, MS, D Eng, PhD); transportation engineering (M Eng, MS, D Eng, PhD); water resources engineering (M Eng, MS, D Eng, PhD). Part-time programs available. *Faculty:* 61. *Students:* 390 full-time (89 women), 42 part-time (6 women); includes 23 minority (2 African Americans, 11 Asian Americans or Pacific Islanders, 10 Hispanic Americans), 281 international. Average age 29. In 2009, 100 master's, 36 doctorates awarded. *Degree requirements:* For master's, thesis (MS); for doctorate, dissertation (PhD), internship (D Eng). *Entrance requirements:* For master's and doctorate, GRE General Test. Additional exam requirements/recommendations for international students: Required—TOEFL. *Application deadline:* Applications are processed on a rolling basis. Application fee: $50 ($75 for international students). Electronic applications accepted. *Expenses:* Tuition, state resident: full-time $3991.32; part-time $221.74 per credit hour. Tuition, nonresident: full-time $9049; part-time $502.74 per credit hour. *Financial support:* In 2009–10, fellowships (averaging $4,500 per year), research assistantships (averaging $14,000 per year), teaching assistantships (averaging $14,400 per year) were awarded; career-related internships or fieldwork and institutionally sponsored loans also available. Financial award application deadline: 4/15; financial award applicants required to submit FAFSA. *Unit head:* Dr. Tony Cahill, Head, 979-845-2438, E-mail: t-cahill@civil.tamu.edu. *Application contact:* Graduate Advisor, 979-845-2498, Fax: 979-862-2800, E-mail: ce-grad@tamu.edu.

Universidad de las Américas–Puebla, Division of Graduate Studies, School of Engineering, Program in Construction Management, Puebla, Mexico. Offers M Adm. Part-time and evening/weekend programs available. *Degree requirements:* For master's, one foreign language, thesis. *Faculty research:* Building structures, budget, project management.

University of Arkansas at Little Rock, Graduate School, College of Business Administration, Little Rock, AR 72204-1099. Offers accountancy (M Acc, Graduate Certificate); business administration (MBA); construction management (Graduate Certificate); management (Graduate Certificate); management information system (MIS); management information systems (Graduate Certificate); management information systems leadership (Graduate Certificate); taxation (MS, Graduate Certificate). *Accreditation:* AACSB. Part-time and evening/weekend programs available. *Entrance requirements:* For master's, GMAT, minimum undergraduate GPA of 2.7. Additional exam requirements/recommendations for international students: Required—TOEFL (minimum score 525 paper-based; 195 computer-based).

University of California, Berkeley, UC Berkeley Extension, Certificate Programs in Engineering, Construction and Facilities Management, Berkeley, CA 94720-1500. Offers construction management (Certificate); HVAC (Certificate); integrated circuit design and techniques (online) (Certificate). Postbaccalaureate distance learning degree programs offered. *Unit head:* Diana Wu, Dean, 510-642-4181. *Application contact:* Engineering, Construction, and Facilities Management, 510-642-4151, E-mail: course@unex.berkeley.edu.

University of Denver, Daniels College of Business, School of Real Estate and Construction Management, Denver, CO 80208. Offers construction management (IMBA, MS); real estate (IMBA, MBA, MS). Part-time programs available. *Faculty:* 7 full-time (0 women), 3 part-time/adjunct (1 woman). *Students:* 32 full-time (5 women), 70 part-time (11 women); includes 9 minority (4 African Americans, 1 American Indian/Alaska Native, 2 Asian Americans or Pacific Islanders, 2 Hispanic Americans), 6 international. Average age 32. 88 applicants, 76% accepted, 41 enrolled. In 2009, 91 master's awarded. *Entrance requirements:* For master's, GMAT. *Application deadline:* For fall admission, 1/15 priority date for domestic students. Applications are processed on a rolling basis. Application fee: $50. Electronic applications accepted. *Expenses:* Tuition: Full-time $34,596; part-time $961 per quarter hour. Required fees: $4 per quarter hour. Tuition and fees vary according to course load, campus/location and program. *Financial support:* In 2009–10, 70 students received support. Career-related internships or fieldwork, Federal Work-Study, institutionally sponsored loans, and scholarships/grants available. Support available to part-time students. Financial award application deadline: 2/15; financial award applicants required to submit FAFSA. *Unit head:* Dr. Mark Levine, Director, 303-871-2142. *Application contact:* Information Contact, 303-871-3416, Fax: 303-871-4466, E-mail: daniels@du.edu.

University of Houston, College of Technology, Department of Engineering Technology, Houston, TX 77204. Offers construction management (M Tech); network communications (M Tech). Part-time and evening/weekend programs available. *Faculty:* 12 full-time (4 women), 4 part-time/adjunct (1 woman). *Students:* 38 full-time (13 women), 30 part-time (8 women); includes 9 minority (5 African Americans, 2 Asian Americans or Pacific Islanders, 2 Hispanic Americans), 39 international. Average age 26. 41 applicants, 78% accepted, 24 enrolled. In 2009, 16 master's awarded. *Degree requirements:* For master's, project or thesis (most programs). *Entrance requirements:* For master's, GRE. Additional exam requirements/recommendations for international students: Required—TOEFL (minimum score 550 paper-based; 79 iBT). *Application deadline:* For fall admission, 7/1 for domestic students, 4/1 for international students; for spring admission, 12/1 for domestic students, 10/1 for international students. Applications are processed on a rolling basis. Application fee: $75 ($150 for international students). Electronic applications accepted. *Expenses:* Tuition, state resident: full-time $7676; part-time $320 per credit hour. Tuition, nonresident: full-time $14,324; part-time $597 per credit hour. Required fees: $3034. *Financial support:* In 2009–10, 7 fellowships with full tuition reimbursements (averaging $10,500 per year), 4 research assistantships with full tuition reimbursements (averaging $10,500 per year), 12 teaching assistantships with full tuition reimbursements (averaging $10,500 per year) were awarded. *Unit head:* Heidar Malki, Chairperson, 713-743-4075, Fax: 713-743-4032, E-mail: malki@uh.edu. *Application contact:* Tiffany Roosa, Graduate Advisor, 713-743-2987, Fax: 713-743-4151, E-mail: troosa@uh.edu.

The University of Kansas, Graduate Studies, School of Engineering, Department of Civil, Environmental, and Architectural Engineering, Program in Construction Management, Lawrence, KS 66045. Offers MCM. Part-time and evening/weekend programs available. *Faculty:* 3 full-time (0 women). *Students:* 1 full-time (0 women), 4 part-time (0 women), 1 international. Average age 33. 9 applicants, 11% accepted, 1 enrolled. In 2009, 3 master's awarded. *Degree requirements:* For master's, thesis or alternative, exam. *Entrance requirements:* For master's, GRE. Additional exam requirements/recommendations for international students: Required—TOEFL. *Application deadline:* For fall admission, 7/1 priority date for domestic students, 3/15 priority date for international students; for spring admission, 12/1 priority date for domestic students, 8/15 priority date for international students. Applications are processed on a rolling basis. Application fee: $45 ($55 for international students). Electronic applications accepted. *Expenses:* Tuition, state resident: full-time $6492; part-time $270.50 per credit hour. Tuition, nonresident: full-time $15,510; part-time $646.25 per credit hour. Required fees: $847; $70.56 per credit hour. Tuition and fees vary according to course load and program. *Financial support:* Fellowships with full tuition reimbursements, research assistantships with full tuition reimbursements, teaching assistantships with full and partial tuition reimbursements, career-related internships or fieldwork available. Financial award application deadline: 2/7. *Faculty research:* Construction engineering, construction management. *Unit head:* Craig D. Adams, Chair, 785-864-2700, Fax: 785-864-5631, E-mail: adamscd@ku.edu. *Application contact:* Bruce M. McEnroe, Graduate Advisor, 785-864-2925, Fax: 785-864-5631, E-mail: mcenroe@ku.edu.

University of Nevada, Las Vegas, Graduate College, Howard R. Hughes College of Engineering, Department of Construction Management, Las Vegas, NV 89154-4054. Offers MS. *Faculty:* 2 full-time (0 women). *Students:* 6 full-time (0 women), 8 part-time (5 women); includes 5 minority (1 American Indian/Alaska Native, 1 Asian American or Pacific Islander, 3 Hispanic Americans), 4 international. Average age 36. 16 applicants, 75% accepted, 6 enrolled. In 2009, 4 master's awarded. *Entrance requirements:* Additional exam requirements/recommendations for international students: Required—TOEFL (minimum score 550 paper-based; 213 computer-based; 80 iBT), IELTS (minimum score 7). *Application deadline:* For fall admission, 2/1 priority date for domestic and international students; for spring admission, 11/15 priority date for domestic students, 10/1 for international students. Applications are processed on a rolling basis. Application fee: $60 ($95 for international students). Electronic applications accepted. *Financial support:* In 2009–10, 3 students received support, including 3 teaching assistantships with partial tuition reimbursements available (averaging $10,000 per year); institutionally sponsored loans, scholarships/grants, health care benefits, and unspecified assistantships also available. Financial award application deadline: 3/1. *Unit head:* Dr. David Shields, Director/ Associate Professor, 702-895-1461, Fax: 702-895-4966, E-mail: david.shields@unlv.edu. *Application contact:* Graduate College Admissions Evaluator, 702-895-3320, Fax: 702-895-4180, E-mail: gradcollege@unlv.edu.

University of New Mexico, Graduate School, School of Engineering, Department of Civil Engineering, Program in Construction Management, Albuquerque, NM 87131-2039. Offers MCM. Part-time programs available. *Faculty:* 18 full-time (3 women), 3 part-time/adjunct (1 woman). *Students:* 2 full-time (0 women), 4 part-time (0 women); includes 3 minority (2 American Indian/Alaska Native, 1 Hispanic American), 1 international. Average age 37. 3 applicants, 33% accepted, 1 enrolled.Terminal master's awarded for partial completion of doctoral program. *Degree requirements:* For master's, comprehensive exam, thesis optional. *Entrance requirements:* For master's, GMAT for MCM, minimum score 500, minimum GPA 3.0, courses in statistics, elements of calculus, engineering economy, construction contracting. Additional exam requirements/recommendations for international students: Required—TOEFL (minimum score 550 paper-based; 213 computer-based). *Application deadline:* For fall admission, 7/15 for domestic students, 3/1 for international students; for spring admission, 11/10 for domestic students, 8/1 for international students. Applications are processed on a rolling basis. Application fee: $50. Electronic applications accepted. *Expenses:* Tuition, state resident: full-time $2098.80; part-time $233.20 per credit hour. Tuition, nonresident: full-time $6650. Required fees: $25 per semester. Tuition and fees vary according to course load, program and reciprocity agreements. *Financial support:* In 2009–10, 4 research assistantships with full tuition reimbursements (averaging $15,000 per year) were awarded; scholarships/grants, health care benefits, and unspecified assistantships also available. Support available to part-time students. Financial award application deadline: 3/1; financial award applicants required to submit FAFSA. *Faculty research:* Applied industry research and training, integration of the design/construction continuum, leadership in project management, life-cycle costing, procurement, production management and productivity management, project benchmarking, project delivery methods, sustainable asset management, sustainable design and construction. *Unit head:* Dr. John C. Stormont, Chair, 505-277-2722, Fax: 505-277-1988, E-mail: jcstorm@unm.edu. *Application contact:* Josie Gibson, Professional Academic Advisor, 505-277-2722, Fax: 505-277-1988, E-mail: civil@unm.edu.

University of Southern California, Graduate School, Viterbi School of Engineering, Sonny Astani Department of Civil Engineering, Los Angeles, CA 90089. Offers applied mechanics (MS); civil engineering (MS, PhD); computer-aided engineering (ME, Graduate Certificate); construction management (MCM); engineering technology commercialization (Graduate Certificate); environmental engineering (MS, PhD); environmental quality management (ME); structural design (ME); sustainable cities (Graduate Certificate); transportation systems (Graduate Certificate). Part-time programs available. Postbaccalaureate distance learning degree programs offered (no on-campus study). *Faculty:* 16 full-time (2 women), 35 part-time/adjunct (5 women). *Students:* 165 full-time (48 women), 65 part-time (16 women); includes 54 minority (40 Asian Americans or Pacific Islanders, 14 Hispanic Americans), 108 international. 451 applicants, 41% accepted, 73 enrolled. In 2009, 74 master's, 10 doctorates awarded. Terminal master's awarded for partial completion of doctoral program. *Degree requirements:* For doctorate, thesis/dissertation. *Entrance requirements:* For master's, GRE General Test; for doctorate, General GRE. *Application deadline:* For fall admission, 3/1 priority date for domestic and international students; for spring admission, 10/1 priority date for domestic and international students. Applications are processed on a rolling basis. Application fee: $85. Electronic applications accepted. *Expenses:* Tuition: Full-time $25,980; part-time $1315 per unit. Required fees: $554. One-time fee: $35 full-time. Full-time tuition and fees vary according to degree level and program. *Financial support:* In 2009–10, fellowships with full tuition reimbursements (averaging $30,000 per year), research assistantships with full tuition reimbursements (averaging $19,250 per year), teaching assistantships with full tuition reimbursements (averaging $19,250 per year) were awarded; career-related internships or fieldwork, scholarships/grants, health care benefits, and unspecified assistantships also available. Financial award application deadline: 12/1; financial award applicants required to submit CSS PROFILE or FAFSA. *Faculty research:* Geotechnical engineering, transportation engineering, structural engineering, construction management, environmental engineering, water resources. Total annual research expenditures: $4.2 million. *Unit head:* Dr. Jean-Pierre Bardet, Chair, 213-740-0609, Fax: 213-744-1426, E-mail: bardet@usc.edu. *Application contact:* Jennifer A. Gerson, Director of Student Services, 213-740-0573, Fax: 213-740-8662, E-mail: jgerson@usc.edu.

University of Southern Mississippi, Graduate School, College of Science and Technology, School of Construction, Hattiesburg, MS 39406-0001. Offers architecture and construction visualization (MS); construction management and technology (MS); logistics management and technology (MS). Part-time programs available. *Faculty:* 6 full-time (0 women). *Students:* 13 full-time (4 women), 7 part-time (2 women); includes 3 minority (all African Americans), 2 international. Average age 31. 19 applicants, 74% accepted, 9 enrolled. In 2009, 13 master's awarded. *Degree requirements:* For master's, comprehensive exam, thesis optional. *Entrance requirements:* For master's, GMAT or GRE General Test, minimum GPA of 2.75 in last 60 hours. Additional exam requirements/recommendations for international students: Required—TOEFL. *Application deadline:* For fall admission, 3/1 priority date for domestic students, 3/1 for international students. Applications are processed on a rolling basis. Application fee: $35. *Expenses:* Tuition, state resident: full-time $5096; part-time $284 per hour. Tuition, nonresident: full-time $13,052; part-time $726 per hour. Required fees: $402. Tuition and fees vary according to course level and course load. *Financial support:* In 2009–10, 7 teaching assistantships (averaging $6,947 per year) were awarded; research assistantships, career-related internships or fieldwork and Federal Work-Study also available. Financial award application deadline: 3/15; financial award applicants required to submit FAFSA. *Faculty research:* Robotics; CAD/CAM; simulation; computer-integrated manufacturing processes; construction scheduling, estimating, and computer systems. *Unit head:* Dr. Desmond Fletcher, Director, 601-266-5185. *Application contact:* Shonna Breland, Graduate Admissions, 601-266-6563.

The University of Texas at El Paso, Graduate School, College of Engineering, Department of Civil Engineering, El Paso, TX 79968-0001. Offers civil engineering (MS, PhD); construction mangement (Certificate); environmental engineering (MEENE, MSENE). Part-time and evening/weekend programs available. *Degree requirements:* For master's, thesis optional. *Entrance requirements:* For master's, GRE General Test, minimum GPA of 3.0. Additional exam requirements/recommendations for international students: Required—TOEFL. Electronic applications accepted. *Faculty research:* On-site wastewater treatment systems, wastewater reuse, disinfection by-product control, water resources, membrane filtration.

University of Washington, Graduate School, College of Built Environments, Department of Construction Management, Seattle, WA 98195. Offers MSCM. Part-time and evening/weekend programs available. *Degree requirements:* For master's, thesis or alternative. *Entrance requirements:* For master's, GRE General Test, minimum GPA of 3.0. Additional exam requirements/recommendations for international students: Required—TOEFL. Electronic applications accepted. *Faculty research:* Business practices, delivery methods, materials, productivity.

Western Carolina University, Graduate School, Kimmel School of Construction Management and Technology, Department of Construction Management, Cullowhee, NC 28723. Offers MCM. Part-time and evening/weekend programs available. Postbaccalaureate distance learning degree programs offered. *Students:* 38 part-time (5 women). Average age 38. 37 applicants, 84% accepted, 22 enrolled. *Entrance requirements:* For master's, GRE or GMAT, appropriate undergraduate degree, resume, letters of recommendation, work experience. Additional exam requirements/recommendations for international students: Required—TOEFL (minimum score 550 paper-based; 270 computer-based; 79 iBT). *Application deadline:* For fall admission, 5/1 priority date for domestic students. Application fee: $45. *Financial support:* In 2009–10, 1 student received support; fellowships, research assistantships with full and partial tuition reimbursements available, teaching assistantships with full and partial tuition reimbursements available, career-related internships or fieldwork, institutionally sponsored loans, traineeships, and unspecified assistantships available. Financial award application deadline: 3/31; financial award applicants required to submit FAFSA. *Faculty research:* Hazardous waste management, energy management and conservation, engineering materials, refrigeration and air conditioning systems. *Unit head:* Dr. Bradford Sims, Head, 828-227-2159, Fax: 828-227-7838, E-mail: bsims@email.wcu.edu. *Application contact:* Admissions Specialist for Construction Management, 828-227-7398, Fax: 828-227-7480, E-mail: gradsch@email.wcu.edu.

Western Michigan University, Graduate College, College of Engineering and Applied Sciences, Department of Civil and Construction Engineering, Kalamazoo, MI 49008. Offers civil engineering (MS), including construction engineering and management, structural engineering, transportation engineering. *Entrance requirements:* For master's, minimum GPA of 3.0.

Worcester Polytechnic Institute, Graduate Studies and Research, Department of Civil and Environmental Engineering, Worcester, MA 01609-2280. Offers civil and environmental engineering (Advanced Certificate, Graduate Certificate); civil engineering (ME, MS, PhD); construction project management (MS); environmental engineering (MS); master builder environmental engineering (M Eng). Part-time and evening/weekend programs available. Postbaccalaureate distance learning degree programs offered (no on-campus study). *Faculty:* 10 full-time (1 woman), 1 part-time/adjunct (0 women). *Students:* 23 full-time (10 women), 53 part-time (14 women). 121 applicants, 79% accepted, 28 enrolled. In 2009, 18 master's, 2 doctorates awarded. *Degree requirements:* For master's, thesis optional; for doctorate, comprehensive exam, thesis/dissertation. *Entrance requirements:* For master's and doctorate, GRE (recommended), 3 letters of recommendation. Additional exam requirements/recommendations for international students: Required—TOEFL (minimum score 550 paper-based; 213 computer-based; 79 iBT), IELTS (minimum score 6.5). *Application deadline:* For fall admission, 1/15 priority date for domestic and international students; for spring admission, 10/15 priority date for domestic and international students. Applications are processed on a rolling basis. Application fee: $70. Electronic applications accepted. *Financial support:* Career-related internships or fieldwork, institutionally sponsored loans, scholarships/grants, and unspecified assistantships available. Financial award application deadline: 1/15. *Faculty research:* Environmental engineering and sustainability, pavement engineering technology, impact mechanics and engineering. *Unit head:* Dr. Tahar El-Korchi, Interim Head, 508-831-5530, Fax: 508-831-5808, E-mail: tek@wpi.edu. *Application contact:* Dr. Paul Mathisen, Graduate Coordinator, 508-831-5530, Fax: 508-831-5808, E-mail: mathisen@wpi.edu.

Energy Management and Policy

Holy Names University, Graduate Division, Department of Business, Oakland, CA 94619-1699. Offers energy and environment management (MBA); finance (MBA); management and leadership (MBA); marketing (MBA); sports management (MBA). Part-time and evening/weekend programs available. *Entrance requirements:* For master's, minimum undergraduate GPA of 2.6 overall, 3.0 in major. Additional exam requirements/recommendations for international students: Required—TOEFL (minimum score 550 paper-based; 213 computer-based; 80 iBT). *Faculty research:* Business ethics, sustainable economics, accounting models, cross-cultural management, diversity in organizations.

New York Institute of Technology, Graduate Division, School of Engineering and Computing Sciences, Program in Energy Management, Old Westbury, NY 11568-8000. Offers energy management (MS); energy technology (Advanced Certificate); environmental management (Advanced Certificate); facilities management (Advanced Certificate). Part-time and evening/weekend programs available. Postbaccalaureate distance learning degree programs offered. *Students:* 53 full-time (8 women), 105 part-time (14 women); includes 38 minority (13 African Americans, 1 American Indian/Alaska Native, 9 Asian Americans or Pacific Islanders, 15 Hispanic Americans), 33 international. Average age 33. In 2009, 25 master's, 15 other advanced degrees awarded. *Degree requirements:* For master's, comprehensive exam, thesis or alternative. *Entrance requirements:* For master's, minimum QPA of 2.85. Additional exam requirements/recommendations for international students: Required—TOEFL (minimum score 550 paper-based; 213 computer-based). *Application deadline:* For fall admission, 7/1 priority date for domestic students; for spring admission, 12/1 priority date for domestic students. Applications are processed on a rolling basis. Application fee: $50. Electronic applications accepted. *Expenses:* Tuition: Part-time $825 per credit. *Financial support:* Fellowships, research assistantships with partial tuition reimbursements, institutionally sponsored loans, tuition waivers (full and partial), and unspecified assistantships available. Support available to part-time students. Financial award applicants required to submit FAFSA. *Unit head:* Dr. Frank Zeman, Director, 212-261-1656, Fax: 212-261-1748, E-mail: fzeman@nyit.edu. *Application contact:* Dr. Jacquelyn Nealon, Vice President for Enrollment Services, 516-686-7925, Fax: 516-686-7597, E-mail: jnealon@nyit.edu.

Energy Management and Policy

Université du Québec, Institut National de la Recherche Scientifique, Graduate Programs, Research Center—Energy, Materials and Telecommunications, Québec, QC G1K 9A9, Canada. Offers energy and materials science (M Sc, PhD); telecommunications (M Sc, PhD). Programs given in French. Part-time programs available. *Faculty:* 37. *Students:* 161 full-time (45 women), 10 part-time (1 woman), 76 international. Average age 32. In 2009, 16 master's, 13 doctorates awarded. *Degree requirements:* For master's, thesis; for doctorate, thesis/dissertation. *Entrance requirements:* For master's, appropriate bachelor's degree, proficiency in French; for doctorate, appropriate master's degree, proficiency in French. *Application deadline:* For fall admission, 3/30 for domestic and international students; for winter admission, 11/1 for domestic and international students. Application fee: $30. *Financial support:* Fellowships, research assistantships, teaching assistantships available. *Faculty research:* New energy sources, plasmas, fusion. *Unit head:* Jean-Claude Kieffer, Director, 450-929-8100, Fax: 450-929-8102, E-mail: kieffer@emt.inrs.ca. *Application contact:* Yvonne Boisvert, Registrar, 418-654-3861, Fax: 418-654-3858, E-mail: registrariat@adm.inrs.ca.

University of California, Berkeley, Graduate Division, Group in Energy and Resources, Berkeley, CA 94720-1500. Offers MA, MS, PhD. *Students:* 60 full-time (32 women). Average age 31. 189 applicants, 12 enrolled. In 2009, 12 master's, 6 doctorates awarded. *Degree requirements:* For master's, project or thesis; for doctorate, one foreign language, thesis/dissertation, qualifying exam. *Entrance requirements:* For master's and doctorate, GRE General Test, minimum GPA of 3.0, 3 letters of recommendation. *Application deadline:* For fall admission, 12/5 for domestic students. Application fee: $70 ($90 for international students). *Financial support:* Unspecified assistantships available. *Faculty research:* Technical, economic, environmental, and institutional aspects of energy conservation in residential and commercial buildings; international patterns of energy use; renewable energy sources; assessment of valuation of energy and environmental resources pricing. *Unit head:* Prof. Daniel Farber, Chair, 510-642-1640, E-mail: erggrad@berkeley.edu. *Application contact:* Bette L. Evans, Student Affairs Officer, 510-642-1750, Fax: 510-642-1085, E-mail: engbarrows@berkeley.edu.

University of Delaware, College of Human Services, Education and Public Policy, Center for Energy and Environmental Policy, Newark, DE 19716. Offers environmental and energy policy (MEEP, PhD); urban affairs and public policy (MA, PhD), including community development and nonprofit leadership (MA), energy and environmental policy (MA), governance, planning and management (PhD), historic preservation (MA), social and urban policy (PhD), technology, environment and society (PhD). *Degree requirements:* For master's, analytical paper or thesis; for doctorate, comprehensive exam, thesis/dissertation. *Entrance requirements:* For master's, GRE General Test, minimum GPA of 3.0; for doctorate, GRE General Test, minimum GPA of 3.5. Additional exam requirements/recommendations for international students: Required—TOEFL. Electronic applications accepted. *Faculty research:* Sustainable development, renewable energy, climate change, environmental policy, environmental justice, disaster policy.

University of Illinois at Urbana–Champaign, Graduate College, College of Agricultural, Consumer and Environmental Sciences, Department of Agricultural and Biological Engineering, Champaign, IL 61820. Offers agricultural engineering (MS, PhD); bioenergy (MS), including professional science. *Faculty:* 19 full-time (2 women). *Students:* 38 full-time (11 women), 10 part-time (1 woman); includes 1 minority (Hispanic American), 33 international. 44 applicants, 18% accepted, 6 enrolled. In 2009, 10 master's, 6 doctorates awarded. *Entrance requirements:* For master's and doctorate, minimum GPA of 3.0. Additional exam requirements/recommendations for international students: Required—TOEFL (minimum score 570 paper-based; 230 computer-based; 88 iBT), or IELTS (minimum score 6.5). *Application deadline:* Applications are processed on a rolling basis. Application fee: $60 ($75 for international students). Electronic applications accepted. *Financial support:* In 2009–10, 6 fellowships, 47 research assistantships were awarded; teaching assistantships, tuition waivers (full and partial) also available. *Unit head:* Kuan Chong Ting, Head, 217-333-3570, Fax: 217-244-0323, E-mail: kcting@illinois.edu. *Application contact:* Ronda Sullivan, Assistant to the Head, 217-333-3570, Fax: 217-244-0323, E-mail: rsully@illinois.edu.

University of Tulsa, Graduate School, Collins College of Business, Master of Business Administration Program, Tulsa, OK 74104-3189. Offers accounting (MBA); business administration (MBA); energy management (MBA); finance (MBA); international business (MBA); management information systems (MBA); taxation (MBA); JD/MBA; MBA/MSCS; MBA/MSF. *Accreditation:* AACSB. Part-time and evening/weekend programs available. *Faculty:* 32 full-time (6 women). *Students:* 59 full-time (26 women), 45 part-time (18 women); includes 13 minority (4 African Americans, 4 American Indian/Alaska Native, 1 Asian American or Pacific Islander, 4 Hispanic Americans), 9 international. Average age 25. 78 applicants, 53% accepted, 30 enrolled. In 2009, 36 master's awarded. *Entrance requirements:* For master's, GMAT. Additional exam requirements/recommendations for international students: Required—TOEFL (minimum score 575 paper-based; 232 computer-based; 90 iBT), IELTS (minimum score 6.5). *Application deadline:* Applications are processed on a rolling basis. Application fee: $40. Electronic applications accepted. *Expenses:* Tuition: Full-time $16,182; part-time $899 per credit hour. Required fees: $4 per credit hour. Tuition and fees vary according to course load. *Financial support:* In 2009–10, 42 students received support, including 5 fellowships (averaging $11,894 per year), 2 research assistantships (averaging $9,322 per year), 35 teaching assistantships (averaging $8,112 per year); institutionally sponsored loans, scholarships/grants, health care benefits, tuition waivers (full and partial), and unspecified assistantships also available. Support available to part-time students. Financial award application deadline: 2/1; financial award applicants required to submit FAFSA. *Faculty research:* Accounting, energy management, finance, international business, management information systems, taxation. *Unit head:* Dr. Markham Collins, Associate Dean of the Collins College of Business, 918-631-2783, Fax: 918-631-2142, E-mail: markham-collins@utulsa.edu. *Application contact:* Dr. Markham Collins, Associate Dean of the Collins College of Business, 918-631-2783, Fax: 918-631-2142, E-mail: markham-collins@utulsa.edu.

University of Washington, Graduate School, College of Forest Resources, Seattle, WA 98195. Offers bioresource science and engineering (MS, PhD); environmental horticulture (MEH); environmental horticulture and urban forestry (MS, PhD); forest ecology (MS, PhD); forest management (MFR); forest soils (MS, PhD); forest systems and bioenergy (MS, PhD); restoration ecology (MS, PhD); social sciences (MS, PhD); sustainable resource management (MS, PhD); wildlife science (MS, PhD); MFR/MAIS; MPA/MS. *Accreditation:* SAF. *Degree requirements:* For master's, thesis (for some programs); for doctorate, comprehensive exam (for some programs), thesis/dissertation. *Entrance requirements:* For master's and doctorate, GRE, minimum GPA of 3.0. Additional exam requirements/recommendations for international students: Required—TOEFL. Electronic applications accepted. *Faculty research:* Ecosystem analysis, silviculture and forest protection, paper science and engineering, environmental horticulture and urban forestry, natural resource policy and economics.

Engineering Management

Air Force Institute of Technology, Graduate School of Engineering and Management, Department of Systems and Engineering Management, Dayton, OH 45433-7765. Offers cost analysis (MS); environmental and engineering management (MS); environmental engineering science (MS); information resource/systems management (MS). *Accreditation:* ABET. Part-time programs available. *Degree requirements:* For master's, thesis. *Entrance requirements:* For master's, GRE, GMAT, minimum GPA of 3.0.

American University of Beirut, Graduate Programs, Faculty of Engineering and Architecture, Beirut, Lebanon. Offers civil engineering (ME, PhD); electrical and computer engineering (ME, PhD); engineering management (MEM); environmental and water resources (ME); environmental and water resources engineering (PhD); environmental technology (MSES); mechanical engineering (ME, PhD); urban design (MUD); urban planning and policy (MUP). Part-time programs available. *Degree requirements:* For master's, one foreign language, comprehensive exam, thesis (for some programs); for doctorate, one foreign language, comprehensive exam, thesis/dissertation, publications. *Entrance requirements:* For master's, letters of recommendation; for doctorate, letters of recommendation, master's degree, transcripts, curriculum vitae, interview. Additional exam requirements/recommendations for international students: Required—TOEFL (minimum score 600 paper-based; 250 computer-based; 100 iBT), IELTS (minimum score 7.5). Electronic applications accepted.

California National University for Advanced Studies, College of Quality and Engineering Management, Northridge, CA 91325. Offers MEM. Part-time programs available. *Entrance requirements:* For master's, minimum GPA of 3.0.

California State Polytechnic University, Pomona, Academic Affairs, College of Engineering, Pomona, CA 91768-2557. Offers civil engineering (MS); electrical engineering (MSEE); engineering (MSE); engineering management (MS); mechanical engineering (MS). Part-time programs available. *Faculty:* 95 full-time (17 women), 71 part-time/adjunct (6 women). *Students:* 36 full-time (3 women), 198 part-time (33 women); includes 104 minority (1 African American, 2 American Indian/Alaska Native, 69 Asian Americans or Pacific Islanders, 32 Hispanic Americans), 42 international. Average age 28. 237 applicants, 49% accepted, 73 enrolled. In 2009, 46 master's awarded. *Degree requirements:* For master's, thesis or comprehensive exam. *Entrance requirements:* For master's, GRE General Test or minimum GPA of 3.0 in upper-level course work. Additional exam requirements/recommendations for international students: Required—TOEFL. *Application deadline:* For fall admission, 5/1 priority date for domestic students; for winter admission, 10/15 priority date for domestic students; for spring admission, 1/2 priority date for domestic students. Applications are processed on a rolling basis. Application fee: $55. Electronic applications accepted. *Expenses:* Tuition, nonresident: full-time $6696; part-time $248 per credit. Required fees: $5487; $3237 per term. Tuition and fees vary according to course load, degree level and program. *Financial support:* In 2009–10, 1 fellowship, 6 research assistantships, 5 teaching assistantships were awarded; career-related internships or fieldwork, Federal Work-Study, institutionally sponsored loans, and unspecified assistantships also available. Support available to part-time students. Financial award application deadline: 3/2; financial award applicants required to submit FAFSA. *Faculty research:* Aerospace; alternative vehicles; communications, computers, and controls; engineering management. Total annual research expenditures: $650,000. *Unit head:* Dr. Edward Hohmann, Dean, 909-869-2472, Fax: 909-869-4370, E-mail: echohmann@csupomona.edu. *Application contact:* Dr. Edward Hohmann, Dean, 909-869-2472, Fax: 909-869-4370, E-mail: echohmann@csupomona.edu.

California State University, East Bay, Academic Programs and Graduate Studies, College of Science, Engineering Department, Hayward, CA 94542-3000. Offers construction management (MS); engineering management (MS). *Faculty:* 4 full-time (2 women). *Students:* 24 full-time (9 women), 61 part-time (17 women); includes 27 minority (6 African Americans, 14 Asian Americans or Pacific Islanders, 7 Hispanic Americans), 33 international. Average age 31. 124 applicants, 59% accepted, 36 enrolled. In 2009, 5 master's awarded. *Entrance requirements:* For master's, GRE or GMAT, minimum GPA of 2.5. Additional exam requirements/recommendations for international students: Required—TOEFL (minimum score 550 paper-based; 213 computer-based). *Application deadline:* For fall admission, 6/30 for domestic and international students. Application fee: $55. Electronic applications accepted. *Financial support:* Federal Work-Study and institutionally sponsored loans available. Support available to part-time students. *Unit head:* Dr. Saeid Motavalli, Chair, 510-885-2654, Fax: 510-885-2678, E-mail: saeid.motavalli@csueastbay.edu. *Application contact:* Donna Wiley, Interim Associate Director, 510-885-2928, Fax: 510-885-4777, E-mail: donna.wiley@csueastbay.edu.

California State University, Long Beach, Graduate Studies, College of Engineering, Department of Mechanical and Aerospace Engineering, Long Beach, CA 90840. Offers aerospace engineering (MSAE); engineering and industrial applied mathematics (PhD); interdisciplinary engineering (MSE); management engineering (MSE); mechanical engineering (MSME). Part-time programs available. *Faculty:* 16 full-time (2 women), 3 part-time/adjunct (0 women). *Students:* 47 full-time (6 women), 75 part-time (9 women); includes 51 minority (5 African Americans, 30 Asian Americans or Pacific Islanders, 16 Hispanic Americans), 28 international. Average age 28. 162 applicants, 63% accepted, 44 enrolled. *Entrance requirements:* Additional exam requirements/recommendations for international students: Required—TOEFL. *Application deadline:* For fall admission, 7/1 for domestic students. Application fee: $55. Electronic applications accepted. *Expenses:* Required fees: $1802 per semester. Part-time tuition and fees vary according to course load. *Financial support:* Career-related internships or fieldwork, Federal Work-Study, institutionally sponsored loans, scholarships/grants, and unspecified assistantships available. Financial award application deadline: 3/2. *Faculty research:* Unsteady turbulent flows, solar energy, energy conversion, CAD/CAM, computer-assisted instruction. *Unit head:* Dr. Hamid Hefazi, Chair, 562-985-1502, Fax: 562-985-1564, E-mail: hefazi@csulb.edu. *Application contact:* Dr. Hamid Rahai, Graduate Advisor, 562-985-5132, Fax: 562-985-4408, E-mail: rahai@csulb.edu.

California State University, Northridge, Graduate Studies, College of Engineering and Computer Science, Department of Manufacturing Systems Engineering and Management, Northridge, CA 91330. Offers engineering automation (MS); engineering management (MS); manufacturing systems engineering (MS); materials engineering (MS). Postbaccalaureate distance learning degree programs offered. *Faculty:* 6 full-time (1 woman), 33 part-time/adjunct (12 women). *Students:* 137 full-time (18 women), 115 part-time (20 women); includes 4 African Americans, 22 Asian Americans or Pacific Islanders, 19 Hispanic Americans, 149 international. Average age 27. 210 applicants, 68% accepted, 69 enrolled. In 2009, 78 master's awarded. *Entrance requirements:* For master's, GRE (if cumulative undergraduate GPA less than 3.0). *Application deadline:* For fall admission, 3/30 for domestic students; for spring admission, 9/30 for domestic students. Application fee: $55. *Unit head:* Prof. Behzad Bavarian, Acting Chair, 818-677-2167. *Application contact:* Prof. Behzad Bavarian, Acting Chair, 818-677-2167.

Case Western Reserve University, School of Graduate Studies, The Case School of Engineering, The Institute for the Integration of Management and Engineering, Cleveland, OH 44106. Offers MEM. *Faculty:* 5 full-time (0 women), 6 part-time/adjunct (2 women). *Students:* 38 full-time (7 women), 1 part-time (0 women); includes 8 minority (4 African Americans, 4 Asian Americans or Pacific Islanders), 11 international. 96 applicants, 89% accepted, 37 enrolled. In 2009, 37 master's awarded. *Entrance requirements:* Additional exam requirements/recommendations for international students: Required—TOEFL (minimum score 100 computer-based), IELTS (minimum score 7.5). *Application deadline:* For fall admission, 2/5 for domestic students, 11/15 priority date for international students; for winter admission, 1/5 for domestic students, 11/15 for international students; for spring admission, 3/5 for domestic students,

11/30 for international students. *Financial support:* In 2009–10, 37 fellowships (averaging $14,300 per year) were awarded; scholarships/grants also available. *Unit head:* Suzette Williamson, Executive Director, 216-368-0598, Fax: 216-368-0144, E-mail: sxwll@cwru.edu. *Application contact:* Ramona David, Program Assistant, 216-368-0596, Fax: 216-368-0144, E-mail: rxd47@cwru.edu.

The Catholic University of America, School of Engineering, Program in Engineering Management, Washington, DC 20064. Offers MSE, Certificate. Part-time programs available. *Faculty:* 5 part-time/adjunct (0 women). *Students:* 16 full-time (5 women), 21 part-time (7 women); includes 6 minority (3 African Americans, 3 Asian Americans or Pacific Islanders), 16 international. Average age 30. 37 applicants, 65% accepted, 14 enrolled. In 2009, 19 master's, 2 other advanced degrees awarded. *Degree requirements:* For master's, thesis optional. *Entrance requirements:* For master's, statement of purpose, official copies of academic transcripts, three letters of recommendation. Additional exam requirements/recommendations for international students: Required—TOEFL (minimum score 580 paper-based; 237 computer-based). *Application deadline:* For fall admission, 8/1 priority date for domestic students, 7/15 for international students; for spring admission, 12/1 priority date for domestic students, 10/15 for international students. Applications are processed on a rolling basis. Application fee: $55. Electronic applications accepted. *Expenses:* Contact institution. *Financial support:* Fellowships, research assistantships, teaching assistantships, Federal Work-Study, scholarships/grants, tuition waivers (full and partial), and unspecified assistantships available. Financial award application deadline: 2/1; financial award applicants required to submit FAFSA. *Faculty research:* Engineering management and organization, project and systems engineering management, technology management. *Unit head:* Jeffrey E. Giangiuli, Director, 202-319-5191, Fax: 202-319-6860, E-mail: giangiuli@cua.edu. *Application contact:* Julie Schwing, Director of Graduate Admissions, 202-319-5057, Fax: 202-319-6533, E-mail: cua-admissions@cua.edu.

Clarkson University, Graduate School, School of Business, Program in Engineering and Global Operations Management, Potsdam, NY 13699. Offers MS. Part-time and evening/weekend programs available. *Students:* 25 part-time (7 women); includes 2 minority (1 Asian American or Pacific Islander, 1 Hispanic American). Average age 40. 5 applicants, 100% accepted, 4 enrolled. In 2009, 14 master's awarded. *Entrance requirements:* For master's, GMAT or GRE, transcripts of all college coursework, resume, personal statement, three letters of recommendation. Additional exam requirements/recommendations for international students: Required—TOEFL (minimum score 550 paper-based; 213 computer-based; 80 iBT), IELTS (minimum score 6.5), TSE required unless TOEFL iBT score is 100 or better. *Application deadline:* For fall admission, 1/30 priority date for domestic and international students; for spring admission, 9/1 priority date for domestic and international students. Applications are processed on a rolling basis. Application fee: $25 ($35 for international students). Electronic applications accepted. *Expenses:* Tuition: Part-time $1074 per credit hour. *Faculty research:* Global supply chain management, business to business marketing, operations strategy, engineering economics process control. *Unit head:* Dr. Kenneth R. DaRin, Director, 315-268-5982, Fax: 315-268-3810, E-mail: kdarin@clarkson.edu. *Application contact:* Karen Fuhr, Assistant to the Graduate Director, 315-268-6613, Fax: 315-268-3810, E-mail: fuhrk@clarkson.edu.

Colorado School of Mines, Graduate School, Division of Economics and Business, Golden, CO 80401. Offers engineering and technology management (MS); mineral economics (MS, PhD). Part-time programs available. *Faculty:* 11 full-time (3 women), 6 part-time/adjunct (0 women). *Students:* 110 full-time (25 women), 18 part-time (3 women); includes 13 minority (4 African Americans, 1 American Indian/Alaska Native, 2 Asian Americans or Pacific Islanders, 6 Hispanic Americans), 32 international. Average age 30. 162 applicants, 92% accepted, 73 enrolled. In 2009, 47 master's, 2 doctorates awarded. *Degree requirements:* For master's, thesis (for some programs); for doctorate, comprehensive exam, thesis/dissertation. *Entrance requirements:* For master's and doctorate, GRE General Test. Additional exam requirements/recommendations for international students: Required—TOEFL (minimum score 550 paper-based; 213 computer-based; 80 iBT). *Application deadline:* For fall admission, 1/15 priority date for domestic and international students; for spring admission, 9/1 priority date for domestic and international students. Application fee: $50 ($70 for international students). Electronic applications accepted. *Expenses:* Tuition, state resident: full-time $10,584; part-time $588 per credit hour. Tuition, nonresident: full-time $24,750; part-time $1375 per credit hour. Required fees: $1654; $827.10 per semester. *Financial support:* In 2009–10, 25 students received support, including 3 fellowships with full tuition reimbursements available (averaging $20,000 per year), research assistantships with full tuition reimbursements available (averaging $20,000 per year), 22 teaching assistantships with full tuition reimbursements available (averaging $20,000 per year); scholarships/grants, health care benefits, and unspecified assistantships also available. Financial award application deadline: 1/15; financial award applicants required to submit FAFSA. *Faculty research:* International trade, resource and environmental economics, energy economics, operations research. Total annual research expenditures: $99,841. *Unit head:* Dr. Rod Eggert, Division Head, 303-273-3981, Fax: 303-273-3416, E-mail: reggert@mines.edu. *Application contact:* Kathleen A. Feighny, Administrative Faculty, 303-273-3979, Fax: 303-273-3416, E-mail: kfeighny@mines.edu.

Columbia University, Fu Foundation School of Engineering and Applied Science, Department of Industrial Engineering and Operations Research, New York, NY 10027. Offers engineering management systems (MS); financial engineering (MS); industrial engineering (Engr); industrial engineering and operations research (MS, Eng Sc D, PhD); MS/MBA. Part-time and evening/weekend programs available. Postbaccalaureate distance learning degree programs offered (no on-campus study). *Faculty:* 13 full-time (1 woman), 3 part-time/adjunct (1 woman). *Students:* 260 full-time (69 women), 173 part-time (50 women); includes 27 minority (1 African American, 24 Asian Americans or Pacific Islanders, 2 Hispanic Americans), 348 international. Average age 25. 1,262 applicants, 35% accepted, 193 enrolled. In 2009, 211 master's, 7 doctorates awarded. *Degree requirements:* For doctorate, thesis/dissertation, oral and written qualifying exams. *Entrance requirements:* For master's, doctorate, and Engr, GRE General Test. Additional exam requirements/recommendations for international students: Required—TOEFL. *Application deadline:* For fall admission, 12/1 priority date for domestic and international students; for spring admission, 10/1 priority date for domestic and international students. Application fee: $70. Electronic applications accepted. *Financial support:* In 2009–10, 49 students received support, including 6 fellowships (averaging $2,500 per year), 23 research assistantships with full tuition reimbursements available (averaging $22,500 per year), 20 teaching assistantships with full tuition reimbursements available (averaging $22,500 per year); career-related internships or fieldwork, health care benefits, and unspecified assistantships also available. Financial award application deadline: 12/1; financial award applicants required to submit FAFSA. *Faculty research:* Combinatorial optimization and mathematical programming; financial engineering; supply chain management and inventory theory; applied probability; queuing theory; scheduling, and simulation. *Unit head:* Dr. Cliff S. Stein, Department Chair; Professor, 212-854-5238, Fax: 212-854-8103, E-mail: cliff@ieor.columbia.edu. *Application contact:* Adina Berrios Brooks, Student Affairs Manager, 212-854-1934, Fax: 212-854-8103, E-mail: admit@ieor.columbia.edu.

Cornell University, Graduate School, Graduate Fields of Engineering, Field of Civil and Environmental Engineering, Ithaca, NY 14853-0001. Offers engineering management (M Eng, MS, PhD); environmental engineering (M Eng, MS, PhD); environmental fluid mechanics and hydrology (M Eng, MS, PhD); environmental systems engineering (M Eng, MS, PhD); geotechnical engineering (M Eng, MS, PhD); remote sensing (M Eng, MS, PhD); structural engineering (M Eng, MS, PhD); structural mechanics (M Eng, MS); transportation engineering (MS, PhD); transportation systems engineering (M Eng); water resource systems (M Eng, MS, PhD). *Faculty:* 40 full-time (7 women). *Students:* 144 full-time (48 women); includes 12 minority (2 African Americans, 1 American Indian/Alaska Native, 5 Asian Americans or Pacific Islanders, 4 Hispanic Americans), 58 international. Average age 25. 454 applicants, 57% accepted, 86 enrolled. In 2009, 69 master's, 5 doctorates awarded. Terminal master's awarded for partial completion of doctoral program. *Degree requirements:* For master's, thesis (MS); for doctorate, comprehensive exam, thesis/dissertation. *Entrance requirements:* For master's and doctorate, GRE General Test (recommended), 2 letters of recommendation. Additional exam requirements/recommendations for international students: Required—TOEFL (minimum score 600 paper-based; 250 computer-based; 77 iBT). *Application deadline:* For fall admission, 1/15 priority date for domestic students; for spring admission, 10/15 for domestic students. Application fee: $70. Electronic applications accepted. *Expenses:* Tuition: Full-time $29,500. Required fees: $70. Full-time tuition and fees vary according to degree level, program and student level. *Financial support:* In 2009–10, 50 students received support, including 6 fellowships with full tuition reimbursements available, 5 research assistantships with full tuition reimbursements available, 1 teaching assistantship with full tuition reimbursement available; institutionally sponsored loans, scholarships/grants, health care benefits, tuition waivers (full and partial), and unspecified assistantships also available. Financial award applicants required to submit FAFSA. *Faculty research:* Environmental engineering, geotechnical engineering remote sensing, environmental fluid mechanics and hydrology, structural engineering. *Unit head:* Director of Graduate Studies, 607-255-7560, Fax: 607-255-9004. *Application contact:* Graduate Field Assistant, 607-255-7560, Fax: 607-255-9004, E-mail: cee_grad@cornell.edu.

Dallas Baptist University, College of Business, Business Administration Program, Dallas, TX 75211-9299. Offers accounting (MBA); business communication (MBA); conflict resolution management (MBA); e-business (MBA); entrepreneurship (MBA); finance (MBA); health care management (MBA); international business (MBA); leading the non-profit organization (MBA); management (MBA); management information systems (MBA); marketing (MBA); project management (MBA); technology and engineering management (MBA). *Accreditation:* ACBSP. Part-time and evening/weekend programs available. *Entrance requirements:* For master's, GMAT, minimum GPA of 3.0. Additional exam requirements/recommendations for international students: Required—TOEFL, IELTS. Electronic applications accepted. *Expenses:* Tuition: Full-time $10,674; part-time $593 per credit hour. *Faculty research:* Sports management, services marketing, retailing, strategic management, financial planning/investments.

Dartmouth College, Thayer School of Engineering, Program in Engineering Management, Hanover, NH 03755. Offers MEM, MBA/MEM. *Degree requirements:* For master's, design experience. *Entrance requirements:* For master's, GRE General Test. Additional exam requirements/recommendations for international students: Required—TOEFL. *Application deadline:* For fall admission, 1/1 priority date for domestic students. Applications are processed on a rolling basis. Application fee: $45. *Financial support:* Fellowships, teaching assistantships, career-related internships or fieldwork, Federal Work-Study, institutionally sponsored loans, and tuition waivers (full and partial) available. Financial award application deadline: 1/15; financial award applicants required to submit CSS PROFILE. *Unit head:* Dr. Joseph J. Helbie, Dean, 603-646-2238, Fax: 603-646-2580, E-mail: joseph.j.helbie@dartmouth.edu. *Application contact:* Candace S. Potter, Graduate Admissions Administrator, 603-646-3844, Fax: 603-646-1620, E-mail: candace.potter@dartmouth.edu.

Drexel University, College of Engineering, Program in Engineering Management, Philadelphia, PA 19104-2875. Offers MS, Certificate. Part-time and evening/weekend programs available. Postbaccalaureate distance learning degree programs offered (no on-campus study). *Degree requirements:* For master's, thesis optional. *Entrance requirements:* For master's, minimum GPA of 3.0. Additional exam requirements/recommendations for international students: Required—TOEFL. Electronic applications accepted. *Faculty research:* Quality, operations research and management, ergonomics, applied statistics.

Duke University, Graduate School, Pratt School of Engineering, Program in Engineering Management, Durham, NC 27708-0586. Offers MEM. *Entrance requirements:* For master's, GRE General Test, resume, 2 letters of recommendation. Additional exam requirements/recommendations for international students: Required—TOEFL. Electronic applications accepted.

Eastern Michigan University, Graduate School, College of Technology, School of Engineering Technology, Program in Engineering Management, Ypsilanti, MI 48197. Offers MS. Part-time and evening/weekend programs available. Postbaccalaureate distance learning degree programs offered (minimal on-campus study). *Students:* 31 full-time (6 women), 118 part-time (21 women); includes 15 minority (7 African Americans, 1 American Indian/Alaska Native, 1 Asian American or Pacific Islander, 6 Hispanic Americans), 33 international. Average age 33. In 2009, 45 master's awarded. *Entrance requirements:* Additional exam requirements/recommendations for international students: Required—TOEFL. *Application deadline:* Applications are processed on a rolling basis. Application fee: $35. Tuition and fees vary according to course level. *Financial support:* Fellowships, research assistantships with full tuition reimbursements, teaching assistantships with full tuition reimbursements, career-related internships or fieldwork, Federal Work-Study, institutionally sponsored loans, scholarships/grants, tuition waivers (partial), and unspecified assistantships available. Support available to part-time students. Financial award applicants required to submit FAFSA. *Unit head:* Dr. Tracy Tillman, Program Coordinator, 734-487-0092, Fax: 734-487-8755, E-mail: tracy.tillman@emich.edu. *Application contact:* Dr. Tracy Tillman, Program Coordinator, 734-487-0092, Fax: 734-487-8755, E-mail: tracy.tillman@emich.edu.

Florida Institute of Technology, Graduate Programs, College of Engineering, Engineering Systems Department, Melbourne, FL 32901-6975. Offers engineering management (MS); systems engineering (MS). Part-time and evening/weekend programs available. *Faculty:* 4 full-time (0 women), 2 part-time/adjunct (0 women). *Students:* 14 full-time (2 women), 129 part-time (31 women); includes 21 minority (7 African Americans, 6 Asian Americans or Pacific Islanders, 8 Hispanic Americans), 16 international. Average age 36. 103 applicants, 69% accepted, 24 enrolled. In 2009, 108 master's awarded. *Degree requirements:* For master's, comprehensive exam (for some programs), thesis optional, portfolio of competencies and summary of career relevance. *Entrance requirements:* For master's, GRE General Test (if GPA less than 3.0), BS in engineering, minimum GPA of 3.0, 2 letters of recommendation, resume, bachelor's degree from ABET-accredited program. Additional exam requirements/recommendations for international students: Required—TOEFL (minimum score 550 paper-based; 213 computer-based; 79 iBT). *Application deadline:* For fall admission, 4/1 for international students; for spring admission, 9/30 for international students. Applications are processed on a rolling basis. Application fee: $50. Electronic applications accepted. *Expenses:* Tuition: Part-time $1015 per credit. Tuition and fees vary according to campus/location and program. *Financial support:* In 2009–10, 1 student received support, including 1 research assistantship with full and partial tuition reimbursement available (averaging $5,000 per year); career-related internships or fieldwork, institutionally sponsored loans, unspecified assistantships, and tuition remissions also available. Support available to part-time students. Financial award application deadline: 3/1; financial award applicants required to submit FAFSA. *Faculty research:* System/software engineering, simulation and analytical modeling, project management, multimedia tools, quality. *Unit head:* Dr. Muzaffar A. Shaikh, Department Head, 321-674-7345, Fax: 321-674-7136, E-mail: mshaikh@fit.edu. *Application contact:* Thomas M. Shea, Director of Graduate Admissions, 321-674-7577, Fax: 321-723-9468, E-mail: tshea@fit.edu.

See Close-Up on page 467.

Gannon University, School of Graduate Studies, College of Engineering and Business, School of Engineering and Computer Science, Program in Engineering Management, Erie, PA 16541-0001. Offers MSEM. Part-time and evening/weekend programs available. *Students:* 24 full-time (1 woman), 7 part-time (0 women), 26 international. Average age 28. 84 applicants, 88% accepted, 19 enrolled. In 2009, 1 master's awarded. *Entrance requirements:* For master's, bachelor's degree in engineering, minimum QPA of 2.5. Additional exam requirements/recommendations for international students: Required—TOEFL (minimum score 79 iBT). *Application deadline:* Applications are processed on a rolling basis. Application fee: $25. Electronic applications accepted. *Expenses:* Tuition: Full-time $13,590; part-time $755 per credit. Required fees: $524; $17 per credit. Tuition and fees vary according to course load, degree level, campus/location and program. *Financial support:* Scholarships/grants available. Financial award application deadline: 7/1; financial award applicants required to submit FAFSA. *Unit head:* Dr. Mahesh Aggarwal, Chair, 814-871-7629, E-mail: affarwal001@gannon.edu.

Engineering Management

Gannon University (continued)

Application contact: Kara Morgan, Assistant Director of Graduate Admissions, 814-871-5831, Fax: 814-871-5827, E-mail: graduate@gannon.edu.

The George Washington University, School of Engineering and Applied Science, Department of Engineering Management and Systems Engineering, Washington, DC 20052. Offers MS, D Sc, App Sc, Engr, Graduate Certificate. Part-time and evening/weekend programs available. *Faculty:* 17 full-time (1 woman), 18 part-time/adjunct (2 women). *Students:* 116 full-time (28 women), 1,181 part-time (290 women); includes 348 minority (152 African Americans, 7 American Indian/Alaska Native, 128 Asian Americans or Pacific Islanders, 61 Hispanic Americans), 121 international. Average age 35. 574 applicants, 93% accepted, 333 enrolled. In 2009, 431 master's, 26 doctorates, 321 other advanced degrees awarded. *Degree requirements:* For master's, thesis optional; for doctorate, one foreign language, thesis/dissertation, final and qualifying exams, submission of articles; for other advanced degree, professional project. *Entrance requirements:* For master's, appropriate bachelor's degree, minimum GPA of 2.7, second semester calculus; for doctorate, appropriate master's degree, minimum GPA of 3.5, 2 letters of recommendation; for other advanced degree, appropriate master's degree, minimum GPA of 3.4. Additional exam requirements/recommendations for international students: Required—TOEFL or George Washington University English as a Foreign Language Test. *Application deadline:* For fall admission, 3/1 for domestic students; for spring admission, 10/1 for domestic students. Applications are processed on a rolling basis. Application fee: $60. *Financial support:* In 2009–10, 35 students received support; fellowships with tuition reimbursements available, research assistantships, teaching assistantships with tuition reimbursements available, career-related internships or fieldwork and institutionally sponsored loans available. Financial award application deadline: 3/1; financial award applicants required to submit FAFSA. *Faculty research:* Artificial intelligence and expert systems, human factors engineering and systems analysis. Total annual research expenditures: $421,800. *Unit head:* Dr. Thomas Mazzuchi, Chair, 202-994-7424, Fax: 202-994-0245, E-mail: mazzu@gwu.edu. *Application contact:* Adina Lav, Marketing, Recruiting and Admissions, 202-994-5827, Fax: 202-994-0909, E-mail: engineering@gwu.edu.

Instituto Tecnológico y de Estudios Superiores de Monterrey, Campus Chihuahua, Graduate Programs, Chihuahua, Mexico. Offers computer systems engineering (Ingeniero); electrical engineering (Ingeniero); electromechanical engineering (Ingeniero); electronic engineering (Ingeniero); engineering administration (MEA); industrial engineering (MIE, Ingeniero); international trade (MIT); mechanical engineering (Ingeniero).

International Technological University, Program in Engineering Management, Santa Clara, CA 95050. Offers MEM.

The Johns Hopkins University, G. W. C. Whiting School of Engineering, Program in Engineering Management, Baltimore, MD 21218-2699. Offers biomaterials (MSEM); communications science (MSEM); computer science (MSEM); fluid mechanics (MSEM); materials science and engineering (MSEM); mechanical engineering (MSEM); mechanics and materials (MSEM); nano-biotechnology (MSEM); nanomaterials and nanotechnology (MSEM); probability and statistics (MSEM); smart product and device design (MSEM); systems analysis, management and environmental policy (MSEM). *Students:* 12 full-time (0 women), 3 international. Average age 23. 66 applicants, 67% accepted. *Entrance requirements:* For master's, GRE, 3 letters of recommendation, resume. Additional exam requirements/recommendations for international students: Required—TOEFL (minimum score 600 paper-based; 250 computer-based; 100 iBT) or IELTS (minimum score 7). *Application deadline:* For fall admission, 1/15 priority date for domestic students, 1/15 for international students; for spring admission, 9/15 priority date for domestic students, 9/15 for international students. Applications are processed on a rolling basis. Application fee: $75. Electronic applications accepted. *Financial support:* Fellowships, health care benefits available. *Unit head:* Dr. Edward R. Scheinerman, Interim Director/Vice Dean for Education, School of Engineering/Professor, Applied Mathematics and Statistics, 410-516-7395, Fax: 410-516-4880, E-mail: ers@jhu.edu. *Application contact:* Dennis McIver, Coordinator of Graduate Admissions, 410-516-8174, Fax: 410-516-0780, E-mail: graduateadmissions@jhu.edu.

Kansas State University, Graduate School, College of Engineering, Department of Industrial and Manufacturing Systems Engineering, Manhattan, KS 66506. Offers engineering management (MEM); industrial engineering (MS, PhD); operations research (MS). Part-time programs available. Postbaccalaureate distance learning degree programs offered. *Faculty:* 9 full-time (1 woman), 2 part-time/adjunct (1 woman). *Students:* 38 full-time (12 women), 48 part-time (14 women); includes 4 minority (1 African American, 1 Asian American or Pacific Islander, 2 Hispanic Americans), 27 international. Average age 30. 85 applicants, 60% accepted, 41 enrolled. In 2009, 20 master's, 1 doctorate awarded. *Degree requirements:* For master's, thesis or alternative; for doctorate, thesis/dissertation. *Entrance requirements:* For master's, GRE General Test, bachelor's degree in engineering, mathematics, or physical science; for doctorate, GRE General Test, master's degree in engineering or industrial manufacturing. Additional exam requirements/recommendations for international students: Required—TOEFL. *Application deadline:* For fall admission, 2/1 priority date for domestic and international students; for spring admission, 8/1 priority date for domestic and international students. Applications are processed on a rolling basis. Application fee: $40 ($55 for international students). Electronic applications accepted. *Financial support:* In 2009–10, 19 research assistantships (averaging $10,372 per year), 1 teaching assistantship with full tuition reimbursement (averaging $12,450 per year) were awarded; Federal Work-Study, institutionally sponsored loans, and scholarships/grants also available. Support available to part-time students. Financial award application deadline: 3/1; financial award applicants required to submit FAFSA. *Faculty research:* Ergonomics, healthcare systems engineering, manufacturing processes, operations research, engineering management. Total annual research expenditures: $484,594. *Unit head:* Bradley Kramer, Head, 785-532-5606, Fax: 785-532-7810, E-mail: bradleyk@ksu.edu. *Application contact:* E. Stanley Lee, Director, 785-532-3730, Fax: 785-532-7810, E-mail: eslee@ksu.edu.

Kettering University, Graduate School, Department of Business, Flint, MI 48504. Offers business administration (MBA); engineering management (MSEM); information technology (MSIT); manufacturing management (MSMM); manufacturing operations (MSMO); operations management (MSOM). *Accreditation:* ACBSP. Part-time and evening/weekend programs available. Postbaccalaureate distance learning degree programs offered (no on-campus study). *Faculty:* 9 full-time (3 women), 4 part-time/adjunct (0 women). *Students:* 12 full-time (5 women), 251 part-time (79 women); includes 42 minority (27 African Americans, 1 American Indian/Alaska Native, 9 Asian Americans or Pacific Islanders, 5 Hispanic Americans), 15 international. Average age 32. 74 applicants, 78% accepted, 31 enrolled. In 2009, 123 master's awarded. *Entrance requirements:* Additional exam requirements/recommendations for international students: Required—TOEFL (minimum score 550 paper-based; 213 computer-based; 79 iBT). *Application deadline:* For fall admission, 9/15 for domestic students, 6/15 for international students; for winter admission, 12/15 for domestic students, 9/15 for international students; for spring admission, 3/15 for domestic students, 12/15 for international students. Applications are processed on a rolling basis. Electronic applications accepted. *Expenses:* Tuition: Full-time $11,120; part-time $695 per credit hour. *Financial support:* In 2009–10, 101 students received support, including fellowships with full tuition reimbursements available (averaging $13,000 per year), research assistantships with full tuition reimbursements available (averaging $13,000 per year), teaching assistantships with full tuition reimbursements available (averaging $13,000 per year); Federal Work-Study, scholarships/grants, and tuition waivers (partial) also available. Support available to part-time students. Financial award application deadline: 7/15. *Unit head:* Dr. Tony Hain, Vice President of Graduate Studies and Corporate Connections, 810-762-9616, Fax: 810-762-9935, E-mail: thain@kettering.edu. *Application contact:* Bonnie Switzer, Admissions Representative, 810-762-7953, Fax: 810-762-9935, E-mail: bswitzer@kettering.edu.

Lamar University, College of Graduate Studies, College of Engineering, Department of Industrial Engineering, Beaumont, TX 77710. Offers engineering management (MEM); industrial engineering (ME, MES, DE). *Faculty:* 7 full-time (0 women). *Students:* 34 full-time (4 women), 8 part-time (1 woman); includes 6 minority (2 African Americans, 3 Asian Americans or Pacific Islanders, 1 Hispanic American), 25 international. Average age 26. 89 applicants, 39% accepted, 9 enrolled. In 2009, 16 master's awarded. *Degree requirements:* For doctorate, thesis/dissertation. *Entrance requirements:* For master's and doctorate, GRE General Test. Additional exam requirements/recommendations for international students: Required—TOEFL. *Application deadline:* For fall admission, 5/15 priority date for domestic students; for spring admission, 10/1 priority date for domestic students. Applications are processed on a rolling basis. Application fee: $25 ($50 for international students). *Financial support:* In 2009–10, 2 fellowships (averaging $6,000 per year), 4 research assistantships (averaging $1,000 per year), 2 teaching assistantships (averaging $4,500 per year) were awarded. Financial award application deadline: 4/1. *Faculty research:* Process simulation, total quality management, ergonomics and safety, scheduling. *Unit head:* Dr. Victor Zaloom, Chair, 409-880-8804, Fax: 409-880-8121. *Application contact:* Dr. Hsing-Wei Chu, Professor, 409-880-8804, Fax: 409-880-8121.

Lawrence Technological University, College of Engineering, Southfield, MI 48075-1058. Offers automotive engineering (MAE); civil engineering (MCE); construction engineering management (MS); electrical and computer engineering (MS); engineering management (ME); industrial engineering (MSIE); manufacturing systems (MEMS, DE); mechanical engineering (MS); mechatronic systems engineering (MS). Part-time and evening/weekend programs available. *Faculty:* 20 full-time (4 women), 12 part-time/adjunct (0 women). *Students:* 15 full-time (4 women), 389 part-time (50 women); includes 57 minority (22 African Americans, 1 American Indian/Alaska Native, 30 Asian Americans or Pacific Islanders, 4 Hispanic Americans), 137 international. Average age 31. 361 applicants, 52% accepted, 108 enrolled. In 2009, 161 master's, 1 doctorate awarded. *Degree requirements:* For master's, thesis (for some programs). *Entrance requirements:* Additional exam requirements/recommendations for international students: Required—TOEFL (minimum score 550 paper-based; 213 computer-based; 79 iBT). *Application deadline:* For fall admission, 8/1 priority date for domestic students, 6/1 for international students; for winter admission, 12/1 priority date for domestic students, 10/1 for international students; for spring admission, 5/1 priority date for domestic students, 3/1 for international students. Applications are processed on a rolling basis. Application fee: $50. Electronic applications accepted. *Expenses:* Tuition: Full-time $11,320; part-time $798 per credit hour. *Financial support:* Federal Work-Study and institutionally sponsored loans available. Support available to part-time students. Financial award application deadline: 4/1; financial award applicants required to submit FAFSA. *Faculty research:* Advanced composite materials in bridges, strengthening existing bridges with carbon and glass fiber sheets, development of drive shafts using composite materials. *Unit head:* Dr. Nabil Grace, Interim Dean, 248-204-2500, Fax: 248-204-2509, E-mail: engrdean@ltu.edu. *Application contact:* Jane Rohrback, Director of Admissions, 248-204-3160, Fax: 248-204-3188, E-mail: admissions@ltu.edu.

Long Island University, C.W. Post Campus, College of Information and Computer Science, Department of Computer Science/Management Engineering, Brookville, NY 11548-1300. Offers information systems (MS); information technology education (MS); management engineering (MS). Part-time and evening/weekend programs available. *Degree requirements:* For master's, comprehensive exam, thesis or alternative. *Entrance requirements:* For master's, bachelor's degree in science, mathematics, or engineering; minimum GPA of 2.5. Additional exam requirements/recommendations for international students: Required—TOEFL (minimum score 500 paper-based; 173 computer-based). Electronic applications accepted. *Faculty research:* Inductive music learning, re-engineering business process, technology and ethics.

Loyola Marymount University, College of Science and Engineering, Department of Systems Engineering and Engineering Management, Program in System Engineering Leadership, Los Anegles, CA 90045-2659. Offers MS, MS/MBA. *Faculty:* 1 full-time (0 women), 5 part-time/adjunct (1 woman). *Students:* 12 full-time (6 women), 4 part-time (1 woman); includes 7 minority (3 Asian Americans or Pacific Islanders, 4 Hispanic Americans). Average age 29. 6 applicants, 67% accepted, 3 enrolled. In 2009, 5 master's awarded. *Degree requirements:* For master's, thesis. *Entrance requirements:* For master's, GMAT, letters of recommendation. Additional exam requirements/recommendations for international students: Required—TOEFL (minimum score 550 paper-based; 213 computer-based; 80 iBT). *Application deadline:* For fall admission, 7/15 for domestic students; for spring admission, 12/15 for domestic students. Applications are processed on a rolling basis. Application fee: $50. Electronic applications accepted. *Financial support:* In 2009–10, 2 students received support. Scholarships/grants and unspecified assistantships available. Support available to part-time students. Financial award application deadline: 6/1; financial award applicants required to submit FAFSA. *Unit head:* Dr. Bohdan W. Oppenheim, Program Director, 310-338-2825, Fax: 310-338-6028, E-mail: boppenheim@lmu.edu. *Application contact:* Chake Kouyoumjian, Associate Dean for Graduate Studies, 310-338-2721, Fax: 310-338-6086, E-mail: chake.kouyoumjian@lmu.edu.

Marquette University, Graduate School, College of Engineering, Department of Mechanical and Industrial Engineering, Milwaukee, WI 53201-1881. Offers engineering management (MS); mechanical engineering (MS, PhD), including manufacturing systems engineering. Part-time and evening/weekend programs available. *Faculty:* 16 full-time (0 women), 3 part-time/adjunct (0 women). *Students:* 26 full-time (4 women), 49 part-time (7 women); includes 3 minority (2 African Americans, 1 Asian American or Pacific Islander), 11 international. Average age 28. 60 applicants, 73% accepted, 16 enrolled. In 2009, 21 master's, 1 doctorate awarded. Terminal master's awarded for partial completion of doctoral program. *Degree requirements:* For master's, thesis; for doctorate, comprehensive exam, thesis/dissertation, qualifying exam. *Entrance requirements:* For master's and doctorate, GRE General Test, minimum GPA of 3.0. Additional exam requirements/recommendations for international students: Required—TOEFL. *Application deadline:* For fall admission, 8/1 priority date for domestic students; for spring admission, 1/1 priority date for domestic students. Applications are processed on a rolling basis. Application fee: $40. Electronic applications accepted. *Financial support:* In 2009–10, 19 students received support, including 5 fellowships with tuition reimbursements available (averaging $11,600 per year), 6 research assistantships with tuition reimbursements available (averaging $11,490 per year), 8 teaching assistantships with tuition reimbursements available (averaging $11,490 per year); Federal Work-Study, institutionally sponsored loans, scholarships/grants, and tuition waivers (full and partial) also available. Support available to part-time students. Financial award application deadline: 2/15. *Faculty research:* Computer-integrated manufacturing, energy conversion, simulation modeling and optimization, applied mechanics, metallurgy. *Unit head:* Dr. Kyle Kim, Chair, 414-288-7259, Fax: 414-288-7790, E-mail: kyle.kim@marquette.edu. *Application contact:* Dr. Nicholas J. Nigro, Director of Graduate Studies, 414-288-3518, Fax: 414-288-7790, E-mail: nicholas.nigro@marquette.edu.

Marshall University, Academic Affairs Division, College of Information Technology and Engineering, Weisberg Division of Engineering and Computer Science, Huntington, WV 25755. Offers engineering (MSE); information systems (MS). Part-time and evening/weekend programs available. *Faculty:* 6 full-time (0 women). *Students:* 20 full-time (6 women), 31 part-time (6 women); includes 3 minority (2 African Americans, 1 Asian American or Pacific Islander), 15 international. Average age 30. In 2009, 15 master's awarded. *Degree requirements:* For master's, final project, oral exam. *Entrance requirements:* For master's, GMAT or GRE General Test, minimum undergraduate GPA of 2.75. Application fee: $40. *Financial support:* Tuition waivers (full) available. Support available to part-time students. Financial award application deadline: 8/1; financial award applicants required to submit FAFSA. *Unit head:* Dr. Bill Pierson, Chair, 304-696-2695, E-mail: pierson@marshall.edu. *Application contact:* Information Contact, 304-746-1900, Fax: 304-746-1902, E-mail: services@marshall.edu.

Massachusetts Institute of Technology, School of Engineering, Engineering Systems Division, Cambridge, MA 02139-4307. Offers engineering and management (SM); engineering systems (SM, PhD); logistics (M Eng); technology and policy (SM); technology, management and policy (PhD); SM/MBA. *Faculty:* 8 full-time (0 women). *Students:* 285 full-time (72 women), 1 part-time (0 women); includes 36 minority (8 African Americans, 19 Asian Americans or Pacific Islanders, 9 Hispanic Americans), 116 international. Average age 31. 874 applicants, 28% accepted, 188 enrolled. In 2009, 143 master's, 11 doctorates awarded. *Degree requirements:* For master's, thesis; for doctorate, comprehensive exam, thesis/dissertation. *Entrance requirements:* For master's and doctorate, GRE General Test or GMAT (for some programs). Additional exam requirements/recommendations for international students: Required—IELTS (minimum score 7.5); Recommended—TOEFL (minimum score 610 paper-based; 255 computer-based; 103 iBT). Application fee: $75. *Expenses:* Contact institution. *Financial support:* In 2009–10, 224 students received support, including 41 fellowships with tuition reimbursements available (averaging $26,522 per year), 95 research assistantships with tuition reimbursements available (averaging $26,506 per year), 17 teaching assistantships with tuition reimbursements available (averaging $21,300 per year); career-related internships or fieldwork, Federal Work-Study, institutionally sponsored loans, scholarships/grants, health care benefits, and unspecified assistantships also available. *Faculty research:* Critical infrastructures, extended enterprises, energy and sustainability, health care delivery, humans and technology, uncertainty and dynamics, design and implementation, networks and flows, policy and standards. Total annual research expenditures: $10.7 million. *Unit head:* Prof. Yossi Sheffi, Director, 617-253-1764, E-mail: esdinquiries@mit.edu. *Application contact:* Graduate Admissions, 617-253-1182, E-mail: esdgrad@mit.edu.

McNeese State University, Doré School of Graduate Studies, College of Engineering and Engineering Technology, Lake Charles, LA 70609. Offers chemical engineering (M Eng); civil engineering (M Eng); electrical engineering (M Eng); engineering management (M Eng); mechanical engineering (M Eng). Part-time and evening/weekend programs available. *Degree requirements:* For master's, thesis or alternative. *Entrance requirements:* For master's, GRE, minimum undergraduate GPA of 3.0. Additional exam requirements/recommendations for international students: Required—TOEFL.

Mercer University, Graduate Studies, Macon Campus, School of Engineering, Macon, GA 31207-0003. Offers biomedical engineering (MSE); computer engineering (MSE); electrical engineering (MSE); engineering management (MSE); environmental engineering (MSE); environmental systems (MS); mechanical engineering (MSE); software engineering (MSE); software systems (MS); technical communications management (MS); technical management (MS). Part-time and evening/weekend programs available. Postbaccalaureate distance learning degree programs offered (no on-campus study). *Faculty:* 19 full-time (4 women), 1 part-time/adjunct (0 women). *Students:* 6 full-time (1 woman), 95 part-time (22 women); includes 22 minority (5 African Americans, 13 Asian Americans or Pacific Islanders, 4 Hispanic Americans), 3 international. Average age 33. In 2009, 42 master's awarded. *Degree requirements:* For master's, thesis or alternative. *Entrance requirements:* For master's, minimum undergraduate GPA of 3.0. Additional exam requirements/recommendations for international students: Required—TOEFL. *Application deadline:* For fall admission, 7/1 for domestic students; for spring admission, 11/15 for domestic students. Applications are processed on a rolling basis. Application fee: $35 ($50 for international students). Electronic applications accepted. *Expenses:* Contact institution. *Financial support:* Federal Work-Study available. *Unit head:* Dr. Wade H. Shaw, Dean, 478-301-2459, Fax: 478-301-5593, E-mail: shaw_wh@mercer.edu. *Application contact:* Greg Lofton, Graduate Program Coordinator, 478-301-5480, Fax: 478-301-5434, E-mail: lofton_g@mercer.edu.

Milwaukee School of Engineering, Rader School of Business, Program in Engineering Management, Milwaukee, WI 53202-3109. Offers MS. Part-time and evening/weekend programs available. *Faculty:* 3 full-time (1 woman), 8 part-time/adjunct (1 woman). *Students:* 2 full-time (0 women), 88 part-time (18 women); includes 7 minority (1 African American, 1 American Indian/Alaska Native, 4 Asian Americans or Pacific Islanders, 1 Hispanic American). Average age 26. 36 applicants, 69% accepted, 13 enrolled. In 2009, 24 master's awarded. *Degree requirements:* For master's, thesis or alternative, thesis defense or capstone project. *Entrance requirements:* For master's, GRE General Test or GMAT, BS in engineering, science, management or related field. Additional exam requirements/recommendations for international students: Required—TOEFL (minimum score 79 iBT). *Application deadline:* Applications are processed on a rolling basis. Application fee: $30. Electronic applications accepted. *Expenses:* Tuition: Part-time $603 per credit. *Financial support:* In 2009–10, 19 students received support, including 2 research assistantships (averaging $15,000 per year). Financial award applicants required to submit FAFSA. *Faculty research:* Operations, project management, quality marketing. *Unit head:* Dr. Bruce Thompson, Director, 414-277-7378, Fax: 414-277-7279, E-mail: thomson@msoe.com. *Application contact:* David E. Tietyen, Graduate Admissions Director, 800-332-6763, Fax: 414-277-7475, E-mail: wp@msoe.edu.

Missouri University of Science and Technology, Graduate School, Department of Engineering Management and Systems Engineering, Rolla, MO 65409. Offers engineering management (MS, DE, PhD); manufacturing engineering (M Eng, MS); systems engineering (MS, PhD). *Degree requirements:* For master's, thesis optional; for doctorate, comprehensive exam. *Entrance requirements:* For master's, GRE (minimum score 1150 verbal and quantitative, 4.5 writing); for doctorate, GRE (minimum score 1100 verbal and quantitative, 3.5 writing). Additional exam requirements/recommendations for international students: Required—TOEFL (minimum score 580 paper-based; 213 computer-based). *Faculty research:* Management of technology, industrial engineering, manufacturing engineering, packaging engineering, quality engineering.

National University, Academic Affairs, School of Engineering and Technology, Department of Applied Engineering, La Jolla, CA 92037-1011. Offers database administration (MS); engineering management (MS); environmental engineering (MS); homeland security and safety engineering (MS); system engineering (MS); wireless communications (MS). Part-time and evening/weekend programs available. Postbaccalaureate distance learning degree programs offered (no on-campus study). *Faculty:* 6 full-time (1 woman), 7 part-time/adjunct (1 woman). *Students:* 61 full-time (16 women), 176 part-time (35 women); includes 54 minority (11 African Americans, 1 American Indian/Alaska Native, 23 Asian Americans or Pacific Islanders, 19 Hispanic Americans), 117 international. Average age 31. 133 applicants, 100% accepted, 83 enrolled. In 2009, 34 master's awarded. *Degree requirements:* For master's, thesis. *Entrance requirements:* For master's, interview, minimum GPA of 2.5. Additional exam requirements/recommendations for international students: Required—TOEFL (minimum score 550 paper-based; 213 computer-based; 79 iBT), IELTS (minimum score 6). *Application deadline:* Applications are processed on a rolling basis. Application fee: $60 ($65 for international students). Electronic applications accepted. *Expenses:* Tuition: Part-time $338 per quarter hour. *Financial support:* Career-related internships or fieldwork, institutionally sponsored loans, scholarships/grants, and tuition waivers (partial) available. Support available to part-time students. Financial award application deadline: 6/30; financial award applicants required to submit FAFSA. *Unit head:* Dr. Shekar Viswanathan, Chair and Associate Professor, 858-309-8416, Fax: 858-309-3420, E-mail: sviswana@nu.edu. *Application contact:* Dominick Giovanniello, Associate Regional Dean—San Diego, 800-NAT-UNIV, Fax: 858-541-7792, E-mail: dgiovann@nu.edu.

New Jersey Institute of Technology, Office of Graduate Studies, Newark College of Engineering, Department of Industrial and Manufacturing Engineering, Program in Engineering Management, Newark, NJ 07102. Offers MS. Part-time and evening/weekend programs available. *Degree requirements:* For master's, thesis or alternative. *Entrance requirements:* For master's, GRE General Test. Additional exam requirements/recommendations for international students: Required—TOEFL (minimum score 550 paper-based; 213 computer-based; 79 iBT). Electronic applications accepted.

New Mexico Institute of Mining and Technology, Graduate Studies, Program in Engineering Management, Socorro, NM 87801. Offers MEM. Part-time programs available.

Northeastern University, College of Engineering, Department of Mechanical, Industrial, and Manufacturing Engineering, Boston, MA 02115-5096. Offers engineering management (MS); industrial engineering (MS, PhD); mechanical engineering (MS, PhD); operations research (MS). Part-time programs available. *Faculty:* 34 full-time (2 women), 7 part-time/adjunct (0 women). *Students:* 270 full-time (56 women), 137 part-time (27 women); includes 4 African Americans, 9 Asian Americans or Pacific Islanders, 3 Hispanic Americans, 182 international. 573 applicants, 75% accepted, 142 enrolled. In 2009, 94 master's, 9 doctorates awarded.

Degree requirements: For master's, thesis (for some programs); for doctorate, thesis/dissertation, departmental qualifying exam. *Entrance requirements:* For master's and doctorate, GRE General Test. Additional exam requirements/recommendations for international students: Required—TOEFL (minimum score 550 paper-based; 213 computer-based; 80 iBT). *Application deadline:* For fall admission, 1/15 priority date for domestic and international students; for spring admission, 11/1 priority date for domestic students. Applications are processed on a rolling basis. Application fee: $50. Electronic applications accepted. *Financial support:* In 2009–10, 79 students received support, including 42 research assistantships with full tuition reimbursements available (averaging $18,320 per year), 37 teaching assistantships with full tuition reimbursements available; fellowships with full tuition reimbursements available, career-related internships or fieldwork, Federal Work-Study, scholarships/grants, health care benefits, and unspecified assistantships also available. Support available to part-time students. Financial award application deadline: 1/15; financial award applicants required to submit FAFSA. *Faculty research:* Dry sliding instabilities, droplet deposition, combustion, manufacturing systems, nano-manufacturing, advanced materials processing, bio-nano robotics, burning speed measurement, virtual environments. *Unit head:* Dr. Hameed Metghalchi, Chairman, 617-373-2973, Fax: 617-373-2921. *Application contact:* Stephen L. Gibson, Associate Director, 617-373-2711, Fax: 617-373-2501, E-mail: grad-eng@coe.neu.edu.

Northwestern University, McCormick School of Engineering and Applied Science, Department of Industrial Engineering and Management Sciences, Program in Engineering Management, Evanston, IL 60208. Offers MEM. Part-time and evening/weekend programs available. *Entrance requirements:* For master's, 3 years of work experience. Additional exam requirements/recommendations for international students: Required—TOEFL (minimum score 600 paper-based; 250 computer-based). Electronic applications accepted. *Faculty research:* Computer simulation, stochastic processes, network flow theory, logistics, statistics, production system design.

Oakland University, Graduate Study and Lifelong Learning, School of Engineering and Computer Science, Department of Industrial and Systems Engineering, Program in Engineering Management, Rochester, MI 48309-4401. Offers MS. *Entrance requirements:* Additional exam requirements/recommendations for international students: Required—TOEFL (minimum score 550 paper-based; 213 computer-based). Electronic applications accepted. *Expenses:* Contact institution.

Old Dominion University, Frank Batten College of Engineering and Technology, Program in Engineering Management, Norfolk, VA 23529. Offers MEM, MS, PhD. Part-time and evening/weekend programs available. Postbaccalaureate distance learning degree programs offered (no on-campus study). *Faculty:* 15 full-time (2 women), 3 part-time/adjunct (0 women). *Students:* 48 full-time (12 women), 249 part-time (33 women); includes 36 minority (16 African Americans, 1 American Indian/Alaska Native, 9 Asian Americans or Pacific Islanders, 10 Hispanic Americans), 46 international. Average age 33. 146 applicants, 86% accepted, 71 enrolled. In 2009, 134 master's, 2 doctorates awarded. *Degree requirements:* For master's, comprehensive exam, thesis optional, project; for doctorate, thesis/dissertation, candidacy exam. *Entrance requirements:* For master's, GRE, minimum GPA of 3.0; for doctorate, GRE, resume, letters of recommendation, minimum GPA of 3.0. Additional exam requirements/recommendations for international students: Required—TOEFL (minimum score 550 paper-based; 213 computer-based; 79 iBT). *Application deadline:* For fall admission, 6/1 priority date for domestic students, 4/15 for international students; for spring admission, 11/1 priority date for domestic students, 2/1 for international students. Applications are processed on a rolling basis. Application fee: $40. Electronic applications accepted. *Expenses:* Tuition, state resident: full-time $8112; part-time $338 per credit. Tuition, nonresident: full-time $20,256; part-time $844 per credit. Required fees: $119 per semester. One-time fee: $50. *Financial support:* In 2009–10, research assistantships with full and partial tuition reimbursements (averaging $20,000 per year), teaching assistantships with full and partial tuition reimbursements (averaging $20,000 per year) were awarded; fellowships, career-related internships or fieldwork, scholarships/grants, and tuition waivers (partial) also available. Support available to part-time students. Financial award application deadline: 2/15; financial award applicants required to submit FAFSA. *Faculty research:* Project management, systems engineering, modeling and simulation, virtual collaborative environments, multidisciplinary designs. Total annual research expenditures: $3.2 million. *Unit head:* Dr. Resit Unal, Chair, 757-683-4558, Fax: 757-683-5640, E-mail: runal@odu.edu. *Application contact:* Dr. Ghaith Rabadi, Graduate Program Director, 757-683-4558, Fax: 757-683-5640, E-mail: enmagpd@odu.edu.

Old Dominion University, Frank Batten College of Engineering and Technology, Program in Engineering Management and Systems Engineering, Norfolk, VA 23529. Offers D Eng. Part-time and evening/weekend programs available. Postbaccalaureate distance learning degree programs offered (no on-campus study). *Faculty:* 15 full-time (2 women), 3 part-time/adjunct (0 women). *Students:* 1 full-time (0 women), 8 part-time (2 women); includes 1 minority (African American). Average age 45. *Degree requirements:* For doctorate, thesis/dissertation, candidacy exam. *Entrance requirements:* For doctorate, GRE, resume, letters of recommendation, minimum GPA of 3.0, interview. Additional exam requirements/recommendations for international students: Required—TOEFL (minimum score 550 paper-based; 213 computer-based; 79 iBT). *Application deadline:* For fall admission, 6/1 priority date for domestic students, 4/15 for international students; for spring admission, 11/1 priority date for domestic students, 2/1 for international students. Applications are processed on a rolling basis. Application fee: $40. Electronic applications accepted. *Expenses:* Tuition, state resident: full-time $8112; part-time $338 per credit. Tuition, nonresident: full-time $20,256; part-time $844 per credit. Required fees: $119 per semester. One-time fee: $50. *Financial support:* In 2009–10, research assistantships with full and partial tuition reimbursements (averaging $20,000 per year), teaching assistantships with full and partial tuition reimbursements (averaging $20,000 per year) were awarded; fellowships, career-related internships or fieldwork and tuition waivers also available. Support available to part-time students. Financial award application deadline: 2/15; financial award applicants required to submit FAFSA. *Faculty research:* Project management, systems engineering, modeling and simulation, virtual collaboration environments, multidisciplinary designs. Total annual research expenditures: $3.2 million. *Unit head:* Dr. Resit Unal, Department Chair, 757-683-4558, Fax: 757-683-5640, E-mail: enmagpd@odu.edu. *Application contact:* Dr. Ghaith Rabadi, Graduate Program Director, 757-683-4558, Fax: 757-683-5640, E-mail: enmagpd@odu.edu.

Point Park University, School of Arts and Sciences, Department of Natural Science and Engineering Technology, Pittsburgh, PA 15222-1984. Offers engineering management (MS). Part-time and evening/weekend programs available. *Degree requirements:* For master's, comprehensive exam (for some programs), thesis or alternative. *Entrance requirements:* For master's, minimum QPA of 2.75, 2 letters of recommendation, minimum B average in engineering technology or a related field. Additional exam requirements/recommendations for international students: Required—TOEFL. Electronic applications accepted. *Expenses:* Tuition: Full-time $11,880; part-time $660 per credit. Required fees: $486; $27 per credit.

Polytechnic University of Puerto Rico, Graduate School, Hato Rey, PR 00919. Offers business administration (MBA), including general studies, management of information systems, management of international enterprises; civil engineering (ME, MS); computer engineering (ME, MS); computer science (MS); electrical engineering (ME, MS); engineering management (MEM); environmental management (MEPM); landscape architecture (M Land Arch); manufacturing competitiveness (MMC, MS); manufacturing engineering (ME, MS). Part-time and evening/weekend programs available. *Entrance requirements:* For master's, 3 letters of recommendation.

Polytechnic University of the Americas–Miami Campus, Graduate School, Miami, FL 33166. Offers business administration (MBA); engineering management (MEM). Part-time and evening/weekend programs available. Postbaccalaureate distance learning degree programs offered (no on-campus study). *Entrance requirements:* For master's, minimum GPA of 3.0. Electronic applications accepted.

Engineering Management

Polytechnic University of the Americas–Orlando Campus, Graduate School, Winter Park, FL 32792. Offers business administration (MBA); civil engineering (MS); computer engineering (MS); electrical engineering (MS); engineering management (MEM). Part-time and evening/weekend programs available. Postbaccalaureate distance learning degree programs offered (no on-campus study). *Entrance requirements:* For master's, minimum GPA of 3.0. Electronic applications accepted.

Portland State University, Graduate Studies, Maseeh College of Engineering and Computer Science, Department of Civil and Environmental Engineering, Portland, OR 97207-0751. Offers civil and environmental engineering (M Eng, MS, PhD); civil and environmental engineering management (M Eng); environmental sciences and resources (PhD); systems science (PhD). Part-time and evening/weekend programs available. *Degree requirements:* For master's, thesis or alternative, oral exam; for doctorate, one foreign language, thesis/dissertation, oral and written exams. *Entrance requirements:* For master's, minimum GPA of 3.0 in upper-division course work, BS in civil engineering or allied field; for doctorate, GRE General Test, GRE Subject Test, minimum GPA of 3.0 in upper-division course work, master's in civil and environmental engineering, 2 years full-time graduate work beyond master's degree. Additional exam requirements/recommendations for international students: Required—TOEFL (minimum score 550 paper-based; 213 computer-based). *Faculty research:* Structures, water resources, geotechnical engineering, environmental engineering, transportation.

Portland State University, Graduate Studies, Maseeh College of Engineering and Computer Science, Department of Engineering and Technology Management, Portland, OR 97207-0751. Offers engineering and technology management (M Eng); engineering management (MS); manufacturing engineering (ME); manufacturing management (M Eng); systems science/engineering management (PhD); MS/MBA; MS/MS. Part-time and evening/weekend programs available. *Degree requirements:* For master's, thesis optional; for doctorate, one foreign language, thesis/dissertation, oral and written exams. *Entrance requirements:* For master's, minimum GPA of 3.0 in upper-division course work, BS degree in civil engineering; for doctorate, GRE General Test, GRE Subject Test, minimum GPA of 3.0 in upper-division course work. Additional exam requirements/recommendations for international students: Required—TOEFL (minimum score 550 paper-based; 213 computer-based). *Faculty research:* Scheduling, hierarchical decision modeling, operations research, knowledge-based information systems.

Portland State University, Graduate Studies, Systems Science Program, Portland, OR 97207-0751. Offers computational intelligence (Certificate); computer modeling and simulation (Certificate); systems science (MS); systems science/anthropology (PhD); systems science/business administration (PhD); systems science/civil engineering (PhD); systems science/economics (PhD); systems science/engineering management (PhD); systems science/general (PhD); systems science/mathematical sciences (PhD); systems science/mechanical engineering (PhD); systems science/psychology (PhD); systems science/sociology (PhD). *Degree requirements:* For doctorate, variable foreign language requirement, thesis/dissertation. *Entrance requirements:* For master's, 2 letters of recommendation; for doctorate, GMAT, GRE General Test, minimum undergraduate GPA of 3.0. Additional exam requirements/recommendations for international students: Required—TOEFL. *Faculty research:* Systems theory and methodology, artificial intelligence neural networks, information theory, nonlinear dynamics/chaos, modeling and simulation.

Rensselaer Polytechnic Institute, Graduate School, Lally School of Management and Technology, Troy, NY 12180-3590. Offers business (MBA); financial engineering and risk analysis (MS); management (MS, PhD); technology, commercialization, and entrepreneurship (MS). *Accreditation:* AACSB. Part-time and evening/weekend programs available. *Faculty:* 47 full-time (11 women), 18 part-time/adjunct (1 woman). *Students:* 145 full-time (46 women), 492 part-time (202 women); includes 152 minority (45 African Americans, 1 American Indian/Alaska Native, 79 Asian Americans or Pacific Islanders, 27 Hispanic Americans), 62 international. Average age 28. 437 applicants, 71% accepted, 196 enrolled. In 2009, 231 master's, 6 doctorates awarded. *Degree requirements:* For doctorate, thesis/dissertation. *Entrance requirements:* For master's, GMAT, 2 letters of recommendation, resume; for doctorate, GMAT or GRE General Test, 2 letters of recommendation. Additional exam requirements/recommendations for international students: Required—TOEFL (minimum score 600 paper-based; 250 computer-based; 100 iBT); Recommended—IELTS (minimum score 7). *Application deadline:* For fall admission, 3/15 priority date for domestic and international students. Applications are processed on a rolling basis. Application fee: $75. Electronic applications accepted. *Expenses:* Tuition: Full-time $38,100. *Financial support:* Fellowships with partial tuition reimbursements, career-related internships or fieldwork, institutionally sponsored loans, and scholarships/grants available. Financial award application deadline: 3/15; financial award applicants required to submit FAFSA. *Faculty research:* Technological entrepreneurship, operations management, new product development and marketing, finance and financial engineering and risk analytics, information systems. *Unit head:* Dr. Iftekhar Hasan, Acting Dean and Cary L. Wellington Professor, 518-276-6586, Fax: 518-276-2665, E-mail: lallymba@rpi.edu. *Application contact:* Michele M. Martens, Manager of Graduate Programs, 518-276-6586, Fax: 518-276-2665, E-mail: lallymba@rpi.edu.

Robert Morris University, Graduate Studies, School of Engineering, Mathematics and Science, Moon Township, PA 15108-1189. Offers engineering management (MS). Part-time and evening/weekend programs available. *Faculty:* 3 full-time (0 women). *Students:* 36 part-time (3 women); includes 2 minority (1 African American, 1 American Indian/Alaska Native), 9 international. Average age 33. 11 applicants, 73% accepted, 7 enrolled. In 2009, 9 master's awarded. *Entrance requirements:* For master's, letters of recommendation. Additional exam requirements/recommendations for international students: Required—TOEFL (minimum score 550 paper-based; 213 computer-based; 79 iBT). *Application deadline:* For fall admission, 7/1 priority date for domestic and international students; for spring admission, 11/1 priority date for domestic and international students. Applications are processed on a rolling basis. Application fee: $35. Electronic applications accepted. *Expenses:* Contact institution. *Financial support:* Federal Work-Study, institutionally sponsored loans, and unspecified assistantships available. Financial award application deadline: 5/1; financial award applicants required to submit FAFSA. *Unit head:* Dr. Joe Iannelli, Department Head, Engineering, 412-397-2514, Fax: 412-397-2593, E-mail: iannelli@rmu.edu. *Application contact:* Deborah Roach, Assistant Dean, Graduate Admissions, 412-397-5200, Fax: 412-397-2425, E-mail: graduateadmissions@rmu.edu.

Rochester Institute of Technology, Graduate Enrollment Services, Kate Gleason College of Engineering, Department of Design, Development and Manufacturing, Program in Product Development, Rochester, NY 14623-5603. Offers MS. Part-time and evening/weekend programs available. *Students:* 37 part-time (3 women); includes 1 Hispanic American, 1 international. Average age 38. 2 applicants, 50% accepted, 1 enrolled. In 2009, 14 master's awarded. *Entrance requirements:* For master's, undergraduate degree in engineering or related field, minimum GPA of 3.0, 5 years experience in product development. Additional exam requirements/recommendations for international students: Required—TOEFL (minimum score 570 paper-based; 230 computer-based; 88 iBT), or IELTS (minimum score 6.5). *Application deadline:* For fall admission, 2/15 priority date for domestic and international students. Application fee: $50. *Expenses:* Contact institution. *Financial support:* Applicants required to submit FAFSA. *Unit head:* Mark Smith, Director, 585-475-7971, Fax: 585-475-7955, E-mail: mpdmail@rit.edu. *Application contact:* Diane Ellison, Assistant Vice President, Graduate Enrollment Services, 585-475-2229, Fax: 585-475-7164, E-mail: gradinfo@rit.edu.

Rochester Institute of Technology, Graduate Enrollment Services, Kate Gleason College of Engineering, Department of Industrial and Systems Engineering, Rochester, NY 14623-5603. Offers engineering management (ME); industrial engineering (ME, MS); manufacturing engineering (ME, MS); systems engineering (ME). Part-time programs available. *Students:* 62 full-time (17 women), 10 part-time (5 women); includes 5 minority (2 African Americans, 2 Asian Americans or Pacific Islanders, 1 Hispanic American), 55 international. Average age 25. 186 applicants, 50% accepted, 40 enrolled. In 2009, 53 master's awarded. *Degree requirements:* For master's, internship. *Entrance requirements:* For master's, GRE, minimum GPA of 3.0. Additional exam requirements/recommendations for international students: Required—TOEFL (minimum score 570 paper-based; 230 computer-based; 88 iBT), or IELTS (minimum score 6.5). *Application deadline:* For fall admission, 2/15 priority date for domestic and international students. Applications are processed on a rolling basis. Application fee: $50. *Expenses:* Tuition: Full-time $31,533; part-time $876 per credit hour. Required fees: $210. *Financial support:* In 2009–10, 63 students received support; research assistantships with partial tuition reimbursements available, teaching assistantships with partial tuition reimbursements available, career-related internships or fieldwork, institutionally sponsored loans, scholarships/grants, tuition waivers (partial), and unspecified assistantships available. Support available to part-time students. Financial award applicants required to submit FAFSA. *Faculty research:* Safety, manufacturing (CAM), simulation. *Unit head:* Dr. Jacqueline Mozrall, Department Head, 585-475-2598, E-mail: ise@rit.edu. *Application contact:* Diane Ellison, Assistant Vice President, Graduate Enrollment Services, 585-475-2229, Fax: 585-475-7164, E-mail: gradinfo@rit.edu.

Rose-Hulman Institute of Technology, Faculty of Engineering and Applied Sciences, Department of Engineering Management, Terre Haute, IN 47803-3999. Offers MS. Part-time and evening/weekend programs available. Postbaccalaureate distance learning degree programs offered (minimal on-campus study). *Faculty:* 5 full-time (0 women). *Students:* 25 full-time (3 women), 44 part-time (12 women); includes 5 minority (1 African American, 3 Asian Americans or Pacific Islanders, 1 Hispanic American), 18 international. Average age 29. 38 applicants, 95% accepted, 24 enrolled. In 2009, 24 master's awarded. *Degree requirements:* For master's, integrated project. *Entrance requirements:* For master's, GRE, minimum GPA of 3.0. Additional exam requirements/recommendations for international students: Required—TOEFL (minimum score 580 paper-based; 237 computer-based; 92 iBT). *Application deadline:* For fall admission, 2/1 priority date for domestic students. Applications are processed on a rolling basis. Application fee: $0. *Expenses:* Tuition: Full-time $33,900; part-time $987 per credit hour. *Financial support:* In 2009–10, 13 students received support; fellowships with full and partial tuition reimbursements available. *Faculty research:* Entrepreneurship, management of technology, manufacturing systems, project management, technology forecasting. *Unit head:* Dr. Richard Stamper, Interim Chairman, 812-877-8956, Fax: 812-877-8878, E-mail: rick.stamper@rose-hulman.edu. *Application contact:* Dr. Daniel J. Moore, Associate Dean of the Faculty, 812-877-8110, Fax: 812-877-8061, E-mail: daniel.j.moore@rose-hulman.edu.

Rowan University, Graduate School, College of Engineering, Program in Engineering Management, Glassboro, NJ 08028-1701. Offers MEM. Part-time and evening/weekend programs available. *Students:* 2 part-time (both women); includes 1 minority (African American). Average age 23. 1 applicant, 100% accepted, 1 enrolled. *Degree requirements:* For master's, thesis. *Entrance requirements:* For master's, GRE General Test. Additional exam requirements/recommendations for international students: Required—TOEFL. *Application deadline:* Applications are processed on a rolling basis. Application fee: $50. Electronic applications accepted. *Expenses:* Tuition, state resident: full-time $10,624; part-time $590 per semester hour. Tuition, nonresident: full-time $10,624; part-time $590 per semester hour. Required fees: $2320; $125 per semester hour. *Financial support:* Career-related internships or fieldwork, scholarships/grants, health care benefits, and unspecified assistantships available. *Unit head:* Dr. Mira Lalovic-Hand, Interim Associate Provost/Director of Graduate School, 856-256-5120, E-mail: lalovic-hand@rowan.edu. *Application contact:* Karen Haynes, Graduate Coordinator, 856-256-4052, E-mail: haynes@rowan.edu.

St. Cloud State University, School of Graduate Studies, College of Science and Engineering, Program in Engineering Management, St. Cloud, MN 56301-4498. Offers MEM. *Faculty:* 6 full-time (0 women). *Students:* 43 full-time (10 women), 59 part-time (12 women); includes 4 minority (all Asian Americans or Pacific Islanders), 85 international. 29 applicants, 97% accepted. *Degree requirements:* For master's, thesis or alternative. *Entrance requirements:* For master's, GRE General Test, minimum GPA of 2.75. Additional exam requirements/recommendations for international students: Required—Michigan English Language Assessment Battery; Recommended—TOEFL (minimum score 550 paper-based; 213 computer-based), IELTS (minimum score 6.5). *Application deadline:* For fall admission, 6/1 priority date for domestic students, 4/1 for international students; for spring admission, 10/1 priority date for domestic students, 8/1 for international students. Applications are processed on a rolling basis. Electronic applications accepted. *Financial support:* Federal Work-Study and unspecified assistantships available. *Unit head:* Dr. Ben Baliga, Coordinator, 320-308-3843, E-mail: baliga@stcloudstate.edu. *Application contact:* Linda Lou Krueger, School of Graduate Studies, 320-308-2113, Fax: 320-308-5371, E-mail: lekrueger@stcloudstate.edu.

Saint Martin's University, Graduate Programs, Program in Engineering Management, Lacey, WA 98503. Offers M Eng Mgt. Part-time and evening/weekend programs available. *Faculty:* 1 full-time (0 women), 1 part-time/adjunct (0 women). *Students:* 8 full-time (1 woman), 4 part-time (all women); includes 2 minority (both Asian Americans or Pacific Islanders), 3 international. Average age 27. 3 applicants, 67% accepted, 1 enrolled. In 2009, 4 master's awarded. *Degree requirements:* For master's, comprehensive exam (for some programs), thesis optional. *Entrance requirements:* For master's, minimum GPA of 2.8 or professional engineer license. Additional exam requirements/recommendations for international students: Required—TOEFL (minimum score 525 paper-based). *Application deadline:* For fall admission, 8/1 priority date for domestic and international students; for spring admission, 12/1 priority date for domestic and international students. Applications are processed on a rolling basis. Application fee: $35. *Expenses:* Tuition: Full-time $12,440; part-time $827 per credit hour. *Financial support:* In 2009–10, 3 students received support; fellowships, research assistantships, Federal Work-Study available. Support available to part-time students. Financial award application deadline: 3/1; financial award applicants required to submit FAFSA. *Faculty research:* Highway safety management, transportation, hydraulics, database structure. *Unit head:* Dr. Anthony de Sam Lazaro, Dean, Engineering, 360-438-4320, Fax: 560-438-4522, E-mail: lazaro@stmartin.edu. *Application contact:* Hopie Lopez, Administrative Assistant, 360-438-4320, Fax: 360-438-4548, E-mail: hlopez@stmartin.edu.

St. Mary's University, Graduate School, Department of Engineering, Program in Engineering Systems Management, San Antonio, TX 78228-8507. Offers MS. Part-time programs available. Postbaccalaureate distance learning degree programs offered (no on-campus study). *Degree requirements:* For master's, comprehensive exam. *Entrance requirements:* For master's, GRE or GMAT. Additional exam requirements/recommendations for international students: Required—TOEFL (minimum score 550 paper-based; 213 computer-based; 80 iBT). Electronic applications accepted. *Expenses:* Tuition: Full-time $8004. Required fees: $536. One-time fee: $5 full-time. Full-time tuition and fees vary according to program.

St. Mary's University, Graduate School, Department of Engineering, Program in Industrial Engineering, San Antonio, TX 78228-8507. Offers engineering computer applications (MS); engineering management (MS); industrial engineering (MS); operations research (MS); JD/MS. Part-time programs available. *Degree requirements:* For master's, comprehensive exam. *Entrance requirements:* For master's, GRE General Test, BS in science or engineering, minimum GPA of 3.0. Additional exam requirements/recommendations for international students: Required—TOEFL (minimum score 550 paper-based; 213 computer-based; 80 iBT). Electronic applications accepted. *Expenses:* Tuition: Full-time $8004. Required fees: $536. One-time fee: $5 full-time. Full-time tuition and fees vary according to program. *Faculty research:* Robotics, artificial intelligence, manufacturing engineering.

Santa Clara University, School of Engineering, Program in Engineering Management, Santa Clara, CA 95053. Offers MS. Part-time and evening/weekend programs available. *Students:* 88 full-time (30 women), 171 part-time (43 women); includes 89 minority (6 African Americans, 71 Asian Americans or Pacific Islanders, 12 Hispanic Americans), 104 international. Average age 29. In 2009, 47 master's awarded. *Degree requirements:* For master's, thesis (for some programs). *Entrance requirements:* For master's, GRE (waiver may be available). Additional exam requirements/recommendations for international students: Required—TOEFL (minimum score 550 paper-based; 213 computer-based; 79 iBT). *Application deadline:* For fall admission, 8/13 for domestic students, 7/16 for international students; for winter admission, 10/29 for domestic students, 9/24 for international students; for spring admission, 2/25 for domestic students, 1/21 for international students. Applications are processed on a rolling basis. Application fee: $60. *Expenses:* Contact institution. *Financial support:* Research assistantships, teaching assistantships available. Financial award application deadline: 3/2; financial award applicants required to submit FAFSA. *Unit head:* Dr. Alex Zecevic, Associate Dean for Graduate Studies, 408-554-2394, E-mail: azecevic@scu.edu. *Application contact:* Stacey Tinker, Director of Enrollment Management, 408-554-4748, Fax: 408-554-4323, E-mail: stinker@scu.edu.

Southern Methodist University, Bobby B. Lyle School of Engineering, Department of Engineering Management, Information, and Systems, Dallas, TX 75275. Offers applied science (MS); engineering management (MSEM, DE); information engineering and management (MSIEM); operations research (MS, PhD); systems engineering (MS, PhD). Part-time and evening/weekend programs available. Postbaccalaureate distance learning degree programs offered. *Faculty:* 10 full-time (3 women), 22 part-time/adjunct (2 women). *Students:* 54 full-time (24 women), 288 part-time (68 women); includes 96 minority (30 African Americans, 2 American Indian/Alaska Native, 35 Asian Americans or Pacific Islanders, 29 Hispanic Americans), 38 international. Average age 33. 125 applicants, 74% accepted, 60 enrolled. In 2009, 128 master's, 3 doctorates awarded. Terminal master's awarded for partial completion of doctoral program. *Degree requirements:* For master's, thesis optional; for doctorate, thesis/dissertation, oral and written qualifying exams. *Entrance requirements:* For master's, minimum GPA of 3.0 in last 2 years; bachelor's degree in engineering, mathematics, sciences, or technical area; for doctorate, GRE General Test (operations research, engineering management), bachelor's degree in related field. Additional exam requirements/recommendations for international students: Required—TOEFL. *Application deadline:* For fall admission, 7/1 for domestic students, 5/15 for international students; for spring admission, 11/15 for domestic students, 9/1 for international students. Applications are processed on a rolling basis. Application fee: $75. *Financial support:* In 2009–10, 8 students received support, including 3 research assistantships with full tuition reimbursements available (averaging $18,000 per year), 9 teaching assistantships with full tuition reimbursements available (averaging $18,000 per year); tuition waivers (full) also available. *Faculty research:* Telecommunications, decision systems, information engineering, operations research, software. Total annual research expenditures: $172,823. *Unit head:* Dr. Richard S. Barr, Chair, 214-768-1772, Fax: 214-768-1112, E-mail: emis@lyle.smu.edu. *Application contact:* Marc Valerin, Director of Graduate and Executive Admissions, 214-768-3042, E-mail: valerin@lyle.smu.edu.

Stanford University, School of Engineering, Department of Management Science and Engineering, Stanford, CA 94305-9991. Offers management science and engineering (MS, PhD). Terminal master's awarded for partial completion of doctoral program. *Degree requirements:* For doctorate, thesis/dissertation, qualification procedure. *Entrance requirements:* For master's and doctorate, GRE General Test. Additional exam requirements/recommendations for international students: Required—TOEFL. Electronic applications accepted. *Expenses:* Tuition: Full-time $37,380; part-time $2760 per quarter. Required fees: $501.

Stevens Institute of Technology, Graduate School, School of Systems and Enterprises, Program in Engineering Management, Hoboken, NJ 07030. Offers M Eng, PhD. *Expenses:* Tuition: Full-time $9900; part-time $1100 per credit. Required fees: $286 per semester.

Stevens Institute of Technology, Graduate School, Wesley J. Howe School of Technology Management, Program in Business Administration, Hoboken, NJ 07030. Offers engineering management (MBA); financial engineering (MBA); information management (MBA); information technology in financial services (MBA); information technology in the pharmaceutical industry (MBA); information technology outsourcing (MBA); pharmaceutical management (MBA); project management (MBA); technology management (MBA); telecommunications management (MBA). *Expenses:* Tuition: Full-time $9900; part-time $1100 per credit. Required fees: $286 per semester.

Syracuse University, L. C. Smith College of Engineering and Computer Science, Program in Engineering Management, Syracuse, NY 13244. Offers MS. Part-time and evening/weekend programs available. *Students:* 62 full-time (23 women), 17 part-time (3 women); includes 2 minority (both Asian Americans or Pacific Islanders), 57 international. Average age 24. 133 applicants, 62% accepted, 38 enrolled. In 2009, 41 master's awarded. *Entrance requirements:* Additional exam requirements/recommendations for international students: Required—TOEFL (minimum score 100 iBT). *Application deadline:* For fall admission, 6/1 priority date for domestic and international students. Applications are processed on a rolling basis. Application fee: $75. Electronic applications accepted. *Expenses:* Tuition: Full-time $26,808; part-time $1117 per credit. Required fees: $1024. *Financial support:* Fellowships with full and partial tuition reimbursements, research assistantships with full and partial tuition reimbursements, teaching assistantships with full and partial tuition reimbursements, tuition waivers (partial) available. Financial award application deadline: 1/1. *Unit head:* Fred Carranti, Program Director, 315-443-4346. *Application contact:* Kathy Datthyn-Madigan, Information Contact, 315-443-4367.

Texas Tech University, Graduate School, College of Engineering, Department of Industrial Engineering, Lubbock, TX 79409. Offers industrial engineering (MSIE, PhD); manufacturing systems engineering (MSMSE); systems and engineering management (MSSEM, PhD). Part-time programs available. *Faculty:* 11 full-time (2 women). *Students:* 85 full-time (19 women), 48 part-time (8 women); includes 9 minority (4 African Americans, 2 Asian Americans or Pacific Islanders, 3 Hispanic Americans), 80 international. Average age 29. 298 applicants, 61% accepted, 24 enrolled. In 2009, 21 master's, 7 doctorates awarded. *Degree requirements:* For master's, thesis or alternative; for doctorate, thesis/dissertation. *Entrance requirements:* For master's and doctorate, GRE General Test, minimum GPA of 3.0. Additional exam requirements/recommendations for international students: Required—TOEFL (minimum score 550 paper-based; 213 computer-based). *Application deadline:* For fall admission, 3/1 priority date for international students; for spring admission, 11/1 priority date for international students. Applications are processed on a rolling basis. Application fee: $50 ($75 for international students). Electronic applications accepted. *Expenses:* Tuition, state resident: full-time $5100; part-time $213 per credit hour. Tuition, nonresident: full-time $11,748; part-time $490 per credit hour. Required fees: $2298; $50 per credit hour. $555 per semester. *Financial support:* In 2009–10, 14 research assistantships with partial tuition reimbursements (averaging $14,979 per year), 10 teaching assistantships with partial tuition reimbursements (averaging $13,050 per year) were awarded; Federal Work-Study and institutionally sponsored loans also available. Support available to part-time students. Financial award application deadline: 4/15; financial award applicants required to submit FAFSA. *Faculty research:* Knowledge and engineering management, environmentally conscious manufacturing, biomechanical simulation, aviation security, supply chain management. Total annual research expenditures: $476,488. *Unit head:* Dr. Pat Patterson, Chair, 806-742-3543, Fax: 806-742-3411, E-mail: pat.patterson@ttu.edu. *Application contact:* Dr. Mario Beruvides, Professor, 806-742-3543, Fax: 806-742-3411, E-mail: mario.beruvides@ttu.edu.

Tufts University, School of Engineering, The Gordon Institute, Medford, MA 02155. Offers MSEM. Part-time programs available. *Faculty:* 9 part-time/adjunct. *Students:* 121 (25 women), 7 international. 83 applicants, 82% accepted, 64 enrolled. In 2009, 35 master's awarded. *Entrance requirements:* Additional exam requirements/recommendations for international students: Required—TOEFL (minimum score 550 paper-based; 213 computer-based; 80 iBT). *Application deadline:* For fall admission, 3/15 priority date for domestic students. Applications are processed on a rolling basis. Application fee: $75. Electronic applications accepted. *Expenses:* Contact institution. *Unit head:* Robert Hannemann, Director, 617-627-3111, Fax: 617-627-3180. *Application contact:* Information Contact, 617-628-5000.

Union Graduate College, School of Engineering and Computer Science, Schenectady, NY 12308-3107. Offers computer science (MS); electrical engineering (MS); engineering and management systems (MS); mechanical engineering (MS). Part-time and evening/weekend programs available. *Faculty:* 24 part-time/adjunct (1 woman). *Students:* 10 full-time (0 women), 60 part-time (7 women); includes 5 minority (1 African American, 1 American Indian/Alaska Native, 2 Asian Americans or Pacific Islanders, 1 Hispanic American), 5 international. Average age 27. 47 applicants, 55% accepted, 25 enrolled. In 2009, 28 master's awarded. *Degree requirements:* For master's, capstone course. *Entrance requirements:* For master's, minimum GPA of 3.0, letters of recommendation. Additional exam requirements/recommendations for international students: Required—TOEFL (minimum score 550 paper-based; 213 computer-based). *Application deadline:* Applications are processed on a rolling basis. Application fee: $60. Electronic applications accepted. *Expenses:* Contact institution. *Financial support:* Research assistantships, Federal Work-Study, scholarships/grants, health care benefits, and tuition waivers (full and partial) available. Support available to part-time students. Financial award applicants required to submit FAFSA. *Unit head:* Robert Kozik, Dean, 515-631-9881, Fax: 518-631-9902, E-mail: kozikr@union.edu. *Application contact:* Diane Trzaskos, Coordinator, Admissions, 518-631-9837, Fax: 518-631-9901, E-mail: trzaskod@uniongraduatecollege.edu.

Université de Sherbrooke, Faculty of Engineering, Programs in Engineering Management, Sherbrooke, QC J1K 2R1, Canada. Offers M Eng, Diploma. Part-time and evening/weekend programs available. *Entrance requirements:* For master's and Diploma, bachelor's degree in engineering, 1 year of practical experience. Electronic applications accepted.

The University of Akron, Graduate School, College of Engineering, Program in Engineering (Management Specialization), Akron, OH 44325. Offers MS. *Students:* 6 full-time (1 woman), 6 part-time (0 women); includes 1 minority (Asian American or Pacific Islander), 3 international. Average age 27. 11 applicants, 55% accepted, 1 enrolled. In 2009, 3 master's awarded. *Degree requirements:* For master's, engineering report. *Entrance requirements:* For master's, GRE, minimum GPA of 2.75, letters of recommendation, resume. Additional exam requirements/recommendations for international students: Required—TOEFL (minimum score 550 paper-based; 213 computer-based; 79 iBT). *Application deadline:* Applications are processed on a rolling basis. Application fee: $30 ($40 for international students). Electronic applications accepted. *Expenses:* Tuition, state resident: full-time $6570; part-time $365 per credit hour. Tuition, nonresident: full-time $11,250; part-time $625 per credit hour. *Unit head:* Dr. Subramaniya Hariharan, Coordinator, 330-972-6580, E-mail: hari@uakron.edu. *Application contact:* Dr. Craig Menzemer, Director of Graduate Studies, 330-972-5536, E-mail: ccmenze@uakron.edu.

The University of Alabama in Huntsville, School of Graduate Studies, College of Engineering, Department of Industrial and Systems Engineering/Engineering Management, Huntsville, AL 35899. Offers industrial and systems engineering (PhD), including engineering management (MSE, PhD), industrial engineering, systems engineering (MSE, PhD); industrial engineering (MSE), including engineering management (MSE, PhD), missile systems engineering, modeling and simulation, rotorcraft systems engineering, systems engineering (MSE, PhD); operations research (MSOR). Part-time and evening/weekend programs available. Postbaccalaureate distance learning degree programs offered (minimal on-campus study). *Faculty:* 6 full-time (2 women). *Students:* 6 full-time (0 women), 138 part-time (37 women); includes 17 minority (14 African Americans, 1 American Indian/Alaska Native, 2 Hispanic Americans), 9 international. Average age 36. 75 applicants, 53% accepted, 29 enrolled. In 2009, 38 master's, 6 doctorates awarded. *Degree requirements:* For master's, comprehensive exam, thesis or alternative, oral and written exams; for doctorate, comprehensive exam, thesis/dissertation, oral and written exams. *Entrance requirements:* For master's and doctorate, GRE General Test, minimum GPA of 3.0. Additional exam requirements/recommendations for international students: Required—TOEFL (minimum score 500 paper-based; 173 computer-based; 62 iBT). *Application deadline:* For fall admission, 7/15 for domestic students, 4/1 for international students; for spring admission, 11/30 for domestic students, 9/1 for international students. Applications are processed on a rolling basis. Application fee: $40 ($50 for international students). Electronic applications accepted. *Expenses:* Tuition, state resident: part-time $355.75 per credit hour. Tuition, nonresident: part-time $847.10 per credit hour. Required fees: $210.80 per semester. Tuition and fees vary according to course load and program. *Financial support:* In 2009–10, 4 students received support, including 4 teaching assistantships with full and partial tuition reimbursements available (averaging $11,733 per year); career-related internships or fieldwork, Federal Work-Study, institutionally sponsored loans, scholarships/grants, health care benefits, and unspecified assistantships also available. Support available to part-time students. Financial award application deadline: 4/1; financial award applicants required to submit FAFSA. *Faculty research:* Engineering management, systems engineering, manufacturing, logistics, simulation. Total annual research expenditures: $19.6 million. *Unit head:* Dr. James Swain, Chair, 256-824-6749, Fax: 256-824-6733, E-mail: jswain@ise.uah.edu. *Application contact:* Kathy Biggs, Graduate Studies Admissions Manager, 256-824-6199, Fax: 256-824-6405, E-mail: deangrad@uah.edu.

University of Alaska Anchorage, School of Engineering, Program in Engineering Management, Anchorage, AK 99508. Offers MS. Part-time and evening/weekend programs available. *Degree requirements:* For master's, comprehensive exam (for some programs), thesis optional. *Entrance requirements:* For master's, BS in engineering or science, work experience in engineering or science. Additional exam requirements/recommendations for international students: Required—TOEFL (minimum score 550 paper-based; 213 computer-based). *Faculty research:* Engineering economy, long-range forecasting, multicriteria design making, project management process and training.

University of Alaska Anchorage, School of Engineering, Program in Science Management, Anchorage, AK 99508. Offers MS. Part-time and evening/weekend programs available. *Degree requirements:* For master's, comprehensive exam (for some programs), thesis (for some programs). *Entrance requirements:* For master's, GRE General Test, BS in engineering or scientific field. Additional exam requirements/recommendations for international students: Required—TOEFL (minimum score 550 paper-based; 213 computer-based). *Faculty research:* Engineering economy, long-range forecasting, multicriteria decision making, project management process and training.

University of Alaska Fairbanks, College of Engineering and Mines, Department of Civil and Environmental Engineering, Engineering and Science Management Program, Fairbanks, AK 99775. Offers engineering management (MS, PhD); science management (MS). Part-time programs available. *Students:* 5 part-time (3 women). Average age 32. 4 applicants, 75% accepted, 3 enrolled. In 2009, 4 master's awarded. *Degree requirements:* For master's, comprehensive exam, thesis or alternative, oral exam; for doctorate, comprehensive exam, thesis/dissertation, oral exam, oral defense. *Entrance requirements:* For doctorate, GRE General Test. Additional exam requirements/recommendations for international students: Required—TOEFL (minimum score 550 paper-based; 213 computer-based; 80 iBT). *Application deadline:* For fall admission, 6/1 for domestic students, 3/1 for international students; for spring admission, 10/15 for domestic students, 9/1 for international students. Applications are processed on a rolling basis. Application fee: $60. Electronic applications accepted. *Expenses:* Tuition, state resident: full-time $7584; part-time $316 per credit. Tuition, nonresident: full-time $15,504; part-time $646 per credit. Required fees: $23 per credit. $135 per semester. Tuition and fees vary according to course level, course load and reciprocity agreements. *Financial support:* Fellowships, research assistantships, teaching assistantships, career-related internships or fieldwork, Federal Work-Study, scholarships/grants, health care benefits, and unspecified assistantships available. Support available to part-time students. Financial award application deadline: 7/1; financial award applicants required to submit FAFSA. *Faculty research:* Traffic studies, decision analysis, application of optimization, transportation safety. *Unit head:* Dr. Robert A. Perkins, Program Coordinator, 907-474-7694, Fax: 907-474-6087, E-mail: raperkins@alaska.edu. *Application contact:* Dr. Robert A. Perkins, Program Coordinator, 907-474-7694, Fax: 907-474-6087, E-mail: raperkins@alaska.edu.

University of Alberta, Faculty of Graduate Studies and Research, Department of Mechanical Engineering, Edmonton, AB T6G 2E1, Canada. Offers engineering management (M Eng); mechanical engineering (M Eng, M Sc, PhD); MBA/M Eng. Part-time programs available. *Faculty:* 33 full-time (1 woman), 1 part-time/adjunct (0 women). *Students:* 144 full-time (17 women), 34 part-time (5 women). 300 applicants, 44% accepted, 76 enrolled. In 2009, 14 master's, 2 doctorates awarded. *Degree requirements:* For master's, thesis; for doctorate, thesis/dissertation. *Entrance requirements:* For master's and doctorate, minimum GPA of 7.0

Engineering Management

University of Alberta *(continued)*
on a 9.0 scale. Additional exam requirements/recommendations for international students: Required—TOEFL (minimum score 580 paper-based; 237 computer-based). *Application deadline:* For fall admission, 3/1 priority date for domestic students; for winter admission, 7/1 priority date for domestic students. Applications are processed on a rolling basis. Tuition and fees charges are reported in Canadian dollars. *Expenses:* Tuition, area resident: Full-time $4626.24 Canadian dollars; part-time $99.72 Canadian dollars per unit. International tuition: $8216 Canadian dollars full-time. Required fees: $3589.92 Canadian dollars; $99.72 Canadian dollars per unit. $215 Canadian dollars per term. *Financial support:* In 2009–10, 14 fellowships, 7 research assistantships, 64 teaching assistantships were awarded; career-related internships or fieldwork, scholarships/grants, and supervisor support also available. Financial award application deadline: 2/1. *Faculty research:* Combustion and environmental issues, advanced materials, computational fluid dynamics, biomedical, acoustics and vibrations. Total annual research expenditures: $1.3 million. *Unit head:* Dr. Zihui Ben Xia, Graduate Coordinator, 780-492-0414, Fax: 403-492-2200. *Application contact:* Gail Anderson, Student Services Assistant, 780-492-0414, Fax: 780-492-2200, E-mail: mecegrad@mail.mece.ualberta.ca.

University of California, Berkeley, Graduate Division, College of Engineering, Department of Civil and Environmental Engineering, Berkeley, CA 94720-1500. Offers engineering and project management (M Eng, MS, D Eng, PhD); environmental engineering (M Eng, MS, D Eng, PhD); geoengineering (M Eng, MS, D Eng, PhD); structural engineering, mechanics and materials (M Eng, MS, D Eng, PhD); transportation engineering (M Eng, MS, D Eng, PhD); M Arch/MS; MCP/MS; MPP/MS. *Students:* 368 full-time (125 women). Average age 27. 921 applicants, 179 enrolled. In 2009, 158 master's, 39 doctorates awarded. *Degree requirements:* For master's, comprehensive exam or thesis (MS); for doctorate, thesis/dissertation, qualifying exam. *Entrance requirements:* For master's, GRE General Test, minimum GPA of 3.0, 3 letters of recommendation; for doctorate, GRE General Test, minimum GPA of 3.5, 3 letters of recommendation. Additional exam requirements/recommendations for international students: Required—TOEFL (minimum score 570 paper-based; 230 computer-based). *Application deadline:* For fall admission, 2/3 for domestic students. Application fee: $70 ($90 for international students). Electronic applications accepted. *Financial support:* Fellowships, research assistantships, teaching assistantships, unspecified assistantships available. *Unit head:* Prof. Lisa Alvarez-Cohen, Chair, 510-643-8739, Fax: 510-643-5264, E-mail: chair@ce.berkeley.edu. *Application contact:* Shelly Okimoto, Graduate Advisor, 510-642-6464, Fax: 510-643-5264, E-mail: aao@ce.berkeley.edu.

University of Colorado at Boulder, Graduate School, College of Engineering and Applied Science, Engineering Management Program, Boulder, CO 80309. Offers operations and logistics (ME); quality and process (ME); research and development (ME). *Students:* 16 full-time (2 women), 98 part-time (27 women); includes 13 minority (8 Asian Americans or Pacific Islanders, 5 Hispanic Americans), 9 international. Average age 35. 36 applicants, 33% accepted, 9 enrolled. In 2009, 42 master's awarded. *Entrance requirements:* For master's, minimum undergraduate GPA of 3.0. *Application deadline:* For fall admission, 2/15 for domestic students, 12/1 for international students; for spring admission, 8/15 for domestic students, 5/1 for international students. Application fee: $50 ($60 for international students). *Financial support:* In 2009–10, 2 fellowships (averaging $3,500 per year), 2 research assistantships (averaging $16,862 per year) were awarded. *Faculty research:* Quality and process, research and development, operations and logistics.

University of Colorado at Colorado Springs, Graduate School, College of Engineering and Applied Science, Department of Mechanical and Aerospace Engineering, Colorado Springs, CO 80933-7150. Offers engineering management (ME); information operations (ME); manufacturing (ME); mechanical engineering (MS); software engineering (ME); space operations (ME); space systems (MS). Part-time and evening/weekend programs available. *Faculty:* 10 full-time (2 women). *Students:* 14 full-time (4 women), 13 part-time (2 women); includes 3 minority (2 Asian Americans or Pacific Islanders, 1 Hispanic American). Average age 30. 39 applicants, 82% accepted, 16 enrolled. In 2009, 6 master's awarded. *Degree requirements:* For master's, thesis optional. *Entrance requirements:* For master's, GRE General Test, bachelor's degree in engineering or related degree, minimum GPA of 3.0. Additional exam requirements/recommendations for international students: Required—TOEFL. *Application deadline:* For fall admission, 5/1 for domestic students; for spring admission, 10/1 for domestic students. Applications are processed on a rolling basis. Application fee: $60 ($75 for international students). *Expenses:* Tuition, state resident: full-time $8922; part-time $639 per credit hour. Tuition, nonresident: full-time $19,372; part-time $1154 per credit hour. Tuition and fees vary according to course level, course load, degree level, program, reciprocity agreements and student level. *Financial support:* Federal Work-Study and scholarships/grants available. Support available to part-time students. Financial award application deadline: 3/1; financial award applicants required to submit FAFSA. *Faculty research:* Neural networks, artificial intelligence, robust control, space operations, space propulsion. *Unit head:* Dr. T. S. Kalkur, Chair, 719-255-3147, Fax: 719-255-3042, E-mail: kalkur@eas.uccs.edu. *Application contact:* Siew Nylund, Academic Adviser, 719-255-3243, Fax: 719-255-3589, E-mail: snylund@eas.uccs.edu.

University of Dayton, Graduate School, School of Engineering, Engineering Management and Systems Department, Dayton, OH 45469-1300. Offers engineering management (MSEM). Part-time and evening/weekend programs available. Postbaccalaureate distance learning degree programs offered (no on-campus study). *Faculty:* 4 full-time (0 women), 4 part-time/adjunct (0 women). *Students:* 61 full-time (17 women), 54 part-time (9 women); includes 19 minority (12 African Americans, 5 Asian Americans or Pacific Islanders, 2 Hispanic Americans), 32 international. Average age 31. 93 applicants, 69% accepted, 30 enrolled. In 2009, 40 master's awarded. *Degree requirements:* For master's, thesis optional. *Entrance requirements:* Additional exam requirements/recommendations for international students: Required—TOEFL (minimum score 550 paper-based; 213 computer-based; 80 iBT). *Application deadline:* For fall admission, 8/1 for domestic students, 3/1 priority date for international students; for winter admission, 7/1 priority date for international students; for spring admission, 1/1 priority date for international students. Applications are processed on a rolling basis. Application fee: $0. Electronic applications accepted. *Expenses:* Tuition: Full-time $8412; part-time $701 per credit hour. Required fees: $325; $65 per course. $25 per semester. Tuition and fees vary according to course load, degree level and program. *Financial support:* Fellowships, research assistantships, teaching assistantships available. Financial award applicants required to submit FAFSA. *Faculty research:* OPS research, simulation, reliability. Total annual research expenditures: $70,621. *Unit head:* Dr. Patrick Sweeney, Chair, 937-229-2238, Fax: 937-229-2698. *Application contact:* Graduate Admissions, 937-229-4411, Fax: 937-229-4729, E-mail: gradadmission@udayton.edu.

University of Detroit Mercy, College of Engineering and Science, Program in Engineering Management, Detroit, MI 48221. Offers M Eng Mgt. Evening/weekend programs available. *Degree requirements:* For master's, thesis or alternative.

University of Idaho, College of Graduate Studies, College of Engineering, Department of Civil Engineering, Program in Engineering Management, Moscow, ID 83844-2282. Offers M Engr. *Students:* 1 full-time, 34 part-time. In 2009, 5 master's awarded. *Expenses:* Tuition, state resident: full-time $6120. Tuition, nonresident: full-time $17,712. *Unit head:* Dr. Richard J. Nielsen, Department Chair. *Application contact:* Dr. Richard J. Nielsen, Department Chair.

The University of Kansas, Graduate Studies, School of Engineering, Program in Engineering Management, Overland Park, KS 66213. Offers MS. Part-time and evening/weekend programs available. Postbaccalaureate distance learning degree programs offered (no on-campus study). *Faculty:* 3 full-time (1 woman), 10 part-time/adjunct (1 woman). *Students:* 6 full-time (0 women), 143 part-time (22 women); includes 26 minority (9 African Americans, 1 American Indian/Alaska Native, 12 Asian Americans or Pacific Islanders, 4 Hispanic Americans), 23 international. Average age 33. 41 applicants, 56% accepted, 19 enrolled. In 2009, 39 master's awarded. *Degree requirements:* For master's, exam. *Entrance requirements:* For master's, minimum GPA of 3.0, 2 years of industrial experience. Additional exam requirements/recommendations for international students: Required—TOEFL (minimum score 600 paper-

based; 250 computer-based; 100 iBT). *Application deadline:* Applications are processed on a rolling basis. Application fee: $45 ($55 for international students). Electronic applications accepted. *Expenses:* Tuition, state resident: full-time $6492; part-time $270.50 per credit hour. Tuition, nonresident: full-time $15,510; part-time $646.25 per credit hour. Required fees: $847; $70.56 per credit hour. Tuition and fees vary according to course load and program. *Faculty research:* Project management, systems analysis, high performance teams, manufacturing systems, strategic analysis. *Unit head:* Herbert R. Tuttle, Director, 913-897-8561, Fax: 913-897-8682, E-mail: emgt@ku.edu. *Application contact:* Parveen Mozaffar, Academic Services Coordinator, 913-897-8560, Fax: 913-897-8682, E-mail: emgt@ku.edu.

University of Louisiana at Lafayette, College of Engineering, Department of Engineering and Technology Management, Lafayette, LA 70504. Offers MSET. Part-time and evening/weekend programs available. *Degree requirements:* For master's, comprehensive exam, thesis or alternative. *Entrance requirements:* For master's, GRE General Test, minimum GPA of 2.85. Additional exam requirements/recommendations for international students: Required—TOEFL (minimum score 550 paper-based; 213 computer-based). Electronic applications accepted. *Faculty research:* Mathematical programming, production management forecasting.

University of Louisville, J.B. Speed School of Engineering, Department of Industrial Engineering, Louisville, KY 40292-0001. Offers engineering management (M Eng); industrial engineering (M Eng, MS, PhD); logistics and distribution (Certificate). *Accreditation:* ABET (one or more programs are accredited). Part-time programs available. *Faculty:* 9 full-time (1 woman). *Students:* 37 full-time (13 women), 35 part-time (7 women); includes 11 minority (6 African Americans, 5 Asian Americans or Pacific Islanders), 19 international. Average age 29. 62 applicants, 61% accepted, 23 enrolled. In 2009, 27 master's, 2 doctorates awarded. Terminal master's awarded for partial completion of doctoral program. *Degree requirements:* For master's, comprehensive exam (for some programs), thesis or alternative; for doctorate, comprehensive exam, thesis/dissertation, minimum GPA of 3.0. *Entrance requirements:* For master's and doctorate, GRE General Test. Additional exam requirements/recommendations for international students: Required—TOEFL (minimum score 550 paper-based; 213 computer-based; 80 iBT). *Application deadline:* For fall admission, 7/12 priority date for domestic and international students; for winter admission, 11/29 priority date for domestic and international students; for spring admission, 3/28 priority date for domestic and international students. Applications are processed on a rolling basis. Application fee: $50. Electronic applications accepted. *Financial support:* In 2009–10, 16 students received support, including 8 fellowships with full tuition reimbursements available (averaging $20,000 per year), 1 research assistantship with full tuition reimbursement available (averaging $20,000 per year), 6 teaching assistantships with full tuition reimbursements available (averaging $20,000 per year). Financial award application deadline: 1/25; financial award applicants required to submit FAFSA. *Faculty research:* Optimization, computer simulation, logistics and distribution, ergonomics and human factors, advanced manufacturing process. Total annual research expenditures: $359,000. *Unit head:* Dr. John S. Usher, Chair, 502-852-6342, Fax: 502-852-5633, E-mail: usher@louisville.edu. *Application contact:* Dr. Michael Day, Associate Dean, 502-852-6195, Fax: 502-852-7294, E-mail: day@louisville.edu.

University of Maryland, Baltimore County, Graduate School, College of Engineering and Information Technology, Department of Computer Science and Electrical Engineering, Program in Engineering Management, Baltimore, MD 21250. Offers MS, Postbaccalaureate Certificate. Part-time programs available. *Students:* 8 full-time (1 woman), 59 part-time (14 women); includes 25 minority (14 African Americans, 1 American Indian/Alaska Native, 8 Asian Americans or Pacific Islanders, 2 Hispanic Americans), 8 international. Average age 29. 42 applicants, 71% accepted, 17 enrolled. In 2009, 10 master's, 5 other advanced degrees awarded. *Degree requirements:* For master's, comprehensive exam (for some programs), thesis optional. *Entrance requirements:* For master's, BS in engineering or information technology with minimum GPA of 3.0. Additional exam requirements/recommendations for international students: Required—TOEFL (minimum score 550 paper-based; 213 computer-based; 80 iBT). *Application deadline:* For fall admission, 7/1 for domestic and international students; for spring admission, 12/1 for domestic and international students. Applications are processed on a rolling basis. Application fee: $50. Electronic applications accepted. *Financial support:* Career-related internships or fieldwork, Federal Work-Study, scholarships/grants, health care benefits, tuition waivers (partial), and unspecified assistantships available. Support available to part-time students. Financial award application deadline: 6/30; financial award applicants required to submit FAFSA. *Faculty research:* Regulatory engineering, environmental engineering, systems engineering, advanced manufacturing, chemical engineering. *Unit head:* Dr. Charles K. Nicholas, Professor and Chair, 410-455-3500, Fax: 410-455-3969, E-mail: nicholas@cs.umbc.edu. *Application contact:* Dr. Ted M. Foster, Professor of Practice and Assistant Dean, COEIT, 410-455-1564, Fax: 410-455-3559, E-mail: tfoster@umbc.edu.

University of Massachusetts Amherst, Graduate School, Interdisciplinary Programs, Program in Industrial Engineering and Business Administration, Amherst, MA 01003. Offers MBA/MSIE. Part-time programs available. *Students:* 4 applicants, 0% accepted, 0 enrolled. *Entrance requirements:* Additional exam requirements/recommendations for international students: Required—TOEFL (minimum score 600 paper-based; 250 computer-based; 100 iBT), IELTS (minimum score 7). *Application deadline:* For fall admission, 1/15 for domestic and international students. Applications are processed on a rolling basis. Application fee: $50 ($65 for international students). Electronic applications accepted. *Expenses:* Tuition, state resident: full-time $2640; part-time $110 per credit. Tuition, nonresident: full-time $9936; part-time $414 per credit. Tuition and fees vary according to course load. *Financial support:* Career-related internships or fieldwork, Federal Work-Study, scholarships/grants, traineeships, health care benefits, tuition waivers (full), and unspecified assistantships available. Support available to part-time students. *Unit head:* Dr. David P. Schmidt, Graduate Program Director, 413-545-3827, Fax: 413-545-1027. *Application contact:* Jean M. Ames, Supervisor of Admissions, 413-545-0722, Fax: 413-577-0010, E-mail: gradadm@grad.umass.edu.

University of Michigan–Dearborn, College of Engineering and Computer Science, Department of Industrial and Manufacturing Systems Engineering, Dearborn, MI 48128-1491. Offers engineering management (MS); industrial and systems engineering (MSE); information systems and technology (MS); information systems engineering (PhD); MBA/MSE. Part-time and evening/weekend programs available. *Faculty:* 14 full-time (0 women), 5 part-time/adjunct (0 women). *Students:* 16 full-time (5 women), 179 part-time (56 women); includes 45 minority (6 African Americans, 26 Asian Americans or Pacific Islanders, 13 Hispanic Americans). Average age 31. 63 applicants, 62% accepted, 37 enrolled. In 2009, 67 master's awarded. *Degree requirements:* For master's, thesis optional. *Entrance requirements:* For master's, bachelor's degree in applied mathematics, computer science, engineering, or physical science; minimum GPA of 3.0. Additional exam requirements/recommendations for international students: Required—TOEFL (minimum score 560 paper-based; 220 computer-based; 84 iBT). *Application deadline:* For fall admission, 8/1 priority date for domestic students, 4/1 for international students; for winter admission, 12/1 priority date for domestic students, 8/1 for international students; for spring admission, 4/1 for domestic students, 12/1 for international students. Applications are processed on a rolling basis. Application fee: $60 ($75 for international students). *Expenses:* Tuition, area resident: Part-time $504.10 per credit hour. Tuition, state resident: part-time $504.10 per credit hour. Tuition, nonresident: part-time $957.90 per credit hour. *Financial support:* Fellowships, research assistantships, teaching assistantships, Federal Work-Study available. Financial award application deadline: 4/1; financial award applicants required to submit FAFSA. *Faculty research:* Health care systems, data and knowledge management, human factors engineering, machine diagnostics, precision machining. *Unit head:* Dr. Armen Zakarian, Chair, 313-593-5361, Fax: 313-593-3692, E-mail: zakarian@umd.umich.edu. *Application contact:* Joey W. Woods, Graduate Program Assistant, 313-593-5361, Fax: 313-593-3692, E-mail: jwwoods@umd.umich.edu.

University of Minnesota, Duluth, Graduate School, Swenson College of Science and Engineering, Department of Mechanical and Industrial Engineering, Duluth, MN 55812-2496. Offers engineering management (MSEM); environmental health and safety (MEHS). Part-time and evening/weekend programs available. Postbaccalaureate distance learning degree programs offered (no on-campus study). *Degree requirements:* For master's, comprehensive exam, thesis or alternative, capstone design project (MSEM), field project (MEHS). *Entrance requirements:* For master's, GRE (MEHS), interview (MEHS), letters of recommendation. Additional exam requirements/recommendations for international students: Required—TOEFL (minimum score 550 paper-based; 213 computer-based). *Faculty research:* Transportation, ergonomics, toxicology, supply chain management, automation and robotics.

University of Nebraska–Lincoln, Graduate College, College of Engineering, Department of Industrial and Management Systems Engineering, Lincoln, NE 68588. Offers engineering management (M Eng); industrial and management systems engineering (MS, PhD); manufacturing systems engineering (MS). Postbaccalaureate distance learning degree programs offered. *Degree requirements:* For master's, thesis optional; for doctorate, comprehensive exam, thesis/dissertation. *Entrance requirements:* For master's and doctorate, GRE. Additional exam requirements/recommendations for international students: Required—TOEFL (minimum score 525 paper-based; 195 computer-based). Electronic applications accepted. *Faculty research:* Ergonomics, occupational safety, quality control, industrial packaging, facility design.

University of New Brunswick Fredericton, School of Graduate Studies, Faculty of Business Administration, Fredericton, NB E3B 5A3, Canada. Offers business administration (MBA); engineering management (MBA); entrepreneurship (MBA); sports and recreation management (MBA); MBA/LL B. Part-time programs available. *Faculty:* 37 full-time (13 women). *Students:* 27 full-time (10 women), 51 part-time (25 women). In 2009, 72 master's awarded. *Degree requirements:* For master's, thesis optional. *Entrance requirements:* For master's, GMAT (550 minimum score), minimum GPA of 3.0; 3-5 years work experience. Additional exam requirements/recommendations for international students: Required—TOEFL (minimum score 580 paper-based; 92 iBT), IELTS (minimum score 7), TOEFL or IELTS. *Application deadline:* For fall admission, 3/1 priority date for domestic students. Applications are processed on a rolling basis. Application fee: $50 Canadian dollars. Tuition and fees charges are reported in Canadian dollars. *Expenses:* Tuition, area resident: Full-time $5562 Canadian dollars; part-time $2781 Canadian dollars per year. Required fees: $49.75 Canadian dollars per term. *Financial support:* In 2009–10, 4 research assistantships (averaging $4,500 per year), 11 teaching assistantships (averaging $2,250 per year) were awarded. *Faculty research:* Strategic management, entrepreneurship, investment practices, marketing and supply chain management, operations management. *Unit head:* Judy Roy, Director of Graduate Studies, 506-458-7307, Fax: 506-453-3561, E-mail: jroy@unb.ca. *Application contact:* Marilyn Davis, Acting Graduate Secretary, 506-453-4766, Fax: 506-453-3561, E-mail: mbacontact@unb.ca.

University of New Haven, Graduate School, Tagliatela College of Engineering, Program in Engineering Management, West Haven, CT 06516-1916. Offers EMS. *Faculty:* 4 part-time/adjunct (1 woman). *Students:* 12 full-time (3 women), 5 part-time (1 woman); includes 4 minority (2 African Americans, 1 Asian American or Pacific Islander, 1 Hispanic American). Average age 39. 6 applicants, 100% accepted, 5 enrolled. In 2009, 2 master's awarded. *Entrance requirements:* For master's, five or more years' experience in a supervisory role in engineering, technical staff support, engineering or systems management, project management, systems engineering, manufacturing, logistics, industrial engineering, military operations, or quality assurance. Additional exam requirements/recommendations for international students: Required—TOEFL (minimum score 520 paper-based; 190 computer-based; 70 iBT); Recommended—IELTS (minimum score 5.5). *Application deadline:* For fall admission, 5/31 for international students; for winter admission, 10/15 for international students; for spring admission, 1/15 for international students. Application fee: $50. *Expenses:* Tuition: Part-time $700 per credit. Required fees: $45 per term. One-time fee: $390 part-time. *Unit head:* Dr. Barry Farbrother, Dean, 203-932-7167. *Application contact:* Eloise Gormley, Director of Graduate Admissions, 203-932-7449, Fax: 203-932-7137, E-mail: gradinfo@newhaven.edu.

University of New Orleans, Graduate School, College of Engineering, Program in Engineering Management, New Orleans, LA 70148. Offers MS, Certificate. *Degree requirements:* For master's, thesis optional. *Entrance requirements:* For master's, GRE General Test, minimum GPA of 3.0. Additional exam requirements/recommendations for international students: Required—TOEFL (minimum score 550 paper-based; 213 computer-based; 79 iBT). Electronic applications accepted.

The University of North Carolina at Charlotte, Graduate School, The William States Lee College of Engineering, Program in Engineering Management, Charlotte, NC 28223-0001. Offers MS. Part-time and evening/weekend programs available. *Faculty:* 4 full-time (1 woman), 3 part-time/adjunct (1 woman). *Students:* 10 full-time (4 women), 17 part-time (4 women); includes 6 minority (4 African Americans, 2 Asian Americans or Pacific Islanders), 7 international. Average age 27. 89 applicants, 55% accepted, 15 enrolled. In 2009, 8 master's awarded. *Degree requirements:* For master's, thesis optional. *Entrance requirements:* For master's, GRE General Test or GMAT. Additional exam requirements/recommendations for international students: Required—TOEFL (minimum score 557 paper-based; 220 computer-based; 83 iBT). *Application deadline:* For fall admission, 7/1 for domestic students, 5/1 for international students; for spring admission, 11/1 for domestic students, 10/1 for international students. Applications are processed on a rolling basis. Application fee: $55. Electronic applications accepted. *Financial support:* In 2009–10, 7 students received support, including 7 teaching assistantships (averaging $7,166 per year); career-related internships or fieldwork, Federal Work-Study, institutionally sponsored loans, scholarships/grants, and unspecified assistantships also available. Support available to part-time students. Financial award application deadline: 4/1; financial award applicants required to submit FAFSA. Total annual research expenditures: $123,395. *Unit head:* Dr. S. Gary Teng, Director, 704-687-3989, Fax: 704-687-3616, E-mail: sgteng@uncc.edu. *Application contact:* Kathy B. Giddings, Director of Graduate Admissions, 704-687-5503, Fax: 704-687-3279, E-mail: gradadm@uncc.edu.

University of Ottawa, Faculty of Graduate and Postdoctoral Studies, Faculty of Engineering, Engineering Management Program, Ottawa, ON K1N 6N5, Canada. Offers engineering management (M Eng); information technology (Certificate); project management (Certificate). *Degree requirements:* For master's, thesis or alternative. *Entrance requirements:* For master's and Certificate, honors degree or equivalent, minimum B average. Electronic applications accepted.

University of St. Thomas, Graduate Studies, School of Engineering, St. Paul, MN 55105-1096. Offers engineering and technology management (Certificate); manufacturing systems (MS); manufacturing systems engineering (MMSE); systems engineering (MS); technology management (MS). *Accreditation:* ABET (one or more programs are accredited). Electronic applications accepted. *Expenses:* Contact institution.

University of Southern California, Graduate School, Viterbi School of Engineering, Department of Aerospace and Mechanical Engineering, Program in Product Development Engineering, Los Angeles, CA 90089. Offers MS. Postbaccalaureate distance learning degree programs offered. *Students:* 8 full-time (0 women), 26 part-time (7 women); includes 8 minority (2 African Americans, 5 Asian Americans or Pacific Islanders, 1 Hispanic American), 10 international. In 2009, 14 master's awarded. Application fee: $85. Electronic applications accepted. *Expenses:* Tuition: Full-time $25,980; part-time $1315 per unit. Required fees: $554. One-time fee: $35 full-time. Full-time tuition and fees vary according to degree level and program. *Unit head:* Dr. Geoffrey Spedding, Chair, 213-740-4132, Fax: 213-740-8071, E-mail: geoff@usc.edu. *Application contact:* Samantha Graves, Student Service Advisor, 213-740-1735, Fax: 213-740-7774, E-mail: smgraves@usc.edu.

University of Southern California, Graduate School, Viterbi School of Engineering, Department of Industrial and Systems Engineering, Los Angeles, CA 90089. Offers digital supply chain management (MS); engineering management (MS); engineering technology communication (Graduate Certificate); health systems operations (Graduate Certificate); industrial and systems engineering (MS, PhD, Engr); manufacturing engineering (MS); operations research engineering (MS); optimization and supply chain management (Graduate Certificate); product development engineering (MS); safety systems and security (MS); systems architecting and engineering (MS, Graduate Certificate); systems safety and security (Graduate Certificate); transportation systems (Graduate Certificate); MS/MBA. Part-time programs available. Postbaccalaureate distance learning degree programs offered (minimal on-campus study). *Faculty:* 11 full-time (2 women), 39 part-time/adjunct (7 women). *Students:* 250 full-time (71 women), 145 part-time (37 women); includes 67 minority (6 African Americans, 2 American Indian/Alaska Native, 39 Asian Americans or Pacific Islanders, 20 Hispanic Americans), 253 international. 679 applicants, 58% accepted, 206 enrolled. In 2009, 98 master's, 7 doctorates awarded. Terminal master's awarded for partial completion of doctoral program. *Degree requirements:* For doctorate, thesis/dissertation. *Entrance requirements:* For master's, GRE General Test; for doctorate, General GRE. *Application deadline:* For fall admission, 3/1 priority date for domestic and international students; for spring admission, 10/1 for domestic students, 10/1 priority date for international students. Applications are processed on a rolling basis. Application fee: $85. Electronic applications accepted. *Expenses:* Tuition: Full-time $25,980; part-time $1315 per unit. Required fees: $554. One-time fee: $35 full-time. Full-time tuition and fees vary according to degree level and program. *Financial support:* In 2009–10, fellowships with full tuition reimbursements (averaging $30,000 per year), research assistantships with full tuition reimbursements (averaging $19,250 per year), teaching assistantships with full tuition reimbursements (averaging $19,250 per year) were awarded; career-related internships or fieldwork, scholarships/grants, health care benefits, and unspecified assistantships also available. Financial award application deadline: 12/1; financial award applicants required to submit CSS PROFILE or FAFSA. *Faculty research:* Health systems, music cognition and retrieval, transportation andlogistics, manufacturing and automation, engineering systems design, risk and economic analysis. Total annual research expenditures: $1.2 million. *Unit head:* Dr. James E. Moore, Chair, 213-740-4885, Fax: 213-740-1120, E-mail: jmoore@usc.edu. *Application contact:* Mary Ordaz, Student Service Advisor, 213-740-4886, Fax: 213-740-1120, E-mail: isedept@usc.edu.

University of South Florida, Graduate School, College of Engineering, Department of Industrial and Management Systems Engineering, Tampa, FL 33620-9951. Offers engineering management (MSEM, MSIE); engineering science (PhD); industrial engineering (MIE, MSIE, PhD). Part-time programs available. Postbaccalaureate distance learning degree programs offered (minimal on-campus study). *Faculty:* 10 full-time (2 women), 6 part-time/adjunct (1 woman). *Students:* 68 full-time (24 women), 67 part-time (12 women); includes 31 minority (10 African Americans, 6 Asian Americans or Pacific Islanders, 15 Hispanic Americans), 49 international. Average age 32. 112 applicants, 63% accepted, 37 enrolled. In 2009, 42 master's, 2 doctorates awarded. Terminal master's awarded for partial completion of doctoral program. *Degree requirements:* For master's, comprehensive exam, thesis (for some programs); for doctorate, comprehensive exam, thesis/dissertation, 2 tools of research as specified by dissertation committee. *Entrance requirements:* For master's, GRE General Test, minimum GPA of 3.0 in last 60 hours of coursework; for doctorate, GRE General Test, minimum GPA of 3.0 in last 60 hours of coursework or in master's program. Additional exam requirements/recommendations for international students: Required—TOEFL (minimum score 550 paper-based; 213 computer-based; 80 iBT). *Application deadline:* For fall admission, 2/15 for domestic students, 1/2 for international students; for spring admission, 10/15 for domestic students, 6/1 for international students. Application fee: $30. Electronic applications accepted. *Financial support:* In 2009–10, teaching assistantships with partial tuition reimbursements (averaging $28,163 per year); tuition waivers (partial) also available. Financial award applicants required to submit FAFSA. *Faculty research:* Bio-Health engineering, engineering health care systems, energy markets, nanotechnology and nanomanufacturing, transportation and logistics, innovation in education. Total annual research expenditures: $1 million. *Unit head:* Dr. Jose Zayas-Castro, Department Chair, 813-974-2269, Fax: 813-974-5953, E-mail: josezaya@usf.edu. *Application contact:* Dr. Michael Weng, Program Coordinator, 813-974-5575, Fax: 813-974-5953, E-mail: mxweng@usf.edu.

The University of Tennessee, Graduate School, College of Engineering, Department of Industrial and Information Engineering, Knoxville, TN 37996. Offers engineering management (MS, PhD); industrial engineering (MS, PhD); reliability and maintainability engineering (MS); MS/MBA. Part-time programs available. Postbaccalaureate distance learning degree programs offered (no on-campus study). *Faculty:* 7 full-time (1 woman), 5 part-time/adjunct (0 women). *Students:* 30 full-time (8 women), 53 part-time (11 women); includes 14 minority (9 African Americans, 2 American Indian/Alaska Native, 3 Asian Americans or Pacific Islanders), 26 international. Average age 25. 77 applicants, 78% accepted, 20 enrolled. In 2009, 13 master's, 4 doctorates awarded. *Degree requirements:* For master's, thesis; for doctorate, comprehensive exam, thesis/dissertation. *Entrance requirements:* For master's, GRE General Test, minimum GPA of 2.7, 3 letters of recommendation; for doctorate, MS, 3 letters of recommendation. Additional exam requirements/recommendations for international students: Required—TOEFL (minimum score 550 paper-based; 213 computer-based). *Application deadline:* For fall admission, 2/1 priority date for domestic and international students; for spring admission, 6/15 priority date for international students. Applications are processed on a rolling basis. Application fee: $35. Electronic applications accepted. *Expenses:* Tuition, state resident: full-time $6826; part-time $380 per semester hour. Tuition, nonresident: full-time $21,844; part-time $1147 per semester hour. Tuition and fees vary according to program. *Financial support:* In 2009–10, 11 research assistantships with full tuition reimbursements (averaging $12,792 per year), 8 teaching assistantships with full tuition reimbursements (averaging $7,044 per year) were awarded; career-related internships or fieldwork, Federal Work-Study, institutionally sponsored loans, health care benefits, and unspecified assistantships also available. Financial award application deadline: 2/1; financial award applicants required to submit FAFSA. *Faculty research:* Dependability and reliability of large computer networks; design of lean, reliable systems; operations research in the automotive industry; sports equipment testing; defense-oriented supply chain modeling. Total annual research expenditures: $488,000. *Unit head:* Dr. R. Bruce Robinson, Interim Head, 865-974-3333, Fax: 865-974-0588, E-mail: rbr@utk.edu. *Application contact:* Dr. Denise Jackson, Graduate Representative, E-mail: djackson@utk.edu.

The University of Tennessee at Chattanooga, Graduate School, College of Engineering and Computer Science, Program in Engineering Management, Chattanooga, TN 37403. Offers engineering management (MS); fundamentals of engineering management (Graduate Certificate); power systems management (Graduate Certificate); project and value management (Graduate Certificate); quality management (Graduate Certificate). Postbaccalaureate distance learning degree programs offered (no on-campus study). *Faculty:* 4 full-time (1 woman). *Students:* 22 full-time (7 women), 69 part-time (11 women); includes 25 minority (12 African Americans, 9 Asian Americans or Pacific Islanders, 4 Hispanic Americans), 12 international. Average age 33. 46 applicants, 67% accepted, 24 enrolled. In 2009, 25 master's, 8 other advanced degrees awarded. *Degree requirements:* For master's, thesis. *Entrance requirements:* For master's, GRE General Test, letters of recommendation; minimum undergraduate GPA of 2.5 overall or 3.0 in senior year. Additional exam requirements/recommendations for international students: Required—TOEFL (minimum score 550 paper-based; 213 computer-based; 79 iBT), IELTS (minimum score 6). *Application deadline:* For fall admission, 8/1 priority date for domestic students, 6/1 for international students; for spring admission, 12/1 priority date for domestic students, 10/1 for international students. Applications are processed on a rolling basis. Application fee: $35. Electronic applications accepted. *Expenses:* Tuition, state resident: full-time $5404; part-time $300 per credit hour. Tuition, nonresident: full-time $16,702; part-time $928 per credit hour. Required fees: $1150; $130 per credit hour. *Financial support:* In 2009–10, 5 research assistantships with full and partial tuition reimbursements (averaging $5,500 per year) were awarded; career-related internships or fieldwork, scholarships/grants, and unspecified assistantships also available. Support available to part-time students. *Faculty research:* Plant layout design, lean manufacturing, six sigma, value management, product development. *Unit head:* Dr. Neslihan Alp, Director, 423-425-4032, Fax: 423-425-5229, E-mail: neslihan-alp@utc.edu. *Application contact:* Dr. Stephanie Bellar, Dean of Graduate Studies, 423-425-4666, Fax: 423-425-5223, E-mail: stephanie-bellar@utc.edu.

The University of Tennessee Space Institute, Graduate Programs, Program in Industrial Engineering (Engineering Management), Tullahoma, TN 37388-9700. Offers engineering

Engineering Management

The University of Tennessee Space Institute (continued)
management (MS, PhD). Part-time programs available. Postbaccalaureate distance learning degree programs offered (no on-campus study). *Faculty:* 2 full-time (1 woman), 7 part-time/adjunct (0 women). *Students:* 5 full-time (2 women), 51 part-time (14 women); includes 10 minority (7 African Americans, 3 American Indian/Alaska Native). 10 applicants, 70% accepted, 5 enrolled. In 2009, 7 master's awarded. *Degree requirements:* For master's, thesis (for some programs). *Entrance requirements:* Additional exam requirements/recommendations for international students: Required—TOEFL (minimum score 550 paper-based; 213 computer-based), IELTS (minimum score 6.5). *Application deadline:* For fall admission, 2/1 for international students; for spring admission, 6/15 for international students. Applications are processed on a rolling basis. Application fee: $35. Electronic applications accepted. *Expenses:* Tuition, state resident: full-time $6826; part-time $380 per hour. Tuition, nonresident: full-time $20,622; part-time $1147 per hour. Required fees: $10 per hour. One-time fee: $90 full-time. *Financial support:* In 2009–10, 2 research assistantships with full tuition reimbursements (averaging $17,791 per year) were awarded; fellowships, career-related internships or fieldwork, Federal Work-Study, institutionally sponsored loans, health care benefits, tuition waivers (full and partial), and unspecified assistantships also available. Financial award applicants required to submit FAFSA. *Unit head:* Dr. Greg Sedrick, Degree Program Chairman, 931-393-7293, Fax: 931-393-7201, E-mail: gsedrick@utsi.edu. *Application contact:* Dee Merriman, Coordinator III, 931-393-7293, Fax: 931-393-7201, E-mail: dmerrima@utsi.edu.

University of Waterloo, Graduate Studies, Faculty of Engineering, Department of Management Sciences, Waterloo, ON N2L 3G1, Canada. Offers applied operations research (MA Sc, MMS, PhD); information systems (MA Sc, MMS, PhD); management of technology (MA Sc, MMS, PhD). Part-time programs available. Postbaccalaureate distance learning degree programs offered (no on-campus study). *Degree requirements:* For master's, research paper or thesis; for doctorate, comprehensive exam, thesis/dissertation. *Entrance requirements:* For master's, GMAT or GRE, honors degree, minimum B average, resume; for doctorate, GMAT or GRE, master's degree, minimum A- average, resumé. Additional exam requirements/recommendations for international students: Required—TOEFL, TWE. *Faculty research:* Operations research, manufacturing systems, scheduling, information systems.

University of Wisconsin–Madison, Graduate School, Wisconsin School of Business, Wisconsin Full-Time MBA Program, Madison, WI 53706-1380. Offers applied corporate finance (MBA); applied security analysis (MBA); arts administration (MBA); brand and product management (MBA); entrepreneurial management (MBA); marketing research (MBA); operations and technology management (MBA); real estate (MBA); risk management and insurance (MBA); strategic human resource management (MBA); strategic management in the life and engineering sciences (MBA); supply chain management (MBA). *Faculty:* 32 full-time (5 women). *Students:* 242 full-time (74 women); includes 47 minority (16 African Americans, 3 American Indian/Alaska Native, 16 Asian Americans or Pacific Islanders, 12 Hispanic Americans), 29 international. Average age 28. 526 applicants, 32% accepted, 117 enrolled. In 2009, 106 master's awarded. *Entrance requirements:* For master's, GMAT, bachelor's or equivalent degree, 2 years of work experience, letters of recommendation. Additional exam requirements/recommendations for international students: Required—TOEFL (minimum score 600 paper-based; 250 computer-based; 100 iBT), IELTS. *Application deadline:* For fall admission, 11/4 for domestic and international students; for winter admission, 2/5 for domestic and international students; for spring admission, 5/26 for domestic students, 4/5 for international students. Applications are processed on a rolling basis. Application fee: $56. Electronic applications accepted. *Expenses:* Tuition, state resident: part-time $594 per credit. Tuition, nonresident: part-time $1504 per credit. Required fees: $65 per credit. Tuition and fees vary according to course load, program and reciprocity agreements. *Financial support:* In 2009–10, 103 students received support, including 13 fellowships with full and partial tuition reimbursements available (averaging $15,000 per year), 53 research assistantships with full tuition reimbursements available (averaging $8,000 per year), 35 teaching assistantships with full tuition reimbursements available (averaging $11,000 per year); scholarships/grants, health care benefits, and unspecified assistantships also available. Financial award application deadline: 4/5; financial award applicants required to submit FAFSA. *Unit head:* Prof. Kenneth A. Kavajecz, Associate Dean of Master's Programs, 608-265-3494, Fax: 608-265-4192, E-mail: kkavajecz@bus.wisc.edu. *Application contact:* Maria Reis, Assistant Director of MBA Marketing and Recruiting, 608-262-4000, Fax: 608-265-4192, E-mail: mreis@bus.wisc.edu.

University of Wisconsin–Milwaukee, Graduate School, College of Engineering and Applied Science, Program in Engineering, Milwaukee, WI 53201-0413. Offers civil engineering (MS); electrical and computer engineering (MS); energy engineering (Certificate); engineering (PhD); engineering management (MS); engineering mechanics (MS); ergonomics (Certificate); industrial and management engineering (MS); manufacturing engineering (MS); materials engineering (MS); mechanical engineering (MS); MUP/MS. Part-time programs available. *Faculty:* 44 full-time (6 women). *Students:* 119 full-time (22 women), 130 part-time (22 women); includes 23 minority (2 African Americans, 14 Asian Americans or Pacific Islanders, 7 Hispanic Americans), 126 international. Average age 32. 231 applicants, 67% accepted, 33 enrolled. In 2009, 29 master's, 14 doctorates awarded. *Degree requirements:* For master's, comprehensive exam (for some programs), thesis or alternative; for doctorate, comprehensive exam, thesis/dissertation, internship. *Entrance requirements:* For master's, GRE, minimum GPA of 2.75; for doctorate, GRE, minimum GPA of 3.5. Additional exam requirements/recommendations for international students: Required—TOEFL (minimum score 550 paper-based; 79 iBT), IELTS (minimum score 6.5). *Application deadline:* For fall admission, 1/1 priority date for domestic students; for spring admission, 9/1 for domestic students. Applications are processed on a rolling basis. Application fee: $45 ($75 for international students). *Expenses:* Tuition, state resident: full-time $8800. Tuition, nonresident: full-time $20,760. Tuition and fees vary according to program and reciprocity agreements. *Financial support:* In 2009–10, 18 research assistantships, 51 teaching assistantships were awarded; fellowships, career-related internships or fieldwork, Federal Work-Study, and unspecified assistantships also available. Support available to part-time students. Financial award application deadline: 4/15. Total annual research expenditures: $2.9 million. *Unit head:* David Yu, Head, 414-229-6169, E-mail: yu@uwm.edu. *Application contact:* Betty Warras, General Information Contact, 414-229-4982, Fax: 414-229-6967, E-mail: bwarras@uwm.edu.

Valparaiso University, Graduate School, College of Business Administration, Valparaiso, IN 46383. Offers business administration (MBA); engineering management (MEM); management (Certificate); JD/MBA; MSN/MBA. *Accreditation:* AACSB. Part-time and evening/weekend programs available. *Faculty:* 15 part-time/adjunct (5 women). *Students:* 21 full-time (6 women), 46 part-time (15 women); includes 7 minority (3 African Americans, 1 Asian American or Pacific Islander, 3 Hispanic Americans), 9 international. Average age 28. In 2009, 29 master's, 6 other advanced degrees awarded. *Entrance requirements:* For master's, GMAT, GRE, minimum GPA of 3.0. Additional exam requirements/recommendations for international students: Required—TOEFL (minimum score 550 paper-based; 213 computer-based; 80 iBT). *Application deadline:* Applications are processed on a rolling basis. Application fee: $30 ($50 for international students). Electronic applications accepted. *Expenses:* Contact institution. *Financial support:* Available to part-time students. Applicants required to submit FAFSA. *Unit head:* Bruce MacLean, Director of Graduate Programs in Management, 219-464-6600, Fax: 219-464-5789, E-mail: bruce.maclean@valpo.edu. *Application contact:* Cindy Scanlan, Assistant Director of Graduate Programs in Management, 219-465-7965, Fax: 219-464-5789, E-mail: cindy.scanlan@valpo.edu.

Virginia Polytechnic Institute and State University, Graduate School, College of Engineering, Department of Industrial and Systems Engineering, Blacksburg, VA 24061. Offers engineering administration (MEA); industrial engineering (M Eng, MS, PhD); operations research (M Eng, MS, PhD); systems engineering (M Eng, MS). *Entrance requirements:* For master's and doctorate, GRE. Additional exam requirements/recommendations for international students: Required—TOEFL (minimum score 550 paper-based; 213 computer-based). Electronic applications accepted.

Virginia Polytechnic Institute and State University, VT Online, Blacksburg, VA 24061. Offers aerospace engineering (MS); business information systems (Graduate Certificate); career and technical education (MS); computer engineering (M Eng, MS); decision support systems (Graduate Certificate); eLearning leadership (MA); electrical engineering (M Eng, MS); engineering administration (MEA); environmental politics and policy (Graduate Certificate); foundations of political analysis (Graduate Certificate); health product risk management (Graduate Certificate); information policy and society (Graduate Certificate); information security (Graduate Certificate); instructional technology (MA); liberal arts (Graduate Certificate); life sciences: health product risk management (MS); natural resources (MNR, Graduate Certificate); networking (Graduate Certificate); nonprofit and nongovernmental organization management (Graduate Certificate); ocean engineering (MS); political science (MA); security studies (Graduate Certificate); software development (Graduate Certificate).

Walden University, Graduate Programs, NTU School of Engineering and Applied Science, Minneapolis, MN 55401. Offers competitive product management (Postbaccalaureate Certificate); engineering management (Postbaccalaureate Certificate); software engineering (MS); software project management (Postbaccalaureate Certificate); software testing (Postbaccalaureate Certificate); systems engineering (MS, Postbaccalaureate Certificate); technical project management (Postbaccalaureate Certificate). Part-time and evening/weekend programs available. Postbaccalaureate distance learning degree programs offered (no on-campus study). *Faculty:* 31 part-time/adjunct. *Students:* 22 full-time (6 women), 120 part-time (14 women); includes 26 minority (19 African Americans, 7 Asian Americans or Pacific Islanders). Average age 38. In 2009, 41 master's awarded. *Degree requirements:* For master's, thesis optional. *Entrance requirements:* For master's, bachelor's degree or equivalent in related field, minimum GPA of 2.5. Additional exam requirements/recommendations for international students: Required—TOEFL (minimum score 550 paper-based; 213 computer-based), IELTS (minimum score 6.5), or Michigan English Language Assessment Battery (minimum score 82). *Application deadline:* Applications are processed on a rolling basis. Application fee: $50. Electronic applications accepted. *Expenses:* Tuition: Full-time $13,665; part-time $560 per credit. Required fees: $1375. Tuition and fees vary according to course load, degree level and program. *Financial support:* Fellowships, Federal Work-Study, scholarships/grants, unspecified assistantships, and family tuition reduction, active duty/veteran tuition reduction, group tuition reduction, interest-free payment plans available. Support available to part-time students. Financial award applicants required to submit FAFSA. *Unit head:* Colin Wightman, Interim Associate Dean, 800-925-3368. *Application contact:* Jennifer Hall, Director of Enrollment, 866-4-WALDEN, E-mail: info@walden.edu.

Walden University, Graduate Programs, School of Management, Minneapolis, MN 55401. Offers applied management and decision sciences (PhD), including accounting, engineering management, finance, general applied management and decision sciences, information systems management, knowledge management, leadership and organizational change, learning management, operations research, self-designed program in applied management and design sciences; business information management (MISM); enterprise information security (MISM); entrepreneurship (MBA, DBA); finance (MBA, DBA); global supply chain management (DBA); healthcare management (MBA); healthcare system improvement (MBA); human resource management (MBA); information systems management (DBA); international business (MBA, DBA); IT strategy and governance (MISM); leadership (MBA, MS, DBA), including entrepreneurship (MS), general management (MS), human resources leadership (MS), innovation and technology (MS), leader development (MS), project management (MS), self-designed (MS), sustainable futures (MS); managing global software and service supply chains (MISM); marketing (MBA, DBA); project management (MBA, MS); risk management (MBA); self-designed (MBA, DBA); social impact management (DBA); sustainable futures (MBA); technology (MBA); technology entrepreneurship (DBA). Part-time and evening/weekend programs available. Postbaccalaureate distance learning degree programs offered (minimal on-campus study). *Faculty:* 17 full-time, 211 part-time/adjunct. *Students:* 3,389 full-time (1,774 women), 815 part-time (482 women); includes 1,969 minority (1,640 African Americans, 36 American Indian/Alaska Native, 123 Asian Americans or Pacific Islanders, 170 Hispanic Americans), 95 international. Average age 41. In 2009, 699 master's, 42 doctorates awarded. *Degree requirements:* For doctorate, thesis/dissertation (for some programs), residency. *Entrance requirements:* For master's, bachelor's degree or equivalent in related field; minimum GPA of 2.5; official transcripts; goal statement; access to computer and Internet; for doctorate, master's degree or equivalent in related field; minimum GPA of 3.0; 3 years of related professional/academic experience (preferred). Additional exam requirements/recommendations for international students: Required—TOEFL (minimum score 550 paper-based; 213 computer-based), IELTS (minimum score 6.5), TOEFL, IELTS, or Michigan English Language Assessment Battery (minimum score 82). *Application deadline:* Applications are processed on a rolling basis. Application fee: $50. Electronic applications accepted. *Expenses:* Tuition: Full-time $13,665; part-time $560 per credit. Required fees: $1375. Tuition and fees vary according to course load, degree level and program. *Financial support:* In 2009–10, 466 students received support; fellowships, Federal Work-Study, scholarships/grants, unspecified assistantships, and family tuition reduction, active duty/veteran tuition reduction, group tuition reduction, interest-free payment plans available. Support available to part-time students. Financial award applicants required to submit FAFSA. *Unit head:* William Schulz, Interim Associate Dean, 800-925-3368. *Application contact:* Jennifer Hall, Director of Enrollment, 866-4-WALDEN, E-mail: info@waldenu.edu.

Washington State University Spokane, Graduate Programs, Program in Engineering Management, Spokane, WA 99210. Offers METM. *Faculty:* 6. *Students:* 19 full-time (7 women). *Degree requirements:* For master's, comprehensive exam (for some programs), thesis (for some programs), project. *Entrance requirements:* For master's, GMAT, minimum GPA of 3.0, 3 letters of recommendation, resume. *Application deadline:* For fall admission, 1/10 priority date for domestic students, 1/10 for international students; for spring admission, 7/1 priority date for domestic students, 7/1 for international students. Application fee: $50. *Expenses:* Tuition, state resident: part-time $423 per credit. Tuition, nonresident: part-time $1032 per credit. *Financial support:* Application deadline: 4/1. *Faculty research:* Operations research for decision analysis quality control and liability, analytical techniques to formulating decisions. *Unit head:* Dr. Hal Rumsey, Program Director, 509-358-7936, E-mail: rumsey@wsu.edu. *Application contact:* Graduate School Admissions, 800-GRADWSU, Fax: 509-335-1949, E-mail: gradsch@wsu.edu.

Wayne State University, College of Engineering, Department of Industrial and Manufacturing Engineering, Program in Engineering Management, Detroit, MI 48202. Offers MS. *Degree requirements:* For master's, thesis optional. *Entrance requirements:* For master's, GRE (if baccalaureate if not from an ABET accredited institution), minimum undergraduate GPA of 2.8; 3 years experience as an engineer or technical leader. Additional exam requirements/recommendations for international students: Required—TOEFL (minimum score 550 paper-based; 213 computer-based); Recommended—TWE (minimum score 6). Electronic applications accepted. *Faculty research:* Technology and change management, quality/reliability, manufacturing systems/infrastructure.

Webster University, College of Arts and Sciences, Department of Biological Sciences, Program in Professional Science Management and Leadership, St. Louis, MO 63119-3194. Offers MA. *Entrance requirements:* Additional exam requirements/recommendations for international students: Required—TOEFL. *Expenses:* Tuition: Part-time $565 per credit hour. Tuition and fees vary according to degree level, campus/location and program.

Western Michigan University, Graduate College, College of Engineering and Applied Sciences, Department of Industrial and Manufacturing Engineering, Program in Engineering Management, Kalamazoo, MI 49008. Offers MS. *Entrance requirements:* For master's, minimum GPA of 3.0.

Widener University, Graduate Programs in Engineering, Program in Engineering Management, Chester, PA 19013-5792. Offers M Eng. Part-time and evening/weekend programs available. *Students:* 3 full-time (0 women), 3 part-time (0 women); includes 1 minority (American Indian/Alaska Native), 3 international. Average age 26. In 2009, 1 master's awarded. *Degree* *requirements:* For master's, thesis optional. *Application deadline:* For fall admission, 8/1 priority date for domestic students; for spring admission, 12/1 for domestic students. Applications are processed on a rolling basis. Application fee: $25 ($300 for international students). *Financial support:* Application deadline: 3/15. *Unit head:* Nora J. Kogut, Assistant Dean,

610-499-4037, Fax: 610-499-4059, E-mail: njkogut@widener.edu. *Application contact:* Christine M. Weist, Assistant to Associate Provost for Graduate Studies, 610-499-4351, Fax: 610-499-4277, E-mail: christine.m.weist@widener.edu.

Ergonomics and Human Factors

Bentley University, McCallum Graduate School of Business, Program in Human Factors in Information Design, Waltham, MA 02452-4705. Offers MSHFID. Part-time and evening/weekend programs available. Postbaccalaureate distance learning degree programs offered (minimal on-campus study). *Faculty:* 65 full-time (24 women), 16 part-time/adjunct (6 women). *Students:* 15 full-time (9 women), 64 part-time (39 women); includes 9 minority (2 African Americans, 4 Asian Americans or Pacific Islanders, 3 Hispanic Americans), 5 international. Average age 34. 50 applicants, 84% accepted, 34 enrolled. *Entrance requirements:* For master's, GMAT or GRE General Test. Additional exam requirements/recommendations for international students: Required—TOEFL (minimum score 600 paper-based; 250 computer-based; 100 iBT) or IELTS (minimum score 7). *Application deadline:* For fall admission, 12/1 priority date for domestic and international students; for spring admission, 10/1 priority date for domestic and international students. Application fee: $50. Electronic applications accepted. *Expenses:* Tuition: Full-time $26,208; part-time $1092 per credit. Required fees: $404. *Financial support:* Application deadline: 6/1; *Faculty research:* Usability engineering, product usability, human-computer interaction, project management, user experience. *Unit head:* Dr. William Gribbons, Director, 781-891-2926, E-mail: wgribbons@bentley.edu. *Application contact:* Sharon Hill, Director of Graduate Admissions, 781-891-2108, Fax: 781-891-2464, E-mail: bentleygraduateadmissions@bentley.edu.

California State University, Long Beach, Graduate Studies, College of Liberal Arts, Department of Psychology, Long Beach, CA 90840. Offers human factors (MS); industrial/organizational psychology (MS); psychology (MA). Part-time and evening/weekend programs available. *Faculty:* 14 full-time (3 women), 4 part-time/adjunct (2 women). *Students:* 41 full-time (30 women), 19 part-time (12 women); includes 23 minority (5 African Americans, 8 Asian Americans or Pacific Islanders, 10 Hispanic Americans). Average age 26. 161 applicants, 25% accepted, 34 enrolled. *Degree requirements:* For master's, comprehensive exam, thesis. *Entrance requirements:* For master's, GRE General Test, GRE Subject Test. *Application deadline:* For fall admission, 3/1 for domestic students. Applications are processed on a rolling basis. Application fee: $55. Electronic applications accepted. *Expenses:* Required fees: $1802 per semester. Part-time tuition and fees vary according to course load. *Financial support:* Federal Work-Study, institutionally sponsored loans, and scholarships/grants available. Financial award application deadline: 3/2. *Faculty research:* Physiological psychology, social and personality psychology, community-clinical psychology, industrial-organizational psychology, developmental psychology. *Unit head:* Dr. Kenneth Green, Chair, 562-985-5049, Fax: 562-985-8004, E-mail: kgreen@csulb.edu. *Application contact:* Dr. Kenneth Green, Chair, 562-985-5049, Fax: 562-985-8004, E-mail: kgreen@csulb.edu.

California State University, Northridge, Graduate Studies, College of Social and Behavioral Sciences, Department of Psychology, Northridge, CA 91330. Offers clinical psychology (MA); general-experimental psychology (MA); human factors and applied experimental psychology (MA). *Faculty:* 27 full-time (16 women), 19 part-time/adjunct (8 women). *Students:* 67 full-time (42 women), 25 part-time (19 women); includes 33 minority (2 African Americans, 9 Asian Americans or Pacific Islanders, 22 Hispanic Americans), 4 international. Average age 27. 173 applicants, 19% accepted, 29 enrolled. In 2009, 18 master's awarded. *Degree requirements:* For master's, thesis. *Entrance requirements:* For master's, GRE General Test, GRE Subject Test, minimum GPA of 3.0, letters of recommendation. Additional exam requirements/recommendations for international students: Required—TOEFL. *Application deadline:* For fall admission, 11/30 for domestic students. Application fee: $55. *Financial support:* Application deadline: 3/1. *Unit head:* Dr. Carrie Saetermoe, Chair, 818-677-3506. *Application contact:* Dr. Carrie Saetermoe, Chair, 818-677-3506.

The Catholic University of America, School of Arts and Sciences, Department of Psychology, Washington, DC 20064. Offers applied experimental psychology (PhD); clinical psychology (PhD); general psychology (MA); human factors (MA); MA/JD. *Accreditation:* APA (one or more programs are accredited). Part-time programs available. *Faculty:* 12 full-time (6 women), 3 part-time/adjunct (0 women). *Students:* 40 full-time (25 women), 38 part-time (33 women); includes 14 minority (5 African Americans, 4 Asian Americans or Pacific Islanders, 5 Hispanic Americans), 1 international. Average age 29. 200 applicants, 36% accepted, 25 enrolled. In 2009, 16 master's, 6 doctorates awarded. *Degree requirements:* For master's, comprehensive exam, thesis (for some programs); for doctorate, comprehensive exam, thesis/dissertation. *Entrance requirements:* For master's, GRE General Test, 3 letters of recommendation; for doctorate, GRE General Test, GRE Subject Test, statement of purpose, official copies of academic transcripts, three letters of recommendation. Additional exam requirements/recommendations for international students: Required—TOEFL (minimum score 580 paper-based; 237 computer-based). *Application deadline:* For fall admission, 8/1 priority date for domestic students, 7/15 for international students; for spring admission, 12/1 priority date for domestic students, 10/15 for international students. Applications are processed on a rolling basis. Application fee: $55. Electronic applications accepted. *Expenses:* Tuition: Full-time $31,740; part-time $1245 per credit hour. Required fees: $50; $25 per semester hour. One-time fee: $425. *Financial support:* Fellowships, research assistantships, teaching assistantships, Federal Work-Study, scholarships/grants, tuition waivers (full and partial), and unspecified assistantships available. Financial award application deadline: 2/1; financial award applicants required to submit FAFSA. *Faculty research:* Clinical psychology, applied cognitive science, psychopathology, cognitive neuroscience, psychotherapy. Total annual research expenditures: $409,988. *Unit head:* Dr. Marc M. Sebrechts, Chair, 202-319-5757, Fax: 202-319-6263, E-mail: sebrechts@cua.edu. *Application contact:* Julie Schwing, Director of Graduate Admissions, 202-319-5057, Fax: 202-319-6533, E-mail: cua-admissions@cua.edu.

Clemson University, Graduate School, College of Business and Behavioral Science, Department of Psychology, Program in Human Factors Psychology, Clemson, SC 29634. Offers PhD. *Students:* 13 full-time (6 women), 2 part-time (both women). Average age 28. 25 applicants, 8% accepted, 1 enrolled. *Degree requirements:* For doctorate, thesis/dissertation. *Entrance requirements:* For doctorate, GRE General Test. Additional exam requirements/recommendations for international students: Required—TOEFL. *Application deadline:* For fall admission, 12/15 for domestic students. Applications are processed on a rolling basis. Application fee: $70 ($80 for international students). Electronic applications accepted. *Expenses:* Contact institution. *Financial support:* In 2009–10, 12 students received support, including 6 research assistantships with partial tuition reimbursements available (averaging $14,217 per year), 6 teaching assistantships with partial tuition reimbursements available (averaging $13,417 per year); fellowships with full and partial tuition reimbursements available, career-related internships or fieldwork, institutionally sponsored loans, scholarships/grants, health care benefits, and unspecified assistantships also available. Support available to part-time students. *Unit head:* Dr. Patrick Raymark, Chair, 864-656-4715, Fax: 864-656-0358, E-mail: praymar@clemson.edu. *Application contact:* Dr. Robert Sinclair, 864-656-3931, Fax: 864-656-0358, E-mail: rsincla@clemson.edu.

Cornell University, Graduate School, Graduate Fields of Human Ecology, Field of Design and Environmental Analysis, Ithaca, NY 14853-0001. Offers applied research in human-environment

relations (MS); facilities planning and management (MS); housing and design (MS); human factors and ergonomics (MS); human-environment relations (MS); interior design (MA, MPS). *Faculty:* 14 full-time (6 women). *Students:* 20 full-time (16 women); includes 3 minority (2 Asian Americans or Pacific Islanders, 1 Hispanic American), 2 international. Average age 27. 43 applicants, 30% accepted, 12 enrolled. In 2009, 3 master's awarded. *Degree requirements:* For master's, thesis. *Entrance requirements:* For master's, GRE General Test, portfolio or slides of recent work; bachelor's degree in interior design, architecture or related design discipline; 2 letters of recommendation. Additional exam requirements/recommendations for international students: Required—TOEFL (minimum score 600 paper-based; 250 computer-based; 105 iBT). *Application deadline:* For fall admission, 2/1 priority date for domestic students. Application fee: $70. Electronic applications accepted. *Expenses:* Tuition: Full-time $29,500. Required fees: $70. Full-time tuition and fees vary according to degree level, program and student level. *Financial support:* In 2009–10, 13 students received support, including 1 fellowship with full tuition reimbursement available, 5 teaching assistantships with full tuition reimbursements available; research assistantships with full tuition reimbursements available, institutionally sponsored loans, scholarships/grants, health care benefits, tuition waivers (full and partial), and unspecified assistantships also available. Financial award applicants required to submit FAFSA. *Faculty research:* Facility planning and management, environmental psychology, housing, interior design, ergonomics and human factors. *Unit head:* Director of Graduate Studies, 607-255-2168, Fax: 607-255-0305. *Application contact:* Graduate Field Assistant, 607-255-2168, Fax: 607-255-0305, E-mail: deagrad@cornell.edu.

Embry-Riddle Aeronautical University, Daytona Beach Campus Graduate Program, Department of Human Factors and Systems, Daytona Beach, FL 32114-3900. Offers human factors engineering (MSHFS); systems engineering (MSHFS). Part-time and evening/weekend programs available. *Faculty:* 5 full-time (2 women). *Students:* 35 full-time (18 women), 13 part-time (7 women); includes 8 minority (3 African Americans, 5 Hispanic Americans). Average age 25. 25 applicants, 68% accepted, 14 enrolled. In 2009, 5 master's awarded. *Degree requirements:* For master's, thesis, practicum, qualifying oral exam. *Entrance requirements:* For master's, minimum GPA of 2.5. Additional exam requirements/recommendations for international students: Required—TOEFL (minimum score 550 paper-based; 213 computer-based; 79 iBT). *Application deadline:* For fall admission, 8/1 priority date for domestic students; for spring admission, 12/1 priority date for domestic students. Applications are processed on a rolling basis. Application fee: $50. *Expenses:* Tuition: Full-time $13,740; part-time $1145 per credit hour. *Financial support:* In 2009–10, 21 students received support, including 3 research assistantships with full and partial tuition reimbursements available (averaging $5,400 per year); teaching assistantships with full and partial tuition reimbursements available, career-related internships or fieldwork and unspecified assistantships also available. Financial award application deadline: 4/15; financial award applicants required to submit FAFSA. *Unit head:* Dr. Shawn Doherty, Program Coordinator, 386-226-6249, Fax: 386-226-7050, E-mail: dohertsh@erau.edu. *Application contact:* Keith Deaton, Director, International and Graduate Admissions, 800-388-3728, Fax: 386-226-7070, E-mail: graduate.admissions@erau.edu.

Florida Institute of Technology, Graduate Programs, College of Aeronautics, Melbourne, FL 32901-6975. Offers airport development and management (MSA); applied aviation safety option (MSA); aviation human factors (MS). Part-time and evening/weekend programs available. *Faculty:* 6 full-time (0 women), 2 part-time/adjunct (0 women). *Students:* 22 full-time (6 women), 21 part-time (5 women); includes 1 minority (Asian American or Pacific Islander), 21 international. Average age 27. 34 applicants, 53% accepted, 9 enrolled. In 2009, 8 master's awarded. *Degree requirements:* For master's, thesis (for some programs). *Entrance requirements:* For master's, GRE, minimum GPA of 3.0. Additional exam requirements/recommendations for international students: Required—TOEFL (minimum score 550 paper-based; 213 computer-based; 79 iBT). *Application deadline:* For fall admission, 4/1 for international students; for spring admission, 9/30 for international students. Applications are processed on a rolling basis. Application fee: $50. Electronic applications accepted. *Expenses:* Tuition: Part-time $1015 per credit. Tuition and fees vary according to campus/location and program. *Financial support:* Career-related internships or fieldwork, institutionally sponsored loans, tuition waivers (partial), and tuition remissions available. Support available to part-time students. Financial award application deadline: 3/1; financial award applicants required to submit FAFSA. *Faculty research:* Aircraft cockpit design, medical human factors, operating room human factors, hypobaric chamber operations and effects, aviation professional education. Total annual research expenditures: $49,349. *Unit head:* Dr. Winston E. Scott, Dean, 321-674-8971, Fax: 321-674-7368, E-mail: wscott@fit.edu. *Application contact:* Thomas M. Shea, Director of Graduate Admissions, 321-674-7577, Fax: 321-723-9468, E-mail: tshea@fit.edu.

See Close-Up on page 107.

Georgia Institute of Technology, Graduate Studies and Research, College of Computing, Atlanta, GA 30332-0001. Offers algorithms, combinatorics, and optimization (PhD); computational science and engineering (MS, PhD); computer science (MS, MSCS, PhD); human computer interaction (MSHCI); human-centered computing (PhD); information security (MS). Part-time programs available. Postbaccalaureate distance learning degree programs offered. Terminal master's awarded for partial completion of doctoral program. *Degree requirements:* For master's, thesis optional; for doctorate, comprehensive exam, thesis/dissertation. *Entrance requirements:* For master's, GRE General Test, GRE Subject Test, minimum GPA of 3.0; for doctorate, GRE General Test, GRE Subject Test, minimum GPA of 3.3. Additional exam requirements/recommendations for international students: Required—TOEFL. *Faculty research:* Computer systems, graphics, intelligent systems and artificial intelligence, networks and telecommunications, software engineering.

Georgia Institute of Technology, Graduate Studies and Research, College of Sciences, School of Psychology, Atlanta, GA 30332-0001. Offers human computer interaction (MSHCI); psychology (MS, MS Psy, PhD), including engineering psychology (PhD), experimental psychology (PhD), industrial/organizational psychology (PhD). Terminal master's awarded for partial completion of doctoral program. *Degree requirements:* For master's, thesis; for doctorate, thesis/dissertation. *Entrance requirements:* For master's and doctorate, GRE General Test, GRE Subject Test, minimum GPA of 3.0. Additional exam requirements/recommendations for international students: Required—TOEFL. Electronic applications accepted. *Faculty research:* Experimental, industrial-organizational, and engineering psychology; cognitive aging and processes; leadership; human factors.

Indiana University Bloomington, School of Health, Physical Education and Recreation, Department of Kinesiology, Bloomington, IN 47405-7000. Offers adapted physical education (MS); applied sport science (MS); athletic administration/sport management (MS); athletic training (MS); biomechanics (MS); ergonomics (MS); exercise physiology (MS); fitness management (MS); human performance (PhD); motor learning/control (MS). Part-time programs available. *Faculty:* 28 full-time (11 women). *Students:* 132 full-time (55 women), 37 part-time (7 women); includes 16 minority (13 African Americans, 1 Asian American or Pacific Islander, 2

Ergonomics and Human Factors

Indiana University Bloomington (continued)
Hispanic Americans), 29 international. Average age 28. 179 applicants, 60% accepted, 72 enrolled. In 2009, 59 master's awarded. Terminal master's awarded for partial completion of doctoral program. *Degree requirements:* For master's, thesis optional; for doctorate, variable foreign language requirement, thesis/dissertation. *Entrance requirements:* For master's, GRE General Test, minimum GPA of 2.8; for doctorate, GRE General Test, minimum graduate GPA of 3.5, undergraduate 3.0. *Application deadline:* For fall admission, 1/1 for international students; for spring admission, 9/1 for international students. Applications are processed on a rolling basis. Application fee: $55 ($65 for international students). *Financial support:* In 2009–10, 71 students received support, including 9 fellowships (averaging $1,400 per year), 28 research assistantships with full tuition reimbursements available (averaging $10,131 per year), 38 teaching assistantships with full tuition reimbursements available (averaging $10,390 per year); career-related internships or fieldwork, Federal Work-Study, institutionally sponsored loans, scholarships/grants, tuition waivers (partial), and fee remissions also available. Financial award application deadline: 3/1. *Faculty research:* Exercise physiology and biochemistry, sports biomechanics, human motor control, adaptation of fitness and exercise to special populations. *Unit head:* Dr. Donetta Cothran, Chairperson, 812-855-3114. *Application contact:* Program Office, 812-855-5523, Fax: 812-855-9417, E-mail: kines@indiana.edu.

New York University, Graduate School of Arts and Science, Department of Environmental Medicine, New York, NY 10012-1019. Offers environmental health sciences (MS, PhD), including biostatistics (PhD), environmental hygiene (MS), epidemiology (PhD), ergonomics and biomechanics (PhD), exposure assessment and health effects (PhD), molecular toxicology/carcinogenesis (PhD), toxicology. Part-time programs available. *Faculty:* 26 full-time (7 women). *Students:* 45 full-time (37 women), 15 part-time (8 women); includes 9 minority (3 African Americans, 3 Asian Americans or Pacific Islanders, 3 Hispanic Americans), 23 international. Average age 31. 60 applicants, 48% accepted, 14 enrolled. In 2009, 11 master's, 10 doctorates awarded. Terminal master's awarded for partial completion of doctoral program. *Degree requirements:* For master's, thesis or alternative; for doctorate, one foreign language, thesis/dissertation, oral and written exams. *Entrance requirements:* For master's and doctorate, GRE General Test, GRE Subject Test, minimum GPA of 3.0; bachelor's degree in biological, physical, or engineering science. Additional exam requirements/recommendations for international students: Required—TOEFL. *Application deadline:* For fall admission, 12/12 for domestic students. Application fee: $90. *Expenses:* Tuition: Full-time $30,528; part-time $1272 per credit. Required fees: $2177. *Financial support:* Fellowships with tuition reimbursements, teaching assistantships with tuition reimbursements, career-related internships or fieldwork, Federal Work-Study, institutionally sponsored loans, and health care benefits available. Financial award application deadline: 12/12; financial award applicants required to submit FAFSA. *Unit head:* Dr. Max Costa, Chair, 845-731-3661, Fax: 845-351-4510, E-mail: ehs@env.med.nyu.edu. *Application contact:* Dr. Jerome J. Solomon, Director of Graduate Studies, 845-731-3661, Fax: 845-351-4510, E-mail: ehs@env.med.nyu.edu.

North Carolina State University, Graduate School, College of Humanities and Social Sciences, Department of Psychology, Raleigh, NC 27695. Offers developmental psychology (PhD); ergonomics and experimental psychology (PhD); industrial/organizational psychology (PhD); psychology in the public interest (PhD); school psychology (PhD). *Accreditation:* APA. *Degree requirements:* For doctorate, comprehensive exam, thesis/dissertation. *Entrance requirements:* For doctorate, GRE General Test, GRE Subject Test (industrial/organizational psychology), MAT (recommended), minimum GPA of 3.0 in major. Electronic applications accepted. *Faculty research:* Cognitive and social development (human factors, families, the workplace, community issues and health, aging).

Old Dominion University, College of Sciences, Doctoral Program in Psychology, Norfolk, VA 23529. Offers applied experimental psychology (PhD); human factors psychology (PhD); industrial/organizational psychology (PhD). *Faculty:* 21 full-time (9 women). *Students:* 24 full-time (17 women), 12 part-time (8 women); includes 2 minority (both Hispanic Americans), 1 international. Average age 29. 60 applicants, 15% accepted, 9 enrolled. In 2009, 4 doctorates awarded. *Degree requirements:* For doctorate, thesis/dissertation, candidacy exam. *Entrance requirements:* For doctorate, GRE General Test, GRE Subject Test, 3 recommendation letters. Additional exam requirements/recommendations for international students: Required—TOEFL (minimum score 550 paper-based). *Application deadline:* For winter admission, 1/5 for domestic and international students. Application fee: $40. Electronic applications accepted. *Expenses:* Tuition, state resident: full-time $8112; part-time $338 per credit. Tuition, nonresident: full-time $20,256; part-time $844 per credit. Required fees: $119 per semester. One-time fee: $50. *Financial support:* In 2009–10, 13 students received support, including 2 fellowships with full tuition reimbursements available (averaging $18,000 per year), research assistantships with full tuition reimbursements available (averaging $12,000 per year), 11 teaching assistantships with full tuition reimbursements available (averaging $12,000 per year). Financial award application deadline: 1/15. *Faculty research:* Human factors, industrial psychology, organizational psychology, applied experimental (health, developmental, quantitative). Total annual research expenditures: $493,384. *Unit head:* Dr. Brian Porter, Graduate Program Director, 757-683-4458, Fax: 757-683-5087, E-mail: bporter@odu.edu. *Application contact:* Dr. Brian Porter, Graduate Program Director, 757-683-4458, Fax: 757-683-5087, E-mail: bporter@odu.edu.

Tufts University, School of Engineering, Department of Mechanical Engineering, Medford, MA 02155. Offers human factors (MS); mechanical engineering (ME, MS, PhD). Part-time programs available. *Faculty:* 13 full-time, 5 part-time/adjunct. *Students:* 73 (18 women); includes 13 minority (1 African American, 10 Asian Americans or Pacific Islanders, 2 Hispanic Americans), 17 international. Average age 27. 82 applicants, 71% accepted, 30 enrolled. In 2009, 25 master's, 2 doctorates awarded. Terminal master's awarded for partial completion of doctoral program. *Degree requirements:* For master's, thesis; for doctorate, thesis/dissertation. *Entrance requirements:* For master's and doctorate, GRE General Test. Additional exam requirements/recommendations for international students: Required—TOEFL (minimum score 550 paper-based; 213 computer-based; 80 iBT). *Application deadline:* For fall admission, 1/15 priority date for domestic students, 12/15 for international students; for spring admission, 10/15 for domestic students, 9/15 for international students. Applications are processed on a rolling basis. Application fee: $75. Electronic applications accepted. *Expenses:* Tuition: Full-time $38,096; part-time $3962 per credit. Required fees: $686; $40 per year. Tuition and fees vary according to course level, course load, degree level, program and student level. *Financial support:* Fellowships with full tuition reimbursements, research assistantships with full and partial tuition reimbursements, teaching assistantships with full and partial tuition reimbursements, Federal Work-Study, scholarships/grants, tuition waivers (partial), and unspecified assistantships available. Financial award application deadline: 1/15; financial award applicants required to submit FAFSA. *Unit head:* Richard Wlezien, Chair, 617-627-3239, Fax: 617-627-3058. *Application contact:* Lorin Polidora, Department Administrator, 617-627-3239.

Université de Montréal, Faculty of Medicine, Programs in Ergonomics, Montréal, QC H3C 3J7, Canada. Offers DESS.

Université du Québec à Montréal, Graduate Programs, Program in Ergonomics in Occupational Health and Safety, Montréal, QC H3C 3P8, Canada. Offers Diploma. Part-time programs available. *Entrance requirements:* For degree, appropriate bachelor's degree or equivalent, proficiency in French.

The University of Alabama, Graduate School, College of Human Environmental Sciences, Program in Human Environmental Science, Tuscaloosa, AL 35487. Offers family financial planning and counseling (MS); interactive technology (MS); quality management (MS); restaurant and meeting management (MS); rural community health (MS); sport management (MS). *Students:* 70 full-time (40 women), 99 part-time (45 women); includes 44 minority (42 African Americans, 2 Hispanic Americans), 1 international. Average age 33. 124 applicants, 71% accepted, 71 enrolled. In 2009, 70 degrees awarded. *Degree requirements:* For master's, comprehensive exam. *Entrance requirements:* For master's, GRE (for some specializations), minimum GPA of 3.0. Additional exam requirements/recommendations for international students: Required—TOEFL. *Application deadline:* Applications are processed on a rolling basis. Application fee: $50 ($60 for international students). Electronic applications accepted. *Expenses:* Tuition, state resident: full-time $7000. Tuition, nonresident: full-time $19,200. *Faculty research:* Hospitality management, sports medicine education, technology and education. *Unit head:* Dr. Milla D. Boschung, Dean, 205-348-6250, Fax: 205-348-1786, E-mail: mboschun@ches.ua.edu. *Application contact:* Dr. Stuart Usdan, Associate Dean, 205-348-6150, Fax: 205-348-3789, E-mail: susdan@ches.ua.edu.

University of Central Florida, College of Engineering and Computer Science, Department of Industrial Engineering and Management Systems, Orlando, FL 32816. Offers applied operations research (Certificate); design for usability (Certificate); industrial engineering (MSIE, PhD); industrial ergonomics and safety (Certificate); project engineering (Certificate); quality assurance (Certificate); systems engineering (Certificate); systems simulation for engineers (Certificate); training simulation (Certificate). Part-time and evening/weekend programs available. *Faculty:* 14 full-time (2 women), 9 part-time/adjunct (6 women). *Students:* 108 full-time (22 women), 143 part-time (54 women); includes 76 minority (21 African Americans, 1 American Indian/Alaska Native, 14 Asian Americans or Pacific Islanders, 40 Hispanic Americans), 64 international. Average age 32. 204 applicants, 66% accepted, 88 enrolled. In 2009, 59 master's, 17 doctorates, 14 other advanced degrees awarded. *Degree requirements:* For master's, thesis; for doctorate, thesis/dissertation, departmental qualifying exam, candidacy exam. *Entrance requirements:* For master's, GRE General Test, minimum GPA of 3.0 in last 60 hours of course work; for doctorate, minimum GPA of 3.5 in last 60 hours of course work. Additional exam requirements/recommendations for international students: Required—TOEFL. *Application deadline:* For fall admission, 7/15 priority date for domestic students; for spring admission, 12/1 priority date for domestic students. Application fee: $30. Electronic applications accepted. *Expenses:* Tuition, state resident: part-time $306.31 per credit hour. Tuition, nonresident: part-time $1099.01 per credit hour. Part-time tuition and fees vary according to degree level and program. *Financial support:* In 2009–10, 20 students received support, including 8 fellowships with partial tuition reimbursements available (averaging $7,600 per year), 9 research assistantships with partial tuition reimbursements available (averaging $12,400 per year), 5 teaching assistantships with partial tuition reimbursements available (averaging $13,000 per year); career-related internships or fieldwork, Federal Work-Study, institutionally sponsored loans, tuition waivers (partial), and unspecified assistantships also available. Financial award application deadline: 3/1; financial award applicants required to submit FAFSA. *Unit head:* Dr. Waldemar Karwowski, Chair, E-mail: wkar@mail.ucf.edu. *Application contact:* Dr. Waldemar Karwowski, Chair, E-mail: wkar@mail.ucf.edu.

University of Cincinnati, Graduate School, College of Medicine, Graduate Programs in Biomedical Sciences, Department of Environmental Health, Cincinnati, OH 45221. Offers environmental and industrial hygiene (MS, PhD); environmental and occupational medicine (MS); environmental genetics and molecular toxicology (MS, PhD); epidemiology and biostatistics (MS, PhD); occupational safety and ergonomics (MS, PhD). *Accreditation:* ABET (one or more programs are accredited). Terminal master's awarded for partial completion of doctoral program. *Degree requirements:* For master's, thesis; for doctorate, thesis/dissertation, qualifying exam. *Entrance requirements:* For master's, GRE General Test, bachelor's degree in science; for doctorate, GRE General Test. Additional exam requirements/recommendations for international students: Required—TOEFL (minimum score 600 paper-based; 250 computer-based; 100 iBT). Electronic applications accepted. *Faculty research:* Carcinogens and mutagenesis, pulmonary studies, reproduction and development.

University of Illinois at Urbana–Champaign, Institute of Aviation, Champaign, IL 61820. Offers human factors (MS). *Faculty:* 5 full-time (1 woman). *Students:* 11 full-time (8 women), 6 international. 18 applicants, 28% accepted, 4 enrolled. In 2009, 3 master's awarded. *Entrance requirements:* For master's, GRE, minimum undergraduate GPA of 3.0 for last 60 hours. Additional exam requirements/recommendations for international students: Required—TOEFL. *Application deadline:* Applications are processed on a rolling basis. Application fee: $60 ($75 for international students). Electronic applications accepted. *Financial support:* In 2009–10, 9 research assistantships, 4 teaching assistantships were awarded; fellowships, tuition waivers (full and partial) also available. *Unit head:* Alex Kirlik, Acting Head, 217-244-8972, E-mail: kirlik@illinois.edu. *Application contact:* Peter Vlach, Information Systems Specialist, 217-265-9456, E-mail: pvlach@illinois.edu.

The University of Iowa, Graduate College, College of Engineering, Department of Industrial Engineering, Iowa City, IA 52242-1316. Offers engineering design and manufacturing (MS, PhD); ergonomics (MS, PhD); information and engineering management (MS, PhD); operations research (MS, PhD); quality engineering (MS, PhD). *Faculty:* 6 full-time (0 women). *Students:* 37 full-time (11 women); includes 3 minority (1 African American, 1 Asian American or Pacific Islander, 1 Hispanic American), 11 international. Average age 28. 65 applicants, 18% accepted, 7 enrolled. In 2009, 7 master's, 3 doctorates awarded. *Degree requirements:* For master's, thesis optional, exam; for doctorate, comprehensive exam, thesis/dissertation, final defense exam. *Entrance requirements:* For master's and doctorate, GRE General Test. Additional exam requirements/recommendations for international students: Required—TOEFL (minimum score 550 paper-based; 213 computer-based; 81 iBT). *Application deadline:* For fall admission, 7/15 for domestic students, 4/15 for international students; for spring admission, 12/1 for domestic students, 10/1 for international students. Applications are processed on a rolling basis. Application fee: $60 ($100 for international students). Electronic applications accepted. *Financial support:* In 2009–10, 2 fellowships with partial tuition reimbursements (averaging $30,450 per year), 22 research assistantships with partial tuition reimbursements (averaging $20,000 per year), 5 teaching assistantships with partial tuition reimbursements (averaging $16,630 per year) were awarded; career-related internships or fieldwork, scholarships/grants, and unspecified assistantships also available. Support available to part-time students. Financial award applicants required to submit FAFSA. *Faculty research:* Operations research; informatics; human factors engineering; manufacturing systems; human-machine interaction. Total annual research expenditures: $4.1 million. *Unit head:* Dr. Lea-Der Chen, Departmental Executive Officer, 319-335-5674, Fax: 319-335-5669, E-mail: lea-der-chen@uiowa.edu. *Application contact:* Jennifer Rumping, Secretary, 319-335-5939, Fax: 319-335-5669, E-mail: indeng@engineering.uiowa.edu.

University of Massachusetts Lowell, School of Health and Environment, Department of Work Environment, Lowell, MA 01854-2881. Offers cleaner production and pollution prevention (MS, Sc D); environmental risk assessment (Certificate); epidemiology (MS, Sc D); ergonomics and safety (MS, Sc D); identification and control of ergonomic hazards (Certificate); job stress and healthy job redesign (Certificate); occupational and environmental hygiene (MS, Sc D); radiological health physics and general work environment protection (Certificate); work environment policy (MS, Sc D). *Accreditation:* ABET (one or more programs are accredited). Part-time programs available. Terminal master's awarded for partial completion of doctoral program. *Degree requirements:* For master's, thesis optional; for doctorate, thesis/dissertation. *Entrance requirements:* For master's and doctorate, GRE General Test. Additional exam requirements/recommendations for international students: Required—TOEFL.

University of Miami, Graduate School, College of Engineering, Department of Industrial Engineering, Program in Occupational Ergonomics and Safety, Coral Gables, FL 33124. Offers environmental health and safety (MS); occupational ergonomics and safety (MSOES). Part-time programs available. *Degree requirements:* For master's, thesis optional. *Entrance requirements:* For master's, GRE General Test, minimum GPA of 3.0. Additional exam requirements/recommendations for international students: Required—TOEFL (minimum score 550 paper-based; 213 computer-based). Electronic applications accepted. *Faculty research:* Noise, heat stress, water pollution.

University of Wisconsin–Milwaukee, Graduate School, College of Engineering and Applied Science, Program in Engineering, Milwaukee, WI 53201-0413. Offers civil engineering (MS); electrical and computer engineering (MS); energy engineering (Certificate); engineering (PhD);

engineering management (MS); engineering mechanics (MS); ergonomics (Certificate); industrial and management engineering (MS); manufacturing engineering (MS); materials engineering (MS); mechanical engineering (MS); MUP/MS. Part-time programs available. *Faculty:* 44 full-time (6 women). *Students:* 119 full-time (22 women), 130 part-time (22 women); includes 23 minority (2 African Americans, 14 Asian Americans or Pacific Islanders, 7 Hispanic Americans), 126 international. Average age 32. 231 applicants, 67% accepted, 33 enrolled. In 2009, 29 master's, 14 doctorates awarded. *Degree requirements:* For master's, comprehensive exam (for some programs), thesis or alternative; for doctorate, comprehensive exam, thesis/ dissertation, internship. *Entrance requirements:* For master's, GRE, minimum GPA of 2.75; for doctorate, GRE, minimum GPA of 3.5. Additional exam requirements/recommendations for international students: Required—TOEFL (minimum score 550 paper-based; 79 iBT), IELTS (minimum score 6.5). *Application deadline:* For fall admission, 1/1 priority date for domestic students; for spring admission, 9/1 for domestic students. Applications are processed on a rolling basis. Application fee: $45 ($75 for international students). *Expenses:* Tuition, state resident: full-time $8800. Tuition, nonresident: full-time $20,760. Tuition and fees vary according to program and reciprocity agreements. *Financial support:* In 2009–10, 18 research assistantships, 51 teaching assistantships were awarded; fellowships, career-related internships or fieldwork, Federal Work-Study, and unspecified assistantships also available. Support available to part-time students. Financial award application deadline: 4/15. Total annual research expenditures: $2.9 million. *Unit head:* David Yu, Head, 414-229-6169, E-mail: yu@uwm.edu. *Application contact:* Betty Warras, General Information Contact, 414-229-4982, Fax: 414-229-6967, E-mail: bwarras@uwm.edu.

University of Wisconsin–Milwaukee, Graduate School, College of Health Sciences, Department of Occupational Therapy, Milwaukee, WI 53201-0413. Offers ergonomics (Certificate); occupational therapy (MS); therapeutic recreation (Certificate). *Accreditation:* AOTA. *Faculty:* 7 full-time (3 women). *Students:* 40 full-time (37 women), 3 part-time (all women), 6 international. Average age 25. 19 applicants, 37% accepted, 1 enrolled. In 2009, 38 master's awarded. *Degree requirements:* For master's, thesis or alternative. *Entrance requirements:* Additional exam requirements/recommendations for international students: Required—TOEFL (minimum score 550 paper-based; 79 iBT), IELTS (minimum score 6.5). *Application deadline:* For fall admission, 1/1 priority date for domestic students; for spring admission, 9/1 for domestic students. Applications are processed on a rolling basis. Application fee: $45 ($75 for international students). *Expenses:* Tuition, state resident: full-time $8800. Tuition, nonresident: full-time $20,760. Tuition and fees vary according to program and reciprocity agreements. *Financial support:* Fellowships, research assistantships, teaching assistantships, unspecified assistantships available. Support available to part-time students. Financial award application deadline: 4/15. Total annual research expenditures: $778,000. *Unit head:* Virginia Stoffel, Chair, 414-229-5583, Fax: 414-229-5100, E-mail: stoffelv@uwm.edu. *Application contact:* Virginia Stoffel, Chair, 414-229-5583, Fax: 414-229-5100, E-mail: stoffelv@uwm.edu.

Wright State University, School of Graduate Studies, College of Engineering and Computer Science, Programs in Engineering, Program in Biomedical and Human Factors Engineering, Dayton, OH 45435. Offers biomedical engineering (MSE); human factors engineering (MSE). Part-time programs available. *Degree requirements:* For master's, thesis or course option alternative. *Entrance requirements:* Additional exam requirements/recommendations for international students: Required—TOEFL. *Faculty research:* Medical imaging, functional electrical stimulation, implantable aids, man-machine interfaces, expert systems.

Wright State University, School of Graduate Studies, College of Science and Mathematics, Department of Psychology, Program in Human Factors and Industrial/Organizational Psychology, Dayton, OH 45435. Offers MS, PhD. *Degree requirements:* For master's, thesis; for doctorate, thesis/dissertation.

Management of Technology

Air Force Institute of Technology, Graduate School of Engineering and Management, Department of Operational Sciences, Dayton, OH 45433-7765. Offers logistics management (MS); operations research (MS, PhD); space operations (MS). Part-time programs available. *Degree requirements:* For master's, thesis; for doctorate, thesis/dissertation. *Entrance requirements:* For doctorate, GRE General Test, minimum GPA of 3.0, U.S. citizenship. *Faculty research:* Optimization, simulation, combat modeling and analysis, reliability and maintainability, resource scheduling.

Alliant International University–San Diego, Marshall Goldsmith School of Management, Business and Management Division, San Diego, CA 92131-1799. Offers business administration (MBA); information and technology management (DBA); international business (MIBA, DBA), including finance (DBA), marketing (DBA); strategic business (DBA); sustainable management (MBA); MBA/MA; MBA/PhD. Part-time and evening/weekend programs available. *Degree requirements:* For doctorate, thesis/dissertation. *Entrance requirements:* For master's, GMAT, minimum GPA of 3.0; for doctorate, GMAT, minimum GPA of 3.3. Additional exam requirements/ recommendations for international students: Required—TOEFL (minimum score 550 paper-based; 213 computer-based), TWE (minimum score 5). Electronic applications accepted. *Faculty research:* Consumer behavior, international business, strategic management, information systems.

Athabasca University, Centre for Innovative Management, St. Albert, AB T8N 1B4, Canada. Offers business administration (MBA); information technology management (MBA), including policing concentration; management (GDM); project management (MBA, GDM). Part-time and evening/weekend programs available. Postbaccalaureate distance learning degree programs offered (no on-campus study). *Faculty:* 9 full-time (6 women), 2 part-time/adjunct (0 women). *Students:* 898 part-time. Average age 36. 297 applicants, 33 enrolled. In 2009, 179 master's, 180 other advanced degrees awarded. *Degree requirements:* For master's, thesis or alternative, applied project. *Entrance requirements:* For master's, 3-8 years of managerial experience, 3 years with undergraduate degree, 5 years managerial experience with professional designation, 8-10 years management experience (on exception). *Application deadline:* For fall admission, 6/15 for domestic and international students; for winter admission, 10/15 for domestic and international students; for spring admission, 2/15 for domestic and international students. Applications are processed on a rolling basis. Application fee: $200. Electronic applications accepted. *Expenses:* Contact institution. *Financial support:* Scholarships/grants available. *Faculty research:* Human resources, project management, operations research, information technology management, corporate stewardship, energy management. *Unit head:* Dr. Alexander Kondra, Dean, 780-418-6582, E-mail: alexk@athabascau.ca. *Application contact:* Shannon Oscroft, Receptionist and Customer Service Representative, 780-459-1144, E-mail: shannono@athabascau.ca.

Boston University, Metropolitan College, Department of Administrative Sciences, Boston, MA 02215. Offers banking and financial management (MSM); business continuity in emergency management (MSM); economics development and tourism management (MSAS); electronic commerce, systems, and technology (MSAS); financial economics (MSAS); human resource management (MSM); innovation and technology (MSAS); insurance management (MSM); international market management (MSM); multinational commerce (MSAS); project management (MSM). *Accreditation:* AACSB. Part-time and evening/weekend programs available. Postbaccalaureate distance learning degree programs offered (no on-campus study). *Students:* 123 full-time (48 women), 204 part-time (92 women); includes 31 minority (10 African Americans, 1 American Indian/Alaska Native, 11 Asian Americans or Pacific Islanders, 9 Hispanic Americans), 146 international. Average age 30. In 2009, 154 master's awarded. *Degree requirements:* For master's, thesis optional. *Entrance requirements:* For master's, 1 year of work experience, minimum GPA of 3.0. Additional exam requirements/recommendations for international students: Required—TOEFL (minimum score 560 paper-based; 220 computer-based; 84 iBT). *Application deadline:* Applications are processed on a rolling basis. Application fee: $70. Electronic applications accepted. *Expenses:* Tuition: Full-time $37,910; part-time $1184 per credit hour. Required fees: $386; $40 per semester. Part-time tuition and fees vary according to class time, course level, degree level and program. *Financial support:* In 2009–10, 15 students received support, including 8 research assistantships (averaging $10,000 per year); career-related internships or fieldwork and Federal Work-Study also available. *Faculty research:* International business, innovative process. *Unit head:* Dr. Kip Becker, Chairman, 617-353-3016, E-mail: adminsc@bu.edu. *Application contact:* Lucille Dicker, Administrative Sciences Department, 617-353-3016, E-mail: adminsc@bu.edu.

California Lutheran University, Graduate Studies, School of Business, Thousand Oaks, CA 91360-2787. Offers business (IMBA); entrepreneurship (MBA, Certificate); finance (MBA, Certificate); financial planning (MBA, Certificate); information systems and technology (MS); information technology management (MBA, Certificate); international business (MBA, Certificate); management and organization behavior (MBA); management and organizational behavior (Certificate); marketing (MBA, Certificate). Evening/weekend programs available. Postbaccalaureate distance learning degree programs offered. *Entrance requirements:* For master's, GMAT, interview, minimum GPA of 3.0. *Expenses:* Contact institution.

California State University, Los Angeles, Graduate Studies, College of Engineering, Computer Science, and Technology, Department of Technology, Los Angeles, CA 90032-8530. Offers industrial and technical studies (MA). Part-time and evening/weekend programs available. *Faculty:* 1 full-time (0 women), 1 part-time/adjunct (0 women). *Students:* 10 full-time (1 woman), 23 part-time (3 women); includes 12 minority (1 African American, 5 Asian Americans or Pacific Islanders, 6 Hispanic Americans), 10 international. Average age 33. 7 applicants, 100% accepted, 7 enrolled. In 2009, 7 master's awarded. *Entrance requirements:* For master's, minimum GPA of 2.5. Additional exam requirements/recommendations for international students: Required—TOEFL (minimum score 550 paper-based). *Application deadline:* For fall admission, 5/1 for domestic and international students. Applications are processed on a rolling basis. Application fee: $55. *Financial support:* Federal Work-Study available. Support available to part-time students. Financial award application deadline: 3/1. *Unit head:* Dr. Benjamin Lee, Chair, 323-343-4550, Fax: 323-343-4571, E-mail: blee10@calstatela.edu. *Application contact:* Dr. Cheryl L. Ney, Associate Vice President for Academic Affairs and Dean of Graduate Studies, 323-343-3820, Fax: 323-343-5653, E-mail: cney@cslanet.calstatela.edu.

Cambridge College, School of Management, Cambridge, MA 02138-5304. Offers business negotiation and conflict resolution (M Mgt); general business (M Mgt); health care informatics (M Mgt); health care management (M Mgt); leadership in human and organizational dynamics (M Mgt); non-profit and public organization management (M Mgt); small business development (M Mgt); technology management (M Mgt). Part-time and evening/weekend programs available. *Faculty:* 4 full-time (3 women), 65 part-time/adjunct (32 women). *Students:* 297 full-time (178 women), 234 part-time (155 women); includes 217 minority (122 African Americans, 53 Asian Americans or Pacific Islanders, 42 Hispanic Americans), 135 international. Average age 39. In 2009, 259 master's awarded. *Degree requirements:* For master's, thesis, seminars. *Entrance requirements:* For master's, resume, 2 professional references. Additional exam requirements/ recommendations for international students: Required—TOEFL (minimum score 550 paper-based; 213 computer-based; 79 iBT); Recommended—IELTS (minimum score 6). *Application deadline:* Applications are processed on a rolling basis. Application fee: $30. Electronic applications accepted. *Expenses:* Contact institution. *Financial support:* In 2009–10, 170 students received support. Career-related internships or fieldwork, Federal Work-Study, and scholarships/grants available. Financial award applicants required to submit FAFSA. *Faculty research:* Negotiation, mediation and conflict resolution; leadership; management of diverse organizations; case studies and simulation methodologies for management education, digital as a second language: social networking for digital immigrants. *Unit head:* Dr. Mary Ann Joseph, Acting Dean, 617-873-0227, E-mail: maryann.joseph@cambridgecollege.edu. *Application contact:* Stephen Lyons, Director of Enrollment, Graduate and N.I.T.E. Programs, 617-868-1000, Fax: 617-349-3561, E-mail: stephen.lyons@cambridgecollege.edu.

Capella University, School of Business and Technology, Minneapolis, MN 55402. Offers accounting (MBA), including system design and programming; business (Certificate), including human resource management (MS, PhD, Certificate), information technology management (MS, PhD, Certificate), leadership (MBA, MS, PhD, Certificate); finance (MBA); general business (MBA); health care management (MBA); information technology (MS, Certificate), including general information technology (MS), information security, network architecture and design (MS), professional projects management (Certificate), project management and leadership (MS), system design and development (MS),); information technology management (MBA); marketing (MBA); organization and management (MBA, MS, PhD), including general business (PhD), general organization and management (MBA, MS), human resource management (MS, PhD, Certificate), information technology management (MS, PhD, Certificate), leadership (MBA, MS, PhD, Certificate); project management (MBA). Part-time and evening/weekend programs available. Postbaccalaureate distance learning degree programs offered (minimal on-campus study). Terminal master's awarded for partial completion of doctoral program. *Degree requirements:* For master's, thesis optional, integrative project; for doctorate, comprehensive exam, thesis/dissertation. *Entrance requirements:* Additional exam requirements/ recommendations for international students: Required—TOEFL (minimum score 550 paper-based; 213 computer-based), TWE (minimum score 4). Electronic applications accepted. *Faculty research:* Business policies: strategic, corporate, and financial management; interplay of technological, organizational and social change.

Carleton University, Faculty of Graduate Studies, Faculty of Engineering and Design, Ottawa-Carleton Institute for Electrical Engineering, Department of Systems and Computer Engineering, Program in Technology Innovation Management, Ottawa, ON K1S 5B6, Canada. Offers M Eng, MA Sc. *Degree requirements:* For master's, thesis optional. *Entrance requirements:* For master's, honors degree. Additional exam requirements/recommendations for international students: Required—TOEFL.

Carnegie Mellon University, Mellon College of Science, Department of Chemistry, Pittsburgh, PA 15213-3891. Offers biotechnology and management (MS); chemistry (PhD), including bioinorganic, bioorganic, organic and materials, biophysics and spectroscopy, computational and theoretical, polymer; colloids, polymers and surfaces (MS). Part-time programs available. Terminal master's awarded for partial completion of doctoral program. *Degree requirements:* For doctorate, thesis/dissertation, departmental qualifying and oral exams, teaching experience. *Entrance requirements:* For master's, GRE General Test; for doctorate, GRE General Test, GRE Subject Test. Additional exam requirements/recommendations for international students: Required—TOEFL. Electronic applications accepted. *Faculty research:* Physical and theoretical chemistry, chemical synthesis, biophysical/bioinorganic chemistry.

Management of Technology

Central Connecticut State University, School of Graduate Studies, School of Technology, Department of Manufacturing and Construction Management, New Britain, CT 06050-4010. Offers construction management (MS, Certificate); lean manufacturing and six sigma (Certificate); supply chain and logistics (Certificate); technology management (MS). Part-time and evening/weekend programs available. *Faculty:* 17 full-time (5 women), 25 part-time/adjunct (1 woman). *Students:* 13 full-time (4 women), 66 part-time (9 women); includes 11 minority (4 African Americans, 4 Asian Americans or Pacific Islanders, 3 Hispanic Americans), 4 international. Average age 33. 46 applicants, 50% accepted, 17 enrolled. In 2009, 27 master's, 1 other advanced degree awarded. *Degree requirements:* For master's, comprehensive exam, thesis or alternative; for Certificate, qualifying exam. *Entrance requirements:* For master's, minimum undergraduate GPA of 2.7. Additional exam requirements/recommendations for international students: Required—TOEFL. *Application deadline:* For fall admission, 7/1 for domestic students; for spring admission, 12/1 for domestic students. Applications are processed on a rolling basis. Application fee: $50. Electronic applications accepted. *Expenses:* Tuition, area resident: Full-time $4662; part-time $440 per credit. Tuition, state resident: full-time $6994; part-time $440 per credit. Tuition, nonresident: full-time $12,988; part-time $440 per credit. Required fees: $3606. One-time fee: $62 part-time. *Financial support:* In 2009–10, 5 students received support, including 3 research assistantships; career-related internships or fieldwork, Federal Work-Study, scholarships/grants, and unspecified assistantships also available. Support available to part-time students. Financial award application deadline: 3/1; financial award applicants required to submit FAFSA. *Faculty research:* All aspects of middle management, technical supervision in the workplace. *Unit head:* Dr. Jacob Kovel, Chair, 860-832-1830. *Application contact:* Dr. Jacob Kovel, Chair, 860-832-1830.

Champlain College, Program in Managing Innovation and Information Technology, Burlington, VT 05402-0670. Offers MS. Part-time programs available. Postbaccalaureate distance learning degree programs offered (no on-campus study). *Entrance requirements:* For master's, at least 2 years experience or equivalent demonstrable competencies in a business environment. Additional exam requirements/recommendations for international students: Required—TOEFL. Electronic applications accepted.

City University of Seattle, Graduate Division, School of Management, Bellevue, WA 98005. Offers accounting (Certificate); change leadership (MBA, Certificate); financial management (MBA, Certificate); general management (MBA); general management-Europe (MBA); global leadership (Certificate); global marketing (MBA); individualized study (MBA); information security (MS); information systems (MBA); leadership (MA); marketing (MBA, Certificate); project management (MBA, MS, Certificate); sustainable business (Certificate); technology management (MBA, MS, Certificate). Part-time and evening/weekend programs available. Postbaccalaureate distance learning degree programs offered (no on-campus study). *Entrance requirements:* Additional exam requirements/recommendations for international students: Required—TOEFL (minimum score 540 paper-based; 207 computer-based); Recommended—IELTS. Electronic applications accepted. *Expenses:* Tuition: Full-time $14,760; part-time $615 per credit. Tuition and fees vary according to program.

Coleman University, Program in Business and Technology Management, San Diego, CA 92123. Offers MS. Evening/weekend programs available. Postbaccalaureate distance learning degree programs offered (no on-campus study). *Entrance requirements:* For master's, bachelor's degree, minimum GPA of 3.0. Additional exam requirements/recommendations for international students: Required—TOEFL (minimum score 500 paper-based; 173 computer-based).

Colorado School of Mines, Graduate School, Division of Economics and Business, Golden, CO 80401. Offers engineering and technology management (MS); mineral economics (MS, PhD). Part-time programs available. *Faculty:* 11 full-time (3 women), 6 part-time/adjunct (0 women). *Students:* 110 full-time (25 women), 18 part-time (3 women); includes 13 minority (4 African Americans, 1 American Indian/Alaska Native, 2 Asian Americans or Pacific Islanders, 6 Hispanic Americans), 32 international. Average age 30. 162 applicants, 92% accepted, 73 enrolled. In 2009, 47 master's, 2 doctorates awarded. *Degree requirements:* For master's, thesis (for some programs); for doctorate, comprehensive exam, thesis/dissertation. *Entrance requirements:* For master's and doctorate, GRE General Test. Additional exam requirements/recommendations for international students: Required—TOEFL (minimum score 550 paper-based; 213 computer-based; 80 iBT). *Application deadline:* For fall admission, 1/15 priority date for domestic and international students; for spring admission, 9/1 priority date for domestic and international students. Application fee: $50 ($70 for international students). Electronic applications accepted. *Expenses:* Tuition, state resident: full-time $10,584; part-time $588 per credit hour. Tuition, nonresident: full-time $24,750; part-time $1375 per credit hour. Required fees: $1654; $827.10 per semester. *Financial support:* In 2009–10, 25 students received support, including 3 fellowships with full tuition reimbursements available (averaging $20,000 per year), research assistantships with full tuition reimbursements available (averaging $20,000 per year), 22 teaching assistantships with full tuition reimbursements available (averaging $20,000 per year); scholarships/grants, health care benefits, and unspecified assistantships also available. Financial award application deadline: 1/15; financial award applicants required to submit FAFSA. *Faculty research:* International trade, resource and environmental economics, energy economics, operations research. Total annual research expenditures: $99,841. *Unit head:* Dr. Rod Eggert, Division Head, 303-273-3981, Fax: 303-273-3416, E-mail: reggert@mines.edu. *Application contact:* Kathleen A. Feighny, Administrative Faculty, 303-273-3979, Fax: 303-273-3416, E-mail: kfeighny@mines.edu.

Colorado Technical University Colorado Springs, Graduate Studies, Program in Management, Colorado Springs, CO 80907-3896. Offers accounting (MBA, MSA); business administration (MBA); finance (MBA); human resources management (MBA); logistics/supply chain management (MBA); management (DM); marketing (MBA); mediation and dispute resolution (MBA); operations management (MBA); project management (MBA); technology management (MBA). Part-time and evening/weekend programs available. Postbaccalaureate distance learning degree programs offered. *Degree requirements:* For master's, thesis or alternative; for doctorate, thesis/dissertation. *Entrance requirements:* For doctorate, minimum graduate GPA of 3.0, 5 years of related work experience. *Faculty research:* Sexual harassment, performance evaluation, critical thinking.

Colorado Technical University Denver, Programs in Business Administration and Management, Greenwood Village, CO 80111. Offers accounting (MBA); business administration (MBA); business administration and management (EMBA); finance (MBA); human resource management (MBA); marketing (MBA); mediation and dispute resolution (MBA); operations management (MBA); project management (MBA); technology management (MBA). Part-time and evening/weekend programs available. *Degree requirements:* For master's, thesis or alternative. *Entrance requirements:* For master's, minimum undergraduate GPA of 3.0, resume.

Colorado Technical University Sioux Falls, Programs in Business Administration and Management, Sioux Falls, SD 57108. Offers business administration (MBA); business management (MSM); health science management (MSM); human resources management (MSM); information technology (MSM); organizational leadership (MSM); project management (MBA); technology management (MBA). Evening/weekend programs available. *Degree requirements:* For master's, thesis optional. *Entrance requirements:* For master's, minimum 2 years work experience, resume.

Columbia University, School of Continuing Education, Program in Technology Management, New York, NY 10027. Offers Exec MS. Part-time and evening/weekend programs available. *Faculty:* 1 full-time (0 women), 11 part-time/adjunct (3 women). *Students:* 3 full-time (0 women), 113 part-time (23 women); includes 55 minority (7 African Americans, 41 Asian Americans or Pacific Islanders, 7 Hispanic Americans), 11 international. Average age 37. *Entrance requirements:* For master's, minimum undergraduate GPA of 3.00. Additional exam requirements/recommendations for international students: Required—American Language Program placement test. *Application deadline:* For fall admission, 6/15 for domestic students. Application fee: $50. Electronic applications accepted. *Financial support:* Institutionally sponsored loans available. *Faculty research:* Information systems, management. *Unit head:* Dennis Green, Director, 212-854-7436, E-mail: dg30@columbia.edu. *Application contact:* Bryce Weinert, Admissions Adviser, 212-854-9666, E-mail: sce-apply@columbia.edu.

Dallas Baptist University, College of Business, Business Administration Program, Dallas, TX 75211-9299. Offers accounting (MBA); business communication (MBA); conflict resolution management (MBA); e-business (MBA); entrepreneurship (MBA); finance (MBA); health care management (MBA); international business (MBA); leading the non-profit organization (MBA); management (MBA); management information systems (MBA); marketing (MBA); project management (MBA); technology and engineering management (MBA). *Accreditation:* ACBSP. Part-time and evening/weekend programs available. *Entrance requirements:* For master's, GMAT, minimum GPA of 3.0. Additional exam requirements/recommendations for international students: Required—TOEFL; IELTS. Electronic applications accepted. *Expenses:* Tuition: Full-time $10,674; part-time $593 per credit hour. *Faculty research:* Sports management, services marketing, retailing, strategic management, financial planning/investments.

DePaul University, College of Computing and Digital Media, Chicago, IL 60604. Offers business information technology (MS); computational finance (MS); computer and information sciences (PhD); computer game development (MS); computer graphics and motion technology (MS); computer science (MS); computer, information and network security (MS), including applied technology; digital cinema (MFA, MS), including information technology project management (MS); e-commerce technology (MS); human-computer interaction (MS); information systems (MS); information technology (MA); information technology project management (MS); software engineering (MS); telecommunications systems (MS); JD/MS. Part-time and evening/weekend programs available. Postbaccalaureate distance learning degree programs offered (no on-campus study). *Faculty:* 78 full-time (16 women), 191 part-time/adjunct (51 women). *Students:* 922 full-time (239 women), 887 part-time (209 women); includes 466 minority (193 African Americans, 3 American Indian/Alaska Native, 162 Asian Americans or Pacific Islanders, 108 Hispanic Americans), 276 international. Average age 31. 853 applicants, 67% accepted, 294 enrolled. In 2009, 444 master's, 4 doctorates awarded. *Degree requirements:* For master's, thesis (for some programs); for doctorate, comprehensive exam, thesis/dissertation. *Entrance requirements:* For master's, GRE or GMAT (MS in computational finance only), bachelor's degree; for doctorate, GRE, master's degree in computer science. Additional exam requirements/recommendations for international students: Required—TOEFL (minimum score 550 paper-based; 213 computer-based), IELTS (minimum score 6.5), Pearson Test of English (minimum score 53). *Application deadline:* For fall admission, 8/15 priority date for domestic students, 6/1 priority date for international students; for winter admission, 12/15 priority date for domestic students, 9/15 priority date for international students; for spring admission, 3/1 priority date for domestic students, 12/15 priority date for international students. Applications are processed on a rolling basis. Application fee: $25. Electronic applications accepted. *Expenses:* Contact institution. *Financial support:* In 2009–10, 69 students received support, including 6 fellowships with full tuition reimbursements available (averaging $25,858 per year), 75 teaching assistantships with full and partial tuition reimbursements available (averaging $5,780 per year); research assistantships, Federal Work-Study, scholarships/grants, tuition waivers (full and partial), and unspecified assistantships also available. Support available to part-time students. Financial award application deadline: 4/30; financial award applicants required to submit FAFSA. *Faculty research:* Bioinformatics, visual computing, graphics and animation, high performance and scientific computing, databases. Total annual research expenditures: $790,000. *Unit head:* Dr. David Miller, Dean, 312-362-8381, Fax: 312-362-5185. *Application contact:* Dr. Liz Friedman, Assistant Dean of Student Services, 312-362-5384, Fax: 312-362-5327, E-mail: efriedm2@cdm.depaul.edu.

East Carolina University, Graduate School, College of Technology and Computer Science, Department of Technology Systems, Greenville, NC 27858-4353. Offers computer network professional (Certificate); industrial technology (MS), including computer networking management, digital communications, industrial distribution and logistics, information security, manufacturing, performance improvement, planning; information assurance (Certificate); occupational safety (MS); technology management (PhD); Website developer (Certificate). *Entrance requirements:* For master's and Certificate, GRE General Test or MAT, minimum GPA of 2.5; for doctorate, GRE General Test, related work experience.

Eastern Michigan University, Graduate School, College of Technology, Program in Technology, Ypsilanti, MI 48197. Offers PhD. Part-time and evening/weekend programs available. *Students:* 17 full-time (6 women), 45 part-time (11 women); includes 10 minority (9 African Americans, 1 Asian American or Pacific Islander), 15 international. Average age 41. In 2009, 3 doctorates awarded. *Degree requirements:* For doctorate, comprehensive exam, thesis/dissertation. *Entrance requirements:* For doctorate, GRE. Additional exam requirements/recommendations for international students: Required—TOEFL. *Application deadline:* For fall admission, 2/15 for domestic and international students; for winter admission, 10/15 for domestic and international students. Applications are processed on a rolling basis. Application fee: $35. Tuition and fees vary according to course level. *Financial support:* Fellowships, research assistantships with full and partial tuition reimbursements, teaching assistantships with full and partial tuition reimbursements, career-related internships or fieldwork, Federal Work-Study, institutionally sponsored loans, scholarships/grants, tuition waivers (partial), and unspecified assistantships available. Support available to part-time students. Financial award applicants required to submit FAFSA. *Unit head:* Dr. Morell Boone, Dean, 734-487-0354, Fax: 734-487-0843, E-mail: morell.boone@emich.edu. *Application contact:* Dr. Morell Boone, 734-487-0354, Fax: 734-487-0843, E-mail: morell.boone@emich.edu.

École Polytechnique de Montréal, Graduate Programs, Department of Mathematics and Industrial Engineering, Montréal, QC H3C 3A7, Canada. Offers ergonomy (M Eng, M Sc A, DESS); mathematical method in CA engineering (M Eng, M Sc A, PhD); operational research (M Eng, M Sc A, PhD); production (M Eng, M Sc A); technology management (M Eng, M Sc A). Part-time programs available. *Degree requirements:* For master's, one foreign language, thesis. *Entrance requirements:* For master's, minimum GPA of 2.75. *Faculty research:* Use of computers in organizations.

Embry-Riddle Aeronautical University Worldwide, Worldwide Headquarters, Program in Technical Management, Daytona Beach, FL 32114-3900. Offers MSTM, MSTM/MBAA. Part-time and evening/weekend programs available. Postbaccalaureate distance learning degree programs offered. *Faculty:* 16 full-time (2 women), 28 part-time/adjunct (9 women). *Students:* 77 full-time (12 women), 34 part-time (6 women); includes 29 minority (8 African Americans, 7 Asian Americans or Pacific Islanders, 14 Hispanic Americans). Average age 39. 30 applicants, 80% accepted, 18 enrolled. In 2009, 64 master's awarded. *Degree requirements:* For master's, thesis (for some programs). *Entrance requirements:* For master's, GMAT. *Application deadline:* Applications are processed on a rolling basis. Application fee: $50. Electronic applications accepted. *Financial support:* In 2009–10, 3 students received support. Applicants required to submit FAFSA. *Unit head:* Dr. Kees Rietsema, Chair, 602-750-0685, E-mail: rietsd37@erau.edu. *Application contact:* Linda Dammer, Director of Admissions, 386-226-6910, Fax: 386-226-6984, E-mail: ecinfo@erau.edu.

Fairfield University, School of Engineering, Fairfield, CT 06824-5195. Offers electrical and computer engineering (MS); management of technology (MS); mechanical engineering (MS); software engineering (MS). Part-time and evening/weekend programs available. *Degree requirements:* For master's, thesis, capstone course. *Entrance requirements:* For master's, interview, minimum GPA of 2.8, resume, 2 recommendations. Additional exam requirements/recommendations for international students: Required—TOEFL (minimum score 550 paper-based; 213 computer-based; 80 iBT). Electronic applications accepted. *Expenses:* Contact institution. *Faculty research:* Vehicle dynamics, image processing, multimedia in instruction, thermal packaging, character recognition, photovoltaics and nanotechnology, Web technology.

Fairleigh Dickinson University, College at Florham, Silberman College of Business, Departments of Management, Marketing, and Entrepreneurial Studies, Program in Management, Madison, NJ 07940-1099. Offers evolving technology (Certificate); management (MBA);

MBA/MA. *Students:* 8 full-time (4 women), 32 part-time (15 women), 3 international. Average age 31. 25 applicants, 56% accepted, 8 enrolled. In 2009, 17 master's awarded. *Application deadline:* Applications are processed on a rolling basis. Application fee: $40.

Florida Institute of Technology, Graduate Programs, College of Business, Online Programs, Melbourne, FL 32901-6975. Offers accounting and finance (MBA); healthcare management (MBA); information technology (MS); information technology management (MBA); management (MBA); marketing (MBA); project management (MBA). Part-time and evening/weekend programs available. Postbaccalaureate distance learning degree programs offered (no on-campus study). *Faculty:* 30 part-time/adjunct (6 women). *Students:* 6 full-time (2 women), 875 part-time (387 women); includes 290 minority (194 African Americans, 6 American Indian/Alaska Native, 44 Asian Americans or Pacific Islanders, 46 Hispanic Americans), 32 international. Average age 37. 329 applicants, 64% accepted, 177 enrolled. In 2009, 33 master's awarded. *Entrance requirements:* For master's, GMAT or resume showing 8 years of supervised experience, 2 letters of recommendation, resume, competency in math past college algebra. Additional exam requirements/recommendations for international students: Required—TOEFL (minimum score 550 paper-based; 213 computer-based; 79 iBT). *Application deadline:* For fall admission, 4/1 for international students; for spring admission, 9/30 for international students. Applications are processed on a rolling basis. Application fee: $50. Electronic applications accepted. *Expenses:* Tuition: Part-time $1015 per credit. Tuition and fees vary according to campus/location and program. *Financial support:* Available to part-time students. Application deadline: 3/1. *Unit head:* Dr. Mary S. Bonhomme, Dean, Florida Tech Online/Associate Provost for Online Learning, 321-674-8883, Fax: 321-674-8216, E-mail: bonhomme@fit.edu. *Application contact:* Carolyn Farrior, Director of Graduate Admissions Online Learning and Off Campus Programs, 321-674-7118, Fax: 321-674-8216, E-mail: cfarrior@fit.edu.

George Mason University, School of Management, Program in Technology Management, Fairfax, VA 22030. Offers MS. Evening/weekend programs available. *Faculty:* 80 full-time (26 women), 57 part-time/adjunct (13 women). *Students:* 37 full-time (10 women); includes 3 minority (1 African American, 1 Asian American or Pacific Islander, 1 Hispanic American), 4 international. Average age 40. In 2009, 46 master's awarded. *Entrance requirements:* For master's, GMAT, 2 letters of recommendation, resume. Additional exam requirements/recommendations for international students: Required—TOEFL, IELTS. *Application deadline:* For spring admission, 10/1 for domestic students. Applications are processed on a rolling basis. Application fee: $75. Electronic applications accepted. *Expenses:* Contact institution. *Financial support:* Application deadline: 3/1; *Faculty research:* Leadership careers in technology oriented businesses, achieving success in the technology marketplace, emphasizing technology leadership and management, technology innovation, commercialization, methods and approaches of systems thinking. *Unit head:* Dr. David Kravitz, Chair, 703-993-1781, E-mail: dkravitz@gmu.edu. *Application contact:* Edward Lewis, Director, 703-993-4833, E-mail: elewis9@gmu.edu.

George Mason University, School of Public Policy, Program in Public Policy, Arlington, VA 22201. Offers MPP, PhD. Part-time programs available. *Faculty:* 61 full-time (14 women), 30 part-time/adjunct (4 women). *Students:* 149 full-time, 369 part-time; includes 51 minority (15 African Americans, 17 Asian Americans or Pacific Islanders, 19 Hispanic Americans), 68 international. Average age 31. 410 applicants, 67% accepted, 147 enrolled. In 2009, 105 master's, 14 doctorates awarded. *Degree requirements:* For master's, thesis or alternative; for doctorate, comprehensive exam, thesis/dissertation. *Entrance requirements:* For master's, GRE exam is required only for students seeking merit-based scholarship consideration, minimum GPA of 3.0, resume, 2 letters of recommendation, goals statement; for doctorate, GMAT or GRE General Test, resume, writing sample, 2 letters of recommendation. Additional exam requirements/recommendations for international students: Required—TOEFL. *Application deadline:* For fall admission, 6/1 priority date for domestic students, 5/1 priority date for international students; for spring admission, 12/1 priority date for domestic students, 11/1 priority date for international students. Applications are processed on a rolling basis. Application fee: $60. Electronic applications accepted. *Expenses:* Contact institution. *Financial support:* In 2009–10, 24 research assistantships with full tuition reimbursements (averaging $16,000 per year) were awarded; career-related internships or fieldwork, Federal Work-Study, scholarships/grants, health care benefits, tuition waivers (partial), and unspecified assistantships also available. Support available to part-time students. Financial award application deadline: 3/1; financial award applicants required to submit FAFSA. *Unit head:* Dr. Catherine Rudder, Director of MPP Program, 703-993-8099, E-mail: spp@gmu.edu. *Application contact:* Leslie Metzger Levin, Assistant Dean of Graduate Admissions and Marketing, 703-993-8099, Fax: 703-993-4876, E-mail: lmetzger@gmu.edu.

The George Washington University, School of Business, Department of Information Systems and Technology Management, Washington, DC 20052. Offers information and decision systems (PhD); information systems (MSIST); information systems development (MSIST); information systems management (MBA); information systems project management (MSIST); management information systems (MSIST); management of science, technology, and innovation (MBA, PhD). Programs also offered in Ashburn and Arlington, VA. Part-time and evening/weekend programs available. *Faculty:* 13 full-time (4 women), 3 part-time/adjunct (1 woman). *Students:* 76 full-time (27 women), 160 part-time (50 women); includes 83 minority (30 African Americans, 1 American Indian/Alaska Native, 39 Asian Americans or Pacific Islanders, 13 Hispanic Americans), 35 international. Average age 33. 217 applicants, 72% accepted, 77 enrolled. In 2009, 117 master's, 7 doctorates awarded. *Entrance requirements:* For master's, GMAT. Additional exam requirements/recommendations for international students: Required—TOEFL. *Application deadline:* For fall admission, 4/1 priority date for domestic students; for spring admission, 10/1 for domestic students. Applications are processed on a rolling basis. Application fee: $60. *Financial support:* In 2009–10, 35 students received support; fellowships, teaching assistantships, career-related internships or fieldwork, Federal Work-Study, institutionally sponsored loans, and tuition waivers available. Financial award application deadline: 4/1. *Faculty research:* Expert systems, decision support systems. *Unit head:* Richard G. Donnelly, Chair, 202-994-4364, E-mail: rgd@gwu.edu. *Application contact:* Kristin Williams, Assistant Vice President for Graduate and Special Enrollment Management, 202-994-0467, Fax: 202-994-0371, E-mail: ksw@gwu.edu.

Georgia Institute of Technology, Graduate Studies and Research, College of Management, Program in Business Administration, Atlanta, GA 30332-0001. Offers accounting (MBA); e-commerce (Certificate); engineering entrepreneurship (MBA); entrepreneurship (Certificate); finance (MBA); information technology management (MBA); international business (MBA, Certificate); management of technology (Certificate); marketing (MBA); operations management (MBA); organizational behavior (MBA); strategic management (MBA). *Accreditation:* AACSB.

Georgia Institute of Technology, Graduate Studies and Research, College of Management, Program in Management of Technology, Atlanta, GA 30332-0001. Offers EMBA. Part-time and evening/weekend programs available. *Degree requirements:* For master's, study abroad. *Entrance requirements:* For master's, GMAT, 5 years of professional work experience. Additional exam requirements/recommendations for international students: Required—TOEFL. Electronic applications accepted. *Expenses:* Contact institution. *Faculty research:* Innovation management, technology analysis, operations management.

Golden Gate University, Ageno School of Business, San Francisco, CA 94105-2968. Offers accounting (MBA); business administration (EMBA, MBA, PMBA, DBA); finance (MBA, MS, Certificate); financial planning (MS, Certificate); human resource management (MBA, MS); human resources management (Certificate); information systems (MS); information technology (MBA); information technology management (Certificate); integrated marketing and communications (MS, Certificate); international business (MBA); management (MBA); marketing (MBA, MS, Certificate); operations management (Certificate); psychology (MA, Certificate); public relations (MS, Certificate); JD/MBA. Part-time and evening/weekend programs available. *Faculty:* 16 full-time (4 women), 241 part-time/adjunct (72 women). *Students:* 380 full-time (193 women), 750 part-time (414 women); includes 480 minority (98 African Americans, 2 American Indian/Alaska Native, 298 Asian Americans or Pacific Islanders, 82 Hispanic Americans), 166 international. Average age 33. 681 applicants, 78% accepted, 270 enrolled. In 2009, 550 master's, 13 doctorates awarded. *Degree requirements:* For doctorate, thesis/dissertation. *Entrance requirements:* For master's, GMAT (MBA), minimum GPA of 2.5 (MS). Additional exam requirements/recommendations for international students: Required—TOEFL. *Application deadline:* For fall admission, 5/15 for international students; for winter admission, 1/15 for international students; for spring admission, 9/15 for international students. Applications are processed on a rolling basis. Application fee: $70 ($110 for international students). Electronic applications accepted. *Expenses:* Contact institution. *Financial support:* Career-related internships or fieldwork, Federal Work-Study, institutionally sponsored loans, and scholarships/grants available. Support available to part-time students. Financial award applicants required to submit FAFSA. *Unit head:* Terry Connelly, Dean, 415-442-6519, Fax: 415-442-5369. *Application contact:* Angela Melero, Enrollment Services, 415-442-7800, Fax: 415-442-7807, E-mail: info@ggu.edu.

Harding University, College of Business Administration, Searcy, AR 72149-0001. Offers accounting (MBA); health care management (MBA); information technology management (MBA); international business (MBA); leadership and organizational management (MBA). *Accreditation:* ACBSP. Part-time and evening/weekend programs available. Postbaccalaureate distance learning degree programs offered (no on-campus study). *Faculty:* 27 part-time/adjunct (6 women). *Students:* 105 full-time (46 women), 140 part-time (66 women); includes 31 minority (18 African Americans, 3 American Indian/Alaska Native, 6 Asian Americans or Pacific Islanders, 4 Hispanic Americans), 43 international. Average age 31. 82 applicants, 96% accepted, 66 enrolled. In 2009, 130 master's awarded. *Degree requirements:* For master's, portfolio. *Entrance requirements:* For master's, minimum GPA of 3.0, 2 letters of recommendation, resume. Additional exam requirements/recommendations for international students: Required—TOEFL (minimum score 550 paper-based; 213 computer-based; 80 iBT). *Application deadline:* For fall admission, 8/1 priority date for domestic and international students; for spring admission, 12/1 priority date for domestic and international students. Applications are processed on a rolling basis. Application fee: $35. *Expenses:* Tuition: Full-time $9720; part-time $540 per credit hour. Required fees: $22 per credit hour. Tuition and fees vary according to course load and program. *Financial support:* In 2009–10, 27 students received support. Unspecified assistantships available. Financial award application deadline: 7/30; financial award applicants required to submit FAFSA. *Unit head:* Glen Metheny, Director of Graduate Studies, 501-279-5851, Fax: 501-279-4805, E-mail: gmetheny@harding.edu. *Application contact:* Melanie Kiihnl, Recruiting Manager/Director of Marketing, 501-279-4523, Fax: 501-279-4805, E-mail: mba@harding.edu.

Harrisburg University of Science and Technology, Program in Project Management, Harrisburg, PA 17101. Offers construction services specialization (MS); governmental services specialization (MS); information technology specialization (MS). Part-time and evening/weekend programs available. *Faculty:* 1 full-time (0 women), 3 part-time/adjunct (0 women). *Students:* 1 full-time (0 women), 21 part-time (4 women); includes 5 minority (2 African Americans, 3 Asian Americans or Pacific Islanders), 2 international. Average age 30. 26 applicants, 92% accepted, 22 enrolled. In 2009, 3 master's awarded. *Entrance requirements:* For master's, BS, BBA. Additional exam requirements/recommendations for international students: Required—TOEFL (minimum score 520 paper-based; 200 computer-based; 80 iBT). *Application deadline:* For fall admission, 8/1 priority date for domestic students, 7/1 priority date for international students. Applications are processed on a rolling basis. Application fee: $0. Electronic applications accepted. *Expenses:* Tuition: Full-time $18,000; part-time $650 per semester hour. *Financial support:* In 2009–10, 7 students received support. Scholarships/grants available. Financial award applicants required to submit FAFSA. *Unit head:* Dr. Amjad Umar, Director and Professor, 717-901-5141, Fax: 717-901-3141, E-mail: aumar@harrisburgu.edu. *Application contact:* Julie Cullings, Information Contact, 717-901-5163, Fax: 717-901-3163, E-mail: admissions@harrisburgu.edu.

Harvard University, Graduate School of Arts and Sciences, Program in Information, Technology and Management, Cambridge, MA 02138. Offers PhD. *Expenses:* Tuition: Full-time $33,696. Required fees: $1126. Full-time tuition and fees vary according to program.

Harvard University, Harvard Business School, Doctoral Programs in Management, Boston, MA 02163. Offers accounting and management (DBA); business economics (PhD); health policy management (PhD); management (DBA); marketing (DBA); organizational behavior (PhD); science, technology and management (PhD); strategy (DBA); technology and operations management (DBA). *Degree requirements:* For doctorate, comprehensive exam (for some programs), thesis/dissertation. *Entrance requirements:* For doctorate, GRE General Test or GMAT. Additional exam requirements/recommendations for international students: Required—TOEFL. *Expenses:* Tuition: Full-time $33,696. Required fees: $1126. Full-time tuition and fees vary according to program.

Hodges University, Graduate Programs, Naples, FL 34119. Offers business administration (MBA); computer information technology (MS); criminal justice (MCJ); education (MPS); information systems management (MIS); interdisciplinary (MPS); law (MPS); management (MSM); professional studies (MPS); psychology (MPS); public administration (MPA). Part-time and evening/weekend programs available. Postbaccalaureate distance learning degree programs offered (no on-campus study). *Faculty:* 14 full-time (4 women), 4 part-time/adjunct (3 women). *Students:* 37 full-time (28 women), 217 part-time (142 women); includes 76 minority (35 African Americans, 5 Asian Americans or Pacific Islanders, 36 Hispanic Americans). Average age 36. 92 applicants, 91% accepted, 81 enrolled. In 2009, 92 master's awarded. *Degree requirements:* For master's, comprehensive exam (for some programs), thesis (for some programs). *Entrance requirements:* For master's, in-house entrance exam. *Application deadline:* Applications are processed on a rolling basis. Application fee: $50. Electronic applications accepted. *Expenses:* Tuition: Full-time $16,605; part-time $615 per credit hour. Required fees: $570. *Financial support:* In 2009–10, 200 students received support. Federal Work-Study and scholarships/grants available. Financial award application deadline: 7/9; financial award applicants required to submit FAFSA. *Unit head:* Terry McMahan, President, 239-513-1122, Fax: 239-598-6253, E-mail: tmcmahan@hodges.edu. *Application contact:* Rita Lampus, Vice President of Student Enrollment Management, 239-513-1122, Fax: 239-598-6253, E-mail: rlampus@hodges.edu.

Idaho State University, Office of Graduate Studies, College of Technology, Department of Human Resource Training and Development, Pocatello, ID 83209-8380. Offers MTD. Part-time and evening/weekend programs available. *Faculty:* 2 full-time (1 woman). *Students:* 14 full-time (6 women), 50 part-time (24 women); includes 4 minority (2 American Indian/Alaska Native, 2 Hispanic Americans), 1 international. Average age 42. 2 applicants, 100% accepted, 1 enrolled. In 2009, 22 master's awarded. *Degree requirements:* For master's, comprehensive exam, thesis optional, statistical procedures. *Entrance requirements:* For master's, GRE or MAT, minimum GPA of 3.0 in upper-division courses. Additional exam requirements/recommendations for international students: Required—TOEFL (minimum score 550 paper-based; 213 computer-based; 80 iBT). *Application deadline:* For fall admission, 7/1 for domestic students, 6/1 for international students; for spring admission, 12/1 for domestic students, 11/1 for international students. Applications are processed on a rolling basis. Application fee: $55. Electronic applications accepted. *Expenses:* Tuition, state resident: full-time $3318; part-time $297 per credit hour. Tuition, nonresident: full-time $13,120; part-time $437 per credit hour. Required fees: $2530. Tuition and fees vary according to program. *Financial support:* Teaching assistantships with full and partial tuition reimbursements, career-related internships or fieldwork, Federal Work-Study, institutionally sponsored loans, scholarships/grants, health care benefits, tuition waivers (full and partial), and unspecified assistantships available. Support available to part-time students. Financial award application deadline: 1/1; financial award applicants required to submit FAFSA. *Faculty research:* Learning styles, instructional methodology, leadership administration. *Unit head:* Dr. Robert Croker, Chair, 208-282-2884, Fax: 208-282-4496, E-mail: crocobe@isu.edu. *Application contact:* Debra K. Ronneburg, Director of Admissions and Student Services, 208-282-2622, Fax: 208-282-5195, E-mail: ctech@isu.edu.

Management of Technology

Illinois State University, Graduate School, College of Applied Science and Technology, Department of Technology, Normal, IL 61790-2200. Offers MS. *Degree requirements:* For master's, thesis or alternative. *Entrance requirements:* For master's, GRE General Test, minimum GPA of 2.8. *Faculty research:* National Center for Engineering and Technology Education, Illinois Manufacturing Extension Center Field Office hosting, model for the professional development of K-12 technology education teachers, Illinois State University Illinois Mathematics and Science Partnership, Illinois University council for career and technical education.

Indiana State University, School of Graduate Studies, Program in Technology Management, Terre Haute, IN 47809. Offers PhD. Postbaccalaureate distance learning degree programs offered (minimal on-campus study). *Degree requirements:* For doctorate, thesis/dissertation. *Entrance requirements:* For doctorate, GRE or GMAT, minimum graduate GPA of 3.5, 6000 hours of occupational experience. Electronic applications accepted. *Faculty research:* Production management, quality control, human resource development, construction project management, lean manufacturing.

Instituto Tecnológico y de Estudios Superiores de Monterrey, Campus Central de Veracruz, Graduate Programs, Córdoba, Mexico. Offers administration (MA); administration of information technologies (MTI); computer sciences (MCC); education (MEE); educational institution administration (MAD); educational technology (MTE); electronic commerce (MCE); finance (MAF); humanistic studies (MEH); international business for Latin America (MNL); marketing (MMT); science (MCP); technology management (MTT). Part-time and evening/weekend programs available. Postbaccalaureate distance learning degree programs offered (minimal on-campus study). *Degree requirements:* For master's, thesis (for some programs). *Entrance requirements:* For master's, PAEP College Board. Electronic applications accepted.

Instituto Tecnológico y de Estudios Superiores de Monterrey, Campus Cuernavaca, Programs in Information Science, Temixco, Mexico. Offers administration of information technology (MATI); computer science (MCC, DCC); information technology (MTI).

Instituto Tecnológico y de Estudios Superiores de Monterrey, Campus Irapuato, Graduate Programs, Irapuato, Mexico. Offers administration (MBA); administration of information technology (MAIT); administration of telecommunications (MAT); architecture (M Arch); computer science (MCS); education (M Ed); educational administration (MEA); educational innovation and technology (DEIT); educational technology (MET); electronic commerce (MBA); environmental administration and planning (MEAP); environmental systems (MES); finances (MBA); humanistic studies (MHS); international management for Latin American executives (MIMLAE); library and information science (MLIS); manufacturing quality management (MMQM); marketing research (MBA).

Iona College, Hagan School of Business, Department of Information and Decision Technology Management, New Rochelle, NY 10801-1890. Offers information systems (MBA, PMC). Part-time and evening/weekend programs available. *Faculty:* 5 full-time (0 women), 2 part-time/adjunct (0 women). *Students:* 4 full-time (1 woman), 15 part-time (6 women); includes 3 minority (2 African Americans, 1 Hispanic American). Average age 33. 3 applicants, 33% accepted, 0 enrolled. In 2009, 10 master's awarded. *Entrance requirements:* For master's, GMAT, 2 letters of recommendation; for PMC, GMAT. Additional exam requirements/recommendations for international students: Required—TOEFL (minimum score 550 paper-based; 213 computer-based). *Application deadline:* Applications are processed on a rolling basis. Application fee: $50. Electronic applications accepted. *Expenses:* Contact institution. *Financial support:* Scholarships/grants, tuition waivers (partial), and unspecified assistantships available. Support available to part-time students. Financial award application deadline: 4/15; financial award applicants required to submit FAFSA. *Faculty research:* Fuzzy sets, risk management, computer security, competence set analysis, investment strategies. *Unit head:* Dr. Robert Richardson, Chairman, 914-637-7726, E-mail: rrichardson@iona.edu. *Application contact:* Jude Fleurismond, Director of MBA Admissions, 914-633-2289, Fax: 914-637-2708, E-mail: jfleurismond@iona.edu.

The Johns Hopkins University, Engineering for Professionals, Part-time Program in Technical Management, Baltimore, MD 21218-2699. Offers MS, Graduate Certificate, Post-Master's Certificate. Part-time and evening/weekend programs available. *Faculty:* 37 part-time/adjunct (13 women). *Students:* 3 full-time (1 woman), 138 part-time (34 women); includes 32 minority (19 African Americans, 1 American Indian/Alaska Native, 7 Asian Americans or Pacific Islanders, 5 Hispanic Americans), 6 international. Average age 36. In 2009, 55 master's awarded. *Application deadline:* Applications are processed on a rolling basis. Application fee: $75. Electronic applications accepted. *Financial support:* Institutionally sponsored loans available. *Unit head:* Dr. Joseph J. Suter, Program Chair, 443-778-5826, E-mail: joseph.suter@jhuapl.edu. *Application contact:* Priyanka Dwivedi, Admissions Manager, 410-516-2300, Fax: 410-579-8049, E-mail: pdwived1@jhu.edu.

Jones International University, School of Business, Centennial, CO 80112. Offers accounting (MBA); business communication (MABC); entrepreneurship (MABC, MBA); finance (MBA); global enterprise management (MBA); health care management (MBA); information security management (MBA); information technology management (MBA); leadership and influence (MABC); leading the customer-driven organization (MABC); negotiation and conflict management (MBA); project management (MABC, MBA). Program only offered online. Part-time and evening/weekend programs available. Postbaccalaureate distance learning degree programs offered (no on-campus study). *Degree requirements:* For master's, capstone project. *Entrance requirements:* For master's, minimum cumulative GPA of 2.5. Additional exam requirements/recommendations for international students: Recommended—TOEFL (minimum score 550 paper-based; 213 computer-based). Electronic applications accepted.

La Salle University, School of Arts and Sciences, Program in Information Technology Leadership, Philadelphia, PA 19141-1199. Offers MS.

Lawrence Technological University, College of Management, Southfield, MI 48075-1058. Offers business administration (MBA, DBA); information systems (MS); information technology (DM); operations management (MS). *Accreditation:* ACBSP. Part-time and evening/weekend programs available. *Faculty:* 14 full-time (6 women), 53 part-time/adjunct (14 women). *Students:* 17 full-time (6 women), 565 part-time (234 women); includes 149 minority (103 African Americans, 2 American Indian/Alaska Native, 37 Asian Americans or Pacific Islanders, 7 Hispanic Americans), 96 international. Average age 34. 353 applicants, 58% accepted, 125 enrolled. In 2009, 263 master's, 5 doctorates awarded. *Degree requirements:* For master's, thesis (for some programs). *Entrance requirements:* For master's, GMAT. Additional exam requirements/recommendations for international students: Required—TOEFL (minimum score 550 paper-based; 213 computer-based; 79 iBT). *Application deadline:* For fall admission, 8/1 priority date for domestic students, 6/1 for international students; for winter admission, 12/1 priority date for domestic students, 10/1 for international students; for spring admission, 5/1 priority date for domestic students, 3/1 for international students. Applications are processed on a rolling basis. Application fee: $50. Electronic applications accepted. *Expenses:* Tuition: Full-time $11,320; part-time $798 per credit hour. *Financial support:* Federal Work-Study and institutionally sponsored loans available. Support available to part-time students. Financial award application deadline: 4/1; financial award applicants required to submit FAFSA. *Unit head:* Dr. Lou DeGennaro, Dean, 248-204-3050, E-mail: degennaro@ltu.edu. *Application contact:* Jane Rohrback, Director of Admissions, 248-204-3160, Fax: 248-204-3188, E-mail: admissions@ltu.edu.

Lewis University, College of Business, Graduate School of Management, Program in Business Administration, Romeoville, IL 60446. Offers accounting (MBA); custom elective option (MBA); e-business (MBA); finance (MBA); healthcare management (MBA); human resources management (MBA); information security (MBA); international business (MBA); management information systems (MBA); marketing (MBA); project management (MBA); technology and operations management (MBA). Part-time and evening/weekend programs available. *Faculty:* 15 full-time (2 women), 18 part-time/adjunct (4 women). *Students:* 120 full-time (64 women),

222 part-time (103 women); includes 97 minority (62 African Americans, 4 Asian Americans or Pacific Islanders, 31 Hispanic Americans), 9 international. Average age 31. In 2009, 84 master's awarded. *Entrance requirements:* For master's, interview, bachelor's degree, resume, 2 recommendations. Additional exam requirements/recommendations for international students: Required—TOEFL (minimum score 550 paper-based; 213 computer-based). *Application deadline:* For fall admission, 8/15 priority date for domestic students, 5/1 priority date for international students; for spring admission, 11/15 priority date for international students. Applications are processed on a rolling basis. Application fee: $40. Electronic applications accepted. *Expenses:* Tuition: Full-time $6480; part-time $720 per credit. One-time fee: $40. Tuition and fees vary according to course load, degree level and program. *Financial support:* Career-related internships or fieldwork, Federal Work-Study, scholarships/grants, and unspecified assistantships available. Financial award application deadline: 5/1; financial award applicants required to submit FAFSA. *Unit head:* Dr. Maureen Culleeney, Academic Program Director, 815-838-0500 Ext. 5631, E-mail: culleema@lewisu.edu. *Application contact:* Michele King, Director of Admission, 815-838-0500 Ext. 5384, E-mail: gsm@lewisu.edu.

Marist College, Graduate Programs, School of Computer Science and Mathematics, Poughkeepsie, NY 12601-1387. Offers information systems (MS, Adv C); software development (MS); technology management (MS). Part-time and evening/weekend programs available. Postbaccalaureate distance learning degree programs offered (minimal on-campus study). *Entrance requirements:* For master's, resume. Additional exam requirements/recommendations for international students: Required—TOEFL (minimum score 550 paper-based; 213 computer-based; 80 iBT); Recommended—IELTS (minimum score 6.5). Electronic applications accepted. *Expenses:* Tuition: Full-time $12,510; part-time $695 per credit hour. *Faculty research:* Data quality, artificial intelligence, imaging, analysis of algorithms, distributed systems and applications.

Marist College, Graduate Programs, School of Management and School of Computer Science and Mathematics, Program in Technology Management, Poughkeepsie, NY 12601-1387. Offers MS. Part-time and evening/weekend programs available. Postbaccalaureate distance learning degree programs offered (minimal on-campus study). *Entrance requirements:* For master's, GMAT or GRE, minimum undergraduate GPA of 3.0, 2 letters of recommendation, resume, professional experience. Additional exam requirements/recommendations for international students: Required—TOEFL (minimum score 550 paper-based; 213 computer-based; 80 iBT); Recommended—IELTS (minimum score 6.5). Electronic applications accepted. *Expenses:* Tuition: Full-time $12,510; part-time $695 per credit hour.

Marquette University, Graduate School, College of Engineering, Department of Biomedical Engineering, Milwaukee, WI 53201-1881. Offers bioinstrumentation/computers (MS, PhD); biomechanics/biomaterials (MS, PhD); functional imaging (PhD); healthcare technologies management (MS); systems physiology (MS, PhD). Part-time and evening/weekend programs available. *Faculty:* 16 full-time (6 women), 3 part-time/adjunct (2 women). *Students:* 64 full-time (21 women), 22 part-time (8 women); includes 6 minority (5 Asian Americans or Pacific Islanders, 1 Hispanic American), 33 international. Average age 27. 132 applicants, 45% accepted, 22 enrolled. In 2009, 19 master's, 3 doctorates awarded. Terminal master's awarded for partial completion of doctoral program. *Degree requirements:* For master's, comprehensive exam, thesis; for doctorate, comprehensive exam, thesis/dissertation, dissertation defense, qualifying exam. *Entrance requirements:* For master's and doctorate, GRE General Test, minimum GPA of 3.0. Additional exam requirements/recommendations for international students: Required—TOEFL. *Application deadline:* For fall admission, 2/15 priority date for domestic students; for spring admission, 11/15 priority date for domestic students. Applications are processed on a rolling basis. Application fee: $40. Electronic applications accepted. *Financial support:* In 2009–10, 50 students received support, including 9 fellowships with full tuition reimbursements available (averaging $24,600 per year), 34 research assistantships with full tuition reimbursements available (averaging $14,500 per year), 7 teaching assistantships with full tuition reimbursements available (averaging $12,306 per year); Federal Work-Study, institutionally sponsored loans, and scholarships/grants also available. Support available to part-time students. Financial award application deadline: 2/15. *Faculty research:* Cell and organ physiology, signal processing, gait analysis, orthopedic rehabilitation engineering, telemedicine. *Unit head:* Dr. Kristina Ropella, Chair, 414-288-3375, Fax: 414-288-7938, E-mail: kristina.ropella@marquette.edu. *Application contact:* Dr. Dean Jeutter, Assistant Chair, 414-288-3375, Fax: 414-288-7938, E-mail: dean.jeutter@marquette.edu.

Marshall University, Academic Affairs Division, College of Information Technology and Engineering, Division of Applied Science and Technology, Program in Technology Management, Huntington, WV 25755. Offers MS. Part-time and evening/weekend programs available. *Faculty:* 2 full-time (0 women), 1 part-time/adjunct (0 women). *Students:* 16 full-time (5 women), 30 part-time (7 women); includes 1 minority (Asian American or Pacific Islander), 14 international. Average age 34. In 2009, 6 master's awarded. *Degree requirements:* For master's, final project, oral exam. *Entrance requirements:* For master's, GRE General Test or GMAT, minimum undergraduate GPA of 2.5. Application fee: $40. *Financial support:* Tuition waivers (full) available. Support available to part-time students. Financial award application deadline: 8/1; financial award applicants required to submit FAFSA. *Unit head:* Dr. Tracy Christofero, Program Coordinator, 304-746-2078, E-mail: christofero@marshall.edu. *Application contact:* Information Contact, 304-746-1900, Fax: 304-746-1902, E-mail: services@marshall.edu.

Mercer University, Graduate Studies, Macon Campus, School of Engineering, Macon, GA 31207-0003. Offers biomedical engineering (MSE); computer engineering (MSE); electrical engineering (MSE); engineering management (MSE); environmental engineering (MSE); environmental systems (MS); mechanical engineering (MSE); software engineering (MSE); software systems (MS); technical communications management (MS); technical management (MS). Part-time and evening/weekend programs available. Postbaccalaureate distance learning degree programs offered (no on-campus study). *Faculty:* 19 full-time (4 women), 1 part-time/adjunct (0 women). *Students:* 6 full-time (1 woman), 95 part-time (22 women); includes 22 minority (5 African Americans, 13 Asian Americans or Pacific Islanders, 4 Hispanic Americans), 3 international. Average age 33. In 2009, 42 master's awarded. *Degree requirements:* For master's, thesis or alternative. *Entrance requirements:* For master's, minimum undergraduate GPA of 3.0. Additional exam requirements/recommendations for international students: Required—TOEFL. *Application deadline:* For fall admission, 7/1 for domestic students; for spring admission, 11/15 for domestic students. Applications are processed on a rolling basis. Application fee: $35 ($50 for international students). Electronic applications accepted. *Expenses:* Contact institution. *Financial support:* Federal Work-Study available. *Unit head:* Dr. Wade H. Shaw, Dean, 478-301-2459, Fax: 478-301-5593, E-mail: shaw_wh@mercer.edu. *Application contact:* Greg Lofton, Graduate Program Coordinator, 478-301-5480, Fax: 478-301-5434, E-mail: lofton_g@mercer.edu.

Meritus University, School of Business, Fredericton, NB E3C 2R2, Canada. Offers global management (MBA); health care management (MBA); human resources management (MBA); information technology management (MBA); marketing (MBA); technology management (MBA). Evening/weekend programs available. Postbaccalaureate distance learning degree programs offered (no on-campus study). *Faculty:* 5 full-time (1 woman), 50 part-time/adjunct (15 women). *Students:* 77 full-time (29 women). Average age 35. *Entrance requirements:* For master's, undergraduate degree or comparable equivalent with minimum cumulative GPA of 2.5; minimum equivalent of two years of full-time, post high-school work experience; current employment. Additional exam requirements/recommendations for international students: Required—TOEFL (minimum score 213 computer-based; 79 iBT), IELTS (minimum score 6.5), or TOEIC (minimum score 750) or Berlitz (minimum score 550). *Application deadline:* Applications are processed on a rolling basis. Application fee: $45. Electronic applications accepted. Tuition and fees charges are reported in Canadian dollars. *Expenses:* Tuition: Full-time $14,400 Canadian dollars. Required fees: $720 Canadian dollars. *Unit head:* Dr. Albert K. S. Wong, Program Chair, Business Administration, 604-657-5465, Fax: 602-643-4624, E-mail: albert.wong@staff.meritusu.ca. *Application contact:* Jeremy S. DeMerchant, Enrolment Manager, 506-443-8413, Fax: 602-759-3688, E-mail: jeremy.demerchant@staff.meritusu.ca.

Murray State University, College of Science, Engineering and Technology, Program in Management of Technology, Murray, KY 42071. Offers MS. Part-time and evening/weekend programs available. *Degree requirements:* For master's, comprehensive exam. *Entrance requirements:* Additional exam requirements/recommendations for international students: Required—TOEFL (computer-based 273) or IELTS. *Faculty research:* Environmental, hydrology, groundworks.

National University, Academic Affairs, School of Business and Management, Department of Leadership and Business Administration, La Jolla, CA 92037-1011. Offers alternative dispute resolution (MBA); e-business (MBA); financial management (MBA); human resource management (MBA); human resources management (MA); international business (MBA); knowledge management (MS); marketing (MBA); organizational leadership (MBA, MS); technology management (MBA). Part-time and evening/weekend programs available. Postbaccalaureate distance learning degree programs offered (no on-campus study). *Faculty:* 4 full-time (2 women), 22 part-time/adjunct (9 women). *Students:* 95 full-time (56 women), 228 part-time (129 women); includes 63 African Americans, 24 Asian Americans or Pacific Islanders, 61 Hispanic Americans, 6 international. Average age 38. 191 applicants, 100% accepted, 131 enrolled. In 2009, 62 master's awarded. *Degree requirements:* For master's, thesis. *Entrance requirements:* For master's, interview, minimum GPA of 2.5. Additional exam requirements/recommendations for international students: Required—TOEFL (minimum score 550 paper-based; 213 computer-based; 79 iBT), IELTS (minimum score 6). *Application deadline:* Applications are processed on a rolling basis. Application fee: $60 ($65 for international students). Electronic applications accepted. *Expenses:* Tuition: Part-time $338 per quarter hour. *Financial support:* Career-related internships or fieldwork, institutionally sponsored loans, scholarships/grants, and tuition waivers (partial) available. Support available to part-time students. Financial award application deadline: 6/30; financial award applicants required to submit FAFSA. *Unit head:* Dr. George Drops, Chair and Professor, 858-642-8438, Fax: 858-642-8406, E-mail: gdrops@nu.edu. *Application contact:* Dominick Giovanniello, Associate Regional Dean—San Diego, 800-NAT-UNIV, Fax: 858-541-7792, E-mail: dgiovann@nu.edu.

National University, Academic Affairs, School of Engineering and Technology, Department of Computer Science and Information Systems, La Jolla, CA 92037-1011. Offers computer science (MS); information systems (MS); software engineering (MS); technology management (MS). Part-time and evening/weekend programs available. Postbaccalaureate distance learning degree programs offered (no on-campus study). *Faculty:* 18 full-time (10 women), 30 part-time/adjunct (7 women). *Students:* 88 full-time (19 women), 163 part-time (31 women); includes 57 minority (24 African Americans, 24 Asian Americans or Pacific Islanders, 9 Hispanic Americans), 111 international. Average age 32. 146 applicants, 100% accepted, 89 enrolled. In 2009, 51 master's awarded. *Degree requirements:* For master's, thesis. *Entrance requirements:* For master's, interview, minimum GPA of 2.5. Additional exam requirements/recommendations for international students: Required—TOEFL (minimum score 550 paper-based; 213 computer-based; 79 iBT), IELTS (minimum score 6). *Application deadline:* Applications are processed on a rolling basis. Application fee: $60 ($65 for international students). Electronic applications accepted. *Expenses:* Tuition: Part-time $338 per quarter hour. *Financial support:* Career-related internships or fieldwork, institutionally sponsored loans, scholarships/grants, and tuition waivers (partial) available. Support available to part-time students. Financial award application deadline: 6/30; financial award applicants required to submit FAFSA. *Unit head:* Dr. Ron Uhlig, Interim Chair and Instructor, 858-309-3412, Fax: 858-309-3420, E-mail: ruhlig@nu.edu. *Application contact:* Dominick Giovanniello, Associate Regional Dean—San Diego, 800-NAT-UNIV, Fax: 858-541-7792, E-mail: dgiovann@nu.edu.

New Jersey Institute of Technology, Office of Graduate Studies, School of Management, Program in Management of Technology, Newark, NJ 07102. Offers MS. Part-time and evening/weekend programs available. Terminal master's awarded for partial completion of doctoral program. *Degree requirements:* For master's, thesis optional. *Entrance requirements:* For master's, GMAT. Additional exam requirements/recommendations for international students: Required—TOEFL (minimum score 550 paper-based; 213 computer-based; 79 iBT). Electronic applications accepted.

North Carolina Agricultural and Technical State University, Graduate School, School of Technology, Department of Graphic Communication Systems and Technological Studies, Greensboro, NC 27411. Offers industrial arts education (MS); technology education (MS); technology management (PhD); vocational-industrial education (MS); workforce development director (MS). *Accreditation:* NCATE (one or more programs are accredited). Part-time and evening/weekend programs available. *Degree requirements:* For master's, comprehensive exam, thesis or alternative, qualifying exam. *Entrance requirements:* For master's, GRE General Test, minimum GPA of 3.0.

North Carolina Agricultural and Technical State University, Graduate School, School of Technology, Department of Manufacturing Systems, Greensboro, NC 27411. Offers industrial technology (MS, MSIT); safety and driver education (MS). Part-time and evening/weekend programs available. *Degree requirements:* For master's, comprehensive exam, thesis or alternative, qualifying exam. *Entrance requirements:* For master's, GRE General Test, minimum GPA of 3.0.

North Carolina State University, Graduate School, College of Textiles, Program in Textile Technology Management, Raleigh, NC 27695. Offers PhD. *Degree requirements:* For doctorate, one foreign language, thesis/dissertation, cumulative exams. *Entrance requirements:* For doctorate, GRE or GMAT. Electronic applications accepted. *Faculty research:* Niche markets, supply chain, globalization, logistics.

Northern Kentucky University, Office of Graduate Programs, College of Informatics, Department of Computer Science, Program in Computer Information Technology, Highland Heights, KY 41099. Offers MSCIT. Part-time and evening/weekend programs available. *Students:* 2 full-time (0 women), 16 part-time (5 women); includes 2 minority (1 African American, 1 Asian American or Pacific Islander), 1 international. Average age 35. 31 applicants, 74% accepted. *Degree requirements:* For master's, thesis optional. *Entrance requirements:* For master's, 3.0 gpa, computer science or related undergraduate degree. Additional exam requirements/recommendations for international students: Required—TOEFL (minimum score 550 paper-based; 213 computer-based; 79 iBT); Recommended—IELTS (minimum score 6.5). *Application deadline:* For fall admission, 8/1 priority date for domestic students, 6/1 for international students; for spring admission, 12/1 priority date for domestic students, 10/1 for international students. Applications are processed on a rolling basis. Application fee: $40. Electronic applications accepted. *Expenses:* Tuition, state resident: full-time $6912; part-time $384 per credit hour. Tuition, nonresident: full-time $12,150; part-time $675 per credit hour. Tuition and fees vary according to course load, program and reciprocity agreements. *Financial support:* Scholarships/grants and unspecified assistantships available. Financial award applicants required to submit FAFSA. *Faculty research:* Data privacy, software security, databasesecurity, mobile and wireless networks, network security. *Unit head:* Dr. Traian Marius Truta, Coordinator, 859-572-7551, E-mail: trutat1@nku.edu. *Application contact:* Dr. Peg Griffin, Director of Graduate Programs, 859-572-6934, Fax: 859-572-6670, E-mail: griffinp@nku.edu.

OGI School of Science & Engineering at Oregon Health & Science University, Graduate Studies, Department of Management in Science and Technology, Beaverton, OR 97006-8921. Offers health care management (Certificate); management in science and technology (MS, Certificate). Part-time and evening/weekend programs available. *Degree requirements:* For master's, thesis. *Entrance requirements:* For master's, 2 years of work experience. Additional exam requirements/recommendations for international students: Recommended—TOEFL (minimum score 625 paper-based; 263 computer-based). Electronic applications accepted.

Old Dominion University, College of Business and Public Administration, Master's Program in Business Administration, Norfolk, VA 23529. Offers business and economic forecasting (MBA); financial analysis and valuation (MBA); information technology and enterprise integration (MBA); international business (MBA); maritime and port management (MBA); public administration (MBA). *Accreditation:* AACSB. Part-time and evening/weekend programs

available. *Faculty:* 66 full-time (15 women), 6 part-time/adjunct (1 woman). *Students:* 81 full-time (27 women), 198 part-time (92 women); includes 46 minority (25 African Americans, 1 American Indian/Alaska Native, 13 Asian Americans or Pacific Islanders, 7 Hispanic Americans), 31 international. Average age 30. 169 applicants, 52% accepted, 61 enrolled. In 2009, 81 master's awarded. *Entrance requirements:* For master's, GMAT, letters of reference, resume, coursework in calculus. Additional exam requirements/recommendations for international students: Required—TOEFL (minimum score 550 paper-based; 213 computer-based; 80 iBT). *Application deadline:* For fall admission, 6/1 priority date for domestic students, 4/15 priority date for international students; for spring admission, 11/1 priority date for domestic students, 10/1 priority date for international students. Applications are processed on a rolling basis. Application fee: $50. Electronic applications accepted. *Expenses:* Tuition, state resident: full-time $8112; part-time $338 per credit. Tuition, nonresident: full-time $20,256; part-time $844 per credit. Required fees: $119 per semester. One-time fee: $50. *Financial support:* In 2009–10, 46 students received support, including 31 research assistantships with partial tuition reimbursements available (averaging $7,000 per year), 3 teaching assistantships with partial tuition reimbursements available (averaging $6,300 per year); career-related internships or fieldwork, scholarships/grants, and unspecified assistantships also available. Support available to part-time students. Financial award application deadline: 2/15; financial award applicants required to submit FAFSA. *Faculty research:* International business, buyer behavior, financial markets, strategy, operations research. *Unit head:* Dr. Bruce Rubin, Graduate Program Director, 757-683-3585, E-mail: mbainfo@odu.edu. *Application contact:* Shanna Wood, MBA Program Manager, 757-683-3585, Fax: 757-683-5750, E-mail: mbainfo@odu.edu.

Oregon Health & Science University, OGI School of Science and Engineering, Department of Management in Science and Technology, Portland, OR 97239-3098. Offers MS. Tuition and fees vary according to course level, course load, degree level, program and reciprocity agreements.

Pacific Lutheran University, Division of Graduate Studies, School of Business, Tacoma, WA 98447. Offers business administration (MBA), including technology and innovation management. *Accreditation:* AACSB. Part-time and evening/weekend programs available. *Entrance requirements:* For master's, GMAT. Additional exam requirements/recommendations for international students: Required—TOEFL (minimum score 550 paper-based; 213 computer-based).

Pacific States University, College of Business, Los Angeles, CA 90006. Offers accounting (MBA); business administration (DBA); finance (MBA); international business (MBA); management of information technology (MBA); real estate management (MBA). Part-time and evening/weekend programs available. Postbaccalaureate distance learning degree programs offered (no on-campus study). *Entrance requirements:* For master's, minimum undergraduate GPA of 2.5 during last 90 hours of course work. Additional exam requirements/recommendations for international students: Required—TOEFL (minimum score 133 computer-based).

Polytechnic Institute of NYU, Department of Finance and Risk Engineering, Brooklyn, NY 11201-2990. Offers financial engineering (MS, Advanced Certificate), including capital markets (MS), computational finance (MS), financial technology (MS); financial technology management (Advanced Certificate); organizational behavior (Advanced Certificate); risk management (Advanced Certificate); technology management (Advanced Certificate). Part-time and evening/weekend programs available. *Faculty:* 6 full-time (1 woman), 20 part-time/adjunct (4 women). *Students:* 196 full-time (71 women), 79 part-time (15 women); includes 28 minority (5 African Americans, 23 Asian Americans or Pacific Islanders), 202 international. Average age 26. 497 applicants, 45% accepted, 85 enrolled. In 2009, 102 master's awarded. *Degree requirements:* For master's, comprehensive exam (for some programs), thesis (for some programs). *Entrance requirements:* For master's, GMAT, minimum B average in undergraduate course work. Additional exam requirements/recommendations for international students: Required—TOEFL (minimum score 550 paper-based; 213 computer-based; 80 iBT); Recommended—IELTS (minimum score 6.5). *Application deadline:* For fall admission, 7/31 priority date for domestic students, 4/30 priority date for international students; for spring admission, 12/31 priority date for domestic students, 11/30 priority date for international students. Applications are processed on a rolling basis. Application fee: $75. Electronic applications accepted. *Expenses:* Tuition: Full-time $21,492; part-time $1194 per credit hour. Required fees: $1160; $204 per course. *Financial support:* Institutionally sponsored loans, scholarships/grants, and unspecified assistantships available. Support available to part-time students. Financial award applicants required to submit FAFSA. *Unit head:* Prof. Charles S. Tapiero, Academic Director, 718-260-3653, Fax: 718-260-3874, E-mail: ctapiero@poly.edu. *Application contact:* JeanCarlo Bonilla, Director of Graduate Enrollment Management, 718-260-3182, Fax: 718-260-3624.

Polytechnic Institute of NYU, Department of Technology Management, Major in Management of Technology, Brooklyn, NY 11201-2990. Offers MS. *Students:* 73 full-time (23 women), 6 part-time (3 women); includes 14 minority (2 African Americans, 9 Asian Americans or Pacific Islanders, 3 Hispanic Americans), 14 international. 91 applicants, 68% accepted, 38 enrolled. In 2009, 42 master's awarded. *Degree requirements:* For master's, comprehensive exam (for some programs), thesis (for some programs). *Entrance requirements:* For master's, GMAT, minimum B average in undergraduate course work. Additional exam requirements/recommendations for international students: Required—TOEFL (minimum score 550 paper-based; 213 computer-based; 80 iBT); Recommended—IELTS (minimum score 6.5). *Application deadline:* For fall admission, 7/31 priority date for domestic students, 4/30 priority date for international students; for spring admission, 12/31 priority date for domestic students, 11/30 priority date for international students. Applications are processed on a rolling basis. Application fee: $75. Electronic applications accepted. *Expenses:* Tuition: Full-time $21,492; part-time $1194 per credit hour. Required fees: $1160; $204 per course. *Financial support:* Institutionally sponsored loans, scholarships/grants, and unspecified assistantships available. Support available to part-time students. Financial award applicants required to submit FAFSA. *Unit head:* Prof. Bharadwaj Rao, Head, 718-260-3617, Fax: 718-260-3874, E-mail: brao@poly.edu. *Application contact:* JeanCarlo Bonilla, Director of Graduate Enrollment Management, 718-260-3182, Fax: 718-260-3624, E-mail: gradinfo@poly.edu.

Polytechnic Institute of NYU, Department of Technology Management, Major in Technology Management, Brooklyn, NY 11201-2990. Offers MBA, PhD. *Students:* 5 full-time (4 women), 2 part-time (0 women); includes 1 minority (Hispanic American), 5 international. 46 applicants, 9% accepted, 1 enrolled. *Entrance requirements:* Additional exam requirements/recommendations for international students: Required—TOEFL (minimum score 550 paper-based; 213 computer-based; 80 iBT); Recommended—IELTS (minimum score 6.5). *Application deadline:* For fall admission, 7/31 priority date for domestic students, 4/30 priority date for international students; for spring admission, 12/31 priority date for domestic students, 11/30 priority date for international students. Applications are processed on a rolling basis. Application fee: $75. Electronic applications accepted. *Expenses:* Tuition: Full-time $21,492; part-time $1194 per credit hour. Required fees: $1160; $204 per course. *Financial support:* Institutionally sponsored loans, scholarships/grants, and unspecified assistantships available. Support available to part-time students. *Unit head:* Bharadwaj Rao, Head, 718-260-3617, Fax: 718-260-3874, E-mail: brao@poly.edu. *Application contact:* JeanCarlo Bonilla, Director of Graduate Enrollment Management, 718-260-3182, Fax: 718-260-3624, E-mail: gradinfo@poly.edu.

Polytechnic Institute of NYU, Long Island Graduate Center, Graduate Programs, Department of Technology Management, Major in Management, Melville, NY 11747. Offers MS. Part-time and evening/weekend programs available. *Faculty:* 5 part-time/adjunct (0 women). *Students:* 2 full-time (0 women), 11 part-time (3 women); includes 4 minority (all Asian Americans or Pacific Islanders), 1 international. 5 applicants, 100% accepted, 5 enrolled. In 2009, 2 master's awarded. *Degree requirements:* For master's, comprehensive exam (for some programs), thesis (for some programs). *Entrance requirements:* Additional exam requirements/recommendations for international students: Required—TOEFL (minimum score 550 paper-based; 213 computer-based; 80 iBT); Recommended—IELTS (minimum score 6.5). *Application deadline:* For fall admission, 7/31 priority date for domestic students, 4/30 priority date for

Management of Technology

Polytechnic Institute of NYU, Long Island Graduate Center (continued)
international students; for spring admission, 12/31 priority date for domestic students, 11/30 priority date for international students. Applications are processed on a rolling basis. Application fee: $75. Electronic applications accepted. *Financial support:* Institutionally sponsored loans, scholarships/grants, and unspecified assistantships available. Support available to part-time students. Financial award applicants required to submit FAFSA. *Unit head:* Dr. Bharadwaj Rao, Department Head, 718-260-3617, E-mail: brao@poly.edu. *Application contact:* JeanCarlo Bonilla, Director of Graduate Enrollment Management, 718-260-3182, Fax: 718-260-3624, E-mail: gradinfo@poly.edu.

Polytechnic Institute of NYU, Long Island Graduate Center, Graduate Programs, Department of Technology Management, Major in Management of Technology, Melville, NY 11747. Offers MS. Part-time and evening/weekend programs available. *Entrance requirements:* Additional exam requirements/recommendations for international students: Required—TOEFL (minimum score 550 paper-based; 213 computer-based; 80 iBT); Recommended—IELTS (minimum score 6.5). *Application deadline:* For fall admission, 7/31 priority date for domestic students, 4/30 priority date for international students; for spring admission, 12/31 priority date for domestic students, 11/30 priority date for international students. Applications are processed on a rolling basis. Application fee: $75. Electronic applications accepted. *Financial support:* Institutionally sponsored loans, scholarships/grants, and unspecified assistantships available. Support available to part-time students. *Unit head:* Dr. Bharadwaj Rao, Department Head, 718-260-3617, E-mail: brao@poly.edu. *Application contact:* JeanCarlo Bonilla, Director of Graduate Enrollment Management, 718-260-3182, Fax: 718-260-3624, E-mail: gradinfo@poly.edu.

Polytechnic Institute of NYU, Westchester Graduate Center, Graduate Programs, Department of Technology Management, Major in Management of Technology, Hawthorne, NY 10532-1507. Offers MS. *Students:* 7 full-time (1 woman), 6 part-time (0 women); includes 4 minority (1 African American, 3 Asian Americans or Pacific Islanders), 3 international. 5 applicants, 100% accepted, 5 enrolled. In 2009, 9 master's awarded. *Entrance requirements:* Additional exam requirements/recommendations for international students: Required—TOEFL (minimum score 550 paper-based; 213 computer-based; 80 iBT); Recommended—IELTS (minimum score 6.5). *Application deadline:* For fall admission, 7/31 priority date for domestic students, 4/30 priority date for international students; for spring admission, 12/31 priority date for domestic students, 11/30 priority date for international students. Applications are processed on a rolling basis. Application fee: $75. Electronic applications accepted. *Financial support:* Institutionally sponsored loans, scholarships/grants, and unspecified assistantships available. Support available to part-time students. *Unit head:* Dr. Bharadwaj Rao, Department Head, 718-260-3617, E-mail: brao@poly.edu. *Application contact:* JeanCarlo Bonilla, Director of Graduate Enrollment Management, 718-260-3182, Fax: 718-260-3624, E-mail: gradinfo@poly.edu.

Polytechnic University of Puerto Rico, Graduate School, Hato Rey, PR 00919. Offers business administration (MBA), including general studies, management of information systems, management of international enterprises; civil engineering (ME, MS); computer engineering (ME, MS); computer science (MS); electrical engineering (ME, MS); engineering management (MEM); environmental management (MEPM); landscape architecture (M Land Arch); manufacturing competitiveness (MMC, MS); manufacturing engineering (ME, MS). Part-time and evening/weekend programs available. *Entrance requirements:* For master's, 3 letters of recommendation.

Portland State University, Graduate Studies, Maseeh College of Engineering and Computer Science, Department of Engineering and Technology Management, Portland, OR 97207-0751. Offers engineering and technology management (M Eng); engineering management (MS); manufacturing engineering (ME); manufacturing management (M Eng); systems science/engineering management (PhD); MS/MBA; MS/MS. Part-time and evening/weekend programs available. *Degree requirements:* For master's, thesis optional; for doctorate, one foreign language, thesis/dissertation, oral and written exams. *Entrance requirements:* For master's, minimum GPA of 3.0 in upper-division course work, BS degree in civil engineering; for doctorate, GRE General Test, GRE Subject Test, minimum GPA of 3.0 in upper-division course work. Additional exam requirements/recommendations for international students: Required—TOEFL (minimum score 550 paper-based; 213 computer-based). *Faculty research:* Scheduling, hierarchical decision modeling, operations research, knowledge-based information systems.

Regis University, College for Professional Studies, School of Management, Denver, CO 80221-1099. Offers accounting (MS); business administration (MBA); computer information technology (MSOL); executive internal management (Certificate); executive leadership (Certificate); finance (MBA); finance and accounting (MBA); human resource management (MSOL); international business (MBA); marketing (MBA); operations management (MBA); organization leadership (MS); organizational leadership (MSOL); project leadership and management (MSOL, Certificate); project management (Certificate); strategic business (Certificate); strategic human resource (Certificate); technical management (Certificate). Offered at Colorado Springs Campus, Northwest Denver Campus, Southeast Denver Campus, Fort Collins Campus, Broomfield Campus, Henderson (Nevada) Campus, and Summerlin (Nevada) Campus and online. Part-time and evening/weekend programs available. Postbaccalaureate distance learning degree programs offered (no on-campus study). *Degree requirements:* For master's, thesis optional, capstone project. *Entrance requirements:* For master's, GMAT or essays, interview, 2 years of full-time business work experience, resume; for Certificate, GMAT. Additional exam requirements/recommendations for international students: Required—TOEFL, TOEFL or university-based test; Recommended—TWE (minimum score 5). Electronic applications accepted. *Faculty research:* Impact of Info Technology on Small Business Regulation of Accounting, International Project financing, Mineral Development, Delivery of Healthcare to rural indigenous communities.

Rollins College, Crummer Graduate School of Business, Winter Park, FL 32789-4499. Offers entrepreneurship (MBA); finance (MBA); international business (MBA); management (MBA); marketing (MBA); operations and technology management (MBA). *Accreditation:* AACSB. Part-time and evening/weekend programs available. Postbaccalaureate distance learning degree programs offered (minimal on-campus study). *Faculty:* 25 full-time (3 women), 8 part-time/adjunct (2 women). *Students:* 277 full-time (105 women), 192 part-time (79 women); includes 95 minority (26 African Americans, 31 Asian Americans or Pacific Islanders, 38 Hispanic Americans), 48 international. Average age 29. 373 applicants, 53% accepted, 140 enrolled. In 2009, 220 master's awarded. *Entrance requirements:* For master's, GMAT. Additional exam requirements/recommendations for international students: Required—TOEFL. *Application deadline:* For fall admission, 6/1 priority date for domestic students; for spring admission, 12/1 for domestic students. Applications are processed on a rolling basis. Application fee: $50. Electronic applications accepted. *Expenses:* Contact institution. *Financial support:* In 2009–10, 95 students received support, including 95 fellowships, 56 research assistantships (averaging $2,400 per year); career-related internships or fieldwork, scholarships/grants, tuition waivers (full), and unspecified assistantships also available. *Faculty research:* Sustainability, world financial markets, international business, market research, strategic marketing. *Unit head:* Dr. Craig M. McAllaster, Dean, 407-646-2249, Fax: 407-646-1550, E-mail: cmcallaster@rollins.edu. *Application contact:* Linda Puritz, Student Admissions Office, 407-646-2405, Fax: 407-646-1550, E-mail: mbaadmissions@rollins.edu.

St. Ambrose University, College of Business, Program in Information Technology Management, Davenport, IA 52803-2898. Offers MSITM. Part-time programs available. *Faculty:* 3 full-time (0 women). *Students:* 2 full-time (both women), 10 part-time (4 women); includes 2 minority (1 African American, 1 Hispanic American). Average age 36. 3 applicants, 33% accepted, 1 enrolled. In 2009, 5 master's awarded. *Degree requirements:* For master's, thesis (for some programs), practica. *Entrance requirements:* For master's, GRE or GMAT, minimum GPA of 2.8. Additional exam requirements/recommendations for international students: Required—TOEFL. *Application deadline:* For fall admission, 8/15 priority date for domestic students; for winter admission, 12/15 priority date for domestic students; for spring admission, 1/1 priority date for domestic students. Applications are processed on a rolling basis. Application fee: $25. Electronic applications accepted. *Expenses:* Tuition: Part-time $702 per credit hour. Tuition and fees vary according to degree level, program and reciprocity agreements. *Financial support:* In 2009–10, 6 students received support; research assistantships with partial tuition reimbursements available, career-related internships or fieldwork, scholarships/grants, and unspecified assistantships available. Financial award application deadline: 3/15; financial award applicants required to submit FAFSA. *Unit head:* Kenneth R. Grenier, Director, 563-333-6173, Fax: 563-333-6268, E-mail: grenierkennethr@sau.edu. *Application contact:* Deborah K. Bennett, Administrative Assistant, 563-333-6266, Fax: 563-333-6268, E-mail: bennettdeborahk@sau.edu.

Santa Clara University, Leavey School of Business, Program in Business Administration, Santa Clara, CA 95053. Offers accounting (MBA); entrepreneurship (MBA); executive MBA (EMBA); finance (MBA); food and agribusiness (MBA); international business (MBA); leading people and organizations (MBA); managing technology and innovation (MBA); marketing management (MBA); supply chain management (MBA). *Accreditation:* AACSB. Part-time and evening/weekend programs available. *Students:* 228 full-time (88 women), 838 part-time (265 women); includes 388 minority (17 African Americans, 2 American Indian/Alaska Native, 326 Asian Americans or Pacific Islanders, 43 Hispanic Americans), 218 international. Average age 31. 486 applicants, 77% accepted, 263 enrolled. In 2009, 317 master's awarded. *Degree requirements:* For master's, thesis or alternative. *Entrance requirements:* For master's, GMAT, GRE. Additional exam requirements/recommendations for international students: Required—TOEFL (minimum score 600 paper-based; 250 computer-based; 100 iBT). *Application deadline:* For fall admission, 6/1 for domestic and international students; for spring admission, 1/19 for domestic students, 1/17 for international students. Applications are processed on a rolling basis. Application fee: $75 ($100 for international students). Electronic applications accepted. *Expenses:* Contact institution. *Financial support:* Fellowships with partial tuition reimbursements, research assistantships with partial tuition reimbursements, career-related internships or fieldwork, Federal Work-Study, institutionally sponsored loans, scholarships/grants, health care benefits, and unspecified assistantships available. Support available to part-time students. Financial award applicants required to submit FAFSA. *Unit head:* Elizabeth B. Ford, Senior Assistant Dean, 408-554-2752, Fax: 408-554-4571, E-mail: eford@scu.edu. *Application contact:* Jennifer W. Taylor, Senior Director, 408-554-4539, Fax: 408-554-4571, E-mail: mbaadmissions@scu.edu.

Seton Hall University, Stillman School of Business, Programs in Business Administration, South Orange, NJ 07079-2697. Offers accounting (MBA); finance (MBA); information technology management (MBA); international business (MBA); management (MBA); marketing (MBA); sport management (MBA). Part-time and evening/weekend programs available. *Faculty:* 57 full-time (13 women), 30 part-time/adjunct (3 women). *Students:* 69 full-time (26 women), 217 part-time (91 women); includes 53 minority (11 African Americans, 35 Asian Americans or Pacific Islanders, 7 Hispanic Americans), 38 international. Average age 29. 286 applicants, 70% accepted, 130 enrolled. In 2009, 110 master's awarded. *Degree requirements:* For master's, 20 hours of community service (Social Responsibility Project). *Entrance requirements:* For master's, GMAT, minimum GPA of 3.0. Additional exam requirements/recommendations for international students: Required—TOEFL (minimum score 607 paper-based; 254 computer-based; 102 iBT), or IELTS, or Pearson Test of English (PTE). *Application deadline:* For fall admission, 5/31 priority date for domestic students, 3/31 priority date for international students; for spring admission, 10/31 priority date for domestic students, 4/30 priority date for international students. Applications are processed on a rolling basis. Application fee: $75. Electronic applications accepted. *Financial support:* In 2009–10, research assistantships with full tuition reimbursements (averaging $34,404 per year); career-related internships or fieldwork, Federal Work-Study, scholarships/grants, and unspecified assistantships also available. Support available to part-time students. Financial award application deadline: 6/30; financial award applicants required to submit FAFSA. *Faculty research:* Financial, hedge funds, international business, legal issues, disclosure and branding. *Unit head:* Dr. Joyce A. Strawser, Associate Dean for Undergraduate and MBA Curricula, 973-761-9225, Fax: 973-761-9217, E-mail: strawsjo@shu.edu. *Application contact:* Catherine Bianchi, Director of Graduate Admissions, 973-761-9262, Fax: 973-761-9208, E-mail: catherine.bianchi@shu.edu.

Simon Fraser University, Graduate Studies, Faculty of Business Administration, Burnaby, BC V5A 1S6, Canada. Offers business administration (EMBA, PhD); financial management (MA); general business (MBA); global asset and wealth management (MBA); management of technology/biotechnology (MBA); MBA/MRM. *Accreditation:* AACSB. Postbaccalaureate distance learning degree programs offered. *Degree requirements:* For master's, thesis or written project. *Entrance requirements:* For master's, minimum GPA of 3.0. Additional exam requirements/recommendations for international students: Required—TOEFL. *Expenses:* Contact institution. *Faculty research:* Leadership, marketing and technology, wealth management.

South Dakota School of Mines and Technology, Graduate Division, College of Engineering, Program in Technology Management, Rapid City, SD 57701-3995. Offers MS. Part-time programs available. *Faculty:* 5 full-time (1 woman). *Students:* 5 full-time (1 woman), 16 part-time (5 women), 3 international. Average age 31. 11 applicants, 73% accepted, 4 enrolled. In 2009, 10 master's awarded. *Entrance requirements:* For master's, GMAT. Additional exam requirements/recommendations for international students: Required—TOEFL, TWE. *Application deadline:* For fall admission, 7/1 priority date for domestic students, 4/1 for international students; for spring admission, 11/1 for domestic students, 9/1 for international students. Applications are processed on a rolling basis. Application fee: $35. Electronic applications accepted. *Expenses:* Tuition, state resident: full-time $3340; part-time $139 per credit hour. Tuition, nonresident: full-time $7060; part-time $294 per credit hour. Required fees: $3270. *Financial support:* In 2009–10, 2 students received support, including 1 fellowship (averaging $2,450 per year), 3 teaching assistantships with partial tuition reimbursements available (averaging $3,800 per year); research assistantships with partial tuition reimbursements available, Federal Work-Study and institutionally sponsored loans also available. Support available to part-time students. Financial award application deadline: 5/15. *Unit head:* Dr. Stuart D. Kellogg, Director, 605-394-1271, E-mail: stuart.kellogg@sdsmt.edu. *Application contact:* Jeannette R. Nilson, Administrative Support Coordinator, Graduate Education, 800-454-8162 Ext. 1206, Fax: 605-394-5360, E-mail: graduate_admissions@sdsmt.edu.

Southeast Missouri State University, School of Graduate Studies, Department of Industrial and Engineering Technology, Cape Girardeau, MO 63701-4799. Offers technology management (MS). Part-time programs available. Postbaccalaureate distance learning degree programs offered (no on-campus study). *Degree requirements:* For master's, comprehensive exam (for some programs), thesis. *Entrance requirements:* For master's, minimum undergraduate GPA of 2.7, undergraduate degree in an engineering, technology, or a related field. Additional exam requirements/recommendations for international students: Required—TOEFL (minimum score 550 paper-based; 213 computer-based); Recommended—IELTS (minimum score 6). Electronic applications accepted. *Expenses:* Tuition, state resident: full-time $4266; part-time $237 per credit hour. Tuition, nonresident: full-time $7506; part-time $417 per credit hour. Required fees: $427; $427. *Faculty research:* Supply chain management, lean manufacturing, energy conservation, telecommunications, graphic communications, ISQ/Q5 9000, SAP (enterprise Resource Planning), automatic control systems.

State University of New York Institute of Technology, School of Business, Program in Business Administration in Technology Management, Utica, NY 13504-3050. Offers technology management (MBA). *Entrance requirements:* For master's, GMAT, minimum GPA of 3.0. Additional exam requirements/recommendations for international students: Required—TOEFL (minimum score 550 paper-based; 213 computer-based). *Faculty research:* Technology management, writing schools, leadership, new products.

Stevens Institute of Technology, Graduate School, Wesley J. Howe School of Technology Management, Doctoral Program in Technology Management, Hoboken, NJ 07030. Offers information management (PhD); technology management (PhD); telecommunications management

(PhD). Part-time and evening/weekend programs available. Postbaccalaureate distance learning degree programs offered (minimal on-campus study). *Entrance requirements:* Additional exam requirements/recommendations for international students: Required—TOEFL. Electronic applications accepted. *Expenses:* Tuition: Full-time $9900; part-time $1100 per credit. Required fees: $286 per semester.

Stevens Institute of Technology, Graduate School, Wesley J. Howe School of Technology Management, Program in Business Administration for Experienced Professionals, Hoboken, NJ 07030. Offers technology management (EMBA). *Expenses:* Tuition: Full-time $9900; part-time $1100 per credit. Required fees: $286 per semester.

Stevens Institute of Technology, Graduate School, Wesley J. Howe School of Technology Management, Program in Management, Hoboken, NJ 07030. Offers general management (MS); global innovation management (MS); human resource management (MS); information management (MS); project management (MS); technology commercialization (MS); technology management (MS). Part-time programs available. *Degree requirements:* For master's, thesis optional. *Entrance requirements:* For master's, GMAT, GRE General Test. Additional exam requirements/recommendations for international students: Required—TOEFL. Electronic applications accepted. *Expenses:* Tuition: Full-time $9900; part-time $1100 per credit. Required fees: $286 per semester. *Faculty research:* Industrial economics.

Stevens Institute of Technology, Graduate School, Wesley J. Howe School of Technology Management, Program in Technology Management for Experienced Professionals, Hoboken, NJ 07030. Offers EMTM, MS, Certificate. Part-time and evening/weekend programs available. Postbaccalaureate distance learning degree programs offered. *Entrance requirements:* For master's, GMAT, GRE General Test. Additional exam requirements/recommendations for international students: Required—TOEFL. Electronic applications accepted. *Expenses:* Contact institution.

Stevens Institute of Technology, Graduate School, Wesley J. Howe School of Technology Management, Program in Telecommunications Management, Hoboken, NJ 07030. Offers business (MS); global innovation management (MS); management of wireless networks (MS); online security, technology and business (MS); project management (MS); technical management (MS); telecommunications management (PhD, Certificate). *Degree requirements:* For master's, thesis optional; for doctorate, thesis/dissertation. *Entrance requirements:* For master's and doctorate, GMAT, GRE General Test. Additional exam requirements/recommendations for international students: Required—TOEFL. Electronic applications accepted. *Expenses:* Tuition: Full-time $9900; part-time $1100 per credit. Required fees: $286 per semester.

Stevenson University, Graduate and Professional Studies Programs, Program in Business and Technology Management, Stevenson, MD 21153. Offers MS. *Degree requirements:* For master's, capstone course.

Stony Brook University, State University of New York, Graduate School, College of Business, Program in Technology Management, Stony Brook, NY 11794. Offers MS. Program conducted mostly in Korea. Evening/weekend programs available. Postbaccalaureate distance learning degree programs offered. In 2009, 39 master's awarded. *Entrance requirements:* For master's, GMAT or GRE General Test, 3 years of work experience, minimum GPA of 3.0, letters of recommendation. Additional exam requirements/recommendations for international students: Required—TOEFL (minimum score 550 paper-based; 213 computer-based). Application fee: $50. *Expenses:* Tuition, state resident: full-time $8370; part-time $349 per credit. Tuition, nonresident: full-time $13,250; part-time $552 per credit. Required fees: $933. *Unit head:* Joseph McDonnell, Interim Dean, 631-632-7180. *Application contact:* Dr. Owen Carroll, Director, Graduate Program, 631-632-7171, E-mail: tcarroll@notes.cc.sunysb.edu.

Stony Brook University, State University of New York, Graduate School, College of Engineering and Applied Sciences, Department of Technology and Society, Program in Global Operations Management, Stony Brook, NY 11794. Offers MS. Postbaccalaureate distance learning degree programs offered. *Application deadline:* For fall admission, 5/1 for domestic students; for spring admission, 11/1 for domestic students. Electronic applications accepted. *Expenses:* Tuition, state resident: full-time $8370; part-time $349 per credit. Tuition, nonresident: full-time $13,250; part-time $552 per credit. Required fees: $933. *Unit head:* David Ferguson, Chairman, 631-632-8770, E-mail: david.ferguson@stonybrook.edu. *Application contact:* Dr. Sheldon Reaven, Graduate Director, 631-632-8765, Fax: 631-632-7809, E-mail: sheldon.raven@sunysb.edu.

Sullivan University, School of Business, Louisville, KY 40205. Offers business administration (MBA); collaborative leadership (MSCL); conflict management (MSCM); dispute resolution (MSDR); executive business administration (EMBA); human resource leadership (MSHRL); information technology (MSMIT); management and information technology (MBIT); pharmacy (Pharm D). Part-time programs available. Postbaccalaureate distance learning degree programs offered (no on-campus study). *Entrance requirements:* Additional exam requirements/recommendations for international students: Required—TOEFL.

Teachers College, Columbia University, Graduate Faculty of Education, Department of Math, Science and Technology, Program in Technology Specialist, New York, NY 10027-6696. Offers MA.

Texas A&M University–Commerce, Graduate School, College of Business and Technology, Department of Industrial Engineering and Technology, Commerce, TX 75429-3011. Offers industrial technology (MS); technology management (MS). Part-time programs available. *Degree requirements:* For master's, comprehensive exam, thesis (for some programs). *Entrance requirements:* For master's, GMAT, GRE General Test. Electronic applications accepted. *Faculty research:* Environmental science, engineering microelectronics, natural sciences.

Texas State University–San Marcos, Graduate School, College of Science, Department of Engineering Technology, San Marcos, TX 78666. Offers industrial technology (MST). Part-time and evening/weekend programs available. *Faculty:* 8 full-time (0 women), 2 part-time/adjunct (0 women). *Students:* 20 full-time (4 women), 18 part-time (3 women); includes 12 minority (2 African Americans, 3 Asian Americans or Pacific Islanders, 7 Hispanic Americans). Average age 29. 14 applicants, 100% accepted, 9 enrolled. In 2009, 7 master's awarded. *Degree requirements:* For master's, comprehensive exam, thesis optional. *Entrance requirements:* For master's, minimum GPA of 2.75 in last 60 hours of undergraduate work. Additional exam requirements/recommendations for international students: Required—TOEFL (minimum score 550 paper-based; 213 computer-based). *Application deadline:* For fall admission, 6/15 priority date for domestic students, 6/1 priority date for international students; for spring admission, 10/15 priority date for domestic students, 10/1 priority date for international students. Applications are processed on a rolling basis. Application fee: $40 ($90 for international students). Electronic applications accepted. *Expenses:* Tuition, state resident: full-time $5784; part-time $241 per credit hour. Tuition, nonresident: part-time $551 per credit hour. Required fees: $1728; $48 per credit hour. $306. Tuition and fees vary according to course load. *Financial support:* In 2009–10, 25 students received support, including 1 research assistantship (averaging $4,928 per year), 4 teaching assistantships (averaging $5,076 per year); career-related internships or fieldwork, Federal Work-Study, and institutionally sponsored loans also available. Support available to part-time students. Financial award application deadline: 4/1; financial award applicants required to submit FAFSA. *Faculty research:* Rapid prototyping, casting technology, statistical process control, spatial abilities and gender. Total annual research expenditures: $3,609. *Unit head:* Dr. Vedaraman Sriraman, Chair, 512-245-2137, Fax: 512-245-3052, E-mail: vs04@txstate.edu. *Application contact:* Dr. Andy Batey, Graduate Adviser, 512-245-2137, Fax: 512-245-3052, E-mail: ab08@txstate.edu.

University at Albany, State University of New York, School of Business, Department of Information Technology Management, Albany, NY 12222-0001. Offers MBA. *Degree requirements:* For master's, field study project. *Entrance requirements:* For master's, GMAT. Additional exam requirements/recommendations for international students: Required—TOEFL (minimum score 550 paper-based; 213 computer-based). Electronic applications accepted. *Faculty research:* Data quality, expert systems, collaborative technology, expert information systems.

University of Advancing Technology, Master of Science Program in Technology, Tempe, AZ 85283-1042. Offers advancing computer science (MS); emerging technologies (MS); game production and management (MS); information assurance (MS); technology leadership (MS). *Degree requirements:* For master's, project or thesis. *Entrance requirements:* Additional exam requirements/recommendations for international students: Required—TOEFL (minimum score 550 paper-based). Electronic applications accepted. *Faculty research:* Artificial intelligence, fractals, organizational management.

The University of Akron, Graduate School, College of Business Administration, Department of Management, Program in Management of Technology, Akron, OH 44325. Offers MBA. *Students:* 5 part-time (2 women), 2 international. Average age 38. 5 applicants, 60% accepted, 3 enrolled. In 2009, 1 master's awarded. *Entrance requirements:* For master's, GMAT, minimum GPA of 2.75, letters of recommendation, resume. Additional exam requirements/recommendations for international students: Required—TOEFL (minimum score 550 paper-based; 213 computer-based; 79 iBT). *Application deadline:* For fall admission, 8/1 for domestic and international students; for spring admission, 12/1 for domestic and international students. Application fee: $30 ($40 for international students). Electronic applications accepted. *Expenses:* Tuition, state resident: full-time $6570; part-time $365 per credit hour. Tuition, nonresident: full-time $11,250; part-time $625 per credit hour. *Unit head:* Dr. R. Ray Gehani, Head, 330-972-8140, E-mail: rgehani@uakron.edu. *Application contact:* Dr. Susan Hanlon, Director of Graduate Business Programs, 330-972-7043, Fax: 330-972-6588, E-mail: shanlon@uakron.edu.

University of Arkansas at Little Rock, Graduate School, College of Business Administration, Little Rock, AR 72204-1099. Offers accountancy (M Acc, Graduate Certificate); business administration (MBA); construction management (Graduate Certificate); management (Graduate Certificate); management information system (MIS); management information systems (Graduate Certificate); management information systems leadership (Graduate Certificate); taxation (MS, Graduate Certificate). *Accreditation:* AACSB. Part-time and evening/weekend programs available. *Entrance requirements:* For master's, GMAT, minimum undergraduate GPA of 2.7. Additional exam requirements/recommendations for international students: Required—TOEFL (minimum score 525 paper-based; 195 computer-based).

University of Bridgeport, School of Engineering, Department of Technology Management, Bridgeport, CT 06604. Offers MS. *Degree requirements:* For master's, thesis optional. *Entrance requirements:* Additional exam requirements/recommendations for international students: Recommended—TOEFL (minimum score 550 paper-based; 213 computer-based; 80 iBT), IELTS (minimum score 6.5). Electronic applications accepted. *Faculty research:* CAD/CAM.

University of Central Missouri, The Graduate School, College of Science and Technology, Warrensburg, MO 64093. Offers applied mathematics (MS); aviation safety (MS); biology (MS); computer science (MS); environmental studies (MA); industrial management (MS); mathematics (MS); technology (MS); technology management (PhD). Part-time programs available. Postbaccalaureate distance learning degree programs offered. *Faculty:* 59. *Students:* 99 full-time (31 women), 85 part-time (37 women). Average age 33. 45 applicants, 96% accepted, 42 enrolled. In 2009, 68 master's awarded. *Entrance requirements:* Additional exam requirements/recommendations for international students: Required—TOEFL (minimum score 550 paper-based; 79 computer-based). *Application deadline:* For fall admission, 6/1 priority date for domestic students, 5/1 for international students; for spring admission, 10/1 priority date for domestic students, 10/1 for international students. Applications are processed on a rolling basis. Application fee: $30 ($75 for international students). Electronic applications accepted. *Expenses:* Tuition, area resident: Part-time $245.80 per credit hour. Tuition, nonresident: part-time $491.60 per credit hour. Required fees: $24.20 per credit hour. Full-time tuition and fees vary according to course load, degree level, campus/location and reciprocity agreements. *Financial support:* In 2009–10, 15 students received support; fellowships with full and partial tuition reimbursements available, research assistantships with full and partial tuition reimbursements available, teaching assistantships with full and partial tuition reimbursements available, career-related internships or fieldwork, Federal Work-Study, scholarships/grants, and administrative and laboratory assistantships available. Support available to part-time students. Financial award application deadline: 3/1; financial award applicants required to submit FAFSA. *Unit head:* Dr. Alice Greife, Dean, 660-543-4450, Fax: 660-543-8031, E-mail: greife@ucmo.edu. *Application contact:* Laurie Delap, Admissions Coordinator, 660-543-4621, Fax: 660-543-4778, E-mail: gradinfo@ucmo.edu.

University of Dallas, Graduate School of Management, Irving, TX 75062-4736. Offers accounting (MBA, MM, MS); business management (MBA, MM); corporate finance (MBA, MM); financial services (MBA); global business (MBA, MM); health services management (MBA, MM); human resource management (MBA, MM); information assurance (MBA, MM, MS); information technology (MBA, MM, MS); information technology service management (MBA, MM, MS); marketing management (MBA, MM); organization development (MBA, MM); project management (MBA, MM); sports and entertainment management (MBA, MM); strategic leadership (MBA, MM); supply chain management (MBA); supply chain management and market logistics (MM). *Accreditation:* ACBSP. Part-time and evening/weekend programs available. Postbaccalaureate distance learning degree programs offered (no on-campus study). *Faculty:* 25 full-time (6 women), 31 part-time/adjunct (6 women). *Students:* 232 full-time (95 women), 923 part-time (365 women); includes 462 minority (184 African Americans, 14 American Indian/Alaska Native, 153 Asian Americans or Pacific Islanders, 111 Hispanic Americans), 184 international. Average age 34. 474 applicants, 85% accepted, 237 enrolled. In 2009, 399 master's awarded. *Entrance requirements:* Additional exam requirements/recommendations for international students: Required—TOEFL. *Application deadline:* Applications are processed on a rolling basis. Application fee: $50. Electronic applications accepted. *Expenses:* Contact institution. *Financial support:* In 2009–10, 399 students received support. Scholarships/grants and unspecified assistantships available. Financial award application deadline: 2/15; financial award applicants required to submit FAFSA. *Unit head:* Alounda Joseph, Director of Enrollment Processes, 972-721-5356, E-mail: admiss@gsm.udallas.edu. *Application contact:* Alounda Joseph, Director of Enrollment Processes, 972-721-5356, E-mail: admiss@gsm.udallas.edu.

University of Delaware, Alfred Lerner College of Business and Economics, Department of Accounting and Management Information Systems and Department of Electrical and Computer Engineering, Program in Information Systems and Technology Management, Newark, DE 19716. Offers MS. Part-time and evening/weekend programs available. *Entrance requirements:* For master's, GRE or GMAT, 2 letters of recommendation, resume, minimum GPA of 2.75. Additional exam requirements/recommendations for international students: Required—TOEFL (minimum score 600 paper-based; 250 computer-based). *Faculty research:* Security, developer trust, XML.

University of Denver, University College, Denver, CO 80208. Offers applied communication (MAS, MPS, Certificate); computer information systems (MAS, Certificate); environmental policy and management (MAS, Certificate); geographic information systems (MAS, Certificate); human resource administration (MPS, Certificate); knowledge and information technologies (MAS); liberal studies (MLS, Certificate); modern languages (MLS, Certificate); organizational leadership (MPS, Certificate); security management (Certificate); technology management (MAS, Certificate), including 21st century strategic management (MAS), international markets (MAS), project management (MAS), research and development management (MAS); telecommunications (MAS, Certificate), including broadband (MAS), telecommunications management and policy (MAS), telecommunications technology (MAS), wireless networks (MAS). Part-time and evening/weekend programs available. Postbaccalaureate distance learning degree programs offered (no on-campus study). *Faculty:* 160 part-time/adjunct (64 women). *Students:* 53 full-time (25 women), 984 part-time (551 women); includes 171 minority (72 African Americans, 10 American Indian/Alaska Native, 33 Asian Americans or Pacific Islanders, 56 Hispanic Americans), 75 international. Average age 36. 537 applicants, 96% accepted, 494 enrolled. In 2009, 229 master's, 109 Certificates awarded. *Entrance requirements:* Additional exam requirements/

Management of Technology

University of Denver (continued)

recommendations for international students: Required—TOEFL (minimum score 550 paper-based; 213 computer-based). *Application deadline:* Applications are processed on a rolling basis. Application fee: $75. Electronic applications accepted. *Expenses:* Contact institution. *Financial support:* Applicants required to submit FAFSA. *Unit head:* Dr. James Davis, Dean, 303-871-2291, Fax: 303-871-4047, E-mail: jdavis@du.edu. *Application contact:* Information Contact, 303-871-3155.

University of Illinois at Urbana–Champaign, Graduate College, College of Business, Department of Business Administration, Champaign, IL 61820. Offers business administration (MS, PhD); technology management (MS). *Accreditation:* AACSB. *Faculty:* 43 full-time (10 women), 8 part-time/adjunct (1 woman). *Students:* 91 full-time (29 women), 8 part-time (4 women); includes 5 minority (all Asian Americans or Pacific Islanders), 77 international. 275 applicants, 33% accepted, 54 enrolled. In 2009, 51 master's, 9 doctorates awarded. *Entrance requirements:* For master's, minimum GPA of 3.0; for doctorate, GMAT or GRE, minimum GPA of 3.0. Additional exam requirements/recommendations for international students: Required—TOEFL (minimum score 550 paper-based; 231 computer-based; 79 iBT) or IELTS (6.5). *Application deadline:* Applications are processed on a rolling basis. Application fee: $60 ($75 for international students). Electronic applications accepted. *Expenses:* Contact institution. *Financial support:* In 2009–10, 23 fellowships, 39 research assistantships, 14 teaching assistantships were awarded; tuition waivers (full and partial) also available. *Unit head:* William J. Qualls, Interim Head, 217-265-0794, Fax: 217-244-7969, E-mail: wqualls@illinois.edu. *Application contact:* J. E. Miller, Coordinator of Graduate Programs, 217-244-8002, Fax: 217-244-7969, E-mail: j-miller@illinois.edu.

University of Maryland University College, Graduate School of Management and Technology, Master of Science in Technology Management Program, Adelphi, MD 20783. Offers MS, Certificate. Offered evenings and weekends only. Part-time and evening/weekend programs available. Postbaccalaureate distance learning degree programs offered (no on-campus study). *Students:* 13 full-time (4 women), 673 part-time (304 women); includes 314 minority (257 African Americans, 4 American Indian/Alaska Native, 32 Asian Americans or Pacific Islanders, 21 Hispanic Americans), 15 international. Average age 38. 160 applicants, 100% accepted, 108 enrolled. In 2009, 157 master's, 75 other advanced degrees awarded. *Degree requirements:* For master's, thesis or alternative. *Application deadline:* Applications are processed on a rolling basis. Application fee: $50. Electronic applications accepted. *Expenses:* Tuition, state resident: full-time $7704; part-time $428 per credit hour. Tuition, nonresident: full-time $11,862; part-time $659 per credit hour. *Financial support:* Federal Work-Study and scholarships/grants available. Support available to part-time students. Financial award application deadline: 6/1; financial award applicants required to submit FAFSA. *Unit head:* Dr. Joyce Shirazi, Director, 240-684-2400, Fax: 240-684-2401, E-mail: jshirazi@umuc.edu. *Application contact:* Coordinator, Graduate Admissions, 800-888-UMUC, Fax: 240-684-2151, E-mail: newgrad@umuc.edu.

University of Miami, Graduate School, College of Engineering, Department of Industrial Engineering, Coral Gables, FL 33124. Offers ergonomics (PhD); industrial engineering (MSIE, PhD); management of technology (MS); occupational ergonomics and safety (MS, MSOES), including environmental health and safety (MS), occupational ergonomics and safety (MSOES); MBA/MSIE. Part-time programs available. *Degree requirements:* For master's, thesis (for some programs); for doctorate, comprehensive exam, thesis/dissertation. *Entrance requirements:* For master's and doctorate, GRE General Test, minimum GPA of 3.0. Additional exam requirements/recommendations for international students: Required—TOEFL (minimum score 550 paper-based; 213 computer-based). *Faculty research:* Logistics, supply chain management, industrial applications of biomechanics and ergonomics, technology management, back pain, aging, operations research, manufacturing, safety, human reliability, energy assessment.

University of Minnesota, Twin Cities Campus, Institute of Technology, Technological Leadership Institute, Program in Management of Technology, Minneapolis, MN 55455-0213. Offers MSMOT. Evening/weekend programs available. *Faculty:* 1 full-time (0 women), 13 part-time/adjunct (0 women). *Students:* 60 full-time (10 women); includes 12 minority (2 African Americans, 9 Asian Americans or Pacific Islanders, 1 Hispanic American), 2 international. Average age 34. 40 applicants, 88% accepted, 30 enrolled. In 2009, 32 master's awarded. *Degree requirements:* For master's, thesis, capstone project. *Entrance requirements:* For master's, 5 years of work experience in high-tech company, preferably in Twin Cities area; demonstrated technological leadership ability. Additional exam requirements/recommendations for international students: Required—TOEFL (minimum score 580 paper-based; 240 computer-based; 90 iBT). *Application deadline:* For fall admission, 6/15 priority date for domestic students, 5/1 for international students. Applications are processed on a rolling basis. Application fee: $75 ($95 for international students). Electronic applications accepted. *Expenses:* Contact institution. *Financial support:* In 2009–10, 14 students received support, including 14 fellowships with partial tuition reimbursements available (averaging $3,250 per year); institutionally sponsored loans and scholarships/grants also available. Financial award application deadline: 7/15; financial award applicants required to submit FAFSA. *Faculty research:* Operations management, strategic management, technology foresight, marketing, business analysis. *Unit head:* Dr. Massond Amin, Director, 612-624-5747, Fax: 612-624-7510. *Application contact:* Ann Bechtell, Admission Associate, 612-624-8826, Fax: 612-624-7510, E-mail: mot-cdtl@umn.edu.

University of New Hampshire, Graduate School, Whittemore School of Business and Economics, Department of Business Administration, Program in Management of Technology, Durham, NH 03824. Offers MS, Postbaccalaureate Certificate. Part-time programs available. *Students:* 10 part-time (1 woman). Average age 46. 13 applicants, 0% accepted, 0 enrolled. In 2009, 27 master's awarded. *Application deadline:* For fall admission, 6/1 for domestic students, 4/1 for international students; for spring admission, 12/1 for domestic students. Application fee: $65. *Expenses:* Tuition, state resident: full-time $10,380; part-time $577 per credit hour. Tuition, nonresident: full-time $24,350; part-time $1002 per credit hour. Required fees: $1550; $387.50 per semester. Tuition and fees vary according to course load and program. *Financial support:* Fellowships, research assistantships, teaching assistantships available. *Application contact:* Holly Hurwitch, Administrative Assistant, 603-862-0277, E-mail: management.technology@unh.edu.

University of New Mexico, Robert O. Anderson Graduate School of Management, Department of Finance, International, Technology and Entrepreneurship, Albuquerque, NM 87131-1221. Offers finance (MBA); international management (MBA); international management in Latin America (MBA); management of technology (MBA). Part-time and evening/weekend programs available. *Faculty:* 12 full-time (0 women), 5 part-time/adjunct (1 woman). *Students:* 46 full-time (18 women), 28 part-time (9 women); includes 31 minority (1 African American, 2 American Indian/Alaska Native, 10 Asian Americans or Pacific Islanders, 18 Hispanic Americans), 7 international. Average age 30. 30 applicants, 97% accepted, 27 enrolled. In 2009, 43 master's awarded. *Entrance requirements:* For master's, GMAT or GRE (can be waived in some instances). Additional exam requirements/recommendations for international students: Required—TOEFL (minimum score 550 paper-based; 213 computer-based; 79 iBT). *Application deadline:* For fall admission, 4/1 priority date for domestic students, 5/1 for international students; for spring admission, 10/1 priority date for domestic students, 10/1 for international students. Applications are processed on a rolling basis. Application fee: $50. Electronic applications accepted. *Expenses:* Tuition, state resident: full-time $2098.80; part-time $233.20 per credit hour. Tuition, nonresident: full-time $6650. Required fees: $25 per semester. Tuition and fees vary according to course load, program and reciprocity agreements. *Financial support:* Fellowships, research assistantships, teaching assistantships, career-related internships or fieldwork, Federal Work-Study, scholarships/grants, and unspecified assistantships available. Support available to part-time students. Financial award application deadline: 6/1. *Faculty research:* Corporate finance, investments, management in Latin America, management of technology, entrepreneurship. *Unit head:* Dr. Raul de Gouvea, Chair, 505-277-6471, Fax:

505-277-7108. *Application contact:* Megan Conner, Academic Advisement Manager, 505-277-3290, Fax: 505-277-8436, E-mail: mconner@mgt.unm.edu.

University of Pennsylvania, School of Engineering and Applied Science, Executive Master's in Technology Management Program, Philadelphia, PA 19104. Offers EMBA. Co-sponsored by The Wharton School. Part-time and evening/weekend programs available. *Students:* 4 full-time (0 women), 126 part-time (18 women); includes 35 minority (7 African Americans, 25 Asian Americans or Pacific Islanders, 3 Hispanic Americans), 4 international. 77 applicants, 56% accepted, 43 enrolled. In 2009, 40 master's awarded. *Application deadline:* For fall admission, 4/1 priority date for domestic students. Application fee: $70. *Expenses:* Tuition: Full-time $25,660; part-time $4758 per course. Required fees: $2152; $270 per course. Tuition and fees vary according to course load, degree level and program.

University of Phoenix, John Sperling School of Business, College of Information Systems and Technology, Phoenix, AZ 85034-7209. Offers e-business (MBA); management (MIS); technology management (MBA). Evening/weekend programs available. *Degree requirements:* For master's, thesis (for some programs). *Entrance requirements:* For master's, 3 years of work experience, minimum undergraduate GPA of 3.0. Additional exam requirements/recommendations for international students: Required—TOEFL (minimum score 550 paper-based; 213 computer-based; 79 iBT). Electronic applications accepted.

University of Phoenix–Atlanta Campus, John Sperling School of Business, College of Information Systems and Technology, Sandy Springs, GA 30350-4153. Offers information systems (MIS); technology management (MBA). Evening/weekend programs available. *Degree requirements:* For master's, thesis (for some programs). *Entrance requirements:* For master's, 3 years of work experience, minimum undergraduate GPA of 3.0. Additional exam requirements/recommendations for international students: Required—TOEFL (minimum score 550 paper-based; 213 computer-based; 79 iBT). Electronic applications accepted.

University of Phoenix–Augusta Campus, College of Information Systems and Technology, Augusta, GA 30909-4583. Offers information systems (MIS); technology management (MBA).

University of Phoenix–Austin Campus, College of Information Systems and Technology, Austin, TX 78759. Offers information systems (MIS); technology management (MBA).

University of Phoenix–Bay Area Campus, John Sperling School of Business, College of Information Systems and Technology, Pleasanton, CA 94588-3677. Offers e-business (MBA); information systems (MIS); technology management (MBA). Evening/weekend programs available. *Degree requirements:* For master's, thesis (for some programs). *Entrance requirements:* For master's, minimum undergraduate GPA of 3.0, 3 years of work experience. Additional exam requirements/recommendations for international students: Required—TOEFL (minimum score 550 paper-based; 213 computer-based; 79 iBT). Electronic applications accepted.

University of Phoenix–Birmingham Campus, College of Information Systems and Technology, Birmingham, AL 35244. Offers information systems (MIS); technology management (MBA).

University of Phoenix–Boston Campus, John Sperling School of Business, College of Information Systems and Technology, Braintree, MA 02184-4949. Offers technology management (MBA). Evening/weekend programs available. *Degree requirements:* For master's, thesis (for some programs). *Entrance requirements:* For master's, minimum GPA of 3.0, 3 years of work experience. Additional exam requirements/recommendations for international students: Required—TOEFL (minimum score 550 paper-based; 213 computer-based; 79 iBT). Electronic applications accepted.

University of Phoenix–Central Florida Campus, John Sperling School of Business, College of Information Systems and Technology, Maitland, FL 32751-7057. Offers management (MIS); technology management (MBA). Evening/weekend programs available. *Degree requirements:* For master's, thesis (for some programs). *Entrance requirements:* For master's, minimum undergraduate GPA of 3.0, 3 years work experience. Additional exam requirements/recommendations for international students: Required—TOEFL (minimum score 550 paper-based; 213 computer-based; 79 iBT). Electronic applications accepted.

University of Phoenix–Central Massachusetts Campus, John Sperling School of Business, College of Information Systems and Technology, Westborough, MA 01581-3906. Offers technology management (MBA). Evening/weekend programs available. *Degree requirements:* For master's, thesis (for some programs). *Entrance requirements:* For master's, minimum undergraduate GPA of 3.0, 3 years of work experience. Additional exam requirements/recommendations for international students: Required—TOEFL (minimum score 550 paper-based; 213 computer-based; 79 iBT). Electronic applications accepted.

University of Phoenix–Central Valley Campus, College of Information Systems and Technology, Fresno, CA 93720-1562. Offers information systems (MIS); technology management (MBA).

University of Phoenix–Charlotte Campus, John Sperling School of Business, College of Information Systems and Technology, Charlotte, NC 28273-3409. Offers information systems (MIS); information systems management (MISM); technology management (MBA). Evening/weekend programs available. *Degree requirements:* For master's, thesis (for some programs). *Entrance requirements:* For master's, minimum undergraduate GPA of 3.0, 3 years work experience. Additional exam requirements/recommendations for international students: Required—TOEFL (minimum score 550 paper-based; 213 computer-based; 79 iBT). Electronic applications accepted.

University of Phoenix–Chattanooga Campus, College of Information Systems and Technology, Chattanooga, TN 37421-3707. Offers information systems (MIS); technology management (MBA). Postbaccalaureate distance learning degree programs offered.

University of Phoenix–Cheyenne Campus, College of Information Systems and Technology, Cheyenne, WY 82009. Offers information systems (MIS); technology management (MBA).

University of Phoenix–Chicago Campus, John Sperling School of Business, College of Information Systems and Technology, Schaumburg, IL 60173-4399. Offers e-business (MBA); information systems (MIS); management (MM); technology management (MBA). Evening/weekend programs available. *Degree requirements:* For master's, thesis (for some programs). *Entrance requirements:* For master's, 3 years of work experience, minimum undergraduate GPA of 3.0. Additional exam requirements/recommendations for international students: Required—TOEFL (minimum score 550 paper-based; 213 computer-based; 79 iBT). Electronic applications accepted.

University of Phoenix–Cincinnati Campus, John Sperling School of Business, College of Information Systems and Technology, West Chester, OH 45069-4875. Offers electronic business (MBA); information systems (MIS); technology management (MBA). Evening/weekend programs available. Postbaccalaureate distance learning degree programs offered. *Degree requirements:* For master's, thesis (for some programs). *Entrance requirements:* For master's, minimum undergraduate GPA of 2.5, 3 years of work experience. Additional exam requirements/recommendations for international students: Required—TOEFL (minimum score 550 paper-based; 213 computer-based; 79 iBT). Electronic applications accepted.

University of Phoenix–Cleveland Campus, John Sperling School of Business, College of Information Systems and Technology, Independence, OH 44131-2194. Offers information management (MIS); technology management (MBA). Evening/weekend programs available. Postbaccalaureate distance learning degree programs offered (no on-campus study). *Degree requirements:* For master's, thesis (for some programs). *Entrance requirements:* For master's, minimum undergraduate GPA of 3.0, 3 years of work experience. Additional exam requirements/recommendations for international students: Required—TOEFL (minimum score 550 paper-based; 213 computer-based; 79 iBT). Electronic applications accepted.

University of Phoenix–Columbia Campus, College of Information Systems and Technology, Columbia, SC 29223. Offers technology management (MBA).

University of Phoenix–Columbus Georgia Campus, John Sperling School of Business, College of Information Systems and Technology, Columbus, GA 31904-6321. Offers e-business (MBA); information systems (MIS); technology management (MBA). Evening/weekend programs available. Postbaccalaureate distance learning degree programs offered. *Degree requirements:* For master's, thesis (for some programs). *Entrance requirements:* For master's, minimum undergraduate GPA of 3.0, 3 years of work experience. Additional exam requirements/recommendations for international students: Required—TOEFL (minimum score 550 paper-based; 213 computer-based; 79 iBT). Electronic applications accepted.

University of Phoenix–Columbus Ohio Campus, John Sperling School of Business, College of Information Systems and Technology, Columbus, OH 43240-4032. Offers information systems (MIS); technology management (MBA). Postbaccalaureate distance learning degree programs offered.

University of Phoenix–Dallas Campus, John Sperling School of Business, College of Information Systems and Technology, Dallas, TX 75251-2009. Offers e-business (MBA); information systems (MIS); technology management (MBA). Evening/weekend programs available. *Degree requirements:* For master's, thesis (for some programs). *Entrance requirements:* For master's, minimum undergraduate GPA of 3.0, 3 years of work experience. Additional exam requirements/recommendations for international students: Required—TOEFL (minimum score 550 paper-based; 213 computer-based; 79 iBT). Electronic applications accepted.

University of Phoenix–Denver Campus, John Sperling School of Business, College of Information Systems and Technology, Lone Tree, CO 80124-5453. Offers e-business (MBA); management (MIS); technology management (MBA). Evening/weekend programs available. Postbaccalaureate distance learning degree programs offered. *Degree requirements:* For master's, thesis (for some programs). *Entrance requirements:* For master's, minimum undergraduate GPA of 3.0, 3 years of work experience. Additional exam requirements/recommendations for international students: Required—TOEFL (minimum score 550 paper-based; 213 computer-based; 79 iBT). Electronic applications accepted.

University of Phoenix–Des Moines Campus, College of Information Systems and Technology, Des Moines, IA 50266. Offers information systems (MIS); technology management (MBA). Postbaccalaureate distance learning degree programs offered.

University of Phoenix–Eastern Washington Campus, John Sperling School of Business, College of Information Systems and Technology, Spokane Valley, WA 99212-2531. Offers technology management (MBA).

University of Phoenix–Harrisburg Campus, College of Information Systems and Technology, Harrisburg, PA 17112. Offers information systems (MIS); technology management (MBA). Postbaccalaureate distance learning degree programs offered.

University of Phoenix–Hawaii Campus, John Sperling School of Business, College of Information Systems and Technology, Honolulu, HI 96813-4317. Offers information systems (MIS); technology management (MBA). Evening/weekend programs available. *Degree requirements:* For master's, thesis (for some programs). *Entrance requirements:* For master's, minimum undergraduate GPA of 3.0, 3 years of work experience. Additional exam requirements/recommendations for international students: Required—TOEFL (minimum score 550 paper-based; 213 computer-based; 79 iBT). Electronic applications accepted.

University of Phoenix–Houston Campus, John Sperling School of Business, College of Information Systems and Technology, Houston, TX 77079-2004. Offers e-business (MBA); information systems (MIS); technology management (MBA). Evening/weekend programs available. Postbaccalaureate distance learning degree programs offered. *Degree requirements:* For master's, comprehensive exam (for some programs), thesis. *Entrance requirements:* For master's, minimum undergraduate GPA of 3.0, 3 years of work experience. Additional exam requirements/recommendations for international students: Required—TOEFL (minimum score 550 paper-based; 213 computer-based; 79 iBT). Electronic applications accepted.

University of Phoenix–Idaho Campus, John Sperling School of Business, College of Information Systems and Technology, Meridian, ID 83642-3014. Offers information systems (MIS); technology management (MBA). Evening/weekend programs available. *Degree requirements:* For master's, thesis (for some programs). *Entrance requirements:* For master's, minimum undergraduate GPA of 3.0, 3 years of work experience. Additional exam requirements/recommendations for international students: Required—TOEFL (minimum score 550 paper-based; 213 computer-based). Electronic applications accepted.

University of Phoenix–Indianapolis Campus, John Sperling School of Business, College of Information Systems and Technology, Indianapolis, IN 46250-932. Offers information systems (MIS); technology management (MBA). Evening/weekend programs available. *Degree requirements:* For master's, thesis (for some programs). *Entrance requirements:* For master's, minimum undergraduate GPA of 3.0, 3 years of work experience. Additional exam requirements/recommendations for international students: Required—TOEFL (minimum score 550 paper-based; 213 computer-based). Electronic applications accepted.

University of Phoenix–Jersey City Campus, College of Information Systems and Technology, Jersey City, NJ 07310. Offers information systems (MIS); technology management (MBA). Postbaccalaureate distance learning degree programs offered.

University of Phoenix–Kansas City Campus, John Sperling School of Business, College of Information Systems and Technology, Kansas City, MO 64131-4517. Offers management (MIS); technology management (MBA). Evening/weekend programs available. *Degree requirements:* For master's, thesis (for some programs). *Entrance requirements:* For master's, minimum undergraduate GPA of 3.0, 3 years of work experience. Additional exam requirements/recommendations for international students: Required—TOEFL (minimum score 550 paper-based; 213 computer-based). Electronic applications accepted.

University of Phoenix–Las Vegas Campus, John Sperling School of Business, College of Information Systems and Technology, Las Vegas, NV 89128. Offers information systems (MIS); technology management (MBA). Evening/weekend programs available. *Degree requirements:* For master's, thesis (for some programs). *Entrance requirements:* For master's, minimum undergraduate GPA of 3.0, 3 years of work experience. Additional exam requirements/recommendations for international students: Required—TOEFL (minimum score 550 paper-based; 213 computer-based; 79 iBT). Electronic applications accepted.

University of Phoenix–Louisiana Campus, John Sperling School of Business, College of Information Systems and Technology, Metairie, LA 70001-2082. Offers information systems/management (MIS); technology management (MBA). Evening/weekend programs available. *Degree requirements:* For master's, thesis (for some programs). *Entrance requirements:* For master's, minimum undergraduate GPA of 3.0, 3 years work experience. Additional exam requirements/recommendations for international students: Required—TOEFL (minimum score 550 paper-based; 213 computer-based). Electronic applications accepted.

University of Phoenix–Louisville Campus, College of Information Systems and Technology, Louisville, KY 40223-3839. Offers technology management (MBA). Postbaccalaureate distance learning degree programs offered.

University of Phoenix–Madison Campus, College of Information Systems and Technology, Madison, WI 53718-2416. Offers information systems (MIS); management (MIS); technology management (MBA).

University of Phoenix–Madison Campus, John Sperling School of Business, College of Information Systems and Technology, Madison, WI 53718-2416. Offers information systems (MIS); technology management (MBA). Evening/weekend programs available. *Degree requirements:* For master's, thesis (for some programs). *Entrance requirements:* For master's, 3 years of work experience, minimum undergraduate GPA of 3.0. Additional exam requirements/recommendations for international students: Required—TOEFL (minimum score 550 paper-based; 213 computer-based; 79 iBT). Electronic applications accepted.

University of Phoenix–Maryland Campus, John Sperling School of Business, College of Information Systems and Technology, Columbia, MD 21045-5424. Offers information systems (MIS); technology management (MBA). Evening/weekend programs available. *Degree requirements:* For master's, thesis (for some programs). *Entrance requirements:* For master's, minimum undergraduate GPA of 3.0, 3 years of work experience. Additional exam requirements/recommendations for international students: Required—TOEFL (minimum score 550 paper-based; 213 computer-based; 79 iBT). Electronic applications accepted.

University of Phoenix–Memphis Campus, College of Information Systems and Technology, Cordova, TN 38018. Offers information systems (MIS); technology management (MBA).

University of Phoenix–Metro Detroit Campus, John Sperling School of Business, College of Information Systems and Technology, Troy, MI 48098-2623. Offers management (MIS); technology management (MBA). Evening/weekend programs available. *Degree requirements:* For master's, thesis (for some programs). *Entrance requirements:* For master's, minimum undergraduate GPA of 3.0, 3 years work experience. Additional exam requirements/recommendations for international students: Required—TOEFL (minimum score 550 paper-based; 213 computer-based; 79 iBT). Electronic applications accepted.

University of Phoenix–Minneapolis/St. Louis Park Campus, College of Information Systems and Technology, St. Louis Park, MN 55426. Offers technology management (MBA).

University of Phoenix–Nashville Campus, John Sperling School of Business, College of Information Systems and Technology, Nashville, TN 37214-5048. Offers technology management (MBA). Evening/weekend programs available. *Degree requirements:* For master's, thesis (for some programs). *Entrance requirements:* For master's, 3 years of work experience, minimum undergraduate GPA of 3.0. Additional exam requirements/recommendations for international students: Required—TOEFL (minimum score 550 paper-based; 213 computer-based; 79 iBT). Electronic applications accepted.

University of Phoenix–New Mexico Campus, John Sperling School of Business, College of Information Systems and Technology, Albuquerque, NM 87113-1570. Offers e-business (MBA); information systems (MS); technology management (MBA). Evening/weekend programs available. *Degree requirements:* For master's, thesis (for some programs). *Entrance requirements:* For master's, minimum undergraduate GPA of 3.0, 3 years of work experience. Additional exam requirements/recommendations for international students: Required—TOEFL (minimum score 550 paper-based; 213 computer-based; 79 iBT). Electronic applications accepted.

University of Phoenix–Northern Nevada Campus, College of Information Systems and Technology, Reno, NV 89521-5862. Offers information systems (MIS); technology management (MBA).

University of Phoenix–Northern Virginia Campus, College of Information Systems and Technology, Reston, VA 20190. Offers information systems and technology (MIS); management (MIS); technology management (MBA).

University of Phoenix–Northwest Arkansas Campus, College of Information Systems and Technology, Rogers, AR 72756-9615. Offers information systems (MIS); technology management (MBA).

University of Phoenix–Oklahoma City Campus, John Sperling School of Business, College of Information Systems and Technology, Oklahoma City, OK 73116-8244. Offers e-business (MBA); technology management (MBA). Evening/weekend programs available. *Degree requirements:* For master's, thesis (for some programs). *Entrance requirements:* For master's, minimum undergraduate GPA of 3.0, 3 years of work experience. Additional exam requirements/recommendations for international students: Required—TOEFL (minimum score 550 paper-based; 213 computer-based; 79 iBT). Electronic applications accepted.

University of Phoenix–Omaha Campus, College of Information Systems and Technology, Omaha, NE 68154-5240. Offers information systems (MIS); technology management (MBA).

University of Phoenix–Oregon Campus, The John Sperling School of Business, College of Information Systems and Technology, Tigard, OR 97223. Offers information systems (MIS); technology management (MBA). Evening/weekend programs available. *Degree requirements:* For master's, thesis (for some programs). *Entrance requirements:* For master's, minimum undergraduate GPA of 2.5, 3 years work experience. Additional exam requirements/recommendations for international students: Required—TOEFL (minimum score 550 paper-based; 213 computer-based; 79 iBT). Electronic applications accepted.

University of Phoenix–Philadelphia Campus, The John Sperling School of Business, College of Information Systems and Technology, Wayne, PA 19087-2121. Offers information systems (MIS); technology management (MBA). Evening/weekend programs available. *Degree requirements:* For master's, thesis (for some programs). *Entrance requirements:* For master's, 3 years of work experience, minimum undergraduate GPA of 3.0. Additional exam requirements/recommendations for international students: Required—TOEFL (minimum score 550 paper-based; 213 computer-based; 79 iBT). Electronic applications accepted.

University of Phoenix–Phoenix Campus, The John Sperling School of Business, College of Information Systems and Technology, Phoenix, AZ 85040-1958. Offers management (MIS); technology management (MBA). Evening/weekend programs available. *Degree requirements:* For master's, thesis (for some programs). *Entrance requirements:* For master's, 3 years of work experience, minimum undergraduate GPA of 3.0. Additional exam requirements/recommendations for international students: Required—TOEFL (minimum score 550 paper-based; 213 computer-based; 79 iBT). Electronic applications accepted.

University of Phoenix–Pittsburgh Campus, John Sperling School of Business, College of Information Systems and Technology, Pittsburgh, PA 15276. Offers e-business (MBA); information systems (MIS); technology management (MBA). Evening/weekend programs available. *Degree requirements:* For master's, thesis (for some programs). *Entrance requirements:* For master's, minimum undergraduate GPA of 3.0, 3 years work experience. Additional exam requirements/recommendations for international students: Required—TOEFL (minimum score 550 paper-based; 213 computer-based; 79 iBT). Electronic applications accepted.

University of Phoenix–Puerto Rico Campus, John Sperling School of Business, College of Information Systems and Technology, Guaynabo, PR 00968. Offers technology management (MBA). Evening/weekend programs available. *Degree requirements:* For master's, thesis (for some programs). *Entrance requirements:* For master's, minimum undergraduate GPA of 3.0, 3 years of work experience. Additional exam requirements/recommendations for international students: Required—TOEFL (minimum score 550 paper-based; 213 computer-based; 79 iBT). Electronic applications accepted.

University of Phoenix–Raleigh Campus, College of Information Systems and Technology, Raleigh, NC 27606. Offers information systems and technology (MIS); management (MIS); technology management (MBA).

University of Phoenix–Richmond Campus, John Sperling School of Business, College of Information Systems and Technology, Richmond, VA 23230. Offers information systems (MIS); technology management (MBA). Evening/weekend programs available. *Degree requirements:*

Management of Technology

University of Phoenix–Richmond Campus *(continued)*
For master's, thesis (for some programs). *Entrance requirements:* For master's, minimum undergraduate GPA of 3.0, 3 years work experience. Additional exam requirements/recommendations for international students: Required—TOEFL (minimum score 500 paper-based; 213 computer-based; 79 iBT). Electronic applications accepted.

University of Phoenix–Sacramento Valley Campus, John Sperling School of Business, College of Information Systems and Technology, Sacramento, CA 95833-3632. Offers management (MIS); technology management (MBA). Evening/weekend programs available. *Degree requirements:* For master's, thesis (for some programs). *Entrance requirements:* For master's, minimum undergraduate GPA of 3.0, 3 years work experience. Additional exam requirements/recommendations for international students: Required—TOEFL (minimum score 550 paper-based; 213 computer-based; 79 iBT). Electronic applications accepted.

University of Phoenix–San Antonio Campus, College of Information Systems and Technology, San Antonio, TX 78230. Offers information systems (MIS); technology management (MBA).

University of Phoenix–San Diego Campus, John Sperling School of Business, College of Information Systems and Technology, San Diego, CA 92123. Offers management (MIS); technology management (MBA). Evening/weekend programs available. *Degree requirements:* For master's, thesis (for some programs). *Entrance requirements:* For master's, minimum undergraduate GPA of 3.0, 3 years work experience. Additional exam requirements/recommendations for international students: Required—TOEFL (minimum score 550 paper-based; 213 computer-based; 79 iBT). Electronic applications accepted.

University of Phoenix–Savannah Campus, College of Information Systems and Technology, Savannah, GA 31405-7400. Offers information systems and technology (MIS); technology management (MBA).

University of Phoenix–Southern Arizona Campus, John Sperling School of Business, College of Information Systems and Technology, Tucson, AZ 85711. Offers information systems (MIS); technology management (MBA). Evening/weekend programs available. *Degree requirements:* For master's, thesis (for some programs). *Entrance requirements:* For master's, minimum undergraduate GPA of 3.0, 3 years of work experience. Additional exam requirements/recommendations for international students: Required—TOEFL (minimum score 550 paper-based; 213 computer-based; 79 iBT). Electronic applications accepted.

University of Phoenix–Southern Colorado Campus, John Sperling School of Business, College of Information Systems and Technology, Colorado Springs, CO 80919-2335. Offers technology management (MBA). Evening/weekend programs available. *Degree requirements:* For master's, thesis (for some programs). *Entrance requirements:* For master's, minimum undergraduate GPA of 3.0, 3 years of work experience. Additional exam requirements/recommendations for international students: Required—TOEFL (minimum score 550 paper-based; 213 computer-based; 79 iBT). Electronic applications accepted.

University of Phoenix–Springfield Campus, College of Information Systems and Technology, Springfield, MO 65804-7211. Offers information systems (MIS); technology management (MBA).

University of Phoenix–Tulsa Campus, John Sperling School of Business, College of Information Systems and Technology, Tulsa, OK 74134-1412. Offers information systems and technology (MIS); technology management (MBA).

University of Phoenix–Utah Campus, John Sperling School of Business, College of Graduate Business and Management, Salt Lake City, UT 84123-4617. Offers accounting (MBA); business administration (MBA); global management (MBA); human resource management (MBA, MM); management (MM); marketing (MBA); technology management (MBA). Evening/weekend programs available. *Degree requirements:* For master's, thesis (for some programs). *Entrance requirements:* For master's, minimum undergraduate GPA of 3.0, 3 years of work experience. Additional exam requirements/recommendations for international students: Required—TOEFL (minimum score 550 paper-based; 213 computer-based; 79 iBT). Electronic applications accepted.

University of Phoenix–Vancouver Campus, John Sperling School of Business, College of Information Systems and Technology, Burnaby, BC V5C 6G9, Canada. Offers technology management (MBA). Evening/weekend programs available. *Degree requirements:* For master's, thesis (for some programs). *Entrance requirements:* For master's, minimum undergraduate GPA of 3.0, 3 years of work experience. Additional exam requirements/recommendations for international students: Required—TOEFL (minimum score 550 paper-based; 213 computer-based; 79 iBT). Electronic applications accepted.

University of Phoenix–Western Washington Campus, College of Information Systems and Technology, Tukwila, WA 98188. Offers information systems (MIS); technology management (MBA). Evening/weekend programs available. *Degree requirements:* For master's, thesis (for some programs). *Entrance requirements:* For master's, minimum undergraduate GPA of 3.0, 3 years of work experience. Additional exam requirements/recommendations for international students: Required—TOEFL (minimum score 550 paper-based; 213 computer-based; 79 iBT). Electronic applications accepted.

University of Phoenix–West Florida Campus, The John Sperling School of Business, College of Information Systems and Technology, Temple Terrace, FL 33637. Offers information systems (MIS); technology management (MBA). Evening/weekend programs available. *Degree requirements:* For master's, thesis (for some programs). *Entrance requirements:* For master's, minimum undergraduate GPA of 3.0, 3 years work experience. Additional exam requirements/recommendations for international students: Required—TOEFL (minimum score 550 paper-based; 213 computer-based; 79 iBT). Electronic applications accepted.

University of St. Thomas, Graduate Studies, School of Engineering, St. Paul, MN 55105-1096. Offers engineering and technology management (Certificate); manufacturing systems (MS); manufacturing systems engineering (MMSE); systems engineering (MS); technology management (MS). *Accreditation:* ABET (one or more programs are accredited). Electronic applications accepted. *Expenses:* Contact institution.

University of Washington, Graduate School, Michael G. Foster School of Business, Seattle, WA 98195-3200. Offers auditing and assurance (MP Acc); business (PhD); business administration (evening) (MBA); business administration (full-time) (MBA); executive business administration (MBA); global business administration (MBA); global executive business administration (MBA); taxation (MP Acc); technology management (MBA); JD/MBA; MBA/MAIS; MBA/MHA. *Accreditation:* AACSB. Part-time and evening/weekend programs available. Terminal master's awarded for partial completion of doctoral program. *Degree requirements:* For doctorate, comprehensive exam, thesis/dissertation. *Entrance requirements:* For master's, GMAT; for doctorate, GMAT, GRE. Additional exam requirements/recommendations for international students: Required—TOEFL (minimum score 600 paper-based; 250 computer-based). Electronic applications accepted. *Expenses:* Contact institution. *Faculty research:* Finance, marketing, organizational behavior, information technology, strategy.

University of Waterloo, Graduate Studies, Centre for Business, Entrepreneurship and Technology, Waterloo, ON N2L 3G1, Canada. Offers MBET. *Entrance requirements:* For master's, honors degree. Additional exam requirements/recommendations for international students: Required—TOEFL (minimum score 550 paper-based; 213 computer-based), TWE. Electronic applications accepted.

University of Waterloo, Graduate Studies, Faculty of Engineering, Department of Management Sciences, Waterloo, ON N2L 3G1, Canada. Offers applied operations research (MA Sc, MMS, PhD); information systems (MA Sc, MMS, PhD); management of technology (MA Sc, MMS, PhD). Part-time programs available. Postbaccalaureate distance learning degree programs offered (no on-campus study). *Degree requirements:* For master's, research paper or thesis; for doctorate, comprehensive exam, thesis/dissertation. *Entrance requirements:* For master's, GMAT or GRE, honors degree, minimum B average, resume; for doctorate, GMAT or GRE, master's degree, minimum A- average, resumé. Additional exam requirements/recommendations for international students: Required—TOEFL, TWE. *Faculty research:* Operations research, manufacturing systems, scheduling, information systems.

University of Wisconsin–Madison, Graduate School, Wisconsin School of Business, Wisconsin Full-Time MBA Program, Madison, WI 53706-1380. Offers applied corporate finance (MBA); applied security analysis (MBA); arts administration (MBA); brand and product management (MBA); entrepreneurial management (MBA); marketing research (MBA); operations and technology management (MBA); real estate (MBA); risk management and insurance (MBA); strategic human resource management (MBA); strategic management in the life and engineering sciences (MBA); supply chain management (MBA). *Faculty:* 32 full-time (5 women). *Students:* 242 full-time (74 women); includes 47 minority (16 African Americans, 3 American Indian/Alaska Native, 16 Asian Americans or Pacific Islanders, 12 Hispanic Americans), 29 international. Average age 28. 526 applicants, 32% accepted, 117 enrolled. In 2009, 106 master's awarded. *Entrance requirements:* For master's, GMAT, bachelor's or equivalent degree, 2 years of work experience, letters of recommendation. Additional exam requirements/recommendations for international students: Required—TOEFL (minimum score 600 paper-based; 250 computer-based; 100 iBT), IELTS. *Application deadline:* For fall admission, 11/4 for domestic and international students; for winter admission, 2/5 for domestic and international students; for spring admission, 5/26 for domestic students, 4/5 for international students. Applications are processed on a rolling basis. Application fee: $56. Electronic applications accepted. *Expenses:* Tuition, state resident: part-time $594 per credit. Tuition, nonresident: part-time $1504 per credit. Required fees: $65 per credit. Tuition and fees vary according to course load, program and reciprocity agreements. *Financial support:* In 2009–10, 103 students received support, including 13 fellowships with full and partial tuition reimbursements available (averaging $15,000 per year), 53 research assistantships with full tuition reimbursements available (averaging $8,000 per year), 35 teaching assistantships with full tuition reimbursements available (averaging $11,000 per year); scholarships/grants, health care benefits, and unspecified assistantships also available. Financial award application deadline: 4/5; financial award applicants required to submit FAFSA. *Unit head:* Prof. Kenneth A. Kavajecz, Associate Dean of Master's Programs, 608-265-3494, Fax: 608-265-4192, E-mail: kkavajecz@bus.wisc.edu. *Application contact:* Maria Reis, Assistant Director of MBA Marketing and Recruiting, 608-262-4000, Fax: 608-265-4192, E-mail: mreis@bus.wisc.edu.

University of Wisconsin–Stout, Graduate School, College of Technology, Engineering, and Management, Program in Technology Management, Menomonie, WI 54751. Offers MS. Part-time programs available. *Degree requirements:* For master's, thesis. *Entrance requirements:* For master's, minimum GPA of 2.75. Additional exam requirements/recommendations for international students: Required—TOEFL (minimum score 500 paper-based; 173 computer-based; 61 iBT). Electronic applications accepted. *Faculty research:* Miniature engines, solid modeling, packaging, lean manufacturing, supply chain management.

University of Wisconsin–Whitewater, School of Graduate Studies, College of Business and Economics, Program in Business Administration, Whitewater, WI 53190-1790. Offers finance (MBA); human resource management (MBA); information technology management (MBA); international business (MBA); management (MBA); marketing (MBA); operations and supply chain management (MBA); technology and training (MBA). *Accreditation:* AACSB. Part-time and evening/weekend programs available. Postbaccalaureate distance learning degree programs offered (no on-campus study). *Degree requirements:* For master's, thesis or alternative. *Entrance requirements:* For master's, GMAT, minimum AACSB index of 1000, minimum GPA of 2.75. Additional exam requirements/recommendations for international students: Required—TOEFL (minimum score 550 paper-based; 213 computer-based). Electronic applications accepted. *Faculty research:* Interface between social institutions and individual behavior, technology and innovation management, occupational mental health, workplace deviance and workplace romance.

Walden University, Graduate Programs, NTU School of Engineering and Applied Science, Minneapolis, MN 55401. Offers competitive product management (Postbaccalaureate Certificate); engineering management (Postbaccalaureate Certificate); software engineering (MS); software project management (Postbaccalaureate Certificate); software testing (Postbaccalaureate Certificate); systems engineering (MS, Postbaccalaureate Certificate); technical project management (Postbaccalaureate Certificate). Part-time and evening/weekend programs available. Postbaccalaureate distance learning degree programs offered (no on-campus study). *Faculty:* 31 part-time/adjunct. *Students:* 22 full-time (6 women), 120 part-time (14 women); includes 26 minority (19 African Americans, 7 Asian Americans or Pacific Islanders). Average age 38. In 2009, 41 master's awarded. *Degree requirements:* For master's, thesis optional. *Entrance requirements:* For master's, bachelor's degree or equivalent in related field, minimum GPA of 2.5. Additional exam requirements/recommendations for international students: Required—TOEFL (minimum score 550 paper-based; 213 computer-based), IELTS (minimum score 6.5), or Michigan English Language Assessment Battery (minimum score 82). *Application deadline:* Applications are processed on a rolling basis. Application fee: $50. Electronic applications accepted. *Expenses:* Tuition: Full-time $13,665; part-time $560 per credit. Required fees: $1375. Tuition and fees vary according to course load, degree level and program. *Financial support:* Fellowships, Federal Work-Study, scholarships/grants, unspecified assistantships, and family tuition reduction, active duty/veteran tuition reduction, group tuition reduction, interest-free payment plans available. Support available to part-time students. Financial award applicants required to submit FAFSA. *Unit head:* Colin Wightman, Interim Associate Dean, 800-925-3368. *Application contact:* Jennifer Hall, Director of Enrollment, 866-4-WALDEN, E-mail: info@walden.edu.

Walden University, Graduate Programs, School of Management, Minneapolis, MN 55401. Offers applied management and decision sciences (PhD), including accounting, engineering management, finance, general applied management and decision sciences, information systems management, knowledge management, leadership and organizational change, learning management, operations research, self-designed program in applied management and design sciences; business information management (MISM); enterprise information security (MISM); entrepreneurship (MBA, DBA); finance (MBA, DBA); global supply chain management (DBA); healthcare management (MBA); healthcare system improvement (MBA); human resource management (MBA); information systems management (DBA); international business (MBA, DBA); IT strategy and governance (MISM); leadership (MBA, MS, DBA), including entrepreneurship (MS), general management (MS), human resources leadership (MS), innovation and technology (MS), leader development (MS), project management (MS), self-designed (MS), sustainable futures (MS); managing global software and service supply chains (MISM); marketing (MBA, DBA); project management (MBA, MS); risk management (MBA); self-designed (MBA, DBA); social impact management (DBA); sustainable futures (MBA); technology (MBA); technology entrepreneurship (DBA). Part-time and evening/weekend programs available. Postbaccalaureate distance learning degree programs offered (minimal on-campus study). *Faculty:* 17 full-time, 211 part-time/adjunct. *Students:* 3,389 full-time (1,774 women), 815 part-time (482 women); includes 1,969 minority (1,640 African Americans, 36 American Indian/Alaska Native, 123 Asian Americans or Pacific Islanders, 170 Hispanic Americans), 95 international. Average age 41. In 2009, 699 master's, 42 doctorates awarded. *Degree requirements:* For doctorate, thesis/dissertation (for some programs), residency. *Entrance requirements:* For master's, bachelor's degree or equivalent in related field; minimum GPA of 2.5; official transcripts; goal statement; access to computer and Internet; for doctorate, master's degree or equivalent in related field; minimum GPA of 3.0; 3 years of related professional/academic experience (preferred). Additional exam requirements/recommendations for international students: Required—TOEFL (minimum score 550 paper-based; 213 computer-based), IELTS (minimum score 6.5), TOEFL, IELTS, or Michigan English Language Assessment Battery (minimum score 82). *Application deadline:* Applications are processed on a rolling basis. Application fee: $50. Electronic applications accepted. *Expenses:* Tuition: Full-time $13,665; part-time $560 per credit. Required fees: $1375. Tuition and fees vary according to course load, degree level and program. *Financial support:* In 2009–10, 466 students received support; fellowships, Federal Work-Study, scholarships/grants, unspecified assistantships, and family tuition reduction, active duty/veteran tuition reduction, group tuition reduction, interest-free payment plans available. Support available to part-time students. Financial award applicants required to submit FAFSA. *Unit head:* William Schulz, Interim Associate Dean, 800-925-3368. *Application contact:* Jennifer Hall, Director of Enrollment, 866-4-WALDEN, E-mail: info@waldenu.edu.

West Chester University of Pennsylvania, Office of Graduate Studies, College of Business and Public Affairs, Department of Marketing, West Chester, PA 19383. Offers business administration: tech-electronic (MBA). Part-time and evening/weekend programs available. *Students:* 2 part-time (1 woman). Average age 44. 1 applicant, 100% accepted, 0 enrolled. In 2009, 2 master's awarded. *Entrance requirements:* For master's, GMAT, statement of professional goals, resume, two letters of reference. Additional exam requirements/recommendations for international students: Required—TOEFL (minimum score 550 paper-based; 213 computer-based; 80 iBT). *Application deadline:* For fall admission, 4/15 for domestic students, 3/15 for international students; for spring admission, 10/15 for domestic students, 9/1 for international students. Applications are processed on a rolling basis. Application fee: $35. Electronic applications accepted. *Expenses:* Tuition, state resident: full-time $6666; part-time $370 per credit. Tuition, nonresident: full-time $10,666; part-time $593 per credit. Required fees: $122.56 per credit. *Financial support:* In 2009–10, research assistantships with full and partial tuition reimbursements (averaging $5,000 per year); unspecified assistantships also available. Support available to part-time students. Financial award application deadline: 2/15; financial award applicants required to submit FAFSA. *Unit head:* Dr. Paul Christ, MBA Director and Graduate Coordinator, 610-425-5000, E-mail: pchrist@wcupa.edu. *Application contact:* Office of Graduate Studies, 610-436-2943, Fax: 610-436-2763, E-mail: gradstudy@wcupa.edu.

Westminster College, The Bill and Vieve Gore School of Business, Salt Lake City, UT 84105-3697. Offers accountancy (M Acc); business administration (MBA, Certificate); technology management (MBATM). *Accreditation:* ACBSP. Part-time and evening/weekend programs available. *Faculty:* 27 full-time (7 women), 28 part-time/adjunct (5 women). *Students:* 189 full-time (36 women), 286 part-time (71 women); includes 32 minority (3 African Americans, 17 Asian Americans or Pacific Islanders, 12 Hispanic Americans), 5 international. Average age 32. 410 applicants, 48% accepted, 167 enrolled. In 2009, 141 master's, 44 other advanced degrees awarded. *Degree requirements:* For master's, international trip, minimum grade of C in all classes. *Entrance requirements:* For master's, GMAT, 2 professional recommendations, employer letter of support, personal resume. Additional exam requirements/recommendations for international students: Required—TOEFL (minimum score 600 paper-based; 214 computer-based; 100 iBT), IELTS (minimum score 7). *Application deadline:* Applications are processed on a rolling basis. Application fee: $40. Electronic applications accepted. *Expenses:* Contact institution. *Financial support:* In 2009–10, 205 students received support. Career-related internships or fieldwork and tuition reimbursement, tuition remission available. Support available to part-time students. Financial award applicants required to submit FAFSA. *Faculty research:* Innovation and entrepreneurship, business strategy and change, financial analysis and capital budgeting, leadership development. Total annual research expenditures: $100,000. *Unit head:* John Groesbeck, Dean, 801-832-2600, Fax: 801-832-3106, E-mail: jgroesbeck@westminstercollege.edu. *Application contact:* Joel Bauman, Vice President of Enrollment Services, 801-832-2200, Fax: 801-832-3101, E-mail: admission@westminstercollege.edu.

Operations Research

Air Force Institute of Technology, Graduate School of Engineering and Management, Department of Operational Sciences, Dayton, OH 45433-7765. Offers logistics management (MS); operations research (MS, PhD); space operations (MS). Part-time programs available. *Degree requirements:* For master's, thesis; for doctorate, thesis/dissertation. *Entrance requirements:* For doctorate, GRE General Test, minimum GPA of 3.0, U.S. citizenship. *Faculty research:* Optimization, simulation, combat modeling and analysis, reliability and maintainability, resource scheduling.

Bowling Green State University, Graduate College, College of Arts and Sciences, Department of Computer Science, Bowling Green, OH 43403. Offers computer science (MS), including operations research, parallel and distributed computing, software engineering. Part-time programs available. *Degree requirements:* For master's, thesis or alternative. *Entrance requirements:* For master's, GRE General Test. Additional exam requirements/recommendations for international students: Required—TOEFL. Electronic applications accepted. *Faculty research:* Artificial intelligence, real time and concurrent programming languages, behavioral aspects of computing, network protocols.

California State University, East Bay, Academic Programs and Graduate Studies, College of Business and Economics, Department of Information Technology Management, Hayward, CA 94542-3000. Offers human resources and organizational behavior (MBA); information technology management (MBA); operations and supply chain management (MBA); strategy and international business (MBA). Part-time and evening/weekend programs available. *Faculty:* 37 full-time (7 women), 8 part-time/adjunct (3 women). *Students:* Average age 32. *Degree requirements:* For master's, comprehensive exam or thesis. *Entrance requirements:* For master's, GMAT, minimum GPA of 2.75. Additional exam requirements/recommendations for international students: Required—TOEFL (minimum score 550 paper-based; 213 computer-based). *Application deadline:* For fall admission, 6/30 for domestic and international students. Application fee: $55. Electronic applications accepted. *Financial support:* Career-related internships or fieldwork, Federal Work-Study, and institutionally sponsored loans available. Support available to part-time students. Financial award application deadline: 3/1; financial award applicants required to submit FAFSA. *Unit head:* Dr. Xinjian Lu, Chair, 510-885-3307, Fax: 510-885-2165, E-mail: xinjian.lu@csueastbay.edu. *Application contact:* Donna Wiley, Interim Associate Director, 510-885-2928, Fax: 510-885-4777.

Carnegie Mellon University, Tepper School of Business, Program in Operations Research, Pittsburgh, PA 15213-3891. Offers PhD. *Degree requirements:* For doctorate, thesis/dissertation. *Entrance requirements:* For doctorate, GMAT or GRE General Test.

Case Western Reserve University, Weatherhead School of Management, Department of Operations, Management Program, Cleveland, OH 44106. Offers operations research (MSM); supply chain (MSM); MBA/MSM. *Accreditation:* AACSB. Part-time and evening/weekend programs available. *Students:* Average age 28. *Entrance requirements:* For master's, GMAT or GRE, 3 letters of recommendation, resume. Additional exam requirements/recommendations for international students: Required—TOEFL (minimum score 600 paper-based; 250 computer-based). Application fee: $100. *Financial support:* Career-related internships or fieldwork, institutionally sponsored loans, scholarships/grants, tuition waivers (partial), and unspecified assistantships available. Financial award application deadline: 3/1. *Faculty research:* Supply chain management, operations management, operations/finance interface optimization, scheduling. *Unit head:* Kamlesh Mathur, Chairman, 216-368-3857, E-mail: kamlesh.mathur@case.edu. *Application contact:* Olivia Seifert, Program Manager, 216-368-2031, Fax: 216-368-5548, E-mail: deborah.bibb@case.edu.

Claremont Graduate University, Graduate Programs, School of Mathematical Sciences, Claremont, CA 91711-6160. Offers computational and systems biology (PhD); computational mathematics and numerical analysis (MA, MS); computational science (PhD); engineering and industrial applied mathematics (PhD); mathematics (PhD); operations research and statistics (MA, MS); physical applied mathematics (MA, MS); pure mathematics (MA, MS); scientific computing (MA, MS); systems and control theory (MA, MS). Part-time programs available. *Faculty:* 5 full-time (0 women), 2 part-time/adjunct (0 women). *Students:* 56 full-time (20 women), 12 part-time (3 women); includes 13 minority (2 African Americans, 6 Asian Americans or Pacific Islanders, 5 Hispanic Americans), 25 international. Average age 33. In 2009, 7 master's, 7 doctorates awarded. Terminal master's awarded for partial completion of doctoral program. *Entrance requirements:* For master's and doctorate, GRE General Test. Additional exam requirements/recommendations for international students: Required—TOEFL (minimum score 550 paper-based; 213 computer-based; 80 iBT). *Application deadline:* For fall admission, 2/1 priority date for domestic students. Applications are processed on a rolling basis. Application fee: $60. Electronic applications accepted. *Expenses:* Tuition: Full-time $35,046; part-time $1524 per credit. Required fees: $161 per semester. *Financial support:* Fellowships, research assistantships, Federal Work-Study, institutionally sponsored loans, scholarships/grants, and tuition waivers (full and partial) available. Support available to part-time students. Financial award application deadline: 2/15; financial award applicants required to submit FAFSA. *Unit head:* John Angus, Dean, 909-621-8080, Fax: 909-607-8261, E-mail: john.angus@cgu.edu. *Application contact:* Susan Townzen, Program Coordinator, 909-621-8080, Fax: 909-607-8261, E-mail: susan.n.townzen@cgu.edu.

Clemson University, Graduate School, College of Engineering and Science, Department of Mathematical Sciences, Clemson, SC 29634. Offers applied and pure mathematics (MS, PhD); computational mathematics (MS, PhD); operations research (MS, PhD); statistics (MS, PhD). Part-time programs available. *Faculty:* 51 full-time (14 women), 9 part-time/adjunct (2 women). *Students:* 92 full-time (39 women), 1 part-time (0 women); includes 3 minority (2 African Americans, 1 American Indian/Alaska Native), 31 international. Average age 26. 134 applicants, 76% accepted, 20 enrolled. In 2009, 36 master's, 13 doctorates awarded. *Degree requirements:* For master's, thesis optional, final project; for doctorate, thesis/dissertation, qualifying exams. *Entrance requirements:* For master's and doctorate, GRE General Test. Additional exam requirements/recommendations for international students: Required—TOEFL. *Application deadline:* For fall admission, 1/15 priority date for domestic students, 2/15 priority date for international students; for spring admission, 10/1 priority date for domestic students, 9/15 priority date for international students. Applications are processed on a rolling basis. Application fee: $70 ($80 for international students). Electronic applications accepted. *Expenses:* Tuition, state resident: full-time $8684; part-time $528 per credit hour. Tuition, nonresident: full-time $15,330; part-time $1078 per credit hour. Required fees: $736; $37 per semester. Part-time tuition and fees vary according to course load and program. *Financial support:* In 2009–10, 85 students received support, including 1 fellowship with full and partial tuition reimbursement available (averaging $10,000 per year), 7 research assistantships with partial tuition reimbursements available (averaging $17,591 per year), 66 teaching assistantships with partial tuition reimbursements available (averaging $18,593 per year); career-related internships or fieldwork, institutionally sponsored loans, scholarships/grants, health care benefits, and unspecified assistantships also available. Support available to part-time students. Financial award application deadline: 4/15. *Faculty research:* Applied and computational analysis, cryptography, discrete mathematics, optimization, statistics. Total annual research expenditures: $535,985. *Unit head:* Dr. Robert L. Taylor, Chair, 864-656-5240, Fax: 864-656-5230, E-mail: rtaylo2@clemson.edu. *Application contact:* Dr. K. B. Kulasekera, Graduate Coordinator, 864-656-5231, Fax: 864-656-5230, E-mail: kk@clemson.edu.

The College of William and Mary, Faculty of Arts and Sciences, Department of Computer Science, Program in Computational Operations Research, Williamsburg, VA 23187-8795. Offers computer science (MS), including operations research. Part-time programs available. *Students:* 17 full-time (4 women); includes 1 minority (Hispanic American), 5 international. Average age 26. 19 applicants, 79% accepted, 10 enrolled. In 2009, 6 master's awarded. *Degree requirements:* For master's, research project. *Entrance requirements:* For master's, GRE General Test, minimum GPA of 2.5. Additional exam requirements/recommendations for international students: Required—TOEFL. *Application deadline:* For fall admission, 3/1 priority date for domestic students, 3/15 priority date for international students; for spring admission, 11/1 for domestic and international students. Applications are processed on a rolling basis. Application fee: $45. Electronic applications accepted. *Expenses:* Tuition, state resident: full-time $6400; part-time $315 per credit hour. Tuition, nonresident: full-time $19,720; part-time $840 per credit hour. Required fees: $4114. *Financial support:* In 2009–10, 13 students received support, including 6 fellowships (averaging $9,000 per year), 7 teaching assistantships with full tuition reimbursements available (averaging $11,500 per year); scholarships/grants, tuition waivers (full), and unspecified assistantships also available. Financial award application deadline: 3/1; financial award applicants required to submit FAFSA. *Faculty research:* Metaheuristics, reliability, optimization, statistics, networks. *Unit head:* Dr. Rex Kincaid, Professor, 757-221-2038, Fax: 757-221-1717, E-mail: rrkinc@math.wm.edu. *Application contact:* Vanessa Godwin, Administrative Director, 757-221-3455, Fax: 757-221-1717, E-mail: cor@cs.wm.edu.

Columbia University, Fu Foundation School of Engineering and Applied Science, Department of Industrial Engineering and Operations Research, New York, NY 10027. Offers engineering management systems (MS); financial engineering (MS); industrial engineering (Engr); industrial engineering and operations research (MS, Eng Sc D, PhD); MS/MBA. Part-time and evening/weekend programs available. Postbaccalaureate distance learning degree programs offered (no on-campus study). *Faculty:* 13 full-time (1 woman), 3 part-time/adjunct (1 woman). *Students:* 260 full-time (69 women), 173 part-time (50 women); includes 27 minority (1 African American, 24 Asian Americans or Pacific Islanders, 2 Hispanic Americans), 348 international. Average age 25. 1,262 applicants, 35% accepted, 193 enrolled. In 2009, 211 master's, 7 doctorates awarded. *Degree requirements:* For doctorate, thesis/dissertation, oral and written qualifying exams. *Entrance requirements:* For master's, doctorate, and Engr, GRE General Test. Additional exam requirements/recommendations for international students: Required—TOEFL. *Application deadline:* For fall admission, 12/1 priority date for domestic and international students; for spring admission, 10/1 priority date for domestic and international students. Application fee: $70. Electronic applications accepted. *Financial support:* In 2009–10, 49 students received support, including 6 fellowships (averaging $2,500 per year), 23 research assistantships with full tuition reimbursements available (averaging $22,500 per year), 20 teaching assistantships with full tuition reimbursements available (averaging $22,500 per year); career-related internships or fieldwork, health care benefits, and unspecified assistantships also available. Financial award application deadline: 12/1; financial award applicants required to submit FAFSA. *Faculty research:* Combinatorial optimization and mathematical programming; financial engineering; supply chain management and inventory theory; applied probability; queuing theory; scheduling, and simulation. *Unit head:* Dr. Cliff S. Stein, Department Chair; Professor, 212-854-5238, Fax: 212-854-8103, E-mail: cliff@ieor.columbia.edu. *Application contact:* Adina Berrios Brooks, Student Affairs Manager, 212-854-1934, Fax: 212-854-8103, E-mail: admit@ieor.columbia.edu.

Cornell University, Graduate School, Graduate Fields of Engineering, Field of Operations Research and Information Engineering, Ithaca, NY 14853-0001. Offers applied probability and statistics (PhD); manufacturing systems engineering (PhD); mathematical programming (PhD); operations research and industrial engineering (M Eng). *Faculty:* 46 full-time (9 women). *Students:* 163 full-time (46 women); includes 20 minority (2 African Americans, 12 Asian Americans or Pacific Islanders, 6 Hispanic Americans), 103 international. Average age 25. 774

Operations Research

Cornell University (continued)

applicants, 29% accepted, 91 enrolled. In 2009, 85 master's, 6 doctorates awarded. *Degree requirements:* For doctorate, comprehensive exam, thesis/dissertation. *Entrance requirements:* For master's and doctorate, GRE General Test, 3 letters of recommendation. Additional exam requirements/recommendations for international students: Required—TOEFL (minimum score 600 paper-based; 250 computer-based; 77 iBT). *Application deadline:* For fall admission, 1/15 for domestic students. Application fee: $70. Electronic applications accepted. *Expenses:* Tuition: Full-time $29,500. Required fees: $70. Full-time tuition and fees vary according to degree level, program and student level. *Financial support:* In 2009–10, 44 students received support, including 6 fellowships with full tuition reimbursements available, 5 teaching assistantships with full tuition reimbursements available; research assistantships with full tuition reimbursements available, institutionally sponsored loans, scholarships/grants, health care benefits, tuition waivers (full and partial), and unspecified assistantships also available. Financial award applicants required to submit FAFSA. *Faculty research:* Mathematical programming and combinatorial optimization, statistics, stochastic processes, mathematical finance, simulation, manufacturing, e-commerce. *Unit head:* Director of Graduate Studies, 607-255-9128, Fax: 607-255-9129. *Application contact:* Graduate Field Assistant, 607-255-9128, Fax: 607-255-9129, E-mail: orie@cornell.edu.

École Polytechnique de Montréal, Graduate Programs, Department of Mathematics and Industrial Engineering, Montréal, QC H3C 3A7, Canada. Offers ergonomy (M Eng, M Sc A, DESS); mathematical method in CA engineering (M Eng, M Sc A, PhD); operational research (M Eng, M Sc A, PhD); production (M Eng, M Sc A); technology management (M Eng, M Sc A). Part-time programs available. *Degree requirements:* For master's, one foreign language, thesis. *Entrance requirements:* For master's, minimum GPA of 2.75. *Faculty research:* Use of computers in organizations.

Florida Institute of Technology, Graduate Programs, College of Business, Extended Studies Division, Melbourne, FL 32901-6975. Offers acquisition and contract management (PMBA); business administration (PMBA); computer information systems (MS); e-business (PMBA); human resource management (PMBA); human resources management (MS); logistics management (MS), including humanitarian and disaster relief logistics; management (MS), including acquisition and contract management, e-business, human resource management, information systems, logistics management, management, transportation management; material acquisition management (MS); project management (MS), including information systems, operations research; public administration (MPA); quality management (MS); space management (MS); space systems (MS); systems management (MS), including information systems, operations research, systems management. Part-time and evening/weekend programs available. Postbaccalaureate distance learning degree programs offered (no on-campus study). *Faculty:* 12 full-time (3 women), 117 part-time/adjunct (20 women). *Students:* 74 full-time (32 women), 1,041 part-time (484 women); includes 343 minority (240 African Americans, 12 American Indian/Alaska Native, 44 Asian Americans or Pacific Islanders, 47 Hispanic Americans), 22 international. Average age 35. 520 applicants, 72% accepted, 279 enrolled. In 2009, 509 master's awarded. *Degree requirements:* For master's, capstone course. *Entrance requirements:* For master's, GMAT or resume showing 8 years of supervised experience, minimum GPA of 3.0, 2 letters of recommendation, resume. Additional exam requirements/recommendations for international students: Required—TOEFL (minimum score 550 paper-based; 213 computer-based; 79 iBT). *Application deadline:* For fall admission, 4/1 for international students; for spring admission, 9/30 for international students. Applications are processed on a rolling basis. Application fee: $50. Electronic applications accepted. *Expenses:* Tuition: Part-time $1015 per credit. Tuition and fees vary according to campus/location and program. *Financial support:* Application deadline: 3/1; *Unit head:* Dr. Clifford Bragdon, Dean, 321-674-8821, Fax: 321-674-7597, E-mail: cbragdon@fit.edu. *Application contact:* Carolyn Farrior, Director of Graduate Admissions Online Learning and Off Campus Programs, 321-674-7118, Fax: 321-674-8216, E-mail: cfarrior@fit.edu.

Florida Institute of Technology, Graduate Programs, College of Science, Department of Mathematical Sciences, Melbourne, FL 32901-6975. Offers applied mathematics (MS, PhD); operations research (MS, PhD). Part-time and evening/weekend programs available. *Faculty:* 11 full-time (1 woman). *Students:* 33 full-time (9 women), 30 part-time (14 women); includes 15 minority (9 African Americans, 3 Asian Americans or Pacific Islanders, 3 Hispanic Americans), 17 international. Average age 34. 75 applicants, 57% accepted, 20 enrolled. In 2009, 19 master's, 3 doctorates awarded. *Degree requirements:* For master's, comprehensive exam (for some programs), thesis optional; for doctorate, comprehensive exam, thesis/dissertation. *Entrance requirements:* For master's, minimum GPA of 3.0, computer literacy; for doctorate, minimum GPA of 3.2, resume, 3 letters of recommendation, statement of objectives. Additional exam requirements/recommendations for international students: Required—TOEFL (minimum score 550 paper-based; 213 computer-based; 79 iBT). *Application deadline:* For fall admission, 4/1 for international students; for spring admission, 9/30 for international students. Applications are processed on a rolling basis. Application fee: $50. Electronic applications accepted. *Expenses:* Tuition: Part-time $1015 per credit. Tuition and fees vary according to campus/location and program. *Financial support:* In 2009–10, 12 students received support, including 1 research assistantship (averaging $8,960 per year), 11 teaching assistantships with full and partial tuition reimbursements available (averaging $9,478 per year); career-related internships or fieldwork, institutionally sponsored loans, tuition waivers (partial), unspecified assistantships, and tuition remissions also available. Support available to part-time students. Financial award application deadline: 3/1; financial award applicants required to submit FAFSA. *Faculty research:* Real analysis, numerical analysis, statistics, data analysis, combinatorics, artificial intelligence, simulation. Total annual research expenditures: $99,058. *Unit head:* Dr. Semem Koksal, Department Head, 321-674-8765, Fax: 321-674-7412, E-mail: skokal@fit.edu. *Application contact:* Thomas M. Shea, Director of Graduate Admissions, 321-674-7577, Fax: 321-723-9468, E-mail: tshea@fit.edu.

George Mason University, Volgenau School of Information Technology and Engineering, Department of Systems Engineering and Operations Research, Fairfax, VA 22030. Offers architecture-based systems integration (Certificate); command, control, communication, computing and intelligence (Certificate); computational modeling (Certificate); discovery, design and innovation (Certificate); military operations research (Certificate); operations research (MS); systems engineering (MS); systems engineering analysis and architecture (Certificate); systems engineering and operations research (PhD); systems engineering of software intensive systems (Certificate). Part-time and evening/weekend programs available. *Faculty:* 17 full-time (4 women), 12 part-time/adjunct (5 women). *Students:* 23 full-time (3 women), 191 part-time (43 women); includes 42 minority (11 African Americans, 2 American Indian/Alaska Native, 17 Asian Americans or Pacific Islanders, 12 Hispanic Americans), 13 international. Average age 37. 156 applicants, 68% accepted, 55 enrolled. In 2009, 41 master's, 1 doctorate, 8 other advanced degrees awarded. *Degree requirements:* For master's, thesis optional; for doctorate, comprehensive exam, thesis/dissertation, qualifying exams. *Entrance requirements:* For master's, GRE General Test, 3 letters of recommendation, resume; for doctorate, GRE, undergraduate and graduate transcripts, 3 letters of reference, resume, statement of career goals and aspirations, self assessment of background. Additional exam requirements/recommendations for international students: Required—TOEFL. *Application deadline:* For fall admission, 3/15 priority date for domestic students, 2/15 priority date for international students; for spring admission, 10/1 for domestic and international students. Application fee: $75. Electronic applications accepted. *Expenses:* Tuition, state resident: full-time $7568; part-time $315.33 per credit hour. Tuition, nonresident: full-time $21,704; part-time $904.33 per credit hour. Required fees: $2184; $91 per credit hour. *Financial support:* In 2009–10, 8 students received support, including 5 research assistantships with full and partial tuition reimbursements available (averaging $9,113 per year), 3 teaching assistantships with full and partial tuition reimbursements available (averaging $10,997 per year); career-related internships or fieldwork, Federal Work-Study, scholarships/grants, unspecified assistantships, and health care benefits (full-time research or teaching assistantship recipients) also available. Support available to part-time students. Financial award application deadline: 3/1; financial award applicants required to submit FAFSA. *Faculty research:* Requirements engineering, signal processing, systems architecture, data fusion. Total annual research expenditures: $1.1 million. *Unit head:* Dr. Ariela Sofer, Chairman, 703-993-1692, Fax: 703-993-1521, E-mail: asofer@gmu.edu. *Application contact:* Dr. K. C. Chang, Graduate Coordinator, 703-993-1639, E-mail: kchang@gmu.edu.

Georgia Institute of Technology, Graduate Studies and Research, College of Engineering, School of Industrial and Systems Engineering, Program in Operations Research, Atlanta, GA 30332-0001. Offers MSOR, PhD. Part-time programs available. *Entrance requirements:* For master's, GRE General Test, minimum GPA of 3.0. Additional exam requirements/recommendations for international students: Required—TOEFL. Electronic applications accepted. *Faculty research:* Linear and nonlinear deterministic models in operations research, mathematical statistics, design of experiments.

Georgia State University, J. Mack Robinson College of Business, Department of Managerial Sciences, Atlanta, GA 30302-3083. Offers business analysis (MBA, MS); decision sciences (PhD); entrepreneurship (MBA); human resources management (MBA, MS); management (MBA, PhD); operations management (MBA, MS); organization change (MS); personnel employee relations (PhD); strategic management (PhD). Part-time and evening/weekend programs available. *Degree requirements:* For doctorate, thesis/dissertation. *Entrance requirements:* For master's and doctorate, GMAT. Additional exam requirements/recommendations for international students: Required—TOEFL (minimum score 610 paper-based; 255 computer-based; 101 iBT). Electronic applications accepted. *Faculty research:* Abusive supervision, entrepreneurship, time series and neural networks, organizational controls, inventory control systems.

HEC Montreal, School of Business Administration, Master of Science Programs in Administration, Program in Business Analytics, Montréal, QC H3T 2A7, Canada. Offers M Sc. Part-time programs available. *Students:* 1 (woman) full-time, 1 part-time (0 women). 5 applicants, 80% accepted, 1 enrolled. *Degree requirements:* For master's, one foreign language, thesis. *Application deadline:* For fall admission, 3/15 for domestic and international students; for winter admission, 9/15 for domestic and international students. Application fee: $77. Electronic applications accepted. Tuition and fees charges are reported in Canadian dollars. *Expenses:* Tuition, area resident: Part-time $65.60 Canadian dollars per credit. Tuition, state resident: full-time $2361.60 Canadian dollars; part-time $183.36 Canadian dollars per credit. Tuition, nonresident: full-time $6601 Canadian dollars; part-time $448.13 Canadian dollars per credit. International tuition: $16,132.68 Canadian dollars full-time. Required fees: $1254.15 Canadian dollars; $28.99 Canadian dollars per course. $91.68 Canadian dollars per term. Tuition and fees vary according to degree level and program. *Financial support:* Research assistantships, teaching assistantships, scholarships/grants available. Financial award application deadline: 10/2. *Unit head:* Claude Laurin, Director, 514-340-6485, Fax: 514-340-5690, E-mail: claude.laurin@hec.ca. *Application contact:* Francine Blais, Administrative Director, 514-340-6112, Fax: 514-340-6411, E-mail: francine.blais@hec.ca.

Idaho State University, Office of Graduate Studies, College of Engineering, Mechanical Engineering Department, Pocatello, ID 83209-8060. Offers measurement and control engineering (MS); mechanical engineering (MS). Part-time programs available. *Faculty:* 15 full-time (1 woman). *Students:* 39 full-time (7 women), 41 part-time (6 women); includes 3 minority (1 African American, 2 Asian Americans or Pacific Islanders), 29 international. Average age 31. In 2009, 7 master's awarded. *Degree requirements:* For master's, comprehensive exam (for some programs), 2 semesters of seminar; thesis or project. *Entrance requirements:* For master's, GRE. Additional exam requirements/recommendations for international students: Required—TOEFL (minimum score 550 paper-based; 213 computer-based; 80 iBT). *Application deadline:* For fall admission, 7/1 for domestic students, 6/1 for international students; for spring admission, 12/1 for domestic students, 11/1 for international students. Applications are processed on a rolling basis. Application fee: $55. Electronic applications accepted. *Expenses:* Tuition, state resident: full-time $3318; part-time $297 per credit hour. Tuition, nonresident: full-time $13,120; part-time $437 per credit hour. Required fees: $2530. Tuition and fees vary according to program. *Financial support:* In 2009–10, 5 research assistantships with full and partial tuition reimbursements (averaging $10,539 per year) were awarded; teaching assistantships with full and partial tuition reimbursements, Federal Work-Study, institutionally sponsored loans, scholarships/grants, health care benefits, tuition waivers (full and partial), and unspecified assistantships also available. Support available to part-time students. Financial award application deadline: 1/1; financial award applicants required to submit FAFSA. *Faculty research:* Modeling and identification of biomedical systems, intelligent systems and adaptive control, active flow control of turbo machinery, validation of advanced computational codes for thermal fluid interactions, development of methodologies for the assessment of passive safety system performance in advanced reactors, alternative energy research (wind, solar, hydrogen). *Unit head:* Dr. George Imel, Chair, 208-282-3732, Fax: 208-282-4538, E-mail: gimel@isu.edu. *Application contact:* Tami Carson, Graduate School Technical Records Specialist, 208-282-2150, Fax: 208-282-4847, E-mail: carstami@isu.edu.

Indiana University–Purdue University Fort Wayne, College of Arts and Sciences, Department of Mathematical Sciences, Fort Wayne, IN 46805-1499. Offers applied mathematics (MS); applied statistics (Certificate); mathematics (MS); operations research (MS); teaching (MAT). Part-time and evening/weekend programs available. *Faculty:* 17 full-time (4 women), 2 part-time/adjunct (1 woman). *Students:* 2 full-time (0 women), 15 part-time (6 women); includes 2 minority (1 American Indian/Alaska Native, 1 Asian American or Pacific Islander), 1 international. Average age 35. 5 applicants, 60% accepted, 3 enrolled. In 2009, 2 master's, 2 other advanced degrees awarded. *Entrance requirements:* For master's, minimum GPA of 3.0, major or minor in mathematics, three letters of recommendation. Additional exam requirements/recommendations for international students: Required—TOEFL (minimum score 550 paper-based; 213 computer-based; 77 iBT); Recommended—TWE. *Application deadline:* For fall admission, 8/1 priority date for domestic students, 7/1 priority date for international students; for spring admission, 12/1 for domestic students, 10/1 for international students. Applications are processed on a rolling basis. Application fee: $55 ($60 for international students). Electronic applications accepted. *Expenses:* Tuition, state resident: full-time $4595; part-time $255 per credit. Tuition, nonresident: full-time $10,963; part-time $609 per credit. Required fees: $528; $29.35 per credit. Tuition and fees vary according to course load. *Financial support:* In 2009–10, 1 research assistantship with partial tuition reimbursement (averaging $12,740 per year), 6 teaching assistantships with partial tuition reimbursements (averaging $12,740 per year) were awarded; scholarships/grants and unspecified assistantships also available. Support available to part-time students. Financial award application deadline: 3/1; financial award applicants required to submit FAFSA. *Faculty research:* Target value, toroidal queen's graph, holomorphic maps. *Unit head:* Dr. David A. Legg, Chair, 260-481-6222, Fax: 260-481-0155, E-mail: legg@ipfw.edu. *Application contact:* Dr. W. Douglas Weakley, Director of Graduate Studies, 260-481-6233, Fax: 260-481-0155, E-mail: weakley@ipfw.edu.

Iowa State University of Science and Technology, Graduate College, College of Engineering, Department of Industrial and Manufacturing Systems Engineering, Ames, IA 50011. Offers industrial engineering (M Eng, MS, PhD); operations research (MS); systems engineering (M Eng). *Faculty:* 12 full-time (2 women). *Students:* 36 full-time (13 women), 39 part-time (7 women); includes 6 minority (3 African Americans, 1 Asian American or Pacific Islander, 2 Hispanic Americans), 34 international. 169 applicants, 21% accepted, 16 enrolled. In 2009, 11 master's, 5 doctorates awarded. *Degree requirements:* For master's, thesis or alternative; for doctorate, thesis/dissertation. *Entrance requirements:* For master's and doctorate, GRE General Test. Additional exam requirements/recommendations for international students: Required—TOEFL (minimum score 550 paper-based; 213 computer-based; 79 iBT) or IELTS (minimum score 6.5). *Application deadline:* For fall admission, 1/15 priority date for international students; for spring admission, 7/15 priority date for international students. Application fee: $40 ($90 for international students). Electronic applications accepted. *Expenses:* Tuition, state resident: full-time $6716. Tuition, nonresident: full-time $8908. Tuition and fees vary according to course level, course load, program and student level. *Financial support:* In 2009–10, 26 research assistantships with full and partial tuition reimbursements (averaging $17,000 per year), 4 teaching assistantships with full and partial tuition reimbursements (averaging $16,000 per year) were awarded; fellowships, scholarships/grants, health care benefits, and unspecified assistantships also available. *Faculty research:* Economic modeling, valuation techniques, robotics, digital controls, systems reliability. *Unit head:* Dr. Gary Mirka, Chair, 515-294-8661, Fax: 515-294-3524. *Application contact:* Dr. Sarah Ryan, Director of Graduate Studies, 515-294-4347, E-mail: smryan@iastate.edu.

The Johns Hopkins University, G. W. C. Whiting School of Engineering, Department of Applied Mathematics and Statistics, Baltimore, MD 21218-2699. Offers computational medicine (PhD); discrete mathematics (MA, MSE, PhD); financial mathematics (MSE); operations research/optimization/decision science (MA, MSE, PhD); statistics/probability/stochastic processes (MA, MSE, PhD). *Faculty:* 17 full-time (3 women), 4 part-time/adjunct (0 women). *Students:* 56 full-time (19 women), 5 part-time (2 women); includes 7 minority (1 African American, 6 Asian Americans or Pacific Islanders), 37 international. Average age 27. 213 applicants, 51% accepted, 16 enrolled. In 2009, 24 master's, 4 doctorates awarded. Terminal master's awarded for partial completion of doctoral program. *Degree requirements:* For master's, thesis (for some programs); for doctorate, thesis/dissertation, oral exam, introductory exam. *Entrance requirements:* For master's and doctorate, GRE General Test, GRE Subject Test. Additional exam requirements/recommendations for international students: Required—TOEFL (minimum score 600 paper-based; 250 computer-based; 100 iBT). *Application deadline:* For fall admission, 1/15 for domestic and international students; for spring admission, 9/15 for domestic and international students. Application fee: $75. Electronic applications accepted. *Financial support:* In 2009–10, 40 students received support, including 3 fellowships with full tuition reimbursements available (averaging $3,000 per year), 13 research assistantships with full tuition reimbursements available (averaging $22,333 per year), 15 teaching assistantships with full tuition reimbursements available (averaging $16,750 per year); Federal Work-Study, institutionally sponsored loans, scholarships/grants, health care benefits, tuition waivers (partial), and unspecified assistantships also available. Financial award application deadline: 1/15. *Faculty research:* Discrete mathematics, probability, statistics, optimization and operations research, scientific computation, financial mathematics. Total annual research expenditures: $1.1 million. *Unit head:* Dr. Daniel Q. Naiman, Chair, 410-516-7203, Fax: 410-516-7459, E-mail: daniel.naiman@jhu.edu. *Application contact:* Kristin Bechtel, Academic Program Coordinator, 410-516-7198, Fax: 410-516-7459, E-mail: kbechtel@jhu.edu.

Kansas State University, Graduate School, College of Engineering, Department of Industrial and Manufacturing Systems Engineering, Manhattan, KS 66506. Offers engineering management (MEM); industrial engineering (MS, PhD); operations research (MS). Part-time programs available. Postbaccalaureate distance learning degree programs offered. *Faculty:* 9 full-time (1 woman), 2 part-time/adjunct (1 woman). *Students:* 38 full-time (12 women), 48 part-time (14 women); includes 4 minority (1 African American, 1 Asian American or Pacific Islander, 2 Hispanic Americans), 27 international. Average age 30. 85 applicants, 60% accepted, 41 enrolled. In 2009, 20 master's, 1 doctorate awarded. *Degree requirements:* For master's, thesis or alternative; for doctorate, thesis/dissertation. *Entrance requirements:* For master's, GRE General Test, bachelor's degree in engineering, mathematics, or physical science; for doctorate, GRE General Test, master's degree in engineering or industrial manufacturing. Additional exam requirements/recommendations for international students: Required—TOEFL. *Application deadline:* For fall admission, 2/1 priority date for domestic and international students; for spring admission, 8/1 priority date for domestic and international students. Applications are processed on a rolling basis. Application fee: $40 ($55 for international students). Electronic applications accepted. *Financial support:* In 2009–10, 19 research assistantships (averaging $10,372 per year), 1 teaching assistantship with full tuition reimbursement (averaging $12,450 per year) were awarded; Federal Work-Study, institutionally sponsored loans, and scholarships/grants also available. Support available to part-time students. Financial award application deadline: 3/1; financial award applicants required to submit FAFSA. *Faculty research:* Ergonomics, healthcare systems engineering, manufacturing processes, operations research, engineering management. Total annual research expenditures: $484,594. *Unit head:* Bradley Kramer, Head, 785-532-5606, Fax: 785-532-7810, E-mail: bradleyk@ksu.edu. *Application contact:* E. Stanley Lee, Director, 785-532-3730, Fax: 785-532-7810, E-mail: eslee@ksu.edu.

Massachusetts Institute of Technology, Operations Research Center, Cambridge, MA 02139-4307. Offers SM, PhD. *Faculty:* 41 full-time (5 women). *Students:* 57 full-time (10 women); includes 7 minority (6 Asian Americans or Pacific Islanders, 1 Hispanic American), 29 international. Average age 26. 175 applicants, 12% accepted, 11 enrolled. In 2009, 5 master's, 8 doctorates awarded. Terminal master's awarded for partial completion of doctoral program. *Degree requirements:* For master's, thesis, writing exam; for doctorate, thesis/dissertation, qualifying exam, general exam, writing exam. *Entrance requirements:* For master's and doctorate, GRE General Test. Additional exam requirements/recommendations for international students: Required—TOEFL (minimum score 600 paper-based; 250 computer-based; 100 iBT), IELTS (minimum score 7). *Application deadline:* For fall admission, 12/15 for domestic and international students. Application fee: $75. Electronic applications accepted. *Financial support:* In 2009–10, 57 students received support, including 8 fellowships (averaging $26,917 per year), 36 research assistantships (averaging $28,190 per year), 10 teaching assistantships (averaging $30,549 per year); Federal Work-Study, institutionally sponsored loans, scholarships/grants, health care benefits, tuition waivers, and unspecified assistantships also available. Financial award application deadline: 12/15. *Faculty research:* Probability, mathematical programming, statistics, stochastic processes and healthcare. *Unit head:* Dr. Dimitris J. Bertsimas, Co-Director, 617-253-3601, Fax: 617-258-9214, E-mail: orc-www@mit.edu. *Application contact:* Laura A. Rose, Admissions Coordinator, 617-253-9303, Fax: 617-258-9214, E-mail: lrose@mit.edu.

Naval Postgraduate School, Graduate Programs, Department of Operations Research, Monterey, CA 93943. Offers MS, PhD. Program only open to commissioned officers of the United States and friendly nations and selected United States federal civilian employees. Part-time programs available. *Degree requirements:* For master's; thesis; for doctorate, one foreign language, thesis/dissertation.

Naval Postgraduate School, Graduate Programs, Program in Undersea Warfare, Monterey, CA 93943. Offers applied science (MS); electrical engineering (MS); engineering acoustics (MS); operations research (MS); physical oceanography (MS). Program only open to commissioned officers of the United States and friendly nations and selected United States federal civilian employees. Part-time programs available. *Degree requirements:* For master's, thesis.

New Mexico Institute of Mining and Technology, Graduate Studies, Department of Mathematics, Socorro, NM 87801. Offers applied math (PhD); mathematics (MS); operations research (MS). *Degree requirements:* For master's, thesis optional; for doctorate, thesis/dissertation. *Entrance requirements:* For master's, GRE General Test. Additional exam requirements/recommendations for international students: Required—TOEFL (minimum score 540 paper-based; 207 computer-based). *Faculty research:* Applied mathematics, differential equations, industrial mathematics, numerical analysis, stochastic processes.

North Carolina State University, Graduate School, College of Engineering and College of Physical and Mathematical Sciences, Program in Operations Research, Raleigh, NC 27695. Offers MOR, MS, PhD. Part-time programs available. *Degree requirements:* For master's, thesis (for some programs), thesis (MS); for doctorate, thesis/dissertation, comprehensive oral and written exams. *Entrance requirements:* For master's, GRE General Test, minimum GPA of 2.7; for doctorate, GRE General Test, minimum GPA of 3.0. Additional exam requirements/recommendations for international students: Required—TOEFL. Electronic applications accepted. *Faculty research:* Queuing analysis, simulation, inventory theory, supply chain management, mathematical programming.

North Carolina State University, Graduate School, College of Management, Institute for Advanced Analytics, Raleigh, NC 27695. Offers analytics (MS). *Entrance requirements:* For master's, GRE General Test. Additional exam requirements/recommendations for international students: Required—TOEFL. Electronic applications accepted.

North Dakota State University, College of Graduate and Interdisciplinary Studies, College of Science and Mathematics, Department of Computer Science, Fargo, ND 58108. Offers computer science (MS, PhD); operations research (MS); software engineering (MS, PhD, Certificate). Part-time programs available. *Faculty:* 14 full-time (1 woman). *Students:* 47 full-time (10 women), 118 part-time (20 women); includes 107 minority (2 African Americans, 104 Asian Americans or Pacific Islanders, 1 Hispanic American). Average age 24. 152 applicants, 63% accepted, 43 enrolled. In 2009, 24 master's, 5 doctorates awarded. *Degree requirements:* For master's, comprehensive exam, thesis optional; for doctorate, thesis/dissertation, qualifying exam. *Entrance requirements:* For master's, minimum GPA of 3.0, BS in computer science or related field; for doctorate, minimum GPA of 3.25, MS in computer science or related field. Additional exam requirements/recommendations for international students: Required—TOEFL (minimum score 550 paper-based; 213 computer-based; 79 iBT). *Application deadline:* For fall admission, 8/15 priority date for domestic students, 8/15 for international students; for spring admission, 12/15 priority date for domestic students, 12/15 for international students. Application fee: $45 ($60 for international students). *Financial support:* In 2009–10, 37 research assistantships with full tuition reimbursements (averaging $10,000 per year), 17 teaching assistantships with full tuition reimbursements (averaging $4,500 per year) were awarded; career-related internships or fieldwork, Federal Work-Study, institutionally sponsored loans, and tuition waivers (full) also available. Financial award application deadline: 4/15. *Faculty research:* Networking, software engineering, artificial intelligence, database, programming languages. Total annual research expenditures: $366,434. *Unit head:* Dr. Brian Slator, Head, 701-231-8562, Fax: 701-231-8255. *Application contact:* Dr. Ken R. Nygard, Graduate Coordinator, 701-231-9460, Fax: 701-231-8255, E-mail: kendall.nygard@ndsu.edu.

Northeastern University, College of Engineering, Department of Mechanical, Industrial, and Manufacturing Engineering, Boston, MA 02115-5096. Offers engineering management (MS); industrial engineering (MS, PhD); mechanical engineering (MS, PhD); operations research (MS). Part-time programs available. *Faculty:* 34 full-time (2 women), 7 part-time/adjunct (0 women). *Students:* 270 full-time (56 women), 137 part-time (27 women); includes 4 African Americans, 9 Asian Americans or Pacific Islanders, 3 Hispanic Americans, 182 international. 573 applicants, 75% accepted, 142 enrolled. In 2009, 94 master's, 9 doctorates awarded. *Degree requirements:* For master's, thesis (for some programs); for doctorate, thesis/dissertation, departmental qualifying exam. *Entrance requirements:* For master's and doctorate, GRE General Test. Additional exam requirements/recommendations for international students: Required—TOEFL (minimum score 550 paper-based; 213 computer-based; 80 iBT). *Application deadline:* For fall admission, 1/15 priority date for domestic and international students; for spring admission, 11/1 priority date for domestic students. Applications are processed on a rolling basis. Application fee: $50. Electronic applications accepted. *Financial support:* In 2009–10, 79 students received support, including 42 research assistantships with full tuition reimbursements available (averaging $18,320 per year), 37 teaching assistantships with full tuition reimbursements available; fellowships with full tuition reimbursements available, career-related internships or fieldwork, Federal Work-Study, scholarships/grants, health care benefits, and unspecified assistantships also available. Support available to part-time students. Financial award application deadline: 1/15; financial award applicants required to submit FAFSA. *Faculty research:* Dry sliding instabilities, droplet deposition, combustion, manufacturing systems, nano-manufacturing, advanced materials processing, bio-nano robotics, burning speed measurement, virtual environments. *Unit head:* Dr. Hameed Metghalchi, Chairman, 617-373-2973, Fax: 617-373-2921. *Application contact:* Stephen L. Gibson, Associate Director, 617-373-2711, Fax: 617-373-2501, E-mail: grad-eng@coe.neu.edu.

Northeastern University, College of Science, Department of Mathematics, Boston, MA 02115-5096. Offers applied mathematics (MS); mathematics (MS, PhD); operations research (MSOR). Part-time and evening/weekend programs available. *Faculty:* 39 full-time (5 women), 15 part-time/adjunct (7 women). *Students:* 52 full-time (17 women), 4 part-time (1 woman); includes 2 Asian Americans or Pacific Islanders, 1 Hispanic American, 28 international. 146 applicants, 76% accepted, 23 enrolled. In 2009, 8 master's, 6 doctorates awarded. *Degree requirements:* For master's, thesis (for some programs); for doctorate, thesis/dissertation, qualifying exams. *Entrance requirements:* For master's and doctorate, GRE Subject Test, GRE General Test. Additional exam requirements/recommendations for international students: Required—TOEFL. *Application deadline:* For fall admission, 2/1 priority date for domestic and international students. Applications are processed on a rolling basis. Application fee: $50. Electronic applications accepted. *Financial support:* In 2009–10, 26 teaching assistantships with tuition reimbursements (averaging $17,345 per year) were awarded; research assistantships with tuition reimbursements, Federal Work-Study, institutionally sponsored loans, tuition waivers (full and partial), and unspecified assistantships also available. Financial award application deadline: 3/1; financial award applicants required to submit FAFSA. *Faculty research:* Algebra and singularities, combinatorics, topology, probability and statistics, geometric analysis and partial differential equations. *Unit head:* Dr. Jerzy Weyman, Graduate Coordinator, 617-373-5513, Fax: 617-373-5658, E-mail: j.weyman@neu.edu. *Application contact:* Jo-Anne Dickinson, Admissions Contact, 617-373-5990, Fax: 617-373-7281, E-mail: gsas@neu.edu.

Northwestern University, McCormick School of Engineering and Applied Science, Department of Industrial Engineering and Management Sciences, Evanston, IL 60208. Offers engineering management (MEM); industrial engineering and management science (MS, PhD); operations research (MS, PhD). MS and PhD admissions and degrees offered through The Graduate School. Terminal master's awarded for partial completion of doctoral program. *Degree requirements:* For master's, comprehensive exam; for doctorate, comprehensive exam, thesis/dissertation. Electronic applications accepted. *Faculty research:* Production, logistics, optimization, simulation, statistics.

Oregon State University, Graduate School, College of Science, Department of Statistics, Corvallis, OR 97331. Offers operations research (MA, MS); statistics (MA, MS, PhD). Part-time programs available. *Faculty:* 10 full-time (4 women). *Students:* 25 full-time (10 women), 2 part-time (both women); includes 3 minority (2 Asian Americans or Pacific Islanders, 1 Hispanic American), 6 international. Average age 30. In 2009, 14 master's, 2 doctorates awarded. *Degree requirements:* For master's, consulting experience; for doctorate, thesis/dissertation, consulting experience. *Entrance requirements:* For master's and doctorate, minimum GPA of 3.0 in last 90 hours. Additional exam requirements/recommendations for international students: Required—TOEFL. *Application deadline:* For fall admission, 2/15 for domestic students. Applications are processed on a rolling basis. Application fee: $50. *Expenses:* Tuition, state resident: full-time $9774; part-time $362 per credit. Tuition, nonresident: full-time $15,849; part-time $587 per credit. Required fees: $1639. Full-time tuition and fees vary according to course load and program. *Financial support:* In 2009–10, 8 research assistantships, 19 teaching assistantships were awarded; Federal Work-Study and institutionally sponsored loans also available. Financial award application deadline: 2/15. *Faculty research:* Analysis of enumerative data, nonparametric statistics, asymptotics, experimental design, generalized regression models, linear model theory, reliability theory, survival analysis, wildlife and general survey methodology. *Unit head:* Dr. Robert T. Smythe, Chair, 541-737-3480, Fax: 541-737-3489, E-mail: smythe@science.oregonstate.edu. *Application contact:* Dr. Alix I. Gitelman, Director of Graduate Studies, 541-737-1987, Fax: 541-737-3489, E-mail: gitelman@science.oregonstate.edu.

Penn State University Park, Graduate School, Intercollege Graduate Programs, State College, University Park, PA 16802-1503. Offers acoustics (M Eng, MS, PhD); bioengineering (MS, PhD); biogeochemistry (dual) (PhD); business administration (MBA); cell and developmental biology (PhD); demography (dual) (MA); ecology (MS, PhD); environmental pollution control (MEPC, MS); genetics (MS, PhD); human dimensions of natural resources and the environment (dual) (MA, MS, PhD); immunology and infectious diseases (MS); integrative biosciences (MS, PhD), including integrative biosciences; materials science and engineering (PhD); operations research (dual) (M Eng, MA, MS, PhD); physiology (MS, PhD); plant physiology (MS, PhD); quality and manufacturing management (MMM). *Students:* 371 full-time (157 women), 22 part-time (7 women). Average age 27. 1,074 applicants, 18% accepted, 130 enrolled. *Entrance requirements:* Additional exam requirements/recommendations for international students: Required—TOEFL (minimum score 550 paper-based; 213 computer-based; 80 iBT). *Application*

Operations Research

Penn State University Park (continued)

deadline: Applications are processed on a rolling basis. Application fee: $45. Electronic applications accepted. *Financial support:* Fellowships, research assistantships, teaching assistantships available. Financial award applicants required to submit FAFSA. *Unit head:* Dr. Regina Vasilatos-Younken, Senior Associate Dean, 814-865-2516, Fax: 814-863-4627, E-mail: rxv@psu.edu. *Application contact:* Cynthia E. Nicosia, Director, Graduate Enrollment Services, 814-865-1795, Fax: 814-865-4627, E-mail: cey1@psu.edu.

Princeton University, Graduate School, School of Engineering and Applied Science, Department of Operations Research and Financial Engineering, Princeton, NJ 08544-1019. Offers M Eng, MSE, PhD. *Faculty:* 14 full-time (1 woman). Terminal master's awarded for partial completion of doctoral program. *Degree requirements:* For master's, thesis (for some programs), thesis required for M.S.E. degree; no thesis required for M.Eng. degree; for doctorate, thesis/dissertation, general exam. *Entrance requirements:* For master's and doctorate, GRE General Test, official transcript(s), 3 letters of recommendation, personal statement. Additional exam requirements/recommendations for international students: Required—TOEFL. *Application deadline:* For fall admission, 12/31 for domestic and international students. Electronic applications accepted. *Financial support:* Fellowships with full tuition reimbursements, research assistantships with full tuition reimbursements, teaching assistantships with full tuition reimbursements, institutionally sponsored loans and health care benefits available. Financial award application deadline: 1/2. *Faculty research:* Applied and computational mathematics; financial mathematics; optimization, queuing theory, and machine learning; statistics and stochastic analysis; transportation and logistics. *Unit head:* Kimberly Lupinacci, Graduate Program Administrator, 609-258-4018, Fax: 609-258-4363, E-mail: orfgrad@princeton.edu. *Application contact:* Michelle Carman, Manager, Graduate Admissions, 609-258-3034, Fax: 609-258-7262, E-mail: gsadmit@princeton.edu.

Rutgers, The State University of New Jersey, New Brunswick, Graduate School-New Brunswick, Program in Operations Research, Piscataway, NJ 08854-8097. Offers PhD. Part-time programs available. *Degree requirements:* For doctorate, comprehensive exam, thesis/dissertation, qualifying exam. *Entrance requirements:* For doctorate, GRE General Test, GRE Subject Test. Electronic applications accepted. *Faculty research:* Mathematical programming, combinatorial optimization, graph theory, stochastic modeling, queuing theory.

St. Mary's University, Graduate School, Department of Engineering, Program in Industrial Engineering, San Antonio, TX 78228-8507. Offers engineering computer applications (MS); engineering management (MS); industrial engineering (MS); operations research (MS); JD/MS. Part-time programs available. *Degree requirements:* For master's, comprehensive exam. *Entrance requirements:* For master's, GRE General Test, BS in science or engineering, minimum GPA of 3.0. Additional exam requirements/recommendations for international students: Required—TOEFL (minimum score 550 paper-based; 213 computer-based; 80 iBT). Electronic applications accepted. *Expenses:* Tuition: Full-time $8004. Required fees: $536. One-time fee: $5 full-time. Full-time tuition and fees vary according to program. *Faculty research:* Robotics, artificial intelligence, manufacturing engineering.

Southern Methodist University, Bobby B. Lyle School of Engineering, Department of Engineering Management, Information, and Systems, Dallas, TX 75275. Offers applied science (MS); engineering management (MSEM, DE); information engineering and management (MSIEM); operations research (MS, PhD); systems engineering (MS, PhD). Part-time and evening/weekend programs available. Postbaccalaureate distance learning degree programs offered. *Faculty:* 10 full-time (3 women), 22 part-time/adjunct (2 women). *Students:* 54 full-time (24 women), 288 part-time (68 women); includes 96 minority (30 African Americans, 2 American Indian/Alaska Native, 35 Asian Americans or Pacific Islanders, 29 Hispanic Americans), 38 international. Average age 33. 125 applicants, 74% accepted, 60 enrolled. In 2009, 128 master's, 3 doctorates awarded. Terminal master's awarded for partial completion of doctoral program. *Degree requirements:* For master's, thesis optional; for doctorate, thesis/dissertation, oral and written qualifying exams. *Entrance requirements:* For master's, minimum GPA of 3.0 in last 2 years; bachelor's degree in engineering, mathematics, sciences, or technical area; for doctorate, GRE General Test (operations research, engineering management), bachelor's degree in related field. Additional exam requirements/recommendations for international students: Required—TOEFL. *Application deadline:* For fall admission, 7/1 for domestic students, 5/15 for international students; for spring admission, 11/15 for domestic students, 9/1 for international students. Applications are processed on a rolling basis. Application fee: $75. *Financial support:* In 2009–10, 8 students received support, including 3 research assistantships with full tuition reimbursements available (averaging $18,000 per year), 9 teaching assistantships with full tuition reimbursements available (averaging $18,000 per year); tuition waivers (full) also available. *Faculty research:* Telecommunications, decision systems, information engineering, operations research, software. Total annual research expenditures: $172,823. *Unit head:* Dr. Richard S. Barr, Chair, 214-768-1772, Fax: 214-768-1112, E-mail: emis@lyle.smu.edu. *Application contact:* Marc Valerin, Director of Graduate and Executive Admissions, 214-768-3042, E-mail: valerin@lyle.smu.edu.

The University of Alabama in Huntsville, School of Graduate Studies, College of Engineering, Department of Industrial and Systems Engineering/Engineering Management, Program in Operations Research, Huntsville, AL 35899. Offers MSOR. Part-time and evening/weekend programs available. Postbaccalaureate distance learning degree programs offered (minimal on-campus study). *Faculty:* 6 full-time (2 women). *Students:* 7 part-time (3 women); includes 2 minority (1 African American, 1 Hispanic American). Average age 32. 10 applicants, 30% accepted, 2 enrolled. In 2009, 2 master's awarded. *Degree requirements:* For master's, comprehensive exam, thesis or alternative, oral and written exams. *Entrance requirements:* For master's, GRE General Test, minimum GPA of 3.0, 6 hours of course work in applied or mathematical statistics and calculus. Additional exam requirements/recommendations for international students: Required—TOEFL (minimum score 500 paper-based; 173 computer-based; 62 iBT). *Application deadline:* For fall admission, 7/15 for domestic students, 4/1 for international students; for spring admission, 11/30 for domestic students, 9/1 for international students. Applications are processed on a rolling basis. Application fee: $40 ($50 for international students). Electronic applications accepted. *Expenses:* Tuition, state resident: part-time $355.75 per credit hour. Tuition, nonresident: part-time $847.10 per credit hour. Required fees: $210.80 per semester. Tuition and fees vary according to course load and program. *Financial support:* Career-related internships or fieldwork, Federal Work-Study, institutionally sponsored loans, scholarships/grants, health care benefits, and unspecified assistantships available. Support available to part-time students. Financial award application deadline: 4/1; financial award applicants required to submit FAFSA. *Faculty research:* Simulation, manufacturing systems, system ergonomics, logistics. *Unit head:* Dr. James Swain, Chair, 256-824-6749, Fax: 256-824-6733, E-mail: jswain@ise.uah.edu. *Application contact:* Kathy Biggs, Manager, 256-824-6199, Fax: 256-824-6405, E-mail: deangrad@uah.edu.

University of Arkansas, Graduate School, College of Engineering, Department of Industrial Engineering, Fayetteville, AR 72701-1201. Offers industrial engineering (MSE, MSIE, PhD); operations management (MS); operations research (MSE, MSOR). *Faculty:* 10 full-time (1 woman), 26 part-time/adjunct (1 woman). *Students:* 46 full-time (17 women), 378 part-time (101 women); includes 85 minority (58 African Americans, 5 American Indian/Alaska Native, 12 Asian Americans or Pacific Islanders, 10 Hispanic Americans), 40 international. In 2009, 204 master's, 7 doctorates awarded. *Degree requirements:* For master's, thesis optional; for doctorate, one foreign language, thesis/dissertation. Application fee: $40 ($50 for international students). *Expenses:* Tuition, state resident: full-time $7355; part-time $356.58 per hour. Tuition, nonresident: full-time $17,401; part-time $775.17 per hour. Required fees: $1203. *Financial support:* In 2009–10, 3 fellowships, 32 research assistantships were awarded; teaching assistantships, career-related internships or fieldwork and Federal Work-Study also available. Support available to part-time students. Financial award application deadline: 4/1; financial award applicants required to submit FAFSA. *Unit head:* Dr. Kim Needy, Departmental

Chair, 479-575-3157, Fax: 479-575-8431, E-mail: kneedy@uark.edu. *Application contact:* Dr. Manuel D. Rossetti, Graduate Coordinator, 479-575-6756, E-mail: rossetti@uark.edu.

The University of British Columbia, Sauder School of Business, Master of Management in Operations Research, Vancouver, BC V6T 1Z1, Canada. Offers operations research (MM). *Degree requirements:* For master's, thesis (for some programs). *Entrance requirements:* For master's, GMAT or GRE, strong quantitative or analytical background, bachelor's degree or recognized equivalent from an accredited university-level institution, minimum of B+ average in undergraduate upper-level course work. Additional exam requirements/recommendations for international students: Required—TOEFL, IELTS or Michigan English Language Assessment Battery. Electronic applications accepted. *Expenses:* Contact institution. *Faculty research:* Operations and Logistics.

University of California, Berkeley, Graduate Division, College of Engineering, Department of Industrial Engineering and Operations Research, Berkeley, CA 94720-1500. Offers M Eng, MS, D Eng, PhD. *Students:* 70 full-time (19 women). Average age 27. 415 applicants, 18 enrolled. In 2009, 28 master's, 6 doctorates awarded. *Degree requirements:* For master's, comprehensive exam or thesis (MS); for doctorate, thesis/dissertation, qualifying exam. *Entrance requirements:* For master's and doctorate, GRE General Test, minimum GPA of 3.0, 3 letters of recommendation. *Application deadline:* For fall admission, 1/5 for domestic students. Application fee: $70 ($90 for international students). *Financial support:* Fellowships, research assistantships, teaching assistantships, career-related internships or fieldwork, Federal Work-Study, tuition waivers (full and partial), and unspecified assistantships available. *Faculty research:* Mathematical programming, robotics and manufacturing, linear and nonlinear optimization, production planning and scheduling, queuing theory. *Unit head:* Prof. Rhonda Righter, Chair, 510-642-5485, Fax: 510-642-1403, E-mail: gradadm@ieor.berkeley.edu. *Application contact:* Anayancy Paz, Student Affairs Officer, 510-642-5485, Fax: 510-642-1403, E-mail: gradadm@ieor.berkeley.edu.

University of Central Florida, College of Engineering and Computer Science, Department of Industrial Engineering and Management Systems, Orlando, FL 32816. Offers applied operations research (Certificate); design for usability (Certificate); industrial engineering (MSIE, PhD); industrial ergonomics and safety (Certificate); project engineering (Certificate); quality assurance (Certificate); systems engineering (Certificate); systems simulation for engineers (Certificate); training simulation (Certificate). Part-time and evening/weekend programs available. *Faculty:* 14 full-time (2 women), 9 part-time/adjunct (6 women). *Students:* 108 full-time (22 women), 143 part-time (54 women); includes 76 minority (21 African Americans, 1 American Indian/Alaska Native, 14 Asian Americans or Pacific Islanders, 40 Hispanic Americans), 64 international. Average age 32. 204 applicants, 66% accepted, 88 enrolled. In 2009, 59 master's, 17 doctorates, 14 other advanced degrees awarded. *Degree requirements:* For master's, thesis; for doctorate, thesis/dissertation, departmental qualifying exam, candidacy exam. *Entrance requirements:* For master's, GRE General Test, minimum GPA of 3.0 in last 60 hours of course work; for doctorate, minimum GPA of 3.5 in last 60 hours of course work. Additional exam requirements/recommendations for international students: Required—TOEFL. *Application deadline:* For fall admission, 7/15 priority date for domestic students; for spring admission, 12/1 priority date for domestic students. Application fee: $30. Electronic applications accepted. *Expenses:* Tuition, state resident: part-time $306.31 per credit hour. Tuition, nonresident: part-time $1099.01 per credit hour. Part-time tuition and fees vary according to degree level and program. *Financial support:* In 2009–10, 20 students received support, including 8 fellowships with partial tuition reimbursements available (averaging $7,600 per year), 9 research assistantships with partial tuition reimbursements available (averaging $12,400 per year), 5 teaching assistantships with partial tuition reimbursements available (averaging $13,000 per year); career-related internships or fieldwork, Federal Work-Study, institutionally sponsored loans, tuition waivers (partial), and unspecified assistantships also available. Financial award application deadline: 3/1; financial award applicants required to submit FAFSA. *Unit head:* Dr. Waldemar Karwowski, Chair, E-mail: wkar@mail.ucf.edu. *Application contact:* Dr. Waldemar Karwowski, Chair, E-mail: wkar@mail.ucf.edu.

University of Colorado at Boulder, Graduate School, College of Engineering and Applied Science, Engineering Management Program, Boulder, CO 80309. Offers operations and logistics (ME); quality and process (ME); research and development (ME). *Students:* 16 full-time (2 women), 98 part-time (27 women); includes 13 minority (8 Asian Americans or Pacific Islanders, 5 Hispanic Americans), 9 international. Average age 35. 36 applicants, 33% accepted, 9 enrolled. In 2009, 42 master's awarded. *Entrance requirements:* For master's, minimum undergraduate GPA of 3.0. *Application deadline:* For fall admission, 2/15 for domestic students, 12/1 for international students; for spring admission, 8/15 for domestic students, 5/1 for international students. Application fee: $50 ($60 for international students). *Financial support:* In 2009–10, 2 fellowships (averaging $3,500 per year), 2 research assistantships (averaging $16,862 per year) were awarded. *Faculty research:* Quality and process, research and development, operations and logistics.

University of Delaware, College of Agriculture and Natural Resources, Operations Research Program, Newark, DE 19716. Offers MS, PhD. Part-time programs available. Terminal master's awarded for partial completion of doctoral program. *Degree requirements:* For master's, thesis, oral exam; for doctorate, thesis/dissertation, qualifying exam. *Entrance requirements:* For master's and doctorate, GRE General Test, 3 letters of recommendation, program language/s, engineering calculus. Additional exam requirements/recommendations for international students: Required—TOEFL. Electronic applications accepted. *Faculty research:* Simulation and modeling-production scheduling and optimization, agricultural production and resource economics, transportation engineering, statistical quality control.

University of Illinois at Chicago, Graduate College, College of Engineering, Department of Mechanical and Industrial Engineering, Program in Industrial Engineering and Operations Research, Chicago, IL 60607-7128. Offers PhD. Part-time programs available. *Degree requirements:* For doctorate, thesis/dissertation. *Entrance requirements:* For doctorate, GRE General Test, minimum GPA of 2.75. Additional exam requirements/recommendations for international students: Required—TOEFL. Electronic applications accepted.

The University of Iowa, Graduate College, College of Engineering, Department of Industrial Engineering, Iowa City, IA 52242-1316. Offers engineering design and manufacturing (MS, PhD); ergonomics (MS, PhD); information and engineering management (MS, PhD); operations research (MS, PhD); quality engineering (MS, PhD). *Faculty:* 6 full-time (0 women). *Students:* 37 full-time (11 women); includes 3 minority (1 African American, 1 Asian American or Pacific Islander, 1 Hispanic American), 11 international. Average age 28. 65 applicants, 18% accepted, 7 enrolled. In 2009, 7 master's, 3 doctorates awarded. *Degree requirements:* For master's, thesis optional, exam; for doctorate, comprehensive exam, thesis/dissertation, final defense exam. *Entrance requirements:* For master's and doctorate, GRE General Test. Additional exam requirements/recommendations for international students: Required—TOEFL (minimum score 550 paper-based; 213 computer-based; 81 iBT). *Application deadline:* For fall admission, 7/15 for domestic students, 4/15 for international students; for spring admission, 12/1 for domestic students, 10/1 for international students. Applications are processed on a rolling basis. Application fee: $60 ($100 for international students). Electronic applications accepted. *Financial support:* In 2009–10, 2 fellowships with partial tuition reimbursements (averaging $30,450 per year), 22 research assistantships with partial tuition reimbursements (averaging $20,000 per year), 5 teaching assistantships with partial tuition reimbursements (averaging $16,630 per year) were awarded; career-related internships or fieldwork, scholarships/grants, and unspecified assistantships also available. Support available to part-time students. Financial award applicants required to submit FAFSA. *Faculty research:* Operations research; informatics; human factors engineering; manufacturing systems; human-machine interaction. Total annual research expenditures: $4.1 million. *Unit head:* Dr. Lea-Der Chen, Departmental Executive Officer, 319-335-5674, Fax: 319-335-5669, E-mail: lea-der-chen@uiowa.edu. *Application contact:* Jennifer Rumping, Secretary, 319-335-5939, Fax: 319-335-5669, E-mail: indeng@engineering.uiowa.edu.

University of Massachusetts Amherst, Graduate School, College of Engineering, Department of Mechanical and Industrial Engineering, Program in Industrial Engineering and Operations Research, Amherst, MA 01003. Offers MS, PhD. Part-time programs available. *Students:* 11 full-time (3 women), 9 part-time (3 women); includes 1 minority (Asian American or Pacific Islander), 12 international. Average age 30. 105 applicants, 38% accepted, 6 enrolled. In 2009, 4 master's, 4 doctorates awarded. Terminal master's awarded for partial completion of doctoral program. *Degree requirements:* For master's, thesis or alternative, project; for doctorate, comprehensive exam, thesis/dissertation. *Entrance requirements:* For master's and doctorate, GRE General Test. Additional exam requirements/recommendations for international students: Required—TOEFL (minimum score 550 paper-based; 213 computer-based; 80 iBT), IELTS (minimum score 6.5). *Application deadline:* For fall admission, 1/15 for domestic and international students; for spring admission, 10/1 for domestic and international students. Applications are processed on a rolling basis. Application fee: $50 ($65 for international students). Electronic applications accepted. *Expenses:* Tuition, state resident: full-time $2640; part-time $110 per credit. Tuition, nonresident: full-time $9936; part-time $414 per credit. Tuition and fees vary according to course load. *Financial support:* Fellowships with full tuition reimbursements, research assistantships with full tuition reimbursements, teaching assistantships with full tuition reimbursements, career-related internships or fieldwork, Federal Work-Study, scholarships/grants, traineeships, health care benefits, tuition waivers, and unspecified assistantships available. Support available to part-time students. Financial award application deadline: 1/15; financial award applicants required to submit FAFSA. *Unit head:* Dr. David P. Schmidt, Graduate Program Director, 413-545-3827, Fax: 413-545-1027. *Application contact:* Jean M. Ames, Supervisor of Admissions, 413-545-0722, Fax: 413-577-0100, E-mail: gradadm@grad.umass.edu.

University of Michigan, Horace H. Rackham School of Graduate Studies, College of Engineering, Department of Industrial and Operations Engineering, Ann Arbor, MI 48109. Offers MS, MSE, PhD, MBA/MS, MBA/MSE. Part-time programs available. *Faculty:* 21 full-time (4 women). *Students:* 178 full-time (46 women), 23 part-time (5 women); includes 22 minority (2 African Americans, 15 Asian Americans or Pacific Islanders, 5 Hispanic Americans), 122 international. 481 applicants, 31% accepted, 73 enrolled. In 2009, 96 master's, 6 doctorates awarded. Terminal master's awarded for partial completion of doctoral program. *Degree requirements:* For doctorate, oral defense of dissertation, preliminary exams, qualifying exam. *Entrance requirements:* For master's, GRE General Test, minimum GPA of 3.2; for doctorate, GRE General Test, minimum GPA of 3.5. Additional exam requirements/recommendations for international students: Required—TOEFL. *Application deadline:* Applications are processed on a rolling basis. Application fee: $60 ($75 for international students). Electronic applications accepted. *Expenses:* Tuition, state resident: full-time $17,286; part-time $1099 per credit hour. Tuition, nonresident: full-time $34,944; part-time $2080 per credit hour. Required fees: $95 per semester. Tuition and fees vary according to course load, degree level and program. *Financial support:* In 2009–10, 71 students received support; fellowships, research assistantships, teaching assistantships, Federal Work-Study, institutionally sponsored loans, scholarships/grants, traineeships, health care benefits, and unspecified assistantships available. Financial award applicants required to submit FAFSA. *Faculty research:* Production/distribution/logistics, financial engineering and enterprise systems, ergonomics (physical and cognitive), stochastic processes, linear and nonlinear optimization, operations research. *Unit head:* Mark Daskin, Chair, 734-764-9422, Fax: 734-764-3451, E-mail: msdaskin@umich.edu. *Application contact:* Matt Irelan, Graduate Student Advisor/Program Coordinator, 734-764-6480, Fax: 734-764-3451, E-mail: mirelan@umich.edu.

The University of North Carolina at Chapel Hill, Graduate School, College of Arts and Sciences, Department of Operations Research, Chapel Hill, NC 27599. Offers MS, PhD. *Degree requirements:* For master's, comprehensive exam; for doctorate, comprehensive exam, thesis/dissertation. *Entrance requirements:* For master's and doctorate, GRE General Test, minimum GPA of 3.0.

University of Southern California, Graduate School, Viterbi School of Engineering, Department of Industrial and Systems Engineering, Los Angeles, CA 90089. Offers digital supply chain management (MS); engineering management (MS); engineering technology communication (Graduate Certificate); health systems operations (Graduate Certificate); industrial and systems engineering (MS, PhD, Engr); manufacturing engineering (MS); operations research engineering (MS); optimization and supply chain management (Graduate Certificate); product development engineering (MS); safety systems and security (MS); systems architecting and engineering (MS, Graduate Certificate); systems safety and security (Graduate Certificate); transportation systems (Graduate Certificate); MS/MBA. Part-time programs available. Postbaccalaureate distance learning degree programs offered (minimal on-campus study). *Faculty:* 11 full-time (2 women), 39 part-time/adjunct (7 women). *Students:* 250 full-time (71 women), 145 part-time (37 women); includes 67 minority (6 African Americans, 2 American Indian/Alaska Native, 39 Asian Americans or Pacific Islanders, 20 Hispanic Americans), 253 international. 679 applicants, 58% accepted, 206 enrolled. In 2009, 98 master's, 7 doctorates awarded. Terminal master's awarded for partial completion of doctoral program. *Degree requirements:* For doctorate, thesis/dissertation. *Entrance requirements:* For master's, GRE General Test; for doctorate, General GRE. *Application deadline:* For fall admission, 3/1 priority date for domestic and international students; for spring admission, 10/1 for domestic students, 10/1 priority date for international students. Applications are processed on a rolling basis. Application fee: $85. Electronic applications accepted. *Expenses:* Tuition: Full-time $25,980; part-time $1315 per unit. Required fees: $554. One-time fee: $35 full-time. Full-time tuition and fees vary according to degree level and program. *Financial support:* In 2009–10, fellowships with full tuition reimbursements (averaging $30,000 per year), research assistantships with full tuition reimbursements (averaging $19,250 per year), teaching assistantships with full tuition reimbursements (averaging $19,250 per year) were awarded; career-related internships or fieldwork, scholarships/grants, health care benefits, and unspecified assistantships also available. Financial award application deadline: 12/1; financial award applicants required to submit CSS PROFILE or FAFSA. *Faculty research:* Health systems, music cognition and retrieval, transportation andlogistics, manufacturing and automation, engineering systems design, risk and economic analysis. Total annual research expenditures: $1.2 million. *Unit head:* Dr. James E. Moore, Chair, 213-740-4885, Fax: 213-740-1120, E-mail: jmoore@usc.edu. *Application contact:* Mary Ordaz, Student Service Advisor, 213-740-4886, Fax: 213-740-1120, E-mail: isedept@usc.edu.

The University of Texas at Austin, Graduate School, Cockrell School of Engineering, Department of Mechanical Engineering, Program in Operations Research and Industrial Engineering, Austin, TX 78712-1111. Offers MS, PhD. *Entrance requirements:* For master's and doctorate, GRE General Test. Additional exam requirements/recommendations for international students: Required—TOEFL.

University of Waterloo, Graduate Studies, Faculty of Engineering, Department of Management Sciences, Waterloo, ON N2L 3G1, Canada. Offers applied operations research (MA Sc, MMS, PhD); information systems (MA Sc, MMS, PhD); management of technology (MA Sc, MMS, PhD). Part-time programs available. Postbaccalaureate distance learning degree programs offered (no on-campus study). *Degree requirements:* For master's, research paper or thesis; for doctorate, comprehensive exam, thesis/dissertation. *Entrance requirements:* For master's, GMAT or GRE, honors degree, minimum B average, resume; for doctorate, GMAT or GRE, master's degree, minimum A- average, resumé. Additional exam requirements/recommendations for international students: Required—TOEFL, TWE. *Faculty research:* Operations research, manufacturing systems, scheduling, information systems.

Virginia Commonwealth University, Graduate School, College of Humanities and Sciences, Department of Mathematics and Applied Mathematics, Program in Statistical Sciences and Operations Research, Richmond, VA 23284-9005. Offers MS, Certificate. *Entrance requirements:* For master's, GRE General Test, GRE Subject Test. Additional exam requirements/recommendations for international students: Required—TOEFL.

Virginia Polytechnic Institute and State University, Graduate School, College of Engineering, Department of Industrial and Systems Engineering, Blacksburg, VA 24061. Offers engineering administration (MEA); industrial engineering (M Eng, MS, PhD); operations research (M Eng, MS, PhD); systems engineering (M Eng, MS). *Entrance requirements:* For master's and doctorate, GRE. Additional exam requirements/recommendations for international students: Required—TOEFL (minimum score 550 paper-based; 213 computer-based). Electronic applications accepted.

Technology and Public Policy

Carnegie Mellon University, Carnegie Institute of Technology, Department of Civil and Environmental Engineering, Pittsburgh, PA 15213. Offers civil and environmental engineering (PhD); advanced infrastructure systems (MS, PhD); civil and environmental engineering (MS); civil and environmental engineering/engineering and public policy (PhD); civil engineering (MS, PhD); computational mechanics (MS, PhD); computational science and engineering (MS, PhD); environmental engineering (MS, PhD); environmental management and science (MS, PhD). Part-time programs available. *Faculty:* 19 full-time (3 women), 13 part-time/adjunct (3 women). *Students:* 118 full-time (48 women), 12 part-time (6 women); includes 15 minority (4 African Americans, 10 Asian Americans or Pacific Islanders, 1 Hispanic American), 78 international. Average age 26. 294 applicants, 75% accepted, 78 enrolled. In 2009, 55 master's, 10 doctorates awarded. Terminal master's awarded for partial completion of doctoral program. *Degree requirements:* For master's, thesis optional; for doctorate, comprehensive exam, thesis/dissertation, qualifying exam, public defense of dissertation. *Entrance requirements:* For master's and doctorate, GRE General Test. Additional exam requirements/recommendations for international students: Required—TOEFL (minimum score 550 paper-based; 213 computer-based; 82 iBT). *Application deadline:* For fall admission, 1/15 priority date for domestic and international students; for spring admission, 9/30 priority date for domestic and international students. Application fee: $65. Electronic applications accepted. *Financial support:* In 2009–10, 102 students received support, including 18 fellowships with full and partial tuition reimbursements available (averaging $22,853 per year), 34 research assistantships with full and partial tuition reimbursements available (averaging $23,661 per year); tuition waivers (partial) and unspecified assistantships also available. Financial award application deadline: 1/15. *Faculty research:* Advanced infrastructure systems; environmental engineering science and management; mechanics, materials, and computing; green design; global sustainable construction. Total annual research expenditures: $4.5 million. *Unit head:* Dr. James H. Garrett, Head, 412-268-2941, Fax: 412-268-7813, E-mail: garrett@cmu.edu. *Application contact:* Maxine A. Leffard, Graduate Program Administrator, 412-268-5673, Fax: 412-268-7813, E-mail: ce-admissions@andrew.cmu.edu.

Carnegie Mellon University, Carnegie Institute of Technology, Department of Engineering and Public Policy, Pittsburgh, PA 15213-3891. Offers PhD. *Degree requirements:* For doctorate, thesis/dissertation. *Entrance requirements:* For doctorate, GRE General Test, BS in physical sciences or engineering. Additional exam requirements/recommendations for international students: Required—TOEFL. *Faculty research:* Issues in energy and environmental policy, IT and telecommunications policy, risk analysis and communication, management of technological innovation, security and engineered civil systems.

See Close-Up on page 465.

Eastern Michigan University, Graduate School, College of Technology, School of Technology Studies, Program in Technology Studies, Ypsilanti, MI 48197. Offers interdisciplinary technology (MLS); technology studies (MS). Part-time and evening/weekend programs available. Postbaccalaureate distance learning degree programs offered (minimal on-campus study). *Students:* 12 full-time (4 women), 78 part-time (17 women); includes 21 minority (19 African Americans, 2 Hispanic Americans), 3 international. Average age 38. In 2009, 19 master's awarded. *Degree requirements:* For master's, thesis optional. *Entrance requirements:* For master's, GRE General Test, minimum GPA of 2.6. Additional exam requirements/recommendations for international students: Required—TOEFL. *Application deadline:* Applications are processed on a rolling basis. Application fee: $35. Tuition and fees vary according to course level. *Financial support:* Fellowships, research assistantships with full tuition reimbursements, teaching assistantships with full tuition reimbursements, career-related internships or fieldwork, Federal Work-Study, institutionally sponsored loans, scholarships/grants, tuition waivers (partial), and unspecified assistantships available. Support available to part-time students. Financial award applicants required to submit FAFSA. *Unit head:* Dr. Denise Pilato, Program Coordinator, 734-487-1161, Fax: 734-487-7690, E-mail: denise.pilato@emich.edu. *Application contact:* Dr. Denise Pilato, Program Coordinator, 734-487-1161, Fax: 734-487-7690, E-mail: denise.pilato@emich.edu.

The George Washington University, Elliott School of International Affairs, Program in International Science and Technology Policy, Washington, DC 20052. Offers MA, JD/MA. Part-time and evening/weekend programs available. *Students:* 18 full-time (6 women), 21 part-time (7 women); includes 7 minority (4 Asian Americans or Pacific Islanders, 3 Hispanic Americans), 7 international. Average age 29. 46 applicants, 80% accepted, 19 enrolled. In 2009, 20 master's awarded. *Degree requirements:* For master's, one foreign language, capstone project. *Entrance requirements:* For master's, GRE General Test. Additional exam requirements/recommendations for international students: Required—TOEFL. *Application deadline:* For fall admission, 2/1 for domestic students; for spring admission, 10/1 for domestic students. Application fee: $60. Electronic applications accepted. *Financial support:* In 2009–10, 15 students received support; fellowships with tuition reimbursements available, research assistantships with tuition reimbursements available, career-related internships or fieldwork, Federal Work-Study, institutionally sponsored loans, and tuition waivers (full and partial) available. Financial award application deadline: 1/15; financial award applicants required to submit FAFSA. *Faculty research:* Science policy, space policy, risk assessment, technology transfer, energy policy. *Unit head:* Dr. Nicholas Vonortas, Director, 202-994-6458, E-mail: vonortas@gwu.edu. *Application contact:* Jeff V. Miles, Director of Graduate Admissions, 202-994-7050, Fax: 202-994-9537, E-mail: esiagrad@gwu.edu.

Massachusetts Institute of Technology, School of Engineering, Engineering Systems Division, Cambridge, MA 02139-4307. Offers engineering and management (SM); engineering systems (SM, PhD); logistics (M Eng); technology and policy (SM); technology, management and policy (PhD); SM/MBA. *Faculty:* 8 full-time (0 women). *Students:* 285 full-time (72 women), 1 part-time (0 women); includes 36 minority (8 African Americans, 19 Asian Americans or Pacific Islanders, 9 Hispanic Americans), 116 international. Average age 31. 874 applicants, 28% accepted, 188 enrolled. In 2009, 143 master's, 11 doctorates awarded. *Degree requirements:* For master's, thesis; for doctorate, comprehensive exam, thesis/dissertation. *Entrance requirements:* For master's and doctorate, GRE General Test or GMAT (for some programs). Additional exam

Technology and Public Policy

Massachusetts Institute of Technology (continued)
requirements/recommendations for international students: Required—IELTS (minimum score 7.5); Recommended—TOEFL (minimum score 610 paper-based; 255 computer-based; 103 iBT). Application fee: $75. *Expenses:* Contact institution. *Financial support:* In 2009–10, 224 students received support, including 41 fellowships with tuition reimbursements available (averaging $26,522 per year), 95 research assistantships with tuition reimbursements available (averaging $26,506 per year), 17 teaching assistantships with tuition reimbursements available (averaging $21,300 per year); career-related internships or fieldwork, Federal Work-Study, institutionally sponsored loans, scholarships/grants, health care benefits, and unspecified assistantships also available. *Faculty research:* Critical infrastructures, extended enterprises, energy and sustainability, health care delivery, humans and technology, uncertainty and dynamics, design and implementation, networks and flows, policy and standards. Total annual research expenditures: $10.7 million. *Unit head:* Prof. Yossi Sheffi, Director, 617-253-1764, E-mail: esdinquiries@mit.edu. *Application contact:* Graduate Admissions, 617-253-1182, E-mail: esdgrad@mit.edu.

Massachusetts Institute of Technology, School of Humanities, Arts, and Social Sciences, Program in Science, Technology, and Society, Cambridge, MA 02139-4307. Offers history, anthropology, and science, technology and society (PhD). *Faculty:* 13 full-time (5 women). *Students:* 28 full-time (16 women); includes 3 minority (1 African American, 2 American Indian/Alaska Native), 7 international. Average age 30. 92 applicants, 4% accepted, 4 enrolled. In 2009, 5 doctorates awarded. *Degree requirements:* For doctorate, comprehensive exam, thesis/dissertation. *Entrance requirements:* For doctorate, GRE General Test. Additional exam requirements/recommendations for international students: Required—TOEFL (minimum score 577 paper-based; 233 computer-based; 90 iBT), IELTS (minimum score 7). *Application deadline:* For fall admission, 1/1 for domestic and international students. Application fee: $75. Electronic applications accepted. *Financial support:* In 2009–10, 26 students received support, including 19 fellowships with tuition reimbursements available (averaging $27,275 per year), 6 teaching assistantships with tuition reimbursements available (averaging $30,736 per year); research assistantships, Federal Work-Study, institutionally sponsored loans, scholarships/grants, traineeships, health care benefits, and unspecified assistantships also available. *Faculty research:* History of science, history of technology, sociology of science and technology, anthropology of science and technology, science, technology, and society. Total annual research expenditures: $543,000. *Unit head:* Prof. David A. Mindell, Director, 617-253-4062, Fax: 617-258-8118, E-mail: stsprogram@mit.edu. *Application contact:* Karen Gardner, Academic Administrator, 617-253-9759, Fax: 617-258-8118, E-mail: hasts@mit.edu.

Rensselaer Polytechnic Institute, Graduate School, School of Humanities and Social Sciences, Department of Science and Technology Studies, Troy, NY 12180-3590. Offers design studies (MS, PhD); policy studies (MS, PhD); science studies (MS, PhD); sustainability studies (MS, PhD); technology studies (MS, PhD). Part-time programs available. *Faculty:* 16 full-time (6 women). *Students:* 21 full-time (8 women), 3 part-time (1 woman); includes 6 Asian Americans or Pacific Islanders. Average age 27. 19 applicants, 42% accepted, 5 enrolled. In 2009, 1 master's, 9 doctorates awarded. Terminal master's awarded for partial completion of doctoral program. *Degree requirements:* For master's, thesis (for some programs); for doctorate, comprehensive exam, thesis/dissertation. *Entrance requirements:* For master's and doctorate, GRE General Test. Additional exam requirements/recommendations for international students: Required—TOEFL (minimum score 600 paper-based; 250 computer-based). *Application deadline:* For fall admission, 1/15 priority date for domestic students, 1/15 for international students. Applications are processed on a rolling basis. Application fee: $75. Electronic applications accepted. *Expenses:* Tuition: Full-time $38,100. *Financial support:* In 2009–10, 22 students received support, including 5 fellowships (averaging $22,000 per year), 1 research assistantship with full tuition reimbursement available (averaging $16,500 per year), 10 teaching assistantships with full tuition reimbursements available (averaging $16,500 per year); career-related internships or fieldwork, institutionally sponsored loans, and tuition waivers (partial) also available. Financial award application deadline: 1/15. *Faculty research:* Communities and technology, social dimensions of IT and biotechnology, ethics and policy, design. Total annual research expenditures: $75,000. *Unit head:* Dr. Sharon Anderson-Gold, Chair, 518-276-8837, Fax: 518-276-2659, E-mail: anders@rpi.edu. *Application contact:* Dr. Edward J. Woodhouse, Director of Graduate Studies, 518-276-8506, Fax: 518-276-2659, E-mail: woodhouse@rpi.edu.

Rochester Institute of Technology, Graduate Enrollment Services, College of Liberal Arts, Department of Science, Technology and Society/Public Policy, Rochester, NY 14623-5603. Offers science, technology and public policy (MS). Part-time programs available. *Students:* 14 full-time (5 women), 3 part-time (2 women); includes 3 minority (2 African Americans, 1 Asian American or Pacific Islander), 2 international. Average age 28. 18 applicants, 89% accepted, 4 enrolled. In 2009, 8 master's awarded. *Degree requirements:* For master's, thesis. *Entrance requirements:* For master's, GRE General Test, minimum GPA of 3.0. Additional exam requirements/recommendations for international students: Required—TOEFL (minimum score 570 paper-based; 230 computer-based; 88 iBT), or IELTS (minimum score 6.5). *Application deadline:* For fall admission, 2/15 priority date for domestic and international students; for winter admission, 11/1 for domestic and international students; for spring admission, 2/1 for domestic and international students. Applications are processed on a rolling basis. Application fee: $50. Electronic applications accepted. *Expenses:* Tuition: Full-time $31,533; part-time $876 per credit hour. Required fees: $210. *Financial support:* In 2009–10, 9 students received support; research assistantships with partial tuition reimbursements available, teaching assistantships with partial tuition reimbursements available, career-related internships or fieldwork, scholarships/grants, and unspecified assistantships available. Support available to part-time students. Financial award applicants required to submit FAFSA. *Faculty research:* Environmental policy, information and communications policy, energy policy, biotechnology policy. *Unit head:* Dr. James Winebrake, Chair, 585-475-4648, Fax: 585-475-2510, E-mail: james.winebrake@rit.edu. *Application contact:* Diane Ellison, Assistant Vice President, Graduate Enrollment Services, 585-475-2229, Fax: 585-475-7164, E-mail: gradinfo@rit.edu.

St. Cloud State University, School of Graduate Studies, College of Science and Engineering, Department of Environmental and Technological Studies, St. Cloud, MN 56301-4498. Offers MS. *Faculty:* 7 full-time (0 women). *Students:* 9 part-time (4 women); includes 1 minority (African American), 2 international. 21 applicants, 90% accepted. In 2009, 14 master's awarded. *Degree requirements:* For master's, thesis or alternative. *Entrance requirements:* For master's, minimum GPA of 2.75. Additional exam requirements/recommendations for international students: Required—TOEFL (minimum score 550 paper-based; 213 computer-based), Michigan English Language Assessment Battery; Recommended—IELTS (minimum score 6.5). *Application deadline:* For fall admission, 6/1 priority date for domestic students, 4/1 for international students; for spring admission, 10/1 priority date for domestic students, 8/1 for international students. Applications are processed on a rolling basis. Application fee: $35. Electronic applications accepted. *Financial support:* Federal Work-Study, scholarships/grants, and unspecified assistantships available. Financial award application deadline: 3/1. *Unit head:* Dr. Michner Bender, Interim Chairperson, 320-308-3891, Fax: 320-308-5122, E-mail: ets@stcloudstate.edu. *Application contact:* Linda Lou Krueger, School of Graduate Studies, 320-308-2113, Fax: 320-308-5371, E-mail: lekrueger@stcloudstate.edu.

Stony Brook University, State University of New York, Graduate School, College of Engineering and Applied Sciences, Department of Technology and Society, Program in Technology, Policy, and Innovation, Stony Brook, NY 11794-3760. Offers PhD. *Degree requirements:* For doctorate, comprehensive exam, thesis/dissertation. *Entrance requirements:* For doctorate, GRE General Test, A minimum undergraduate grade point average of 3.0. Additional exam requirements/recommendations for international students: Required—TOEFL. *Application deadline:* For fall admission, 2/1 for domestic and international students. *Expenses:* Tuition, state resident: full-time $8370; part-time $349 per credit. Tuition, nonresident: full-time $13,250; part-time $552 per credit. Required fees: $933. *Unit head:* David Ferguson. *Application contact:* Dr. Sheldon Reaven, Graduate Director, 631-632-8765, Fax: 631-632-7809, E-mail: sheldon.reaven@sunysb.edu.

University of Minnesota, Twin Cities Campus, Graduate School, Hubert H. Humphrey Institute of Public Affairs, Program in Science, Technology, and Environmental Policy, Minneapolis, MN 55455-0213. Offers MS, JD/MS. Part-time programs available. *Faculty:* 33 full-time (14 women), 29 part-time/adjunct (15 women). *Students:* 15 full-time (5 women), 9 part-time (4 women); includes 3 minority (all Asian Americans or Pacific Islanders), 2 international. Average age 26. 24 applicants, 75% accepted, 12 enrolled. In 2009, 10 master's awarded. *Degree requirements:* For master's, thesis. *Entrance requirements:* For master's, GRE General Test, undergraduate training in the biological or physical sciences or engineering, minimum undergraduate GPA of 3.0. Additional exam requirements/recommendations for international students: Required—TOEFL (minimum score 600 paper-based; 250 computer-based; 100 iBT). *Application deadline:* For fall admission, 4/1 for domestic and international students. Applications are processed on a rolling basis. Application fee: $75 ($95 for international students). Electronic applications accepted. *Financial support:* In 2009–10, 6 students received support, including fellowships with full and partial tuition reimbursements available (averaging $8,500 per year), research assistantships with full and partial tuition reimbursements available (averaging $5,270 per year), teaching assistantships with full and partial tuition reimbursements available (averaging $5,270 per year); career-related internships or fieldwork, Federal Work-Study, scholarships/grants, health care benefits, tuition waivers (full and partial), and unspecified assistantships also available. Financial award application deadline: 1/5. *Faculty research:* Economics, history, philosophy, and politics of science and technology; organization and management of science and technology. Total annual research expenditures: $5.1 million. *Unit head:* Dr. Deborah Swackhamer, Head, 612-624-3800, Fax: 612-626-0002, E-mail: hhhadmit@umn.edu. *Application contact:* Julie Harrold, Director of Admissions, 612-626-7229, Fax: 612-626-0002, E-mail: hhhadmit@umn.edu.

University of South Africa, College of Human Sciences, Pretoria, South Africa. Offers adult education (M Ed); African languages (MA, PhD); African politics (MA, PhD); Afrikaans (MA, PhD); ancient history (MA, PhD); ancient Near Eastern studies (MA, PhD); anthropology (MA, PhD); applied linguistics (MA); Arabic (MA, PhD); archaeology (MA); art history (MA); Biblical archaeology (MA); Biblical studies (M Th, D Th, PhD); Christian spirituality (M Th, D Th); church history (M Th, D Th); classical studies (MA, PhD); clinical psychology (MA); communication (MA, PhD); comparative education (M Ed, Ed D); consulting psychology (D Admin, D Com, PhD); curriculum studies (M Ed, Ed D); development studies (M Admin, MA, D Admin, PhD); didactics (M Ed, Ed D); education (M Tech); education management (M Ed, Ed D); educational psychology (M Ed); English (MA); environmental education (M Ed); French (MA, PhD); German (MA, PhD); Greek (MA); guidance and counseling (M Ed); health studies (MA, PhD), including health sciences education (MA), health services management (MA), medical and surgical nursing science (critical care general) (MA), midwifery and neonatal nursing science (MA), trauma and emergency care (MA); history (MA, PhD); history of education (Ed D); inclusive education (M Ed, Ed D); information and communications technology policy and regulation (MA); information science (MA, MIS, PhD); international politics (MA, PhD); Islamic studies (MA, PhD); Italian (MA, PhD); Judaica (MA, PhD); linguistics (MA, PhD); mathematical education (M Ed); mathematics education (MA); missiology (M Th, D Th); modern Hebrew (MA, PhD); musicology (MA, MMus, D Mus, PhD); natural science education (M Ed); New Testament (M Th, D Th); Old Testament (D Th); pastoral therapy (M Th, D Th); philosophy (MA); philosophy of education (M Ed, Ed D); politics (MA, PhD); Portuguese (MA, PhD); practical theology (M Th, D Th); psychology (MA, MS, PhD); psychology of education (M Ed, Ed D); public health (MA); religious studies (MA, D Th, PhD); Romance languages (MA); Russian (MA, PhD); Semitic languages (MA, PhD); social behavior studies in HIV/AIDS (MA); social science (mental health) (MA); social science in development studies (MA); social science in psychology (MA); social science in social work (MA); social science in sociology (MA); social work (MSW, DSW, PhD); socio-education (M Ed, Ed D); sociolinguistics (MA); sociology (MA, PhD); Spanish (MA, PhD); systematic theology (M Th, D Th); TESOL (teaching English to speakers of other languages) (MA); theological ethics (M Th, D Th); theory of literature (MA, PhD); urban ministries (D Th); urban ministry (M Th).

The University of Texas at Austin, Graduate School, Program in Technology Commercialization, Austin, TX 78712-1111. Offers MS. Twelve month program, beginning in May, with classes held every other Friday and Saturday. Evening/weekend programs available. Postbaccalaureate distance learning degree programs offered (no on-campus study). *Degree requirements:* For master's, year-long global teaming project. *Entrance requirements:* For master's, GRE General Test, or GMAT. Additional exam requirements/recommendations for international students: Required—TOEFL (minimum score 550 paper-based; 213 computer-based; 79 iBT). Electronic applications accepted. *Expenses:* Contact institution. *Faculty research:* Technology transfer; entrepreneurship; commercialization; research, development and innovation.

Western Illinois University, School of Graduate Studies, College of Business and Technology, Department of Engineering Technology, Macomb, IL 61455-1390. Offers manufacturing engineering systems (MS). Part-time programs available. *Students:* 14 full-time (1 woman), 7 part-time (0 women); includes 1 minority (African American), 10 international. Average age 25. 20 applicants, 75% accepted. In 2009, 10 master's awarded. *Degree requirements:* For master's, thesis or alternative. *Entrance requirements:* Additional exam requirements/recommendations for international students: Required—TOEFL (minimum score 550 paper-based; 213 computer-based; 80 iBT). *Application deadline:* Applications are processed on a rolling basis. Application fee: $30. Electronic applications accepted. *Expenses:* Tuition, state resident: full-time $4486; part-time $249.21 per credit hour. Tuition, nonresident: full-time $8972; part-time $498.42 per credit hour. Required fees: $72.62 per credit hour. *Financial support:* In 2009–10, 9 students received support, including 9 research assistantships with full tuition reimbursements available (averaging $7,280 per year). Financial award applicants required to submit FAFSA. *Unit head:* Dr. Ray Diez, Chairperson, 309-298-1091. *Application contact:* Evelyn Hoing, Assistant Director of Graduate Studies, 309-298-1806, Fax: 309-298-2345, E-mail: grad-office@wiu.edu.

Carnegie Mellon

CARNEGIE MELLON UNIVERSITY

Department of Engineering and Public Policy

Program of Study

A broad range of critical problems require analysis and skills at the interface between technology and society. The graduate program in the Department of Engineering and Public Policy is designed to prepare students to adapt and extend the perspectives and tools of engineering and science to these problems. While students receive a considerable amount of training and experience in social science and in techniques of social analysis, the Department's philosophical and methodological roots remain in engineering.

The primary degree offered is a research-oriented Ph.D. In preparing for the Ph.D., students may elect to earn a joint M.S. with one of the traditional engineering departments. Terminal M.S. programs are not recommended.

Graduate students take three types of courses: engineering and science courses, primarily offered by the engineering departments of Carnegie Institute of Technology (the College of Engineering); courses in social sciences and social analysis offered by the H. John Heinz III College, the School of Humanities and Social Sciences, and the Tepper School of Business; and courses offered by the Department of Engineering and Public Policy, including, at a minimum, a one-semester course in project management and a four-course sequence on applied policy analysis. Candidates for the Ph.D. degree should expect to spend at least three years or the equivalent in graduate study. Part-time Ph.D. degree candidates must devote at least one academic year to full-time graduate study.

The Department of Engineering and Public Policy subscribes firmly to the belief that the Ph.D. is a research degree. Research undertaken in fulfillment of the requirements for a Ph.D. must make a fundamental and generalizable contribution toward the definition, understanding, or solution of a class of problems in the area of technology and public policy. While faculty members assist students in defining and developing their research problems, responsibility in this area lies primarily with the student.

Faculty research and interest are currently focused on policy problems in energy and environmental systems; information and communication; risk analysis and communication; and the management of technical innovation and R&D policy. The Department also addresses issues in technology and economic development, focusing in particular on China, India, Mexico, and Brazil; the domestic security aspects of engineered civil systems; and various issues in technology, organizations, and social networks. The Department frequently undertakes the development of new software tools for the support of policy analysis and research and sometimes studies issues in arms control and defense policy. Faculty members maintain many close ties in their areas of interest with industrial and public sector organizations, and many members act as consultants to industry and government agencies. Students are encouraged to make full use of these faculty ties in defining and developing their research problems.

Specific details on degree requirements are included in the descriptive literature available from the Department.

Research Facilities

The University has excellent computer and library facilities. In addition, research facilities are available through the Heinz College, the Tepper School of Business, the Robotics Institute, and the Institute for Complex Engineered Systems.

Financial Aid

The Department strives to provide financial aid for the majority of its qualified doctoral students.

Cost of Study

Tuition is $36,700 for the 2010–11 academic year.

Living and Housing Costs

The estimated cost for living expenses for 2010–11, including housing, transportation, books and supplies, and incidentals, is $25,600. All graduate students live off campus in areas near the University.

Student Group

The graduate enrollment at Carnegie Mellon University totals more than 5,000 students, who come from colleges and universities throughout the United States and from many countries. In 2009, more than 2,000 graduate degrees were awarded, including 245 doctorates. The current enrollment in the Department is 83 graduate students and 90 undergraduates.

Student Outcomes

Since 1978, 184 students have graduated with a Ph.D. degree and 36 have graduated with an M.S. degree. Graduates are currently employed in policy research in think tanks, consulting firms, and nongovernmental organizations (24 percent); as university faculty members and postdoctoral research fellows (44 percent); in private-sector firms (16 percent); and in government and national labs (16 percent).

Location

Pittsburgh offers many valuable resources to students working on problems in the area of technology and society. It is a dynamic, working city that has been revitalized in the past few decades and has developed an outstanding cultural life. Excellent cultural opportunities are available, including museums, orchestras, opera, drama, and dance, and there are active groups in the fine arts and folk crafts. The city has a good botanical garden, a zoo, many fine parks, and excellent public radio and television. The countryside around Pittsburgh provides opportunities for outdoor activities in all seasons.

The University and The Department

Carnegie Mellon University has developed an international reputation as an outstanding environment in which to conduct interdisciplinary research on problems in the area of technology and society. The Department of Engineering and Public Policy maintains a vigorous intellectual interaction with the engineering departments and special programs of the Carnegie Institute of Technology, the School of Computer Science, the H. John Heinz III College, the College of Humanities and Social Sciences, and the Tepper School of Business. In addition to these, the University includes the Mellon College of Science and the College of Fine Arts.

Applying

All entering students must hold the equivalent of an undergraduate degree in engineering, physical science, or mathematics. Students with education or experience beyond the bachelor's degree are particularly encouraged to apply. Applications are welcome at any time, but they are usually processed between December and March for fall admission. Students are urged to take the General Test of the Graduate Record Examinations (the test is required for international students). In addition to filing the formal application, each student is asked to submit a letter describing his or her background and probable area(s) of research interest. Correspondence about the details of the program is encouraged.

Correspondence and Information

Victoria Finney, Graduate Program Administrator
Department of Engineering and Public Policy
Carnegie Mellon University
Pittsburgh, Pennsylvania 15213
Phone: 412-268-2670
E-mail: eppadmt@andrew.cmu.edu
Web site: http://www.epp.cmu.edu/

Carnegie Mellon University

THE FACULTY AND THEIR RESEARCH

Peter Adams, Professor of Civil and Environmental Engineering and of Engineering and Public Policy; Ph.D., Caltech. Climatic effects of atmospheric particulate matter (aerosols), global and regional models of atmospheric chemistry, air quality in developing countries.

Jay Apt, Professor of Technology, Tepper School of Business, and of Engineering and Public Policy; Executive Director, Carnegie Mellon Electricity Industry Center; Ph.D., MIT. Structure, economics, and control of the electric power system; public communication of natural and human-caused planetary change.

V. S. Arunachalam, Distinguished Service Professor of Engineering and Public Policy; Ph.D., Wales. Technology for economic development, energy and communication technology.

Inês L. Azevedo, Research Assistant Professor of Engineering and Public Policy; Ph.D., Carnegie Mellon. Energy and climate policy, decision-making under uncertainty, sustainable energy systems.

Alfred Blumstein, J. Erik Jonsson University Professor of Urban Systems and Operations Research, H. John Heinz III College, and Professor of Engineering and Public Policy; Ph.D., Cornell. Methodologies for public systems analysis, criminology, and criminal justice.

Serguey Braguinsky, Associate Professor of Social and Decision Sciences and of Engineering and Public Policy; Ph.D., Keio (Japan). Economics of innovation, entrepreneurship, and growth; development economics; institutional economics.

Wändi Bruine de Bruin, Assistant Professor of Social and Decision Sciences and of Engineering and Public Policy; Ph.D., Carnegie Mellon. Judgment and decision making, risk perception and communication, individual differences in decision-making competence, health decision making, environmental decision making.

Kathleen M. Carley, Professor of Computation, Organization, and Society; Engineering and Public Policy; Social and Decision Sciences; the Heinz College; and the Tepper School of Business; Ph.D., Harvard. Dynamic network analysis, multiagent systems, complexity, diffusion, and knowledge management.

Elizabeth A. Casman, Associate Research Professor of Engineering and Public Policy; Ph.D., Johns Hopkins. Environmental and microbial risk assessment, infectious disease transmission, health policy, risk communication, water resources.

Jared L. Cohon, President of Carnegie Mellon; Professor of Civil and Environmental Engineering and of Engineering and Public Policy; Ph.D., MIT. Environmental and energy systems analysis, multi-criteria decision making.

Lorrie Faith Cranor, Associate Professor of Computer Science and of Engineering and Public Policy; D.Sc., Washington (St. Louis). Usable privacy and security, online privacy, privacy enhancing technology, usability of privacy and security software, technology policy, social impact of computers.

Neil M. Donahue, Professor of Chemistry, Chemical Engineering, and Engineering and Public Policy; Ph.D., MIT. Chemical processes in air pollution and fine particles.

David J. Farber, Distinguished Career Professor of the School of Computer Science and of Public Policy; D.Sc. (hon.), Stevens. Information and telecommunication technology and policy.

Pedro Ferreira, Assistant Research Professor of Engineering and Public Policy and of the Heinz College; Ph.D., Carnegie Mellon. Telecommunications technology, policy and management; economics of information technology and networks.

Paul S. Fischbeck, Professor of Social and Decision Sciences and of Engineering and Public Policy; Ph.D., Stanford. Bayesian decision theory, geographic information systems, subjective probability assessment, system reliability, military decision making.

Baruch Fischhoff, Howard Heinz University Professor of Social and Decision Sciences and of Engineering and Public Policy; Ph.D., Hebrew (Jerusalem). Judgment and decision making, risk management, risk perception and communication, environmental benefits assessment, historical and expert judgment, adolescent decision making, homeland security, medical decision making, political and behavioral foundations of formal analysis.

Eden S. Fisher, Professor of the Practice of Engineering and Public Policy and Executive Director of Engineering and Technology Innovation Management Program; Ph.D., Carnegie Mellon. Technology planning, innovation management, design for sustainability, innovation education.

Erica R. H. Fuchs, Assistant Professor of Engineering and Public Policy; Ph.D., MIT. Geography of design; international technology and operations management; innovation and industrial policy; automotive and semiconductor telecom/computing industries, especially optoelectronics; China.

W. Michael Griffin, Executive Director of the Green Design Institute; Assistant Research Professor of Engineering and Public Policy and of the Tepper School of Business; Ph.D., Rhode Island. Impacts of production of chemicals and fuels via fermentation from renewable resources; the biodegradation of materials.

Alex Hills, Distinguished Service Professor of Engineering and Public Policy; Ph.D., Carnegie Mellon. Telecommunications in the developing world; remote and rural telecommunications systems; wireless communications technology, including LAN, MAN, and WAN; telecommunications policy and regulation.

David A. Hounshell, David M. Roderick Professor of Technology and Social Change; Professor of Social and Decision Sciences and of Engineering and Public Policy; Ph.D., Delaware. Innovation of environmental technologies, industrial research and development, industrialization of regions, history of science, technology, and business.

Marija D. Ilic, Professor of Electrical and Computer Engineering and of Engineering and Public Policy; D.Sc., Washington (St. Louis). Modeling and control of electric power and other large-scale systems.

Paulina Jaramillo, Assistant Research Professor of Engineering and Public Policy; Executive Director of the RenewElec Project; Ph.D., Carnegie Mellon. Energy system analysis, life cycle assessment, green design, renewable electricity.

Lester B. Lave, Harry B. and James H. Higgins University Professor of Economics; Professor of Engineering and Public Policy; Director of the Green Design Institute; Ph.D., Harvard. Alternative automobile fuels, life-cycle analysis, nanotechnology, sustainability, electricity deregulation.

Deanna H. Matthews, Assistant Teaching Professor and Associate Department Head for Undergraduate Affairs, Engineering and Public Policy; Ph.D., Carnegie Mellon. Life-cycle assessment, green design, K–12 engineering and science education.

H. Scott Matthews, Professor of Civil and Environmental Engineering and of Engineering and Public Policy; Ph.D., Carnegie Mellon. Design for environment, life-cycle assessment of energy, transportation and information infrastructure, energy sensing.

Sean T. McCoy, Project Manager, CCS Regulatory Project; Research Engineer, Engineering and Public Policy; Ph.D., Carnegie Mellon. Technical and regulatory issues in carbon capture and sequestration, engineering analysis of fossil energy systems, risk assessment, life-cycle assessment.

Francis C. McMichael, Professor Emeritus, Departments of Civil and Environmental Engineering and of Engineering and Public Policy; Ph.D., Caltech. Industrial and municipal solid-waste management, landfills, product design for the environment, engineering economics, risk analysis, source reduction, and recycling.

Jeremy J. Michalek, Associate Professor of Mechanical Engineering and of Engineering and Public Policy; Ph.D., Michigan. Systems optimization, design for market systems, green design, and environmental policy.

Benoît Morel, Associate Teaching Professor of Engineering and Public Policy; Ph.D., Geneva. Cyber security, international security, nonlinear dynamical modeling, environmental studies, arms control (technical aspects), space policy, complexity theory.

M. Granger Morgan, University and Lord Chair Professor of Engineering; Head, Department of Engineering and Public Policy; Professor of Electrical and Computer Engineering and of the Heinz College; Co-Director of the Carnegie Mellon Electricity Industry Center; Ph.D., California, San Diego. Technology and public policy, analysis and treatment of uncertainty, health and environmental risk analysis and communication, climate decision making, electric power systems and policy.

Spyros N. Pandis, Research Professor of Chemical Engineering and of Engineering and Public Policy; Ph.D., Caltech. Air pollution, atmospheric chemistry, aerosol science.

Jon M. Peha, Professor of Engineering and Public Policy and of Electrical and Computer Engineering; Ph.D., Stanford. Technical and policy issues of telecommunications, including telephone and computer networks, spectrum management, public safety and homeland security, e-commerce, Internet payment systems, information technology for developing countries.

Adrian Perrig, Professor of Electrical and Computer Engineering and of Engineering and Public Policy; Ph.D., Carnegie Mellon. Computer and communications security, applied cryptography, trusted computing technologies, secure operating systems.

Henry R. Piehler, Professor Emeritus of Materials Sciences and Engineering, of Engineering and Public Policy, and of Biomedical Engineering; Sc.D., MIT. Deformation processing and the mechanical behavior of materials, powder processing, clad, coated, and composite materials, biomaterials and medical devices, product liability litigation and standardization processes, productivity and innovation.

Allen L. Robinson, Professor of Mechanical Engineering and of Engineering and Public Policy; Ph.D., Berkeley. Air pollution, atmospheric chemistry, aerosol science, climate change, biomass energy.

Edward S. Rubin, Professor of Engineering and Public Policy and of Mechanical Engineering; Director of the Center for Energy and Environmental Studies; Ph.D., Stanford. Integrated energy–environmental–economic modeling and analysis of electric power systems, global climate change mitigation, carbon sequestration, environmental technology innovation.

Marvin A. Sirbu, Professor of Engineering and Public Policy, Industrial Administration, and Electrical and Computer Engineering; D.Sc., MIT. Telecommunication technology, policy and management regulation and industrial structure, economic impacts of information and communication technologies.

Mitchell J. Small, The H. John Heinz III Professor of Environmental Engineering; Professor and Associate Department Head for Graduate Affairs of Engineering and Public Policy; Professor of Civil and Environmental Engineering; Ph.D., Michigan. Environmental policy, math modeling, water and air quality, statistical analysis, soil and ground water monitoring data, uncertainty analysis.

Sarosh M. Talukdar, Professor Emeritus of Electrical and Computer Engineering and of Engineering and Public Policy; Ph.D., Purdue. Electrical power systems, autonomous agents, distributed control, market design.

Joel A. Tarr, Richard S. Caliguiri University Professor of History and Policy; Professor of History, Engineering and Public Policy, and the Heinz College; Ph.D.; Northwestern. Development of the urban infrastructure, urban technology, environmental trends, problems, and regulatory policies.

Francisco Veloso, Associate Professor of Engineering and Public Policy; Ph.D., MIT. Technology policy and management, supply chain decisions, innovation and entrepreneurship, automotive industry.

Jay Whitacre, Assistant Professor of Materials Science and Engineering and of Engineering and Public Policy; Ph.D., Michigan. Sustainable energy solutions with a focus on both materials and policy issues surrounding energy generation and storage technology.

Additional information on this list of faculty members, as well as adjunct and other faculty members, can be found on the Department Web site at http://www.epp.cmu.edu/.

FLORIDA INSTITUTE OF TECHNOLOGY

College of Engineering
Master of Science in Engineering Management
Master of Science in Systems Engineering

Program of Study

The College of Engineering (COE) at Florida Tech offers two programs of study. The Master of Science in Engineering Management (M.S.E.M.) degree prepares students in contemporary issues in technical and management areas faced by project/team leaders, supervising engineers, or scientists in high-technology and traditional industries. The Master of Science in Systems Engineering (M.S.S.E.) degree prepares students to be able to integrate system components. System engineering emphasizes the process aspects of a product or service. The programs feature learning flexibility by preparing programs of study that are individually crafted for each student. Course offerings include such modern courses as quality engineering, project engineering, systems engineering, engineering modeling and design, product development to address practical cases and issues in the industry, systems life cycle, design and risk analysis, and operations research.

The interdisciplinary nature of both programs, which attracts students from all areas of engineering, sciences, mathematics, technology, and computing, focuses on learning experiences in leadership and management along with technical areas such as system requirements, design, and development.

Special projects in EM and EM internship provide hands-on learning experiences in the working world. Student feedback is very favorable from these internships completed at industrial, government, and service organizations. The Capstone Design Projects course in M.S.S.E. integrates learning experiences from all courses. Both programs use the proper tools in training and preparing today's engineering or science graduates to become tomorrow's leaders and executives and as such it serves as a natural career path.

Earning the M.S.E.M. degree requires a minimum of 30 credit hours. The program requires five courses from the technical area and five courses from management. The EM program offers twelve courses, either technical, management, or both. Courses need to be taken from other engineering or science disciplines as well. The M.S.S.E. degree requires a total of 30 credits. Five courses are the required systems engineering courses and the remaining five courses are electives from technical disciplines.

Research Facilities

For technical courses in respective disciplines, the College of Engineering's extensive research facilities are available for students.

Financial Aid

A prospective student with excellent scholastic record may apply for an assistantship with the COE engineering disciplines. Eligible U.S. citizens may qualify for federal/or state financial aid.

Cost of Study

Tuition is $1040 per graduate credit hour in 2010–11. New students must pay a tuition deposit of $300, which is deducted from the semester's tuition charges.

Living and Housing Costs

On-campus housing (dormitories and apartments) is available for full-time single and married graduate students, but priority for dormitory room is given to undergraduate students. Many apartment complexes and related houses are available near the campus.

Student Outcomes

All M.S.E.M. and M.S.S.E. graduates find a job soon after graduation. Job opportunities span many disciplines. Many graduates are placed in local high-technology corporations within the U.S.

Location

Melbourne is located on the east coast of Florida. The climate is extremely pleasant, and opportunities for outdoor recreation abound. The John F. Kennedy Space Center and Disney World/EPCOT are nearby and the Atlantic beaches are within 3 miles of campus.

The Institute

Florida Institute of Technology was founded in 1958 by a group of scientists and engineers pioneering America's space program in Cape Canaveral. The environmental remote sensing program utilizes the technology developed by the space program. Florida Tech has rapidly developed into a residential institution and is the only independent technological university in the Southeast. It is supported by the community and industry and is the recipient of many research grants and contracts, a number of which provide financial support for graduate students. The campus covers 175 acres and includes a beautiful botanical garden and an internationally known collection of palm trees.

Applying

Applicants for either degree program must possess a bachelor's degree from an ABET-accredited engineering program. Applicants with B.S. degrees in physical science, mathematics, and computer science are also considered.

Forms and instructions for applying for admission and assistantship are sent on request. Admission is possible at the beginning of any semester, but admission in the fall semester is recommended. It is advantageous to apply early. Entering students are expected to have had undergraduate courses in general chemistry, organic chemistry, analytical chemistry, calculus, physics, and biology as well as a year or more of advanced science courses. The GRE General Test is required for admission.

Correspondence and Information

Department of Engineering Systems
College of Engineering
Florida Institute of Technology
150 West University Boulevard
Melbourne, Florida 32901
Phone: 321-674-7132
Fax: 321-674-7136
E-mail: des@fit.edu
Web site: http://www.fit.edu/AcadRes/se

Graduate Admissions Office
Florida Institute of Technology
150 West University Boulevard
Melbourne, Florida 32901
Phone: 321-674-8027
          800-944-4348 (toll-free in the U.S.)
Fax: 321-723-9468
E-mail: grad-admission@fit.edu
Web site: http://www.fit.edu/grad

Florida Institute of Technology

THE FACULTY AND RESEARCH AREAS

William W. Arrasmith, Associate Professor; Ph.D., Air Force Tech.
Carmo A. D'Cruz, Associate Professor; D.Eng., Southern Methodist.
Muzaffar A. Shaikh, Professor and Head; Ph.D., Illinois at Urbana-Champaign.
Wade H. Shaw, Professor; Ph.D. Clemson; PE.
Barry L. Webster, Associate Professor; Ph.D., Florida Tech.

Research Interests
Design of experiments.
Process engineering and flow modeling to reduce complexity.
Project scheduling using constrained optimization.
Science/operations research.
Simulation and modeling.
Software engineering.
Software engineering cost estimation.
Statistical process control.
System life cycle.
Systems engineering.
System testing.

Dr. Muzaffar A. Shaikh.

Working in the EM studio.

Section 16
Materials Sciences and Engineering

This section contains a directory of institutions offering graduate work in materials sciences and engineering, followed by an in-depth entry submitted by an institution that chose to prepare a detailed program description. Additional information about programs listed in the directory but not augmented by an in-depth entry may be obtained by writing directly to the dean of a graduate school or chair of a department at the address given in the directory.

For programs offering related work, see also in this book *Agricultural Engineering and Bioengineering, Biomedical Engineering and Biotechnology, Engineering and Applied Sciences,* and *Geological, Mineral/Mining, and Petroleum Engineering.* In another guide in this series: ***Graduate Programs in the Physical Sciences, Mathematics, Agricultural Sciences, the Environment & Natural Resources***
See *Chemistry* and *Geosciences*

CONTENTS

Ceramic Sciences and Engineering

Alfred University, Graduate School, New York State College of Ceramics, School of Engineering, Alfred, NY 14802-1205. Offers biomedical materials engineering science (MS); ceramic engineering (MS); ceramics (PhD); electrical engineering (MS); glass science (MS, PhD); materials science and engineering (MS, PhD); mechanical engineering (MS). *Degree requirements:* For master's, thesis; for doctorate, thesis/dissertation. *Entrance requirements:* Additional exam requirements/recommendations for international students: Required—TOEFL (minimum score 590 paper-based; 243 computer-based). Electronic applications accepted. *Expenses:* Contact institution. *Faculty research:* Fine-particle technology, x-ray diffraction, superconductivity, electronic materials.

Missouri University of Science and Technology, Graduate School, Department of Materials Science and Engineering, Rolla, MO 65409. Offers ceramic engineering (MS, DE, PhD); metallurgical engineering (MS, PhD). *Degree requirements:* For master's, thesis optional; for doctorate, comprehensive exam. *Entrance requirements:* For master's, GRE (minimum combined score 1100, 600 verbal, 3.5 writing); for doctorate, GRE (minimum score: quantitative 600, writing 3.5). Additional exam requirements/recommendations for international students: Required—TOEFL (minimum score 570 paper-based; 230 computer-based).

Rensselaer Polytechnic Institute, Graduate School, School of Engineering, Department of Materials Science and Engineering, Troy, NY 12180. Offers ceramics and glass science (M Eng, MS, PhD); composites (M Eng, MS, PhD); electronic materials (M Eng, MS, PhD); metallurgy (M Eng, MS, PhD); polymers (M Eng, MS, PhD). Part-time and evening/weekend programs available. *Faculty:* 16 full-time (2 women). *Students:* 54 full-time (11 women), 4 part-time (1 woman); includes 7 minority (all Asian Americans or Pacific Islanders), 30 international. Average age 24. 234 applicants, 14% accepted, 14 enrolled. In 2009, 10 master's, 6 doctorates awarded. Terminal master's awarded for partial completion of doctoral program. *Degree requirements:* For master's, thesis; for doctorate, comprehensive exam, thesis/dissertation. *Entrance requirements:* For master's and doctorate, GRE. Additional exam requirements/recommendations for international students: Required—TOEFL (minimum score 570 paper-based; 230 computer-based; 88 iBT). *Application deadline:* For fall admission, 1/15 priority date for domestic and international students; for spring admission, 8/31 priority date for domestic and international students. Applications are processed on a rolling basis. Application fee: $75. Electronic applications accepted. *Expenses:* Tuition: Full-time $38,100. *Financial support:* In 2009–10, 50 students received support, including fellowships with full tuition reimbursements available (averaging $24,750 per year), 40 research assistantships with full tuition reimbursements available (averaging $24,750 per year), 13 teaching assistantships with full tuition reimbursements available (averaging $24,750 per year); career-related internships or fieldwork, institutionally sponsored loans, and unspecified assistantships also available. Financial award application deadline: 2/1. *Faculty research:* Materials processing, nanostructural materials, materials for microelectronics, composite materials, computational materials. Total annual research expenditures: $5 million. *Unit head:* Dr. Robert Hull, Department Head, 518-276-6373, Fax: 518-276-8554, E-mail: hullr2@rpi.edu. *Application contact:* Dr. Pawel Keblinski, Admissions Coordinator, 518-276-6858, Fax: 518-276-8554, E-mail: keblip@rpi.edu.

University of Cincinnati, Graduate School, College of Engineering, Department of Chemical and Materials Engineering, Program in Materials Science and Metallurgical Engineering, Cincinnati, OH 45221. Offers ceramic science and engineering (MS, PhD); materials science and engineering (MS, PhD); metallurgical engineering (MS, PhD); polymer science and engineering (MS, PhD). Evening/weekend programs available. *Degree requirements:* For master's, thesis optional; for doctorate, one foreign language, comprehensive exam, thesis/dissertation, oral English proficiency exam. *Entrance requirements:* For master's and doctorate, GRE General Test, BS in related field, minimum undergraduate GPA of 3.0. Additional exam requirements/recommendations for international students: Required—TOEFL (minimum score 550 paper-based; 213 computer-based). Electronic applications accepted. *Expenses:* Contact institution.

Electronic Materials

Colorado School of Mines, Graduate School, Department of Metallurgical and Materials Engineering, Golden, CO 80401. Offers materials science (MS, PhD); metallurgical and materials engineering (ME, MS, PhD). Part-time programs available. *Faculty:* 34 full-time (3 women), 4 part-time/adjunct (0 women). *Students:* 54 full-time (13 women), 6 part-time (1 woman); includes 6 minority (1 American Indian/Alaska Native, 4 Asian Americans or Pacific Islanders, 1 Hispanic American), 8 international. Average age 30. 84 applicants, 26% accepted, 14 enrolled. In 2009, 18 master's, 8 doctorates awarded. *Degree requirements:* For master's, thesis (for some programs); for doctorate, comprehensive exam, thesis/dissertation. *Entrance requirements:* For master's and doctorate, GRE General Test. Additional exam requirements/recommendations for international students: Required—TOEFL (minimum score 550 paper-based; 213 computer-based; 80 iBT). *Application deadline:* For fall admission, 1/15 priority date for domestic and international students; for spring admission, 9/1 priority date for domestic and international students. Application fee: $50 ($70 for international students). Electronic applications accepted. *Expenses:* Tuition, state resident: full-time $10,584; part-time $588 per credit hour. Tuition, nonresident: full-time $24,750; part-time $1375 per credit hour. Required fees: $1654; $827.10 per semester. *Financial support:* In 2009–10, 3 fellowships with full tuition reimbursements (averaging $20,000 per year), 64 research assistantships with full tuition reimbursements (averaging $20,000 per year), 8 teaching assistantships with full tuition reimbursements (averaging $20,000 per year) were awarded; scholarships/grants, health care benefits, and unspecified assistantships also available. Financial award application deadline: 1/15; financial award applicants required to submit FAFSA. Total annual research expenditures: $6.9 million. *Unit head:* Dr. Michael Kaufman, Interim Department Head, 303-273-3009, Fax: 303-273-3795, E-mail: mkaufman@mines.edu. *Application contact:* Peggy Cook, Program Assistant, 303-273-3660, Fax: 303-273-3795, E-mail: pcook@mines.edu.

Massachusetts Institute of Technology, School of Engineering, Department of Materials Science and Engineering, Cambridge, MA 02139-4307. Offers archaeological materials (PhD, Sc D); bio- and polymeric materials (PhD, Sc D); electronic, photonic and magnetic materials (PhD, Sc D); emerging, fundamental and computational studies in materials science (Sc D); emerging, fundamental, and computational studies in materials science (PhD); materials engineering (Mat E); materials science and engineering (M Eng, SM, PhD, Sc D); metallurgical engineering (Met E); structural and environmental materials (PhD, Sc D); SM/MBA. *Faculty:* 36 full-time (8 women). *Students:* 222 full-time (62 women); includes 32 minority (3 African Americans, 21 Asian Americans or Pacific Islanders, 8 Hispanic Americans), 125 international. Average age 26. 459 applicants, 23% accepted, 63 enrolled. In 2009, 35 master's, 28 doctorates awarded. Terminal master's awarded for partial completion of doctoral program. *Degree requirements:* For master's and other advanced degree, thesis; for doctorate, comprehensive exam, thesis/dissertation. *Entrance requirements:* For master's and doctorate, GRE General Test. Additional exam requirements/recommendations for international students: Required—IELTS (minimum score 5.5); Recommended—TOEFL (minimum score 577 paper-based; 233 computer-based; 90 iBT). *Application deadline:* For fall admission, 1/1 for domestic and international students. Application fee: $75. Electronic applications accepted. *Financial support:* In 2009–10, 222 students received support, including 55 fellowships with tuition reimbursements available (averaging $22,387 per year), 135 research assistantships with tuition reimbursements available (averaging $27,287 per year), 10 teaching assistantships with tuition reimbursements available (averaging $30,736 per year); career-related internships or fieldwork, Federal Work-Study, institutionally sponsored loans, scholarships/grants, health care benefits, and unspecified assistantships also available. *Faculty research:* Thermodynamics and kinetics of phase transformations, structure of all materials classes: metals, ceramics, semiconductors, polymers, biomaterials, influence of processing on materials structure, structure, property relationships (electrical, magnetic, optical, mechanical). Total annual research expenditures: $22.6 million. *Unit head:* Prof. Edwin L. Thomas, Department Head, 617-253-3300, Fax: 617-252-1775. *Application contact:* Angelita Mireles, Graduate Admissions, 617-253-3302, E-mail: dmse-admissions@mit.edu.

Northwestern University, McCormick School of Engineering and Applied Science, Department of Electrical Engineering and Computer Science and Department of Materials Science and Engineering, Program in Electronic Materials, Evanston, IL 60208. Offers MS, PhD, Certificate. Part-time programs available. Terminal master's awarded for partial completion of doctoral program. *Degree requirements:* For master's, thesis; for doctorate, comprehensive exam, thesis/dissertation. *Faculty research:* Electronic optical magnetic materials and devices.

Northwestern University, McCormick School of Engineering and Applied Science, Department of Materials Science and Engineering, Evanston, IL 60208. Offers electronic materials (Certificate); materials science and engineering (MS, PhD). Admissions and degrees offered through The Graduate School. Part-time programs available. Terminal master's awarded for partial completion of doctoral program. *Degree requirements:* For master's, oral thesis defense; for doctorate, oral defense of dissertation, preliminary evaluation, qualifying exam. Electronic applications accepted. *Faculty research:* Metallurgy, ceramics, polymers, electronic materials, biomaterials.

Princeton University, Princeton Institute for the Science and Technology of Materials (PRISM), Princeton, NJ 08544-1019. Offers materials (PhD).

University of Arkansas, Graduate School, Interdisciplinary Program in Microelectronics and Photonics, Fayetteville, AR 72701-1201. Offers MS, PhD. *Students:* 12 full-time (0 women), 35 part-time (4 women); includes 5 minority (4 African Americans, 1 Hispanic American), 20 international. 29 applicants, 59% accepted. In 2009, 11 master's, 7 doctorates awarded. *Degree requirements:* For doctorate, thesis/dissertation. Application fee: $40 ($50 for international students). *Expenses:* Tuition, state resident: full-time $7355; part-time $356.58 per hour. Tuition, nonresident: full-time $17,401; part-time $775.17 per hour. Required fees: $1203. *Financial support:* In 2009–10, 8 fellowships with tuition reimbursements, 9 research assistantships, 4 teaching assistantships were awarded. Financial award application deadline: 4/1; financial award applicants required to submit FAFSA. *Unit head:* Dr. Ken Vickers, Head, 479-575-2875, Fax: 479-575-4580, E-mail: vickers@uark.edu. *Application contact:* Graduate Admissions, 479-575-6246, Fax: 479-575-5908, E-mail: gradinfo@uark.edu.

Materials Engineering

Arizona State University, Graduate College, Ira A. Fulton School of Engineering, School of Materials, Tempe, AZ 85287. Offers materials science and engineering (MS, MSE, PhD); semiconductor processing and packaging (MSE). *Degree requirements:* For doctorate, thesis/dissertation. *Entrance requirements:* For doctorate, GRE.

Auburn University, Graduate School, Ginn College of Engineering, Department of Mechanical Engineering, Program in Materials Engineering, Auburn University, AL 36849. Offers M Mtl E, MS, PhD. *Faculty:* 29 full-time (0 women), 2 part-time/adjunct (0 women). *Students:* 16 full-time (6 women), 33 part-time (8 women); includes 1 minority (African American), 33 international. Average age 31. 62 applicants, 15% accepted, 5 enrolled. In 2009, 5 master's, 6 doctorates awarded. *Degree requirements:* For master's, thesis (MS), oral exam; for doctorate, one foreign language, thesis/dissertation. *Entrance requirements:* For master's and doctorate, GRE General Test. *Application deadline:* For fall admission, 7/7 for domestic students; for spring admission, 11/24 for domestic students. Applications are processed on a rolling basis. Application fee: $50 ($60 for international students). Electronic applications accepted. *Expenses:* Tuition, state resident: full-time $6240. Tuition, nonresident: full-time $18,720. International tuition: $18,938 full-time. Required fees: $492. Tuition and fees vary according to course load, program and reciprocity agreements. *Financial support:* Fellowships, research assistantships, teaching assistantships, Federal Work-Study available. Support available to part-time students. Financial award application deadline: 3/15; financial award applicants required to submit FAFSA. *Faculty research:* Smart materials. *Unit head:* Dr. Bryan Chin, Head, 334-844-3322. *Application contact:* Dr. George Flowers, Dean of the Graduate School, 334-844-2125.

Boise State University, Graduate College, College of Engineering, Department of Materials Science and Engineering, Boise, ID 83725-0399. Offers M Engr, MS. *Expenses:* Tuition, state resident: full-time $3106; part-time $209 per credit. Tuition, nonresident: part-time $284 per credit.

Boston University, College of Engineering, Division of Materials Science and Engineering, Boston, MA 02215. Offers MS, PhD. Part-time programs available. *Students:* 21 full-time (4 women), 2 part-time (both women); includes 2 minority (1 Asian American or Pacific Islander, 1 Hispanic American), 12 international. Average age 26. 82 applicants, 44% accepted, 10 enrolled. In 2009, 2 master's, 1 doctorate awarded. Terminal master's awarded for partial completion of doctoral program. *Degree requirements:* For master's, thesis optional; for doctorate, comprehensive exam, thesis/dissertation. *Entrance requirements:* For master's and doctorate, GRE General Test. Additional exam requirements/recommendations for international students: Required—TOEFL (minimum score 550 paper-based; 213 computer-based; 84 iBT), IELTS (minimum score 6). *Application deadline:* For fall admission, 4/1 for domestic and international students; for spring admission, 10/1 for domestic and international students. Applications are processed on a rolling basis. Application fee: $70. Electronic applications accepted. *Expenses:* Tuition: Full-time $37,910; part-time $1184 per credit hour. Required fees: $386; $40 per semester. Part-time tuition and fees vary according to class time, course level, degree level and program. *Financial support:* In 2009–10, 19 students received support, including 4 fellowships with full tuition reimbursements available (averaging $27,600 per year), 12 research assistantships with full tuition reimbursements available (averaging $18,400 per year), 3 teaching assistantships with full tuition reimbursements available (averaging $18,400 per year); career-related internships or fieldwork, Federal Work-Study, institutionally sponsored loans, scholarships/grants, traineeships, and health care benefits also available. Financial award application deadline: 1/15; financial award applicants required to submit FAFSA. *Faculty research:* Biomaterials; electronic and photonic materials; materials for energy and environment; nanomaterials. *Unit head:* Dr. Uday Pal, Division Head, 617-353-7708, Fax: 617-353-5548, E-mail: upal@bu.edu. *Application contact:* Cheryl Kelley, Director of Graduate Programs, 617-353-9760, Fax: 617-353-0259, E-mail: enggrad@bu.edu.

California State University, Northridge, Graduate Studies, College of Engineering and Computer Science, Department of Manufacturing Systems Engineering and Management, Northridge, CA 91330. Offers engineering automation (MS); engineering management (MS); manufacturing systems engineering (MS); materials engineering (MS). Postbaccalaureate distance learning degree programs offered. *Faculty:* 6 full-time (1 woman), 33 part-time/adjunct (12 women). *Students:* 137 full-time (18 women), 115 part-time (20 women); includes 4 African Americans, 22 Asian Americans or Pacific Islanders, 19 Hispanic Americans, 149 international. Average age 27. 210 applicants, 68% accepted, 69 enrolled. In 2009, 78 master's awarded. *Entrance requirements:* For master's, GRE (if cumulative undergraduate GPA less than 3.0). *Application deadline:* For fall admission, 3/30 for domestic students; for spring admission, 9/30 for domestic students. Application fee: $55. *Unit head:* Prof. Behzad Bavarian, Acting Chair, 818-677-2167. *Application contact:* Prof. Behzad Bavarian, Acting Chair, 818-677-2167.

Carleton University, Faculty of Graduate Studies, Faculty of Engineering and Design, Department of Mechanical and Aerospace Engineering, Ottawa, ON K1S 5B6, Canada. Offers aerospace engineering (M Eng, MA Sc, PhD); materials engineering (M Eng, MA Sc); mechanical engineering (M Eng, MA Sc, PhD). *Degree requirements:* For master's, thesis optional; for doctorate, thesis/dissertation. *Entrance requirements:* For master's, honors degree; for doctorate, MA Sc or M Eng. Additional exam requirements/recommendations for international students: Required—TOEFL. *Faculty research:* Thermal fluids engineering, heat transfer, vehicle engineering.

Carnegie Mellon University, Carnegie Institute of Technology, Department of Materials Science and Engineering, Pittsburgh, PA 15213-3891. Offers MS, PhD. Part-time programs available. Terminal master's awarded for partial completion of doctoral program. *Degree requirements:* For master's, exam; for doctorate, thesis/dissertation, qualifying exam. *Entrance requirements:* For master's and doctorate, GRE General Test. Additional exam requirements/recommendations for international students: Required—TOEFL. *Faculty research:* Materials characterization, process metallurgy, high strength alloys, growth kinetics, ceramics.

Case Western Reserve University, School of Graduate Studies, The Case School of Engineering, Department of Materials Science and Engineering, Cleveland, OH 44106. Offers materials science and engineering (MS, PhD). Part-time programs available. Postbaccalaureate distance learning degree programs offered (no on-campus study). *Faculty:* 10 full-time (0 women). *Students:* 50 full-time (11 women), 7 part-time (2 women), 45 international. In 2009, 11 master's, 4 doctorates awarded. Terminal master's awarded for partial completion of doctoral program. *Degree requirements:* For master's, thesis (for some programs); for doctorate, thesis/dissertation, qualifying exam, teaching experience. *Entrance requirements:* For master's and doctorate, GRE General Test. Additional exam requirements/recommendations for international students: Required—TOEFL. *Application deadline:* For fall admission, 2/15 priority date for domestic students; for spring admission, 9/15 for domestic students. Applications are processed on a rolling basis. Application fee: $50. *Financial support:* Fellowships with full and partial tuition reimbursements, research assistantships with full and partial tuition reimbursements, teaching assistantships available. Financial award application deadline: 4/30; financial award applicants required to submit FAFSA. *Faculty research:* Surface hardening of steels and other alloys, chemistry and structure of surfaces, microstructural and mechanical property characterization, materials for energy applications, thermodynamics and kinetics of materials, performance and reliability of materials. Total annual research expenditures: $7.4 million. *Unit head:* Dr. James D. McGuffin-Cawley, Department Chair, 216-368-6482, Fax: 216-368-4224, E-mail: emse.info@case.edu. *Application contact:* Kathleen Bates, Academic Administration Manager, 216-368-3840, Fax: 216-368-3209, E-mail: esme.info@case.edu.

Clemson University, Graduate School, College of Engineering and Science, School of Materials Science and Engineering, Programs in Materials Science and Engineering, Clemson, SC 29634. Offers MS, PhD. Part-time programs available. *Students:* 57 full-time (19 women), 3 part-time (0 women), 33 international. Average age 27. 84 applicants, 51% accepted, 15 enrolled. In 2009, 2 master's, 5 doctorates awarded. Terminal master's awarded for partial completion of doctoral program. *Degree requirements:* For master's, thesis; for doctorate, comprehensive exam, thesis/dissertation. *Entrance requirements:* For master's and doctorate, GRE General Test. Additional exam requirements/recommendations for international students: Required—TOEFL. *Application deadline:* For fall admission, 2/1 for domestic students; for spring admission, 9/1 for domestic students. Applications are processed on a rolling basis. Application fee: $70 ($80 for international students). Electronic applications accepted. *Expenses:* Tuition, state resident: full-time $8684; part-time $528 per credit hour. Tuition, nonresident: full-time $15,330; part-time $1078 per credit hour. Required fees: $736; $37 per semester. Part-time tuition and fees vary according to course load and program. *Financial support:* In 2009–10, 2 fellowships with full and partial tuition reimbursements (averaging $18,000 per year), 41 research assistantships with partial tuition reimbursements (averaging $20,295 per year), 1 teaching assistantship with partial tuition reimbursement (averaging $18,500 per year) were awarded; career-related internships or fieldwork, institutionally sponsored loans, scholarships/grants, health care benefits, and unspecified assistantships also available. Support available to part-time students. Financial award applicants required to submit FAFSA. *Faculty research:* Composites, fibers, ceramics, metallurgy, biomaterials, semiconductors. *Unit head:* Dr. Kathleen Richardson, Chair and Director of the School of Materials Science and Engineering, 864-656-3311, Fax: 864-656-5973, E-mail: richar3@clemson.edu. *Application contact:* Dr. Gary C. Lickfield, Graduate Program Coordinator, 864-656-5964, Fax: 864-656-5973, E-mail: lgary@clemson.edu.

Colorado School of Mines, Graduate School, Department of Metallurgical and Materials Engineering, Golden, CO 80401. Offers materials science (MS, PhD); metallurgical and materials engineering (ME, MS, PhD). Part-time programs available. *Faculty:* 34 full-time (3 women), 4 part-time/adjunct (0 women). *Students:* 54 full-time (13 women), 6 part-time (1 woman); includes 6 minority (1 American Indian/Alaska Native, 4 Asian Americans or Pacific Islanders, 1 Hispanic American), 8 international. Average age 30. 84 applicants, 26% accepted, 14 enrolled. In 2009, 18 master's, 8 doctorates awarded. *Degree requirements:* For master's, thesis (for some programs); for doctorate, comprehensive exam, thesis/dissertation. *Entrance requirements:* For master's and doctorate, GRE General Test. Additional exam requirements/recommendations for international students: Required—TOEFL (minimum score 550 paper-based; 213 computer-based; 80 iBT). *Application deadline:* For fall admission, 1/15 priority date for domestic and international students; for spring admission, 9/1 priority date for domestic and international students. Application fee: $50 ($70 for international students). Electronic applications accepted. *Expenses:* Tuition, state resident: full-time $10,584; part-time $588 per

credit hour. Tuition, nonresident: full-time $24,750; part-time $1375 per credit hour. Required fees: $1654; $827.10 per semester. *Financial support:* In 2009–10, 3 fellowships with full tuition reimbursements (averaging $20,000 per year), 64 research assistantships with full tuition reimbursements (averaging $20,000 per year), 8 teaching assistantships with full tuition reimbursements (averaging $20,000 per year) were awarded; scholarships/grants, health care benefits, and unspecified assistantships also available. Financial award application deadline: 1/15; financial award applicants required to submit FAFSA. Total annual research expenditures: $6.9 million. *Unit head:* Dr. Michael Kaufman, Interim Department Head, 303-273-3009, Fax: 303-273-3795, E-mail: mkaufman@mines.edu. *Application contact:* Peggy Cook, Program Assistant, 303-273-3660, Fax: 303-273-3795, E-mail: pcook@mines.edu.

Columbia University, Fu Foundation School of Engineering and Applied Science, Department of Applied Physics and Applied Mathematics, New York, NY 10027. Offers applied physics (Eng Sc D); applied physics and applied mathematics (MS, PhD, Engr); materials science and engineering (MS, Eng Sc D, PhD); medical physics (MS). Part-time programs available. Postbaccalaureate distance learning degree programs offered (no on-campus study). *Faculty:* 19 full-time (1 woman), 3 part-time/adjunct (1 woman). *Students:* 127 full-time (24 women), 44 part-time (7 women); includes 12 minority (2 African Americans, 1 American Indian/Alaska Native, 8 Asian Americans or Pacific Islanders, 1 Hispanic American), 73 international. Average age 27. 300 applicants, 35% accepted, 45 enrolled. In 2009, 31 master's, 10 doctorates awarded. Terminal master's awarded for partial completion of doctoral program. *Degree requirements:* For master's, comprehensive exam; for doctorate, thesis/dissertation, qualifying exam. *Entrance requirements:* For master's, GRE General Test, GRE Subject Test (strongly recommended); for doctorate, GRE General Test, GRE Subject Test (physics); for Engr, GRE General Test. Additional exam requirements/recommendations for international students: Required—TOEFL. *Application deadline:* For fall admission, 12/1 priority date for domestic and international students; for spring admission, 10/1 priority date for domestic and international students. Application fee: $70. Electronic applications accepted. *Financial support:* In 2009–10, 70 students received support, including 4 fellowships with full and partial tuition reimbursements available, 50 research assistantships with full tuition reimbursements available (averaging $30,000 per year), 18 teaching assistantships with full tuition reimbursements available (averaging $30,000 per year); health care benefits and unspecified assistantships also available. Financial award application deadline: 12/1; financial award applicants required to submit FAFSA. *Faculty research:* Plasma, solid state, optical and laser physics; atmospheric, oceanic and earth physics; computational math and applied mathematics; materials science and engineering. *Unit head:* Dr. Irving P. Herman, Professor and Chair, 212-854-4457, E-mail: seasinfo.apam@columbia.edu. *Application contact:* Montserrat Fernandez-Pinkley, Student Services Coordinator, 212-854-4457, Fax: 212-854-8257, E-mail: mf2157@columbia.edu.

Cornell University, Graduate School, Graduate Fields of Engineering, Field of Materials Science and Engineering, Ithaca, NY 14853-0001. Offers materials engineering (M Eng, PhD); materials science (M Eng, PhD). *Faculty:* 46 full-time (6 women). *Students:* 67 full-time (23 women); includes 15 minority (2 African Americans, 9 Asian Americans or Pacific Islanders, 4 Hispanic Americans), 26 international. Average age 26. 312 applicants, 35% accepted, 1 enrolled. In 2009, 21 master's, 10 doctorates awarded. *Degree requirements:* For doctorate, comprehensive exam, thesis/dissertation. *Entrance requirements:* For master's and doctorate, GRE General Test, 3 letters of recommendation. Additional exam requirements/recommendations for international students: Required—TOEFL (minimum score 550 paper-based; 213 computer-based; 77 iBT). *Application deadline:* For fall admission, 1/15 priority date for domestic students. Application fee: $70. Electronic applications accepted. *Expenses:* Tuition: Full-time $29,500. Required fees: $70. Full-time tuition and fees vary according to degree level, program and student level. *Financial support:* In 2009–10, 48 students received support, including 2 fellowships with full tuition reimbursements available, 7 research assistantships with full tuition reimbursements available, 1 teaching assistantship with full tuition reimbursement available; institutionally sponsored loans, scholarships/grants, health care benefits, tuition waivers (full and partial), and unspecified assistantships also available. Financial award applicants required to submit FAFSA. *Faculty research:* Ceramics, complex fluids, glass, metals, polymers semiconductors. *Unit head:* Director of Graduate Studies, 607-255-9159, Fax: 607-255-2365. *Application contact:* Graduate Field Assistant, 607-255-9159, Fax: 607-255-2365, E-mail: matsci@cornell.edu.

Dalhousie University, Faculty of Engineering, Department of Materials Engineering, Halifax, NS B3H 1Z1, Canada. Offers M Eng, MA Sc, PhD. *Faculty:* 5 full-time (0 women), 2 part-time/adjunct (0 women). *Students:* 3 full-time (0 women). 6 applicants, 33% accepted. In 2009, 2 master's awarded. *Degree requirements:* For master's, thesis; for doctorate, thesis/dissertation. *Entrance requirements:* Additional exam requirements/recommendations for international students: Required—TOEFL, IELTS, CANTEST, CAEL, or Michigan English Language Assessment Battery. *Application deadline:* For fall admission, 6/1 for domestic students, 4/1 for international students; for winter admission, 11/15 for domestic students, 8/31 for international students; for spring admission, 2/28 for domestic students, 12/31 for international students. Applications are processed on a rolling basis. Application fee: $70. Electronic applications accepted. *Financial support:* Fellowships, research assistantships, teaching assistantships, scholarships/grants and traineeships available. *Faculty research:* Ceramic and metal matrix composites, electron microscopy, electrolysis in molten salt, fracture mechanics, electronic materials. *Unit head:* Dr. Michael Pegg, Head, 902-494-3252, Fax: 902-420-0219, E-mail: michael.pegg@dal.ca. *Application contact:* Dr. Georges Kipouros, Graduate Coordinator, 902-494-6100, Fax: 902-494-0219, E-mail: peas.grad@dal.ca.

Dartmouth College, Thayer School of Engineering, Program in Materials Sciences and Engineering, Hanover, NH 03755. Offers MS, PhD. *Degree requirements:* For master's, thesis; for doctorate, thesis/dissertation, candidacy oral exam. *Entrance requirements:* For master's and doctorate, GRE General Test. *Application deadline:* For fall admission, 1/1 priority date for domestic students. Application fee: $45. *Financial support:* Fellowships, research assistantships, teaching assistantships, career-related internships or fieldwork, Federal Work-Study, institutionally sponsored loans, and tuition waivers (full and partial) available. Financial award application deadline: 1/15. *Faculty research:* Electronic and magnetic materials, microstructural evolution, biomaterials and nanostructures, laser-material interactions, nano composites. Total annual research expenditures: $2.4 million. *Unit head:* Dr. Joseph J. Helbie, Dean, 603-646-2238, Fax: 603-646-2580, E-mail: joseph.j.helbie@dartmouth.edu. *Application contact:* Candace S. Potter, Graduate Admissions Administrator, 603-646-3844, Fax: 603-646-1620, E-mail: candace.potter@dartmouth.edu.

Drexel University, College of Engineering, Department of Materials Engineering, Philadelphia, PA 19104-2875. Offers MS, PhD. Part-time and evening/weekend programs available. Terminal master's awarded for partial completion of doctoral program. *Degree requirements:* For master's, thesis or alternative; for doctorate, thesis/dissertation. *Entrance requirements:* For master's, minimum GPA of 3.0; for doctorate, minimum GPA of 3.0, MS. Additional exam requirements/recommendations for international students: Required—TOEFL. Electronic applications accepted. *Faculty research:* Composite science; polymer and biomedical engineering; solidification; near net shape processing, including powder metallurgy.

Florida International University, College of Engineering and Computing, Department of Mechanical and Materials Engineering, Miami, FL 33199. Offers materials science and engineering (MS, PhD); mechanical engineering (MS, PhD). Part-time and evening/weekend programs available. *Faculty:* 17 full-time (2 women). *Students:* 46 full-time (7 women), 19 part-time (5 women); includes 18 minority (3 African Americans, 1 Asian American or Pacific Islander, 14 Hispanic Americans), 44 international. Average age 28. 89 applicants, 20% accepted, 16 enrolled. In 2009, 19 master's, 8 doctorates awarded. Terminal master's awarded for partial completion of doctoral program. *Degree requirements:* For master's, thesis or alternative; for doctorate, comprehensive exam, thesis/dissertation. *Entrance requirements:* For master's, GRE (depending on program), 3 letters of recommendation, minimum undergraduate GPA of 3.0 in upper level course; for doctorate, GRE minimum of 1150 with GRE verbal at least 450 and GRE quantitative at least 650, for someone with BS only:

Materials Engineering

Florida International University (continued)
minimum undergraduate GPA of 3.0 in upper-level coursework, 3 letters of recommendation, letter of intent; for someone with MS: in addition to the above requirements for someone having a BS degree, the MS GPA must be a minimum of 3.3. Additional exam requirements/recommendations for international students: Required—TOEFL (minimum score 550 paper-based; 80 iBT), or IELTS (minimum score 6.5). *Application deadline:* For fall admission, 6/1 for domestic students, 4/1 for international students; for spring admission, 10/1 for domestic students, 9/1 for international students. Applications are processed on a rolling basis. Application fee: $30. Electronic applications accepted. *Expenses:* Tuition, state resident: full-time $8008; part-time $4004 per year. Tuition, nonresident: full-time $20,104; part-time $10,052 per year. Required fees: $298; $149 per term. *Financial support:* In 2009–10, 7 fellowships (averaging $25,000 per year), 13 research assistantships (averaging $20,000 per year), 19 teaching assistantships (averaging $20,000 per year) were awarded; institutionally sponsored loans, scholarships/grants, and unspecified assistantships also available. Financial award application deadline: 3/1; financial award applicants required to submit FAFSA. *Faculty research:* Mechanics and materials, fluid/thermal/energy, design and manufacturing, materials science engineering. Total annual research expenditures: $3.8 million. *Unit head:* Dr. Cesar Levy, Chair, Mechanical and Materials Engineering Department, 305-348-0104, Fax: 305-348-1932, E-mail: cesar.levy@fiu.edu. *Application contact:* Maria Parrilla, Graduate Admissions Assistant, 305-348-1890, Fax: 305-348-6142, E-mail: grad_eng@fiu.edu.

Georgia Institute of Technology, Graduate Studies and Research, College of Engineering, School of Materials Science and Engineering, Atlanta, GA 30332-0001. Offers biomedical engineering (MS Bio E); materials science and engineering (MS, PhD); polymers (MS Poly). Terminal master's awarded for partial completion of doctoral program. *Degree requirements:* For master's, thesis (for some programs); for doctorate, comprehensive exam, thesis/dissertation. *Entrance requirements:* For master's and doctorate, GRE General Test. Additional exam requirements/recommendations for international students: Required—TOEFL (minimum score 620 paper-based; 260 computer-based). Electronic applications accepted. *Faculty research:* Nanomaterials, biomaterials, computational materials science, mechanical behavior, advanced engineering materials.

Illinois Institute of Technology, Graduate College, Armour College of Engineering, Department of Mechanical, Materials and Aerospace Engineering, Chicago, IL 60616-3793. Offers manufacturing engineering (MME, MS); materials science and engineering (MMME, MS, PhD); mechanical and aerospace engineering (MMAE, MS, PhD). Part-time programs available. Terminal master's awarded for partial completion of doctoral program. *Degree requirements:* For master's, comprehensive exam (for some programs), thesis (for some programs); for doctorate, comprehensive exam, thesis/dissertation. *Entrance requirements:* For master's and doctorate, GRE General Test, minimum undergraduate GPA of 3.0. Additional exam requirements/recommendations for international students: Required—TOEFL (minimum score 550 paper-based; 213 computer-based; 80 iBT). Electronic applications accepted. *Expenses:* Tuition: Full-time $17,550; part-time $888 per credit hour. Required fees: $850; $7.50 per credit hour. One-time fee: $50 full-time. Full-time tuition and fees vary according to program. *Faculty research:* Active flow control, bio-fluid dynamics, acoustics and separated flows, digital design and manufacturing and high performance materials, two-phase flows in micro scales and combustion-driven MEMS, global positioning systems, experimental and computational solid mechanics.

Instituto Tecnológico y de Estudios Superiores de Monterrey, Campus Estado de México, Professional and Graduate Division, Estado de Mexico, Mexico. Offers administration of information technologies (MITA); architecture (M Arch); business administration (GMBA, MBA); computer sciences (MCS, PhD); education (M Ed); educational institution administration (MAD); educational technology and innovation (PhD); electronic commerce (MEC); environmental systems (MS); finance (MAF); humanistic studies (MHS); information sciences and knowledge management (MISKM); information systems (MS); manufacturing systems (MS); marketing (MEM); quality systems and productivity (MS); science and materials engineering (PhD); telecommunications management (MTM). Part-time programs available. Postbaccalaureate distance learning degree programs offered (minimal on-campus study). *Degree requirements:* For master's, one foreign language, thesis (for some programs); for doctorate, one foreign language, thesis/dissertation. *Entrance requirements:* For master's, E-PAEP 500, interview; for doctorate, E-PAEP 500, research proposal. Additional exam requirements/recommendations for international students: Required—TOEFL (minimum score 550 paper-based). *Faculty research:* Surface treatments by plasmas, mechanical properties, robotics, graphical computing, mechatronics security protocols.

Iowa State University of Science and Technology, Graduate College, College of Engineering and College of Liberal Arts and Sciences, Department of Materials Science and Engineering, Ames, IA 50011. Offers MS, PhD. *Faculty:* 24 full-time (2 women), 1 part-time/adjunct (0 women). *Students:* 63 full-time (16 women), 5 part-time (1 woman); includes 4 minority (1 African American, 1 American Indian/Alaska Native, 1 Asian American or Pacific Islander, 1 Hispanic American), 36 international. 137 applicants, 12% accepted, 16 enrolled. In 2009, 9 master's, 10 doctorates awarded. *Degree requirements:* For master's, thesis; for doctorate, thesis/dissertation. *Entrance requirements:* Additional exam requirements/recommendations for international students: Required—TOEFL (minimum score 550 paper-based; 79 iBT) or IELTS (minimum score 6.5). *Application deadline:* For fall admission, 1/15 priority date for domestic and international students; for spring admission, 8/15 priority date for domestic and international students. Application fee: $40 ($90 for international students). Electronic applications accepted. *Expenses:* Tuition, state resident: full-time $6716. Tuition, nonresident: full-time $8908. Tuition and fees vary according to course level, course load, program and student level. *Financial support:* In 2009–10, 57 research assistantships with full and partial tuition reimbursements (averaging $17,300 per year), 3 teaching assistantships with full and partial tuition reimbursements (averaging $17,300 per year) were awarded; fellowships, scholarships/grants, health care benefits, and unspecified assistantships also available. *Unit head:* Dr. Richard Lesar, Chair, 515-294-1841, Fax: 515-204-5444, E-mail: gradmse@iastate.edu. *Application contact:* Dr. Alan Russell, Director of Graduate Education, 515-294-3204, E-mail: gradmse@iastate.edu.

The Johns Hopkins University, Engineering for Professionals, Part-time Program in Materials Science and Engineering, Baltimore, MD 21218-2699. Offers M Mat SE, MSE. Part-time and evening/weekend programs available. *Faculty:* 6 part-time/adjunct (1 woman). *Students:* 1 full-time (0 women), 12 part-time (7 women); includes 5 minority (4 African Americans, 1 Asian American or Pacific Islander). Average age 27. *Application deadline:* Applications are processed on a rolling basis. Application fee: $75. Electronic applications accepted. *Financial support:* Institutionally sponsored loans available. *Unit head:* Dr. Robert C. Cammarata, Program Chair, 410-516-5462, Fax: 410-516-5293, E-mail: rcc@jhu.edu. *Application contact:* Priyanka Dwivedi, Admissions Manager, 410-516-2300, Fax: 410-579-8049, E-mail: pdwived1@jhu.edu.

The Johns Hopkins University, G. W. C. Whiting School of Engineering, Department of Materials Science and Engineering, Baltimore, MD 21218-2699. Offers M Mat SE, MSE, PhD. Part-time and evening/weekend programs available. *Faculty:* 14 full-time (3 women), 1 part-time/adjunct (0 women). *Students:* 45 full-time (12 women), 2 part-time (1 woman); includes 8 minority (2 African Americans, 4 Asian Americans or Pacific Islanders, 2 Hispanic Americans), 16 international. Average age 28. 130 applicants, 17% accepted, 10 enrolled. In 2009, 16 master's, 6 doctorates awarded. Terminal master's awarded for partial completion of doctoral program. *Degree requirements:* For master's, thesis, oral exam; for doctorate, thesis/dissertation, oral exam, thesis defense. *Entrance requirements:* For master's and doctorate, GRE General Test. Additional exam requirements/recommendations for international students: Required—TOEFL (minimum score 600 paper-based; 250 computer-based). *Application deadline:* For fall admission, 1/17 priority date for domestic and international students; for spring admission, 10/15 priority date for domestic and international students. Application fee: $0 ($75 for international students). Electronic applications accepted. *Financial support:* In 2009–10, 5 fellowships with full tuition reimbursements (averaging $30,000 per year), 29 research assistantships with full tuition reimbursements (averaging $27,200 per year), 4 teaching assistantships with full tuition reimbursements (averaging $27,200 per year) were awarded; Federal Work-Study, institutionally sponsored loans, health care benefits, tuition waivers (full), and unspecified assistantships also available. Financial award application deadline: 3/14. *Faculty research:* Thin films, nanomaterials, biomaterials, materials characterization, electronic materials. Total annual research expenditures: $3.7 million. *Unit head:* Dr. Howard E. Katz, Chair, 410-516-6141, Fax: 410-516-5293, E-mail: hekatz@jhu.edu. *Application contact:* Jeanine Majewski, Academic Coordinator, 410-516-8760, Fax: 410-516-5293, E-mail: dmse.admissions@jhu.edu.

The Johns Hopkins University, G. W. C. Whiting School of Engineering, Program in Engineering Management, Baltimore, MD 21218-2699. Offers biomaterials (MSEM); communications science (MSEM); computer science (MSEM); fluid mechanics (MSEM); materials science and engineering (MSEM); mechanical engineering (MSEM); mechanics and materials (MSEM); nano-biotechnology (MSEM); nanomaterials and nanotechnology (MSEM); probability and statistics (MSEM); smart product and device design (MSEM); systems analysis, management and environmental policy (MSEM). *Students:* 12 full-time (0 women), 3 international. Average age 23. 66 applicants, 67% accepted. *Entrance requirements:* For master's, GRE, 3 letters of recommendation, resume. Additional exam requirements/recommendations for international students: Required—TOEFL (minimum score 600 paper-based; 250 computer-based; 100 iBT) or IELTS (minimum score 7). *Application deadline:* For fall admission, 1/15 priority date for domestic students, 1/15 for international students; for spring admission, 9/15 priority date for domestic students, 9/15 for international students. Applications are processed on a rolling basis. Application fee: $75. Electronic applications accepted. *Financial support:* Fellowships, health care benefits available. *Unit head:* Dr. Edward R. Scheinerman, Interim Director/Vice Dean for Education, School of Engineering/Professor, Applied Mathematics and Statistics, 410-516-7395, Fax: 410-516-4880, E-mail: ers@jhu.edu. *Application contact:* Dennis McIver, Coordinator of Graduate Admissions, 410-516-8174, Fax: 410-516-0780, E-mail: graduateadmissions@jhu.edu.

Lehigh University, P.C. Rossin College of Engineering and Applied Science, Department of Materials Science and Engineering, Bethlehem, PA 18015. Offers materials science and engineering (M Eng, MS, PhD); photonics (MS); polymer science/engineering (M Eng, MS, PhD); MBA/E. Part-time programs available. *Faculty:* 13 full-time (3 women). *Students:* 26 full-time (3 women), 4 part-time (2 women), 15 international. Average age 26. 163 applicants, 4% accepted, 2 enrolled. In 2009, 2 master's, 4 doctorates awarded. *Degree requirements:* For master's, thesis; for doctorate, comprehensive exam, thesis/dissertation. *Entrance requirements:* For master's and doctorate, GRE General Test, minimum GPA of 3.0. Additional exam requirements/recommendations for international students: Required—TOEFL. *Application deadline:* For fall admission, 1/15 priority date for domestic students, 1/15 for international students; for spring admission, 12/1 priority date for domestic students, 12/1 for international students. Applications are processed on a rolling basis. Application fee: $65. Electronic applications accepted. *Financial support:* In 2009–10, 27 students received support, including 5 fellowships with full and partial tuition reimbursements available (averaging $22,400 per year), 21 research assistantships with full tuition reimbursements available (averaging $22,449 per year), 6 teaching assistantships with partial tuition reimbursements available (averaging $17,512 per year); career-related internships or fieldwork, Federal Work-Study, institutionally sponsored loans, scholarships/grants, and unspecified assistantships also available. Support available to part-time students. Financial award application deadline: 1/15. *Faculty research:* Metals, ceramics, crystals, polymers, fatigue crack propagation. Total annual research expenditures: $4 million. *Unit head:* Dr. Helen Chan, Chairperson, 610-758-5554, Fax: 610-758-4244, E-mail: hmc0@lehigh.edu. *Application contact:* Anne Marie Lobley, Graduate Administrative Coordinator, 610-758-4222, Fax: 610-758-4244, E-mail: amme@lehigh.edu.

Massachusetts Institute of Technology, School of Engineering, Department of Civil and Environmental Engineering, Cambridge, MA 02139-4307. Offers biological oceanography (PhD, Sc D); chemical oceanography (PhD, Sc D); civil and environmental engineering (M Eng, SM, PhD, Sc D); civil and environmental systems (PhD, Sc D); civil engineering (PhD, Sc D, CE); coastal engineering (PhD, Sc D); construction engineering and management (PhD, Sc D); environmental biology (PhD, Sc D); environmental chemistry (PhD, Sc D); environmental engineering (PhD, Sc D); environmental fluid mechanics (PhD, Sc D); geotechnical and geoenvironmental engineering (PhD, Sc D); hydrology (PhD, Sc D); information technology (PhD, Sc D); oceanographic engineering (PhD, Sc D); structures and materials (PhD, Sc D); transportation (PhD, Sc D); SM/MBA. *Faculty:* 36 full-time (5 women). *Students:* 190 full-time (59 women); includes 22 minority (2 African Americans, 14 Asian Americans or Pacific Islanders, 6 Hispanic Americans), 103 international. Average age 26. 478 applicants, 25% accepted, 76 enrolled. In 2009, 72 master's, 14 doctorates awarded. *Degree requirements:* For master's and CE, thesis; for doctorate, comprehensive exam, thesis/dissertation. *Entrance requirements:* For master's and doctorate, GRE General Test. Additional exam requirements/recommendations for international students: Required—TOEFL (minimum score 577 paper-based; 233 computer-based; 90 iBT), IELTS (minimum score 7). *Application deadline:* For fall admission, 1/2 for domestic and international students. Application fee: $75. Electronic applications accepted. *Financial support:* In 2009–10, 185 students received support, including 40 fellowships with tuition reimbursements available (averaging $27,725 per year), 97 research assistantships with tuition reimbursements available (averaging $28,035 per year), 21 teaching assistantships with tuition reimbursements available (averaging $24,802 per year); career-related internships or fieldwork, Federal Work-Study, institutionally sponsored loans, scholarships/grants, health care benefits, and unspecified assistantships also available. *Faculty research:* Environmental chemistry, environmental microbiology, environmental fluid mechanics and coastal engineering, geotechnical engineering and geomechanics, hydrology and hydroclimatology, mechanics of materials and structures, operations research/supply chain, transportation. Total annual research expenditures: $16.6 million. *Unit head:* Prof. Andrew Whittle, Department Head, 617-253-7101. *Application contact:* Patricia Glidden, Graduate Admissions Coordinator, 617-253-7119, Fax: 617-258-6775, E-mail: cee-admissions@mit.edu.

Massachusetts Institute of Technology, School of Engineering, Department of Materials Science and Engineering, Cambridge, MA 02139-4307. Offers archaeological materials (PhD, Sc D); bio- and polymeric materials (PhD, Sc D); electronic, photonic and magnetic materials (PhD, Sc D); emerging, fundamental and computational studies in materials science (Sc D); emerging, fundamental, and computational studies in materials science (PhD); materials engineering (Mat E); materials science and engineering (M Eng, SM, PhD, Sc D); metallurgical engineering (Met E); structural and environmental materials (PhD, Sc D); SM/MBA. *Faculty:* 36 full-time (8 women). *Students:* 222 full-time (62 women); includes 32 minority (3 African Americans, 21 Asian Americans or Pacific Islanders, 8 Hispanic Americans), 125 international. Average age 26. 459 applicants, 23% accepted, 63 enrolled. In 2009, 35 master's, 28 doctorates awarded. Terminal master's awarded for partial completion of doctoral program. *Degree requirements:* For master's and other advanced degree, thesis; for doctorate, comprehensive exam, thesis/dissertation. *Entrance requirements:* For master's and doctorate, GRE General Test. Additional exam requirements/recommendations for international students: Required—IELTS (minimum score 5.5); Recommended—TOEFL (minimum score 577 paper-based; 233 computer-based; 90 iBT). *Application deadline:* For fall admission, 1/1 for domestic and international students. Application fee: $75. Electronic applications accepted. *Financial support:* In 2009–10, 222 students received support, including 55 fellowships with tuition reimbursements available (averaging $22,387 per year), 135 research assistantships with tuition reimbursements available (averaging $27,287 per year), 10 teaching assistantships with tuition reimbursements available (averaging $30,736 per year); career-related internships or fieldwork, Federal Work-Study, institutionally sponsored loans, scholarships/grants, health care benefits, and unspecified assistantships also available. *Faculty research:* Thermodynamics and kinetics of phase transformations, structure of all materials classes: metals, ceramics, semiconductors, polymers, biomaterials, influence of processing on materials structure, structure, property relationships (electrical, magnetic, optical, mechanical). Total annual research expenditures:

$22.6 million. *Unit head:* Prof. Edwin L. Thomas, Department Head, 617-253-3300, Fax: 617-252-1775. *Application contact:* Angelita Mireles, Graduate Admissions, 617-253-3302, E-mail: dmse-admissions@mit.edu.

McGill University, Faculty of Graduate and Postdoctoral Studies, Faculty of Engineering, Department of Civil Engineering and Applied Mechanics, Montréal, QC H3A 2T5, Canada. Offers environmental engineering (M Eng, M Sc, PhD); fluid mechanics (M Sc); fluid mechanics and hydraulic engineering (M Eng, PhD); materials engineering (M Eng, PhD); rehabilitation of urban infrastructure (M Eng, PhD); soil behavior (M Eng, PhD); soil mechanics and foundations (M Eng, PhD); structures and structural mechanics (M Eng, PhD); water resources (M Sc); water resources engineering (M Eng, PhD).

McGill University, Faculty of Graduate and Postdoctoral Studies, Faculty of Engineering, Department of Mining and Materials Engineering, Montréal, QC H3A 2T5, Canada. Offers materials engineering (M Eng, PhD); mining engineering (M Eng, M Sc, PhD, Diploma).

McMaster University, School of Graduate Studies, Faculty of Engineering, Department of Materials Science and Engineering, Hamilton, ON L8S 4M2, Canada. Offers materials engineering (M Eng, MA Sc, PhD); materials science (M Eng, PhD). *Degree requirements:* For master's, thesis; for doctorate, comprehensive exam, thesis/dissertation. *Entrance requirements:* Additional exam requirements/recommendations for international students: Required—TOEFL (minimum score 550 paper-based; 213 computer-based). *Faculty research:* Localized corrosion of metals and alloys, electron microscopy, polymer synthesis and characterization, polymer reaction kinetics and engineering, polymer process modeling.

Michigan State University, The Graduate School, College of Engineering, Department of Chemical Engineering and Materials Science, East Lansing, MI 48824. Offers chemical engineering (MS, PhD); materials science and engineering (MS, PhD). *Entrance requirements:* Additional exam requirements/recommendations for international students: Required—TOEFL. Electronic applications accepted.

Michigan Technological University, Graduate School, College of Engineering, Department of Materials Science and Engineering, Houghton, MI 49931. Offers MS, PhD. Part-time programs available. Terminal master's awarded for partial completion of doctoral program. *Degree requirements:* For master's, comprehensive exam; for doctorate, comprehensive exam, thesis/dissertation. *Entrance requirements:* For master's, GRE. Additional exam requirements/recommendations for international students: Required—TOEFL (minimum score 550 paper-based; 213 computer-based). Electronic applications accepted. *Expenses:* Contact institution. *Faculty research:* Structure/property/processing relationships, microstructural characterization, alloy design, electronic/magnetic/photonic materials, materials and manufacturing processes.

New Jersey Institute of Technology, Office of Graduate Studies, College of Science and Liberal Arts, Department of Chemistry and Environmental Science, Program in Materials Science and Engineering, Newark, NJ 07102. Offers MS, PhD. Part-time and evening/weekend programs available. Terminal master's awarded for partial completion of doctoral program. *Degree requirements:* For master's, thesis; for doctorate, thesis/dissertation. *Entrance requirements:* For master's, GRE General Test; for doctorate, GRE General Test, minimum graduate GPA of 3.5. Additional exam requirements/recommendations for international students: Required—TOEFL (minimum score 550 paper-based; 213 computer-based; 79 iBT). Electronic applications accepted.

New Mexico Institute of Mining and Technology, Graduate Studies, Department of Materials Engineering, Socorro, NM 87801. Offers MS, PhD. *Degree requirements:* For master's, thesis; for doctorate, thesis/dissertation. *Entrance requirements:* For master's, GRE General Test; for doctorate, GRE General Test, GRE Subject Test. Additional exam requirements/recommendations for international students: Required—TOEFL (minimum score 540 paper-based; 207 computer-based). *Faculty research:* Thin films, ceramics, damage studies from radiation, corrosion shock.

North Carolina State University, Graduate School, College of Engineering, Department of Materials Science and Engineering, Raleigh, NC 27695. Offers MMSE, MS, PhD. *Degree requirements:* For master's, thesis; for doctorate, thesis/dissertation. Electronic applications accepted. *Faculty research:* Processing and properties of wide band gap semiconductors, ferroelectric thin-film materials, ductility of nanocrystalline materials, computational materials science, defects in silicon-based devices.

Northwestern University, McCormick School of Engineering and Applied Science, Department of Materials Science and Engineering, Evanston, IL 60208. Offers electronic materials (Certificate); materials science and engineering (MS, PhD). Admissions and degrees offered through The Graduate School. Part-time programs available. Terminal master's awarded for partial completion of doctoral program. *Degree requirements:* For master's, oral thesis defense; for doctorate, oral defense of dissertation, preliminary evaluation, qualifying exam. Electronic applications accepted. *Faculty research:* Metallurgy, ceramics, polymers, electronic materials, biomaterials.

The Ohio State University, Graduate School, College of Engineering, Department of Materials Science and Engineering, Columbus, OH 43210. Offers MS, PhD. *Faculty:* 26. *Students:* 74 full-time (19 women), 35 part-time (9 women); includes 3 minority (1 Asian American or Pacific Islander, 2 Hispanic Americans), 55 international. Average age 26. In 2009, 15 master's, 19 doctorates awarded. *Degree requirements:* For master's, thesis; for doctorate, thesis/dissertation. *Entrance requirements:* For master's and doctorate, GRE (for graduates of foreign universities and holders of non-engineering degrees). Additional exam requirements/recommendations for international students: Recommended—TOEFL (minimum score 600 paper-based; 250 computer-based). *Application deadline:* For fall admission, 8/15 priority date for domestic students, 7/1 priority date for international students; for winter admission, 12/1 priority date for domestic students, 11/1 priority date for international students; for spring admission, 3/1 priority date for domestic students, 2/1 priority date for international students. Applications are processed on a rolling basis. Application fee: $40 ($50 for international students). Electronic applications accepted. *Expenses:* Tuition, state resident: full-time $10,683. Tuition, nonresident: full-time $25,923. Tuition and fees vary according to course load and program. *Financial support:* In 2009–10, fellowships (averaging $43,000 per year), research assistantships (averaging $40,700 per year) were awarded; teaching assistantships, career-related internships or fieldwork, scholarships/grants, and unspecified assistantships also available. *Faculty research:* Computational materials modeling, biomaterials, metallurgy, ceramics, advanced alloys/composites. Total annual research expenditures: $10 million. *Unit head:* Suliman A. Dregia, Graduate Studies Committee Chair, 614-688-3050, Fax: 614-292-4668, E-mail: dregia.1@osu.edu. *Application contact:* 614-292-9444, Fax: 614-292-3895, E-mail: domestic.grad@osu.edu.

Penn State University Park, Graduate School, College of Earth and Mineral Sciences, Department of Materials Science and Engineering, State College, University Park, PA 16802-1503. Offers MS, PhD.

Penn State University Park, Graduate School, Intercollege Graduate Programs, State College, University Park, PA 16802-1503. Offers acoustics (M Eng, MS, PhD); bioengineering (MS, PhD); biogeochemistry (dual) (PhD); business administration (MBA); cell and developmental biology (PhD); demography (dual) (MA); ecology (MS, PhD); environmental pollution control (MEPC, MS); genetics (MS, PhD); human dimensions of natural resources and the environment (dual) (MA, MS, PhD); immunology and infectious diseases (MS); integrative biosciences (MS, PhD), including integrative biosciences; materials science and engineering (PhD); operations research (dual) (M Eng, MA, MS, PhD); physiology (MS, PhD); plant physiology (MS, PhD); quality and manufacturing management (MMM). *Students:* 371 full-time (157 women), 22 part-time (7 women). Average age 27. 1,074 applicants, 18% accepted, 130 enrolled. *Entrance requirements:* Additional exam requirements/recommendations for international students: Required—TOEFL (minimum score 550 paper-based; 213 computer-based; 80 iBT). *Application*

deadline: Applications are processed on a rolling basis. Application fee: $45. Electronic applications accepted. *Financial support:* Fellowships, research assistantships, teaching assistantships available. Financial award applicants required to submit FAFSA. *Unit head:* Dr. Regina Vasilatos-Younken, Senior Associate Dean, 814-865-2516, Fax: 814-863-4627, E-mail: rxv@psu.edu. *Application contact:* Cynthia E. Nicosia, Director, Graduate Enrollment Services, 814-865-1795, Fax: 814-865-4627, E-mail: cey1@psu.edu.

Purdue University, College of Engineering, School of Materials Engineering, West Lafayette, IN 47907. Offers MSMSE, PhD. Part-time programs available. *Entrance requirements:* For master's and doctorate, minimum GPA of 3.0. Additional exam requirements/recommendations for international students: Required—TOEFL (minimum score 550 paper-based; 213 computer-based; 77 iBT); Recommended—TWE. Electronic applications accepted. *Faculty research:* Electronic behavior, mechanical behavior, thermodynamics, kinetics, phase transformations.

Rensselaer Polytechnic Institute, Graduate School, School of Engineering, Department of Materials Science and Engineering, Troy, NY 12180. Offers ceramics and glass science (M Eng, MS, PhD); composites (M Eng, MS, PhD); electronic materials (M Eng, MS, PhD); metallurgy (M Eng, MS, PhD); polymers (M Eng, MS, PhD). Part-time and evening/weekend programs available. *Faculty:* 16 full-time (2 women). *Students:* 54 full-time (11 women), 4 part-time (1 woman); includes 7 minority (all Asian Americans or Pacific Islanders), 30 international. Average age 24. 234 applicants, 14% accepted, 14 enrolled. In 2009, 10 master's, 6 doctorates awarded. Terminal master's awarded for partial completion of doctoral program. *Degree requirements:* For master's, thesis; for doctorate, comprehensive exam, thesis/dissertation. *Entrance requirements:* For master's and doctorate, GRE. Additional exam requirements/recommendations for international students: Required—TOEFL (minimum score 570 paper-based; 230 computer-based; 88 iBT). *Application deadline:* For fall admission, 1/15 priority date for domestic and international students; for spring admission, 8/31 priority date for domestic and international students. Applications are processed on a rolling basis. Application fee: $75. Electronic applications accepted. *Expenses:* Tuition: Full-time $38,100. *Financial support:* In 2009–10, 50 students received support, including fellowships with full tuition reimbursements available (averaging $24,750 per year), 40 research assistantships with full tuition reimbursements available (averaging $24,750 per year), 13 teaching assistantships with full tuition reimbursements available (averaging $24,750 per year); career-related internships or fieldwork, institutionally sponsored loans, and unspecified assistantships also available. Financial award application deadline: 2/1. *Faculty research:* Materials processing, nanostructural materials, materials for microelectronics, composite materials, computational materials. Total annual research expenditures: $5 million. *Unit head:* Dr. Robert Hull, Department Head, 518-276-6373, Fax: 518-276-8554, E-mail: hullr2@rpi.edu. *Application contact:* Dr. Pawel Keblinski, Admissions Coordinator, 518-276-6858, Fax: 518-276-8554, E-mail: keblip@rpi.edu.

Rochester Institute of Technology, Graduate Enrollment Services, College of Science, Center for Materials Science and Engineering, Rochester, NY 14623-5603. Offers MS. Part-time and evening/weekend programs available. *Students:* 9 full-time (4 women), 10 part-time (1 woman), 13 international. Average age 29. 33 applicants, 61% accepted, 4 enrolled. In 2009, 8 master's awarded. *Degree requirements:* For master's, thesis or project. *Entrance requirements:* For master's, GRE (recommended), minimum GPA of 3.0. Additional exam requirements/recommendations for international students: Required—TOEFL (minimum score 575 paper-based; 233 computer-based; 90 iBT), or IELTS (minimum score 6.5). *Application deadline:* For fall admission, 2/15 priority date for domestic and international students; for winter admission, 11/1 for domestic students, 10/1 for international students; for spring admission, 2/1 for domestic students, 1/1 for international students. Applications are processed on a rolling basis. Application fee: $50. Electronic applications accepted. *Expenses:* Tuition: Full-time $31,533; part-time $876 per credit hour. Required fees: $210. *Financial support:* In 2009–10, 10 students received support; research assistantships with partial tuition reimbursements available, teaching assistantships with partial tuition reimbursements available, career-related internships or fieldwork, scholarships/grants, tuition waivers (partial), and unspecified assistantships available. Support available to part-time students. Financial award application deadline: 7/29; financial award applicants required to submit FAFSA. *Faculty research:* VUV modification of polymers, stress and morphology of sputtered copper films, MRI applications to materials problems. *Unit head:* Dr. K. S. V. Santhanam, Program Director, 585-475-2920, E-mail: ksssch@rit.edu. *Application contact:* Diane Ellison, Assistant Vice President, Graduate Enrollment Services, 585-475-2229, Fax: 585-475-7164, E-mail: gradinfo@rit.edu.

Rutgers, The State University of New Jersey, New Brunswick, Graduate School-New Brunswick, Program in Materials Science and Engineering, Piscataway, NJ 08854-8097. Offers MS, PhD. Part-time programs available. *Degree requirements:* For master's, thesis; for doctorate, comprehensive exam, thesis/dissertation. *Entrance requirements:* For master's and doctorate, GRE General Test. Electronic applications accepted. *Faculty research:* Ceramic processing, nanostructured materials, electrical and structural ceramics, fiber optics.

San Jose State University, Graduate Studies and Research, Charles W. Davidson College of Engineering, Department of Chemical and Materials Engineering, Program in Materials Engineering, San Jose, CA 95192-0001. Offers MS. Part-time programs available. *Students:* 15 full-time (8 women), 26 part-time (10 women); includes 8 minority (1 African American, 7 Asian Americans or Pacific Islanders), 16 international. Average age 29. 40 applicants, 48% accepted, 9 enrolled. In 2009, 9 master's awarded. *Degree requirements:* For master's, thesis or alternative. *Entrance requirements:* For master's, GRE. Additional exam requirements/recommendations for international students: Required—TOEFL. *Application deadline:* For fall admission, 6/29 for domestic students; for spring admission, 11/30 for domestic students. Applications are processed on a rolling basis. Application fee: $59. Electronic applications accepted. *Financial support:* In 2009–10, 3 teaching assistantships were awarded; career-related internships or fieldwork, Federal Work-Study, and institutionally sponsored loans also available. Support available to part-time students. Financial award applicants required to submit FAFSA. *Faculty research:* Electronic materials, thin films, electron microscopy, fiber composites, polymeric materials.

Santa Clara University, School of Engineering, Department of Mechanical Engineering, Santa Clara, CA 95053. Offers controls (Certificate); dynamics (Certificate); materials engineering (Certificate); mechanical design analysis (Certificate); mechanical engineering (MS, PhD, Engineer); mechatronics systems engineering (Certificate); technology jump-start (Certificate); thermofluids (Certificate). Part-time and evening/weekend programs available. *Students:* 36 full-time (5 women), 61 part-time (10 women); includes 27 minority (1 American Indian/Alaska Native, 22 Asian Americans or Pacific Islanders, 4 Hispanic Americans), 15 international. Average age 28. In 2009, 17 master's awarded. *Degree requirements:* For master's, thesis (for some programs); for doctorate, thesis/dissertation; for other advanced degree, thesis. *Entrance requirements:* For master's, GRE (waiver may be available); for doctorate, GRE, master's degree or equivalent; for other advanced degree, master's degree, published paper. Additional exam requirements/recommendations for international students: Required—TOEFL (minimum score 550 paper-based; 213 computer-based; 79 iBT). *Application deadline:* For fall admission, 8/13 for domestic students, 7/16 for international students; for winter admission, 10/29 for domestic students, 9/24 for international students; for spring admission, 2/25 for domestic students, 1/21 for international students. Applications are processed on a rolling basis. Application fee: $60. *Expenses:* Contact institution. *Financial support:* Research assistantships, teaching assistantships available. Financial award application deadline: 3/2; financial award applicants required to submit FAFSA. *Faculty research:* Development of Small Satellite Design, Tests and Operations Technology. Total annual research expenditures: $585,448. *Unit head:* Dr. Alex Zecevic, Associate Dean for Graduate Studies, 408-554-2394, E-mail: azecevic@scu.edu. *Application contact:* Stacey Tinker, 408-554-4748, Fax: 408-554-4323, E-mail: stinker@scu.edu.

South Dakota School of Mines and Technology, Graduate Division, College of Engineering, Doctoral Program in Materials Engineering and Science, Rapid City, SD 57701-3995. Offers

Materials Engineering

South Dakota School of Mines and Technology (continued)

PhD. Part-time programs available. *Faculty:* 6 full-time (0 women), 1 part-time/adjunct (0 women). *Students:* 10 full-time (1 woman), 4 part-time (0 women), 9 international. Average age 35. 11 applicants, 64% accepted, 1 enrolled. In 2009, 5 doctorates awarded. *Degree requirements:* For doctorate, thesis/dissertation. *Entrance requirements:* For doctorate, GRE General Test, minimum graduate GPA of 3.0, 3 letters of recommendation. Additional exam requirements/recommendations for international students: Required—TOEFL, TWE. *Application deadline:* For fall admission, 7/1 priority date for domestic students, 4/1 for international students; for spring admission, 11/1 for domestic students, 9/1 for international students. Applications are processed on a rolling basis. Application fee: $35. Electronic applications accepted. *Expenses:* Tuition, state resident: full-time $3340; part-time $139 per credit hour. Tuition, nonresident: full-time $7060; part-time $294 per credit hour. Required fees: $3270. *Financial support:* In 2009–10, 1 fellowship (averaging $1,000 per year), 6 research assistantships with partial tuition reimbursements (averaging $15,390 per year), teaching assistantships with partial tuition reimbursements (averaging $4,482 per year) were awarded; Federal Work-Study and institutionally sponsored loans also available. Support available to part-time students. Financial award application deadline: 5/15. *Faculty research:* Thermophysical properties of solids, development of multiphase materials and composites, concrete technology, electronic polymer materials. *Unit head:* Dr. Jon Kellar, Chair, 605-394-2343, E-mail: jon.kellar@sdsmt.edu. *Application contact:* Jeannette R. Nilson, Administrative Support Coordinator, Graduate Education, 800-454-8162 Ext. 1206, Fax: 605-394-5360, E-mail: graduate_admissions@sdsmt.edu.

South Dakota School of Mines and Technology, Graduate Division, College of Engineering, Master's Program in Materials Engineering and Science, Rapid City, SD 57701-3995. Offers chemistry (MS); metallurgical engineering (MS); physics (MS). *Faculty:* 6 full-time (0 women), 1 part-time/adjunct (0 women). *Students:* 9 full-time (1 woman), 9 part-time (2 women), 8 international. Average age 26. 9 applicants, 56% accepted, 1 enrolled. In 2009, 4 master's awarded. *Entrance requirements:* For master's, GRE General Test. Additional exam requirements/recommendations for international students: Required—TOEFL, TWE. *Application deadline:* For fall admission, 7/1 priority date for domestic students, 4/1 for international students; for spring admission, 11/1 for domestic students, 9/1 for international students. Applications are processed on a rolling basis. Application fee: $35. Electronic applications accepted. *Expenses:* Tuition, state resident: full-time $3340; part-time $139 per credit hour. Tuition, nonresident: full-time $7060; part-time $294 per credit hour. Required fees: $3270. *Financial support:* In 2009–10, 15 research assistantships with partial tuition reimbursements (averaging $11,400 per year), 11 teaching assistantships with partial tuition reimbursements (averaging $4,063 per year) were awarded; fellowships also available. Financial award application deadline: 5/15. *Unit head:* Dr. Jon Kellar, Chair, 605-394-2343, E-mail: jon.kellar@sdsmt.edu. *Application contact:* Jeannette R. Nilson, Administrative Support Coordinator, Graduate Education, 800-454-8162 Ext. 1206, Fax: 605-394-5360, E-mail: graduate_admissions@sdsmt.edu.

Stanford University, School of Engineering, Department of Materials Science and Engineering, Stanford, CA 94305-9991. Offers MS, PhD, Eng. Terminal master's awarded for partial completion of doctoral program. *Degree requirements:* For doctorate, thesis/dissertation; for Eng, thesis. *Entrance requirements:* For master's, doctorate, and Eng, GRE General Test. Additional exam requirements/recommendations for international students: Required—TOEFL. Electronic applications accepted. *Expenses:* Tuition: Full-time $37,380; part-time $2760 per quarter. Required fees: $501.

State University of New York at Binghamton, Graduate School, Thomas J. Watson School of Engineering and Applied Science and School of Arts and Sciences, Materials Science and Engineering Program, Binghamton, NY 13902-6000. Offers MS, PhD. *Students:* 20 full-time (8 women), 26 part-time (2 women); includes 4 minority (all Asian Americans or Pacific Islanders), 34 international. Average age 30. 30 applicants, 53% accepted, 11 enrolled. In 2009, 2 master's, 3 doctorates awarded. Application fee: $60. *Financial support:* In 2009–10, 13 students received support, including 1 fellowship with full tuition reimbursement available (averaging $16,500 per year), 5 research assistantships with full tuition reimbursements available (averaging $16,500 per year), 6 teaching assistantships with full tuition reimbursements available (averaging $16,500 per year); career-related internships or fieldwork, Federal Work-Study, institutionally sponsored loans, scholarships/grants, health care benefits, and unspecified assistantships also available. Financial award applicants required to submit FAFSA. *Unit head:* Dr. Stanley Whittingham, Director, 607-777-4623, E-mail: stanwhit@binghamton.edu. *Application contact:* Victoria Williams, Recruiting and Admissions Coordinator, 607-777-2151, Fax: 607-777-2501, E-mail: vwilliam@binghamton.edu.

Stevens Institute of Technology, Graduate School, Charles V. Schaefer Jr. School of Engineering, Department of Chemical Engineering and Materials Science, Program in Materials Science, Hoboken, NJ 07030. Offers M Eng, PhD. *Expenses:* Tuition: Full-time $9900; part-time $1100 per credit. Required fees: $286 per semester.

Stony Brook University, State University of New York, Graduate School, College of Engineering and Applied Sciences, Department of Materials Science and Engineering, Stony Brook, NY 11794. Offers MS, PhD. *Faculty:* 12 full-time (2 women), 3 part-time/adjunct (0 women). *Students:* 65 full-time (23 women), 8 part-time (1 woman); includes 14 minority (3 African Americans, 9 Asian Americans or Pacific Islanders, 2 Hispanic Americans), 50 international. Average age 28. 81 applicants, 52% accepted. In 2009, 13 master's, 12 doctorates awarded. *Degree requirements:* For master's, thesis or alternative; for doctorate, comprehensive exam, thesis/dissertation. *Entrance requirements:* For master's and doctorate, GRE General Test, minimum undergraduate GPA of 3.0. Additional exam requirements/recommendations for international students: Required—TOEFL. *Application deadline:* For fall admission, 1/15 for domestic students. Application fee: $60. *Expenses:* Tuition, state resident: full-time $8370; part-time $349 per credit. Tuition, nonresident: full-time $13,250; part-time $552 per credit. Required fees: $933. *Financial support:* In 2009–10, 21 research assistantships, 7 teaching assistantships were awarded; fellowships also available. *Faculty research:* Electronic materials, biomaterials, synchrotron topography. Total annual research expenditures: $2.4 million. *Unit head:* Dr. Michael Dudley, Chairman, 631-632-8484. *Application contact:* Dr. Miriam Rafailovich, Director, 631-632-8484, Fax: 631-632-8052, E-mail: mrafailovich.nsf@notes.cc.sunysb.edu.

Texas A&M University, College of Engineering, Zachry Department of Civil Engineering, College Station, TX 77843. Offers construction engineering and management (M Eng, MS, D Eng, PhD); environmental engineering (M Eng, MS, D Eng, PhD); geotechnical engineering (M Eng, MS, D Eng, PhD); materials engineering (M Eng, MS, D Eng, PhD); ocean engineering (M Eng, MS, D Eng, PhD); structural engineering (M Eng, MS, D Eng, PhD); transportation engineering (M Eng, MS, D Eng, PhD); water resources engineering (M Eng, MS, D Eng, PhD). Part-time programs available. *Faculty:* 61. *Students:* 390 full-time (89 women), 42 part-time (6 women); includes 23 minority (2 African Americans, 11 Asian Americans or Pacific Islanders, 10 Hispanic Americans), 281 international. Average age 29. In 2009, 100 master's, 36 doctorates awarded. *Degree requirements:* For master's, thesis (MS); for doctorate, dissertation (PhD), internship (D Eng). *Entrance requirements:* For master's and doctorate, GRE General Test. Additional exam requirements/recommendations for international students: Required—TOEFL. *Application deadline:* Applications are processed on a rolling basis. Application fee: $50 ($75 for international students). Electronic applications accepted. *Expenses:* Tuition, state resident: full-time $3991.32; part-time $221.74 per credit hour. Tuition, nonresident: full-time $9049; part-time $502.74 per credit hour. *Financial support:* In 2009–10, fellowships (averaging $4,500 per year), research assistantships (averaging $14,000 per year), teaching assistantships (averaging $14,400 per year) were awarded; career-related internships or fieldwork and institutionally sponsored loans also available. Financial award application deadline: 4/15; financial award applicants required to submit FAFSA. *Unit head:* Dr. Tony Cahill, Head, 979-845-2438, E-mail: t-cahill@civil.tamu.edu. *Application contact:* Graduate Advisor, 979-845-2498, Fax: 979-862-2800, E-mail: ce-grad@tamu.edu.

Tuskegee University, Graduate Programs, College of Engineering, Architecture and Physical Sciences, Program in Material Science and Engineering, Tuskegee, AL 36088. Offers PhD. *Students:* 8 full-time (3 women), 1 part-time (0 women); includes 4 minority (all African Americans), 3 international. Average age 30. 5 applicants, 20% accepted, 1 enrolled. *Entrance requirements:* Additional exam requirements/recommendations for international students: Required—TOEFL (minimum score 500 paper-based; 69 computer-based). *Application deadline:* For fall admission, 7/15 for domestic students. Applications are processed on a rolling basis. Application fee: $25 ($35 for international students). *Expenses:* Tuition: Full-time $15,630; part-time $940 per credit hour. Required fees: $650. *Financial support:* Application deadline: 4/15. *Unit head:* Dr. Shaik Jeelani, Head, 334-727-8375. *Application contact:* Dr. Robert L. Laney, Vice President/Director of Admissions and Enrollment Management, 334-727-8580, Fax: 334-727-5750, E-mail: planey@tuskegee.edu.

The University of Alabama, Graduate School, College of Engineering, Department of Metallurgical and Materials Engineering, Tuscaloosa, AL 35487. Offers MS Met E, PhD. *Faculty:* 7 full-time (1 woman). *Students:* 25 full-time (2 women), 2 part-time (0 women); includes 2 minority (1 African American, 1 Hispanic American), 15 international. Average age 27. 31 applicants, 35% accepted, 10 enrolled. In 2009, 1 master's, 1 doctorate awarded. *Median time to degree:* Of those who began their doctoral program in fall 2001, 100% received their degree in 8 years or less. *Degree requirements:* For master's, thesis or alternative; for doctorate, thesis/dissertation. *Entrance requirements:* For master's, GRE General Test, minimum GPA of 3.0 in last 60 hours; for doctorate, GRE General Test, minimum graduate GPA of 3.0, graduate degree. Additional exam requirements/recommendations for international students: Required—TOEFL (minimum score 550 paper-based; 213 computer-based). *Application deadline:* For fall admission, 7/1 priority date for domestic students. Applications are processed on a rolling basis. Application fee: $50 ($60 for international students). Electronic applications accepted. *Expenses:* Tuition, state resident: full-time $7000. Tuition, nonresident: full-time $19,200. *Financial support:* In 2009–10, 3 fellowships (averaging $15,000 per year), 14 research assistantships (averaging $14,700 per year), 6 teaching assistantships (averaging $12,250 per year) were awarded; Federal Work-Study and unspecified assistantships also available. *Faculty research:* Thermodynamics, molten metals processing, casting and solidification, mechanical properties of materials, thin films and nanostructures, electrochemistry, corrosion and alloy development. Total annual research expenditures: $1.4 million. *Unit head:* Dr. Ramana G. Reddy, Head and ACIPCO Professor, 205-348-4246, Fax: 205-348-2164. *Application contact:* Dr. Su Gupta, Associate Professor, 205-348-4272, Fax: 205-348-2164, E-mail: sgupta@eng.ua.edu.

The University of Alabama at Birmingham, School of Engineering, Program in Materials Engineering, Birmingham, AL 35294. Offers MS Mt E, PhD. *Degree requirements:* For master's, comprehensive exam, project/thesis; for doctorate, comprehensive exam, thesis/dissertation. *Entrance requirements:* For master's and doctorate, GRE General Test. Electronic applications accepted. *Faculty research:* Casting metallurgy, microgravity solidification, thin film techniques, ceramics/glass processing, biomedical materials processing.

University of Alberta, Faculty of Graduate Studies and Research, Department of Chemical and Materials Engineering, Edmonton, AB T6G 2E1, Canada. Offers chemical engineering (M Eng, M Sc, PhD); materials engineering (M Eng, M Sc, PhD); process control (M Eng, M Sc, PhD); welding (M Eng). Part-time programs available. Postbaccalaureate distance learning degree programs offered (minimal on-campus study). *Faculty:* 30 full-time (3 women), 16 part-time/adjunct (0 women). *Students:* 60 full-time (14 women), 19 part-time (2 women). Terminal master's awarded for partial completion of doctoral program. *Degree requirements:* For master's, thesis; for doctorate, thesis/dissertation. *Application deadline:* For fall admission, 2/1 priority date for domestic students. Tuition and fees charges are reported in Canadian dollars. *Expenses:* Tuition, area resident: Full-time $4626.24 Canadian dollars; part-time $99.72 Canadian dollars per unit. International tuition: $8216 Canadian dollars full-time. Required fees: $3589.92 Canadian dollars; $99.72 Canadian dollars per unit. $215 Canadian dollars per term. *Financial support:* In 2009–10, 79 students received support, including 35 research assistantships (averaging $18,000 per year); career-related internships or fieldwork and scholarships/grants also available. *Faculty research:* Advanced materials and polymers, catalytic and reaction engineering, mineral processing, physical metallurgy, fluid mechanics. Total annual research expenditures: $4.2 million. *Unit head:* Dr. William McCaffrey, Graduate Coordinator, 780-492-1823, Fax: 403-492-2881, E-mail: chemical.materials@ualberta.ca. *Application contact:* Dr. William McCaffrey, Graduate Coordinator, 780-492-1823, Fax: 403-492-2881, E-mail: chemical.materials@ualberta.ca.

The University of Arizona, Graduate College, College of Engineering, Department of Materials Science and Engineering, Tucson, AZ 85721. Offers MS, PhD. Part-time programs available. *Faculty:* 12. *Students:* 29 full-time (14 women), 28 part-time (11 women); includes 5 minority (4 Asian Americans or Pacific Islanders, 1 Hispanic American), 19 international. Average age 30. 82 applicants, 20% accepted, 6 enrolled. In 2009, 5 master's, 5 doctorates awarded. *Degree requirements:* For master's, thesis (for some programs); for doctorate, comprehensive exam, thesis/dissertation. *Entrance requirements:* For master's and doctorate, GRE General Test, 3 letters of recommendation, statement of purpose. Additional exam requirements/recommendations for international students: Required—TOEFL (minimum score 550 paper-based; 213 computer-based). *Application deadline:* Applications are processed on a rolling basis. Application fee: $75. Electronic applications accepted. *Expenses:* Tuition, state resident: full-time $9028. Tuition, nonresident: full-time $24,890. *Financial support:* In 2009–10, 20 research assistantships with full tuition reimbursements (averaging $18,093 per year), 1 teaching assistantship with full tuition reimbursement (averaging $15,176 per year) were awarded; institutionally sponsored loans, scholarships/grants, health care benefits, tuition waivers (full), and unspecified assistantships also available. Financial award application deadline: 12/31. *Faculty research:* High-technology ceramics, optical materials, electronic materials, chemical metallurgy, science of materials. Total annual research expenditures: $1.9 million. *Unit head:* Dr. Joseph H. Simmons, Head, 520-621-6070, Fax: 520-621-8059, E-mail: simmons@mse.arizona.edu. *Application contact:* Information Contact, 520-626-6762, Fax: 520-621-8059, E-mail: msed@email.arizona.edu.

The University of British Columbia, Faculty of Applied Science, Department of Materials Engineering, Vancouver, BC V6T 1Z1, Canada. Offers materials and metallurgy (M Sc, PhD); metals and materials engineering (MA Sc, PhD). *Degree requirements:* For master's, comprehensive exam, thesis; for doctorate, comprehensive exam, thesis/dissertation. *Entrance requirements:* Additional exam requirements/recommendations for international students: Required—TOEFL (minimum score 560 paper-based; 220 computer-based; 83 iBT). Electronic applications accepted. *Faculty research:* Electroslag melting, mathematical modeling, solidification and hydrometallurgy.

University of California, Berkeley, Graduate Division, College of Engineering, Department of Materials Science and Engineering, Berkeley, CA 94720-1500. Offers engineering (M Eng, MS, D Eng, PhD); engineering science (M Eng, MS, PhD). *Faculty:* 15 full-time. *Students:* 87 full-time (33 women). Average age 27. 273 applicants, 15 enrolled. In 2009, 14 master's, 18 doctorates awarded. *Degree requirements:* For master's, comprehensive exam or thesis (MS); for doctorate, comprehensive exam, thesis/dissertation, qualifying exam. *Entrance requirements:* For master's and doctorate, GRE General Test, minimum GPA of 3.0, 3 letters of recommendation. Additional exam requirements/recommendations for international students: Required—TOEFL (minimum score 230 computer-based). *Application deadline:* For fall admission, 12/10 for domestic students. Application fee: $70 ($90 for international students). *Financial support:* Fellowships, research assistantships, teaching assistantships, unspecified assistantships available. *Faculty research:* Ceramics, biomaterials, structural, electronic, magnetic and optical materials. *Unit head:* Prof. Robert Ritchie, Chair, 510-642-3801, Fax: 510-643-5792. *Application contact:* Janene Carol Martinez, Student Affairs Officer, 510-642-0716, Fax: 510-643-5792, E-mail: gradoffice@lists.berkeley.edu.

University of California, Davis, College of Engineering, Program in Materials Science and Engineering, Davis, CA 95616. Offers MS, PhD. Terminal master's awarded for partial completion of doctoral program. *Degree requirements:* For master's, comprehensive exam (for some programs), thesis (for some programs); for doctorate, comprehensive exam, thesis/dissertation. *Entrance requirements:* Additional exam requirements/recommendations for international students: Required—TOEFL (minimum score 550 paper-based; 213 computer-based).

University of California, Irvine, Office of Graduate Studies, School of Engineering, Department of Chemical Engineering and Materials Science, Irvine, CA 92697. Offers chemical and biochemical engineering (MS, PhD); materials science and engineering (MS, PhD). Part-time programs available. *Students:* 78 full-time (24 women), 7 part-time (2 women); includes 22 minority (1 American Indian/Alaska Native, 19 Asian Americans or Pacific Islanders, 2 Hispanic Americans), 37 international. Average age 27. 281 applicants, 25% accepted, 25 enrolled. In 2009, 26 master's, 4 doctorates awarded. Terminal master's awarded for partial completion of doctoral program. *Degree requirements:* For doctorate, thesis/dissertation. *Entrance requirements:* For master's and doctorate, GRE General Test, minimum GPA of 3.0, 3 letters of recommendation. Additional exam requirements/recommendations for international students: Required—TOEFL (minimum score 550 paper-based; 213 computer-based). *Application deadline:* For fall admission, 1/15 priority date for domestic students, 1/15 for international students. Applications are processed on a rolling basis. Application fee: $70 ($90 for international students). Electronic applications accepted. *Financial support:* In 2009–10, fellowships with tuition reimbursements (averaging $14,656 per year); research assistantships with full tuition reimbursements, teaching assistantships with tuition reimbursements, institutionally sponsored loans, traineeships, health care benefits, and unspecified assistantships also available. Financial award application deadline: 3/1; financial award applicants required to submit FAFSA. *Faculty research:* Molecular biotechnology, nano-bio-materials, biophotonics, synthesis, superplasticity and mechanical behavior, characterization of advanced and nanostructural materials. *Unit head:* Dr. Stanley Grant, Director, 949-824-8277, Fax: 949-824-2541, E-mail: sbgrant@uci.edu. *Application contact:* Beatrice Mei, Graduate Coordinator, 949-824-3887, Fax: 949-824-2541, E-mail: bmei@uci.edu.

University of California, Irvine, Office of Graduate Studies, School of Engineering, Program in Materials Engineering and Manufacturing Technology, Irvine, CA 92697. Offers engineering (MS, PhD). Part-time programs available. *Students:* 51 full-time (16 women), 6 part-time (2 women); includes 9 minority (all Asian Americans or Pacific Islanders), 31 international. Average age 27. 163 applicants, 26% accepted, 20 enrolled. In 2009, 16 master's, 2 doctorates awarded. *Entrance requirements:* For master's and doctorate, GRE General Test, 3 letters of recommendation, minimum GPA of 3.0. Additional exam requirements/recommendations for international students: Required—TOEFL (minimum score 550 paper-based; 213 computer-based). *Application deadline:* For fall admission, 1/15 priority date for domestic students, 1/15 for international students. Applications are processed on a rolling basis. Application fee: $70 ($90 for international students). Electronic applications accepted. *Financial support:* In 2009–10, fellowships with tuition reimbursements (averaging $14,656 per year); research assistantships with full tuition reimbursements, teaching assistantships with tuition reimbursements, institutionally sponsored loans, traineeships, health care benefits, and unspecified assistantships also available. Financial award application deadline: 3/1; financial award applicants required to submit FAFSA. *Faculty research:* Advanced materials, microelectronic and photonic devices and packaging, biomedical devices, MEMS, thin film materials, nanotechnology. *Unit head:* Dr. Farghalli A. Mohamed, Director, 949-824-5807, Fax: 949-824-3440, E-mail: famohame@uci.edu. *Application contact:* Frank Shi, Professor, 949-824-5362, Fax: 949-824-2541, E-mail: fgshi@uci.edu.

University of California, Los Angeles, Graduate Division, Henry Samueli School of Engineering and Applied Science, Department of Materials Science and Engineering, Los Angeles, CA 90095-1595. Offers MS, PhD. *Faculty:* 11 full-time (2 women). *Students:* 91 full-time (25 women); includes 16 minority (1 African American, 12 Asian Americans or Pacific Islanders, 3 Hispanic Americans), 51 international. In 2009, 14 master's, 7 doctorates awarded. *Degree requirements:* For master's, comprehensive exam or thesis; for doctorate, thesis/dissertation, qualifying exams. *Entrance requirements:* For master's, GRE General Test, minimum GPA of 3.0; for doctorate, GRE General Test, minimum GPA of 3.25. Additional exam requirements/recommendations for international students: Required—TOEFL (minimum score 560 paper-based; 220 computer-based). *Application deadline:* For fall admission, 12/15 for domestic and international students. Application fee: $70 ($90 for international students). Electronic applications accepted. *Financial support:* In 2009–10, 24 fellowships, 250 research assistantships, 35 teaching assistantships were awarded; Federal Work-Study, institutionally sponsored loans, and tuition waivers (full and partial) also available. Financial award application deadline: 1/15; financial award applicants required to submit FAFSA. Total annual research expenditures: $5.1 million. *Unit head:* Dr. Jenn-Ming Yang, Chair, 310-825-2758, E-mail: jyang@seas.ucla.edu. *Application contact:* Paradee Chularee, Student Affairs Officer, 310-825-8913, Fax: 310-206-7353, E-mail: paradee@ea.ucla.edu.

University of California, Riverside, Graduate Division, Graduate Materials Science and Engineering Program, Riverside, CA 92521-0102. Offers MS, PhD.

University of California, Santa Barbara, Graduate Division, College of Engineering, Department of Materials, Santa Barbara, CA 93106-5050. Offers materials science and engineering (MS, PhD); MS/PhD. *Faculty:* 35 full-time (3 women). *Students:* 105 full-time (27 women). Average age 26. 291 applicants, 22% accepted, 15 enrolled. In 2009, 4 master's, 15 doctorates awarded. Terminal master's awarded for partial completion of doctoral program. *Degree requirements:* For master's, comprehensive exam, thesis or alternative; for doctorate, comprehensive exam, thesis/dissertation. *Entrance requirements:* For master's, GRE General Test, 3 letters of recommendation, resume/curriculum vitae; for doctorate, GRE General Test, 3 letters of recommendation, statement of purpose, personal achievements/contributions statement, resume/curriculum vitae, transcripts for post-secondary institutions attended. Additional exam requirements/recommendations for international students: Required—TOEFL (minimum score 600 paper-based; 213 computer-based; 100 iBT) or IELTS (minimum score 7). *Application deadline:* For fall admission, 1/5 for domestic and international students; for winter admission, 11/1 for domestic and international students; for spring admission, 1/1 for domestic and international students. Application fee: $70 ($90 for international students). Electronic applications accepted. *Financial support:* In 2009–10, 100 students received support, including 52 fellowships with full and partial tuition reimbursements available (averaging $8,600 per year), 91 research assistantships with full and partial tuition reimbursements available (averaging $12,200 per year), 23 teaching assistantships with partial tuition reimbursements available (averaging $2,200 per year); career-related internships or fieldwork, Federal Work-Study, institutionally sponsored loans, scholarships/grants, traineeships, health care benefits, and unspecified assistantships also available. Financial award application deadline: 1/28; financial award applicants required to submit FAFSA. *Faculty research:* Electronic materials, structural materials, inorganic materials, macromolecular materials, biomolecular materials. *Unit head:* Dr. James S. Speck, Chair, 805-893-8005, Fax: 805-893-8486, E-mail: speck@mrl.ucsb.edu. *Application contact:* Constance Callinicos, Student Affairs Officer, 805-893-4601, Fax: 805-893-8486, E-mail: callinic@engineering.ucsb.edu.

University of Central Florida, College of Engineering and Computer Science, Department of Mechanical, Materials, and Aerospace Engineering, Program in Materials Science and Engineering, Orlando, FL 32816. Offers MSMSE, PhD. *Students:* 50 full-time (9 women), 14 part-time (3 women); includes 8 minority (1 American Indian/Alaska Native, 2 Asian Americans or Pacific Islanders, 5 Hispanic Americans), 3 international. Average age 29. 61 applicants, 34% accepted, 14 enrolled. In 2009, 10 master's, 8 doctorates awarded. *Degree requirements:* For master's, thesis or alternative; for doctorate, thesis/dissertation, candidacy exam, departmental qualifying exam. *Application deadline:* For fall admission, 7/15 priority date for domestic students; for spring admission, 12/1 priority date for domestic students. Application fee: $30. Electronic applications accepted. *Expenses:* Tuition, state resident: part-time $306.31 per credit hour. Tuition, nonresident: part-time $1099.01 per credit hour. Part-time tuition and fees vary according to degree level and program. *Financial support:* In 2009–10, 41 students received support, including 12 fellowships (averaging $2,200 per year), 42 research assistantships (averaging $9,700 per year), 2 teaching assistantships (averaging $9,700 per year).

University of Cincinnati, Graduate School, College of Engineering, Department of Chemical and Materials Engineering, Cincinnati, OH 45221. Offers chemical engineering (MS, PhD); materials science and metallurgical engineering (MS, PhD), including ceramic science and engineering, materials science and engineering, metallurgical engineering, polymer science and engineering. Part-time and evening/weekend programs available. Terminal master's awarded for partial completion of doctoral program. *Degree requirements:* For master's, thesis; for doctorate, thesis/dissertation. *Entrance requirements:* For master's and doctorate, GRE General Test. Additional exam requirements/recommendations for international students: Required—TOEFL. Electronic applications accepted. *Faculty research:* Process synthesis, aerosol processes, clean coal technology, membrane technology.

University of Cincinnati, Graduate School, College of Engineering, Department of Chemical and Materials Engineering, Program in Materials Science and Metallurgical Engineering, Program in Materials Science and Engineering, Cincinnati, OH 45221. Offers MS, PhD. Evening/weekend programs available. *Degree requirements:* For master's, thesis optional; for doctorate, one foreign language, comprehensive exam, thesis/dissertation, oral English proficiency exam. *Entrance requirements:* For master's and doctorate, GRE General Test, BS in related field, minimum undergraduate GPA of 3.0. Additional exam requirements/recommendations for international students: Required—TOEFL. Electronic applications accepted. *Faculty research:* Polymer characterization, surface analysis, and adhesion; mechanical behavior of high-temperature materials; composites; electrochemistry of materials.

University of Connecticut, Graduate School, School of Engineering, Department of Metallurgy and Materials Engineering, Storrs, CT 06269. Offers MS, PhD. *Faculty:* 31 full-time (4 women). *Students:* 89 full-time (29 women), 22 part-time (3 women); includes 12 minority (3 African Americans, 5 Asian Americans or Pacific Islanders, 4 Hispanic Americans), 56 international. Average age 28. 211 applicants, 11% accepted, 19 enrolled. In 2009, 12 master's, 9 doctorates awarded. Terminal master's awarded for partial completion of doctoral program. *Degree requirements:* For master's, comprehensive exam, thesis or alternative; for doctorate, thesis/dissertation. *Entrance requirements:* For master's and doctorate, GRE General Test, GRE Subject Test. Additional exam requirements/recommendations for international students: Required—TOEFL (minimum score 550 paper-based; 213 computer-based). *Application deadline:* For fall admission, 2/1 priority date for domestic and international students; for spring admission, 11/1 for domestic students, 10/1 for international students. Applications are processed on a rolling basis. Application fee: $55. Electronic applications accepted. *Expenses:* Tuition, state resident: full-time $4725; part-time $525 per credit. Tuition, nonresident: full-time $12,267; part-time $1363 per credit. Required fees: $346 per semester. Tuition and fees vary according to course load. *Financial support:* In 2009–10, 80 research assistantships with full tuition reimbursements, 4 teaching assistantships with full tuition reimbursements were awarded; fellowships, Federal Work-Study, scholarships/grants, health care benefits, and unspecified assistantships also available. Financial award application deadline: 2/1; financial award applicants required to submit FAFSA. *Faculty research:* Microsegregation and coarsening, fatigue crack, electron-dislocation interaction. *Unit head:* Harris L. Marcus, Director, 860-486-4623, Fax: 860-486-4745, E-mail: hmarcus@ims.uconn.edu. *Application contact:* Harris L. Marcus, Director, 860-486-4623, Fax: 860-486-4745, E-mail: hmarcus@ims.uconn.edu.

University of Dayton, Graduate School, School of Engineering, Department of Materials Engineering, Dayton, OH 45469-1300. Offers MS Mat E, DE, PhD. Part-time and evening/weekend programs available. *Faculty:* 2 full-time (0 women), 8 part-time/adjunct (0 women). *Students:* 50 full-time (17 women), 10 part-time (0 women); includes 7 minority (5 African Americans, 1 Asian American or Pacific Islander, 1 Hispanic American), 14 international. Average age 32. 63 applicants, 56% accepted, 14 enrolled. In 2009, 16 master's, 5 doctorates awarded. *Degree requirements:* For master's, thesis optional; for doctorate, variable foreign language requirement, thesis/dissertation, departmental qualifying exam. *Entrance requirements:* Additional exam requirements/recommendations for international students: Required—TOEFL (minimum score 550 paper-based; 213 computer-based; 80 iBT). *Application deadline:* For fall admission, 8/1 for domestic students, 3/1 priority date for international students; for winter admission, 7/1 priority date for international students; for spring admission, 1/1 priority date for international students. Applications are processed on a rolling basis. Application fee: $0 ($50 for international students). Electronic applications accepted. *Expenses:* Tuition: Full-time $8412; part-time $701 per credit hour. Required fees: $325; $65 per course. $25 per semester. Tuition and fees vary according to course load, degree level and program. *Financial support:* In 2009–10, 1 fellowship (averaging $27,500 per year), 20 research assistantships with full tuition reimbursements (averaging $15,000 per year) were awarded. Financial award applicants required to submit FAFSA. *Faculty research:* Ultra-fine microstructure by rapid hot-compaction of Armstrong-process titanium powder, diffusion during synthesis of titanium alloys by means of power metallurgy. Total annual research expenditures: $37,397. *Unit head:* Dr. Daniel Eylon, Director, 937-229-2679, E-mail: deylon@udayton.edu. *Application contact:* Graduate Admissions, 937-229-4411, Fax: 937-229-4729, E-mail: gradadmission@udayton.edu.

University of Delaware, College of Engineering, Department of Materials Science and Engineering, Newark, DE 19716. Offers MMSE, PhD. Terminal master's awarded for partial completion of doctoral program. *Degree requirements:* For master's, thesis; for doctorate, thesis/dissertation. *Entrance requirements:* For master's and doctorate, GRE General Test, 3 letters of recommendation, minimum GPA of 3.2. Additional exam requirements/recommendations for international students: Required—TOEFL. Electronic applications accepted. *Faculty research:* Thin films and self assembly, drug delivery and tissue engineering, biomaterials and nanocomposites, semiconductor and oxide interfaces, electronic and magnetic materials.

University of Denver, School of Engineering and Computer Science, Department of Mechanical and Materials Engineering, Denver, CO 80208. Offers bioengineering (MS); engineering (MS, PhD); materials science (PhD); mechanical engineering (MS); mechatronics (MS). *Faculty:* 9 full-time (1 woman), 2 part-time/adjunct (1 woman). *Students:* 1 full-time (0 women), 17 part-time (12 women), 3 international. Average age 31. 46 applicants, 61% accepted, 12 enrolled. In 2009, 9 master's awarded. *Expenses:* Tuition: Full-time $34,596; part-time $961 per quarter hour. Required fees: $4 per quarter hour. Tuition and fees vary according to course load, campus/location and program. *Financial support:* In 2009–10, 3 research assistantships (averaging $11,000 per year), 5 teaching assistantships (averaging $11,000 per year) were awarded. *Faculty research:* Aerosols, biomechanics, composite materials, photo optics, drug delivery. Total annual research expenditures: $565,000. *Unit head:* Dr. Maciej Kumosa, Chair, 303-871-3807. *Application contact:* Dr. Maciej Kumosa, Chair, 303-871-3807.

University of Florida, Graduate School, College of Engineering, Department of Materials Science and Engineering, Gainesville, FL 32611. Offers ME, MS, PhD, Engr, JD/MS. *Degree requirements:* For master's and Engr, thesis optional; for doctorate, thesis/dissertation. *Entrance requirements:* For master's and doctorate, GRE General Test, minimum GPA of 3.0; for Engr, GRE General Test. Additional exam requirements/recommendations for international students: Required—TOEFL (minimum score 550 paper-based; 213 computer-based). Electronic applications accepted. *Faculty research:* Polymeric materials, electronic materials, glass, biomaterials, composites.

University of Idaho, College of Graduate Studies, College of Engineering, Department of Materials Science and Engineering, Moscow, ID 83844-2282. Offers materials science and engineering (MS, PhD), including materials science and engineering (PhD), metallurgical engineering (MS); metallurgical engineering (MS). *Students:* 4 full-time, 3 part-time. In 2009, 5 master's, 1 doctorate awarded. *Degree requirements:* For doctorate, one foreign language, thesis/dissertation. *Entrance requirements:* For master's, minimum GPA of 2.8; for doctorate, minimum undergraduate GPA of 2.8, 3.0 graduate. *Application deadline:* For fall admission, 8/1 for domestic students; for spring admission, 12/15 for domestic students. Application fee: $55 ($60 for international students). *Expenses:* Tuition, state resident: full-time $6120. Tuition, nonresident: full-time $17,712. *Financial support:* Fellowships, research assistantships, teaching

Materials Engineering

University of Idaho (continued)
assistantships, career-related internships or fieldwork available. Financial award application deadline: 2/15. *Faculty research:* Ventilation, rock mechanics, operations, production. *Unit head:* Dr. Wudneh Admassu, Chair, 208-885-6376, E-mail: wadmassu@uidaho.edu. *Application contact:* Dr. Wudneh Admassu, Chair, 208-885-6376, E-mail: wadmassu@uidaho.edu.

University of Illinois at Chicago, Graduate College, College of Engineering, Department of Civil and Materials Engineering, Chicago, IL 60607-7128. Offers civil engineering (MS, PhD); materials engineering (MS, PhD). Evening/weekend programs available. *Degree requirements:* For master's, thesis (for some programs); for doctorate, thesis/dissertation, preliminary and qualifying exams. *Entrance requirements:* For master's and doctorate, GRE General Test, minimum GPA of 3.0. Additional exam requirements/recommendations for international students: Required—TOEFL. Electronic applications accepted. *Faculty research:* Transportation and geotechnical engineering, damage and anisotropic behavior, steel processing.

University of Illinois at Urbana–Champaign, Graduate College, College of Engineering, Department of Materials Science and Engineering, Champaign, IL 61820. Offers MS, PhD, MS/MBA, PhD/MBA. *Faculty:* 25 full-time (3 women), 1 part-time/adjunct (0 women). *Students:* 154 full-time (38 women), 5 part-time (1 woman); includes 20 minority (18 Asian Americans or Pacific Islanders, 2 Hispanic Americans), 84 international. 336 applicants, 23% accepted, 29 enrolled. In 2009, 5 master's, 29 doctorates awarded. *Entrance requirements:* For master's and doctorate, GRE, minimum GPA of 3.0. Additional exam requirements/recommendations for international students: Required—TOEFL (minimum score 613 paper-based; 257 computer-based; 103 iBT), or IELTS (minimum score 7). *Application deadline:* Applications are processed on a rolling basis. Application fee: $60 ($75 for international students). Electronic applications accepted. *Financial support:* In 2009–10, 18 fellowships, 135 research assistantships, 20 teaching assistantships were awarded; tuition waivers (full and partial) also available. *Unit head:* Robert S. Averback, Interim Head, 217-333-4302, Fax: 217-333-2736, E-mail: averback@illinois.edu. *Application contact:* Michelle L. Malloch, Office Support Associate, 217-333-8517, Fax: 217-333-2736, E-mail: malloch@illinois.edu.

University of Maryland, College Park, Academic Affairs, A. James Clark School of Engineering, Department of Continuing and Distance Learning in Engineering, Professional Program in Engineering, College Park, MD 20742. Offers aerospace engineering (M Eng); chemical engineering (M Eng); civil engineering (M Eng); electrical engineering (M Eng); engineering (Certificate); fire protection engineering (M Eng); materials science and engineering (M Eng); mechanical engineering (M Eng); reliability engineering (M Eng); systems engineering (M Eng). Part-time and evening/weekend programs available. Postbaccalaureate distance learning degree programs offered. *Students:* 50 full-time (15 women), 234 part-time (41 women); includes 91 minority (36 African Americans, 39 Asian Americans or Pacific Islanders, 16 Hispanic Americans), 45 international. 137 applicants, 69% accepted, 77 enrolled. In 2009, 103 master's awarded. *Entrance requirements:* For master's, 3 letters of recommendation. *Application deadline:* For fall admission, 8/15 for domestic students, 1/10 for international students; for spring admission, 12/15 for domestic students, 6/1 for international students. Applications are processed on a rolling basis. Application fee: $60. Electronic applications accepted. *Expenses:* Tuition, area resident: Part-time $471 per credit hour. Tuition, state resident: part-time $471 per credit hour. Tuition, nonresident: part-time $1016 per credit hour. Required fees: $337.04 per term. *Financial support:* In 2009–10, 2 research assistantships with tuition reimbursements (averaging $19,561 per year), 9 teaching assistantships with tuition reimbursements (averaging $16,849 per year) were awarded; fellowships, Federal Work-Study and scholarships/grants also available. Support available to part-time students. Financial award applicants required to submit FAFSA. *Unit head:* Dr. George Syrmos, Director, 301-405-3633, Fax: 301-314-3305, E-mail: syrmos@umd.edu. *Application contact:* Dean of Graduate School, 301-405-0376, Fax: 301-314-9305.

University of Maryland, College Park, Academic Affairs, A. James Clark School of Engineering, Department of Materials and Nuclear Engineering, Materials Science and Engineering Program, College Park, MD 20742. Offers MS, PhD. Part-time and evening/weekend programs available. Postbaccalaureate distance learning degree programs offered. *Faculty:* 67 full-time (10 women), 2 part-time/adjunct (1 woman). *Students:* 70 full-time (20 women), 9 part-time (3 women); includes 18 minority (7 African Americans, 6 Asian Americans or Pacific Islanders, 5 Hispanic Americans), 23 international. 208 applicants, 14% accepted, 14 enrolled. In 2009, 1 master's, 7 doctorates awarded. *Degree requirements:* For master's, comprehensive exam, thesis optional, research paper; for doctorate, thesis/dissertation, oral exam. *Entrance requirements:* For master's and doctorate, GRE General Test, minimum B+ average in undergraduate course work. Additional exam requirements/recommendations for international students: Required—TOEFL. *Application deadline:* For fall admission, 2/1 for domestic and international students; for spring admission, 8/1 for domestic students, 6/1 for international students. Applications are processed on a rolling basis. Application fee: $60. Electronic applications accepted. *Expenses:* Tuition, area resident: Part-time $471 per credit hour. Tuition, state resident: part-time $471 per credit hour. Tuition, nonresident: part-time $1016 per credit hour. Required fees: $337.04 per term. *Financial support:* In 2009–10, 6 fellowships (averaging $14,203 per year), 39 research assistantships (averaging $23,611 per year), 8 teaching assistantships (averaging $22,242 per year) were awarded. Financial award applicants required to submit FAFSA. *Unit head:* Robert Briber, Chair, 301-405-7313, E-mail: rbriber@umd.edu. *Application contact:* Dean of Graduate School, 301-405-0376, Fax: 301-314-9305.

University of Maryland, College Park, Academic Affairs, A. James Clark School of Engineering, Department of Mechanical Engineering, College Park, MD 20742. Offers electronic packaging and reliability (MS, PhD); manufacturing and design (MS, PhD); mechanics and materials (MS, PhD); reliability engineering (M Eng, MS, PhD); thermal and fluid sciences (MS, PhD). Part-time and evening/weekend programs available. Postbaccalaureate distance learning degree programs offered. *Faculty:* 84 full-time (5 women), 14 part-time/adjunct (1 woman). *Students:* 217 full-time (37 women), 76 part-time (13 women); includes 39 minority (11 African Americans, 2 American Indian/Alaska Native, 18 Asian Americans or Pacific Islanders, 8 Hispanic Americans), 140 international. 420 applicants, 21% accepted, 64 enrolled. In 2009, 40 master's, 33 doctorates awarded. *Degree requirements:* For master's, thesis optional; for doctorate, thesis/dissertation, qualifying exam. *Entrance requirements:* For master's, GRE General Test, 3 letters of recommendation; for doctorate, GRE General Test, minimum GPA of 3.0. Additional exam requirements/recommendations for international students: Required—TOEFL. *Application deadline:* For fall admission, 5/15 for domestic students, 2/1 for international students; for spring admission, 10/1 for domestic students, 6/1 for international students. Applications are processed on a rolling basis. Application fee: $60. Electronic applications accepted. *Expenses:* Tuition, area resident: Part-time $471 per credit hour. Tuition, state resident: part-time $471 per credit hour. Tuition, nonresident: part-time $1016 per credit hour. Required fees: $337.04 per term. *Financial support:* In 2009–10, 7 fellowships with full and partial tuition reimbursements (averaging $13,060 per year), 168 research assistantships with tuition reimbursements (averaging $23,703 per year), 10 teaching assistantships with tuition reimbursements (averaging $18,884 per year) were awarded; Federal Work-Study and scholarships/grants also available. Support available to part-time students. Financial award applicants required to submit FAFSA. *Faculty research:* Injection molding, electronic packaging, fluid mechanics, product engineering. Total annual research expenditures: $15 million. *Unit head:* Dr. Avram Bar-Cohen, Chairman, 301-405-3173, Fax: 301-314-9477, E-mail: abc@umd.edu. *Application contact:* Dr., Graduate Director, 301-405-0376.

University of Massachusetts Lowell, James B. Francis College of Engineering, Department of Plastics Engineering, Lowell, MA 01854-2881. Offers elastomers (Graduate Certificate); medical plastics design and manufacturing (Graduate Certificate); plastics design (Graduate Certificate); plastics engineering (MS Eng, D Eng, PhD), including coatings and adhesives (MS Eng), plastics materials (MS Eng), plastics processing (MS Eng), product design (MS Eng); plastics engineering fundamentals (Graduate Certificate); plastics materials (Graduate Certificate); plastics processing (Graduate Certificate); polymer science/plastics engineering (PhD). Part-time programs available. Terminal master's awarded for partial completion of doctoral program. *Degree requirements:* For master's, thesis optional; for doctorate, comprehensive exam, thesis/dissertation. *Entrance requirements:* For master's and doctorate, GRE General Test. Additional exam requirements/recommendations for international students: Required—TOEFL.

University of Michigan, Horace H. Rackham School of Graduate Studies, College of Engineering, Department of Materials Science and Engineering, Ann Arbor, MI 48109. Offers MS, PhD. Part-time programs available. *Faculty:* 19 full-time (4 women). *Students:* 106 full-time (33 women), 1 (woman) part-time; includes 19 minority (3 African Americans, 12 Asian Americans or Pacific Islanders, 4 Hispanic Americans), 40 international. 332 applicants, 23% accepted, 34 enrolled. In 2009, 14 master's, 9 doctorates awarded. *Degree requirements:* For master's, thesis, oral defense of thesis; for doctorate, thesis/dissertation, oral defense of dissertation, written exam. *Entrance requirements:* For master's, GRE General Test, minimum GPA of 3.0 in related field; for doctorate, GRE General Test, minimum GPA of 3.0 in related field, master's degree. Additional exam requirements/recommendations for international students: Required—TOEFL. *Application deadline:* Applications are processed on a rolling basis. Application fee: $60 ($75 for international students). Electronic applications accepted. *Expenses:* Tuition, state resident: full-time $17,286; part-time $1099 per credit hour. Tuition, nonresident: full-time $34,944; part-time $2080 per credit hour. Required fees: $95 per semester. Tuition and fees vary according to course load, degree level and program. *Financial support:* Fellowships, research assistantships, teaching assistantships available. Financial award applicants required to submit FAFSA. *Faculty research:* Soft materials (polymers, biomaterials); computational materials science; structural materials; electronic and optical materials; nanocomposite materials. *Unit head:* Peter Green, Department Chair, 734-763-2445, Fax: 734-763-4788. *Application contact:* Renee Hilgendorf, Graduate Program Coordinator, 734-763-9790, Fax: 734-763-4788, E-mail: reneeh@umich.edu.

See Close-Up on page 493.

University of Minnesota, Twin Cities Campus, Institute of Technology, Department of Chemical Engineering and Materials Science, Program in Materials Science and Engineering, Minneapolis, MN 55455-0132. Offers M Mat SE, MS Mat SE, PhD. Part-time programs available. Terminal master's awarded for partial completion of doctoral program. *Degree requirements:* For master's, thesis; for doctorate, thesis/dissertation. *Entrance requirements:* For master's and doctorate, GRE General Test. *Faculty research:* Fracture micromechanics, hydrogen embrittlement, polymer physics, microelectric materials, corrosion science.

University of Nebraska–Lincoln, Graduate College, College of Engineering, Department of Mechanical Engineering, Lincoln, NE 68588. Offers chemical and materials engineering (PhD); mechanical engineering (MS, PhD), including materials science engineering (MS), metallurgical engineering (MS). *Degree requirements:* For master's, thesis optional; for doctorate, comprehensive exam, thesis/dissertation. *Entrance requirements:* For master's and doctorate, GRE General Test. Additional exam requirements/recommendations for international students: Required—TOEFL (minimum score 550 paper-based; 213 computer-based). Electronic applications accepted. *Faculty research:* Robotics for planetary exploration, vehicle crashworthiness, transient heat conduction, laser beam/particle interactions.

See Close-Up on page 527.

University of Nevada, Las Vegas, Graduate College, Howard R. Hughes College of Engineering, Department of Mechanical Engineering, Las Vegas, NV 89154-4027. Offers aerospace engineering (MS); biomedical engineering (MS); materials and nuclear engineering (MS); mechanical engineering (MS, PhD). Part-time programs available. *Faculty:* 17 full-time (0 women), 10 part-time/adjunct (0 women). *Students:* 39 full-time (4 women), 28 part-time (6 women); includes 10 minority (1 African American, 8 Asian Americans or Pacific Islanders, 1 Hispanic American), 28 international. Average age 30. 64 applicants, 83% accepted, 22 enrolled. In 2009, 13 master's, 7 doctorates awarded. *Degree requirements:* For master's, comprehensive exam, thesis (for some programs), project; for doctorate, comprehensive exam, thesis/dissertation. *Entrance requirements:* For master's and doctorate, GRE General Test. Additional exam requirements/recommendations for international students: Required—TOEFL (minimum score 550 paper-based; 213 computer-based; 80 iBT), IELTS (minimum score 7). *Application deadline:* For fall admission, 5/1 priority date for domestic and international students; for spring admission, 10/1 priority date for domestic and international students. Applications are processed on a rolling basis. Application fee: $60 ($95 for international students). Electronic applications accepted. *Financial support:* In 2009–10, 37 students received support, including 21 research assistantships with partial tuition reimbursements available (averaging $13,335 per year), 16 teaching assistantships with partial tuition reimbursements available (averaging $11,000 per year); institutionally sponsored loans, scholarships/grants, health care benefits, and unspecified assistantships also available. Financial award application deadline: 3/1. *Unit head:* Dr. Woosoon Yim, Chair/Professor, 702-895-0956, Fax: 702-895-3936, E-mail: wy@me.unlv.edu. *Application contact:* Graduate College Admissions Evaluator, 702-895-3320, Fax: 702-895-4180, E-mail: gradcollege@unlv.edu.

University of Nevada, Reno, Graduate School, College of Engineering, Department of Chemical and Materials Engineering, Program in Materials Science and Engineering, Reno, NV 89557. Offers MS, PhD. Terminal master's awarded for partial completion of doctoral program. *Degree requirements:* For master's, thesis; for doctorate, one foreign language, thesis/dissertation. *Entrance requirements:* For master's, minimum GPA of 2.75; for doctorate, GRE, minimum GPA of 3.0. Additional exam requirements/recommendations for international students: Required—TOEFL (minimum score 500 paper-based; 173 computer-based; 61 iBT), IELTS (minimum score 6). Electronic applications accepted. *Faculty research:* Hydrometallurgy, applied surface chemistry, mineral processing, mineral bioprocessing, ceramics.

University of Pennsylvania, School of Engineering and Applied Science, Department of Materials Science and Engineering, Philadelphia, PA 19104. Offers MSE, PhD, MSE/MBA. Part-time programs available. *Faculty:* 15 full-time (4 women), 2 part-time/adjunct (0 women). *Students:* 70 full-time (18 women), 6 part-time (1 woman); includes 5 minority (all Asian Americans or Pacific Islanders), 48 international. 268 applicants, 26% accepted, 34 enrolled. In 2009, 20 master's, 7 doctorates awarded. Terminal master's awarded for partial completion of doctoral program. *Degree requirements:* For master's, thesis; for doctorate, thesis/dissertation. *Entrance requirements:* Additional exam requirements/recommendations for international students: Required—TOEFL. *Application deadline:* For fall admission, 6/1 priority date for domestic students, 5/1 priority date for international students; for spring admission, 11/1 priority date for domestic students, 10/1 priority date for international students. Applications are processed on a rolling basis. Application fee: $70. Electronic applications accepted. *Expenses:* Tuition: Full-time $25,660; part-time $4758 per course. Required fees: $2152; $270 per course. Tuition and fees vary according to course load, degree level and program. *Financial support:* Fellowships, research assistantships, teaching assistantships, institutionally sponsored loans, scholarships/grants, traineeships, health care benefits, and unspecified assistantships available. *Faculty research:* Advanced metallic, ceramic, and polymeric materials for device applications; micromechanics and structure of interfaces; thin film electronic materials; physics and chemistry of solids.

The University of Tennessee, Graduate School, College of Engineering, Department of Materials Science and Engineering, Program in Materials Science and Engineering, Knoxville, TN 37996. Offers MS, PhD. *Faculty:* 13 full-time (1 woman), 7 part-time/adjunct (1 woman). *Students:* 62 full-time (12 women), 7 part-time (1 woman); includes 4 minority (3 African Americans, 1 Asian American or Pacific Islander), 45 international. Average age 24. 119 applicants, 19% accepted, 13 enrolled. In 2009, 10 master's, 13 doctorates awarded. *Degree requirements:* For master's, thesis or alternative; for doctorate, comprehensive exam, thesis/dissertation. *Entrance requirements:* For master's and doctorate, minimum GPA of 3.0. Additional exam requirements/recommendations for international students: Required—TOEFL (minimum score 550 paper-based; 213 computer-based). *Application deadline:* For fall admission, 2/1 priority date for domestic and international students; for spring admission, 6/15 priority date for international students. Applications are processed on a rolling basis. Application fee: $35. Electronic applications accepted. *Expenses:* Tuition, state resident: full-time $6826; part-time $380 per semester hour. Tuition, nonresident: full-time $21,844; part-time $1147 per semester hour. Tuition and fees vary according to program. *Financial support:* In 2009–10, 2 students received support, including 2 fellowships with full tuition reimbursements available (averaging $8,892 per year), 63 research assistantships with full tuition reimbursements available (averaging $19,812 per year), 12 teaching assistantships with full tuition reimbursements available (averaging $17,580 per year); career-related internships or fieldwork, Federal Work-Study, institutionally sponsored loans, health care benefits, and unspecified assistantships also available. Financial award application deadline: 3/1; financial award applicants required to submit FAFSA. *Faculty research:* Biomaterials; functional materials electronic, magnetic and optical; high temperature materials; mechanical behavior of materials; neutron materials science. Total annual research expenditures: $4.1 million. *Unit head:* Dr. George Pharr, Head, 865-974-5336, Fax: 865-974-4115, E-mail: pharr@utk.edu. *Application contact:* Dr. Masood Parang, Associate Dean of Student Affairs, 865-974-2454, Fax: 865-974-9871, E-mail: mparang@utk.edu.

The University of Tennessee Space Institute, Graduate Programs, Program in Materials Science and Engineering, Tullahoma, TN 37388-9700. Offers MS. *Faculty:* 4 full-time (1 woman). *Students:* 5 full-time (0 women); includes 1 minority (Asian American or Pacific Islander), 2 international. 3 applicants, 67% accepted, 2 enrolled. In 2009, 1 master's awarded. *Entrance requirements:* Additional exam requirements/recommendations for international students: Required—TOEFL (minimum score 550 paper-based; 213 computer-based; 80 iBT), IELTS (minimum score 6.5). *Application deadline:* For fall admission, 2/1 for international students; for spring admission, 6/15 for international students. Applications are processed on a rolling basis. Application fee: $35. Electronic applications accepted. *Expenses:* Tuition, state resident: full-time $6826; part-time $380 per hour. Tuition, nonresident: full-time $20,622; part-time $1147 per hour. Required fees: $10 per hour. One-time fee: $90 full-time. *Financial support:* In 2009–10, 1 fellowship (averaging $850 per year), 5 research assistantships with full tuition reimbursements (averaging $17,791 per year) were awarded; career-related internships or fieldwork, Federal Work-Study, institutionally sponsored loans, health care benefits, tuition waivers (full and partial), and unspecified assistantships also available. *Unit head:* Dr. William Hofmeister, Degree Program Chairman, 931-393-7466, Fax: 931-454-2271, E-mail: whofmeis@utsi.edu. *Application contact:* Dee Merriman, Coordinator III, 931-393-7293, Fax: 931-393-7201, E-mail: dmerrima@utsi.edu.

The University of Texas at Arlington, Graduate School, College of Engineering, Department of Materials Science and Engineering, Arlington, TX 76019. Offers M Engr, MS, PhD. Part-time programs available. *Faculty:* 6 full-time (0 women), 8 part-time/adjunct (0 women). *Students:* 57 full-time (12 women), 15 part-time (4 women); includes 5 minority (1 African American, 4 Asian Americans or Pacific Islanders), 64 international. 27 applicants, 100% accepted, 11 enrolled. In 2009, 11 master's, 3 doctorates awarded. Terminal master's awarded for partial completion of doctoral program. *Degree requirements:* For master's, comprehensive exam (for some programs), thesis optional; for doctorate, comprehensive exam, thesis/dissertation. *Entrance requirements:* For master's, GRE General Test, minimum GPA of 3.0; for doctorate, GRE General Test, minimum GPA of 3.5. Additional exam requirements/recommendations for international students: Required—TOEFL (minimum score 550 paper-based; 213 computer-based). *Application deadline:* For fall admission, 6/6 for domestic students, 4/4 for international students; for spring admission, 10/17 for domestic students, 9/5 for international students. Applications are processed on a rolling basis. Application fee: $35 ($50 for international students). *Financial support:* In 2009–10, 4 fellowships (averaging $1,000 per year), 10 research assistantships (averaging $16,000 per year), 13 teaching assistantships (averaging $16,000 per year) were awarded; scholarships/grants and unspecified assistantships also available. Financial award application deadline: 6/1; financial award applicants required to submit FAFSA. *Faculty research:* Electronic materials, conductive polymer, composites biomaterial, structural materials. Total annual research expenditures: $400,000. *Unit head:* Dr. Efstathios Meletis, Chair, 817-272-2398, Fax: 817-272-2538, E-mail: meletis@uta.edu. *Application contact:* Dr. Pranesh B. Aswath, Graduate Adviser, 817-272-7108, Fax: 817-272-2538, E-mail: aswath@uta.edu.

The University of Texas at Austin, Graduate School, Cockrell School of Engineering, Program in Materials Science and Engineering, Austin, TX 78712-1111. Offers MS, PhD. Part-time programs available. *Degree requirements:* For master's, thesis (for some programs); for doctorate, thesis/dissertation. *Entrance requirements:* For master's and doctorate, GRE General Test. Additional exam requirements/recommendations for international students: Required—TOEFL (minimum score 550 paper-based; 213 computer-based). Electronic applications accepted.

The University of Texas at Dallas, Erik Jonsson School of Engineering and Computer Science, Programs in Materials Science and Engineering, Richardson, TX 75080. Offers MS, PhD. Part-time and evening/weekend programs available. *Faculty:* 8 full-time (1 woman). *Students:* 40 full-time (9 women), 6 part-time (3 women); includes 3 minority (all Hispanic Americans), 28 international. Average age 27. 38 applicants, 55% accepted, 12 enrolled. In 2009, 5 master's, 1 doctorate awarded. *Degree requirements:* For master's, thesis or major design project; for doctorate, thesis/dissertation. *Entrance requirements:* For master's, GRE General Test, minimum GPA of 3.0 in related bachelor's degree; for doctorate, GRE General Test, minimum GPA of 3.5. Additional exam requirements/recommendations for international students: Required—TOEFL (minimum score 550 paper-based; 213 computer-based). *Application deadline:* For fall admission, 7/15 for domestic students, 5/1 priority date for international students; for spring admission, 11/15 for domestic students, 9/1 priority date for international students. Applications are processed on a rolling basis. Application fee: $50 ($100 for international students). Electronic applications accepted. *Expenses:* Tuition, state resident: full-time $11,068; part-time $461 per credit hour. Tuition, nonresident: full-time $21,178; part-time $882 per credit hour. Tuition and fees vary according to course load. *Financial support:* In 2009–10, 37 research assistantships with full tuition reimbursements (averaging $17,708 per year) were awarded; fellowships, teaching assistantships with full tuition reimbursements, career-related internships or fieldwork, Federal Work-Study, institutionally sponsored loans, scholarships/grants, and unspecified assistantships also available. Support available to part-time students. Financial award application deadline: 4/30; financial award applicants required to submit FAFSA. *Faculty research:* Advanced micro and nanoelectronics; nanotechnology; micro and nanomanipulation; organic electronics; physical, chemical and bio-sensors; materials characterization; energy generation and storage. *Unit head:* Dr. Yves Chabal, Department Head, 972-883-5751, E-mail: chabal@utdallas.edu. *Application contact:* Suzanne Potts, Administrative Assistant, 972-883-5755, Fax: 972-883-2813, E-mail: gradecs@utdallas.edu.

The University of Texas at El Paso, Graduate School, College of Engineering, Department of Metallurgical and Materials Engineering, El Paso, TX 79968-0001. Offers materials science and engineering (PhD); metallurgical and materials engineering (MS). Part-time and evening/weekend programs available. *Degree requirements:* For master's, thesis. *Entrance requirements:* For master's, GRE General Test. Additional exam requirements/recommendations for international students: Required—TOEFL. Electronic applications accepted.

The University of Texas at El Paso, Graduate School, Interdisciplinary Program in Materials Science and Engineering, El Paso, TX 79968-0001. Offers PhD. Part-time and evening/weekend programs available. *Students:* 20 (6 women); includes 11 minority (2 African Americans, 1 Asian American or Pacific Islander, 8 Hispanic Americans), 8 international. Average age 34. In 2009, 5 doctorates awarded. *Degree requirements:* For doctorate, thesis/dissertation. *Entrance requirements:* For doctorate, GRE, letters of recommendation. Additional exam requirements/recommendations for international students: Required—TOEFL; Recommended—IELTS. *Application deadline:* For fall admission, 8/1 priority date for domestic students, 3/1 for international students; for spring admission, 11/1 priority date for domestic students, 9/1 for international students. Applications are processed on a rolling basis. Application fee: $45 ($80 for international students). Electronic applications accepted. *Financial support:* In 2009–10, research assistantships with partial tuition reimbursements (averaging $22,500 per year), teaching assistantships with partial tuition reimbursements (averaging $1,800 per year) were awarded; fellowships with partial tuition reimbursements, institutionally sponsored loans, scholarships/grants, health care benefits, tuition waivers (partial), and unspecified assistantships also available. Support available to part-time students. Financial award application deadline: 3/15; financial award applicants required to submit FAFSA. *Unit head:* Dr. Lawrence E. Murr, Director, 915-747-8002, Fax: 915-747-8036, E-mail: fekberg@utep.edu. *Application contact:* Dr. Patricia D. Witherspoon, Dean of the Graduate School, 915-747-5491, Fax: 915-747-5788, E-mail: withersp@utep.edu.

University of Toronto, School of Graduate Studies, Physical Sciences Division, Faculty of Applied Science and Engineering, Department of Materials Science and Engineering, Toronto, ON M5S 1A1, Canada. Offers M Eng, MA Sc, PhD. Part-time programs available. *Degree requirements:* For master's, thesis (for some programs), oral presentation/thesis defense (MA Sc), qualifying exam; for doctorate, thesis/dissertation. *Entrance requirements:* For master's, BA Sc or B Sc degree in materials science and engineering, 2 letters of reference; for doctorate, MA Sc degree or equivalent, 2 letters of reference, minimum B+ average in last 2 years. Additional exam requirements/recommendations for international students: Required—TOEFL (minimum score 580 paper-based), TWE (minimum score 4).

University of Utah, The Graduate School, College of Engineering, Department of Materials Science and Engineering, Salt Lake City, UT 84112. Offers MS, PhD. *Faculty:* 8 full-time (1 woman), 1 part-time/adjunct (0 women). *Students:* 28 full-time (4 women), 13 part-time (2 women); includes 1 minority (Asian American or Pacific Islander), 28 international. Average age 30. 77 applicants, 16% accepted, 10 enrolled. In 2009, 4 master's, 2 doctorates awarded. Terminal master's awarded for partial completion of doctoral program. *Degree requirements:* For master's, thesis; for doctorate, thesis/dissertation, exam. *Entrance requirements:* For master's, GRE General Test, minimum GPA of 3.0; for doctorate, GRE General Test, minimum GPA of 3.0. Additional exam requirements/recommendations for international students: Required—TOEFL (minimum score 570 paper-based; 230 computer-based; 88 iBT), IELTS (minimum score 6.5). *Application deadline:* For fall admission, 4/1 for domestic and international students; for spring admission, 11/1 for domestic and international students. Applications are processed on a rolling basis. Application fee: $55 ($65 for international students). Electronic applications accepted. *Expenses:* Tuition, state resident: full-time $4004; part-time $1674 per semester. Tuition, nonresident: full-time $14,134; part-time $5915 per semester. Required fees: $324 per semester. Tuition and fees vary according to course load, degree level and program. *Financial support:* In 2009–10, 25 research assistantships (averaging $20,000 per year) were awarded; career-related internships or fieldwork and Federal Work-Study also available. Financial award application deadline: 2/5; financial award applicants required to submit FAFSA. *Faculty research:* Solid oxide fuel cells, computational nanostructures, computational polymers, biomaterials, electronic materials, nanomaterials. Total annual research expenditures: $3 million. *Unit head:* Dr. Anil V. Virkar, Chair, 801-581-6863, Fax: 801-581-4816, E-mail: anil.virkar@utah.edu. *Application contact:* Ashley Christensen, Academic Program Specialist, 801-581-6863, Fax: 801-581-4816, E-mail: ashley.christensen@utah.edu.

University of Washington, Graduate School, College of Engineering, Department of Materials Science and Engineering, Seattle, WA 98195-2120. Offers materials science and engineering (MS, MSE, MSMSE, PhD); materials science and engineering nanotechnology (PhD). Part-time programs available. *Faculty:* 15 full-time (2 women), 6 part-time/adjunct (1 woman). *Students:* 95 full-time (32 women), 8 part-time (2 women); includes 18 minority (2 African Americans, 1 American Indian/Alaska Native, 12 Asian Americans or Pacific Islanders, 3 Hispanic Americans), 48 international. Average age 30. 194 applicants, 12% accepted, 9 enrolled. In 2009, 4 master's, 10 doctorates awarded. *Degree requirements:* For master's, comprehensive exam, thesis; for doctorate, comprehensive exam, thesis/dissertation. *Entrance requirements:* For master's and doctorate, GRE General Test, minimum GPA of 3.0. Additional exam requirements/recommendations for international students: Required—TOEFL (minimum score 600 paper-based; 250 computer-based; 70 iBT). *Application deadline:* For fall admission, 1/15 priority date for domestic and international students. Application fee: $65. Electronic applications accepted. *Financial support:* In 2009–10, 3 students received support, including 12 fellowships with full tuition reimbursements available, 42 research assistantships with full tuition reimbursements available (averaging $16,380 per year), 13 teaching assistantships with full tuition reimbursements available (averaging $16,380 per year); career-related internships or fieldwork, Federal Work-Study, institutionally sponsored loans, scholarships/grants, health care benefits, unspecified assistantships, and stipend supplements also available. Financial award application deadline: 1/15. *Faculty research:* Biomimetics and biomaterials; electronic, optical and magnetic materials; eco-materials and materials for energy applications; ceramics, metals, composites, and polymers. Total annual research expenditures: $7.4 million. *Unit head:* Dr. Alex Jen, Professor and Chair, 206-543-2600, Fax: 206-543-3100, E-mail: ajen@uw.edu. *Application contact:* Kathleen A. Elkins, Academic Counselor, 206-616-6581, Fax: 206-543-3100, E-mail: kelkins@uw.edu.

The University of Western Ontario, Faculty of Graduate Studies, Physical Sciences Division, Faculty of Engineering, London, ON N6A 5B8, Canada. Offers chemical and biochemical engineering (ME Sc, PhD); civil and environmental engineering (M Eng, ME Sc, PhD); electrical and computer engineering (M Eng, ME Sc, PhD); mechanical and materials engineering (M Eng, ME Sc, PhD). Part-time programs available. Terminal master's awarded for partial completion of doctoral program. *Degree requirements:* For master's, thesis; for doctorate, thesis/dissertation. *Entrance requirements:* For master's, minimum B average; for doctorate, minimum B+ average. *Faculty research:* Wind, geotechnical, chemical reactor engineering, applied electrostatics, biochemical engineering.

University of Windsor, Faculty of Graduate Studies, Faculty of Engineering, Department of Mechanical, Automotive, and Materials Engineering, Windsor, ON N9B 3P4, Canada. Offers engineering materials (M Eng, MA Sc, PhD); mechanical engineering (M Eng, MA Sc, PhD). Part-time programs available. *Degree requirements:* For master's, thesis; for doctorate, comprehensive exam, thesis/dissertation. *Entrance requirements:* For master's, minimum B average; for doctorate, master's degree, minimum B average. Additional exam requirements/recommendations for international students: Required—TOEFL (minimum score 600 paper-based; 250 computer-based). Electronic applications accepted. *Faculty research:* Thermofluids, applied mechanics, materials engineering.

University of Wisconsin–Madison, Graduate School, College of Engineering, Department of Materials Science and Engineering, Madison, WI 53706-1380. Offers materials engineering (MS, PhD). Part-time programs available. *Faculty:* 13 full-time (3 women). *Students:* 4 full-time (1 woman); includes 1 minority (Asian American or Pacific Islander), 1 international. Average age 25. 34 applicants, 3% accepted, 1 enrolled. Terminal master's awarded for partial completion of doctoral program. *Degree requirements:* For master's, thesis; for doctorate, comprehensive exam, thesis/dissertation. *Entrance requirements:* For master's and doctorate, GRE General Test. Additional exam requirements/recommendations for international students: Required—TOEFL (minimum score 580 paper-based; 237 computer-based). *Application deadline:* For fall admission, 7/1 priority date for domestic students; for spring admission, 11/15 priority date for domestic students. Applications are processed on a rolling basis. Application fee: $56. Electronic applications accepted. *Expenses:* Tuition, state resident: part-time $594 per credit. Tuition, nonresident: part-time $1504 per credit. Required fees: $65 per credit. Tuition and fees vary according to course load, program and reciprocity agreements. *Financial support:* In 2009–10, 1 fellowship with tuition reimbursement (averaging $20,760 per year), 3 research assistantships with tuition reimbursements (averaging $20,184 per year) were awarded; teaching assistantships with tuition reimbursements. Financial award application deadline: 1/15. *Faculty research:* Materials characterization, electronic materials, metallurgy, computational materials science, nanotechnology. Total annual research expenditures: $7.2 million. *Unit head:* Dr. Susan Elizabeth Babcock, Chair, 608-262-1821, Fax: 608-262-8353, E-mail: msaedept@engr.wisc.edu. *Application contact:* Diana J. Rhoads, University Services Program Associate B, 608-263-1795, Fax: 608-262-8353, E-mail: rhoads@engr.wisc.edu.

Materials Engineering

University of Wisconsin–Milwaukee, Graduate School, College of Engineering and Applied Science, Program in Engineering, Milwaukee, WI 53201-0413. Offers civil engineering (MS); electrical and computer engineering (MS); energy engineering (Certificate); engineering (PhD); engineering management (MS); engineering mechanics (MS); ergonomics (Certificate); industrial and management engineering (MS); manufacturing engineering (MS); materials engineering (MS); mechanical engineering (MS); MUP/MS. Part-time programs available. *Faculty:* 44 full-time (6 women). *Students:* 119 full-time (22 women), 130 part-time (22 women); includes 23 minority (2 African Americans, 14 Asian Americans or Pacific Islanders, 7 Hispanic Americans), 126 international. Average age 32. 231 applicants, 67% accepted, 33 enrolled. In 2009, 29 master's, 14 doctorates awarded. *Degree requirements:* For master's, comprehensive exam (for some programs), thesis or alternative; for doctorate, comprehensive exam, thesis/dissertation, internship. *Entrance requirements:* For master's, GRE, minimum GPA of 2.75; for doctorate, GRE, minimum GPA of 3.5. Additional exam requirements/recommendations for international students: Required—TOEFL (minimum score 550 paper-based; 79 iBT), IELTS (minimum score 6.5). *Application deadline:* For fall admission, 1/1 priority date for domestic students; for spring admission, 9/1 for domestic students. Applications are processed on a rolling basis. Application fee: $45 ($75 for international students). *Expenses:* Tuition, state resident: full-time $8800. Tuition, nonresident: full-time $20,760. Tuition and fees vary according to program and reciprocity agreements. *Financial support:* In 2009–10, 18 research assistantships, 51 teaching assistantships were awarded; fellowships, career-related internships or fieldwork, Federal Work-Study, and unspecified assistantships also available. Support available to part-time students. Financial award application deadline: 4/15. Total annual research expenditures: $2.9 million. *Unit head:* David Yu, Head, 414-229-6169, E-mail: yu@uwm.edu. *Application contact:* Betty Warras, General Information Contact, 414-229-4982, Fax: 414-229-6967, E-mail: bwarras@uwm.edu.

Virginia Polytechnic Institute and State University, Graduate School, College of Engineering, Department of Materials Science and Engineering, Blacksburg, VA 24061. Offers M Eng, MS, PhD. *Entrance requirements:* For master's and doctorate, GRE. Additional exam requirements/recommendations for international students: Required—TOEFL (minimum score 550 paper-based; 213 computer-based). Electronic applications accepted.

Washington State University, Graduate School, College of Engineering and Architecture, School of Mechanical and Materials Engineering, Program in Material Science Engineering, Pullman, WA 99164. Offers MS. *Faculty:* 29. *Students:* 27 full-time (6 women), 3 part-time (1 woman); includes 5 minority (1 African American, 1 American Indian/Alaska Native, 2 Asian Americans or Pacific Islanders, 1 Hispanic American), 13 international. 133 applicants, 10% accepted, 3 enrolled. *Degree requirements:* For master's, comprehensive exam (for some programs), thesis. *Entrance requirements:* For master's, GRE, Apply Graduate School, statement of purpose, three letters of recommendation, student interest profile, student interest profile, transcripts. Additional exam requirements/recommendations for international students: Required—TOEFL, IELTS. *Application deadline:* For fall admission, 1/10 for domestic and international students; for spring admission, 7/1 for domestic and international students. Applications are processed on a rolling basis. Application fee: $50. Electronic applications accepted. *Financial support:* In 2009–10, fellowships (averaging $2,500 per year), research assistantships with tuition reimbursements (averaging $13,917 per year) were awarded. Financial award application deadline: 2/10. Total annual research expenditures: $2.2 million. *Unit head:* Dr. Matthew McCluskey, Chair, 509-509-335-5356, Fax: 509-335-4662, E-mail: mattmcc@wsu.edu. *Application contact:* Graduate School Admissions, 800-GRADWSU, Fax: 509-335-1949, E-mail: gradsch@wsu.edu.

Wayne State University, College of Engineering, Department of Chemical Engineering and Materials Science, Program in Materials Science and Engineering, Detroit, MI 48202. Offers materials science and engineering (MS, PhD); polymer engineering (Certificate). Part-time programs available. Terminal master's awarded for partial completion of doctoral program. *Degree requirements:* For master's, thesis optional; for doctorate, thesis/dissertation. *Entrance requirements:* For master's, GRE (if applying for financial support), recommendations; resume; for doctorate, GRE (if applying for financial support), recommendations; resumè, personal statement. Additional exam requirements/recommendations for international students: Required—TOEFL (minimum score 550 paper-based; 213 computer-based); Recommended—TWE (minimum score 6). Electronic applications accepted. *Faculty research:* Polymer science, rheology, fatigue in metals, metal matrix composites, ceramics.

Worcester Polytechnic Institute, Graduate Studies and Research, Department of Mechanical Engineering, Program in Materials Science and Engineering, Worcester, MA 01609-2280. Offers MS, PhD. Part-time and evening/weekend programs available. *Faculty:* 4 full-time (0 women), 1 part-time/adjunct (0 women). *Students:* 26 full-time (12 women), 17 part-time (6 women). 68 applicants, 72% accepted, 17 enrolled. In 2009, 6 master's, 2 doctorates awarded. *Degree requirements:* For master's, thesis; for doctorate, comprehensive exam, thesis/dissertation. *Entrance requirements:* For master's and doctorate, GRE General Test (recommended), 3 letters of recommendation. Additional exam requirements/recommendations for international students: Required—TOEFL (minimum score 550 paper-based; 213 computer-based; 79 iBT), IELTS (minimum score 6.5). *Application deadline:* For fall admission, 2/1 priority date for domestic students; for spring admission, 10/15 priority date for domestic students. Applications are processed on a rolling basis. Application fee: $70. Electronic applications accepted. *Financial support:* Career-related internships or fieldwork, institutionally sponsored loans, scholarships/grants, and unspecified assistantships available. Financial award application deadline: 1/15. *Faculty research:* Metals processing, nanomaterials, reliability analysis, surface metrology, biopolymers. *Unit head:* Dr. Richard D. Sisson, Director, 508-831-5633, Fax: 508-831-5178, E-mail: sisson@wpi.edu. *Application contact:* Rita Shilansky, Graduate Secretary, 508-831-5633, Fax: 508-831-5178, E-mail: rita@wpi.edu.

Wright State University, School of Graduate Studies, College of Engineering and Computer Science, Programs in Engineering, Program in Mechanical and Materials Engineering, Dayton, OH 45435. Offers materials science and engineering (MSE); mechanical engineering (MSE). *Degree requirements:* For master's, thesis or course option alternative. *Entrance requirements:* Additional exam requirements/recommendations for international students: Required—TOEFL.

Materials Sciences

Air Force Institute of Technology, Graduate School of Engineering and Management, Department of Aeronautics and Astronautics, Dayton, OH 45433-7765. Offers aeronautical engineering (MS, PhD); astronautical engineering (MS, PhD); materials science (MS, PhD); space operations (MS); systems engineering (MS, PhD). *Accreditation:* ABET (one or more programs are accredited). Part-time programs available. *Degree requirements:* For master's, thesis; for doctorate, thesis/dissertation. *Entrance requirements:* For master's and doctorate, GRE General Test, minimum GPA of 3.0, U.S. citizenship. *Faculty research:* Computational fluid dynamics, experimental aerodynamics, computational structural mechanics, experimental structural mechanics, aircraft and spacecraft stability and control.

Air Force Institute of Technology, Graduate School of Engineering and Management, Department of Engineering Physics, Dayton, OH 45433-7765. Offers applied physics (MS, PhD); electro-optics (MS, PhD); materials science (PhD); nuclear engineering (MS, PhD); space physics (MS). Part-time programs available. *Degree requirements:* For master's, thesis; for doctorate, thesis/dissertation. *Entrance requirements:* For master's and doctorate, GRE General Test, minimum GPA of 3.0, U.S. citizenship. *Faculty research:* High-energy lasers, space physics, nuclear weapon effects, semiconductor physics.

Alabama Agricultural and Mechanical University, School of Graduate Studies, School of Arts and Sciences, Department of Physics, Huntsville, AL 35811. Offers physics (MS, PhD), including applied physics (PhD), materials science (PhD), optics/lasers (PhD). Part-time and evening/weekend programs available. *Degree requirements:* For doctorate, thesis/dissertation. *Entrance requirements:* For master's and doctorate, GRE General Test. Additional exam requirements/recommendations for international students: Required—TOEFL (minimum score 500 paper-based; 173 computer-based; 61 iBT). Electronic applications accepted.

Alfred University, Graduate School, New York State College of Ceramics, School of Engineering, Alfred, NY 14802-1205. Offers biomedical materials engineering science (MS); ceramic engineering (MS); ceramics (PhD); electrical engineering (MS); glass science (MS, PhD); materials science and engineering (MS, PhD); mechanical engineering (MS). *Degree requirements:* For master's, thesis; for doctorate, thesis/dissertation. *Entrance requirements:* Additional exam requirements/recommendations for international students: Required—TOEFL (minimum score 590 paper-based; 243 computer-based). Electronic applications accepted. *Expenses:* Contact institution. *Faculty research:* Fine-particle technology, x-ray diffraction, superconductivity, electronic materials.

Arizona State University, Graduate College, Ira A. Fulton School of Engineering, School of Materials, Tempe, AZ 85287. Offers materials science and engineering (MS, MSE, PhD); semiconductor processing and packaging (MSE). *Degree requirements:* For doctorate, thesis/dissertation. *Entrance requirements:* For doctorate, GRE.

Boston University, College of Engineering, Division of Materials Science and Engineering, Boston, MA 02215. Offers MS, PhD. Part-time programs available. *Students:* 21 full-time (4 women), 2 part-time (both women); includes 2 minority (1 Asian American or Pacific Islander, 1 Hispanic American), 12 international. Average age 26. 82 applicants, 44% accepted, 10 enrolled. In 2009, 2 master's, 1 doctorate awarded. Terminal master's awarded for partial completion of doctoral program. *Degree requirements:* For master's, thesis optional; for doctorate, comprehensive exam, thesis/dissertation. *Entrance requirements:* For master's and doctorate, GRE General Test. Additional exam requirements/recommendations for international students: Required—TOEFL (minimum score 550 paper-based; 213 computer-based; 84 iBT), IELTS (minimum score 6). *Application deadline:* For fall admission, 4/1 for domestic and international students; for spring admission, 10/1 for domestic and international students. Applications are processed on a rolling basis. Application fee: $70. Electronic applications accepted. *Expenses:* Tuition: Full-time $37,910; part-time $1184 per credit hour. Required fees: $386; $40 per semester. Part-time tuition and fees vary according to class time, course level, degree level and program. *Financial support:* In 2009–10, 19 students received support, including 4 fellowships with full tuition reimbursements available (averaging $27,600 per year), 12 research assistantships with full tuition reimbursements available (averaging $18,400 per year), 3 teaching assistantships with full tuition reimbursements available (averaging $18,400 per year); career-related internships or fieldwork, Federal Work-Study, institutionally sponsored loans, scholarships/grants, traineeships, and health care benefits also available. Financial award application deadline: 1/15; financial award applicants required to submit FAFSA. *Faculty research:* Biomaterials; electronic and photonic materials; materials for energy and environment; nanomaterials. *Unit head:* Dr. Uday Pal, Division Head, 617-353-7708, Fax: 617-353-5548, E-mail: upal@bu.edu. *Application contact:* Cheryl Kelley, Director of Graduate Programs, 617-353-9760, Fax: 617-353-0259, E-mail: enggrad@bu.edu.

Brown University, Graduate School, Division of Engineering, Program in Materials Science and Engineering, Providence, RI 02912. Offers Sc M, PhD. *Degree requirements:* For doctorate, thesis/dissertation, preliminary exam.

California Institute of Technology, Division of Engineering and Applied Science, Option in Materials Science, Pasadena, CA 91125-0001. Offers MS, PhD. *Faculty:* 6 full-time (2 women). *Students:* 55 full-time (11 women). 175 applicants, 16% accepted, 14 enrolled. In 2009, 5 master's, 8 doctorates awarded. *Degree requirements:* For doctorate, thesis/dissertation. *Application deadline:* For fall admission, 1/15 for domestic students. Application fee: $0. *Financial support:* In 2009–10, 18 fellowships, 27 research assistantships, 7 teaching assistantships were awarded. *Faculty research:* Mechanical properties, physical properties, kinetics of phase transformations, metastable phases, transmission electron microscopy. *Unit head:* Dr. Brent Fultz, Option Representative, 626-395-2170, E-mail: btf@caltech.edu. *Application contact:* Natalie Gilmore, Assistant Dean of Graduate Studies, 626-395-3812, Fax: 626-577-9246, E-mail: ngilmore@caltech.edu.

Carnegie Mellon University, Carnegie Institute of Technology, Department of Materials Science and Engineering, Pittsburgh, PA 15213-3891. Offers MS, PhD. Part-time programs available. Terminal master's awarded for partial completion of doctoral program. *Degree requirements:* For master's, exam; for doctorate, thesis/dissertation, qualifying exam. *Entrance requirements:* For master's and doctorate, GRE General Test. Additional exam requirements/recommendations for international students: Required—TOEFL. *Faculty research:* Materials characterization, process metallurgy, high strength alloys, growth kinetics, ceramics.

Case Western Reserve University, School of Graduate Studies, The Case School of Engineering, Department of Materials Science and Engineering, Cleveland, OH 44106. Offers materials science and engineering (MS, PhD). Part-time programs available. Postbaccalaureate distance learning degree programs offered (no on-campus study). *Faculty:* 10 full-time (0 women). *Students:* 50 full-time (11 women), 7 part-time (2 women), 45 international. In 2009, 11 master's, 4 doctorates awarded. Terminal master's awarded for partial completion of doctoral program. *Degree requirements:* For master's, thesis (for some programs); for doctorate, thesis/dissertation, qualifying exam, teaching experience. *Entrance requirements:* For master's and doctorate, GRE General Test. Additional exam requirements/recommendations for international students: Required—TOEFL. *Application deadline:* For fall admission, 2/15 priority date for domestic students; for spring admission, 9/15 for domestic students. Applications are processed on a rolling basis. Application fee: $50. *Financial support:* Fellowships with full and partial tuition reimbursements, research assistantships with full and partial tuition reimbursements, teaching assistantships available. Financial award application deadline: 4/30; financial award applicants required to submit FAFSA. *Faculty research:* Surface hardening of steels and other alloys, chemistry and structure of surfaces, microstructural and mechanical property characterization, materials for energy applications, thermodynamics and kinetics of materials, performance and reliability of materials. Total annual research expenditures: $7.4 million. *Unit head:* Dr. James D. McGuffin-Cawley, Department Chair, 216-368-6482, Fax: 216-368-4224, E-mail: emse.info@case.edu. *Application contact:* Kathleen Bates, Academic Administration Manager, 216-368-3840, Fax: 216-368-3209, E-mail: esme.info@case.edu.

Central Michigan University, College of Graduate Studies, College of Science and Technology, Department of Physics, Program in the Science of Advanced Materials, Mount Pleasant, MI 48859. Offers PhD. *Degree requirements:* For doctorate, comprehensive exam, thesis/dissertation. *Entrance requirements:* For doctorate, GRE. Electronic applications accepted. *Faculty research:* Electronic properties of nanomaterials, polymers for energy and for environmental applications, inorganic materials synthesis, magnetic properties from first-principles, and nano devices for biomedical applications and environmental remediation.

Clemson University, Graduate School, College of Engineering and Science, School of Materials Science and Engineering, Programs in Materials Science and Engineering, Clemson, SC 29634. Offers MS, PhD. Part-time programs available. *Students:* 57 full-time (19 women), 3 part-time (0 women), 33 international. Average age 27. 84 applicants, 51% accepted, 15 enrolled. In 2009, 2 master's, 5 doctorates awarded. Terminal master's awarded for partial completion of doctoral program. *Degree requirements:* For master's, thesis; for doctorate, comprehensive exam, thesis/dissertation. *Entrance requirements:* For master's and doctorate, GRE General Test. Additional exam requirements/recommendations for international students: Required—TOEFL. *Application deadline:* For fall admission, 2/1 for domestic students; for spring admission, 9/1 for domestic students. Applications are processed on a rolling basis. Application fee: $70 ($80 for international students). Electronic applications accepted. *Expenses:* Tuition, state resident: full-time $8684; part-time $528 per credit hour. Tuition, nonresident: full-time $15,330; part-time $1078 per credit hour. Required fees: $736; $37 per semester. Part-time tuition and fees vary according to course load and program. *Financial support:* In 2009–10, 2 fellowships with full and partial tuition reimbursements (averaging $18,000 per year), 41 research assistantships with partial tuition reimbursements (averaging $20,295 per year), 1 teaching assistantship with partial tuition reimbursement (averaging $18,500 per year) were awarded; career-related internships or fieldwork, institutionally sponsored loans, scholarships/grants, health care benefits, and unspecified assistantships also available. Support available to part-time students. Financial award applicants required to submit FAFSA. *Faculty research:* Composites, fibers, ceramics, metallurgy, biomaterials, semiconductors. *Unit head:* Dr. Kathleen Richardson, Chair and Director of the School of Materials Science and Engineering, 864-656-3311, Fax: 864-656-5973, E-mail: richar3@clemson.edu. *Application contact:* Dr. Gary C. Lickfield, Graduate Program Coordinator, 864-656-5964, Fax: 864-656-5973, E-mail: lgary@clemson.edu.

Colorado School of Mines, Graduate School, Department of Metallurgical and Materials Engineering, Golden, CO 80401. Offers materials science (MS, PhD); metallurgical and materials engineering (ME, MS, PhD). Part-time programs available. *Faculty:* 34 full-time (3 women), 4 part-time/adjunct (0 women). *Students:* 54 full-time (13 women), 6 part-time (1 woman); includes 6 minority (1 American Indian/Alaska Native, 4 Asian Americans or Pacific Islanders, 1 Hispanic American), 8 international. Average age 30. 84 applicants, 26% accepted, 14 enrolled. In 2009, 18 master's, 8 doctorates awarded. *Degree requirements:* For master's, thesis (for some programs); for doctorate, comprehensive exam, thesis/dissertation. *Entrance requirements:* For master's and doctorate, GRE General Test. Additional exam requirements/ recommendations for international students: Required—TOEFL (minimum score 550 paper-based; 213 computer-based; 80 iBT). *Application deadline:* For fall admission, 1/15 priority date for domestic and international students; for spring admission, 9/1 priority date for domestic and international students. Application fee: $50 ($70 for international students). Electronic applications accepted. *Expenses:* Tuition, state resident: full-time $10,584; part-time $588 per credit hour. Tuition, nonresident: full-time $24,750; part-time $1375 per credit hour. Required fees: $1654; $827.10 per semester. *Financial support:* In 2009–10, 3 fellowships with full tuition reimbursements (averaging $20,000 per year), 64 research assistantships with full tuition reimbursements (averaging $20,000 per year), 8 teaching assistantships with full tuition reimbursements (averaging $20,000 per year) were awarded; scholarships/grants, health care benefits, and unspecified assistantships also available. Financial award application deadline: 1/15; financial award applicants required to submit FAFSA. Total annual research expenditures: $6.9 million. *Unit head:* Dr. Michael Kaufman, Interim Department Head, 303-273-3009, Fax: 303-273-3795, E-mail: mkaufman@mines.edu. *Application contact:* Peggy Cook, Program Assistant, 303-273-3660, Fax: 303-273-3795, E-mail: pcook@mines.edu.

Colorado School of Mines, Graduate School, Program in Materials Science, Golden, CO 80401. Offers MS, PhD. Part-time programs available. *Students:* 54 full-time (11 women), 6 part-time (2 women); includes 4 minority (3 Asian Americans or Pacific Islanders, 1 Hispanic American), 22 international. Average age 29. 61 applicants, 33% accepted, 9 enrolled. In 2009, 14 master's, 3 doctorates awarded. *Degree requirements:* For master's, thesis (for some programs); for doctorate, comprehensive exam, thesis/dissertation. *Entrance requirements:* For master's and doctorate, GRE General Test. Additional exam requirements/recommendations for international students: Required—TOEFL (minimum score 550 paper-based; 213 computer-based; 80 iBT). *Application deadline:* For fall admission, 1/15 priority date for domestic and international students; for spring admission, 9/1 priority date for domestic and international students. Application fee: $50 ($70 for international students). Electronic applications accepted. *Expenses:* Tuition, state resident: full-time $10,584; part-time $588 per credit hour. Tuition, nonresident: full-time $24,750; part-time $1375 per credit hour. Required fees: $1654; $827.10 per semester. *Financial support:* In 2009–10, 53 students received support, including fellowships with full tuition reimbursements available (averaging $20,000 per year), 45 research assistantships with full tuition reimbursements available (averaging $20,000 per year), 8 teaching assistantships with full tuition reimbursements available (averaging $20,000 per year); scholarships/grants, health care benefits, and unspecified assistantships also available. Financial award application deadline: 1/15; financial award applicants required to submit FAFSA. *Faculty research:* Ceramics processing, solar and electronic materials, optical properties of surfaces and interfaces, materials synthesis, metal and alloy processing. *Unit head:* Dr. Michael Kaufman, Interim Department Head, 303-273-3009, Fax: 303-273-3795, E-mail: mkaufman@mines.edu. *Application contact:* Peggy Cook, Administrative Assistant, 303-273-3660, Fax: 303-273-3795, E-mail: pcook@mines.edu.

Columbia University, Fu Foundation School of Engineering and Applied Science, Department of Applied Physics and Applied Mathematics, New York, NY 10027. Offers applied physics (Eng Sc D); applied physics and applied mathematics (MS, PhD, Engr); materials science and engineering (MS, Eng Sc D, PhD); medical physics (MS). Part-time programs available. Post-baccalaureate distance learning degree programs offered (no on-campus study). *Faculty:* 19 full-time (1 woman), 3 part-time/adjunct (1 woman). *Students:* 127 full-time (24 women), 44 part-time (7 women); includes 12 minority (2 African Americans, 1 American Indian/Alaska Native, 8 Asian Americans or Pacific Islanders, 1 Hispanic American), 73 international. Average age 27. 300 applicants, 35% accepted, 45 enrolled. In 2009, 31 master's, 10 doctorates awarded. Terminal master's awarded for partial completion of doctoral program. *Degree requirements:* For master's, comprehensive exam; for doctorate, thesis/dissertation, qualifying exam. *Entrance requirements:* For master's, GRE General Test, GRE Subject Test (strongly recommended); for doctorate, GRE General Test, GRE Subject Test (physics); for Engr, GRE General Test. Additional exam requirements/recommendations for international students: Required—TOEFL. *Application deadline:* For fall admission, 12/1 priority date for domestic and international students; for spring admission, 10/1 priority date for domestic and international students. Application fee: $70. Electronic applications accepted. *Financial support:* In 2009–10, 70 students received support, including 4 fellowships with full and partial tuition reimbursements available, 50 research assistantships with full tuition reimbursements available (averaging $30,000 per year), 18 teaching assistantships with full tuition reimbursements available (averaging $30,000 per year); health care benefits and unspecified assistantships also available. Financial award application deadline: 12/1; financial award applicants required to submit FAFSA. *Faculty research:* Plasma, solid state, optical and laser physics; atmospheric, oceanic and earth physics; computational math and applied mathematics; materials science and engineering. *Unit head:* Dr. Irving P. Herman, Professor and Chair, 212-854-4457, E-mail: seasinfo.apam@columbia.edu. *Application contact:* Montserrat Fernandez-Pinkley, Student Services Coordinator, 212-854-4457, Fax: 212-854-8257, E-mail: mf2157@columbia.edu.

Cornell University, Graduate School, Graduate Fields of Engineering, Field of Materials Science and Engineering, Ithaca, NY 14853-0001. Offers materials engineering (M Eng, PhD); materials science (M Eng, PhD). *Faculty:* 46 full-time (6 women). *Students:* 67 full-time (23 women); includes 15 minority (2 African Americans, 9 Asian Americans or Pacific Islanders, 4 Hispanic Americans), 26 international. Average age 26. 312 applicants, 35% accepted, 1 enrolled. In 2009, 21 master's, 10 doctorates awarded. *Degree requirements:* For doctorate,

comprehensive exam, thesis/dissertation. *Entrance requirements:* For master's and doctorate, GRE General Test, 3 letters of recommendation. Additional exam requirements/recommendations for international students: Required—TOEFL (minimum score 550 paper-based; 213 computer-based; 77 iBT). *Application deadline:* For fall admission, 1/15 priority date for domestic students. Application fee: $70. Electronic applications accepted. *Expenses:* Tuition: Full-time $29,500. Required fees: $70. Full-time tuition and fees vary according to degree level, program and student level. *Financial support:* In 2009–10, 48 students received support, including 2 fellowships with full tuition reimbursements available, 7 research assistantships with full tuition reimbursements available, 1 teaching assistantship with full tuition reimbursement available; institutionally sponsored loans, scholarships/grants, health care benefits, tuition waivers (full and partial), and unspecified assistantships also available. Financial award applicants required to submit FAFSA. *Faculty research:* Ceramics, complex fluids, glass, metals, polymers semiconductors. *Unit head:* Director of Graduate Studies, 607-255-9159, Fax: 607-255-2365. *Application contact:* Graduate Field Assistant, 607-255-9159, Fax: 607-255-2365, E-mail: matsci@cornell.edu.

Dartmouth College, Thayer School of Engineering, Program in Materials Sciences and Engineering, Hanover, NH 03755. Offers MS, PhD. *Degree requirements:* For master's, thesis; for doctorate, thesis/dissertation, candidacy oral exam. *Entrance requirements:* For master's and doctorate, GRE General Test. *Application deadline:* For fall admission, 1/1 priority date for domestic students. Application fee: $45. *Financial support:* Fellowships, research assistantships, teaching assistantships, career-related internships or fieldwork, Federal Work-Study, institutionally sponsored loans, and tuition waivers (full and partial) available. Financial award application deadline: 1/15. *Faculty research:* Electronic and magnetic materials, microstructural evolution, biomaterials and nanostructures, laser-material interactions, nano composites. Total annual research expenditures: $2.4 million. *Unit head:* Dr. Joseph J. Helbie, Dean, 603-646-2238, Fax: 603-646-2580, E-mail: joseph.j.helbie@dartmouth.edu. *Application contact:* Candace S. Potter, Graduate Admissions Administrator, 603-646-3844, Fax: 603-646-1620, E-mail: candace.potter@dartmouth.edu.

Duke University, Graduate School, Pratt School of Engineering, Department of Mechanical Engineering and Materials Science, Durham, NC 27708. Offers materials science (MS, PhD); mechanical engineering (MS, PhD); JD/MS. Part-time programs available. *Faculty:* 26 full-time. *Students:* 55 full-time (11 women); includes 5 minority (4 Asian Americans or Pacific Islanders, 1 Hispanic American), 19 international. 200 applicants, 20% accepted, 17 enrolled. In 2009, 10 master's, 9 doctorates awarded. Terminal master's awarded for partial completion of doctoral program. *Degree requirements:* For master's, thesis optional; for doctorate, thesis/dissertation. *Entrance requirements:* For master's and doctorate, GRE General Test. Additional exam requirements/recommendations for international students: Required—TOEFL (minimum score 550 paper-based; 213 computer-based; 83 iBT), IELTS (minimum score 7). *Application deadline:* For fall admission, 12/8 priority date for domestic and international students; for spring admission, 11/1 for domestic students. Application fee: $75. Electronic applications accepted. *Financial support:* Fellowships, research assistantships, teaching assistantships, Federal Work-Study available. Financial award application deadline: 12/31. *Unit head:* Stefan Zauscher, Director of Graduate Studies, 919-660-5360, Fax: 919-660-8963, E-mail: kparrish@duke.edu. *Application contact:* Cynthia Robertson, Associate Dean for Enrollment Services, 919-684-3913, E-mail: grad-admissions@duke.edu.

Florida State University, The Graduate School, College of Arts and Sciences, Department of Chemistry and Biochemistry, Tallahassee, FL 32306-4390. Offers analytical chemistry (MS, PhD); biochemistry (MS, PhD); inorganic chemistry (MS, PhD); materials chemistry (MS, PhD); organic chemistry (MS, PhD); physical chemistry (MS, PhD). *Faculty:* 40 full-time (6 women), 3 part-time/adjunct (0 women). *Students:* 150 full-time (47 women), 9 part-time (6 women); includes 16 minority (5 African Americans, 1 American Indian/Alaska Native, 5 Asian Americans or Pacific Islanders, 5 Hispanic Americans), 68 international. Average age 25. 286 applicants, 21% accepted, 28 enrolled. In 2009, 7 master's, 15 doctorates awarded. Terminal master's awarded for partial completion of doctoral program. *Degree requirements:* For master's, comprehensive exam (for some programs), thesis (for some programs), cumulative and diagnostic exams; for doctorate, comprehensive exam (for some programs), thesis/dissertation, cumulative and diagnostic exams. *Entrance requirements:* For master's and doctorate, GRE General Test, minimum B average in undergraduate course work. Additional exam requirements/recommendations for international students: Required—TOEFL (minimum score 550 paper-based; 213 computer-based; 80 iBT). *Application deadline:* For fall admission, 12/15 for domestic and international students; for spring admission, 9/15 for domestic and international students. Applications are processed on a rolling basis. Application fee: $30. Electronic applications accepted. *Expenses:* Tuition, state resident: full-time $7413.36. Tuition, nonresident: full-time $22,567. *Financial support:* In 2009–10, 150 students received support, including fellowships with full tuition reimbursements available (averaging $19,000 per year), 52 research assistantships with full tuition reimbursements available (averaging $19,000 per year), 100 teaching assistantships with full tuition reimbursements available (averaging $19,000 per year); career-related internships or fieldwork, Federal Work-Study, institutionally sponsored loans, and traineeships also available. Financial award application deadline: 12/15; financial award applicants required to submit FAFSA. *Faculty research:* Materials synthesis including polymers, natural products; catalysis, NMR; mass spectrometry; optical spectroscopy, scattering techniques, computational chemistry, separation technology; nanostructured materials including metallic, semiconducting and magnetic nanocrystals; nanoscience interfaced with biology; supramolecular materials for solar energy conversion. Total annual research expenditures: $5.5 million. *Unit head:* Dr. Joseph Schlenoff, Chairman, 850-644-5195, Fax: 850-644-8281, E-mail: schlen@chem.fsu.edu. *Application contact:* Dr. Tyler McQuade, Chair, Graduate Admissions Committee, 888-525-9286, Fax: 850-644-0465, E-mail: gradinfo@chem.fsu.edu.

Florida State University, The Graduate School, Interdisciplinary Program in Materials Science, Tallahassee, FL 32306. Offers computational materials science and mechanics (MS); functional materials (MS); nanoscale materials, composite materials, and interfaces (MS); polymers and bio-inspired materials (MS). *Faculty:* 38 full-time (5 women). *Students:* 6 full-time (1 woman), 2 international. *Degree requirements:* For master's, thesis. *Entrance requirements:* For master's, GRE General Test (minimum score 1100 verbal and quantitative), minimum GPA of 3.0, letters of recommendation. Additional exam requirements/recommendations for international students: Required—TOEFL (minimum score 550 paper-based; 213 computer-based; 80 iBT). *Application deadline:* For fall admission, 7/1 for domestic and international students; for winter admission, 11/1 for domestic and international students; for spring admission, 3/1 for domestic and international students. Applications are processed on a rolling basis. Electronic applications accepted. *Expenses:* Tuition, state resident: full-time $7413.36. Tuition, nonresident: full-time $22,567. *Financial support:* Fellowships, research assistantships, teaching assistantships available. Financial award application deadline: 1/15; financial award applicants required to submit FAFSA. *Faculty research:* Magnetism and magnetic materials, composites, superconductors, polymers, computations. *Unit head:* Prof. Eric Hellstrom, Director, 850-645-7489, Fax: 850-645-7754, E-mail: hellstrom@asc.magnet.fsu.edu. *Application contact:* Todd Kramer, Admissions Coordinator, 850-410-6161, Fax: 850-410-6486, E-mail: krameto@eng.fsu.edu.

Georgetown University, Graduate School of Arts and Sciences, Department of Chemistry, Washington, DC 20057. Offers analytical chemistry (PhD); biochemistry (PhD); computational chemistry (PhD); inorganic chemistry (PhD); materials chemistry (PhD); organic chemistry (PhD); physical chemistry (PhD); theoretical chemistry (PhD). Terminal master's awarded for partial completion of doctoral program. *Degree requirements:* For doctorate, comprehensive exam, thesis/dissertation. *Entrance requirements:* For doctorate, GRE General Test. Additional exam requirements/recommendations for international students: Required—TOEFL.

The George Washington University, Columbian College of Arts and Sciences, Department of Chemistry, Washington, DC 20052. Offers analytical chemistry (MS, PhD); inorganic chemistry (MS, PhD); materials science (MS, PhD); organic chemistry (MS, PhD); physical chemistry (MS, PhD). Part-time and evening/weekend programs available. *Faculty:* 15 full-time (4 women),

Materials Sciences

The George Washington University (continued)

7 part-time/adjunct (3 women). *Students:* 19 full-time (12 women), 12 part-time (7 women); includes 4 minority (2 Asian Americans or Pacific Islanders, 2 Hispanic Americans), 12 international. Average age 28. 45 applicants, 49% accepted, 6 enrolled. In 2009, 2 master's, 4 doctorates awarded. Terminal master's awarded for partial completion of doctoral program. *Degree requirements:* For master's, comprehensive exam, thesis or alternative; for doctorate, thesis/dissertation, general exam. *Entrance requirements:* For master's and doctorate, GRE General Test, interview, minimum GPA of 3.0. Additional exam requirements/recommendations for international students: Required—TOEFL (minimum score 550 paper-based; 213 computer-based; 80 iBT). *Application deadline:* For fall admission, 1/15 priority date for domestic and international students; for spring admission, 9/1 priority date for domestic and international students. Applications are processed on a rolling basis. Application fee: $60. Electronic applications accepted. *Financial support:* In 2009–10, 27 students received support; fellowships with tuition reimbursements available, research assistantships, teaching assistantships with tuition reimbursements available, Federal Work-Study and tuition waivers available. Financial award application deadline: 1/15. *Unit head:* Dr. Michael King, Chair, 202-994-6488. *Application contact:* Information Contact, E-mail: gwchem@www.gwu.edu.

Illinois Institute of Technology, Graduate College, Armour College of Engineering, Department of Mechanical, Materials and Aerospace Engineering, Chicago, IL 60616-3793. Offers manufacturing engineering (MME, MS); materials science and engineering (MMME, MS, PhD); mechanical and aerospace engineering (MMAE, MS, PhD). Part-time programs available. Terminal master's awarded for partial completion of doctoral program. *Degree requirements:* For master's, comprehensive exam (for some programs), thesis (for some programs); for doctorate, comprehensive exam, thesis/dissertation. *Entrance requirements:* For master's and doctorate, GRE General Test, minimum undergraduate GPA of 3.0. Additional exam requirements/recommendations for international students: Required—TOEFL (minimum score 550 paper-based; 213 computer-based; 80 iBT). Electronic applications accepted. *Expenses:* Tuition: Full-time $17,550; part-time $888 per credit hour. Required fees: $850; $7.50 per credit hour. One-time fee: $50 full-time. Full-time tuition and fees vary according to program. *Faculty research:* Active flow control, bio-fluid dynamics, acoustics and separated flows, digital design and manufacturing and high performance materials, two-phase flows in micro scales and combustion-driven MEMS, global positioning systems, experimental and computational solid mechanics.

Illinois Institute of Technology, Graduate College, College of Science and Letters, Department of Biological, Chemical and Physical Sciences, Chemistry Division, Chicago, IL 60616-3793. Offers analytical chemistry (M Ch); chemistry (M Chem, MS, PhD); materials and chemical synthesis (M Ch). Part-time and evening/weekend programs available. Postbaccalaureate distance learning degree programs offered (no on-campus study). Terminal master's awarded for partial completion of doctoral program. *Degree requirements:* For master's, comprehensive exam, thesis (for some programs); for doctorate, comprehensive exam, thesis/dissertation. *Entrance requirements:* For master's and doctorate, GRE General Test, minimum undergraduate GPA of 3.0. Additional exam requirements/recommendations for international students: Required—TOEFL (minimum score 550 paper-based; 213 computer-based; 80 iBT). Electronic applications accepted. *Expenses:* Tuition: Full-time $17,550; part-time $888 per credit hour. Required fees: $850; $7.50 per credit hour. One-time fee: $50 full-time. Full-time tuition and fees vary according to program. *Faculty research:* Organic synthesis for cancer-therapy, nano-materials for environmental/medical applications, single protein/cell functions and dynamics, polymer chemistry.

Instituto Tecnológico y de Estudios Superiores de Monterrey, Campus Estado de México, Professional and Graduate Division, Estado de Mexico, Mexico. Offers administration of information technologies (MITA); architecture (M Arch); business administration (GMBA, MBA); computer sciences (MCS, PhD); education (M Ed); educational institution administration (MAD); educational technology and innovation (PhD); electronic commerce (MEC); environmental systems (MS); finance (MAF); humanistic studies (MHS); information sciences and knowledge management (MISKM); information systems (MS); manufacturing systems (MS); marketing (MEM); quality systems and productivity (MS); science and materials engineering (PhD); telecommunications management (MTM). Part-time programs available. Postbaccalaureate distance learning degree programs offered (minimal on-campus study). *Degree requirements:* For master's, one foreign language, thesis (for some programs); for doctorate, one foreign language, thesis/dissertation. *Entrance requirements:* For master's, E-PAEP 500, interview; for doctorate, E-PAEP 500, research proposal. Additional exam requirements/recommendations for international students: Required—TOEFL (minimum score 550 paper-based). *Faculty research:* Surface treatments by plasmas, mechanical properties, robotics, graphical computing, mechatronics security protocols.

Iowa State University of Science and Technology, Graduate College, College of Engineering and College of Liberal Arts and Sciences, Department of Materials Science and Engineering, Ames, IA 50011. Offers MS, PhD. *Faculty:* 24 full-time (2 women), 1 part-time/adjunct (0 women). *Students:* 63 full-time (16 women), 5 part-time (1 woman); includes 4 minority (1 African American, 1 American Indian/Alaska Native, 1 Asian American or Pacific Islander, 1 Hispanic American), 36 international. 137 applicants, 12% accepted, 16 enrolled. In 2009, 9 master's, 10 doctorates awarded. *Degree requirements:* For master's, thesis; for doctorate, thesis/dissertation. *Entrance requirements:* Additional exam requirements/recommendations for international students: Required—TOEFL (minimum score 550 paper-based; 79 iBT) or IELTS (minimum score 6.5). *Application deadline:* For fall admission, 1/15 priority date for domestic and international students; for spring admission, 8/15 priority date for domestic and international students. Application fee: $40 ($90 for international students). Electronic applications accepted. *Expenses:* Tuition, state resident: full-time $6716. Tuition, nonresident: full-time $8908. Tuition and fees vary according to course level, course load, program and student level. *Financial support:* In 2009–10, 57 research assistantships with full and partial tuition reimbursements (averaging $17,300 per year), 3 teaching assistantships with full and partial tuition reimbursements (averaging $17,300 per year) were awarded; fellowships, scholarships/grants, health care benefits, and unspecified assistantships also available. *Unit head:* Dr. Richard Lesar, Chair, 515-294-1841, Fax: 515-204-5444, E-mail: gradmse@iastate.edu. *Application contact:* Dr. Alan Russell, Director of Graduate Education, 515-294-3204, E-mail: gradmse@iastate.edu.

Jackson State University, Graduate School, School of Science and Technology, Department of Technology and Industrial Arts, Jackson, MS 39217. Offers hazardous materials management (MS); industrial arts education (MS Ed). Part-time and evening/weekend programs available. *Degree requirements:* For master's, comprehensive exam, thesis or alternative. *Entrance requirements:* For master's, GRE General Test. Additional exam requirements/recommendations for international students: Required—TOEFL.

The Johns Hopkins University, Engineering for Professionals, Part-time Program in Materials Science and Engineering, Baltimore, MD 21218-2699. Offers M Mat SE, MSE. Part-time and evening/weekend programs available. *Faculty:* 6 part-time/adjunct (1 woman). *Students:* 1 full-time (0 women), 12 part-time (7 women); includes 5 minority (4 African Americans, 1 Asian American or Pacific Islander). Average age 27. *Application deadline:* Applications are processed on a rolling basis. Application fee: $75. Electronic applications accepted. *Financial support:* Institutionally sponsored loans available. *Unit head:* Dr. Robert C. Cammarata, Program Chair, 410-516-5462, Fax: 410-516-5293, E-mail: rcc@jhu.edu. *Application contact:* Priyanka Dwivedi, Admissions Manager, 410-516-2300, Fax: 410-579-8049, E-mail: pdwived1@jhu.edu.

The Johns Hopkins University, G. W. C. Whiting School of Engineering, Department of Materials Science and Engineering, Baltimore, MD 21218-2699. Offers M Mat SE, MSE, PhD. Part-time and evening/weekend programs available. *Faculty:* 14 full-time (3 women), 1 part-time/adjunct (0 women). *Students:* 45 full-time (12 women), 2 part-time (1 woman); includes 8 minority (2 African Americans, 4 Asian Americans or Pacific Islanders, 2 Hispanic Americans), 16 international. Average age 28. 130 applicants, 17% accepted, 10 enrolled. In 2009, 16 master's, 6 doctorates awarded. Terminal master's awarded for partial completion of doctoral program. *Degree requirements:* For master's, thesis, oral exam; for doctorate, thesis/dissertation, oral exam, thesis defense. *Entrance requirements:* For master's and doctorate, GRE General Test. Additional exam requirements/recommendations for international students: Required—TOEFL (minimum score 600 paper-based; 250 computer-based). *Application deadline:* For fall admission, 1/17 priority date for domestic and international students; for spring admission, 10/15 priority date for domestic and international students. Application fee: $0 ($75 for international students). Electronic applications accepted. *Financial support:* In 2009–10, 5 fellowships with full tuition reimbursements (averaging $30,000 per year), 29 research assistantships with full tuition reimbursements (averaging $27,200 per year), 4 teaching assistantships with full tuition reimbursements (averaging $27,200 per year) were awarded; Federal Work-Study, institutionally sponsored loans, health care benefits, tuition waivers (full), and unspecified assistantships also available. Financial award application deadline: 3/14. *Faculty research:* Thin films, nanomaterials, biomaterials, materials characterization, electronic materials. Total annual research expenditures: $3.7 million. *Unit head:* Dr. Howard E. Katz, Chair, 410-516-6141, Fax: 410-516-5293, E-mail: hekatz@jhu.edu. *Application contact:* Jeanine Majewski, Academic Coordinator, 410-516-8760, Fax: 410-516-5293, E-mail: dmse.admissions@jhu.edu.

The Johns Hopkins University, G. W. C. Whiting School of Engineering, Program in Engineering Management, Baltimore, MD 21218-2699. Offers biomaterials (MSEM); communications science (MSEM); computer science (MSEM); fluid mechanics (MSEM); materials science and engineering (MSEM); mechanical engineering (MSEM); mechanics and materials (MSEM); nano-biotechnology (MSEM); nanomaterials and nanotechnology (MSEM); probability and statistics (MSEM); smart product and device design (MSEM); systems analysis, management and environmental policy (MSEM). *Students:* 12 full-time (0 women), 3 international. Average age 23. 66 applicants, 67% accepted. *Entrance requirements:* For master's, GRE, 3 letters of recommendation, resume. Additional exam requirements/recommendations for international students: Required—TOEFL (minimum score 600 paper-based; 250 computer-based; 100 iBT) or IELTS (minimum score 7). *Application deadline:* For fall admission, 1/15 priority date for domestic students, 1/15 for international students; for spring admission, 9/15 priority date for domestic students, 9/15 for international students. Applications are processed on a rolling basis. Application fee: $75. Electronic applications accepted. *Financial support:* Fellowships, health care benefits available. *Unit head:* Dr. Edward R. Scheinerman, Interim Director/Vice Dean for Education, School of Engineering/Professor, Applied Mathematics and Statistics, 410-516-7395, Fax: 410-516-4880, E-mail: ers@jhu.edu. *Application contact:* Dennis McIver, Coordinator of Graduate Admissions, 410-516-8174, Fax: 410-516-0780, E-mail: graduateadmissions@jhu.edu.

Lehigh University, P.C. Rossin College of Engineering and Applied Science, Department of Materials Science and Engineering, Bethlehem, PA 18015. Offers materials science and engineering (M Eng, MS, PhD); photonics (MS); polymer science/engineering (M Eng, MS, PhD); MBA/E. Part-time programs available. *Faculty:* 13 full-time (3 women). *Students:* 26 full-time (3 women), 4 part-time (2 women), 15 international. Average age 26. 163 applicants, 4% accepted, 2 enrolled. In 2009, 2 master's, 4 doctorates awarded. *Degree requirements:* For master's, thesis; for doctorate, comprehensive exam, thesis/dissertation. *Entrance requirements:* For master's and doctorate, GRE General Test, minimum GPA of 3.0. Additional exam requirements/recommendations for international students: Required—TOEFL. *Application deadline:* For fall admission, 1/15 priority date for domestic students, 1/15 for international students; for spring admission, 12/1 priority date for domestic students, 12/1 for international students. Applications are processed on a rolling basis. Application fee: $65. Electronic applications accepted. *Financial support:* In 2009–10, 27 students received support, including 5 fellowships with full and partial tuition reimbursements available (averaging $22,400 per year), 21 research assistantships with full tuition reimbursements available (averaging $22,449 per year), 6 teaching assistantships with partial tuition reimbursements available (averaging $17,512 per year); career-related internships or fieldwork, Federal Work-Study, institutionally sponsored loans, scholarships/grants, and unspecified assistantships also available. Support available to part-time students. Financial award application deadline: 1/15. *Faculty research:* Metals, ceramics, crystals, polymers, fatigue crack propagation. Total annual research expenditures: $4 million. *Unit head:* Dr. Helen Chan, Chairperson, 610-758-5554, Fax: 610-758-4244, E-mail: hmc0@lehigh.edu. *Application contact:* Anne Marie Lobley, Graduate Administrative Coordinator, 610-758-4222, Fax: 610-758-4244, E-mail: amme@lehigh.edu.

Massachusetts Institute of Technology, School of Engineering, Department of Materials Science and Engineering, Cambridge, MA 02139-4307. Offers archaeological materials (PhD, Sc D); bio- and polymeric materials (PhD, Sc D); electronic, photonic and magnetic materials (PhD, Sc D); emerging, fundamental and computational studies in materials science (Sc D); emerging, fundamental, and computational studies in materials science (PhD); materials engineering (Mat E); materials science and engineering (M Eng, SM, PhD, Sc D); metallurgical engineering (Met E); structural and environmental materials (PhD, Sc D); SM/MBA. *Faculty:* 36 full-time (8 women). *Students:* 222 full-time (62 women); includes 32 minority (3 African Americans, 21 Asian Americans or Pacific Islanders, 8 Hispanic Americans), 125 international. Average age 26. 459 applicants, 23% accepted, 63 enrolled. In 2009, 35 master's, 28 doctorates awarded. Terminal master's awarded for partial completion of doctoral program. *Degree requirements:* For master's and other advanced degree, thesis; for doctorate, comprehensive exam, thesis/dissertation. *Entrance requirements:* For master's and doctorate, GRE General Test. Additional exam requirements/recommendations for international students: Required—IELTS (minimum score 5.5); Recommended—TOEFL (minimum score 577 paper-based; 233 computer-based; 90 iBT). *Application deadline:* For fall admission, 1/1 for domestic and international students. Application fee: $75. Electronic applications accepted. *Financial support:* In 2009–10, 222 students received support, including 55 fellowships with tuition reimbursements available (averaging $22,387 per year), 135 research assistantships with tuition reimbursements available (averaging $27,287 per year), 10 teaching assistantships with tuition reimbursements available (averaging $30,736 per year); career-related internships or fieldwork, Federal Work-Study, institutionally sponsored loans, scholarships/grants, health care benefits, and unspecified assistantships also available. *Faculty research:* Thermodynamics and kinetics of phase transformations, structure of all materials classes: metals, ceramics, semiconductors, polymers, biomaterials, influence of processing on materials structure, structure, property relationships (electrical, magnetic, optical, mechanical). Total annual research expenditures: $22.6 million. *Unit head:* Prof. Edwin L. Thomas, Department Head, 617-253-3300, Fax: 617-252-1775. *Application contact:* Angelita Mireles, Graduate Admissions, 617-253-3302, E-mail: dmse-admissions@mit.edu.

McMaster University, School of Graduate Studies, Faculty of Engineering, Department of Materials Science and Engineering, Hamilton, ON L8S 4M2, Canada. Offers materials engineering (M Eng, MA Sc, PhD); materials science (M Eng, PhD). *Degree requirements:* For master's, thesis; for doctorate, comprehensive exam, thesis/dissertation. *Entrance requirements:* Additional exam requirements/recommendations for international students: Required—TOEFL (minimum score 550 paper-based; 213 computer-based). *Faculty research:* Localized corrosion of metals and alloys, electron microscopy, polymer synthesis and characterization, polymer reaction kinetics and engineering, polymer process modeling.

Michigan State University, The Graduate School, College of Engineering, Department of Chemical Engineering and Materials Science, East Lansing, MI 48824. Offers chemical engineering (MS, PhD); materials science and engineering (MS, PhD). *Entrance requirements:* Additional exam requirements/recommendations for international students: Required—TOEFL. Electronic applications accepted.

Missouri State University, Graduate College, College of Natural and Applied Sciences, Department of Physics, Astronomy, and Materials Science, Springfield, MO 65897. Offers materials science (MS); physics, astronomy, and materials science (MNAS); secondary education (MS Ed), including physics. Part-time programs available. *Faculty:* 13 full-time (0 women). *Students:* 6 full-time (2 women), 7 part-time (1 woman), 3 international. Average age 31. 12

applicants, 58% accepted, 6 enrolled. In 2009, 12 master's awarded. *Degree requirements:* For master's, comprehensive exam, thesis. *Entrance requirements:* For master's, GRE (MS, MNAS), minimum undergraduate GPA of 3.0 (MS and MNAS), 9-12 teaching certification (MS Ed). Additional exam requirements/recommendations for international students: Required—TOEFL (minimum score 550 paper-based; 213 computer-based; 79 iBT). *Application deadline:* For fall admission, 7/20 priority date for domestic students, 5/1 for international students; for spring admission, 12/20 priority date for domestic students, 9/1 for international students. Applications are processed on a rolling basis. Application fee: $35 ($50 for international students). Electronic applications accepted. *Expenses:* Tuition, state resident: full-time $3852; part-time $214 per credit hour. Tuition, nonresident: full-time $7524; part-time $418 per credit hour. Required fees: $696; $172 per semester. Tuition and fees vary according to course level, course load, degree level and program. *Financial support:* In 2009–10, 8 teaching assistantships with full tuition reimbursements (averaging $8,834 per year) were awarded; research assistantships with full tuition reimbursements, Federal Work-Study, institutionally sponsored loans, scholarships/grants, and unspecified assistantships also available. Financial award application deadline: 3/31; financial award applicants required to submit FAFSA. *Faculty research:* Nanocomposites, ferroelectricity, infrared focal plane array sensors, biosensors, pulsating stars. *Unit head:* Dr. Robert Patterson, Head, 417-836-5131, Fax: 417-836-6226, E-mail: physics@missouristate.edu. *Application contact:* Eric Eckert, Coordinator of Admissions and Recruitment, 417-836-5331, Fax: 417-836-6200, E-mail: ericeckertn@missouristate.edu.

New Jersey Institute of Technology, Office of Graduate Studies, College of Science and Liberal Arts, Department of Chemistry and Environmental Science, Program in Materials Science and Engineering, Newark, NJ 07102. Offers MS, PhD. Part-time and evening/weekend programs available. Terminal master's awarded for partial completion of doctoral program. *Degree requirements:* For master's, thesis; for doctorate, thesis/dissertation. *Entrance requirements:* For master's, GRE General Test; for doctorate, GRE General Test, minimum graduate GPA of 3.5. Additional exam requirements/recommendations for international students: Required—TOEFL (minimum score 550 paper-based; 213 computer-based; 79 iBT). Electronic applications accepted.

Norfolk State University, School of Graduate Studies, School of Science and Technology, Department of Chemistry, Norfolk, VA 23504. Offers materials science (MS). *Entrance requirements:* Additional exam requirements/recommendations for international students: Required—TOEFL (minimum score 500 paper-based).

North Carolina State University, Graduate School, College of Engineering, Department of Materials Science and Engineering, Raleigh, NC 27695. Offers MMSE, MS, PhD. *Degree requirements:* For master's, thesis; for doctorate, thesis/dissertation. Electronic applications accepted. *Faculty research:* Processing and properties of wide band gap semiconductors, ferroelectric thin-film materials, ductility of nanocrystalline materials, computational materials science, defects in silicon-based devices.

North Dakota State University, College of Graduate and Interdisciplinary Studies, Interdisciplinary Program in Materials and Nanotechnology, Fargo, ND 58108. Offers PhD. *Students:* 3 full-time (0 women), 2 part-time (0 women), all international. In 2009, 1 doctorate awarded. *Entrance requirements:* For doctorate, GRE General Test. Additional exam requirements/recommendations for international students: Required—TOEFL (minimum score 525 paper-based; 197 computer-based; 71 iBT). Application fee: $45 ($60 for international students). *Unit head:* Dr. Daniel Kroll, Director, 701-231-8968, E-mail: daniel.kroll@ndsu.edu. *Application contact:* Dr. Daniel Kroll, Director, 701-231-8968, E-mail: daniel.kroll@ndsu.edu.

Northwestern University, McCormick School of Engineering and Applied Science, Department of Civil and Environmental Engineering, Evanston, IL 60208-3109. Offers environmental engineering and science (MS, PhD); geotechnical engineering (MS, PhD); mechanics of materials and solids (MS, PhD); project management (MS, PhD); structural engineering and materials (MS, PhD); theoretical and applied mechanics (MS, PhD), including fluid mechanics, solid mechanics; transportation systems analysis and planning (MS, PhD). MS and PhD admissions and degrees offered through The Graduate School. Part-time programs available. *Faculty:* 25 full-time (2 women), 3 part-time/adjunct (1 woman). *Students:* 63 full-time (19 women), 3 part-time (0 women); includes 7 minority (1 African American, 3 Asian Americans or Pacific Islanders, 3 Hispanic Americans), 34 international. Average age 22. 149 applicants, 30% accepted, 23 enrolled. In 2009, 11 master's, 11 doctorates awarded. Terminal master's awarded for partial completion of doctoral program. *Degree requirements:* For master's, thesis (for some programs); for doctorate, thesis/dissertation. *Entrance requirements:* For master's and doctorate, GRE General Test, minimum 2 letters of recommendation, transcripts from all academic institutions attended. Additional exam requirements/recommendations for international students: Required—TOEFL (minimum score 600 paper-based; 250 computer-based; 100 iBT), IELTS (minimum score 7), TOEFL (minimum score iBT 26). *Application deadline:* For fall admission, 12/31 for domestic and international students. Application fee: $75. Electronic applications accepted. *Financial support:* In 2009–10, 55 students received support, including fellowships with full tuition reimbursements available (averaging $15,390 per year), research assistantships with full tuition reimbursements available (averaging $17,892 per year), 23 teaching assistantships with full tuition reimbursements available (averaging $15,867 per year); career-related internships or fieldwork, institutionally sponsored loans, scholarships/grants, and health care benefits also available. Financial award application deadline: 12/31; financial award applicants required to submit FAFSA. *Faculty research:* Environmental engineering and science, geotechnics, mechanics of materials and solids, structural engineering and materials, transportation systems analysis and planning. Total annual research expenditures: $5.8 million. *Unit head:* Jianmin Qu, Chair, 847-467-4528, Fax: 847-491-4011, E-mail: j-qu@northwestern.edu. *Application contact:* Janet Soule, Academic Coordinator, 847-491-7462, Fax: 847-491-4011, E-mail: civil-info@northwestern.edu.

Northwestern University, McCormick School of Engineering and Applied Science, Department of Materials Science and Engineering, Evanston, IL 60208. Offers electronic materials (Certificate); materials science and engineering (MS, PhD). Admissions and degrees offered through The Graduate School. Part-time programs available. Terminal master's awarded for partial completion of doctoral program. *Degree requirements:* For master's, oral thesis defense; for doctorate, oral defense of dissertation, preliminary evaluation, qualifying exam. Electronic applications accepted. *Faculty research:* Metallurgy, ceramics, polymers, electronic materials, biomaterials.

The Ohio State University, Graduate School, College of Engineering, Department of Materials Science and Engineering, Columbus, OH 43210. Offers MS, PhD. *Faculty:* 26. *Students:* 74 full-time (19 women), 35 part-time (9 women); includes 3 minority (1 Asian American or Pacific Islander, 2 Hispanic Americans), 55 international. Average age 26. In 2009, 15 master's, 19 doctorates awarded. *Degree requirements:* For master's, thesis; for doctorate, thesis/dissertation. *Entrance requirements:* For master's and doctorate, GRE (for graduates of foreign universities and holders of non-engineering degrees). Additional exam requirements/recommendations for international students: Recommended—TOEFL (minimum score 600 paper-based; 250 computer-based). *Application deadline:* For fall admission, 8/15 priority date for domestic students, 7/1 priority date for international students; for winter admission, 12/1 priority date for domestic students, 11/1 priority date for international students; for spring admission, 3/1 priority date for domestic students, 2/1 priority date for international students. Applications are processed on a rolling basis. Application fee: $40 ($50 for international students). Electronic applications accepted. *Expenses:* Tuition, state resident: full-time $10,683. Tuition, nonresident: full-time $25,923. Tuition and fees vary according to course load and program. *Financial support:* In 2009–10, fellowships (averaging $43,000 per year), research assistantships (averaging $40,700 per year) were awarded; teaching assistantships, career-related internships or fieldwork, scholarships/grants, and unspecified assistantships also available. *Faculty research:* Computational materials modeling, biomaterials, metallurgy, ceramics, advanced alloys/composites. Total annual research expenditures: $10 million. *Unit head:* Suliman A. Dregia, Graduate Studies Committee Chair, 614-688-3050, Fax: 614-292-4668, E-mail: dregia.1@osu.edu. *Application contact:* 614-292-9444, Fax: 614-292-3895, E-mail: domestic.grad@osu.edu.

Oregon State University, Graduate School, College of Engineering, School of Mechanical, Industrial, and Manufacturing Engineering, Program in Materials Science, Corvallis, OR 97331. Offers MAIS, MS, PhD. *Students:* 26 full-time (9 women), 2 part-time (0 women); includes 2 minority (1 Asian American or Pacific Islander, 1 Hispanic American), 11 international. Average age 30. In 2009, 2 master's, 3 doctorates awarded. *Degree requirements:* For master's, thesis or alternative. *Entrance requirements:* For master's, GRE General Test, minimum GPA of 3.0 in last 90 hours of course work. Additional exam requirements/recommendations for international students: Required—TOEFL (minimum score 550 paper-based; 213 computer-based). *Application deadline:* For fall admission, 3/1 for domestic students. Applications are processed on a rolling basis. Application fee: $50. *Expenses:* Tuition, state resident: full-time $9774; part-time $362 per credit. Tuition, nonresident: full-time $15,849; part-time $587 per credit. Required fees: $1639. Full-time tuition and fees vary according to course load and program. *Financial support:* Fellowships, research assistantships, teaching assistantships, Federal Work-Study and institutionally sponsored loans available. Support available to part-time students. Financial award application deadline: 2/1. *Unit head:* Dr. William Warnes, Director, 541-737-2016, Fax: 541-737-2600, E-mail: matsci@oregonstate.edu. *Application contact:* Dr. William Warnes, Director, 541-737-2016, Fax: 541-737-2600, E-mail: matsci@oregonstate.edu.

Penn State University Park, Graduate School, College of Earth and Mineral Sciences, Department of Materials Science and Engineering, State College, University Park, PA 16802-1503. Offers MS, PhD.

Penn State University Park, Graduate School, Intercollege Graduate Programs, State College, University Park, PA 16802-1503. Offers acoustics (M Eng, MS, PhD); bioengineering (MS, PhD); biogeochemistry (dual) (PhD); business administration (MBA); cell and developmental biology (PhD); demography (dual) (MA); ecology (MS, PhD); environmental pollution control (MEPC, MS); genetics (MS, PhD); human dimensions of natural resources and the environment (dual) (MA, MS, PhD); immunology and infectious diseases (MS); integrative biosciences (MS, PhD), including integrative biosciences; materials science and engineering (PhD); operations research (dual) (M Eng, MA, MS, PhD); physiology (MS, PhD); plant physiology (MS, PhD); quality and manufacturing management (MMM). *Students:* 371 full-time (157 women), 22 part-time (7 women). Average age 27. 1,074 applicants, 18% accepted, 130 enrolled. *Entrance requirements:* Additional exam requirements/recommendations for international students: Required—TOEFL (minimum score 550 paper-based; 213 computer-based; 80 iBT). *Application deadline:* Applications are processed on a rolling basis. Application fee: $45. Electronic applications accepted. *Financial support:* Fellowships, research assistantships, teaching assistantships available. Financial award applicants required to submit FAFSA. *Unit head:* Dr. Regina Vasilatos-Younken, Senior Associate Dean, 814-865-2516, Fax: 814-863-4627, E-mail: rxv@psu.edu. *Application contact:* Cynthia E. Nicosia, Director, Graduate Enrollment Services, 814-865-1795, Fax: 814-865-4627, E-mail: cey1@psu.edu.

Polytechnic Institute of NYU, Department of Mechanical and Aerospace Engineering, Major in Materials Science, Brooklyn, NY 11201-2990. Offers MS. Part-time and evening/weekend programs available. *Students:* 1 (woman) full-time, all international. 7 applicants, 43% accepted, 1 enrolled. *Degree requirements:* For master's, comprehensive exam (for some programs), project or thesis. *Entrance requirements:* Additional exam requirements/recommendations for international students: Required—TOEFL (minimum score 550 paper-based; 213 computer-based; 80 iBT); Recommended—IELTS (minimum score 6.5). *Application deadline:* For fall admission, 7/31 priority date for domestic students, 4/30 priority date for international students; for spring admission, 12/31 priority date for domestic students, 11/30 priority date for international students. Applications are processed on a rolling basis. Application fee: $75. Electronic applications accepted. *Expenses:* Tuition: Full-time $21,492; part-time $1194 per credit hour. Required fees: $1160; $204 per course. *Financial support:* Fellowships, research assistantships, teaching assistantships, institutionally sponsored loans, scholarships/grants, and unspecified assistantships available. Support available to part-time students. Financial award applicants required to submit FAFSA. *Faculty research:* Studies of materials for aerospace, electronics, and energy-related applications; alloy hardening; deformation and fracture; phase transformations. *Unit head:* Dr. George Vradis, Head, 718-260-3875, Fax: 718-260-3532, E-mail: gvradis@poly.edu. *Application contact:* JeanCarlo Bonilla, Director of Graduate Enrollment Management, 718-260-3182, Fax: 718-260-3624, E-mail: gradinfo@poly.edu.

Princeton University, Princeton Institute for the Science and Technology of Materials (PRISM), Princeton, NJ 08544-1019. Offers materials (PhD).

Rensselaer Polytechnic Institute, Graduate School, School of Engineering, Department of Materials Science and Engineering, Troy, NY 12180. Offers ceramics and glass science (M Eng, MS, PhD); composites (M Eng, MS, PhD); electronic materials (M Eng, MS, PhD); metallurgy (M Eng, MS, PhD); polymers (M Eng, MS, PhD). Part-time and evening/weekend programs available. *Faculty:* 16 full-time (2 women). *Students:* 54 full-time (11 women), 4 part-time (1 woman); includes 7 minority (all Asian Americans or Pacific Islanders), 30 international. Average age 24. 234 applicants, 14% accepted, 14 enrolled. In 2009, 10 master's, 6 doctorates awarded. Terminal master's awarded for partial completion of doctoral program. *Degree requirements:* For master's, thesis; for doctorate, comprehensive exam, thesis/dissertation. *Entrance requirements:* For master's and doctorate, GRE. Additional exam requirements/recommendations for international students: Required—TOEFL (minimum score 570 paper-based; 230 computer-based; 88 iBT). *Application deadline:* For fall admission, 1/15 priority date for domestic and international students; for spring admission, 8/31 priority date for domestic and international students. Applications are processed on a rolling basis. Application fee: $75. Electronic applications accepted. *Expenses:* Tuition: Full-time $38,100. *Financial support:* In 2009–10, 50 students received support, including fellowships with full tuition reimbursements available (averaging $24,750 per year), 40 research assistantships with full tuition reimbursements available (averaging $24,750 per year), 13 teaching assistantships with full tuition reimbursements available (averaging $24,750 per year); career-related internships or fieldwork, institutionally sponsored loans, and unspecified assistantships also available. Financial award application deadline: 2/1. *Faculty research:* Materials processing, nanostructural materials, materials for microelectronics, composite materials, computational materials. Total annual research expenditures: $5 million. *Unit head:* Dr. Robert Hull, Department Head, 518-276-6373, Fax: 518-276-8554, E-mail: hullr2@rpi.edu. *Application contact:* Dr. Pawel Keblinski, Admissions Coordinator, 518-276-6858, Fax: 518-276-8554, E-mail: keblip@rpi.edu.

Rice University, Graduate Programs, George R. Brown School of Engineering, Department of Mechanical Engineering and Materials Science, Houston, TX 77251-1892. Offers materials science (MMS, MS, PhD); mechanical engineering (MME, MS, PhD); MBA/ME. Part-time programs available. *Faculty:* 16 full-time (2 women), 8 part-time/adjunct (0 women). *Students:* 56 full-time (13 women), 9 part-time (1 woman); includes 13 minority (2 African Americans, 2 Asian Americans or Pacific Islanders, 9 Hispanic Americans), 35 international. Average age 24. 270 applicants, 13% accepted, 26 enrolled. In 2009, 4 master's, 3 doctorates awarded. Terminal master's awarded for partial completion of doctoral program. *Degree requirements:* For master's, comprehensive exam, thesis; for doctorate, comprehensive exam, thesis/dissertation. *Entrance requirements:* For master's and doctorate, GRE General Test, minimum GPA of 3.0. Additional exam requirements/recommendations for international students: Required—TOEFL (minimum score 600 paper-based; 250 computer-based; 90 iBT), IELTS (minimum score 7). *Application deadline:* For fall admission, 2/1 priority date for domestic and international students; for spring admission, 11/15 priority date for domestic students, 11/1 priority date for international students. Applications are processed on a rolling basis. Application fee: $70. Electronic applications accepted. *Financial support:* In 2009–10, 41 students received support, including 9 fellowships with full tuition reimbursements available (averaging $14,000 per year), 31 research assistantships with full tuition reimbursements available (averaging

Materials Sciences

Rice University (continued)
$14,000 per year), 1 teaching assistantship with full tuition reimbursement available (averaging $14,000 per year). Financial award application deadline: 2/1. *Faculty research:* Heat transfer, biomedical engineering, fluid dynamics, aero-astronautics, control systems/robotics, materials science. Total annual research expenditures: $2.2 million. *Unit head:* Dr. Enrique V. Barrera, Chair, 713-348-4906, Fax: 713-348-5423, E-mail: mems@rice.edu. *Application contact:* Judith D. Farhat, Graduate Coordinator, 713-348-3582, Fax: 713-348-5423, E-mail: mems@rice.edu.

Rochester Institute of Technology, Graduate Enrollment Services, College of Science, Center for Materials Science and Engineering, Rochester, NY 14623-5603. Offers MS. Part-time and evening/weekend programs available. *Students:* 9 full-time (4 women), 10 part-time (1 woman), 13 international. Average age 29. 33 applicants, 61% accepted, 4 enrolled. In 2009, 8 master's awarded. *Degree requirements:* For master's, thesis or project. *Entrance requirements:* For master's, GRE (recommended), minimum GPA of 3.0. Additional exam requirements/recommendations for international students: Required—TOEFL (minimum score 575 paper-based; 233 computer-based; 90 iBT), or IELTS (minimum score 6.5). *Application deadline:* For fall admission, 2/15 priority date for domestic and international students; for winter admission, 11/1 for domestic students, 10/1 for international students; for spring admission, 2/1 for domestic students, 1/1 for international students. Applications are processed on a rolling basis. Application fee: $50. Electronic applications accepted. *Expenses:* Tuition: Full-time $31,533; part-time $876 per credit hour. Required fees: $210. *Financial support:* In 2009–10, 10 students received support; research assistantships with partial tuition reimbursements available, teaching assistantships with partial tuition reimbursements available, career-related internships or fieldwork, scholarships/grants, tuition waivers (partial), and unspecified assistantships available. Support available to part-time students. Financial award application deadline: 7/29; financial award applicants required to submit FAFSA. *Faculty research:* VUV modification of polymers, stress and morphology of sputtered copper films, MRI applications to materials problems. *Unit head:* Dr. K. S. V. Santhanam, Program Director, 585-475-2920, E-mail: kssssch@rit.edu. *Application contact:* Diane Ellison, Assistant Vice President, Graduate Enrollment Services, 585-475-2229, Fax: 585-475-7164, E-mail: gradinfo@rit.edu.

Royal Military College of Canada, Division of Graduate Studies and Research, Engineering Division, Program in Chemical and Materials Science, Kingston, ON K7K 7B4, Canada. Offers M Sc, PhD. *Degree requirements:* For master's, thesis; for doctorate, comprehensive exam, thesis/dissertation. *Entrance requirements:* For master's, honours degree with second-class standing; for doctorate, master's degree. Electronic applications accepted.

Rutgers, The State University of New Jersey, New Brunswick, Graduate School-New Brunswick, Program in Materials Science and Engineering, Piscataway, NJ 08854-8097. Offers MS, PhD. Part-time programs available. *Degree requirements:* For master's, thesis; for doctorate, comprehensive exam, thesis/dissertation. *Entrance requirements:* For master's and doctorate, GRE General Test. Electronic applications accepted. *Faculty research:* Ceramic processing, nanostructured materials, electrical and structural ceramics, fiber optics.

School of the Art Institute of Chicago, Graduate Division, Department of Fiber and Material Studies, Chicago, IL 60603-3103. Offers MFA. *Accreditation:* NASAD. *Entrance requirements:* Additional exam requirements/recommendations for international students: Required—TOEFL, IELTS.

South Dakota School of Mines and Technology, Graduate Division, College of Engineering, Doctoral Program in Materials Engineering and Science, Rapid City, SD 57701-3995. Offers PhD. Part-time programs available. *Faculty:* 6 full-time (0 women), 1 part-time/adjunct (0 women). *Students:* 10 full-time (1 woman), 4 part-time (0 women), 9 international. Average age 35. 11 applicants, 64% accepted, 1 enrolled. In 2009, 5 doctorates awarded. *Degree requirements:* For doctorate, thesis/dissertation. *Entrance requirements:* For doctorate, GRE General Test, minimum graduate GPA of 3.0, 3 letters of recommendation. Additional exam requirements/recommendations for international students: Required—TOEFL, TWE. *Application deadline:* For fall admission, 7/1 priority date for domestic students, 4/1 for international students; for spring admission, 11/1 for domestic students, 9/1 for international students. Applications are processed on a rolling basis. Application fee: $35. Electronic applications accepted. *Expenses:* Tuition, state resident: full-time $3340; part-time $139 per credit hour. Tuition, nonresident: full-time $7060; part-time $294 per credit hour. Required fees: $3270. *Financial support:* In 2009–10, 1 fellowship (averaging $1,000 per year), 6 research assistantships with partial tuition reimbursements (averaging $15,390 per year), teaching assistantships with partial tuition reimbursements (averaging $4,482 per year) were awarded; Federal Work-Study and institutionally sponsored loans also available. Support available to part-time students. Financial award application deadline: 5/15. *Faculty research:* Thermophysical properties of solids, development of multiphase materials and composites, concrete technology, electronic polymer materials. *Unit head:* Dr. Jon Kellar, Chair, 605-394-2343, E-mail: jon.kellar@sdsmt.edu. *Application contact:* Jeannette R. Nilson, Administrative Support Coordinator, Graduate Education, 800-454-8162 Ext. 1206, Fax: 605-394-5360, E-mail: graduate_admissions@sdsmt.edu.

South Dakota School of Mines and Technology, Graduate Division, College of Engineering, Master's Program in Materials Engineering and Science, Rapid City, SD 57701-3995. Offers chemistry (MS); metallurgical engineering (MS); physics (MS). *Faculty:* 6 full-time (0 women), 1 part-time/adjunct (0 women). *Students:* 9 full-time (1 woman), 9 part-time (2 women), 8 international. Average age 26. 9 applicants, 56% accepted, 1 enrolled. In 2009, 4 master's awarded. *Entrance requirements:* For master's, GRE General Test. Additional exam requirements/recommendations for international students: Required—TOEFL, TWE. *Application deadline:* For fall admission, 7/1 priority date for domestic students, 4/1 for international students; for spring admission, 11/1 for domestic students, 9/1 for international students. Applications are processed on a rolling basis. Application fee: $35. Electronic applications accepted. *Expenses:* Tuition, state resident: full-time $3340; part-time $139 per credit hour. Tuition, nonresident: full-time $7060; part-time $294 per credit hour. Required fees: $3270. *Financial support:* In 2009–10, 15 research assistantships with partial tuition reimbursements (averaging $11,400 per year), 11 teaching assistantships with partial tuition reimbursements (averaging $4,063 per year) were awarded; fellowships also available. Financial award application deadline: 5/15. *Unit head:* Dr. Jon Kellar, Chair, 605-394-2343, E-mail: jon.kellar@sdsmt.edu. *Application contact:* Jeannette R. Nilson, Administrative Support Coordinator, Graduate Education, 800-454-8162 Ext. 1206, Fax: 605-394-5360, E-mail: graduate_admissions@sdsmt.edu.

Stanford University, School of Engineering, Department of Materials Science and Engineering, Stanford, CA 94305-9991. Offers MS, PhD, Eng. Terminal master's awarded for partial completion of doctoral program. *Degree requirements:* For doctorate, thesis/dissertation; for Eng, thesis. *Entrance requirements:* For master's, doctorate, and Eng, GRE General Test. Additional exam requirements/recommendations for international students: Required—TOEFL. Electronic applications accepted. *Expenses:* Tuition: Full-time $37,380; part-time $2760 per quarter. Required fees: $501.

State University of New York at Binghamton, Graduate School, Thomas J. Watson School of Engineering and Applied Science and School of Arts and Sciences, Materials Science and Engineering Program, Binghamton, NY 13902-6000. Offers MS, PhD. *Students:* 20 full-time (8 women), 26 part-time (2 women); includes 4 minority (all Asian Americans or Pacific Islanders), 34 international. Average age 30. 30 applicants, 53% accepted, 11 enrolled. In 2009, 2 master's, 3 doctorates awarded. Application fee: $60. *Financial support:* In 2009–10, 13 students received support, including 1 fellowship with full tuition reimbursement available (averaging $16,500 per year), 5 research assistantships with full tuition reimbursements available (averaging $16,500 per year), 6 teaching assistantships with full tuition reimbursements available (averaging $16,500 per year); career-related internships or fieldwork, Federal Work-Study, institutionally sponsored loans, scholarships/grants, health care benefits, and unspecified assistantships also available. Financial award applicants required to submit FAFSA. *Unit head:* Dr. Stanley Whittingham, Director, 607-777-4623, E-mail: stanwhit@binghamton.edu. *Application contact:* Victoria Williams, Recruiting and Admissions Coordinator, 607-777-2151, Fax: 607-777-2501, E-mail: vwilliam@binghamton.edu.

Stony Brook University, State University of New York, Graduate School, College of Engineering and Applied Sciences, Department of Materials Science and Engineering, Stony Brook, NY 11794. Offers MS, PhD. *Faculty:* 12 full-time (2 women), 3 part-time/adjunct (0 women). *Students:* 65 full-time (23 women), 8 part-time (1 woman); includes 14 minority (3 African Americans, 9 Asian Americans or Pacific Islanders, 2 Hispanic Americans), 50 international. Average age 28. 81 applicants, 52% accepted. In 2009, 13 master's, 12 doctorates awarded. *Degree requirements:* For master's, thesis or alternative; for doctorate, comprehensive exam, thesis/dissertation. *Entrance requirements:* For master's and doctorate, GRE General Test, minimum undergraduate GPA of 3.0. Additional exam requirements/recommendations for international students: Required—TOEFL. *Application deadline:* For fall admission, 1/15 for domestic students. Application fee: $60. *Expenses:* Tuition, state resident: full-time $8370; part-time $349 per credit. Tuition, nonresident: full-time $13,250; part-time $552 per credit. Required fees: $933. *Financial support:* In 2009–10, 21 research assistantships, 7 teaching assistantships were awarded; fellowships also available. *Faculty research:* Electronic materials, biomaterials, synchrotron topography. Total annual research expenditures: $2.4 million. *Unit head:* Dr. Michael Dudley, Chairman, 631-632-8484. *Application contact:* Dr. Miriam Rafailovich, Director, 631-632-8484, Fax: 631-632-8052, E-mail: mrafailovich.nsf@notes.cc.sunysb.edu.

Texas A&M Health Science Center, Baylor College of Dentistry, Graduate Division, Department of Biomaterials Science, College Station, TX 77840. Offers MS. Part-time programs available. *Degree requirements:* For master's, thesis. *Entrance requirements:* For master's, GRE General Test, DDS or DMD or BS in engineering. Additional exam requirements/recommendations for international students: Required—TOEFL. *Faculty research:* Titanium casting for dental applications, mechanical properties of dental ceramics, metal-ceramic adhesion, fatigue failure of dental implants, orthodontic materials, laser welding.

Trent University, Graduate Studies, Program in Materials Science, Peterborough, ON K9J 7B8, Canada. Offers M Sc.

Université du Québec, Institut National de la Recherche Scientifique, Graduate Programs, Research Center—Energy, Materials and Telecommunications, Québec, QC G1K 9A9, Canada. Offers energy and materials science (M Sc, PhD); telecommunications (M Sc, PhD). Programs given in French. Part-time programs available. *Faculty:* 37. *Students:* 161 full-time (45 women), 10 part-time (1 woman), 76 international. Average age 32. In 2009, 16 master's, 13 doctorates awarded. *Degree requirements:* For master's, thesis; for doctorate, thesis/dissertation. *Entrance requirements:* For master's, appropriate bachelor's degree, proficiency in French; for doctorate, appropriate master's degree, proficiency in French. *Application deadline:* For fall admission, 3/30 for domestic and international students; for winter admission, 11/1 for domestic and international students. Application fee: $30. *Financial support:* Fellowships, research assistantships, teaching assistantships available. *Faculty research:* New energy sources, plasmas, fusion. *Unit head:* Jean-Claude Kieffer, Director, 450-929-8100, Fax: 450-929-8102, E-mail: kieffer@emt.inrs.ca. *Application contact:* Yvonne Boisvert, Registrar, 418-654-3861, Fax: 418-654-3858, E-mail: registrariat@adm.inrs.ca.

University at Buffalo, the State University of New York, Graduate School, School of Dental Medicine, Graduate Programs in Dental Medicine, Department of Oral Diagnostic Sciences, Buffalo, NY 14260. Offers biomaterials (MS). Part-time programs available. *Degree requirements:* For master's, thesis. *Entrance requirements:* Additional exam requirements/recommendations for international students: Required—TOEFL (minimum score 79 iBT). Electronic applications accepted. *Faculty research:* Bioengineering, surface science, bioadhesion, regulatory sterilization.

The University of Alabama, Graduate School, College of Engineering and College of Arts and Sciences, Tri-Campus Materials Science PhD Program, Tuscaloosa, AL 35487. Offers PhD. *Students:* 7 full-time (2 women); includes 1 minority (African American), 5 international. Average age 26. In 2009, 1 degree awarded. *Median time to degree:* Of those who began their doctoral program in fall 2001, 100% received their degree in 8 years or less. *Degree requirements:* For doctorate, comprehensive exam, thesis/dissertation. *Entrance requirements:* For doctorate, GRE General Test. Additional exam requirements/recommendations for international students: Required—TOEFL (minimum score 550 paper-based; 213 computer-based). *Application deadline:* For fall admission, 2/28 priority date for domestic and international students; for spring admission, 10/30 priority date for domestic students, 9/30 priority date for international students. Applications are processed on a rolling basis. Application fee: $50 ($60 for international students). Electronic applications accepted. *Expenses:* Tuition, state resident: full-time $7000. Tuition, nonresident: full-time $19,200. *Financial support:* In 2009–10, 4 research assistantships with full tuition reimbursements (averaging $19,500 per year) were awarded; career-related internships or fieldwork and unspecified assistantships also available. Financial award application deadline: 2/28. *Faculty research:* Magnetic multilayers, metals casting, molecular electronics, conducting polymers, metals physics, electrodeposition. *Unit head:* Prof. Garry Warren, Campus Coordinator, 205-348-4337, E-mail: gwarren@coe.eng.ua.edu. *Application contact:* Dr. David A. Francko, Dean, 205-348-8280, Fax: 205-348-0400, E-mail: dfrancko@ua.edu.

The University of Alabama at Birmingham, School of Engineering, Joint Materials Science PhD Program, Birmingham, AL 35294. Offers PhD. *Degree requirements:* For doctorate, thesis/dissertation. *Entrance requirements:* For doctorate, GRE General Test. Electronic applications accepted. *Faculty research:* Biocompatibility studies with biomaterials, microgravity solidification of proteins and metals, analysis of microelectronic materials, thin film analysis using TEM.

The University of Alabama in Huntsville, School of Graduate Studies, Interdisciplinary Studies, Interdisciplinary Program in Materials Science, Huntsville, AL 35899. Offers MS, PhD. Part-time and evening/weekend programs available. *Faculty:* 31 full-time (4 women). *Students:* 3 full-time (2 women), 3 part-time (0 women), 5 international. Average age 33. 4 applicants, 75% accepted, 1 enrolled. In 2009, 2 master's awarded. *Degree requirements:* For master's, comprehensive exam, thesis or alternative, oral and written exams; for doctorate, comprehensive exam, thesis/dissertation, oral and written exams. *Entrance requirements:* For master's, GRE General Test, minimum GPA of 3.0; for doctorate, GRE General Test, bachelor's degree in engineering or physical science, minimum GPA of 3.0. Additional exam requirements/recommendations for international students: Required—TOEFL (minimum score 500 paper-based; 173 computer-based; 62 iBT). *Application deadline:* For fall admission, 7/15 for domestic students, 4/1 for international students; for spring admission, 11/30 for domestic students, 9/1 for international students. Applications are processed on a rolling basis. Application fee: $40 ($50 for international students). Electronic applications accepted. *Expenses:* Tuition, state resident: part-time $355.75 per credit hour. Tuition, nonresident: part-time $847.10 per credit hour. Required fees: $210.80 per semester. Tuition and fees vary according to course load and program. *Financial support:* In 2009–10, 5 students received support, including 1 research assistantship with full and partial tuition reimbursement available (averaging $12,000 per year), 2 teaching assistantships with full and partial tuition reimbursements available (averaging $11,116 per year); career-related internships or fieldwork, Federal Work-Study, institutionally sponsored loans, scholarships/grants, health care benefits, tuition waivers, and unspecified assistantships also available. Support available to part-time students. Financial award application deadline: 4/1; financial award applicants required to submit FAFSA. *Faculty research:* Materials structure and properties, materials processing, mechanical behavior, macromolecular materials, electronic, optical, and magnetic materials. *Unit head:* Dr. Michael Banish, Coordinator, 256-824-6810, Fax: 256-824-6349, E-mail: banishm@uah.edu. *Application contact:* Kathy Biggs, Graduate Studies Admissions Manager, 256-824-6199, Fax: 256-824-6405, E-mail: deangrad@uah.edu.

The University of Arizona, Graduate College, College of Engineering, Department of Materials Science and Engineering, Tucson, AZ 85721. Offers MS, PhD. Part-time programs available.

Faculty: 12. *Students:* 29 full-time (14 women), 28 part-time (11 women); includes 5 minority (4 Asian Americans or Pacific Islanders, 1 Hispanic American), 19 international. Average age 30. 82 applicants, 20% accepted, 6 enrolled. In 2009, 5 master's, 5 doctorates awarded. *Degree requirements:* For master's, thesis (for some programs); for doctorate, comprehensive exam, thesis/dissertation. *Entrance requirements:* For master's and doctorate, GRE General Test, 3 letters of recommendation, statement of purpose. Additional exam requirements/ recommendations for international students: Required—TOEFL (minimum score 550 paper-based; 213 computer-based). *Application deadline:* Applications are processed on a rolling basis. Application fee: $75. Electronic applications accepted. *Expenses:* Tuition, state resident: full-time $9028. Tuition, nonresident: full-time $24,890. *Financial support:* In 2009–10, 20 research assistantships with full tuition reimbursements (averaging $18,093 per year), 1 teaching assistantship with full tuition reimbursement (averaging $15,176 per year) were awarded; institutionally sponsored loans, scholarships/grants, health care benefits, tuition waivers (full), and unspecified assistantships also available. Financial award application deadline: 12/31. *Faculty research:* High-technology ceramics, optical materials, electronic materials, chemical metallurgy, science of materials. Total annual research expenditures: $1.9 million. *Unit head:* Dr. Joseph H. Simmons, Head, 520-621-6070, Fax: 520-621-8059, E-mail: simmons@mse.arizona.edu. *Application contact:* Information Contact, 520-626-6762, Fax: 520-621-8059, E-mail: msed@email.arizona.edu.

The University of British Columbia, Faculty of Applied Science, Department of Materials Engineering, Vancouver, BC V6T 1Z1, Canada. Offers materials and metallurgy (M Sc, PhD); metals and materials engineering (MA Sc, PhD). *Degree requirements:* For master's, comprehensive exam, thesis; for doctorate, comprehensive exam, thesis/dissertation. *Entrance requirements:* Additional exam requirements/recommendations for international students: Required—TOEFL (minimum score 560 paper-based; 220 computer-based; 83 iBT). Electronic applications accepted. *Faculty research:* Electroslag melting, mathematical modeling, solidification and hydrometallurgy.

University of California, Berkeley, Graduate Division, College of Engineering, Department of Materials Science and Engineering, Berkeley, CA 94720-1500. Offers engineering (M Eng, MS, D Eng, PhD); engineering science (M Eng, MS, PhD). *Faculty:* 15 full-time. *Students:* 87 full-time (33 women). Average age 27. 273 applicants, 15 enrolled. In 2009, 14 master's, 18 doctorates awarded. *Degree requirements:* For master's, comprehensive exam or thesis (MS); for doctorate, comprehensive exam, thesis/dissertation, qualifying exam. *Entrance requirements:* For master's and doctorate, GRE General Test, minimum GPA of 3.0, 3 letters of recommendation. Additional exam requirements/recommendations for international students: Required—TOEFL (minimum score 230 computer-based). *Application deadline:* For fall admission, 12/10 for domestic students. Application fee: $70 ($90 for international students). *Financial support:* Fellowships, research assistantships, teaching assistantships, unspecified assistantships available. *Faculty research:* Ceramics, biomaterials, structural, electronic, magnetic and optical materials. *Unit head:* Prof. Robert Ritchie, Chair, 510-642-3801, Fax: 510-643-5792. *Application contact:* Janene Carol Martinez, Student Affairs Officer, 510-642-0716, Fax: 510-643-5792, E-mail: gradoffice@lists.berkeley.edu.

University of California, Davis, College of Engineering, Program in Materials Science and Engineering, Davis, CA 95616. Offers MS, PhD. Terminal master's awarded for partial completion of doctoral program. *Degree requirements:* For master's, comprehensive exam (for some programs), thesis (for some programs); for doctorate, comprehensive exam, thesis/dissertation. *Entrance requirements:* Additional exam requirements/recommendations for international students: Required—TOEFL (minimum score 550 paper-based; 213 computer-based).

University of California, Irvine, Office of Graduate Studies, School of Engineering, Department of Chemical Engineering and Materials Science, Irvine, CA 92697. Offers chemical and biochemical engineering (MS, PhD); materials science and engineering (MS, PhD). Part-time programs available. *Students:* 78 full-time (24 women), 7 part-time (2 women); includes 22 minority (1 American Indian/Alaska Native, 19 Asian Americans or Pacific Islanders, 2 Hispanic Americans), 37 international. Average age 27. 281 applicants, 25% accepted, 25 enrolled. In 2009, 26 master's, 4 doctorates awarded. Terminal master's awarded for partial completion of doctoral program. *Degree requirements:* For doctorate, thesis/dissertation. *Entrance requirements:* For master's and doctorate, GRE General Test, minimum GPA of 3.0, 3 letters of recommendation. Additional exam requirements/recommendations for international students: Required—TOEFL (minimum score 550 paper-based; 213 computer-based). *Application deadline:* For fall admission, 1/15 priority date for domestic students, 1/15 for international students. Applications are processed on a rolling basis. Application fee: $70 ($90 for international students). Electronic applications accepted. *Financial support:* In 2009–10, fellowships with tuition reimbursements (averaging $14,656 per year); research assistantships with full tuition reimbursements, teaching assistantships with tuition reimbursements, institutionally sponsored loans, traineeships, health care benefits, and unspecified assistantships also available. Financial award application deadline: 3/1; financial award applicants required to submit FAFSA. *Faculty research:* Molecular biotechnology, nano-bio-materials, biophotonics, synthesis, superplasticity and mechanical behavior, characterization of advanced and nanostructural materials. *Unit head:* Dr. Stanley Grant, Director, 949-824-8277, Fax: 949-824-2541, E-mail: sbgrant@uci.edu. *Application contact:* Beatrice Mei, Graduate Coordinator, 949-824-3887, Fax: 949-824-2541, E-mail: bmei@uci.edu.

University of California, Irvine, Office of Graduate Studies, School of Physical Sciences, Department of Chemistry and Department of Physics and Astronomy, Program in Chemical and Materials Physics (CHAMP), Irvine, CA 92697. Offers MS, PhD. *Students:* 25 full-time (7 women); includes 5 minority (4 Asian Americans or Pacific Islanders, 1 Hispanic American), 2 international. Average age 27. 22 applicants, 18% accepted, 1 enrolled. In 2009, 7 master's, 4 doctorates awarded. *Degree requirements:* For doctorate, thesis/dissertation. *Entrance requirements:* For master's and doctorate, GRE General Test, GRE Subject Test, minimum GPA of 3.0. *Application deadline:* For fall admission, 1/15 priority date for domestic students, 1/15 for international students. Applications are processed on a rolling basis. Application fee: $70 ($90 for international students). Electronic applications accepted. *Financial support:* Fellowships, research assistantships with full tuition reimbursements, teaching assistantships, institutionally sponsored loans, traineeships, health care benefits, and unspecified assistantships available. Financial award application deadline: 3/1; financial award applicants required to submit FAFSA. *Unit head:* Dr. Kenneth Janda, Chemistry Graduate Advisor, 949-824-5266. *Application contact:* Jim Rutledge, Advisor, 949-824-5141, E-mail: jrutledg@uci.edu.

University of California, Los Angeles, Graduate Division, Henry Samueli School of Engineering and Applied Science, Department of Materials Science and Engineering, Los Angeles, CA 90095-1595. Offers MS, PhD. *Faculty:* 11 full-time (2 women). *Students:* 91 full-time (25 women); includes 16 minority (1 African American, 12 Asian Americans or Pacific Islanders, 3 Hispanic Americans), 51 international. In 2009, 14 master's, 7 doctorates awarded. *Degree requirements:* For master's, comprehensive exam or thesis; for doctorate, thesis/dissertation, qualifying exams. *Entrance requirements:* For master's, GRE General Test, minimum GPA of 3.0; for doctorate, GRE General Test, minimum GPA of 3.25. Additional exam requirements/recommendations for international students: Required—TOEFL (minimum score 560 paper-based; 220 computer-based). *Application deadline:* For fall admission, 12/15 for domestic and international students. Application fee: $70 ($90 for international students). Electronic applications accepted. *Financial support:* In 2009–10, 24 fellowships, 250 research assistantships, 35 teaching assistantships were awarded; Federal Work-Study, institutionally sponsored loans, and tuition waivers (full and partial) also available. Financial award application deadline: 1/15; financial award applicants required to submit FAFSA. Total annual research expenditures: $5.1 million. *Unit head:* Dr. Jenn-Ming Yang, Chair, 310-825-2758, E-mail: jyang@seas.ucla.edu. *Application contact:* Paradee Chularee, Student Affairs Officer, 310-825-8913, Fax: 310-206-7353, E-mail: paradee@ea.ucla.edu.

University of California, Riverside, Graduate Division, Graduate Materials Science and Engineering Program, Riverside, CA 92521-0102. Offers MS, PhD.

University of California, San Diego, Office of Graduate Studies, Materials Science and Engineering Program, La Jolla, CA 92093. Offers MS, PhD. *Degree requirements:* For doctorate, thesis/dissertation. *Entrance requirements:* For master's and doctorate, GRE General Test, minimum GPA of 3.0. Additional exam requirements/recommendations for international students: Required—TOEFL. Electronic applications accepted.

University of California, Santa Barbara, Graduate Division, College of Engineering, Department of Materials, Santa Barbara, CA 93106-5050. Offers materials science and engineering (MS, PhD); MS/PhD. *Faculty:* 35 full-time (3 women). *Students:* 105 full-time (27 women). Average age 26. 291 applicants, 22% accepted, 15 enrolled. In 2009, 4 master's, 15 doctorates awarded. Terminal master's awarded for partial completion of doctoral program. *Degree requirements:* For master's, comprehensive exam, thesis or alternative; for doctorate, comprehensive exam, thesis/dissertation. *Entrance requirements:* For master's, GRE General Test, 3 letters of recommendation, resume/curriculum vitae; for doctorate, GRE General Test, 3 letters of recommendation, statement of purpose, personal achievements/contributions statement, resume/curriculum vitae, transcripts for post-secondary institutions attended. Additional exam requirements/recommendations for international students: Required—TOEFL (minimum score 600 paper-based; 213 computer-based; 100 iBT) or IELTS (minimum score 7). *Application deadline:* For fall admission, 1/5 for domestic and international students; for winter admission, 11/1 for domestic and international students; for spring admission, 1/1 for domestic and international students. Application fee: $70 ($90 for international students). Electronic applications accepted. *Financial support:* In 2009–10, 100 students received support, including 52 fellowships with full and partial tuition reimbursements available (averaging $8,600 per year), 91 research assistantships with full and partial tuition reimbursements available (averaging $12,200 per year), 23 teaching assistantships with partial tuition reimbursements available (averaging $2,200 per year); career-related internships or fieldwork, Federal Work-Study, institutionally sponsored loans, scholarships/grants, traineeships, health care benefits, and unspecified assistantships also available. Financial award application deadline: 1/28; financial award applicants required to submit FAFSA. *Faculty research:* Electronic materials, structural materials, inorganic materials, macromolecular materials, biomolecular materials. *Unit head:* Dr. James S. Speck, Chair, 805-893-8005, Fax: 805-893-8486, E-mail: speck@mrl.ucsb.edu. *Application contact:* Constance Callinicos, Student Affairs Officer, 805-893-4601, Fax: 805-893-8486, E-mail: callinic@engineering.ucsb.edu.

University of Central Florida, College of Engineering and Computer Science, Department of Mechanical, Materials, and Aerospace Engineering, Program in Materials Science and Engineering, Orlando, FL 32816. Offers MSMSE, PhD. *Students:* 50 full-time (9 women), 14 part-time (3 women); includes 8 minority (1 American Indian/Alaska Native, 2 Asian Americans or Pacific Islanders, 5 Hispanic Americans), 3 international. Average age 29. 61 applicants, 34% accepted, 14 enrolled. In 2009, 10 master's, 8 doctorates awarded. *Degree requirements:* For master's, thesis or alternative; for doctorate, thesis/dissertation, candidacy exam, departmental qualifying exam. *Application deadline:* For fall admission, 7/15 priority date for domestic students; for spring admission, 12/1 priority date for domestic students. Application fee: $30. Electronic applications accepted. *Expenses:* Tuition, state resident: part-time $306.31 per credit hour. Tuition, nonresident: part-time $1099.01 per credit hour. Part-time tuition and fees vary according to degree level and program. *Financial support:* In 2009–10, 41 students received support, including 12 fellowships (averaging $2,200 per year), 42 research assistantships (averaging $9,700 per year), 2 teaching assistantships (averaging $9,700 per year).

University of Cincinnati, Graduate School, College of Engineering, Department of Chemical and Materials Engineering, Cincinnati, OH 45221. Offers chemical engineering (MS, PhD); materials science and metallurgical engineering (MS, PhD), including ceramic science and engineering, materials science and engineering, metallurgical engineering, polymer science and engineering. Part-time and evening/weekend programs available. Terminal master's awarded for partial completion of doctoral program. *Degree requirements:* For master's, thesis; for doctorate, thesis/dissertation. *Entrance requirements:* For master's and doctorate, GRE General Test. Additional exam requirements/recommendations for international students: Required—TOEFL. Electronic applications accepted. *Faculty research:* Process synthesis, aerosol processes, clean coal technology, membrane technology.

University of Cincinnati, Graduate School, College of Engineering, Department of Chemical and Materials Engineering, Program in Materials Science and Metallurgical Engineering, Program in Materials Science and Engineering, Cincinnati, OH 45221. Offers MS, PhD. Evening/weekend programs available. *Degree requirements:* For master's, thesis optional; for doctorate, one foreign language, comprehensive exam, thesis/dissertation, oral English proficiency exam. *Entrance requirements:* For master's and doctorate, GRE General Test, BS in related field, minimum undergraduate GPA of 3.0. Additional exam requirements/ recommendations for international students: Required—TOEFL. Electronic applications accepted. *Faculty research:* Polymer characterization, surface analysis, and adhesion; mechanical behavior of high-temperature materials; composites; electrochemistry of materials.

University of Connecticut, Graduate School, School of Engineering, Department of Chemical, Materials and Biomolecular Engineering, Field of Materials Science and Engineering, Storrs, CT 06269. Offers MS, PhD. *Faculty:* 36 full-time (6 women). *Students:* 18 full-time (10 women), 1 part-time (0 women); includes 2 minority (both Hispanic Americans), 15 international. Average age 30. 17 applicants, 6% accepted, 1 enrolled. In 2009, 1 master's awarded. Terminal master's awarded for partial completion of doctoral program. *Degree requirements:* For master's, comprehensive exam; for doctorate, thesis/dissertation. *Entrance requirements:* For master's and doctorate, GRE General Test, GRE Subject Test. Additional exam requirements/ recommendations for international students: Required—TOEFL (minimum score 550 paper-based; 213 computer-based). *Application deadline:* For fall admission, 2/1 priority date for domestic and international students; for spring admission, 11/1 for domestic students, 10/1 for international students. Applications are processed on a rolling basis. Application fee: $55. Electronic applications accepted. *Expenses:* Tuition, state resident: full-time $4725; part-time $525 per credit. Tuition, nonresident: full-time $12,267; part-time $1363 per credit. Required fees: $346 per semester. Tuition and fees vary according to course load. *Financial support:* In 2009–10, 16 research assistantships with full tuition reimbursements were awarded; fellowships, teaching assistantships with full tuition reimbursements, Federal Work-Study, scholarships/ grants, health care benefits, and unspecified assistantships also available. Financial award application deadline: 2/1; financial award applicants required to submit FAFSA. *Unit head:* Mark Aindow, Program Director, 860-486-2644, Fax: 860-486-2959, E-mail: m.aindow@uconn.edu. *Application contact:* Mark Aindow, Program Director, 860-486-2644, Fax: 860-486-2959, E-mail: m.aindow@uconn.edu.

University of Connecticut, Institute of Materials Science, Storrs, CT 06269. Offers MS, PhD. *Expenses:* Tuition, state resident: full-time $4725; part-time $525 per credit. Tuition, nonresident: full-time $12,267; part-time $1363 per credit. Required fees: $346 per semester. Tuition and fees vary according to course load. *Application contact:* Anne K. Lanzit, Associate Director of Graduate Admissions, 860-486-3617, Fax: 860-486-6739, E-mail: anne.lanzit@uconn.edu.

University of Delaware, College of Engineering, Department of Materials Science and Engineering, Newark, DE 19716. Offers MMSE, PhD. Terminal master's awarded for partial completion of doctoral program. *Degree requirements:* For master's, thesis; for doctorate, thesis/dissertation. *Entrance requirements:* For master's and doctorate, GRE General Test, 3 letters of recommendation, minimum GPA of 3.2. Additional exam requirements/ recommendations for international students: Required—TOEFL. Electronic applications accepted. *Faculty research:* Thin films and self assembly, drug delivery and tissue engineering, biomaterials and nanocomposites, semiconductor and oxide interfaces, electronic and magnetic materials.

University of Florida, Graduate School, College of Engineering, Department of Materials Science and Engineering, Gainesville, FL 32611. Offers ME, MS, PhD, Engr, JD/MS. *Degree requirements:* For master's and Engr, thesis optional; for doctorate, thesis/dissertation. *Entrance requirements:* For master's and doctorate, GRE General Test, minimum GPA of 3.0; for Engr, GRE General Test. Additional exam requirements/recommendations for international students:

Materials Sciences

University of Florida (continued)
Required—TOEFL (minimum score 550 paper-based; 213 computer-based). Electronic applications accepted. *Faculty research:* Polymeric materials, electronic materials, glass, biomaterials, composites.

University of Idaho, College of Graduate Studies, College of Engineering, Department of Materials Science and Engineering, Program in Materials Science and Engineering, Moscow, ID 83844-2282. Offers materials science and engineering (PhD), including mining engineering; metallurgical engineering (MS). *Students:* 6 full-time, 1 part-time. In 2009, 5 master's, 1 doctorate awarded. *Expenses:* Tuition, state resident: full-time $6120. Tuition, nonresident: full-time $17,712. *Unit head:* Dr. Wudneh Admassu, Chair, 208-885-6376. *Application contact:* Dr. Wudneh Admassu, Chair, 208-885-6376.

University of Illinois at Urbana–Champaign, Graduate College, College of Engineering, Department of Materials Science and Engineering, Champaign, IL 61820. Offers MS, PhD, MS/MBA, PhD/MBA. *Faculty:* 25 full-time (3 women), 1 part-time/adjunct (0 women). *Students:* 154 full-time (38 women), 5 part-time (1 woman); includes 20 minority (18 Asian Americans or Pacific Islanders, 2 Hispanic Americans), 84 international. 336 applicants, 23% accepted, 29 enrolled. In 2009, 5 master's, 29 doctorates awarded. *Entrance requirements:* For master's and doctorate, GRE, minimum GPA of 3.0. Additional exam requirements/recommendations for international students: Required—TOEFL (minimum score 613 paper-based; 257 computer-based; 103 iBT), or IELTS (minimum score 7). *Application deadline:* Applications are processed on a rolling basis. Application fee: $60 ($75 for international students). Electronic applications accepted. *Financial support:* In 2009–10, 18 fellowships, 135 research assistantships, 20 teaching assistantships were awarded; tuition waivers (full and partial) also available. *Unit head:* Robert S. Averback, Interim Head, 217-333-4302, Fax: 217-333-2736, E-mail: averback@illinois.edu. *Application contact:* Michelle L. Malloch, Office Support Associate, 217-333-8517, Fax: 217-333-2736, E-mail: malloch@illinois.edu.

University of Kentucky, Graduate School, College of Engineering, Program in Materials Science, Lexington, KY 40506-0032. Offers materials science and engineering (MSMAE, PhD). *Degree requirements:* For master's, comprehensive exam, thesis optional; for doctorate, comprehensive exam, thesis/dissertation. *Entrance requirements:* For master's, GRE General Test, minimum undergraduate GPA of 2.75; for doctorate, GRE General Test, minimum undergraduate GPA of 3.0. Additional exam requirements/recommendations for international students: Required—TOEFL (minimum score 550 paper-based; 213 computer-based). Electronic applications accepted. *Faculty research:* Physical and mechanical metallurgy, computational material engineering, polymers and composites, high-temperature ceramics, powder metallurgy.

University of Maryland, College Park, Academic Affairs, A. James Clark School of Engineering, Department of Continuing and Distance Learning in Engineering, Professional Program in Engineering, College Park, MD 20742. Offers aerospace engineering (M Eng); chemical engineering (M Eng); civil engineering (M Eng); electrical engineering (M Eng); engineering (Certificate); fire protection engineering (M Eng); materials science and engineering (M Eng); mechanical engineering (M Eng); reliability engineering (M Eng); systems engineering (M Eng). Part-time and evening/weekend programs available. Postbaccalaureate distance learning degree programs offered. *Students:* 50 full-time (15 women), 234 part-time (41 women); includes 91 minority (36 African Americans, 39 Asian Americans or Pacific Islanders, 16 Hispanic Americans), 45 international. 137 applicants, 69% accepted, 77 enrolled. In 2009, 103 master's awarded. *Entrance requirements:* For master's, 3 letters of recommendation. *Application deadline:* For fall admission, 8/15 for domestic students, 1/10 for international students; for spring admission, 12/15 for domestic students, 6/1 for international students. Applications are processed on a rolling basis. Application fee: $60. Electronic applications accepted. *Expenses:* Tuition, area resident: Part-time $471 per credit hour. Tuition, state resident: part-time $471 per credit hour. Tuition, nonresident: part-time $1016 per credit hour. Required fees: $337.04 per term. *Financial support:* In 2009–10, 2 research assistantships with tuition reimbursements (averaging $19,561 per year), 9 teaching assistantships with tuition reimbursements (averaging $16,849 per year) were awarded; fellowships, Federal Work-Study and scholarships/grants also available. Support available to part-time students. Financial award applicants required to submit FAFSA. *Unit head:* Dr. George Syrmos, Director, 301-405-3633, Fax: 301-314-3305, E-mail: syrmos@umd.edu. *Application contact:* Dean of Graduate School, 301-405-0376, Fax: 301-314-9305.

University of Maryland, College Park, Academic Affairs, A. James Clark School of Engineering, Department of Materials and Nuclear Engineering, Materials Science and Engineering Program, College Park, MD 20742. Offers MS, PhD. Part-time and evening/weekend programs available. Postbaccalaureate distance learning degree programs offered. *Faculty:* 67 full-time (10 women), 2 part-time/adjunct (1 woman). *Students:* 70 full-time (20 women), 9 part-time (3 women); includes 18 minority (7 African Americans, 6 Asian Americans or Pacific Islanders, 5 Hispanic Americans), 23 international. 208 applicants, 14% accepted, 14 enrolled. In 2009, 1 master's, 7 doctorates awarded. *Degree requirements:* For master's, comprehensive exam, thesis optional, research paper; for doctorate, thesis/dissertation, oral exam. *Entrance requirements:* For master's and doctorate, GRE General Test, minimum B+ average in undergraduate course work. Additional exam requirements/recommendations for international students: Required—TOEFL. *Application deadline:* For fall admission, 2/1 for domestic and international students; for spring admission, 8/1 for domestic students, 6/1 for international students. Applications are processed on a rolling basis. Application fee: $60. Electronic applications accepted. *Expenses:* Tuition, area resident: Part-time $471 per credit hour. Tuition, state resident: part-time $471 per credit hour. Tuition, nonresident: part-time $1016 per credit hour. Required fees: $337.04 per term. *Financial support:* In 2009–10, 6 fellowships (averaging $14,203 per year), 39 research assistantships (averaging $23,611 per year), 8 teaching assistantships (averaging $22,242 per year) were awarded. Financial award applicants required to submit FAFSA. *Unit head:* Robert Briber, Chair, 301-405-7313, E-mail: rbriber@umd.edu. *Application contact:* Dean of Graduate School, 301-405-0376, Fax: 301-314-9305.

University of Michigan, Horace H. Rackham School of Graduate Studies, College of Engineering, Department of Materials Science and Engineering, Ann Arbor, MI 48109. Offers MS, PhD. Part-time programs available. *Faculty:* 19 full-time (4 women). *Students:* 106 full-time (33 women), 1 (woman) part-time; includes 19 minority (3 African Americans, 12 Asian Americans or Pacific Islanders, 4 Hispanic Americans), 40 international. 332 applicants, 23% accepted, 34 enrolled. In 2009, 14 master's, 9 doctorates awarded. *Degree requirements:* For master's, thesis, oral defense of thesis; for doctorate, thesis/dissertation, oral defense of dissertation, written exam. *Entrance requirements:* For master's, GRE General Test, minimum GPA of 3.0 in related field; for doctorate, GRE General Test, minimum GPA of 3.0 in related field, master's degree. Additional exam requirements/recommendations for international students: Required—TOEFL. *Application deadline:* Applications are processed on a rolling basis. Application fee: $60 ($75 for international students). Electronic applications accepted. *Expenses:* Tuition, state resident: full-time $17,286; part-time $1099 per credit hour. Tuition, nonresident: full-time $34,944; part-time $2080 per credit hour. Required fees: $95 per semester. Tuition and fees vary according to course load, degree level and program. *Financial support:* Fellowships, research assistantships, teaching assistantships available. Financial award applicants required to submit FAFSA. *Faculty research:* Soft materials (polymers, biomaterials); computational materials science; structural materials; electronic and optical materials; nanocomposite materials. *Unit head:* Peter Green, Department Chair, 734-763-2445, Fax: 734-763-4788. *Application contact:* Renee Hilgendorf, Graduate Program Coordinator, 734-763-9790, Fax: 734-763-4788, E-mail: reneeh@umich.edu.

See Close-Up on page 493.

University of Minnesota, Twin Cities Campus, Institute of Technology, Department of Chemical Engineering and Materials Science, Program in Materials Science and Engineering, Minneapolis, MN 55455-0132. Offers M Mat SE, MS Mat SE, PhD. Part-time programs available. Terminal master's awarded for partial completion of doctoral program. *Degree requirements:* For master's, thesis; for doctorate, thesis/dissertation. *Entrance requirements:* For master's

and doctorate, GRE General Test. *Faculty research:* Fracture micromechanics, hydrogen embrittlement, polymer physics, microelectric materials, corrosion science.

University of Nebraska–Lincoln, Graduate College, College of Arts and Sciences, Department of Chemistry, Lincoln, NE 68588. Offers analytical chemistry (PhD); biochemistry (PhD); chemistry (MS); inorganic chemistry (PhD); materials chemistry (PhD); organic chemistry (PhD); physical chemistry (PhD). *Degree requirements:* For master's, one foreign language, thesis optional, departmental qualifying exam; for doctorate, one foreign language, comprehensive exam, thesis/dissertation, departmental qualifying exams. *Entrance requirements:* For master's and doctorate, GRE. Additional exam requirements/recommendations for international students: Required—TOEFL (minimum score 550 paper-based; 213 computer-based). Electronic applications accepted. *Faculty research:* Bioorganic and bioinorganic chemistry, biophysical and bioanalytical chemistry, structure-function of DNA and proteins, organometallics, mass spectrometry.

University of New Brunswick Fredericton, School of Graduate Studies, Faculty of Engineering, Department of Civil Engineering, Fredericton, NB E3B 5A3, Canada. Offers construction engineering and management (M Eng, M Sc E, PhD); environmental engineering (M Eng, M Sc E, PhD); environmental studies (M Eng); geotechnical engineering (M Eng, M Sc E, PhD); groundwater/hydrology (M Eng, M Sc E, PhD); materials (M Eng, M Sc E, PhD); pavements (M Eng, M Sc E, PhD); structures (M Eng, M Sc E, PhD); transportation (M Eng, M Sc E, PhD). Part-time programs available. *Faculty:* 18 full-time (1 woman), 1 (woman) part-time/adjunct. *Students:* 42 full-time (9 women), 18 part-time (2 women). In 2009, 11 master's, 4 doctorates awarded. *Degree requirements:* For master's, thesis, proposal; for doctorate, comprehensive exam, thesis/dissertation, Qualifying exam; Proposal; 27 credit hours of courses. *Entrance requirements:* For master's, Minimum GPA of 3.0; BScE in Civil Engineering or related engineering degree.; for doctorate, Minimum GPA of 3.0; Candidates are normally required to have a graduate degree in engineering or applied science. Additional exam requirements/recommendations for international students: Required—TOEFL (minimum score 580 paper-based; 237 computer-based), TWE (minimum score 4), or IELTS (minimum score 7.5). *Application deadline:* For fall admission, 5/1 priority date for domestic students; for winter admission, 11/1 priority date for domestic students. Applications are processed on a rolling basis. Application fee: $50 Canadian dollars. Tuition and fees charges are reported in Canadian dollars. *Expenses:* Tuition, area resident: Full-time $5562 Canadian dollars; part-time $2781 Canadian dollars per year. Required fees: $49.75 Canadian dollars per term. *Financial support:* In 2009–10, 51 research assistantships (averaging $7,000 per year), 43 teaching assistantships (averaging $2,000 per year) were awarded; career-related internships or fieldwork and scholarships/grants also available. *Faculty research:* Construction engineering and management, concrete materials and structural engineering, transportation and asset management, geotechnical engineering, water and environmental engineering. *Unit head:* Dr. Eric Hildebrand, Director of Graduate Studies, 506-453-5113, Fax: 506-453-3568, E-mail: ktm@unb.ca. *Application contact:* Joyce Moore, Graduate Secretary, 506-452-6127, Fax: 506-453-3568, E-mail: civil-grad@unb.ca.

University of New Hampshire, Graduate School, College of Engineering and Physical Sciences, Program in Materials Science, Durham, NH 03824. Offers MS, PhD. *Faculty:* 3 full-time (0 women). *Students:* 7 full-time (5 women), 5 part-time (1 woman), 10 international. Average age 28. 23 applicants, 35% accepted, 2 enrolled. In 2009, 2 master's, 1 doctorate awarded. *Degree requirements:* For master's, thesis or alternative. *Entrance requirements:* For master's, GRE. Additional exam requirements/recommendations for international students: Required—TOEFL (minimum score 550 paper-based; 213 computer-based; 80 iBT). *Application deadline:* For fall admission, 4/1 priority date for domestic students, 4/1 for international students. Applications are processed on a rolling basis. Application fee: $65. Electronic applications accepted. *Expenses:* Tuition, state resident: full-time $10,380; part-time $577 per credit hour. Tuition, nonresident: full-time $24,350; part-time $1002 per credit hour. Required fees: $1550; $387.50 per semester. Tuition and fees vary according to course load and program. *Financial support:* In 2009–10, 11 students received support, including 10 research assistantships, 1 teaching assistantship; fellowships, Federal Work-Study, scholarships/grants, and tuition waivers (full and partial) also available. Support available to part-time students. Financial award application deadline: 2/15. *Unit head:* Dr. Olof Echt, Chairperson, 603-862-2669. *Application contact:* Katie Makem-Boucher, Administrative Assistant, 603-862-2669, E-mail: materials.science@unh.edu.

The University of North Carolina at Chapel Hill, Graduate School, Curriculum in Applied and Materials Science, Chapel Hill, NC 27599. Offers materials science (MS, PhD). Terminal master's awarded for partial completion of doctoral program. *Degree requirements:* For doctorate, thesis/dissertation. *Entrance requirements:* For master's, GRE General Test, minimum GPA of 3.0; for doctorate, GRE General Test. Electronic applications accepted. *Faculty research:* Scanning tunneling microscopy, magnetic resonance, carbon nanotubes, thin films, biomaterials, nano-materials, nanotechnology, polymeric materials, electronic and optic materials, tissue engineering.

University of North Texas, Robert B. Toulouse School of Graduate Studies, College of Engineering, Department of Materials Science and Engineering, Denton, TX 76203. Offers MS, PhD. Part-time programs available. *Degree requirements:* For master's, comprehensive exam, thesis optional; for doctorate, thesis/dissertation. *Entrance requirements:* For master's and doctorate, GRE General Test. Additional exam requirements/recommendations for international students: Required—proof of English language proficiency required for non-native English speakers; Recommended—TOEFL (minimum score 550 paper-based; 213 computer-based). *Application deadline:* Applications are processed on a rolling basis. Application fee: $50 ($75 for international students). Electronic applications accepted. *Expenses:* Tuition, state resident: full-time $4298; part-time $239 per contact hour. Tuition, nonresident: full-time $9878; part-time $549 per contact hour. Required fees: $265 per contact hour. *Financial support:* Fellowships, research assistantships with tuition reimbursements, teaching assistantships, scholarships/grants available. *Faculty research:* Polymers, electronic materials, ceramics, metals, nanomaterials. *Application contact:* Graduate Advisor, 940-369-7714, Fax: 940-565-4824.

University of Pennsylvania, School of Engineering and Applied Science, Department of Materials Science and Engineering, Philadelphia, PA 19104. Offers MSE, PhD, MSE/MBA. Part-time programs available. *Faculty:* 15 full-time (4 women), 2 part-time/adjunct (0 women). *Students:* 70 full-time (18 women), 6 part-time (1 woman); includes 5 minority (all Asian Americans or Pacific Islanders), 48 international. 268 applicants, 26% accepted, 34 enrolled. In 2009, 20 master's, 7 doctorates awarded. Terminal master's awarded for partial completion of doctoral program. *Degree requirements:* For master's, thesis; for doctorate, thesis/dissertation. *Entrance requirements:* Additional exam requirements/recommendations for international students: Required—TOEFL. *Application deadline:* For fall admission, 6/1 priority date for domestic students, 5/1 priority date for international students; for spring admission, 11/1 priority date for domestic students, 10/1 priority date for international students. Applications are processed on a rolling basis. Application fee: $70. Electronic applications accepted. *Expenses:* Tuition: Full-time $25,660; part-time $4758 per course. Required fees: $2152; $270 per course. Tuition and fees vary according to course load, degree level and program. *Financial support:* Fellowships, research assistantships, teaching assistantships, institutionally sponsored loans, scholarships/grants, traineeships, health care benefits, and unspecified assistantships available. *Faculty research:* Advanced metallic, ceramic, and polymeric materials for device applications; micromechanics and structure of interfaces; thin film electronic materials; physics and chemistry of solids.

University of Pittsburgh, School of Engineering, Department of Mechanical Engineering and Materials Science, Pittsburgh, PA 15260. Offers MSME, PhD. Part-time programs available. Postbaccalaureate distance learning degree programs offered. *Faculty:* 28 full-time (5 women), 32 part-time/adjunct (2 women). *Students:* 90 full-time (14 women), 87 part-time (10 women); includes 7 minority (2 African Americans, 1 American Indian/Alaska Native, 4 Asian Americans or Pacific Islanders), 47 international. 363 applicants, 25% accepted, 44 enrolled. In 2009, 24 master's, 9 doctorates awarded. Terminal master's awarded for partial completion of doctoral program. *Degree requirements:* For master's, thesis optional; for doctorate, comprehensive exam, thesis/dissertation, final oral exams. *Entrance requirements:* For master's and doctorate, minimum QPA of 3.0. Additional exam requirements/recommendations for international students: Required—TOEFL (minimum score 550 paper-based; 230 computer-based). *Application deadline:* For fall admission, 3/1 priority date for domestic students; for spring admission, 7/1 priority date for domestic students. Applications are processed on a rolling basis. Application fee: $50. Electronic applications accepted. *Expenses:* Tuition, state resident: full-time $16,402; part-time $665 per credit. Tuition, nonresident: full-time $28,694; part-time $1175 per credit. Required fees: $690; $175 per term. Tuition and fees vary according to program. *Financial support:* In 2009–10, 75 students received support, including 6 fellowships with full tuition reimbursements available (averaging $20,772 per year), 46 research assistantships with full tuition reimbursements available (averaging $22,000 per year), 28 teaching assistantships with full tuition reimbursements available (averaging $21,000 per year); scholarships/grants and tuition waivers (full and partial) also available. Financial award application deadline: 4/15. *Faculty research:* Smart materials and structure solid mechanics, computational fluid dynamics, multiphase bio-fluid dynamics, mechanical vibration analysis. Total annual research expenditures: $5.1 million. *Unit head:* Dr. Minking K. Chyu, Chairman, 412-624-9784, Fax: 412-624-4846. *Application contact:* Dr. Patrick Smelinski, Graduate Coordinator, 412-624-9788, Fax: 412-624-4846, E-mail: pat.smel@pitt.edu.

University of Rochester, The College, School of Engineering and Applied Sciences, Program in Materials Science, Rochester, NY 14627. Offers MS, PhD. Terminal master's awarded for partial completion of doctoral program. *Degree requirements:* For master's, comprehensive exam, thesis optional; for doctorate, thesis/dissertation, preliminary and qualifying exams. *Entrance requirements:* For master's and doctorate, GRE. Additional exam requirements/recommendations for international students: Required—TOEFL.

University of Southern California, Graduate School, Viterbi School of Engineering, Mork Family Department of Chemical Engineering and Materials Science, Los Angeles, CA 90089. Offers chemical engineering (MS, PhD, Engr); materials science (MS, PhD, Engr); petroleum engineering (MS, PhD, Engr); smart oilfield technologies (MS, Graduate Certificate). Part-time programs available. Postbaccalaureate distance learning degree programs offered (no on-campus study). *Faculty:* 17 full-time (3 women), 14 part-time/adjunct (1 woman). *Students:* 182 full-time (63 women), 70 part-time (23 women); includes 33 minority (8 African Americans, 18 Asian Americans or Pacific Islanders, 7 Hispanic Americans), 170 international. 443 applicants, 37% accepted, 72 enrolled. In 2009, 37 master's, 19 doctorates, 4 other advanced degrees awarded. Terminal master's awarded for partial completion of doctoral program. *Degree requirements:* For doctorate, thesis/dissertation. *Entrance requirements:* For master's, GRE General Test; for doctorate, General GRE. *Application deadline:* For fall admission, 3/1 priority date for domestic and international students; for spring admission, 10/1 priority date for domestic and international students. Applications are processed on a rolling basis. Application fee: $85. Electronic applications accepted. *Expenses:* Contact institution. *Financial support:* In 2009–10, 12 fellowships with full tuition reimbursements (averaging $30,000 per year), 70 research assistantships with full tuition reimbursements (averaging $19,250 per year), 29 teaching assistantships with full tuition reimbursements (averaging $19,250 per year) were awarded; career-related internships or fieldwork, scholarships/grants, health care benefits, and unspecified assistantships also available. Financial award application deadline: 12/1; financial award applicants required to submit CSS PROFILE or FAFSA. *Faculty research:* Heterogeneous materials and porous media, statistical mechanics, molecular simulation, polymer science and engineering, advanced materials, reaction engineering and catalysis, membrane processes and separation, biochemical engineering, cell culture, bioreactor modeling, petroleum engineering. Total annual research expenditures: $8.8 million. *Unit head:* Dr. Theodore Tsotsis, Chair, 213-740-2069, Fax: 213-740-8053, E-mail: tsotsis@usc.edu. *Application contact:* Petra P. Sapir, Student Service Advisor, 213-740-6011, Fax: 213-740-7797, E-mail: ppearce@usc.edu.

The University of Tennessee, Graduate School, College of Engineering, Department of Materials Science and Engineering, Program in Materials Science and Engineering, Knoxville, TN 37996. Offers MS, PhD. *Faculty:* 13 full-time (1 woman), 7 part-time/adjunct (1 woman). *Students:* 62 full-time (12 women), 7 part-time (1 woman); includes 4 minority (3 African Americans, 1 Asian American or Pacific Islander), 45 international. Average age 24. 119 applicants, 19% accepted, 13 enrolled. In 2009, 10 master's, 13 doctorates awarded. *Degree requirements:* For master's, thesis or alternative; for doctorate, comprehensive exam, thesis/dissertation. *Entrance requirements:* For master's and doctorate, minimum GPA of 3.0. Additional exam requirements/recommendations for international students: Required—TOEFL (minimum score 550 paper-based; 213 computer-based). *Application deadline:* For fall admission, 2/1 priority date for domestic and international students; for spring admission, 6/15 priority date for international students. Applications are processed on a rolling basis. Application fee: $35. Electronic applications accepted. *Expenses:* Tuition, state resident: full-time $6826; part-time $380 per semester hour. Tuition, nonresident: full-time $21,844; part-time $1147 per semester hour. Tuition and fees vary according to program. *Financial support:* In 2009–10, 2 students received support, including 2 fellowships with full tuition reimbursements available (averaging $8,892 per year), 63 research assistantships with full tuition reimbursements available (averaging $19,812 per year), 12 teaching assistantships with full tuition reimbursements available (averaging $17,580 per year); career-related internships or fieldwork, Federal Work-Study, institutionally sponsored loans, health care benefits, and unspecified assistantships also available. Financial award application deadline: 3/1; financial award applicants required to submit FAFSA. *Faculty research:* Biomaterials; functional materials electronic, magnetic and optical; high temperature materials; mechanical behavior of materials; neutron materials science. Total annual research expenditures: $4.1 million. *Unit head:* Dr. George Pharr, Head, 865-974-5336, Fax: 865-974-4115, E-mail: pharr@utk.edu. *Application contact:* Dr. Masood Parang, Associate Dean of Student Affairs, 865-974-2454, Fax: 865-974-9871, E-mail: mparang@utk.edu.

The University of Tennessee, Graduate School, College of Engineering, Department of Mechanical, Aerospace and Biomedical Engineering, Program in Engineering Science, Knoxville, TN 37996. Offers applied artificial intelligence (MS); composite materials (MS, PhD); computational mechanics (MS, PhD); engineering science (MS, PhD); fluid mechanics (MS, PhD); industrial engineering (PhD); optical engineering (MS, PhD); solid mechanics (MS, PhD); MS/MBA. Part-time programs available. *Students:* 9 full-time (0 women), 4 part-time (1 woman); includes 2 minority (both African Americans), 2 international. Average age 34. 5 applicants, 60% accepted, 1 enrolled. In 2009, 2 master's awarded. *Degree requirements:* For master's, thesis or alternative; for doctorate, comprehensive exam, thesis/dissertation. *Entrance requirements:* For master's and doctorate, GRE, minimum GPA of 2.7. Additional exam requirements/recommendations for international students: Required—TOEFL (minimum score 550 paper-based; 213 computer-based). *Application deadline:* For fall admission, 2/1 priority date for domestic and international students; for spring admission, 6/15 priority date for international students. Applications are processed on a rolling basis. Application fee: $35. Electronic applications accepted. *Expenses:* Tuition, state resident: full-time $6826; part-time $380 per semester hour. Tuition, nonresident: full-time $21,844; part-time $1147 per semester hour. Tuition and fees vary according to program. *Financial support:* In 2009–10, 1 student received support, including 5 research assistantships with full tuition reimbursements available (averaging $14,628 per year), 2 teaching assistantships with full tuition reimbursements available (averaging $10,104 per year); fellowships, career-related internships or fieldwork, Federal Work-Study, institutionally sponsored loans, health care benefits, and unspecified assistantships also available. Financial award application deadline: 2/1; financial award applicants required to submit FAFSA. *Faculty research:* Thermal science, computational mechanics, computational fluid dynamics, micro/nano-scale science and engineering for bio-systems. *Unit head:* Dr. William Hamel, Head, 865-974-5115, Fax: 865-974-5274, E-mail: whamel@utk.edu. *Application contact:* Dr. Gary V. Smith, Chair, Graduate Programs Committee, 865-974-5271, E-mail: gvsmith@utk.edu.

The University of Tennessee Space Institute, Graduate Programs, Program in Materials Science and Engineering, Tullahoma, TN 37388-9700. Offers MS. *Faculty:* 4 full-time (1 woman). *Students:* 5 full-time (0 women); includes 1 minority (Asian American or Pacific Islander), 2 international. 3 applicants, 67% accepted, 2 enrolled. In 2009, 1 master's awarded. *Entrance requirements:* Additional exam requirements/recommendations for international students: Required—TOEFL (minimum score 550 paper-based; 213 computer-based; 80 iBT), IELTS (minimum score 6.5). *Application deadline:* For fall admission, 2/1 for international students; for spring admission, 6/15 for international students. Applications are processed on a rolling basis. Application fee: $35. Electronic applications accepted. *Expenses:* Tuition, state resident: full-time $6826; part-time $380 per hour. Tuition, nonresident: full-time $20,622; part-time $1147 per hour. Required fees: $10 per hour. One-time fee: $90 full-time. *Financial support:* In 2009–10, 1 fellowship (averaging $850 per year), 5 research assistantships with full tuition reimbursements (averaging $17,791 per year) were awarded; career-related internships or fieldwork, Federal Work-Study, institutionally sponsored loans, health care benefits, tuition waivers (full and partial), and unspecified assistantships also available. *Unit head:* Dr. William Hofmeister, Degree Program Chairman, 931-393-7466, Fax: 931-454-2271, E-mail: whofmeis@utsi.edu. *Application contact:* Dee Merriman, Coordinator III, 931-393-7293, Fax: 931-393-7201, E-mail: dmerrima@utsi.edu.

The University of Texas at Arlington, Graduate School, College of Engineering, Department of Materials Science and Engineering, Arlington, TX 76019. Offers M Engr, MS, PhD. Part-time programs available. *Faculty:* 6 full-time (0 women), 8 part-time/adjunct (0 women). *Students:* 57 full-time (12 women), 15 part-time (4 women); includes 5 minority (1 African American, 4 Asian Americans or Pacific Islanders), 64 international. 27 applicants, 100% accepted, 11 enrolled. In 2009, 11 master's, 3 doctorates awarded. Terminal master's awarded for partial completion of doctoral program. *Degree requirements:* For master's, comprehensive exam (for some programs), thesis optional; for doctorate, comprehensive exam, thesis/dissertation. *Entrance requirements:* For master's, GRE General Test, minimum GPA of 3.0; for doctorate, GRE General Test, minimum GPA of 3.5. Additional exam requirements/recommendations for international students: Required—TOEFL (minimum score 550 paper-based; 213 computer-based). *Application deadline:* For fall admission, 6/6 for domestic students, 4/4 for international students; for spring admission, 10/17 for domestic students, 9/5 for international students. Applications are processed on a rolling basis. Application fee: $35 ($50 for international students). *Financial support:* In 2009–10, 4 fellowships (averaging $1,000 per year), 10 research assistantships (averaging $16,000 per year), 13 teaching assistantships (averaging $16,000 per year) were awarded; scholarships/grants and unspecified assistantships also available. Financial award application deadline: 6/1; financial award applicants required to submit FAFSA. *Faculty research:* Electronic materials, conductive polymer, composites biomaterial, structural materials. Total annual research expenditures: $400,000. *Unit head:* Dr. Efstathios Meletis, Chair, 817-272-2398, Fax: 817-272-2538, E-mail: meletis@uta.edu. *Application contact:* Dr. Pranesh B. Aswath, Graduate Adviser, 817-272-7108, Fax: 817-272-2538, E-mail: aswath@uta.edu.

The University of Texas at Austin, Graduate School, Cockrell School of Engineering, Program in Materials Science and Engineering, Austin, TX 78712-1111. Offers MS, PhD. Part-time programs available. *Degree requirements:* For master's, thesis (for some programs); for doctorate, thesis/dissertation. *Entrance requirements:* For master's and doctorate, GRE General Test. Additional exam requirements/recommendations for international students: Required—TOEFL (minimum score 550 paper-based; 213 computer-based). Electronic applications accepted.

The University of Texas at Dallas, Erik Jonsson School of Engineering and Computer Science, Programs in Materials Science and Engineering, Richardson, TX 75080. Offers MS, PhD. Part-time and evening/weekend programs available. *Faculty:* 8 full-time (1 woman). *Students:* 40 full-time (9 women), 6 part-time (3 women); includes 3 minority (all Hispanic Americans), 28 international. Average age 27. 38 applicants, 55% accepted, 12 enrolled. In 2009, 5 master's, 1 doctorate awarded. *Degree requirements:* For master's, thesis or major design project; for doctorate, thesis/dissertation. *Entrance requirements:* For master's, GRE General Test, minimum GPA of 3.0 in related bachelor's degree; for doctorate, GRE General Test, minimum GPA of 3.5. Additional exam requirements/recommendations for international students: Required—TOEFL (minimum score 550 paper-based; 213 computer-based). *Application deadline:* For fall admission, 7/15 for domestic students, 5/1 priority date for international students; for spring admission, 11/15 for domestic students, 9/1 priority date for international students. Applications are processed on a rolling basis. Application fee: $50 ($100 for international students). Electronic applications accepted. *Expenses:* Tuition, state resident: full-time $11,068; part-time $461 per credit hour. Tuition, nonresident: full-time $21,178; part-time $882 per credit hour. Tuition and fees vary according to course load. *Financial support:* In 2009–10, 37 research assistantships with full tuition reimbursements (averaging $17,708 per year) were awarded; fellowships, teaching assistantships with full tuition reimbursements, career-related internships or fieldwork, Federal Work-Study, institutionally sponsored loans, scholarships/grants, and unspecified assistantships also available. Support available to part-time students. Financial award application deadline: 4/30; financial award applicants required to submit FAFSA. *Faculty research:* Advanced micro and nanoelectronics; nanotechnology; micro and nanomanipulation; organic electronics; physical, chemical and bio-sensors; materials characterization; energy generation and storage. *Unit head:* Dr. Yves Chabal, Department Head, 972-883-5751, E-mail: chabal@utdallas.edu. *Application contact:* Suzanne Potts, Administrative Assistant, 972-883-5755, Fax: 972-883-2813, E-mail: gradecs@utdallas.edu.

The University of Texas at El Paso, Graduate School, College of Engineering, Department of Metallurgical and Materials Engineering, El Paso, TX 79968-0001. Offers materials science and engineering (PhD); metallurgical and materials engineering (MS). Part-time and evening/weekend programs available. *Degree requirements:* For master's, thesis. *Entrance requirements:* For master's, GRE General Test. Additional exam requirements/recommendations for international students: Required—TOEFL. Electronic applications accepted.

The University of Texas at El Paso, Graduate School, Interdisciplinary Program in Materials Science and Engineering, El Paso, TX 79968-0001. Offers PhD. Part-time and evening/weekend programs available. *Students:* 20 (6 women); includes 11 minority (2 African Americans, 1 Asian American or Pacific Islander, 8 Hispanic Americans), 8 international. Average age 34. In 2009, 5 doctorates awarded. *Degree requirements:* For doctorate, thesis/dissertation. *Entrance requirements:* For doctorate, GRE, letters of recommendation. Additional exam requirements/recommendations for international students: Required—TOEFL; Recommended—IELTS. *Application deadline:* For fall admission, 8/1 priority date for domestic students, 3/1 for international students; for spring admission, 11/1 priority date for domestic students, 9/1 for international students. Applications are processed on a rolling basis. Application fee: $45 ($80 for international students). Electronic applications accepted. *Financial support:* In 2009–10, research assistantships with partial tuition reimbursements (averaging $22,500 per year), teaching assistantships with partial tuition reimbursements (averaging $1,800 per year) were awarded; fellowships with partial tuition reimbursements, institutionally sponsored loans, scholarships/grants, health care benefits, tuition waivers (partial), and unspecified assistantships also available. Support available to part-time students. Financial award application deadline: 3/15; financial award applicants required to submit FAFSA. *Unit head:* Dr. Lawrence E. Murr, Director, 915-747-8002, Fax: 915-747-8036, E-mail: fekberg@utep.edu. *Application contact:* Dr. Patricia D. Witherspoon, Dean of the Graduate School, 915-747-5491, Fax: 915-747-5788, E-mail: withersp@utep.edu.

University of Toronto, School of Graduate Studies, Physical Sciences Division, Faculty of Applied Science and Engineering, Department of Materials Science and Engineering, Toronto, ON M5S 1A1, Canada. Offers M Eng, MA Sc, PhD. Part-time programs available. *Degree requirements:* For master's, thesis (for some programs), oral presentation/thesis defense (MA Sc), qualifying exam; for doctorate, thesis/dissertation. *Entrance requirements:* For master's, BA Sc or B Sc degree in materials science and engineering, 2 letters of reference; for doctorate, MA Sc degree or equivalent, 2 letters of reference, minimum B+ average in last 2 years.

Materials Sciences

University of Toronto (continued)

Additional exam requirements/recommendations for international students: Required—TOEFL (minimum score 580 paper-based), TWE (minimum score 4).

University of Utah, The Graduate School, College of Engineering, Department of Materials Science and Engineering, Salt Lake City, UT 84112. Offers MS, PhD. *Faculty:* 8 full-time (1 woman), 1 part-time/adjunct (0 women). *Students:* 28 full-time (4 women), 13 part-time (2 women); includes 1 minority (Asian American or Pacific Islander), 28 international. Average age 30. 77 applicants, 16% accepted, 10 enrolled. In 2009, 4 master's, 2 doctorates awarded. Terminal master's awarded for partial completion of doctoral program. *Degree requirements:* For master's, thesis; for doctorate, thesis/dissertation, exam. *Entrance requirements:* For master's, GRE General Test, minimum GPA of 3.0; for doctorate, GRE General Test, minimum GPA of 3.0. Additional exam requirements/recommendations for international students: Required—TOEFL (minimum score 570 paper-based; 230 computer-based; 88 iBT), IELTS (minimum score 6.5). *Application deadline:* For fall admission, 4/1 for domestic and international students; for spring admission, 11/1 for domestic and international students. Applications are processed on a rolling basis. Application fee: $55 ($65 for international students). Electronic applications accepted. *Expenses:* Tuition, state resident: full-time $4004; part-time $1674 per semester. Tuition, nonresident: full-time $14,134; part-time $5915 per semester. Required fees: $324 per semester. Tuition and fees vary according to course load, degree level and program. *Financial support:* In 2009–10, 25 research assistantships (averaging $20,000 per year) were awarded; career-related internships or fieldwork and Federal Work-Study also available. Financial award application deadline: 2/5; financial award applicants required to submit FAFSA. *Faculty research:* Solid oxide fuel cells, computational nanostructures, computational polymers, biomaterials, electronic materials, nanomaterials. Total annual research expenditures: $3 million. *Unit head:* Dr. Anil V. Virkar, Chair, 801-581-6863, Fax: 801-581-4816, E-mail: anil.virkar@utah.edu. *Application contact:* Ashley Christensen, Academic Program Specialist, 801-581-6863, Fax: 801-581-4816, E-mail: ashley.christensen@utah.edu.

University of Vermont, Graduate College, College of Engineering and Mathematics, Program in Materials Science, Burlington, VT 05405. Offers MS, PhD. *Students:* 13 (3 women), 9 international. 15 applicants, 47% accepted, 3 enrolled. In 2009, 1 master's awarded. *Degree requirements:* For master's, thesis or alternative; for doctorate, thesis/dissertation. *Entrance requirements:* Additional exam requirements/recommendations for international students: Required—TOEFL (minimum score 550 paper-based; 213 computer-based; 80 iBT). *Application deadline:* For fall admission, 4/1 priority date for domestic students. Applications are processed on a rolling basis. Application fee: $40. Electronic applications accepted. *Expenses:* Tuition, area resident: Part-time $508 per credit hour. Tuition, state resident: part-time $508 per credit hour. Tuition, nonresident: part-time $1281 per credit hour. *Financial support:* Research assistantships, teaching assistantships available. Financial award application deadline: 3/1. *Unit head:* Dr. R. Hendrick, Coordinator, 802-656-2644. *Application contact:* Dr. R. Hendrick, Coordinator, 802-656-2644.

University of Virginia, School of Engineering and Applied Science, Department of Materials Science and Engineering, Charlottesville, VA 22903. Offers materials science (MMSE, MS, PhD). Part-time programs available. Postbaccalaureate distance learning degree programs offered (no on-campus study). *Faculty:* 21 full-time (1 woman). *Students:* 44 full-time (13 women), 1 (woman) part-time; includes 8 minority (2 African Americans, 5 Asian Americans or Pacific Islanders, 1 Hispanic American), 9 international. Average age 27. 167 applicants, 11% accepted, 8 enrolled. In 2009, 10 master's, 9 doctorates awarded. Terminal master's awarded for partial completion of doctoral program. *Degree requirements:* For master's, comprehensive exam, thesis (for some programs); for doctorate, comprehensive exam, thesis/dissertation. *Entrance requirements:* For master's and doctorate, GRE General Test, three recommendations. Additional exam requirements/recommendations for international students: Required—TOEFL. *Application deadline:* For fall admission, 1/15 for domestic and international students. Applications are processed on a rolling basis. Application fee: $60. Electronic applications accepted. *Financial support:* Fellowships, research assistantships, teaching assistantships available. Financial award application deadline: 1/15; financial award applicants required to submit FAFSA. *Faculty research:* Environmental effects on material behavior, electronic materials, metals, polymers, tribology. *Unit head:* William C. Johnson, Chair, 434-982-5641, Fax: 434-982-5660. *Application contact:* Kathryn C. Thornton, Assistant Dean for Graduate Programs, 434-924-3897, Fax: 434-982-2214, E-mail: seas-grad-admission@cs.virginia.edu.

University of Washington, Graduate School, College of Engineering, Department of Aeronautics and Astronautics, Seattle, WA 98195-2400. Offers aeronautics and astronautics (MSAA, PhD); composite materials and structures (MAE, MAECMS). Part-time programs available. Postbaccalaureate distance learning degree programs offered (no on-campus study). *Faculty:* 19 full-time (1 woman), 4 part-time/adjunct (0 women). *Students:* 66 full-time (12 women), 80 part-time (7 women); includes 20 minority (1 African American, 10 Asian Americans or Pacific Islanders, 9 Hispanic Americans), 26 international. Average age 27. 187 applicants, 65% accepted, 65 enrolled. In 2009, 26 master's, 5 doctorates awarded. *Degree requirements:* For master's, thesis optional; for doctorate, comprehensive exam, thesis/dissertation. *Entrance requirements:* For master's, GRE General Test, minimum GPA of 3.0; for doctorate, GRE General Test, minimum GPA of 3.4, research advisor. Additional exam requirements/recommendations for international students: Required—TOEFL (minimum score 580 paper-based; 237 computer-based; 70 iBT), TOEFL iBT (listening, writing and reading sections). *Application deadline:* For fall admission, 1/15 priority date for domestic students, 11/1 priority date for international students; for winter admission, 10/1 priority date for domestic students; for spring admission, 2/1 priority date for domestic students. Applications are processed on a rolling basis. Application fee: $65. Electronic applications accepted. *Financial support:* In 2009–10, 2 students received support, including 9 fellowships (averaging $15,624 per year), 35 research assistantships with full tuition reimbursements available (averaging $17,217 per year), 9 teaching assistantships with full tuition reimbursements available (averaging $13,725 per year); career-related internships or fieldwork, Federal Work-Study, health care benefits, tuition waivers (full), and unspecified assistantships also available. Financial award application deadline: 1/15. *Faculty research:* Space systems, aircraft systems, energy systems, composites/structures, fluid dynamics, controls. Total annual research expenditures: $7 million. *Unit head:* Dr. Adam P. Bruckner, Professor and Chair, 206-543-1950, Fax: 206-543-0217, E-mail: bruckner@aa.washington.edu. *Application contact:* Wanda Frederick, Manager of Graduate Programs and External Relations, 206-616-1113, Fax: 206-543-0217, E-mail: wanda@aa.washington.edu.

University of Washington, Graduate School, College of Engineering, Department of Materials Science and Engineering, Seattle, WA 98195-2120. Offers materials science and engineering (MS, MSE, MSMSE, PhD); materials science and engineering nanotechnology (PhD). Part-time programs available. *Faculty:* 15 full-time (2 women), 6 part-time/adjunct (1 woman). *Students:* 95 full-time (32 women), 8 part-time (2 women); includes 18 minority (2 African Americans, 1 American Indian/Alaska Native, 12 Asian Americans or Pacific Islanders, 3 Hispanic Americans), 48 international. Average age 30. 194 applicants, 12% accepted, 9 enrolled. In 2009, 4 master's, 10 doctorates awarded. *Degree requirements:* For master's, comprehensive exam, thesis; for doctorate, comprehensive exam, thesis/dissertation. *Entrance requirements:* For master's and doctorate, GRE General Test, minimum GPA of 3.0. Additional exam requirements/recommendations for international students: Required—TOEFL (minimum score 600 paper-based; 250 computer-based; 70 iBT). *Application deadline:* For fall admission, 1/15 priority date for domestic and international students. Application fee: $65. Electronic applications accepted. *Financial support:* In 2009–10, 3 students received support, including 12 fellowships with full tuition reimbursements available, 42 research assistantships with full tuition reimbursements available (averaging $16,380 per year), 13 teaching assistantships with full tuition reimbursements available (averaging $16,380 per year); career-related internships or fieldwork, Federal Work-Study, institutionally sponsored loans, scholarships/grants, health care benefits, unspecified assistantships, and stipend supplements also available. Financial award application deadline: 1/15. *Faculty research:* Biomimetics and biomaterials; electronic, optical and magnetic materials; eco-materials and materials for energy applications; ceramics, metals, composites, and polymers. Total annual research expenditures: $7.4 million. *Unit head:* Dr. Alex Jen, Professor and Chair, 206-543-2600, Fax: 206-543-3100, E-mail: ajen@uw.edu. *Application contact:* Kathleen A. Elkins, Academic Counselor, 206-616-6581, Fax: 206-543-3100, E-mail: kelkins@uw.edu.

University of Wisconsin–Madison, Graduate School, College of Engineering, Materials Science Program, Madison, WI 53706-1380. Offers MS, PhD. Part-time programs available. *Faculty:* 74 full-time (14 women). *Students:* 97 full-time (19 women); includes 51 minority (1 American Indian/Alaska Native, 36 Asian Americans or Pacific Islanders, 14 Hispanic Americans). Average age 29. 415 applicants, 8% accepted, 10 enrolled. In 2009, 13 master's, 10 doctorates awarded. Terminal master's awarded for partial completion of doctoral program. *Degree requirements:* For master's, thesis or alternative; for doctorate, comprehensive exam, thesis/dissertation. *Entrance requirements:* For master's and doctorate, GRE General Test. Additional exam requirements/recommendations for international students: Required—TOEFL (minimum score 550 paper-based; 213 computer-based; 80 iBT). *Application deadline:* For fall admission, 7/1 for domestic and international students; for spring admission, 11/1 for domestic and international students. Applications are processed on a rolling basis. Application fee: $56. Electronic applications accepted. *Expenses:* Tuition, state resident: part-time $594 per credit. Tuition, nonresident: part-time $1504 per credit. Required fees: $65 per credit. Tuition and fees vary according to course load, program and reciprocity agreements. *Financial support:* In 2009–10, 9 fellowships with full tuition reimbursements (averaging $22,224 per year), 87 research assistantships with full tuition reimbursements (averaging $20,184 per year), 1 teaching assistantship with tuition reimbursement (averaging $28,175 per year) were awarded; traineeships, health care benefits, and unspecified assistantships also available. Financial award application deadline: 1/15. *Faculty research:* Electronic materials, polymers and biomaterials, nanotechnology and nanoscience, structural and mechanical materials, magnetic and superconducting materials, ceramics, metals, computational and theoretical modeling of materials, photonics and optical materials, materials for energy or environmental technology. *Unit head:* Ray Vanderby, Director, 608-265-3032, Fax: 608-262-8353, E-mail: matsciad@engr.wisc.edu. *Application contact:* Diana J. Rhoads, University Services Program Associate B, 608-263-1795, Fax: 608-262-8353, E-mail: rhoads@engr.wisc.edu.

Vanderbilt University, School of Engineering, Interdisciplinary Program in Materials Science, Nashville, TN 37240-1001. Offers M Eng, MS, PhD. Part-time programs available. *Faculty:* 43 full-time (6 women), 2 part-time/adjunct (0 women). *Students:* 38 full-time (10 women); includes 10 minority (5 African Americans, 1 American Indian/Alaska Native, 4 Asian Americans or Pacific Islanders), 7 international. Average age 26. 73 applicants, 12% accepted, 6 enrolled. In 2009, 1 master's, 2 doctorates awarded. Terminal master's awarded for partial completion of doctoral program. *Degree requirements:* For master's, thesis; for doctorate, thesis/dissertation. *Entrance requirements:* For master's and doctorate, GRE General Test. *Application deadline:* For fall admission, 1/15 for domestic students; for spring admission, 11/1 for domestic students. Application fee: $0. Electronic applications accepted. *Financial support:* In 2009–10, 8 fellowships with tuition reimbursements (averaging $30,000 per year), 10 research assistantships with tuition reimbursements (averaging $19,800 per year), 8 teaching assistantships with tuition reimbursements (averaging $18,000 per year) were awarded; institutionally sponsored loans and tuition waivers (partial) also available. Support available to part-time students. Financial award application deadline: 1/15. *Faculty research:* Nanostructure materials, materials physics, surface and interface science, materials synthesis, biomaterials. *Unit head:* Dr. Timothy P. Hanusa, Director, 615-322-4667, Fax: 615-322-3202, E-mail: t.hanusa@vanderbilt.edu. *Application contact:* Sarah R. Satterwhite, Administrative Assistant, 615-343-6868, Fax: 615-322-3202, E-mail: sarah.m.ross@vanderbilt.edu.

Virginia Polytechnic Institute and State University, Graduate School, College of Engineering, Department of Materials Science and Engineering, Blacksburg, VA 24061. Offers M Eng, MS, PhD. *Entrance requirements:* For master's and doctorate, GRE. Additional exam requirements/recommendations for international students: Required—TOEFL (minimum score 550 paper-based; 213 computer-based). Electronic applications accepted.

Washington State University, Graduate School, College of Engineering and Architecture, School of Mechanical and Materials Engineering, Program in Material Science Engineering, Pullman, WA 99164. Offers MS. *Faculty:* 29. *Students:* 27 full-time (6 women), 3 part-time (1 woman); includes 5 minority (1 African American, 1 American Indian/Alaska Native, 2 Asian Americans or Pacific Islanders, 1 Hispanic American), 13 international. 133 applicants, 10% accepted, 3 enrolled. *Degree requirements:* For master's, comprehensive exam (for some programs), thesis. *Entrance requirements:* For master's, GRE, Apply Graduate School, statement of purpose, three letters of recommendation, student interest profile, student interest profile, transcripts. Additional exam requirements/recommendations for international students: Required—TOEFL, IELTS. *Application deadline:* For fall admission, 1/10 for domestic and international students; for spring admission, 7/1 for domestic and international students. Applications are processed on a rolling basis. Application fee: $50. Electronic applications accepted. *Financial support:* In 2009–10, fellowships (averaging $2,500 per year), research assistantships with tuition reimbursements (averaging $13,917 per year) were awarded. Financial award application deadline: 2/10. Total annual research expenditures: $2.2 million. *Unit head:* Dr. Matthew McCluskey, Chair, 509-509-335-5356, Fax: 509-335-4662, E-mail: mattmcc@wsu.edu. *Application contact:* Graduate School Admissions, 800-GRADWSU, Fax: 509-335-1949, E-mail: gradsch@wsu.edu.

Washington State University, Graduate School, College of Sciences, Program in Materials Science, Pullman, WA 99164. Offers PhD. *Degree requirements:* For doctorate, comprehensive exam, thesis/dissertation, oral exam, written exam. *Entrance requirements:* For doctorate, minimum GPA of 3.0, 3 letters of recommendation. Additional exam requirements/recommendations for international students: Required—TOEFL. *Faculty research:* Thin films, materials characterization, mechanical properties, materials processing, electrical and optical behavior.

Wayne State University, College of Engineering, Department of Chemical Engineering and Materials Science, Program in Materials Science and Engineering, Detroit, MI 48202. Offers materials science and engineering (MS, PhD); polymer engineering (Certificate). Part-time programs available. Terminal master's awarded for partial completion of doctoral program. *Degree requirements:* For master's, thesis optional; for doctorate, thesis/dissertation. *Entrance requirements:* For master's, GRE (if applying for financial support), recommendations; resume; for doctorate, GRE (if applying for financial support), recommendations; resumé, personal statement. Additional exam requirements/recommendations for international students: Required—TOEFL (minimum score 550 paper-based; 213 computer-based); Recommended—TWE (minimum score 6). Electronic applications accepted. *Faculty research:* Polymer science, rheology, fatigue in metals, metal matrix composites, ceramics.

Worcester Polytechnic Institute, Graduate Studies and Research, Department of Mechanical Engineering, Program in Materials Process Engineering, Worcester, MA 01609-2280. Offers MS. Part-time and evening/weekend programs available. *Students:* 1 part-time (0 women). 4 applicants, 100% accepted, 0 enrolled. In 2009, 2 master's awarded. *Degree requirements:* For master's, thesis optional. *Entrance requirements:* For master's, 3 letters of recommendation. Additional exam requirements/recommendations for international students: Required—TOEFL (minimum score 550 paper-based; 213 computer-based). *Application deadline:* For fall admission, 1/15 priority date for domestic and international students; for spring admission, 10/15 priority date for domestic and international students. Applications are processed on a rolling basis. Application fee: $70. Electronic applications accepted. *Financial support:* Application deadline: 1/15. *Unit head:* Dr. Richard D. Sisson, Director, 508-831-5633, Fax: 508-831-5178, E-mail: sisson@wpi.edu. *Application contact:* Rita Shilansky, Graduate Secretary, 508-831-5633, Fax: 508-831-5178, E-mail: rita@wpi.edu.

Worcester Polytechnic Institute, Graduate Studies and Research, Department of Mechanical Engineering, Program in Materials Science and Engineering, Worcester, MA 01609-2280.

Offers MS, PhD. Part-time and evening/weekend programs available. *Faculty:* 4 full-time (0 women), 1 part-time/adjunct (0 women). *Students:* 26 full-time (12 women), 17 part-time (6 women). 68 applicants, 72% accepted, 17 enrolled. In 2009, 6 master's, 2 doctorates awarded. *Degree requirements:* For master's, thesis; for doctorate, comprehensive exam, thesis/dissertation. *Entrance requirements:* For master's and doctorate, GRE General Test (recommended), 3 letters of recommendation. Additional exam requirements/recommendations for international students: Required—TOEFL (minimum score 550 paper-based; 213 computer-based; 79 iBT), IELTS (minimum score 6.5). *Application deadline:* For fall admission, 2/1 priority date for domestic students; for spring admission, 10/15 priority date for domestic students. Applications are processed on a rolling basis. Application fee: $70. Electronic applications accepted. *Financial support:* Career-related internships or fieldwork, institutionally sponsored loans, scholarships/grants, and unspecified assistantships available. Financial award application deadline: 1/15. *Faculty research:* Metals processing, nanomaterials, reliability analysis, surface metrology, biopolymers. *Unit head:* Dr. Richard D. Sisson, Director, 508-831-5633, Fax: 508-831-5178, E-mail: sisson@wpi.edu. *Application contact:* Rita Shilansky, Graduate Secretary, 508-831-5633, Fax: 508-831-5178, E-mail: rita@wpi.edu.

Wright State University, School of Graduate Studies, College of Engineering and Computer Science, Programs in Engineering, Program in Mechanical and Materials Engineering, Dayton, OH 45435. Offers materials science and engineering (MSE); mechanical engineering (MSE). *Degree requirements:* For master's, thesis or course option alternative. *Entrance requirements:* Additional exam requirements/recommendations for international students: Required—TOEFL.

Metallurgical Engineering and Metallurgy

Colorado School of Mines, Graduate School, Department of Metallurgical and Materials Engineering, Golden, CO 80401. Offers materials science (MS, PhD); metallurgical and materials engineering (ME, MS, PhD). Part-time programs available. *Faculty:* 34 full-time (3 women), 4 part-time/adjunct (0 women). *Students:* 54 full-time (13 women), 6 part-time (1 woman); includes 6 minority (1 American Indian/Alaska Native, 4 Asian Americans or Pacific Islanders, 1 Hispanic American), 8 international. Average age 30. 84 applicants, 26% accepted, 14 enrolled. In 2009, 18 master's, 8 doctorates awarded. *Degree requirements:* For master's, thesis (for some programs); for doctorate, comprehensive exam, thesis/dissertation. *Entrance requirements:* For master's and doctorate, GRE General Test. Additional exam requirements/recommendations for international students: Required—TOEFL (minimum score 550 paper-based; 213 computer-based; 80 iBT). *Application deadline:* For fall admission, 1/15 priority date for domestic and international students; for spring admission, 9/1 priority date for domestic and international students. Application fee: $50 ($70 for international students). Electronic applications accepted. *Expenses:* Tuition, state resident: full-time $10,584; part-time $588 per credit hour. Tuition, nonresident: full-time $24,750; part-time $1375 per credit hour. Required fees: $1654; $827.10 per semester. *Financial support:* In 2009–10, 3 fellowships with full tuition reimbursements (averaging $20,000 per year), 64 research assistantships with full tuition reimbursements (averaging $20,000 per year), 8 teaching assistantships with full tuition reimbursements (averaging $20,000 per year) were awarded; scholarships/grants, health care benefits, and unspecified assistantships also available. Financial award application deadline: 1/15; financial award applicants required to submit FAFSA. Total annual research expenditures: $6.9 million. *Unit head:* Dr. Michael Kaufman, Interim Department Head, 303-273-3009, Fax: 303-273-3795, E-mail: mkaufman@mines.edu. *Application contact:* Peggy Cook, Program Assistant, 303-273-3660, Fax: 303-273-3795, E-mail: pcook@mines.edu.

Columbia University, Fu Foundation School of Engineering and Applied Science, Department of Earth and Environmental Engineering, New York, NY 10027. Offers earth and environmental engineering (MS, Eng Sc D, PhD); metallurgical engineering (Engr); mining engineering (Engr); MS/MBA. Part-time programs available. Postbaccalaureate distance learning degree programs offered (minimal on-campus study). *Faculty:* 7 full-time (0 women), 4 part-time/adjunct (1 woman). *Students:* 50 full-time (19 women), 20 part-time (7 women); includes 3 minority (1 African American, 1 American Indian/Alaska Native, 1 Asian American or Pacific Islander), 33 international. Average age 28. 149 applicants, 25% accepted, 18 enrolled. In 2009, 12 master's, 4 doctorates awarded. Terminal master's awarded for partial completion of doctoral program. *Degree requirements:* For master's, thesis; for doctorate, thesis/dissertation, qualifying exam. *Entrance requirements:* For master's, doctorate, and Engr, GRE General Test. Additional exam requirements/recommendations for international students: Required—TOEFL. *Application deadline:* For fall admission, 12/1 priority date for domestic and international students; for spring admission, 10/1 priority date for domestic and international students. Application fee: $70. Electronic applications accepted. *Financial support:* In 2009–10, 39 students received support, including 6 fellowships with full and partial tuition reimbursements available (averaging $16,478 per year), 26 research assistantships with full tuition reimbursements available (averaging $27,733 per year), 7 teaching assistantships with full tuition reimbursements available (averaging $22,500 per year); health care benefits and unspecified assistantships also available. Financial award application deadline: 12/1; financial award applicants required to submit FAFSA. *Faculty research:* Sustainable energy and materials, waste to energy, water resources and climate risks, environmental health engineering, life cycle analysis. *Unit head:* Dr. Klaus S. Lackner, Department Chair; Maurice Ewing and J. Lamar Worzel Professor of Geophysics, 212-854-0304, Fax: 212-854-7081, E-mail: kl2010@columbia.edu. *Application contact:* Peter Rennee, Department Administrator, 212-854-7065, Fax: 212-854-7081, E-mail: pr99@columbia.edu.

Massachusetts Institute of Technology, School of Engineering, Department of Materials Science and Engineering, Cambridge, MA 02139-4307. Offers archaeological materials (PhD, Sc D); bio- and polymeric materials (PhD, Sc D); electronic, photonic and magnetic materials (PhD, Sc D); emerging, fundamental and computational studies in materials science (Sc D); emerging, fundamental, and computational studies in materials science (PhD); materials engineering (Mat E); materials science and engineering (M Eng, SM, PhD, Sc D); metallurgical engineering (Met E); structural and environmental materials (PhD, Sc D); SM/MBA. *Faculty:* 36 full-time (8 women). *Students:* 222 full-time (62 women); includes 32 minority (3 African Americans, 21 Asian Americans or Pacific Islanders, 8 Hispanic Americans), 125 international. Average age 26. 459 applicants, 23% accepted, 63 enrolled. In 2009, 35 master's, 28 doctorates awarded. Terminal master's awarded for partial completion of doctoral program. *Degree requirements:* For master's and other advanced degree, thesis; for doctorate, comprehensive exam, thesis/dissertation. *Entrance requirements:* For master's and doctorate, GRE General Test. Additional exam requirements/recommendations for international students: Required—IELTS (minimum score 5.5); Recommended—TOEFL (minimum score 577 paper-based; 233 computer-based; 90 iBT). *Application deadline:* For fall admission, 1/1 for domestic and international students. Application fee: $75. Electronic applications accepted. *Financial support:* In 2009–10, 222 students received support, including 55 fellowships with tuition reimbursements available (averaging $22,387 per year), 135 research assistantships with tuition reimbursements available (averaging $27,287 per year), 10 teaching assistantships with tuition reimbursements available (averaging $30,736 per year); career-related internships or fieldwork, Federal Work-Study, institutionally sponsored loans, scholarships/grants, health care benefits, and unspecified assistantships also available. *Faculty research:* Thermodynamics and kinetics of phase transformations, structure of all materials classes: metals, ceramics, semiconductors, polymers, biomaterials, influence of processing on materials structure, structure, property relationships (electrical, magnetic, optical, mechanical). Total annual research expenditures: $22.6 million. *Unit head:* Prof. Edwin L. Thomas, Department Head, 617-253-3300, Fax: 617-252-1775. *Application contact:* Angelita Mireles, Graduate Admissions, 617-253-3302, E-mail: dmse-admissions@mit.edu.

Michigan Technological University, Graduate School, College of Engineering, Department of Materials Science and Engineering, Houghton, MI 49931. Offers MS, PhD. Part-time programs available. Terminal master's awarded for partial completion of doctoral program. *Degree requirements:* For master's, comprehensive exam; for doctorate, comprehensive exam, thesis/dissertation. *Entrance requirements:* For master's, GRE. Additional exam requirements/recommendations for international students: Required—TOEFL (minimum score 550 paper-based; 213 computer-based). Electronic applications accepted. *Expenses:* Contact institution. *Faculty research:* Structure/property/processing relationships, microstructural characterization, alloy design, electronic/magnetic/photonic materials, materials and manufacturing processes.

Missouri University of Science and Technology, Graduate School, Department of Materials Science and Engineering, Rolla, MO 65409. Offers ceramic engineering (MS, DE, PhD); metallurgical engineering (MS, PhD). *Degree requirements:* For master's, thesis optional; for doctorate, comprehensive exam. *Entrance requirements:* For master's, GRE (minimum combined score 1100, 600 verbal, 3.5 writing); for doctorate, GRE (minimum score: quantitative 600, writing 3.5). Additional exam requirements/recommendations for international students: Required—TOEFL (minimum score 570 paper-based; 230 computer-based).

Montana Tech of The University of Montana, Graduate School, Metallurgical/Mineral Processing Engineering Programs, Butte, MT 59701-8997. Offers MS. Part-time programs available. *Faculty:* 5 full-time (0 women). *Students:* 6 full-time (2 women), 2 part-time (1 woman); includes 1 minority (American Indian/Alaska Native). 6 applicants, 67% accepted, 1 enrolled. In 2009, 1 master's awarded. *Degree requirements:* For master's, comprehensive exam (for some programs), thesis optional. *Entrance requirements:* For master's, GRE General Test, minimum GPA of 3.0. Additional exam requirements/recommendations for international students: Required—TOEFL (minimum score 525 paper-based; 195 computer-based; 71 iBT). *Application deadline:* For fall admission, 4/1 priority date for domestic students, 3/1 priority date for international students; for spring admission, 10/1 priority date for domestic students, 7/1 priority date for international students. Applications are processed on a rolling basis. Application fee: $30. Electronic applications accepted. *Expenses:* Tuition, state resident: full-time $5068; part-time $319 per credit. Tuition, nonresident: full-time $14,815; part-time $875 per credit. Tuition and fees vary according to course load and campus/location. *Financial support:* In 2009–10, 5 students received support, including 5 teaching assistantships with partial tuition reimbursements available (averaging $6,000 per year); research assistantships with partial tuition reimbursements available, career-related internships or fieldwork, tuition waivers (full and partial), and unspecified assistantships also available. Financial award application deadline: 4/1; financial award applicants required to submit FAFSA. *Faculty research:* Stabilizing hazardous waste, decontamination of metals by melt refining, ultraviolet enhancement of stabilization reactions, extractive metallurgy, fuel cells. *Unit head:* Dr. Courtney Young, Department Head, 406-496-4158, Fax: 406-496-4664, E-mail: cyoung@mtech.edu. *Application contact:* Cindy Dunstan, Administrator, Graduate School, 406-496-4304, Fax: 406-496-4710, E-mail: cdunstan@mtech.edu.

The Ohio State University, Graduate School, College of Engineering, Program in Welding Engineering, Columbus, OH 43210. Offers MS, MWE, PhD. *Faculty:* 25. *Students:* 13 full-time (1 woman), 21 part-time (3 women); includes 3 minority (all Asian Americans or Pacific Islanders), 10 international. Average age 29. In 2009, 16 master's, 1 doctorate awarded. *Degree requirements:* For master's, thesis optional; for doctorate, thesis/dissertation. *Entrance requirements:* For master's and doctorate, GRE General Test or engineering degree. Additional exam requirements/recommendations for international students: Recommended—TOEFL (minimum score 600 paper-based; 250 computer-based). *Application deadline:* For fall admission, 8/15 priority date for domestic students, 7/1 priority date for international students; for winter admission, 12/1 priority date for domestic students, 11/1 priority date for international students; for spring admission, 3/1 priority date for domestic students, 2/1 priority date for international students. Applications are processed on a rolling basis. Application fee: $40 ($50 for international students). Electronic applications accepted. *Expenses:* Tuition, state resident: full-time $10,683. Tuition, nonresident: full-time $25,923. Tuition and fees vary according to course load and program. *Financial support:* Fellowships, research assistantships, teaching assistantships, Federal Work-Study and institutionally sponsored loans available. Support available to part-time students. *Unit head:* Avraham Benatar, Graduate Studies Committee Chair, 614-292-2466, Fax: 614-292-7852, E-mail: benatar.1@osu.edu. *Application contact:* 614-292-9444, Fax: 614-292-3895, E-mail: domestic.grad@osu.edu.

Rensselaer Polytechnic Institute, Graduate School, School of Engineering, Department of Materials Science and Engineering, Troy, NY 12180. Offers ceramics and glass science (M Eng, MS, PhD); composites (M Eng, MS, PhD); electronic materials (M Eng, MS, PhD); metallurgy (M Eng, MS, PhD); polymers (M Eng, MS, PhD). Part-time and evening/weekend programs available. *Faculty:* 16 full-time (2 women). *Students:* 54 full-time (11 women), 4 part-time (1 woman); includes 7 minority (all Asian Americans or Pacific Islanders), 30 international. Average age 24. 234 applicants, 14% accepted, 14 enrolled. In 2009, 10 master's, 6 doctorates awarded. Terminal master's awarded for partial completion of doctoral program. *Degree requirements:* For master's, thesis; for doctorate, comprehensive exam, thesis/dissertation. *Entrance requirements:* For master's and doctorate, GRE. Additional exam requirements/recommendations for international students: Required—TOEFL (minimum score 570 paper-based; 230 computer-based; 88 iBT). *Application deadline:* For fall admission, 1/15 priority date for domestic and international students; for spring admission, 8/31 priority date for domestic and international students. Applications are processed on a rolling basis. Application fee: $75. Electronic applications accepted. *Expenses:* Tuition: Full-time $38,100. *Financial support:* In 2009–10, 50 students received support, including fellowships with full tuition reimbursements available (averaging $24,750 per year), 40 research assistantships with full tuition reimbursements available (averaging $24,750 per year), 13 teaching assistantships with full tuition reimbursements available (averaging $24,750 per year); career-related internships or fieldwork, institutionally sponsored loans, and unspecified assistantships also available. Financial award application deadline: 2/1. *Faculty research:* Materials processing, nanostructural materials, materials for microelectronics, composite materials, computational materials. Total annual research expenditures: $5 million. *Unit head:* Dr. Robert Hull, Department Head, 518-276-6373, Fax: 518-276-8554, E-mail: hullr2@rpi.edu. *Application contact:* Dr. Pawel Keblinski, Admissions Coordinator, 518-276-6858, Fax: 518-276-8554, E-mail: keblip@rpi.edu.

South Dakota School of Mines and Technology, Graduate Division, College of Engineering, Master's Program in Materials Engineering and Science, Rapid City, SD 57701-3995. Offers chemistry (MS); metallurgical engineering (MS); physics (MS). *Faculty:* 6 full-time (0 women), 1 part-time/adjunct (0 women). *Students:* 9 full-time (1 woman), 9 part-time (2 women), 8 international. Average age 26. 9 applicants, 56% accepted, 1 enrolled. In 2009, 4 master's awarded. *Entrance requirements:* For master's, GRE General Test. Additional exam requirements/recommendations for international students: Required—TOEFL, TWE. *Application deadline:* For fall admission, 7/1 priority date for domestic students, 4/1 for international students; for spring admission, 11/1 for domestic students, 9/1 for international students. Applications are processed on a rolling basis. Application fee: $35. Electronic applications

Metallurgical Engineering and Metallurgy

South Dakota School of Mines and Technology (continued)
accepted. *Expenses:* Tuition, state resident: full-time $3340; part-time $139 per credit hour. Tuition, nonresident: full-time $7060; part-time $294 per credit hour. Required fees: $3270. *Financial support:* In 2009–10, 15 research assistantships with partial tuition reimbursements (averaging $11,400 per year), 11 teaching assistantships with partial tuition reimbursements (averaging $4,063 per year) were awarded; fellowships also available. Financial award application deadline: 5/15. *Unit head:* Dr. Jon Kellar, Chair, 605-394-2343, E-mail: jon.kellar@sdsmt.edu. *Application contact:* Jeannette R. Nilson, Administrative Support Coordinator, Graduate Education, 800-454-8162 Ext. 1206, Fax: 605-394-5360, E-mail: graduate_admissions@sdsmt.edu.

Université Laval, Faculty of Sciences and Engineering, Department of Mining, Metallurgical and Materials Engineering, Programs in Metallurgical Engineering, Québec, QC G1K 7P4, Canada. Offers M Sc, PhD. Terminal master's awarded for partial completion of doctoral program. *Degree requirements:* For master's, thesis; for doctorate, comprehensive exam, thesis/dissertation. *Entrance requirements:* For master's and doctorate, knowledge of French and English. Electronic applications accepted.

The University of Alabama, Graduate School, College of Engineering, Department of Metallurgical and Materials Engineering, Tuscaloosa, AL 35487. Offers MS Met E, PhD. *Faculty:* 7 full-time (1 woman). *Students:* 25 full-time (2 women), 2 part-time (0 women); includes 2 minority (1 African American, 1 Hispanic American), 15 international. Average age 27. 31 applicants, 35% accepted, 10 enrolled. In 2009, 1 master's, 1 doctorate awarded. *Median time to degree:* Of those who began their doctoral program in fall 2001, 100% received their degree in 8 years or less. *Degree requirements:* For master's, thesis or alternative; for doctorate, thesis/dissertation. *Entrance requirements:* For master's, GRE General Test, minimum GPA of 3.0 in last 60 hours; for doctorate, GRE General Test, minimum graduate GPA of 3.0, graduate degree. Additional exam requirements/recommendations for international students: Required—TOEFL (minimum score 550 paper-based; 213 computer-based). *Application deadline:* For fall admission, 7/1 priority date for domestic students. Applications are processed on a rolling basis. Application fee: $50 ($60 for international students). Electronic applications accepted. *Expenses:* Tuition, state resident: full-time $7000. Tuition, nonresident: full-time $19,200. *Financial support:* In 2009–10, 3 fellowships (averaging $15,000 per year), 14 research assistantships (averaging $14,700 per year), 6 teaching assistantships (averaging $12,250 per year) were awarded; Federal Work-Study and unspecified assistantships also available. *Faculty research:* Thermodynamics, molten metals processing, casting and solidification, mechanical properties of materials, thin films and nanostructures, electrochemistry, corrosion and alloy development. Total annual research expenditures: $1.4 million. *Unit head:* Dr. Ramana G. Reddy, Head and ACIPCO Professor, 205-348-4246, Fax: 205-348-2164. *Application contact:* Dr. Su Gupta, Associate Professor, 205-348-4272, Fax: 205-348-2164, E-mail: sgupta@eng.ua.edu.

The University of British Columbia, Faculty of Applied Science, Department of Materials Engineering, Vancouver, BC V6T 1Z1, Canada. Offers materials and metallurgy (M Sc, PhD); metals and materials engineering (MA Sc, PhD). *Degree requirements:* For master's, comprehensive exam, thesis; for doctorate, comprehensive exam, thesis/dissertation. *Entrance requirements:* Additional exam requirements/recommendations for international students: Required—TOEFL (minimum score 560 paper-based; 220 computer-based; 83 iBT). Electronic applications accepted. *Faculty research:* Electroslag melting, mathematical modeling, solidification and hydrometallurgy.

University of Cincinnati, Graduate School, College of Engineering, Department of Chemical and Materials Engineering, Cincinnati, OH 45221. Offers chemical engineering (MS, PhD); materials science and metallurgical engineering (MS, PhD), including ceramic science and engineering, materials science and engineering, metallurgical engineering, polymer science and engineering. Part-time and evening/weekend programs available. Terminal master's awarded for partial completion of doctoral program. *Degree requirements:* For master's, thesis; for doctorate, thesis/dissertation. *Entrance requirements:* For master's and doctorate, GRE General Test. Additional exam requirements/recommendations for international students: Required—TOEFL. Electronic applications accepted. *Faculty research:* Process synthesis, aerosol processes, clean coal technology, membrane technology.

University of Cincinnati, Graduate School, College of Engineering, Department of Chemical and Materials Engineering, Program in Materials Science and Metallurgical Engineering, Program in Metallurgical Engineering, Cincinnati, OH 45221. Offers MS, PhD. *Degree requirements:* For master's, thesis optional; for doctorate, one foreign language, comprehensive exam, thesis/dissertation, oral English proficiency exam. *Entrance requirements:* For master's and doctorate, GRE General Test, BS in related field, minimum undergraduate GPA of 3.0. Additional exam requirements/recommendations for international students: Required—TOEFL. Electronic applications accepted. *Faculty research:* Polymer characterization, surface analysis, and adhesion; high-temperature coatings and physical chemistry of materials.

University of Connecticut, Graduate School, School of Engineering, Department of Metallurgy and Materials Engineering, Storrs, CT 06269. Offers MS, PhD. *Faculty:* 31 full-time (4 women). *Students:* 89 full-time (29 women), 22 part-time (3 women); includes 12 minority (3 African Americans, 5 Asian Americans or Pacific Islanders, 4 Hispanic Americans), 56 international. Average age 28. 211 applicants, 11% accepted, 19 enrolled. In 2009, 12 master's, 9 doctorates awarded. Terminal master's awarded for partial completion of doctoral program. *Degree requirements:* For master's, comprehensive exam, thesis or alternative; for doctorate, thesis/dissertation. *Entrance requirements:* For master's and doctorate, GRE General Test, GRE Subject Test. Additional exam requirements/recommendations for international students: Required—TOEFL (minimum score 550 paper-based; 213 computer-based). *Application deadline:* For fall admission, 2/1 priority date for domestic and international students; for spring admission, 11/1 for domestic students, 10/1 for international students. Applications are processed on a rolling basis. Application fee: $55. Electronic applications accepted. *Expenses:* Tuition, state resident: full-time $4725; part-time $525 per credit. Tuition, nonresident: full-time $12,267; part-time $1363 per credit. Required fees: $346 per semester. Tuition and fees vary according to course load. *Financial support:* In 2009–10, 80 research assistantships with full tuition reimbursements, 4 teaching assistantships with full tuition reimbursements were awarded; fellowships, Federal Work-Study, scholarships/grants, health care benefits, and unspecified assistantships also available. Financial award application deadline: 2/1; financial award applicants required to submit FAFSA. *Faculty research:* Microsegregation and coarsening, fatigue crack, electron-dislocation interaction. *Unit head:* Harris L. Marcus, Director, 860-486-4623, Fax: 860-486-4745, E-mail: hmarcus@ims.uconn.edu. *Application contact:* Harris L. Marcus, Director, 860-486-4623, Fax: 860-486-4745, E-mail: hmarcus@ims.uconn.edu.

University of Idaho, College of Graduate Studies, College of Engineering, Department of Materials Science and Engineering, Program in Materials Science and Engineering, Moscow, ID 83844-2282. Offers materials science and engineering (PhD), including mining engineering; metallurgical engineering (MS). *Students:* 6 full-time, 1 part-time. In 2009, 5 master's, 1 doctorate awarded. *Expenses:* Tuition, state resident: full-time $6120. Tuition, nonresident: full-time $17,712. *Unit head:* Dr. Wudneh Admassu, Chair, 208-885-6376. *Application contact:* Dr. Wudneh Admassu, Chair, 208-885-6376.

University of Idaho, College of Graduate Studies, College of Engineering, Department of Materials Science and Engineering, Program in Metallurgical Engineering, Moscow, ID 83844-2282. Offers MS. *Students:* 1 part-time. *Entrance requirements:* For master's, minimum GPA of 2.8. *Application deadline:* For fall admission, 8/1 for domestic students; for spring admission, 12/15 for domestic students. Application fee: $55 ($60 for international students). *Expenses:* Tuition, state resident: full-time $6120. Tuition, nonresident: full-time $17,712. *Financial support:* Application deadline: 2/15. *Unit head:* Dr. Wudneh Admassu, Chair, 208-885-6376. *Application contact:* Dr. Wudneh Admassu, Chair, 208-885-6376.

University of Nebraska–Lincoln, Graduate College, College of Engineering, Department of Mechanical Engineering, Lincoln, NE 68588. Offers chemical and materials engineering (PhD); mechanical engineering (MS, PhD), including materials science engineering (MS), metallurgical engineering (MS). *Degree requirements:* For master's, thesis optional; for doctorate, comprehensive exam, thesis/dissertation. *Entrance requirements:* For master's and doctorate, GRE General Test. Additional exam requirements/recommendations for international students: Required—TOEFL (minimum score 550 paper-based; 213 computer-based). Electronic applications accepted. *Faculty research:* Robotics for planetary exploration, vehicle crashworthiness, transient heat conduction, laser beam/particle interactions.

See Close-Up on page 527.

University of Nevada, Reno, Graduate School, College of Engineering, Department of Chemical and Materials Engineering, Program in Materials Science and Engineering, Reno, NV 89557. Offers MS, PhD. Terminal master's awarded for partial completion of doctoral program. *Degree requirements:* For master's, thesis; for doctorate, one foreign language, thesis/dissertation. *Entrance requirements:* For master's, minimum GPA of 2.75; for doctorate, GRE, minimum GPA of 3.0. Additional exam requirements/recommendations for international students: Required—TOEFL (minimum score 500 paper-based; 173 computer-based; 61 iBT), IELTS (minimum score 6). Electronic applications accepted. *Faculty research:* Hydrometallurgy, applied surface chemistry, mineral processing, mineral bioprocessing, ceramics.

The University of Texas at El Paso, Graduate School, College of Engineering, Department of Metallurgical and Materials Engineering, El Paso, TX 79968-0001. Offers materials science and engineering (PhD); metallurgical and materials engineering (MS). Part-time and evening/weekend programs available. *Degree requirements:* For master's, thesis. *Entrance requirements:* For master's, GRE General Test. Additional exam requirements/recommendations for international students: Required—TOEFL. Electronic applications accepted.

University of Utah, The Graduate School, College of Mines and Earth Sciences, Department of Metallurgical Engineering, Salt Lake City, UT 84112. Offers ME, MS, PhD. Part-time programs available. *Faculty:* 8 full-time (0 women). *Students:* 41 full-time (11 women), 11 part-time (1 woman); includes 4 minority (3 Asian Americans or Pacific Islanders, 1 Hispanic American), 42 international. Average age 29. 31 applicants, 68% accepted, 13 enrolled. In 2009, 11 master's, 11 doctorates awarded. Terminal master's awarded for partial completion of doctoral program. *Degree requirements:* For master's, comprehensive exam (ME), thesis (MS); for doctorate, thesis/dissertation. *Entrance requirements:* For master's and doctorate, GRE General Test (recommended), minimum GPA of 3.0. Additional exam requirements/recommendations for international students: Required—TOEFL (minimum score 530 paper-based; 173 computer-based), or IELTS. *Application deadline:* For fall admission, 4/1 for domestic students, 4/1 priority date for international students; for spring admission, 11/1 priority date for domestic and international students. Applications are processed on a rolling basis. Application fee: $55 ($65 for international students). Electronic applications accepted. *Expenses:* Tuition, state resident: full-time $4004; part-time $1674 per semester. Tuition, nonresident: full-time $14,134; part-time $5915 per semester. Required fees: $324 per semester. Tuition and fees vary according to course load, degree level and program. *Financial support:* In 2009–10, 46 research assistantships with full and partial tuition reimbursements (averaging $15,634 per year) were awarded; fellowships with full and partial tuition reimbursements, teaching assistantships with full and partial tuition reimbursements, institutionally sponsored loans also available. Financial award application deadline: 2/15; financial award applicants required to submit FAFSA. *Faculty research:* Physical metallurgy, mathematical modeling, mineral processing, chemical metallurgy nanoscience and technology. Total annual research expenditures: $2.8 million. *Unit head:* Dr. Jan D. Miller, Chair, 801-581-5160, Fax: 801-581-4937, E-mail: jan.miller@utah.edu. *Application contact:* Kay Argyle, Executive Secretary, 801-581-6386, Fax: 801-581-4937, E-mail: kay.argyle@utah.edu.

Wayne State University, College of Engineering, Department of Chemical Engineering and Materials Science, Detroit, MI 48202. Offers chemical engineering (MS, PhD); hazardous waste (MS, Certificate), including environmental auditing (Certificate), hazardous materials management on public lands (Certificate), hazardous waste control (Certificate), hazardous waste management (MS); materials science and engineering (MS, PhD, Certificate), including materials science and engineering (MS, PhD), polymer engineering (Certificate); metallurgical engineering (MS, PhD). Part-time programs available. Terminal master's awarded for partial completion of doctoral program. *Degree requirements:* For master's, thesis optional; for doctorate, thesis/dissertation. *Entrance requirements:* For master's, GRE (if applying for financial support), letters of recommendation; resume; for doctorate, GRE (if applying for financial support), recommendations; resumè personal statement. Additional exam requirements/recommendations for international students: Required—TOEFL (minimum score 550 paper-based; 213 computer-based), TWE (minimum score 6). Electronic applications accepted. *Faculty research:* Polymer solutions and processing, catalysis, environmental transport, waste minimization, transport in biological systems.

Polymer Science and Engineering

California Polytechnic State University, San Luis Obispo, College of Science and Mathematics, Department of Chemistry and Biochemistry, San Luis Obispo, CA 93407. Offers polymers and coating science (MS). Part-time programs available. *Faculty:* 3 full-time (0 women), 1 (woman) part-time/adjunct. *Students:* 2 full-time (1 woman), 2 part-time (1 woman); includes 1 minority (African American). Average age 23. 5 applicants, 80% accepted, 3 enrolled. In 2009, 5 master's awarded. *Degree requirements:* For master's, comprehensive oral exam. *Entrance requirements:* For master's, minimum GPA of 2.5 in last 90 quarter units of course work. Additional exam requirements/recommendations for international students: Required—TOEFL (minimum score 550 paper-based; 213 computer-based), or IELTS (minimum score 6). *Application deadline:* For fall admission, 7/1 for domestic students, 11/30 for international students; for winter admission, 11/1 for domestic students, 6/30 for international students; for spring admission, 2/1 for domestic students. Applications are processed on a rolling basis. Application fee: $55. Electronic applications accepted. *Expenses:* Tuition, nonresident: full-time $11,160; part-time $248 per unit. Required fees: $7134; $1553 per quarter. *Financial support:* Career-related internships or fieldwork, Federal Work-Study, and scholarships/grants available. Support available to part-time students. Financial award application deadline: 3/2; financial award applicants required to submit FAFSA. *Faculty research:* Polymer physical chemistry and analysis, polymer synthesis, coatings formulation. *Unit head:* Dr. Ray Fernando, Graduate Coordinator, 805-756-2395, Fax: 805-756-5500, E-mail: rhfernan@calpoly.edu. *Application contact:* Dr. James Maraviglia, Assistant Vice President for Admissions, Recruitment and Financial Aid, 805-756-2311, Fax: 805-756-5400, E-mail: admissions@calpoly.edu.

Carnegie Mellon University, Carnegie Institute of Technology, Department of Chemical Engineering and Department of Chemistry, Program in Colloids, Polymers and Surfaces, Pittsburgh, PA 15213-3891. Offers MS. Part-time and evening/weekend programs available. *Entrance requirements:* For master's, GRE General Test, GRE Subject Test. Additional exam requirements/recommendations for international students: Required—TOEFL. *Faculty research:* Surface phenomena, polymer rheology, solubilization phenomena, colloid transport phenomena, polymer synthesis.

Carnegie Mellon University, Mellon College of Science, Department of Chemistry, Pittsburgh, PA 15213-3891. Offers biotechnology and management (MS); chemistry (PhD), including bioinorganic, bioorganic, organic and materials, biophysics and spectroscopy, computational and theoretical, polymer; colloids, polymers and surfaces (MS). Part-time programs available. Terminal master's awarded for partial completion of doctoral program. *Degree requirements:* For doctorate, thesis/dissertation, departmental qualifying and oral exams, teaching experience. *Entrance requirements:* For master's, GRE General Test; for doctorate, GRE General Test, GRE Subject Test. Additional exam requirements/recommendations for international students: Required—TOEFL. Electronic applications accepted. *Faculty research:* Physical and theoretical chemistry, chemical synthesis, biophysical/bioinorganic chemistry.

Case Western Reserve University, School of Graduate Studies, The Case School of Engineering, Department of Macromolecular Science and Engineering, Cleveland, OH 44106. Offers MS, PhD, MD/PhD. Part-time programs available. *Faculty:* 14 full-time (4 women). *Students:* 45 full-time (13 women), 5 part-time (1 woman); includes 6 minority (1 African American, 1 American Indian/Alaska Native, 3 Asian Americans or Pacific Islanders, 1 Hispanic American), 23 international. In 2009, 1 master's, 7 doctorates awarded. Terminal master's awarded for partial completion of doctoral program. *Degree requirements:* For master's, thesis; for doctorate, thesis/dissertation, qualifying exam, teaching experience. *Entrance requirements:* For master's and doctorate, GRE General Test. Additional exam requirements/recommendations for international students: Required—TOEFL. *Application deadline:* For fall admission, 2/28 priority date for domestic students; for spring admission, 10/1 priority date for domestic students. Applications are processed on a rolling basis. Application fee: $50. *Financial support:* Fellowships with full tuition reimbursements, research assistantships with full and partial tuition reimbursements, teaching assistantships available. Financial award applicants required to submit FAFSA. *Faculty research:* Synthesis and molecular design; processing, modeling and simulation, structure-property relationships. Total annual research expenditures: $5.3 million. *Unit head:* Dr. David Schiraldi, Department Chair, 216-368-4243, Fax: 216-368-4202, E-mail: das44@case.edu. *Application contact:* Kathleen Bates, Academic Administration Manager, 216-368-3840, Fax: 216-368-3209, E-mail: tls4@case.edu.

Cornell University, Graduate School, Graduate Fields of Engineering, Field of Chemical Engineering, Ithaca, NY 14853-0001. Offers advanced materials processing (M Eng, MS, PhD); applied mathematics and computational methods (M Eng, MS, PhD); biochemical engineering (M Eng, MS, PhD); chemical reaction engineering (M Eng, MS, PhD); classical and statistical thermodynamics (M Eng, MS, PhD); fluid dynamics, rheology and biorheology (M Eng, MS, PhD); heat and mass transfer (M Eng, MS, PhD); kinetics and catalysis (M Eng, MS, PhD); polymers (M Eng, MS, PhD); surface science (M Eng, MS, PhD). *Faculty:* 29 full-time (2 women). *Students:* 95 full-time (30 women); includes 9 minority (1 African American, 5 Asian Americans or Pacific Islanders, 3 Hispanic Americans), 41 international. Average age 25. 317 applicants, 38% accepted, 46 enrolled. In 2009, 22 master's, 17 doctorates awarded. *Degree requirements:* For master's, thesis (MS); for doctorate, comprehensive exam, thesis/dissertation. *Entrance requirements:* For master's and doctorate, GRE General Test, 2 letters of recommendation. Additional exam requirements/recommendations for international students: Required—TOEFL (minimum score 600 paper-based; 237 computer-based; 77 iBT). *Application deadline:* For fall admission, 1/15 priority date for domestic students. Application fee: $70. Electronic applications accepted. *Expenses:* Tuition: Full-time $29,500. Required fees: $70. Full-time tuition and fees vary according to degree level, program and student level. *Financial support:* In 2009–10, 67 students received support, including 3 fellowships with full tuition reimbursements available, 3 research assistantships with full tuition reimbursements available; teaching assistantships with full tuition reimbursements available, institutionally sponsored loans, scholarships/grants, health care benefits, tuition waivers (full and partial), and unspecified assistantships also available. Financial award applicants required to submit FAFSA. *Faculty research:* Biochemical, biomedical and metabolic engineering; fluid and polymer dynamics; surface science and chemical kinetics; electronics materials; microchemical systems and nanotechnology. *Unit head:* Director of Graduate Studies, 607-255-4550. *Application contact:* Graduate Field Assistant, 607-255-4550, E-mail: dgs@cheme.cornell.edu.

Cornell University, Graduate School, Graduate Fields of Human Ecology, Field of Textiles, Ithaca, NY 14853-0001. Offers apparel design (MA, MPS); fiber science (MS, PhD); polymer science (MS, PhD); textile science (MS, PhD). *Faculty:* 17 full-time (7 women). *Students:* 21 full-time (16 women); includes 1 minority (Hispanic American), 12 international. Average age 30. 26 applicants, 19% accepted, 3 enrolled. In 2009, 1 master's, 4 doctorates awarded. *Degree requirements:* For master's, thesis (MA, MS), project paper (MPS); for doctorate, comprehensive exam, thesis/dissertation. *Entrance requirements:* For master's, GRE General Test, 2 letters of recommendation, portfolio (functional apparel design); for doctorate, GRE General Test, 2 letters of recommendation. Additional exam requirements/recommendations for international students: Required—TOEFL (minimum score 600 paper-based; 250 computer-based; 77 iBT). *Application deadline:* For fall admission, 3/1 for domestic students; for spring admission, 10/1 for domestic students. Application fee: $70. Electronic applications accepted. *Expenses:* Tuition: Full-time $29,500. Required fees: $70. Full-time tuition and fees vary according to degree level, program and student level. *Financial support:* In 2009–10, 19 students received support, including 2 teaching assistantships with full tuition reimbursements available; fellowships with full tuition reimbursements available, research assistantships with full tuition reimbursements available, institutionally sponsored loans, scholarships/grants, health care benefits, tuition waivers (full and partial), and unspecified assistantships also available. Financial award applicants required to submit FAFSA. *Faculty research:* Apparel design, consumption, mass customization, 3-D body scanning. *Unit head:* Director of Graduate Studies, 607-255-3151, Fax: 607-255-1093. *Application contact:* Graduate Field Assistant, 607-255-3151, Fax: 607-255-1093, E-mail: textiles_grad@cornell.edu.

DePaul University, College of Liberal Arts and Sciences, Department of Chemistry, Chicago, IL 60614. Offers biochemistry (MS); chemistry (MS); polymer chemistry and coatings technology (MS). Part-time and evening/weekend programs available. *Faculty:* 13 full-time (7 women), 4 part-time/adjunct (1 woman). *Students:* 14 full-time (7 women), 9 part-time (4 women); includes 6 minority (2 African Americans, 3 Asian Americans or Pacific Islanders, 1 Hispanic American), 1 international. Average age 27. 6 applicants, 100% accepted, 4 enrolled. In 2009, 2 master's awarded. *Degree requirements:* For master's, thesis (for some programs), oral exam (for selected programs). *Entrance requirements:* For master's, GRE Subject Test (chemistry), GRE General Test, BS in chemistry or equivalent. Additional exam requirements/recommendations for international students: Required—TOEFL (minimum score 590 paper-based; 243 computer-based). *Application deadline:* For fall admission, 7/15 for domestic students, 5/1 for international students; for winter admission, 11/15 for domestic students, 9/1 for international students; for spring admission, 2/15 for domestic students, 12/1 for international students. Applications are processed on a rolling basis. Application fee: $40. Electronic applications accepted. *Expenses:* Tuition: Full-time $37,525; part-time $620 per credit hour. *Financial support:* In 2009–10, 4 students received support, including 6 teaching assistantships with partial tuition reimbursements available (averaging $9,000 per year). Financial award application deadline: 6/1. *Faculty research:* Computational chemistry, organic synthesis, inorganic synthesis, polymer synthesis, biochemistry. Total annual research expenditures: $30,000. *Unit head:* Dr. Richard F. Niedziela, Chair, 773-325-7307, Fax: 773-325-7421, E-mail: rniedzie@condor.depaul.edu. *Application contact:* Dr. Matthew Dintzner, Director of Graduate Studies, 773-325-4726, Fax: 773-325-7421, E-mail: mdintzne@depaul.edu.

Eastern Michigan University, Graduate School, College of Technology, School of Engineering Technology, Program in Polymers and Coatings Technology, Ypsilanti, MI 48197. Offers polymer technology (MS). Part-time and evening/weekend programs available. Postbaccalaureate distance learning degree programs offered (minimal on-campus study). *Students:* 4 full-time (3 women), 22 part-time (6 women); includes 2 minority (1 African American, 1 Asian American or Pacific Islander), 14 international. Average age 29. In 2009, 4 master's awarded. *Degree requirements:* For master's, thesis optional. *Entrance requirements:* For master's, GRE General Test, BS in chemistry, minimum GPA of 2.6. Additional exam requirements/recommendations for international students: Required—TOEFL. *Application deadline:* Applications are processed on a rolling basis. Application fee: $35. Tuition and fees vary according to course level. *Financial support:* Fellowships, research assistantships with full tuition reimbursements, teaching assistantships with full tuition reimbursements, career-related internships or fieldwork, Federal Work-Study, institutionally sponsored loans, scholarships/grants, tuition waivers (partial), and unspecified assistantships available. Support available to part-time students. Financial award applicants required to submit FAFSA. *Unit head:* Dr. Jamil Baghdachi, Program Coordinator, 734-487-3192, Fax: 734-487-8755, E-mail: jamil.baghdachi@emich.edu. *Application contact:* Dr. Jamil Baghdachi, Program Coordinator, 734-487-3192, Fax: 734-487-8755, E-mail: jamil.baghdachi@emich.edu.

Florida State University, The Graduate School, Interdisciplinary Program in Materials Science, Tallahassee, FL 32306. Offers computational materials science and mechanics (MS); functional materials (MS); nanoscale materials, composite materials, and interfaces (MS); polymers and bio-inspired materials (MS). *Faculty:* 38 full-time (5 women). *Students:* 6 full-time (1 woman), 2 international. *Degree requirements:* For master's, thesis. *Entrance requirements:* For master's, GRE General Test (minimum score 1100 verbal and quantitative), minimum GPA of 3.0, letters of recommendation. Additional exam requirements/recommendations for international students: Required—TOEFL (minimum score 550 paper-based; 213 computer-based; 80 iBT). *Application deadline:* For fall admission, 7/1 for domestic and international students; for winter admission, 11/1 for domestic and international students; for spring admission, 3/1 for domestic and international students. Applications are processed on a rolling basis. Electronic applications accepted. *Expenses:* Tuition, state resident: full-time $7413.36. Tuition, nonresident: full-time $22,567. *Financial support:* Fellowships, research assistantships, teaching assistantships available. Financial award application deadline: 1/15; financial award applicants required to submit FAFSA. *Faculty research:* Magnetism and magnetic materials, composites, superconductors, polymers, computations. *Unit head:* Prof. Eric Hellstrom, Director, 850-645-7489, Fax: 850-645-7754, E-mail: hellstrom@asc.magnet.fsu.edu. *Application contact:* Todd Kramer, Admissions Coordinator, 850-410-6161, Fax: 850-410-6486, E-mail: krameto@eng.fsu.edu.

Georgia Institute of Technology, Graduate Studies and Research, College of Engineering, Multidisciplinary Program in Polymers, Atlanta, GA 30332-0001. Offers MS Poly. *Degree requirements:* For master's, thesis. *Entrance requirements:* For master's, minimum GPA of 2.7. Additional exam requirements/recommendations for international students: Required—TOEFL.

Georgia Institute of Technology, Graduate Studies and Research, College of Engineering, School of Polymer, Textile, and Fiber Engineering, Atlanta, GA 30332-0001. Offers polymer, textile and fiber engineering (MS, PhD); polymers (MS Poly). *Degree requirements:* For master's, thesis (for some programs); for doctorate, comprehensive exam, thesis/dissertation. *Entrance requirements:* For master's, GRE, minimum GPA of 2.7; for doctorate, GRE, minimum GPA of 3.0. Additional exam requirements/recommendations for international students: Required—TOEFL (minimum score 550 paper-based; 213 computer-based). Electronic applications accepted. *Faculty research:* Energy conservation, environmental control, engineered fibrous structures, polymer synthesis and degradation, high performance organic-carbon-ceramic fibers.

Lehigh University, College of Arts and Sciences, Department of Chemistry, Bethlehem, PA 18015. Offers chemistry (MS, PhD); polymer science and engineering (MS, PhD). Part-time programs available. Postbaccalaureate distance learning degree programs offered (no on-campus study). *Faculty:* 15 full-time (2 women), 1 part-time/adjunct (0 women). *Students:* 36 full-time (17 women), 83 part-time (40 women); includes 15 minority (2 African Americans, 1 American Indian/Alaska Native, 6 Asian Americans or Pacific Islanders, 6 Hispanic Americans), 12 international. Average age 29. 92 applicants, 45% accepted, 35 enrolled. In 2009, 31 master's, 2 doctorates awarded. Terminal master's awarded for partial completion of doctoral program. *Degree requirements:* For master's, comprehensive exam, thesis; for doctorate, comprehensive exam, thesis/dissertation. *Entrance requirements:* Additional exam requirements/recommendations for international students: Required—TOEFL (minimum score 230 computer-based). *Application deadline:* For fall admission, 1/15 priority date for domestic and international students. Applications are processed on a rolling basis. Application fee: $65. Electronic applications accepted. *Financial support:* In 2009–10, 3 fellowships with full tuition reimbursements (averaging $20,000 per year), 8 research assistantships with full tuition reimbursements (averaging $20,000 per year), 19 teaching assistantships with full tuition reimbursements (averaging $20,000 per year) were awarded; career-related internships or fieldwork, Federal Work-Study, institutionally sponsored loans, scholarships/grants, tuition waivers (full and partial), and unspecified assistantships also available. Support available to part-time students. Financial award application deadline: 1/15. *Faculty research:* Materials chemistry, biological chemistry, surface chemistry, nano science. Total annual research expenditures: $3.3 million. *Unit head:* Prof. Robert A. Flowers, Professor/Chair, 610-758-3470, Fax: 610-758-6536, E-mail: rof2@lehigh.edu. *Application contact:* Dr. Rebecca Miller, Graduate Coordinator, 610-758-3471, Fax: 610-758-6536, E-mail: inluchem@lehigh.edu.

Lehigh University, College of Arts and Sciences, Department of Physics, Bethlehem, PA 18015. Offers photonics (MS); physics (MS, PhD); polymer science (MS, PhD). Part-time programs available. *Faculty:* 17 full-time (1 woman), 1 part-time/adjunct (0 women). *Students:* 48 full-time (13 women), 1 part-time (0 women); includes 1 minority (African American), 19 international. Average age 26. 100 applicants, 13% accepted, 9 enrolled. In 2009, 6 doctorates awarded. *Degree requirements:* For doctorate, comprehensive exam, thesis/dissertation. *Entrance requirements:* Additional exam requirements/recommendations for international students: Required—TOEFL (minimum score 213 computer-based; 85 iBT). *Application deadline:* For fall admission, 2/15 priority date for domestic and international students. Applications are processed on a rolling basis. Application fee: $65. Electronic applications accepted. *Financial support:* In 2009–10, 47 students received support, including 4 fellowships with full tuition reimbursements available (averaging $23,000 per year), 23 research assistantships with full tuition reimbursements available (averaging $22,180 per year), 20 teaching assistantships with full tuition reimbursements available (averaging $22,180 per year); career-related internships or fieldwork, Federal Work-Study, institutionally sponsored loans, scholarships/grants, tuition waivers (full and partial), and unspecified assistantships also available. Support available to part-time students. Financial award application deadline: 1/15. *Faculty research:* Condensed matter physics; atomic, molecular and optical physics; plasma physics; nonlinear optics and photonics; astronomy and astrophysics. Total annual research expenditures: $2.9 million. *Unit head:* Dr. Volkmar Dierolf, Chair, 610-758-3915, Fax: 610-758-5730, E-mail: vod2@lehigh.edu. *Application contact:* Dr. Ivan Biaggio, Graduate Admissions Officer, 610-758-4916, Fax: 610-758-5730, E-mail: ivb2@lehigh.edu.

Lehigh University, P.C. Rossin College of Engineering and Applied Science and College of Arts and Sciences, Center for Polymer Science and Engineering, Bethlehem, PA 18015. Offers M Eng, MS, PhD. Part-time and evening/weekend programs available. Postbaccalaureate distance learning degree programs offered (no on-campus study). *Faculty:* 1 part-time/adjunct (0 women). *Students:* 4 full-time (1 woman), 9 part-time (2 women); includes 1 minority (Asian American or Pacific Islander), 2 international. Average age 34. 45 applicants, 0% accepted, 0 enrolled. In 2009, 2 master's, 1 doctorate awarded. Terminal master's awarded for partial

Polymer Science and Engineering

Lehigh University (continued)
completion of doctoral program. *Degree requirements:* For master's, thesis (for some programs); for doctorate, thesis/dissertation. *Entrance requirements:* For master's and doctorate, GRE General Test. Additional exam requirements/recommendations for international students: Required—TOEFL (minimum score 550 paper-based; 213 computer-based; 82 iBT). *Application deadline:* For fall admission, 7/15 for domestic students, 1/15 for international students; for spring admission, 12/1 for domestic and international students. Applications are processed on a rolling basis. Application fee: $65. Electronic applications accepted. *Financial support:* In 2009–10, 5 students received support, including fellowships (averaging $17,667 per year), 5 research assistantships (averaging $26,670 per year), teaching assistantships (averaging $17,667 per year); Royal Thai scholarship also available. Financial award application deadline: 1/15. *Faculty research:* Polymer colloids, polymer coatings, blends and composites, polymer interfaces, emulsion polymer. *Unit head:* Dr. Raymond A. Pearson, Director, 610-758-3857, Fax: 610-758-3526, E-mail: rp02@lehigh.edu. *Application contact:* James E. Roberts, Chair, Polymer Education Committee, 610-758-4841, Fax: 610-758-6536, E-mail: jer1@lehigh.edu.

Lehigh University, P.C. Rossin College of Engineering and Applied Science, Department of Materials Science and Engineering, Bethlehem, PA 18015. Offers materials science and engineering (M Eng, MS, PhD); photonics (MS); polymer science/engineering (M Eng, MS, PhD); MBA/E. Part-time programs available. *Faculty:* 13 full-time (3 women). *Students:* 26 full-time (3 women), 4 part-time (2 women), 15 international. Average age 26. 163 applicants, 4% accepted, 2 enrolled. In 2009, 2 master's, 4 doctorates awarded. *Degree requirements:* For master's, thesis; for doctorate, comprehensive exam, thesis/dissertation. *Entrance requirements:* For master's and doctorate, GRE General Test, minimum GPA of 3.0. Additional exam requirements/recommendations for international students: Required—TOEFL. *Application deadline:* For fall admission, 1/15 priority date for domestic students, 1/15 for international students; for spring admission, 12/1 priority date for domestic students, 12/1 for international students. Applications are processed on a rolling basis. Application fee: $65. Electronic applications accepted. *Financial support:* In 2009–10, 27 students received support, including 5 fellowships with full and partial tuition reimbursements available (averaging $22,400 per year), 21 research assistantships with full tuition reimbursements available (averaging $22,449 per year), 6 teaching assistantships with partial tuition reimbursements available (averaging $17,512 per year); career-related internships or fieldwork, Federal Work-Study, institutionally sponsored loans, scholarships/grants, and unspecified assistantships also available. Support available to part-time students. Financial award application deadline: 1/15. *Faculty research:* Metals, ceramics, crystals, polymers, fatigue crack propagation. Total annual research expenditures: $4 million. *Unit head:* Dr. Helen Chan, Chairperson, 610-758-5554, Fax: 610-758-4244, E-mail: hmc0@lehigh.edu. *Application contact:* Anne Marie Lobley, Graduate Administrative Coordinator, 610-758-4222, Fax: 610-758-4244, E-mail: amme@lehigh.edu.

Lehigh University, P.C. Rossin College of Engineering and Applied Science, Department of Mechanical Engineering and Mechanics, Bethlehem, PA 18015. Offers applied mathematics (MS, PhD); computational engineering and mechanics (MS, PhD); mechanical engineering (M Eng, MS, PhD, MBA/E); polymer science/engineering (M Eng, MS, PhD, MBA/E); MBA/E. Part-time and evening/weekend programs available. Postbaccalaureate distance learning degree programs offered. *Faculty:* 20 full-time (0 women). *Students:* 85 full-time (12 women), 32 part-time (3 women); includes 4 minority (1 African American, 2 Asian Americans or Pacific Islanders, 1 Hispanic American), 51 international. Average age 27. 320 applicants, 29% accepted, 45 enrolled. In 2009, 23 master's, 6 doctorates awarded. Terminal master's awarded for partial completion of doctoral program. *Degree requirements:* For master's, thesis; for doctorate, thesis/dissertation, general exam. *Entrance requirements:* Additional exam requirements/recommendations for international students: Required—TOEFL (minimum score 550 paper-based; 213 computer-based; 79 iBT). *Application deadline:* For fall admission, 7/15 for domestic and international students; for spring admission, 12/1 for domestic and international students. Applications are processed on a rolling basis. Application fee: $75. Electronic applications accepted. *Financial support:* In 2009–10, 30 students received support, including 8 fellowships with full and partial tuition reimbursements available (averaging $21,060 per year), 24 research assistantships with full and partial tuition reimbursements available (averaging $20,700 per year), 18 teaching assistantships with full and partial tuition reimbursements available (averaging $21,060 per year); unspecified assistantships also available. Financial award application deadline: 1/15. *Faculty research:* Thermofluids, dynamic systems, CAD/CAM, computational mechanics, solid mechanics. Total annual research expenditures: $3.1 million. *Unit head:* Dr. D. Gary Harlow, Chairman, 610-758-4102, Fax: 610-758-6224, E-mail: dgh0@lehigh.edu. *Application contact:* Jo Ann M. Casciano, Graduate Coordinator, 610-758-4107, Fax: 610-758-6224, E-mail: jmc4@lehigh.edu.

Massachusetts Institute of Technology, School of Engineering, Department of Materials Science and Engineering, Cambridge, MA 02139-4307. Offers archaeological materials (PhD, Sc D); bio- and polymeric materials (PhD, Sc D); electronic, photonic and magnetic materials (PhD, Sc D); emerging, fundamental and computational studies in materials science (Sc D); emerging, fundamental, and computational studies in materials science (PhD); materials engineering (Mat E); materials science and engineering (M Eng, SM, PhD, Sc D); metallurgical engineering (Met E); structural and environmental materials (PhD, Sc D); SM/MBA. *Faculty:* 36 full-time (8 women). *Students:* 222 full-time (62 women); includes 32 minority (3 African Americans, 21 Asian Americans or Pacific Islanders, 8 Hispanic Americans), 125 international. Average age 26. 459 applicants, 23% accepted, 63 enrolled. In 2009, 35 master's, 28 doctorates awarded. Terminal master's awarded for partial completion of doctoral program. *Degree requirements:* For master's and other advanced degree, thesis; for doctorate, comprehensive exam, thesis/dissertation. *Entrance requirements:* For master's and doctorate, GRE General Test. Additional exam requirements/recommendations for international students: Required—IELTS (minimum score 5.5); Recommended—TOEFL (minimum score 577 paper-based; 233 computer-based; 90 iBT). *Application deadline:* For fall admission, 1/1 for domestic and international students. Application fee: $75. Electronic applications accepted. *Financial support:* In 2009–10, 222 students received support, including 55 fellowships with tuition reimbursements available (averaging $22,387 per year), 135 research assistantships with tuition reimbursements available (averaging $27,287 per year), 10 teaching assistantships with tuition reimbursements available (averaging $30,736 per year); career-related internships or fieldwork, Federal Work-Study, institutionally sponsored loans, scholarships/grants, health care benefits, and unspecified assistantships also available. *Faculty research:* Thermodynamics and kinetics of phase transformations, structure of all materials classes: metals, ceramics, semiconductors, polymers, biomaterials, influence of processing on materials structure, structure, property relationships (electrical, magnetic, optical, mechanical). Total annual research expenditures: $22.6 million. *Unit head:* Prof. Edwin L. Thomas, Department Head, 617-253-3300, Fax: 617-252-1775. *Application contact:* Angelita Mireles, Graduate Admissions, 617-253-3302, E-mail: dmse-admissions@mit.edu.

North Carolina State University, Graduate School, College of Textiles, Program in Fiber and Polymer Science, Raleigh, NC 27695. Offers PhD. *Degree requirements:* For doctorate, one foreign language, thesis/dissertation, cumulative exams. *Entrance requirements:* For doctorate, GRE. Electronic applications accepted. *Faculty research:* Polymer science, fiber mechanics, medical textiles, nanotechnology.

North Dakota State University, College of Graduate and Interdisciplinary Studies, College of Science and Mathematics, Department of Coatings and Polymeric Materials, Fargo, ND 58108. Offers MS, PhD. Part-time programs available. *Students:* 24 full-time (6 women), 1 part-time (0 women), 19 international. Terminal master's awarded for partial completion of doctoral program. *Degree requirements:* For master's, thesis, cumulative exams; for doctorate, comprehensive exam, thesis/dissertation, cumulative exams. *Entrance requirements:* For master's and doctorate, BS in chemistry or chemical engineering, minimum GPA of 3.0. Additional exam requirements/recommendations for international students: Required—TOEFL (minimum score 550 paper-based; 213 computer-based). *Application deadline:* Applications are processed on a rolling basis. Application fee: $45 ($60 for international students). Electronic

applications accepted. *Financial support:* Fellowships, research assistantships with full tuition reimbursements, teaching assistantships with full tuition reimbursements, Federal Work-Study, institutionally sponsored loans, scholarships/grants, health care benefits, and tuition waivers (full) available. Support available to part-time students. Financial award application deadline: 3/15. *Faculty research:* Nanomaterials, combinatorial materials science. Total annual research expenditures: $1.2 million. *Unit head:* Dr. Stuart Croll, Chair, 701-231-7633, Fax: 701-231-8439. *Application contact:* Dr. Dean C. Webster, Assistant Professor, 701-231-8709, Fax: 701-231-8439, E-mail: dean.webster@ndsu.edu.

Polytechnic Institute of NYU, Department of Chemical and Biological Engineering, Major in Polymer Science and Engineering, Brooklyn, NY 11201-2990. Offers MS. *Students:* 1 (woman) full-time, all international. *Degree requirements:* For master's, comprehensive exam (for some programs), thesis (for some programs). *Entrance requirements:* Additional exam requirements/recommendations for international students: Required—TOEFL (minimum score 550 paper-based; 213 computer-based; 80 iBT); Recommended—IELTS (minimum score 6.5). *Application deadline:* For fall admission, 7/31 priority date for domestic students, 4/30 priority date for international students; for spring admission, 12/31 priority date for domestic students, 10/30 priority date for international students. Applications are processed on a rolling basis. Application fee: $75. Electronic applications accepted. *Expenses:* Tuition: Full-time $21,492; part-time $1194 per credit hour. Required fees: $1160; $204 per course. *Unit head:* Dr. Walter Zurawsky, Department Head, 718-260-3600. *Application contact:* JeanCarlo Bonilla, Dir. Graduate Enrollment Management, 718-260-3182, Fax: 718-260-3624.

Rensselaer Polytechnic Institute, Graduate School, School of Engineering, Department of Materials Science and Engineering, Troy, NY 12180. Offers ceramics and glass science (M Eng, MS, PhD); composites (M Eng, MS, PhD); electronic materials (M Eng, MS, PhD); metallurgy (M Eng, MS, PhD); polymers (M Eng, MS, PhD). Part-time and evening/weekend programs available. *Faculty:* 16 full-time (2 women). *Students:* 54 full-time (11 women), 4 part-time (1 woman); includes 7 minority (all Asian Americans or Pacific Islanders), 30 international. Average age 24. 234 applicants, 14% accepted, 14 enrolled. In 2009, 10 master's, 6 doctorates awarded. Terminal master's awarded for partial completion of doctoral program. *Degree requirements:* For master's, thesis; for doctorate, comprehensive exam, thesis/dissertation. *Entrance requirements:* For master's and doctorate, GRE. Additional exam requirements/recommendations for international students: Required—TOEFL (minimum score 570 paper-based; 230 computer-based; 88 iBT). *Application deadline:* For fall admission, 1/15 priority date for domestic and international students; for spring admission, 8/31 priority date for domestic and international students. Applications are processed on a rolling basis. Application fee: $75. Electronic applications accepted. *Expenses:* Tuition: Full-time $38,100. *Financial support:* In 2009–10, 50 students received support, including fellowships with full tuition reimbursements available (averaging $24,750 per year), 40 research assistantships with full tuition reimbursements available (averaging $24,750 per year), 13 teaching assistantships with full tuition reimbursements available (averaging $24,750 per year); career-related internships or fieldwork, institutionally sponsored loans, and unspecified assistantships also available. Financial award application deadline: 2/1. *Faculty research:* Materials processing, nanostructural materials, materials for microelectronics, composite materials, computational materials. Total annual research expenditures: $5 million. *Unit head:* Dr. Robert Hull, Department Head, 518-276-6373, Fax: 518-276-8554, E-mail: hullr2@rpi.edu. *Application contact:* Dr. Pawel Keblinski, Admissions Coordinator, 518-276-6858, Fax: 518-276-8554, E-mail: keblip@rpi.edu.

Stevens Institute of Technology, Graduate School, Charles V. Schaefer Jr. School of Engineering, Department of Chemistry, Chemical Biology and Biomedical Engineering, Hoboken, NJ 07030. Offers analytical chemistry (PhD, Certificate); bioinformatics (PhD, Certificate); biomedical chemistry (Certificate); biomedical engineering (M Eng, Certificate); chemical biology (MS, PhD, Certificate); chemical physiology (Certificate); chemistry (MS, PhD); organic chemistry (PhD); physical chemistry (PhD); polymer chemistry (PhD, Certificate). Part-time and evening/weekend programs available. Postbaccalaureate distance learning degree programs offered (no on-campus study). Terminal master's awarded for partial completion of doctoral program. *Degree requirements:* For master's, thesis or alternative; for doctorate, one foreign language, thesis/dissertation; for Certificate, project or thesis. *Entrance requirements:* Additional exam requirements/recommendations for international students: Required—TOEFL. Electronic applications accepted. *Expenses:* Tuition: Full-time $9900; part-time $1100 per credit. Required fees: $286 per semester. *Faculty research:* Biochemical reaction engineering, polymerization engineering, reactor design, biochemical process control and synthesis.

The University of Akron, Graduate School, College of Engineering, Program in Engineering (Polymer Specialization), Akron, OH 44325. Offers MS. *Students:* 2 full-time (0 women), both international. Average age 27. 7 applicants, 14% accepted, 0 enrolled. *Degree requirements:* For master's, thesis. *Entrance requirements:* For master's, GRE, minimum GPA of 2.75, letters of recommendation, resume. Additional exam requirements/recommendations for international students: Required—TOEFL (minimum score 550 paper-based; 213 computer-based; 79 iBT). *Application deadline:* Applications are processed on a rolling basis. Application fee: $30 ($40 for international students). Electronic applications accepted. *Expenses:* Tuition, state resident: full-time $6570; part-time $365 per credit hour. Tuition, nonresident: full-time $11,250; part-time $625 per credit hour. *Unit head:* Dr. Subramaniya Hariharan, Coordinator, 330-972-6580, E-mail: hari@uakron.edu. *Application contact:* Dr. Craig Menzemer, Director of Graduate Studies, 330-972-5536, E-mail: ccmenze@uakron.edu.

The University of Akron, Graduate School, College of Polymer Science and Polymer Engineering, Department of Polymer Engineering, Akron, OH 44325. Offers MS, PhD. Part-time and evening/weekend programs available. *Faculty:* 14 full-time (1 woman), 1 part-time/adjunct (0 women). *Students:* 71 full-time (19 women), 11 part-time (1 woman); includes 2 minority (both African Americans), 60 international. Average age 28. 107 applicants, 17% accepted, 13 enrolled. In 2009, 3 master's, 12 doctorates awarded. *Degree requirements:* For master's, thesis, basic engineering exam; for doctorate, one foreign language, thesis/dissertation, candidacy exam. *Entrance requirements:* For master's, GRE, bachelor's degree in engineering or physical science, minimum GPA of 2.75 (3.0) in last two years, letters of recommendation; for doctorate, GRE, bachelor's degree in engineering or physical science, minimum GPA of 2.75 (3.0 in last two years), letters of recommendation. Additional exam requirements/recommendations for international students: Required—TOEFL (minimum score 550 paper-based; 213 computer-based; 79 iBT). *Application deadline:* For fall admission, 1/15 priority date for domestic and international students. Applications are processed on a rolling basis. Application fee: $30 ($40 for international students). Electronic applications accepted. *Expenses:* Tuition, state resident: full-time $6570; part-time $365 per credit hour. Tuition, nonresident: full-time $11,250; part-time $625 per credit hour. *Financial support:* In 2009–10, 67 research assistantships with full tuition reimbursements, 2 teaching assistantships with full tuition reimbursements were awarded; unspecified assistantships also available. *Faculty research:* Processing and properties of multi-functional polymeric materials, nanomaterials and nanocomposites, micro and nano-scale materials processing, novel self-assembled polymeric materials for energy applications, coating materials and coating technology. Total annual research expenditures: $4.5 million. *Unit head:* Dr. Sadhan Jana, Chair, 330-972-8293, E-mail: janas@uakron.edu. *Application contact:* Sarah Thorley, Coordinator of Academic Program, 330-972-8845, E-mail: sarah3@uakron.edu.

The University of Akron, Graduate School, College of Polymer Science and Polymer Engineering, Department of Polymer Science, Akron, OH 44325. Offers MS, PhD. Part-time and evening/weekend programs available. *Faculty:* 13 full-time (3 women), 1 part-time/adjunct (0 women). *Students:* 81 full-time (21 women), 19 part-time (8 women); includes 2 minority (1 African American, 1 Asian American or Pacific Islander), 70 international. Average age 28. 130 applicants, 15% accepted, 17 enrolled. In 2009, 2 master's, 11 doctorates awarded. Terminal master's awarded for partial completion of doctoral program. *Degree requirements:* For master's, thesis; for doctorate, one foreign language, thesis/dissertation, cumulative exam, seminars. *Entrance requirements:* For master's, GRE, minimum GPA of 2.75, letters of recommendation;

for doctorate, GRE, minimum GPA of 2.75, letters of recommendation, personal statement. Additional exam requirements/recommendations for international students: Required—TOEFL (minimum score 550 paper-based; 213 computer-based; 79 iBT). *Application deadline:* For fall admission, 12/1 priority date for domestic students, 12/15 priority date for international students. Application fee: $30 ($40 for international students). Electronic applications accepted. *Expenses:* Tuition, state resident: full-time $6570; part-time $365 per credit hour. Tuition, nonresident: full-time $11,250; part-time $625 per credit hour. *Financial support:* In 2009–10, 2 fellowships with full tuition reimbursements, 72 research assistantships with full tuition reimbursements were awarded; scholarships/grants also available. *Faculty research:* Synthesis of polymers, structure of polymers, physical properties of polymers, engineering and technological properties of polymers, elastomers. Total annual research expenditures: $6.8 million. *Unit head:* Dr. Ali Dhinojwala, Chair, 330-972-6246, E-mail: ali4@uakron.edu. *Application contact:* Melissa Bowman, Coordinator, Academic Programs, 330-972-7532, E-mail: mb8@uakron.edu.

University of Cincinnati, Graduate School, College of Engineering, Department of Chemical and Materials Engineering, Program in Materials Science and Metallurgical Engineering, Cincinnati, OH 45221. Offers ceramic science and engineering (MS, PhD); materials science and engineering (MS, PhD); metallurgical engineering (MS, PhD); polymer science and engineering (MS, PhD). Evening/weekend programs available. *Degree requirements:* For master's, thesis optional; for doctorate, one foreign language, comprehensive exam, thesis/dissertation, oral English proficiency exam. *Entrance requirements:* For master's and doctorate, GRE General Test, BS in related field, minimum undergraduate GPA of 3.0. Additional exam requirements/recommendations for international students: Required—TOEFL (minimum score 550 paper-based; 213 computer-based). Electronic applications accepted. *Expenses:* Contact institution.

University of Connecticut, Institute of Materials Science, Polymer Program, Storrs, CT 06269-3136. Offers polymer science and engineering (MS, PhD). Part-time programs available. Terminal master's awarded for partial completion of doctoral program. *Degree requirements:* For master's, thesis (for some programs); for doctorate, one foreign language, comprehensive exam, thesis/dissertation. *Entrance requirements:* For master's and doctorate, GRE General Test. Additional exam requirements/recommendations for international students: Required—TOEFL (minimum score 550 paper-based; 213 computer-based; 80 iBT), IELTS (minimum score 6.5). Electronic applications accepted. *Expenses:* Tuition, state resident: full-time $4725; part-time $525 per credit. Tuition, nonresident: full-time $12,267; part-time $1363 per credit. Required fees: $346 per semester. Tuition and fees vary according to course load. *Faculty research:* Nanomaterials and nanotechnology, biomaterials and sensors, synthesis, electronic/photonic materials, solar cells and fuel cells, structure and function of proteins, biodegradable polymers, molecular simulations, drug targeting and delivery.

University of Massachusetts Amherst, Graduate School, College of Natural Sciences, Department of Polymer Science and Engineering, Amherst, MA 01003. Offers MS, PhD. *Faculty:* 18 full-time (1 woman). *Students:* 85 full-time (32 women), 15 part-time (5 women); includes 4 minority (all Asian Americans or Pacific Islanders), 49 international. Average age 26. 184 applicants, 21% accepted, 16 enrolled. In 2009, 26 master's, 12 doctorates awarded. Terminal master's awarded for partial completion of doctoral program. *Degree requirements:* For master's, thesis or alternative; for doctorate, comprehensive exam, thesis/dissertation. *Entrance requirements:* For master's and doctorate, GRE General Test. Additional exam requirements/recommendations for international students: Required—TOEFL (minimum score 550 paper-based; 213 computer-based; 80 iBT), IELTS (minimum score 6.5). *Application deadline:* For fall admission, 2/1 for domestic and international students. Applications are processed on a rolling basis. Application fee: $50 ($65 for international students). Electronic applications accepted. *Expenses:* Tuition, state resident: full-time $2640; part-time $110 per credit. Tuition, nonresident: full-time $9936; part-time $414 per credit. Tuition and fees vary according to course load. *Financial support:* In 2009–10, 16 fellowships with full tuition reimbursements (averaging $20,671 per year), 116 research assistantships with full tuition reimbursements (averaging $17,136 per year), 11 teaching assistantships with full tuition reimbursements (averaging $1,715 per year) were awarded; career-related internships or fieldwork, Federal Work-Study, scholarships/grants, traineeships, health care benefits, tuition waivers (full), and unspecified assistantships also available. Support available to part-time students. Financial award application deadline: 2/1. *Unit head:* Dr. Alfred J. Crosby, Graduate Program Director, 413-577-9120, Fax: 413-545-0082. *Application contact:* Jean M. Ames, Supervisor of Admissions, 413-545-0722, Fax: 413-577-0010, E-mail: gradadm@grad.umass.edu.

University of Massachusetts Lowell, College of Arts and Sciences, Department of Chemistry, Program in Polymer Science, Lowell, MA 01854-2881. Offers MS. *Degree requirements:* For master's, thesis. *Entrance requirements:* For master's, GRE General Test. Electronic applications accepted.

University of Massachusetts Lowell, James B. Francis College of Engineering, Department of Plastics Engineering, Lowell, MA 01854-2881. Offers elastomers (Graduate Certificate); medical plastics design and manufacturing (Graduate Certificate); plastics design (Graduate Certificate); plastics engineering (MS Eng, D Eng, PhD), including coatings and adhesives (MS Eng), plastics materials (MS Eng), plastics processing (MS Eng), product design (MS Eng); plastics engineering fundamentals (Graduate Certificate); plastics materials (Graduate Certificate); plastics processing (Graduate Certificate); polymer science/plastics engineering (PhD). Part-time programs available. Terminal master's awarded for partial completion of doctoral program. *Degree requirements:* For master's, thesis optional; for doctorate, comprehensive exam, thesis/dissertation. *Entrance requirements:* For master's and doctorate, GRE General Test. Additional exam requirements/recommendations for international students: Required—TOEFL.

University of Missouri–Kansas City, College of Arts and Sciences, Department of Chemistry, Kansas City, MO 64110-2499. Offers analytical chemistry (MS, PhD); inorganic chemistry (MS, PhD); organic chemistry (MS, PhD); physical chemistry (MS, PhD); polymer chemistry (MS, PhD). PhD (interdisciplinary) offered through the School of Graduate Studies. Part-time and evening/weekend programs available. *Faculty:* 16 full-time (3 women), 1 part-time/adjunct (0 women). *Students:* 7 part-time (4 women), 2 international. Average age 32. 30 applicants, 67% accepted. In 2009, 1 master's awarded. *Degree requirements:* For master's, thesis (for some programs); for doctorate, thesis/dissertation. *Entrance requirements:* For master's, equivalent of American Chemical Society approved bachelor's degree in chemistry; for doctorate, GRE General Test, equivalent of American Chemical Society approved bachelor's degree in chemistry. Additional exam requirements/recommendations for international students: Required—TOEFL (minimum score 550 paper-based; 213 computer-based; 80 iBT), TWE. *Application deadline:* For fall admission, 4/15 for domestic and international students; for spring admission, 10/15 for domestic and international students. Applications are processed on a rolling basis. Application fee: $45 ($50 for international students). Electronic applications accepted. *Expenses:* Tuition, state resident: full-time $5378; part-time $299 per credit hour. Tuition, nonresident: full-time $13,881; part-time $771 per credit hour. Required fees: $641; $71 per credit hour. Tuition and fees vary according to course load and program. *Financial support:* In 2009–10, 8 research assistantships with partial tuition reimbursements (averaging $17,973 per year), 17 teaching assistantships with partial tuition reimbursements (averaging $17,179 per year) were awarded; Federal Work-Study, institutionally sponsored loans, and scholarships/grants also available. Support available to part-time students. Financial award application deadline: 3/1; financial award applicants required to submit FAFSA. *Faculty research:* Molecular spectroscopy, characterization and synthesis of materials and compounds, computational chemistry, natural products, drug delivery systems and anti-tumor agents. Total annual research expenditures: $1 million. *Unit head:* Dr. Kathleen V. Kilway, Chair, 816-235-2289, Fax: 816-235-5502. *Application contact:* Graduate Recruiting Committee, 816-235-2272, Fax: 816-235-5502, E-mail: umkc-chemdept@umkc.edu.

University of Southern Mississippi, Graduate School, College of Science and Technology, School of Polymers and High Performance Materials, Hattiesburg, MS 39406-0001. Offers polymer science (MS); polymer science and engineering (PhD). *Faculty:* 14 full-time (1 woman), 1 part-time/adjunct (0 women). *Students:* 66 full-time (18 women), 9 part-time (3 women); includes 3 minority (1 American Indian/Alaska Native, 1 Asian American or Pacific Islander, 1 Hispanic American), 25 international. Average age 28. 54 applicants, 24% accepted, 8 enrolled. In 2009, 6 master's, 9 doctorates awarded. *Degree requirements:* For master's, comprehensive exam, thesis; for doctorate, comprehensive exam, thesis/dissertation, original proposal. *Entrance requirements:* For master's, GRE General Test, minimum GPA of 2.75; for doctorate, GRE General Test, minimum GPA of 3.5. Additional exam requirements/recommendations for international students: Required—TOEFL. *Application deadline:* For fall admission, 3/1 priority date for domestic students, 3/1 for international students. Applications are processed on a rolling basis. Application fee: $35. *Expenses:* Tuition, state resident: full-time $5096; part-time $284 per hour. Tuition, nonresident: full-time $13,052; part-time $726 per hour. Required fees: $402. Tuition and fees vary according to course level and course load. *Financial support:* In 2009–10, 60 research assistantships (averaging $20,000 per year), 15 teaching assistantships (averaging $10,000 per year) were awarded; fellowships also available. Financial award application deadline: 3/15; financial award applicants required to submit FAFSA. *Faculty research:* Water-soluble polymers; polymer composites; coatings; solid-state, laser-initiated polymerization. *Unit head:* Dr. Marek Urban, Chair, 601-266-4868, Fax: 601-266-6178. *Application contact:* Dr. Robert B. Moore, Graduate Coordinator, 601-266-4868.

University of South Florida, Graduate School, College of Arts and Sciences, Department of Chemistry, Tampa, FL 33620-9951. Offers computational chemistry (PhD); analytical chemistry (MS, PhD); biochemistry (MS, PhD); computational chemistry (MS); environmental chemistry (MS, PhD); inorganic chemistry (MS, PhD); organic chemistry (MS); physical chemistry (MS, PhD); polymer chemistry (PhD). Part-time programs available. *Faculty:* 25 full-time (4 women). *Students:* 113 full-time (36 women), 15 part-time (11 women); includes 19 minority (5 African Americans, 6 Asian Americans or Pacific Islanders, 8 Hispanic Americans), 58 international. Average age 32. 112 applicants, 30% accepted, 21 enrolled. In 2009, 8 master's, 11 doctorates awarded. Terminal master's awarded for partial completion of doctoral program. *Degree requirements:* For master's, comprehensive exam, thesis (for some programs); for doctorate, 2 foreign languages, comprehensive exam, thesis/dissertation. *Entrance requirements:* For master's, GRE General Test or GMAT, minimum GPA of 3.0. Additional exam requirements/recommendations for international students: Required—TOEFL (minimum score 550 paper-based; 213 computer-based). *Application deadline:* For fall admission, 2/15 priority date for domestic students, 1/2 priority date for international students; for spring admission, 10/1 priority date for domestic students, 6/1 priority date for international students. Applications are processed on a rolling basis. Application fee: $30. Electronic applications accepted. *Financial support:* In 2009–10, teaching assistantships with tuition reimbursements (averaging $27,522 per year); unspecified assistantships also available. Financial award application deadline: 6/30. *Faculty research:* Synthesis, bio-organic chemistry, bioinorganic chemistry, environmental chemistry, NMR. Total annual research expenditures: $3.2 million. *Unit head:* Dr. Randy Larsen, Chairperson, 813-974-4129, Fax: 813-974-3203, E-mail: rlarsen@cas.usf.edu. *Application contact:* Patricia Muisener, Director, 813-974-1730, Fax: 813-974-3203, E-mail: muisener@cas.usf.edu.

The University of Tennessee, Graduate School, College of Engineering, Department of Materials Science and Engineering, Program in Polymer Engineering, Knoxville, TN 37996. Offers MS, PhD. *Faculty:* 6 full-time (1 woman). *Students:* 9 full-time (2 women); includes 1 minority (African American), 6 international. Average age 24. 22 applicants, 14% accepted, 1 enrolled. In 2009, 1 master's awarded. *Degree requirements:* For master's, thesis or alternative; for doctorate, comprehensive exam, thesis/dissertation. *Entrance requirements:* For master's and doctorate, minimum GPA of 2.7. Additional exam requirements/recommendations for international students: Required—TOEFL (minimum score 550 paper-based; 213 computer-based). *Application deadline:* For fall admission, 2/1 priority date for domestic and international students; for spring admission, 6/15 priority date for international students. Applications are processed on a rolling basis. Application fee: $35. Electronic applications accepted. *Expenses:* Tuition, state resident: full-time $6826; part-time $380 per semester hour. Tuition, nonresident: full-time $21,844; part-time $1147 per semester hour. Tuition and fees vary according to program. *Financial support:* In 2009–10, 2 students received support, including 1 fellowship (averaging $8,892 per year), 9 research assistantships with full tuition reimbursements available (averaging $19,812 per year), 2 teaching assistantships with full tuition reimbursements available (averaging $18,708 per year); career-related internships or fieldwork, Federal Work-Study, institutionally sponsored loans, health care benefits, and unspecified assistantships also available. Financial award application deadline: 3/1; financial award applicants required to submit FAFSA. *Faculty research:* Polymer chemistry, processing, and characterization. Total annual research expenditures: $1.9 million. *Unit head:* Dr. George Pharr, Head, 865-974-5336, Fax: 865-974-4115, E-mail: pharr@utk.edu. *Application contact:* Dr. Masood Parang, Associate Dean of Student Affairs, 865-974-2454, Fax: 865-974-9871, E-mail: mparang@utk.edu.

University of Wisconsin–Madison, Graduate School, College of Engineering, Department of Mechanical Engineering, Madison, WI 53706-1380. Offers energy systems (ME); engine systems (ME); mechanical engineering (MS, PhD); polymers (ME). Part-time programs available. Postbaccalaureate distance learning degree programs offered (no on-campus study). *Faculty:* 33 full-time (3 women), 1 part-time/adjunct (0 women). *Students:* 178 full-time (20 women), 27 part-time (2 women); includes 19 minority (3 African Americans, 9 Asian Americans or Pacific Islanders, 7 Hispanic Americans). Average age 25. 613 applicants, 29% accepted, 72 enrolled. In 2009, 36 master's, 22 doctorates awarded. Terminal master's awarded for partial completion of doctoral program. *Degree requirements:* For master's, thesis optional; for doctorate, thesis/dissertation, qualifying exam, preliminary exam. *Entrance requirements:* For master's, GRE, BS in mechanical engineering or related field, minimum GPA of 3.0 in last 60 hours of course work; for doctorate, GRE, BS in mechanical engineering or related field, minimum undergraduate GPA of 3.0 in last 60 hours of course work. Additional exam requirements/recommendations for international students: Required—TOEFL (minimum score 550 paper-based; 213 computer-based; 80 iBT). *Application deadline:* For fall admission, 5/1 for domestic students, 6/1 for international students; for spring admission, 11/30 for domestic students, 10/1 for international students. Applications are processed on a rolling basis. Application fee: $56. Electronic applications accepted. *Expenses:* Tuition, state resident: part-time $594 per credit. Tuition, nonresident: part-time $1504 per credit. Required fees: $65 per credit. Tuition and fees vary according to course load, program and reciprocity agreements. *Financial support:* In 2009–10, 12 fellowships with full tuition reimbursements (averaging $22,224 per year), 138 research assistantships with full tuition reimbursements (averaging $19,596 per year), 36 teaching assistantships with full tuition reimbursements (averaging $8,595 per year) were awarded; career-related internships or fieldwork, institutionally sponsored loans, scholarships/grants, traineeships, health care benefits, and unspecified assistantships also available. *Faculty research:* Design and manufacturing, materials processing, combustion, energy systems nanotechnology. Total annual research expenditures: $10 million. *Unit head:* Roxann L. Engelstad, Chair, 608-262-5745, Fax: 608-265-2316, E-mail: engelsta@engr.wisc.edu. *Application contact:* Roxann L. Engelstad, Chair, 608-262-5745, Fax: 608-265-2316, E-mail: engelsta@engr.wisc.edu.

Wayne State University, College of Engineering, Department of Chemical Engineering and Materials Science, Program in Materials Science and Engineering, Detroit, MI 48202. Offers materials science and engineering (MS, PhD); polymer engineering (Certificate). Part-time programs available. Terminal master's awarded for partial completion of doctoral program. *Degree requirements:* For master's, thesis optional; for doctorate, thesis/dissertation. *Entrance requirements:* For master's, GRE (if applying for financial support), recommendations; resume; for doctorate, GRE (if applying for financial support), recommendations; resumé, personal statement. Additional exam requirements/recommendations for international students: Required—TOEFL (minimum score 550 paper-based; 213 computer-based); Recommended—TWE (minimum score 6). Electronic applications accepted. *Faculty research:* Polymer science, rheology, fatigue in metals, metal matrix composites, ceramics.

UNIVERSITY OF MICHIGAN

College of Engineering
Department of Materials Science and Engineering

Programs of Study

The Department of Materials Science and Engineering offers Master of Science in Engineering (M.S.E.) and Ph.D. programs leading to degrees in materials science and engineering. Students may emphasize work in various materials categories or phenomena, although the Department encourages a broad graduate educational experience. Course offerings include basic materials courses in structure of materials, thermodynamics, diffusion, phase transformations, mechanical behavior, and materials characterization. Courses also exist in many areas of special interest, such as corrosion, composites, deformation processing, and failure analysis. The M.S.E. degree, typically completed in one to two years, requires 30 credit hours of graduate study. A research project of up to 6 credit hours or a master's thesis of 9–11 credit hours is included within this total and often forms the basis for the student's Ph.D. written examination. The Ph.D. degree, usually completed in four to five years beyond the B.S. degree, requires 18 credit hours of courses beyond the M.S.E. degree, passing grades on a written examination based on advanced undergraduate and graduate-level course material, a research-based oral examination, satisfactory completion of research, and defense of the doctoral dissertation. A precandidate must complete at least 18 credit hours of graded graduate course work registered as a Rackham student while in residence on the Ann Arbor campus. Master's students must complete at least one-half of the minimum required credit hours on the home campus. Each student is also required to complete one teaching assignment prior to the completion of the Ph.D. degree.

Faculty interests are diverse (see the reverse of this page) and fall into five main categories: inorganic materials, organic and biomaterials, electronic materials, structural materials, and computational materials science. Many additional research activities exist in collaboration with other departments and graduate programs.

Research Facilities

The Department occupies approximately 50,000 square feet, primarily in the H. H. Dow Building, but also in the adjacent G. G. Brown Building and the nearby Space Research and Gerstacker Buildings. Research facilities include world-class laboratories for electron microscopy and X-ray diffraction, ion-beam characterization and modification of materials, thin-film deposition, and solid-state device research. Modern instrumentation is added regularly. The Electron Microbeam Analysis Laboratory (EMAL) is a user facility that provides a broad spectrum of analytical equipment for the microstructural and microchemical characterization of materials. The facility includes two dual-beam focused ion beam (FIB) systems; four scanning electron microscopes (SEM); two environmental SEMs; three transmission electron microscopes (TEM) equipped with STEM, XEDS, and EELS; one X-ray photoelectron spectroscopy (XPS) system; and two atomic force microscopes (AFM). The J. D. Hanawalt X-ray Diffraction Laboratory offers several Rigaku, Phillips, and Siemens X-ray diffractometers. The Michigan Ion Beam Laboratory includes facilities for Rutherford backscattering spectrometry, ion channeling, nuclear reaction analysis, elastic recoil detection, and ion implantation for most of the elements of the periodic table, over a wide energy range. The Lurie Nanofabrication Facility offers complete capabilities for the fabrication and characterization of solid-state materials, devices, and circuits using silicon and compound semiconductors, and organic materials.

Financial Aid

Qualified applicants are eligible for fellowships and teaching or research assistantships that pay stipends of up to $25,041 per calendar year in 2009–10 plus tuition remission and some fringe benefits. Students funded by faculty advisers as research assistants work on research problems that are appropriate for their thesis topic. Teaching and research assistantships carry certain defined responsibilities that are adjusted to the needs of the student and the Department.

Cost of Study

The 2009–10 tuition fee for full-time students was $9845 per term for Michigan residents and $18,528 per term for nonresidents.

Living and Housing Costs

A residence hall contract for room and board for the 2009–10 fall and winter terms ranged in cost from $9192 for a double to $10,970 for a single. Family housing units cost from $896 per month for an unfurnished one-bedroom unit to $1229 per month for a furnished three-bedroom unit. Prices include all utilities except telephone.

Many graduate students live in privately owned off-campus housing, which varies in expense depending on its proximity to the University. Food costs and local restaurant prices are typical of those in smaller cities in the Midwest.

Student Group

The Department has 112 full-time graduate students and 4 part-time students from local industry and research laboratories. Approximately 60 percent of the students are from the United States, and 40 percent are from abroad. Most students receive financial aid from the Department. The Department also has about 130 undergraduate students. The College of Engineering currently enrolls 8,160 students in twelve engineering departments/divisions and more than sixty engineering fields of study. The current total student enrollment on the Ann Arbor campus is 56,000. The student-based Michigan Materials Society is very active.

Location

Ann Arbor is a cultural and cosmopolitan community of approximately 105,000 about 40 miles west of Detroit in southeastern Michigan. Ann Arbor offers world-class orchestras, dance companies, dramatic artists, and musical performers throughout the year. The internationally renowned May Festival of classical music and the Ann Arbor Folk Festival are held annually. Ann Arbor art fairs attract 500,000 patrons from across the nation every July. Recreational facilities are extensive, both on campus and throughout the community.

The University and The College

The University of Michigan, one of the nation's most distinguished state universities, is internationally recognized in all of its schools and colleges. The 6,180 faculty members and 41,674 students work in a modern environment that includes more than 275 research units. Michigan consistently ranks as a national leader in total research expenditures. The College of Engineering, of which the Department is a part, awards about 1,198 B.S., 758 M.S., and 255 Ph.D. degrees annually. There are 349 faculty members, 500 supporting staff members, 91 research faculty, and more than 65,000 alumni. Many of the programs in the College are rated among the ten best in the nation, and the College itself is often ranked among the top five engineering schools and colleges.

Applying

Applications are accepted for either the fall (September) or winter (January) terms; however, most students are admitted in the fall term. Applications for fall admission should be received by December 15 if financial support is required. Additional information on admission may be obtained from the Department or from the Horace H. Rackham School of Graduate Studies.

Correspondence and Information

Graduate Program Office
Department of Materials Science and Engineering
College of Engineering
University of Michigan
Ann Arbor, Michigan 48109-2136
Phone: 734-763-9790
Web site: http:// www.mse.engin.umich.edu

Horace H. Rackham School of Graduate Studies
Mail Office
University of Michigan
Ann Arbor, Michigan 48109

University of Michigan

THE FACULTY AND THEIR RESEARCH

Michael Atzmon, Professor of Materials Science and Engineering and Nuclear Engineering and Radiological Sciences; Ph.D., Caltech, 1985. Materials thermodynamics and kinetics, nanocrystalline and amorphous metal alloys.

Akram Boukai, Assistant Professor of Materials Science and Engineering; Ph.D., Caltech, 2008. Growth and characterization of nanomaterials for energy and electronic applications.

Rodney C. Ewing, Professor of Materials Science and Engineering, Geological Sciences and Nuclear Engineering and Radiological Sciences; Ph.D., Stanford, 1974. Radiation effects in complex ceramics and minerals, crystal chemistry of actinides, nuclear materials.

Steven Forrest, Professor of Materials Science and Engineering, Electrical Engineering and Computer Science, Physics, and Vice President for Research; Ph.D., Michigan, 1979.

Amit K. Ghosh, Professor of Materials Science and Engineering and Mechanical Engineering; Ph.D., MIT, 1972. Superplasticity, deformation processing, advanced metallic materials, composites and laminates, friction stir processing.

Sharon C. Glotzer, Professor of Materials Science and Engineering, Chemical Engineering, and Physics; Ph.D., Boston University, 1993. Soft materials, polymers, dense liquids, glasses, colloids, and liquid crystals.

Rachel S. Goldman, Professor of Materials Science and Engineering, Electrical Engineering and Computer Science, and Physics; Ph.D., California, San Diego, 1995. Atomic-scale design of electronic materials; strain relaxation, alloy formation, and diffusion; correlations between microstructure and electronic and optical properties of semiconductor films, nanostructures, and heterostructures.

Peter Green, Professor and Chair of Materials Science and Engineering; Ph.D., Cornell, 1985. Structure, phase behavior and dynamics of bulk and thin polymer films and polymer nanocomposite systems.

John W. Halloran, Alfred Holmes White Collegiate Professor of Materials Science and Engineering; Ph.D., MIT, 1977. Ceramic processing, high-temperature superconductors, engineering ceramics.

J. Wayne Jones, Professor of Materials Science and Engineering; Ph.D., Vanderbilt, 1977. High-temperature materials, fracture, fatigue and creep properties.

John Kieffer, Professor of Materials Science and Engineering; Ph.D., Clausthal (Germany), 1985. Structural assembly and dynamic response of materials at the nanoscale.

Jinsang Kim, Associate Professor of Materials Science and Engineering and Chemical Engineering; Ph.D., MIT, 2001. Molecular design, synthesis, modification, and self-assembly of smart polymers for biomedical and optoelectronic applications.

Nicholas Kotov, Professor of Materials Science and Engineering and Chemical Engineering; Ph.D., Moscow State, 1990. Applications of nanostructured materials to biology and medicine, self-organization of nanocolloidal systems.

Joerg Lahann, Professor of Materials Science and Engineering; Ph.D., RWTH Aachen,1998. Designer surfaces, advanced polymers, biomimetic materials, microfluidic devices, engineered cellular microenvironments, nanoscale self-assembly.

Richard M. Laine, Professor of Materials Science and Engineering, Macromolecular Science and Engineering, and Chemistry; Ph.D., USC, 1973. Inorganic and organometallic precursors, materials chemistry, catalysis.

Victor Li, Professor of Materials Science and Engineering and Civil and Environmental Engineering; Ph.D., Brown, 1981. Fiber reinforced cementitious composites, micromechanics, self-healing design, sustainable material development.

Brian Love, Professor of Materials Science and Engineering; Ph.D., SMU, 1990. Structure/property relationships in polymers, photopolymerization, dispersions and sedimentation, chemorheology, biomaterials.

John F. Mansfield, Associate Research Scientist; Ph.D., Bristol (England), 1983. Analytical electron microscopy of metals, semiconductors, and superconductors.

Jyotirmoy Mazumder, Robert H. Lurie Professor of Materials Science and Engineering and Mechanical Engineering; Ph.D., Imperial College (London), 1978. Laser-aided manufacturing, atom to application for nonequilibrium synthesis, mathematical modeling, spectroscopic and optical diagnostics of laser materials interaction.

Joanna Mirecki Millunchick, Associate Professor of Materials Science and Engineering; Ph.D., Northwestern, 1995. Correlation of structural and theoretical aspects of materials to optical and electrical properties via photoluminescence, hall mobility, and resistivity measurements; fabrication of novel microelectronic devices.

Xiaoqing Pan, Professor of Materials Science and Engineering; Ph.D., Saarlandes (Germany), 1991. High-resolution electron microscopy, structural-property relationships of materials interfaces, thin-film growth and characterization.

Richard E. Robertson, Professor of Materials Science and Engineering and Macromolecular Science and Engineering; Ph.D., Caltech, 1960. Polymer structure, molecular dynamics and fracture, fiber composite properties, composite design and manufacturing.

Anne Marie Sastry, Professor of Materials Science and Engineering and Mechanical Engineering; Ph.D., Cornell, 1994. Percolation phenomena in multiphase materials; assembly and self-assembly in biomaterials, damage progression in diabetic nerves, modeling of intracellular transport, design of porous structures for energy devices.

Max Shtein, Assistant Professor of Materials Science and Engineering; Ph.D., Princeton, 2004. Structure-property relationships of organic semiconductors and their application to electronic and optoelectronic devices.

Katsuyo Thornton, Assistant Professor of Materials Science and Engineering; Ph.D., Chicago, 1997. Computational and theoretical investigations of the evolution of microstructures and nanostructures and their effects on materials properties.

Michael D. Thouless, Professor of Materials Science and Engineering and Mechanical Engineering and Applied Mechanics; Ph.D., Berkeley, 1984. Mechanical properties of materials, mechanics of thin films, coatings and interfaces, toughening of polymers, mechanical properties of adhesives.

Anish Tuteja, Assistant Professor of Materials Science and Engineering; Ph.D., Michigan State, 2006. Understanding and engineering functional nanoparticle-polymeric systems in which nanoparticles are used to imbue specific surface and bulk properties, soft materials, surface and interfacial science, wettability, polymer nanocomposites, liquid-liquid separations.

Anton Van der Ven, Assistant Professor of Materials Science and Engineering; Ph.D., MIT, 2000. Electronic structure methods (density functional theory), with techniques from statistical mechanics to calculate thermodynamic and kinetic properties of new materials.

Lumin Wang, Professor of Materials Science and Engineering and Nuclear Engineering and Radiological Sciences, and Director of Electron Microbeam Analysis Laboratory, Ph.D., Wisconsin–Madison, 1988. Radiation effects, Ion-beam processing of nanostructured materials, transmission electron microscopy.

Gary S. Was, Professor of Materials Science and Engineering, and Nuclear Engineering and Radiological Sciences; Sc.D., MIT, 1980. Ion-solid interactions, radiation effects, stress corrosion cracking, hydrogen embrittlement.

Steven M. Yalisove, Professor; Ph.D., Pennsylvania, 1986. Thin-film materials, surface analytical and ion-beam techniques, surface and interface structures.

Section 17
Mechanical Engineering and Mechanics

This section contains a directory of institutions offering graduate work in mechanical engineering and mechanics, followed by in-depth entries submitted by institutions that chose to prepare detailed program descriptions. Additional information about programs listed in the directory but not augmented by an in-depth entry may be obtained by writing directly to the dean of a graduate school or chair of a department at the address given in the directory.

For programs offering related work, see also in this book *Engineering and Applied Sciences, Management of Engineering and Technology,* and *Materials Sciences and Engineering.* In another guide in this series:

Graduate Programs in the Physical Sciences, Mathematics, Agricultural Sciences, the Environment & Natural Resources
See *Geosciences* and *Physics*

CONTENTS

Mechanical Engineering

Alfred University, Graduate School, New York State College of Ceramics, School of Engineering, Alfred, NY 14802-1205. Offers biomedical materials engineering science (MS); ceramic engineering (MS); ceramics (PhD); electrical engineering (MS); glass science (MS, PhD); materials science and engineering (MS, PhD); mechanical engineering (MS). *Degree requirements:* For master's, thesis; for doctorate, thesis/dissertation. *Entrance requirements:* Additional exam requirements/recommendations for international students: Required—TOEFL (minimum score 590 paper-based; 243 computer-based). Electronic applications accepted. *Expenses:* Contact institution. *Faculty research:* Fine-particle technology, x-ray diffraction, superconductivity, electronic materials.

American University of Beirut, Graduate Programs, Faculty of Engineering and Architecture, Beirut, Lebanon. Offers civil engineering (ME, PhD); electrical and computer engineering (ME, PhD); engineering management (MEM); environmental and water resources (ME); environmental and water resources engineering (PhD); environmental technology (MSES); mechanical engineering (ME, PhD); urban design (MUD); urban planning and policy (MUP). Part-time programs available. *Degree requirements:* For master's, one foreign language, comprehensive exam, thesis (for some programs); for doctorate, one foreign language, comprehensive exam, thesis/dissertation, publications. *Entrance requirements:* For master's, letters of recommendation; for doctorate, letters of recommendation, master's degree, transcripts, curriculum vitae, interview. Additional exam requirements/recommendations for international students: Required—TOEFL (minimum score 600 paper-based; 250 computer-based; 100 iBT), IELTS (minimum score 7.5). Electronic applications accepted.

American University of Sharjah, Graduate Programs, Sharjah, United Arab Emirates. Offers business (EMBA, GEMPA, MBA); chemical engineering (MS Ch E); civil engineering (MSCE); computer engineering (MS); electrical engineering (MSEE); mechanical engineering (MSME); mechatronics engineering (MS); public administration (MPA); teaching English to speakers of other languages (MA); translation and interpreting (MA); urban planning (MUP). Part-time and evening/weekend programs available. *Faculty:* 59 full-time (4 women), 5 part-time/adjunct (1 woman). *Students:* 101 full-time (44 women), 218 part-time (95 women). Average age 27. 184 applicants, 83% accepted, 92 enrolled. In 2009, 97 master's awarded. *Entrance requirements:* For master's, GMAT (MBA). Additional exam requirements/recommendations for international students: Required—TOEFL (minimum score 550 paper-based; 213 computer-based; 80 iBT), TWE (minimum score 5). *Application deadline:* For fall admission, 7/30 priority date for domestic students, 7/15 priority date for international students; for spring admission, 12/31 priority date for domestic students, 12/16 for international students. Applications are processed on a rolling basis. Application fee: $300. Electronic applications accepted. Tuition charges are reported in United Arab Emirates dirhams. *Expenses:* Tuition: Part-time 3250 United Arab Emirates dirhams per credit hour. *Financial support:* In 2009–10, 63 students received support, including 28 research assistantships with tuition reimbursements available, 35 teaching assistantships with tuition reimbursements available. *Faculty research:* Chemical engineering, civil engineering, computer engineering, electrical engineering, linguistics, translation. *Unit head:* Ghada S. Sami, Admissions Manager, 971-65151006 Ext. 1006, Fax: 971-65151020, E-mail: graduateadmission@aus.edu. *Application contact:* Ghada S. Sami, Admissions Manager, 971-65151006 Ext. 1006, Fax: 971-65151020, E-mail: graduateadmission@aus.edu.

Arizona State University, Graduate College, College of Technology and Innovation, Department of Mechanical and Manufacturing Engineering Technology, Tempe, AZ 85287. Offers MS. Part-time and evening/weekend programs available. *Degree requirements:* For master's, thesis or applied project and oral defense, final examination. *Entrance requirements:* For master's, resume, industrial experience beyond bachelor degree (recommended). Additional exam requirements/recommendations for international students: Required—TOEFL (minimum score 550 paper-based; 213 computer-based; 83 iBT); Recommended—TWE. Electronic applications accepted. *Faculty research:* Manufacturing modeling and simulation 'smart' and composite materials, optimization of turbine engines, machinability and manufacturing processes design, fuel cells and other alternative energy sources.

Arizona State University, Graduate College, Ira A. Fulton School of Engineering, Department of Mechanical and Aerospace Engineering, Tempe, AZ 85287. Offers aerospace engineering (MS, MSE, PhD); mechanical engineering (MS, MSE, PhD). *Degree requirements:* For master's, thesis or alternative; for doctorate, thesis/dissertation. *Entrance requirements:* For master's and doctorate, GRE General Test.

Auburn University, Graduate School, Ginn College of Engineering, Department of Mechanical Engineering, Auburn University, AL 36849. Offers materials engineering (M Mtl E, MS, PhD); mechanical engineering (MME, MS, PhD). Part-time programs available. *Faculty:* 29 full-time (0 women), 2 part-time/adjunct (0 women). *Students:* 65 full-time (10 women), 85 part-time (10 women); includes 7 minority (3 African Americans, 1 American Indian/Alaska Native, 2 Asian Americans or Pacific Islanders, 1 Hispanic American), 89 international. Average age 28. 237 applicants, 41% accepted, 21 enrolled. In 2009, 14 master's, 11 doctorates awarded. *Degree requirements:* For master's, thesis (for some programs); for doctorate, one foreign language, thesis/dissertation. *Entrance requirements:* For master's and doctorate, GRE General Test. *Application deadline:* For fall admission, 7/7 for domestic students; for spring admission, 11/24 for domestic students. Applications are processed on a rolling basis. Application fee: $50 ($60 for international students). *Expenses:* Tuition, state resident: full-time $6240. Tuition, nonresident: full-time $18,720. International tuition: $18,938 full-time. Required fees: $492. Tuition and fees vary according to course load, program and reciprocity agreements. *Financial support:* Fellowships, research assistantships, teaching assistantships, Federal Work-Study available. Support available to part-time students. Financial award application deadline: 3/15; financial award applicants required to submit FAFSA. *Faculty research:* Engineering mechanics, experimental mechanics, engineering design, engineering acoustics, engineering optics. *Unit head:* Dr. David Dyer, Chair, 334-844-4820. *Application contact:* Dr. George Flowers, Dean of the Graduate School, 334-844-2125.

Baylor University, Graduate School, School of Engineering and Computer Science, Department of Engineering, Waco, TX 76798. Offers biomedical engineering (MSBE); electrical and computer engineering (MSECE); engineering (ME); mechanical engineering (MSME). *Faculty:* 14 full-time (1 woman). *Students:* 19 full-time (1 woman), 5 part-time (1 woman); includes 4 minority (1 African American, 1 Asian American or Pacific Islander, 2 Hispanic Americans), 8 international. In 2009, 8 master's awarded. *Unit head:* Dr. Mike Thompson, Graduate Director, 254-710-4188. *Application contact:* Linda Keer, Administrative Assistant, 254-710-4188, Fax: 254-710-3870, E-mail: linda_kerr@baylor.edu.

Boise State University, Graduate College, College of Engineering, Department of Mechanical and Biomedical Engineering, Boise, ID 83725-0399. Offers mechanical engineering (M Engr, MS). Part-time and evening/weekend programs available. *Degree requirements:* For master's, thesis. *Entrance requirements:* For master's, GRE General Test, minimum GPA of 3.0. Additional exam requirements/recommendations for international students: Required—TOEFL. Electronic applications accepted. *Expenses:* Tuition, state resident: full-time $3106; part-time $209 per credit. Tuition, nonresident: part-time $284 per credit.

Boston University, College of Engineering, Department of Mechanical Engineering, Boston, MA 02215. Offers global manufacturing (MS); manufacturing (MS); mechanical (MS, PhD); MS/MBA. Part-time programs available. Postbaccalaureate distance learning degree programs offered (no on-campus study). *Faculty:* 42 full-time (7 women). *Students:* 89 full-time (17 women), 18 part-time (6 women); includes 13 minority (2 African Americans, 1 American Indian/Alaska Native, 8 Asian Americans or Pacific Islanders, 2 Hispanic Americans), 48 international. Average age 25. 222 applicants, 29% accepted, 32 enrolled. In 2009, 34 master's, 7 doctorates awarded. Terminal master's awarded for partial completion of doctoral program. *Degree requirements:* For master's, thesis optional; for doctorate, comprehensive exam, thesis/dissertation. *Entrance requirements:* For master's and doctorate, GRE General Test.

Additional exam requirements/recommendations for international students: Required—TOEFL (minimum score 550 paper-based; 213 computer-based; 84 iBT), IELTS (minimum score 6). *Application deadline:* For fall admission, 4/1 for domestic and international students; for spring admission, 10/1 for domestic and international students. Applications are processed on a rolling basis. Application fee: $70. Electronic applications accepted. *Expenses:* Tuition: Full-time $37,910; part-time $1184 per credit hour. Required fees: $386; $40 per semester. Part-time tuition and fees vary according to class time, course level, degree level and program. *Financial support:* In 2009–10, 74 students received support, including 8 fellowships with full tuition reimbursements available (averaging $27,600 per year), 43 research assistantships with full tuition reimbursements available (averaging $18,400 per year), 18 teaching assistantships with full tuition reimbursements available (averaging $18,400 per year); career-related internships or fieldwork, Federal Work-Study, institutionally sponsored loans, scholarships/grants, and health care benefits also available. Financial award application deadline: 1/15; financial award applicants required to submit FAFSA. *Faculty research:* Acoustics, ultrasound, and vibrations; biomechanics; dynamics, control, and robotics; energy and thermofluid sciences; MEMS and nanotechnology. Total annual research expenditures: $11 million. *Unit head:* Dr. Ronald A. Roy, Chairman, 617-353-2814, Fax: 617-353-5866, E-mail: ronroy@bu.edu. *Application contact:* Cheryl Kelley, Director of Graduate Programs, 617-353-9760, Fax: 617-353-0259, E-mail: enggrad@bu.edu.

Bradley University, Graduate School, College of Engineering and Technology, Department of Mechanical Engineering, Peoria, IL 61625-0002. Offers MSME. Part-time and evening/weekend programs available. *Degree requirements:* For master's, comprehensive exam, thesis optional. *Entrance requirements:* For master's, minimum GPA of 3.0. Additional exam requirements/recommendations for international students: Required—TOEFL (minimum score 550 paper-based; 213 computer-based; 79 iBT). *Faculty research:* Ground-coupled heat pumps, robotic end-effectors, power plant optimization.

Brigham Young University, Graduate Studies, Ira A. Fulton College of Engineering and Technology, Department of Mechanical Engineering, Provo, UT 84602. Offers MS, PhD. *Faculty:* 26 full-time (1 woman), 1 part-time/adjunct (0 women). *Students:* 59 full-time (4 women), 62 part-time (6 women); includes 1 American Indian/Alaska Native, 2 Hispanic Americans, 10 international. Average age 27. 73 applicants, 73% accepted, 41 enrolled. In 2009, 23 master's, 5 doctorates awarded. Terminal master's awarded for partial completion of doctoral program. *Degree requirements:* For master's, thesis; for doctorate, comprehensive exam, thesis/dissertation. *Entrance requirements:* For master's, GRE General Test, minimum GPA of 3.0 in last 60 hours of upper division course work; for doctorate, GRE General Test, minimum GPA in last 60 hours of upper division course work. Additional exam requirements/recommendations for international students: Required—TOEFL (minimum score 580 paper-based; 85 iBT), or IELTS (minimum score 7). *Application deadline:* For fall admission, 1/15 for domestic and international students; for winter admission, 9/15 for domestic and international students; for spring admission, 1/15 for domestic and international students. Application fee: $50. Electronic applications accepted. *Expenses:* Tuition: Full-time $5580; part-time $301 per credit hour. Tuition and fees vary according to student's religious affiliation. *Financial support:* In 2009–10, 3 students received support, including 10 fellowships with full tuition reimbursements available (averaging $5,000 per year), 63 research assistantships with full tuition reimbursements available (averaging $11,000 per year), 36 teaching assistantships with full and partial tuition reimbursements available (averaging $4,720 per year); scholarships/grants and unspecified assistantships also available. Financial award application deadline: 1/15; financial award applicants required to submit FAFSA. *Faculty research:* Combustion, composite materials, advanced design methods and optimization, electronics heat transfer, acoustic noise controls and robotics. Total annual research expenditures: $1.2 million. *Unit head:* Dr. Timothy W. McLain, Chair, 801-422-2625, Fax: 801-422-0516, E-mail: tmclaine@et.byu.edu. *Application contact:* Miriam Busch, Graduate Advisor, 801-422-2624, Fax: 801-422-0516, E-mail: mbusch@byu.edu.

Brown University, Graduate School, Division of Engineering, Program in Mechanics of Solids, Providence, RI 02912. Offers Sc M, PhD. *Degree requirements:* For doctorate, thesis/dissertation, preliminary exam.

Bucknell University, Graduate Studies, College of Engineering, Department of Mechanical Engineering, Lewisburg, PA 17837. Offers MS, MSME. Part-time programs available. *Degree requirements:* For master's, thesis. *Entrance requirements:* For master's, GRE General Test, GRE Subject Test, minimum GPA of 2.8. Additional exam requirements/recommendations for international students: Required—TOEFL. *Faculty research:* Heat pump performance, microprocessors in heat engine testing, computer-aided design.

California Institute of Technology, Division of Engineering and Applied Science, Option in Mechanical Engineering, Pasadena, CA 91125-0001. Offers MS, PhD, Engr. *Faculty:* 6 full-time (1 woman). *Students:* 47 full-time (13 women). 288 applicants, 8% accepted, 10 enrolled. In 2009, 6 master's, 9 doctorates awarded. *Degree requirements:* For doctorate, thesis/dissertation. *Application deadline:* For fall admission, 1/1 for domestic students. Application fee: $0. *Financial support:* In 2009–10, 19 fellowships, 24 research assistantships, 7 teaching assistantships were awarded. *Faculty research:* Design, mechanics, thermal and fluids engineering, jet propulsion. *Unit head:* Dr. Kaushik Bhattacharya, Executive Officer, 626-395-8306, E-mail: bhatta@caltech.edu. *Application contact:* Natalie Gilmore, Assistant Dean of Graduate Studies, 626-395-3812, Fax: 626-577-9246, E-mail: ngilmore@caltech.edu.

California Polytechnic State University, San Luis Obispo, College of Engineering, Department of Mechanical Engineering, San Luis Obispo, CA 93407. Offers MS. Part-time programs available. *Faculty:* 9 full-time (1 woman). *Students:* 25 full-time (2 women), 6 part-time (1 woman); includes 14 minority (1 American Indian/Alaska Native, 7 Asian Americans or Pacific Islanders, 6 Hispanic Americans), 1 international. Average age 26. 30 applicants, 73% accepted, 16 enrolled. In 2009, 14 master's awarded. *Degree requirements:* For master's, comprehensive exam (for some programs), thesis (for some programs). *Entrance requirements:* For master's, GRE, minimum GPA of 3.0 in last 90 quarter units of course work, 3 letters of recommendation. Additional exam requirements/recommendations for international students: Required—TOEFL (minimum score 550 paper-based; 213 computer-based), or IELTS (minimum score 6). *Application deadline:* For fall admission, 7/1 for domestic students, 11/30 for international students; for winter admission, 11/1 for domestic students, 6/30 for international students; for spring admission, 2/1 for domestic students. Applications are processed on a rolling basis. Application fee: $55. Electronic applications accepted. *Expenses:* Tuition, nonresident: full-time $11,160; part-time $248 per unit. Required fees: $7134; $1553 per quarter. *Financial support:* Fellowships, research assistantships, teaching assistantships, career-related internships or fieldwork, Federal Work-Study, and scholarships/grants available. Support available to part-time students. Financial award application deadline: 3/2; financial award applicants required to submit FAFSA. *Faculty research:* Mechatronics, robotics, thermosciences, mechanics and stress analysis, composite materials. *Unit head:* Dr. Saeed Niku, Graduate Coordinator, 805-756-1376, Fax: 805-756-1137, E-mail: sniku@calpoly.edu. *Application contact:* Dr. Saeed Niku, Graduate Coordinator, 805-756-1376, Fax: 805-756-1137, E-mail: sniku@calpoly.edu.

California State Polytechnic University, Pomona, Academic Affairs, College of Engineering, Pomona, CA 91768-2557. Offers civil engineering (MS); electrical engineering (MSEE); engineering (MSE); engineering management (MS); mechanical engineering (MS). Part-time programs available. *Faculty:* 95 full-time (17 women), 71 part-time/adjunct (6 women). *Students:* 36 full-time (3 women), 198 part-time (33 women); includes 104 minority (1 African American, 2 American Indian/Alaska Native, 69 Asian Americans or Pacific Islanders, 32 Hispanic Americans), 42 international. Average age 28. 237 applicants, 49% accepted, 73 enrolled. In 2009, 46 master's awarded. *Degree requirements:* For master's, thesis or comprehensive exam. *Entrance requirements:* For master's, GRE General Test or minimum GPA of 3.0 in upper-level course work. Additional exam requirements/recommendations for international students: Required—TOEFL. *Application deadline:* For fall admission, 5/1 priority date for domestic students; for winter admission, 10/15 priority date for domestic students; for spring admission, 1/2 priority date for domestic students. Applications are processed on a rolling basis. Application fee: $55. Electronic applications accepted. *Expenses:* Tuition, nonresident: full-time $6696; part-time $248 per credit. Required fees: $5487; $3237 per term. Tuition and fees vary according to course load, degree level and program. *Financial support:* In 2009–10, 1 fellowship, 6 research assistantships, 5 teaching assistantships were awarded; career-related internships or fieldwork, Federal Work-Study, institutionally sponsored loans, and unspecified assistantships also available. Support available to part-time students. Financial award application deadline: 3/2; financial award applicants required to submit FAFSA. *Faculty research:* Aerospace; alternative vehicles; communications, computers, and controls; engineering management. Total annual research expenditures: $650,000. *Unit head:* Dr. Edward Hohmann, Dean, 909-869-2472, Fax: 909-869-4370, E-mail: echohmann@csupomona.edu. *Application contact:* Dr. Edward Hohmann, Dean, 909-869-2472, Fax: 909-869-4370, E-mail: echohmann@csupomona.edu.

California State University, Fresno, Division of Graduate Studies, College of Engineering and Computer Science, Program in Mechanical Engineering, Fresno, CA 93740-8027. Offers MS. Offered at Edwards Air Force Base. Part-time programs available. *Degree requirements:* For master's, thesis or alternative. *Entrance requirements:* For master's, GRE General Test, minimum GPA of 2.7. Additional exam requirements/recommendations for international students: Required—TOEFL. Electronic applications accepted. *Faculty research:* Flowmeter calibration, digital camera calibration.

California State University, Fullerton, Graduate Studies, College of Engineering and Computer Science, Department of Mechanical Engineering, Fullerton, CA 92834-9480. Offers MS. Part-time programs available. *Students:* 13 full-time (1 woman), 34 part-time (2 women); includes 16 minority (1 American Indian/Alaska Native, 9 Asian Americans or Pacific Islanders, 6 Hispanic Americans), 18 international. Average age 28. 82 applicants, 49% accepted, 15 enrolled. In 2009, 8 master's awarded. *Degree requirements:* For master's, comprehensive exam, project or thesis. *Entrance requirements:* For master's, minimum undergraduate GPA of 2.5. Application fee: $55. *Expenses:* Tuition, nonresident: full-time $11,160; part-time $373 per credit. Required fees: $1440 per term. Tuition and fees vary according to course load, degree level and program. *Financial support:* Career-related internships or fieldwork, Federal Work-Study, institutionally sponsored loans, and scholarships/grants available. Support available to part-time students. Financial award application deadline: 3/1; financial award applicants required to submit FAFSA. *Unit head:* Dr. Hossein Moini, Chair, 657-278-4304. *Application contact:* Admissions/Applications, 657-278-2371.

California State University, Long Beach, Graduate Studies, College of Engineering, Department of Mechanical and Aerospace Engineering, Long Beach, CA 90840. Offers aerospace engineering (MSAE); engineering and industrial applied mathematics (PhD); interdisciplinary engineering (MSE); management engineering (MSE); mechanical engineering (MSME). Part-time programs available. *Faculty:* 16 full-time (2 women), 3 part-time/adjunct (0 women). *Students:* 47 full-time (6 women), 75 part-time (9 women); includes 51 minority (5 African Americans, 30 Asian Americans or Pacific Islanders, 16 Hispanic Americans), 28 international. Average age 28. 162 applicants, 63% accepted, 44 enrolled. *Entrance requirements:* Additional exam requirements/recommendations for international students: Required—TOEFL. *Application deadline:* For fall admission, 7/1 for domestic students. Application fee: $55. Electronic applications accepted. *Expenses:* Required fees: $1802 per semester. Part-time tuition and fees vary according to course load. *Financial support:* Career-related internships or fieldwork, Federal Work-Study, institutionally sponsored loans, scholarships/grants, and unspecified assistantships available. Financial award application deadline: 3/2. *Faculty research:* Unsteady turbulent flows, solar energy, energy conversion, CAD/CAM, computer-assisted instruction. *Unit head:* Dr. Hamid Hefazi, Chair, 562-985-1502, Fax: 562-985-1564, E-mail: hefazi@csulb.edu. *Application contact:* Dr. Hamid Rahai, Graduate Advisor, 562-985-5132, Fax: 562-985-4408, E-mail: rahai@csulb.edu.

California State University, Los Angeles, Graduate Studies, College of Engineering, Computer Science, and Technology, Department of Mechanical Engineering, Los Angeles, CA 90032-8530. Offers MS. Part-time and evening/weekend programs available. *Faculty:* 3 full-time (1 woman), 2 part-time/adjunct (1 woman). *Students:* 23 full-time (8 women), 51 part-time (3 women); includes 29 minority (2 African Americans, 12 Asian Americans or Pacific Islanders, 15 Hispanic Americans), 41 international. Average age 28. 20 applicants, 100% accepted, 12 enrolled. In 2009, 19 master's awarded. *Degree requirements:* For master's, comprehensive exam or thesis. *Entrance requirements:* For master's, minimum GPA of 2.75. Additional exam requirements/recommendations for international students: Required—TOEFL (minimum score 550 paper-based). *Application deadline:* For fall admission, 5/1 for domestic and international students. Applications are processed on a rolling basis. Application fee: $55. Electronic applications accepted. *Financial support:* Federal Work-Study available. Support available to part-time students. Financial award application deadline: 3/1. *Faculty research:* Mechanical design, thermal systems, solar-powered vehicle. *Unit head:* Dr. Darrell Guillaume, Chair, 323-343-4490, Fax: 323-343-5004, E-mail: dguilla@calstatela.edu. *Application contact:* Dr. Cheryl L. Ney, Associate Vice President for Academic Affairs and Dean of Graduate Studies, 323-343-3820, Fax: 323-343-5653, E-mail: cney@cslanet.calstatela.edu.

California State University, Northridge, Graduate Studies, College of Engineering and Computer Science, Department of Mechanical Engineering, Northridge, CA 91330. Offers MS. Part-time and evening/weekend programs available. *Faculty:* 8 full-time (0 women), 11 part-time/adjunct (1 woman). *Students:* 49 full-time (3 women), 30 part-time (3 women); includes 1 African American, 7 Asian Americans or Pacific Islanders, 10 Hispanic Americans, 31 international. Average age 27. 194 applicants, 62% accepted, 44 enrolled. In 2009, 13 master's awarded. *Degree requirements:* For master's, thesis or project. *Entrance requirements:* Additional exam requirements/recommendations for international students: Required—TOEFL. *Application deadline:* For fall admission, 11/30 for domestic students. Application fee: $55. *Financial support:* Application deadline: 3/1. *Unit head:* Dr. Hamid Johari, Chair, 818-677-2187. *Application contact:* Dr. Hamid Johari, Chair, 818-677-2187.

California State University, Sacramento, Graduate Studies, College of Engineering and Computer Science, Department of Mechanical Engineering, Sacramento, CA 95819. Offers MS. Evening/weekend programs available. *Degree requirements:* For master's, thesis or alternative, writing proficiency exam. *Entrance requirements:* Additional exam requirements/recommendations for international students: Required—TOEFL. Electronic applications accepted.

Carleton University, Faculty of Graduate Studies, Faculty of Engineering and Design, Department of Mechanical and Aerospace Engineering, Ottawa, ON K1S 5B6, Canada. Offers aerospace engineering (M Eng, MA Sc, PhD); materials engineering (M Eng, MA Sc); mechanical engineering (M Eng, MA Sc, PhD). *Degree requirements:* For master's, thesis optional; for doctorate, thesis/dissertation. *Entrance requirements:* For master's, honors degree; for doctorate, MA Sc or M Eng. Additional exam requirements/recommendations for international students: Required—TOEFL. *Faculty research:* Thermal fluids engineering, heat transfer, vehicle engineering.

Carnegie Mellon University, Carnegie Institute of Technology, Department of Mechanical Engineering, Pittsburgh, PA 15213-3891. Offers MS, PhD. Part-time and evening/weekend programs available. Terminal master's awarded for partial completion of doctoral program. *Degree requirements:* For master's, thesis (for some programs); for doctorate, thesis/dissertation (for some programs), qualifying exam. *Entrance requirements:* For master's and doctorate, GRE General Test. Additional exam requirements/recommendations for international students: Required—TOEFL. *Faculty research:* Combustion, design, fluid, and thermal sciences; computational fluid dynamics; energy and environment; solid mechanics; systems and controls; materials and manufacturing.

Case Western Reserve University, School of Graduate Studies, The Case School of Engineering, Department of Mechanical and Aerospace Engineering, Cleveland, OH 44106. Offers MS, PhD, MD/PhD. Part-time programs available. Postbaccalaureate distance learning degree programs offered (no on-campus study). *Faculty:* 13 full-time (3 women). *Students:* 60 full-time (9 women), 16 part-time (2 women); includes 6 minority (2 African Americans, 1 American Indian/Alaska Native, 3 Asian Americans or Pacific Islanders), 26 international. In 2009, 11 master's, 5 doctorates awarded. *Degree requirements:* For master's, thesis (for some programs); for doctorate, thesis/dissertation, qualifying exam, teaching experience. *Entrance requirements:* For master's and doctorate, GRE General Test. Additional exam requirements/recommendations for international students: Required—TOEFL. *Application deadline:* For fall admission, 7/1 priority date for domestic students. Applications are processed on a rolling basis. Application fee: $50. *Financial support:* Fellowships with full and partial tuition reimbursements, research assistantships with full and partial tuition reimbursements, teaching assistantships, institutionally sponsored loans and tuition waivers (full and partial) available. Financial award application deadline: 3/1; financial award applicants required to submit FAFSA. *Faculty research:* Musculoskeletal biomechanics, combustion diagnostics and computation, mechanical behavior of advanced materials and nanostructures, biorobotics. Total annual research expenditures: $7.8 million. *Unit head:* Dr. Iwan Alexander, Department Chair, 216-368-6045, Fax: 216-368-6445, E-mail: ida2@case.edu. *Application contact:* Carla Wilson, Student Affairs Coordinator, 216-368-4580, Fax: 216-368-3007, E-mail: cxw75@case.edu.

The Catholic University of America, School of Engineering, Department of Mechanical Engineering, Washington, DC 20064. Offers active control and smart materials/systems (MME, MSE, PhD); combustion (MME, MSE, D Engr); computational fluid dynamics (MME, MSE, D Engr); controls (MME, MSE, D Engr, PhD); dynamics (MME, MSE, PhD); electronic packaging (MME, MSE, PhD); human thermal comfort (MME, MSE, D Engr, PhD); HVAC and refrigeration (MME, MSE, D Engr, PhD); MEMS (MSE, D Engr, PhD); nano-mechanics (MME, D Engr, PhD); thermal/fluid sciences (MME, MSE, D Engr, PhD); vibrations (MSE, D Engr, PhD). Part-time programs available. *Faculty:* 6 full-time (0 women), 4 part-time/adjunct (0 women). *Students:* 8 full-time (2 women), 13 part-time (0 women); includes 1 minority (Hispanic American), 3 international. Average age 30. 20 applicants, 60% accepted, 9 enrolled. In 2009, 6 master's, 1 doctorate awarded. *Degree requirements:* For master's, thesis (for some programs); for doctorate, comprehensive exam, thesis/dissertation, oral exams. *Entrance requirements:* For master's, statement of purpose, official copies of academic transcripts, three letters of recommendation; for doctorate, 3 letters of recommendation. Additional exam requirements/recommendations for international students: Required—TOEFL (minimum score 580 paper-based; 237 computer-based). *Application deadline:* For fall admission, 8/1 priority date for domestic students, 7/15 for international students; for spring admission, 12/1 priority date for domestic students, 10/15 for international students. Applications are processed on a rolling basis. Application fee: $55. Electronic applications accepted. *Expenses:* Contact institution. *Financial support:* Fellowships, research assistantships, teaching assistantships, Federal Work-Study, scholarships/grants, tuition waivers (full and partial), and unspecified assistantships available. Financial award application deadline: 2/1; financial award applicants required to submit FAFSA. *Faculty research:* Fluid mechanics, dynamics, acoustics, computational mechanics, solar winds. Total annual research expenditures: $523,041. *Unit head:* Dr. Sen Nieh, Chair, 202-319-5171, Fax: 202-319-5173, E-mail: nieh@cua.edu. *Application contact:* Julie Schwing, Director of Graduate Admissions, 202-319-5057, Fax: 202-319-6533, E-mail: cua-admissions@cua.edu.

City College of the City University of New York, Graduate School, Grove School of Engineering, Department of Mechanical Engineering, New York, NY 10031-9198. Offers ME, MS, PhD. Part-time programs available. *Degree requirements:* For master's, thesis optional; for doctorate, one foreign language, comprehensive exam, thesis/dissertation. *Entrance requirements:* For master's and doctorate, GRE General Test. Additional exam requirements/recommendations for international students: Required—TOEFL (minimum score 500 paper-based; 173 computer-based). *Faculty research:* Bio-heat and mass transfer, bone mechanics, fracture mechanics, heat transfer in computer parts, mechanisms design.

Clarkson University, Graduate School, Wallace H. Coulter School of Engineering, Department of Mechanical and Aeronautical Engineering, Potsdam, NY 13699. Offers mechanical engineering (ME, MS, PhD). Part-time programs available. *Faculty:* 24 full-time (3 women). *Students:* 64 full-time (8 women); includes 1 minority (Hispanic American), 32 international. Average age 27. 93 applicants, 76% accepted, 22 enrolled. In 2009, 10 master's, 9 doctorates awarded. Terminal master's awarded for partial completion of doctoral program. *Degree requirements:* For master's, thesis; for doctorate, comprehensive exam, thesis/dissertation, departmental qualifying exam. *Entrance requirements:* For master's, GRE, resume, 3 letters of recommendation; for doctorate, GRE, transcripts of all college coursework, resume, personal statement, three letters of recommendation. Additional exam requirements/recommendations for international students: Required—TOEFL (minimum score 550 paper-based; 213 computer-based; 80 iBT), IELTS (minimum score 6.5). *Application deadline:* For fall admission, 1/30 priority date for domestic and international students; for spring admission, 9/1 priority date for domestic and international students. Applications are processed on a rolling basis. Application fee: $25 ($35 for international students). Electronic applications accepted. *Expenses:* Tuition: Part-time $1074 per credit hour. *Financial support:* In 2009–10, 54 students received support, including 2 fellowships (averaging $30,000 per year), 34 research assistantships (averaging $20,190 per year), 12 teaching assistantships (averaging $20,190 per year); scholarships/grants, tuition waivers (partial), and unspecified assistantships also available. *Faculty research:* Renewable energy, indoor and outdoor pollution, materials processing in space, application of nanomaterials and nanocomposites, gas filtration. Total annual research expenditures: $1.8 million. *Unit head:* Dr. Daryush K. Aidun, Department Chair, 315-268-6518, Fax: 315-268-6695, E-mail: dka@clarkson.edu. *Application contact:* Kelly Sharlow, Assistant to the Dean, 315-268-7929, Fax: 315-268-4494, E-mail: ksharlow@clarkson.edu.

Clemson University, Graduate School, College of Engineering and Science, Department of Mechanical Engineering, Program in Automotive Engineering, Clemson, SC 29634. Offers MS, PhD. *Students:* 70 full-time (5 women), 4 part-time (0 women); includes 2 minority (both African Americans), 43 international. Average age 26. 114 applicants, 82% accepted, 30 enrolled. In 2009, 8 master's awarded. *Degree requirements:* For master's, one foreign language, industrial internship; for doctorate, one foreign language, thesis/dissertation. *Entrance requirements:* For master's, GRE; for doctorate, GRE, MS or 2 years post-bachelor's experience. Additional exam requirements/recommendations for international students: Required—TOEFL. *Application deadline:* Applications are processed on a rolling basis. Application fee: $70 ($80 for international students). Electronic applications accepted. *Expenses:* Contact institution. *Financial support:* In 2009–10, 29 students received support, including 3 fellowships with partial tuition reimbursements available (averaging $14,500 per year), 24 research assistantships with partial tuition reimbursements available (averaging $18,277 per year); career-related internships or fieldwork, institutionally sponsored loans, scholarships/grants, traineeships, health care benefits, and unspecified assistantships also available. Support available to part-time students. Financial award application deadline: 2/1. *Faculty research:* Systems integration, manufacturing product design/development/vehicle electronics. *Unit head:* Dr. Donald Beasley, Mechanical Engineering Department Chair, 864-656-5622, Fax: 864-656-4435, E-mail: debsl@exchange.clemson.edu. *Application contact:* Dr. Mohammed Omar, Coordinator, 864-656-5537, Fax: 864-656-4435, E-mail: momar@clemson.edu.

Clemson University, Graduate School, College of Engineering and Science, Department of Mechanical Engineering, Program in Mechanical Engineering, Clemson, SC 29634. Offers MS, PhD. *Students:* 161 full-time (17 women), 16 part-time (1 woman); includes 7 minority (4 African Americans, 3 Asian Americans or Pacific Islanders), 116 international. Average age 25. 296 applicants, 74% accepted, 56 enrolled. In 2009, 34 master's, 6 doctorates awarded. *Degree requirements:* For master's, thesis; for doctorate, thesis/dissertation. *Entrance requirements:* For master's and doctorate, GRE General Test. Additional exam requirements/recommendations for international students: Required—TOEFL. *Application deadline:* Applications are processed on a rolling basis. Application fee: $70 ($80 for international students).

Mechanical Engineering

Clemson University (continued)
Electronic applications accepted. *Expenses:* Contact institution. *Financial support:* In 2009–10, 117 students received support, including 2 fellowships with full and partial tuition reimbursements available (averaging $7,833 per year), 76 research assistantships with partial tuition reimbursements available (averaging $15,991 per year), 5 teaching assistantships with partial tuition reimbursements available (averaging $13,379 per year); career-related internships or fieldwork, institutionally sponsored loans, scholarships/grants, health care benefits, and unspecified assistantships also available. Support available to part-time students. Financial award applicants required to submit FAFSA. *Unit head:* Dr. Donald Beasley, Coordinator, 864-656-5622, Fax: 864-656-4435, E-mail: debsl@exchange.clemson.edu. *Application contact:* Dr. Richard Miller, Coordinator, 864-656-6248, Fax: 864-656-4435, E-mail: rm@clemson.edu.

Cleveland State University, College of Graduate Studies, Fenn College of Engineering, Department of Civil and Environmental Engineering, Cleveland, OH 44115. Offers accelerated program civil engineering (MS); accelerated program environmental engineering (MS); civil engineering (MS, D Eng); engineering mechanics (MS); environmental engineering (MS). Part-time and evening/weekend programs available. *Degree requirements:* For master's, project or thesis; for doctorate, comprehensive exam, thesis/dissertation, candidacy and qualifying exams. *Entrance requirements:* For master's, GRE General Test, GRE Subject Test, minimum GPA of 2.75; for doctorate, GRE General Test, GRE Subject Test, minimum GPA of 3.25. Additional exam requirements/recommendations for international students: Required—TOEFL (minimum score 525 paper-based; 197 computer-based). *Faculty research:* Solid-waste disposal, constitutive modeling, transportation, safety engineering.

Cleveland State University, College of Graduate Studies, Fenn College of Engineering, Department of Mechanical Engineering, Cleveland, OH 44115. Offers MS, D Eng. Part-time programs available. *Degree requirements:* For master's, project or thesis; for doctorate, thesis/dissertation, candidacy and qualifying exams. *Entrance requirements:* For master's, GRE General Test, minimum GPA of 3.0; for doctorate, GRE General Test, minimum GPA of 3.25. Additional exam requirements/recommendations for international students: Required—TOEFL (minimum score 525 paper-based; 197 computer-based). *Faculty research:* Fluid piezoelectric sensors, laser-optical inspection simulation of forging and forming processes, multiphase flow and heat transfer, turbulent flows.

Colorado State University, Graduate School, College of Engineering, Department of Mechanical Engineering, Fort Collins, CO 80523-1374. Offers ME, MS, PhD. Part-time programs available. Postbaccalaureate distance learning degree programs offered (minimal on-campus study). *Faculty:* 20 full-time (2 women), 1 part-time/adjunct (0 women). *Students:* 50 full-time (7 women), 55 part-time (4 women); includes 12 minority (2 African Americans, 2 American Indian/Alaska Native, 5 Asian Americans or Pacific Islanders, 3 Hispanic Americans), 27 international. Average age 30. 110 applicants, 40% accepted, 23 enrolled. In 2009, 18 master's, 2 doctorates awarded. *Degree requirements:* For master's, comprehensive exam, thesis, oral exam; for doctorate, comprehensive exam, thesis/dissertation, preliminary exams, diagnostic exams, defense as final exam. *Entrance requirements:* For master's, GRE General Test (minimum score 1200 verbal and quantitative, 4.5 analytical), minimum GPA of 3.0, BS/BA from ABET accredited institution, 3 letters of recommendation, curriculum vitae, resume; for doctorate, GRE General Test (minimum score of 1200 on Verbal and Quantitative sections and 4.5 on the Analytical section), minimum GPA of 3.0, 3 letters of recommendation, curriculum vitae, department application, statement of purpose, resume. Additional exam requirements/recommendations for international students: Required—TOEFL (minimum score 550 paper-based; 213 computer-based; 80 iBT). *Application deadline:* For fall admission, 1/15 priority date for domestic and international students; for spring admission, 4/1 priority date for domestic and international students. Application fee: $50. Electronic applications accepted. *Expenses:* Tuition, state resident: full-time $6434; part-time $359.10 per credit. Tuition, nonresident: full-time $18,116; part-time $1006.45 per credit. Required fees: $1496; $83 per credit. *Financial support:* In 2009–10, 52 students received support, including 6 fellowships with tuition reimbursements available (averaging $13,164 per year), 30 research assistantships with tuition reimbursements available (averaging $12,284 per year), 16 teaching assistantships with tuition reimbursements available (averaging $9,602 per year); Federal Work-Study, scholarships/grants, and unspecified assistantships also available. Financial award application deadline: 1/15; financial award applicants required to submit FAFSA. *Faculty research:* Advanced materials processing and plasma engineering, energy conversion, dynamic and industrial systems, motorsport engineering, bioengineering. Total annual research expenditures: $4.7 million. *Unit head:* Dr. Allan T. Kirkpatrick, Head, 970-491-6559, Fax: 970-491-3827, E-mail: allan.kirkpatrick@colostate.edu. *Application contact:* Karen Mueller, Graduate Coordinator, 970-491-3872, Fax: 970-491-3827, E-mail: karen.mueller@colostate.edu.

Columbia University, Fu Foundation School of Engineering and Applied Science, Department of Mechanical Engineering, New York, NY 10027. Offers MS, Eng Sc D, PhD, Engr. PhD offered through the Graduate School of Arts and Sciences. Part-time programs available. Postbaccalaureate distance learning degree programs offered (no on-campus study). *Faculty:* 8 full-time (0 women), 5 part-time/adjunct (0 women). *Students:* 115 full-time (21 women), 37 part-time (6 women); includes 21 minority (4 African Americans, 13 Asian Americans or Pacific Islanders, 4 Hispanic Americans), 85 international. Average age 26. 267 applicants, 62% accepted, 64 enrolled. In 2009, 32 master's, 6 doctorates awarded. *Degree requirements:* For doctorate, thesis/dissertation, qualifying exam. *Entrance requirements:* For master's, GRE General Test, minimum GPA of 3.3; for doctorate and Engr, GRE General Test. Additional exam requirements/recommendations for international students: Required—TOEFL. *Application deadline:* For fall admission, 12/1 priority date for domestic and international students; for spring admission, 10/1 priority date for domestic and international students. Application fee: $70. Electronic applications accepted. *Financial support:* In 2009–10, 17 students received support, including 1 fellowship with full tuition reimbursement available (averaging $36,000 per year), 2 research assistantships with full tuition reimbursements available (averaging $30,000 per year), 14 teaching assistantships with full tuition reimbursements available (averaging $30,000 per year); health care benefits and unspecified assistantships also available. Financial award application deadline: 12/1; financial award applicants required to submit FAFSA. *Faculty research:* Biomechanics, solid mechanics, molecular biology, energy and tribology. *Unit head:* Dr. Y. Lawrence Yao, Professor and Department Chair, 212-854-2887, Fax: 212-854-3304, E-mail: yly1@columbia.edu. *Application contact:* Sandra Morris, Department Administrator, 212-854-6269, Fax: 212-854-3304, E-mail: swm16@columbia.edu.

Concordia University, School of Graduate Studies, Faculty of Engineering and Computer Science, Department of Mechanical and Industrial Engineering, Montréal, QC H3G 1M8, Canada. Offers composites (M Eng); industrial engineering (M Eng, MA Sc); mechanical engineering (M Eng, MA Sc, PhD, Certificate); software systems for industrial engineering (Certificate). *Degree requirements:* For master's, variable foreign language requirement, thesis or alternative; for doctorate, comprehensive exam, thesis/dissertation. *Faculty research:* Mechanical systems, fluid control systems, thermofluids engineering and robotics, industrial control systems.

Cooper Union for the Advancement of Science and Art, Albert Nerken School of Engineering, New York, NY 10003-7120. Offers chemical engineering (ME); civil engineering (ME); electrical engineering (ME); mechanical engineering (ME). Part-time programs available. *Faculty:* 27 full-time (1 woman), 15 part-time/adjunct (2 women). *Students:* 66 full-time (8 women), 20 part-time (1 woman); includes 30 minority (2 African Americans, 1 American Indian/Alaska Native, 19 Asian Americans or Pacific Islanders, 8 Hispanic Americans), 10 international. Average age 24. 80 applicants, 90% accepted, 56 enrolled. In 2009, 18 master's awarded. *Degree requirements:* For master's, thesis. *Entrance requirements:* For master's, GRE, BE, minimum GPA of 3.5. Additional exam requirements/recommendations for international students: Required—TOEFL (minimum score 600 paper-based; 250 computer-based; 100 iBT). *Application deadline:* For fall admission, 5/1 for domestic and international students. Applications are processed on a rolling basis. Application fee: $65. *Expenses:* Tuition: Full-time $35,000. Required fees: $1650. *Financial support:* Fellowships with tuition reimbursements, career-related internships or fieldwork, Federal Work-Study, tuition waivers (full), and all admitted students receive full-tuition scholarships available. Support available to part-time students. Financial award application deadline: 5/1; financial award applicants required to submit CSS PROFILE or FAFSA. *Faculty research:* Civil infrastructure, imaging and sensing technology, biomedical engineering, encryption technology, process engineering. *Unit head:* Dr. Simon Ben-Avi, Dean, 212-353-4285, E-mail: benavi@cooper.edu. *Application contact:* Student Contact, 212-353-4120, E-mail: admissions@cooper.edu.

Cornell University, Graduate School, Graduate Fields of Engineering, Field of Mechanical Engineering, Ithaca, NY 14853-0001. Offers biomechanical engineering (M Eng, MS, PhD); combustion (M Eng, MS, PhD); energy and power systems (M Eng, MS, PhD); fluid mechanics (M Eng, MS, PhD); heat transfer (M Eng, MS, PhD); materials and manufacturing engineering (M Eng, MS, PhD); mechanical systems and design (M Eng, MS, PhD); multiphase flows (M Eng, MS, PhD). *Faculty:* 51 full-time (5 women). *Students:* 139 full-time (26 women); includes 20 minority (1 African American, 12 Asian Americans or Pacific Islanders, 7 Hispanic Americans), 43 international. Average age 24. 469 applicants, 36% accepted, 86 enrolled. In 2009, 47 master's, 7 doctorates awarded. Terminal master's awarded for partial completion of doctoral program. *Degree requirements:* For master's, project (M Eng), thesis (MS); for doctorate, one foreign language, comprehensive exam, thesis/dissertation, 2 semesters of teaching experience. *Entrance requirements:* For master's and doctorate, GRE General Test, 3 letters of recommendation. Additional exam requirements/recommendations for international students: Required—TOEFL (minimum score 550 paper-based; 213 computer-based; 77 iBT). *Application deadline:* For fall admission, 1/15 for domestic students; for spring admission, 11/1 for domestic students. Application fee: $70. Electronic applications accepted. *Expenses:* Tuition: Full-time $29,500. Required fees: $70. Full-time tuition and fees vary according to degree level, program and student level. *Financial support:* In 2009–10, 47 students received support, including 25 fellowships with full tuition reimbursements available, 8 research assistantships with full tuition reimbursements available, 1 teaching assistantship with full tuition reimbursement available; institutionally sponsored loans, scholarships/grants, health care benefits, tuition waivers (full and partial), and unspecified assistantships also available. Financial award applicants required to submit FAFSA. *Faculty research:* Combustion and heat transfer, fluid mechanics and CFD, system dynamics and control, biomechanics, manufacturing. *Unit head:* Director of Graduate Studies, 607-255-5250. *Application contact:* Graduate Field Assistant, 607-255-5250, E-mail: maegrad@cornell.edu.

Dalhousie University, Faculty of Engineering, Department of Mechanical Engineering, Halifax, NS B3J 2X4, Canada. Offers M Eng, MA Sc, PhD. *Faculty:* 13 full-time (0 women), 2 part-time/adjunct (0 women). *Students:* 35 full-time (6 women), 5 part-time (0 women). Average age 31. 64 applicants, 77% accepted. In 2009, 9 master's, 1 doctorate awarded. *Degree requirements:* For master's, thesis; for doctorate, thesis/dissertation. *Entrance requirements:* Additional exam requirements/recommendations for international students: Required—TOEFL, IELTS, CANTEST, CAEL, or Michigan English Language Assessment Battery. *Application deadline:* For fall admission, 6/1 for domestic students, 4/1 for international students; for winter admission, 10/31 for domestic students, 8/31 for international students; for spring admission, 2/28 for domestic students, 12/31 for international students. Applications are processed on a rolling basis. Application fee: $70. Electronic applications accepted. *Financial support:* Fellowships, research assistantships, teaching assistantships, scholarships/grants and unspecified assistantships available. *Faculty research:* Fluid dynamics and energy, system dynamics, naval architecture, MEMS, space structures. *Unit head:* Dr. Ismet Ugursal, Head, 902-494-3917, Fax: 902-423-6711, E-mail: mechanical.engineering@dal.ca. *Application contact:* Dr. Alex Kalamkarov, Graduate Coordinator, 902-494-, Fax: 902-423-6711, E-mail: andrew.warkentin@dal.ca.

Dartmouth College, Thayer School of Engineering, Program in Mechanical Engineering, Hanover, NH 03755. Offers MS, PhD. *Degree requirements:* For master's, thesis; for doctorate, thesis/dissertation, candidacy oral exam. *Entrance requirements:* For master's and doctorate, GRE General Test. *Application deadline:* For fall admission, 1/1 priority date for domestic students. Application fee: $45. *Financial support:* Fellowships, research assistantships, teaching assistantships, career-related internships or fieldwork, Federal Work-Study, institutionally sponsored loans, and tuition waivers (full and partial) available. Financial award application deadline: 1/15. *Faculty research:* Tribology, dynamics and control systems, thermal science and energy conversion, fluid mechanics and multi-phase flow, mobile robots. Total annual research expenditures: $826,257. *Unit head:* Dr. Joseph J. Helbie, Dean, 603-646-2238, Fax: 603-646-2580, E-mail: joseph.j.helbie@dartmouth.edu. *Application contact:* Candace S. Potter, Graduate Admissions Administrator, 603-646-3844, Fax: 603-646-1620, E-mail: candace.potter@dartmouth.edu.

Drexel University, College of Engineering, Department of Mechanical Engineering and Mechanics, Philadelphia, PA 19104-2875. Offers mechanical engineering (MS, PhD). Part-time and evening/weekend programs available. Terminal master's awarded for partial completion of doctoral program. *Degree requirements:* For master's, thesis optional; for doctorate, thesis/dissertation. *Entrance requirements:* For master's, minimum GPA of 3.0, BS in engineering or science; for doctorate, minimum GPA of 3.5, MS in engineering or science. Additional exam requirements/recommendations for international students: Required—TOEFL. Electronic applications accepted. *Faculty research:* Composites, dynamic systems and control, combustion and fuels, biomechanics, mechanics and thermal fluid sciences.

Duke University, Graduate School, Pratt School of Engineering, Department of Mechanical Engineering and Materials Science, Durham, NC 27708. Offers materials science (MS, PhD); mechanical engineering (MS, PhD); JD/MS. Part-time programs available. *Faculty:* 26 full-time. *Students:* 55 full-time (11 women); includes 5 minority (4 Asian Americans or Pacific Islanders, 1 Hispanic American), 19 international. 200 applicants, 20% accepted, 17 enrolled. In 2009, 10 master's, 9 doctorates awarded. Terminal master's awarded for partial completion of doctoral program. *Degree requirements:* For master's, thesis optional; for doctorate, thesis/dissertation. *Entrance requirements:* For master's and doctorate, GRE General Test. Additional exam requirements/recommendations for international students: Required—TOEFL (minimum score 550 paper-based; 213 computer-based; 83 iBT), IELTS (minimum score 7). *Application deadline:* For fall admission, 12/8 priority date for domestic and international students; for spring admission, 11/1 for domestic students. Application fee: $75. Electronic applications accepted. *Financial support:* Fellowships, research assistantships, teaching assistantships, Federal Work-Study available. Financial award application deadline: 12/31. *Unit head:* Stefan Zauscher, Director of Graduate Studies, 919-660-5360, Fax: 919-660-8963, E-mail: kparrish@duke.edu. *Application contact:* Cynthia Robertson, Associate Dean for Enrollment Services, 919-684-3913, E-mail: grad-admissions@duke.edu.

École Polytechnique de Montréal, Graduate Programs, Department of Mechanical Engineering, Montréal, QC H3C 3A7, Canada. Offers aerothermics (M Eng, M Sc A, PhD); applied mechanics (M Eng, M Sc A, PhD); tool design (M Eng, M Sc A, PhD). Part-time and evening/weekend programs available. *Degree requirements:* For master's, one foreign language, thesis; for doctorate, one foreign language, thesis/dissertation. *Entrance requirements:* For master's, minimum GPA of 2.75; for doctorate, minimum GPA of 3.0. *Faculty research:* Noise control and vibration, fatigue and creep, aerodynamics, composite materials, biomechanics, robotics.

Embry-Riddle Aeronautical University, Daytona Beach Campus Graduate Program, Department of Mechanical Engineering, Daytona Beach, FL 32114-3900. Offers MSME. *Faculty:* 4 full-time (0 women). *Students:* 17 full-time (3 women), 2 part-time (0 women); includes 2 minority (1 African American, 1 American Indian/Alaska Native), 5 international. Average age 25. 17 applicants, 65% accepted, 10 enrolled. *Degree requirements:* For master's, thesis. *Entrance requirements:* Additional exam requirements/recommendations for international students: Required—TOEFL (minimum score 550 paper-based; 213 computer-based; 79 iBT). *Application deadline:* For fall admission, 8/1 priority date for domestic students; for spring admission, 12/1 priority date for domestic students. Applications are processed on a rolling basis. Application fee: $50. *Expenses:* Tuition: Full-time $13,740; part-time $1145 per credit hour. *Financial support:* In 2009–10, 10 students received support, including 3 research assistantships (averaging $6,000 per year), 5 teaching assistantships (averaging $6,000 per year). Financial award applicants required to submit FAFSA. *Unit head:* Dr. Maj Mirmirani, College of Engineering Dean, 386-226-6889. *Application contact:* Keith Deaton, Associate Director, International and Graduate Admissions, 800-388-3728, Fax: 386-226-7070, E-mail: graduate.admissions@erau.edu.

Fairfield University, School of Engineering, Fairfield, CT 06824-5195. Offers electrical and computer engineering (MS); management of technology (MS); mechanical engineering (MS); software engineering (MS). Part-time and evening/weekend programs available. *Degree requirements:* For master's, thesis, capstone course. *Entrance requirements:* For master's, interview, minimum GPA of 2.8, resume, 2 recommendations. Additional exam requirements/recommendations for international students: Required—TOEFL (minimum score 550 paper-based; 213 computer-based; 80 iBT). Electronic applications accepted. *Expenses:* Contact institution. *Faculty research:* Vehicle dynamics, image processing, multimedia in instruction, thermal packaging, character recognition, photovoltaics and nanotechnology, Web technology.

Florida Agricultural and Mechanical University, Division of Graduate Studies, Research, and Continuing Education, FAMU-FSU College of Engineering, Department of Mechanical Engineering, Tallahassee, FL 32307-3200. Offers MS, PhD. *Faculty:* 21 full-time (1 woman). *Students:* 7 full-time (4 women), 2 part-time (1 woman); includes 8 minority (all African Americans), 1 international. In 2009, 2 doctorates awarded. *Degree requirements:* For master's, thesis optional; for doctorate, comprehensive exam, thesis/dissertation. *Entrance requirements:* For master's, GRE General Test, minimum GPA of 3.0. Additional exam requirements/recommendations for international students: Required—TOEFL (minimum score 550 paper-based; 213 computer-based). *Application deadline:* For fall admission, 7/1 for domestic students, 3/1 for international students. Application fee: $20. *Faculty research:* Fluid mechanical and heat transfer, thermodynamics, dynamics and controls, mechanics and materials. *Unit head:* Dr. Ching Shih, Chairperson, 850-410-6100. *Application contact:* Dr. Chanta M. Haywood, Dean of Graduate Studies, Research, and Continuing Education, 850-599-3315, Fax: 850-599-3727.

Florida Atlantic University, College of Engineering and Computer Science, Department of Mechanical Engineering, Boca Raton, FL 33431-0991. Offers MS, PhD. Part-time and evening/weekend programs available. *Faculty:* 11 full-time (0 women). *Students:* 27 full-time (8 women), 5 part-time (0 women); includes 6 minority (1 Asian American or Pacific Islander, 5 Hispanic Americans), 11 international. Average age 30. 35 applicants, 69% accepted, 12 enrolled. In 2009, 8 master's, 2 doctorates awarded. Terminal master's awarded for partial completion of doctoral program. *Degree requirements:* For master's, thesis optional; for doctorate, thesis/dissertation, qualifying exam. *Entrance requirements:* For master's and doctorate, GRE General Test, minimum GPA of 3.0. Additional exam requirements/recommendations for international students: Required—TOEFL. *Application deadline:* For fall admission, 7/1 priority date for domestic students, 2/15 for international students; for spring admission, 11/1 for domestic students, 7/15 for international students. Applications are processed on a rolling basis. Application fee: $30. *Expenses:* Tuition, state resident: full-time $7055; part-time $293.94 per credit hour. Tuition, nonresident: full-time $22,096; part-time $920.66 per credit hour. *Financial support:* Fellowships, research assistantships, teaching assistantships, career-related internships or fieldwork, Federal Work-Study, and unspecified assistantships available. Support available to part-time students. Financial award application deadline: 4/1; financial award applicants required to submit FAFSA. *Faculty research:* Fault detection and diagnostics, computational fluid mechanics, composite materials, two-phase flows, helicopter dynamics. *Unit head:* Dr. Oren Masory, Chairman, 561-297-3478, Fax: 561-297-2825. *Application contact:* Dr. G. Cai, Graduate Advisor, 561-297-3428, Fax: 561-297-2825, E-mail: caig@fau.edu.

Florida Institute of Technology, Graduate Programs, College of Engineering, Mechanical and Aerospace Engineering Department, Melbourne, FL 32901-6975. Offers aerospace engineering (MS, PhD); mechanical engineering (MS, PhD). Part-time programs available. *Faculty:* 13 full-time (1 woman). *Students:* 58 full-time (1 woman), 34 part-time (3 women); includes 7 minority (1 African American, 3 Asian Americans or Pacific Islanders, 3 Hispanic Americans), 42 international. Average age 27. 206 applicants, 59% accepted, 43 enrolled. In 2009, 14 master's, 1 doctorate awarded. *Degree requirements:* For master's, comprehensive exam (for some programs), thesis optional; for doctorate, comprehensive exam, thesis/dissertation, oral section of written exam, complete program of significant original research. *Entrance requirements:* For master's, GRE General Test, minimum GPA of 3.0, bachelor's degree from an ABET-accredited program; for doctorate, GRE General Test, 3 letters of recommendation, minimum GPA of 3.5, resume, statement of objectives. Additional exam requirements/recommendations for international students: Required—TOEFL (minimum score 550 paper-based; 213 computer-based; 79 iBT). *Application deadline:* For fall admission, 4/1 for international students; for spring admission, 9/30 for international students. Applications are processed on a rolling basis. Application fee: $50. Electronic applications accepted. *Expenses:* Tuition: Part-time $1015 per credit. Tuition and fees vary according to campus/location and program. *Financial support:* In 2009–10, 15 students received support, including 4 research assistantships with full and partial tuition reimbursements available (averaging $3,002 per year), 11 teaching assistantships with full and partial tuition reimbursements available (averaging $3,041 per year); career-related internships or fieldwork, institutionally sponsored loans, tuition waivers (partial), unspecified assistantships, and tuition remissions also available. Support available to part-time students. Financial award application deadline: 3/1; financial award applicants required to submit FAFSA. *Faculty research:* Dynamic systems, robotics, and controls; structures, solid mechanics, and materials; thermal-fluid sciences, optical tomography, composite/recycled materials. Total annual research expenditures: $731,514. *Unit head:* Dr. Pei-feng Hsu, Department Head, 321-674-8092, Fax: 321-674-8813, E-mail: phsu@fit.edu. *Application contact:* Thomas M. Shea, Director of Graduate Admissions, 321-674-7577, Fax: 321-723-9468, E-mail: tshea@fit.edu.

See Close-Up on page 521.

Florida International University, College of Engineering and Computing, Department of Mechanical and Materials Engineering, Miami, FL 33199. Offers materials science and engineering (MS, PhD); mechanical engineering (MS, PhD). Part-time and evening/weekend programs available. *Faculty:* 17 full-time (2 women). *Students:* 46 full-time (7 women), 19 part-time (5 women); includes 18 minority (3 African Americans, 1 Asian American or Pacific Islander, 14 Hispanic Americans), 44 international. Average age 28. 89 applicants, 20% accepted, 16 enrolled. In 2009, 19 master's, 8 doctorates awarded. Terminal master's awarded for partial completion of doctoral program. *Degree requirements:* For master's, thesis or alternative; for doctorate, comprehensive exam, thesis/dissertation. *Entrance requirements:* For master's, GRE (depending on program), 3 letters of recommendation, minimum undergraduate GPA of 3.0 in upper level course; for doctorate, GRE minimum of 1150 with GRE verbal at least 450 and GRE quantitative at least 650, for someone with BS only: minimum undergraduate GPA of 3.0 in upper-level coursework, 3 letters of recommendation, letter of intent; for someone with MS: in addition to the above requirements for someone having a BS degree, the MS GPA must be a minimum of 3.3. Additional exam requirements/recommendations for international students: Required—TOEFL (minimum score 550 paper-based; 80 iBT), or IELTS (minimum score 6.5). *Application deadline:* For fall admission, 6/1 for domestic students, 4/1 for international students; for spring admission, 10/1 for domestic students, 9/1 for international students. Applications are processed on a rolling basis. Application fee: $30. Electronic applications accepted. *Expenses:* Tuition, state resident: full-time $8008; part-time $4004 per year. Tuition, nonresident: full-time $20,104; part-time $10,052 per year. Required fees: $298; $149 per term. *Financial support:* In 2009–10, 7 fellowships (averaging $25,000 per year), 13 research assistantships (averaging $20,000 per year), 19 teaching assistantships (averaging $20,000 per year) were awarded; institutionally sponsored loans, scholarships/grants, and unspecified assistantships also available. Financial award application deadline: 3/1; financial award applicants required to submit FAFSA. *Faculty research:* Mechanics

and materials, fluid/thermal/energy, design and manufacturing, materials science engineering. Total annual research expenditures: $3.8 million. *Unit head:* Dr. Cesar Levy, Chair, Mechanical and Materials Engineering Department, 305-348-0104, Fax: 305-348-1932, E-mail: cesar.levy@fiu.edu. *Application contact:* Maria Parrilla, Graduate Admissions Assistant, 305-348-1890, Fax: 305-348-6142, E-mail: grad_eng@fiu.edu.

Florida State University, The Graduate School, FAMU-FSU College of Engineering, Department of Mechanical Engineering, Tallahassee, FL 32306. Offers MS, PhD. Part-time programs available. Postbaccalaureate distance learning degree programs offered (no on-campus study). Terminal master's awarded for partial completion of doctoral program. *Degree requirements:* For master's, thesis optional; for doctorate, thesis/dissertation. *Entrance requirements:* For master's, GRE General Test, minimum GPA of 3.0, resume, letters of recommendation; for doctorate, GRE General Test, minimum graduate GPA of 3.0, official transcripts, personal statement, resume, letters of recommendation. Additional exam requirements/recommendations for international students: Required—TOEFL (minimum score 550 paper-based; 213 computer-based; 80 iBT), IELTS (minimum score 6.5), Michigan English Language Assessment Battery (minimum score 77). *Application deadline:* For fall admission, 5/1 for domestic and international students; for spring admission, 10/1 for domestic and international students. Applications are processed on a rolling basis. Application fee: $30. Electronic applications accepted. *Expenses:* Tuition, state resident: full-time $7413.36. Tuition, nonresident: full-time $22,567. *Financial support:* In 2009–10, fellowships with full tuition reimbursements (averaging $24,000 per year); research assistantships with full tuition reimbursements, teaching assistantships with full tuition reimbursements, career-related internships or fieldwork, institutionally sponsored loans, scholarships/grants, health care benefits, tuition waivers (partial), and unspecified assistantships also available. Support available to part-time students. *Faculty research:* Fluid mechanics, superconductivity, experimental and theoretical solid mechanics, computational mechanics of materials, intelligent robotic systems. *Unit head:* Dr. Cesar Luongo, Associate Chair, 850-644-1095, Fax: 850-410-6337, E-mail: luongo@magnet.fsu.edu. *Application contact:* George Green, Coordinator of Graduate Studies, 850-410-6330, Fax: 850-410-6337, E-mail: ggreen@eng.fsu.edu.

Gannon University, School of Graduate Studies, College of Engineering and Business, School of Engineering and Computer Science, Program in Mechanical Engineering, Erie, PA 16541-0001. Offers MSME. Part-time and evening/weekend programs available. *Students:* 26 full-time (1 woman), 19 part-time (2 women), 34 international. Average age 24. 131 applicants, 77% accepted, 8 enrolled. In 2009, 47 master's awarded. *Degree requirements:* For master's, comprehensive exam, thesis or project. *Entrance requirements:* For master's, bachelor's degree in mechanical engineering, minimum QPA of 2.5. Additional exam requirements/recommendations for international students: Required—TOEFL (minimum score 79 iBT). *Application deadline:* Applications are processed on a rolling basis. Application fee: $25. Electronic applications accepted. *Expenses:* Tuition: Full-time $13,590; part-time $755 per credit. Required fees: $524; $17 per credit. Tuition and fees vary according to course load, degree level, campus/location and program. *Financial support:* Career-related internships or fieldwork, scholarships/grants, traineeships, and unspecified assistantships available. Financial award application deadline: 7/1; financial award applicants required to submit FAFSA. *Unit head:* Dr. Mahesh Aggarwal, Chair, 814-871-7629, E-mail: affarwal001@gannon.edu. *Application contact:* Kara Morgan, Assistant Director of Graduate Admissions, 814-871-5831, Fax: 814-871-5827, E-mail: graduate@gannon.edu.

The George Washington University, School of Engineering and Applied Science, Department of Mechanical and Aerospace Engineering, Washington, DC 20052. Offers MS, D Sc, App Sc, Engr, Graduate Certificate. Part-time and evening/weekend programs available. *Faculty:* 11 full-time (0 women), 10 part-time/adjunct (1 woman). *Students:* 30 full-time (6 women), 36 part-time (7 women); includes 9 minority (2 African Americans, 1 American Indian/Alaska Native, 6 Asian Americans or Pacific Islanders), 27 international. Average age 29. 84 applicants, 93% accepted, 18 enrolled. In 2009, 11 master's, 6 doctorates awarded. *Degree requirements:* For master's, thesis optional; for doctorate, thesis/dissertation, final and qualifying exams. *Entrance requirements:* For master's, appropriate bachelor's degree, minimum GPA of 3.0; for doctorate, appropriate bachelor's or master's degree, minimum GPA of 3.4, GRE if highest earned degree is BS; for other advanced degree, appropriate master's degree, minimum GPA of 3.0. Additional exam requirements/recommendations for international students: Required—TOEFL or George Washington University English as a Foreign Language Test. *Application deadline:* For fall admission, 3/1 priority date for domestic students; for spring admission, 10/1 for domestic students. Applications are processed on a rolling basis. Application fee: $60. *Financial support:* In 2009–10, 51 students received support; fellowships with tuition reimbursements available, research assistantships, teaching assistantships with tuition reimbursements available, career-related internships or fieldwork and institutionally sponsored loans available. Financial award application deadline: 3/1; financial award applicants required to submit FAFSA. *Unit head:* Dr. Michael Plesniak, Chairman, 202-994-6749, E-mail: maeng@gwu.edu. *Application contact:* Adina Lav, Marketing, Recruiting and Admissions, 202-994-5827, Fax: 202-994-0909, E-mail: engineering@gwu.edu.

Georgia Institute of Technology, Graduate Studies and Research, College of Engineering, George W. Woodruff School of Mechanical Engineering, Program in Mechanical Engineering, Atlanta, GA 30332-0001. Offers biomedical engineering (MS Bio E); mechanical engineering (MS, MSME, PhD). Part-time programs available. Postbaccalaureate distance learning degree programs offered (no on-campus study). Terminal master's awarded for partial completion of doctoral program. *Degree requirements:* For master's, thesis optional; for doctorate, comprehensive exam, thesis/dissertation. *Entrance requirements:* For master's and doctorate, GRE General Test, minimum GPA of 3.0. Additional exam requirements/recommendations for international students: Required—TOEFL. Electronic applications accepted. *Faculty research:* Automation and mechatronics; computer-aided engineering and design; micro-electronic mechanical systems; heat transfer, combustion and energy systems; fluid mechanics.

Georgia Southern University, Jack N. Averitt College of Graduate Studies, Allen E. Paulson College of Science and Technology, Department of Mechanical and Electrical Engineering Technology, Statesboro, GA 30460. Offers M Tech, MSAE. Part-time and evening/weekend programs available. *Students:* 31 full-time (6 women), 17 part-time (4 women); includes 15 minority (13 African Americans, 2 Hispanic Americans), 5 international. Average age 27. 25 applicants, 100% accepted, 25 enrolled. In 2009, 3 master's awarded. *Degree requirements:* For master's, comprehensive exam, thesis optional. *Entrance requirements:* For master's, GRE. Additional exam requirements/recommendations for international students: Required—TOEFL (minimum score 550 paper-based; 213 computer-based; 80 iBT). *Application deadline:* For fall admission, 3/1 priority date for domestic and international students; for spring admission, 10/1 priority date for domestic students, 10/1 for international students. Applications are processed on a rolling basis. Application fee: $50. Electronic applications accepted. *Expenses:* Tuition, state resident: full-time $5040; part-time $210 per credit hour. Tuition, nonresident: full-time $20,136; part-time $839 per credit hour. Required fees: $1644. *Financial support:* In 2009–10, 28 students received support, including 4 research assistantships with partial tuition reimbursements available (averaging $7,200 per year); tuition waivers (partial) and unspecified assistantships also available. Financial award application deadline: 4/15; financial award applicants required to submit FAFSA. *Faculty research:* Interdisciplinary research in computational mechanics, experimental and computational biofuel combustion and tribology, mechatronics and control, thermomechanical and thermofluid finite element modeling, information technology. *Unit head:* Dr. Mohammad S. Davoud, Director, 912-478-0540, Fax: 912-478-1455, E-mail: mdavoud@georgiasouthern.edu. *Application contact:* Dr. Charles Ziglar, Coordinator for Graduate Student Recruitment, 912-478-5384, Fax: 912-478-0740, E-mail: gradadmissions@georgiasouthern.edu.

Graduate School and University Center of the City University of New York, Graduate Studies, Program in Engineering, New York, NY 10016-4039. Offers biomedical engineering (PhD); chemical engineering (PhD); civil engineering (PhD); electrical engineering (PhD); mechanical engineering (PhD). *Faculty:* 68 full-time (1 woman). *Students:* 115 full-time (33

Mechanical Engineering

Graduate School and University Center of the City University of New York (continued)

women), 8 part-time (2 women); includes 17 minority (5 African Americans, 8 Asian Americans or Pacific Islanders, 4 Hispanic Americans), 68 international. Average age 34. 119 applicants, 48% accepted, 26 enrolled. In 2009, 30 doctorates awarded. *Degree requirements:* For doctorate, thesis/dissertation. *Entrance requirements:* For doctorate, GRE General Test. Additional exam requirements/recommendations for international students: Required—TOEFL. Application fee: $125. Electronic applications accepted. *Financial support:* In 2009–10, 61 fellowships, 10 teaching assistantships were awarded; research assistantships, Federal Work-Study, institutionally sponsored loans, and tuition waivers (full and partial) also available. Financial award application deadline: 2/1; financial award applicants required to submit FAFSA. *Unit head:* Dr. Mumtaz Kassir, Executive Officer, 212-650-8031, Fax: 212-650-8029, E-mail: kassir@ce-mail.engr.ccny.cuny.edu. *Application contact:* Les Gribben, Director of Admissions, 212-817-7470, Fax: 212-817-1624, E-mail: lgribben@gc.cuny.edu.

See Close-Up on page 69.

Grand Valley State University, Padnos College of Engineering and Computing, School of Engineering, Allendale, MI 49401-9403. Offers electrical and computer engineering (MSE); manufacturing operations (MSE); mechanical engineering (MSE); product design and manufacturing engineering (MSE). Part-time and evening/weekend programs available. *Faculty:* 6 full-time (0 women). *Students:* 8 full-time (1 woman), 37 part-time (4 women), 4 international. Average age 30. 21 applicants, 86% accepted, 10 enrolled. In 2009, 12 master's awarded. *Degree requirements:* For master's, project or thesis. *Entrance requirements:* For master's, engineering degree, minimum GPA of 3.0. Additional exam requirements/recommendations for international students: Required—TOEFL. *Application deadline:* Applications are processed on a rolling basis. Application fee: $30. Electronic applications accepted. *Financial support:* In 2009–10, 11 students received support, including 3 fellowships (averaging $1,083 per year), 9 research assistantships with full tuition reimbursements available (averaging $7,304 per year); career-related internships or fieldwork, Federal Work-Study, institutionally sponsored loans, scholarships/grants, and unspecified assistantships also available. *Faculty research:* Digital signal processing, computer aided design, computer aided manufacturing, manufacturing simulation, biomechanics, product design. Total annual research expenditures: $300,000. *Unit head:* Dr. Charles Standridge, Acting Director, 616-331-6750, Fax: 616-331-7215, E-mail: standric@gvsu.edu. *Application contact:* Dr. Pranod Chaphalkar, Graduate Director, 616-331-6843, Fax: 616-331-7215, E-mail: chaphalp@gvsu.edu.

Howard University, College of Engineering, Architecture, and Computer Sciences, School of Engineering and Computer Science, Department of Mechanical Engineering, Washington, DC 20059-0002. Offers M Eng, PhD. *Degree requirements:* For master's, comprehensive exam, thesis; for doctorate, one foreign language, comprehensive exam, thesis/dissertation, 2 terms of residency. *Entrance requirements:* For master's and doctorate, GRE General Test, minimum GPA of 3.0. Additional exam requirements/recommendations for international students: Required—TOEFL (minimum score 213 computer-based). Electronic applications accepted. *Faculty research:* The dynamics and control of large flexible space structures, optimization of space structures.

Idaho State University, Office of Graduate Studies, College of Engineering, Mechanical Engineering Department, Pocatello, ID 83209-8060. Offers measurement and control engineering (MS); mechanical engineering (MS). Part-time programs available. *Faculty:* 15 full-time (1 woman). *Students:* 39 full-time (7 women), 41 part-time (6 women); includes 3 minority (1 African American, 2 Asian Americans or Pacific Islanders), 29 international. Average age 31. In 2009, 7 master's awarded. *Degree requirements:* For master's, comprehensive exam (for some programs), 2 semesters of seminar; thesis or project. *Entrance requirements:* For master's, GRE. Additional exam requirements/recommendations for international students: Required—TOEFL (minimum score 550 paper-based; 213 computer-based; 80 iBT). *Application deadline:* For fall admission, 7/1 for domestic students, 6/1 for international students; for spring admission, 12/1 for domestic students, 11/1 for international students. Applications are processed on a rolling basis. Application fee: $55. Electronic applications accepted. *Expenses:* Tuition, state resident: full-time $3318; part-time $297 per credit hour. Tuition, nonresident: full-time $13,120; part-time $437 per credit hour. Required fees: $2530. Tuition and fees vary according to program. *Financial support:* In 2009–10, 5 research assistantships with full and partial tuition reimbursements (averaging $10,539 per year) were awarded; teaching assistantships with full and partial tuition reimbursements, Federal Work-Study, institutionally sponsored loans, scholarships/grants, health care benefits, tuition waivers (full and partial), and unspecified assistantships also available. Support available to part-time students. Financial award application deadline: 1/1; financial award applicants required to submit FAFSA. *Faculty research:* Modeling and identification of biomedical systems, intelligent systems and adaptive control, active flow control of turbo machinery, validation of advanced computational codes for thermal fluid interactions, development of methodologies for the assessment of passive safety system performance in advanced reactors, alternative energy research (wind, solar, hydrogen). *Unit head:* Dr. George Imel, Chair, 208-282-3732, Fax: 208-282-4538, E-mail: gimel@isu.edu. *Application contact:* Tami Carson, Graduate School Technical Records Specialist, 208-282-2150, Fax: 208-282-4847, E-mail: carstami@isu.edu.

Illinois Institute of Technology, Graduate College, Armour College of Engineering, Department of Mechanical, Materials and Aerospace Engineering, Chicago, IL 60616-3793. Offers manufacturing engineering (MME, MS); materials science and engineering (MMME, MS, PhD); mechanical and aerospace engineering (MMAE, MS, PhD). Part-time programs available. Terminal master's awarded for partial completion of doctoral program. *Degree requirements:* For master's, comprehensive exam (for some programs), thesis (for some programs); for doctorate, comprehensive exam, thesis/dissertation. *Entrance requirements:* For master's and doctorate, GRE General Test, minimum undergraduate GPA of 3.0. Additional exam requirements/recommendations for international students: Required—TOEFL (minimum score 550 paper-based; 213 computer-based; 80 iBT). Electronic applications accepted. *Expenses:* Tuition: Full-time $17,550; part-time $888 per credit hour. Required fees: $850; $7.50 per credit hour. One-time fee: $50 full-time. Full-time tuition and fees vary according to program. *Faculty research:* Active flow control, bio-fluid dynamics, acoustics and separated flows, digital design and manufacturing and high performance materials, two-phase flows in micro scales and combustion-driven MEMS, global positioning systems, experimental and computational solid mechanics.

Indiana University–Purdue University Fort Wayne, College of Engineering, Technology, and Computer Science, Department of Engineering, Fort Wayne, IN 46805-1499. Offers computer engineering (MS); electrical engineering (MS); mechanical engineering (MS); systems engineering (MS). Part-time programs available. *Faculty:* 15 full-time (3 women). *Students:* 4 full-time (0 women), 29 part-time (5 women); includes 2 minority (1 African American, 1 Asian American or Pacific Islander), 5 international. Average age 29. 13 applicants, 92% accepted, 7 enrolled. In 2009, 1 master's awarded. *Entrance requirements:* For master's, minimum GPA of 3.0. Additional exam requirements/recommendations for international students: Required—TOEFL (minimum score 550 paper-based; 213 computer-based; 77 iBT); Recommended—TWE. *Application deadline:* For fall admission, 7/15 priority date for domestic students, 3/1 priority date for international students; for spring admission, 12/1 priority date for domestic students, 9/1 priority date for international students. Applications are processed on a rolling basis. Application fee: $55 ($60 for international students). Electronic applications accepted. *Expenses:* Tuition, state resident: full-time $4595; part-time $255 per credit. Tuition, nonresident: full-time $10,963; part-time $609 per credit. Required fees: $528; $29.35 per credit. Tuition and fees vary according to course load. *Financial support:* In 2009–10, 1 research assistantship with partial tuition reimbursement (averaging $12,740 per year), 3 teaching assistantships with partial tuition reimbursements (averaging $12,740 per year) were awarded. Financial award application deadline: 3/1; financial award applicants required to submit FAFSA. *Faculty research:* Synthesis technique, Markov parameters. Total annual research expenditures: $57,918. *Unit head:* Dr. Donald Mueller, Chair, 260-481-5707, Fax: 260-481-6281, E-mail: mueller@engr.ipfw.edu. *Application contact:* Dr. Donald Mueller, Chair, 260-481-5707, Fax: 260-481-6281, E-mail: mueller@engr.ipfw.edu.

Indiana University–Purdue University Indianapolis, School of Engineering and Technology, Department of Mechanical Engineering, Indianapolis, IN 46202-2896. Offers biomedical engineering (MS Bm E); computer-aided mechanical engineering (Certificate); mechanical engineering (MSME, PhD). Part-time programs available. *Students:* 11 full-time (0 women), 43 part-time (13 women); includes 5 minority (1 African American, 2 Asian Americans or Pacific Islanders, 2 Hispanic Americans), 29 international. Average age 27. 6 applicants, 0% accepted, 0 enrolled. In 2009, 13 master's awarded. *Degree requirements:* For master's, thesis optional. *Entrance requirements:* For master's, GRE. Additional exam requirements/recommendations for international students: Required—TOEFL. *Application deadline:* For fall admission, 7/1 for domestic students. Application fee: $55 ($65 for international students). *Financial support:* Fellowships with tuition reimbursements, research assistantships with full and partial tuition reimbursements, tuition waivers (full and partial) available. Financial award application deadline: 3/1. *Faculty research:* Computational fluid dynamics, heat transfer, finite-element methods, composites, biomechanics. *Unit head:* Dr. Hasan Akay, Chairman, 317-274-9717, Fax: 317-274-9744. *Application contact:* Valerie Diemer, Graduate Program, 317-278-4960, Fax: 317-278-1671, E-mail: grad@engr.iupui.edu.

Instituto Tecnológico y de Estudios Superiores de Monterrey, Campus Chihuahua, Graduate Programs, Chihuahua, Mexico. Offers computer systems engineering (Ingeniero); electrical engineering (Ingeniero); electromechanical engineering (Ingeniero); electronic engineering (Ingeniero); engineering administration (MEA); industrial engineering (MIE, Ingeniero); international trade (MIT); mechanical engineering (Ingeniero).

Instituto Tecnológico y de Estudios Superiores de Monterrey, Campus Monterrey, Graduate and Research Division, Programs in Engineering, Monterrey, Mexico. Offers applied statistics (M Eng); artificial intelligence (PhD); automation engineering (M Eng); chemical engineering (M Eng); civil engineering (M Eng); electrical engineering (M Eng); electronic engineering (M Eng); environmental engineering (M Eng); industrial engineering (M Eng, PhD); manufacturing engineering (M Eng); mechanical engineering (M Eng); systems and quality engineering (M Eng). Part-time and evening/weekend programs available. Terminal master's awarded for partial completion of doctoral program. *Degree requirements:* For master's, one foreign language, thesis; for doctorate, one foreign language, thesis/dissertation. *Entrance requirements:* For master's, EXADEP; for doctorate, GRE, master's degree in related field. Additional exam requirements/recommendations for international students: Required—TOEFL. *Faculty research:* Flexible manufacturing cells, materials, statistical methods, environmental prevention, control and evaluation.

Iowa State University of Science and Technology, Graduate College, College of Engineering, Department of Mechanical Engineering, Ames, IA 50011. Offers mechanical engineering (MS, PhD); mechanical engineering (coursework only) (M Eng); systems engineering (M Eng). *Faculty:* 31 full-time (3 women), 1 (woman) part-time/adjunct. *Students:* 124 full-time (16 women), 53 part-time (2 women); includes 15 minority (4 African Americans, 2 American Indian/Alaska Native, 7 Asian Americans or Pacific Islanders, 2 Hispanic Americans), 69 international. 209 applicants, 27% accepted, 41 enrolled. In 2009, 27 master's, 14 doctorates awarded. *Degree requirements:* For master's, thesis or alternative; for doctorate, thesis/dissertation. *Entrance requirements:* For master's and doctorate, GRE General Test, resume. Additional exam requirements/recommendations for international students: Required—TOEFL (minimum score 550 paper-based; 79 iBT) or IELTS (minimum score 6.5). *Application deadline:* For fall admission, 1/10 priority date for domestic and international students; for spring admission, 7/10 priority date for domestic and international students. Application fee: $40 ($90 for international students). Electronic applications accepted. *Expenses:* Tuition, state resident: full-time $6716. Tuition, nonresident: full-time $8908. Tuition and fees vary according to course level, course load, program and student level. *Financial support:* In 2009–10, 76 research assistantships with full and partial tuition reimbursements (averaging $15,000 per year), 23 teaching assistantships with full and partial tuition reimbursements (averaging $16,000 per year) were awarded; fellowships, scholarships/grants, health care benefits, and unspecified assistantships also available. *Unit head:* Dr. Thomas Heindel, Interim Chair, 515-294-3891, E-mail: megradinfo@iastate.edu. *Application contact:* Dr. Sriram Sundararajan, Director of Graduate Education, 515-294-1050, E-mail: megradinfo@iastate.edu.

The Johns Hopkins University, Engineering for Professionals, Part-time Program in Mechanical Engineering, Baltimore, MD 21218-2699. Offers MME. Part-time and evening/weekend programs available. *Faculty:* 9 part-time/adjunct (0 women). *Students:* 2 full-time (0 women), 83 part-time (14 women); includes 14 minority (5 African Americans, 7 Asian Americans or Pacific Islanders, 2 Hispanic Americans). Average age 26. In 2009, 25 master's awarded. *Application deadline:* Applications are processed on a rolling basis. Application fee: $75. Electronic applications accepted. *Financial support:* Institutionally sponsored loans available. *Unit head:* Dr. K. T. Ramesh, Program Chair, 410-516-7735, Fax: 410-516-7254, E-mail: ramesh@jhu.edu. *Application contact:* Priyanka Dwivedi, Admissions Manager, 410-516-2300, Fax: 410-579-8049, E-mail: pdwived1@jhu.edu.

The Johns Hopkins University, G. W. C. Whiting School of Engineering, Department of Mechanical Engineering, Baltimore, MD 21218-2681. Offers MSE, PhD. *Faculty:* 18 full-time (3 women), 13 part-time/adjunct (1 woman). *Students:* 85 full-time (17 women), 2 part-time (1 woman); includes 6 minority (1 African American, 4 Asian Americans or Pacific Islanders, 1 Hispanic American), 38 international. Average age 26. 235 applicants, 38% accepted, 30 enrolled. In 2009, 18 master's, 17 doctorates awarded. Terminal master's awarded for partial completion of doctoral program. *Degree requirements:* For master's, thesis (for some programs); for doctorate, comprehensive exam, thesis/dissertation, oral exam. *Entrance requirements:* For master's and doctorate, GRE General Test. Additional exam requirements/recommendations for international students: Required—TOEFL or IELTS. *Application deadline:* For fall admission, 12/15 priority date for domestic and international students; for spring admission, 10/15 priority date for domestic and international students. Application fee: $25. Electronic applications accepted. *Financial support:* In 2009–10, 55 students received support, including 13 fellowships with full tuition reimbursements available (averaging $25,320 per year), 42 research assistantships with full tuition reimbursements available (averaging $24,621 per year); Federal Work-Study, institutionally sponsored loans, scholarships/grants, health care benefits, tuition waivers (partial), and unspecified assistantships also available. Support available to part-time students. Financial award application deadline: 12/15. *Faculty research:* Microscale/nanoscale science and engineering, computational engineering, aerospace and marine systems, robotics and human-machine interaction, energy and the environment, mechanics and materials. Total annual research expenditures: $5.1 million. *Unit head:* Dr. Kevin Hemker, Chair, 410-516-6451, Fax: 410-516-7254, E-mail: hemker@jhu.edu. *Application contact:* Mike Bernard, Academic Program Administrator, 410-516-7154, Fax: 410-516-7254, E-mail: megrad@jhu.edu.

The Johns Hopkins University, G. W. C. Whiting School of Engineering, Program in Engineering Management, Baltimore, MD 21218-2699. Offers biomaterials (MSEM); communications science (MSEM); computer science (MSEM); fluid mechanics (MSEM); materials science and engineering (MSEM); mechanical engineering (MSEM); mechanics and materials (MSEM); nano-biotechnology (MSEM); nanomaterials and nanotechnology (MSEM); probability and statistics (MSEM); smart product and device design (MSEM); systems analysis, management and environmental policy (MSEM). *Students:* 12 full-time (0 women), 3 international. Average age 23. 66 applicants, 67% accepted. *Entrance requirements:* For master's, GRE, 3 letters of recommendation, resume. Additional exam requirements/recommendations for international students: Required—TOEFL (minimum score 600 paper-based; 250 computer-based; 100 iBT) or IELTS (minimum score 7). *Application deadline:* For fall admission, 1/15 priority date for domestic students, 1/15 for international students; for spring admission, 9/15 priority date for domestic students, 9/15 for international students. Applications are processed on a rolling basis. Application fee: $75. Electronic applications accepted. *Financial support:* Fellowships, health care benefits available. *Unit head:* Dr. Edward R. Scheinerman, Interim Director/Vice Dean for Education, School of Engineering/Professor, Applied Mathematics and Statistics, 410-516-7395, Fax: 410-516-4880, E-mail: ers@jhu.edu. *Application contact:* Dennis McIver, Coordinator of Graduate Admissions, 410-516-8174, Fax: 410-516-0780, E-mail: graduateadmissions@jhu.edu.

Kansas State University, Graduate School, College of Engineering, Department of Mechanical and Nuclear Engineering, Manhattan, KS 66506. Offers mechanical engineering (MS, PhD); nuclear engineering (MS, PhD). *Faculty:* 21 full-time (1 woman), 3 part-time/adjunct (0 women). *Students:* 35 full-time (11 women), 51 part-time (4 women); includes 5 minority (1 African American, 1 American Indian/Alaska Native, 2 Asian Americans or Pacific Islanders, 1 Hispanic American), 32 international. Average age 28. 68 applicants, 38% accepted, 22 enrolled. In 2009, 11 master's, 2 doctorates awarded. *Degree requirements:* For master's, thesis or alternative; for doctorate, comprehensive exam, thesis/dissertation. *Entrance requirements:* For master's, GRE General Test, minimum GPA of 3.0 in physics, mathematics, and chemistry; for doctorate, GRE General Test, master's degree in mechanical engineering. Additional exam requirements/recommendations for international students: Required—TOEFL. *Application deadline:* For fall admission, 2/1 priority date for domestic and international students; for spring admission, 7/1 priority date for domestic students, 8/1 priority date for international students. Applications are processed on a rolling basis. Application fee: $40 ($55 for international students). Electronic applications accepted. *Financial support:* In 2009–10, 44 research assistantships (averaging $15,984 per year), 4 teaching assistantships with full and partial tuition reimbursements (averaging $14,916 per year) were awarded; career-related internships or fieldwork, Federal Work-Study, institutionally sponsored loans, and scholarships/grants also available. Support available to part-time students. Financial award application deadline: 3/1; financial award applicants required to submit FAFSA. *Faculty research:* Radiation detection and protection, heat and mass transfer, machine design, control systems, nuclear reactor physics and engineering. Total annual research expenditures: $2.3 million. *Unit head:* Donald Fenton, Head, 785-532-2321, Fax: 785-532-7057, E-mail: fenton@ksu.edu. *Application contact:* Steve Eckels, Director, 785-532-2283, Fax: 785-532-7057, E-mail: grad@mne.ksu.edu.

Kettering University, Graduate School, Mechanical Engineering Department, Flint, MI 48504. Offers automotive systems (MS Eng); computer aided engineering simulation (MS Eng); mechanical cognate (MS Eng); mechanical design (MS Eng); sustainable energy and hybrid technology (MS Eng). Part-time and evening/weekend programs available. Postbaccalaureate distance learning degree programs offered (no on-campus study). *Faculty:* 14 full-time (1 woman). *Students:* 8 full-time (0 women), 35 part-time (7 women); includes 2 minority (1 Asian American or Pacific Islander, 1 Hispanic American), 8 international. Average age 26. 6 applicants, 67% accepted, 2 enrolled. In 2009, 20 master's awarded. *Degree requirements:* For master's, thesis optional. *Entrance requirements:* Additional exam requirements/recommendations for international students: Required—TOEFL (minimum score 550 paper-based; 213 computer-based; 79 iBT). *Application deadline:* For fall admission, 9/15 for domestic students, 6/15 for international students; for winter admission, 12/15 for domestic students, 9/15 for international students; for spring admission, 3/15 for domestic students, 12/15 for international students. Applications are processed on a rolling basis. Application fee: $0. Electronic applications accepted. *Expenses:* Tuition: Full-time $11,120; part-time $695 per credit hour. *Financial support:* In 2009–10, 24 students received support, including fellowships with full tuition reimbursements available (averaging $13,000 per year), research assistantships with full tuition reimbursements available (averaging $13,000 per year), teaching assistantships with full tuition reimbursements available (averaging $13,000 per year); Federal Work-Study, scholarships/grants, and tuition waivers (partial) also available. Support available to part-time students. Financial award application deadline: 7/15; financial award applicants required to submit CSS PROFILE or FAFSA. *Faculty research:* Fuel cells, chemical agents, crash safety, bio-gas, sustainable energy. Total annual research expenditures: $3.9 million. *Unit head:* Dr. K. Joel Berry, Head, 810-762-7833, Fax: 810-762-7860, E-mail: jberry@kettering.edu. *Application contact:* Bonnie Switzer, Graduate Admissions Officer, 810-762-7953, Fax: 810-762-9935, E-mail: bswitzer@kettering.edu.

Lamar University, College of Graduate Studies, College of Engineering, Department of Mechanical Engineering, Beaumont, TX 77710. Offers ME, MES, DE. Part-time programs available. *Faculty:* 7 full-time (0 women). *Students:* 59 full-time (1 woman), 29 part-time (1 woman); includes 2 minority (both Asian Americans or Pacific Islanders), 57 international. Average age 23. 105 applicants, 36% accepted, 27 enrolled. In 2009, 39 master's, 2 doctorates awarded. Terminal master's awarded for partial completion of doctoral program. *Degree requirements:* For master's, comprehensive exam (for some programs), thesis (for some programs); for doctorate, thesis/dissertation. *Entrance requirements:* For master's and doctorate, GRE General Test. Additional exam requirements/recommendations for international students: Required—TOEFL. *Application deadline:* For fall admission, 5/15 priority date for domestic students; for spring admission, 10/1 priority date for domestic students. Applications are processed on a rolling basis. Application fee: $25 ($50 for international students). *Financial support:* In 2009–10, 2 fellowships (averaging $7,200 per year), 4 research assistantships, 5 teaching assistantships were awarded; tuition waivers (partial) also available. Financial award application deadline: 4/1. *Faculty research:* Materials combustion, mechanical and multiphysics study in micro-electronics structural instability/reliability mechanics of micro electronics. *Unit head:* Dr. Malur N. Srinivasan, Chair, 409-880-8094, Fax: 409-880-8121, E-mail: srinivasmn@hal.lamar.edu. *Application contact:* Dr. James L. Thomas, Director of Recruitment, 409-880-7870, Fax: 409-880-8121, E-mail: thomasjl@hal.lamar.edu.

Lawrence Technological University, College of Engineering, Southfield, MI 48075-1058. Offers automotive engineering (MAE); civil engineering (MCE); construction engineering management (MS); electrical and computer engineering (MS); engineering management (ME); industrial engineering (MSIE); manufacturing systems (MEMS, DE); mechanical engineering (MS); mechatronic systems engineering (MS). Part-time and evening/weekend programs available. *Faculty:* 20 full-time (4 women), 12 part-time/adjunct (0 women). *Students:* 15 full-time (4 women), 389 part-time (50 women); includes 57 minority (22 African Americans, 1 American Indian/Alaska Native, 30 Asian Americans or Pacific Islanders, 4 Hispanic Americans), 137 international. Average age 31. 361 applicants, 52% accepted, 108 enrolled. In 2009, 161 master's, 1 doctorate awarded. *Degree requirements:* For master's, thesis (for some programs). *Entrance requirements:* Additional exam requirements/recommendations for international students: Required—TOEFL (minimum score 550 paper-based; 213 computer-based; 79 iBT). *Application deadline:* For fall admission, 8/1 priority date for domestic students, 6/1 for international students; for winter admission, 12/1 priority date for domestic students, 10/1 for international students; for spring admission, 5/1 priority date for domestic students, 3/1 for international students. Applications are processed on a rolling basis. Application fee: $50. Electronic applications accepted. *Expenses:* Tuition: Full-time $11,320; part-time $798 per credit hour. *Financial support:* Federal Work-Study and institutionally sponsored loans available. Support available to part-time students. Financial award application deadline: 4/1; financial award applicants required to submit FAFSA. *Faculty research:* Advanced composite materials in bridges, strengthening existing bridges with carbon and glass fiber sheets, development of drive shafts using composite materials. *Unit head:* Dr. Nabil Grace, Interim Dean, 248-204-2500, Fax: 248-204-2509, E-mail: engrdean@ltu.edu. *Application contact:* Jane Rohrback, Director of Admissions, 248-204-3160, Fax: 248-204-3188, E-mail: admissions@ltu.edu.

Lehigh University, P.C. Rossin College of Engineering and Applied Science, Department of Mechanical Engineering and Mechanics, Bethlehem, PA 18015. Offers applied mathematics (MS, PhD); computational engineering and mechanics (MS, PhD); mechanical engineering (M Eng, MS, PhD, MBA/E); polymer science/engineering (M Eng, MS, PhD, MBA/E); MBA/E. Part-time and evening/weekend programs available. Postbaccalaureate distance learning degree programs offered. *Faculty:* 20 full-time (0 women). *Students:* 85 full-time (12 women), 32 part-time (3 women); includes 4 minority (1 African American, 2 Asian Americans or Pacific Islanders, 1 Hispanic American), 51 international. Average age 27. 320 applicants, 29% accepted, 45 enrolled. In 2009, 23 master's, 6 doctorates awarded. Terminal master's awarded for partial completion of doctoral program. *Degree requirements:* For master's, thesis; for doctorate, thesis/dissertation, general exam. *Entrance requirements:* Additional exam requirements/recommendations for international students: Required—TOEFL (minimum score 550 paper-based; 213 computer-based; 79 iBT). *Application deadline:* For fall admission, 7/15 for domestic and international students; for spring admission, 12/1 for domestic and international students. Applications are processed on a rolling basis. Application fee: $75. Electronic applications accepted. *Financial support:* In 2009–10, 30 students received support, including 8 fellowships with full and partial tuition reimbursements available (averaging $21,060 per year), 24 research assistantships with full and partial tuition reimbursements available (averaging $20,700 per year), 18 teaching assistantships with full and partial tuition reimbursements available (averaging $21,060 per year); unspecified assistantships also available. Financial award application deadline: 1/15. *Faculty research:* Thermofluids, dynamic systems, CAD/CAM, computational mechanics, solid mechanics. Total annual research expenditures: $3.1 million. *Unit head:* Dr. D. Gary Harlow, Chairman, 610-758-4102, Fax: 610-758-6224, E-mail: dgh0@lehigh.edu. *Application contact:* Jo Ann M. Casciano, Graduate Coordinator, 610-758-4107, Fax: 610-758-6224, E-mail: jmc4@lehigh.edu.

Louisiana State University and Agricultural and Mechanical College, Graduate School, College of Engineering, Department of Mechanical Engineering, Baton Rouge, LA 70803. Offers MSME, PhD. Part-time programs available. *Faculty:* 27 full-time (1 woman). *Students:* 97 full-time (13 women), 9 part-time (0 women); includes 8 minority (6 African Americans, 2 Asian Americans or Pacific Islanders), 75 international. Average age 28. 106 applicants, 51% accepted, 17 enrolled. In 2009, 13 master's, 8 doctorates awarded. Terminal master's awarded for partial completion of doctoral program. *Degree requirements:* For master's, thesis; for doctorate, thesis/dissertation. *Entrance requirements:* For master's and doctorate, GRE General Test, minimum GPA of 3.0. Additional exam requirements/recommendations for international students: Required—TOEFL (minimum score 550 paper-based; 213 computer-based; 79 iBT) or IELTS (minimum score 6.5). *Application deadline:* For fall admission, 1/25 priority date for domestic students, 2/15 priority date for international students; for spring admission, 10/15 for international students. Applications are processed on a rolling basis. Application fee: $50 ($70 for international students). Electronic applications accepted. *Financial support:* In 2009–10, 93 students received support, including 11 fellowships with full and partial tuition reimbursements available (averaging $24,378 per year), 64 research assistantships with partial tuition reimbursements available (averaging $16,834 per year), 23 teaching assistantships with partial tuition reimbursements available (averaging $10,658 per year); Federal Work-Study, institutionally sponsored loans, health care benefits, tuition waivers (full and partial), and unspecified assistantships also available. Financial award applicants required to submit FAFSA. *Faculty research:* Computer-aided design, thermal and fluid sciences materials engineering, fluid mechanics, combustion and microsystems engineering. Total annual research expenditures: $2.2 million. *Unit head:* Dr. Dimitris Nikitopoulos, Chair, 225-578-5900, E-mail: medimi@egateway.lsu.edu. *Application contact:* Dr. Eyassu Woldesnbet, Graduate Adviser, 225-578-5900, Fax: 225-578-5924, E-mail: woldesen@me.lsu.edu.

Louisiana Tech University, Graduate School, College of Engineering and Science, Department of Mechanical Engineering, Ruston, LA 71272. Offers MS, PhD. Part-time programs available. Terminal master's awarded for partial completion of doctoral program. *Degree requirements:* For master's, thesis; for doctorate, thesis/dissertation. *Entrance requirements:* For master's, GRE General Test, minimum GPA of 3.0 in last 60 hours; for doctorate, minimum graduate GPA of 3.25 (with MS) or GRE General Test. Additional exam requirements/recommendations for international students: Required—TOEFL. *Faculty research:* Engineering management, facilities planning, thermodynamics, automated manufacturing, micromanufacturing.

Loyola Marymount University, College of Science and Engineering, Department of Mechanical Engineering, Program in Mechanical Engineering, Los Angeles, CA 90045-2659. Offers MSE. *Faculty:* 9 full-time (0 women), 1 part-time/adjunct (0 women). *Students:* 19 full-time (4 women), 6 part-time (1 woman); includes 10 minority (3 African Americans, 6 Asian Americans or Pacific Islanders, 1 Hispanic American), 2 international. Average age 25. 16 applicants, 63% accepted, 8 enrolled. In 2009, 6 master's awarded. *Entrance requirements:* For master's, letters of recommendation, undergraduate degree in mechanical engineering or related field from ABET-accredited university, computer proficiency. Additional exam requirements/recommendations for international students: Required—TOEFL (minimum score 550 paper-based; 213 computer-based; 80 iBT). *Application deadline:* Applications are processed on a rolling basis. Application fee: $50. Electronic applications accepted. *Financial support:* In 2009–10, 12 students received support. Federal Work-Study, scholarships/grants, and laboratory assistantships available. Support available to part-time students. Financial award application deadline: 6/1; financial award applicants required to submit FAFSA. Total annual research expenditures: $78,981. *Unit head:* Dr. Matthew T. Siniawski, Graduate Director, 310-338-5849, E-mail: matthew.siniawski@lmu.edu. *Application contact:* Chake H. Kouyoumjian, Associate Dean of Graduate Admissions, 310-338-2721, Fax: 310-338-6086, E-mail: ckouyoum@lmu.edu.

Manhattan College, Graduate Division, School of Engineering, Program in Mechanical Engineering, Riverdale, NY 10471. Offers MS. Part-time and evening/weekend programs available. *Degree requirements:* For master's, thesis or alternative. *Entrance requirements:* For master's, GRE (recommended), minimum GPA of 3.0. Additional exam requirements/recommendations for international students: Required—TOEFL (minimum score 550 paper-based; 213 computer-based; 79 iBT). *Faculty research:* Thermal analysis of rocket thrust chambers, quality of wood, biomechanics/structural analysis of cacti, orthodontic research.

Marquette University, Graduate School, College of Engineering, Department of Mechanical and Industrial Engineering, Milwaukee, WI 53201-1881. Offers engineering management (MS); mechanical engineering (MS, PhD), including manufacturing systems engineering. Part-time and evening/weekend programs available. *Faculty:* 16 full-time (0 women), 3 part-time/adjunct (0 women). *Students:* 26 full-time (4 women), 49 part-time (7 women); includes 3 minority (2 African Americans, 1 Asian American or Pacific Islander), 11 international. Average age 28. 60 applicants, 73% accepted, 16 enrolled. In 2009, 21 master's, 1 doctorate awarded. Terminal master's awarded for partial completion of doctoral program. *Degree requirements:* For master's, thesis; for doctorate, comprehensive exam, thesis/dissertation, qualifying exam. *Entrance requirements:* For master's and doctorate, GRE General Test, minimum GPA of 3.0. Additional exam requirements/recommendations for international students: Required—TOEFL. *Application deadline:* For fall admission, 8/1 priority date for domestic students; for spring admission, 1/1 priority date for domestic students. Applications are processed on a rolling basis. Application fee: $40. Electronic applications accepted. *Financial support:* In 2009–10, 19 students received support, including 5 fellowships with tuition reimbursements available (averaging $11,600 per year), 6 research assistantships with tuition reimbursements available (averaging $11,490 per year), 8 teaching assistantships with tuition reimbursements available (averaging $11,490 per year); Federal Work-Study, institutionally sponsored loans, scholarships/grants, and tuition waivers (full and partial) also available. Support available to part-time students. Financial award application deadline: 2/15. *Faculty research:* Computer-integrated manufacturing, energy conversion, simulation modeling and optimization, applied mechanics, metallurgy. *Unit head:* Dr. Kyle Kim, Chair, 414-288-7259, Fax: 414-288-7790, E-mail: kyle.kim@marquette.edu. *Application contact:* Dr. Nicholas J. Nigro, Director of Graduate Studies, 414-288-3518, Fax: 414-288-7790, E-mail: nicholas.nigro@marquette.edu.

Massachusetts Institute of Technology, School of Engineering, Department of Mechanical Engineering, Cambridge, MA 02139-4307. Offers manufacturing (M Eng); mechanical engineering (SM, PhD, Sc D, Mech E); naval architecture and marine engineering (SM, PhD, Sc D); naval engineering (Naval E); ocean engineering (SM, PhD, Sc D), including); oceanographic engineering (SM, PhD, Sc D); SM/MBA. *Faculty:* 68 full-time (8 women). *Students:* 489 full-time (80 women); includes 58 minority (7 African Americans, 3 American Indian/Alaska Native, 30 Asian Americans or Pacific Islanders, 18 Hispanic Americans), 211 international. Average age 27. 966 applicants, 24% accepted, 144 enrolled. In 2009, 110 master's, 45 doctorates, 9 other advanced degrees awarded. Terminal master's awarded for

Mechanical Engineering

Massachusetts Institute of Technology *(continued)*
partial completion of doctoral program. *Degree requirements:* For master's and other advanced degree, thesis; for doctorate, comprehensive exam, thesis/dissertation. *Entrance requirements:* For master's, doctorate, and other advanced degree, GRE General Test. Additional exam requirements/recommendations for international students: Required—TOEFL (minimum score 577 paper-based; 233 computer-based; 91 iBT), IELTS (minimum score 7), IELTS preferred. *Application deadline:* For fall admission, 12/15 for domestic and international students. Application fee: $75. Electronic applications accepted. *Financial support:* In 2009–10, 453 students received support, including 76 fellowships with tuition reimbursements available (averaging $22,340 per year), 312 research assistantships with tuition reimbursements available (averaging $26,967 per year), 35 teaching assistantships with tuition reimbursements available (averaging $29,932 per year); career-related internships or fieldwork, Federal Work-Study, institutionally sponsored loans, scholarships/grants, health care benefits, and unspecified assistantships also available. *Faculty research:* Mechanics: modeling, experimentation and computation, design, manufacturing, product development, controls, instrumentation, robotics, energy science and engineering, ocean science and engineering, bioengineering, micro and nano engineering. Total annual research expenditures: $39 million. *Unit head:* Prof. Mary C. Boyce, Department Head, 617-253-2201, Fax: 617-258-6156, E-mail: mehq@mit.edu. *Application contact:* Graduate Office, 617-253-2291, Fax: 617-258-5802, E-mail: megradoffice@mit.edu.

McGill University, Faculty of Graduate and Postdoctoral Studies, Faculty of Engineering, Department of Mechanical Engineering, Montréal, QC H3A 2T5, Canada. Offers aerospace (M Eng); manufacturing management (MMM); mechanical engineering (M Eng, M Sc, PhD).

McMaster University, School of Graduate Studies, Faculty of Engineering, Department of Mechanical Engineering, Hamilton, ON L8S 4M2, Canada. Offers M Eng, MA Sc, PhD. M Eng degree offered as part of the Advanced Design and Manufacturing Institute (ADMI) group collaboration with the University of Toronto, University of Western Ontario, and University of Waterloo. *Degree requirements:* For master's, thesis; for doctorate, comprehensive exam, thesis/dissertation. *Entrance requirements:* Additional exam requirements/recommendations for international students: Required—TOEFL (minimum score 550 paper-based; 213 computer-based). *Faculty research:* Manufacturing engineering, dimensional metrology, micro-fluidics, multi-phase flow and heat transfer, process modeling simulation.

McNeese State University, Doré School of Graduate Studies, College of Engineering and Engineering Technology, Lake Charles, LA 70609. Offers chemical engineering (M Eng); civil engineering (M Eng); electrical engineering (M Eng); engineering management (M Eng); mechanical engineering (M Eng). Part-time and evening/weekend programs available. *Degree requirements:* For master's, thesis or alternative. *Entrance requirements:* For master's, GRE, minimum undergraduate GPA of 3.0. Additional exam requirements/recommendations for international students: Required—TOEFL.

Memorial University of Newfoundland, School of Graduate Studies, Faculty of Engineering and Applied Science, St. John's, NL A1C 5S7, Canada. Offers civil engineering (M Eng, PhD); electrical and computer engineering (M Eng, PhD); mechanical engineering (M Eng, PhD); ocean and naval architecture engineering (M Eng, PhD). Part-time programs available. *Degree requirements:* For master's, thesis; for doctorate, comprehensive exam, thesis/dissertation, oral thesis defense. *Entrance requirements:* For master's, 2nd class degree; for doctorate, master's degree in engineering. Electronic applications accepted. *Faculty research:* Engineering analysis, environmental and hydrotechnical studies, manufacturing and robotics, mechanics, structures and materials.

Mercer University, Graduate Studies, Macon Campus, School of Engineering, Macon, GA 31207-0003. Offers biomedical engineering (MSE); computer engineering (MSE); electrical engineering (MSE); engineering management (MSE); environmental engineering (MSE); environmental systems (MS); mechanical engineering (MSE); software engineering (MSE); software systems (MS); technical communications management (MS); technical management (MS). Part-time and evening/weekend programs available. Postbaccalaureate distance learning degree programs offered (no on-campus study). *Faculty:* 19 full-time (4 women), 1 part-time/adjunct (0 women). *Students:* 6 full-time (1 woman), 95 part-time (22 women); includes 22 minority (5 African Americans, 13 Asian Americans or Pacific Islanders, 4 Hispanic Americans), 3 international. Average age 33. In 2009, 42 master's awarded. *Degree requirements:* For master's, thesis or alternative. *Entrance requirements:* For master's, minimum undergraduate GPA of 3.0. Additional exam requirements/recommendations for international students: Required—TOEFL. *Application deadline:* For fall admission, 7/1 for domestic students; for spring admission, 11/15 for domestic students. Applications are processed on a rolling basis. Application fee: $35 ($50 for international students). Electronic applications accepted. *Expenses:* Contact institution. *Financial support:* Federal Work-Study available. *Unit head:* Dr. Wade H. Shaw, Dean, 478-301-2459, Fax: 478-301-5593, E-mail: shaw_wh@mercer.edu. *Application contact:* Greg Lofton, Graduate Program Coordinator, 478-301-5480, Fax: 478-301-5434, E-mail: lofton_g@mercer.edu.

Michigan State University, The Graduate School, College of Engineering, Department of Mechanical Engineering, East Lansing, MI 48824. Offers engineering mechanics (MS, PhD); mechanical engineering (MS, PhD). *Entrance requirements:* For master's, GRE General Test. Additional exam requirements/recommendations for international students: Required—TOEFL. Electronic applications accepted.

Michigan Technological University, Graduate School, College of Engineering, Department of Mechanical Engineering-Engineering Mechanics, Program in Mechanical Engineering, Houghton, MI 49931. Offers mechanical engineering (MS); mechanical engineering-engineering mechanics (PhD). Part-time programs available. Postbaccalaureate distance learning degree programs offered (minimal on-campus study). Terminal master's awarded for partial completion of doctoral program. *Degree requirements:* For master's, comprehensive exam (for some programs), thesis (for some programs); for doctorate, comprehensive exam, thesis/dissertation. *Entrance requirements:* For master's, GRE; for doctorate, GRE, MS (preferred). Additional exam requirements/recommendations for international students: Required—TOEFL (minimum score 637 paper-based; 270 computer-based). Electronic applications accepted. *Expenses:* Contact institution.

Mississippi State University, Bagley College of Engineering, Department of Mechanical Engineering, MS State, MS 39762. Offers engineering (PhD), including mechanical engineering; mechanical engineering (MS). Part-time programs available. Postbaccalaureate distance learning degree programs offered (minimal on-campus study). *Faculty:* 17 full-time (1 woman). *Students:* 62 full-time (9 women), 10 part-time (0 women); includes 4 minority (all African Americans), 22 international. Average age 28. 75 applicants, 33% accepted, 21 enrolled. In 2009, 10 master's, 7 doctorates awarded. *Degree requirements:* For master's, thesis optional, oral exam; for doctorate, thesis/dissertation, qualifying exam, preliminary exam, dissertation defense. *Entrance requirements:* For master's and doctorate, GRE General Test, minimum GPA of 2.75. Additional exam requirements/recommendations for international students: Required—TOEFL (minimum score 550 paper-based; 213 computer-based; 79 iBT); Recommended—IELTS (minimum score 6.5). *Application deadline:* For fall admission, 7/1 for domestic students, 5/1 for international students; for spring admission, 11/1 for domestic students, 9/1 for international students. Applications are processed on a rolling basis. Application fee: $40. Electronic applications accepted. *Expenses:* Tuition, state resident: full-time $2575.50; part-time $286.25 per credit hour. Tuition, nonresident: full-time $6510; part-time $723.50 per credit hour. Tuition and fees vary according to course load. *Financial support:* In 2009–10, 26 research assistantships with full tuition reimbursements (averaging $12,363 per year), 2 teaching assistantships with full tuition reimbursements (averaging $13,500 per year) were awarded; career-related internships or fieldwork, Federal Work-Study, institutionally sponsored loans, scholarships/grants, and unspecified assistantships also available. Financial award application deadline: 4/1; financial award applicants required to submit FAFSA. *Faculty research:* Fatigue and fracture, heat transfer, fluid dynamics, manufacturing systems, materials. Total annual research expenditures:

$9.5 million. *Unit head:* Dr. Steve Daniewicz, Professor and Interim Head, 662-325-7322, Fax: 662-325-7223, E-mail: daniewicz@me.msstate.edu. *Application contact:* Dr. Rogelio Luck, Professor and Graduate Coordinator, 662-325-7307, Fax: 662-325-7223, E-mail: luck@me.msstate.edu.

Missouri University of Science and Technology, Graduate School, Department of Mechanical and Aerospace Engineering, Rolla, MO 65409. Offers aerospace engineering (MS, PhD); mechanical engineering (MS, DE, PhD). Part-time and evening/weekend programs available. Terminal master's awarded for partial completion of doctoral program. *Degree requirements:* For master's, thesis optional; for doctorate, comprehensive exam, thesis/dissertation. *Entrance requirements:* For master's, GRE General Test (minimum score 1100 verbal and quantitative, writing 3.5), minimum GPA of 3.0; for doctorate, GRE General Test (minimum score: verbal and quantitative 1100, writing 3.5), minimum GPA of 3.5. Additional exam requirements/recommendations for international students: Required—TOEFL. Electronic applications accepted. *Faculty research:* Dynamics and controls, acoustics, computational fluid dynamics, space mechanics, hypersonics.

Montana State University, College of Graduate Studies, College of Engineering, Department of Mechanical and Industrial Engineering, Bozeman, MT 59717. Offers engineering (PhD), including industrial engineering option, mechanical engineering option; industrial and management engineering (MS); mechanical engineering (MS). Part-time programs available. *Faculty:* 18 full-time (2 women), 4 part-time/adjunct (1 woman). *Students:* 20 full-time (3 women), 21 part-time (1 woman); includes 2 minority (1 American Indian/Alaska Native, 1 Asian American or Pacific Islander), 9 international. Average age 26. 44 applicants, 48% accepted, 8 enrolled. In 2009, 13 master's awarded. *Degree requirements:* For master's, comprehensive exam, thesis, oral exams; for doctorate, comprehensive exam, thesis/dissertation, qualifying exam. *Entrance requirements:* For master's and doctorate, GRE General Test. Additional exam requirements/recommendations for international students: Required—TOEFL (minimum score 550 paper-based; 213 computer-based). *Application deadline:* For fall admission, 7/15 priority date for domestic students, 5/15 priority date for international students; for spring admission, 12/1 priority date for domestic students, 10/1 priority date for international students. Applications are processed on a rolling basis. Application fee: $30. Electronic applications accepted. *Expenses:* Tuition, state resident: full-time $5635; part-time $3492 per year. Tuition, nonresident: full-time $17,212; part-time $7865.10 per year. Required fees: $1441.05; $153.15 per credit. Tuition and fees vary according to course load and program. *Financial support:* In 2009–10, 30 students received support, including 2 fellowships with full tuition reimbursements available (averaging $18,000 per year), 14 research assistantships with full and partial tuition reimbursements available (averaging $9,493 per year), 22 teaching assistantships with full and partial tuition reimbursements available (averaging $4,782 per year); scholarships/grants and unspecified assistantships also available. Financial award application deadline: 3/1; financial award applicants required to submit FAFSA. *Faculty research:* Design and manufacture; energy systems, materials and structures, measurement systems, systems modeling. Total annual research expenditures: $1.3 million. *Unit head:* Dr. Chris Jenkins, Head, 406-994-2203, Fax: 406-994-6292, E-mail: cjenkins@me.montana.edu. *Application contact:* Dr. Carl A. Fox, Vice Provost for Graduate Education, 406-994-4145, Fax: 406-994-7433, E-mail: gradstudy@montana.edu.

Naval Postgraduate School, Graduate Programs, Department of Mechanical and Astronautical Engineering, Monterey, CA 93943. Offers MS, D Eng, PhD, Eng. Program only open to commissioned officers of the United States and friendly nations and selected United States federal civilian employees. *Accreditation:* ABET (one or more programs are accredited). Part-time programs available. Postbaccalaureate distance learning degree programs offered. *Degree requirements:* For master's and Eng, thesis; for doctorate, one foreign language, thesis/dissertation.

New Jersey Institute of Technology, Office of Graduate Studies, Newark College of Engineering, Department of Mechanical Engineering, Newark, NJ 07102. Offers MS, PhD, Engineer. Part-time and evening/weekend programs available. Terminal master's awarded for partial completion of doctoral program. *Degree requirements:* For master's, thesis optional; for doctorate, thesis/dissertation. *Entrance requirements:* For master's, GRE General Test; for doctorate, GRE General Test, minimum graduate GPA of 3.5. Additional exam requirements/recommendations for international students: Required—TOEFL (minimum score 550 paper-based; 213 computer-based; 79 iBT). Electronic applications accepted. *Faculty research:* Energy systems, structural mechanics, electromechanical systems.

New Mexico State University, Graduate School, College of Engineering, Department of Mechanical Engineering, Las Cruces, NM 88003-8001. Offers MSME, PhD. Postbaccalaureate distance learning degree programs offered (no on-campus study). *Faculty:* 14 full-time (1 woman). *Students:* 50 full-time (6 women), 5 part-time (0 women); includes 5 minority (1 African American, 4 Hispanic Americans), 31 international. Average age 27. 74 applicants, 78% accepted, 24 enrolled. In 2009, 7 master's awarded. *Degree requirements:* For master's, thesis (for some programs); for doctorate, thesis/dissertation, 2 research tools. *Entrance requirements:* For master's, minimum GPA of 3.0; for doctorate, qualifying exam, minimum GPA of 3.0. *Application deadline:* For fall admission, 7/1 priority date for domestic students; for spring admission, 11/1 for domestic students. Applications are processed on a rolling basis. Application fee: $30 ($50 for international students). Electronic applications accepted. *Expenses:* Tuition, state resident: full-time $4080; part-time $223 per credit. Tuition, nonresident: full-time $14,256; part-time $647 per credit. Required fees: $1278; $639 per semester. *Financial support:* In 2009–10, 24 research assistantships with partial tuition reimbursements (averaging $14,745 per year), 13 teaching assistantships with partial tuition reimbursements (averaging $14,038 per year) were awarded; fellowships with partial tuition reimbursements, career-related internships or fieldwork, Federal Work-Study, scholarships/grants, and health care benefits also available. Support available to part-time students. Financial award application deadline: 3/1. *Faculty research:* Computational mechanics; robotics; CAD/CAM; control, dynamics, and solid mechanics; interconnection engineering; heat transfer; composites. *Unit head:* Dr. Thomas Burton, Head, 575-646-3501, Fax: 575-646-6111, E-mail: tdburton@nmsu.edu. *Application contact:* Dr. Thomas Burton, Head, 575-646-3501, Fax: 575-646-6111, E-mail: tdburton@nmsu.edu.

North Carolina Agricultural and Technical State University, Graduate School, College of Engineering, Department of Mechanical and Chemical Engineering, Greensboro, NC 27411. Offers chemical engineering (MS Ch E); mechanical engineering (MSME, PhD). Part-time programs available. *Degree requirements:* For master's, comprehensive exam, thesis optional, dual exam, qualifying exam, thesis defense; for doctorate, thesis/dissertation. *Entrance requirements:* For doctorate, GRE. *Faculty research:* Composites, smart materials and sensors, mechanical systems modeling and finite element analysis, computational fluid dynamics and engine research, design and manufacturing.

North Carolina State University, Graduate School, College of Engineering, Department of Mechanical and Aerospace Engineering, Program in Mechanical Engineering, Raleigh, NC 27695. Offers MS, PhD. Part-time programs available. Postbaccalaureate distance learning degree programs offered (no on-campus study). *Degree requirements:* For master's, thesis optional, oral exam; for doctorate, thesis/dissertation, oral and preliminary exams. *Entrance requirements:* For master's and doctorate, GRE General Test. Additional exam requirements/recommendations for international students: Required—TOEFL (minimum score 550 paper-based; 213 computer-based). Electronic applications accepted. *Faculty research:* Vibration and control, fluid dynamics, thermal sciences, structures and materials, aerodynamics acoustics.

See Close-Up on page 523.

North Dakota State University, College of Graduate and Interdisciplinary Studies, College of Engineering and Architecture, Department of Mechanical Engineering and Applied Mechanics, Fargo, ND 58108. Offers MS, PhD. Part-time programs available. *Faculty:* 15 full-time (1 woman), 1 part-time/adjunct (0 women). *Students:* 20 full-time (3 women), 20 part-time (1 woman), 23 international. Average age 28. 39 applicants, 49% accepted, 3 enrolled. In 2009, 13 master's awarded. *Degree requirements:* For master's, thesis; for doctorate, comprehensive exam, thesis/dissertation. *Entrance requirements:* For master's and doctorate, minimum GPA of 3.0. Additional exam requirements/recommendations for international students: Required—TOEFL (minimum score 550 paper-based). *Application deadline:* For fall admission, 7/1 priority date for domestic students, 5/1 priority date for international students; for spring admission, 12/1 priority date for domestic students, 9/1 priority date for international students. Applications are processed on a rolling basis. Application fee: $45 ($60 for international students). Electronic applications accepted. *Financial support:* In 2009–10, 20 students received support, including research assistantships with full tuition reimbursements available (averaging $9,000 per year), teaching assistantships with full tuition reimbursements available (averaging $9,000 per year); career-related internships or fieldwork, Federal Work-Study, and institutionally sponsored loans also available. Financial award application deadline: 2/15. *Faculty research:* Thermodynamics, finite element analysis, automotive systems, robotics, nanotechnology. Total annual research expenditures: $530,000. *Unit head:* Dr. Alan Kallmeyer, Chair, 701-231-8836, Fax: 701-231-8913, E-mail: alan.kallmeyer@ndsu.edu. *Application contact:* Dr. David A. Wittrock, Dean, 701-231-7033, Fax: 701-231-6524.

Northeastern University, College of Engineering, Department of Mechanical, Industrial, and Manufacturing Engineering, Boston, MA 02115-5096. Offers engineering management (MS); industrial engineering (MS, PhD); mechanical engineering (MS, PhD); operations research (MS). Part-time programs available. *Faculty:* 34 full-time (2 women), 7 part-time/adjunct (0 women). *Students:* 270 full-time (56 women), 137 part-time (27 women); includes 4 African Americans, 9 Asian Americans or Pacific Islanders, 3 Hispanic Americans, 182 international. 573 applicants, 75% accepted, 142 enrolled. In 2009, 94 master's, 9 doctorates awarded. *Degree requirements:* For master's, thesis (for some programs); for doctorate, thesis/dissertation, departmental qualifying exam. *Entrance requirements:* For master's and doctorate, GRE General Test. Additional exam requirements/recommendations for international students: Required—TOEFL (minimum score 550 paper-based; 213 computer-based; 80 iBT). *Application deadline:* For fall admission, 1/15 priority date for domestic and international students; for spring admission, 11/1 priority date for domestic students. Applications are processed on a rolling basis. Application fee: $50. Electronic applications accepted. *Financial support:* In 2009–10, 79 students received support, including 42 research assistantships with full tuition reimbursements available (averaging $18,320 per year), 37 teaching assistantships with full tuition reimbursements available; fellowships with full tuition reimbursements available, career-related internships or fieldwork, Federal Work-Study, scholarships/grants, health care benefits, and unspecified assistantships also available. Support available to part-time students. Financial award application deadline: 1/15; financial award applicants required to submit FAFSA. *Faculty research:* Dry sliding instabilities, droplet deposition, combustion, manufacturing systems, nano-manufacturing, advanced materials processing, bio-nano robotics, burning speed measurement, virtual environments. *Unit head:* Dr. Hameed Metghalchi, Chairman, 617-373-2973, Fax: 617-373-2921. *Application contact:* Stephen L. Gibson, Associate Director, 617-373-2711, Fax: 617-373-2501, E-mail: grad-eng@coe.neu.edu.

Northern Arizona University, Graduate College, College of Engineering, Forestry and Natural Sciences, Programs in Engineering, Flagstaff, AZ 86011. Offers civil engineering (MSE); computer science (MSE); electrical engineering (MSE); environmental engineering (MSE); mechanical engineering (MSE). Postbaccalaureate distance learning degree programs offered (no on-campus study). *Faculty:* 43 full-time (11 women). *Students:* 30 full-time (4 women), 9 part-time (0 women); includes 6 minority (4 American Indian/Alaska Native, 1 Asian American or Pacific Islander, 1 Hispanic American), 10 international. Average age 28. 42 applicants, 55% accepted, 12 enrolled. In 2009, 4 master's awarded. *Degree requirements:* For master's, thesis. *Entrance requirements:* Additional exam requirements/recommendations for international students: Required—TOEFL (minimum score 550 paper-based; 213 computer-based; 80 iBT), IELTS (minimum score 7). *Application deadline:* For fall admission, 3/1 priority date for domestic students, 9/1 priority date for international students; for spring admission, 9/15 priority date for domestic students. Applications are processed on a rolling basis. Application fee: $65. Electronic applications accepted. *Financial support:* In 2009–10, 9 research assistantships with partial tuition reimbursements, 9 teaching assistantships with partial tuition reimbursements were awarded; career-related internships or fieldwork, Federal Work-Study, scholarships/grants, health care benefits, and unspecified assistantships also available. Support available to part-time students. Financial award application deadline: 3/30; financial award applicants required to submit FAFSA. *Unit head:* Dr. Ernesto Penado, Chair, 928-523-9453, Fax: 928-523-2300, E-mail: ernesto.penado@nau.edu. *Application contact:* Dieter Otte, Coordinator, 928-523-0876, Fax: 928-523-2300, E-mail: dieter.otte@nau.edu.

Northern Illinois University, Graduate School, College of Engineering and Engineering Technology, Department of Mechanical Engineering, De Kalb, IL 60115-2854. Offers MS. Part-time programs available. *Faculty:* 9 full-time (0 women). *Students:* 43 full-time (2 women), 23 part-time (3 women); includes 2 minority (both Asian Americans or Pacific Islanders), 53 international. Average age 23. 147 applicants, 50% accepted, 24 enrolled. In 2009, 13 master's awarded. *Degree requirements:* For master's, comprehensive exam, thesis optional. *Entrance requirements:* For master's, GRE General Test, minimum GPA of 2.75. Additional exam requirements/recommendations for international students: Required—TOEFL (minimum score 550 paper-based; 213 computer-based). *Application deadline:* For fall admission, 6/1 for domestic students, 5/1 for international students; for spring admission, 11/1 for domestic students, 10/1 for international students. Applications are processed on a rolling basis. Application fee: $30. Electronic applications accepted. *Expenses:* Tuition, state resident: full-time $6576; part-time $274 per credit hour. Tuition, nonresident: full-time $13,152; part-time $548 per credit hour. Required fees: $1813; $75.53 per credit hour. Part-time tuition and fees vary according to course load. *Financial support:* In 2009–10, 4 research assistantships with full tuition reimbursements, 18 teaching assistantships with full tuition reimbursements were awarded; fellowships with full tuition reimbursements, Federal Work-Study, scholarships/grants, tuition waivers (full), and staff assistantships also available. Support available to part-time students. Financial award applicants required to submit FAFSA. *Faculty research:* Robotics, nonlinear dynamic systems, piezo mechanics, quartz resonators, sheet metal forming. *Unit head:* Dr. Simon Song, Chair, 815-753-9970, Fax: 815-753-0416, E-mail: smsong@ceet.niu.edu. *Application contact:* Graduate School Office, 815-753-0395, E-mail: gradsch@niu.edu.

Northwestern University, McCormick School of Engineering and Applied Science, Department of Mechanical Engineering, Evanston, IL 60208. Offers manufacturing engineering (MME); mechanical engineering (MS, PhD). MS, PhD admissions and degrees offered through The Graduate School. Part-time programs available. Terminal master's awarded for partial completion of doctoral program. *Degree requirements:* For master's, thesis or alternative; for doctorate, thesis/dissertation. Electronic applications accepted. *Faculty research:* Experimental, theoretical and computational mechanics of materials; fluid mechanics; manufacturing processes; robotics and control; micro-electromechanical systems and nanotechnology.

Oakland University, Graduate Study and Lifelong Learning, School of Engineering and Computer Science, Department of Mechanical Engineering, Rochester, MI 48309-4401. Offers MS, PhD. Part-time and evening/weekend programs available. *Entrance requirements:* For master's, minimum GPA of 3.0 for unconditional admission. Additional exam requirements/recommendations for international students: Required—TOEFL (minimum score 550 paper-based; 213 computer-based). Electronic applications accepted. *Expenses:* Contact institution. *Faculty research:* Efficient reliability-based design optimization and robust design methods, mechanical loading and Bunc, automotive research, industrial mentorship.

The Ohio State University, Graduate School, College of Engineering, Department of Mechanical Engineering, Columbus, OH 43210. Offers engineering mechanics (MS, PhD); mechanical engineering (MS, PhD), nuclear engineering (MS, PhD). *Faculty:* 62. *Students:* 236 full-time (35 women), 60 part-time (7 women); includes 20 minority (4 African Americans, 8 Asian Americans or Pacific Islanders, 8 Hispanic Americans), 120 international. Average age 26. In 2009, 66 master's, 25 doctorates awarded. *Degree requirements:* For doctorate, thesis/dissertation. *Entrance requirements:* For master's, GRE General Test or U.S. engineering degree with minimum GPA of 3.3; for doctorate, GRE General Test or U.S. engineering degree with minimum GPA of 3.75. Additional exam requirements/recommendations for international students: Recommended—TOEFL (minimum score 600 paper-based; 250 computer-based). *Application deadline:* For fall admission, 8/15 priority date for domestic students, 7/1 priority date for international students; for winter admission, 12/1 priority date for domestic students, 11/1 priority date for international students; for spring admission, 3/1 priority date for domestic students, 2/1 priority date for international students. Applications are processed on a rolling basis. Application fee: $40 ($50 for international students). Electronic applications accepted. *Expenses:* Tuition, state resident: full-time $10,683. Tuition, nonresident: full-time $25,923. Tuition and fees vary according to course load and program. *Financial support:* Fellowships, research assistantships, teaching assistantships, career-related internships or fieldwork, Federal Work-Study, institutionally sponsored loans, and unspecified assistantships available. Support available to part-time students. *Unit head:* Vish Subramaniam, Graduate Studies Committee Chair, E-mail: subramaniam.1@osu.edu. *Application contact:* 614-292-9444, Fax: 614-292-3895, E-mail: domestic.grad@osu.edu.

Ohio University, Graduate College, Russ College of Engineering and Technology, Department of Mechanical Engineering, Athens, OH 45701-2979. Offers biomedical engineering (MS); mechanical engineering (MS, PhD), including CAD/CAM (MS), design (MS), energy (MS), manufacturing (MS), materials (MS), robotics (MS), thermofluids (MS). Part-time programs available. *Faculty:* 12 full-time (1 woman). *Students:* 24 full-time (2 women), 4 part-time (0 women); includes 1 minority (Hispanic American), 9 international. 34 applicants, 47% accepted, 8 enrolled. In 2009, 7 master's awarded. *Degree requirements:* For master's, comprehensive exam (for some programs), thesis; for doctorate, comprehensive exam, thesis/dissertation. *Entrance requirements:* For master's, GRE, BS in engineering or science, minimum GPA of 2.8; for doctorate, GRE. Additional exam requirements/recommendations for international students: Required—TOEFL (minimum score 550 paper-based; 80 iBT) or IELTS Academic (minimum score 6.5). *Application deadline:* For fall admission, 2/15 priority date for domestic and international students. Applications are processed on a rolling basis. Application fee: $50 ($55 for international students). Electronic applications accepted. *Expenses:* Tuition, state resident: full-time $7839; part-time $323 per quarter hour. Tuition, nonresident: full-time $15,831; part-time $654 per quarter hour. Required fees: $2931. *Financial support:* In 2009–10, research assistantships with tuition reimbursements (averaging $14,000 per year), teaching assistantships with tuition reimbursements (averaging $14,000 per year) were awarded; career-related internships or fieldwork, Federal Work-Study, institutionally sponsored loans, tuition waivers (full and partial), and unspecified assistantships also available. Financial award application deadline: 2/15; financial award applicants required to submit FAFSA. *Faculty research:* Biomedical, energy and the environment, materials and manufacturing, bioengineering. *Unit head:* Dr. Greg Kremer, Chairman, 740-593-1561, Fax: 740-593-0476, E-mail: kremer@bobcat.ent.ohiou.edu. *Application contact:* Dr. Frank F. Kraft, Graduate Chairman, 740-597-1478, Fax: 740-593-0476, E-mail: kraft@ohio.edu.

Ohio University, Graduate College, Russ College of Engineering and Technology, Program in Mechanical and Systems Engineering, Athens, OH 45701-2979. Offers industrial (PhD); mechanical (PhD). *Faculty:* 40 full-time (1 woman), 1 part-time/adjunct (0 women). *Students:* 15 full-time (2 women), 4 part-time (0 women), 13 international. 13 applicants, 54% accepted, 1 enrolled. In 2009, 4 doctorates awarded. *Degree requirements:* For doctorate, comprehensive exam, thesis/dissertation. *Entrance requirements:* For doctorate, GRE General Test, MS in engineering or related field. Additional exam requirements/recommendations for international students: Required—TOEFL (minimum score 550 paper-based; 80 iBT) or IELTS Academic (minimum score 6.5). *Application deadline:* For fall admission, 3/15 priority date for domestic and international students. Applications are processed on a rolling basis. Application fee: $50 ($55 for international students). Electronic applications accepted. *Expenses:* Tuition, state resident: full-time $7839; part-time $323 per quarter hour. Tuition, nonresident: full-time $15,831; part-time $654 per quarter hour. Required fees: $2931. *Financial support:* In 2009–10, 4 research assistantships with full tuition reimbursements (averaging $14,000 per year) were awarded; Federal Work-Study, institutionally sponsored loans, and unspecified assistantships also available. Financial award application deadline: 3/15; financial award applicants required to submit FAFSA. *Faculty research:* Material processing, expert systems, environmental geotechnical manufacturing, thermal systems, robotics. Total annual research expenditures: $1.8 million. *Unit head:* Dr. James Rankin, Associate Dean for Research and Graduate Studies, 740-593-1482, Fax: 740-593-0659, E-mail: rankinj@ohio.edu. *Application contact:* Dr. James Rankin, Associate Dean for Research and Graduate Studies, 740-593-1482, Fax: 740-593-0659, E-mail: rankin@ohio.edu.

Oklahoma State University, College of Engineering, Architecture and Technology, School of Mechanical and Aerospace Engineering, Stillwater, OK 74078. Offers mechanical and aerospace engineering (MS, PhD); mechanical engineering (MS, PhD). Postbaccalaureate distance learning degree programs offered. *Faculty:* 26 full-time (2 women), 1 part-time/adjunct (0 women). *Students:* 82 full-time (10 women), 98 part-time (5 women); includes 2 minority (1 American Indian/Alaska Native, 1 Asian American or Pacific Islander), 149 international. Average age 26. 233 applicants, 19% accepted, 21 enrolled. In 2009, 42 master's, 6 doctorates awarded. *Degree requirements:* For master's, thesis or alternative; for doctorate, comprehensive exam, thesis/dissertation. *Entrance requirements:* For master's and doctorate, GRE or GMAT. Additional exam requirements/recommendations for international students: Required—TOEFL (minimum score 550 paper-based; 79 iBT). *Application deadline:* For fall admission, 3/1 priority date for international students; for spring admission, 8/1 priority date for international students. Applications are processed on a rolling basis. Application fee: $40 ($75 for international students). Electronic applications accepted. *Expenses:* Tuition, state resident: full-time $3716; part-time $154.85 per credit hour. Tuition, nonresident: full-time $14,448; part-time $602 per credit hour. Required fees: $1772; $73.85 per credit hour. One-time fee: $50. Tuition and fees vary according to course load and campus/location. *Financial support:* In 2009–10, 110 research assistantships (averaging $10,410 per year), 60 teaching assistantships (averaging $7,702 per year) were awarded; career-related internships or fieldwork, Federal Work-Study, scholarships/grants, health care benefits, tuition waivers (partial), and unspecified assistantships also available. Support available to part-time students. Financial award application deadline: 3/1; financial award applicants required to submit FAFSA. *Unit head:* Dr. Lawrence L. Hoberock, Head, 405-744-5900, Fax: 405-744-7873. *Application contact:* Dr. Gordon Emslie, Dean, 405-744-6368, Fax: 405-744-0355, E-mail: grad-i@okstate.edu.

Old Dominion University, Frank Batten College of Engineering and Technology, Program in Mechanical Engineering, Norfolk, VA 23529. Offers design and manufacturing (ME); mechanical engineering (ME, MS, D Eng, PhD). Part-time and evening/weekend programs available. Postbaccalaureate distance learning degree programs offered (no on-campus study). *Faculty:* 15 full-time (2 women). *Students:* 30 full-time (5 women), 44 part-time (11 women); includes 12 minority (2 African Americans, 7 Asian Americans or Pacific Islanders, 3 Hispanic Americans), 31 international. Average age 29. 59 applicants, 44% accepted, 18 enrolled. In 2009, 17 master's, 1 doctorate awarded. *Degree requirements:* For master's, comprehensive exam, thesis optional; for doctorate, thesis/dissertation, candidacy exam. *Entrance requirements:* For master's, GRE, minimum GPA of 3.0; for doctorate, GRE, minimum GPA of 3.5. Additional exam requirements/recommendations for international students: Required—TOEFL (minimum score 550 paper-based; 213 computer-based). *Application deadline:* For fall admission, 6/1 for domestic students, 2/15 priority date for international students; for spring admission, 11/1 for domestic students, 10/1 for international students. Applications are processed on a rolling basis. Application fee: $40 ($50 for international students). Electronic applications accepted. *Expenses:* Tuition, state resident: full-time $8112; part-time $338 per credit. Tuition, nonresident: full-time $20,256; part-time $844 per credit. Required fees: $119 per semester. One-time fee: $50. *Financial support:* In 2009–10, 31 students received support, including 5 fellowships with partial tuition reimbursements available (averaging $16,000 per year), 11 research assistantships with partial tuition reimbursements available (averaging $15,000 per year), 15 teaching assistantships with partial tuition reimbursements available (averaging $6,400 per year); career-

Mechanical Engineering

Old Dominion University (continued)
related internships or fieldwork, institutionally sponsored loans, scholarships/grants, and unspecified assistantships also available. Financial award application deadline: 2/15; financial award applicants required to submit FAFSA. *Faculty research:* Computational applied mechanics, manufacturing, experimental stress analysis, systems dynamics and control, mechanical design. Total annual research expenditures: $975,887. *Unit head:* Dr. Jen-Kuang Huang, Chair, 757-683-3734, Fax: 757-683-5344, E-mail: jhuang@odu.edu. *Application contact:* Dr. Gene Hou, Graduate Program Director, 757-683-3728, Fax: 757-683-5344, E-mail: megpd@odu.edu.

Oregon State University, Graduate School, College of Engineering, School of Mechanical, Industrial, and Manufacturing Engineering, Corvallis, OR 97331. Offers human systems engineering (MS, PhD); industrial engineering (MS, PhD); information systems engineering (MS, PhD); manufacturing engineering (M Engr); manufacturing systems engineering (MS, PhD); materials science (MAIS, MS, PhD); mechanical engineering (MS, PhD); nano/micro fabrication (MS, PhD). Part-time programs available. Postbaccalaureate distance learning degree programs offered (minimal on-campus study). *Faculty:* 26 full-time (2 women), 2 part-time/adjunct (1 woman). *Students:* 136 full-time (25 women), 12 part-time (2 women); includes 11 minority (3 African Americans, 4 Asian Americans or Pacific Islanders, 4 Hispanic Americans), 46 international. Average age 29. 53 applicants, 42% accepted, 13 enrolled. In 2009, 26 master's, 10 doctorates awarded. *Degree requirements:* For master's, thesis or alternative; for doctorate, thesis/dissertation. *Entrance requirements:* For master's, placement exam, minimum GPA of 3.0 in last 90 hours of course work; for doctorate, GRE, placement exam, minimum GPA of 3.0 in last 90 hours of course work. Additional exam requirements/recommendations for international students: Required—TOEFL (minimum score 550 paper-based; 213 computer-based). *Application deadline:* For fall admission, 3/1 for domestic students. Applications are processed on a rolling basis. Application fee: $50. *Expenses:* Tuition, state resident: full-time $9774; part-time $362 per credit. Tuition, nonresident: full-time $15,849; part-time $587 per credit. Required fees: $1639. Full-time tuition and fees vary according to course load and program. *Financial support:* In 2009–10, 10 research assistantships with full tuition reimbursements (averaging $11,124 per year), 8 teaching assistantships with full tuition reimbursements (averaging $7,020 per year) were awarded; fellowships with full tuition reimbursements, institutionally sponsored loans and instructorships also available. Support available to part-time students. Financial award application deadline: 2/1. *Faculty research:* Computer-integrated manufacturing, human factors, robotics, decision support systems, simulation modeling and analysis. Total annual research expenditures: $1.3 million. *Unit head:* Dr. Belinda A. Batten, Head, 541-737-3441, Fax: 541-737-2600, E-mail: info-mime@oregonstate.edu. *Application contact:* Jean Robinson, Graduate Records Specialist, 541-737-7009, Fax: 541-737-2600, E-mail: jean.robinson@oregonstate.edu.

Penn State University Park, Graduate School, College of Engineering, Department of Mechanical and Nuclear Engineering, State College, University Park, PA 16802-1503. Offers M Eng, MS, PhD. *Faculty research:* Reactor safety, radiation damage, advanced controls, radiation instrumentation, computational methods.

Polytechnic Institute of NYU, Department of Mechanical and Aerospace Engineering, Major in Mechanical Engineering, Brooklyn, NY 11201-2990. Offers MS, PhD. Part-time and evening/weekend programs available. *Students:* 49 full-time (7 women), 11 part-time (3 women); includes 6 minority (2 African Americans, 4 Asian Americans or Pacific Islanders), 37 international. 175 applicants, 48% accepted, 36 enrolled. In 2009, 16 master's, 3 doctorates awarded. *Degree requirements:* For master's, comprehensive exam (for some programs), thesis (for some programs); for doctorate, comprehensive exam, thesis/dissertation. *Entrance requirements:* For master's, BE or BS in engineering, physics, chemistry, mathematical sciences, or biological sciences or MBA. Additional exam requirements/recommendations for international students: Required—TOEFL (minimum score 550 paper-based; 213 computer-based; 80 iBT); Recommended—IELTS (minimum score 6.5). *Application deadline:* For fall admission, 7/31 priority date for domestic students, 4/30 priority date for international students; for spring admission, 12/31 priority date for domestic students, 11/30 priority date for international students. Applications are processed on a rolling basis. Application fee: $75. Electronic applications accepted. *Expenses:* Tuition: Full-time $21,492; part-time $1194 per credit hour. Required fees: $1160; $204 per course. *Financial support:* Institutionally sponsored loans, scholarships/grants, and unspecified assistantships available. Support available to part-time students. Financial award applicants required to submit FAFSA. *Unit head:* Dr. George Vradis, Head, 718-260-3875, Fax: 718-260-3532, E-mail: gvradis@poly.edu. *Application contact:* JeanCarlo Bonilla, Director of Graduate Enrollment Management, 718-260-3182, Fax: 718-260-3624, E-mail: gradinfo@poly.edu.

Polytechnic Institute of NYU, Long Island Graduate Center, Graduate Programs, Department of Mechanical and Aerospace Engineering, Melville, NY 11747. Offers aeronautics and astronautics (MS); industrial engineering (MS); manufacturing engineering (MS); mechanical engineering (MS). Part-time and evening/weekend programs available. *Students:* 1 (woman) part-time. Average age 25. In 2009, 2 master's awarded. *Degree requirements:* For master's, comprehensive exam (for some programs), thesis (for some programs). *Entrance requirements:* Additional exam requirements/recommendations for international students: Required—TOEFL (minimum score 550 paper-based; 213 computer-based; 80 iBT); Recommended—IELTS (minimum score 6.5). *Application deadline:* For fall admission, 7/31 priority date for domestic students, 4/30 priority date for international students; for spring admission, 12/31 priority date for domestic students, 11/30 priority date for international students. Applications are processed on a rolling basis. Application fee: $75. Electronic applications accepted. *Financial support:* In 2009–10, 16 fellowships with tuition reimbursements (averaging $1,394 per year) were awarded; research assistantships with tuition reimbursements, institutionally sponsored loans, scholarships/grants, and unspecified assistantships also available. Support available to part-time students. Financial award applicants required to submit FAFSA. *Faculty research:* UV filter, fuel efficient hydrodynamic containment for gas core fission, turbulent boundary layer research. *Unit head:* Dr. George Vradis, Department Head, 718-260-3875, E-mail: gvradis@duke.poly.edu. *Application contact:* JeanCarlo Bonilla, Director of Graduate Enrollment Management, 718-260-3182, Fax: 718-260-3624, E-mail: gradinfo@poly.edu.

Portland State University, Graduate Studies, Maseeh College of Engineering and Computer Science, Department of Mechanical Engineering, Portland, OR 97207-0751. Offers M Eng, MS, PhD. Part-time and evening/weekend programs available. *Degree requirements:* For master's, thesis or alternative; for doctorate, one foreign language, thesis/dissertation, oral and written exams. *Entrance requirements:* For master's, minimum GPA of 3.0 in upper-division course work, BS in mechanical engineering or allied field; for doctorate, GRE General Test, GRE Subject Test, minimum GPA of 3.0 in upper-division course work. Additional exam requirements/recommendations for international students: Required—TOEFL (minimum score 550 paper-based; 213 computer-based). *Faculty research:* Mechanical system modeling, indoor air quality, manufacturing process, computational fluid dynamics, building science.

Portland State University, Graduate Studies, Systems Science Program, Portland, OR 97207-0751. Offers computational intelligence (Certificate); computer modeling and simulation (Certificate); systems science (MS); systems science/anthropology (PhD); systems science/business administration (PhD); systems science/civil engineering (PhD); systems science/economics (PhD); systems science/engineering management (PhD); systems science/general (PhD); systems science/mathematical sciences (PhD); systems science/mechanical engineering (PhD); systems science/psychology (PhD); systems science/sociology (PhD). *Degree requirements:* For doctorate, variable foreign language requirement, thesis/dissertation. *Entrance requirements:* For master's, 2 letters of recommendation; for doctorate, GMAT, GRE General Test, minimum undergraduate GPA of 3.0. Additional exam requirements/recommendations for international students: Required—TOEFL. *Faculty research:* Systems theory and methodology, artificial intelligence neural networks, information theory, nonlinear dynamics/chaos, modeling and simulation.

Princeton University, Graduate School, School of Engineering and Applied Science, Department of Mechanical and Aerospace Engineering, Princeton, NJ 08544. Offers M Eng, MSE, PhD. *Faculty:* 23 full-time (2 women). Terminal master's awarded for partial completion of doctoral program. *Degree requirements:* For master's, thesis (MSE); for doctorate, thesis/dissertation, general exam. *Entrance requirements:* For master's, GRE General Test, 3 letters of recommendation; for doctorate, GRE General Test, official transcript(s), 3 letters of recommendation, personal statement. Additional exam requirements/recommendations for international students: Required—TOEFL. *Application deadline:* For fall admission, 12/15 for domestic and international students. Application fee: $90. Electronic applications accepted. *Financial support:* Fellowships with full tuition reimbursements, research assistantships with full tuition reimbursements, teaching assistantships with full tuition reimbursements, institutionally sponsored loans and health care benefits available. *Faculty research:* Bioengineering and bio-mechanics; combustion, energy conversion, and climate; fluid mechanics, dynamics, and control systems; lasers and applied physics; materials and mechanical systems. *Unit head:* Jessica O'Leary, Graduate Program Administrator, 609-258-4683, Fax: 609-258-6109, E-mail: maegrad@princeton.edu. *Application contact:* Michelle Carman, Manager of Graduate Admissions, 609-258-3034, Fax: 609-258-7262, E-mail: gsadmit@princeton.edu.

Purdue University, College of Engineering, School of Mechanical Engineering, West Lafayette, IN 47907-2088. Offers MS, MSE, MSME, PhD, Certificate. MS and PhD degree programs in biomedical engineering offered jointly with School of Electrical and Computer Engineering and School of Chemical Engineering. Part-time programs available. Postbaccalaureate distance learning degree programs offered (no on-campus study). *Entrance requirements:* For master's and doctorate, GRE General Test, minimum GPA of 3.2. Additional exam requirements/recommendations for international students: Required—TOEFL (minimum score 575 paper-based; 233 computer-based; 77 iBT); Recommended—TWE. Electronic applications accepted. *Faculty research:* Design, manufacturing, thermal/fluid sciences, mechanics, electromechanical systems.

Purdue University Calumet, Graduate School, School of Engineering, Mathematics, and Science, Department of Engineering, Hammond, IN 46323-2094. Offers computer engineering (MSE); electrical engineering (MSE); engineering (MS); mechanical engineering (MSE). Evening/weekend programs available. *Entrance requirements:* Additional exam requirements/recommendations for international students: Required—TOEFL.

Queen's University at Kingston, School of Graduate Studies and Research, Faculty of Applied Science, Department of Mechanical and Materials Engineering, Kingston, ON K7L 3N6, Canada. Offers M Eng, M Sc, M Sc Eng, PhD. Part-time programs available. *Degree requirements:* For master's, thesis optional; for doctorate, comprehensive exam, thesis/dissertation. *Entrance requirements:* Additional exam requirements/recommendations for international students: Required—TOEFL. Electronic applications accepted. *Faculty research:* Dynamics and control systems, manufacturing and design, materials and engineering, heat transferring fluid dynamics, energy systems and combustion.

Rensselaer at Hartford, Department of Engineering, Program in Mechanical Engineering, Hartford, CT 06120-2991. Offers ME, MS. Part-time and evening/weekend programs available. *Faculty:* 3 full-time (0 women), 8 part-time/adjunct (0 women). *Students:* 1 full-time (0 women), 212 part-time (33 women); includes 34 minority (4 African Americans, 21 Asian Americans or Pacific Islanders, 9 Hispanic Americans). Average age 34. 76 applicants, 79% accepted, 60 enrolled. In 2009, 36 master's awarded. *Degree requirements:* For master's, thesis optional. *Entrance requirements:* For master's, GRE. Additional exam requirements/recommendations for international students: Required—TOEFL (minimum score 600 paper-based; 250 computer-based; 100 iBT). *Application deadline:* For fall admission, 8/30 priority date for domestic students, 8/1 priority date for international students. Applications are processed on a rolling basis. Application fee: $75. *Expenses:* Tuition: Full-time $31,800; part-time $1325 per credit hour. *Financial support:* Research assistantships, tuition waivers (full and partial) and unspecified assistantships available. Financial award applicants required to submit FAFSA. *Unit head:* Dr. Ernesto Gutierrez-Miravete, 860-548-2464, E-mail: gutiee@rpi.edu. *Application contact:* Kristin Galligan, Director, Enrollment Management and Marketing, 860-548-2480, Fax: 860-548-7823, E-mail: info@ewp.rpi.edu.

Rensselaer Polytechnic Institute, Graduate School, School of Engineering, Department of Mechanical, Aerospace, and Nuclear Engineering, Program in Mechanical Engineering, Troy, NY 12180-3590. Offers M Eng, MS, PhD. Part-time programs available. Postbaccalaureate distance learning degree programs offered. *Faculty:* 21 full-time (4 women), 4 part-time/adjunct (0 women). *Students:* 122 full-time (14 women), 9 part-time (1 woman); includes 7 minority (2 African Americans, 5 Hispanic Americans), 71 international. Average age 27. 285 applicants, 45% accepted, 30 enrolled. In 2009, 14 master's, 7 doctorates awarded. *Degree requirements:* For master's, thesis (for some programs); for doctorate, thesis/dissertation. *Entrance requirements:* For master's and doctorate, GRE. Additional exam requirements/recommendations for international students: Required—TOEFL (minimum score 600 paper-based; 250 computer-based; 100 iBT). *Application deadline:* For fall admission, 1/15 priority date for domestic and international students; for spring admission, 1/15 for domestic and international students. Applications are processed on a rolling basis. Application fee: $75. Electronic applications accepted. *Expenses:* Tuition: Full-time $38,100. *Financial support:* In 2009–10, 51 students received support, including 6 fellowships with full tuition reimbursements available (averaging $22,000 per year), 51 research assistantships with full tuition reimbursements available (averaging $16,500 per year), 33 teaching assistantships with full tuition reimbursements available (averaging $16,500 per year); career-related internships or fieldwork, tuition waivers, and unspecified assistantships also available. Financial award application deadline: 2/1. *Faculty research:* Tribology, advanced composite materials, energy and combustion systems, computer-aided and optimal design, manufacturing. Total annual research expenditures: $3.7 million. *Unit head:* Dr. Timothy Wei, Head, 518-276-6351, Fax: 518-276-6025, E-mail: weit@rpi.edu. *Application contact:* Dr. Thierry A. Blanchet, Associate Chair for Graduate Studies, 518-276-8697, Fax: 518-276-2623, E-mail: blanct@rpi.edu.

Rice University, Graduate Programs, George R. Brown School of Engineering, Department of Mechanical Engineering and Materials Science, Houston, TX 77251-1892. Offers materials science (MMS, MS, PhD); mechanical engineering (MME, MS, PhD); MBA/ME. Part-time programs available. *Faculty:* 16 full-time (2 women), 8 part-time/adjunct (0 women). *Students:* 56 full-time (13 women), 9 part-time (1 woman); includes 13 minority (2 African Americans, 2 Asian Americans or Pacific Islanders, 9 Hispanic Americans), 35 international. Average age 24. 270 applicants, 13% accepted, 26 enrolled. In 2009, 4 master's, 3 doctorates awarded. Terminal master's awarded for partial completion of doctoral program. *Degree requirements:* For master's, comprehensive exam, thesis; for doctorate, comprehensive exam, thesis/dissertation. *Entrance requirements:* For master's and doctorate, GRE General Test, minimum GPA of 3.0. Additional exam requirements/recommendations for international students: Required—TOEFL (minimum score 600 paper-based; 250 computer-based; 90 iBT), IELTS (minimum score 7). *Application deadline:* For fall admission, 2/1 priority date for domestic and international students; for spring admission, 11/15 priority date for domestic students, 11/1 priority date for international students. Applications are processed on a rolling basis. Application fee: $70. Electronic applications accepted. *Financial support:* In 2009–10, 41 students received support, including 9 fellowships with full tuition reimbursements available (averaging $14,000 per year), 31 research assistantships with full tuition reimbursements available (averaging $14,000 per year), 1 teaching assistantship with full tuition reimbursement available (averaging $14,000 per year). Financial award application deadline: 2/1. *Faculty research:* Heat transfer, biomedical engineering, fluid dynamics, aero-astronautics, control systems/robotics, materials science. Total annual research expenditures: $2.2 million. *Unit head:* Dr. Enrique V. Barrera, Chair, 713-348-4906, Fax: 713-348-5423, E-mail: mems@rice.edu. *Application contact:* Judith D. Farhat, Graduate Coordinator, 713-348-3582, Fax: 713-348-5423, E-mail: mems@rice.edu.

Rochester Institute of Technology, Graduate Enrollment Services, College of Applied Science and Technology, Department of Electrical, Computer and Telecommunications Engineering

Technology, Program in Manufacturing and Mechanical Systems Integration, Rochester, NY 14623-5603. Offers MS. Part-time and evening/weekend programs available. *Students:* 17 full-time (2 women), 14 part-time (0 women); includes 2 Hispanic Americans, 11 international. Average age 30. 18 applicants, 78% accepted, 12 enrolled. In 2009, 9 master's awarded. *Degree requirements:* For master's, thesis. *Entrance requirements:* For master's, GRE, minimum GPA of 3.0. Additional exam requirements/recommendations for international students: Required—TOEFL (minimum score 550 paper-based; 213 computer-based; 79 iBT), or IELTS (minimum score 6.5). *Application deadline:* For fall admission, 2/15 priority date for domestic and international students; for winter admission, 11/1 for domestic and international students; for spring admission, 2/1 for domestic and international students. Applications are processed on a rolling basis. Application fee: $50. *Expenses:* Tuition: Full-time $31,533; part-time $876 per credit hour. Required fees: $210. *Financial support:* In 2009–10, 26 students received support; research assistantships with partial tuition reimbursements available, teaching assistantships with partial tuition reimbursements available, career-related internships or fieldwork, scholarships/grants, and unspecified assistantships available. Support available to part-time students. Financial award application deadline: 2/15; financial award applicants required to submit FAFSA. *Unit head:* Dr. S. Manian Ramkumar, Program Chair, 585-475-6081, Fax: 585-475-5227, E-mail: smrmet@rit.edu. *Application contact:* Diane Ellison, Assistant Vice President, Graduate Enrollment Services, 585-475-2229, Fax: 585-475-7164, E-mail: gradinfo@rit.edu.

Rochester Institute of Technology, Graduate Enrollment Services, Kate Gleason College of Engineering, Department of Mechanical Engineering, Rochester, NY 14623-5603. Offers ME, MS. Part-time programs available. *Students:* 62 full-time (8 women), 26 part-time (4 women); includes 5 minority (2 American Indian/Alaska Native, 1 Asian American or Pacific Islander, 2 Hispanic Americans), 18 international. Average age 26. 108 applicants, 56% accepted, 29 enrolled. In 2009, 67 master's awarded. *Degree requirements:* For master's, thesis optional. *Entrance requirements:* For master's, GRE, minimum GPA of 3.0. Additional exam requirements/recommendations for international students: Required—TOEFL (minimum score 570 paper-based; 230 computer-based; 88 iBT), or IELTS (minimum score 6.5). *Application deadline:* For fall admission, 2/15 priority date for domestic and international students; for winter admission, 10/15 for domestic and international students; for spring admission, 2/1 for domestic and international students. Applications are processed on a rolling basis. Application fee: $50. Electronic applications accepted. *Expenses:* Tuition: Full-time $31,533; part-time $876 per credit hour. Required fees: $210. *Financial support:* In 2009–10, 86 students received support; research assistantships with partial tuition reimbursements available, teaching assistantships with partial tuition reimbursements available, career-related internships or fieldwork, institutionally sponsored loans, scholarships/grants, and unspecified assistantships available. Support available to part-time students. Financial award applicants required to submit FAFSA. *Faculty research:* Aerospace systems, unmanned aircraft design, fabrication and testing, automotive systems, assistive device technologies, artificial organ engineering, biomedical device engineering, microscale heat and mass transfer, thermoelectric energy, energy systems for developing countries. *Unit head:* Dr. Edward Hensel, Department Head, 585-475-5181, Fax: 585-475-7710, E-mail: echeme@rit.edu. *Application contact:* Diane Ellison, Assistant Vice President, Graduate Enrollment Services, 585-475-2229, Fax: 585-475-7164, E-mail: gradinfo@rit.edu.

Rose-Hulman Institute of Technology, Faculty of Engineering and Applied Sciences, Department of Mechanical Engineering, Terre Haute, IN 47803-3999. Offers MS. Part-time programs available. Postbaccalaureate distance learning degree programs offered (minimal on-campus study). *Faculty:* 25 full-time (4 women). *Students:* 7 full-time (1 woman), 10 part-time (0 women); includes 2 minority (both Asian Americans or Pacific Islanders), 5 international. Average age 24. 8 applicants, 100% accepted, 3 enrolled. In 2009, 6 master's awarded. *Degree requirements:* For master's, thesis. *Entrance requirements:* For master's, GRE, minimum GPA of 3.0. Additional exam requirements/recommendations for international students: Required—TOEFL (minimum score 580 paper-based; 237 computer-based; 92 iBT). *Application deadline:* For fall admission, 2/1 priority date for domestic students. Applications are processed on a rolling basis. Application fee: $0. *Expenses:* Tuition: Full-time $33,900; part-time $987 per credit hour. *Financial support:* In 2009–10, 3 students received support; fellowships with full and partial tuition reimbursements available, research assistantships with full and partial tuition reimbursements available, institutionally sponsored loans, scholarships/grants, and tuition waivers (full and partial) available. *Faculty research:* Dynamics of large flexible space structures, finite-element analysis, system simulation and optimization, mechanical design, fracture mechanics and fatigue. Total annual research expenditures: $356,737. *Unit head:* Dr. David J. Purdy, Chairman, 812-877-8320, Fax: 812-877-3198. *Application contact:* Dr. Daniel J. Moore, Associate Dean of the Faculty, 812-877-8110, Fax: 812-877-8061, E-mail: daniel.j.moore@rose-hulman.edu.

Rowan University, Graduate School, College of Engineering, Department of Mechanical Engineering, Glassboro, NJ 08028-1701. Offers MS. Part-time and evening/weekend programs available. *Faculty:* 5 full-time (0 women). *Students:* 5 full-time (0 women), 2 part-time (0 women); includes 1 minority (Hispanic American). Average age 24. 4 applicants, 75% accepted, 2 enrolled. In 2009, 4 master's awarded. *Entrance requirements:* For master's, GRE General Test. Additional exam requirements/recommendations for international students: Required—TOEFL. *Application deadline:* Applications are processed on a rolling basis. Application fee: $50. Electronic applications accepted. *Expenses:* Tuition, state resident: full-time $10,624; part-time $590 per semester hour. Tuition, nonresident: full-time $10,624; part-time $590 per semester hour. Required fees: $2320; $125 per semester hour. *Unit head:* Dr. Dianne Dorland, Dean, 856-256-5301. *Application contact:* Dr. Ralph Dusseau, Program Adviser, 856-256-5332.

Royal Military College of Canada, Division of Graduate Studies and Research, Engineering Division, Department of Mechanical Engineering, Kingston, ON K7K 7B4, Canada. Offers M Eng, MA Sc, PhD. *Degree requirements:* For master's, thesis; for doctorate, comprehensive exam, thesis/dissertation. *Entrance requirements:* For master's, honours degree with second-class standing; for doctorate, master's degree. Electronic applications accepted.

Rutgers, The State University of New Jersey, New Brunswick, Graduate School-New Brunswick, Program in Mechanical and Aerospace Engineering, Piscataway, NJ 08854-8097. Offers design and control (MS, PhD); fluid mechanics (MS, PhD); solid mechanics (MS, PhD); thermal sciences (MS, PhD). Part-time and evening/weekend programs available. *Degree requirements:* For master's, thesis (for some programs); for doctorate, thesis/dissertation. *Entrance requirements:* For master's, GRE General Test, BS in mechanical/aerospace engineering or related field; for doctorate, GRE General Test, MS in mechanical/aerospace engineering or related field. Additional exam requirements/recommendations for international students: Required—TOEFL. Electronic applications accepted. *Faculty research:* Combustion, propulsion, thermal transport, crystal plasticity, optimization, fabrication, nanoidentation.

St. Cloud State University, School of Graduate Studies, College of Science and Engineering, Program in Mechanical Engineering, St. Cloud, MN 56301-4498. Offers MS. *Faculty:* 6 full-time (0 women). *Students:* 4 full-time (0 women), 3 part-time (0 women), 6 international. 1 applicant, 0% accepted. In 2009, 1 master's awarded. *Degree requirements:* For master's, thesis or alternative. *Entrance requirements:* For master's, GRE General Test, minimum GPA of 2.75. Additional exam requirements/recommendations for international students: Required—Michigan English Language Assessment Battery; Recommended—TOEFL (minimum score 550 paper-based; 213 computer-based), IELTS (minimum score 6.5). *Application deadline:* For fall admission, 6/1 priority date for domestic students, 4/1 for international students; for spring admission, 10/1 priority date for domestic students, 8/1 for international students. Applications are processed on a rolling basis. Application fee: $35. Electronic applications accepted. *Financial support:* Federal Work-Study, scholarships/grants, and unspecified assistantships available. *Unit head:* Dr. Ken Miller, Coordinator, 320-308-5522, E-mail: kmiller@stcloudstate.edu. *Application contact:* Linda Lou Krueger, School of Graduate Studies, 320-308-2113, Fax: 320-308-5371, E-mail: lekrueger@stcloudstate.edu.

San Diego State University, Graduate and Research Affairs, College of Engineering, Department of Mechanical Engineering, San Diego, CA 92182. Offers engineering sciences and applied mechanics (PhD); manufacture and design (MS); mechanical engineering (MS). Evening/weekend programs available. *Degree requirements:* For master's, comprehensive exam (for some programs), thesis (for some programs); for doctorate, thesis/dissertation. *Entrance requirements:* For master's, GRE General Test; for doctorate, GRE, 3 letters of recommendation. Additional exam requirements/recommendations for international students: Required—TOEFL. Electronic applications accepted. *Faculty research:* Energy analysis and diagnosis, seawater pump design, space-related research.

San Jose State University, Graduate Studies and Research, Charles W. Davidson College of Engineering, Department of Mechanical and Aerospace Engineering, Program in Mechanical Engineering, San Jose, CA 95192-0001. Offers MS. Part-time programs available. *Students:* 68 full-time (6 women), 61 part-time (3 women); includes 43 minority (5 African Americans, 32 Asian Americans or Pacific Islanders, 6 Hispanic Americans), 57 international. Average age 27. 129 applicants, 50% accepted, 36 enrolled. In 2009, 31 master's awarded. *Degree requirements:* For master's, thesis optional. *Entrance requirements:* For master's, GRE. Additional exam requirements/recommendations for international students: Required—TOEFL. *Application deadline:* For fall admission, 6/29 for domestic students; for spring admission, 11/30 for domestic students. Applications are processed on a rolling basis. Application fee: $59. Electronic applications accepted. *Financial support:* Teaching assistantships available. Financial award applicants required to submit FAFSA. *Faculty research:* Gas dynamics, mechanics/vibrations, heat transfer, structural analysis, two-phase fluid flow. *Unit head:* Dr. Raghu Agarwal, Graduate Coordinator, 408-924-3845. *Application contact:* Dr. Raghu Agarwal, Graduate Coordinator, 408-924-3845.

Santa Clara University, School of Engineering, Department of Mechanical Engineering, Santa Clara, CA 95053. Offers controls (Certificate); dynamics (Certificate); materials engineering (Certificate); mechanical design analysis (Certificate); mechanical engineering (MS, PhD, Engineer); mechatronics systems engineering (Certificate); technology jump-start (Certificate); thermofluids (Certificate). Part-time and evening/weekend programs available. *Students:* 36 full-time (5 women), 61 part-time (10 women); includes 27 minority (1 American Indian/Alaska Native, 22 Asian Americans or Pacific Islanders, 4 Hispanic Americans), 15 international. Average age 28. In 2009, 17 master's awarded. *Degree requirements:* For master's, thesis (for some programs); for doctorate, thesis/dissertation; for other advanced degree, thesis. *Entrance requirements:* For master's, GRE (waiver may be available); for doctorate, GRE, master's degree or equivalent; for other advanced degree, master's degree, published paper. Additional exam requirements/recommendations for international students: Required—TOEFL (minimum score 550 paper-based; 213 computer-based; 79 iBT). *Application deadline:* For fall admission, 8/13 for domestic students, 7/16 for international students; for winter admission, 10/29 for domestic students, 9/24 for international students; for spring admission, 2/25 for domestic students, 1/21 for international students. Applications are processed on a rolling basis. Application fee: $60. *Expenses:* Contact institution. *Financial support:* Research assistantships, teaching assistantships available. Financial award application deadline: 3/2; financial award applicants required to submit FAFSA. *Faculty research:* Development of Small Satellite Design, Tests and Operations Technology. Total annual research expenditures: $585,448. *Unit head:* Dr. Alex Zecevic, Associate Dean for Graduate Studies, 408-554-2394, E-mail: azecevic@scu.edu. *Application contact:* Stacey Tinker, 408-554-4748, Fax: 408-554-4323, E-mail: stinker@scu.edu.

South Carolina State University, School of Graduate Studies, Department of Civil and Mechanical Engineering Technology, Orangeburg, SC 29117-0001. Offers transportation (MS). Part-time and evening/weekend programs available. *Degree requirements:* For master's, comprehensive exam, thesis, departmental qualifying exam. *Entrance requirements:* For master's, GRE. Electronic applications accepted. *Expenses:* Tuition, state resident: part-time $470 per credit hour. Tuition, nonresident: part-time $924 per credit hour. *Faculty research:* Societal competence, relationship of parent-child interaction to adult, rehabilitation evaluation, vocation, language assessment of rural children.

South Dakota School of Mines and Technology, Graduate Division, College of Engineering, Department of Mechanical Engineering, Rapid City, SD 57701-3995. Offers MS. Part-time programs available. *Faculty:* 10 full-time (0 women), 2 part-time/adjunct (0 women). *Students:* 9 full-time (1 woman), 6 part-time (1 woman), 2 international. Average age 27. 17 applicants, 59% accepted, 4 enrolled. In 2009, 7 master's awarded. *Entrance requirements:* Additional exam requirements/recommendations for international students: Required—TOEFL, TWE. *Application deadline:* For fall admission, 7/1 priority date for domestic students, 4/1 for international students; for spring admission, 11/1 for domestic students, 9/1 for international students. Applications are processed on a rolling basis. Application fee: $35. Electronic applications accepted. *Expenses:* Tuition, state resident: full-time $3340; part-time $139 per credit hour. Tuition, nonresident: full-time $7060; part-time $294 per credit hour. Required fees: $3270. *Financial support:* In 2009–10, fellowships (averaging $16,000 per year), research assistantships with partial tuition reimbursements (averaging $13,531 per year), teaching assistantships with partial tuition reimbursements (averaging $5,638 per year) were awarded; Federal Work-Study and institutionally sponsored loans also available. Support available to part-time students. Financial award application deadline: 5/15. *Faculty research:* Advanced composite materials, robotics, computer-integrated manufacturing, enhanced heat transfer, dynamic systems controls. Total annual research expenditures: $5,533. *Unit head:* Dr. Michael Langerman, Chair, 605-394-2408, E-mail: michael.langerman@sdsmt.edu. *Application contact:* Jeannette R. Nilson, Administrative Support Coordinator, Graduate Education, 800-454-8162 Ext. 1206, Fax: 605-394-5360, E-mail: graduate_admissions@sdsmt.edu.

South Dakota State University, Graduate School, College of Engineering, Department of Mechanical Engineering, Brookings, SD 57007. Offers engineering (MS). Part-time programs available. *Degree requirements:* For master's, thesis (for some programs), oral exam. *Entrance requirements:* Additional exam requirements/recommendations for international students: Required—TOEFL (minimum score 525 paper-based; 197 computer-based; 71 iBT). *Faculty research:* Thermo-fluid science, solid mechanics and dynamics, industrial and quality control engineering, bioenergy.

Southern Illinois University Carbondale, Graduate School, College of Engineering, Department of Mechanical Engineering and Energy Processes, Carbondale, IL 62901-4701. Offers MS. *Degree requirements:* For master's, comprehensive exam, thesis or alternative. *Entrance requirements:* For master's, GRE General Test, minimum GPA of 2.7. Additional exam requirements/recommendations for international students: Required—TOEFL. *Faculty research:* Coal conversion and processing, combustion, materials science and engineering, mechanical system dynamics.

Southern Illinois University Edwardsville, Graduate Studies and Research, School of Engineering, Department of Mechanical and Industrial Engineering, Program in Mechanical Engineering, Edwardsville, IL 62026-0001. Offers MS. Part-time programs available. *Students:* 11 full-time (1 woman), 8 part-time (2 women), 13 international. Average age 26. 37 applicants, 65% accepted. In 2009, 10 master's awarded. *Degree requirements:* For master's, comprehensive exam (for some programs), thesis (for some programs). *Entrance requirements:* Additional exam requirements/recommendations for international students: Required—TOEFL (minimum score 550 paper-based; 213 computer-based; 79 iBT), IELTS (minimum score 6.5). *Application deadline:* For fall admission, 7/23 for domestic students, 6/1 for international students; for spring admission, 12/11 for domestic students, 10/1 for international students. Applications are processed on a rolling basis. Application fee: $30. Electronic applications accepted. *Expenses:* Tuition, state resident: part-time $1252.50 per semester. Tuition, nonresident: part-time $3131.25 per semester. Required fees: $586.85 per semester. Tuition and fees vary according to course load. *Financial support:* In 2009–10, 1 research assistantship with full tuition reimbursement (averaging $8,064 per year), 14 teaching assistantships with full tuition reimbursements (averaging $8,064 per year) were awarded; career-related internships or fieldwork, Federal

Mechanical Engineering

Southern Illinois University Edwardsville (continued)

Work-Study, institutionally sponsored loans, scholarships/grants, traineeships, and unspecified assistantships also available. Support available to part-time students. Financial award application deadline: 3/1; financial award applicants required to submit FAFSA. *Unit head:* Dr. Kegin Gu, Chair, 618-650-3389, E-mail: kgu@siue.edu. *Application contact:* Dr. Terry Yan, Program Director, 618-650-3463, E-mail: xyan@siue.edu.

Southern Methodist University, Bobby B. Lyle School of Engineering, Department of Mechanical Engineering, Dallas, TX 75205. Offers electronic and optical packaging (MS); manufacturing systems management (MS); mechanical engineering (MSME, PhD). Part-time and evening/weekend programs available. Postbaccalaureate distance learning degree programs offered (no on-campus study). *Faculty:* 13 full-time (2 women), 6 part-time/adjunct (0 women). *Students:* 30 full-time (9 women), 42 part-time (6 women); includes 10 minority (1 African American, 3 Asian Americans or Pacific Islanders, 6 Hispanic Americans), 22 international. Average age 30. 53 applicants, 98% accepted, 52 enrolled. In 2009, 15 master's, 6 doctorates awarded. Terminal master's awarded for partial completion of doctoral program. *Degree requirements:* For master's, thesis optional; for doctorate, thesis/dissertation, oral and written qualifying exams, oral final exam. *Entrance requirements:* For master's, GRE General Test, minimum GPA of 3.0 in last 2 years; bachelor's degree in engineering, mathematics, or sciences; for doctorate, preliminary counseling exam, minimum graduate GPA of 3.0, bachelor's degree in related field. Additional exam requirements/recommendations for international students: Required—TOEFL. *Application deadline:* For fall admission, 7/1 for domestic students, 5/15 for international students; for spring admission, 11/15 for domestic students, 9/1 for international students. Applications are processed on a rolling basis. Application fee: $75. *Financial support:* In 2009–10, 17 students received support, including 10 research assistantships with full and partial tuition reimbursements available (averaging $16,000 per year), 7 teaching assistantships with full and partial tuition reimbursements available (averaging $16,000 per year); Federal Work-Study, institutionally sponsored loans, and tuition waivers (full and partial) also available. Financial award applicants required to submit FAFSA. *Faculty research:* Design, systems, and controls; thermal and fluid sciences. Total annual research expenditures: $774,564. *Unit head:* Dr. Volkan Otugen, Chairman, 214-768-3200, Fax: 214-768-1473, E-mail: otugen@engr.smu.edu. *Application contact:* Marc Valerin, Director of Graduate and Executive Admissions, 214-768-3042, E-mail: valerin@engr.smu.edu.

Stanford University, School of Engineering, Department of Mechanical Engineering, Stanford, CA 94305-9991. Offers biomechanical engineering (MS); mechanical engineering (MS, PhD, Eng); product design (MS). *Degree requirements:* For doctorate, thesis/dissertation; for Eng, thesis. *Entrance requirements:* For master's, GRE General Test, undergraduate degree in engineering, math or sciences; for doctorate and Eng, GRE General Test, MS in engineering, math or sciences. Additional exam requirements/recommendations for international students: Required—TOEFL. *Expenses:* Tuition: Full-time $37,380; part-time $2760 per quarter. Required fees: $501.

See Close-Up on page 525.

State University of New York at Binghamton, Graduate School, Thomas J. Watson School of Engineering and Applied Science, Department of Mechanical Engineering, Binghamton, NY 13902-6000. Offers M Eng, MS, PhD. Part-time and evening/weekend programs available. *Faculty:* 13 full-time (0 women), 2 part-time/adjunct (0 women). *Students:* 38 full-time (2 women), 31 part-time (4 women); includes 5 minority (4 Asian Americans or Pacific Islanders, 1 Hispanic American), 37 international. Average age 27. 59 applicants, 63% accepted, 20 enrolled. In 2009, 12 master's, 5 doctorates awarded. *Degree requirements:* For master's, thesis or alternative; for doctorate, thesis/dissertation. *Entrance requirements:* For master's and doctorate, GRE General Test, GRE Subject Test. Additional exam requirements/recommendations for international students: Required—TOEFL. *Application deadline:* For fall admission, 4/15 priority date for domestic students, 1/15 priority date for international students; for spring admission, 11/1 for domestic students, 10/1 priority date for international students. Applications are processed on a rolling basis. Application fee: $60. Electronic applications accepted. *Financial support:* In 2009–10, 55 students received support, including 39 research assistantships with full tuition reimbursements available (averaging $16,500 per year), 14 teaching assistantships with full tuition reimbursements available (averaging $16,500 per year); fellowships with full tuition reimbursements available, career-related internships or fieldwork, Federal Work-Study, institutionally sponsored loans, scholarships/grants, health care benefits, and unspecified assistantships also available. Financial award application deadline: 2/15; financial award applicants required to submit FAFSA. *Unit head:* Dr. James M. Pitarresi, Chairperson, 607-777-4037, E-mail: jmp@binghamton.edu. *Application contact:* Victoria Williams, Recruiting and Admissions Coordinator, 607-777-2151, Fax: 607-777-2501, E-mail: vwilliam@binghamton.edu.

Stevens Institute of Technology, Graduate School, Charles V. Schaefer Jr. School of Engineering, Department of Mechanical Engineering, Hoboken, NJ 07030. Offers advanced manufacturing (Certificate); air pollution technology (Certificate); computational fluid mechanics and heat transfer (Certificate); design and production management (Certificate); integrated product development (M Eng), including armament engineering, computer and electrical engineering, manufacturing technologies, systems reliability and design; mechanical engineering (M Eng, PhD), including manufacturing systems (M Eng), pharmaceutical manufacturing systems (M Eng), product design (M Eng), thermal engineering (M Eng); pharmaceutical manufacturing (M Eng, MS, Certificate); power generation (Certificate); product architecture and engineering (M Eng); robotics and control (Certificate); structural analysis and design (Certificate); vibration and noise control (Certificate). Part-time and evening/weekend programs available. Terminal master's awarded for partial completion of doctoral program. *Degree requirements:* For master's, thesis optional; for doctorate, variable foreign language requirement, thesis/dissertation; for Certificate, project or thesis. *Entrance requirements:* Additional exam requirements/recommendations for international students: Required—TOEFL. Electronic applications accepted. *Expenses:* Tuition: Full-time $9900; part-time $1100 per credit. Required fees: $286 per semester. *Faculty research:* Acoustics, incineration, CAD/CAM, computational fluid dynamics and heat transfer, robotics.

Stony Brook University, State University of New York, Graduate School, College of Engineering and Applied Sciences, Department of Mechanical Engineering, Stony Brook, NY 11794. Offers MS, PhD. Evening/weekend programs available. *Faculty:* 20 full-time (2 women), 1 part-time/adjunct (0 women). *Students:* 47 full-time (4 women), 28 part-time (2 women); includes 12 minority (1 African American, 10 Asian Americans or Pacific Islanders, 1 Hispanic American), 40 international. Average age 27. 141 applicants, 24% accepted. In 2009, 17 master's, 6 doctorates awarded. *Degree requirements:* For master's, thesis or alternative; for doctorate, comprehensive exam, thesis/dissertation. *Entrance requirements:* For master's, GRE General Test, minimum GPA of 3.0; for doctorate, GRE General Test, minimum GPA of 3.5. Additional exam requirements/recommendations for international students: Required—TOEFL. *Application deadline:* For fall admission, 1/15 for domestic students. Application fee: $60. *Expenses:* Tuition, state resident: full-time $8370; part-time $349 per credit. Tuition, nonresident: full-time $13,250; part-time $552 per credit. Required fees: $933. *Financial support:* In 2009–10, 12 research assistantships, 14 teaching assistantships were awarded; fellowships also available. *Faculty research:* Atmospheric sciences, thermal fluid sciences, solid mechanics. Total annual research expenditures: $1.6 million. *Unit head:* Dr. Fu-Pen Chiang, Chairman, 631-632-8310. *Application contact:* Dr. John Kincaid, Director, 631-632-8305, Fax: 631-632-8720, E-mail: jkincaid@ccmail.sunysb.edu.

Syracuse University, L. C. Smith College of Engineering and Computer Science, Program in Mechanical and Aerospace Engineering, Syracuse, NY 13244. Offers MS, PhD. *Students:* 67 full-time (14 women), 16 part-time (2 women); includes 6 minority (4 Asian Americans or Pacific Islanders, 2 Hispanic Americans), 59 international. Average age 27. 143 applicants, 48% accepted, 28 enrolled. In 2009, 27 master's, 3 doctorates awarded. *Degree requirements:* For master's, project or thesis; for doctorate, thesis/dissertation. *Entrance requirements:* For master's and doctorate, GRE General Test. Additional exam requirements/recommendations for international students: Required—TOEFL (minimum score 100 iBT). *Application deadline:* For fall admission, 6/1 priority date for domestic and international students. Applications are processed on a rolling basis. Application fee: $75. Electronic applications accepted. *Expenses:* Tuition: Full-time $26,808; part-time $1117 per credit. Required fees: $1024. *Financial support:* Fellowships with full tuition reimbursements, research assistantships with full and partial tuition reimbursements, teaching assistantships with full and partial tuition reimbursements, scholarships/grants and tuition waivers (partial) available. Financial award application deadline: 1/1. *Faculty research:* Solid mechanics and materials, fluid mechanics, thermal sciences, controls and robotics. *Unit head:* Dr. Alan Levy, Chair, 315-443-4311, Fax: 315-443-9099. *Application contact:* Kathy Datthyn-Madigan, Information Contact, 315-443-4367, E-mail: kjdatthy@syr.edu.

Temple University, Graduate School, College of Engineering, Department of Mechanical Engineering, Philadelphia, PA 19122-6096. Offers MSE. Part-time and evening/weekend programs available. *Degree requirements:* For master's, thesis optional. *Entrance requirements:* For master's, GRE General Test, minimum GPA of 3.0. Additional exam requirements/recommendations for international students: Required—TOEFL (minimum score 550 paper-based; 213 computer-based; 79 iBT). Electronic applications accepted. *Faculty research:* Rapid solidification by melt spinning, microfracture analysis of dental materials, failure detection methods.

Tennessee Technological University, Graduate School, College of Engineering, Department of Mechanical Engineering, Cookeville, TN 38505. Offers MS, PhD. Part-time programs available. *Faculty:* 25 full-time (2 women). *Students:* 13 full-time (0 women), 9 part-time (0 women); includes 7 minority (1 African American, 6 Asian Americans or Pacific Islanders). Average age 28. 39 applicants, 38% accepted, 7 enrolled. In 2009, 10 master's awarded. *Degree requirements:* For master's, thesis. *Entrance requirements:* For master's, GRE. Additional exam requirements/recommendations for international students: Required—TOEFL (minimum score 550 paper-based; 79 iBT), IELTS (minimum score 5.5). *Application deadline:* For fall admission, 8/1 for domestic students, 5/1 for international students; for spring admission, 12/1 for domestic students, 10/1 for international students. Application fee: $25 ($30 for international students). Electronic applications accepted. *Expenses:* Tuition, state resident: full-time $7034; part-time $368 per credit hour. *Financial support:* In 2009–10, fellowships (averaging $8,000 per year), 20 research assistantships (averaging $8,190 per year), 8 teaching assistantships (averaging $6,711 per year) were awarded. Financial award application deadline: 4/1. *Faculty research:* Energy-related systems, design, acoustics and acoustical systems. *Unit head:* Dr. Darrell A. Hoy, Interim Chairperson, 931-372-3233, Fax: 931-372-3497. *Application contact:* Shelia K. Kendrick, Coordinator of Graduate Studies, 931-372-3808, Fax: 931-372-3497, E-mail: skendrick@tntech.edu.

Texas A&M University, College of Engineering, Department of Mechanical Engineering, College Station, TX 77843. Offers M Eng, MS, D Eng, PhD. *Faculty:* 58. *Students:* 416 full-time (76 women), 46 part-time (7 women); includes 43 minority (11 African Americans, 1 American Indian/Alaska Native, 13 Asian Americans or Pacific Islanders, 18 Hispanic Americans), 325 international. Average age 24. In 2009, 93 master's, 25 doctorates awarded. *Degree requirements:* For master's, thesis (MS); for doctorate, dissertation (PhD). *Entrance requirements:* For master's, GRE General Test, minimum undergraduate GPA of 3.0; for doctorate, GRE General Test, minimum graduate GPA of 3.5. Additional exam requirements/recommendations for international students: Required—TOEFL (minimum score 570 paper-based). *Application deadline:* For fall admission, 2/1 priority date for domestic students; for spring admission, 11/1 for domestic students. Applications are processed on a rolling basis. Application fee: $50 ($75 for international students). Electronic applications accepted. *Expenses:* Tuition, state resident: full-time $3991.32; part-time $221.74 per credit hour. Tuition, nonresident: full-time $9049; part-time $502.74 per credit hour. *Financial support:* In 2009–10, fellowships with partial tuition reimbursements (averaging $5,000 per year), research assistantships with partial tuition reimbursements (averaging $14,000 per year), teaching assistantships (averaging $14,000 per year) were awarded; institutionally sponsored loans also available. Financial award application deadline: 3/1; financial award applicants required to submit FAFSA. *Faculty research:* Thermal/fluid sciences, materials/manufacturing and controls systems. *Unit head:* Dr. Sai Lau, Head, 979-845-5337, E-mail: slau@mengr.tamu.edu. *Application contact:* Kim Moses, Senior Academic Advisor, 979-845-1270, Fax: 979-845-3081, E-mail: kmoses@mengr.tamu.edu.

Texas A&M University–Kingsville, College of Graduate Studies, College of Engineering, Department of Mechanical and Industrial Engineering, Program in Mechanical Engineering, Kingsville, TX 78363. Offers ME, MS. *Degree requirements:* For master's, comprehensive exam, thesis or alternative. *Entrance requirements:* For master's, GRE General Test, minimum GPA of 3.0. Additional exam requirements/recommendations for international students: Required—TOEFL. *Faculty research:* Intelligent systems and controls; neural networks and fuzzy logic; robotics and automation; biomass, cogeneration, and enhanced heat transfer.

Texas Tech University, Graduate School, College of Engineering, Department of Mechanical Engineering, Lubbock, TX 79409. Offers MSME, PhD. Part-time programs available. *Faculty:* 22 full-time (3 women). *Students:* 73 full-time (11 women), 36 part-time (4 women); includes 3 minority (1 Asian American or Pacific Islander, 2 Hispanic Americans), 68 international. Average age 29. 184 applicants, 21% accepted, 16 enrolled. In 2009, 34 master's, 10 doctorates awarded. *Degree requirements:* For master's, thesis or alternative; for doctorate, thesis/dissertation. *Entrance requirements:* For master's and doctorate, GRE General Test, minimum GPA of 3.0. Additional exam requirements/recommendations for international students: Required—TOEFL (minimum score 550 paper-based; 213 computer-based). *Application deadline:* For fall admission, 3/1 priority date for international students; for spring admission, 11/1 priority date for international students. Applications are processed on a rolling basis. Application fee: $50 ($75 for international students). Electronic applications accepted. *Expenses:* Tuition, state resident: full-time $5100; part-time $213 per credit hour. Tuition, nonresident: full-time $11,748; part-time $490 per credit hour. Required fees: $2298; $50 per credit hour. $555 per semester. *Financial support:* In 2009–10, 6 research assistantships with partial tuition reimbursements (averaging $16,168 per year) were awarded; teaching assistantships with partial tuition reimbursements, Federal Work-Study and institutionally sponsored loans also available. Support available to part-time students. Financial award application deadline: 4/15; financial award applicants required to submit FAFSA. *Faculty research:* Dynamics and control, energy systems, materials, experimental and computational fluid mechanics, bioengineering. Total annual research expenditures: $1 million. *Unit head:* Dr. Jharna Chaudhuri, Chair, 806-742-3563, Fax: 806-742-3540, E-mail: jharna.chandhuri@ttu.edu. *Application contact:* Dr. Sira P. Parameswaran, Graduate Advisor, 806-742-3563 Ext. 247, Fax: 806-742-3540, E-mail: sira.parameswaran@ttu.edu.

Trine University, Allen School of Engineering and Technology, Angola, IN 46703-1764. Offers civil engineering (ME); mechanical engineering (ME). Part-time and evening/weekend programs available. *Degree requirements:* For master's, comprehensive exam, thesis. *Faculty research:* CAD, computer aided MFG, computer numerical control, parametric modeling, megatronics.

Tufts University, School of Engineering, Department of Mechanical Engineering, Medford, MA 02155. Offers human factors (MS); mechanical engineering (ME, MS, PhD). Part-time programs available. *Faculty:* 13 full-time, 5 part-time/adjunct. *Students:* 73 (18 women); includes 13 minority (1 African American, 10 Asian Americans or Pacific Islanders, 2 Hispanic Americans), 17 international. Average age 27. 82 applicants, 71% accepted, 30 enrolled. In 2009, 25 master's, 2 doctorates awarded. Terminal master's awarded for partial completion of doctoral program. *Degree requirements:* For master's, thesis; for doctorate, thesis/dissertation. *Entrance requirements:* For master's and doctorate, GRE General Test. Additional exam requirements/recommendations for international students: Required—TOEFL (minimum score 550 paper-based; 213 computer-based; 80 iBT). *Application deadline:* For fall admission, 1/15 priority date for domestic students, 12/15 for international students; for spring admission, 10/15 for domestic students, 9/15 for international students. Applications are processed on a rolling basis. Application fee: $75. Electronic applications accepted. *Expenses:* Tuition: Full-time $38,096; part-time $3962 per credit. Required fees: $686; $40 per year. Tuition and fees vary according to course level, course load, degree level, program and student level. *Financial support:* Fellowships with full tuition reimbursements, research assistantships with full and partial tuition reimbursements, teaching assistantships with full and partial tuition reimbursements, Federal Work-Study, scholarships/grants, tuition waivers (partial), and unspecified assistantships available. Financial award application deadline: 1/15; financial award applicants required to submit FAFSA. *Unit head:* Richard Wlezien, Chair, 617-627-3239, Fax: 617-627-3058. *Application contact:* Lorin Polidora, Department Administrator, 617-627-3239.

Tuskegee University, Graduate Programs, College of Engineering, Architecture and Physical Sciences, Department of Mechanical Engineering, Tuskegee, AL 36088. Offers MSME. *Faculty:* 11 full-time (0 women). *Students:* 23 full-time (7 women), 2 part-time (0 women); includes 8 minority (7 African Americans, 1 Hispanic American), 15 international. Average age 29. In 2009, 11 master's awarded. *Degree requirements:* For master's, thesis or alternative. *Entrance requirements:* For master's, GRE General Test, GRE Subject Test. Additional exam requirements/recommendations for international students: Required—TOEFL (minimum score 500 paper-based; 69 computer-based). *Application deadline:* For fall admission, 7/15 for domestic students. Applications are processed on a rolling basis. Application fee: $25 ($35 for international students). *Expenses:* Tuition: Full-time $15,630; part-time $940 per credit hour. Required fees: $650. *Financial support:* Fellowships, research assistantships, teaching assistantships, career-related internships or fieldwork, Federal Work-Study, and institutionally sponsored loans available. Support available to part-time students. Financial award application deadline: 4/15. *Faculty research:* Superalloys, fatigue and surface machinery, energy management, solar energy. *Unit head:* Dr. Pradosh Ray, Head, 334-727-8989. *Application contact:* Dr. Robert L. Laney, Vice President/Director of Admissions and Enrollment Management, 334-727-8580, Fax: 334-727-5750, E-mail: planey@tuskegee.edu.

Union Graduate College, School of Engineering and Computer Science, Schenectady, NY 12308-3107. Offers computer science (MS); electrical engineering (MS); engineering and management systems (MS); mechanical engineering (MS). Part-time and evening/weekend programs available. *Faculty:* 24 part-time/adjunct (1 woman). *Students:* 10 full-time (0 women), 60 part-time (7 women); includes 5 minority (1 African American, 1 American Indian/Alaska Native, 2 Asian Americans or Pacific Islanders, 1 Hispanic American), 5 international. Average age 27. 47 applicants, 55% accepted, 25 enrolled. In 2009, 28 master's awarded. *Degree requirements:* For master's, capstone course. *Entrance requirements:* For master's, minimum GPA of 3.0, letters of recommendation. Additional exam requirements/recommendations for international students: Required—TOEFL (minimum score 550 paper-based; 213 computer-based). *Application deadline:* Applications are processed on a rolling basis. Application fee: $60. Electronic applications accepted. *Expenses:* Contact institution. *Financial support:* Research assistantships, Federal Work-Study, scholarships/grants, health care benefits, and tuition waivers (full and partial) available. Support available to part-time students. Financial award applicants required to submit FAFSA. *Unit head:* Robert Kozik, Dean, 515-631-9881, Fax: 518-631-9902, E-mail: kozikr@union.edu. *Application contact:* Diane Trzaskos, Coordinator, Admissions, 518-631-9837, Fax: 518-631-9901, E-mail: trzaskod@uniongraduatecollege.edu.

Université de Moncton, Faculty of Engineering, Program in Mechanical Engineering, Moncton, NB E1A 3E9, Canada. Offers M Sc A. *Degree requirements:* For master's, thesis, proficiency in French. *Faculty research:* Composite materials, thermal energy systems, control systems, fluid mechanics and heat transfer, CAD/CAM and robotics.

Université de Sherbrooke, Faculty of Engineering, Department of Mechanical Engineering, Sherbrooke, QC J1K 2R1, Canada. Offers M Sc A, PhD. *Degree requirements:* For master's, one foreign language, thesis; for doctorate, comprehensive exam, thesis/dissertation. *Entrance requirements:* For master's, bachelor's degree in engineering or equivalent; for doctorate, master's degree in engineering or equivalent. Electronic applications accepted. *Faculty research:* Acoustics, aerodynamics, vehicle dynamics, composite materials, heat transfer.

Université Laval, Faculty of Sciences and Engineering, Department of Mechanical Engineering, Programs in Mechanical Engineering, Québec, QC G1K 7P4, Canada. Offers M Sc, PhD. Part-time programs available. Terminal master's awarded for partial completion of doctoral program. *Degree requirements:* For master's, thesis; for doctorate, comprehensive exam, thesis/dissertation. *Entrance requirements:* For master's and doctorate, knowledge of French. Electronic applications accepted.

University at Buffalo, the State University of New York, Graduate School, School of Engineering and Applied Sciences, Department of Mechanical and Aerospace Engineering, Buffalo, NY 14260. Offers aerospace engineering (MS, PhD); mechanical engineering (MS, PhD). Part-time programs available. *Faculty:* 26 full-time (4 women), 8 part-time/adjunct (0 women). *Students:* 204 full-time (19 women), 66 part-time (8 women); includes 17 minority (3 African Americans, 11 Asian Americans or Pacific Islanders, 3 Hispanic Americans), 148 international. Average age 27. 773 applicants, 17% accepted, 90 enrolled. In 2009, 59 master's, 10 doctorates awarded. Terminal master's awarded for partial completion of doctoral program. *Degree requirements:* For master's, comprehensive exam, project or thesis; for doctorate, thesis/dissertation. *Entrance requirements:* For master's and doctorate, GRE General Test, GRE Subject Test. Additional exam requirements/recommendations for international students: Required—TOEFL (minimum score 79 iBT). *Application deadline:* For fall admission, 1/15 for domestic and international students; for spring admission, 9/15 for domestic and international students. Applications are processed on a rolling basis. Application fee: $50. *Financial support:* In 2009-10, 157 students received support, including 5 fellowships with full tuition reimbursements available (averaging $28,900 per year), 25 research assistantships with full tuition reimbursements available (averaging $24,000 per year), 30 teaching assistantships with full tuition reimbursements available (averaging $20,900 per year); Federal Work-Study, institutionally sponsored loans, tuition waivers (partial), and unspecified assistantships also available. Financial award application deadline: 1/15; financial award applicants required to submit FAFSA. *Faculty research:* Fluid and thermal sciences, systems and design, mechanics and materials. Total annual research expenditures: $6.2 million. *Unit head:* Dr. Gary Dargush, Chair, 716-645-2593, Fax: 716-645-2883, E-mail: gdargush@buffalo.edu. *Application contact:* Dr. Zonglu (Susan) Hua, Director of Graduate Studies, 716-645-1471, Fax: 716-645-3875, E-mail: zhua@buffalo.edu.

The University of Akron, Graduate School, College of Engineering, Department of Mechanical Engineering, Akron, OH 44325. Offers MS, PhD. Part-time and evening/weekend programs available. *Faculty:* 19 full-time (1 woman), 11 part-time/adjunct (0 women). *Students:* 54 full-time (11 women), 28 part-time (2 women); includes 2 minority (1 African American, 1 Asian American or Pacific Islander), 39 international. Average age 27. 82 applicants, 49% accepted, 19 enrolled. In 2009, 15 master's, 2 doctorates awarded. Terminal master's awarded for partial completion of doctoral program. *Degree requirements:* For master's, thesis optional; for doctorate, one foreign language, thesis/dissertation, candidacy exam, qualifying exam. *Entrance requirements:* For master's, GRE, minimum GPA of 2.75, letters of recommendation; for doctorate, GRE, minimum GPA of 3.0 with bachelor's degree, 3.5 with master's degree; letters of recommendation; personal statement. Additional exam requirements/recommendations for international students: Required—TOEFL (minimum score 550 paper-based; 213 computer-based; 79 iBT). *Application deadline:* Applications are processed on a rolling basis. Application fee: $30 ($40 for international students). Electronic applications accepted. *Expenses:* Tuition, state resident: full-time $6570; part-time $365 per credit hour. Tuition, nonresident: full-time $11,250; part-time $625 per credit hour. *Financial support:* In 2009-10, 2 fellowships with full tuition reimbursements, 8 research assistantships with full tuition reimbursements, 32 teaching assistantships with full tuition reimbursements were awarded. *Faculty research:* Materials science, tribology and lubrication, vibration and dynamic analysis, solid mechanics, MEMS and NEMS, bio-mechanics. Total annual research expenditures: $1 million. *Unit head:* Dr. Celal Batur, Chair, 330-972-7367, E-mail: batur@uakron.edu. *Application contact:* Dr. Celal Batur, Chair, 330-972-7367, E-mail: batur@uakron.edu.

The University of Alabama, Graduate School, College of Engineering, Department of Mechanical Engineering, Tuscaloosa, AL 35487. Offers MS, PhD. Part-time programs available. *Faculty:* 17 full-time (1 woman). *Students:* 47 full-time (5 women), 7 part-time (0 women); includes 6 minority (3 African Americans, 3 Asian Americans or Pacific Islanders), 24 international. Average age 28. 59 applicants, 39% accepted, 14 enrolled. In 2009, 12 master's, 2 doctorates awarded. Terminal master's awarded for partial completion of doctoral program. *Median time to degree:* Of those who began their doctoral program in fall 2001, 100% received their degree in 8 years or less. *Degree requirements:* For master's, comprehensive exam, thesis (for some programs); for doctorate, comprehensive exam, thesis/dissertation. *Entrance requirements:* For master's, GRE General Test (waived for ABET accredited engineering degree), minimum GPA of 3.0; for doctorate, GRE General Test (waived for ABET-accredited engineering degree), minimum GPA of 3.0 with MS, 3.3 without MS. Additional exam requirements/recommendations for international students: Required—TOEFL (minimum score 600 paper-based). *Application deadline:* For fall admission, 7/1 priority date for domestic students, 1/15 priority date for international students; for spring admission, 11/1 priority date for domestic students, 6/1 priority date for international students. Applications are processed on a rolling basis. Application fee: $50 ($60 for international students). Electronic applications accepted. *Expenses:* Tuition, state resident: full-time $7000. Tuition, nonresident: full-time $19,200. *Financial support:* In 2009-10, 32 students received support, including 5 fellowships with full tuition reimbursements available (averaging $15,000 per year), 14 research assistantships with full tuition reimbursements available (averaging $15,000 per year), 13 teaching assistantships with full tuition reimbursements available (averaging $12,000 per year); career-related internships or fieldwork and unspecified assistantships also available. Financial award application deadline: 3/30. *Faculty research:* Thermal/fluids, robotics, numerical modeling, energy conservation, energy and combustion systems, internal combustion engines, manufacturing, vehicular systems, solid mechanics and materials. Total annual research expenditures: $2.1 million. *Unit head:* Dr. Robert P. Taylor, Head and Professor, 205-348-4078, Fax: 205-348-6419, E-mail: btaylor2@eng.ua.edu. *Application contact:* Dr. Will Schreiber, Coordinator and Professor, 205-348-1650, Fax: 205-348-6419, E-mail: wschreiber@eng.ua.edu.

The University of Alabama at Birmingham, School of Engineering, Program in Mechanical Engineering, Birmingham, AL 35294. Offers MSME.

The University of Alabama in Huntsville, School of Graduate Studies, College of Engineering, Department of Mechanical and Aerospace Engineering, Huntsville, AL 35899. Offers aerospace engineering (MSE), including missile systems engineering, rotorcraft systems engineering; mechanical engineering (MSE, PhD). Part-time and evening/weekend programs available. *Faculty:* 17 full-time (2 women), 3 part-time/adjunct (0 women). *Students:* 44 full-time (8 women), 109 part-time (13 women); includes 11 minority (4 African Americans, 1 American Indian/Alaska Native, 3 Asian Americans or Pacific Islanders, 3 Hispanic Americans), 19 international. Average age 30. 112 applicants, 71% accepted, 47 enrolled. In 2009, 25 master's, 4 doctorates awarded. *Degree requirements:* For master's, comprehensive exam, thesis or alternative, oral and written exams; for doctorate, comprehensive exam, thesis/dissertation, oral and written exams. *Entrance requirements:* For master's, GRE General Test, BSE, minimum GPA of 3.0; for doctorate, GRE General Test, minimum GPA of 3.0. Additional exam requirements/recommendations for international students: Required—TOEFL (minimum score 500 paper-based; 173 computer-based; 62 iBT). *Application deadline:* For fall admission, 7/15 for domestic students, 4/1 for international students; for spring admission, 1/30 for domestic students, 9/1 for international students. Applications are processed on a rolling basis. Application fee: $40 ($50 for international students). Electronic applications accepted. *Expenses:* Tuition, state resident: part-time $355.75 per credit hour. Tuition, nonresident: part-time $847.10 per credit hour. Required fees: $210.80 per semester. Tuition and fees vary according to course load and program. *Financial support:* In 2009-10, 29 students received support, including 14 research assistantships with full and partial tuition reimbursements available (averaging $12,975 per year), 15 teaching assistantships with full and partial tuition reimbursements available (averaging $10,400 per year); career-related internships or fieldwork, Federal Work-Study, institutionally sponsored loans, scholarships/grants, health care benefits, and unspecified assistantships also available. Support available to part-time students. Financial award application deadline: 4/1; financial award applicants required to submit FAFSA. *Faculty research:* Combustion, fluid dynamics, materials and structures, propulsion, laser diagnostics. Total annual research expenditures: $4.7 million. *Unit head:* Dr. Kader Frendi, Chair, 256-824-6154, Fax: 256-824-6758, E-mail: frendi@mae.uah.edu. *Application contact:* Kathy Biggs, Graduate Studies Admissions Manager, 256-824-6199, Fax: 256-824-6405, E-mail: deangrad@uah.edu.

University of Alaska Fairbanks, College of Engineering and Mines, Department of Mechanical Engineering, Fairbanks, AK 99775-5905. Offers engineering (PhD); mechanical engineering (MS). Part-time programs available. *Faculty:* 9 full-time (0 women), 1 part-time/adjunct (0 women). *Students:* 9 full-time (3 women), 3 part-time (1 woman); includes 2 minority (1 African American, 1 Asian American or Pacific Islander), 6 international. Average age 29. 17 applicants, 29% accepted, 5 enrolled. In 2009, 3 master's, 1 doctorate awarded. Terminal master's awarded for partial completion of doctoral program. *Degree requirements:* For master's, comprehensive exam, thesis or alternative; for doctorate, comprehensive exam, thesis/dissertation, oral exam, oral defense. *Entrance requirements:* For master's and doctorate, GRE General Test. Additional exam requirements/recommendations for international students: Required—TOEFL (minimum score 550 paper-based; 213 computer-based; 80 iBT). *Application deadline:* For fall admission, 6/1 for domestic students, 3/1 for international students; for spring admission, 10/15 for domestic students, 9/1 for international students. Applications are processed on a rolling basis. Application fee: $60. Electronic applications accepted. *Expenses:* Tuition, state resident: full-time $7584; part-time $316 per credit. Tuition, nonresident: full-time $15,504; part-time $646 per credit. Required fees: $23 per credit. $135 per semester. Tuition and fees vary according to course level, course load and reciprocity agreements. *Financial support:* In 2009-10, 2 research assistantships (averaging $13,004 per year), 5 teaching assistantships (averaging $7,088 per year) were awarded; fellowships, career-related internships or fieldwork, Federal Work-Study, scholarships/grants, health care benefits, and unspecified assistantships also available. Support available to part-time students. Financial award application deadline: 7/1; financial award applicants required to submit FAFSA. *Faculty research:* Cold regions engineering, fluid mechanics, heat transfer, energy systems, indoor air quality. *Unit head:* Dr. Jonah Lee, Department Chair, 907-474-7136, Fax: 907-474-6141, E-mail: fymech@uaf.edu. *Application contact:* Dr. Jonah Lee, Department Chair, 907-474-7136, Fax: 907-474-6141, E-mail: fymech@uaf.edu.

University of Alberta, Faculty of Graduate Studies and Research, Department of Mechanical Engineering, Edmonton, AB T6G 2E1, Canada. Offers engineering management (M Eng); mechanical engineering (M Eng, M Sc, PhD); MBA/M Eng. Part-time programs available. *Faculty:* 33 full-time (1 woman), 1 part-time/adjunct (0 women). *Students:* 144 full-time (17 women), 34 part-time (5 women). 300 applicants, 44% accepted, 76 enrolled. In 2009, 14 master's, 2 doctorates awarded. *Degree requirements:* For master's, thesis; for doctorate, thesis/dissertation. *Entrance requirements:* For master's and doctorate, minimum GPA of 7.0 on a 9.0 scale. Additional exam requirements/recommendations for international students: Required—TOEFL (minimum score 580 paper-based; 237 computer-based). *Application deadline:* For fall admission, 3/1 priority date for domestic students; for winter admission, 7/1 priority date for domestic students. Applications are processed on a rolling basis. Tuition and fees charges are reported in Canadian dollars. *Expenses:* Tuition, area resident: Full-time $4626.24 Canadian dollars; part-time $99.72 Canadian dollars per unit. International tuition: $8216 Canadian dollars full-time. Required fees: $3589.92 Canadian dollars; $99.72 Canadian dollars per unit. $215 Canadian dollars per term. *Financial support:* In 2009-10, 14 fellowships, 7 research assistantships, 64 teaching assistantships were awarded; career-related internships or fieldwork, scholarships/grants, and supervisor support also available. Financial award application deadline: 2/1. *Faculty research:* Combustion and environmental issues, advanced materials, computational fluid dynamics, biomedical, acoustics and vibrations. Total annual research expenditures: $1.3 million. *Unit head:* Dr. Zihui Ben Xia, Graduate Coordinator, 780-492-0414, Fax: 403-492-2200. *Application contact:* Gail Anderson, Student Services Assistant, 780-492-0414, Fax: 780-492-2200, E-mail: mecegrad@mail.mece.ualberta.ca.

Mechanical Engineering

The University of Arizona, Graduate College, College of Engineering, Department of Aerospace and Mechanical Engineering, Program in Mechanical Engineering, Tucson, AZ 85721. Offers MS, PhD. Part-time programs available. *Students:* 46 full-time (10 women), 12 part-time (2 women); includes 4 minority (1 Asian American or Pacific Islander, 3 Hispanic Americans), 34 international. Average age 26. 64 applicants, 69% accepted, 16 enrolled. In 2009, 23 master's, 5 doctorates awarded. *Degree requirements:* For master's, thesis or alternative; for doctorate, one foreign language, thesis/dissertation. *Entrance requirements:* For master's and doctorate, GRE General Test, minimum GPA of 3.25, 3 letters of recommendation, statement of purpose. Additional exam requirements/recommendations for international students: Required—TOEFL (minimum score 550 paper-based; 213 computer-based; 79 iBT). *Application deadline:* For fall admission, 6/1 for domestic students, 12/1 for international students; for spring admission, 10/1 for domestic students, 6/1 for international students. Applications are processed on a rolling basis. Application fee: $75. Electronic applications accepted. *Expenses:* Tuition, state resident: full-time $9028. Tuition, nonresident: full-time $24,890. *Financial support:* Research assistantships, teaching assistantships, unspecified assistantships available. *Faculty research:* Fluid mechanics, structures, computer-aided design, stability and control, probabilistic design. *Unit head:* Dr. Ara Arabyan, Interim Department Head, 520-621-2116, Fax: 520-621-8191, E-mail: arabyan@email.arizona.edu. *Application contact:* Barbara Heefner, Graduate Secretary, 520-621-4692, Fax: 520-621-8191, E-mail: heefner@email.arizona.edu.

University of Arkansas, Graduate School, College of Engineering, Department of Mechanical Engineering, Fayetteville, AR 72701-1201. Offers MSE, MSME, PhD. Part-time programs available. Postbaccalaureate distance learning degree programs offered. *Students:* 20 full-time (0 women), 20 part-time (1 woman); includes 4 minority (2 African Americans, 1 Asian American or Pacific Islander, 1 Hispanic American), 24 international. 51 applicants, 47% accepted. In 2009, 5 master's, 2 doctorates awarded. *Degree requirements:* For master's, thesis optional; for doctorate, one foreign language, thesis/dissertation. Application fee: $40 ($50 for international students). *Expenses:* Tuition, state resident: full-time $7355; part-time $356.58 per hour. Tuition, nonresident: full-time $17,401; part-time $775.17 per hour. Required fees: $1203. *Financial support:* In 2009–10, 3 fellowships, 18 research assistantships, 7 teaching assistantships were awarded; career-related internships or fieldwork and Federal Work-Study also available. Support available to part-time students. Financial award application deadline: 4/1; financial award applicants required to submit FAFSA. *Unit head:* Dr. Joseph Rencis, Departmental Chair, 479-575-3153, Fax: 479-575-6982, E-mail: jjrencis@uark.edu. *Application contact:* Dr. Rick Couvillion, Graduate Coordinator, 479-575-4155, E-mail: rjc@uark.edu.

University of Bridgeport, School of Engineering, Department of Mechanical Engineering, Bridgeport, CT 06604. Offers MS. *Degree requirements:* For master's, thesis optional. *Entrance requirements:* Additional exam requirements/recommendations for international students: Recommended—TOEFL (minimum score 550 paper-based; 213 computer-based; 80 iBT), IELTS (minimum score 6.5). Electronic applications accepted. *Faculty research:* Residual stress in composite material resins, helicopter composite structure and dynamic components, water spray cooling, heat transfer.

The University of British Columbia, Faculty of Applied Science, Program in Mechanical Engineering, Vancouver, BC V6T 1Z1, Canada. Offers M Eng, MA Sc, PhD. *Degree requirements:* For master's, thesis; for doctorate, comprehensive exam, thesis/dissertation, 33 credits beyond bachelor's degree. *Entrance requirements:* For master's, bachelor's degree, minimum B+ average; for doctorate, master's degree, minimum B+ average. Additional exam requirements/recommendations for international students: Required—TOEFL (minimum score 580 paper-based; 237 computer-based; 93 iBT), IELTS (minimum score 6.5), GRE (recommended); Recommended—TWE. Electronic applications accepted. *Faculty research:* Applied mechanics, manufacturing, robotics and controls, thermodynamics and combustion, fluid/aerodynamics, acoustics.

University of Calgary, Faculty of Graduate Studies, Schulich School of Engineering, Department of Mechanical and Manufacturing Engineering, Calgary, AB T2N 1N4, Canada. Offers M Eng, M Sc, PhD. *Degree requirements:* For master's, thesis (for some programs); for doctorate, thesis/dissertation, candidacy exam. *Entrance requirements:* For master's, minimum GPA of 3.0; for doctorate, minimum GPA of 3.3. Additional exam requirements/recommendations for international students: Required—TOEFL (minimum score 550 paper-based; 213 computer-based), IELTS (minimum score 7). *Faculty research:* Thermofluids, solid mechanics, materials, biomechanics, manufacturing.

University of California, Berkeley, Graduate Division, College of Engineering, Department of Mechanical Engineering, Berkeley, CA 94720-1500. Offers M Eng, MS, D Eng, PhD. *Students:* 328 full-time (70 women). Average age 27. 897 applicants, 60 enrolled. In 2009, 90 master's, 41 doctorates awarded. *Degree requirements:* For master's, comprehensive exam or thesis (MS); for doctorate, thesis/dissertation, preliminary and qualifying exams. *Entrance requirements:* For master's and doctorate, GRE General Test, minimum GPA of 3.0, 3 letters of recommendation. Additional exam requirements/recommendations for international students: Required—TOEFL. *Application deadline:* For fall admission, 12/5 for domestic students. Application fee: $70 ($90 for international students). *Financial support:* Fellowships, unspecified assistantships available. *Unit head:* Prof. Albert P. Pisano, Chair, 510-642-1338, Fax: 510-642-6163. *Application contact:* Patricia Giddings, Graduate Assistant, 510-642-5084, Fax: 510-642-6163, E-mail: mech@me.berkeley.edu.

University of California, Davis, College of Engineering, Program in Mechanical and Aeronautical Engineering, Davis, CA 95616. Offers aeronautical engineering (M Engr, MS, D Engr, PhD, Certificate); mechanical engineering (M Engr, MS, D Engr, PhD, Certificate); M Engr/MBA. *Degree requirements:* For master's, comprehensive exam (for some programs), thesis (for some programs); for doctorate, thesis/dissertation. *Entrance requirements:* For master's and doctorate, GRE General Test, minimum GPA of 3.0. Additional exam requirements/recommendations for international students: Required—TOEFL (minimum score 550 paper-based; 213 computer-based). Electronic applications accepted.

University of California, Irvine, Office of Graduate Studies, School of Engineering, Department of Mechanical and Aerospace Engineering, Irvine, CA 92697. Offers MS, PhD. Part-time programs available. *Students:* 113 full-time (21 women), 11 part-time (2 women); includes 32 minority (23 Asian Americans or Pacific Islanders, 9 Hispanic Americans), 52 international. Average age 27. 343 applicants, 27% accepted, 38 enrolled. In 2009, 31 master's, 17 doctorates awarded. Terminal master's awarded for partial completion of doctoral program. *Degree requirements:* For doctorate, thesis/dissertation. *Entrance requirements:* For master's, GRE General Test, minimum GPA of 3.0. 3 letters of recommendation; for doctorate, GRE General Test, minimum GPA of 3.0, 3 letters of recommendation. Additional exam requirements/recommendations for international students: Required—TOEFL (minimum score 550 paper-based; 213 computer-based). *Application deadline:* For fall admission, 1/15 priority date for domestic students, 1/15 for international students. Applications are processed on a rolling basis. Application fee: $70 ($90 for international students). Electronic applications accepted. *Financial support:* In 2009–10, fellowships with tuition reimbursements (averaging $14,656 per year); research assistantships with full tuition reimbursements, teaching assistantships with tuition reimbursements, institutionally sponsored loans, traineeships, health care benefits, and unspecified assistantships also available. Financial award application deadline: 3/1; financial award applicants required to submit FAFSA. *Faculty research:* Thermal and fluid sciences, combustion and propulsion, control systems, robotics, lightweight structures. *Unit head:* Dr. Simitri Papamoschoy, Chair, 949-824-6590, Fax: 949-824-3726. *Application contact:* Leslie Noel, Graduate Coordinator, 949-824-7984, Fax: 949-824-8585, E-mail: lknoel@uci.edu.

University of California, Los Angeles, Graduate Division, Henry Samueli School of Engineering and Applied Science, Department of Mechanical and Aerospace Engineering, Program in Mechanical Engineering, Los Angeles, CA 90095-1597. Offers MS, PhD. *Students:* 205 full-time (27 women); includes 58 minority (2 African Americans, 46 Asian Americans or Pacific Islanders, 10 Hispanic Americans), 75 international. 336 applicants, 46% accepted, 63 enrolled. In 2009, 51 master's, 24 doctorates awarded. *Degree requirements:* For master's, comprehensive exam or thesis; for doctorate, thesis/dissertation, qualifying exams. *Entrance requirements:* For master's, GRE General Test, minimum GPA of 3.0; for doctorate, GRE General Test, minimum GPA of 3.25. Additional exam requirements/recommendations for international students: Required—TOEFL (minimum score 560 paper-based; 220 computer-based). *Application deadline:* For fall admission, 1/5 for domestic and international students; for winter admission, 10/1 for domestic students; for spring admission, 12/31 for domestic students. Application fee: $70 ($90 for international students). Electronic applications accepted. *Financial support:* Fellowships, research assistantships, teaching assistantships, Federal Work-Study, institutionally sponsored loans, and tuition waivers (full and partial) available. Financial award application deadline: 1/5; financial award applicants required to submit FAFSA. *Unit head:* Dr. Adrienne Lavine, Chair, 310-825-7468. *Application contact:* Angie Castillo, Student Affairs Officer, 310-825-7793, Fax: 310-206-4830, E-mail: angie@ea.ucla.edu.

University of California, Merced, Division of Graduate Studies, School of Natural Sciences, Merced, CA 95343. Offers applied mathematics (MS, PhD); biological engineering and small-scale technologies (MS, PhD); environmental systems (MS, PhD); mechanical engineering and applied mechanics (MS, PhD); physics and chemistry (PhD); quantitative and systems biology (MS, PhD). *Expenses:* Tuition, nonresident: full-time $15,102. Required fees: $10,919.

University of California, Riverside, Graduate Division, Department of Mechanical Engineering, Riverside, CA 92521. Offers MS, PhD. Part-time programs available. Terminal master's awarded for partial completion of doctoral program. *Degree requirements:* For master's, comprehensive exam or thesis, seminar in mechanical engineering; for doctorate, comprehensive exam, thesis/dissertation, seminar in mechanical engineering. *Entrance requirements:* Additional exam requirements/recommendations for international students: Required—TOEFL (minimum score 550 paper-based; 213 computer-based; 80 iBT). *Faculty research:* Advanced robotics and machine design, air quality modeling group, computational fluid dynamics, computational mechanics and materials, biomaterials and nanotechnology laboratory.

University of California, San Diego, Office of Graduate Studies, Department of Mechanical and Aerospace Engineering, Program in Mechanical Engineering, La Jolla, CA 92093. Offers MS, PhD. Part-time programs available. *Degree requirements:* For master's, comprehensive exam or thesis; for doctorate, thesis/dissertation, qualifying exam. *Entrance requirements:* For master's and doctorate, GRE General Test, minimum GPA of 3.0. Additional exam requirements/recommendations for international students: Required—TOEFL. Electronic applications accepted. *Faculty research:* Combustion engineering, environmental mechanics, magnetic recording, materials processing, computational fluid dynamics.

University of California, Santa Barbara, Graduate Division, College of Engineering, Department of Mechanical Engineering, Santa Barbara, CA 93106-5070. Offers computational science and engineering (PhD); mechanical engineering (MS, PhD); MS/PhD. *Faculty:* 33 full-time (4 women), 5 part-time/adjunct (0 women). *Students:* 74 full-time (15 women). Average age 27. 204 applicants, 21% accepted, 15 enrolled. In 2009, 2 master's, 15 doctorates awarded. *Degree requirements:* For master's, thesis; for doctorate, comprehensive exam, thesis/dissertation. *Entrance requirements:* For master's, GRE, 3 letters of recommendation, statement of purpose, personal achievements/contributions statement, resume/curriculum vitae, transcripts for post-secondary institutions attended; for doctorate, GRE General Test, 3 letters of recommendation, resume/curriculum vitae. Additional exam requirements/recommendations for international students: Required—TOEFL (minimum score 550 paper-based; 213 computer-based; 80 iBT) or IELTS (minimum score 7). *Application deadline:* For fall admission, 1/1 for domestic and international students. Application fee: $70 ($90 for international students). Electronic applications accepted. *Financial support:* In 2009–10, 72 students received support, including 29 fellowships with full and partial tuition reimbursements available (averaging $11,500 per year), 55 research assistantships with full and partial tuition reimbursements available (averaging $10,800 per year), 40 teaching assistantships with partial tuition reimbursements available (averaging $7,100 per year); Federal Work-Study, institutionally sponsored loans, scholarships/grants, health care benefits, tuition waivers (full and partial), and unspecified assistantships also available. Financial award application deadline: 1/1; financial award applicants required to submit FAFSA. *Faculty research:* Micro/nanoscale technology; computational science and engineering; dynamics, controls and robotics; thermofluid sciences, solid mechanics, materials, and structures. Total annual research expenditures: $4.9 million. *Unit head:* Prof. Kimberly Turner, Chair, 805-893-5106, Fax: 805-893-8486, E-mail: turner@engineering.ucsb.edu. *Application contact:* Laura Reynolds, Staff Graduate Program Advisor, 805-893-2239, Fax: 805-893-8651, E-mail: meegrad@engineering.ucsb.edu.

University of Central Florida, College of Engineering and Computer Science, Department of Mechanical, Materials, and Aerospace Engineering, Program in Mechanical Engineering, Orlando, FL 32816. Offers mechanical engineering (MSME, PhD). *Students:* 66 full-time (7 women), 50 part-time (3 women); includes 24 minority (2 African Americans, 8 Asian Americans or Pacific Islanders, 14 Hispanic Americans), 32 international. Average age 28. 110 applicants, 72% accepted, 49 enrolled. In 2009, 12 master's, 8 doctorates awarded. *Degree requirements:* For master's, thesis or alternative; for doctorate, thesis/dissertation, candidacy exam, departmental qualifying exam. *Application deadline:* For fall admission, 7/15 priority date for domestic students; for spring admission, 12/1 priority date for domestic students. Electronic applications accepted. *Expenses:* Tuition, state resident: part-time $306.31 per credit hour. Tuition, nonresident: part-time $1099.01 per credit hour. Part-time tuition and fees vary according to degree level and program. *Financial support:* In 2009–10, 46 students received support, including 8 fellowships (averaging $7,200 per year), 31 research assistantships (averaging $8,100 per year), 22 teaching assistantships (averaging $6,600 per year); career-related internships or fieldwork, institutionally sponsored loans, scholarships/grants, tuition waivers (partial), and unspecified assistantships also available.

University of Cincinnati, Graduate School, College of Engineering, Department of Mechanical, Industrial and Nuclear Engineering, Program in Mechanical Engineering, Cincinnati, OH 45221. Offers MS, PhD. Evening/weekend programs available. Terminal master's awarded for partial completion of doctoral program. *Degree requirements:* For master's, oral exam or thesis defense; for doctorate, variable foreign language requirement, thesis/dissertation. *Entrance requirements:* For master's and doctorate, GRE General Test. Additional exam requirements/recommendations for international students: Required—TOEFL (minimum score 575 paper-based; 233 computer-based). Electronic applications accepted. *Faculty research:* Signature analysis, structural analysis, energy, design, robotics.

University of Colorado at Boulder, Graduate School, College of Engineering and Applied Science, Department of Mechanical Engineering, Boulder, CO 80309. Offers ME, MS, PhD. Part-time programs available. *Faculty:* 23 full-time (5 women). *Students:* 172 full-time (25 women), 28 part-time (7 women); includes 22 minority (1 African American, 2 American Indian/Alaska Native, 12 Asian Americans or Pacific Islanders, 7 Hispanic Americans), 53 international. Average age 26. 274 applicants, 42% accepted, 54 enrolled. In 2009, 36 master's, 10 doctorates awarded. Terminal master's awarded for partial completion of doctoral program. *Degree requirements:* For master's, comprehensive exam, thesis optional; for doctorate, comprehensive exam, thesis/dissertation, final and preliminary exams. *Entrance requirements:* For master's and doctorate, minimum undergraduate GPA of 3.0. Additional exam requirements/recommendations for international students: Required—TOEFL. *Application deadline:* For fall admission, 1/15 priority date for domestic students, 12/1 for international students; for spring admission, 10/15 for domestic students, 9/1 for international students. Applications are processed on a rolling basis. Application fee: $50 ($60 for international students). *Financial support:* In 2009–10, 37 fellowships with full tuition reimbursements (averaging $11,900 per year), 72 research assistantships with full tuition reimbursements (averaging $16,054 per year), 18 teaching assistantships with full tuition reimbursements (averaging $14,537 per year) were awarded; career-related internships or fieldwork also available. Financial award application deadline: 1/15. *Faculty research:* Thermal science, fluid mechanics, solid mechanics, materials science, interactive design and manufacturing. Total annual research expenditures: $7.4 million.

University of Colorado at Colorado Springs, Graduate School, College of Engineering and Applied Science, Department of Mechanical and Aerospace Engineering, Colorado Springs, CO 80933-7150. Offers engineering management (ME); information operations (ME); manufacturing (ME); mechanical engineering (MS); software engineering (ME); space operations (ME); space systems (MS). Part-time and evening/weekend programs available. *Faculty:* 10 full-time (2 women). *Students:* 14 full-time (4 women), 13 part-time (2 women); includes 3 minority (2 Asian Americans or Pacific Islanders, 1 Hispanic American). Average age 30. 39 applicants, 82% accepted, 16 enrolled. In 2009, 6 master's awarded. *Degree requirements:* For master's, thesis optional. *Entrance requirements:* For master's, GRE General Test, bachelor's degree in engineering or related degree, minimum GPA of 3.0. Additional exam requirements/recommendations for international students: Required—TOEFL. *Application deadline:* For fall admission, 5/1 for domestic students; for spring admission, 10/1 for domestic students. Applications are processed on a rolling basis. Application fee: $60 ($75 for international students). *Expenses:* Tuition, state resident: full-time $8922; part-time $639 per credit hour. Tuition, nonresident: full-time $19,372; part-time $1154 per credit hour. Tuition and fees vary according to course level, course load, degree level, program, reciprocity agreements and student level. *Financial support:* Federal Work-Study and scholarships/grants available. Support available to part-time students. Financial award application deadline: 3/1; financial award applicants required to submit FAFSA. *Faculty research:* Neural networks, artificial intelligence, robust control, space operations, space propulsion. *Unit head:* Dr. T. S. Kalkur, Chair, 719-255-3147, Fax: 719-255-3042, E-mail: kalkur@eas.uccs.edu. *Application contact:* Siew Nylund, Academic Adviser, 719-255-3243, Fax: 719-255-3589, E-mail: snylund@eas.uccs.edu.

University of Colorado Denver, College of Engineering and Applied Science, Department of Mechanical Engineering, Denver, CO 80217-3364. Offers M Eng, MS. Part-time and evening/weekend programs available. *Students:* 7 full-time (0 women), 31 part-time (4 women); includes 6 minority (2 African Americans, 2 Asian Americans or Pacific Islanders, 2 Hispanic Americans), 8 international. 41 applicants, 59% accepted, 14 enrolled. In 2009, 9 master's awarded. *Degree requirements:* For master's, comprehensive exam, thesis or alternative. *Entrance requirements:* For master's, GRE. Additional exam requirements/recommendations for international students: Required—TOEFL (minimum score 525 paper-based; 197 computer-based). *Application deadline:* For fall admission, 4/1 for domestic students; for spring admission, 10/1 for domestic students. Applications are processed on a rolling basis. Application fee: $50 ($75 for international students). Electronic applications accepted. *Financial support:* Research assistantships, teaching assistantships, career-related internships or fieldwork and Federal Work-Study available. Financial award application deadline: 4/1; financial award applicants required to submit FAFSA. *Unit head:* Dr. Sam Welch, Chair, 303-556-8488, Fax: 303-556-6371, E-mail: sam.welch@ucdenver.edu. *Application contact:* Petrina Mazza, Program Assistant, 303-556-8516, Fax: 303-556-6371, E-mail: petrina.mazza@ucdenver.edu.

University of Connecticut, Graduate School, School of Engineering, Department of Mechanical Engineering, Storrs, CT 06269. Offers MS, PhD. *Faculty:* 35 full-time (1 woman). *Students:* 74 full-time (9 women), 27 part-time (2 women); includes 7 minority (3 African Americans, 4 Asian Americans or Pacific Islanders), 45 international. Average age 28. 190 applicants, 16% accepted, 19 enrolled. In 2009, 13 master's, 4 doctorates awarded. Terminal master's awarded for partial completion of doctoral program. *Degree requirements:* For master's, comprehensive exam, thesis or alternative; for doctorate, thesis/dissertation. *Entrance requirements:* For master's and doctorate, GRE General Test, GRE Subject Test. Additional exam requirements/recommendations for international students: Required—TOEFL (minimum score 550 paper-based; 213 computer-based). *Application deadline:* For fall admission, 2/1 priority date for domestic and international students; for spring admission, 11/1 for domestic students, 10/1 for international students. Applications are processed on a rolling basis. Application fee: $55. Electronic applications accepted. *Expenses:* Tuition, state resident: full-time $4725; part-time $525 per credit. Tuition, nonresident: full-time $12,267; part-time $1363 per credit. Required fees: $346 per semester. Tuition and fees vary according to course load. *Financial support:* In 2009–10, 59 research assistantships with full tuition reimbursements, 8 teaching assistantships with full tuition reimbursements were awarded; fellowships, Federal Work-Study, scholarships/grants, health care benefits, and unspecified assistantships also available. Financial award application deadline: 2/1; financial award applicants required to submit FAFSA. *Faculty research:* Design, applied mechanics, dynamics and control, energy and thermal sciences, manufacturing. *Unit head:* Baki Cetegen, Head, 860-486-2966, Fax: 860-486-5088, E-mail: cetegen@engr.uconn.edu. *Application contact:* Michael W. Renfro, Director of Graduate Studies, 860-486-5937, Fax: 860-486-5088, E-mail: renfro@engr.uconn.edu.

University of Dayton, Graduate School, School of Engineering, Department of Mechanical and Aerospace Engineering, Dayton, OH 45469-1300. Offers aerospace engineering (MSAE, DE, PhD); mechanical engineering (MSME, DE, PhD); renewable and clean energy (MS). Part-time programs available. Postbaccalaureate distance learning degree programs offered (no on-campus study). *Faculty:* 15 full-time (2 women), 13 part-time/adjunct (1 woman). *Students:* 83 full-time (16 women), 29 part-time (5 women); includes 13 minority (6 African Americans, 3 Asian Americans or Pacific Islanders, 4 Hispanic Americans), 32 international. Average age 30. 80 applicants, 50% accepted, 24 enrolled. In 2009, 24 master's, 5 doctorates awarded. Terminal master's awarded for partial completion of doctoral program. *Degree requirements:* For master's, thesis optional; for doctorate, variable foreign language requirement, thesis/dissertation, departmental qualifying exam. *Entrance requirements:* Additional exam requirements/recommendations for international students: Required—TOEFL (minimum score 550 paper-based; 213 computer-based; 80 iBT). *Application deadline:* For fall admission, 8/1 priority date for domestic students, 6/1 priority date for international students; for winter admission, 9/1 priority date for international students; for spring admission, 3/1 priority date for international students. Applications are processed on a rolling basis. Application fee: $0. Electronic applications accepted. *Expenses:* Tuition: Full-time $8412; part-time $701 per credit hour. Required fees: $325; $65 per course. $25 per semester. Tuition and fees vary according to course load, degree level and program. *Financial support:* In 2009–10, 25 students received support, including 2 fellowships with full tuition reimbursements available (averaging $27,500 per year), 22 research assistantships with full tuition reimbursements available (averaging $12,000 per year), 1 teaching assistantship (averaging $9,000 per year). Financial award applicants required to submit FAFSA. *Faculty research:* Jet engine combustion, surface coating friction and wear, aircraft thermal management, aerospace fuels, energy efficient buildings, energy efficient manufacturing, renewable energy. Total annual research expenditures: $1.2 million. *Unit head:* Dr. Kevin Hallinan, Chair, 937-229-2835, Fax: 937-229-4766, E-mail: kevin.hallinan@udayton.edu. *Application contact:* Graduate Admissions, 937-229-4411, Fax: 937-229-4729, E-mail: gradadmission@udayton.edu.

University of Delaware, College of Engineering, Department of Mechanical Engineering, Newark, DE 19716. Offers MEM, MSME, PhD. Part-time programs available. Terminal master's awarded for partial completion of doctoral program. *Degree requirements:* For master's, thesis (for some programs); for doctorate, thesis/dissertation. *Entrance requirements:* For master's and doctorate, GRE General Test. Additional exam requirements/recommendations for international students: Required—TOEFL (minimum score 600 paper-based; 250 computer-based). Electronic applications accepted. *Faculty research:* Biomedical engineering, clean energy, composites and nanotechnology, robotics and controls, fluid mechanics.

University of Denver, School of Engineering and Computer Science, Department of Mechanical and Materials Engineering, Denver, CO 80208. Offers bioengineering (MS); engineering (MS, PhD); materials science (PhD); mechanical engineering (MS); mechatronics (MS). *Faculty:* 9 full-time (1 woman), 2 part-time/adjunct (1 woman). *Students:* 1 full-time (0 women), 17 part-time (12 women), 3 international. Average age 31. 46 applicants, 61% accepted, 12 enrolled. In 2009, 9 master's awarded. *Expenses:* Tuition: Full-time $34,596; part-time $961 per quarter hour. Required fees: $4 per quarter hour. Tuition and fees vary according to course load, campus/location and program. *Financial support:* In 2009–10, 3 research assistantships (averaging $11,000 per year), 5 teaching assistantships (averaging $11,000 per year) were awarded. *Faculty research:* Aerosols, biomechanics, composite materials, photo optics, drug delivery. Total annual research expenditures: $565,000. *Unit head:* Dr. Maciej Kumosa, Chair, 303-871-3807. *Application contact:* Dr. Maciej Kumosa, Chair, 303-871-3807.

University of Detroit Mercy, College of Engineering and Science, Department of Mechanical Engineering, Detroit, MI 48221. Offers mechanical engineering (ME, DE). Evening/weekend programs available. *Degree requirements:* For doctorate, thesis/dissertation. *Faculty research:* CAD/CAM.

University of Florida, Graduate School, College of Engineering, Department of Mechanical and Aerospace Engineering, Gainesville, FL 32611. Offers aerospace engineering (ME, MS, PhD, Engr); mechanical engineering (ME, MS, PhD, Engr). Part-time programs available. *Degree requirements:* For master's, thesis (for some programs); for doctorate, thesis/dissertation; for Engr, thesis. *Entrance requirements:* For master's and doctorate, GRE General Test, minimum GPA of 3.0; for Engr, GRE General Test. Additional exam requirements/recommendations for international students: Required—TOEFL (minimum score 550 paper-based; 213 computer-based). Electronic applications accepted. *Faculty research:* Thermal sciences, design, controls and robotics, manufacturing, energy transport and utilization.

University of Hawaii at Manoa, Graduate Division, College of Engineering, Department of Mechanical Engineering, Honolulu, HI 96822. Offers MS, PhD. Part-time programs available. *Faculty:* 12 full-time (0 women), 8 part-time/adjunct (1 woman). *Students:* 31 full-time (4 women), 10 part-time (1 woman); includes 9 minority (8 Asian Americans or Pacific Islanders, 1 Hispanic American), 19 international. Average age 26. 33 applicants, 67% accepted, 13 enrolled. In 2009, 8 master's, 2 doctorates awarded. *Degree requirements:* For master's, comprehensive exam, thesis; for doctorate, comprehensive exam, thesis/dissertation. *Entrance requirements:* For master's and doctorate, GRE General Test. Additional exam requirements/recommendations for international students: Required—TOEFL (minimum score 550 paper-based; 213 computer-based; 79 iBT), IELTS (minimum score 5). *Application deadline:* For fall admission, 3/1 for domestic students, 1/15 for international students; for spring admission, 9/1 for domestic students, 8/1 for international students. Applications are processed on a rolling basis. Application fee: $60. *Expenses:* Tuition, state resident: full-time $8900; part-time $372 per credit. Tuition, nonresident: full-time $21,400; part-time $898 per credit. Required fees: $207 per semester. *Financial support:* In 2009–10, 1 student received support, including 4 fellowships (averaging $1,000 per year), 21 research assistantships (averaging $19,178 per year), 5 teaching assistantships (averaging $15,558 per year); tuition waivers (full) also available. Financial award application deadline: 8/31; financial award applicants required to submit FAFSA. *Faculty research:* Materials and manufacturing; mechanics, systems and control; thermal and fluid sciences. Total annual research expenditures: $472,000. *Application contact:* Ronald Knapp, Graduate Chairperson, 808-956-7167, Fax: 808-956-2373, E-mail: knapp@hawaii.edu.

University of Houston, Cullen College of Engineering, Department of Mechanical Engineering, Houston, TX 77204. Offers MME, MSME, PhD. Part-time and evening/weekend programs available. *Faculty:* 23 full-time (1 woman), 1 (woman) part-time/adjunct. *Students:* 63 full-time (6 women), 29 part-time (5 women); includes 9 minority (1 African American, 4 Asian Americans or Pacific Islanders, 4 Hispanic Americans), 59 international. Average age 27. 129 applicants, 50% accepted, 27 enrolled. In 2009, 12 master's, 9 doctorates awarded. Terminal master's awarded for partial completion of doctoral program. *Degree requirements:* For master's, thesis (for some programs); for doctorate, thesis/dissertation, departmental qualifying exam. *Entrance requirements:* For master's and doctorate, GRE General Test. Additional exam requirements/recommendations for international students: Required—TOEFL. *Application deadline:* For fall admission, 5/1 for domestic students, 3/1 for international students; for spring admission, 11/1 for domestic students, 10/1 for international students. Application fee: $25 ($75 for international students). *Expenses:* Tuition, state resident: full-time $7676; part-time $320 per credit hour. Tuition, nonresident: full-time $14,324; part-time $597 per credit hour. Required fees: $3034. *Financial support:* In 2009–10, 1 fellowship with full tuition reimbursement (averaging $12,300 per year), 45 research assistantships with full tuition reimbursements (averaging $12,300 per year), 20 teaching assistantships with full tuition reimbursements (averaging $12,300 per year) were awarded; career-related internships or fieldwork, Federal Work-Study, institutionally sponsored loans, scholarships/grants, health care benefits, and unspecified assistantships also available. Support available to part-time students. Financial award application deadline: 3/10. *Unit head:* Dr. David Zimmerman, Interim Chairperson, 713-743-4520, Fax: 713-743-4503, E-mail: dzimmerman@uh.edu. *Application contact:* Trina Johnson, Academic Advisor, 713-743-4505, Fax: 713-743-3722, E-mail: tajohnson@uh.edu.

University of Illinois at Chicago, Graduate College, College of Engineering, Department of Mechanical and Industrial Engineering, Chicago, IL 60607-7128. Offers energy engineering (MEE); industrial engineering (MS); industrial engineering and operations research (PhD); mechanical engineering (MS, PhD), including fluids engineering, mechanical analysis and design, thermomechanical and power engineering. Part-time programs available. *Degree requirements:* For doctorate, thesis/dissertation. *Entrance requirements:* For master's and doctorate, GRE General Test, minimum GPA of 2.75. Additional exam requirements/recommendations for international students: Required—TOEFL. Electronic applications accepted.

University of Illinois at Urbana–Champaign, Graduate College, College of Engineering, Department of Mechanical Science and Engineering, Champaign, IL 61820. Offers mechanical engineering (MS, PhD); theoretical and applied mechanics (MS, PhD); MS/MBA. *Faculty:* 54 full-time (4 women), 2 part-time/adjunct (0 women). *Students:* 331 full-time (38 women), 34 part-time (5 women); includes 28 minority (1 African American, 18 Asian Americans or Pacific Islanders, 9 Hispanic Americans), 189 international. 488 applicants, 39% accepted, 95 enrolled. In 2009, 48 master's, 32 doctorates awarded. Terminal master's awarded for partial completion of doctoral program. *Entrance requirements:* For master's, GRE General Test, minimum GPA of 3.25; for doctorate, GRE General Test, minimum GPA of 3.5. Additional exam requirements/recommendations for international students: Required—TOEFL (minimum score 613 paper-based; 257 computer-based; 103 iBT), v. *Application deadline:* Applications are processed on a rolling basis. Application fee: $60 ($75 for international students). Electronic applications accepted. *Financial support:* In 2009–10, 37 fellowships, 271 research assistantships, 90 teaching assistantships were awarded; tuition waivers (full and partial) also available. *Faculty research:* Combustion and propulsion, design methodology, dynamic systems and controls, energy transfer, materials behavior and processing, manufacturing systems operations, management. *Unit head:* Placid Mathew Ferreira, Head, 217-333-0639, Fax: 217-244-6534, E-mail: pferreir@illinois.edu. *Application contact:* Kathy A. Smith, Admissions and Records Officer, 217-244-4539, Fax: 217-244-6534, E-mail: smith15@illinois.edu.

The University of Iowa, Graduate College, College of Engineering, Department of Mechanical Engineering, Iowa City, IA 52242-1316. Offers MS, PhD. *Faculty:* 15 full-time (1 woman). *Students:* 58 full-time (7 women); includes 3 minority (1 African American, 2 Asian Americans or Pacific Islanders), 36 international. Average age 27. 103 applicants, 27% accepted, 12 enrolled. In 2009, 12 master's, 9 doctorates awarded. *Degree requirements:* For master's, thesis optional, oral exam (if no thesis); for doctorate, comprehensive exam, thesis/dissertation. *Entrance requirements:* For master's and doctorate, GRE. Additional exam requirements/recommendations for international students: Required—TOEFL (minimum score 550 paper-based; 213 computer-based; 81 iBT). *Application deadline:* For fall admission, 7/15 for domestic students, 4/15 for international students; for spring admission, 12/1 for domestic students, 10/1 for international students. Applications are processed on a rolling basis. Application fee: $60 ($100 for international students). Electronic applications accepted. *Financial support:* In 2009–10, 1 fellowship with partial tuition reimbursement (averaging $26,438 per year), 55 research assistantships with partial tuition reimbursements (averaging $21,930 per year), 18 teaching assistantships with partial tuition reimbursements (averaging $16,575 per year) were awarded; traineeships and unspecified assistantships also available. Financial award applicants required to submit FAFSA. *Faculty research:* Computer simulation methodology; biomechanics; dynamics; solid mechanics; fluid dynamics. Total annual research expenditures: $8.3 million. *Unit head:* Dr. Lea-Der Chen, Departmental Executive Officer, 319-335-5674, Fax: 319-335-5669, E-mail:

Mechanical Engineering

The University of Iowa (continued)

lea-der-chen@uiowa.edu. *Application contact:* Jennifer Rumping, Secretary, 319-335-5668, Fax: 319-335-5669, E-mail: mech_eng@engineering.uiowa.edu.

The University of Kansas, Graduate Studies, School of Engineering, Department of Mechanical Engineering, Lawrence, KS 66045. Offers MS, DE, PhD. Part-time programs available. *Faculty:* 17 full-time (4 women). *Students:* 41 full-time (7 women), 6 part-time (0 women), 17 international. Average age 25. 70 applicants, 37% accepted, 13 enrolled. In 2009, 6 master's, 2 doctorates awarded. *Degree requirements:* For master's, thesis or alternative, exam; for doctorate, comprehensive exam, thesis/dissertation. *Entrance requirements:* For master's, minimum GPA of 3.0; for doctorate, minimum GPA of 3.5. Additional exam requirements/recommendations for international students: Required—TOEFL. *Application deadline:* For fall admission, 6/1 priority date for domestic students, 3/31 priority date for international students; for spring admission, 11/1 priority date for domestic students, 9/30 priority date for international students. Applications are processed on a rolling basis. Application fee: $45 ($55 for international students). Electronic applications accepted. *Expenses:* Tuition, state resident: full-time $6492; part-time $270.50 per credit hour. Tuition, nonresident: full-time $15,510; part-time $646.25 per credit hour. Required fees: $847; $70.56 per credit hour. Tuition and fees vary according to course load and program. *Financial support:* Fellowships with full and partial tuition reimbursements, research assistantships with full and partial tuition reimbursements, teaching assistantships with full and partial tuition reimbursements, career-related internships or fieldwork available. Financial award application deadline: 5/15. *Faculty research:* Heat transfer, energy analysis, computer-aided design, biomedical engineering, computational mathematics. *Unit head:* Ronald Dougherty, Chair, 785-864-3181, E-mail: kume@ku.edu. *Application contact:* Glen Marotz, Associate Dean, 785-864-2941, Fax: 785-864-5445, E-mail: gama@ku.edu.

University of Kentucky, Graduate School, College of Engineering, Program in Mechanical Engineering, Lexington, KY 40506-0032. Offers MSME, PhD. *Degree requirements:* For master's, comprehensive exam, thesis optional; for doctorate, comprehensive exam, thesis/dissertation. *Entrance requirements:* For master's, GRE General Test, minimum undergraduate GPA of 2.75; for doctorate, GRE General Test, minimum undergraduate GPA of 3.0. Additional exam requirements/recommendations for international students: Required—TOEFL (minimum score 550 paper-based; 213 computer-based). Electronic applications accepted. *Faculty research:* Combustion, computational fluid dynamics, design and systems, manufacturing, thermal and fluid sciences.

University of Louisiana at Lafayette, College of Engineering, Department of Mechanical Engineering, Lafayette, LA 70504. Offers MSE. Evening/weekend programs available. *Degree requirements:* For master's, comprehensive exam, thesis or alternative. *Entrance requirements:* For master's, GRE General Test, BS in mechanical engineering, minimum GPA of 2.85. Additional exam requirements/recommendations for international students: Required—TOEFL (minimum score 550 paper-based; 213 computer-based). Electronic applications accepted. *Faculty research:* CAD/CAM, machine design and vibration, thermal science.

University of Louisville, J.B. Speed School of Engineering, Department of Mechanical Engineering, Louisville, KY 40292-0001. Offers M Eng, MS, PhD. *Accreditation:* ABET (one or more programs are accredited). Part-time programs available. *Faculty:* 16 full-time (5 women), 1 part-time/adjunct (0 women). *Students:* 78 full-time (10 women), 24 part-time (2 women); includes 7 minority (5 Asian Americans or Pacific Islanders, 2 Hispanic Americans), 15 international. Average age 27. 29 applicants, 69% accepted, 11 enrolled. In 2009, 48 master's, 2 doctorates awarded. Terminal master's awarded for partial completion of doctoral program. *Degree requirements:* For master's, comprehensive exam (for some programs), thesis or alternative; for doctorate, comprehensive exam, thesis/dissertation, minimum GPA of 3.0. *Entrance requirements:* For master's and doctorate, GRE General Test. Additional exam requirements/recommendations for international students: Required—TOEFL (minimum score 550 paper-based; 213 computer-based; 80 iBT). *Application deadline:* For fall admission, 7/12 priority date for domestic and international students; for winter admission, 11/29 priority date for domestic and international students; for spring admission, 3/28 priority date for domestic and international students. Applications are processed on a rolling basis. Application fee: $50. Electronic applications accepted. *Financial support:* In 2009–10, 21 students received support, including 3 fellowships with full tuition reimbursements available (averaging $20,000 per year), 8 research assistantships with full tuition reimbursements available (averaging $19,000 per year), 9 teaching assistantships with full tuition reimbursements available (averaging $20,000 per year). Financial award application deadline: 1/25; financial award applicants required to submit FAFSA. *Faculty research:* Aerospace and automotive engineering, air pollution control, biomechanics and rehabilitation engineering, computer-aided design, micro and nanotechnology. Total annual research expenditures: $1.6 million. *Unit head:* Dr. Glen Prater, Chair, 502-852-6331, Fax: 502-852-6053, E-mail: gprater@louisville.edu. *Application contact:* Dr. Michael Day, Associate Dean, 502-852-6195, Fax: 502-852-7294, E-mail: day@louisville.edu.

University of Maine, Graduate School, College of Engineering, Department of Mechanical Engineering, Orono, ME 04469. Offers MS, PhD. *Faculty:* 10 full-time (0 women), 1 part-time/adjunct (0 women). *Students:* 16 full-time (1 woman), 8 part-time (1 woman); includes 1 minority (Asian American or Pacific Islander), 8 international. Average age 31. 27 applicants, 41% accepted, 7 enrolled. In 2009, 2 master's awarded. *Degree requirements:* For master's, thesis (for some programs). *Entrance requirements:* For master's and doctorate, GRE General Test. Additional exam requirements/recommendations for international students: Required—TOEFL. *Application deadline:* For fall admission, 2/1 priority date for domestic students. Applications are processed on a rolling basis. Application fee: $65. Electronic applications accepted. *Financial support:* In 2009–10, 17 research assistantships with tuition reimbursements (averaging $16,800 per year), 2 teaching assistantships with tuition reimbursements (averaging $12,790 per year) were awarded; Federal Work-Study and tuition waivers (full and partial) also available. Financial award application deadline: 3/1. *Faculty research:* Higher order beam and plate theories, dynamic response of structural systems, heat transfer in window systems, forced convection heat transfer in gas turbine passages, effect of parallel space heating systems on utility load management. *Unit head:* Dr. Moshen Shahinpoor, Chair, 207-581-2120, Fax: 207-581-2379. *Application contact:* Scott G. Delcourt, Associate Dean of the Graduate School, 207-581-3291, Fax: 207-581-3232, E-mail: graduate@maine.edu.

University of Manitoba, Faculty of Graduate Studies, Faculty of Engineering, Department of Mechanical and Manufacturing Engineering, Winnipeg, MB R3T 2N2, Canada. Offers M Eng, M Sc, PhD. *Degree requirements:* For master's, thesis; for doctorate, thesis/dissertation.

University of Maryland, Baltimore County, Graduate School, College of Engineering and Information Technology, Department of Mechanical Engineering, Baltimore, MD 21250. Offers mechanical engineering (MS, PhD). Part-time programs available. *Faculty:* 16 full-time (4 women), 7 part-time/adjunct (2 women). *Students:* 58 full-time (10 women), 37 part-time (6 women); includes 18 minority (10 African Americans, 5 Asian Americans or Pacific Islanders, 3 Hispanic Americans), 40 international. Average age 27. 52 applicants, 71% accepted, 26 enrolled. In 2009, 11 master's, 7 doctorates awarded. *Degree requirements:* For master's, comprehensive exam (for some programs), thesis (for some programs); for doctorate, comprehensive exam, thesis/dissertation. *Entrance requirements:* For master's, GRE General Test, minimum GPA of 3.0; for doctorate, GRE General Test, minimum overall GPA of 3.3; bachelor's degree in mechanical, aerospace, civil, industrial, or chemical engineering. Additional exam requirements/recommendations for international students: Required—TOEFL (minimum score 550 paper-based; 250 computer-based; 80 iBT). *Application deadline:* For fall admission, 6/1 for domestic students, 1/1 for international students; for spring admission, 11/1 for domestic students, 6/1 for international students. Applications are processed on a rolling basis. Application fee: $50. Electronic applications accepted. *Financial support:* In 2009–10, 25 research assistantships with full tuition reimbursements (averaging $20,500 per year), 18 teaching assistantships with full tuition reimbursements (averaging $17,000 per year) were awarded; fellowships with full tuition reimbursements, career-related internships or fieldwork, Federal Work-Study, scholarships/grants, health care benefits, tuition waivers (partial), and unspecified assistantships also available. Support available to part-time students. Financial award application deadline: 6/30; financial award applicants required to submit FAFSA. *Faculty research:* Design and manufacturing, thermal fluids, solid mechanics and materials, biomechanics. Total annual research expenditures: $2.9 million. *Unit head:* Dr. Shlomo Carmi, Professor and Chair, 410-455-3313, Fax: 410-455-1052, E-mail: carmi@umbc.edu. *Application contact:* Dr. L. D. Timmie Topoleski, Director, 410-455-3302, Fax: 410-455-1052, E-mail: topoleski@umbc.edu.

University of Maryland, College Park, Academic Affairs, A. James Clark School of Engineering, Department of Continuing and Distance Learning in Engineering, Professional Program in Engineering, College Park, MD 20742. Offers aerospace engineering (M Eng); chemical engineering (M Eng); civil engineering (M Eng); electrical engineering (M Eng); engineering (Certificate); fire protection engineering (M Eng); materials science and engineering (M Eng); mechanical engineering (M Eng); reliability engineering (M Eng); systems engineering (M Eng). Part-time and evening/weekend programs available. Postbaccalaureate distance learning degree programs offered. *Students:* 50 full-time (15 women), 234 part-time (41 women); includes 91 minority (36 African Americans, 39 Asian Americans or Pacific Islanders, 16 Hispanic Americans), 45 international. 137 applicants, 69% accepted, 77 enrolled. In 2009, 103 master's awarded. *Entrance requirements:* For master's, 3 letters of recommendation. *Application deadline:* For fall admission, 8/15 for domestic students, 1/10 for international students; for spring admission, 12/15 for domestic students, 6/1 for international students. Applications are processed on a rolling basis. Application fee: $60. Electronic applications accepted. *Expenses:* Tuition, area resident: Part-time $471 per credit hour. Tuition, state resident: part-time $471 per credit hour. Tuition, nonresident: part-time $1016 per credit hour. Required fees: $337.04 per term. *Financial support:* In 2009–10, 2 research assistantships with tuition reimbursements (averaging $19,561 per year), 9 teaching assistantships with tuition reimbursements (averaging $16,849 per year) were awarded; fellowships, Federal Work-Study and scholarships/grants also available. Support available to part-time students. Financial award applicants required to submit FAFSA. *Unit head:* Dr. George Syrmos, Director, 301-405-3633, Fax: 301-314-3305, E-mail: syrmos@umd.edu. *Application contact:* Dean of Graduate School, 301-405-0376, Fax: 301-314-9305.

University of Maryland, College Park, Academic Affairs, A. James Clark School of Engineering, Department of Mechanical Engineering, College Park, MD 20742. Offers electronic packaging and reliability (MS, PhD); manufacturing and design (MS, PhD); mechanics and materials (MS, PhD); reliability engineering (M Eng, MS, PhD); thermal and fluid sciences (MS, PhD). Part-time and evening/weekend programs available. Postbaccalaureate distance learning degree programs offered. *Faculty:* 84 full-time (5 women), 14 part-time/adjunct (1 woman). *Students:* 217 full-time (37 women), 76 part-time (13 women); includes 39 minority (11 African Americans, 2 American Indian/Alaska Native, 18 Asian Americans or Pacific Islanders, 8 Hispanic Americans), 140 international. 420 applicants, 21% accepted, 64 enrolled. In 2009, 40 master's, 33 doctorates awarded. *Degree requirements:* For master's, thesis optional; for doctorate, thesis/dissertation, qualifying exam. *Entrance requirements:* For master's, GRE General Test, 3 letters of recommendation; for doctorate, GRE General Test, minimum GPA of 3.0. Additional exam requirements/recommendations for international students: Required—TOEFL. *Application deadline:* For fall admission, 5/15 for domestic students, 2/1 for international students; for spring admission, 10/1 for domestic students, 6/1 for international students. Applications are processed on a rolling basis. Application fee: $60. Electronic applications accepted. *Expenses:* Tuition, area resident: Part-time $471 per credit hour. Tuition, state resident: part-time $471 per credit hour. Tuition, nonresident: part-time $1016 per credit hour. Required fees: $337.04 per term. *Financial support:* In 2009–10, 7 fellowships with full and partial tuition reimbursements (averaging $13,060 per year), 168 research assistantships with tuition reimbursements (averaging $23,703 per year), 10 teaching assistantships with tuition reimbursements (averaging $18,884 per year) were awarded; Federal Work-Study and scholarships/grants also available. Support available to part-time students. Financial award applicants required to submit FAFSA. *Faculty research:* Injection molding, electronic packaging, fluid mechanics, product engineering. Total annual research expenditures: $15 million. *Unit head:* Dr. Avram Bar-Cohen, Chairman, 301-405-3173, Fax: 301-314-9477, E-mail: abc@umd.edu. *Application contact:* Dr., Graduate Director, 301-405-0376.

University of Massachusetts Amherst, Graduate School, College of Engineering, Department of Mechanical and Industrial Engineering, Program in Mechanical Engineering, Amherst, MA 01003. Offers MS, PhD. Part-time programs available. *Students:* 62 full-time (13 women), 16 part-time (3 women); includes 3 minority (2 Asian Americans or Pacific Islanders, 1 Hispanic American), 38 international. Average age 26. 177 applicants, 43% accepted, 26 enrolled. In 2009, 15 master's, 4 doctorates awarded. Terminal master's awarded for partial completion of doctoral program. *Degree requirements:* For master's, thesis, project; for doctorate, comprehensive exam, thesis/dissertation. *Entrance requirements:* For master's and doctorate, GRE General Test. Additional exam requirements/recommendations for international students: Required—TOEFL (minimum score 550 paper-based; 213 computer-based; 80 iBT), IELTS (minimum score 6.5). *Application deadline:* For fall admission, 1/15 for domestic and international students; for spring admission, 10/1 for domestic and international students. Applications are processed on a rolling basis. Application fee: $50 ($65 for international students). Electronic applications accepted. *Expenses:* Tuition, state resident: full-time $2640; part-time $110 per credit. Tuition, nonresident: full-time $9936; part-time $414 per credit. Tuition and fees vary according to course load. *Financial support:* Fellowships with full tuition reimbursements, research assistantships with full tuition reimbursements, teaching assistantships with full tuition reimbursements, career-related internships or fieldwork, Federal Work-Study, scholarships/grants, traineeships, health care benefits, tuition waivers, and unspecified assistantships available. Support available to part-time students. Financial award application deadline: 1/15; financial award applicants required to submit FAFSA. *Unit head:* Dr. David P. Schmidt, Director, 413-545-3827, Fax: 413-545-1027. *Application contact:* Jean M. Ames, Supervisor of Admissions, 413-545-0722, Fax: 413-577-0100, E-mail: gradadml@grad.umass.edu.

University of Massachusetts Amherst, Graduate School, Interdisciplinary Programs, Program in Mechanical Engineering and Business Administration, Amherst, MA 01003. Offers MSME/MBA. Part-time programs available. *Students:* 2 applicants, 50% accepted, 0 enrolled. *Entrance requirements:* Additional exam requirements/recommendations for international students: Required—TOEFL (minimum score 600 paper-based; 250 computer-based; 100 iBT), IELTS (minimum score 7). *Application deadline:* For fall admission, 1/15 for domestic and international students. Applications are processed on a rolling basis. Application fee: $50 ($65 for international students). Electronic applications accepted. *Expenses:* Tuition, state resident: full-time $2640; part-time $110 per credit. Tuition, nonresident: full-time $9936; part-time $414 per credit. Tuition and fees vary according to course load. *Financial support:* Career-related internships or fieldwork, Federal Work-Study, scholarships/grants, traineeships, health care benefits, tuition waivers (full), and unspecified assistantships available. Support available to part-time students. *Unit head:* Dr. David P. Schmidt, Graduate Program Director, 413-545-3827, Fax: 413-545-1027. *Application contact:* Jean M. Ames, Supervisor of Admissions, 413-545-0722, Fax: 413-577-0010, E-mail: gradadm@grad.umass.edu.

University of Massachusetts Dartmouth, Graduate School, College of Engineering, Program in Mechanical Engineering, North Dartmouth, MA 02747-2300. Offers MS. Part-time programs available. *Faculty:* 11 full-time (1 woman). *Students:* 20 full-time (3 women), 13 part-time (0 women); includes 1 minority (Hispanic American), 16 international. Average age 25. 33 applicants, 70% accepted, 10 enrolled. In 2009, 5 master's awarded. *Degree requirements:* For master's, thesis or alternative. *Entrance requirements:* For master's, GRE General Test, minimum undergraduate GPA of 3.0, 3 letters of recommendation. Additional exam requirements/recommendations for international students: Required—TOEFL (minimum score 500 paper-based). *Application deadline:* For fall admission, 4/20 priority date for domestic students, 2/20 priority date for international students; for spring admission, 11/15 priority date for domestic students, 9/15 priority date for international students. Applications are processed on a rolling basis. Application fee: $40 ($60 for international students). Electronic applications accepted. *Expenses:* Tuition, state resident: full-time $2071; part-time $86.29 per credit. Tuition, nonresident: full-time $8099; part-time $337.46 per credit. Required fees: $9446. Tuition and fees vary according to class time, course load and reciprocity agreements. *Financial support:*

In 2009–10, 12 research assistantships with full tuition reimbursements (averaging $7,964 per year), 7 teaching assistantships with full tuition reimbursements (averaging $8,827 per year) were awarded; Federal Work-Study and unspecified assistantships also available. Support available to part-time students. Financial award application deadline: 3/1. *Faculty research:* Biopreservation, fiber-reinforced polymeric composites, heat exchanger optimization, nano-scale surface embrittlement of textile fibers. Total annual research expenditures: $421,000. *Unit head:* Dr. John Rice, Director, 508-999-8498, E-mail: jrice@umassd.edu. *Application contact:* Elan Turcotte-Shamski, Graduate Admissions Officer, 508-999-8604, Fax: 508-999-8183, E-mail: graduate@umassd.edu.

University of Massachusetts Lowell, James B. Francis College of Engineering, Department of Mechanical Engineering, Lowell, MA 01854-2881. Offers MS Eng, D Eng, PhD. Part-time programs available. *Degree requirements:* For master's, thesis or alternative; for doctorate, 2 foreign languages, comprehensive exam, thesis/dissertation. *Entrance requirements:* For master's and doctorate, GRE General Test. Additional exam requirements/recommendations for international students: Required—TOEFL (minimum score 560 paper-based; 215 computer-based). Electronic applications accepted. *Faculty research:* Composites, heat transfer.

University of Memphis, Graduate School, Herff College of Engineering, Department of Mechanical Engineering, Memphis, TN 38152. Offers design and mechanical engineering (MS); energy systems (MS); industrial engineering (MS); mechanical engineering (PhD); mechanical systems (MS); power systems (MS). Part-time programs available. *Faculty:* 8 full-time (0 women). *Students:* 3 full-time (1 woman), 8 part-time (0 women); includes 2 minority (both African Americans), 5 international. Average age 30. 11 applicants, 64% accepted, 3 enrolled. In 2009, 5 master's awarded. Terminal master's awarded for partial completion of doctoral program. *Degree requirements:* For master's, comprehensive exam, thesis; for doctorate, comprehensive exam, thesis/dissertation. *Entrance requirements:* For master's, GRE General Test, BS in mechanical engineering, minimum undergraduate GPA of 3.0. *Application deadline:* For fall admission, 8/1 for domestic students; for spring admission, 12/1 for domestic students. Application fee: $35 ($60 for international students). *Expenses:* Tuition, state resident: full-time $6246; part-time $347 per credit hour. Tuition, nonresident: full-time $15,894; part-time $883 per credit hour. Required fees: $1160. Full-time tuition and fees vary according to course load, degree level and program. *Financial support:* In 2009–10, 6 students received support; fellowships with full tuition reimbursements available, research assistantships with full tuition reimbursements available, teaching assistantships with full tuition reimbursements available, career-related internships or fieldwork, Federal Work-Study, scholarships/grants, and unspecified assistantships available. Financial award application deadline: 2/15; financial award applicants required to submit FAFSA. *Faculty research:* Computational fluid dynamics, computational mechanics, integrated design, nondestructive testing, operations research. *Unit head:* Dr. John I. Hochstein, Chair, 901-678-2173, Fax: 901-678-5459, E-mail: jhochste@memphis.edu. *Application contact:* Dr. Teong Tan, Graduate Studies Coordinator, 901-678-3264, Fax: 901-678-5459, E-mail: ttan@memphis.edu.

University of Miami, Graduate School, College of Engineering, Department of Mechanical and Aerospace Engineering, Coral Gables, FL 33124. Offers MSME, PhD. Part-time programs available. *Degree requirements:* For master's, thesis (for some programs); for doctorate, comprehensive exam, thesis/dissertation. *Entrance requirements:* For master's and doctorate, GRE General Test, minimum GPA of 3.0. Additional exam requirements/recommendations for international students: Required—TOEFL (minimum score 550 paper-based; 213 computer-based). Electronic applications accepted. *Faculty research:* Internal combustion engines, heat transfer, hydrogen energy, controls, fuel cells.

University of Michigan, Horace H. Rackham School of Graduate Studies, College of Engineering, Department of Mechanical Engineering, Ann Arbor, MI 48109. Offers MSE, PhD. Part-time programs available. *Faculty:* 58 full-time (10 women). *Students:* 394 full-time (57 women), 21 part-time (2 women); includes 30 minority (7 African Americans, 11 Asian Americans or Pacific Islanders, 12 Hispanic Americans), 261 international. 1,013 applicants, 33% accepted, 125 enrolled. In 2009, 124 master's, 50 doctorates awarded. Terminal master's awarded for partial completion of doctoral program. *Degree requirements:* For master's, thesis optional; for doctorate, thesis/dissertation, oral defense of dissertation, preliminary and qualifying exams. *Entrance requirements:* For master's, GRE General Test, undergraduate degree in same or relevant field; for doctorate, GRE General Test. Additional exam requirements/recommendations for international students: Required—TOEFL (minimum score 560 paper-based; 220 computer-based). *Application deadline:* Applications are processed on a rolling basis. Application fee: $60 ($75 for international students). Electronic applications accepted. *Expenses:* Tuition, state resident: full-time $17,286; part-time $1099 per credit hour. Tuition, nonresident: full-time $34,944; part-time $2080 per credit hour. Required fees: $95 per semester. Tuition and fees vary according to course load, degree level and program. *Financial support:* Fellowships, research assistantships, teaching assistantships, institutionally sponsored loans, health care benefits, tuition waivers (full), and unspecified assistantships available. *Faculty research:* Design and manufacturing, systems and controls, combustion and heat transfer, materials and solid mechanics, dynamics and vibrations, biosystems, fluid mechanics, microsystems, environmental sustainabilities. *Unit head:* Kon-Well Wang, Department Chair, 734-764-8464, E-mail: kwwang@umich.edu. *Application contact:* Cynthia Quann-White, Graduate Admissions and Program Coordinator, 734-763-9223, Fax: 734-647-7303, E-mail: me.grad.application@umich.edu.

University of Michigan–Dearborn, College of Engineering and Computer Science, Department of Mechanical Engineering, Dearborn, MI 48128. Offers MSE. Part-time and evening/weekend programs available. Postbaccalaureate distance learning degree programs offered (no on-campus study). *Faculty:* 17 full-time (1 woman), 2 part-time/adjunct (0 women). *Students:* 4 full-time (0 women), 64 part-time (7 women); includes 7 minority (2 African Americans, 4 Asian Americans or Pacific Islanders, 1 Hispanic American), 14 international. Average age 25. 47 applicants, 81% accepted, 18 enrolled. In 2009, 28 master's awarded. *Degree requirements:* For master's, thesis optional. *Entrance requirements:* For master's, BS in mechanical engineering and/or applied mathematics, minimum GPA of 3.0 or equivalent. Additional exam requirements/recommendations for international students: Required—TOEFL (minimum score 560 paper-based; 220 computer-based; 84 iBT), or IELTS, or Michigan English Language Assessment Battery exam. *Application deadline:* For fall admission, 7/1 priority date for domestic students, 4/1 for international students; for winter admission, 11/15 priority date for domestic students, 8/1 for international students; for spring admission, 4/1 priority date for domestic students, 12/1 for international students. Applications are processed on a rolling basis. Application fee: $60 ($75 for international students). *Expenses:* Tuition, area resident: Part-time $504.10 per credit hour. Tuition, state resident: part-time $504.10 per credit hour. Tuition, nonresident: part-time $957.90 per credit hour. *Financial support:* In 2009–10, 12 students received support, including 7 research assistantships with full tuition reimbursements available (averaging $14,700 per year), 12 teaching assistantships (averaging $3,400 per year); Federal Work-Study, scholarships/grants, health care benefits, and unspecified assistantships also available. Financial award application deadline: 4/1; financial award applicants required to submit FAFSA. *Faculty research:* Combustion, fatigue, fracture/damage mechanics, noise and vibration, vehicle climate control. *Unit head:* Dr. Ben Q. Li, Chair, 313-593-5241, Fax: 313-593-3851, E-mail: benqli@umich.edu. *Application contact:* Rebekah S. Awood, Graduate Secretary, 313-593-5241, Fax: 313-593-3851, E-mail: rsdew@umd.umich.edu.

University of Minnesota, Twin Cities Campus, Institute of Technology, Department of Mechanical Engineering, Minneapolis, MN 55455-0213. Offers industrial engineering (MSIE, PhD); mechanical engineering (MSME, PhD). Part-time programs available. *Degree requirements:* For doctorate, thesis/dissertation. *Entrance requirements:* For master's, GRE General Test, minimum GPA of 3.0; for doctorate, GRE General Test.

University of Missouri, Graduate School, College of Engineering, Department of Mechanical and Aerospace Engineering, Columbia, MO 65211. Offers MS, PhD. *Degree requirements:* For master's, thesis; for doctorate, one foreign language, thesis/dissertation. *Entrance requirements:* For master's and doctorate, GRE General Test, minimum GPA of 3.0. Additional exam requirements/recommendations for international students: Required—TOEFL (minimum score 500 paper-based; 173 computer-based; 61 iBT).

University of Missouri–Kansas City, School of Computing and Engineering, Kansas City, MO 64110-2499. Offers civil engineering (MS); computer and electrical engineering (PhD); computer science (MS), including bioinformatics, software engineering, telecommunications networking; computer science and informatics (PhD); computing (PhD); electrical engineering (MS); engineering (PhD); mechanical engineering (MS); telecommunications (PhD). PhD (interdisciplinary) offered through the School of Graduate Studies. Part-time programs available. *Faculty:* 40 full-time (5 women), 28 part-time/adjunct (0 women). *Students:* 230 full-time (46 women), 158 part-time (31 women); includes 20 minority (5 African Americans, 12 Asian Americans or Pacific Islanders, 3 Hispanic Americans), 313 international. Average age 24. 484 applicants, 64% accepted, 106 enrolled. In 2009, 144 master's awarded. *Degree requirements:* For doctorate, thesis/dissertation. *Entrance requirements:* For master's, GRE General Test, minimum GPA of 3.0, 3 letters of recommendations from professors; for doctorate, GRE General Test, minimum GPA of 3.5. Additional exam requirements/recommendations for international students: Required—TOEFL (minimum score 550 paper-based; 213 computer-based; 80 iBT). *Application deadline:* For fall admission, 1/15 priority date for domestic students, 1/15 for international students. Applications are processed on a rolling basis. Application fee: $45 ($50 for international students). *Expenses:* Tuition, state resident: full-time $5378; part-time $299 per credit hour. Tuition, nonresident: full-time $13,881; part-time $771 per credit hour. Required fees: $641; $71 per credit hour. Tuition and fees vary according to course load and program. *Financial support:* In 2009–10, 29 research assistantships with partial tuition reimbursements (averaging $15,040 per year), 10 teaching assistantships with partial tuition reimbursements (averaging $12,118 per year) were awarded; career-related internships or fieldwork, Federal Work-Study, scholarships/grants, tuition waivers (partial), and unspecified assistantships also available. Support available to part-time students. Financial award application deadline: 3/1; financial award applicants required to submit FAFSA. *Faculty research:* Algorithms, bioinformatics and medical informatics, biomechanics/biomaterials, civil engineering materials, networking and telecommunications, thermal science. Total annual research expenditures: $1.4 million. *Unit head:* Dr. Kevin Z. Truman, Dean, 816-235-2399, Fax: 816-235-5159. *Application contact:* Dr. Kevin Z. Truman, Dean, 816-235-2399, Fax: 816-235-5159.

University of Nebraska–Lincoln, Graduate College, College of Engineering, Department of Mechanical Engineering, Lincoln, NE 68588. Offers chemical and materials engineering (PhD); mechanical engineering (MS, PhD), including materials science engineering (MS), metallurgical engineering (MS). *Degree requirements:* For master's, thesis optional; for doctorate, comprehensive exam, thesis/dissertation. *Entrance requirements:* For master's and doctorate, GRE General Test. Additional exam requirements/recommendations for international students: Required—TOEFL (minimum score 550 paper-based; 213 computer-based). Electronic applications accepted. *Faculty research:* Robotics for planetary exploration, vehicle crashworthiness, transient heat conduction, laser beam/particle interactions.

See Close-Up on page 527.

University of Nevada, Las Vegas, Graduate College, Howard R. Hughes College of Engineering, Department of Mechanical Engineering, Las Vegas, NV 89154-4027. Offers aerospace engineering (MS); biomedical engineering (MS); materials and nuclear engineering (MS); mechanical engineering (MS, PhD). Part-time programs available. *Faculty:* 17 full-time (0 women), 10 part-time/adjunct (0 women). *Students:* 39 full-time (4 women), 28 part-time (6 women); includes 10 minority (1 African American, 8 Asian Americans or Pacific Islanders, 1 Hispanic American), 28 international. Average age 30. 64 applicants, 83% accepted, 22 enrolled. In 2009, 13 master's, 7 doctorates awarded. *Degree requirements:* For master's, comprehensive exam, thesis (for some programs), project; for doctorate, comprehensive exam, thesis/dissertation. *Entrance requirements:* For master's and doctorate, GRE General Test. Additional exam requirements/recommendations for international students: Required—TOEFL (minimum score 550 paper-based; 213 computer-based; 80 iBT), IELTS (minimum score 7). *Application deadline:* For fall admission, 5/1 priority date for domestic and international students; for spring admission, 10/1 priority date for domestic and international students. Applications are processed on a rolling basis. Application fee: $60 ($95 for international students). Electronic applications accepted. *Financial support:* In 2009–10, 37 students received support, including 21 research assistantships with partial tuition reimbursements available (averaging $13,335 per year), 16 teaching assistantships with partial tuition reimbursements available (averaging $11,000 per year); institutionally sponsored loans, scholarships/grants, health care benefits, and unspecified assistantships also available. Financial award application deadline: 3/1. *Unit head:* Dr. Woosoon Yim, Chair/Professor, 702-895-0956, Fax: 702-895-3936, E-mail: wy@me.unlv.edu. *Application contact:* Graduate College Admissions Evaluator, 702-895-3320, Fax: 702-895-4180, E-mail: gradcollege@unlv.edu.

University of Nevada, Reno, Graduate School, College of Engineering, Department of Mechanical Engineering, Reno, NV 89557. Offers MS, PhD. Terminal master's awarded for partial completion of doctoral program. *Degree requirements:* For master's, thesis optional; for doctorate, thesis/dissertation. *Entrance requirements:* For master's, GRE General Test, minimum GPA of 2.75; for doctorate, GRE General Test, minimum GPA of 3.0. Additional exam requirements/recommendations for international students: Required—TOEFL (minimum score 500 paper-based; 173 computer-based; 61 iBT), IELTS (minimum score 6). Electronic applications accepted. *Faculty research:* Composite, solid, fluid, thermal, and smart materials.

University of New Brunswick Fredericton, School of Graduate Studies, Faculty of Engineering, Department of Mechanical Engineering, Fredericton, NB E3B 5A3, Canada. Offers applied mechanics (M Eng, M Sc E, PhD); mechanical engineering (M Eng, M Sc E, PhD). Part-time programs available. *Faculty:* 14 full-time (1 woman), 9 part-time/adjunct (0 women). *Students:* 36 full-time (8 women), 2 part-time (1 woman). In 2009, 6 master's, 2 doctorates awarded. *Degree requirements:* For master's, thesis; for doctorate, comprehensive exam, thesis/dissertation, qualifying exam. *Entrance requirements:* For master's, minimum GPA of 3.0; successful completion of BScE degree; for doctorate, Qualifying Examinations, minimum GPA of 3.0;successful completion of MScE degree. Additional exam requirements/recommendations for international students: Required—TOEFL (minimum score 550 paper-based), IELTS, TWE (minimum score 4). *Application deadline:* For fall admission, 3/1 priority date for domestic students. Applications are processed on a rolling basis. Application fee: $50 Canadian dollars. Tuition and fees charges are reported in Canadian dollars. *Expenses:* Tuition, area resident: Full-time $5562 Canadian dollars; part-time $2781 Canadian dollars per year. Required fees: $49.75 Canadian dollars per term. *Financial support:* In 2009–10, 50 teaching assistantships (averaging $4,200 per year) were awarded; research assistantships. *Faculty research:* Analysis of gross motor activities as a means of assessing upper limb prosthesis; distance determination algorithms and their applications, void nucleation in automotive aluminum alloy. *Unit head:* Dr. Andrew Gerber, Director of Graduate Studies, 506-458-7194, Fax: 506-453-5025, E-mail: agerber@unb.ca. *Application contact:* Susan Shea-Perrott, Graduate Secretary, 506-458-7742, Fax: 506-453-5025, E-mail: susan@unb.ca.

University of New Hampshire, Graduate School, College of Engineering and Physical Sciences, Department of Mechanical Engineering, Durham, NH 03824. Offers mechanical engineering (MS, PhD); systems design (PhD). Part-time programs available. *Faculty:* 14 full-time (1 woman). *Students:* 26 full-time (6 women), 25 part-time (3 women), 16 international. Average age 29. 35 applicants, 71% accepted, 16 enrolled. In 2009, 3 master's, 2 doctorates awarded. *Degree requirements:* For master's, thesis or alternative; for doctorate, thesis/dissertation. *Entrance requirements:* For master's and doctorate, GRE. Additional exam requirements/recommendations for international students: Required—TOEFL (minimum score 550 paper-based; 213 computer-based; 80 iBT). *Application deadline:* For fall admission, 4/1 priority date for domestic students, 4/1 for international students; for spring admission, 12/1 for domestic students. Applications are processed on a rolling basis. Application fee: $25. Electronic applications accepted. *Expenses:* Tuition, state resident: full-time $10,380; part-time $577 per

Mechanical Engineering

University of New Hampshire (continued)
credit hour. Tuition, nonresident: full-time $24,350; part-time $1002 per credit hour. Required fees: $1550; $387.50 per semester. Tuition and fees vary according to course load and program. *Financial support:* In 2009–10, 32 students received support, including 1 fellowship, 17 research assistantships, 12 teaching assistantships; Federal Work-Study, scholarships/grants, and tuition waivers (full and partial) also available. Support available to part-time students. Financial award application deadline: 2/15. *Faculty research:* Solid mechanics, dynamics, materials science, dynamic systems, automatic control. *Unit head:* Dr. Todd Gross, Chairperson, 603-862-2445. *Application contact:* Tracey Harvey, Administrative Assistant, 603-862-1353, E-mail: mechanical.engineering@unh.edu.

University of New Haven, Graduate School, Tagliatela College of Engineering, Program in Mechanical Engineering, West Haven, CT 06516-1916. Offers MS. Part-time and evening/weekend programs available. *Faculty:* 6 full-time (1 woman), 2 part-time/adjunct (0 women). *Students:* 9 full-time (0 women), 19 part-time (2 women); includes 3 minority (1 African American, 2 Asian Americans or Pacific Islanders), 11 international. Average age 28. 52 applicants, 77% accepted, 4 enrolled. In 2009, 22 master's awarded. *Degree requirements:* For master's, thesis or alternative. *Entrance requirements:* Additional exam requirements/recommendations for international students: Required—TOEFL (minimum score 520 paper-based; 190 computer-based; 70 iBT); Recommended—IELTS (minimum score 5.5). *Application deadline:* For fall admission, 5/31 for international students; for winter admission, 10/15 for international students; for spring admission, 1/15 for international students. Applications are processed on a rolling basis. Application fee: $50. Electronic applications accepted. *Expenses:* Tuition: Part-time $700 per credit. Required fees: $45 per term. One-time fee: $390 part-time. *Financial support:* Research assistantships with partial tuition reimbursements, teaching assistantships with partial tuition reimbursements, career-related internships or fieldwork, Federal Work-Study, scholarships/grants, tuition waivers, and unspecified assistantships available. Support available to part-time students. Financial award applicants required to submit FAFSA. *Unit head:* Dr. Konstantine Lambrakis, Coordinator, 203-932-7408. *Application contact:* Eloise Gormley, Director of Graduate Admissions, 203-932-7449, Fax: 203-932-7137, E-mail: gradinfo@newhaven.edu.

University of New Mexico, Graduate School, School of Engineering, Department of Mechanical Engineering, Albuquerque, NM 87131-2039. Offers MS, PhD. Part-time programs available. *Faculty:* 16 full-time (1 woman), 7 part-time/adjunct (0 women). *Students:* 47 full-time (6 women), 35 part-time (4 women); includes 27 minority (1 African American, 1 American Indian/Alaska Native, 1 Asian American or Pacific Islander, 24 Hispanic Americans), 17 international. Average age 29. 72 applicants, 43% accepted, 24 enrolled. In 2009, 22 master's, 5 doctorates awarded. Terminal master's awarded for partial completion of doctoral program. *Degree requirements:* For master's, thesis or alternative; for doctorate, comprehensive exam, thesis/dissertation. *Entrance requirements:* For master's and doctorate, GRE General Test, 3 letters of recommendation. Additional exam requirements/recommendations for international students: Required—TOEFL (minimum score 575 paper-based; 213 computer-based; 90 iBT). *Application deadline:* For fall admission, 7/30 for domestic students, 3/1 for international students; for spring admission, 11/30 for domestic students, 8/1 for international students. Applications are processed on a rolling basis. Application fee: $50. Electronic applications accepted. *Expenses:* Tuition, state resident: full-time $2098.80; part-time $233.20 per credit hour. Tuition, nonresident: full-time $6650. Required fees: $25 per semester. Tuition and fees vary according to course load, program and reciprocity agreements. *Financial support:* In 2009–10, 8 students received support, including 3 fellowships with tuition reimbursements available (averaging $2,000 per year), 20 research assistantships with full and partial tuition reimbursements available (averaging $24,000 per year), 6 teaching assistantships with full tuition reimbursements available (averaging $23,000 per year); scholarships/grants, health care benefits, and unspecified assistantships also available. Financial award application deadline: 3/1; financial award applicants required to submit FAFSA. *Faculty research:* Engineering mechanics and materials (including solid mechanics and materials science), mechanical sciences and engineering (including dynamic systems, controls and robotics), thermal sciences and engineering. Total annual research expenditures: $811,981. *Unit head:* Dr. Juan C. Heinrich, Chairperson, 505-277-2761, Fax: 505-277-1571, E-mail: heinrich@unm.edu. *Application contact:* Dr. Nader D. Ebrahimi, Director of Graduate Programs, 505-277-2761, Fax: 505-277-1571, E-mail: ebrahimi@unm.edu.

University of New Orleans, Graduate School, College of Engineering, Concentration in Mechanical Engineering, New Orleans, LA 70148. Offers MS. *Degree requirements:* For master's, thesis optional. *Entrance requirements:* For master's, GRE General Test, minimum GPA of 3.0. Additional exam requirements/recommendations for international students: Required—TOEFL (minimum score 550 paper-based; 213 computer-based; 79 iBT). Electronic applications accepted. *Faculty research:* Two-phase flow instabilities, thermal-hydrodynamic modeling, solar energy, heat transfer from sprays, boundary integral techniques in mechanics.

The University of North Carolina at Charlotte, Graduate School, The William States Lee College of Engineering, Department of Mechanical Engineering and Engineering Science, Charlotte, NC 28223-0001. Offers mechanical engineering (MSE, MSME, PhD). Evening/weekend programs available. *Faculty:* 12 full-time (7 women), 2 part-time/adjunct (0 women). *Students:* 54 full-time (8 women), 34 part-time (4 women); includes 4 minority (3 African Americans, 1 Asian American or Pacific Islander), 51 international. Average age 26. 25 applicants, 72% accepted, 4 enrolled. In 2009, 17 master's, 8 doctorates awarded. *Degree requirements:* For master's, thesis; for doctorate, thesis/dissertation. *Entrance requirements:* For master's, GRE General Test, minimum GPA of 3.0 in undergraduate major, 2.75 overall; for doctorate, GRE General Test, 3 letters of reference from faculty or professionals. Additional exam requirements/recommendations for international students: Required—TOEFL (minimum score 557 paper-based; 220 computer-based; 83 iBT). *Application deadline:* For fall admission, 7/1 for domestic students, 5/1 for international students; for spring admission, 11/1 for domestic students, 10/1 for international students. Applications are processed on a rolling basis. Application fee: $55. Electronic applications accepted. *Financial support:* In 2009–10, 47 students received support, including 4 fellowships (averaging $29,382 per year), 13 research assistantships (averaging $9,104 per year), 30 teaching assistantships (averaging $10,151 per year); career-related internships or fieldwork, Federal Work-Study, institutionally sponsored loans, scholarships/grants, and unspecified assistantships also available. Support available to part-time students. Financial award application deadline: 4/1; financial award applicants required to submit FAFSA. *Faculty research:* Precision metrology, bioengineering/cell preservation, computational mechanics/computational modeling, materials processing, precision design. Total annual research expenditures: $2.1 million. *Unit head:* Dr. Scott Smith, Chair, 704-687-8350, Fax: 704-687-8345, E-mail: kssmith@uncc.edu. *Application contact:* Kathy B. Giddings, Director of Graduate Admissions, 704-687-5503, Fax: 704-687-3279, E-mail: gradadm@uncc.edu.

University of North Dakota, Graduate School, School of Engineering and Mines, Department of Mechanical Engineering, Grand Forks, ND 58202. Offers M Engr, MS. Part-time programs available. *Degree requirements:* For master's, comprehensive exam, thesis or alternative. *Entrance requirements:* For master's, GRE General Test, minimum GPA of 3.0 (MS), minimum GPA of 2.5 (M Engr). Additional exam requirements/recommendations for international students: Required—TOEFL (minimum score 550 paper-based; 213 computer-based; 79 iBT), IELTS (minimum score 6.5). Electronic applications accepted. *Faculty research:* Energy conversion, dynamics, control, manufacturing processes with special emphasis on machining, stress vibration analysis.

University of North Florida, College of Computing, Engineering, and Construction, Jacksonville, FL 32224. Offers civil engineering (MSCE); computer and information sciences (MS); electrical engineering (MSEE); mechanical engineering (MSME). Part-time programs available. *Faculty:* 35 full-time (6 women). *Students:* 21 full-time (4 women), 64 part-time (11 women); includes 22 minority (6 African Americans, 9 Asian Americans or Pacific Islanders, 7 Hispanic Americans), 10 international. Average age 31. 82 applicants, 45% accepted, 14 enrolled. In 2009, 6 master's awarded. *Degree requirements:* For master's, thesis optional. *Entrance requirements:* For master's, GRE General Test, minimum GPA of 3.0 in last 60 hours of course work. Additional exam requirements/recommendations for international students: Required—TOEFL (minimum score 500 paper-based; 173 computer-based). *Application deadline:* For fall admission, 7/1 priority date for domestic students, 5/1 for international students; for spring admission, 11/1 priority date for domestic students, 10/1 for international students. Applications are processed on a rolling basis. Application fee: $30. Electronic applications accepted. *Expenses:* Tuition, state resident: full-time $6649.20; part-time $277.05 per credit hour. Tuition, nonresident: full-time $22,970; part-time $957.08 per credit hour. Required fees: $985; $41.03 per credit hour. *Financial support:* In 2009–10, 20 students received support, including 5 research assistantships (averaging $5,009 per year), 3 teaching assistantships (averaging $2,844 per year); Federal Work-Study and tuition waivers (partial) also available. Support available to part-time students. Financial award application deadline: 4/1; financial award applicants required to submit FAFSA. *Faculty research:* Parallel and distributed computing, networks, generic programming, algorithms, artificial intelligence. Total annual research expenditures: $2.2 million. *Unit head:* Dr. Neal Coulter, Dean, 904-620-1350, E-mail: ncoulter@unf.edu. *Application contact:* Dr. Roger Eggen, Director of Graduate Studies for Computer Science, 904-320-2985, Fax: 904-620-2988, E-mail: ree@unf.edu.

University of Notre Dame, Graduate School, College of Engineering, Department of Aerospace and Mechanical Engineering, Notre Dame, IN 46556. Offers aerospace and mechanical engineering (M Eng, PhD); aerospace engineering (MS Aero E); mechanical engineering (MEME, MSME). Terminal master's awarded for partial completion of doctoral program. *Degree requirements:* For master's, comprehensive exam, thesis or alternative; for doctorate, thesis/dissertation, candidacy exam. *Entrance requirements:* For master's and doctorate, GRE General Test. Additional exam requirements/recommendations for international students: Required—TOEFL (minimum score 600 paper-based; 250 computer-based; 80 iBT). Electronic applications accepted. *Faculty research:* Aerodynamics/fluid dynamics, design and manufacturing, controls/robotics, solid mechanics or biomechanics/biomaterials.

University of Oklahoma, Graduate College, College of Engineering, School of Aerospace and Mechanical Engineering, Program in Mechanical Engineering, Norman, OK 73019. Offers MS, PhD. Part-time programs available. *Students:* 39 full-time (4 women), 27 part-time (2 women); includes 5 minority (2 African Americans, 1 American Indian/Alaska Native, 2 Hispanic Americans), 31 international. 31 applicants, 94% accepted, 12 enrolled. In 2009, 15 master's, 1 doctorate awarded. Terminal master's awarded for partial completion of doctoral program. *Degree requirements:* For master's, comprehensive exam, thesis or alternative; for doctorate, comprehensive exam, thesis/dissertation optional, combined general and qualifying exam. *Entrance requirements:* For master's, GRE General Test, BS in engineering or physical sciences; for doctorate, GRE General Test, MS in mechanical engineering or equivalent. Additional exam requirements/recommendations for international students: Required—TOEFL (minimum score 600 paper-based; 250 computer-based). *Application deadline:* For fall admission, 6/1 priority date for domestic students, 4/1 for international students; for spring admission, 11/1 for domestic students, 9/1 for international students. Applications are processed on a rolling basis. Application fee: $40 ($90 for international students). Electronic applications accepted. *Expenses:* Tuition, state resident: full-time $3744; part-time $156 per credit hour. Tuition, nonresident: full-time $13,577; part-time $565.70 per credit hour. Required fees: $2415; $90.10 per credit hour. *Financial support:* In 2009–10, 42 students received support. Career-related internships or fieldwork, health care benefits, and unspecified assistantships available. Financial award application deadline: 3/1; financial award applicants required to submit FAFSA. *Faculty research:* Dynamics, controls and robotics, materials design and manufacturing, structures, thermal-fluid systems. *Unit head:* Farrokh Mistree, Director, 405-325-5011, Fax: 405-325-1088, E-mail: farrokh.mistree@ou.edu. *Application contact:* Dr. Ramkumar Parthasarathy, Graduate Liaison, 405-325-1753, Fax: 405-325-1088, E-mail: rparthasarathy@ou.edu.

University of Ottawa, Faculty of Graduate and Postdoctoral Studies, Faculty of Engineering, Ottawa-Carleton Institute for Mechanical and Aerospace Engineering, Ottawa, ON K1N 6N5, Canada. Offers M Eng, MA Sc, PhD. *Degree requirements:* For master's, thesis or alternative; for doctorate, thesis/dissertation, seminar series, qualifying exam. *Entrance requirements:* For master's, honors degree or equivalent, minimum B average; for doctorate, master's degree, minimum B+ average. Electronic applications accepted. *Faculty research:* Fluid mechanics-heat transfer, solid mechanics, design, manufacturing and control.

University of Pennsylvania, School of Engineering and Applied Science, Department of Mechanical Engineering and Applied Mechanics, Philadelphia, PA 19104. Offers applied mechanics (MSE, PhD); mechanical engineering (MSE, PhD). Part-time programs available. *Faculty:* 25 full-time (4 women), 7 part-time/adjunct (0 women). *Students:* 77 full-time (9 women), 18 part-time (3 women); includes 9 minority (2 African Americans, 6 Asian Americans or Pacific Islanders, 1 Hispanic American), 42 international. 236 applicants, 28% accepted, 32 enrolled. In 2009, 18 master's, 9 doctorates awarded. *Degree requirements:* For master's, thesis optional; for doctorate, thesis/dissertation. *Entrance requirements:* Additional exam requirements/recommendations for international students: Required—TOEFL. *Application deadline:* For fall admission, 1/2 priority date for domestic students. Applications are processed on a rolling basis. Application fee: $70. Electronic applications accepted. *Expenses:* Tuition: Full-time $25,660; part-time $4758 per course. Required fees: $2152; $270 per course. Tuition and fees vary according to course load, degree level and program. *Financial support:* Fellowships, research assistantships, teaching assistantships, institutionally sponsored loans, scholarships/grants, traineeships, health care benefits, and unspecified assistantships available. *Faculty research:* Heat transfer, fluid mechanics, energy conversion, solid mechanics, dynamics of mechanisms and robots.

University of Pittsburgh, School of Engineering, Department of Mechanical Engineering and Materials Science, Pittsburgh, PA 15260. Offers MSME, PhD. Part-time programs available. Postbaccalaureate distance learning degree programs offered. *Faculty:* 28 full-time (5 women), 32 part-time/adjunct (2 women). *Students:* 90 full-time (14 women), 87 part-time (10 women); includes 7 minority (2 African Americans, 1 American Indian/Alaska Native, 4 Asian Americans or Pacific Islanders), 47 international. 363 applicants, 25% accepted, 44 enrolled. In 2009, 24 master's, 9 doctorates awarded. Terminal master's awarded for partial completion of doctoral program. *Degree requirements:* For master's, thesis optional; for doctorate, comprehensive exam, thesis/dissertation, final oral exams. *Entrance requirements:* For master's and doctorate, minimum QPA of 3.0. Additional exam requirements/recommendations for international students: Required—TOEFL (minimum score 550 paper-based; 230 computer-based). *Application deadline:* For fall admission, 3/1 priority date for domestic students; for spring admission, 7/1 priority date for domestic students. Applications are processed on a rolling basis. Application fee: $50. Electronic applications accepted. *Expenses:* Tuition, state resident: full-time $16,402; part-time $665 per credit. Tuition, nonresident: full-time $28,694; part-time $1175 per credit. Required fees: $690; $175 per term. Tuition and fees vary according to program. *Financial support:* In 2009–10, 75 students received support, including 6 fellowships with full tuition reimbursements available (averaging $20,772 per year), 46 research assistantships with full tuition reimbursements available (averaging $22,000 per year), 28 teaching assistantships with full tuition reimbursements available (averaging $21,000 per year); scholarships/grants and tuition waivers (full and partial) also available. Financial award application deadline: 4/15. *Faculty research:* Smart materials and structure solid mechanics, computational fluid dynamics, multiphase bio-fluid dynamics, mechanical vibration analysis. Total annual research expenditures: $5.1 million. *Unit head:* Dr. Minking K. Chyu, Chairman, 412-624-9784, Fax: 412-624-4846. *Application contact:* Dr. Patrick Smelinski, Graduate Coordinator, 412-624-9788, Fax: 412-624-4846, E-mail: pat.smel@pitt.edu.

University of Puerto Rico, Mayagüez Campus, Graduate Studies, College of Engineering, Department of Mechanical Engineering, Mayagüez, PR 00681-9000. Offers ME, MS. Part-time programs available. *Degree requirements:* For master's, comprehensive exam, thesis. *Entrance requirements:* For master's, BS degree in mechanical engineering or the equivalent; minimum GPA of 2.75, 3.0 in field of specialty. Additional exam requirements/recommendations for international students: Required—TOEFL. *Faculty research:* Metallurgy, hybrid vehicles, manufacturing, thermal and fluid sciences, HVAC.

University of Rochester, The College, School of Engineering and Applied Sciences, Department of Mechanical Engineering, Rochester, NY 14627. Offers MS, PhD. Part-time programs available. Terminal master's awarded for partial completion of doctoral program. *Degree requirements:* For master's, comprehensive exam, thesis optional; for doctorate, thesis/dissertation, preliminary and qualifying exams. *Entrance requirements:* For master's and doctorate, GRE. Additional exam requirements/recommendations for international students: Required—TOEFL.

University of Saskatchewan, College of Graduate Studies and Research, College of Engineering, Department of Mechanical Engineering, Saskatoon, SK S7N 5A2, Canada. Offers M Sc, PhD. *Degree requirements:* For master's, thesis (for some programs); for doctorate, thesis/dissertation. *Entrance requirements:* For master's and doctorate, GRE. Additional exam requirements/recommendations for international students: Required—TOEFL. Tuition and fees charges are reported in Canadian dollars. *Expenses:* Tuition, area resident: Full-time $3000 Canadian dollars; part-time $500 Canadian dollars per term. Required fees: $700 Canadian dollars; $100 Canadian dollars per term.

University of South Alabama, Graduate School, College of Engineering, Department of Mechanical Engineering, Mobile, AL 36688-0002. Offers MSME. *Degree requirements:* For master's, project or thesis. *Entrance requirements:* For master's, GRE General Test, BS in engineering, minimum GPA of 3.0. *Expenses:* Tuition, state resident: part-time $218 per contact hour. Required fees: $1102 per year.

University of South Carolina, The Graduate School, College of Engineering and Computing, Department of Mechanical Engineering, Columbia, SC 29208. Offers ME, MS, PhD. Part-time and evening/weekend programs available. Postbaccalaureate distance learning degree programs offered. *Degree requirements:* For master's, thesis (for some programs); for doctorate, thesis/dissertation. *Entrance requirements:* For master's and doctorate, GRE General Test. Additional exam requirements/recommendations for international students: Required—TOEFL (minimum score 600 paper-based; 250 computer-based). Electronic applications accepted. *Faculty research:* Heat exchangers, computer vision measurements in solid mechanics and bio-mechanics, robot dynamics and control.

University of Southern California, Graduate School, Viterbi School of Engineering, Department of Aerospace and Mechanical Engineering, Los Angeles, CA 90089. Offers aerospace and mechanical engineering: computational fluid and solid mechanics (MS); aerospace and mechanical engineering: dynamics and control (MS); aerospace engineering (MS, PhD, Engr), including aerospace engineering (PhD, Engr); mechanical engineering (MS, PhD, Engr), including mechanical engineering (PhD, Engr); product development engineering (MS). Part-time programs available. Postbaccalaureate distance learning degree programs offered. *Faculty:* 24 full-time (3 women), 19 part-time/adjunct (2 women). *Students:* 186 full-time (22 women), 192 part-time (35 women); includes 89 minority (9 African Americans, 60 Asian Americans or Pacific Islanders, 20 Hispanic Americans), 119 international. 499 applicants, 48% accepted, 107 enrolled. In 2009, 107 master's, 11 doctorates, 1 other advanced degree awarded. Terminal master's awarded for partial completion of doctoral program. *Degree requirements:* For doctorate, thesis/dissertation. *Entrance requirements:* For master's and doctorate, General GRE Test. *Application deadline:* For fall admission, 3/1 priority date for domestic and international students; for spring admission, 10/1 priority date for domestic and international students. Applications are processed on a rolling basis. Application fee: $85. Electronic applications accepted. *Expenses:* Tuition: Full-time $25,980; part-time $1315 per unit. Required fees: $554. One-time fee: $35 full-time. Full-time tuition and fees vary according to degree level and program. *Financial support:* In 2009–10, fellowships with full tuition reimbursements (averaging $30,000 per year), research assistantships with full tuition reimbursements (averaging $19,250 per year), teaching assistantships with full tuition reimbursements (averaging $19,250 per year) were awarded; career-related internships or fieldwork, scholarships/grants, traineeships, health care benefits, and unspecified assistantships also available. Financial award application deadline: 12/1; financial award applicants required to submit CSS PROFILE or FAFSA. *Faculty research:* Mechanics and materials, aerodynamics of air/ground vehicles, gas dynamics; aerosols, astronautics and space science, geophysical and microgravity flows, planetary physics, power MEMs and MEMS vacuum pumps, heat transfer and combustion. Total annual research expenditures: $3.9 million. *Unit head:* Dr. Geoffrey Spedding, Chair, 213-740-4132, Fax: 213-740-8071, E-mail: geoff@usc.edu. *Application contact:* Samantha Graves, Student Service Advisor, 213-740-1735, Fax: 213-740-7774, E-mail: smgraves@usc.edu.

University of South Florida, Graduate School, College of Engineering, Department of Mechanical Engineering, Tampa, FL 33620-9951. Offers ME, MME, MSES, MSME, PhD. Part-time programs available. *Faculty:* 14 full-time (1 woman). *Students:* 49 full-time (6 women), 17 part-time (1 woman); includes 15 minority (4 African Americans, 7 Asian Americans or Pacific Islanders, 4 Hispanic Americans), 20 international. Average age 32. 80 applicants, 68% accepted, 30 enrolled. In 2009, 18 master's, 3 doctorates awarded. Terminal master's awarded for partial completion of doctoral program. *Degree requirements:* For master's, comprehensive exam, thesis or alternative; for doctorate, comprehensive exam, thesis/dissertation, 2 tools of research as specified by dissertation committee. *Entrance requirements:* For master's, GRE General Test (minimum score 1100 verbal and quantitative), minimum GPA of 3.0 in last 60 hours of coursework, BSME or equivalent; for doctorate, GRE General Test (minimum score: 1100 Verbal and Quantitative), BSME, MSME or equivalent. Additional exam requirements/recommendations for international students: Required—TOEFL (minimum score 550 paper-based; 213 computer-based). *Application deadline:* For fall admission, 2/15 for domestic students, 1/2 for international students; for spring admission, 10/15 for domestic students, 6/1 for international students. Application fee: $30. Electronic applications accepted. *Financial support:* In 2009–10, teaching assistantships with partial tuition reimbursements (averaging $28,613 per year). Financial award applicants required to submit FAFSA. *Faculty research:* Robot sensors, rehabilitation engineering, mechatronics, vibrations, composites. Total annual research expenditures: $2.4 million. *Application contact:* Muhammad Rahman, Director, 813-974-5625, Fax: 813-974-3539, E-mail: rahman@eng.usf.edu.

The University of Tennessee, Graduate School, College of Engineering, Department of Mechanical, Aerospace and Biomedical Engineering, Program in Mechanical Engineering, Knoxville, TN 37996. Offers MS, PhD, MS/MBA. Part-time programs available. *Faculty:* 16 full-time (0 women), 4 part-time/adjunct (0 women). *Students:* 40 full-time (0 women), 42 part-time (2 women); includes 4 minority (2 African Americans, 2 Asian Americans or Pacific Islanders), 21 international. Average age 30. 127 applicants, 62% accepted, 20 enrolled. In 2009, 16 master's, 6 doctorates awarded. *Degree requirements:* For master's, thesis or alternative; for doctorate, comprehensive exam, thesis/dissertation. *Entrance requirements:* For master's and doctorate, GRE, minimum GPA of 2.7. Additional exam requirements/recommendations for international students: Required—TOEFL (minimum score 550 paper-based; 213 computer-based). *Application deadline:* For fall admission, 2/1 priority date for domestic and international students; for spring admission, 6/15 priority date for international students. Applications are processed on a rolling basis. Application fee: $35. Electronic applications accepted. *Expenses:* Tuition, state resident: full-time $6826; part-time $380 per semester hour. Tuition, nonresident: full-time $21,844; part-time $1147 per semester hour. Tuition and fees vary according to program. *Financial support:* In 2009–10, 11 students received support, including 4 fellowships with full tuition reimbursements available (averaging $13,692 per year), 30 research assistantships with full tuition reimbursements available (averaging $14,628 per year), 11 teaching assistantships with full tuition reimbursements available (averaging $10,104 per year); career-related internships or fieldwork, Federal Work-Study, institutionally sponsored loans, health care benefits, and unspecified assistantships also available. Financial award application deadline: 2/1; financial award applicants required to submit FAFSA. *Faculty research:* Automotive systems and technology, combustion and emissions, alternative fuels. Total annual research expenditures: $1.7 million. *Unit head:* Dr. William Hamel, Head, 865-974-5115, Fax: 865-974-5274, E-mail: whamel@utk.edu. *Application contact:* Dr. Gary V. Smith, Chair, Graduate Programs Committee, 865-974-5271, E-mail: gvsmith@utk.edu.

The University of Tennessee at Chattanooga, Graduate School, College of Engineering and Computer Science, Program in Engineering, Chattanooga, TN 37403. Offers chemical (MS Engr); civil (MS Engr); computational (MS Engr); electrical (MS Engr); industrial (MS Engr); mechanical (MS Engr). Part-time and evening/weekend programs available. *Faculty:* 8 full-time (0 women). *Students:* 22 full-time (7 women), 30 part-time (3 women); includes 9 minority (4 African Americans, 4 Asian Americans or Pacific Islanders, 1 Hispanic American), 9 international. Average age 29. 59 applicants, 59% accepted, 19 enrolled. In 2009, 9 master's awarded. *Degree requirements:* For master's, comprehensive exam, thesis or alternative, engineering project. *Entrance requirements:* For master's, GRE General Test, minimum undergraduate GPA of 2.5 or 3.0 in last 30 hours of coursework. Additional exam requirements/recommendations for international students: Required—TOEFL (minimum score 550 paper-based; 213 computer-based; 79 iBT), IELTS (minimum score 6). *Application deadline:* For fall admission, 8/1 priority date for domestic students, 6/1 for international students; for spring admission, 12/1 priority date for domestic students, 10/1 for international students. Applications are processed on a rolling basis. Application fee: $35. Electronic applications accepted. *Expenses:* Tuition, state resident: full-time $5404; part-time $300 per credit hour. Tuition, nonresident: full-time $16,702; part-time $928 per credit hour. Required fees: $1150; $130 per credit hour. *Financial support:* In 2009–10, 23 research assistantships with full and partial tuition reimbursements (averaging $5,500 per year) were awarded; career-related internships or fieldwork, scholarships/grants, and unspecified assistantships also available. Support available to part-time students. *Faculty research:* Quality control and reliability engineering, financial management, thermal science, energy conservation, structural analysis. Total annual research expenditures: $2.6 million. *Unit head:* Dr. Neslihan Alp, Director, 423-425-4032, Fax: 423-425-5229, E-mail: neslihan-alp@utc.edu. *Application contact:* Dr. Stephanie Bellar, Dean of Graduate Studies, 423-425-4666, Fax: 423-425-5223, E-mail: stephanie-bellar@utc.edu.

The University of Tennessee Space Institute, Graduate Programs, Program in Mechanical Engineering, Tullahoma, TN 37388-9700. Offers MS, PhD. Part-time programs available. *Faculty:* 2 full-time (0 women), 7 part-time/adjunct (0 women). *Students:* 7 full-time (0 women), 20 part-time (0 women); includes 1 minority (African American), 3 international. 8 applicants, 75% accepted, 3 enrolled. In 2009, 2 master's awarded. Terminal master's awarded for partial completion of doctoral program. *Degree requirements:* For master's, thesis (for some programs); for doctorate, one foreign language, thesis/dissertation. *Entrance requirements:* For master's and doctorate, GRE General Test. Additional exam requirements/recommendations for international students: Required—TOEFL (minimum score 550 paper-based; 213 computer-based), IELTS (minimum score 6.5). *Application deadline:* For fall admission, 2/1 for international students; for spring admission, 6/15 for international students. Applications are processed on a rolling basis. Application fee: $35. Electronic applications accepted. *Expenses:* Tuition, state resident: full-time $6826; part-time $380 per hour. Tuition, nonresident: full-time $20,622; part-time $1147 per hour. Required fees: $10 per hour. One-time fee: $90 full-time. *Financial support:* In 2009–10, 1 fellowship (averaging $700 per year), 7 research assistantships with full tuition reimbursements (averaging $17,791 per year) were awarded; career-related internships or fieldwork, Federal Work-Study, institutionally sponsored loans, health care benefits, tuition waivers (full and partial), and unspecified assistantships also available. Financial award applicants required to submit FAFSA. *Unit head:* Dr. Basil Antar, Degree Program Chairman, 931-393-7471, Fax: 931-393-7444, E-mail: bantar@utsi.edu. *Application contact:* Dee Merriman, Coordinator III, 931-393-7293, Fax: 931-393-7201, E-mail: dmerrima@utsi.edu.

The University of Texas at Arlington, Graduate School, College of Engineering, Department of Mechanical and Aerospace Engineering, Program in Mechanical Engineering, Arlington, TX 76019. Offers M Engr, MS, PhD. Part-time and evening/weekend programs available. Postbaccalaureate distance learning degree programs offered (minimal on-campus study). *Students:* 87 full-time (10 women), 58 part-time (8 women); includes 18 minority (3 African Americans, 7 Asian Americans or Pacific Islanders, 8 Hispanic Americans), 94 international. 145 applicants, 96% accepted, 43 enrolled. In 2009, 24 master's, 4 doctorates awarded. Terminal master's awarded for partial completion of doctoral program. *Degree requirements:* For master's, thesis optional; for doctorate, comprehensive exam, thesis/dissertation. *Entrance requirements:* For master's, GRE General Test, minimum GPA of 3.0; for doctorate, GRE General Test, minimum GPA of 3.5. Additional exam requirements/recommendations for international students: Required—TOEFL (minimum score 550 paper-based; 213 computer-based). *Application deadline:* For fall admission, 6/6 for domestic students, 4/4 for international students; for spring admission, 10/17 for domestic students, 9/5 for international students. Applications are processed on a rolling basis. Application fee: $35 ($50 for international students). *Financial support:* In 2009–10, 61 students received support, including 9 fellowships (averaging $1,000 per year), 12 research assistantships (averaging $12,000 per year), 14 teaching assistantships (averaging $14,000 per year); institutionally sponsored loans, scholarships/grants, health care benefits, and unspecified assistantships also available. Financial award application deadline: 6/1; financial award applicants required to submit FAFSA. *Unit head:* Dr. Erian Armanios, Chair, 817-272-2062, Fax: 817-272-5010, E-mail: armanios@uta.edu. *Application contact:* Dr. Roger D. Goolsby, Graduate Adviser, 817-272-2006, Fax: 817-272-2952, E-mail: goolsby@uta.edu.

The University of Texas at Austin, Graduate School, Cockrell School of Engineering, Department of Mechanical Engineering, Austin, TX 78712-1111. Offers mechanical engineering (MS, PhD); operations research and industrial engineering (MS, PhD). *Entrance requirements:* For master's and doctorate, GRE General Test. Additional exam requirements/recommendations for international students: Required—TOEFL.

The University of Texas at Dallas, Erik Jonsson School of Engineering and Computer Science, Program in Mechanical Engineering, Richardson, TX 75080. Offers MSME. Part-time and evening/weekend programs available. *Faculty:* 17 full-time (2 women). *Students:* 4 full-time (0 women), 2 part-time (0 women); includes 2 minority (both Asian Americans or Pacific Islanders), 3 international. Average age 29. 36 applicants, 42% accepted, 5 enrolled. *Degree requirements:* For master's, thesis or major design project. *Entrance requirements:* For master's, GRE General Test, minimum GPA of 3.0 in related bachelor's degree. Additional exam requirements/recommendations for international students: Required—TOEFL (minimum score 550 paper-based; 213 computer-based). *Application deadline:* For fall admission, 7/15 for domestic students, 5/1 priority date for international students; for spring admission, 11/15 for domestic students, 9/1 priority date for international students. Application fee: $50 ($100 for international students). *Expenses:* Tuition, state resident: full-time $11,068; part-time $461 per credit hour. Tuition, nonresident: full-time $21,178; part-time $882 per credit hour. Tuition and fees vary according to course load. *Financial support:* In 2009–10, 1 teaching assistantship with full tuition reimbursement (averaging $14,850 per year) was awarded; fellowships, research assistantships with full tuition reimbursements, career-related internships or fieldwork, Federal Work-Study, institutionally sponsored loans, scholarships/grants, and unspecified assistantships also available. Support available to part-time students. Financial award application deadline: 4/30; financial award applicants required to submit FAFSA. *Faculty research:* Nanomaterials and nanoelectronic devices, industrially relevant plasmas, nonlinear systems and controls, semiconductor and oxide surfaces, electronic materials-dielectrics, thermofluids, nanofabrication, control systems. *Unit head:* Dr. Mario Rotea, Department Head, 972-883-4663, Fax: 972-883-2813, E-mail: rotea@utdallas.edu. *Application contact:* Dr. Matthew Goeckner, Associate Department Head, 972-883-4293, Fax: 972-883-2813, E-mail: gradecs@utdallas.edu.

The University of Texas at El Paso, Graduate School, College of Engineering, Department of Mechanical Engineering, El Paso, TX 79968-0001. Offers MS. Part-time and evening/weekend programs available. *Students:* 52 (4 women); includes 20 minority (2 Asian Americans or Pacific Islanders, 18 Hispanic Americans), 30 international. Average age 34. In 2009, 16 master's awarded. *Degree requirements:* For master's, thesis optional. *Entrance requirements:* For master's, GRE, minimum GPA of 3.0, letter of reference. Additional exam requirements/recommendations for international students: Required—TOEFL; Recommended—IELTS.

Mechanical Engineering

The University of Texas at El Paso (continued)

Application deadline: For fall admission, 8/1 priority date for domestic students, 3/1 for international students; for spring admission, 11/1 priority date for domestic students, 9/1 for international students. Applications are processed on a rolling basis. Application fee: $45 ($80 for international students). Electronic applications accepted. *Financial support:* In 2009–10, research assistantships with partial tuition reimbursements (averaging $21,125 per year), teaching assistantships with partial tuition reimbursements (averaging $16,900 per year) were awarded; fellowships with partial tuition reimbursements, institutionally sponsored loans, scholarships/grants, health care benefits, tuition waivers (partial), and unspecified assistantships also available. Support available to part-time students. Financial award application deadline: 3/15; financial award applicants required to submit FAFSA. *Unit head:* Dr. Louis Everett, Chair, 915-747-5450 Ext. 7987, Fax: 915-747-5019, E-mail: leverett@utep.edu. *Application contact:* Dr. Patricia D. Witherspoon, Dean of the Graduate School, 915-747-5491, Fax: 915-747-5788, E-mail: withersp@utep.edu.

The University of Texas at San Antonio, College of Engineering, Department of Mechanical Engineering, San Antonio, TX 78249-0617. Offers MSME. Part-time and evening/weekend programs available. *Faculty:* 13 full-time (1 woman), 4 part-time/adjunct (0 women). *Students:* 48 full-time (11 women), 40 part-time (7 women); includes 19 minority (5 Asian Americans or Pacific Islanders, 14 Hispanic Americans), 42 international. Average age 27. 60 applicants, 87% accepted, 33 enrolled. In 2009, 19 master's awarded. *Degree requirements:* For master's, comprehensive exam (for some programs), thesis (for some programs). *Entrance requirements:* For master's, GRE General Test, minimum GPA of 3.0 in last 60 hours of undergraduate degree. Additional exam requirements/recommendations for international students: Required—TOEFL (minimum score 500 paper-based; 173 computer-based; 61 iBT), IELTS (minimum score 5). *Application deadline:* For fall admission, 7/1 for domestic students, 4/1 for international students; for spring admission, 11/1 for domestic students, 9/1 for international students. Applications are processed on a rolling basis. Application fee: $45 ($80 for international students). Electronic applications accepted. *Expenses:* Tuition: state resident: full-time $3975; part-time $221 per contact hour. Tuition, nonresident: full-time $13,947; part-time $775 per contact hour. Required fees: $1853. *Financial support:* In 2009–10, 33 students received support, including 1 fellowship (averaging $42,000 per year), 26 research assistantships (averaging $12,257 per year); career-related internships or fieldwork, scholarships/grants, tuition waivers, and unspecified assistantships also available. Support available to part-time students. Financial award application deadline: 3/31. Total annual research expenditures: $1.1 million. *Unit head:* Dr. Can Saygin, Graduate Advisor, 210-458-7614, E-mail: can.saygin@utsa.edu. *Application contact:* Dr. Dorothy A. Flannagan, Dean of the Graduate School, 210-458-4330, Fax: 210-458-4332, E-mail: dorothy.flannagan@utsa.edu.

The University of Texas at Tyler, College of Engineering and Computer Science, Department of Mechanical Engineering, Tyler, TX 75799-0001. Offers MS. Part-time and evening/weekend programs available. *Faculty:* 7 full-time (2 women). *Students:* 5 full-time (0 women), 3 part-time (0 women); includes 2 minority (1 African American, 1 Asian American or Pacific Islander), 1 international. Average age 30. 7 applicants, 71% accepted, 1 enrolled. In 2009, 1 master's awarded. *Degree requirements:* For master's, engineering project. *Entrance requirements:* For master's, GRE or GMAT, bachelor's degree in engineering. *Application deadline:* For fall admission, 10/30 for domestic students; for spring admission, 5/30 for domestic students. Applications are processed on a rolling basis. Application fee: $0 ($50 for international students). *Expenses:* Tuition, state resident: part-time $665 per semester hour. Tuition, nonresident: part-time $942 per semester hour. Part-time tuition and fees vary according to degree level and program. *Financial support:* Research assistantships with partial tuition reimbursements, scholarships/grants available. Financial award application deadline: 7/1; financial award applicants required to submit FAFSA. *Faculty research:* Mechatronics vibration analysis, fluid dynamics, electronics and instrumentation, manufacturing processes, optics, computational fluid dynamics, signal processing, high voltage related studies, real time systems, semiconductors. Total annual research expenditures: $100,000. *Unit head:* Dr. Yueh-Jaw Lin, Chair, 903-566-7468, E-mail: yjlin@uttyler.edu. *Application contact:* Dr. Yueh-Jaw Lin, Chair, 903-566-7468, E-mail: yjlin@uttyler.edu.

The University of Texas–Pan American, College of Science and Engineering, Department of Mechanical Engineering, Edinburg, TX 78539. Offers MS. *Expenses:* Tuition, state resident: full-time $3630.60; part-time $201.70 per credit hour. Tuition, nonresident: full-time $8617; part-time $478.70 per credit hour. Required fees: $806.50.

The University of Toledo, College of Graduate Studies, College of Engineering, Department of Mechanical, Industrial, and Manufacturing Engineering, Toledo, OH 43606-3390. Offers industrial engineering (MS, PhD); mechanical engineering (MS, PhD). Part-time programs available. Postbaccalaureate distance learning degree programs offered (minimal on-campus study). *Degree requirements:* For master's, thesis optional; for doctorate, thesis/dissertation, qualifying exam. *Entrance requirements:* For master's, GRE General Test, minimum GPA of 3.0; for doctorate, GRE General Test, minimum GPA of 3.3. Additional exam requirements/recommendations for international students: Required—TOEFL (minimum score 550 paper-based; 213 computer-based; 80 iBT). Electronic applications accepted. *Faculty research:* Computational and experimental thermal sciences, manufacturing process and systems, mechanics, materials, design, quality and management engineering systems.

University of Toronto, School of Graduate Studies, Physical Sciences Division, Faculty of Applied Science and Engineering, Department of Mechanical and Industrial Engineering, Toronto, ON M5S 1A1, Canada. Offers M Eng, MA Sc, PhD. Part-time programs available. *Degree requirements:* For master's, thesis (for some programs), oral exam/thesis defense (MA Sc); for doctorate, thesis/dissertation, thesis defense, qualifying examination. *Entrance requirements:* For master's, GRE (recommended), minimum B+ average in last 2 years of undergraduate study, 2 letters of reference, resume, must be a Canadian citizen or a permanent resident (M Eng); for doctorate, GRE (recommended), minimum B+ average, 2 letters of reference, resumé. Additional exam requirements/recommendations for international students: Required—TOEFL (580 paper-based, 237 computer-based), Michigan English Language Assessment Battery (85), IELTS (7) or COPE (4).

University of Tulsa, Graduate School, College of Engineering and Natural Sciences, Department of Mechanical Engineering, Tulsa, OK 74104-3189. Offers ME, MSE, PhD. Part-time programs available. *Faculty:* 10 full-time (0 women). *Students:* 29 full-time (3 women), 12 part-time (5 women); includes 2 minority (1 Asian American or Pacific Islander, 1 Hispanic American), 24 international. Average age 27. 45 applicants, 71% accepted, 17 enrolled. In 2009, 9 master's awarded. *Degree requirements:* For master's, thesis (MSE); for doctorate, thesis/dissertation. *Entrance requirements:* For master's and doctorate, GRE General Test. Additional exam requirements/recommendations for international students: Required—TOEFL (minimum score 550 paper-based; 213 computer-based; 80 iBT), IELTS (minimum score 6). *Application deadline:* Applications are processed on a rolling basis. Application fee: $40. Electronic applications accepted. *Expenses:* Tuition: Full-time $16,182; part-time $899 per credit hour. Required fees: $4 per credit hour. Tuition and fees vary according to course load. *Financial support:* In 2009–10, 31 students received support, including 5 fellowships with full and partial tuition reimbursements available (averaging $900 per year), 22 research assistantships with full and partial tuition reimbursements available (averaging $13,444 per year), 9 teaching assistantships with full and partial tuition reimbursements available (averaging $9,467 per year); career-related internships or fieldwork, Federal Work-Study, scholarships/grants, health care benefits, tuition waivers (full and partial), and unspecified assistantships also available. Support available to part-time students. Financial award application deadline: 2/1; financial award applicants required to submit FAFSA. *Faculty research:* Erosion and corrosion, solid mechanics, composite material, computational fluid dynamics, coiled tubing mechanics. Total annual research expenditures: $5.9 million. *Unit head:* Dr. Edmund F. Rybicki, Chairperson, 918-631-2996, Fax: 918-631-2397, E-mail: ed-rybicki@utulsa.edu. *Application contact:* Dr. Siamack A. Shirazi, Adviser, 918-631-3001, Fax: 918-631-2397, E-mail: grad@utulsa.edu.

University of Utah, The Graduate School, College of Engineering, Department of Mechanical Engineering, Salt Lake City, UT 84112. Offers M Phil, MS, PhD. Part-time programs available. *Faculty:* 26 full-time (4 women), 5 part-time/adjunct (0 women). *Students:* 129 full-time (9 women), 82 part-time (7 women); includes 10 minority (1 American Indian/Alaska Native, 4 Asian Americans or Pacific Islanders, 5 Hispanic Americans), 68 international. Average age 28. 167 applicants, 64% accepted, 57 enrolled. In 2009, 47 master's, 9 doctorates awarded. Terminal master's awarded for partial completion of doctoral program. *Degree requirements:* For master's, comprehensive exam (for some programs), thesis (for some programs); for doctorate, comprehensive exam, thesis/dissertation, qualifying exam. *Entrance requirements:* For master's and doctorate, GRE General Test, minimum GPA of 3.0, statement of purpose, 3 letters of recommendation. Additional exam requirements/recommendations for international students: Required—TOEFL (minimum score 590 paper-based; 243 computer-based; 96 iBT). *Application deadline:* For fall admission, 4/1 priority date for domestic students, 12/1 priority date for international students; for spring admission, 11/1 priority date for domestic students. Application fee: $55 ($65 for international students). Electronic applications accepted. *Expenses:* Contact institution. *Financial support:* In 2009–10, 94 students received support, including 11 fellowships with full tuition reimbursements available (averaging $24,972 per year), 50 research assistantships with full and partial tuition reimbursements available (averaging $12,640 per year), 33 teaching assistantships with full and partial tuition reimbursements available (averaging $11,200 per year); institutionally sponsored loans, traineeships, health care benefits, and unspecified assistantships also available. Financial award application deadline: 1/15; financial award applicants required to submit FAFSA. *Faculty research:* Thermal science and energy systems, robotics, design and fatigue, automated manufacturing, ergonomics and safety. Total annual research expenditures: $2.5 million. *Unit head:* Dr. Timothy Ameel, Chair, 801-585-9730, Fax: 801-585-9826, E-mail: ameel@mech.utah.edu. *Application contact:* Dr. Donald Bloswick, Director of Graduate Studies, 801-581-4163, Fax: 801-585-9826, E-mail: bloswick@mech.utah.edu.

University of Vermont, Graduate College, College of Engineering and Mathematics, Department of Mechanical Engineering, Burlington, VT 05405. Offers MS, PhD. *Students:* 32 (9 women); includes 1 minority (Asian American or Pacific Islander), 8 international. 44 applicants, 50% accepted, 13 enrolled. In 2009, 3 master's, 2 doctorates awarded. *Degree requirements:* For master's, thesis; for doctorate, thesis/dissertation. *Entrance requirements:* Additional exam requirements/recommendations for international students: Required—TOEFL (minimum score 550 paper-based; 213 computer-based; 80 iBT). *Application deadline:* For fall admission, 2/1 priority date for domestic students. Applications are processed on a rolling basis. Application fee: $40. Electronic applications accepted. *Expenses:* Tuition, area resident: Part-time $508 per credit hour. Tuition, state resident: part-time $508 per credit hour. Tuition, nonresident: part-time $1281 per credit hour. *Financial support:* Fellowships, research assistantships, teaching assistantships available. Financial award application deadline: 3/1. *Unit head:* Dr. Jeff Marshall, Director, 802-656-3333. *Application contact:* Prof. Douglas Fletcher, Coordinator, 802-656-3333.

University of Victoria, Faculty of Graduate Studies, Faculty of Engineering, Department of Mechanical Engineering, Victoria, BC V8W 2Y2, Canada. Offers M Eng, MA Sc, PhD. Part-time programs available. *Degree requirements:* For master's, thesis (for some programs); for doctorate, thesis/dissertation, candidacy exam. *Entrance requirements:* For master's, minimum B average in undergraduate course work. Additional exam requirements/recommendations for international students: Required—TOEFL (minimum score 575 paper-based; 233 computer-based), IELTS (minimum score 7). Electronic applications accepted. *Faculty research:* CAD/CAM, energy systems, cryofuels, fuel cell technology, computational mechanics.

University of Virginia, School of Engineering and Applied Science, Department of Mechanical and Aerospace Engineering, Charlottesville, VA 22903. Offers ME, MS, PhD. Postbaccalaureate distance learning degree programs offered (no on-campus study). *Faculty:* 24 full-time (3 women). *Students:* 77 full-time (11 women), 5 part-time (0 women); includes 4 minority (1 African American, 2 Asian Americans or Pacific Islanders, 1 Hispanic American), 24 international. Average age 27. 190 applicants, 15% accepted, 22 enrolled. In 2009, 17 master's, 9 doctorates awarded. *Degree requirements:* For master's, thesis (MS); for doctorate, comprehensive exam, thesis/dissertation. *Entrance requirements:* For master's and doctorate, GRE General Test, 3 letters of recommendation. Additional exam requirements/recommendations for international students: Required—TOEFL (minimum score 650 paper-based; 250 computer-based; 90 iBT), IELTS (minimum score 7). *Application deadline:* For fall admission, 8/1 for domestic students, 4/1 for international students; for winter admission, 12/1 for domestic students, 8/1 for international students; for spring admission, 5/1 for domestic students, 1/1 for international students. Applications are processed on a rolling basis. Application fee: $60. Electronic applications accepted. *Financial support:* Fellowships, research assistantships, teaching assistantships available. Financial award application deadline: 1/15; financial award applicants required to submit FAFSA. *Faculty research:* Solid mechanics, dynamical systems and control, thermofluids. *Unit head:* Hossein Haj-Hariri, Chair, 434-924-7424, Fax: 434-982-2037, E-mail: mae-adm@virginia.edu. *Application contact:* Graduate Secretary, 434-924-7425, Fax: 434-982-2037, E-mail: mae-adm@virginia.edu.

University of Washington, Graduate School, College of Engineering, Department of Mechanical Engineering, Seattle, WA 98195-2600. Offers MS, MSE, MSME, PhD. Part-time programs available. Postbaccalaureate distance learning degree programs offered (minimal on-campus study). *Faculty:* 35 full-time (5 women), 18 part-time/adjunct (4 women). *Students:* 131 full-time (24 women), 101 part-time (21 women); includes 36 minority (3 African Americans, 1 American Indian/Alaska Native, 24 Asian Americans or Pacific Islanders, 8 Hispanic Americans), 55 international. Average age 24. 206 applicants, 94% accepted, 70 enrolled. In 2009, 37 master's, 10 doctorates awarded. *Degree requirements:* For master's, comprehensive exam (for some programs), thesis optional; for doctorate, comprehensive exam, thesis/dissertation. *Entrance requirements:* For master's and doctorate, GRE General Test. Additional exam requirements/recommendations for international students: Required—TOEFL (minimum score 580 paper-based; 237 computer-based; 70 iBT). *Application deadline:* For fall admission, 1/15 priority date for domestic students, 11/1 for international students; for winter admission, 10/1 for domestic students, 9/1 for international students; for spring admission, 2/1 for domestic students, 1/1 for international students. Applications are processed on a rolling basis. Application fee: $65. Electronic applications accepted. *Financial support:* In 2009–10, 7 students received support, including 15 fellowships with partial tuition reimbursements available (averaging $5,490 per year), 71 research assistantships with full tuition reimbursements available (averaging $16,146 per year), 20 teaching assistantships with full tuition reimbursements available (averaging $13,734 per year); Federal Work-Study and health care benefits also available. Financial award application deadline: 1/15; financial award applicants required to submit FAFSA. *Faculty research:* Environmentally sensitive energy conversion; health systems and biotechnology; mechatronics; advanced materials, structures and manufacturing. Total annual research expenditures: $7.6 million. *Unit head:* Dr. Mark Tuttle, Professor and Chair, 206-685-6665, Fax: 206-685-8047, E-mail: tuttle@u.washington.edu. *Application contact:* Dr. Steve Shen, Professor, 206-543-5718, Fax: 206-685-8047, E-mail: ishen@u.washington.edu.

University of Waterloo, Graduate Studies, Faculty of Engineering, Department of Mechanical and Mechatronics Engineering, Waterloo, ON N2L 3G1, Canada. Offers mechanical engineering (M Eng, MA Sc, PhD); mechanical engineering design and manufacturing (M Eng). Part-time and evening/weekend programs available. *Degree requirements:* For master's, research paper or thesis; for doctorate, comprehensive exam, thesis/dissertation. *Entrance requirements:* For master's, honors degree, minimum B average, resume; for doctorate, master's degree, minimum A- average, resumé. Additional exam requirements/recommendations for international students: Required—TOEFL (minimum score 550 paper-based; 213 computer-based), TWE (minimum score 4). Electronic applications accepted. *Faculty research:* Fluid mechanics, thermal engineering, solid mechanics, automation and control, materials engineering.

The University of Western Ontario, Faculty of Graduate Studies, Physical Sciences Division, Faculty of Engineering, London, ON N6A 5B8, Canada. Offers chemical and biochemical engineering (ME Sc, PhD); civil and environmental engineering (M Eng, ME Sc, PhD); electrical and computer engineering (M Eng, ME Sc, PhD); mechanical and materials engineering (M Eng, ME Sc, PhD). Part-time programs available. Terminal master's awarded for partial completion of doctoral program. *Degree requirements:* For master's, thesis; for doctorate, thesis/dissertation. *Entrance requirements:* For master's, minimum B average; for doctorate, minimum B+ average. *Faculty research:* Wind, geotechnical, chemical reactor engineering, applied electrostatics, biochemical engineering.

University of Windsor, Faculty of Graduate Studies, Faculty of Engineering, Department of Mechanical, Automotive, and Materials Engineering, Windsor, ON N9B 3P4, Canada. Offers engineering materials (M Eng, MA Sc, PhD); mechanical engineering (M Eng, MA Sc, PhD). Part-time programs available. *Degree requirements:* For master's, thesis; for doctorate, comprehensive exam, thesis/dissertation. *Entrance requirements:* For master's, minimum B average; for doctorate, master's degree, minimum B average. Additional exam requirements/recommendations for international students: Required—TOEFL (minimum score 600 paper-based; 250 computer-based). Electronic applications accepted. *Faculty research:* Thermofluids, applied mechanics, materials engineering.

University of Wisconsin–Madison, Graduate School, College of Engineering, Department of Mechanical Engineering, Madison, WI 53706-1380. Offers energy systems (ME); engine systems (ME); mechanical engineering (MS, PhD); polymers (ME). Part-time programs available. Postbaccalaureate distance learning degree programs offered (no on-campus study). *Faculty:* 33 full-time (3 women), 1 part-time/adjunct (0 women). *Students:* 178 full-time (20 women), 27 part-time (2 women); includes 19 minority (3 African Americans, 9 Asian Americans or Pacific Islanders, 7 Hispanic Americans). Average age 25. 613 applicants, 29% accepted, 72 enrolled. In 2009, 36 master's, 22 doctorates awarded. Terminal master's awarded for partial completion of doctoral program. *Degree requirements:* For master's, thesis optional; for doctorate, thesis/dissertation, qualifying exam, preliminary exam. *Entrance requirements:* For master's, GRE, BS in mechanical engineering or related field, minimum GPA of 3.0 in last 60 hours of course work; for doctorate, GRE, BS in mechanical engineering or related field, minimum undergraduate GPA of 3.0 in last 60 hours of course work. Additional exam requirements/recommendations for international students: Required—TOEFL (minimum score 550 paper-based; 213 computer-based; 80 iBT). *Application deadline:* For fall admission, 5/1 for domestic students, 6/1 for international students; for spring admission, 11/30 for domestic students, 10/1 for international students. Applications are processed on a rolling basis. Application fee: $56. Electronic applications accepted. *Expenses:* Tuition, state resident: part-time $594 per credit. Tuition, nonresident: part-time $1504 per credit. Required fees: $65 per credit. Tuition and fees vary according to course load, program and reciprocity agreements. *Financial support:* In 2009–10, 12 fellowships with full tuition reimbursements (averaging $22,224 per year), 138 research assistantships with full tuition reimbursements (averaging $19,596 per year), 36 teaching assistantships with full tuition reimbursements (averaging $8,595 per year) were awarded; career-related internships or fieldwork, institutionally sponsored loans, scholarships/grants, traineeships, health care benefits, and unspecified assistantships also available. *Faculty research:* Design and manufacturing, materials processing, combustion, energy systems nanotechnology. Total annual research expenditures: $10 million. *Unit head:* Roxann L. Engelstad, Chair, 608-262-5745, Fax: 608-265-2316, E-mail: engelsta@engr.wisc.edu. *Application contact:* Roxann L. Engelstad, Chair, 608-262-5745, Fax: 608-265-2316, E-mail: engelsta@engr.wisc.edu.

University of Wisconsin–Milwaukee, Graduate School, College of Engineering and Applied Science, Program in Engineering, Milwaukee, WI 53201-0413. Offers civil engineering (MS); electrical and computer engineering (MS); energy engineering (Certificate); engineering (PhD); engineering management (MS); engineering mechanics (MS); ergonomics (Certificate); industrial and management engineering (MS); manufacturing engineering (MS); materials engineering (MS); mechanical engineering (MS); MUP/MS. Part-time programs available. *Faculty:* 44 full-time (6 women). *Students:* 119 full-time (22 women), 130 part-time (22 women); includes 23 minority (2 African Americans, 14 Asian Americans or Pacific Islanders, 7 Hispanic Americans), 126 international. Average age 32. 231 applicants, 67% accepted, 33 enrolled. In 2009, 29 master's, 14 doctorates awarded. *Degree requirements:* For master's, comprehensive exam (for some programs), thesis or alternative; for doctorate, comprehensive exam, thesis/dissertation, internship. *Entrance requirements:* For master's, GRE, minimum GPA of 2.75; for doctorate, GRE, minimum GPA of 3.5. Additional exam requirements/recommendations for international students: Required—TOEFL (minimum score 550 paper-based; 79 iBT), IELTS (minimum score 6.5). *Application deadline:* For fall admission, 1/1 priority date for domestic students; for spring admission, 9/1 for domestic students. Applications are processed on a rolling basis. Application fee: $45 ($75 for international students). *Expenses:* Tuition, state resident: full-time $8800. Tuition, nonresident: full-time $20,760. Tuition and fees vary according to program and reciprocity agreements. *Financial support:* In 2009–10, 18 research assistantships, 51 teaching assistantships were awarded; fellowships, career-related internships or fieldwork, Federal Work-Study, and unspecified assistantships also available. Support available to part-time students. Financial award application deadline: 4/15. Total annual research expenditures: $2.9 million. *Unit head:* David Yu, Head, 414-229-6169, E-mail: yu@uwm.edu. *Application contact:* Betty Warras, General Information Contact, 414-229-4982, Fax: 414-229-6967, E-mail: bwarras@uwm.edu.

University of Wyoming, College of Engineering and Applied Sciences, Department of Mechanical Engineering, Laramie, WY 82070. Offers MS, PhD. Terminal master's awarded for partial completion of doctoral program. *Degree requirements:* For master's, thesis; for doctorate, thesis/dissertation. *Entrance requirements:* For master's, GRE General Test (minimum score 900), minimum GPA of 3.0; for doctorate, GRE General Test (minimum score: 1000), minimum GPA of 3.0. Additional exam requirements/recommendations for international students: Required—TOEFL (minimum score 550 paper-based; 215 computer-based). Electronic applications accepted. *Faculty research:* Composite materials, thermal and fluid sciences, continuum mechanics, material science.

Utah State University, School of Graduate Studies, College of Engineering, Department of Mechanical and Aerospace Engineering, Logan, UT 84322. Offers aerospace engineering (MS, PhD); mechanical engineering (ME, MS, PhD). Terminal master's awarded for partial completion of doctoral program. *Degree requirements:* For master's, thesis (for some programs); for doctorate, thesis/dissertation. *Entrance requirements:* For master's, GRE General Test, minimum GPA of 3.0; for doctorate, GRE General Test, minimum GPA of 3.3. Additional exam requirements/recommendations for international students: Required—TOEFL. *Faculty research:* In-space instruments, cryogenic cooling, thermal science, space structures, composite materials.

Vanderbilt University, School of Engineering, Department of Mechanical Engineering, Nashville, TN 37240-1001. Offers M Eng, MS, PhD. MS and PhD offered through the Graduate School. Part-time programs available. *Faculty:* 16 full-time (1 woman). *Students:* 53 full-time (13 women); includes 1 minority (African American), 19 international. Average age 27. 188 applicants, 7% accepted, 6 enrolled. In 2009, 7 master's, 8 doctorates awarded. Terminal master's awarded for partial completion of doctoral program. *Degree requirements:* For master's, comprehensive exam, thesis; for doctorate, comprehensive exam, thesis/dissertation. *Entrance requirements:* For master's and doctorate, GRE General Test. Additional exam requirements/recommendations for international students: Required—TOEFL (minimum score 550 paper-based; 220 computer-based); Recommended—TWE (minimum score 4). *Application deadline:* For fall admission, 1/15 for domestic students; for spring admission, 11/1 for domestic students. Applications are processed on a rolling basis. Application fee: $0. Electronic applications accepted. *Financial support:* In 2009–10, 6 fellowships with full tuition reimbursements (averaging $24,516 per year), 28 research assistantships with full tuition reimbursements (averaging $22,916 per year), 10 teaching assistantships with full tuition reimbursements (averaging $22,316 per year) were awarded; institutionally sponsored loans, health care benefits, and tuition waivers (full) also available. Support available to part-time students. Financial award application deadline: 1/15. *Faculty research:* Active noise and vibration control, robotics, mesoscale and microscale energy conversions, laser diagnostics, combustion. Total annual research expenditures: $3.1 million. *Unit head:* Dr. Robert W. Pitz, Chair, 615-322-2413, Fax: 615-343-6687, E-mail: robert.w.pitz@vanderbilt.edu. *Application contact:* Dr. Nilanjan Sarkar, Director of Graduate Studies, 615-343-7219, Fax: 615-343-6687, E-mail: nilanjan.sarkar@vanderbilt.edu.

Villanova University, College of Engineering, Department of Electrical and Computer Engineering, Program in Electrical Engineering, Villanova, PA 19085-1699. Offers communication systems engineering (Certificate); electric power systems (Certificate); electrical engineering (MSEE); electro mechanical systems (Certificate); high frequency systems (Certificate); intelligent systems (Certificate); wireless and digital communications (Certificate). Part-time and evening/weekend programs available. *Degree requirements:* For master's, thesis optional. *Entrance requirements:* For master's, GRE General Test (for applicants with degrees from foreign universities), BEE, minimum GPA of 3.0. Additional exam requirements/recommendations for international students: Required—TOEFL (minimum score 600 paper-based; 250 computer-based; 100 iBT). *Expenses:* Tuition: Part-time $630 per credit. Required fees: $60 per credit. Part-time tuition and fees vary according to degree level and program. *Faculty research:* Signal processing, communications, antennas, devices.

Villanova University, College of Engineering, Department of Mechanical Engineering, Villanova, PA 19085-1699. Offers electro-mechanical systems (Certificate); machinery dynamics (Certificate); mechanical engineering (MSME); thermofluid systems (Certificate). Part-time and evening/weekend programs available. Postbaccalaureate distance learning degree programs offered (no on-campus study). *Entrance requirements:* For master's, GRE General Test (for applicants with degrees from foreign universities), BME, minimum GPA of 3.0. Additional exam requirements/recommendations for international students: Required—TOEFL (minimum score 600 paper-based; 250 computer-based; 100 iBT). Electronic applications accepted. *Expenses:* Tuition: Part-time $630 per credit. Required fees: $60 per credit. Part-time tuition and fees vary according to degree level and program. *Faculty research:* Composite materials, power plant systems, fluid mechanics, automated manufacturing, dynamic analysis.

Virginia Commonwealth University, Graduate School, School of Engineering, Department of Mechanical Engineering, Richmond, VA 23284-9005. Offers MS, PhD.

Virginia Polytechnic Institute and State University, Graduate School, College of Engineering, Department of Mechanical Engineering, Blacksburg, VA 24061. Offers M Eng, MS, PhD. *Entrance requirements:* For master's and doctorate, GRE General Test. Additional exam requirements/recommendations for international students: Required—TOEFL (minimum score 600 paper-based; 250 computer-based). Electronic applications accepted. *Faculty research:* Turbomachinery, CAD/CAM, thermofluid sciences, controls, mechanical system dynamics.

Washington State University, Graduate School, College of Engineering and Architecture, School of Mechanical and Materials Engineering, Program in Mechanical Engineering, Pullman, WA 99164. Offers MS, PhD. Part-time programs available. *Faculty:* 32. *Students:* 57 full-time (11 women), 18 part-time (3 women); includes 3 minority (2 African Americans, 1 Hispanic American), 42 international. Average age 32. 137 applicants, 28% accepted, 15 enrolled. In 2009, 11 master's, 3 doctorates awarded. Terminal master's awarded for partial completion of doctoral program. *Degree requirements:* For master's, comprehensive exam (for some programs), thesis (for some programs), oral exam; for doctorate, comprehensive exam, thesis/dissertation, oral exam, qualifying exam. *Entrance requirements:* For master's, GRE (recommended), minimum GPA of 3.0, resume, 3 letters of recommendation with evaluation forms, student interest profile; for doctorate, minimum GPA of 3.4, resume, 3 letters of recommendation with evaluation forms, student interest profile. Additional exam requirements/recommendations for international students: Required—TOEFL, IELTS. *Application deadline:* For fall admission, 1/10 priority date for domestic students, 1/10 for international students; for spring admission, 7/1 priority date for domestic students, 7/1 for international students. Applications are processed on a rolling basis. Application fee: $50. Electronic applications accepted. *Financial support:* In 2009–10, 38 students received support, including 3 fellowships (averaging $3,252 per year), 19 research assistantships with full tuition reimbursements available (averaging $13,917 per year), 15 teaching assistantships with full tuition reimbursements available (averaging $13,056 per year); career-related internships or fieldwork, Federal Work-Study, institutionally sponsored loans, scholarships/grants, health care benefits, and unspecified assistantships also available. Financial award application deadline: 4/1; financial award applicants required to submit FAFSA. *Faculty research:* Thermal and fluid sciences, solid mechanics, manufacturing, MEMS, computer-aided design. Total annual research expenditures: $2.2 million. *Unit head:* Dr. Hussein M. Zbib, Director, 509-335-8654, Fax: 509-335-4662, E-mail: director@mme.wsu.edu. *Application contact:* Graduate School Admissions, 800-GRADWSU, Fax: 509-335-1949, E-mail: gradsch@wsu.edu.

Washington State University Tri-Cities, Graduate Programs, College of Engineering and Computer Science, Richland, WA 99352. Offers computer science (MS, PhD); electrical and computer engineering (PhD); electrical engineering (MS); mechanical engineering (MS, PhD). Part-time programs available. *Faculty:* 28. *Students:* 4 full-time (0 women), 25 part-time (8 women); includes 2 minority (both African Americans), 1 international. *Degree requirements:* For master's, comprehensive exam, thesis (for some programs); for doctorate, comprehensive exam, thesis/dissertation, oral exam. *Entrance requirements:* For master's and doctorate, GRE, minimum GPA of 3.0, 3 letters of recommendation. Additional exam requirements/recommendations for international students: Required—TOEFL (minimum score 550 paper-based; 213 computer-based). *Application deadline:* For fall admission, 1/10 priority date for domestic students, 1/10 for international students; for spring admission, 7/1 priority date for domestic students, 7/1 for international students. Application fee: $50. *Expenses:* Tuition, state resident: part-time $423 per credit. Tuition, nonresident: part-time $1032 per credit. *Financial support:* Application deadline: 3/1. *Faculty research:* Positive ion track structure, biological systems computer simulations. *Unit head:* Dr. Ali Saberi, Chair, 509-372-7178, E-mail: sidra@eecs.wsu.edu. *Application contact:* Dr. Scott Hudson, Associate Director, 509-372-7254, Fax: 509-335-1949, E-mail: hudson@tricity.wsu.edu.

Washington State University Vancouver, Graduate Programs, School of Engineering and Computer Science, Vancouver, WA 98686. Offers computer science (MS); mechanical engineering (MS). Part-time programs available. *Faculty:* 9. *Students:* 14 full-time (1 woman), 5 part-time (1 woman); includes 1 minority (Asian American or Pacific Islander), 5 international. In 2009, 4 master's awarded. *Degree requirements:* For master's, comprehensive exam (for some programs), thesis, research project. *Entrance requirements:* For master's, minimum GPA of 3.0, 3 letters of recommendation with evaluation forms, resume. Additional exam requirements/recommendations for international students: Required—TOEFL (minimum score 550 paper-based). *Application deadline:* For fall admission, 1/10 priority date for domestic students, 1/10 for international students; for spring admission, 7/1 priority date for domestic students, 7/1 for international students. Applications are processed on a rolling basis. Application fee: $50. *Expenses:* Tuition, state resident: full-time $4228; part-time $423 per credit. Tuition, nonresident: full-time $10,322; part-time $1032 per credit. *Financial support:* In 2009–10, research assistantships with full tuition reimbursements (averaging $14,634 per year), teaching assistantships with full tuition reimbursements (averaging $13,383 per year) were awarded; health care benefits and unspecified assistantships also available. Financial award application deadline: 2/15. *Faculty research:* Software design, artificial intelligence, sensor networks, robotics, nanotechnology. Total annual research expenditures: $3.4 million. *Unit head:* Dr. Hakan Gurocak, Director, 360-546-9637, Fax: 360-546-9438, E-mail: hgurocak@vancouver.wsu.edu. *Application contact:* Peggy Moore, Academic Coordinator, 360-546-9638, Fax: 360-546-9438, E-mail: moorep@vancouver.wsu.edu.

Washington University in St. Louis, Henry Edwin Sever Graduate School of Engineering and Applied Science, Department of Mechanical, Aerospace and Structural Engineering, St. Louis, MO 63130-4899. Offers MS, D Sc, PhD. Part-time programs available. Terminal master's awarded for partial completion of doctoral program. *Degree requirements:* For master's, thesis optional; for doctorate, thesis/dissertation optional. *Entrance requirements:* For master's, GRE; for doctorate, GRE General Test, departmental qualifying exam. *Faculty research:* Aerosols

Mechanical Engineering

Washington University in St. Louis (continued)
science and technology, applied mechanics, biomechanics and biomedical engineering, design, dynamic systems, combustion science, composite materials, materials science.

Wayne State University, College of Engineering, Department of Mechanical Engineering, Detroit, MI 48202. Offers MS, PhD. *Degree requirements:* For master's, thesis optional; for doctorate, thesis/dissertation. *Entrance requirements:* For master's, GRE (if BS degree is not from an ABET accredited university), minimum undergraduate GPA of 3.0; for doctorate, GRE, minimum graduate GPA of 3.5. Additional exam requirements/recommendations for international students: Required—TOEFL (minimum score 550 paper-based; 213 computer-based); Recommended—TWE (minimum score 6). Electronic applications accepted. *Faculty research:* Acoustics and vibrations/noise control, engine combustion and emission controls, advanced materials and structures, computational fluid mechanics, material processing and manufacturing.

Western Michigan University, Graduate College, College of Engineering and Applied Sciences, Department of Mechanical and Aeronautical Engineering, Kalamazoo, MI 49008. Offers mechanical engineering (MSE, PhD). Part-time programs available. *Degree requirements:* For master's, thesis optional; for doctorate, thesis/dissertation, oral exam. *Entrance requirements:* For master's, minimum GPA of 3.0; for doctorate, GRE General Test, minimum GPA of 3.0. *Faculty research:* Computational fluid dynamics, manufacturing process designs, composite materials, thermal fluid flow, experimental stress analysis.

Western New England College, School of Engineering, Department of Mechanical Engineering, Springfield, MA 01119. Offers MSE. Part-time and evening/weekend programs available. *Faculty:* 7 full-time (1 woman). *Students:* 11 part-time (1 woman). Average age 29. In 2009, 5 master's awarded. *Degree requirements:* For master's, comprehensive exam, thesis optional. *Entrance requirements:* For master's, GRE, bachelor's degree in engineering or related field. *Application deadline:* Applications are processed on a rolling basis. Application fee: $30. *Expenses:* Tuition: Part-time $552 per credit hour. Part-time tuition and fees vary according to program. *Financial support:* Available to part-time students. Application deadline: 4/1; *Faculty research:* Low-loss fluid mixing, flow separation delay and alleviation, high-lift airfoils, ejector research, compact heat exchangers. *Unit head:* Dr. Said Dini, Chair, 413-782-1272, E-mail: sdini@wnec.edu. *Application contact:* Douglas Kenyon, Assistant Vice President, Graduate Studies and Continuing Education, 413-782-1249, Fax: 413-782-1779, E-mail: ce@wnec.edu.

West Virginia University, College of Engineering and Mineral Resources, Department of Mechanical and Aerospace Engineering, Program in Mechanical Engineering, Morgantown, WV 26506. Offers MSME, PhD. Part-time programs available. Terminal master's awarded for partial completion of doctoral program. *Degree requirements:* For master's, thesis; for doctorate, comprehensive exam, thesis/dissertation, qualifying exam, proposal and defense. *Entrance requirements:* For master's and doctorate, GRE Subject Test, minimum GPA of 3.0, 3 references. Additional exam requirements/recommendations for international students: Required—TOEFL. *Faculty research:* Thermal sciences, material sciences, automatic controls, mechanical/structure design.

Wichita State University, Graduate School, College of Engineering, Department of Mechanical Engineering, Wichita, KS 67260. Offers MS, PhD. Part-time programs available. *Expenses:* Tuition, state resident: full-time $4247; part-time $235.95 per credit hour. Tuition, nonresident: full-time $11,171; part-time $620.60 per credit hour. Required fees: $34; $3.60 per credit hour. $17 per term. Tuition and fees vary according to campus/location and program. *Unit head:* Dr. David Koert, Acting Chair, 316-978-3402, Fax: 316-978-3236, E-mail: david.koert@wichita.edu. *Application contact:* Dr. T. S. Ravigururajan, Graduate Coordinator, 316-978-3402, E-mail: ts.ravi@wichita.edu.

Widener University, Graduate Programs in Engineering, Program in Mechanical Engineering, Chester, PA 19013-5792. Offers M Eng. Part-time and evening/weekend programs available. *Students:* 4 full-time (0 women), 1 part-time (0 women); includes 1 minority (Asian American or Pacific Islander), 3 international. Average age 27. In 2009, 1 master's awarded. *Degree requirements:* For master's, thesis optional. *Application deadline:* For fall admission, 8/1 priority date for domestic students; for spring admission, 12/1 for domestic students. Applications are processed on a rolling basis. Application fee: $25 ($300 for international students). *Financial support:* Teaching assistantships with full tuition reimbursements, unspecified assistantships available. Financial award application deadline: 3/15. *Faculty research:* Computational fluid mechanics, thermal and solar engineering, energy conversion, composite materials, solid mechanics. *Unit head:* Dr. Maria Slomiana, Chairman, 610-499-4062, Fax: 610-449-4059, E-mail: maria.slomiana@widener.edu. *Application contact:* Dr. Maria Slomiana, Chairman, 610-499-4062, Fax: 610-449-4059, E-mail: maria.slomiana@widener.edu.

Woods Hole Oceanographic Institution, MIT/WHOI Joint Program in Oceanography/Applied Ocean Science and Engineering, Woods Hole, MA 02543-1541. Offers applied ocean sciences (PhD); biological oceanography (PhD, Sc D); chemical oceanography (PhD, Sc D); civil and environmental and oceanographic engineering (PhD); electrical and oceanographic engineering (PhD); geochemistry (PhD); geophysics (PhD); marine biology (PhD); marine geochemistry (PhD, Sc D); marine geology (PhD, Sc D); marine geophysics (PhD); mechanical and oceanographic engineering (PhD); ocean engineering (PhD); oceanographic engineering (M Eng, MS, PhD, Sc D, Eng); paleoceanography (PhD); physical oceanography (PhD, Sc D). Terminal master's awarded for partial completion of doctoral program. *Degree requirements:* For master's and Eng, thesis (for some programs); for doctorate, thesis/dissertation. *Entrance requirements:* For master's, GRE General Test; for doctorate, GRE General Test, GRE Subject Test. Additional exam requirements/recommendations for international students: Required—TOEFL. Electronic applications accepted.

Worcester Polytechnic Institute, Graduate Studies and Research, Department of Mechanical Engineering, Worcester, MA 01609-2280. Offers manufacturing engineering (MS, PhD); materials process engineering (MS); materials science and engineering (MS, PhD); mechanical engineering (MS, PhD). Part-time and evening/weekend programs available. Postbaccalaureate distance learning degree programs offered (minimal on-campus study). *Faculty:* 21 full-time (0 women), 1 part-time/adjunct (0 women). *Students:* 60 full-time (9 women), 40 part-time (6 women). 130 applicants, 92% accepted, 48 enrolled. In 2009, 36 master's, 6 doctorates awarded. *Degree requirements:* For master's, thesis optional; for doctorate, comprehensive exam, thesis/dissertation. *Entrance requirements:* For master's, GRE (recommended), BS in mechanical engineering or related field, 3 letters of recommendation; for doctorate, GRE (recommended), MS in mechanical engineering or related field, 3 letters of recommendation, statement of purpose. Additional exam requirements/recommendations for international students: Required—TOEFL (minimum score 550 paper-based; 213 computer-based; 79 iBT), IELTS (minimum score 6.5). *Application deadline:* For fall admission, 1/15 priority date for domestic and international students; for spring admission, 10/15 priority date for domestic and international students. Applications are processed on a rolling basis. Application fee: $70. Electronic applications accepted. *Financial support:* Career-related internships or fieldwork, institutionally sponsored loans, scholarships/grants, and unspecified assistantships available. Financial award application deadline: 1/15. *Faculty research:* Theoretical, numerical and experimental work in rarefied gas and plasma dynamics; electric propulsion; multiphase flows; rotating flows; turbomachinery; fluid-structure interactions; structural analysis; nonlinear dynamics and control; cooperative control in network systems; random vibrations; biomechanics and biomaterials; mesh generation for biomedical imaging; robotics and biorobotics; materials processing; mechanics of granular materials; laser holography; MEMS; computer-aided engineering. *Application contact:* Dr. Mark Richman, Graduate Coordinator, 508-831-5556, Fax: 508-831-5680, E-mail: mrichman@wpi.edu.

Wright State University, School of Graduate Studies, College of Engineering and Computer Science, Programs in Engineering, Program in Mechanical and Materials Engineering, Dayton, OH 45435. Offers materials science and engineering (MSE); mechanical engineering (MSE). *Degree requirements:* For master's, thesis or course option alternative. *Entrance requirements:* Additional exam requirements/recommendations for international students: Required—TOEFL.

Yale University, Graduate School of Arts and Sciences, School of Engineering and Applied Science, Department of Mechanical Engineering, New Haven, CT 06520. Offers MS, PhD. Terminal master's awarded for partial completion of doctoral program. *Degree requirements:* For doctorate, thesis/dissertation, exam. *Entrance requirements:* For master's and doctorate, GRE General Test. Additional exam requirements/recommendations for international students: Required—TOEFL. *Faculty research:* Mechanics of fluids, mechanics of solids/material science.

Youngstown State University, Graduate School, College of Science, Technology, Engineering and Mathematics, Department of Mechanical Engineering, Youngstown, OH 44555-0001. Offers MSE. Part-time and evening/weekend programs available. *Degree requirements:* For master's, thesis optional. *Entrance requirements:* For master's, minimum GPA of 2.75 in field. Additional exam requirements/recommendations for international students: Required—TOEFL. *Faculty research:* Kinematics and dynamics of machines, computational and experimental heat transfer, machine controls and mechanical design.

Mechanics

Brown University, Graduate School, Division of Engineering, Program in Mechanics of Solids, Providence, RI 02912. Offers Sc M, PhD. *Degree requirements:* For doctorate, thesis/dissertation, preliminary exam.

California Institute of Technology, Division of Engineering and Applied Science, Option in Applied Mechanics, Pasadena, CA 91125-0001. Offers MS, PhD. *Faculty:* 2 full-time (0 women). *Students:* 2 full-time (1 woman). 6 applicants, 17% accepted, 1 enrolled. In 2009, 1 master's, 2 doctorates awarded. *Degree requirements:* For doctorate, thesis/dissertation. *Application deadline:* For fall admission, 1/1 for domestic students. Application fee: $0. *Financial support:* In 2009–10, 1 fellowship, 1 research assistantship were awarded; teaching assistantships. *Faculty research:* Elasticity, mechanics of quasi-static and dynamic fracture, dynamics and mechanical vibrations, stability and control. *Unit head:* Dr. Thomas H. Heaton, Option Representative, 626-395-4232, E-mail: heaton@caltech.edu. *Application contact:* Natalie Gilmore, Assistant Dean of Graduate Studies, 626-395-3812, Fax: 626-577-9246, E-mail: ngilmore@caltech.edu.

California State University, Fullerton, Graduate Studies, College of Engineering and Computer Science, Department of Civil Engineering and Engineering Mechanics, Fullerton, CA 92834-9480. Offers MS. Part-time programs available. *Students:* 63 full-time (15 women), 61 part-time (14 women); includes 55 minority (2 African Americans, 44 Asian Americans or Pacific Islanders, 9 Hispanic Americans), 20 international. Average age 30. 136 applicants, 66% accepted, 42 enrolled. In 2009, 27 master's awarded. *Degree requirements:* For master's, comprehensive exam, project or thesis. *Entrance requirements:* For master's, minimum undergraduate GPA of 2.5. Application fee: $55. *Expenses:* Tuition, nonresident: full-time $11,160; part-time $373 per credit. Required fees: $1440 per term. Tuition and fees vary according to course load, degree level and program. *Financial support:* Career-related internships or fieldwork, Federal Work-Study, institutionally sponsored loans, and scholarships/grants available. Support available to part-time students. Financial award application deadline: 3/1; financial award applicants required to submit FAFSA. *Faculty research:* Soil-structure interaction, finite-element analysis, computer-aided analysis and design. *Unit head:* Dr. Pinaki Chakrabarti, Chair, 657-278-3016. *Application contact:* Admissions/Applications, 657-278-2371.

Carnegie Mellon University, Carnegie Institute of Technology, Department of Civil and Environmental Engineering, Pittsburgh, PA 15213. Offers civil and environmental engineering (PhD); advanced infrastructure systems (MS, PhD); civil and environmental engineering (MS); civil and environmental engineering/engineering and public policy (PhD); civil engineering (MS, PhD); computational mechanics (MS, PhD); computational science and engineering (MS, PhD); environmental engineering (MS, PhD); environmental management and science (MS, PhD). Part-time programs available. *Faculty:* 19 full-time (3 women), 13 part-time/adjunct (3 women). *Students:* 118 full-time (48 women), 12 part-time (6 women); includes 15 minority (4 African Americans, 10 Asian Americans or Pacific Islanders, 1 Hispanic American), 78 international. Average age 26. 294 applicants, 75% accepted, 78 enrolled. In 2009, 55 master's, 10 doctorates awarded. Terminal master's awarded for partial completion of doctoral program. *Degree requirements:* For master's, thesis optional; for doctorate, comprehensive exam, thesis/dissertation, qualifying exam, public defense of dissertation. *Entrance requirements:* For master's and doctorate, GRE General Test. Additional exam requirements/recommendations for international students: Required—TOEFL (minimum score 550 paper-based; 213 computer-based; 82 iBT). *Application deadline:* For fall admission, 1/15 priority date for domestic and international students; for spring admission, 9/30 priority date for domestic and international students. Application fee: $65. Electronic applications accepted. *Financial support:* In 2009–10, 102 students received support, including 18 fellowships with full and partial tuition reimbursements available (averaging $22,853 per year), 34 research assistantships with full and partial tuition reimbursements available (averaging $23,661 per year); tuition waivers (partial) and unspecified assistantships also available. Financial award application deadline: 1/15. *Faculty research:* Advanced infrastructure systems; environmental engineering science and management; mechanics, materials, and computing; green design; global sustainable construction. Total annual research expenditures: $4.5 million. *Unit head:* Dr. James H. Garrett, Head, 412-268-2941, Fax: 412-268-7813, E-mail: garrett@cmu.edu. *Application contact:* Maxine A. Leffard, Graduate Program Administrator, 412-268-5673, Fax: 412-268-7813, E-mail: ce-admissions@andrew.cmu.edu.

The Catholic University of America, School of Engineering, Department of Civil Engineering, Washington, DC 20064. Offers environmental engineering (MCE, MSE, D Engr, PhD, Certificate); environmental engineering and management (MCE, MSE, PhD, Certificate); environmental engineering and management (D Engr); fluid and solid mechanics (MCE, MSE, PhD, Certificate); geotechnical engineering (MCE, MSE, PhD, Certificate); management of construction (MCE, MSE, D Engr, PhD); structural engineering (MSE, D Engr, PhD); systems engineering (MSE, D Engr, PhD, Certificate). Part-time programs available. *Faculty:* 5 full-time (0 women), 7 part-time/adjunct (1 woman). *Students:* 7 full-time (3 women), 18 part-time (5 women); includes 6 minority (3 African Americans, 3 Hispanic Americans), 11 international. Average age 32. 36 applicants, 47% accepted, 9 enrolled. In 2009, 8 master's, 2 doctorates awarded. *Degree requirements:* For master's, thesis optional; for doctorate, comprehensive exam, thesis/dissertation. *Entrance requirements:* For master's and doctorate, statement of purpose, official copies of academic transcripts, three letters of recommendation. Additional exam requirements/

recommendations for international students: Required—TOEFL (minimum score 580 paper-based; 237 computer-based). *Application deadline:* For fall admission, 8/1 priority date for domestic students, 7/15 for international students; for spring admission, 12/1 priority date for domestic students, 10/15 for international students. Applications are processed on a rolling basis. Application fee: $55. Electronic applications accepted. *Expenses:* Contact institution. *Financial support:* Fellowships, research assistantships, teaching assistantships, Federal Work-Study, scholarships/grants, tuition waivers (full and partial), and unspecified assistantships available. Financial award application deadline: 2/1; financial award applicants required to submit FAFSA. *Faculty research:* Geotechnical engineering, solid mechanics, construction engineering and management, environmental engineering, structural engineering. Total annual research expenditures: $438,834. *Unit head:* Dr. Lu Sun, Chair, 202-319-5164, Fax: 202-319-6677, E-mail: sunl@cua.edu. *Application contact:* Julie Schwing, Director of Graduate Admissions, 202-319-5057, Fax: 202-319-6533, E-mail: cua-admissions@cua.edu.

Columbia University, Fu Foundation School of Engineering and Applied Science, Department of Civil Engineering and Engineering Mechanics, New York, NY 10027. Offers civil engineering (MS, Eng Sc D, PhD, Engr); construction engineering and management (MS); engineering mechanics (MS, Eng Sc D, PhD, Engr). Part-time programs available. Postbaccalaureate distance learning degree programs offered (no on-campus study). *Faculty:* 10 full-time (1 woman), 4 part-time/adjunct (0 women). *Students:* 89 full-time (24 women), 48 part-time (16 women); includes 17 minority (2 African Americans, 8 Asian Americans or Pacific Islanders, 7 Hispanic Americans), 72 international. Average age 27. 221 applicants, 54% accepted, 48 enrolled. In 2009, 38 master's, 1 doctorate awarded. Terminal master's awarded for partial completion of doctoral program. *Degree requirements:* For doctorate, thesis/dissertation, qualifying exam. *Entrance requirements:* For master's, doctorate, and Engr, GRE General Test. Additional exam requirements/recommendations for international students: Required—TOEFL. *Application deadline:* For fall admission, 12/1 priority date for domestic and international students; for spring admission, 10/1 priority date for domestic and international students. Application fee: $70. Electronic applications accepted. *Financial support:* In 2009–10, 29 students received support, including 5 fellowships with full tuition reimbursements available (averaging $33,518 per year), 12 research assistantships with full tuition reimbursements available (averaging $32,761 per year), 12 teaching assistantships with full tuition reimbursements available (averaging $32,761 per year); health care benefits also available. Financial award application deadline: 12/1; financial award applicants required to submit FAFSA. *Faculty research:* Motion monitoring of Manhattan Bridge, lightweight concrete panels, simulation of life of well sealant, intercultural knowledge system dynamics, corrosion monitoring of New York City bridges. *Unit head:* Dr. Upmanu Lall, Interim Chairman and Professor, 212-854-8905, Fax: 212-854-7081, E-mail: lall@civil.columbia.edu. *Application contact:* Rene B. Testa, Professor, 212-854-3143, Fax: 212-854-6267, E-mail: testa@civil.columbia.edu.

Cornell University, Graduate School, Graduate Fields of Engineering, Field of Theoretical and Applied Mechanics, Ithaca, NY 14853-0001. Offers advanced composites and structures (M Eng); dynamics and space mechanics (MS, PhD); fluid mechanics (MS, PhD); mechanics of materials (MS, PhD); solid mechanics (MS, PhD). *Faculty:* 26 full-time (2 women). *Students:* 32 full-time (7 women); includes 2 minority (both Asian Americans or Pacific Islanders), 21 international. Average age 25. 43 applicants, 26% accepted, 4 enrolled. In 2009, 3 master's, 9 doctorates awarded. *Degree requirements:* For master's, thesis (MS); for doctorate, one foreign language, comprehensive exam, thesis/dissertation, teaching experience. *Entrance requirements:* For master's and doctorate, GRE General Test, 3 letters of recommendation. Additional exam requirements/recommendations for international students: Required—TOEFL (minimum score 600 paper-based; 237 computer-based; 77 iBT). *Application deadline:* For fall admission, 1/15 for domestic students. Application fee: $70. Electronic applications accepted. *Expenses:* Tuition: Full-time $29,500. Required fees: $70. Full-time tuition and fees vary according to degree level, program and student level. *Financial support:* In 2009–10, 2 fellowships with full tuition reimbursements, 1 teaching assistantship with full tuition reimbursement were awarded; research assistantships with full tuition reimbursements, institutionally sponsored loans, scholarships/grants, health care benefits, and unspecified assistantships also available. *Faculty research:* Biomathematics, bio-fluids, animal locomotion; non-linear dynamics, celestial mechanics, control; mechanics of materials, computational mechanics; experimental mechanics; non-linear elasticity, granular materials, phase transitions. *Unit head:* Director of Graduate Studies, 607-255-5062, Fax: 607-255-2011. *Application contact:* Graduate Field Assistant, 607-255-5062, Fax: 607-255-2011, E-mail: tam_grad@cornell.edu.

Drexel University, College of Engineering, Department of Mechanical Engineering and Mechanics, Philadelphia, PA 19104-2875. Offers mechanical engineering (MS, PhD). Part-time and evening/weekend programs available. Terminal master's awarded for partial completion of doctoral program. *Degree requirements:* For master's, thesis optional; for doctorate, thesis/dissertation. *Entrance requirements:* For master's, minimum GPA of 3.0, BS in engineering or science; for doctorate, minimum GPA of 3.5, MS in engineering or science. Additional exam requirements/recommendations for international students: Required—TOEFL. Electronic applications accepted. *Faculty research:* Composites, dynamic systems and control, combustion and fuels, biomechanics, mechanics and thermal fluid sciences.

École Polytechnique de Montréal, Graduate Programs, Department of Mechanical Engineering, Montréal, QC H3C 3A7, Canada. Offers aerothermics (M Eng, M Sc A, PhD); applied mechanics (M Eng, M Sc A, PhD); tool design (M Eng, M Sc A, PhD). Part-time and evening/weekend programs available. *Degree requirements:* For master's, one foreign language, thesis; for doctorate, one foreign language, thesis/dissertation. *Entrance requirements:* For master's, minimum GPA of 2.75; for doctorate, minimum GPA of 3.0. *Faculty research:* Noise control and vibration, fatigue and creep, aerodynamics, composite materials, biomechanics, robotics.

Georgia Institute of Technology, Graduate Studies and Research, College of Engineering, School of Civil and Environmental Engineering, Program in Engineering Science and Mechanics, Atlanta, GA 30332-0001. Offers MS, MSESM, PhD. Part-time programs available. Terminal master's awarded for partial completion of doctoral program. *Degree requirements:* For doctorate, thesis/dissertation. *Entrance requirements:* For master's, GRE; for doctorate, GRE, minimum GPA of 3.2. Additional exam requirements/recommendations for international students: Required—TOEFL. *Faculty research:* Bioengineering, structural mechanics, solid mechanics, dynamics.

Iowa State University of Science and Technology, Graduate College, College of Engineering, Department of Aerospace Engineering and Engineering Mechanics, Ames, IA 50011. Offers aerospace engineering (M Eng, MS, PhD); engineering mechanics (M Eng, MS, PhD). *Faculty:* 28 full-time (1 woman), 3 part-time/adjunct (0 women). *Students:* 50 full-time (7 women), 2 part-time (0 women); includes 4 minority (3 Asian Americans or Pacific Islanders, 1 Hispanic American), 33 international. 121 applicants, 24% accepted, 18 enrolled. In 2009, 15 master's, 8 doctorates awarded. *Degree requirements:* For master's, thesis (for some programs); for doctorate, thesis/dissertation. *Entrance requirements:* For master's and doctorate, GRE General Test, resume. Additional exam requirements/recommendations for international students: Required—TOEFL (minimum score 550 paper-based; 80 iBT) or IELTS (minimum score 6.5). *Application deadline:* For fall admission, 1/1 priority date for domestic and international students; for spring admission, 9/1 priority date for domestic and international students. Application fee: $40 ($90 for international students). Electronic applications accepted. *Expenses:* Tuition, state resident: full-time $6716. Tuition, nonresident: full-time $8908. Tuition and fees vary according to course level, course load, program and student level. *Financial support:* In 2009–10, 30 research assistantships with full and partial tuition reimbursements (averaging $15,000 per year), 18 teaching assistantships with full and partial tuition reimbursements (averaging $15,000 per year) were awarded; fellowships, scholarships/grants, health care benefits, and unspecified assistantships also available. *Unit head:* Dr. Thomas Rudolphi, Interim Chair, 515-294-5666, E-mail: aere_@iastate.edu. *Application contact:* Dr. Alric Rothmayer, Director of Graduate Education, 515-294-8851, E-mail: aere_info@iastate.edu.

The Johns Hopkins University, G. W. C. Whiting School of Engineering, Program in Engineering Management, Baltimore, MD 21218-2699. Offers biomaterials (MSEM); communications science (MSEM); computer science (MSEM); fluid mechanics (MSEM); materials science and engineering (MSEM); mechanical engineering (MSEM); mechanics and materials (MSEM); nano-biotechnology (MSEM); nanomaterials and nanotechnology (MSEM); probability and statistics (MSEM); smart product and device design (MSEM); systems analysis, management and environmental policy (MSEM). *Students:* 12 full-time (0 women), 3 international. Average age 23. 66 applicants, 67% accepted. *Entrance requirements:* For master's, GRE, 3 letters of recommendation, resume. Additional exam requirements/recommendations for international students: Required—TOEFL (minimum score 600 paper-based; 250 computer-based; 100 iBT) or IELTS (minimum score 7). *Application deadline:* For fall admission, 1/15 priority date for domestic students, 1/15 for international students; for spring admission, 9/15 priority date for domestic students, 9/15 for international students. Applications are processed on a rolling basis. Application fee: $75. Electronic applications accepted. *Financial support:* Fellowships, health care benefits available. *Unit head:* Dr. Edward R. Scheinerman, Interim Director/Vice Dean for Education, School of Engineering/Professor, Applied Mathematics and Statistics, 410-516-7395, Fax: 410-516-4880, E-mail: ers@jhu.edu. *Application contact:* Dennis McIver, Coordinator of Graduate Admissions, 410-516-8174, Fax: 410-516-0780, E-mail: graduateadmissions@jhu.edu.

Lehigh University, P.C. Rossin College of Engineering and Applied Science, Department of Mechanical Engineering and Mechanics, Bethlehem, PA 18015. Offers applied mathematics (MS, PhD); computational engineering and mechanics (MS, PhD); mechanical engineering (M Eng, MS, PhD, MBA/E); polymer science/engineering (M Eng, MS, PhD, MBA/E); MBA/E. Part-time and evening/weekend programs available. Postbaccalaureate distance learning degree programs offered. *Faculty:* 20 full-time (0 women). *Students:* 85 full-time (12 women), 32 part-time (3 women); includes 4 minority (1 African American, 2 Asian Americans or Pacific Islanders, 1 Hispanic American), 51 international. Average age 27. 320 applicants, 29% accepted, 45 enrolled. In 2009, 23 master's, 6 doctorates awarded. Terminal master's awarded for partial completion of doctoral program. *Degree requirements:* For master's, thesis; for doctorate, thesis/dissertation, general exam. *Entrance requirements:* Additional exam requirements/recommendations for international students: Required—TOEFL (minimum score 550 paper-based; 213 computer-based; 79 iBT). *Application deadline:* For fall admission, 7/15 for domestic and international students; for spring admission, 12/1 for domestic and international students. Applications are processed on a rolling basis. Application fee: $75. Electronic applications accepted. *Financial support:* In 2009–10, 30 students received support, including 8 fellowships with full and partial tuition reimbursements available (averaging $21,060 per year), 24 research assistantships with full and partial tuition reimbursements available (averaging $20,700 per year), 18 teaching assistantships with full and partial tuition reimbursements available (averaging $21,060 per year); unspecified assistantships also available. Financial award application deadline: 1/15. *Faculty research:* Thermofluids, dynamic systems, CAD/CAM, computational mechanics, solid mechanics. Total annual research expenditures: $3.1 million. *Unit head:* Dr. D. Gary Harlow, Chairman, 610-758-4102, Fax: 610-758-6224, E-mail: dgh0@lehigh.edu. *Application contact:* Jo Ann M. Casciano, Graduate Coordinator, 610-758-4107, Fax: 610-758-6224, E-mail: jmc4@lehigh.edu.

Louisiana State University and Agricultural and Mechanical College, Graduate School, College of Engineering, Department of Civil and Environmental Engineering, Baton Rouge, LA 70803. Offers environmental engineering (MSCE, PhD); geotechnical engineering (MSCE, PhD); structural engineering and mechanics (MSCE, PhD); transportation engineering (MSCE, PhD); water resources (MSCE, PhD). Part-time programs available. *Faculty:* 28 full-time (2 women). *Students:* 74 full-time (18 women), 37 part-time (6 women); includes 9 minority (1 American Indian/Alaska Native, 5 Asian Americans or Pacific Islanders, 3 Hispanic Americans), 59 international. Average age 31. 104 applicants, 63% accepted, 31 enrolled. In 2009, 16 master's, 13 doctorates awarded. *Degree requirements:* For master's, thesis optional; for doctorate, one foreign language, thesis/dissertation. *Entrance requirements:* For master's and doctorate, GRE General Test, minimum GPA of 3.0. Additional exam requirements/recommendations for international students: Required—TOEFL (minimum score 550 paper-based; 213 computer-based; 79 iBT) or IELTS (minimum score 6.5). *Application deadline:* For fall admission, 1/25 priority date for domestic students, 5/15 for international students; for spring admission, 10/15 for international students. Applications are processed on a rolling basis. Application fee: $50 ($70 for international students). Electronic applications accepted. *Financial support:* In 2009–10, 74 students received support, including 2 fellowships with full and partial tuition reimbursements available (averaging $16,672 per year), 65 research assistantships with full and partial tuition reimbursements available (averaging $11,242 per year); teaching assistantships with full and partial tuition reimbursements available, career-related internships or fieldwork, institutionally sponsored loans, scholarships/grants, and health care benefits also available. Financial award application deadline: 3/1; financial award applicants required to submit FAFSA. *Faculty research:* Mechanics and structures, environmental, geotechnical transportation, water resources. Total annual research expenditures: $2.4 million. *Unit head:* Dr. George Z. Voyiadjis, Chair/Boyd Professor, 225-578-8668, Fax: 225-578-9176, E-mail: cegzv@lsu.edu. *Application contact:* Dr. Donald Dean Adrian, Professor, 225-578-8636, E-mail: dadrian@lsu.edu.

McGill University, Faculty of Graduate and Postdoctoral Studies, Faculty of Engineering, Department of Civil Engineering and Applied Mechanics, Montréal, QC H3A 2T5, Canada. Offers environmental engineering (M Eng, M Sc, PhD); fluid mechanics (M Sc); fluid mechanics and hydraulic engineering (M Eng, PhD); materials engineering (M Eng, PhD); rehabilitation of urban infrastructure (M Eng, PhD); soil behavior (M Eng, PhD); soil mechanics and foundations (M Eng, PhD); structures and structural mechanics (M Eng, PhD); water resources (M Sc); water resources engineering (M Eng, PhD).

Michigan State University, The Graduate School, College of Engineering, Department of Mechanical Engineering, East Lansing, MI 48824. Offers engineering mechanics (MS, PhD); mechanical engineering (MS, PhD). *Entrance requirements:* For master's, GRE General Test. Additional exam requirements/recommendations for international students: Required—TOEFL. Electronic applications accepted.

Michigan Technological University, Graduate School, College of Engineering, Department of Mechanical Engineering-Engineering Mechanics, Program in Engineering Mechanics, Houghton, MI 49931. Offers MS. Part-time programs available. *Degree requirements:* For master's, comprehensive exam (for some programs), thesis (for some programs). *Entrance requirements:* For master's, GRE. Additional exam requirements/recommendations for international students: Required—TOEFL (minimum score 637 paper-based; 270 computer-based). Electronic applications accepted. *Expenses:* Contact institution.

Missouri University of Science and Technology, Graduate School, Department of Civil, Architectural, and Environmental Engineering, Rolla, MO 65409. Offers civil engineering (MS, DE, PhD); construction engineering (MS, DE, PhD); environmental engineering (MS); fluid mechanics (MS, DE, PhD); geotechnical engineering (MS, DE, PhD); hydrology and hydraulic engineering (MS, DE, PhD). Part-time and evening/weekend programs available. Terminal master's awarded for partial completion of doctoral program. *Degree requirements:* For master's, thesis optional; for doctorate, comprehensive exam, thesis/dissertation. *Entrance requirements:* For master's, GRE General Test (minimum combined score 1100), minimum GPA of 3.0; for doctorate, GRE General Test (minimum score: verbal and quantitative 400, writing 3.5), minimum GPA of 3.0. Additional exam requirements/recommendations for international students: Required—TOEFL. Electronic applications accepted. *Faculty research:* Earthquake engineering, structural optimization and control systems, structural health monitoring/damage detection, soil-structure interaction, soil mechanics and foundation engineering.

Montana State University, College of Graduate Studies, College of Engineering, Department of Civil Engineering, Bozeman, MT 59717. Offers civil engineering (MS); construction engineering management (MCEM); engineering (PhD), including applied mechanics option, civil engineering option. Part-time programs available. *Faculty:* 19 full-time (2 women), 2 part-time/adjunct (0 women). *Students:* 24 full-time (7 women), 16 part-time (3 women); includes 1 minority

Mechanics

Montana State University (continued)

(American Indian/Alaska Native), 1 international. Average age 26. 36 applicants, 50% accepted, 16 enrolled. In 2009, 15 master's, 2 doctorates awarded. *Degree requirements:* For master's, comprehensive exam, thesis (for some programs); for doctorate, comprehensive exam, thesis/dissertation. *Entrance requirements:* For master's and doctorate, GRE General Test. Additional exam requirements/recommendations for international students: Required—TOEFL (minimum score 550 paper-based; 213 computer-based). *Application deadline:* For fall admission, 7/15 priority date for domestic students, 5/15 priority date for international students; for spring admission, 12/1 priority date for domestic students, 10/1 priority date for international students. Applications are processed on a rolling basis. Application fee: $30. Electronic applications accepted. *Expenses:* Tuition, state resident: full-time $5635; part-time $3492 per year. Tuition, nonresident: full-time $17,212; part-time $7865.10 per year. Required fees: $1441.05; $153.15 per credit. Tuition and fees vary according to course load and program. *Financial support:* In 2009–10, 15 students received support, including 1 research assistantship with partial tuition reimbursement available (averaging $24,000 per year), 5 teaching assistantships with partial tuition reimbursements available (averaging $8,000 per year); scholarships/grants and tuition waivers (partial) also available. Financial award application deadline: 3/1; financial award applicants required to submit FAFSA. *Faculty research:* Snow and ice mechanics, biofilm engineering, transportation, structural and geo materials, water resources. Total annual research expenditures: $714,709. *Unit head:* Dr. Brett Gunnick, Head, 406-994-2111, Fax: 406-994-6105, E-mail: bgunnick@ce.montana.edu. *Application contact:* Dr. Carl A. Fox, Vice Provost for Graduate Education, 406-994-4145, Fax: 406-994-7433, E-mail: gradstudy@montana.edu.

New Mexico Institute of Mining and Technology, Graduate Studies, Program in Engineering Science in Mechanics, Socorro, NM 87801. Offers advanced mechanics (MS); explosives engineering (MS). *Degree requirements:* For master's, thesis (for some programs). *Entrance requirements:* For master's, GRE General Test. Additional exam requirements/recommendations for international students: Required—TOEFL (minimum score 540 paper-based; 207 computer-based). *Faculty research:* Vibrations, fluid-structure interactions.

North Dakota State University, College of Graduate and Interdisciplinary Studies, College of Engineering and Architecture, Department of Mechanical Engineering and Applied Mechanics, Fargo, ND 58108. Offers MS, PhD. Part-time programs available. *Faculty:* 15 full-time (1 woman), 1 part-time/adjunct (0 women). *Students:* 20 full-time (3 women), 20 part-time (1 woman), 23 international. Average age 28. 39 applicants, 49% accepted, 3 enrolled. In 2009, 13 master's awarded. *Degree requirements:* For master's, thesis; for doctorate, comprehensive exam, thesis/dissertation. *Entrance requirements:* For master's and doctorate, minimum GPA of 3.0. Additional exam requirements/recommendations for international students: Required—TOEFL (minimum score 550 paper-based). *Application deadline:* For fall admission, 7/1 priority date for domestic students, 5/1 priority date for international students; for spring admission, 12/1 priority date for domestic students, 9/1 priority date for international students. Applications are processed on a rolling basis. Application fee: $45 ($60 for international students). Electronic applications accepted. *Financial support:* In 2009–10, 20 students received support, including research assistantships with full tuition reimbursements available (averaging $9,000 per year), teaching assistantships with full tuition reimbursements available (averaging $9,000 per year); career-related internships or fieldwork, Federal Work-Study, and institutionally sponsored loans also available. Financial award application deadline: 2/15. *Faculty research:* Thermodynamics, finite element analysis, automotive systems, robotics, nanotechnology. Total annual research expenditures: $530,000. *Unit head:* Dr. Alan Kallmeyer, Chair, 701-231-8836, Fax: 701-231-8913, E-mail: alan.kallmeyer@ndsu.edu. *Application contact:* Dr. David A. Wittrock, Dean, 701-231-7033, Fax: 701-231-6524.

Northwestern University, McCormick School of Engineering and Applied Science, Department of Civil and Environmental Engineering, Program in Theoretical and Applied Mechanics, Evanston, IL 60208. Offers fluid mechanics (MS, PhD); solid mechanics (MS, PhD). Admissions and degrees offered through The Graduate School. Terminal master's awarded for partial completion of doctoral program. *Degree requirements:* For master's, thesis; for doctorate, thesis/dissertation. *Entrance requirements:* For master's, GRE General Test, minimum 2 letters of recommendation; for doctorate, GRE General Test, minimum 2 letters of recommendation, transcripts from all academic institutions attended. Additional exam requirements/recommendations for international students: Required—TOEFL (minimum score 600 paper-based; 250 computer-based; 100 iBT), IELTS (minimum score 7), TOEFL (internet-based) speaking score of 26. Electronic applications accepted. *Faculty research:* Composite materials, computational mechanics, fracture and damage mechanics, geophysics, nondestructive evaluation.

The Ohio State University, Graduate School, College of Engineering, Department of Mechanical Engineering, Program in Engineering Mechanics, Columbus, OH 43210. Offers MS, PhD. *Degree requirements:* For master's, thesis optional; for doctorate, thesis/dissertation. *Entrance requirements:* Additional exam requirements/recommendations for international students: Recommended—TOEFL (minimum score 600 paper-based; 250 computer-based). Electronic applications accepted. *Expenses:* Tuition, state resident: full-time $10,683. Tuition, nonresident: full-time $25,923. Tuition and fees vary according to course load and program.

Ohio University, Graduate College, Russ College of Engineering and Technology, Department of Civil Engineering, Athens, OH 45701-2979. Offers civil engineering (PhD); construction (MS); environmental (MS); geotechnical and geoenvironmental (MS); mechanics (MS); structures (MS); transportation (MS); water resources and structures (MS). Part-time programs available. *Faculty:* 13 full-time (3 women), 3 part-time/adjunct (0 women). *Students:* 18 full-time (2 women), 2 part-time (1 woman), 13 international. 22 applicants, 68% accepted, 1 enrolled. In 2009, 7 master's awarded. *Degree requirements:* For master's, comprehensive exam (for some programs), thesis or alternative; for doctorate, comprehensive exam, thesis/dissertation. *Entrance requirements:* For master's, GRE General Test, minimum GPA of 3.0, 3 letters of recommendation; for doctorate, GRE General Test. Additional exam requirements/recommendations for international students: Required—TOEFL (minimum score 550 paper-based; 80 iBT) or IELTS Academic (minimum score 6.5). *Application deadline:* For fall admission, 5/1 priority date for domestic students, 2/1 priority date for international students; for winter admission, 8/1 priority date for domestic students, 4/1 priority date for international students; for spring admission, 2/1 priority date for domestic students, 7/1 priority date for international students. Applications are processed on a rolling basis. Application fee: $50 ($55 for international students). Electronic applications accepted. *Expenses:* Tuition, state resident: full-time $7839; part-time $323 per quarter hour. Tuition, nonresident: full-time $15,831; part-time $654 per quarter hour. Required fees: $2931. *Financial support:* Research assistantships with full tuition reimbursements, teaching assistantships with full tuition reimbursements, Federal Work-Study, institutionally sponsored loans, scholarships/grants, and unspecified assistantships available. Financial award application deadline: 3/15; financial award applicants required to submit FAFSA. *Faculty research:* Noise abatement, materials and environment, highway infrastructure, subsurface investigation, (pavements, pipes, bridges, etc.). Total annual research expenditures: $1.2 million. *Unit head:* Dr. Gayle F. Mitchell, Chair, 740-593-0430, Fax: 740-593-0625, E-mail: mitchelg@ohio.edu. *Application contact:* Dr. Shad M. Sargand, Graduate Chair, 740-593-1465, Fax: 740-593-0625, E-mail: sargand@ohio.edu.

Penn State University Park, Graduate School, College of Engineering, Department of Engineering Science and Mechanics, State College, University Park, PA 16802-1503. Offers M Eng, MS, PhD.

Rutgers, The State University of New Jersey, New Brunswick, Graduate School-New Brunswick, Program in Mechanics, Piscataway, NJ 08854-8097. Offers MS, PhD. Part-time programs available. Terminal master's awarded for partial completion of doctoral program. *Degree requirements:* For master's, thesis optional, qualifying exam; for doctorate, thesis/dissertation, qualifying exam. *Entrance requirements:* For master's and doctorate, GRE General Test, GRE Subject Test (recommended). Additional exam requirements/recommendations for international students: Required—TOEFL. Electronic applications accepted. *Faculty research:* Continuum mechanics, constitutive theory, thermodynamics, visolasticity, liquid crystal theory.

San Diego State University, Graduate and Research Affairs, College of Engineering, Department of Aerospace Engineering and Engineering Mechanics, San Diego, CA 92182. Offers aerospace engineering (MS); engineering mechanics (MS); engineering sciences and applied mechanics (PhD); flight dynamics (MS); fluid dynamics (MS). Terminal master's awarded for partial completion of doctoral program. *Degree requirements:* For master's, comprehensive exam (for some programs), thesis (for some programs); for doctorate, thesis/dissertation. *Entrance requirements:* For master's, GRE General Test; for doctorate, GRE, 3 letters of recommendation. Additional exam requirements/recommendations for international students: Required—TOEFL. Electronic applications accepted. *Faculty research:* Organized structures in post-stall flow over wings/three dimensional separated flow, airfoil growth effect, probabilities, structural mechanics.

Southern Illinois University Carbondale, Graduate School, College of Engineering, Department of Civil and Environmental Engineering, Carbondale, IL 62901-4701. Offers civil engineering (MS). *Degree requirements:* For master's, comprehensive exam, thesis. *Entrance requirements:* For master's, minimum GPA of 2.7. Additional exam requirements/recommendations for international students: Required—TOEFL. *Faculty research:* Composite materials, wastewater treatment, solid waste disposal, slurry transport, geotechnical engineering.

Southern Illinois University Carbondale, Graduate School, College of Engineering, Program in Engineering Science, Carbondale, IL 62901-4701. Offers electrical systems (PhD); fossil energy (PhD); mechanics (PhD). *Degree requirements:* For doctorate, thesis/dissertation. *Entrance requirements:* For doctorate, GRE General Test, minimum GPA of 3.5. Additional exam requirements/recommendations for international students: Required—TOEFL.

The University of Alabama, Graduate School, College of Engineering, Department of Aerospace Engineering and Mechanics, Tuscaloosa, AL 35487. Offers aerospace engineering (MAE); engineering science and mechanics (MES, PhD). Part-time programs available. Post-baccalaureate distance learning degree programs offered (no on-campus study). *Faculty:* 14 full-time (1 woman). *Students:* 26 full-time (5 women), 21 part-time (4 women); includes 1 minority (Hispanic American), 19 international. Average age 27. 52 applicants, 52% accepted, 20 enrolled. In 2009, 8 degrees awarded. Terminal master's awarded for partial completion of doctoral program. *Degree requirements:* For master's, comprehensive exam (for some programs), thesis (for some programs); for doctorate, comprehensive exam, thesis/dissertation, 1 year residency. *Entrance requirements:* For master's and doctorate, GRE, minimum undergraduate GPA of 3.0. Additional exam requirements/recommendations for international students: Required—TOEFL (minimum score 550 paper-based). *Application deadline:* For fall admission, 7/1 priority date for domestic students, 1/15 priority date for international students; for spring admission, 11/1 priority date for domestic students, 6/1 priority date for international students. Applications are processed on a rolling basis. Application fee: $50 ($60 for international students). Electronic applications accepted. *Expenses:* Tuition, state resident: full-time $7000. Tuition, nonresident: full-time $19,200. *Financial support:* In 2009–10, 18 students received support, including fellowships with full tuition reimbursements available (averaging $20,000 per year), research assistantships with full tuition reimbursements available (averaging $18,375 per year), teaching assistantships with full tuition reimbursements available (averaging $18,375 per year); Federal Work-Study, institutionally sponsored loans, scholarships/grants, health care benefits, and unspecified assistantships also available. Financial award application deadline: 2/15. *Faculty research:* Intelligent computer systems, genetic algorithms, neural networks, impact and penetration mechanics, spacecraft dynamics and controls. Total annual research expenditures: $753,882. *Unit head:* Dr. Stanley E. Jones, Interim Department Head and Cudworth Professor, 205-348-7242, Fax: 205-348-7240, E-mail: sejones@eng.ua.edu. *Application contact:* Dr. John E. Jackson, Professor, 205-348-7306, Fax: 208-348-7240, E-mail: johnjackson@eng.ua.edu.

The University of Arizona, Graduate College, College of Engineering, Department of Civil Engineering and Engineering Mechanics, Tucson, AZ 85721. Offers civil engineering (MS, PhD); engineering mechanics (MS, PhD). Part-time programs available. *Faculty:* 11. *Students:* 38 full-time (11 women), 23 part-time (3 women); includes 9 minority (3 American Indian/Alaska Native, 3 Asian Americans or Pacific Islanders, 3 Hispanic Americans), 33 international. Average age 30. 74 applicants, 46% accepted, 7 enrolled. In 2009, 7 master's, 6 doctorates awarded. *Degree requirements:* For master's, thesis; for doctorate, thesis/dissertation, departmental qualifying exam. *Entrance requirements:* For master's, GRE General Test, 3 letters of recommendation, statement of purpose; for doctorate, GRE General Test, minimum GPA of 3.5, 3 letters of recommendation, statement of purpose. Additional exam requirements/recommendations for international students: Required—TOEFL (minimum score 550 paper-based; 213 computer-based; 79 iBT). *Application deadline:* For fall admission, 6/1 for domestic students, 12/1 for international students; for spring admission, 10/1 for domestic students, 6/1 for international students. Applications are processed on a rolling basis. Application fee: $75. Electronic applications accepted. *Expenses:* Tuition, state resident: full-time $9028. Tuition, nonresident: full-time $24,890. *Financial support:* In 2009–10, 27 research assistantships with full tuition reimbursements (averaging $18,074 per year), 7 teaching assistantships with full tuition reimbursements (averaging $18,074 per year) were awarded; institutionally sponsored loans, scholarships/grants, health care benefits, tuition waivers (partial), and unspecified assistantships also available. Financial award application deadline: 4/6. *Faculty research:* Constitutive modeling, rehabilitation of structures, groundwater, earthquake engineering, hazardous waste treatment. Total annual research expenditures: $1.1 million. *Unit head:* Kevin E. Lansey, Department Head, 520-621-6564, E-mail: lansey@engr.arizona.edu. *Application contact:* Graduate Coordinator, 520-621-2266, Fax: 520-621-2550, E-mail: ceemg@engr.arizona.edu.

University of California, Berkeley, Graduate Division, College of Engineering, Department of Civil and Environmental Engineering, Berkeley, CA 94720-1500. Offers engineering and project management (M Eng, MS, D Eng, PhD); environmental engineering (M Eng, MS, D Eng, PhD); geoengineering (M Eng, MS, D Eng, PhD); structural engineering, mechanics and materials (M Eng, MS, D Eng, PhD); transportation engineering (M Eng, MS, D Eng, PhD); M Arch/MS; MCP/MS; MPP/MS. *Students:* 368 full-time (125 women). Average age 27. 921 applicants, 179 enrolled. In 2009, 158 master's, 39 doctorates awarded. *Degree requirements:* For master's, comprehensive exam or thesis (MS); for doctorate, thesis/dissertation, qualifying exam. *Entrance requirements:* For master's, GRE General Test, minimum GPA of 3.0, 3 letters of recommendation; for doctorate, GRE General Test, minimum GPA of 3.5, 3 letters of recommendation. Additional exam requirements/recommendations for international students: Required—TOEFL (minimum score 570 paper-based; 230 computer-based). *Application deadline:* For fall admission, 2/3 for domestic students. Application fee: $70 ($90 for international students). Electronic applications accepted. *Financial support:* Fellowships, research assistantships, teaching assistantships, unspecified assistantships available. *Unit head:* Prof. Lisa Alvarez-Cohen, Chair, 510-643-8739, Fax: 510-643-5264, E-mail: chair@ce.berkeley.edu. *Application contact:* Shelly Okimoto, Graduate Advisor, 510-642-6464, Fax: 510-643-5264, E-mail: aao@ce.berkeley.edu.

University of California, Merced, Division of Graduate Studies, School of Natural Sciences, Merced, CA 95343. Offers applied mathematics (MS, PhD); biological engineering and small-scale technologies (MS, PhD); environmental systems (MS, PhD); mechanical engineering and applied mechanics (MS, PhD); physics and chemistry (PhD); quantitative and systems biology (MS, PhD). *Expenses:* Tuition, nonresident: full-time $15,102. Required fees: $10,919.

University of California, San Diego, Office of Graduate Studies, Department of Mechanical and Aerospace Engineering, Program in Applied Mechanics, La Jolla, CA 92093. Offers MS, PhD. Part-time programs available. *Degree requirements:* For master's, comprehensive exam or thesis; for doctorate, thesis/dissertation, qualifying exam. *Entrance requirements:* For master's and doctorate, GRE General Test, minimum GPA of 3.0. Additional exam requirements/recommendations for international students: Required—TOEFL. Electronic applications accepted.

Faculty research: Combustion engineering, environmental mechanics, magnetic recording, materials processing, computational fluid dynamics.

University of Cincinnati, Graduate School, College of Engineering, Department of Aerospace Engineering and Engineering Mechanics, Cincinnati, OH 45221. Offers MS, PhD. Part-time programs available. Terminal master's awarded for partial completion of doctoral program. *Degree requirements:* For master's, project or thesis; for doctorate, thesis/dissertation. *Entrance requirements:* For master's and doctorate, GRE General Test. Additional exam requirements/recommendations for international students: Required—TOEFL (minimum score 550 paper-based; 213 computer-based). Electronic applications accepted. *Faculty research:* Computational fluid mechanics/propulsion, large space structures, dynamics and guidance of VTOL vehicles.

University of Dayton, Graduate School, School of Engineering, Department of Civil and Environmental Engineering, Dayton, OH 45469-1300. Offers engineering mechanics (MSEM); environmental engineering (MSCE); geotechnical engineering (MSCE); structural engineering (MSCE); transport engineering (MSCE); water resources engineering (MSCE). Part-time programs available. *Faculty:* 8 full-time (2 women), 1 part-time/adjunct (0 women). *Students:* 10 full-time (6 women), 8 part-time (1 woman); includes 3 minority (all African Americans), 7 international. Average age 29. 35 applicants, 49% accepted, 6 enrolled. In 2009, 3 master's awarded. *Degree requirements:* For master's, thesis optional. *Entrance requirements:* Additional exam requirements/recommendations for international students: Required—TOEFL (minimum score 550 paper-based; 213 computer-based; 80 iBT). *Application deadline:* For fall admission, 8/1 for domestic students, 3/1 priority date for international students; for winter admission, 7/1 priority date for international students; for spring admission, 1/1 priority date for international students. Applications are processed on a rolling basis. Application fee: $0 ($50 for international students). Electronic applications accepted. *Expenses:* Tuition: Full-time $8412; part-time $701 per credit hour. Required fees: $325; $65 per course. $25 per semester. Tuition and fees vary according to course load, degree level and program. *Financial support:* In 2009–10, 3 research assistantships (averaging $10,780 per year), 4 teaching assistantships with partial tuition reimbursements (averaging $5,110 per year) were awarded. Financial award applicants required to submit FAFSA. *Faculty research:* Physical modeling of hydraulic systems, finite element methods, mechanics of composite materials, transportation systems safety, high-velocity wear. Total annual research expenditures: $421,839. *Unit head:* Dr. Donald V. Chase, Interim Chair, 937-229-3847, Fax: 937-229-3491, E-mail: donald.chase@notes.udayton.edu. *Application contact:* Graduate Admissions, 937-229-4411, Fax: 937-229-4729, E-mail: gradadmission@udayton.edu.

University of Illinois at Urbana–Champaign, Graduate College, College of Engineering, Department of Mechanical Science and Engineering, Champaign, IL 61820. Offers mechanical engineering (MS, PhD); theoretical and applied mechanics (MS, PhD); MS/MBA. *Faculty:* 54 full-time (4 women), 2 part-time/adjunct (0 women). *Students:* 331 full-time (38 women), 34 part-time (5 women); includes 28 minority (1 African American, 18 Asian Americans or Pacific Islanders, 9 Hispanic Americans), 189 international. 488 applicants, 39% accepted, 95 enrolled. In 2009, 48 master's, 32 doctorates awarded. Terminal master's awarded for partial completion of doctoral program. *Entrance requirements:* For master's, GRE General Test, minimum GPA of 3.25; for doctorate, GRE General Test, minimum GPA of 3.5. Additional exam requirements/recommendations for international students: Required—TOEFL (minimum score 613 paper-based; 257 computer-based; 103 iBT), v. *Application deadline:* Applications are processed on a rolling basis. Application fee: $60 ($75 for international students). Electronic applications accepted. *Financial support:* In 2009–10, 37 fellowships, 271 research assistantships, 90 teaching assistantships were awarded; tuition waivers (full and partial) also available. *Faculty research:* Combustion and propulsion, design methodology, dynamic systems and controls, energy transfer, materials behavior and processing, manufacturing systems operations, management. *Unit head:* Placid Mathew Ferreira, Head, 217-333-0639, Fax: 217-244-6534, E-mail: pferreir@illinois.edu. *Application contact:* Kathy A. Smith, Admissions and Records Officer, 217-244-4539, Fax: 217-244-6534, E-mail: smith15@illinois.edu.

University of Maryland, College Park, Academic Affairs, A. James Clark School of Engineering, Department of Mechanical Engineering, College Park, MD 20742. Offers electronic packaging and reliability (MS, PhD); manufacturing and design (MS, PhD); mechanics and materials (MS, PhD); reliability engineering (M Eng, MS, PhD); thermal and fluid sciences (MS, PhD). Part-time and evening/weekend programs available. Postbaccalaureate distance learning degree programs offered. *Faculty:* 84 full-time (5 women), 14 part-time/adjunct (1 woman). *Students:* 217 full-time (37 women), 76 part-time (13 women); includes 39 minority (11 African Americans, 2 American Indian/Alaska Native, 18 Asian Americans or Pacific Islanders, 8 Hispanic Americans), 140 international. 420 applicants, 21% accepted, 64 enrolled. In 2009, 40 master's, 33 doctorates awarded. *Degree requirements:* For master's, thesis optional; for doctorate, thesis/dissertation, qualifying exam. *Entrance requirements:* For master's, GRE General Test, 3 letters of recommendation; for doctorate, GRE General Test, minimum GPA of 3.0. Additional exam requirements/recommendations for international students: Required—TOEFL. *Application deadline:* For fall admission, 5/15 for domestic students, 2/1 for international students; for spring admission, 10/1 for domestic students, 6/1 for international students. Applications are processed on a rolling basis. Application fee: $60. Electronic applications accepted. *Expenses:* Tuition, area resident: Part-time $471 per credit hour. Tuition, state resident: part-time $471 per credit hour. Tuition, nonresident: part-time $1016 per credit hour. Required fees: $337.04 per term. *Financial support:* In 2009–10, 7 fellowships with full and partial tuition reimbursements (averaging $13,060 per year), 168 research assistantships with tuition reimbursements (averaging $23,703 per year), 10 teaching assistantships with tuition reimbursements (averaging $18,884 per year) were awarded; Federal Work-Study and scholarships/grants also available. Support available to part-time students. Financial award applicants required to submit FAFSA. *Faculty research:* Injection molding, electronic packaging, fluid mechanics, product engineering. Total annual research expenditures: $15 million. *Unit head:* Dr. Avram Bar-Cohen, Chairman, 301-405-3173, Fax: 301-314-9477, E-mail: abc@umd.edu. *Application contact:* Dr., Graduate Director, 301-405-0376.

University of Massachusetts Lowell, College of Arts and Sciences, Department of Physics and Applied Physics, Program in Applied Physics, Lowell, MA 01854-2881. Offers applied mechanics (PhD); applied physics (MS, PhD), including optical sciences (MS). Terminal master's awarded for partial completion of doctoral program. *Degree requirements:* For master's, thesis; for doctorate, 2 foreign languages, thesis/dissertation. *Entrance requirements:* For master's, GRE General Test, 3 letters of reference; for doctorate, GRE General Test, transcripts, 3 letters of reference. Additional exam requirements/recommendations for international students: Required—TOEFL.

University of Minnesota, Twin Cities Campus, Institute of Technology, Department of Aerospace Engineering and Mechanics, Minneapolis, MN 55455-0213. Offers aerospace engineering (M Aero E); aerospace engineering and mechanics (MS, PhD). Part-time programs available. *Degree requirements:* For doctorate, thesis/dissertation. *Entrance requirements:* Additional exam requirements/recommendations for international students: Required—TOEFL (minimum score 550 paper-based; 213 computer-based). Electronic applications accepted. *Faculty research:* Fluid mechanics, solid and continuum fluid mechanics, computational mechanics, aerospace systems.

University of Nebraska–Lincoln, Graduate College, College of Engineering, Department of Engineering Mechanics, Lincoln, NE 68588. Offers MS, PhD. *Degree requirements:* For master's, thesis optional; for doctorate, comprehensive exam, thesis/dissertation. *Entrance requirements:* For master's and doctorate, GRE. Additional exam requirements/recommendations for international students: Required—TOEFL (minimum score 550 paper-based; 213 computer-based). Electronic applications accepted. *Faculty research:* Polymer mechanics, piezoelectric materials, meshless methods, smart materials, fracture mechanics.

University of New Brunswick Fredericton, School of Graduate Studies, Faculty of Engineering, Department of Mechanical Engineering, Fredericton, NB E3B 5A3, Canada. Offers applied mechanics (M Eng, M Sc E, PhD); mechanical engineering (M Eng, M Sc E, PhD). Part-time programs available. *Faculty:* 14 full-time (1 woman), 9 part-time/adjunct (0 women). *Students:* 36 full-time (8 women), 2 part-time (1 woman). In 2009, 6 master's, 2 doctorates awarded. *Degree requirements:* For master's, thesis; for doctorate, comprehensive exam, thesis/dissertation, qualifying exam. *Entrance requirements:* For master's, minimum GPA of 3.0; successful completion of BScE degree; for doctorate, Qualifying Examinations, minimum GPA of 3.0;successful completion of MScE degree. Additional exam requirements/recommendations for international students: Required—TOEFL (minimum score 550 paper-based), IELTS, TWE (minimum score 4). *Application deadline:* For fall admission, 3/1 priority date for domestic students. Applications are processed on a rolling basis. Application fee: $50 Canadian dollars. Tuition and fees charges are reported in Canadian dollars. *Expenses:* Tuition, area resident: Full-time $5562 Canadian dollars; part-time $2781 Canadian dollars per year. Required fees: $49.75 Canadian dollars per term. *Financial support:* In 2009–10, 50 teaching assistantships (averaging $4,200 per year) were awarded; research assistantships. *Faculty research:* Analysis of gross motor activities as a means of assessing upper limb prosthesis; distance determination algorithms and their applications, void nucleation in automotive aluminum alloy. *Unit head:* Dr. Andrew Gerber, Director of Graduate Studies, 506-458-7194, Fax: 506-453-5025, E-mail: agerber@unb.ca. *Application contact:* Susan Shea-Perrott, Graduate Secretary, 506-458-7742, Fax: 506-453-5025, E-mail: susan@unb.ca.

University of Pennsylvania, School of Engineering and Applied Science, Department of Mechanical Engineering and Applied Mechanics, Philadelphia, PA 19104. Offers applied mechanics (MSE, PhD); mechanical engineering (MSE, PhD). Part-time programs available. *Faculty:* 25 full-time (4 women), 7 part-time/adjunct (0 women). *Students:* 77 full-time (9 women), 18 part-time (3 women); includes 9 minority (2 African Americans, 6 Asian Americans or Pacific Islanders, 1 Hispanic American), 42 international. 236 applicants, 28% accepted, 32 enrolled. In 2009, 18 master's, 9 doctorates awarded. *Degree requirements:* For master's, thesis optional; for doctorate, thesis/dissertation. *Entrance requirements:* Additional exam requirements/recommendations for international students: Required—TOEFL. *Application deadline:* For fall admission, 1/2 priority date for domestic students. Applications are processed on a rolling basis. Application fee: $70. Electronic applications accepted. *Expenses:* Tuition: Full-time $25,660; part-time $4758 per course. Required fees: $2152; $270 per course. Tuition and fees vary according to course load, degree level and program. *Financial support:* Fellowships, research assistantships, teaching assistantships, institutionally sponsored loans, scholarships/grants, traineeships, health care benefits, and unspecified assistantships available. *Faculty research:* Heat transfer, fluid mechanics, energy conversion, solid mechanics, dynamics of mechanisms and robots.

University of Southern California, Graduate School, Viterbi School of Engineering, Sonny Astani Department of Civil Engineering, Los Angeles, CA 90089. Offers applied mechanics (MS); civil engineering (MS, PhD); computer-aided engineering (ME, Graduate Certificate); construction management (MCM); engineering technology commercialization (Graduate Certificate); environmental engineering (MS, PhD); environmental quality management (ME); structural design (ME); sustainable cities (Graduate Certificate); transportation systems (Graduate Certificate). Part-time programs available. Postbaccalaureate distance learning degree programs offered (no on-campus study). *Faculty:* 16 full-time (2 women), 35 part-time/adjunct (5 women). *Students:* 165 full-time (48 women), 65 part-time (16 women); includes 54 minority (40 Asian Americans or Pacific Islanders, 14 Hispanic Americans), 108 international. 451 applicants, 41% accepted, 73 enrolled. In 2009, 74 master's, 10 doctorates awarded. Terminal master's awarded for partial completion of doctoral program. *Degree requirements:* For doctorate, thesis/dissertation. *Entrance requirements:* For master's, GRE General Test; for doctorate, General GRE. *Application deadline:* For fall admission, 3/1 priority date for domestic and international students; for spring admission, 10/1 priority date for domestic and international students. Applications are processed on a rolling basis. Application fee: $85. Electronic applications accepted. *Expenses:* Tuition: Full-time $25,980; part-time $1315 per unit. Required fees: $554. One-time fee: $35 full-time. Full-time tuition and fees vary according to degree level and program. *Financial support:* In 2009–10, fellowships with full tuition reimbursements (averaging $30,000 per year), research assistantships with full tuition reimbursements (averaging $19,250 per year), teaching assistantships with full tuition reimbursements (averaging $19,250 per year) were awarded; career-related internships or fieldwork, scholarships/grants, health care benefits, and unspecified assistantships also available. Financial award application deadline: 12/1; financial award applicants required to submit CSS PROFILE or FAFSA. *Faculty research:* Geotechnical engineering, transportation engineering, structural engineering, construction management, environmental engineering, water resources. Total annual research expenditures: $4.2 million. *Unit head:* Dr. Jean-Pierre Bardet, Chair, 213-740-0609, Fax: 213-744-1426, E-mail: bardet@usc.edu. *Application contact:* Jennifer A. Gerson, Director of Student Services, 213-740-0573, Fax: 213-740-8662, E-mail: jgerson@usc.edu.

The University of Tennessee, Graduate School, College of Engineering, Department of Mechanical, Aerospace and Biomedical Engineering, Program in Engineering Science, Knoxville, TN 37996. Offers applied artificial intelligence (MS); composite materials (MS, PhD); computational mechanics (MS, PhD); engineering science (MS, PhD); fluid mechanics (MS, PhD); industrial engineering (PhD); optical engineering (MS, PhD); solid mechanics (MS, PhD); MS/MBA. Part-time programs available. *Students:* 9 full-time (0 women), 4 part-time (1 woman); includes 2 minority (both African Americans), 2 international. Average age 34. 5 applicants, 60% accepted, 1 enrolled. In 2009, 2 master's awarded. *Degree requirements:* For master's, thesis or alternative; for doctorate, comprehensive exam, thesis/dissertation. *Entrance requirements:* For master's and doctorate, GRE, minimum GPA of 2.7. Additional exam requirements/recommendations for international students: Required—TOEFL (minimum score 550 paper-based; 213 computer-based). *Application deadline:* For fall admission, 2/1 priority date for domestic and international students; for spring admission, 6/15 priority date for international students. Applications are processed on a rolling basis. Application fee: $35. Electronic applications accepted. *Expenses:* Tuition, state resident: full-time $6826; part-time $380 per semester hour. Tuition, nonresident: full-time $21,844; part-time $1147 per semester hour. Tuition and fees vary according to program. *Financial support:* In 2009–10, 1 student received support, including 5 research assistantships with full tuition reimbursements available (averaging $14,628 per year), 2 teaching assistantships with full tuition reimbursements available (averaging $10,104 per year); fellowships, career-related internships or fieldwork, Federal Work-Study, institutionally sponsored loans, health care benefits, and unspecified assistantships also available. Financial award application deadline: 2/1; financial award applicants required to submit FAFSA. *Faculty research:* Thermal science, computational mechanics, computational fluid dynamics, micro/nano-scale science and engineering for bio-systems. *Unit head:* Dr. William Hamel, Head, 865-974-5115, Fax: 865-974-5274, E-mail: whamel@utk.edu. *Application contact:* Dr. Gary V. Smith, Chair, Graduate Programs Committee, 865-974-5271, E-mail: gvsmith@utk.edu.

The University of Tennessee Space Institute, Graduate Programs, Program in Engineering Sciences and Mechanics, Tullahoma, TN 37388-9700. Offers engineering sciences (MS, PhD); mechanics (MS, PhD). Part-time programs available. *Faculty:* 2 full-time (0 women), 2 part-time/adjunct (0 women). *Students:* 3 full-time (0 women), 1 (woman) part-time. 1 applicant, 0% accepted, 0 enrolled. In 2009, 1 master's awarded. *Degree requirements:* For master's, thesis (for some programs); for doctorate, one foreign language, thesis/dissertation. *Entrance requirements:* Additional exam requirements/recommendations for international students: Required—TOEFL (minimum score 550 paper-based; 213 computer-based), IELTS (minimum score 6.5). *Application deadline:* For fall admission, 2/1 for international students; for spring admission, 6/15 for international students. Applications are processed on a rolling basis. Application fee: $35. Electronic applications accepted. *Expenses:* Tuition, state resident: full-time $6826; part-time $380 per hour. Tuition, nonresident: full-time $20,622; part-time $1147 per hour. Required fees: $10 per hour. One-time fee: $90 full-time. *Financial support:* In 2009–10, 3 research assistantships with full tuition reimbursements (averaging $17,791 per year) were awarded; fellowships with full and partial tuition reimbursements, career-related internships or fieldwork, Federal Work-Study, institutionally sponsored loans, health care benefits, tuition waivers (full and partial), and unspecified assistantships also available. Financial

Mechanics

The University of Tennessee Space Institute *(continued)*
award applicants required to submit FAFSA. *Unit head:* Dr. Basil Antar, Degree Program Chairman, 931-393-7471, Fax: 931-393-7444, E-mail: bantar@utsi.edu. *Application contact:* Dee Merriman, Coordinator III, 931-393-7293, Fax: 931-393-7201, E-mail: dmerrima@utsi.edu.

The University of Texas at Austin, Graduate School, Cockrell School of Engineering, Department of Aerospace Engineering and Engineering Mechanics, Program in Engineering Mechanics, Austin, TX 78712-1111. Offers MS, PhD. *Degree requirements:* For doctorate, one foreign language, thesis/dissertation, qualifying exam. *Entrance requirements:* For master's and doctorate, GRE General Test.

University of Wisconsin–Madison, Graduate School, College of Engineering, Department of Engineering Physics, Madison, WI 53706-1380. Offers engineering mechanics (MS, PhD); nuclear engineering and engineering physics (MS, PhD). Part-time programs available. Post-baccalaureate distance learning degree programs offered (minimal on-campus study). *Faculty:* 21 full-time (1 woman), 8 part-time/adjunct (2 women). *Students:* 88 full-time (8 women), 4 part-time (0 women); includes 5 minority (1 African American, 2 Asian Americans or Pacific Islanders, 2 Hispanic Americans). Average age 25. 152 applicants, 54% accepted, 19 enrolled. In 2009, 18 master's, 8 doctorates awarded. Terminal master's awarded for partial completion of doctoral program. *Degree requirements:* For master's, thesis optional; for doctorate, thesis/dissertation. *Entrance requirements:* For master's and doctorate, GRE General Test, minimum GPA of 3.0 in last 60 hours, appropriate bachelor's degree. Additional exam requirements/recommendations for international students: Required—TOEFL (minimum score 600 paper-based; 245 computer-based). *Application deadline:* For fall admission, 1/15 priority date for domestic students. Applications are processed on a rolling basis. Application fee: $56. Electronic applications accepted. *Expenses:* Tuition, state resident: part-time $594 per credit. Tuition, nonresident: part-time $1504 per credit. Required fees: $65 per credit. Tuition and fees vary according to course load, program and reciprocity agreements. *Financial support:* In 2009–10, 78 students received support, including 7 fellowships with full tuition reimbursements available (averaging $20,760 per year), 71 research assistantships with full tuition reimbursements available (averaging $19,596 per year), 10 teaching assistantships with full tuition reimbursements available (averaging $12,894 per year); career-related internships or fieldwork, Federal Work-Study, and institutionally sponsored loans also available. Support available to part-time students. Financial award application deadline: 1/15. *Faculty research:* Fission reactor engineering and safety, plasma physics and fusion technology, plasma processing and ion implantation, nanotechnology, engineering mechanics and astronautics. Total annual research expenditures: $12.4 million. *Unit head:* Dr. Michael L. Corradini, Chair, 608-263-1646, Fax: 608-263-7451, E-mail: corradini@engr.wisc.edu. *Application contact:* Dr. Michael L. Corradini, Chair, 608-263-1646, Fax: 608-263-7451, E-mail: corradini@engr.wisc.edu.

University of Wisconsin–Milwaukee, Graduate School, College of Engineering and Applied Science, Program in Engineering, Milwaukee, WI 53201-0413. Offers civil engineering (MS); electrical and computer engineering (MS); energy engineering (Certificate); engineering (PhD); engineering management (MS); engineering mechanics (MS); ergonomics (Certificate); industrial and management engineering (MS); manufacturing engineering (MS); materials engineering (MS); mechanical engineering (MS); MUP/MS. Part-time programs available. *Faculty:* 44 full-time (6 women). *Students:* 119 full-time (22 women), 130 part-time (22 women); includes 23 minority (2 African Americans, 14 Asian Americans or Pacific Islanders, 7 Hispanic Americans), 126 international. Average age 32. 231 applicants, 67% accepted, 33 enrolled. In 2009, 29 master's, 14 doctorates awarded. *Degree requirements:* For master's, comprehensive exam (for some programs), thesis or alternative; for doctorate, comprehensive exam, thesis/dissertation, internship. *Entrance requirements:* For master's, GRE, minimum GPA of 2.75; for doctorate, GRE, minimum GPA of 3.5. Additional exam requirements/recommendations for international students: Required—TOEFL (minimum score 550 paper-based; 79 iBT), IELTS (minimum score 6.5). *Application deadline:* For fall admission, 1/1 priority date for domestic students; for spring admission, 9/1 for domestic students. Applications are processed on a rolling basis. Application fee: $45 ($75 for international students). *Expenses:* Tuition, state resident: full-time $8800. Tuition, nonresident: full-time $20,760. Tuition and fees vary according to program and reciprocity agreements. *Financial support:* In 2009–10, 18 research assistantships, 51 teaching assistantships were awarded; fellowships, career-related internships or fieldwork, Federal Work-Study, and unspecified assistantships also available. Support available to part-time students. Financial award application deadline: 4/15. Total annual research expenditures: $2.9 million. *Unit head:* David Yu, Head, 414-229-6169, E-mail: yu@uwm.edu. *Application contact:* Betty Warras, General Information Contact, 414-229-4982, Fax: 414-229-6967, E-mail: bwarras@uwm.edu.

Virginia Polytechnic Institute and State University, Graduate School, College of Engineering, Department of Engineering Science and Mechanics, Blacksburg, VA 24061. Offers engineering mechanics (MS, PhD). Part-time programs available. Terminal master's awarded for partial completion of doctoral program. *Degree requirements:* For master's, thesis optional; for doctorate, comprehensive exam, thesis/dissertation, 45 credit hours. *Entrance requirements:* For master's and doctorate, GRE General Test. Additional exam requirements/recommendations for international students: Required—TOEFL (minimum score 550 paper-based; 213 computer-based). Electronic applications accepted. *Faculty research:* Solid mechanics and materials, fluid mechanics, dynamics and vibrations, composite materials, computational mechanics and finite element methods.

FLORIDA INSTITUTE OF TECHNOLOGY

College of Engineering
Mechanical and Aerospace Engineering Programs

Programs of Study

The graduate program in mechanical engineering has four areas of specialization: dynamic systems, robotics, and controls; structures, solid mechanics, and materials; thermal-fluid sciences; and biomedical engineering. The graduate program in aerospace engineering has three areas of specialization, which include aerodynamics and fluid dynamics, aerospace structures and materials, and combustion and propulsion. The master's degree requires 30 semester credit hours of course work, which may include 6 semester credit hours of thesis. The Ph.D. degree is offered in the same areas of specialization for each program for students who wish to carry out advanced research. The Ph.D. is conferred primarily in recognition of creative accomplishments and ability to independently investigate scientific or engineering problems. The work should consist of advanced studies and research leading to a significant contribution to the knowledge in a particular subject.

Research Facilities

Located in the Fluid Mechanics and Aerodynamics Laboratory are two low-speed wind tunnels used for boundary layer studies and a shock tube for compressible flow studies. Instrumentation includes hot-wire anemometry, pressure scanning systems, flow visualization, and computerized data acquisition. The Heat Transfer Laboratory includes experimentation of buoyancy effects and combustion, emission, radiation effects in porous ceramic burners, and various energy conversion systems. The nearby Kennedy Space Center, Florida Solar Energy Center, and aerospace firms also provides the opportunity for collaborative energy research. The Structural Mechanics Laboratory includes ovens and axial test, vibration, and instrumented low-energy impact systems to study the mechanical behavior of advanced composite and recycled plastic materials. The Dynamic Systems and Controls Laboratory provides a facility for research work on machinery diagnostics and mechatronics. In addition, the Robotics Laboratory provides advanced robot research capabilities. Research in biomedical material processing and bioheat transfer applications is conducted in the Laser, Optics, and Instrumentation Laboratory.

Financial Aid

Graduate student assistantships, awarded each year to a limited number of highly qualified entering students, provide full tuition beginning in the fall semester, plus a stipend for the 2010–11 academic year. Assistants are assigned duties related to both undergraduate instruction and faculty research.

Cost of Study

Tuition is $1040 per credit hour in 2010–11. There is a tuition deposit of $300 for new students. Book costs are estimated at $550 per year.

Living and Housing Costs

Room and board on campus cost approximately $4500 per semester in 2010–11. On-campus housing (dormitories and apartments) is available for full-time single and married graduate students, but priority for dormitory rooms is given to undergraduate students. Many apartment complexes and rental houses are available near the campus.

Student Group

Graduate students constitute more than one half of the approximately 4,100 students at Florida Tech's Melbourne campus. Only about one fourth of the students are from the state of Florida; the remainder are from all parts of the United States and from many other countries. There are 60 graduate students in the Mechanical and Aerospace Engineering Programs.

Student Outcomes

Graduates of the program obtained positions in various companies, such as Boeing, Siemens, Earth Tech, EG&G, Harris Corp., Honeywell Aircraft Systems, I-NET, Johnson Controls World Services, Lockheed Martin, Loral Aerospace, MCNC, NASA, Northrop Grumman, Rosemount Inc., Piper Aircraft, United Space Alliance, United Technologies, U.S. Air Force Civilian Personnel, and U.S. Navy Civilian Personnel.

Location

The greater Melbourne metropolitan area is located on Florida's "Space Coast," south of the Kennedy Space Center and Cape Canaveral Air Force Station. The climate is mild both winter and summer, with abundant sunshine and little variation in temperature. Opportunities for recreation include extensive ocean beaches; the Indian River, an attractive saltwater lagoon between the campus and the ocean; the St. Johns River and Lake Washington, west of Melbourne; and central Florida's numerous commercial attractions in Orlando. There are also outstanding entertainment, shopping, and housing facilities in the Melbourne area.

The Institute

In response to a need for specialized and advanced educational opportunities, Florida Institute of Technology was founded in 1958 by a group of scientists and engineers pioneering America's space program at Cape Canaveral. Florida Tech has rapidly developed into a residential institution that is the largest private technological university in the Southeast. Supported by community and industry, Florida Tech is currently the recipient of many research grants and contracts, a number of which provide financial support for graduate students. The campus is situated on 175 acres of partially wooded and beautifully landscaped grounds.

Applying

Forms for applying for admission and assistantships are sent on request. Admission in the fall semester is recommended, but full-time students may also enter in the spring semester, and part-time students may enter in any semester. Full-time students entering in the spring should plan a reduced course load in their first semester. International students should apply at least six months in advance. Assistantship applications and all supporting material must be received by March 1.

Correspondence and Information

Dr. Pei-feng Hsu, Head
Department of Mechanical and Aerospace Engineering
Florida Institute of Technology
150 West University Boulevard
Melbourne, Florida 32901
Phone: 321-674-8092
E-mail: vborton@fit.edu
Web site: http://coe.fit.edu/mae

Office of Graduate Admissions
Florida Institute of Technology
150 West University Boulevard
Melbourne, Florida 32901-6975
Phone: 321-674-8027
E-mail: grad-admissions@fit.edu
Web site: http://www.fit.edu

Florida Institute of Technology

THE FACULTY AND THEIR RESEARCH

Mark Archambault, Assistant Professor; Ph.D., Stanford. Fluid dynamics, spray and particulate dynamics, liquid droplet modeling, rocket and air-breathing propulsion, modeling and simulation of rocket engine chambers and fuel injectors, hydrogen fuel cell modeling, computational fluid dynamics (CFD).

Youngsik Choi, Assistant Professor; Ph.D., Purdue. Nanomachining, biomanufacturing processes, mechanical design, precision engineering, superfinish hard machining, nanomechanics, fracture mechanics.

David C. Fleming, Associate Professor; Ph.D., Maryland. Structural mechanics, advanced composite materials, crashworthy aerospace vehicle design, finite-element analysis.

Hector Gutierrez, Associate Professor; Ph.D., North Carolina State. Dynamic systems, mechatronics, magnetic suspension systems, electromechanical energy conversion, precision motion control, nonlinear control, characterization and control of novel actuators (electromagnetic, magneto-rheological).

Pei-feng Hsu, Professor; Ph.D., Texas at Austin. Radiative and multimode heat transfer, numerical methods, premixed combustion modeling in porous ceramics, radiative properties of microscale and nanoscale devices, heat exchangers and thermal systems design.

Daniel R. Kirk, Associate Professor; Ph.D., MIT. Propulsion, air-breathing and rocket engine modeling, nuclear thermal rocket propulsion, experimental and computational fluid dynamics, low-gravity fluid dynamics and slosh, structure of internal and vortical flows, transient compressible flow and shock tube experimentation, combustion, reacting shear layers, heat transfer, aeroacoustics, blast field and blast-induced traumatic brain injury modeling.

Pierre Larochelle, Professor; Ph.D., California, Irvine. Theoretical kinematics, mechanism and machine design, robotics, dynamics and controls of mechanical systems, computer-aided design.

Taeyoung Lee, Assistant Professor; Ph.D., Michigan. Geometric mechanics and control, geometric numerical integration, nonlinear control, adaptive control, estimation, neural network, multibody systems.

Mary Helen McCay, Research Professor; Ph.D., Florida. Metallurgy, crystal growth, laser interaction with materials.

T. Dwayne McCay, Professor and Provost; Ph.D., Auburn. Low-density gas dynamics, high-speed flows, propulsion systems, laser interaction with materials.

Kunal Mitra, Professor; Ph.D., Polytechnic. Thermal-fluid sciences, lasers for biomedical and material processing applications, thermal radiation, bio-heat transfer, heat conduction, nanobiosensors, solar energy and nanomaterials-based photovoltaic systems.

Razvan Rusovici, Assistant Professor; Ph.D., Virginia Tech. Smart materials and structures, structural dynamics, instrumentation, experimental modal analysis, finite-element analysis, turbomachinery, bioengineering structures.

Paavo Sepri, Associate Professor; Ph.D., California, San Diego. Fluid mechanics, turbulence, convective heat transfer, boundary layers, aerodynamics, wind-tunnel testing, droplet combustion, computational fluid dynamics.

Yahya I. Sharaf-Eldeen, Associate Professor; Ph.D., Ohio State; Ph.D., Oklahoma State. Modeling, simulation, and design of dynamic systems; advanced dynamics, vibration, and design of machinery; thermal-fluid sciences and energy/power systems.

Chelakara S. Subramanian, Professor; Ph.D., Newcastle (Australia). Experimental fluid mechanics, turbulence measurements and modeling, wireless instrumentation, data processing techniques, wind-tunnel experimentation, flow instabilities, structure of complex turbulent flows, boundary layer receptivity.

Bo Yang, Associate Professor; Ph.D., Houston. Nanomechanics, fabrication of semiconductor nanodevices, composites, fracture mechanics, Green's functions, boundary-element method, multiscale modeling.

Shengyuan Yang, Assistant Professor; Ph.D., Illinois at Urbana-Champaign. Cell and tissue mechanobiology, microelectromechanical and nanoelectromechanical systems (MEMS/NEMS), sensors and actuators, mechanics of materials.

RESEARCH AREAS

Fluid Mechanics and Aerodynamics

Turbulence research within the mechanical and aerospace engineering programs is being carried out experimentally in topics such as boundary layers with embedded vortices, spinning objects, passive control of flow separation, and the effect of unsteadiness on shear-layer instabilities. Theoretical and computational research is being pursued to characterize flow instabilities, leaks of cryogenic fluids, turbulent boundary-layer structure, aerodynamic interactions, moisture transport, internal flow configurations, and pressure and temperature sensitive paints. Research is also underway in wind engineering and advanced instrumentation.

Structures, Solid Mechanics, and Materials

Efforts in mechanics and materials engineering focus on characterizing the mechanical behavior of composite materials and on the design and manufacture of structures made of them. The relationship between microstructure and macroscopic behavior is being studied to better understand the effects of environmental conditions on the constituents of composite materials. Research is being conducted experimentally by the application of static and dynamic loads, including impact and vibration on composite and biomaterials, leading to an understanding of damage mechanisms. Computational models are being developed for predicting the mechanical performance of structures for the propagation of delaminations, for the optimization of composite structure geometries, and for improving vehicle crashworthiness.

Dynamic Systems, Robotics, and Mechatronics

Research in the design and control of machine systems and other generalized systems is being pursued along both theoretical and practical avenues. Recent research contributions have been made in the synthesis and analysis of spatial and spherical mechanisms. Along the experimental avenue, research is being conducted in the monitoring and diagnosis of vibration and flutter in rotating machinery, dynamic systems, and control and mechatronics. Other research topics include magnetic suspension systems, electromechanical energy conversion, and precision motion control.

Thermal Sciences and Propulsion

In the disciplines of energy, heat transfer, and combustion, research programs address aspects relevant to steady-state and transient radiative transfer in thermal and biomedical applications; advanced computational methods for solving problems in radiative transport, bio–heat transfer, mixed-mode heat transfer, and electronic cooling applications; combustion in porous ceramics; aerospace propulsion; modeling of fuel spray dynamics; automotive combustion; issues related to environmental pollution and energy; liquid rocket propulsion system modeling and analysis; low-gravity propellant thermal stratification and slosh computational and experiments for future space vehicles; 6-degree-of-freedom flight dynamics, controls, and heat transfer modeling of launch vehicles; combustion chamber modeling and kinetics; modeling of advanced reactor concepts for nuclear thermal rocket propulsion; 6-degree-of-freedom thrust measurement of existing and new solid rocket motor concepts; microscale rocket and air-breathing engines.

NC STATE UNIVERSITY

NORTH CAROLINA STATE UNIVERSITY

College of Engineering
Department of Mechanical and Aerospace Engineering

Programs of Study

The Department of Mechanical and Aerospace Engineering (MAE) at North Carolina State University is the largest in the state and among the largest and most prominent in the nation. The MAE Department is housed in a new state-of-the-art building on the University's beautiful Centennial Campus. The strengths of the Department lie in the thermal sciences, particularly thermal fluids, fluid mechanics, and combustion; mechanical sciences, including manufacturing mechanics, structural dynamics, and materials and controls; and the aerospace sciences, particularly aerodynamics, aircraft design, space flight dynamics, space systems design, hypersonics, propulsion, flight research using UAVs, and computational fluid dynamics. The Department offers the Master of Science (M.S.) degree in both mechanical engineering (ME) and aerospace engineering (AE) with a thesis or nonthesis option and the Doctor of Philosophy (Ph.D.) degree in both ME and AE. Nonthesis M.S. degrees in both mechanical engineering and aerospace engineering are offered through distance education. The Department also offers an accelerated B.S./M.S. degree in both mechanical engineering and aerospace engineering and an "enroute Ph.D." program that provides a direct path from the B.S. degree to the Ph.D., awarding the M.S. "enroute" to the Ph.D.

Research Facilities

The Department houses several facilities that support research activities. Included in these facilities are instruments and equipment associated with the centers and laboratories of the MAE Department. The Precision Engineering Center is a multidisciplinary research center that performs research in metrology (sensors and measurement systems), innovative precision fabrication processes, and real-time process control. The Flight Research Laboratory conducts state-of-the-art research in UAV propulsion integration and control. Laboratory facilities in Aerospace Engineering include computational hypersonic aerodynamics and propulsion, spacecraft structures, navigation and control, and composite materials and fabrication.

The Sound and Vibration Laboratory encompasses a range of graduate research activities in the areas of acoustics and mechanical vibration. The laboratory has a new large anechoic chamber as well as computational and data acquisition equipment. The Adaptive Structures Laboratory conducts basic and applied research on shape memory alloys. The Optical Sensing and Monitoring Laboratory conducts research in fiber optic sensors for structural health monitoring of composite structures. The Computational Fluid-Particle Dynamics Laboratory conducts research in areas such as two-phase flow, blood rheology, microscale flows, particle dynamics, and cell biology.

The Applied Energy Research Laboratory conducts research in experimental fluid mechanics, heat transfer, and combustion, and collaborates with the North Carolina Solar Center on alternative energy initiatives. As a facility established to promote the implementation of solar technologies, the North Carolina Solar Center, operating in conjunction with the NCSU Solar House, has a variety of resources that support this function. The Energy analysis and Diagnostic Laboratory conducts research and development in energy efficiency as well as alternative energy sources.

Financial Aid

The Department of Mechanical and Aerospace Engineering offers a number of graduate research and teaching assistantships ranging from $13,275 to $26,000 per year. A limited number of fellowships are also available.

Cost of Study

Tuition and fees for full-time study in 2010–11 are $3522.65 per semester for North Carolina residents and $9546.65 per semester for nonresidents. Students taking fewer than 9 credits pay reduced amounts. Both North Carolina State residents and out-of-state students appointed as teaching or research assistants have all tuition and health insurance covered.

Living and Housing Costs

On-campus dormitory facilities are provided for unmarried graduate students. In 2010–11, the rent for double rooms starts at $2330 per semester. Accommodations in the newest residence hall for graduate students cost $2650 per semester (Wolf Village). Apartments for married students in King Village rent for $560 per month for a studio, $620 for a one-bedroom apartment, and $715 for a two-bedroom apartment.

Student Group

The Department of Mechanical and Aerospace Engineering has an enrollment of 1,417 undergraduate students and 305 graduate students. Most graduate students find full- or part-time support through fellowships, assistantships, and special duties with research organizations in the area.

Location

Raleigh, the state capital, has a population of 392,083. Nearby is the Research Triangle Park, one of the largest and fastest-growing research institutions of its type in the country. The Raleigh metro area population is 1,428,171. The University's concert series has more subscribers than any other in the United States. Excellent sports and recreational facilities are also available.

The University and The College

North Carolina State University is the principal technological institution of the University of North Carolina System. Its largest schools are the Colleges of Engineering, Agriculture and Life Sciences, Physical and Mathematical Sciences, and Humanities and Social Sciences. Total enrollment in the Department of Mechanical and Aerospace Engineering is 1,722. A strong cooperative relationship exists with nearby Duke University and the University of North Carolina at Chapel Hill, as well as with the Research Triangle Park. The Department has 39 tenure track faculty members and 6 instructors with professorial rank. Some of their current research areas are listed on the back of this page.

Applying

Application submission deadlines for fall and spring semesters, respectively, are June 25 and November 25 for U.S. citizens and March 1 and July 15 for international applicants. Application forms may be downloaded from http://www2.acs.ncsu.edu/grad/applygrad.htm. Electronic submission of applications is required. An applicant desiring to visit the campus may request information concerning travel allowances by writing to the Director of Graduate Programs. Students may apply for fellowships or assistantships in their application for admission. For further information, students should write to the University address.

Correspondence and Information

Director of Graduate Programs
Department of Mechanical and Aerospace Engineering
North Carolina State University
Box 7910
Raleigh, North Carolina 27695-7910
Phone: 919-515-3026
Web site: http://www.mae.ncsu.edu/

North Carolina State University

THE FACULTY AND THEIR RESEARCH

G. D. Buckner, Associate Professor; Ph.D., Texas at Austin, 1996. Electromechanical systems; intelligent system identification and control; applications, including active vehicle suspension systems, magnetic bearings, and machine operations. (e-mail: greg_buckner@ncsu.edu)

F. R. DeJarnette, Professor; Ph.D., Virginia Tech, 1965. Engineering and computational methods in aerothermodynamics. (e-mail: dejar@eos.ncsu.edu)

T. A. Dow, Professor; Ph.D., Northwestern, 1972. Precision mechanism/machine design, process development (machining, grinding, polishing), actuator design/control (mechatronic, piezoelectric); metrology, nanotechnology. (e-mail: thomas_dow@ncsu.edu)

T. Echekki, Associate Professor; Ph.D., Stanford, 1993. Direct numerical simulation and large eddy simulation of turbulent combustion, combustion theory and dynamics. (e-mail: techekk@eos.ncsu.edu)

H. M. Eckerlin, Professor; Ph.D., North Carolina State, 1972. Industrial energy conservation/management, solar-active/passive/photovoltaic, renewable energy, steam generation, incineration. (e-mail: eckerlin@eos.ncsu.edu)

J. R. Edwards Jr., Professor; Ph.D., North Carolina State, 1993. CFD, 2-D and 3-D compressible flows, chemically reacting and multiphase flows, turbulence modeling. (e-mail: jredward@eos.ncsu.edu)

J. W. Eischen, Associate Professor; Ph.D., Stanford, 1986. Computational solid mechanics, elasticity, fracture mechanics, structural dynamics. (e-mail: eischen@eos.ncsu.edu)

T. Fang, Assistant Professor; Ph.D., Illinois, 2007. Combustion and propulsion, internal combustion engines, exhaust emissions and air pollution control, alternative fuels, renewable energy, spray and atomization, laser diagnostics for reacting flows, energy conversion systems. (e-mail: tfang2@ncsu.edu)

S. Ferguson, Assistant Professor; Ph.D., Buffalo, 2008. Design theory, reconfigurability, multidisciplinary/multiobjective optimization. (e-mail: smfergu2@ncsu.edu)

A. Gopalarathnam, Associate Professor; Ph.D., Illinois at Urbana-Champaign, 1999. Applied aerodynamics, flight mechanics, aircraft design, design methodologies. (e-mail: agopalar@eos.ncsu.edu)

R. D. Gould, Professor and Head; Ph.D., Purdue, 1987. Experimental heat transfer, electronic cooling, fluid mechanics, combustion, turbulence, nonintrusive optical diagnostics. (e-mail: gould@eos.ncsu.edu)

C. E. Hall Jr., Associate Professor; Ph.D., Ohio State, 1986. Flight dynamics and control, nonlinear control theory, RPV system design and flight testing. (e-mail: chall@skyraider.mae.ncsu.edu)

H. A. Hassan, Professor; Ph.D., Illinois at Urbana-Champaign, 1956. Fluid mechanics, aerodynamics, combustion, transition, turbulence, Monte Carlo methods, CFD. (e-mail: hassan@eos.ncsu.edu)

H. Y. Huang, Assistant Professor; Ph.D., Pittsburgh, 2004. Degradation mechanisms in rechargeable battery cathode materials via theoretical and computational approaches. (e-mail: hshuang@ncsu.edu)

X. Jiang, Assistant Professor; Ph.D., Tsinghua (Beijing), 1997. High-frequency ultrasound bioimaging, developing electromechanical devices for extreme environments, new smart-material structures for energy conversion (harvesting, sensing, actuation). (e-mail: xjiang5@ncsu.edu)

R. F. Keltie, Professor; Ph.D., North Carolina State, 1978. Structural acoustics, vibration of rib-stiffened structures, acoustic radiation, mechanical vibrations. (e-mail: keltie@eos.ncsu.edu)

E. C. Klang, Associate Professor; Ph.D., Virginia Tech, 1983. Automotive engineering, analytical and experimental studies of composite materials, aerospace structural analysis. (e-mail: klang@eos.ncsu.edu)

C. Kleinstreuer, Professor; Ph.D., Vanderbilt, 1977. Computational biofluid mechanics; convection heat and mass transfer; two-phase flow, including microfluidics and system optimization. (e-mail: ck@eos.ncsu.edu; Web site: http://www.mae.ncsu.edu/research/ck_CFPDlab)

A. V. Kuznetsov, Associate Professor; Ph.D., Russian Academy of Sciences, 1992. Heat transfer and fluid flow in porous media, modeling of solidification processing, macrosegregation and processes in the mushy zone during solidification of binary alloys. (e-mail: avkuznet@eos.ncsu.edu)

H. Luo, Associate Professor; Ph.D., Paris VI, 1989. Computational fluid dynamics, numerical methods, shock waves, parallel computing, multimaterial flows, mesh generation methods. (e-mail: hluo2@ncsu.edu)

K. M. Lyons, Associate Professor; Ph.D., Yale, 1994. Experimental combustion, laser diagnostics, jet flames, turbulent mixing. (e-mail: lyons@eos.ncsu.edu)

A. P. Mazzoleni, Associate Professor; Ph.D., Wisconsin–Madison, 1992. Dynamics, vibrations, nonlinear systems, astronautics, spacecraft design. (e-mail: a_mazzoleni@ncsu.edu)

R. T. Nagel, Professor, Associate Department Head and Director of the Graduate Program; Ph.D., Connecticut, 1980. Acoustics, aeroacoustics, active noise control, experimental fluid mechanics. (e-mail: nagel@eos.ncsu.edu)

G. Ngaile, Assistant Professor; Ph.D., Kumamoto (Japan), 1999. Tribology in manufacturing, modeling and optimization of manufacturing processes, material characterization, tool design. (e-mail: gngaile@unity.ncsu.edu)

K. J. Peters, Associate Professor; Ph.D., Michigan, 1996. Optical fiber sensors, structural health monitoring, composite materials. (e-mail: kjpeters@eos.ncsu.edu)

A. Rabiei, Associate Professor; Ph.D., Tokyo, 1997. Fracture mechanics, materials science, reliability and nondestructive evaluation of materials and structures, thin-film coatings, MEMS. (e-mail: arabiei@eos.ncsu.edu)

M. K. Ramasubramanian, Associate Professor; Ph.D., Syracuse, 1987. Design, manufacturing, mechanics, behavior of paper and short-fiber composites, mechatronics design, unmanned autonomous vehicles, automotive mechatronics. (e-mail: rammk@eos.ncsu.edu)

P. I. Ro, Professor; Ph.D., MIT, 1989. Precision mechatronics, robotics, manufacturing automation, control theory, vehicle dynamics. (e-mail: ro@eos.ncsu.edu)

W. L. Roberts, Professor; Ph.D., Michigan, 1992. Experimental combustion, laser diagnostics, propulsion, turbulence-chemistry interactions. (e-mail: bill_roberts@eos.ncsu.edu)

A. Saveliev, Associate Professor; Ph.D., Moscow Institute of Physics and Technology, 1988, Non-thermal plasmas for pollution control and material synthesis, energy systems, fuel processing and gasification. (e-mail: avsaveli@ncsu.edu)

S. Seelecke, Associate Professor; Ph.D., Berlin Technical, 1999. Shape memory/autoadaptive materials, thermophysics of materials. (e-mail: stefan_seelecke@ncsu.edu)

L. M. Silverberg, Professor and Director of Undergraduate Programs, IMSE; Ph.D., Virginia Tech, 1983. Structural electrodynamics and control, electromechanical systems. (e-mail: silver@eos.ncsu.edu)

J. S. Strenkowski, Professor; Ph.D., Virginia, 1976. Finite-element analysis, nonlinear stresses, structural dynamics, computer-aided design and optimization. (e-mail: jsstren@eos.ncsu.edu)

R. H. Tolson, Langley Professor; Ph.D., Old Dominion, 1990. Space flight orbital and rigid body mechanics, guidance, navigation and control; planetary atmospheric aero-assisted mission aerodynamics and atmospheric modeling. (e-mail: rhtolson@ncsu.edu).

J. F. Tu, Professor; Ph.D., Michigan, 1991. Laser material processing, high speed machining/spindle technology, monitoring and modeling of manufacturing processes, precision engineering, control systems, mechatronics. (e-mail: jftu@unity.ncsu.edu)

T. Ward, Assistant Professor; Ph.D., California, Santa Barbara, 2003. Heat/mass transfer in multiphase flows, fluid mixing, electro-hydromechanics and dynamical systems. (e-mail: tward@ncsu.edu)

F. Wu, Associate Professor; Ph.D., Berkeley, 1995. Robust and gain-scheduling control, control theory, applications including automotive engine, aircraft and missile control, smart-structure control. (e-mail: fwu@eos.ncsu.edu)

F. G. Yuan, Professor; Ph.D., Illinois at Urbana-Champaign, 1986. Structural health monitoring, microsensor design, failure analysis, fracture and life prediction of advanced materials and structures. (e-mail: yuan@eos.ncsu.edu)

Y. Zhu, Assistant Professor; Ph.D., Northwestern, 2005. MEMS/NEMS design, fabrication, and characterization; mechanics and material issues in nanostructures and thin films; experimental solid mechanics. (e-mail: yong_zhu@ncsu.edu).

M. A. Zikry, Professor; Ph.D., California, San Diego, 1990. Dynamics plasticity and fracture, constitutive relations for solids, computational solid mechanics. (e-mail: zikry@eos.ncsu.edu)

EMERITUS PROFESSORS

E. M. Afify, J. A. Bailey, M. A. Boles, J. A. Edwards, F. J. Hale, F. D. Hart, T. H. Hodgson, R. R. Johnson, J. W. Leach, D. J. Maday, D. S. McRae, J. C. Mulligan, J. N. Perkins, L. H. Royster, F. O. Smetana, F. Y. Sorrell, G. D. Walberg, C. F. Zorowski.

STANFORD UNIVERSITY

Department of Mechanical Engineering

Programs of Study	The Department of Mechanical Engineering is administratively organized into five groups: Biomechanical Engineering (BME); Design; Flow Physics and Computational Engineering (FPCE); Mechanics and Computation; and Thermosciences. Academic programs range from the general program in mechanical engineering to programs with particular concentrations such as product design and biomechanical engineering.
	The Biomechanical Engineering (BME) program has teaching and research activities which focus primarily on musculoskeletal biomechanics, neuromuscular biomechanics, cardiovascular biomechanics, and rehabilitation engineering. Research in other areas, including hearing, ocean, plant, and vision biomechanics, exists in collaboration with associated faculty in biology, engineering, and medicine. The Biomechanical Engineering program has particularly strong research interactions with the Mechanics and Computation and the Design groups, and the departments of Functional Restoration, Neurology, Radiology, and Surgery in the School of Medicine.
	The Design Group emphasizes cognitive skill development for creative design. It is concerned with automatic control, computer-aided design, creativity, design aesthetics, design for manufacturability, design research, experimental stress analysis, fatigue and fracture mechanics, finite element analysis, human factors, kinematics, manufacturing systems, microcomputers in design, micro-electromechanics systems (MEMS), robotics, and vehicle dynamics. The Design Group offers undergraduate and graduate programs in product design (jointly with the Department of Art and Art History) and is centrally involved in the founding of Stanford's new Hasso Plattner Institute of Design.
	The Flow Physics and Computational Engineering Group (FPCE) is developing new theories, models, and computational tools for accurate engineering design analysis and control of complex flows (including acoustics, chemical reactions, interactions with electromagnetic waves, plasmas, and other phenomena) of interest in aerodynamics, electronics cooling, environment engineering, materials processing, planetary entry, propulsion and power systems, and other areas. A significant emphasis of FPCE research is on modeling and analysis of physical phenomena in engineering systems. FPCE students and research staff are developing new methods and tools for generation, access, display, interpretation, and post-processing of large databases resulting from numerical simulations of physical systems. Research in FPCE ranges from advanced simulation of complex turbulent flows to active flow control. The FPCE faculty teaches graduate and undergraduate courses in acoustics, aerodynamics, computational fluid mechanics, computational mathematics, fluid mechanics, combustion, and thermodynamics and propulsion.
	The Mechanics and Computational Group covers biomechanics, continuum mechanics, dynamics, experimental and computational mechanics, finite element analysis, fluid dynamics, fracture mechanics, micromechanics, nanotechnology, and simulation-based design. Qualified students can work as research project assistants, engaging in thesis research in working association with the faculty director and fellow students. Projects include analysis, synthesis, and control of systems; biomechanics; flow dynamics of liquids and gases; fracture and micro-mechanics, vibrations, and nonlinear dynamics; and original theoretical, computational, and experimental investigations in the strength and deformability of elastic and inelastic elements of machines and structures.
	The Thermosciences Group conducts experimental and analytical research on both fundamental and applied topics in the general area of thermal and fluid systems. Research strengths include high Reynolds number flows, microfluidics, combustion and reacting flows, multiphase flow and combustion, plasma sciences, gas physics and chemistry, laser diagnostics, microscale heat transfer, convective heat transfer, and energy systems. Research motivation comes from applications including air-breathing and space propulsion, bioanalytical systems, pollution control, electronics fabrication and cooling, stationary and mobile energy systems, biomedical systems, and materials processing. There is a strong emphasis on fundamental experiments leading towards advances in modeling, optimization, and control of complex systems.
Research Facilities	Excellent research facilities are available at the University. Some of the resources used by the Department include the following: Biomimetics and Dexterous Manipulation Lab, BioMotion Research Laboratory, d'Arbeloff Undergraduate Research and Teaching Lab, Design Observatory, Dynamic Design Lab, Design Research Laboratory, Engine Research Lab, Heat Transfer and Turbulence Mechanics Lab (HTTM), High Temperature Gas Dynamics Lab (HTGL), Internal Combustion Engine Lab, Mechanical Dissection Lab, Mechanical Testing Lab, Microscale Mechanical Engineering Labs, Microscale Thermal and Mechanical Characterization Lab (MTMC), Neuromuscular Biomechanics Laboratory, Product Realization Laboratory, Robotic Locomotion Lab, Rapid Prototyping Lab for Energy and Biology, Shock Tube Lab, Soft Tissue Biomechanics Laboratory, Spray Combustion Lab, Stanford Microsystems Laboratory, Stanford Plasma Physics Laboratory, Telerobotics Lab, and UQLAB: Uncertainty Quantification in Computational Engineering.
Financial Aid	Each year, the Department awards several graduate fellowships, primarily to entering master's degree candidates who have indicated their desire to ultimately pursue a Ph.D. These awards are based on merit. Fellowships normally provide full tuition and a living-expense stipend for the five-quarter period of study leading to the master's degree. Research assistantships are normally available to students at the post–master's degree level and occasionally for master's degree candidates. Loans based on financial need are available to U.S. citizens.
Cost of Study	In 2009–10, tuition is $8930 for 8 to 10 units and $13,740 per quarter for 11 to 18 units. Other fees, such as student health insurance, student association, and a one-time document fee, are also required.
Living and Housing Costs	Per the University's estimated graduate student expense budget for 2010–11, a single graduate student living on campus for nine months can expect to spend $24,336 ($31,424 for twelve months) in rent, medical insurance, local transportation, food, and personal items. Students living off campus should add 10–15 percent to the total living allowance.
Student Group	The Department has approximately 250 doctoral students and 250 master's students from all parts of the nation and the world. Approximately 40 to 50 doctoral degrees and 170 master's degrees are awarded each year.
Location	The campus, extending from the wooded area surrounding Palo Alto to the foothills of the Coast Range, offers a great variety of recreational activities. The University is surrounded by the Stanford Industrial Park and San Francisco's busy suburbs. San Francisco, with its theaters, galleries, and restaurants, is 30 miles to the north. There is boating on nearby San Francisco Bay, and Pacific beaches are a 45-minute drive to the west. The Sierra Nevada snow country is a 4-hour drive east. The wine-producing areas of the state, the Gold Rush country, and Monterey, Carmel, and the Big Sur areas are within easy reach of the campus.
The University	Stanford University was founded in 1885 by Senator and Mrs. Leland Stanford and has an international reputation as an outstanding educational institution. Stanford has a long-standing tradition of academic excellence in the engineering and physical science fields and has produced many prominent engineers and scientists. The University's atmosphere is an unusual blend of a pleasant and uncrowded environment, a spirited and dynamic student body and faculty, and unswerving standards of academic excellence.
Applying	Completed applications for the M.S. program and the Ph.D. program, including transcripts, letters of recommendation, and GRE General Test scores, must be received by December 7. Students should take the GRE General Test no later than September/October to ensure that the scores are received by Stanford by this date. Decisions on financial awards are made by the Admissions Committee on the basis of review of the candidate's application and supplementary credentials.
Correspondence and Information	Indrani Gardella, Student Services Manager Patrick Ferguson, Admissions Specialist Brittany Voelker, Student Services Specialist Mechanical Engineering Department Building 530, Room 125 Stanford University Stanford, California 94305-3030 Phone: 650-724-7660 Fax: 650-723-4882 E-mail: meinquiry@stanford.edu Web site: http://me.stanford.edu/

Stanford University

THE FACULTY AND THEIR AREAS OF RESEARCH

Biomechanical Engineering
Thomas Andriacchi, Professor of Mechanical Engineering and Orthopedic Surgery; Ph.D., Illinois, 1974.
Gary S. Beaupre, Consulting Professor of Mechanical Engineering and Orthopedic Surgery; Ph.D., Stanford, 1983.
Dennis R. Carter, Professor of Mechanical Engineering; Ph.D., Stanford, 1976.
Scott L. Delp, Associate Professor of Mechanical Engineering and Chairman, Bioengineering; Ph.D., Stanford, 1990.
Marc E. Levenston, Associate Professor of Mechanical Engineering; Ph.D., Stanford, 1995.
R. Lane Smith, Ph.D., Professor (Research), by courtesy, and Associate Professor (Research) of Orthopedic Surgery.
Charles Taylor, Associate Professor of Bioengineering and, by courtesy, Associate Professor of Mechanical Engineering; Ph.D., Stanford, 1996.
Felix Zajac, Professor Emeritus of Mechanical Engineering and Orthopedic Surgery (School of Medicine); Ph.D., Stanford, 1968.

Design
Banny Banerjee, Associate Professor (Teaching) of Mechanical Engineering; M.S., Stanford, 2000.
David W. Beach, Professor (Teaching) of Mechanical Engineering; M.S., Stanford, 1972.
Bill Burnett, Consulting Assistant Professor of Mechanical Engineering and Executive Director for the Product Design Program; M.S., Stanford, 1982.
J. Edward Carryer, Consulting Associate Professor of Mechanical Engineering; Ph.D., Stanford, 1992.
Mark R. Cutkosky, Professor of Mechanical Engineering and Associate Chair for Design and Manufacturing; Ph.D., Carnegie Mellon, 1985.
J. Christian Gerdes, Associate Professor of Mechanical Engineering; Ph.D., Berkeley, 1996.
David M. Kelley, Professor of Mechanical Engineering; M.S., Stanford, 1978.
Thomas W. Kenny, Professor of Mechanical Engineering; Ph.D., Berkeley, 1989.
Larry J. Leifer, Professor of Mechanical Engineering and of Neurology (School of Medicine); Ph.D., Stanford, 1969.
Drew V. Nelson, Professor of Mechanical Engineering; Ph.D., Stanford, 1978.
Friedrich B. Prinz, Professor and Chair of Mechanical Engineering and Materials Science; Ph.D., Vienna, 1975.
Bernard Roth, Professor of Mechanical Engineering; Ph.D., Columbia, 1962.
Sheri D. Sheppard, Professor of Mechanical Engineering; Ph.D., Michigan, 1985.
Kenneth J. Waldron, Professor (Research) of Mechanical Engineering; Ph.D., Stanford, 1969.

Flow Physics, Computation and Engineering
Eric Darve, Assistant Professor of Mechanical Engineering; Ph.D., Paris VI (Curie), 1999.
John Eaton, Professor and Department Vice Chairman; Ph.D., Stanford, 1980.
Gianluca Iaccarino, Assistant Professor of Mechanical Engineering; Ph.D., Bari (Italy), 2005.
Sanjiva Lele, Professor of Aeronautics and Astronautics and of Mechanical Engineering; Ph.D., Cornell, 1985.
Parviz Moin, Professor of Mechanical Engineering; Ph.D., Stanford, 1978.
Eric Shaqfeh, Professor of Chemical Engineering and Mechanical Engineering; Ph.D., Stanford, 1986.

Mechanics and Computation
David M. Barnett, Professor of Mechanical Engineering and Materials Science; Ph.D., Stanford, 1967.
Wei Cai, Assistant Professor of Mechanical Engineering; Ph.D., MIT, 2001.
Eric Darve, Assistant Professor of Mechanical Engineering; Ph.D., Paris VI (Curie), 1999.
Charbel Farhat, Professor (also with ICME); Ph.D., Berkeley, 1986.
Ellen Kuhl, Assistant Professor of Mechanical Engineering; Dr.-Ing. habil., Kaiserslautern (Germany), 2004.
Adrian Lew, Assistant Professor of Mechanical Engineering; Ph.D., Caltech, 2003.
Peter M. Pinsky, Professor of Mechanical Engineering; Ph.D., Berkeley, 1981.
Beth Pruitt, Assistant Professor of Mechanical Engineering; Ph.D., Stanford, 2002.
Charles R. Steele, Professor Emeritus of Mechanical Engineering and of Aeronautics and Astronautics; Ph.D., Stanford, 1960.

Thermosciences
Craig T. Bowman, Professor of Mechanical Engineering; Ph.D., Princeton, 1966.
Mark A. Cappelli, Professor of Mechanical Engineering; Ph.D., Toronto, 1987.
John Eaton, Professor and Department Vice Chairman; Ph.D., Stanford, 1980.
Christopher F. Edwards, Associate Professor of Mechanical Engineering; Ph.D., Berkeley, 1985.
Kenneth E. Goodson, Professor of Mechanical Engineering; Ph.D., MIT, 1993.
Ronald K. Hanson, Professor of Mechanical Engineering; Ph.D., Stanford, 1968.
Charles H. Kruger Jr., Professor of Mechanical Engineering; D.I.C., Imperial College (London), 1957; Ph.D., MIT, 1960.
Reginald E. Mitchell, Associate Professor of Mechanical Engineering; Sc.D., MIT, 1975.
Juan Santiago, Associate Professor of Mechanical Engineering; Ph.D., Illinois, 1995.
Xiaolin Zheng, Assistant Professor of Mechanical Engineering; Ph.D., Princeton, 2006.

UNIVERSITY OF NEBRASKA–LINCOLN

College of Engineering
Department of Mechanical Engineering

Programs of Study

The Department of Mechanical Engineering offers programs leading to the M.S. and Ph.D. degrees. There are three primary areas of emphasis within the Department: thermal/fluids engineering, systems and design engineering, and materials science engineering. The Department offers a broad program of study leading to the M.S. in mechanical engineering. The thesis-based program requires 24 hours of course work and at least 6 hours of thesis credit. Students may obtain an M.S. in mechanical engineering with a specialization in metallurgical engineering or, by taking a stronger materials course concentration, with a specialization in materials science engineering. It typically takes nineteen months to complete the master's program.

Students in the doctoral program may obtain the Doctor of Philosophy in engineering with a designated field of either mechanical engineering or chemical and materials engineering. A Ph.D. supervisory committee, in consultation with the student, arranges an appropriate program of doctoral course work. After the course work is substantially completed, the graduate student must pass a written comprehensive exam administered by the supervisory committee. In addition to the course work, doctoral students must complete a written Ph.D. dissertation with an oral presentation and defense. It typically requires three years of study after the M.S. to complete the Ph.D., but an M.S. is not required for admission.

Research Facilities

There are eight specialized research laboratories in the Department of Mechanical Engineering. The Computational Thermal-Fluid Sciences Laboratory is a state-of-the-art workstation facility for research using finite-difference, finite-element, and Green's functions methods applied to problems in fluid flow, heat transfer, combustion, and DNA replication. Design, simulation, and crash testing of roadside safety hardware are conducted at the Midwest Roadside Safety Facility. The Robotics and Mechatronics Laboratory performs research on surgical, industrial, planetary, mobile, and highway maintenance robots. The Central Facility for Electron Microscopy provides hands-on access, with training, to comprehensive, well-equipped electron microscopes, sample preparation, and related computing for surface and nanoscale observation and characterization of materials. It is supported by the University's Nebraska Center for Materials and Nanoscience. Measurement and characterization of the mechanical and physical properties of materials is the purview of the Physical/Mechanical Materials Characterization Laboratory. In the Thin Film Laboratory research is conducted on thin-film deposition and characterization, while work in the X-Ray Diffraction Laboratory focuses on powder and single-crystal X-ray diffraction.

Financial Aid

Approximately 65 percent of the Department's full-time graduate students are currently supported by research assistantships, teaching assistantships, and/or fellowships. Applicants with degrees from U.S. institutions and highly qualified international students are considered for such awards on a competitive basis. In addition to a monthly stipend, students holding research or teaching assistantships receive a tuition waiver so they pay only program and facilities fees.

Cost of Study

Tuition in 2007–08 for Nebraska residents was $261.75 per credit hour. For nonresident students, it was $705.75 per credit hour. Fees are based on the number of hours the student is enrolled; to calculate, refer to http://studentaccounts.unl.edu/tuitionfee/tandfa1011.shtml. Students are expected to pay the program and facilities fees, library fee, engineering fee, course fees, registration fee, and international fees. N-Card charges and late fees may apply.

Living and Housing Costs

On-campus room and board costs in the 2010–11 academic year range from $6500 to $7649. Rates for married student housing range from $475 to $600 per month, depending on size and location. For more information on campus housing, visit http://www.unl.edu/housing/family. Privately owned rental units within walking distance are also readily available; these units are advertised by the owners.

Student Group

The Department of Mechanical Engineering has approximately 52 full-time and 5 part-time graduate students. Approximately 65 percent of the mechanical engineering graduate students are supported either by the Department or research. The student population is diverse; currently 60 percent of the students in the Department are international.

Student Outcomes

M.S. and Ph.D. graduates readily find positions in a wide range of academic institutions, government agencies, consulting firms, and industries. National and international employers include Black & Veatch, Boeing, Caterpillar, Ford, General Electric, General Motors, Goodyear, Honda, Intel, McDonnell-Douglas, and Toyota. M.S. graduates also continue on to a Ph.D. at the University of Nebraska or elsewhere.

Location

Lincoln is located in the Great Plains and has the reputation of being one of the Midwest's most beloved cities with a population of more than 250,000 people. As Nebraska's state capitol and a University community, Lincoln provides the amenities of a big city and the serenity of country living. The city offers fine culinary and artistic experiences, a live music scene, numerous parks and bike trails, golf courses, and a friendly Midwestern attitude. The continental climate varies by season; winters are cold but relatively dry, and summers are hot and humid.

The University and The Department

The University of Nebraska–Lincoln (UNL) is the largest component of the University of Nebraska system. UNL began as a land-grant university chartered in 1869 and granted its first engineering degree in 1882. Mechanical engineering is one of eleven departments in the college and is the only mechanical engineering program in the state of Nebraska. The student population on the Lincoln campus is over 23,000 students and over 2,450 of those students are enrolled in engineering programs. Current enrollment in the Department of Mechanical Engineering is over 370 students.

Applying

Applications for an M.S. degree should specify the Department of Mechanical Engineering and the area of interest (thermal/fluids, systems/design, materials). Ph.D. applicants should specify engineering and the field area of mechanical engineering or of chemical and materials engineering. Ph.D. applicants need not have an M.S. degree.

Applicants to the M.S. or Ph.D. programs in mechanical engineering should have a B.S. degree in mechanical engineering or in a closely related field of engineering, science, or math.

Applicants to the M.S. in mechanical engineering with a metallurgical or materials specialization or the Ph.D. in engineering in the field of chemical and materials engineering are expected to have a B.S. degree in mechanical engineering or materials science or in a closely related field of engineering or science.

International applicants without degrees from U.S. institutions are required to take the TOEFL and GRE General Test. Faculty members in an applicant's area of interest evaluate each application on an individual basis. Applications are evaluated as they arrive, and full processing of an application may take about two months. Applicants who lack the background that is a prerequisite for required courses in their chosen program are informed of any required prerequisite courses in their letter of offer of admission.

Correspondence and Information

Dr. John D. Reid
Professor and Graduate Chair
Department of Mechanical Engineering
University of Nebraska–Lincoln
N121 SEC
Lincoln, Nebraska 68588-0656
Phone: 402-472-3084
Fax: 402-472-1465
E-mail: megrad@unl.edu
Web site: http://www.engr.unl.edu/me/

University of Nebraska–Lincoln

THE FACULTY AND THEIR RESEARCH

J. P. Barton, Professor; Ph.D., Stanford, 1980. Laser beam/particle interactions, acoustics, electromagnetic wave theory, high-temperature gas dynamics, fluid mechanics, experimental methods, data acquisition and analysis.

K. Coen-Brown, Lecturer; M.S., Nebraska, 1989. Engineering education in the field of engineering graphics and computer modeling: computer-aided drafting and design, solid modeling, rendering, animation, and other three-dimensional visualization techniques.

K. D. Cole, Associate Professor; Ph.D., Michigan State, 1986. Heat transfer and diffusion theory, Green's functions and symbolic computation, numerical modeling, thermal sensor technology, thermal conductivity measurements.

L. E. Ehlers, Associate Professor Emeritus; Ph.D., Oklahoma State, 1969. Fluid flow, wind energy, vibrations.

S. M. Farritor, Professor; Ph.D., MIT, 1998. Robotics for planetary exploration, design and control of mobile robot systems, industrial robot programming, mobile robot planning, modular design, computer-aided creative design.

J. Huang, Assistant Professor; Ph.D., UCLA, 2007. Polymer solar cells, organic field-effect transistors, organic photodetectors, organic spintronics, polymer light emitting diodes, nano-based sensors and capacitors.

G. Gogos, Professor; Ph.D., Pennsylvania, 1986. Computational heat transfer and fluid flow; perturbation methods; fundamental processes associated with vaporizing/combusting sprays with applications in liquid-fueled rocket engines, gas turbines, diesel engines, and industrial furnaces (evaporation/combustion of moving droplets, subcritical and supercritical droplet evaporation, transition of envelop to wake flames in burning droplets, droplet interactions, interaction of sprays and buoyant diffusion flames); natural convection; heat transfer and material deposition in rotational molding.

L. Gu, Assistant Professor, Ph.D., Florida, 2004. Computational mechanics with experimental validation, multiscale modeling, fluid-structure interaction, material characterization, traumatic brain injury, vascular mechanics including vascular remodeling, mechanism of in-stent restenosis and atherosclerosis, minimally invasive medical device design.

D. L. Johnson, Professor Emeritus; Ph.D., Nebraska, 1968. Corrosion/degradation and hydrogen permeation and diffusion in metallic and nonmetallic systems, metallurgical thermochemistry.

D. Y. S. Lou, Ludwickson Professor; Sc.D., MIT, 1967. Rarefied gas dynamics, heat conduction in rarefied gases, solar energy, thermal curing of composite materials, thermal manufacturing process analysis, thermal modeling of pulse combustors, heat transfer in phase change materials.

C. A. Nelson, Associate Professor; Ph.D., Purdue, 2005. Design and analysis of robotic and mechanical systems, robot-assisted surgery, design of novel medical devices, modular design, applied graph theory, rehabilitation engineering.

R. C. Nelson, Professor Emeritus; D.Sc., Colorado School of Mines, 1951. Powder metallurgy; biomaterials; the mechanical behavior of materials, including failure analysis.

J. D. Reid, Professor; Ph.D., Michigan State, 1990. Vehicle crashworthiness and roadside safety design, analysis, and simulation; vehicle dynamics; nonlinear, large deformation, finite-element analysis; computer simulation.

B. W. Robertson, Professor; Ph.D., Glasgow, 1979. Nanoscale and nanostructured materials; electron beam–induced fabrication of materials with nm-scale resolution; development and application of characterization methods and instrumentation for quantitative nm-scale electron microscopy and spectroscopy; plasma enhanced chemical vapor deposition of boron-carbide materials; novel materials for electronic, magnetic, and neutron detection, extreme radiation, and extreme temperature applications.

J. E. Shield, Professor; Ph.D., Iowa State, 1992. Microstructural evolution in materials during processing, rapid solidification processing, structure/property relationships in magnetic materials, order/disorder transformations in materials, nucleation and growth, materials characterization by X-ray and electron diffraction and electron microscopy.

W. M. Szydlowski, Associate Professor; Ph.D., Warsaw Technical, 1975. Analysis and synthesis of mechanisms, computer simulation of mechanical systems, dynamics of machinery (mechanical impact and mechanisms of intermittent motion with clearances in particular), redundant constraints in large mechanical systems, application of genetic algorithms to synthesis of mechanisms.

C. W. S. To, Professor; Ph.D., Southampton, 1980. Sound and vibration studies (acoustic pulsation in pipelines, railway noise and vibration, signal analysis, structural dynamics, random vibration, nonlinear and chaotic vibration), solid mechanics (linear and nonlinear finite-element methods with application to laminated composite shell structures and modeling of aorta dissection), system dynamics (nonlinear and rigid-body dynamics), controls (deterministic and stochastic), nanomechanics.

Z. Zhang, Associate Professor; Ph.D., Penn State, 2000. Numerical and experimental study of the laser-induced plasma and its application to pulsed laser deposition of thin films, numerical modeling of diesel particulate filters and other after-treatment devices, blast wave mitigation devices.

Section 18
Ocean Engineering

This section contains a directory of institutions offering graduate work in ocean engineering, followed by an in-depth entry submitted by an institution that chose to prepare a detailed program description. Additional information about programs listed in the directory but not augmented by an in-depth entry may be obtained by writing directly to the dean of a graduate school or chair of a department at the address given in the directory.

For programs offering related work, see also in this book *Civil and Environmental Engineering* and *Engineering and Applied Sciences*. In the other guides in this series:

Graduate Programs in the Biological Sciences
See *Marine Biology*
Graduate Programs in the Physical Sciences, Mathematics, Agricultural Sciences, the Environment & Natural Resources
See *Environmental Sciences and Management* and *Marine Sciences and Oceanography*

CONTENTS

Ocean Engineering

Florida Atlantic University, College of Engineering and Computer Science, Department of Ocean Engineering, Boca Raton, FL 33431-0991. Offers MS, PhD. Part-time and evening/weekend programs available. *Faculty:* 13 full-time (0 women), 1 part-time/adjunct (0 women). *Students:* 40 full-time (8 women), 19 part-time (4 women); includes 3 minority (2 African Americans, 1 Hispanic American), 27 international. Average age 28. 51 applicants, 57% accepted, 13 enrolled. In 2009, 6 master's, 2 doctorates awarded. Terminal master's awarded for partial completion of doctoral program. *Degree requirements:* For master's, thesis (for some programs); for doctorate, comprehensive exam, thesis/dissertation, qualifying exam. *Entrance requirements:* For master's and doctorate, GRE General Test, minimum GPA of 3.0. Additional exam requirements/recommendations for international students: Required—TOEFL. *Application deadline:* For fall admission, 7/1 priority date for domestic students, 2/15 for international students; for spring admission, 11/1 for domestic students, 7/15 for international students. Applications are processed on a rolling basis. Application fee: $30. *Expenses:* Tuition, state resident: full-time $7055; part-time $293.94 per credit hour. Tuition, nonresident: full-time $22,096; part-time $920.66 per credit hour. *Financial support:* In 2009–10, research assistantships (averaging $15,000 per year); career-related internships or fieldwork, Federal Work-Study, scholarships/grants, and unspecified assistantships also available. Financial award application deadline: 1/10; financial award applicants required to submit FAFSA. *Faculty research:* Marine materials and corrosion, ocean structures, marine vehicles, acoustics and vibrations, hydrodynamics, coastal engineering. *Unit head:* Dr. Manhar Dhanak, Chairman, 954-924-7000, Fax: 954-924-7270, E-mail: dhanak@oe.fau.edu. *Application contact:* Dr. Manhar Dhanak, Chairman, 954-924-7000, Fax: 954-924-7270, E-mail: dhanak@oe.fau.edu.

Florida Institute of Technology, Graduate Programs, College of Engineering, Department of Marine and Environmental Systems, Program in Ocean Engineering, Melbourne, FL 32901-6975. Offers MS, PhD. Part-time programs available. *Students:* Average age 29. *Degree requirements:* For master's, thesis optional; for doctorate, comprehensive exam, thesis/dissertation, departmental qualifying exams. *Entrance requirements:* For master's, minimum GPA of 3.0; for doctorate, minimum GPA of 3.3, resume. *Application deadline:* Applications are processed on a rolling basis. Electronic applications accepted. *Expenses:* Tuition: Part-time $1015 per credit. Tuition and fees vary according to campus/location and program. *Financial support:* Research assistantships with full and partial tuition reimbursements, teaching assistantships with full and partial tuition reimbursements, career-related internships or fieldwork and tuition remissions available. Financial award application deadline: 3/1; financial award applicants required to submit FAFSA. *Faculty research:* Underwater technology, materials and structures, coastal processes and engineering, marine vehicles and ocean systems, naval architecture. Total annual research expenditures: $645,441. *Unit head:* Dr. Andrew Zborowski, Chair, 321-674-7304, Fax: 321-674-7212, E-mail: zborowsk@fit.edu. *Application contact:* Carolyn P. Shea.

See Close-Up on page 533.

Massachusetts Institute of Technology, School of Engineering, Department of Mechanical Engineering, Cambridge, MA 02139-4307. Offers manufacturing (M Eng); mechanical engineering (SM, PhD, Sc D, Mech E); naval architecture and marine engineering (SM, PhD, Sc D); naval engineering (Naval E); ocean engineering (SM, PhD, Sc D), including); oceanographic engineering (SM, PhD, Sc D); SM/MBA. *Faculty:* 68 full-time (8 women). *Students:* 489 full-time (80 women); includes 58 minority (7 African Americans, 3 American Indian/Alaska Native, 30 Asian Americans or Pacific Islanders, 18 Hispanic Americans), 211 international. Average age 27. 966 applicants, 24% accepted, 144 enrolled. In 2009, 110 master's, 45 doctorates, 9 other advanced degrees awarded. Terminal master's awarded for partial completion of doctoral program. *Degree requirements:* For master's and other advanced degree, thesis; for doctorate, comprehensive exam, thesis/dissertation. *Entrance requirements:* For master's, doctorate, and other advanced degree, GRE General Test. Additional exam requirements/recommendations for international students: Required—TOEFL (minimum score 577 paper-based; 233 computer-based; 91 iBT), IELTS (minimum score 7), IELTS preferred. *Application deadline:* For fall admission, 12/15 for domestic and international students. Application fee: $75. Electronic applications accepted. *Financial support:* In 2009–10, 453 students received support, including 76 fellowships with tuition reimbursements available (averaging $22,340 per year), 312 research assistantships with tuition reimbursements available (averaging $26,967 per year), 35 teaching assistantships with tuition reimbursements available (averaging $29,932 per year); career-related internships or fieldwork, Federal Work-Study, institutionally sponsored loans, scholarships/grants, health care benefits, and unspecified assistantships also available. *Faculty research:* Mechanics: modeling, experimentation and computation, design, manufacturing, product development, controls, instrumentation, robotics, energy science and engineering, ocean science and engineering, bioengineering, micro and nano engineering. Total annual research expenditures: $39 million. *Unit head:* Prof. Mary C. Boyce, Department Head, 617-253-2201, Fax: 617-258-6156, E-mail: mehq@mit.edu. *Application contact:* Graduate Office, 617-253-2291, Fax: 617-258-5802, E-mail: megradoffice@mit.edu.

Memorial University of Newfoundland, School of Graduate Studies, Faculty of Engineering and Applied Science, St. John's, NL A1C 5S7, Canada. Offers civil engineering (M Eng, PhD); electrical and computer engineering (M Eng, PhD); mechanical engineering (M Eng, PhD); ocean and naval architecture engineering (M Eng, PhD). Part-time programs available. *Degree requirements:* For master's, thesis; for doctorate, comprehensive exam, thesis/dissertation, oral thesis defense. *Entrance requirements:* For master's, 2nd class degree; for doctorate, master's degree in engineering. Electronic applications accepted. *Faculty research:* Engineering analysis, environmental and hydrotechnical studies, manufacturing and robotics, mechanics, structures and materials.

OGI School of Science & Engineering at Oregon Health & Science University, Graduate Studies, Science and Technology Center for Coastal and Land Margin Research, Beaverton, OR 97006-8921. Offers M Sc, PhD. Part-time programs available. *Entrance requirements:* For master's and doctorate, GRE General Test. Additional exam requirements/recommendations for international students: Required—TOEFL. Electronic applications accepted. *Faculty research:* Coastal marine observation and prediction science and technology.

Oregon State University, Graduate School, College of Engineering, School of Civil and Construction Engineering, Program in Coastal and Ocean Engineering, Corvallis, OR 97331. Offers M Oc E, MS, PhD. Part-time programs available. *Students:* 7 full-time (3 women), 1 (woman) part-time, 1 international. Average age 26. In 2009, 4 master's awarded. *Degree requirements:* For master's, thesis or alternative. *Entrance requirements:* For master's, GRE General Test, minimum GPA of 3.0 in last 90 hours. Additional exam requirements/recommendations for international students: Required—TOEFL. *Application deadline:* For fall admission, 3/1 priority date for domestic students. Application fee: $50. *Expenses:* Tuition, state resident: full-time $9774; part-time $362 per credit. Tuition, nonresident: full-time $15,849; part-time $587 per credit. Required fees: $1639. Full-time tuition and fees vary according to course load and program. *Financial support:* Fellowships, research assistantships, teaching assistantships, career-related internships or fieldwork and institutionally sponsored loans available. Support available to part-time students. Financial award application deadline: 2/1. *Faculty research:* Beach erosion and coastal protection, loads on sea-based structures, ocean wave mechanics, wave forces on structures, breakwater behavior. *Unit head:* Dr. Merrick C. Haller, Coordinator, 541-737-9141, Fax: 541-737-3052, E-mail: hallerm@engr.orst.edu. *Application contact:* Kathy Westberg, CCE Graduate Advising School Operations Manager, 541-737-1786, Fax: 541-737-3052, E-mail: kathy.westberg@oregonstate.edu.

Princeton University, Graduate School, Department of Geosciences, Princeton, NJ 08544-1019. Offers atmospheric and oceanic sciences (PhD); geosciences (PhD); ocean sciences and marine biology (PhD). *Degree requirements:* For doctorate, one foreign language, thesis/dissertation. *Entrance requirements:* For doctorate, GRE General Test. Additional exam requirements/recommendations for international students: Required—TOEFL (minimum score 600 paper-based; 250 computer-based). Electronic applications accepted. *Faculty research:* Biogeochemistry, climate science, earth history, regional geology and tectonics, solid–earth geophysics.

Stevens Institute of Technology, Graduate School, Charles V. Schaefer Jr. School of Engineering, Department of Civil, Environmental, and Ocean Engineering, Program in Ocean Engineering, Hoboken, NJ 07030. Offers M Eng, PhD. *Degree requirements:* For master's, thesis optional; for doctorate, variable foreign language requirement, thesis/dissertation. *Entrance requirements:* For doctorate, GRE. Additional exam requirements/recommendations for international students: Required—TOEFL. Electronic applications accepted. *Expenses:* Tuition: Full-time $9900; part-time $1100 per credit. Required fees: $286 per semester. *Faculty research:* Estuarine oceanography, hydrodynamic and environmental processes, wave/ship interaction.

Texas A&M University, College of Engineering, Zachry Department of Civil Engineering, College Station, TX 77843. Offers construction engineering and management (M Eng, MS, D Eng, PhD); environmental engineering (M Eng, MS, D Eng, PhD); geotechnical engineering (M Eng, MS, D Eng, PhD); materials engineering (M Eng, MS, D Eng, PhD); ocean engineering (M Eng, MS, D Eng, PhD); structural engineering (M Eng, MS, D Eng, PhD); transportation engineering (M Eng, MS, D Eng, PhD); water resources engineering (M Eng, MS, D Eng, PhD). Part-time programs available. *Faculty:* 61. *Students:* 390 full-time (89 women), 42 part-time (6 women); includes 23 minority (2 African Americans, 11 Asian Americans or Pacific Islanders, 10 Hispanic Americans), 281 international. Average age 29. In 2009, 100 master's, 36 doctorates awarded. *Degree requirements:* For master's, thesis (MS); for doctorate, dissertation (PhD), internship (D Eng). *Entrance requirements:* For master's and doctorate, GRE General Test. Additional exam requirements/recommendations for international students: Required—TOEFL. *Application deadline:* Applications are processed on a rolling basis. Application fee: $50 ($75 for international students). Electronic applications accepted. *Expenses:* Tuition, state resident: full-time $3991.32; part-time $221.74 per credit hour. Tuition, nonresident: full-time $9049; part-time $502.74 per credit hour. *Financial support:* In 2009–10, fellowships (averaging $4,500 per year), research assistantships (averaging $14,000 per year), teaching assistantships (averaging $14,400 per year) were awarded; career-related internships or fieldwork and institutionally sponsored loans also available. Financial award application deadline: 4/15; financial award applicants required to submit FAFSA. *Unit head:* Dr. Tony Cahill, Head, 979-845-2438, E-mail: t-cahill@civil.tamu.edu. *Application contact:* Graduate Advisor, 979-845-2498, Fax: 979-862-2800, E-mail: ce-grad@tamu.edu.

University of Alaska Anchorage, School of Engineering, Program in Civil Engineering, Anchorage, AK 99508. Offers civil engineering (MCE, MS); port and coastal engineering (Certificate). Part-time and evening/weekend programs available. *Degree requirements:* For master's, thesis (for some programs). *Entrance requirements:* For master's, bachelor's degree in engineering. Additional exam requirements/recommendations for international students: Required—TOEFL (minimum score 550 paper-based; 213 computer-based). *Faculty research:* Structural engineering, engineering education, astronomical observations related to engineering.

University of California, San Diego, Office of Graduate Studies, Department of Electrical and Computer Engineering, La Jolla, CA 92093. Offers applied ocean science (MS, PhD); applied physics (MS, PhD); communication theory and systems (MS, PhD); computer engineering (MS, PhD); electrical engineering (M Eng); electronic circuits and systems (MS, PhD); intelligent systems, robotics and control (MS, PhD); photonics (MS, PhD); signal and image processing (MS, PhD). MS only offered to students who have been admitted to the PhD program. *Entrance requirements:* For master's and doctorate, GRE General Test. Electronic applications accepted.

University of California, San Diego, Office of Graduate Studies, Department of Mechanical and Aerospace Engineering, Program in Applied Ocean Science, La Jolla, CA 92093. Offers MS, PhD. Part-time programs available. *Degree requirements:* For master's, comprehensive exam or thesis; for doctorate, thesis/dissertation, qualifying exam. *Entrance requirements:* For master's and doctorate, GRE General Test, minimum GPA of 3.0. Additional exam requirements/recommendations for international students: Required—TOEFL. Electronic applications accepted.

University of Delaware, College of Engineering, Department of Civil and Environmental Engineering, Newark, DE 19716. Offers environmental engineering (MAS, MCE, PhD); geotechnical engineering (MAS, MCE, PhD); ocean engineering (MAS, MCE, PhD); structural engineering (MAS, MCE, PhD); transportation engineering (MAS, MCE, PhD); water resource engineering (MAS, MCE, PhD). Part-time programs available. Terminal master's awarded for partial completion of doctoral program. *Degree requirements:* For master's, thesis; for doctorate, thesis/dissertation. *Entrance requirements:* For master's and doctorate, GRE General Test. Additional exam requirements/recommendations for international students: Required—TOEFL. Electronic applications accepted. *Faculty research:* Structural engineering and mechanics; transportation engineering; ocean engineering; soil mechanics and foundation; water resources and environmental engineering.

University of Florida, Graduate School, College of Engineering, Department of Civil and Coastal Engineering, Gainesville, FL 32611. Offers civil engineering (MCE, MS, PhD, Engr); coastal and oceanographic engineering (ME, MS, PhD, Engr). Part-time programs available. *Degree requirements:* For master's and Engr, thesis optional; for doctorate, thesis/dissertation. *Entrance requirements:* For master's and doctorate, GRE General Test, minimum GPA of 3.0. Additional exam requirements/recommendations for international students: Required—TOEFL (minimum score 550 paper-based; 213 computer-based). Electronic applications accepted.

University of Hawaii at Manoa, Graduate Division, School of Ocean and Earth Science and Technology, Department of Ocean and Resources Engineering, Honolulu, HI 96822. Offers MS, PhD. *Accreditation:* ABET (one or more programs are accredited). Part-time programs available. *Faculty:* 19 full-time (3 women), 6 part-time/adjunct (1 woman). *Students:* 27 full-time (6 women), 3 part-time (0 women); includes 6 minority (5 Asian Americans or Pacific Islanders, 1 Hispanic American), 9 international. Average age 27. 38 applicants, 55% accepted, 9 enrolled. In 2009, 5 master's, 3 doctorates awarded. *Degree requirements:* For master's, thesis optional, exams; for doctorate, comprehensive exam, thesis/dissertation, exams. *Entrance requirements:* For master's and doctorate, GRE General Test. Additional exam requirements/recommendations for international students: Required—TOEFL (minimum score 560 paper-based; 220 computer-based; 83 iBT), IELTS (minimum score 5). *Application deadline:* For fall admission, 3/15 for domestic students, 2/15 for international students; for spring admission, 9/15 for domestic students, 8/15 for international students. Application fee: $60. *Expenses:* Tuition, state resident: full-time $8900; part-time $372 per credit. Tuition, nonresident: full-time $21,400; part-time $898 per credit. Required fees: $207 per semester. *Financial support:* In 2009–10, 1 fellowship (averaging $1,200 per year), 23 research assistantships (averaging $21,013 per year), 2 teaching assistantships (averaging $19,818 per year) were awarded; institutionally sponsored loans and tuition waivers (full) also available. Financial award application deadline: 3/1. *Faculty research:* Coastal and harbor engineering, near shore environmental ocean engineering, marine structures/naval architecture. Total annual research expenditures: $2.2 million. *Application contact:* John C. Wiltshire, Graduate Chairperson, 808-956-7572, Fax: 808-956-3498, E-mail: johnw@soest.hawaii.edu.

University of Michigan, Horace H. Rackham School of Graduate Studies, College of Engineering, Department of Naval Architecture and Marine Engineering, Ann Arbor, MI 48109. Offers concurrent marine design (M Eng); naval architecture and marine engineering (MS, MSE, PhD, Mar Eng, Nav Arch); MBA/MSE. Part-time programs available. *Faculty:* 12 full-time (2 women). *Students:* 74 full-time (13 women), 1 part-time (0 women); includes 3 minority (1 African American, 1 Asian American or Pacific Islander, 1 Hispanic American), 32 international.

Ocean Engineering

104 applicants, 64% accepted, 37 enrolled. In 2009, 12 master's, 6 doctorates awarded. Terminal master's awarded for partial completion of doctoral program. *Degree requirements:* For master's, thesis (for some programs); for doctorate, comprehensive exam, thesis/dissertation, oral defense of dissertation, preliminary exams (written and oral); for other advanced degree, comprehensive exam, thesis, oral defense of thesis. *Entrance requirements:* For master's, GRE General Test (for financial award applicants); for doctorate, GRE General Test, master's degree; for other advanced degree, GRE General Test. Additional exam requirements/recommendations for international students: Required—TOEFL (minimum score 560 paper-based; 220 computer-based). *Application deadline:* Applications are processed on a rolling basis. Application fee: $60 ($75 for international students). Electronic applications accepted. *Expenses:* Tuition, state resident: full-time $17,286; part-time $1099 per credit hour. Tuition, nonresident: full-time $34,944; part-time $2080 per credit hour. Required fees: $95 per semester. Tuition and fees vary according to course load, degree level and program. *Financial support:* Fellowships, research assistantships, teaching assistantships, career-related internships or fieldwork, Federal Work-Study, institutionally sponsored loans, scholarships/grants, and unspecified assistantships available. *Faculty research:* System and structural reliability, design and analysis of offshore structures and vehicles, marine systems design, remote sensing of ship wakes and sea surfaces, marine hydrodynamics, nonlinear seakeeping analysis. *Unit head:* Dr. Armin W. Troesch, Chair, 734-763-6644, Fax: 734-936-8820, E-mail: kdrake@engin.umich.edu. *Application contact:* Nathalie Fiveland, Unit Administrator, 734-936-0566, Fax: 734-936-8820, E-mail: fiveland@umich.edu.

University of New Hampshire, Graduate School, College of Engineering and Physical Sciences, Program in Ocean Engineering, Durham, NH 03824. Offers ocean engineering (MS, PhD); ocean mapping (MS, Postbaccalaureate Certificate). *Faculty:* 13 full-time (1 woman). *Students:* 12 full-time (5 women), 4 part-time (0 women); includes 1 minority (Hispanic American), 10 international. Average age 30. 17 applicants, 76% accepted, 8 enrolled. In 2009, 2 master's, 1 doctorate, 4 other advanced degrees awarded. *Degree requirements:* For master's, thesis. *Entrance requirements:* Additional exam requirements/recommendations for international students: Required—TOEFL (minimum score 550 paper-based; 213 computer-based; 80 iBT). *Application deadline:* For fall admission, 4/1 priority date for domestic students; for spring admission, 12/1 for domestic students. Applications are processed on a rolling basis. Application fee: $65. Electronic applications accepted. *Expenses:* Tuition, state resident: full-time $10,380; part-time $577 per credit hour. Tuition, nonresident: full-time $24,350; part-time $1002 per credit hour. Required fees: $1550; $387.50 per semester. Tuition and fees vary according to course load and program. *Financial support:* In 2009–10, 11 students received support, including 10 research assistantships, 1 teaching assistantship; fellowships, Federal Work-Study, scholarships/grants, and tuition waivers (full and partial) also available. Support available to part-time students. Financial award application deadline: 2/15. *Unit head:* Dr. Kenneth Baldwin, Chairperson, 603-862-1898. *Application contact:* Jennifer Bedsole, Information Contact, 603-862-0672, E-mail: ocean.engineering@unh.edu.

University of Rhode Island, Graduate School, College of Engineering, Department of Ocean Engineering, Narragansett, RI 02882. Offers MS, PhD. Part-time programs available. *Faculty:* 8 full-time (1 woman), 1 part-time/adjunct (0 women). *Students:* 18 full-time (3 women), 16 part-time (4 women), 8 international. In 2009, 3 master's awarded. *Degree requirements:* For master's, comprehensive exam (for some programs), thesis optional; for doctorate, comprehensive exam, thesis/dissertation. *Entrance requirements:* For master's and doctorate, 2 letters of recommendation. Additional exam requirements/recommendations for international students: Required—TOEFL (minimum score 550 paper-based; 213 computer-based). *Application*

deadline: For fall admission, 7/15 for domestic students, 2/1 for international students; for spring admission, 11/15 for domestic students, 7/15 for international students. Application fee: $65. Electronic applications accepted. *Expenses:* Tuition, state resident: full-time $8828; part-time $490 per credit hour. Tuition, nonresident: full-time $22,100; part-time $1228 per credit hour. Required fees: $1118; $57 per semester. Tuition and fees vary according to program. *Financial support:* In 2009–10, 3 research assistantships with full and partial tuition reimbursements (averaging $10,535 per year), 3 teaching assistantships with full and partial tuition reimbursements (averaging $11,806 per year) were awarded. Financial award application deadline: 2/1; financial award applicants required to submit FAFSA. *Faculty research:* Telepresence technology for high bandwidth ship-to-shore link, wave-induced sediment transport, tsunami impact, geohazards, acoustical oceanography, underwater vehicle mechanical and control system design, deep sea drilling. Total annual research expenditures: $746,333. *Unit head:* Dr. James H. Miller, Chairman, 401-874-6540, Fax: 401-874-6837, E-mail: miller@uri.edu. *Application contact:* Dr. Christopher Baxter, Associate Professor, 401-874-6575, Fax: 401-874-6837, E-mail: baxter@oce.uri.edu.

Virginia Polytechnic Institute and State University, Graduate School, College of Engineering, Department of Aerospace and Ocean Engineering, Blacksburg, VA 24061. Offers aerospace engineering (M Eng, MS, PhD); ocean engineering (MS). *Entrance requirements:* For master's and doctorate, GRE. Additional exam requirements/recommendations for international students: Required—TOEFL (minimum score 550 paper-based; 213 computer-based), GRE. Electronic applications accepted. *Faculty research:* Aerodynamics, flight mechanics, vehicle structures, space mechanics and design.

Virginia Polytechnic Institute and State University, VT Online, Blacksburg, VA 24061. Offers aerospace engineering (MS); business information systems (Graduate Certificate); career and technical education (MS); computer engineering (M Eng, MS); decision support systems (Graduate Certificate); eLearning leadership (MA); electrical engineering (M Eng, MS); engineering administration (MEA); environmental politics and policy (Graduate Certificate); foundations of political analysis (Graduate Certificate); health product risk management (Graduate Certificate); information policy and society (Graduate Certificate); information security (Graduate Certificate); instructional technology (MA); liberal arts (Graduate Certificate); life sciences: health product risk management (MS); natural resources (MNR, Graduate Certificate); networking (Graduate Certificate); nonprofit and nongovernmental organization management (Graduate Certificate); ocean engineering (MS); political science (MA); security studies (Graduate Certificate); software development (Graduate Certificate).

Woods Hole Oceanographic Institution, MIT/WHOI Joint Program in Oceanography/Applied Ocean Science and Engineering, Woods Hole, MA 02543-1541. Offers applied ocean sciences (PhD); biological oceanography (PhD, Sc D); chemical oceanography (PhD, Sc D); civil and environmental and oceanographic engineering (PhD); electrical and oceanographic engineering (PhD); geochemistry (PhD); geophysics (PhD); marine biology (PhD); marine geochemistry (PhD, Sc D); marine geology (PhD, Sc D); marine geophysics (PhD); mechanical and oceanographic engineering (PhD); ocean engineering (PhD); oceanographic engineering (M Eng, MS, PhD, Sc D, Eng); paleoceanography (PhD); physical oceanography (PhD, Sc D). Terminal master's awarded for partial completion of doctoral program. *Degree requirements:* For master's and Eng, thesis (for some programs); for doctorate, thesis/dissertation. *Entrance requirements:* For master's, GRE General Test; for doctorate, GRE General Test, GRE Subject Test. Additional exam requirements/recommendations for international students: Required—TOEFL. Electronic applications accepted.

FLORIDA INSTITUTE OF TECHNOLOGY

Department of Marine and Environmental Systems
Ocean Engineering Program

Programs of Study

The Florida Institute of Technology Department of Marine and Environmental Systems offers graduate courses and research opportunities that lead to the Master of Science and Doctor of Philosophy in ocean engineering. The ocean engineering degree offers specialization in coastal processes, coastal engineering, hydrographic engineering, marine vehicles and ocean systems, materials and structures, naval architecture, and underwater technology. The Department also offers graduate programs in oceanography, with options in chemical, biological, physical, and geological oceanography; and in coastal zone management. The master's degree in oceanography is offered in thesis and nonthesis options.

Research Facilities

Florida Institute of Technology is conveniently located on the Atlantic coast in central Florida and has marine laboratories and field research sites both on the Indian River Lagoon and at an oceanfront marine research facility. The Evinrude Marine Operations Center, just 5 minutes from campus, houses a fleet of small outboard-powered craft and medium-sized work boats. These boats are available to students and faculty members for teaching and research in the freshwater tributaries and the Indian River Lagoon.

The university regularly charters UNOLS vessels for offshore teaching and research.

Florida Tech's oceanfront marine research facility, the Vero Beach Marine Laboratory, located just 40 minutes from campus, provides facilities that include flowing seawater from the Atlantic Ocean and supports research in such areas as aquaculture, biofouling, and corrosion.

On campus, Departmental teaching and research facilities include a computer-aided design center and graduate research computer facilities for design, data analysis, numerical modeling, and other teaching and research activities. The ocean engineering program provides facilities for structural and pressure testing and a laboratory for biofouling and corrosion research. The marine geology laboratory provides facilities for core boring and sediment analysis, beach and hydrographic surveying, and oceanographic instrumentation for coastal research activities. In the past few years, developments in the coastal engineering area include a wave channel and an ROV construction and test facility. Separate laboratories are available for biological, chemical, physical, geological, and instrumentation investigations. In addition, high-pressure, hydroacoustics, fluid dynamics, and optical facilities are available in the Department. An electron microscope is also available for research work.

About 1 hour from campus is the Harbor Branch Oceanographic Institute of Florida Atlantic University; scientists and engineers there pursue their own research and development activities and interact with Florida Tech's students and faculty members on projects of mutual interest. Graduate students, especially those having an interest in submersibles, exploratory equipment, and instrumentation, frequently have the opportunity to conduct research with the HBOI staff and to utilize facilities at the institution.

Financial Aid

Graduate teaching and research assistantships and endowed fellowships are available to qualified students. Typical stipends range from $13,000 upward for twelve months for approximately half-time duties; most assistantships include tuition.

Cost of Study

For 2010–11, tuition is $1040 per semester credit hour. Tuition is paid for some graduate students.

Living and Housing Costs

Room and board on campus cost approximately $4500 per semester in 2010–11. On-campus housing (dormitories and apartments) is available for full-time single and married graduate students, but priority for dormitory rooms is given to undergraduate students. Many apartment complexes and rental houses are available near the campus.

Student Group

The College of Engineering has 450 graduate students. The Department of Marine and Environmental Systems has 250 students of which one third are graduate students.

Student Outcomes

Graduates of the Ocean Engineering Program are employed by such facilities as the Naval Sea Systems Command, the Naval Surface Warfare Center, the Naval Undersea Warfare Center, the Naval Research Lab, Newport News Shipbuilding, the U.S. Army Corps of Engineers, the American Bureau of Shipping, Digicon, LCT, NOAA, Autec, Tracor Marine, G. M. Selby & Associates, the U.S. Navy, the U.S. Coast Guard, Quantic Engineering & Logistics, Underwater Engineering Services, Biospherical Instruments Inc., Oceaneering International Inc., and EG&G.

Location

The campus is located in Melbourne, on Florida's east coast. The area, located 4 miles from Atlantic Ocean beaches, has a year-round subtropical climate. The area's economy is supported by a well-balanced mix of industries in electronics, aviation, light manufacturing, optics, maritime communications, agriculture, meteorology, and tourism. Many industries support activities at the Kennedy Space Center.

The Institute

Florida Institute of Technology is a distinctive, independent university founded in 1958 by a group of scientists and engineers to fulfill a need for specialized advanced educational opportunities on the Space Coast of Florida. Florida Tech is the only independent technological university in the Southeast. Supported by both industry and the community, Florida Tech is the recipient of many research grants and contracts, a number of which provide financial support for graduate students.

Applying

Forms and instructions for applying for admission and assistantships are sent on request. Admission is possible at the beginning of any semester, but admission in the fall semester is recommended. It is advantageous to apply early.

Correspondence and Information

Dr. George A. Maul, Department Head
Ocean Engineering Program
Florida Institute of Technology
Melbourne, Florida 32901-6975
Phone: 321-674-8096
Fax: 321-674-7212
E-mail: dmes@fit.edu
Web site: http://coe.fit.edu/dmes/ocean.php

Office of Graduate Admission
Florida Institute of Technology
Melbourne, Florida 32901-6988
Phone: 321-674-8027
800-944-4348 (toll-free in the U.S.)
Fax: 321-723-9468
E-mail: grad-admissions@fit.edu
Web site: http://www.fit.edu

Florida Institute of Technology

THE FACULTY AND THEIR RESEARCH

Lee Harris, Associate Professor and Acting Program Chair; Ph.D., Florida; PE. Coastal engineering, coastal structures, hydrographic surveying, beach erosion and control, physical oceanography, ports, harbors, marinas.

Steven M. Jachec, Assistant Professor; Ph.D., Stanford; PE. Environmental fluid mechanics, coastal engineering, turbulence modeling.

Prasanta Sahoo, Associate Professor; Ph.D., Rostock (Germany). Hydrodynamics, numerical modeling of hull designs, naval architecture.

Geoffrey W. J. Swain, Professor; Ph.D., Southampton. Materials corrosion, biofouling, offshore technology, ship operations.

Stephen L. Wood, Assistant Professor; Ph.D., Oregon State; PE. Design of underwater vehicles, robotic systems development, navigation and control.

Andrew Zborowski, Professor and Chair (Emeritus); Ph.D., Gdansk (Poland). Ship hydrodynamics, marine structures, ship model tank studies, ship propulsion, dynamics of marine vehicles, high-speed craft design.

Adjunct Faculty

A. M. Clark, Ph.D.; CSnetNTL.com.

D. P. Reichard, Ph.D.; Structural Composites, Inc.

Eric D. Thosteson, Assistant Professor; Ph.D., Florida; PE. Coastal and nearshore engineering.

Section 19
Paper and Textile Engineering

This section contains a directory of institutions offering graduate work in paper and textile engineering, followed by in-depth entries submitted by institutions that chose to prepare detailed program descriptions. Additional information about programs listed in the directory but not augmented by an in-depth entry may be obtained by writing directly to the dean of a graduate school or chair of a department at the address given in the directory.

For programs offering related work, see also in this book *Engineering and Applied Sciences* and *Materials Sciences and Engineering*. In another guide in this series:

Graduate Programs in the Humanities, Arts & Social Sciences
See *Family and Consumer Sciences (Clothing and Textiles)*

CONTENTS

Program Directories

Paper and Pulp Engineering

Miami University, Graduate School, School of Engineering and Applied Science, Department of Paper and Chemical Engineering, Oxford, OH 45056. Offers MS. *Students:* 9 full-time (4 women), 8 international. *Entrance requirements:* For master's, GRE General Test, minimum undergraduate GPA of 3.0 during previous 2 years or 2.75 overall. Additional exam requirements/recommendations for international students: Required—TOEFL. Application fee: $50. *Expenses:* Tuition, state resident: full-time $11,280. Tuition, nonresident: full-time $24,912. Required fees: $516. *Financial support:* Fellowships, research assistantships, teaching assistantships, Federal Work-Study, health care benefits, tuition waivers (full), and unspecified assistantships available. Financial award application deadline: 3/1. *Unit head:* Dr. Shashi Lalvani, Chair, 513-529-0760, Fax: 513-529-0761, E-mail: paper@muohio.edu. *Application contact:* Dr. Douglas Coffin, Graduate Director, 513-529-0760, Fax: 513-529-0761, E-mail: paper@muohio.edu.

North Carolina State University, Graduate School, College of Natural Resources, Department of Wood and Paper Science, Raleigh, NC 27695. Offers MS, MWPS, PhD. Postbaccalaureate distance learning degree programs offered. *Degree requirements:* For master's, thesis optional; for doctorate, thesis/dissertation. *Entrance requirements:* For master's and doctorate, GRE General Test. Additional exam requirements/recommendations for international students: Required—TOEFL. Electronic applications accepted. *Faculty research:* Pulping, bleaching, recycling, papermaking, drying of wood.

Oregon State University, Graduate School, College of Forestry, Department of Wood Science and Engineering, Corvallis, OR 97331. Offers forest products (MAIS, MF, MS, PhD); wood science and technology (MF, MS, PhD). *Accreditation:* SAF (one or more programs are accredited). Part-time programs available. *Faculty:* 9 full-time (1 woman). *Students:* 35 full-time (17 women), 2 part-time (1 woman); includes 3 minority (1 Asian American or Pacific Islander, 2 Hispanic Americans), 7 international. Average age 33. In 2009, 7 master's, 4 doctorates awarded. *Degree requirements:* For master's, thesis (for some programs); for doctorate, thesis/dissertation. *Entrance requirements:* For master's and doctorate, GRE General Test, minimum GPA of 3.0 in last 90 hours. Additional exam requirements/recommendations for international students: Required—TOEFL. *Application deadline:* For fall admission, 3/1 priority date for domestic students. Applications are processed on a rolling basis. Application fee: $50. *Expenses:* Tuition, state resident: full-time $9774; part-time $362 per credit. Tuition, nonresident: full-time $15,849; part-time $587 per credit. Required fees: $1639. Full-time tuition and fees vary according to course load and program. *Financial support:* Fellowships, research assistantships, career-related internships or fieldwork, Federal Work-Study, and institutionally sponsored loans available. Support available to part-time students. Financial award application deadline: 2/1. *Faculty research:* Biodeterioration and preservation, timber engineering, process engineering and control, composite materials science, anatomy, chemistry and physical properties. *Unit head:* Dr. Thomas E. McLain, Head, 541-737-4224, Fax: 541-737-3385, E-mail: thomas.mclain@oregonstate.edu. *Application contact:* George Swanson, Program Support Coordinator, 541-737-4206, Fax: 541-737-3385, E-mail: george.swanson@oregonstate.edu.

State University of New York College of Environmental Science and Forestry, Department of Paper and Bioprocess Engineering, Syracuse, NY 13210-2779. Offers environmental and resources engineering (MPS, MS, PhD). *Degree requirements:* For master's, thesis; for doctorate, comprehensive exam, thesis/dissertation. *Entrance requirements:* For master's and doctorate, GRE General Test, minimum GPA of 3.0. Additional exam requirements/recommendations for international students: Required—TOEFL (minimum score 550 paper-based; 213 computer-based; 80 iBT), IELTS (minimum score 6).

Western Michigan University, Graduate College, College of Engineering and Applied Sciences, Department of Paper Engineering, Chemical Engineering, and Imaging, Kalamazoo, MI 49008. Offers paper and imaging science and engineering (MS, PhD). *Degree requirements:* For master's, thesis optional; for doctorate, one foreign language, comprehensive exam, thesis/dissertation. *Entrance requirements:* For master's, minimum GPA of 3.0. *Faculty research:* Fiber recycling, paper machine wet end operations, paper coating.

Textile Sciences and Engineering

Auburn University, Graduate School, Interdepartmental Programs, Interdepartmental Program in Integrated Textile and Apparel Sciences, Auburn University, AL 36849. Offers PhD. *Faculty:* 23 full-time (16 women), 1 (woman) part-time/adjunct. *Students:* 12 full-time (5 women), 12 part-time (9 women); includes 3 minority (1 African American, 2 Asian Americans or Pacific Islanders), 16 international. Average age 29. 33 applicants, 55% accepted, 2 enrolled. In 2009, 3 doctorates awarded. *Application deadline:* For fall admission, 7/7 for domestic students; for spring admission, 11/24 for domestic students. Applications are processed on a rolling basis. Application fee: $50 ($60 for international students). *Expenses:* Tuition, state resident: full-time $6240. Tuition, nonresident: full-time $18,720. International tuition: $18,938 full-time. Required fees: $492. Tuition and fees vary according to course load, program and reciprocity agreements. *Financial support:* Research assistantships, Federal Work-Study available. Support available to part-time students. Financial award application deadline: 3/15; financial award applicants required to submit FAFSA. *Faculty research:* Design and utilization of textile products, engineering and technology of textile production, textile material science, textile chemistry, use of resources. *Unit head:* Dr. Royall M. Broughton, Graduate Program Officer, 334-844-4123, E-mail: royalb@eng.auburn.edu. *Application contact:* Dr. George Flowers, Dean of the Graduate School, 334-844-2125.

Cornell University, Graduate School, Graduate Fields of Human Ecology, Field of Textiles, Ithaca, NY 14853-0001. Offers apparel design (MA, MPS); fiber science (MS, PhD); polymer science (MS, PhD); textile science (MS, PhD). *Faculty:* 17 full-time (7 women). *Students:* 21 full-time (16 women); includes 1 minority (Hispanic American), 12 international. Average age 30. 26 applicants, 19% accepted, 3 enrolled. In 2009, 1 master's, 4 doctorates awarded. *Degree requirements:* For master's, thesis (MA, MS), project paper (MPS); for doctorate, comprehensive exam, thesis/dissertation. *Entrance requirements:* For master's, GRE General Test, 2 letters of recommendation, portfolio (functional apparel design); for doctorate, GRE General Test, 2 letters of recommendation. Additional exam requirements/recommendations for international students: Required—TOEFL (minimum score 600 paper-based; 250 computer-based; 77 iBT). *Application deadline:* For fall admission, 3/1 for domestic students; for spring admission, 10/1 for domestic students. Application fee: $70. Electronic applications accepted. *Expenses:* Tuition: Full-time $29,500. Required fees: $70. Full-time tuition and fees vary according to degree level, program and student level. *Financial support:* In 2009–10, 19 students received support, including 2 teaching assistantships with full tuition reimbursements available; fellowships with full tuition reimbursements available, research assistantships with full tuition reimbursements available, institutionally sponsored loans, scholarships/grants, health care benefits, tuition waivers (full and partial), and unspecified assistantships also available. Financial award applicants required to submit FAFSA. *Faculty research:* Apparel design, consumption, mass customization, 3-D body scanning. *Unit head:* Director of Graduate Studies, 607-255-3151, Fax: 607-255-1093. *Application contact:* Graduate Field Assistant, 607-255-3151, Fax: 607-255-1093, E-mail: textiles_grad@cornell.edu.

Georgia Institute of Technology, Graduate Studies and Research, College of Engineering, School of Polymer, Textile, and Fiber Engineering, Atlanta, GA 30332-0001. Offers polymer, textile and fiber engineering (MS, PhD); polymers (MS Poly). *Degree requirements:* For master's, thesis (for some programs); for doctorate, comprehensive exam, thesis/dissertation. *Entrance requirements:* For master's, GRE, minimum GPA of 2.7; for doctorate, GRE, minimum GPA of 3.0. Additional exam requirements/recommendations for international students: Required—TOEFL (minimum score 550 paper-based; 213 computer-based). Electronic applications accepted. *Faculty research:* Energy conservation, environmental control, engineered fibrous structures, polymer synthesis and degradation, high performance organic-carbon-ceramic fibers.

North Carolina State University, Graduate School, College of Textiles, Department of Textile and Apparel Technology and Management, Raleigh, NC 27695. Offers MS, MT. *Degree requirements:* For master's, thesis optional. *Entrance requirements:* For master's, GRE. Electronic applications accepted. *Faculty research:* Textile and apparel products and processes, management systems, nonwovens, process simulation, structure design and analysis.

North Carolina State University, Graduate School, College of Textiles, Department of Textile Engineering, Chemistry, and Science, Program in Textile Chemistry, Raleigh, NC 27695. Offers MS. *Degree requirements:* For master's, thesis optional. *Entrance requirements:* For master's, GRE. Electronic applications accepted. *Faculty research:* Color science, polymer science, dye chemistry, fiber formation, wet processing technology.

North Carolina State University, Graduate School, College of Textiles, Department of Textile Engineering, Chemistry, and Science, Program in Textile Engineering, Raleigh, NC 27695. Offers MS. *Degree requirements:* For master's, thesis optional. *Entrance requirements:* For master's, GRE. Electronic applications accepted. *Faculty research:* Electro-mechanical design, inventory and supply chain control, textile composites, biomedical textile appliations, pollution prevention.

North Carolina State University, Graduate School, College of Textiles, Program in Fiber and Polymer Science, Raleigh, NC 27695. Offers PhD. *Degree requirements:* For doctorate, one foreign language, thesis/dissertation, cumulative exams. *Entrance requirements:* For doctorate, GRE. Electronic applications accepted. *Faculty research:* Polymer science, fiber mechanics, medical textiles, nanotechnology.

Philadelphia University, School of Engineering and Textiles, Program in Textile Engineering, Philadelphia, PA 19144. Offers MS, PhD. Part-time programs available. *Entrance requirements:* For master's, GRE, minimum GPA of 2.8; for doctorate, master's degree. Additional exam requirements/recommendations for international students: Required—TOEFL (minimum score 550 paper-based; 213 computer-based; 79 iBT). Electronic applications accepted.

University of Massachusetts Dartmouth, Graduate School, College of Engineering, Department of Materials and Textiles, North Dartmouth, MA 02747-2300. Offers textile chemistry (MS); textile technology (MS). Part-time programs available. *Faculty:* 6 full-time (0 women). *Students:* 5 full-time (0 women), 4 part-time (0 women), all international. Average age 25. 15 applicants, 80% accepted, 3 enrolled. In 2009, 4 master's awarded. *Degree requirements:* For master's, thesis. *Entrance requirements:* For master's, GRE General Test, 3 letters of recommendation. Additional exam requirements/recommendations for international students: Required—TOEFL (minimum score 500 paper-based). *Application deadline:* For fall admission, 4/20 priority date for domestic students, 2/20 priority date for international students; for spring admission, 11/15 priority date for domestic students, 9/15 priority date for international students. Applications are processed on a rolling basis. Application fee: $40 ($60 for international students). Electronic applications accepted. *Expenses:* Tuition, state resident: full-time $2071; part-time $86.29 per credit. Tuition, nonresident: full-time $8099; part-time $337.46 per credit. Required fees: $9446. Tuition and fees vary according to class time, course load and reciprocity agreements. *Financial support:* In 2009–10, 4 research assistantships with full tuition reimbursements (averaging $7,792 per year), 1 teaching assistantship with full tuition reimbursement (averaging $6,000 per year) were awarded; Federal Work-Study also available. Support available to part-time students. Financial award application deadline: 3/1; financial award applicants required to submit FAFSA. *Faculty research:* Flock fundamentals, nanofibers, bioactive fabrics, high stress elastic materials, nano-engineered fire resistant composite fibers. Total annual research expenditures: $992,000. *Unit head:* Dr. Qinguo Fan, Director, 508-999-8452, Fax: 508-999-9139, E-mail: fqinguo@umassd.edu. *Application contact:* Elan Turcotte-Shamski, Graduate Admissions Officer, 508-999-8604, Fax: 508-999-8183, E-mail: graduate@umassd.edu.

The University of Texas at Austin, Graduate School, College of Natural Sciences, School of Human Ecology, Program in Textile and Apparel Technology, Austin, TX 78712-1111. Offers MS.

Section 20
Telecommunications

This section contains a directory of institutions offering graduate work in telecommunications, followed by an in-depth entry submitted by an institution that chose to prepare a detailed program description. Additional information about programs listed in the directory but not augmented by an in-depth entry may be obtained by writing directly to the dean of a graduate school or chair of a department at the address given in the directory.

For programs offering related work, see also in this book *Computer Science and Information Technology* and *Engineering and Applied Sciences*. In the other guides in this series:

Graduate Programs in the Humanities, Arts & Social Sciences
See *Communication and Media*
Graduate Programs in Business, Education, Health, Information Studies, Law & Social Work
See *Business Administration and Management*

CONTENTS

Program Directories

Close-Up

Telecommunications

The American University of Athens, The School of Graduate Studies, Athens, Greece. Offers biomedical sciences (MS); business (MBA); business communication (MA); computer sciences (MS); engineering and applied sciences (MS); politics and policy making (MA); systems engineering (MS); telecommunications (MS). *Entrance requirements:* For master's, resum&e, 2 recommendation letters. Additional exam requirements/recommendations for international students: Required—TOEFL (minimum score 550 paper-based; 213 computer-based). *Faculty research:* Nanotechnology, environmental sciences, rock mechanics, human skin studies, Monte Carlo algorithms and software.

Ball State University, Graduate School, College of Communication, Information, and Media, Department of Telecommunications, Muncie, IN 47306-1099. Offers digital storytelling (MA).

Boston University, Metropolitan College, Department of Computer Science, Program in Telecommunications, Boston, MA 02215. Offers MS. Part-time and evening/weekend programs available. *Faculty:* 1 full-time (0 women), 4 part-time/adjunct (0 women). *Students:* 1 full-time (0 women), 11 part-time (2 women); includes 1 minority (Asian American or Pacific Islander), 3 international. Average age 36. 4 applicants, 100% accepted, 4 enrolled. *Entrance requirements:* For master's, 3 letters of recommendation, resume. Additional exam requirements/recommendations for international students: Required—TOEFL or IELTS. *Application deadline:* For fall admission, 6/1 priority date for domestic and international students; for winter admission, 10/1 priority date for domestic and international students; for spring admission, 3/1 priority date for domestic and international students. Applications are processed on a rolling basis. Application fee: $70. Electronic applications accepted. *Expenses:* Tuition: Full-time $37,910; part-time $1184 per credit hour. Required fees: $386; $40 per semester. Part-time tuition and fees vary according to class time, course level, degree level and program. *Financial support:* Research assistantships with partial tuition reimbursements, career-related internships or fieldwork, Federal Work-Study, and institutionally sponsored loans available. Support available to part-time students. Financial award applicants required to submit FAFSA. *Unit head:* Dr. Lubomir Chitkushev, Chairman, 617-353-2566, Fax: 617-353-2367, E-mail: csinfo@bu.edu. *Application contact:* Camille Grace Kardoose, Program Coordinator, 617-353-2566, Fax: 617-353-2367, E-mail: cgkardoo@bu.edu.

The Catholic University of America, School of Engineering, Department of Electrical Engineering and Computer Science, Washington, DC 20064. Offers antennas and electromagnetic propagation (MEE, MSCS, D Engr); bioimaging (MEE, MSCS, PhD); bioinformatics and intelligent information systems (MEE, D Engr, PhD); distributed and real-time systems (MEE, MSCS, D Engr, PhD); high speed communications and networking (MSCS, D Engr, PhD); information security (MEE, MSCS, PhD); micro-optics (MEE, MSCS, D Engr, PhD); signal and image processing (MEE, MSCS, D Engr). Part-time programs available. *Faculty:* 7 full-time (2 women), 6 part-time/adjunct (0 women). *Students:* 10 full-time (4 women), 50 part-time (7 women); includes 10 minority (3 African Americans, 4 Asian Americans or Pacific Islanders, 3 Hispanic Americans), 12 international. Average age 34. 50 applicants, 54% accepted, 11 enrolled. In 2009, 10 master's awarded. *Degree requirements:* For master's, thesis or alternative; for doctorate, comprehensive exam, thesis/dissertation, qualifying exam, oral exams. *Entrance requirements:* For master's, statement of purpose, official copies of academic transcripts, three letters of recommendation; for doctorate, 3 letters of recommendation. Additional exam requirements/recommendations for international students: Required—TOEFL (minimum score 580 paper-based; 237 computer-based). *Application deadline:* For fall admission, 8/1 priority date for domestic students, 7/15 for international students; for spring admission, 12/1 priority date for domestic students, 10/15 for international students. Applications are processed on a rolling basis. Application fee: $55. Electronic applications accepted. *Expenses:* Contact institution. *Financial support:* Fellowships, research assistantships, teaching assistantships, Federal Work-Study, scholarships/grants, tuition waivers (full and partial), and unspecified assistantships available. Financial award application deadline: 2/1; financial award applicants required to submit FAFSA. *Faculty research:* Signal and image processing, computer communications, robotics, intelligent controls, bioelectromagnetics. Total annual research expenditures: $1.2 million. *Unit head:* Dr. Phillip Regalia, Chair, 202-319-5879, Fax: 202-319-5195, E-mail: regalia@cua.edu. *Application contact:* Julie Schwing, Director of Graduate Admissions, 202-319-5057, Fax: 202-319-6533, E-mail: cua-admissions@cua.edu.

Claremont Graduate University, Graduate Programs, School of Information Systems and Technology, Claremont, CA 91711-6160. Offers electronic commerce (MS, PhD); health information management (MS); information systems (Certificate); knowledge management (MS, PhD); systems development (MS, PhD); telecommunications and networking (MS, PhD); MBA/MS. Part-time programs available. *Faculty:* 6 full-time (1 woman), 1 part-time/adjunct (0 women). *Students:* 78 full-time (28 women), 35 part-time (11 women); includes 32 minority (8 African Americans, 1 American Indian/Alaska Native, 16 Asian Americans or Pacific Islanders, 7 Hispanic Americans), 32 international. Average age 38. In 2009, 31 master's, 11 doctorates, 1 other advanced degree awarded. *Degree requirements:* For doctorate, comprehensive exam, thesis/dissertation, portfolio. *Entrance requirements:* For master's and doctorate, GMAT, GRE General Test. Additional exam requirements/recommendations for international students: Required—TOEFL (minimum score 550 paper-based; 213 computer-based; 80 iBT). *Application deadline:* For fall admission, 2/1 priority date for domestic students. Applications are processed on a rolling basis. Application fee: $60. Electronic applications accepted. *Expenses:* Tuition: Full-time $35,046; part-time $1524 per credit. Required fees: $161 per semester. *Financial support:* Fellowships, research assistantships, teaching assistantships, Federal Work-Study, institutionally sponsored loans, and scholarships/grants available. Support available to part-time students. Financial award application deadline: 2/15; financial award applicants required to submit FAFSA. *Faculty research:* GPSS, man-machine interaction, organizational aspects of computing, implementation of information systems, information systems practice. *Unit head:* Terry Ryan, Dean, 909-607-9591, Fax: 909-621-8564, E-mail: terry.ryan@cgu.edu. *Application contact:* Matt Hutter, Director of External Affairs, 909-621-3180, Fax: 909-621-8564, E-mail: matt.hutter@cgu.edu.

DePaul University, College of Computing and Digital Media, Chicago, IL 60604. Offers business information technology (MS); computational finance (MS); computer and information sciences (PhD); computer game development (MS); computer graphics and motion technology (MS); computer science (MS); computer, information and network security (MS), including applied technology; digital cinema (MFA, MS), including information technology project management (MS); e-commerce technology (MS); human-computer interaction (MS); information systems (MS); information technology (MA); information technology project management (MS); software engineering (MS); telecommunications systems (MS); JD/MS. Part-time and evening/weekend programs available. Postbaccalaureate distance learning degree programs offered (no on-campus study). *Faculty:* 78 full-time (16 women), 191 part-time/adjunct (51 women). *Students:* 922 full-time (239 women), 887 part-time (209 women); includes 466 minority (193 African Americans, 3 American Indian/Alaska Native, 162 Asian Americans or Pacific Islanders, 108 Hispanic Americans), 276 international. Average age 31. 853 applicants, 67% accepted, 294 enrolled. In 2009, 444 master's, 4 doctorates awarded. *Degree requirements:* For master's, thesis (for some programs); for doctorate, comprehensive exam, thesis/dissertation. *Entrance requirements:* For master's, GRE or GMAT (MS in computational finance only), bachelor's degree; for doctorate, GRE, master's degree in computer science. Additional exam requirements/recommendations for international students: Required—TOEFL (minimum score 550 paper-based; 213 computer-based), IELTS (minimum score 6.5), Pearson Test of English (minimum score 53). *Application deadline:* For fall admission, 8/15 priority date for domestic students, 6/1 priority date for international students; for winter admission, 12/15 priority date for domestic students, 9/15 priority date for international students; for spring admission, 3/1 priority date for domestic students, 12/15 priority date for international students. Applications are processed on a rolling basis. Application fee: $25. Electronic applications accepted. *Expenses:* Contact institution. *Financial support:* In 2009–10, 69 students received support, including 6 fellowships with full tuition reimbursements available (averaging $25,858 per year), 75 teaching assistantships with full and partial tuition reimbursements available (averaging $5,780 per year); research assistantships, Federal Work-Study, scholarships/grants, tuition waivers (full and partial), and unspecified assistantships also available. Support available to part-time students. Financial award application deadline: 4/30; financial award applicants required to submit FAFSA. *Faculty research:* Bioinformatics, visual computing, graphics and animation, high performance and scientific computing, databases. Total annual research expenditures: $790,000. *Unit head:* Dr. David Miller, Dean, 312-362-8381, Fax: 312-362-5185. *Application contact:* Dr. Liz Friedman, Assistant Dean of Student Services, 312-362-5384, Fax: 312-362-5327, E-mail: efriedm2@cdm.depaul.edu.

Drexel University, College of Engineering, Department of Electrical and Computer Engineering, Program in Telecommunications Engineering, Philadelphia, PA 19104-2875. Offers MSEE. *Entrance requirements:* For master's, BS in electrical engineering or physics, minimum GPA of 3.0. Additional exam requirements/recommendations for international students: Required—TOEFL. Electronic applications accepted.

Florida International University, College of Engineering and Computing, Department of Electrical and Computer Engineering, Miami, FL 33175. Offers computer engineering (MS); electrical engineering (MS, PhD); telecommunications and networking (MS). Part-time and evening/weekend programs available. *Faculty:* 17 full-time (0 women). *Students:* 95 full-time (17 women), 70 part-time (11 women); includes 54 minority (11 African Americans, 8 Asian Americans or Pacific Islanders, 35 Hispanic Americans), 98 international. Average age 28. 319 applicants, 12% accepted, 38 enrolled. In 2009, 83 master's, 6 doctorates awarded. Terminal master's awarded for partial completion of doctoral program. *Degree requirements:* For master's, thesis optional; for doctorate, comprehensive exam, thesis/dissertation. *Entrance requirements:* For master's, minimum undergraduate GPA of 3.0 in upper-level coursework, resume, letters of recommendation, letter of intent; for doctorate, GRE General Test, minimum graduate GPA of 3.3, resume, letters of recommendation, letter of intent. Additional exam requirements/recommendations for international students: Required—TOEFL (minimum score 550 paper-based; 80 iBT). *Application deadline:* For fall admission, 6/1 for domestic students, 4/1 for international students; for spring admission, 10/1 for domestic students, 9/1 for international students. Applications are processed on a rolling basis. Application fee: $30. Electronic applications accepted. *Expenses:* Tuition, state resident: full-time $8008; part-time $4004 per year. Tuition, nonresident: full-time $20,104; part-time $10,052 per year. Required fees: $298; $149 per term. *Financial support:* In 2009–10, 4 fellowships (averaging $25,000 per year), 17 research assistantships (averaging $20,474 per year), 36 teaching assistantships (averaging $20,474 per year) were awarded; institutionally sponsored loans, scholarships/grants, and unspecified assistantships also available. Financial award application deadline: 3/1; financial award applicants required to submit FAFSA. Total annual research expenditures: $1.5 million. *Unit head:* Dr. Kang Yen, Chair, Electrical and Computer Engineering Department, 305-348-3037, Fax: 305-348-3707, E-mail: yenk@fiu.edu. *Application contact:* Maria Parrilla, Graduate Admissions Assistant, 305-348-1980, Fax: 305-348-6142, E-mail: grad_eng@fiu.edu.

Florida International University, College of Engineering and Computing, School of Computing and Information Sciences, Program in Telecommunications and Networking, Miami, FL 33175. Offers MS. Part-time and evening/weekend programs available. *Students:* 11 full-time (1 woman), 31 part-time (7 women); includes 22 minority (5 African Americans, 1 Asian American or Pacific Islander, 16 Hispanic Americans), 16 international. Average age 31. 88 applicants, 8% accepted, 7 enrolled. In 2009, 25 master's awarded. *Entrance requirements:* For master's, minimum undergraduate GPA of 3.0 in the upper level coursework. Additional exam requirements/recommendations for international students: Required—TOEFL (minimum score 550 paper-based; 80 iBT). *Application deadline:* For fall admission, 6/1 for domestic students, 4/1 for international students; for spring admission, 10/1 for domestic students, 9/1 for international students. Applications are processed on a rolling basis. Application fee: $30. Electronic applications accepted. *Expenses:* Tuition, state resident: full-time $8008; part-time $4004 per year. Tuition, nonresident: full-time $20,104; part-time $10,052 per year. Required fees: $298; $149 per term. *Financial support:* Institutionally sponsored loans and scholarships/grants available. Financial award application deadline: 3/1; financial award applicants required to submit FAFSA. *Faculty research:* Wireless networks and mobile computing, high-performance routers and switches, network centric middleware components, distributed systems, networked databases. *Unit head:* Dr. Jainendra Navlakha, Director, School of Computing and Information Sciences, 305-348-2026, Fax: 305-348-3549, E-mail: navlakha@cis.fiu.edu. *Application contact:* Maria Parrilla, Graduate Admissions Assistant, 305-348-1890, Fax: 305-348-6142, E-mail: grad_eng@fiu.edu.

Franklin Pierce University, Graduate Studies, Rindge, NH 03461-0060. Offers emerging network technology (Graduate Certificate); health practice management (MBA, Graduate Certificate); human resource management (MBA); human resources management (Graduate Certificate); information technology management (MS); leadership (MBA, DA), including transformational leadership (DA); nursing (MS); physical therapy (DPT); physician assistant (MPAS); sports facilities management (MS); teacher education (M Ed). *Accreditation:* APTA. Part-time programs available. Postbaccalaureate distance learning degree programs offered (no on-campus study). *Faculty:* 27 full-time (16 women), 18 part-time/adjunct (4 women). *Students:* 296 full-time (172 women), 249 part-time (165 women); includes 18 minority (5 African Americans, 7 Asian Americans or Pacific Islanders, 6 Hispanic Americans), 31 international. Average age 38. 227 applicants, 97% accepted, 185 enrolled. In 2009, 76 master's, 46 doctorates awarded. *Degree requirements:* For master's, Program specific. Concentrated original research projects; student teaching, fieldwork and/or internship; leadership project.; for doctorate, concentrated original research projects, clinical fieldwork and/or internship, leadership project. *Entrance requirements:* For master's, minimum GPA of 2.5 GPA, 3 letters of recommendation; for doctorate, Demonstrated success at previous academic institutions (GPA of 2.5 or higher), cover letter, 3 letters of recommendation, personal mission statement. Interview. Writing sample required for Doctor of Arts program. Additional exam requirements/recommendations for international students: Required—TOEFL (minimum score 550 paper-based; 195 computer-based). *Application deadline:* Applications are processed on a rolling basis. Application fee: $0. Electronic applications accepted. *Expenses:* Tuition: Part-time $1560 per course. Part-time tuition and fees vary according to degree level, campus/location and program. *Financial support:* In 2009–10, 36 students received support, including 22 teaching assistantships with full and partial tuition reimbursements available; career-related internships or fieldwork and unspecified assistantships also available. Support available to part-time students. Financial award applicants required to submit FAFSA. *Faculty research:* Evidence based practice in sports physical therapy, human resource management in economic crisis, leadership in nursing, innovation in sports facility management, differentiated learning and understanding by design. *Unit head:* Dr. Robert G. Goddard, Assistant Dean, 603-899-4361, Fax: 603-229-4580, E-mail: goddardr@franklinpierce.edu. *Application contact:* 800-325-1090, Fax: 603-898-0827, E-mail: gpsadmin@franklinpierce.edu.

George Mason University, Volgenau School of Information Technology and Engineering, Department of Electrical and Computer Engineering, Fairfax, VA 22030. Offers advanced networking protocols for telecommunications (Certificate); communications and networking (Certificate); computer engineering (MS); computer forensics (MS); electrical and computer engineering (PhD); electrical engineering (MS); network technology and applications (Certificate); networks, system integration and testing (Certificate); signal processing (Certificate); telecom systems modeling (Certificate); telecommunications (MS); telecommunications forensics and security (Certificate); VLSI design/manufacturing (Certificate); wireless communication (Certificate). Part-time and evening/weekend programs available. *Faculty:* 29 full-time (4 women), 37 part-time/adjunct (5 women). *Students:* 115 full-time (18 women), 308 part-time (46 women); includes 84 minority (17 African Americans, 51 Asian Americans or Pacific Islanders, 16 Hispanic Americans), 179 international. Average age 29. 461 applicants, 67% accepted, 105 enrolled. In 2009, 157 master's, 6 doctorates, 61 other advanced degrees awarded. *Degree* *requirements:* For master's, thesis optional; for doctorate, comprehensive exam, thesis or scholarly paper. *Entrance requirements:* For master's, GMAT or GRE General Test, letters of recommendation, resume; for doctorate, GRE/GMAT, personal goal statement, 2 transcripts, letter of recommendation. Additional exam requirements/recommendations for international students: Required—TOEFL. *Application deadline:* For fall admission, 7/15 priority date for domestic and international students; for spring admission, 12/2 for domestic students, 12/1 for international students. Applications are processed on a rolling basis. Application fee: $75. Electronic applications accepted. *Expenses:* Tuition, state resident: full-time $7568; part-time $315.33 per credit hour. Tuition, nonresident: full-time $21,704; part-time $904.33 per credit hour. Required fees: $2184; $91 per credit hour. *Financial support:* In 2009–10, 64 students received support, including 2 fellowships with full tuition reimbursements available (averaging $18,000 per year), 22 research assistantships with full and partial tuition reimbursements available (averaging $8,469 per year), 42 teaching assistantships with full and partial tuition reimbursements available (averaging $6,291 per year); career-related internships or fieldwork, Federal Work-Study, scholarships/grants, unspecified assistantships, and health care benefits (full-time research or teaching assistantship recipients) also available. Support available to part-time students. Financial award application deadline: 3/1; financial award applicants required to submit FAFSA. *Faculty research:* Communication networks, signal processing, system failure diagnosis, multiprocessors, material processing using microwave energy. Total annual research expenditures: $3 million. *Unit head:* Dr. Andre Manitius, Chairperson, 703-993-1569, Fax: 703-993-1601, E-mail: ece@gmu.edu. *Application contact:* Jessica Skinner, Associate Dean, 703-993-1569, E-mail: jskinne6@gmu.edu.

The George Washington University, School of Engineering and Applied Science, Department of Electrical and Computer Engineering, Washington, DC 20052. Offers electrical and computer engineering (MS, D Sc); telecommunication and computers (MS). Part-time and evening/weekend programs available. *Faculty:* 23 full-time (2 women), 6 part-time/adjunct (0 women). *Students:* 98 full-time (19 women), 132 part-time (14 women); includes 33 minority (12 African Americans, 1 American Indian/Alaska Native, 18 Asian Americans or Pacific Islanders, 2 Hispanic Americans), 126 international. Average age 30. 293 applicants, 88% accepted, 64 enrolled. In 2009, 54 master's, 5 doctorates awarded. *Degree requirements:* For master's, thesis optional; for doctorate, comprehensive exam, thesis/dissertation, dissertation defense, qualifying exam. *Entrance requirements:* For master's, appropriate bachelor's degree, minimum GPA of 3.0; for doctorate, appropriate bachelor's or master's degree, minimum GPA of 3.3, GRE if highest earned degree is BS. Additional exam requirements/recommendations for international students: Required—TOEFL or George Washington University English as a Foreign Language Test. *Application deadline:* For fall admission, 3/1 priority date for domestic students; for spring admission, 10/1 for domestic students. Applications are processed on a rolling basis. Application fee: $60. *Financial support:* In 2009–10, 39 students received support; fellowships with tuition reimbursements available, research assistantships, teaching assistantships with tuition reimbursements available, career-related internships or fieldwork and institutionally sponsored loans available. Financial award application deadline: 3/1; financial award applicants required to submit FAFSA. *Faculty research:* Computer graphics, multimedia systems. *Unit head:* Can E. Korman, Chair, 202-994-4952, E-mail: korman@gwu.edu. *Application contact:* Adina Lav, Marketing, Recruiting and Admissions, 202-994-5827, Fax: 202-994-0909, E-mail: engineering@gwu.edu.

Illinois Institute of Technology, Graduate College, Armour College of Engineering, Department of Electrical and Computer Engineering, Chicago, IL 60616-3793. Offers biomedical imaging and signals (MBMI); computer engineering (MS, PhD); electrical and computer engineering (MECE); electrical engineering (MS, PhD); electricity markets (MEM); manufacturing engineering (MME, MS); network engineering (MNE); power engineering (MPE); telecommunications and software engineering (MTSE); VLSI and microelectronics (MVM). Part-time and evening/weekend programs available. Terminal master's awarded for partial completion of doctoral program. *Degree requirements:* For master's, comprehensive exam, thesis (for some programs); for doctorate, comprehensive exam, thesis/dissertation. *Entrance requirements:* For master's and doctorate, GRE General Test, minimum undergraduate GPA of 3.0. Additional exam requirements/recommendations for international students: Required—TOEFL (minimum score 550 paper-based; 213 computer-based; 80 iBT). Electronic applications accepted. *Expenses:* Tuition: Full-time $17,550; part-time $888 per credit hour. Required fees: $850; $7.50 per credit hour. One-time fee: $50 full-time. Full-time tuition and fees vary according to program. *Faculty research:* Communications and signal processing, computers and digital systems, electronics and electromagnetics, power and control systems.

Illinois Institute of Technology, Graduate College, College of Science and Letters, Department of Computer Science, Chicago, IL 60616-3793. Offers computer science (MCS, MS, PhD); teaching (MST); telecommunications and software engineering (MTSE); MS/M Ch E. Part-time and evening/weekend programs available. Postbaccalaureate distance learning degree programs offered (no on-campus study). Terminal master's awarded for partial completion of doctoral program. *Degree requirements:* For master's, thesis (for some programs); for doctorate, comprehensive exam, thesis/dissertation. *Entrance requirements:* For master's and doctorate, GRE General Test, minimum undergraduate GPA of 3.0. Additional exam requirements/recommendations for international students: Required—TOEFL (minimum score 550 paper-based; 213 computer-based; 80 iBT). Electronic applications accepted. *Expenses:* Tuition: Full-time $17,550; part-time $888 per credit hour. Required fees: $850; $7.50 per credit hour. One-time fee: $50 full-time. Full-time tuition and fees vary according to program. *Faculty research:* Information retrieval, parallel and distributed computing, networking, algorithms, natural language processing.

Indiana University Bloomington, University Graduate School, College of Arts and Sciences, Department of Telecommunications, Program in Telecommunications, Bloomington, IN 47405-7000. Offers MA, MS. *Students:* 34 full-time (14 women); includes 6 minority (3 African Americans, 2 Asian Americans or Pacific Islanders, 1 Hispanic American), 13 international. Average age 28. 32 applicants, 72% accepted, 15 enrolled. In 2009, 17 master's awarded. *Degree requirements:* For master's, comprehensive exam (for some programs), thesis (for some programs). *Entrance requirements:* For master's, GRE General Test. Application fee: $50 ($60 for international students). *Unit head:* Tamera Theodore, Graduate Secretary, 812-855-2017, E-mail: ttheodor@indiana.edu. *Application contact:* Tamera Theodore, Graduate Secretary, 812-855-2017, E-mail: ttheodor@indiana.edu.

Instituto Tecnologico de Santo Domingo, Graduate School, Santo Domingo, Dominican Republic. Offers applied linguistics (MA); construction administration (M Mgmt); corporate finance (M Mgmt); education (M Ed); engineering (M Eng), including data telecommunications, industrial engineering, logistics and supply chain, maintenance engineering, sanitary and environmental engineering, structural engineering; environmental science (M En S), including environmental education, environmental management, marine and coastal ecosystems, natural resources management; family therapy (MA); food science and technology (MS); human development (MA); human resources administration (M Mgmt); international business (M Mgmt); labor risks (M Mgmt); management (M Mgmt); marketing (M Mgmt); mathematics (MS); organizational development (M Mgmt); planning and taxation (M Mgmt); psychology (MA); social science (M Ed); upper management (M Mgmt). *Entrance requirements:* For master's, birth certificate, minimum GPA of 2.0.

Iona College, School of Arts and Science, Program in Computer Science, New Rochelle, NY 10801-1890. Offers computer science (MS); telecommunications (MS). Part-time and evening/weekend programs available. *Faculty:* 10 full-time (4 women), 3 part-time/adjunct (0 women). *Students:* 25 part-time (5 women); includes 6 minority (3 African Americans, 3 Hispanic Americans), 1 international. Average age 36. 18 applicants, 72% accepted, 8 enrolled. In 2009, 7 master's awarded. *Degree requirements:* For master's, thesis or alternative. *Entrance requirements:* For master's, minimum GPA of 3.0. Additional exam requirements/recommendations for international students: Required—TOEFL (minimum score 550 paper-based; 213 computer-based). *Application deadline:* Applications are processed on a rolling basis. Application fee: $50. Electronic applications accepted. *Expenses:* Contact institution. *Financial support:* Tuition waivers (partial) and unspecified assistantships available. Support available to part-time students. Financial award application deadline: 4/15; financial award applicants required to submit FAFSA. *Faculty research:* Telecommunications, expert systems, graph isomorphism, algorithms, formal verification of hardware. *Unit head:* Dr. Robert Schiaffino, Chair, 914-633-2338, E-mail: rschiaffino@iona.edu. *Application contact:* Veronica Jarek-Prinz, Director of Graduate Admissions, 914-633-2420, Fax: 914-633-2277, E-mail: vjarekprinz@iona.edu.

The Johns Hopkins University, Engineering for Professionals, Part-Time Program in Computer Science, Baltimore, MD 21218-2699. Offers bioinformatics (MS); computer science (MS, Post-Master's Certificate); telecommunications and networking (MS). Part-time and evening/weekend programs available. Postbaccalaureate distance learning degree programs offered (no on-campus study). *Faculty:* 58 part-time/adjunct (5 women). *Students:* 25 full-time (3 women), 411 part-time (65 women); includes 103 minority (27 African Americans, 65 Asian Americans or Pacific Islanders, 11 Hispanic Americans), 8 international. Average age 29. In 2009, 174 master's, 2 other advanced degrees awarded. *Application deadline:* Applications are processed on a rolling basis. Application fee: $75. Electronic applications accepted. *Financial support:* Institutionally sponsored loans available. *Unit head:* Dr. Ralph D. Semmel, Program Chair, 443-778-6179, E-mail: ralph.semmel@jhuapl.edu. *Application contact:* Priyanka Dwivedi, Admissions Manager, 410-516-2300, Fax: 410-579-8049, E-mail: pdwived1@jhu.edu.

Michigan State University, The Graduate School, College of Communication Arts and Sciences, Department of Telecommunication, Information Studies, and Media, East Lansing, MI 48824. Offers digital media arts and technology (MA); information and telecommunication management (MA); information, policy and society (MA); serious game design (MA). *Entrance requirements:* Additional exam requirements/recommendations for international students: Required—TOEFL. Electronic applications accepted.

National University, Academic Affairs, School of Engineering and Technology, Department of Applied Engineering, La Jolla, CA 92037-1011. Offers database administration (MS); engineering management (MS); environmental engineering (MS); homeland security and safety engineering (MS); system engineering (MS); wireless communications (MS). Part-time and evening/weekend programs available. Postbaccalaureate distance learning degree programs offered (no on-campus study). *Faculty:* 6 full-time (1 woman), 7 part-time/adjunct (1 woman). *Students:* 61 full-time (16 women), 176 part-time (35 women); includes 54 minority (11 African Americans, 1 American Indian/Alaska Native, 23 Asian Americans or Pacific Islanders, 19 Hispanic Americans), 117 international. Average age 31. 133 applicants, 100% accepted, 83 enrolled. In 2009, 34 master's awarded. *Degree requirements:* For master's, thesis. *Entrance requirements:* For master's, interview, minimum GPA of 2.5. Additional exam requirements/recommendations for international students: Required—TOEFL (minimum score 550 paper-based; 213 computer-based; 79 iBT), IELTS (minimum score 6). *Application deadline:* Applications are processed on a rolling basis. Application fee: $60 ($65 for international students). Electronic applications accepted. *Expenses:* Tuition: Part-time $338 per quarter hour. *Financial support:* Career-related internships or fieldwork, institutionally sponsored loans, scholarships/grants, and tuition waivers (partial) available. Support available to part-time students. Financial award application deadline: 6/30; financial award applicants required to submit FAFSA. *Unit head:* Dr. Shekar Viswanathan, Chair and Associate Professor, 858-309-8416, Fax: 858-309-3420, E-mail: sviswana@nu.edu. *Application contact:* Dominick Giovanniello, Associate Regional Dean—San Diego, 800-NAT-UNIV, Fax: 858-541-7792, E-mail: dgiovann@nu.edu.

Ohio University, Graduate College, Scripps College of Communication, J. Warren McClure School of Information and Telecommunication Systems, Athens, OH 45701-2979. Offers MCTP. Part-time programs available. *Faculty:* 8 full-time (1 woman). *Students:* 10 full-time (3 women), 4 part-time (0 women); includes 2 minority (both Asian Americans or Pacific Islanders), 10 international. 23 applicants, 74% accepted, 3 enrolled. In 2009, 17 master's awarded. *Degree requirements:* For master's, comprehensive exam (for some programs), thesis (for some programs). *Entrance requirements:* For master's, GRE or GMAT, 3.0(on 4.10 scale) cumulative GPA. Additional exam requirements/recommendations for international students: Required—TOEFL (minimum score 550 paper-based; 80 iBT) or IELTS Academic (minimum score 6.5). *Application deadline:* For fall admission, 2/1 priority date for domestic students, 12/15 priority date for international students. Applications are processed on a rolling basis. Application fee: $50 ($55 for international students). Electronic applications accepted. *Expenses:* Tuition, state resident: full-time $7839; part-time $323 per quarter hour. Tuition, nonresident: full-time $15,831; part-time $654 per quarter hour. Required fees: $2931. *Financial support:* Research assistantships with full and partial tuition reimbursements, institutionally sponsored loans and unspecified assistantships available. Financial award application deadline: 2/1; financial award applicants required to submit FAFSA. *Faculty research:* Voice and data networks, with special emphasis on the interaction of technology and policy issues in the successful design, deployment, and operation of complex networks and information systems. Total annual research expenditures: $200,000. *Unit head:* Philip D. Campbell, Associate Professor and Director, 740-593-4907, Fax: 740-593-4889, E-mail: campbell@ohio.edu. *Application contact:* Dr. Phyllis W. Bernt, Professor and Associate Director for Graduate Studies, 740-593-0020, Fax: 740-593-4889, E-mail: bernt@ohio.edu.

Pace University, Seidenberg School of Computer Science and Information Systems, New York, NY 10038. Offers computer communications and networks (Certificate); computer science (MS); computing studies (DPS); information systems (MS); Internet technologies for e-commerce (MS); Internet technology (MS); object-oriented programming (Certificate); security and information assurance (Certificate); software development and engineering (MS); telecommunications (MS, Certificate). Part-time and evening/weekend programs available. *Students:* 122 full-time (37 women), 424 part-time (131 women); includes 188 minority (76 African Americans, 1 American Indian/Alaska Native, 65 Asian Americans or Pacific Islanders, 46 Hispanic Americans), 110 international. Average age 35. 352 applicants, 89% accepted, 128 enrolled. In 2009, 137 master's, 11 doctorates, 3 other advanced degrees awarded. *Entrance requirements:* For master's, GRE General Test. Additional exam requirements/recommendations for international students: Required—TOEFL. *Application deadline:* For fall admission, 7/31 priority date for domestic students; for spring admission, 11/30 for domestic students. Applications are processed on a rolling basis. Application fee: $70. Electronic applications accepted. *Expenses:* Contact institution. *Financial support:* Research assistantships, career-related internships or fieldwork available. Support available to part-time students. Financial award applicants required to submit FAFSA. *Unit head:* Dr. Constance Knapp, Interim Dean, 914-773-3750, Fax: 914-773-3533, E-mail: cknapp@pace.edu. *Application contact:* Joanna Broda, Director of Graduate Admissions, 914-422-4283, Fax: 914-422-4287, E-mail: gradwp@pace.edu.

Polytechnic Institute of NYU, Department of Electrical and Computer Engineering, Major in Telecommunication Networks, Brooklyn, NY 11201-2990. Offers MS. Part-time and evening/weekend programs available. *Students:* 51 full-time (8 women), 41 part-time (4 women); includes 15 minority (3 African Americans, 8 Asian Americans or Pacific Islanders, 4 Hispanic Americans), 52 international. 134 applicants, 72% accepted, 41 enrolled. In 2009, 16 master's awarded. *Degree requirements:* For master's, comprehensive exam (for some programs), thesis (for some programs). *Entrance requirements:* For master's, BS in electrical engineering. Additional exam requirements/recommendations for international students: Required—TOEFL (minimum score 550 paper-based; 213 computer-based; 80 iBT); Recommended—IELTS (minimum score 6.5). *Application deadline:* For fall admission, 7/31 priority date for domestic students, 4/30 priority date for international students; for spring admission, 12/31 priority date for domestic students, 11/30 priority date for international students. Applications are processed on a rolling basis. Application fee: $75. Electronic applications accepted. *Expenses:* Tuition: Full-time $21,492; part-time $1194 per credit hour. Required fees: $1160; $204 per course. *Financial support:* Fellowships, research assistantships, teaching assistantships, institutionally sponsored loans, scholarships/grants, and unspecified assistantships available. Support available to part-time students. Financial award applicants required to submit FAFSA. *Unit head:* Dr.

Telecommunications

Polytechnic Institute of NYU *(continued)*
Jonathan Chao, Head, 718-260-3478, Fax: 718-260-3302, E-mail: chao@poly.edu. *Application contact:* JeanCarlo Bonilla, Director of Graduate Enrollment Management, 718-260-3182, Fax: 718-260-3624.

Polytechnic Institute of NYU, Long Island Graduate Center, Graduate Programs, Department of Electrical and Computer Engineering, Major in Telecommunication Networks, Melville, NY 11747. Offers MS. Part-time and evening/weekend programs available. *Students:* 1 full-time (0 women), 8 part-time (1 woman); includes 3 minority (1 American Indian/Alaska Native, 1 Asian American or Pacific Islander, 1 Hispanic American), 2 international. 3 applicants, 100% accepted, 3 enrolled. In 2009, 1 master's awarded. *Degree requirements:* For master's, comprehensive exam (for some programs), thesis (for some programs). *Entrance requirements:* Additional exam requirements/recommendations for international students: Required—TOEFL (minimum score 550 paper-based; 213 computer-based; 80 iBT); Recommended—IELTS (minimum score 6.5). *Application deadline:* For fall admission, 7/31 priority date for domestic students, 4/30 priority date for international students; for spring admission, 12/31 priority date for domestic students, 11/30 priority date for international students. Applications are processed on a rolling basis. Application fee: $75. Electronic applications accepted. *Financial support:* Institutionally sponsored loans, scholarships/grants, and unspecified assistantships available. Support available to part-time students. Financial award applicants required to submit FAFSA. *Unit head:* Dr. Jonathan Chao, Department Head, 718-260-3302, E-mail: chao@poly.edu. *Application contact:* JeanCarlo Bonilla, Director of Graduate Enrollment Management, 718-260-3182, Fax: 718-260-3624, E-mail: gradinfo@poly.edu.

Polytechnic Institute of NYU, Westchester Graduate Center, Graduate Programs, Department of Electrical and Computer Engineering, Major in Telecommunication Networks, Hawthorne, NY 10532-1507. Offers MS. Part-time and evening/weekend programs available. *Students:* 3 full-time (0 women), 2 part-time (0 women), 3 international. 2 applicants, 100% accepted, 2 enrolled. *Degree requirements:* For master's, thesis (for some programs). *Entrance requirements:* Additional exam requirements/recommendations for international students: Required—TOEFL (minimum score 550 paper-based; 213 computer-based; 80 iBT); Recommended—IELTS (minimum score 6.5). *Application deadline:* For fall admission, 7/31 priority date for domestic students, 4/30 priority date for international students; for spring admission, 12/31 priority date for domestic students, 11/30 priority date for international students. Applications are processed on a rolling basis. Application fee: $75. Electronic applications accepted. *Financial support:* Institutionally sponsored loans, scholarships/grants, and unspecified assistantships available. Support available to part-time students. *Unit head:* Dr. Jonathan Chao, Department Head, 718-260-3302, E-mail: chao@poly.edu. *Application contact:* JeanCarlo Bonilla, Director of Graduate Enrollment Management, 718-260-3182, Fax: 718-260-3624, E-mail: gradinfo@poly.edu.

Rochester Institute of Technology, Graduate Enrollment Services, College of Applied Science and Technology, Department of Electrical, Computer and Telecommunications Engineering Technology, Program of Telecommunications Engineering Technology, Rochester, NY 14623-5603. Offers MS. Part-time and evening/weekend programs available. Postbaccalaureate distance learning degree programs offered (no on-campus study). *Students:* 38 full-time (16 women), 21 part-time (4 women); includes 1 African American, 1 Hispanic American, 43 international. Average age 30. 127 applicants, 50% accepted, 16 enrolled. In 2009, 22 master's awarded. *Degree requirements:* For master's, thesis or alternative. *Entrance requirements:* For master's, GRE. Additional exam requirements/recommendations for international students: Required—TOEFL (minimum score 570 paper-based; 230 computer-based; 89 iBT), or IELTS (minimum score 6.5). *Application deadline:* For fall admission, 2/15 priority date for domestic and international students; for winter admission, 11/1 for domestic and international students; for spring admission, 2/1 for domestic and international students. Applications are processed on a rolling basis. Application fee: $50. Electronic applications accepted. *Expenses:* Tuition: Full-time $31,533; part-time $876 per credit hour. Required fees: $210. *Financial support:* In 2009–10, 47 students received support; research assistantships with partial tuition reimbursements available, teaching assistantships, career-related internships or fieldwork, scholarships/grants, and unspecified assistantships available. Support available to part-time students. Financial award application deadline: 2/15; financial award applicants required to submit FAFSA. *Unit head:* Warren Koontz, Program Chair, 585-475-2179, Fax: 585-475-2178, E-mail: ectet@rit.edu. *Application contact:* Diane Ellison, Assistant Vice President, Graduate Enrollment Services, 585-475-2229, Fax: 585-475-7164, E-mail: gradinfo@rit.edu.

Roosevelt University, Graduate Division, College of Arts and Sciences, Department of Computer Science and Telecommunications, Program in Telecommunications, Chicago, IL 60605. Offers MST. Part-time and evening/weekend programs available. *Entrance requirements:* For master's, GRE. *Faculty research:* Coding theory, mathematical models, network design, simulation models.

Saint Mary's University of Minnesota, Schools of Graduate and Professional Programs, Graduate School of Business and Technology, Information Technology Management Program, Winona, MN 55987-1399. Offers MS. *Unit head:* Viki Kimsal, Director, E-mail: vkimsal@smumn.edu. *Application contact:* Yasin Alsaidi, Director of Admissions for Graduate and Professional Programs, 612-728-5207, Fax: 612-728-5121, E-mail: yalsaidi@smumn.edu.

Southern Methodist University, Bobby B. Lyle School of Engineering, Department of Electrical Engineering, Dallas, TX 75275-0338. Offers electrical engineering (MSEE, PhD); telecommunications (MS). Part-time and evening/weekend programs available. Postbaccalaureate distance learning degree programs offered (no on-campus study). *Faculty:* 14 full-time (1 woman), 7 part-time/adjunct (1 woman). *Students:* 71 full-time (15 women), 94 part-time (21 women); includes 28 minority (7 African Americans, 15 Asian Americans or Pacific Islanders, 6 Hispanic Americans), 101 international. Average age 28. 270 applicants, 49% accepted, 46 enrolled. In 2009, 52 master's, 5 doctorates awarded. Terminal master's awarded for partial completion of doctoral program. *Degree requirements:* For master's, thesis optional; for doctorate, thesis/dissertation, oral and written qualifying exams, oral final exam. *Entrance requirements:* For master's, GRE General Test, minimum GPA of 3.0 in last 2 years; bachelor's degree in engineering, mathematics, or sciences; for doctorate, preliminary counseling exam, minimum GPA of 3.0, bachelor's degree in related field. Additional exam requirements/recommendations for international students: Required—TOEFL. *Application deadline:* For fall admission, 7/1 priority date for domestic students, 5/15 for international students; for spring admission, 11/15 for domestic students, 9/1 for international students. Applications are processed on a rolling basis. Application fee: $75. Electronic applications accepted. *Financial support:* In 2009–10, 38 students received support, including 22 research assistantships with full tuition reimbursements available (averaging $19,200 per year), 16 teaching assistantships with full tuition reimbursements available (averaging $14,400 per year); unspecified assistantships also available. Financial award application deadline: 5/15; financial award applicants required to submit FAFSA. *Faculty research:* Mobile communications, optical communications, digital signal processing, photonics. *Unit head:* Dr. Marc P. Christensen, Chair, 214-768-3113, Fax: 214-768-3573, E-mail: mpc@lyle.smu.edu. *Application contact:* Marc Valerin, Director of Graduate and Executive Admissions, 214-768-3042, Fax: 214-768-3778, E-mail: valerin@lyle.smu.edu.

State University of New York Institute of Technology, School of Information Systems and Engineering Technology, Program in Telecommunications, Utica, NY 13504-3050. Offers MS. Part-time and evening/weekend programs available. *Degree requirements:* For master's, thesis, project or capstone. *Entrance requirements:* For master's, GRE General Test, minimum GPA of 3.0, letters of recommendation (3). Additional exam requirements/recommendations for international students: Required—TOEFL (minimum score 550 paper-based; 213 computer-based). *Faculty research:* Network design/simulation/management, wireless telecommunication systems, international telecommunications policy and management, information assurance, disaster recovery.

Stevens Institute of Technology, Graduate School, Wesley J. Howe School of Technology Management, Program in Telecommunications Management, Hoboken, NJ 07030. Offers business (MS); global innovation management (MS); management of wireless networks (MS); online security, technology and business (MS); project management (MS); technical management (MS); telecommunications management (PhD, Certificate). *Degree requirements:* For master's, thesis optional; for doctorate, thesis/dissertation. *Entrance requirements:* For master's and doctorate, GMAT, GRE General Test. Additional exam requirements/recommendations for international students: Required—TOEFL. Electronic applications accepted. *Expenses:* Tuition: Full-time $9900; part-time $1100 per credit. Required fees: $286 per semester.

Stratford University, School of Graduate Studies, Falls Church, VA 22043. Offers accounting (MS); business administration (IMBA, MBA); enterprise business management (MS); entrepreneurial management (MS); information assurance (MS); information systems (MS); software engineering (MS); telecommunications (MS). Part-time and evening/weekend programs available. Postbaccalaureate distance learning degree programs offered (no on-campus study). *Faculty:* 35 full-time (15 women), 115 part-time/adjunct (25 women). *Students:* 944 full-time (430 women), 15 part-time (5 women). Average age 26. 950 applicants, 45% accepted, 415 enrolled. In 2009, 412 master's awarded. *Degree requirements:* For master's, comprehensive exam, capstone project. *Entrance requirements:* For master's, baccalaureate degree. Additional exam requirements/recommendations for international students: Required—TOEFL (minimum score 500 paper-based; 173 computer-based; 61 iBT). *Application deadline:* Applications are processed on a rolling basis. Application fee: $50. Electronic applications accepted. *Expenses:* Tuition: Full-time $10,530; part-time $390 per credit. Tuition and fees vary according to course load. *Financial support:* Federal Work-Study available. Financial award applicants required to submit FAFSA. *Unit head:* Dr. Habib Khan, Chief Academic Officer, 703-821-8570 Ext. 3305, Fax: 703-734-5335, E-mail: hkhan@stratford.edu. *Application contact:* James Ray, Director of Admissions, 703-821-8570 Ext. 3021, Fax: 703-734-5339, E-mail: jray@stratford.edu.

Syracuse University, School of Information Studies, Program in Telecommunications and Network Management, Syracuse, NY 13244. Offers MS, MS/CAS. Part-time and evening/weekend programs available. Postbaccalaureate distance learning degree programs offered (minimal on-campus study). *Students:* 47 full-time (5 women), 23 part-time (5 women); includes 9 minority (2 African Americans, 1 American Indian/Alaska Native, 1 Asian American or Pacific Islander, 5 Hispanic Americans), 38 international. Average age 29. 136 applicants, 71% accepted, 33 enrolled. In 2009, 22 master's awarded. *Degree requirements:* For master's, internship or research project. *Entrance requirements:* For master's, GRE General Test. Additional exam requirements/recommendations for international students: Required—TOEFL (minimum score 100 iBT). *Application deadline:* For fall admission, 2/1 priority date for domestic and international students; for spring admission, 10/15 priority date for domestic and international students. Applications are processed on a rolling basis. Application fee: $75. Electronic applications accepted. *Expenses:* Tuition: Full-time $26,808; part-time $1117 per credit. Required fees: $1024. *Financial support:* Fellowships with tuition reimbursements, research assistantships with tuition reimbursements, teaching assistantships with tuition reimbursements, career-related internships or fieldwork, Federal Work-Study, and tuition waivers (partial) available. Financial award application deadline: 1/1. *Faculty research:* Multimedia, information resources management. *Unit head:* Martha Garcia-Marillo, Director, 315-443-1829, Fax: 315-443-6886, E-mail: mgarciam@syr.edu. *Application contact:* Susan Corieri, Director of Enrollment Management, 315-443-2575, E-mail: ist@syr.edu.

Universidad del Turabo, Graduate Programs, School of Engineering, Program in Telecommunication and Network Administration, Gurabo, PR 00778-3030. Offers MS. *Students:* 9 full-time (1 woman), 34 part-time (3 women); includes 37 Hispanic Americans. Average age 32. 32 applicants, 81% accepted, 18 enrolled. In 2009, 10 master's awarded. *Unit head:* David Mendez, Head, 787-743-7979. *Application contact:* Virginia Gonzalez, Admissions Officer, 787-746-3009.

Université du Québec, Institut National de la Recherche Scientifique, Graduate Programs, Research Center—Energy, Materials and Telecommunications, Québec, QC G1K 9A9, Canada. Offers energy and materials science (M Sc, PhD); telecommunications (M Sc, PhD). Programs given in French. Part-time programs available. *Faculty:* 37. *Students:* 161 full-time (45 women), 10 part-time (1 woman), 76 international. Average age 32. In 2009, 16 master's, 13 doctorates awarded. *Degree requirements:* For master's, thesis; for doctorate, thesis/dissertation. *Entrance requirements:* For master's, appropriate bachelor's degree, proficiency in French; for doctorate, appropriate master's degree, proficiency in French. *Application deadline:* For fall admission, 3/30 for domestic and international students; for winter admission, 11/1 for domestic and international students. Application fee: $30. *Financial support:* Fellowships, research assistantships, teaching assistantships available. *Faculty research:* New energy sources, plasmas, fusion. *Unit head:* Jean-Claude Kieffer, Director, 450-929-8100, Fax: 450-929-8102, E-mail: kieffer@emt.inrs.ca. *Application contact:* Yvonne Boisvert, Registrar, 418-654-3861, Fax: 418-654-3858, E-mail: registrariat@adm.inrs.ca.

University of Alberta, Faculty of Graduate Studies and Research, Department of Electrical and Computer Engineering, Edmonton, AB T6G 2E1, Canada. Offers communications (M Eng, M Sc, PhD); computer engineering (M Eng, M Sc, PhD); electromagnetics (M Eng, M Sc, PhD); nanotechnology and microdevices (M Eng, M Sc, PhD); power/power electronics (M Eng, M Sc, PhD); systems (M Eng, M Sc, PhD). *Faculty:* 42 full-time (3 women), 12 part-time/adjunct (0 women). *Students:* 252 full-time (28 women), 65 part-time (10 women). Average age 26. 1,500 applicants, 5% accepted. Terminal master's awarded for partial completion of doctoral program. *Degree requirements:* For master's, thesis; for doctorate, thesis/dissertation. *Entrance requirements:* Additional exam requirements/recommendations for international students: Required—TOEFL. *Application deadline:* For fall admission, 4/30 for domestic students; for winter admission, 8/30 for domestic students. Applications are processed on a rolling basis. Application fee: $0 Canadian dollars. Electronic applications accepted. Tuition and fees charges are reported in Canadian dollars. *Expenses:* Tuition, area resident: Full-time $4626.24 Canadian dollars; part-time $99.72 Canadian dollars per unit. International tuition: $8216 Canadian dollars full-time. Required fees: $3589.92 Canadian dollars; $99.72 Canadian dollars per unit. $215 Canadian dollars per term. *Financial support:* In 2009–10, 80 students received support; fellowships, research assistantships, teaching assistantships, scholarships/grants available. *Faculty research:* Controls, communications, microelectronics, electromagnetics. Total annual research expenditures: $3 million Canadian dollars. *Unit head:* Dr. H. J. Marquez, Chair, 780-492-0161, Fax: 780-492-1811. *Application contact:* Michelle Vaage, Graduate Student Advisor, 780-492-0161, Fax: 780-492-1811, E-mail: gradinfo@ece.ualberta.ca.

University of Arkansas, Graduate School, College of Engineering, Department of Electrical Engineering, Fayetteville, AR 72701-1201. Offers electrical engineering (MSEE, PhD); telecommunications engineering (MS Tc E). *Students:* 24 full-time (0 women), 58 part-time (5 women); includes 2 minority (both African Americans), 56 international. In 2009, 16 master's, 5 doctorates awarded. *Degree requirements:* For master's, thesis optional; for doctorate, one foreign language, thesis/dissertation. *Entrance requirements:* For master's and doctorate, GRE General Test. Application fee: $40 ($50 for international students). *Expenses:* Tuition, state resident: full-time $7355; part-time $356.58 per hour. Tuition, nonresident: full-time $17,401; part-time $775.17 per hour. Required fees: $1203. *Financial support:* In 2009–10, 10 fellowships with tuition reimbursements, 52 research assistantships, 4 teaching assistantships were awarded; career-related internships or fieldwork and Federal Work-Study also available. Support available to part-time students. Financial award application deadline: 4/1; financial award applicants required to submit FAFSA. *Unit head:* Dr. Juan Balda, Department Chair, 479-575-3005, Fax: 479-575-7967, E-mail: jbalda@uark.edu. *Application contact:* Dr. Randy Brown, Graduate Coordinator, 479-575-6581, E-mail: rlb02@uark.edu.

University of California, San Diego, Office of Graduate Studies, Department of Electrical and Computer Engineering, La Jolla, CA 92093. Offers applied ocean science (MS, PhD); applied physics (MS, PhD); communication theory and systems (MS, PhD); computer engineering (MS, PhD); electrical engineering (M Eng); electronic circuits and systems (MS,

PhD); intelligent systems, robotics and control (MS, PhD); photonics (MS, PhD); signal and image processing (MS, PhD). MS only offered to students who have been admitted to the PhD program. *Entrance requirements:* For master's and doctorate, GRE General Test. Electronic applications accepted.

University of California, Santa Cruz, Division of Graduate Studies, Jack Baskin School of Engineering, Program in Computer Engineering, Santa Cruz, CA 95064. Offers computer engineering (MS, PhD); network engineering (MS). *Degree requirements:* For doctorate, one foreign language, comprehensive exam, thesis/dissertation, oral exams. *Entrance requirements:* For master's and doctorate, GRE General Test, GRE Subject Test. *Faculty research:* Computer-aided design of digital systems.

University of Colorado at Boulder, Graduate School, College of Engineering and Applied Science, Interdisciplinary Telecommunications Program, Boulder, CO 80309. Offers MS, JD/MS, MBA/MS. Part-time programs available. Postbaccalaureate distance learning degree programs offered. *Students:* 90 full-time (13 women), 56 part-time (15 women); includes 13 minority (3 African Americans, 9 Asian Americans or Pacific Islanders, 1 Hispanic American), 101 international. Average age 28. 153 applicants, 58% accepted, 39 enrolled. In 2009, 70 master's awarded. *Degree requirements:* For master's, comprehensive exam, thesis or alternative. *Entrance requirements:* For master's, minimum undergraduate GPA of 3.0. *Application deadline:* For fall admission, 6/15 priority date for domestic students, 3/15 for international students; for spring admission, 11/1 for domestic students, 10/1 for international students. Applications are processed on a rolling basis. Application fee: $50 ($60 for international students). *Financial support:* In 2009–10, 14 fellowships (averaging $1,709 per year), 2 research assistantships (averaging $12,197 per year) were awarded; career-related internships or fieldwork also available. *Faculty research:* Technology, planning, and management of telecommunications systems.

University of Denver, University College, Denver, CO 80208. Offers applied communication (MAS, MPS, Certificate); computer information systems (MAS, Certificate); environmental policy and management (MAS, Certificate); geographic information systems (MAS, Certificate); human resource administration (MPS, Certificate); knowledge and information technologies (MAS); liberal studies (MLS, Certificate); modern languages (MLS, Certificate); organizational leadership (MPS, Certificate); security management (Certificate); technology management (MAS, Certificate), including 21st century strategic management (MAS), international markets (MAS), project management (MAS), research and development management (MAS); telecommunications (MAS, Certificate), including broadband (MAS), telecommunications management and policy (MAS), telecommunications technology (MAS), wireless networks (MAS). Part-time and evening/weekend programs available. Postbaccalaureate distance learning degree programs offered (no on-campus study). *Faculty:* 160 part-time/adjunct (64 women). *Students:* 53 full-time (25 women), 984 part-time (551 women); includes 171 minority (72 African Americans, 10 American Indian/Alaska Native, 33 Asian Americans or Pacific Islanders, 56 Hispanic Americans), 75 international. Average age 36. 537 applicants, 96% accepted, 494 enrolled. In 2009, 229 master's, 109 Certificates awarded. *Entrance requirements:* Additional exam requirements/recommendations for international students: Required—TOEFL (minimum score 550 paper-based; 213 computer-based). *Application deadline:* Applications are processed on a rolling basis. Application fee: $75. Electronic applications accepted. *Expenses:* Contact institution. *Financial support:* Applicants required to submit FAFSA. *Unit head:* Dr. James Davis, Dean, 303-871-2291, Fax: 303-871-4047, E-mail: jdavis@du.edu. *Application contact:* Information Contact, 303-871-3155.

University of Hawaii at Manoa, Graduate Division, College of Social Sciences, School of Communications, Program in Telecommunication and Information Resource Management, Honolulu, HI 96822. Offers Graduate Certificate. Part-time programs available. *Students:* 1 part-time (0 women). Average age 32. In 2009, 5 Graduate Certificates awarded. *Entrance requirements:* Additional exam requirements/recommendations for international students: Required—TOEFL (minimum score 500 paper-based; 173 computer-based; 61 iBT), IELTS (minimum score 5). *Application deadline:* For fall admission, 5/1 for domestic and international students; for spring admission, 10/1 for domestic and international students. Application fee: $60. *Expenses:* Tuition, state resident: full-time $8900; part-time $372 per credit. Tuition, nonresident: full-time $21,400; part-time $898 per credit. Required fees: $207 per semester. *Application contact:* Norman Okamura, Director, 808-956-2895, Fax: 808-956-5591, E-mail: tirm@hawaii.edu.

University of Houston, College of Technology, Department of Engineering Technology, Houston, TX 77204. Offers construction management (M Tech); network communications (M Tech). Part-time and evening/weekend programs available. *Faculty:* 12 full-time (4 women), 4 part-time/adjunct (1 woman). *Students:* 38 full-time (13 women), 30 part-time (8 women); includes 9 minority (5 African Americans, 2 Asian Americans or Pacific Islanders, 2 Hispanic Americans), 39 international. Average age 26. 41 applicants, 78% accepted, 24 enrolled. In 2009, 16 master's awarded. *Degree requirements:* For master's, project or thesis (most programs). *Entrance requirements:* For master's, GRE. Additional exam requirements/recommendations for international students: Required—TOEFL (minimum score 550 paper-based; 79 iBT). *Application deadline:* For fall admission, 7/1 for domestic students, 4/1 for international students; for spring admission, 12/1 for domestic students, 10/1 for international students. Applications are processed on a rolling basis. Application fee: $75 ($150 for international students). Electronic applications accepted. *Expenses:* Tuition, state resident: full-time $7676; part-time $320 per credit hour. Tuition, nonresident: full-time $14,324; part-time $597 per credit hour. Required fees: $3034. *Financial support:* In 2009–10, 7 fellowships with full tuition reimbursements (averaging $10,500 per year), 4 research assistantships with full tuition reimbursements (averaging $10,500 per year), 12 teaching assistantships with full tuition reimbursements (averaging $10,500 per year) were awarded. *Unit head:* Heidar Malki, Chairperson, 713-743-4075, Fax: 713-743-4032, E-mail: malki@uh.edu. *Application contact:* Tiffany Roosa, Graduate Advisor, 713-743-2987, Fax: 713-743-4151, E-mail: troosa@uh.edu.

University of Louisiana at Lafayette, College of Engineering, Department of Electrical and Computer Engineering, Program in Telecommunications, Lafayette, LA 70504. Offers MSTC. *Degree requirements:* For master's, thesis or alternative. *Entrance requirements:* For master's, GRE General Test, minimum GPA of 2.75. Additional exam requirements/recommendations for international students: Required—TOEFL (minimum score 550 paper-based; 213 computer-based). Electronic applications accepted.

University of Maryland, College Park, Academic Affairs, A. James Clark School of Engineering, Department of Electrical and Computer Engineering, Program in Telecommunications, College Park, MD 20742. Offers MS. Part-time and evening/weekend programs available. *Students:* 107 full-time (37 women), 17 part-time (3 women); includes 17 minority (6 African Americans, 9 Asian Americans or Pacific Islanders, 2 Hispanic Americans), 103 international. 314 applicants, 46% accepted, 49 enrolled. In 2009, 47 master's awarded. *Degree requirements:* For master's, thesis or alternative. *Entrance requirements:* For master's, GRE General Test, minimum GPA of 3.0, professional experience. Additional exam requirements/recommendations for international students: Required—TOEFL. *Application deadline:* For fall admission, 5/1 for domestic students, 2/1 for international students. Applications are processed on a rolling basis. Application fee: $60. Electronic applications accepted. *Expenses:* Tuition, area resident: Part-time $471 per credit hour. Tuition, state resident: part-time $471 per credit hour. Tuition, nonresident: part-time $1016 per credit hour. Required fees: $337.04 per term. *Financial support:* In 2009–10, 9 research assistantships (averaging $18,457 per year), 30 teaching assistantships (averaging $16,574 per year) were awarded. Financial award applicants required to submit FAFSA. *Unit head:* Asante Dumisani Shakuur, Associate Director, 301-405-8189, Fax: 301-314-9324, E-mail: ashakuur@eng.umd.edu. *Application contact:* Dean of Graduate School, 301-405-0358, Fax: 301-314-9305.

See Close-Up on page 545.

University of Massachusetts Dartmouth, Graduate School, College of Engineering, Department of Electrical and Computer Engineering, North Dartmouth, MA 02747-2300. Offers acoustics (Postbaccalaureate Certificate); communications (Postbaccalaureate Certificate); computer engineering (MS, PhD); computer systems engineering (Postbaccalaureate Certificate); digital signal processing (Postbaccalaureate Certificate); electrical engineering (MS, PhD); electrical engineering systems (Postbaccalaureate Certificate). Part-time programs available. *Faculty:* 18 full-time (3 women), 4 part-time/adjunct (0 women). *Students:* 39 full-time (11 women), 42 part-time (8 women); includes 8 minority (2 African Americans, 5 Asian Americans or Pacific Islanders, 1 Hispanic American), 46 international. Average age 28. 99 applicants, 80% accepted, 26 enrolled. In 2009, 34 master's, 1 doctorate, 3 other advanced degrees awarded. *Degree requirements:* For master's, culminating project or thesis; for doctorate, comprehensive exam, thesis/dissertation. *Entrance requirements:* For master's, GRE General Test, minimum undergraduate GPA of 3.0, 3 letters or recommendation; for doctorate, GRE. Additional exam requirements/recommendations for international students: Required—TOEFL (minimum score 550 paper-based; 213 computer-based). *Application deadline:* For fall admission, 2/1 priority date for domestic students, 12/1 for international students; for spring admission, 11/1 priority date for domestic students, 9/1 for international students. Applications are processed on a rolling basis. Application fee: $40 ($60 for international students). Electronic applications accepted. *Expenses:* Tuition, state resident: full-time $2071; part-time $86.29 per credit. Tuition, nonresident: full-time $8099; part-time $337.46 per credit. Required fees: $9446. Tuition and fees vary according to class time, course load and reciprocity agreements. *Financial support:* In 2009–10, 2 fellowships with full tuition reimbursements (averaging $16,000 per year), 14 research assistantships with full tuition reimbursements (averaging $11,096 per year), 9 teaching assistantships with full tuition reimbursements (averaging $12,500 per year) were awarded; Federal Work-Study and unspecified assistantships also available. Support available to part-time students. Financial award application deadline: 3/1; financial award applicants required to submit FAFSA. *Faculty research:* Speech acoustics, marine applications, signals and systems, applies electromagnetics, intelligent agency. Total annual research expenditures: $935,000. *Unit head:* Dr. Karen Payton, Director, 508-999-8434, Fax: 508-999-8489, E-mail: kpayton@umassd.edu. *Application contact:* Elan Turcotte-Shamski, Graduate Admissions Officer, 508-999-8604, Fax: 508-999-8183, E-mail: graduate@umassd.edu.

University of Missouri–Kansas City, School of Computing and Engineering, Kansas City, MO 64110-2499. Offers civil engineering (MS); computer and electrical engineering (PhD); computer science (MS), including bioinformatics, software engineering, telecommunications networking; computer science and informatics (PhD); computing (PhD); electrical engineering (MS); engineering (PhD); mechanical engineering (MS); telecommunications (PhD). PhD (interdisciplinary) offered through the School of Graduate Studies. Part-time programs available. *Faculty:* 40 full-time (5 women), 28 part-time/adjunct (0 women). *Students:* 230 full-time (46 women), 158 part-time (31 women); includes 20 minority (5 African Americans, 12 Asian Americans or Pacific Islanders, 3 Hispanic Americans), 313 international. Average age 24. 484 applicants, 64% accepted, 106 enrolled. In 2009, 144 master's awarded. *Degree requirements:* For doctorate, thesis/dissertation. *Entrance requirements:* For master's, GRE General Test, minimum GPA of 3.0, 3 letters of recommendations from professors; for doctorate, GRE General Test, minimum GPA of 3.5. Additional exam requirements/recommendations for international students: Required—TOEFL (minimum score 550 paper-based; 213 computer-based; 80 iBT). *Application deadline:* For fall admission, 1/15 priority date for domestic students, 1/15 for international students. Applications are processed on a rolling basis. Application fee: $45 ($50 for international students). *Expenses:* Tuition, state resident: full-time $5378; part-time $299 per credit hour. Tuition, nonresident: full-time $13,881; part-time $771 per credit hour. Required fees: $641; $71 per credit hour. Tuition and fees vary according to course load and program. *Financial support:* In 2009–10, 29 research assistantships with partial tuition reimbursements (averaging $15,040 per year), 10 teaching assistantships with partial tuition reimbursements (averaging $12,118 per year) were awarded; career-related internships or fieldwork, Federal Work-Study, scholarships/grants, tuition waivers (partial), and unspecified assistantships also available. Support available to part-time students. Financial award application deadline: 3/1; financial award applicants required to submit FAFSA. *Faculty research:* Algorithms, bioinformatics and medical informatics, biomechanics/biomaterials, civil engineering materials, networking and telecommunications, thermal science. Total annual research expenditures: $1.4 million. *Unit head:* Dr. Kevin Z. Truman, Dean, 816-235-2399, Fax: 816-235-5159. *Application contact:* Dr. Kevin Z. Truman, Dean, 816-235-2399, Fax: 816-235-5159.

University of Oklahoma, Graduate College, College of Engineering, Department of Electrical and Computer Engineering, Program in Telecommunication Systems Engineering, Tulsa, OK 74135. Offers MS. Part-time programs available. *Students:* 3 full-time (2 women), all international. 8 applicants, 88% accepted, 1 enrolled. In 2009, 7 master's awarded. *Entrance requirements:* Additional exam requirements/recommendations for international students: Required—TOEFL (minimum score 550 paper-based; 213 computer-based). *Application deadline:* For fall admission, 4/1 for domestic and international students; for spring admission, 11/1 for domestic students, 9/1 for international students. Application fee: $40 ($90 for international students). Electronic applications accepted. *Expenses:* Tuition, state resident: full-time $3744; part-time $156 per credit hour. Tuition, nonresident: full-time $13,577; part-time $565.70 per credit hour. Required fees: $2415; $90.10 per credit hour. *Financial support:* In 2009–10, 2 students received support. Career-related internships or fieldwork, scholarships/grants, health care benefits, tuition waivers (partial), and unspecified assistantships available. *Faculty research:* Optical communications and networks, wireless communications and networking, telecommunications security, photonic systems, information theory. *Unit head:* Dr. James Sluss, Director, 405-325-4721, Fax: 405-325-7066, E-mail: sluss@ou.edu. *Application contact:* Pramode Verma, Director/Graduate Liaison, 918-660-3236, Fax: 918-660-3238, E-mail: pverma@ou.edu.

University of Oklahoma, Graduate College, Gaylord College of Journalism and Mass Communication, Program in Journalism and Mass Communication, Norman, OK 73019-0390. Offers advertising and public relations (MA); information gathering and distribution (MA); mass communication management and policy (MA); professional writing (MA); telecommunication and new technology (MA). Part-time programs available. *Students:* 34 full-time (18 women), 43 part-time (23 women); includes 13 minority (4 African Americans, 5 American Indian/Alaska Native, 4 Hispanic Americans), 9 international. 45 applicants, 42% accepted, 9 enrolled. *Degree requirements:* For master's, thesis optional. *Entrance requirements:* For master's, GRE General Test, minimum GPA of 3.2, 9 hours of course work in journalism, course work in statistics. Additional exam requirements/recommendations for international students: Required—TOEFL (minimum score 600 paper-based; 250 computer-based), TWE (minimum score 5). *Application deadline:* For fall admission, 2/1 for domestic students, 4/1 for international students; for spring admission, 11/1 for domestic students, 9/1 for international students. Application fee: $40 ($90 for international students). Electronic applications accepted. *Expenses:* Tuition, state resident: full-time $3744; part-time $156 per credit hour. Tuition, nonresident: full-time $13,577; part-time $565.70 per credit hour. Required fees: $2415; $90.10 per credit hour. *Financial support:* In 2009–10, 43 students received support, including 4 fellowships (averaging $5,000 per year); career-related internships or fieldwork, scholarships/grants, health care benefits, and unspecified assistantships also available. *Faculty research:* Organizational management, rhetorical analysis, international public relations, digital production, normative theory. *Unit head:* Dr. Joe Foote, Dean, 405-325-2721, Fax: 405-325-7565, E-mail: jfoote@ou.edu. *Application contact:* Kelly Storm, Graduate Advisor, 405-325-2722, Fax: 405-325-7565, E-mail: kstorm@ou.edu.

University of Oklahoma—Tulsa, Program in Telecommunications Engineering, Tulsa, OK 74135-2512. Offers MS. *Degree requirements:* For master's, project.

University of Pennsylvania, School of Engineering and Applied Science, Telecommunications and Networking Program, Philadelphia, PA 19104. Offers MSE. Part-time programs available. *Students:* 62 full-time (8 women), 7 part-time (0 women); includes 1 minority (African American), 64 international. 125 applicants, 65% accepted, 45 enrolled. In 2009, 13 master's awarded. *Application deadline:* For fall admission, 6/1 for domestic students, 5/1 for international students; for spring admission, 11/1 for domestic students, 10/1 for international

Telecommunications

University of Pennsylvania (continued)
students. Application fee: $70. Electronic applications accepted. *Expenses:* Tuition: Full-time $25,660; part-time $4758 per course. Required fees: $2152; $270 per course. Tuition and fees vary according to course load, degree level and program.

University of Pittsburgh, School of Information Sciences, Telecommunications and Networking Program, Pittsburgh, PA 15260. Offers telecommunications (MST, PhD, Certificate). Part-time and evening/weekend programs available. *Faculty:* 6 full-time (0 women), 2 part-time/adjunct (1 woman). *Students:* 49 full-time (8 women), 13 part-time (2 women); includes 1 minority (African American), 50 international. 66 applicants, 77% accepted, 17 enrolled. In 2009, 18 master's, 5 doctorates, 1 other advanced degree awarded. *Degree requirements:* For master's, thesis optional; for doctorate, comprehensive exam, thesis/dissertation. *Entrance requirements:* For master's, GRE General Test, undergraduate degree with minimum GPA of 3.0; previous course work in computer programming, calculus, and probability; for doctorate, GRE, master's degree; minimum GPA of 3.3; course work in computer programming, calculus, and probability; for Certificate, MSIS, MST from accredited university. Additional exam requirements/recommendations for international students: Required—TOEFL (minimum score 550 paper-based; 213 computer-based; 80 iBT). *Application deadline:* For fall admission, 1/15 priority date for domestic and international students; for winter admission, 9/15 priority date for domestic students, 6/15 for international students; for spring admission, 1/15 priority date for domestic students, 12/15 priority date for international students. Applications are processed on a rolling basis. Application fee: $50. Electronic applications accepted. *Expenses:* Contact institution. *Financial support:* Fellowships with full and partial tuition reimbursements, research assistantships with full and partial tuition reimbursements, teaching assistantships, career-related internships or fieldwork, scholarships/grants, health care benefits, tuition waivers (full and partial), and unspecified assistantships available. Financial award application deadline: 1/15; financial award applicants required to submit FAFSA. *Faculty research:* Telecommunication systems, telecommunications policy, network design and management, wireless information systems, network security. *Unit head:* Dr. David Tipper, Program Chair, 412-624-9421, Fax: 412-624-2788, E-mail: tipper@tele.pitt.edu. *Application contact:* Shabana Reza, Student Recruiting Coordinator, 412-624-3988, Fax: 412-624-5231, E-mail: teleinq@sis.pitt.edu.

University of Southern California, Graduate School, Viterbi School of Engineering, Department of Industrial and Systems Engineering, Los Angeles, CA 90089. Offers digital supply chain management (MS); engineering management (MS); engineering technology communication (Graduate Certificate); health systems operations (Graduate Certificate); industrial and systems engineering (MS, PhD, Engr); manufacturing engineering (MS); operations research engineering (MS); optimization and supply chain management (Graduate Certificate); product development engineering (MS); safety systems and security (MS); systems architecting and engineering (MS, Graduate Certificate); systems safety and security (Graduate Certificate); transportation systems (Graduate Certificate); MS/MBA. Part-time programs available. Postbaccalaureate distance learning degree programs offered (minimal on-campus study). *Faculty:* 11 full-time (2 women), 39 part-time/adjunct (7 women). *Students:* 250 full-time (71 women), 145 part-time (37 women); includes 67 minority (6 African Americans, 2 American Indian/Alaska Native, 39 Asian Americans or Pacific Islanders, 20 Hispanic Americans), 253 international. 679 applicants, 58% accepted, 206 enrolled. In 2009, 98 master's, 7 doctorates awarded. Terminal master's awarded for partial completion of doctoral program. *Degree requirements:* For doctorate, thesis/dissertation. *Entrance requirements:* For master's, GRE General Test; for doctorate, General GRE. *Application deadline:* For fall admission, 3/1 priority date for domestic and international students; for spring admission, 10/1 for domestic students, 10/1 priority date for international students. Applications are processed on a rolling basis. Application fee: $85. Electronic applications accepted. *Expenses:* Tuition: Full-time $25,980; part-time $1315 per unit. Required fees: $554. One-time fee: $35 full-time. Full-time tuition and fees vary according to degree level and program. *Financial support:* In 2009–10, fellowships with full tuition reimbursements (averaging $30,000 per year), research assistantships with full tuition reimbursements (averaging $19,250 per year), teaching assistantships with full tuition reimbursements (averaging $19,250 per year) were awarded; career-related internships or fieldwork, scholarships/grants, health care benefits, and unspecified assistantships also available. Financial award application deadline: 12/1; financial award applicants required to submit CSS PROFILE or FAFSA. *Faculty research:* Health systems, music cognition and retrieval, transportation andlogistics, manufacturing and automation, engineering systems design, risk and economic analysis. Total annual research expenditures: $1.2 million. *Unit head:* Dr. James E. Moore, Chair, 213-740-4885, Fax: 213-740-1120, E-mail: jmoore@usc.edu. *Application contact:* Mary Ordaz, Student Service Advisor, 213-740-4886, Fax: 213-740-1120, E-mail: isedept@usc.edu.

The University of Texas at Dallas, Erik Jonsson School of Engineering and Computer Science, Programs in Electrical Engineering, Richardson, TX 75080. Offers computer engineering (MS, PhD); electrical engineering (MSEE, PhD); microelectronics (MSEE, PhD); telecommunications (MSEE, MSTE, PhD). Part-time and evening/weekend programs available. *Faculty:* 43 full-time (3 women), 3 part-time/adjunct (0 women). *Students:* 391 full-time (78 women), 160 part-time (23 women); includes 86 minority (14 African Americans, 59 Asian Americans or Pacific Islanders, 13 Hispanic Americans), 383 international. Average age 27. 1,292 applicants, 31% accepted, 168 enrolled. In 2009, 149 master's, 14 doctorates awarded. *Degree requirements:* For master's, thesis or major design project; for doctorate, thesis/dissertation. *Entrance requirements:* For master's, GRE General Test, minimum GPA of 3.0 in related bachelor's degree; for doctorate, GRE General Test, minimum GPA of 3.5. Additional exam requirements/recommendations for international students: Required—TOEFL (minimum score 550 paper-based; 213 computer-based). *Application deadline:* For fall admission, 7/15 for domestic students, 5/1 priority date for international students; for spring admission, 11/15 for domestic students, 9/1 priority date for international students. Applications are processed on a rolling basis. Application fee: $50 ($100 for international students). Electronic applications accepted. *Expenses:* Tuition, state resident: full-time $11,068; part-time $461 per credit hour. Tuition, nonresident: full-time $21,178; part-time $882 per credit hour. Tuition and fees vary according to course load. *Financial support:* In 2009–10, 1 fellowship with full tuition reimbursement (averaging $18,000 per year), 116 research assistantships with full tuition reimbursements (averaging $17,579 per year), 41 teaching assistantships with full tuition reimbursements (averaging $17,516 per year) were awarded; Federal Work-Study, institutionally sponsored loans, scholarships/grants, unspecified assistantships, and co-op positions also available. Support available to part-time students. Financial award application deadline: 4/30; financial award applicants required to submit FAFSA. *Faculty research:* Communications and signal processing, solid-state devices and circuits, digital systems, optical devices, materials and systems, lasers and photonics. *Unit head:* Dr. John H. L. Hansen, Head, 972-883-2910, Fax: 972-883-2710, E-mail: john.hansen@utdallas.edu. *Application contact:* Kathy Gribble, Coordinator, 972-883-2649, Fax: 972-883-2813, E-mail: gradecs@utdallas.edu.

Widener University, Graduate Programs in Engineering, Program Telecommunications Engineering, Chester, PA 19013-5792. Offers M Eng. Part-time and evening/weekend programs available. *Students:* 4 full-time (0 women), 6 part-time (0 women), 4 international. Average age 30. In 2009, 1 master's awarded. *Degree requirements:* For master's, thesis optional. *Application deadline:* For fall admission, 8/1 priority date for domestic students; for spring admission, 12/1 for domestic students. Applications are processed on a rolling basis. Application fee: $25 ($300 for international students). *Financial support:* Teaching assistantships with full tuition reimbursements, unspecified assistantships available. Financial award application deadline: 3/15. *Faculty research:* Signal and image processing, electromagnetics, telecommunications and computer network. *Unit head:* Dr. Bryen E. Lorenz, Chairman, Department of Electrical/Telecommunication Engineering, 610-499-4064, Fax: 610-499-4059, E-mail: bryen.f.lorenz@widener.edu. *Application contact:* Dr. Bryen E. Lorenz, Chairman, Department of Electrical/Telecommunication Engineering, 610-499-4064, Fax: 610-499-4059, E-mail: bryen.f.lorenz@widener.edu.

Telecommunications Management

Alaska Pacific University, Graduate Programs, Business Administration Department, Programs in Information and Communication Technology, Anchorage, AK 99508-4672. Offers MBAICT. Part-time and evening/weekend programs available. *Degree requirements:* For master's, capstone course. *Entrance requirements:* For master's, GMAT or GRE General Test, minimum GPA of 3.0.

Capitol College, Graduate Programs, Laurel, MD 20708-9759. Offers business administration (MBA); computer science (MS); electrical engineering (MS); information and telecommunications systems management (MS); information architecture (MS); network security (MS). Part-time and evening/weekend programs available. Postbaccalaureate distance learning degree programs offered (no on-campus study). *Entrance requirements:* For master's, minimum GPA of 3.0. Electronic applications accepted.

Carnegie Mellon University, Carnegie Institute of Technology, Information Networking Institute, Pittsburgh, PA 15213. Offers information networking (MS); information security technology and management (MS); information technology—information security (MS); information technology—mobility (MS); information technology—software management (MS). *Degree requirements:* For master's, thesis optional. *Entrance requirements:* For master's, GRE General Test, bachelor's degree in computer science, computer engineering, or electrical engineering, or related technology degree; programming skills (C/C++ fluency for some programs). Additional exam requirements/recommendations for international students: Required—TOEFL. *Faculty research:* Computer forensics and incident response; dependable systems, embedded systems, mobile systems, and sensor networks; computer and information networks, network and information security, human and socio-economic factors in secure system design; wireless sensor networks, survivable embedded systems, signal processing/compression; strategic management, international strategic management, group dynamics and decision-making structures, simulated competitive environments.

Concordia University, School of Graduate Studies, Faculty of Engineering and Computer Science, Concordia Institute for Information Systems Engineering (CIISE), Montréal, QC H3G 1M8, Canada. Offers 3D graphics and game development (Certificate); information systems security (M Eng, MA Sc); quality systems engineering (M Eng, MA Sc); service engineering and network management (Certificate).

George Mason University, Volgenau School of Information Technology and Engineering, Department of Electrical and Computer Engineering, Fairfax, VA 22030. Offers advanced networking protocols for telecommunications (Certificate); communications and networking (Certificate); computer engineering (MS); computer forensics (MS); electrical and computer engineering (PhD); electrical engineering (MS); network technology and applications (Certificate); networks, system integration and testing (Certificate); signal processing (Certificate); telecom systems modeling (Certificate); telecommunications (MS); telecommunications forensics and security (Certificate); VLSI design/manufacturing (Certificate); wireless communication (Certificate). Part-time and evening/weekend programs available. *Faculty:* 29 full-time (4 women), 37 part-time/adjunct (5 women). *Students:* 115 full-time (18 women), 308 part-time (46 women); includes 84 minority (17 African Americans, 51 Asian Americans or Pacific Islanders, 16 Hispanic Americans), 179 international. Average age 29. 461 applicants, 67% accepted, 105 enrolled. In 2009, 157 master's, 6 doctorates, 61 other advanced degrees awarded. *Degree requirements:* For master's, thesis optional; for doctorate, comprehensive exam, thesis or scholarly paper. *Entrance requirements:* For master's, GMAT or GRE General Test, letters of recommendation, resume; for doctorate, GRE/GMAT, personal goal statement, 2 transcripts, letter of recommendation. Additional exam requirements/recommendations for international students: Required—TOEFL. *Application deadline:* For fall admission, 7/15 priority date for domestic and international students; for spring admission, 12/2 for domestic students, 12/1 for international students. Applications are processed on a rolling basis. Application fee: $75. Electronic applications accepted. *Expenses:* Tuition, state resident: full-time $7568; part-time $315.33 per credit hour. Tuition, nonresident: full-time $21,704; part-time $904.33 per credit hour. Required fees: $2184; $91 per credit hour. *Financial support:* In 2009–10, 64 students received support, including 2 fellowships with full tuition reimbursements available (averaging $18,000 per year), 22 research assistantships with full and partial tuition reimbursements available (averaging $8,469 per year), 42 teaching assistantships with full and partial tuition reimbursements available (averaging $6,291 per year); career-related internships or fieldwork, Federal Work-Study, scholarships/grants, unspecified assistantships, and health care benefits (full-time research or teaching assistantship recipients) also available. Support available to part-time students. Financial award application deadline: 3/1; financial award applicants required to submit FAFSA. *Faculty research:* Communication networks, signal processing, system failure diagnosis, multiprocessors, material processing using microwave energy. Total annual research expenditures: $3 million. *Unit head:* Dr. Andre Manitius, Chairperson, 703-993-1569, Fax: 703-993-1601, E-mail: ece@gmu.edu. *Application contact:* Jessica Skinner, Associate Dean, 703-993-1569, E-mail: jskinne6@gmu.edu.

Hawai'i Pacific University, College of Business Administration, Program in Information Systems, Honolulu, HI 96813. Offers knowledge management (MSIS); software engineering (MSIS); telecommunications security (MSIS). *Faculty:* 9 full-time (2 women), 3 part-time/adjunct (1 woman). *Students:* 54 full-time (14 women), 60 part-time (17 women); includes 50 minority (4 African Americans, 40 Asian Americans or Pacific Islanders, 6 Hispanic Americans), 49 international. Average age 32. In 2009, 52 master's awarded. *Expenses:* Tuition: Full-time $12,600; part-time $700 per credit hour. Tuition and fees vary according to program. *Unit head:* Dr. Gordon Jones, Dean, 808-544-1181, Fax: 808-544-0247, E-mail: gjones@hpu.edu. *Application contact:* Danny Lam, Assistant Director of Graduate Admissions, 808-544-1135, Fax: 808-544-0280, E-mail: graduate@hpu.edu.

Instituto Tecnológico y de Estudios Superiores de Monterrey, Campus Ciudad de México, Division of Engineering and Architecture, Ciudad de Mexico, Mexico. Offers management (MA); telecommunications (MA). Part-time and evening/weekend programs available. Postbaccalaureate distance learning degree programs offered (minimal on-campus study). *Faculty research:* Telecommunications; informatics; technology development; computer systems.

Instituto Tecnológico y de Estudios Superiores de Monterrey, Campus Ciudad Obregón, Program in Administration of Telecommunications, Ciudad Obregón, Mexico. Offers MAT.

Instituto Tecnológico y de Estudios Superiores de Monterrey, Campus Estado de México, Professional and Graduate Division, Estado de Mexico, Mexico. Offers administration of information technologies (MITA); architecture (M Arch); business administration (GMBA, MBA); computer sciences (MCS, PhD); education (M Ed); educational institution administration (MAD); educational technology and innovation (PhD); electronic commerce (MEC); environmental systems (MS); finance (MAF); humanistic studies (MHS); information sciences and knowledge management (MISKM); information systems (MS); manufacturing systems (MS); marketing (MEM); quality systems and productivity (MS); science and materials engineering (PhD); telecommunications management (MTM). Part-time programs available. Postbaccalaureate distance learning degree programs offered (minimal on-campus study). *Degree requirements:* For master's, one foreign language, thesis (for some programs); for doctorate, one foreign language, thesis/dissertation. *Entrance requirements:* For master's, E-PAEP 500, interview; for doctorate, E-PAEP 500, research proposal. Additional exam requirements/recommendations for international students: Required—TOEFL (minimum score 550 paper-based). *Faculty research:* Surface treatments by plasmas, mechanical properties, robotics, graphical computing, mechatronics security protocols.

Instituto Tecnológico y de Estudios Superiores de Monterrey, Campus Irapuato, Graduate Programs, Irapuato, Mexico. Offers administration (MBA); administration of information technology (MAIT); administration of telecommunications (MAT); architecture (M Arch); computer science (MCS); education (M Ed); educational administration (MEA); educational innovation and technology (DEIT); educational technology (MET); electronic commerce (MBA); environmental administration and planning (MEAP); environmental systems (MES); finances (MBA); humanistic studies (MHS); international management for Latin American executives (MIMLAE); library and information science (MLIS); manufacturing quality management (MMQM); marketing research (MBA).

Morgan State University, School of Graduate Studies, College of Liberal Arts, Department of Telecommunications Management, Baltimore, MD 21251. Offers MS. *Degree requirements:* For master's, comprehensive exam. *Entrance requirements:* For master's, GRE. Additional exam requirements/recommendations for international students: Required—TOEFL (minimum score 550 paper-based; 213 computer-based).

Murray State University, College of Business and Public Affairs, Program in Telecommunications Systems Management, Murray, KY 42071. Offers MS. *Entrance requirements:* For master's, GMAT or GRE. Additional exam requirements/recommendations for international students: Required—TOEFL (minimum score 213 computer-based). *Faculty research:* Network security, emergency management communications, network economies.

Northeastern University, College of Engineering, Program in Telecommunication Systems Management, Boston, MA 02115-5096. Offers MS. Part-time programs available. *Students:* 106 full-time (24 women), 5 part-time (1 woman), 103 international. Average age 25. 135 applicants, 73% accepted, 35 enrolled. In 2009, 49 master's awarded. *Entrance requirements:* For master's, GRE General Test. Additional exam requirements/recommendations for international students: Required—TOEFL (minimum score 550 paper-based; 213 computer-based). *Application deadline:* For fall admission, 1/15 for domestic and international students. Applications are processed on a rolling basis. Application fee: $50. Electronic applications accepted. *Financial support:* In 2009–10, 2 students received support, including 1 fellowship (averaging $18,320 per year), 1 research assistantship (averaging $18,320 per year); teaching assistantships, career-related internships or fieldwork, Federal Work-Study, scholarships/grants, health care benefits, tuition waivers, and unspecified assistantships also available. Support available to part-time students. Financial award application deadline: 1/15; financial award applicants required to submit FAFSA. *Faculty research:* Information theory, wireless grids, IP telephony architecture. *Unit head:* Dr. Peter O'Reilly, Director, 617-373-5548, Fax: 617-373-2501. *Application contact:* Stephen L. Gibson, Associate Director, 617-373-2711, Fax: 617-373-2501, E-mail: grad-eng@coe.neu.edu.

Oklahoma State University, William S. Spears School of Business, Department of Management Science and Information Systems, Stillwater, OK 74078. Offers management information systems (MS); management science and information systems (PhD); telecommunications management (MS). Part-time programs available. Postbaccalaureate distance learning degree programs offered. *Faculty:* 15 full-time (2 women), 1 part-time/adjunct (0 women). *Students:* 75 full-time (25 women), 80 part-time (17 women); includes 7 minority (1 African American, 4 American Indian/Alaska Native, 2 Asian Americans or Pacific Islanders), 100 international. Average age 29. 251 applicants, 38% accepted, 41 enrolled. In 2009, 58 master's awarded. *Degree requirements:* For master's, thesis or alternative; for doctorate, comprehensive exam, thesis/dissertation. *Entrance requirements:* For master's and doctorate, GRE or GMAT. Additional exam requirements/recommendations for international students: Required—TOEFL (minimum score 550 paper-based; 79 iBT). *Application deadline:* For fall admission, 3/1 priority date for international students; for spring admission, 8/1 priority date for international students. Applications are processed on a rolling basis. Application fee: $40 ($75 for international students). Electronic applications accepted. *Expenses:* Tuition, state resident: full-time $3716; part-time $154.85 per credit hour. Tuition, nonresident: full-time $14,448; part-time $602 per credit hour. Required fees: $1772; $73.85 per credit hour. One-time fee: $50. Tuition and fees vary according to course load and campus/location. *Financial support:* In 2009–10, 2 research assistantships (averaging $6,720 per year), 14 teaching assistantships (averaging $13,962 per year) were awarded; career-related internships or fieldwork, Federal Work-Study, scholarships/grants, health care benefits, tuition waivers (partial), and unspecified assistantships also available. Support available to part-time students. Financial award application deadline: 3/1; financial award applicants required to submit FAFSA. *Unit head:* Dr. Rick Wilson, Head, 405-744-3551, Fax: 405-744-5180. *Application contact:* Dr. Gordon Emslie, Dean, 405-744-6368, Fax: 405-744-0355, E-mail: grad-i@okstate.edu.

Polytechnic Institute of NYU, Department of Technology Management, Major in Telecommunications and Information Management, Brooklyn, NY 11201-2990. Offers MS. *Students:* 3 full-time (1 woman), 1 part-time (0 women); includes 1 minority (American Indian/Alaska Native). 10 applicants, 60% accepted, 1 enrolled. In 2009, 7 master's awarded. *Degree requirements:* For master's, comprehensive exam (for some programs), thesis (for some programs). *Entrance requirements:* For master's, GMAT, minimum B average in undergraduate course work. Additional exam requirements/recommendations for international students: Required—TOEFL (minimum score 550 paper-based; 213 computer-based; 80 iBT); Recommended—IELTS (minimum score 6.5). *Application deadline:* For fall admission, 7/31 priority date for domestic students, 4/30 priority date for international students; for spring admission, 12/31 priority date for domestic students, 11/30 priority date for international students. Applications are processed on a rolling basis. Application fee: $75. Electronic applications accepted. *Expenses:* Tuition: Full-time $21,492; part-time $1194 per credit hour. Required fees: $1160; $204 per course. *Financial support:* Institutionally sponsored loans, scholarships/grants, and unspecified assistantships available. Support available to part-time students. Financial award applicants required to submit FAFSA. *Unit head:* Prof. Bharadwaj Rao, Head, 718-260-3617, Fax: 718-260-3874, E-mail: ro@poly.edu. *Application contact:* JeanCarlo Bonilla, Director of Graduate Enrollment Management, 718-260-3182, Fax: 718-260-3624, E-mail: gradinfo@poly.edu.

San Diego State University, Graduate and Research Affairs, College of Professional Studies and Fine Arts, School of Communication, San Diego, CA 92182. Offers advertising and public relations (MA); critical-cultural studies (MA); interaction studies (MA); intercultural and international studies (MA); new media studies (MA); news and information studies (MA); telecommunications and media management (MA). *Degree requirements:* For master's, thesis. *Entrance requirements:* For master's, GRE General Test, 3 letters of recommendation. Additional exam requirements/recommendations for international students: Required—TOEFL. Electronic applications accepted.

Santa Clara University, School of Engineering, Department of Electrical Engineering, Santa Clara, CA 95053. Offers analog circuit design (Certificate); ASIC design and test (Certificate); data storage technologies (Certificate); digital signal processing (Certificate); electrical engineering (MS, PhD, Engineer); fundamentals of electrical engineering (Certificate); microwave and antennas (Certificate); telecommunications management (Certificate). Part-time and evening/weekend programs available. *Degree requirements:* For master's, thesis or alternative; for doctorate, thesis/dissertation; for other advanced degree, thesis. *Entrance requirements:* For master's, GRE General Test, minimum GPA of 2.75; for doctorate, GRE General Test, GRE Subject Test, master's degree or equivalent; for other advanced degree, master's degree, published paper. Additional exam requirements/recommendations for international students: Required—TOEFL. Electronic applications accepted. *Expenses:* Contact institution.

Stevens Institute of Technology, Graduate School, Wesley J. Howe School of Technology Management, Doctoral Program in Technology Management, Hoboken, NJ 07030. Offers information management (PhD); technology management (PhD); telecommunications management (PhD). Part-time and evening/weekend programs available. Postbaccalaureate distance learning degree programs offered (minimal on-campus study). *Entrance requirements:* Additional exam requirements/recommendations for international students: Required—TOEFL. Electronic applications accepted. *Expenses:* Tuition: Full-time $9900; part-time $1100 per credit. Required fees: $286 per semester.

Stevens Institute of Technology, Graduate School, Wesley J. Howe School of Technology Management, Program in Business Administration, Hoboken, NJ 07030. Offers engineering management (MBA); financial engineering (MBA); information management (MBA); information technology in financial services (MBA); information technology in the pharmaceutical industry (MBA); information technology outsourcing (MBA); pharmaceutical management (MBA); project management (MBA); technology management (MBA); telecommunications management (MBA). *Expenses:* Tuition: Full-time $9900; part-time $1100 per credit. Required fees: $286 per semester.

Stevens Institute of Technology, Graduate School, Wesley J. Howe School of Technology Management, Program in Information Systems, Hoboken, NJ 07030. Offers computer science (MS); e-commerce (MS); enterprise systems (MS); entrepreneurial information technology (MS); information architecture (MS); information management (MS, Certificate); information security (MS); information technology in financial services industry (MS); information technology in the pharmaceutical industry (MS); information technology outsourcing management (MS); project management (MS, Certificate); software engineering (MS); telecommunications (MS). *Degree requirements:* For master's, thesis optional. *Entrance requirements:* For master's, GMAT, GRE General Test. Additional exam requirements/recommendations for international students: Required—TOEFL. Electronic applications accepted. *Expenses:* Tuition: Full-time $9900; part-time $1100 per credit. Required fees: $286 per semester.

Stevens Institute of Technology, Graduate School, Wesley J. Howe School of Technology Management, Program in Telecommunications Management, Hoboken, NJ 07030. Offers business (MS); global innovation management (MS); management of wireless networks (MS); online security, technology and business (MS); project management (MS); technical management (MS); telecommunications management (PhD, Certificate). *Degree requirements:* For master's, thesis optional; for doctorate, thesis/dissertation. *Entrance requirements:* For master's and doctorate, GMAT, GRE General Test. Additional exam requirements/recommendations for international students: Required—TOEFL. Electronic applications accepted. *Expenses:* Tuition: Full-time $9900; part-time $1100 per credit. Required fees: $286 per semester.

Strayer University, Graduate Studies, Washington, DC 20005-2603. Offers accounting (MS); acquisition (MBA); business administration (MBA); communications technology (MS); educational management (M Ed); finance (MBA); health services administration (MHSA); hospitality and tourism management (MBA); human resource management (MBA); information systems (MS), including computer security management, decision support system management, enterprise resource management, network management, software engineering management, systems development management; management (MBA); management information systems (MS); marketing (MBA); professional accounting (MS), including accounting information systems, controllership, taxation; public administration (MPA); supply chain management (MBA); technology in education (M Ed). Programs also offered at campus locations in Birmingham, AL; Chamblee, GA; Cobb County, GA; Morrow, GA; White Marsh, MD; Charleston, SC; Columbia, SC; Greensboro, NC; Greenville, SC; Lexington, KY; Louisville, KY; Nashville, TN; North Raleigh, NC; Washington, DC. Part-time and evening/weekend programs available. Postbaccalaureate distance learning degree programs offered (minimal on-campus study). *Degree requirements:* For master's, thesis. *Entrance requirements:* For master's, GMAT, GRE General Test, bachelor's degree from an accredited college or university, minimum undergraduate GPA of 2.75. Electronic applications accepted.

Syracuse University, School of Information Studies, Program in Information Systems and Telecommunications Management, Syracuse, NY 13244. Offers CAS. Part-time and evening/weekend programs available. Postbaccalaureate distance learning degree programs offered. *Students:* 1 full-time (0 women), 7 part-time (3 women); includes 3 minority (2 African Americans, 1 Hispanic American). Average age 36. 15 applicants, 80% accepted, 3 enrolled. In 2009, 5 CASs awarded. *Entrance requirements:* Additional exam requirements/recommendations for international students: Required—TOEFL (minimum score 100 iBT). *Application deadline:* For fall admission, 2/1 priority date for domestic and international students; for spring admission, 10/15 priority date for domestic and international students. Applications are processed on a rolling basis. Application fee: $75. Electronic applications accepted. *Expenses:* Tuition: Full-time $26,808; part-time $1117 per credit. Required fees: $1024. *Financial support:* Application deadline: 1/1; *Unit head:* David Dischiave, Director, 315-443-4681, Fax: 315-443-6886, E-mail: ddischia@syr.edu. *Application contact:* Susan Corieri, Director of Enrollment Management, 315-443-2575, E-mail: ist@syr.edu.

Syracuse University, School of Information Studies, Program in Telecommunications and Network Management, Syracuse, NY 13244. Offers MS, MS/CAS. Part-time and evening/weekend programs available. Postbaccalaureate distance learning degree programs offered (minimal on-campus study). *Students:* 47 full-time (5 women), 23 part-time (5 women); includes 9 minority (2 African Americans, 1 American Indian/Alaska Native, 1 Asian American or Pacific Islander, 5 Hispanic Americans), 38 international. Average age 29. 136 applicants, 71% accepted, 33 enrolled. In 2009, 22 master's awarded. *Degree requirements:* For master's, internship or research project. *Entrance requirements:* For master's, GRE General Test. Additional exam requirements/recommendations for international students: Required—TOEFL (minimum score 100 iBT). *Application deadline:* For fall admission, 2/1 priority date for domestic and international students; for spring admission, 10/15 priority date for domestic and international students. Applications are processed on a rolling basis. Application fee: $75. Electronic applications accepted. *Expenses:* Tuition: Full-time $26,808; part-time $1117 per credit. Required fees: $1024. *Financial support:* Fellowships with tuition reimbursements, research assistantships with tuition reimbursements, teaching assistantships with tuition reimbursements, career-related internships or fieldwork, Federal Work-Study, and tuition waivers (partial) available. Financial award application deadline: 1/1. *Faculty research:* Multimedia, information resources management. *Unit head:* Martha Garcia-Marillo, Director, 315-443-1829, Fax: 315-443-6886, E-mail: mgarciam@syr.edu. *Application contact:* Susan Corieri, Director of Enrollment Management, 315-443-2575, E-mail: ist@syr.edu.

University of Colorado at Boulder, Graduate School, College of Engineering and Applied Science, Interdisciplinary Telecommunications Program, Boulder, CO 80309. Offers MS, JD/MS, MBA/MS. Part-time programs available. Postbaccalaureate distance learning degree programs offered. *Students:* 90 full-time (13 women), 56 part-time (15 women); includes 13 minority (3 African Americans, 9 Asian Americans or Pacific Islanders, 1 Hispanic American), 101 international. Average age 28. 153 applicants, 58% accepted, 39 enrolled. In 2009, 70 master's awarded. *Degree requirements:* For master's, comprehensive exam, thesis or alternative. *Entrance requirements:* For master's, minimum undergraduate GPA of 3.0. *Application deadline:* For fall admission, 6/15 priority date for domestic students, 3/15 for international students; for spring admission, 11/1 for domestic students, 10/1 for international students. Applications are processed on a rolling basis. Application fee: $50 ($60 for international students). *Financial support:* In 2009–10, 14 fellowships (averaging $1,709 per year), 2 research assistantships

Telecommunications Management

University of Colorado at Boulder (continued)

(averaging $12,197 per year) were awarded; career-related internships or fieldwork also available. *Faculty research:* Technology, planning, and management of telecommunications systems.

University of Denver, University College, Denver, CO 80208. Offers applied communication (MAS, MPS, Certificate); computer information systems (MAS, Certificate); environmental policy and management (MAS, Certificate); geographic information systems (MAS, Certificate); human resource administration (MPS, Certificate); knowledge and information technologies (MAS); liberal studies (MLS, Certificate); modern languages (MLS, Certificate); organizational leadership (MPS, Certificate); security management (Certificate); technology management (MAS, Certificate), including 21st century strategic management (MAS), international markets (MAS), project management (MAS), research and development management (MAS); telecommunications (MAS, Certificate), including broadband (MAS), telecommunications management and policy (MAS), telecommunications technology (MAS), wireless networks (MAS). Part-time and evening/weekend programs available. Postbaccalaureate distance learning degree programs offered (no on-campus study). *Faculty:* 160 part-time/adjunct (64 women). *Students:* 53 full-time (25 women), 984 part-time (551 women); includes 171 minority (72 African Americans, 10 American Indian/Alaska Native, 33 Asian Americans or Pacific Islanders, 56 Hispanic Americans), 75 international. Average age 36. 537 applicants, 96% accepted, 494 enrolled. In 2009, 229 master's, 109 Certificates awarded. *Entrance requirements:* Additional exam requirements/recommendations for international students: Required—TOEFL (minimum score 550 paper-based; 213 computer-based). *Application deadline:* Applications are processed on a rolling basis. Application fee: $75. Electronic applications accepted. *Expenses:* Contact institution. *Financial support:* Applicants required to submit FAFSA. *Unit head:* Dr. James Davis, Dean, 303-871-2291, Fax: 303-871-4047, E-mail: jdavis@du.edu. *Application contact:* Information Contact, 303-871-3155.

University of New Haven, Graduate School, School of Business, Program in Business Administration, West Haven, CT 06516-1916. Offers accounting (MBA, Certificate), including CPA (MBA); business management (Certificate); business policy and strategy (MBA); finance (MBA), including CFA; global marketing (MBA); human resource management (Certificate); human resources management (MBA); international business (Certificate); marketing (Certificate); sports management (MBA); telcommunications management (Certificate); MBA/MPA. Part-time and evening/weekend programs available. *Faculty:* 26 full-time (3 women), 23 part-time/adjunct (5 women). *Students:* 302 full-time (120 women), 194 part-time (101 women); includes 109 minority (56 African Americans, 3 American Indian/Alaska Native, 28 Asian Americans or Pacific Islanders, 22 Hispanic Americans), 110 international. Average age 31. 372 applicants, 83% accepted, 172 enrolled. In 2009, 194 master's, 31 other advanced degrees awarded. *Degree requirements:* For master's, thesis or alternative. *Entrance requirements:* For master's, GMAT. Additional exam requirements/recommendations for international students: Required—TOEFL (minimum score 520 paper-based; 190 computer-based; 70 iBT), IELTS (minimum score 5.5). *Application deadline:* For fall admission, 5/31 for international students; for winter admission, 10/15 for international students; for spring admission, 1/15 for international students. Applications are processed on a rolling basis. Application fee: $50. Electronic applications accepted. *Expenses:* Contact institution. *Financial support:* Research assistantships with partial tuition reimbursements, teaching assistantships with partial tuition reimbursements, Federal Work-Study, scholarships/grants, health care benefits, tuition waivers, and unspecified assistantships available. Support available to part-time students. Financial award applicants required to submit FAFSA. *Unit head:* Charles Coleman, Chairman, 203-932-7375. *Application contact:* Eloise Gormley, Director of Graduate Admissions, 203-932-7449, Fax: 203-932-7137, E-mail: gradinfo@newhaven.edu.

University of Pennsylvania, School of Engineering and Applied Science, Telecommunications and Networking Program, Philadelphia, PA 19104. Offers MSE. Part-time programs available. *Students:* 62 full-time (8 women), 7 part-time (0 women); includes 1 minority (African American), 64 international. 125 applicants, 65% accepted, 45 enrolled. In 2009, 13 master's awarded. *Application deadline:* For fall admission, 6/1 for domestic students, 5/1 for international students; for spring admission, 11/1 for domestic students, 10/1 for international students. Application fee: $70. Electronic applications accepted. *Expenses:* Tuition: Full-time $25,660; part-time $4758 per course. Required fees: $2152; $270 per course. Tuition and fees vary according to course load, degree level and program.

University of San Francisco, School of Business and Professional Studies, Masagung Graduate School of Management, Program in Business Administration, San Francisco, CA 94117-1080. Offers business economics (MBA); e-business (MBA); entrepreneurship (MBA); finance (MBA); international business (MBA); management (MBA); marketing (MBA); telecommunications management and policy (MBA); JD/MBA; MSN/MBA. *Accreditation:* AACSB. *Faculty:* 17 full-time (4 women), 16 part-time/adjunct (7 women). *Students:* 278 full-time (140 women), 18 part-time (10 women); includes 94 minority (5 African Americans, 1 American Indian/Alaska Native, 69 Asian Americans or Pacific Islanders, 19 Hispanic Americans), 53 international. Average age 30. 410 applicants, 70% accepted, 133 enrolled. In 2009, 137 master's awarded. *Entrance requirements:* For master's, GMAT, minimum undergraduate GPA of 3.2. Additional exam requirements/recommendations for international students: Required—TOEFL. *Application deadline:* For fall admission, 7/1 priority date for domestic students; for spring admission, 11/30 for domestic students. Applications are processed on a rolling basis. Application fee: $55 ($65 for international students). *Expenses:* Tuition: Full-time $19,710; part-time $1095 per unit. Part-time tuition and fees vary according to degree level, campus/location and program. *Financial support:* In 2009–10, 155 students received support; fellowships available. Financial award application deadline: 3/2; financial award applicants required to submit FAFSA. *Faculty research:* International financial markets, technology transfer licensing, international marketing, strategic planning. Total annual research expenditures: $50,000. *Unit head:* Kelly Brookes, Director, 415-422-2221, Fax: 415-422-6315. *Application contact:* Director, MBA Program, 415-422-2221, Fax: 415-422-6315, E-mail: mba@usfca.edu.

University of South Africa, College of Human Sciences, Pretoria, South Africa. Offers adult education (M Ed); African languages (MA, PhD); African politics (MA, PhD); Afrikaans (MA, PhD); ancient history (MA, PhD); ancient Near Eastern studies (MA, PhD); anthropology (MA, PhD); applied linguistics (MA); Arabic (MA, PhD); archaeology (MA); art history (MA); Biblical archaeology (MA); Biblical studies (M Th, D Th, PhD); Christian spirituality (M Th, D Th); church history (M Th, D Th); classical studies (MA, PhD); clinical psychology (MA); communication (MA, PhD); comparative education (M Ed, Ed D); consulting psychology (D Admin, D Com, PhD); curriculum studies (M Ed, Ed D); development studies (M Admin, MA, D Admin, PhD); didactics (M Ed, Ed D); education (M Tech); education management (M Ed, Ed D); educational psychology (M Ed); English (MA); environmental education (M Ed); French (MA, PhD); German (MA, PhD); Greek (MA); guidance and counseling (M Ed); health studies (MA, PhD), including health sciences education (MA), health services management (MA), medical and surgical nursing science (critical care general) (MA), midwifery and neonatal nursing science (MA), trauma and emergency care (MA); history (MA, PhD); history of education (Ed D); inclusive education (M Ed, Ed D); information and communications technology policy and regulation (MA); information science (MA, MIS, PhD); international politics (MA, PhD); Islamic studies (MA, PhD); Italian (MA, PhD); Judaica (MA, PhD); linguistics (MA, PhD); mathematical education (M Ed); mathematics education (MA); missiology (M Th, D Th); modern Hebrew (MA, PhD); musicology (MA, MMus, D Mus, PhD); natural science education (M Ed); New Testament (M Th, D Th); Old Testament (D Th); pastoral therapy (M Th, D Th); philosophy (MA); philosophy of education (M Ed, Ed D); politics (MA, PhD); Portuguese (MA, PhD); practical theology (M Th, D Th); psychology (MA, MS, PhD); psychology of education (M Ed, Ed D); public health (MA); religious studies (MA, D Th, PhD); Romance languages (MA); Russian (MA, PhD); Semitic languages (MA, PhD); social behavior studies in HIV/AIDS (MA); social science (mental health) (MA); social science in development studies (MA); social science in psychology (MA); social science in social work (MA); social science in sociology (MA); social work (MSW, DSW, PhD); socio-education (M Ed, Ed D); sociolinguistics (MA); sociology (MA, PhD); Spanish (MA, PhD); systematic theology (M Th, D Th); TESOL (teaching English to speakers of other languages) (MA); theological ethics (M Th, D Th); theory of literature (MA, PhD); urban ministries (D Th); urban ministry (M Th).

University of Wisconsin–Stout, Graduate School, College of Technology, Engineering, and Management, Program in Information and Communication Technologies, Menomonie, WI 54751. Offers MS. Part-time programs available. Postbaccalaureate distance learning degree programs offered (minimal on-campus study). *Degree requirements:* For master's, thesis. *Entrance requirements:* For master's, minimum GPA of 2.75. Additional exam requirements/recommendations for international students: Required—TOEFL (minimum score 500 paper-based; 173 computer-based; 61 iBT). Electronic applications accepted.

Webster University, George Herbert Walker School of Business and Technology, Department of Business, St. Louis, MO 63119-3194. Offers business (MA); business and organizational security management (MBA); computer resources and information management (MBA); environmental management (MBA); finance (MA, MBA); health services management (MBA); human resources development (MBA); human resources management (MBA); international business (MA, MBA); management and leadership (MBA); marketing (MBA); procurement and acquisitions management (MBA); telecommunications management (MBA). Part-time and evening/weekend programs available. Postbaccalaureate distance learning degree programs offered (no on-campus study). *Faculty:* 9 full-time, 430 part-time/adjunct. *Students:* 1,190 full-time (543 women), 4,226 part-time (2,159 women); includes 2,110 minority (1,448 African Americans, 20 American Indian/Alaska Native, 310 Asian Americans or Pacific Islanders, 332 Hispanic Americans), 2,176 international. Average age 34. In 2009, 2,021 master's awarded. *Degree requirements:* For master's, comprehensive exam (for some programs), thesis (for some programs). *Entrance requirements:* Additional exam requirements/recommendations for international students: Required—TOEFL. *Application deadline:* Applications are processed on a rolling basis. Application fee: $35 ($50 for international students). *Expenses:* Tuition: Part-time $565 per credit hour. Tuition and fees vary according to degree level, campus/location and program. *Financial support:* Federal Work-Study available. Support available to part-time students. Financial award application deadline: 4/1; financial award applicants required to submit FAFSA. *Unit head:* Dr. Debbie Psihountas, Chair, 314-246-7553 Ext. 7017, Fax: 314-968-7077, E-mail: buschair@webster.edu. *Application contact:* Matt Nolan, Assoc., V.P.—Enrollment Management / Dean of Admissions, Fax: 314-968-7116, E-mail: gadmit@webster.edu.

Webster University, George Herbert Walker School of Business and Technology, Department of Management, St. Louis, MO 63119-3194. Offers business and organizational security management (MA); computer resources and information management (MA); environmental management (MS); government contracting (Certificate); health care management (MA); health services management (MA); human resources development (MA); human resources management (MA); management (DM); management and leadership (MA); marketing (MA); nonprofit management (Certificate); procurement and acquisitions management (MA); public administration (MA); quality management (MA); space systems operations management (MS); telecommunications management (MA). Part-time and evening/weekend programs available. Postbaccalaureate distance learning degree programs offered (no on-campus study). *Faculty:* 16 full-time, 781 part-time/adjunct. *Students:* 1,369 full-time (610 women), 5,182 part-time (3,047 women); includes 3,460 minority (2,835 African Americans, 38 American Indian/Alaska Native, 169 Asian Americans or Pacific Islanders, 418 Hispanic Americans), 80 international. Average age 37. In 2009, 2,491 master's, 13 doctorates, 68 other advanced degrees awarded. *Degree requirements:* For master's, thesis (for some programs); for doctorate, thesis/dissertation, written exam. *Entrance requirements:* For doctorate, GMAT, 3 years of work experience, MBA. Additional exam requirements/recommendations for international students: Required—TOEFL. *Application deadline:* Applications are processed on a rolling basis. Application fee: $25 ($50 for international students). *Expenses:* Tuition: Part-time $565 per credit hour. Tuition and fees vary according to degree level, campus/location and program. *Financial support:* Federal Work-Study available. Support available to part-time students. Financial award application deadline: 4/1; financial award applicants required to submit FAFSA. *Unit head:* Jim Brasfield, Chair, 314-961-2660 Ext. 7063, Fax: 314-968-7077, E-mail: mgtchair@webster.edu. *Application contact:* Matt Nolan, Assoc. V.P.—Enrollment Management / Dean of Admissions, Fax: 314-968-7116, E-mail: gadmit@webster.edu.

UNIVERSITY OF MARYLAND, COLLEGE PARK

Cross-Disciplinary Master's Program in Telecommunications

Program of Study

The master's program in telecommunications (ENTS) at the University of Maryland is designed to provide students with the professional skills needed to advance a successful career in telecommunications. The program is cross-disciplinary in nature and combines fresh, cutting-edge technical courses with management, regulatory, and public policy instruction—creating a telecommunications professional who is technically savvy, business-minded, and acutely in tune with the policy issues that surround a constantly changing industry. The curriculum was carefully developed with the guidance of telecommunication industry leaders. Since its inception, new state-of-the-art classes have been added each year to keep pace with the technological advancements of the telecommunications industry. In terms of wireless and networking, classes focus on topics such as VoIP, IP network design, cellular hardware, GSM networks, Wi-Fi networks, CDMA, and OFDM technologies. A sampling of the information security courses offered includes cryptography, system security, network security, and CISSP.

Requirements for the M.S. in telecommunications include completing 33 credit hours of course work with a cumulative grade point average of at least 3.0/4.0. These 33 credits include eight core courses, two elective courses, and 3 credit hours for a project. The program can be pursued either full-time or part-time. Classes are scheduled in the evening to accommodate full-time working students,

Additional details regarding the program of study or degree requirements can be found on the University's Web site, http://telecom.umd.edu.

Research Facilities

Students can use several research facilities at the University of Maryland, including the program's own telecommunications lab. The telecommunications lab is a state-of-the-art facility that contains innovative tools and resources for both engineering and business instruction. Software applications featured include Crystal Ball, OPNET Modeler, Premium Solver, MaxPlan, Satellite Toolkit, Pathloss, and Pro-Scout drive test equipment. Students also have access to some resources at the University's Department of Electrical and Computer Engineering and School of Business. The campus has an extensive library system for both technical and business research.

Financial Aid

Financial aid is not available.

Cost of Study

Tuition is currently $905 per credit.

Living and Housing Costs

Boarding and lodging are available in many private homes and apartments in College Park and its surrounding area. A database of accommodations is maintained by the University's Off-Campus Housing Services.

Student Group

There were 124 students registered in the program during the fall 2009 semester, of whom 109 were full-time and 15 were part-time. There were 104 international students and 40 women.

Student Outcomes

Graduates of the program are currently making their mark at companies like Verizon, Booz Allen Hamilton, Hughes Network Systems, and Texas Instruments, as well as government agencies like the Federal Communications Commission and the National Security Agency.

Location

The University of Maryland is located along the thriving Washington-Baltimore corridor, one of the most prosperous and fastest-growing technology areas in the United States. The area is home to more than 3,000 high-tech companies, and more than half of the nation's Internet traffic is carried on the communication lines of local industry. This proximity to such a vibrant region offers students a wealth of opportunities in the telecom industry.

The University

The University of Maryland (also known as UM or UMD), is a public university located in College Park, Maryland, just outside Washington, D.C. The Clark School's graduate programs collectively rank seventeenth in the nation according to *U.S. News & World Report*'s listing of America's Best Graduate Schools 2010. The Clark School is ranked ninth in the nation among public universities and is the top public graduate engineering program in the Mid-Atlantic area. In 2009 the Institute of Higher Education and Center for World-Class Universities ranked the Clark School fourteenth in the world among all engineering programs.

Applying

Applicants must have a regionally accredited baccalaureate degree with a cumulative average of a B grade or better. Students applying generally hold degrees in engineering, computer science, and other technical fields. In the statement of purpose, successful applicants articulate a desire to enroll in a program that combines both technical and business aspects of telecommunications rather than traditional electrical engineering or M.B.A. programs. All applicants must have successfully completed calculus 1, calculus 2, and differential equations prior to gaining admission into the program. Application deadlines are May 1 (February 1 for international students) for the fall semester and October 1 (June 1 for international students) for the spring semester. All applicants are required to apply online at http://www.gradschool.umd. edu. In addition to submitting an online application for admission, a copy of the applicant's college transcripts and three letters of recommendation are required for evaluation.

Correspondence and Information

Master's Program in Telecommunications (ENTS)
University of Maryland
2433 A. V. Williams Building
College Park, Maryland 20742

Phone: 301-405-3682
Fax: 301-314-9324
E-mail: ece-entsinfo@umd.edu
Web site: http://telecom.umd.edu

University of Maryland, College Park

THE FACULTY

Department of Electrical and Computer Engineering
Michael Dellomo, ENTS Academic Adviser; Ph.D., Johns Hopkins.
Kamran Etemad, Ph.D., Maryland.
Mehdi Kalantari, ENTS Academic Director; Ph.D., Maryland.
Sheldon Wolk, Ph.D., Maryland.

Robert H. Smith School of Business
Jahangir Bouromand, ENTS Business Adviser; Ph.D., Syracuse.
Henry C. Boyd III, Tyser Teaching Fellow and Academic Director, Black & Decker TOBE Program; Ph.D., Duke.
David J. Kressler, Ph.D., Michigan.
Subramanian Raghavan, Ph.D., MIT.
William Rand, Ph.D., Michigan.
Donald R. Riley, Ph.D., Purdue.

APPENDIXES

APPENDIXES

Institutional Changes
Since the 2010 Edition

Following is an alphabetical listing of institutions that have recently closed, merged with other institutions, or changed their names or status. In the case of a name change, the former name appears first, followed by the new name.

Agnes Scott College (Decatur, GA): no longer offers graduate degrees

American Graduate School of International Relations and Diplomacy (Paris, France): name changed to American Graduate School in Paris

Antioch University McGregor (Yellow Springs, OH): name changed to Antioch University Midwest

Arizona State University at the Downtown Phoenix Campus (Phoenix, AZ): will be included with main campus Arizona State University (Tempe, AZ) by request from the institution

Arizona State University at the Polytechnic Campus (Mesa, AZ): will be included with main campus Arizona State University (Tempe, AZ) by request from the institution

Arizona State University at the West campus (Phoenix, AZ): [will be included with main campus Arizona State University (Tempe, AZ) by request from the institution

Arkansas State University (State University, AR): name changed to Arkansas State University–Jonesboro

Asbury College (Wilmore, KY): name changed to Asbury University

Australasian College of Health Sciences (Portland, OR): name changed to American College of Healthcare Sciences

Baker College Center for Graduate Studies (Flint, MI): name changed to Baker College Center for Graduate Studies–Online

Baltimore Hebrew University (Baltimore, MD): now a unit of Towson University (Towson, MD)

Beacon University (Columbus, GA): closed

Belhaven College (Jackson, MS): name changed to Belhaven University

Beth Benjamin Academy of Connecticut (Stamford, CT): no longer offers graduate degrees

Bethel College (McKenzie, TN): name changed to Bethel University

Bridgewater State College (Bridgewater, MA): name changed to Bridgewater State University

British American College London (London, United Kingdom): name changed to Regent's American College London

The Chicago School of Professional Psychology: Downtown Los Angeles Campus (Los Angeles, CA): name changed to The Chicago School of Professional Psychology at Downtown Los Angeles

The Chicago School of Professional Psychology: Grayslake Campus (Grayslake, IL): name changed to The Chicago School of Professional Psychology at Grayslake

The Cleveland Institute of Art (Cleveland, OH): no longer offers graduate degrees

Coleman College (San Diego, CA): name changed to Coleman University

Columbia Union College (Takoma Park, MD): name changed to Washington Adventist University

Dell'Arte School of Physical Theatre (Blue Lake, CA): name changed to Dell'Arte International School of Physical Theatre

DeVry University (San Francisco, CA): closed

Fitchburg State College (Fitchburg, MA): name changed to Fitchburg State University

George Meany Center for Labor Studies–The National Labor College (Silver Spring, MD): name changed to National Labor College

Hebrew Theological College (Skokie, IL): no longer offers graduate degrees

International University in Geneva (Geneva, Switzerland): no longer accredited by agency recognized by USDE or CHEA

Joint Military Intelligence College (Washington, DC): name changed to National Defense Intelligence College

Kent State University, Stark Campus (Canton, OH): name changed to Kent State University at Stark

Lancaster Bible College (Lancaster, PA): name changed to Lancaster Bible College & Graduate School

Leadership Institute of Seattle (Kenmore, WA): is now part of Saybrook University (San Francisco, CA)

New England School of Law (Boston, MA): name changed to New England Law-Boston

Otterbein College (Westerville, OH): name changed to Otterbein University

Pepperdine University (Los Angeles, CA): will be included with Pepperdine University (Malibu, CA) by request from the institution

The Protestant Episcopal Theological Seminary in Virginia (Alexandria, VA): name changed to Virginia Theological Seminary

Reinhardt College (Waleska, GA): name changed to Reinhardt University

Robert Morris College (Chicago, IL): name changed to Robert Morris University Illinois

St. Petersburg Theological Seminary (St. Petersburg, FL): no longer accredited by agency recognized by USDE or CHEA

Saybrook Graduate School and Research Center (San Francisco, CA): name changed to Saybrook University

Shorter College (Rome, GA): name changed to Shorter University

Southeastern University (Washington, DC): closed

Southern New England School of Law (North Dartmouth, MA): is now part of University of Massachusetts Dartmouth (North Dartmouth, MA)

Trinity Episcopal School for Ministry (Ambridge, PA): name changed to Trinity School for Ministry

University of Missouri–Columbia (Columbia, MO): name changed to University of Missouri

University of Phoenix–Renton Learning Center (Renton, WA): name changed to University of Phoenix–Western Washington Campus

University of Phoenix–Wisconsin Campus (Brookfield, WI): now listed as University of Phoenix–Madison Campus (Madison, WI)

West Liberty State University (West Liberty, WV): name changed to West Liberty University

World Medicine Institute: College of Acupuncture and Herbal Medicine (Honolulu, HI): name changed to World Medicine Institute of Acupuncture and Herbal Medicine

Abbreviations Used in the Guides

The following list includes abbreviations of degree names used in the profiles in the 2011 edition of the guides. Because some degrees (e.g., Doctor of Education) can be abbreviated in more than one way (e.g., D.Ed. or Ed.D.), and because the abbreviations used in the guides reflect the preferences of the individual colleges and universities, the list may include two or more abbreviations for a single degree.

Degrees

A Mus D	Doctor of Musical Arts
AC	Advanced Certificate
AD	Artist's Diploma Doctor of Arts
ADP	Artist's Diploma
Adv C	Advanced Certificate
Adv M	Advanced Master
AGC	Advanced Graduate Certificate
AGSC	Advanced Graduate Specialist Certificate
ALM	Master of Liberal Arts
AM	Master of Arts
AMBA	Accelerated Master of Business Administration
AMRS	Master of Arts in Religious Studies
APC	Advanced Professional Certificate
App Sc	Applied Scientist
App Sc D	Doctor of Applied Science
Au D	Doctor of Audiology
B Th	Bachelor of Theology
CAES	Certificate of Advanced Educational Specialization
CAGS	Certificate of Advanced Graduate Studies
CAL	Certificate in Applied Linguistics
CALS	Certificate of Advanced Liberal Studies
CAMS	Certificate of Advanced Management Studies
CAPS	Certificate of Advanced Professional Studies
CAS	Certificate of Advanced Studies
CASPA	Certificate of Advanced Study in Public Administration
CASR	Certificate in Advanced Social Research
CATS	Certificate of Achievement in Theological Studies
CBHS	Certificate in Basic Health Sciences
CBS	Graduate Certificate in Biblical Studies
CCJA	Certificate in Criminal Justice Administration
CCSA	Certificate in Catholic School Administration
CCTS	Certificate in Clinical and Translational Science
CE	Civil Engineer
CEM	Certificate of Environmental Management
CET	Certificate in Educational Technologies
CGS	Certificate of Graduate Studies
Ch E	Chemical Engineer
CM	Certificate in Management
CMH	Certificate in Medical Humanities
CMM	Master of Church Ministries
CMS	Certificate in Ministerial Studies
CNM	Certificate in Nonprofit Management
CP	Certificate in Performance
CPASF	Certificate Program for Advanced Study in Finance
CPC	Certificate in Professional Counseling Certificate in Publication and Communication
CPH	Certificate in Public Health
CPM	Certificate in Public Management
CPS	Certificate of Professional Studies
CScD	Doctor of Clinical Science
CSD	Certificate in Spiritual Direction
CSS	Certificate of Special Studies
CTS	Certificate of Theological Studies
CURP	Certificate in Urban and Regional Planning
D Admin	Doctor of Administration
D Arch	Doctor of Architecture
D Com	Doctor of Commerce
D Div	Doctor of Divinity
D Ed	Doctor of Education
D Ed Min	Doctor of Educational Ministry
D Eng	Doctor of Engineering
D Engr	Doctor of Engineering
D Env	Doctor of Environment
D Env M	Doctor of Environmental Management
D Law	Doctor of Law
D Litt	Doctor of Letters
D Med Sc	Doctor of Medical Science
D Min	Doctor of Ministry
D Miss	Doctor of Missiology
D Mus	Doctor of Music
D Mus A	Doctor of Musical Arts
D Phil	Doctor of Philosophy

D Ps	Doctor of Psychology
D Sc	Doctor of Science
D Sc D	Doctor of Science in Dentistry
D Sc IS	Doctor of Science in Information Systems
D Sc PA	Doctor of Science in Physician Assistant Studies
D Th	Doctor of Theology
D Th P	Doctor of Practical Theology
DA	Doctor of Accounting Doctor of Arts
DA Ed	Doctor of Arts in Education
DAH	Doctor of Arts in Humanities
DAOM	Doctorate in Acupuncture and Oriental Medicine
DAST	Diploma of Advanced Studies in Teaching
DBA	Doctor of Business Administration
DBL	Doctor of Business Leadership
DBS	Doctor of Buddhist Studies
DC	Doctor of Chiropractic
DCC	Doctor of Computer Science
DCD	Doctor of Communications Design
DCL	Doctor of Civil Law Doctor of Comparative Law
DCM	Doctor of Church Music
DCN	Doctor of Clinical Nutrition
DCS	Doctor of Computer Science
DDN	Diplôme du Droit Notarial
DDS	Doctor of Dental Surgery
DE	Doctor of Education Doctor of Engineering
DED	Doctor of Economic Development
DEIT	Doctor of Educational Innovation and Technology
DEL	Doctor of Executive Leadership
DEM	Doctor of Educational Ministry
DEPD	Diplôme Études Spécialisées
DES	Doctor of Engineering Science
DESS	Diplôme Études Supérieures Spécialisées
DFA	Doctor of Fine Arts
DGP	Diploma in Graduate and Professional Studies
DH Ed	Doctor of Health Education
DH Sc	Doctor of Health Sciences
DHA	Doctor of Health Administration
DHCE	Doctor of Health Care Ethics
DHL	Doctor of Hebrew Letters Doctor of Hebrew Literature

DHS	Doctor of Health Science Doctor of Human Services
DHSc	Doctor of Health Science
Dip CS	Diploma in Christian Studies
DIT	Doctor of Industrial Technology
DJ Ed	Doctor of Jewish Education
DJS	Doctor of Jewish Studies
DLS	Doctor of Liberal Studies
DM	Doctor of Management Doctor of Music
DMA	Doctor of Musical Arts
DMD	Doctor of Dental Medicine
DME	Doctor of Manufacturing Management Doctor of Music Education
DMEd	Doctor of Music Education
DMFT	Doctor of Marital and Family Therapy
DMH	Doctor of Medical Humanities
DML	Doctor of Modern Languages
DMM	Doctor of Music Ministry
DMP	Doctorate in Medical Physics
DMPNA	Doctor of Management Practice in Nurse Anesthesia
DN Sc	Doctor of Nursing Science
DNAP	Doctor of Nurse Anesthesia Practice
DNP	Doctor of Nursing Practice
DNS	Doctor of Nursing Science
DO	Doctor of Osteopathy
DPA	Doctor of Public Administration
DPC	Doctor of Pastoral Counseling
DPDS	Doctor of Planning and Development Studies
DPH	Doctor of Public Health
DPM	Doctor of Plant Medicine Doctor of Podiatric Medicine
DPPD	Doctor of Policy, Planning, and Development
DPS	Doctor of Professional Studies
DPT	Doctor of Physical Therapy
DPTSc	Doctor of Physical Therapy Science
Dr DES	Doctor of Design
Dr PH	Doctor of Public Health
Dr Sc PT	Doctor of Science in Physical Therapy
DRSc	Doctor of Regulatory Science
DS	Doctor of Science
DS Sc	Doctor of Social Science
DSJS	Doctor of Science in Jewish Studies

DSL	Doctor of Strategic Leadership
DSN	Doctor of Science in Nursing
DSW	Doctor of Social Work
DTL	Doctor of Talmudic Law
DV Sc	Doctor of Veterinary Science
DVM	Doctor of Veterinary Medicine
EAA	Engineer in Aeronautics and Astronautics
ECS	Engineer in Computer Science
Ed D	Doctor of Education
Ed DCT	Doctor of Education in College Teaching
Ed M	Master of Education
Ed S	Specialist in Education
Ed Sp	Specialist in Education
Ed Sp PTE	Specialist in Education in Professional Technical Education
EDM	Executive Doctorate in Management
EDSPC	Education Specialist
EE	Electrical Engineer
EJD	Executive Juris Doctor
EMBA	Executive Master of Business Administration
EMFA	Executive Master of Forensic Accounting
EMHA	Executive Master of Health Administration
EMIB	Executive Master of International Business
EML	Executive Master of Leadership
EMPA	Executive Master of Public Administration Executive Master of Public Affairs
EMS	Executive Master of Science
EMTM	Executive Master of Technology Management
Eng	Engineer
Eng Sc D	Doctor of Engineering Science
Engr	Engineer
Ex Doc	Executive Doctor of Pharmacy
Exec Ed D	Executive Doctor of Education
Exec MBA	Executive Master of Business Administration
Exec MPA	Executive Master of Public Administration
Exec MPH	Executive Master of Public Health
Exec MS	Executive Master of Science
G Dip	Graduate Diploma
GBC	Graduate Business Certificate
GCE	Graduate Certificate in Education
GDM	Graduate Diploma in Management
GDPA	Graduate Diploma in Public Administration
GDRE	Graduate Diploma in Religious Education

GEMBA	Global Executive Master of Business Administration
GEMPA	Gulf Executive Master of Public Administration
GM Acc	Graduate Master of Accountancy
GMBA	Global Master of Business Administration
GPD	Graduate Performance Diploma
GSS	Graduate Special Certificate for Students in Special Situations
IEMBA	International Executive Master of Business Administration
IM Acc	Integrated Master of Accountancy
IMA	Interdisciplinary Master of Arts
IMBA	International Master of Business Administration
IMES	International Masters in Environmental Studies
Ingeniero	Engineer
JCD	Doctor of Canon Law
JCL	Licentiate in Canon Law
JD	Juris Doctor
JSD	Doctor of Juridical Science Doctor of Jurisprudence Doctor of the Science of Law
JSM	Master of Science of Law
L Th	Licenciate in Theology
LL B	Bachelor of Laws
LL CM	Master of Laws in Comparative Law
LL D	Doctor of Laws
LL M	Master of Laws
LL M in Tax	Master of Laws in Taxation
LL M CL	Master of Laws (Common Law)
LL M/MBA	Master of Laws/Master of Business Administration
LL M/MNM	Master of Laws/Master of Nonprofit Management
M Ac	Master of Accountancy Master of Accounting Master of Acupuncture
M Ac OM	Master of Acupuncture and Oriental Medicine
M Acc	Master of Accountancy Master of Accounting
M Acct	Master of Accountancy Master of Accounting
M Accy	Master of Accountancy
M Actg	Master of Accounting
M Acy	Master of Accountancy
M Ad	Master of Administration
M Ad Ed	Master of Adult Education
M Adm	Master of Administration

M Adm Mgt	Master of Administrative Management
M Admin	Master of Administration
M ADU	Master of Architectural Design and Urbanism
M Adv	Master of Advertising
M Aero E	Master of Aerospace Engineering
M AEST	Master of Applied Environmental Science and Technology
M Ag	Master of Agriculture
M Ag Ed	Master of Agricultural Education
M Agr	Master of Agriculture
M Anesth Ed	Master of Anesthesiology Education
M App Comp Sc	Master of Applied Computer Science
M App St	Master of Applied Statistics
M Appl Stat	Master of Applied Statistics
M Aq	Master of Aquaculture
M Ar	Master of Architecture
M Arc	Master of Architecture
M Arch	Master of Architecture
M Arch I	Master of Architecture I
M Arch II	Master of Architecture II
M Arch E	Master of Architectural Engineering
M Arch H	Master of Architectural History
M Bioethics	Master in Bioethics
M Biomath	Master of Biomathematics
M Ch	Master of Chemistry
M Ch E	Master of Chemical Engineering
M Chem	Master of Chemistry
M Cl D	Master of Clinical Dentistry
M Cl Sc	Master of Clinical Science
M Comp E	Master of Computer Engineering
M Comp Sc	Master of Computer Science
M Coun	Master of Counseling
M Dent	Master of Dentistry
M Dent Sc	Master of Dental Sciences
M Des	Master of Design
M Des S	Master of Design Studies
M Div	Master of Divinity
M Ec	Master of Economics
M Econ	Master of Economics
M Ed	Master of Education
M Ed T	Master of Education in Teaching
M En	Master of Engineering Master of Environmental Science
M En S	Master of Environmental Sciences
M Eng	Master of Engineering
M Eng Mgt	Master of Engineering Management
M Engr	Master of Engineering
M Env	Master of Environment
M Env Des	Master of Environmental Design
M Env E	Master of Environmental Engineering
M Env Sc	Master of Environmental Science
M Fin	Master of Finance
M Geo E	Master of Geological Engineering
M Geoenv E	Master of Geoenvironmental Engineering
M Geog	Master of Geography
M Hum	Master of Humanities
M Hum Svcs	Master of Human Services
M IBD	Master of Integrated Building Delivery
M IDST	Master's in Interdisciplinary Studies
M Kin	Master of Kinesiology
M Land Arch	Master of Landscape Architecture
M Litt	Master of Letters
M Man	Master of Management
M Mat SE	Master of Material Science and Engineering
M Math	Master of Mathematics
M Med Sc	Master of Medical Science
M Mgmt	Master of Management
M Mgt	Master of Management
M Min	Master of Ministries
M Mtl E	Master of Materials Engineering
M Mu	Master of Music
M Mus	Master of Music
M Mus Ed	Master of Music Education
M Music	Master of Music
M Nat Sci	Master of Natural Science
M Oc E	Master of Oceanographic Engineering
M Pet E	Master of Petroleum Engineering
M Pharm	Master of Pharmacy
M Phil	Master of Philosophy
M Phil F	Master of Philosophical Foundations
M Pl	Master of Planning
M Plan	Master of Planning
M Pol	Master of Political Science
M Pr Met	Master of Professional Meteorology
M Prob S	Master of Probability and Statistics

M Psych	Master of Psychology
M Pub	Master of Publishing
M Rel	Master of Religion
M Sc	Master of Science
M Sc A	Master of Science (Applied)
M Sc AHN	Master of Science in Applied Human Nutrition
M Sc BMC	Master of Science in Biomedical Communications
M Sc CS	Master of Science in Computer Science
M Sc E	Master of Science in Engineering
M Sc Eng	Master of Science in Engineering
M Sc Engr	Master of Science in Engineering
M Sc F	Master of Science in Forestry
M Sc FE	Master of Science in Forest Engineering
M Sc Geogr	Master of Science in Geography
M Sc N	Master of Science in Nursing
M Sc OT	Master of Science in Occupational Therapy
M Sc P	Master of Science in Planning
M Sc Pl	Master of Science in Planning
M Sc PT	Master of Science in Physical Therapy
M Sc T	Master of Science in Teaching
M SEM	Master of Sustainable Environmental Management
M Serv Soc	Master of Social Service
M Soc	Master of Sociology
M Sp Ed	Master of Special Education
M Stat	Master of Statistics
M Sw En	Master of Software Engineering
M Sys Sc	Master of Systems Science
M Tax	Master of Taxation
M Tech	Master of Technology
M Th	Master of Theology
M Tox	Master of Toxicology
M Trans E	Master of Transportation Engineering
M Urb	Master of Urban Planning
M Vet Sc	Master of Veterinary Science
MA	Master of Administration Master of Arts
MA Comm	Master of Arts in Communication
MA Ed	Master of Arts in Education
MA Ed Ad	Master of Arts in Educational Administration
MA Ext	Master of Agricultural Extension
MA Islamic	Master of Arts in Islamic Studies
MA Military Studies	Master of Arts in Military Studies
MA Min	Master of Arts in Ministry
MA Miss	Master of Arts in Missiology
MA Past St	Master of Arts in Pastoral Studies
MA Ph	Master of Arts in Philosophy
MA Psych	Master of Arts in Psychology
MA Sc	Master of Applied Science
MA Sp	Master of Arts (Spirituality)
MA Strategic Intelligence	Master of Arts in Strategic Intelligence
MA Th	Master of Arts in Theology
MA-R	Master of Arts (Research)
MAA	Master of Administrative Arts Master of Applied Anthropology Master of Applied Arts Master of Arts in Administration
MAAAP	Master of Arts Administration and Policy
MAAE	Master of Arts in Art Education
MAAT	Master of Arts in Applied Theology Master of Arts in Art Therapy
MAB	Master of Agribusiness
MABC	Master of Arts in Biblical Counseling Master of Arts in Business Communication
MABE	Master of Arts in Bible Exposition
MABL	Master of Arts in Biblical Languages
MABM	Master of Agribusiness Management
MABS	Master of Arts in Biblical Studies
MABT	Master of Arts in Bible Teaching
MAC	Master of Accountancy Master of Accounting Master of Arts in Communication Master of Arts in Counseling
MACC	Master of Arts in Accountancy Master of Arts in Christian Counseling Master of Arts in Clinical Counseling
MACCM	Master of Arts in Church and Community Ministry
MACCT	Master of Accounting
MACE	Master of Arts in Christian Education
MACFM	Master of Arts in Children's and Family Ministry
MACH	Master of Arts in Church History
MACIS	Master of Accounting and Information Systems
MACJ	Master of Arts in Criminal Justice
MACL	Master of Arts in Christian Leadership

MACM	Master of Arts in Christian Ministries Master of Arts in Christian Ministry Master of Arts in Church Music Master of Arts in Counseling Ministries
MACN	Master of Arts in Counseling
MACO	Master of Arts in Counseling
MAcOM	Master of Acupuncture and Oriental Medicine
MACP	Master of Arts in Counseling Psychology
MACS	Master of Arts in Catholic Studies
MACSE	Master of Arts in Christian School Education
MACT	Master of Arts in Christian Thought Master of Arts in Communications and Technology
MAD	Master in Educational Institution Administration Master of Art and Design
MADR	Master of Arts in Dispute Resolution
MADS	Master of Animal and Dairy Science Master of Applied Disability Studies
MAE	Master of Aerospace Engineering Master of Agricultural Economics Master of Agricultural Education Master of Architectural Engineering Master of Art Education Master of Arts in Education Master of Arts in English Master of Automotive Engineering
MAECMS	Master of Aerospace Engineering in Composite Materials and Structures
MAEd	Master of Arts Education
MAEL	Master of Arts in Educational Leadership
MAEM	Master of Arts in Educational Ministries
MAEN	Master of Arts in English
MAEP	Master of Arts in Economic Policy
MAES	Master of Arts in Environmental Sciences
MAESL	Master of Arts in English as a Second Language
MAET	Master of Arts in English Teaching
MAF	Master of Arts in Finance
MAFE	Master of Arts in Financial Economics
MAFLL	Master of Arts in Foreign Language and Literature
MAFM	Master of Accounting and Financial Management
MAFS	Master of Arts in Family Studies
MAG	Master of Applied Geography
MAGU	Master of Urban Analysis and Management
MAH	Master of Arts in Humanities
MAHA	Master of Arts in Humanitarian Assistance Master of Arts in Humanitarian Studies
MAHCM	Master of Arts in Health Care Mission
MAHG	Master of American History and Government
MAHL	Master of Arts in Hebrew Letters
MAHN	Master of Applied Human Nutrition
MAHSR	Master of Applied Health Services Research
MAIA	Master of Arts in International Administration
MAIB	Master of Arts in International Business
MAICS	Master of Arts in Intercultural Studies
MAIDM	Master of Arts in Interior Design and Merchandising
MAIH	Master of Arts in Interdisciplinary Humanities
MAIPCR	Master of Arts in International Peace and Conflict Management
MAIR	Master of Arts in Industrial Relations
MAIS	Master of Arts in Intercultural Studies Master of Arts in Interdisciplinary Studies Master of Arts in International Studies
MAIT	Master of Administration in Information Technology Master of Applied Information Technology
MAJ	Master of Arts in Journalism
MAJ Ed	Master of Arts in Jewish Education
MAJCS	Master of Arts in Jewish Communal Service
MAJE	Master of Arts in Jewish Education
MAJS	Master of Arts in Jewish Studies
MAL	Master in Agricultural Leadership
MALA	Master of Arts in Liberal Arts
MALD	Master of Arts in Law and Diplomacy
MALED	Master of Arts in Literacy Education
MALER	Master of Arts in Labor and Employment Relations
MALM	Master of Applied Leadership and Management Master of Arts in Leadership Evangelical Mobilization
MALP	Master of Arts in Language Pedagogy
MALPS	Master of Arts in Liberal and Professional Studies
MALS	Master of Arts in Liberal Studies
MALT	Master of Arts in Learning and Teaching
MAM	Master of Acquisition Management Master of Agriculture and Management Master of Applied Mathematics Master of Arts in Management Master of Arts in Ministry Master of Arts Management Master of Avian Medicine
MAMB	Master of Applied Molecular Biology
MAMC	Master of Arts in Mass Communication Master of Arts in Ministry and Culture Master of Arts in Ministry for a Multicultural Church
MAME	Master of Arts in Missions/Evangelism

MAMFC	Master of Arts in Marriage and Family Counseling
MAMFCC	Master of Arts in Marriage, Family, and Child Counseling
MAMFT	Master of Arts in Marriage and Family Therapy
MAMM	Master of Arts in Ministry Management
MAMS	Master of Applied Mathematical Sciences
	Master of Arts in Ministerial Studies
	Master of Arts in Ministry and Spirituality
MAMT	Master of Arts in Mathematics Teaching
MAN	Master of Applied Nutrition
MANP	Master of Applied Natural Products
MANT	Master of Arts in New Testament
MAOM	Master of Acupuncture and Oriental Medicine
	Master of Arts in Organizational Management
MAOT	Master of Arts in Old Testament
MAP	Master of Applied Psychology
	Master of Arts in Planning
	Master of Public Administration
	Masters of Psychology
MAP Min	Master of Arts in Pastoral Ministry
MAPA	Master of Arts in Public Administration
MAPC	Master of Arts in Pastoral Counseling
MAPE	Master of Arts in Political Economy
MAPL	Master of Arts in Pastoral Leadership
MAPM	Master of Arts in Pastoral Ministry
	Master of Arts in Pastoral Music
	Master of Arts in Practical Ministry
MAPP	Master of Arts in Public Policy
MAPPS	Master of Arts in Asia Pacific Policy Studies
MAPS	Master of Arts in Pastoral Counseling/Spiritual Formation
	Master of Arts in Pastoral Studies
	Master of Arts in Public Service
MAPT	Master of Practical Theology
MAPW	Master of Arts in Professional Writing
MAR	Master of Arts in Religion
Mar Eng	Marine Engineer
MARC	Master of Arts in Rehabilitation Counseling
MARE	Master of Arts in Religious Education
MARL	Master of Arts in Religious Leadership
MARS	Master of Arts in Religious Studies

MAS	Master of Accounting Science
	Master of Actuarial Science
	Master of Administrative Science
	Master of Advanced Study
	Master of Aeronautical Science
	Master of American Studies
	Master of Applied Science
	Master of Applied Statistics
	Master of Architectural Studies
	Master of Archival Studies
MASA	Master of Advanced Studies in Architecture
MASD	Master of Arts in Spiritual Direction
MASE	Master of Arts in Special Education
MASF	Master of Arts in Spiritual Formation
MASJ	Master of Arts in Systems of Justice
MASL	Master of Arts in School Leadership
MASLA	Master of Advanced Studies in Landscape Architecture
MASM	Master of Aging Services Management
	Master of Arts in Specialized Ministries
MASP	Master of Applied Social Psychology
	Master of Arts in School Psychology
MASPAA	Master of Arts in Sports and Athletic Administration
MASS	Master of Applied Social Science
	Master of Arts in Social Science
MAST	Master of Arts in Science Teaching
MASW	Master of Aboriginal Social Work
MAT	Master of Arts in Teaching
	Master of Arts in Theology
	Master of Athletic Training
	Masters in Administration of Telecommunications
Mat E	Materials Engineer
MATCM	Master of Acupuncture and Traditional Chinese Medicine
MATDE	Master of Arts in Theology, Development, and Evangelism
MATDR	Master of Territorial Management and Regional Development
MATE	Master of Arts for the Teaching of English
MATESL	Master of Arts in Teaching English as a Second Language
MATESOL	Master of Arts in Teaching English to Speakers of Other Languages
MATF	Master of Arts in Teaching English as a Foreign Language/Intercultural Studies
MATFL	Master of Arts in Teaching Foreign Language
MATH	Master of Arts in Therapy
MATI	Master of Administration of Information Technology

MATL	Master of Arts in Teaching of Languages Master of Arts in Transformational Leadership
MATM	Master of Arts in Teaching of Mathematics
MATS	Master of Arts in Theological Studies Master of Arts in Transforming Spirituality
MATSL	Master of Arts in Teaching a Second Language
MAUA	Master of Arts in Urban Affairs
MAUD	Master of Arts in Urban Design
MAURP	Master of Arts in Urban and Regional Planning
MAW	Master of Arts in Worship
MAWL	Master of Arts in Worship Leadership
MAWSHP	Master of Arts in Worship
MAYM	Master of Arts in Youth Ministry
MB	Master of Bioinformatics
MBA	Master of Business Administration
MBA-EP	Master of Business Administration–Experienced Professionals
MBAA	Master of Business Administration in Aviation
MBAE	Master of Biological and Agricultural Engineering Master of Biosystems and Agricultural Engineering
MBAH	Master of Business Administration in Health
MBAi	Master of Business Administration–International
MBAICT	Master of Business Administration in Information and Communication Technology
MBAPA	Master of Business Administration–Physician Assistant
MBATM	Master of Business Administration in Technology Management
MBC	Master of Building Construction
MBE	Master of Bilingual Education Master of Bioengineering Master of Biological Engineering Master of Biomedical Engineering Master of Business and Engineering Master of Business Economics Master of Business Education
MBET	Master of Business, Entrepreneurship and Technology
MBiotech	Master of Biotechnology
MBIT	Master of Business Information Technology
MBL	Master of Business Law Master of Business Leadership
MBLE	Master in Business Logistics Engineering
MBMI	Master of Biomedical Imaging and Signals

MBMSE	Master of Business Management and Software Engineering
MBS	Master of Behavioral Science Master of Biblical Studies Master of Biological Science Master of Biomedical Sciences Master of Bioscience Master of Building Science
MBSI	Master of Business Information Science
MBT	Master of Biblical and Theological Studies Master of Biomedical Technology Master of Biotechnology Master of Business Taxation
MC	Master of Communication Master of Counseling Master of Cybersecurity
MC Ed	Master of Continuing Education
MC Sc	Master of Computer Science
MCA	Master of Arts in Applied Criminology Master of Commercial Aviation
MCAM	Master of Computational and Applied Mathematics
MCC	Master of Computer Science
MCCS	Master of Crop and Soil Sciences
MCD	Master of Communications Disorders Master of Community Development
MCE	Master in Electronic Commerce Master of Christian Education Master of Civil Engineering Master of Control Engineering
MCEM	Master of Construction Engineering Management
MCH	Master of Chemical Engineering
MCHE	Master of Chemical Engineering
MCIS	Master of Communication and Information Studies Master of Computer and Information Science Master of Computer Information Systems
MCIT	Master of Computer and Information Technology
MCJ	Master of Criminal Justice
MCJA	Master of Criminal Justice Administration
MCL	Master in Communication Leadership Master of Canon Law Master of Comparative Law
MCM	Master of Christian Ministry Master of Church Music Master of City Management Master of Communication Management Master of Community Medicine Master of Construction Management Master of Contract Management Masters of Corporate Media

ABBREVIATIONS USED IN THE GUIDES

MCMS	Master of Clinical Medical Science
MCP	Master in Science
	Master of City Planning
	Master of Community Planning
	Master of Counseling Psychology
	Master of Cytopathology Practice
MCPC	Master of Arts in Chaplaincy and Pastoral Care
MCPD	Master of Community Planning and Development
MCRP	Master of City and Regional Planning
MCRS	Master of City and Regional Studies
MCS	Master of Christian Studies
	Master of Clinical Science
	Master of Combined Sciences
	Master of Communication Studies
	Master of Computer Science
	Master of Consumer Science
MCSE	Master of Computer Science and Engineering
MCSL	Master of Catholic School Leadership
MCSM	Master of Construction Science/Management
MCST	Master of Science in Computer Science and Information Technology
MCTP	Master of Communication Technology and Policy
MCTS	Master of Clinical and Translational Science
MCVS	Master of Cardiovascular Science
MD	Doctor of Medicine
MDA	Master of Development Administration
	Master of Dietetic Administration
MDB	Master of Design-Build
MDE	Master of Developmental Economics
	Master of Distance Education
	Master of the Education of the Deaf
MDH	Master of Dental Hygiene
MDM	Master of Digital Media
MDP	Master of Development Practice
MDR	Master of Dispute Resolution
MDS	Master of Dental Surgery
ME	Master of Education
	Master of Engineering
	Master of Entrepreneurship
	Master of Evangelism
ME Sc	Master of Engineering Science
MEA	Master of Educational Administration
	Master of Engineering Administration
MEAP	Master of Environmental Administration and Planning
MEBT	Master in Electronic Business Technologies
MEC	Master of Electronic Commerce
MECE	Master of Electrical and Computer Engineering
Mech E	Mechanical Engineer
MED	Master of Education of the Deaf
MEDS	Master of Environmental Design Studies
MEE	Master in Education
	Master of Electrical Engineering
	Master of Energy Engineering
	Master of Environmental Engineering
MEEM	Master of Environmental Engineering and Management
MEENE	Master of Engineering in Environmental Engineering
MEEP	Master of Environmental and Energy Policy
MEERM	Master of Earth and Environmental Resource Management
MEH	Master in Humanistic Studies
	Master of Environmental Horticulture
MEHS	Master of Environmental Health and Safety
MEIM	Master of Entertainment Industry Management
MEL	Master of Educational Leadership
	Master of English Literature
MELP	Master of Environmental Law and Policy
MEM	Master of Ecosystem Management
	Master of Electricity Markets
	Master of Engineering Management
	Master of Environmental Management
	Master of Marketing
MEME	Master of Engineering in Manufacturing Engineering
	Master of Engineering in Mechanical Engineering
MEMS	Master of Engineering in Manufacturing Systems
MENG	Master of Arts in English
MENVEGR	Master of Environmental Engineering
MEP	Master of Engineering Physics
MEPC	Master of Environmental Pollution Control
MEPD	Master of Education–Professional Development
	Master of Environmental Planning and Design
MEPM	Master of Environmental Protection Management
MER	Master of Employment Relations
MES	Master of Education and Science
	Master of Engineering Science
	Master of Environmenta and Sustainability
	Master of Environmental Science
	Master of Environmental Studies
	Master of Environmental Systems
	Master of Special Education
MESM	Master of Environmental Science and Management
MET	Master of Education in Teaching
	Master of Educational Technology
	Master of Engineering Technology
	Master of Entertainment Technology
	Master of Environmental Toxicology
Met E	Metallurgical Engineer

METM	Master of Engineering and Technology Management
MF	Master of Finance Master of Forestry
MFA	Master of Financial Administration Master of Fine Arts
MFAM	Master in Food Animal Medicine
MFAS	Master of Fisheries and Aquatic Science
MFAW	Master of Fine Arts in Writing
MFC	Master of Forest Conservation
MFCS	Master of Family and Consumer Sciences
MFE	Master of Financial Economics Master of Financial Engineering Master of Forest Engineering
MFG	Master of Functional Genomics
MFHD	Master of Family and Human Development
MFM	Master of Financial Mathematics
MFMS	Masters in Food Microbiology and Safety
MFPE	Master of Food Process Engineering
MFR	Master of Forest Resources
MFRC	Master of Forest Resources and Conservation
MFS	Master of Food Science Master of Forensic Sciences Master of Forest Science Master of Forest Studies Master of French Studies
MFSA	Master of Forensic Sciences Administration
MFST	Master of Food Safety and Technology
MFT	Master of Family Therapy Master of Food Technology
MFWB	Master of Fishery and Wildlife Biology
MFWCB	Master of Fish, Wildlife and Conservation Biology
MFWS	Master of Fisheries and Wildlife Sciences
MFYCS	Master of Family, Youth and Community Sciences
MG	Master of Genetics
MGA	Master of Governmental Administration
MGD	Master of Graphic Design
MGE	Master of Gas Engineering Master of Geotechnical Engineering
MGEM	Master of Global Entrepreneurship and Management
MGH	Master of Geriatric Health
MGIS	Master of Geographic Information Science Master of Geographic Information Systems
MGM	Master of Global Management
MGP	Master of Gestion de Projet
MGPS	Master of Global Policy Studies

MGS	Master of Gerontological Studies Master of Global Studies
MH	Master of Humanities
MH Ed	Master of Health Education
MH Sc	Master of Health Sciences
MHA	Master of Health Administration Master of Healthcare Administration Master of Hospital Administration Master of Hospitality Administration
MHAD	Master of Health Administration
MHB	Master of Human Behavior
MHCA	Master of Health Care Administration
MHCI	Master of Human-Computer Interaction
MHCL	Master of Health Care Leadership
MHE	Master of Health Education Master of Human Ecology
MHE Ed	Master of Home Economics Education
MHEA	Masters of Higher Education Administration
MHHS	Master of Health and Human Services
MHI	Master of Health Informatics Master of Healthcare Innovation
MHIIM	Master of Health Informatics and Information Management
MHIS	Master of Health Information Systems
MHK	Master of Human Kinetics
MHL	Master of Hebrew Literature
MHMS	Master of Health Management Systems
MHP	Master of Health Physics Master of Heritage Preservation Master of Historic Preservation
MHPA	Master of Heath Policy and Administration
MHPE	Master of Health Professions Education
MHR	Master of Human Resources
MHRD	Master in Human Resource Development
MHRIR	Master of Human Resources and Industrial Relations
MHRLR	Master of Human Resources and Labor Relations
MHRM	Master of Human Resources Management
MHS	Master of Health Science Master of Health Sciences Master of Health Studies Master of Hispanic Studies Master of Human Services Master of Humanistic Studies
MHSA	Master of Health Services Administration
MHSM	Master of Health Sector Management Master of Health Systems Management
MI	Master of Instruction

MI Arch	Master of Interior Architecture
MI St	Master of Information Studies
MIA	Master of Interior Architecture Master of International Affairs
MIAA	Master of International Affairs and Administration
MIAM	Master of International Agribusiness Management
MIB	Master of International Business
MIBA	Master of International Business Administration
MICM	Master of International Construction Management
MID	Master of Industrial Design Master of Industrial Distribution Master of Interior Design Master of International Development
MIE	Master of Industrial Engineering
MIH	Master of Integrative Health
MIHTM	Master of International Hospitality and Tourism Management
MIJ	Master of International Journalism
MILR	Master of Industrial and Labor Relations
MiM	Master in Management
MIM	Master of Industrial Management Master of Information Management Master of International Management
MIMLAE	Master of International Management for Latin American Executives
MIMS	Master of Information Management and Systems Master of Integrated Manufacturing Systems
MIP	Master of Infrastructure Planning Master of Intellectual Property
MIPER	Master of International Political Economy of Resources
MIPP	Master of International Policy and Practice Master of International Public Policy
MIPS	Master of International Planning Studies
MIR	Master of Industrial Relations Master of International Relations
MIS	Master of Industrial Statistics Master of Information Science Master of Information Systems Master of Integrated Science Master of Interdisciplinary Studies Master of International Service Master of International Studies
MISE	Master of Industrial and Systems Engineering
MISKM	Master of Information Sciences and Knowledge Management
MISM	Master of Information Systems Management

MIT	Master in Teaching Master of Industrial Technology Master of Information Technology Master of Initial Teaching Master of International Trade Master of Internet Technology
MITA	Master of Information Technology Administration
MITM	Master of International Technology Management
MITO	Master of Industrial Technology and Operations
MJ	Master of Journalism Master of Jurisprudence
MJ Ed	Master of Jewish Education
MJA	Master of Justice Administration
MJM	Master of Justice Management
MJS	Master of Judicial Studies Master of Juridical Science
MKM	Master of Knowledge Management
ML	Master of Latin
ML Arch	Master of Landscape Architecture
MLA	Master of Landscape Architecture Master of Liberal Arts
MLAS	Master of Laboratory Animal Science Master of Liberal Arts and Sciences
MLAUD	Master of Landscape Architecture in Urban Development
MLD	Master of Leadership Development Master of Leadership Studies
MLE	Master of Applied Linguistics and Exegesis
MLER	Master of Labor and Employment Relations
MLERE	Master of Land Economics and Real Estate
MLHR	Master of Labor and Human Resources
MLI	Master of Legal Institutions
MLI Sc	Master of Library and Information Science
MLIS	Master of Library and Information Science Master of Library and Information Studies
MLM	Master of Library Media
MLOS	Masters in Leadership and Organizational Studies
MLRHR	Master of Labor Relations and Human Resources
MLS	Master of Leadership Studies Master of Legal Studies Master of Liberal Studies Master of Library Science Master of Life Sciences
MLSP	Master of Law and Social Policy
MLT	Master of Language Technologies

MM	Master of Management
	Master of Ministry
	Master of Missiology
	Master of Music
MM Ed	Master of Music Education
MM Sc	Master of Medical Science
MM St	Master of Museum Studies
MMA	Master of Marine Affairs
	Master of Media Arts
	Master of Musical Arts
MMAE	Master of Mechanical and Aerospace Engineering
MMAS	Master of Military Art and Science
MMB	Master of Microbial Biotechnology
MMBA	Managerial Master of Business Administration
MMC	Master of Manufacturing Competitiveness
	Master of Mass Communications
	Master of Music Conducting
MMCM	Master of Music in Church Music
MMCSS	Masters of Mathematical Computational and Statistical Sciences
MME	Master of Manufacturing Engineering
	Master of Mathematics Education
	Master of Mathematics for Educators
	Master of Mechanical Engineering
	Master of Medical Engineering
	Master of Mining Engineering
	Master of Music Education
MMF	Master of Mathematical Finance
MMFT	Master of Marriage and Family Therapy
MMG	Master of Management
MMH	Master of Management in Hospitality
	Master of Medical Humanities
MMI	Master of Management of Innovation
MMIS	Master of Management Information Systems
MMM	Master of Manufacturing Management
	Master of Marine Management
	Master of Medical Management
MMME	Master of Metallurgical and Materials Engineering
MMP	Master of Management Practice
	Master of Marine Policy
	Master of Medical Physics
	Master of Music Performance
MMPA	Master of Management and Professional Accounting
MMQM	Master of Manufacturing Quality Management
MMR	Master of Marketing Research
MMRM	Master of Marine Resources Management

MMS	Master of Management Science
	Master of Management Studies
	Master of Manufacturing Systems
	Master of Marine Studies
	Master of Materials Science
	Master of Medical Science
	Master of Medieval Studies
	Master of Modern Studies
MMSE	Master of Manufacturing Systems Engineering
MMSM	Master of Music in Sacred Music
MMT	Master in Marketing
	Master of Management
	Master of Music Teaching
	Master of Music Therapy
	Masters in Marketing Technology
MMus	Master of Music
MN	Master of Nursing
	Master of Nutrition
MN NP	Master of Nursing in Nurse Practitioner
MNA	Master of Nonprofit Administration
	Master of Nurse Anesthesia
MNAL	Master of Nonprofit Administration and Leadership
MNAS	Master of Natural and Applied Science
MNCM	Master of Network and Communications Management
MNE	Master of Network Engineering
	Master of Nuclear Engineering
MNL	Master in International Business for Latin America
MNM	Master of Nonprofit Management
MNO	Master of Nonprofit Organization
MNPL	Master of Not-for-Profit Leadership
MNPS	Master of New Professional Studies
MNpS	Master of Nonprofit Studies
MNR	Master of Natural Resources
MNRES	Master of Natural Resources and Environmental Studies
MNRM	Master of Natural Resource Management
MNRS	Master of Natural Resource Stewardship
MNS	Master of Natural Science
MO	Master of Oceanography
MOD	Master of Organizational Development
MOGS	Master of Oil and Gas Studies
MOH	Master of Occupational Health
MOL	Master of Organizational Leadership
MOM	Master of Oriental Medicine
MOR	Master of Operations Research

MOT	Master of Occupational Therapy	**MPPPM**	Master of Plant Protection and Pest Management
MP	Master of Physiology Master of Planning	**MPPUP**	Master of Public Policy and Urban Planning
MP Ac	Master of Professional Accountancy	**MPRTM**	Master of Parks, Recreation, and Tourism Management
MP Acc	Master of Professional Accountancy Master of Professional Accounting Master of Public Accounting	**MPS**	Master of Pastoral Studies Master of Perfusion Science Master of Planning Studies Master of Political Science Master of Preservation Studies Master of Professional Studies Master of Public Service
MP Aff	Master of Public Affairs		
MP Th	Master of Pastoral Theology		
MPA	Master of Physician Assistant Master of Professional Accountancy Master of Professional Accounting Master of Public Administration Master of Public Affairs		
		MPSA	Master of Public Service Administration
		MPSRE	Master of Professional Studies in Real Estate
MPAC	Masters in Professional Accounting	**MPT**	Master of Pastoral Theology Master of Physical Therapy
MPAID	Master of Public Administration and International Development	**MPVM**	Master of Preventive Veterinary Medicine
MPAP	Master of Physician Assistant Practice Master of Public Affairs and Politics	**MPW**	Master of Professional Writing Master of Public Works
MPAS	Master of Physician Assistant Science Master of Physician Assistant Studies Master of Public Art Studies	**MQF**	Master of Quantitative Finance
		MQM	Master of Quality Management
		MQS	Master of Quality Systems
MPC	Master of Pastoral Counseling Master of Professional Communication Master of Professional Counseling	**MR**	Master of Recreation Master of Retailing
		MRA	Master in Research Administration
MPD	Master of Product Development Master of Public Diplomacy	**MRC**	Master of Rehabilitation Counseling
		MRCP	Master of Regional and City Planning Master of Regional and Community Planning
MPDS	Master of Planning and Development Studies		
MPE	Master of Physical Education Master of Power Engineering	**MRD**	Master of Rural Development
		MRE	Master of Religious Education
MPEM	Master of Project Engineering and Management	**MRED**	Master of Real Estate Development
MPH	Master of Public Health	**MREM**	Master of Resource and Environmental Management
MPHE	Master of Public Health Education		
MPHTM	Master of Public Health and Tropical Medicine	**MRLS**	Master of Resources Law Studies
MPIA	Master of Public and International Affairs Master Program in International Affairs	**MRM**	Master of Resources Management
		MRP	Master of Regional Planning
MPM	Master of Pastoral Ministry Master of Pest Management Master of Policy Management Master of Practical Ministries Master of Project Management Master of Public Management	**MRS**	Master of Religious Studies
		MRSc	Master of Rehabilitation Science
		MS	Master of Science
		MS Cmp E	Master of Science in Computer Engineering
		MS Kin	Master of Science in Kinesiology
MPNA	Master of Public and Nonprofit Administration	**MS Acct**	Master of Science in Accounting
MPOD	Master of Positive Organizational Development	**MS Accy**	Master of Science in Accountancy
MPP	Master of Public Policy	**MS Aero E**	Master of Science in Aerospace Engineering
MPPA	Master of Public Policy Administration Master of Public Policy and Administration	**MS Ag**	Master of Science in Agriculture
		MS Arch	Master of Science in Architecture
MPPAL	Master of Public Policy, Administration and Law	**MS Arch St**	Master of Science in Architectural Studies
MPPM	Master of Public and Private Management Master of Public Policy and Management		

MS Bio E	Master of Science in Bioengineering
	Master of Science in Biomedical Engineering
MS Bm E	Master of Science in Biomedical Engineering
MS Ch E	Master of Science in Chemical Engineering
MS Chem	Master of Science in Chemistry
MS Cp E	Master of Science in Computer Engineering
MS Eco	Master of Science in Economics
MS Econ	Master of Science in Economics
MS Ed	Master of Science in Education
MS El	Master of Science in Educational Leadership and Administration
MS En E	Master of Science in Environmental Engineering
MS Eng	Master of Science in Engineering
MS Engr	Master of Science in Engineering
MS Env E	Master of Science in Environmental Engineering
MS Exp Surg	Master of Science in Experimental Surgery
MS Int A	Master of Science in International Affairs
MS Mat E	Master of Science in Materials Engineering
MS Mat SE	Master of Science in Material Science and Engineering
MS Met E	Master of Science in Metallurgical Engineering
MS Metr	Master of Science in Meteorology
MS Mgt	Master of Science in Management
MS Min	Master of Science in Mining
MS Min E	Master of Science in Mining Engineering
MS Mt E	Master of Science in Materials Engineering
MS Otal	Master of Science in Otalrynology
MS Pet E	Master of Science in Petroleum Engineering
MS Phys	Master of Science in Physics
MS Phys Op	Master of Science in Physiological Optics
MS Poly	Master of Science in Polymers
MS Psy	Master of Science in Psychology
MS Pub P	Master of Science in Public Policy
MS Sc	Master of Science in Social Science
MS Sp Ed	Master of Science in Special Education
MS Stat	Master of Science in Statistics
MS Surg	Master of Science in Surgery
MS Tax	Master of Science in Taxation
MS Tc E	Master of Science in Telecommunications Engineering
MS-R	Master of Science (Research)
MSA	Master of School Administration
	Master of Science Administration
	Master of Science in Accountancy
	Master of Science in Accounting
	Master of Science in Administration
	Master of Science in Aeronautics
	Master of Science in Agriculture
	Master of Science in Anesthesia
	Master of Science in Architecture
	Master of Science in Aviation
	Master of Sports Administration
MSA Phy	Master of Science in Applied Physics
MSAA	Master of Science in Astronautics and Aeronautics
MSAAE	Master of Science in Aeronautical and Astronautical Engineering
MSABE	Master of Science in Agricultural and Biological Engineering
MSAC	Master of Science in Acupuncture
MSACC	Master of Science in Accounting
MSaCS	Master of Science in Applied Computer Science
MSAE	Master of Science in Aeronautical Engineering
	Master of Science in Aerospace Engineering
	Master of Science in Applied Economics
	Master of Science in Applied Engineering
	Master of Science in Architectural Engineering
	Master of Science in Art Education
MSAL	Master of Sport Administration and Leadership
MSAM	Master of Science in Applied Mathematics
MSANR	Master of Science in Agriculture and Natural Resources Systems Management
MSAPM	Master of Security Analysis and Portfolio Management
MSAS	Master of Science in Applied Statistics
	Master of Science in Architectural Studies
MSAT	Master of Science in Accounting and Taxation
	Master of Science in Advanced Technology
	Master of Science in Athletic Training
MSAUS	Master of Science in Architectural Urban Studies
MSB	Master of Science in Bible
	Master of Science in Business
MSBA	Master of Science in Business Administration
MSBAE	Master of Science in Biological and Agricultural Engineering
	Master of Science in Biosystems and Agricultural Engineering
MSBC	Master of Science in Building Construction
MSBE	Master of Science in Biological Engineering
	Master of Science in Biomedical Engineering
MSBENG	Master of Science in Bioengineering

MSBIT	Master of Science in Business Information Technology
MSBM	Master of Sport Business Management
MSBME	Master of Science in Biomedical Engineering
MSBMS	Master of Science in Basic Medical Science
MSBS	Master of Science in Biomedical Sciences
MSC	Master of Science in Commerce
	Master of Science in Communication
	Master of Science in Computers
	Master of Science in Counseling
	Master of Science in Criminology
MSCA	Master of Science in Construction Administration
MSCC	Master of Science in Christian Counseling
	Master of Science in Community Counseling
MSCD	Master of Science in Communication Disorders
	Master of Science in Community Development
MSCE	Master of Science in Civil Engineering
	Master of Science in Clinical Epidemiology
	Master of Science in Computer Engineering
	Master of Science in Continuing Education
MSCEE	Master of Science in Civil and Environmental Engineering
MSCF	Master of Science in Computational Finance
MSChE	Master of Science in Chemical Engineering
MSCI	Master of Science in Clinical Investigation
	Master of Science in Curriculum and Instruction
MSCIS	Master of Science in Computer and Information Systems
	Master of Science in Computer Information Science
	Master of Science in Computer Information Systems
MSCIT	Master of Science in Computer Information Technology
MSCJ	Master of Science in Criminal Justice
MSCJA	Master of Science in Criminal Justice Administration
MSCJS	Master of Science in Crime and Justice Studies
MSCL	Master of Science in Collaborative Leadership
MSCLS	Master of Science in Clinical Laboratory Studies
MSCM	Master of Science in Conflict Management
	Master of Science in Construction Management
MScM	Master of Science in Management
MSCM	Master of Supply Chain Management
MSCP	Master of Science in Clinical Psychology
	Master of Science in Computer Engineering
	Master of Science in Counseling Psychology
MSCPE	Master of Science in Computer Engineering

MSCPharm	Master of Science in Pharmacy
MSCPI	Master in Strategic Planning for Critical Infrastructures
MSCRP	Master of Science in City and Regional Planning
	Master of Science in Community and Regional Planning
MSCS	Master of Science in Clinical Science
	Master of Science in Computer Science
MSCSD	Master of Science in Communication Sciences and Disorders
MSCSE	Master of Science in Computer Science and Engineering
MSCTE	Master of Science in Career and Technical Education
MSD	Master of Science in Dentistry
	Master of Science in Design
	Master of Science in Dietetics
MSDD	Master of Software Design and Development
MSDM	Master of Design Methods
MSDR	Master of Dispute Resolution
MSE	Master of Science Education
	Master of Science in Economics
	Master of Science in Education
	Master of Science in Engineering
	Master of Science in Engineering Management
	Master of Software Engineering
	Master of Special Education
	Master of Structural Engineering
MSECE	Master of Science in Electrical and Computer Engineering
MSED	Master of Sustainable Economic Development
MSEE	Master of Science in Electrical Engineering
	Master of Science in Environmental Engineering
MSEH	Master of Science in Environmental Health
MSEL	Master of Science in Educational Leadership
	Master of Science in Executive Leadership
MSEM	Master of Science in Engineering Management
	Master of Science in Engineering Mechanics
	Master of Science in Environmental Management
MSENE	Master of Science in Environmental Engineering
MSEO	Master of Science in Electro-Optics
MSEP	Master of Science in Economic Policy
	Master of Science in Engineering Physics
MSEPA	Masters of Science in Economics and Policy Analysis
MSES	Master of Science in Embedded Software Engineering
	Master of Science in Engineering Science
	Master of Science in Environmental Science
	Master of Science in Environmental Studies

MSESM	Master of Science in Engineering Science and Mechanics
MSET	Master of Science in Education in Educational Technology
	Master of Science in Engineering Technology
MSETM	Master of Science in Environmental Technology Management
MSEV	Master of Science in Environmental Engineering
MSEVH	Master of Science in Environmental Health and Safety
MSF	Master of Science in Finance
	Master of Science in Forestry
MSFA	Master of Science in Financial Analysis
MSFAM	Master of Science in Family Studies
MSFCS	Master of Science in Family and Consumer Science
MSFE	Master of Science in Financial Engineering
MSFOR	Master of Science in Forestry
MSFP	Master of Science in Financial Planning
MSFS	Master of Science in Financial Sciences
	Master of Science in Forensic Science
MSFSB	Master of Science in Financial Services and Banking
MSFT	Master of Science in Family Therapy
MSGC	Master of Science in Genetic Counseling
MSGL	Master of Science in Global Leadership
MSH	Master of Science in Health
	Master of Science in Hospice
MSHA	Master of Science in Health Administration
MSHCA	Master of Science in Health Care Administration
MSHCI	Master of Science in Human Computer Interaction
MSHCPM	Master of Science in Health Care Policy and Management
MSHE	Master of Science in Health Education
MSHES	Master of Science in Human Environmental Sciences
MSHFID	Master of Science in Human Factors in Information Design
MSHFS	Master of Science in Human Factors and Systems
MSHI	Master of Science in Health Informatics
MSHP	Master of Science in Health Professions
	Master of Science in Health Promotion
MSHR	Master of Science in Human Resources
MSHRL	Master of Science in Human Resource Leadership
MSHRM	Master of Science in Human Resource Management
MSHROD	Master of Science in Human Resources and Organizational Development
MSHS	Master of Science in Health Science
	Master of Science in Health Services
	Master of Science in Health Systems
	Master of Science in Homeland Security
MSHT	Master of Science in History of Technology
MSI	Master of Science in Instruction
MSIA	Master of Science in Industrial Administration
	Master of Science in Information Assurance and Computer Security
MSIB	Master of Science in International Business
MSIDM	Master of Science in Interior Design and Merchandising
MSIDT	Master of Science in Information Design and Technology
MSIE	Master of Science in Industrial Engineering
	Master of Science in International Economics
MSIEM	Master of Science in Information Engineering and Management
MSIID	Master of Science in Information and Instructional Design
MSIM	Master of Science in Information Management
	Master of Science in International Management
	Master of Science in Investment Management
MSIMC	Master of Science in Integrated Marketing Communications
MSIR	Master of Science in Industrial Relations
MSIS	Master of Science in Information Science
	Master of Science in Information Systems
	Master of Science in Interdisciplinary Studies
MSISE	Master of Science in Infrastructure Systems Engineering
MSISM	Master of Science in Information Systems Management
MSISPM	Master of Science in Information Security Policy and Management
MSIST	Master of Science in Information Systems Technology
MSIT	Master of Science in Industrial Technology
	Master of Science in Information Technology
	Master of Science in Instructional Technology
MSITM	Master of Science in Information Technology Management
MSJ	Master of Science in Journalism
	Master of Science in Jurisprudence
MSJE	Master of Science in Jewish Education
MSJFP	Master of Science in Juvenile Forensic Psychology
MSJJ	Master of Science in Juvenile Justice
MSJPS	Master of Science in Justice and Public Safety

MSJS	Master of Science in Jewish Studies		**MSN-R**	Master of Science in Nursing (Research)
MSK	Master of Science in Kinesiology		**MSNA**	Master of Science in Nurse Anesthesia
MSKM	Master of Science in Knowledge Management		**MSNE**	Master of Science in Nuclear Engineering
MSL	Master of School Leadership		**MSNED**	Master of Science in Nurse Education
	Master of Science in Leadership		**MSNM**	Master of Science in Nonprofit Management
	Master of Science in Limnology			
	Master of Strategic Leadership		**MSNS**	Master of Science in Natural Science
	Master of Studies in Law			Master's of Science in Nutritional Science
MSLA	Master of Science in Landscape Architecture		**MSOD**	Master of Science in Organizational Development
	Master of Science in Legal Administration		**MSOEE**	Master of Science in Outdoor and Environmental Education
MSLD	Master of Science in Land Development			
MSLS	Master of Science in Legal Studies		**MSOES**	Master of Science in Occupational Ergonomics and Safety
	Master of Science in Library Science			
MSLSCM	Master of Science in Logistics and Supply Chain Management		**MSOH**	Master of Science in Occupational Health
			MSOL	Master of Science in Organizational Leadership
MSLT	Master of Second Language Teaching		**MSOM**	Master of Science in Operations Management
MSM	Master of Sacred Ministry			Master of Science in Organization and Management
	Master of Sacred Music			
	Master of School Mathematics			Master of Science in Oriental Medicine
	Master of Science in Management		**MSOR**	Master of Science in Operations Research
	Master of Science in Mathematics			
	Master of Science in Organization Management		**MSOT**	Master of Science in Occupational Technology
	Master of Security Management			Master of Science in Occupational Therapy
MSMA	Master of Science in Marketing Analysis		**MSP**	Master of Science in Pharmacy
MSMAE	Master of Science in Materials Engineering			Master of Science in Planning
MSMC	Master of Science in Mass Communications			Master of Science in Psychology
				Master of Speech Pathology
MSME	Master of Science in Mathematics Education		**MSPA**	Master of Science in Physician Assistant
	Master of Science in Mechanical Engineering			Master of Science in Professional Accountancy
MSMFE	Master of Science in Manufacturing Engineering		**MSPAS**	Master of Science in Physician Assistant Studies
MSMFT	Master of Science in Marriage and Family Therapy		**MSPC**	Master of Science in Professional Communications
MSMIS	Master of Science in Management Information Systems			Master of Science in Professional Counseling
MSMIT	Master of Science in Management and Information Technology		**MSPE**	Master of Science in Petroleum Engineering
			MSPG	Master of Science in Psychology
MSMM	Master of Science in Manufacturing Management		**MSPH**	Master of Science in Public Health
MSMO	Master of Science in Manufacturing Operations		**MSPHR**	Master of Science in Pharmacy
MSMOT	Master of Science in Management of Technology		**MSPM**	Master of Science in Professional Management
				Master of Science in Project Management
MSMS	Master of Science in Management Science		**MSPNGE**	Master of Science in Petroleum and Natural Gas Engineering
	Master of Science in Medical Sciences			
MSMSE	Master of Science in Manufacturing Systems Engineering		**MSPS**	Master of Science in Pharmaceutical Science
	Master of Science in Material Science and Engineering			Master of Science in Political Science
	Master of Science in Mathematics and Science Education			Master of Science in Psychological Services
			MSPT	Master of Science in Physical Therapy
MSMT	Master of Science in Management and Technology		**MSpVM**	Master of Specialized Veterinary Medicine
	Master of Science in Medical Technology		**MSR**	Master of Science in Radiology
				Master of Science in Reading
MSMus	Master of Sacred Music		**MSRA**	Master of Science in Recreation Administration
MSN	Master of Science in Nursing		**MSRC**	Master of Science in Resource Conservation

MSRE	Master of Science in Real Estate Master of Science in Religious Education
MSRED	Master of Science in Real Estate Development
MSRLS	Master of Science in Recreation and Leisure Studies
MSRMP	Master of Science in Radiological Medical Physics
MSRS	Master of Science in Rehabilitation Science
MSS	Master of Science in Software Master of Social Science Master of Social Services Master of Software Systems Master of Sports Science Master of Strategic Studies
MSSA	Master of Science in Social Administration
MSSCP	Master of Science in Science Content and Process
MSSE	Master of Science in Software Engineering Master of Science in Space Education Master of Science in Special Education
MSSEM	Master of Science in Systems and Engineering Management
MSSI	Master of Science in Security Informatics Master of Science in Strategic Intelligence
MSSL	Master of Science in Strategic Leadership
MSSLP	Master of Science in Speech-Language Pathology
MSSM	Master of Science in Sports Medicine
MSSP	Master of Science in Social Policy
MSSPA	Master of Science in Student Personnel Administration
MSSS	Master of Science in Safety Science Master of Science in Systems Science
MSST	Master of Science in Security Technologies
MSSW	Master of Science in Social Work
MSSWE	Master of Science in Software Engineering
MST	Master of Science and Technology Master of Science in Taxation Master of Science in Teaching Master of Science in Technology Master of Science in Telecommunications Master of Science Teaching
MSTC	Master of Science in Technical Communication Master of Science in Telecommunications
MSTCM	Master of Science in Traditional Chinese Medicine
MSTE	Master of Science in Telecommunications Engineering Master of Science in Transportation Engineering
MSTM	Master of Science in Technical Management
MSTOM	Master of Science in Traditional Oriental Medicine
MSUD	Master of Science in Urban Design

MSW	Master of Social Work
MSWE	Master of Software Engineering
MSWREE	Master of Science in Water Resources and Environmental Engineering
MSX	Master of Science in Exercise Science
MT	Master of Taxation Master of Teaching Master of Technology Master of Textiles
MTA	Master of Tax Accounting Master of Teaching Arts Master of Tourism Administration
MTCM	Master of Traditional Chinese Medicine
MTD	Master of Training and Development
MTE	Master in Educational Technology Master of Teacher Education
MTESOL	Master in Teaching English to Speakers of Other Languages
MTHM	Master of Tourism and Hospitality Management
MTI	Master of Information Technology
MTIM	Masters of Trust and Investment Management
MTL	Master of Talmudic Law
MTM	Master of Technology Management Master of Telecommunications Management Master of the Teaching of Mathematics
MTMH	Master of Tropical Medicine and Hygiene
MTOM	Master of Traditional Oriental Medicine
MTP	Master of Transpersonal Psychology
MTPC	Master of Technical and Professional Communication
MTS	Master of Theological Studies
MTSC	Master of Technical and Scientific Communication
MTSE	Master of Telecommunications and Software Engineering
MTT	Master in Technology Management
MTX	Master of Taxation
MUA	Master of Urban Affairs
MUD	Master of Urban Design
MUEP	Master of Urban and Environmental Planning
MUP	Master of Urban Planning
MUPDD	Master of Urban Planning, Design, and Development
MUPP	Master of Urban Planning and Policy
MUPRED	Masters of Urban Planning and Real Estate Development
MURP	Master of Urban and Regional Planning Master of Urban and Rural Planning

MUS	Master of Urban Studies	Psya D	Doctor of Psychoanalysis
MVM	Master of VLSI and microelectronics	Re Dir	Director of Recreation
MVP	Master of Voice Pedagogy	Rh D	Doctor of Rehabilitation
MVPH	Master of Veterinary Public Health	S Psy S	Specialist in Psychological Services
MVS	Master of Visual Studies	Sc D	Doctor of Science
MWC	Master of Wildlife Conservation	Sc M	Master of Science
MWE	Master in Welding Engineering	SCCT	Specialist in Community College Teaching
MWPS	Master of Wood and Paper Science	ScDPT	Doctor of Physical Therapy Science
MWR	Master of Water Resources	SD	Doctor of Science Specialist Degree
MWS	Master of Women's Studies	SJD	Doctor of Juridical Science
MZS	Master of Zoological Science	SLPD	Doctor of Speech-Language Pathology
Nav Arch	Naval Architecture	SLS	Specialist in Library Science
Naval E	Naval Engineer	SM	Master of Science
ND	Doctor of Naturopathic Medicine	SM Arch S	Master of Science in Architectural Studies
NE	Nuclear Engineer	SM Vis S	Master of Science in Visual Studies
Nuc E	Nuclear Engineer	SMBT	Master of Science in Building Technology
OD	Doctor of Optometry	SP	Specialist Degree
OTD	Doctor of Occupational Therapy	Sp C	Specialist in Counseling
PBME	Professional Master of Biomedical Engineering	Sp Ed	Specialist in Education
PD	Professional Diploma	Sp LIS	Specialist in Library and Information Science
PGC	Post-Graduate Certificate	SPA	Specialist in Arts
PGD	Postgraduate Diploma	SPCM	Special in Church Music
Ph L	Licentiate of Philosophy	Spec	Specialist's Certificate
Pharm D	Doctor of Pharmacy	Spec M	Specialist in Music
PhD	Doctor of Philosophy	SPEM	Special in Educational Ministries
PhD Otal	Doctor of Philosophy in Otalrynology	SPS	School Psychology Specialist
Phd Surg	Doctor of Philosophy in Surgery	Spt	Specialist Degree
PhDEE	Doctor of Philosophy in Electrical Engineering	SPTH	Special in Theology
PM Sc	Professional Master of Science	SSP	Specialist in School Psychology
PMBA	Professional Master of Business Administration	STB	Bachelor of Sacred Theology
PMC	Post Master Certificate	STD	Doctor of Sacred Theology
PMD	Post-Master's Diploma	STL	Licentiate of Sacred Theology
PMS	Professional Master of Science Professional Master's Degree	STM	Master of Sacred Theology
Post-Doctoral MS	Post-Doctoral Master of Science	TDPT	Transitional Doctor of Physical Therapy
		Th D	Doctor of Theology
PPDPT	Postprofessional Doctor of Physical Therapy	Th M	Master of Theology
PSM	Professional Master of Science Professional Science Master's	VMD	Doctor of Veterinary Medicine
		WEMBA	Weekend Executive Master of Business Administration
Psy D	Doctor of Psychology	XMA	Executive Master of Arts
Psy M	Master of Psychology	XMBA	Executive Master of Business Administration
Psy S	Specialist in Psychology		

INDEXES

Close-Ups and Displays

Directories and Subject Areas

Following is an alphabetical listing of directories and subject areas. Also listed are cross-references for subject area names not used in the directory structure of the guides, for example, "Arabic (*see* Near and Middle Eastern Languages)."

Graduate Programs in the Humanities, Arts & Social Sciences

Addictions/Substance Abuse Counseling
Administration (*see* Arts Administration; Public Administration)
African-American Studies
African Languages and Literatures (*see* African Studies)
African Studies
Agribusiness (*see* Agricultural Economics and Agribusiness)
Agricultural Economics and Agribusiness
Alcohol Abuse Counseling (*see* Addictions/Substance Abuse Counseling)
American Indian/Native American Studies
American Studies
Anthropology
Applied Arts and Design—General
Applied Economics
Applied History (*see* Public History)
Applied Social Research
Arabic (*see* Near and Middle Eastern Languages)
Arab Studies (*see* Near and Middle Eastern Studies)
Archaeology
Architectural History
Architecture
Archives Administration (*see* Public History)
Area and Cultural Studies (*see* African-American Studies; African Studies; American Indian/Native American Studies; American Studies; Asian-American Studies; Asian Studies; Canadian Studies; Cultural Studies; East European and Russian Studies; Ethnic Studies; Folklore; Gender Studies; Hispanic Studies; Holocaust Studies; Jewish Studies; Latin American Studies; Near and Middle Eastern Studies; Northern Studies; Pacific Area/Pacific Rim Studies; Western European Studies; Women's Studies)
Art/Fine Arts
Art History
Arts Administration
Arts Journalism
Art Therapy
Asian-American Studies
Asian Languages
Asian Studies
Behavioral Sciences (*see* Psychology)
Bible Studies (*see* Religion; Theology)
Biological Anthropology
Black Studies (*see* African-American Studies)
Broadcasting (*see* Communication; Film, Television, and Video Production)
Broadcast Journalism
Building Science
Canadian Studies
Celtic Languages
Ceramics (*see* Art/Fine Arts)
Child and Family Studies
Child Development
Chinese

Chinese Studies (*see* Asian Languages; Asian Studies)
Christian Studies (*see* Missions and Missiology; Religion; Theology)
Cinema (*see* Film, Television, and Video Production)
City and Regional Planning (*see* Urban and Regional Planning)
Classical Languages and Literatures (*see* Classics)
Classics
Clinical Psychology
Clothing and Textiles
Cognitive Psychology (*see* Psychology—General; Cognitive Sciences)
Cognitive Sciences
Communication—General
Community Affairs (*see* Urban and Regional Planning; Urban Studies)
Community Planning (*see* Architecture; Environmental Design; Urban and Regional Planning; Urban Design; Urban Studies)
Community Psychology (*see* Social Psychology)
Comparative and Interdisciplinary Arts
Comparative Literature
Composition (*see* Music)
Computer Art and Design
Conflict Resolution and Mediation/Peace Studies
Consumer Economics
Corporate and Organizational Communication
Corrections (*see* Criminal Justice and Criminology)
Counseling (*see* Counseling Psychology; Pastoral Ministry and Counseling)
Counseling Psychology
Crafts (*see* Art/Fine Arts)
Creative Arts Therapies (*see* Art Therapy; Therapies—Dance, Drama, and Music)
Criminal Justice and Criminology
Cultural Studies
Dance
Decorative Arts
Demography and Population Studies
Design (*see* Applied Arts and Design; Architecture; Art/Fine Arts; Environmental Design; Graphic Design; Industrial Design; Interior Design; Textile Design; Urban Design)
Developmental Psychology
Diplomacy (*see* International Affairs)
Disability Studies
Drama Therapy (*see* Therapies—Dance, Drama, and Music)
Dramatic Arts (*see* Theater)
Drawing (*see* Art/Fine Arts)
Drug Abuse Counseling (*see* Addictions/Substance Abuse Counseling)
Drug and Alcohol Abuse Counseling (*see* Addictions/Substance Abuse Counseling)
East Asian Studies (*see* Asian Studies)
East European and Russian Studies
Economic Development
Economics
Educational Theater (*see* Theater; Therapies—Dance, Drama, and Music)
Emergency Management
English
Environmental Design
Ethics
Ethnic Studies
Ethnomusicology (*see* Music)
Experimental Psychology
Family and Consumer Sciences—General
Family Studies (*see* Child and Family Studies)
Family Therapy (*see* Child and Family Studies; Clinical Psychology; Counseling Psychology; Marriage and Family Therapy)
Filmmaking (*see* Film, Television, and Video Production)
Film Studies (*see* Film, Television, and Video Production)

Film, Television, and Video Production
Film, Television, and Video Theory and Criticism
Fine Arts (*see* Art/Fine Arts)
Folklore
Foreign Languages (*see* specific language)
Foreign Service (*see* International Affairs; International Development)
Forensic Psychology
Forensic Sciences
Forensics (*see* Speech and Interpersonal Communication)
French
Gender Studies
General Studies (*see* Liberal Studies)
Genetic Counseling
Geographic Information Systems
Geography
German
Gerontology
Graphic Design
Greek (*see* Classics)
Health Communication
Health Psychology
Hebrew (*see* Near and Middle Eastern Languages)
Hebrew Studies (*see* Jewish Studies)
Hispanic Studies
Historic Preservation
History
History of Art (*see* Art History)
History of Medicine
History of Science and Technology
Holocaust and Genocide Studies
Home Economics (*see* Family and Consumer Sciences—General)
Homeland Security
Household Economics, Sciences, and Management (*see* Family and Consumer Sciences—General)
Human Development
Humanities
Illustration
Industrial and Labor Relations
Industrial and Organizational Psychology
Industrial Design
Interdisciplinary Studies
Interior Design
International Affairs
International Development
International Economics
International Service (*see* International Affairs; International Development)
International Trade Policy
Internet and Interactive Multimedia
Interpersonal Communication (*see* Speech and Interpersonal Communication)
Interpretation (*see* Translation and Interpretation)
Islamic Studies (*see* Near and Middle Eastern Studies; Religion)
Italian
Japanese
Japanese Studies (*see* Asian Languages; Asian Studies; Japanese)
Jewelry (*see* Art/Fine Arts)
Jewish Studies
Journalism
Judaic Studies (*see* Jewish Studies; Religion)
Labor Relations (*see* Industrial and Labor Relations)
Landscape Architecture
Latin American Studies
Latin (*see* Classics)
Law Enforcement (*see* Criminal Justice and Criminology)
Liberal Studies
Lighting Design
Linguistics

Literature (*see* Classics; Comparative Literature; specific language)
Marriage and Family Therapy
Mass Communication
Media Studies
Medical Illustration
Medieval and Renaissance Studies
Metalsmithing (*see* Art/Fine Arts)
Middle Eastern Studies (*see* Near and Middle Eastern Studies)
Military and Defense Studies
Mineral Economics
Ministry (*see* Pastoral Ministry and Counseling; Theology)
Missions and Missiology
Motion Pictures (*see* Film, Television, and Video Production)
Museum Studies
Music
Musicology (*see* Music)
Music Therapy (*see* Therapies—Dance, Drama, and Music)
National Security
Native American Studies (*see* American Indian/Native American Studies)
Near and Middle Eastern Languages
Near and Middle Eastern Studies
Near Environment (*see* Family and Consumer Sciences)
Northern Studies
Organizational Psychology (*see* Industrial and Organizational Psychology)
Oriental Languages (*see* Asian Languages)
Oriental Studies (*see* Asian Studies)
Pacific Area/Pacific Rim Studies
Painting (*see* Art/Fine Arts)
Pastoral Ministry and Counseling
Philanthropic Studies
Philosophy
Photography
Playwriting (*see* Theater; Writing)
Policy Studies (*see* Public Policy)
Political Science
Population Studies (*see* Demography and Population Studies)
Portuguese
Printmaking (*see* Art/Fine Arts)
Product Design (*see* Industrial Design)
Psychoanalysis and Psychotherapy
Psychology—General
Public Administration
Public Affairs
Public History
Public Policy
Public Speaking (*see* Mass Communication; Rhetoric; Speech and Interpersonal Communication)
Publishing
Regional Planning (*see* Architecture; Urban and Regional Planning; Urban Design; Urban Studies)
Rehabilitation Counseling
Religion
Renaissance Studies (*see* Medieval and Renaissance Studies)
Rhetoric
Romance Languages
Romance Literatures (*see* Romance Languages)
Rural Planning and Studies
Rural Sociology
Russian
Scandinavian Languages
School Psychology
Sculpture (*see* Art/Fine Arts)
Security Administration (*see* Criminal Justice and Criminology)
Slavic Languages
Slavic Studies (*see* East European and Russian Studies; Slavic Languages)
Social Psychology

Social Sciences
Sociology
Southeast Asian Studies (*see* Asian Studies)
Soviet Studies (*see* East European and Russian Studies; Russian)
Spanish
Speech and Interpersonal Communication
Sport Psychology
Studio Art (*see* Art/Fine Arts)
Substance Abuse Counseling (*see* Addictions/Substance Abuse Counseling)
Survey Methodology
Sustainable Development
Technical Communication
Technical Writing
Telecommunications (*see* Film, Television, and Video Production)
Television (*see* Film, Television, and Video Production)
Textile Design
Textiles (*see* Clothing and Textiles; Textile Design)
Thanatology
Theater
Theater Arts (*see* Theater)
Theology
Therapies—Dance, Drama, and Music
Translation and Interpretation
Transpersonal and Humanistic Psychology
Urban and Regional Planning
Urban Design
Urban Planning (*see* Architecture; Urban and Regional Planning; Urban Design; Urban Studies)
Urban Studies
Video (*see* Film, Television, and Video Production)
Visual Arts (*see* Applied Arts and Design; Art/Fine Arts; Film, Television, and Video Production; Graphic Design; Illustration; Photography)
Western European Studies
Women's Studies
World Wide Web (*see* Internet and Interactive Multimedia)
Writing

Graduate Programs in the Biological Sciences

Anatomy
Animal Behavior
Bacteriology
Behavioral Sciences (*see* Biopsychology; Neuroscience; Zoology)
Biochemistry
Biological and Biomedical Sciences—General
Biological Chemistry (*see* Biochemistry)
Biological Oceanography (*see* Marine Biology)
Biophysics
Biopsychology
Botany
Breeding (*see* Botany; Plant Biology; Genetics)
Cancer Biology/Oncology
Cardiovascular Sciences
Cell Biology
Cellular Physiology (*see* Cell Biology; Physiology)
Computational Biology
Conservation (*see* Conservation Biology; Environmental Biology)
Conservation Biology
Crop Sciences (*see* Botany; Plant Biology)
Cytology (*see* Cell Biology)
Developmental Biology
Dietetics (*see* Nutrition)
Ecology
Embryology (*see* Developmental Biology)

Endocrinology (*see* Physiology)
Entomology
Environmental Biology
Evolutionary Biology
Foods (*see* Nutrition)
Genetics
Genomic Sciences
Histology (*see* Anatomy; Cell Biology)
Human Genetics
Immunology
Infectious Diseases
Laboratory Medicine (*see* Immunology; Microbiology; Pathology)
Life Sciences (*see* Biological and Biomedical Sciences)
Marine Biology
Medical Microbiology
Medical Sciences (*see* Biological and Biomedical Sciences)
Medical Science Training Programs (*see* Biological and Biomedical Sciences)
Microbiology
Molecular Biology
Molecular Biophysics
Molecular Genetics
Molecular Medicine
Molecular Pathogenesis
Molecular Pathology
Molecular Pharmacology
Molecular Physiology
Molecular Toxicology
Neural Sciences (*see* Biopsychology; Neurobiology; Neuroscience)
Neurobiology
Neuroendocrinology (*see* Biopsychology; Neurobiology; Neuroscience; Physiology)
Neuropharmacology (*see* Biopsychology; Neurobiology; Neuroscience; Pharmacology)
Neurophysiology (*see* Biopsychology; Neurobiology; Neuroscience; Physiology)
Neuroscience
Nutrition
Oncology (*see* Cancer Biology/Oncology)
Organismal Biology (*see* Biological and Biomedical Sciences; Zoology)
Parasitology
Pathobiology
Pathology
Pharmacology
Photobiology of Cells and Organelles (*see* Botany; Cell Biology; Plant Biology)
Physiological Optics (*see* Physiology)
Physiology
Plant Biology
Plant Molecular Biology
Plant Pathology
Plant Physiology
Pomology (*see* Botany; Plant Biology)
Psychobiology (*see* Biopsychology)
Psychopharmacology (*see* Biopsychology; Neuroscience; Pharmacology)
Radiation Biology
Reproductive Biology
Sociobiology (*see* Evolutionary Biology)
Structural Biology
Systems Biology
Teratology
Theoretical Biology (*see* Biological and Biomedical Sciences)
Therapeutics (*see* Pharmacology)
Toxicology
Translational Biology
Tropical Medicine (*see* Parasitology)
Virology

Wildlife Biology (*see* Zoology)
Zoology

Graduate Programs in the Physical Sciences, Mathematics, Agricultural Sciences, the Environment & Natural Resources

Acoustics
Agricultural Sciences
Agronomy and Soil Sciences
Analytical Chemistry
Animal Sciences
Applied Mathematics
Applied Physics
Applied Statistics
Aquaculture
Astronomy
Astrophysical Sciences (*see* Astrophysics; Atmospheric Sciences; Meteorology; Planetary and Space Sciences)
Astrophysics
Atmospheric Sciences
Biological Oceanography (*see* Marine Affairs; Marine Sciences; Oceanography)
Biomathematics
Biometry
Biostatistics
Chemical Physics
Chemistry
Computational Sciences
Condensed Matter Physics
Dairy Science (*see* Animal Sciences)
Earth Sciences (*see* Geosciences)
Environmental Management and Policy
Environmental Sciences
Environmental Studies (*see* Environmental Management and Policy)
Experimental Statistics (*see* Statistics)
Fish, Game, and Wildlife Management
Food Science and Technology
Forestry
General Science (*see* specific topics)
Geochemistry
Geodetic Sciences
Geological Engineering (*see* Geology)
Geological Sciences (*see* Geology)
Geology
Geophysical Fluid Dynamics (*see* Geophysics)
Geophysics
Geosciences
Horticulture
Hydrogeology
Hydrology
Inorganic Chemistry
Limnology
Marine Affairs
Marine Geology
Marine Sciences
Marine Studies (*see* Marine Affairs; Marine Geology; Marine Sciences; Oceanography)
Mathematical and Computational Finance
Mathematical Physics
Mathematical Statistics (*see* Applied Statistics; Statistics)
Mathematics
Meteorology

Mineralogy
Natural Resource Management (*see* Environmental Management and Policy; Natural Resources)
Natural Resources
Nuclear Physics (*see* Physics)
Ocean Engineering (*see* Marine Affairs; Marine Geology; Marine Sciences; Oceanography)
Oceanography
Optical Sciences
Optical Technologies (*see* Optical Sciences)
Optics (*see* Applied Physics; Optical Sciences; Physics)
Organic Chemistry
Paleontology
Paper Chemistry (*see* Chemistry)
Photonics
Physical Chemistry
Physics
Planetary and Space Sciences
Plant Sciences
Plasma Physics
Poultry Science (*see* Animal Sciences)
Radiological Physics (*see* Physics)
Range Management (*see* Range Science)
Range Science
Resource Management (*see* Environmental Management and Policy; Natural Resources)
Solid-Earth Sciences (*see* Geosciences)
Space Sciences (*see* Planetary and Space Sciences)
Statistics
Theoretical Chemistry
Theoretical Physics
Viticulture and Enology
Water Resources

Graduate Programs in Engineering & Applied Sciences

Aeronautical Engineering (*see* Aerospace/Aeronautical Engineering)
Aerospace/Aeronautical Engineering
Aerospace Studies (*see* Aerospace/Aeronautical Engineering)
Agricultural Engineering
Applied Mechanics (*see* Mechanics)
Applied Science and Technology
Architectural Engineering
Artificial Intelligence/Robotics
Astronautical Engineering (*see* Aerospace/Aeronautical Engineering)
Automotive Engineering
Aviation
Biochemical Engineering
Bioengineering
Bioinformatics
Biological Engineering (*see* Bioengineering)
Biomedical Engineering
Biosystems Engineering
Biotechnology
Ceramic Engineering (*see* Ceramic Sciences and Engineering)
Ceramic Sciences and Engineering
Ceramics (*see* Ceramic Sciences and Engineering)
Chemical Engineering
Civil Engineering
Computer and Information Systems Security
Computer Engineering
Computer Science
Computing Technology (*see* Computer Science)
Construction Engineering
Construction Management

Database Systems
Electrical Engineering
Electronic Materials
Electronics Engineering (*see* Electrical Engineering)
Energy and Power Engineering
Energy Management and Policy
Engineering and Applied Sciences
Engineering and Public Affairs (*see* Technology and Public Policy)
Engineering and Public Policy (*see* Energy Management and Policy; Technology and Public Policy)
Engineering Design
Engineering Management
Engineering Mechanics (*see* Mechanics)
Engineering Metallurgy (*see* Metallurgical Engineering and Metallurgy)
Engineering Physics
Environmental Design (*see* Environmental Engineering)
Environmental Engineering
Ergonomics and Human Factors
Financial Engineering
Fire Protection Engineering
Food Engineering (*see* Agricultural Engineering)
Game Design and Development
Gas Engineering (*see* Petroleum Engineering)
Geological Engineering
Geophysics Engineering (*see* Geological Engineering)
Geotechnical Engineering
Hazardous Materials Management
Health Informatics
Health Systems (*see* Safety Engineering; Systems Engineering)
Highway Engineering (*see* Transportation and Highway Engineering)
Human-Computer Interaction
Human Factors (*see* Ergonomics and Human Factors)
Hydraulics
Hydrology (*see* Water Resources Engineering)
Industrial Engineering (*see* Industrial/Management Engineering)
Industrial/Management Engineering
Information Science
Internet Engineering
Macromolecular Science (*see* Polymer Science and Engineering)
Management Engineering (*see* Engineering Management; Industrial/ Management Engineering)
Management of Technology
Manufacturing Engineering
Marine Engineering (*see* Civil Engineering)
Materials Engineering
Materials Sciences
Mechanical Engineering
Mechanics
Medical Informatics
Metallurgical Engineering and Metallurgy
Metallurgy (*see* Metallurgical Engineering and Metallurgy)
Mineral/Mining Engineering
Nanotechnology
Nuclear Engineering
Ocean Engineering
Operations Research
Paper and Pulp Engineering
Petroleum Engineering
Pharmaceutical Engineering
Plastics Engineering (*see* Polymer Science and Engineering)
Polymer Science and Engineering
Public Policy (*see* Energy Management and Policy; Technology and Public Policy)
Reliability Engineering
Robotics (*see* Artificial Intelligence/Robotics)
Safety Engineering
Software Engineering
Solid-State Sciences (*see* Materials Sciences)

Structural Engineering
Surveying Science and Engineering
Systems Analysis (*see* Systems Engineering)
Systems Engineering
Systems Science
Technology and Public Policy
Telecommunications
Telecommunications Management
Textile Sciences and Engineering
Textiles (*see* Textile Sciences and Engineering)
Transportation and Highway Engineering
Urban Systems Engineering (*see* Systems Engineering)
Waste Management (*see* Hazardous Materials Management)
Water Resources Engineering

Graduate Programs in Business, Education, Health, Information Studies, Law & Social Work

Accounting
Actuarial Science
Acupuncture and Oriental Medicine
Acute Care/Critical Care Nursing
Administration (*see* Business Administration and Management; Educational Administration; Health Services Management and Hospital Administration; Industrial and Manufacturing Management; Nursing and Healthcare Administration; Pharmaceutical Administration; Sports Management)
Adult Education
Adult Nursing
Advanced Practice Nursing (*see* Family Nurse Practitioner Studies)
Advertising and Public Relations
Agricultural Education
Alcohol Abuse Counseling (*see* Counselor Education)
Allied Health—General
Allied Health Professions (*see* Clinical Laboratory Sciences/Medical Technology; Clinical Research; Communication Disorders; Dental Hygiene; Emergency Medical Services; Occupational Therapy; Physical Therapy; Physician Assistant Studies; Rehabilitation Sciences)
Allopathic Medicine
Anesthesiologist Assistant Studies
Art Education
Athletics Administration (*see* Kinesiology and Movement Studies)
Athletic Training and Sports Medicine
Audiology (*see* Communication Disorders)
Aviation Management
Banking (*see* Finance and Banking)
Bioethics
Business Administration and Management—General
Business Education
Child-Care Nursing (*see* Maternal and Child/Neonatal Nursing)
Chiropractic
Clinical Laboratory Sciences/Medical Technology
Clinical Research
Communication Disorders
Community College Education
Community Health
Community Health Nursing
Computer Education
Continuing Education (*see* Adult Education)
Counseling (*see* Counselor Education)
Counselor Education
Curriculum and Instruction
Dental and Oral Surgery (*see* Oral and Dental Sciences)

Dental Assistant Studies (*see* Dental Hygiene)
Dental Hygiene
Dental Services (*see* Dental Hygiene)
Dentistry
Developmental Education
Distance Education Development
Drug Abuse Counseling (*see* Counselor Education)
Early Childhood Education
Educational Leadership and Administration
Educational Measurement and Evaluation
Educational Media/Instructional Technology
Educational Policy
Educational Psychology
Education—General
Education of the Blind (*see* Special Education)
Education of the Deaf (*see* Special Education)
Education of the Gifted
Education of the Hearing Impaired (*see* Special Education)
Education of the Learning Disabled (*see* Special Education)
Education of the Mentally Retarded (*see* Special Education)
Education of the Physically Handicapped (*see* Special Education)
Education of Students with Severe/Multiple Disabilities
Education of the Visually Handicapped (*see* Special Education)
Electronic Commerce
Elementary Education
Emergency Medical Services
English as a Second Language
English Education
Entertainment Management
Entrepreneurship
Environmental and Occupational Health
Environmental Education
Environmental Law
Epidemiology
Exercise and Sports Science
Exercise Physiology (*see* Kinesiology and Movement Studies)
Facilities and Entertainment Management
Family Nurse Practitioner Studies
Finance and Banking
Food Services Management (*see* Hospitality Management)
Foreign Languages Education
Forensic Nursing
Foundations and Philosophy of Education
Gerontological Nursing
Guidance and Counseling (*see* Counselor Education)
Health Education
Health Law
Health Physics/Radiological Health
Health Promotion
Health-Related Professions (*see* individual allied health professions)
Health Services Management and Hospital Administration
Health Services Research
Hearing Sciences (*see* Communication Disorders)
Higher Education
HIV/AIDS Nursing
Home Economics Education
Hospice Nursing
Hospital Administration (*see* Health Services Management and Hospital Administration)
Hospitality Management
Hotel Management (*see* Travel and Tourism)
Human Resources Development
Human Resources Management
Human Services
Industrial Administration (*see* Industrial and Manufacturing Management)
Industrial and Manufacturing Management
Industrial Education (*see* Vocational and Technical Education)
Industrial Hygiene

Information Studies
Instructional Technology (*see* Educational Media/Instructional Technology)
Insurance
International and Comparative Education
International Business
International Commerce (*see* International Business)
International Economics (*see* International Business)
International Health
International Trade (*see* International Business)
Investment and Securities (*see* Business Administration and Management; Finance and Banking; Investment Management)
Investment Management
Junior College Education (*see* Community College Education)
Kinesiology and Movement Studies
Laboratory Medicine (*see* Clinical Laboratory Sciences/Medical Technology)
Law
Legal and Justice Studies
Leisure Services (*see* Recreation and Park Management)
Leisure Studies
Library Science
Logistics
Management (*see* Business Administration and Management)
Management Information Systems
Management Strategy and Policy
Marketing
Marketing Research
Maternal and Child Health
Maternal and Child/Neonatal Nursing
Mathematics Education
Medical Imaging
Medical Nursing (*see* Medical/Surgical Nursing)
Medical Physics
Medical/Surgical Nursing
Medical Technology (*see* Clinical Laboratory Sciences/Medical Technology)
Medicinal and Pharmaceutical Chemistry
Medicinal Chemistry (*see* Medicinal and Pharmaceutical Chemistry)
Medicine (*see* Allopathic Medicine; Naturopathic Medicine; Osteopathic Medicine; Podiatric Medicine)
Middle School Education
Midwifery (*see* Nurse Midwifery)
Movement Studies (*see* Kinesiology and Movement Studies)
Multilingual and Multicultural Education
Museum Education
Music Education
Naturopathic Medicine
Nonprofit Management
Nuclear Medical Technology (*see* Clinical Laboratory Sciences/Medical Technology)
Nurse Anesthesia
Nurse Midwifery
Nurse Practitioner Studies (*see* Family Nurse Practitioner Studies)
Nursery School Education (*see* Early Childhood Education)
Nursing Administration (*see* Nursing and Healthcare Administration)
Nursing and Healthcare Administration
Nursing Education
Nursing—General
Nursing Informatics
Occupational Education (*see* Vocational and Technical Education)
Occupational Health (*see* Environmental and Occupational Health; Occupational Health Nursing)
Occupational Health Nursing
Occupational Therapy
Oncology Nursing
Optometry
Oral and Dental Sciences
Oral Biology (*see* Oral and Dental Sciences)

Oral Pathology (*see* Oral and Dental Sciences)
Organizational Behavior
Organizational Management
Oriental Medicine and Acupuncture (*see* Acupuncture and Oriental Medicine)
Orthodontics (*see* Oral and Dental Sciences)
Osteopathic Medicine
Parks Administration (*see* Recreation and Park Management)
Pediatric Nursing
Pedontics (*see* Oral and Dental Sciences)
Perfusion
Personnel (*see* Human Resources Development; Human Resources Management; Organizational Behavior; Organizational Management; Student Affairs)
Pharmaceutical Administration
Pharmaceutical Chemistry (*see* Medicinal and Pharmaceutical Chemistry)
Pharmaceutical Sciences
Pharmacy
Philosophy of Education (*see* Foundations and Philosophy of Education)
Physical Education
Physical Therapy
Physician Assistant Studies
Physiological Optics (*see* Vision Sciences)
Podiatric Medicine
Preventive Medicine (*see* Community Health and Public Health)
Project Management
Psychiatric Nursing
Public Health—General
Public Health Nursing (*see* Community Health Nursing)
Public Relations (*see* Advertising and Public Relations)
Quality Management
Quantitative Analysis
Radiological Health (*see* Health Physics/Radiological Health)
Reading Education
Real Estate
Recreation and Park Management
Recreation Therapy (*see* Recreation and Park Management)
Rehabilitation Sciences

Rehabilitation Therapy (*see* Physical Therapy)
Religious Education
Remedial Education (*see* Special Education)
Restaurant Administration (*see* Hospitality Management)
School Nursing
Science Education
Secondary Education
Social Sciences Education
Social Studies Education (*see* Social Sciences Education)
Social Work
Special Education
Speech-Language Pathology and Audiology (*see* Communication Disorders)
Sports Management
Sports Medicine (*see* Athletic Training and Sports Medicine)
Sports Psychology and Sociology (*see* Kinesiology and Movement Studies)
Student Affairs
Substance Abuse Counseling (*see* Counselor Education)
Supply Chain Management
Surgical Nursing (*see* Medical/Surgical Nursing)
Sustainability Management
Systems Management (*see* Management Information Systems)
Taxation
Teacher Education (*see* specific subject areas)
Teaching English as a Second Language (*see* English as a Second Language)
Technical Education (*see* Vocational and Technical Education)
Teratology (*see* Environmental and Occupational Health)
Therapeutics (*see* Pharmaceutical Sciences; Pharmacy)
Transcultural Nursing
Transportation Management
Travel and Tourism
Urban Education
Veterinary Medicine
Veterinary Sciences
Vision Sciences
Vocational and Technical Education
Vocational Counseling (*see* Counselor Education)
Women's Health Nursing

Directories and Subject Areas in This Book

NOTES

NOTES

NOTES

NOTES

NOTES

NOTES

NOTES

NOTES

NOTES

NOTES

NOTES

NOTES

NOTES